CHILTON'S TRUCK and VAN SERVICE MANUAL

Gasoline and Diesel Engines

Publisher Kerry A. Freeman, S.A.E.
Editor-In-Chief Dean F. Morgantini, S.A.E. □ **Managing Editor** David H. Lee, A.S.E., S.A.E.
Senior Editor Richard J. Rivele, S.A.E. □ **Senior Editor** Nick D'Andrea □ **Senior Editor** Ron Webb
Project Manager Peter M. Conti, Jr. □ **Project Manager** Ken Grabowski, A.S.E.
Project Manager Richard T. Smith
Service Editors Lawrence C. Braun, S.A.E., A.S.C., Robert E. Doughten, Thomas G. Gaeta
Jacques Gordon, Michael L. Grady, Martin J. Gunther, Steve Horner, Neil Leonard, A.S.E.,
James R. Marotta, Robert McAnally, Steven Morgan, James B. Steele,
Larry E. Stiles, Jim Taylor, Anthony Tortorici, A.S.E., S.A.E.
Editorial Consultants Edward K. Shea, S.A.E., Stan Stephenson

Manager of Manufacturing John J. Cantwell
Production Manager W. Calvin Settle, Jr., S.A.E
Assistant Production Manager Andrea Steiger
Mechanical Artist Marsha Park Herman
Mechanical Artist Lorraine Martinelli
Special Projects Peter Kaprielyan

Sales Director Donald A Wright □ **Assistant** Jacquelyn T. Powers
Regional Sales Managers Joseph Andrews, Jr., David Flaherty, Larry W. Marshall

OFFICERS
President Gary R. Ingersoll
Senior Vice President, Book Publishing & Research Ronald A. Hoxter

CHILTON BOOK COMPANY
ONE OF THE ABC PUBLISHING COMPANIES,
A PART OF CAPITAL CITIES/ABC, INC.
Manufactured in USA • Chilton Way, Radnor, Pa. 19089
ISBN 0–8019–7688–X 2345678901 0987654321 ISSN 0742–0331

SAFETY NOTICE

Proper service and repair procedures are vital to the safe, reliable operation of all motor vehicles, as well as the personal safety of those performing repairs. This manual outlines procedures for servicing and repairing vehicles using safe effective methods. The procedures contain many NOTES, CAUTIONS and WARNINGS which should be followed along with standard safety procedures to eliminate the possibility of personal injury or improper service which could damage the vehicle or compromise its safety.

It is important to note that repair procedures and techniques, tools and parts for servicing motor vehicles, as well as the skill and experience of the individual performing the work vary widely. It is not possible to anticipate all of the conceivable ways or conditions under which vehicles may be serviced, or to provide cautions as to all of the possible hazards that may result. Standard and accepted safety precautions and equipment should be used when handling toxic or flammable fluids, and safety goggles or other protection should be used during cutting, grinding, chiseling, prying, or any other process that can cause material removal or projectiles.

Some procedures require the use of tools specially designed for a specific purpose. Before substituting another tool or procedure, you must be completely satisfied that neither your personal safety, nor the performance of the vehicle will be endangered.

PARTS LISTINGS

Part numbers listed in this reference are not recommendations by Chilton for any product by brand name. They are references that can be used with interchange manuals and aftermarket supplier catalogs to locate each brand supplier's discrete part number.

Although information in this manual is based on industry sources and is as complete as possible at the time of publication, the possibility exists that some car manufacturers made later changes which could not be included here. While striving for total accuracy, Chilton Book Company cannot assume responsibility for any errors, changes, or omissions that may occur in the compilation of this data.

INDEX

BEFORE SERVICING, SEE THE SAFETY NOTICE AT THE FRONT OF THE BOOK

ENGINE IDENTIFICATION CODES BY VIN NUMBER
S/T Truck Series, Astro Vans, 10-30, 1500-3500 Series Light Duty Trucks

Engine Cu. In. (Liter)	Cylinders ●	'80	'81	'82	'83	'84	'85	'86
				GASOLINE				
119 (1.9)	L4	—	—	A	A	A	A	A
121 (2.0)	L4	—	—	Y	Y	Y	—	—
151 (2.5)	L4	—	—	—	—	—	E	E
173 (2.8)	V6	—	—	B	B	B	B	B
263 (4.3)	V6	—	—	—	—	—	N	N
250 (4.1)	L6	D	D	D	D	D	D	D
292 (4.8)	L6	T	T	T	T	T	T	T
305 (5.0)①	V8	—	F	F	F	F	F	F
305 (5.0)②	V8	G	H	H	H	H	H	H
350 (5.7)③	V8	P	P	P	P	—	—	—
350 (5.7)④	V8	L	L	L	L	L	L	L
350 (5.7)⑤	V8	—	M	M	M	M	M	M
400 (6.6)	V8	R	—	—	—	—	—	—
454 (7.4)	V8	W	W	W	W	W	W	W
454 (7.4)	V8	S	—	—	—	—	—	—
				DIESEL				
366 (6.0)	V8	B	B	B	B	B	B	B
135 (2.2)	L4	—	—	—	—	S	S	S
350 (5.7)	V8	Z	Z	—	—	—	—	—
378 (6.2)⑥	V8	—	—	C	C	C	C	C
378 (6.2)⑦	V8	—	—	J	J	J	J	J

NOTE: A combination Vehicle Identification Number and rating plate used on all models is located on the left door lock pillar of C, K and G models. On forward control models, it is attached to the dash and toe panel. The Vehicle Identification Number is stamped on a plate which is attached to the left top of the instrument panel on C, K and G models, and is visible through the windshield. On P models, the plate is attached to the front of the dash and toe panel to the left of the steering column. The third symbol of the Vehicle Identification Number is the engine code. Refer to the chart for the corresponding engine cubic inch displacement.

① California only—W/Electronic Spark Control
② 49 States—Less Electronic Spark Control
③ W/2 bbl carburetor
④ W/light duty emission package
⑤ W/heavy duty emission package
⑥ W/light duty emission package
⑦ W/heavy duty emission package

ENGINE	FIRST DESIGN CODES			SECOND DESIGN CODES		
	Federal Emissions	California Emissions	Canada and Export Emissions	Federal Emissions	California Emissions	Canada and Export Emissions
6.0L (366) RPO L86	AAX AAU AAW	AAM AAK AAT	A8A A8B A8C	ABK ABM ABR APJ APK APL	ABU ABY ABZ ABL ABX	T6F T6H T6L
7.0L (427) RPO L43	ACF ACB ACA	ACF ACB ACA	A8D A8H A8F	ACT ACW ACX	—	All First Design

1985 Emission system availability Mark IV engines

ENGINE IDENTIFICATION CODE BY VIN NUMBER
40 through 90 Series, 4000 through 9000 Series (Medium and Heavy Duty Trucks)

Engine	'80	'81	'82	'83	'84	'85	'86
292 Cu. In. Gasoline	T	T	T	T	T	T	T
350 Cu. In. Gasoline	A	A	A	A	A	A	A
366 Cu. In. Gasoline	B	B	B	B	B	B	B
427 Cu. In. Gasoline	E	E	E	E	E	E②	E②
454 Cu. In. Gasoline	S	S	S	S	S	—	—
3406 Caterpillar Inline 6 Cyl. Diesel	R	R	R	R	R	R	R
3208 Caterpillar V-8 Diesel	Y	Y	Y	Y	Y	Y	Y
Cummins KT-450 Inline 6 Cyl. Diesel	C	C	C	C	C	C	C
Cummins Turbocharged 6 Cyl. Diesel	C	C	C	C	C	C	C
Cummins V-8 Diesel (10L)	C	C	C	W	W	W	W
Detroit Diesel 4-53 Series	D	D	D	V	V		
Detroit Diesel 6-71 Series	I	I		Z	Z	Z	Z
Detroit Diesel V6-92 Series	J	J	J	J	J	J	J
Detroit Diesel V-8, 8.2L	G①	G①	G①	G①	G①	G①	G①
Detroit Diesel 8V-71 Series	H	H	H	H	H	—	—
Detroit Diesel V8-92	K	K	K	K	K	K	K
Deutz BF6L913 Diesel	—	—	—	L	L	L	L
Isuzu 5.8 L Diesel	—	—	—	—	—	N	N

NOTE: The Vehicle Identification Number (VIN) plate for all 40-70, 4000-7000 series trucks is located on the top of the instrument panel and is visible from the driver's side (left) by looking through the windshield. A combination Vehicle Identification and Rating plate is used on 80-90, 8500-9000 series trucks and is attached to the left-hand door pillar on most models. Bus models have their plates attached to the air intake plenum panel. The fifth symbol of the VIN number represents the engine code for 1980 medium and heavy duty vehicles, while the eighth symbol represents the engine code for 1981 and later medium and heavy duty vehicles.

① Detroit Diesel 8.2 N—VIN F
② Also designated VIN D

Printed in U.S.A. 4-6334 061884 4-4JB673 15516776

SERVICE PARTS IDENTIFICATION

V.I.N. 1GBHC34M7EV138562 **W/BASE** NONE

V.I.N. VEHICLE IDENTIFICATION NUMBER

NOTE: THE OPTIONAL EQUIPMENT LISTED BELOW HAS BEEN INSTALLED ON THIS VEHICLE. FOR PROPER IDENTIFICATION OF REPLACEMENT PARTS BE SURE TO SPECIFY THE APPLICABLE OPTION NUMBERS.

OPTION NO.	DESCRIPTION	OPTION NO.	DESCRIPTION
MODEL #	CC31403	A52	SEAT ASM BENCH
B3W	ADVANCE PRICE SHEET	C7A	GVW RATING(10000 LB)
C91	LAMP DOME	DG5	MIRROR-SEN[illegible]WEST
D1Y	GEAR-SPEEDOMETER	E1A	ADAPTER-SP[illegible]DOMETER
E6W	SLEEVE-SPEEDOMETER	E9Z	LES[illegible] KEY O[illegible] SPEEDMTR
F59	STABILIZER-FRONT	GMC	[illegible]SSE[illegible]LY P[illegible]C TRK
GQ1	RR AXLE STANDARD RAT	GT5	[illegible]LE[illegible]EAR ([illegible])
G60	AUXILIARY REAR SPRIN	[illegible]B8	[illegible]AK[illegible] HYDRA[illegible]IC
K19	REACTOR SYSTEM-[illegible]	[illegible]1	[illegible]NER[illegible]OR D[illegible]COTRON
LT9	ENGINE V8 [illegible] 7L [illegible] C	[illegible]4	[illegible]ANS[illegible]SSION [illegible] M
M20	TRANS[illegible] 4 [illegible] M	N[illegible]5	EMISS[illegible]S[illegible] FEDE
N41	STEER[illegible]NG-[illegible]AUL[illegible]	R[illegible]	CONVER[illegible] DUAL
SLM	[illegible]STO[illegible]K OR[illegible] PR[illegible]	U[illegible]	BATTERY-HEAVY DUTY
U[illegible]	L[illegible]-ROOF [illegible]ER	U3[illegible]	CIGARETTE LIGHTER
V[illegible]	RA[illegible]TOR-[illegible] DU[illegible]	V7[illegible]	STATEMENT OF VEHICLE
X[illegible]	TIR[illegible].50-[illegible] TU[illegible]	YD7	FRT AXLE USED WITH R
Y[illegible]	PRE[illegible]ATIO[illegible] NE[illegible] VE[illegible]I	YPG	TIRE-7.50-16D ON/OFF
ZN[illegible]	SPR[illegible] [illegible]HED GVW	ZW9	BASE BODY OR CHASSIS
ZY[illegible]	COL[illegible]R [illegible] SOLID	Z53	GAUGE VOLTMTR/OILPRS
03U	COL[illegible]R COMB-SOLID	12L	COLOR COMB-WHITE
77I	[illegible]NTERIOR TRIM-	77V	INTERIOR TRIM DARK M
	WGT-2717-1654-4140		GREAT LAK
	OCR-E9999 -G003		

IMPORTANT: RETAIN THIS LABEL AS PERMANENT RECORD

EXAMPLE

GENERAL ENGINE SPECIFICATIONS

Cu. In. Displacement (Liter)	Year	Bore × Stroke (in.)	Firing Order	Horsepower @ rpm	Torque @ rpm	Compression Ratio	Carburetor	Valve Lifter Type	Normal Oil Pressure (psi)④
				FOUR CYLINDER					
119 (1.9L)	'82–'86	3.42 × 3.23	1-3-4-2	82 @ 4600	101 @ 3000	8.4:1	2V	Mech	57
121 (2.0L)	'82–'84	3.50 × 3.15	1-3-4-2	83 @ 4600	108 @ 2400	9.3:1	2V	Hyd.	45
151 (2.5L)	'85–'86	4.0 × 3.0	1-3-4-2	92 @ 4400	132 @ 2800	9.0:1	TBI	Hyd.	—
				SIX CYLINDER					
250 (4.1L)	'80–'86	3.88 × 3.53	1-5-3-6-2-4	115 @ 3600 ①	200 @ 2000 ②	8.3:1	2V	Hyd.	40–60
292 (4.8L)	'80–'86	3.88 × 4.12	1-5-3-6-2-4	115 @ 3600 ③	215 @ 1600 ③	7.8:1	1V	Hyd.	40–60
173 (2.8L) V6	'82–'86	3.50 × 2.99	1-2-3-4-5-6	110 @ 4800	145 @ 2100	8.5:1	2V	Hyd.	50–65
263 (4.3L) V6	'85–'86	4.0 × 3.48	1-6-5-4-3-2	150 @ 4000	225 @ 2400	9.3:1	2V	Hyd.	—
				EIGHT CYLINDER					
305 (5.0L)	'80–'86	3.74 × 3.48	1-8-4-3-6-5-7-2	160 @ 4400 ⑤	235 @ 2000 ⑥	9.2:1 ⑦	4V	Hyd.	45
350 (5.7L)	'80–'86 (Fed.)	4.00 × 3.48	1-8-4-3-6-5-7-2	165 @ 3800	275 @ 1600	8.2:1	4V	Hyd.	45
350 (5.7L)	'80–'86 (Calif.)	4.00 × 3.48	1-8-4-3-6-5-7-2	155 @ 4000 ⑧	240 @ 2800 ⑨	8.2:1	4V	Hyd.	45
366 (6.0L)	'80–'86 (Single Exh.)	3.94 × 3.76	1-8-4-3-6-5-7-2	180 @ 4000	290 @ 2400	7.6:1	4V	Hyd.	40–55
366 (6.0L)	'80–'86 (Dual Exh.)	3.94 × 3.76	1-8-4-3-6-5-7-2	190 @ 4000	305 @ 2400	7.6:1	4V	Hyd.	40–55
400 (6.6L)	'80 (Fed.)	4.13 × 3.75	1-8-4-3-6-5-7-2	185 @ 3600	300 @ 2400	8.5:1	4V	Hyd.	40–55
400 (6.6L)	'80 (Calif.)	4.13 × 3.75	1-8-4-3-6-5-7-2	170 @ 3600	305 @ 1600	8.5:1	4V	Hyd.	40–55
427 (7.0L)	'80–'86	4.25 × 3.76	1-8-4-3-6-5-7-2	220 @ 4000	360 @ 2400	7.5:1	4V	Hyd.	40–55
454 (7.4L)	'80–'84	4.25 × 4.00	1-8-4-3-6-5-7-2	230 @ 3800	360 @ 2800	7.9:1	4V	Hyd.	40–55
				DIESEL					
137 (2.2L)	'84–'86	3.46 × 3.32	1-3-4-2	62 @ 4300	96 @ 2200	21:1	FI	Mech	60
350 (5.7L)	'80–'81	4.06 × 3.38	1-8-4-3-6-5-7-2	105 @ 3200	200 @ 1600	22.1:1	FI	Hyd.	35
379 (6.2L)	'82–'86	3.98 × 3.82	1-8-4-3-6-5-7-2	130 @ 3600 ⑩	240 @ 2000 ⑪	21.3:1	FI	Hyd.	35

① 110 @ 3600 Calif. light and medium duty emission
② 200 @ 2000 Calif. light and medium duty emission
③ Heavy duty emission
④ @ 2000 rpm
⑤ 155 @ 4000 (Calif.)
⑥ 245 @ 1600 (Calif.)
⑦ 8.6:1 (Calif.)
⑧ 160 @ 3800 Heavy duty emission
⑨ 250 @ 2800 Heavy duty emission
⑩ 135 @ 3600 Heavy duty emission
⑪ 240 @ 2000 Heavy duty emission

1980 GASOLINE ENGINE TUNE-UP SPECIFICATIONS

(All engines use hydraulic valve lifters.)

Engine Displacement And Model Identification	Ignition Timing B.T.D.C. Degrees	Spark Plug Type & Gap	Solenoid Screw (rpm)	Curb Idle (rpm)③	Fast Idle (rpm)	Carburetor Identification	Distributor②		Vacuum & Mechanical Advance	
							Dist. Model	Vacuum Model	Vacuum Advance (In Crank Degrees @ Inches of Vacuum)	Mechanical Advance (Crank Degrees @ Engine rpm)
4.1 L (250 C.I.D.) (Vin D) Fed./Manual C-10, C-20 G-10, 20, K-10 G-1500, 2500 K-1500	10°	R46TS (.035)	450 (N)	750 (N)	2000 (N)	17080621 17080623	1110755	690	0° @ 5″ 16° @ 11.5″	0° @ 1100 14° @ 2300 24° @ 4100
4.1 L (250 C.I.D.) (Vin D) Calif./Manual C-10, G10, C20, G20 C-1500, G1500 C2500, G2500	10°	R46TS (.035)	425 (N)	750 (N)	2000 (N)	17080721 17080723	1110747	620	0° @ 4″ 15° @ 12″	0° @ 1100 14° @ 2300 24° @ 4100
4.1 L (250 C.I.D.) (Vin D) Fed./Auto. C-10,20 G-10, 20, K10 C-1500, 2500 G-1500, 2500 K-1500	10°	R46TS (.035)	450 (D)	650 (D)	2200 (P) or (N)	17080622 17080626	1110717 1110755	690	0° @ 5″ 16° @ 11.5″	0° @ 1100 14° @ 2300 24° @ 4100
4.1 L (250 C.I.D.) (Vin D) Calif./Auto. C-10; G10 C-1500, G1500	10°	R46TS (.035)	425 (D)	600 (D)	2200 (P) or (N)	17080720	1110749	626	0° @ 4″ 10° @ 8″	0° @ 1100 7° @ 2300 16° @ 4200
4.1 L (250 C.I.D.) Vin (D) Calif./Auto. C-20, G20 C-2500, G-2500	8°	R46TS (.035)	425	600	2200 (P) or (N)	17080722	1110717	621	0° @ 4″ 18° @ 12″	0° @ 1100 14° @ 2300 24° @ 4100
4.8 L (292 C.I.D.) (Vin T) Nation./Manual CK-30, P10, 20, 30 CK20 CK3500, P-1500, 2500, 3500, CK-2500	8°	R44T (.025)	—	700 (N)	2400 (N)	17080009	1110753	626	0° @ 4″ 10° @ 8″	0° @ 1100 14° @ 2300 24° @ 4100
4.8 L (292 C.I.D.) (Vin T) Nation./Auto. CK-30, P-10, 20, 30 CK20 CK-3509, P-1500, 2500, 3500, CK2500	8°	R44T (.035)	—	700 (N)	2400 (P) or (N)	17080009 17080359	1110753	626	0° @ 4″ 10° @ 8″	0° @ 1100 14° @ 2300 24° @ 4100

1980 GASOLINE ENGINE TUNE-UP SPECIFICATIONS

(All engines use hydraulic valve lifters.)

Engine Displacement And Model Identification	Ignition Timing B.T.D.C. Degrees	Spark Plug Type & Gap	Solenoid Screw (rpm)	Curb Idle (rpm)③	Fast Idle (rpm)	Carburetor Identification	Distributor②		Vacuum & Mechanical Advance	
							Dist. Model	Vacuum Model	Vacuum Advance (In Crank Degrees @ Inches of Vacuum)	Mechanical Advance (Crank Degrees @ Engine rpm)
5.0 L (305 C.I.D.) (Vin U) Fed./Manual CKG-10, 1500	8° 6°	R45TS (.045)	700 (N)	600 (N)	1300 (N)	17080143 17080144	1103381 1103369	691 644	0° @ 3″ 10° @ 7.5″ 0° @ 3″ 16° @ 6.5″	0° @ 1200 8° @ 2000 20° @ 4200
5.0 L (305 C.I.D.) (Vin U) Fed./Auto. C-10, 1500	8°	R45TS (.045)	600 (D)	500 (D)	1600 (P) or (N)	17080142 17080144	1103369 1103381	644 691	0° @ 3″ 16° @ 6.5″ 0° @ 3″ 20° @ 7.5″	0° @ 1200 8° @ 2000 20° @ 4200
5.0 L (305 C.I.D.) (Vin U) Fed./Auto. G-10, 1500	8°	R45TS (.045)	600 (D)	500 (D)	1600 (P) or (N)	17080100 17080102	1103369	644	0° @ 3″ 16° @ 6.5″	0° @ 1200 8° @ 2000 20° @ 4200
5.7 L (350 C.I.D.) (Vin L) Calif./Auto. C10, 20, C1500, 2500	8°	R45TS (.045)	600 (D)	500 (D)	1600 (P) or (N)	17080506 17080508	1103436 1103435	691 644	0° @ 3″ 10° @ 7.5″ 0° @ 3″ 16° @ 6.5″	0° @ 1100 12° @ 1600 16° @ 2400 22° @ 4600
5.7 L (350 C.I.D.) (Vin L) Nation./Auto. CK10, 20 CK1500, 2500	8°	R45TS (.045)	600 (D)	500 (D)	1600 (P) or (N)	17080290 17080292 17080506 17080508	1103436 1103372 1103435	691 604 644	0° @ 3″ 20° @ 7.5″ 0° @ 4″ 14° @ 8″ 0° @ 3″ 16° @ 6.5″	0° @ 1100 12° @ 1600 16° @ 2400 22° @ 4600
5.7 L (350 C.I.D.) (Vin L) Nation./Auto C10, 20, C1500, 2500	6°	R45TS (.045)	600 (D)	500 (D)	1600 (P) or (N)	17080295 17080224 17080525 17080523	1103339	626	0° @ 4″ 10° @ 8″	0° @ 1100 12° @ 1600 16° @ 2400 22° @ 4600
5.7 L (350 C.I.D.) (Vin L) Calif./Auto G10, 20 G1500, 2500	8°	R45TS (.045)	600 (D)	500 (D)	1600 (P) or (N)	17080506 17080508	1103339 1103436	626 691	0° @ 4″ 10° @ 8″ 0° @ 3″ 20° @ 7.5″	0° @ 1100 12° @ 1600 16° @ 2400 22° @ 4600
6.6 L (400 C.I.D.) (Vin R) Fed./Auto G20, G2500	4°	R45TS (.045)	600 (D)	500 (D)	1600	17080227 17080226	1103439	604	0° @ 4″ 14° @ 8″	0° @ 1000 8° @ 1600 19° @ 3450
6.6 L (400 C.I.D.) (Vin R) Calif./Auto. G20, G2500	4°	R45TS (.045)	600 (D)	500 (D)	1600 (P) or (N)	17080527 17080528	1103423	665	0° to 4″ 15° @ 10″	0° @ 1000 8° @ 1600 19° @ 3450
5.7 L (350 C.I.D.) (Vin M) Fed./Man. CKG 20, 30, CKG 2500, 3500	4°	R44T (.045)	1500①	700 (N)	1900 (N)	17080213	1103375	626	0° @ 4″ 10° @ 8″	0° @ 1150 17° @ 2900 22° @ 4200

1980 GASOLINE ENGINE TUNE-UP SPECIFICATIONS

(All engines use hydraulic valve lifters.)

Engine Displacement And Model Identification	Ignition Timing B.T.D.C. Degrees	Spark Plug Type & Gap	Solenoid Screw (rpm)	Curb Idle (rpm)③	Fast Idle (rpm)	Carburetor Identification	Distributor② Dist. Model	Distributor② Vacuum Model	Vacuum & Mechanical Advance: Vacuum Advance (In Crank Degrees @ Inches of Vacuum)	Vacuum & Mechanical Advance: Mechanical Advance (Crank Degrees @ Engine rpm)
5.7 L (350 C.I.D.) (Vin M) Calif./Man. CKG 20, 30 P30 CKG 2500, 3500, P-3500	6°	R44T (.045)	1500①	700 (N)	1900 (N)	17080513	1103420	681	0° @ 10″ 10° @ 13″	0° @ 1800 24° @ 4000
5.7 L (350 C.I.D.) (Vin M) Fed./Man. P20, 30, P2500, 3500	4°	R44T (0.45)	1600①	700 (N)	1900 (N)	17080213	1103375	626	0° @ 4″ 10° @ 8″	0° @ 1150 17° @ 2900 22° @ 4200
5.7 L (350 C.I.D.) (Vin L) Fed./Manual K10, 20, 1500, 2500	8°	R45TS (0.45)	—	700 (N)	1300 (N)	17080205	1103436	691	0° @ 3″ 2° @ 7.5″	0° @ 1100 12° @ 1600 16° @ 2400 22° @ 4600
5.7 L (350 C.I.D.) (Vin L) Fed./Manual C10, 20 G10, 20 C1500, 2500 G1500, 2500	8°	R45TS (.045)	—	700 (N)	1300 (N)	1708021	1103372	604	0° @ 4″ 14° @ 8″	0° @ 1100 12° @ 1600 16° @ 2400 22° @ 4600
5.7 L (350 C.I.D.) (Vin L) Calif./Manual K10, C20, K1500, C2500	8°	R45TS (.045)	—	700 (N)	1300 (N)	17080524	1103339	626	0° @ 4″ 10° @ 8″	0° @ 1100 12° @ 1600 16° @ 2400 22° @ 4600
5.7 L (350 C.I.D.) (Vin L) Nation./Manual C10, C1500	8°	R45TS (.045)	—	700 (N)	1600 (N)	17080291 17080503	1103435	644	0° @ 3″ 16° @ 6.5″	0° @ 1100 12° @ 1600 16° @ 2400 22° @ 4600
5.7 L (350 C.I.D.) (Vin L) Nation./Manual C10, 20, C1500, 2500	6°	R45TS (.045)	—	700 (N)	1600 (N)	17080201 17080526	1103339	626	0° @ 4″ 10° @ 8″	0° @ 1100 12° @ 1600 16° @ 2500 22° @ 4600
5.7 L (350 C.I.D.) (Vin L) Fed./Manual K10, K1500	8°	R45TS (.045)	—	700 (N)	1600 (N)	17080291	1103436	691	0° @ 3″ 2° @ 7.5″	0° @ 1100 12° @ 1600 16° @ 2400 22° @ 4600
5.7 L (350 C.I.D.) (Vin L) Fed./Auto. C10, 20, C1500, C2500 G10, 20, G1500, C2500	8°	R45TS (.045)	600 (D)	500 (D)	1600 (P) or (N)	17080205 17080206	1103372	604	0° @ 4″ 14° @ 8″	0° @ 1100 12° @ 1600 16° @ 2400 22° @ 4600

1980 GASOLINE ENGINE TUNE-UP SPECIFICATIONS

(All engines use hydraulic valve lifters.)

Engine Displacement And Model Identification	Ignition Timing B.T.D.C. Degrees	Spark Plug Type & Gap	Solenoid Screw (rpm)	Curb Idle (rpm)③	Fast Idle (rpm)	Carburetor Identification	Distributor② Dist. Model	Distributor② Vacuum Model	Vacuum & Mechanical Advance: Vacuum Advance (In Crank Degrees @ Inches of Vacuum)	Vacuum & Mechanical Advance: Mechanical Advance (Crank Degrees @ Engine rpm)
5.7 L (350 C.I.D.) (Vin M) Fed./Auto CK20, 30, CK2500 G30, G3500, P20, 30, P2500, 3500 G30, G3500	4°	R44T (.045)	1600①	700 (N)	1900 (N)	17080213	1103375	626	0° @ 4″ 10° @ 8″	0° @ 1150 17° @ 2900 22° @ 4200
						17080215	1103439	604	0° @ 4″ 14° @ 8″	0° @ 1000 8° @ 1600 19° @ 3450
5.7 L (350 C.I.D.) (Vin M) Calif./Auto. CK10, 30, CK1500, 3500	6°	R44T (.045)	1500①	700 (N)	1900 (N)	17080513 17080515	1103420	681	0° @ 10″ 10° @ 13″	0° @ 1800 24° @ 4000
6.6 L (400 C.I.D.) (Vin X) Fed./Auto. K20, 30, K2500, 3500 G30, G3500	4°	R44T (.045)	1600①	700 (N)	1900 (N)	17080229	1103375	626	0° to 4″ 10° @ 8″	0° @ 1150 17° @ 2900 22° @ 4200
6.6 L (400 C.I.D.) (Vin X) Calif./Auto K20, 30, K2500, 3500 G30, G3500	6°	R44T (.045)	1500①	700 (N)	1900 (N)	17080529	1103420	681	0° @ 10″ 10° @ 13″	0° @ 1800 24° @ 4000
7.4 L (454 C.I.D.) (Vin W) Nation./Auto./Man. C20, 30, C2500, 3500 P30, P3500	4°	R44T (.045)	1500①	700 (N)	1900 (N)	17080212 17080213	1103376	682	0° @ 8″ 10° @ 13″	0° @ 1100 14° @ 2800 20° @ 4200

NOTE: See the underhood emission control sticker before making any adjustments. Sticker values must be used if they disagree with the specifications in this chart. Always verify engine and truck model before performing any service (see text for details).

—Not Applicable
P-Park
N-Neutral
D-Drive
① TRC actuator speed (non-governed)
② All engines use electronic ignition system. Use distributor model numbers to select correct performance specifications when testing.
③ Carburetor mixture adjustment is not normally part of tune-up, except on 4.8 liter (292 cu. in.) engine. If adjustment is required, see underhood emission control sticker for proper procedure.

1981 GASOLINE ENGINE TUNE-UP SPECIFICATIONS

(All engines use hydraulic valve lifters)

Engine and Emission Family	Emission Label Code	Ignition Timing B.T.D.C. Degrees	Spark Plug Type & Gap	Solenoid Screw (rpm)	Curb Idle (rpm)	Fast Idle③ (rpm)	Carburetor Part Number	Distributor② Dist. Model	Distributor② Vacuum Model	Vacuum & Mechanical Advance: Vacuum Advance (In Crank Degrees @ Inches of Vacuum)	Vacuum & Mechanical Advance: Mechanical Advance (Crank Degrees @ Engine rpm)
4.1 L (250 C.I.D.) Manual Trans. Federal Sales C-10, C1500	ACR ACS	10°	R45TS (.035)	450 (N)	750 (N)	2000 (N)	17081621 17081629	1110589 1111388	644 691	0° @ 3″ 16° @ 6.5″ 0° @ 3″ 20° @ 7.5″	0° @ 1100 14° @ 2300 24° @ 4100
4.1 L (250 C.I.D.) Manual Trans. Federal Sales K-10, K1500	ACR ACS	10°	R46TS (.035)	450 (N)	750 (N)	2000 (N)	17081625 17081633	1110590 1110753	665 626	0° @ 4″ 15° @ 10″	0° @ 1100 14° @ 2300 24° @ 4100
4.1L (250 C.I.D.) Manual Trans. Federal Sales G10,20,G1500, 2500	ACS ADA	10°	R46TS (.035)	450 (N)	750 (N) LABEL 800 (N) ADA	2000 (N)	17081623 17081627	1110589	644	0° @ 3″ 16° @ 6.5″	0° @ 1100 14° @ 2300 24° @ 4100
4.1 L (250 C.I.D.) Manual Trans Calif. Sales C-10, C1500	ACW AWA ACK AWB	10°	R46TS (.035)	450 (N)	750 (N)	2000 (N)	17081721	1110749	626	0° @ 4″ 10° @ 8″	0° @ 1100 7° @ 2300 16° @ 4200
4.1L (250 C.I.D.) Manual Trans. Calif. & Fed. Sales G-10, G20, G30 G1500,G2500, G3500	ACX ADB AFA	10°	R46TS (.035)	450 (N)	750 (N)	2000 (N)	17081727 G10, G1500 17081725 G20, 30 G2500, G3500	1110749	626	0° @ 4″ 10° @ 8″	0° @ 1100 7° @ 2300 16° @ 4200
4.1 L (250 C.I.D.) Auto Trans. Federal Sales C-10, 20 K-10 C-1500, C2500, K1500	ACT AUU ACU	10°	R46TS (.035)	450 (D)	650 (D)	2200 (P or N)	17081622	1110589	644	0° @ 3″ 16° @ 6.5″	0° @ 1100 14° @ 2300 24° @ 4100
4.1 L (250 C.I.D.) Auto Trans. Federal Sales G-10, 20 G1500, G2500	ADC AAC	8°	R46TS (.035)	450 (D)	650 (D) 700 (D) AAC	2200 (P or N)	17081624 17081626	1110589	644	0° @ 3″ 16° @ 6.5″	0° @ 1100 14° @ 2300 24° @ 4100
4.1L (250 C.I.D.) Auto Trans. Calif. Sales C-10, B1500	ACY AWC ACZ AWD	10°	R46TS (.035)	450 (D)	650 (D)	2200 (P or N)	17081720	1110749	626	0° @ 4″ 10° @ 8″	0° @ 1100 7° @ 2300 16° @ 4200
4.1 L (250 C.I.D.) Auto Trans. Calif. & Fed. Sales G10, 20, 30 G1500, G2500, G3500	ACZ ADD AFB	10°	R46TS (.035)	450 (D)	650 (D)	2200 (P or N)	17081726	1110749	626	0° @ 4″ 10° @ 8″	0° @ 1100 7° @ 2300 16° @ 4200

1981 GASOLINE ENGINE TUNE-UP SPECIFICATIONS

(All engines use hydraulic valve lifters)

Engine Displacement and Model Identification	Emission Label Code	Ignition Timing B.T.D.C. Degrees	Spark Plug Type & Gap	Solenoid Screw (rpm)	Curb Idle (rpm)	Fast Idle③ (rpm)	Carburetor Part Number	Distributor② Dist. Model	Distributor② Vacuum Model	Vacuum & Mechanical Advance: Vacuum Advance (In Crank Degrees @ Inches of Vacuum)	Vacuum & Mechanical Advance: Mechanical Advance (Crank Degrees @ Engine rpm)
4.8 L (292 C.I.D.) Manual Trans. Nation Wide CK20, 30; P20, 30 CK2500, CK3500 P2500, P3500	ADF ADM ADH	8°	R44T (.035)	450 (N)	700 (N)①	2400 (N)	17081309 17081680	1110753	626	0° @ 4″ 10° @ 8″	0° @ 1100 14° @ 2300 24° @ 4100
4.8L (292 C.I.D.) Auto Trans. Nation Wide Sales CKP20, 30 CKP2500, 3500	ADF ADM ADH	8°	R44T (.035)	450 (N)	700 (N)	2400 (N)	17081309 17081680	1110753	626	0° @ 4″ 10° @ 8″	0° @ 1100 14° @ 2300 24° @ 4100
5.0L (305 C.I.D.) Manual Trans. Federal Sales C-10, C1500	AAA	8°	R45TS (.045)	700 (N)	600 (N)	1300 (N)	17081143 17081145 w/AC	1103381	691	0° @ 3″ 10° @ 7.5″	0° @ 1200 8° @ 2000 20° @ 4200
5.0L (305 C.I.D.) Manual Trans. Federal Sales G10, 20, 1500, 2500	AAA	8°	R45TS (.045)	700 (N)	600 (N)	1300 (N)	17081101 17081103 w/AC	1103369	644	0° @ 3″ 16° @ 6.5″	0° @ 1200 8° @ 2000 20° @ 4200
5.0L (305 C.I.D.) Auto Trans. Federal Sales C10, G10, 20 C-1500, G-1500, G-2500	AAB	8°	R45TS (.045)	600 (D)	500 (D)	1600 (P or N)	17081142 17081144 w/AC	1103381	691	0° @ 3″ 10° @ 7.5″	0° @ 1200 8° @ 2000 20° @ 4200
5.0L (305 C.I.D.) Manual Trans. Federal Sales C-10, C1500	AAF	4°	R45TS (.045)	—	700 (N)	1300 (N)	17081201	1103464	Elect Spark Control	—	—
5.0L (305 C.I.D.) Manual Trans. Federal Sales C-10, 20, K10 C1500, C2500, K1500	AAM AAR	4°	R45TS (.045)	—	700 (N)	1300 (N)	17081220	1103464	Elect Spark Control	—	—
5.0L (305 C.I.D.) Manual Trans. Federal Sales C-10, C1500	AUS	4°	R45TS (.045)	—	600 (N)	1500 (N)	17081200	1103465	Elect Spark Control	—	—
5.0L (305 C.I.D.) Manual Trans. Federal Sales G10, 20, 1500, 2500	AAJ	6°	R45TS (.045)	—	700 (N)	1300 (N)	17081220	1103464	Elect Spark Control	—	—

1981 GASOLINE ENGINE TUNE-UP SPECIFICATIONS

(All engines use hydraulic valve lifters)

Engine Displacement and Model Identification	Emission Label Code	Ignition Timing B.T.D.C. Degrees	Spark Plug Type & Gap	Solenoid Screw (rpm)	Curb Idle (rpm)	Fast Idle③ (rpm)	Carburetor Part Number	Distributor②		Vacuum & Mechanical Advance	
								Dist. Model	Vacuum Model	Vacuum Advance (In Crank Degrees @ Inches of Vacuum)	Mechanical Advance (Crank Degrees @ Engine rpm)
5.0L (305 C.I.D.) Auto Trans. Federal Sales C-10, C1500	AAH	4°	R45TS (.045)	—	500 (D)	1600 (P) or (N)	17081206 w/AC 17081205	1103464	Elect Spark Control	—	—
5.0L (305 C.I.D.) Auto Trans. Federal Sales C-10, 20; K-10 C1500,C2500, K1500	AAN AAS	6° 2°	R45TS (.045)	—	500 (D)	1600 (P) or (N)	17081227 17081226 w/AC	1103464	Elect Spark Control	—	—
5.0L (305 C.I.D.) Auto Trans. Federal Sales G10, 20 G1500,G2500	AAK	4°	R45TS (.045)	—	500 (D)	1600 (P) or (N)	17081227 17081226 w/AC	1103464	Elect Spark Control	—	—
5.0L (305 C.I.D.) Auto Trans. Calif. Sales C-10, C1500	ACC AWF ACD ACF	8°	R45TS (.045)	650 (D)	550 (D)	1800 (P) or (N)	17081526 w/AC 17081524	1103432	620	0° @ 4″ 15° @ 12″	0° @ 1000 10° @ 2000 14° @ 4000
5.7L (350 C.I.D.) Manual Trans. Federal Sales C-10; K-10, 20 C1500, K1500, K2500	AAT	8°	R45TS (.045)	—	700 (N)	1300 (N)	17081291	1103353	624	0° @ 4″ 20° @ 10″	0° @ 1100 12° @ 1600 16° @ 2400 22° @ 4600
5.7L (350 C.I.D.) Manual Trans. Federal Sales G-10, 20, G1500, G2500	AAW	8°	R45TS (.045)	—	700 (N)	1300 (N)	17081291	1103353	624	0° @ 4″ 20° @ 10″	0° @ 1100 12° @ 1600 16° @ 2400 22° @ 4600
5.7L (350 C.I.D.) Auto Trans. Federal Sales C-10, K-10, 20 C-1500, K-1500, K-2500	AAU	8°	R45TS (.045)	600 (D)	500 (D)	1600 (P) or (N)	17081290 17081292 w/AC	1103353	624	0° @ 4″ 20° @ 10″	0° @ 1100 12° @ 1600 16° @ 2400 22° @ 4600
5.7L (350 C.I.D.) Auto Trans. Federal Sales G-10, 20, G1500, 2500	AAK	8°	R45TS (.045)	600 (D)	500 (D)	1600 (P) or (N)	17081290 17081292 w/AC	1103353	624	0° @ 4″ 20° @ 10″	0° @ 1100 12° @ 1600 16° @ 2400 22° @ 4600
5.7L (350 C.I.D.) Auto Trans. Calif. Sales CK-10, CK1500	AAZ AAD	6°	R45TS (.045)	650 (D)	550 (D)	1800 (P) or (N)	17081506 17081508 w/AC	1103433	620	0° @ 4″ 15° @ 12″	0° @ 1100 12° @ 1600 16° @ 2400 22° @ 4600
5.7L (350 C.I.D.) Auto Trans. Calif. Sales CK-20, CK2500	AAZ AAD	6° 8°	R45TS (.045)	650 (D)	550 (D)	1600 (P or N)	17081506 17081508 w/AC	1103433 1103339	620 626	0° @ 4″ 15° @ 12″ 0° @ 4″ 10° @ 8″	0° @ 1100 12° @ 1600 16° @ 2400 22° @ 4600

1981 GASOLINE ENGINE TUNE-UP SPECIFICATIONS

(All engines use hydraulic valve lifters)

Engine Displacement and Model Identification	Emission Label Code	Ignition Timing B.T.D.C. Degrees	Spark Plug Type & Gap	Solenoid Screw (rpm)	Curb Idle (rpm)	Fast Idle③ (rpm)	Carburetor Part Number	Distributor②		Vacuum & Mechanical Advance	
								Dist. Model	Vacuum Model	Vacuum Advance (In Crank Degrees @ Inches of Vacuum)	Mechanical Advance (Crank Degrees @ Engine rpm)
5.7L (350 C.I.D.) Calif. Sales G10, 20, G1500, 2500	ACA ACB	8°	R45TS (.045)	650 (D)	550 (D)	1800 (P or N)	17081506 17081508 w/AC	1103433	620	0° @ 4″ 15° @ 12″	0° @ 1100 12° @ 1600 16° @ 2400 22° @ 4600
5.7L (350 C.I.D.) Manual Trans. Federal Sales CK-20, CK2500	ACJ	4°	R44T (.045)	1600①	700 (N)	1900 (N)	17080213	1103375	620	0° @ 4″ 10° @ 8″	0° @ 1150 17° @ 2900 22° @ 4200
5.7L (350 C.I.D.) Manual Trans. Federal Sales G-30, G3500	ACJ ACM	4°	R44T (.045)	1600①	700 (N)	1900 (N)	17080298	1103375	620	0° @ 4″ 14° @ 8″ 0° @ 3″ 16° @ 6.5″	0° @ 1150 17° @ 2900 22° @ 4200
5.7L (350 C.I.D.) Manual Trans. Calif. Sales CK-20, 30 CK2500, CK3500	ACK	6°	R44T (.045)	1500①	700 (N)	1900 (N)	17080507	1103420	681	0° @ 10″ 10° @ 13″	0° @ 1800 24° @ 4000
5.7L (350 C.I.D.) Manual Trans. Calif. Sales G-30, G3500	ACK	6°	R44T (.045)	1500①	700 (N)	1900 (N)	17080507	1103420	681	0° @ 10″ 10° @ 13″	0° @ 1800 24° @ 4000
5.7L (350 C.I.D.) Manual Trans. Federal Sales P-20, 30, P2500, P3500	ACJ ACM	4°	R44T (.045)	1600①	700 (N)	1900 (N)	17080213	1103375	626	0° @ 4″ 10° @ 8″	0° @ 1150 17° @ 2900 22° @ 4200
5.7L (350 C.I.D.) Manual Trans. Calif. Sales P-30, P3500	ACK	6°	R44T (.045)	1500①	700 (N)	1900 (N)	17080513	1103420	681	0° @ 10″ 10° @ 13″	0° @ 1800 24° @ 4000
5.7L (350 C.I.D.) Auto Trans. Federal Sales CK-20, 30, CK2500, CK3500	ACJ	4°	R44T (.045)	1600①	700 (N)	1900 (N)	17080213	1103375	626	0° @ 4″ 10° @ 8″	0° @ 1150 17° @ 2900 22° @ 4200
5.7L (350 C.I.D.) Auto Trans. Federal Sales G-30, G30	ACJ ACM	4°	R44T (.045)	1600①	700 (N)	1900 (N)	17080298	1103375	681	0° @ 4″ 10° @ 8″	0° @ 1150 17° @ 2900 22° @ 4200
5.7L (350 C.I.D.) Auto Trans. Calif. Sales CK-20, 30, CK2500, CK3500	ACK	6°	R44T (.045)	1500①	700 (N)	1900 (N)	17080513	1103420	681	0° @ 4″ 15° @ 10″	0° @ 1000 17° @ 1600 22° @ 4200
5.7L (350 C.I.D.) Auto Trans. Calif. Sales G-30, G3500	ACK	6°	R44T (.045)	1500①	700 (N)	1900 (N)	17080507	1103420	681	0° @ 4″ 15° @ 10″	0° @ 1000 17° @ 1600 22° @ 4200

1981 GASOLINE ENGINE TUNE-UP SPECIFICATIONS

(All engines use hydraulic valve lifters)

Engine Displacement and Model Identification	Emission Label Code	Ignition Timing B.T.D.C. Degrees	Spark Plug Type & Gap	Solenoid Screw (rpm)	Curb Idle (rpm)	Fast Idle③ (rpm)	Carburetor Part Number	Distributor② Dist. Model	Distributor② Vacuum Model	Vacuum & Mechanical Advance: Vacuum Advance (In Crank Degrees @ Inches of Vacuum)	Vacuum & Mechanical Advance: Mechanical Advance (Crank Degrees @ Engine rpm)
5.7L (350 C.I.D.) Auto Trans. Federal Sales P-30, P3500	ACJ ACM	4°	R44T (.045)	1600①	700 (N)	1900 (N)	17080213 17080215	1103375	626	0° @ 4″ 14° @ 8″	0° @ 1000 8° @ 1600 19° @ 3450
5.7L (350 C.I.D.) Auto Trans. Calif. Sales P-30, P3500	ACK	6°	R44T (.045)	1500①	700 (N)	1900 (N)	17080513	1103420	681	0° @ 4″ 15° @ 10″	0° @ 1000 17° @ 1600 22° @ 4200
7.4L (454 C.I.D.) Manual Trans. Nationwide C-20, 30; K-30 C-2500, C-3500, K-3500	ADJ ADK	4°	R44T (.045)	1500 ①	700 (N)	1900 (N)	17080212 17080512	1103376	682	0° @ 8″ 10° @ 13″	0° @ 1100 14° @ 2800 20° @ 4200
7.4L (454 C.I.D.) Auto Trans. Nationwide P-30, P3500	ADJ ADK	4°	R44T (.045)	1500①	700 (N)	1900 (N)	17080212 17080512	1103376	682	0° @ 8″ 10° @ 13″	0° @ 1100 14° @ 2800 20° @ 4200

NOTE: See the underhood emission control sticker before making any adjustments. Sticker valves must be used if they disagree with the specifications listed in the chart. Always verify engine and truck model before performing any service (see text for details).

— Not Applicable
P - Park
N - Neutral
D - Drive

① Throttle Return Control speed

② All engines use electronic ignition systems. See text for details on types, operation and testing. Use distributor model numbers when selecting performance valves for testing.

③ See underhood emission sticker before attempting any carburetor mixture adjustments.

1982 GASOLINE ENGINE TUNE-UP SPECIFICATIONS

Cu. In. Displacement (Liter)	Spark Plug Type (orig.)	Spark Plug Gap (in.)	Distributor Type	Ignition Timing (Degrees)	TRC Speed (rpm)⑨	Valve Clearance Int.	Valve Clearance Ext.	Fuel Pump Press (psi)	Curb Idle Speed (rpm) Man.	Curb Idle Speed (rpm) Auto.
119 (1.9L)	R42XLS	.040	Electronic	6B	—	.006	.010	3.0	800	900
121 (2.0L)	R42CTS	.035	Electronic	12B ①	—	Hydraulic ⑧		5.0	750	700
173 (2.8L)	R42TS	.040	Electronic	Mt-6B At-10B	—	Hydraulic ⑧		7.0	1000	750
250 (4.1L)	①	①	Electronic	①	—	Hydraulic ②		4–6	①	①

1982 GASOLINE ENGINE TUNE-UP SPECIFICATIONS

Cu. In. Displace-ment (Liter)	Spark Plug Type (orig.)	Spark Plug Gap (in.)	Distributor Type	Ignition Timing (Degrees)	TRC Speed (rpm)⑨	Valve Clearance Int.	Valve Clearance Ext.	Fuel Pump Press (psi)	Curb Idle Speed (rpm) Man.	Curb Idle Speed (rpm) Auto.
292 (4.8L)	R44T	.035	Electronic	8B ③	1500	Hydraulic ②		4–6	700	700
305 (5.0L)	R45TS	.045	Electronic	①	—	Hydraulic ②		7–9	①	①
350 (5.7L)	R44T	0.045	Electronic	4B ④	1400 ⑤	Hydraulic ②		7–9	700 ⑥	700 ⑥
366 (6.0L)	R43T	0.045	Electronic	8B	1400	Hydraulic ②		7–9	700 ⑦	700 ⑦
427 (7.0L)	R42T	0.045	Electronic	8B	1400	Hydraulic ②		7–9	700 ⑦	700 ⑦
454 (7.4L)	R44T	0.045	Electronic	①	①	Hydraulic ②		4–6	①	①

Note: See the underhood emission control sticker before making any adjustments. Sticker values must be used if they disagree with the specifications listed in the chart.

— Not Applicable

① See underhood sticker
② One turn down from zero lash
③ With distributor vacuum hose disconnected and plugged
④ Non-governed California engines — 2BTDC
⑤ Non-governed California engines — 1500 rpm
⑥ With A/C ON, if equipped
⑦ With A/C OFF, if equipped
⑧ 1½ turns down from zero lash
⑨ Throttle Return Control setting

1983 GASOLINE ENGINE TUNE-UP SPECIFICATIONS

Cu. In. Displace-ment (Liter)	Spark Plug Type (orig.)	Spark Plug Gap (in.)	Distributor Type	Ignition Timing (Degrees)	TRC Speed (rpm)⑨	Valve Clearance Int.	Valve Clearance Ext.	Pump Fuel Press (psi)	Curb Idle Speed (rpm) Std.	Curb Idle Speed (rpm) Auto.
119 (1.9L)	R42XLS	.040	Electronic ②	6B	—	.006	.010	3.0	800	900
121 (2.0L)	R42CTS	.035	Electronic	①	—	Hydraulic ③		5.0	①	①
173 (2.8L)	R42TS	.040	Electronic	16B ①	—	Hydraulic ③		7.0	700	650 ④
250 (4.1L)	R45TS	.045	Electronic	①	—	Hydraulic ⑤		4–6	①	①
292 (4.8L)	R44T	.035	Electronic	8B	1500	Hydraulic ⑤		4–6	700	700
305 (5.0L)	R45TS	.045	Electronic	①	—	Hydraulic ⑤		7–9	①	①
350 (5.7L)	R45TS ⑥	.045	Electronic	4B	1400	Hydraulic ⑤		7–9	700 ⑧	700 ⑧
366 (6.0L)	R43T	.045	Electronic	8B	1400	Hydraulic ⑤		7–9	700 ⑦	700 ⑦

1983 GASOLINE ENGINE TUNE-UP SPECIFICATIONS

Cu. In. Displacement (Liter)	Spark Plug Type (orig.)	Spark Plug Gap (in.)	Distributor Type	Ignition Timing (Degrees)	TRC Speed (rpm) ⑨	Valve Clearance Int.	Valve Clearance Ext.	Pump Fuel Press (psi)	Curb Idle Speed (rpm) Std.	Curb Idle Speed (rpm) Auto.
427 (7.0L)	R42T	.045	Electronic	8B	1400	Hydraulic ⑤		7–9	700 ⑦	700 ⑦
454 (7.4L)	R44T	.045	Electronic	①	①	Hydraulic ⑤		4–6	①	①

NOTE: See the underhood emission control sticker before making any adjustments. Sticker values must be used if they disagree with the specifications listed in the chart. Check for high or low altitude specifications before adjusting idle speed or timing.

— Not applicable
B - Before Top Dead Center
① See underhood sticker
② Air gap 0.12-0.02 in.
③ 1½ turns down from zero lash
④ Automatic in Drive
⑤ One turn down from zero lash
⑥ R44T on heavy duty engines
⑦ With A/C OFF, if equipped
⑧ With A/C ON, if equipped
⑨ Throttle Return Control setting

1984 GASOLINE ENGINE TUNE-UP SPECIFICATIONS

Cu. In. Displacement (Liter)	Spark Plug Type (orig.)	Spark Plug Gap (in.)	Distributor Type	Ignition Timing (Degrees)	TRC Speed (rpm)	Valve Clearance Int.	Valve Clearance Ext.	Pump Fuel Press (psi)	Curb Idle Speed (rpm) Std.	Curb Idle Speed (rpm) Auto.
119 (1.9L)	R42XLS	.040	Electronic	6BTDC	—	.006	.010	3.0	800	900
121 (2.0L)	R42CTS	.035	Electronic	①	—	Hydraulic ③		5.0	①	①
173 (2.8L)	R42TS	.040	Electronic	①	—	Hydraulic ③		7.0	①	①
250 (4.1L)	R45TS	.045	Electronic	①	—	Hydraulic ②		4–6	①	①
292 (4.8L)	R44T	.035	Electronic	①	1500	Hydraulic ②		4–6	①	①
305 (5.0L)	R45TS	.045	Electronic	①	—	Hydraulic ②		7–9	①	①
350 (5.7L)	R45TS	.045	Electronic	①	1400 ④	Hydraulic ②		7–9	①	①
454 (7.4L)	R44T	.045	Electronic	①	①	Hydraulic ②		4–6	①	①

NOTE: See the underhood emission control sticker before making any adjustments. Sticker values must be used if they disagree with the specifications listed in the chart. Check for high or low altitude specifications before adjusting idle speed or timing.

— Not applicable
① See underhood emission sticker for specifications and procedure
② One turn down from zero lash
③ 1½ turns down from zero lash
④ California engines (non-governed)—1500 rpm

GASOLINE ENGINE TUNE-UP SPECIFICATIONS
1985–86

Cu. IN. Displacement (Liter)	Spark Plug Type (orig.)	Spark Plug Gap (in.)①	Distributor Type	Ignition Timing (Degrees)	Valve Clearance		Pump Fuel Press (psi)	Curb Idle Speed (rpm)	
					Int.	Ext.		Std.	Auto.
119 (1.9)	R42XLS	.040	Elect.	②	.006	.010	4–6.5	③	
151 (2.5)	R43TSX	.040	Elect.	②	Hyd.	④	4–6.5	③	
173 (2.8)	R43CTS	.040	Elect.	②	Hyd.	⑥	4–6.5	③	
263 (4.3)	R43CTS	.040	Elect.	②	Hyd.	⑤	4–6.5	③	
250 (4.1)	R45TS	.045	Elect.	②	Hyd.	⑤	4–6.5	③	
292 (4.8)	R43CTS	.035	Elect.	②	Hyd.	⑤	4–6.5	③	
305 (5.0)	R45TS	.045	Elect.	②	Hyd.	⑤	4–6.5	③	
350 (5.7)	R45TS	.045	Elect.	②	Hyd.	⑤	4–6.5	③	
366 (6.0)	R43T	.045	Elect.	②	Hyd.	⑤	4–6.5	③	
427 (7.0)	R42T	.045	Elect.	②	Hyd.	⑤	4–6.5	③	
454 (7.4)	R44T	.045	Elect.	②	Hyd.	⑤	4–6.5	③	

Note: See the underhood emission control sticker before making any adjustments. Sticker values must be used if they disagree with the specifications listed in the chart. Check for high or low altitude specifications before adjusting idle speed or timing.
Replacement Vehicle Emission Control Label can be obtained by Vehicle Identification Number, through GM Parts Network.
① See underhood emission sticker for spark plug gap
② Refer to Underhood emission sticker for specifications and timing procedure
③ Idle speed, ECM controlled—not adjustable, ECM controls idle
Idle speed, Non-ECM controlled—refer to underhood emission sticker
④ Torque rocker arm stud nut to 20 ft. lbs.
⑤ One turn down from zero lash
⑥ One and one/half turns down from zero lash

FIRING ORDERS

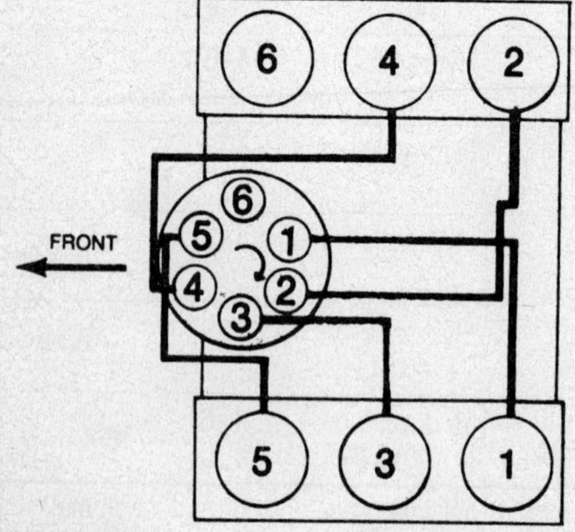

173 CID V6 engine
Firing order: 1-2-3-4-5-6 (© General Motors Corp.)

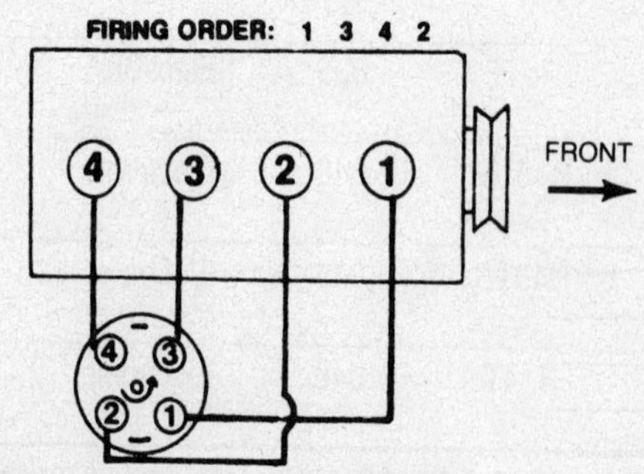

119 CID 4 cylinder
Firing order: 1-3-4-2 (© General Motors Corp.)

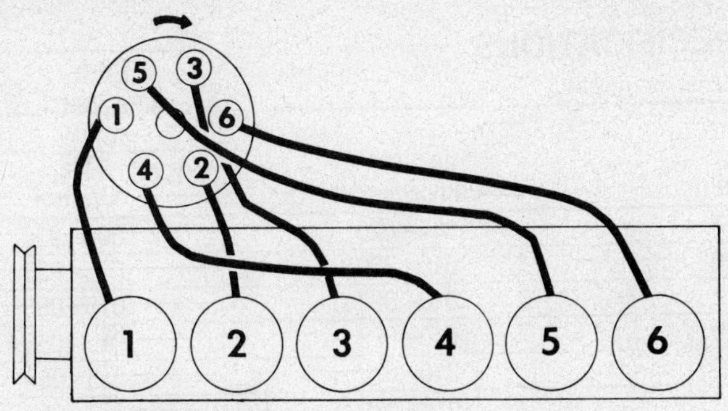

250 and 292 6-cylinder
Firing order: 1-5-3-6-2-4 (© General Motors Corp.)

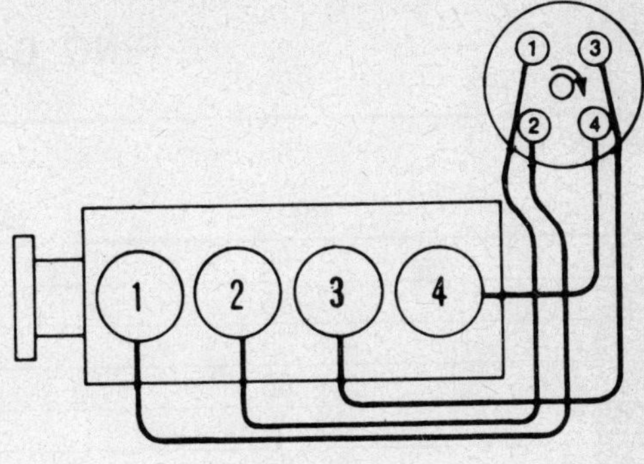

Firing order—4 cyl 121 cu. in.

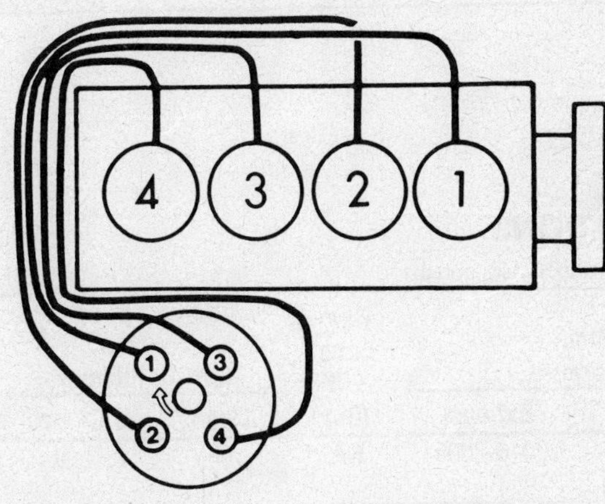

151-L4 Engine
Firing Order: 1-3-4-2 (© General Motors Corp.)

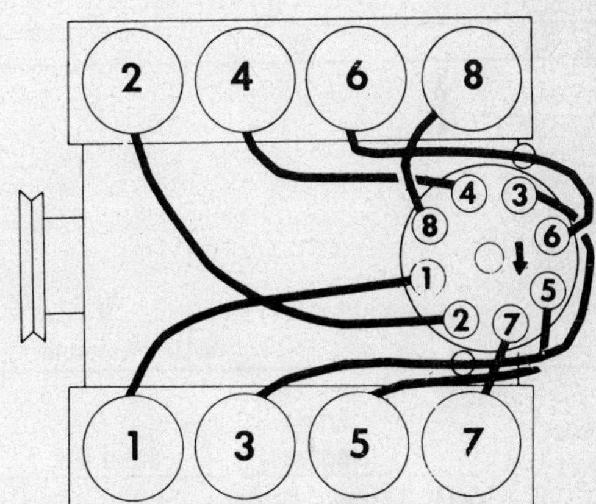

305, 350, 366, 400 and 454 cu. in. engines
Firing Order: 1-8-4-3-6-5-7-2 (© General Motors Corp.)

RING SIDE CLEARANCE

(All measurements in inches.)

Engine cu. in. (liter)	Year	Top Compression	Bottom Compression	Oil Control
119 (1.9L)	'82–'86	.0000–.0059	.0000–.0059	.0000–.0059
121 (2.0L)	'82–'86	.0012–.0027	.0012–.0027	.0000–.0078
151 (2.5L)	'84–'86	.0015–.0030	.0015–.0030	—
263 (4.3L)	'84–'86	.0012–.0032	.0012–.0032	.002–.007
250 (4.1L)	'80–'86	.0012–.0027	.0012–.0032	.0000–.0050
292 (4.8L)	'80–'86	.0020–.0040	.0020–.0040	.0005–.0055
173 (2.8L)	'80–'86	.0012–.0027	.0015–.0037	.0078 max.
305 (5.0L)	'80–'86	.0012–.0032	.0012–.0032	.002–.007
350 (5.7L)	'80–'86	.0012–.0032	.0012–.0032	.002–.007
366 (6.0L)	'80–'86	.0018–.0032	.0018–.0032	.0020–.0035
400 (6.6L)	'80	.0012–.0032	.0012–.0032	.002–.007
454 (7.4L)	'80–'86	.0017–.0032	.0017–.0032	.005–.0065

RING GAP SPECIFICATIONS

(All measurements in inches.)

Engine cu. in. (Liter)	Year	Top Compression	Bottom Compression	Oil Control
119 (1.9L)	'82–'86	.014–.020	.014–.020	.008–.035
121 (2.0L)	'82–'86	.010–.020	.010–.020	.015–.055
151 (2.5L)	'84–'86	.010–.022	.010–.027	.015–.055
263 (4.3L)	'84–'86	.010–.025	.010–.025	.015–.055
250 (4.1L)	'80–'86	.010–.020	.010–.020	.015–.055
292 (4.8L)	'80–'86	.010–.020	.010–.020	.015–.055
173 (2.8L)	'82–'86	.010–.020	.010–.020	.020–.055
305 (5.0L)	'80–'86	.010–.020	.010–.025	.015–.055
350 (5.7L)	'80–'86	.010–.020	.013–.025	.015–.055
366 (6.0L)	'80–'86	.010–.020	.010–.020	.010–.023
400 (6.6L)	'80	.010–.020	.010–.025	.015–.055
454 (7.4L)	'80–'86	.010–.020	.010–.020	.015–.055

VALVE SPECIFICATIONS

(All measurements in inches unless otherwise noted.)

Cu. Displacement (Liter)	Year	Angle (Degrees) Face	Angle (Degrees) Seat	Stem Dia. Int.	Stem Dia. Exh.	Stem Clearance Intake	Stem Clearance Exhaust	Cam Lobe Lift (in.)	Valve Spring Tension (lbs @ inches) Open	Valve Spring Tension (lbs @ inches) Closed
119 (1.9L)	'82–'86	45	45 ①	.3102 MAX	.3091 MAX	.0009–② .0022 ③	.0015–.0031	NA	④	④
121 (2.0L)	'82–'86	45	46	—	—	.0011–.0026	.0013–.0030	6.67	182 @ 1.32	77 @ 1.60
250 (4.1L)	'80–'86	45	46	.342	.3413	.0010–.0027	.0015–.0032	.2217	170 @ 1.26	60 @ 1.66
151 (2.5L)	'85–'86	45	46	0.3418–0.3425	0.3418–0.3425	0.0010–0.0027	0.0010–0.0027	.398	122–180 @ 1.254	78–86 @ 1.66
263 (4.3L)	'85–'86	45	46	—	—	0.0010–0.0027	0.0010–0.0027	⑤	194–206 @ 1.25	76–84 @ 1.70
292 (4.8L)	'80–'86	45	46	.342	.3413	.0010–.0027	.0015–.0032	.2315	175 @ 1.26	82 @ 1.66
173 (2.8L)	'82–'86	45	46	—	—	.0010–.0025	.0010–.0025	⑥	195 @ 1.18	88 @ 1.58
305 (5.0L)	'80–'86	45	46	.341	.341	.0010–.0027	.0010–.0027	⑦	⑧	⑨
350 (5.7L)	'80–'86	45	46	.341	.341	.0010–.0027	.0010–.0027	⑩	⑧	⑨
366 (6.0L)	'80–'86	45	46	.3718	.372	.0010–.0027	.0012–.0029	.234	220 @ 1.40	90 @ 1.80
400 (6.6L)	'80	45	46	.371	.371	.0010–.0027	.0012–.0029	⑩	⑧	⑨
454 (7.4L)	'80–'86	45	46	.372	.371	.0010–.0027	.0012–.0029	.234	300 @ 1.38	80 @ 1.88

Note: See the Tune-Up Specifications Chart for valve clearance adjustment
—Not applicable, use oversize valves if stem clearance is excessive

① Valve seats are removable inserts
② Maximum allowable clearance:
Intake—.1298 in.
Exhaust—.0097 in.
③ Valve guides are replaceable
④ Spring test: Inner—18 @ 1.516
Outer—32 @ 1.614
⑤ Exhaust .390 in.
Intake .375 in.
⑥ Intake—.231 in.
Exhaust—.263 in.
⑦ Intake—.2484 in.
Exhaust—.2667 in.
⑧ Intake 200 @ 1.25
Exhaust—200 @ 1.16
⑨ Intake—80 @ 1.70
Exhaust—80 @ 1.61
⑩ Intake—.260
Exhaust—.273

CRANKSHAFT BEARING JOURNAL SPECIFICATIONS

(All measurements in inches.)

Cu. In. Displacement (Liter)	Year	Main Bearing Journals: Journal Diameter	Main Bearing Journals: Oil Clearance	Main Bearing Journals: Shaft End-Play	Thrust on No.	Connecting Rod Bearing Journals: Journal Diameter	Connecting Rod Bearing Journals: Oil Clearance	Connecting Rod Bearing Journals: Rod Side Clearance
FOUR CYLINDER								
119 (1.9L)	'82–'86	2.1555–2.205	.0008–.0025	.0024–.0094	3	1.8799–1.9290	.0007–.0030	.0137 max
121 (2.0L)	'82–'86	①	②	.0019–.0082	4	1.9983–1.993	.0009–.0031	.0039–.0149
151 (2.5L)	'85–'86	2.300	.0005–.0022	.0035–.0085	5	2.000	.0005–.0026	.006–.022
SIX CYLINDER								
250 (4.1L)	'80–'86	2.2979–2.9994	③	.002–.006	Rear	1.999–2.000	.0010–.0030	.006–.0017
292 (4.8L)	'80–'86	2.2979–2.2994	③	.002–.006	5	2.099–2.100	.0010–.0030	.006–.017
173 V-6 (2.8L)	'82–'86	2.4937–2.4946	.0017–.0030	.002–.007	3	1.9994–1.9983	.0014–.0035	.0063–.0173
263 (4.3L)	'85–'86	⑪	⑫	.002–.006	4	2.2497–2.2487	.002–.003	.007–.015
EIGHT CYLINDER								
305 (5.0L)	'80–'86	④	⑤	.002–.006	5	2.0988–2.0998	.0013–.0035	.008–.014
350 (5.7L)	'80–'86	④	⑤	.002–.006	5	2.0988–2.0998	.0013–.0035	.008–.014
366 (6.0L)	'80–'86	2.7481–2.749⑦	.0013–.0025⑥	.006–.010	5	2.1985–2.1995	.0014–.0030	.019–.025
400 (6.6L)	'80	⑦	⑤	.002–.006	5	2.0988–2.0998	.0013–.0035	.008–.014
454 (4.8L)	'80–'86	2.7485–2.7494⑨	.0013–.0025⑩	.006–.010	5	2.1985–2.1995	.0009–.0025	.013–.023

① Nos. 1–4: 2.4944–2.4954
No. 5: 2.4936–2.4946

② Nos. 1–4: .0010–.0023
No. 5: .0018–.0031

③ Nos. 1–6: .0010–.0024
No. 7: .0016–.0035

④ No. 1: 2.4484–2.4493
Nos. 2–4: 2.4481–2.4490
No. 5: 2.4479–2.4488

⑤ No. 1: .0008–.0020 (.002 max)
Nos. 2–4: .0011–.0023 (.0025 max)
No. 5: .0017–.0032 (.0035 max)

⑥ Not Used

⑦ Nos. 1–4: 2.6484–2.6493
No. 5: 2.6479–2.6488

⑧ Rear: 2.7473–2.7483

⑨ Nos. 2–4: 2.7481–2.7490
No. 5: 2.7478–2.7488

⑩ No. 5: .0024–.0040

⑪ Front 2.4484–2.4493
Inter. 2.4481–2.4490
Rear 2.4479–2.4.488

⑫ Front 0.001–0.0015
Inter. 0.001–0.0020
Rear 0.0025–0.0030

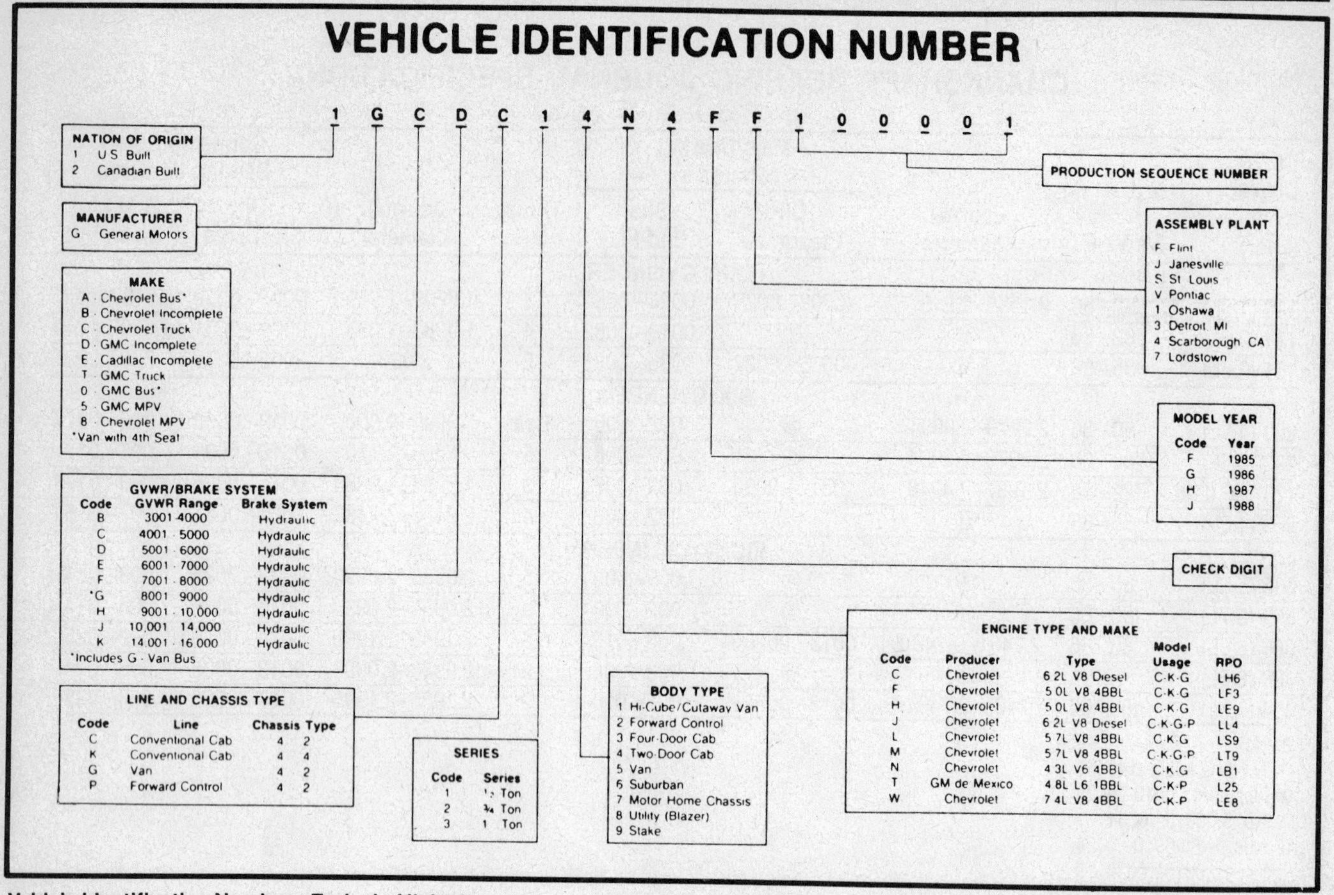

VEHICLE IDENTIFICATION NUMBER
1 G C D C 1 4 N 4 F F 1 0 0 0 0 1
NATION OF ORIGIN
1 U S Built
2 Canadian Built
MANUFACTURER
G General Motors
MAKE
A Chevrolet Bus*
B Chevrolet Incomplete
C Chevrolet Truck
D GMC Incomplete
E Cadillac Incomplete
T GMC Truck
0 GMC Bus*
5 GMC MPV
8 Chevrolet MPV
*Van with 4th Seat
GVWR/BRAKE SYSTEM
Code GVWR Range Brake System
B 3001-4000 Hydraulic
C 4001-5000 Hydraulic
D 5001-6000 Hydraulic
E 6001-7000 Hydraulic
F 7001-8000 Hydraulic
*G 8001-9000 Hydraulic
H 9001-10,000 Hydraulic
J 10,001-14,000 Hydraulic
K 14,001-16,000 Hydraulic
*Includes G-Van Bus
LINE AND CHASSIS TYPE
Code Line Chassis Type
C Conventional Cab 4 2
K Conventional Cab 4 4
G Van 4 2
P Forward Control 4 2
SERIES
Code Series
1 ½ Ton
2 ¾ Ton
3 1 Ton
BODY TYPE
1 Hi-Cube/Cutaway Van
2 Forward Control
3 Four-Door Cab
4 Two-Door Cab
5 Van
6 Suburban
7 Motor Home Chassis
8 Utility (Blazer)
9 Stake
PRODUCTION SEQUENCE NUMBER
ASSEMBLY PLANT
F Flint
J Janesville
S St Louis
V Pontiac
1 Oshawa
3 Detroit MI
4 Scarborough CA
7 Lordstown
MODEL YEAR
Code Year
F 1985
G 1986
H 1987
J 1988
CHECK DIGIT
ENGINE TYPE AND MAKE
Code Producer Type Model Usage RPO
C Chevrolet 6.2L V8 Diesel C-K-G LH6
F Chevrolet 5.0L V8 4BBL C-K-G LF3
H Chevrolet 5.0L V8 4BBL C-K-G LE9
J Chevrolet 6.2L V8 Diesel C-K-G-P LL4
L Chevrolet 5.7L V8 4BBL C-K-G LS9
M Chevrolet 5.7L V8 4BBL C-K-G-P LT9
N Chevrolet 4.3L V6 4BBL C-K-G LB1
T GM de Mexico 4.8L L6 1BBL C-K-P L25
W Chevrolet 7.4L V8 4BBL C-K-P LE8

Vehicle Identification Number—Typical of light duty trucks and vans (© General Motors Corp.)

GM Make Identifiers
GVWR And Brake Systems
Series Code
Cab Type Code
Chassis Type Code
Engine Code
Check Digit
Model Year Code
Plant Code
Sequential Numbers
1 G T D 6 D 4 A 9 E V 5 5 5 0 0 1
1-United States
2-Canada
G-General Motors
T-GMC
C-CHEV.
D-GMC Incomplete vehicle
8-Chev Incomplete vehicle
Code GVWR Range Brake System
A 9001-10000 Hydraulic
B 10001-14000 Hydraulic
C 14001-16000 Hydraulic
D 14001-16000 Air
E 16001-19500 Hydraulic
F 16001-19500 Air
G 19501-23500 Hydraulic
H 19501-23500 Air
J 23501-26000 Hydraulic
K 23501-26000 Air
L 26001-33000 Hydraulic
M 26001-33000 Air
N 33001-40500 Hydraulic
P 33001-40500 Air
R 40501-48500 Hydraulic
S 40501-48500 Air
T 48501-58000 Air
CODE SERIES
4 4500
5 5000
6 6000
7 7000
CODE DESCRIPTION CAB TYPE
D Medium Conv. 97.5 BBC
P Bus Chassis Flat Back Cowl
S Buss Chassis other than Flat Back Cowl
T Forward Control Chassis Only
2 Medium Conv. Steel 97.5-other than Cab Chassis
Code Description
1 4X2 2 Axles 1 Driving
2 4X4 2 Axles 2 Driving
4 6X4 3 Axles 2 Driving
1984
V-Pontiac
5-London
CODE DESCRIPTION
A GM 5.7 Liter V8 Gasoline
B GM 6.0 Liter V8 Gasoline
E GM 7.0 Liter V8 Gasoline
F GM 8.2N Diesel
G GM 8.2T Diesel
L Deutz BF6L913 Diesel
T GM 4.8 Liter Gasoline
Y Caterpillar 3208 Diesel

Vehicle Identification Number—Typical of medium and heavy duty trucks (© General Motors Corp.)

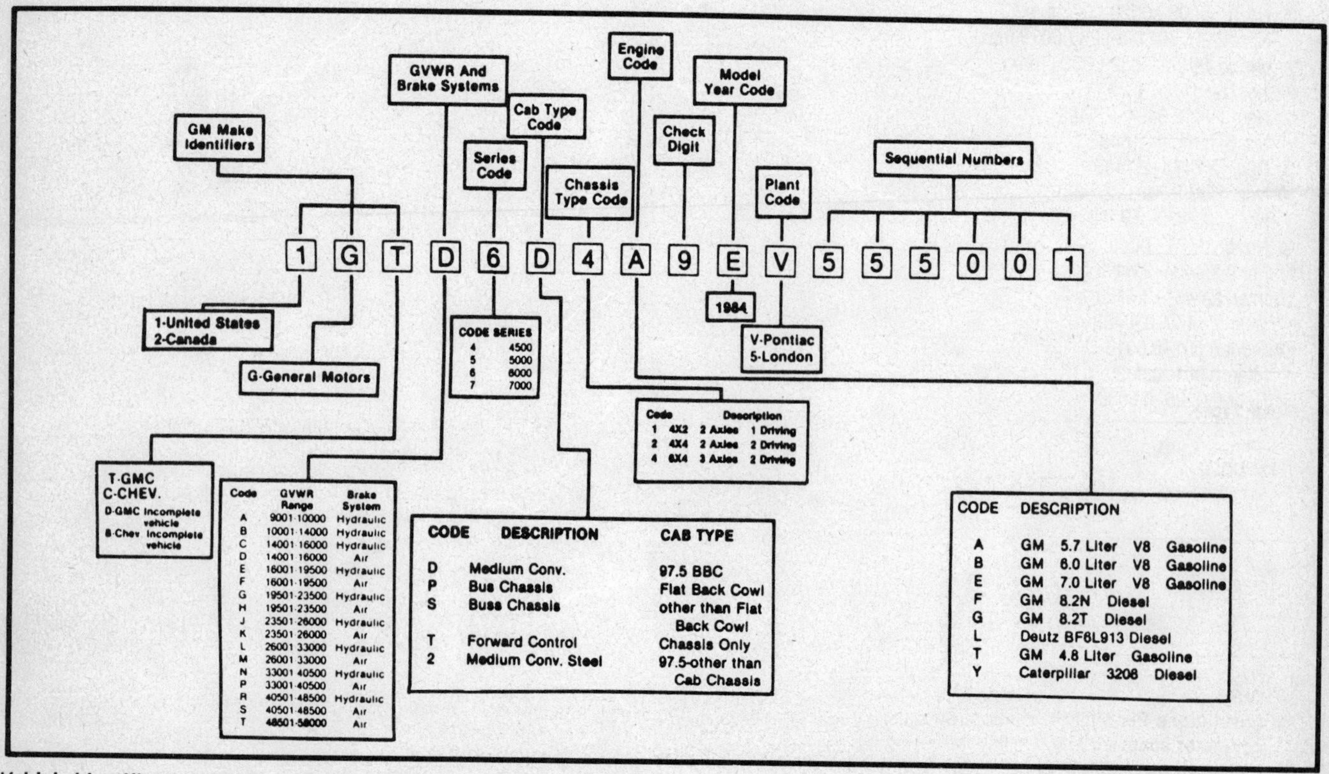

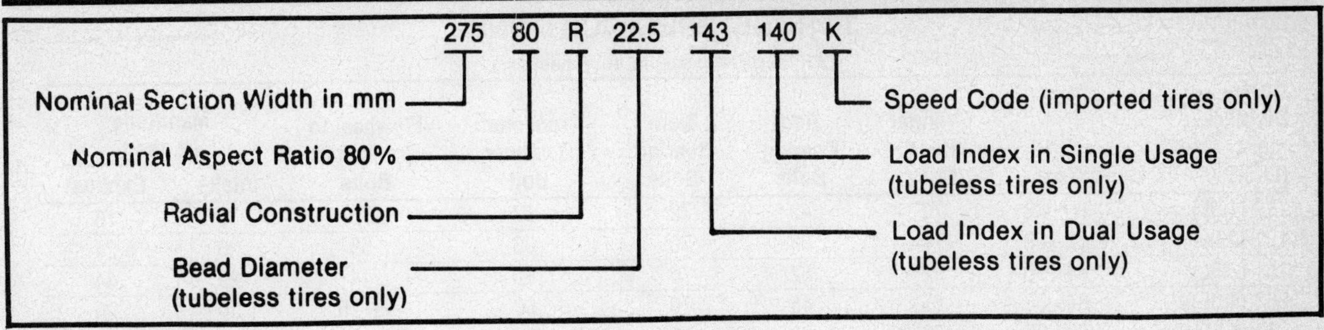

Metric radial tire identification

METRIC RADIAL TIRE LOAD AND INFLATION TABLE

Loads Per Axle (lbs. and kg) at Different Pressures 2 Tires: (S) Single, 4 Tires: (D) Dual

(Inflation Pressures psi and kPa)

(Tubeless) Tire Size and Ply Rating		psi	60	65	70	75	80	85	90	95	100	105	110	115	120
		kPa	410	450	480	520	550	590	620	660	690	720	760	790	830
255/70R22.5 136/133	lbs.	S	6,175	6,590	7,000	7,410	7,820	8,235	8,645	9,055	9,470	9,880			
		D	11,460	12,205	12,950	13,695	14,440	15,180	15,930	16,670	17,415	18,160			
	kg	S	2 800	2 990	3 175	3 360	3 550	3 735	3 920	4 110	4 295	4 480			
		D	5 200	5 535	5 875	6 210	6 550	6 885	7 225	7 560	7 900	8 240			
275/80R22.5 143/140	lbs.	S			8,870	9,385	9,900	10,430	10,940	11,510	12,010				
		D			15,970	16,895	17,820	18,770	19,690	20,720	22,040				
	kg	S			4 023	4 256	4 490	4 730	4 961	5 220	5 447				
		D			7 243	7 662	8 082	8 512	8 930	9 397	9 995				
13/75R22.5	lbs.	S						12,090	12,730	13,360	13,940	14,620	15,220	16,000	
		D						21,670	22,830	23,960	24,990	26,210	27,290	28,640	
	kg	S						5 480	5 770	6 060	6 320	6 630	6 900	7 260	
		D						9 830	10 360	10 870	11 340	11 890	12 380	12 990	
315/80R22.5 154/149	lbs.	S			10,800	11,430	12,090	12,810	13,350	13,990	14,620	15,260	15,900	16,540	
		D			18,700	19,800	20,900	22,000	23,120	24,220	25,320	26,420	27,540	28,640	
	kg	S			4 900	5 180	5 470	5 760	6 050	6 350	6 630	6 920	7 210	7 500	
		D			8 480	8 980	9 480	9 980	10 490	10 990	11 480	11 980	12 490	12 990	
275/80R24.5 143/140	lbs.	S			8,870	9,385	9,900	10,430	10,940	11,510	12,010				
		D			15,970	16,895	17,820	18,770	19,690	20,720	22,040				
	kg	S			4 023	4 256	4 490	4 730	4 961	5 220	5 447				
		D			7 243	7 662	8 082	8 512	8 930	9 397	9 995				
285/75R24.5	lbs.	S								5,215	5,425	5,675	5,840	6,045	**6,175(G)**
		D								5,025	5,205	5,400	**5,675(G)**		
	kg	S								2 365	2 460	2 574	2 649	2 742	2 800
		D								2 279	2 360	2 449	2 574		
295/75R22.5	lbs.	S								5,155	5,370	5,575	5,780	5,980	**6,175(G)**
		D								4,970	5,155	5,340	**6,765(G)**		
	kg	S								2 338	2 435	2 528	2 621	2 712	2 800
		D								2 254	2 338	2 422	3 068		
(Tube Type)															
13/80R20	lbs.	S					11,380	11,990	12,570	13,220	13,720	14,420	15,000	16,000	
		D					20,490	22,050	23,170	24,300	25,420	26,500	27,630	28,640	
	kg	S					5 160	5 440	5 700	6 000	6 240	6 540	6 800	7 260	
		D					9 290	10 000	10 510	11 020	11 530	12 020	12 530	12 990	
14/80R20	lbs.	S						13,420	14,040	14,790	15,400	16,080	16,790	17,750	18,080
		D						24,180	25,300	26,640	27,750	28,970	30,250	31,970	32,560
	kg.	S						6 090	6 370	6 710	6 990	7 290	7 620	8 050	8 200
		D						10 970	11 480	12 080	12 590	13 140	13 720	14 500	14 770

NOTES:

1. Revolutions Per Mile: If a change over the Pilote tires changes the revolutions per mile of the existing wheels by more than 3%, and odometer adapter is recommended.
2. Letters in parenthesis denote load range for which bold face loads are maximum. (G) replaces 14 ply rating.

TORQUE SPECIFICATIONS

(All measurements in foot pounds.)

Cu. In. Displacement (Liter)	Year	Cylinder Head Bolts	Rod Bearing Bolts	Main Bearing Bolts	Crankshaft Balancer Bolt	Flywheel to Crankshaft Bolts	Manifolds (ft. lbs.)	
							Intake	Exhaust
119 (1.9L)	'82–'86	72	43	72	87	76	30	16
121 (2.0L)	'82–'86	70	38	70	85	55	26	24
151 (2.5L)	'84–'86	92	32	70	160	44	29	44
263 (4.3L)	'84–'86	65	45	70	60	55–75	30	20
250 (4.1L)	'80–'86	95	35	65	Pressed on	60	①	①
292 (4.8L)	'80–'86	95	40	65	60	110	①	①
173 (2.8L)	'82–'86	70	37	70	84	55	23	25
305 (V8) (5.0L)	'80–'86	65	45	80②	60	60	30	20
350 (5.7L)	'80–'86	65	45	80②	60	60	30	20③
366 (6.0L)	'80–'86	80	④	105	85	65	30	17
454 (7.4L)	'80–'86	80	50	110	85	65	30	20
400 (6.6L)	'80	65	45	70	80	60	30	30

① Exhaust 30 ft. lbs.
Exhaust to intake 45 ft. lbs.
Manifold to cylinder head 40 ft. lbs.
② Intermediate outer bolts 70 ft. lbs.
③ Inside bolts 30 ft. lbs.
④ 7/16" 67–73 ft. lbs.

FRONT END ALIGNMENT

How To Determine Caster Angle

ALL MODELS – EXCEPT S/T TRUCKS AND ASTRO VANS

1. With the vehicle on a level surface, determine the frame angle using a bubble protractor or clinometer.
2. Determine the caster angle reading from the alignment equipment.
3. To determine the actual (corrected) caster angle with various frame angles and caster angle readings from the alignment equipment, one of the following rules will apply from the next steps.
4. Example A – A "down in the rear" frame angle must be subtracted from a positive caster angle reading.
5. Example B – An "up in rear" frame angle must be added to a positive caster angle reading.
6. Example C – A "down in rear" frame angle must be added to a negative caster angle reading.
7. Example D – An "up in rear" frame angle must be subtracted from a negative caster angle reading.
8. Dimension "A" or "BC"is obtained by measuring 90 degrees from the lower surface of the crossmember and to the inboard rear corner of the jounce bumper bracket.
9. Using dimension "A"or"BC" and the caster, camber and wheel toe–in chart, find the recommended caster angle.

NOTE: If the actual corrected caster angle does not correspond to a recommended caster angle within ± 1 degree, make the necessary shim changes to bring the actual corrected caster angle in line with the recommended caster angle.

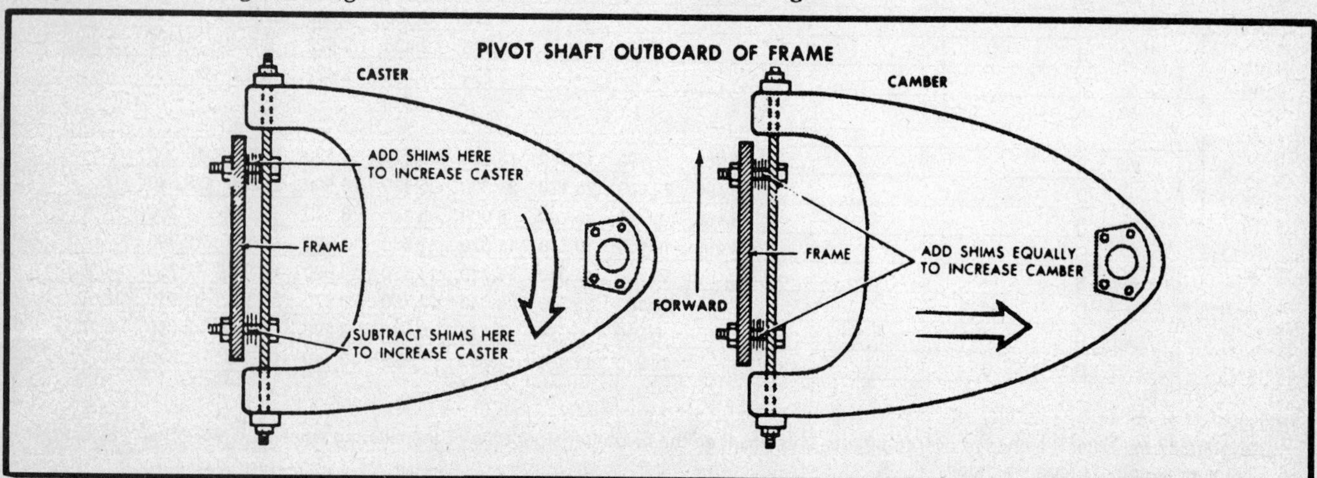

Typical caster, camber shim adjustment procedure (© General Motors Corp.)

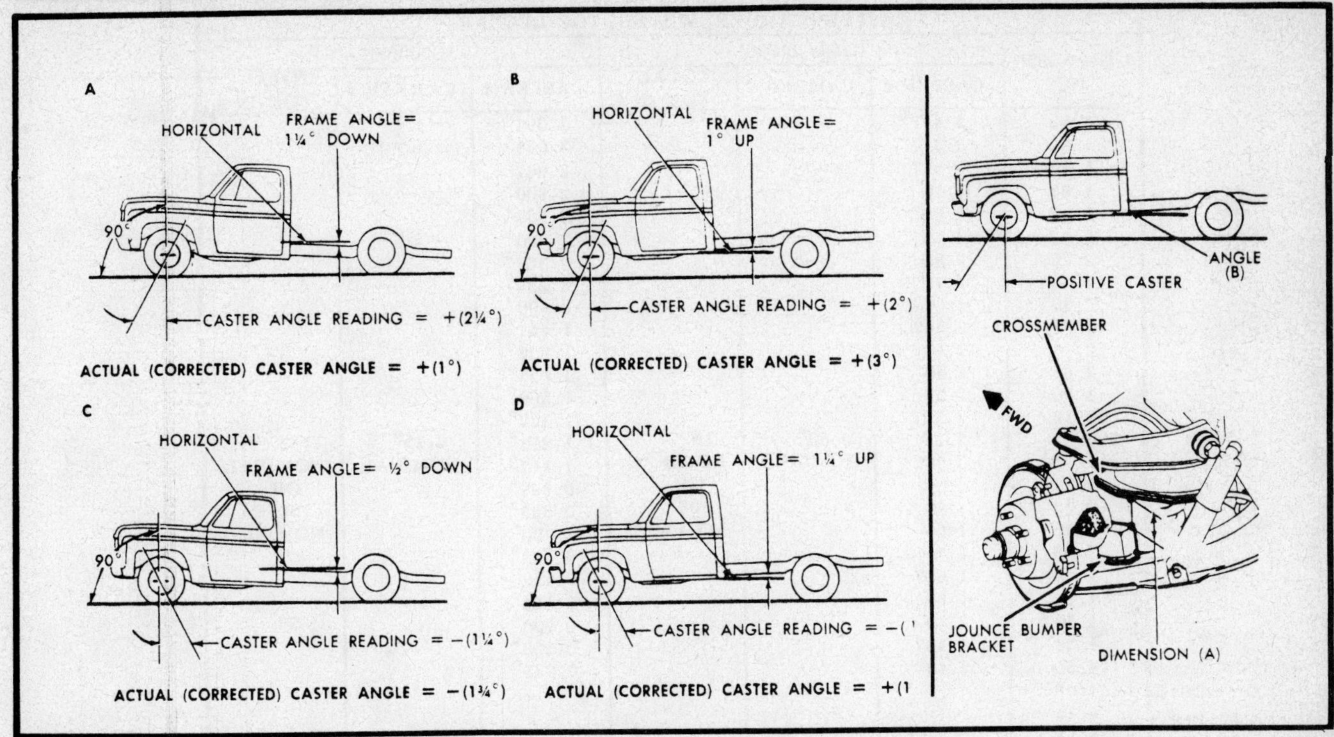

CASTER, CAMBER, WHEEL, TOE-IN CHART •

DIM. "BC" (C Models only)	C100(00)			C200+300(00)			K100+200+300(00)		
	CASTER #	CAMBER #	TOTAL TOE-IN #	CASTER #	CAMBER #	TOTAL TOE-IN #	CASTER #	CAMBER #	TOTAL TOE-IN #
2.50	3.65 •	.70° NOMINAL	.18 IN. NOMINAL OR .366 NOMINAL	1.507	0° 15' NOMINAL .25°	.366 NOMINAL	+8° NOMINAL (Reference no means of adjustment provided)	+1° 30' NOMINAL (Reference no means of adjustment provided)	0' NOMINAL
2.62	3.55			1.370					
2.75	3.45			1.224					
2.88	3.30			1.061					
3.00	3.15			.928					
3.12	3.00			.766					
3.25	2.85			.612					
3.38	2.75			.474					
3.50	2.60			.328					
3.62	2.45			.186					
3.75	2.35			.114					
3.88	2.20			.046					
4.00	2.05			-.011					
4.12	1.90			-.084					
4.25	1.75			-.152					
4.38	1.65			-.605					
4.50	1.50			-.746					
4.62	1.35			-.866					
4.75	1.25			-.999					
4.88	1.10			-1.126					
5.00	1.00			-1.246					
5.12	.90			-1.350					
5.25	.75			-1.440					
5.38	.60			-1.542					
5.50	.50			-1.638					
5.62	.35			-1.747					
5.75	.25			-1.849					
5.88	.15			-1.944					
6.00	0								

CONVERSION TABLE FOR MINUTES TO DECIMAL OF DEGREES

Min.	Deg.	Min.	Deg.	Min.	Deg.	Min.	Deg.	Min.	Deg.
1'	.0167°	13'	.2167°	25'	.4167°	37'	.6167°	49'	.8167°
2'	.0333	14'	.2333	26'	.4333	38'	.6333	50'	.8333
3'	.0500	15'	.2500	27'	.4500	39'	.6500	51'	.8500
4'	.0667	16'	.2667	28'	.4667	40'	.6667	52'	.8667
5'	.0833	17'	.2833	29'	.4833	41'	.6833	53'	.8833
6'	.1000	18'	.3000	30'	.5000	42'	.7000	54'	.9000
7'	.1167	19'	.3167	31'	.5167	43'	.7167	55'	.9167
8'	.1333	20'	.3333	32'	.5333	44'	.7333	56'	.9333
9'	.1500	21'	.3500	33'	.5500	45'	.7500	57'	.9500
10'	.1667	22'	.3667	34'	.5667	46'	.7667	58'	.9667
11'	.1833	23'	.3833	35'	.5833	47'	.7833	59'	.9833
12'	.2000	24'	.4000	36'	.6000	48'	.8000		

• Use in conjunction with Tolerances Chart at right.
See appropriate Alignment Sheet.
⊕ Use with Caster, Camber, Wheel Toe-in Chart above.
★ Left & Right to be Equal within 0°30'
◆ Left & Right to be Equal within 1°0'

CASTER, CAMBER, WHEEL TOE-IN ALIGNMENT SETTING TOLERANCES C000(00) ⊕

	FACTORY		FIELD SERVICE (Ref.)	
	TARGET (Ref.)	AUDIT (Eng. Spec.)	CHECK	RE-SET
CASTER	±.5°★	±1.0° ◆	±1.0° ◆	±.5°★
CAMBER	±.5°★	±.75° ◆	±.75° ◆	±.5°★
TOTAL TOE-IN #	±.06 IN. ±.116°	±.12 IN. ±.232°	±.12 IN. ±.232°	±.06 IN. ±.116°

Caster, camber, toe-in chart for 1985 and later, 2 and 4 wheel drive, full size pick-up trucks, Blazer/Jimmy and Suburban models (© General Motors Corp.)

CASTER, CAMBER, WHEEL, TOE-IN CHART•

DIMENSION "BC"	G100+200(00) CASTER ♯	G100+200(00) CAMBER ♯	G100+200(00) TOTAL TOE-IN ♯	G300(00) CASTER ♯	G300(00) CAMBER ♯	G300(00) TOTAL TOE-IN ♯
1.50	3.417°			3.094°		
1.62	3.317°			3.034°		
1.75	3.217°			2.967°		
1.88	3.10°			2.800°		
2.00	3.00°			2.667°		
2.12	2.95°			2.500°		
2.25	2.85°			2.367°		
2.38	2.75°			2.233°		
2.50	2.667°			2.100°		
2.62	2.567°			1.967°		
2.75	2.48°			1.833°		
2.88	2.40°			1.633°		
3.00	2.33			1.500°		
3.12	2.317°			1.367°		
3.25	2.15	0.50° NOMINAL	.18" NOMINAL OR .36° NOMINAL	1.233°	0.25° NOMINAL	.18" NOMINAL OR .36° NOMINAL
3.38	2.066			1.117°		
3.50	2.00			0.967°		
3.62	1.88			0.833°		
3.75	1.80			0.700°		
3.88	1.73			0.583°		
4.00	1.667			0.450°		
4.12	1.60			0.333°		
4.25	1.53			0.200°		
4.38	1.467			0.100°		
4.50	1.40			-0.033°		
4.62						
4.75						
4.88						
5.00						
5.12						
5.25						
5.38						
5.50						
5.62						

CASTER, CAMBER, WHEEL TOE-IN ALIGNMENT SETTING TOLERANCES ⊕

	FACTORY	
	TARGET (Ref)	AUDIT (Eng Spec)
CASTER ♯	±0.50° ★	±1.00° ◆
CAMBER ♯	±0.50° ★	±0.75° ◆
TOTAL TOE-IN♯	±.06 IN. ±.116°	±.12 IN. ±.232°
	FIELD SERVICE (Ref)	
	CHECK	RE-SET
CASTER ♯	±1.00° ◆	±0.50° ★
CAMBER ♯	±0.75° ◆	±0.50° ★
TOTAL TOE-IN♯	±.12 IN. ±.232°	±.06 IN. ±.116°

- • Use in conjunction with Tolerances Chart above.
- ♯ See appropriate Alignment Sheet
- ⊕ Use with Caster, Camber, Wheel Toe-in Chart at left.
- ★ Left & Right to be Equal within 0.50°.
- ◆ Left & Right to be Equal within 1.00°.

Caster, camber, toe-in chart for 1985 and later full size Van models (© General Motors Corp.)

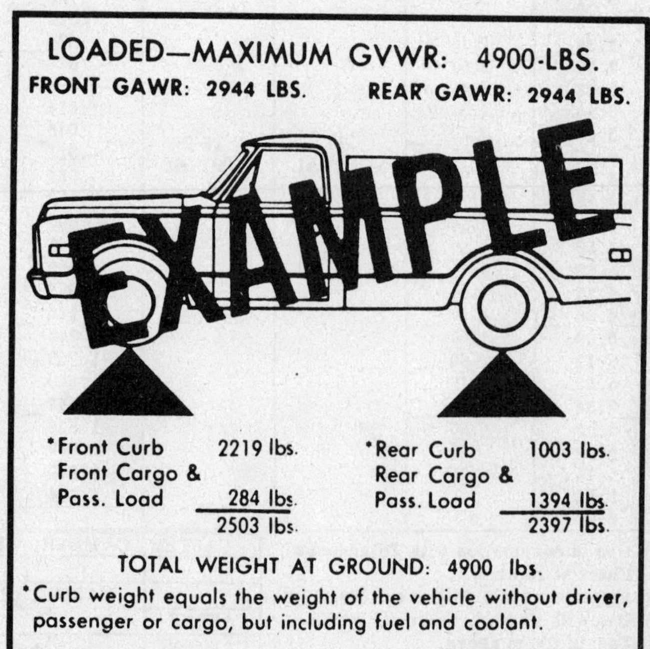

LOADED—MAXIMUM GVWR: 4900-LBS.
FRONT GAWR: 2944 LBS.
REAR GAWR: 2944 LBS.
EXAMPLE
*Front Curb 2219 lbs.
Front Cargo & Pass. Load 284 lbs.
2503 lbs.
*Rear Curb 1003 lbs.
Rear Cargo & Pass. Load 1394 lbs.
2397 lbs.
TOTAL WEIGHT AT GROUND: 4900 lbs.
*Curb weight equals the weight of the vehicle without driver, passenger or cargo, but including fuel and coolant.

Typical vehicle loading condition (© General Motors Corp.)

WHEEL ALIGNMENT SPECIFICATIONS
'80–'84 Light Duty Trucks

Vehicle Identification		Caster @ Height Measurement (Degrees) Suspension Height Measurement							Camber (Degrees)				
Chevrolet Year Model (A)	GMC Model (A)	1 1/2	2	2 1/2	3	3 1/2	3 3/4	4	Min.	Pref.	Max.	Toe-In (Inches)	Toe-In (Millimeters)
1982–84													
S-10(4 × 2)	S-15(4 × 2)	①	①	①	①	①	①	①	0	13/16	1 5/8	1/8	3.2
S-10(4 × 4)	S-15(4 × 4)	①	①	①	①	①	①	①	0	13/16	1 5/8	1/8	3.2
1982–84													
C-10	C-1500	—	—	3 5/8	3 1/8	2 5/8	2 3/8	2	0	11/16	1 3/8	3/16 ± 1/8	4.8 ± 3.2
C-20,30	C-2500,3500	—	—	1 1/2	1 5/16	5/16	1/8	0	−1/2	3/16	7/8	3/16 ± 1/8	4.8 ± 3.2
1982–84													
K-10,20	K-1500,2500	—	—	8	8	8	8	8	5/16	1	1 11/16	3/16 ± 1/8	4.8 ± 3.2
K-30	K-3500	—	—	8	8	8	8	8	−3/16	1/2	1 3/16	3/16 ± 1/8	4.8 ± 3.2
1982–84													
G-10,20	G-1500,2500	3 1/2	3 1/8	2 11/16	2 3/8	2 1/8	1 15/16	1 7/8	−3/16	1/2	1 3/16	3/16 ± 1/8	4.8 ± 3.2
G-30	G-3500	2 7/8	2 3/16	1 5/8	1	1/2	3/16	0	−1/2	3/16	7/8	3/16 ± 1/8	4.8 ± 3.2
1982–84													
P-10	P1500	—	—	2 5/16	1 11/16	1 3/16	15/16	5/8	−1/2	3/16	7/8	3/16 ± 1/8	4.8 ± 3.2
P-20,30	P-2500,3500	—	—	2 5/16	1 11/16	1 3/16	15/16	5/8	−1/2	3/16	7/8	3/16 ± 1/8	4.8 ± 3.2
1982–84													
P30 Motor Home	P-3500 Motor Home	—	—	5 1/2	5	4 3/8	4 1/8	3 7/8	−1/2	3/16	7/8	5/16 ± 1/8	7.9 ± 3.2
1980–81													
G-10,20	G-1500,2500	3 1/2	3 1/8	2 11/16	2 13/32	2 1/8	1 13/16	—	−3/16	1/2	1 3/16	3/16 ± 1/8	4.8 ± 3.2
G-30	G-3500	2 3/16	2 3/16	1 5/8	1	1/2	0	—	−1/2	3/16	7/8	3/16 ± 1/8	4.8 ± 3.2
1980–81													
C-10	C-1500	—	—	2 13/32	1 13/16	1 3/16	11/16	3/16	−1/2	3/16	1 7/8	3/16 ± 1/8	4.8 ± 3.2
C-20,30	C-2500,3500	—	—	1 1/2	23/32	5/16	0	−11/16	−1/2	3/16	7/8	3/16 ± 1/8	4.8 ± 3.2
K-10,20	K-1500,2500	—	—	8	8	8	8	8	5/16	1	1 11/16	0 ± 1/8	0 ± 3.2
K-30	K-3500	—	—	8	8	8	8	8	−3/16	1/2	1 3/16	0 ± 1/8	0 ± 3.2
P-10	P-1500	—	—	2 5/16	1 11/16	1 3/16	5/8	1/8	−1/2	3/16	7/8	3/16 ± 1/8	4.8 ± 3.2
P-20,30(B)	P-2500,3500(B)	—	2 23/32	2 11/16	1 11/16	1 3/16	5/8	3/16	−1/2	3/16	7/8	3/16 ± 1/8	4.8 ± 3.2

With vehicle level, measure frame angle with a bubble protractor. Record the suspension height measurement.
a. Subtract an up-in-rear frame angle from a positive caster specification.
b. Subtract a down-in-rear frame angle from a negative caster specification.
c. Add an up-in-rear frame angle to a negative caster specification.
d. Add a down-in-rear frame angle to a positive caster specification.
(A) Vehicle height must be checked and corrected before alignment is performed.
① 1° Min. 2° Pref. 3° Max.

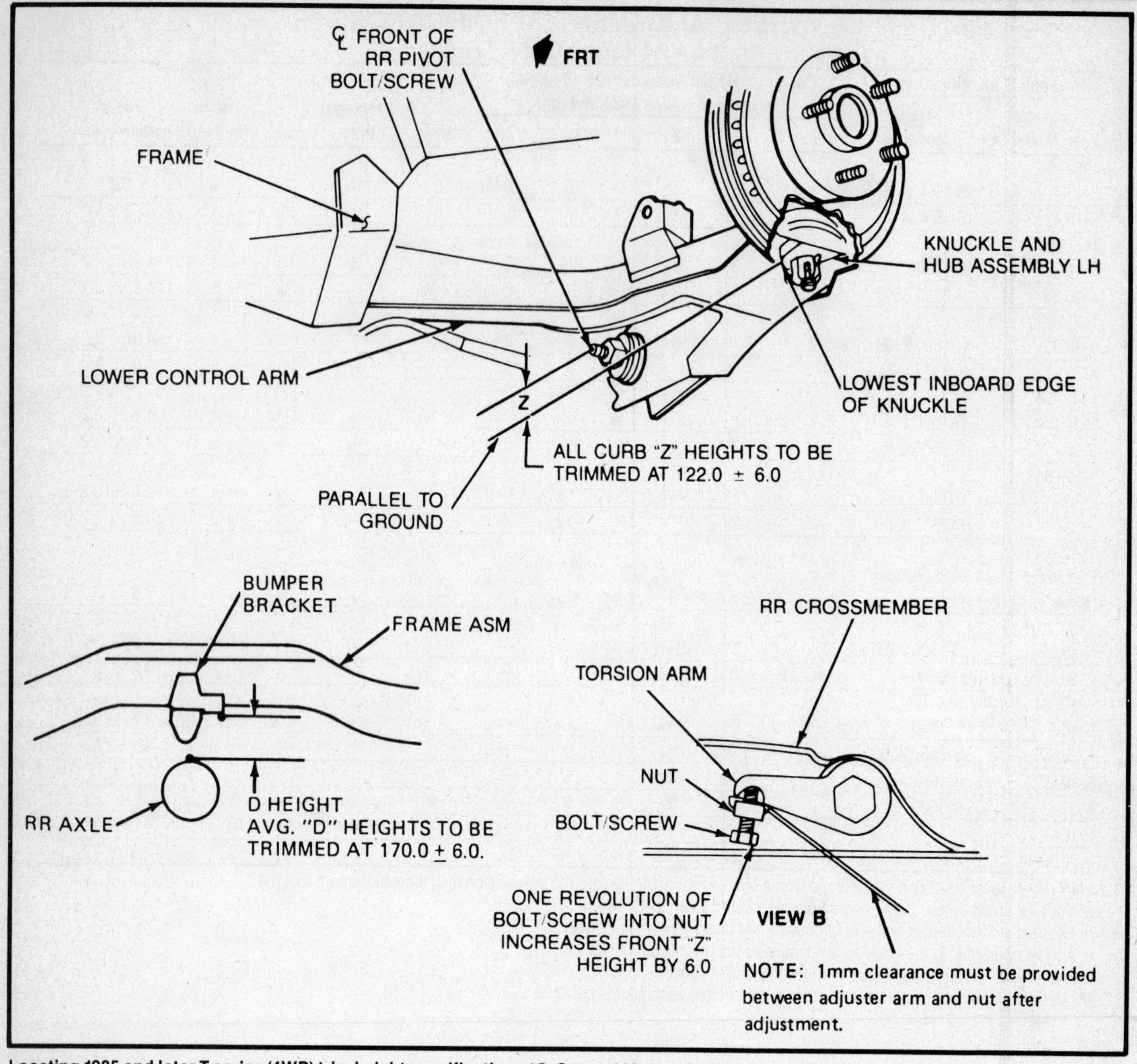

Locating 1985 and later T series (4WD) trim height specifications (© General Motors Corp.)

FRONT SUSPENSION ALIGNMENT
1985 and Later

To Align (A):	Service Checking	Service Setting
	T SERIES (4WD)	
Caster	+2.0° ± 1.0° (C)	+2.0 ± .50° (B)
Camber	+.8° ± .80° (C)	+.8° ± .50° (B)
Toe-in (degrees-per wheel)	+.15° ± .10° (D)	+.15° ± .05° (D)

Front Suspension Alignment 1985 and Later

To Align (A):	Service Checking	Service Setting
S-SERIES TRUCKS AND BLAZERS		
Caster	+2.0° ± 1.0° (C)	+2.0° ± .50° (B)
Camber	+.8° ± .80° (C)	+.8° ± .50° (B)
Toe-In (Degrees-Per Wheel)	+.15° ± .10° (D)	+.15° ± .05° (D)
ASTRO VANS		
Caster①	+2.7° ± 1.0° (C)	+2.7° ± .50° (B)
Camber	+.94° ± .80° (C)	+.94° ± .50° (B)
Toe (Degrees-Per Wheel)	+.15° ± .10° (D)	+.15° ± .05° (D)

① Caster set relative to ground.

S–SERIES TRUCKS (2WD) AND ASTRO VANS

To find trim height specifications ("Z" dimension), lift the front bumper of the vehicle up approximately 38.0mm. Gently remove hands and let vehicle settle. Repeat twice for a total of three times. Measure dimension "Z" each time. Dimension "Z" is the difference between an imaginary horizontal line from the lower inboard corner of a ball joint and an imaginary horizotal line from the centerline of the lower arm inner bolt head. "Z" dimension is the average of the high and low measurements.

T–SERIES TRUCKS (4WD)

To find trim height specifications ("Z" dimension), lift the front bummer of the vehicle up approximately 38.0mm. Gently remove hands and let vehicle settle. Repeat twice for a total of three times. Measure dimension "Z" each time. Push the front bumper down approximately 38.0mm. Gently remove the hands and let the vehicle rise on its own. Repeat the procedure twice more for a total of three times, measuring "Z" dimension each time. True height is the average of the high and the low measurements. "Z " dimension is the difference between an imaginary line from the knuckle and the left hand hub assembly and an imaginary line from the center of the right rear pivot bolt/screw on the lower control arm. To adjust the torsion rod, a bolt is provided to trim the curb height at 122.0 ± 6.0mm from the lower imaginary lower "Z" line.

NOTE: 1mm clearance must be provided between the adjuster arm and nut after the torsion bar adjustment.

ELECTRICAL

Distributor

Detailed information on direction of distributor rotation, cylinder numbering, firing order, air gap, timing, spark plugs and idle speed will be found in the Specifications section. Overhaul and diagnosis procedures are found in the Unit Repair section.

NOTE: Specifications listed on underhood Vehicle Emission Information label should be checked before any adjustment. Label values should be used, if different from specification charts.

H.E.I. SYSTEM

All V8, V6 and Inline 6 cylinder General Motors Corp. gasoline engines use the High Energy Ignition (HEI) system, combining all ignition components in one unit. The coil is in the distributor cap and connects directly to the rotor. There is no resistor wire from the ignition switch to the distributor. The module and pick-up coil replace the conventional breaker points. The module automatically controls the dwell, stretching it with increased engine speed. The system also features a longer spark duration due to the greater amount of energy stored in the primary coil. The electronic module is replaced if defective. Centrifugal and vacuum advance mechanisms are used on distributors without Electronic Spark Control (ESC).

Some engines use an HEI/EST distributor. All spark timing changes in the HEI/EST distributor are accomplished electronically by the Electronic Control Module (ECM), which monitors information from various engine sensors, computes the desired spark timing and signals the distributor to change the ignition timing accordingly. When this system is used, no vacuum or mechanical advances are used. An additional electronic control (ESC) is used on vehicles equipped with an LE9 (H in VIN number)engine. The Electronic Spark Control system is a closed loop system that controls engine detonation by modifying the spark advance when detonation occurs, after which the spark control will revert to EST. The amount of re-

WHEEL ALIGNMENT SPECIFICATIONS
Medium And Heavy Duty Trucks

Axle Model (Lbs. Rate) ⑩	Year	Axle⑩	Camber②③		Caster②③	Toe-In④⑥⑦	Angles Turning		King Pin Inclination	
			L.H.	R.H.			Inside	Outside	Left	Right
5000	'80–'86	F-050	+1½°	+1½°	+2½°	⅛"–¼"	⑤	⑤	7°10′	7°10′
5500	'80–'86	F-055	+1½°	+1½°	+2½°	⅛"–¼"	⑤	⑤	7°10′	7°10′
7000	'80–'86	F-070	+1½°	+1½°	+2½°	⅛"–¼°	⑤	⑤	7°10′	7°10′
9000	'80–'86	F-090	+¼°	−¼°	+2½°	⅛"–¼"	⑤	⑤	5¾°	6¼°
9000	'80–'86	F-120	+¼°	+¼°	+2½°	⅛"–¼"	⑤	⑤	5¾°	6½°⑨
					STEEL TILT (T)					
7000	'80–'86	F-070	+1½°	+1½°	+4°	⅛"–¼"	⑤	⑤	7°10′	7°10′
9000	'80–'86	F-090⑧	+½°	−¼°	+4°	⅛"–¼"	⑤	⑤	5¾"	6¼°
9000	'80–'86	F-120⑧	+½°	+¼°	+4°	⅛"–¼"	⑤	⑤	5¾°	6¼°
1200	'80–'86	F-120⑧	+½°	+¼°	+4°	⅛"–¼"	⑤	⑤	5¾°	6¼°
	'80–'86	FL931	+¾°	+¼°	0 + 1½°	⅛"–¼"	⑤	⑤	5¾°	6¼°
	'80–'86	FF933	+¾°	+¾°	0 + 1½°	⅛"–¼"	⑤	⑤	5¾°	6¼°

With vehicle level, measure frame angle with a bubble protractor. Record the suspension height measurement.

a. Subtract an up-in-rear frame angle from a positive caster specification.

b. Subtract a down-in-rear frame angle from a negative caster specification.

c. Add an up-in-rear frame angle to a negative caster specification.

d. Add a down-in-rear frame angle to a positive caster specification.

(A) Vehicle height must be checked and corrected before alignment is performed.

① Not used

② Caster and camber must not vary more than ½° from side to side.

③ A reading of ± ½° from specified setting is acceptable.

④ Always set toe-in after caster and camber adjustments.

⑤ Adjustment to stop screw must provide ⅝" minimum clearance of tire with any chassis components, regardless of maximum turning angles.

⑥ Toe-in measurements must be made at the horizontal axis of the wheel. If, for any reason, the vehicle has been jacked up, it will be necessary to neutralize the front suspension. Roll the vehicle forward 12 to 15 feet. By doing so, all tolerances in the front suspension will be taken up, and the suspension will then be in normal operating position (neutralized).

⑦ Vehicles equipped with steel belted radial tires will have zero toe-in.

⑧ 12,000 lbs. axle rated at 9,000 lbs.

⑨ '80–'82, right side king-pin-inclination is 5¾°.

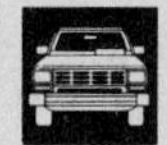

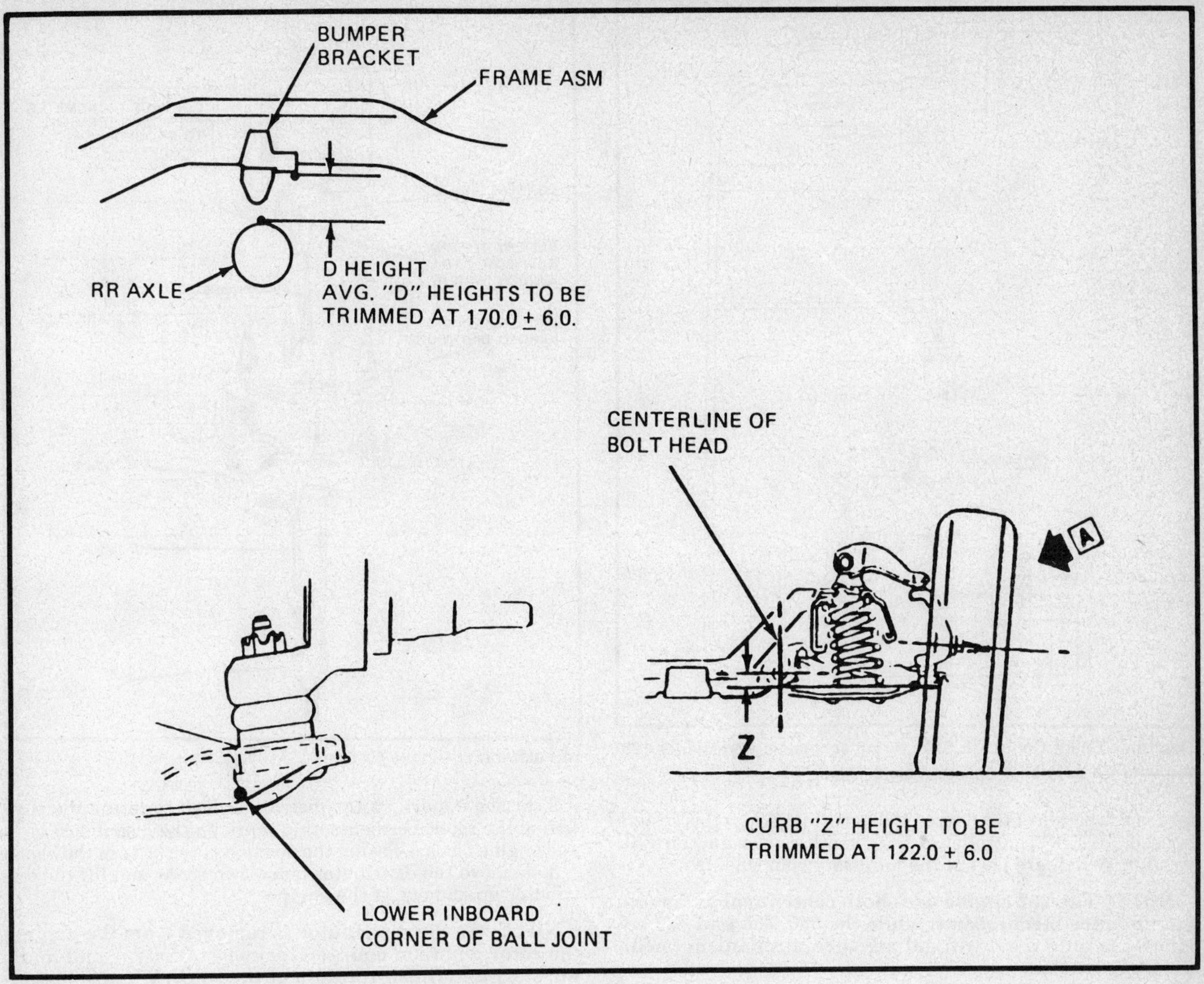

BUMPER BRACKET
FRAME ASM
RR AXLE
D HEIGHT
AVG. "D" HEIGHTS TO BE TRIMMED AT 170.0 ± 6.0.
CENTERLINE OF BOLT HEAD
A
Z
CURB "Z" HEIGHT TO BE TRIMMED AT 122.0 ± 6.0
LOWER INBOARD CORNER OF BALL JOINT

Locating 1985 and later S series trim height specifications (© General Motors Corp.)

CENTERLINE OF BOLT HEAD
℄ WHEELS
A
Z
VERTICAL
POSITIVE CAMBER
LOWER INBOARD CORNER OF BALL JOINT

Locating 1985 and later Astro van trim height specifications (© General Motors Corp.)

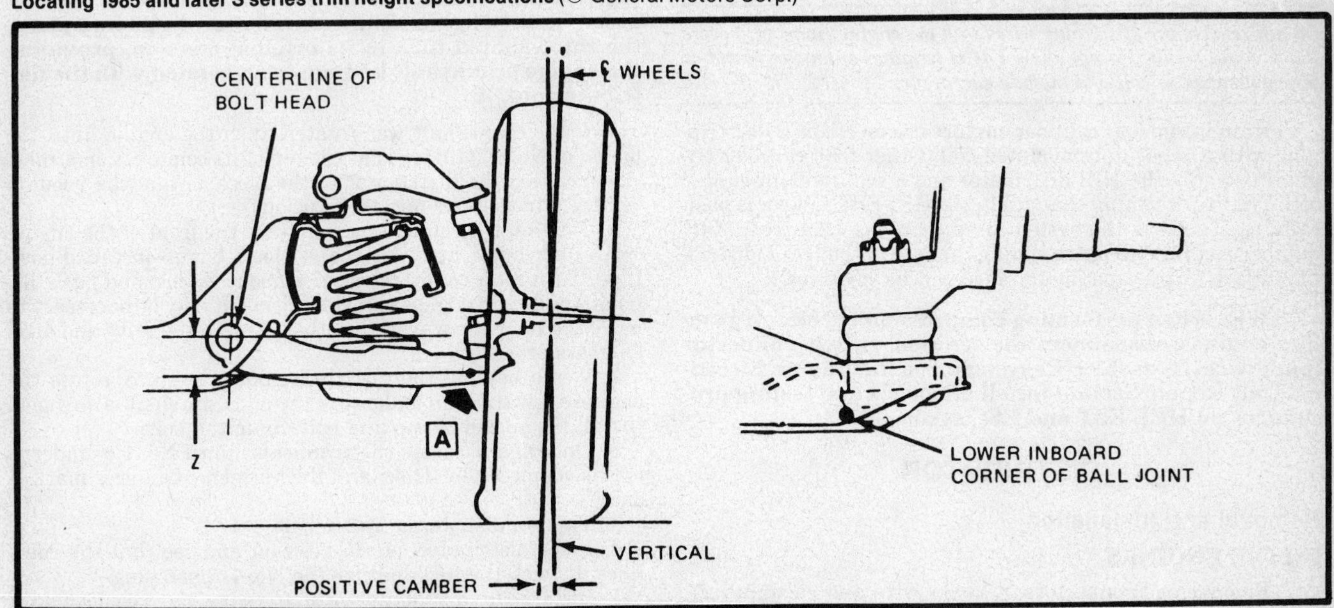

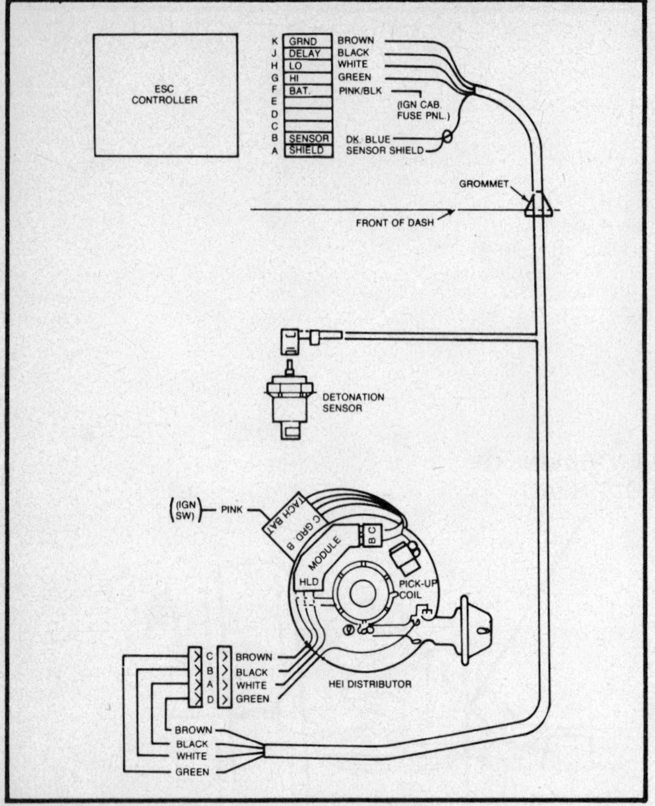

Electronic Spark Control (E.S.C.) wiring schematic—typical for 1981 and later CK series (© General Motors Corp.)

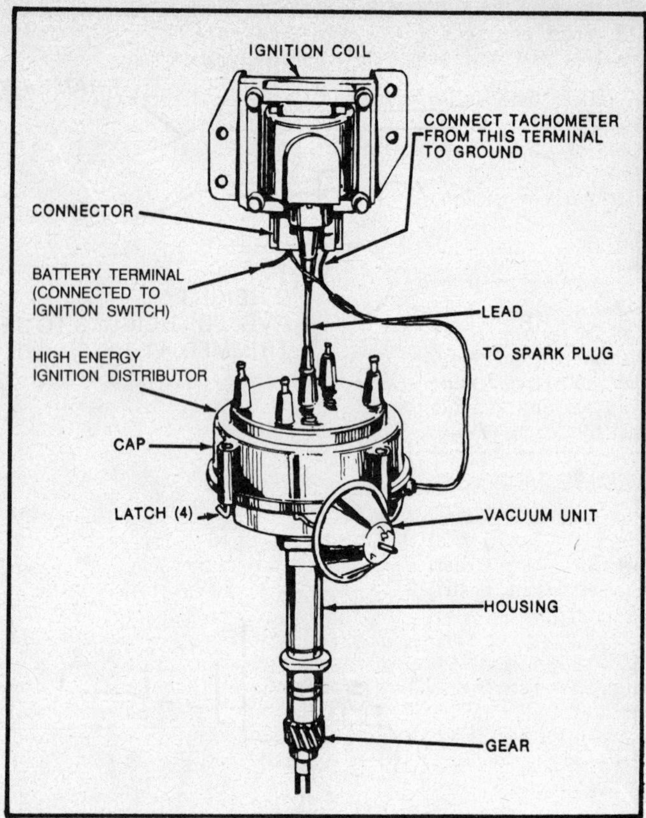

HEI distributor—inline (© General Motors Corp.)

tard is a function of the degree of detonation. When this system is used, an ESC controller, a ESC knock sensor and an ESC vacuum switch are part of the necessary components.

NOTE: The 292 engine uses both centrifugal and vacuum advance mechanisms, while the 350, 366 and 427 engines use only a centrifugal advance mechanism (medium duty trucks).

CAUTION

Do not remove the spark plug wires with the engine running. Severe shock could result. Do not allow TACH terminal to touch ground or severe damage to coil and module can occur.

Certain inline four cylinder engines use an HEI/EST distributor with a separately mounted coil. Other four cylinder engines use only the HEI distributor and a separately mounted coil. The spark timing changes in the HEI/EST system is basically the same as the system used with the LE9 (H in VIN number) engine. All spark timing changes in the H.E.I. distributor are done by vacuum and mechanical advances.

NOTE: When performing compression checks on gasoline engines, disconnect the ignition switch connector (pink wire) from the HEI system. See the Engine Electrical Unit Repair Section for all diagnosis and testing procedures on HEI, EST and ESC systems.

DISTRIBUTOR

Removal and Installation

INLINE ENGINES

1. Remove coil connectors, primary wire and vacuum line. Disconnect ignition switch feed wire and remove distributor cap.
2. Scribe a mark on the distributor body, locating the position of the rotor. Scribe another mark on the distributor body and engine block, showing the position of the body in the block.
3. Remove the distributor hold-down screw and lift the distributor up and out of the engine.

NOTE: As the distributor is removed from the engine, the rotor will turn counterclockwise. Observe and mark the start and finish rotation of the rotor. When reinstalling, position the rotor at the last mark and set the distributor into the engine. As the distributor drops into place, the rotor should turn to its original position, providing the engine crankshaft had not been rotated with the distributor out.

4. If the crankshaft was rotated, turn the engine until the piston of No. 1 cylinder is at the top of its compression stroke.
5. Position the distributor in the block so that the vacuum control unit is in its normal position.
6. Position the rotor to point toward the front of the engine (with distributor held out of the block, but in installed position). Turn rotor counterclockwise about $\frac{1}{8}$ turn and push distributor down to engage camshaft drive. It may be necessary to move the rotor one way or the other to mesh the drive and driven gears properly.
7. While holding the distributor down in place, rotate the engine a few times to make sure the oil pump shaft is engaged. Install hold-down clamp and bolt. Snug the bolt.
8. Once again, rotate the crankshaft until No. 1 cylinder is on the compression stroke and the harmonic balancer mark is on 0°.
9. Tighten distributor clamp bolt.
10. Place distributor cap in position and see that the rotor lines up with the terminal for the No. 1 spark plug.
11. Install cap, distributor primary wire, ignition feed wire and coil connectors. Check all secondary wires in the cap towers.

12. Start engine and set timing according to the Tune-up chart, or instructions on underhood sticker.

NOTE: The Vehicle Emission Information label will be found in the engine compartment sheet metal, support bars or on the air cleaner assembly. If none are found, new decals can be obtained through General Motors Parts Division, by VIN number.

13. Reconnect vacuum hose to vacuum control assembly.

CAUTION

When using an auxiliary starter switch for bumping the engine into position for timing or compression test, the primary distributor lead must be disconnected from the negative post of the ignition coil and the ignition switch must be on. Failure to do this may cause damage to the grounding circuit in the ignition switch. This will also prevent the sudden starting of engine and possible serious injury.

V6 AND V8 ENGINES

If it becomes necessary to remove the distributor, carefully mark the position of the rotor so that, if the engine is not turned after the distributor is taken out, the rotor can be returned to the position from which it was removed without difficulty.

1. To remove the distributor, take off the carburetor air cleaner, ignition feed wire, coil connectors and disconnect the coil primary wire and the vacuum line. Remove the distributor cap and take out the single hold-down bolt located under the distributor body. Mark the position of the rotor to the body and the body relative to the block and then work the distributor up out of the block.

CAUTION

Do not allow the TACH terminal to touch ground or serious damage to the module and coil can occur.

NOTE: Proceed with Step 2 if crankshaft was rotated.

2. Remove No. 1 spark plug and, with finger on plug hole, crank the engine until compression is felt in No. 1 cylinder. Continue cranking until pointer lines up with the timing mark on the crankshaft pulley.
3. Position distributor in opening of the block in normal installed attitude; have rotor pointing to front of engine.
4. Turn the rotor counterclockwise about $\frac{1}{8}$ of a turn (from straight front toward the left cylinder bank). Push the distributor down to engage the camshaft and while holding, turn the engine with the starter so that distributor shaft engages the oil pump shaft.
5. Return engine to compression stroke of No. 1 piston with timing mark on pulley aligned with the pointer. Install the cap being sure the rotor points to the contact for No. 1 spark plug. Connect the timing light and check that spark occurs as timing mark and pointer are aligned. Refer to underhood sticker for timing procedure.

TIMING LIGHT CONNECTIONS—H.E.I. SYSTEM

Timing light connections should be made in parallel using an adapter at the distributor No. 1 terminal, or an inductive pick-up. DO NOT pierce the wire.

NOTE: On some engines, it is necessary to disconnect the EST connector to set the timing. See the underhood sticker for details.

TACHOMETER CONNECTIONS—H.E.I. SYSTEM

There is a "tach" terminal on the distributor cap or on the re-

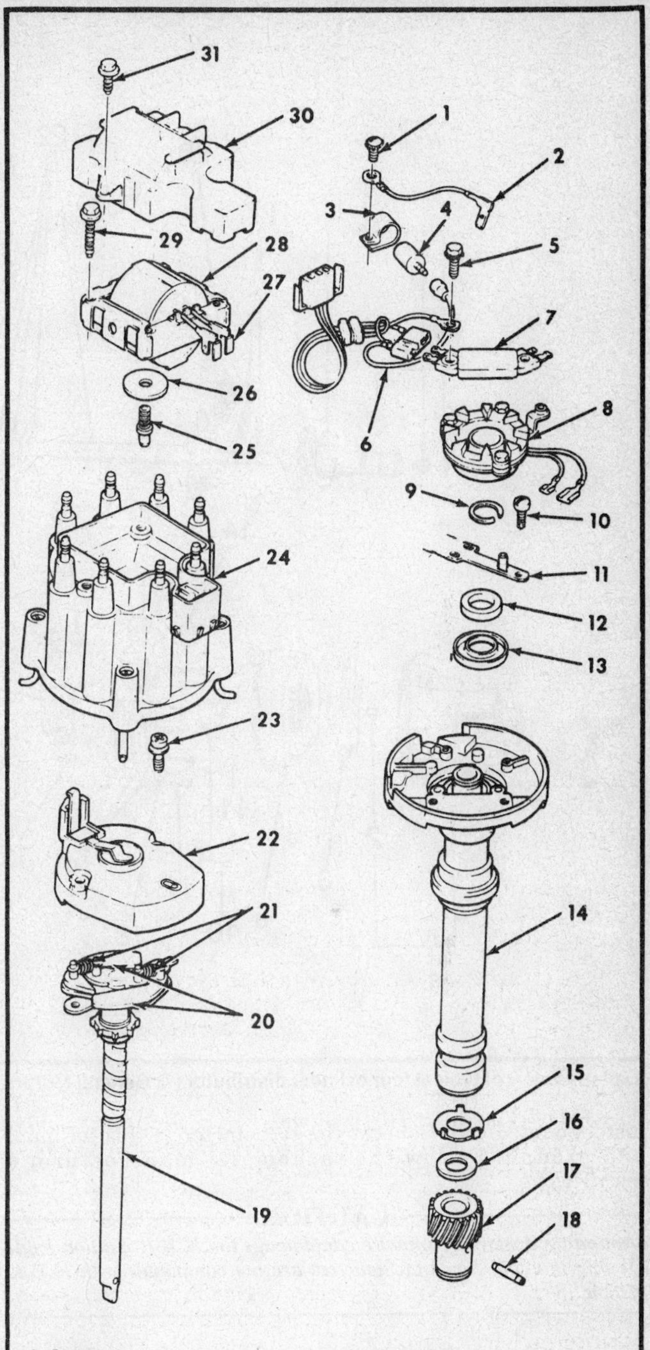

1 Screw
2 Wiring Lead
3 Capacitor Clamp
4 Capacitor
5 Screw
6 Wiring Harness Module Leads
7 Module
8 Pick-Up Coil Magnet Assembly
9 Thin "C" Washer
10 Screw
11 Plastic Retainer
12 Felt Washer
13 Felt Retainer
14 Housing
15 Thrust Washer
16 Shim
17 Driven Gear
18 Roll Pin
19 Shaft
20 "Centrifugal Advance" Weights
21 Springs
22 Rotor
23 Screw
24 Cap
25 Spring & Button Assembly
26 Seal
27 Coil Terminals
28 Coil
29 Screw
30 Cover
31 Screw

HEI distributor w/o vacuum advance—V8 engine—typical
(© General Motors Corp.)

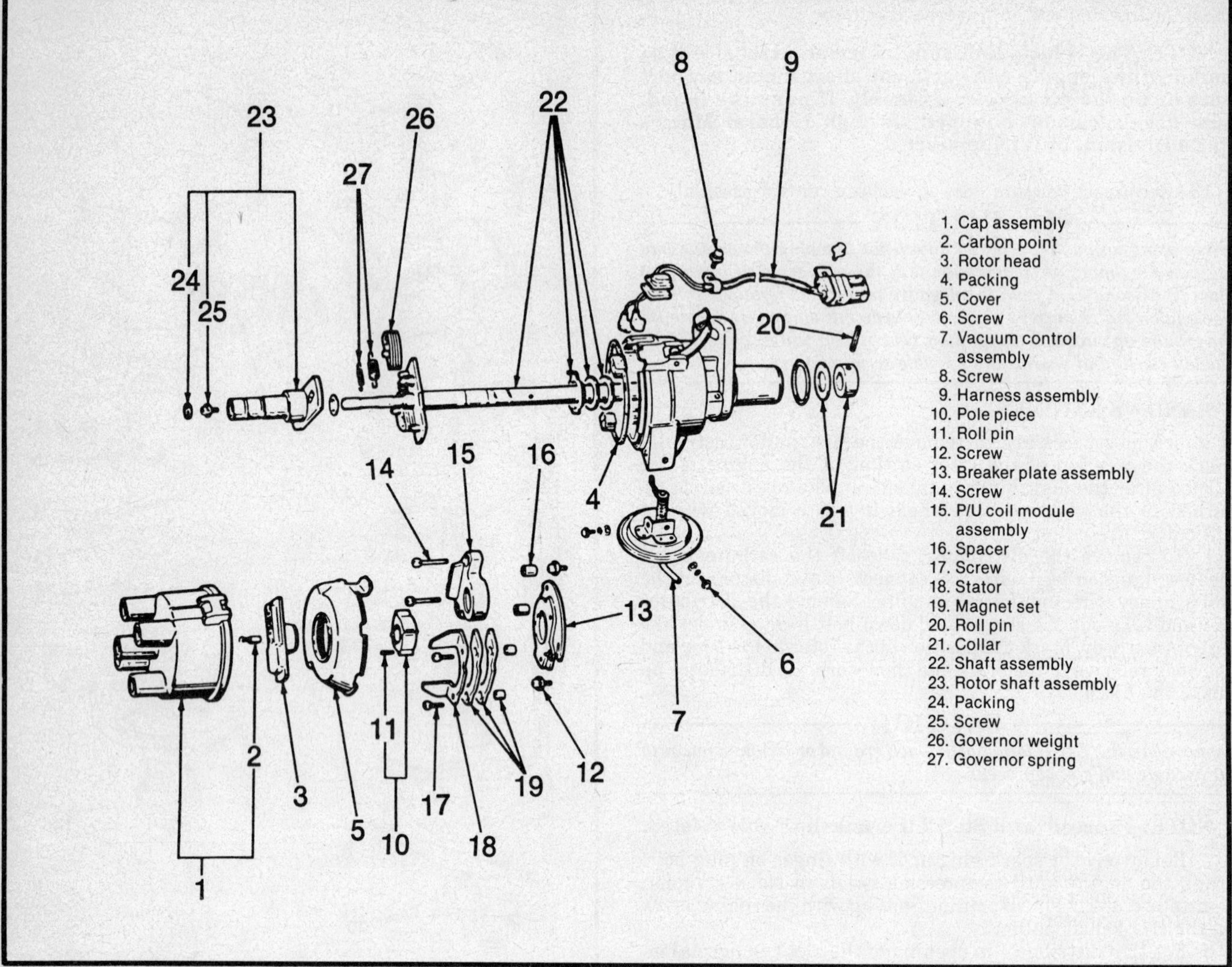

Exploded view of typical four cylinder distributor (© General Motors Corp.)

mote-mounted coil. Connect the tachometer to this terminal and ground. Follow the tachometer manufacturer's instructions.

CAUTION

Grounding the tach terminal could damage the H.E.I. ignition module and the coil. Some tachometers are not compatible with H.E.I. system.

IGNITION TIMING

On H.E.I. systems, connect the timing light in parallel at the No. 1 tower on the distributor cap. Disconnect the distributor spark advance hose and plug the vacuum opening. Start the engine and run it at idle speed. Aim the timing light at the degree scale just over the harmonic balancer. The markings on the scale are in 2° increments with the greatest number of markings on the *before* side of the 0. Adjust the timing by loosening the securing clamp and rotating the distributor until the desired ignition advance is achieved, then tighten the clamp. To advance the timing, rotate the distributor opposite to the normal direction of rotor rotation. Retard the timing by rotating the distributor in the normal direction of rotor rotation.

NOTE: See underhood sticker for exact procedure. EST connector may have to be disconnected.

Alternator

NOTE: Repair and test details on the alternator and its regulators are covered in the Unit Repair section. The following is a general removal and installation procedure.

Removal and Installation

1. Disconnect the battery ground strap at battery to prevent damaging diodes or wiring harness.
2. Disconnect wiring leads at Delcotron.
3. Remove the alternator brace bolt (if power steering equipped, loosen pump brace and mount nuts), then detach drive belt(s).
4. Support the alternator and remove alternator mount bolt or bolts and remove the alternator from vehicle.

The upper radiator fan shroud must be removed before the alternator can be removed from the Astro Vans.

5. Reverse the removal procedure to install, then adjust drive belt(s).
6. If no belt tension tool is available, force alternator away from the engine until fan belt has $^{5}/_{16}$ in. deflection when forced downward from normal position with light pressure applied between the alternator and the fan. When adjusting belt tension, never apply pressure against either end frame.

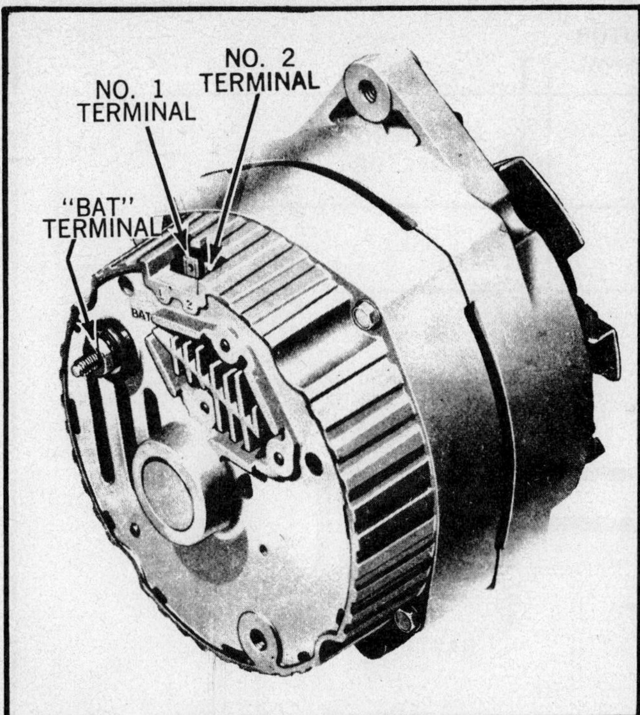

Alternator wiring terminals (© General Motors Corp.)

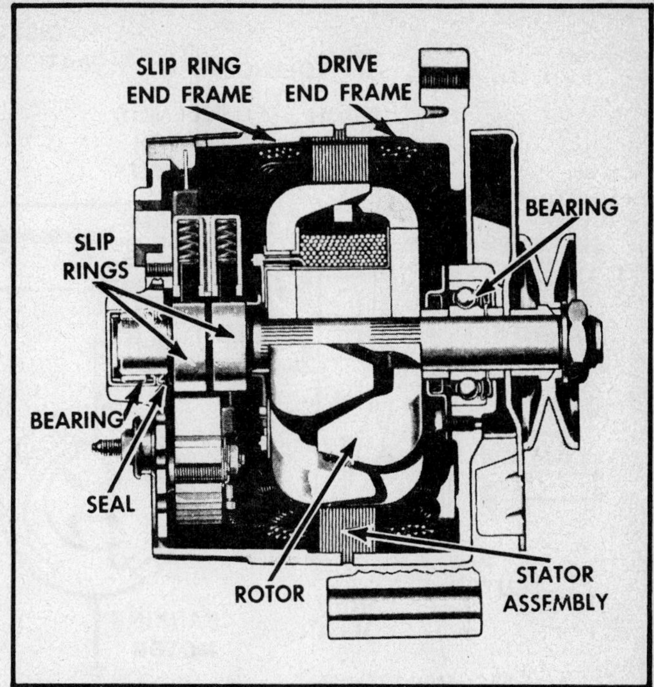

Cross section of alternator (© General Motors Corp.)

CAUTION

Since the Delcotron and regulator are designed for use on a single polarity system, the following precautions must be observed:

1. Never operate the Delcotron on uncontrolled open circuit (output terminal disconnected). Be sure that all connections in the circuit are clean and tight.
2. Do not short across or ground any of the terminals on the Delcotron regulator.
3. Do not attempt to polarize the Delcotron.
4. Do not use test lamps of more than 12 volts for checking diode continuity.
5. Avoid long soldering times when replacing diodes or transistors. Prolonged heat is damaging to these units.

Starter

NOTE: General information on the starting systems will be found in the Electrical chapter of the Unit Repair section.

Removal and Installation

The following procedure is a general guide for all vehicles and will vary slightly depending on the truck series and model. (On forward control trucks and vans, the vehicle must be raised and supported.)

1. Disconnect battery ground cable at the battery.
2. Disconnect engine wiring harness and battery leads at solenoid terminals.

It may be necessary to first lower starter from the engine to gain access to the wiring harness and cable connections at the solenoid.

3. Remove starter mounting bolts and retaining nuts and disengage starter assembly from the flywheel housing. Light duty gasoline powered engines use conventional nose housing or pad mounting. Intermediate and heavy duty use conventional flange. On these, scribe mark on flange and flywheel housing as nose housing can be mounted in several positions.

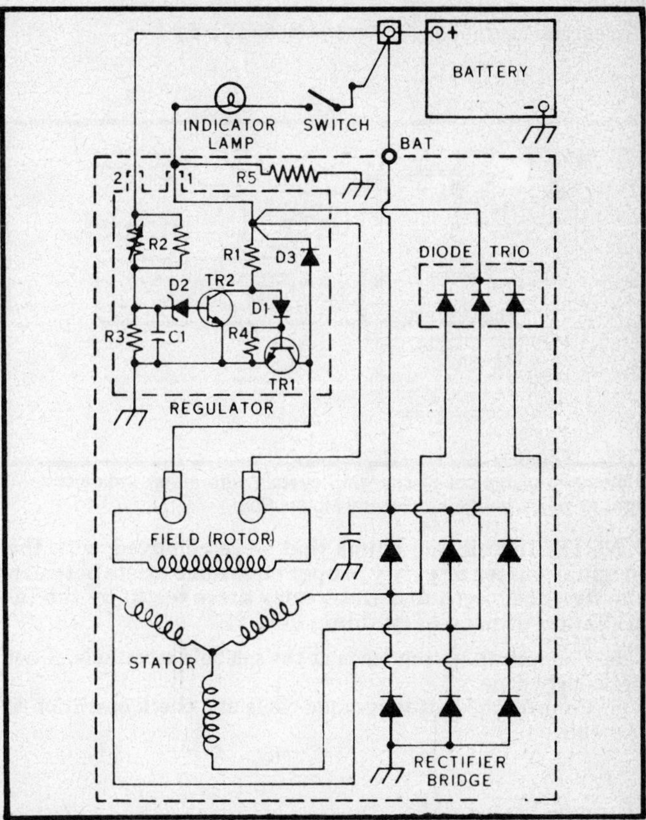

Schematic of internal regulator and alternator electrical circuits—typical of 10-SI, 15-SI and 27-SI alternator series (© General Motors Corp.)

4. Position starter motor assembly (install wires and cable if disconnected after starter was removed from engine), to the flywheel housing and install the mounting bolts and retaining nuts. Torque the mounting bolts to 25–35 ft. lbs

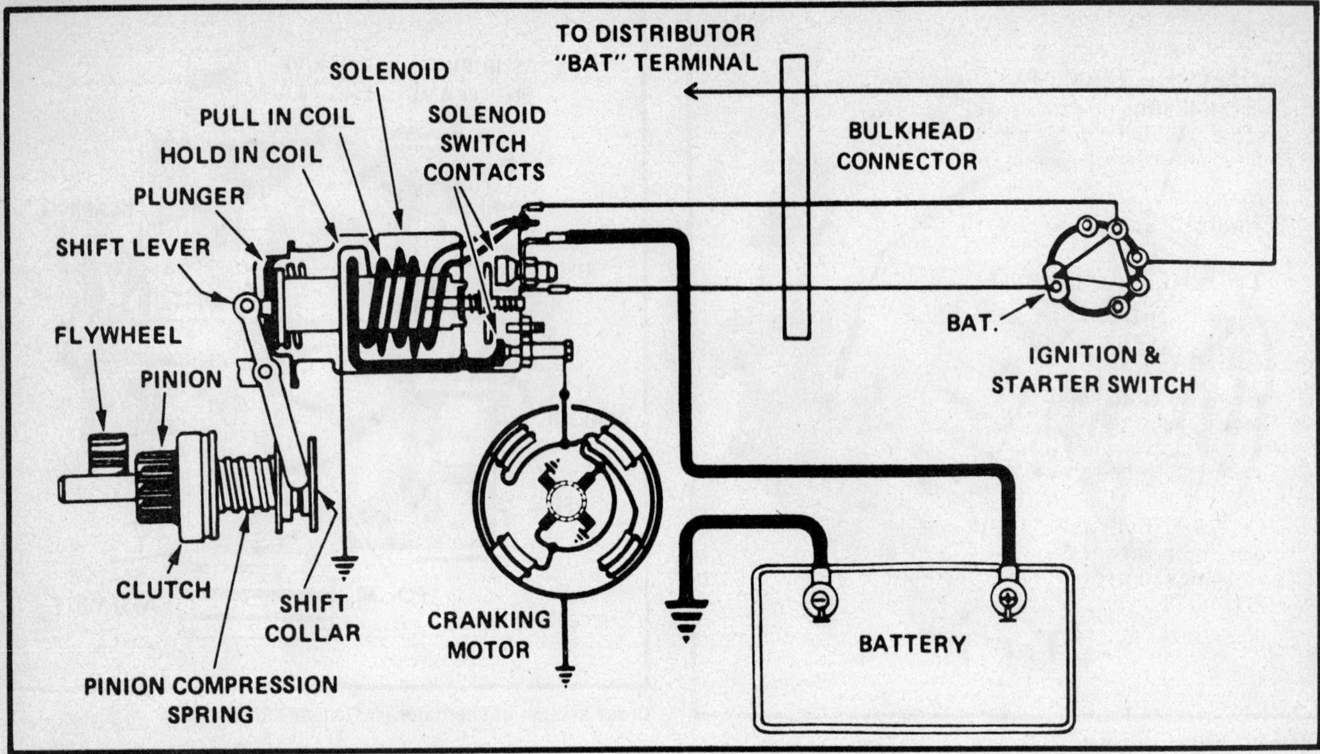

Typical cranking circuit (© General Motors Corp.)

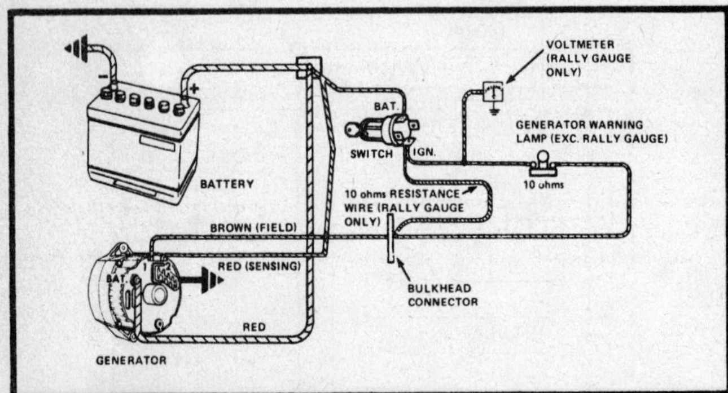

Schematic of typical SI charging system with either indicator light or ralley gauge (© General Motors Corp.)

NOTE: Install any shims that were removed with the original starter or verify proper clearance exists between the flywheel teeth and the starter drive teeth, by the installation of necessary shim pack.

5. Connect all wiring leads at the solenoid terminals, if not previously done.
6. Connect the battery ground cable and check operation of the unit.

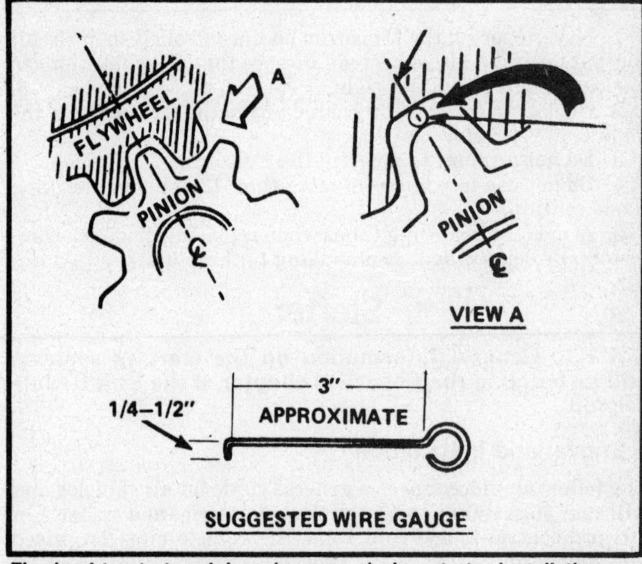

Flywheel to starter pinion clearance during starter installation (© General Motors Corp.)

BRAKES

Specific information will be found in Unit Repair section on adjustments, bleeding, master cylinder and wheel cylinder overhaul procedures and trouble shooting.

Refer to Power Brake section for details concerning power brakes.

Master Cylinders

TWIN (BRAKE AND CLUTCH) TYPE MASTER CYLINDER

Removal

1. Disconnect clutch and brake pedal return springs.
2. Detach push rod boots from cylinders.
3. Remove clutch and brake hydraulic lines.
4. Remove three bolts holding cylinder to dash and slide cylinder off push rod.

NOTE: Wipe hydraulic fittings clean and place dry cloth under lines to absorb any fluid spillage. Cover fittings and lines to prevent any foreign matter from entering system.

Installation

1. Place new gaskets and push rod boots over cylinder tubes.
2. Hold cylinder next to dash and insert push rods, making sure they are centered.
3. Bolt assembly loosely to dash. This freedom of assembly will allow hydraulic lines to be started in cylinder without stripping fittings.
4. Tighten assembly and hydraulic lines securely.
5. Replace the pedal return springs.
6. Fill reservoir and bleed both clutch and brake cylinders.
7. Check pedal free play and operation.

STANDARD CONVENTIONAL SINGLE MASTER CYLINDER

Removal

1. Clean area at fitting and place dry cloth under line to absorb leakage.
2. Disconnect hydraulic line at cylinder and cover ends with clean cloth to prevent any foreign matter from entering system.
3. Disconnect push rod from pedal.
4. Remove the two nuts and washers holding cylinder to firewall. Remove Cylinder.

Installation

1. Position cylinder at dash, align push rod through boot and secure loosely. This freedom of assembly will allow hydraulic line and push rod to be installed with minimum of effort.
2. Tighten nuts and line. Check free play.
3. Fill cylinder and bleed. Bleeding can be accomplished by slowly pressing down on brake pedal and at same time tightening the hydraulic line fitting. Any air still trapped in line at fitting can be expelled by pressing hard on brake pedal to a point of just below free play. By having a slight pressure on pedal, the piston is held forward enough to clear ports in reservoir and check valve is held off its seat, so air can be released.
4. Final check of fluid and brake operation.

STANDARD DUAL MASTER CYLINDER

Removal

1. Clean area at fittings and place dry cloth under lines to absorb leakage.

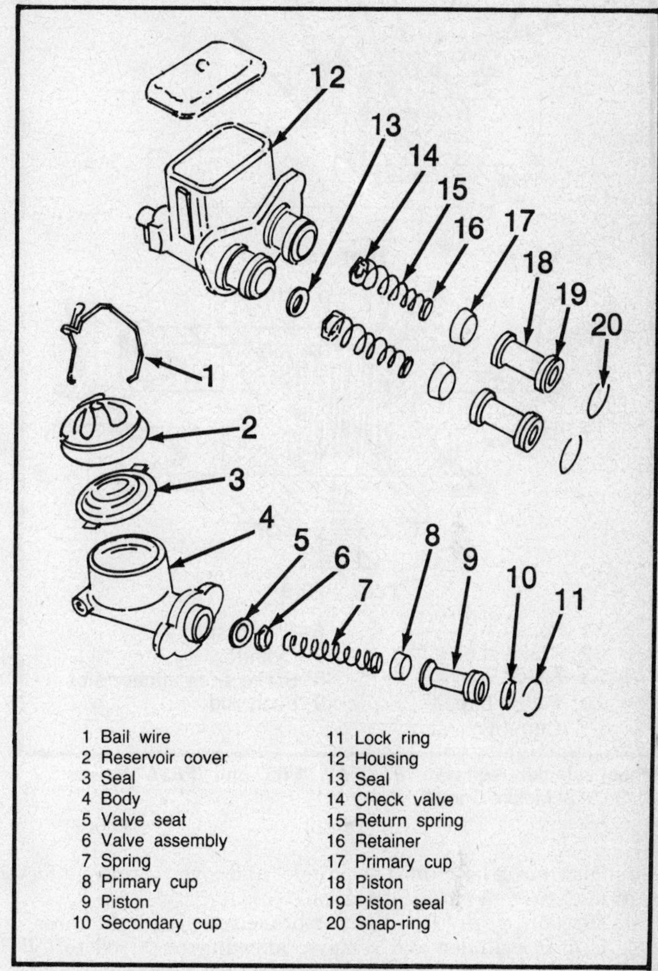

Single and clutch assist master cylinders

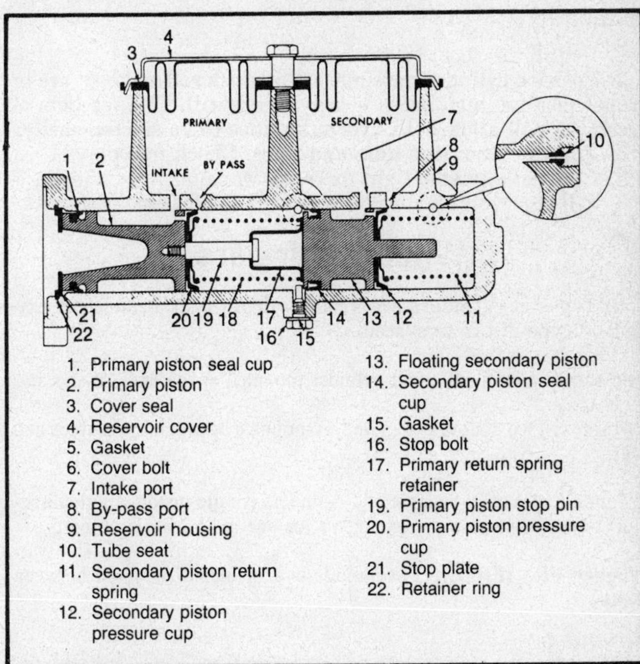

Typical split system master cylinder (© General Motors Corp.)

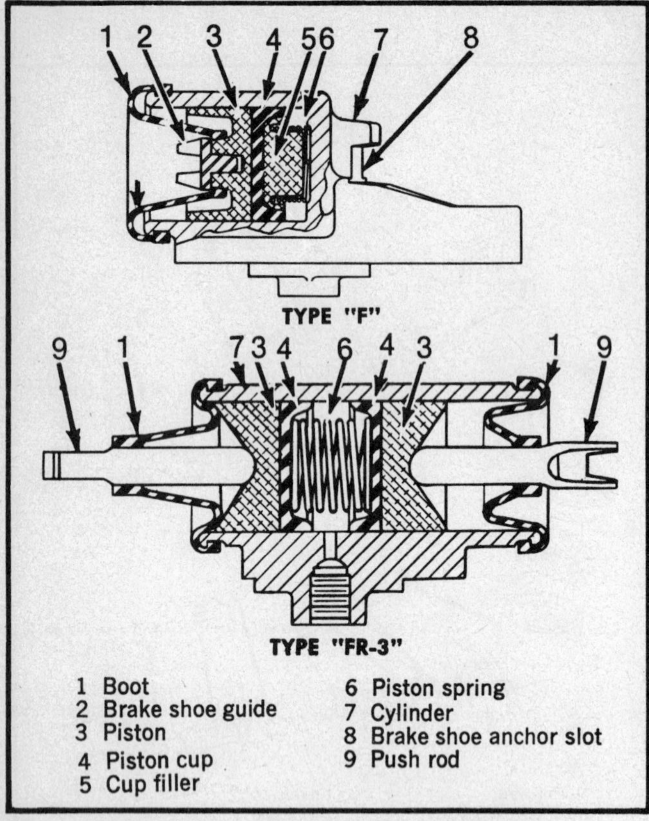

Wheel cylinder used with "F", "FA", "FR3" and "FR3A" brakes (© General Motors Corp.)

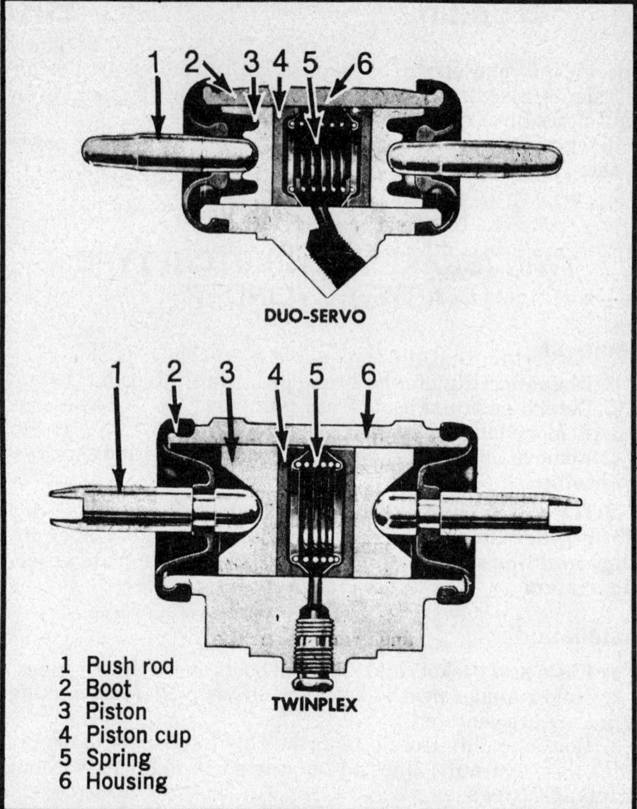

Duo servo and Twin Plex cylinders (© General Motors Corp.)

2. Disconnect both lines at cylinder and cover to prevent foreign matter from entering system.
3. Disconnect any stop light or brake warning light wires.
4. Unbolt cylinder and remove, allowing push rod to fall loose.

Installation

1. Install new boot on push rod.
2. Position cylinder making certain push rod and boot are in proper position and fasten loosely to firewall. This freedom of assembly will allow both hydraulic lines to be started easily.
3. Tighten mounting nuts and lines. Check free play.
4. Connect any stop light or brake warning light wires.
5. Fill reservoir and bleed. Test brakes before moving truck.

Wheel Cylinders

Four types of cylinders are used on drum-type brakes, identified by type of brake system.

Duo servo: One double-end cylinder mounted at toe ends of shoes.

Twinplex: Two double-end cylinders mounted between shoes at toe and heel.

Wagner F (FA): Two single end cylinders (single piston, single direction) mounted so as to be an anchor for one and powering other.

Wagner FR3 (FR3A): Two double-end cylinders mounted between shoes.

Removal

1. Jack up axle and support. Remove wheel and drum.

NOTE: To remove drum, it may be necessary to back off brake adjustment. Also, if equipped with rear drum, release hand brake cable, if so equipped.

CAUTION

To gain access to adjusting starwheel, a knockout lanced area is located in web of drum or brake support plate. After knocking out metal, be sure to clean all metal particles from brake compartment. A new cover plug must be installed.

2. Release shoe return springs and spread shoes to clear wheel cylinder links. Make sure any lubricant or brake fluid does not get on facings by covering same.
3. At front: Disconnect metal line from flexible hose and remove hose if accessible or remove hose later after cylinder is removed. At rear: Disconnect metal line from cylinder.
4. Remove shield over cylinder and connecting line between cylinders, if so equipped.
5. Remove cap screws and washers holding cylinder to backing plate. Remove cylinder being careful of any fluid spillage.

Installation

1. Clean mounting surface and reverse above procedures.
2. Bleed and readjust brakes. Check pedal before moving vehicle.

NOTE: Twinplex upper and lower cylinders are not interchangeable due to position of connector tube openings. Upper cylinder has threaded bleeder valve opening drilled at outer edge of bore. Wagner F & FA two wheel cylinder (upper and lower) are identical, however cylinders on right and left brakes have opposite castings. Wagner FR3 & FR3A upper and lower cylinders on both right and left brakes are interchangeable.

Bleeding Hydraulic Brakes

PRESSURE BLEEDING

LIGHT DUTY TRUCKS

NOTE: The manufacturer specifically advises that the pressure bleeding equipment be of the diaphragm type, i.e., there must be a rubber diaphragm between the air supply and the brake fluid to prevent contaminants, such as air, moisture, oil, etc., from entering the hydraulic system. Furthermore, the equipment used must be capable of exerting 20 to 30 psi hydraulic pressure on the brake system.

1. Be certain that the brake fluid in the bleeder equipment is at the operating level.
2. Remove all dirt from the top of the master cylinder and remove the cylinder cover and rubber diaphragm.
3. Attach a brake bleeder adapter tool for the frame mounted boosters to the master cylinder.
4. Connect a hose from the bleeder equipment to the bleeder adapter and open the release valve on the bleeder equipment.

NOTE: The combination valve (front brake metering valve) must be held in the open position while bleeding. Install tool, Kent Moore J–23709 or an equivalent device with the open slot under the mounting bolt and pushing in on the pin in the end of the valve.

5. Bleed the brakes in the following order:10–20–30 Series, Astro Van and S/T Series – right rear, left rear, right front and left front.

NOTE: Bleed combination valve before bleeding the wheel cylinders or calipers on the S/T Series.

6. Fill a transparent container with a sufficient amount of brake fluid to ensure that the submerged end of the bleeder hose will remain below the surface of the fluid.
7. Place a brake bleeder wrench over the first bleeder valve and install one end of the bleeder hose over the valve.
8. Place the loose end of the bleeder hose in the container of brake fluid. Make sure that the hose end remains submerged in the brake fluid.
9. Open the bleeder valve by turning the bleeder wrench $^3/_4$ turn counterclockwise and allow fluid to flow until no air is seen in the fluid.
10. Close the bleeder valve tightly and proceed in the same manner with the remaining bleeder valves until there is no longer any air in the brake system.
11. Disconnect the brake bleeder equipment from the adapter at the master cylinder and remove the adapter from the master cylinder.
12. Fill the master cylinder reservoir(s) to within $^1/_4$ in. of the top rim and install the master cylinder diaphragm and cover.

MEDIUM DUTY TRUCKS

CAUTION

Stop engine and relieve vacuum or exhaust pressure from system before following procedures.

1. Make certain fluid in pressure tank is above the petcock outlet and that tank is charged with 40–50 psi of air.
2. Clean dirt from around master cylinder filler cap. Connect pressure tank hose to filler cap or cover opening. Bleed air from hose before tightening connection. Open valves at both ends.
3. Bleed slave cylinder and control valve first (when used). Slip end of bleeder hose over bleeder valve no. 1 and place other end in glass jar containing enough hydraulic fluid to cover end of hose. Open bleeder valve with wrench and observe flow of fluid. On 40–50 and 4000–5000 series vehicles, start engine and make at least two power brake applications with bleeder valve open to force air out of slave cylinder. Close bleeder valve as soon as bubbles stop and fluid flows in solid stream. Stop engine and relieve vacuum from system.
4. Bleed valve No. 2 (on power cylinder control valve), then bleed wheel cylinders in sequence. Repeat bleeding operations at power cylinder. On 40–50 and 4000–5000 series vehicles, repeat power brake applications with engine running as in Step 3. If, after bleeding the pedal "feel" is not satisfactory, inspect residual check valve in the master cylinder and the check valve in the power cylinder piston. Improper operation of either or both of these valves will result in same pedal "feel" as air in the system, since malfunction permits recirculation of fluid through compensating line and back to master cylinder reservoir. Refer to applicable procedures for repair.

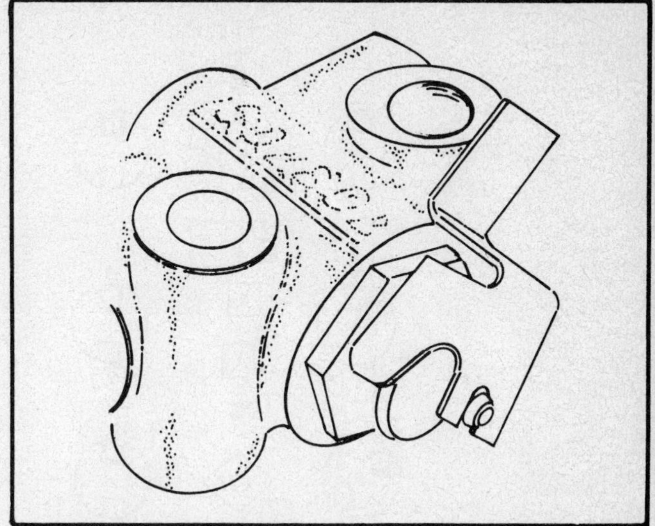

Metering valve held in the open position—medium duty trucks w/disc brakes

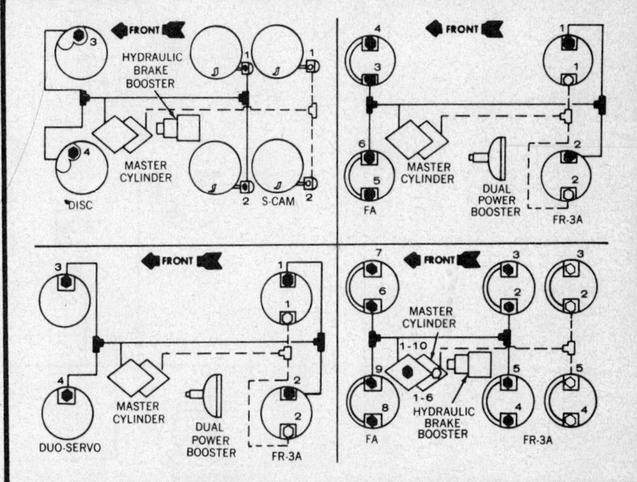

Typical hydraulic brake bleeding sequence, medium duty trucks (© General Motors Corp.)

MEDIUM DUTY TRUCKS w/DISC BRAKES

The pressure bleeding procedure for medium duty trucks with disc brakes is essentially the same as the procedure for light duty trucks with the following exceptions.

1. Install special tool, Kent Moore J–23774–01 or an equivalent tool on the metering valve, which is located at the frame crossmember. This step is necessary to hold the metering valve

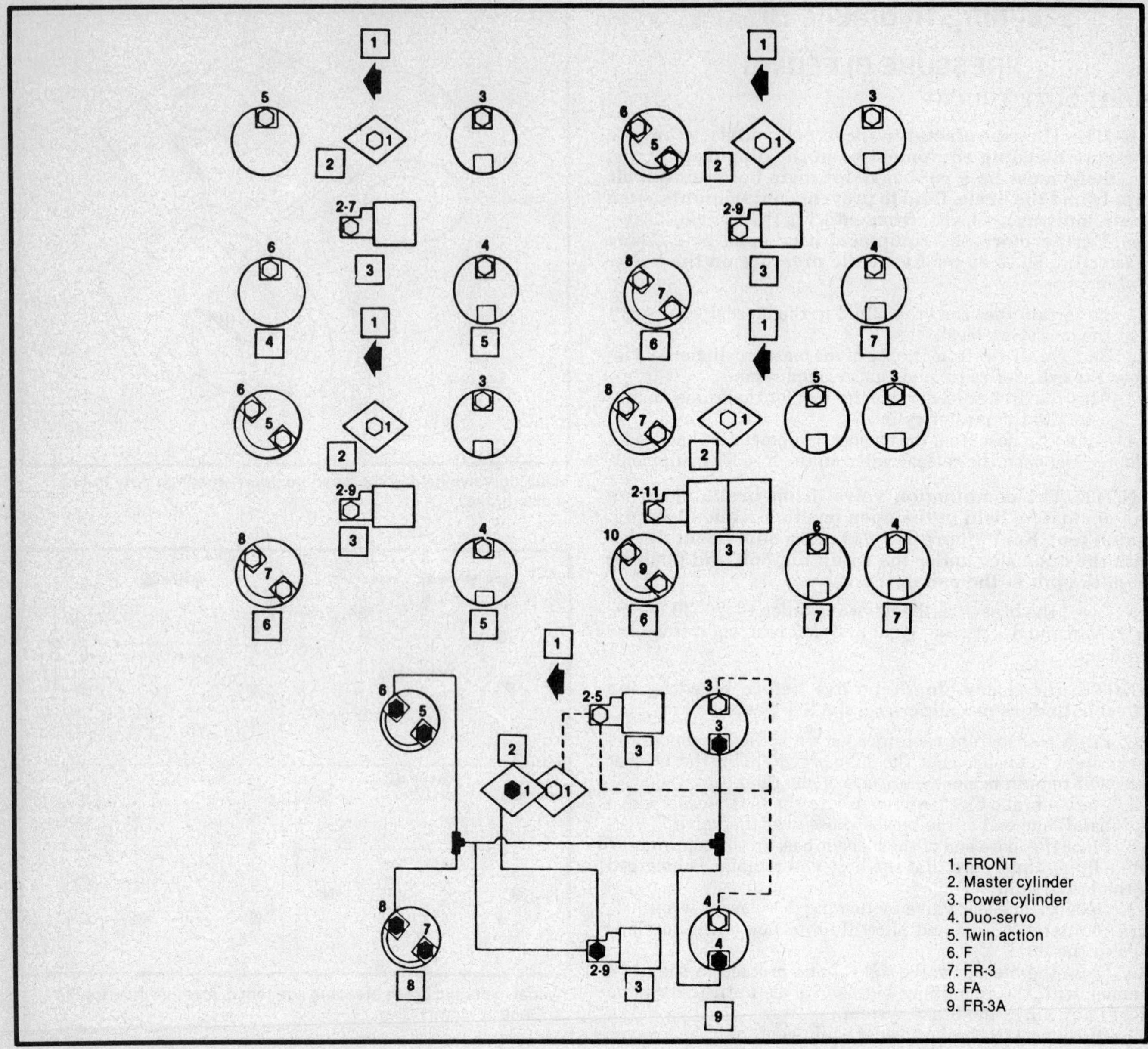

Medium truck hydraulic brake bleeding sequence, equipped with vacuum power booster cylinder (© General Motors Corp.)

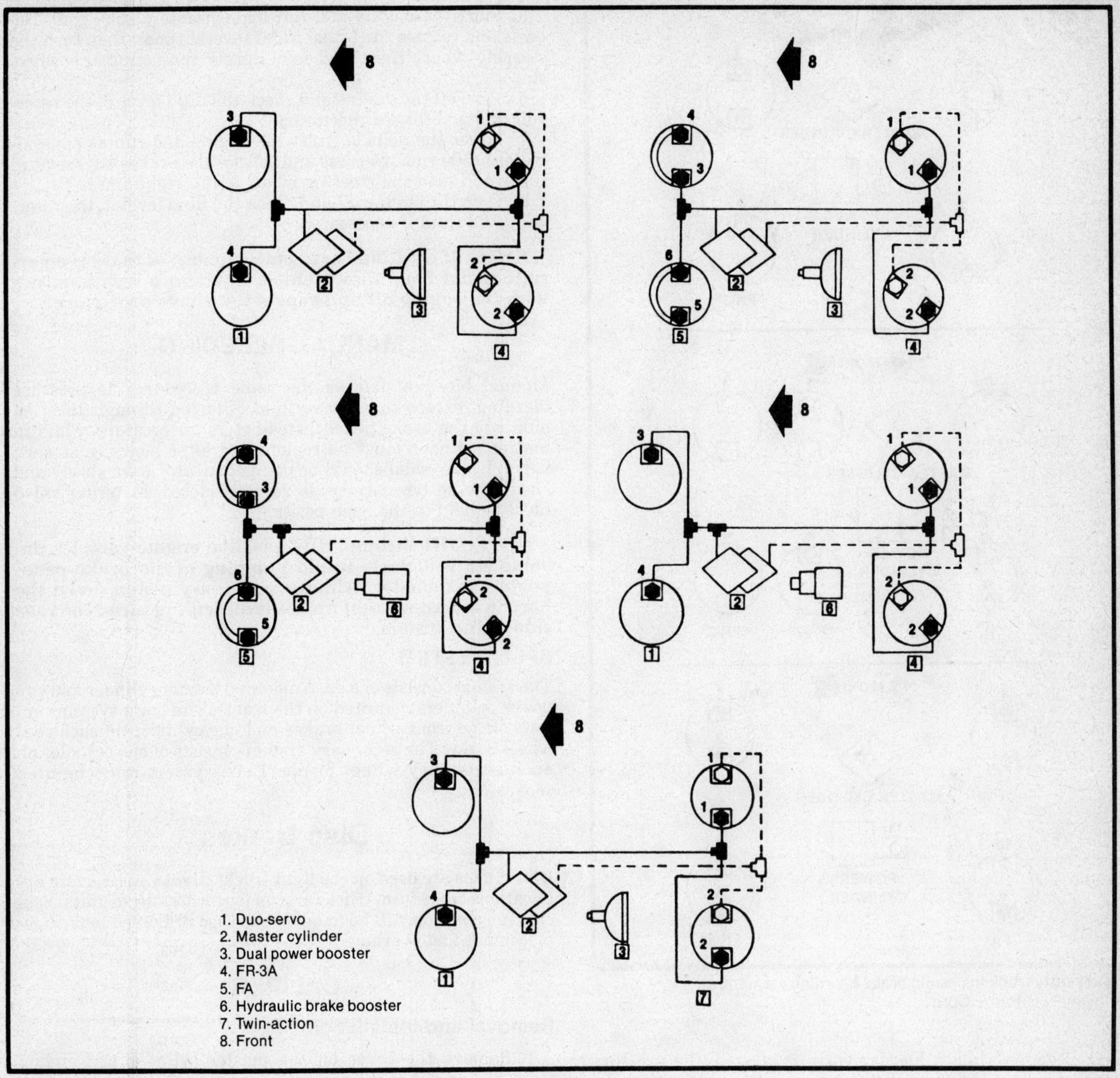

1. Duo-servo
2. Master cylinder
3. Dual power booster
4. FR-3A
5. FA
6. Hydraulic brake booster
7. Twin-action
8. Front

Medium truck hydraulic brake bleeding sequence, equipped with dual power or hydraulic booster (© General Motors Corp.)

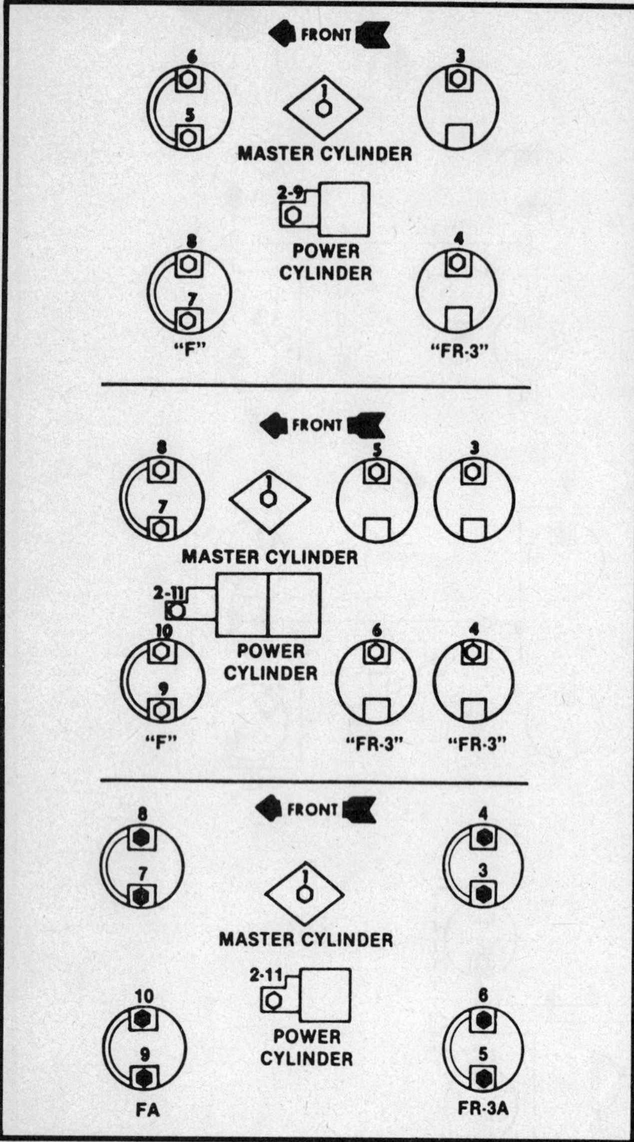

Heavy duty truck hydraulic brake bleeding sequence
(© General Motors Corp.)

open, because when a bleeder valve is opened, the pressure drops, allowing the metering valve to close, which stops the flow of fluid to the front brakes.

2. Install a brake bleeder adapter tool on the master cylinder.
3. Begin bleeding the system at the valve nearest the master cylinder, then proceed to the next nearest and so on until all of the valves have been bled. If the master cylinder has bleeder valves, bleed these valves first.

HYDRO–BOOST SYSTEM

Bleeding

MEDIUM AND HEAVY DUTY TRUCKS

1. Fill the power steering pump to the proper level.
2. Start the engine for approximately two seconds. Check the fluid and add if necessary.
3. Repeat Step 2 until the fluid level remains constant.
4. Raise the front end of the vehicle so that the tires are clear of the ground.
5. Start the engine and run approximately 1500 rpm. Depress and release the brake pedal several times, then turn the steering wheel right and left, lightly contacting the wheel stops.
6. Turn off the engine and check the fluid level in the reservoir and add fluid, if necessary.
7. Lower the vehicle, start the engine and run at approximately 1500 rpm. Depress and release the brake pedal several times and turn the steering wheel to full right and left.
8. Turn the engine off and check the fluid level in the reservoir. Add fluid if necessary.

NOTE: If the fluid is extremely foamy, or there is an erratic pedal feel, allow vehicle to stand a few moments with the engine off and repeat the above procedure.

MANUAL BLEEDING

Manual bleeding follows the same procedures as pressure bleeding, except that brake fluid is forced through lines by pumping the brake pedal instead of by air pressure. Fluid in master cylinder must be replenished after bleeding at each valve. Brake pedal should be pumped up and down slowly and should be on downstroke as valve is closed. Metering valve must be held in the open position.

NOTE: JB1 through JB6 gasoline engine vehicles (incomplete vehicles)–Rapid pumping of the brake pedal pushes the master cylinder secondary piston down the bore in a manner that makes it difficult to bleed the rear side of the system.

SPLIT SYSTEM

The system consists of a dash mounted master cylinder and two power cylinders mounted on the frame. The main system consists of the front wheel brakes and one cylinder on each rear wheel brake. The secondary system consists of one cylinder on each secondary wheel brake. Each system must be bled separately.

Disc Brakes

Disc brakes are used on the light trucks, light vans, certain applications of meduim trucks and on four wheel drive units. Specific information will be found in the Disc Brake sections on replacement and overhaul.

CALIPER

Removal and Installation

1. Remove the cover on the master cylinder and siphon enough fluid out of the reservoirs to bring the level to ⅓ full. This step prevents spilling fluid when the piston is pushed back.
2. Raise and support the vehicle. Remove the front wheels and tires.
3. Push the brake piston back into its bore using a C-clamp to pull the caliper outward.
4. Remove the two bolts which hold the caliper and then lift the caliper off the disc.

CAUTION

Do not let the caliper assembly hang by the brake hose.

5. Remove the inboard and outboard shoe.

NOTE: If the pads are to be reinstalled, mark them 'inside' and 'outside".

6. Remove the pad support spring from the piston.
7. Remove the two sleeves from the inside ears of the caliper and the 4 rubber bushings from the grooves in the caliper ears.

8. Remove the hose from the steel brake line and tape the fittings to prevent foreign material from entering the line or the hoses.
9. Remove the retainer from the hose fitting.
10. Remove the hose from the frame bracket and pull off the caliper with the hose attached.

NOTE: Check the inside of the caliper for fluid leakage; if so, the caliper should be overhauled or replaced.

CAUTION

Do not use compressed air to clean the inside of the caliper as this may unseat the dust boot.

11. Connect the brake line to start reinstallation. Lubricate the sleeves, rubber bushings, bushing grooves and the end of the mounting bolts, using silicone lubricant.
12. Install new bushings in the caliper ears along with new sleeves. The sleeve should be replaced so that the end toward the shoe is flush with the machined surface of the ear.
13. Position the support spring and the inner pad into the center cavity of the piston. The outboard pad has ears which are bent over to keep the pad in position while the inboard pad has ears on the top end which fit over the caliper retaining bolts. A spring which is inside the brake piston holds the bottom edge of the inboard pad.
14. Push down on the inner pad until it lays flat against the caliper. It is important to push the piston all the way into the caliper, if new linings are installed, or the caliper will not fit over the rotor.
15. Position the outboard pad with the ears of the pad over the caliper ears and the tab at the bottom engaged in the caliper cutout.
16. With the two pads in position, place the caliper over the brake disc and align the holes in the caliper with those of the mounting bracket.

CAUTION

Make certain that the brake hose is not twisted or kinked.

17. Install the mounting bracket bolts through the sleeves in the inboard caliper ears and through the mounting bracket, making sure that the ends of the bolts pass under the retaining ears on the inboard pad.
18. Tighten the mounting bolts to 35 ft. lbs After installing both sides, pump the brake pedal to seat the pads against the rotor. With the brakes applied, use a pair of channel lock pliers or similar tool, to bend over the upper ears of the outer pad so it not loose on the caliper.
19. Install the front wheel and lower the truck.
20. Add fluid to the master cylinder reservoirs until the fluid is $\frac{1}{4}$ in. from the top.
21. Test the brake pedal by pumping it to obtain a "hard" pedal. Check the fluid level again and add fluid as necessary. Do not move the vehicle until a "hard" pedal is obtained.

Power Brakes

POWER HYDRAULIC

Specific information will be found in Power Brake section on adjustments, bleeding, overhaul and trouble shooting.

Various vacuum/hydraulic or air/over/hydraulic brake systems are used, although sizes and shapes differ, the basic function is the same.

DUAL POWER BRAKE SYSTEM

MEDUIM DUTY CONVENTIONAL CAB

The Dual Power Brake system is a system which utilizes two power boosting units in series to provide the power assist necessary to stop the vehicle. This is accomplished by combining a vacuum operated booster with a hydraulically operated booster in tandem arrangement with a standard dual master cylinder. Assist power generated by the vacuum booster is transmitted forward to the hydraulic booster, where the apply power is, again, assisted or augmented by the hydraulic booster. Doubly assisted power available at the hydraulic booster is transmitted to the master cylinder, thereby developing hydraulic pressure up to a maximum of approximately 600 psi. Refer to the Unit Repair Brake section of this manual for more specific overhaul and troubleshooting information.

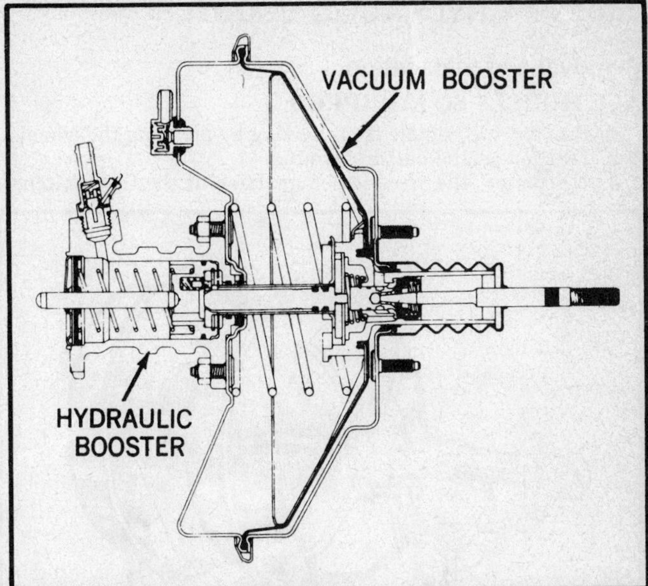

Dual power booster (© General Motors Corp.)

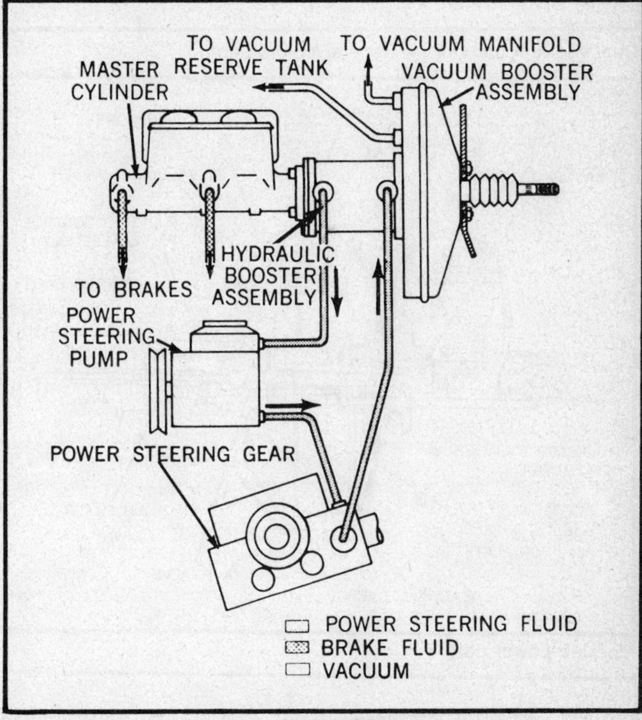

Dual power brake system (© General Motors Corp.)

NOTE: The entire dual power assembly may be removed as one unit (master cylinder, hydraulic booster and vacuum booster), induividual units, or in combination of units.

HYDRAULIC BOOSTER

Removal and Installation

ALL MODELS SO EQUIPPED

1. Prevent the vehicle from moving by blocking the wheels.
2. Disconnect the battery ground.
3. Disconnect the electrical connection at the flow switch.

Dual vacuum booster (© General Motors Corp.)

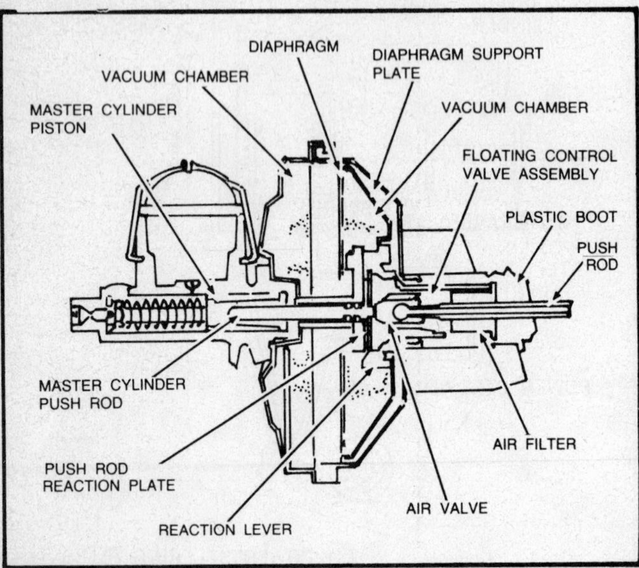

Moraine power unit

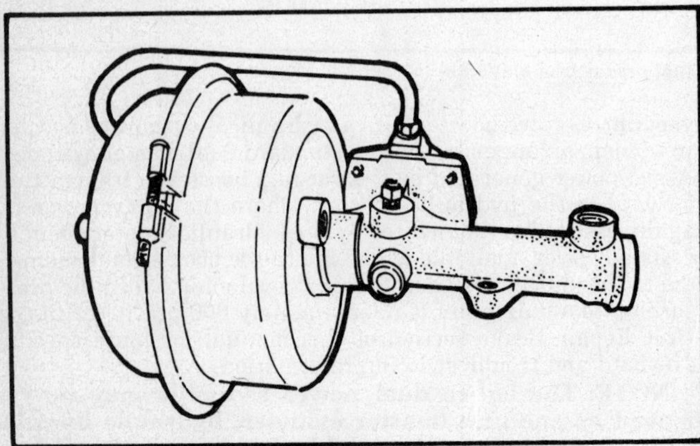

Hy-Power vacuum booster

NOTE: It is advised that a container of suitable size be placed under the master cylinder and booster assembly prior to disconnecting any fluid lines.

4. Remove, if necessary, the brake line clamps, clips and supports to allow movement of the master cylinder.
5. Remove the master cylinder mounting bolts and position the master cylinder out of the way.

NOTE: Support the master cylinder in an upright position in order to relieve strain on the brake lines and prevent spillage of hydraulic fluid.

6. Disconnect the fluid lines at the booster inlet and flow switch.
7. Remove the nuts which secure the hydraulic booster to the vacuum booster and remove the hydraulic booster.
8. Install in the reverse order of removal.
9. Torque the hydraulic booster to vacuum booster retaining nuts to 23 ft. lbs
10. Torque the master cylinder mounting bolts to 23 ft. lbs
11. Bleed the system.
12. Connect the battery ground.

VACUUM BOOSTER

Removal and Installation

1. Prevent the vehicle from moving by blocking the wheels.
2. Disconnect the battery ground.
3. Remove, if necessary, the brake line clamps, clips and support to allow movement of the master cylinder.
4. Remove the three nuts which retain the hydraulic booster to the vacuum booster.
5. Position the master cylinder and hydraulic booster out of the way.

NOTE: Support the master cylinder and hydraulic booster in an upright position in order to relive strain on the hydraulic lines and prevent spillage of hydraulic fluid.

6. Disconnect the vacuum hose from the check valve.
7. Disconnect the vacuum hose at the elbow.
8. Position the vacuum hose out of the way in order to prevent contamination.
9. Disconnect the push rod (apply rod) at the brake pedal.
10. Working from inside the cab, remove the four mounting studs which secure the vacuum booster to the cab. Pull the booster away from the cowl and remove it from the vehicle.
11. Install in the reverse order of removal.

NOTE: It will be necessary to gauge the hydraulic booster piston push rod. For information concerning the gauging procedure, refer to the Brake portion of the Unit Repair section.

12. Torque the vacuum booster mounting stud nuts to 18 ft. lbs
13. Torque the hydraulic booster to vacuum booster mounting nuts to 23 ft. lbs

MASTER–VAC

The Master–Vac, a self contained hydraulic and vacuum unit, is used on meduim duty trucks. This hydrovac is of the diaphragm type. The multi-vac-unit was designed for use with the low input-high, output system, while the newer hydrovac is used in equal displacement system. In equal displacement hydraulic system the fluid displaced by the master cylinder is equal to the fluid displaced by the power cylinder. Vacuum powered cylinders on 40–50–60, 4000–5000–6000 series with hydraulic brakes, are either single or tandem diaphragms. The tandem diaphragm unit is used with single master cylinder. Two single type diaphragm units are used with dual master cylinder units, utilizing one for each master cylinder system.

SINGLE DIAPHRAGM HYDROVAC

The Single Diaphragm Hydrovac is a self contained vacuum hydraulic power brake unit designed for use on a vehicle with a vacuum source, such as the intake manifold vacuum of a conventional gasoline engine. The Hydrovac is comprised of three basic elements:

1. A vacuum power chamber which consists of a power diaphragm and a push rod that connects the power diaphragm to the hydraulic piston.
2. A hydraulic cylinder (slave cylinder), which contains a hydraulic piston with a drilled passage, to permit the filling of the hydraulic cylinder and return of the fluid to the master cylinder upon release of the brakes.
3. A vacuum control valve built integrally with the hydraulic cylinder which controls the power output of the vacuum power chamber in accordance with the hydraulic pressure developed with the vehicle master cylinder.

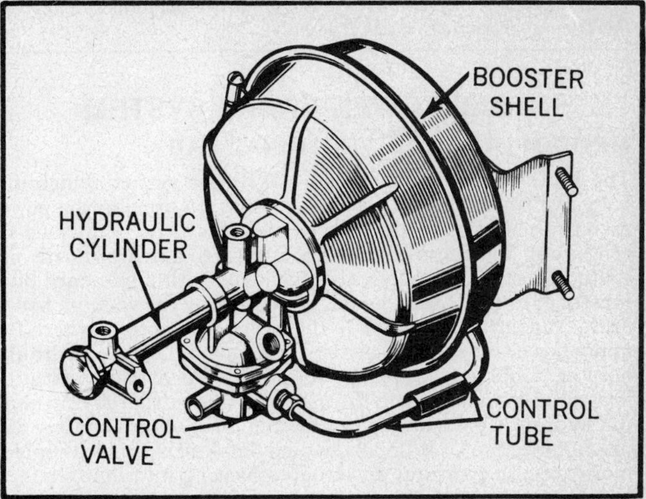

Single diaphragm Hydrovac (© General Motors Corp.)

POWER CYLINDER

Removal

NOTE: Wipe hydraulic fittings clean. Place dry cloth under lines to absorb any fluid leakage and cover the lines to keep system clean.

1. Disconnect push rod clevis at pedal. If clearance hole in dash is not large enough, remove clevis and mark position.
2. Remove vacuum hose and check valve.
3. Disconnect hydraulic lines, if necessary.
4. Remove any stop light wires.
5. Remove 4 nuts and washers holding unit to firewall. Remove unit and bracket.

Installation

1. Mount unit in place and install loosely. Secure push rod to pedal and check free-play.
2. Tighten mounting nuts and hydraulic lines.
3. Install vacuum line.
4. Connect any stop light wire.
5. Bleed brakes. Bench-bleed unit before installing. Bleed valve nearest to shell first, on units with two bleeder valves.

CAUTION

Pressure bleeding must be done with engine off (no vacuum). In manual bleeding, use engine vacuum. Start engine, allowing vacuum to build up.

6. Check brakes and stoplight before moving vehicle.
7. Units requiring lubrication, remove $\frac{1}{8}$ in. pipe plug in front end of shell (engine off). Fill with vacuum cylinder oil until oil runs out filler hole.

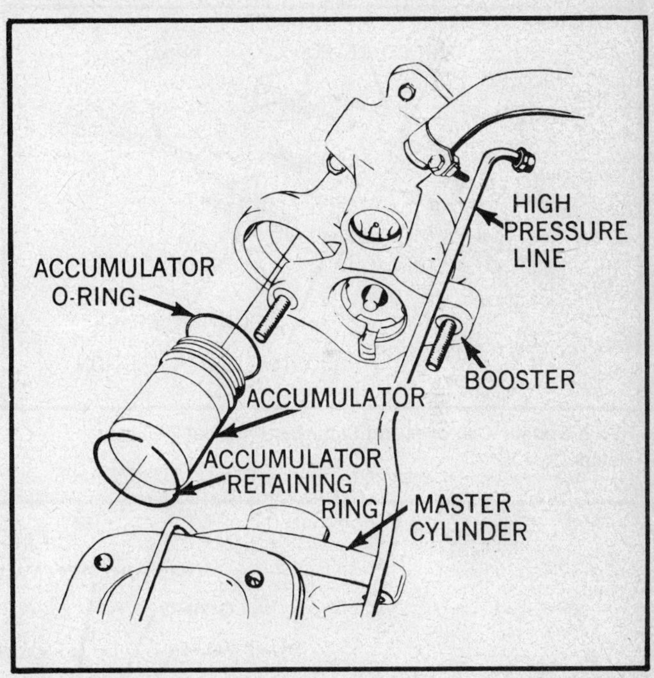

Compressed gas type accumular installation (© General Motors Corp.)

HYDRO-BOOST

Specific information will be found in the Power Brake portion of the Unit Repair section on adjustments, overhauling and troubleshooting.

The Hydro-boost system was designed to eliminate the need for the remote frame mounted boosters. It utilizes power steering fluid in place of engine vacuum to provide a power assist that operates a dual master cylinder brake system. A spring accumulator is used in conjunction with the hydraulic brake booster. The accumulator is a sealed hydraulic cylinder with a port at each end.

CAUTION

The accumulator used on hydro-boost vehicles contains compressed gas. DO NOT apply heat to the accumulator. NEVER attempt to repair an inoperative accumulator; always replace the accumulator with a new unit. In order to dispose of an inoperative accumulator, drill a

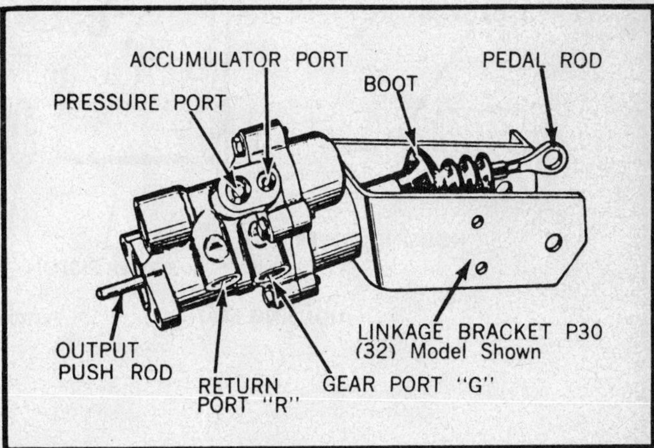

Hydro-boost—typical (© General Motors Corp.)

$^1/_{16}$ in. diameter hole through the end of the accumulator can opposite the O-ring. (compressed gas type only).

DUAL POWER BRAKE SYSTEM

MEDIUM DUTY CONVENTIONAL CAB

The Dual Power Brake System (DPB) is a system which utilizes two power boosting units in series, to provide the power assist necessary to stop the vehicle. This is accomplished by combining a vacuum operated booster with a hydraulically operated booster in tandem arrangement, with a standard dual master cylinder. Assist power, generated by the vacuum booster, is transmitted forward to the hydraulic booster, where the apply power is, again, assisted or augmented by the hydraulic booster. Doubly assisted power, available at the hydraulic booster, is transmitted to the master cylinder, thereby developing hydraulic pressure up to a maximum of approximately 600 psi. Refer to the Unit Repair section (Brakes) of this manual for more specific overhaul and troubleshooting information.

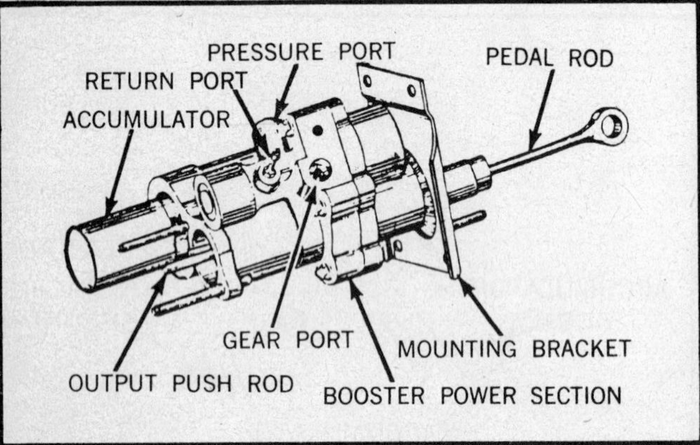

Hydro-Boost—Cab over and Suburban—typical (© General Motors Corp.)

NOTE: The entire dual power assembly may be removed as one unit (master cylinder, hydraulic booster and vacuum booster), individual units, or combinations of units.

HYDRAULIC BRAKE BOOSTER

Removal and Installation

MOTOR HOME CHASSIS

1. Make sure all pressure is discharged from the accumulator by depressing and releasing the brake pedal several times.
2. Raise the vehicle on a hoist.
3. Clean all the dirt from the booster at the hydraulic line connections and master cylinder.
4. Remove the nuts and lockwashers that secure the master cylinder to the booster and support bracket. Support the master cylinder leaving the hydraulic lines attached to the master cylinder.
5. Disconnect and plug the hydraulic lines from the booster ports.
6. Remove the cotter pin, nut, bolt and washers that secure the operating lever to the vertical brake rod.
7. Remove the six nuts, lockwashers and bolts that secure the booster linkage bracket to the front and rear support brackets, then slide the booster off the rear support studs and remove the booster from the vehicle.
8. Remove the cotter pin, nut, washer and bolt that secures the operating lever to the pedal rod.
9. Remove the brake pedal rod lever nut and bolt and then remove the lever, sleeve and bushings.
10. To install reverse the removal procedures. Bleed the booster-power steering hydraulic system and check the brake pedal and stoplamp switch adjustment.

CONVENTIONAL CAB AND SUBURBAN

1. Make sure all pressure is discharged from the accumulator by depressing and releasing the brake pedal several times.
2. Remove the nuts and lockwashers that secure the master cylinder to the booster and support bracket. Support the master cylinder leaving the hydraulic lines attached to the master cylinder.

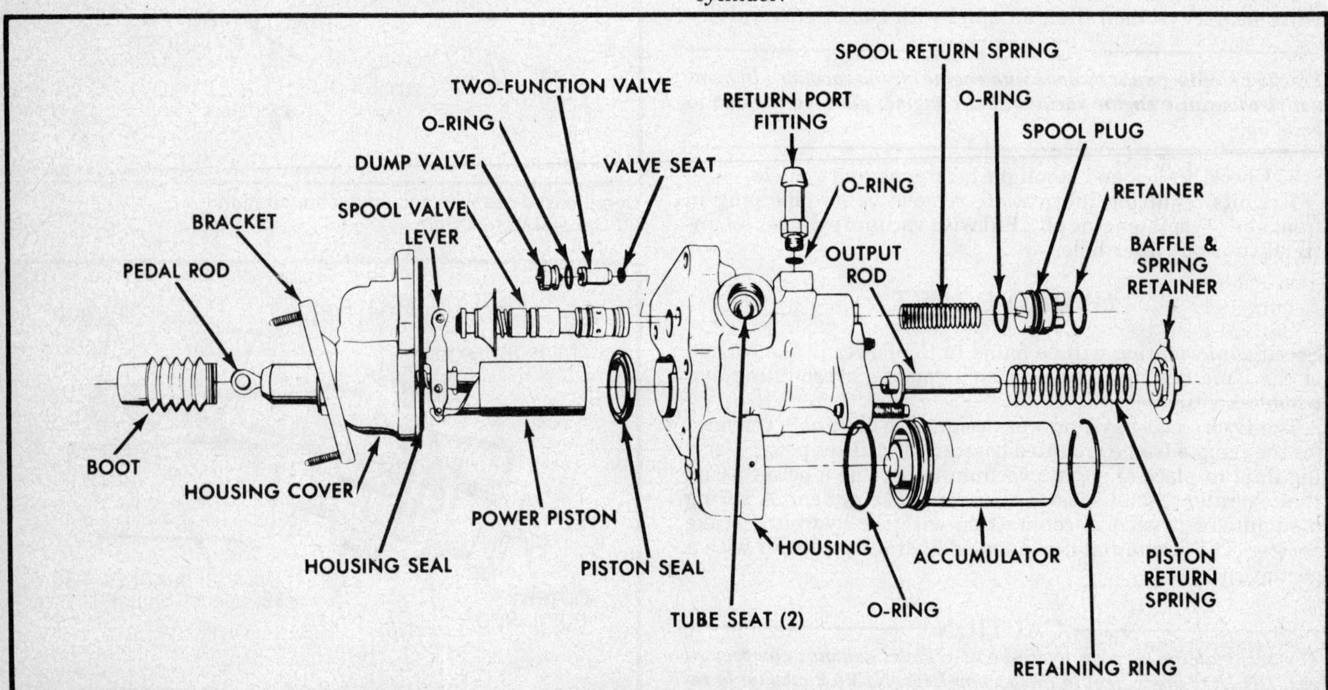

Exploded view of Bendix Hydro-boost brake unit (© General Motors Corp.)

3. Remove the booster pedal push rod cotter pin and washer and disconnect the push rod from the brake pedal.
4. Remove the booster support bracket.
5. Remove the booster bracket to dash panel or support bracket nuts and remove the booster assembly.
6. To install reverse the removal procedure. Bleed the booster-power steering hydraulic system and check brake pedal and stoplamp switch adjustment.

FORWARD CONTROL CHASSIS AND VANS

1. Make sure all pressure is discharged from the accumulator by depressing and releasing the brake pedal several times.
2. Clean all the dirt from the booster at the hydraulic line connections and master cylinder.
3. Remove the nuts and lockwashers that secure the master cylinder to the booster and the support bracket. Support the master cylinder leaving the hydraulic lines attached to the master cylinder.
4. Remove the booster pedal push rod cotter pin and washer and disconnect the push rod from the booster bracket pivot lever.
5. Remove the booster support braces.
6. Remove the booster bracket nuts and remove the booster.
7. To install, reverse the removal procedure. Bleed the booster-power steering hydraulic system and check the brake pedal and stoplamp switch adjustment.

BRAKE PEDAL

Adjustment

MOTOR HOME CHASSIS

1. With brake pedal pull back spring installed, brake pedal hard into bumper, brake master cylinder assembly and brake pedal rod lever at full return, install the preassembled brake pedal rod assembly (rod end at boot) and adjust to 31.75 in..
2. Turn the brake pedal rod end and adjust the free pedal travel to 0.06–0.36 in.
3. Fasten the boot to the floor pan assembly and compress the boot to 2.54 in. installed height.

FORWARD CONTROL CHASSIS (P and G Models)

1. Adjust the length of the pedal rod to 10.32 in. on G models.
2. Adjust the length of the pedal rod to 9.90 in. on P models.

NOTE: The brake pedal push rod is not adjustable on conventional cab models.

ELECTRO-HYDRAULIC

The booster unit is hydraulically operated with an electrical pump attached as a back-up unit in the event of primary pump failure. The booster system features a dual braking system, increased pressure output, excellent pedal feel, separate hydraulic pump and an electrically powered back-up system.

The hydraulic booster is powered by a standard power steering vane type pump.

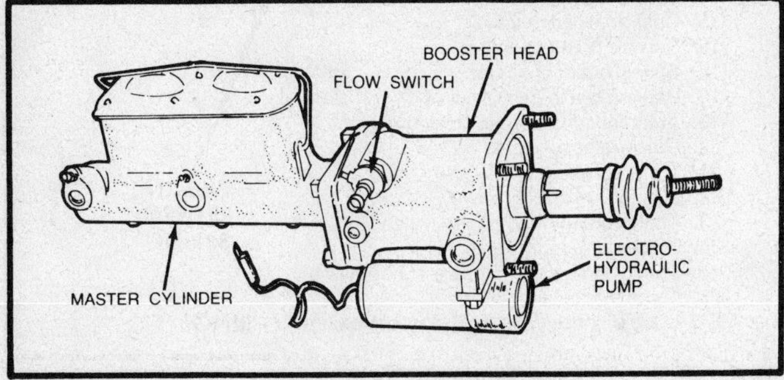

Electro-Hydraulic brake booster and master cylinder

ELECTRO-HYDRAULIC PUMP

NOTE: The pump may be removed from the booster assembly while in the vehicle.

Removal

1. Block vehicle wheels.
2. Disconnect battery ground.
3. Disconnect E.H. pump lead.
4. Position a container to catch fluid and remove bracket-to-booster $^9/_{16}$ in. hex-head bolt.
5. Remove two $^9/_{16}$ in. hex head mounting bolts. Remove pump and two O-rings.

Installation

1. To install reverse the removal procedure. Use new O-rings and torque the two $^3/_8$–16 × $1^1/_8$ in. mounting bolts to 16–30 ft. lbs

BOOSTER ASSEMBLY

Removal

CONVENTIONAL CAB

1. Block vehicle wheels.
2. Disconnect battery ground cable.
3. Disconnect electrical leads to E.H. pump and flow switch.

NOTE: Booster head may be removed from vehicle without removing master cylinder and disconnecting brake lines. Remove two nuts retaining brake line clips to line support. Remove bolt and clips in booster head. Remove four $^9/_{16}$ in. hex head master cylinder to booster head mounting bolts and move master cylinder forward from booster. Secure in an upright position. Complete booster assembly removal procedure following:

4. Disconnect hydraulic lines from booster. Use a container to catch fluid. Do not reuse fluid.
5. Remove cotter key from push rod pin. Remove nut and bolt from pedal push rod eye. Thread push rod and nut from booster push rod.
6. Remove line and hose supports from booster head.

NOTE: Use care when proceeding to next two steps. This is a heavy unit (approximately 50 pounds, including master cylinder) and should be handled as such. After removing from vehicle, use care in handling so that flow switch or E.H. pump is not damaged and bail or cover on master cylinder is not damaged.

7. Remove two $^3/_8$–24 thread hex-head nuts and washers from inside cab at dash panel.
8. Remove upper two mounting bolts and washers from booster head at dash. Remove booster assembly.
9. Remove four $^9/_{16}$ in. hex-head bolts, which attach brake master cylinder to booster head. Remove master cylinder, gasket and brake line support.

Installation

1. To install, reverse the removal procedure. Torque the four $^3/_8$–16 × $1^3/_8$ in. hex-head bolts, attaching the master cylinder to the booster head, to 16–30 ft. lbs The two hex-nuts on the $^3/_8$–24 in. studs are torqued to 25–30 ft. lbs The two mounting bolts are torqued to 25–30 ft. lbs

Removal

TILT CAB

1. Block vehicle wheels.
2. Disconnect battery ground cable.
3. Disconnect electrical lead to E.H. pump.

4. Disconnect hydraulic lines from booster and master cylinder. Use a suitable container to catch fluid. Do not reuse fluid.
5. Loosen nuts on each end of push rod extension. Turn extension until free of booster push rod. Bellcrank ball joint may have to be removed to facilitate turning extension.
6. Remove two 9/16 in. hex-head bolts and nuts retaining support to cab sill.
7. Remove two 9/16 in. hex-head bolts and nuts retaining bracket to sill.
8. Remove booster assembly. Move push rod end forward and down while revolving unit to clear E.H. pump, support and bracket.
9. Remove four 9/16 in. hex-head bolts which attach brake master cylinder to booster head and remove master cylinder and gasket.
10. The installation is the reverse of the removal procedure.

FLOW SWITCH

Removal and Installation

1. Position container to catch fluid from disconnected hose at flow switch.
2. Loosen outer hose clamp at switch and remove hydraulic line from hose. Drain fluid into previously placed container. Do not reuse fluid.
3. Loosen inner hose clamp at switch and remove hose.
4. Disconnect electrical lead to switch.
5. Remove switch using a one-inch thin blade wrench.
6. Installation is the reverse of removal. Use a new O-ring seal and torque to 20–30 ft. lbs

STOP LAMP SWITCH

Adjustment

1. Release the brake pedal to its normal position.
2. Loosen the switch locknut and rotate the switch in its bracket. Electrical contact should be made when pedal travel is 3/8–5/8 in..

Air Brakes

Specific information will be found in Air Brake Unit Repair section on adjustments, overhauling and troubleshooting.

Full air brakes completely replace all hydraulic parts with more durable components, capable of producing and using greater braking energy.

Brakes are applied by pushing on the pedal, which controls the application valve. Varying amounts of pressurized air will fill the brake chambers depending on brake pedal travel. Cam type shoe actuators (wedge type on stopmaster) are connected to push rods attached to diaphragms in the brake chamber. When air pressure is passed to brake chambers, the diaphragm then converts air pressure energy to mechanical force, the pressured diaphragms move the cam type actuators (wedge type on stopmaster), spreading the brake shoes and thereby applying brakes.

When the brake pedal (application valve) is released, a rapid discharge of air pressure from brake chambers is necessary to speed brake shoe release. A front and rear quick release valve aids in this function.

Many safety devices are used. A low air pressure warning buzzer sounds when pressure falls below a safe level. An air pressure gauge on dash shows the air pressure in system. Normal air pressure, for brake application, is at least 70 lbs. "Wet" and "dry" reserve tanks (also called primary and secondary), serve to remove moisture from air and also to provide a reserve of braking power. Drain cocks in tanks are provided to drain condensation. A pressure relief valve on the "wet" tank will release pressures over 150 lbs. A check valve located ahead of "wet" tank will retain air pressure in event of compressor failure or leaks.

Components of Air Brake System

COMPRESSOR

NOTE: Belt driven on gas engines and usually gear driven on diesel.

The air compressor serves only to supply and maintain sufficient pressure for brakes and air operated accessories. When pressure in system reaches top of normal range, an unloading valve opens and nullifies compressor action.

The average compressor is a single stage, reciprocating piston type, usually one cylinder. Larger units are two cylinders. Compressors are lubricated by the engine lubricating system.

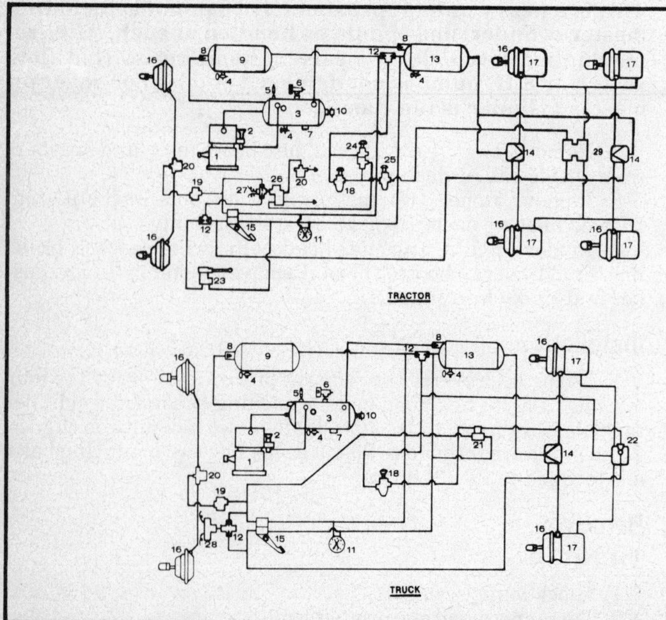

1. Air compressor
2. Governor
3. Supply reservoir
4. Drain cock
5. Safety valve
6. Pressure protection valve
7. Automatic drain valve
8. Single check valve
9. Reservoir—front system
10. Low pressure switch
11. Dual air gauge
12. Double check valve
13. Reservoir—rear system
14. Wheel lock control modulator (or service relay valve)
15. Dual application valve
16. Service brake chamber
17. Spring brake chamber
18. Parking brake control valve
19. Automatic front brake limiting valve
20. Quick release valve
21. Spring brake control valve
22. Spring brake relay valve
23. Trailer brake hand control valve
24. Trailer air supply valve
25. Tractor-only parking brake control valve
26. Tractor protection valve
27. Double check valve and stoplight switch
28. Stoplight switch
29. Combination quick release/double check valve

Typical air brake plumbing schematic on truck and tractor (© General Motors Corp.)

NOTE: In the event of freezing weather, water cooled compressors must be drained as well as engine block, or protected with sufficient anti-freeze solution .

GOVERNOR

The governor controls the load and unload mechanisms to automatically maintain maximum and minimum air pressures in reservoirs. Pressure ranges or settings are adjustable. The governor, by regulating the load and unloading mechanism, establishes an intermittent compressor pumping cycle.

BRAKE CONTROL (APPLICATION) VALVE (FOOT OPERATED)

Provides quick and sensitive control of air pressure (force) from reservoir to brake chambers. The amount of force applied to brakes is proportional to the amount of pedal depression.

RESERVOIR(S)

"Wet and Dry" tanks serve to remove moisture and provide a sufficient reserve of air under pressure for several brake applications (safety factor). Drain cocks are provided to drain condensed moisture. A dash mounted gauge will show amount of reservoir pressure.

SAFETY VALVE

The safety valve is usually mounted on reservoir, allowing air to escape when air pressure exceeds a predetermined setting and is adjustable.

CHECK VALVE

The check valve is located between "Wet" tank and compressor to retain air pressure in the event of compression (compressor or lines) failure.

LOW PRESSURE SIGNAL

The low pressure signal is a safety device (buzzer), which sounds when air pressure is absent or low.

AIR GAUGE

The air gauge is located on instrument panel and shows air pressure in system. It works in conjunction with low pressure switch to warn of low pressure.

PRESSURE PROTECTION VALVE

The pressure protection valve is mounted in the delivery port of application valve. Its function is to close all air lines to auxiliary systems in event of loss of air pressure.

RELAY VALVE

A relay valve is used as a relay station to speed the application and release of brakes because of long air lines and volume of air necessary. A relay valve is usually at rear wheels. It is connected to application valve and meters air directly to rear brake chambers from an auxiliary reservoir.

QUICK RELEASE VALVE

When brake pedal is released, a rapid discharge of air is necessary to speed the return of brake shoes. Two quick release valves are used, one with front brake chambers and one with rear brake chambers.

MOISTURE EJECTOR VALVE

The moisture ejector valve is mounted on a bracket on the cab step support, close to the wet air tank. The valve operates when brakes are applied and released to evacuate moisture from system.

BRAKE CHAMBERS

The brake chambers converts energy of compressed air into mechanical force required for brake application.

CAM TYPE

Air, admitted by control valve, enters brake chamber and pressurizes diaphragm with attached push rod. Push rod rotates lever arm of slack adjuster exerting a turning force on camshaft with an "S" design on end. This "S" cam operates between rollers on free ends of brake shoes and serves to expand shoes. Adjustment is manual at slack adjusters.

WEDGE TYPE

Features two brake chambers per wheel. Wedge type actuators, operating between roller assemblies, force *each* shoe evenly against drum. Stop-master brakes have automatic adjusters and do not need slack adjusters. *Fail-Safe* and *Super Fail-Safe* can be operated by either air or springs sure, with additional features such as spring applied parking brake and is a safety factor in event of air brake failure.

NOTE: These units have a manual release bolt, in center of chamber cap, to permit safe handling for service. See note and caution under R&R.

SLACK ADJUSTER

Used with cam type brakes to provide convenient means of adjustment for brake lining wear. With brakes applied, the angle formed by slack adjuster lever and brake chamber push rod should be approximately 90 degrees and all adjusters to be about the same angle. Excessive travel of push rod shortens the life of chamber diaphragms and also results in slow braking re-

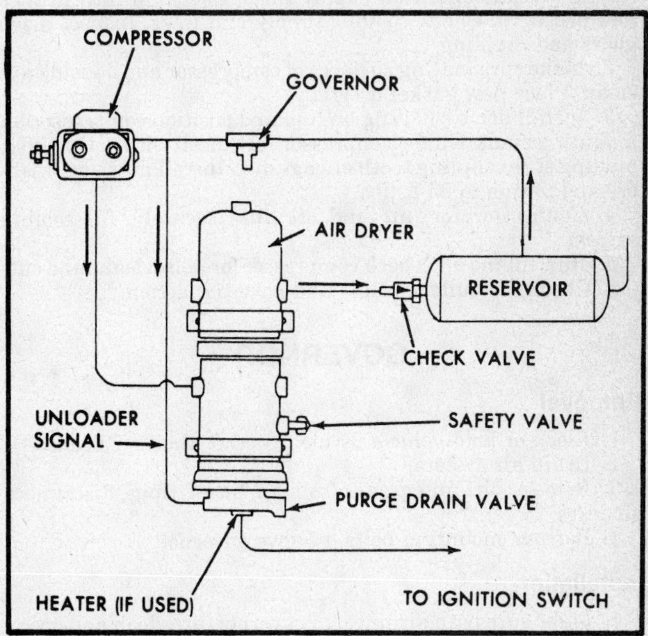

Typical air brake air dryer installation (© General Motors Corp.)

sponse. Some slack adjusters have a locking sleeve, which engages head of worm shaft adjusting bolt, that must be pushed in to clear bolt head in order to make brake adjustments. Re-engage sleeve when finished.

BELT DRIVEN COMPRESSOR

Removal

1. Block or hold vehicle by means other than air brakes.
2. Drain air from system, usually at reservoirs.
3. If water cooled, drain cooling system.
4. Disconnect ALL lines. (air, water and oil).
5. Loosen belt adjusting stud and remove drive belt.
6. Remove mounting bolts, remove compressor.

Installation

1. Run engine briefly to clear and check oil supply lines. Clean oil return lines and passages. Check coolant supply and lines (if used).
2. Clean mounting surface and replace gasket, be sure oil holes in gasket are aligned.
3. Install compressor with mounting cap screws loose, compressor will be movable to allow fittings on lines to be started.
4. Make sure air cleaner is cleaned and properly installed.
5. Align compressor, check drive belt.
6. Tighten mounting bolts and adjust belt tension.
7. Tighten all lines, fill cooling system if drained.
8. Run engine and check compressor for noises, leaks and output. Soapy water will help pin-point any air leaks. Check build-up time and governor.

GEAR DRIVEN COMPRESSOR

Removal

1. Block or hold vehicle by means other than air brakes.
2. Drain air from system.
3. Drain engine block.
4. Disconnect all lines (air, water, oil).
5. Remove four nuts and washers from mounting studs, pull compressor back off studs and remove.

Installation

1. Clear and check oil supply lines. Check oil return lines and passages. Check coolant supply and lines. Inspect drive gears and coupling.
2. Make sure mating surfaces of compressor and housing are clean. Place new gasket on studs.
3. Install drive coupling on hub and position compressor on mounting studs. Guide compressor into mesh with driven disc, making sure coupling teeth engage disc. Install nuts and washers and torque to 65 ft. lbs
4. Connect water, air and oil lines securely, fill cooling system.
5. Run engine and check compressor for noise, leaks and output. Check air build-up time and governor action.

GOVERNOR

Removal

1. Block or hold vehicle by means other than air brakes.
2. Drain air system.
3. Remove dirt and grease from air line fittings, disconnect air lines.
4. Remove mounting bolts, remove governor.

Installation

1. Make sure both air lines, to governor, are clean and open.
2. Place governor in position with exhaust port towards ground, tighten bolts finger-tight allowing unit to move. Start fittings.
3. After fittings are started, tighten governor mounting bolts then securely tighten fittings.
4. Test governor and check for leaks.

APPLICATION CONTROL VALVE

Removal

1. Block or hold vehicle by means other than air brakes.
2. Exhaust air system.
3. Remove all lines and wires.
4. Remove pedal clevis pin and pedal.
5. Remove mounting bolts, remove valve.

Installation

1. Mount valve in position, fasten loosely.
2. Start all fittings, connect stoplight wires.

NOTE: Keep any sealant compound off first two threads of fittings.

3. Tighten mounting bolts, then securely tighten all lines.
4. Replace pedal.
5. Run engine and charge air system.
6. Check all fittings with pedal depressed with soapy water solution.
7. Check and adjust pedal free play.
8. Check valve action.

RESERVOIR

Removal

1. Block or hold vehicle by means other than air brakes.
2. Exhaust air system, open drain cocks.
3. Disconnect all air lines, remove drain cock and valves.
4. Remove mounting bracket bolts and nuts, remove tank.

CAUTION

Where inside of reservoir is sludged and steam is used to clean, do not plug up reservoir or use excessive steam pressure.

NOTE: In cold weather, more attention should be given to draining of moisture.

Installation

1. Install reservoir in place loosely.
2. Start all fittings, valves and drain cock.
3. Tighten all mounting bolts and nuts to make sure reservoir does not vibrate in service. (Vibration causes premature line failures).
4. Securely tighten all lines, drain cock and valves.
5. Run engine, charge air system.
6. Check for leaks.

VALVES, SIGNALS and GAUGES

Removal

1. Block or hold vehicle by means other than air brakes.
2. Exhaust air system, make certain ignition is off.
3. Clean work area, remove any wires, air lines and brackets. Remove unit.

Installation

1. Position replacement unit in system, making certain of any markings showing air flow direction and secure.
2. Connect any wires and air lines.
3. Run engine and charge air system.
4. Test for leaks and operation of unit.

CAM TYPE CHAMBER (USES SLACK ADJUSTERS, ONE PER WHEEL)

Removal

1. Disconnect air hose from chamber.
2. Remove clevis pin from yoke.
3. Remove nuts and washers from mounting studs.
4. Remove chamber.

Installation

1. Place chamber on mounting bracket and secure with stud nuts and lock washers.
2. Connect air hose.
3. Install slack adjuster yoke clevis pin, after adjusting for minimum travel.

NOTE: Angle made by push rod and slack adjuster lever should not be less than 90°, brakes applied. Lock yoke with locking nut. Push rod travel should be as short as possible without brakes dragging.

4. Check for leaks and possible brake shoe adjustment.

WEDGE TYPE CHAMBER (TWO PER WHEEL)

Removal

1. Block or hold vehicle by means other than air brakes.
2. Disconnect air hose from chamber.
3. Remove lock washer tangs from notches in spanner nut and spider housing.
4. Loosen spanner nut and unscrew air chamber from housing.

Installation

1. Screw air chamber in spider housing until it "bottoms", then back off (no more than one turn) until chamber air port aligns with air hose. The plastic guide will assure proper position of wedge. Lock brake chamber in position with spanner nut and lock washer.
2. Start engine, charge air system, check for leaks. Pump brake pedal to allow automatic adjusters to adjust brakes.

NOTE: When brakes are equipped with "fail-safe" brake chambers, cage power spring before starting any disassembly or removal of wheels or drums to avoid possible injury. When a vehicle is disabled, due to low or lost air pressure, cage power spring before attempting to move the vehicle. Cage the power spring by rotating the release bolt approximately 18 to 21 turns clockwise. Caging and uncaging can be made easier by applying air pressure, 65 lbs. needed (if possible). This takes spring load off release bolt.

CAUTION

Before removing or caging brake chamber, block wheels since parking brake will not be applied.

SLACK ADJUSTER

Removal

1. Remove clevis pin at lever.
2. Remove lock ring and washer on splined camshaft (some front slack adjusters are held on by a retaining screw).
3. Slide adjuster off splined shaft.

Installation

1. Make sure spacer washers are in place (if used).

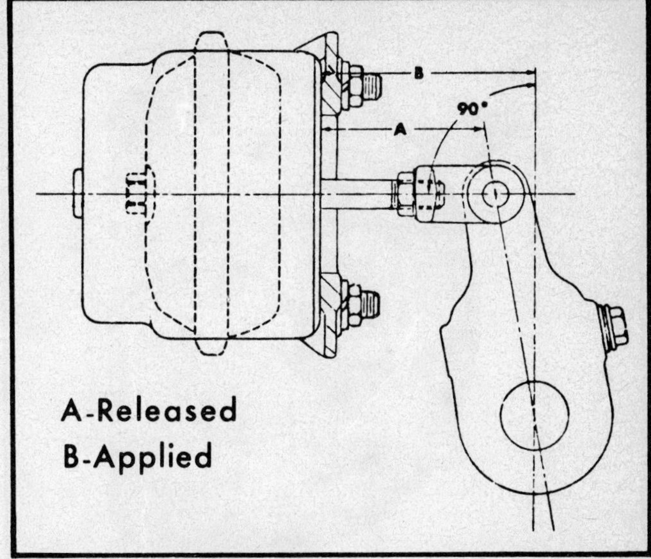

Slack adjuster and pushrod angle (© General Motors Corp.)

2. Slide slack adjuster on splined camshaft, lock in place with snap-ring and washer. If held on by retaining screw, allow 0.010 in. end-play. Stake edge of screw to lock.
3. Connect yoke clevis pin. Angle made by push rod and slack adjuster lever should NOT be less than 90° brakes applied. Push rod travel should be as short as possible without brakes dragging.
4. Lubricate adjuster.

Parking Brake Systems

HY-PARK SYSTEM

The Hy-Park brake system is comprise basically of a hydraulic service brake system in conjuction with a hydraulically released, spring applied parking brake.

Hydraulic brake fluid from the master cylinder is used to actuate the rear S-cam service brakes. A hydraulic pump (power steering pump on medium duty trucks) delivers power steering fluid, under pressure, to compress the power spring in the Hy-Park acuator (chamber). Application and release of the parking brake is controlled by a hand valve, which is located in the cab. The rear brake is a conventional S-cam brake such as the type found on vehicles equipped with air brakes. Refer to the Unit Repair section (Brakes) of this manual for specific repair information.

Caging Hy-Park Actuator Power Spring

CAUTION

Failure to properly cage the spring before removal or disassembly could result in serious personal injury, as the load on the compressed power spring is approximately 2,000 pounds.

NOTE: Two special release studs, nuts and washers will be needed to cage one power spring (illustration).

CAGING WITH ENGINE OPERATING

1. Prevent the vehicle from moving by blocking the wheels or by whatever means is safe and convenient.
2. Start the engine.
3. Release the parking brakes by using the cab control valve.
4. Install a washer on a release stud and thread a nut on the stud for a few turns.

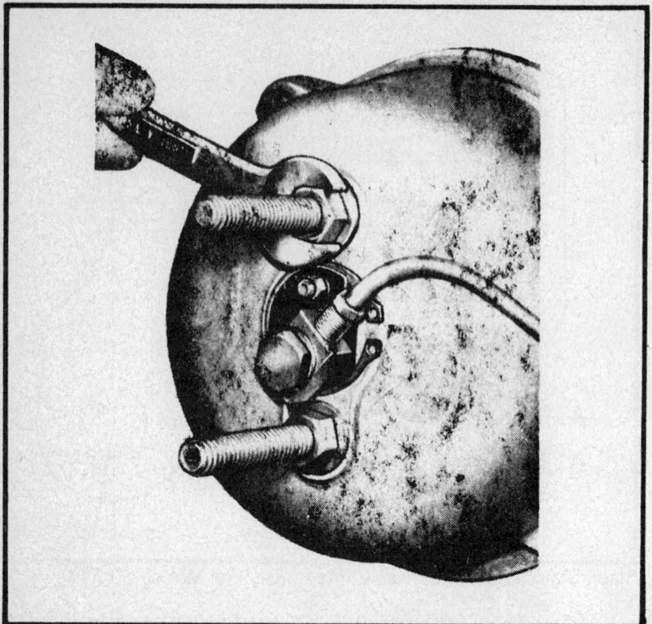

Release studs—installed (© General Motors Corp.)

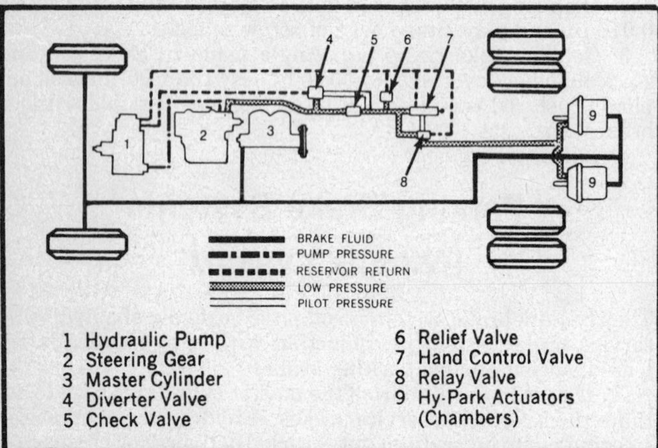

Hy-Park brake system—typical (© General Motors Corp.)

5. Remove the dust caps from the slots in the rear of the actuator and insert a release stud, nut and washer assembly until there is metal to metal contact. Do not force.

6. Turn the release study 1/4 turn clockwise and pull outward to engage the stud in the recess in the diaphragm support assembly.

7. While pulling outward on the release stud with a slight force, try rotating the stud in either direction. If the stud has been properly installed, it will not turn. Continue holding the stud firmly in this position.

8. Thread the nut on the stud until the nut and washer contact the rear housing. Hand tighten to ensure that there is a firm contact.

9. Repeat Steps 4 through 8 for the other release stud assembly.

NOTE: If the system has been operating properly, i.e., if the power spring has been hydraulically compressed, then the release studs are now in position to properly contain (cage) the power spring and the engine may be shut off. With the engine not running and the parking brake applied, the power spring will begin to expand, but it will be prevented from expanding as the release studs now hold the spring in the caged position.

10. Continue tightening the release stud nuts until the diaphragm support assembly bottoms out against the rear housing.

CAGING WITH ENGINE NOT OPERATING

In the event of a parking brake hydraulic system malfunction, manually release the parking brakes and cage the power spring by following the steps of the previous procedure noting the following exceptions.

1. Only start the nut onto the threads of the release stud. This is done because almost the full length of the studs will be required to reach the diaphragm support assembly.

2. Tighten the release nuts in an alternate and gradual manner until the power spring is compressed. Continue tightening the release stud nuts until the diaphragm support assembly bottoms out against the rear housing.

CAUTION

Failure to tighten the release stud nuts alternately could cause the sleeve and diaphragm support assembly to tilt and bind in the housing.

NOTE: Bottoming out will occur when the extension of the end of the stud beyond the housing is approximately 2 7/8 in.

HY-PARK ACTUATOR

Removal and Installation

CAUTION

The Hy-Park actuator houses two types of hydraulic fluid: brake fluid and power steering fluid. These two very different types of hydraulic fluid are not compatible and should not be allowed to come into contact with one another, nor should they be allowed to come into contact with components of the system for which they are not intended. If, at any time during removal or installation, either fluid contacts a rubber sealing component of the wrong system, i.e., should power steering fluid contaminate the apply piston double lip seal, or, if brake fluid should contaminate the actuator diaphragm or boot, then the affected seal(s) should be discarded, as the fluid will attack the seal and cause it to deteriorate. If care is not exercised to isolate these two fluids, then inevitable deterioration will result, causing leakage at the seals and eventual system malfunction.

1. Prevent the vehicle from moving by blocking the wheels.
2. Disconnect the battery ground.
3. Disconnect the brake fluid line from the piston housing, located at the rear of the actuator.
4. Disconnect the power steering fluid line from the front of the housing.

NOTE: After disconnecting the fluid lines, cover the openings immediately to contain the fluid and prevent contamination.

5. Disconnect the push rod clevis pin from the slack adjuster.
6. Remove the nuts and lock washers from the mounting studs.
7. Remove the actuator from the mounting bracket.
8. Drain all remaining fluid.
9. Install in the reverse order of removal.

NOTE: During installation, position the actuator so that the brake bleeder valve is above the brake line.

RELAY VALVE

Removal and Installation

1. Disconnect the battery ground.
2. Pull the control valve knob outward and set the parking brakes.
3. Disconnect the return line.

4. Disconnect the remaining lines.

NOTE: Cap all open lines.

5. Remove the two, valve-to-frame, attaching bolts and nuts on conventional cab models. Remove the two, valve-to-support, attaching bolts and nuts on aluminum conventional cab models.
6. Disconnect the actuator delivery lines from the base of the valve and remove the valve.
7. Remove the bracket from the valve.
8. Install in the reverse order of removal.

PRESSURE RELIEF VALVE

Removal and Installation

1. Disconnect the battery ground.
2. Disconnect the hydraulic lines at the valve and plug the lines.
3. Remove the bracket-to-frame attaching bolts and nuts.
4. Install in the reverse order of removal.
5. Torque the valve mounting bolt nuts to 75 inch lbs.

CHECK VALVE

Removal and Installation

1. Disconnect the battery ground.
2. Disconnect the lines from the "T" fitting on the end of the valve.
3. Remove the fittings from the "T" as necessary.
4. Remove the check valve by unscrewing it in a counterclockwise direction.
5. Remove the "T" from the check valve.
6. Install in the reverse order of removal.

DIVERTER VALVE

Removal and Installation

1. Disconnect the battery ground.
2. Disconnect the return line.
3. Disconnect the pilot line.

NOTE: Cap all open lines.

4. For conventional cab models, remove the check valve and then thread the diverter valve from the pressure line. For aluminum conventional cab models, turn the valve down 90 degrees, turn the valve outwards 180 degrees and thread the diverter valve from the bushing and elbow.

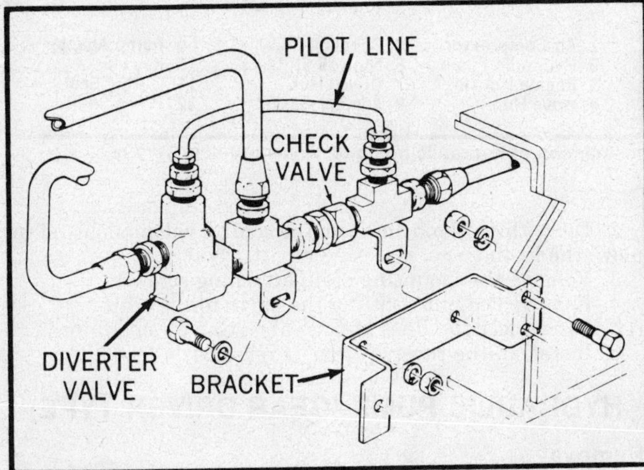

Installation of check and diverter valves—medium duty conventional cab (© General Motors Corp.)

NOTE: In order to allow movement of the line to provide clearance for valve movement, it may be necessary to remove the clip on the hydraulic pressure line to the booster.

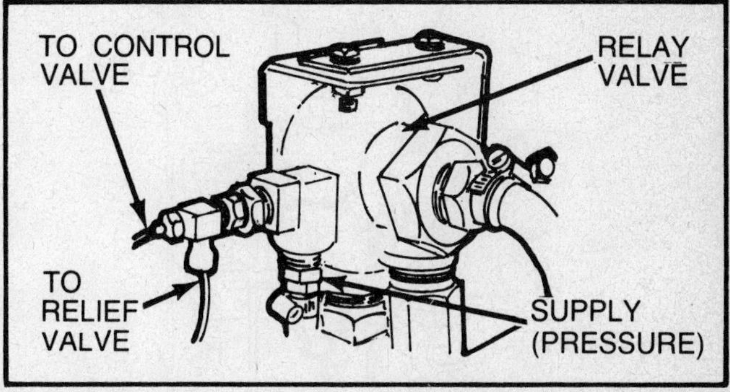

Relay valve—installed on aluminum conventional cab (© General Motors Corp.)

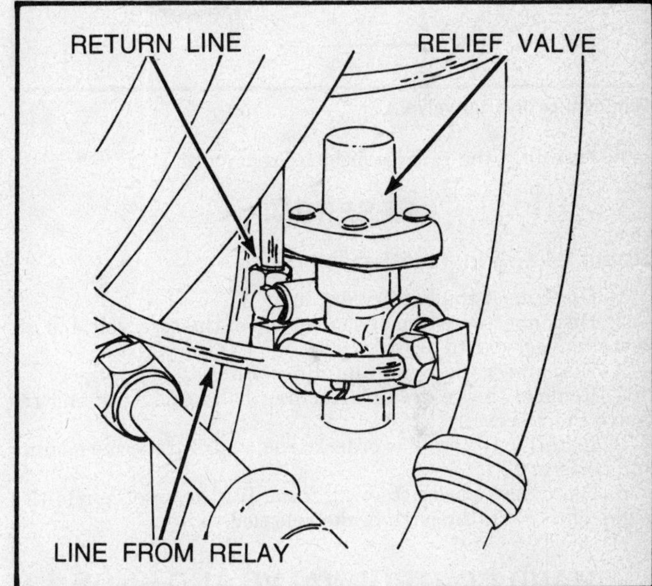

Pressure relief valve—installed on aluminum conventional cab (© General Motors Corp.)

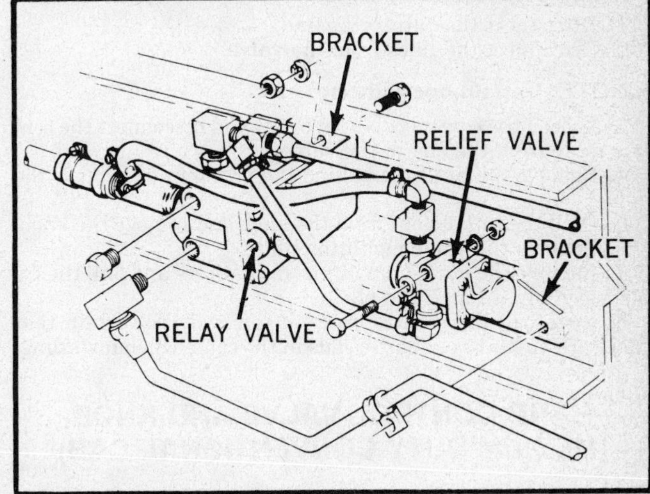

Pressure relief and relay valves—installed on medium duty conventional cab (© General Motors Corp.)

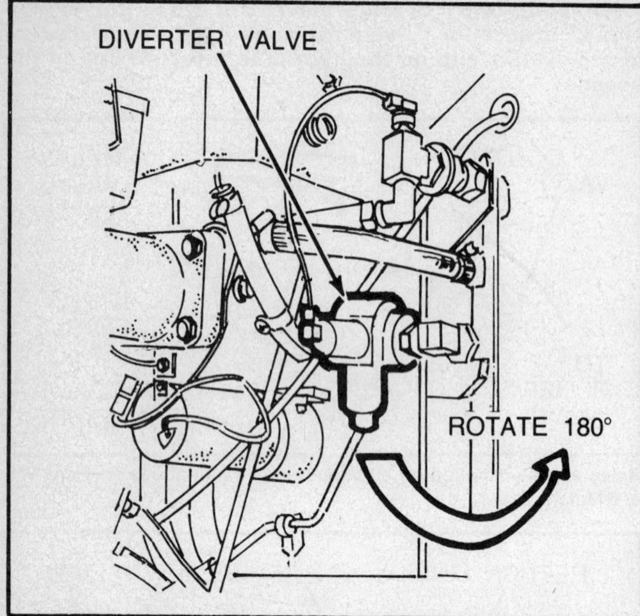

Removal of diverter valve

5. Install in the reverse order of removal.

RESERVOIR

Removal and Installation

1. Disconnect the battery ground.
2. Disconnect one line at the bottom of the reservoir and allow the reservoir to drain.
3. Disconnect the remaining lines. Plug all open lines.
4. Remove the reservoir attaching bolts and nuts and remove the reservoir.
5. Install in the reverse order of removal. Torque the mounting bolts to 27 ft. lbs
6. Using new power steering fluid, fill the reservoir to the sight glass with the park brake released.

HAND CONTROL VALVE AND KNOB (ALUMINUM CONVENTIONAL CAB)

Removal and Installation

1. Disconnect the battery ground.
2. Disconnect the lines from the valve.

NOTE: Cap all open lines.

3. Loosen the control cable set screw and disconnect the control cable from the end of the valve.
4. Remove the nut from behind the bracket and remove the valve.
5. Drill the roll pin out from the knob and remove the knob.
6. Remove the valve mounting plate.
7. Remove the hexagonal nut from the plate and pull the cable assembly through the plate.
8. Install in the reverse order of removal. Be certain that there are no kinks or sharp bends in the cable when installing.

HAND CONTROL VALVE AND KNOB (MEDIUM DUTY CONVENTIONAL CAB)

Removal and Installation

1. Disconnect the battery ground.

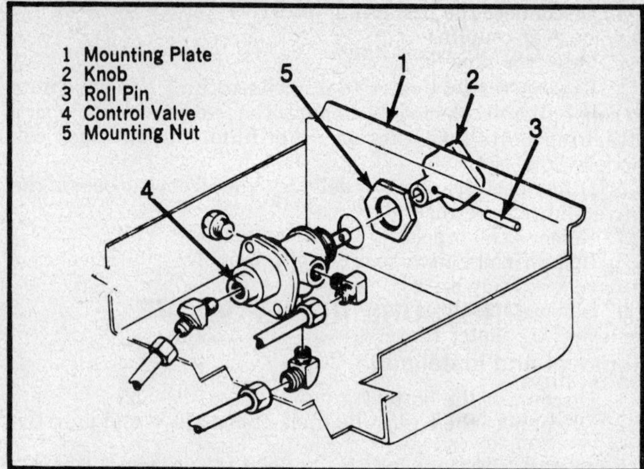

Installation of control valve—medium duty conventional cab (© General Motors Corp.)

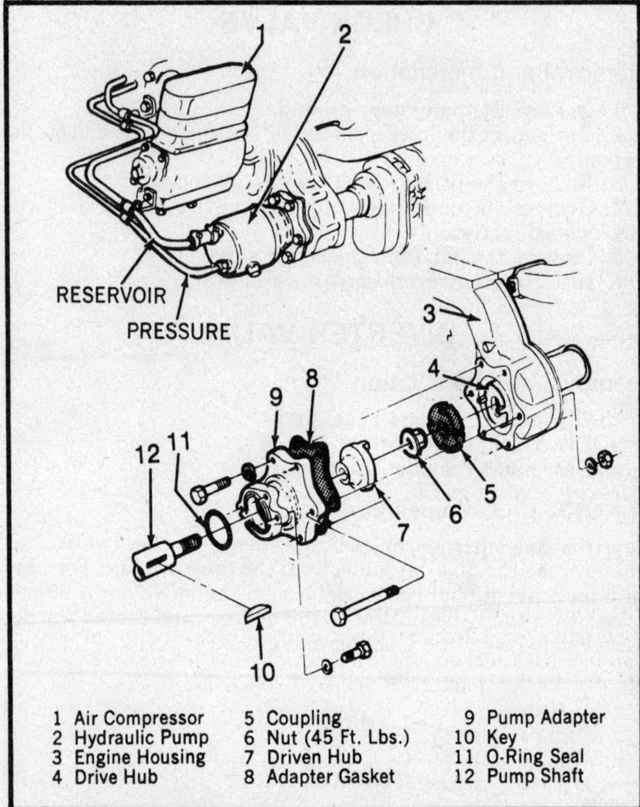

Installation of hydraulic pump (© General Motors Corp.)

2. Drive the roll pin out from the control valve knob and remove the knob.
3. Remove the mounting plate attaching screws.
4. Remove the nut securing the valve to the plate.
5. Disconnect the lines at the valve. Cap all open lines.
6. Install in the reverse order of removal.

HYDRAULIC PUMP (GEAR DRIVEN TYPE)

Removal

1. Disconnect the battery ground.
2. Remove the engine access cover from inside the cab.

3. Disconnect the exhaust pipe from the exhaust manifold and the rear coupling.
4. Move the pipe forward and away from the pump.
5. Disconnect the lines at the pump. Cap all open lines.
6. Remove the six pump-to-engine attaching bolts and discard the mounting gasket.
7. Remove the coupling from the pump drive hub.

NOTE: The coupling may remain on the engine drive hub.

8. Remove the $^3/_4$ in. hexagonal nut from the pump shaft and remove the pump drive hub.
9. Remove the three, adapter-to-pump, attaching bolts and remove the adapter from the pump. Discard the seal ring.

Installation

1. Position a new seal ring in the adapter housing groove.
2. Position the adapter in its correct position on the pump and install the three attaching bolts and washers. Torque the bolts to 27 ft. lbs
3. Position the pump drive hub over the pump shaft and Woodruff key.
4. Thread the hexagonal nut onto the pump shaft and torque to 45 ft. lbs
5. Install the coupling on the pump drive hub and position a new gasket on the adapter flange.
6. Position the pump assembly onto the engine and install the six attaching bolts and washers. Make sure that the slots in the coupling are aligned with the tabs on the engine drive hub. Torque the nuts and bolts to 27 ft. lbs
7. Connect all fluid lines to the pump.
8. Install the exhaust pipe.
9. Connect the battery ground.
10. Install the engine access cover.

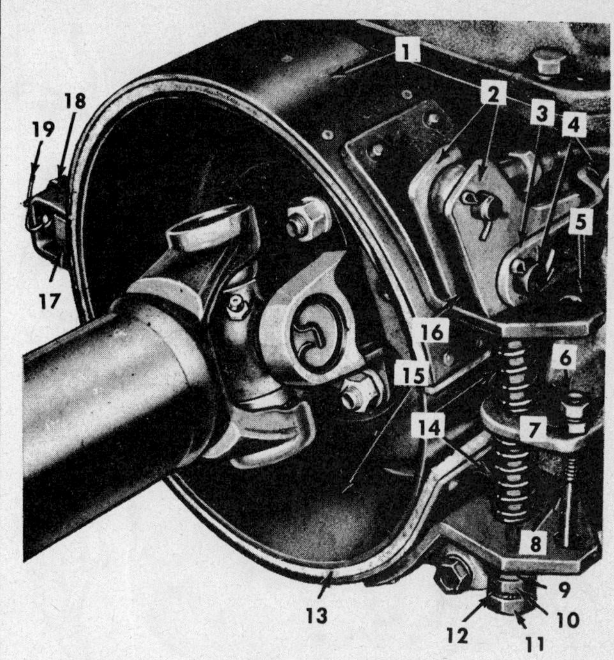

Contracting band (external) parking brake (© General Motors Corp.)

PARKING BRAKE

Adjustment

NOTE: Except in case of an emergency, set parking brake only after vehicle is brought to a complete stop. Parking brakes are not designed to take the place of service brakes.

DRIVE SHAFT–BAND TYPE

This type, using external band and drum mounted on rear of transmission, provides a hand controlled brake independent of service brakes. The band with lining, is centered on transmission bracket (anchor) and both sides are arranged to contract equally. Brake is actuated by lever and rod, or cable, to a cam and "J" bolt.

1. Block wheels and release hand brake.
2. Remove locking wire from anchor bolt and adjust to obtain 0.010 in. clearance between lining and drum. Rewire anchor.
3. Loosen lock nut on locating bolt and tighten adjusting nut until there is a clearance of 0.020 in. between lining and drum. Measure clearance about 3 inches from end of lining. Tighten lock nut.
4. Loosen lock nut on adjusting "J" bolt and tighten adjusting nut to obtain a clearance of 0.020 in. approximately 3 inches from end of lining. Tighten lock nut.
5. Check hand brake operation by applying lever. If more than $^1/_2$ the number of notches on sector are needed to lock the propeller shaft, make final adjustment on lever rod, at clevis end. Remove blocks.

PROPELLER SHAFT–SHOE TYPE

Hand brake drum is mounted on rear of transmission with internal and external shoes (DUO-GRIP) or with two internal expanding shoes. Shoes are forced against drum by lever and cam actuated by cable. Propeller shaft brakes lock the driveline for parking.

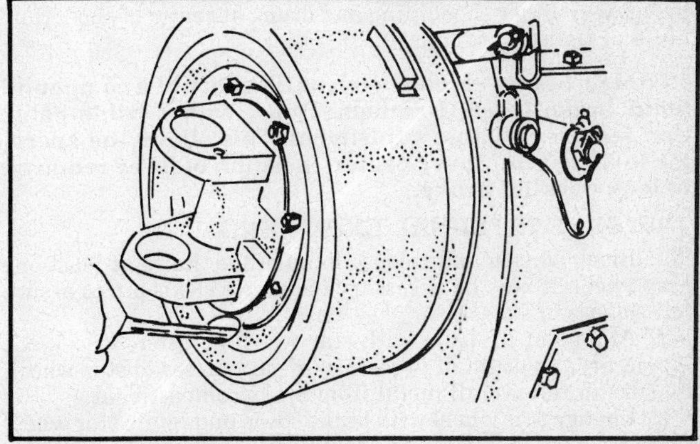

Internal expanding type adjustment

DUO-GRIP

1. Block wheels and release hand brake.
2. Loosen lock nut and tighten adjusting bolt to obtain 0.010 in. clearance between outer shoe lining and drum at this point. Hold bolt and lock nut securely.

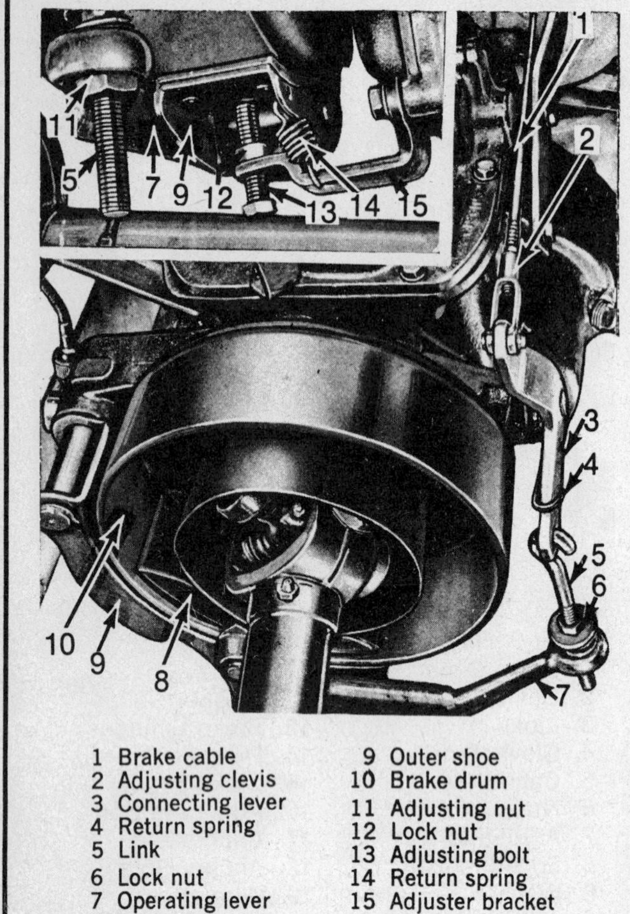

Two shoe (Duo Grip) parking brake (© General Motors Corp.)

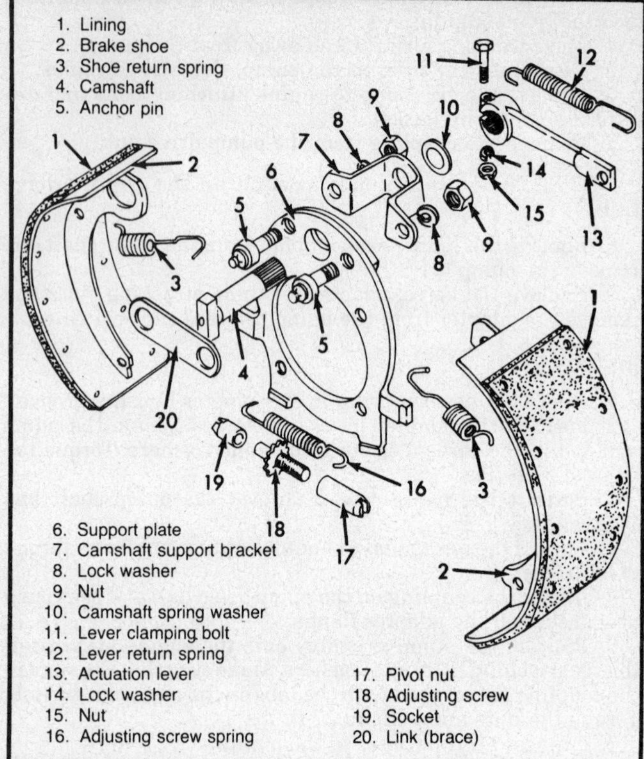

Internal expanding type brake (© General Motors Corp.)

3. Loosen lock nut and tighten adjusting nut to obtain 0.010 in. between inner shoe lining and drum, at center of shoe. Hold nut and tighten nut.

NOTE: Some vehicles, such as tilt cab, use a compound hand brake lever (Orscheln Type), with flexible cable that features a cable adjustment. This allows the operator to adjust the "over-center" position of lever required to lock parking brake.

TWO SHOE INTERNAL EXPANDING

1. Block wheels and release hand brake. Raise at least one rear wheel. It may be necessary to remove clevis pin to assure full release of shoes.
2. Align slot in drum with star wheel adjuster. Knock out lanced area in drum, if necessary to gain access to star wheel. Be sure to remove all metal from brake compartment.
3. Engage star wheel with brake spoon and rotate star wheel to obtain a 0.010 in. clearance between lining and drum. Shoes can be expanded so as to lock drum then backed off 5 notches, similar to a wheel adjustment. Check drum for free rotation after adjustment.
4. Replace clevis, install drum hole cover, remove jack and blocks.

FOOT CONTROLLED, REAR WHEEL CABLE TYPE (EXCEPT S–SERIES TRUCKS AND SMALL VANS)

Hand lever or foot pedal operated, cable actuated, rear wheel service brakes are used for parking brakes.

1. Block front wheels and apply hand brake four notches from released position.
2. Jack up both rear wheels.
3. With all cables, linkage and pull back spring in place, loosen cable adjusting lock nut and tighten adjusting nut until a slight drag is felt when rotating rear wheels. Tighten lock nut.
4. Fully release parking brake and check both rear wheels. No drag should be present.
5. Remove jack and blocks.

NOTE: Adjustment of cable should only be made when service brakes are in full adjustment. Cables should be lubricated when rear drums are off.

ORSCHELN TYPE

1. Turn the adjusting knob on the parking brake lever counterclockwise to its stop.
2. Apply the parking brake.
3. Raise the vehicle and support safely.
4. Loosen the nut on the intermediate cable equalizer and adjust the nut to give a slight drag at the rear wheels.
5. Readjust the parking brake lever knob to give a definite snap–over–center feel.

S–SERIES TRUCKS, ASTRO/SAFARI AND BLAZER/ JIMMY

Adjustment of parking brake system is necessary whenever the parking brake cables have been disconnected.

1. Set parking brake pedal at specified number of clicks:
2 wheel drive pickups, Astro/Safari and Blazer/Jimmy = 2 clicks
4 wheel drive pickups and Blazer/Jimmy = 3 clicks
2. Raise and safely support vehicle.

Some pick–up trucks will have an intermediate cable guide bracket. This must be removed before making any parking brake cable adjustments

3. Tighten the equalizer nut until the the rear wheels will not rotate without excessive force in a forward direction.
4. Back off the equalizer nut until there is moderate drag when the rear wheels are rotated in a forward direction. Reinstall the cable guide, if removed.

NOTE: The cables are not to be adjusted to tightly as brake drag will result.

5. Release the parking brake and rotate the rear wheels. There should be no brake drag.
6. Lower the vehicle and verify parking brake adjustment.

REAR WHEEL–AIR BRAKE

NOTE: For Stopmaster fail-safe and super fail-safe information, see brake chamber section. (automatic adjusters)

ANCHORLOK

Anchorlok chamber is mounted "piggy back" on service chamber. It contains a diaphragm under air pressure (60 pounds or more) to contain a powerful spring in compression in normal operation. When air pressure drops below 60 pounds, the coiled spring starts to move out. If air pressure continues to drop, the spring will keep expanding to apply brakes until at approximately 30 pounds, the spring will have applied the brakes sufficiently to bring the vehicle to a safe, even stop.

To permit moving vehicle when air pressure is not available to compress spring, a caging tool, consisting of a stud and nut will be found stored on service chamber housing. Remove rubber plug in center of anchorlok and insert stud $\frac{1}{4}$ turn. Turning nut on stud will cage spring.

CAUTION

Cage spring before removing or servicing anchorlock.

TRU-STOP (DISC TYPE)

This type brake is used only on models equipped with an auxiliary transmission. It uses a ventilated brake disc which is mounted between the propeller shaft flange and the auxiliary transmission shaft companion flange. The brake shoes are mounted in the opposed positions with the brake disc between. When the brake is applied, the shoes are forced against the disc.

1. Disconnect the brake cable or rod clevis from the brake lever.
2. Tighten the adjusting nut until the spring exerts enough pressure to bring the lever against the front lever arm.
3. Insert a $\frac{1}{32}$ in. shim between the rear shoe lining and brake disc.
4. Tighten the adjusting nut until the front shoe lining is firmly against the disc yet still allowing removal of the shim.
5. Make sure that the tensions spring is in place. Make sure that both linings are parallel with the disc by adjusting the parallel adjusting screws. This provides $\frac{1}{64}$ inch clearance between the front and rear shoe linings and brake disc at all points.

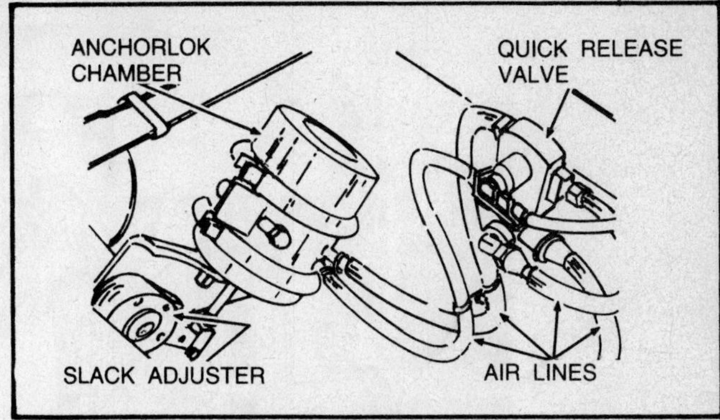

Anchor lock brake chamber—installed

Spring compressor assembly—installed (© General Motors Corp.)

6. Check to see that brake lever in the cab is in the full released position. Adjust the clevis on the brake cable as necessary, to permit installation of the clevis pin through the clevis and brake lever, without changing position of the lever. Install the clevis pin and cotter pin.
7. Make sure the lock nuts on the brake cable and adjusting screws are firmly tightened.

STOPGARD SPRING BRAKE CHAMBER

The "Stopgard" chamber is used as a service brake chamber and an emergency brake, in case of air pressure loss and a spring-applied parking brake. It consists of two separate air chambers, each having its own diaphragm and push rod, an adapter case and clamps.

1
2
3
4
3
4
5
7
8
7
8
10
9
6
15
14
13
16
17
12
11

1 Brake support bracket
2 Parallel adjusting screws
3 Front lever arm pin
4 Pin retaining screw
5 Brake cable clevis
6 Brake lever
7 Brake shoe pin retainer
8 Brake shoe pin
9 Front brake shoe
10 Rear brake shoe
11 Front lever arm
12 Brake disc
13 Tension spring
14 Spring
15 Rear lever arm
16 Adjusting nut
17 Tie rod

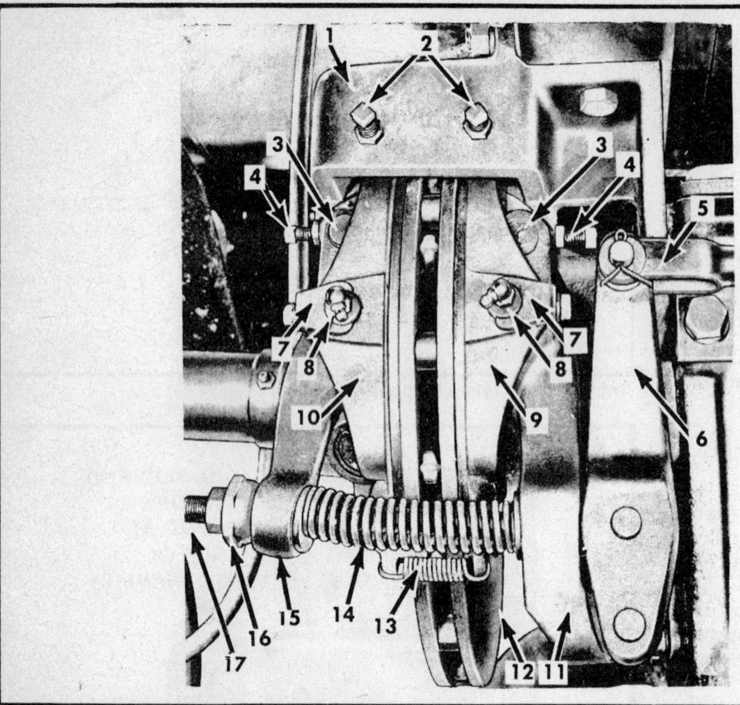

Tru-Stop parking brake (© General Motors Corp.)

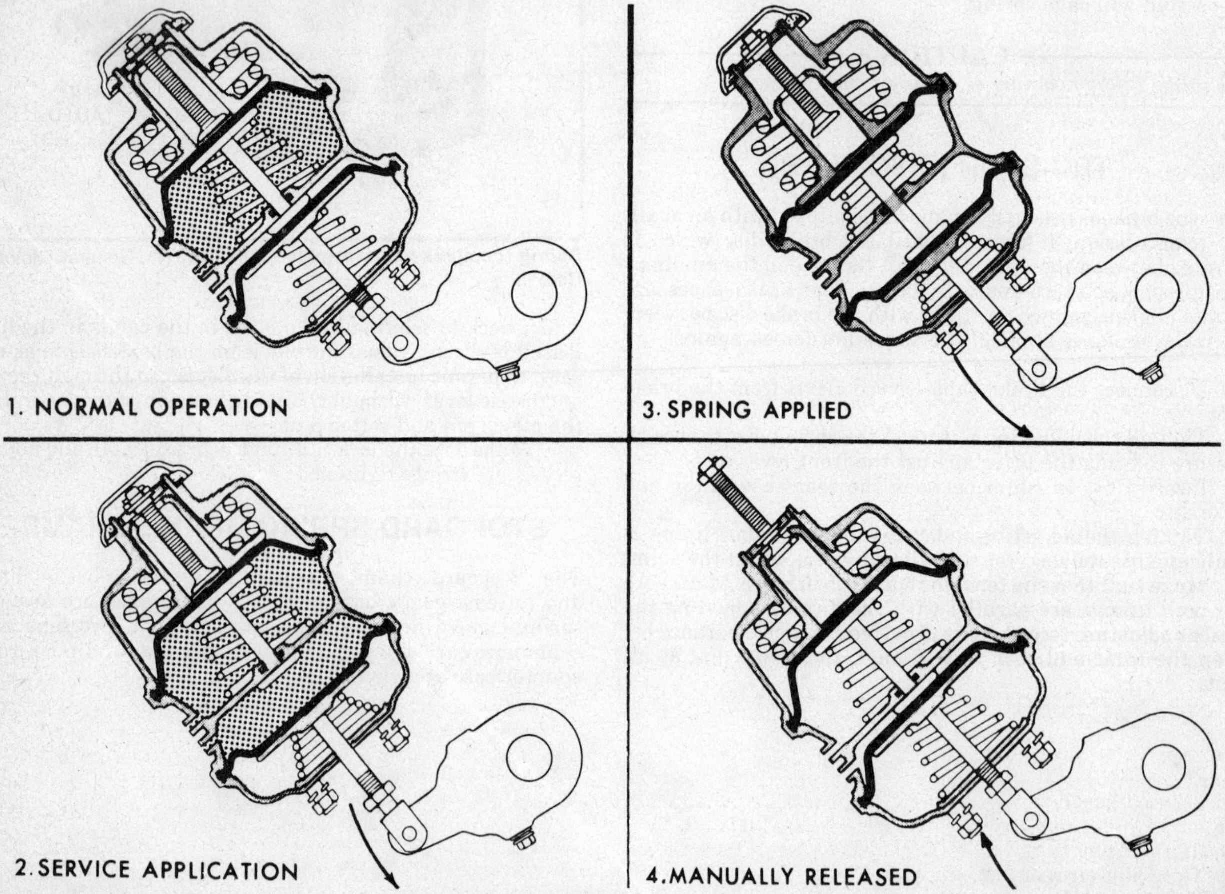

1. NORMAL OPERATION
3. SPRING APPLIED
2. SERVICE APPLICATION
4. MANUALLY RELEASED

Stopgard brake chamber operation (© General Motors Corp.)

FUEL SYSTEM

This section contains brief information on removal, installation and minor external adjustments. For more detailed information, see Carburetor Unit Repair section.

Carburetor

Various carburetors are designed to meet requirements of engine, transmission and vehicle; therefore, carburetors may look alike, but are not always interchangeable. All carburetors have conventional float, idle, low speed, power or high speed and accelerating circuits with either manual or automatic chokes.

NOTE: Some symptoms may indicate carburetor trouble, but in reality, the symptoms maybe resulting from other engine related problems. Before any extensive repairs on carburetor, check engine condition, heat riser, intake manifold and ignition components.

Removal

1. Remove air cleaner.
2. Disconnect fuel, vacuum, spark control and governor lines. Mark as required.
3. Disconnect choke and hand throttle controls, if equipped.
4. Disconnect throttle and automatic transmission linkage at carburetor. Remove pull back spring.
5. Remove mounting nuts and washers.
6. Lift carburetor off manifold and drain. Discard gasket.

Installation

1. Clean carburetor mounting surface.
2. Install new gasket on manifold. Be sure vacuum port and gasket slots are aligned.
3. Place carburetor on manifold, reconnect and finger-tight all lines before evenly tightening carburetor mounting nuts.
4. Tighten all lines.
5. Reconnect choke and hand throttle controls (if equipped), replace throttle and automatic transmission linkage, reconnect all vacuum and electrical lines. Connect pull back spring. Check choke and throttle operation.
6. Install air cleaner.
7. Start engine and warm to operating temperature.
8. Adjust idle mixture and idle speed screws with choke fully open. See Unit Repair section for procedures.

CAUTION

Do not force idle mixture screw against seat as this will damage needle. On transmission controlled spark engines (TCS), fast idle adjustment must be set with electrical leads disconnected at solenoid and transmission in neutral.

NOTE: If possible (safely), fill carburetor bowl before installing. This will save time and battery drain as well as reducing possible backfiring. Check all filters. For idle speed and mixture adjustments (see Tune-Up decal) in the engine compartment. For all other adjustments, refer to the appropriate carburetor in the Unit Repair section.

Electric Choke Heater/Oil Pressure Switch

All carbureted gasoline engines without gauge instrumentation, have a two-terminal oil pressure switch (sending unit) for controlling current to the electric choke heater. This switch and its associated circuitry also provides for the illumination of the "Oil" or "Check Engine" indicator lamp. On vehicles with gauges, a choke heater relay is sometimes used for the illumination of the "Choke" warning indicator.

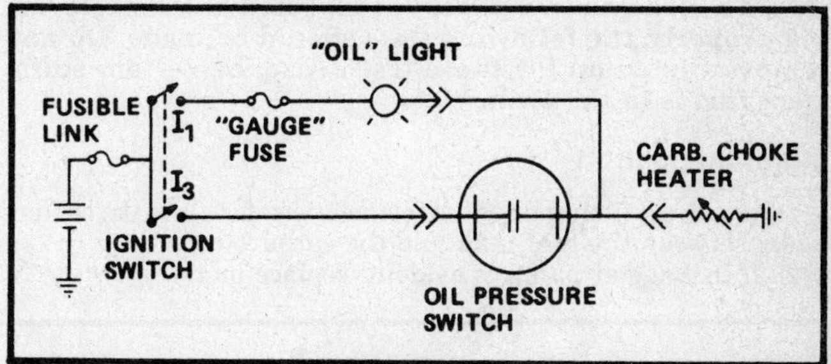

Electric choke heater wiring schematic (© General Motors Corp.)

Note: The instrument panel "Check Engine" light is an integral part of the Computer Command Control (CCC) system, if the vehicle is equipped with the system and must be considered when the indicator light is illuminated.

If "Oil" telltale lamp illuminates with engine running, it could indicate one or more of the following:

1. Loss of oil pressure.
2. Loss of choke heater voltage.
3. Blown gauge fuse.

Electric Choke Heater Checking Procedure

1. Allow choke to cool so that when throttle is opened slightly, choke blade fully closes. This check must be performed with engine not running and at an ambient temperature of 140°F. to 80°F. (60°C. to 27°C.).
2. Start engine and determine time for choke blade to reach full open position. (Start timer when engine starts).
3. If the choke blade fails to open fully within 3.5 minutes, proceed with Steps 4–6 below.
4. Check voltage at the choke heater connection. (Engine must be running). If the voltage is approximately 12–15 volts, replace the electrical choke unit.
5. If the voltage is low or zero, check all wires and connections. If any connections in the oil pressure switch circuitry are faulty or if the oil pressure switch is failed open, the oil warning light will be on with the engine running. Repair wires or connections as required.
6. If all wiring and connections are good, replace oil pressure switch. No gasket is used between the choke cover and the choke housing because of grounding requirements.

CAUTION

Choke housing and hot air inlet pipe may be hot enough to cause burns.

Fuel Pump

Two types of pumps are used, mechanical and electric. Mechanical pump is diaphragm type, consisting of a single fuel chamber or a combination fuel and vacuum chambers. In-line engines actuate the pump by an eccentric lobe on camshaft, V6 engines have an eccentric attached to front of camshaft, V8 engines use a push rod between eccentric lobe on camshaft and pump rocker arm. Electrical pumps are used with Throttle Bore Injection (TBI), certain step fuel tanks or as stand-by emergency units.

NOTE: In order to minimize the possibility of vapor lock, some fuel pumps are equipped with a special metering outlet for a vapor return system. Any vapor which forms is returned to the fuel tank along with hot fuel through a separate line.

DIAGNOSIS OF CAMSHAFT DRIVEN FUEL PUMP

NOTE: When a fuel pump is suspected of not performing properly, the following tests should be made. Do not remove the pump for these tests. Also, be certain sufficient fuel is in the tank.

Initial Inspection

1. Check all fitting lines and connections for air leaks or fuel leaks between the fuel tank and the carburetor.
2. If leakage at pump is evident, replace pump.

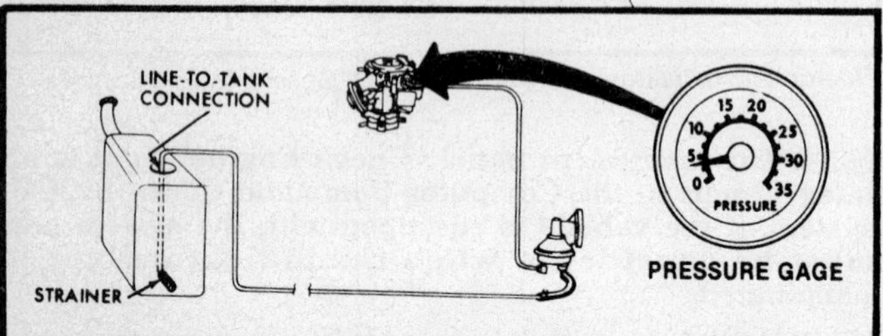

Pressure test of mechanical fuel pump (© General Motors Corp.)

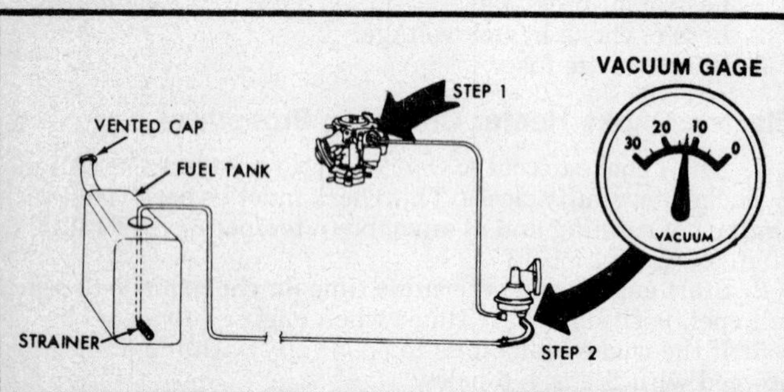

Vacuum test of mechanical fuel pump (© General Motors Corp.)

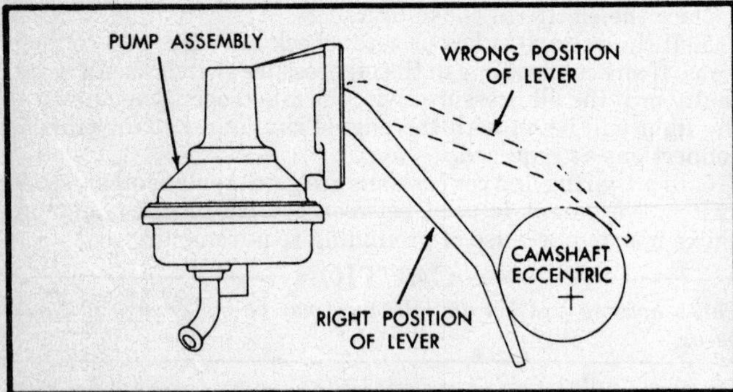

Fuel pump installation (© General Motors Corp.)

Vacuum Test

1. Disconnect fuel line at carburetor.
2. Disconnect pump inlet line hose and, if necessary, apply vise-grips to prevent siphoning. Install vacuum gauge at inlet of pump.
3. With engine idling (using fuel in carburetor), vacuum should register a minimum of 15 in.Hg. If satisfactory, proceed to "Pressure Test."
4. Less than 15 in.Hg., replace pump.

Pressure Test

1. Reconnect all fuel lines and run engine to fill carburetor. Shut off engine.
2. Disconnect the fuel line at the carburetor, then install pressure gauge into end of fuel line. (If pump has a vapor return line, pinch the line hose closed.)
3. With engine idling, gauge should indicate 4–6.5 psi.
4. If less than 4 psi, check line from pump to carburetor for restriction. If restricted, clean or replace. If not restricted, install new pump.
5. If pressure is OK, determine if fuel can be pulled up to pump freely. Shut off engine. Disconnect fuel line from fuel tank and pump. (See Note below.) Blow air from pump end of line to determine if fuel will flow through line. If not restricted, proceed to other areas, such as gas tank or carburetor. The fuel pump is not at fault.

NOTE: Failure to disconnect the fuel line at the tank prior to blowing the line out with air will damage the tank strainer.

Removal

DIAPHRAGM TYPE

1. Disconnect fuel lines at pump. Be ready to cap gas feed line should it be necessary (trucks without shut-off valve).
2. Remove two cap screws and washers holding pump to block. Remove pump and mounting gasket. Be careful of push rod on V8's.

Installation

1. Rotate engine crankshaft to position camshaft lobe on lowest point.
2. Check feed line for restrictions.
3. On V8s, place heavy grease on one end of push rod and slide into position.
4. Hold fuel pump, with new gasket, in position and start two cap screws finger tight.

CAUTION

Be sure rocker arm contacts eccentric in correct position.

5. Start fuel line fittings, using flexibility of pump to insure against crossing threads.
6. Tighten mounting bolts and lines. Start engine and check for leaks. (open shut-off valve, if closed)

ELECTRICAL FUEL PUMP

Fuel pressure Relief Procedure (W/TBI)

1. Remove the fuse marked "FUEL PUMP"from the fuse block in the passenger compartment.
2. Start the engine and run until the fuel, under pressure, is exhausted from the lines. When the engine stops, engage the starter again for approximately three (3) seconds to assure the release of fuel pressure.
3. After necessary checks and repairs are accomplished, replace the fuse with the ignition in the OFF position.

Pressure Test (W/TBI)

1. Remove the air cleaner and plug the thermal vacuum port on the throttle body unit.
2. Install a gauge assembly between the TBI unit and the fuel filter, using necessary pipes or fittings.
3. Start the engine and observe the fuel pressure reading, which should be between 9–13 psi. Excess fuel is returned to the tank.

NOTE: The fuel pump will remain on as long as the engine is cranking or running and the ECM is receiving HEI distributor reference pulses. If no reference pulses are sent to the ECMN, it will shut off current to the fuel pump within two (2) seconds after the key is turned to the ON position. Should no-start problems occur, refer to Chilton's Electronic Control Service manual for test procedures.

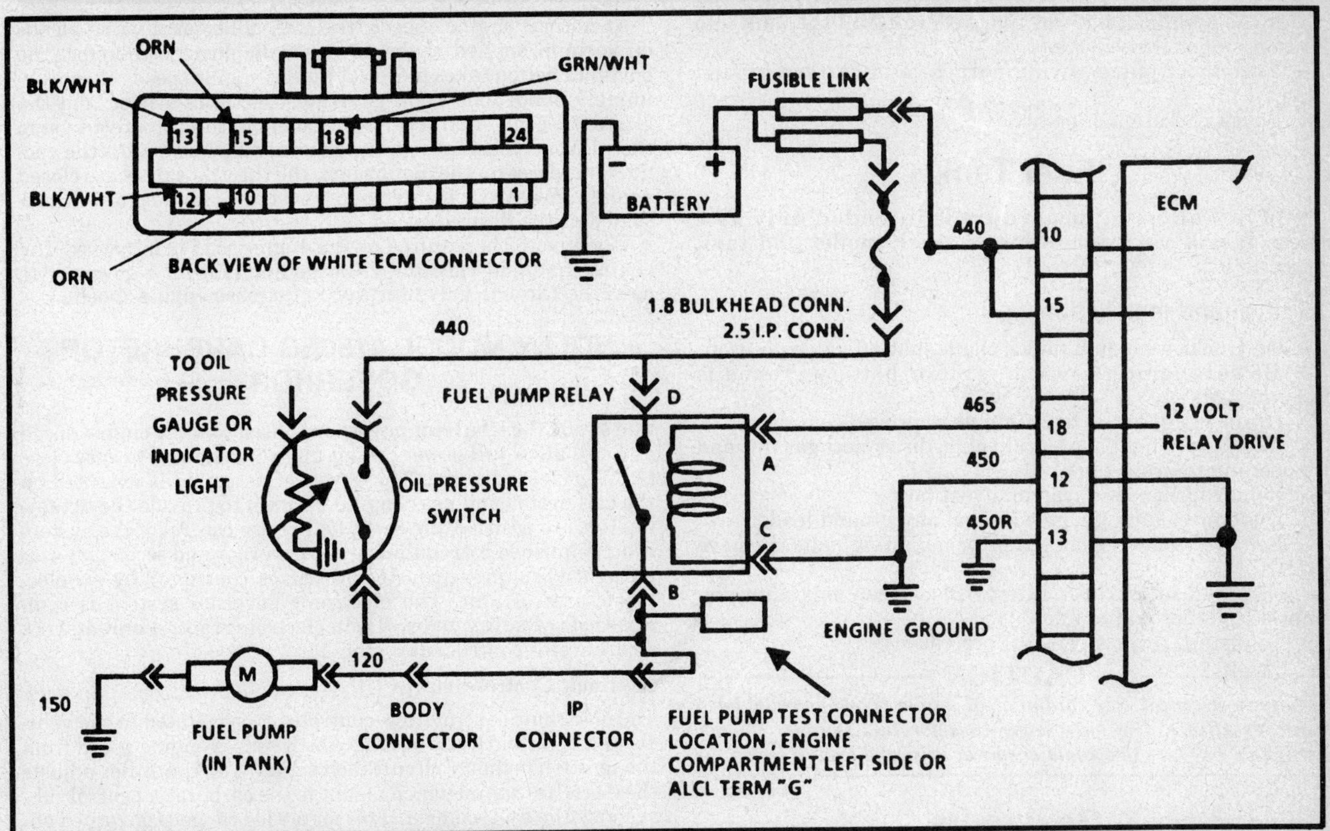

Electrical schematic of 2.5L engine with TBI system (© General Motors Corp.)

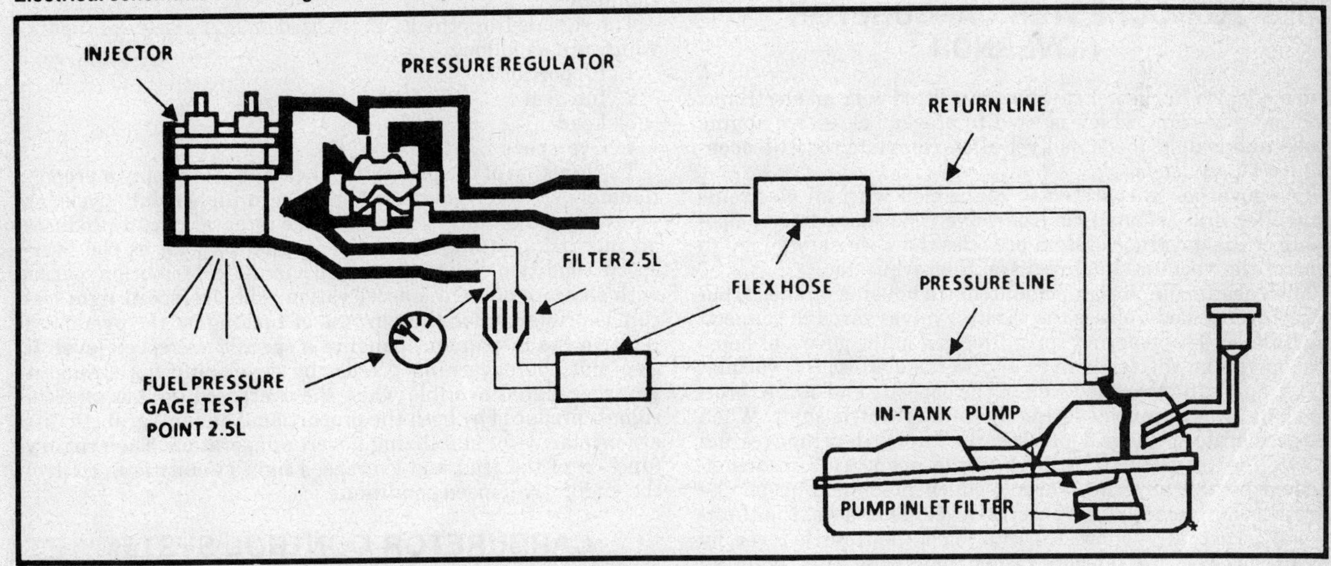

Fuel system diagram, 2.5L engine with TBI system (© General Motors Corp.)

4. Remove the gauge and replace original piping between the TBI unit and the fuel filter.
5. Reinstall the air cleaner assembly and unplug the thermal vacuum port on the throttle body unit.

Removal

ELECTRIC TYPE

Note: It may be necessary to raise the vehicle, support safely and remove the gasoline tank.

1. Disconnect battery ground cable.
2. Disconnect wiring harness from pump connector.
3. Remove fuel line from pump.
4. Remove bolts and washers from pump to tank or turn cam lock ring counterclockwise and remove the pump from tank.

Installation

1. Carefully position pump into tank opening. Reconnect fuel outlet line to fitting.
2. Install attaching bolts and torque to 4–6 ft. lbs or install the cam lock ring in a clockwise rotation to lock pump to tank.

3. If the gasoline tank was removed, reinstall the tank into position, under the vehicle.
4. Reconnect pump wiring harness and battery ground cable.
5. Check operation of pump.

Fuel Tank

NOTE: Following procedure is intended only as a guide. It will vary according to truck model and tank type.

Removal and Installation

1. On trucks with dual tanks, check shut-off valve position.
2. Be sure ignition switch is off or battery ground is disconnected.
3. Drain the gasoline tank into an approved container.
4. If tank does not have a drain plug, disconnect gas line and use opening to drain tank.
5. Remove filler neck, cap and vent hose.
6. Disconnect tank gauge wire and any ground lead.
7. Remove tank support straps or mounting bolts. Remove tank.
8. Clean all lines, check filters. (Blow clean only after disconnecting other end of line).
9. To install, reverse removal procedures.

CAUTION

Do not use electrical drop cord in area. A bulb breakage could have disastrous effects. Use only safety cans for fuel storage. Do not overtighten lines, as this could distort or twist and lead to leaks.

Governors

2G ROCHESTER CARBURETOR GOVERNOR

The model 2G Rochester carburetor is fitted with an electronic/vacuum governor, which is used to prevent excessive engine speed under light loads and yet allow complete throttle opening for heavy loads.

The governor is operated in connection with an electronic controller and solenoid control valve. The electronic components of the governor system provides the necessary signal to control the vacuum diaphragm on the carburetor.

The vacuum diaphragm, mounted in a housing on the carburetor throttle body, closes the throttle valves through connecting linkage. The governor spring, located in the governor housing, opens the throttle valves and works against the vacuum diaphragm. The throttle lever on the opposite end of the throttle shaft is not connected directly to the throttle shaft. When the accelerator pedal is depressed, the throttle lever moves and allows the primary throttle valves to open. This is accomplished by the governor spring, which holds a tang on the throttle shaft, against the throttle lever. Therefore, the throttle valves actually follows the rotation of the throttle lever, by the governor spring tension, rather than being directly forced open, as on the conventional carburetor.

In operation, manifold vacuum is supplied to the top side of the governor diaphragm, through a passage in the housing, which leads to manifold vacuum directly beneath the throttle valves. Calibrated restrictions are used in this passage to control the amount of vacuum applied to the diaphragm. A vacuum line connects the diaphragm cover on the governor housing, to the solenoid control valve. The solenoid control valve , which acts as a vacuum bleed valve, receives its signal from the electronic controller. The electronic controller is wired to the HEI distributor and relates a tachometer signal back to the solenoid control valve, to regulate vacuum at the carburetor governor diaphragm.

At normal engine speeds, the solenoid control valve bleeds off vacuum applied to the governor diaphragm, therefore, no governor action takes place. At higher engine speeds of approximately 3800–4000 rpm, governor control is needed and the electronic controller acts on the solenoid control valve to stop the vacuum bleeding from the governor diaphragm. As the vacuum increases on the diaphragm, the throttle valves are closed against govern spring tension and the engine rpm is maintained at the desired speed.

When power is required as the engine load is increased, the engine manifold vacuum will drop and allow the governor to open the throttle valve further to increase engine speed.

HOLLY MODEL 4150EG CARBURETOR GOVERNOR

The 4150EG carburetor governor is used to limit engine speed and still allow full power output upon demand, up to very close to full governed speed. The governor assembly is mounted on the carburetor and uses engine vacuum to provide the actuating force to position the throttle. Precise control of the system is accomplished by regulating the governor and secondary diaphragm vacuum with solenoid valves controlled by an electronic control unit. The electronic governor system is comprised of two subsystems, (1), an electronic control unit and (2), a carburetor control subsystem.

Electronic Control Unit (ECU)

The electronic control unit (controller), is mounted in the vehicle and is a solid state device, which senses engine speed from the ignition primary circuit tach signal. The controller adjusts the electrical signal which is sent to the carburetor control subsystem. The ECU compensates for a wide range of governed engine conditions and it varies, depending upon engine conditions.

The signals from the ECU is based on four electrical inputs, which are as follows;

1. Proportional
2. Integral
3. Lead
4. Overspeed light

The function of the proportional circuit is to supply a proportionately stronger governor signal, at a higher duty cycle, as an overspeed condition worsens. The integral circuit produces an increasing stronger governor signal as long as the overspeed condition exists. The lead circuit contribution varies with the rate of engine acceleration. The overspeed light circuit is primarily for the purpose of turning on the overspeed light on the instrument panel at a specific overspeed level. It also aids the governing process by developing the strongest governor signal availble when the overspeed light is on. The signals produced by both the proportional and integral circuits are primarily for stabilizing governor operation. The primary function of the lead and overspeed light circuits is to control the engine overspeed conditions.

CARBURETOR CONTROL SYSTEM

The purpose of the carburetor control subsystem is to convert the electronic signal received from the ECU, into a mechanical force. This mechanical force holds the throttle at the correct position to obtain the desired engine speed. The components responsible for this function are the Electronic Governor Solenoid/Cover assembly and the Governor Control Mechanism.

ELECTRONIC GOVERNOR SOLENOID AND COVER ASSEMBLY

Two solenoid control valves are located within the Electronic Governor Solenoid and Cover Assembly.

1. Governor Control Valve—This valve is normally spring loaded closed below governor speed, sealing off the vacuum

source in the carburetor and at the same time, allowing atmosphere pressure to be applied to the governor diaphragm. With no governor signal being developed against the governor diaphragm, the primary throttle plates will follow the operator's foot pressure due to the force from the governor spring. During the higher speed condition, when the governor is being called for by the ECU, the governor control valve cycles electromagnetically between its conical seat the the flat seal on its opposite end. This cycling mixes the vacuum with atmospheric pressure and creates a vacuum signal on the governor diaphragm. The increased governor vacuum level causes the primary throttle to become governed, opposing the governor spring force.

2. Secondary Control Valve – This valve is a spring loaded, normally closed valve sealing the secondary diaphragm vacuum from atmospheric pressure. At speeds below the governed speed, the secondaries operate normally. As the governed speed is attained, the secondary control valve cycles electromagnetically on and off its seat in response to the ECU signal. When the secondary control valve cycles, it allows atmospheric pressure to bleed into the secondary throttle diaphragm vacuum chamber. This causes the secondary throttle to modulate or fully close as the governor action demands.

GOVERNOR CONTROL MECHANISM

The primary purpose of the governor control mechanism is to convert the regulated governor vacuum into a throttle position which will provide the proper engine governed speed.

This is done with the following components;

1. Throttle–to–throttle shaft clutch
2. Governor vacuum supply restrictions
3. Governor diaphragm and linkage
4. Governor spring

The purpose of the throttle to throttle shaft clutch mechanism is to allow the governor system to overcome the throttle position held by the operator during engine overspeed conditions. Governor vacuum supply restrictions consists of a venturi vacuum restriction and a manifold vacuum restriction. The purpose of these restrictions are to give the governor control valve a properly balanced governor vacuum supply. The governor diaphragm and its associated linkage is the means by which a vacuum is converted into a mechanical force to close the throttle. The governor spring has two functions, it loads the throttle shaft against the throttle–to–throttle shaft clutch mechanism and it is used as a governor calibration tool, imposing a precise counterforce against the governor diaphragm during governor operations.

NOTE: Governor rpm is preset at the factory and is not adjustable. Any deviation from normal operation will require testing of the system.

DIAGNOSIS OF GOVERNOR ASSEMBLY

ALL CARBURETOR GOVERNORS

The following checks should be made initially in response to any complaint about the governor operation.

1. Check the throttle linkage and the carburetor primary throttle plates for a proper wide open position (open throttle plates) and proper idle position (closed throttle plates).
2. Check the vacuum hose from the governor solenoid assembly to the secondary diaphragm housing for proper attachments, leaks, etc.
3. Check the governor solenoid and cover assembly attachment to the governor housing for secure assembly.
4. Check the secondary operating lever and shaft assembly to ensure that its properly connected and operating freely.
5. Check the electrical connections for breaks or loose wires at the harness–to–ECU junction and also at the harness–to–carburetor "pigtail" junction.

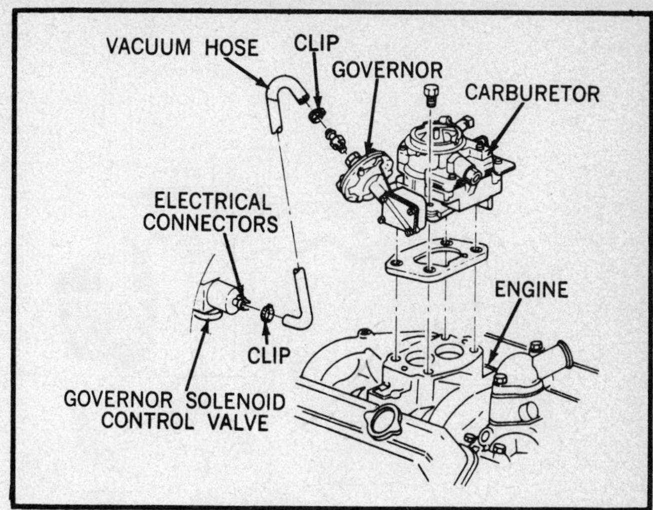

Governor solenoid control valve (© General Motors Corp.)

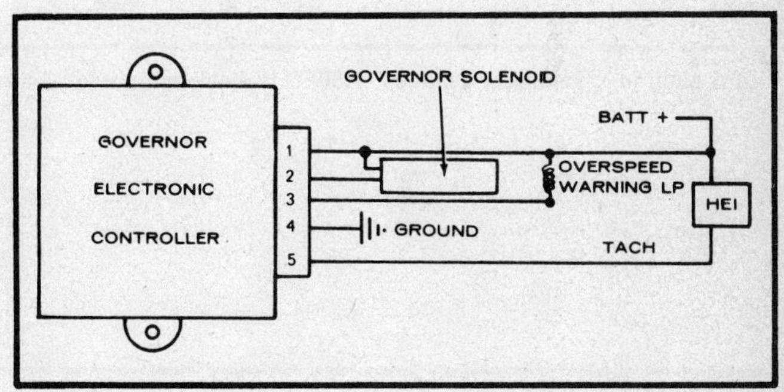

Governor electronic controller—wiring schematic—typical (© General Motors Corp.)

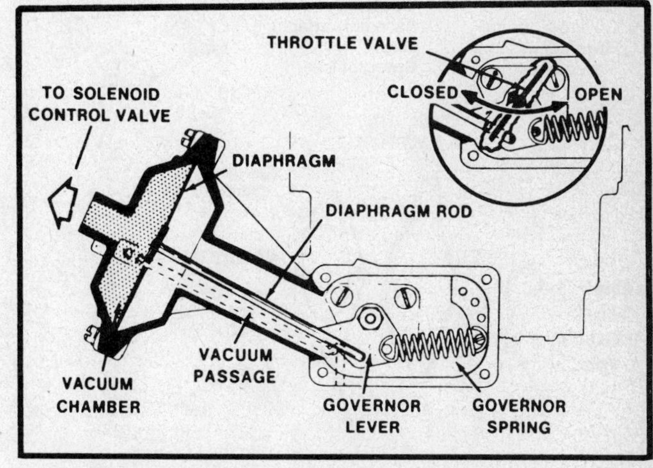

Cross section of vacuum type governor assembly (© General Motors Corp.)

SOLENOID CONTROL VALVE

Testing

ALL CARBURETOR MODELS

1. Disconnect the battery ground.
2. Disconnect the wiring harness from the solenoid control valve at the governor.
3. Measure the resistance across the solenoid terminals with an ohmmeter.

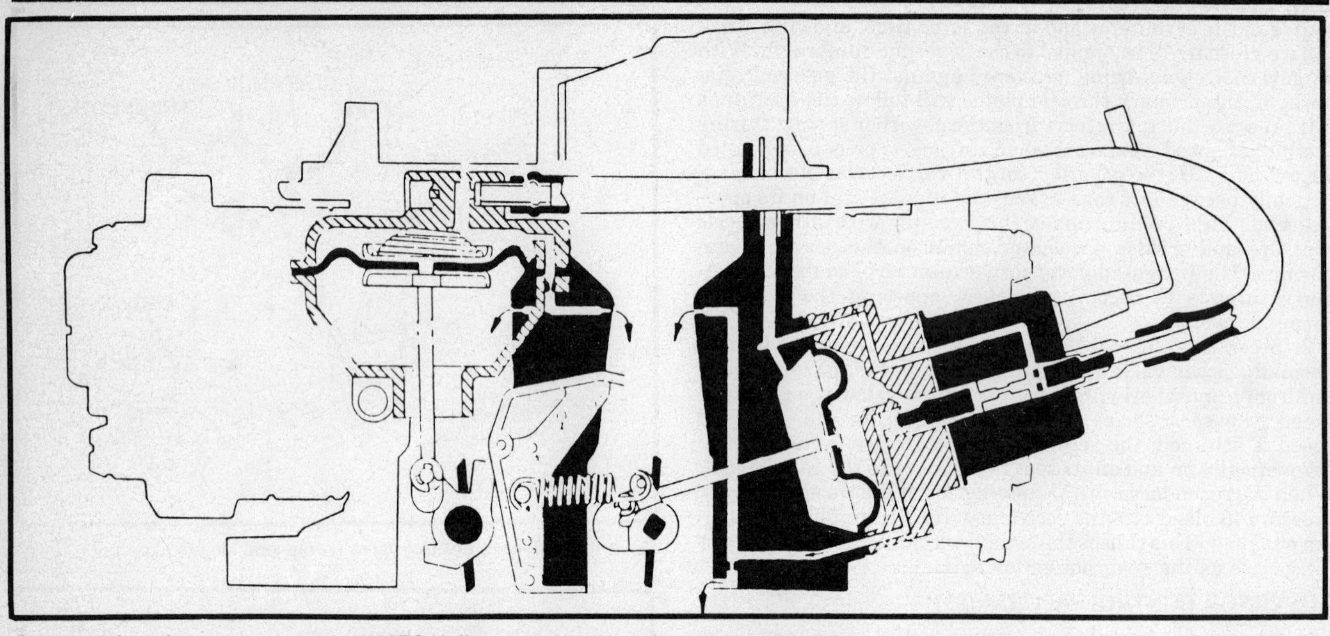

Cross section of vacuum passages, 4150EG Holley governor (© General Motors Corp.)

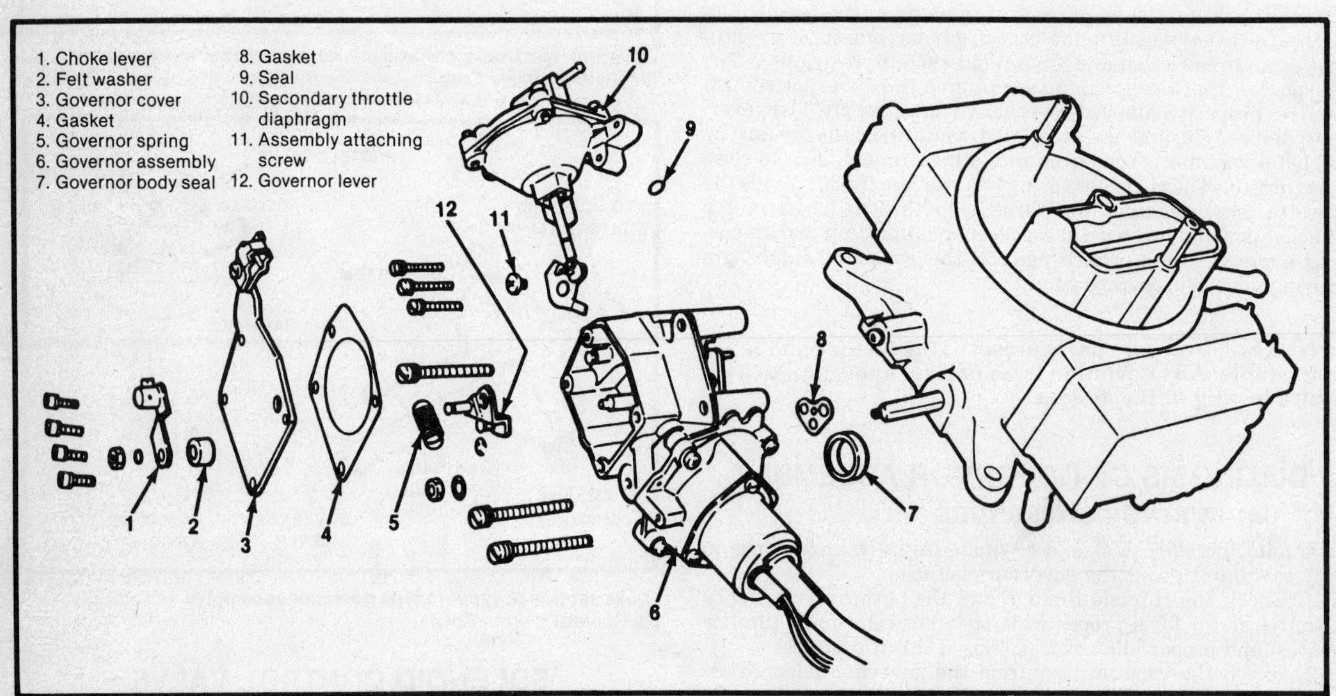

4150EG Holley carburetor governor components (© General Motors Corp.)

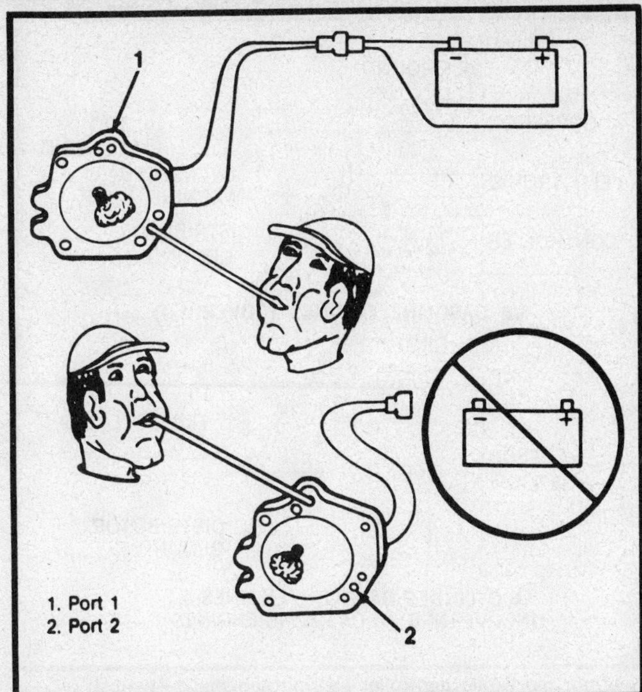

Testing governor solenoid passages (© General Motors Corp.)

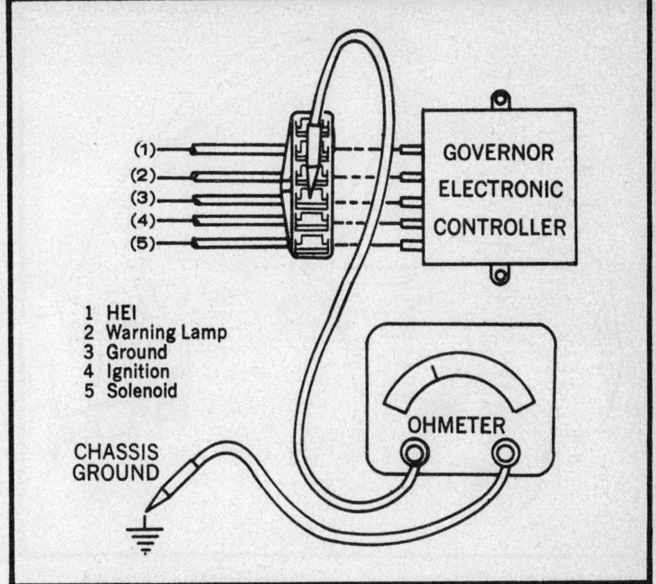

Governor electronic controller terminal connector identification and checking circuit with ohmmeter (© General Motors Corp.)

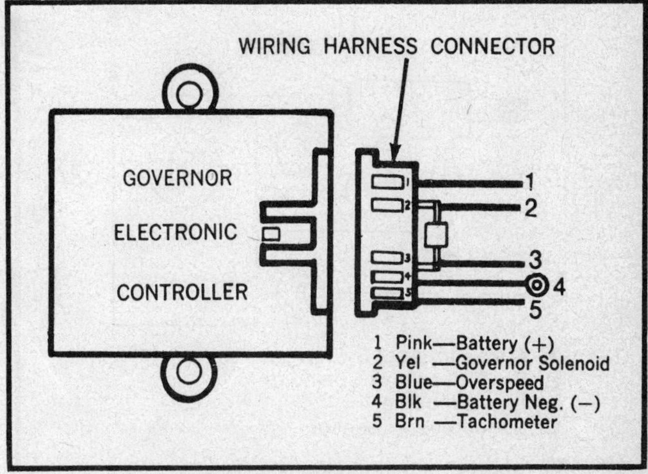

Terminal connector wiring identification (© General Motors Corp.)

NOTE: Resistance for the two barrel carburetor should be 25–35 ohms. and resistance for the four barrel carburetor should be 47–53 ohms.

4. Replace the solenoid control valve if the measured resistance is not within these limits.

NOTE: If the measured resistance is below these limits, the controller may be damaged. Perform the electronic controller test.

5. To test for an internal short circuit, connect one lead of the ohmmeter to either terminal of the valve and the other to the metal case of the valve. The resistance should be 800 ohms or higher. If the resistance is lower than 800 ohms, then a short circuit condition probably exists within the valve. If the measured resistance falls within the required limits, then proceed to check for proper governor operation.
6. Check the governor solenoid and cover assembly by removing it from the carburetor at the four screw attachment to the governor housing.
7. Energize the solenoid by applying 12 volts across the pigtail. Blow into the governor vent port and check the secondary hose fitting for discharge of air. The port should be open.
8. Cap the secondary fitting and repeat the previous test. The passage should now be closed.
9. Blow into the governor supply port and check the angled diaphragm port for discharge. The passage should be open.
10. Cover the angled diaphragm port and repeat the previous test. The passage should now be closed.

NOTE: Should any of the previous tests of the governor solenoid and cover assembly not be correct, the entire assembly must be replaced.

ELECTRONIC CONTROLLER

Testing

1. Disconnect the battery ground.
2. Disconnect the wiring harness from the electronic controller. The electronic controller is located under the left side dash panel.
3. Attach one lead of an ohmmeter to the ground terminal in the wiring harness connector and the other lead to the chassis ground. The measured resistance should be less than 3 ohms.

NOTE: If there is an open circuit between the connector and the chassis ground, look for a problem in the ground wire connectors and terminals.

4. Connect the battery ground.
5. Turn the ignition switch to the ON position, but do not start the engine.
6. Using a voltmeter, measure the voltage between the ground terminal in the harness connector and the terminals connecting the HEI tachometer, the solenoid control valve and ignition (battery +). The reading at all four terminals should be equivalent to battery voltage. If the reading at any of these terminals is less than battery voltage, then check the appropriate circuit for damage, corrosion, or poor insulation. Repair damaged or defective circuitry.

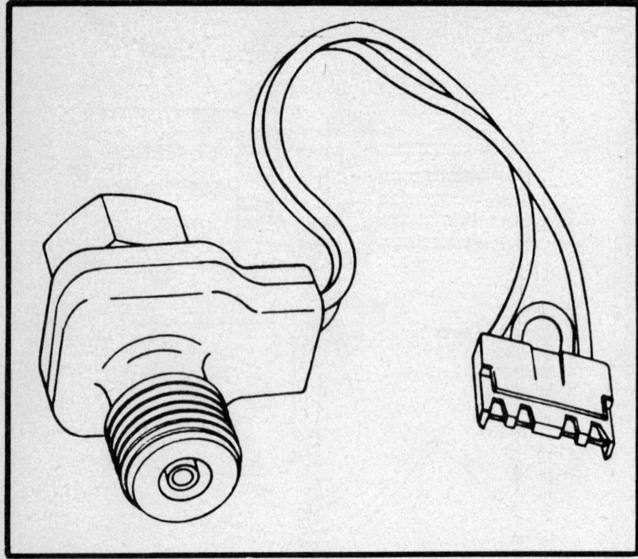

Typical road speed governor circuit (© General Motors Corp.)

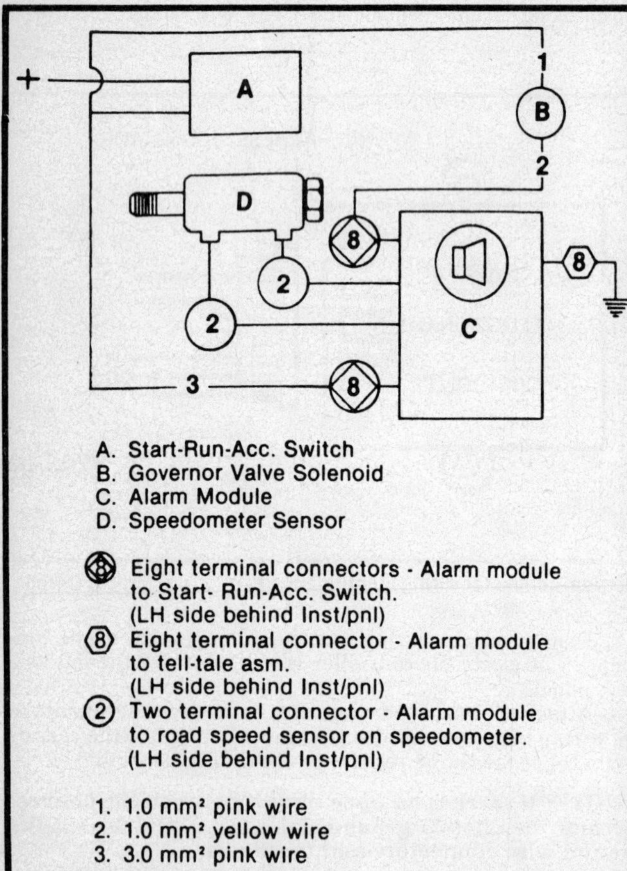

Speed transducer used at speedometer assembly
(© General Motors Corp.)

NOTE: Allow for a very slight voltage drop between the battery voltage and the reading at the voltmeter, as this may only be the result of minor resistance in the chassis ground circuit.

7. Turn the engine control off and using and ohmmeter,

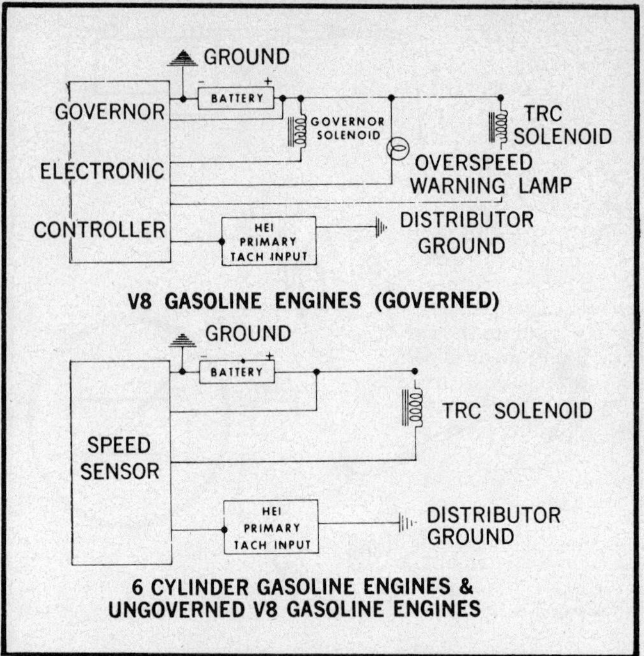

Governor electronic controller—wiring schematic—typical
(© General Motors Corp.)

check the signal input wire for continuity between the distributor tach connector and the electronic controller harness connector.

8. If, after checking the wiring harness, solenoid control valve, tubing, electrical fuse and governor, the governor still does not govern properly, then replace the electronic controller.

OVERSPEED WARNING SYSTEM

This system was designed to alert the driver of excessive engine speeds such as would be caused by down-hill operation when the wheels may begin to drive the engine.

A red warning lamp, located in the instrument panel will light when activated by a signal from the governor electronic controller.

When the ignition key is returned from the START position, the ignition switch ground circuit is broken and the light will go out. The warning lamp will remain unlighted until the engine rpm reaches the predetermined governed speed.

NOTE: Some ungoverned V8 and 6 cylinder engines are equipped with a similar sensing device which is designed to warn the operator of excessive engine speeds.

ROAD SPEED GOVERNOR

SCHOOL BUS MODELS

This type of governor control allows the operator of the vehicle to use the maximum power of the engine up to the governed speed of the vehicle. The vehicle speed transducer sends a signal to the governor module. When the predetermined vehicle speed is reached, the governor electronic controller sends a signal to the governor solenoid, which activates the carburetor governor.

The vehicle speed transducer is located on the back of the speedometer. The governor electronic controller is located on the left kickpanel. The governor solenoid control valve is located on the dash panel.

COOLING SYSTEM

All models, except the Deutz Diesel engine, which is air cooled, have pressurized cooling system, thermostatically controlled coolant bypass and the system sealed by a radiator cap. The system is designed to operate with coolant's boiling point raised (approximately 3 degrees for every pound of pressure), which increases efficiency of radiator. Pressure cap contains both pressure and vacuum relief valves, spring loaded. Pressure valve allows excess pressure out the overflow and into a coolant recovery container. The vacuum valve opens as the system cools down, drawing the coolant stored in the recovery container, back into the system, therefore maintaining a constant level. Thermostat is pellet or poppet construction, designed to open and close at predetermined temperatures and incorporates a by-pass. Two types of cores are used, down-flow or cross-flow, according to vehicle needs and design.

Water Pump

The water pump is belt driven, centrifugal vane impeller type. Bearings are permanently lubricated and sealed against water and dirt. Pump requires no maintenance, other than keeping bottom drain hole open.

Removal and Installation

S/T MODELS WITH 1.9L ENGINE

1. Disconnect the negative battery cable.
2. Remove the bolts holding the lower cover and remove the cover.
3. Drain the cooling system below the level of the water pump.
4. Non-air conditioned models – Remove the four nuts retaining the engine fan and remove the fan.
5. Air conditioned models:
   a. Remove the air pump and alternator mounting bolts. Remove the fan and air pump drive belt by pivoting the air pump and alternator in towards the engine.
   b. Remove the bolts retaining the fan and pulley, remove the fan together with the fan pulley and air pump drive pulley.
   c. Remove the retaining bolts attaching the fan set plate and fan pulley. Remove the set plate and pulley.
6. Remove the six bolts retaining the water pump to the engine block and remove the pump assembly.
7. Clean the mounting surface on water pump and engine block. Install gasket, if included with pump.

NOTE: Certain pumps do not use a sealing gasket, but rely upon RTV sealant.

8. Install the water pump and tighten the bolts evenly.
9. Complete the installation in the reverse order of removal. Fill the system with coolant, start the engine and check for leakage.

Removal and Installation

S/T MODELS WITH 2.5L ENGINE

1. Disconnect the negative battery cable.
2. Remove the necessary accessory drive belts.
3. Remove the upper fan shroud.
4. Drain the cooling system below the level of the water pump.
5. Remove the fan and pump pulley.
6. Remove the radiator hose and heater hoses.
7. Remvoe the retaining bolts and remove the water pump from the engine block.
8. Clean the surfaces of the water pump and engine block. Apply sealant on the water pump and install pump into the engine block. Apply sealant to the bolts and torque to 15 ft. lbs
9. Complete the installation in the reverse order of removal. Fill the system with coolant, start the engine and check for leakage.

Removal and Installation

S/T MODELS WITH 2.2L ENGINE

1. Disconnect the negative battery cable and drain the cooling system below the level of the water pump.
2. Disconnect the power steering reservoir at the fan shroud. Remove the upper fan shroud.
3. Remove the drive belts and the fan blades.
4. Disconnect the radiator pipe at the front cover. Remove the A/C compressor.
5. Disconnect the radiator and heater hoses at the right side of the water pump.
6. Disconnect the PCV valve at the rocker cover and remove the air cleaner assembly.
7. Remove the heater pipe at the intake stove.
8. Disconnect the heater hose at the left side of the water pump and disconnect the alternator adjusting strap from the pump assembly.
9. Remove the water pump retaining bolts and remove the pump from the engine block.
10. Clean the water pump and engine block surfaces. Install new gasket and install the pump assembly.
11. Seal the pump bolts and torque to 24–38 ft. lbs
12. Complete the assembly, fill the system with coolant, start the engine and check for leakage.

Removal and Installation

S/T MODELS WITH 2.8L ENGINE

ASTRO/SAFARI VANS WITH 4.3L and 2.5L ENGINES

1. Remove the negative battery cable.
2. Drain the coolant below the water pump level
3. Remove the fan shroud as necessary and remove the fan blades.
4. Remove the retaining bolts and remove the water pump assembly.
5. Clean the water pump and block surfaces. Install new gasket and install the water pump.
6. Tighten the bolts securely, complete the assembly, fill the cooling system, start the engine and check for coolant leakages.

Removal and Installation

10–30, 15–35 SERIES – C,K,G AND P MODELS WITH L6 AND V8 ENGINES

NOTE: In some cases, the radiator shroud will have to be relocated or removed to gain access to the fan retaining bolts. Relocate or remove as required.

1. Disconnect the negative battery cable and drain the cooling system below the water pump level.
2. Remove the accessory drive belts.
3. Remove the fan to water pump hub (or fan clutch to water pump hub) attaching bolts or nuts. Remove the fan and pulley.
4. Remove the lower radiator hose and the heater hose from the water pump. On 7.4L engines, remove the by–pass hose.
5. Remove the retaining bolts and remove the water pump.

NOTE: If the alternator adjusting brackets are bolted to the engine with one of the water pump retaining bolts, it will be necessary to loosen the alternator adjusting bolt and move the braces away from the water pump.

6. Clean the surface of the water pump and engine block. Install new gasket on L6 engine water pumps and place a bead of

RTV sealant on the V8 engine water pumps. Install the pump to the engine block. Torque the bolts to 15 ft. lbs

7. Complete the assembly, fill the system with coolant, start the engine and check for leakage.

Removal and Installation

10–30,15–35 SERIES, C,K,G AND P MODELS WITH DIESEL ENGINE

1. Disconnect the negative battery cable and drain the cooling system below the water pump level.
2. Remove the fan and fan shroud. Drain the cooling system below the level of the water pump.
3. If equipped with A/C, remove the A/C hose bracket nuts.
4. Remove the oil fill tube.
5. Remove the alternator pivot bolt and remove the belt.
6. Remove the alternator lower bracket and the power steering belt.
7. Remove the power steering pump and move it aside.
8. Remove the A/C belt, if equipped.
9. Disconnect the by–pass hose and lower radiator hose.
10. Remove the retaining bolts and remove the water pump assembly.
11. If new pump is being installed, be sure plate to pump gasket is in place.
12. Apply sealer to water pump and/or engine block. Install water pump and retaining bolts. Complete the assembly, fill the system with coolant, start the engine and check for leakage.

NOTE: The procedures for the removal and installation of water pumps on the 5.7L, 6.0L, 7.0L and 4.8L engines, used on meduim trucks, are basically the same as outlined for the V8 engine equipped 10–30, 15–35 Series.

Heater Core

NOTE: Due to the many truck models, the following procedure is a general removal and installation outline for the heater core, with or without air conditioning and does not include Van models. It is advisable to refer to Chilton's 1985 Auto Heating and Air Conditioning Manual for correct removal and installation procedures. Care should be exercised when removing any air distribution duct assembly, to avoid breakage of the housing due to hidden screws. Reinstall any sealer that is broken or removed during the disassembly.

Removal and Installation

WITH AIR CONDITIONING

1. Disconnect the negative battery cable and drain the cooling system. Plug the heater core outlets to avoid leakage.
2. Remove the glove box and door assembly.
3. Remove the center duct to selector duct and instrument panel screws. Remove the center lower and upper ducts.
4. Disconnect the Bowden cable at the temperature door.
5. Remove the nuts from the three selector duct studs, projecting into the engine compartment.
6. Remove the selector duct to dash panel screw, (inside the vehicle).
7. Pull the duct assembly rearward to clear the dash panel by the heater core tubes.
8. Lower the unit to gain access to the electrical and vacuum harnesses and disconnect them.
9. Remove the duct assembly from the vehicle. Remove the core straps and remove the heater core.
10. To install, reverse the procedure. Refill the cooling system, start the engine and check the heater system for proper operation.

WITHOUT AIR CONDITIONING

1. Disconnect the negative battery cable, drain the coolant and plug the core tubes.
2. Remove the nuts from the distribution duct studs projecting into the engine compartment.
3. Remove the glove box and door assemblies and disconnect the temperature and air-defrost cable.
4. Remove the floor outlet, the defroster duct to air distribution duct screws and the distribution duct to dash panel screws.
5. Pull the assembly to the rear and remove the wiring harness.
6. Remove the heater distribution unit from the vehicle and remove the core retaining screws.
7. Remove the heater core from the distribution unit.
8. To install, reverse the procedure. Refill the cooling system, start the engine and check the heater system for proper operation.

Clutch Drive Fan Assemblies

FLUID COUPLING TYPE

To ease engine power drain at higher speeds because of fan and water pump operation, drive clutch assemblies are used on most General Motors Corporation light truck models. These units consists of a fluid coupling, filled with silicone oil and temperature sensitive bi-metal spring which disengages the fan when it is not required for cooling.

Because of the large usage of the fluid coupling type fan control on the varied G.M. model engines, the following diagnosis outline is presented to aid the technician in determining malfunctions of the unit.

NOISE

Fan noise is sometimes evident under the following normal conditions:

1. Noise can be heard when the clutch is engaged for maximum cooling.
2. Noise can be heard during the first few minutes after start-up, until the clutch can re-distribute the silicone fluid back to its normal disengaged operating condition after overnight settling.

Fan noise or an excessive roar will generally occur continuously. However, under all high engine speed conditions (2500 rpm and up), if the clutch assembly is locked up due to an internal failure, the roar will increase and decrease in tone with the engine speed. If the fan clutch cannot be rotated by hand or there is a rough grating feel as the fan is turned, the clutch assembly should be replaced.

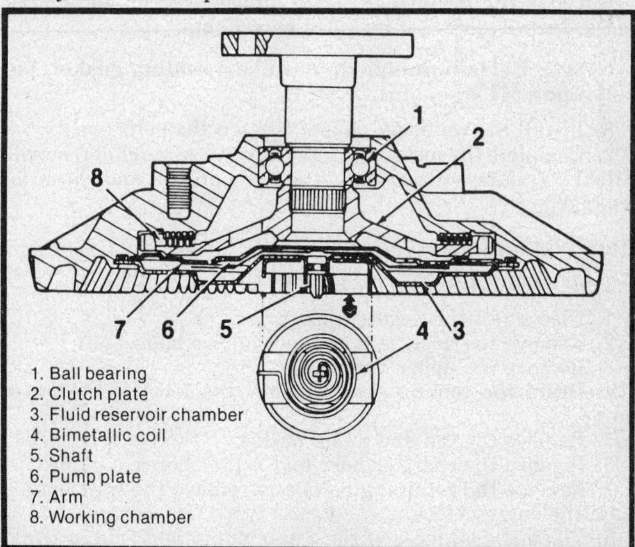

Cross section of fan clutch coil and components used with light duty vehicles (© General Motors Corp.)

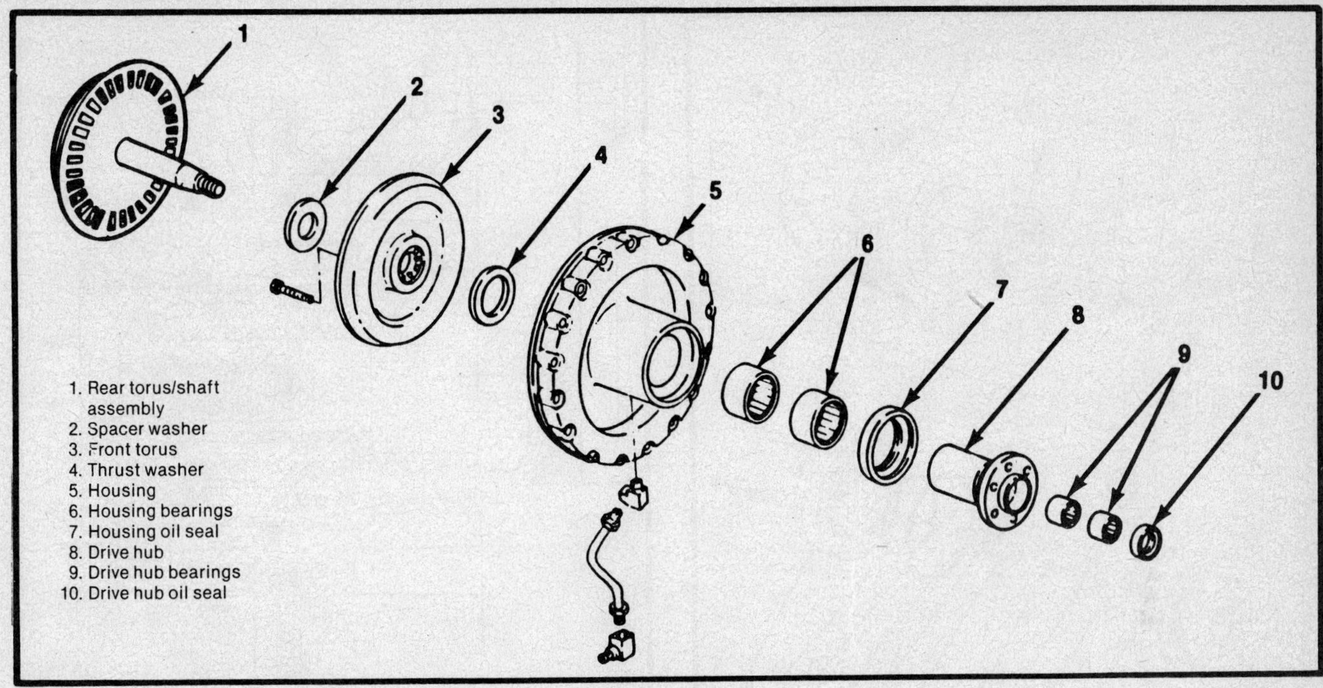

Exploded view of GM fluid fan clutch components (© General Motors Corp.)

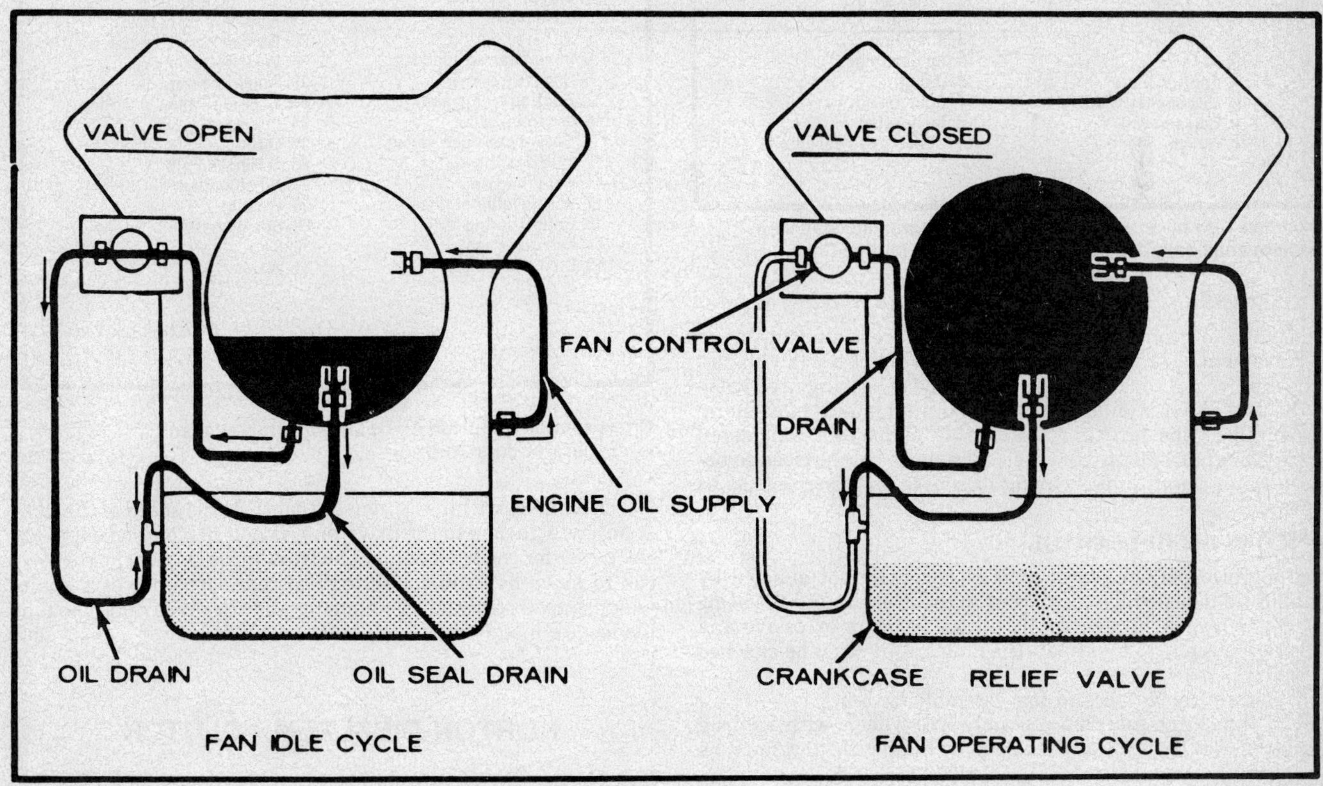

Fluid fan operation schematic (© General Motors Corp.)

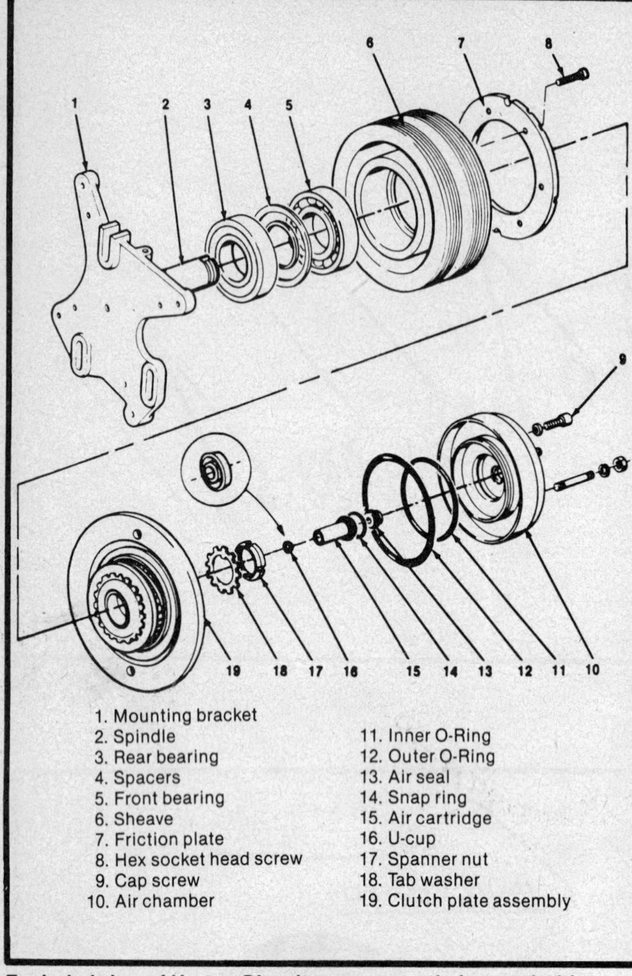

Exploded view of Horton Dieseltemp automatic fan used with medium and heavy duty vehicles (© General Motors Corp.)

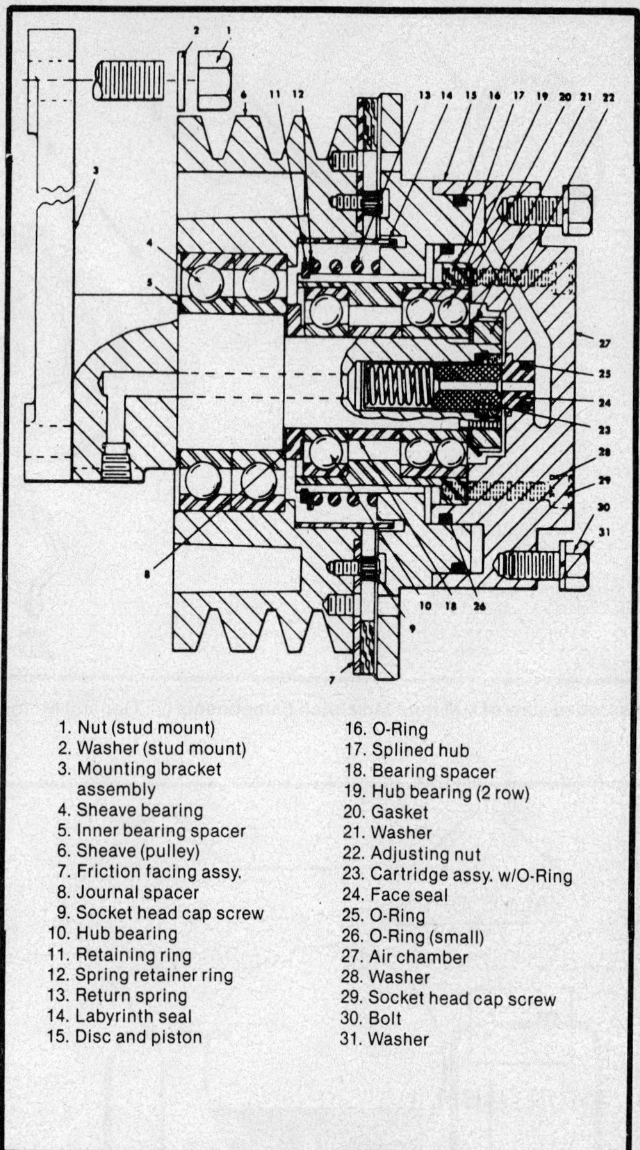

Cross section of Horton Air Operated automatic fan (© General Motors Corp.)

LOOSENESS

Under various temperature conditions, there is a visible lateral movement that can be observed at the tip of the fan blades. This is a normal condition due to the type of bearing used within the unit. Approximately $1/4$ in. maximum lateral movement, measured at the fan tip, is allowable and is not considered cause for replacement. However, care must be exercised to observe water pump shaft/bearing looseness and to correct as as required.

SILICONE FLUID LEAKAGE

The operation of the clutch unit is generally not affected by small fluid leaks which may occur in the area around the bearing assembly. If the degree of leakage appears excessive and the engine tends to overheat, the clutch unit must be checked as follows;

1. Rotate the clutch and fan assembly by hand.
2. If the clutch and fan assembly free-wheels with no drag (revolves over five times when spun by hand), the unit must be replaced.

GMC TYPE AUTOMATIC FAN CLUTCH

The GMC fluid fan clutch operates by using engine oil to provide a coupling between a drive torus and a driven torus. Oil is supplied by engine oil pressure. The amount of oil allowed to drain from the assembly is controlled by a thermostatic valve. This valve is linked to the engine coolant.

The oil level within the housing controls the speed of the fan. A pulley, attached to the drive hub, is belt driven and supplies the power for the front torus. The front torus causes the rear torus to move by fluid coupling. The rear torus drives a shaft which extends through the housing and the drive hub. The fan blades are mounted to this shaft.

HORTON DIESLTEMP CLUTCH

The Horton Diesltemp clutch assembly is an OFF/ON air clutch which controls the engine temperature by engaging and disengaging the cooling fan as signalled by a sensor valve. When the air pressure is applied to the clutch, a clutch plate connected to the fan, is moved against a friction plate, which is attached to the drive belt sleeve. This action causes a direct mechanical link-up between the drive belt and the fan. Rotating friction is low because ball bearings are used throughout the assembly.

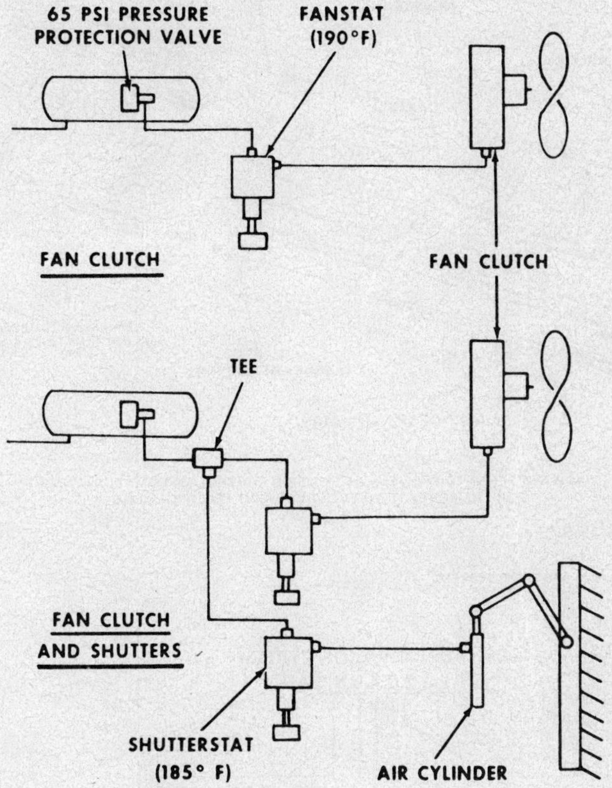

Diagram of air clutch installation—typical (© General Motors Corp.)

HORTON 9 INCH SINGLE PLATE FAN CLUTCH

The Horton 9 in. single plate fan clutch is an OFF/ON air clutch which controls the engine temperature by engaging and disengaging the cooling fan as signalled by a sensor valve. When air pressure is applied to the clutch, a clutch plate connected to the fan, is moved aginst a friction plate which is attached to the drive belt sleeve. This causes a direct mechanical link-up between the drive belt and the fan. Rotating friction is low because ball bearings are used throughout the assembly.

HORTON DUAL PLATE FAN CLUTCH

The Horton dual plate fan clutch works with air pressure. When the thermovalve opens, air pressure is applied to the clutch. The air enters the mounting bracket, passes through the air seal and moves the pistons with the friction surfaces, against the pressure plates, thus engaging the clutch and causing the fan to rotate.

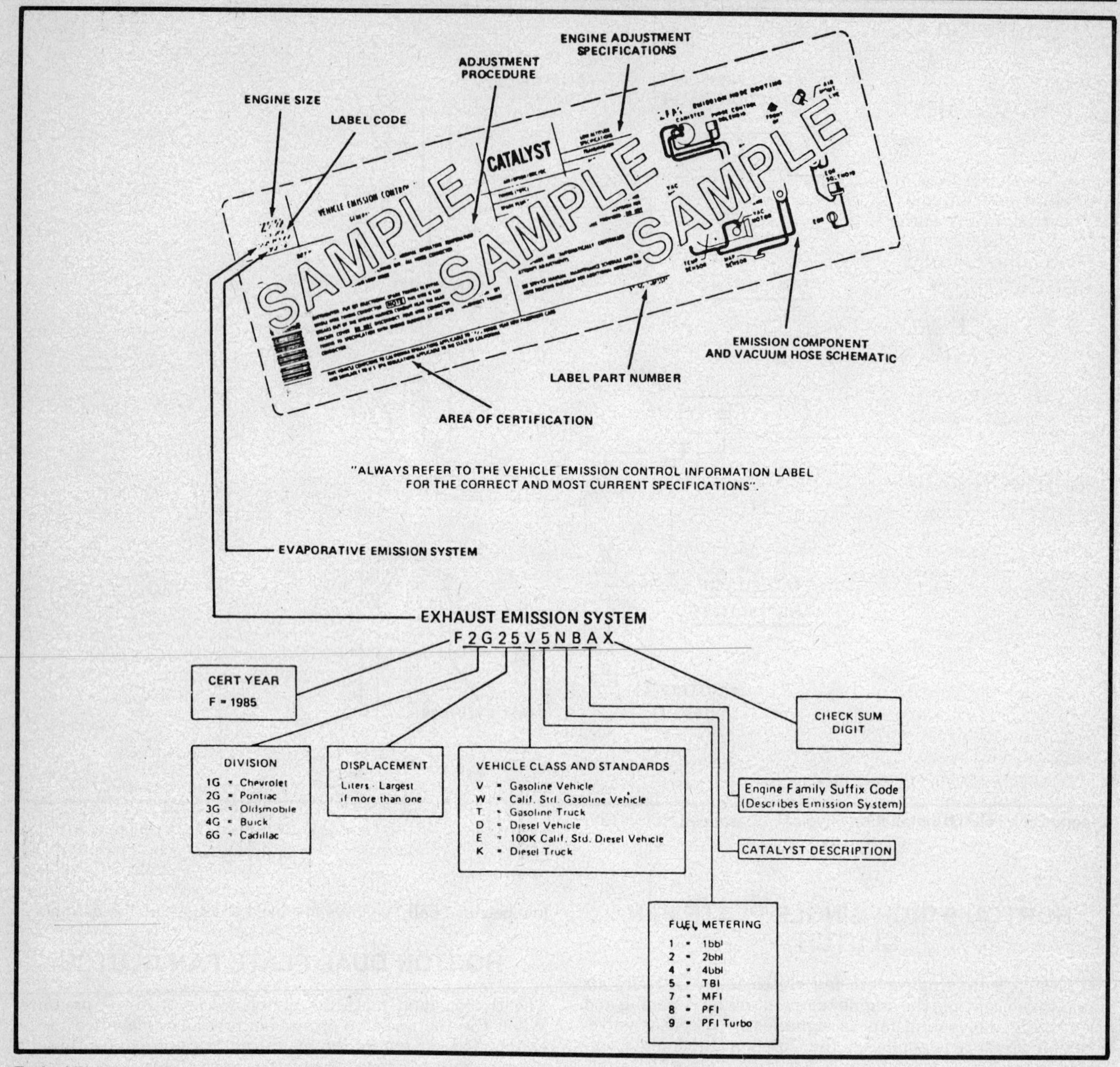

Typical Emission Information label and decoding examples (© General Motors Corp.)

EMISSION CONTROL SYSTEMS

Emission control systems are designed to control the emissions of hydrocarbons (HC), carbon monoxide (CO) and oxides of nitrogen (NOx), at the levels specified by the federal and state governments. Emission control systems vary in their usage, in relation to the engine, transmission and series application.

Vehicle Emission Control Information Label

The Vehicle Emission Control Information Label contains important emission specifications and setting procedures. In the upper left corner of the label is the exhaust emission information, which identifies the year, the manufacturing division of the engine, the displacement in liters, the class of vehicle and the type of fuel metering. Also, there is an illustrated emission component and vacuum hose schematic. This label is located in the engine compartment of every General Motors Corporation Vehicle. If the label has been removed, mulilated or destroyed, it can be ordered by Vehicle Identification Number (VIN) through the parts division (WDDGM) of General Motors Corporation.

NOTE: The basic units are covered in the Emission Control section of the Unit Repair section.

Emission Control Systems and Components

S/T TRUCK MODELS WITH 1.9L ENGINE–VIN CODE A

Air injection reactor system (AIR)
Exhaust gas recirculation system (EGR)
Thermostatically controlled air induction system (TAC)
Positive crankcase ventilation system (PCV)
Evaporative Emission Control System (EEC)
Catalytic converter

S/T TRUCK MODELS WITH 2.2L DIESEL ENGINE–VIN CODE S

Positive crankcase ventilation system (PCV)
Electronic exhaust gas recirculation system, California only (EEGR)

S/T TRUCK MODELS, ASTRO/SAFARI VANS WITH 2.5L ENGINE–VIN CODE E

Evaporative emission control system (EEC)
Exhaust gas recirculation system (EGR)
Positive crankcase ventilation system (PCV)
Thermostatic air cleaner assembly (TAC)
Catalytic Converter
Computer command control system (CCC)
Controls:
Fuel control (TBI)
Electronic spark timing (EST)
A/C clutch control
Transmission converter clutch (TCC)
Manual transmission shift light

S/T TRUCKS WITH 2.8L ENGINE–VIN CODE B

FEDERAL

Positive crankcase ventilation system(PCV)
Exhaust gas recirculation system (ERG)
Thermostatic air cleaner assembly (TAC)
Early fuel evaporator (EFE)
Air injector reactor (AIR)
Catalytic converter

CALIFORNIA

Positive crankcase ventilation system (PCV)
Exhaust gas recirculation system (EGR)
Thermostatic air cleaner (TAC)
Early fuel evaporation system (EFE)
Catalytic Converter
Computer command control system (CCC)
Controls:
Fuel control system (EFI)
Electronic spark timing(EST)
A/C clutch control
Air injection reaction (AIR)
Transmission converter clutch(TCC)

ASTRO/SAFARI VAN MODELS WITH 4.3L ENGINE–VIN CODE N

FEDERAL

Positive crankcase ventilation system (PCV)
Exhaust gas recirculation system (EGR)
Thermostatic air cleaner (TAC)
Early fuel evaporation system (EFE)
Air injection reaction system
Evaporation emission control system (EEC)
Catalytic converter

CALIFORNIA

Positive crankcase ventilation system (PCV)
Exhaust gas recirculation system(EGR)
Thermostatic air cleaner(TAC)
Catalytic converter
Computer Command control system (CCC)
Controls:
Fuel control (EFI)
Air injection reaction (AIR)
Evaporative emission control system (EEC)
Electronic spark timing (EST)
Electronic spark control (ESC)
Transmission converter clutch (TCC)

10–30, 15–35 AND MEDIUM TRUCK MODELS

LIGHT/HEAVY DUTY EMISSION CLASSIFICATION

All series truck models under 8501 lbs. gross vehicle weight rating (GVWR) are classified as light duty emissions and any truck models over the 8501 lbs. gross vehicle weight rating (GVWR) are classified as heavy duty emissions. Each vehicle will have an included recommended maintenance schedule for the emission components that are included with the vehicle and engine combination, for the area that the vehicle is to be operated in, such as 49 States, California and/or High Altitude.

ENGINE CLASSIFICATION

NOTE: The following list of engines should only be used as a guide for vehicle applications. The usage of engines in light or heavy duty emission application could change from year to year or from vehicle to vehicle.

LIGHT DUTY EMISSION

4.3L Engine–VIN number N
5.0L Engine–VIN number F
5.0L Engine–VIN number H
5.7L Engine–VIN number L
5.7L Diesel Engine–VIN number Z
6.2L Diesel Engine–VIN number C

HEAVY DUTY EMISSION

4.8L Engine–VIN number T
5.7L Engine–VIN number M
5.7L Engine–VIN number P
5.7L Engine–VIN number L
6.0L Engine–VIN number B
7.0L Engine–VIN number E
7.4L Engine–VIN number S
6.2L Diesel Engine–VIN number C

EMISSION COMPONENTS

NOTE: All engines have the following emission controls or modifications as noted.

Positive crankcase emission control system (PCV)
Exhaust gas recirculation system (EGR)
Thermostatic air cleaner (TAC)
Air injection reaction (AIR)
Early fuel evaporation (EFE), Except 4.8L engine
The 4.3L, 5.0L and 5.7L engines for California have Computer Command Control (CCC) system which controls the following functions.

Fuel control system (EFI)
Air injection reaction (AIR)
Exhaust gas recirculation (EGR)
Evaporative emission control system (EEC)
Electronic spark timing (EST)
Electronic spark control (EST)
Transmission converter clutch (TCC)

All vehicles/engines units for California have an Evaporative Emission Control system included in the assembly.

The 4.3L, 5.0L and 5.7L engines (other than in California), have Evaporative Emission Control system.

A throttle return control (TRC) system is used on heavy duty emission vehicle/engine units.

EVAPORATIVE EMISSION SYSTEM

This system was designed to reduce fuel vapor emissions that are normally vented into the atmosphere from the gas tank and the carburetor fuel bowl, through the use of a carbon canister and liquid-vapor separator.

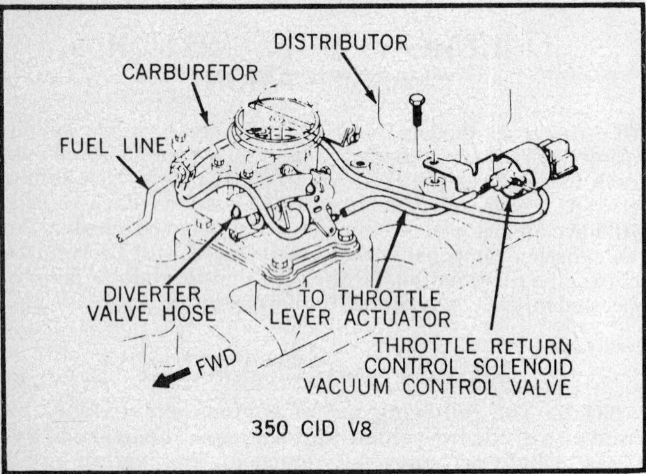

Location of solenoid vacuum control valve—V8 engines
(© General Motors Corp.)

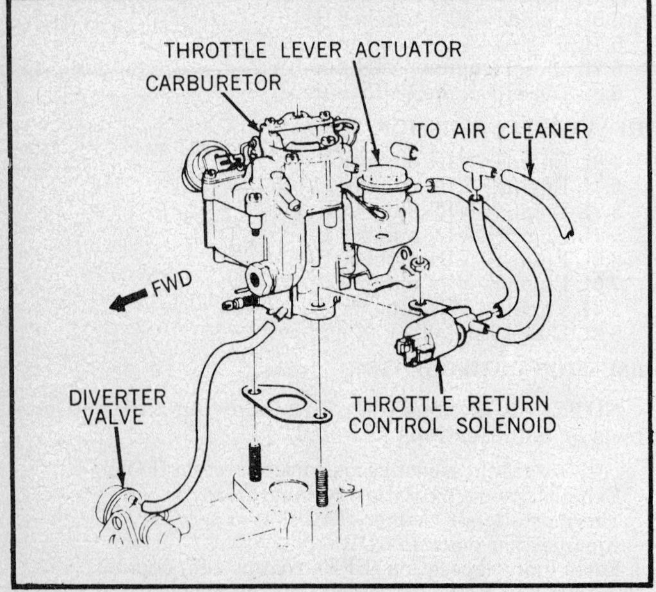

Location of solenoid vacuum control valve—6 cylinder engine
(© General Motors Corp.)

THROTTLE RETURN CONTROL SYSTEM (TRC)

Ordinarily, engine deceleration is controlled by the operator of the vehicle, as he regulates the throttle blade position through a system of accelerator linkage components. This sytem, though thoroughly operational, is not entirely efficient. In conventional carburetion systems, there is usually some mechanical force which opposes accelerate application, i.e., there is some device which returns the throttle blade to the idle position whenever the accelerator is released. This is, in a great many cases, accomplished with the aid of a return spring.

Even though the accelerator return spring is an effective decelerator, it, neverthless, contributes to pollution because of its rapid rate of deceleration. If the throttle blade is rapidly returned to idle, a very low pressure develops in the intake manifold area. When this happens, an unnecessarily high proportion of liquid fuel is drawn into the combustion area and then exhausted before complete burning can occur. Also, when wheel rotation, transmitted through the differential and transmission, drives the engine (coasting), very high manifold vacuum levels are attained and again, an unnecessarily high volume of liquid fuel is introduced into the combustion area.

In order to overcome the problem of rapid deceleration and non-volatile fuel consumption during coasting, the TCR system has been installed on some V-8 and 6 cylinder engines. The system consists of three major components; they are the throttle lever actuator, solenoid vacuum control valve and the electronic speed sensor.

The throttle lever actuator, located at the carburetor, is vacuum operated and controls the position of the primary throttle plates a preset amount in excess of curb idle when engine vacuum is applied to it.

The electronic speed sensor monitors engine speed at the distributor and will supply a continuous electrical signal to the solenoid vacuum control valve whenever speed is in excess of the present value.

The solenoid vacuum control valve is an ON/OFF vacuum valve which is held open above a present engine speed by a signal from the electronic speed sensor. When this happens, vacuum at the throttle lever actuator causes the actuator to open the throttle blade, only slightly, admitting more air to ensure more complete burning of the air/fuel mixture.

NOTE: TRC activation value is 1825 rpm ±65 rpm. Deactivation value is at least 10 rpm below activation, or not less than 1700 rpm.

TRC System Test

THROTTLE LEVER ACTUATOR OPERATES OUTSIDE NORMAL RPM RANGE:

1. Connect a tachometer to the distributor TACH terminal.
2. Start the engine and shift the transmission into neutral.
3. Advance the throttle until the engine speed is 1890 rpm. The throttle lever actuator should be extended at this speed.
4. Decrease the engine speed to 1700 rpm. The throttle lever actuator should be retracted at this speed.
5. If the throttle lever actuator operates outside of the 1890–1700 rpm range, then the electronic speed sensor is out of calibration and should be replaced.

THROTTLE LEVER DOES NOT OPERATE AT ANY SPEED:

1. Start the engine and shift the transmission into neutral.
2. Connect the negative lead of a voltmeter to the engine ground and insert the positive lead into the connector cavities of either the solenoid control valve or the electronic speed sensor. In either case the voltage should measure 12–14 volts.
3. If the voltage measured at the speed sensor is approximately equivalent to battery voltage (12–14 volts), but the voltage measured at the solenoid control valve is 0, then a

problem exists somewhere in the engine wiring harness. Repair is necessary.

4. If the voltage measured at either device is 0 (no voltage), then check the engine harness connections at the distributor and/or the bulkhead connector. Repair as necessary.

5. If battery voltage is present at both the solenoid control valve and the speed sensor, then connect one end of a jumper wire to the solenoid control valve-to-speed sensor connecting wire terminal at the solenoid vacuum control valve and the other end of the jumper wire to ground. With the engine running, the throttle lever actuator should extend.

6. If the throttle lever actuator does not extend, then disconnect the actuator vacuum hose at the solenoid vacuum control valve side port. Check for any blockage or obstruction in the port. Clean as necessary.

7. If there is no vacuum obstruction in the vacuum line (vacuum passage is clear), then replace the solenoid vacuum control valve.

8. If the actuator extends after performing Step no. 5, then connect one end of a jumper wire to the solenoid control valve-to-speed sensor connecting wire terminal at the speed sensor and the other end of the jumper wire to ground. If the throttle lever actuator does not extend, then repair the wire which connects the speed sensor to the solenoid vacuum control valve. If the actuator does extend, then connect one lead of the voltmeter to the speed sensor ground wire at the speed sensor and the other lead to ground. The voltmeter should indicate 0 volts (no voltage drop). If any voltage is indicated on the voltmeter, then there is resistance in the speed sensor-to-ground circuit, or, possibly, an open circuit. Repair as necessary.

THROTTLE LEVER ACTUATOR EXTENDED AT ALL SPEEDS

1. Disconnect the wire connector from the solenoid vacuum control valve.

2. If the actuator remains in the extended position, then check the solenoid side vacuum port for blockage. Clean as necessary.

3. Reattach the wire connector and the vacuum hose to the solenoid control valve and recheck system operation.

4. If the actuator remains in the extended position, again, disconnect the wire connector from the solenoid vacuum control valve. If the actuator does not retract, then replace the solenoid vacuum control valve.

5. If the actuator retracts with the solenoid control valve wire connector disconnected, then reattach the connector and disconnect the speed sensor wire connector. If the actuator retracts from the extended position, then replace the speed sensor. If the actuator does not retract, then a short circuit condition (to ground) probably exists in the solenoid-to-speed sensor wire located within the wiring harness. Repair as necessary.

Testing Throttle Lever Actuator

NOTE: The throttle lever actuator can be vacuum leak tested in the conventional manner by using an ordinary vacuum and pump/gauge tool.

1. Disconnect the valve-to-actuator vacuum hose at the solenoid vacuum control valve.

2. Connect the disconnected end of the vacuum hose to a vacuum hand pump/gauge tool or any external vacuum source equipped with a vacuum gauge.

3. Manually, check the throttle linkage, lever and shaft for binding or sticking. Repair as necessary.

4. Start the engine with the transmission in neutral and operate until normal operating temperature is reached. Note the idle rpm.

5. Apply vacuum (20 in.Hg.) to the actuator.

6. Manually, open the throttle slightly and allow the throttle to close against the extended actuator plunger. Again note the engine rpm.

7. Open the actuator vacuum hose to atmospheric pressure

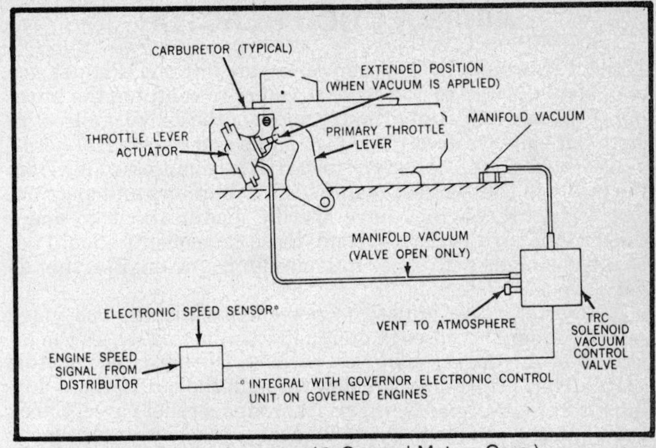

Throttle return control system (© General Motors Corp.)

(vacuum cancelled) and reapply vacuum (20 in.Hg.). DO NOT assist the actuator. Note the increase in engine rpm.

8. If the rpm noted in Step no. 7 is not within 150 rpm of that noted in Step no. 6, then the actuator plunger may be binding due to foreign material, corrosion, etc. Also, the actuator diaphragm tension may have weakened. Correct any binding condition. Replace the actuator if proved to be weak.

9. Again, open the actuator vacuum hose to atmospheric pressure (vacuum cancelled). The engine speed should return to within 50 rpm of the idle speed noted in Step no. 4. If not, the plunger may be binding. If the binding condition cannot be repaired, then replace the actuator.

10. If the engine rpm noted in Step no. 6 is not within the specified TRC speed range, then adjust the throttle lever actuator (see chart).

TRC Idle Speed Adjustment

NOTE: Check the throttle linkage, lever and shaft to be certain that they are free from binding or sticking.

1. Disconnect the valve-to-acuator vacuum hose at the solenoid vacuum control valve.

2. Connect the disconnected end of the vacuum hose to a vacuum hand pump/gauge tool or any external vacuum source equipped with a vacuum gauge.

3. Apply vacuum (20 in.Hg.) to the actuator.

4. Manually, open the throttle slightly and allow the throttle to close against the extended actuator plunger. Note the engine rpm.

5. Adjust by turning the actuator plunger screw on 350 CID and 292 CID engines, or by loosening the jam nut on the mounting bracket for the 366, 427 and 454 CID engines and turning the actuator body in the appropriate direction. Repeat Steps no. 3 and 4 until the specified speed range is obtained.

EXHAUST GAS RECIRCULATION SYSTEM

This system helps reduce nitrogen oxides emitted by the engine exhaust. This is accomplished by releasing small amounts of exhaust gas into the cylinders by means of the E.G.R. valve. This lowers the peak combustion temperatures, reducing the amounts of oxides produced.

A backpressure EGR valve is used on light duty emission class engines. The valve opening is determined by the amount of vacuum received from a ported source on the carburetor and the amount of backpressure in the exhaust system.

Two different types of backpressure EGR valves are used. A positive transducer valve and a negative transducer valve. The negative transduced backpressure valve is used on engines with a relatively low backpressure to provide the desired opening point and flow rate.

The EGR system requires the use of unleaded fuel.

AIR INJECTION REACTOR

The A.I.R. system injects compressed air into the exhaust system, close enough to the exhaust valves to continue the burning of the normally unburned segment of the exhaust gases. To do this it employs an air injection pump and a system of hoses, valves, tubes, etc., necessary to carry the compressed air from the pump to the exhaust manifolds. Carburetors and distributors for A.I.R. engines have specific modifications to adapt them to the air injection system; these components should not be interchanged with those intended for use on engines that do not have the system.

A diverter valve is used to prevent backfiring. The valve senses sudden increases in manifold vacuum and ceases the injection of air during fuel-rich periods. During coasting, this valve diverts the entire air flow through the muffler and during high engines speeds, expels it through a relief valve. Check valves in the system prevent exhaust gases from entering the pump.

EARLY FUEL EVAPORATION SYSTEM

Engine models are equipped with this system to reduce engine warm-up time, improve driveability and reduce emissions. On start-up, a vacuum motor acts to close a heat valve in the exhaust manifold which causes exhaust gases to enter the intake manifold heat riser passages. Incoming fuel mixture is then heated and more complete fuel evaporation is provided during warm-up.

CATALYTIC CONVERTERS

The converters are used to oxidize hydrocarbons (HC) and carbon monoxide (CO).
The catalysts are made of noble metals (platinum and palladium) which are bonded to either a monolithic (one-piece) element or to individual pellets. The catalyst causes the HC and CO to break down without taking part in the reaction; hence, a catalyst life of 50,000 miles is expected.

Some engines equipped with the converters require an air injection pump to supply air for the reaction; others will not.

For more detailed information, refer to the Unit Repair section.

NOTE: Some models are equipped with a Closed Loop emission control system that uses an oxygen sensor and three-way catalyst.

PULSE AIR INJECTION REACTION SYSTEM (P.A.I.R.)

The Pulse Air Injection Reactor System consists of four pulse air check valves. The check valves are connected by tubes to the exhaust ports. The firing of the engine creates a pulsating flow of exhaust gases which are positive or negative pressure. A negative pressure at the pulse air valves results in the flow of fresh air into the exhaust system. If pressure is positive the check valve is forced closed and no exhaust gas will flow past the valve into the fresh air supply line.

A deceleration valve is used on some L6 and California V8 models to prevent backfiring in the exhaust system during deceleration. When deceleration causes a sudden vacuum increase in the vacuum signal line, the pressure differential on the diaphragm will overcome the closing force of the spring, opening the valve and bleeding air into the intake manifold.

Air trapped in the chamber above the vacuum diaphragm will bleed at a calibrated rate through the delay valve portion of the integral "Check and Delay Valve," reducing the vacuum acting on the diaphragm. When the vacuum load on the diaphragm and the spring load become equal, the valve assembly will close, shutting off the air flow into the intake manifold.

The check valve portion of the "Check and Delay Valve" provides quick balancing of chamber pressure when a sudden decrease in vacuum is caused by acceleration rather than deceleration.

THERMOSTATIC AIR CLEANER (THERMAC)

The Thermostatic Air Cleaner (THERMAC) is on all engines. The TAC uses a damper door in the air cleaner inlet, controlled by a vacuum diaphragm motor to mix pre-heated and non preheated air entering the air cleaner to maintain a controlled air temperature into the carburetor. The vacuum motor is modulated by a temperature sensor in the air cleaner. The pre-heating of the air cleaner inlet air allows leaner carburetor and choke calibrations resulting in lower emission levels, while maintaining good driveability. The pre-heated air is obtained by drawing inlet air through stove attached to the exhaust manifold.

CARBURETOR CALIBRATION

While the carburetor's main function is to provide the engine with a combustible air/fuel mixture, the carburetor calibration is critical to maintaining proper emission levels.

The carburetor's idle, off-idle, main metering, power enrichment and accelerating pump systems are calibrated to provide the best possible combination of engine performance, fuel economy and exhaust emission control. Carburetor adjustments and service must be performed using the recommended procedures to insure engine exhaust emission levels remain within official limits.

COMPUTER COMMAND CONTROL

The Computer Command Control system is an electronically controlled exhaust emission system that monitors many different engine/vehicle functions and can control various operations including the transmission converter clutch. The system has back-up programs in the event of a failure to alert or instruct the operator through a CHECK ENGINE lamp on the instrument panel. This lamp will light indicating a fault in the system and will remain on until the problem is corrected. This same lamp through an integral diagnostic system, will aid the technician in locating the cause of a problem.

The system helps to lower exhaust emissions while maintaining good fuel economy and driveability. The system control the following operations:

1. Fuel Control System
2. Electronic Spark Timing (EST)
3. Air Management
4. Early Fuel Evaporation
5. Transmission Converter Clutch

Trouble Code "Test" Lead

The trouble code "TEST" lead terminal is mounted in a 12 terminal connector is used at assembly to evaluate the system and is known as the Assembly Line Diagnostic Link (ALDL) or Assembly Line Communication Link (ALCL). With the ignition "ON", jumper the "test" terminal-to-ground terminal.

Grounding this terminal signals the ECM to flash any trouble codes stored in memory. For information on trouble codes and diagnosis procedures, see the Unit Repair section or Chilton's Electronic Engine Control Manual.

ENGINE ASSEMBLIES

Engine Removal and Installation

S/T SERIES TRUCKS

1.9L (VIN A) and 2.5L (VIN E) GASOLINE ENGINES

NOTE: Due to the varied engine-transmission combinations used in the GMC and Chevrolet truck line, the procedures for removal and installation of the engines are given as a general outline. It may be necessary to alter the procedures somewhat to compensate.

1. Raise the hood and disconnect the battery cables.
2. Drain the cooling system.
3. Remove the air cleaner assembly and vacuum hoses. Mark the vacuum hoses for reinstallation. Remove the A/C compressor, if equipped and lay aside.
4. Disconnect all hoses, tubing and electrical leads from the engine and mark them for reinstallation. Remove the power steering pump, if equipped and lay aside.
5. Remove the radiator and fan blade assembly.
6. Disconnect the exhaust pipe from the exhaust manifold. Disconnect the oxygen sensor wire.
7. Raise the vehicle and, if equipped with a manual transmission, remove the clutch return spring and cable. If equipped, remove the skid plate. Drain the engine oil pan. Remove the strut rods on 2-wheel drive models.
8. Remove the starter motor and fasten it to the frame rail with a piece of wire.
9. Remove the flywheel cover pan. Remove the crossmember and disconnect the transmission cooler lines on 4 wheel drive models.
10. Remove flexplate to converter retaining bolts, is equipped with auto transmission. Remove the bell housing bolts and support the transmission.
11. Lift the engine slightly and remove the engine mount nuts.
12. Make certain that all lines, hoses, wires and cables have been disconnected from the engine and the frame.
13. Lower the vehicle and support the transmission. Remove the engine from the vehicle with the front of the engine raised slightly.
14. Installation is the reverse of removal.

S/T SERIES TRUCKS

Removal and Installation

2.8L V6 (VIN B) ENGINE – TWO WHEEL DRIVE

NOTE: The following procedure is to be used as a general guide for engine removal and installation. Depending upon options, modifications, etc., changes in the removal and installation outline may have to be considered.

1. Disconnect the battery and remove the hood.
2. Drain the cooling system, disconnect the radiator hose, the overflow hose and the upper fan shroud.
3. Disconnect the transmission cooler lines at the radiator, if equipped and remove the radiator.
4. Remove the fan assembly.
5. Disconnect the heater hoses and remove the air cleaner.
6. Disconnect the vacuum hoses and the necessary wires at the firewall, ground wires and the main electrical feed wires.
7. Disconnect the throttle cable and cruise control cable.
8. Remove the distributor cap and raise the vehicle. Support safely.
9. Remove the converter to exhaust pipe bolts. Remove the exhaust manifolds from both sides.
10. Remove the strut rods at the bell housing. Remove the flywheel cover.
11. Remove the torque converter bolts, if equipped with auto transmission.
12. Disconnect the shield from the rear of the catalytic converter. Remove the converter hanger at the exhaust pipe.
13. Remove the lower fan shroud and disconnect the fuel hoses at the fuel pump.
14. Remove the two outer air dam bolts and remove the left hand body mount bolts.
15. Install jackstands as required and raise the body.
16. Remove the bellhousing bolts and lower the body.
17. Remove the motor mount through bolts and remove the jackstands.
18. Lower the vehicle and disconnect the A/C compressor, if equipped.
19. Disconnect the power steering pump and install a lifting device onto the engine.
20. Support the transmission with a floor jack and remove the engine from the vehicle.
21. The installation of the engine assembly is the reverse of the removal procedure.

S/T TRUCK 4X4 MODELS

Removal and Installation

2.8L V6 (VIN B) ENGINE WITH MANUAL TRANSMISSIONS

NOTE: The following procedure is to be used as a general guide for engine removal and installation. Depending upon options, modifications, etc., changes in the removal and installation outline may have to be considered.

1. Remove the hood, disconnect the battery and remove.
2. Remove the air cleaner assembly and drain the cooling system.
3. Remove the upper fan shroud and remove the radiator hoses from the radiator. Remove the radiator from the vehicle.
4. Remove the fan and fan clutch. Remove the A/C compressor (if equipped) and lay aside.
5. Remove the power steering pump (if equipped) and lay aside.
6. Disconnect the fuel lines, the vacuum lines and the electrical wiring.

NOTE: Tag the various hoses, if required, for identification during installation procedures.

7. Disconnect the accelerator and cruise control (if equipped), cables and the heater hoses at the engine.
8. Disconnect the negative ground strap at the bulkhead. Disconnect the engine wiring harness at the bulkhead connector, if necessary.
9. Remove the lower fan shroud and the main feed wire at the bulkhead.
10. Remove the distributor cap and the diverter valve.
11. From inside the cab, remove the shifter boot, the transfer case shifter and the transmission shift lever assembly.
12. Raise the vehicle and support safely.
13. Remove the front skid plate, the rear skid plate and the front splash shield.
14. Drain both the transfer case and the transmission into a suitable container.
15. Remove the rear propeller shaft and disconnect the speedometer cable.
16. Disconnect the front propeller shaft at the transfer case. Disconnect the shift linkage and vacuum hoses at the case.

17. Disconnect the parking brake cable and remove the rear transmission mount. Remove the catalytic converter bracket.
18. Support the transfer case safely and remove the case bolts. Remove the transfer case from the vehicle.
19. Remove the crossmember.
20. Disconnect the back-up light wire and clip. Remove the clutch slave cylinder attaching bolts and lay the cylinder aside.
21. Remove the transmission retaining bolts and remove the transmission from the vehicle.
22. Remove the clutch release bearing and remove the inspection cover.
23. Remove the left hand body mount bolts and loosen the left hand radiator support bolt.
24. Raise the left side of the body and install a block of wood.
25. Remove the bellhousing and disconnect the exhaust at the converter and manifold.
26. Disconnect the clutch cross shaft at the frame.
27. Remove the starter bolts, the starter wires and the starter.
28. Remove the engine mount bolts, install a lifting device to the engine and remove the engine from the vehicle
29. To install the engine into the vehicle, reverse the removal procedure.

Removal and Installation

2.8L V6 (VIN B) ENGINE WITH AUTOMATIC TRANSMISSION

NOTE: The following procedure is to be used as a general guide for engine removal and installation. Depending upon options, modifications, etc., changes in the removal and installation outline may have to be considered.

1. Remove the hood and the battery from the vehicle.
2. Raise the vehicle and support safely.
3. On Blazer models, remove the body mounts. On chassis cab models, remove two body mounts.
4. Remove the front air dam end bolts.
5. Raise the body from the frame enough to gain access to the top transmission bolts and remove the bolts.
6. Lower body and remove the remaining transmission to engine mounting bolts.
7. Remove the 2nd crossmember bolts and remove the crossmember.
8. Disconnect the exhaust at the manifold and disconnect the catalytic converter hanger.
9. Remove the torque converter cover bolts.
10. Disconnect the front propeller shaft at the front differential.
11. Remove the torque converter cover and disconnect the oil cooler lines at the engine retaining clips.
12. Remove the engine mount bolts and remove the flexplate to torque converter bolts.
13. Remove the front splash shield and the lower fan shroud bolts.
14. Lower the vehicle and drain the cooling system into a suitable container.
15. Remove the upper fan shroud and disconnect the radiator hoses at the radiator. Disconnect the transmission oil cooler lines at the radiator and remove the radiator from the vehicle.
16. Remove the fan assembly.
17. Remove the air cleaner assembly and if equipped with A/C, remove the A/C compressor and lay aside.
18. If equipped with power steering, remove the pump and lay aside.
19. Disconect the fuel lines, the necessary vacuum lines, wires and emission hoses.
20. Disconnect the accelerator, TV cables and cruise control cables, if equipped.
21. Disconnect engine wiring harness at the bulkhead connector and the heater hoses at the engine.
22. Support the transmission securely. Install an engine lifting device and carefully remove the engine from the vehicle.
23. To install the engine into the vehicle, reverse the removal procedure.

S/T SERIES TRUCKS

Removal and Installation

2.2L (VIN S) DIESEL ENGINE (2 AND 4 WHEEL DRIVE)

NOTE: The following procedure is to be used as a general guide for engine removal and installation. Depending upon options, modifications, etc., changes in the removal and installation outline may have to be considered.

1. Remove the engine hood, disconnect and remove the battery.
2. Disconnect the exhaust pipe at the manifold.
3. Remove the power steering reservoir.
4. Remove the upper fan shroud.
5. Remove under cover and drain the cooling system by opening the drain plugs on the radiator and on the cylinder block. Disconnect the radiator hoses and remove the radiator.
6. Remove the fan and the lower fan shroud.
7. Disconnect the heater hoses at the engine.
8. Remove the PCV valve at the cylinder head. Remove the air cleaner assembly.
9. Loosen the compressor drive belts by moving the power steering oil pump or idler (if so equipped). Evacuate the A/C system and disconnect the A/C manifold at the compressor. Seal the opening.
10. Disconnect the power steering pump from the engine.
11. Disconnect necessary wires from the engine assembly. Tag the wires for easier assembly.
12. Disconnect vacuum hoses and rear air cleaner bracket.
13. Disconnect the accelerator control cable from the injection pump side.
14. Remove the starter bolts, starter wires and the starter from the engine.
15. Disconnect the fuel hoses from the injection pump.
16. Remove the shifter boot and the shifter.
17. Raise the vehicle and support safely.
18. Remove the right hand motor mount through bolt.
19. Disconnect the lower clutch cable and disconnect the clutch bellcrank at the frame.
20. Disconnect the back-up light switch wires and the speedometer cable at the transmission.
21. Remove the drive shaft.
22. Remove the transmission mount nut and support the transmission.
23. Remove the transmission crossmember.
24. Remove the transmission to bell housing bolts and remove the transmission.
25. Remove the transmission bell housing to engine bolts and remove the bellhousing.
26. Lower the vehicle, disconnect the upper clutch cable and remove the bellcrank.
27. Install a lifting device on the engine, remove the left hand motor mount through bolt and disconnect the battery ground cable at the engine block.
28. Carefully remove the engine from the vehicle.
29. For installation of the engine assembly, reverse the removal procedure.

ASTRO VAN

2.5L (VIN E) ENGINE

NOTE: The following procedure is to be used as a general guide for engine removal and installation. Depend-

ing upon options, modifications, etc., changes in the removal and installation outline may have to be considered.

1. Remove the battery and engine cover.
2. Drain the radiator into a suitable container.
3. Remove the headlamp bezel and remove the grille.
4. Remove the radiator lower close-up panel.
5. Remove the radiator support brace and the lower tie bar. Remove the cross brace and the hood latch assembly.
6. Remove the upper core support. Disconnect the radiator hoses at the radiator.
7. Remove the radiator filler panels.
8. Remove the radiator and fan shroud as an assembly.
9. Disconnect the engine wiring harness at the bulkhead connector.
10. Disconnect the wiring harness at the ECM and pull through the bulkhead.
11. Disconnect the heater hoses at the heater core. Disconnect the accelerator cable.
12. Disconnect the battery ground strap at the cylinder head.
13. Disconnect the canister purge hose and remove the air cleaner with adapter.
14. Raise the vehicle and support safely. Disconnect the exhaust pipe at the manifold.
15. Disconnect the wiring harness at the transmission and frame.
16. Disconnect the wires at the starter and remove the starter assembly.
17. Remove the flywheel shield.
18. Disconnect the fuel hoses and remove the engine mount through bolts.
19. Remove the bell housing bolts and lower the vehicle.
20. Remove the soil filler neck and the thermostat outlet.
21. Install a suitable engine lifting device, support the transmission and remove the engine from the vehicle.
22. To install the engine into the vehicle, reverse the removal procedure.

ASTRO VAN

Removal and Installation

4.3L (VIN N) ENGINE

NOTE: The following procedure is to be used as a general guide for engine removal and installation. Depending upon options, modifications, etc., changes in the removal and installation outline may have to be considered.

1. Disconnect the battery and remove. Drain the cooling system into a suitable container.
2. Raise the vehicle and support safely.
3. Disconnect the exhaust pipes at the manifolds.
4. Disconnect the strut rods at the flywheel inspection cover. Remove the torque converter bolts.
5. Disconnect the starter wires at the starter and remove the starter assembly.
6. Place a container and remove the oil filter.
7. Disconnect the wires and fuel hoses at the transmission and frame.
8. Disconnect the lower transmission cooler line at the radiator.
9. Disconnect the lower engine oil cooler line at the radiator.
10. Remove the lower fan shroud bolts, the engine mount bolts and the bell housing bolts.
11. Lower the vehicle.
12. Remove the headlamp bezel and the grille assembly.
13. Remove the radiator lower close out panel.
14. Remove the radiator support brace and the lower tie bar. Remove the hood latch assembly.
15. Disconnect the master cylinder and lay aside.
16. Remove the upper fan shroud and the upper radiator core support.
17. Disconnect the radiator hose at the radiator. Disconnect the upper transmission oil cooler line and the upper engine oil cooler line from the radiator.
18. Remove the radiator from the vehicle.
19. Discharge the A/C system and remove the radiator filler panels.
20. Remove the engine cover and remove the A/C brace at the rear of the compressor.
21. Disconnect A/C hose at the accumulator. Remove the A/C compressor and bracket.
22. Remove the power steering pump.
23. Disconnect the necessary vacuum hoses and wiring harness at the bulkhead.
24. Remove the right kick panel and disconnect the harness at the ESC module. Push the harness through the bulkhead.
25. Remove the distributor cap and the A/C accumulator.
26. Disconnect the fuel lines at the carburetor.
27. Remove the diverter valve and the horn.
28. Disconnect the transmission dipstick tube and the heater hose at the heater core.
29. Remove the A.I.R. check valves.
30. Install a suitable engine lifting device, support the transmission and remove the engine from the vehicle.
31. To install the engine into the vehicle, reverse the removal procedure.

10–30, 15–35 MODEL PICK-UPS AND FOUR WHEEL DRIVE (C–K SERIES)

Removal

IN-LINE 6 CYLINDER ENGINE, 4.1L (VIN D) AND/OR 4.8L (VIN T)

NOTE: The following procedure is to be used as a general guide for engine removal and installation. Depending upon options, modifications, etc., changes in the removal and installation outline may have to be considered.

1. Disconnect and remove battery.
2. Drain cooling system into a suitable container.
3. Disconnect the accelerator cable from the carburetor throttle lever and if equipped with automatic transmission, remove the detent cable from the throttle lever.
4. Remove air cleaner and ducts.
5. Disconnect all wiring from the engine.
6. Remove the radiator hoses from the radiator and the heater hoses from the engine.
7. Remove the radiator from the vehicle. Remove the fan and water pump pulley.
8. Disconnect the fuel line from the fuel pump.
9. Remove the vehicle hood after scribing hood hinge locations.
10. Raise the vehicle and support safely.
11. Remove the starter bolts, wiring and remove the starter assembly.
12. Remove the flywheel or torque converter splash shield, as applicable.
13. Disconnect the exhaust pipe from the exhaust manifold and wire to the frame.
14. Support the engine and remove the engine mount through bolts. If equipped with an automatic transmission, remove the flex plate bolts. If equipped with four wheel drive, remove the strut rods at the engine mounts.
15. Remove the bell housing to engine retaining bolts and with the lifting device attached to the engine, remove the engine from the vehicle.
16. To install the engine into the vehicle, reverse the removal procedure.

10–30, 15–35 MODEL PICK-UPS AND FOUR WHEEL DRIVE (C–K SERIES)

Removal and Installation

5.0L(VIN F&H), 5.7L(VIN L&M) V8 ENGINES AND 4.3L V6 (VIN N)

NOTE: The following procedure is to be used as a general guide for engine removal and installation. Depending upon options, modifications, etc., changes in the removal and installation outline may have to be considered.

1. Remove the hood assembly. Disconnect the battery cables and remove the battery.
2. Drain the cooling system into a suitable container.
3. Remove the air cleaner assembly and all the accessory drive belts.
4. Remove the fan and water pump pulley.
5. Disconnect the upper and lower radaitor hoses at the engine.
6. Disconnect the heater hoses at the engine and if equipped with automatic transmission, disconnect the cooler lines at the radiator.
7. Remove the radiator and shroud assembly.
8. Disconnect the accelerator linkage and detent cable from the carburetor.
9. If equipped with A/C, remove the compressor and lay aside.
10. If equipped with power steering, remove the pump from the engine and lay aside.
11. Remove the engine wiring harness from the engine components.
12. Disconnect the fuel line at the fuel pump.
13. Disconnect the vacuum lines from the intake manifold.
14. Raise the vehicle and support safely.
15. Drain the engine oil pan and disconnect the exhaust pipe from the exhaust manifold.
16. On four wheel drive models with automatic transmission, remove the strut rods from the engine mounts.
17. Remove the flywheel or converter splash pan, as applicable.
18. Disconnect the wiring along the right pan rail, the gas gauge wire and disconnect the wiring from the starter. Remove the starter retaining bolts and remove the starter.
19. If equipped with automatic transmission, remove the converter to flex plate attaching bolts.
20. Support the transmission and remove the bell housing to engine bolts, leaving one or more loosely to support weight. Remove the lower engine mount bracket to frame bolts.
21. Lower the vehicle.
22. Attach a lifting device to the engine, remove the remaining bell housing bolt(s) and remove the engine from the vehicle.
23. To install the engine into the vehicle, reverse the removal procedure.

10–30, 15–35 MODEL PICK-UPS AND FOUR WHEEL DRIVE (C–K SERIES)

Removal and Installation

7.4L MARK IV Engines (VIN W)

NOTE: The following procedure is to be used as a general guide for engine removal and installation. Depending upon options, modifications, etc., changes in the removal and installation outline may have to be considered.

1. Remove the hood assembly, disconnect the battery cables and remove the battery.
2. Drain the cooling system into a suitable container.
3. Disconnect the radiator and heater hoses at the engine. Remove the radiator and shroud assembly.
4. Disconnect the engine wiring harness. Mark wires as required to ease assembly.
5. Disconnect the accelerator linkage, the fuel lines and all vacuum lines from the engine. Mark the lines as required to ease assembly.
6. Remove the power steering and A/C compressor assemblies, if equipped and lay aside.
7. Raise the vehicle and support safely. Drain the engine oil pan.
8. Disconnect the exhaust pipe from the exhaust manifold.
9. Remove the starter bolts, wires and remove the starter assembly.
10. Remove the flywheel splash shield or converter housing cover, as appicable.
11. If equipped with automatic transmission, remove the converter to flex plate bolts.
12. Remove the bell housing to engine bolts, leaving one or more loosely to support weight.
13. Lower the vehicle and install a lifting device onto the engine.
14. Support the transmission with a floor jack and raise the engine slightly.
15. Remove the engine mount to engine brackets, the remaining bell housing bolt(s) and remove the engine assembly from the vehicle.
16. To install the engine, reverse the removal procedure.

10–30, 15–35 MODEL PICK-UPS AND FOUR WHEEL DRIVE (C–K SERIES)

Removal and Installation

5.7L V8 DIESEL ENGINE (VIN Z)

NOTE: The following procedure is to be used as a general guide for engine removal and installation. Depending upon options, modifications, etc., changes in the removal and installation outline may have to be considered.

1. Remove the hood from the vehicle, scribing the hinge locations for ease of installation.
2. Remove the air cleaner and install the screened safety cover.
3. Drain the engine coolant into a suitable container.
4. Disconnect the battery cables and remove the batteries from the vehicle. Disconnect the ground cables at the engine as required.
5. Disconnect the radiator hoses, cooler lines heater hoses, vacuum hoses and power steering pump hoses at the steering gear assembly.
6. Remove the A/C compressor with brackets and hoses attached. Remove the fuel hose from the fuel pump and all necessary wiring.
7. Remove the hairpin clip at the bellcrank. Remove the throttle cable from the intake manifold bracket and position the cable away from the engine.
8. Remove the upper radiator support and the radiator from the vehicle.
9. Raise the vehicle and support safely.
10. Disconnect the exhaust pipes from the manifolds.
11. Disconnect the torque converter cover and three bolts holding the converter to the flywheel.
12. Remove the engine mount through bolts. Support engine safely.
13. Remove three bolts on the right side from the bell housing to engine. Disconnect the starter wiring and remove the starter.
14. Lower the vehicle and safely support the transmission.

15. Install a lifting device to the engine and remove the three left side engine to bell housing bolts. Remove the engine from the vehicle.
16. To install the engine into the vehicle, reverse the removal procedure.

10–30, 15–35 MODEL PICK-UPS AND FOUR WHEEL DRIVE (C–K SERIES)

Removal and Installation

6.2L V8 DIESEL ENGINE (VIN J)

NOTE: The following procedure is to be used as a general guide for engine removal and installation. Depending upon options, modifications, etc., changes in the removal and installation outline may have to be considered.

1. Remove the hood and scribe the hinges for ease of installation.
2. Disconnect the batteries and remove from the vehicle.
3. Raise the vehicle and support safely.
4. Remove the transmission dust cover and disconnect the torque converter from the flexplate.
5. Disconnect the exhaust pipes from the manifolds.
6. Remove the starter bolts, the starter wires and remove the starter.
7. Remove the transmission bell housing to engine bolts, leaving one or more loosely to prevent separation.
8. Remove the right and left engine mount bolts.
9. Disconnect the block heaters, remove the wiring harness, transmission oil cooler lines and the front battery cable clamp at the oil pan.
10. Disconnect the fuel lines, the oil cooler lines at the engine block and the lower fan shroud bolts.
11. Lower the vehicle and drain the engine coolant into a suitable container.
12. Remove the air cleaner assembly with resonator and the primary filter from, the cowl.
13. Disconnect the ground cable from the alternator bracket. Disconnect the alternator wires and clips.
14. Disconnect the TPS,EGR–EPR, fuel cut-off at the injection pump.
15. Remove the harness from the clips at the rocker covers and disconnect the glow plugs.
16. Disconnect the EGR–EPR solenoids, glow plugs, controller, temperature sender and move the harness aside.
17. Disconnect the ground strap on the left side.
18. Remove the fan assembly, the upper radiator hoses at the engine and the fan shroud.
19. Remove the power steering pump and belt. remove the reservoir and lay the pump and reservoir aside.
20. Disconnect the vacuum lines at the cruise servo and accelerator cable at the injection pump.
21. Disconnect the heater hoses and the oil cooler lines at the engine.
22. Disconnect the lower radiator hose, the oil cooler lines, the heater hose, the automatic transmission cooler lines and the overflow hose at the radiator.
23. Remove the upper radiator cover and remove the radiator from the vehicle.
24. Remove the detent cable, install a lifting device, remove the loose bolt(s) in the bell housing to engine and remove the engine from the vehicle while supporting the transmission.
25. To install the engine into the vehicle, reverse the removal procedure.

10–30, 15–35 MODEL VANS (G SERIES)

Removal and Installation

IN-LINE 6 CYLINDER ENGINE, 4.1L (VIN D)

NOTE: The following procedure is to be used as a general guide for engine removal and installation. Depending upon options, modifications, etc., changes in the removal and installation outline may have to be considered.

1. Disconnect the battery cables and remove the battery.
2. Drain the cooling system into a suitable container and remove the engine cover.
3. Remove the air cleaner assembly from the carburetor.
4. If equipped with A/C, evacuate the system and remove the A/C compressor.
5. Disconnect the carburetor linkage and remove the carburetor from the manifold.
6. Remove the grille and the cross brace from the front of the vehicle.
7. Remove the windshield washer and the A/C vacuum reservoir, if equipped.
8. Remove the radiator hoses from the radiator and remove the radiator to radiator support attaching brackets. Remove the transmission cooling lines from the radiator, if equipped. Remove the radiator.

NOTE: If equipped with A/C, remove the condensor to radiator supports and swing the condensor out of the way.

9. Remove the heater hoses from the engine.
10. Disconnect the wiring harness from the engine components. Mark the wires for ease of assembly, if necessary.
11. Raise the vehicle and support safely.
12. Remove the fuel line from the fuel pump and drain the crankcase.
13. Remove the propeller shaft and plug the transmission end.
14. Remove the exhaust pipe from the manifold, disconnect the speedometer cable and remove the linkage from the transmission.
15. Remove the transmission mount bolts. If equipped with manual transmission, disconnect the clutch linkage and remove the clutch cross shaft.
16. Remove the engine through bolts.
17. Lower the vehicle and install a lifting device to the engine/transmission assembly.
18. Raise the engine slightly and remove the right hand engine mount from the engine.
19. Carefully remove the engine/transmission assembly from the vehicle.
20. Install the engine/transmission assembly into the vehicle in the reverse order of the removal procedure.

10–30, 15–35 MODEL VANS (G SERIES)

5.0L (VIN F&H), 5.7L (VIN L&M) V8 ENGINES AND 4.3L V6 (VIN N)

NOTE: The following procedure is to be used as a general guide for engine removal and installation. Depending upon options, modifications, etc., changes in the removal and installation outline may have to be considered.

1. Disconnect the battery and remove from the vehicle.
2. Remove the glove box and the engine cover.
3. Drain the engine coolant into a suitable container.
4. Remove the outside air duct and the power steering reservoir bracket.
5. Disconnect the hood release cable.
6. Remove the upper fan shroud bolts and disconnect the overflow hoses.
7. Disconnect the transmission cooler lines and the radiator hoses. Remove the radiator.
8. Remove the upper fan shroud and the fan/pully assembly.
9. Remove the air cleaner and the cruise control servo.

10. Disconnect the brake vacuum line, the accelerator and T.V. cables. Disconnect the fuel line and vacuum lines at the carburetor. Remove the carburetor from the engine.
11. Remove the distributor cap and the diverter valve assembly.
12. Disconnect the coolant hose at the intake manifold. Disconnect the PCV valve.
13. Disconnect the necessary vacuum lines, the necessary wiring and harness connectors from the components. Identify each with tags, as necessary, for ease of assembly.
14. Discharge the A/C system. Disconnect the A/C brace and remove the compressor.
15. Disconnect the upper half of the engine dipstick tube. Remove the oil filler tube and remove the transmission dipstick tube.
16. Disconnect the accelerator cable at the dipstick and disconnect the fuel hoses at the fuel pump.
17. Disconnect the power steering pump and remove the A/C idler pulley.
18. Remove the headlamp bezels and the grille.
19. Remove the upper radiator support. Remove the lower fan shroud and the lower filler panel.
20. Remove hood latch support.
21. Disconnect the lines at the condensor and remove the condensor from the vehicle.
22. Raise and support the vehicle safely.
23. Drain the crankcase and disconnect the exhaust pipes at the manifolds.
24. Disconnect the strut rods at the flywheel cover and remove the cover.
25. Disconnect the starter wiring and remove the starter assembly.
26. Disconnect the necessary wires from engine/transmission assembly.
27. Remove the flexplate to torque converter bolts.
28. Remove the bell housing bolts, leaving one or more loosely in their bores.
29. Remove the engine mount through bolts and carefully lower the vehicle.
30. Install a lifting device to the engine, support the transmission, remove the remaining bell housing bolts and carefully, remove the engine from the vehicle.
31. To install the engine into the vehicle, reverse the removal procedure.

10–30, 15–35 MODEL VANS (G SERIES)

Removal and Installation

6.2L V8 DIESEL ENGINE (VIN J)

NOTE: The following procedure is to be used as a general guide for engine removal and installation. Depending upon options, modifications, etc., changes in the removal and installation outline may have to be considered.

1. Disconnect batteries and remove from the vehicle.
2. Remove the headlamp bezels and the grille. Remove the front bumper assembly, along with the lower valence panel.
3. Remove the hood latch and the coolant recovery bottle.
4. Remove the upper fan shroud and the upper tie bar.
5. Remove the engine cover.
6. If equipped with A/C, discharge the A/C system, disconnect and seal the lines.
7. Remove the condensor, the low coolant wire and drain the engine coolant into a suitable container.
8. Disconnect the transmission and engine oil cooler lines from the radiator.
9. Disconnect the upper and lower radiator hoses at the radiator. Remove the radiator from the vehicle.
10. Remove the fan assembly from the water pump.
11. Remove the fuel injection pump assembly from the engine.

NOTE: If unfamilar with the removal and installation of the fuel injection pump, refer to the appropriate diesel engine chapter in the Unit Repair section.

12. Raise the vehicle and support safely.
13. Disconnect the exhaust pipe at the manifolds. Remove the converter inspection cover.
14. Remove the flex plate to torque converter retaining bolts.
15. Remove the engine mount through bolts.
16. Disconnect the block heater at the element and disconnect the ground wire to block.
17. Remove the bell housing to cylinder case bolts, loosely leaving one or more to prevent accidental separation.
18. Remove the starter assembly and lower the vehicle.
19. If equipped with cruise control, remove the cruise control transducer.
20. If equipped with A/C, remove the rear A/C compressor brace and disconnect the lines. Remove the brackets and the compressor from the engine.
21. Remove the power steering pump and lay aside.
22. Remove the oil fill tube upper bracket and the glow plug relay.
23. Disconnect the oil pressure sender and loam.
24. Remove the air cleaner resonator and bracket.
25. Remove the transmission fill tube nut and lay aside. Disconnect the heater, radiator and bypass hoses at the crossover.
26. Disconnect the fuel lines at the fuel pump.
27. Install a lifting device to the engine and carefully remove the engine from the vehicle.

NOTE: A lifting device adapter, part number Kent Moore J–33888, is available to connect a common lifting device to the 6.2L Diesel engine.

28. To install the engine into the vehicle, reverse the removal procedure.

STEP VANS

Removal

ALL ENGINES

NOTE: The following procedure is to be used as a general guide for engine removal and installation. Depending upon options, modifications, etc., changes in the removal and installation outline may have to be considered. The Deutz Air Cooled Diesel engine removal and installation procedure can be derived from this outline by substituting the various steps as required. The removal of the heater hoses will allow engine oil leakage, since engine oil is used for in-cab heating purposes.

1. Disconnect battery and remove.
2. Drain cooling system and the engine oil.
3. Remove engine box, drivers seat, floor panels at stepwalls, floor panel around steering column and pedals and inspection plate on firewall above engine box.
4. Remove air cleaner (and any ducts).
5. Remove the upper and lower radiator hoses. Remove the radiator and shroud.
6. Loosen fan belt and remove fan blades.
7. Remove engine splash pans (if used).
8. Disconnect neutral safety wire at automatic transmission or at the clutch pedal safety switch.
9. Disconnect all heater hoses from the engine.
10. Disconnect wires at:
   a. Starter solenoid.
   b. Delcotron.
   c. Emission components

d. Temperature switch.
e. Oil pressure switch.
f. Coil.

11. Disconnect:
 a. Accelerator linkage.
 b. Choke cable at carburetor, if equipped.
 c. Fuel line to pump.
 d. Air compressor, if equipped
 e. Oil pressure gauge line, if equipped.
 f. Air conditioning system, if equipped.
 g. Vacuum or airlines.
 h. Power steering lines, if equipped.
 i. Engine ground straps.
 j. Exhaust pipe (support if necessary).

12. Remove clutch cross-shaft or disconnect clutch slave cylinder (if so equipped).

13. Remove oil fill tube and dipstick; also transmission dipstick and tube, plug holes (if used).

14. Remove rocker arm cover(s) and attach engine lift tool.

15. With the vehicle raised and supported safely, push arm of engine lift crane in right side door opening. Attach to lifting device or sling and take engine weight off mounts.

CAUTION

Make final check that all necessary disconnects have been made.

16. Support transmission and remove shift controls (cover opening), speedometer cable (plug hole), transmission spark control switch wire and oil cooler lines (if used).

17. Remove propeller shaft at transmission. Plug extension housing to prevent leakage.

18. Remove 2 top transmission to clutch housing cap screws and insert 2 headless guide bolts.

19. Remove 2 lower transmission to clutch housing cap screws and slide transmission back until clear of clutch disc. When transmission is free from engine, lower and remove from under vehicle.

20. Lower vehicle carefully with engine lifting device still attached to the engine. Remove engine mounting bolts, front and rear.

21. Raise engine slightly and push forward to clear crossmember, then lift up and remove engine through door opening.

Installation

A careful check of clutch components should be made. Install in reverse order of removal, fill cooling system and crankcase (check transmission). Start engine and check for leaks and operation. Adjust engine as required and road test.

TILT CAB

Removal

ALL ENGINES

NOTE: The following procedure is to be used as a general guide for engine removal and installation. Depending upon options, modifications, etc., changes in the removal and installation outline may have to be considered.

1. Tilt cab to expose engine area and secure.
2. Block wheels and exhaust air (if so equipped).
3. Disconnect battery ground cable.
4. Drain cooling system.
5. Drain crankcase.
6. Remove air cleaner and any ducts.
7. Remove radiator and heater hoses.
8. Remove radiator support and shroud assembly.
9. Disconnect hoses and remove surge tank.
10. Disconnect choke cable at carburetor.
11. Disconnect hand throttle at carburetor.
12. Disconnect shift linkage at control island.
13. Remove control island bolts and swing island out of way.
14. Remove both right and left island supports.
15. Disconnect cab safety lock and remote cab support.
16. Disconnect parking brake cable, if required.
17. Remove any engine splash shields.
18. Disconnect wires at:
 a. Starter solenoid.
 b. Delcotron.
 c. Temperature sender.
 d. Oil pressure sender.
 e. Coil.
 f. Governor speed warning.
 g. Transmission controlled spark solenoid at carburetor.
19. Remove:
 a. Accelerator linkage.
 b. Fuel line to pump.
 c. Lines or wires to dash gauges.
 d. Vacuum or air lines at engine.
 e. Power steering lines at pump (if equipped).
 f. Engine ground straps.
 g. Exhaust pipe or crossover pipe (support if necessary).
20. Remove fan blades, pulley and support bracket assembly.
21. Remove clutch cross-shaft or disconnect clutch slave cylinder.
22. Remove rocker arm covers and install lift tool or sling.
23. Hoist engine and take engine weight off motor mounts.

NOTE: According to work to be performed, select either of the following procedures.

REMOVAL OF ENGINE AND TRANSMISSION AS A UNIT

24. Disconnect speedometer (and plug).

25. Disconnect shift linkage at transmission (cover opening).

26. Disconnect any clutch linkage not yet removed.

27. Disconnect and drop propeller shaft at transmission, also any power take-off or auxiliary transmission couplings (cover or plug all openings).

28. Disconnect oil cooler lines, if equipped.

29. On Roadrangers, remove air lines and parking brake drum (if used).

30. Remove all engine mounting bolts and raise slightly to support transmission weight.

CAUTION

Make final check that all necessary disconnects have been made.

31. Remove any transmission to support bolts.

32. Raise engine and transmission assembly out of chassis as a unit.

REMOVAL OF ENGINE ONLY

33. Support transmission, remove flywheel under-pan and disconnect from engine.

NOTE: If possible, install transmission guide pins in top (transmission to clutch housing) holes to allow engine to slide forward to clear clutch disc splines. This will prevent bending clutch hub.

34. Remove all engine mounting bolts.

CAUTION

Make final check that all necessary disconnects have been made.

35. Raise slightly and pull forward until clear of transmission.

36. Continue to raise engine until high enough to clear chassis.

Installation

Install in reverse order of removal, fill cooling system and crankcase (check transmission). Start engine and check for leaks and operation. Make any minor adjustments and road test.

NOTE: Engine removal and installation procedures for meduim and heavy duty trucks are not outlined because of the numerous engines used in the vehicles and their mounting within the chassis. Usual disconnects of engine components are done with the engine in the vehicle and the complete unit lifted directly from the chassis frame rails. Because of the extreme weight of the assembly, care must be exercised to prevent damage or personal injury to occur.

Engine Manifolds

NOTE: Since all diesel engine disassembly and repair procedures require specialized tools and training, see the Chilton Diesel Engine Service manual for all overhaul and adjustment procedures.

COMBINATION MANIFOLD

Removal

IN-LINE ENGINES

1. Remove air cleaner (and any ducts).
2. Disconnect throttle controls, rods, linkage and return spring.
3. Disconnect fuel and vacuum lines at carburetor, also choke cable or control (if used).
4. Disconnect crankcase ventilation valve, vacuum brake or transmission spark control hoses (if used).
5. Remove carburetor.
6. Remove oil filter support bracket and swing filter to one side (if so equipped).
7. Disconnect exhaust pipe at flange and support if necessary (discard gasket or packing).
8. Remove manifold attaching bolts and clamps, remove manifold assembly (be careful of locating rings). Discard gaskets.

Installation

Reverse removal procedures after cleaning all gasket surfaces, checking for cracks, check heat riser and alignment. Lay straight edge on manifold to head surface to check. If intake and exhaust are not in line, loosen center bolts where they are joined and do not tighten until assembly is bolted to head, then retighten). Install finger-tight, check that pilot or locating rings and gaskets are in place, then torque to specifications in proper sequence. Warm engine, adjust idle and check for leaks.

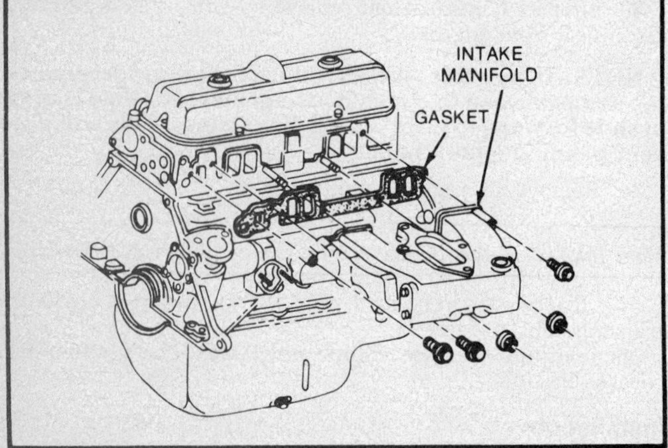

Removing intake manifold—typical 4 cylinder

INTAKE MANIFOLD

Removal and Installation

4–119 CU.IN. (1.9L)

1. Disconnect the battery ground cable and remove the air cleaner assembly.
2. Remove the EGR pipe clamp bolt at the rear of the cylinder head.
3. Raise the vehicle and remove the EGR pipe from the intake and exhaust manifolds.
4. Remove the EGR valve and bracket assembly from the intake manifold.
5. Lower the vehicle and drain the cooling system.
6. Remove the upper coolant hoses from the manifold.
7. Disconnect the accelerator linkage, vacuum lines, electrical wiring and fuel line from the intake manifold.
8. Remove the retaining nuts and remove the manifold from the cylinder head.
9. Remove the lower heater hose while holding the manifold away from the engine. Remove the manifold from the vehicle.
10. Installation is the reverse of removal.

Removal and Installation

4–121 CU.IN. (2.0L)

1. Disconnect the negative battery cable.
2. Remove the air cleaner. Drain the cooling system.
3. Tag and disconnect all necessary vacuum lines and wires. Remove the idler pulley.
4. Remove the A.I.R. drive belt. If equipped with power steering, remove the drive belt and then remove the pump with the lines attached. Position the pump out of the way.
5. Remove the AI.R. bracket-to-intake manifold bolt. Remove the air pump pulley.

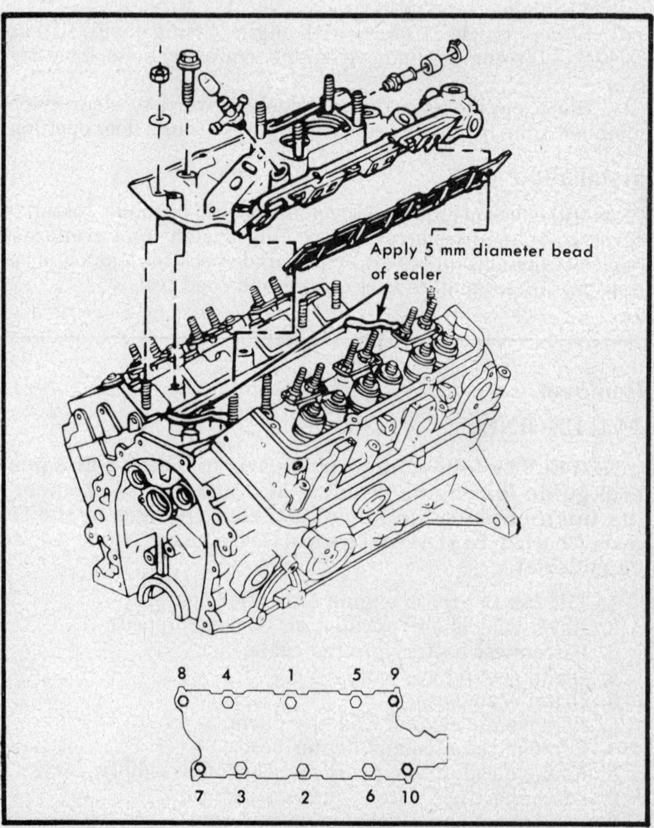

Intake manifold installation—173 CID V6 engine (© General Motors Corp.)

6. If equipped with power steering, remove the A.I.R. thru-bolt and then the power steering adjusting bracket.
7. Loosen the lower bolt on the air pump mounting bracket so that the bracket will rotate.
8. Disconnect the fuel line at the carburetor. Disconnect the carburetor linkage and then remove the carburetor.
9. Lift off the Early Fuel Evaporation (EFE) heater grid.
10. Remove the distributor.
11. Remove the mounting bolts and nuts and remove the intake manifold. Make sure to disconnect the heater hose and condenser from the bottom of the intake manifold before you lift it all the way out.
12. Using a new gasket, replace the manifold, tightening the nuts and bolts to specification.
13. Installation of the remaining components is in the reverse order of removal.
14. Adjust all necessary drive belts and check the ignition timing.

Removal and Installation

4-151 CU.IN.(2.5L, ASTRO/SAFARI VANS)

1. Disconnect the negative battery cable.
2. Remove the glove box assembly and the engine cover.
3. Remove the air cleaner assembly.
4. Drain the cooling system.
5. Disconnect the vacuum pipe rail at the exhaust and thermostat housing.
6. Disconnect the electrical and vacuum connections, as required. Tag the connection for ease of installation.
7. Disconnect the accelerator cable at the TBI unit.
8. Disconnect the vacuum and fuel lines at the intake manifold. Disconnect the heater hoses at the intake manifold.
9. Remove the alternator bracket attaching bolts and lay the alternator aside. Remove the ignition coil at the head/intake.
10. Remove the intake manifold retaining bolts and remove the intake manifold.
11. To install the manifold, reverse the removal procedure. Refer to the specifications for bolt torque.

Removal and Installation

V6–173 CU.IN.(2.8L)

1. Remove the rocker covers.
2. Drain the cooling system.
3. If equpped, remove the AIR pump and bracket.
4. Remove the distributor cap. Mark the position of the ignition rotor in relation to the distributor body and remove the distributor. Do not crank the engine with the distributor removed.
5. Remove the heater and radiator hoses from the intake manifold.
6. Remove the power brake vacuum hose.
7. Disconnect and label the vacuum hose. Remove the EFE pipe from the rear of the manifold.
8. Remove the carburetor linkage. Disconnect and plug the fuel line.
9. Remove the manifold retaining bolts and nuts.
10. Remove the intake manifold. Remove and discard the gaskets and scrape off the old silicone seal from the front and rear ridges.
11. The gaskets are marked for right and left side installation; do not interchange them. Clean the sealing surface of the engine block and apply a $^{3}/_{16}$ in. bead of silicone sealer to each ridge.
12. Install the new gaskets onto the heads. The gaskets will have to be cut slightly to fit past the center pushrods. Do not cut any more material than necessary. Hold the gaskets in place by extending the ridge bead of sealer $^{1}/_{4}$ in. onto the gasket ends.
13. Install the intake manifold. The area between the ridges and the manifold should be completely sealed.
14. Install the retaining bolts and nuts and tighten in sequence to 23 ft. lbs Do not overtighten; the manifold is made from aluminum and can be warped or cracked with excessive force.
15. The rest of installation is the reverse of removal. Adjust the ignition timing after installation and check the coolant level after the engine has warmed up.

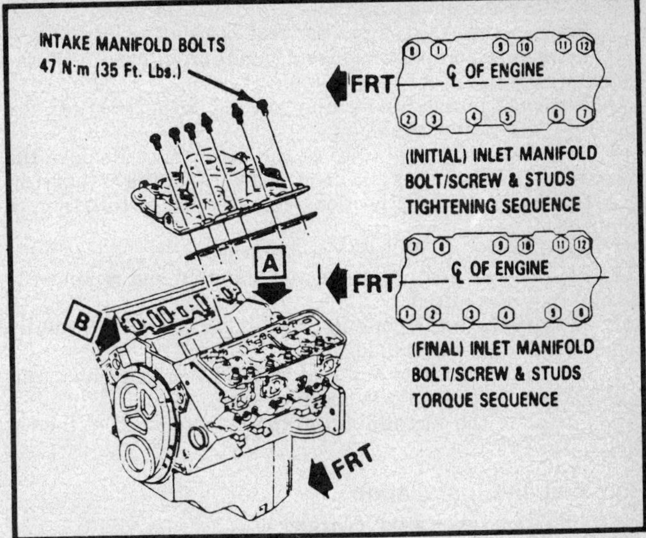

Intake manifold torque sequence for 4.3L engine (© General Motors Corp.)

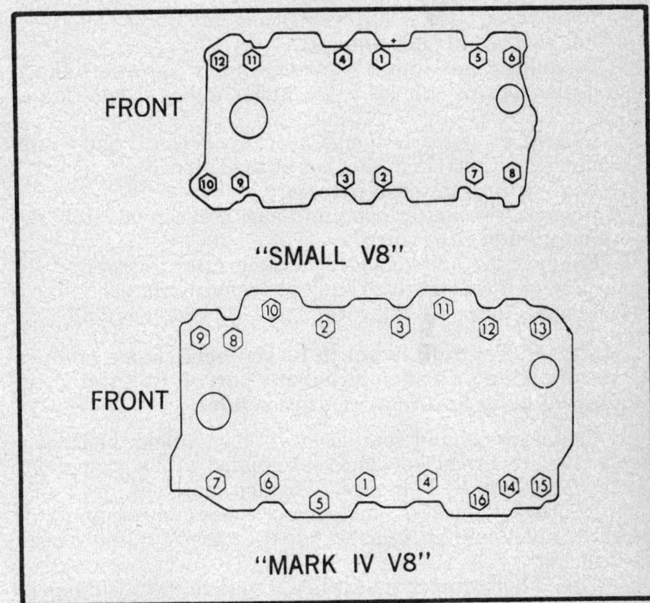

Intake manifold—bolt torquing sequence (© General Motors Corp.)

Removal and Installation

V6–263 CU.IN.(4.3L, ASTRO/SAFARI VANS)

1. Disconnect the battery ground cable.
2. Remove the engine cover and the air cleaner assembly.
3. Drain the cooling system into a suitable container.
4. Remove the distributor cap and secondary wires.
5. Disconnect the ESC connector and after marking the distributor location in relation to the crankshaft/camshaft, remove the distributor.

6. Remove the detent and accelerator cables.
7. Remove the A/C compressor rear brace.
8. Remove the transmission and engine oil filler tubes at the alternator brace.
9. Remove the A/C idler pulley at the alternator brace. Remove the alternator brace.
10. Disconnect the fuel lines at the carburetor. Remove the necessary vacuum hoses and electrical wires at the carburetor. Tag the hoses and connections for ease of installation, if required.
11. Remove the A.I.R. hoses and brackets.
12. Remove the heater hose at the manifold and remove the carburetor, if required.
13. Remove the intake manifold retaining bolts and carefully remove the intake manifold.
14. Install new gaskets and seal with RTV. Install the manifold and torque the bolts to specifications.
15. Complete the installation in the reverse order of the removal procedure.

Removal and Installation

V8 ENGINES (EXCEPT DIESEL)

1. Drain radiator, remove top hose at thermostat housing, also any bypass or heater hoses.
2. Remove battery ground cable.
3. Remove carburetor air cleaner and any ducts.
4. Remove oil fill tube and cap.
5. Disconnect gas line, all vacuum hoses, throttle linkage and return spring, choke cable and crankcase ventilation valve.
6. Disconnect wires to temperature sender, coil and transmission spark controlled solenoid (if so equipped).
7. Remove carburetor, if necessary.
8. Remove distributor cap and mark position of rotor. Remove distributor, if required.
9. Exhaust air and remove air compressor, disconnect oil drain line at manifold (if so equipped and interferes).
10. Remove manifold attaching bolts, remove manifold.

NOTE: If manifold is not to be replaced, some components can be left on such as carburetor, oil fill tube, thermostat housing and temperature sender.

11. Clean gasket and seal surfaces on manifold, block and heads. Install new gaskets and seals, coated with a good sealer particularly at water passages. Position manifold, use guide pins to prevent gaskets moving and check mating angle at heads. (Angle could be incorrect due to excessive cylinder head resurfacing).
12. Install bolts finger tight, then torque to specifications in proper sequence. Reverse the removal procedures fill radiator, warm engine, adjust timing and carburetor idle if necessary and check for leaks.

EXHAUST MANIFOLD

Removal

V6, V8 ENGINES

1. Use a good liquid penetrant freely on attaching bolts and nuts.
2. Remove the carburetor heater, if so equipped.
3. Remove exhaust pipe (support if necessary).
4. Open French locks and remove manifold attaching bolts.

NOTE: A $^9/_{16}$ in., thin wall, 6 point socket sharpened at leading edges, placed over head of bolt, then tapped with hammer, will speed the opening of French locks.

5. Remove Delcotron (on left side), remove manifold.

NOTE: On 366 and 427 engines, the spark plugs must also be removed before removing manifold.

Installation

Clean mating surfaces, install new gaskets where used, check heat riser and check for cracks. Reverse removal procedures. Start engine and check for leaks.

Removal and Installation

4-119 CU.IN. (1.9L)

1. Disconnect the battery ground cable and remove the air cleaner assembly.
2. Remove the EGR pipe clamp bolt at the rear of the cylinder head.
3. Raise the vehicle and remove the EGR pipe from the intake and exhaust manifolds.
4. Separate the exhaust pipe from the manifold.
5. Remove the manifold shield and remove the heat stove.
6. Remove the manifold retaining nuts and remove the manifold from the engine.
7. Installation is the reverse of removal.

Removal and Installation

4-121 CU.IN. (2.0L)

1. Disconnect the negative battery cable.
2. Remove the air cleaner. Remove the exhaust manifold shield. Raise and support the front of the vehicle.
3. Disconnect the exhaust pipe at the manifold and then lower the vehicle.
4. Disconnect the air management-to-check valve hose and remove the bracket. Disconnect the oxygen sensor lead wire.
5. Remove the alternator belt. Remove the alternator adjusting bolts, loosen the pivot bolt and pivot the alternator upward.
6. Remove the alternator brace and the A.I.R. pipes bracket bolt.
7. Unscrew the mounting bolts and remove the exhaust manifold. The manifold should be removed with the A.I.R. plumbing as an assembly. If the manifold is to be replaced, transfer the plumbing to the new one.
8. Clean the mating surfaces on the manifold and the head, position the manifold and tighten the bolts to the proper specifications.
9. Installation of the remaining components is in the reverse order of removal.

Removal and Installation

4-151 CU.IN. (2.5L, ASTRO/SAFARI VANS)

1. Disconnect the negative battery cable.
2. Remove the glove box and the engine cover assembly.
3. Remove the exhaust stove pipe at the manifold.
4. Disconnect the oxygen sensor wire.
5. Raise and safely support the vehicle.
6. Disconnect the exhaust pipe at the exhaust manifold.
7. Remove the rear A/C compressor bracket.
8. Remove the exhaust manifold bolts and remove the manifold.
9. To install, reverse the removal procedure. Torque the bolts to specifications

Cylinder Head

CAUTION

H/D engines may have sodium-cooled exhaust valves installed as OEM or aftermarket components. Sodium-cooled valves must not be discarded with other scrap metal. If a sodium-cooled valve is accidentally broken, the sodium will react violently with water, resulting in fire and explosion. Serious burns will result if sodium or sodium oxide comes in contact with the skin.

NOTE: When working on vans, the engine cover assembly must be removed and other necessary components removed or layed aside, to gain access to the cylinder heads. Protect the interior of the vans to prevent grease, dirt or other substances from soiling carpets, seats and etc.

Removal and Installation

4–119 CU.IN. (1.9L)

1. Remove cam cover.
2. Remove EGR pipe clamp bolt at rear of cylinder head.
3. Raise vehicle on hoist.
4. Disconnect exhaust pipe at exhaust manifold.
5. Lower vehicle on hoist.
6. Drain cooling system.
7. Disconnect heater hoses at intake manifold and at front of cylinder head.
8. Remove A/C and/or P/S compressor or pump and lay them aside.
9. Disconnect accelerator linkage at carburetor, fuel line at carburetor, all necessary electrical connections, spark plug wires and necessary vacuum lines.
10. Rotate camshaft until #4 cylinder is in firing position. Remove distributor cap and mark rotor to housing relationship. Remove the distributor.
11. Remove the fuel pump.
12. Lock the shoe on automatic adjuster in fully retracted position by depressing the adjuster lock lever with a screwdriver or equivalent in direction as indicated in the drawing.
13. Remove timing sprocket to camshaft bolt and remove the sprocket and the fuel pump drive cam from the camshaft. Keep the sprocket on the chain damper and tensioner. Do not remove the sprocket from the chain.
14. Disconnect AIR hose and check valve at air manifold.
15. Remove cylinder head to timing cover bolts.
16. Remove cylinder head bolts using Extension Bar Wrench J–24239–01; remove bolts in progressional sequence, beginning with the outer bolts.
17. With the aid of an assistant, remove cylinder head, intake and exhaust manifold as an assembly.
18. Clean all gasket material from cylinder head and block surfaces.

NOTE: The gasket surfaces on both the head and block must be clean of any foreign matter and free of nicks or heavy scratches. Cylinder bolt threads in the block and threads on the bolts must be cleaned (dirt will affect bolt torque).

19. Place new gasket over dowel pins with "TOP" side of gasket up.
20. Reverse removal Steps 1–17.
21. Tighten cylinder head bolts a little at a time in the sequence shown, torque to 60 ft. lbs and then retighten to specified torque of 72 ft. lbs.

Removal and Installation

4–121 CU.IN. (2.0L)

NOTE: The engine should be "overnight" cold before removing the cylinder head.

1. Disconnect the negative battery cable.
2. Drain the engine coolant into a suitable container.
3. Remove the air cleaner. Raise and support the front of the vehicle safely.
4. Remove the exhaust shield. Disconnect the exhaust pipe.
5. Remove the heater hose from the intake manifold and then lower the car.
6. Unscrew the mounting bolts and remove the engine lift bracket (includes air management).

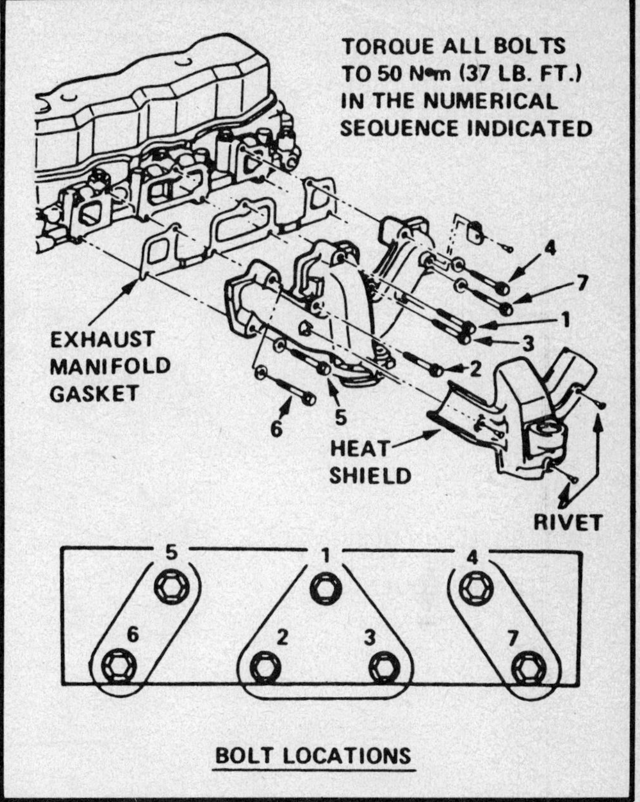

Exhaust manifold bolt torque sequence for 2.5L engine (© General Motors Corp.)

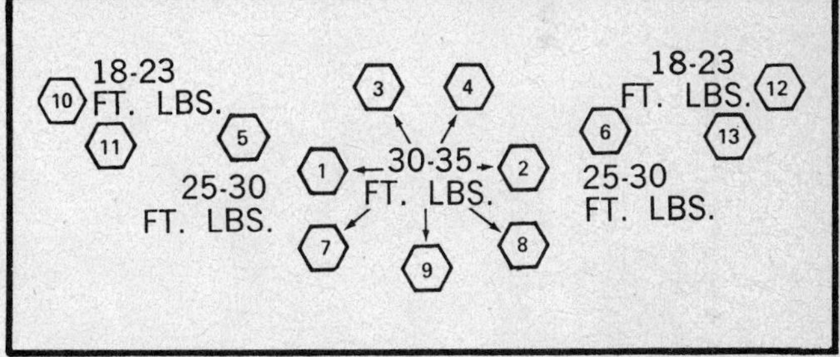

Exhaust manifold to cylinder head tightening sequence—6 cylinder (© General Motors Corp.)

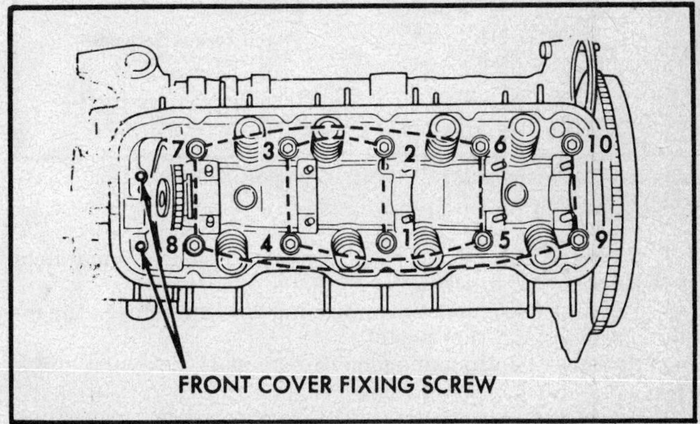

1.9 liter head bolt torque sequence

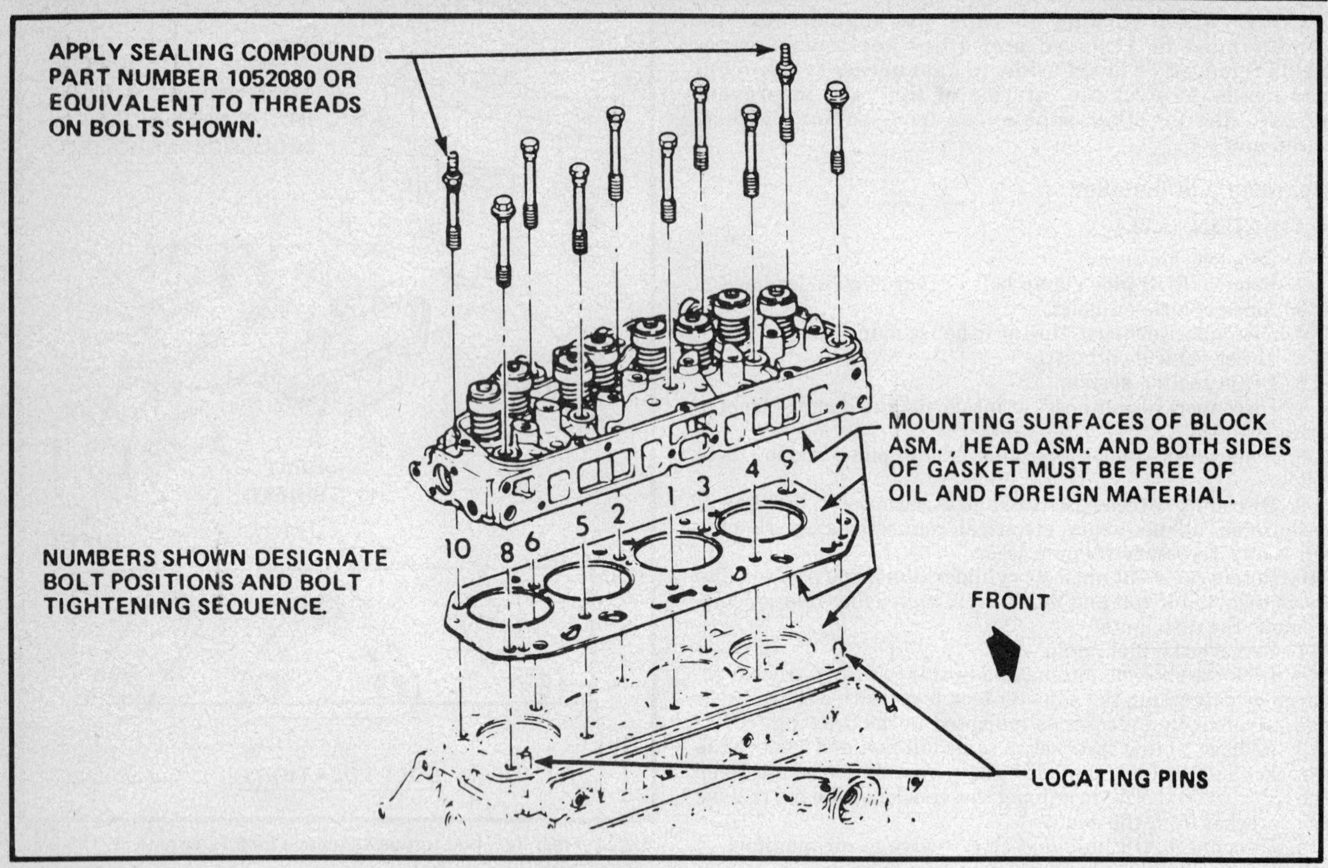

APPLY SEALING COMPOUND PART NUMBER 1052080 OR EQUIVALENT TO THREADS ON BOLTS SHOWN.
MOUNTING SURFACES OF BLOCK ASM., HEAD ASM. AND BOTH SIDES OF GASKET MUST BE FREE OF OIL AND FOREIGN MATERIAL.
NUMBERS SHOWN DESIGNATE BOLT POSITIONS AND BOLT TIGHTENING SEQUENCE.
FRONT
LOCATING PINS
10 8 6 5 2 1 3 4 9 7

Cylinder head bolt torque sequence for 2.5L 4L engine (© General Motors Corp.)

Head Torque Sequence
6 2 3 7
5 1 4 8

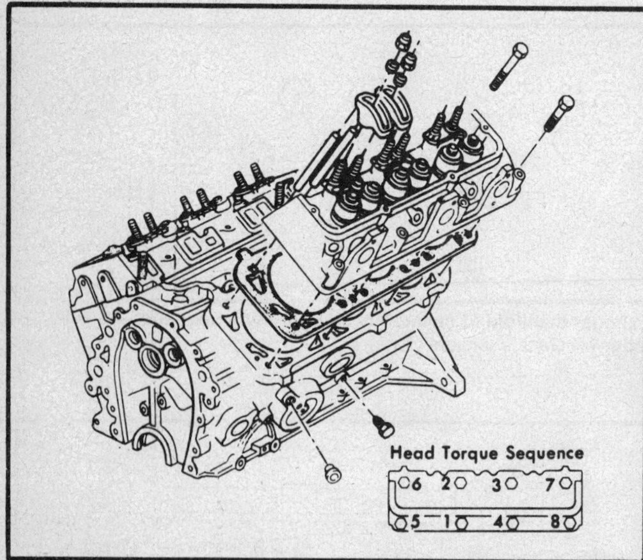

Cylinder head installation—173 CID V6 engine (© General Motors Corp.)

ADJUST SCREW
ROCKER ARM
THICKNESS GAGE
VALVE STEM
VALVE STEM END CAP

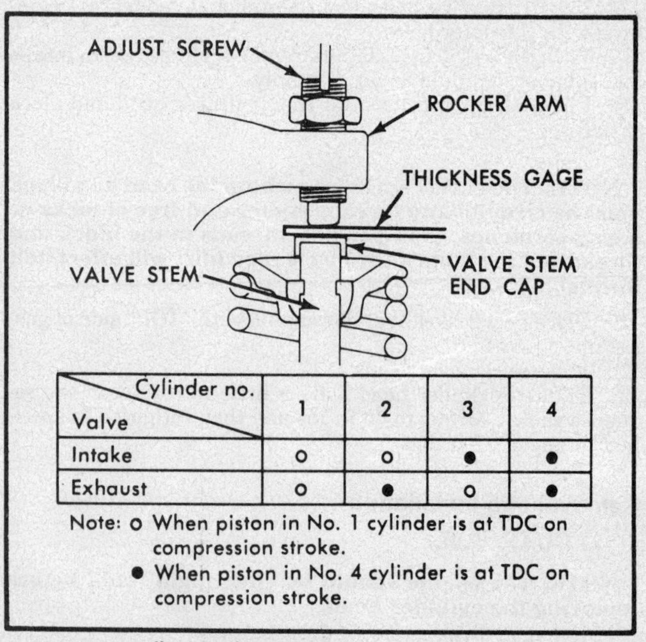

Valve \ Cylinder no.	1	2	3	4
Intake	o	o	●	●
Exhaust	o	●	o	●

Note: o When piston in No. 1 cylinder is at TDC on compression stroke.
● When piston in No. 4 cylinder is at TDC on compression stroke.

1.9 liter valve adjustment sequence

7. Remove the distributor. Disconnect the vacuum manifold at the alternator bracket.
8. Tag and disconnect the remaining vacuum lines at the intake manifold and thermostat.
9. Remove the air management pipe at the exhaust check valve.
10. Disconnect the accelerator linkage at the carburetor and then remove the linkage bracket.
11. Tag and disconnect all necessary wires. Remove the upper radiator hose at the thermostat.
12. Remove the bolt attaching the dipstick tube and hot water bracket.
13. Remove the idler pulley. Remove the A.I.R. and power steering pump drive belts.

14. Remove the A.I.R. bracket-to-intake manifold bolt. If equipped with power steering, remove the air pump pulley, the A.I.R. thru-bolt and the power steering adjusting bracket.
15. Loosen the A.I.R. mounting bracket lower bolt so that the bracket will rotate.
16. Disconnect and plug the fuel line at the carburetor.
17. Remove the alternator. Remove the alternator brace from the head and then remove the upper mounting bracket.
18. Remove the cylinder head cover. Remove the rocker arms and push rods.
19. Remove the cylinder head bolts in the order given in the illustration. Remove the cylinder head with the carburetor, intake and exhaust manifolds still attached. To install, the gasket surfaces on both the head and the block must be clean of any foreign matter and free of any nicks or heavy scratches. Cylinder bolt threads in the block and the bolt must be clean.
20. Place a new cylinder head gasket in position over the dowel pins on the block. Carefully guide the cylinder head into position.
21. Coat the cylinder bolts with sealing compound and install them finger tight.
22. Using a torque wrench, gradually tighten the bolts in the sequence shown in the illustration to the proper specifications.
23. Installation of the remaining components is in the reverse order of removal.

Removal and Installation

INLINE 6 CYL ENGINES

1. Drain cooling system and remove battery ground strap at head.
2. Remove air cleaner and any ducts.
3. Remove choke cable, accelerator rod and return spring, fuel and vacuum lines at carburetor.
4. Remove manifold to head bolts and clamps, pull manifold and carburetor assembly clear of head and support.
5. Remove fuel and vacuum lines from retaining clip at thermostat housing.
6. Disconnect temperature sender wire, remove wiring harness from rocker cover clip. Remove coil wires and coil.
7. Remove top radiator hose, at thermostat housing.
8. Remove spark plug wires and distributor cap.
9. Remove rocker arm cover.

CAUTION

Never pry rocker arm cover loose. Bump cover rearward in a gasket shearing manner.

10. Engines with rocker arm shafts, back off adjusting nuts, rotate rocker arm to clear push rod and remove push rods. Engines using pedestal rocker arms, remove rocker arm ball nuts, arms and push rods.
11. Remove push rod cover.
12. Remove cylinder head bolts, cylinder head and discard gasket.

NOTE: Place rocker arm mechanism and cylinder head bolts in a rack so they can be re-installed in same locations. (mated) Check cylinder head for warpage with a straight edge. Inspect for cracks and burnt valves.

13. Reverse removal procedures and adjust valves after cleaning gasket surfaces. Engines using a steel (shim) gasket, coat both sides with a good sealer, bead side up. Do not reuse gaskets. Cylinder head bolt threads in block and threads on bolts must be clean. Coat threads on bolts with sealer before installing.
14. Tighten each cylinder head bolt a little at a time, in correct sequence, until specified torque is reached.
15. Engines using composition (steel asbestos) gaskets must have heads retorqued after warm-up. (retightening heads effects valve lash) Refer to specifications at beginning of this section for nut tightening sequence.

NOTE: Refer to the head gasket accompanying instructions as to installation. Different gasket manufacturing companies require special procedures to avoid head gasket failure.

Removal and Installation

V6, V8 ENGINES

1. Drain the cooling system into a suitable container. Remove intake manifold (with carburetor) and and if clearance is not sufficient, the exhaust manifold.

NOTE: Differences in components, braces and brackets will exist between the right and left cylinder head. This removal and installation procedure should be used as a guide only and modifications to the procedure steps must be considered.

2. Loosen belt and remove power steering pump (if so equipped). Remove A/C compressor and/or brackets.
3. Remove rocker arm covers.

CAUTION

Never pry rocker arm cover loose. Bump cover rearward in a gasket shearing manner.

4. Loosen rocker arm adjusting nut, turn rocker arm to clear push rods and remove push rods or remove rocker arm assemblies. Place the pushrods and rocker arm components in sequence so that they can be installed in same location (mated).
5. Remove cylinder head bolts, cylinder head and discard gasket.
6. Check cylinder head for warpage with a straight edge. Inspect for cracks and burnt valves.
7. Reverse removal procedures and adjust valves, after cleaning gasket surfaces. If heads are to be resurfaced, check alignment at intake manifold.

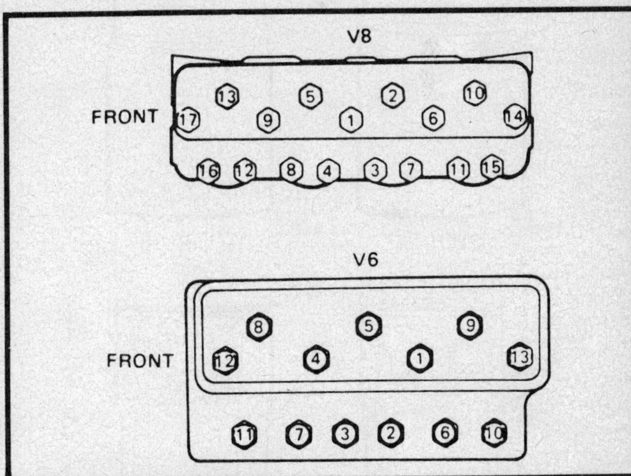

Cylinder head bolt torque sequence for 4.3L V6, 5.0L and 5.7L V8 engines (© General Motors Corp.)

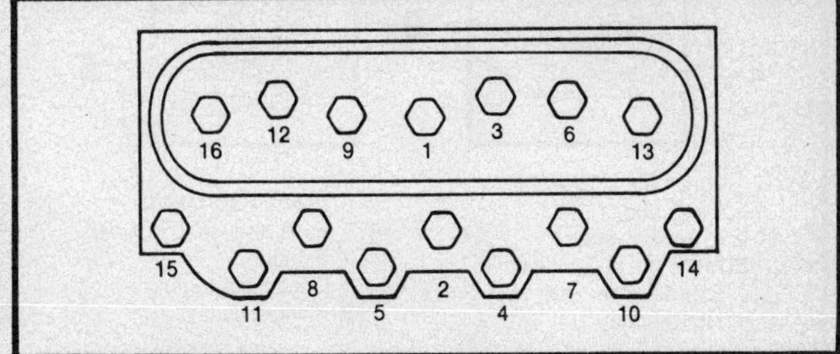

Torquing sequence—366, 400, 427 and 454 V8 engines (© General Motors Corp.)

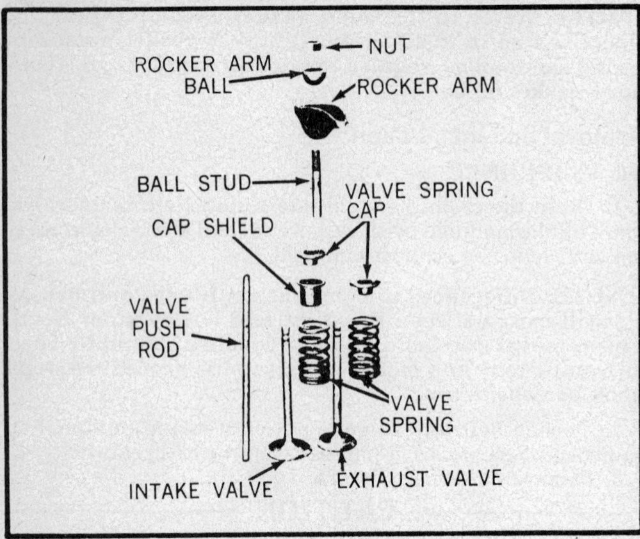

Valve system—V8 engines (© General Motors Corp.)

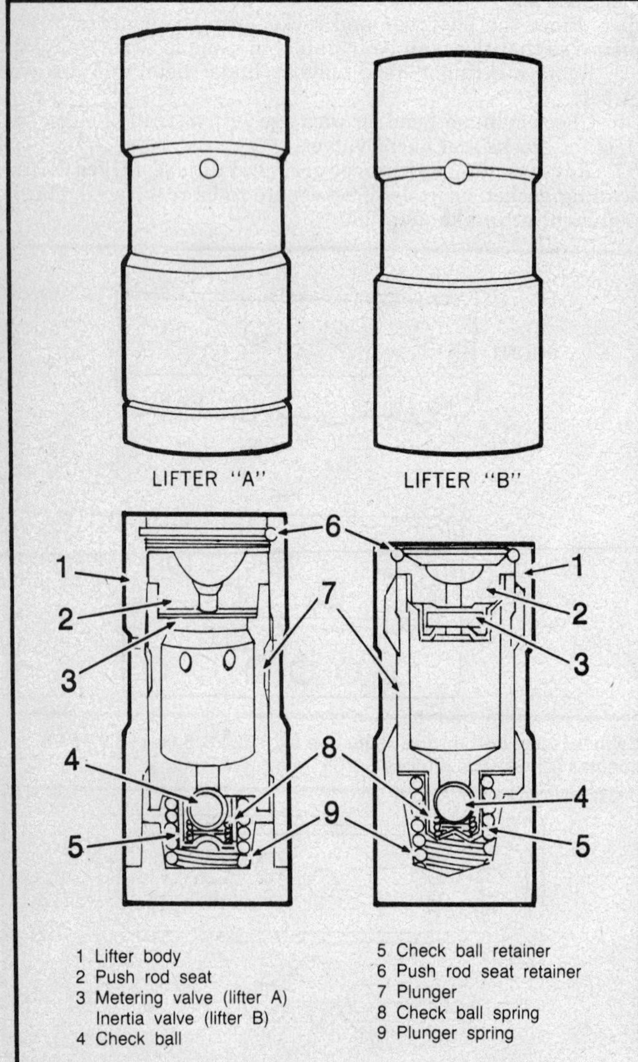

Hydraulic valve lifters

8. Cylinder head bolt threads in block and threads on bolts must be clean, coat threads with sealer. Tighten each cylinder head bolt a little at a time, in correct sequence, until specified torque is reached.

9. Engines using steel (shim) gasket, coat both sides with a good sealer, bead side up. Engines using composition (steel asbestos) gaskets must be retorqued after warm-up (retightening heads effects valve lash).

NOTE: Refer to the head gasket accompanying instructions as to installation. Different gasket manufacturing companies require special procedures to avoid head gasket failure.

10. Refer to specifications at beginning of this section for nut tightening sequence.

Valve System

HYDRAULIC LIFTERS

NOTE: Refer to Diesel Engine Section in the Unit Repair section for valve information on the 2.2L, 5.7L and the 6.2L diesel engines. The 1.9L gasoline engine requires manual valve clearance adjustment (room temperature) with specification of 0.006 in. for the intake valves and 0.010 in. for the exhaust valve. The 2.5L gasoline engine requires the rocker arm stud nut to be tightened to 20 ft. lbs torque, with no other adjustment available.

Adjustments

ALL, EXCEPT 1.9L AND 2.5L ENGINES

ENGINE RUNNING

1. Run engine to normalize and stabilize oil temperature, remove rocker cover(s) bump off. Do not pry off. Leave old gasket on head to aid against oil overflow or use oil deflector clips.

2. Reduce engine idle as low as possible, tighten cylinder head bolts (and rocker supports if used). Check camshaft lobe lift.

3. Back off rocker arm adjusting nut until rocker arm starts to clatter, then turn nut down slowly until clatter stops. This is zero lash position.

4. Turn adjusting nut down $\frac{1}{4}$ turn and pause 10 seconds until engine runs smoothly. Repeat operation 3 (2.8L – 5) more times until 1 (2.8L – 1 $\frac{1}{}$full turn down from zero lash position is reached.

NOTE: 2.8L V6 engine valves are adjusted to 1 $\frac{1}{2}$ turns.

Valve spring installation—inline and small V8 engines
(© General Motors Corp.)

CAUTION

This 1 (2.8L – 1 ½ turn pre-load adjustment must be done slowly and in stages to allow hydraulic lifter to adjust itself to prevent possibility of internal interference or bent push rods.

5. Repeat for each valve, the use of a vacuum gauge is recommended.
6. Install new rocker cover gaskets and torque rocker covers. Reset engine idle.

ENGINE NOT RUNNING

1. Remove rocker cover(s).
2. Tighten cylinder head bolts (and rocker arm supports if used).
3. Disconnect primary wire at negative terminal of coil.
4. Mark distributor housing with chalk at each spark plug tower (double mark No. 1 cylinder).
5. Remove distributor cap and crank engine until rotor points to No. 1 chalk mark. (No. 1 cylinder is approximately at TDC and both valves can be adjusted). Valve adjustment is made by backing off rocker arm nut until push rod can be rotated and then slowly tightened until push rod does not turn. This is zero lash position. Turn adjusting nut down 1 (2.8L – 1 ½) full turn to complete adjustment.

NOTE: 2.8L V6 Engine valves are adjusted to 1 ½ turns.

6. Adjust the remaining valves, one cylinder at a time (following firing order) in same manner.
7. Install distributor cap.
8. Install new rocker cover gasket(s) and torque rocker cover(s) bolts.

VALVE ADJUSTMENT

1.9 LITER OHC

1. Check the rocker arm shaft bracket nuts for looseness and retighten as necessary before adjusting the valve clearances. Rocker arm shaft bracket nut torque is 16 ft. lbs
2. Bring either the No. 1 or No. 4 piston to top dead center on the compression stroke. Do this by turning the crankshaft to align timing mark on crankshaft pulley with pointer.
3. Hold crankshaft in above position and adjust clearance of the valves indicated. Measurement should be taken at the clearance between rocker arm and valve stem.
4. Turn crankshaft one full turn and adjust clearance of remaining valves. Standard valve clearances, at room temperature are:
   Intake Valve: 0.006 in. (0.15mm)
   Exhaust Valve: 0.010 in. (0.25mm)

INLINE 6 CYLINDER, V6 and V8 ENGINES WHERE APPLICABLE

NOTE: Adjust valves when lifter is on base circle of camshaft lobe.

1. Crank engine until mark on torsional damper lines up with "O" mark on the timing tab. The engine should also be in the #1 firing position. This may be determined by placing fingers on the #1 rocker arms as the mark on the damper comes near the "O" mark. If the valves are not moving, the engine is in the #1 firing position. If the valves move as the mark comes up to the timing tab, the engine is in opposite cylinder firing position and should be rotated one revolution to reach the #1 position.
2. With the engine in the #1 firing position, the following valves may be adjusted.

V6 Engines
- Exhaust: 1, 2, 3
- Intake: 1, 5, 6

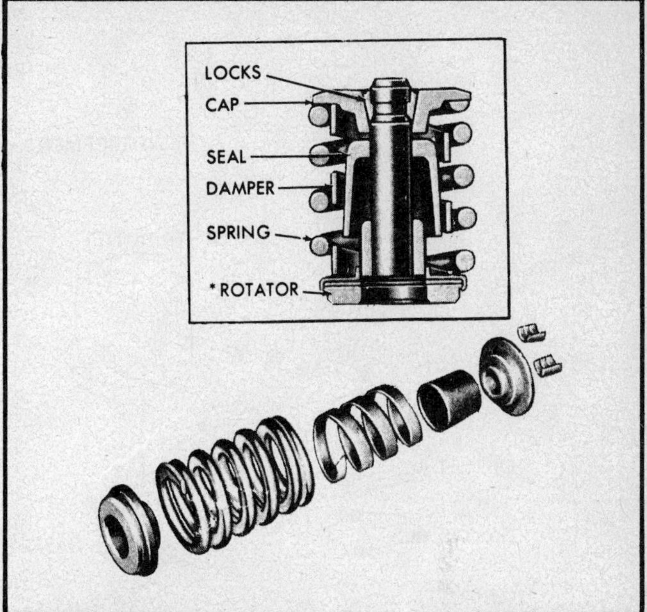

Exhaust valve spring installation—Mark IV V8 engines (© General Motors Corp.)

Valve adjustment (© General Motors Corp.)

Inline 6 Cylinder Engines
- Exhaust: 1, 3, 5
- Intake: 1, 2, 4

V8 Engines
- Exhaust: 1, 3, 4, 8
- Intake: 1, 2, 5, 7

3. Back out adjusting nut until lash is felt at the push rod, then turn in adjusting nut until all lash is removed (This can be determined by rotating push rod while turning adjusting nut). When lash has been removed, turn adjusting nut in 1½ additional turns (to center lifter plunger).
4. Crank the engine one revolution until the timing tab "O" mark and torsional damper mark are again in alignment. This is the #4 firing position. With the engine in this position, the following valves may be adjusted:

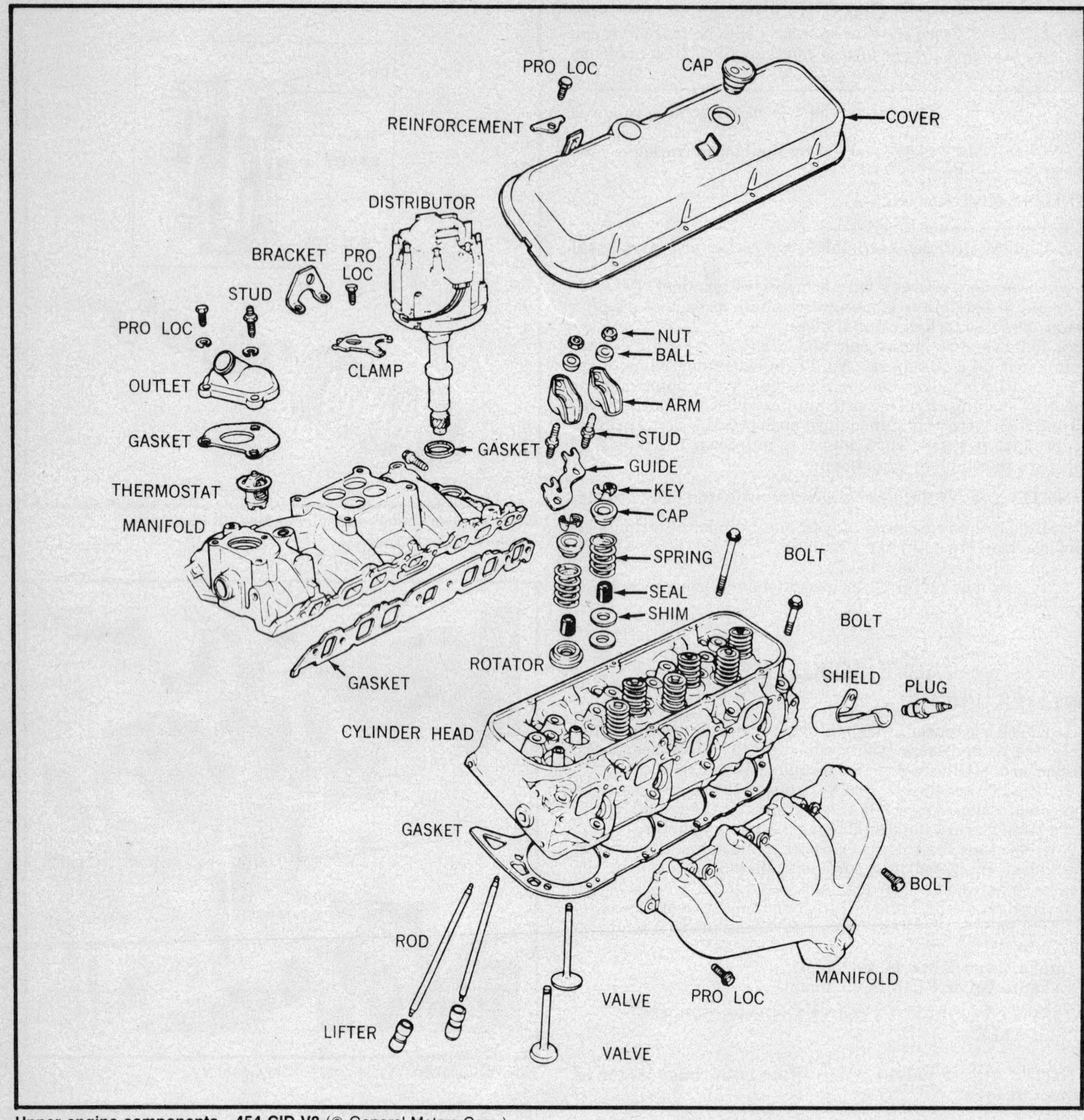

Upper engine components—454 CID V8 (© General Motors Corp.)

V6 Engines
- Exhaust: 4, 5, 6
- Intake: 2, 3, 4

Inline 6 Cylinder Engines
- Exhaust: 2, 4, 6
- Intake: 3, 5, 6

V8 Engines
- Exhaust: 2, 5, 6, 7
- Intake: 3, 4, 6, 8

5. Install rocker arm covers.
6. Start engine and check timing and idle speed.

NOTE: Refer to the firing order diagrams for cylinder location and firing orders.

ROCKER ARMS

Rocker arms on all pushrod engines are trough shaped, pressed steel levers that transfer lifter motion to valves. Rocker arms are supported on individual pedestals and have an oval hole in center to fit over stud and pivot on ball seats. Oil is fed to rocker arms by means of hollow push rods. Whenever arms or ball seats are being installed, coat all bearing surfaces with engine oil.

Rocker arm studs are pressed in cylinder head and are available in oversize for replacement.

CAUTION

Do not try to press oversized stud in head without reaming stud hole first.

Pressed in studs can be replaced by a stud threaded on both ends. Head is to be threaded in stud hole to accept threaded stud.

CHECKING ENGINE CAM LOBE LIFT

ALL ENGINES

If improper valve operation is indicated, measure the lift of each push rod in consecutive order and record the readings.

1. Remove the valve ROCKER ARM Mechanism, as previously outlined.
2. Position indicator with ball socket adapter (tool J-8520) on push rod. Make sure push rod is in the lifter socket.
3. Rotate the crankshaft slowly in the direction of rotation until the lifter is on the heel of the cam lobe. At this point, the push rod is in its lowest position.
4. Set the dial indicator on zero, then rotate the crankshaft slowly, or attach an auxiliary starter switch and "bump" the engine over, until the push rod is in the fully raised position.
5. Compare the total lift recorded from the dial indicator with the specifications.
6. If camshaft readings for all lobes are within specifications, remove dial indicator assembly.
7. Install and adjust valve mechanism, as previously outlined.

ENGINE VALVE TIMING

Inspection

ALL ENGINES

1. Remove the rocker arm cover(s).
2. Turn the crankshaft so that the crankshaft pulley timing mark is at the "O" mark on the pointer and the No. 1 cylinder is ready to fire.
3. To verify that number one cylinder is on its firing stroke, rotate the crankshaft counterclockwise $\frac{1}{8}$ of a turn before TDC and then rotate the crankshaft clockwise slowly through the TDC position, while observing the valves and rocker arms on the companion cylinder of number one. As the crankshaft is rotated, the exhaust valve will be ending its closing stroke, while the intake valve will just begin to open. This indicates that number one cylinder is on its firing stroke.
4. Companion cylinders are as follows:

Inline four cylinder engines with firing order 1–3–4–2
Cylinders 1 and 4
Cylinders 3 and 2

2.8L V6 Engine with firing order 1–2–3–4–5–6
Cylinders 1 and 4
Cylinders 2 and 5
Cylinders 3 and 6

4.3L V6 Engine with firing order 1–6–5–4–3–2
Cylinders 1 and 4
Cylinders 6 and 3
Cylinders 5 and 2

Inline Six cylinder Engines with firing order 1–5–3–6–2–4
Cylinders 1 and 6
Cylinders 5 and 2
Cylinders 3 and 4

V8 Engines with firing order 1–8–4–3–6–5–7–2
Cylinders 1 and 6
Cylinders 8 and 5
Cylinders 4 and 7
Cylinders 3 and 2

5. If the exhaust or intake valves on the companion cylinder do not open and close as outlined in Step 3 when the crankshaft pulley is moved through TDC, the camshaft is out of time, which is usually caused by either stripped gears or a stretched timing chain.
6. Verification of which cylinder is in its firing position can be made by observing the distributor rotor and its positioning towards either number one cylinder or its companion cylinder. Should the crankshaft and camshaft timing be correct and the distributor rotor incorrect, indications of a distributor gear or shaft malfunction would be indicated.
7. To verify valve timing, turn the crankshaft 180 degrees and repeat Steps 2 and 3.

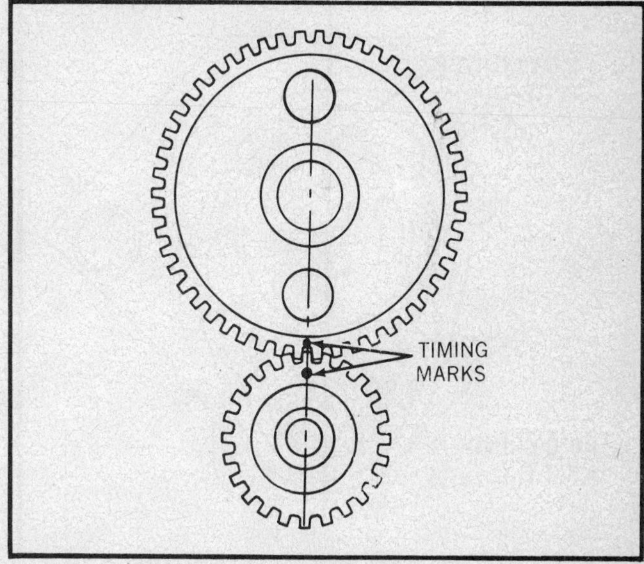

Timing mark alignment—inline engines (© General Motors Corp.)

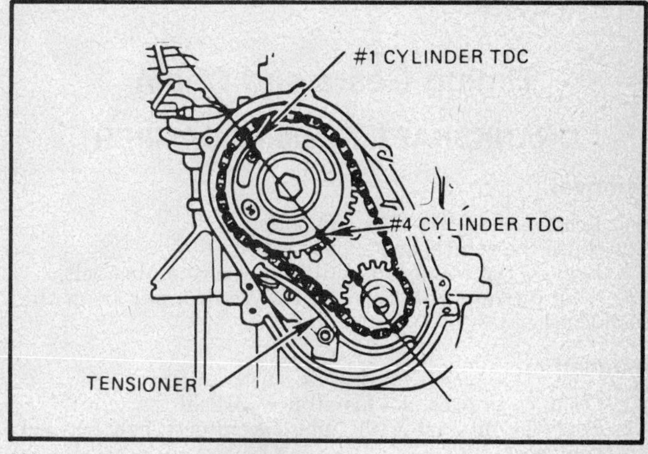

121 cu. in. timing chain alignment

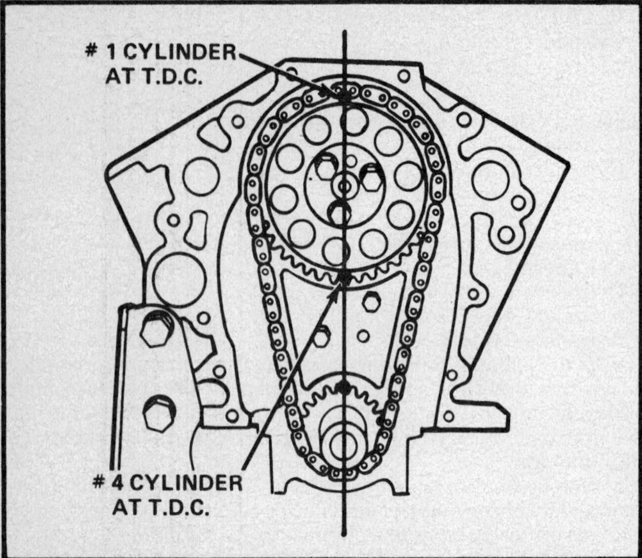

Camshaft sprocket alignment marks—typical of V6 engines (© General Motors Corp.)

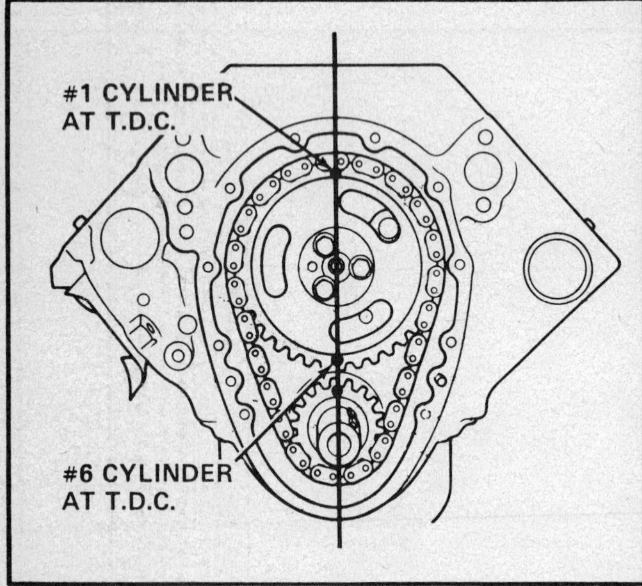

Valve timing—V8 engines (© General Motors Corp.)

Timing Gears and Chain

CRANKSHAFT Torsional DAMPER

Removal

1. Remove the drive belts and pulley.
2. Raise the vehicle and support safely.
3. Remove the crankshaft pully and the retaining bolt.
4. Use puller type tool to remove damper from the crankshaft.

Installation

1. Clean cover area and install new oil seal.
2. Coat the oil seal with light oil, inspect hub for seal (grooved) wear.
3. Position damper (or hub) on crankshaft, aligning keyway and tap lightly into position.
4. Pull damper (or hub) into position with damper installing tool. Install the retaining bolt and washer. (Make sure damper retaining bolt has good thread engagement before applying force). Torque to specifications.

CAUTION

The inertial weight section of the torsional damper is assembled to the hub with a rubber type material. The installation procedure, using the special installing tools, must be used or movement of the inertia weight section on the hub will destroy the tuning of the torsional damper.

5. Reverse balance of removal steps.

TIMING COVER OIL SEAL

Replacement

1. Remove torsional damper.
2. Pry old seal out, be careful not to mar crankshaft or bend cover.
3. Install new seal (lip of seal toward block), tap lightly into position. Coat seal with oil.
4. Reverse removal procedures.

TIMING GEAR

Replacement

INLINE ENGINES (EXCEPT 1.9L OHC)

NOTE: When necessary to install a new crankshaft gear, the camshaft should be removed. However, the gear can be removed from camshaft without removing camshaft from engine. Cam gear can be split and hub section pulled off, but extreme care must be taken not to allow any impact, either removing or installing gear, on the shaft. Camshaft must be totally blocked so as not to allow any movement to disturb oil sealing welsh plug at camshaft rear bearing.

Removal

1. Drain and remove radiator.
2. Remove front end sheet metal or grille.
3. Remove damper or pulley.
4. Remove oil pan, if required.
5. Remove timing case cover (2 bolts inside oil pan at front main bearing cap).
6. Remove rocker arm covers and remove lifters.
7. Remove fuel pump and distributor (mark position of rotor).
8. Align timing gear marks (check rotor mark) then remove 2 thrust plate screws by reaching through 2 holes in cam gear.
9. Remove camshaft and gear assembly by pulling and turning shaft carefully so lobes will not mar bearings and will clear lifters.
10. Use press to remove cam gear, using caution not to damage thrust plate by Woodruff key.
11. Clean all gasket surfaces and inspect.
12. Check camshaft alignment and lobes for wear. Check camshaft bearings in block, check crank gear and if equipped, the oil spray nozzle.

Installation

1. Support camshaft at back end of front bearing in a press, place thrust plate over end of shaft, install Woodruff key in keyway, align cam gear with key and press gear on shaft until clearance at thrust plate (and front end of front bearing) is 0.001–0.003 in..

NOTE: Coat lobes and bearing surfaces with engine oil supplement.

2. Install camshaft and gear assembly in block, turning shaft carefully so lobes clear bearings.
3. Turn camshaft and mesh timing marks, tighten thrust plate.
4. Check cam gear for runout (should not exceed 0.005 in.).
5. Check backlash at gears. (0.004–0.006 in.).
6. Reverse remaining removal procedures.
7. Fill radiator, oil reservoir and start engine. Adjust valves, check timing and inspect for leaks.

TIMING CHAIN

Removal and Installation

4–119 CU. IN. (1.9 LITER)

1. Remove front cover assembly.
2. Lock the shoe on automatic adjuster in fully retracted position by depressing the shoe with a pry bar type tool and turning the adjuster lock lever towards the engine block to lock the lever.
3. Remove timing chain from crankshaft sprocket.
4. Check timing sprockets for wear or damage. If crankshaft sprocket must be replaced, remove sprocket and pinion gear from crankshaft using Puller J–25031.
5. Check timing chain for wear or damage; replace as necessary. Measure distance (L) with chain stretched with a pull of approximately 98 N (22 lbs.). Standard (L) value is 381mm (15.00 in.); replace chain if (L) is greater than 385mm (15.16 in.).
6. Remove attaching bolt and remove automatic chain adjuster.
7. Check that the shoe becomes locked when shoe is pushed in with the lock lever released.
8. Check that lock is released when the shoe is pushed in. The adjuster assembly must be replaced if rack teeth are found to be worn excessively.
9. Remove "E" clip and remove chain tensioner. Check tensioner for wear or damage; replace as necessary.
10. Inspect tensioner pin for wear or damage. If replacement is necessary, remove pin from cylinder block using locking pliers. Lubricate NEW pin tensioner with clean engine oil. Start new pin in block, place tensioner over appropriate pin. Place "E" clip on pin and then tap pin into block, using a hammer, until clip just clears tensioner. Check tensioner and adjuster for freedom of rotation on pins.
11. Inspect guide for wear or damage and plugged lower oil jet. If replacement or cleaning is necessary, remove guide bolts, guide and oil jet. Install new guide and upper attaching bolt. Install lower oil jet and bolt so that oil port is pointed toward crankshaft as shown.
12. Install timing sprocket and pinion gear (groove side toward front cover). Align key grooves with key on crankshaft, then drive into position using Installating Tool J–26587.
13. Turn crankshaft so that key is turned toward cylinder head side (#1 and #4 pistons at top dead center).
14. Install the timing chain by aligning mark plate on chain with mark on crankshaft timing sprocket. The side of the chain with the mark plate is on the front side and the side of chain with the most links between mark plates is on the chain guide side. Keep the timing chain engaged with the camshaft timing sprocket until the camshaft timing sprocket is installed on camshaft.
15. Install the camshaft timing sprocket so that marked side of sprocket faces forward and so that the triangular mark aligns with the chain mark plate.
16. Install the automatic chain adjuster.
17. Release lock by depressing the shoe on adjusted by hand and check to make certain the chain is properly tensioned when lock is released.
18. Install front cover assembly.

4–121 CU. IN.

1. Remove the front cover as previously detailed.
2. Place the No. 1 piston at TDC of the compression stroke so that the marks on the camshaft and crankshaft sprockets are in alignment.
3. Loosen the timing chain tensioner nut as far as possible without actually removing it.
4. Remove the camshaft sprocket bolts and remove the sprocket and chain together. If the sprocket does not slide from the camshaft easily, a light blow with a soft mallet at the lower edge of the sprocket will dislodge it.
5. Use a gear puller (J–2288–8–20) and remove the crank-

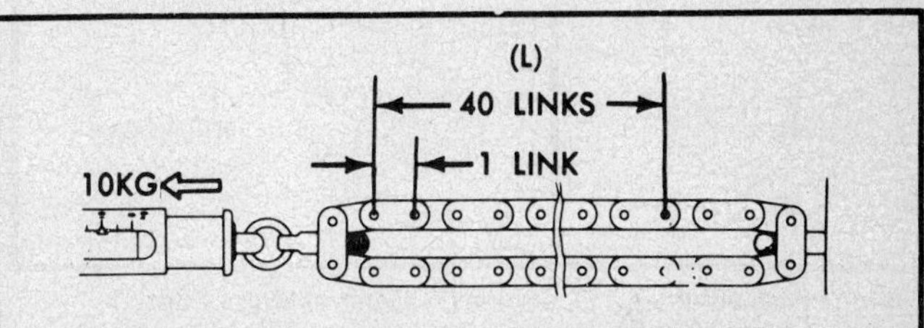

Checking timing chain for wear—4 cyl 119 cu. in. shown

Depressing lock lever, 1.9L engine (© General Motors Corp.)

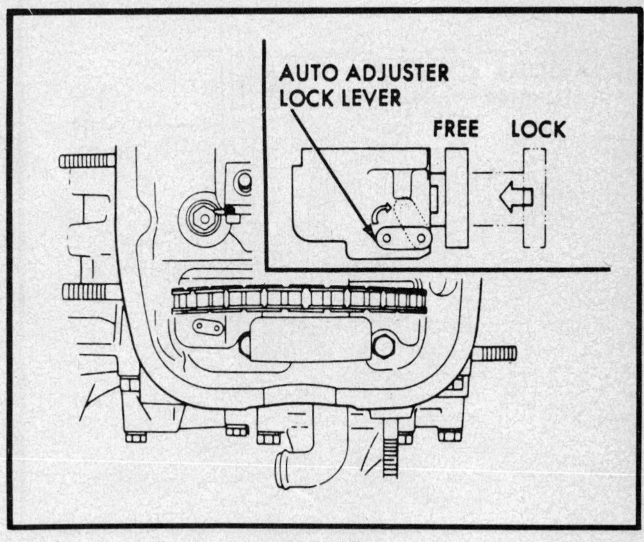

Locking the chain adapter, 1.9L engine (© General Motors Corp.)

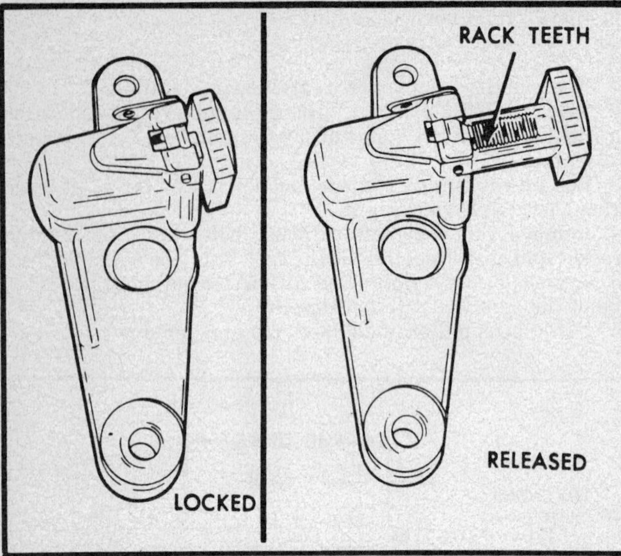

Timing chain adjuster, 1.9L engine (© General Motors Corp.)

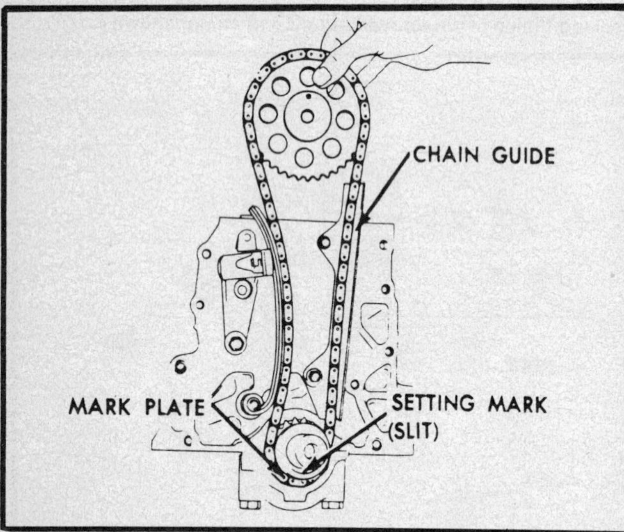

Timing chain guide, tensioner and adjuster, 1.9L engine (© General Motors Corp.)

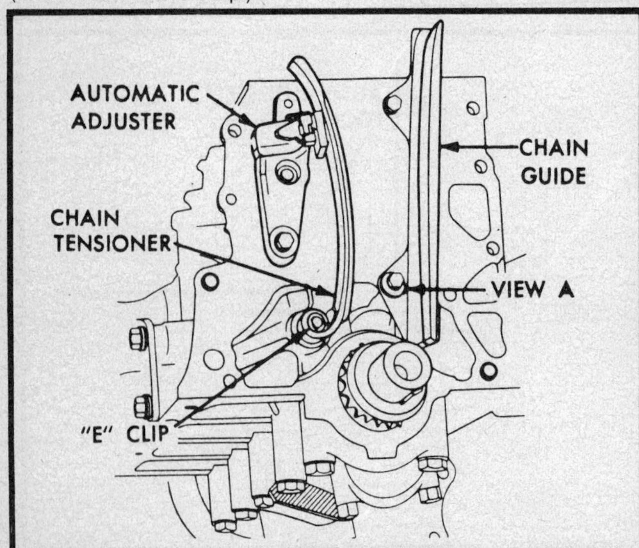

Alignment of timing chain, 1.9L engine (© General Motors Corp.)

shaft sprocket.

6. Press the crankshaft sprocket back onto the crankshaft.
7. Install the timing chain over the camshaft sprocket and then around the crankshaft sprocket. Make sure that the marks on the two sprockets are in alignment. Lubricate the thrust surface with Molykote or its equivalent.
8. Align the dowel in the camshaft with the dowel hole in the sprocket and then install the sprocket onto the camshaft. Use the mounting bolts to draw the sprocket onto the camshaft and then tighten them to 27–33 ft.lb.
9. Lubricate the timing chain with clean engine oil. Tighten the chain tensioner.
10. Installation of the remaining components is in the reverse order of removal.

Removal and Installation

6–173 CU.IN.

1. To replace the chain, remove the crankcase front cover. This will allow access to the timing chain. Crank the engine until the marks punched on both sprockets are closest to one another and in line between the shaft centers.
2. Take out the three bolts that hold the camshaft sprocket to the camshaft. This sprocket is a light press fit on the camshaft and will come off readily. It is located by a dowel. The chain comes off with the camshaft sprocket. A gear puller will be required to remove the camshaft sprocket.
3. Without disturbing the position of the engine, mount the new crank sprocket on the shaft, then mount the chain over the camshaft sprocket. Arrange the camshaft sprocket in such a way that the timing marks will line up between the shaft centers and the camshaft locating dowel will enter the dowel hole in the cam sprocket.
4. Place the cam sprocket, with its chain mounted over it, in position on the front of the camshaft and pull up with the three bolts that hold it to the camshaft.
5. After the sprockets are in place, turn the engine two full revolutions to make certain that the timing marks are in correct alignment between the shaft centers.
6. Complete the assembly in the reverse order of the removal procedure.

Removal

V6, V8 ENGINES

1. Drain and remove radiator.
2. Remove torsional damper.
3. Remove oil pan (V8 engine), if required.
4. Remove water pump or pulley if necessary.
5. Remove timing case cover.
6. Align timing marks.
7. Remove camshaft sprocket bolts.
8. Remove sprocket and chain.

NOTE: Sprocket is a light press fit on the camshaft. If sprocket is tight, tap lightly with plastic hammer on lower edge of sprocket.

9. Clean all gasket and seal areas and inspect.
10. Check teeth on both sprockets for wear.

Installation

1. Suspend chain on camshaft sprocket with timing mark in approximate position.
2. Place chain over crankshaft sprocket and position camshaft sprocket on dowel. Recheck timing marks.
3. Draw camshaft sprocket in place using the three mounting bolts. Torque to specifications.

CAUTION

Do not drive sprocket on camshaft as welsh plug at rear of camshaft can be dislodged.

4. Lubricate chain with engine oil and be sure oil slinger is in place.
5. Reverse removal procedures.
6. Fill radiator, add engine oil and start engine. Check for leaks.

Check for Worn Chain

1. Expose distributor and raise the vehicle to gain working clearance. Support the vehicle safely.
2. Remove distributor cap, loosen or remove spark plugs.
3. Move crankshaft pulley in either direction, until distributor rotor moves. Mark distributor housing and balancer at this point.
4. Move crankshaft pulley in opposite direction until distributor rotor moves again and remark both units.
5. Marks in excess of 4° apart, 2 graduations (usually) on balancer, indicate excess wear and chain and/or gears should be replaced.

NOTE: With the front cover off the engine, move the timing chain back and forth. If the chain can be moved in excess of $^5/_8$ in., the chain and/or gears should be replaced

Pistons and Connecting Rods

PISTONS

Pistons are of various designs, flat, cup, hump and dome. Heads are usually notched or stamped with an arrow to indicate front. Oversize pistons are available for all engines.

CONNECTING RODS

Rod forging and cap have mating numbers and must be on same side when installed or cap is on "backwards." Rod number on in-line engines go to camshaft side. Numbers on "V" engines go to outside of block. The oil spurt (cylinder wall oiling) hole goes toward camshaft. On in-line engines, the spurt hole and number are both on camshaft side. On "V" engines, the spurt hole is in center, toward camshaft and numbers to outside.

Removal

1. Drain cooling system and remove cylinder head(s).
2. Drain crankcase oil and remove oil pan.
3. Remove any ridge and/or deposits from upper end of cylinder bores with a ridge reamer.

NOTE: Move piston to bottom of its travel and place a cloth on top of piston to collect cuttings. After ridge and or deposits are removed turn crankshaft until piston is at top of its stroke and carefully remove cloth with its cuttings.

4. Check connecting rods and pistons for cylinder number identification and if necessary, mark them.
5. Remove connecting rod nuts and caps. Push rods away from crankshaft and install caps and nuts loosely to their respective rods.

NOTE: Connecting rod caps and nuts may have to be installed onto the rod after the piston/rod assembly is removed from the engine block.

6. Push piston and rod assemblies away from crankshaft and out of cylinders.

Installation

1. Lightly coat pistons, rings and cylinder walls with light engine oil, making sure everything is clean and free of dirt and foreign material.

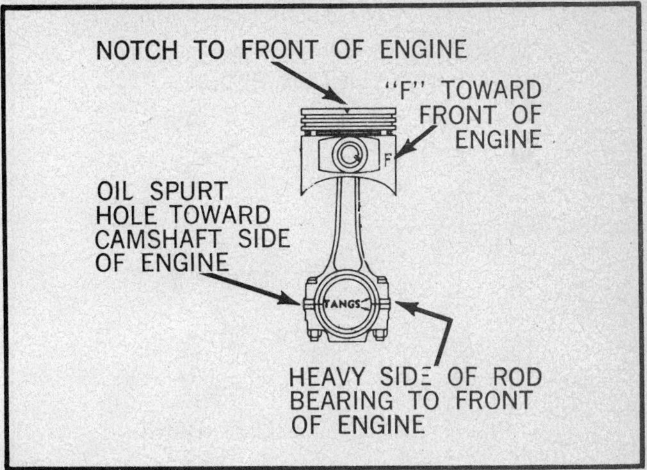

Correct relationship of piston and rod on 250 engine (© General Motors Corp.)

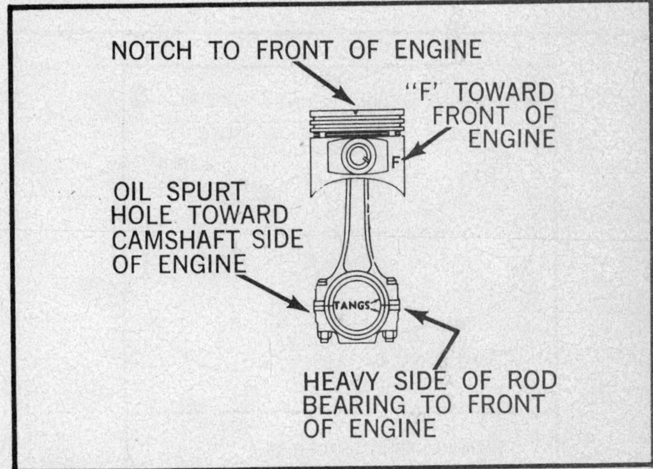

Correct relationship of piston and rod on 292 engines (© General Motors Corp.)

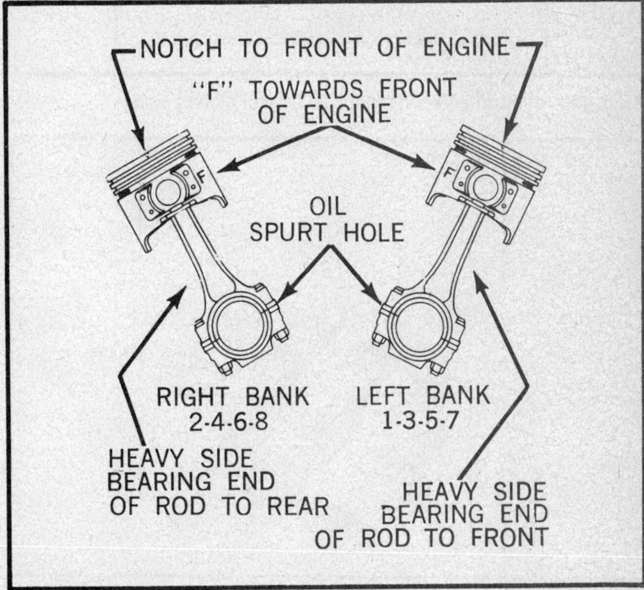

Correct relationship of piston and rod on 307, 305 and 350 engines (© General Motors Corp.)

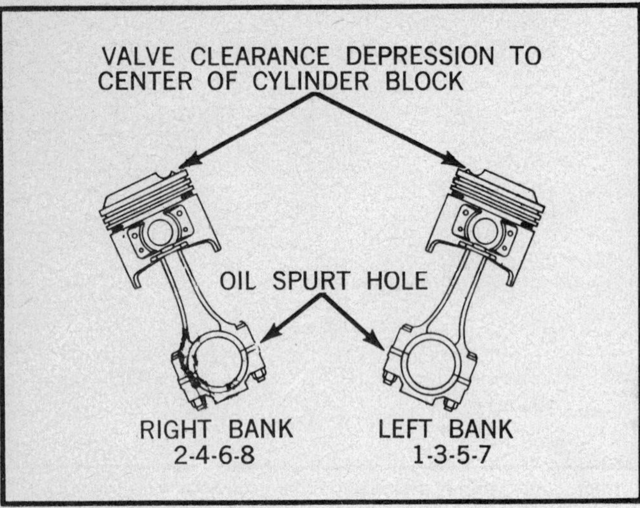

Correct relationship of piston and rod on 366, 400, 427 and 454 engines (© General Motors Corp.)

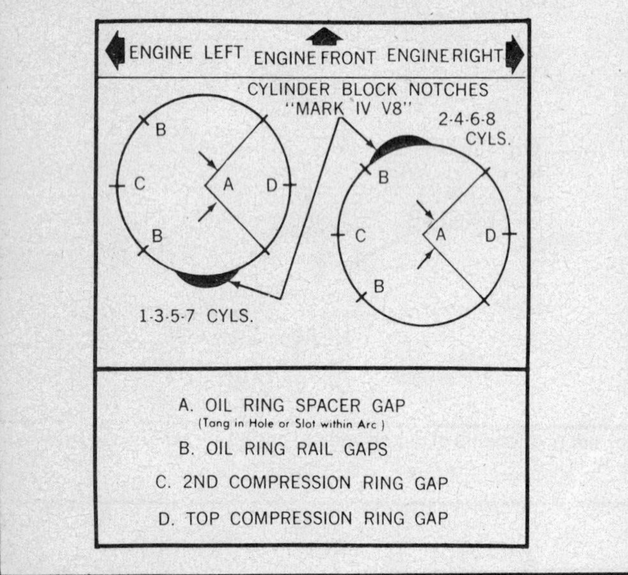

Ring gap location—V8—typical (© General Motors Corp.)

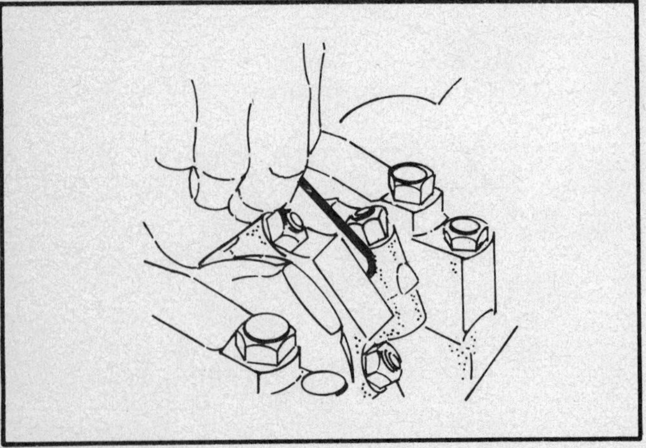

Measuring connecting rod side clearance—V8 engines (© General Motors Corp.)

2. With bearing caps removed and ring compressor tool installed, install each piston in its respective bore.
3. Install bearing caps and check bearing clearance.
4. Install oil pan gaskets, seals and oil pan.
5. Install cylinder head gasket(s) and head(s).
6. Refill crankcase and cooling system and check for leaks.

Piston Rings

Piston rings are available in standard size as well as .020 in., .030 in. and .040 in. oversizes.

Removal

1. With pistons removed from cylinders, remove piston rings by expanding them and sliding them off piston.
2. Clean piston ring grooves by removing all particles of carbon. Check for burrs or nicks that might cause rings to hang up.

Installation

Follow instructions in ring package for installation onto piston.

Main and Rod Bearings

Main bearings and connecting rod bearings are replaceable inserts, precision fit and held in place by locking tangs. Excessive bearing clearances reduce oil pressure. Never replace the lower half of any bearing without replacing the upper half. Do not file any bearing cap. Make sure, on main bearings, the upper half oil hole is aligned. Be certain oil passages in the crankshaft are open. Mark rod caps and upper forgings, also main caps and block, in numerical order to aid in reassembly. Rod

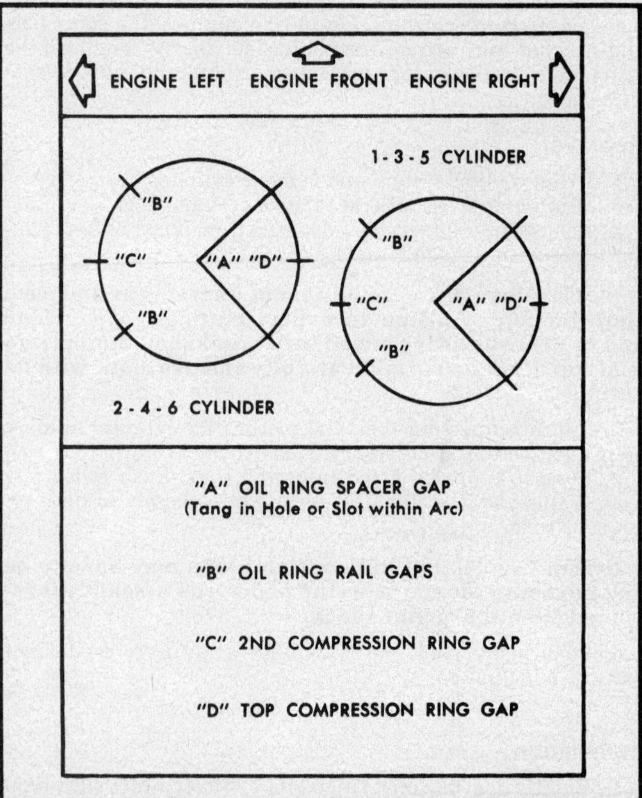

Piston ring gap locations—V6 engine (© General Motors Corp.)

bearings are available in standard size as well as 0.001 in., 0.002 in., 0.010 in. and 0.020 in. undersizes. Main bearings are furnished in standard size and 0.001 in., 0.002 in., 0.009 in., 0.010 in., 0.020 in. and 0.030 in. undersizes.

ROD BEARING

Replacement

1. Drain crankcase oil and remove oil pan.
2. Remove connecting rod bearing cap.
3. Wipe bearing shell and crankpin clean of oil.
4. Inspect bearings for evidence of wear or damage. (Bearings showing the above should not be installed).
5. Measure crankpin for out-of-round or taper with a micrometer. If within specifications, measure bearing clearance with plastigage or its equivalent.
6. Install bearing in connecting rod and cap.
7. Coat bearing surface with oil, install rod cap and torque nuts to specifications.
8. Rotate crankshaft after bearing adjustment, to be sure bearings are not too tight. Check side clearance.
9. Install oil pan gaskets, seals and oil pan.

MAIN BEARING

Replacement

NOTE: Main bearings may be replaced with or without removing crankshaft. Engine must be removed on S-series trucks.

ENGINE IN VEHICLE

1. Drain crankcase oil and remove oil pan.
2. Remove oil pump.
3. Loosen or remove spark plugs for easier crankshaft rotation.
4. Starting with rear main bearing, remove bearing cap and wipe oil from journal and cap.
5. Inspect bearings for evidence of wear or damage.
6. Measure bearing clearance with plastigage or its equivalent. The crankshaft should be supported at damper and flywheel to remove clearance from upper bearing. Total clearance can then be measured between lower bearing and journal.
7. Remove bearing shell from cap.
8. On in-line engine crankshaft, rear main bearing journal has no oil hole. Replace rear main bearing upper half as follows:
   a. Use a small drift punch and hammer to start upper bearing half rotating out of block.
   b. Use a pair of pliers (with taped jaws) to hold bearing thrust surface to oil slinger and rotate crankshaft to remove bearing.
   c. Oil new selected size upper bearing and insert plate (unnotched) and between crankshaft and indented or notched side of block.
   d. Use pliers as in removing to rotate bearing into place. The last ¼ movement may be done by holding just the slinger with pliers or tap in place with a drift punch.
9. All other crankshaft journals (in-line and "V" models) have oil holes. Replace main bearing upper half as follows:
   a. Install a main bearing removing and installing tool in oil hole in crankshaft journal.

   NOTE: If such a tool is not available, a cotter pin (with head flattened) may be used.

   b. Rotate crankshaft clockwise as viewed from front of engine. This will roll upper bearing out of block.
   c. Oil new selected size upper bearing and insert plain (unnotched) end between crankshaft and indented or notched side of block. Rotate bearing into place and remove tool from oil hole in crankshaft journal.
10. Oil new lower bearing and install in bearing cap.
11. Install main bearing cap according to markings. Torque bearing cap bolts to specifications.
12. Install oil pump and oil pan. Refill crankcase. Install and tighten spark plugs.

REAR MAIN BEARING OIL SEAL

Replacement

ENGINE IN VEHICLE (ALL EXCEPT S–SERIES)

1. Raise vehicle and drain oil.
2. Remove oil pan and oil pump. See oil pan and oil pump removal.
3. Remove rear main cap and discard seal.
4. Loosen all mains (except no. 1) and block crankshaft down for maximum clearance at rear main.

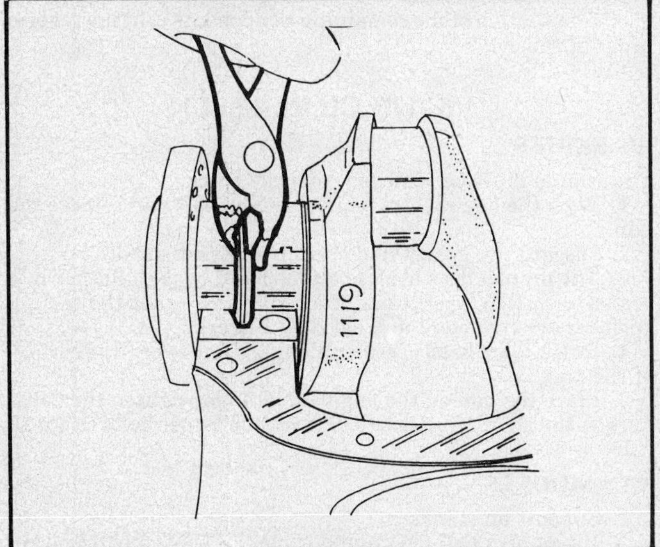

Removing upper half of rear main bearing (© General Motors Corp.)

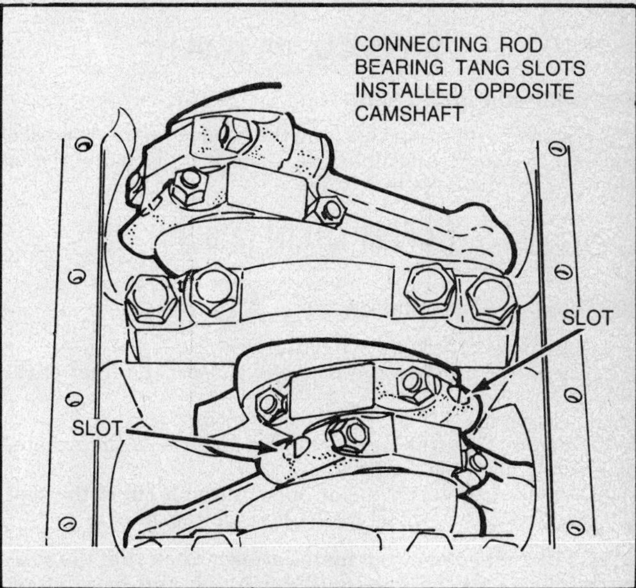

Connecting rods installed—V8 engines (© General Motors Corp.)

5. Use wooden dowel, so as not to mar journal, tap lightly until seal can be gripped and removed. Rotating shaft may help.
6. Molded type seal: Insert new upper half, lubricated with light sealer, into channel and apply firm pressure with hammer handle until seal is centered. (Lip of seal facing toward front of engine.) Install lower half of oil seal in cap (lip toward front), lubricate lip with oil and install cap.
7. Torque all mains, check for drag.
8. Replace oil pump, oil pan and add oil.
9. Start engine and check for leaks.

NOTE: The 1.9L OHC engine uses a one-piece seal that is installed with driver J-22928-A, or equivalent.

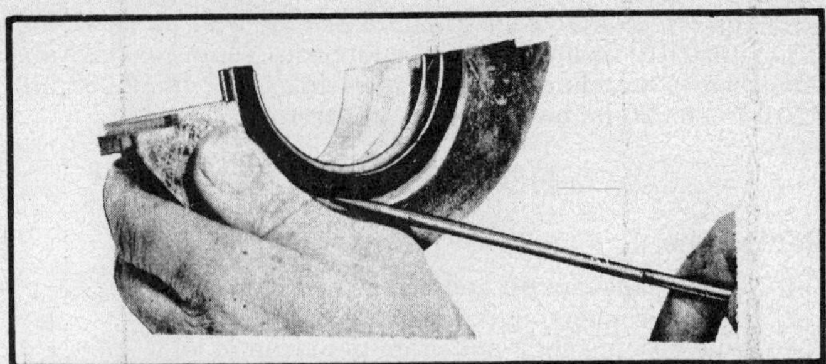

Removing lower half of rear oil seal (© General Motors Corp.)

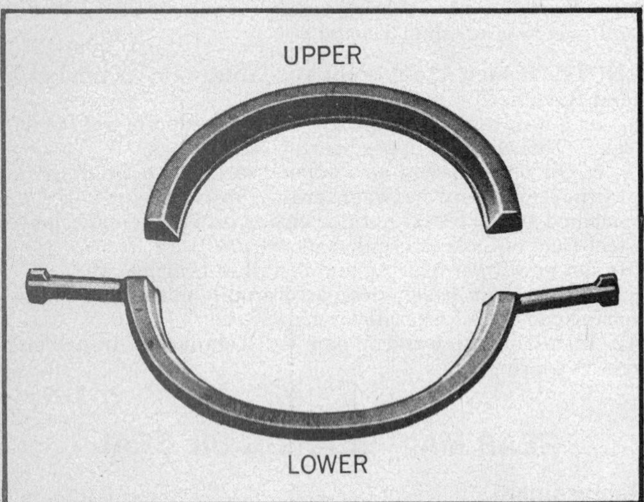

Rear main oil seal—6 cylinder engines (© General Motors Corp.)

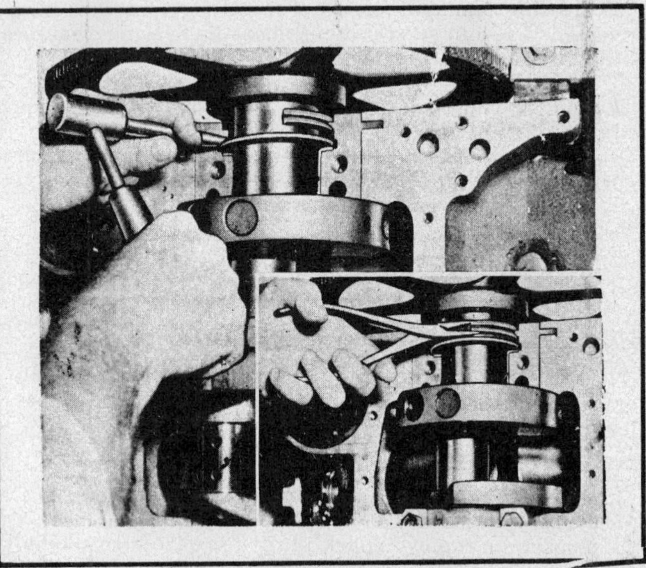

Rear main oil seal removal (© General Motors Corp.)

ENGINE LUBRICATION

Oil Pan

L4-119 CU. IN. (1.9L)

Removal and Installation

The engine must be removed from the vehicle before removal of the oil pan can be accomplished. Upon installation of the oil pan, tighten the bolts to 4 ft. lbs

L4-121 CU.IN (2.0L)

Removal and Installation

1. Disconnect the negative battery cable.
2. Drain the crankcase. Raise and support the front of the vehicle.
3. Remove the A/C brace if so equipped.
4. Remove the exhaust shield and disconnect the exhaust pipe at the manifold
5. Remove the starter motor and position it out of the way.
6. Remove the flywheel cover. Remove the oil pan.

NOTE: Prior to oil pan installation, check that the sealing surfaces on the pan, cylinder block and front cover are clean and free of oil. If installing the old pan, be sure that all old RTV has been removed.

7. Apply a $\frac{1}{8}$ in. bead of RTV sealant to the oil pan sealing surface. Use a new oil pan rear seal and install the pan in place. Tighten the bolts to 9-13 ft. lbs
8. Installation of the remaining components is in the reverse order of removal.

V6-173 CU.IN. (2.8L)

S/T SERIES

The engine must be removed from the truck.

1. With the engine on a work stand, unbolt and remove the pan.
2. Discard the gasket and clean the gasket surfaces.
3. The oil pan does not use a preformed gasket. Rather it is sealed with RTV gasket material. Make sure that the sealing surfaces are free of oil and old RTV material.
4. Run a $\frac{1}{8}$ in. bead of sealer along the entire sealing surface of the pan.
5. Place the pan on the engine and finger tighten the bolts. Torque the smaller bolts to 6-9 ft.lb.; the larger bolts to 15-22 ft.lb.

VAN MODELS

1. Support on stands.
2. Disconnect battery ground cable, loosen fan belt and remove radiator shroud top belt.
3. Remove radiator fan and pulley.

4. Raise vehicle, clean road dirt from oil pan.
5. Drain oil, replace drain plug gasket.
6. Remove engine splash shields if equipped.
7. Remove starter, leave electrical connections intact, swing out of way.
8. Automatic transmission models: Remove oil cooler lines and converter pan.
9. Remove front motor mount bolts.
10. Remove accessory drive pulley (if used).
11. Engines with radiator shroud: Drain radiator, remove lower radiator hose, remove lower shroud bolts and lower shroud out of way.
12. Using a jack, raise and support front of engine.
13. Remove crossmember to frame bolts, remove crossmember.
14. Remove oil pan bolts, remove oil pan.

CAUTION

If any prolonged operations are planned (with pan off), it would be safer to re-install crossmember and lower engine on mounts.

15. Reverse removal steps to install after cleaning gasket and seal surfaces.
16. Lower vehicle, fill crankcase and radiator, start engine and check for leaks.

NOTE: Use gasket sealer as a retainer to hold side gaskets in place on block. Bolts in front cover should be installed last. They are installed at an angle and holes line up after rest of pan bolts are tightened.

10–3500 SERIES

1. Raise front of vehicle and support on stands.
2. Drain oil, replace drain plug gasket.
3. Remove converter pan on automatic transmission.
4. Remove battery ground cable, remove starter (leave electrical connections intact and swing aside).
5. If necessary, remove front motor mount bolts, using a block of wood under oil pan, raise engine with a jack high enough to insert blocks at motor mounts.
6. Remove oil pan and discard gaskets and seals.
7. Reverse removal steps to install after cleaning all gasket and seal surfaces.
8. Lower vehicle, fill crankcase to level, start engine and check for leaks.

NOTE: Use gasket sealer as a retainer to hold side gaskets in place on block.

L4–152 CU.IN. (2.5L)

Removal and Installation

S/T TRUCKS (4X4)

1. Disconnect the negative battery cable.
2. Disconnect the power steering reservoir at the fan shroud.
3. Remove the upper fan shroud and the dipstick.
4. Raise the vehicle and support safely. Drain the oil pan.
5. Disconnect the brake lines clips at the cross member and remove the cross member from the vehicle.
6. Disconnect the transmission cooler lines at the flywheel cover, if equipped.
7. Disconnect the exhaust pipe at the manifold.
8. Disconnect the catalytic converter hanger, remove one bolt and loosen the other.
9. Remove the flywheel cover and the drive shaft splash shield.
10. Mark the position of the idler arm to frame and remove the attaching bolts.
11. Remove the steering gear bolts and pull the steering gear, with linkage, forward.
12. Remove the differential housing mounting bolts at the bracket on the right hand side and at the frame on the left hand side. Move the housing forward.
13. Remove the starter assembly and lay aside.
14. Loosen the starter brace to block.
15. Disconnect the front prop shaft at the drive pinion.
16. Remove the engine mount through bolts and support the engine.
17. Remove the oil pan bolts, raise the engine and remove the oil pan assembly.
18. To install the oil pan, use a ⅛ bead of RTV sealer on the clean surface of the entire oil pan sealing flange.
19. Install the oil pan retaining bolts and complete the assembly in the reverse order of the removal procedure.

Removal and Installation

S/T TRUCK MODELS (4X2) AND ASTRO VAN

NOTE: The oil pan removal for the Astro Van models is basically the same as for the S/T truck models. Slight variations from the procedure will have to be accomplished.

1. Disconnect the battery negative cable.
2. Raise the vehicle and support safely. Drain the engine oil.
3. Remove the strut rods and the torque converter cover bolts.
4. Disconnect the exhaust pipe at the catalytic converter hanger.
5. Disconnect the exhaust pipe at the manifold and remove the torque converter cover.
6. Disconnect the starter brace at the engine block and remove the starter.
7. Disconnect the transmission oil cooler lines at the oil pan.
8. Remove the oil pan retaining bolts and remove the oil pan.
9. To install the oil pan, use a ⅛ bead of RTV sealer on the clean surface of the entire oil pan sealing flange. Complete the assembly in the reverse of the removal procedure.

V6–363 CU.IN. (4.3L)

Removal and Installation

ASTRO VAN

1. Disconnect the negative battery cable.
2. Raise the vehicle and support safely. Drain the engine oil.
3. Disconnect the exhaust pipes at the manifolds.
4. Remove the engine strut rods at the inspection cover.
5. Remove the flywheel inspection cover.
6. Remove the starter assembly and set aside.
7. Remove the engine mount trim bolts.
8. Place a suitable jack on the engine and raise to gain working clearance.
9. Remove the oil pan retaining bolts and remove the oil pan.
10. To install the oil pan, use new gaskets, place to the engine block and install the retaining screws.
11. Complete the assembly by reversing the removal procedure.

IN-LINE 6 CYLINDER ENGINE

Removal and Installation

ALL MODELS

1. Disconnect the negative battery cable.
2. Raise the vehicle and support safely. Drain the engine oil.
3. Remove the starter assembly.
4. Remove the flywheel splash pan or converter housing underpan, as applicable.
5. Remove the engine mount through bolts from the engine front mounts. Raise the engine and install the through bolt

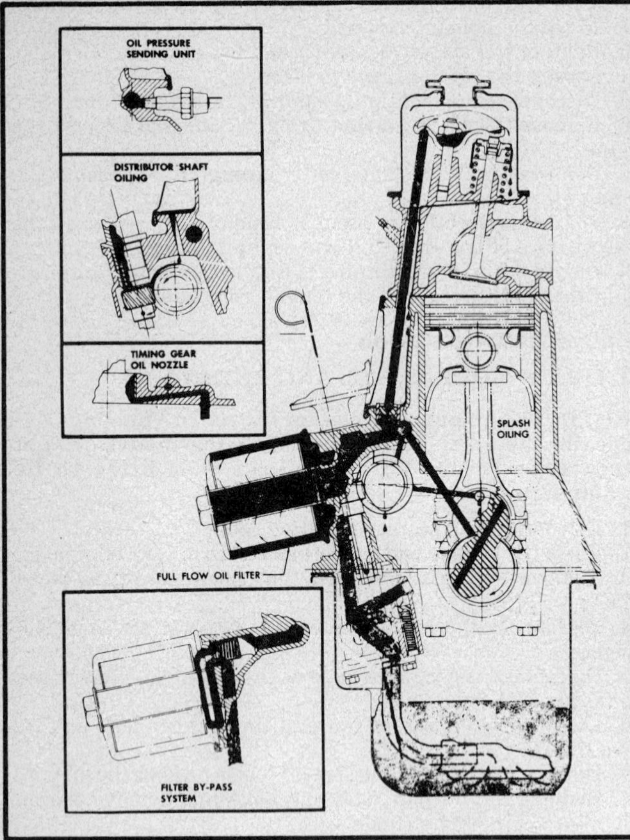

Engine lubrication—inline 6 cylinder engines (© General Motors Corp.)

into the mount only. Lower the engine.

6. Remove the oil pan retaining bolts and remove the oil pan.
7. To install the oil pan, install a new gasket and position to the engine. Install the retaining bolts and torque to 80 INCH lbs.
8. Complete the assembly in the reverse order of the the removal procedure.

V6 ENGINE—263 CU.IN.(4.3L), V8 ENGINES—305 CU.IN. (5.0L) and 350 CU.IN. (5.7L)

Removal and Installation

10–3500 SERIES

1. Disconnect the negative battery cable.
2. Raise the vehicle and support safely. Drain the engine oil.
3. On vehicles with A/T transmission, remove the converter housing under pan.
4. On V6 models, remove the strut rods at the flywheel cover.
5. On V6 models, remove the starter assembly.
6. On four wheel drive vehicles with A/T, remove the strut rods at the engine mounts.
7. Remove the oil pan retaining bolts and the oil pan.
8. To install the oil pan, use new gaskets and reverse the removal procedure.

V8 ENGINES (LARGE BLOCK)

Removal and Installation

ALL MODELS

1. Disconnect the negative battery cable.
2. Loosen the fan shroud and remove the air cleaner assembly.

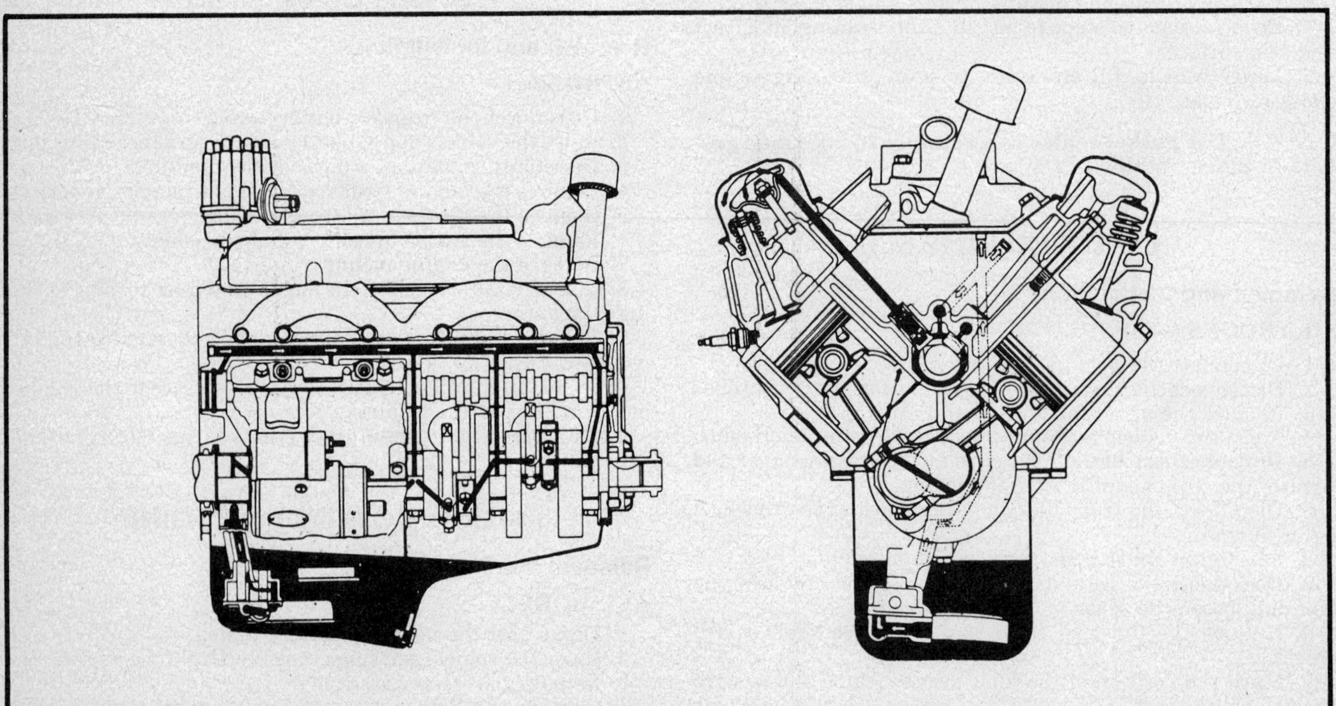

Engine lubrication—305, 350 cu. in. engines (© General Motors Corp.)

3. Remove the distributor cap.
4. Raise the vehicle and support safely. Drain the engine oil.
5. If equipped with manual transmission, remove the starter assembly.
6. Remove the torque converter cover or the clutch cover as applicable.
7. Remove the oil filter.
8. On gauge equipped vehicles, remove the oil pressure line from the side of the engine block to avoid crushing of the line when raising the engine.
9. Remove the engine mount through bolt and raise the engine with a suitable jack.
10. Remove the oil pan retaining bolts and remove the engine oil pan.
11. To install the oil pan, use new gasket and position the pan to the engine block. Install the retaining bolts.
12. Complete the assembly in the reverse of the removal procedure.

Oil Pump

The pumps used are distributor driven gear or trochoid type. On in-line engines, pump is mounted on cylinder block while on "V" engines, the pump is mounted on rear main cap inside oil pan. Pump gears and body are usually not serviced separately. If the components are not available, the pump should be replaced as a unit. A baffle, incorporated on the pickup screen, eliminates oil pressure loss due to surging of the oil within the oil pan as the vehicle is operated.

Removal and Installation (All Models)

1. Remove oil pan.
2. In-line engines—Remove oil suction pipe at housing.

CAUTION

Do not disturb screen on pick up pipe.

3. Remove two flange mounting bolts, remove pump.
4. Reverse removal steps to install, using new pan gasket, watch slot alignment with distributor tang. Torque all bolts to specifications.

NOTE: Pump should slide easily into place, if not, remove and relocate slot. Pack oil pump gear cavity with petroleum jelly.

5. Refill with oil, start engine and check for leaks.

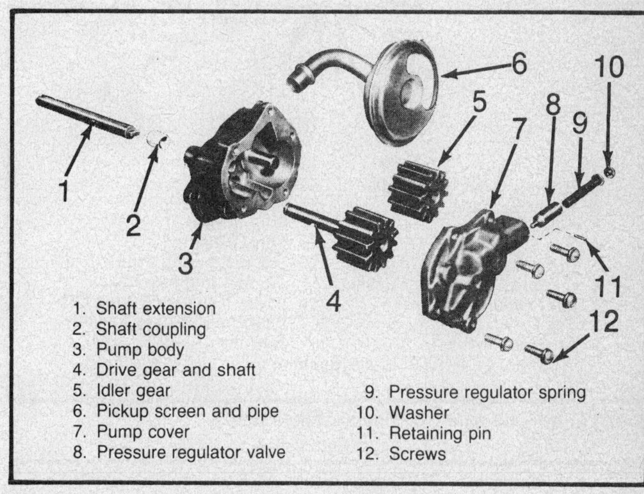

Oil pump—V8 engines (© General Motors Corp.)

FRONT SUSPENSION

General instructions covering the front suspension and how to repair and adjust it are given in the Unit Repair Section.

Figures covering the caster, camber, toe-in, kingpin inclination and turning radius can be found in the Wheel Alignment table of this section.

I-Beam Front Axle

This type of front axle is a one-piece steel forging in which dowel pins are installed to locate spring seats. Both ends of the axle are machined to accept the steering knuckle and kingpin assemblies and the kingpin inclination is a built-in angle.

SPRING

Removal and Installation

1. Wire brush all road dirt from threaded areas on U bolts, shock absorbers and stabilizer links, apply a good penetrant on threads.
2. Disconnect shock and stabilizer link at lower bracket.
3. Loosen both spring U bolts.
4. Using jack under I-beam, raise front of vehicle and support at frame side rail with stand. Finish removing U bolts and rebound bumper. Lower jack until spring clears I-beam or tire rests on ground. Remove any caster wedges (shims) and set aside for installation.

NOTE: Thick end of shim goes to rear of vehicle for increased caster.

5. Remove front spring eye bolt.
6. Remove rear shackle (and hanger cam if equipped).
7. Remove spring, inspect hangers and spring seat (center bolt index).
8. Reverse removal procedures to install after placing spring on axle with center bolt head indexed in seat and caster shims in place. Torque all nuts and lubricate.
9. Align front end assembly if the caster wedge had been removed.

STEERING KNUCKLE AND KINGPIN ASSEMBLY F–050, F–055, F–070 AND F–070D AXLES

CAUTION

Steering knuckle bushings are of a split type and are constructed of thermoplastic polyester. Bushings can be cleaned in most conventional solvents, except ketone or chlorinated types.

1. Support the frame of the vehicle in a raised position, high enough so that the tires clear the floor.
2. Remove the wheels, hubs and bearings.
3. Remove brake components as necessary.
4. Disconnect the tie-rod from the steering arm.
5. Remove the two lower steering arm-to-axle flange bolts and swing the steering arm out of the way.
6. Remove the two upper bolts from the axle flange and remove the brake backing plate.

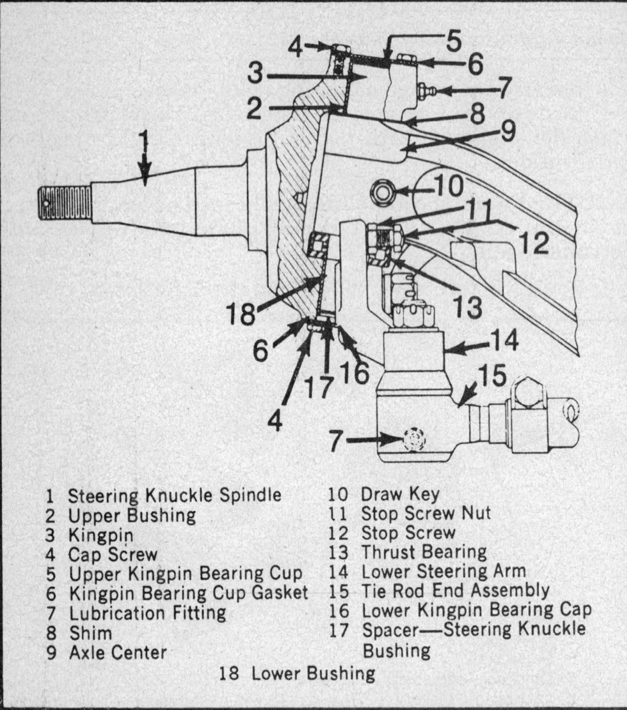

F-050 and F-055 axle (© General Motors Corp.)

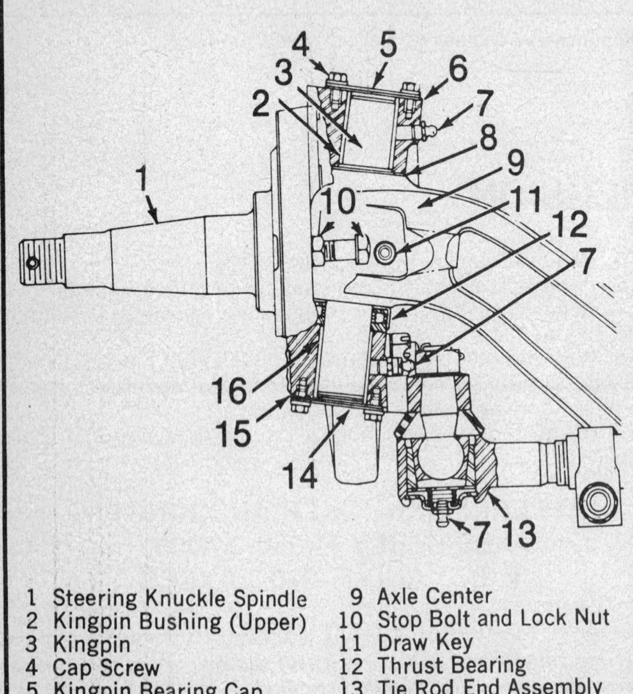

F-070 axle (© General Motors Corp.)

7. Remove the kingpin draw key nut and washer.
8. Thread the draw key nut onto the draw key far enough to protect the threads from damage.
9. Drive the draw key loose by striking the nut with a brass hammer.
10. Finish driving the draw key out with a brass drift.
11. Remove the kingpin bearing cap screws.
12. Remove the kingpin bearing caps and gaskets.
13. Using a brass hammer, drive the kingpin out of the axle.
14. Remove the steering knuckle, thrust bearing, shims and the O-ring.

NOTE: Steering knuckle bushings can be hand pressed into the knuckle bore until flush with the top.

Installation

1. Position the steering knuckle on the axle and insert the thrust bearing.
2. Install a new O-ring seal at the bottom of the upper bushing.
3. Align the steering knuckle yoke, axle end and the thrust bearing to accept the kingpin; start the kingpin through the top of the assembly.
4. With the axle center firmly secured, jack up the steering knuckle until there is zero clearance between the steering knuckle lower yoke, thrust bearing and the axle center.
5. Check the clearance between the top of the axle center and the knuckle upper yoke. Select shims which will provide the correct thrust clearance as indicated in the Front Axle Specification Chart.
6. From the top, insert the kingpin through the steering knuckle yoke, shim, thrust bearing and axle center end. Press the kingpin down until the machined slot in the kingpin aligns with the draw key hole.
7. Insert the draw key into the axle center and install the washer and nut.

CAUTION

If, after tightening the draw key nut, the kingpin is not secured, then replace the draw key.

NOTE: On models using steering knuckle bushing spacer, install spacer at lower end of the kingpin.

8. Using new gaskets, install upper and lower kingpin bearing caps and cap screws.
9. Lubricate the kingpin with chassis lubricant.
10. Secure the brake backing plate to the axle flange with the top two axle flange bolts.
11. Swing the steering arm into position and secure it to the axle flange with two lower flange bolts.
12. Install brake components.
13. Install hubs and bearings.
14. Install wheels.
15. Lower the vehicle and check front end alignment. Make necessary adjustments.

STEERING KNUCKLE AND KINGPIN ASSEMBLY F–090 AXLE (F–120, F–120D AXLE SIMILAR)

NOTE: The steering knuckle is supported on a solid kingpin which is tapered at the center. The kingpin bushing is constructed of steel and the knuckle bushings are constructed of steel backed bronze.

Removal

1. Support the frame of the vehicle in a raised position, high enough so that the tires clear the floor.
2. Remove the wheels, hubs and bearings.
3. Remove brake components as necessary.
4. Disconnect steering linkage components as necessary.
5. Remove the axle flange-to-steering knuckle bolts and remove the brake backing plate.

6. Remove the dust cap and gasket.
7. Remove the lower expansion plug retainer and plug.

NOTE: If the plug does not remove freely after the retainer has been removed, it will come out along with the kingpin when the kingpin is driven out.

8. Remove the cotter pin, kingpin nut and the steel washer.
9. Drive the kingpin down and out of the axle with a brass drift.
10. Remove the steering knuckle, thrust bearing and spacers from the axle.

NOTE: Bushing replacement can be accomplished with the use of an arbor press.

Installation

1. With the steering knuckle positioned on the axle center end, insert the thrust bearing assembly between the lower face of the axle center and the steering knuckle lower yoke.

NOTE: Be sure that the retainer is on top of the bearing with the lip of the retainer facing down.

2. Align the knuckle yoke and axle center to accept the kingpin.
3. With the axle center firmly secured, jack up the steering knuckle until there is zero clearance between the steering knuckle lower yoke, thrust bearing and the axle center.
4. Check the clearance between the top face of the axle center end and the face of the upper steering knuckle yoke. Select shims which will provide the correct thrust clearance as indicated in the Front Axle Specification Chart.

NOTE: Kingpin, kingpin bore and component parts must be thoroughly cleaned and dry.

5. Insert the kingpin up through the bottom yoke of the steering knuckle and drive it into place with a soft hammer.
6. Position the kingpin bushing over the kingpin and press into place. Bushing must be flush with the knuckle.
7. Install the kingpin nut and cotter pin.
8. Install a new inverted expansion plug in the lower hole.
9. Install the plug retainer. Retainer must be seated securely in groove.
10. Install the kingpin dust cap and gasket.
11. Connect steering linkage components.
12. Install backing plate to axle flange.
13. Install brake components.
14. Install the hubs, bearings and wheels.

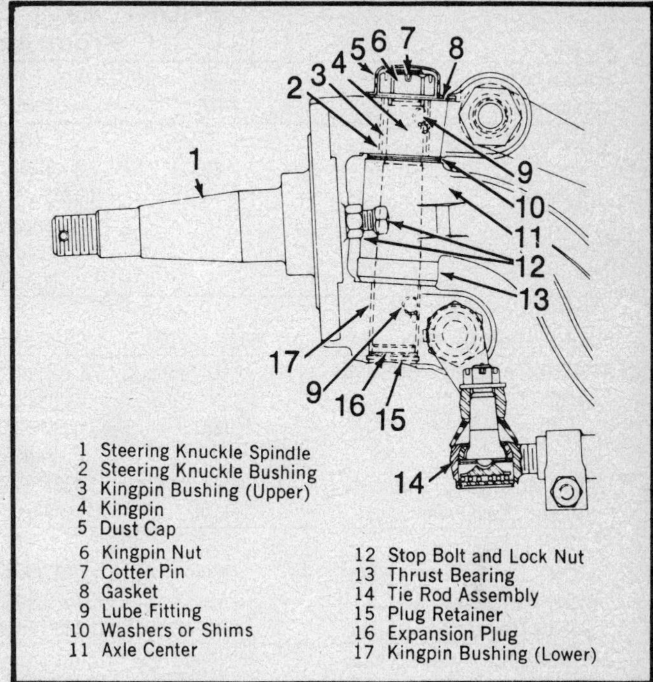

F-090 axle (© General Motors Corp.)

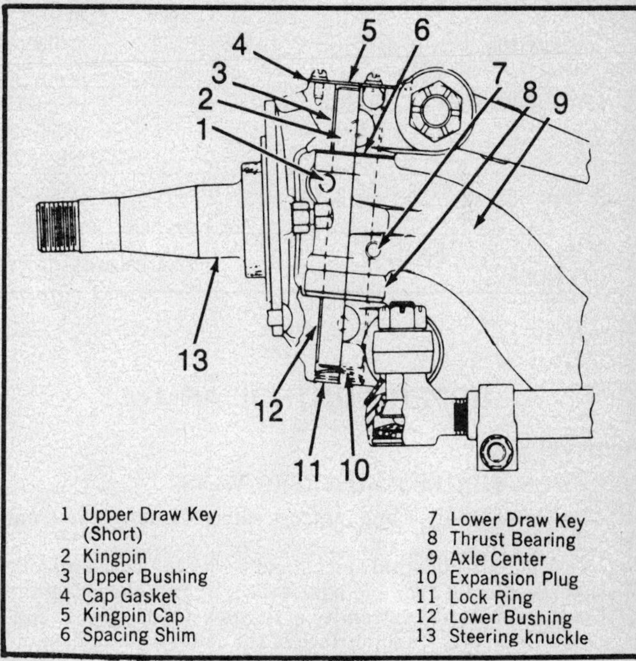

F-120 axle (© General Motors Corp.)

Independent Front Suspension

This suspension consists of upper and lower control arms, pivoting on steel threaded bushings on upper and lower control arm inner shafts which are attached to the crossmember. Control arms are connected to the steering knuckle by ball joints. A coil spring is seated between the upper and lower control arms, thus the lower control arm is the load carrying member.

NOTE: Astro Vans and S-series 2wd front suspension is similar to standard size Vans and Pickups. 4wd models use a torsion bar type front suspension.

COIL SPRING

Removal and Installation

1. Raise vehicle and place stands under frame, allowing control arm to hang free.
2. Disconnect shock absorber (and stabilizer if used) at lower end.
3. Using a floor jack under center of lower control arm inner shaft, raise and remove tension from shaft.

CAUTION

Install a safety chain through arm and spring.

4. Remove both clamps or "U" bolts securing inner shaft to crossmember.
5. Release jack very cautiously, slowly lowering arm with spring until spring is free. Remove safety chain, remove spring.
6. Inspect front end especially at ball joints and both upper and lower control arm inner shaft bushings.
7. Reverse removal steps to install spring. Use a long tapered drift to align holes of inner control arm shaft and crossmember while slowly jacking arm into place.

FRONT AXLE SPECIFICATIONS

Front Axle Models

Front Axle Component	F-070	F-090	F-120 & F-120D	FF-933	FL-931
KINGPIN					
Length	7.89″	8.750″	9.38″	10.392″	11.212″
Diameter	1.2492″–1.2496″	1.1855″–1.1865″ (upper) 1.4330″–1.4340″ (lower)	1.7445″–1.7455″	1.7930″–1.7940″	1.9980″–1.9990″
STEERING KNUCKLE					
Bushing Bore Diameter	1.3682″–1.3702″	1.560″–1.562″	1.876″–1.878″	1.919″–1.921″	2.124″–2.126″
STEERING KNUCKLE BUSHING					
Length	1.88″	1.709″–1.729″ (upper) 1.990″–2.010″ (lower)	2.240″	2.812″	2.625′
I.D. After Reaming or Burnishing	1.2496″–1.2526″	1.4365″–1.4375″	1.7465″–1.7485″	1.7965″–1.7975″	2.001″–2.003″
Installed Depth From Center	Flush	Flush	0.135″ Min.	See Text	See Text
KINGPIN SLEEVE					
Length	—	1.9063″	—	—	—
Inside Diameter	—	1.1870″–1.1880″	—	—	—
Outside Diameter	—	1.4330″–1.4340″		—	—
STEERING KNUCKLE TO AXLE CENTER CLEARANCE					
In Service Check	0.001″–0.010″ (0.03–0.25mm)	0.004″–0.012″ (0.10–0.30mm)	0.005″–0.015″ (0.13–0.38mm)	0.065″ (1.70mm) maximum	0.065″ (1.70mm) maximum
At Assembly	0.015″–0.030″ (0.38–0.76mm)	0.015″–0.030″ (0.38–0.76mm)	0.015″–0.030″ (0.38–0.76mm)	0.005–0.025″ (0.12–0.65mm)	0.005–0.025″ (0.12–0.64mm)
SPACING WASHERS AVAILABLE	—	0.114″–0.116″ white	0.0478″	—	—
	—	0.121″–0.123″ yellow	—	—	—
	—	0.128″–0.130″ blue	—	—	—
SHIM WASHERS AVAILABLE	0.005″ (0.13mm)	0.005″ (0.13mm) 0.010″ (0.25mm)	0.010″ (0.25mm) 0.015″ (0.38mm)	0.005″ (0.13mm) 0.010″ (0.25mm)	0.005″ (0.13mm) 0.010″ (0.25mm)
STOP SCREW ADJUSTMENT (ALL MODELS)	Adjustment must provide 5/8″ (16mm) minimum clearance from tire to any chassis component.				

UPPER CONTROL ARM

Removal

EXCEPT S–SERIES AND ASTRO VANS

1. Raise the vehicle and support safely. Remove the front wheels.
2. Position an adjustable jackstand under the outboard side of the lower control arm and adjust the height of the jackstand so that the uppermost extremity of the jackstand comes in contact with the metal undersurface of the lower control arm.
3. Remove the cotter pin from the upper control arm ball joint stud and nut.
4. Loosen the stud nut approximately one full turn.
5. If the ball joint stud does not unseat from the steering knuckle, it may be necessary to press the control arm and ball joint stud away from the knuckle, using a tool designed for that purpose.
6. Remove the nut from the ball stud and swing the upper control arm up and away from the steering knuckle.

NOTE: It may be necessary to remove the brake caliper assembly from the steering knuckle in order to facilitate upper control arm removal and installation.

7. Remove the nuts securing the control arm pivot shaft to the frame and remove the control arm.
8. Tape the alignment shims together and tag them in order to properly relocate them during installation.

Installation

NOTE: Special pivot shaft aligning washers must be positioned with the concave and convex sides together.

1. Situate the upper control arm against its normal mounting position and install the pivot shaft nuts. Do not tighten the nuts.
2. Install the alignment shims in their respective positions as noted during removal.

NOTE: Tighten the nut on the thinner shim pack first. This will improve shaft to frame clamping force and torque retention.

4. Insert the ball joint stud into the bore and the steering knuckle and install the nut and cotter pin.
5. Install the brake caliper assembly.
6. Remove the adjustable jackstand from under the lower control arm.
7. Install the wheel and tire assembly.
8. The vehicle may now be positioned to check front end alignment.

NOTE: Ordinarily, a shim pack will leave at least two threads of the bolt exposed beyond the nut. If, in order to properly align the front wheels, it is necessary to build the shim pack beyond the two thread minimum, then check for damaged control arms and related parts. The difference, in thickness, between the front shim pack and the rear shim pack must not exceed 0.03 inches. The front shim pack must be at least 0.24 inches.

LOWER CONTROL ARM

Removal

EXCEPT S-SERIES AND ASTRO VANS

1. Raise the vehicle and support safely. Remove the front coil spring (see Coil Spring/Removal and Installation).
2. Support the disconnected inboard end of the lower control arm after the spring is removed.
3. Remove the cotter pin from the lower ball joint stud and loosen the stud nut approximately one full turn.
4. Press the control arm and ball joint stud away from the steering knuckle, using a tool designed for that purpose.

NOTE: It may be necessary to remove the brake caliper assembly from the steering knuckle in order to facilitate lower control arm removal and installation.

5. Remove the lower control arm.

Installation

1. Insert the lower ball joint stud through the steering knuckle and tighten the nut.
2. Install the coil spring and reattach the inboard end of the lower control arm to the crossmember.
3. Be sure that the ball joint stud nut is properly tightened and install the cotter pin.
4. Install the brake caliper assembly.
5. Remove the vehicle from the hoist.

NOTE: It is always advisable that the front end alignment be checked after any component of the front suspension has been replaced.

UPPER CONTROL ARM

Removal

S-SERIES AND ASTRO VANS

1. Note the location of the shims. Alignment shims are to be installed in the same position from which they were removed. Remove nuts and shims. Raise front of vehicle and support lower control arm with floor stands.

CAUTION

Floor jack must remain under control arm spring seat during removal and installation to retain spring and control arm in position.

Since the weight of the vehicle is used to relieve spring tension on the upper control arm, the floor stands must be positioned between the spring seats and ball joints of the lower control arms for maximum leverage.

2. Remove wheel, then loosen the upper ball joint from the steering knuckle as previously outlined.
3. Support hub assembly to prevent weight from damaging brake hose.
4. It is necessary to remove the upper control arm attaching bolts to allow clearance to remove upper control arm assembly.
5. Remove upper control arm.

Installation

1. Position upper control arm attaching bolts loosely in the frame and install pivot shaft on the attaching bolts.

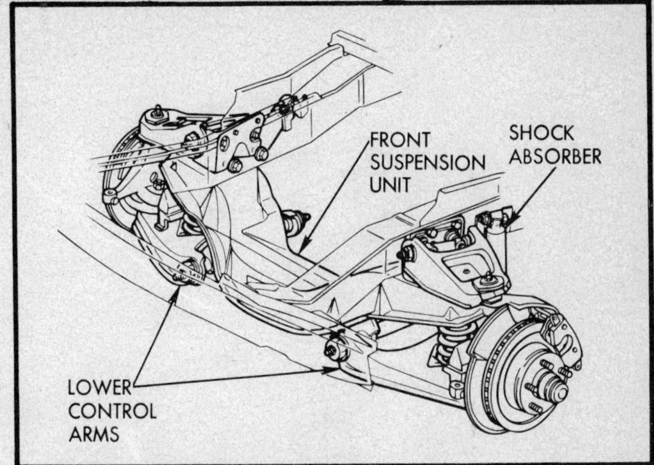

Coil spring suspension (© General Motors Corp.)

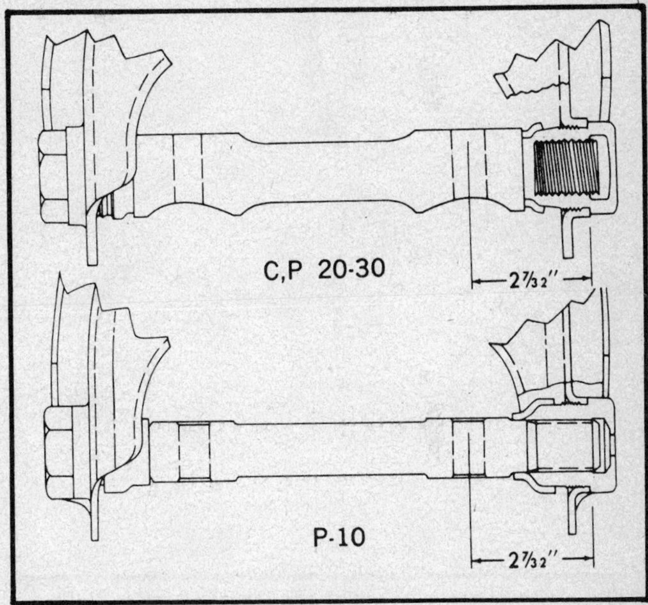

Correctly positioned upper control arm steel bushings (© General Motors Corp.)

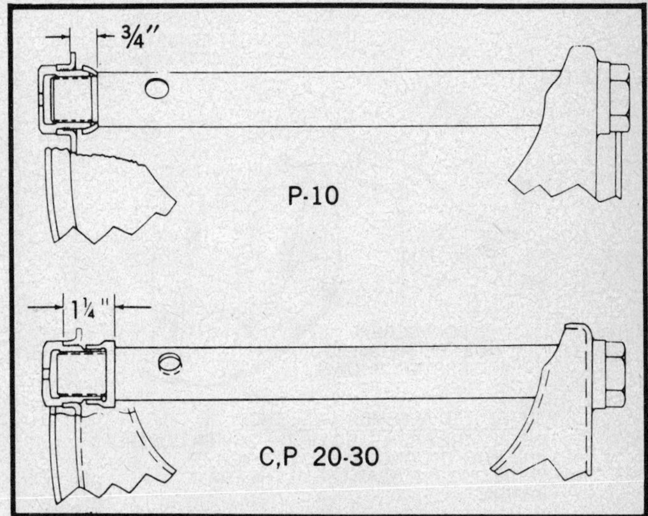

Correctly positioned lower control arm steel bushings (© General Motors Corp.)

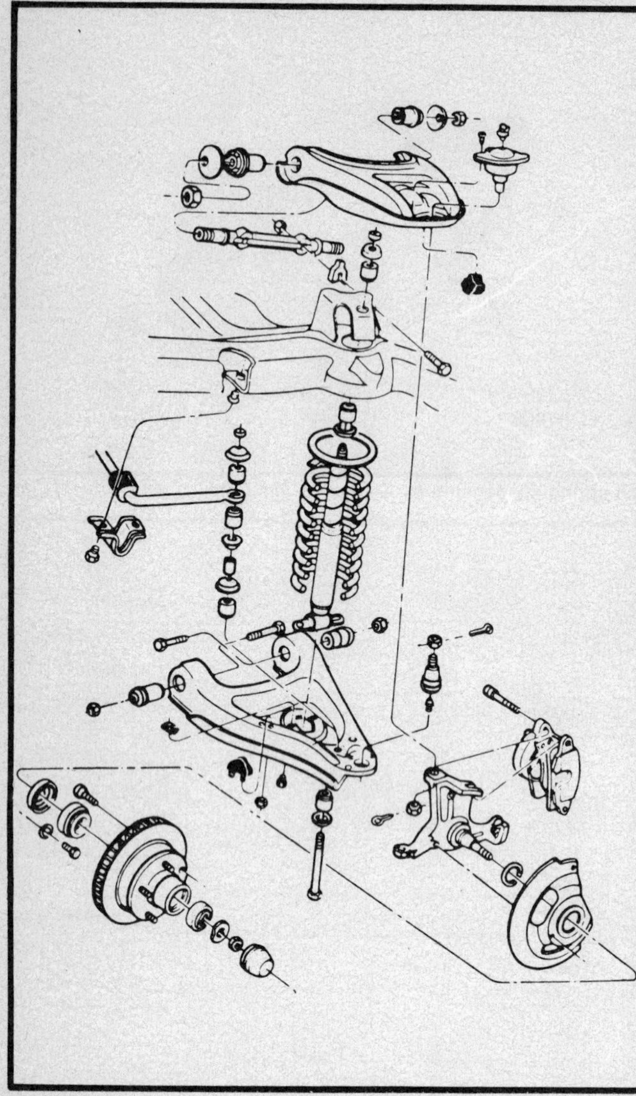

Exploded view of front suspension components, S series (2WD) and Astro van models (© General Motors Corp.)

The inner pivot bolts must be installed with the bolt heads to the front (on the front bushing) and to the rear (on the rear bushing).

2. Install alignment shims in their original position between the pivot shaft and frame on their respective bolts. Torque nuts to 45 ft. lbs

3. Remove the temporary support from the hub assembly, then connect ball joint to steering knuckle as previously outlined.

4. Install wheel, then check wheel alignment and adjust if necessary.

LOWER CONTROL ARM

Removal

S-SERIES AND ASTRO VANS

1. Remove coil spring as described earlier in this section.
2. Remove the lower ball joint stud as previously outlined.
3. After stud breaks loose, hold up on lower control arm. Remove control arm.
4. Guide lower control arm out of opening in splash shield with a putty knife or similar tool.

Installation

1. Install lower ball joint stud into knuckle. Install nut as previously outlined.
2. Install spring.
3. Check front alignment. Reset as required.

STABILIZER BAR

Removal and Installation

S-SERIES AND ASTRO VANS

1. Raise the vehicle and support safely.
2. Disconnect each side of stabilizer linkage by removing nut from link bolt, pull bolt from linkage and remove retainers, grommets and spacer.
3. Remove bracket to frame or body bolts and remove stabilizer shaft, rubber bushings and brackets.
4. To replace, reverse sequence of operations, being sure to install with the identification forming on the right side of the vehicle. The rubber bushings should be positioned squarely in the brackets with the slit in the bushings facing the front of car. Torque stabilizer link nut to 13 ft. lbs and bracket bolts to 24 ft. lbs

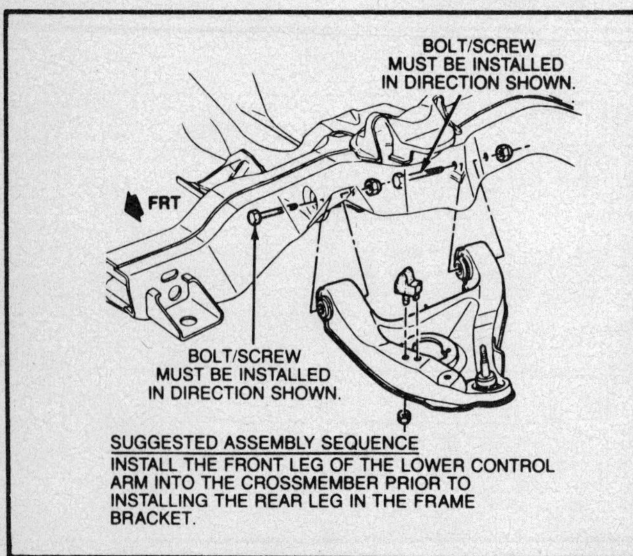
BOLT/SCREW MUST BE INSTALLED IN DIRECTION SHOWN.
FRT
BOLT/SCREW MUST BE INSTALLED IN DIRECTION SHOWN.
SUGGESTED ASSEMBLY SEQUENCE
INSTALL THE FRONT LEG OF THE LOWER CONTROL ARM INTO THE CROSSMEMBER PRIOR TO INSTALLING THE REAR LEG IN THE FRAME BRACKET.

Lower control arm assembly on S–series

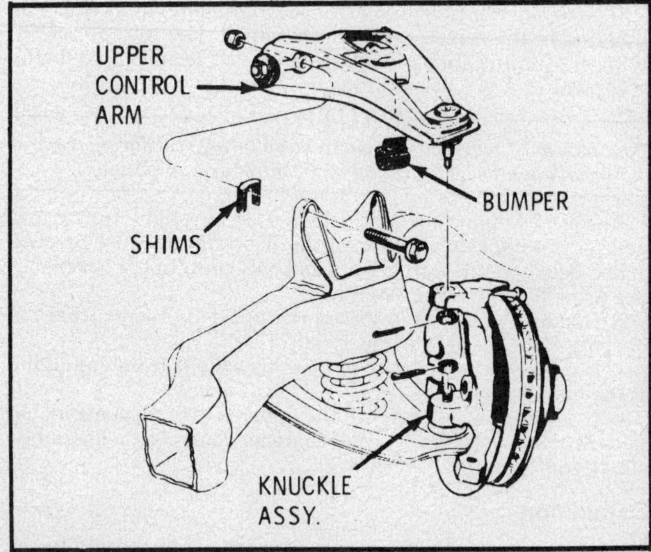
UPPER CONTROL ARM
BUMPER
SHIMS
KNUCKLE ASSY.

Upper control arm assembly on S–series

TORSION BAR

Removal and Installation

S–SERIES 4WD

1. Raise the vehicle and support safely.
2. Remove torsion bar adjusting screw.
3. Remove support retainer attaching nuts and bolts.
4. Slide torsion bar forward in lower control arm until torsion bar clears support. Pull down on bar and remove from control arm.
5. Installation is the reverse of removal.

NOTE: Count the number of turns when removing the torsion bar for easy reinstallation. Apply lubricant to top of adjusting arm and adjusting bolt for easy reinstallation. Also apply lubricant to hex ends of torsion bar.

BALL JOINT

Removal and Installation

UPPER

1. Place jack under lower control arm, at coil spring and raise vehicle.
2. Remove tire, wheel and drum or rotor assembly.
3. Remove upper ball stud nut and break the stud taper from the steering knuckle by rapping sides of knuckle flats at stud. Separate stud from knuckle.

NOTE: Support the knuckle assembly to prevent weight of the assembly from damaging the brake hose.

4. Remove rivets and bolt in new ball joint. Rivets can be chiseled off, ground off or drilled out.

CAUTION

Use special hardened bolts only when installing joint (furnished with joint).

5. Reverse remaining removal steps to complete installation.

LOWER

1. Jack vehicle at lower control arm spring seat and remove tire, wheel and drum or rotor assembly. Support with jack stands under frame, keeping the jack under the spring seat.
2. Remove ball stud nut at knuckle, use stud jack or rap stud loose from knuckle.
3. Press out ball joint. Press new ball joint into arm. Make sure ball joint assembly is fully seated and square with arm. Check inner shaft bushings.
4. Reverse remaining removal steps to complete installation.

WHEEL BEARINGS

Removal, Packing, Installation

WITH LOCKING HUBS

NOTE: This procedure requires snapring pliers and a special hub nut wrench and does not apply to S/T–series trucks. The 4WD S/T series trucks have front sealed wheel bearings, which are pre-adjusted and require no lubrication.

1. Remove the wheel and tire.
2. For $^1/_2$ and $^3/_4$ ton trucks with lock front hubs: lock the hubs. Remove the outer retaining plate Allen head bolts and take off the plate, O-ring and knob. Take out the large snapring inside the hub and remove the outer clutch retaining ring and actuating cam body. This is a lot easier with snapring pliers. Relieve pressure on the axle shaft snapring and remove it. Take out the axle shaft sleeve and clutch ring assembly and the inner clutch ring and bushing assembly. Remove the spring and retainer plate.
3. If the vehicle doesn't have locking front hubs, remove the hub cap and snapring. Next, remove the drive gear and pressure spring. To prevent the spring from popping out, place a hand over the drive gear and use a screwdriver to pry the gear out. Remove the spring.
4. Remove the wheel bearing outer lock nut, lock ring and wheel bearing inner adjusting nut. A special wrench is required.
5. Remove the brake disc assembly and outer wheel bearing. Remove the spring retainer plate if you don't have locking hubs.
6. Remove the oil seal and inner bearing cone from the hub using a brass drift and hammer. Discard the oil seal. Use the drift to remove the inner and outer bearing cups.

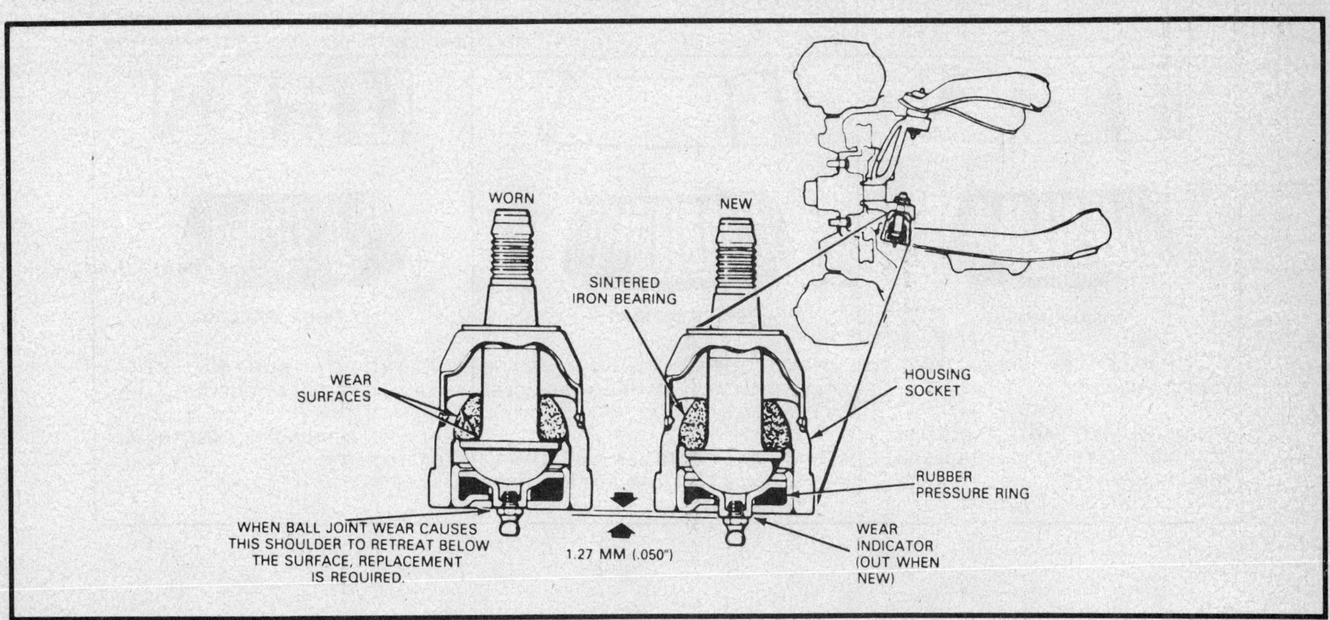

Ball joint wear indicators (© General Motors Corp.)

FRONT WHEEL BEARING DIAGNOSIS

CONSIDER THE FOLLOWING FACTORS WHEN DIAGNOSING BEARING CONDITION:

1. GENERAL CONDITION OF ALL PARTS DURING DISASSEMBLY AND INSPECTION.
2. CLASSIFY THE FAILURE WITH THE AID OF THE ILLUSTRATIONS.
3. DETERMINE THE CAUSE.
4. MAKE ALL REPAIRS FOLLOWING RECOMMENDED PROCEDURES.

GOOD BEARING

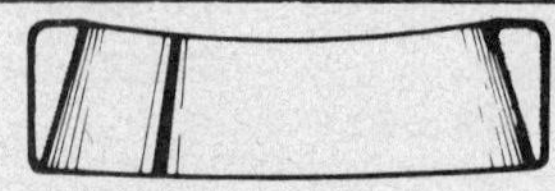

BENT CAGE

CAGE DAMAGE DUE TO IMPROPER HANDLING OR TOOL USAGE.

REPLACE BEARING.

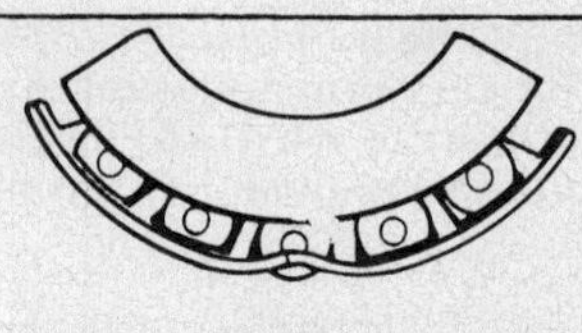

BENT CAGE

CAGE DAMAGE DUE TO IMPROPER HANDLING OR TOOL USAGE.

REPLACE BEARING.

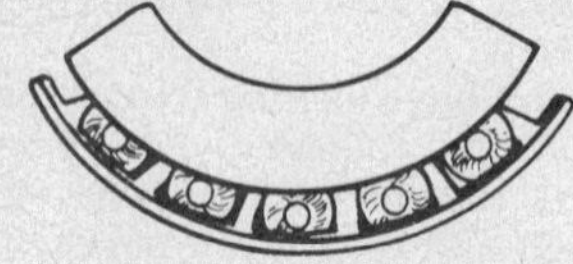

GALLING

METAL SMEARS ON ROLLER ENDS DUE TO OVERHEAT, LUBRICANT FAILURE OR OVERLOAD.

REPLACE BEARING – CHECK SEALS AND CHECK FOR PROPER LUBRICATION.

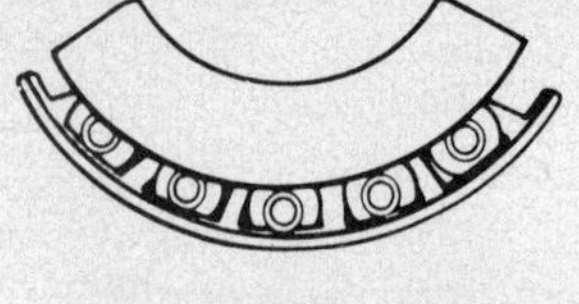
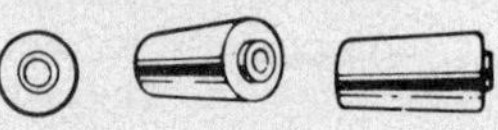

ABRASIVE STEP WEAR

PATTERN ON ROLLER ENDS CAUSED BY FINE ABRASIVES.

CLEAN ALL PARTS AND HOUSINGS, CHECK SEALS AND BEARINGS AND REPLACE IF LEAKING, ROUGH OR NOISY.

ETCHING

BEARING SURFACES APPEAR GRAY OR GRAYISH BLACK IN COLOR WITH RELATED ETCHING AWAY OF MATERIAL USUALLY AT ROLLER SPACING.

REPLACE BEARINGS – CHECK SEALS AND CHECK FOR PROPER LUBRICATION.

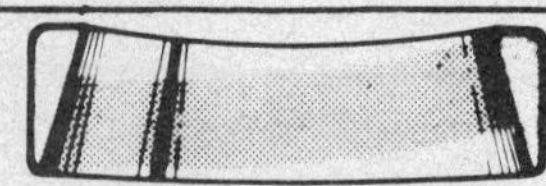

MISALIGNMENT

OUTER RACE MISALIGNMENT DUE TO FOREIGN OBJECT.

CLEAN RELATED PARTS AND REPLACE BEARING. MAKE SURE RACES ARE PROPERLY SEATED.

INDENTATIONS

SURFACE DEPRESSIONS ON RACE AND ROLLERS CAUSED BY HARD PARTICLES OF FOREIGN MATERIAL.

CLEAN ALL PARTS AND HOUSINGS, CHECK SEALS AND REPLACE BEARINGS IF ROUGH OR NOISY.

FATIGUE SPALLING

FLAKING OF SURFACE METAL RESULTING FROM FATIGUE.

REPLACE BEARING – CLEAN ALL RELATED PARTS.

FRONT WHEEL BEARING DIAGNOSIS

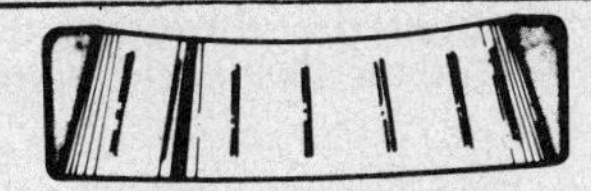

BRINELLING

SURFACE INDENTATIONS IN RACEWAY CAUSED BY ROLLERS EITHER UNDER IMPACT LOADING OR VIBRATION WHILE THE BEARING IS NOT ROTATING.

REPLACE BEARING IF ROUGH OR NOISY.

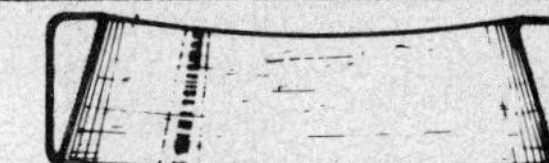

CAGE WEAR

WEAR AROUND OUTSIDE DIAMETER OF CAGE AND ROLLER POCKETS CAUSED BY ABRASIVE MATERIAL AND INEFFICIENT LUBRICATION. CHECK SEALS AND REPLACE BEARINGS.

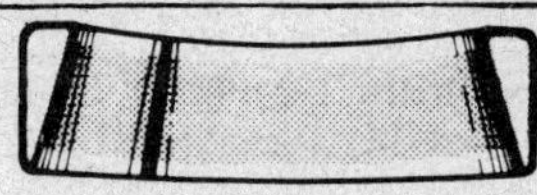

ABRASIVE ROLLER WEAR

PATTERN ON RACES AND ROLLERS CAUSED BY FINE ABRASIVES.

CLEAN ALL PARTS AND HOUSINGS, CHECK SEALS AND BEARINGS AND REPLACE IF LEAKING, ROUGH OR NOISY.

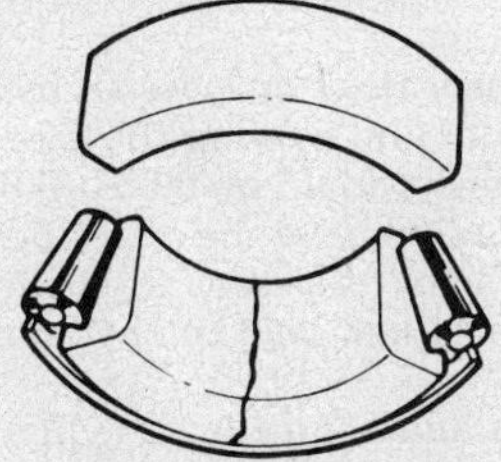

CRACKED INNER RACE

RACE CRACKED DUE TO IMPROPER FIT, COCKING, OR POOR BEARING SEATS.

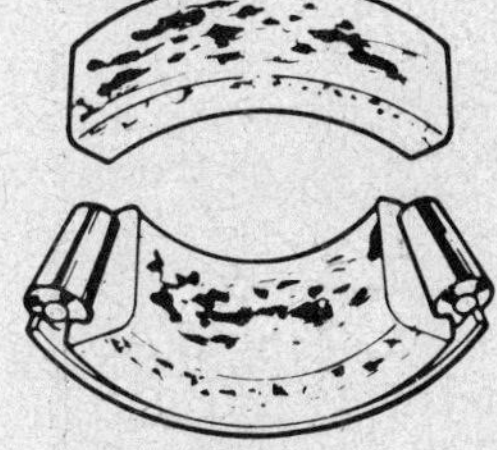

SMEARS

SMEARING OF METAL DUE TO SLIPPAGE, SLIPPAGE CAN BE CAUSED BY POOR FITS, LUBRICATION, OVERHEATING, OVERLOADS OR HANDLING DAMAGE.

REPLACE BEARINGS, CLEAN RELATED PARTS AND CHECK FOR PROPER FIT AND LUBRICATION.

REPLACE SHAFT IF DAMAGED.

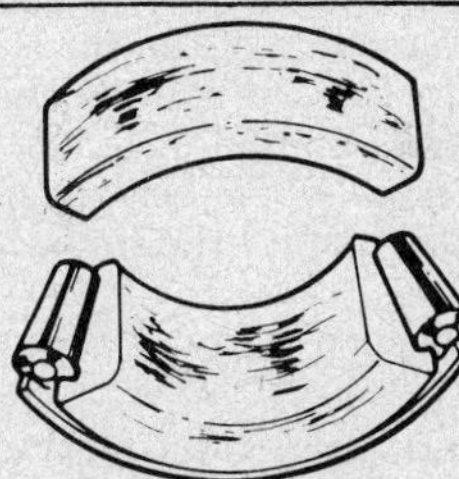

FRETTAGE

CORROSION SET UP BY SMALL RELATIVE MOVEMENT OF PARTS WITH NO LUBRICATION.

REPLACE BEARING. CLEAN RELATED PARTS. CHECK SEALS AND CHECK FOR PROPER LUBRICATION.

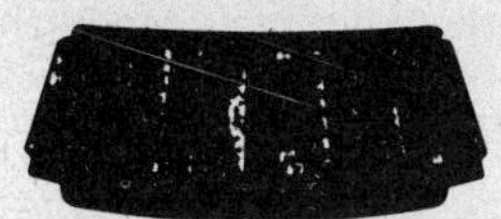

HEAT DISCOLORATION

HEAT DISCOLORATION CAN RANGE FROM FAINT YELLOW TO DARK BLUE RESULTING FROM OVERLOAD OR INCORRECT LUBRICANT.

EXCESSIVE HEAT CAN CAUSE SOFTENING OF RACES OR ROLLERS.

TO CHECK FOR LOSS OF TEMPER ON RACES OR ROLLERS A SIMPLE FILE TEST MAY BE MADE. A FILE DRAWN OVER A TEMPERED PART WILL GRAB AND CUT META, WHEREAS, A FILE DRAWN OVER A HARD PART WILL GLIDE READILY WITH NO METAL CUTTING.

REPLACE BEARINGS IF OVER HEATING DAMAGE IS INDICATED. CHECK SEALS AND OTHER PARTS.

STAIN DISCOLORATION

DISCOLORATION CAN RANGE FROM LIGHT BROWN TO BLACK CAUSED BY INCORRECT LUBRICANT OR MOISTURE.

RE-USE BEARINGS IF STAINS CAN BE REMOVED BY LIGHT POLISHING OR IF NO EVIDENCE OF OVERHEATING IS OBSERVED.

CHECK SEALS AND RELATED PARTS FOR DAMAGE.

7. Check the condition of the spindle bearing. Unbolt the spindle and tap it with a soft hammer to break it loose. Remove the spindle and check the condition of the thrust washer, replacing it if worn. Now you can remove the oil seal and spindle roller bearing.

NOTE: The spindle bearings must be greased each time the wheel bearings are serviced.

8. Clean all parts in solvent, dry and check for wear or damage.
9. Pack both wheel bearings (and the spindle bearing) using wheel bearing grease. Place a healthy glob of grease in the palm of one hand and force the edge of the bearing into it so that grease fills the bearing. Do this until the whole bearing is packed. Grease packing tools are available to make this job easier.
10. To reassemble the spindle: drive the repacked bearing into the spindle and install the grease seal onto the slinger with the lip toward the spindle. It would be best to replace the axle shaft slinger when the spindle seal is replaced.

If you are using the improved seals, fill the seal end of the spindle with grease. If not, apply grease only to the lip of the seal. Install the thrust washer over the axle shaft. On late 1982 models, the chamfered side of the thrust washer should be toward the slinger. Replace the spindle and torque the nuts to 33 ft. lbs for 1980 models and 65 ft. lbs for 1981 and later.

11. To reassemble the wheel bearings: drive the outer bearing cup into the hub, replace the inner bearing cup and insert the repacked bearing.
12. Install the disc or drum and outer wheel bearing to the spindle.
13. Adjust the bearings by rotating the hub and torquing the inner adjusting nut to 50 ft. lbs, then loosening it and retorquing to 35 ft. lbs Next, back the nut off $^3/_8$ turn or less. Turn the nut to the nearest hole in the lockwasher. Install the outer locknut and torque to a minimum of 80 ft. lbs for 1980, 160–205 ft. lbs for 1981 and later $^1/_2$ and $^3/_4$ ton and 65 ft. lbs on 1 ton vehicles. There should be 0.001–0.010 in. bearing end play.This can be measured with a dial indicator.
14. Replace the brake components.
15. Lubricate the locking hub components with high temperature grease. Lubrication must be applied to prevent component failure. For $^1/_2$ ton and 1980 and later $^3/_4$ and 1 ton models, install the spring retainer plate with the flange side facing the bearing outer cup. Install the pressure spring with the large end against the spring retaining plate. The spring is an interference fit; when seated, its end extends past the spindle nuts by approximately $^7/_8$ in. Place the inner clutch ring and bushing assembly into the axle shaft sleeve and clutch ring assembly and install that as an assembly onto the axle shaft. Press in on this assembly and install the axle shaft ring.

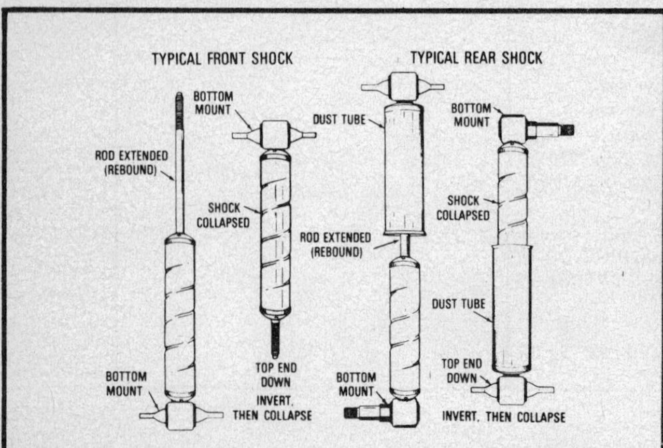

Purging air from shock absorbers (© General Motors Corp.)

Removal & Installation

S/T-SERIES TRUCKS

NOTE: The S/T series trucks have sealed front wheel bearings which are pre-adjusted and require no lubrication. They are replaced as an assembly, should it be required.

1. Raise the front of the vehicle and support safely. Remove the wheel assembly, caliper and rotor.
2. Remove the cotter pin, the locking cap, washer and the axle nut from the axle end.
3. Remove the hub and bearing assembly. It may be necessary to employ a puller to remove the hub from the axle.
4. To install the hub and bearing, reverse the removal procedure. The axle nut should be torqued to 174 ft. lbs

NOTE: Do not back off the axle nut to install the new cotter pin.

DRUM OR ROTOR TYPE ADJUSTABLE WHEEL BEARINGS

Adjustment

1. Check the bearing for a tight or loose fit by gripping the wheel at the top and bottom and moving the wheel in and out on the spindle. The end play should be 0.001–0.005 in..
2. If adjustment is needed, remove the cotter pin and tighten the spindle nut to 12 ft. lbs to fully seat the bearings.
3. Loosen the nut until either hole in the spindle lines up with the slot in the nut.
4. Install the cotter pin and bend the ends against the nut. The end play should be between 0.001 and 0.005 in..
5. Install the dust cover and wheel cover, if equipped.

Shock Absorbers

Shock absorbers are used to dampen the rebound of the two types of springs used: coil and leaf.

LEAF TYPE

The top of the shock absorbers are mounted to the frame and the bottom is usually mounted to the U bolt bracket at the axle area or to a bracket welded to the axle housing.

COIL SPRING

FRONT

The shock absorbers are usually attached to the lower control arm at the bottom and to the frame rail at the top. On some models, the shock absorbers may be mounted through the coil spring.

REAR

The top of the shock absorber is mounted to the body or to a crossmember with the bottom mounted to a stud or bracket welded or mounted on the axle housing.

Removal and Replacement

Removal and replacement is accomplished by the removing of the attaching retainers at the top and bottom of the shock absorber and withdrawing the shock. Replacement is the reverse of removal. Air should be purged from the shock absorber by extending it in the upright position and then inverting and collapsing the shock.

Front Drive Axle

The front axle is a hypoid type gear unit equipped with either ball joint or kingpin steering knuckles and is powered through a transfer case which may be one of two types. A full-time four wheel drive unit is used mainly with V8 engines and automatic transmission. The other type is a conventional part-time four wheel drive system.

A yoke and a trunnion universal joint, as part of the drive axle, allows a continuous power flow to each wheel, regardless of the turning angle.

Free-wheeling hubs are available on the front wheels, except those vehicles equipped with the full time four wheel drive transfer case.

For repairs to the hypoid gear unit, refer to the Unit Repair section.

LEAF SPRING

Removal

1. Raise the vehicle and support safely.
2. Position an adjustable jack under the front axle.
3. Situate the axle so that all tension is removed from the spring.
4. Remove shackle retaining bolt (upper).
5. Remove the front eye bolt from the spring.
6. Remove the U-bolt nuts and remove the spring, lower plate and spring pads.
7. Remove the spring-to-shackle bolt and remove the bushings and shackle.

Installation

1. Install the shackle bushings in the spring and attach the shackle. Do not tighten bolt.
2. Place the upper cushion on the spring.
3. Position the front of the spring in its mounted position at the frame and install the bolt. Do not tighten bolt.
4. Position the shackle bushings in the frame and attach the rear shackle. Do not tighten bolt.
5. Install the lower spring pad.
6. Install the spring retainer plate. Tighten bolts.
7. Tighten front and rear spring eye and shackle bolts.
8. Lower the vehicle. Recheck the tightness of the bolts and nuts.

AUTOMATIC LOCKING HUBS

1981 AND LATER

The automatic locking hub engages or disengages to lock the front axle shaft to the hub of the front wheel. Engagement occurs whenever the vehicle is operated in four-wheel drive. Disengagement occurs whenever two-wheel drive has been selected and the vehicle is moved rearward. Disengagement will not occur when the vehicle is moved rearward if four-wheel drive is selected and the hub has already been engaged.

The outer clutch housing is splined to the wheel. The hub sleeve is splined to the front axle shaft. The clutch gear is splined to the hub sleeve. Engagement occurs when the clutch gear is moved on the splines of the hub sleeve to engage the internal teeth of the outer clutch housing.

The cam surface of the steel inner cage forces the cam follower and clutch gear to move outward toward the cover and into engagement with the clutch teeth of the outer clutch housing. A lug on the inside of the drag sleeve retainer washer keys the washer to the axle and two lock nuts retain this washer in position on the axle. Cutouts in the drag sleeve engage the four tabs on the drag sleeve retainer washer to hold the drag sleeve in a fixed position with respect to the axle shaft. The one way clutch spring (called a brake band) is positioned over the serrated portion of the drag sleeve.

Engagement is accomplished (when four-wheel drive is selected) by the movement of the drag sleeve, causing one of the tangs of the brake band to engage the steel outer cage and rotate the cage which will cause the cam ramp to move the clutch gear into mesh with the outer clutch housing. One of the tangs of the brake band is used for engagement when the vehicle is moving forward. The other tang is used to engage reverse when the vehicle is moving rearward.

Disengagement is accomplished (when two-wheel drive has been selected) by the reverse movement of the wheel causing the clutch gear, hub sleeve and cam follower to rotate. The cam follower moves against the lugs of the plastic outer cage, causing the cage to rotate and move to the disengaged condition. The release spring then moves the clutch gear out of mesh with the outer clutch housing to disengage the wheel from the axle shaft.

Preliminary Checking

Before disassembling a unit for complaint of abnormal noise, read the following:

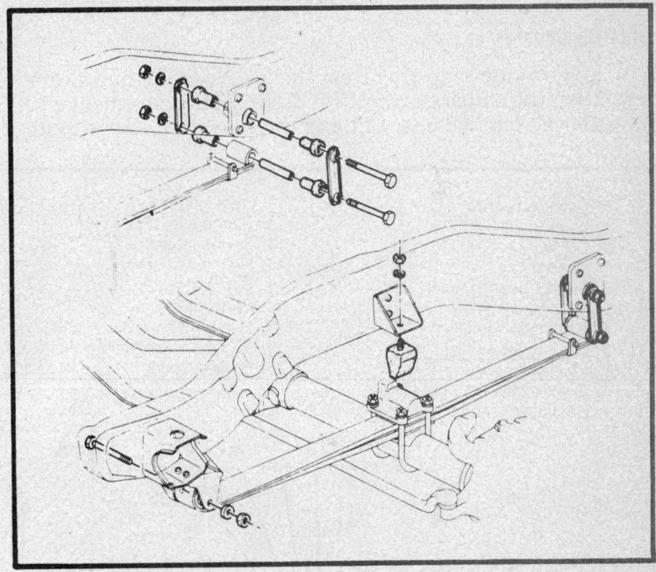

Spring assembly—front drive axle (© General Motors Corp.)

TIGHTENING SEQUENCE

1. INSTALL ALL FOUR NUTS TO UNIFORM ENGAGEMENT ON U-BOLTS TO RETAIN AND POSITION ANCHOR POSITION (PERPENDICULAR TO PLATE IN DESIGN AXIS OF U-BOLTS).
2. TORQUE NUTS IN POSITIONS 1 AND 3 TO 10-25 FT. LBS.
3. TORQUE ALL NUTS TO FULL TORQUE IN FOLLOWING SEQUENCE: 2-4-1-3

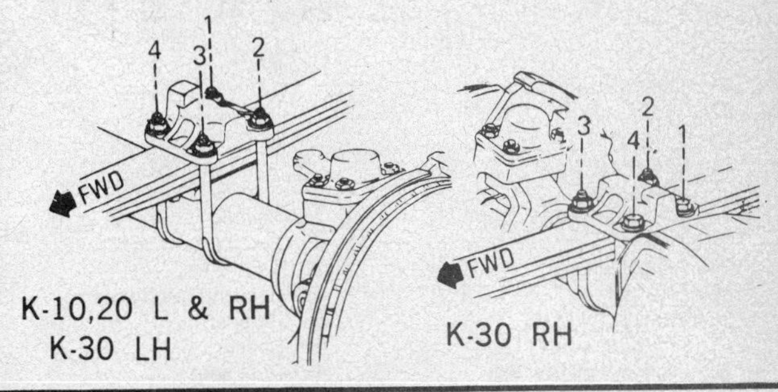

U-bolt tightening sequence—front drive axle (© General Motors Corp.)

1. To obtain all-wheel drive, the transfer case lever must be placed in (4L) or (4H), at which time the hub locks will automatically engage.

2. To unlock (free wheel) the hubs, shift the transfer case lever to (2H), then slowly reverse vehicle direction approximately ten feet.

3. Incomplete shift from 2WD to 4WD, or disengagement of only one hub lock may cause an abnormal sound from the front axle. Shift to 4WD to stop the noise, then unlock the hubs as described previously.

Removal Of Hub From Wheel

1. Remove the retaining screws which hold the cover to the outer clutch housing.

2. Remove the cover, seal, seal bridge and the bearing components.

3. Using needle nose pliers, compress the retaining wire ring and pull the remaining components from the wheel.

Disassembly

1. Remove the snap-ring from the groove of the hub sleeve.

2. Turn the clutch gear until it drops into engagement with the outer clutch housing. Lift and cock the drag sleeve to unlock the tangs of the brake band from the window of the inner cage and remove the drag sleeve and brake assembly.

CAUTION

Do not remove the brake band from the drag sleeve. To do so would change the spring tension of the brake band by over expanding the coils, effecting the operation of the hub.

3. Remove the snap-ring from the groove in the outer clutch housing.

4. Use a pointed probe to pry the plastic outer cage free of the inner cage while the inner cage is being removed.

5. Pry the plastic outer cage tabs free from the groove in the outer clutch housing and remove the outer cage.

6. Remove the clutch sleeve and attached components from the outer clutch housing.

7. Compress the return spring and hold the spring in the compressed position with fabricated clamps. Position the entire assembly in a bench vise so that the vise holds both ends of the clutch sleeve. Remove the retaining ring.

8. Slowly remove the clamps with the unit still in the vise. Slowly open the vise jaws to permit the release of the return spring tension, in a controlled manner. Remove the retainer seat, spring and spring support washers from the hub sleeve.

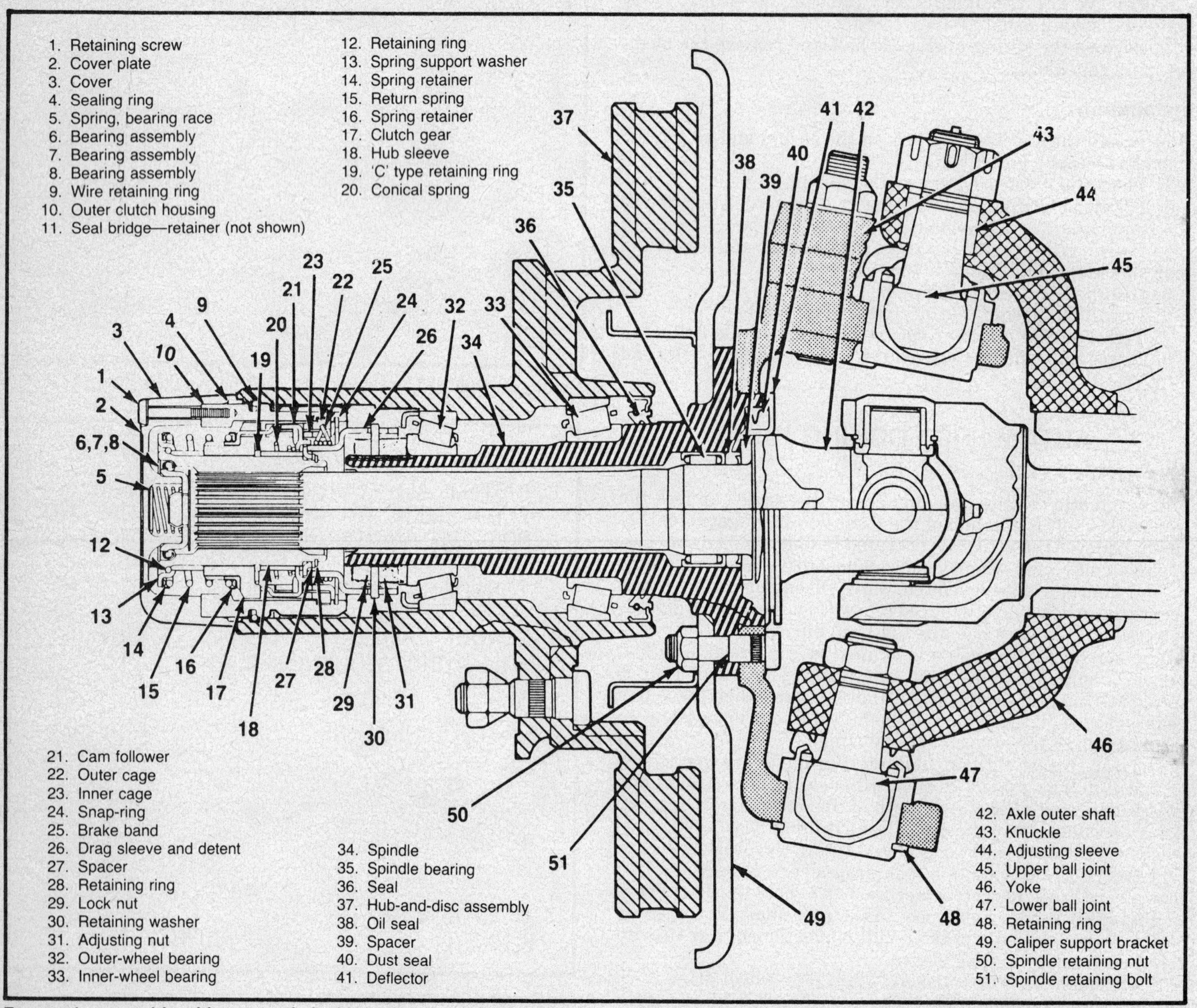

Front axle assembly with automatic locking hubs and ball joints—1981–82 K series (© General Motors Corp.)

9. Remove the "C" type retaining ring from the clutch sleeve.

NOTE: It is necessary to position the sleeve assembly so that the C-ring ends are aligned with the legs of the cam follower, allowing removal between the two legs.

10. Remove the conical spring from between the cam follower and the clutch gear.
11. Separate the cam follower from the clutch gear.

Assembly

1. Snap the tangs of the cam follower over the flats of the clutch gear.
2. Compress the conical spring and slide it into position with the large diameter of the spring located against the clutch gear.
3. Position the clutch gear assembly over the splines of the hub sleeve. The teeth of the cam follower should be located at the end of the hub sleeve which has no splines. The clutch gear and spring should slide freely over the splines of the hub sleeve.
4. Assemble the "C" shaped retainer ring in the groove of the hub sleeve.
5. Install the spring retainer over each end of the return spring. Place one end of the spring against the shoulder of the clutch gear.

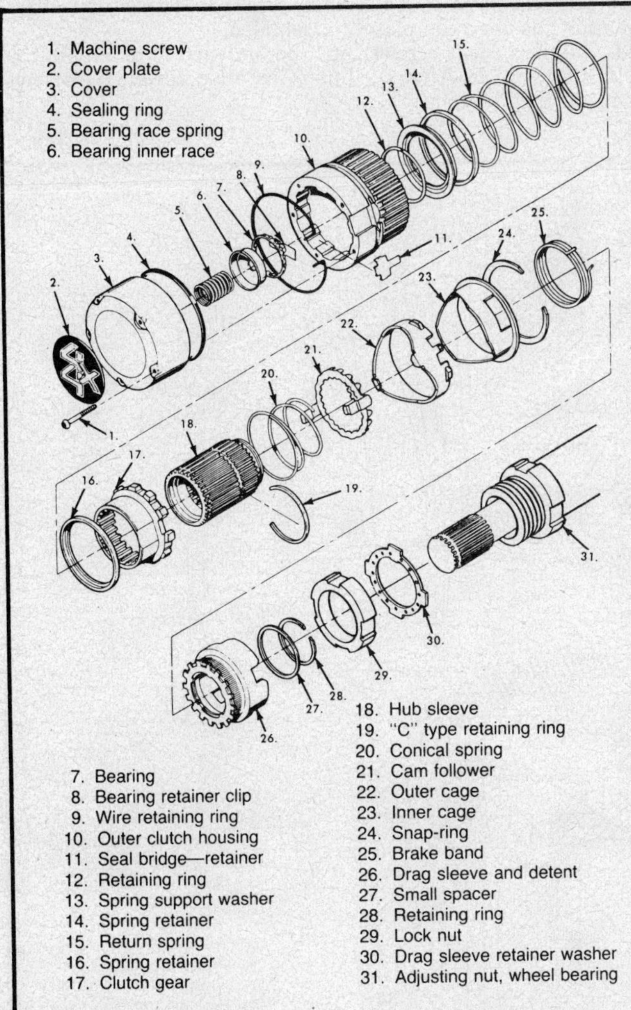

Exploded view of automatic locking hubs, front wheel drive (© General Motors Corp.)

6. Position the spring support washer against the retainer on the end of the spring. Compress the return spring and assemble the retainer ring in the groove of the hub sleeve. Two "C" shaped clamps may be used to retain the return spring while the retainer ring is being assembled.
7. Install the pre-assembled components into the outer housing. The cam follower should be positioned with the two legs directly outboard.
8. Screw three cover screws into three holes of the outer clutch housing.

NOTE: These three screws will support the component to permit the clutch hub to drop down so that the tangs of the brake band can be assembled.

9. Install the plastic outer cage into the outer clutch housing with the ramps facing towards the cam follower. The small external tabs of the plastic cage should be located in the wide groove of the outer clutch housing.
10. Assemble the steel inner cage into the outer cage, aligning the tab of the outer cage with the "window" of the inner cage.
11. Assemble the retaining ring into the groove of the outer clutch housing above the outer cage.
12. Assemble the tangs of the brake band with one tang on each side of the lug on the outer cage, which is located in the "window" of the steel inner cage.

NOTE: The brake band and the drag sleeve are serviced as an assembly.

13. Remove the three screws and rest the end of the hub sleeve on a suitable support. Assemble the washer and snapring above the drag sleeve.
14. As the hub is assembled to the vehicle, assemble the wire retaining ring in the groove in the unsplined end of the outer clutch housing.

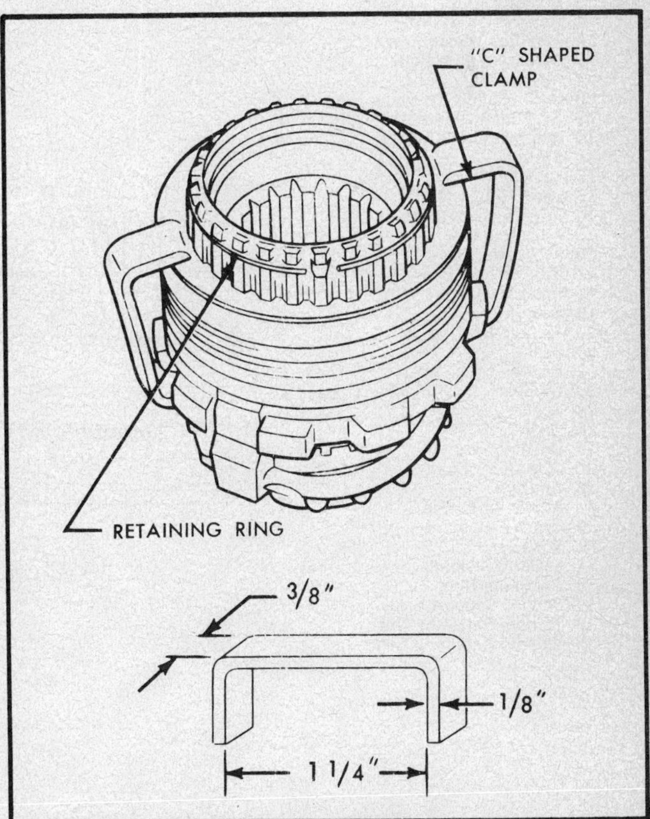

Fabricated "C" shaped clamps (© General Motors Corp.)

1. Retaining plate bolts
2. Washer
3. Hub ring retaining knob
4. Actuator knob O-ring
5. Actuator knob
6. O-ring
7. Internal snap-ring
8. Outer clutch retaining ring
9. Actuating cam body
10. Axle shaft snap-ring
11. Axle shaft sleeve and ring
12. Inner clutch ring
13. Pressure spring
14. Spring retainer plate

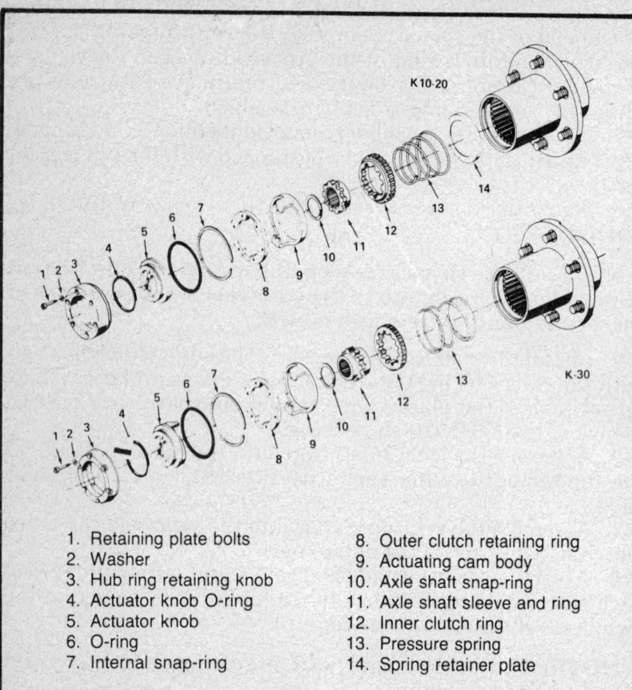

Exploded view of free-wheeling hub (© General Motors Corp.)

NOTE: The tangs of the retainer ring should point away from the splined end of the clutch housing.

15. Hold the tangs of the wire retainer together and assemble the two bent down tabs of the seal bridge over the tangs. The seal bridge will hold the retainer ring in a clamped condition in the groove of the outer clutch housing. Assemble the O-ring in the groove of the outer clutch housing and over the seal bridge.
16. Assemble the bearing over the inner race and lubricate.

NOTE: The steel balls should be visible when the bearing is properly installed.

17. Snap the bearing retainer clip into the hole in the outer race.
18. Assemble the bearing and retainer assembly in the end of the hub sleeve. Assemble the sealing ring over the outer clutch housing.
19. Assemble the bearing race spring into the bore in the cover.
20. Assemble the cover and spring assembly. Align the hole in the cover to the holes in the outer clutch housing and assemble the five screws.
21. Place the O-ring over the seal bridge to prevent it from jumping out of position during the handling prior to the hub bearing being installed in the vehicle.

NOTE: This O-ring may be left on, but is not necessary.

22. The hub sleeve and attached parts should turn freely after the unit has been completely assembled.
23. The five cover screws must be loosened to assemble the hub to the vehicle. After the hub is installed, torque the screws to 40–50 inch lbs.

1 Retaining Plate
2 O-Ring
3 Actuator Knob
4 Retaining Plate Bolt
5 Axle Shaft Snap Ring
6 Actuating Cam Body
7 Internal Snap Ring
8 Outer Clutch Retaining Ring
9 Axle Shaft Sleeve And Clutch Ring
10 Inner Clutch Ring
11 Spring
12 Lock Nut
13 Lock-Adjust. Nut
14 Pin-Adjust. Nut
15 Adjusting Nut
16 Pressure Plate
17 Outer-Wheel Bearing
18 Inner-Wheel Bearing
19 Spindle
20 Spindle Bearing
21 Seal
22 Hub-And-Disc Assy.
23 Oil Seal
24 Spacer
25 Dust Seal
26 Deflector
27 Axle Outer Shaft
28 Knuckle
29 Adjusting Sleeve
30 Upper Ball Joint
31 Yoke
32 Lower Ball Joint
33 Retaining Ring
34 Caliper Support Brkt.
35 Spindle Retaining Nut
36 Spindle Retaining Bolt

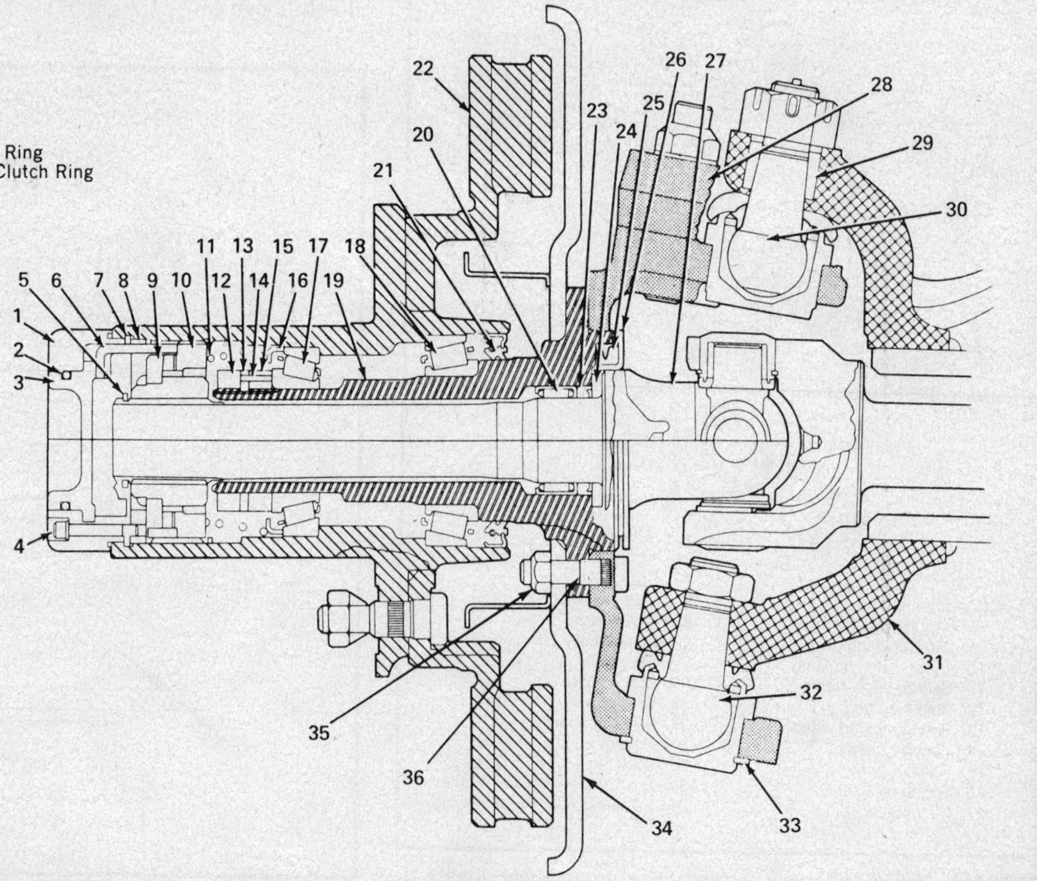

Steering knuckle/ball joint assembly w/free-wheeling hub (© General Motors Corp.)

LOCKED HUB (FULL-TIME)

Removal

K10–30, K1500–3500

1. Remove the hub cap and the snap-ring.
2. Remove the drive gear and pressure spring, if equipped.
3. Remove the wheel bearing outer lock nut, lock ring and the wheel bearing inner adjusting nut.
4. Remove the hub and disc assembly.
5. Remove the outer wheel bearing and the spring retainer plate.
6. Drive the inner bearing cone and oil seal from the hub with the use of a brass drift. Discard the oil seal.
7. Using a brass drift, remove the inner and outer bearing cups.

Installation

1. Install the outer wheel bearing cup into the wheel hub.
2. Install the inner wheel bearing cup into the wheel hub.
3. Pack the wheel bearing cone with a suitable wheel bearing grease (high melting point type).
4. Install the cone into the cup.
5. Install a new grease seal into the inboard end of the hub.
6. Lubricate the wheel bearings; install the hub and disc and the bearings on the spindle.
7. While rotating the hub and disc, torque the inner adjusting nut to 50 ft. lbs
8. Back off the inner adjusting nut.
9. While rotating the hub and disc, torque the inner adjusting nut to 35 ft. lbs
10. Again, back off the inner adjusting nut a maximum of $^3/_8$ turn.
    a. K15, K25, K10, K20 models: Assemble the adjusting nut lock by aligning the nearest hole in lock with the adjusting nut pin. Install the outer lock nut torque to 80 ft. lbs.
    b. K30, K35 models: Assemble the lockwasher and outer locknut. Torque the outer locknut to 65 ft. lbs Bend one tab of the lockwasher over the inner nut a minimum of 30 degrees. Bend one tab of the lockwasher over the outer nut a minimum of 60 degrees.

NOTE: End play for all models is 0.001–0.010 in.

11. Install the pressure spring, drive gear, snap-ring and hub cap.

FREE-WHEELING HUB—PART-TIME

CURRENT MODELS

The engagement and disengagement of free-wheeling hubs is a manual operation which must be performed at each front wheel. The transfer case control lever must be in 2-wheel drive position when locking or unlocking hubs. Both hubs must be in the fully locked or fully unlocked position. They must not be in the free-wheeling position when low all-wheeldrive is used as the additional torque output in this position can subject the rear axle to severe strain and rear axle failure may result.

Removal

K10–20, K1500–2500

1. Turn the actuator to the LOCK position.
2. Raise the vehicle on a hoist.
3. Remove the six retaining plate bolts.
4. Remove the retaining plate, actuator knob and O-ring.
5. Remove the internal snap-ring, outer clutch retaining ring and actuating cam body.
6. Remove the axle shaft snap-ring.

NOTE: It may be necessary to first relieve pressure from the axle shaft snap-ring.

7. Remove the wheel bearing outer lock nut and lock ring.
8. Remove the wheel bearing inner adjusting nut.
9. Remove the hub and disc assembly, outer wheel bearing and the spring retainer plate.
10. Drive the inner bearing cone and oil seal from the hub with a brass drift. Discard the oil seal.
11. Using a brass drift, remove the inner and outer bearing cups.

Installation

NOTE: All parts should be lubricated with an ample amount of high speed grease prior to installation.

1. Install the outer wheel bearing cup into the wheel hub.
2. Install the inner wheel bearing cup into the wheel hub.
3. Pack the wheel bearing cone with a suitable wheel bearing grease (high melting point type).
4. Install the cone into the cup.
5. Lubricate the wheel bearings; install the hub and disc and the bearings on the spindle.
6. While rotating the hub and disc, torque the inner adjusting nut to 50 ft. lbs
7. Back off the inner adjustment nut.
8. While rotating the hub and disc, torque the inner adjusting nut to 35 ft. lbs
9. Again, back off the inner adjusting nut a maximum of $^3/_8$ turn.
10. Assemble the adjusting nut lock by aligning the nearest hole in lock with the adjusting nut pin.
11. Install outer lock nut and torque to 50 ft. lbs

NOTE: Hub end play should be 0.001–0.010 in..

12. Install the spring retainer plate over the spindle nuts with the flange side facing the bearing and seat the retainer against the bearing outer cup.
13. Install the pressure spring.

NOTE: The large diameter of the spring seats against the retaining plate. When the spring is seated, it extends past the spindle nuts by approximately $^7/_8$ in..

14. Install the inner clutch ring and bushing into the axle shaft sleeve and clutch ring; install unit as an assembly onto the axle shaft.
15. While pressing in on the assembly, install the axle shaft snap-ring.

NOTE: To facilitate snap-ring installation, thread a $^7/_{16}$ × 20 bolt in the end of the axle shaft and pull outward on the axle shaft.

16. Install the actuating cam body. Cam faces outward.
17. Install the outer clutch retaining ring and the internal snap-ring.
18. Install the O-ring on the retaining plate.
19. Install the actuating knob and retaining plate.

NOTE: Actuating knob should be installed in the LOCK position. The grooves in the knob must fit into the actuator cam body.

20. Install the six cover bolts and seals. Torque bolts to 30 ft. lbs
21. Turn the actuating knob to the FREE position and check free-wheeling operation.
22. Remove vehicle from hoist.

FRONT AXLE ASSEMBLY

NOTE: This procedure does not apply to S-series trucks.

Removal

1. Disconnect the drive shaft from the front axle. Raise the

vehicle far enough to take the weight off the front springs and place the jack stands under the truck frame.

2. Disconnect the connecting rod at the steering arms.

3. Disconnect the brake hoses at the frame fittings and cover all open ends.

4. Disconnect the shock absorbers at the axle brackets.

5. Disconnect the axle vent tube clip at the differential housing.

6. Unfasten the U-bolts, raise the truck further, as necessary and roll the axle out from underneath.

Installation

1. With truck on axle stands, roll the axle under the truck. Lower the truck until axle and truck are in proper relative positions. Again support the vehicle with axle stands.

2. Attach the shock absorbers to the axle brackets. Connect the brake hoses to the frame fittings and fill and bleed the brake system.

3. Attach the steering connecting rod at the steering arms.

4. Connect the drive axle to the front differential.

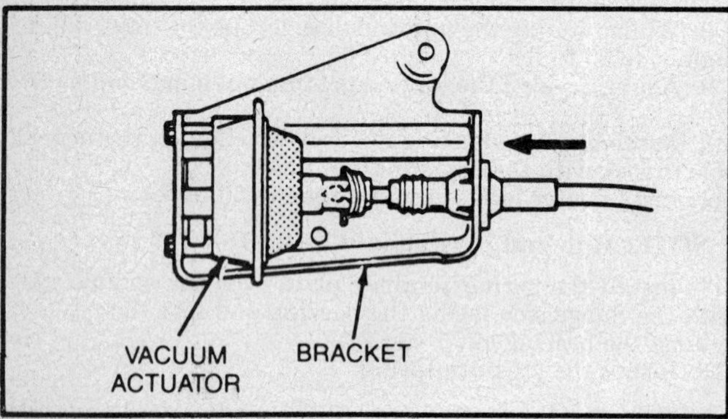

Cable–to–vacuum actuator attachment

AXLE SHAFT ASSEMBLY

Removal

1. Remove the free-wheeling hubs as outlined, if so equipped.

2. Remove the wheel bearing outer lock nut, lock ring and inner adjusting nut.

3. Remove the hub assembly from the spindle.

4. Remove the spindle retaining bolts and tap the end of the spindle with a soft faced hammer, to separate the spindle from the knuckle.

5. Remove the axle shaft and joint assembly by pulling outward on the shaft.

6. Repairs to the wheel hub assembly and to the axle universal joint can be accomplished at this time.

Installation

1. Install a new grease seal onto the slinger of the axle shaft, with the lip of the seal facing toward the spindle.

2. Install the axle shaft into the housing and engage the splines with the pinion side gears of the differential.

3. Place the bronze thrust washer on the axle shaft with the chamfered edge towards the slinger and install the spindle onto the knuckle.

4. Torque the spindle nuts to 45 ft. lbs and assemble the hub to the spindle. Torque the inner adjustment nut to 50 ft. lbs while rotating the hub. Back off the inner nut an additional $^3/_8$ of a turn maximum.

5. Assemble the lock washer and the outer lock nut to the spindle. Torque the outer lock nut to 50 ft. lbs minimum. The hub should have 0.001–0.010 in. end play.

6. If the vehicle is equipped with free-wheeling hubs, refer to the installation procedure for correct installation and if not equipped, install the hub cap assembly.

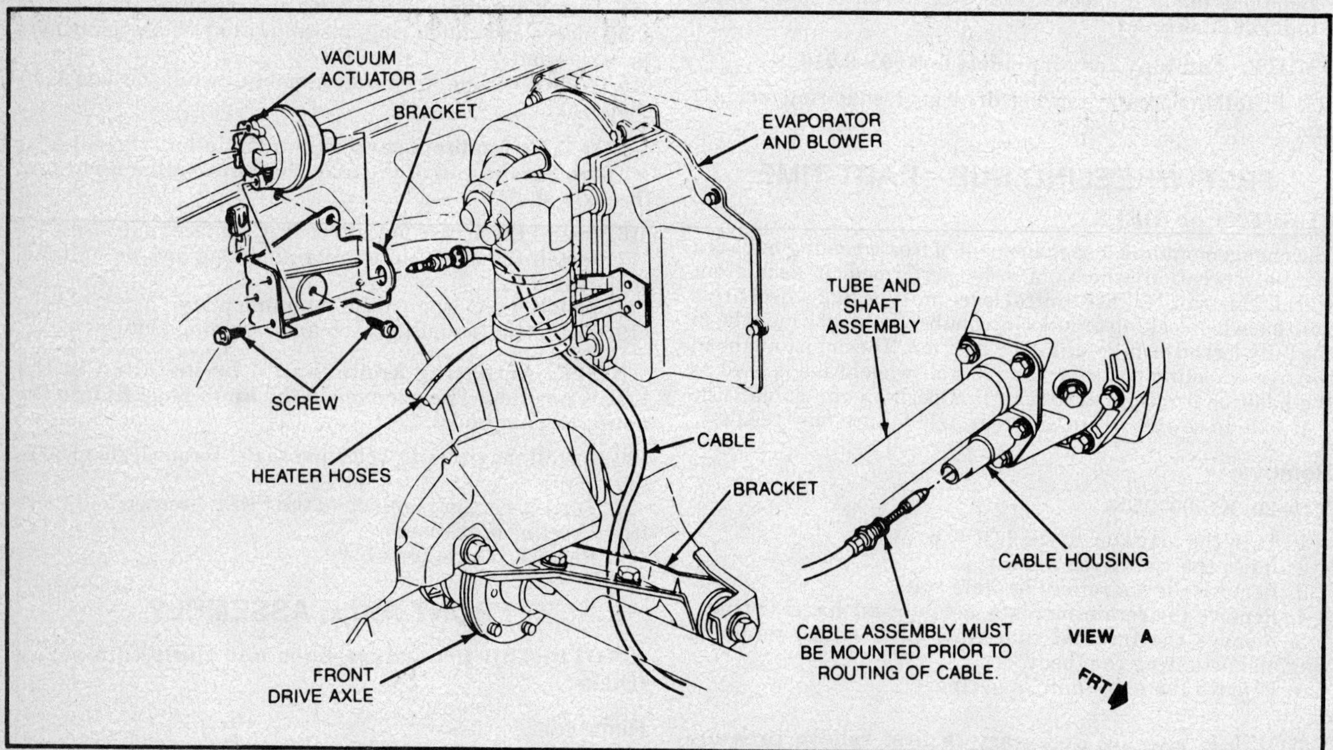

Vacuum actuator assembly

TUBE/SHAFT ASSEMBLY

Removal

S/T–Series Trucks

1. Disconnect negative battery cable.
2. Disconnect shift cable from vacuum actuator by disengaging locking spring. Then push actuator diaphragm in to release cable.
3. Unlock steering wheel at steering column so linkage is free to move.
4. Raise vehicle. If twin post hoist is used, place jack stands under frame and lower front post hoist.
5. Remove front wheels.
6. Remove engine drive belt shield.
7. Remove front axle skid plate (if equipped).
8. Place support under right hand lower control arm and disconnect right hand upper ball joint, then remove support so control arm will hang free.
9. Disconnect right hand drive axle shaft from tube assembly by removing six bolts.

   Keep axle from turning by inserting a drift through opening in top of brake caliper into corresponding vane of brake rotor.
10. Disconnect four wheel drive indicator light electrical connection from switch.
11. Remove three bolts securing cable and switch housing to carrier and pull housing away to gain access to cable locking spring. Do not unscrew cable coupling nut unless cable is being replaced.
12. Disconnect cable from shift fork shaft by lifting spring over slot in shift fork.
13. Remove two bolts securing tube bracket to frame.
14. Remove remaining two upper bolts securing tube assembly to carrier.
15. Remove tube assembly by working around drive axle. Be careful not to allow sleeve, thrust washers, connector and output shaft to fall out of carrier or be damaged when removing tube.

Installation

1. Install sleeve, thrust washers, connector and output shaft in carrier. Apply sealer #1052357, Locktite 514 or equivalent on tube to carrier surface.

   Be sure to install thrust washer. Apply grease to washer to hold it in place during assembly.
2. Install tube and shaft assembly to carrier and install bolt at one o'clock position but do not torque. Pull assembly down and install cable and switch housing and remaining four bolts. Torque all bolts to 45–60 ft. lb.
3. Install two bolts securing tube to frame and torque.
4. Check operation of four wheel drive mechanism using Tool J–33799. Insert tool into shift fork and check for rotation of axle shaft.
5. Remove tool and install shift cable switch housing by pushing cable through into fork shaft hole. Cable will automatically snap in place.
6. Connect four wheel drive indicator light electrical connection to switch.
7. Install support under right hand lower control arm to raise arm and connect upper ball joint.

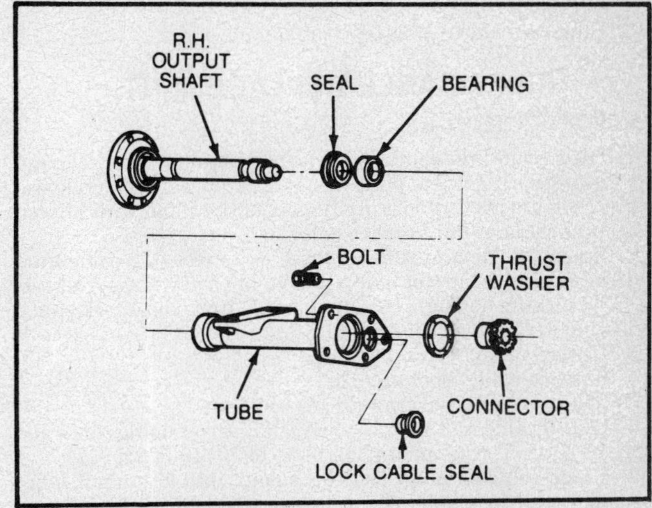

Right side output shaft and tube

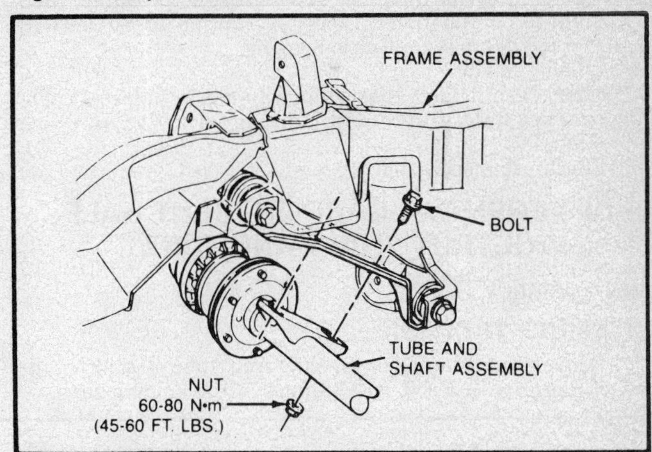

Tube–to–frame attachment

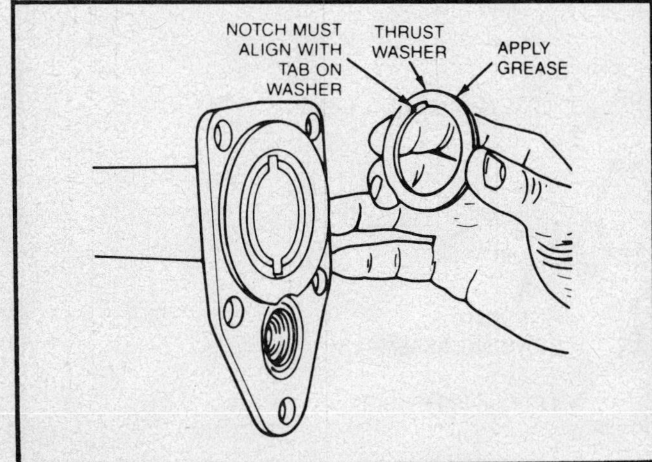

Thrust washer installation

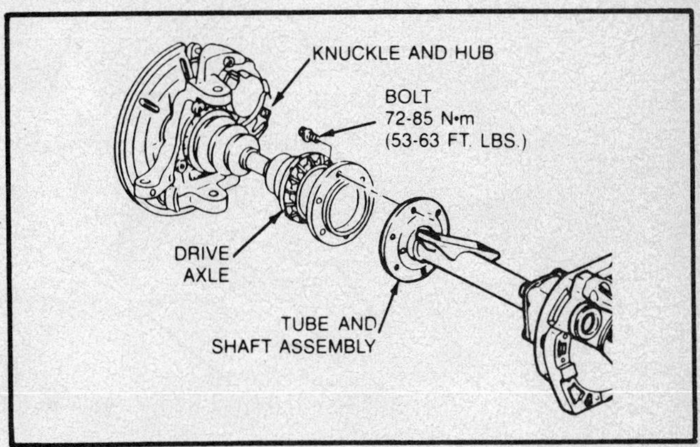

Drive axle bolts

8. Install right-hand drive axle to axle tube by installing one bolt first, then, rotate axle to install remaining five bolts. Hold axle from turning by inserting a drift through opening in top of brake caliper into corresponding vane of brake rotor. Tighten bolts to 53–63 ft. lb.
9. Install front axle skid plate, if equipped.
10. Install engine drive belt shield.
11. Install front wheels.
12. Lower vehicle.
13. Connect shift cable to vacuum actuator by pushing cable end into vacuum actuator shaft hole. Cable will snap in place automatically.
14. Connect negative battery cable.

SHIFT CABLE REPLACEMENT

S/T–SERIES TRUCKS

1. Disengage shift cable from vacuum actuator by disengaging locking spring, then, push actuator diaphragm in to release cable. Squeeze the two locking fingers of the cable with pliers, then pull cable out of bracket hole.
2. Raise vehicle and remove three bolts securing cable and switch housing to carrier and pull housing away to gain access to cable locking spring. Disconnect cable from shaft fork shaft by lifting spring over slot in shift fork.
3. Unscrew cable from housing.
4. Remove cable from vehicle.
5. Install cable observing proper routing.
6. Install cable and switch housing to carrier using three attaching bolts. Torque mounting bolts to 30–40 ft. lbs
7. Guide cable through switch housing into fork shaft hole and push cable in. Cable will automatically snap in place. Start turning coupling nut by hand, to avoid cross threading, then torque nut to 71–106 in. lbs. Do not overtorque nut as this will cause thread damage to plastic housing.
8. Lower vehicle.
9. Connect shift cable to vacuum actuator by pressing cable into bracket hole. Cable and housing will snap in place automatically.
10. Check cable operation.

DIFFERENTIAL CARRIER RIGHT HALF OUTPUT SHAFT AND TUBE

Disassembly

S/T–SERIES TRUCKS

1. Remove right-hand output shaft from tube by striking inside of flange with a soft face hammer while holding tube.
2. Remove output shaft tube seal by prying out of tube.
3. Remove output shaft tube bearing using J–29369–2.
4. Remove differential shift cable housing seal by driving out with a punch or similar tool.

Assembly

1. Install output shaft tube bearing using tool J–33844. Tool must be flush with tube when bearing is correctly installed.
2. Install output shaft tube seal using tool J–33893. Flange of seal must be flush with tube outer surface when seal is installed.
3. Install output shaft into tube and seat by striking flange with a soft face hammer.
4. Install differential shift cable housing seal using J–33799.

STEERING KNUCKLE

Removal

S–SERIES

1. Raise front of vehicle and support with floor stands under front lift points. Remove wheel.

Spring tension is needed to assist in breaking ball joint studs loose from steering knuckle. Do not place stands under lower control arm.

2. Remove caliper.
3. Remove hub and rotor assembly.
4. Remove the three bolts attaching shield to knuckle.
5. Remove tie-rod end from knuckle using Tool J–6627 or equivalent.
6. Carefully remove knuckle seal if knuckle is to be replaced.
7. Remove ball studs from steering knuckle using tool J–23742 or equivalent.

CAUTION

Floor jack must remain under control arm spring seat during removal and installation to retain spring and control arm in position.

8. Position a floor jack under lower control arm near spring seat and raise jack until it just supports lower control arm.
9. Raise upper control arm to disengage ball joint stud from knuckle.
10. Raise knuckle from lower ball joint stud and remove knuckle.

Inspection

Inspect the tapered hole in the steering knuckle. Remove any

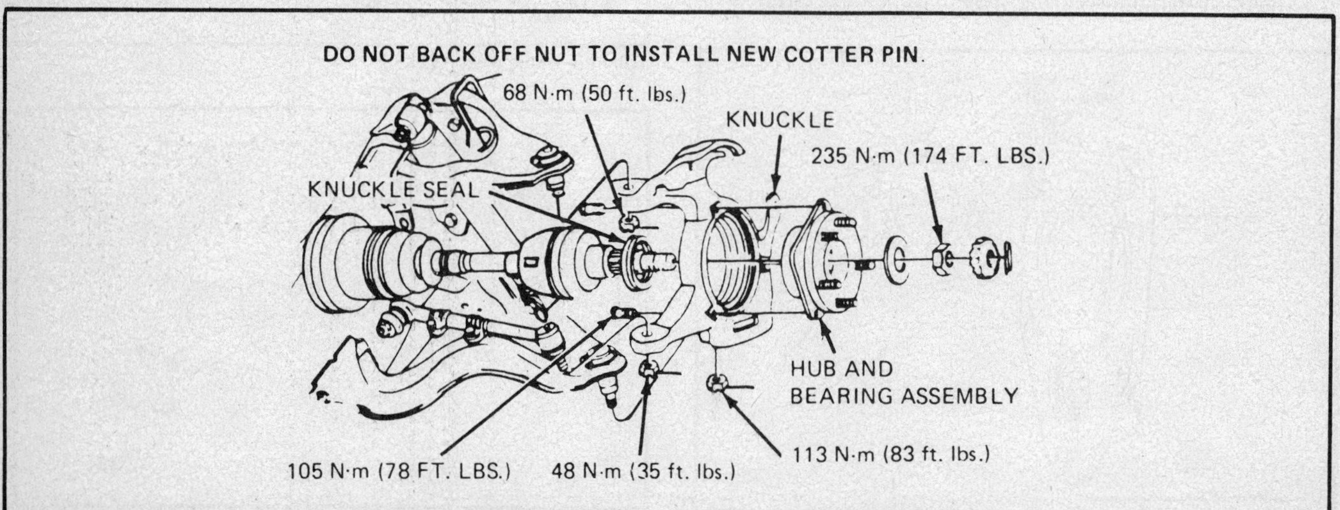

Removal of hub, bearing assembly, knuckle and seal on S–series

dirt. If out-of-roundness, deformation, or damage is noted, the knuckle MUST be replaced.

Installation

1. Insert upper and lower ball joint studs into knuckle and install nuts.
2. Install shield to knuckle seal and splash shield. Torque attaching bolts to 10 ft. lbs
3. Install tie rod end into knuckle. Install tool J–29193 or equivalent and torque to 15 ft. lbs. Remove tool and install nut to 40 ft. lbs.
4. Replace wheel bearings. Install hub and disc assembly.
5. Adjust wheel bearings. Install caliper.
6. Install remaining parts in reverse order of removal.

STEERING KNUCKLE—WITH BALL JOINTS

Removal

K10, 20, K1500, 2500

1. With the spindle and axle removed, as previously outlined, disconnect the tie rod end from the steering arm.
2. If necessary for working clearance, remove the steering arm from the knuckle.

NOTE: If the steering arm is removed, discard the three self-locking nuts and replace them with new self-locking nuts upon assembly.

3. Remove the upper and lower ball joint retaining nuts.

NOTE: The upper ball joint stud and nut have a cotter pin retainer, while the lower ball point stud and nut have none.

4. With a wedge type tool, separate the lower ball joint stud from the knuckle. Repeat this operation for the upper ball joint stud.
5. Remove the snap-ring retainer from the lower ball joint. With the aid of a C-clamp tool, press the lower ball joint from the knuckle.

NOTE: The lower ball joint must be removed before any service can be performed on the upper ball joint.

6. With the aid of the C-clamp tool, press the upper ball joint from the knuckle. Replacement of the knuckle can be accomplished at this point in the disassembly.

Installation

1. Press the lower ball joint into the knuckle with the aid of the "C" type tool and install the snap-ring retainer on the lower ball joint.
2. Install the upper ball joint into the knuckle with the aid of the C-clamp tool.
3. Position the ball joint studs in their respective openings on the yoke and install the new nuts finger tight.

NOTE: The castellated nut is placed on the upper ball joint stud.

4. Torque the lower ball joint stud nut to 70 ft. lbs while exerting upward pressure on the knuckle.
5. Torque the upper ball joint stud adjusting sleeve to 50 ft. lbs using a spanner type socket.
6. Torque the upper ball joint stud nut to 100 ft. lbs Apply additional torque if necessary to align the cotter pin hole in the nut and stud.
7. Reassemble the steering arm, if removed, tie rod ends, spindle, axle and hub as outlined previously.
8. Torque the steering arm nuts to 90 ft. lbs and the tie rod nut to 45 ft. lbs and install the cotter pin.

STEERING KNUCKLE—WITH KING PINS

Removal

K30, K3500

1. Remove the hub and spindle.

NOTE: It may be necessary to tap lightly on the spindle with a rawhide hammer in order to free it from the knuckle.

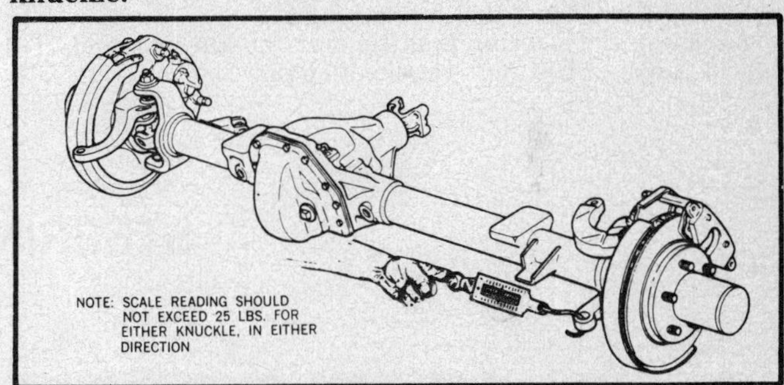

Checking front drive axle ball joint adjustment (© General Motors Corp.)

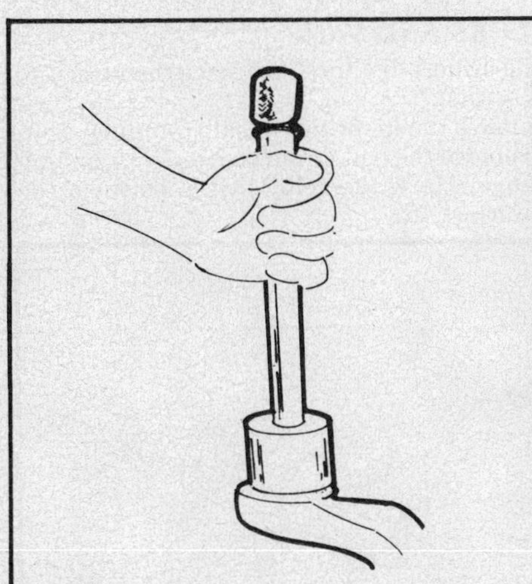

Installing oil seal—front drive yoke w/ king pins

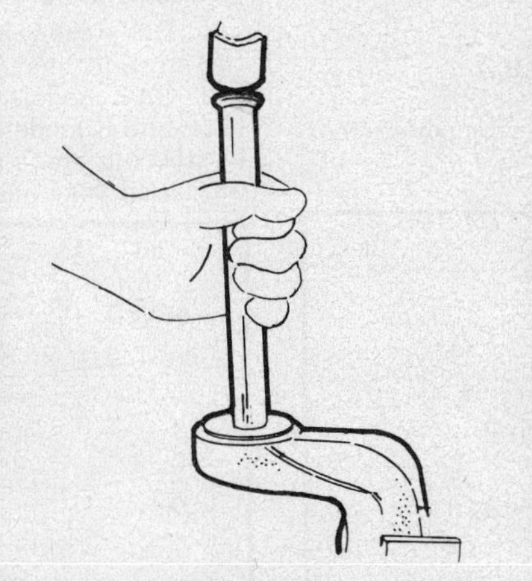

Installing grease retainer—front drive yoke w/king pins

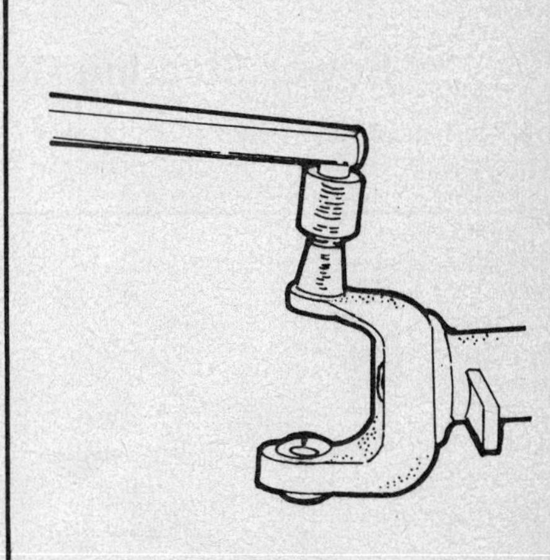

Installing upper king pin—front drive axle

2. Remove the four cap nuts from the upper king pin.

NOTE: Spring pressure will force the cap up.

3. Remove the cap, spring and gasket. Discard the gasket.
4. Remove the four cap screws from the lower king pin bearing.
5. Remove the cap and the lower king pin.
6. Remove the upper king pin bushing.
7. Remove the knuckle from the yoke.
8. Remove the king pin felt seal.
9. Remove the upper king pin from the yoke with a very large breaker bar and any suitable adapter designed to fit the king pin.

NOTE: Considerable force will be required to remove the king pin from the yoke as the king pin is originally torqued to 500–600 ft. lbs

10. Remove the lower king pin bearing cup, cone, grease retainer and seal. Discard the seal. Discard the grease retainer if damaged.

Installation

1. Install the lower king pin bearing cup and a new grease retainer.
2. Fill the grease retainer with grease.
3. Lubricate the bearing cone with grease. Install the bearing cone.
4. Install a new oil seal for the lower king pin bearing.

NOTE: The oil seal will protrude slightly from the surface of the yoke flange when fully installed.

5. Install the upper king pin and torque to 500–600 ft. lbs
6. Assemble the felt seal to the king pin.
7. Position the steering knuckle over the king pin and install the tapered bushing over the king pin.
8. Install the lower king pin and the lower bearing cap. Torque the cap screws to 70–90 ft. lbs
9. Position the compression spring over the upper king pin bushing.
10. Install the upper bearing cap with a new gasket. Torque the nuts to 70–90 ft. lbs

BALL JOINT

Adjustment

K10, 20, K1500, 2500

1. Raise the vehicle on a hoist.
2. Disconnect the connecting rod and the tie rod to allow the steering knuckle to move freely.
3. Attach a spring scale to the tie rod mounting hole of the steering arm.
4. Move the knuckle to the straight-ahead position.
5. Determine the right angle pull required to keep the knuckle turning after initial movement from standing still. The pull should not exceed 25 lbs. for each knuckle assembly.
6. If the effort required to maintain turning movement is in excess of 25 lbs., then remove the upper ball stud nut and loosen the ball stud adjusting sleeve as required. Tighten the ball stud nut and recheck the turning effort.

WHEEL BEARING

Adjustment

Refer to the Installation procedures under Locked Hub-Full Time or Free-Wheeling Hub-Part-Time for the corresponding wheel bearing adjustment instructions.

Non-driving front wheel axle bearings should have an end play of 0.001–0.005 in..

STEERING GEAR

Manual Steering Gear

Instructions covering the overhaul of the steering gear will be found in the Unit Repair section.

Power Steering Gears

Troubleshooting and repair instructions covering power steering gears are given in the Unit Repair section.

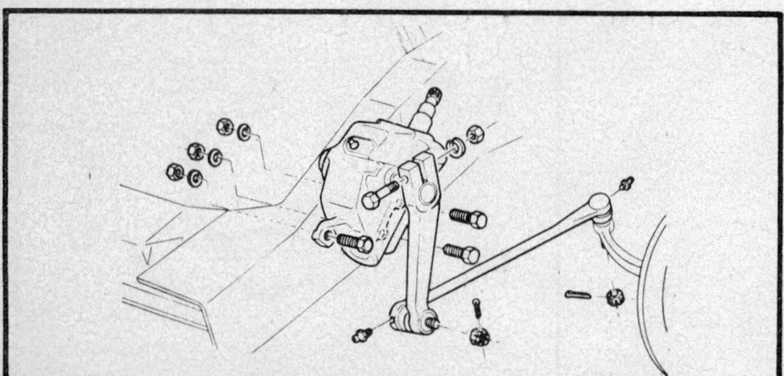

Manually operated steering gear—P models (© General Motors Corp.)

Manual Steering Gear Assembly

Removal

LIGHT DUTY TRUCKS AND VANS

1. Drive the vehicle a short distance and move the wheels to the straight ahead position.
2. On P models, remove the lower universal joint pinch bolt. On C and K models, remove the bolts from the flexible coupling to steering shaft flange. Mark the relationship between the universal yoke and wormshaft.

Manually operated steering gear—C and K models (© General Motors Corp.)

3. Mark the relationship between the pitman arm and the pitman shaft and remove the pitman shaft nut or pitman arm pinch bolt.
4. Remove the pitman arm from the shaft with a special puller.
5. Remove the bolts between steering gear and frame. Remove the steering gear.
6. On C and K models, remove the flexible coupling pinch bolt and remove the coupling from the wormshaft.

Installation

1. On C and K models:
a. Install the flexible coupling onto the steering gear wormshaft. The flats in the coupling and on the shaft must line up. Then, push the coupling onto the shaft until the wormshaft bottoms on the coupling reinforcement. Install the pinch bolt.

NOTE: The coupling bolt must pass through the shaft undercut.

b. Position the steering gear, guiding the coupling bolt into the steering shaft flange.
c. Install the steering gear to frame bolts. Torque to 65 ft. lbs
d. In cases where plastic spacers are used on the flexible coupling alignment pins, make sure they are bottomed on the pins, torque the flange bolt nuts and then remove the spacers.
e. If plastic spacers are not used, center the pins in the steering shaft flange slots and install and torque the flange bolt nuts.
2. On P models:
a. Position the steering gear, guiding wormshaft into the U-joint assembly. Line up the marks made at removal. In cases where a new steering gear is being installed, line up the mark on the wormshaft with the slit in the yoke of the U-joint.
b. Install the steering gear to frame bolts and torque to 65 ft. lbs
c. Install and torque the universal joint pinch bolt. Make sure the bolt passes through the shaft undercut.
3. Install the pitman arm onto the shaft, lining up marks made at removal. Install the shaft nut or pinch bolt and torque to 140 ft. lbs

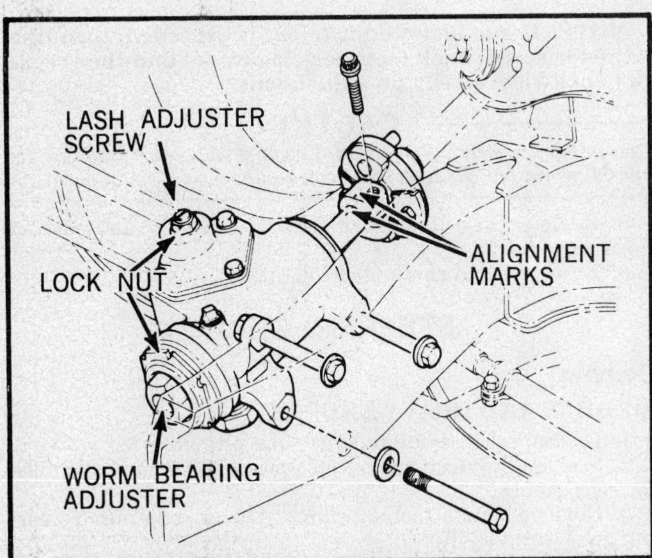

Steering gear adjustments—typical (© General Motors Corp.)

Adjustments

ON VEHICLE

1. Check tire pressure and inspect steering linkage.
2. Check gear housing for lubricant, tighten cover side plate.
3. Check steering gear housing to frame rail bolts.
4. Set wheels in straight ahead position.

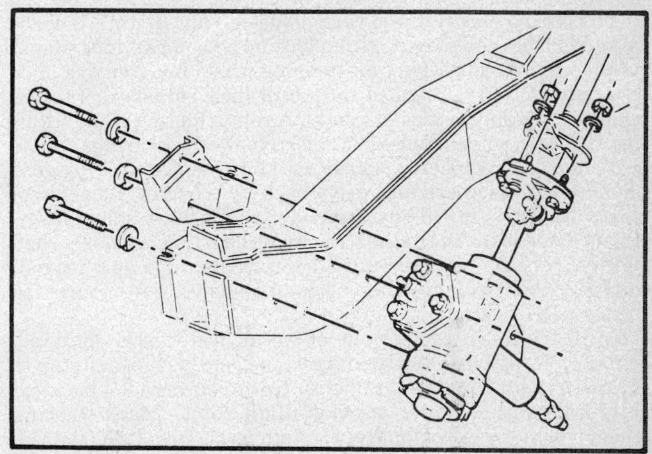

Manually operated steering gear—G and P models (© General Motors Corp.)

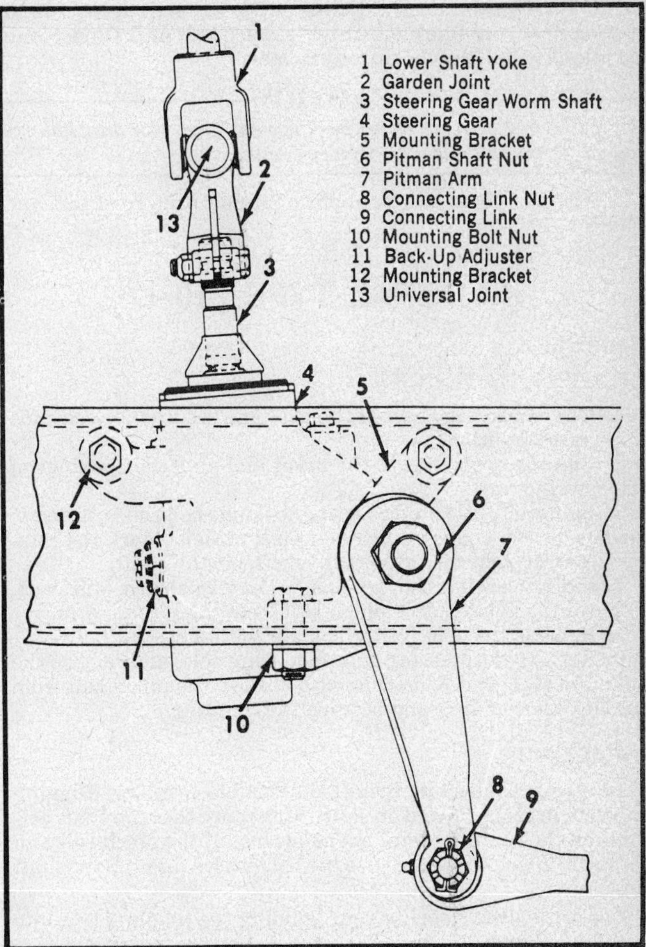

Manually operated steering gear installed—steel tilt (© General Motors Corp.)

5. Disconnect drag link from pitman arm, remove pitman arm on vans.

6. Loosen sector (cross) shaft lock nut and back off lash adjuster ¼ turn. This lessens steering worm bearing load by reducing tooth mesh contact.

7. Check load on steering gear by measuring pull on steering wheel with scale. Pull is measured at rim of wheel with scale tangent to rim of wheel (½ to 3 lbs. pull according to size of truck).

8. If pull is not within limits, adjust worm bearings. Loosen worm bearing lock nut and turn adjusting nut in until there is no perceptible end play. Tighten lock nut. Using an inch-pound torque wrench and socket on steering wheel nut (remove horn wire and button), measure torque (3 inch pounds to 14 inch pounds according to size of truck). A rough feeling when rotating steering wheel indicates defective worm bearings. Some early heavy duty steering gears use shims under steering gear housing top cover and also use a back-up adjuster. Removal of shims decreases worm bearing end play. Back-up adjuster setting is made last. After adjusting worm bearings and lash, then tighten back-up adjuster until adjuster bottoms against ball nut return guide clamp, then back-off adjuster ⅛ to ¼ turn and secure with lock nut.

9. After proper adjustment of worm bearings is obtained, center steering wheel by turning wheel gently from one stop to the other, counting the number of turns. Turn wheel back exactly half way to center position (high point). Mark steering wheel rim at top or bottom center with tape. Turn lash (slotted) adjuster clockwise to take out all lash in gear teeth and tighten lock nut. Check steering free play.

NOTE: If maximum adjustment is exceeded, turn lash adjuster screw back (counter-clockwise) and then come in (clockwise) slowly on adjustment.

CAUTION

Do not bounce steering wheel hard against stops with drag link removed, worm ball guide damage can result.

10. Connect drag link or replace pitman arm, road test and check steering.

INTEGRAL TYPE 710–D

Removal

LIGHT DUTY TRUCKS

1. Disconnect the hoses at the gear and secure the open ends in a raised position.

2. Cap the open ends of the hoses and plug the openings of the steering unit.

3. Remove the flexible coupling to flange bolts on G, C and K models, or the U-joint pinch bolt on P models. Mark the relationship between the universal yoke and stub shaft.

4. Mark the relationship between the pitman arm and shaft. Remove the shaft nut or pinch bolt from the pitman arm.

5. Remove the arm from the shaft with a special puller.

6. Remove the steering gear mounting bolts and remove the gear. On G, C and K models, also remove the pinch bolt from the flexible coupling and remove the coupling.

Installation

1. Where applicable, install the flexible coupling, aligning the flats in coupling and on shaft. Make sure the stub shaft bottoms on the coupling reinforcement. Install the pinch bolt and torque to 18 in. lbs. Make sure the bolt passes through the shaft undercut.

2. Position the steering gear, guiding the coupling bolt into the shaft flange.

3. Install the mounting bolts and torque to 65 ft. lbs (110 ft. lbs on G series).

4. If plastic spacers are used in the flexible coupling, make sure they are bottomed on the pins, tighten the flange bolt nuts to 18 in. lbs. (20 ft. lbs on P series) and then remove the spacers. Where plastic spacers are not used, center the pins in the steering shaft flange slots and install the bolt nuts and torque as above.

5. On P Models:

a. Position the steering gear, guiding the stub shaft into the U-joint assembly and lining up marks made at removal or, with a new unit, lining up the mark on the stub shaft with the mark on the universal yoke.

b. Install the gear to frame bolts and torque to 65 ft. lbs

c. Install the U-joint pinch bolt and torque to 20 ft. lbs Make sure the bolt passes through the shaft undercut.

6. Install the pitman arm, lining up the marks made at removal. Install the shaft nut or pinch bolt and torque to 180 ft. lbs on C series, 90 ft. lbs on K series and 180 ft. lbs on G and P series.

7. Remove the plugs and caps from the fluid fittings and reinstall both hoses.

TYPE 710–D

Adjustments

LIGHT DUTY TRUCKS

Power steering gear is adjusted in the same manner as manual steering gear however, sector lash adjustment is the only power steering gear adjustment that can be made on the vehicle. In order to make this adjustment, it is necessary to check the combined valve drag and worm bearing preload.

1. Check power steering fluid level, check belt tension and hose for leaks or kinks.

2. Remove drag link from pitman arm.

3. Disconnect horn wire, remove horn button assembly.

4. Center steering wheel – turn through its full travel then locate wheel at center of its travel.

5. Loosen sector lash adjusting screw locknut and back off (slotted) adjusting screw to the limit of its travel.

6. Check combined valve drag and worm bearing preload with inch-pound torque wrench and socket on steering shaft nut, by rotating wheel approximately 20° in each direction. Note highest reading.

7. Tighten sector lash adjusting screw until torque at steering wheel meets specifications (4 to 18 inch pounds according to truck size). Secure lock nut.

NOTE: If maximum adjustment is exceeded, turn lash adjuster screw back (counter-clockwise) and then come in (clockwise) slowly on adjustment.

CAUTION

Do not bounce steering wheel hard against stops with drag link removed, worm ball guide damage can result.

8. Replace drag link, horn button assembly and connect horn wire.

9. Road test and check steering.

STEERING GEAR

Removal

MEDIUM AND HEAVY TRUCKS

1. Disconnect steering linkage from pitman arm.

2. Scribe alignment marks on worm shaft and clamp yoke for reassembly.

3. Remove bolts attaching clamp yoke or coupling to steering gear worm shaft.

4. Remove pitman arm nut and washer, then use a puller to remove arm.

5. Remove attaching bolts, nuts and washers, then remove steering gear.

Installation

1. Turn steering wheel to straight-ahead position and center steering gear.
2. Position the steering gear, matching the alignment marks.
3. Install attaching bolts, washers and nuts.
4. Connect clamp yoke or coupling to steering gear worm shaft with attaching parts and torque to specifications.
5. Align pitman arm and shaft; press arm onto shaft and torque to specifications.

Power Steering Gear

INTEGRAL TYPE 553–D

Removal

MEDIUM AND HEAVY TRUCKS

1. Mark steering gear worm shaft and clamp yoke or coupling for reassembly.

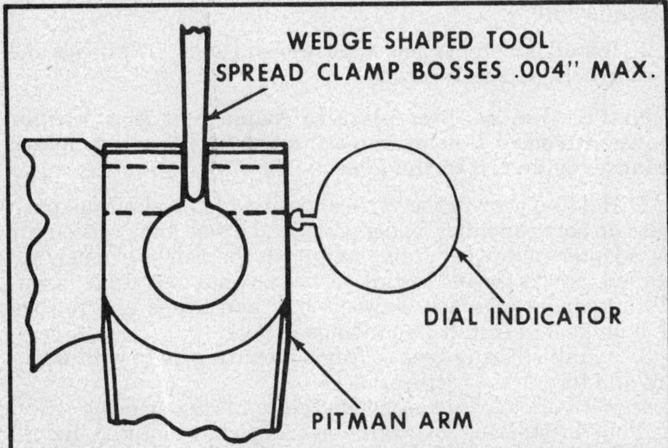

Pitman arm removal—dial indicator and wedge shape tool installed (© General Motors Corp.)

2. Remove connecting rod from pitman arm.
3. Remove attaching pinch bolt, nuts and washers from pitman arm; press pitman arm from shaft.
4. Drain as much fluid as possible from steering gear.
5. Disconnect all tubes from the control valve ports. Plug all tubes and cover all ports to prevent any dirt from entering the system.
6. Remove attaching bolts, nuts and washers from the steering gear and control valve assembly. Remove steering gear.

Installation

1. Center steering wheel and steering gear.
2. Install steering gear by reversing the removal procedure. Make certain to match all alignment marks and to torque all nuts to specifications.
3. Bleed the system and fill reservoir to the proper level.

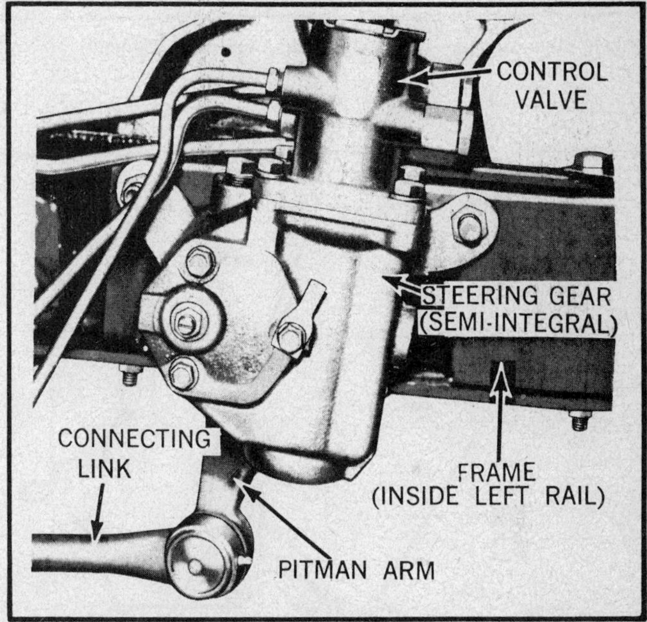

Semi-integral power steering gear—steel tilt cab (© General Motors Corp.)

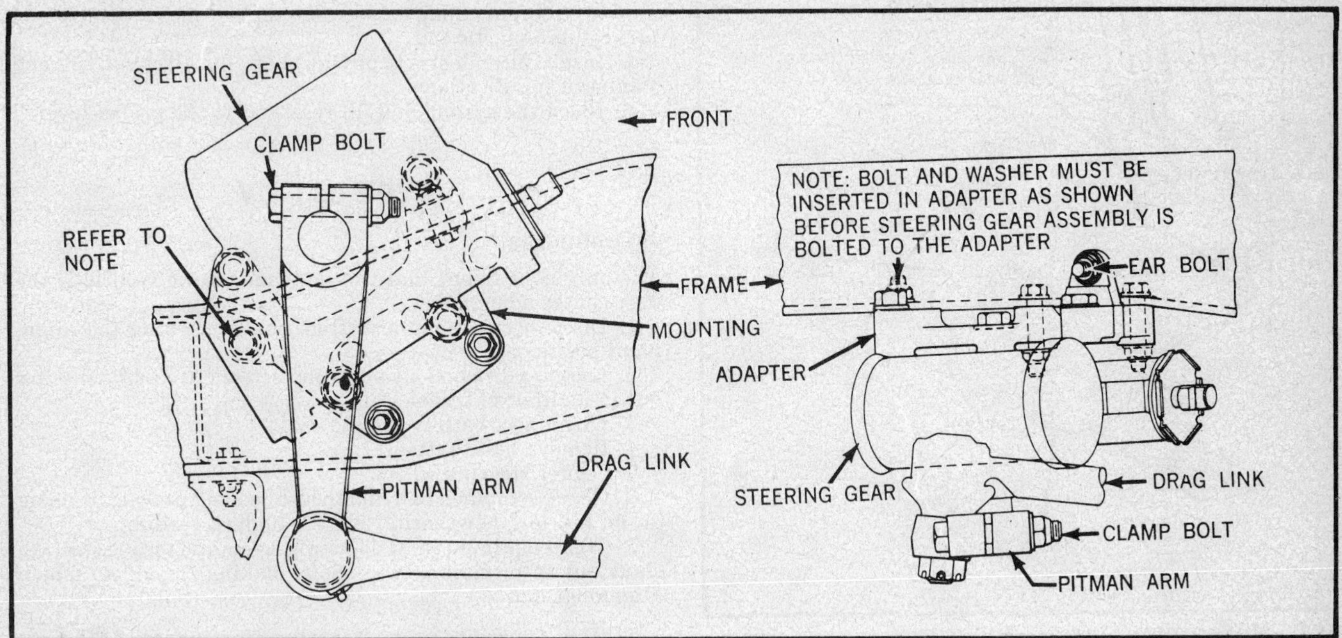

Integral power steering gear (© General Motors Corp.)

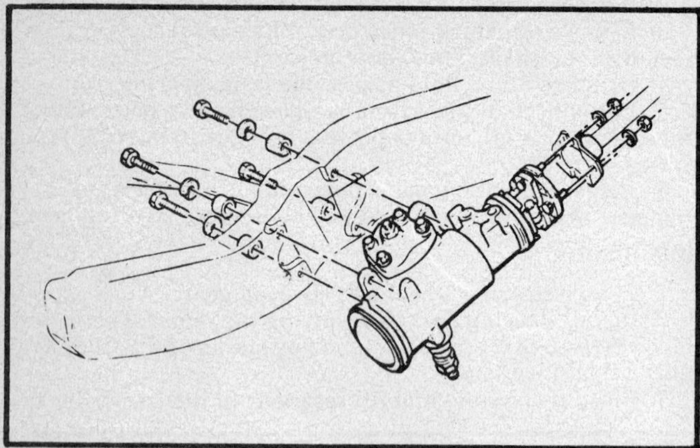

Power steering gear—light duty trucks—typical (© General Motors Corp.)

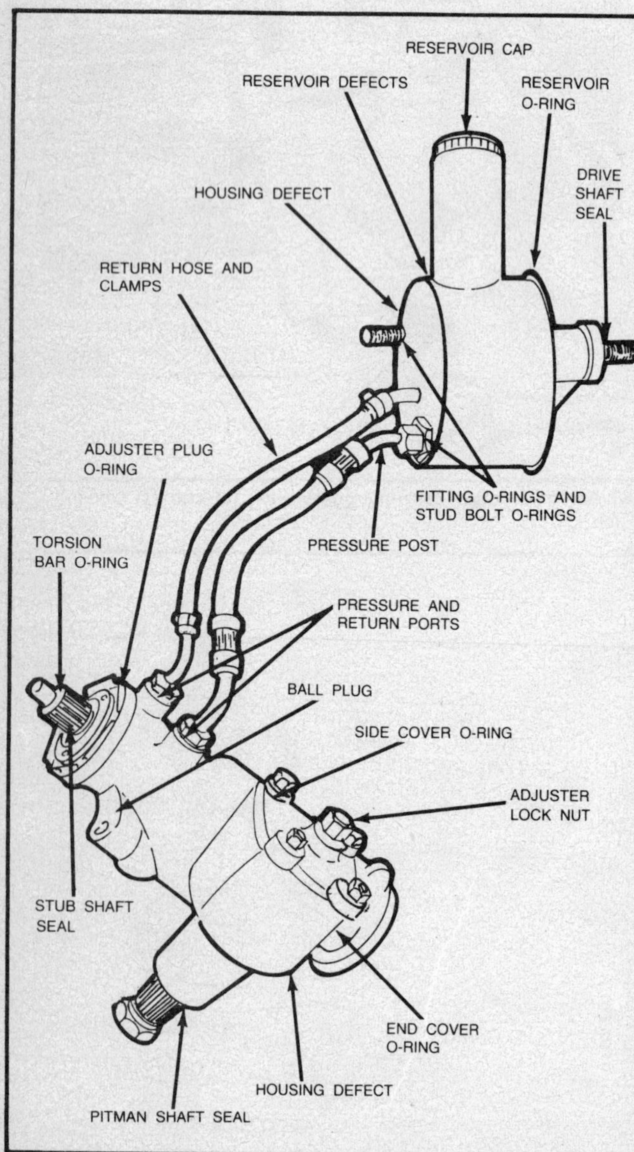

Potential leakage areas—light duty power steering system

INTEGRAL TYPE 710–D

Removal

1. Center steering gear by positioning tires straight ahead and remove pitman arm clamp bolt.
2. Install pitman arm puller and remove pitman arm.

NOTE: It may be necessary to spread the pitman arm clamp bosses slightly to remove arm. Install a dial indicator as shown. Insert a wedge shaped tool and spread clamp bosses 0.004 in.

3. Remove pot joint to stub shaft clamp bolt (conventional cab) or carden joint to stub shaft clamp bolt (school bus model). Remove steering column plastic cap and metal cover at dash. Remove column clamp cap screws. Pull steering shaft up until shaft coupling clears stub shaft.
4. Remove steering gear mounting bolts. It will be necessary to use two technicians to remove ear bolt as shown.
5. Disconnect lines from steering gear and plug lines. Turn gear in a vertical position (stub shaft up) and work gear down between frame and inner fender panel and remove gear.
6. Remove adapter to gear bolts.

Installation

1. Install adapter to gear with washers under bolt heads and torque bolts to specifications.

NOTE: One adapter plate to frame bolt and washer (lower forward bolt as shown) must be installed before adapter is bolted to the gear.

2. Holding gear in the vertical position (stub shaft up) push gear up between inner fender panel and frame and position ear on adapter plate over frame and push the bolt previously installed into frame and install washer and nut only finger tight. With gear loose, reach between gear and frame and remove line plugs and install line fittings to gear.
3. Install steering gear to frame mounting bolts with washers and torque to specifications.
4. With one technician inside cab centering steering wheel and one at steering gear with steering gear centered, install pot joint or carden joint over stub shaft. Push steering shaft down until coupling lines up with the cross groove in stub shaft. Install clamp bolt and adjust pot joint to 3.08 in. Tighten steering column clamp cap screws, replace metal cover panel and column plastic cap.
5. Install pitman arm to pitman shaft, install clamp bolt and torque to specifications.
6. Bleed the system and fill reservoir to the proper level.

TYPE 533–DV

Adjustments

The only adjustment that can be made on the vehicle is the over-center adjustment.

1. Disconnect pitman arm from shaft, marking the alignment positions.
2. Loosen pitman shaft adjusting screw nut and turn screw out to its limit of travel.
3. Disconnect battery ground cable.
4. Remove horn button.
5. Center steering wheel.
6. Check combined ball and thrust bearing preload by using an in. lbs. torque wrench. Note the highest reading.
7. Tighten pitman shaft adjusting screw and torque steering shaft nut to pitman arm to shaft, making certain to match alignment marks.

NOTE: There are no on-vehicle adjustments of the type 710–D steering gears.

Power Cylinders

Power cylinders are used to assist in lowering the steering effort for the vehicle operator. Two types are used, side mounted and axle mounted.

The side mounted unit is attached to the frameside rail at one end and to the pitman arm at the other end. The axle mounted cylinder is attached to the front axle at one end and to the steering tie rod at the other.

A control valve mounted on the steering gear housing, directs oil pressure from the belt driven oil pump to either the right or left sides of the piston within the power cylinder, depending upon the turn being made. If a hydraulic failure occurs with this type unit, the steering reverts to manual with no hydraulic assist.

Overhaul of the power cylinder is detailed in the Power Steering section of the Unit General Repair section.

Removal and Installation

Removal and installation of the power cylinder is accomplished by the removal of the power cylinder hydraulic lines and the attaching bolts at each end of the cylinder. A container should be placed under the lines to catch the fluid that will drain from the lines.

To install the cylinder, reverse the procedure, fill the power steering reservoir and bleed the system of air.

Bleeding Hydraulic System

LIGHT DUTY TRUCKS

1. Fill the reservoir to the proper level and allow the fluid to stand for at least two minutes; any air bubbles trapped in the fluid will rise and separate from the fluid.
2. Operate the engine for a few seconds.
3. Add fluid as needed.
4. Repeat the above until the fluid level remains constant.
5. Support the front of the vehicle in the raised position, so that the wheels are off of the ground.
6. Increase the engine speed to approximately 1500 rpm.
7. Operate the steering mechanism from right to left, contacting the steering stops only lightly.
8. Add fluid as needed.
9. Lower the vehicle to the ground and turn the wheels from full right to full left.

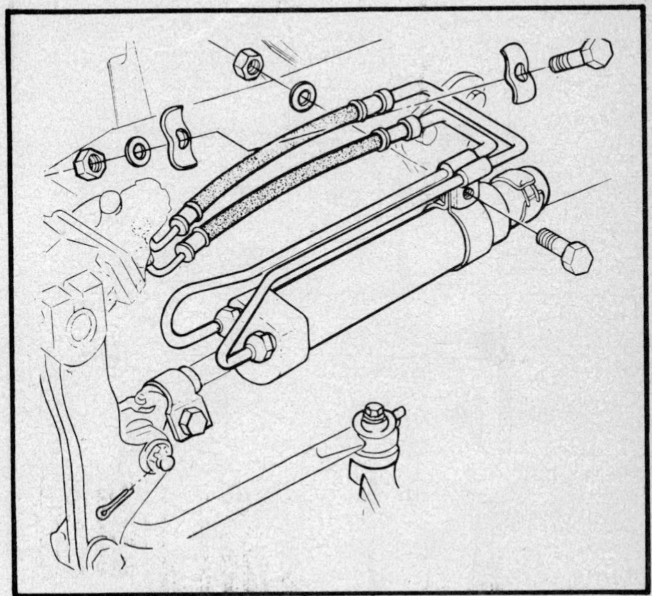

Side mounted power steering cylinder (© General Motors Corp.)

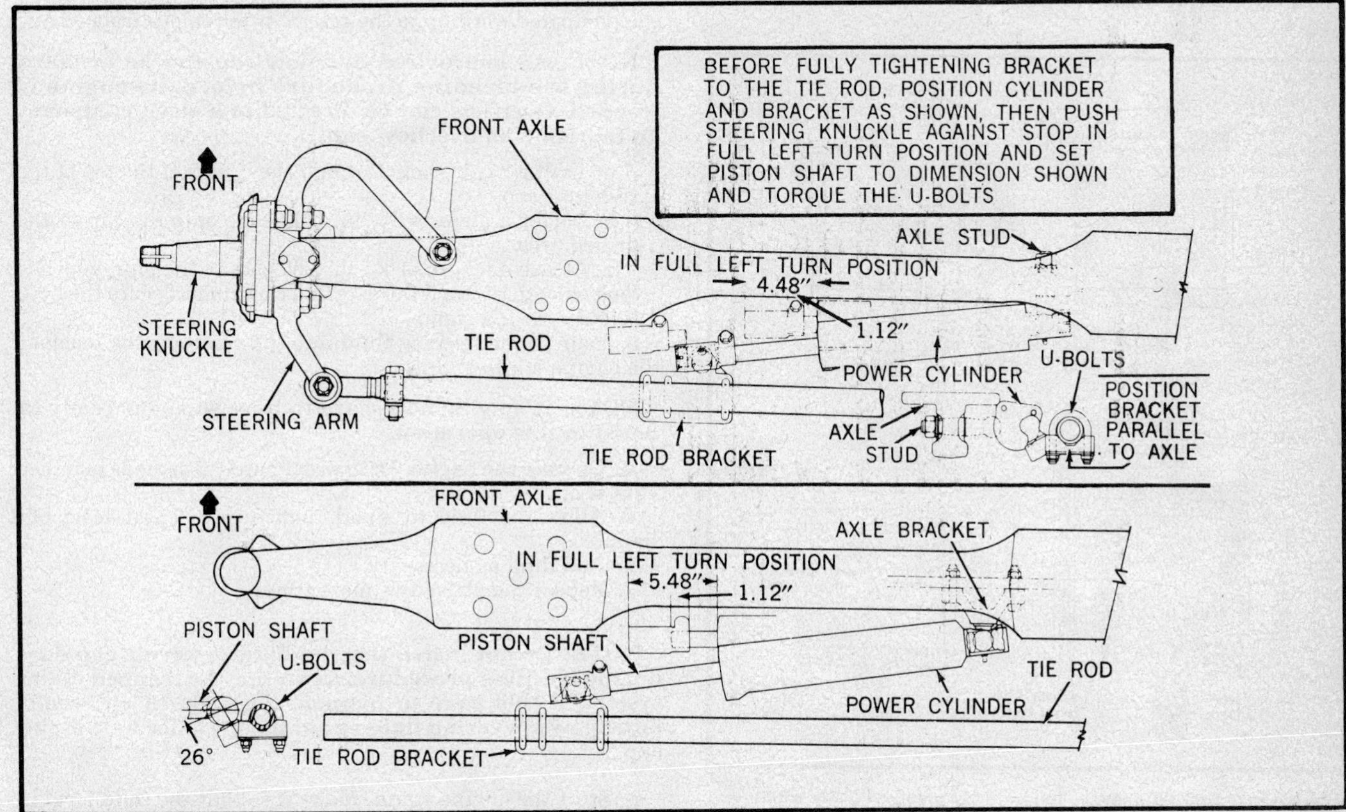

Installation and adjustment (to axle) of power cylinder—steel tilt cab (© General Motors Corp.)

10. Add fluid as needed.
11. Repeat all of the above steps as many times as necessary. Keep adding fluid as needed.

NOTE: If, after repeated attempts to bleed the system, air is still present in the fluid (fluid is foamy), then check the hydraulic system for leaks.

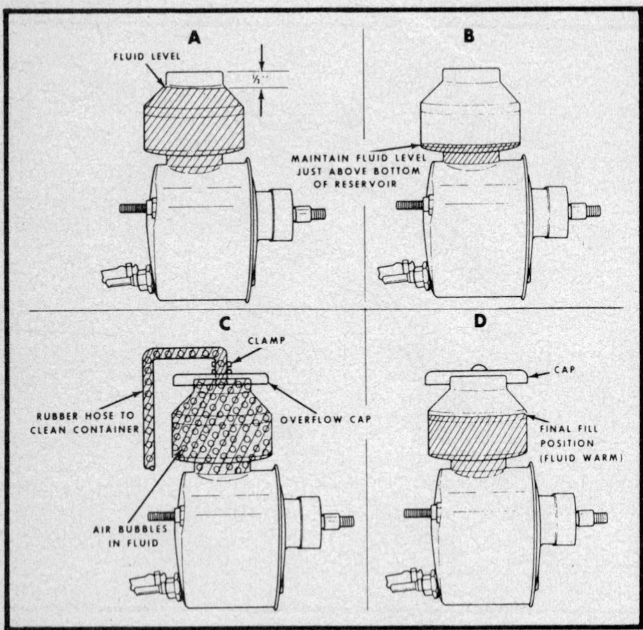

Integral reservoir fluid level—follow in alphabetical order when bleeding hydraulic system (© General Motors Corp.)

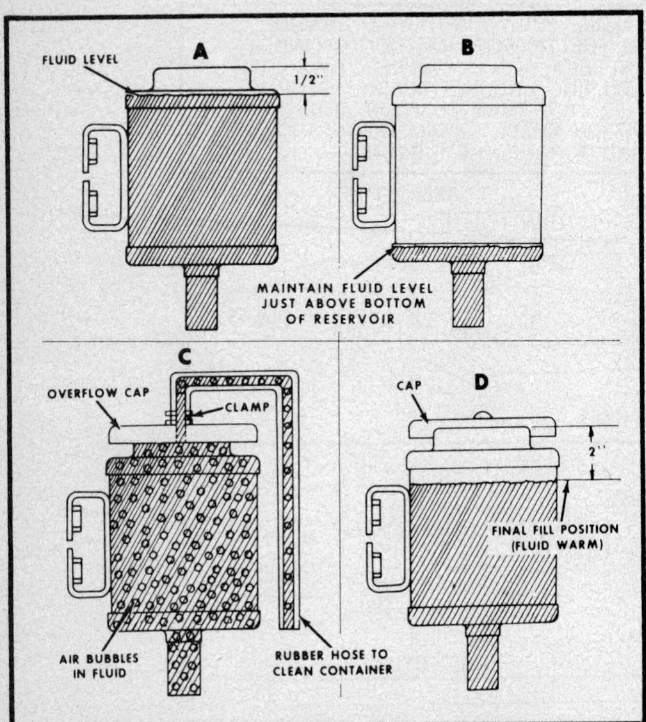

Remote reservoir fluid level—follow in alphabetical order when bleeding hydraulic system (© General Motors Corp.)

SEMI-INTEGRAL SYSTEM

Bleeding

MEDIUM AND HEAVY DUTY TRUCKS

1. Fill the fluid reservoir to the proper level: Fluid level mark on integral pumps; half full on remote mounted reservoir.
2. Allow the fluid to stand undisturbed for at least two minutes.
3. Operate the engine for a few seconds.
4. Add fluid as needed.
5. Repeat the above steps until the fluid level remains constant.
6. Support the front of the vehicle in the raised position, so that the wheels are off of the ground.
7. Operate the steering mechanism from stop to stop. Continue this operation until fluid is noticeably clear and free of air bubbles.
8. Add fluid as needed.
9. Increase the engine speed to approximately 1500 rpm and again, operate the steering mechanism from stop to stop. Continue until the fluid is clear.
10. Lower the vehicle to the ground.

NOTE: If, after repeated attempts to bleed the system, air is still present in the fluid (fluid is foamy), then check the hydraulic system for leaks.

INTEGRAL SYSTEM

Bleeding

MEDIUM DUTY TRUCKS

1. Remove the drag link at the pitman arm.
2. Fill the reservoir to within one-half inch of the top with power steering fluid and leave the cap off. On vehicles equipped with a remote reservoir, squeeze the hose starting at the pump and work up to the reservoir to remove trapped air.

NOTE: An improvised overflow cap can be installed during the bleeding procedure before the engine is stopped. Overflow can be directed to a clean container. To fabricate an overflow cap:

a. Drill a $^{3}/_{16}$ in. hole through the center of the top of the reservoir cap.
b. Solder a piece of $^{3}/_{16}$ in. O.D. pipe onto the cap at the drilled area.
c. Attach a length of $^{3}/_{16}$ in. I.D. hose to the pipe, which is long enough to reach the external container. Secure the hose in place with a clamp.

3. Pour power steering fluid into the reservoir the moment the engine starts.

NOTE: It may be necessary to have someone ready to assist in this operation.

4. Operate the engine for approximately 3 seconds and then shut it off.
5. Allow the fluid to stand undisturbed for at least one minute.
6. Add fluid as necessary.
7. Repeat the above two more times.

NOTE: Do not install the standard reservoir cap during the bleeding procedure, as air may be trapped in the system. If this were to happen, the trapped air would force power steering fluid out of the breather hole in the cap.

8. Start the engine again. Make sure that the fluid level is up to the bottom of the reservoir.

NOTE: The fluid level should be maintained at the bottom of the reservoir to prevent pump aeration during the bleeding procedure.

9. On vehicles equipped with a hydraulic brake booster, pump the brake pedal a minimum of 3 times with the engine running. This will purge air from the booster.
10. Allow the engine to idle and operate the steering mechanism in one direction, either full right or full left, against the stop. Turn the steering away from the stop only slightly and return it to the stop. Repeat this operation 5 times. Do not force the steering against the stop, as this may damage the pump.
11. Repeat Step 10 for the opposite side.
12. Maintain the fluid level at a point just above the bottom of the reservoir.
13. Center the steering wheel and allow the engine to idle. Install the overflow cap.
14. Shut the engine off. Air will bubble out through the overflow cap.
15. Remove the cap and start the engine.
16. Add fluid as needed to maintain the fluid level just above the bottom of the reservoir.
17. Repeat Steps 3–16 as many times as necessary, until there is no more than a one in. rise in the fluid level with the engine shut off.
18. Start the engine and center the steering wheel.
19. Connect the drag link to the pitman arm.
20. Idle the engine at approximately 1500 rpm and operate the steering mechanism from stop to stop.
21. Shut the engine off and fill the reservoir to the proper level.

CLUTCH

Clutches used on inline engines are single (driven) disc with either of two types of pressure (drive) plates, diaphragm or coil spring. "V" engines use a single disc with coil spring pressure plate. Heavy duty clutches use two discs. The two plate clutch consists of three basic assemblies, the cover with rear pressure plate assembly, front pressure plate and two discs. The front pressure plate, located between the two driven discs, has two friction surfaces and is coupled to rear pressure plate through steel drive straps bolted at each of its four driving bosses. Diaphragm spring covers operate with light pedal pressure while coil spring levers combine operating ease and high torque capacity. The operating controls are either mechanical or hydraulic. Discs have torsion spring centers.

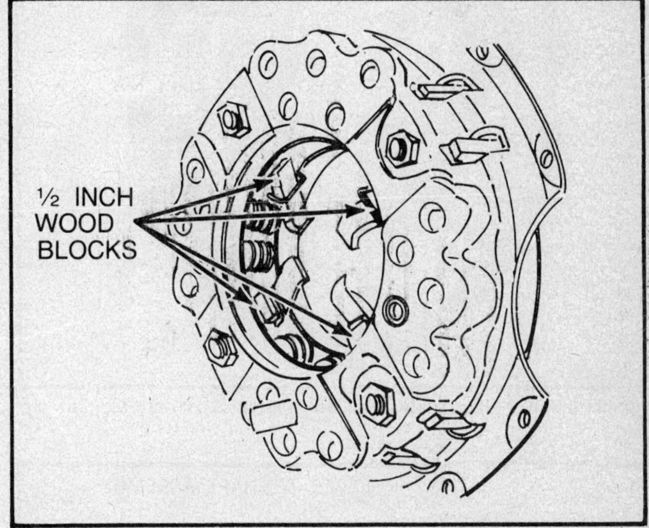

Wooden blocks installed between release levers and cover

Clutch Assembly

Removal and Installation

ALL MODELS

1. Remove transmission.
2. Block clutch fingers down on coil spring covers for additional clearance. On heavy duty clutches use blocks between release bearing and spring plate hub. On Lipe-Rollaway use bolts and washer in three holes provided.
3. Disconnect pedal linkage and fork arm pull back springs.
4. Disconnect slave cylinder from fork arm (if equipped).
5. Remove release bearing from fork arm or disconnect grease hose and remove bearing assembly from yoke.
6. Remove fork arm from ball stud or remove yoke and shaft.
7. Fork arm ball stud can be removed if necessary.
8. Punch mark cover and flywheel for alignment if cover assembly is to be re-used.
9. Loosen cover bolts a turn or two at a time to prevent cover distortion. Support cover and disc with pilot tool (or sling) to prevent damage to clutch when last cover bolt is removed. A good practice on heavy units is to remove one cover bolt and install a support stud. Rotate flywheel and locate stud at top, loosen all other bolts evenly until pressure is released from disc(s). Disc(s) can be removed and marked for positions. Remove remaining cover bolts and slide cover assembly off stud. Stud will also aid in installation.
10. Clean flywheel and pressure plates, check for scores and heat cracks. Excessive bluing indicates abnormally high operating temperatures. Torque flywheel bolts.
11. Check pilot bearing or bushing (lubricate sparingly), check splines on clutch shaft, check release bearing (do not wash bearing).

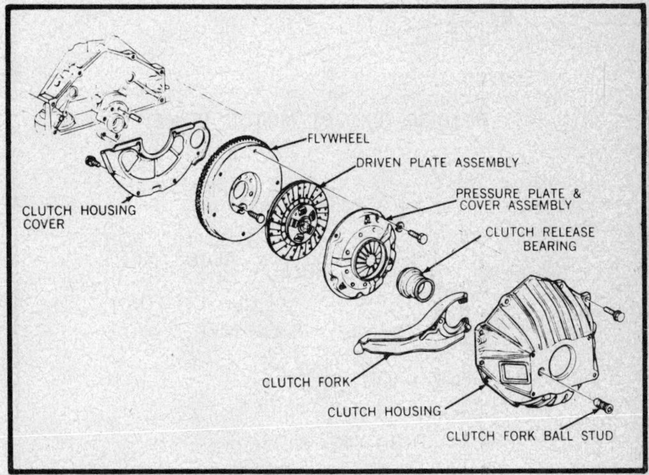

Clutch system components (© General Motors Corp.)

12. Reverse removal steps to install. Use pilot tool or dummy shaft to align disc(s). Be certain of disc's position in relation to flywheel. Tighten cover bolts evenly. Do not try to pull clutch into place with impact wrench. This procedure can crack or break pilot shoulders on bolts. Lubricate with a light coat of grease, fork arm ball seat and inside of release bearing. Make sure spring retainer (if used) for release fork ball stud is in correct position. Install retainer with high side up, away from bottom of ball socket and with open end of retainer horizontal. After clutch and transmission are installed and clutch pedal free travel adjusted, check disc(s) for release. This can be done by putting transmission in gear and pulling down slowly on clutch pedal while applying torque to transmission propeller shaft flange. If release can be felt, then complete installation.

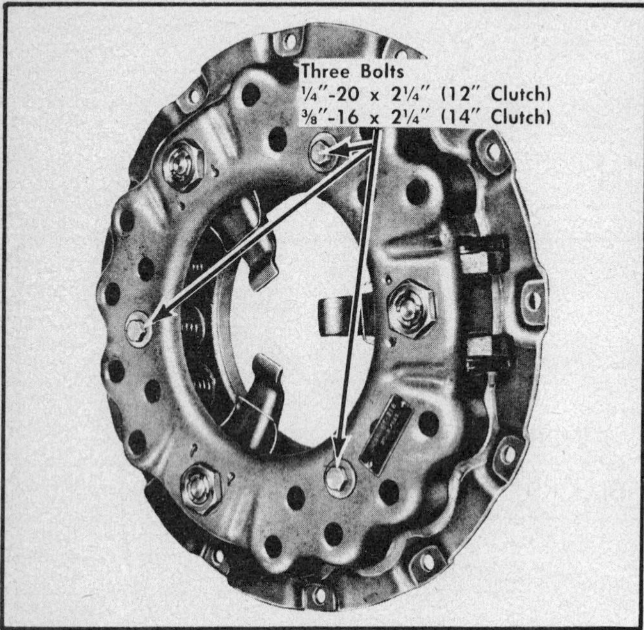

Lipe clutch hold-down bolts installed—typical (© General Motors Corp.)

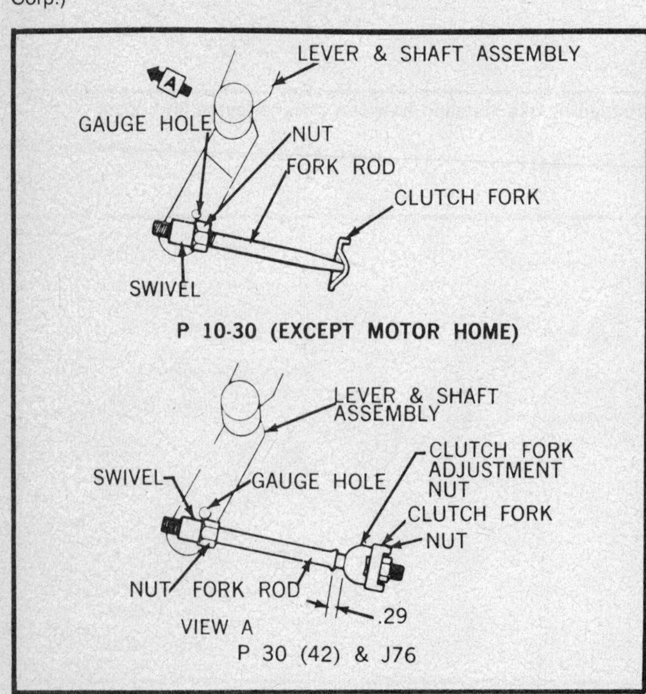

Free pedal travel—P models (© General Motors Corp.)

FREE PEDAL TRAVEL

Adjustment

This adjustment is for the amount of pedal travel (measured at pedal) before clutch release bearing contacts the levers, or fingers of a coil spring cover or the diaphragm spring of a diaphragm clutch cover. This is called free-play. With normal clutch wear the amount of free-play is reduced and in time this will cause the release bearing to be in constant contact with the cover. This in turn will cause clutch disc slippage resulting in premature failure of disc and release bearing. It is necessary to maintain sufficient free pedal travel for clutch efficiency and long life.

S-SERIES TRUCKS

1. Lift up on the pedal to allow the self adjuster to adjust the cable length.
2. Depress the pedal several times to set the pawl into mesh with the detent teeth.
3. Check the linkage for lost motion caused by loose or worn swivels, mounting brackets or a damaged cable.

C, K AND P MODELS (EXCEPT P-30, P-3500 W/J76)

1. Disconnect the clutch fork return spring.
2. Rotate the clutch lever assembly until the clutch pedal stops against the rubber bumper on the brake pedal bracket.
3. Position the clutch fork so that the release bearing lightly contacts the pressure plate levers.
4. Loosen the apply rod lock nut and adjust the rod length so that the swivel slips easily into the gauge hole (upper hole) on the clutch lever.
5. Continue lengthening the push rod until all lash is removed from the clutch linkage.
6. Remove the swivel from the gauge hole and insert it into the lower hole on the clutch lever.
7. Install the washers and cotter pin. Tighten the lock nut.
8. Install the clutch fork return spring. Check clutch pedal free travel.

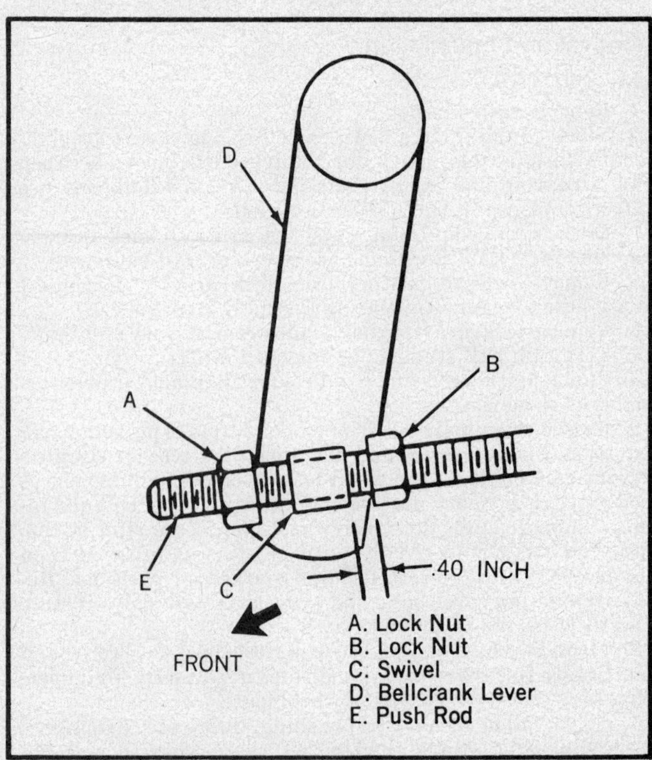

Clutch linkage adjustment (© General Motors Corp.)

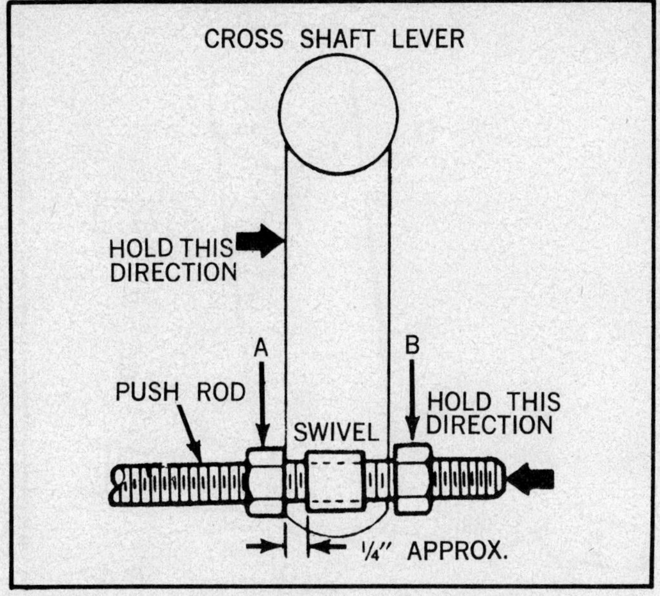

Free travel adjustment—G models (© General Motors Corp.)

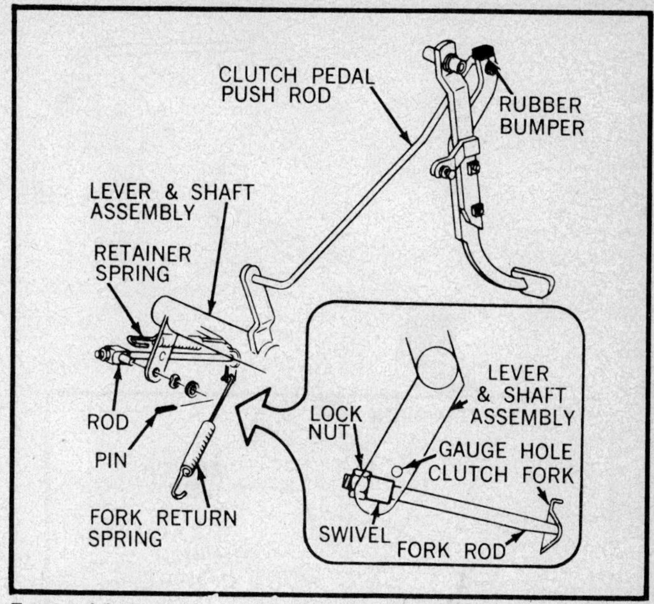

Free pedal travel—C and K models (© General Motors Corp.)

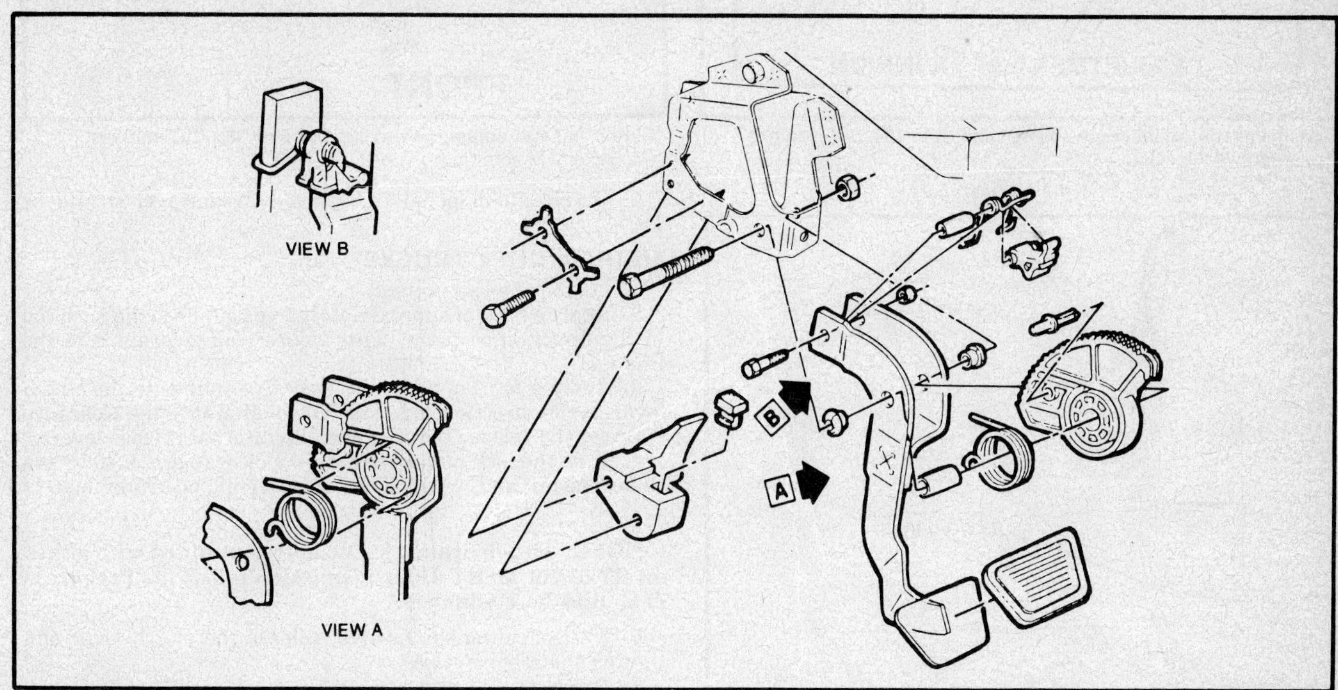

Self–adjusting clutch mechanism

NOTE: Pedal travel for C and K models should be $1^3/_8$–$1^5/_8$ inches; pedal travel for P models should be $1^1/_4$–$1^1/_2$ inches.

P–30, P–3500 W/J76

1. Disconnect the clutch fork return spring.
2. Loosen the lock nut at the apply rod swivel.
3. Move the clutch fork rearward to remove all clearance between the release bearing and the pressure plate levers.
4. Rotate the clutch lever assembly until the clutch pedal stops against the bumper on the brake pedal bracket.
5. Adjust the apply rod until the distance between the shoulder on the apply rod and the adjustment nut is approximately $^1/_4$–$^5/_{16}$ (0.29) in..
6. Tighten the lock nut and install the return spring.
7. Check clutch pedal free travel. Free travel should be $1^3/_8$–$1^5/_8$ inches.

G MODELS

1. Check linkage for excessive wear.
2. Disconnect fork arm return spring.
3. Back off locknut "A" at least $^1/_2$ in. from swivel.
4. Hold fork push rod against fork to keep release bearing touching fingers (or diaphragm). Push rod will slide through swivel at cross shaft.
5. Adjust nut "B" to obtain approximately $^3/_{16}$ in. to $^1/_4$ in. clearance between nut "B" and swivel.
6. Release push rod, connect pull back spring at fork and tighten nut "A" to lock swivel against nut "B".

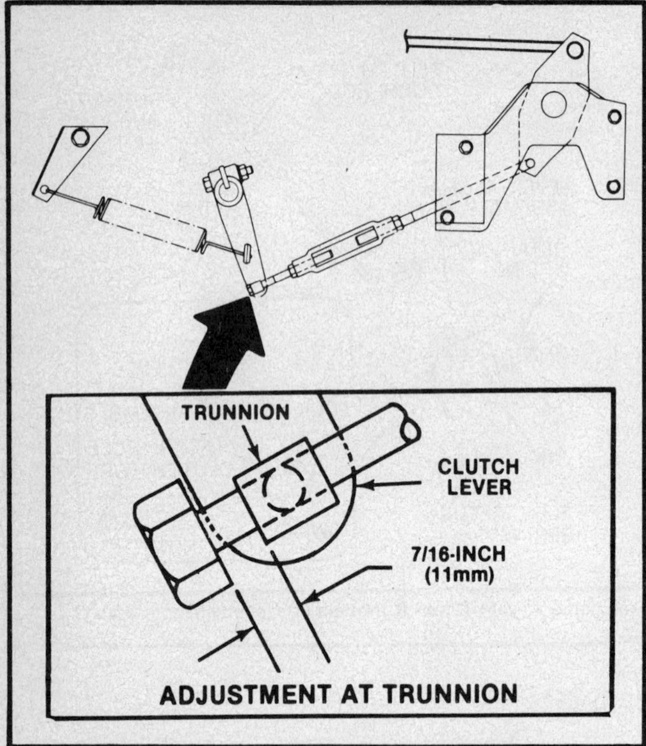

Clutch linkage adjustment—diesel and 400–454 CID engines
(© General Motors Corp.)

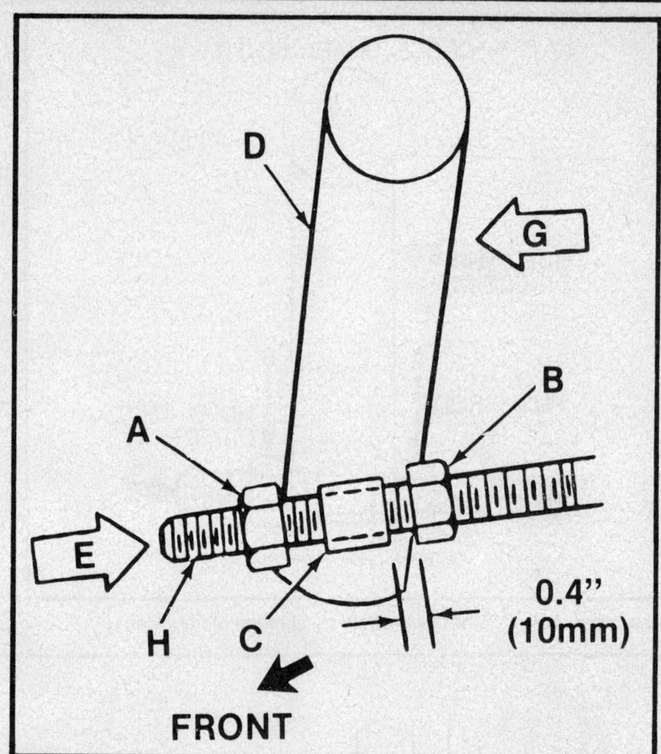

Clutch linkage adjustment—292, 350 and 366 CID engines
(© General Motors Corp.)

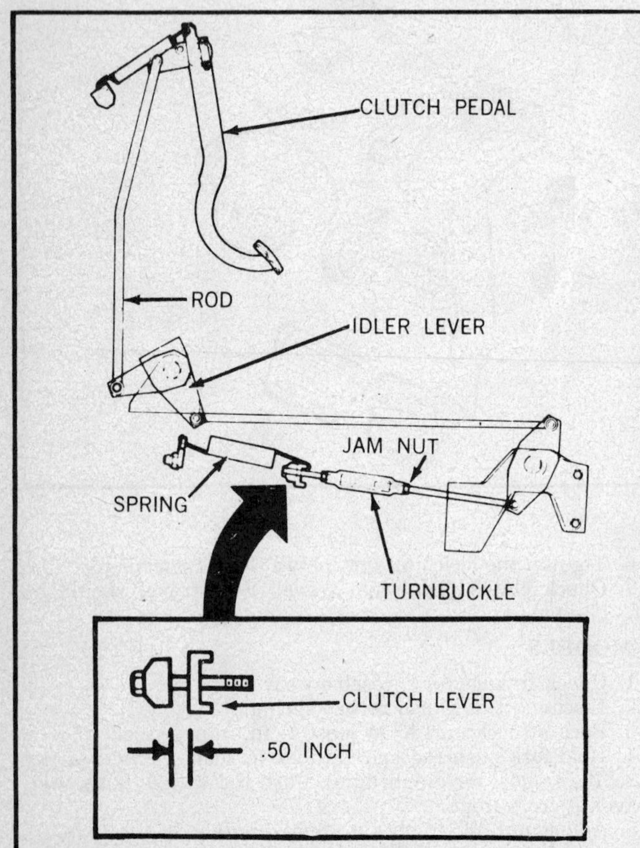

Clutch linkage adjustment—medium duty steel cab w/427 V8, 454 V8 and 4-53T engines (© General Motors Corp.)

7. Check clutch pedal free travel. Free travel should be $1^1/_4$–$1^1/_2$ inches.

MEDIUM DUTY TRUCKS

1. Loosen the lock nuts.
2. Apply a force of approximately five pounds to the push rod in the direction of arrow (E) to take up all clearances in the linkage.
3. Apply a force of approximately five pounds to the clutch lever in the direction of arrow (G) to eliminate the clearance between the release bearing and the internal release levers.
4. Turn the lock nut (B) to obtain a clearance of 0.40 in. between the nut and swivel. Free travel should be approximately $^3/_4$–1 in..

NOTE: The clearance for vehicles equipped with either an RT 613 or an RT 610 transmission is 0.45 in.. Free travel should be $1^7/_8$ inches.

5. While holding the nut (B), release the clutch lever and tighten the other nut (A).
6. Check clutch operation.

SLAVE CYLINDER PUSH ROD

Adjustment

1. Disconnect the slave cylinder return spring.
2. Push the slave cylinder push rod into the slave cylinder, until it bottoms.
3. Move the clutch fork in the direction away from the slave cylinder. This will bring the release bearing into contact with the clutch release levers.
4. Check the clearance between the wedge and the adjusting nut. Clearances should be as follows:
5. Loosen the jam nut and the adjusting nut.
6. Turn the adjusting nut to obtain the proper clearance and then tighten the jam nut against the adjusting nut.
7. Connect the return spring and check clutch operation.

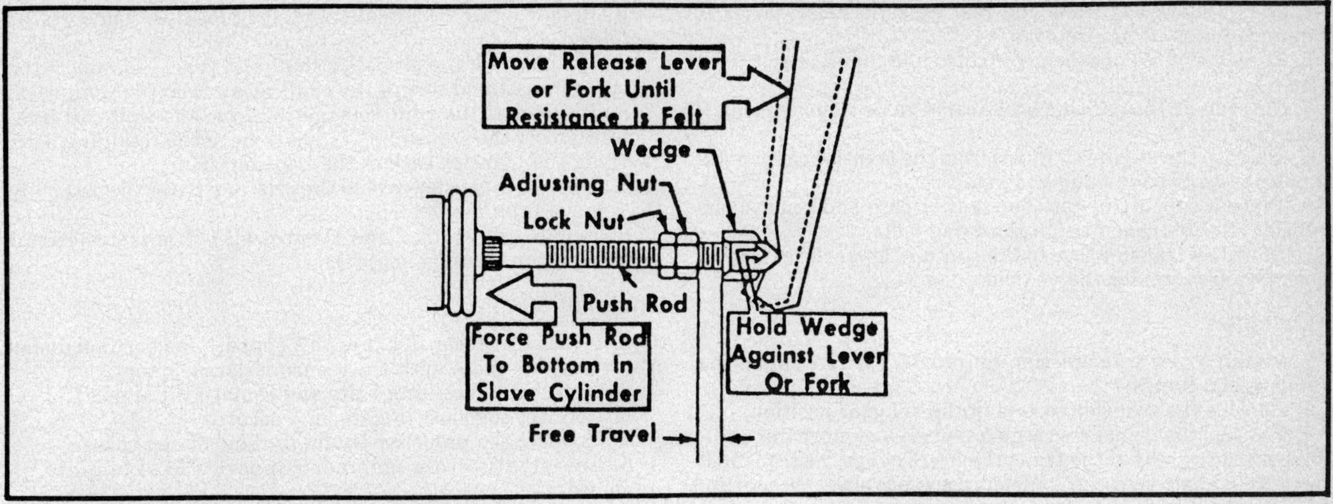

Clutch slave cylinder adjustment (© General Motors Corp.)

COVER ASSEMBLIES

While no wear adjustment is needed (except Spicer), original settings at time of manufacture must be retained for good clutch operation. If a diaphragm clutch cover fails to release properly, after first checking pedal travel, pedal lash and linkage for looseness, replace the cover assembly.

TRANSFER CASE

NOTE: Information on repair and overhaul of the transfer case can be found in the Unit Repair section.

MODEL 207

NOTE: The S–Series uses a model 207 transfer case.

Removal

1. Shift transfer case into 4 Hi.
2. Disconnect negative cable at battery.
3. Raise vehicle and remove skid plate.
4. Drain lubricant from transfer case.
5. Mark transfer case front output shaft yoke and propeller shaft for assembly reference. Disconnect front propeller shaft from transfer case.
6. Mark rear axle yoke and propeller shaft for assembly reference. Remove rear propeller shaft.
7. Disconnect speedometer cable and vacuum harness at transfer case. Remove shift lever from transfer case.
8. Remove catalytic converter hanger bolts at converter.
9. Raise transmission and transfer case and remove transmission mount attaching bolts. Remove mount and catalytic converter hanger and lower transmission and transfer case.
10. Support transfer case and remove transfer case attaching bolts.

NOTE: On vehicles equipped with an automatic transmission, it will be necessary to remove the shift lever bracket mounting bolts from the transfer case adapter in order to remove the upper left transfer case attaching bolt.

11. Separate transfer case from adapter (auto) or extension housing (man.) and remove from vehicle.

Installation

1. Position new gasket on the transfer case.
2. Install transfer case, aligning splines of input shaft with transmission and slide transfer case forward until seated against transmission.
3. Install transfer case attaching bolts and torque to specification. On vehicles equipped with automatic transmission, reinstall shift lever bracket bolts.
4. Raise transmission and transfer case and install mount and hanger bracket. Install attaching bolts and torque to specification.
5. Install catalytic converter hanger bolts at converter and torque to specification.
6. Attach shift lever at transfer case. Connect speedometer cable and vacuum harness at transfer case.
7. Connect the front and install the rear propeller shaft. Be sure to align reference marks made during removal.
8. Fill transfer case with Dexron® II.
9. Install skid plate and lower vehicle.
10. Connect negative cable at battery.
11. Road test vehicle, check to make sure vehicle shifts and operates into all ranges.

MODEL 208

Removal

SERIES K10–20, K1500–2500

1. Place the shift lever in the 4H position.
2. Raise and support the vehicle safely.
3. Drain the lubricant from the transfer case.
4. Disconnect the shift lever swivel.

5. Match-mark the front and rear propeller shaft yokes to the propeller shaft and remove.
6. Disconnect the speedometer cable and the indicator light wire.
7. Disconnect the parking brake cable guide from its pivot, if necessary.
8. Remove the engine strut rod from the transfer case on automatic transmission equipped vehicles.
9. Place a support under the transfer case and remove the transfer case-to-transmission retaining bolts.
10. Move the transfer case to the rear and lower the assembly to remove from under the vehicle.

Installation

1. Install a new transmission-to-transfer case gasket on the transmission flange.
2. Be sure the transfer case is in the 4H gear position.
3. Position the transfer case on a support and move into position behind the rear of the transmission. Engage the transmission output shaft with the transfer case input shaft by rotating the yoke of the transfer case output shaft.
4. Move the transfer case forward until the case seats flush against the rear of the transmission and install the retaining bolts.
5. Connect the speedometer cable to the transfer case. Install the indicator light wire.
6. Install the propeller shafts to the previously marked positions on the yokes.
7. Remove the support from under the transfer case and connect the parking brake cable, if removed previously.
8. Install the shift lever swivel and secure.
9. Connect the strut rod to the transfer case from the automatic transmission, if equipped.
10. Fill the transfer case with lubricant (Dexron® II) to its proper level and lower the vehicle.

MODEL 205

Removal

SERIES K30 AND K3500

1. Raise and support the vehicle safely. Drain the lubricant from the transfer case.
2. Disconnect the speedometer cable.
3. Remove the skid plate and crossmember supports as required.
4. Match-mark the propeller shaft and yoke. Disconnect the propeller shaft and secure the shaft away from the work area.
5. Disconnect the shift linkage rod from the shift rail link.
6. Support the transfer case and remove the retaining bolts holding the transfer case to the transmission.
7. Move the transfer case to the rear and lower the assembly to remove from the vehicle.
8. Repair as required and remove all old gasket material from the transmission adaptor.

Installation

1. Position the transfer case on a support and position under the vehicle to mate with the transmission adapter.
2. Install the retaining bolts and remove the support.
3. Connect the shift linkage and secure.
4. Connect the propeller shafts to their mated yokes.
5. Install the cross member support and skid plate, if removed.
6. Connect the speedometer cable and fill the transfer case with lubricant (Dexron® II).
7. Lower the vehicle from the safety supports.

SHIFT LINKAGE

Adjustment

MODEL 207

1. Loosen the transfer case switch bolt and the case shift lever pivot bolt.
2. Shift the transfer case to the 4H position.
3. Remove the console and slide the boot up the lever.
4. Install a $^5/_{16}$ in. drill bit through the shifter and into the switch bracket.
5. Install a bolt at the case lever to lock it in position.
6. Tighten the switch bracket bolt to 30 ft. lb. and the shifter pivot bolt to 100 ft.lb.
7. Remove the bolt installed to lock the lever.
8. Remove the drill bit. Check the linkage action.

MODELS 208 AND 205

1. Place transfer case shift in "4 Hi" detent.
2. Mate shift lever and linkage to transfer case detent. Tighten lock nuts.

MANUAL TRANSMISSION

Troubleshooting and repair of manual transmission are covered in the Unit Repair section.

LIGHT DUTY TRANSMISSION—76MM 3 AND 4 SPEEDS

Removal

ALL, EXCEPT REGULAR SIZED VAN, JIMMY, S-SERIES AND BLAZER WITH 4 WHEEL DRIVE

1. Raise vehicle and support on jack stands.
2. Drain transmission.
3. Disconnect speedometer cable and electrical connections at transmission.
4. Disconnect shift control levers from transmission.
5. Disconnect parking brake lever and controls (if used).
6. Remove drive shaft after marking position of shaft to flange.
7. Position jack under transmission to support weight of transmission.
8. Remove crossmember. Visually inspect to see if other equipment, brackets or lines, must be removed to permit removal of transmission.

NOTE: Mark position of crossmember when removing to prevent incorrect installation.

9. Remove flywheel housing underpan.
10. Remove the top two transmission to housing bolts and insert two guide pins.

NOTE: The use of guide pins will not only support the transmission but will prevent damage to the clutch disc. Guide pins can be made by taking two bolts, the same as those just removed only longer and cutting off the heads. (Slot for screwdriver)

11. Remove two remaining bolts and slide transmission straight back from engine. Use care to keep the transmission drive gear straight in line with clutch disc hub.

NOTE: Be sure to support release bearing when removing transmission to avoid having bearing fall into flywheel housing.

12. When transmission is free from engine, move from under vehicle.

Installation

1. Place transmission on guide pins, slide forward starting main drive gear into clutch disc's splines.

NOTE: Place transmission in gear and rotate transmission flange or output yoke to aid entry of main drive gear into disc's splines. Make sure clutch release bearing is in position.

2. Install two lower transmission mounting bolts and flywheel lower pan (if equipped).
3. Remove guide pins and install upper mounting bolts.
4. Install propeller shaft, watch align marks.
5. Connect parking brake, back-up lamp and T.S.C. switch (if used).
6. Connect shift levers, see section on adjustment if needed.
7. Connect speedometer cable, refill transmission.
8. Lower vehicle and road test.

LIGHT DUTY TRANSMISSION—77.5MM 3, 4 AND 5 SPEEDS

Removal & Installation

S/T–SERIES TRUCKS

NOTE: On 4-wheel drive TRUCK models, see Transfer Case Removal and Installation.

1. Disconnect the battery ground.
2. Remove the upper starter retaining nut.
3. Remove the shift lever boot attaching screws and slide the boot up the shift lever.
4. Disconnect the shift lever at the transmission.
5. Disconnect the electrical connector at the transmission.
6. Raise and support the vehicle safely.
7. Remove the driveshaft.
8. Disconnect the exhaust pipe at the manifold.
9. Disconnect the speedometer cable and electrical connector at the transmission.
10. Disconnect the clutch cable at the transmission.
11. Place a floor jack under the transmission to take up its weight.
12. Remove the transmission mount bolts.
13. Remove the catalytic converter hanger.
14. Remove the crossmember.
15. Remove the lower dust cover bolts.
16. Remove the lower starter bolt.
17. Unbolt the transmission from the engine and lower it on the jack.
18. Installation is the reverse of removal. Torque the transmission-to-engine bolts to 25 ft. lb. on the 4 cylinder and 55 ft. lb. on the 6 cylinder. Torque the transmission mount-to-transmission bolts to 35 ft. lb.; the crossmember-to-frame bolts to 25 ft. lb.; the dust cover bolts to 7 ft. lb.

77MM 4–SPEED AND 5–SPEED

Removal and Installation

S/T–SERIES TRUCKS

NOTE: On 4-wheel drive models, see Transfer Case Removal and Installation.

1. Disconnect the battery ground.
2. Remove the shift lever boot screws and slide the boot up the lever.
3. Shift the transmission into neutral and remove the shift lever.
4. Raise and support the vehicle safely.
5. Remove the driveshaft.
6. Disconnect the speedometer cable and wiring at the transmission.
7. Disconnect the clutch cable at the transmission.
8. Place a floor jack under the transmission and take up its weight. Remove the transmission mount bolts.
9. Remove the catalytic converter hanger, if required,
10. Remove the crossmember. On Astro vans, remove the transmission support braces.
11. Remove the dust cover bolts.
12. Unbolt the transmission from the bell housing and lower the jack. It will be necessary to pull the transmission back a ways to clear the clutch. Installation is the reverse of removal. Lightly grease the input shaft splines with chassis lube.

89MM 4 SPEED

Removal

REGULAR SIZED VANS AND 2 WHEEL DRIVE TRUCKS

1. Place heavy cardboard between radiator core and fan blades as a precautionary measure.
2. Raise and support vehicle on stands or hoist, drain transmission.
3. Disconnect speedometer cable at transmission.
4. Disconnect parking brake and back-up lamp connections.
5. Disconnect propeller shaft and power take off (if equipped).
6. **3 speed (column shift):**
   a. Remove shift controls from transmission.

   4 speed (floor shift):
   a. Remove floor mat.
   b. Remove floor pan.
   c. Place transmission in neutral and remove gearshift lever by sliding open side of tool over lever, engage lugs of tool in the open slot of retainer, press down on tool and turn to left to disengage the lugs on retainer. Cover transmission opening. Be careful of pivot pin.
   d. Remove reverse lever cable and bracket at transmission.

   4 speed (column shift):
   a. Remove shift controls from levers.
   b. Remove reverse lever cable and bracket at transmission.

7. Remove clutch shaft frame bolts and accelerator linkage at manifold bellcrank.
8. Place jack under bell housing and raise enough to relieve weight at transmission rear support.
9. Remove transmission rear support crossmember or on early models, remove support bolt and lower engine carefully to allow transmission rear mount to clear support bracket.
10. Position jack under transmission and adjust to carry weight of transmission (if 4 speed).
11. Remove 2 top transmission to bell housing bolts and install 2 guide pins to prevent damaging clutch disc.
12. Remove two lower transmission mounting bolts.
13. Visually inspect to determine if other equipment or lines need to be removed.
14. Slide transmission back on guide pins, four speed units aided by jack (support release bearing), until transmission clears engine. Remove transmission from under vehicle.

CAUTION

If other work is to be performed, support engine more securely after transmission is removed.

Installation

1. Clean bell housing and transmission mating surfaces, lightly lubricate main drive gear bearing retainer and clutch pilot bushing or bearing. Make sure release bearing is in position.
2. Move transmission into position on guide pins, shift transmission into any gear.
3. Slide transmission forward rotating transmission flange or yoke to aid entry of main drive gear into clutch disc splines.
4. Install two lower transmission mounting bolts. Remove guide pins and install two upper mounting bolts. Remove transmission jack.
5. Carefully raise engine and transmission to normal position and install transmission rear mounting bolt or crossmember. Remove jack from under bell housing. Remove cardboard from radiator.
6. Connect speedometer cable, parking brake, back-up light and T.S.C. switch (if equipped).
7. Connect propeller shaft and power take off (if equipped).
8. Connect clutch shaft and accelerator linkage.
9. Reinstall shift controls on transmission or gearshift lever on four speed. Install reverse cable and bracket. See section on shift linkage adjustment if needed.
10. Replace floor mat and floor pans on four speed units.
11. Refill transmission, lower vehicle and road test.

89MM 4 SPEED

Removal and Installation

4 WHEEL DRIVE, INCLUDING BLAZER AND JIMMY

1. Floor shift models.
   a. Remove shift lever boots and retainers on both transfer case and transmission.
   b. Remove floor mat or carpet, seat and accelerator pedal, as required.
   c. Center console models: remove center outlet from heater distributor duct and remove console.
   d. Remove transmission floor cover, shift transfer case lever into neutral and rotate floor cover approximately 90° while lifting to clear transfer case lever.
   e. Slide open side of tool over transmission gearshift lever, engage lugs of tool in open slot of retainer, press down and turn counter-clockwise to remove lever. Do same for transfer case lever. Be careful of any pivot pins. Cover transmission openings.
2. Raise vehicle and support safely.
3. Drain transmission and transfer case.
4. Disconnect back-up light and electrical connections.
5. Disconnect parking brake, if used.
6. Disconnect speedometer cable (at transfer case on some models).
7. Disconnect front and rear auxiliary drive shafts at transfer case and tie up out of work area.
8. Remove bolts attaching transfer case to adapter (remove side access cover to reach two bolts).
9. Support rear of engine with jack.
10. Support transfer case on cradle or dolly. Remove two transmission adapter mounting bolts.
11. Remove transfer case mounting bolts, remove transfer case (all except Blazer and Jimmy).
12. Column shift models:
    a. Disconnect shift control rods from levers at transmission.
    b. On 4 speed, remove reverse cable and bracket at transmission.
13. Remove two upper transmission mounting bolts and install two guide pins (longer bolts with heads cut off and slotted). Use of guide pins will prevent damage to clutch disc.
14. Remove flywheel under pan and remove two lower transmission mounting bolts.
15. On V8 engines, remove exhaust crossover pipe.
16. On Blazer and Jimmy, remove transmission frame crossmember bolts. Remove crossmember (rotating to clear frame rails).
17. Visually inspect to determine if other equipment or lines need to be removed.
18. Slide transmission and adapter (transmission with transfer case on Blazer or Jimmy) back on guide pins, aided by transmission dolly, until main drive gear clears clutch (watch clutch release bearing), remove from under vehicle.
19. Lubricate pilot bushing or bearing, make sure clutch release bearing is in position, use guide pins to align transmission and rotate main drive gear to enter clutch disc splines without forcing. Reverse removal procedures to install.

HEAVY DUTY TRANSMISSIONS

The procedures required to remove and install the transmissions covered in this section are dependent upon types of cabs, engines and chassis used, also what equipment is available in repair shop. Other operations may be necessary if vehicle has special equipment; therefore, procedures contained herein will serve only as a guide. It is important to note that vehicles covered in this section will have either an "apron" or "S.A.E. 2" type of flywheel housing. The apron type is identified by sheet metal pan, also note it is a one piece housing. The "S.A.E. 2" type completely surrounds the flywheel. A separate clutch housing is used in addition to the flywheel housing. Transmission replacement procedures are different for each type of flywheel housing used.

Removal

1. Drain transmission.
2. On transmission equipped with remote controls:
   a. Disconnect control rods from shift levers at transmission.
3. On transmissions with a conventional floor gearshift lever.
   a. Remove steering jacket grommet from floor and slide grommet up mast jacket out of way (if used).
   b. Remove floor mat and accelerator pedal.
   c. Disconnect and remove parking brake lever.
   d. Remove transmission floor pan(s), place gearshift lever in neutral.
   e. Remove gearshift lever (and control tower on some models).

NOTE: On models with New Process Transmissions, remove lever by sliding open side of tool over lever. Engage lugs of tool in open slot of retainer, press down on tool and turn to left to disengage lugs on retainer. Lift lever out of cover, be careful of pivot pin. Cover opening in transmission.

On Spicer models, press down on shift lever cup and drive locking pin out of lever. Lift off cup, spring, cap and seal. Remove snap-ring from groove on lever housing and tap out slotted pin. Lift lever out of housing and cover opening.

On Clark models, remove shift lever housing cover to transmission bolts. Lift lever and control tower from transmission. Cover transmission opening.

On air control shift models, bleed air tanks, remove range shift lines at air valve on transmission. Remove gearshift lever and control tower assembly from transmission. Cover transmission opening and tape or plug air valves.

4. Disconnect and drop propeller shaft at transmission.

5. If unit is equipped with power take-off, disconnect drive shaft and controls.
6. Remove reverse shift control cable and bracket on 4 speed units.
7. Disconnect any clutch control linkage on transmission.
8. Disconnect speedometer cable at transmission.
9. Remove engine ground strap and back up lamp switch.
10. Place transmission jack into position and adjust to carry weight of transmission. Use locking chain to secure transmission to jack.

NOTE: On vehicles which have rear engine mountings attached to the clutch housing (except "apron" type flywheel housing models), position a jack under flywheel housing and adjust to carry the weight of the engine. Remove rear engine mounts.

11. Remove bolts attaching transmission to rear crossmember support brackets (if used).
12. Remove clutch housing-to-flywheel housing bolts (except on "apron" type flywheel housing models).

NOTE: On models with "apron" type flywheel housing, remove flywheel housing under pan (also access panel on Spicer) and transmission to flywheel housing bolts. The use of guidepins in two top holes of "apron" type flywheel housing or in two top side holes on "S.A.E." type will maintain alignment during both removal and installation of transmission.

13. Visually inspect to determine if other equipment or lines must be removed.
14. Move transmission straight back, using guide pins to keep transmission main drive gear in alignment with clutch disc, until free from engine. Be sure to support clutch release bearing during removal of transmission. Lower transmission and move from under the vehicle.

Installation

1. Clean transmission mating surfaces and apply a light film of grease to main drive gear bearing retainer and clutch pivot bearing.
2. Place transmission on jack and move into position.
3. On "apron" type, place clutch release bearing and support assembly inside flywheel housing. Be sure clutch fork engages bearing. On "S.A.E. 2" type, make sure clutch release bearing is in position.
4. Using guide pins to align transmission main drive gear with clutch disc, move transmission forward rotating main drive gear so gear can enter clutch disc splines without forcing.
5. Reverse removal procedures to install.

NOTE: On transmissions having remote controls make the following control island shift mechanism adjustments if necessary.

1. Place transmission selector and shift levers in neutral.
2. Adjust selector and shift rods to provide 90° angle at the lower end of the gearshift lever to the control island panel. Adjustment is made by rotating the adjustable clevis at either the control island or transmission end of the selector and shift rods. Tighten lock nuts.
3. Check adjustments by moving gearshift lever through shift pattern.

NOTE: On 4 speed transmissions with reverse idler eccentric. To adjust the position of the reverse idler gear, the transmission must be fully assembled except for power take-off cover. Then proceed as follows:

1. Loosen the eccentric nut and rotate the eccentric, using a screwdriver in the slot with end of eccentric, until slot with dot on end is to the rear. This places the reverse idler in its extreme rear position and will provide for maximum engagement when the transmission is shifted into reverse.
2. Shift transmission into second. Check for interference between reverse idler and first and reverse gear. If interference exists, rotate eccentric in a counter-clockwise direction to obtain approximately $1/32$ in. clearance. This clearance can be checked through the power take-off opening.
4. Shift transmission into reverse and check clearance between reverse idler gear and transmission case. If necessary, rotate the eccentric an additional amount, in counter-clockwise direction, to obtain running clearance at this point.
5. Tighten eccentric nut and lock.
6. Install power take-off cover and new gasket.

TRANSMISSION SHIFT LINKAGE

Adjustment

3 SPEED COLUMN

1. Raise vehicle and support on stands.
2. Disconnect control rods at transmission levers.
3. Place transmission shift levers in neutral (neutral detents in cover must be fully engaged).
4. Place gearshift lever in neutral, on early models remove housing cover at base of mast jacket and make sure shifter gates and inner levers are aligned. If alignment is off, loosen first and reverse control rod swivel clamp at housing outer lever and adjust swivel until shifter gates are aligned.
5. Adjust swivels on control rods until swivels (or rods) enter transmission shift lever holes. Make sure levers remain in neutral position. Lock control rods.
6. Lower vehicle and move gearshift lever through all gear positions to check (keep clutch pedal depressed to aid shifting).

4 SPEED COLUMN SHIFT, EXCEPT VAN

1. Place gearshift lever in neutral. Raise vehicle on hoist.
2. Disconnect first and second shift rod from cross shaft lever. Disconnect third and fourth shift rod from transmission le-

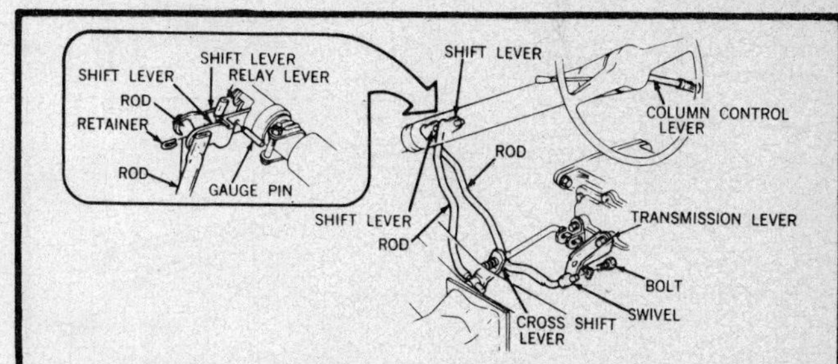

Column shift linkage—C and K models (© General Motors Corp.)

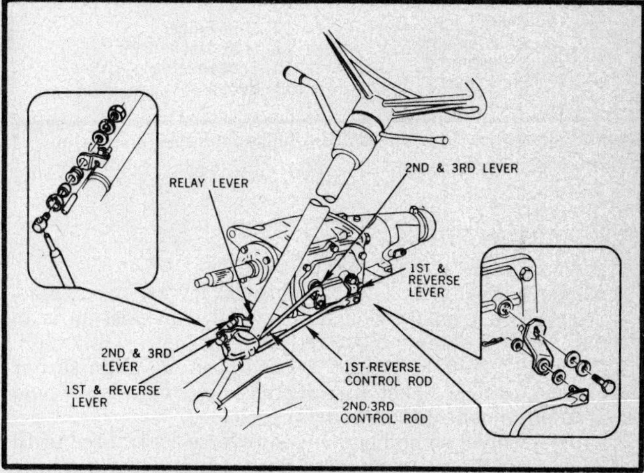

Column shift linkage—G models (© General Motors Corp.)

ver. Disconnect reverse cable from reverse lever by removing "C" clip. Manually shift all transmission controls into neutral, including reverse lever.

3. Remove engine splash shield. Install a fabricated pin (see illustration for details) through upper control shaft bracket into cutouts in shift levers and into hole provided at base of control shaft as shown.

4. Adjust swivel on end of first and second rod to freely enter cross shaft lever hole. Reconnect rod to lever.

5. Adjust swivel on end of third and fourth rod to freely enter transmission lever. Reconnect rod to lever.

6. Adjust swivel on end of reverse cable to freely enter reverse lever hole. If more adjustment is needed at swivel, adjust cable assembly by using cable to bracket attaching nuts. Install washer and C-clip. Tighten swivel lock nut.

7. Remove fabricated pin, replace splash shield, lower vehicle and move gearshift lever through all gear positions to check. Depressing clutch pedal will aid in shifting.

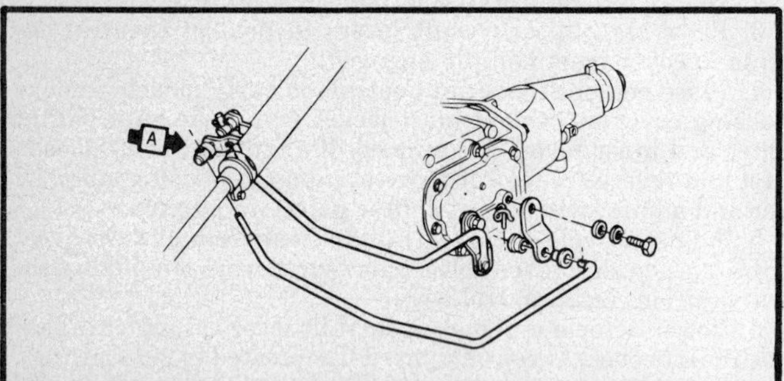

Column shift linkage—P models (© General Motors Corp.)

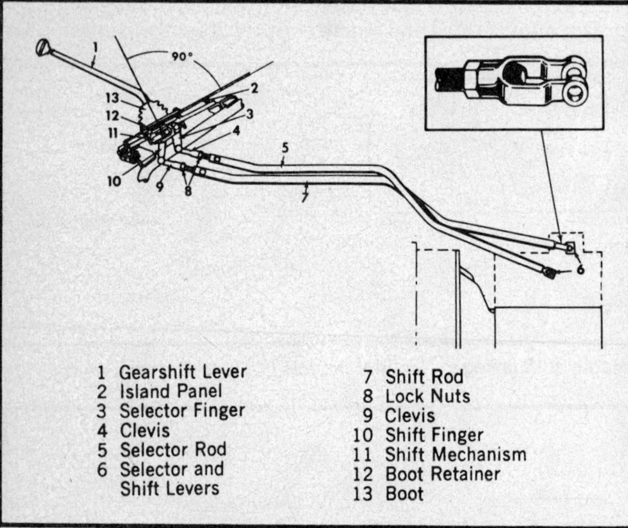

Gearshift linkage w/dual rod control—tilt cab models (© General Motors Corp.)

VAN COLUMN SHIFT

1. Raise vehicle and support on stands.
2. Remove control rods at transmission levers.
3. Move both transmission levers until transmission is in neutral. Neutral detents must be fully engaged.
4. Move gearshift lever into neutral position, align shifter relay levers on mast jacket, install pin in holes of levers to hold levers in alignment and in neutral position.
5. Adjust swivel on end of low and reverse control rod until swivel enters transmission lever freely, lock with retaining ring, tighten swivel locknut.

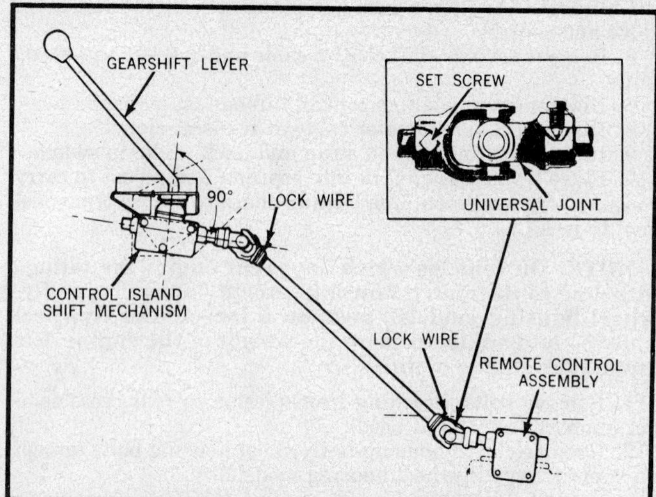

Gearshift linkage w/two piece shift rod—tilt cab models (© General Motors Corp.)

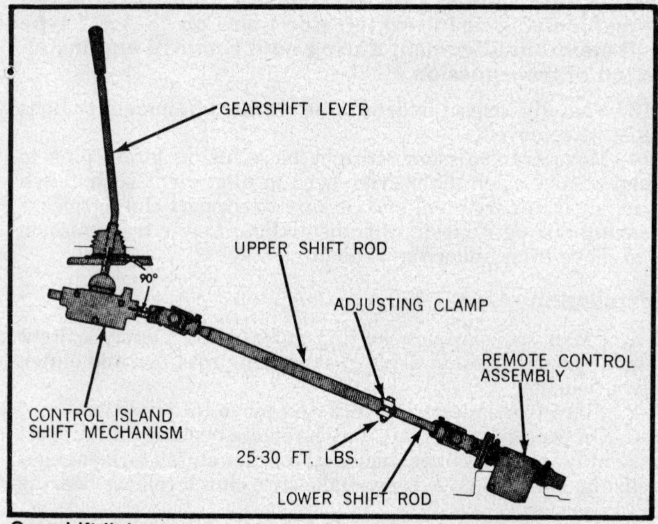

Gearshift linkage w/one piece shift rod-tilt cab models (© General Motors Corp.)

6. Similarly, install second and third control rod, be sure levers remain in neutral.
7. Lower vehicle and move gearshift lever through all gear positions to check. Keep clutch pedal depressed to aid in shifting.

TILT CAB (W/DUAL ROD CONTROL)

1. Position the transmission selector and shift levers in NEUTRAL.

NOTE: The position of the selector and shift levers (in NEUTRAL) is critical and must be maintained throughout the adjustment procedure.

2. Disconnect the clevis of either control rod (both if necessary) at the transmission and rotate the clevis(es) to the length required to bring the lower end of the gearshift lever into a 90 degree relationship with the control island panel.
3. Connect the control rods to the transmission.
4. Check adjustment by shifting through the gear ranges.

TILT CAB (W/ONE-PIECE SHIFT ROD)

1. Shift the transmission into NEUTRAL and tilt the cab forward.

2. Remove the lock wire and set screw from the U-joint at the shift rod.
3. Secure the gearshift lever to maintain a 90 degree angle between the lower end of the lever and the control island shift mechanism. Adjust the position of both U-joints to retain the 90 degree angle.
4. Install the set screw and the lock wire.

TILT CAB (W/TWO-PIECE SHIFT ROD)

NOTE: This operation is similar to the one for tilt cabs equipped with a one-piece shift rod. The only difference is the point of adjustment. On vehicles equipped with the two-piece shift rod, the adjustment is made by loosening the adjusting clamp to achieve the 90 degree gearshift lever angle and then tightening the clamp to retain the angle.

Auxiliary Transmissions

The Spicer auxiliary transmission is supported at the front by a support bracket attached to the frame side rails and at the rear by a support beam attached to frame brackets. The gears are shifted by a lever in the cab, which is interconnected to the auxiliary transmission with control rods. The hand brake and speedometer drive gear are located at the rear of the transmission.

Removal

1. Drain the lubricant.
2. Disconnect and support the propeller shafts from the input and output ends of the transmission.
3. Disconnect the shift control rods from the front of the transmission.
4. Disconnect the speedometer cable from the adapter at the rear of the transmission.
5. Disconnect the parking brake linkage if applicable.
6. Remove all connections to the auxiliary transmission power take-off.
7. Place a suitable dolly or jack under the transmission and adjust its position so it can safely carry the weight.
8. Disconnect the front and rear mountings and lower the transmission away from the chassis.

Installation

1. Make sure the tapered surface of the front mounts face the front of the vehicle as shown in the illustration.
2. Move the transmission into position under the vehicle and adjust the front and rear height. (See Alignment Data Chart.)
3. Torque the attaching parts to the proper specifications (See torque specification chart)
4. Reconnect the propeller shafts to the input and output ends of the transmission.

NOTE: It is important that all angles of the driveline be checked with a bevel protractor. Also the auxiliary transmission must be the same as the engine and main transmission. Adjustments may be made by raising or lowering the front or rear of the auxiliary transmission or by adding plates, washers, spacers etc. (See Driveshaft Alignment in U-joints-Drive Line section).

5. Connect the power take-off, if applicable.
6. Connect the parking brake linkage.
7. Connect the speedometer cable to the adapter at the rear of the transmission.
8. Connect the shift control rods and adjust if necessary.
9. Refill the transmission with the recommended lubricant.

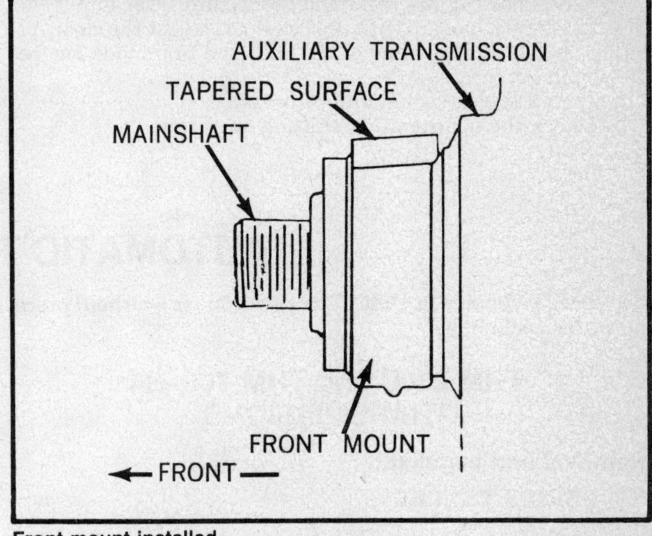

Front mount installed

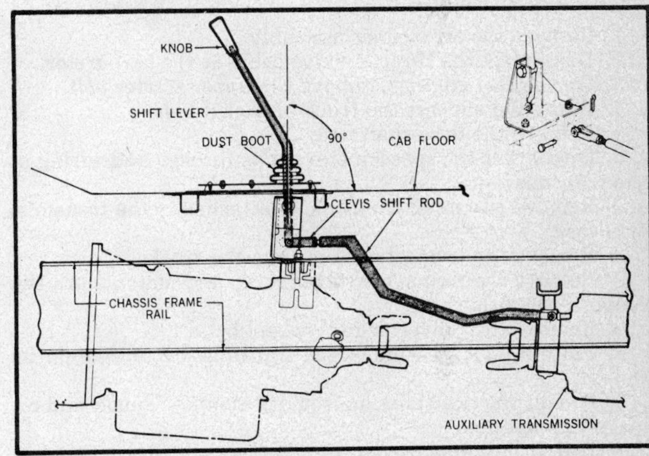

Gearshift linkage—auxiliary transmission AT-1202 (© General Motors Corp.)

AUXILIARY TRANSMISSION SHIFT LINKAGE

Adjustment

SP6041 AND SP7041

1. Disconnect the control rods from the shift control tower under the cab.
2. Place the auxiliary transmission gearshift lever and shift rods in the "Neutral" position.
3. Adjust the length of each control rod by rotating its adjustable clevis to provide a free clevis pin fit.
4. Reconnect the control rods to the control tower and shift the transmission through its entire shift pattern.
5. Replace any worn or damaged cotter pins, tighten the locknuts firmly and lubricate the control linkage.

AT1202

1. Remove the clevis pin and disconnect the control rod from the shift lever.

NOTE: Make sure that the shift lever mounting bracket bolts are tight.

2. Place the transmission shift rail in the NEUTRAL position.

3. While holding the lower end of the shift lever in a 90 degree angle relationship with the cab floor, adjust the clevis position on the threaded end of the shift rod to provide for free clevis pin entry.
4. Install the clevis pin and cotter pin.
5. Check the transmission shifting operation.

NOTE: Check for free pin rotation in each gear. If the pin does not turn freely, then a binding condition exists. Readjust the clevis if necessary.

6. Tighten the jam nut against the clevis and spread the cotter pin ends to retain the pin.

AUTOMATIC TRANSMISSION

See specific chapter in Unit Repair section for overhaul procedures for each make.

THM 200C and THM 700–R4 TRANSMISSIONS

Removal and Installation

S/T–SERIES TRUCKS

NOTE: On 4-wheel drive models, see Transfer Case Removal and Installation.

1. Remove the air cleaner assembly.
2. Disconnect the throttle valve cable at the carburetor.
3. On the L–4 engines, remove the upper starter bolt.
4. Raise and support the truck on jackstands.
5. Remove the driveshaft.
6. Disconnect the speedometer cable, linkage and wiring at the transmission.
7. Remove any other components attached to the transmission case.
8. Remove the exhaust system from the truck.
9. Remove the torque converter cover and match-mark the converter and flywheel.
10. Remove the converter-to-flywheel bolts.
11. Place a floor jack under the transmission to take up its weight.
12. Unbolt the transmission from its mounts. Unbolt and remove the mounts.
13. Lower the transmission slightly to gain access to the fluid cooler lines. Disconnect and cap these lines.
14. Disconnect the throttle valve cable.
15. Place a jack or jackstand under the engine for support.
16. Unbolt the transmission from the engine. Lower the assembly to gain access to the oil cooler lines and to the T.V. cable connections.
17. Pull the transmission rearward to disengage it and lower it from the truck.

NOTE: Take care to avoid dropping the converter.

18. Installation is the reverse of removal. Match up the mating marks on the converter.

THM 350C, THM 700–R4

Removal

CAUTION

The temperature of the transmission fluid, after the vehicle has been in operation, can exceed 350 degrees F.

EXCEPT 4 WHEEL DRIVE VEHICLES

1. With vehicle on hoist drain by removing pan or drain plug (if so equipped).

NOTE: Fluid can be drained after transmission is removed if so desired.

2. Remove the vacuum modulator line and speedometer cable from the transmission and secure out of way.
3. Remove detent cable and manual control lever from the transmission.
4. Disconnect the drive shaft and remove.
5. Place suitable jack or other support under transmission and secure transmission to it.
6. At transmission extension disconnect rear engine mount and then remove support crossmember.
7. Remove converter underpan. Place marks on the flywheel and converter to insure proper installation and then remove the flywheel-to-converter bolts.
8. Support engine at oil pan rail with jack capable of supporting the weight of the engine when transmission is removed.
9. Lower rear of the transmission slightly so that upper, housing-to-engine, transmission bolts can be reached with a long extension and universal socket. Remove upper bolts.

NOTE: Have an assistant watch upper engine parts to make sure everything clears when rear of transmission is being lowered.

10. Remove remaining transmission-to-housing bolts.
11. Remove transmission by moving it slightly to the rear and downward. Remove from under vehicle.

CAUTION

Watch converter when removing transmission to be sure that it moves with transmission. If it does not move pry it free from flywheel before proceeding any further.

NOTE: On those vehicles so equipped, disconnection of the catalytic converter may be necessary to provide adequate clearance for transmission removal.

NOTE: Keep transmission front upward when removing transmission to prevent converter from falling out. Install converter holding tool after removal from engine.

For overhaul procedures,see Unit Repair section.

Installation

1. Mount transmission on transmission lifting device.
2. Remove converter holding tool.

CAUTION

Do not permit converter to move forward after removal of holding tool.

3. Raise transmission into place at rear of engine and install transmission case to engine upper mounting bolts, then install remainder of the mounting bolts.
4. Remove support from beneath engine, then raise rear of transmission to final position.
5. If scribed during removal, align scribe marks on flywheel and converter cover. Install converter to flywheel attaching nuts and bolts.
6. Install converter underpan.
7. Reinstall transmission support crossmember to transmission and frame.

8. Remove transmission lift equipment.
9. Connect propeller shaft to transmission.
10. Connect manual control lever rod and detent cable to transmission.
11. Connect vacuum modulator line and speedometer drive cable to transmission.
12. Lower vehicle.
13. Refill transmission.
14. Check transmission for proper operation and for leakage. Check and, if necessary, adjust linkage.
15. Remove vehicle from hoist.

THM 350C

Removal

4 WHEEL DRIVE VEHICLES

1. With vehicle on hoist drain by removing pan or drain plug (if so equipped).

NOTE: Fluid can be drained after transmission removal if so desired.

2. Remove shift lever and rod from transfer case.
3. Remove speedometer cable and vacuum modulator line from transmission and secure out of way.
4. Disconnect detent cable and manual control lever rod from transmission.
5. Remove front and rear drive shafts from transfer case.
6. Place jack or other support under transfer case and remove transmission-to-adapter case bolts.
7. Place jack or other support under transmission and secure transmission to it.
8. Remove transfer case-to-frame bracket bolts and remove transfer case.
9. On V8 engines, remove exhaust crossover pipe.
10. Disconnect and remove rear transmission crossmember.
11. Remove converter underpan. Place marks on the flywheel and converter to insure proper installation and then remove the flywheel-to-converter bolts.
12. Support engine at oil pan rail with jack capable of supporting engine weight when transmission is removed.
13. Lower rear of transmission slightly so that upper housing-to-engine transmission bolts can be removed with a long extension and universal socket. Remove upper bolts.

NOTE: Have an assistant watch upper engine parts to make sure everything clears when transmission is lowered.

14. Remove the remaining transmission-to-housing bolts.
15. Remove the transmission by moving it slightly to the rear and downward. Remove from under vehicle.

CAUTION

Watch converter when removing transmission to make sure converter moves with transmission. If it does not, pry it loose from flywheel before proceeding any further.

NOTE: Keep transmission front upwards when removing from engine to prevent converter holding tool after removal from engine. See Unit Repair section for overhaul procedures.

Installation

1. Mount transmission on transmission lifting equipment installed on jack or other lifting device.
2. Remove converter holding tool.

CAUTION

Do not permit converter to move forward after removal of holding tool.

3. Raise transmission into place at rear of engine and install transmission case to engine upper mounting bolts, then install remainder of the mounting bolts.
4. Remove support from beneath engine, then raise rear of transmission to final position.
5. If scribed during removal, align scribe marks on flywheel and converter cover. Install converter to flywheel attaching bolts.
6. Install flywheel cover.
7. Place transfer case and adapter assembly at rear of transmission on suitable lift equipment and install transfer case to frame bracket attaching bolts.
8. Reinstall transmission to transfer case adapter attaching bolts and remove lift equipment.
9. Connect front and rear axle propeller shafts to transfer case.
10. Install exhaust system cross pipe.
11. Connect manual control lever rod and detent cable to transmission.
12. Connect vacuum modulator line and speedometer drive cable to transmission.
13. Assemble rod on transfer case shift lever before installing rod to transfer case shift linkage.
14. Lower vehicle.
15. Refill transmission.
16. Check transmission for proper operation and for leakage. Check and if necessary, adjust linkage.
17. Remove from hoist.

THM 400

Removal and Installation

REGULAR SIZED VANS AND TRUCKS

NOTE: Before raising the vehicle, disconnect the battery and release the parking brake.

1. Raise vehicle and support safely.
2. Remove propeller shaft.
3. Disconnect speedometer cable, electrical lead to case connector, vacuum line at modulator and oil cooler pipes.
4. Disconnect shift control linkage.
5. Support transmission with transmission jack.
6. Disconnect rear mount from frame crossmember.
7. Remove two bolts at each end of frame crossmember and remove crossmember.
8. Remove converter under pan.
9. Remove converter to flywheel bolts.
10. Loosen exhaust pipe to manifold bolts approximately $\frac{1}{4}$ in. and lower transmission until jack is barely supporting it.
11. Remove transmission to engine mounting bolts and remove oil filler tube at transmission.
12. Raise transmission to its normal position, support engine with jack and slide transmission rearward from engine and lower it away from vehicle.

CAUTION

Use converter holding tool when lowering transmission or keep rear of transmission lower than front so as not to lose converter.

The installation of the transmission is the reverse of the removal with the following additional steps.

Before installing the flex plate to converter bolts, make certain that the weld nuts on the converter are flush with the flex plate and the converter rotates freely by hand in this position. Then, hand start all three bolts and tighten finger tight before torquing to specification. This will insure proper converter alignment.

NOTE: After installation of transmission check linkage for proper adjustment and check for leaks.

THM 700–R4

Removal and Installation

ASTRO/SAFARI VANS

1. Open the hood and disconnect the negative battery cable.
2. Remove the inner engine cover.
3. Disconnect the T.V. cable at its upper end.
4. Raise the vehicle and support safely.
5. match-mark and remove the propeller shaft.
6. Disconnect the speedometer cable and all electrical leads or connections at the transmission.
7. Disconnect the shift linkage at the transmission.
8. Remove the transmission support brace attaching bolts at the converter cover.
9. Disconnect the exhaust cross over pipe from the exhaust manifolds.
10. Remove the converter cover and match-mark the flywheel to the torque converter. Remove the bolts or nuts.
11. Position a transmission lifting jack or its equivalent, under the transmission and raise slightly.
12. Remove the transmission crossmember mounting bolts, slide it rearward and remove from the vehicle.
13. Lower the rear of the transmission to gain access to the oil cooler lines and the T.V. cable attachment.
14. Disconnect the lines and the T.V. cable. Cap all openings.
15. Support the engine with a suitable tool and remove the transmission to engine bolts.
16. Carefully pull the transmission rearward and down to clear the underneath of the vehicle. Install the converter holding tool and remove the transmission from the vehicle.
17. The installation of the transmission is the reverse of the removal procedure.
18. Upon installation, verify no leakages are present and all connection have been properly installed.

Automatic Transmission

Draining and Refilling

TYPICAL OF ALL MODELS

CAUTION

The temperature of the transmission fluid, after the vehicle has been in operation, can exceed 350 degrees F.

1. Raise the vehicle and support safely.
2. Place a fluid receptacle under the transmission pan. Remove the pan attaching bolts from the front and side of the pan.
3. Loosen the rear pan attaching bolts approximately four turns and pry the pan loose to allow the fluid to drain.
4. Remove the remaining pan screws and remove the pan and gasket. Discard the gasket.
5. Remove the strainer to valve body screws and remove the strainer (filter) and gasket and discard.

NOTE: On the 400 transmissions, remove the filter retaining bolt, filter and intake pipe O-ring. When installing, replace the filter and the intake pipe O-ring. Tighten the retaining bolt to 10 ft. lbs

6. Install the new strainer and gasket and install the strainer to valve body screws and tighten.
7. Install a new gasket on the oil pan and install the oil pan. Tighten the pan bolts to 12 ft. lbs torque. Connect and tighten the filler tube.
8. Lower the vehicle and install 2.5 quarts of transmission fluid into the transmission and start the engine.
9. Move the selector lever through the detents for each range. Add fluid to bring the level to ¼ in. below the ADD mark on the dipstick.

THM 200C, 350C, 400 and 700 R–4

SHIFT LINKAGE

Adjustment

S/T SERIES TRUCKS AND ASTRO/SAFARI VANS

With the selector lever in Park, the parking pawl should engage and immobilize the transmission. The pointer on the indicator quadrant should line up properly with the indicated gear position in all ranges. To adjust the linkage, raise and support the truck on jackstands. Place the selector in Park. Loosen the locknut on the linkage arm at the transmission and make sure that the transmission lever is fully in the Park position. Tighten the locknut.

CABS, SUBURBANS, 4-WHEEL DRIVE, FORWARD CONTROL EXC. VANS

1. Place gearshift lever in Drive (D), as determined by transmission detent. Obtain Drive position by rotating transmission lever counterclockwise to low detent, then clockwise two detent positions to Drive.
2. Loosen adjustment swivel at mast jacket lever and rotate transmission lever so that it contacts the Drive stop in the steering column.
3. Tighten swivel and recheck adjustment.
4. Readjust indicator pointer, if necessary, to agree with transmission detent positions.
5. Readjust neutral safety switch, if necessary.

REGULAR SIZED VANS

1. The shift tube and lever assembly must be free in the mast jacket.
2. Set transmission lever in Neutral position by one of the following optional methods.

NOTE: Obtain Neutral position by moving transmission lever counter-clockwise to "LI" detent, then clockwise three detent positions to Neutral or obtain Neutral position by moving transmission lever clockwise to the Park detent then counter-clockwise two detents to Neutral.

3. Set the column shift lever in Neutral position. This is obtained by rotating shift lever until it locks into mechanical stop in the column assembly.

NOTE: Do not use indicator pointer as a reference to position the shift lever.

4. Attach rod (A) to shaft assembly (B) as shown.
5. Slide swivel (D) and clamp (E) onto rod (A) align the column shift lever and loosely attach as shown.
6. Hold column lever against Neutral stop Park position side.
7. Tighten nut (F) to 18 ft. lbs
8. Readjust indicator needle if necessary to agree with the transmission detent positions.
9. Readjust neutral start switch if necessary to provide the correct relationship to the transmission detent positions.

CAUTION

Any inaccuracies in the above adjustments may result in premature failure of the transmission due to operation without controls in full detent position. Such operation results in reduced oil pressure and partial engagement of clutches.

DETENT CABLE

Adjustment

THM 350C

1. Disengage the snap lock on the detent cable.

2. Place the carburetor in the wide open position.
3. Holding the carburetor in the wide open position, push the snap lock on the detent cable downward until the top is flush with the cable.

DETENT CABLE

Adjustment

IN-LINE ENGINES

1. After installation into transmission, install cable fitting into engine bracket.

CAUTION

Slider must not ratchet through the fitting before or during assembly into bracket. Use the readjustment procedure to correct this condition.

2. Install cable terminal to carburetor lever.
3. Open carburetor lever to "full throttle stop" position to automatically adjust slider on cable to correct setting.

CAUTION

Lock tab must not be depressed during this operation.

4. Release carburetor lever.

DETENT CABLE READJUSTMENT PROCEDURE

In case readjustment is necessary because of inadvertent adjustment before or during assembly, or for repair, perform the following:

1. Depress and hold metal lock tab.
2. Move slider back through fitting in direction away from carburetor lever until slider stops against fitting.
3. Release metal lock tab.
4. Repeat Steps 2–4 of adjustment procedure.

V8 ENGINES EXCEPT WITH THM 350C

1. After installation into transmission, install cable fitting into engine bracket.

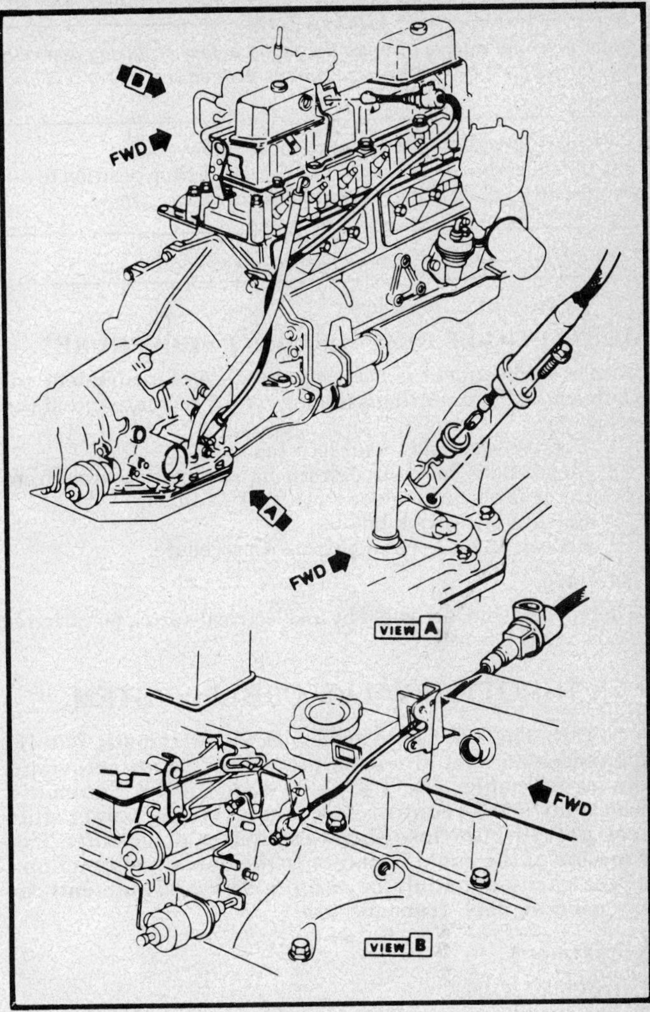

Detent cable adjustment—in-line engines (© General Motors Corp.)

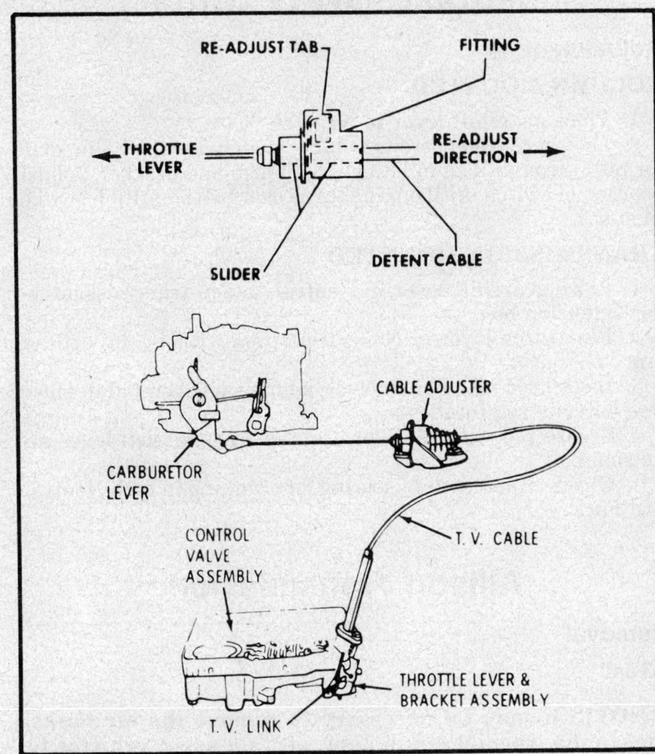

Throttle valve cable adjustment point

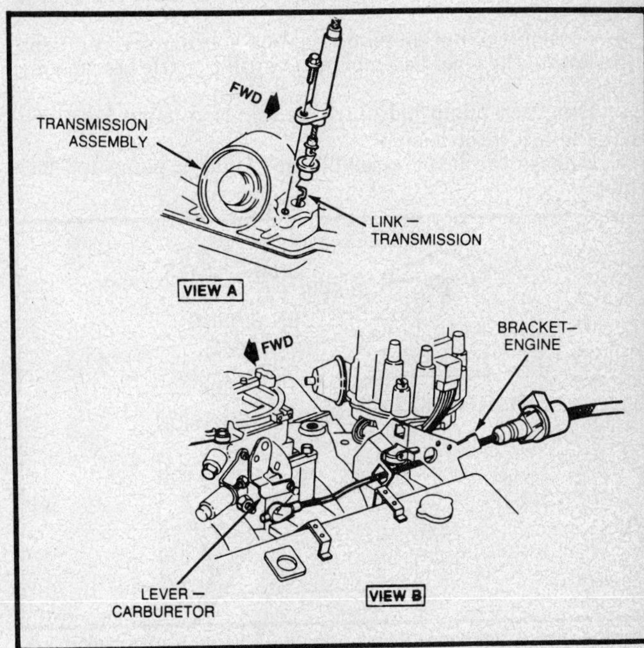

Detent cable adjustment—V8 engines (© General Motors Corp.)

CAUTION

Slider must not ratchet through the fitting before or during assembly into bracket. Use the re-adjustment procedure to correct this condition.

2. Install cable terminal to carburetor lever.
3. Open carburetor lever to Full Throttle Stop position to automatically adjust slider on cable to correct setting.

CAUTION

Lock tab must not be depressed during this operation.

4. Release carburetor lever.

DETENT CABLE READJUSTMENT PROCEDURE

In case readjustment is necessary because of inadvertent adjustment before or during assembly, or for repair, perform the following:

1. Depress and hold metal lock tab.
2. Move slider back through fitting in direction away from carburetor lever until slider stops against fitting.
3. Release metal lock tab.
4. Repeat Steps 2–4 of adjustment procedure.

THM 400

A detent solenoid, activated by an electrical switch on carburetor, controls downshifts.

THROTTLE VALVE CABLE SYSTEM

NOTE: The T.V. Cable used with the Automatic 700–4R transmission should not be thought of as an automatic downshift cable. The T.V. cable used on the Automatic 200C and 700–R4 controls line pressure, shift points, shift feel, part throttle downshifts and detent downshifts. The function of the cable is similar to the combined functions of the vacuum modulator and the downshift (detent) cable used on 350C transmission.

Adjustment

DIESEL ENGINE

1. Stop Engine.
2. Remove cruise control rod (if so equipped).
3. Disconnect transmission T.V. cable terminal from throttle assembly.
4. Loosen lock nut on pump rod and shorten several turns.
5. Rotate the lever assembly to the full throttle position and hold.
6. Lengthen pump rod until the injection pump lever contacts the full throttle stop.
7. Release the lever assembly and tighten pump rod lock nut.

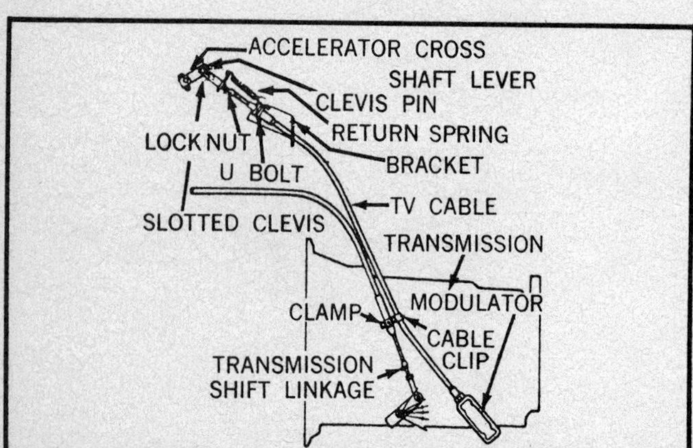

Throttle valve linkage—diesel engine—Allison transmission (© General Motors Corp.)

8. Remove the pump rod from the lever assembly.
9. Reconnect the transmission T.V. cable terminal to throttle assembly.
10. Depress and hold the metal re-adjust tab on the cable upper end. Move the slider through the fitting in the direction away from the lever assembly until the slider stops against the fitting.
11. Release the tab, rotate the lever assembly to the full throttle stop and release the lever assembly.
12. Reconnect the pump rod (and cruise control throttle rod if so equipped).
13. If equipped with cruise control, adjust the servo throttle rod to minimum slack (engine off) then put clip in first free hole closet to the bellcrank, but within the servo bail.

GAS ENGINE WITH SELF-ADJUSTING CABLE

1. Stop engine.
2. Depress re-adjust tab. Move slider back through fitting in direction away from throttle body until slider stops against fitting.
3. Release re-adjust tab.
4. Open carburetor lever to "full throttle stop" position to automatically adjust cable. Release carburetor lever.
5. Check cable for sticking and binding.Road test vehicle. If delayed or only full throttle shifts still occur, proceed with the following:

Remove the oil pan and inspect the throttle lever and bracket assembly. Check that the T.V. exhaust valve lifter rod is not distorted and not binding in the control valve assembly or spacer plate. The T.V. exhaust check ball must move up and down as the lifter does. Also, be sure lifter spring holds the lifter rod up against the bottom of the control valve assembly. Make sure T.V. plunger is not stuck. Inspect transmission for correct throttle lever to cable link. If the T.V. cable is adjusted too short or not adjusted at all, it will result in raising the line pressure and shift points. It may also limit the carburetor opening to prevent full throttle operation.

NEUTRAL SAFETY SWITCH

Adjustment

COLUMN MOUNTED

1. Place gearshift lever in Neutral.
2. Loosen retainer screws holding switch, install $^3/_{32}$ in. drill (or pin) through hole in lower switch arm and bracket. Adjust position of switch until engine turns over (with ignition switch in start).

TRANSMISSION MOUNTED

1. Place gearshift lever in Neutral, loosen transmission lever extension bolt.
2. Pin switch lever in Neutral position with $^3/_{32}$ in. drill or pin.
3. Install rod into switch lever, adjust swivel on rod to allow free entry of rod into lever.
4. Secure rod with retainer, tighten transmission lever extension bolt.
5. Check adjustment by testing for cranking in both Neutral and Park.

Allison Transmission

Removal

AT540

NOTE: It may be necessary to remove the air tanks, fuel tanks, special equipment, etc., on some vehicles to provide clearance before the transmission is removed.

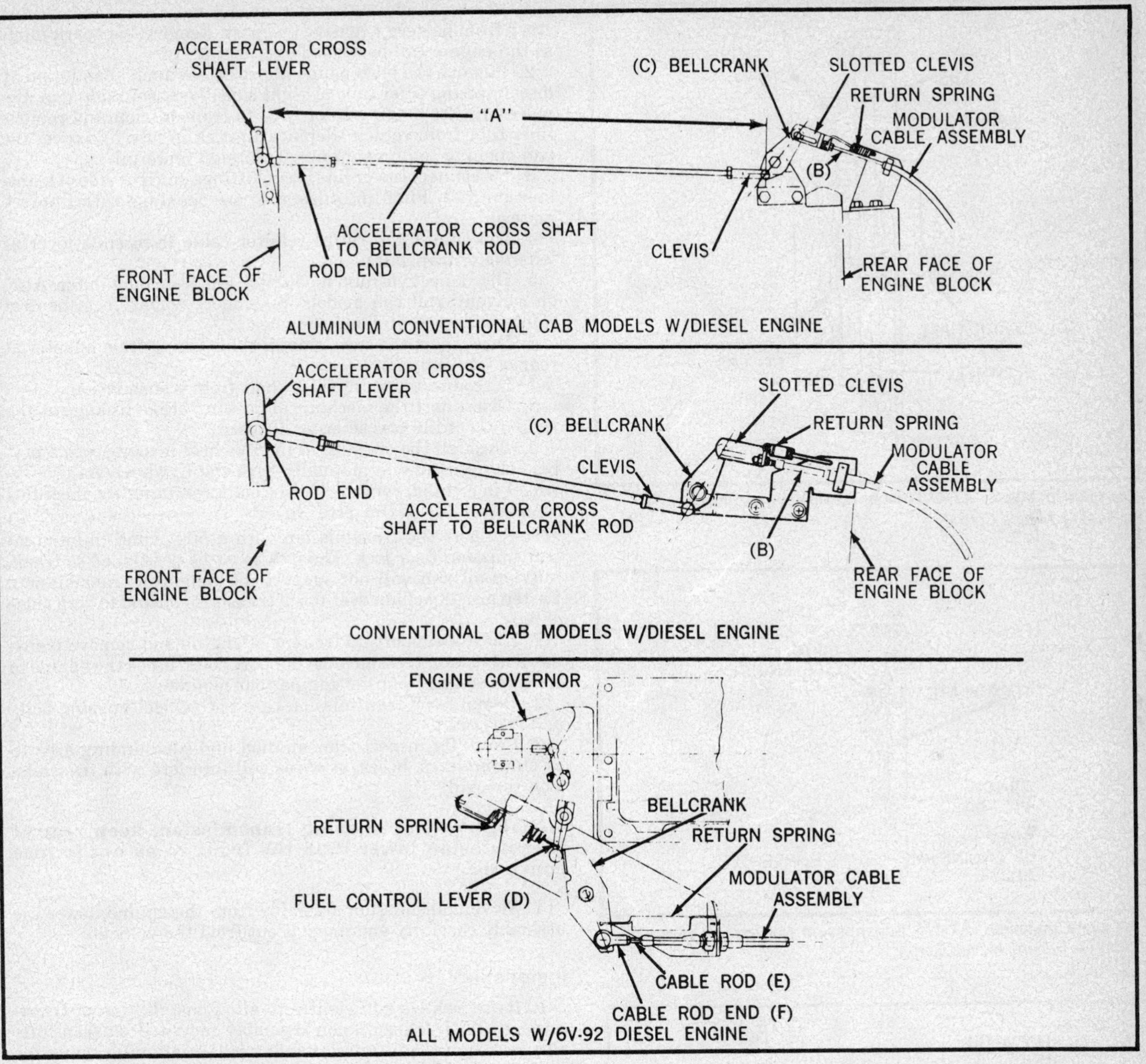

ACCELERATOR CROSS SHAFT LEVER
"A"
(C) BELLCRANK
SLOTTED CLEVIS
RETURN SPRING
MODULATOR CABLE ASSEMBLY
(B)
ACCELERATOR CROSS SHAFT TO BELLCRANK ROD
CLEVIS
FRONT FACE OF ENGINE BLOCK
ROD END
REAR FACE OF ENGINE BLOCK
ALUMINUM CONVENTIONAL CAB MODELS W/DIESEL ENGINE
ACCELERATOR CROSS SHAFT LEVER
SLOTTED CLEVIS
(C) BELLCRANK
RETURN SPRING
MODULATOR CABLE ASSEMBLY
CLEVIS
ROD END
ACCELERATOR CROSS SHAFT TO BELLCRANK ROD
(B)
FRONT FACE OF ENGINE BLOCK
REAR FACE OF ENGINE BLOCK
CONVENTIONAL CAB MODELS W/DIESEL ENGINE
ENGINE GOVERNOR
BELLCRANK
RETURN SPRING
RETURN SPRING
MODULATOR CABLE ASSEMBLY
FUEL CONTROL LEVER (D)
CABLE ROD (E)
CABLE ROD END (F)
ALL MODELS W/6V-92 DIESEL ENGINE

Throttle valve linkage adjustment (© General Motors Corp.)

THROTTLE RETURN SPRING
ADJUSTING SCREWS
.05"
THROTTLE LEVER (WIDE OPEN POSITION)
DOWNSHIFT SWITCH (PLUNGER FULLY DEPRESSED)

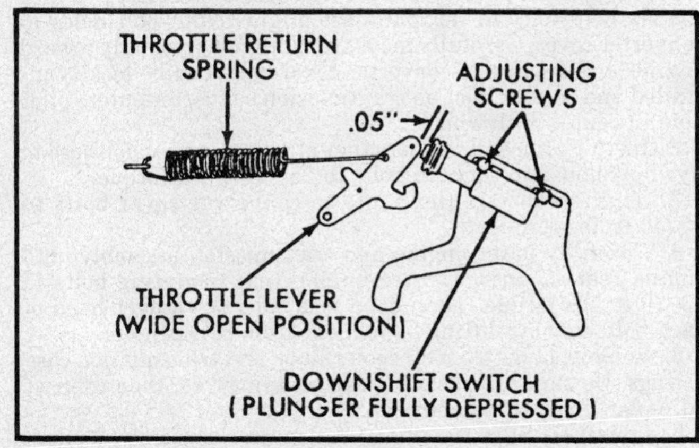

Downshift linkage AT-475 transmission (© General Motors Corp.)

FRAME
50-60 FT.LBS.
FRONT
ENGINE REAR SUPPORT
VIEW A
TRANSMISSION EXTENSION
65-85 FT.LBS.
MOUNTING ASSEMBLY
BEND TABS DOWN AFTER ASSEMBLY
SPACER
40-50 FT.LBS.
REINFORCEMENT
VIEW A

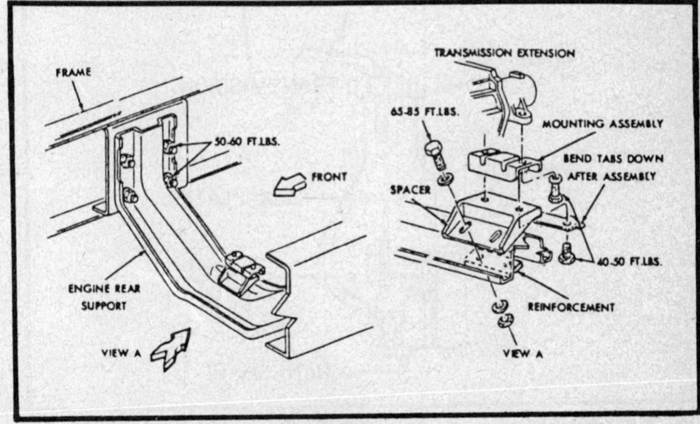

Engine rear mounting—AT-475 transmission (© General Motors Corp.)

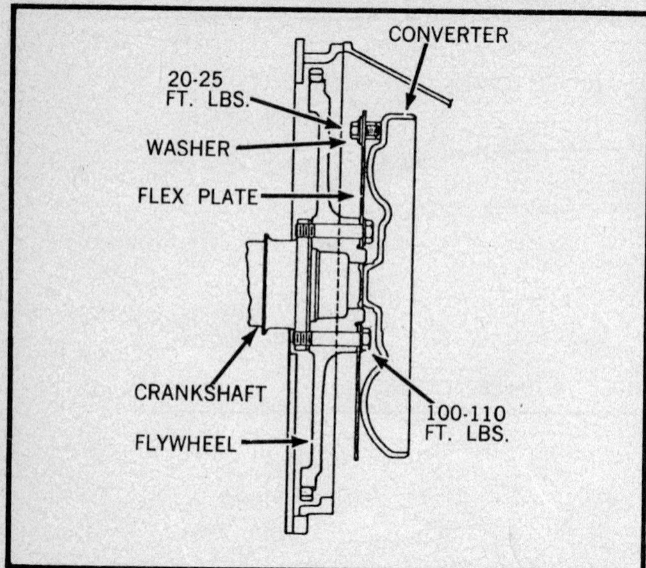

Flex plate installed—AT-475 transmission w/V6 engines (© General Motors Corp.)

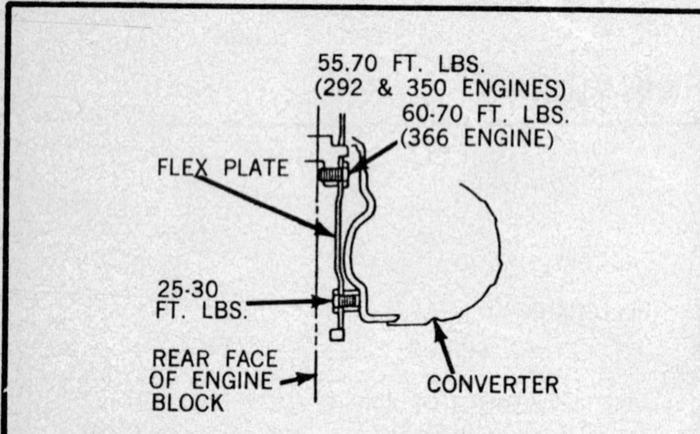

Flex plate installed—AT-475 transmission (all except V6 engines) (© General Motors Corp.)

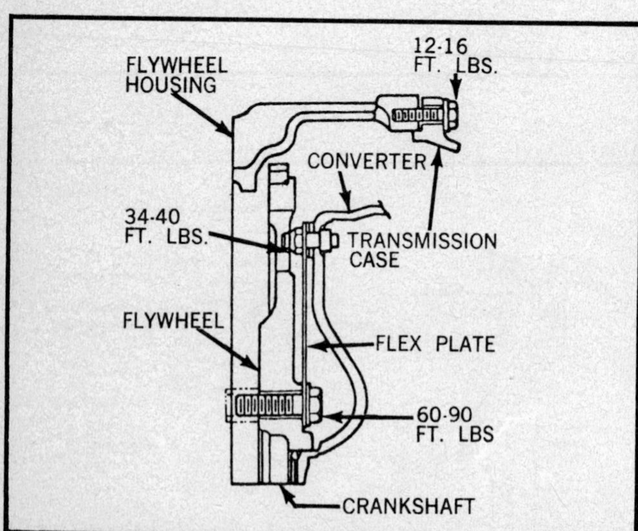

Flex plate installation—MT-640 and MT-650 series (© General Motors Corp.)

1. Block vehicle so that it cannot move. Disconnect ground strap from battery negative (−) post. Remove the spark plugs so the engine can be turned over manually.
2. Remove the level gauge (dipstick). Drain transmission by disconnecting filler tube at right side of transmission pan. Remove bracket holding filler tube to transmission and remove filler tube from vehicle. Replace dipstick in tube and cover the pan opening to prevent entry of foreign material.
3. Disconnect cooler lines from fittings on right side of transmission case. Plug line ends and case openings with lint-free material.
4. Disconnect the range selector cable from shift lever at left-side of transmission.
5. Disconnect vacuum modulator line from modulator. Also, on conventional cab models, disconnect wiring from neutral safety and back-up lamp switches.
6. Disconnect the speedometer shaft fitting from adapter at rear of transmission.
7. Disconnect the propeller shaft from transmission.
8. Disconnect the mechanical parking brake linkage at the right side of the transmission (if used).
9. Through the opening in the flywheel housing, use a pry-bar, as necessary to manually turn the flywheel. As the flywheel is rotated, remove the six bolts retaining flywheel flex plate assembly to converter cover.
10. Support the transmission with a 500-pound (minimum) transmission floor jack. The jack must be positioned so transmission oil pan will not support the weight of transmission. Fasten a safety chain over top of transmission and to both sides of jack.
11. Place a support under rear of engine and remove transmission case-to-crossmember support bolts. Raise the engine to remove weight from the engine rear mounts.
12. Remove the transmission case-to-flywheel housing bolts and washers.
13. Carefully inspect transmission and surrounding area to be sure no lines, hoses, or wires will interfere with transmission removal.

NOTE: When removing transmission, keep rear of transmission lower than the front so as not to lose converter.

14. Move transmission assembly from the engine, lower the assembly carefully and move it out from the vehicle.

Installation

1. Raise vehicle sufficiently to allow installation of transmission. With transmission assembly mounted on transmission jack move transmission into position aligning converter with flywheel. Check for and clean away any foreign material in flywheel pilot hole, flywheel flex-plate assembly and front face of transmission case. Rotate flywheel as necessary so that the six bolt holes in flex-plate are aligned with bolt holes in converter cover. Carefully move transmission assembly toward engine so flex-plate-to-converter cover bolts can be loosely installed and so that pilot on transmission converter enters pilot hole in center of flywheel.
2. Install bolts and washers that attach transmission case to flywheel housing. Tighten bolts to 25–30 ft. lbs torque.
3. Tighten the six flex-plate-to-converter cover bolts to 35–40 ft. lbs torque.
4. Carefully lower engine and transmission assembly onto engine rear mounts. Tighten engine rear mounting bolts to 60–70 ft. lbs torque. Then bend lock tabs down over head of each bolt. Remove lifting equipment from beneath vehicle.
5. Remove plugs from oil cooler lines and transmission case fittings. Be sure fittings are clean and lint-free, then connect oil cooler lines to transmission.
6. Install oil filler tube and bracket on right side of transmission. Install oil level gauge (dipstick).

7. Connect the speedometer shaft fitting to adapter at rear of transmission.
8. Connect propeller shaft to transmission.
9. Connect parking brake linkage (if used) at side of transmission.
10. Connect the range selector cable to shift lever at left side of transmission.
11. Connect the vacuum modulator line to modulator. Also, on conventional cab models, connect wiring to neutral safety and back-up lamp switches.

NOTE: Make sure the ignition switch is in the off position before proceeding to the next step.

12. Install spark plugs and connect battery ground strap, previously disconnected.
13. Connect any other lines, hoses, or wires which were disconnected to aid in transmission removal.
14. Adjust the shift linkage. (See Shift Linkage Adjustment).
15. Refill the transmission with the proper lubricant.

Removal

MT640, 643, MT650, 653

NOTE: It may be necessary to remove the air tanks, fuel tanks, special equipment, etc., on some vehicles to provide clearance before the transmission is removed.

1. Block vehicle so that it cannot move. Disconnect ground strap from battery negative (−) post. Remove the spark plugs so the engine can be turned over manually.
2. Remove the level gauge (dipstick). Drain transmission by disconnecting filler tube at right side of transmission pan. Remove bracket holding filler tube to transmission and remove filler tube from vehicle. Replace dipstick in tube and cover the pan opening to prevent entry of foreign materials.
3. Disconnect cooler lines from fittings on right side of transmission case. Plug line ends and case openings with lint-free material.
4. Disconnect shift cable from shift lever at left side of transmission.
5. Disconnect vacuum modulator line from modulator. Also, disconnect wiring from back-up lamp switch (right side of transmission) and neutral safety switch (left side of transmission).
6. Disconnect the speedometer shaft fitting from adapter at rear of transmission.
7. Disconnect the propeller shaft from transmission.
8. Disconnect the mechanical parking brake linkage at the right side of the transmission (if used).
9. Through access opening in the flywheel housing, use a pry bar, as necessary to manually turn the flywheel. As the flywheel is rotated, remove the six nuts retaining flex-plate assembly to converter cover.

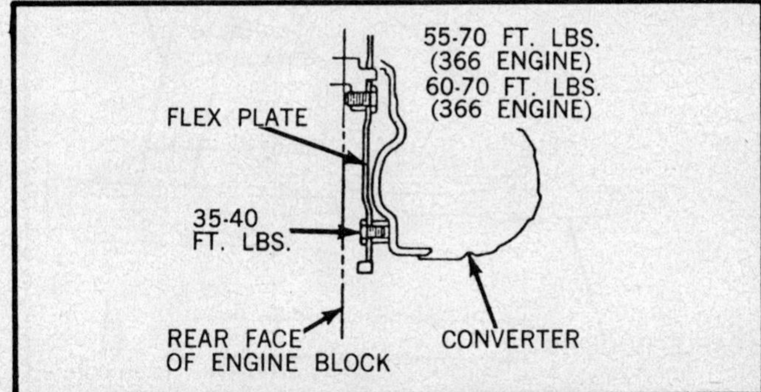

Flex plate installation—V8 engine—AT-540 series (© General Motors Corp.)

10. Support the transmission with a 750-pound (minimum rating) transmission floor jack. The jack must be positioned so transmission oil pan will not support the weight of transmission. Fasten a safety chain over top of transmission and to both sides of jack.
11. Place a support under rear of engine and remove transmission case-to-crossmember support bolts. Raise the engine to remove weight from the engine rear mounts.

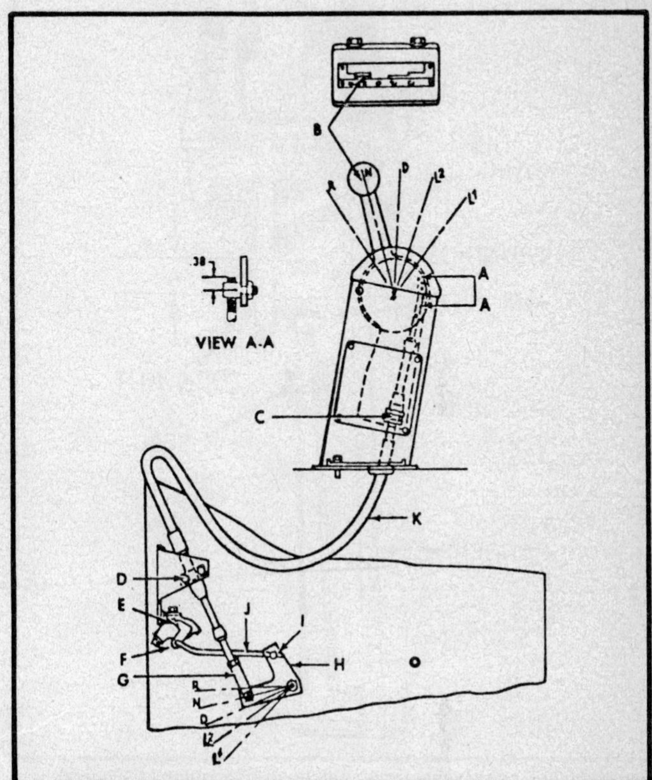

Shift linkage—AT-475 transmission (© General Motors Corp.)

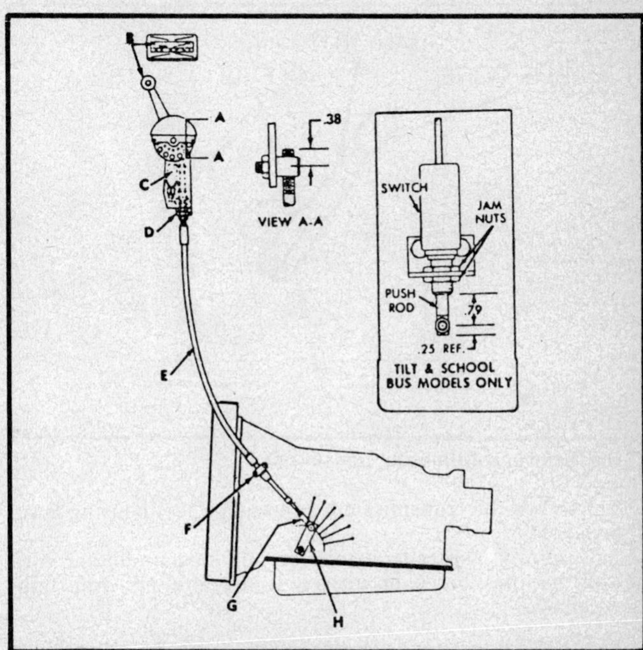

Shift linkage—AT-540 series transmission (© General Motors Corp.)

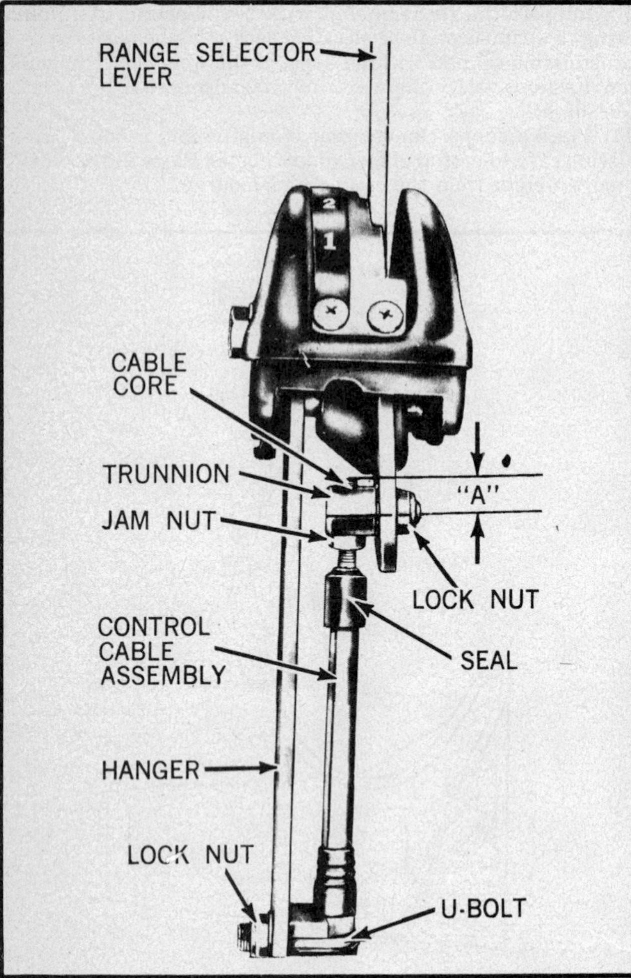

Trunnion and cable assembly—Allison transmission (© General Motors Corp.)

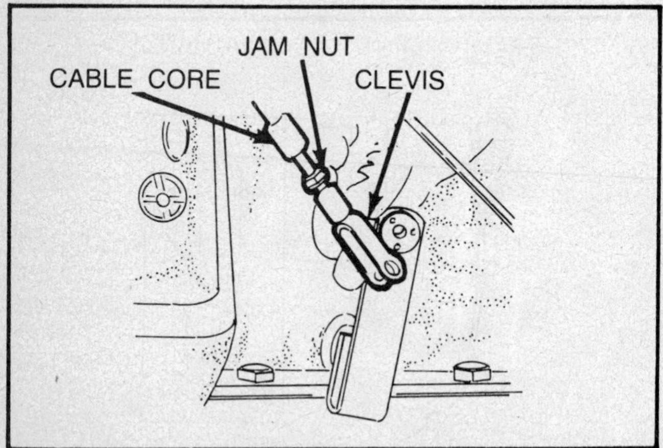

Clevis adjustment—Allison transmission

12. Remove the transmission case-to-flywheel housing bolts and washers.
13. Carefully inspect transmission and surrounding area to be sure no lines, hoses, or wires will interfere with transmission removal.

NOTE: When removing transmission keep rear of transmission lower than the front so as not to lose converter.

14. Move transmission assembly from the engine, lower the assembly carefully and move it out from the vehicle.

Installation

1. Raise vehicle sufficiently to allow installation of transmission. With transmission assembly mounted on transmission jack move transmission into position aligning converter with flywheel. Check for and clean away any foreign material in flywheel pilot hole, flex-plate assembly and front face of transmission case. Rotate flywheel as necessary so that the six studs in converter cover are aligned with holes in flex plate. Carefully move transmission assembly toward engine so flex-plate-to-converter cover nuts can be loosely installed and so that pilot on transmission converter enters pilot hole in center of flywheel.
2. Install bolts and washers that attach transmission case-to-flywheel housing. Tighten bolts to 12–16 ft. lbs torque.
3. Tighten the six flex-plate-to-converter cover nuts to 34–40 ft. lbs torque.
4. Carefully lower engine and transmission assembly onto engine rear mounts. Tighten engine rear mounting nuts to 190–210 ft. lbs torque. Remove lifting equipment from beneath vehicle.
5. Remove plugs from oil cooler lines and transmission case fittings. Be sure fittings are clean and lint-free, then connect oil cooler lines-to-transmission.
6. Install oil filler tube and bracket on right side of transmission. Install oil level gauge (dipstick).
7. Connect the speedometer shaft fitting to adapter at rear of transmission.
8. Connect propeller shaft to transmission.
9. Connect parking brake linkage (if used) at side of transmission.
10. Connect shift cable to shift lever at left side of transmission.
11. Connect the vacuum modulator line to modulator. Also, connect wiring to neutral safety switch (left side of transmission) and back-up lamp switch (right side of transmission).

NOTE: Make sure the ignition switch is in the off position before proceeding to the next step.

12. Install spark plugs and connect battery ground strap, previously disconnected.
13. Connect any other lines, hoses, or wires which were disconnected to aid in transmission removal.
14. Adjust the shift linkage. (see Shift Linkage Adjustment)
15. Refill the transmission with the proper lubricant.

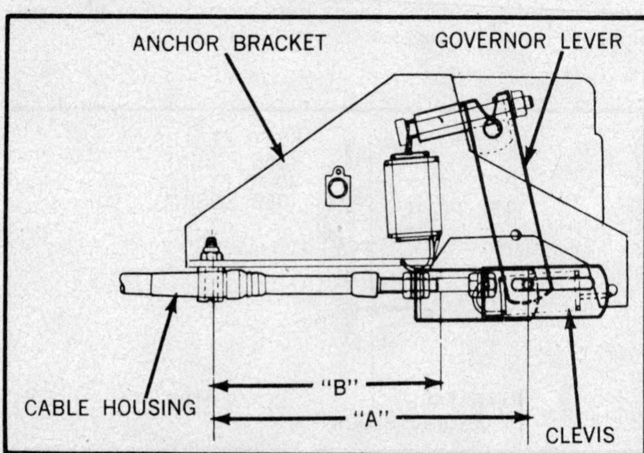

Throttle valve linkage adjustment—medium duty trucks (© General Motors Corp.)

TRANSMISSION SHIFT LINKAGE

Adjustment

AT540, MT640, 643 GAS AND DIESEL ENGINES

1. Disconnect clevis from transmission shift lever by removing cotter pin and clevis pin.
2. Disconnect control cable from anchor point at bracket on transmission and remove cable retainer clips from underside of cab.
3. Remove four cross recess screws retaining range selector cover to tower or bracket, depending on truck model. Lift range selector assembly out to inspect cable attachment at range selector lever and hanger.
4. Check cable at trunnion for dimension "A" as shown. This dimension is necessary to allow for proper cable length at clevis. If adjustment is necessary, remove cable from range selector lever and hanger assembly as follows:
   a. Remove ½–inch locknut from trunnion.
   b. Disconnect cable from anchor point on hanger by removing two locknuts and U-bolt.

NOTE: Locknuts can be removed and reinstalled up to six times before their replacement becomes necessary.

   c. Mark location of trunnion. Remove trunnion with attached cable core from lever.

CAUTION

The trunnion has been placed in the proper hole at the factory. Any change in the location could cause vehicle operation to be dangerous.

5. With control cable removed, loosen jam nut at trunnion.

NOTE: Do not use pliers on cable core when loosening jam nut or when adjusting trunnion. Cable core finish may be damaged resulting in cable core seal damage.

6. Turn trunnion clockwise, or counterclockwise to attain dimension "A". Tighten jam nut against trunnion.
7. Install trunnion in its original hole and tighten locknut securely.
8. Anchor cable to hanger with U-bolt, washers and locknuts. Tighten locknuts 3–5 ft. lbs torque.
9. Install shift control cover in tower or bracket depending on truck model. Install four cross recess screws. Tighten screws 3–5 ft. lbs torque. Install cable clips to underside of cab.
10. Anchor cable to bracket at transmission. Tighten two cross recess screws securely.
11. Locate transmission shift lever in Reverse position.

NOTE: Reverse position is full counterclockwise (except on AT 475 movement of lever.

12. Locate range selector lever against stop in Reverse position.
13. Loosen jam nut at clevis. Turn clevis clockwise or counterclockwise on threaded cable core until holes in clevis align with hole in shift lever. Install clevis pin, note that pin should enter freely, if it does not, adjust clevis slightly by ½ turn in each direction until pin does enter freely.
14. Turn clevis one full turn clockwise to allow for cable backlash.
15. Connect clevis to shift lever with clevis pin and a new cotter pin, but do not spread cotter pin at this time.
16. Move the range selector lever through all drive ranges. The transmission detents should fully engage just before the range selector lever hits the stops incorporated in the shift control cover.

MODEL MT 653

NOTE: If the shift linkage cannot be adjusted satisfactorily, it may be necessary to replace the shift linkage cable.

1. Move the range selector against the stop in the Reverse position.
2. Remove the cotter pin from the shift lever clevis and disconnect the clevis.
3. Place the shift lever in the Reverse position.
4. Loosen the jam nut and turn the clevis until the holes in the clevis align with the hole in the shift lever. The clevis pin should install easily.
5. Turn the clevis one full turn clockwise to allow for cable backlash.
6. Connect the clevis pin to the shift lever. Install the clevis pin and the cotter pin.
7. Check shifter operation.

NOTE: The transmission detents should fully engage just before the range selector lever contacts the stops in the shift control cover.

THROTTLE VALVE LINKAGE

Adjustment

MEDIUM DUTY TRUCKS W/DIESEL ENGINE

NOTE: Make sure that the throttle valve cable housing is secured to the control anchor bracket.

1. Disconnect the throttle valve cable clevis from the governor lever.
2. Measure distance "A" (6 ⅝ inches) with the governor lever in the idle position. Adjust if necessary and torque the clamp bolt to 9 ft. lbs
3. Disconnect the clevis and lever return springs.
4. Move the governor lever to the full throttle position and hold. Check for free pin entry.

NOTE: The hole in the lever must align at the forward end of the slot with free pin entry. Adjust the position of the clevis accordingly and tighten the jam nut against the clevis.

6. Connect the clevis and governor lever return springs. Check lever operation.

CONVENTIONAL CAB MODELS W/DIESEL ENGINE

NOTE: Make sure that the cable assembly is properly secured at the support bracket.

1. Disconnect the cable return spring and clevis from the bellcrank.
2. Measure distance "A": 33 $^5/_{32}$ inches for aluminum conventional cabs and 29 ⅝ inches for steel conventional cabs.

NOTE: If distance "A" is correct and valve operation is normal, adjustment is not necessary.

3. Disconnect the rod end from the accelerator cross shaft lever.
4. Loosen the jam nut and adjust the rod to the desired length by turning the rod end.
5. Tighten the jam nut and install the rod end on the accelerator lever. Torque the attaching nut to 11 ft. lbs.
6. Push the modulator cable end (with clevis) toward the modulator and against the stop.
7. With the bellcrank in the accelerator idle position, install the upper end of the slot (in clevis) against the clevis pin in the bellcrank. Decrease the overall length of the cable by turning the clevis adjusting nuts 3 complete turns; locate the lower end of the cable in the modulator a distance of ⅛ in. from the stop.
8. Install the cotter pin through the clevis pin.
9. Tighten the jam nut against the clevis and install the return spring.
10. Check the operation of the linkage assembly.

ALL MODELS W/6V–92 ENGINE

NOTE: Make sure that the cable assembly is properly secured at the support bracket. Be sure that the bellcrank bolt is tight.

1. Rotate the fuel control lever to the full throttle position.
2. Pull cable "E" until it is bottomed out.
3. Adjust the cable rod end to permit free pin entry in the bellcrank.
4. Check linkage for proper return to the idle position.
5. Check cable travel "E": $1^3/_{16}$ in. minimum and $1^9/_{16}$ in. maximum.

NEUTRAL SAFETY AND BACKUP LAMP SWITCH

Adjustment

ALLISON – (AT450) TRANSMISSION TILT AND SCHOOLBUS MODELS

NOTE: Shift linkage adjustment should be performed as described previously, prior to adjustment of the neutral safety and backup lamp switch.

1. Block driving wheels, apply parking brake and perform the following to prevent the vehicle from accidentally starting.

NOTE: Pull the secondary wire out of center socket in the distributor cap and ground wire to prevent possible damage to coil.

2. Move selector lever (B) to "N" (Neutral) position. Then, loosen jam nuts and adjust length of push rod to dimension shown.
3. With switch push rod properly adjusted, tighten jam nuts securely.
4. Check each range position of shift linkage to make sure the starter does not operate with the selector lever in any position other than "N". Have assistant check for proper operation of back-up lights with selector lever in "R". If necessary readjust switch.
5. Reconnect secondary wire to distributor cap.

NOTE: The neutral safety and back-up lamp switches are non-adjustable on the Allison-MT–640, 643, MT–650, 653 trans. and all diesel engines with automatic transmissions.

FLUID AND FILTER

Replacement

AT AND MT MODELS

1. Have the transmission at normal operating temperature (160 to 220 degrees F) and the transmission in neutral.
2. Remove the fill tube from the pan or the drain plug from the right side of the transmission pan. Allow the fluid to drain into a large container.

NOTE: Do not allow the fluid to spill and splash. Burns can result.

3. Remove the pan bolts, loosen and remove the pan and gasket. Discard the gasket.
4. Remove the one screw that retains the filter, remove the filter and discard.

NOTE: Later models will have a suction tube that separates from the filter. Retain the tube for use with the new filter, the tubes will have a sealring. Replace with a new sealring upon installation.

5. To clean or replace the governor feed screen, the valve body must be removed on the AT Models and the screen taken from the governor feed bore. Refer to the valve body removal and installation procedures outlined in the Unit Repair section. The MT models have discontinued the use of the primary governor screen and if one is found in the governor feed tube area of the valve body, discard it.
6. The MT models have the main governor screen located in the rear cover. Early models will have a screen to be cleaned and reinstalled while the later models will have a replaceable cartridge type filter.

NOTE: The screen or filter is inserted into the rear cover open end first.

7. Retain the screen or filter with the plug or cap.
8. Install the new filter, suction tube and seal ring in the sump area and secure with the retaining bolt. Torque to 10 to 15 ft. lbs for the MT models and 10 to 13 ft. lbs for the AT models.
9. Install the pan with a new gasket. Torque the pan bolts to 10 to 15 ft. lbs for the MT models and 10 to 13 ft. lbs for the AT models.
10. Install the filler tube or drain plug into the transmission on pan.
11. Install 10 quarts of transmission fluid into the AT models and 15 quarts into the MT models. Start the engine, check for leaks, move the selector through the gear positions and recheck the fluid level of the transmission and refill to the full mark on the dipstick.

DRIVE SHAFT

Tubular type drive shafts and needle bearing type universal joints are used on all model trucks. An internally splined sleeve which compensates for variation in distance between rear axle and transmission is located at the forward end of single or rear shafts.

The number of shafts used is dependent upon the wheel base of the vehicle. On vehicles which use two or more shafts, each shaft (except the rear) is supported near its splined end in a rubber cushioned ball bearing which is mounted in a bracket attached to a frame cross member. The ball bearing is a permanently sealed and lubricated type.

An extended-life universal joint, which does not require periodic inspection and lubrication, has been incorporated in many applications.

This extended-life universal joint is identified by the absence of the lubrication fitting, which is present on all trunnions not equipped with the extended-life feature.

A lubrication fitting is also provided on each sliding sleeve to lubricate the splines. A plug is staked into the yoke end of sleeve to retain lubricant and a small hole is drilled in the end of this plug to relieve trapped air. The opposite end of the sleeve is sealed by means of a cork packing in a retainer which screws on the end of the sleeve.

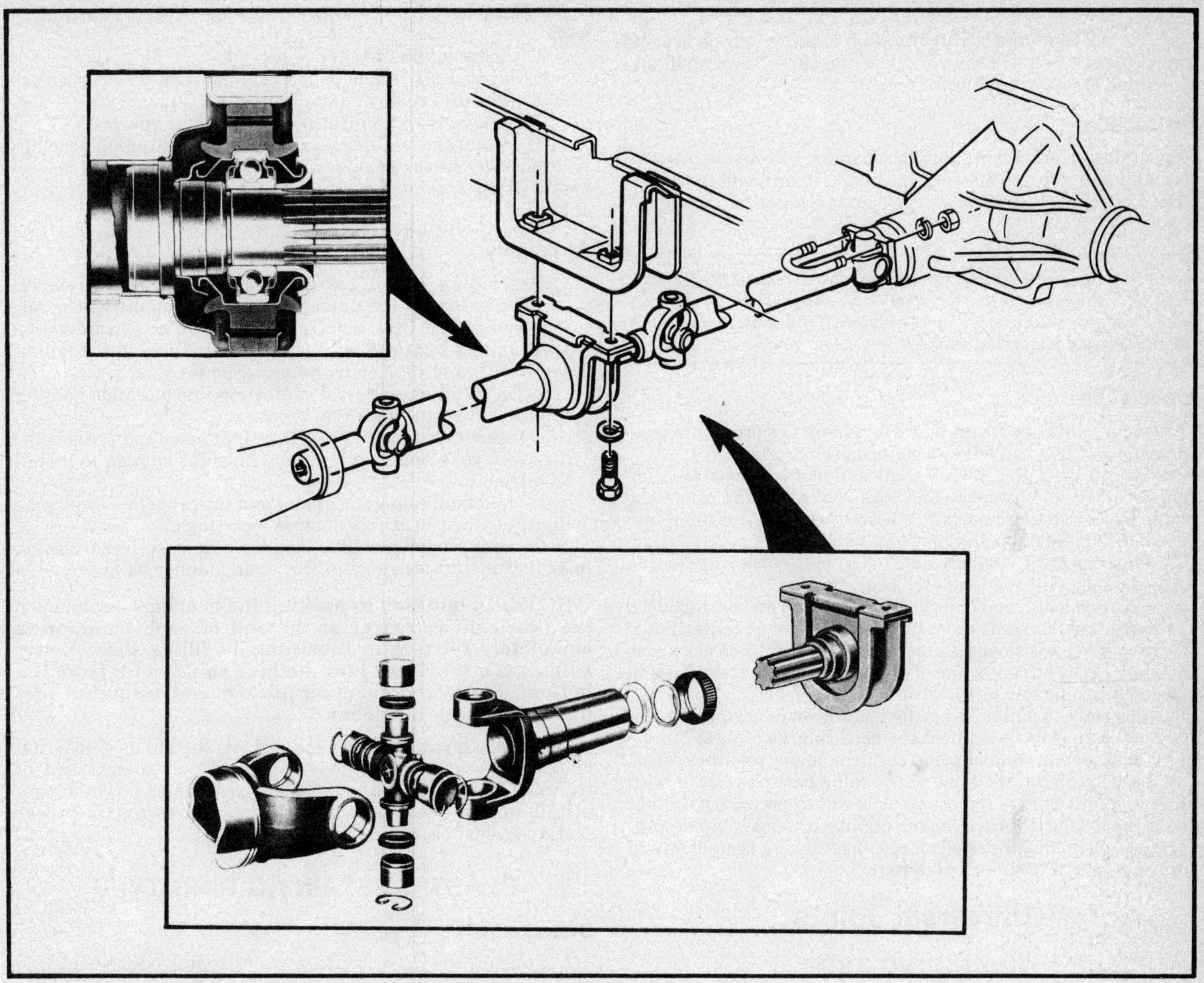

Propeller shafts, universal joints and bearing supports (© General Motors Corp.)

SHAFT ASSEMBLY

Removal

SINGLE OR REAR

Remove rear trunnion "U" clamps, lower the rear of shaft and pull back to disengage the sleeve at front of shaft. Remove shaft from under vehicle.

FRONT

Remove four front flange nuts at transmission and, if equipped with intermediate shaft, remove the rear trunnion U-clamps. Remove nuts and lock washers attaching bearing support to frame crossmember and pull shaft assembly from vehicle.

INTERMEDIATE OR REAR INTERMEDIATE SHAFT

Remove the front trunnion U-clamps and the bearing support mounting bolt nuts and lock washers. Lower the front of the shaft and pull forward to disengage splines at rear of shaft. Remove shaft and bearing support assembly from under vehicle.

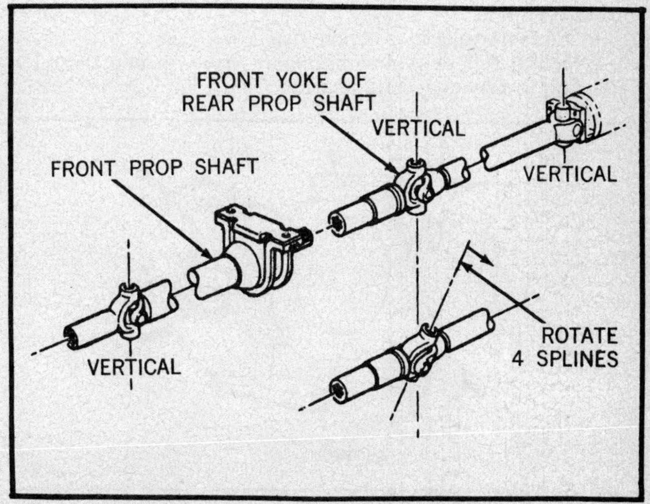

Aligning universal joints (© General Motors Corp.)

FRONT INTERMEDIATE SHAFT

Remove the front and rear trunnion U-clamps and the bearing support mounting bolt nuts and lock washers. Lower shaft and bearing support assembly from vehicle.

Inspection

Wash ends of propeller shaft in cleaning solvent, inspect for damage and excessive wear on splines, trunnions and bearings. Examine sleeve seal, washer and retainer for damage or deterioration.

CAUTION

When trunnion bearing U-clamps are removed to remove the propeller shaft, tape the bearings to keep them clean and from becoming damaged. Propeller shaft guards may be removed, if necessary, by removing nut at each end of the guard.

Installation

Drive shafts may be installed by reversing the procedure used in removal when the following steps are observed.

1. Before installing a rear shaft and sleeve assembly, slide seal retainer, steel washer and cork seal on spline of mating shaft. Assemble these parts to sleeve by turning retainer onto sleeve after rear propeller shaft is installed.
2. Over torquing U-clamp nuts will result in bearing cap distortion which will reduce roller bearing life.
3. To prevent excessive driveline vibration on some models, the rear propeller shaft must be installed so that centerline of sleeve yoke is positioned from vertical to 7 splines clockwise from vertical. The centerline of either yoke at the transmission end is perpendicular to the ground.
4. The shaft to pinion flange fastener is an important attaching part in that it could affect the performance of vital components and systems and/or could result in major repair expense. It must be replaced with one of the same part number or with an equivalent part if replacement becomes necessary. Do not use a replacement part of lesser quality or substitute design. Torque values must be used as specified during reassembly to assure proper retention of this part.

Universal Joints

SNAP-RING TYPE

Disassembly

1. Remove trunnion bearings from propeller shaft yoke as follows:
   a. Remove lock rings from yoke and lubrication fitting from trunnion.
   b. Support yoke in a bench vise.
   c. Using soft drift and hammer, drive on one trunnion bearing to drive opposite bearing from yoke.

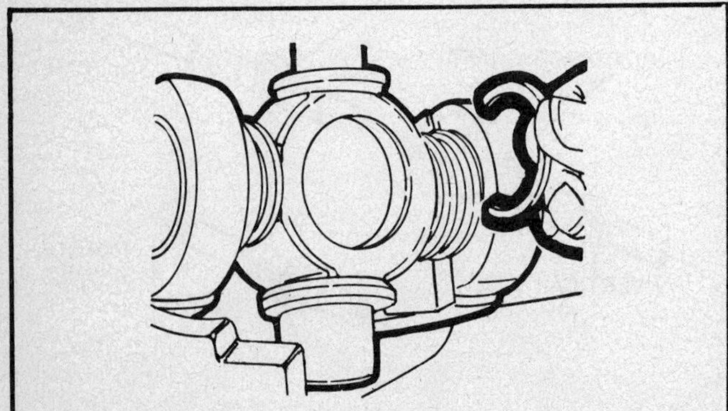

Installing snap ring to retain trunnion

NOTE: The bearing cap cannot be driven completely out.

   d. Grasp cap in vise and work out.
   e. Support other side of yoke and drive other bearing cap from yoke and remove as in Step d.
   f. Remove trunnion from propeller shaft yoke.
2. If equipped with sliding sleeve, remove trunnion bearings from sleeve yoke in the same manner as above. Remove seal retainer from end of sleeve and pull seal and washer from retainer.

Assembly

1. Assemble trunnion bearings to propeller shaft as follows:
   a. On extended-life universal joints when performing service operations that require disassembly of the universal joint, repack bearings with grease as outlined in the following NOTE and replace trunnion assembly dust seals.
   b. On all other universal joints lubricate trunnion bearing rollers and install new seal rings.
   c. Insert trunnion in propeller shaft yoke and press bearings into yoke and over trunnion hubs far enough to install lock rings.
   d. Hold trunnion in one hand and tap propeller shaft yoke lightly to seat bearings against lock rings.
2. On rear propeller shafts, install sleeve yoke over trunnion hubs and install bearings in the same manner as above.

NOTE: In addition to packing the bearings, make sure the lubricant reservoir at the end of each trunnion is completely filled with lubricant. In filling these reservoirs, pack lubricant into the hole so as to fill from the bottom. This will prevent air pockets and ensure an adequate supply of lubricant.

To replace trunnion dust seal, remove the old dust seal and place new seal on trunnion—cavity of seal toward end of trunnion—press seal onto trunnion exercising caution during installation to prevent seal distortion and to assure proper seating of seal on trunnion.

PLASTIC RETAINING RING TYPE

Disassembly

1. Support the drive shaft in a horizontal position in line with the base plate of a press. Place the universal joint so that the lower ear of the shaft yoke is support on a 1 ⅛ in. socket. Place the cross press, J–9522–3 or equivalent, on the open horizontal bearing cups and press the lower bearing cup out of the yoke ear. This will shear the plastic retaining the lower bearing cup.
2. If the bearing cup is not completely removed, lift the cross and insert spacer J–9522–5 or equivalent, between the seal and bearing cup being removed.

   Complete the removal of the bearing cup, by pressing it out of the yoke.
3. Rotate the drive shaft, shear the opposite plastic retainer and press the opposite bearing cup out of the yoke as before, using spacer J–9522.
4. Disengage the cross from the yoke and remove.

NOTE: Production universal joints cannot be reassembled. There are no bearing retainer grooves in production bearing cups. Discard all universal joint parts removed.

5. Remove the remains of the sheared plastic bearing retainer from the ears of the yoke. This will aid in reassembly of the service joint bearing cups. It usually is easier to remove plastic if a small pin or punch is first driven through the injection holes.
6. If the front universal joint is being serviced, remove the pair of bearing cups from the slip yoke in the same manner.

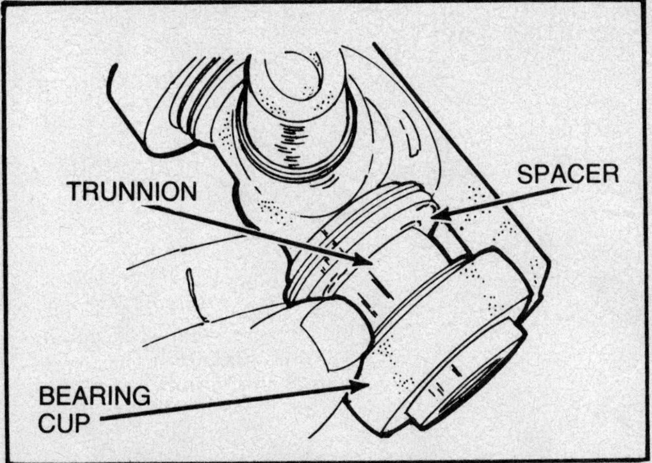

Using spacer to remove bearing cup—plastic retaining ring type

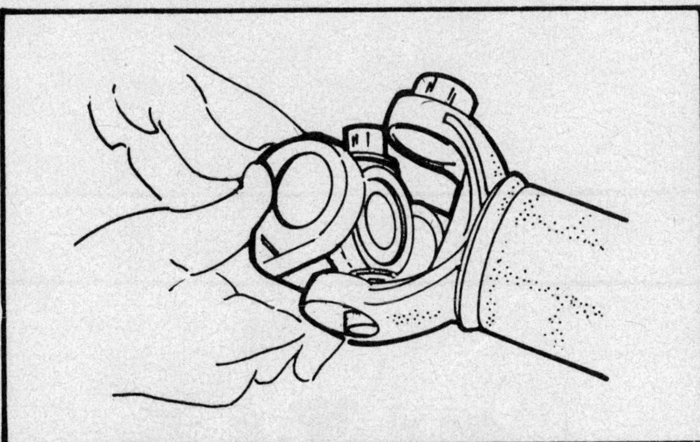
Installing trunnion into yoke—plastic retaining ring type

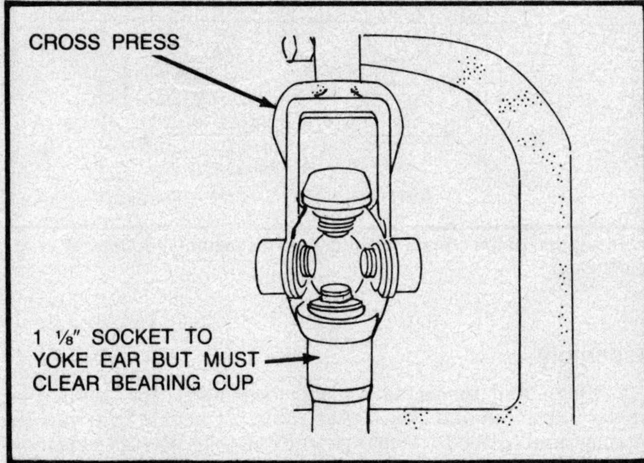

Pressing out bearing cup—plastic retaining ring type

Assembly

1. A universal joint service kit is used when reassembling this joint. This kit includes one pregreased cross assembly, four service bearing cup assemblies with seals, needle rollers, washers, grease and four bearing retainers.
2. Make sure that the seals are in place on the service bearing cups to hold the needle rollers in place for handling.

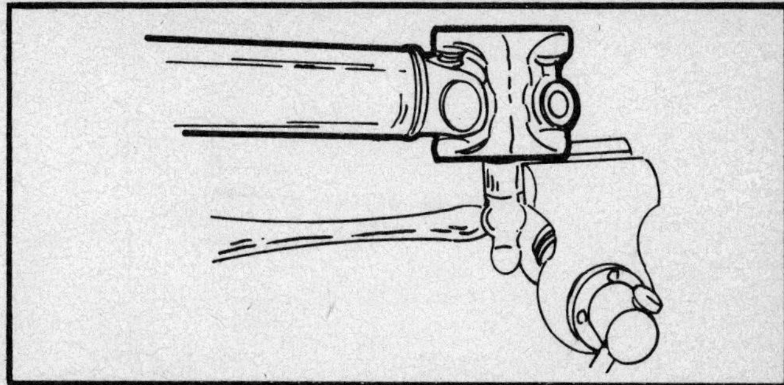
Driving yoke away from bearing cup

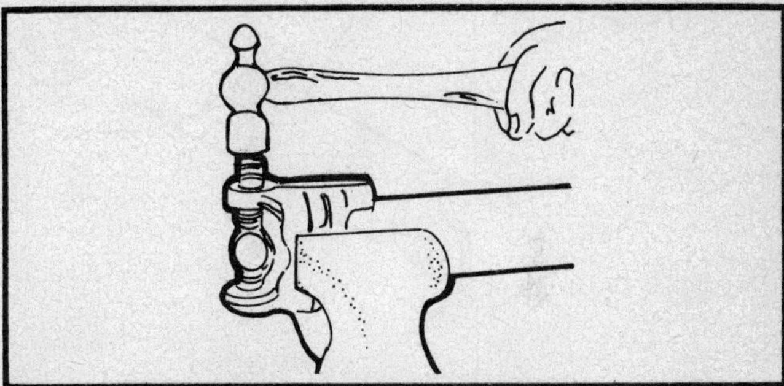
Driving out constant velocity joint bearing cups

3. Remove all of the remains of the sheared plastic bearing retainers from the grooves in the yokes. The sheared plastic may prevent the bearing cups from being pressed into place and this prevents the bearing retainers from being properly sealed.
4. Install one bearing cup part way into one side of the yoke and turn this yoke ear to the bottom.
5. Insert cross into yoke so that the trunnion seats freely into bearing cup.
6. Install opposite bearing cup part way. Make sure that both trunnions are started straight and true into both bearing cups.
7. Press against opposite bearing cups, working the cross all of the time to check for free movement of the trunnions in the bearings. If there isn't, stop pressing and recheck needle rollers to determine if one or more of them has been tipped under the end of the trunnion.
8. As soon as one bearing retainer groove clears the inside of the yoke, stop pressing and snap the bearing retainer into place.
9. Continue to press until the opposite bearing retainer can be snapped into place. If difficulty is encountered, strike the yoke firmly with a hammer to aid in seating bearing retainers. This springs the yoke ears slightly.
10. Assemble the other half of the universal joint in the same manner.
11. Check the freedom of rotation of both sets of trunnions of the cross. If too tight, again rap the yoke ears as described above. This will loosen the bearings and help seat the bearing retainers.

CONSTANT VELOCITY JOINT

Disassembly

1. Remove front propeller shaft from vehicle.
2. Remove rear trunnion snap-rings from center yoke. Remove grease fitting.
3. Place propeller shaft in vise and drive one rear trunnion bearing cap from center yoke until it protrudes approximately $^3/_8$ in..

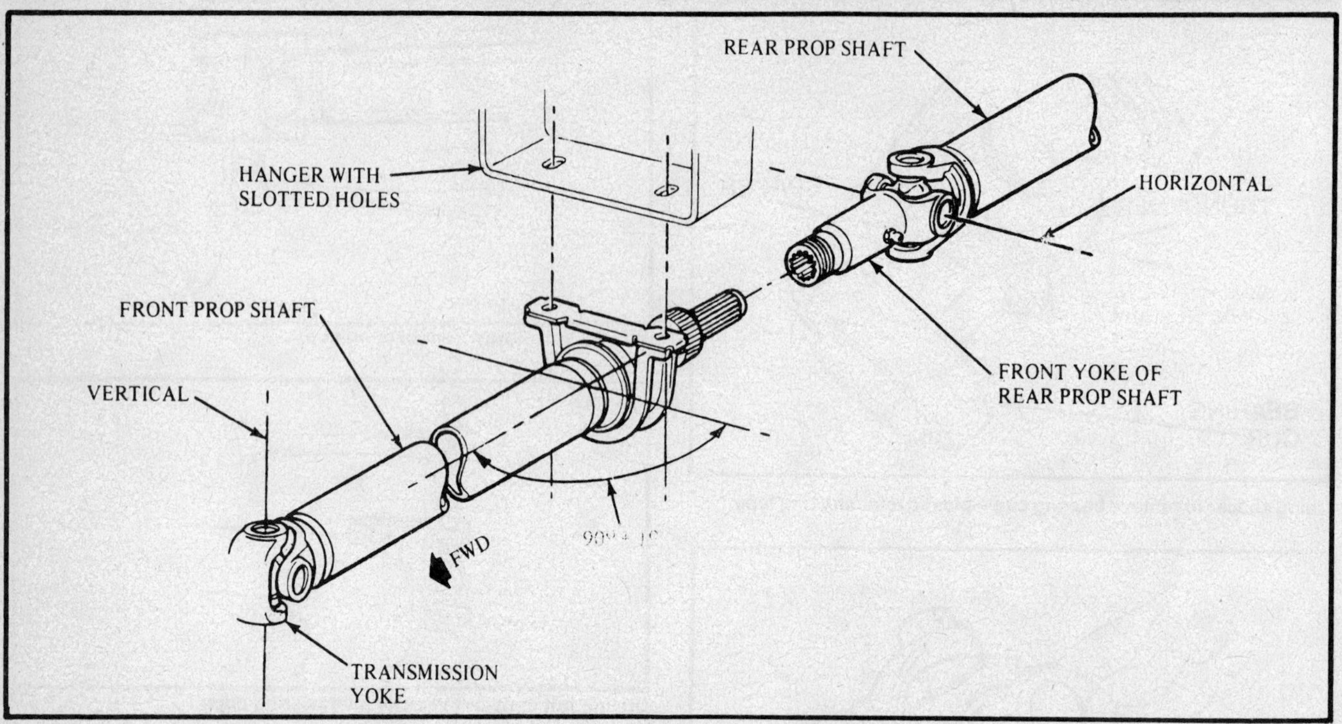

Center bearing support installation, typical (© General Motors Corp.)

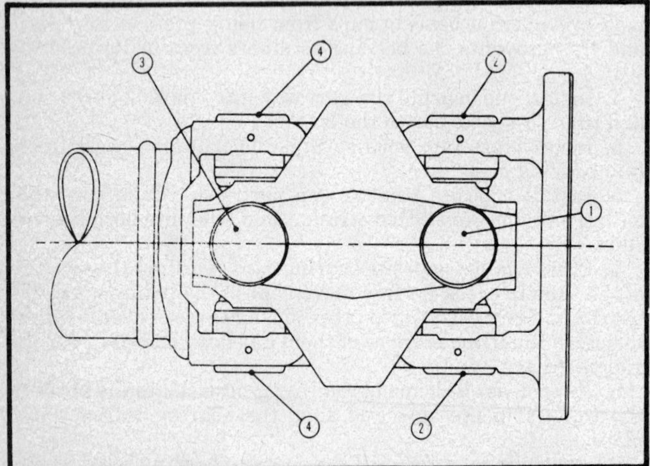
Constant velocity joint bearing cap removal sequence (© General Motors Corp.)

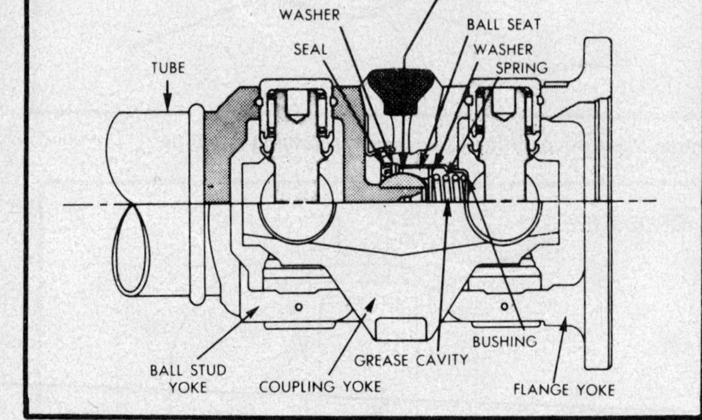

Cross section of the constant velocity joint assembly (© General Motors Corp.)

NOTE: Keep rear portion of propeller shaft up to avoid interference of rear yoke half with center yoke.

4. Once the bearing cap protrudes $^3/_8$ in., release vise. Grasp protruding portion of cap in vise and drive on center yoke until cap is removed. Remove cap seal by prying off with a thin screwdriver.
5. Repeat Steps 3 and 4 for remaining bearing caps.
6. Once the center yoke caps have been removed, remove rear yoke half bearing caps. Remove rear trunnion.
7. Gently pull rear yoke half from propeller shaft. Remove all loose needle bearings. Remove spring seal.
8. Remove front trunnion from center and front yoke in same manner as described in Steps 2, 3 and 4.

NOTE: Before front trunnion can be removed all four bearing caps must be removed.

Assembly

1. Clean and inspect all needle bearings, caps, seals, fittings, trunnions and yokes. Assemble all needle bearings in caps; assemble needle bearings in front yoke. Retain bearings with a heavy grease. Assemble seals to bearing caps.
2. Place front trunnion in drive shaft. Place center yoke on front trunnion. Install one bearing cap and seal assembly in front yoke. Drive in to a depth that the snapring can be installed. Install snapring. Install remaining cap and seal in front yoke. Install snapring.
3. Install front trunnion bearing caps in center yoke in same manner.
4. With front trunnion completely installed, install seal on propeller shaft (large face first). Gently slip rear yoke half on propeller shaft using care not to upset rollers. Insert rear trunnion in center yoke. Install rear yoke half bearing caps on rear

trunnion. Install one rear trunnion bearing cap in center yoke and press into yoke until snapring can be installed. Install remaining cap and snapring.

5. Before assembly is reinstalled in vehicle, grease universal at all three (3) fittings (2 conventional type and one, in rear yoke half), that requires a needle nose grease gun adapter.

Bearing Support

Removal

1. Remove dust shield or, if equipped with flange, remove cotter pin and nut and pull flange and deflector assembly from shaft.
2. Pull support bracket from rubber cushion and pull cushion from bearing.
3. Pull bearing assembly from shaft. Remove grease retainers and slingers (if used) from bearing.
4. Remove inner deflector from shaft if replacement is necessary.

NOTE: The ball bearing is a permanently sealed and lubricated type.

Installation

1. Install inner deflector on propeller shaft, if removed and prick punch deflector at two opposite points to make sure it is tight on shaft.
2. Pack retainers with grease. Insert a slinger (if used) inside one retainer and press this retainer over bearing outer race.

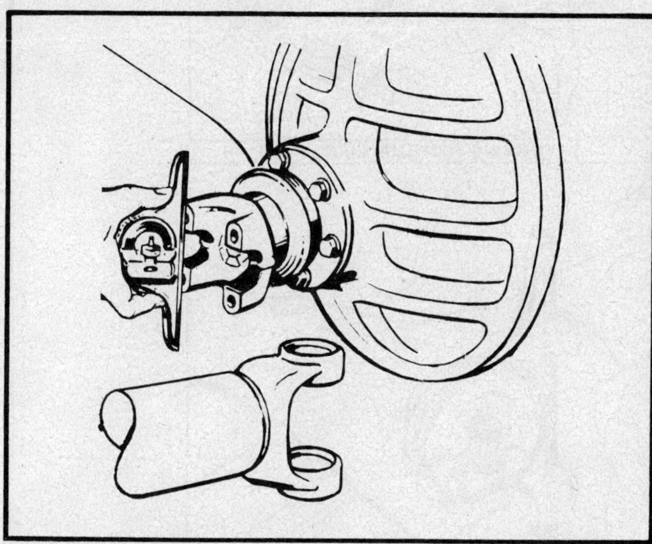

Method of checking pinion angle (single speed rear)—typical (© General Motors Corp.)

3. Start bearing and slinger assembly straight on shaft journal. Support propeller shaft and, using suitable length of pipe over splined end of shaft, press bearing and inner slinger against shoulder on shaft.
4. Install second slinger on shaft and press second retainer over bearing outer race.
5. Install dust shield over shaft, small diameter first and press into position against outer slinger or, if equipped with flange, install flange and deflector assembly as follows:
   a. Install deflector on flange, if removed and prick punch at two opposite points to make sure it is tight on flange.
   b. Align centerline of flange yoke with centerline of propeller shaft yoke and start flange straight on splines of shaft with end of flange against slinger.
   c. Install retaining nut and tighten to 160–180 ft. lbs torque. Install cotter pin.
6. Force rubber cushion onto bearing and coat outside diameter of cushion with brake fluid.
7. Force bracket onto cushion.

DRIVE SHAFT

Alignment

Correct drive line angles are necessary to prevent excessive torsional vibrations, especially tandem rear axle models. On some vehicles adjustable auxiliary transmission mountings are provided for adjusting the angle of the various drive line components. On vehicles not having adjustable auxiliary transmission mountings and adjustable torque rods at rear axles, proper adjustment of the angle of the drive line components must be accomplished by the use of spacers or shims at the frame crossmember or hangers. All angles must be checked with a maximum amount of exactness. The use of a bubble level is not sufficient, a bevel protractor must be used. The vehicle should be checked on a reasonably flat surface.

Clean machined surface at rear of (main) transmission to check engine (and transmission) angle. This is the key angle and auxiliary transmission (if equipped) and rear axle pinion must be set to this angle. Make sure all drive line components from (main) transmission to rear axle are properly centered. Clean dirt and paint off machined surface of propeller shaft yoke, make sure surface is free of nicks or burrs. Set bevel protractor to zero, place protractor on yoke surface at right angle to propeller shaft and rotate shaft until bubble is centered in glass. Reposition protractor on yoke, in-line with propeller shaft and note shaft angle.

Shaft angle must be held within a maximum of 1° less than engine. Check rear axles on machined surfaces on differential carrier housing, at right angle to pinion shaft. Make sure protractor is held straight up to get correct angle. On rear axles that do not have a machined surface it will be necessary to remove propeller shaft. Rotate the pinion yoke into a vertical position, clean the four machined ends of yoke of dirt, paint, nicks and burrs. Place the protractor across ends of yoke, on either side and in as close as possible to a vertical position. Rear axle angle should be same as engine.

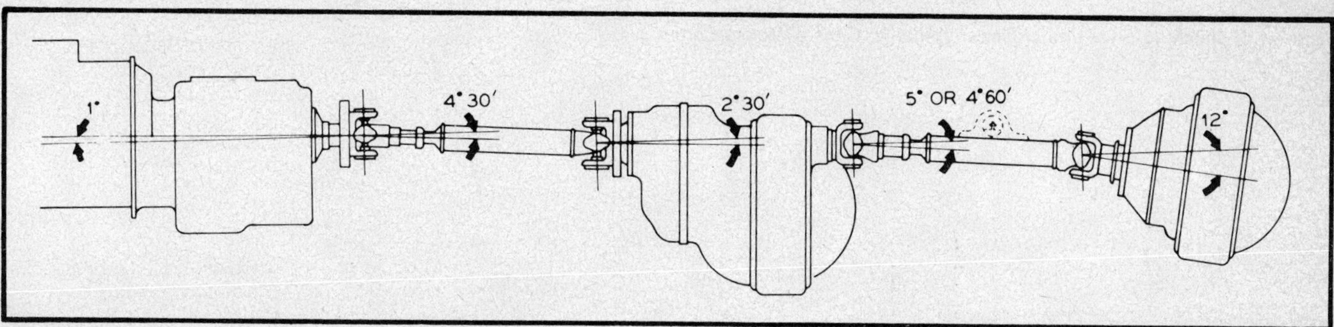

Typical sketch for recording drive line angles. Substitute recorded angle measurements where required (© General Motors Corp.)

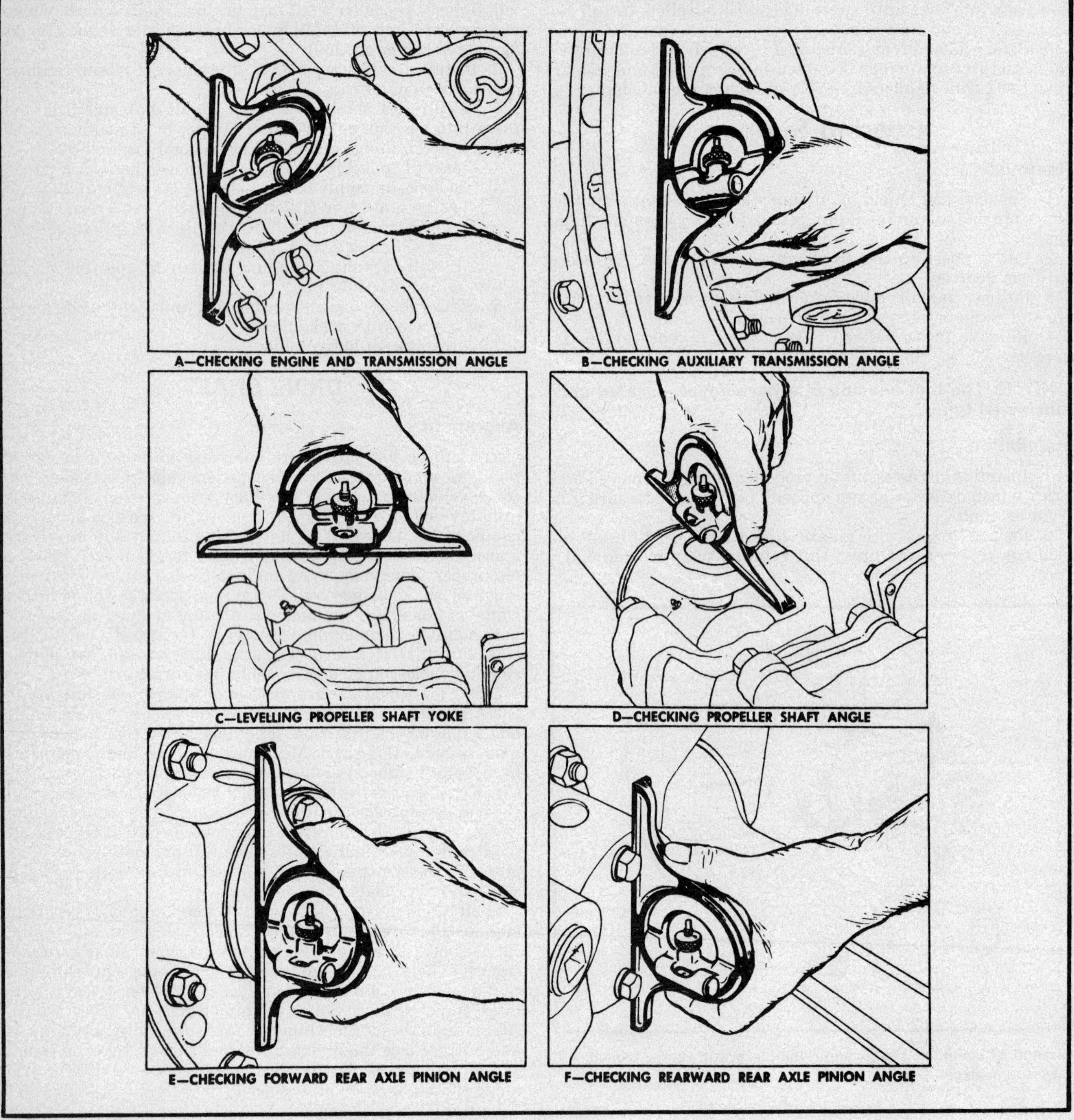

A—CHECKING ENGINE AND TRANSMISSION ANGLE
B—CHECKING AUXILIARY TRANSMISSION ANGLE
C—LEVELLING PROPELLER SHAFT YOKE
D—CHECKING PROPELLER SHAFT ANGLE
E—CHECKING FORWARD REAR AXLE PINION ANGLE
F—CHECKING REARWARD REAR AXLE PINION ANGLE

Method of checking drive line angles—typical (© General Motors Corp.)

REAR AXLE

Semi-Floating Axles Single Speed

Two types of rear axles are used. The removable carrier type with Hotchkiss drive and the Salisbury type with an integral carrier.

The following applies to both rear axles except where noted.

The drive pinion is mounted on two preloaded taper roller bearings. The ring gear is bolted to the differential case which is mounted on preloaded taper roller bearings. There are two side gears and two differential pinion gears.

AXLE SHAFT

Removal

7½, 8½, 8⅞, 9½ INCH RING GEAR

1. Remove the brake drum.
2. Drain lubricant from the differential and remove the housing cover.
3. Remove the differential pinion shaft lock screw, pinion shaft and axle shaft spacer.
4. Push the axle shaft in and remove the C-washer from the inner end of the axle shaft.
5. Remove the axle shaft from the housing.

Installation

NOTE: If a new axle shaft is to be installed.

1. Position the axle shaft gasket to the axle shaft flange.
2. Apply appropriate sealer to both sides of the gasket and axle shaft oil deflector.
3. Install the axle shaft oil deflector over the gasket aligning the oil pocket with the notch in the flange.
4. Insert six special axle shaft bolts and force the heads down to the deflector.
5. Peen the end of the shoulder on the bolts into the countersink around the bolt holes in the flange.
6. Slide the axle shaft into place.

CAUTION

Exercise care that the splines on the end of the shaft do not cut the axle shaft oil seal and that they engage with the splines of the differential side gears.

7. Install the C-washer on the inner end of the shaft.
8. Pry the shafts apart so that the C-washers are seated in the counterbore in the differential side gears and install the pinion gears.
9. Select the proper axle shaft spacer to give free fit to 0.014 in. maximum clearance between the end of the axle shaft and the spacer.
10. Install the spacer and pinion shaft, locking in place with the special screw.
11. Install the axle housing cover and gasket and refill the differential.
12. Install the drum and wheel.
13. Road test for leaks and noise.

Full Floating Axles

SINGLE SPEED

The rear axle is a full floating type with hypoid ring gear and pinion. The full floating construction enables removal of the axle shafts without removing the truck load or jacking up the rear axle. The drive pinion is straddle mounted being supported at the rear end on a roller bearing and at the front end on a double row bearing.

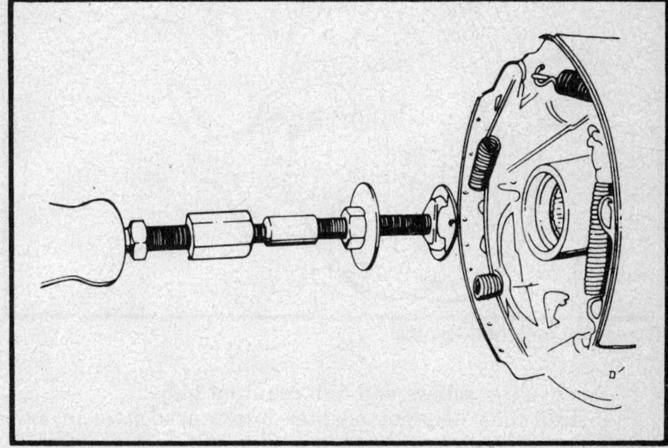

Bearing and oil seal removal (© General Motors Corp.)

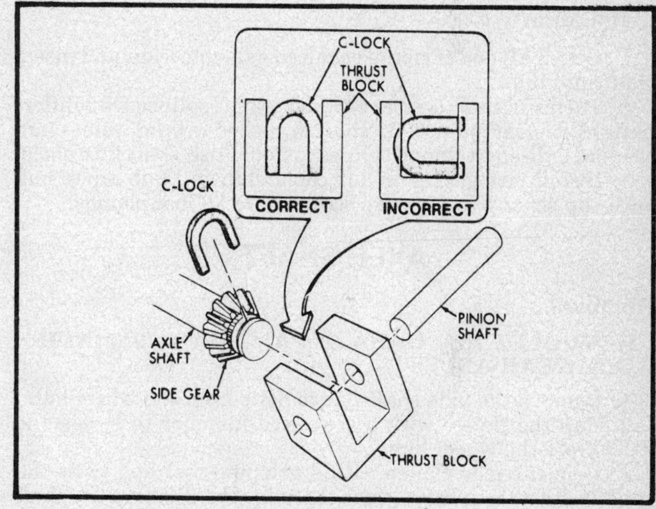

Correct "C" lock position (© General Motors Corp.)

The ring gear is bolted to the differential case and some models are provided with a ring gear thrust pad to prevent distortion when starting under heavy loads.

Some models have a two pinion differential while others have a four pinion differential.

TWO-SPEED

The two-speed axle is available in varied weight capacities. In low gear, torque is transmitted to the differential case through the planetary pinions. The straddle mounted drive pinion and the ring gears operate to produce the high range reduction, the planet and sun gears being locked to revolve with the ring gear.

Some models have a two way vacuum system for axle shifts. Other models use an electric shift system.

Maintenance and adjustments for the two speed axle are performed the same as those outlined for the single-speed axles.

SPLINE DRIVE TYPE AXLE SHAFT

12¼ INCH RING GEAR

Removal

Procedure for removal of axle shafts is same with assembly removed or installed in the vehicle.

Removing lock nut—typical

1. Remove cap screws and hub cap from hub.
2. Install slide hammer adapter into tapped hole in axle flange.
3. Install slide hammer into adapter and remove axle shaft.

Installation

1. Dip small end of splined shaft in axle lubricant and insert shaft into hub.
2. Turn shaft as necessary to index shaft splines with differential side gear splines. As shaft is pushed inward, rotate hub to align axle shaft flange splines to hub. Push shaft into place.
3. Install new gasket on hub cap and install hub cap to hub with cap screws. Torque cap screws 15 to 20 foot-pounds.

AXLE SHAFT

Removal

CHEVROLET 10½, DANA 10½ AND DANA 9¾ INCH RING, GEAR AXLES

1. Remove the axle shaft flange bolts from the wheel hub.
2. Rap the flange with a soft faced hammer to loosen the shaft from the wheel hub.
3. Grip the axle flange with a gripping tool and twist the shaft to start the removal from the axle tube. Remove the shaft from the tube.

Installation

1. Install a new hub gasket on the axle shaft and push the axle shaft into the axle tube.
2. Engage the shaft splines with the splines of the differential side gear. Align the gasket and install the hub/flange bolts.
3. Torque the bolts to specifications.

SEMI-FLOATING AXLE SHAFT BEARING OR OIL SEAL

Removal

1. Remove the wheel, drum and axle shaft (see Axle Shaft Removal).
2. Using a slide hammer, remove the bearing, bearing retainer and oil seal.
3. Inspect the bore and dress out the old stake points.

Installation

1. Using the proper driver, place the oil seal, bearing and inside bearing retainer on the driver in that order.
2. Place a light coat of sealer on the outside of the seal to insure proper sealing of the seal in the housing bore.
3. Start the bearing into the axle housing and tap the tool with a hammer to seat the parts.
4. Remove the driver and stake the oil seal in place with a punch.
5. Assemble the axle shafts (see Axle Shaft Installation).

Removal

DOWEL EQUIPPED

1. Remove the axle shaft flange–to–hub nuts.
2. Strike the flange with a lead hammer to loosen the flange and dowels.
3. Remove the tapered dowels from the studs and pull the axle shaft from the housing.

Installation

1. Clean the old gasket from the wheel hub and axle shaft flange and install a new gasket over the hub studs.
2. Install the axle shaft so that the splines are aligned with the differential side gear and the flange holes index over the hub studs.
3. Install the tapered dowel over each hub stud. Install and tighten the stud nuts to 80–100 ft. lbs

HUB AND DRUM

Removal

1. Remove the wheel assembly and axle shaft (see Axle Shaft Removal).
2. Disengage the tang of the nut lock from the slot or flat of the adjusting nut and remove the nut lock. Using an appropriate tool, remove the adjusting nut.

NOTE: On 5,200 through 15,000 lb. axles, remove the thrust washer from the housing tube.

3. Pull the hub and drum assembly straight off the axle housing.

NOTE: On 11,000 through 17,000 lb. axles avoid dropping the outer bearing inner race and roller assembly.

Installation

On the 15,000 lb. axle with 4 in. brakes, install the inner bearing oil seal in the inner bearing race and position the bearing race on the axle housing.

1. Using a smooth cup grease, pack the bearings and apply a light coat of grease to the inside of the bearing hub and the outside of the axle housing tube.
2. Install the hub and drum assembly on the axle housing, exercise care so as not to damage the oil seal or dislocate other internal componants.
3. On the 11,000, 13,500 and 15,000 with 15 × 4 in. brake and the 17,000 lb. (single speed) axles, place the outer bearing on the axle housing and press firmly into the hub.
4. On 5,200 through 15,000 lb. with 4 in. brake axles, install the thrust washer so that the tang is in the keyway on the axle housing.

BEARING AND BEARING CUP

Replacement

Replace the inner cup (all axles) and outer bearing cup for 17,000 lb. axle as follows:

1. Place an appropriate press-out tool behind the bearing cup, index the tool in provided notches and press out the cup.

NOTE: The hub outer bearing (all axles except 17,000 lb. axle) cannot be replaced with the inner bearings in position; therefore, replace the outer bearings (if required) before proceeding.

2. Position the cup in the hub, with the thick edge of the cup toward the shoulder of the hub. Using an applicable cup installer, press the cup into the hub until it seats on the hub shoulder.

Replace the outer bearing assembly (all axles except 17,000 lb.) as follows:

NOTE: The inner bearing assembly must be removed before attempting to replace the outer bearing.

1. Using a punch, tap the bearing outer race away from the bearing retaining ring from the hub.
2. On 5,200 and 7,200 lb. axles, remove the outer bearing by using a brass drift. On 11,000, 13,500 and 15,000 lb. axles, remove the bearings by driving on the axle spacer, using the splined flange cut from an old axle.
3. On 11,000, 13,500 and 15,000 lb. axles place the axle shaft spacer in the hub first. Place the inner race and roller assembly in the hub, larger O.D. towards the outer end of the hub. Position the bearing cup in the hub, then end of the cup toward the outer end of the hub. Press the cup into the hub, install the retainer ring, then press the cup into positive contact with the retainer ring.

NOTE: The bearing cup to retainer ring seating is essential to assure accurate wheel bearing adjustment.

WHEEL HUB OIL SEAL

Replacement

Pry out the old seal from the hub bore. Pack the cavity between the new seal lips with wheel bearing grease. Position the seal in the hub bore and press the seal into the bore until it is properly seated.

With the exception of the 15,000 lb. axle with 15 × 4 in. brakes, the seal should be installed flush with the end of the hub. On the 15,000 lb. axle with 15 × 4 in. brakes the seal should be installed so that it makes contact with the bearing race.

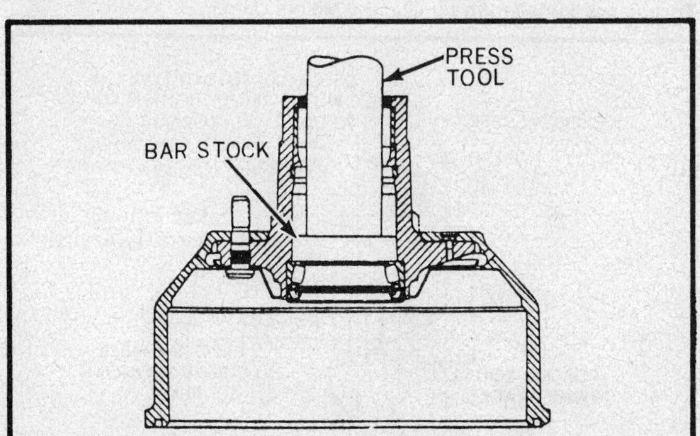

Removing hub inner bearing cup (© General Motors Corp.)

PINION FLANGE, OIL DEFLECTOR AND/OR OIL SEAL

Replacement

1. Raise the vehicle and support the frame on stand jacks, allow the axle to drop for clearance and expand the brake shoes on one wheel to lock the wheel.
2. Check the free wheel for freedom of rotation.
3. Separate the rear universal, tape the trunnion bearings to the joint and lower the rear of the propeller shaft.
4. Using a one inch torque wrench and proper socket on the pinion flange nut, rotate the pinion through several complete revolutions and record the torque required to keep the pinion turning. If the old flange is to be installed, mark the pinion and flange for reassembly in the same relative position.
5. Hold the pinion flange, remove the pinion flange nut and special washer. Discard the nut and use a new one upon reassembly.
6. Remove the pinion flange. Pry the old oil seal out of the case.
7. Inspect the pinion flange for smooth oil seal surface or worn drive splines. Replace if necessary.
8. Install a new flange oil deflector if the deflector is damaged.
9. Soak the new seal in light engine oil before installation. Wipe the outside of the seal and coat the outside with sealer.
10. Install the new seal using the proper driver.
11. Install the pinion flange, aligning the marks on the pinion and flange if the old flange is being used. If the flange does not go on the shaft easily, pull the flange on the shaft using a special tool. Remove the special tool and install the special washer and new nut.
12. Tighten the nut to remove end play and continue alternately tightening and checking preload with an inch pound torque wrench until it is the same as recorded in Step 4.
13. Readjust the brake on the locked wheel.
14. Connect the propeller shaft, lower the vehicle and road test for leaks and noise.

DIFFERENTIAL CARRIER

Removal

1. Drain the lubricant from the differential.
2. Remove the axle shafts.
3. Disconnect the rear universal joint and swing the propeller shaft to one side.
4. On two speed axles, remove the electric or vacuum lines.
5. Remove the bolts and lockwashers which retain the carrier assembly to the axle housing. Support the differential housing with a floor jack and roll it from under the truck. For overhaul, see Unit Section.

Installation

1. Clean the axle housing and differential housing gasket surfaces and place a new gasket over the axle housing.
2. Assemble the carrier to the axle housing, install the lockwashers and bolts and tighten securely.

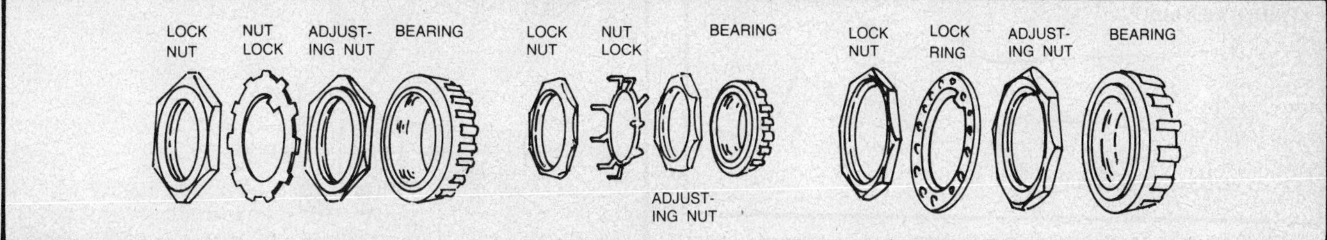

Typical lock types used on rear axle wheel bearing nuts—full floating axle system

3. Assemble the rear universal joint.
4. On two speed axles, connect the electric or vacuum lines.
5. Install the axle shafts.

DRIVE PINION OIL SEAL

Replacement

1. Disconnect the propeller shaft and remove the pinion flange and deflector.
2. Remove the bolts retaining the oil seal retainer to the carrier and withdraw the retainer from the pinion.
3. Pry the old seal from the bore.
4. Clean all foreign matter from the retainer.
5. Pack the cavity of the new seal with a high melting point bearing lubricant, position the seal on an installer.
6. Press the seal into the retainer until it bottoms against the shoulder.
7. Position the seal retainer over the pinion. Install and tighten the retaining bolts.
8. Reinstall the pinion flange and propeller shaft.

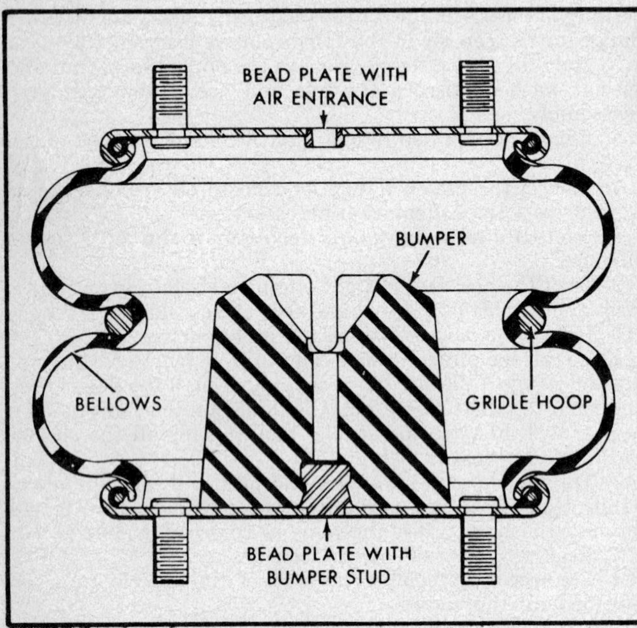

Air suspension bellows (© General Motors Corp.)

Rear Axle Assembly

3,500 AND 5,500 LBS CAPACITY AXLE

Removal

1. Raise truck and support rear axle to relieve load from springs, tie-rod and shock absorbers.
2. Disconnect tie-rod at axle (when used).
3. Disconnect driveshaft.

NOTE: Secure bearing caps to trunnion with tape.

4. Disconnect shock absorbers.
5. Disconnect vent hose.
6. Disconnect brake hose on axle housing. Remove brake drum and disconnect parking brake cable.
7. Make certain coil springs (when used) are compressed, then remove U-bolts, spacers and clamp plates.

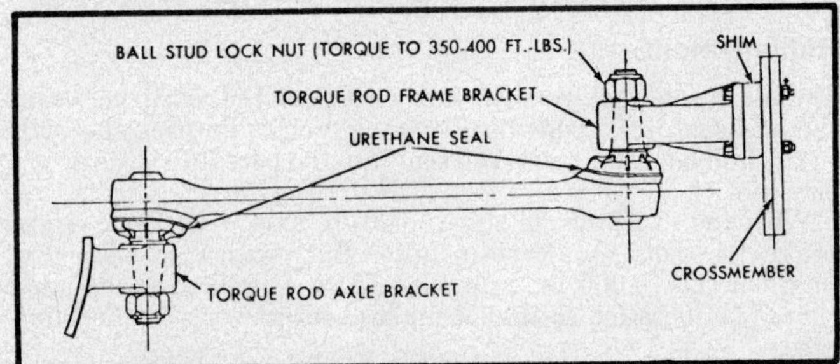

Torque rod installation (© General Motors Corp.)

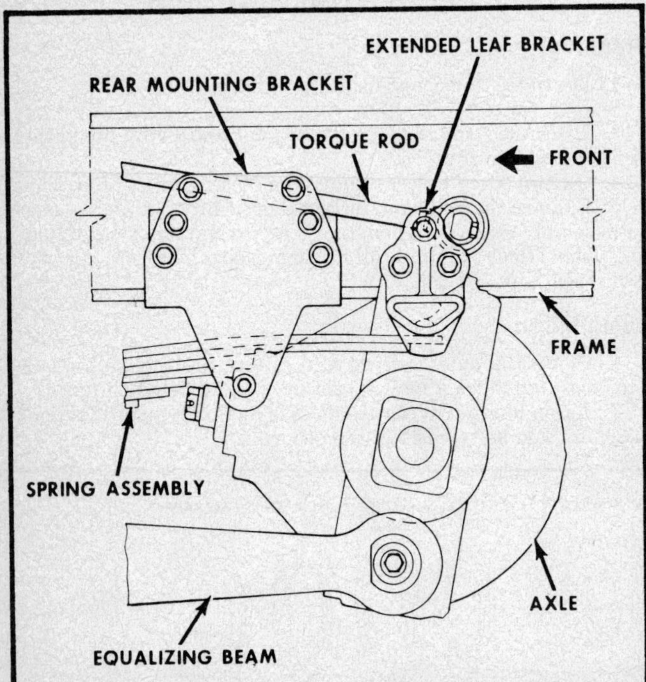

Hendrickson tandem rear axle suspension—model UE-340 (© General Motors Corp.)

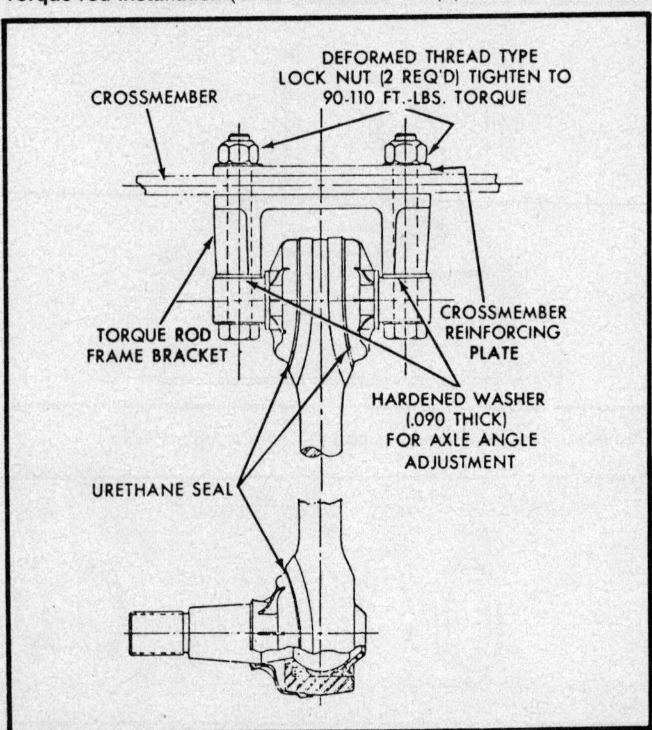

Straddle type torque rod (© General Motors Corp.)

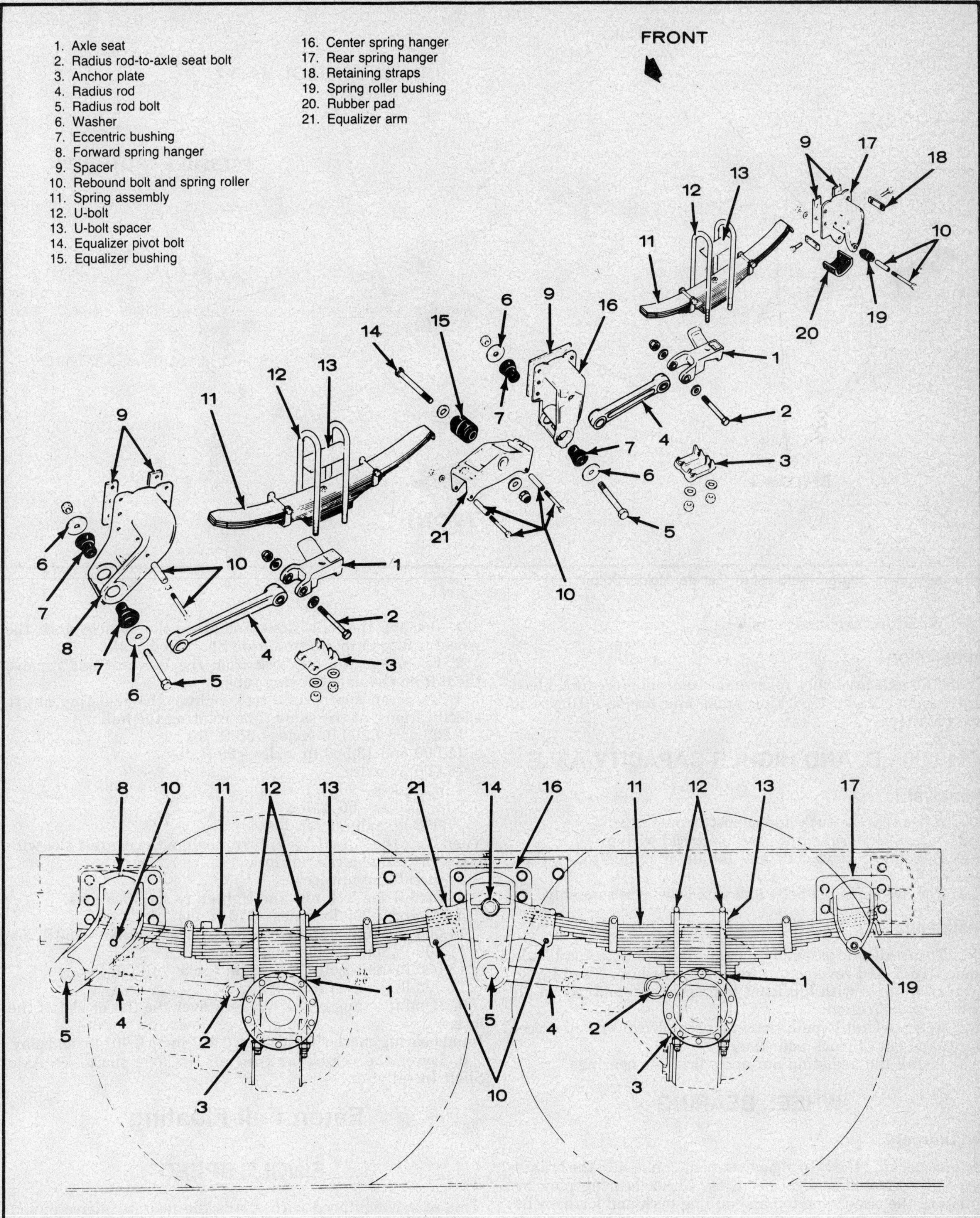

Reyco tandem rear axle suspension

(© General Motors Corp.)

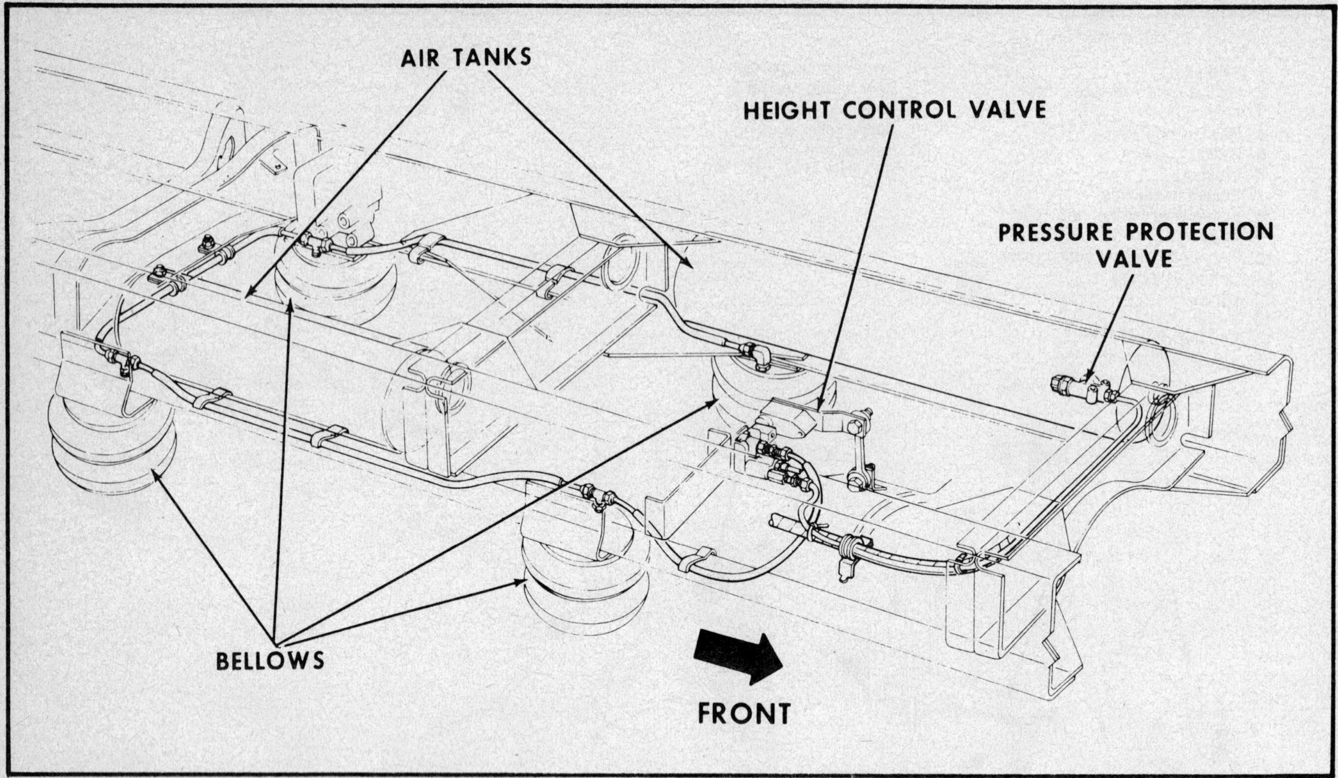

Air suspension diagram—typical (© General Motors Corp.)

8. Withdraw axle assembly.

Installation

To install axle assembly, reverse the removal procedure, bleed brake system, adjust parking brake and torque all bolts to specifications.

11,000 LB. AND HIGHER CAPACITY AXLE

Removal

1. Raise rear of truck and support frame rails.
2. Disconnect brake lines and electrical wiring.
3. Disconnect driveshaft and torque or radius rods (when used).
4. Remove spring U-bolts and withdraw axle assembly.

Installation

1. To install axle assembly, mount wheels and tires, roll axle under truck and reverse the removal procedure. Bleed brake system, fill axle with lubricant to proper level and torque all bolts to specifications.
2. Refer to Unit Repair section for complete overhaul procedures and out of truck adjustments.
3. Install the adjusting nut and adjust the bearings.

WHEEL BEARING

Adjustment

Before checking the bearing adjustment, make sure the brakes are fully released and do not drag. Check bearing play by grasping the tire at the top and pulling back and forth, or by using a pry bar under the tire. If the bearings are properly adjusted, movement of the brake drum in relation to the brake flange plate will be barely noticeable and the wheel will turn freely. If movement is excessive, adjust the bearings as follows:

1. Remove the axle shaft and raise the vehicle until the wheel is free to rotate (see Axle Shaft Removal).
2. Disengage the nut lock from the lock nut and remove them from the axle housing tube.
3. Using an appropriate tool, tighten the adjusting nut to specifications, at the same time rotating the hub.
   5,200 and 7,200 lb. axles – 55 ft. lbs
   11,000 and 13,500 lb. axles – 90 ft. lbs
   15,000 lb. axle
   4 in. brakes – 90 ft. lbs
   5 in. brakes – 50 ft. lbs
   17,000 lb. axle – 65 ft. lbs

Then back the nut off $\frac{1}{8}$–$\frac{1}{4}$ turn to align the nearest slot with the short tang on the nut lock.

3. Install the nut lock.
4. Install the lock nut and tighten to specifications.
   5,200 and 7,200 lb. axles – 175 ft. lbs
   11,000 and 15,000 lb. axles with 15 × 4 in. brake – 250 ft. lbs
   13,500 lb. axle – 135 ft. lbs
   15,000 lb. axle with 15 × 5 in. brake – 135 ft. lbs
   17,000 lb. axle – 135 ft. lbs
5. Bend the tang of the nut lock over the flat or slot of the lock nut.

Final bearing check should show 0.001 in. to 0.007 in. end play.

6. Lower the vehicle and install the axle shaft (see Axle Shaft Installation).

Eaton Full Floating

SINGLE SPEED

This axle is equipped with a straddle mounted drive pinion. Pinion bearings are of the opposed tapered roller bearing type.

A straight roller type pilot bearing is pressed onto the inner end of the drive pinion and seats in the bore of the differential case.

The differential carrier assembly may be removed, while the axle is still installed in the truck, after the axle shafts have been removed.

The differential is a conventional four pinion type. On early models the ring gear is riveted to the differential case. On later models the ring gear is bolted to the differential case.

Some models have a thrust pad mounted on the end of an adjusting screw which is threaded into an opening in the differential carrier. This thrust pad limits the deflection of the drive gear under severe loads.

Axle shaft, oil seal, wheel bearings, pinion seal and differential removal and installation are performed the same as those outlined for Chevrolet axles. Refer to Rear Axle (Chevrolet).

For overhaul, see Unit Repair section.

TWO SPEED

The differential and planetary assembly is installed in a two-piece support case. The ring gear is installed between the halves of the support case and retained in place by the same bolts which fasten the support case halves together.

The planetary assembly is composed of a high speed clutch plate and four planetary pinions.

An electric power shifting arrangement is used to assist in making ratio changes. For schematic of Electric Shift see Chevrolet Two Speed Axle.

Axle shaft, oil seal, wheel bearings, pinion seal and differential removal and installation are performed the same as those outlined for Chevrolet Axles. Refer to Rear Axle (Chevrolet).

For overhaul, see Unit Repair section.

Tandem Axle

The Hendrickson type tandem axle suspension uses equalizing beams to tie the front to the rear axle and to permit independent vertical movement of each axle. The torque rods are used to maintain proper drive line alignment and to stabilize the driving and braking forces. Bolts are used on some models to hold the spring to the top saddle pad, while U-bolts are used on other models.

NOTE: When major overhaul is required, the complete tandem axle should be removed as a unit. The torque rods, springs, equalizing beam and other parts may be removed separately as required.

CAUTION

Block the vehicle securely before removal of the assembly to avoid rolling or pivoting at the equalizer beams when the torque rods are disconnected. The use of a helper is suggested, along with proper lifting tools so that personal injury does not occur.

Removal and Installation

1. Block all wheels and disconnect all applicable brake lines or hoses, differential lock lines, or electrical wiring from the rear axles.
2. Remove the rebound bolts from the rear spring brackets.
3. Remove all nuts and washers from the front spring brackets.
4. If equipped with ball stud torque rods, remove the stud nuts and tap each ball stud loose with a soft hammer. Remove the ball studs from the axle brackets.
5. If equipped with straddle mount torque rods, remove the mounting bolts from the rear axle bracket.
6. Support the rear axle differential with a floor jack and disconnect the drive shaft from the forward rear axle.
7. Using a hoist, raise the rear of the frame high enough to clear the tandem axle assembly. Roll the assembly out from under the frame.
8. Installation is the reverse of removal.

REAR SUSPENSION

Leaf Spring Type

Removal

LIGHT DUTY TRUCKS AND VANS

1. Jack the vehicle at the frame to relieve tension on the spring.
2. Remove the U-bolt retaining nuts and withdraw the U-bolts.
3. Loosen the shackle bolts and remove the lower bolt.
4. Remove the nut and bolt securing the spring to the front hanger.
5. Remove the spring from the vehicle.

Installation

1. Position the spring assembly and spacers if so equipped, on the axle housing.

NOTE: On springs with metal encased pressed in type bushings the shackle assembly must be attached to the rear spring eye before installing the shackle to the rear hanger.

2. Position the U-bolts and loosely install the U-bolt retaining nuts.
3. Jack as required to align the spring eyes with the front hanger and rear shackle, install the eye bolts.
4. Lower the vehicle.
5. Tighten the U-bolt retaining nuts alternately and evenly to properly seat the spring and tighten the front hanger and rear shackle bolts.

Removal

MEDIUM DUTY TRUCKS

1. Raise vehicle frame to take weight off the spring. Make sure vehicle is supported safely.
2. Remove rear wheels to provide access to spring assembly.
3. Safely support axle on floor jack.
4. Install a C-clamp on radius leaf, to relieve load on radius eye bolt on 45 Series vehicles.
5. On 45 Series at the front and rear hanger, remove rebound pin retainer bolt, then remove retainer. Install suitable puller into tapped hole at end of rebound pin, then remove pin.
6. Remove spring U-bolt nuts, shock absorber bracket (when used), U-bolt anchor plate and U-bolts and U-bolt spacer, then lower axle slightly.
7. Remove spring eye on radius bolt nut and washer, then remove spring eye bolt from spring eye or radius leaf.

NOTE: When tapered shim is used, the position of shim thin and thick edge should be noted so that shim can be installed properly at assembly.

Installation

1. Set spring assembly and tapered shim or spacer (if used) at axle pad.

NOTE: Tapered shim must be installed on axle in same position that was noted at removal.

2. Install U-bolt spacer over center bolt.
3. Seat U-bolts in spacer grooves, then secure spring to axle by installing anchor plates, shock absorber bracket (when used) and nuts on U-bolts.
4. Lower frame until ends of spring enter the hanger and touch the cam surface of hanger. Compress radius leaf with C-clamp until radius leaf eye and hanger holes are aligned and torque to specifications.
5. Remove C-clamp from radius leaf.
6. Install rebound pin at front and rear hangers. Install rebound pin retainer and secure with retainer bolt.
7. Install wheels.
8. Remove blocking and lower frame to place weight on springs. Check U-bolt nuts for proper torque.

Removal and Installation

SINGLE OR TANDEM AXLES SPRINGS – HEAVY DUTY

1. Raise the rear of the vehicle, place floor jacks under the axle(s) and remove the dual wheels from the hubs to facilitate the removal of the spring eye pin and to expose the other nuts and bolts.
2. Remove the saddle cap stud nuts and/or spring U-bolts.
3. Remove the rebound pin locks or retainers and then remove the rebound pins.
4. Remove the eye bolts or radius lead pin clamp bolts, then remove the lubrication fitting from the inner end of the pin, if equipped.
5. Remove the pins from the springs and lower the axle(s) or raise the frame until the spring will clear the brackets.
6. Remove the spring from the vehicle.
7. The installation is in the reverse of the removal procedure.
8. Torque the U-bolts or saddle cap stud nuts to specifications after the vehicle is lowered to the floor.

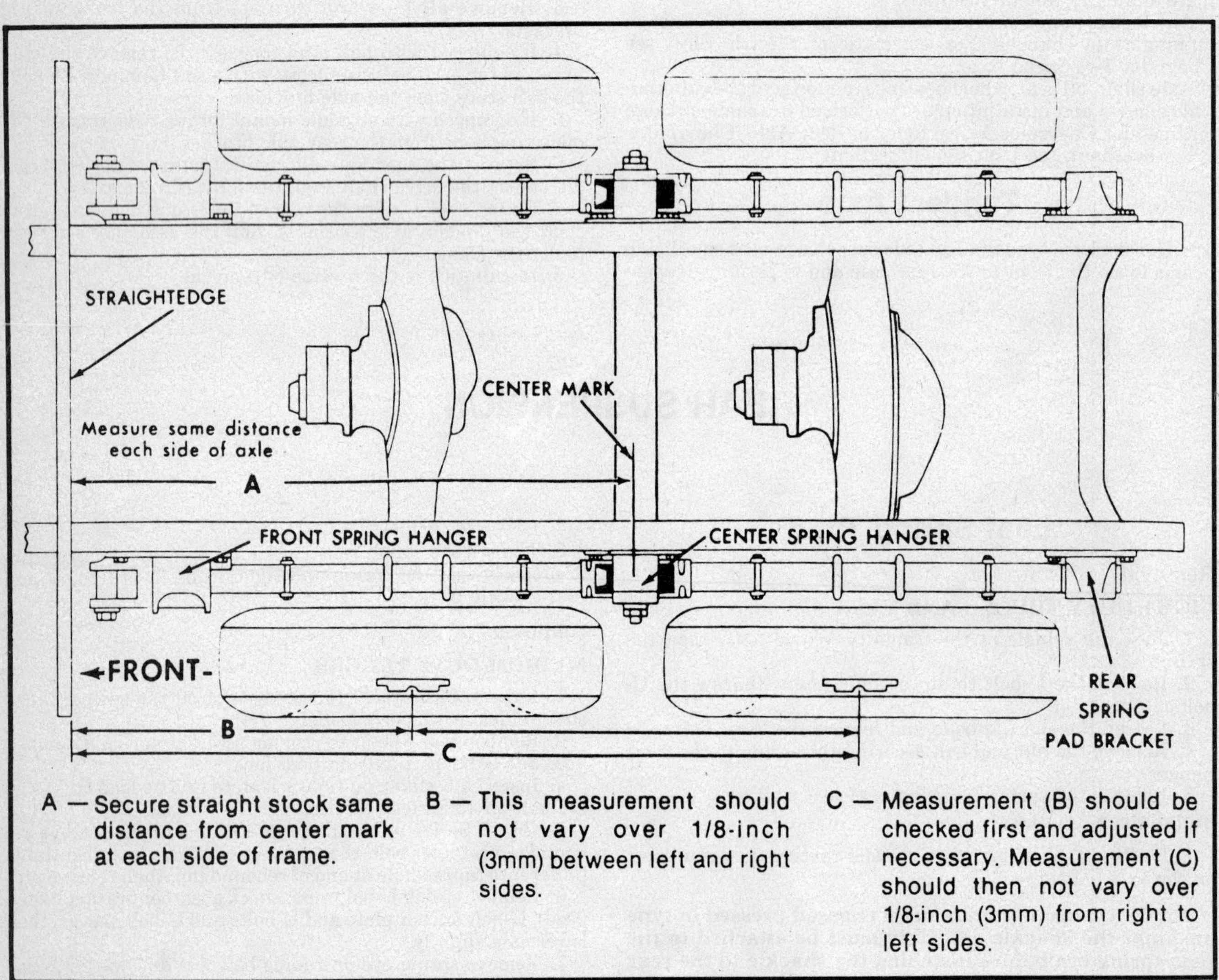
STRAIGHTEDGE
CENTER MARK
Measure same distance each side of axle
A
FRONT SPRING HANGER
CENTER SPRING HANGER
←FRONT-
REAR SPRING PAD BRACKET
B
C
A — Secure straight stock same distance from center mark at each side of frame.
B — This measurement should not vary over 1/8-inch (3mm) between left and right sides.
C — Measurement (B) should be checked first and adjusted if necessary. Measurement (C) should then not vary over 1/8-inch (3mm) from right to left sides.

Reyco tandem axle alignment diagram—typical

INDEX

BEFORE SERVICING, SEE THE SAFETY NOTICE AT THE FRONT OF THE BOOK

MODEL IDENTIFICATION
Dodge/Plymouth Trucks, Vans, Ramcharger, Trailduster, Pick-ups

B 100	Dodge Tradesman Van
B 100	Dodge Sportsman Wagon
B 200	Dodge Sportsman Van
B 200	Dodge Sportsman Wagon
B 300	Dodge Tradesman Van
B 300	Dodge Sportsman Wagon
PB 100	Plymouth Voyager Wagon
PB 200	Plymouth Voyager Wagon
PB 300	Plymouth Voyager Wagon
CB 300	Front section—Kary Van
CB 400	Front section—Kary Van
AW 100	Ramcharger—4 wheel drive
PW 100	Trailduster—4 wheel drive
AD 100	Ramcharger—2 wheel drive
PD 100	Trailduster—2 wheel drive
D 100	Dodge pick-up—2 wheel drive
D 150	Dodge pick-up—2 wheel drive
D 200	Dodge pick-up—2 wheel drive
RD 200	Dodge rail—track—2 wheel drive
D 300	Dodge pick-up—2 wheel drive
W 100	Dodge pick-up—4 wheel drive
W 200	Dodge pick-up—4 wheel drive
W 300	Dodge pick-up—4 wheel drive
W 400	Dodge pick-up—4 wheel drive
T 110	Rampage pick-up—Front drive
T 110	Scamp pick-up—Front drive
T 115	Voyager (Plymouth)
T 115	Caravan (Dodge)

ENGINE IDENTIFICATION

Engine	Years Available	Engine Make
	GASOLINE ENGINES	
4-104.7	'82–'83	Own
4-135	'82–'84	Own
4-155.9	'84	Mitsubishi
6-225	'80–'84	Own
V8-318	'80–'84	Own
V8-360	'80–'84	Own
	DIESEL ENGINES	
6-243	'83–'86	Mitsubishi

1981 AND LATER ENGINE IDENTIFICATION CODE
Light Duty Trucks

(Beginning with 1981 the (V.I.N.) vehicle identification number consists of 17 digits. The number plate is located on the upper left corner of the instrument panel, near the windshield. The engine identification code will be the 8th digit (letter) from the left.)

Engine	Cu. in. Displacement	Liters	Carburetor
C	135	2.2①	1-bbl
G	155.9	2.6①	1-bbl
E	225	3.7	1-bbl
P	318	5.2	2-bbl
M	318	5.2	4-bbl
S	360	5.9	2-bbl
T	360	5.9	4-bbl
U	360	5.9	4-bbl②
V	360	5.9	4-bbl③

① Transverse mount front wheel drive engine
② H.D.S.E.—Heavy duty single exhaust
③ H.D.D.E.—Heavy duty dual exhaust

GENERAL ENGINE SPECIFICATIONS

Year	Engine Displacement (cu. in.)	Estimated Horsepower (@ rpm)④	Estimated Torque @ rpm (ft. lbs.)④	Bore and Stroke (in.)	Compression Ratio	Oil Pressure (psi @ rpm)
'80–'81	6-225	90 @ 3600①	160 @ 1600	3.40 × 4.12	8.4:1	35–65 @ 2000
	8-318②	120 @ 3600	245 @ 1600	3.91 × 3.31	8.5:1	35–65 @ 2000
	8-318③	155 @ 4000	240 @ 2000	3.91 × 3.31	8.5:1	35–65 @ 2000
	8-360②	130 @ 3200	255 @ 2000	4.00 × 3.58	8.4:1	35–65 @ 2000
	8-360③	185 @ 4000	275 @ 2000	4.00 × 3.58	8.0:1	35–65 @ 2000
'82–'84	4-104.7	—	—	3.13 × 3.40	—	60–90 @ 2000
	4-135	84 @ 4800	111 @ 2400	3.44 × 3.62	8.5:1	50 @ 2000
	4-155.9	92 @ 4500	131 @ 2500	3.59 × 3.86	8.2:1	56 @ 2000
	6-225	90 @ 3600	160 @ 1600	3.40 × 4.12	8.4:1	35–65 @ 2000
	8-318②	120 @ 3600	245 @ 1600	3.91 × 3.31	8.5:1	35–65 @ 2000
	8-318③	155 @ 4000	240 @ 2000	3.91 × 3.31	8.5:1	35–65 @ 2000
	8-360②	130 @ 3200	255 @ 2000	4.00 × 3.58	8.4:1	35–65 @ 2000
	8-360③	185 @ 4000	275 @ 2000	4.00 × 3.58	8.0:1	35–65 @ 2000

GENERAL ENGINE SPECIFICATIONS

Year	Engine Displacement (cu. in.)	Estimated Horsepower (@ rpm)④	Estimated Torque @ rpm (ft. lbs.)④	Bore and Stroke (in.)	Compression Ratio	Oil Pressure (psi @ rpm)
'85–'86	Refer to Underhood Specifications Sticker					

① 10 more hp with two barrel carburetor
② 2 barrel carb
③ 4 barrel carb
④ Horsepower and torque are SAE net figures. They are measured at the rear of the transmission with all accessories installed and operating. Since the figures may vary when a given engine is installed in different models, some ratings are representative rather than exact.

TUNE-UP SPECIFICATIONS

Year	Engine No. Cyl. Displacement (cu in.)	Spark Plugs Original Type	Spark Plugs Gap (in.)	Distributor Point Dwell (deg)	Distributor Point Gap (in.)	Ignition Timing (±2°) (deg)▲ MT	Ignition Timing (±2°) (deg)▲ AT	Intake Valve Opens (deg)	Fuel Pump Pressure (psi)	Compression Pressure (psi)	Idle Speed (rpm) MT	Idle Speed (rpm) AT	Valve Clearance (in.) In	Valve Clearance (in.) Ex
'80	6-225 LD	560PR	.035	Elec.	Elec.	12B	12B	16B	3.5–5.0	100 (Min.)	600㉓	600㉓	.010	.020
	6-225 MD Calif.	560PR	.035	Elec.	Elec.	12B	12B	16B	3.5–5.0	100 (Min.)	800	800	.010	.020
	6-225 HD Canada	560PR	.035	Elec.	Elec.	12B	12B	16B	3.5–5.0	100 (Min.)	650	650	.010	.020
	V8-318 LD㉔	64PR	.035	Elec.	Elec.	12B	12B	10B	5.0–7.0	100 (Min.)	600	600	Hyd.	Hyd.
	V8-318 LD㉕	64PR	.035	Elec.	Elec.	10B	10B	10B	5.0–7.0	100 (Min.)	750	750	Hyd.	Hyd.
	V8-318 MD Calif.	64PR	.035	Elec.	Elec.	10B	10B	10B	5.0–7.0	100 (Min.)	750	750	Hyd.	Hyd.
	V8-318 HD	64PR	.035	Elec.	Elec.	8B㉖	8B㉖	10B	5.0–7.0	100 (Min.)	750	750	Hyd.	Hyd.
	V8-360 Canada	65PR	.035	Elec.	Elec.	—	4B㉔	18B	5.0–7.0	100 (Min.)	—	750	Hyd.	Hyd.
	V8-360 Canada	65PR	.035	Elec.	Elec.	12B	12B㉗	18B	5.0–7.0	100 (Min.)	650	650	Hyd.	Hyd.
	V8-360 LD㉖	65PR	.035	Elec.	Elec.	12B	12B	18B	5.0–7.0	100 (Min.)	650	650	Hyd.	Hyd.
	V8-360 LD㉖	65PR	.035	Elec.	Elec.	—	10B	18B	5.0–7.0	100 (Min.)	—	750	Hyd.	Hyd.
	V8-360 MD㉚	65PR	.035	Elec.	Elec.	10B	10B	18B	5.0–7.0	100 (Min.)	750	750	Hyd.	Hyd.
	V8-360 HD㉚	65PR	.035	Elec.	Elec.	10B	10B	18B	5.0–7.0	100 (Min.)	750	750	Hyd.	Hyd.
	V8-360 HD	65PR	.035	Elec.	Elec.	4B	4B	18B	5.0–7.0	100 (Min.)	700	700	Hyd.	Hyd.
'81	6-225 LD	560PR	.035	Elec.	Elec.	12B	16B	6B	3.5–5.0	100 (Min.)	㉛	㉛	Hyd.	Hyd.
	6-225 HD	560PR	.035	Elec.	Elec.	12B	16B	6B	3.5–5.0	100 (Min.)	750	750	Hyd.	Hyd.
	V8-318 LD㉔	64PR	.035	Elec.	Elec.	10B	16B	10B	5.0–7.0	100 (Min.)	650㉜	650	Hyd.	Hyd.
	V8-318 HD Canada㉔	64PR	.035	Elec.	Elec.	2A	2A	10B	5.0–7.0	100 (Min.)	750	750	Hyd.	Hyd.
	V8-318 LD㉕	64PR	.035	Elec.	Elec.	12B	16B㉝	10B	5.0–7.0	100 (Min.)	750	750	Hyd.	Hyd.
	V8-318 HD㉕	64PR	.035	Elec.	Elec.	12B	12B	10B	5.0–7.0	100 (Min.)	750	750	Hyd.	Hyd.
	V8-360-1 LD㉕	64PR	.035	Elec.	Elec.	12B	16B	18B	5.0–7.0	100 (Min.)	600㉞	625㉞	Hyd.	Hyd.
	V8-360-1 HD㉔	64PR	.035	Elec.	Elec.	—	4B	18B	5.0–7.0	100 (Min.)	—	750	Hyd.	Hyd.
	V8-360-1 HD㉕	64PR	.035	Elec.	Elec.	—	4B	18B	5.0–7.0	100 (Min.)	—	700	Hyd.	Hyd.
	V8-360-3 HD	73SR	.035	Elec.	Elec.	—	4B㉟	18B	5.0–7.0	100 (Min.)	—	700	Hyd.	Hyd.
	V8-360-3 HD	73SR	.035	Elec.	Elec.	—	10B㊱	18B	5.0–7.0	100 (Min.)	—	750	Hyd.	Hyd.
'82	4-104.7(1.7)	65PR	.035	Elec.	Elec.	12B	20B	14B	4.5–6.0	—	㊲	㊲	.012	.020
	4-135.0(2.2)	65PR	.035	Elec.	Elec.	12B	12B	12BV	4.5–6.0	130–150	850	900	Hyd.	Hyd.
	6-225 LD	560PR	.035	Elec.	Elec.	12B	16B	6B	3.5–5.0	100	㉛	㉛	Hyd.	Hyd.
	6-225 HD	560PR	.035	Elec.	Elec.	12B	16B	6B	3.5–5.0	100	750	750	Hyd.	Hyd.
	V8-318 LD㉔	64PR	.035	Elec.	Elec.	10B	16B	10B	5.0–7.0	100	650	650	Hyd.	Hyd.
	V8-318 HD㉕	64PR	.035	Elec.	Elec.	12B	12B	10B	5.0–7.0	100	750	750	Hyd.	Hyd.
	V8-360 LD㉔	64PR	.035	Elec.	Elec.	—	4B	18B	5.0–7.0	100	600	625	Hyd.	Hyd.
	V8-360 HD㉕	64PR	.035	Elec.	Elec.	—	4B	18B	5.0–7.0	100	750	750	Hyd.	Hyd.
	V8-360 HD㉕	64PR	.035	Elec.	Elec.	—	4B	18B	5.0–7.0	100	700	700	Hyd.	Hyd.

TUNE-UP SPECIFICATIONS

Year	Engine No. Cyl. Displacement (cu in.)	Spark Plugs Original Type	Spark Plugs Gap (in.)	Distributor Point Dwell (deg)	Distributor Point Gap (in.)	Ignition Timing (±2°) (deg)▲ MT	Ignition Timing (±2°) (deg)▲ AT	Intake Valve Opens (deg)	Fuel Pump Pressure (psi)	Compression Pressure (psi)	Idle Speed (rpm) MT	Idle Speed (rpm) AT	Valve Clearance (in.) In	Valve Clearance (in.) Ex
'83	4-104.7(1.7)	65PR	.035	Elec.	Elec.	12B	20B	14B	4.5–6.0	—	㊲	㊲	.012	.020
	4-135.0(2.2)	65PR	.035	Elec.	Elec.	12B	12B	14B	4.5–6.0	100 (Min.)	800㊷	800㊷	Hyd.	Hyd.
	6-225	560PR	.035	Elec.	Elec.	12B	16B	6B	3.5–5.0	100 (Min.)	㊴	㊴	Hyd.	Hyd.
	8-318㉔	64PR	.035	Elec.	Elec.	12B㊱	12B㊱	10B	4.75–6.25	100 (Min.)	㊵	㊵	Hyd.	Hyd.
	8-318㉕	64PR	.035	Elec.	Elec.	12B㊶	12B㊶	10B	4.75–6.25	100 (Min.)	750	750	Hyd.	Hyd.
	8-360㉔	65PR	.035	Elec.	Elec.	—	4B	18B	5.0–7.0	100 (Min.)	—	750	Hyd.	Hyd.
'84–'85	Refer to Underhood Specifications Sticker													

NOTE: The underhood specifications sticker often reflects tune-up specifications changes made in production. Sticker figures must be used if they disagree with those in this chart.

NOTE: All Canadian specifications are the same as Federal specifications unless noted otherwise.

—Not Applicable
▲ With vacuum advance disconnected and plugged
B Before Top Dead Center
A After Top Dead Center
CAP Cleaner Air Package
Fed. All states except California
Calif. California only
(Min.) Minimum
Hyd. Hydraulic valve lifters; no service adjustment
LD Light duty emissions
HD Heavy duty emissions
Elec. Electronic ignition
① through ㉑ Not Used
㉒ Static
㉓ Canada; MT & AT: 675
㉔ 2 barrel carb.
㉕ 4 barrel carb.
㉖ Canada HD engine w/2 bbl: 2A
㉗ Canada w/4 bbl. and distributor 4111487: 10B
㉘ Distributor; 4111947
㉙ Distributor; 4111487
㉚ California
㉛ Federal; 600
California: 800
Canada; 725
㉜ Canada; 750
㉝ Canada; 10B
㉞ California; 750
㉟ Distributor; 4091661
㊱ Distributor; 4111950
㊲ Use the information from the emission control label on the vehicle.
㊳ High Alt: 16B
Calif: 16B
㊴ Fed. 1-bbl: 600 MT, 650 AT
Calif: 750 All
Canada 1-bbl: 725 MT, 750 AT
All 2-bbl: 700
㊵ Fed. & Canada: 750
High Alt. & Calif: 700
㊶ H.D. Engines: 8B
㊷ High Alt: 900
㊸ California: 10B
㊹ California: 750

FIRING ORDERS

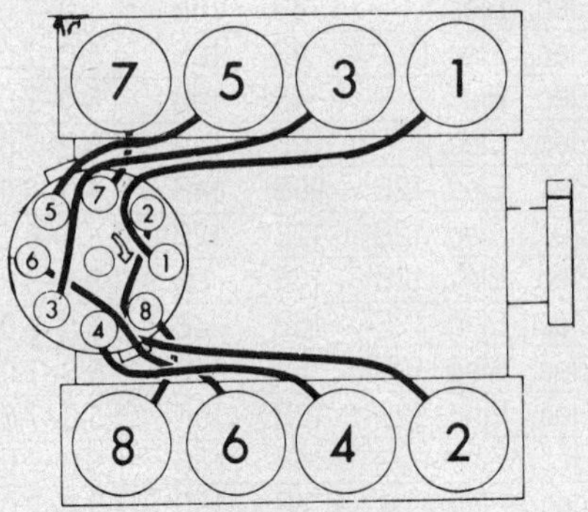

318, 360 V8 engines

FIRING ORDERS

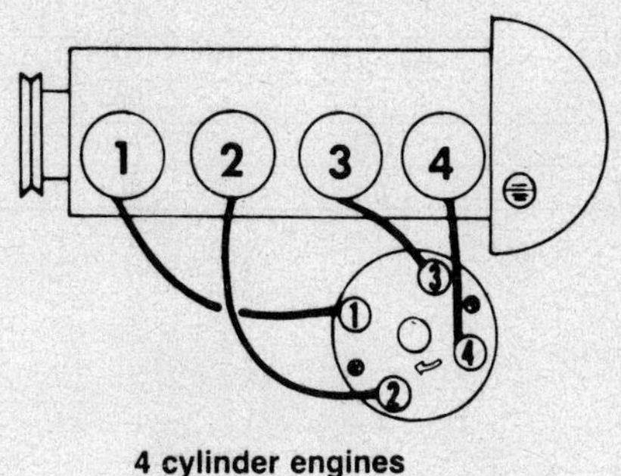

4 cylinder engines

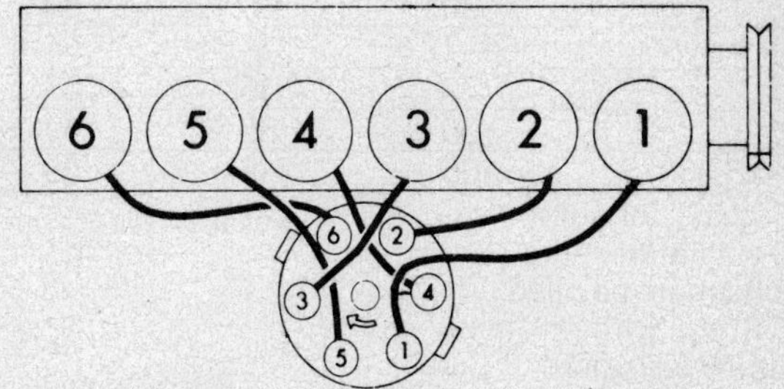

6-cylinder engine

PISTON CLEARANCE

Year	Engine Displacement (cu in.)	Measured at top of Skirt (in.)
'80–'86	6-225	.0005–.0015
	V8-318	.0005–.0015
	V8-360	.0005–.0015
	4-104.7	.0004–.0015
	4-135.0	.0005–.0240
	4-155.9	.0008–.0016

RING SIDE CLEARANCE

Year	Engine Displacement (cu in.)	Top Compression (in.)		Bottom Compression (in.)		Oil Control (in.) Steel	
		Min	Max	Min	Max	Min	Max
'80–'86	4-104.7	.0016	.0028	.0008	.0020	.0008	.0020
	4-135.0	.0016	.0028	.0008	.0020	.0008	.0020
	4-155.9	.0015	.0031	.0015	.0037	—	—
	6-225	.0015	.0030	.0015	.0030	.0002	.0050
	8-318	.0015	.0030	.0015	.0030	.0002	.0050
	8-360	.0015	.0030	.0015	.0030	.0002	.0050

Note: Side clearance for all rings in the diesel engine is .001–.002

TORQUE SPECIFICATIONS

Engine Displacement (cu in.)	Cylinder Head Bolts	Rod Bearing Bolts	Main Bearing Bolts	Crankshaft Bolt	Flywheel-to-Crankshaft Bolts	Manifold Intake	Manifold Exhaust
4-104.7	60 ⑤	25	47	58	55 ⑥	—	—
4-135	30 ⑤	40 ⑤	30 ⑤	50	55	15	15
4-155.9	65–72 ⑦	33–34	55–61	80–94	94–101 ⑥	11–14	11–14
6-225	70	45	85	Press fit	55	20 ②	10
Diesel	90 ③	65 ③	69 ③④	289	80	—	—
8-318, 8-360	105	45	85	100	55	40	20 ①

① 15 ft. lbs. for nuts
② 80 and later—stud-30; nut-20
③ Bolts must be oiled
④ 80 ft. lbs. with "H" mark
⑤ plus 1/4 turn more
⑥ Alt drive plate—84-90 ft. lbs.
⑦ Hot engine—73-79 ft. lbs.

RING GAP

Year	Engine Displacement (cu in.)	Top Compression (in.) Min	Top Compression (in.) Max	Bottom Compression (in.) Min	Bottom Compression (in.) Max	Oil Control (in.) Steel Min	Oil Control (in.) Steel Max
'80–'86	4-104.7	.012	.018	.012	.018	.016	.055
	4-135.0	.011	.021	.011	.021	.016	.055
	4-155.9	.010	.018	.010	.018	.0078	.035
	6-225	.010	.020	.010	.020	.015	.055
	8-318	.010	.020	.010	.020	.015	.055
	8-360	.010	.020	.010	.020	.015	.055

Note: Gap on all rings in the diesel engine is .012–.020

VALVE SPECIFICATIONS

Year	Engine Displacement (cu in.)	Seat Angle (deg)	Face Angle (deg)	Spring Test Pressure (lbs. @ in.)	Spring Installed Height (in.)	Stem-to-Guide Clearance (in.) Intake	Stem-to-Guide Clearance (in.) Exhaust	Stem Diameter (in.) Intake	Stem Diameter (in.) Exhaust
'80–'83	4-104.7	45	①	②	③	.002–.003	.002–.003	.3140	.3130
'82–'84	4-135.0	45	45	175 @ 1.22	1.65	.001–.003	.002–.004	.312–.313	.311–.312
'84–'86	4-155.9	45	45	61 @ 15.9	1.59	.0012–.0024	.0020–.0035	.315	.315
'80–'84	6-225	45	④	137–150 @ 1 5/16	1 11/16	.001–.003	.002–.004	.372–.373	.371–.372
Diesel	6-243	45	45	NA	1 49/64	.002–.003	.003–.004	.314	.314
'80–'86	8-318	45	45	⑤	⑥	.001–.003	.002–.004	.372–.373	.371–.372
'80–'86	8-360	45	45	⑤	⑥	.001–.003	.002–.004	.372–.373	.371–.372

NA—Not Available
① Intake; 45°33′
Exhaust; 43°33′
② Outer; 101 @ .878
Inner; 49 @ .720
③ Outer; 1.28
Inner; 1.13
④ Intake; 45°
Exhaust; 43°
⑤ Intake; 170–184 @ 1 5/16
Exhaust; 181–197 @ 1 1/16
⑥ Intake; 1 11/16
Exhaust; 1 33/64

WHEEL ALIGNMENT SPECIFICATIONS

Year	Model	Caster (Deg.)①	Camber (Deg.)	Toe-In (in.)	Kingpin Inclination (Deg.)
'80	D100	0 to +½	0 to +½	1/16–⅛	—
'80–'82	B, PB, MB100, 200, 300, AD150, D150, D350, 450	½②	+¼	1/16–⅛	—
'82	B150, 250, 350, PB150, 250, 350, MB250, 350, 450, CB350, 450	2¼	½	⅛	—
'80–'84	D200	0 to +½	0 to +½	1/16–⅛	—
'80–'86	W150, 200, 250③	3	1½	0–⅛	7½
'80	D300	0 to +½	0 to +½	1/16–⅛	—
'80–'86	W250, 300, 350③	3	½	0–⅛	8½

① No load
② 2¼ with power steering
③ Use W300 figures ro W200, 250 with Spicer 60 or 70F front axle

NOTE: Ramcharger and Trailduster service procedures are the same as those for conventional trucks, except where specific and separate procedures are given.

DISTRIBUTOR

Distributor—All Types

Removal

1. Disconnect primary lead wire at coil. On electronic ignition, disconnect the distributor lead wire at the connector.
2. Disconnect vacuum hose at distributor or vacuum controller.
3. On the Holley distributor, disconnect tachometer drive and governor inlet and outlet lines.
4. Unfasten distributor cap retaining clips and remove distributor cap.

NOTE: The spark plug and coil wires used on the 2.2L 4 cyl. engine are fitted with a forked type connector. The forked clip must be depressed before the wires can be removed from the cap.

5. Scribe a line on the distributor housing and engine block to indicate positioning of the rotor and housing.
6. Remove distributor hold-down clamp or screw.
7. Carefully lift out distributor assembly.

NOTE: Do not disturb engine position.

Installation

1. If the crankshaft has not been rotated, insert distributor into block with the rotor and body aligned to the previously scribed marks. Make sure O-ring seal is in groove of shank.

NOTE: Distributors on 6 cylinder engines have the drive gear mounted on the bottom of the distributor shaft and a slight rotation will occur when installing. Allow for

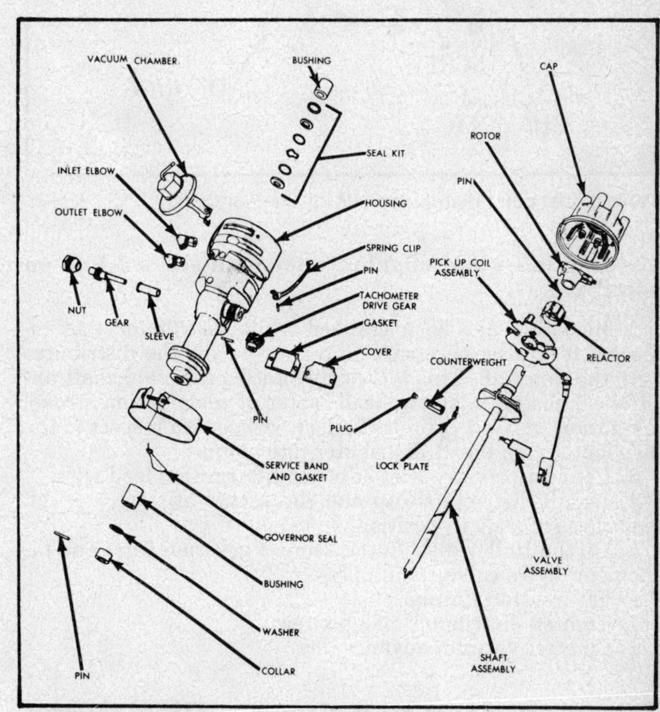

Exploded view of Holley electronic distributor
(© Chrysler Corp.)

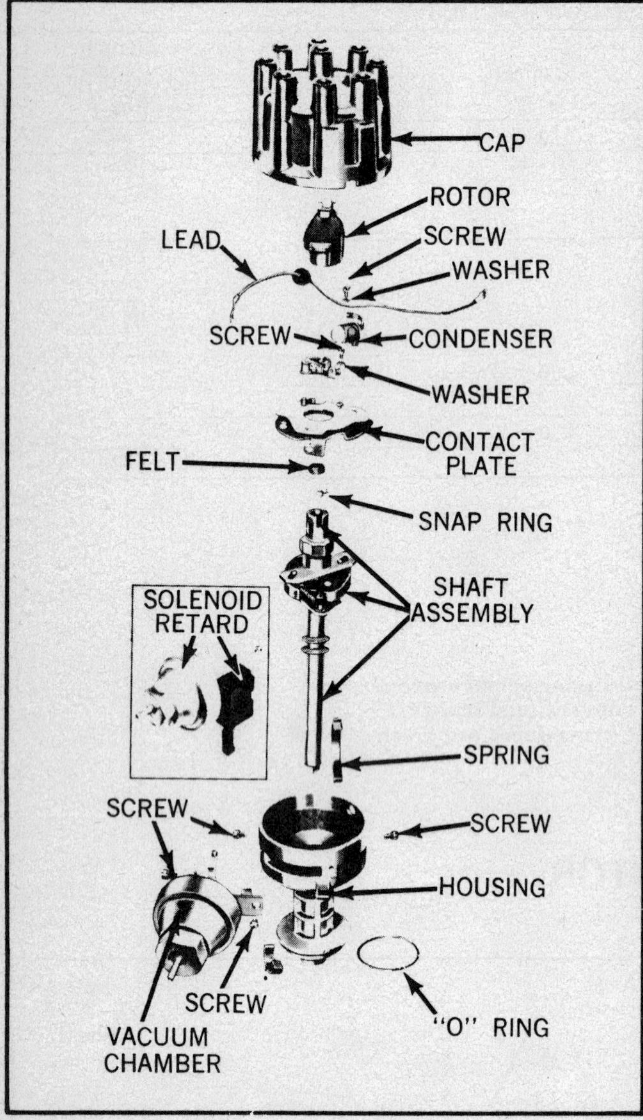

Typical dual point distributor—V8 (© Chrysler Corp.)

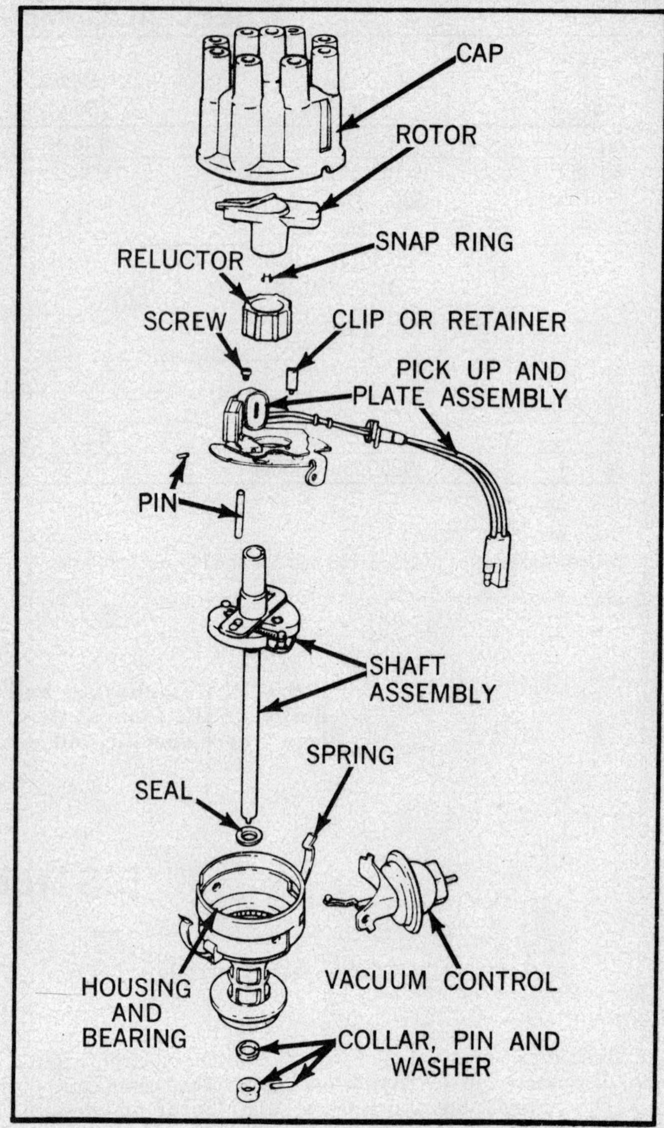

V8 electronic ignition distributor (© Chrysler Corp.)

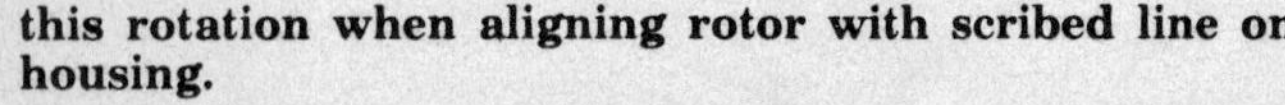
this rotation when aligning rotor with scribed line on housing.

2. If engine has been cranked while distributor was removed, it will be necessary to correctly time the distributor with the camshaft. This is done by rotating the crankshaft until No. 1 piston is at top dead center of compression stroke. With rotor in No. 1 cylinder firing position with respect to the distributor cap, insert distributor into engine.
3. Connect primary lead or electronic ignition lead wire.
4. Install distributor cap and check that all high tension leads are securely in position.
5. On the Holley distributor, connect governor lines and tachometer drive cable.
6. Set ignition timing.
7. Tighten distributor clamp screw.
8. Connect vacuum advance line.

Electronic Ignition System Distributor

No internal distributor maintenance is required with this system; it does not use contact points or a condenser. This system is easily identified by a double wire lead from the distributor and a control unit in the engine compartment.

NOTE: The dwell meter is of no significance in servicing the ignition system and since dwell is non-adjustable, no changes should be attempted.

ELECTRONIC IGNITION DISTRIBUTOR AIR GAP ADJUSTMENT

This adjustment is not required at regular intervals. It is not a normal tune-up service. Air gap is not adjustable on the 4 cylinder engines.

1. Release the spring clips and remove the distributor cap. Pull off the rotor.
2. Align one reluctor tooth with the pick-up coil tooth by turning the engine. The reluctor is the six or eight-toothed ring around the distributor shaft.
3. Insert an 0.008 in. nonmagnetic (brass) feeler gauge between the reluctor tooth and the pick-up coil tooth.

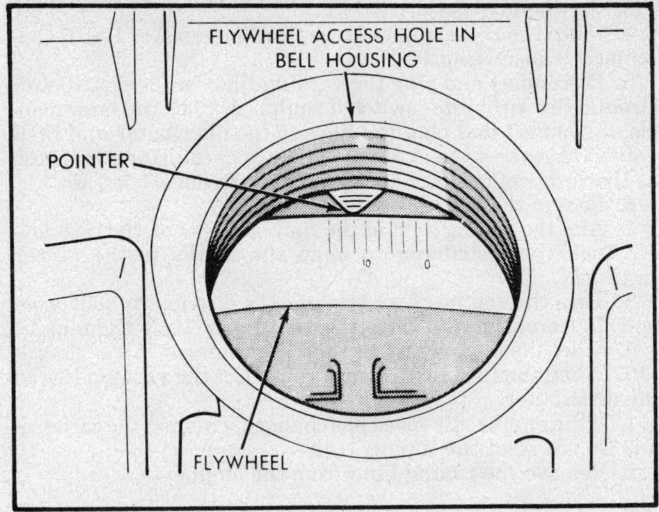

Manual A-412 transaxle timing mark location (© Chrysler Corp.)

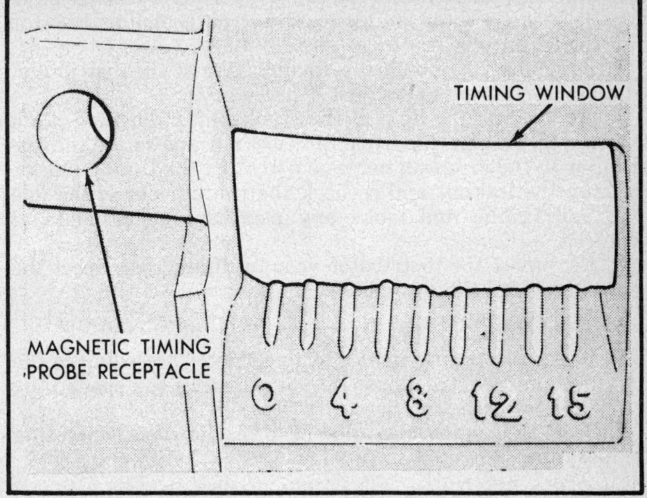

All manual transaxle except A-412—timing mark location (© Chrysler Corp.)

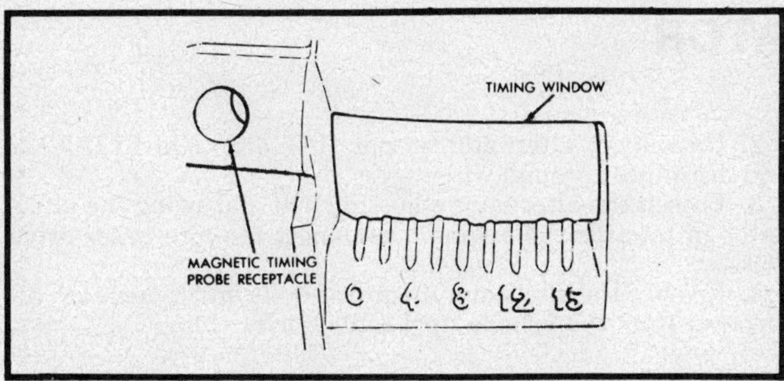

135 (2.2L) timing mark location (© Chrysler Corp.)

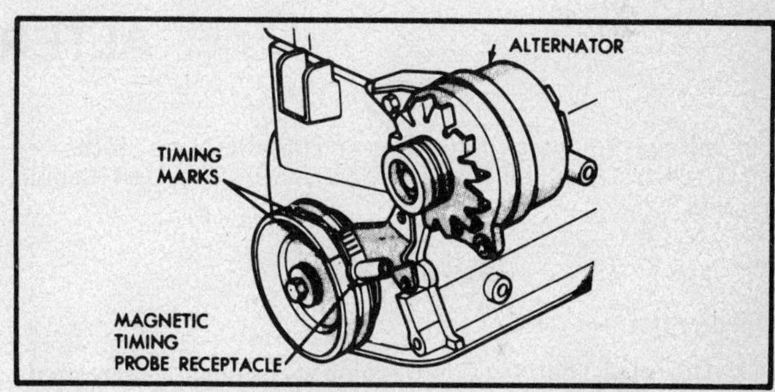

155.9 (2.6L) timing mark location (© Chrysler Corp.)

4. Loosen the hold-down screw and adjust the gap using the screwdriver slot in the mounting plate. Contact should be made between the reluctor tooth, the feeler gauge, and the pick-up coil tooth.
5. Tighten the hold-down screw.
6. Remove the feeler gauge. No force should be required.
7. Check the gap with a 0.010 in. nonmagnetic feeler gauge. It should not fit; don't force it into the gap.
8. Turn the distributor shaft and apply vacuum to the vacuum advance unit. If it is adjusted properly and nothing is bent, the pick-up coil tooth will not hit the reluctor teeth.

NOTE: Some applications will have a dual pick-up coil in the distributor. A cranking and starting pick-up is identified by a two prong male connector at the distributor. The pick-up used during engine running, will have a single male-female connector. Set the air gap on the cranking and starting pick-up at 0.006 inch and the air gap on the running pick-up at 0.012 inch up to 1984 and 0.008 in. for later models.

IGNITION TIMING

On all engines except, Rampage front wheel drive, the timing plate is located on the timing case (front) cover and the timing mark is on the crankshaft pulley damper. On all models the ignition is timed to the No. 1 cylinder spark plug. Always remove and plug the vacuum advance line when setting ignition timing.

The Rampage transaxle timing marks can be seen through a hole in the transmission bell housing. The A–412 manual transaxle has the timing degrees on the flywheel. All other transaxles have the timing degrees marked on a timing window in the bell housing.

Adjustment

135 (2.2L) 4 CYLINDER

1. Connect a timing light according to the manufacturers instructions.
2. Run the engine to normal operating temperature.
3. Make sure that the idle speed is correct.
4. Loosen the distributor hold down bolt so the distributor can be rotated.
5. Ground the carburetor switch (if equipped). Disconnect and plug the vacuum lines to the distributor. If the vehicle is equipped with electronic spark control computer, disconnect the vacuum advance line at the computer.
6. Remove the timing hole access cover and aim the timing light at the hole in the clutch housing. Rotate the distributor until the timing marks are aligned.
7. Tighten the distributor hold down bolt and recheck the timing. Check and adjust the idle speed if necessary.

156 (2.6L) 4 CYLINDER

1. Locate, clean and mark the timing scale and pointer on the crank pulley and front cover.
2. Connect a timing light and tachometer to the engine according to the manufacturers instructions. Start the engine and allow it to reach normal operating temperature..

3. Open the throttle and release it to check for linkage binding. Be sure the throttle linkage idle screw is against the stop and the carburetor is off fast idle.
4. Disconnect and plug the vacuum line at the distributor. Check the idle rpm and adjust if necessary.
5. Aim the timing light at the crankshaft pulley and check the timing. Loosen the distributor locknut and rotate the distributor in the direction necessary to align the timing marks. Tighten the locknut and recheck the timing. Check the idle rpm and timing and make any necessary adjustments as required.
6. Reconnect the distributor vacuum lines. Disconnect the tachometer and timing light.

6 AND 8 CYLINDERS

1. Connect a timing light and tachometer according to the manufacturers instructions. Do not puncture the spark plug wires or boot with a probe.
2. Start the engine and allow it to reach normal operating temperature.
3. Set the idle speed.
4. Place the trnasmission in neutral (manual) or PARK (automatic transmissions)
5. Disconnect and plug the vacuum lines at the distributor. Ground the carburetor switch if equipped. 1981 and later models, disconnect and plug the lines to the distributor and EGR valve. Disconnect the PCV valve and vapor canister purge hose at the carburetor end. Leave both open to underhood air.
6. Loosen the distributor hold down bolt.
7. Aim the timing light at the timing marks on the case cover. Turn the distributor to align the marks to the proper setting.
8. Turn the engine off and tighten the distributor hold down bolt. Be careful not to move the distributor while tightening.
9. Start the engine and recheck the timing.
10. When the timing is correct, reconnect the vacuum line to the distributor.
11. If the engine idle speed has changed, readjust the carburetor. Do not reset the timing.
12. Remove the timing light from the engine.

ALTERNATOR

For voltage regulator circuit tests and for alternator off-the-vehicle service, see The Electrical Section in The Unit Repair Section.

Alternator

Removal

1. Disconnect battery ground cable at the negative terminal.

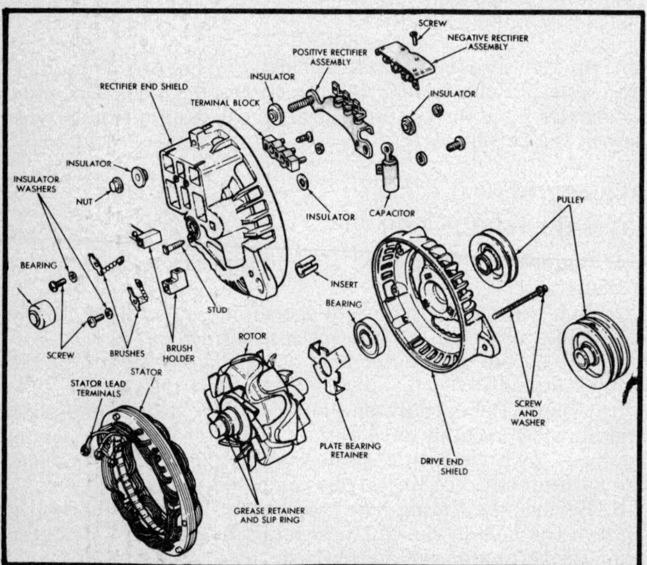

Exploded view of alternator (© Chrysler Corp.)

2. Disconnect alternator output BAT and field FLD leads and disconnect ground wire.
3. Loosen the alternator adjusting bolt and swing the alternator in towards the engine. Disconnect the alternator drive belt.
4. Remove the alternator mounting bolts and remove the alternator from the vehicle from the vehicle.

Installation

1. Install alternator and adjust drive belt.
2. Connect output BAT and field FLD leads and connect ground wire.
3. Connect battery ground cable.
4. Start engine, and observe alternator operation.
5. Test current output and adjust regulator voltage setting, if necessary. See Electrical section.

NOTE: Late models use a non-adjustable sealed electronic regulator.

Voltage Regulator

ELECTRONIC VOLTAGE REGULATOR

Removal and Installation

1. Release the spring clips and pull off the regulator wiring plug.
2. Unbolt and remove the regulator.
3. Installation is the reverse of removal. Be sure that the spring clips engage the wiring plug.

STARTER

For starter motor overhaul procedures see the Electrical section in the Unit Repair Section.

Gasoline Engine

Removal and Installation

1. Disconnect the battery ground cable.
2. Remove the cable at the starter. Remove the heat shield clamp and heat shield if equipped.
3. If the solenoid is mounted on the starter, disconnect the wires at the solenoid terminals.
4. Remove the starter to flywheel housing mounting bolts. Remove automatic transmission oil cooler tube bracket off the stud if necessary. Remove the starter and removable seal if so equipped.
5. Before installing the starter, make sure the starter and flywheel housing mounting surfaces are free of dirt and oil. These surfaces must be clean.
6. Install the starter to flywheel housing removable seal if so equipped.
7. Position the starter to the flywheel housing and, if necessary, install the automatic transmission oil cooler bracket. Install mounting bolts. Tighten securely.

NOTE: When tightening the mounting bolt and nut on the starter hold the starter away from the engine for correct alignment.

8. If the solenoid is mounted on the starter, connect the wires to the solenoid terminals.
9. Connect the cable to the starter terminal.
10. Connect the battery ground cable and test operation of the starter for proper engine cranking.

Diesel Engine

Removal and Installation

1. Disconnect the negative battery cable at the battery. Raise the vehicle on a hoist.
2. Disconnect the battery and solenoid wiring at the starter. Remove the bolt, nut and washer securing the starter to the engine.
3. Remove the starter and the solenoid from the engine as an assembly.
4. Before installing the starter, be sure that the mounting surfaces on the drive-end housing and the flywheel housing are free of dirt and oil to ensure a good electrical contact.
5. To install the starter, reverse the removal procedures.

NOTE: When tightening attaching bolt and nut, hold the starter away from the flywheel housing to ensure proper alignment.

6. Connect the battery ground cable and test the operation of the starter for proper engine cranking.

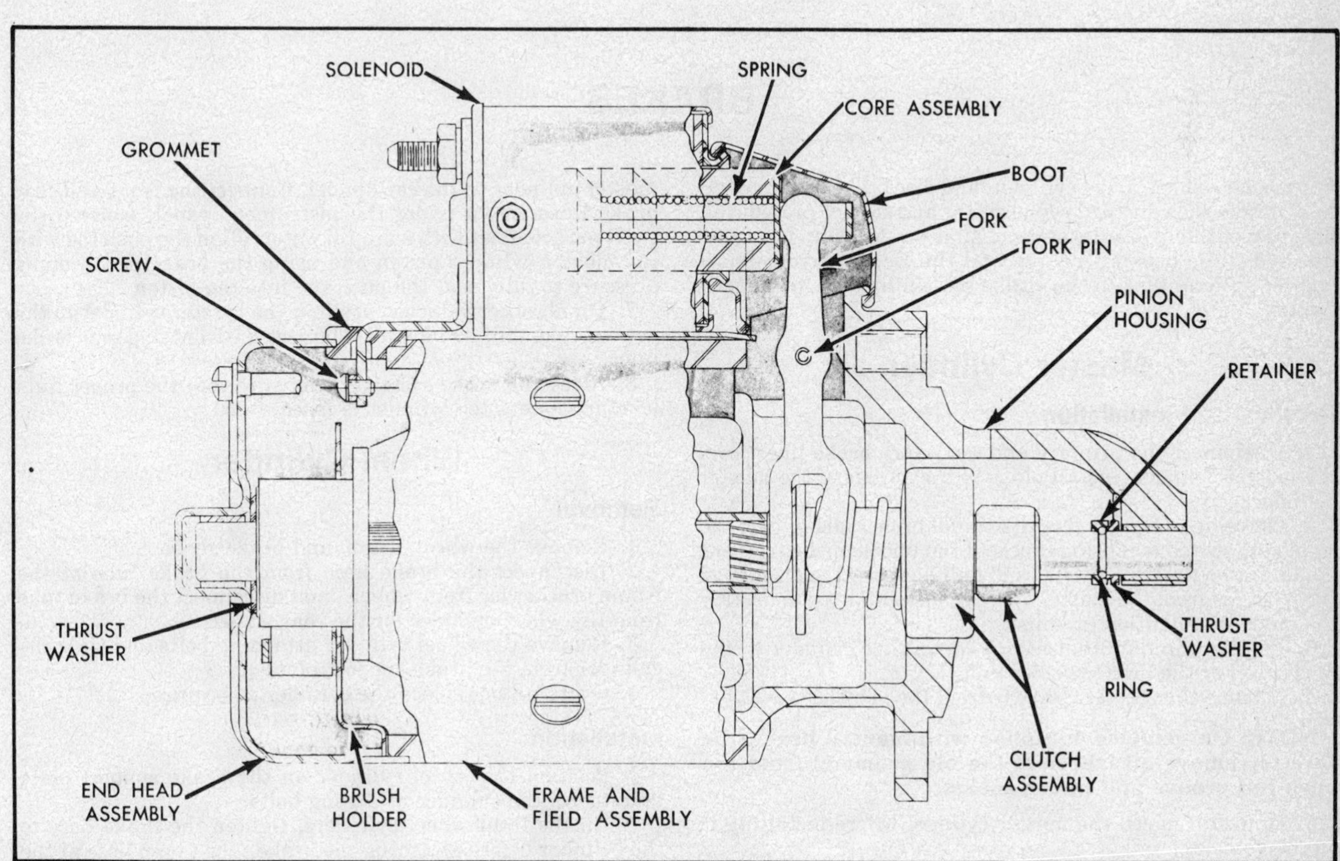

Starter motor (direct drive type) (© Chrysler Corp.)

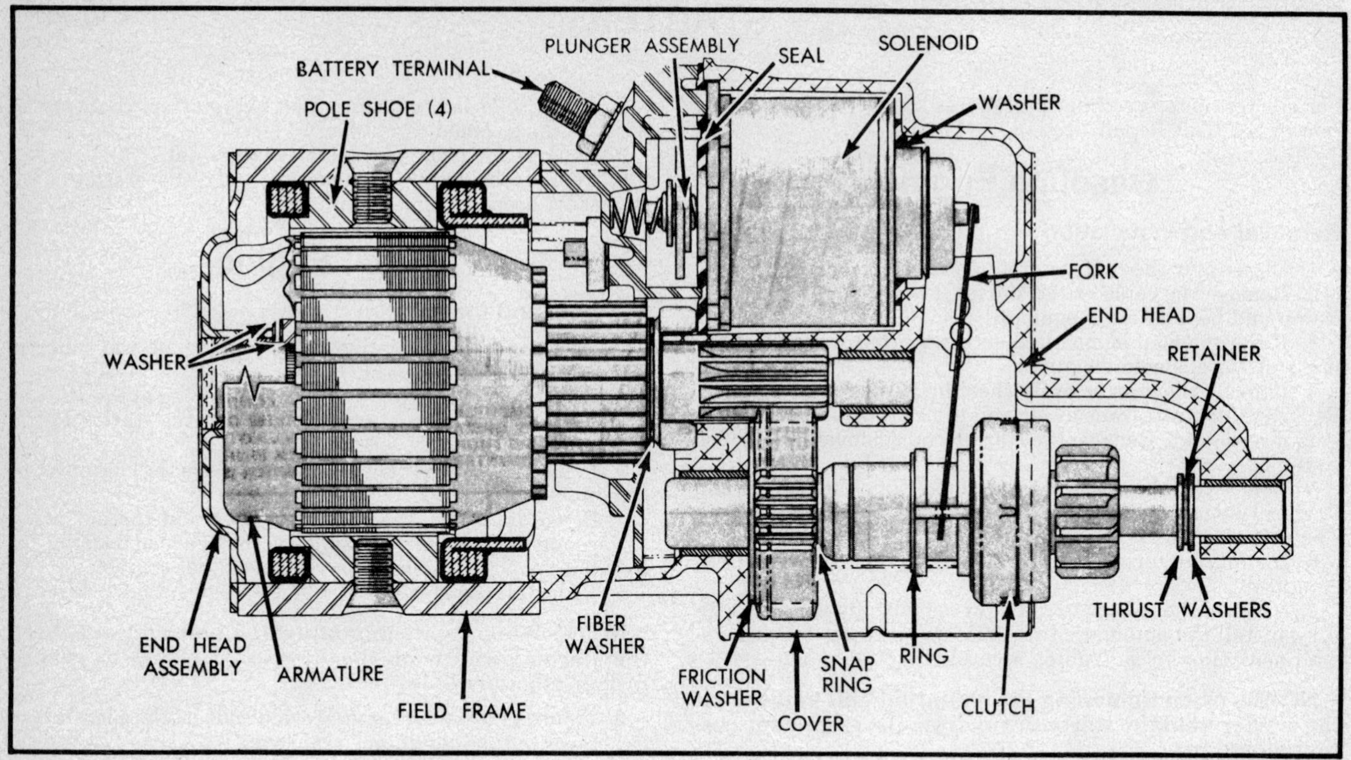

Starter motor (reduction gear type) (© Chrysler Corp.)

BRAKES

For master, wheel, slave cylinder, and disc brake caliper overhaul, brake shoe and pad replacement and service procedures, bleeding of the hydraulic system, dual master cylinder, vacuum-hydraulic booster system and the Bendix hydro-boost booster system refer to the Brake section in the Unit Repair section.

Master Cylinder

Removal and Installation

1. Disconnect the primary and secondary brake lines from the master cylinder. Install plugs in the outlets of the master cylinder.
2. On vehicles equipped with manual brakes, disconnect the stop lamp switch mounting bracket from under the instrument panel. Grasp the brake pedal and pull backward to disengage the push rod from the master cylinder piston. This will destroy the push rod retention grommet.
3. Remove the nuts that attach the master cylinder to the cowl panel or the brake booster unit.
4. Remove the master cylinder from the vehicle.

NOTE: On vehicles equipped with manual brakes be sure to remove all traces of the old grommet from the push rod groove and piston socket.

5. To install, bleed the master cylinder before installing it on the vehicle.
6. On vehicles equipped with manual brakes, install a new push rod grommet onto the push rod. Position and install the master cylinder to the cowl panel. Connect the front and rear brake lines. From under the instrument panel, moisten the push rod grommet with a drop of water, align the push rod with the master cylinder piston and using the brake pedal, apply pressure to fully seat the push rod into the piston.
7. On all other vehicles, position the master cylinder to the power brake unit and install. Connect the front and rear brake lines.
8. Bleed the brake system, being sure that the proper fluid level in the master cylinder is maintained.

Wheel Cylinder

Removal

1. Remove the wheel, drum, and brake shoes.
2. Disconnect the brake hose from the brake tube at the frame bracket for front wheels, and disconnect the brake tube from the wheel cylinder for the rear wheels.
3. Remove the wheel cylinder attaching bolts and slide the cylinder from the brake support plate.
4. Overhaul or replace the cylinder as required.

Installation

1. Position the wheel cylinder on the brake support plate and install the cylinder attaching bolts.
2. On the front wheel cylinders, tighten the brake hose to the cylinder before attaching the brake tube to the hose at the frame location. Tighten the attaching bolts.
3. With the rear wheel cylinder loose on the brake support

COVER
GASKET
PISTON
RETAINER
SCREW
BAIL
SEATS
MASTER
CYLINDER BODY
SECONDARY SYSTEM COMPONENTS
(REAR BRAKES)
PRIMARY SYSTEM
COMPONENTS
(FRONT BRAKES)
PISTON
RETURN
SPRING
CUP RETAINER
PRIMARY CUP
"O" RING
SEAL OR CUP
PRIMARY
PISTON
ASSEMBLY
PRIMARY
CUP
PISTON
RETAINER
SNAP RING
CHECK FLOW WASHER
DISC BRAKE
SECONDARY
PISTON
SECONDARY
CUP
SECONDARY
CUP

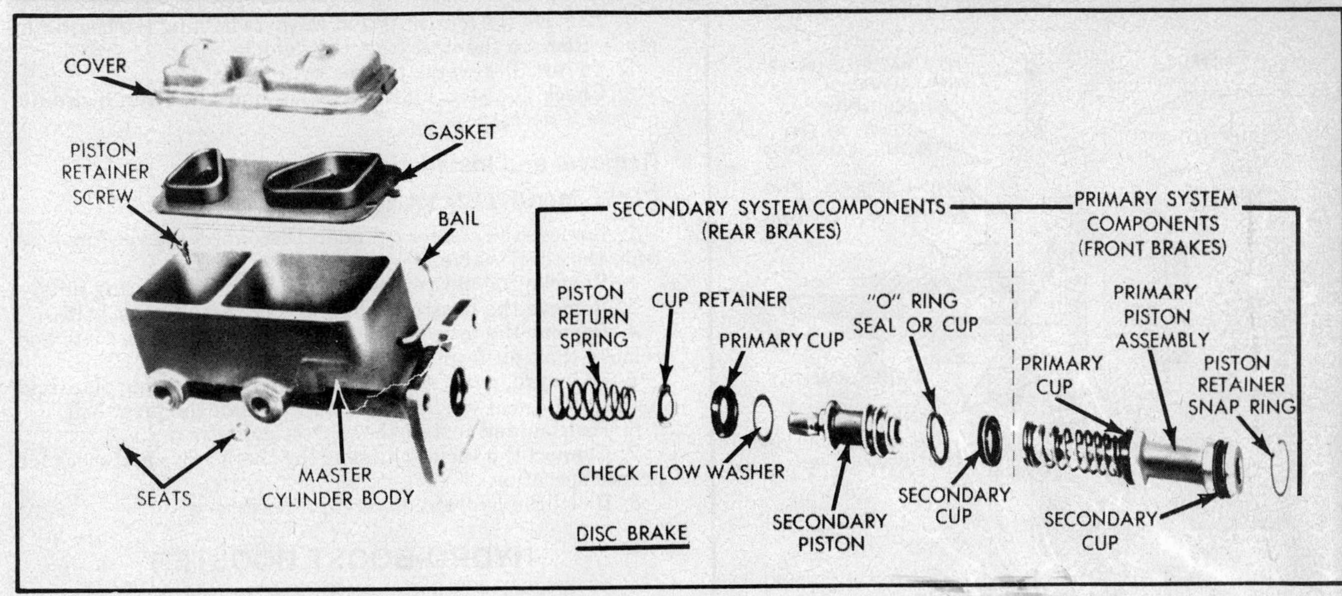

Exploded view of typical tandem master cylinder (© Chrysler Corp.)

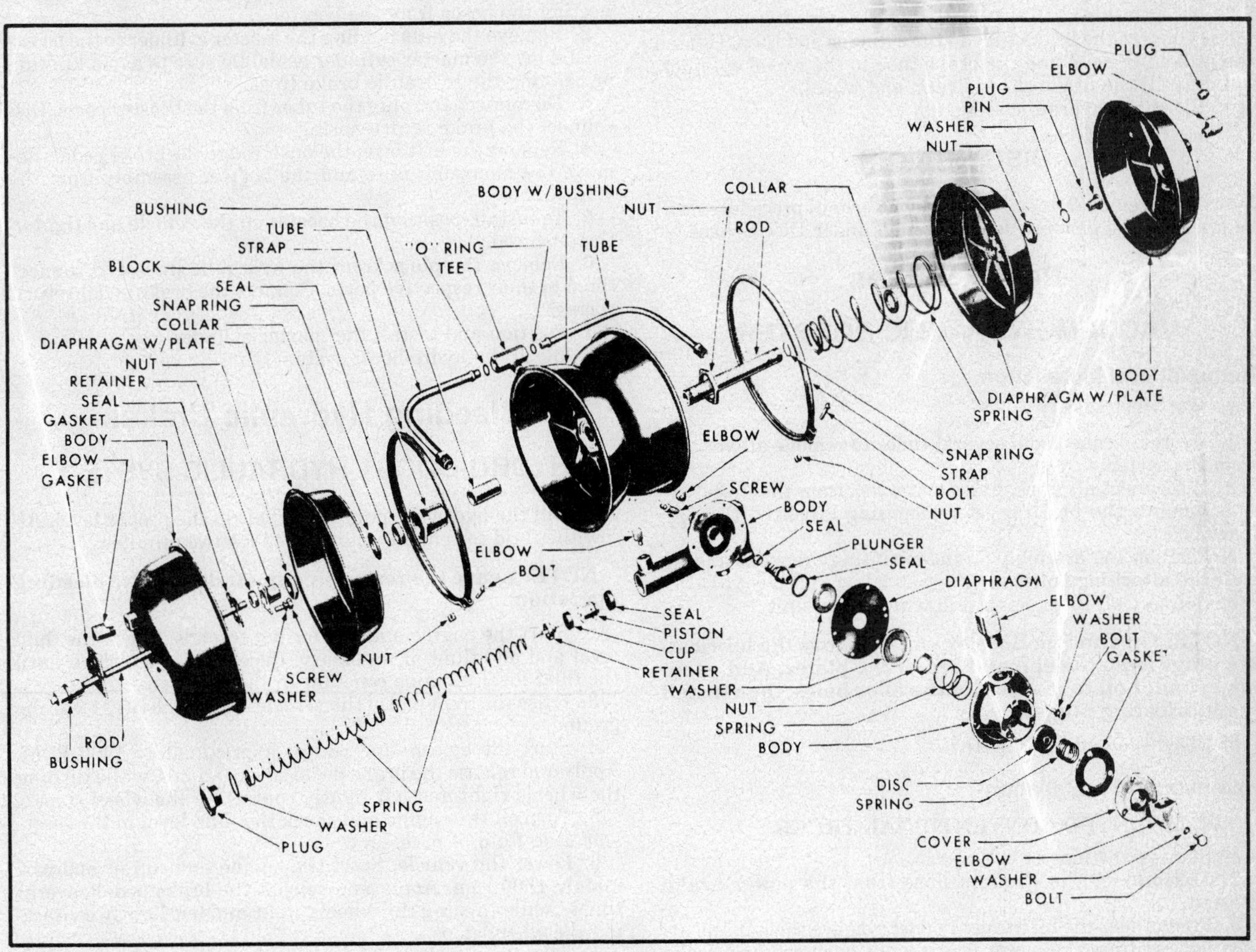

PLUG
ELBOW
PLUG
PIN
WASHER
NUT
BODY W/BUSHING
COLLAR
NUT
ROD
BUSHING
TUBE
STRAP
"O" RING
TEE
TUBE
BLOCK
SEAL
SNAP RING
COLLAR
DIAPHRAGM W/PLATE
NUT
RETAINER
SEAL
GASKET
BODY
ELBOW
GASKET
BODY
DIAPHRAGM W/PLATE
SPRING
ELBOW
SNAP RING
STRAP
BOLT
NUT
SCREW
BODY
SEAL
PLUNGER
SEAL
DIAPHRAGM
ELBOW
BOLT
ELBOW
WASHER
BOLT
GASKET
SEAL
PISTON
CUP
RETAINER
WASHER
NUT
SPRING
BODY
NUT
SCREW
WASHER
ROD
BUSHING
SPRING
WASHER
PLUG
DISC
SPRING
COVER
ELBOW
WASHER
BOLT

Exploded view of double diaphragm power brake unit (© Chrysler Corp.)

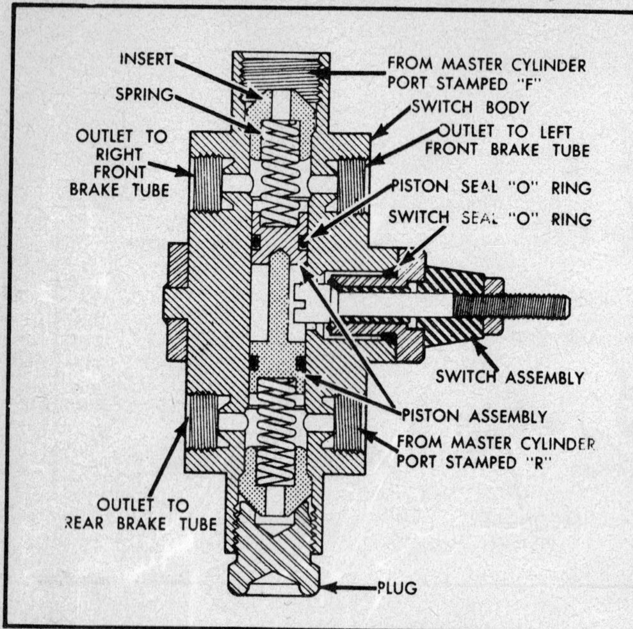

Dual brake system safety switch (© Chrysler Corp.)

plate, connect the brake tube to the cylinder and then, tighten the attaching bolts and the brake tube to the wheel cylinder.

4. Install the brake shoes, drum, and wheel.
5. Bleed the hydraulic system.

DISC BRAKES

Disc brake removal, installation, and overhaul procedures will be found in the general Repair Section under Disc Brakes.

Power Brakes

VACUUM HYDRAULIC BOOSTER

Removal and Installation

FRAME MOUNTED

1. Depress brake pedal several times to remove all vacuum from the system.
2. Disconnect all lines, hoses and wires from the unit.
3. Remove the brake booster mounting brackets, then remove booster.
4. Position the assembly on the mounting brackets, and install the attaching bolts.
5. Connect all lines, hoses and wires to the unit.

NOTE: On Tandem Booster units, remove the lubricating plugs from the end and center the plates. Add vacuum cylinder oil to the level of the filler holes, then install the lubricating plugs.

6. Bleed the hydraulic system.

Removal and Installation

COWL MOUNTED CONVENTIONAL TRUCK

1. Remove the master cylinder.
2. Disconnect the vacuum hose from the power brake booster.
3. From under the instrument panel, remove the nut and attaching bolt from the power brake input push rod and brake pedal blade.
4. Remove the four nuts and washers holding the booster in place. Remove the unit from the vehicle.
5. To install, reverse the removal procedures.
6. Check the stop light operation and bleed the hydraulic system if necessary.

Removal and Installation

COWL MOUNTED VANS

1. Remove the master cylinder. Disconnect the vacuum hose from the check valve.
2. Remove the master cylinder to booster mounting nuts.
3. Remove the booster-to-hub and bellcrank pivot bolt.
4. Remove the mounting nuts from the mounting plate and remove the unit from the vehicle.
5. To install, position the booster on the mounting plate and install the coned washers and nuts. Install the pivot bolt.
6. Position and install the master cylinder.
7. Connect the vacuum hose to the check valve and check for proper operation.
8. Bleed the hydraulic system if necessary.

HYDRO-BOOST BOOSTER

Removal and Installation

1. Pump the brake pedal several times to be sure that all pressure is discharged from the accumulator prior to disconnecting the hoses from the booster.
2. Remove the nuts holding the master cylinder to the booster and lay the master cylinder aside. Be sure to avoid kinking or bending the hydraulic brake lines.
3. Disconnect and plug the tubes from the booster ports. Disconnect the brake return spring.
4. Remove the bolt from the push rod to the brake pedal. Remove the mounting nuts and the booster assembly from the vehicle.
5. To install, position the booster on the vehicle and tighten the push rod.
6. Remove the plugs from the hydraulic lines and connect them to their respective ports. Connect the brake pedal return spring.
7. Position and install the master cylinder.
8. Bleed the hydro-boost system.

Bleeding Hydraulic Brakes

HYDRO-BOOST HYDRAULIC SYSTEM

1. Fill the hydraulic pump reservoir to the proper level. Allow the fluid to remain undisturbed for two minutes.

NOTE: Leave the reservoir cap off during the bleeding operation.

2. Start the engine and run for ten seconds. Check the fluid level and add fluid, if necessary. Repeat this procedure until the fluid level remains constant in the reservoir.
3. Raise the front end of the vehicle so that the tires clear the ground.
4. Start the engine and run at approximately 1500 RPM. Apply and release the brake pedal several times, while turning the wheels right and left lightly contacting the wheel stops.
5. Turn off the engine and check the fluid level in the reservoir. Add fluid, if necessary.
6. Lower the vehicle. Start the engine and run at approximately 1500 rpm. Apply and release the brake pedal several times, while turning the wheels right and left lightly contacting the wheel stops.
7. Turn the engine off and check the fluid level in the reservoir, add if necessary.

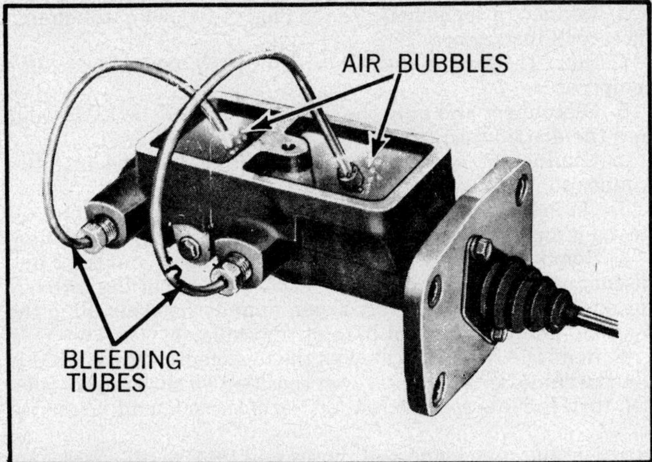

Bleeding dual master cylinder (© Chrysler Corp.)

NOTE: If fluid is extremely foamy, allow the vehicle to stand for an hour with the engine off. If fluid level is low repeat the process again.

8. Replace the cover on the reservoir.

NOTE: When using a pressure tank to bleed disc brakes, the hold off valve must be held open to the front brakes. Chrysler special tool C-4121 or equivalent can be used to hold open the valve.

CAUTION

Never use a wedge or rigid clamp to depress the hold off valve. This could damage the valve, resulting in complete loss of front brakes.

Stop Light Switch

Adjustment

The stop light switch is located behind the brake pedal and adjustment is possible by moving the switch and the bracket assembly in either direction.

Parking Brake

REAR WHEEL CABLE TYPE

In this system, the rear wheel brakes also act as parking brakes. They are operated mechanically by a lever and strut connected to a steel cable. This cable is connected to the rear wheel brake cables via an equalizer.

Removal

1. Raise the vehicle, release the brakes, and remove the rear wheels.
2. Remove the brake drum from the rear axle.
3. Remove the brake shoe return spring and brake shoe retaining springs.
4. Remove the brake shoe strut and spring from the support plate.
5. Disconnect the cable from the operating arm.
6. Compress the retainers on the end of the cable housing and remove the cables from the support plate.
7. Remove the retaining bolt and nut from the cable bracket. Remove the clips at the frame bracket.
8. Disconnect the cable from the equalizer bar, and remove the assembly.

Installation

1. Lubricate the cable with short fiber grease at the point of contact.
2. Insert the cable and housing into the frame bracket and install the retaining clips.
3. Engage the end with the equalizer bar.
4. Insert the rear end of the cable and housing into the brake support plate. Make sure the housing retainers lock firmly in place.
5. Insert the end of the cable into the brake shoe operating lever and install the brake shoes.
6. Install the retaining springs, return springs, brake drum, and wheel.
7. Connect the brake cable bracket.
8. Adjust the brakes and cable.

Adjustment

1. Inspect all components and correct any deficiencies such as rust, kinks, or bent parts.
2. Raise the vehicle on a lift and release the brake.
3. Loosen the adjustment until both cables have slack.
4. Tighten the cable adjuster until a slight drag is felt while rotating the wheel. Loosen the adjuster until there is no drag, then back off two turns.
5. Apply the brake several times, then recheck the adjustment.

FUEL SYSTEM

Carburetor specifications, exploded views, and basic adjustments are found in the Unit Repair Section under Carburetor Repairs.

Carburetor

Removal and Installation

The following is a general removal procedure for all carburetors.

1. Disconnect the battery ground cable.
2. Remove the air cleaner. On the 2.6L carburetered engine, remove the air intake housing from the air horn.
3. Remove the fuel tank pressure-vacuum filler cap. The tank could be under a small amount of pressure. On the 2.6L carbureted engine, drain the radiator until the coolant level is below the carburetor, and then disconnect the coolant hoses at the carburetor.
4. Disconnect and plug the fuel lines. Use two wrenches to avoid twisting the fuel line. A container is also useful to catch any fuel which spills from the lines.
5. Disconnect the throttle and choke linkage and all wiring.
6. Tag and disconnect any vacuum lines preventing access to the carburetor mounting bolts.
7. Remove the mounting bolts.
8. Carefully remove the carburetor from the engine and carry it in a level position to a clean work place.
9. Installation is the reverse of removal. Adjust the curb idle speed. Be sure to refill the cooling system is necessary.

Fuel Pump

Removal and Installation

1. Disconnect the fuel lines from the inlet and output sides of the fuel pump.
2. Plug these lines to prevent gasoline from leaking out.
3. Unbolt the retaining bolts from the fuel pump and remove the fuel pump from the engine.
4. Remove the old gasket from the engine and/or fuel pump. Note that on the 2.2L engine there is a spacer with a gasket on either side.
5. Clean all mounting surfaces.
6. Using a new gasket, install the fuel pump. Installation is the reverse of removal. The 2.2L engine will require the use of 2 gaskets.

Idle Speed and Mixture Adjustment

4–CYLINDER 1.7L AND 2.2L ENGINES

1. Set the parking brake and place the transmission in neutral.
2. Turn off all the lights and accessories.

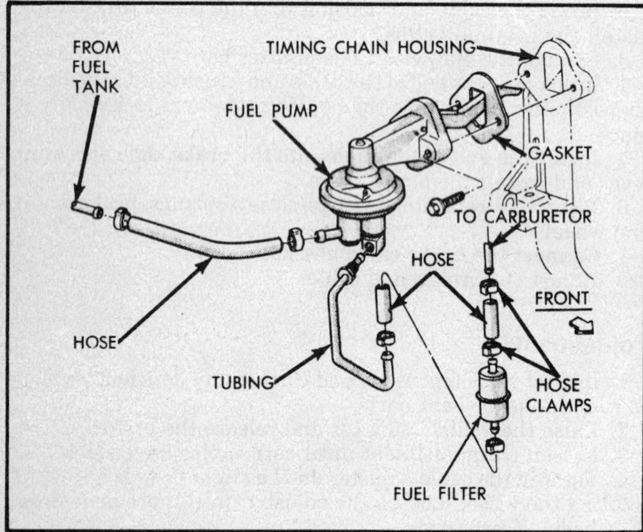

318 and 360 engine fuel pump details (© Chrysler Corp.)

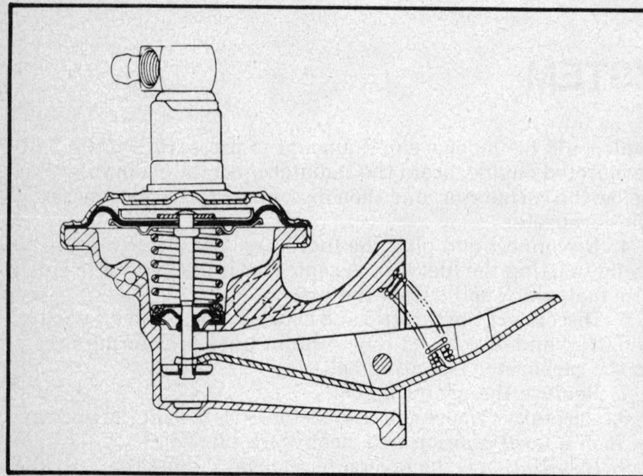

Fuel pump 6 cylinder (© Chrysler Corp.)

3. Connect a tachometer to the engine following the manufacturer's instructions.
4. Start the engine and allow it to reach normal operating temperature.
5. Disconnect and plug the vacuum hoses to the EGR valve and the distributor.
6. Unplug the connector at the radiator fan and install a jumper so it will run continuously.
7. On models equipped with the fuel control computer, connect a jumper wire between the carburetor switch and ground.
8. Remove the PCV from the rubber molded connector and disconnect the purge hose to the vapor canister at the carburetor end. Leave the PCV valve open to underhood air. Plug the $^{3}/_{16}$ inch diameter control hose at the canister.
9. Read the RPM indicated on the tachometer. If the RPM is not the same as the idle set rpm specified on the emissions label, turn the idle speed screw (on top of the solenoid) to correct it.
10. Unplug and connect all hoses and replace all wires.

4 CYLINDER 2.6L ENGINE

1. Set the parking brake and place the transmission in neutral.
2. Turn off all the lights and accessories and disconnect the cooling fan.
3. Connect a tachometer to the engine following the manufacturer's instructions.
4. Start the engine and allow it to reach normal operating temperature.
5. Check the timing and adjust if necessary.
6. Remove the timing light and read the rpm indicated on the tachometer. It is not the same as the curb idle specified on the emission label adjust the idle speed adjusting screw. The screw is accessable through the hole in the choke cover plate using a long narrow screwdriver at a 45° angle inwards.
7. After adjusting the curb idle speed, press the A/C button on. With the compressor running, set the engine speed to 900 rpm by turning the idle up adjusting screw. The idle up adjusting screw is accessible through a hole in the choke cover plate using a long narrow shaft screwdriver at a 45° angle downwards.
8. Turn the engine off, disconnect the tachometer and reconnect the cooling fan.

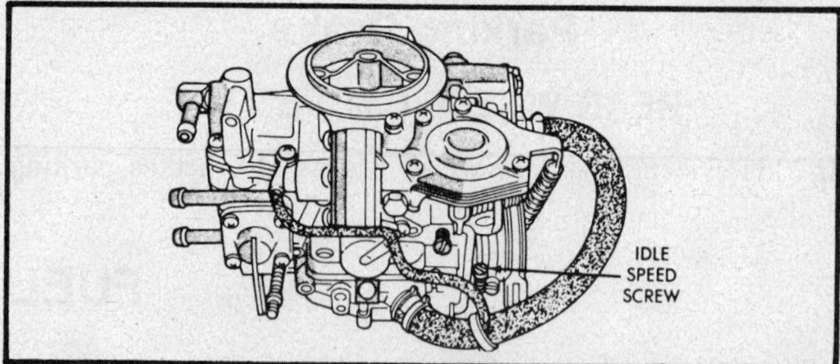

Idle speed adjusting—155.9 (2.6L) engines (© Chrysler Corp.)

6–CYLINDER AND V8 ENGINES

NOTE: Adjust with the air cleaner installed.

1. Run the engine at fast idle to stabilize engine temperature.
2. Make sure that the choke plate is fully released.
3. Attach a tachometer to the engine. With electronic ignition, connect the meter to the negative primary coil terminal and to a ground.

NOTE: Not all tachometers or dwell/tachometers will work with electronic ignition; some may be damaged. Check the manufacturer's instructions carefully.

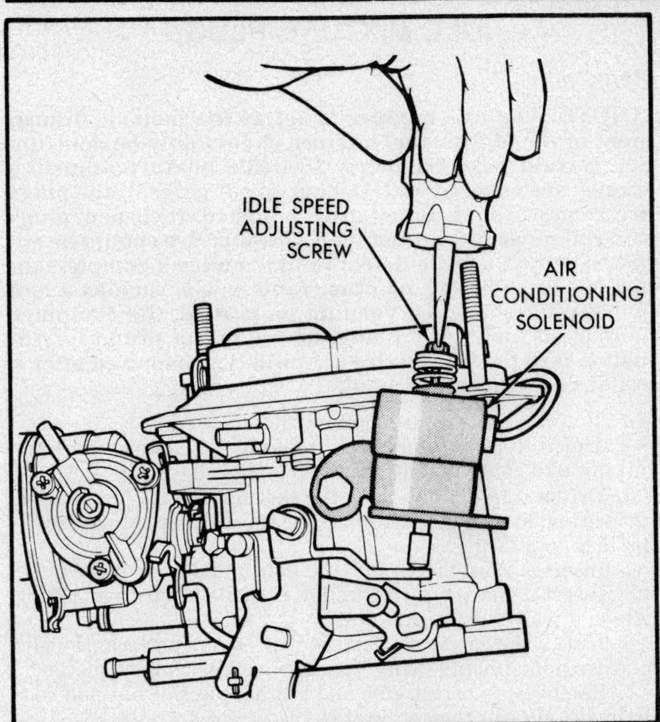

Rampage idle speed adjustment (© Chrysler Corp.)

4. Connect an exhaust analyzer to the engine and insert the probe as far into the tailpipe as possible. On vehicles with dual exhaust, insert the probe into the left tailpipe as this is the side without the heat riser valve.
5. Check ignition timing and adjust it as required.
6. If the truck has air conditioning, turn the air conditioner off. On six-cylinder engines, turn the headlights on high beam.
7. Place the manual transmission in neutral; put the automatic in Park. Make sure the hot idle compensator valve (if any) on the carburetor is fully seated in the closed position.
8. Turn the engine idle speed adjustment screw in or out to adjust idle speed to specification. If the carburetor has an electric solenoid, turn the solenoid adjusting screw in or out to obtain the specified rpm. Then, adjust the curb idle speed screw until it just touches the stop on the carburetor body. Now, back the curb idle speed adjusting screw out one full turn.
9. Turn each idle mixture adjustment screw, wait 30 seconds and observe the reading on the exhaust gas analyzer. Continue this procedure until the meter indicates a definite increase in the richness of the mixture.

NOTE: This step is very important. A carburetor that is set too lean will cause the exhaust gas analyzer to give a false reading indicating a rich mixture. Because of this, the carburetor must be known to have a rich mixture to verify the reading on the exhaust gas analyzer.

10. After verifying the reading obtained on the meter, adjust the mixture screws to get an air/fuel ratio of 14.2:1. Turn the mixture screws clockwise (leaner) to raise the meter reading or counterclockwise (richer) to lower the meter reading.

NOTE: Adjust to get the air/fuel ratio and percentage of CO indicated on the engine compartment sticker.

IDLE SPEED SOLENOID

Adjustment

This solenoid is energized whenever the ignition circuit is on. Its function is to allow the throttle plates to close farther when the ignition is switched off, thereby preventing engine overrunning.

1. Start the engine and allow it to reach normal operating temperature. Connect a tachometer according to the manufacturers instructions.
2. With the engine running, adjust the solenoid screw to the proper rpm.
3. Adjust the slow curb idle screw until the screw end just contacts the stop on the carburetor body. Back the screw off one full turn.
4. Test the above procedure by disconnecting the solenoid wire at the connector. Be sure not to let the lead short to the engine. The solenoid should de-energize and idle speed should drop down below normal. Now reconnect the wire. After you reconnect the solenoid, move the throttle linkage by hand since the solenoid isn't strong enough to move it.

ELECTRONIC THROTTLE CONTROL

CARTER ELECTRONIC THROTTLE CONTROL

1. Energize ETC solenoid (separate electrical connector and apply 12 volt current to BLUE wire connector).

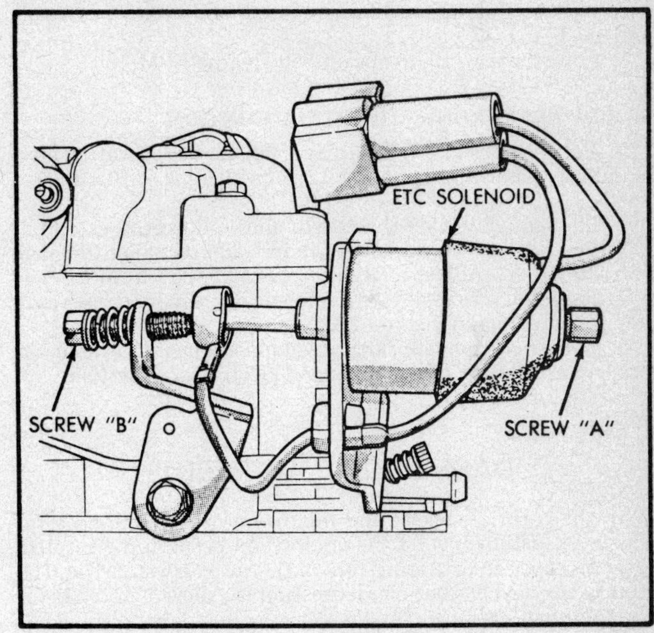

Location of adjusting screw "B" (© Chrysler Corp.)

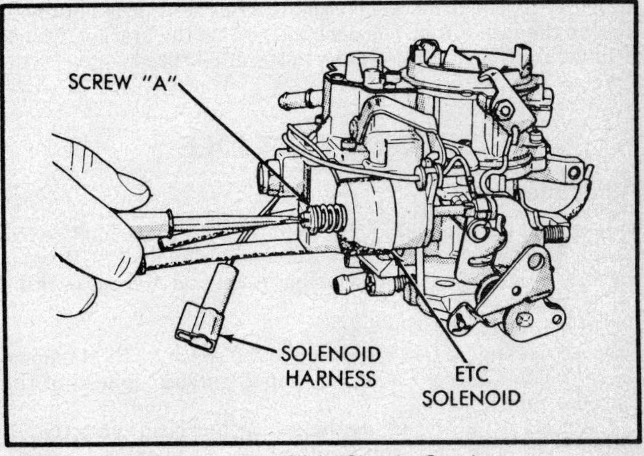

Location of adjusting screw "A" (© Chrysler Corp.)

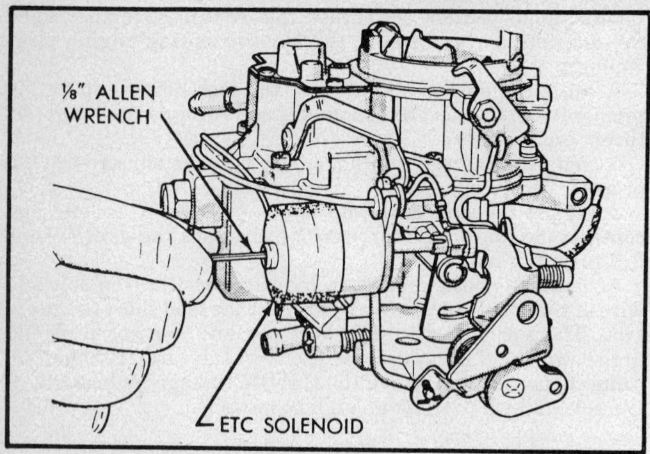

Adjusting engine idle speed after adjusting screw "A" is removed (© Chrysler Corp.)

2. Momentarily open throttle to allow plunger to extend from solenoid (plunger will extend and hold position but will not "push").
3. Adjust screw "B" to obtain 850 Engine RPM.

HOLLY ELECTRONIC THROTTLE CONTROL

1. Remove screw "A". Energize solenoid, by separating electrical connector and applying 12 volts current to BLUE wire spade.
2. Momentarily open throttle to allow plunger to extend.
3. Position ⅛ inch allen wrench into adjusting nut (through screw hole "A". Adjust engine idle speed to 850 RPM.
4. Reinstall screw "A", with solenoid de-energized reset curb idle speed using only screw "A".
5. Remove tachometer and any jumper wires. Check for the proper installation of all hoses and electrical connections.

DASHPOT ADJUSTMENT

With the curb idle speed and mixture properly set and a tachometer installed, start the engine and position the throttle lever so that the actuating tab on the lever is contacting the stem of the dashpot but not depressing it. Allow 30 seconds for the engine to stabilize. The tachometer should read 2300 RPM with throttle lever in this position.

To adjust setting, loosen the lock nut and screw the dashpot in or out as required. When the desired setting is obtained, tighten the lock nut on the dashpot against the bracket. Check to make sure curb idle returns to specified speed.

ENGINE FAST IDLE

Adjustment

1. Adjust engine fast idle to conform with Emission Control Label. Disconnect and plug both distributor and EGR valve vacuum hoses. Place transmission in neutral and set parking brake.
2. Remove air cleaner top.
3. Adjust engine fast idle speed to the specified RPM (shown on Emission Control Label) on Step 2 (second highest) of the fast idle cam.
4. Reconnect all hoses, as the engine has been correctly adjusted for proper Emission Control.

IDLE MIXTURE PLUGS

Removal

NOTE: The idle mixture is set at the factory. Adjustment of the idle air fuel mixture should only be done under certain circumstances. The idle mixture adjusting screws are covered with tamper-proof plugs. If the plugs are removed and the mixture adjusted, then new plugs and roll pins must be installed. The mixture should be adjusted only if an idle defect remains after a complete diagnosis reveals that no other fault exists, such as a bad spark plug wire or a vacuum leak. Also, the computer controlled fuel system must be operating properly. Adjustment to the idle mixture should be performed after a major carburetor overhaul.

1. Remove the carburetor from the engine.
2. Hold the carburetor in a suitable fixture for removing the roll pin and concealment plug.
3. Drill a small pilot hole in the casting into the base gasket surface and at a 45° angle toward the concealment plug. Redrill the hole to a larger size.
4. Insert a blunt punch into the hole and drive out the plug.
5. Insert a sharp punch through the idle mixture adjusting hole and slide out the roll pin.
6. Install the carburetor on the engine and perform the idle mixture adjustments using the propane enrichment method.
7. Remove the carburetor and install the roll pin and concealment plug in the carburetor.
8. Install the carburetor.

PROPANE ENRICHMENT

Adjustment

EXCEPT 2.2L 4 CYLINDER

1. Place the transmission in neutral position and set the parking brake. Turn all lights and accessories off. Connect a tachometer and a timing light to the engine. Start the engine and allow it to warm up on the second stop of the fast idle cam. Do this until normal operation temperature is reached, then return the engine to idle.
2. Disconnect and plug the EGR vacuum hose and the distributor vacuum hose. Check the engine timing and adjust if necessary, Disconnect the heated air door vacuum hose at the carburetor nipple and in it's place, install the propane supply hose. On 440 Cu. In. engines without the heated air system, insert the propane supply hose 12 in. into the air cleaner snorkel. Make sure that the propane bottle is in an upright and safe position. Remove the PCV valve from the cylinder head cover and disconnect the purge hose to the vapor canister at the carburetor end. Leave both open to underhood air.
3. Open the propane main flow valve. With the air cleaner in place, slowly open the propane metering valve until the maximum engine rpm is reached. When too much propane is added, the engine rpm will decrease. Fine tune the metering valve to obtain the highest engine rpm.
4. With the propane still flowing, adjust the idle speed screw to attain the propane rpm specified on the emissions label. If there has been a change in the maximum rpm, readjust the idle speed screw to the specified propane rpm.
5. Turn off the propane main valve and allow the engine speed to stabalize. With the air cleaner in place, slowly adjust the idle air mixture screws to achieve the smoothest idle at the specified idle set rpm. Pause between adjustments to allow the engine speed to stablize. If it appears necessary to remove the limiter caps to reach the idle set rpm, first check for engine malfunctions and vacuum leaks. If idle limiter caps are removed, service caps must be installed with the tang against the maximum rich stop.

6. Turn the propane main valve on. If the maximum speed is more than 25 rpm different than the specified propane rpm, repeat Steps 3 through 6.

7. Turn both the propane main valve and the metering valve off. Remove the tachometer. Remove the propane supply hose and reinstall the heated air door vacuum hose (except models without heated air). Unplug and reinstall the vacuum hose to the EGR valve and to the distributor.

8. Replace the PCV valve. Reconnect the canister purge hose to it's proper place. A variation in the engine RPM may occur, but do not readjust.

2.2L 4 CYLINDER

1. Remove the concealment plug. Set the parking brake. Make sure that the transaxle is in neutral. Turn off all accessories and lights.

2. Connect a tachometer to the engine. Start the engine and allow it to warm up while on the second step of the fast idle cam. When the engine reaches normal operating temperature, open the throttle and bring the engine down to normal idle speed.

3. Unplug the radiator fan connector (front wheel drive vehicles only) and jumper it so the fan runs continuously. Remove the PCV valve from the crankcase vent and allow it to draw underhood air. If the vehicle has an oxygen sensor, unplug the oxygen feedback system test connector located on the left fender shield.

4. Disconnect the vacuum harness from the CVSCC valve and plug both hoses. Disconnect the wiring from the kicker solenoid on the left fender shield.

5. Check to make sure the two propane valves are fully closed and that the bottle is upright and in a safe location. Disconnect the vacuum hose leading to the heated air sensor at the three way connector. Connect the propane hose from the propane bottle in place of this hose.

6. Open the main propane valve. Very gradually and slowly open the propane metering valve while watching the tachometer reading until maximum rpm is reached. The air cleaner must remain in place during this procedure.

CAUTION

Opening the propane metering valve rapidly will usually cause the carburetor setting to jump to a rich condition and slow the engine down.

7. Refering to the engine compartment sticker, adjust the idle speed screw (located on top of the carburetor solenoid) to get the rpm specified for propane enrichment. Increase the engine rpm to 2,500 for 15 seconds. Then, allow the engine to return to idle. Report the last part of Step 6 in order to optimize the rpm. If this raises rpm, repeat the idle speed adjustment.

8. Turn off the main propane valve and allow the engine rpm to stabilize. Adjust the idle mixture screw to get the specified idle set rpm.

9. Turn off both propane valves. Disconnect the propane tank and reconnect the vacuum hose. Replace the concealment plug. Reverse all remaining portions of Steps 1–4.

FUEL TANK

Removal

VANS AND WAGONS

1. Disconnect the battery ground cable.
2. Remove the fuel tank filler cap.
3. Raise the vehicle and support safely. Pump all fuel from the tank into an approved holding tank.
4. Disconnect the fuel line and wire lead to the gauge unit. Remove the ground strap.
5. Remove the vent hose shield and the hose clamps from the hoses running to the vapor vent tube.
6. Remove the filler tube hose clamps and disconnect the hose from the tank.
7. Place a transmission jack under the center of the tank and apply sufficient pressure to support the tank.
8. Disconnect the two J-bolts and remove the retaining straps at the rear of the tank. Lower the tank from the vehicle. Feed the two vent tube hoses and filler tube vent hose through the grommets in the frame as the tank is being lowered. Remove the tank gauge unit.

Installation

1. Inspect the fuel filter, and if it is clogged or damaged, replace it.
2. Insert a new gasket in the recess of the fuel gauge opening and slide the gauge into the tank. Align the positioning tangs on the gauge with those on the tank. Install the lock ring, and tighten securely.
3. Position the tank on a transmission jack and hoist it into place, feeding the vent hoses through the grommets on the way up.
4. Connect the J-bolts and retaining straps, and tighten to 40 inch lbs. Remove the jack.
5. Connect the filler tube and all vent hoses.
6. Connect the fuel supply line, ground strap, and gauge unit wire lead.
7. Refill the tank and inspect it for leaks. Connect the battery ground cable.

Removal

PICKUPS RAMCHARGER AND TRAIL DUSTER

1. If there is a tank skid plate, remove it.
2. Disconnect the battery ground cable.
3. Remove the tank filler cap.
4. Pump or siphon the contents of the tank into a safe container. Siphoning should not be started by mouth. Only fuel-safe pumps should be used.
5. Raise the vehicle on a hoist and disconnect the fuel line and tank sending unit wire. Remove the ground strap or wire.
6. Remove the hose clamps from the vent dome hose.
7. Remove the filler tube hose clamps. Detach the hoses from the tank.
8. Support the tank with a padded transmission jack.
9. Disconnect the two J-bolts and remove the straps at the rear of the tank.
10. Remove the tank gauge sending unit.

Installation

1. Use a new tank gauge sending unit gasket. Check the filter on the end of the fuel suction tube.
2. Use a new or undamaged tank to frame insulator. Raise the tank into position.
3. Connect the J-bolts and retaining straps. Tighten the bolts until about 0.97 in. of threads protrude.
4. Connect the filler tube and all hoses. Tighten the clamps.
5. Connect the fuel line, ground strap or wire, and tank sending unit wire. Make sure that all fuel line heat shields are in place.
6. Reconnect the battery ground cable and replace the skid plate.

Removal

RAMPAGE AND SCAMP

1. Disconnect the battery ground cable.
2. Remove the fuel tank filler cap before disconnecting any lines. The tank could be under a small pressure.
3. Disconnect fuel supply hose at right front shock tower and siphon the gasoline from the tank into a safely marked container.

4. Remove the screws that hold the filler tube to the inner and outer quarter panel.

5. Remove the right rear tire and wheel and disconnect the wiring and lines from the tank.

6. Remove the exhaust pipe to fuel tank shield and allow it to rest on the exhuast pipe.

7. Use a padded transmission jack to support the fuel tank while removing the fuel tank straps.

8. Lower the tank slightly and carefully work the filler tube from the tank.

9. Lower the fuel tank, disconnect the vapor separator valve hose and remove the fuel tank and insulator pad from the vehicle.

Installation

1. Position the fuel tank on a padded transmission jacks. Connect the vapor separator rollover valve hose and set the insulator pad on the fuel tank.

CAUTION

Do not pinch the vapor vent hose between the tank and the floor pan.

2. Raise the tank into position and install the filler tube into the tank.

3. Install the exhaust pipe to fuel tank shield.

4. Install the fuel tank straps and torque the nuts to 250 inch lbs. (23.2 Nm). Do not twist or bend the straps during installation or tightening.

5. Connect all fuel lines and wiring. Install the right rear tire and wheel.

6. Install the filler tube mounting screws and torque them to 17 inch lbs. (1.9 Nm).

7. Fill the fuel tank, replace cap, connect the battery ground cable and check system operation.

COOLING SYSTEM

Water Pump

Removal and Installation

6 CYLINDER AND V8 ENGINES

1. Drain the cooling system and remove the fan belt and fan shroud. Remove the radiator if necessary.

2. Unscrew fan blade bolts and remove fan blade, spacers and bolts as an assembly.

Silicone drive fans must be kept in their normal attitude. If the shaft points down, silicone fluid will contaminate the fan drive bearing.

3. Position the six-cylinder lower clamp in the center of the by-pass hose. Disconnect or remove heater and radiator hoses.

4. Remove water pump retaining bolts and remove water pump assembly.

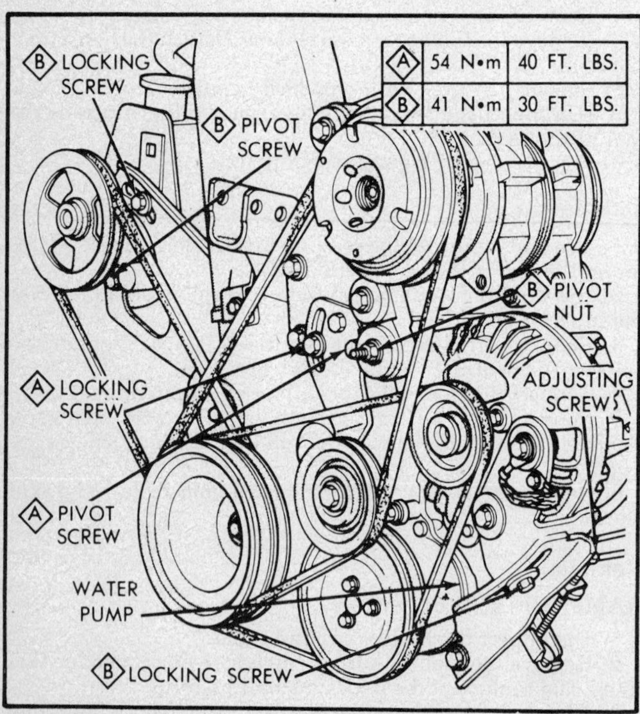

Accessory drive belt arrangement on the 2.2L engine (© Chrysler Corp.)

NOTE: On air conditioned equipped vehicles with V8 engines, the compressor clutch assembly and the front mounting brackets may have to be removed to allow for the removal of the water pump assembly.

5. Install a new by-pass hose if necessary, with clamps positioned in the center of the hose.

6. Use a new gasket and install water pump. Install and tighten pump retaining bolts to 30 ft. lbs. Position by-pass hose clamps. Install the heater and radiator hoses.

7. Install fan blade, spacer and bolt assembly. Start all bolts, then tighten to 15–18 ft. lbs.

8. Install fan belt and adjust belt tension. Fill cooling system. Start the engine and check for leaks.

Removal

RAMPAGE & SCAMP 4 CYLINDER (1.7L) ENGINE

1. Drain cooling system.

2. Move compressor from engine brackets and set aside. Do not discharge.

3. Remove the alternator completely.

4. Remove water pump pulley.

5. If so equipped, disconnect diverter valve hose at diverter valve, remove rear air pump bracket and the front air pump bracket.

6. Remove alternator bracket attached to the water pump.

7. Remove water pump by disconnecting lower radiator hose, bypass hose and unbolting timing belt cover bolt and two top water pump bolts.

Installation

1. Install the water pump, attaching the top two screws loosely.

2. Install the air pump rear and front brackets and the alternator bracket.

NOTE: Follow the sequence for tightening of air pump brackets or early failure may occur.

3. Tighten the two upper water pump attaching bolts to 250 inch lbs. (30 Nm). Next, tighten the two front air pump brackets to the water pump bolts, the upper one to 250 inch lbs. (30 Nm), the lower one to 50 ft. lbs. (68 Nm). Next, install the air pump and tighten the two bolts to 24 ft. lbs. (35 Nm). Next, tighten the two rear air pump brackets and lower water pump to engine bolts to 250 inch lbs. (30 Nm).

4. Install air pump plumbing, bypass hose, and lower radiator hose.

5. Install water pump pulley.
6. Install alternator and refill the cooling system.

Removal

4 CYLINDER (2.2L) ENGINES

1. Drain cooling system.
2. Remove upper radiator hose.
3. Remove air conditioning compressor from engine brackets and set aside. Do not discharge the system.
4. Remove alternator and lay aside.
5. Remove water pump by disconnecting lower radiator hose, bypass hose and four water pump to engine attaching bolts.

Installation

1. Install water pump on engine. Tighten top water pump bolts to 250 inch lbs. (30 Nm) and the lower bolt to 50 ft. lbs. (68 Nm).
2. Install the bypass hose and lower radiator hose.
3. Install alternator and air conditioning compressor.
4. Install upper radiator hose.
5. Refill the cooling system.

Removal

4 CYLINDER (2.6L) ENGINES

1. Drain cooling system.
2. Remove the radiator hose, bypass hose and heater hose from the water pump.
3. Remove the drive pulley shield.
4. Remove the locking screw and pivot screws.
5. Remove the drive belt and lift off the water pump.

Installation

1. Installation is the reverse of removal. Tighten mounting bolts to 80 inch lbs. Tighten locking screw and pivot screws to 204 inch lbs. Tighten drive pulley shield to 105 inch lbs.

Heater Core

Removal and Installation

VANS AND WAGONS WITHOUT AIR CONDITIONING

1. Disconnect the battery ground cable.
2. Drain the radiator.
3. Cover the alternator with a waterproof cover.
4. Disconnect the blower motor resistor and ground wires from the heater.
5. Disconnect and plug the heater core hoses.
6. Disconnect the control cables.
7. Remove the retaining screws from the water valve. Do not disconnect the hoses from the water valve; place the water valve with hoses attached to one side.
8. Remove the blower motor cooler tube.
9. Remove the nuts holding the housing to the mounting studs and tip the complete unit out through the hood opening.

To remove the heater core:

10. Remove the 3 retaining nuts and lift the blower assembly out of the housing.
11. Remove the 4 cover retaining nuts and lift the cover off the housing.
12. Remove the 4 core retaining screws and lift the core out of the housing.
13. Installation is the reverse of removal. Fill the cooling system.
14. Let the engine warm up with the heater on, then check the coolant level.

VANS AND WAGONS WITH FACTORY AIR CONDITIONING

The air conditioning system must be discharged to remove the heater core.

1. Disconnect the battery ground cable and drain the coolant.
2. Remove the grille, condenser, and radiator.
3. Place a waterproof cover over the alternator.
4. Disconnect the heater hoses at the water valve and remove the valve and bracket. Disconnect and cap the refrigerant lines.
5. Remove the glovebox, spot cooler bezel, and appearance shield.
6. Working through the glovebox opening, remove the evaporator housing to firewall screws and nuts.
7. Remove the wiper motor. Detach all evaporator housing vacuum and electrical connections. Detach the blower motor cooling hose and the drain hoses.
8. Remove the two 2 $^1/_4$ in. bolts from the crossbar and the four screws from the seal plate on the front of the housing. Separate the evaporator and blower motor housings, remove the evaporator housing.
9. Remove the receiver drier and cap all the openings. Carefully pry the heater core out, leaving the air seal at the front intact.
10. On installation, connect the hoses to the core. Position the evaporator housing on top of the blower housing. Install the mounting screws and nuts.
11. Position the crossbar under the lip on the blower housing opening and install the two 2$^1/_4$ in. bolts. Install the four seal plate screws at the front of the housing.
12. Replace the wiper motor and connect the vacuum and electrical lines. Connect the blower motor cooler hose and the drain hoses.
13. Connect the heater hoses to the water valve.
14. Install the receiver drier and connect the refrigerant lines.
15. Install the radiator, condenser, and grille.
16. Replace the glovebox, spot cooler bezel, and appearance shield.
17. Install the battery ground cable and fill the cooling system. Let the engine warm up with the heater on, then check the coolant. Charge the air conditioner.

RAMPAGE AND SCAMP WITHOUT AIR CONDITIONING

1. Disconnect battery and drain radiator.
2. Disconnect blower motor wiring connector.
3. Remove ash tray receiver receptacle.
4. Depress tab on temperature control cable flag and pull temperature control cable out of receiver on heater assembly.
5. Remove glovebox and door assembly.
6. Disconnect heater hoses and seal heater core tube openings.
7. Remove the two nuts fastening heater assembly to dash panel.
8. Remove wire connector from blower motor resistor block.
9. Remove screw attaching heater support brace to instrument panel.
10. Remove heater support bracket nut. Disconnect strap from plenum stud and lower the heater assembly from under the instrument panel.
11. Depress tab on flag and pull mode door control cable out of receiver on heater assembly.
12. Move the heater unit towards right side of vehicle and then out from under instrument panel.
13. Set the assembly on a work bench and remove the left heater outlet duct.
14. Remove the blower motor assembly and the outside air and defroster door cover.

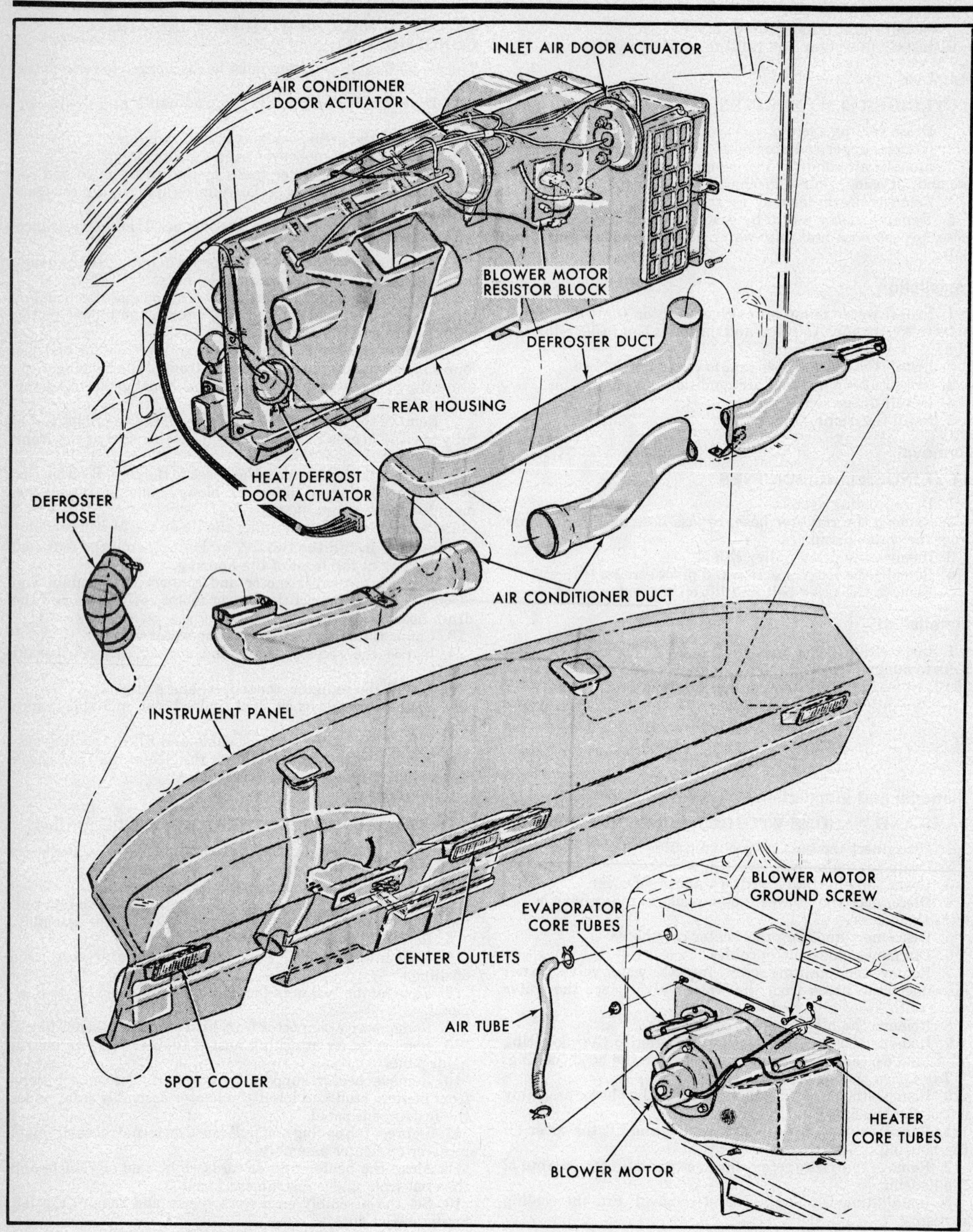

Typical heater and evaporator assembly (© Chrysler Corp.)

15. Remove the center defroster door, screw, and screw retaining plate.
16. Lift the defroster door control rod out of the assembly and remove the heater core cover screws.
17. Remove the heater core cover and lift the heater core out of the assembly.
18. Installation is the reverse of removal. Refill the radiator and test the systems operation.

RAMPAGE AND SCAMP WITH AIR CONDITIONING

1. Discharge the air conditioning system and drain the engine coolant. Disconnect the battery fusible link.
2. Disconnect heater hoses at heater core. Plug heater core tube openings to prevent coolant from spilling out when assembly is removed.
3. Disconnect vacuum lines at engine intake manifold and at water valve.
4. Remove the "H" type expansion valve.
5. Remove the clamp and condensation drain tube.
6. Remove evaporator heater assembly to dash retaining nuts and depress the tab on the control cable flag and pull the flag out of the receiver on the heater assembly.
7. Remove the glovebox and disconnect the vacuum harness from the heater A/C control. Disconnect the blower and anti-diesel relay wires.
8. Remove the passenger side instrument panel trim bezel.
9. Remove the center air distribution duct from the instrument panel. Remove the defroster duct adapter and the panel support bracket.
10. Remove the drivers side cowl lower panel and remove the drivers side instrument panel pivot bracket screw.
11. Remove the lower instrument panel screws at the steering column.
12. Pull back the carpet from under the heater assembly. Remove the nut from the heater assembly to plenum mounting brace and blower motor ground wire.
13. Lift the heater assembly and remove the brace from its stud.
14. While lifting the heater assembly, pull it away from the cowl. At the same time pull the lower instrument panel out enough for the heater assembly to be removed. This operation may take two people.
15. Place the heater assembly on a work bench and remove the mode door actuator from the cover.
16. Remove the attaching screws and lift the heater assembly cover and mode door from the assembly.
17. Remove the heater core bracket retaining screw, bracket and heater core from the assembly.
18. Installation is the reverse of removal. Evacuate and recharge the air conditioning and refill the cooling system. Check the operation of the heating and air conditioning systems. Check the system for proper operation and system leaks. Repair as necessary.

ENGINE

Engine overhaul procedures can be found in the "Engine Rebuilding" section of this manual.

Emission Controls

Two basic approaches to emission control have been used on Dodge/Plymouth engines. The first is engine design modifications, which apply to some extent to all engines. The second is a group of specific emission control systems, the application of which varies with model and power train. Those models rated under a specific GVW are subject to stricter light-duty emission regulations, and therefore use more of these systems.

ENGINE DESIGN MODIFICATIONS

Engine design modifications have been made from model year

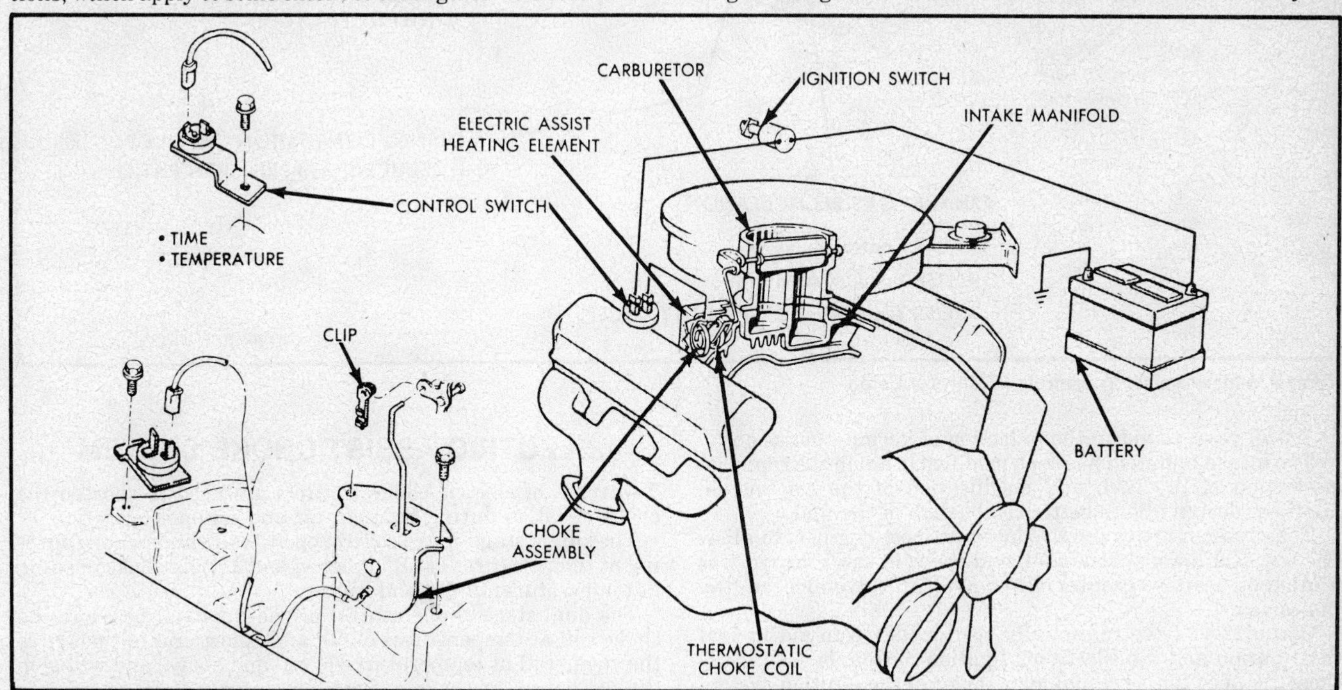

Electric assist choke system (© Chrysler Corp.)

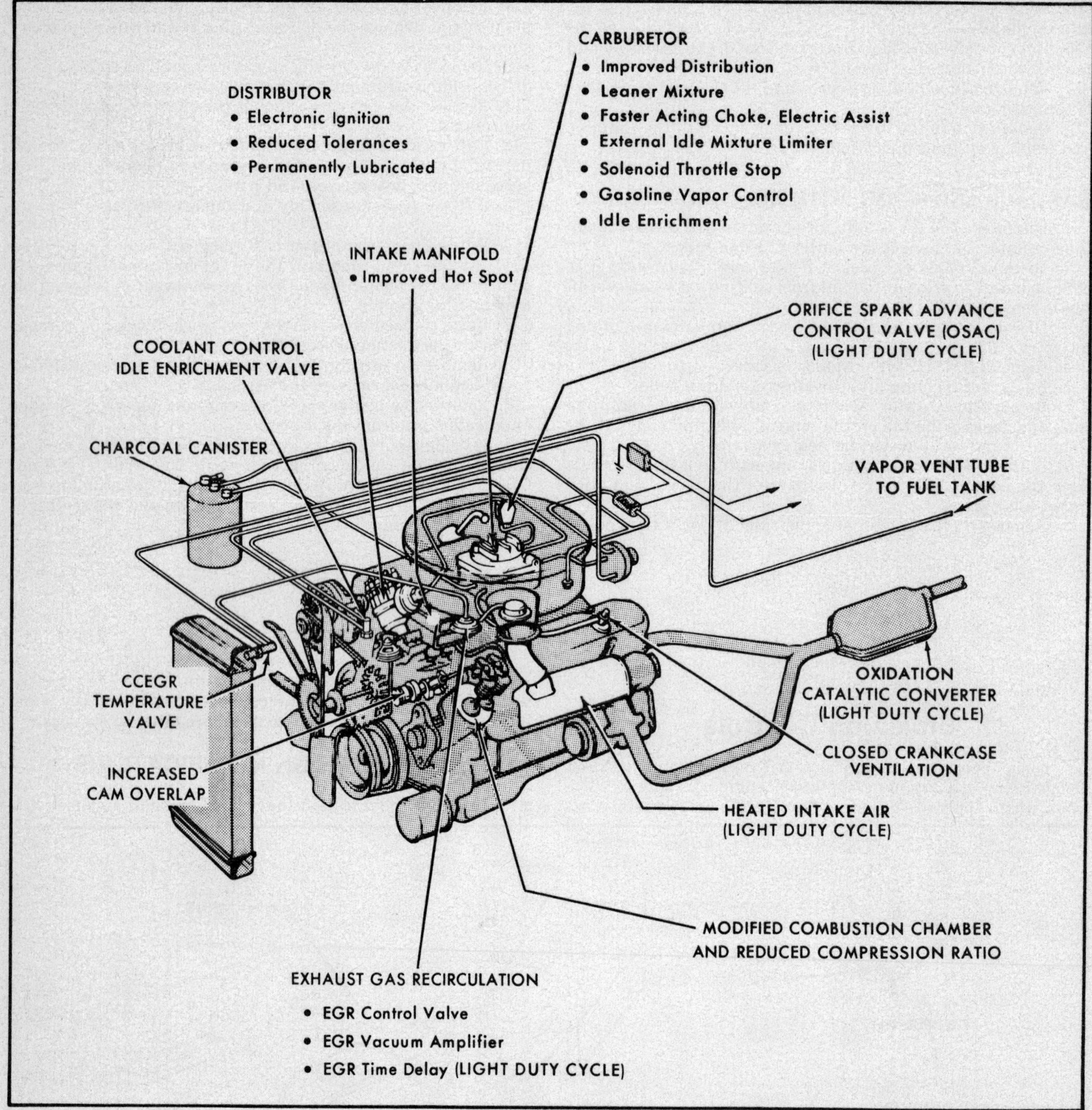

Typical vehicle emission controls (© Chrysler Corp.)

to model year, to aid in the reduction of harmful emissions.

The intake manifold has been modified to aid in the rapid vaporization of the fuel, and modification of the combustion chamber design allows better combustion of the fuel.

Compression ratios were reduced on most engines, to allow the use of a lower octane fuel, and the cam shaft design was changed to allow greater valve overlap to reduce engine emissions.

Carburetors have continually been modified to aid in fuel distribution and the Electronic Ignition System is used to reduce the need for continual adjustment of the ignition system and also provides for better and more precise spark.

ELECTRIC ASSIST CHOKE SYSTEM

Two types of electric choke controls are used to shorten the choke duration during both winter and summer operation.

The single stage choke control operates a slower choke opening at temperatures of 58° or below and a rapid choke opening at temperatures of 68° and higher.

The dual stage choke control provides partial power to the choke coil at temperatures of 58° and below, and full power to the choke coil at temperatures of 68° and above, and will stop the current to the choke coil at temperatures of approximately 130° and higher.

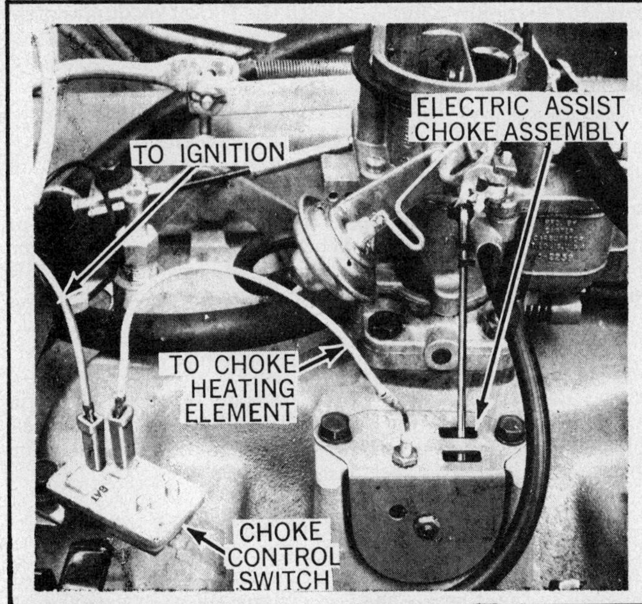

Typical electric choke system (© Chrysler Corp.)

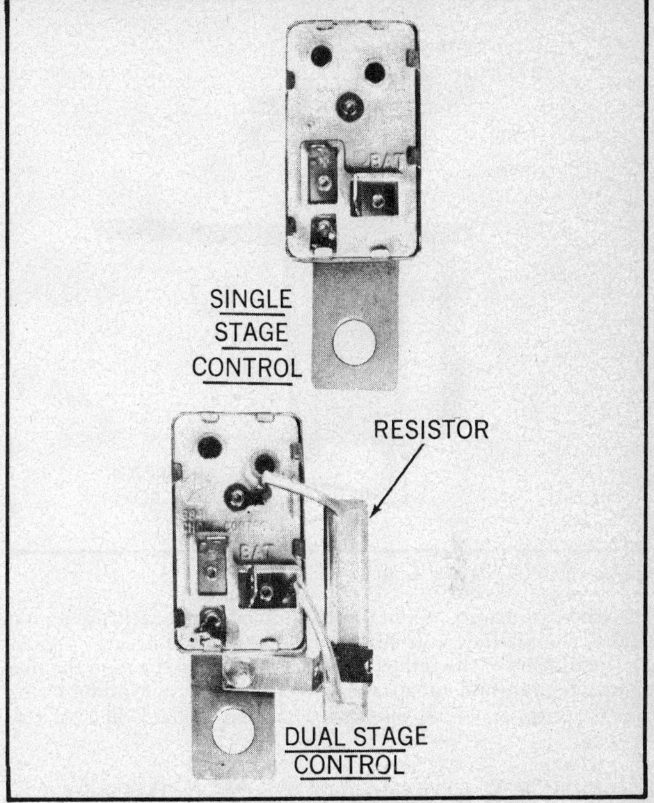

Two types of electric choke controls (© Chrysler Corp.)

Engines started in the winter will experience three levels of current to the choke coil from the dual choke control. Low during the engine warmup, high after the engine warmup, and none after the engine reaches normal operating temperatures. Engines started in summer weather will not have the low system in operation, nor will an engine that is restarted when hot, have a high system in operation.

NOTE: All temperature readings are in Fahrenheit.

Single Stage Control Switch Test

1. Remove the BAT connector from the control unit.
2. Connect a test lamp to the small terminal of the control to ground.
3. Start the engine and warm it up to normal operating temperature.
4. Reconnect the BAT terminal wire to its post on the control and observe the test lamp.
5. The test lamp should light. It may remain on for a few seconds or for a longer duration, but must not remain on for over five minutes. If so, replace the control switch.

Dual Stage Control Switch Test

1. The test procedure is the same for the dual stage control switch as for the single stage switch, except the brightness or intensity of the test lamp should match that of battery current during the test. If the intensity is less, or the light remains on for over five minutes, the control switch is defective and should be replaced.

Choke Heating Element Test

1. Disconnect the electric heating element wire at the control switch.
2. Connect an ohmmeter lead to the crimped junction of the element wire at the choke end, avoiding connection with the heater casing. Ground the other lead of the ohmmeter.
3. Resistance of twelve ohms is acceptable. Replace the unit if resistance is outside this range.
4. Make sure choke linkage moves freely when hot and when cold.

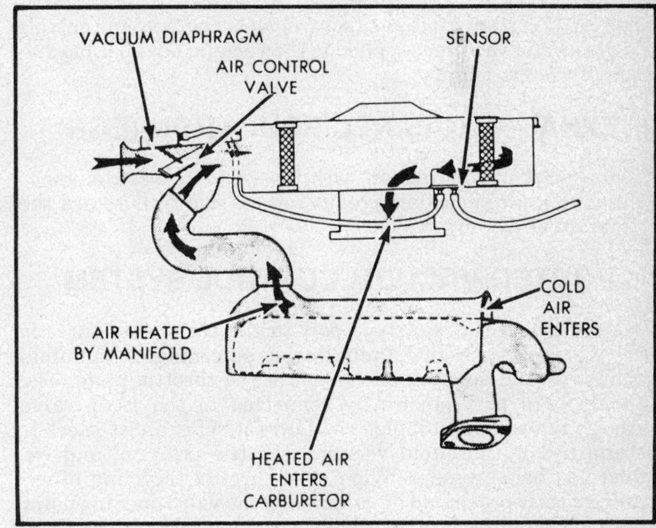

Heated air inlet system (© Chrysler Corp.)

HEATED AIR INTAKE SYSTEM

The carburetor air preheater is a device which is part of the air cleaner and which keeps the air entering the carburetor at about 100°F when underhood temperatures are less than 100°F. By using this device, the carburetor can be calibrated much leaner to improve engine warm-up characteristics.

The heated air intake system is basically a two circuit airflow system. When underhood temperatures are less than 100°F, the air will flow into the stove, through a flexible connector, into the adapter on the bottom of the snorkel, and then

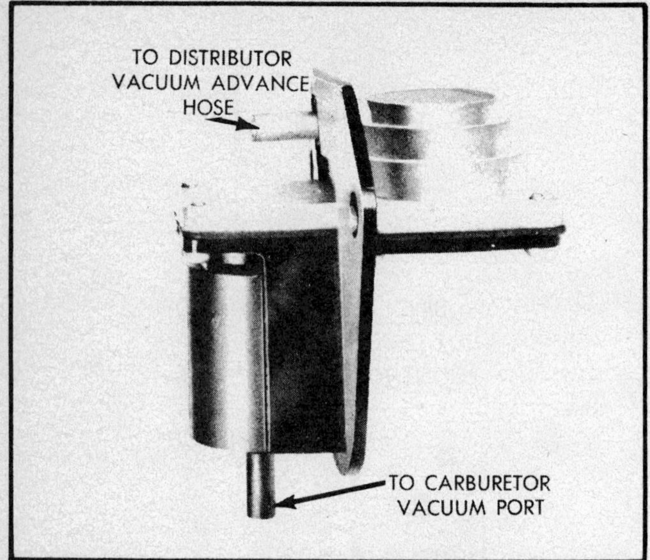

OSAC valve (© Chrysler Corp.)

into the carburetor. When the underhood temperature is above 100°F, the air-flow will be through the snorkel.

Modulation of the induction air is performed through the use of intake manifold vacuum, a temperature sensor, and a vacuum diaphragm which operates the heat control door in the snorkel.

ORIFICE SPARK ADVANCE CONTROL (OSAC)

The OSAC system is used to control NO. The system controls the amount of vacuum supplied to the vacuum advance mechanism of the distributor.

EXHAUST GAS RECIRCULATION (EGR)

EGR is used in conjunction with the vacuum spark advance control to limit peak flame temperatures and thus retard the formation of nitrous oxides.

PORTED VACUUM CONTROL SYSTEM

This system uses a slot type port in the carburetor throttle body which is exposed to an increasing percentage of manifold vacuum by the opening movement of the throttle plate. The throttle bore port is directly connected to the EGR valve through an external nipple. The flow rate of exhaust gases is determined by manifold vacuum, throttle position, and exhaust gas backpressure. Wide open throttle recycling of exhaust gases is prevented by calibrating the valve opening point above manifold vacuum available at wide open throttle, since port vacuum cannot exceed manifold vacuum.

VENTURI VACUUM CONTROL SYSTEM

This system uses a vacuum tap at the throat of the carburetor venturi to provide a control signal. Because the signal is so low however, a vacuum amplifier is used to increase the strength of the signal. The amplifier uses stored manifold vacuum to provide the source for amplification. Elimination of EGR at wide open throttle is accomplished by a "dump" diaphragm which compares venturi and manifold vacuum to determine when wide open throttle is achieved. At wide open throttle, the internal reservoir is "dumped", limiting the output of the EGR valve to manifold vacuum. As with the ported vacuum control system, the valve opening point is set above the manifold vacuum available at wide open throttle, permitting the valve to be closed at wide open throttle.

COOLANT CONTROL EXHAUST GAS RECIRCULATION VALUE

Trucks with EGR are equipped with a CCEGR valve located in the top of the radiator tank. When coolant in the top radiator tank reaches 65°F, the valve opens to apply vacuum to the EGR valve to recirculate exhaust gases.

EGR DELAY SYSTEM

Some trucks are equipped with an EGR delay system, which is an electrical timer on the dash to control an engine mounted solenoid. The timer prevents exhaust gas recirculation for about 35 seconds after the ignition is turned on.

AIR INJECTION SYSTEM

This system adds a controlled amount of air through special passages in the cylinder head, to exhaust gases in the exhaust ports, causing oxidation of the gases and thereby reducing carbon monoxide and hydro-carbon emissions to the required levels.

The air injection system consists of a belt-driven air pump, rubber hose, a check valve to protect the hoses and pump from hot gases, injection tubes, and a combination diverter/pressure relief valve assembly.

EVAPORATIVE CONTROL SYSTEM

The function of the evaporative control system is to prevent the emission of raw gasoline vapors from the fuel tank and carburetor into the atmosphere. When fuel evaporates in the tank or float bowl, the vapors pass through lines and into the charcoal canister where they are temporarily stored until they can be drawn into the intake manifold and burned. A vacuum port located in the base of the carburetor governs vapor flow from the canister to the engine.

CLOSED CRANKCASE VENTILATION SYSTEM

The closed PCV system operates as follows:

In place of a vented oil filler cap, an air intake line is installed between the carburetor air filter and a crankcase opening in the valve cover.

A sealed oil filler cap and dipstick are used.

A separate PCV air filter is used. The filter is located where the intake air line connects to the valve cover.

Under normal engine operation, air enters through the intake line from the air filter. Under heavy acceleration, any excess vapors back up through the air intake line and are forced to mix with incoming air into the carburetor and are burned in the combustion chamber. Back-up fumes cannot escape into the atmosphere, creating a closed system.

The PCV valve is used to control the rate at which crankcase vapors are returned to the intake manifold. The action of the valve plunger is controlled by intake manifold vacuum and the spring. During deceleration and idle, when manifold vacuum is high, it overcomes the tension of the valve spring and the plunger bottoms in the manifold end of the valve housing. Because of the valve construction, it reduces the passage of vapors to the intake manifold. When the engine is lightly accelerated or operated at constant speed, spring tension matches intake

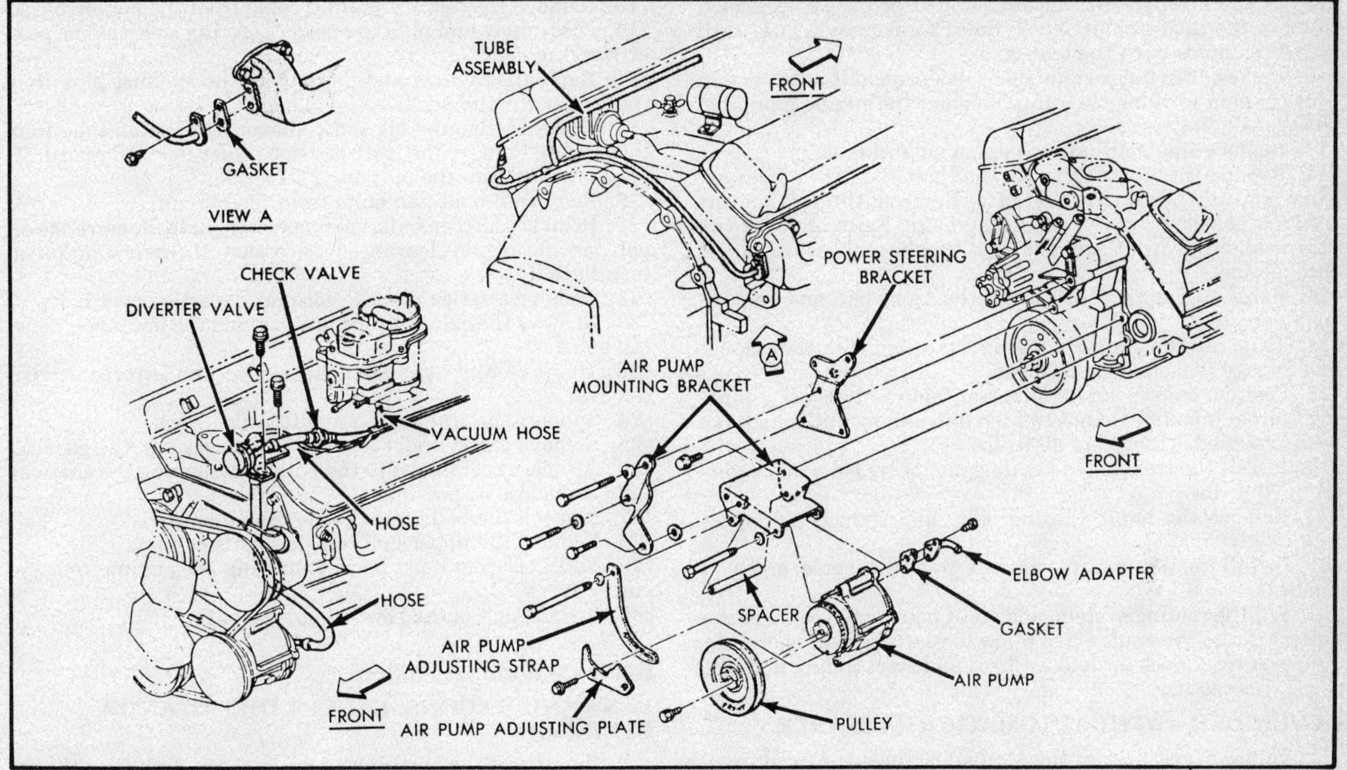

Air injection system—360 engine shown (© Chrysler Corp.)

manifold vacuum pull and the plunger takes a mid-position in the valve body, allowing more vapors to flow into the manifold.

CATALYTIC CONVERTER

Most 1980 and later models rated under a specific GVW, are equipped with catalytic converters. These devices are used to oxidize excess carbon monoxide (CO) and hydrocarbons (HC) in the exhaust system before they can escape out the tailpipe and into the atmosphere. The converter is installed in front of the mufflers, under the vehicle, and protected by a heat shield.

The expected catalyst life is 50,000 miles, provided that the engine is kept in tune and unleaded fuel is used.

To keep the catalyst from being overheated by an overly rich mixture during deceleration, a catalyst protection system (CPS) is sometimes used. The system consists of a throttle positioner solenoid (not to be confused with the idle stop solenoid), a control box, and an engine rpm sensor.

Any time that the engine speed is more than 2,000 rpm, the solenoid is energized and keeps the throttle from fully closing, thus preventing the deceleration mixture from becoming too rich.

Engine Assembly

Removal and Installation

4 CYLINDER – WITH MANUAL TRANSAXLE

1. Scribe the hood hinge outlines on the hood and remove the hood.
2. Drain the cooling system. Disconnect the battery cables and remove the battery.
3. Remove all water hoses from the radiator and engine. Remove the radiator and cooling fan assembly.
4. Remove the air cleaner, duct and hose assembly. Label vacuum hoses for reinstallation identification.

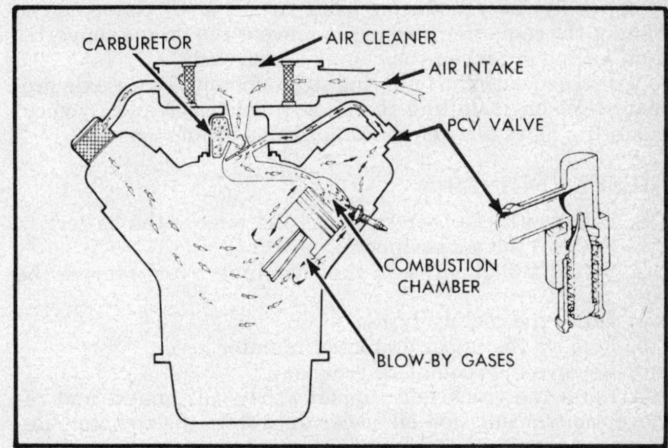

Closed crankcase ventilation system (© Chrysler Corp.)

5. Remove the A/C compressor and mounting brackets. Leave the hoses attached and position the compressor out of the way.
6. Remove the power steering pump and brackets. Leave the hoses attached and position the pump out of the way.
7. Position a suitable container under the oil filter to catch any spilled oil and remove the oil filter.
8. Tag and disconnect all electrical connectors that will interfere with engine removal. Disconnect the fuel lines, accelerator linkage, heater hoses and air pump hoses.
9. Remove the alternator. Disconnect the clutch cable from the throwout bearing arm.
10. Remove the lower transaxle case lower cover. Disconnect the exhaust pipe from the exhaust manifold.
11. Remove the starter motor. Install a suitable jack under the transaxle assembly.

12. Install an engine lifting sling and attach to a chain hoist. Remove the lifting chain slack. Raise transmission jack until contact is made with the transaxle.
13. Remove the inner right side splash shield if necessary in order to gain working clearance. Remove the engine ground to chassis bonding strap.
14. Remove the transaxle to engine mounting bolts.
15. Remove the "through" nut(s) and bolt(s) from the front engine mount and anti-roll struts. Remove the left mount through bolt or insulator mounting bolts. Raise or lower the engine slightly with the chain hoist to relieve pressure on the through bolts.
16. Raise engine, separate from the transaxle and remove from vehicle.
17. To install the engine; lower into position with chain hoist and engage transaxle main drive.
18. Position engine against the transaxle and install mounting "through bolts". Do not tighten until all mount bolts have been installed. Tighten to 40 ft. lbs.
19. Install the transaxle to engine mounting bolts and tighten to 70 ft. lbs.
20. Remove the engine lifting sling and transaxle support jack.
21. Install remaining components in the reverse order of removal.
22. Fill the cooling system, add oil (if necessary), connect the battery. Start the engine and allow to reach normal operating temperature. Check for leaks. Check and reset timing and idle speed if necessary.

4 CYLINDER – WITH AUTOMATIC TRANSAXLE

1. Follow Steps 1–10 of the Manual Transaxle procedure.
2. Remove the lower transaxle case lower cover, mark converter and flywheel for installation reference. Remove the converter to flywheel mounting bolts. Attach a "C" clamp on the front of the converter housing to prevent the torque converter from falling out when the engine is removed.
3. Proceed with the following steps of manual transaxle procedure. When installing the engine, converter and flywheel mounting holes and reference marks must line up.

DIESEL ENGINES

1. Disconnect the battery cables and remove the battery.
2. Remove the air cleaner.
3. Scribe matchmarks on the hood hinges and remove the hood.
4. Drain the cooling system.
5. Remove the upper and lower radiator hoses.
6. Remove the coolant reserve tank.
7. Raise the truck and support safely. Disconnect and remove the transmission oil cooler lines from the radiator. Remove the lower radiator and fan shroud mounting screws.
8. Lower the truck and remove the upper radiator and fan shroud mounting screws and remove the radiator and the fan shroud.
9. Disconnect the heater hoses from the engine and position them out of the working area.
10. Disconnect the speedometer cable housing from the engine.
11. Tag and disconnect the electrical connections at the alternator, temperature sending unit, starter relay-to-solenoid wires, the oil gauge sending unit and the injection pump control motor. Set the wiring harness aside.
12. Disconnect and plug the fuel line at the transfer pump inlet. Disconnect and cap return line at the injector lines bleedback connection.
13. Disconnect and remove the injection pump linkage. Disconnect and remove the accelerator and throttle cable linkage.
14. Disconnect the starter motor wire from the solenoid. Remove the starter motor.
15. Remove the battery ground cable from the engine block.
16. Disconnect and plug the power steering hoses at the power steering gear.
17. Raise the vehicle and disconnect the exhaust pipe from the exhaust manifold.
18. Drain the engine oil and remove the dipstick tube from the oil pan. Remove the transmission cooler line and road draft tube bracket from the oil pan.
19. Remove the oil pan bolts from the oil pan.
20. Remove the transmission inspection plate. Remove the oil pan on vans to gain clearance if necessary. Use a new gasket on installation.
21. Remove the flex plate-to-torque converter cover bolts.
22. Remove the exhaust pipe bracket and the lower bell housing bolts.
23. Remove any other brackets that can interfere with removal.
24. Support the transmission with a floor jack.
25. Remove the cylinder head (valve) cover and the gasket.
26. Attach a boom hoist to the engine, wrapping the chain as tight and close as possible.
27. Remove the bolts from the engine mounts.
28. Remove the upper bell housing bolts.
29. Roll the boom hoist back, removing the engine from the van or truck.
30. Installation is the reverse of removal.

Removal and Installation

VANS AND WAGONS, EXCEPT DIESEL AND 4 CYLINDER

1. Disconnect the battery and drain the coolant from the radiator and engine block. Drain the engine oil. On V8s, remove the oil filter.
2. Remove the engine cover, air cleaner, and starter.
3. Remove the front bumper, grille, and support brace. Disconnect both radiator hoses and remove the radiator and support brace as a unit.
4. Remove the power steering and air pumps with the hoses attached and lay them aside.
5. Tag and disconnect the throttle linkage, heater and vacuum hoses and all electrical connections to the ignition, alternator, and all other electrical connections.
6. Remove the alternator, fan, pulley, and drive belts.
7. Remove the heater blower motor.
8. Remove and plug the inlet line to the fuel pump.
9. Remove the oil dipstick tube. On V8s, remove the intake manifold and left exhaust manifold. If equipped with air conditioning, remove the right side valve cover.
10. To provide clearance for engine removal, the oil pan and transmission must be removed.
11. Raise the engine slightly in preparation for transmission removal. Support it with an engine lifting fixture.
12. Raise the vehicle and support safely. Remove the starter and distributor.
13. Remove the driveshaft and engine rear support. Remove the rear support by removing the rear mount through-bolt and the U-shaped bracket from the crossmember. Remove the insulator from the bottom face of the transmission housing.
14. If equipped with an automatic transmission, remove the transmission intact with the filler tube and the torque converter separated from the drive plate.
15. Raise the rear of the engine approximately 2 in. and remove the clutch or drive plate and the flywheel. On V8s, position the cut-out in the crankshaft flange at 3 o'clock. Remove the oil pan screws and lower the oil pan far enough to reach inside and turn the oil pump pick-up tube slightly to the right to clear the pan. Remove the oil pan.
16. Lower the vehicle.
17. Using a boom hoist or equivalent, attached to the engine

with the shortest hook-up possible, take up all tension and support the engine.

18. Remove the engine front mounts and insulators.
19. Carefully remove the engine from the vehicle.
20. Installation is the reverse of removal. Check all fluid levels and perform all tune-up adjustments if the engine was rebuilt.

NOTE: If the engine was rebuilt or new camshaft or lifters installed, add 1 quart of engine oil supplement to aid break-in. This should be left in the engine for at least 500 miles.

CONVENTIONAL TRUCKS

1. Drain the coolant.
2. Remove the battery.
3. Mark the outline of the hinges on the hood and remove it.
4. Discharge the air conditioning system safely. Disconnect and cap the compressor lines.
5. Tag and disconnect the wiring at the alternator, coil, temperature and oil pressure sending units, starter relay, and engine ground strap.
6. Remove the air cleaner and carburetor. Install an engine lifting fixture.
7. Remove the distributor cap, rotor, and spark plug wires.
8. Disconnect and cap the fuel line.
9. Remove the fan and radiator.
10. Detach the exhaust pipe, driveshaft, linkage, and oil cooler lines.
11. Support the rear of the engine and remove the engine rear crossmember and transmission.
12. Unbolt the engine mount and lift the engine out from the vehicle.

PICKUPS, RAMCHARGER AND TRAIL DUSTER

1. Drain the coolant from the radiator and cylinder block.
2. Disconnect the battery ground cable. Remove the battery on V8 models.
3. Scribe the outline of the hood hinges and remove the hood.
4. If the vehicle is equipped with air conditioning, remove the compressor with lines attached and lay it aside. Do not disconnect any refrigerant lines. Bodily injury could result.
5. Disconnect the electrical connections at the alternator, ignition coil, temperature and oil pressure sending units, starter-to-sole-noid, and engine/body ground.
6. Remove the air cleaner and carburetor. Install an engine lifting fixture.
7. Remove the distributor cap and rotor.
8. Disconnect and plug the fuel pump line.
9. Disconnect the radiator and heater hoses. Disconnect and plug the oil cooler lines.
10. Remove the fan, spacer, fluid drive, and radiator. Do not store the fan drive unit with the shaft pointing downward. Fluid will leak out.
11. Raise the vehicle and support the rear of the engine.
12. Disconnect the exhaust pipes at the manifolds.
13. Remove the starter on V8 models.
14. Remove the automatic transmission dust cover and attach a C-clamp to the front bottom of the torque converter housing to prevent it from failing out. Remove the drive plate bolts from the torque converter. On manual transmission models, remove the rear crossmember, transmission, transfer case and adapter. The transfer case can be left in place on six-cylinder models.
15. Support the transmission and remove the transmission attaching bolts.
16. Lower the truck and attach a hoist to the engine.
17. Remove the front motor mount bolt stud nuts and washers.
18. Carefully remove the engine.
19. Installation is the reverse of removal. Fill the engine with coolant and fresh oil. Adjust the transmission linkage, carburetor, and ignition timing.

V8 intake manifold tightening sequence (© Chrysler Corp.)

Intake Manifold

Removal and Installation

4 CYLINDER (2.6L) ENGINE

1. Disconnect the negative battery cable.
2. Drain the cooling system and disconnect the hoses from the water pump to the intake manifold.
3. Disconnect the carburetor air horn adapter and move to one side.
4. Disconnect the vacuum hoses and throttle linkage from the carburetor.
5. Disconnect the fuel inlet line at the fuel filter.
6. Remove the fuel filter and fuel pump and move to one side.
7. Remove the intake manifold retaining nuts and washers and remove the manifold.
8. Installation is the reverse of removal. Tighten the retaining nuts to 150 inch lbs.

V-8 ENGINES

1. Drain cooling system and disconnect battery.
2. Remove alternator, carburetor air cleaner, and fuel line.
3. Disconnect accelerator linkage.
4. Remove vacuum control between carburetor and distributor.
5. Remove the distributor cap and wires.
6. Disconnect coil wires, temperature sending unit wire, heater hoses and bypass hose.
7. Remove intake manifold, ignition coil and carburetor as an assembly.
8. Installation is the reverse of the above procedure. Tighten the intake manifold to head bolts in the sequence illustrated, from center alternating out.
9. Tighten the exhaust manifold mounting nuts.

Exhaust Manifold

Removal and Installation

4 CYLINDER (2.6L) ENGINE

1. Disconnect the battery.
2. Remove the air cleaner.
3. Remove the belt from the power steering pump.
4. Raise the vehicle and make sure it is supported safely.
5. Remove the exhaust pipe from the manifold or converter.
6. Disconnect the air injection tube assembly from the ex-

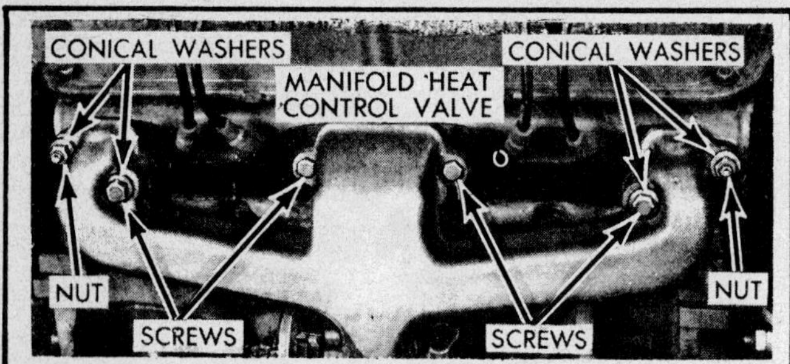

Installing 318 and 360 exhaust manifold (© Chrysler Corp.)

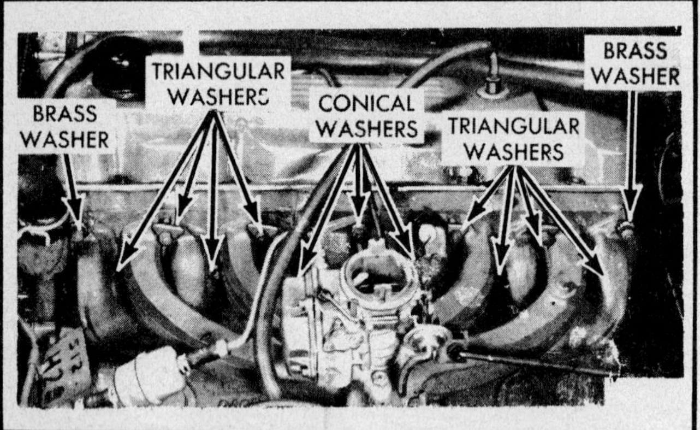

Intake and exhaust manifold installation—6-cylinder (© Chrysler Corp.)

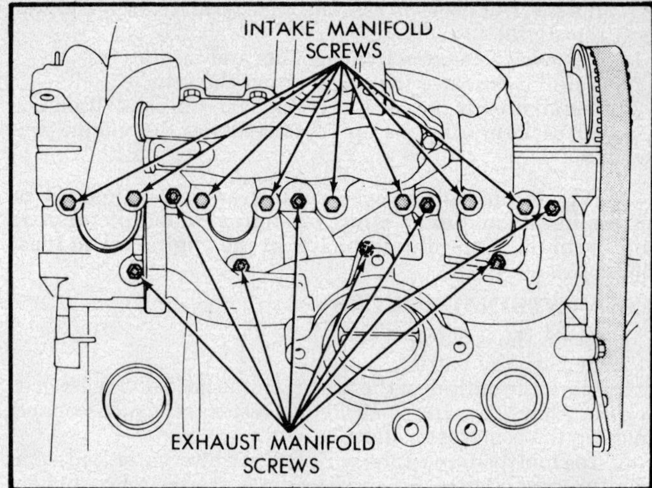

Rampage 2.2L intake and exhaust attaching points (© Chrysler Corp.)

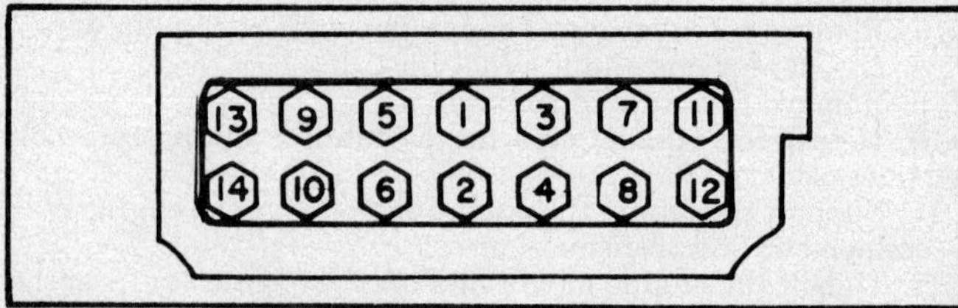

6-cylinder head bolt tightening sequences (© Chrysler Corp.)

haust manifold and lower the vehicle.

7. Remove the power steering pump assembly and move to one side.
8. Remove the heat cowl from the exhaust manifold.
9. Remove the exhaust manifold retaining nuts and remove the assembly from the vehicle.
10. Remove the carburetor air heater from the manifold.
11. Separate the exhaust manifold from the catalytic converter by removing the retaining screws.
12. Installation is the reverse of removal. Use a new gasket between the exhaust manifold and the front catalytic converter and torque the mounting screws to 24 ft. lbs. Use a new manifold gasket and coat the cylinder head side lightly with sealer. Torque the manifold center mounting nuts to 150 inch lbs. then torque the outer mounting nuts to 150 inch lbs.

V–8 ENGINES

1. Disconnect the exhaust manifold at the flange where it mates to the exhaust pipe.
2. If the vehicle is equipped with air injection and/or a carburetor-heated air stove, remove them.
3. Remove the exhaust manifold by removing the securing bolts and washers. To reach these bolts, it may be necessary to jack the engine slightly off its front mounts. When the exhaust manifold is removed, sometimes the securing studs will screw out with the nuts. If this occurs, the studs must be replaced with the aid of sealing compound on the coarse thread ends. If this is not done, water leaks may develop at the studs.
4. To install, reverse the removal procedures.

Combination Manifold

Removal and Installation

6–CYLINDER ENGINES

1. Remove the air cleaner, lines and tubes to the carburetor.
2. Disconnect all the linkages to the carburetor and remove the carburetor from the manifold.
3. Disconnect the exhaust pipe from the manifold, remove the manifold attaching washers and retaining nuts, and remove the manifold from the cylinder head.
4. Separate the exhaust manifold from the intake manifold if necessary, and install a new gasket between the two upon reassembly.

NOTE: Do not tighten the three securing bolts until the manifold assembly has been installed on the cylinder head.

5. Position the manifold on the cylinder head using a new gasket, and install the conical and triangular washers, the retaining nuts, and torque the retaining nuts and the three securing bolts to the specified torque.
6. Attach the exhaust pipe to the exhaust manifold flange.
7. Install the carburetor and attach all the lines, tubes, and linkages. Install the air cleaner assembly.

Removal and Installation

4 CYLINDER (2.2L) ENGINE

1. Disconnect the battery and drain the cooling system.
2. Remove the air cleaner and disconnect all vacuum lines, electrical wiring and fuel lines from the carburetor. Remove the throttle linkage.
3. Loosen the power steering pump and remove the drive belt. Remove the power brake vacuum hose from the intake manifold.
4. On vehicles equipped with A.I.R., remove the coupling hose from the diverter valve to exhaust manifold air injection tube assembly.
5. Remove the water hoses from the water crossover and raise the vehicle. Remove the exhaust pipe from the manifold.
6. Remove the intake manifold support bracket and the EGR tube.
7. On vehicles equipped with A.I.R., remove the four air in-

jection tube bolts and remove the air injection tube assembly from the exhaust manifold.

8. Remove the intake manifold and then remove the exhaust manifold.

9. If necessary remove the water crossover cover from the intake manifold.

10. Installation is the reverse of removal. Use new manifold gaskets. Tighten the exhaust manifold from the center and progress outward to both ends. Torque the manifold nuts to 16.7 ft. lbs. (23 Nm) and repeat the sequence until all bolts are torqued to specification.

11. Tighten the intake manifold bolts from the center of the head, progressing outward to both ends. Torque the bolts to 16.7 ft. lbs. (23 Nm) and repeat the sequence until all bolts are torqued to specification.

Cylinder Head

Removal and Installation

6-CYLINDER ENGINE

1. Drain cooling system.
2. Remove air cleaner and fuel line.
3. Remove vacuum line at carburetor and distributor.
4. Disconnect accelerator linkage.
5. Disconnect spark plug wires by pulling boot straight out in line with plugs.
6. Disconnect heater hose and by-pass hose clamp.
7. Disconnect temperature sending wire.
8. Disconnect exhaust pipe at exhaust manifold flange. Disconnect diverter valve vacuum line on engines with air pump.
9. Remove intake and exhaust manifolds.
10. Remove closed vent system (PCV) and rocker cover.
11. Remove rocker shaft assembly.
12. Remove pushrods in sequence and mark them in such a way that they may be put back into their original positions.
13. Remove head bolts.
14. Remove spark plugs.
15. To install, clean all gasket surfaces of cylinder block and cylinder head and install spark plugs.
16. Check all surfaces with a straightedge if there is any reason to suspect leakage.
17. Install gasket, using sealer, and cylinder head.
18. Install cylinder head attaching bolts. Tighten all bolts in the sequence illustrated to 50 ft. lbs. torque, then repeat tightening sequence torquing to 70 ft. lbs.
19. Install rocker arms and shaft assembly. The special bolt goes to the rear. Install rocker shaft retainers between rocker arms so they seat on rocker shaft and not on extended bushing of rocker arm. Be sure to install long retainer in center position only. Tighten bolts to 25 ft. lbs. Tighten the special bolt to 200 inch lbs.
20. Loosen the 3 bolts holding intake manifold to exhaust manifold. This is necessary for proper alignment.
21. Install the manifolds as detailed under manifold removal and installation.
22. Connect heater hose and by-pass hose clamp.
23. Connect heat indicator sending unit wire, the accelerator linkage and spark plug wires.
24. Install the vacuum control tube from carburetor to distributor. Install the air tube assembly with a new gasket to the head, tightening it to 100 inch lbs. Install the diverter valve vacuum line.
25. Connect exhaust pipe to exhaust manifold flange.
26. Install fuel line and carburetor air cleaner.
27. Fill cooling system, start and warm up engine, and adjust valve tappet clearance.
28. Install valve cover using new gasket, tightening retaining nuts to 3–4 ft. lbs.
29. Install crankcase ventilation system.

Removal and Installation

4 CYLINDER ENGINES (INCLUDES RAMPAGE AND SCAMP)

1. Drain cooling system.
2. Remove air cleaner and fuel line.
3. Remove vacuum line at carburetor and distributor.
4. Disconnect accelerator linkage.
5. Disconnect spark plug wires by pulling boot straight out in line with plugs.
6. Disconnect heater hose and bypass hose clamp.
7. Disconnect temperature sending wire.
8. Disconnect exhaust pipe at exhaust manifold flange. Disconnect diverter valve vacuum line on engines with air pump.
9. Remove intake and exhaust manifolds.
10. Remove closed vent system (PCV) and rocker cover.
11. Remove rocker shaft assembly.

NOTE: On 4 cylinder engines, always mark the rocker arms for reinstallation in the same position. Also, remove the nuts and caps a little at a time, to avoid damaging the thrust and bearing surfaces. Care should be exercised not to cock the camshaft during removal and installation.

12. Remove pushrods in sequence and mark them in such a way that they may be put back into their original positions.
13. Remove head bolts.
14. To install, clean all gasket surfaces of cylinder block and cylinder head.
15. Check all surfaces with a straightedge if there is any reason to suspect leakage.
16. Install gasket, using sealer, and cylinder head.
17. Install cylinder head attaching bolts. Tighten all bolts in the sequence illustrated to 50 ft. lbs. torque, then repeat tightening sequence torquing to 70 ft. lbs.

NOTE: Follow the 2.2L, 4 cylinder head bolt torque sequence and use a 4 step tightening procedure.

a. 30 ft. lbs.
b. 45 ft. lbs.
c. 45 ft. lbs. again
d. $^1/_4$ final turn of each bolt

18. Install rocker arms and shaft assembly with the oil hole on the end of the shaft on top and to the front. The special bolt goes to the rear. Install rocker shaft retainers between rocker arms so they seat on rocker shaft and not on extended bushing of rocker arm. Be sure to install long retainer in center position only. Tighten the special bolt to 200 inch lbs.
19. Loosen the 3 bolts holding intake manifold to exhaust manifold. This is necessary for proper alignment.
20. Install the manifolds as detailed under manifold removal and installation.
21. Connect heater hose and by-pass hose clamp.
22. Connect heat indicator sending unit wire, the accelerator linkage and spark plug wires.
23. Install the vacuum control tube from carburetor to distributor.
24. Install the air tube assembly with a new gasket to the head, tightening it to 100 inch lbs.
25. Install the diverter valve vacuum line.
26. Connect exhaust pipe to exhaust manifold flange.
27. Install fuel line and carburetor air cleaner.
28. Fill cooling system, start and warm up engine, and adjust valve tappet clearance.
29. Install valve cover using new gasket, tightening retaining nuts to 3–4 ft. lbs.
30. Install crankcase ventilation system.

Removal and Installation

V8 ENGINES

1. Drain cooling system and disconnect battery.

2. Remove alternator, air cleaner and fuel line.
3. Disconnect accelerator linkage.
4. Remove vacuum control hose between carburetor and distributor.
5. Remove cooling and heater hoses from head and, if so equipped, remove air compressor.
6. Remove distributor cap and high tension leads as an assembly.
7. Remove heat indicator sending unit wire.
8. Remove crankcase ventilation system and valve covers.
9. Remove spark plugs.
10. Remove intake manifold, carburetor and, if attached to manifold, ignition coil as an assembly.
11. Remove tappet chamber cover.
12. Remove exhaust manifolds.
13. Remove rocker arms and shaft assemblies.
14. Remove pushrods and identify to insure installation in original location.
15. Remove cylinder head bolts and cylinder heads.
16. Before installing cylinder heads, clean all gasket surfaces of block and heads.
17. Inspect all surfaces with a straightedge if there is any indication of leakage.
18. Coat new head gaskets with sealant and install on block.
19. Install cylinder head and head bolts. Tighten bolts in the sequence illustrated, first to 50 ft. lbs. torque, then in sequence again to the specified torque.

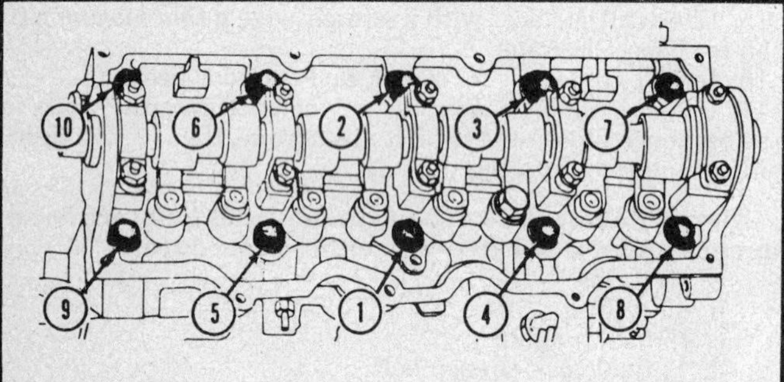

Rampage 2.2L cylinder head bolt tightening sequence (© Chrysler Corp.)

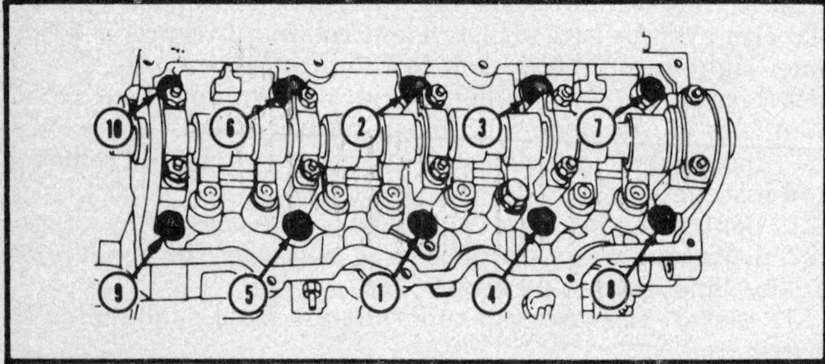

Cylinder head torque sequence—135 (2.2L) engine (© Chrysler Corp.)

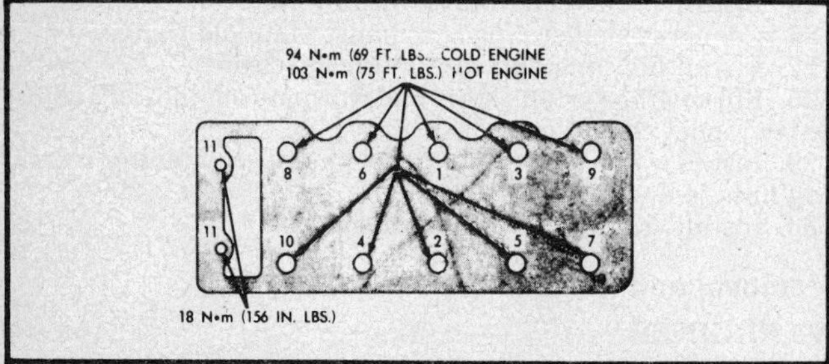

Cylinder head torque sequence—155.9 (2.6L) engine (© Chrysler Corp.)

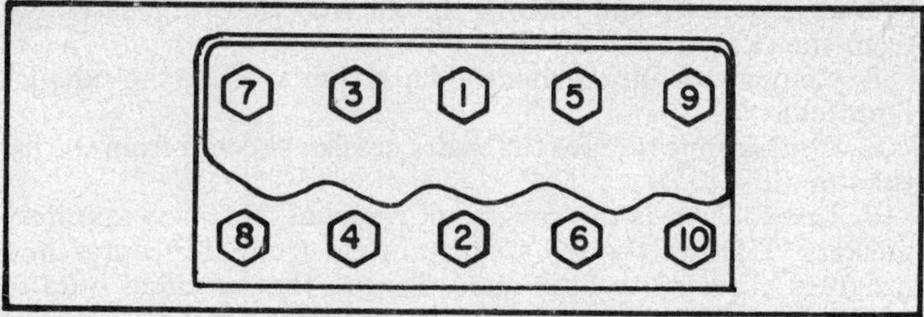

Cylinder head tightening sequence—360 and smaller V8 (© Chrysler Corp.)

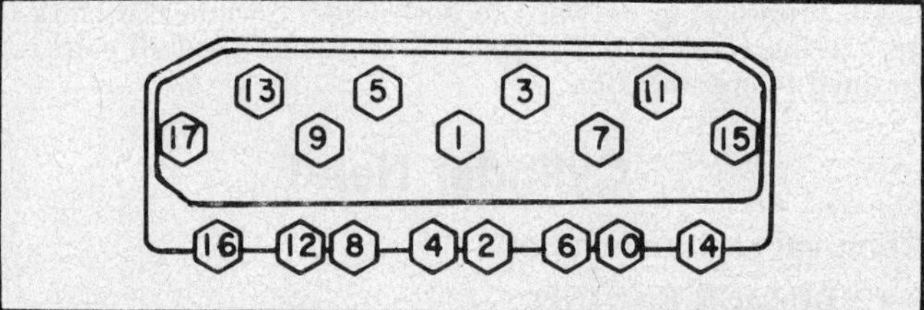

Cylinder head tightening sequence–400, 440 engines (© Chrysler Corp.)

CAUTION

Do not retighten cylinder head bolts after engine has been operated if embossed steel head gaskets are used.

20. Inspect pushrods for wear or bending and install in original positions. Use an aligning rod.
21. Install rocker shaft assembly making sure long stamped steel retainers are in the No. 2 and No. 4 positions. Tighten rocker shaft mounting bolts to 25 ft. lbs. (17 ft. lbs. on 318 and 360 cu. in. engine) torque. On the 318 and 360 cu. in. engines, make sure the "NOTCH" end of the rocker assemblies are pointing toward the centerline of the engine and toward the front on the left bank and toward the rear on the right bank.
22. Install tappet chamber cover. Tighten bolts to 7–8 ft. lbs. torque.
23. Install exhaust manifolds. Use new gaskets. Tighten bolts to the specified torque.
24. Set correct gap on spark plugs.
25. Install intake manifold and carburetor assembly, tightening bolts from center outward, first to 25 ft. lbs. torque, then again to correct torque (see Torque Specifications at the beginning of this section). On the 318 cu. in. engine, coat the gaskets with sealant and install with bead down. On 360 cu. in. engines, do not use any sealer on side composition gaskets.
26. Install distributor cap and high tension leads.
27. Connect vacuum control hose between distributor and carburetor, throttle linkage, heat indicator sending unit wire, heater and coolant hoses, fuel line and, if so equipped, manual choke cable.
28. Install rocker cover, using new gasket. Tighten bolts to 3–4 ft. lbs. torque.
29. Install crankcase ventilation system and air cleaner.
30. Install alternator and drive belts. Install air compressor if so equipped.
31. Fill cooling system and install or connect battery.

Valve Rocker Arm Shaft Assembly

Removal and Installation

4 CYLINDER (2.2L) ENGINE

CAUTION

When depressing the valve spring with Chrysler tool 4682, or the equivalent, the valve locks can become dislocated. Check and make sure both locks are fully seated in the valve grooves and retainer.

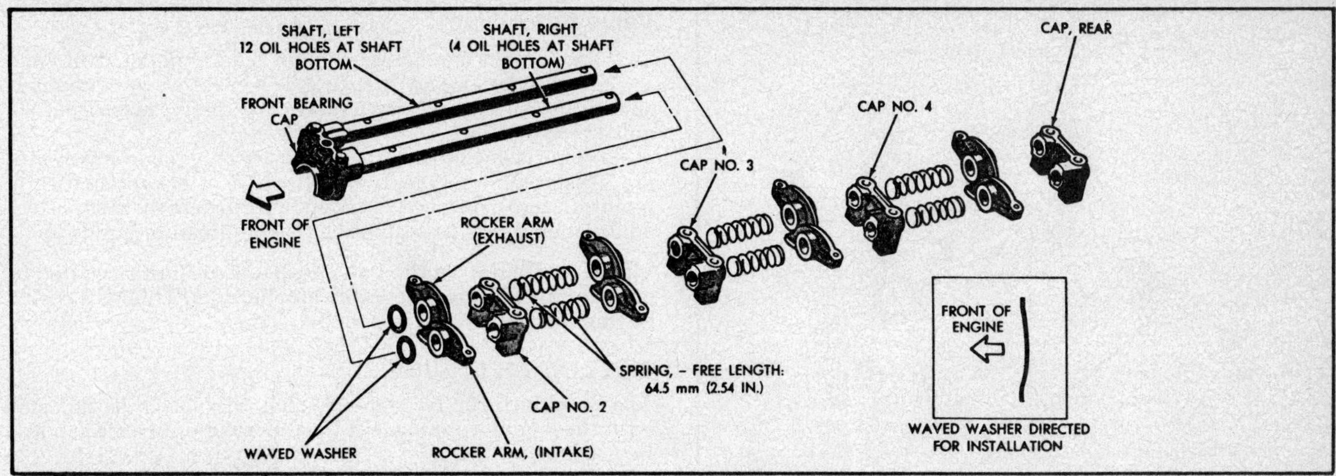

155.9 (2.6L) engine—rocker arm and shaft assembly (© Chrysler Corp.)

1. Remove the valve cover.
2. Rotate the camshaft until the lobe base is on the rocker arm that is to be removed.
3. Slightly depress the valve spring using Chrysler tool 4682 or equivalent. Slide the rocker off the lash adjuster and valve tip and remove. Label the rocker arms for position identification. Proceed to next rocker arm and repeat Step 2 and 3. Install in reverse order. Check the valve keys, be sure they are not dislocated.

4 CYLINDER (2.6L) ENGINE

1. Turn the engine until No. 1 piston is at TDC (top dead center) of the compression stroke. Remove the distributor cap and confirm that the rotor tip is pointed at the No. 1 plug wire location. Disconnect the negative battery cable. Remove the distributor.
2. Remove the water pump cover (upper shield) and valve cover.
3. Confirm that No. 1 piston is at TDC of the compression stroke. Take white paint and mark the timing chain in line with the camshaft sprocket timing mark.
4. Remove the camshaft sprocket bolt, distributor drive gear and sprocket with chain meshed. Secure sprocket and chain in holder.
5. Loosen the camshaft bearing bracket and rocker arm assembly mounting bolts. Start at each end and work toward the center. Do not remove the retaining bolts. When all retaining bolts are loose, lift assembly from the cylinder head.
6. Remove the bolts from the camshaft bearing caps and remove the rocket shafts and arms. Keep all parts in order. Note the way the rocker shafts, rocker arms, springs and wave washers are mounted, the left shaft has 12 oil holes which face down. The right shaft has 4 oil holes that face down.
7. Lubricate all parts and assemble in reverse order. Secure the assembled shafts in position with retaining bolts through the cam bearing caps and install on head.

6-CYLINDER ENGINE

1. Remove the closed ventilation system.
2. Remove the evaporative control system.
3. Remove the valve cover with its gasket.
4. Turn out the rocker arm and shaft assembly securing bolts and remove the rocker arm and shaft.
5. Reverse the above for installation. The oil hole on the end of the shaft must be on the top and point toward the front of the engine to provide proper lubrication to the rocker arms. The special bolt goes to the rear. Torque the rocker arm bolts to 25 ft. lbs. and adjust the valves.

Removal and Installation

V8 ENGINES

1. Disconnect the spark plug wires.
2. Disconnect the closed ventilation and evaporative control system.
3. Remove the valve covers with their gaskets.
4. Remove the rocker shaft bolts and retainers, and lift off the rocker arm assembly.

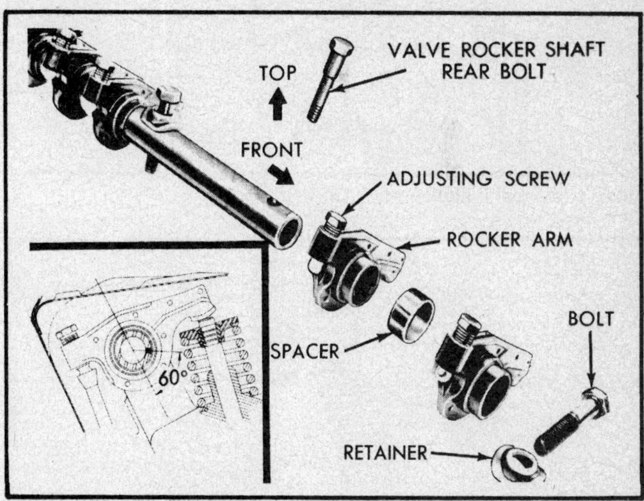

6 cylinder rocker arm shaft (© Chrysler Corp.)

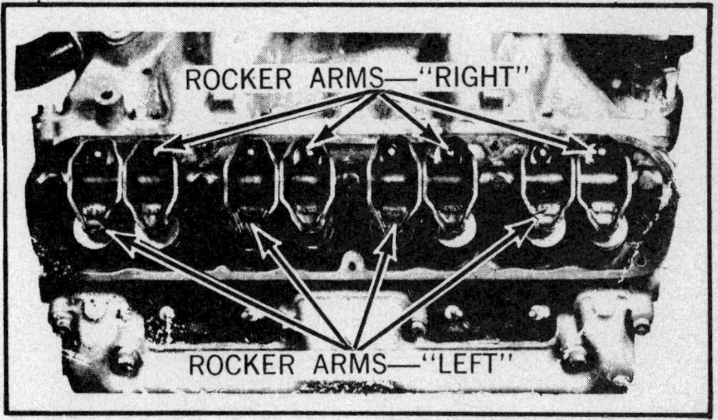

Proper rocker arm location on shaft (© Chrysler Corp.)

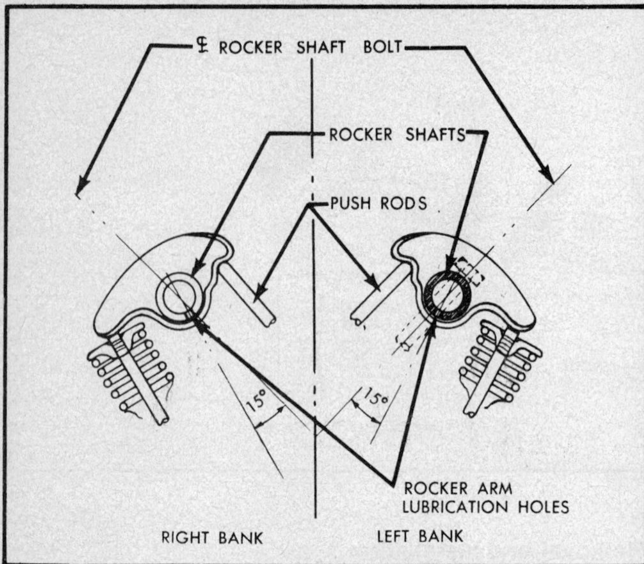

The rocker arm lubrication holes should be aligned as illustrated on the 400 and 440 engines (© Chrysler Corp.)

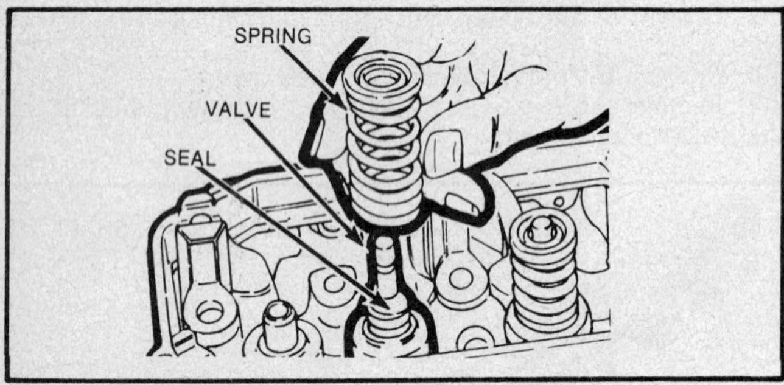

Valve stem seal installation (© Chrysler Corp.)

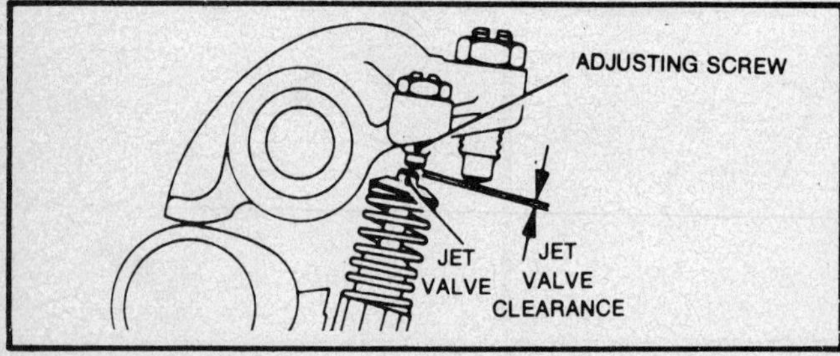

Adjusting the jet valve on 155.9 (2.6L) engines (© Chrysler Corp.)

5. Reverse the above procedure to install. The notch on the end of both rocker shafts on the 318 and 360 should point to the engine centerline and toward the front of the engine on the left cylinder head, or toward the rear on the right cylinder head. Torque the rocker shaft bolts to 17 ft. lbs.

VALVE ARRANGEMENT

4 CYLINDER ENGINE
Drivers to passenger side
E I E I I E I E

6 CYLINDER ENGINE
Front to rear as follows
E I E I E I I E I E I E

V8 ENGINE
Right
E I I E E I I E
Left
E I I E E I I E

Valve Adjustment

This adjustment is required only on the 4 cylinder (2.6L) and the six-cylinder engine. It should be done at every tune-up. It should also be done whenever there is excessive noise from the valve mechanism.

No valve lash adjustment is necessary or possible on any other Chrysler built engine. Hydraulic valve lifters automatically maintain zero clearance. After engine reassembly these lifters adjust themselves as soon as engine oil pressure builds up.

NOTE: Do not set the valve lash closer than specified in an attempt to quiet the valve mechanism. This will result in burned valve.

6 CYLINDER ENGINE

The manufacturer recommends that the valves be adjusted with the engine running, but the following procedure can also be used.

1. The engine must be at normal operating temperature. Mark the crankshaft pulley into three equal 120° segments, starting at the TDC mark.
2. Remove the valve (rocker) cover and the distributor cap.
3. Set the engine at TDC on the No. 1 cylinder by aligning the mark on the crankshaft pulley with the 0° mark on the timing cover pointer. The distributor rotor should point at the position of the No. 1 spark plug wire in the distributor cap. Both rocker arms on the No. 1 cylinder should be free to move slightly. If all this isn't the case, you have No. 6 cylinder at TDC and will have to turn the engine 360° in the normal direction of rotation.
4. The lash is measured between the rocker arm and the end of the valve.
5. To check the lash, insert the correct size feeler gauge between the rocker arm and the valve. Press down lightly on the other end of the rocker arm. If the gauge cannot be inserted, loosen the self-locking adjustment nut on top of the rocker arm. Tighten the nut until the gauge can just be inserted and withdrawn without buckling.
6. After both valves for the No. 1 cylinder are adjusted, turn the engine so that the pulley turns 120° in the normal direction of rotation (clockwise). The distributor rotor will turn 60°, since it turns at half engine speed.
7. Check that the rocker arms are free and adjust the valves for the next cylinder in the firing order, (5). The firing order is 1–5–3–6–2–4.
8. Turn the engine 120° to adjust each of the remaining cylinders in the firing order. When you are done the engine will have made two complete revolutions (720°) and the rotor one complete revolution (360°).
9. Replace the rocker cover with a new gasket. Replace the distributor cap. Start the engine and check for leaks.
10. Replace the rocker cover with a new gasket. Replace the distributor cap. Start the engine and check for leaks.

4 CYLINDER (2.6L) ENGINE

NOTE: A jet valve is added on USA models. The jet valve adjuster is located on the intake valve rocker arm and must be adjusted before the intake valve.

1. Start the engine and allow it to reach normal operating temperature.

NOTE: Do not run the engine with the rocker arm cover removed, oil will be sprayed onto the hot exhaust manifold.

2. Shut off engine and remove the rocker arm cover.
3. Watch the valve operation on No. 1 cylinder (No. 1 cylinder on transverse mounted engines is on the driver's side) while turning the crankshaft to close the exhaust valve and have the intake valve just begin to open. This places the No. 4

cylinder on TDC of its firing stroke and permits the adjustment of the valves.

4. Jet valves must be adjusted before the intake valve.

a. Loosen the intake valve lock nut and back off the adjustment screw two or more turns.

b. Loosen the lock nut on the jet valve adjusting screw. Turn the jet valve adjusting screw counterclockwise and insert a 0.006 in. feeler gauge between the valve stem and the adjusting screw.

c. Tighten the adjusting screw until it touches the feeler gauge. The jet valve spring is weak, be careful not to force the jet valve in.

d. After adjustment is made, hold the adjusting screw with a screwdriver and tighten the lock nut.

5. Proceed to adjust the intake and the exhaust valves on the same cylinder as the jet valve you finished adjusting. Adjust by loosening the locknut and passing a feeler gauge of the correct thickness between the bottom of the rocker arm and top of the valve stem. If the clearance is too great or too small, turn the adjusting screw until the gauge will pass through with a slight drag. Tighten the locknut and proceed to the next valve. Refer to the chart in Step 3 for the adjusting sequence.

Exhaust Valve Closing	Adjust
No. 1 cylinder	No. 4 cylinder valves
No. 2 cylinder	No. 3 cylinder valves
No. 3 cylinder	No. 2 cylinder valves
No. 4 cylinder	No. 1 cylinder valves

Timing Belt Cover and Sprockets

Removal and Installation

4 CYLINDER (2.2L) ENGINE

1. Loosen the alternator lock screw and adjusting screw. Remove the drive belt.
2. Remove the power steering pump lock screw. Remove the pivot bolt and nut. Remove the drive belt. Remove the power steering pump and mounting bracket. The hoses need not be disconnected, locate the pump out of the way.
3. Loosen and remove the water pump pulley mounting screws and remove the pulley.
4. From under the vehicle remove the right inner splash shield.
5. Remove the crankshaft pulley.
6. The upper part of the timing cover is retained by nuts, the lower part is retained with screws. Remove the fasteners and the two halves of the timing cover.
7. Installation is the reverse of the removal procedure.

TIMING BELT

Removal and Installation

1. Follow Steps 1–6 of the Timing Cover Removal and Installation section.
2. Place a jack under the engine with a piece of wood separating it from the jacking point.

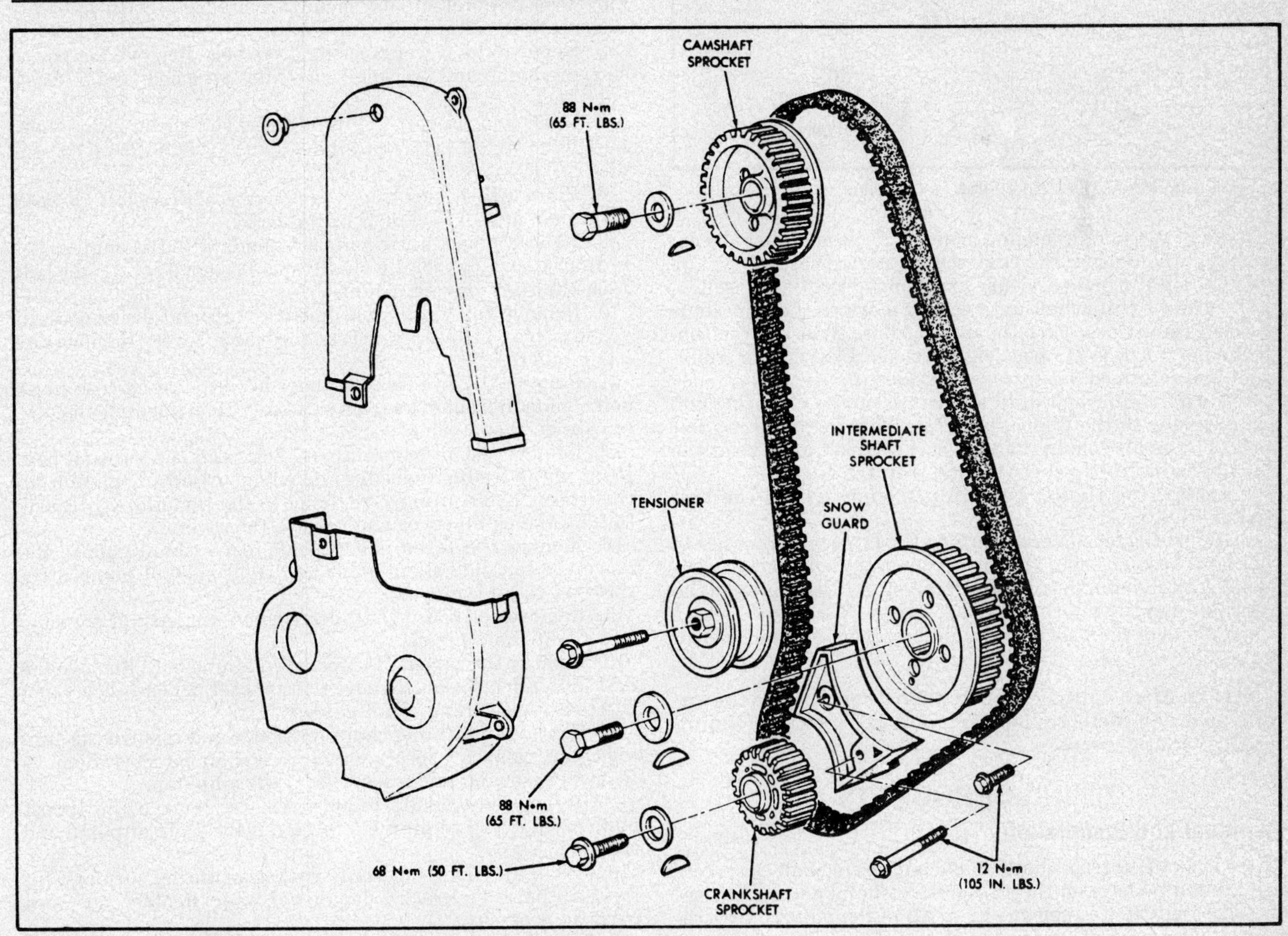

Timing belt and components—135 (2.2L) engine (© Chrysler Corp.)

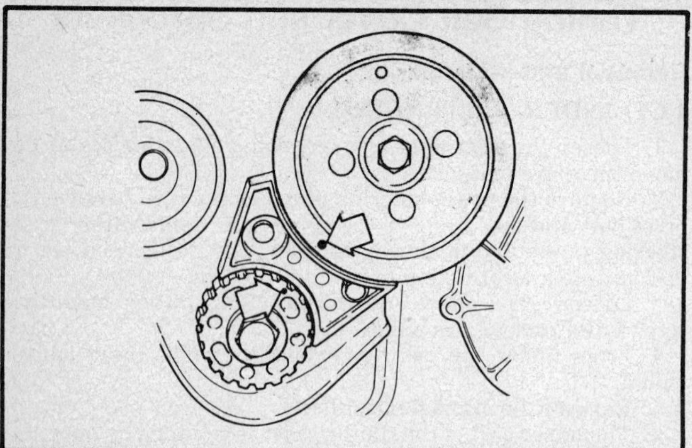

Crankshaft and intermediate shaft timing alignment—135 (2.2L) engine (© Chrysler Corp.)

Camshaft timing—135 (2.2L) engine (© Chrysler Corp.)

3. Remove the right engine mounting bolt and raise the engine slightly. Be sure the engine is supported securely.
4. Loosen the belt tensioner and remove the timing belt.
5. Turn the crankshaft until the dot mark on the sprocket is at about two o'clock. Turn the intermediate shaft sprocket until the dot mark is at about eight o'clock. Line up the crankshaft and intermediate sprocket marks.
6. Turn the camshaft until the arrows on the mounting hub are in line with the front (no. 1) camshaft retaining cap flat spots. The small hole in the camshaft sprocket must be at the top and be in a vertical center line with the engine.
7. Install the timing belt. Adjust and tighten the belt tensioner.
8. Adjust the tensioner by turning the large tensioner hex to the right. Tension should be correct when the belt can be twisted 90° with the thumb and the forefinger, midway between the camshaft and the intermediate sprocket.
9. Complete the belt installation by reversing the removal steps.

NOTE: After applying the belt tensioner, rotate the engine two complete revolutions and recheck the timing marks for alignment.

TIMING SPROCKETS

Removal and Installation

The camshaft, intermediate shaft, and crankshaft sprockets are located by keys on their respective shafts and each is retained by a bolt. To remove any or all of the pulleys, first remove the timing belt cover and belt and then use the following procedure.

NOTE: When removing the crankshaft pulley, don't remove the four socket head bolts which retain the outer belt pulley to the timing belt pulley.

1. Remove the center bolt.
2. Gently pry the pulley off the shaft.
3. If the pulley is stubborn in coming off, use a gear puller. Don't hammer on the pulley.
4. Remove the pulley and key.
5. Install the pulley in the reverse order of removal.
6. Tighten the center bolt to 58 ft. lbs.
7. Install the timing belt, check valve timing, tension belt, and install the cover.

Timing Chain, Cover, "Silent Shafts" and Tensioner

Removal and Installation

4 CYLINDER (2.6L) ENGINE

1. Bring the engine to No. 1 piston at TDC (top dead center) of the compression stroke.
2. Disconnect the negative battery cable. Remove the air cleaner assembly.
3. Remove the alternator drive belt. Tag and disconnect the spark plug wires from the plugs, free wires from supports. Remove the distributor with cap and wires attached.
4. Remove the air conditioner compressor drive belt. Remove the compressor and mounting brackets, with lines attached; and position out of the way.
5. Remove the power steering drive belt. Remove the power steering pump and brackets, with lines attached, and position out of the way.
6. Raise and support the front of the vehicle on jackstands.
7. Remove the right front inner splash shield. Drain the engine oil. Remove the crankshaft pulley.
8. Place a floor jack under the engine with a piece of wood mounted between jack and lifting point.
9. Raise the jack until contact is made with the engine. Relieve pressure by jacking slightly and remove the center bolt from the right engine mount.
10. Remove the engine oil dipstick. Tag and disconnect all vacuum hoses that run across the valve cover. Remove the valve cover.
11. Remove the two front cylinder head to timing case cover bolts (bolts in front of the cam sprocket). Do not loosen any other cylinder head bolts.
12. Remove the oil pan retaining bolts and lower the oil pan. Remove the timing indicator and engine mounting plate from the timing chain case cover. Remove the remaining bolts retaining the chain cover and remove the cover.
13. Remove the three "silent shaft" drive chain guides. Remove the left side silent shaft and right side oil pump drive sprocket retaining bolts.
14. Remove the silent shaft drive chain, crankshaft sprocket and silent shaft sprockets.
15. Remove the camshaft sprocket retaining bolt. Remove the distributor drive gear. Remove the sprocket holder bracket and right and left timing chain guides.
16. Depress the timing chain tensioner and remove the timing chain, camshaft sprocket and crankshaft sprocket. Remove tensioner, spring, and washer from the oil pump.
17. If the silent shafts require service, remove the thrust plate or oil pump retaining screws, remove plate or pump and shaft.
18. Clean all parts, especially gasket mounting surfaces. Inspect all parts for cracks, damage or wear. Replace the worn parts as necessary.
19. Install the left side silent shaft and thrust plate with a new O-ring. Tighten the retaining bolts to 71 inch lbs.

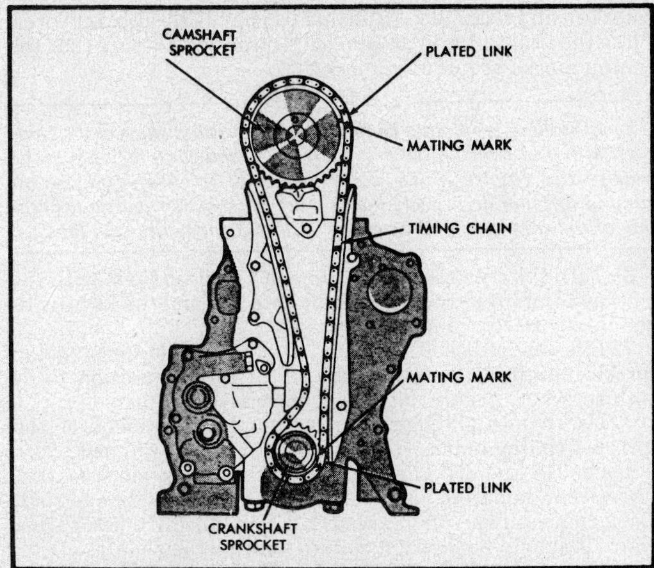

Timing gears and chain alignment—155.9 (2.6L) engine (© Chrysler Corp.)

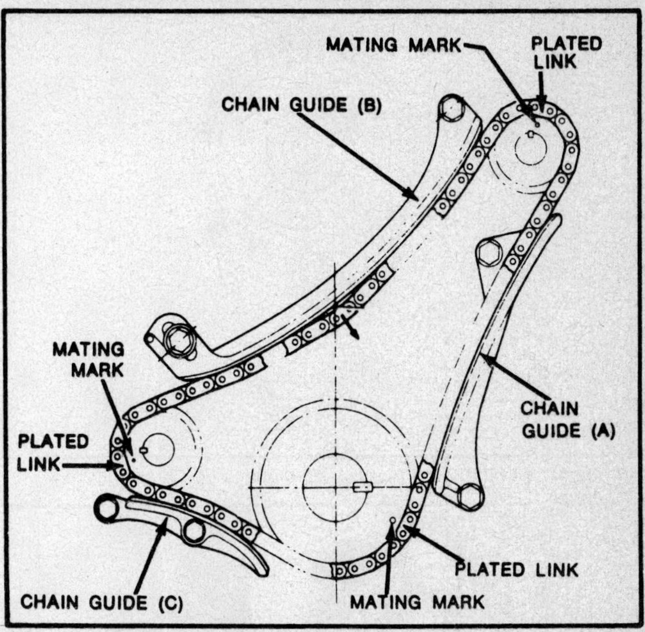

"Silent Shaft" balance system timing mark alignment—155.9 (2.6L) engine (© Chrysler Corp.)

20. Install the right side silent shaft, prime the oil pump with fresh oil and install. Tighten the retaining bolts to 71 inch lbs.

NOTE: Use a part of bolts without heads to act as guides when installing the silent shaft thrust plate or oil pump. When plate or pump is installed, remove the guide bolts and install regular bolts.

21. Verify that No. 1 piston is at TDC on the compression stroke (keyway at approx. 3 o'clock). Make sure the dowel pin hole on the front of the camshaft is in the vertical position at 12 o'clock.
22. Install the cam sprocket holder. Install the right and left chain guides. Install the tensioner spring, washer and shoe on the oil pump body.
23. Position the crankshaft and camshaft sprockets on the timing chain with timing marks aligned. The crank and camshaft sprockets have a punch mark on one gear tooth. The timing chain is equipped with two plated links. The marked tooth on each gear should be installed in the plated link.
24. Using both hands, lift the gears and chain with marks aligned. Slide the gears onto their respective shafts with dowel hole and keyway in proper position. Verify gear marks and plated links are aligned.
25. Install the dowel pin, distributor drive gear and sprocket bolt on the camshaft. Torque bolt to 40 ft. lbs.
26. Install the silent shaft chain drive sprocket on the crankshaft.
27. Install the oil pump and silent shaft drive sprockets in the silent drive chain with the punch marked tooth on each sprocket inserted into the plated links on the timing chain.
28. Hold the sprockets and chain with both hands, lift and align the remaining plated link with the punch marked tooth on the crankshaft sprocket.
29. Install plated link over the punch marked tooth on the crank sprocket. Install the silent shaft and oil pump sprocket with plated links and marked tooth aligned.
30. Tighten oil pump and silent shaft sprocket bolts to 25 ft. lbs.
31. Install the silent shaft chain guides. Do not tighten the mounting bolts at this time.
32. After the guides are installed loosely, tighten the mounting bolts on chain Guide A.
33. Tighten the mounting bolts on chain Guide C. Shake the chain on all of the sprockets to ensure snug seating.

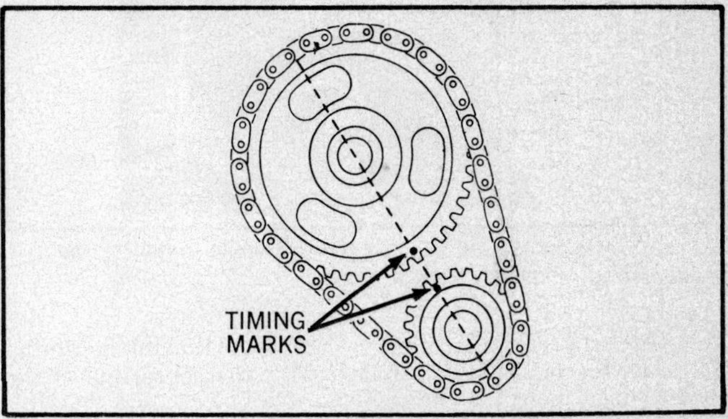

Alignment of timing gear marks—6 cylinder (© Chrysler Corp.)

34. Adjust chain guide B so that slack is pulled in the direct of arrow F in the illustration. The clearance between the chain guide and links should be between 0.04 and 0.14 inches. Tighten the chain Guide B mounting bolts.
35. Fit new cover case gaskets to the chain case. Trim gaskets as require for snug fit at the top and bottom. Coat the gaskets with sealer and install case cover.
36. Installation from this point is in the reverse order of removal.

Timing Cover and Chain or Belt

Removal and Installation

6-CYLINDER ENGINES

1. Drain the cooling system and disconnect the battery.
2. Remove the radiator and fan.
3. With a puller, remove the vibration damper.
4. Loosen the oil pan bolts to allow clearance, and remove the timing case cover and gasket.
5. Slide the crankshaft oil slinger off the front of the crankshaft.
6. Remove the camshaft sprocket bolt.
7. Remove the timing chain with the camshaft sprocket.

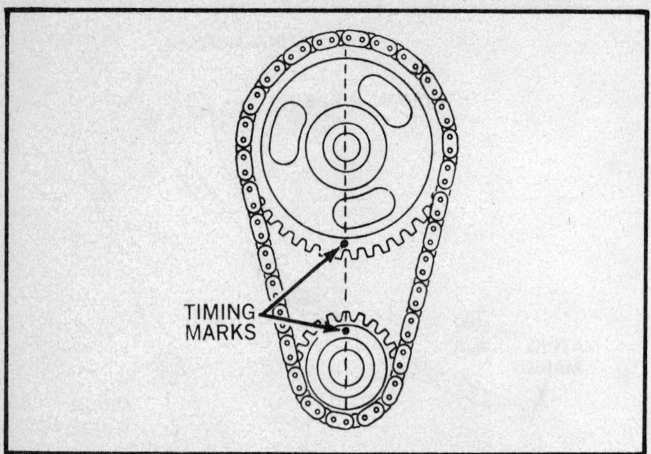

Alignment of timing gear marks—V8 engines (© Chrysler Corp.)

The V8 camshaft should be held forward while installing the chain and sprockets (© Chrysler Corp.)

8. On installation: Turn the crankshaft to line up the timing mark on the crankshaft sprocket with the centerline of the camshaft (without the chain).
9. Install the camshaft sprocket and chain. Align the timing marks.
10. Torque the camshaft sprocket bolt to 35 ft. lbs.
11. Replace the oil slinger.
12. Reinstall the timing case cover with a new gasket and torque the bolts to 17 ft. lbs. Retighten the engine oil pan to 17 ft. lbs.
13. Press the vibration damper back on.
14. Replace the radiator and hoses.
15. Refill the cooling system.

Removal and Installation

V8 ENGINES

1. Disconnect the battery and drain the cooling system. Remove the radiator.
2. Remove the vibration damper pulley. Unbolt and remove the vibration damper with a puller. On 318 and 360 engines, remove the fuel lines and fuel pump, then loosen the oil pan bolts and remove the front bolt on each side.
3. Remove the timing gear cover and the crankshaft oil slinger.
4. On 318 and 360 engines, remove the camshaft sprocket lockbolt, securing cup washer, and fuel pump eccentric. Remove the timing chain with both sprockets.
5. To begin the installation procedure, place the camshaft and crankshaft sprockets on a flat surface with the timing indicators on an imaginary centerline through both sprocket bores. Place the timing chain around both sprockets. Be sure that the timing marks are in alignment.

CAUTION

When installing the timing chain, have an assistant support the camshaft with a suitable tool to prevent it from contacting the plug in the rear of the engine block. Remove the distributor and the oil pump/distributor drive gear. Position the suitable tool against the rear side of the cam gear and be careful not to damage the cam lobes.

6. Turn the crankshaft and camshaft to align them with the keyway location in the crankshaft sprocket and the keyway or dowel hole in the camshaft sprocket.
7. Lift the sprockets and timing chain while keeping the sprockets tight against the chain in the correct position. Slide both sprockets evenly onto their respective shafts.
8. Use a straightedge to measure the alignment of the sprocket timing marks. They must be perfectly aligned.
9. On 318 and 360 engines, install the fuel pump eccentric, cup washer, and camshaft sprocket lockbolt and torque to 35 ft. lbs. If camshaft end play exceeds 0.010 in., install a new thrust plate. It should be 0.002–0.006 in. with the new plate.

CHECKING TIMING CHAIN SLACK

1. Position a scale next to the timing chain to detect any movement in the chain.
2. Place a torque wrench and socket on the camshaft sprocket attaching bolt. Apply either 30 ft. lbs. (if the cylinder heads are installed on the engine) or 15 ft. lbs. (cylinder heads removed) of force to the bolt and rotate the bolt in the direction of crankshaft rotation in order to remove all slack from the chain.
3. While applying torque to the camshaft sprocket bolt, the crankshaft should not be allowed to rotate. It may be necessary to block the crankshaft to prevent rotation.
4. Position the scale over the edge of a timing chain link and apply an equal amount of torque in the opposite direction. If the movement of the chain exceeds $\frac{1}{8}$ in., replace the chain.

TIMING GEAR COVER SEAL

Replacement

NOTE: A seal remover and installer tool is required to prevent seal damage.

1. Using a seal puller, separate the seal from the retainer.
2. Pull the seal from the case.
3. To install the seal place it face down in the case with the seal lips downward.
4. Seat the seal tightly against the cover face. There should be a maximum clearance of 0.0014 in. between the seal and the cover. Be careful not to over-compress the seal.

4 CYLINDER ENGINES

1. Remove the timing belt cover, loosen the tensioner and remove the timing belt.
2. Remove the sprocket of the seal to be replaced; crankshaft, intermediate shaft or camshaft.
3. On the 2.2L engine use special tool C–4679 or equivalent to remove the seal.
4. On the 2.2L engines with steel cased seals use a light coat of Loctite® stud and bearing mount (P/N 4057987), or equivalent. If the seal is rubber cased, use a solution of soap and water to lubricate it for installation. Install the 2.2L seals with special tool C-4680 or equivalent.
5. Install the timing belt and adjust the tension.
6. Install the timing belt cover and all related components.

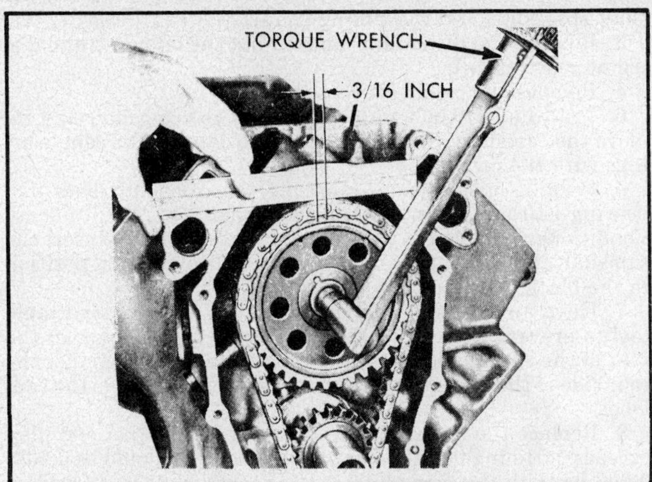

Measuring timing chain stretch (© Chrysler Corp.)

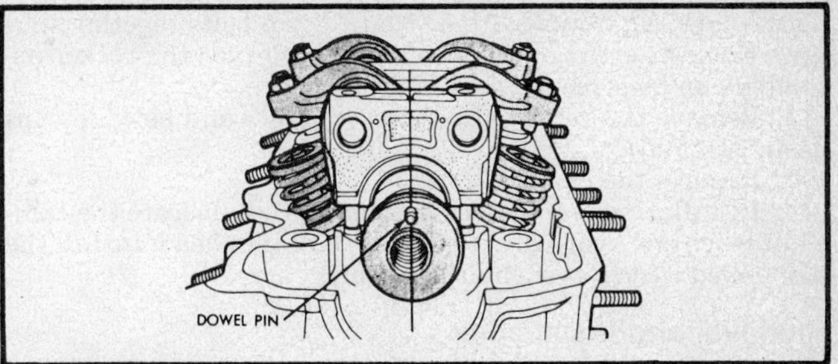

Camshaft alignment—155.9 (2.6L) engine (© Chrysler Corp.)

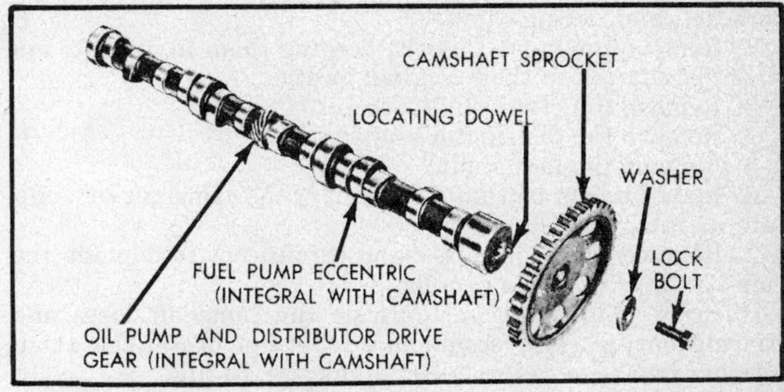

Camshaft—6 cylinder engines (© Chrysler Corp.)

VALVE TIMING OPERATION

6-CYLINDER

1. Rotate the crankshaft until no. 6 exhaust valve is closing and no. 6 intake valve is opening.
2. Install a dial indicator so that the indicator pointer contacts the valve spring retainer on the No. 1 intake valve parallel to the axis of the valve stem.
3. Turn the no. 1 intake adjusting screw in one complete turn to remove the lash. Adjust the dial indicator to zero.
4. Rotate the crankshaft clockwise (normal running direction) until the valve has lifted 0.029 inch.
5. The timing of the crankshaft pulley should now read from 12 degrees BTDC to DC. Readjust lash.

NOTE: If the reading is not within specified limits, inspect the sprocket index marks, inspect the timing chain for wear, and inspect the accuracy of the "DC" mark on the timing indicator.

318, 360, CU. IN. ENGINE

1. Turn the crankshaft until the no. 6 exhaust valve is closing and the no. 6 intake valve is opening.
2. Insert a ¼ inch spacer between the rocker arm pad and the stem tip of the no. 1 intake valve. Allow the spring load to bleed the tappet down, giving, in effect, a solid tappet.
3. Install a dial indicator so that the plunger contacts the valve spring retainer as nearly perpendicular as possible. Zero the indicator.
4. Rotate the crankshaft clockwise (normal running direction) until the valve has lifted 0.010 inch for 318 cu. in. engines.

NOTE: Do not turn the crankshaft any further clockwise as the valve spring might bottom and result in damage.

5. The timing of the crankshaft pulley should now read from 10 degrees BTDC to 2 degrees ATDC. Remove the spacer.

NOTE: If the reading is not within the specified limits, check the sprocket index marks, inspect the timing chain for wear, and check the accuracy of the "DC" mark on the timing indicator.

Camshaft

Removal and Installation

4 CYLINDER (2.2L) ENGINE

1. Remove the valve cover.
2. Remove the timing belt covers, loosen the tensioner and remove the timing belt.
3. Remove the camshaft sprocket and use special tool C-4679 or equivalent to remove the camshaft seal.
4. Mark the rocker arms for re-installation in the same position.
5. Loosen the bearing caps a little at a time on each cap, but do not remove the nuts.
6. Use a soft mallet to break the camshaft free.
7. Remove the nuts evenly a little at a time from each cap.

NOTE: Cocking the camshaft during removal or installation could cause damage to the cam or bearing thrust surfaces.

8. Check the bearing cap oil holes for blockage.
9. Align the bearing caps in sequence with no. 1 at the timing belt end and no. 5 at the transmission end of the head. The arrows on the caps no. 1, 2, 3 and 4 must point in the direction of the timing belt.
10. Apply anaerobic form-in-place gasket to no. 1 and no. 5 bearing caps. Install the bearing caps before installing the camshaft seals.
11. Install the camshaft seal using tool C-4680 or equivalent. Install the timing belt and cover.
12. Install the related front of engine components. Install the valve cover using a new gasket.

4 CYLINDER (2.6L) ENGINE

1. Remove the breather hoses and purge hose.
2. Remove the air cleaner and fuel line.
3. Remove the fuel pump. Remove the distributor.
4. Disconnect the spark plug cables.
5. Remove the rocker cover.
6. Remove the breather and semi-circular seal.
7. After slightly loosening the camshaft sprocket bolt, turn the crankshaft until No. 1 piston is at Top Dead Center on compression stroke (both valves closed).
8. Remove the camshaft sprocket bolt and distributor drive gear.
9. Remove the camshaft sprocket with chain and allow it to rest on the camshaft sprocket holder.
10. Remove the camshaft bearing cup tightening bolts. Do

not remove the front and rear bearing cap bolts together, but keep them inserted in the bearing caps so that the rocker assembly can be removed as a unit.

11. Remove the rocker arms, rocker shafts and bearing caps as an assembly.

12. Remove the camshaft.

13. Installation is the reverse of removal. Lubricate the camshaft lobes and bearings and fit camshaft into head. Install the assembled rocker arm shaft assembly.

Removal and Installation

6 CYLINDER ENGINE

1. Remove the cylinder head, timing gear cover, camshaft sprocket, and timing chain.
2. Remove the valve tappets, keeping them in order to ensure installation in their original locations.
3. Remove the crankshaft sprocket.
4. Remove the distributor and oil pump.
5. Remove the fuel pump.
6. Install a long bolt into the front of the camshaft to facilitate its removal.
7. Remove the camshaft, being careful not to damage the cam bearings with the cam lobes.
8. Prior to installation, lubricate the camshaft lobes and bearing journals. It is recommended that 1 pt. of crankcase conditioner be added to the initial crankcase oil fill.
9. Install the camshaft in the engine block. From this point, reverse the removal procedure.

Removal and Installation

V8 ENGINES

1. Remove the intake manifold, cylinder head covers, rocker arm assemblies, push rods, and valve tappets, keeping them in order to insure the installation in their original locations.
2. Remove the timing gear cover, the camshaft and crankshaft sprockets, and the timing chain.
3. Remove the distributor and lift out the oil pump and distributor driveshaft.
4. Remove the camshaft thrust plate.
5. Install a long bolt into the front of the camshaft and remove the camshaft, being careful not to damage the cam bearings with the cam lobes.
6. Prior to installation, lubricate the camshaft lobes and bearing journals. It is recommended that 1 pt. of Crankcase Conditioner be added to the initial crankcase oil fill. Insert the camshaft into the engine block within 2 in. of its final position in the block.
7. Have an assistant support the camshaft with a suitable tool to prevent the camshaft from contacting the plug in the rear of the engine block. Position the suitable tool against the rear side of the cam gear and be careful not to damage the cam lobes.
8. Replace the camshaft thrust plate. If camshaft end play exceeds 0.010 in., install a new thrust plate. It should be 0.002-0.006 in. with the new plate.
9. Install the timing chain and sprockets, timing gear cover, and pulley.
10. Install the tappets, pushrods, rocker arms, and cylinder head covers. Install fuel pump, if removed.
11. Install the distributor and oil pump driveshaft. Install the distributor.
12. After starting the engine, adjust the ignition timing.

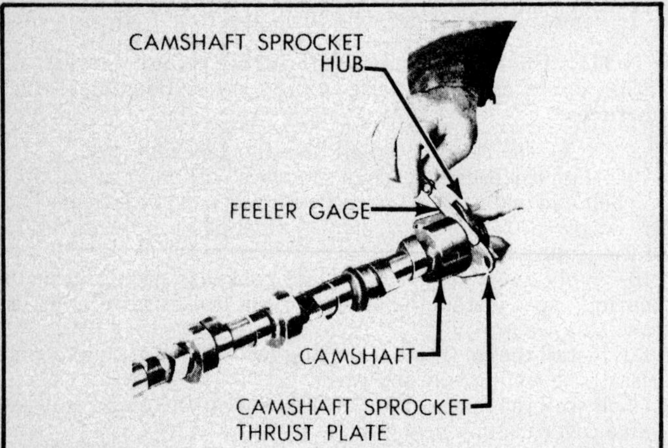

Measuring camshaft end play (© Chrysler Corp.)

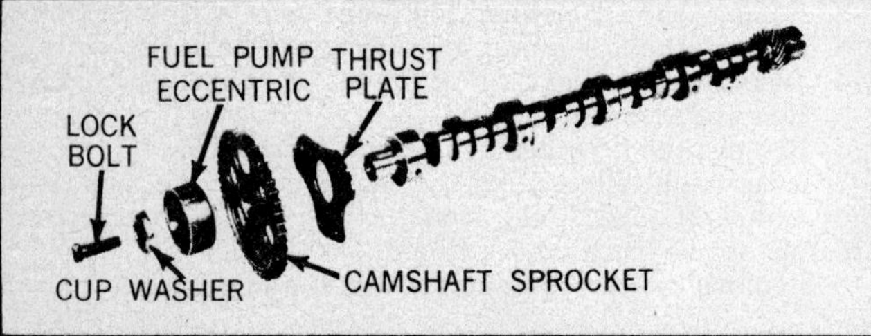

Typical V8 camshaft and sprocket assembly—318/360 shown (© Chrysler Corp.)

Pistons and Connecting Rods

4 CYLINDER ENGINES

The piston crown is marked with an arrow which must point toward the drive belt end of the engine when installed. The connecting rod and cap are marked with rectangular forge marks which must be mated when assembled and which must be on the intermediate shaft side of the engine when installed.

6 AND 8 CYLINDER ENGINES

The notch on the top of each piston must face the front of the engine. To position the connecting rod correctly, the oil squirt hole should point to the right-side on all six-cylinder engines. On all V8 engines, the larger chamfer of the lower connecting rod bore must face to the rear on the right bank and to the front on the left bank.

Main Bearings

Detailed procedures for fitting main and rod bearings can be found in the Engine Rebuilding Section.

4 CYLINDER ENGINE

The bearing caps should be numbered no. 1 through no. 5 for correct installation. The no. 1 bearing cap should be on the drive belt end of the engine and the no. 5 cap on the transmission end of the engine. Install the no. 1, 2, 4 and 5 bearing shells with the lubrication groove in the crankcase. The new main bearing maximum clearance is 0.003 inch. The new thrust bearing maximum end play is 0.007 inch.

6 CYLINDER ENGINE

The maximum allowable bearing clearance is 0.001". No. 1, no. 2 and no. 4 lower inserts are interchangeable. No. 2 and No. 4 upper inserts are interchangeable. No. 1 upper insert has a chamfer on the tab side for timing chain oiling and is identified by the red mark on the edge of the insert. No. 3 upper and lower inserts are flanged. Bearing caps are not interchangeable and are numbered for correct installation. Maximum end play is 0.0085". Replace no. 3 (thrust) bearing if end play exceeds that amount.

V8 ENGINE

A Maltese cross stamped on the engine (except on the 318 and 360) numbering pad indicates that the engine is equipped with a crankshaft which has one or more connecting rods and/or main bearing journal finished 0.001" undersize. The position of the undersize journal(s) is stamped on a machine surface of the no. 3 counterweight. The letter "R" or "M" signifies whether the undersize journal is a rod or main, and the number following the letter indicates which one it is. A Maltese cross with an "X" indicates that all those journals are 0.010" undersize. On the 318 and 360 engines, 0.001 in. undersize journals are indicated by marks on the no. 8 crankshaft counterweight. If the "R" or "M" is followed by "X", all those journals are 0.010 in. undersize.

Upper and lower bearing inserts are not interchangeable on any of the V8 engines due to oil hole and V-groove in the uppers. On the 318 and 360 cu. in. engine lower bearing halves no. 1, no. 2 and no. 4 are interchangeable; no. 1, no. 2 and no. 4 upper bearing halves are interchangeable. No. 3 bearing is the thrust bearing and no. 5 is the wider rear main bearing.

Remove main bearing caps one at a time and check clearance. Check number of cap for proper location.

On the 318 and 360 cu. in. engine, the rear main bearing lower seal is held in place by the rear main bearing cap. Note that the oil pump is mounted on this cap and that there is a hollow dowel which must be in place when the cap is installed.

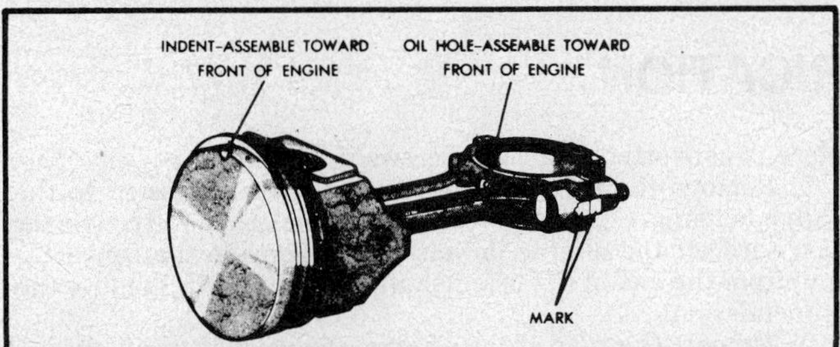

135 (2.2L) engine piston installation (© Chrysler Corp.)

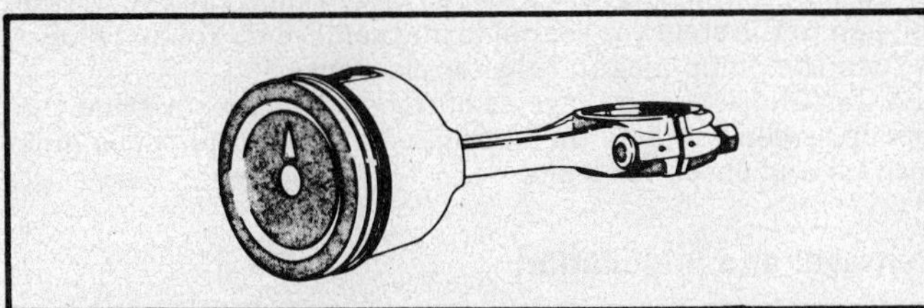

155.9 (2.6L) engine piston installation (mark faces front) (© Chrysler Corp.)

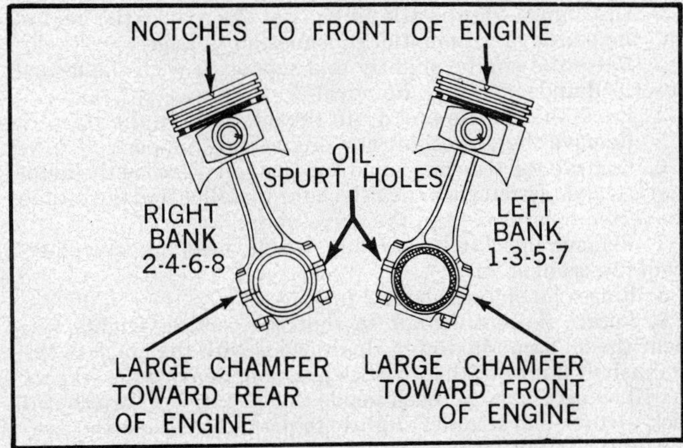

Relation of piston to rod—V8 engines (© Chrysler Corp.)

Crankshaft Main Bearing

Removal and Installation

ALL MODELS

1. Drain the engine oil and remove the oil pan.
2. Mark the bearing caps before removing them.
3. Remove the bearing caps one at a time. Remove the upper half of the bearing by inserting a suitable tool into the oil hole of the crankshaft.
4. Slowly rotate the crankshaft clockwise forcing out the up-

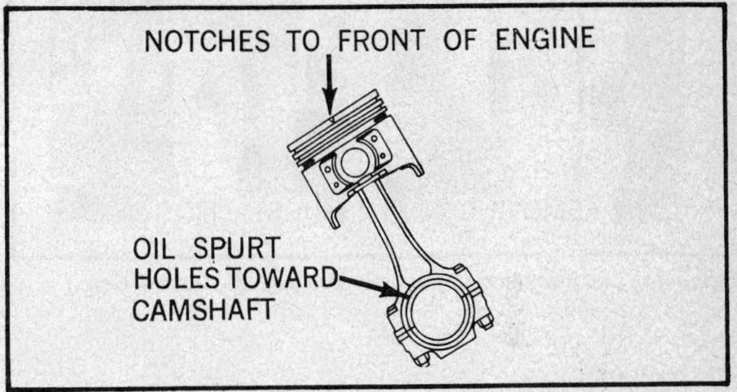

Relation of piston to rod—6 cylinder engines (© Chrysler Corp.)

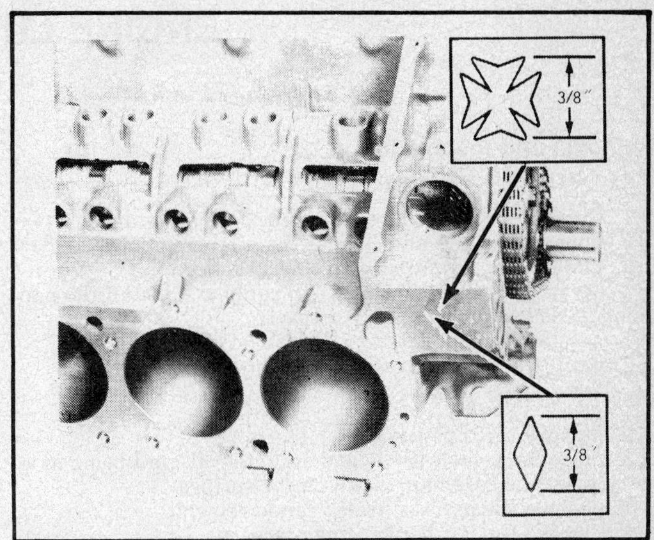

The engine number pad shows marks which indicate undersize crankshaft journals—except 318 and 360 engines (© Chrysler Corp.)

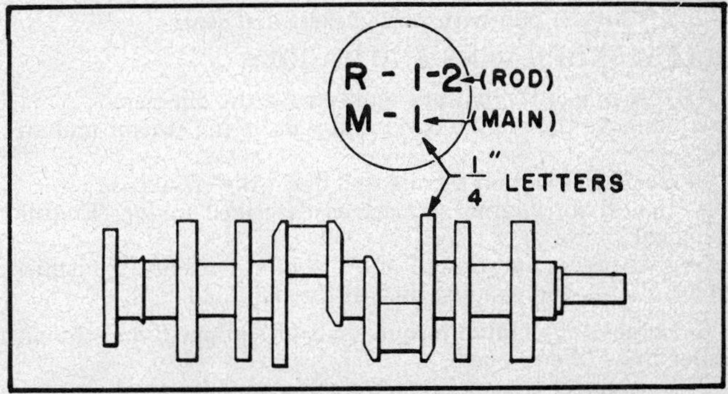

Location of undersize markings on counterweight; 318 and 360 engines are marked on the no. 8 counterweight (© Chrysler Corp.)

Removing and installing upper main bearings (© Chrysler Corp.)

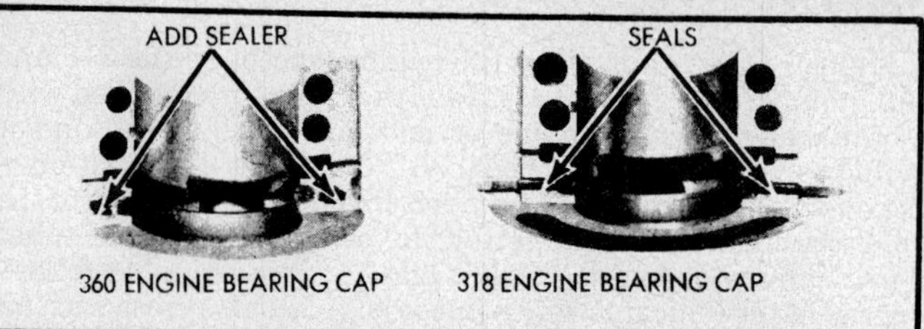

Typical rear main bearing caps (© Chrysler Corp.)

per half of the bearing shell.

NOTE: Only one main bearing should be selectively fitted while all other main bearing caps are properly torqued. When installing a new upper bearing shell, slightly chamfer the sharp edges from the plain side.

5. To install, start the bearing in place, and insert a suitable tool into the oil hole of the crankshaft. Slowly rotate the crankshaft counter-clockwise sliding the bearing into position. Remove the tool.
6. Continue the installation in the reverse order of the removal.
7. Fill the engine with the proper grade engine oil. Start the engine and check for leaks.

ENGINE LUBRICATION

Oil Pan

Removal and Installation

4 CYLINDER ENGINES

1. Raise and safely support the truck on jack stands.
2. Support the pan and remove the attaching bolts.
3. Lower the pan and discard the gaskets.
4. Clean all gasket surfaces thoroughly and install the pan using gasket sealer and a new gasket.
5. Torque the pan bolts to 7 ft. lbs.
6. Refill the pan, start the engine, and check for leaks.

CONVENTIONAL TRUCKS

1. Remove the dipstick.
2. Raise the vehicle safely and drain the oil. On I-beam axle models, let the axle hang down on the springs.
3. Remove the optional frame reinforcement.
4. Remove the left bellhousing brace.
5. Unbolt the pan and lower it.
6. On installation, make sure that the six cylinder oil pickup screen contacts the bottom of the pan and that it is $1\frac{1}{8}$ in. from the inside edge of the block.
7. Install the pan with new gaskets and seals.

SIX CYLINDER VANS AND WAGONS

1. Disconnect the battery and remove the dipstick.
2. Remove the engine cover and remove the starter and air cleaner.
3. Raise the van on a hoist and drain the crankcase oil.
4. Install an engine support as described under "Engine Removal."
5. Disconnect and tie out of the way: driveshaft, transmission linkage, and exhaust pipe at the manifold.
6. Remove the clutch torque shaft (if equipped) and the oil cooler lines (if equipped).
7. Disconnect the speedometer cable and electrical connections to the transmission.
8. Remove the support bracket, inspection plate, and drive plate-to-converter attaching screws if equipped.
9. Remove the bolts which attach the transmission to the clutch housing. Carefully work the transmission and converter rearward off the engine dowels and disengage the converter hub from the end of the crankshaft if so equipped. Remove the transmission.
10. Support the rear of the engine and raise it two inches.
11. Remove the oil pan attaching bolts. Positioning the crankshaft so that the counterweights will clear the pan, rotate the pan to the steering gear side and remove it. You may have to turn the pump pickup tube for clearance.
12. Installation is the reverse of removal. Make sure that the pickup screen contacts the bottom of the pan. Fill the engine with oil and check for leaks.

Removal and Installation

V8 VANS AND WAGONS

1. Disconnect the battery ground cable. Remove the dipstick and tube, engine cover, and air cleaner.
2. Disconnect the throttle linkage at the rear of the engine and the clutch or automatic transmission linkage.
3. Raise the engine slightly and support it with the device described under "Engine Removal".
4. Raise the vehicle and drain the oil. Remove the starter.
5. Remove the driveshaft and engine rear support.
6. Remove the transmission from the van. Remove the automatic transmission with the filler tube installed and the torque converter separated from the drive plate.
7. Remove the clutch assembly and flywheel (or driveplate) from the crankshaft.
8. Raise the engine about 2 in.
9. Rotate the crankshaft so that the counterweights will clear the oil pan. Maximum clearance is with the notch in the crankshaft flange at the 3 o'clock position. Remove the oil pan. It will be necessary to reach inside the oil pan and turn the oil pick-up tube and strainer slightly to the right to clear the pan.
10. Installation is the reverse of removal. Be sure to check all fluid levels and be sure that there are no leaks.

Removal and Installation

TWO-WHEEL DRIVE PICKUPS RAMCHARGER AND TRAIL DUSTER

1. Disconnect the negative battery cable. Remove the oil dipstick.
2. Raise and support the vehicle safely.
3. Drain the oil from the vehicle.
4. Remove the torque converter or clutch housing brace.
5. Remove the exhaust pipe, if necessary, in order to gain working clearance.
6. Remove the oil pan bolts and remove the pan.
7. Installation is the reverse of removal.

FOUR-WHEEL DRIVE PICKUPS RAMCHARGER AND TRAIL DUSTER

1. Raise the vehicle and support safely.
2. Remove the two front engine mounting bolts.
3. Remove the left-side support, connecting the converter housing and cylinder block.
4. Raise the engine approximately 2 in.
5. Drain oil.
6. Remove the oil pan bolts, lower pan down and to the rear. (Do not turn oil pickup out of position).

Oil Pump

Removal and Installation

4 CYLINDER (1.7L) ENGINES

1. Disconnect the negative battery cable.
2. Raise and support the vehicle safely. Drain the engine oil and remove the oil pan and gasket.
3. Remove the hex head retaining bolts from the oil pump assembly.
4. Pull the pump assembly down from the engine.
5. Installation is the reverse of the removal procedure. Pump indexing is not required.

4 CYLINDER (2.2L) ENGINES

1. Disconnect the negative battery cable.
2. Drain the engine oil and remove the oil pan and gasket.
3. Remove two mounting bolts and pull the oil pump assembly from the engine block.
4. Install the pump with the shaft in bore until the pump mounting face contacts the engine block. Rotate the pump body if necessary to engage the drive gear shaft to the distributor shaft.

NOTE: Pump indexing is not required.

5. Install the two pump bolts and tighten the shorter bolt to 7 ft. lbs. and the longer to 14 ft. lbs.
6. Install the oil pan, using a new gasket and fill the crankcase with the proper grade and quantity of oil.
7. Run the engine and check for oil leaks.

OIL PUMP CLEARANCE CHECKING

1.7L ENGINE

1. Check the oil pump end play with a straight edge across gear end face and a feeler gauge between the straight edge and the gears. The minimum end play is 0.001 inch and the maximum is 0.006 inch.
2. Check the drive to driven gear backlash, with a feeler gauge inserted between the gears. If the backlash is not within 0.002 inch–0.008 inch, then replace the gears.

4 CYLINDER 2.2L ENGINES

1. Check the end play with a straight edge and feeler gauge.

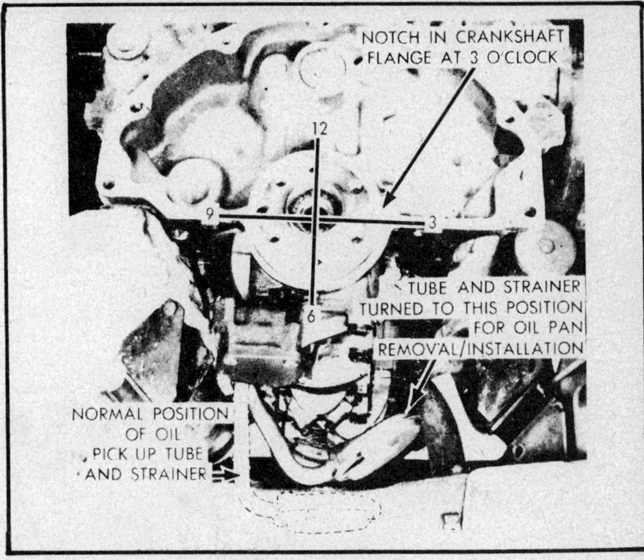

The crankshaft and oil pick up tube positioned for oil pan removal and installation (© Chrysler Corp.)

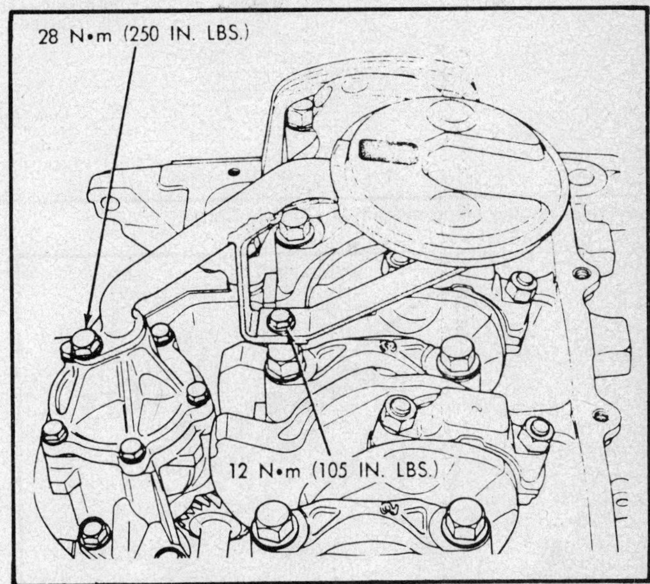

Rampage 2.2L oil pick up (© Chrysler Corp.)

Check end-play to a minimum of 0.001 inch and a maximum of 0.006 inch.

2. Check the outer pump rotor for a maximum thickness of 0.825 inch and a minimum outer diameter of 2.469 inch.
3. Check between the inner and outer rotors, with a feeler gauge for a maximum of 0.01 inch of clearance.
4. Check between the outer rotor and pump body, with a feeler gauge for a maximum clearance of 0.014 inch.

Removal and Installation

6-CYLINDER ENGINES

The rotor type oil pump is externally mounted on the rear right-hand (camshaft) side of the engine and is gear driven (helical) from the camshaft. The oil filter screws into the pump body.

1. Remove oil pump mounting bolts and remove pump and filter assembly from engine.
2. Disassemble the oil pump (drive gear must be pressed off)

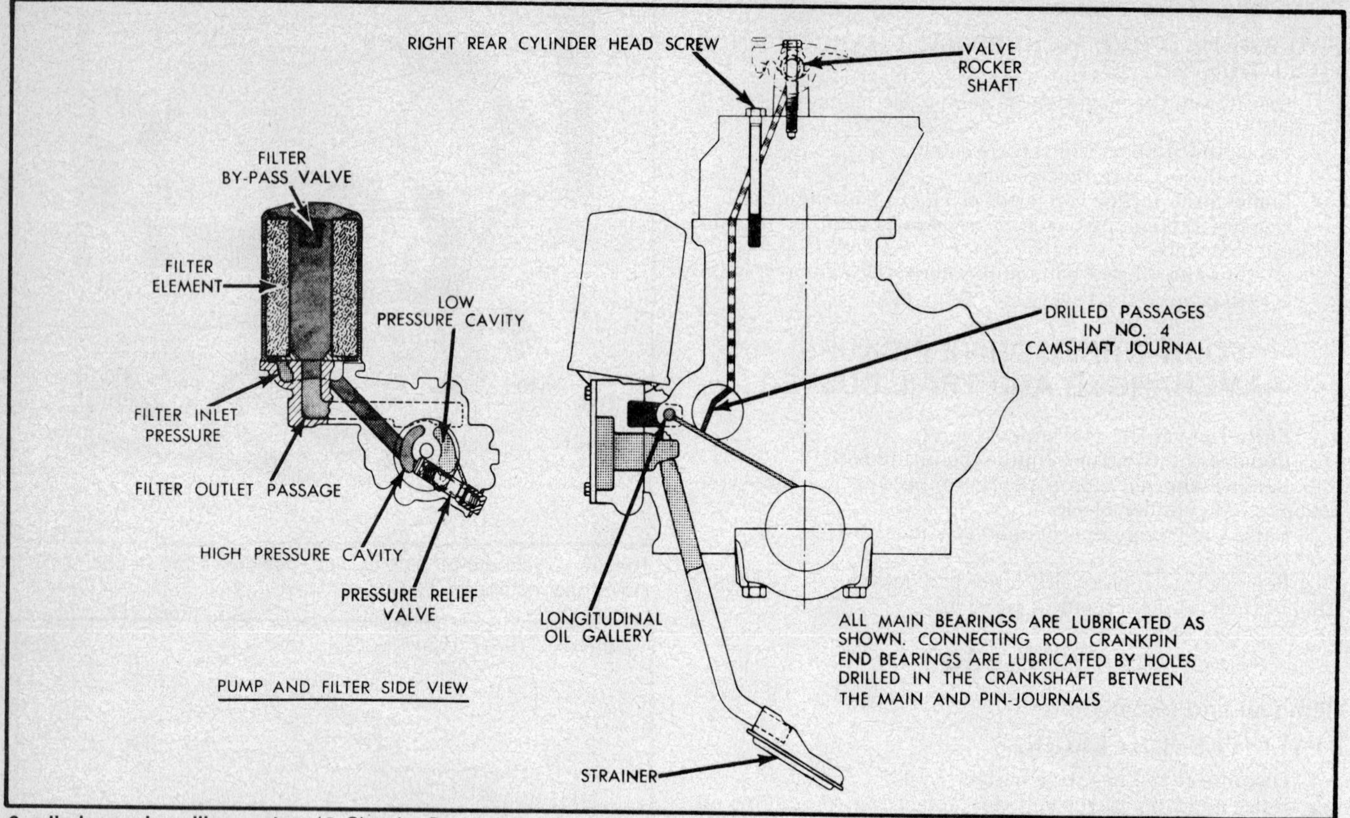

RIGHT REAR CYLINDER HEAD SCREW
VALVE ROCKER SHAFT
FILTER BY-PASS VALVE
FILTER ELEMENT
LOW PRESSURE CAVITY
DRILLED PASSAGES IN NO. 4 CAMSHAFT JOURNAL
FILTER INLET PRESSURE
FILTER OUTLET PASSAGE
HIGH PRESSURE CAVITY
PRESSURE RELIEF VALVE
LONGITUDINAL OIL GALLERY
ALL MAIN BEARINGS ARE LUBRICATED AS SHOWN. CONNECTING ROD CRANKPIN END BEARINGS ARE LUBRICATED BY HOLES DRILLED IN THE CRANKSHAFT BETWEEN THE MAIN AND PIN-JOURNALS
PUMP AND FILTER SIDE VIEW
STRAINER

6 cylinder engine oiling system (© Chrysler Corp.)

STAND-PIPE
BODY
GASKET
DRIVE GEAR
INNER ROTOR AND SHAFT
OUTER ROTOR
SEAL RING
COVER
VALVE
SPRING
SCREW AND LOCKWASHER
PLUG
GASKET
SCREW AND LOCKWASHER

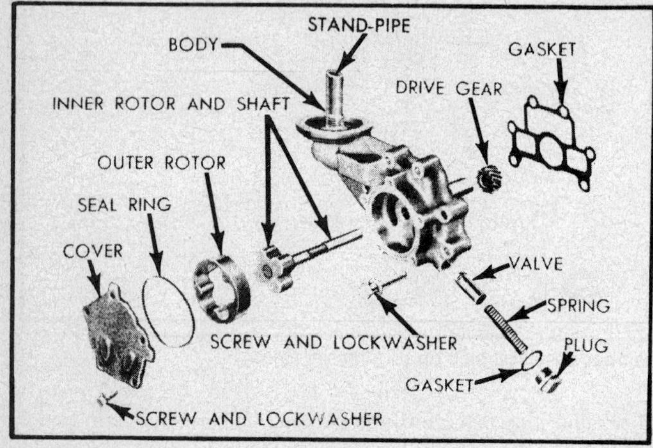

6 cylinder oil pump (© Chrysler Corp.)

and inspect the following clearances: maximum cover wear is 0.0015"; outer rotor to body maximum clearance is 0.014"; maximum clearance between rotors is 0.010". Inspect the pressure relief valve for scoring and free operation. Relief valve spring should have a free length of $2^1/_4$ in.

3. Install new oil seal rings between cover and body, tightening cover attaching bolts to 95 inch lbs.

4. Install oil pump to engine block using a new gasket and tightening mounting bolts to 200 inch lbs.

Removal and Installation

318 AND 360 CU. IN. ENGINES

NOTE: It is necessary to remove the oil pan, and to remove the oil pump from the rear main bearing cap to service the oil pump.

1. Drain the engine oil and remove the oil pan.
2. Remove the oil pump mounting bolts and remove the oil pump from the rear main bearing cap.
3. To remove the relief valve, drill a $^1/_8$ inch hole into the relief valve retainer cap and insert a self-threading sheet metal screw into the cap. Clamp the screw into a vise and while supporting the oil pump, remove the cap by tapping the pump body using a soft hammer. Discard the retainer cap and remove the spring and the relief valve.
4. Remove the oil pump cover and lockwashers, and lift off the cover. Discard the oil ring seal. Remove the pump rotor and shaft, and lift out the outer rotor.

NOTE: Wash all parts in solvent and inspect for damage or wear. The mating surfaces of the oil pump cover should be smooth. Replace the pump assembly if this is not the case.

5. Lay a straight edge across the pump cover surface and if a 0.0015 inch feeler gauge can be inserted between the cover and the straight edge, the pump assembly should be replaced. Measure the thickness and the diameter of the outer rotor. If the outer rotor thickness measures 0.825 inch or less (0.943 inch or less on 360 cu. in. engines 1980) or if the diameter is 2.469 inches or less, replace the outer rotor. If the inner rotor measures 0.825 inch or less, (0.943 inch or less on 360 cu. in. engines 1980) then the inner rotor and shaft assembly must be replaced.
6. Slide the outer rotor into the pump body, do this by pressing it to one side with your fingers and measure the clearance between the rotor and the pump body. If the measurement is 0.014 inch or more, replace the oil pump assembly. Install the inner rotor and shaft into the pump body. If the clearance between the inner and outer rotors is 0.010 inch or more, replace the shaft and both rotors.

6 cylinder oil pump pick up screen on conventional trucks must be positioned 1⅛ inch from the inside edge of the block (© Chrysler Corp.)

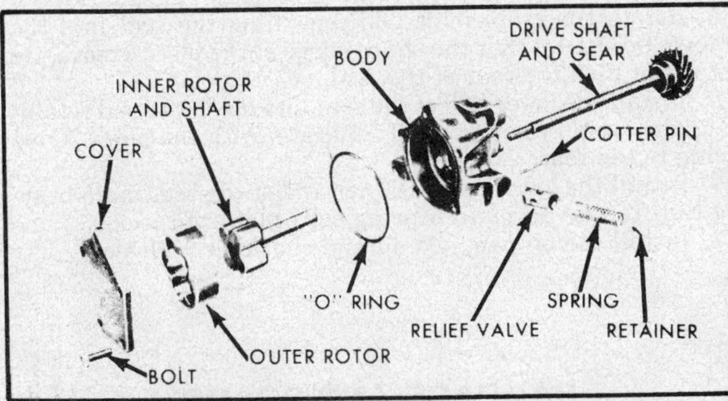

318 and 360 V8 oil pump (© Chrysler Corp.)

7. Place a straight edge across the face of the pump, between the bolt holes. If a feeler gauge of 0.004 inch or more can be inserted between the rotors and the straight edge, replace the pump assembly.

8. Inspect the oil pressure relief valve plunger for scoring and free operation in its bore. Small marks may be removed with 400-grit wet or dry sandpaper.

9. The relief valve spring has a free length of 2–2⅞ inch. Replace the spring if it fails to meet this specification.

10. To install, assemble the oil pump, using new parts as required. Tighten the cover bolts to 95 inch lbs.

11. Prime the oil pump before installation by filling the rotor cavity with engine oil. Install the oil pump on the engine and tighten attaching bolts to 30 ft. lbs.

12. Continue the installation in the reverse order of the removal.

13. Fill the engine with the proper grade motor oil. Start the engine and check for leaks.

Rear Main Bearing Oil Seal

Replacement

4 CYLINDER (2.2L) ENGINE

The rear main seal is located in a housing on the rear of the block. To replace the seal it is necessary to remove the engine.

1. Remove the transaxle and flywheel. Before running the transaxle, align the dimple on the flywheel with the pointer on the flywheel housing. The transaxle will not mate with the engine during installation unless this alignment is observed.
2. Very carefully, pry the old seal out of the support ring.

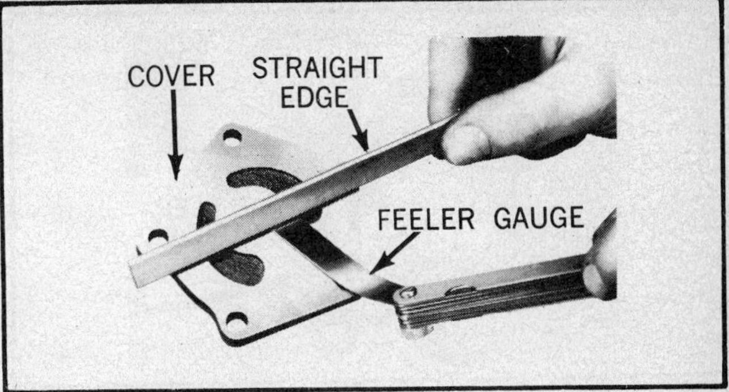

Measuring oil pump cover wear—typical (© Chrysler Corp.)

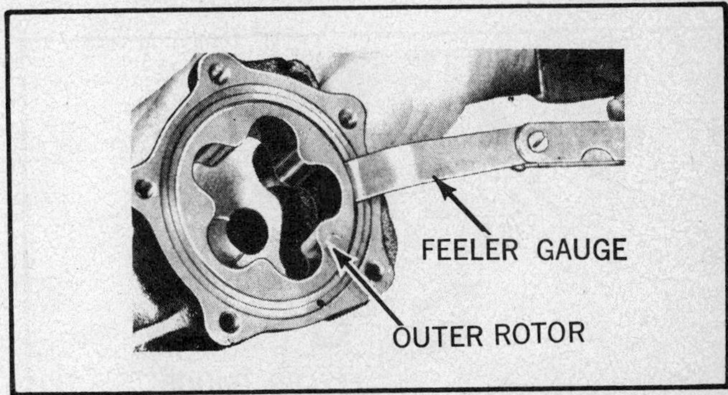

Measuring the outer rotor clearance—typical (© Chrysler Corp.)

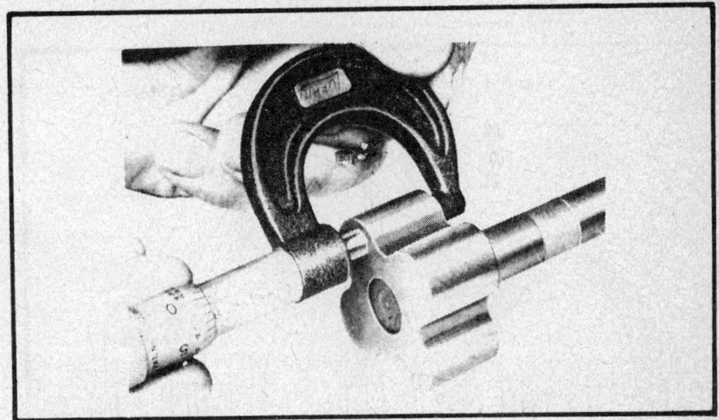

Measuring the inner rotor clearance—typical (© Chrysler Corp.)

3. Coat the new seal with clean engine oil and press it into place with a flat piece of metal. Take great care not to scratch the seal or crankshaft.
4. Install the flywheel and transaxle.

4 CYLINDER (2.6L) ENGINE

The rear main oil seal is located in a housing on the rear of the block. To replace the seal, remove the transaxle, and do the work from underneath the vehicle or remove the engine and do the work on the bench.

1. Remove the housing from the block.
2. Remove the separator from the housing.
3. Pry out the old seal.
4. Lightly oil the replacement seal. The oil seal should be installed so that the seal plate fits into the inner contact surface of the seal case. Install the separator with the oil holes facing down.

6 CYLINDER AND V8 ENGINES

Service replacement seals are of the split rubber type composition. This type of seal makes it possible to replace the upper

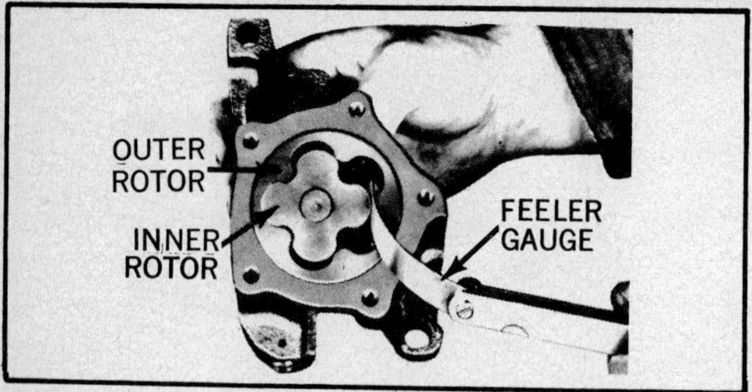

Measuring the clearance between the rotors—typical (© Chrysler Corp.)

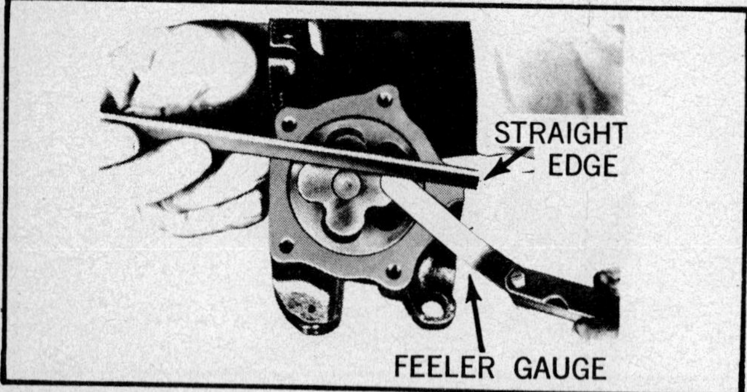

Measuring the clearance over the rotors—typical (© Chrysler Corp.)

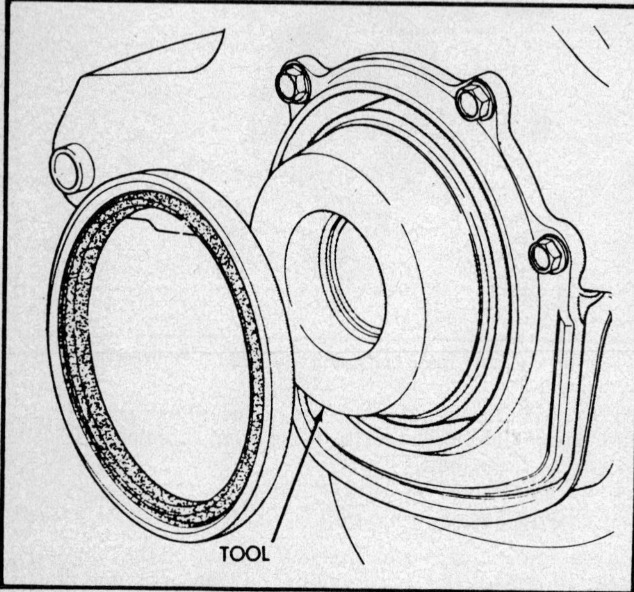

Rampage 2.2L rear oil seal installation (© Chrysler Corp.)

rear seal without removing the crankshaft. The seal must be used as an upper and lower set and cannot be used with the rope type seal.

NOTE: Rope type seals are included in overhaul gasket sets, for use when the crankshaft has been removed, on all engines, except the 360 V8, which uses only the composition seal.

The following procedure is for removing the rope type rear main seal and replacing it with the rubber type seal.

1. Remove the oil pan, and both the rear seal retainer and the rear main bearing cap, if separate.
2. Remove the lower rope seal from the cap or retainer by prying the seal out of the groove.
3. With the use of suitable tools, either pull or push the seal from its seal, while rotating the crankshaft, being careful not to damage the surface of the journal. If necessary, loosen all the main bearing caps slightly, to lower the crankshaft, which will aid in the removal and replacement of the seal.
4. Clean and lubricate the crankshaft journal. Hold the seal tight against the crankshaft with the painted stripe to the rear, and install the seal into the block groove.
5. Rotate the crankshaft while pushing the seal into the groove. Be careful that the sharp edges of the block groove. Do not cut or nick the rear of the seal.
6. Install the lower half of the seal into the lower seal retainer or the main bearing cap, if separate, with the paint stripe facing to the rear.
7. Install the lower seal retainer and/or the rear main bearing cap. Torque all main bearing caps to specifications.
8. Install the oil pan, add oil and check for oil leaks.

RAMPAGE AND SCAMP

Replacement (Front Wheel Drive)

The transaxle must be removed from Rampage applications before the rear bearing main oil seal can be removed.

4 CYLINDER (2.7L) ENGINE

1. Pry out the rear main bearing oil seal with a suitable prying tool.

CAUTION

Do not nick or damage the crankshaft flange seal surface.

2. Place special tool C-4681 or equivalent on the crankshaft.
3. Lightly coat the outer diameter of the new seal with Loctite® stud and bearing mount or equivalent.
4. Place the seal over the special tool and tap it into place, using a plastic hammer.

4 CYLINDER (2.6L) ENGINE

Refer to timing chain cover, silent shaft procedures for oil pump removal.

FRONT SUSPENSION

WHEEL BEARINGS

Adjustment

D100, D200, AND D300

1. While rotating the wheel, tighten the adjusting nut to 360-480 inch pounds.
2. With the wheel at rest, back off the adjusting nut to completely release the bearing preload.
3. Finger tighten the adjusting nut, and install the lock nut and the cotter key.

NOTE: End-play of 0.0001-0.003 inch is acceptable. If this measurement is obtained, then the wheel bearing adjustment is satisfactory.

Front Drive Axle (4WD)

Removal and Installation

1. Raise the truck and install stands under the frame rails, behind the front springs.
2. Disconnect front driveshaft at drive pinion yoke.
3. Disconnect steering linkage at drag link.
4. Disconnect front shock absorbers and brake line at frame. Disconnect the sway bar link assembly from the spring clip plate.
5. Remove nuts from the spring hold down bolts and remove axle assembly from under vehicle.
6. To install, place axle assembly under vehicle and line up spring center bolts with locating hole in axle housing pad.
7. Install spring clips or spring U-bolts, new lock washer and nuts.
8. Connect the shock absorbers, and the brake line at the frame.
9. Connect the steering linkage to the drag link, and the driveshaft to the pinion yoke. Check lubricants and bleed the brakes.
10. Lower the vehicle and test the operation.

Front Drive Axle Shaft and Joint Assembly

MODEL 44FBJ (W/O LOCKING HUBS)

Removal

1. Remove wheel cover. Remove cotter key and loosen outer axle shaft nut.
2. Raise vehicle and support safely. Remove wheel and tire assembly.
3. Remove caliper retainer and anti-rattle spring assemblies. Remove caliper from disc by sliding out and away from disc. Hang caliper out of the way. Remove inboard shoe.

NOTE: Do not allow caliper to hang or be supported by hydraulic brake hose. Support the brake caliper using wire or other suitable device.

4. Remove outer axle shaft nut and washer.
5. Through hole in rotor assembly remove retainer bolts. Position Puller Tool over wheel studs and install wheel nuts. Tighten main screw of tool to remove hub, rotor, bearings, retainer and outer seal as an assembly.
6. Remove wheel nuts and Puller from hub and rotor assembly.
7. Remove the brake caliper adapter from the knuckle.
8. Position a pry bar behind the inner axle shaft yoke and push the bearings out of the knuckle.

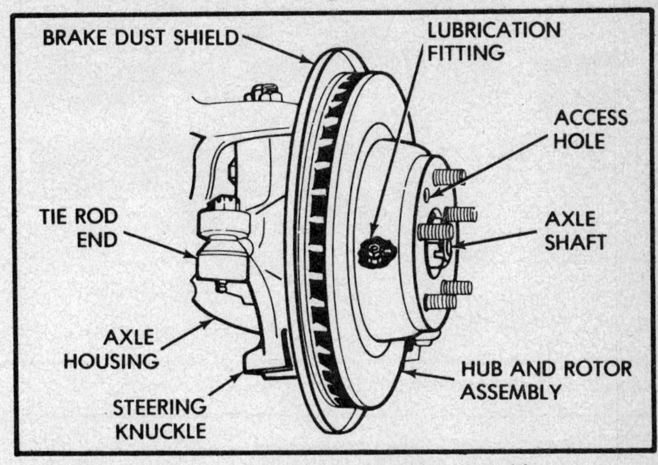

Location of various components on the joint assembly (© Chrysler Corp.)

Removing hub and rotor assembly (© Chrysler Corp.)

9. Remove the "O" ring from the knuckle (if so equipped) and discard.
10. Carefully remove the axle shaft assembly. Remove seal and slinger from shaft.

Installation

1. Inspect the outer axle shaft seal surface for grooving. If the surface is grooved, repair or replace knuckle.
2. Install brake dust shield (if removed), tighten mounting bolts to 160 inch lbs. (18 Nm).
3. Apply RTV sealer to the seal surface of the axle shaft.
4. Using Driver Tool, install the seal slinger onto the outer axle shaft.
5. Install lip seal on the slinger with the lip toward the axle shaft spline.
6. Carefully insert axle shaft into the housing so as not to damage the differential seal at the side gears.
7. Insert a pry bar through the axle shaft "U" joint and wedge it so that the axle shaft is in all the way and cannot be moved out.
8. Using Adaptor Tool and Driver Tool carefully install the seal cup until bottomed in the knuckle.

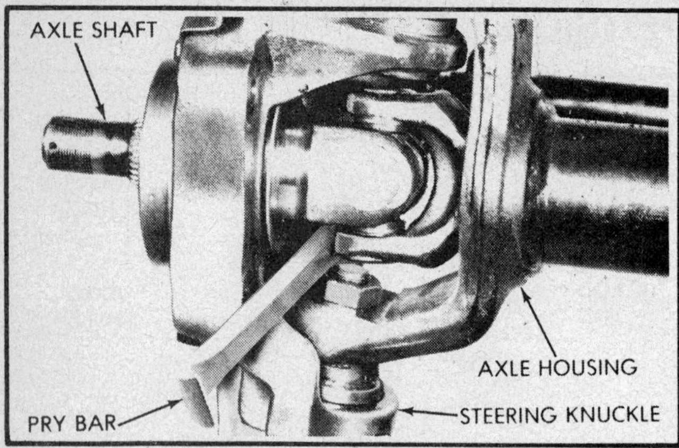

Using pry bar to hold axle (© Chrysler Corp.)

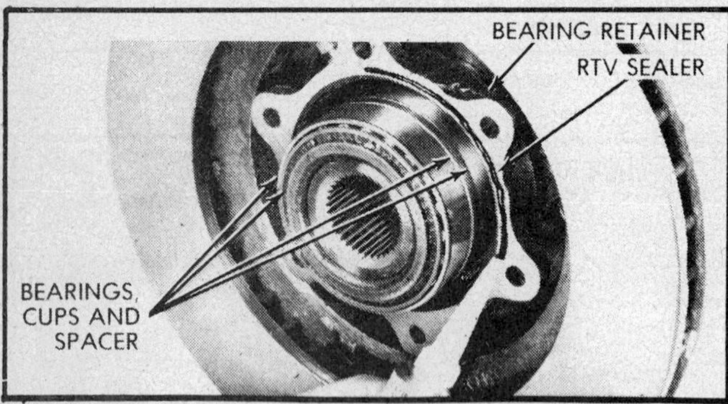

Installing RTV sealer to the bearing retainer face (© Chrysler Corp.)

NOTE: A small amount of wheel bearing grease on the Adaptor face will aid in holding the cup in position. Do not remove the tool at this time.

9. Apply a $\frac{1}{4}$ inch (6mm) bead of RTV sealer to the retainer face on the chamfer (this takes the place of the "O" ring discarded at disassembly).

10. Carefully remove seal installing tool from the knuckle bore so that the outer axle shaft remains centered.

NOTE: If the shaft is disturbed, check to make sure that the lip seal is still riding inside the cup. Correct if necessary.

11. Position the bearing retainer on the knuckle so that the lube fitting is facing directly forward. This is extremely important.

12. Install the hub, rotor, retainer and bearing assembly on the knuckle and tighten retainer plate bolts to 30 ft.lb. (41 Nm) using a criss-cross method to position it evenly.

13. Install brake adapter and tighten mounting bolts to 85 ft.lb. (115 Nm).

14. Remove pry bar from "U" joint and install axle shaft washer and nut. Tighten nut to 100 ft.lb. (136 Nm), continue to tighten nut until next slot in nut aligns with cotter key hole in axle shaft. Install cotter key.

15. Insert a grease gun through the access hole in the hub and rotor assembly into the lube fitting. Fill with Multi-Purpose Grease, until grease flows through the new inner seal (observe at the "U" joint area). Remove lube gun and rotate hub and rotor several times. Reinstall grease gun and apply until grease flows from at least 50% of the seal diameter.

16. Locate inboard brake shoe on adapter with shoe flanges in adapter ways. Slowly slide caliper assembly into position in adapter and over disc. Align caliper on machined ways of adapter.

NOTE: Be careful not to pull the dust boot from its grooves as the piston and boot slide over the inboard shoe.

17. Install anti-rattle springs and retaining clips and torque to 180 in.lb. (20 Nm).

NOTE: The inboard shoe anti-rattle spring must always be installed on top of the retainer spring plate.

18. Install wheel and tire assembly. Tighten nuts to 110 ft.lb. (149 Nm). Install wheel covers, lower vehicle and test operation.

MODEL 44FBJ (WITH LOCKING HUBS)

Removal

1. Remove locking hub assembly.
2. Raise vehicle and support safely. Remove wheel and tire assembly.
3. Remove caliper retainer and anti-rattle spring assemblies. Remove caliper from disc by sliding out and away from disc. Hang caliper out of the way. Remove inboard shoe.

NOTE: Do not allow caliper to hang or be supported by hydraulic brake hose. Support the brake caliper using a length of wire or other suitable device.

4. Remove outer axle shaft lock nut washer and nut.
5. Remove rotor and bearing assembly.
6. Remove six nuts which fasten splash shield and spindle to knuckle.
7. Remove splash shield and spindle.
8. Remove the brake caliper adaptor from the knuckle.
9. Carefully remove the axle shaft assembly. Remove seal and stone shield (if equipped) from shaft.

Installation

1. Install lip seal on the axle shaft stone shield with the lip toward the axle shaft spline.
2. Carefully insert axle shaft into the housing so as not to damage the differential seal at the side gears.
3. Install spindle and brake splash shield. Install 6 new nuts and tighten to 25-30 ft.lb. (34-41 Nm).
4. Install the rotor, outer bearing, nut, washer and locknut onto spindle. Tighten as specified.
5. Install brake adapter and tighten mounting bolts to 85 ft.lb. (115 Nm).
6. Locate inboard brake shoe on adapter with shoe flanges in adapter ways. Slowly slide caliper assembly into position in adapter and over disc. Align caliper on machined ways of adapter.

NOTE: Be careful not to pull the dust boot from its grooves as the piston and boot slide over the inboard shoe.

7. Install anti-rattle springs and retaining clips and torque to 180 ft.lb. (20 Nm). The inboard shoe anti-rattle spring must always be installed on top of the retainer spring plate. Install locking hub assembly.
8. Install wheel and tire assembly. Tighten nuts to 110 ft.lb. (149 Nm). Install wheel covers. Remove jack stands, lower vehicle and test operation.

Removal

1. Block brake pedal in the up position.
2. Raise vehicle and support safely.
3. Remove wheel and tire assembly.
4. Remove allen screw holding caliper to adapter.
5. Tap adapter lock and spring from between caliper and adapter.

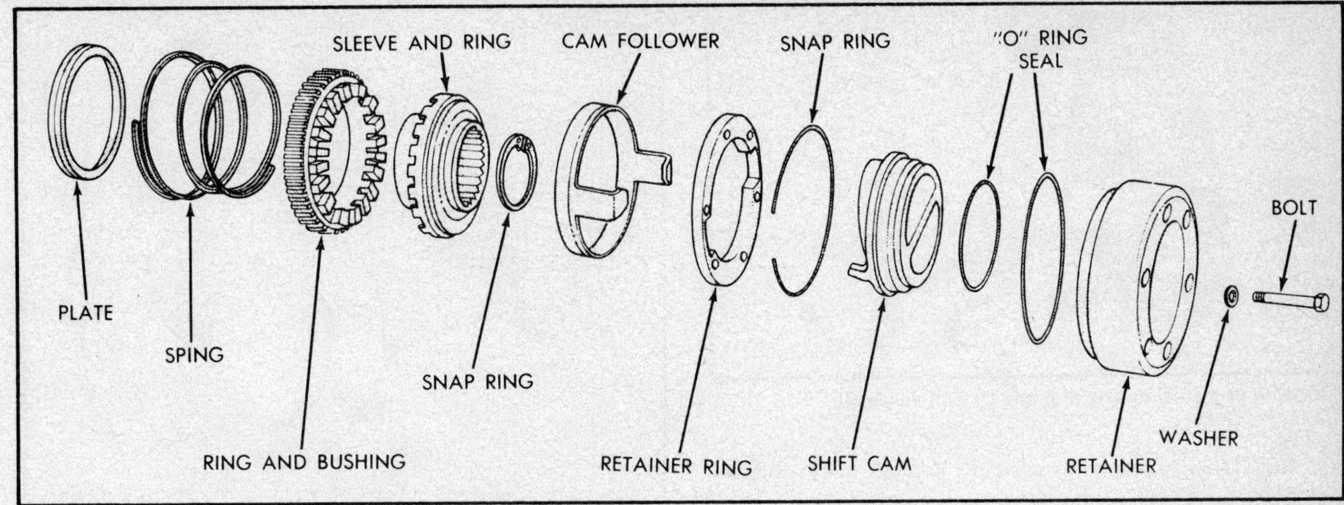

Exploded view of locking hub assembly (© Chrysler Corp.)

6. Carefully separate caliper from adapter. Hang caliper out of the way. Inner brake shoe will remain on adapter.

NOTE: Do not allow caliper to hang or be supported by hydraulic brake hose.

7. Remove hub cap and snap ring.
8. Remove flange nuts and lockwashers. Remove drive flange and discard gasket, or remove locking hub if so equipped.
9. Straighten tang on lock ring and remove outer lock nut, lock ring, inner lock nut and outer bearing. Carefully slide hub and rotor assembly from spindle.
10. Remove inner brake shoe from adapter.
11. Remove nuts and washers holding brake splash shield, brake adapter and spindle to steering knuckle.
12. Remove spindle from knuckle. Slide inner and outer axle shaft complete with bronze spacer, seal and slinger from axle.

Installation

1. Slide axle shaft into position. Position bronze spacer on axle shaft with chamfer facing toward universal joint.
2. Install spindle, brake adapter and brake splash shield. Install washers and nuts and tighten to 50 to 70 ft.lb. (68 to 95 Nm).
3. Position inner brake shoe on adapter.
4. Carefully install hub and rotor assembly onto spindle. Install outer bearing and inner lock nut. Tighten to 50 ft.lb. to seat bearings, back off lock nut and retighten to 30 to 40 ft.lb. (88 Nm) while rotating hub and rotor. Back nut off 135° to 150°. Assemble lock ring and outer lock nut. Tighten lock nut to 65 ft.lb. (88 Nm) minimum. Bend one tang of lock ring over inner lock nut and one tang of lock ring over outer lock nut. Final bearing end play to be 0.001-0.010 inch (0.025-0.254mm).
5. Install new gasket on hub. Install drive flange, lock washers and nuts. Tighten to 30 to 40 ft.lb. (41 to 54 Nm). Install snap ring. Install hub cap, or install locking hub if so equipped.
6. Carefully position caliper onto adapter. Position adapter lock and spring between caliper and adapter and tap into position. Install allen screw and tighten to 12 to 18 ft.lb. (16 to 24 Nm).
7. Install wheel and tire assembly. Tighten nuts to 75 ft.lb. (102 Nm).
8. Remove jack stands, lower vehicle, remove block from brake pedal and test vehicle operation.

Steering Knuckle, Spindle and Ball Joint

MODEL 44FBJ (WITH LOCKING HUBS)

Removal and Disassembly

1. Remove locking hub assembly.

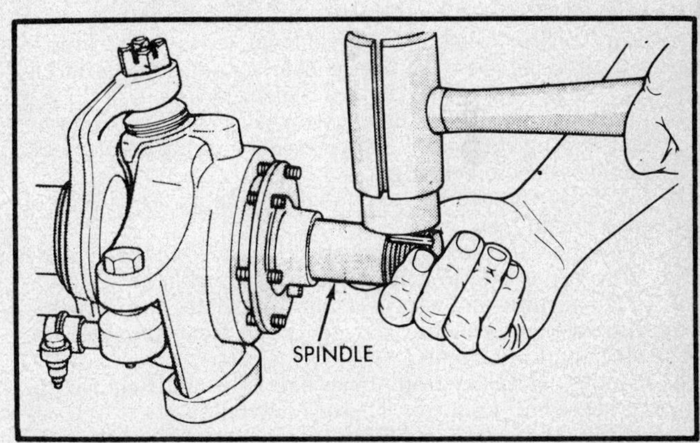

Removing spindle from steering knuckle (© Chrysler Corp.)

Removing or installing spindle and splash shield (© Chrysler Corp.)

Removing or installing axle shft and U–joint assembly
(© Chrysler Corp.)

2. Raise vehicle and support safely. Remove wheel and tire assembly.
3. Remove caliper retainer and anti-rattle spring assemblies. Remove caliper from disc by sliding out and away from disc. Hang caliper out of the way. Remove inboard shoe.

NOTE: Do not allow caliper to hang or be supported by hydraulic brake hose. Support the brake caliper with wire.

4. Remove braking disc.
5. Remove brake caliper adapter from the knuckle.
6. Remove the torque prevailing nuts and washers from the spindle to steering knuckle attaching bolts. Remove the brake splash shield.
7. Using a soft faced hammer, hit spindle lightly to break it free from steering knuckle. Upon removal, examine the bronze spacer located between the needle bearing and shaft joint assembly. If wear is evident, replace the spacer.
8. Place spindle in vise having soft jaws. Do not clamp on bearing carrying surfaces. Remove needle bearing grease seal.
9. Remove needle bearings.
10. Carefully remove the axle shaft assembly. Remove seal and stone shield from shaft.
11. Disconnect tie rod from steering knuckle from the left side only. Disconnect drag link from steering knuckle arm.
12. Remove nuts and cone washers from steering knuckle arm. Tap steering knuckle arm to loosen from knuckle. Remove steering knuckle arm.
13. Remove cotter key from upper ball joint nut. Remove upper and lower ball joint nut. Discard lower nut.
14. Using a brass drift and hammer separate steering knuckle from axle housing yoke. Remove and discard sleeve from upper ball joint joke on axle housing.

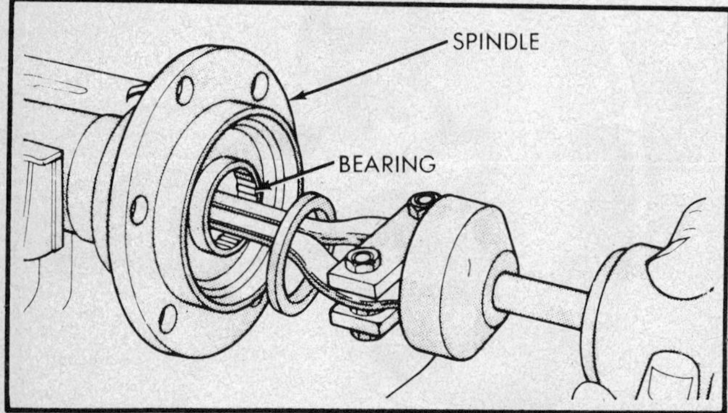

Removing needle bearing from the spindle assembly
(© Chrysler Corp.)

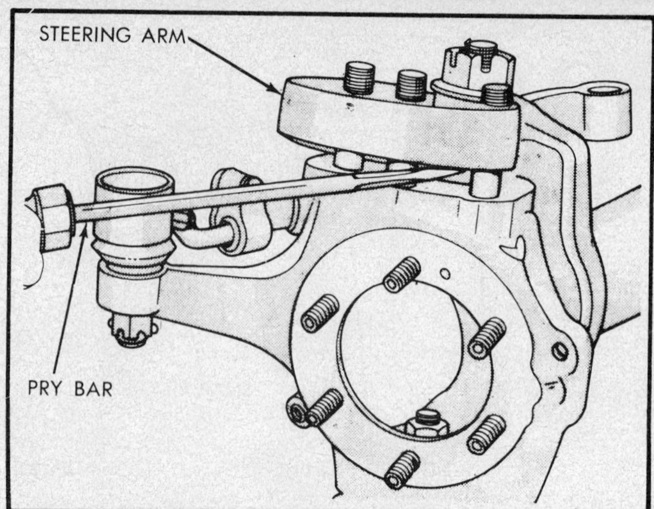

Removing steering knuckle arm (© Chrysler Corp.)

15. Position steering knuckle upside down in a vise and remove snap ring from lower ball joint with snap ring pliers.
16. Press lower ball joint from steering knuckle. Press upper ball joint from steering knuckle. Replace ball joints if any looseness or end play exists.
17. Clean all components with a suitable solvent and blow dry with compressed air. Inspect all parts for burrs, chips, wear or cracks. Replace necessary parts at assembly.

Assembly and Installation

1. Position steering knuckle right side up in a vise. Carefully press lower ball joint into position. Install snap ring.
2. Carefully press upper ball joint into position. Install new boots on both ball joints. Remove steering knuckle from vise.
3. Screw new sleeve into upper ball joint yoke on axle housing leaving about two threads showing at the top.
4. Position steering knuckle on axle housing yoke and install lower ball joint nut. Tighten to 80 ft. lb. (108 Nm).
5. Tighten sleeve in upper ball joint yoke to 40 ft.lb. (54 Nm). Install upper ball joint nut and tighten to 100 ft.lb. (136 Nm). Align cotter key hole in stud with slot in castellated nut, if slot and hole are not aligned continue to tighten nut until aligned. Do not loosen to align. Install cotter key.
6. Position steering knuckle arm over studs on steering knuckle. Install cone washer and nuts. Tighten nuts to 90 ft.lb. (122 Nm). Assemble drag link to steering knuckle arm. Install nut and tighten to 60 ft.lb. (81 Nm). Install cotter key.
7. Assemble tie rod end to steering knuckle. Install nut and tighten to 45 ft. lb. (61 Nm). Install cotter key.
8. Install lip seal on the stone shield with the lip toward the axle shaft spline.
9. Carefully insert axle shaft into the housing so as not to damage the differential seal at the side gears.
10. Assemble new needle bearings into spindle.
11. Install a new grease seal. Fill the seal area of the spindle and thrust face area of shaft and seal with Multi-purpose Grease.
12. Position new bronze spacer on axle shaft, install spindle and brake splash shield.
13. Install new nuts, tighten to 25-35 ft. lbs. (34-41 Nm).
14. Mount braking disc assembly and outer wheel bearing cone onto spindle.
15. Install wheel bearing nuts and locking washer.
16. Install locking hub assembly.
17. Install brake adapter and tighten mounting bolts to 85 ft. lbs. (115 Nm).
18. Locate inboard brake shoe on adapter with shoe flanges in

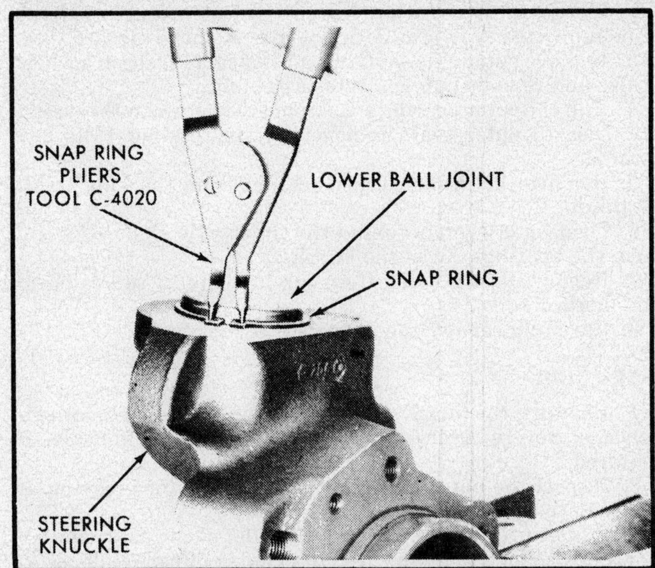

Removing or installing snap ring on the lower ball joint
(© Chrysler Corp.)

adapter ways. Slowly slide caliper assembly into position in adapter and over disc. Align caliper on machined ways of adapter. Be careful not to pull the dust boot from its grooves as the piston and boot slide over the inboard shoe.

19. Install anti-rattle springs and retaining clips and torque to 180 inch lbs. (20 Nm): The inboard shoe anti-rattle spring must always be installed on top of the retainer spring plate.

20. Install wheel and tire assembly. Tighten nuts to 110 ft. lbs. (149 Nm). Install wheel covers. Remove jack stands, lower vehicle and test operation.

Steering Knuckle

MODEL 60

Removal

1. Block brake pedal in the up position.
2. Raise vehicle and support safely. Install jack stands.
3. Remove wheel and tire assembly.
4. Remove allen screw holding caliper to adapter.
5. Tap adapter lock and spring from between caliper and adapter.
6. Carefully separate caliper from adapter. Hang caliper out of the way. Inner brake shoe will remain on adapter.

NOTE: Do not allow caliper to hang or be supported by hydraulic brake hose.

7. Remove hub cap. Remove snap ring.
8. Remove flange nuts and lock washers. Remove drive flange and discard gasket, or remove locking hub if so equipped.
9. Straighten tang on lock ring and remove outer lock nut, lock ring, inner lock nut and outer bearing. Carefully slide hub and rotor assembly from spindle.
10. Remove inner brake shoe from adaptor.
11. Remove nuts and washers holding brake splash shield, brake adapter and spindle to steering knuckle.
12. Remove spindle from knuckle. Slide inner and outer axle shaft complete with bronze spacer, seal and slinger from axle.
13. Remove cotter key and nut from tie rod. Disconnect tie rod from steering knuckle. Remove cotter key and nut from drag link. Disconnect drag link from steering knuckle arm.
14. Remove nuts and upper knuckle cap (left side steering knuckle arm). Discard gasket. Remove spring and upper socket sleeve.
15. Remove capscrews from lower knuckle cap. Work cap free from knuckle and housing.
16. To remove knuckle from housing, swing out at the bottom, then lift up and off upper socket pin.
17. Loosen and remove upper socket pin. Remove seal.
18. Press lower ball socket assembly from axle housing.
19. Clean all components with a suitable solvent and blow dry with compressed air. Inspect all parts for burrs, chips, wear, flat spots or cracks. Replace necessary parts at assembly.

Installation

1. Lubricate lower ball socket assembly with Multi-Mileage Lubricant.
2. Press seal and lower bearing cup into axle housing. Press lower bearing and seal into axle housing.
3. Install upper socket pin and tighten to 500 to 600 ft. lbs. (668 to 813 Nm). Install seal over socket pin.
4. Position steering knuckle over socket pin. Fill lower socket cavity with lubricant. Work lower knuckle cap into place on knuckle and housing. Install capscrews and tighten to 70 to 90 ft. lbs. (95 to 122 Nm).
5. Liberally lubricate upper socket pin with lubricant. Align upper socket sleeve in keyway of steering knuckle and slide into position.
6. Install new gasket over upper steering knuckle studs. Position spring over sleeve. Install cap (left side steering knuckle arm). Install nuts and tighten to 70 to 90 ft. lbs. (95 to 122 Nm).
7. Left side only connect drag link to steering knuckle arm and install nut. Tighten to 60 ft. lbs. (81 Nm). Install cotter key.
8. Connect tie rod to steering knuckle and install nut. Tighten to 45 ft. lbs. (61 Nm). Install cotter key.
9. Slide axle shaft into position. Position bronze spacer on axle shaft with chamfer facing toward universal joint.
10. Install spindle, brake adapter and brake splash shield. Install washers and nuts and tighten to 50 to70 ft. lbs. (68 to 95 Nm).
11. Position inner brake shoe on adapter.
12. Carefully install hub and rotor assembly onto spindle. Install outer bearing and inner lock nut. Tighten to 50 ft. lbs. (68 Nm) to seat bearings. Back off lock nut and retighten to 30 to 40 ft. lbs. (41 to 54 Nm) while rotating hub and rotor. Back nut off 135° to 150°. Assemble lock ring and outer lock nut. Tighten lock nut to 65 ft. lbs. (88 Nm) minimum. Bend one tang of lock ring over inner lock nut and one tang of lock ring over outer lock nut. Final bearing end play to be 0.001 to 0.010 inch (0.025 to 0.254mm).
13. Install new gasket on hub. Install drive flange, lockwashers and nuts. Tighten to 30 to 40 ft. lbs. (41 to 54 Nm). Install snap ring. Install hub cap, or install locking hub if so equipped.
14. Carefully position caliper onto adapter. Position adapter lock and spring between caliper and adapter and tap into position. Install allen screw and tighten to 12 to 18 ft. lbs. (16 to 24 Nm).
15. Install wheel and tire assembly. Tighten nuts to 75 ft. lbs. (102 Nm).
16. Lubricate at all fittings. Remove jack stands, lower vehicle, remove block from brake pedal and test vehicle operation.

Steering Knuckle Arm

MODEL 60

Removal

1. Raise vehicle and support safely.
2. Turn wheels to the left. Remove cotter key and nut and disconnect drag link.

3. Remove three steering knuckle arm to steering knuckle mounting nuts and cone washers. Tap steering knuckle arm to loosen. Remove steering knuckle arm.

Installation

1. Position steering knuckle arm on steering knuckle. Install cone washers and nuts. Tighten nuts to 90 ft. lbs. (122 Nm).
2. Install drag link to steering knuckle arm. Install nut and tighten to 60 ft. lbs. (81 Nm). Install cotter key.
3. Remove jack stands. Lower vehicle and test operation.

Servicing Rotor Hub or Bearings

1. Block brake pedal in the up position.
2. Raise vehicle and support safely.
3. Remove wheel and tire assembly.
4. Remove allen screw holding caliper to adapter.
5. Tap adapter lock and spring from between caliper and adapter.
6. Carefully separate caliper from adapter. Hang caliper out of the way. Inner brake shoe will remain on adapter.

NOTE: Do not allow caliper to hang or be supported by hydraulic brake hose.

7. Remove hub cap. Remove snap ring.
8. Remove flange nuts and lockwashers. Remove drive flange and discard gasket, or remove locking hub if so equipped.
9. Straighten tang on lock ring and remove outer lock nut, lock ring, inner lock nut and outer bearing. Carefully slide hub and rotor assembly from spindle.
10. Remove oil seal and inner bearing from hub.
11. Clean bearings and interior of hub, removing all old grease.
12. If bearings and cups are to be replaced. Remove cups from the hub with a brass drift or use suitable remover.
13. Replace bearing cups with a suitable installer.
14. Install inner bearing in grease coated hub and install new seal with a seal installer tool. Exercise extreme care not to damage seals when installing.
15. Carefully install hub and rotor assembly onto grease coated spindle. Install outer bearing and inner lock nut.
16. Tighten to 50 ft. lbs. (68 Nm) to seat bearings, back off lock nut and retighten to 30 to 40 ft. lbs. (41 to 54 Nm) while rotating hub and rotor. Back nut off 135° to 150°. Assemble lock ring and outer lock nut. Tighten lock nut to 65ft. lbs. (88 Nm) minimum. Bend one tang of lock ring over inner lock nut and one tang of lock ring over outer lock nut. Final bearing end play to be 0.001 to 0.010 inch (0.025 to 0.254mm).
17. Install new gasket on hub. Install drive flange, lockwashers and nuts. Tighten to 30 to 40 ft. lbs. Install snap ring. Install hub cap, or install locking hub if equipped.
18. Carefully position caliper onto adapter. Position adapter lock and spring between caliper and adapter and tap into position. Install allen screw and tighten to 12 to 18 ft. lbs. (16-24 Nm).
19. Install wheel and tire assembly. Tighten nuts to 75 ft. lbs. (102 Nm).

Servicing Rotor, Hub or Bearings

MODEL 44 FBJ

Removal and Disassembly

1. Raise vehicle to a comfortable working height and install jack stands. Remove wheel.
2. Remove caliper retainer and anti-rattle spring assemblies. Remove caliper from disc by sliding out and away from disc. Hang caliper out of the way. Do not allow caliper to hang or be supported by hydraulic brake hose. Remove inboard shoe.
3. Remove outer axle shaft nut and washer. Position a wheel puller and remove hub and rotor assembly.
4. Pull the outer bearing cone from the hub and rotor assembly. Discard outer seal. Remove the six retainer bolts and retainer.
5. Remove the brake caliper adapter from the knuckle (if required).
6. Position a pry bar behind the inner axle shaft yoke and push the bearings out of the knuckle.
7. Remove the "O" ring from the knuckle (if so equipped) and discard.
8. Carefully remove the axle shaft assembly.

Inspection

1. Examine the knuckle bore and inner seal surface for evidence of severe wear or damage. Replace the knuckle, if required.
2. Inspect the outer axle shaft seal surface for grooving. If the surface is grooved, repair as follows:
   a. Measure in from the yoke shoulder of the axle approximately $^3/_8$ inch (9.5mm). Using a center punch, stake at $^1/_4$ inch (6mm) intervals around the circumference of the shaft. This will size the shaft to insure a tight fit of the inner seal slinger.
3. Check for proper bearing clamp as follows:
   a. Install the bearing cups and spacer into the knuckle bore.
   b. Position the bearing retainer onto the steering knuckle. Install retainer bolts and tighten to 30 ft. lbs.
   c. Insert a 0.004 inch (0.101mm) feeler gauge between the knuckle and the retainer at a point approximately midway between the retainer mounting ears.

NOTE: The brake dust shield may have to be removed to complete this check. If 0.004 (0.101mm) clearance cannot be obtained at each measuring point, the knuckle must be replaced.

   d. Remove retainer plate, bearing cups and spacer. Install brake dust shield (if removed), tighten mounting bolts to 160 inch lbs. (18 Nm).

Assembly and Installation

1. Apply RTV sealer to the seal surface of the axle shaft.
2. Using Driver, Tool C-4398-1, or equivalent install the seal slinger onto the outer axle shaft.
3. Install lip seal on the slinger with the lip toward the axle shaft spline.
4. Carefully insert axle shaft into the housing so as not to damage the differential seal at the side gears.
5. Insert a pry bar through the axle shaft "U" joint and wedge so that the axle shaft is in all the way and cannot be moved out.
6. Using Adapter, Tool C-4398-2 and Driver, Tool C-4398-1 or equivalent carefully install the seal cup until bottomed in the knuckle.

NOTE: A small amount of wheel bearing grease on the Adapter face will aid in holding the cup in position. Do not remove the tool at this time.

7. Install new outer seal in retainer plate. Locate retainer plate over hub of rotor assembly.
8. Pack wheel bearings with Multi-Purpose Grease.
9. Carefully press outer bearing onto hub.
10. Place grease coated outer bearing cup over outer bearing cone followed by spacer, grease coated inner bearing cup and inner bearing cone. Carefully press into position.
11. Apply a $^1/_4$ inch (6mm) bead of RTV sealer to the retainer face on the chamfer, (this takes the place of the "O" ring dis-

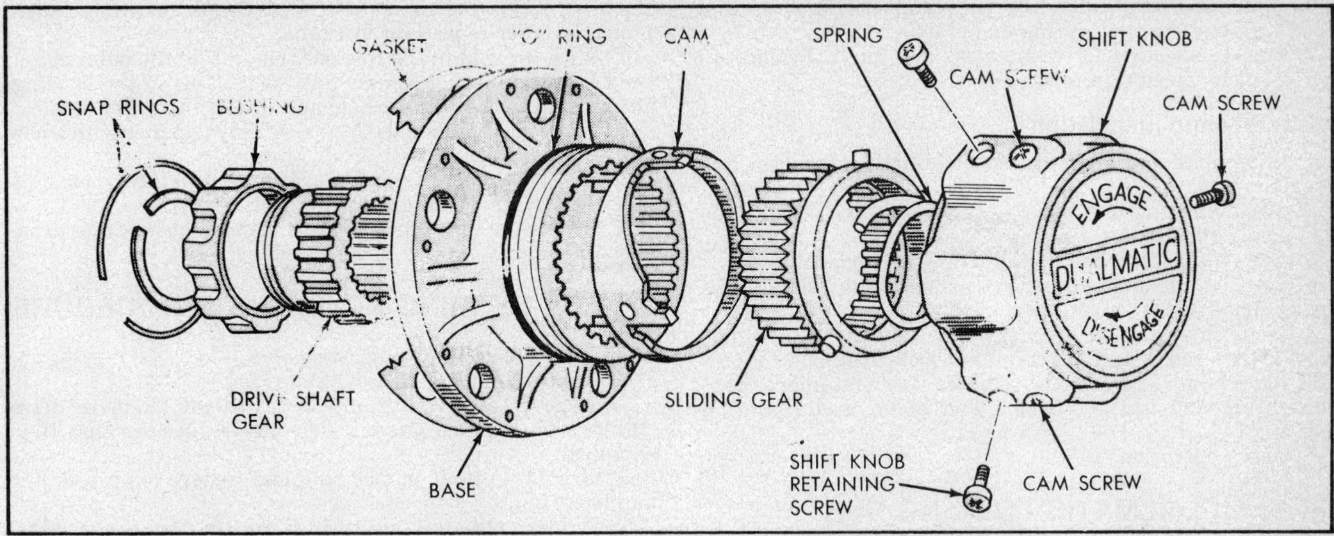

Exploded view of Dualmatic locking hub (© Chrysler Corp.)

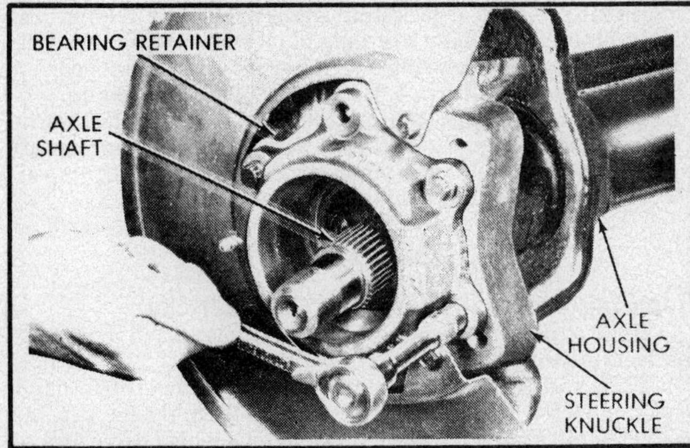

Removing the bearing retainer bolts (© Chrysler Corp.)

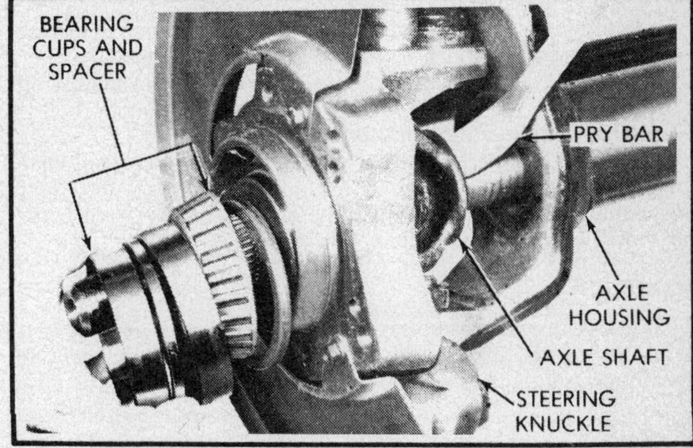

Removing the bearing assembly from the steering knuckle (© Chrysler Corp.)

carded at disassembly).

12. Carefully remove seal installing tool from the knuckle bore so that the outer axle shaft remains centered.

NOTE: If the shaft is disturbed, check to make sure that the lip seal is still riding inside the cup. Correct if necessary.

13. Position the bearing retainer in the hub and rotor so that the lube fitting is facing directly forward. This is extremely important.
14. Assemble the hub and rotor to the knuckle and tighten retainer plate bolts to 30ft. lbs. (41 Nm) using a criss-cross method to position it evenly.
15. Install brake adapter and tighten mounting bolts to 85 ft. lbs. (115 Nm).
16. Remove pry bar from "U" joint and install axle shaft washer and nut. Tighten nut to 100 ft. lbs. (136 Nm), continue to tighten nut until next slot in nut aligns with cotter key hole in axle shaft. Install cotter key.

Front Wheel Locking Hubs

DANA FRONT LOCKING HUBS (MANUAL)

Removal and Disassembly

1. Place hub in lock position. Remove allen head mounting bolts and washers.
2. Carefully remove retainer, O-ring seal and knob. Separate knob from retainer.
3. Remove large internal snap-ring. Slide retainer ring and cam from hub.
4. While pressing against sleeve and ring assembly, remove

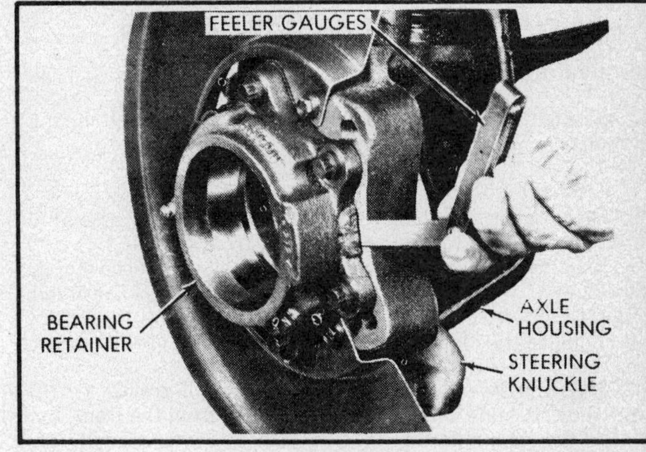

Measuring retainer to steering knuckle clearance (© Chrysler Corp.)

axle shaft snap-ring. Relieve pressure and remove sleeve and ring, ring and bushing, spring and plate.

5. Inspect all parts for wear, nicks and burrs. Replace all parts which appear questionable.

Assembly and Installation

1. Slide plate and spring (large coils first) into wheel hub housing.
2. Assemble ring and bushing, sleeve and bushing. Slide complete assembly into housing.
3. Compress spring and install axle shaft snap-ring.
4. Position cam and retainer in housing and install large internal snap-ring.
5. Place small O-ring seal on knob, lubricate with waterproof grease and install in retainer at lock position.
6. Place large O-ring seal on retainer. Align retainer and retainer ring and install washers and allen head mounting screws.
7. Check operation.

DUALMATIC LOCKING HUB

Removal and Disassembly

1. Turn shift knob to "engage" position.
2. Apply pressure to the face of shift knob, remove the three screws spaced 120° apart and nearest to the flange.
3. With an outward pull, remove shift knob from mounting base.
4. Remove snap ring from axle shaft.
5. Remove capscrews and lockwashers from mounting base flange.
6. Separate and remove locking hub assembly from rotor hub; remove and discard gasket.

Inspection

Wash parts in mineral spirits and blow dry with compressed air. Examine splines shift knob, cam, sliding gear, drive shaft gear, and mounting base for damage.

Assembly

Lubricate parts lightly with Multi-Purpose lubricant.

1. Position new gasket and locking hub onto rotor hub.
2. Install attaching capscrews and lock washers; tighten to 30ft. lbs. (41-54 Nm).
3. Install axle shaft snap ring.
4. Position shift knob on mounting base. Align splines by pushing inward on shift knob and turning it clockwise to lock it in position.
5. Install and tighten three shift knob retaining screws.

WARN FRONT LOCKING HUBS

Removal and Installation

1. Straighten the lock tabs and remove the six hub mounting bolts.
2. Tap the hub gently with a mallet to remove it.
3. Separate the clutch assembly from the body assembly.
4. Remove the snap ring from the rear of the body assembly. Slip the axle shaft hub out of the body from the front.
5. Remove the allen screw from the inner side of the clutch, and remove the dial assembly from the front side of the clutch housing assembly.
6. Remove the clutch assembly from the rear of the housing complete with the roller pins.
7. Coat the moving parts with a waterproof grease.
8. Slide the axle shaft hub into the body from the front, and replace the snap ring.
9. Replace the dial assembly and the inner clutch. Tighten the allen screw and stake the edge of the screw with a center punch in order to prevent loosening.
10. With the dial in the free position, rotate the outer clutch body into the inner assembly until it bottoms in the housing. Bring it up to the nearest hole and install the roller pins.
11. Position the hub and clutch assembly together with a new gasket in between.
12. Position the hub assembly over the end of the axle and replace the hub mounting bolts and lock tabs.
13. Torque the bolts 30-35 ft. lbs. and bend the lock tabs to anchor the bolts.

WHEEL BEARING ADJUSTING PROCEDURE

1. Raise vehicle and support safely.
2. Remove hub cap. Remove snap ring.
3. Remove flange nuts and lock washers. Remove drive flange and discard gasket, or remove locking hub if so equipped.
4. Straighten tang on lock ring and remove outer lock nut and lock ring.
5. Tighten inner lock nut to 50 ft. lbs. (68 Nm) to seat bearings, back off lock nut and retighten to 30–40 ft. lbs. (41 to 54 Nm) while rotating assembly. Back nut off 135° to 150°. Assemble lock ring and outer lock nut. Tighten lock nut to 65 ft. lbs. (88 Nm) minimum. Bend one tang of lock ring over inner lock nut and one tang of lock ring over outer lock nut. Final bearing adjustment to be 0.001 to 0.010 inch (0.025 to 0.254mm).
6. Install new gasket on hub. Install drive flange, lockwashers and nuts. Tighten to 30 to 40ft. lbs. (41 to 54 Nm). Install snap ring. Install hub cap, or install locking hub if so equipped.
7. Lower vehicle and test vehicle operation.

AUTOMATIC HUBS

Preparing Automatic Hubs for Disassembly

1. Shift transfer case lever into four wheel drive to engage and lock hubs.
2. Shift the transfer case lever into two wheel drive and slowly move the vehicle backwards approximately six feet. Incomplete shift from two wheel drive to four wheel drive or disengagement of only one hub lock may cause an abnormal sound from the axle.
3. Shift to four wheel drive to stop the noise, then shift to two wheel drive to unlock the hub.

Remove Hub from Wheel

1. Using a Torx T-25 driver, remove the five cover screws. Remove cover and bearing race spring assembly, sealing ring, seal bridge retainer, and bearing components.
2. Squeeze the tangs of the wire retaining ring together with a needle nose pliers and pull the remaining components of the automatic locking hub from the wheel.

Assemble Hub to Wheel

1. Make sure that the drag sleeve retainer washer is in position between the wheel bearing adjusting nut and the lock nut. Tighten the lock nut as specified.

NOTE: Before installing the automatic locking hub, make sure that the spacer and retaining ring are in position on the axle shaft.

2. Install the automatic locking hub into the wheel hub aligning the drag sleeve slots with the tabs on the drag sleeve retainer washer.

Align the outer clutch housing splines with the splines of the wheel hub.

3. Loosen the cover screws three or four turns and push in on the cover to allow the retaining ring to expand into the rotor hub groove.

4. Tighten cover screws to 40-50 inch lbs. (4.52-5.65 Nm) using a Torx T-25 driver.

Disassembling Hub

To disassemble, the hub must be unlocked. If hub is locked when removed from the wheel, hold the hub sleeve and rotate the drag sleeve in either direction to unlock.

1. With the cover removed, turn the clutch gear until it drops to engage with the outer clutch housing.
2. Lift and tilt the drag sleeve and detent to free the brake band tangs from the rectangular opening in the inner cage. Remove the drag sleeve and detent, and brake band assembly.

NOTE: Never remove the brake band from the drag sleeve and detent as the brake band spring tension may be affected.

3. Remove retaining ring from outer clutch housing groove.
4. Using a small screw driver, pry plastic outer cage free from inner cage and remove inner cage.
5. Pry free and remove the plastic outer cage from the outer clutch housing.
6. Remove the clutch gear and hub sleeve assembly from the outer clutch housing.
7. Compress the clutch gear return spring and remove the retaining ring from the clutch gear hub sleeve.

CAUTION

To prevent injury, use a spring compressor to hold spring securely.

8. Carefully release the spring to its normal extended length. Remove the spring support washer, return spring retainers and return spring from the hub sleeve.
9. Remove the "C" type retaining ring from the hub sleeve, remove clutch gear, spring, and cam follower.

Cleaning and Inspection

1. Wash all parts with cleaning solvent; dry with compressed air.
2. Check cover for cracks or porous condition.
3. Check seats of cover screws in cover for pitting, or a tapered, countersunk condition.
4. Examine wire retaining ring for kinks, bends and size (0.088 min.-0.094 max.).
5. Check brake band for distortion or wear.
6. Inspect the teeth on clutch gear and cam follower for wear and broken teeth.
7. Check drag sleeve and drag sleeve retainer washer for cracks or wear.

Lubrication

The automatic locking hub requires lubrication at approximately 24,000 mile intervals.

1. Dip all parts with the exception of the bearing and race assembly, and the brake band and drag sleeve assembly, in automatic transmission fluid.
2. Allow the excess transmission fluid to drip off before proceeding to assemble the unit.
3. Repack the bearing race, and retainer with Lubricant.
4. Lubricate the brake band and drag sleeve using 1.5 grams (0.05 oz.) of lubricant.

Reassembling Hub

1. Snap the cam follower legs over the tooth gaps at the flat surfaces of the clutch gear.

NOTE: Do not pry the legs of the cam follower apart.

2. Compress and slide the conical spring into position between the cam follower and the clutch gear having the large diameter of the spring contacting the face of the clutch gear.
3. Install the assembled cam follower, conical spring, and clutch gear assembly onto the hub sleeve having the teeth of the cam follower near the step at the end of the hub sleeve.
4. Position the "C" type retaining ring between the clutch gear and the cam follower, then snap it into place in the groove of the hub sleeve.
5. Place a spring retainer at the end of the return spring and position the spring and retainer in the clutch gear.
6. Install a spring retainer and the spring support washer on the remaining end of the return spring. Compress the return spring, install the retainer ring into the ring groove at the end of the hub sleeve.
7. Install the clutch gear and hub sleeve assembly (spring support washer end first) into the outer clutch housing.
8. For support during the assembling operation, screw three of the cover screws into the outer clutch housing face.
9. Position the plastic outer cage into the outer clutch housing, having the ramps of the plastic outer cage near the cam follower. Carefully work the outer cage into the outer clutch housing until the small external tabs of the plastic cage locates in the wide groove of the outer clutch housing.
10. Install the steel inner cage into the outer cage, aligning the lug of the outer cage with the rectangular opening of the inner cage.
11. Install the retaining ring into the outer clutch housing groove to lock the outer cage into place.
12. Service the brake band and drag sleeve as an assembly. After lubricating, as described previously, position one of the two brake band tangs on each side of the outer cage lug which is located at the rectangular opening of the steel inner cage. If necessary, tilt the drag sleeve while engaging the brake band tangs. When correctly positioned, the brake band tangs will be engaged one on each side of the outer cage lug, and the drag sleeve teeth will be in mesh with the teeth of the cam follower.
13. Remove the three screws from the outer clutch housing which had been previously installed for support during the reassembly procedure. Install the spacer and retaining ring to lock the drag sleeve into position. After making certain that the spacer and retaining ring are in position on axle shaft, install the automatic locking hub onto the vehicle.
14. Position the wire retaining ring in the groove machined in the outer clutch housing surface having the retainer tangs pointing away from the splines.
15. Holding the tangs of the wire retainer together, assemble the seal bridge over the tangs positioned in such a manner that the bent down tabs of the seal bridge clamp the wire retainer tangs together.
16. Install the "O" ring in the outer clutch housing groove and over the seal bridge.
17. Position the bearing over the inner race, lubricate as described previously. Assemble into position, then snap the bearing retainer clip into the hole in the inner race.
18. Install the bearing and retainer assembly into the end of the hub sleeve. Install the sealing ring over the outer clutch housing.
19. Position the bearing race spring into the bore in the cover.
20. Install the spring and cover assembly, install the five screws and tighten to 40-50 inch lbs. (4.5-5.6 Nm) using a Torx T-25 driver.

NOTE: The "O" ring installed previously to hold the seal bridge in position during assembly, may be left on, but is not required.

21. After assembling is completed, the hub should turn freely.

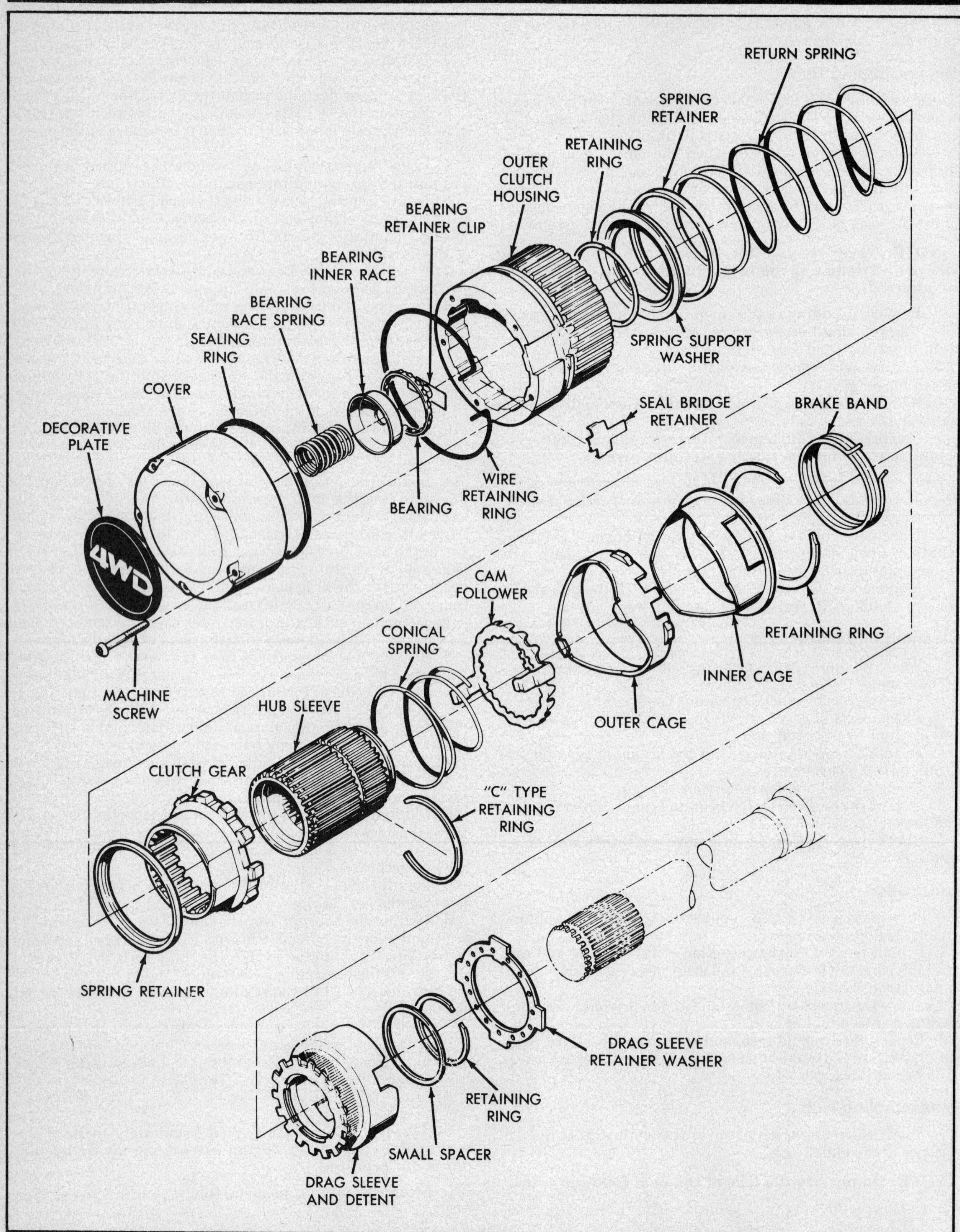

Exploded view of Automatic locking hub (© Chrysler Corp.)

AUTOMATIC LOCKING HUB DIAGNOSIS

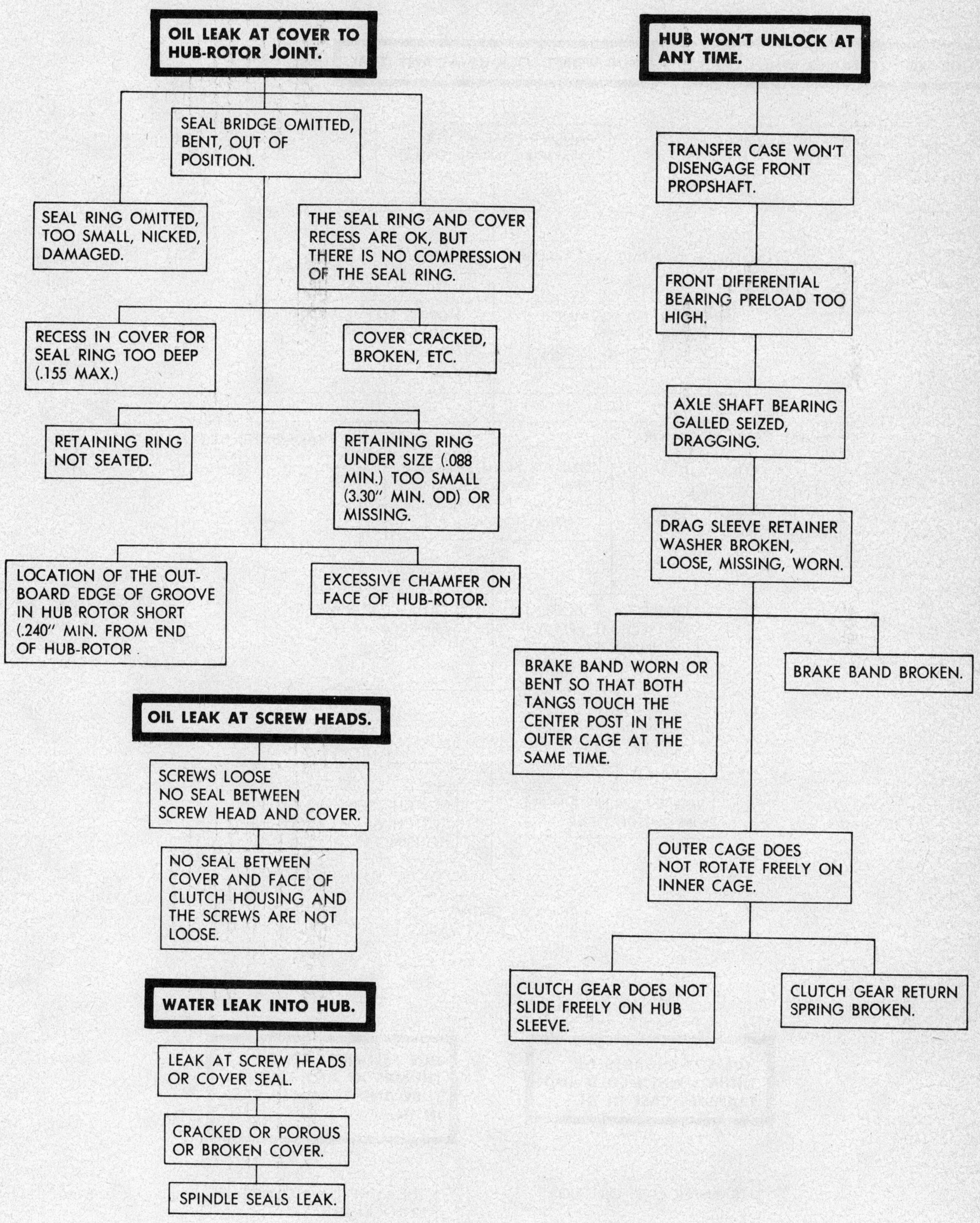
OIL LEAK AT COVER TO HUB-ROTOR JOINT.
SEAL BRIDGE OMITTED, BENT, OUT OF POSITION.
SEAL RING OMITTED, TOO SMALL, NICKED, DAMAGED.
THE SEAL RING AND COVER RECESS ARE OK, BUT THERE IS NO COMPRESSION OF THE SEAL RING.
RECESS IN COVER FOR SEAL RING TOO DEEP (.155 MAX.)
COVER CRACKED, BROKEN, ETC.
RETAINING RING NOT SEATED.
RETAINING RING UNDER SIZE (.088 MIN.) TOO SMALL (3.30" MIN. OD) OR MISSING.
LOCATION OF THE OUT-BOARD EDGE OF GROOVE IN HUB ROTOR SHORT (.240" MIN. FROM END OF HUB-ROTOR
EXCESSIVE CHAMFER ON FACE OF HUB-ROTOR.
OIL LEAK AT SCREW HEADS.
SCREWS LOOSE NO SEAL BETWEEN SCREW HEAD AND COVER.
NO SEAL BETWEEN COVER AND FACE OF CLUTCH HOUSING AND THE SCREWS ARE NOT LOOSE.
WATER LEAK INTO HUB.
LEAK AT SCREW HEADS OR COVER SEAL.
CRACKED OR POROUS OR BROKEN COVER.
SPINDLE SEALS LEAK.
HUB WON'T UNLOCK AT ANY TIME.
TRANSFER CASE WON'T DISENGAGE FRONT PROPSHAFT.
FRONT DIFFERENTIAL BEARING PRELOAD TOO HIGH.
AXLE SHAFT BEARING GALLED SEIZED, DRAGGING.
DRAG SLEEVE RETAINER WASHER BROKEN, LOOSE, MISSING, WORN.
BRAKE BAND WORN OR BENT SO THAT BOTH TANGS TOUCH THE CENTER POST IN THE OUTER CAGE AT THE SAME TIME.
BRAKE BAND BROKEN.
OUTER CAGE DOES NOT ROTATE FREELY ON INNER CAGE.
CLUTCH GEAR DOES NOT SLIDE FREELY ON HUB SLEEVE.
CLUTCH GEAR RETURN SPRING BROKEN.

AUTOMATIC LOCKING HUB DIAGNOSIS

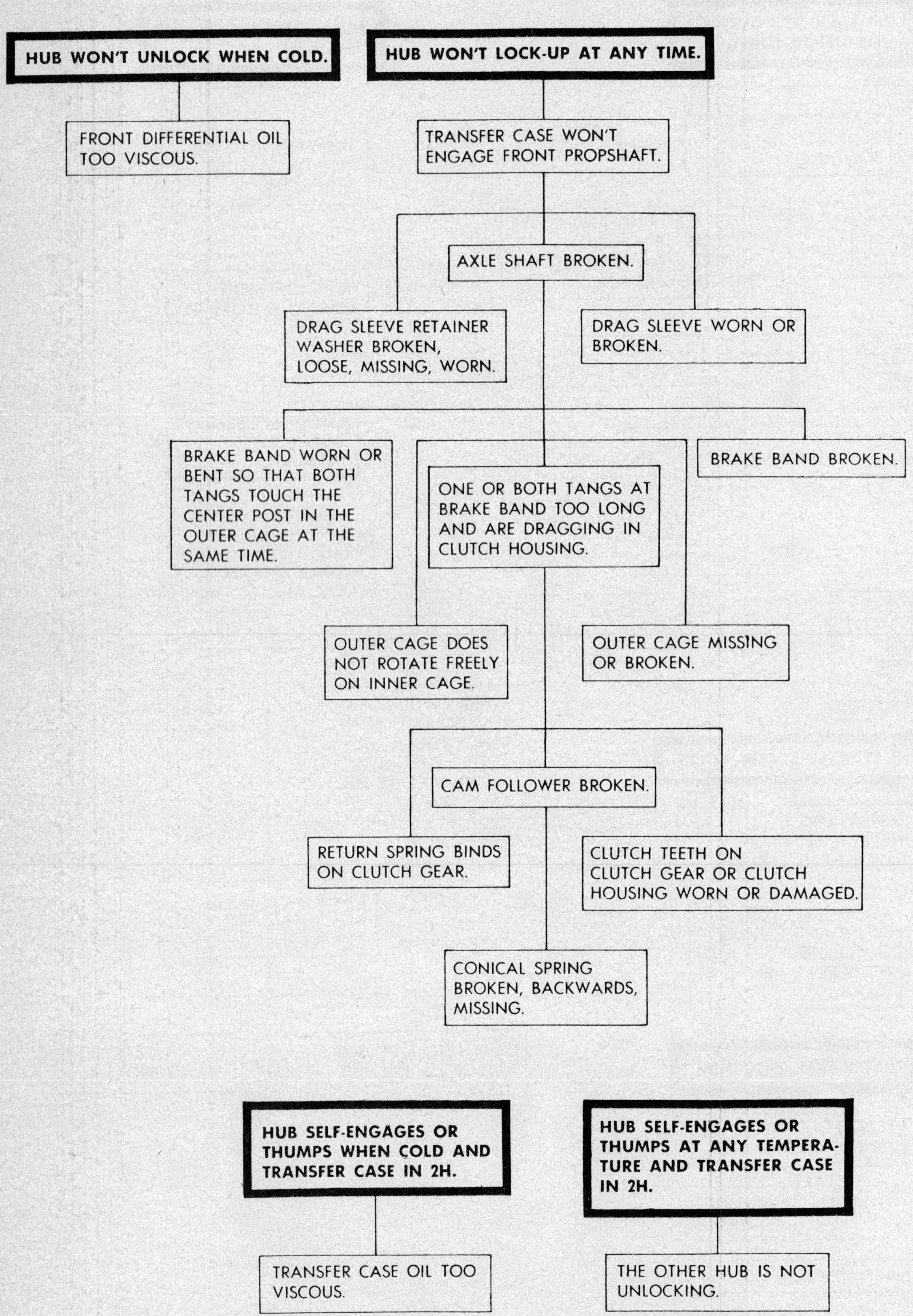

INDEPENDENT FRONT SUSPENSION

NOTE: These procedures apply to all vans, wagons, and conventional trucks with independent front suspension.

COIL SPRING

Removal and Installation

1. Raise the vehicle and support it safely.
2. Remove the wheel.
3. Remove the shock absorber and upper shock absorber bushing bushing and sleeve.
4. If equipped, remove the sway bar.
5. Remove the strut.
6. Install a spring compressor and tighten finger-tight.
7. Remove the cotter pins and ball joint nuts.
8. Install a ball joint breaker tool and turn the threaded portion of the tool to lock it against the lower stud.
9. Spread the tool to place the lower stud under pressure, then strike the steering knuckle sharply with a hammer to free the stud. Do not attempt to force the stud out of the steering knuckle with the tool.
10. Remove the tool. Slowly release the spring compressor until all tension is relieved from the spring.
11. Remove the spring compressor and spring.
12. Installation is the reverse of removal. Compress the spring until the ball joint can be properly positioned in the steering knuckle.

SHOCK ABSORBER

Removal and Installation

1. Raise and support the vehicle with jackstands positioned at the extreme front ends of the frame rails.
2. Remove the wheel.
3. Remove the upper nut and retainer.
4. Remove the two lower mounting bolts.
5. Remove the shock absorber.
6. Installation is the reverse of removal.

UPPER CONTROL ARM

Removal and Installation

NOTE: Any time the control arm is removed, it is necessary to align the front end.

1. Raise and support the vehicle with jackstands under the frame rails.
2. Remove the wheel.
3. Remove the shock absorber and shock absorber upper bushing and sleeve.
4. Install a spring compressor and tighten it finger-tight.
5. Remove the cotter pins and ball joint nuts.
6. Install a ball joint breaker and turn the threaded portion of the tool, locking it securely against the upper stud. Spread the tool enough to place the upper ball joint under pressure and strike the steering knuckle sharply to loosen the stud. Do not attempt to remove the stud from the steering knuckle with the tool.
7. Remove the tool.
8. Remove the eccentric pivot bolts, after making their relative positions in the control arm.
9. Remove the upper control arm.
10. Installation is the reverse of removal. Tighten the ball joint nuts to 135ft. lbs. Tighten the eccentric pivot bolts to 70ft. lbs.
11. Adjust the caster and camber.

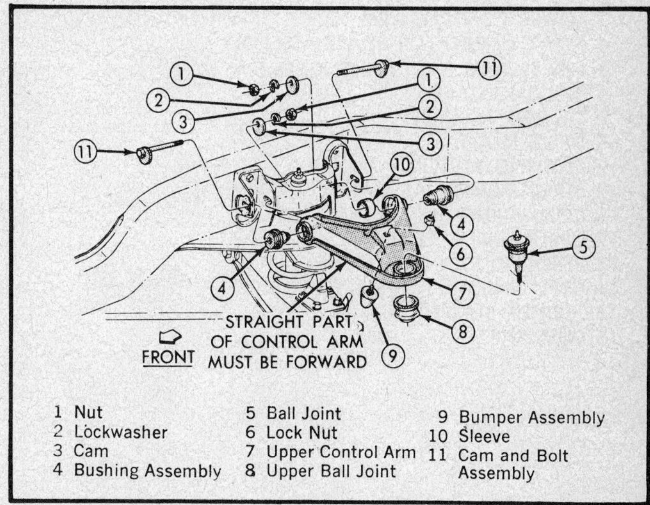

Upper control arm details (© Chrysler Corp.)

LOWER CONTROL ARM

Removal and Installation

1. Follow the procedure outlined under "Coil Spring Removal and Installation."
2. Remove the mounting bolt from the crossmember.
3. Remove the lower control arm from the vehicle.
4. Installation is the reverse of removal. After the vehicle has been lowered to the ground, tighten the mounting bolt to 210 ft. lbs.

LOWER BALL JOINT

Removal and Installation

1. Remove the lower control arm.
2. Remove the ball joint seal.
3. Using an arbor press and a sleeve, press the ball joint from the control arm.
4. Installation is the reverse of removal. Be sure that the ball joint is fully seated. Install a new ball joint seal.
5. Install the lower control arm. Be sure to install the ball joint cotter pins.

UPPER BALL JOINT

Removal and Installation

1. Install a jack under the outer end of the lower control arm and raise the vehicle.
2. Remove the wheel.
3. Remove the ball joint nuts. Using a ball joint breaker, loosen the upper ball joint.
4. Unscrew the ball joint from the control arm.
5. Screw a new ball joint into the control arm and tighten 125 ft. lbs.
6. Install the new ball joint seal, using a 2 in. socket. Be sure that the seal is seated on the ball joint housing.
7. Insert the ball joint into the steering knuckle and install the ball joint nuts. Tighten the nuts to 135ft. lbs. and install the cotter pins.
8. Install the wheel and lower the truck to the ground.

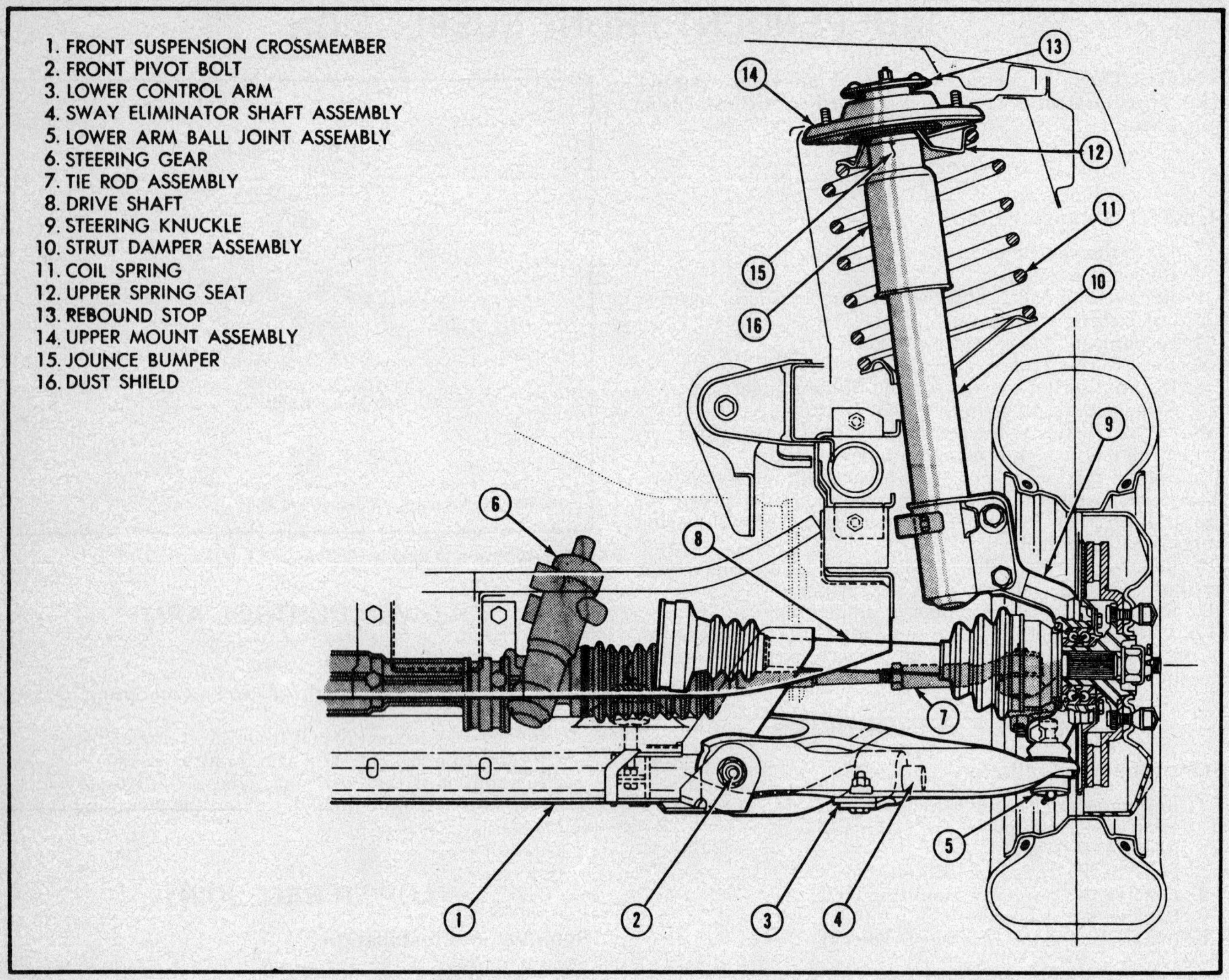

1. FRONT SUSPENSION CROSSMEMBER
2. FRONT PIVOT BOLT
3. LOWER CONTROL ARM
4. SWAY ELIMINATOR SHAFT ASSEMBLY
5. LOWER ARM BALL JOINT ASSEMBLY
6. STEERING GEAR
7. TIE ROD ASSEMBLY
8. DRIVE SHAFT
9. STEERING KNUCKLE
10. STRUT DAMPER ASSEMBLY
11. COIL SPRING
12. UPPER SPRING SEAT
13. REBOUND STOP
14. UPPER MOUNT ASSEMBLY
15. JOUNCE BUMPER
16. DUST SHIELD

Rampage front suspension—front wheel drive with struts (© Chrysler Corp.)

FRONT ADJUSTING BOLT
REAR ADJUSTING BOLT
CASTER
+
+
CAMBER
FRONT
SIDE

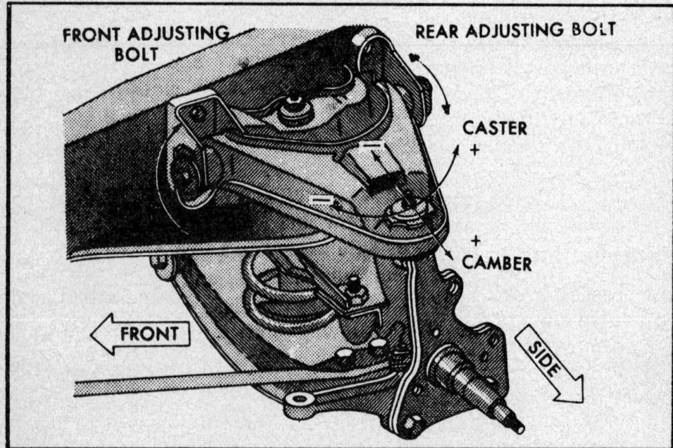

Independent front suspension alignment points (© Chrysler Corp.)

Wheel Bearings

It is recommended that the front wheel bearings be cleaned, inspected and repacked periodically and as soon as possible after the front hubs have been submerged in water.

NOTE: Sodium based grease is not compatible with lithium based grease. Be careful not to mix the two types. If unsure of the present grease being used in the bearings, clean all of the old grease from the hub assembly before installing any new grease.

Front Wheel Drive

STRUT ASSEMBLY

Removal and Installation

1. Loosen the wheel lug nuts.
2. Raise the vehicle and remove the wheel assembly.
3. Mark the camber cam to damper bracket position before removing the cam adjusting bolt.
4. Remove the cam adjusting bolt, the through bolt and the brake hose to damper bracket retaining screw.
5. Remove the strut damper to fender shield (strut tower) mounting nut and washer assembly.
6. Install strut assembly into fender (strut tower) and install nut and washer assemblies. Torque the retaining nuts to 20 ft. lbs. (27 Nm).

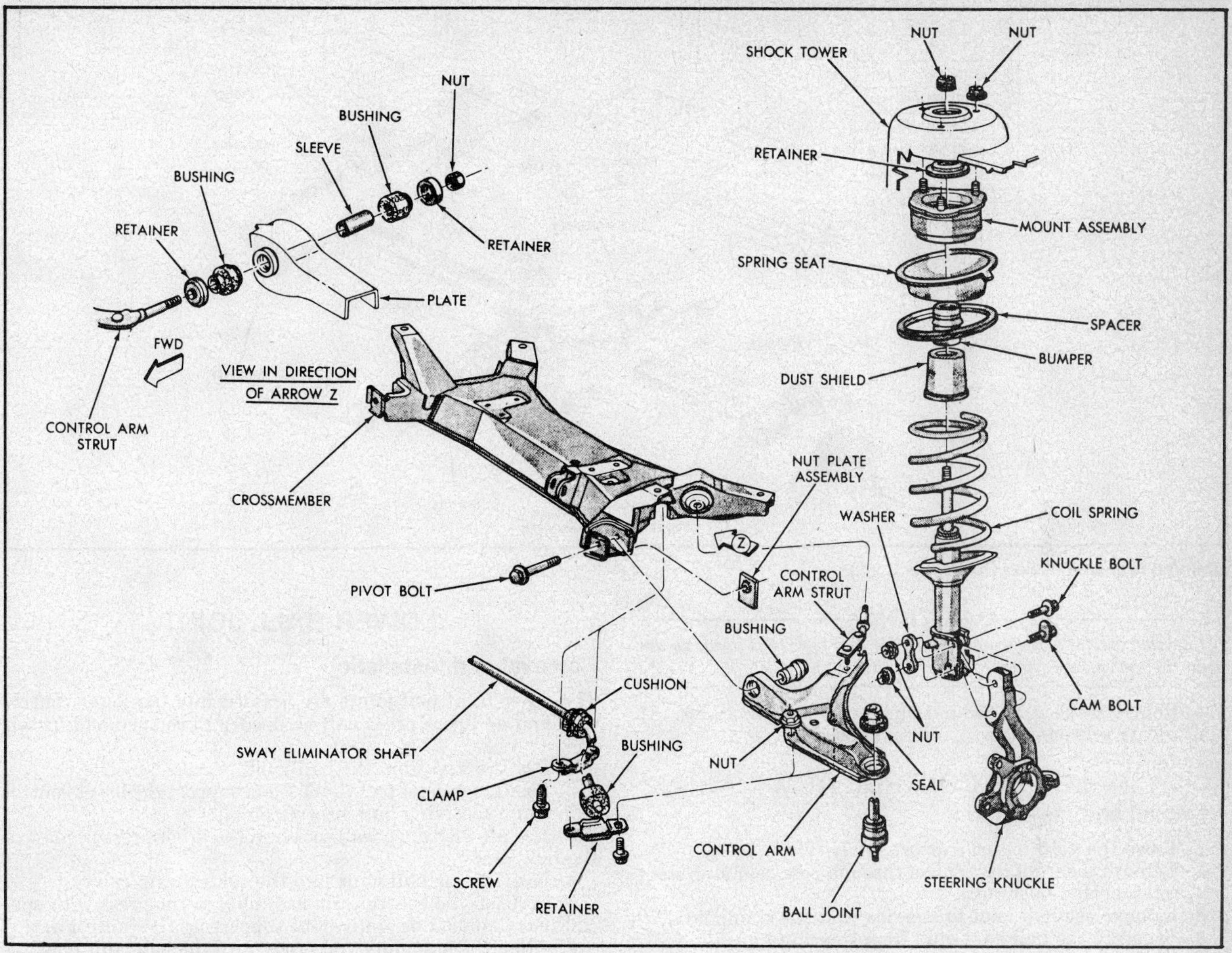

Mini-Van front suspension (© Chrysler Corp.)

7. Position the steering knuckle neck into the strut damper bracket, install the cam adjusting and through bolts.

8. Attach the brake hose retainer to the damper bracket, torque the screws to 10 ft. lbs. (13 Nm).

9. Adjust the camber to the original marked position.

10. Place a 4 inch or larger "C" clamp on the strut and knuckle. Tighten the clamp just enough to eliminate any looseness between the knuckle and the strut. Recheck the alignment marks and tighten the bolts to 45 ft. lbs. (61 Nm). Turn the bolts an additional ¼ turn (90°) beyond the specified torque.

11. Install the wheel and tire assembly. Torque the wheel nuts to 80 ft. lbs. (108 Nm).

STRUT TYPE COIL SPRING

Removal and Installation

1. Use a coil spring compressor (strut type) to compress the coil spring.

2. Hold the strut rod while removing the strut rod.

3. Remove the strut damper mount assembly and the coil spring.

NOTE: If both strut springs are to be removed and reinstalled, mark them so they can be returned to their original position.

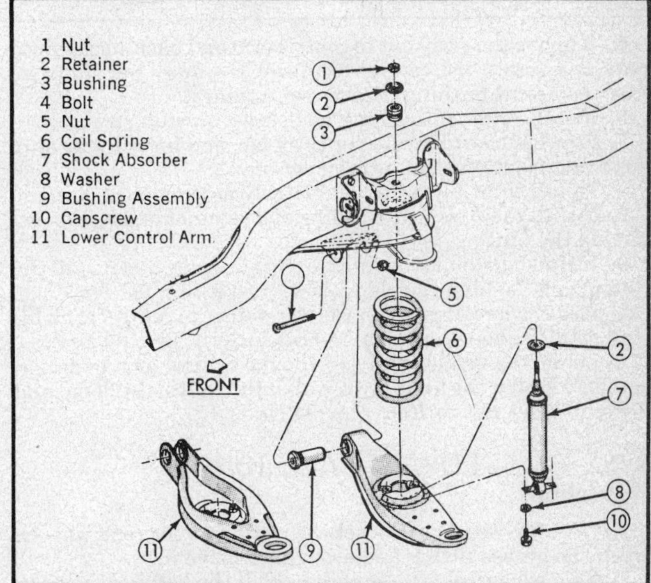

Lower control details (© Chrysler Corp.)

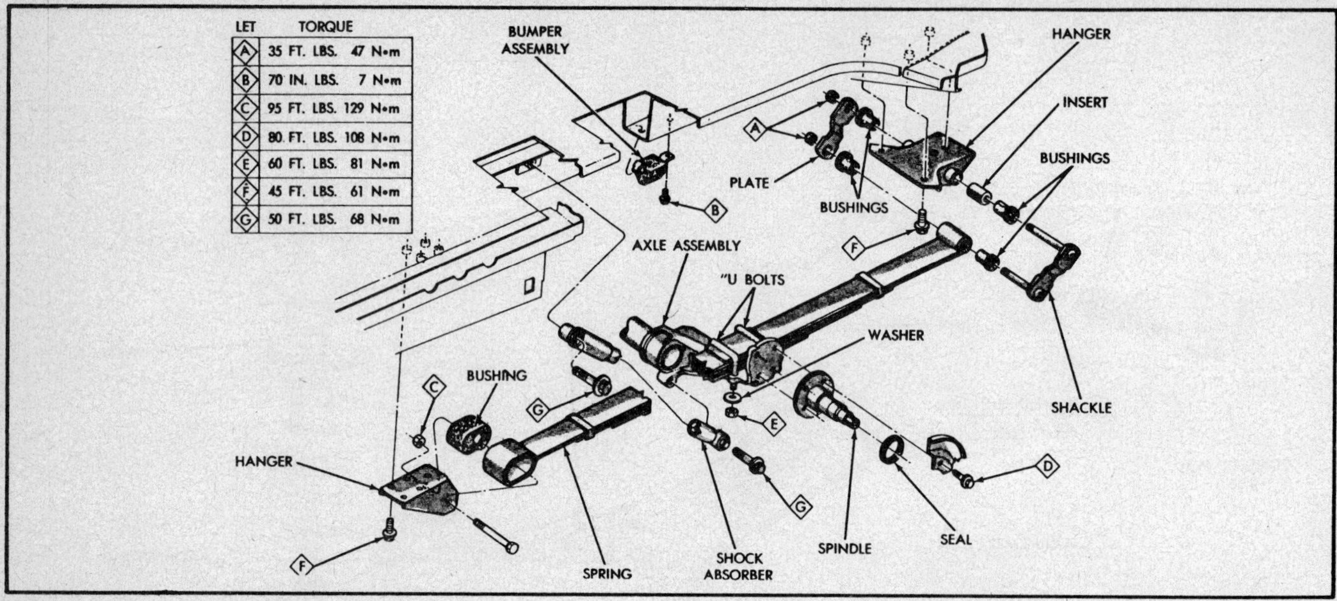

Mini-Van rear suspension (© Chrysler Corp.)

CAUTION

If Chrysler special tool spring compressor tool L-4514 is used, do not open the tool jaws beyond 9 1/4 inches (230mm).

4. Reinstall the strut rod nut and torque it to 60 ft. lbs. (81 Nm) before releasing the spring compressor.

LOWER CONTROL ARM

Removal and Installation

1. Raise the vehicle and support safely.
2. Remove the front inner pivot through bolt, rear stub strut nut, retainer and bushing.
3. Remove the ball joint to steering knuckle clamp bolt.
4. Separate the ball joint stud from steering knuckle.

CAUTION

Do not pull the steering knuckle away from the vehicle, while the ball joint is disconnected, it can separate the inner C/V joint.

5. Remove the sway bar to control arm end bushing retainer nuts and rotate the control arm over the sway bar. Remove rear stub strut bushing, sleeve and retainer.
6. Install retainer, bushing and sleeve on stub strut.
7. Position control arm over sway bar and install rear stub strut and front pivot into crossmember.
8. Install front pivot bolt and loosely assemble the nut.
9. Install the stub strut bushing and retainer and loosely assemble the nut.
10. Install ball joint stud into steering knuckle and install the clamp bolt. Tighten the clamp bolt to 50 ft. lbs. (67 Nm).
11. Position sway bar end bushing retainer to control arm. Install retainer bolts and tighten nuts to 22 ft. lbs. (30 Nm).
12. Lower the vehicle and support the control arm to design height. Tighten the front pivot bolt to 105 ft. lbs. (142 Nm) and the stub strut nut to 70 ft. lbs. (94 Nm).

LOWER BALL JOINT

Inspection

1. With the weight of the vehicle resting on the road wheels, grasp the grease fitting and attempt to move it.
2. No mechanical force is necessary. If the ball joint is worn the grease fitting will move easily. Replace worn ball joints.

LOWER BALL JOINT

Removal and Installation

The lower front ball joints are pressed into the lower control arm and an arbor press will be needed to remove and install them.

1. Pry the seal from the ball joint.
2. Position special tool C-4699-2 to support the lower control arm while receiving ball joint assembly.
3. Use a 1 inch deep wall socket in the arbor press to remove the ball joint.
4. Position the ball joint into the control arm cavity.
5. Position the control arm assembly in the press with special tool C-4699-1 or equivalent supporting the control arm.
6. Align the assembly and press until the ball joint housing ledge stops against control arm cavity down flange.
7. Support the ball joint housing with special tool C-4699-2 or equivalent and position a new seal over the ball joint stud.
8. Using an 1 1/2 inch socket in an arbor press force the seal to seat against the control arm.

WHEEL BEARING

Adjustment

1. Remove the wheel and tire assembly.
2. Remove the hub lock nut cotter pin and lock nut.
3. Loosen the hub nut and apply the brakes.
4. With brakes applied, tighten hub nut to 180 ft. lbs. (245 Nm).
5. Install nut lock and new cotter pin. Wrap cotter pin tightly against nut lock.
6. Install wheel and tire assembly and tighten wheel nuts to 80 ft. lbs. (108 Nm).

DRIVE AXLES A-412 MANUAL TRANSMISSION

Removal and Installation

1. Remove the cotter pin and nut lock.
2. Loosen hub nut and wheel nuts while vehicle is on floor and brakes applied.

3. Raise vehicle and remove hub nut and wheel and tire assembly.
4. Remove the clamp bolt securing ball joint stud into the steering knuckle.
5. Separate the ball joint stud from the steering knuckle by prying against the knuckle leg and control arm. Do not damage the ball joint or C/V joint boots.
6. Separate out C/V joint splined shaft from hub by holding C/V housing while moving knuckle hub assembly away.
7. Remove the plastic caps from the allen head screws by prying under the cap and against the inner joint flange.

NOTE: The separated outer joint and shaft must be supported during inner joint separation. Tie the assembly to the control arm during the operation.

8. Using special tool L-4550 or equivalent remove the allen head screws attaching the inner C/V joint to the transaxle drive flange. Wipe foreign material from C/V joint and drive flange.
9. Release the outer C/V joint from the control arm.
10. Remove the driveshaft assembly carefully in order to reduce loss of special lubricant from the inner C/V joint. Hold both the inner and outer housings parallel and rotate the outer assembly down while pivoting inner housing up at the drive flange.

NOTE: The drive shaft installed acts as a bolt and secures the hub/bearing assembly. If the vehicle is to be supported or moved on its wheels, install a bolt through the hub to insure that the hub bearing assembly cannot loosen.

11. Replace any lost lubricant with Chrysler part number 4131389 or equivalent.
12. Wipe grease from the joint housing, face, screw holes and transaxle drive flange face before installation.
13. Support assembly vertically inner housing up to retain special lubricant. Do not move inner joint in or out during assembly to drive flange. Pumping action can force lubricant out of the joint.
14. Position inner housing to drive flange and rotate assembly up. Locate the inner housing in the drive flange. Tie the outer end of the drive shaft to the control arm during assembly of the inner end.
15. Install the allen head screws to secure the inner joint to drive axle flange. Torque the screws to 36.6 ft. lbs. (50 Nm).

NOTE: Failure to torque the flange screws to the specified torque may result in loosening during operation.

16. Untie the outer end of the drive shaft and push the hub assembly out far enough to install the outer C/V joint shaft into the hub.
17. Install the knuckle assembly on the ball joint stud.
18. Install and tighten the clamp bolt to 50 ft. lbs. (68 Nm).

NOTE: The steering knuckle clamp bolt is a prevailing torque type and must be replaced with the original and/or equivalent bolt.

19. Install the washer and hub nut. With brakes applied tighten the nut to 180 ft. lbs. (245 Nm).
20. Install lock and cotter pin.

DRIVE AXLES, ALL EXCEPT A-412 TRANSAXLE

Removal and Installation

The inboard C/V joints have stub shafts splined into the differential side gears. The two different types of axles are retained either by spring force or by circlips on the end of the shafts. The clip type axles require the removal of the differential cover to remove the axle shaft. The spring loaded type shafts do not require removal of the differential cover.

1. On the clip type axles, remove drain plug, drain the lubricant and remove the differential cover.
2. On the right side (passenger side) remove the speedometer pinion.
3. Rotate the driveshaft to expose the circlip tangs. A relief (flat) is machined on the end of the shaft to accommodate the circlip tangs.
4. With needle nose pliers, compress the circlip tangs. Pry the shaft into the side gear splined cavity. The circlip will be compressed into the cavity with the shaft.
5. Remove the clamp bolt securing the ball joint stud into the steering knuckle.
6. Separate the ball joint stud from the steering knuckle by prying against the knuckle leg and control arm. Do not damage

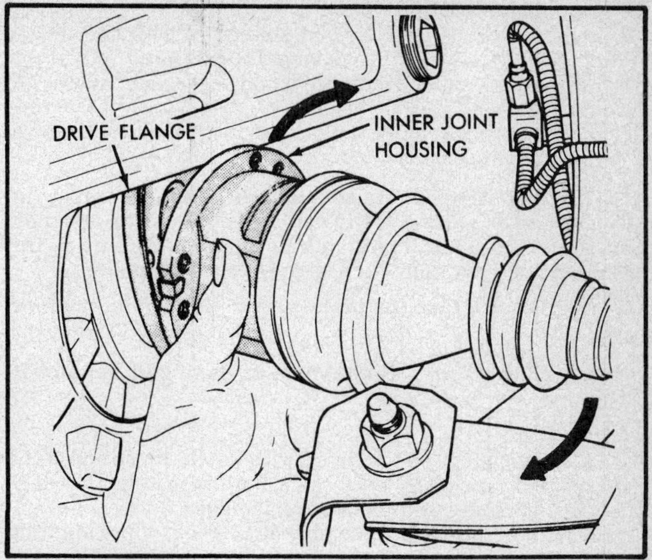

Removing the Rampage drive axle—tilt up to retain lubricant (© Chrysler Corp.)

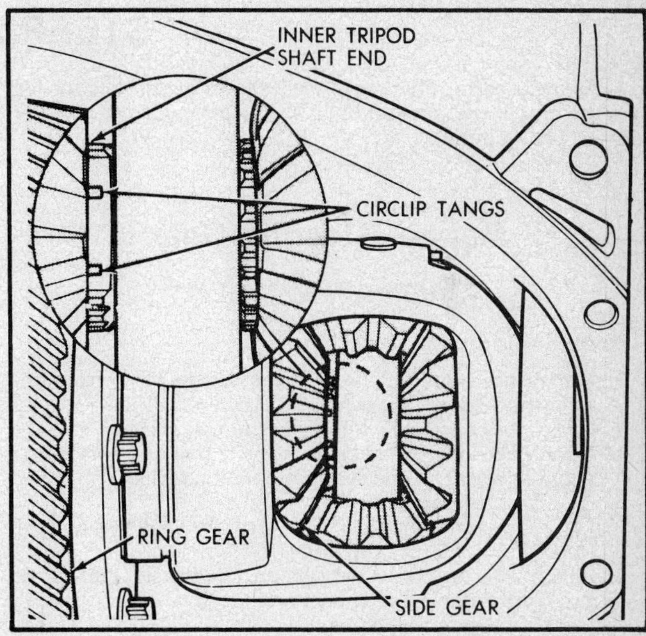

Clip type retained drive axle—Rampage (© Chrysler Corp.)

the ball joint or C/V joint boots.

7. Separate the outer C/V joint splined shaft from hub by holding C/V housing while moving knuckle (hub) assembly away. Do not pry on or otherwise damage the wear sleeve on the outer C/V joint.

8. Support the assembly at the C/V joint housings. Remove by pulling outward on the inner joint jousing.

NOTE: The drive shaft acts as a bolt and secures the hub/bearing assembly. If the vehicle is to be supported or moved on its wheels, install a bolt through the hub to insure that the hub bearing assembly cannot loosen.

9. Install new circlips on the inner joint shaft before installation.

NOTE: If the wear sleeve is bent or damaged, replace it before installing the axle shaft.

10. Align the tangs on the circlip with the flattened end of the shaft before inserting into transaxle. Failure to align the tangs can cause jamming and component damage.

11. Hold the inner joint assembly at housing, while aligning and guiding the inner joint spline into the transaxle.

12. Check the clip type axle for locking of the circlip in the proper position.

13. Push the knuckle (hub) assembly out and install the splined outer C/V joint shaft in the hub.

14. Install the knuckle assembly on the ball joint stud.

NOTE: The steering knuckle clamp bolt is the prevailing torque type and the original or exact equivalent must be reinstalled.

15. Install and tighten clamp bolt to 50 ft. lbs. (68 Nm).

16. Install the speedometer pinion.

17. If the differential cover was removed, apply a $^1/_8$ inch bead of gasket material, RTV to the gasket surface of the differential cover.

18. Install the differential cover and torque the retaining screws to 13.8 ft. lbs. (19 Nm).

19. Fill the differential to the bottom of the plug hole with Dexron® type automatic transmission fluid.

20. Install the washer and a new hub nut, apply the brakes and torque the hub nut to 180 ft. lbs. (245 Nm).

21. Install a lock and new cotter pin on the hub nut.

22. Install the wheel and tire assembly and torque the lug nuts to 80 ft. lbs. (108 Nm).

STEERING GEAR

Refer to the Steering chapter in the General Repair Section for the overhaul of the manual and power steering gears and the power steering pump.

Manual Steering Gear

SAGINAW MODELS

Removal and Installation

1. Unbolt the coupling clamp at the bottom of the column.
2. Remove the steering gear arm nut.
3. Use a puller to remove the steering gear arm.
4. Unbolt the steering gear from the frame and remove it.
5. Align the gear in the straight-ahead position.
6. Bolt the steering gear to the frame.
7. Make sure the front wheels are straight ahead and install the steering arm but not the nut.
8. If both wheels and steering gear are in the straight-ahead position, install the steering arm nut.
9. Install the coupling clamp.

NOTE: On models with the Saginaw 553 steering box, you will have to slide the column up to install the coupling.

Removal and Installation

PICKUPS, RAMCHARGER AND TRAIL DUSTER

1. Remove the two bolts from the wormshaft coupling.
2. Remove the steering arm from the steering gear using a suitable tool.
3. Remove the steering gear-to-frame bolts and remove the unit from the vehicle.
4. To install, position the steering gear to the frame and install the mounting bolts.
5. Install the steering arm and place the front wheels in the straight ahead position.
6. Place the steering wheel in the straight ahead position.
7. Install the wormshaft-to-column coupling bolts.

VANS AND WAGONS

Removal and Installation

1. Disconnect the negative battery cable.
2. Raise the vehicle on a hoist and support safely. Disconnect the "rubber and fabric" coupling (leaving the lower half of the coupling on the wormshaft).
3. Disconnect the shift linkage at the steering column.
4. Remove the steering arm retaining nut and washer. With a suitable tool remove the steering arm from the sector shaft.
5. Remove the three gear mounting bolts. Lower the vehicle from the hoist and remove the toe plate and column support bolts.
6. Disconnect the wiring and remove the column assembly.
7. Raise the vehicle on the hoist and remove the steering gear through the opening on the inboard side of the frame. (It may be helpful to remove the three bolts from the left idle arm bracket and move the bracket out of the way to provide additional clearance.)

NOTE: If the lower half of the steering coupling was removed from the gear, reinstall it on the wormshaft and secure it with a roll pin before installing the gear into the vehicle.

8. From underneath the vehicle, place the steering gear in position and install the three mounting bolts.
9. Reinstall the idler arm bracket, if removed.
10. Install the steering arm on the sector shaft. Install the washer and retaining nut.
11. Install the steering column assembly. Connect the steering column wiring. Install the shift linkage at the steering column.
12. Connect the steering shaft coupling at the wormshaft.
13. Connect the battery.

MANUAL AND POWER STEERING GEAR

Removal and Installation

FRONT WHEEL DRIVE

1. Remove the front wheels.

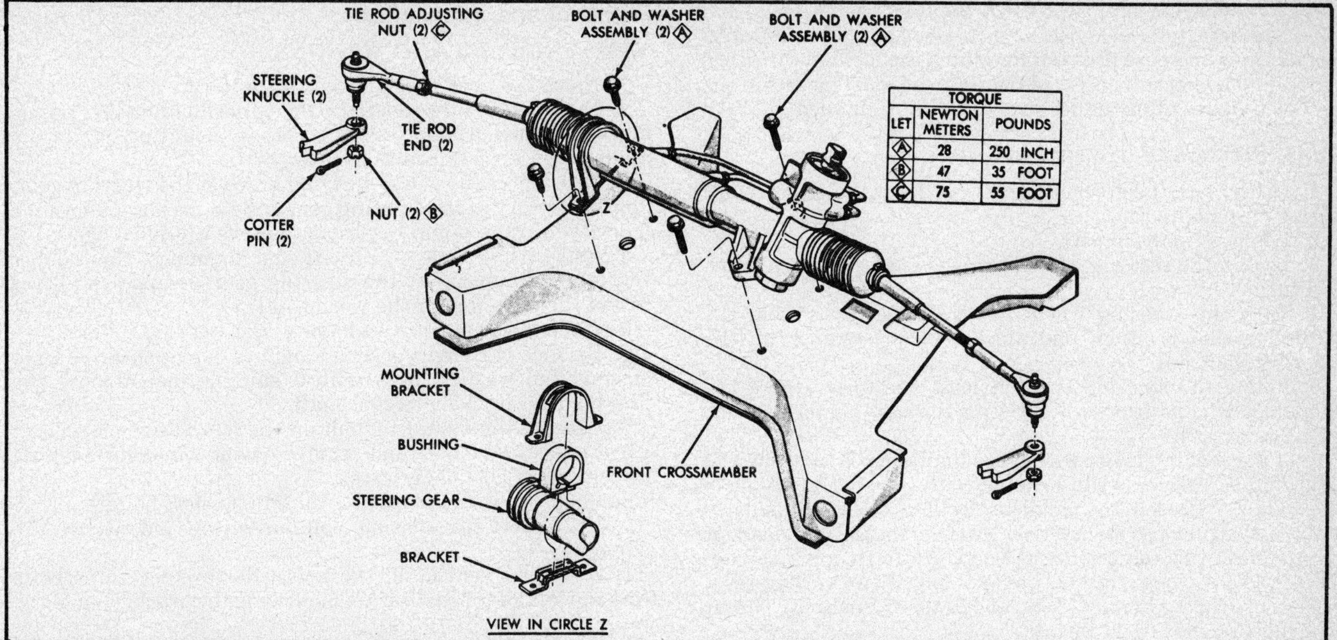

Typical steering assembly mounting—Mini-Van (© Chrysler Corp.)

2. Remove the tie rod ends, using a suitable puller.
3. Drive out the lower roll pin attaching the pinion shaft to the lower universal joint. Use a back up counter weight, to protect the universal joint, while driving the roll pin.
4. Support the front suspension crossmember with a hydraulic jack. Remove the two rear nuts attaching the crossmember to the frame. Loosen the two front bolts attaching the crossmember to frame and lower the crossmember slightly for access to the boot seal shields.
5. Remove the splash shields and boot seal shields.
6. On power steering models remove the hoses from the steering gear box.
7. Disconnect the tie rod ends from the steering knuckles and remove the bolts attaching the gear to the front suspension crossmember.
8. Remove the gear from driver's side of vehicle.
9. Installation is the reverse of removal.
10. Torque the steering gear to crossmember bolts to 20.8 ft. lbs. (28 Nm).

WORM BEARING PRELOAD

Adjustment

SAGINAW MODEL 525

1. Disconnect and remove the steering gear arm from the sector shaft using a suitable tool.
2. Remove the horn pad.
3. Loosen the sector shaft adjusting screw lock nut, and back out the adjusting screw one half to two turns.
4. Turn the steering wheel to the right stop theh back it off one half turn and place a torque wrench on the steering shaft nut.
5. Rotate the steering shaft from the right stop toward the straight ahead position, while testing the rotating torque with the torque wrench. The torque required to keep the wheel moving should be between 4 to 6 inch lbs.
6. If this reading is not within the specified limits, adjustment can be made as follows, with the gear in or out of the vehicle: Loosen the adjuster locknut. Turn the adjuster plug clockwise to increase preload or counterclockwise to decrease preload. While holding the adjuster plug from turning, tighten the locknut securely, then reset the worm bearing preload.

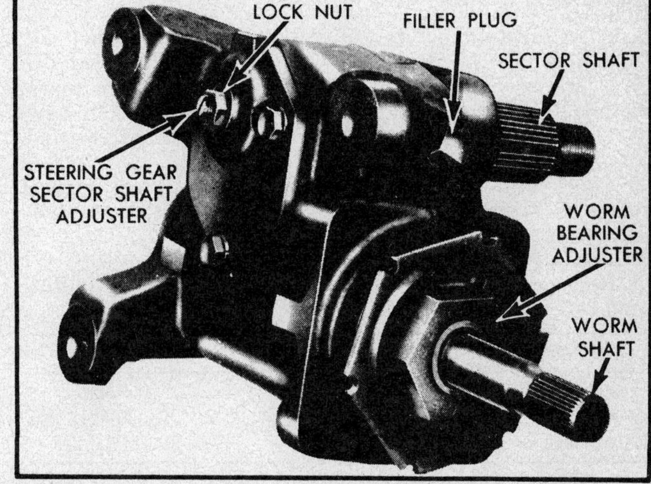

Model 553 Saginaw steering gear (© Chrysler Corp.)

SAGINAW MODEL 553

1. Remove the steering arm from the steering gear sector shaft.
2. Loosen the sector shaft adjuster screw locknut, and back out the adjuster screw (approx. two turns).
3. Turn the steering wheel two complete turns from the straight-ahead position.

NOTE: Do not turn the steering wheel hard against the stops in the gear when the steering gear arm is disconnected as internal damage could result.

4. Using a torque wrench and a $^3/_4$ inch socket (12 point), rotate the steering worm shaft at least one turn (toward straight-ahead position). The torque required to keep the worm shaft moving should be between 13 and 18 inch lbs. If the reading is not within these limits, adjustment is necessary.

5. To adjust the preload, loosen the adjuster lock nut and turn the adjuster clockwise to increase preload, or counterclockwise to decrease preload. Retighten the locknut to 70-100 ft. lbs. and recheck the preload. The preload must be within the specified limits after the locknut has been tightened.

Vans, Pickups and Wagons

1. Disconnect the steering gear arm from the sector shaft with a suitable tool.
2. Remove the horn pad.
3. Loosen the sector shaft adjusting screw lock nut (approx. two turns).
4. Turn the steering wheel two complete turns from the straight-ahead position, and place a torque wrench on the steering shaft nut.
5. Rotate the steering shaft at least one turn toward the straight-ahead position, while testing the rotating torque with a torque wrench.
6. If the reading is not within the limits specified below, the following adjustments can be made with the gear in or out of the vehicle. Loosen the adjuster locknut. Use an adjuster wrench and turn the adjuster clockwise to increase preload, or counterclockwise to decrease preload. While stopping the adjuster from turning, tighten the lock nut securely, then reset the worm bearing preload. 1980 and Later Worm Shaft Thrust Bearing Preload: 16-24 inch lbs.

CROSS OR SECTOR GEAR MESH

Adjustment

This adjustment is made only after worm bearing preload is adjusted. Steering arm is still removed from cross (sector) shaft.

1. Center steering wheel (wormshaft) by counting turns from full right to full left and counting back exactly half way.
2. Loosen locknut on cross (sector) shaft adjusting screw and turn adjusting screw in until all lash is gone.
3. Check torque required to move steering wheel (torque wrench on steering wheel nut) through high-spot (center) position.
4. Readjust if necessary and retighten locknut.
5. Reinstall steering arm on cross (sector) shaft and tighten clamp bolt to 85 ft. lbs. torque.

Cross or Sector Gear Mesh	in. lbs.
Saginaw 525	14 Total
Saginaw 553	25–29 Total
Vans and Wagons	8¼–11¼ Total

Power Steering Gear

INTEGRAL TYPE

Removal and Installation

CONVENTIONAL TRUCKS

1. Center the steering gear.
2. Pull off the steering gear arm with a suitable tool.
3. Disconnect the pressure and return hoses.
4. Disconnect the steering shaft coupling.
5. Unbolt the gear from the frame and remove it.
6. Install the mounting bolts finger tight on installation.
7. Connect the coupling. Align the gear to the frame to prevent binding; tighten the bolts.
8. Connect the pressure and return hoses.
9. Center the steering gear, make sure the wheels are straight ahead, replace the steering arm and nut.
10. Idle the engine and turn the steering wheel gently from stop to stop to bleed the system of air.

Removal and Installation

VANS, PICKUPS AND WAGONS

1. Raise the hood and remove the battery.
2. Disconnect the wires from the windshield washer pump. Remove the windshield washer reservoir mounting screws and position the reservoir out of the way.
3. Disconnect the power steering hoses at the steering gear. Cap the fittings at the steering gear and tie the hoses above the fluid level in the pump reservoir to prevent oil leakage.
4. Raise the vehicle on a hoist and disconnect the "rubber and fabric" coupling at the steering gear (leaving the lower half of the coupling on the wormshaft).
5. Disconnect the shift linkage at the steering column.
6. Remove the steering arm shield if so equipped. Remove the nut and washer, then with a suitable tool, remove the steering arm from the sector shaft.
7. Remove the mounting bolt on the left side of the gear.
8. Lower the vehicle and remove one of the two remaining steering gear mounting bolts.
9. Remove the toe plate and column support bolts.
10. Disconnect the steering column wiring and remove the assembly.
11. Raise the vehicle on the hoist. Remove the three bolts from the left idler arm bracket and swing the bracket out of the way.
12. Remove the remaining bolt and the steering gear from underneath of the vehicle, through the opening on the inboard side of the frame.

NOTE: Before installing the steering gear into the vehicle, install the coupling half on the wormshaft and secure it with the roll pin.

13. From the underside of the vehicle, place the steering gear into position on the mounting bracket and install the three mounting bolts.
14. Continue the installation in the reverse order of the removal.
15. Lower the vehicle, start the engine and turn the steering wheel several times from stop to stop to bleed the system of air.
16. Stop the engine and check the fluid level, correct if necessary. Inspect for leaks.

Adjustment

SECTOR ADJUSTMENT, VANS, PICKUPS AND WAGONS

1. Disconnect the center link from the steering gear arm.
2. Start the engine and allow to run at normal idle speed.
3. Rotate the steering wheel from lock to lock. Carefully count the number of turns required, then rotate the wheel back, exactly to the midpoint of its travel.
4. Loosen the adjusting screw until backlash in the steering gear arm becomes apparent.

NOTE: Backlash is felt by holding the end of the steering gear arm lightly between your thumb and forefinger.

5. Tighten the adjusting screw just enough so that the backlash disappears. Continue to tighten the screw for another $^3/_8$ to $^1/_2$ turn from this point. Tighten the locknut to 28 ft. lbs.
6. Attach the center link to the steering gear arm.

POWER STEERING PUMP

Removal and Installation

EXCEPT FRONT WHEEL DRIVE

1. Loosen pump lower mounting and locking bolts and remove the belt.

2. Place a container under pump and disconnect both pump hoses.
3. Remove mounting and locking bolts and remove pump and brackets.
4. To install, position pump on engine and install retaining and locking bolts.
5. Install drive belt and adjust. Tighten pump brackets to 30 ft. lbs. torque.
6. Connect pressure and return hoses, routing them in the same position they were in before removal.
7. Fill pump reservoir.
8. Start engine and turn steering wheel all the way left and right to bleed the system. Stop engine and recheck fluid level, refilling if necessary.

FRONT WHEEL DRIVE

1. Disconnect the power steering hoses from the pump.
2. Remove the adjusting bolt and slip off the belt.
3. Support the pump, remove the mounting bolts and lift out the pump.
4. Installation is the reverse of removal. Adjust the belt to specifications.

CLUTCH

REMOVAL AND INSTALLATION

ALL MODELS-EXCEPT FRONT WHEEL DRIVE

1. Raise the vehicle and support safely.
2. Support the engine on a suitable jack.
3. Remove the crossmember if necessary.
4. Remove the transmission. Remove the transfer case if equipped.
5. Remove the clutch housing pan if equipped.
6. Remove the clutch fork, clutch bearing and sleeve assembly if not removed from the transmission.
7. Mark the position of the clutch cover and flywheel. Remove the clutch cover retaining bolts, loosening them evenly so as not to distort the clutch cover.
8. Pull the pressure plate assembly clear of the flywheel and, while supporting the pressure plate, slide the clutch disc from between the flywheel and the pressure plate.
9. To install, clean all working surfaces of the flywheel and pressure plate.
10. Grease radius at the back of the bushing.
11. Rotate the clutch cover and pressure plate assembly for maximum clearance between flywheel and frame crossmember if crossmember was not removed during clutch removal.
12. Tilt top edge of clutch cover and pressure plate assembly back and move it up into the clutch housing. Support clutch cover and pressure plate assembly and slide clutch disc into position.
13. Position clutch disc and plate against flywheel and insert spare transmission main drive gear shaft or clutch installing tool through clutch disc hub and into main. drive bearing.
14. Rotate clutch cover until the punch marks on cover and flywheel line up.
15. Bolt cover loosely to flywheel. Tighten cover bolts a few turns at a time, in progression, until tight. Then tighten bolts to 20 ft. lbs. torque.
16. Install transmission.
17. Install frame crossmembers and insulator, tighten all bolts.

REMOVAL

FRONT WHEEL DRIVE WITH A–412 MANUAL TRANS.

1. Remove the tranxaxle. Refer to the Manual Transmission Removal and Installation procedure in this section.
2. Diagonally loosen bolts attaching flywheel to pressure plate. Back off bolts, one or two turns at a time, in succession, to avoid bending the cover flange.
3. Remove flywheel and clutch disc from pressure plate.
4. Remove retaining ring and release plate.
5. Use special tool L-4533 or equivalent to center the clutch disc and install the disc and flywheel onto the pressure plate.
6. Install the flywheel to pressure plate bolts. Torque the bolts to 15 ft. lbs. (20 Nm).
7. Install the transaxle and adjust the clutch free play.

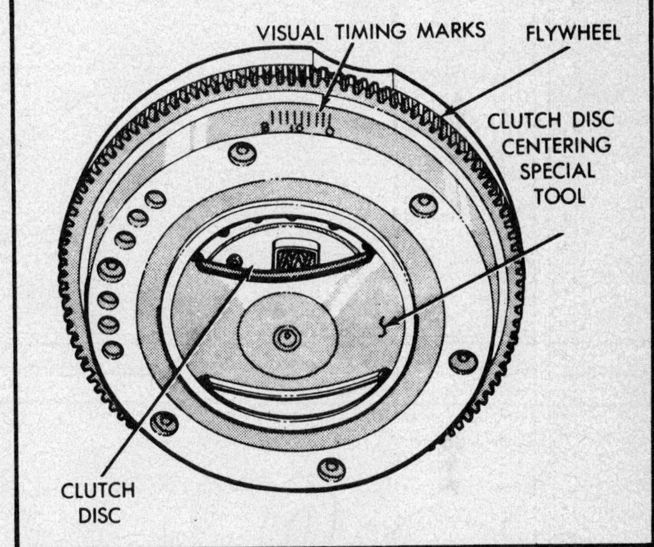

A-412 manual transaxle clutch centering tool (© Chrysler Corp.)

Removal

FRONT WHEEL DRIVE WITH A–460 MANUAL TRANS.

1. Remove the transaxle. See the Manual Transmission part of this Dodge Truck section.
2. Mark clutch cover and flywheel, to maintain their same relative positions when re-installing them.
3. Insert clutch disc aligning tool C-4676 or equivalent through the clutch disc hub to prevent clutch disc from falling and damaging the facings.
4. Loosen the clutch cover attaching bolts one or two turns at a time, in succession, to avoid bending the cover flange.
5. Remove the clutch pressure plate and cover assembly and disc from flywheel. Handle carefully to avoid contaminating the friction surfaces.
6. Remove the clutch release shaft and slide release bearing assembly off the input shaft seal retainer.
7. Remove the fork from the release bearing thrust plate.

Installation

1. Installation is the reverse of removal.
2. Mount the clutch assembly on the flywheel, being careful to properly align dowels and the alignment marks made before removal.

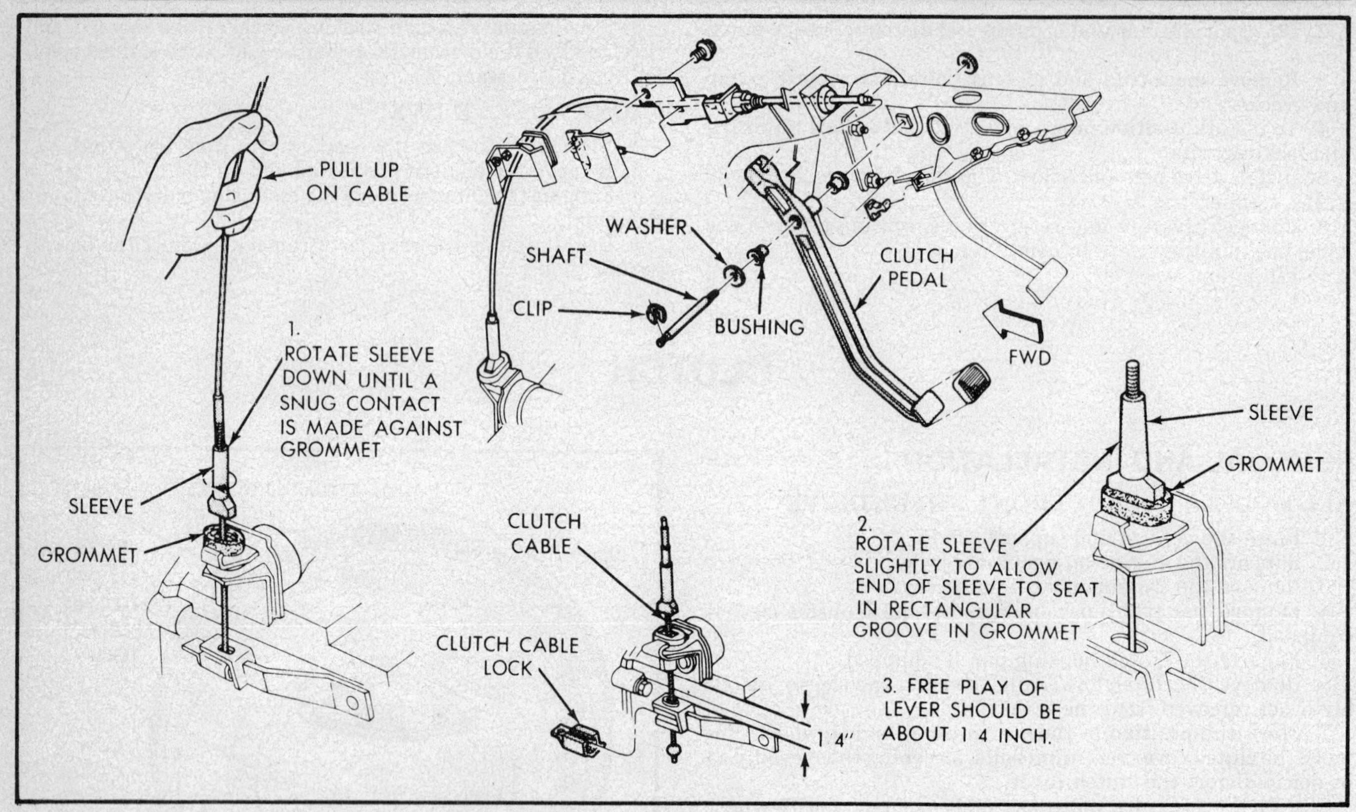
PULL UP ON CABLE
1. ROTATE SLEEVE DOWN UNTIL A SNUG CONTACT IS MADE AGAINST GROMMET
SLEEVE
GROMMET
WASHER
SHAFT
CLIP
BUSHING
CLUTCH PEDAL
FWD
SLEEVE
GROMMET
CLUTCH CABLE
CLUTCH CABLE LOCK
2. ROTATE SLEEVE SLIGHTLY TO ALLOW END OF SLEEVE TO SEAT IN RECTANGULAR GROOVE IN GROMMET
3. FREE PLAY OF LEVER SHOULD BE ABOUT 1 4 INCH.
1 4"

Adjusting clutch free play on the A-412 manual transaxle (© Chrysler Corp.)

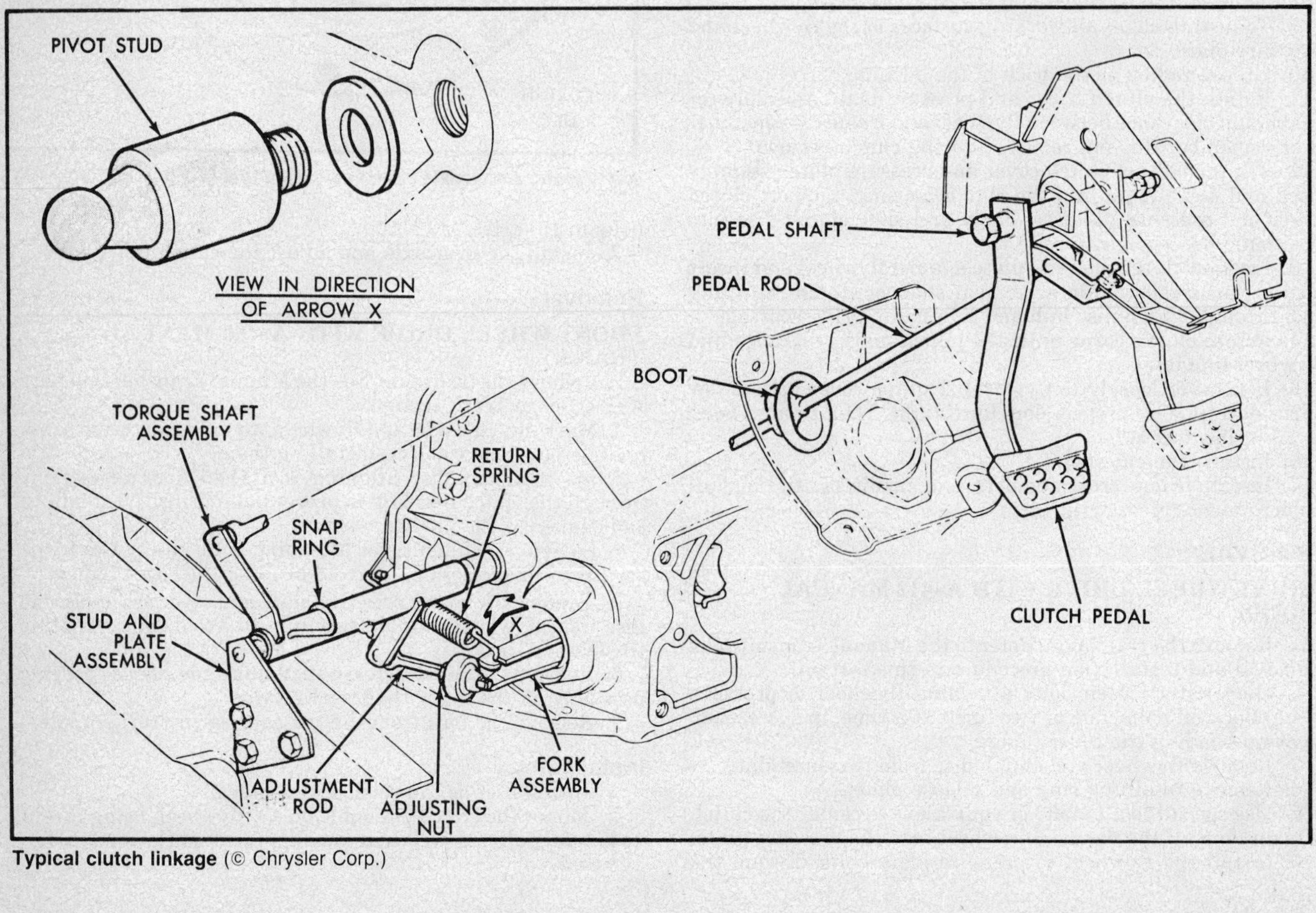

PIVOT STUD
VIEW IN DIRECTION OF ARROW X
PEDAL SHAFT
PEDAL ROD
BOOT
TORQUE SHAFT ASSEMBLY
RETURN SPRING
SNAP RING
STUD AND PLATE ASSEMBLY
X
CLUTCH PEDAL
FORK ASSEMBLY
ADJUSTMENT ROD
ADJUSTING NUT

Typical clutch linkage (© Chrysler Corp.)

3. Apply pressure to the alignment tool C-4676 or equivalent to center the tip of the tool into the crankshaft and the sliding cone into the clutch fingers while snugging the clutch attaching bolts sufficiently to hold the disc in position.
4. To avoid distortion of the clutch cover, turn the bolts in a few turns at a time alternately until they are all seated. tighten them to 21 ft. lbs. (28 Nm.).
5. Remove the clutch disc alignment tool C-4676.

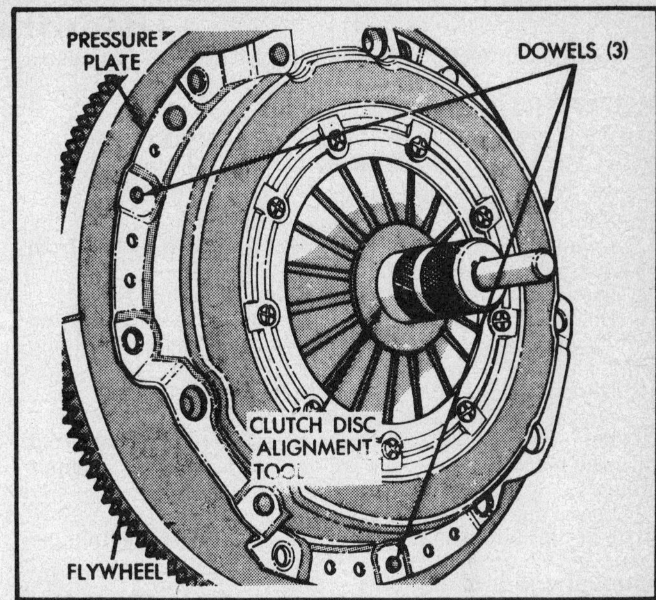

A-460 manual transaxle clutch centering tool (© Chrysler Corp.)

MECHANICAL CLUTCH LINKAGE

Adjustment

The only adjustment required is pedal free-play. Adjust the clutch actuating fork rod by turning the self-locking adjusting nut to provide $^1/_8$ in. ($^3/_{32}$ in. on vans and wagons) free movement at the end of the fork. This will provide the recommended $1^1/_2$ in. (1 in. on vans, wagons, Ramcharger and Trailduster) freeplay at the pedal. On Rampage applications with A-412 transmissions, adjust the free play at the end of the clutch cable to $^1/_4$ inch and lock the lever to cable with the clutch cable locking clip. The Rampage & Scamp A-460, A-465 and A-525 transmissions have automatic clutch linkage adjustment.

Bleeding Hydraulic Clutch System

1. Clean away dirt from around master cylinder reservoir filler cap, remove cap and fill reservoir. Make sure to check reservoir frequently during bleeding process and fill when necessary.
2. Clean bleeder valve on valve cylinder and attach bleeder hose to valve.
3. Place other end of hose in jar half full of brake fluid.
4. Bleed intermittently as clutch pedal is being depressed by opening and closing bleeder valve. Continue bleeding until no air bubbles come from bleeder hose.

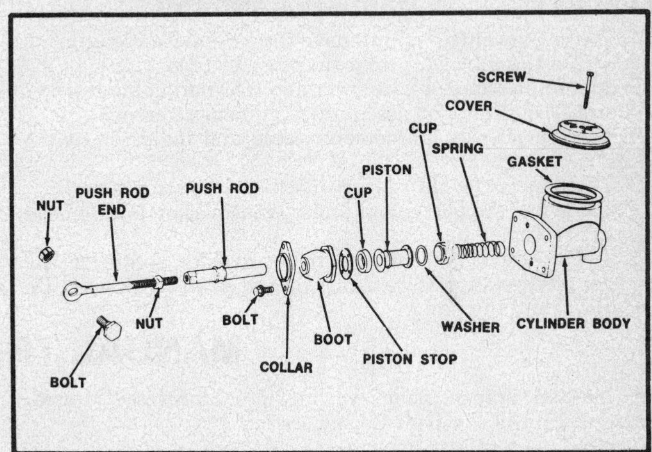

Exploded view of clutch master cylinder (© Chrysler Corp.)

CLUTCH MASTER CYLINDER

Removal and Installation

1. Remove pedal return spring.
2. Disconnect push rod end at clutch pedal and hydraulic fluid line at master cylinder.
3. Unbolt master cylinder from firewall.
4. Installation is the reverse of the above procedure. Adjust master cylinder push rod to 0.010" free play. Bleed hydraulic system.

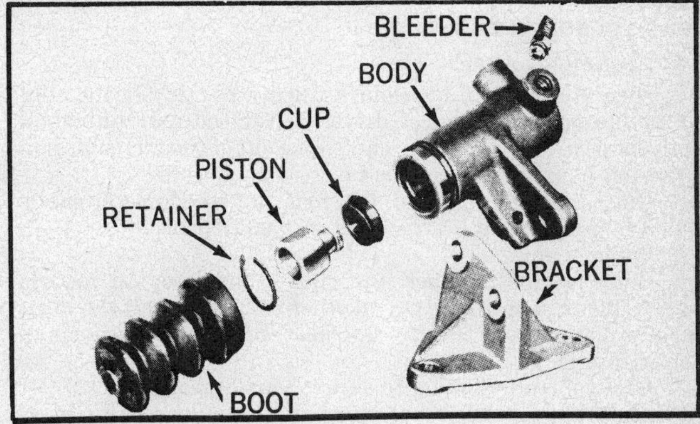

Clutch slave cylinder (© Chrysler Corp.)

CLUTCH SLAVE CYLINDER

Removal and Installation

Slave cylinder is located on the right side of the clutch housing. Disconnect hydraulic line, then remove cylinder mounting bolts. After installation, be sure to bleed hydraulic system and adjust as described above.

TRANSFER CASE

See Unit Repair Section for Transfer Case overhaul procedure

Removal and Installation

MODELS W250, W350, W450, W100, W200 AND W300 PICKUPS, RAMCHARGER AND TRAIL DUSTER

1. Raise and support the truck.
2. Remove the skid plate, if any.
3. Drain the transfer case by removing the bottom bolt from the front output rear cover.
4. Disconnect the speedometer cable.
5. Disconnect the front and rear output shafts. Suspend these from a convenient location; do not allow them to hang free.
6. Disconnect the shift rods at the transfer case.
7. Support the transfer case.
8. Remove the adaptor-to-transfer case mounting bolts and move the transfer case rearward to disengage the front input splines.
9. Lower and remove the transfer case.
10. Installation is the reverse of removal. Adjust the linkage.

Removal and Installation

MODELS W150, W250, PW150 and AW150 PICKUPS, RAMCHARGER, TRAILDUSTER AND 4 x 4

1. Raise the vehicle and remove the skid plate if equipped.
2. Drain the lubricant from the transfer case.
3. Mark the transfer case front and rear output shaft yokes and propeller shafts for assembly alignment reference.
4. Disconnect the speedometer cable and indicator switch wires.
5. Disconnect the shift lever link from operating lever.
6. Place and support stand under transmission and remove the rear crossmember.
7. Disconnect the front and rear propeller shafts at the transfer case yokes. Secure shafts to frame rails with wire. Do not allow shafts to hang.
8. Disconnect the parking brake cable guide from the pivot locted on the right frame rail, if necessary.
9. Remove the bolts attaching exhaust pipe support bracket to transfer case, if necessary.
10. Remove the transfer case-to-transmission bolts.
11. Move the transfer case assembly rearward until free of the transmission output shaft and remove assembly.
12. Remove all gasket material from the rear of the transmission adapter housing.
13. Installation is the reverse of removal.

NOTE: Do not install any transfer case attaching bolts until the transfer is completely seated against the transmission.

14. Torque the transfer case attaching bolts to 40 ft. lbs. (54 Nm). Torque the shift lever locknut to 18 ft. lbs. (24 Nm).
15. Fill the transfer case with Dexron® II type oil.
16. Lower the vehicle.

Linkage Adjustment

MODELS W100, 200, 300 PICKUPS, RAMCHARGER AND TRAILDUSTER

1. Loosen the lockscrews in both swivel rod clamps at the shifter assembly. The rods must be free to slide in the swivels.
2. Place the selector lever in the cab in neutral and insert alignment rod through the alignment holes in the shifter housing.
3. Place the range shift lever (outboard lever) on the transfer case in the neutral position.
4. Place the locknut shift lever on the transfer case (the inboard lever) in the unlocked position.
5. Retighten the rod swivel screws.
6. Remove the alignment rod from the shifter housing.

NOTE: The W250, W350, W450, W150, PW 150 and AW150 shift linkage is not adjustable.

MANUAL TRANSMISSION

For Manual Transmission overhaul procedures see Manual Transmission in the Unit Repair section

3-SPEED 2WD MODELS

Removal and Installation

1. Drain lubricant.
2. Disconnect and match-mark the driveshaft. On the sliding spline type, disconnect driveshaft at the rear universal joint, then carefully pull the shaft yoke out of the transmission extension housing. Do not nick or scratch splines.
3. Disconnect gearshift control rods and speedometer cable.
4. Remove backup light switch if so equipped.
5. Support engine.
6. Remove crossmember and rubber insulator on models with A-390 transmission. On all other models, unbolt the insulator or mount from the crossmember. Support the transmission with a jack.
7. Remove transmission to clutch housing bolts.
8. Slide transmission rearward until pinion shaft clears clutch completely, then lower transmission from vehicle.
9. Installation is the reverse order of the above procedure. Before inserting transmission driveshaft into clutch, make sure clutch housing bore, disc and face are aligned. Tighten clutch housing to transmission bolts to 50ft. lbs. torque.
10. Fill with lubricant.
11. Adjust shift linkage.
12. Road test.

4-SPEED 2WD MODELS

Removal and Installation

1. Shift transmission into any gear.
2. Disconnect universal joint and loosen yoke retaining nut.
3. Disconnect parking brake (if so equipped) and speedometer cables at transmission.
4. Remove lever retainer by pressing down, rotating retainer counterclockwise slightly, then releasing.
5. Remove lever and its springs and washers.
6. Support the rear of the engine and remove the crossmember. Remove transmission to clutch bell housing retaining bolts and pull transmission rearward until drive pinion clears clutch, then remove transmission.
7. To install, place 1/2 teaspoon of short fibre grease in pinion shaft pilot bushing, taking care not to get any grease on flywheel face.
8. Align clutch disc and backing plate with a spare drive pinion shaft or clutch aligning tool, then carefully install transmission.
9. Install transmission to bell housing bolts, tightening to 50ft. lbs. torque. Replace the crossmember.
10. Install gear shift lever, shift into any gear and tighten yoke nut to 95-105ft. lbs. torque.
11. Install universal joint, speedometer cable and brake cable.
12. Adjust clutch.
13. Install transmission drain plug and fill transmission with lubricant.

14. Road test.

3 AND 4-SPEED-4WD MODELS

Removal and Installation

1. Raise and support the truck.
2. Remove the skid plate, if any.
3. Disconnect the speedometer cable.
4. Disconnect and match-mark the front and rear driveshafts. Suspend each shaft from a convenient place; do not allow them to hang free.
5. Disconnect the shift rods at the transfer case. On 4-speed transmissions, remove the shift lever retainer by pressing down and turning it counterclockwise. Remove the shift lever springs and washers.
6. Remove the rear driveshaft. Matchmark the driveshaft and rear U-joints before removing the driveshaft.
7. Support the transfer case.
8. Remove the extension-to-transfer case mounting bolts.
9. Move the transfer case rearward to disengage the front input shaft spline.
10. Lower and remove the transfer case.
11. Disconnect the back-up light switch.
12. Support the engine.
13. Support the transmission.
14. Remove the transmission crossmember.
15. Remove the transmission-to-clutch housing bolts.
16. Slide the transmission rearward until the mainshaft clears the clutch disc.
17. Lower and remove the transmission.
18. Installation is the reverse of removal. The transmission pilot bushing in the end of the crankshaft requires high-temperature grease. Multipurpose grease should be used. Do not lubricate the end of the mainshaft, clutch splines, or clutch release levers. Adjust the gearshift linkage on 3-speed transmissions.

OVERDRIVE, FOUR SPEED

Removal and Installation

1. Disconnect the negative battery cable.
2. Remove the retaining screws from the floor pan boot and slide the boot up and off the shift lever.
3. Remove the shift lever, retaining clips, washers, and control rods from the shift unit.
4. Remove the two bolts and washers which secure the shift unit to mounting plate on the extension housing and remove the unit.
5. Drain the fluid from the transmission.
6. Disconnect the speedometer cable and backup light switch leads.
8. Install engine support fixture C-3487-A or equivalent. Be sure that the support points are tight against the oil pan flange.
9. Raise engine slightly with the support fixture. Disconnect the extension housing from the center crossmember.
10. Support the transmission with a suitable jack and remove the center crossmember.
11. Remove the transmission to clutch housing bolts. Slide the transmission toward the rear until drive pinion shaft clears the clutch disc, before lowering the transmission. Remove the transmission.
12. Installation is the reverse of removal. Use high temperature multi-purpose grease on the pilot bushing in the end of the crankshaft, around the inner end of the pinion shaft pilot bushing in the flywheel and on the pinion bearing retainer release bearing area. Do not lubricate the end of the pinion shaft, clutch disc splines or clutch release levers.
13. Torque the clutch housing bolts to 50 ft. lbs. (68 Nm). Tighten the corssmember bolts to 30 ft. lbs. (41 Nm). Torque engine and transmission mounts to 50 ft. lbs. (68 Nm).
14. Fill the transmission with Dexron II® (or equivalent) automatic transmission fluid.
15. Road test the vehicle.

Locally fabricated engine support fixture—A-412 transaxle removal (© Chrysler Corp.)

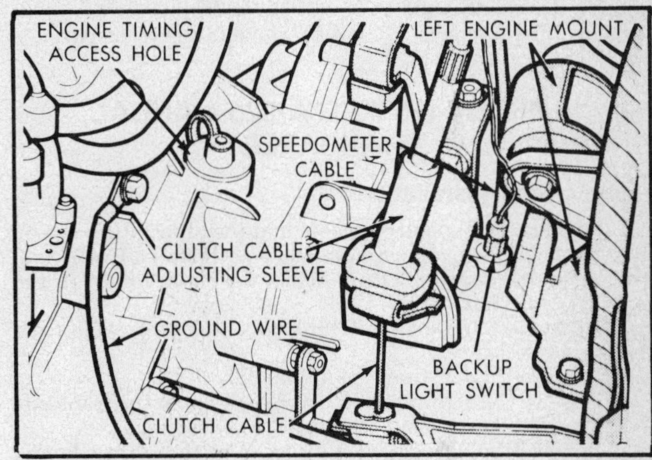

A-412 transaxle removal—engine compartment components to be removed. (© Chrysler Corp.)

MANUAL TRANSAXLE

Removal and Installation

A-412 MANUAL TRANSAXLE

1. Disconnect the battery negative cable.
2. Discsonnect the shift linkage rods and remove the starter wires.
3. Disconnect the back-up light switch wire and remove the starter motor.
4. Disconnect the clutch cable and remove the speedometer adaptor and pinion from the transaxle.
5. Support the engine with a locally fabricated support fixture.
6. Loosen the left wheel hub nut, raise the vehicle and disconnect the right drive shaft and tie it out of the way.
7. Remove the driveshaft, secure it out of the way.
8. Remove the left splash shield and the small dust cover at the bell housing.
9. Remove the large dust cover bolts t the bell housing and drain the fluid from the transaxle.
10. Place a transmission jack under the transaxle and chain it in place.
11. Remove the bolt from the left engine mount and the trans-

axle to engine bolt.

12. Slide the transaxle assembly to the left and the rear of the vehicle until the mainshaft clears clutch. Lower the transaxle and remove it from the vehicle.

13. Installation is the reverse of removal.

14. Adjust the clutch pedal free play to $^1/_2$ inch.

15. Adjust the gearshift linkage by placing the gearshift lever in neutral at the 3-4 position and loosening the clamp on the shift tube. Align the tab on the slider with the hole on the blocker bracket. Place a $^3/_4$ inch (19mm) spacer between the slider and the blocker bracket. Tighten the clamp on the shift tube and remove the spacer.

NOTE: No significant upward force should be exerted while tightening the shift tube clamp nut.

16. Align the marks on the flywheel with the indicator located in the timing access hole of the engine.

17. Torque the engine mounting bolts to 40 ft. lbs. (54 Nm) and the driveshaft bolts to 35 ft. lbs. (47 Nm).

18. Install 1.5 quarts of GL-4 gearlube in the transaxle.

19. Road test the vehicle.

A-460, A-465 AND A-525 MANUAL TRANSAXLE

Removal and Installation

1. Disconnect the battery cable and install a lifting eye on number 4 cylinder exhaust manifold bolt. Install a locally fabricated engine support fixture across the shock towers in the engine compartment.

2. Disconnect the gearshift linkage and clutch cable from the transaxle.

3. Remove the left front splash shield.

4. Remove the right and left drive shafts from the transaxle and support them. Do not let the drive axles hang free.

5. Remove the anti-rotational link from the transaxle and support the transmission with a transmission jack. Install a chain around the jack and transmission for safety.

6. Remove the speedometer adaptor and pinion from the transaxle.

7. Remove the engine mount from the front crossmember and the front mount insulator through bolt. Remove the upper ball housing bolts.

8. Remove the left engine mount and remove the lower bell housing bolts.

9. Pry the transaxle away from the engine and lower the assembly from the vehicle.

10. Installation is the reverse of removal. Refill the transaxle with Dexron®II or equivalent automatic transmission fluid. Adjust the clutch free play and transmission linkage.

11. Torque the engine mounting bolts to 40 ft. lbs. (54 Nm). Torque the transmission to cylinder block bolts to 70 ft. lbs. (95 Nm). Torque the hub nut to 180 ft. lbs. (245 Nm) and torque the lug nuts to 80 ft. lbs. (108 Nm).

Locally fabricated engine support fixture—A-460 transaxle removal (© Chrysler Corp.)

SHIFT LINKAGE

Adjustment

CONVENTIONAL TRUCKS

1. Remove both shift rod swivels from the transmission shift levers. Make sure transmission shift levers are in neutral (middle detent) position.

2. Move shift lever to line up locating slots in bottom of steering column shift housing and bearing housing. Install suitable tool in slot, if any.

3. Place a suitable tool between crossover blade and second-third lever at steering column so that both lever pins are engaged by crossover blade.

4. Set first-reverse lever on transmission to reverse position (rotate clockwise).

5. Adjust first-reverse rod by loosening clamp bolt and sliding swivel along rod so it will enter first-reverse lever at transmission. Install washers and clip.Tighten swivel bolt.

6. Remove gearshift housing locating tool and shift column lever into neutral position.

7. Adjust second-third rod swivel by loosening clamp bolt and sliding swivel along rod so it will enter second-third lever at transmission. Install washers and clip. Tighten swivel bolt.

8. Remove tool from crossover blade at steering column, and shift through all gears to check adjustment and crossover smoothness.

VANS AND WAGONS A-230 AND A-250

1. Adjust the length of the 2-3 shift rod so the position of the shift lever on the steering column will be correct.

2. Assemble the 1st-reverse and 2-3 shift rods, and place each in its normal position, secured with a clip. Loosen both swivel clamp bolts.

3. Move the 2-3 shift lever into 3rd position (this means moving the forward lever forward). Move the steering column lever until it is about five degrees above the horizontal. Tighten the shift rod swivel clamp bolt.

4. Shift the transmission to neutral. Place a suitable tool between the crossover blade and the 2-3 lever at the steering column so that both lever pins are engaged by the crossover blade.

5. Set the 1st-reverse lever in neutral. tighten the swivel clamp bolt.

6. Remove the tool from the crossover blade, and check all shifts for smoothness.

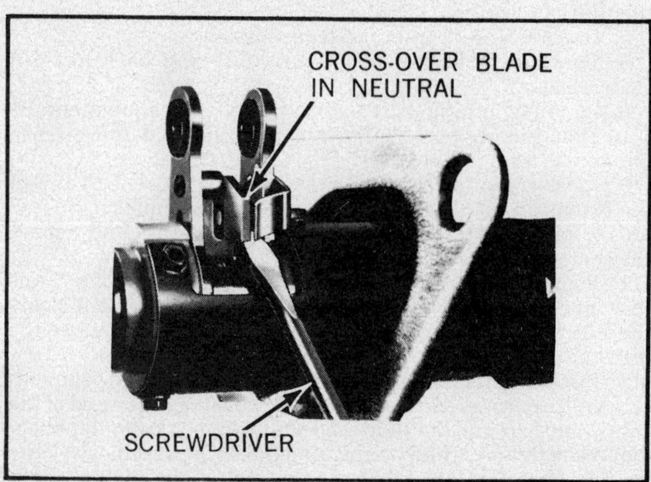

Holding the three speed column shift linkage in the neutral position (© Chrysler Corp.)

PICKUPS, RAMCHARGER AND TRAILDUSTER A- 230

1. Remove both shift rod swivels from the transmission shift levers. Make sure that the transmission shift levers are in the neutral position (middle detent).
2. Move the shift lever to line up the locating slots in the bottom of the steering column shift housing and bearing housing.
3. Place a suitable tool between the crossover blade and the 2nd and 3rd lever at the steering column, so that both lever pins are engaged by the crossover blade.
4. Set the 1st-reverse lever on the transmission to the reverse position (rotate clockwise).
5. Adjust the 1st-reverse rod swivel by loosening the clamp bolt and sliding the swivel along the rod so it will enter the 1st-reverse lever at the transmission. Install the washers and the clip. Tighten the swivel bolt.
6. Remove the gearshift housing locating tool, and shift the transmission into the neutral position.
7. Adjust the 2nd-3rd rod swivel by loosening the clamp bolt and sliding the swivel along the rod so it will enter the 2nd-3rd lever at the transmission. Install the washer and the clip.Tighten the swivel bolt.
8. Remove the tool from the crossover blade at the steering column and shift the transmission through all the gears to check the adjustment and the crossover smoothness.

FRONT WHEEL DRIVE A-412 TRANSAXLE

1. Place the gearshift lever in neutral at 3-4 position.
2. Loosen the clamp on the shift tube and align the tab on the slider with the hole on the blocker bracket.
3. Place a $^3/_4$ inch (19mm) spacer between the slider and blocker bracket.
4. Tighten the clamp on the shift tube and then remove the spacer.

NOTE: Do not exert any significant force upward on the shift tube nut, while tightening the clamp.

FRONT WHEEL DRIVE A-460, A-465, A-525 MANUAL TRANSAXLE

1. Working over the left front fender, remove the lock pin from the transaxle selector shaft housing.
2. Reverse the lock pin (so the long end is down) and insert the pin into the same threaded hole while pushing the selector shaft into the selector housing. This operation locks the selector shaft in the 1-2 neutral position.
3. Raise the vehicle on a hoist and loosen the clamp bolt that secures the gearshift tube to the gearshift connector.
4. Check to see that the gearshift connector slides and turns freely in the gearshift tube.
5. Position the shifter mechanism connector assembly so that the isolator is contacting the upstanding flange and the rib on the isolator is aligned for and aft with the hole in the blockout bracket. Hold the connector isolator in this position while tightening the clamp bolt on the gearshift tube to 14.1ft. lbs. (19 Nm).

NOTE: No significant force should be exerted upward on the linkage, while tightening the clamp.

6. Remove the lock pin from the selector shaft housing and reinstall it in a reversed position. Torque the lock pin to 8.4ft. lbs. (12 Nm).
7. Check the first to reverse shifting and for the blockout into reverse.

MANUAL TRANSMISSION (435, 445 MODELS,) AND OVERDRIVE

1. Install the floor shift lever aligning tool to hold the levers in the neutral crossover position.
2. With all rods removed from the transmission shift levers, place the levers in the neutral detent positions.
3. Rotate the threaded shift rods to make the length exactly right to enter the transmission levers. Start with the 1-2 shift rod (it may be necessary to pull clip at shifter end to rotate this rod).
4. Replace the washers and clips. Remove the aligning tool and test the shifting action.

MODELS A-390, A-230

1. Loosen both shift rod swivels. Make sure that the transmission shift levers are in the neutral position (middle detent).
2. Move the shift lever to line up the locating slots in the bottom of the steering column shift housing and bearing housing. Install a suitable tool in the slot.
3. Place a suitable tool between the crossover blade and the 2nd-3d lever at the steering column so that both lever pins are engaged by the crossover blade.
4. Tighten both rod swivel bolts. Remove the gearshift housing locating tool.
5. Remove the tool from the crossover blade at the steering column and shift the transmission through all gears to check adjustment and crossover smoothness.
6. Check for proper operation of the steering column lock in reverse. With the proper linkage adjustment, the ignition should lock in reverse only, with hands off the gearshift lever.

AUTOMATIC TRANSMISSION

Removal

LOADFLITE

1. Remove the transmission and converter as an assembly; otherwise the coverter drive plate, pump bushing, and oil seal will be damaged. The drive plate will not support a load. Therefore, none of the weight of the transmission should be allowed to rest on the plate during removal. Remove the transfer case, as necessary.
2. Attach a remote control starter switch to the starter solenoid so the engine can be rotated from under the vehicle.
3. Disconnect high tension cable from the ignition coil.
4. Remove cover plate from in front of the converter assembly to provide access to the converter drain plug and mounting bolts.
5. Rotate engine to bring drain plug to "6 o'clock" position. Drain the converter and transmission.
6. Mark converter and drive plate to aid in reassembly.
7. Rotate the engine with the remote control switch to locate two converter to drive plate bolts at 5 and 7 o'clock positions. Remove the two bolts, rotate engine again and remove the other two bolts.
8. Disconnect battery ground cable. Remove engine to transmission struts, if necessary. The exhaust system on some models may have to be dropped.
9. Remove the starter.
10. Remove wire from the neutral starting switch.
11. Remove gearshift cable or rod from the transmission and the lever.
12. Disconnect the throttle rod from left side of transmission.
13. Disconnect the oil cooler lines at transmission and remove the oil filler tube. Disconnect the speedometer cable.
14. Disconnect the driveshaft.
15. Install engine support fixture to hold up the rear of the engine.
16. Raise transmission slightly with jack to relieve load and remove support bracket or crossmember. Remove all bell housing bolts and carefully work transmission and converter rearward off engine dowels and disengage converter hub from end of crankshaft.

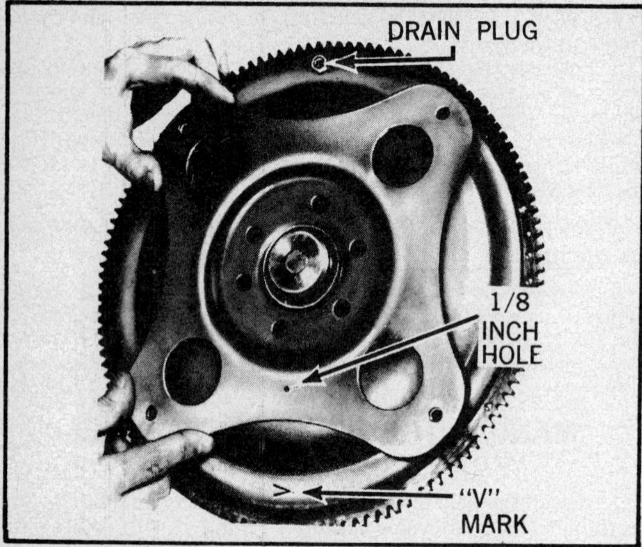

Converter and drive plate markings typical (© Chrysler Corp.)

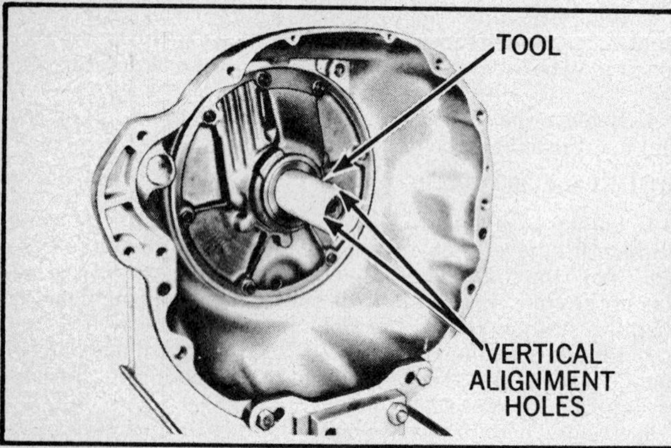

Aligning the pump rotors (© Chrysler Corp.)

CAUTION

Attach a small C-clamp to edge of bell housing to hold converter in place during transmission removal; otherwise the front pump bushing might be damaged.

Installation

NOTE: Install transmission and converter as an assembly. The drive plate will not support a load. Do not allow weight of transmission to rest on the plate during installation.

1. Rotate pump rotors until the rotor lugs are vertical.
2. Carefully slide converter assembly over input shaft and reaction shaft. Make sure converter impeller shaft slots are also vertical and fully engaged front pump inner rotor lugs.
3. Use a "C" clamp on edge of converter housing to old converter in place during transmission installation.
4. Converter drive plate should be free of distortion and drive plate to crankshaft bolts tightened to 55 ft. lbs. torque.
5. Using a jack, position transmission and converter assembly in alignment with engine.
6. Rotate converter so mark on converter (made during removal) will align with mark on drive plate. The offset holes in plate are located next to the $^1/_8$ in. hole in inner circle of the plate. A stamped "V" mark identified the offset hole in converter front cover. Carefully work transmission assembly forward over engine block dowels with converter hub entering the crankshaft opening.
7. Install converter housing to engine bolts and tighten to 28ft. lbs.
8. Install the two lower drive plate to converter bolts and tighten to 270 inch lbs. torque.
9. Install engine to transmission struts, if required. Install starting motor and connect battery ground cable.
10. Rotate engine and install two remaining drive plate to converter bolts.
11. Install crossmember and tighten attaching bolts to 90 ft. lbs. torque. Lower transmission so that extension housing is aligned and rests on the rear mount. Install bolts and tighten to 40 ft. lbs. torque.
12. Remove transmission jack and engine support fixture, then install tie-bars under the transmission.
13. Replace the driveshaft.
14. Connect oil coolerlines, install oil filler tube and connect the speedometer cable.
15. Connect gearshift cable or rod and torqueshaft assembly to the transmission case to the lever.
16. Connect throttle rod to the lever at left side of transmission bell housing.
17. Connect wire to back-up and neutral starting switch.
18. Install cover plate in front of the converter assembly.
19. Refill transmission with fluid.
20. Adjust throttle and shift linkage.

AUTOMATIC TRANSAXLE

Removal and Installation

FRONT WHEEL DRIVE

The transaxle removal does not require engine removal. The transaxle and converter must be removed as an assembly. Leaving the weight of the transaxle on the drive plate during removal or installation could damage the plate. Leaving the converter with the engine, could damage the drive plate, pump bushing or oil seal.

1. Disconnect the negative battery cable.
2. Disconnect the throttle and shift linkage from the transaxle.
3. Loosen the hub nut on both front wheels (vehicle on the floor and brakes applied).
4. Raise the vehicle and remove the front wheels.
5. Remove the left fender well splash shield

NOTE: If the axle shafts are held in the differential by circlips, drain the differential and remove the cover. If the axles are retained by spring pressure the differential cover need not be removed.

6. Remove the speedometer adaptor, cable, and pinion.
7. Remove the front sway bar and the lower ball joint to steering knuckle bolts. Pry the ball joints from the steering knuckles.
8. Remove the drive shaft from the hub. Do not let the drive shaft hang. Tie the drive shaft to the steering knuckle.
9. If equipped rotate the drive shafts to expose the circlip ends. Observe the flat surface on the inner ends of the axle tripod shafts. Squeeze the circlip ends together, while prying the drive shaft out of the side gear.
10. Support both ends of the drive shaft and remove from the transaxle.
11. Match mark the torque converter and drive plate. Remove the torque converter mounting bolts. Remove the access plug in the right fender splash shield, to rotate the engine crankshaft, to gain access to the torque converter bolts.
12. Remove the lower cooler tube and neutral/park safety switch wire.
13. Remove the engine mount bracket from the front

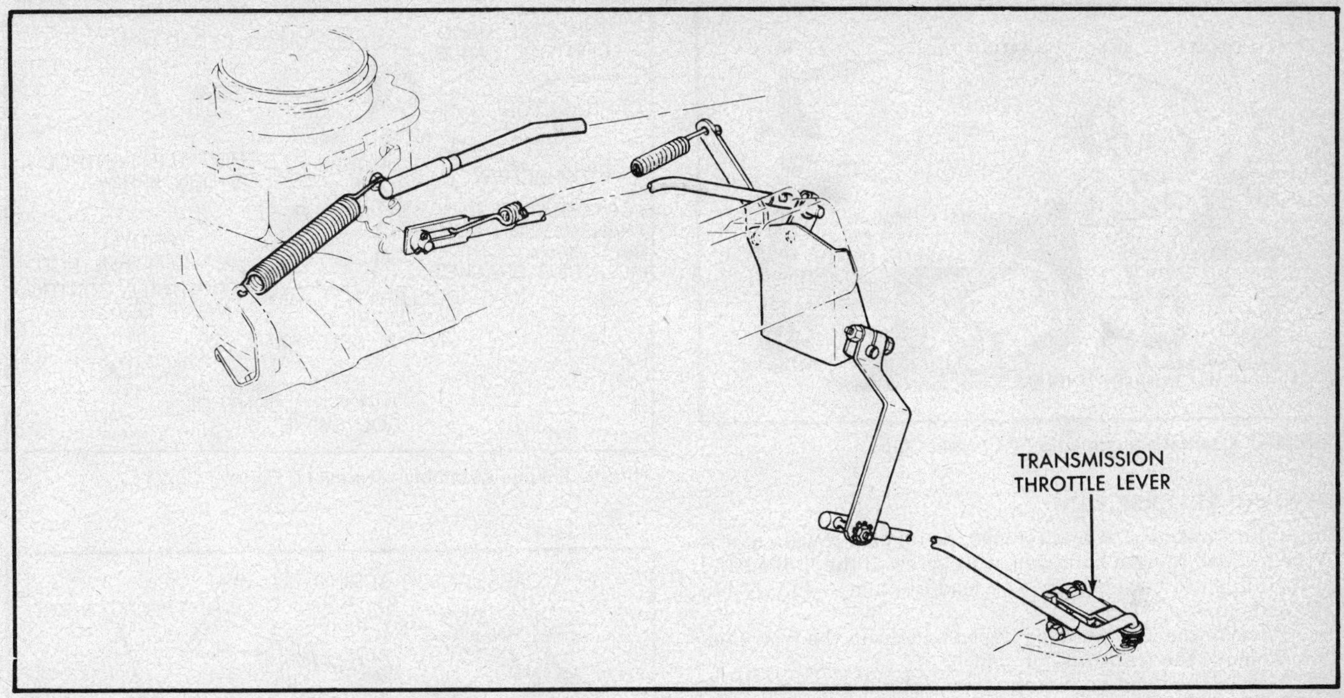

Loadflite® transmission kickdown throttle linkage—V8 conventional truck (© Chrysler Corp.)

crossmember.

14. Remove the front mount insulator through bolt and the bell housing bolts.

15. Set a transmission jack under the transmission and wrap a safety chain around the jack and transmission.

16. Remove the left engine mount and remove the lower bell housing bolts.

17. Pry the transaxle and converter away from the engine and lower the assembly from the vehicle.

18. Installation is the reverse of removal. Fill the differential with 2.37 pints of Dexron® or equivalent automatic transmission fluid. Torque the flex plate to torque converter to 40 ft. lbs. (54 Nm). Tighten the transmission to cylinder block to 70 ft. lbs. (95 Nm), and motor mounts to 40 ft. lbs. (54 Nm).

SHIFT LINKAGE

Adjustment

LOADFLITE

1. Place the gearshift lever in the Park position.
2. Move the shift control lever on the transmission all the way to the rear (in the Park detent).
3. Set the adjustable rod to the proper length and install it with no load in either direction. Tighten the swivel bolt.
4. The shift linkage must be free of binding and be positive in all positions. Make sure that the engine can start only when the gearshift lever is in the Park or Neutral position. Be sure that the gearshift lever will not jump into an unwanted gear.

AUTOMATIC TRANSAXLE

1. Place the gearshift lever in the "P" (PARK) position and loosen the adjusting bolt.
2. Pull the shift lever by hand all the way to the front detent position (PARK) with a load of 10 pounds. While maintaining the 10 pounds of pull on the shift lever, tighten the lock nut bolt to 7.5 ft. lbs. (10 Nm).
3. Check for proper adjustment as follows:
   a. The detent position for neutral and drive should be within limits of the hand lever gate stops.

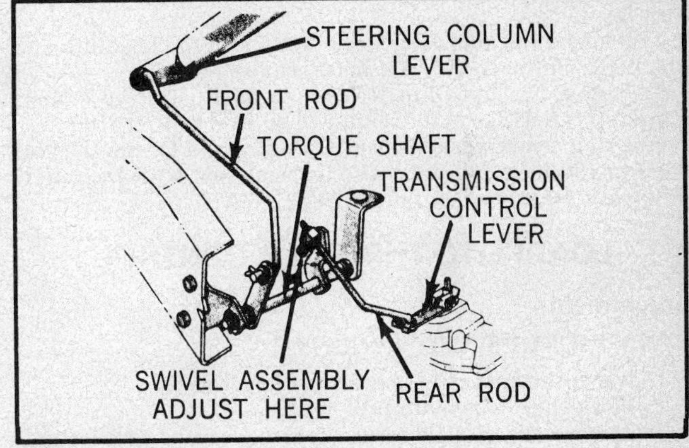

Typical Loadflite® transmission shift linkage (© Chrysler Corp.)

   b. Key starting must occur only when the shift lever is in park or neutral.

LOADFLITE AND AUTOMATIC TRANSAXLE

Band Adjustment

KICKDOWN BAND

The kickdown band adjusting screw is located on the left-hand side of the transmission case near the throttle lever shaft (top front of the transaxle case).

1. Loosen the locknut and back off about five turns. Be sure that the adjusting screw is free in the case.
2. Torque the adjusting screw to 72 inch lbs. (8.1 Nm).
3. Back off the adjusting screw 2 turns. On six-cylinder engines and V8s back off $2^1/_2$ turns. On V8 van and wagon, and A-345 four speed, back off 2 turns. On Rampage transaxle A-404, back off 3 turns and on the Rampage A-413, A-470 back off $2^3/_4$ turns. Hold the adjusting screw and torque the locknut to 35 ft. lbs. (47 Nm).

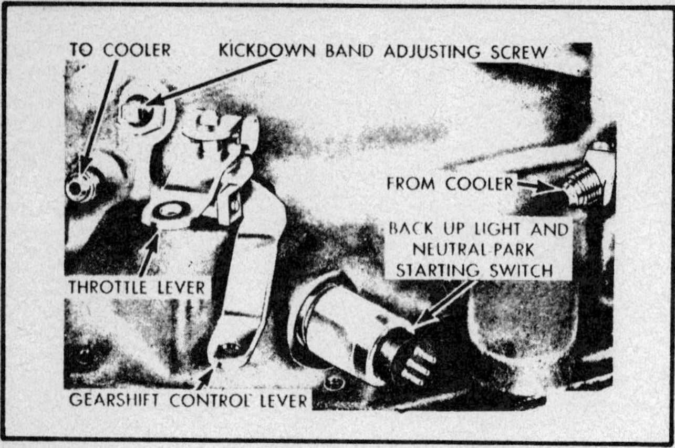

Loadflite® external adjustments (© Chrysler Corp.)

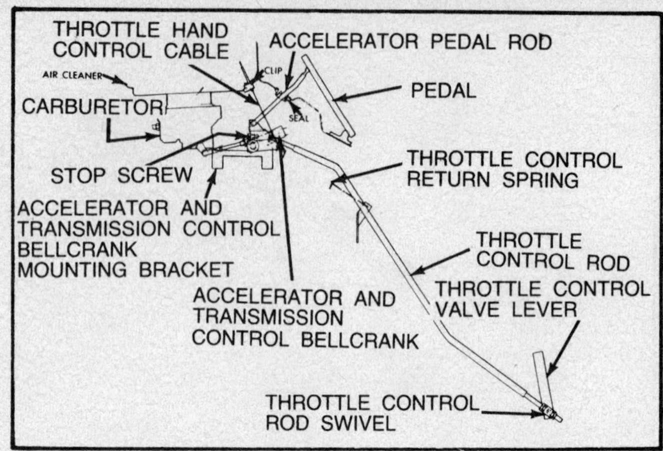

Throttle linkage assembly—typical (© Chrysler Corp.)

LOW AND REVERSE BAND

Drain the transmission and remove the oil pan, to gain access to the low and reverse band adjusting screw. If the A-404 band is worn it must be replaced. The loadflite and A-413, A-470 transaxle are adjustable.

1. Remove the skid plate equipped and drain the transmission. Remove the transmission pan.
2. Loosen the band adjusting screw locknut and back it off about five turns.
3. On Loadflite torque the adjusting screw to 72 inch lbs. On the Rampage A-413 and A-470 torque the adjusting screw to 41 inch lbs. (5 Nm).
4. Back off the adjusting screw 2 turns on the Loadflite and $3^1/_2$ turns on the A-413, A-470 transaxles.
5. Torque the Loadflite locknut to 30 ft. lbs. (40.7 Nm). Torque the A-413, A-470 locknut to 20 ft. lbs. (27.1 Nm).
6. Using a new gasket, install the pan and torque the pan bolts to 150 inch lbs. Refill the transmission with Dexron®II automatic transmission fluid.

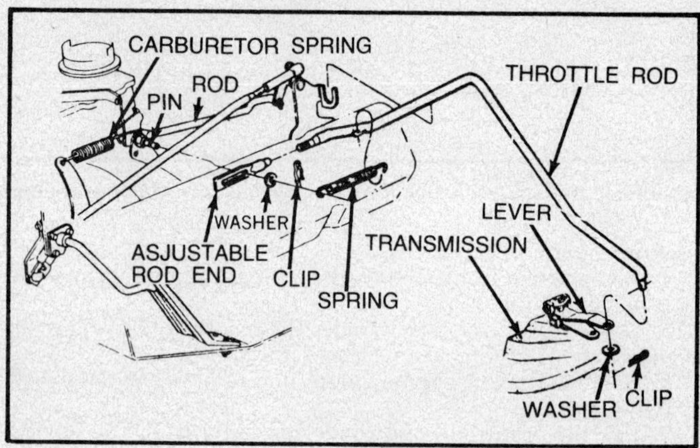

Typical Loadflite® transmission kickdown throttle linkage—V8 (© Chrysler Corp.)

LOADFLITE THROTTLE CONTROL

Adjustments

VANS, PICKUPS AND WAGONS

1. Warm the engine to operating temperature.
2. Block the choke plate fully open.
3. Remove the throttle return spring from the carburetor.
4. Remove the clip, washer and slotted throttle rod from the carburetor pin.
5. Rotate the threaded end of the rod so that the rear edge of the slot in the rod contacts the carburetor pin when the transmission throttle lever is held forward against its stop.
6. Install the washer and clip to retain the throttle rod to the carburetor.
7. Install the throttle rod return spring.
8. Check the transmission linkage for freedom of operation and unblock the choke plate, if necessary.

AUTOMATIC TRANSAXLE

Make the throttle cable adjustment with the engine at operating temperature or the choke disconnected to insure that the carburetor is off fast idle cam.

1. Loosen the adjustment bracket lock screw.
2. The bracket must slide freely in its slot.
3. Hold the throttle lever firmly rearward against its internal stop and tighten the adjusting bracket lock screw to 105 inch lbs. (12 Nm).
4. Install the choke linkage if it was disconnected during the adjustment.

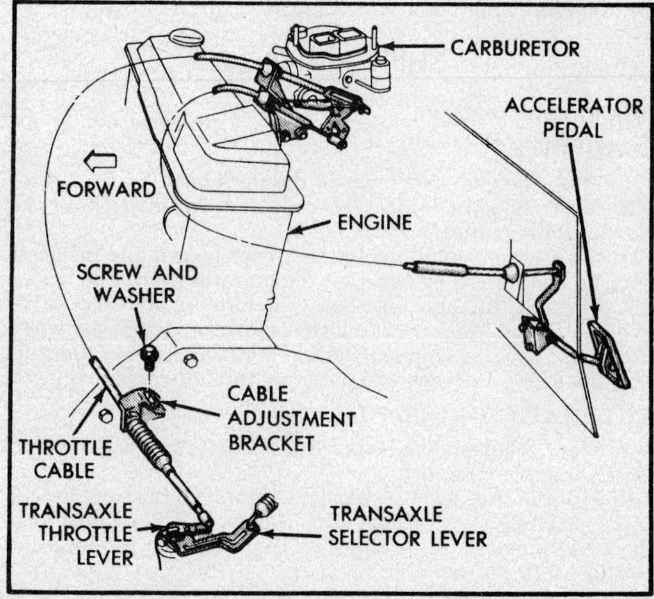

Rampage automatic transmission throttle control—typical (© Chrysler Corp.)

NEUTRAL START SWITCH

Adjustment

LOADFLITE AND AUTOMATIC TRANSAXLE

The neutral safety switch is mounted on the transmission case. When the gearshift lever is placed in either the Park or Neutral position, a cam, which is attached to the transmission throttle lever inside the transmission, contacts the neutral safety switch and provides a ground to complete the starter solenoid circuit.

The back-up light switch is incorporated into the neutral safety switch. The center terminal is for the neutral safety switch ad the two outer terminals are for the back-up lamps.

There is no adjustment for the switch. If a malfunction occurs, the switch must be removed and replaced.

To remove the switch, disconnect the electrical leads and unscrew the switch. Use a drain pan to catch the transmission fluid. Using a new seal, install the new switch and torque it to 24 ft. lbs. Refill the transmission.

TRANSMISSION OIL PAN AND FILTER

Removal and Installation

1. Operate the transmission until it is thoroughly warmed up.
2. Remove the skidplate, if any. Unbolt the pan. Be ready with a large container to drain the fluid.

NOTE: If the fluid removed smells burnt, serous transmission troubles, probably due to overheating should be suspected.

3. Remove the access plate in front of the torque converter. Rotate the engine clockwise to bring the converter drain to the bottom. Position the container under the converter, remove the drain plug, and allow the fluid to drain. Drain the housing on the A-345. Replace the converter drain plug and torque it to 110 inch lbs. for a $^{7}/_{16}$ in. head plug and 90 inch lbs. for a $^{5}/_{16}$ in. plug. Install the access plate.
4. Unscrew and discard the filter.
5. Install a new filter. The proper torque is 35 inch lbs.
6. Clean out the pan, being extremely careful not to leave any lint from rags inside.
7. Replace the pan with a new gasket. Tighten the bolts to 150 inch lbs. in a crisscross pattern.
8. Pour six quarts (eight on the A-345) of the proper type automatic transmission fluid through the dipstick tube.
9. Start the engine in Neutral and let it idle for two minutes or more.
10. Hold your foot on the Brake and shift through D,2,1 and R and back to N.
11. Add enough fluid to bring the level to the ADD ONE PINT mark.
12. Operate the vehicle until the transmission is thoroughly warmed up, then check the level. It should be between FULL and ADD ONE PINT. Add fluid as necessary.

NOTE: The manufacturer recommends automatic transmission sealer be added to reduce fluid leakage resulting from hardening or shrinking of the seals in high-mileage vehicles.

DRIVESHAFT, U-JOINTS

Driveshaft

SINGLE SECTION TYPE

Removal and Installation

This driveshaft has a universal joint at either end and no external supports.

1. Raise and support the truck with the rear higher.
2. Matchmark the shaft and pinion flange to assure proper balance at installation.
3. Remove both rear U-joint roller and bushing clamps from the rear axle pinion flange. Do not disturb the retaining strap which holds the bushing assemblies on the J-joint cross.

NOTE: Do not allow the driveshaft to hang during removal. Suspend it from the frame with a piece of wire. Before removing the driveshaft, raise the rear end of the truck to prevent loss of transmission fluid.

4. Slide the driveshaft, with the front sliding yoke, off the transmission output shaft.
5. Installation is the reverse of removal. Align the matchmarks made during removal.

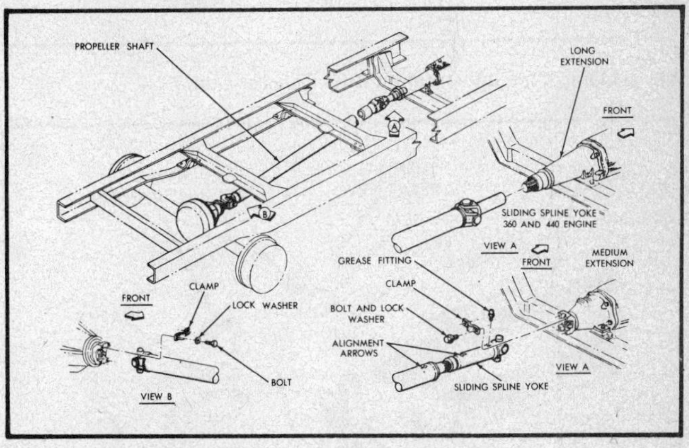

Single section driveshaft (© Chrysler Corp.)

TWO-SECTION TYPE

Removal and Installation

This driveshaft has a universal joint at either end, with a third universal joint and a support bearing at the center bearing spline and slip yoke.

1. Matchmark the shaft and the rear axle pinion hub yoke. Matchmark the center bearing spline and slip yoke.

NOTE: Do not allow the driveshaft to hang down during removal. Suspend it from the frame. Raise the rear of the truck to prevent loss of transmission fluid.

2. Remove both rear U-joint roller and bushing assembly clamps from the rear axle pinion yoke. Do not disturb the retaining strap used to hold the bushing assemblies on the U-joint cross.
3. Slide the rear half of the shaft off the front shaft splines at the center bearing. Remove the rear half.
4. At the transmission end of the front half, remove the bushing retaining bolts and clamps, after matchmarking. If there is a driveshaft brake, there will be flange nuts.
5. Unbolt the center bearing mounting nuts and bolts and remove the front half of the shaft.

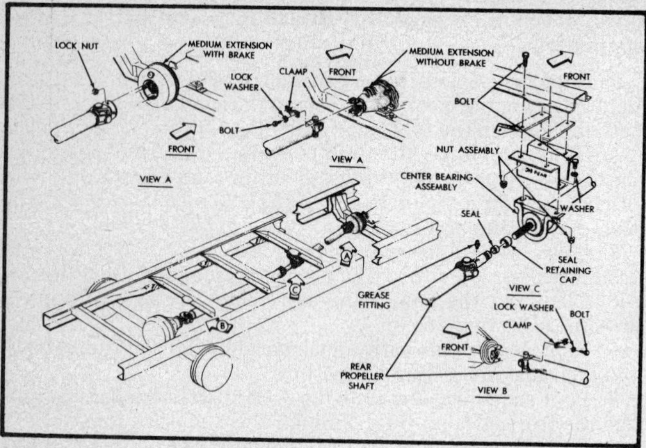

Two-section driveshaft (© Chrysler Corp.)

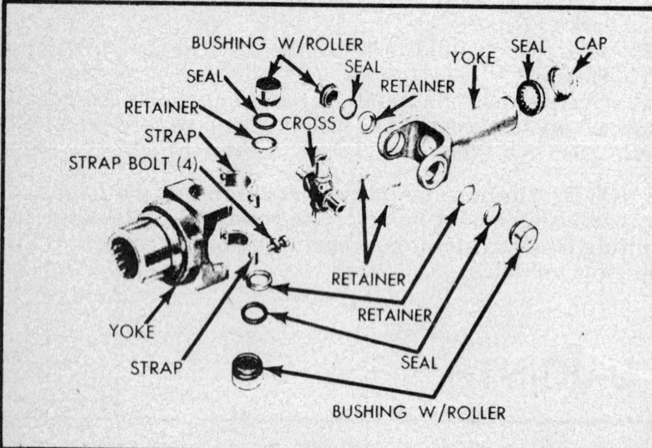

Strap clamp type universal joint (© Chrysler Corp.)

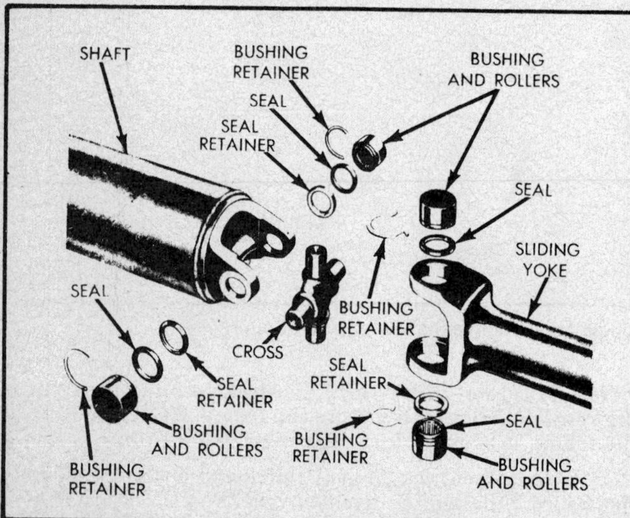

Lock ring type universal joint (© Chrysler Corp.)

6. On installation, align the matchmarks at the transmission and start all the bolts and nuts at the front U-joint and the center support bearing.
7. Tighten $^{1}/_{4}$ in. clamp bolts to 170 inch lbs., and $^{5}/_{16}$ in. bolts to 300 inch lbs. Tighten driveshaft brake flange nuts to 35 ft. lbs. Leave the center bearing bolts just snug.
8. Align the rear shaft matchmarks and slide the yoke onto the front shaft splines.
9. Align the rear U-joint matchmarks and install bushing clamps and bolts. Tighten the bolts to the torque given in Step 7. Grease the joints and splines.
10. Jack up the rear wheels and let the engine drive the shaft. The center support bearing will align itself.
11. Tighten the center bearing bolts to 50 ft. lbs.

FOUR-WHEEL DRIVE FRONT DRIVESHAFT

Removal and Installation

1. Remove the four flange retaining bolts and lockwashers from the constant velocity U-joint at the transfer case. Mark the parts to reinstall them in the same position. To prevent the constant velocity joint from turning while removing the nuts, use a press bar.
2. Remove the nuts and lockwashers from the U-bolts at the differential flange and remove the U-bolts.
3. Support the driveshaft and separate the U-joint at the front of the driveshaft joint backward to clear the flange. The driveshaft should never be allow to hand by either universal joint.
4. Remove the driveshaft.
5. Installation is the reverse of removal.

Universal Joint

LOCK RING AND THE SNAP-RING TYPE

Replacement

The lock-ring and the snap ring type universal joints are basically the same, except for the locations of the retainers. The lock-ring retainers hold the bearing cups in the yoke by being installed in a machined groove on the bearing cup, which is located on the inner side of the yoke when the joint is assembled.

The snap-ring type retainer holds the bearing cup in the yoke by being installed in a machined groove in the upper area of the bearing bore of the yoke.

The disassembly and assembly are as follows:

1. Hammer the bushings (roller cups) slightly inward to relieve pressure on the retainers. Remove the retainers.
2. Place the yoke in a vise with a socket bigger than the bushing on one side and one smaller than the bushing on the other side.
3. Apply pressure, forcing one busing out into the larger socket.
4. Reverse the vise and socket arrangement to remove the other bushing and the cross.
5. On installation, press the new bushings in just far enough to install the retainer.

STRAP CLAMP TYPE (REAR AXLE YOKE)

Removal and Installation

Unbolt strap bolts and remove straps, bushings, seals and washer retainers. Install new components as required. When assembling, grease bearings. Install with grease fitting parallel to other fittings in drive train. Tighten strap bolts to 20 ft. lbs. torque.

CONSTANT VELOCITY U-JOINT

Removal and Installation

This is the double universal joint used in the front driveshaft

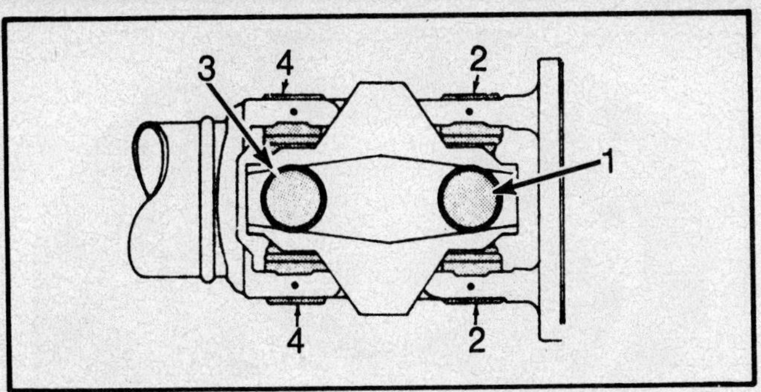

Constant velocity joint bearing cup removal sequence (© Chrysler Corp.)

on four-wheel drive models. These are disassembled in the same way as the snap-ring type U-joint. Original equipment U-joints are held together by plastic retainers which shear when pressed out. The bearing cups in the center part of the joint should be pressed out before those in the yoke. Original equipment constant velocity joints cannot be reassembled. Replacement part kits have bearing cups with grooves for retaining rings.

SLIP JOINTS

Removal and Installation

When reassembling slip joints make sure that arrows stamped on each side are matched. This will assure proper universal joint alignment.

REAR AXLE

See the Unit Repair Section for overhaul procedures for rear axles.

Axle Assembly

Removal and Installation

1. Raise vehicle and support at front of rear springs.
2. Block brake pedal in the up position.
3. Remove rear wheels.
4. Disconnect hydraulic brake hose at "T" fitting or at each wheel.
5. Disconnect parking brake cable.

NOTE: To insure proper drive line balance when reassembling, make scribe marks on the driveshaft universal joint and differential pinion flange before removal.

6. Disconnect driveshaft at rear universal joint bearing clamps and secure with wire to prevent damage to front universal joint.
7. Disconnect shock absorbers and remove rear spring nuts and U-bolts.
8. Remove assembly from vehicle.
9. To install, position rear axle assembly spring pads over the spring center bolts.
10. Install U-bolts and tighten nuts securely.
11. Connect shock absorbers.
12. Connect parking brake cable.
13. Connect hydraulic brake lines. Install brake drums and adjust. Bleed hydraulic brake system.
14. Connect driveshaft universal joint in its original position, matching scribe marks made during removal. Tighten universal joint clamp bolts.

Differential Service

For service and overhaul procedures on differentials see Drive Axles in the Unit Repair section.

Axle Shaft

Removal and Installation

$8^3/_8$ AND $9^1/_4$ IN AXLES

NOTE: There is no provision for axle shaft end-play adjustment on this axle.

1. Raise the vehicle and remove the rear wheels.

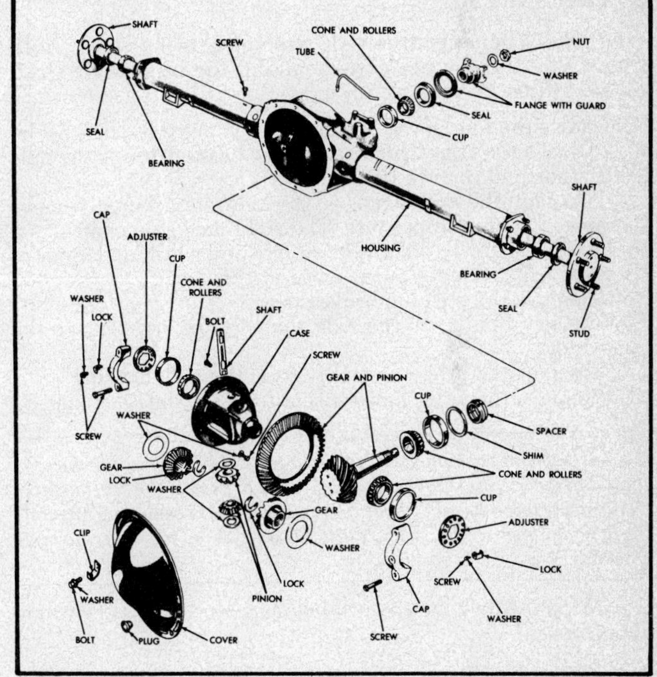

$8^3/_8$ inch rear axle, the $9^1/_4$ inch is similar (© Chrysler Corp.)

2. Clean all dirt from the housing cover and remove the housing cover to drain the lubricant.
3. Remove the brake drum.
4. Rotate the differential case until the differential pinion shaft lockscrew can be removed. Remove the lockscrew and pinion shaft.
5. Push the axle shafts toward the center of the vehicle and remove the C-locks from the grooves on the axle shafts.
6. Pull the axle shafts from the housing, being careful not to damage the bearing which remains in the housing.
7. Inspect the axle shaft and bearings and replace any doubtful parts. Whenever the axle shaft is replaced, the bearings should also be replaced.
8. Remove the axle shaft seal from the bore in the housing.
9. Remove the axle shaft bearing from the housing.
10. Check the bearing shoulder in the axle housing for imperfections, and should be corrected.

11. Clean the axle shaft bearing cavity.
12. Install the axle shaft bearing seal. It should be seated beyond the end of the flange face.
14. Insert the axle shaft, making sure that the splines do not damage the seal. Be sure that the splines are properly engaged with the differential side gear splines.
15. Install the C-locks in the grooves on the axle shafts. Pull the shafts outward so that the C-locks seat in the counterbore of the differential side gears.
16. Install the differential pinion shaft through the case and pinions. Install the lockscrew and secure it in position.
17. Install the cover and a new gasket.

NOTE: Replacement gaskets may not be available for differential covers. In this case, the use of a gel type nonsticking sealant is recommended.

Be sure that the rear axle ratio identification tag is replaced under one of the cover bolts. Refill the axle with the specified lubricant to $^1/_2$ in. below the filler plug hole. Do not overfill.
18. Install the brake drum and wheel.
19. Lower the vehicle to the ground and test the operation of the brakes.

8 $^3/_4$ IN. AXLES

NOTE: Whenever this axle assembly is serviced, both the brake support plate gaskets and the inner axle shaft oil seal must be renewed.

1. Raise the rear of the vehicle and remove the rear wheels.
2. Detach the clips which secure the brake drum to the axle shaft studs and remove the brake drum.
3. Through the access hole in the axle shaft flange, remove the axle shaft retaining nuts. The right-side axle shaft has a threaded adjuster in the retainer plate and a lock under one of its studs which should be removed at this time.
4. Remove the parking brake strut.
5. Attach a puller to the axle shaft flange and remove the axle shaft.
6. Remove the brake assembly from the axle housing.
7. Remove the axle shaft oil seal from the axle housing.

CAUTION

It is advisable to position some sort of a protective sleeve over the axle shaft seal surface next to the bearing collar to protect the seal surface. Never use a torch or other heat source as an aid in removing any axle shaft components; this will result in serious damage to the axle assembly.

8. Wipe the axle housing seal bore clean. Install a new axle shaft oil seal.

NOTE: All 8 $^3/_4$ in. rear axle shaft bearings are packed with a special lubricant at the factory. If the roller bearing must be repacked, the factory lubricant must be washed out. The service lubricant is not compatible with the factory lubricant.

9. Place the axle shaft retainer retaining collar i a vise. With the chisel, cut deeply into the retaining collar at 90° intervals. Remove the retainer.
10. Remove the bearing roller retainer flange by cutting off the lower edge with a chisel.
11. Grind or file a section off the flange of the inner bearing cone and remove the bearing rollers.
12. Pull the bearing roller retainer down as much as possible and cut it off with side cutters.
13. Remove the roller bearing cup with its protective sleeves.
14. To prevent damage to the seal journal when the bearing cone is removed, protect the journal with a single wrap of 0.002 in. thick shim stock held in place by a rubber band.
15. Use a puller, remove the bearing cone. Remove the seal in the bearing retainer plate and replace it.

Grind the flange off the inner cone to remove the $^3/_4$ inch axle bearing rollers (© Chrysler Corp.)

16. To assemble the axle, first install the retainer plate and seal assembly on the axle shaft.
17. Grease the wheel bearings and install them.
18. Install a new axle shaft bearing cup, cone, and collar on the shaft. Check the axle shaft seal journal for imperfections and if necessary, polish with No. 600 crocus cloth.
19. Thoroughly clean the axle housing flange face and brake support. Install a new rubber/asbestos gasket onto the axle housing studs. Next, install the brake support assembly on the left side of the axle housing.
20. Lightly grease the outside edge of the bearing cup. Install the bearing cup in the bearing bore.
21. Replace the foam gasket on the studs of the left-side axle housing and very carefully slide the axle shaft assembly through the oil seal and engage the splines of the differential side gear.
22. Using a non-metallic hammer, lightly tap the axle shaft bearing in the recess end of the axle shaft to position the axle housing. Install the retainer plate over the axle housing studs and, starting with the bottom securing nut, torque the nuts to 30-35 ft. lbs.
23. Repeat Steps 19-22 for the right side axle housing.
24. At the right side of the axle housing, back off the threaded adjuster until the inner face of the adjuster is flush with the inner face of the retainer plate. Very carefully slide the axle shaft assembly through the oil seal and engage the splines of the differential side gear. Then repeat Step 22.
25. Mount a dial indicator on the left brake support. Turn the adjuster clockwise until both wheel bearings are seated and there is zero end play in the axle shafts. Back off the adjuster about four notches to establish proper endplay (0.008-0.018).
26. Lightly tap the end of the left axle shaft with a non-metallic hammer. This will seat the right wheel bearing cup against the adjuster. Turn the axle shaft several times so that a rue endplay reading is obtained.
27. Remove one retainer plate nut and install the adjuster lock. If the lock tab does not mate with the notch in the adjuster, turn the adjuster slightly until it does. Refit the nut and torque it to 30-35 ft. lbs.
28. Recheck the axle shaft end-play. If it is not within specifications, repeat the adjustments. When the adjustment is complete, remove the dial indicator.
29. Install the parking brake strut. Replace the brake drum and retaining clips.
30. Install the rear wheels and lower the vehicle.

RAMPAGE AND SCAMP

The Rampage and Scamp front wheel drive pickup uses removable axle spindles bolted to the axle and spring plate assembly.

Removal and Installation

1. Raise the vehicle on a hoist. Remove the wheel and tire

assembly.

2. Using floor stands under the axle assembly, relieve the weight of the rear leaf springs.

3. Disconnect the rear proportioning valve spring.

4. Pry the grease cap from the drum and remove the cotter pin nut lock.

5. Remove the bearing adjustment nut and the brake drum.

6. Remove the parking brake cable bracket. Disconnect the cable from the shoe lever. Using a hole clamp to compress the brake cable retainer, pull the retainer out of the backing plate. Remove the hose clamp, when the cable is free of the backing plate. Remove the hose clamp, when the cable is free of the backing plate.

7. Remove the five brake assembly and spindle retaining bolts. Remove the spindle axle.

8. Installation is the reverse of removal. Torque the brake assembly and spindle mounting bolts to 45 ft. lbs. (61 Nm). Torque the bearing adjusting nut to 20-25 ft. lbs. (27-34 Nm).

9. Re-install the spring on the proportioning valve and adjust the valve:

a. Loosen spring adjusting bracket nuts A and B.

b. Push the valve lever rearward until it bottoms and hold it there.

c. Rotate the spring adjusting bracket rearward until all free play has been removed from the spring. Do not stretch the spring. Hold the adjusting bracket in position and release the valve lever. Tighten the lower adjusting bracket nut temporarily to hold adjusting bracket in position.

d. Mark the position of the adjusting bracket lower nut on the bracket support.

e. Loosen the lower adjusting bracket nut and rotate the adjusting bracket rearward so that the lower nut is $^1/_8$ inch (3mm) forward of the no free play position. Tighten the lower nut to 250 inch lbs. Do not move the adjusting bracket. Tighten the upper adjusting bracket nut to 250 inch lbs.

Wheel Bearing

Adjustment

SEMI-FLOATING AXLES

NOTE: Both of the rear wheels must be off the ground to measure and set the axle shaft end play.

1. Remove the tire, wheel and drum assembly. Remove the adjuster lock from the right shaft.

2. Using the dial indicator mounted on the left brake support, turn the adjuster clockwise until both wheel bearings are seated and there is zero end play in the axle shafts. Back off the adjuster counterclockwise approximately four notches to establish an axle shaft end play of 0.005-0.0015 inch.

3. Tap the end of the left axle shaft lightly with a non-metallic mallet to seat the right wheel bearing cup against the adjuster. Rotate the axle shaft several revolutions so that a true end play reading is indicated. Install the adjuster lock. If the tab on the lock does not mate with the notch in the adjuster, turn the adjuster slightly until it does. Install and tighten the nut.

4. Recheck the axle shaft end play. If it is not within the tolerance of 0.005-0.0015 inch, repeat the procedure.

5. Remove the dial indicator, install the drum, wheel tire and assembly and lower the vehicle.

RAMPAGE AND SCAMP

1. Raise the vehicle and support safely. Remove the wheel and tire assembly.

2. Pry off the grease cap, remove the cotter pin and remove the nut lock.

3. Check the adjusting nut torque to 20-25 ft. lbs. (27-34 Nm), while rotating the hub and drum. Back off the adjusting nut completely to release the bearing preload. Finger tighten the adjusting nut.

4. Position the nut lock with one pair of slots in line with the cotter pin hole. Install the cotter pin. Check the end play to 0.001-0.003 in. (0.025-0.076mm). Clean and install the grease cap.

5. Install the wheel and lower the vehicle.

FULL-FLOATING AXLES

1. Raise the wheel to be adjusted and remove the axle shaft, gasket or seal.

2. Straighten the tang on the lock ring, if so equipped and using a suitable wrench, remove the outer lock nut and lock ring.

3. While revolving the wheel and tire tighten the inner nut until a slight bid is evident. Back off the nut $^1/_6$ of a turn so that the wheel will rotate freely without excessive end play.

4. Install the lock ring and the outer nut.

NOTE: Be careful in tightening the outer nut not to force the inner nut forward on the threads affecting the adjustment.

5. Bend the tang on the lock ring if so equipped. Install a new gasket or seal. Install the axle shaft. Lower the vehicle.

REAR SUSPENSION

Rear Spring

Removal and Installation

CONVENTIONAL TRUCKS, 100–300

1. Raise rear of truck until weight is removed from springs, wheels just touching the floor.

NOTE: Truck must be lifted by jack or hoist under frame side rail at crossmember behind the axle being careful not to bend flange of side rail.

2. Place stands under side frame members as a safety precaution.

3. Remove nuts, lockwashers and U-bolts securing spring to axle.

4. Remove spring shackle bolts, shackle and spring front bolt, then remove spring.

5. To install, position spring on axle so spring center bolt enters locating hole in axle housing pad.

6. Line up spring front eye with bolt hole in bracket and install spring bolt and nut.

7. Install the rear shackle, bolts and nuts. Tighten shackle bolt nut until slack is taken up.

8. On headless type spring bolts install the bolts with lock bolt groove lined up with lock bolt hole in bracket. Install lock bolt and tighten lock bolt nut. Install lubrication fittings.

9. Install U-bolts, new lockwashers and nuts, tightening until nuts push lockwashers against axle. Align auxiliary spring parallel with main spring.

10. Remove stands from under vehicle, lower truck so weight is resting on wheels. Tighten U-bolt nuts, spring eye nuts and shackle bolt nuts.

11. Lubricate spring bolts and shackle bolts with chassis lubricant when equipped with lubrication fittings.

VANS, PICKUPS AND WAGONS

1. Raise the vehicle until springs are accessible. Support safely.
2. Remove U-bolt nuts, U-bolts, and plate.
3. Remove the front pivot bolt nut. Remove the bolt.
4. Remove the rear shackle bolt nuts. Remove the shackle plate.
5. Remove the outer shackle and bolt assembly from the hanger. Remove the spring. On vehicles equipped with one piece shackles, remove the nut, remove the shackle to spring bolt, and remove the spring.
6. To install, position the spring and shackle assembly in the rear hanger.
7. Install the shackle plates and nuts, tightening the nuts to 40 ft. lbs. On vehicles with the one piece shackle, first position the spring to the shackle, and then install the bolt and nut.
8. Position the spring in the front pivot hanger and install the bolt and nut.
9. Position the spring properly on the axle ad install the U-bolt plate.
10. Install the U-bolts and nuts. Make sure that shackled end of the spring is above the shackle bracket pivot.
11. Lower the vehicle to the floor, and tighten all nuts.

Installing New Leaf

1. Clamp spring in a vise, remove center bolt and bend clamp type clips back from spring leafs.
2. Insert long drive in center bolt hole and release vise slowly.
3. Remove assembly from vise and replace broken leaf.
4. Place spring assembly in vise, slowly tightening vise while holding spring leaves in alignment with drift.
5. Remove drift and install new center bolt.
6. Install nut, tightening to 15 ft. lbs. torque.
7. Remove spring from vise.

Removal and Installation

FRONT WHEEL DRIVE–PICKUPS

1. Raise the vehicle and support safely.
2. Using floor stands under the axle assembly, raise axle assembly to relieve the weight of the rear springs.
3. Disconnect the rear brake proportioning valve spring. Disconnect the lower ends of the rear shock absorbers at the axle brackets.
4. Loosen and remove the "U" bolt nuts and remove the "U" bolts and spring plate.
5. Lower the rear axle assembly, allowing the rear springs to hang free.
6. Loosen and remove the front pivot bolt from the front spring hanger.
7. Loosen and remove rear spring shackle nuts and remove shackles from spring.
8. To install, assemble the shackle and bushings in the rear end of the spring. Install the rear spring hanger, start the shackle bolt nuts. Do not tighten.
9. Raise the front of the spring and install the pivot bolt and nut, do not tighten.
10. Raise the axle assembly into correct position with the axle centered under spring center bolts.
11. Install the spring plate and "U" bolts. Tighten the U-bolt nuts to 60 ft. lbs. (81 Nm).
12. Install the shock absorbers and retaining nuts.
13. Lower the vehicle to the floor and with full weight on the wheels, tighten component fasteners as follows:
    a. Front pivot bolt: 115 ft. lbs. (155 Nm).
    b. Shackle nuts: 35 ft. lbs. (47 Nm).
    c. Shock absorber nut: 20 ft. lbs. (27 Nm).
14. Connect the rear brake proportioning valve spring and adjust the valve.

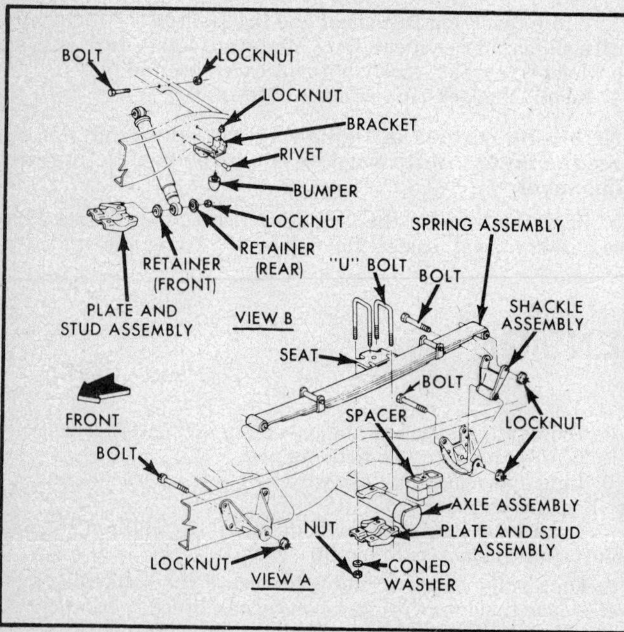

Rear suspension Ramcharger and Trail Duster (© Chrysler Corp.)

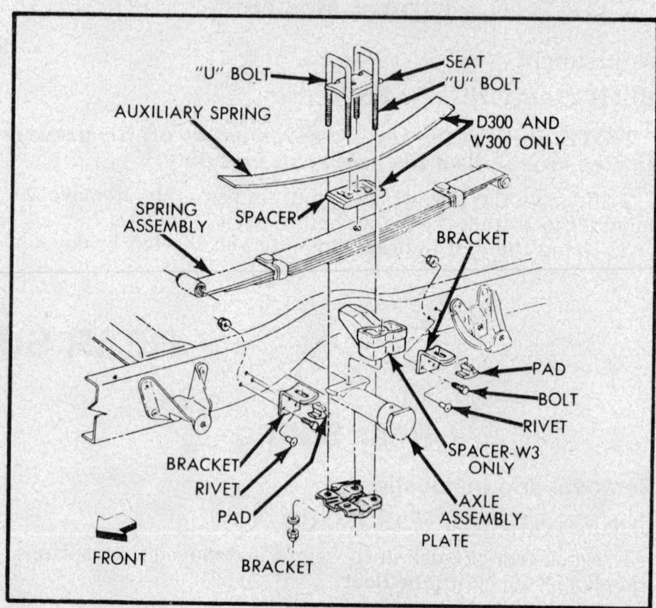

Rear suspension—W200, W300 and D300 shown (© Chrysler Corp.)

INDEX

BEFORE SERVICING, SEE THE SAFETY NOTICE AT THE FRONT OF THE BOOK

FORD MOTOR COMPANY TRUCKS AND VANS

ENGINE IDENTIFICATION

C.I.D.	Liter	C.I.D.	Liter
122	2.0	255	4.1
140	2.3	302	5.0
173	2.8	351	5.8
179	2.9		
300	4.9	400	6.6
232	3.8	460	7.5

GENERAL ENGINE SPECIFICATIONS

Cu. In. Displacement	Year	Bore and Stroke	Firing Order	Developed Horse Power @ rpm	Developed Torque @ rpm	Compression Ratio	Carburetor	Valve Lifter Type	Normal Oil Pressure (p.s.i.)
				FOUR CYLINDER					
122	'83–'86	3.52 × 3.13	1-3-4-2	73 @ 4000	107 @ 2406	9.0:1	1V	Hyd.	40–60
140	'83–'86	3.78 × 3.13	1-3-4-2	79 @ 3800⑦	124 @ 2400⑧	9.0:1	1V	Hyd.	40–60
				SIX CYLINDER					
173-V6	'83–'85	3.66 × 2.70	1-4-2-5-3-6	115 @ 4600	150 @ 2600	8.7:1	2V	Mech.	40–60
179-V6	'86	3.66 × 2.83	1-4-2-5-3-6	140 @ 4600	170 @ 2600	9.3:1	FI	Hyd.	40–60
300	'80–'86	4.00 × 3.98	1-5-3-6-2-4	120 @ 3400①	229 @ 1400②	8.0:1③	1V	Hyd.	40–60
232-V6	'82–'84	3.81 × 3.39	1-4-2-5-3-6	112 @ 4000	175 @ 2600	8.6:1	2V	Hyd.	54–59
				EIGHT CYLINDER					
255	'81–'82	3.68 × 3.00	1-5-4-2-6-3-7-8	111 @ 3400	194 @ 1600	8.2:1	2V	Hyd.	40–60
302	'80–'84	4.00 × 3.00	1-5-4-2-6-3-7-8	④	⑤	8.0:1⑥	2V	Hyd.	40–60
351W	'80–'85	4.00 × 3.50	1-3-7-2-6-5-4-8	N.A.	N.A.	N.A.	2V	Hyd.	40–65
351M	'79	4.00 × 3.50	1-3-7-2-6-5-4-8	N.A.	N.A.	N.A.	2V	Hyd.	50–75
351	'83–'85	4.00 × 3.50	1-3-7-2-6-5-4-8	210 @ 4000	305 @ 2800	8.3:1	4V	Hyd.	40–65
400	'80–'82	4.00 × 4.00	1-3-7-2-6-5-4-8	N.A.	N.A.	N.A.	2V	Hyd.	50–75
460	'80–'86	4.36 × 3.85	1-5-4-2-6-3-7-8	N.A.	N.A.	N.A.	4V	Hyd.	40–65

① '80–'81: Bronco, F-100, 250 (49 States)—119 @ 3200
E-100, 250 (49 States)—115 @ 3200
All Calif. 116 @ 3200
'82: N.A.

② '80–'81: Bronco, F-100, 250 (49 States)—243 @ 1200
E-100, 250 (49 States)—241 @ 1200
All Calif.—244 @ 1200
'82: N.A.

③ '81–'82: 8.9:1

④ '80–'81: Bronco, F-100, 250 (49 States)—137 @ 3600
E-100, 250 (49 States)—138 @ 3600
Bronco, F-150 (4 × 4), 250, E-100-250 Calif.: 136 @ 3600
F-100, 150 (4 × 2) Calif.: 133 @ 3400
'82: N.A.

⑤ '80–'81: Bronco, F-100, 250 (49 States)—239 @ 1800
E-100, 250 (49 States)—242 @ 1800
Bronco, F-150 (4 × 4) Calif.—235 @ 2000
'82: N.A.

⑥ '79:
'80–'82: 8.4:1

⑦ Automatic Trans; 82 @ 4200

⑧ Automatic Trans; 126 @ 2200

TUNE-UP SPECIFICATIONS
1980

(For 1980 Tune-Up Specifications consult the Vehicle Emissions Control Label, which is located on the engine of the vehicle. This decal will contain a calibration number which when used in conjunction with the chart below will yield the required tune-up information. If the information given in this chart disagrees with the information on the decal, use the information on the decal.)

Calibration	Spark Plug Gap	Ignition Timing	Fast Idle rpm High Cam	Fast Idle rpm Kick Down	Curb Idle Rpm A/C① Off/On	Curb Idle Rpm Non A/C	Tsp Off Rpm A/C	Tsp Off Rpm Non A/C
9-51G-RO	.042–.046	6°BTDC	—	1600	700	700	500	500
9-51J-RO	.042–.046	6°BTDC	—	1600	700	700	500	500
9-51K-RO	.042–.046	6°BTDC	—	1600	700	700	500	500
9-51L-RO	.042–.046	6°BTDC	—	1600	700	700	500	500
9-51M-RO	.042–.046	6°BTDC	—	1600	700	700	500	500
9-51S-RO	.042–.046	6°BTDC	—	1600	700	700	500	500
9-51T-RO	.042–.046	6°BTDC	—	1600	700	700	500	500
9-52G-RO	.042–.046	10°BTDC	—	1600	550	550	500	500
9-52J-RO	.042–.046	10°BTDC	—	1600	550	550	500	500
9-52L-RO	.042–.046	10°BTDC	—	1600	550	550	500	500
9-52M-RO	.042–.046	10°BTDC	—	1600	550	550	500	500
9-53G-RO	.042–.046	6°BTDC	2000	—	700	700	—	—
9-53H-RO	.042–.046	4°BTDC	2000	—	700	700	—	—
9-54G-RO	.042–.046	8°BTDC	2000	—	600	600	550	550
9-54H-RO	.042–.046	6°BTDC	2000	—	600	600	550	550
9-54J-RO	.042–.046	6°BTDC	2000	—	600	600	550	550
9-54R-RO	.042–.046	6°BTDC	2000	—	600	600	550	550
9-54S-RO	.042–.046	8°BTDC	2000	—	650	650	550	550
9-54T-RO	.042–.046	6°BTDC	2000	—	600	600	550	550
9-54U-RO	.042–.046	6°BTDC	2000	—	650	650	550	550
9-59H-RO	.042–.046	10°BTDC	2000	—	650	650	—	—
9-59J-RO	.042–.046	10°BTDC	2000	—	650	650	—	—
9-59K-RO	.042–.046	10°BTDC	2000	—	650	650	—	—
9-59S-RO	.042–.046	8°BTDC	2000	—	650	650	—	—
9-59T-RO	.042–.046	10°BTDC	2000	—	650	650	—	—
9-60G-RO	.042–.046	6°BTDC	2000	—	550	550	—	—
9-60H-RO	.042–.046	6°BTDC	2000	—	550	550	—	—
9-60J-RO	.042–.046	6°BTDC	2000	—	550	550	—	—
9-60L-RO	.042–.046	6°BTDC	2000	—	550	550	—	—
9-60M-RO	.042–.046	6°BTDC	2000	—	550	550	—	—
9-60S-RO	.042–.046	10°BTDC	2100	—	550	550	—	—
9-61G-RO	.042–.046	10°BTDC	2000	—	650	650	—	—
9-61H-RO	.042–.046	10°BTDC	2000	—	650	650	—	—
9-62J-RO	.042–.046	6°BTDC	1900	—	550	550	—	—
9-62M-RO	.042–.046	6°BTDC	1900	—	550	550	—	—
9-63H-RO	.042–.046	4°BTDC	—	1500	800	800	500	500
9-64G-RO	.042–.046	10°BTDC	2200	—	600	600	500	500
9-64H-RO	.042–.046	12°BTDC	2200	—	600	600	500	500
9-64S-RO	.042–.046	8°BTDC	2200	—	600	600	500	500
9-66G-RO	.042–.046	14°BTDC	—	1600	650	650	800②	800
7-76J-R11	.042–.046	6°BTDC	—	1700	650	650	525②	525
7-93J-RO	.042–.046	10°BTDC	2500	—	600	600	—	—
7-95J-RO	.042–.046	10°BTDC	2500	—	600	600	—	—
9-71J-RO	.042–.046	6°BTDC	1750	—	600	600	—	—
9-72J-RO	.042–.046	12°BTDC	2000	—	600	600	500	500
9-73-RO	.042–.046	3°BTDC	1750	—	600	600	—	—
9-74J-RO	.042–.046	3°BTDC	2000	—	600	600	500	500
9-77J-RO	.042–.046	12°BTDC	—	1600	700	700	500	500
9-77M-RO	.042–.046	12°BTDC	2550	—	—	700	—	500

TUNE-UP SPECIFICATIONS 1980

(For 1980 Tune-Up Specifications consult the Vehicle Emissions Control Label, which is located on the engine of the vehicle. This decal will contain a calibration number which when used in conjunction with the chart below will yield the required tune-up information. If the information given in this chart disagrees with the information on the decal, use the information on the decal.)

Calibration	Spark Plug Gap	Ignition Timing	Fast Idle rpm High Cam	Fast Idle rpm Kick Down	Curb Idle Rpm A/C ① Off/On	Curb Idle Rpm Non A/C	Tsp Off Rpm A/C	Tsp Off Rpm Non A/C
9-78J-RO	.042–.046	12°BTDC	—	1600	550	550	500	500
9-83G-RO	.042–.046	6°BTDC	2200	—	—	600	—	—
9-83H-RO	.042–.046	2°BTDC	2500	—	—	600	—	—
9-87G-RO	.042–.046	8°BTDC	2700	—	—	600	—	—
9-97J-RO	.042–.046	8°BTDC	—	1600	650	—	—	—
9-97J-R11	.042–.046	8°BTDC	—	1600	650	—	—	—

① Only for A/C-TSP equipment, A/C compressor electromagnetic clutch deenergized.

TUNE-UP SPECIFICATIONS 1981

For 1981 Tune-Up Specifications consult the Vehicle Emissions Control Label, which is located on the engine of the vehicle. This decal will contain a calibration number which when used in conjunction with the chart below will yield the required tune-up information. If the information given in this chart disagrees with the information on the decal, use the information on the decal.

Calibration Number	Engine	Spark Plug Gap	Ignition Timing °BTDC	Timing RPM	Fast Idle RPM High CAM	Fast Idle RPM Kick Down	Curb Idle RPM A/C On	Curb Idle RPM A/C Off	Curb Idle RPM Non A/C
1-57G-R1	4.2L	.042-.046	4	800	2200	—	—	—	750
1-57G-R10	4.2L	.042-.046	4	800	2050	—	—	—	700
1-58-R0	4.2L	.042-.046	10	800	2000	—	—	—	575
1-51D-R0	4.9L	.042-.046	6	800	—	1400	700	600	600
1-51D-R10	4.9L	.042-.046	6	800	—	1250	650	550	550
1-51D-R12	4.9L	.042-.046	6	800	—	1250	650	550	550
1-51E-R0	4.9L	.042-.046	6	800	—	1400	700	600	600
1-51F-R0	4.9L	.042-.046	6	800	—	1250	650	550	550
1-51G-R0	4.9L	.042-.046	6	800	—	1250	650	550	550
1-51H-R0	4.9L	.042-.046	6	800	—	1250	650	550	550
1-51K-R0	4.9L	.042-.046	6	800	—	1250	650	550	550
1-51L-R0	4.9L	.042-.046	6	800	—	1250	650	550	550
1-51E-R10	4.9L	.042-.046	6	800	—	1400	700	600	600
1-51F-R10	4.9L	.042-.046	6	800	—	1250	650	550	550
1-51G-R10	4.9L	.042-.046	6	800	—	1250	650	550	550
1-51H-R10	4.9L	.042-.046	6	800	—	1250	650	550	550
1-51K-R10	4.9L	.042-.046	6	800	—	1250	650	550	550
1-51L-R10	4.9L	.042-.046	6	800	—	1250	650	550	550
1-51S-R0	4.9L	.042-.046	6	800	—	1400	700	600	600
1-51S-R10	4.9L	.042-.046	6	800	—	1250	650	550	550
1-51T-R0	4.9L	.042-.046	6	800	—	120	650	550	550
1-52G-R0	4.9L	.042-.046	10	800	—	1400	—	—	550

TUNE-UP SPECIFICATIONS
1981

For 1981 Tune-Up Specifications consult the Vehicle Emissions Control Label, which is located on the engine of the vehicle. This decal will contain a calibration number which when used in conjunction with the chart below will yield the required tune-up information. If the information given in this chart disagrees with the information on the decal, use the information on the decal.

Calibration Number	Engine	Spark Plug Gap	Ignition Timing °BTDC	Timing RPM	Fast Idle RPM High CAM	Fast Idle RPM Kick Down	Curb Idle RPM A/C On	Curb Idle RPM A/C Off	Curb Idle RPM Non A/C
1-52H-R0	4.9L	.042-.046	10	800	—	1250	—	—	500
1-52K-R0	4.9L	.042-.046	10	800	—	1250	—	—	500
1-52L-R0	4.9L	.042-.046	10	800	—	1250	—	—	500
1-52G-R10	4.9L	.042-.046	10	800	—	1400	—	—	550
1-52H-R10	4.9L	.042-.046	10	800	—	1250	—	—	500
1-52K-R10	4.9L	.042-.046	10	800	—	1250	—	—	500
1-52L-R10	4.9L	.042-.046	10	800	—	1250	—	—	500
1-52S-R0	4.9L	.042-.046	10	800	—	1400	—	—	550
1-52T-R0	4.9L	.042-.046	10	800	—	1250	—	—	550
5-77-R1	4.9L	.042-.046	10	800	—	1500	—	—	600(A)
5-78-R1	4.9L	.042-.046	10	800	—	1500	—	—	700(M)
9-77J-R12	4.9L	.042-.046	12	800	1600	—	—	—	700
9-77S-R10	4.9L	.042-.046	10	800	1600	—	—	—	700
1-59H-R10	5.8L	.042-.046	10	800	1850	—	600	—	600
1-59K-R10	5.8L	.042-.046	10	800	1850	—	600	—	600
1-60A-R0	5.8L	.042-.046	6	800	2200	—	—	—	—
1-60B-R0	5.8L	.042-.046	6	800	2200	—	—	—	—
1-60H-R1	5.8L	.042-.046	6	800	2000	—	625	550	550
1-60J-R0	5.8L	.042-.046	6	800	2000	—	625	550	550
1-60K-R0	5.8L	.042-.046	6	800	2000	—	625	550	550
1-60A-R10	5.8L	.042-.046	6	800	2000	—	625	550	550
1-60B-R10	5.8L	.042-.046	6	800	1850	—	575	500	500
1-60H-R10	5.8L	.042-.046	6	800	1850	—	575	500	500
1-60J-R10	5.8L	.042-.046	6	800	1850	—	575	500	500
1-60K-R10	5.8L	.042-.046	6	800	1850	—	575	500	500
1-63T-R0	5.8L	.042-.046	—	—	1700	—	—	—	—
1-64A-R0	5.8L	.042-.046	8	800	2000	—	625	550	550
1-64G-R1	5.8L	.042-.046	10	600	2000	—	625	550	550
1-64H-R2	5.8L	.042-.046	10	600	2000	—	625	550	550
1-64R-R1	5.8L	.042-.046	—	—	1650	—	—	—	—
1-64S-R0	5.8L	.042-.046	—	—	1500	—	—	—	—
1-64T-R0	5.8L	.042-.046	—	—	1500	—	—	—	—
7-76J-R11	5.8L	.042-.046	6	800	1700	—	—	—	600
9-71J-R10	5.8L	.042-.046	10	800	1750	—	—	—	600
9-71J-R11	5.8L	.042-.046	10	800	1750	—	—	—	600

TUNE-UP SPECIFICATIONS
1981

For 1981 Tune-Up Specifications consult the Vehicle Emissions Control Label, which is located on the engine of the vehicle. This decal will contain a calibration number which when used in conjunction with the chart below will yield the required tune-up information. If the information given in this chart disagrees with the information on the decal, use the information on the decal.

Calibration Number	Engine	Spark Plug Gap	Ignition Timing °BTDC	Timing RPM	Fast Idle RPM High CAM	Fast Idle RPM Kick Down	Curb Idle RPM A/C On	Curb Idle RPM A/C Off	Curb Idle RPM Non A/C
9-72J-R11	5.8L	.042-.046	10	800	2000	—	—	—	600
9-72J-R12	5.8L	.042-.046	10	800	2000	—	—	—	600
9-83G-R12	6.1L	.042-.046	6	800	2200	—	—	—	600
9-83H-R11	6.1L	.042-.046	6	800	2500	—	—	—	600
9-83H-R14	6.1L	.042-.046	2	800	2500	—	—	—	600
9-73J-R11	6.6L	.042-.046	6	800	1750	—	—	—	600
9-73J-R12	6.6L	.042-.046	6	800	1750	—	—	—	600
9-74J-R11	6.6L	.042-.046	3	800	2000	—	—	—	600
9-74J-R12	6.6L	.042-.046	6	800	2000	—	—	—	600
9-87G-R11	7.0L	.042-.046	6	800	2700	—	—	—	600
9-97J-R0	7.5L	.042-.046	8	800	1600	—	—	—	650
7-93J-R0	7.8L	.038-.042	10	800	2500	—	—	—	600
7-95J-R0	8.8L	.038-.042	10	800	2500	—	—	—	600
9-78J-R0	4.9L	.042-.046	12	800	—	1500	—	—	550
9-78J-R11	4.9L	.042-.046	12	800	1600	—	—	—	550
1-53D-R0	5.0L	.042-.046	8	800	2200	—	—	—	700
1.53F-R0	5.0L	.042-.046	8	800	2050	—	—	—	650
1-53G-R0	5.0L	.042-.046	8	800	2050	—	—	—	650
1-53H-R0	5.0L	.042-0.46	8	800	2050	—	—	—	650
1-53K-R0	5.0L	.042-.046	8	800	2050	—	—	—	650
1-53D-R10	5.0L	.042-.046	8	800	2200	—	—	—	700
1-53G-R10	5.0L	.042-.046	8	800	2050	—	—	—	650
1-53K-R10	5.0L	.042-.046	8	800	2050	—	—	—	650
1-53D-R12	5.0L	.042-.046	8	800	2050	—	—	—	650
1-53F-R11	5.0L	.042-.046	8	800	2050	—	—	—	650
1-53G-R12	5.0L	.042-.046	8	800	2050	—	—	—	650
1-53H-R11	5.0L	.042-.046	8	800	2050	—	—	—	650
1-53K-R13	5.0L	.042-.046	8	800	2050	—	—	—	650
1-54D-R1	5.0L	.042-.046	8	800	2000	—	—	—	575
1-54K-R0	5.0L	.042-.046	8	800	1850	—	—	—	525
1-54F-R0	5.0L	.042-.046	8	800	2000	—	—	—	575
1-54G-R0	5.0L	.042-.046	8	800	2000	—	—	—	575
1-54H-R0	5.0L	.042-.046	8	800	2000	—	—	—	575
1-54L-R2	5.0L	.042-.046	8	800	2000	—	—	—	575
1-54L-R10	5.0L	.042-.046	8	800	1850	—	—	—	525
1-54P-R0	5.0L	.042-.046	—	—	1350	—	—	—	—

TUNE-UP SPECIFICATIONS 1981

For 1981 Tune-Up Specifications consult the Vehicle Emissions Control Label, which is located on the engine of the vehicle. This decal will contain a calibration number which when used in conjunction with the chart below will yield the required tune-up information. If the information given in this chart disagrees with the information on the decal, use the information on the decal.

Calibration Number	Engine	Spark Plug Gap	Ignition Timing °BTDC	Timing RPM	Fast Idle RPM		Curb Idle RPM		
					High CAM	Kick Down	A/C On	A/C Off	Non A/C
1-54R-R0	5.0L	.042-.046	—	—	1350	—	—	—	—
1-54P-R10	5.0L	.042-.046	—	—	1350	—	—	—	—
1-54R-R10	5.0L	.042-.046	—	—	1200	—	—	—	—
7-79-R1	5.0L	.042-.046	6	800	—	1250	—	—	750
7-80-R0	5.0L	.042-.046	6	800	—	1500	—	—	650
1-59A-R0	5.8L	.042-.046	10	800	2000	—	650	—	650
1-59B-R0	5.8L	.042-.046	10	800	2000	—	650	—	650
1-59G-R0	5.8L	.042-.046	10	800	2000	—	650	—	650
1-59H-R0	5.8L	.042-.046	10	800	2000	—	650	—	650
1-59K-R0	5.8L	.042-.046	10	800	2000	—	650	—	650
1-59A-R10	5.8L	.042-.046	10	800	2000	—	650	—	650
1-59B-R10	5.8L	.042-.046	10	800	1850	—	600	—	600
1-59G-R10	5.8L	.042-.046	10	800	1850	—	600	—	600

TUNE-UP SPECIFICATIONS 1982

For 1982 Tune-Up Specifications consult the Vehicle Emissions Control Label, which is located on the engine of the vehicle. This decal will contain a calibration number which when used in conjunction with the chart below will yield the required tune-up information. If the information in this chart disagrees with the information on the decal, use the information on the decal.

Calibration	Engine	Spark Plug Gap	Ignition Timing	Fast Idle RPM	Curb Idle RPM
2-55D-R0	3.8L	.042-.046	10° BTDC	2100	750①
2-56D-R0	3.8L	.042-.046	12° BTDC	2200	600①
2-56D-R10	3.8L	.042-.046	12° BTDC	2200	700①
2-57G-R0	4.2L	.042-.046	8° BTDC	2250	750①
2-58H-R0	4.2L	.042-.046	8° BTDC	2000	700①
2-51D-R0	4.9L	.042-.046	6° BTDC	1400	700②
2-51E-R0	4.9L	.042-.046	6° BTDC	1400	700②
2-51F-R0	4.9L	.042-.046	6° BTDC	1400	700②
2-51G-R0	4.9L	.042-.046	6° BTDC	1400	700②
2-51K-R0	4.9L	.042-.046	6° BTDC	1400	700②
2-51L-R0	4.9L	.042-.046	6° BTDC	1400	700③
2-51P-R0	4.9L	.042-.046	10° BTDC	1600	500③
2-51P-R10	4.9L	.042-.046	12° BTDC	1600	500③
2-51S-R0	4.9L	.042-.046	6° BTDC	1600	700③
2-51T-R0	4.9L	.042-.046	6° BTDC	1600	700③
2-51X-R0	4.9L	.042-.046	10° BTDC	1400	700③

TUNE-UP SPECIFICATIONS
1982

For 1982 Tune-Up Specifications consult the Vehicle Emissions Control Label, which is located on the engine of the vehicle. This decal will contain a calibration number which when used in conjunction with the chart below will yield the required tune-up information. If the information in this chart disagrees with the information on the decal, use the information on the decal.

Calibration	Engine	Spark Plug Gap	Ignition Timing	Fast Idle RPM	Curb Idle RPM
2-51Y-R0	4.9L	.042-.046	10° BTDC	1400	—
2-52G-R0	4.9L	.042-.046	10° BTDC	1400	550
2-52H-R0	4.9L	.042-.046	10° BTDC	1400	550
2-52K-R0	4.9L	.042-.046	10° BTDC	1400	550
2-52L-R0	4.9L	.042-.046	10° BTDC	1400	550
2-52S-R0	4.9L	.042-.046	10° BTDC	1400	550
2-52T-R0	4.9L	.042-.046	10° BTDC	1400	550
2-52Y-R0	4.9L	.042-.046	14° BTDC	1400	—
2-53D-R0	5.0L	.042-.046	8° BTDC	2000	700
2-53F-R0	5.0L	.042-.046	8° BTDC	2000	700
2-53G-R0	5.0L	.042-.046	8° BTDC	2000	700
2-53H-R0	5.0L	.042-.046	8° BTDC	2000	700
2-53K-R0	5.0L	.042-.046	8° BTDC	2000	700
2-53X-R1	5.0L	.042-.046	8° BTDC	2000	730
2-54D-R0	5.0L	.042-.046	8° BTDC	2000	650
2-54F-R0	5.0L	.042-.046	8° BTDC	2000	575
2-54G-R0	5.0L	.042-.046	8° BTDC	2000	650
2-54H-R0	5.0L	.042-.046	8° BTDC	2000	575
2-54K-R0	5.0L	.042-.046	8° BTDC	2000	650
2-54L-R0	5.0L	.042-.046	8° BTDC	2000	650
2-54P-R0	5.0L	.042-.046	—	1350	—
2-54R-R0	5.0L	.042-.046	—	1350	—
2-54X-R1	5.0L	.042-.046	12° BTDC	2100	650
1-63T-R0	5.8L	.042-.046	—	1700	—
1-63T-R10B	5.8L	.042-.046	—	1700	—
1-64H-R2	5.8L	.042-.046	10° BTDC	2000	625
1-64R-R1	5.8L	.042-.046	—	1650	—
1-64S-R0	5.8L	.042-.046	—	1650	—
1-64T-R0	5.8L	.042-.046	—	1650	—
1-64T-R10	5.8L	.042-.046	—	1650	—
2-63Y-R10B	5.8L	.042-.046	—	1700	—
2-64X-R0	5.8L	.042-.046	14° BTDC	2000	625
2-64Y-R10B	5.8L	.042-.046	—	1650	—
9-77J-R12	4.9L	.042-.046	12° BTDC	1600	—
9-77G-R10	4.9L	.042-.046	10° BTDC	1600	—
9-78J-R0	4.9L	.042-.046	12° BTDC	1600	—
9-78J-R11	4.9L	.042-.046	12° BTDC	1600	—
2-75J-R17	5.8L	.042-.046	5° BTDC	1500	700④

TUNE-UP SPECIFICATIONS 1982

For 1982 Tune-Up Specifications consult the Vehicle Emissions Control Label, which is located on the engine of the vehicle. This decal will contain a calibration number which when used in conjunction with the chart below will yield the required tune-up information. If the information in this chart disagrees with the information on the decal, use the information on the decal.

Calibration	Engine	Spark Plug Gap	Ignition Timing	Fast Idle RPM	Curb Idle RPM
2-76J-R17	5.8L	.042-.046	5° BTDC	1500	—
7-75J-R14	5.8L	.042-.046	6° BTDC	1500	700④
7-76J-R11	5.8L	.042-.046	6° BTDC	1700	—
7-76J-R13	5.8L	.042-.046	12° BTDC	1600	500
7-76J-R14	5.8L	.042-.046	6° BTDC	1700	—
7-76J-R15	5.8L	.042-.046	6° BTDC	1700	—
9-83G-R12	6.1L	.042-.046	6° BTDC	2200	600
9-83H-R11	6.1L	.042-.046	6° BTDC	2500	600
9-83H-R14	6.1L	.042-.046	2° BTDC	2500	600
9-73J-R11	6.6L	.042-.046	6° BTDC	1750	600④
9-73J-R12	6.6L	.042-.046	6° BTDC	1750	600④
9-73J-R13	6.6L	.042-.046	6° BTDC	1750	600④
9-73J-R14	6.6L	.042-.046	6° BTDC	1750	600④
9-74J-R11	6.6L	.042-.046	6° BTDC	2000	—
9-74J-R12	6.6L	.042-.046	6° BTDC	2000	—
9-74J-R13	6.6L	.042-.046	3° BTDC	2000	—
9-74J-R14	6.6L	.042-.046	6° BTDC	2000	—
9-87G-R11	7.0L	.042-.046	6° BTDC	—	600
9-97J-R12	7.5L	.042-.046	8° BTDC	—	650

①A/C on—50 RPM Less if NON A/C
②A/C on—600 NON A/C
③100 RPM Less for NON A/C or A/C off
④NON A/C.

TUNE-UP SPECIFICATIONS 1983

(For 1983 Tune-Up Specifications consult the Vehicle Emissions Control Label, which is located on the engine of the vehicle. This decal will contain a calibration number which when used in conjunction with the chart below will yield the required tune-up information. If the information given in this chart disagrees with the information on the decal, use the information on the decal.)

Calibration	Engine	Spark Plug Gap	Ignition Timing	Fast Idle RPM	Curb Idle RPM
3-41D-R01	2.0L	.032-.036	6° BTDC	2000	800
3-41D-R10	2.0L	.032-.036	6° BTDC	2000	800
3-41P-R02	2.0L	.032-.036	6° BTDC	2000	800
3-41P-R11	2.0L	.032-.036	6° BTDC	2000	800
3-41P-R12	2.0L	.032-.036	6° BTDC	2000	800
3-49S-R01	2.3L	.032-.036	6° BTDC	2000	850①
3-49S-R10	2.3L	.032-.036	6° BTDC	2000	850①
3-49S-R11	2.3L	.032-.036	6° BTDC	2000	850①
3-49X-R01	2.3L	.032-.036	10° BTDC	2000	850

TUNE-UP SPECIFICATIONS
1983

(For 1983 Tune-Up Specifications consult the Vehicle Emissions Control Label, which is located on the engine of the vehicle. This decal will contain a calibration number which when used in conjunction with the chart below will yield the required tune-up information. If the information given in this chart disagrees with the information on the decal, use the information on the decal.)

Calibration	Engine	Spark Plug Gap	Ignition Timing	Fast Idle RPM	Curb Idle RPM
3-49X-R11	2.3L	.032-.036	10° BTDC	2000	850
3-50S-R01	2.3L	.032-.036	8° BTDC	2000	750
3-50S-R01	2.3L	.032-.036	8° BTDC	2000	800
3-50X-R10	2.3L	.032-.036	8° BTDC	2000	800
3-50X-R11	2.3L	.032-.036	10° BTDC	2000	800
3-49G-R20	2.3L	.042-.046	6° BTDC	2000	850①
3-49H-R17	2.3L	.042-.046	6° BTDC	2000	850①
3-49S-R16	2.3L	.042-.046	6° BTDC	2000	850①
3-49T-R20	2.3L	.042-.046	6° BTDC	2000	850①
3-49T-R20	2.3L	.042-.046	6° BTDC	2000	850①
3-49Y-R19	2.3L	.042-.046	10° BTDC	2000	850①
3-50S-R18	2.3L	.042-.046	6° BTDC	2000	800
3-50Y-R18	2.3L	.042-.046	10° BTDC	2000	800
4-61F-R00	2.8L	.042-.046	10° BTDC	3000	850-900②
4-62D-R00	2.8L	.042-.046	10° BTDC	3000	850-900②
4-62S-R01	2.8L	.042-.046	10° BTDC	3000	850-900②
4-62S-R10	2.8L	.042-.046	10° BTDC	3000	800-900③
3-55D-R00	3.8L	.042-.046	2° BTDC	1300	550
3-56D-R00	3.8L	.042-.046	10° BTDC	2200	550
3-51D-R00	4.9L	.042-.046	6° BTDC	1600	700④
3-51E-R01	4.9L	.042-.046	6° BTDC	1600	700④
3-51F-R00	4.9L	.042-.046	6° BTDC	1600	700④
3-51G-R00	4.9L	.042-.046	6° BTDC	1600	700④
3-51H-R00	4.9L	.042-.046	6° BTDC	1600	700④
3-51K-R00	4.9L	.042-.046	6° BTDC	1600	700④
3-51L-R00	4.9L	.042-.046	6° BTDC	1600	700④
3-51P-R00	4.9L	.042-.046	10° BTDC	1600	500
3-51R-R00	4.9L	.042-.046	6° BTDC	1600	700④
3-51R-R10	4.9L	.042-.046	6° BTDC	1600	700④
3-51S-R00	4.9L	.042-.046	6° BTDC	1600	700④
3-51S-R10	4.9L	.042-.046	6° BTDC	1600	700④
3-51T-R00	4.9L	.042-.046	6° BTDC	1600	700④
3-51T-R10	4.9L	.042-.046	6° BTDC	1600	700④
3-51V-R00	4.9L	.042-.046	10° BTDC	1600	700④
3-51X-R00	4.9L	.042-.046	10° BTDC	1600	700④
3-51Z-R00	4.9L	.042-.046	10° BTDC	1600	700④
3-52E-R00	4.9L	.042-.046	10° BTDC	1600	600⑤
3-52F-R00	4.9L	.042-.046	10° BTDC	1600	600⑤

TUNE-UP SPECIFICATIONS 1983

(For 1983 Tune-Up Specifications consult the Vehicle Emissions Control Label, which is located on the engine of the vehicle. This decal will contain a calibration number which when used in conjunction with the chart below will yield the required tune-up information. If the information given in this chart disagrees with the information on the decal, use the information on the decal.)

Calibration	Engine	Spark Plug Gap	Ignition Timing	Fast Idle RPM	Curb Idle RPM
3-52G-R00	4.9L	.042-.046	10° BTDC	1600	600⑤
3-52K-R00	4.9L	.042-.046	10° BTDC	1600	600⑤
3-52R-R00	4.9L	.042-.046	10° BTDC	1600	600⑤
3-52R-R10	4.9L	.042-.046	10° BTDC	1600	600⑤
3-52S-R00	4.9L	.042-.046	10° BTDC	1600	600⑤
3-52S-R10	4.9L	.042-.046	10° BTDC	1600	600⑤
3-52T-R00	4.9L	.042-.046	10° BTDC	1600	600⑤
3-52T-R10	4.9L	.042-.046	10° BTDC	1600	600⑤
3-52V-R00	4.9L	.042-.046	14° BTDC	1600	600⑤
3-52Y-R00	4.9L	.042-.046	14° BTDC	1600	600⑤
3-52Z-R00	4.9L	.042-.046	14° BTDC	1600	600⑤
3-53F-R00	5.0L	.042-.046	8° BTDC	2100	700⑥
3-53G-R00	5.0L	.042-.046	8° BTDC	2100	700⑥
3-531L-R00	5.0L	.042-.046	8° BTDC	2100	700⑥
3-53L-R00	5.0L	.042-.046	8° BTDC	2100	700⑥
3-53W-R00	5.0L	.042-.046	12° BTDC	2100	700⑥
3-53Y-R00	5.0L	.042-.046	12° BTDC	2100	700⑥
3-53Z-R00	5.0L	.042-.046	12° BTDC	2100	700⑥
3-54E-R00	5.0L	.042-.046	8° BTDC	2250	675⑦
3-54F-R00	5.0L	.042-.046	8° BTDC	2250	675⑦
3-54J-R00	5.0L	.042-.046	8° BTDC	2250	675⑦
3-54L-R00	5.0L	.042-.046	8° BTDC	2250	675⑦
3-54P-R00	5.0L	.042-.046	8° BTDC	2000	575
3-54R-R00	5.0L	.042-.046	8° BTDC	2000	575
3-54T-R00	5.0L	.042-.046	8° BTDC	2000	575
3-54W-R00	5.0L	.042-.046	12° BTDC	2250	600⑧
3-54Y-R00	5.0L	.042-.046	12° BTDC	2250	675⑦
3-54Z-R00	5.0L	.042-.046	12° BTDC	2250	675⑦
1-63T-R15B	5.8L	.042-.046	—	2000	1400⑨
1-63Y-R14B	5.8L	.042-.046	—	2000	1400⑨
2-64Y-R14B	5.8L	.042-.046	—	2000	1400⑨
1-63T-R12	5.8L	.042-.046	—	1700	750
1-63T-R13	5.8L	.042-.046	—	1700	750
1-64H-R02	5.8L	.042-.046	10° BTDC	2000	625⑩
1-64T-R12	5.8L	.042-.046	—	1650	600
1-64T-R13	5.8L	.042-.046	—	1650	600
2-63Y-R11	5.8L	.042-.046	—	1700	750
2-63Y-R12	5.8L	.042-.046	—	1700	750

TUNE-UP SPECIFICATIONS
1983

(For 1983 Tune-Up Specifications consult the Vehicle Emissions Control Label, which is located on the engine of the vehicle. This decal will contain a calibration number which when used in conjunction with the chart below will yield the required tune-up information. If the information given in this chart disagrees with the information on the decal, use the information on the decal.)

Calibration	Engine	Spark Plug Gap	Ignition Timing	Fast Idle RPM	Curb Idle RPM
2-64X-R00	5.8L	.042-.046	14° BTDC	2000	625⑩
2-64Y-R11	5.8L	.042-.046	—	1650	600
2-64Y-R12	5.8L	.042-.046	—	1650	600
5-77-R01	4.9L	.042-.046	10° BTDC	1500	600⑪
5-78-R01	4.9L	.042-.046	10° BTDC	1500	600⑪
9-77J-R12	4.9L	.042-.046	12° BTDC	1600	700
9-77S-R10	4.9L	.042-.046	10° BTDC	1600	700
9-78J-R00	4.9L	.042-.046	12° BTDC	1600	550
9-78J-R11	4.9L	.042-.046	12° BTDC	1600	550
7-79-R01	5.0L	.042-.046	6° BTDC	1250	750
7-80-R00	5.0L	.042-.046	6° BTDC	1600	650
2-75A-R10	5.8L	.042-.046	8° BTDC	1500	650
2-75J-R20	5.8L	.042-.046	8° BTDC	1500	650
2-76A-R10	5.8L	.042-.046	8° BTDC	1500	650
2-76J-R20	5.8L	.042-.046	8° BTDC	1500	650
9-83G-R12	6.1L	.042-.046	6° BTDC	2200	600
9-83G-R14	6.1L	.042-.046	6° BTDC	1600	600
9-83H-R11	6.1L	.042-.046	6° BTDC	2500	600
9-83H-R14	6.1L	.042-.046	2° BTDC	2500	600
9-87G-R11	7.0L	.042-.046	6° BTDC	2700	600
9-97J-R13	7.5L	.042-.046	8° BTDC	1600	600
9-98S-R00	7.5L	.042-.046	6° BTDC	1500	600

①800—w/o Power Steering
②750-800—Auto. Trans.
③700-800—Auto Trans.
④600—Non A/c or A/c off
⑤550—Non A/c or A/c off
⑥800—A/c on
⑦600—Non A/c or A/c off
⑧675—A/c on
⑨900—Throttle solenoid on, 600 throttle solenoid off
⑩550—A/c off and Non A/c
⑪700—Manual Trans.

TUNE-UP SPECIFICATIONS
1984

(For 1984 Tune-Up Specifications consult the Vehicle Emissions Control Label, which is located on the engine of the vehicle. This decal will contain a calibration number which when used in conjunction with the chart below will yield the required tune-up information. If the information given in this chart disagrees with the information on the decal, use the information on the decal.)

Calibration	Engine	Spark Plug Gap	Ignition Timing	Fast Idle RPM	Curb Idle RPM
3-41P-R15	2.0L	.032-.036	8° BTDC	2000	800
3-41S-R18	2.0L	.032-.036	9° BTDC	2000	800
3-49G-R20	2.3L	.042-.046	6° BTDC	2000	850①
3-49G-R20	2.3L	.042-.046	6° BTDC	2200	850①
3-49G-R17	2.3L	.042-.046	6° BTDC	2000	850①
3-49S-R16	2.3L	.042-.046	6° BTDC	2000	850①
3-49T-R20	2.3L	.042-.046	6° BTDC	2000	850①
3-49Y-R20	2.3L	.042-.046	10° BTDC	2000	850①
3-50H-R18	2.3L	.042-.046	6° BTDC	2000	800
3-50S-R18	2.3L	.042-.046	6° BTDC	2000	800
3-50Y-R18	2.3L	.042-.046	10° BTDC	2000	800
4-61F-R00	2.8L	.042-.046	10° BTDC	3000	800-900②
4-61F-R10	2.8L	.042-.046	10° BTDC	3000	800-900②
4-61G-R00	2.8L	.042-.046	10° BTDC	3000	700-800
4-61K-R01	2.8L	.042-.046	10° BTDC	3000	850-950②
4-61S-R00	2.8L	.042-.046	10° BTDC	3000	800-900②
4-62D-R00	2.8L	.042-.046	10° BTDC	3000	800-900②
4-62D-R10	2.8L	.042-.046	10° BTDC	3000	800-900②
4-62S-R01	2.8L	.042-.046	10° BTDC	3000	800-900②
4-62S-R10	2.8L	.042-.046	10° BTDC	3000	800-900②
4-51D-R01	4.9L	.042-.046	10° BTDC	1600	600-700③
4-51E-R00	4.9L	.042-.046	10° BTDC	1600	600-700③
4-51K-R00	4.9L	.042-.046	10° BTDC	1600	600-700③
4-51L-R00	4.9L	.042-.046	10° BTDC	1600	600-700③
4-51R-R00	4.9L	.042-.046	10° BTDC	1600	600-700③
4-51S-R00	4.9L	.042-.046	10° BTDC	1600	600-700③
4-51S-R01	4.9L	.042-.046	10° BTDC	1600	600-700③
4-51S-R02	4.9L	.042-.046	10° BTDC	1600	600-700③
4-51T-R00	4.9L	.042-.046	10° BTDC	1600	600-700③
4-51Z-R00	4.9L	.042-.046	10° BTDC	1600	600-700③
4-52L-R00	4.9L	.042-.046	10° BTDC	1600	600-700③
4-52R-R00	4.9L	.042-.046	10° BTDC	1600	600-700③
4-52S-R00	4.9L	.042-.046	10° BTDC	1600	600-700③
4-52T-R00	4.9L	.042-.046	10° BTDC	1600	600-700③
4-52W-R00	4.9L	.042-.046	10° BTDC	1600	600-700③
4-53F-R00	5.0L	.042-.046	8° BTDC	2100	800④
4-53F-R10	5.0L	.042-.046	8° BTDC	2100	800④
4-53G-R00	5.0L	.042-.046	8° BTDC	2100	800④

TUNE-UP SPECIFICATIONS
1984

(For 1984 Tune-Up Specifications consult the Vehicle Emissions Control Label, which is located on the engine of the vehicle. This decal will contain a calibration number which when used in conjunction with the chart below will yield the required tune-up information. If the information given in this chart disagrees with the information on the decal, use the information on the decal.)

Calibration	Engine	Spark Plug Gap	Ignition Timing	Fast Idle RPM	Curb Idle RPM
4-53G-R10	5.0L	.042-.046	8° BTDC	2100	800④
4-53K-R00	5.0L	.042-.046	8° BTDC	2100	800④
4-53K-R10	5.0L	.042-.046	8° BTDC	2100	800④
4-53Z-R00	5.0L	.042-.046	8° BTDC	2100	800④
4-53Z-R10	5.0L	.042-.046	8° BTDC	2100	800④
4-54E-R00	5.0L	.042-.046	8° BTDC	2100	800④
4-54E-R10	5.0L	.042-.046	8° BTDC	2100	800④
4-54J-R00	5.0L	.042-.046	8° BTDC	2100	800④
4-54J-R10	5.0L	.042-.046	8° BTDC	2100	800④
4-54L-R00	5.0L	.042-.046	8° BTDC	2100	800④
4-54L-R10	5.0L	.042-.046	8° BTDC	2100	800④
4-54R-R00	5.0L	.042-.046	10° BTDC	2000	575
4-54R-R10	5.0L	.042-.046	10° BTDC	2000	575
4-54T-R00	5.0L	.042-.046	10° BTDC	2000	575
4-54T-R10	5.0L	.042-.046	10° BTDC	2000	575
4-54W-R00	5.0L	.042-.046	12° BTDC	2100	675⑤
4-54W-R10	5.0L	.042-.046	12° BTDC	2100	675⑤
4-63H-R00	5.8L	.042-.046	10° BTDC	2000	750
4-64H-R00	5.8L	.042-.046	10° BTDC	2000	600
4-64H-R00	5.8L	.042-.046	10° BTDC	2000	600
4-64T-R00	5.8L	.042-.046	10° BTDC	2000	600
4-64T-R00	5.8L	.042-.046	10° BTDC	2000	600
4-64Y-R00	5.8L	.042-.046	10° BTDC	2000	600
5-77-R01	4.9L	.042-.046	10° BTDC	1500	600⑥
5-78-R01	4.9L	.042-.046	10° BTDC	1500	600⑥
9-77J-R12	4.9L	.042-.046	12° BTDC	1600	700⑦
9-78J-R00	4.9L	.042-.046	12° BTDC	1600	550
9-78J-R11	4.9L	.042-.046	12° BTDC	1600	550
7-79-R01	5.0L	.042-.046	6° BTDC	1500	750⑧
7-80-R00	5.0L	.042-.046	6° BTDC	1500	750⑧
2-75A-R10	5.8L	.042-.046	8° BTDC	1500	800⑧
2-75J-R20	5.8L	.042-.046	8° BTDC	1500	700⑧
2-76A-R10	5.8L	.042-.046	8° BTDC	1500	800⑧
2-76J-R20	5.8L	.042-.046	8° BTDC	1500	700⑧
9-83G-R12	6.1L	.042-.046	6° BTDC	2200	600
9-83G-R14	6.1L	.042-.046	6° BTDC	1600	600
9-83H-R11	6.1L	.042-.046	6° BTDC	2500	600
9-87G-R11	7.0L	.042-.046	6° BTDC	2700	600

TUNE-UP SPECIFICATIONS
1984

(For 1984 Tune-Up Specifications consult the Vehicle Emissions Control Label, which is located on the engine of the vehicle. This decal will contain a calibration number which when used in conjunction with the chart below will yield the required tune-up information. If the information given in this chart disagrees with the information on the decal, use the information on the decal.)

Calibration	Engine	Spark Plug Gap	Ignition Timing	Fast Idle RPM	Curb Idle RPM
9-97J-R10	7.5L	.042-.046	8° BTDC	1600	800⑨
3-98S-R10	7.5L	.042-.046	8° BTDC	1600	800⑨
4-98S-R00	7.5L	.042-.046	8° BTDC	1600	800⑨
4-37A-R00	2.0L	—	—	1450	725-775
4-37B-R00	2.0L	—	—	1450	725-775
3-47D-R00	2.2L	—	—	1450	780-830
4-68J-R00	6.9L	—	—	—	650-700
4-68X-R00	6.9L	—	—	—	650-700

①800 without P/S
②700-800 RPM—Auto. Trans. in DRIVE
③550-650 RPM—Auto Trans. in DRIVE
④700—Non a/c or A/C off
⑤600—Non a/c or A/C off
⑥700—Manual Trans.
⑦600—TSP off
⑧650—"D" auto trans; 525—TSP off
⑨650—DRIVE

TUNE-UP SPECIFICATIONS
1985–86

(For 1985–86 Tune-Up Specifications consult the Vehicle Emissions Control Label, which is located on the engine of the vehicle. This decal will contain a calibration number which when used in conjunction with the chart below will yield the required tune-up information. If the information given in this chart disagrees with the information on the decal, use the information on the decal.)

Calibration	Engine	Spark Plug Gap	Ignition Timing*	Fast Idle rpm	Curb Idle rpm
5-41D-R00	2.0L	.042–.046	6°	1700	775–825
5-41D-R10	2.0L	.042–.046	6°	1700	775–825
5-49F-R01	2.3L	.042–.046	10°	—	575–725
5-49S-R01	2.3L	.042–.046	10°	—	575–725
5-50H-R02	2.3L	.042–.046	10°	—	625–775
5-50S-R02	2.3L	.042–.046	10°	—	625–775
5-61F-R01	2.8L	.042–.046	10°	3000	800–900①
5-61S-R01	2.8L	.042–.046	14°	3200	800–900①
5-62E-R01	2.8L	.042–.046	10°	3000	800–900①
5-62R-R01	2.8L	.042–.046	10°	3000	800–900①
4-51R-R00	4.9L	.042–.046	10°	1600	600–700②
4-51S-R02	4.9L	.042–.046	10°	1600	600–700②
4-51T-R00	4.9L	.042–.046	10°	1600	600–700②
4-52G-R00	4.9L	.042–.046	10°	1600	600–700②
4-52G-R10	4.9L	.042–.046	10°	1600	600–700①
4-52L-R00	4.9L	.042–.046	10°	1600	600–700②
4-52L-R10	4.9L	.042–.046	10°	1600	600–700②
4-52R-R00	4.9L	.042–.046	10°	1600	600–700②
4-52S-R00	4.9L	.042–.046	10°	1600	600–700②
4-52S-R10	4.9L	.042–.046	10°	1600	600–700②
4-52T-R00	4.9L	.042–.046	10°	1600	600–700②
5-51D-R00	4.9L	.042–.046	10°	1600	600–700②
5-51E-R00	4.9L	.042–.046	10°	1600	600–700②
5-51F-R00	4.9L	.042–.046	10°	1600	600–700②

TUNE-UP SPECIFICATIONS
1985–86

(For 1985–86 Tune-Up Specifications consult the Vehicle Emissions Control Label, which is located on the engine of the vehicle. This decal will contain a calibration number which when used in conjunction with the chart below will yield the required tune-up information. If the information given in this chart disagrees with the information on the decal, use the information on the decal.)

Calibration	Engine	Spark Plug Gap	Ignition Timing*	Fast Idle rpm	Curb Idle rpm
5-51H-R00	4.9L	.042–.046	10°	1600	600–700②
5-51K-R00	4.9L	.042–.046	10°	1600	600–700②
5-51L-R00	4.9L	.042–.046	10°	1600	600–700②
5-51V-R00	4.9L	.042–.046	10°	1600	600–700②
5-51Z-R00	4.9L	.042–.046	10°	1600	600–700②
5-52E-R00	4.9L	.042–.046	10°	1600	600–700②
5-52K-R00	4.9L	.042–.046	10°	1600	600–700②
5-52W-R00	4.9L	.042–.046	10°	1600	600–700②
5-52Y-R00	4.9L	.042–.046	10°	1600	600–700②
4-54R-R12	5.0L	.042–.046	10°	2000	575D
4-454R-R13	5.0L	.042–.046	10°	2000	575D
4-54R-R14	5.0L	.042–.046	10°	2000	575D
5-53D-R00	5.0L	.042–.046	10°	—	—
5-53D-R01	5.0L	.042–.046	8°	—	—
5-53F-R00	5.0L	.042–.046	10°	—	—
5-53F-R01	5.0L	.042–.046	8°	—	—
5-53H-R00	5.0L	.042–.046	10°	—	—
5-53H-R01	5.0L	.042–.046	8°	—	—
5-54Q-R00	5.0L	.042–.046	10°	—	—
5-54Q-R01	5.0L	.042–.046	10°	—	—
5-54S-R00	5.0L	.042–.046	10°	—	—
5-54S-R01	5.0L	.042–.046	10°	—	—
5-54W-R00	5.0L	.042–.046	10°	—	—
5-54X-R00	5.0L	.042–.046	10°	—	—
4-64G-R00	5.8L(F)	.042–.046	10°	1900	650D
4-64G-R02	5.8L(F)	.042–.046	10°	1900	650D
4-64G-R02	5.8L(E)	.042–.046	10°	1900	650D
4-64T-R00	5.8L(F)	.042–.046	10°	2000	600D
4-64T-R00	5.8L(E)	.042–.046	10°	2000	600D
4-64Z-R10	5.8L(F)	.042–.046	14°	1900	650D
4-64Z-R10	5.8L(E)	.042–.046	14°	1900	650D
5-63H-R00	5.8L	.042–.046	10°	2000	700
5-63Y-R00	5.8L	.042–.046	10°	2000	700

* All settings Before Top Dead Center
① 700–800 in Drive A/T
② 550–650 in Drive A/T

FIRING ORDERS

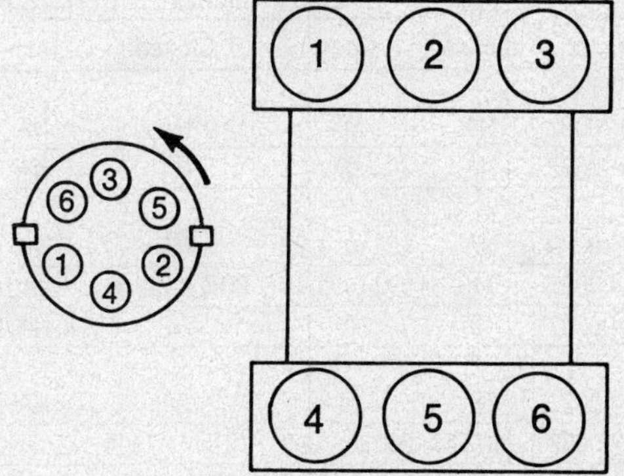

232(3.8L) V6

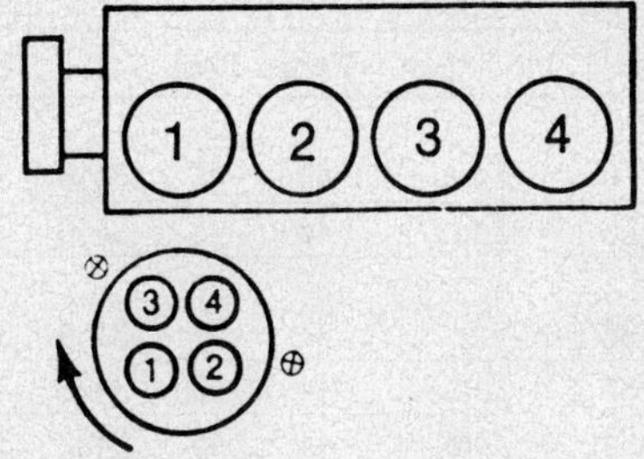

122(2.0L) and 140(2.3L) 4 cylinder

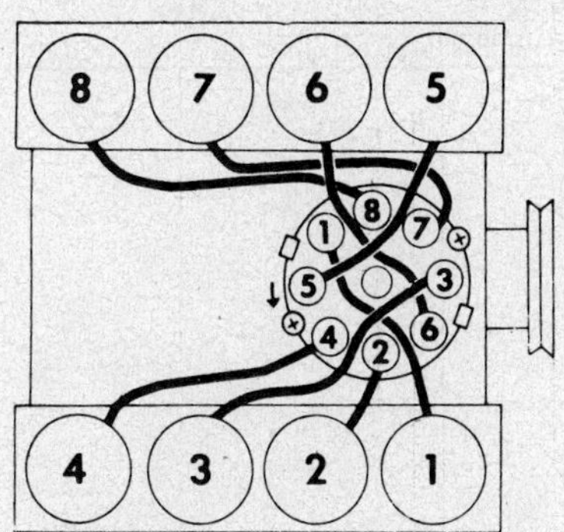

255, 302, 360, 390, 460 V8

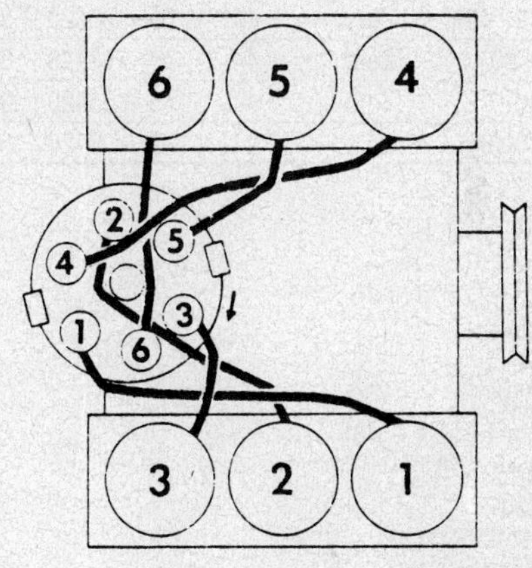

173(2.8L) V6

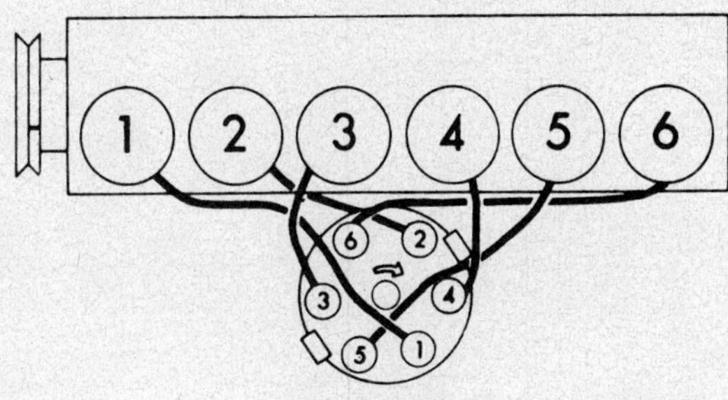

300 6-cylinder

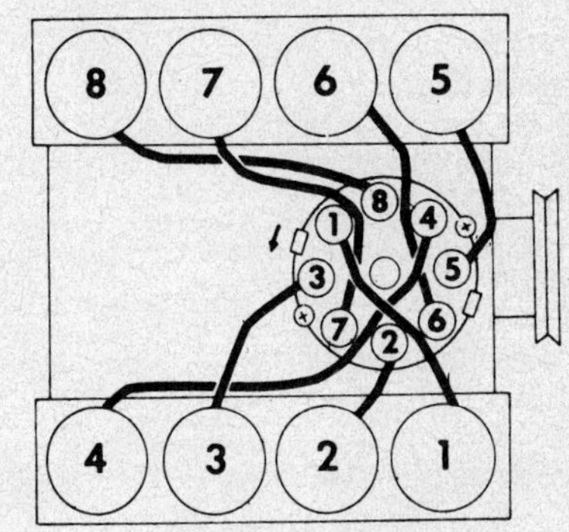

351W, 351M, 400 V8

VALVE SPECIFICATIONS

Cu. In. Displacement	Year	Lash (Hot) Inches Int.	Lash (Hot) Inches Exh.	Angle Degree Face	Angle Degree Seat	Stem Dia. Inches Int.	Stem Dia. Inches Exh.	Stem Clearance Intake	Stem Clearance Exhaust	Valve Lift Inches	Valve Spring Lbs. @ Inches Open	Valve Spring Lbs. @ Inches Closed	Spring Free Length Inch
FOUR CYLINDER													
122	'83–'86	Zero		44	45	.3416	.3411	.0010–.0027	.0015–.0032	NA	①	NA	NA
140	'83–'86	Zero		44	45	.3416	.3411	.0010–.0027	.0015–.0032	NA	②	NA	NA
SIX CYLINDER													
173V6	'83–'86	③		44	45	.3159	.3149	.0008–.0025	.0008–.0035	NA	152 @ 1.22	NA	NA
300	'80–'86	Zero		44	45	.3420	.3420	.0010–.0027	.0010–.0027	.249	192 @ 1.18	80 @ 158④	1.99⑤
232V6	'82–'84	Zero		44	45	.3422	.3415	.0010–.0025	.0015–.0032	⑥	⑦	⑧	NA
EIGHT CYLINDER													
255	'81–'82	Zero		46	45	.3420	.3415	.0010–.0027	.0010–.0027	⑨	⑩	⑪	NA
302	'80–'86	Zero		44	45	.3420	.3415	.0010–.0027	.0015–.0032	.2375⑫	200 @ 1.36	78 @ 1.78⑬	2.04⑭
351 W	'79–'86	Zero		44	45	.3420	.3415	.0010–.0027	.0015–.0032	.2600	200 @ 1.35	78 @ 1.78	2.04⑭
351 M	'80	Zero		44	45	.3420	.3415	.0010–.0027	.0015–.0032	.2350⑭	226 @ 1.39	80 @ 1.82⑬	2.06
400	'80–'82	Zero		44	45	.3420	.3415	.0010–.0027	.0015–.0032	.2480	225 @ 1.39	80 @ 1.82⑮	2.06
460	'80–'86	Zero		44	45	.3420	.3420	.0010–.0027	.0010–.0027	.2530	252 @ 1.33	80 @ 1.81	2.070

① Intake: 71–79 @ 1.52
Exhaust: 142–156 @ 1.12
② Intake: 71–79 @ 1.56
Exhaust: 159–175 @ 1.16
③ Cold Adjustment
Intake: .014
Exhaust: .016
④ Intake Open: 1.95 @ 1.30
Closed: 80 @ 1.70
⑤ Exhaust: 1.87
⑥ Intake: 0.415 in.
Exhaust: 0.417 in.
⑦ Loaded: 215 lbs @ 1.39 in.
75 lbs @ 1.70 in.
⑧ Assembled height 1.70–1.78 in.
⑨ Intake: .2375 in.
Exhaust: .2474 in.
⑩ Intake: 74–82 lbs @ 1.78 in.
190–212 lbs @ 1.36 in.
Exhaust: 76–84 lbs @ 1.60 in.
190–210 lbs @ 1.20 in.
⑪ Intake: 204 in.
Exhaust: 1.85 in.
⑫ Exhaust: .2474 in
⑬ Exhaust: Opened: 200 @ 120
Closed: 80 @ 160
⑭ Exhaust 1.85 in.
⑮ '80: Exhaust closed 84 @ 1.68 in.

CRANKSHAFT BEARING JOURNAL SPECIFICATIONS

(Inches)

Cu. In. Displace-ment	Year	Main Bearing Journals: Journal Diameter	Main Bearing Journals: Oil Clearance	Shaft End-play	Thrust On No.	Connecting Rod Bearing Journals: Journal Diameter	Connecting Rod Bearing Journals: Oil Clearance (max)	Connecting Rod Bearing Journals: Side Clearance
				FOUR CYLINDER				
122	'83–'86	2.3982–2.3990	.0008–.0015	.004–.008	3	2.0472	.0008–.0015	.0035–.0105
140	'83–'86	2.3982–2.3990	.0008–.0015	.004–.008	3	2.0472	.0008–.0015	.0035–.0105
				SIX CYLINDER				
173V6	'83–'85	2.2441	.0008–.0015	.012	3	2.1260	.0006–.0016	.004–.011
300		2.3982–2.3990	.0009–.0028	.004–.008	5	2.1228–2.1236	.0009–.0027	.006–.013
232-V6	'82–'84	2.5190	.0009–.0027	.004–.008	3	2.3107	.0009–.0027	.004–.011
				EIGHT CYLINDER				
255	'81–'82	2.2490	.0005–.0024 ①	.004–.008	3	2.1232	.0008–.0025	.010–.020
302	'80–'86	2.2482–2.2490	.0005–.0015 ④	.004–.008	3	2.1228–2.1236	.0010–.0015	.010–.020
351W	'80–'86	2.9994–3.0002	②	.004–.008	3	2.3103–2.3111	.0008–.0026	.010–.020
351M	'80	2.9994–3.0002	.0008–.0025 ③	.004–.008	3	2.3103–2.3111	.0008–.0025	.010–.020
400	'80–'82	2.9994–3.0002	.0008–.0025 ③	.004–.008	3	2.3103–2.3111	.0008–.0025	.010–.020
460	'80–'86	2.9994–3.0002	.0008–.0015 ③	.004–.008	3	2.4992–2.5000	.008–.0015	.010–.020

① No. 1 .0001–.0020.
② No. 1—.0005–.0015;
All others .0008–.0015.
③ Maximum
④ No. 1—.0001–.0015

PISTON AND RING SPECIFICIATIONS

All measurements given in inches

Year	Engine	Piston to Bore Clearance	Ring Side Clearance: Top Compression	Ring Side Clearance: Bottom Compression	Ring Side Clearance: Oil Control	Ring Gap: Top Compression	Ring Gap: Bottom Compression	Ring Gap: Oil Control ①
'83–'86	4-122	.0014–.0022	.0020–.0040	.0020–.0040	snug	.0100–.0200	.0100–.0200	.015–.055
'83–'86	4-134	.0021–.0031	.0020–.0035	.0016–.0031	.0012–.0028	.0157–.0217	.0118–.0157	.0138–.0217
'83–'86	4-140	.0014–.0022	.0020–.0040	.0020–.0040	snug	.0100–.0200	.0100–.0200	.015–.055
'83–'86	6-173	.0011–.0019	.0020–.0033	.0020–.0033	snug	.0150–.0230	.0150–.0230	.015–.055
'82–'84	6-232	.0014–.0022	.0020–.0040	.0020–.0040	snug	.0100–.0200	.0100–.0200	.015–.055
'80–'86	6-300	.0014–.0022	.0019–.0036	.0020–.0040	snug	.0100–.0200	.0100–.0200	.010–.035
'82	8-255	.0014–.0024	.0020–.0040	.0020–.0040	snug	.0100–.0200	.0100–.0200	.015–.055
'80–'86	8-302	.0018–.0026	.0020–.0040	.0020–.0040	snug	.010–.020	.0100–.0200	.015–.035
'80	8-351M	.0014–.0022	.0019–.0036	.0020–.0040	snug	.010–.020	.0100–.0200	.010–.035
'80–'86	8-351W	.0022–.0030	.0019–.0036	.0020–.0040	snug	.010–.020	.0100–.0200	.015–.035
'80–'82	8-400	.0014–.0022	.0019–.0036	.0020–.0040	snug	.0100–.0200	.0100–.0200	.015–.035
'80–'86	8-460	.0022–.0300	.0019–.0036	.0020–.0040	snug	.0100–.0200	.0100–.0200	.010–.035
'83–'86	8-420	.0055–.0075	.0020–.0040	.0020–.0040	.0010–.0030	.0140–.0240	.0100–.0240	.0600–.0700

① Steel rails

TORQUE SPECIFICATIONS

Cu. In. Displacement	Year	Cylinder Head Bolts (Ft. Lbs.)	Rod Bearing Bolts (Ft. Lbs.)	Main Bearing Bolts (Ft. Lbs.)	Crankshaft Balancer Bolt (Ft. Lbs.)	Flywheel to Crankshaft Bolts (Ft. Lbs.)	Manifold (Ft. Lbs.) Intake	Manifold (Ft. Lbs.) Exhaust
FOUR CYLINDER								
122	'83–'86	⑲	⑳	㉑	100–120	56–64	14–21⑱	14–21⑱
140	'83–'86	⑲	⑳	㉑	100–120	56–64	14–21⑱	14–21⑱
SIX CYLINDER								
173-V6	'83–'86	⑰	19–24	65–75	85–96	47–52	15–18⑱	20–30⑱
300		70–85②	40–45	60–70	130–150	75–85	22–32	28–33
232-V6	'82–'86	74⑮	31–36	65–81	93–121	54–64	18–20	15–22
EIGHT CYLINDER								
255-V8	'81–'82	65–72⑯	19–24	60–70	70–90	75–85	23–25	18–24
302	'80–'86	65–72③	19–24	95–105	70–90	75–85	23–25	18–24
351 W	'80–'86	65–70⑧	19–24⑨	60–70⑪	70–90	75–90	23–25	18–24
351 M	'80	95–105④	40–45	35–45⑪	70–90	75–85	⑤	18–24
370	'80–'86	70–140⑭	45–50	95–105	150–175	75–85	22–32	28–33
400	'80–'82	95–105④	40–45	35–45⑪	70–90	75–85	⑤	18–24
429	'80–'86	70–140⑭	45–50	95–105	150–175	75–85	22–32	28–33
460	'80–'86	130–140	40–45	95–105	70–90	75–85	25–30	28–33
477/475	'80–'81	170–180⑥	60–65	130–150	130–175	100–110	25–32	22–32

① Not used.
② Torque in steps; first to 55 ft. lbs., then to 65, final 70–85.
③ Torque in steps; first to 55–65 ft. lbs., then to 65–72.
④ Torque in steps; first to 75, then 95, final 105 ft. lbs.
⑤ ⅜ in-22-32 ft. lbs.; 5/16″-17-25 ft. lbs.
⑥ Torque in steps; first to 140 ft. lbs., then to 160 ft. lbs., final 170–180 ft. lbs.
⑦ Not used.
⑧ Not used.
⑨ '80 (40–45)
⑩ Not used
⑪ '80 (95–105)
⑫ '80 torque in steps first to 70, then to 80, final to 90
⑭ '80 torque in steps; first to 70–80; then to 100–110; final to 130–140
⑮ Torque in four steps–47, 55, 63 and 74 ft. lbs.–back off bolt 2–3 turns and repeat torque steps.
⑯ Torque in two steps–55–65, then to 65–72 ft. lbs.
⑰ Torque in three steps:
a) 29–40 ft. lbs.
b) 40–51 ft. lbs.
c) 70–85 ft. lbs.
⑱ Re-check after engine is warm.
⑲ Torque in two steps:
a) 50–60 ft. lbs.
b) 80–90 ft. lbs.
⑳ Torque in two steps:
a) 25–30 ft. lbs.
b) 30–36 ft. lbs.
㉑ Torque in two steps:
a) 50–60 ft. lbs.
b) 80–90 ft. lbs.

OIL PUMP CLEARANCES

(Inches)

Engine Cu. In.	Year	Relief Valve Spring Pressure Lbs. @ Specified Length	Driveshaft to Housing Clearance	Relief Valve to Housing Clearance	Rotor Assembly End Clearance	Outer Race to Housing Clearance
122	'83–'86	15.2–17.2 @ 1.20	.0015–.0030	.0015–.0030	.004 Max	.001–.013
140	'83–'86	15.2–17.2 @ 1.20	.0015–.0030	.0015–.0030	.004 Max.	.001–.013
176-V6	'83–'86	13.6–14.7 @ 1.39	.0015–.0030	.0015–.0030	.004 Max.	.001–.013
300	'80–'86	2.06–22.6 @ 2.49	.0015–.0030	.0015–.0030	.001–.004	.001–.013
232-V6	'82–'86	17.1–15.2 @ 1.20	.0015–.0030	.0017–.0029	—	—
255	'81–'82	10.6–12.2 @ 1.74	.0015–.0030	.0015–.0030	.004 Max.	.001–.013
302	'80–'86	10.6–12.2 @ 1.704	.0015–.0030	.0015–.0030	.001–.004	.001–.013
351W	'80–'82	18.2–20.2 @ 2.49	.0015–.0030	.0015–.0030	.001–.004	.001–.013
370	'80–'86	20.6–22.6 @ 2.49	.0015–.0030	.0015–.0030	.001–.004	.001–.013
400	'80–'82	20.6–22.6 @ 2.49	.0015–.0030	.0015–.0030	.001–.004	.001–.013
429	'80–'86	20.6–22.6 @ 2.49	.0015–.0030	.0015–.0030	.001–.004	.001–.013
460	'80–'86	20.6–22.6 @ 2.49	.0015–.0030	.0015–.0030	.001–.004	.001–.013
401/477/475/534	'80–'82	10.7–11.9 @ 1.07	.0015–.0030	.0015–.0030	.001–.004	.006–.011

ENGINE CODE SPECIFICATIONS
Gasoline Engine Codes

The Engine Identification Code letter is the fourth character in the vehicle identification number for Ford vehicles. See the chart below for code letter information.

	Model Year and Engine Code						
Engines	'80	'81	'82	'83	'84	'85	'86
122-4	—	—	—	K	K	K	K
140-4	—	—	—	Z	Z	Z	Z
173-V6	—	—	—	S	S	S	—
179-V6	—	—	—	—	—	—	④
300-6 Cylinder 1V	E	E	E①	Y	Y	Y	Y
232-V6	—	—	3	3	3	—	—
255-V8	—	D	D	—	—	—	—
302-V8	F	F	F	F	F	F	F
351-V8	G	G②	W	G	G	G③	G
400-V8	Z	Z	Z	—	—		
460-V8 Econoline	L	L	L	L	L	L	L
Light Truck	L	L	L	L	L	L	L

① Gasoline engine for LP conversion
② W = E-100 Windsor only, E-150 less leaded fuel
G = E-150, with lead fuel E-250, E-350
③ 4 bbL.
④ Not available at time of publication

FRONT WHEEL ALIGNMENT SPECIFICATIONS
Light Duty Vehicles

Year, Model	Ride Height		Caster ⑥ (Degrees)		Camber (Degrees)		Toe-In	Toe-In
	Min.	Max.	Min.	Max.	Min.	Max.	(Inches)	(Millimeters)
1983–86			④	④				
Ranger,	2 3/4	3 1/4	4 1/2	7	−1	1	1/32	0.8
4 × 2 ①③⑥	3 1/4	3 1/2	4	6 1/2	−1/2	1 3/4	1/32	0.8
	3 1/2	4	3 3/8	5 7/8	0	2 3/8	1/32	0.8
	4	4 1/4	2 5/8	5 1/8	3/4	3	1/32	0.8
	4 1/4	4 3/4	2	4 1/2	1 1/2	3 3/4	1/32	0.8
1983–86			④	④	④	④		
Ranger Bronco II	2 3/4	3 1/4	5	8	−1	1/2	1/32	0.8
4 × 4 ①③⑥	3 1/4	3 1/2	4	7	−0	1 1/2	1/32	0.8
	3 1/2	4	3	6	1/2	2	1/32	0.8
	4	4 1/4	2 1/2	5 1/2	1 1/4	2 3/4	1/32	0.8
	4 1/4	4 3/4	1 3/4	5	2	3 3/4	1/32	0.8
1983–86			④	④				
F250, 350, 4 × 2 ①③Ⓐ	2 1/2	2 3/4	5 1/2	7	−1/2	1/2	1/32	0.8
	2 3/4	3 1/4	5	6	−1/2	1 1/2	1/32	0.8
	3 1/4	3 1/2	4	5	1/4	2 1/4	1/32	0.8
	3 1/2	4	3	4	1	3	1/32	0.8
	4	4 1/4	⑦	⑦	2	3 1/2	1/32	0.8
1981–82			④	④	④	④		
F-250, 350, 4 × 2 ①③	2	2 1/4	5 3/4	9	−2 1/2	0	1/32	0.8
	2 1/4	2 3/4	4 3/4	8	−1 1/2	1	1/32	0.8
	2 1/4	3 1/4	3 3/4	7	−1/4	1 3/4	1/32	0.8
	3 1/4	3 3/4	2 3/4	6	1/4	2 3/4	1/32	0.8
	3 1/2	4	1 3/4	5	1	3 1/2	1/32	0.8
	4	4 1/4	3/4	4	2	4 1/2	1/32	0.8
1983–86			④	④	④	④		
F-250, 350, 4 × 4	5	5 1/2	3 1/16	5 1/8	−1 3/4	3/4	1/32	0.8
①③Ⓐ	5 1/2	6	3 1/8	5 1/4	−3/4	1 3/4	1/32	0.8
	6	6 1/4	3 1/4	5 3/8	1/4	3	1/32	0.8
	6 1/4	6 3/4	3 3/8	5 1/2	1 1/2	4	1/32	0.8
	6 3/4	7	3 1/2	5 1/2	2 1/2	4 1/4	1/32	0.8

FRONT WHEEL ALIGNMENT SPECIFICATIONS
Light Duty Vehicles

Year, Model	Ride Height Min.	Ride Height Max.	Caster ⑥ (Degrees) Min.	Caster ⑥ (Degrees) Max.	Camber (Degrees) Min.	Camber (Degrees) Max.	Toe-In (Inches)	Toe-In (Millimeters)
1981–82			④	④				
F-250, 350 4 × 4	4 3/4	5	3	5	4 3/4	5	1/32	0.8
①③	5	5 1/2	3 1/8	5 1/8	– 1 3/4	3/4	1/32	0.8
	5 1/2	6	3 1/8	5 1/8	– 3/4	1 3/4	1/32	0.8
	6	6 1/4	3 1/4	5 1/4	1/4	2 3/4	1/32	0.8
	6 1/4	6 3/4	3 3/8	5 3/8	1 1/4	4	1/32	0.8
	6 3/4	7	3 1/2	5 1/2	2 1/2	5	1/32	0.8
1983–86	3 3/4	4	—	—	– 3/4	3/4	1/32	0.8
E-100, 150 ①③	4	4 1/2	4 1/2	5 1/4	– 5/8	1 5/8	1/32	0.8
	4 1/2	5	3 1/4	4	3/8	2 5/8	1/32	0.8
	5	5 1/2	2	2 3/4	1 1/4	3 5/8	1/32	0.8
	5 1/2	5 3/4	3/4	2 1/4	2 1/4	4 1/8	1/32	0.8
1981–82	3 1/4	3 1/2	6 1/4	8	– 1 3/4	– 1/4	1/32	0.8
E-100, 150 ①③	3 1/2	3 3/4	5 3/4	7 1/4	– 1 1/2	1/4	1/32	0.8
	3 3/4	4	5	6 3/4	– 1	3/4	1/32	0.8
	4	4 1/4	4 1/2	5 3/4	– 1/2	1 1/4	1/32	0.8
	4 1/4	4 1/2	4	5 1/4	0	1 3/4	1/32	0.8
	4 1/2	4 3/4	3 1/4	4 1/2	1/2	2 1/4	1/32	0.8
	4 3/4	5	2 1/2	4	1	2 3/4	1/32	0.8
	5	5 1/4	2	3 1/4	1 1/2	3 1/4	1/32	0.8
	5 1/4	5 1/2	1 1/2	2 3/4	2	3 3/4	1/32	0.8
1983–86			④	④				
F-100, 150,	2 3/4	3 1/4	5 1/2	7 1/2	– 1 1/2	3/4	1/32	0.8
4 × 2 ①③Ⓐ	3 1/4	3 1/2	5	6	– 3/4	1 1/2	1/32	0.8
	3 1/2	4	4 1/4	5 1/4	1/4	2 1/2	1/32	0.8
	4	4 1/4	3 1/4	4 1/4	1	3 1/2	1/32	0.8
	4 1/4	4 3/4	2 1/2	3 1/2	2	4 1/2	1/32	0.8

FRONT WHEEL ALIGNMENT SPECIFICATIONS
Light Duty Vehicles

Year, Model	Ride Height Min.	Ride Height Max.	Caster ⑥ (Degrees) Min.	Caster ⑥ (Degrees) Max.	Camber (Degrees) Min.	Camber (Degrees) Max.	Toe-In (Inches)	Toe-In (Millimeters)
1981–82			④	④	④	④		
F-100, F-150 4 × 2 ①③	2 1/4	2 3/4	6	10	– 3	– 1/2	1/32	0.8
	2 3/4	3 1/4	5	9	– 2	1/2	1/32	0.8
	3 1/4	3 1/2	4	8	– 1 1/4	1 1/4	1/32	0.8
	3 1/2	4	3	7	– 1/4	2 1/4	1/32	0.8
	4	4 1/4	2	6	1/2	3	1/32	0.8
	4 1/4	4 3/4	1	5	1 1/2	4	1/32	0.8
1980			④	④	④	④		
F-100, 150 4 × 2 ①②	2 1/4	2 3/4	6	10	– 3	– 1/2	3/32	2.4
	2 3/4	3 1/4	5	9	– 2	1/2	3/32	2.4
	3 1/4	3 1/2	4	8	– 1 1/4	1 1/4	3/32	2.4
	3 1/2	4	3	7	– 1/4	2 1/4	3/32	2.4
	4	4 1/4	2	6	– 1/2	3	3/32	2.4
	4 1/4	4 3/4	1	5	1 1/2	4	3/32	2.4
1981–82			④	④				
F-150, Bronco 4 × 4 ①③	2 3/4	3 1/4	6	9	– 2 1/2	– 1/4	1/32	0.8
	3 1/4	3 1/2	5	8	– 1 3/4	1/2	1/32	0.8
	3 1/2	4	4	7	– 3/4	1 1/2	1/32	0.8
	4	4 1/4	3	6	0	2 1/4	1/32	0.8
	4 1/4	4 3/4	2	5	1	3 1/4	1/32	0.8
	4 3/4	5	1	4	1 3/4	4	1/32	0.8
1983–86			④	④				
F-150, Bronco 4 × 4 ①③	3 1/4	3 1/2	6	7	– 1 1/2	3/4	1/32	0.8
	3 1/2	4	5	6	– 3/4	1 3/4	1/32	0.8
	4	4 1/4	4	5	1/4	2 3/4	1/32	0.8
	4 1/4	4 3/4	3	4	1 1/4	3 1/2	1/32	0.8
1980			④	④				
F-150, Bronco 4 × 4 ①②	2 3/4	3 1/4	6	9	– 2 1/2	– 1/4	3/32	2.4
	3 1/4	3 1/2	5	8	– 1 3/4	1/2	3/32	2.4
	3 1/2	4	4	7	– 3/4	1 1/2	3/32	2.4
	4	4 1/4	3	6	0	2 1/4	3/32	2.4
	4 1/4	4 3/4	2	5	1	3 1/4	3/32	2.4
	4 3/4	5	1	4	1 3/4	4	3/32	2.4
1983–86	3 3/4	4	—	—	– 5/8	7/8	1/32	0.8
E-250, 350 ①③	4	4 1/2	7 1/4	8	– 1/2	1 7/8	1/32	0.8
	4 1/2	5	6	6 3/4	1/2	2 7/8	1/32	0.8
	5	5 1/2	4 3/4	5 1/2	1 1/2	3 7/8	1/32	0.8
	5 1/2	5 3/4	3 1/4	4	2 1/2	4 3/8	1/32	0.8
1980–82	3 1/4	3 1/2	9	10 1/2	– 1 3/4	– 1/4	1/32	0.8
E-250, 350 ①③	3 1/2	3 3/4	8 1/2	9 3/4	– 1 1/2	1/4	1/32	0.8
	3 3/4	4	7 7/8	9	– 1	3/4	1/32	0.8
	4	4 1/4	7 1/8	8 1/2	– 1/2	1 1/4	1/32	0.8
	4 1/4	4 1/2	6 1/2	7 3/4	0	1 3/4	1/32	0.8
	4 1/2	4 3/4	5 3/4	7	1/2	2 1/4	1/32	0.8
	4 3/4	5	5 1/4	6 1/2	1	2 3/4	1/32	0.8
	5	5 1/4	4 5/8	6	1 1/2	3 1/4	1/32	0.8
	5 1/4	5 1/2	4	5 1/2	2	3 3/4	1/32	0.8

FRONT WHEEL ALIGNMENT SPECIFICATIONS
Light Duty Vehicles

Year, Model	Ride Height Min.	Ride Height Max.	Caster ⑥ (Degrees) Min.	Caster ⑥ (Degrees) Max.	Camber (Degrees) Min.	Camber (Degrees) Max.	Toe-In (Inches)	Toe-In (Millimeters)
1980			④	④	④	④		
F-250, 350 4 × 2 ①③	2	2 1/4	5 1/4	9	− 2 1/2	0	1/32	0.8
	2 1/4	2 3/4	4 3/4	8	− 1 1/2	1	1/32	0.8
	2 3/4	2 1/4	3 3/4	7	− 3/4	1 3/4	1/32	0.8
	3 1/4	3 1/2	2 3/4	6	1/4	2 3/4	1/32	0.8
	3 1/2	4	1 3/4	5	1	3 1/2	1/32	0.8
	4	4 1/4	3/4	4	2	4 1/2	1/32	0.8
1980			④	④				
F-250, 350 4 × 4 ①②	4 1/4	4 3/4	3 1/2	5 3/4	− 4	− 1 1/4	3/32	2.4
	4 3/4	5	3 1/4	5 1/2	− 2 3/4	0	3/32	2.4
	5	5 1/2	3	5 1/4	− 1 1/2	1 1/4	3/32	2.4
	5 1/2	6	2 3/4	5	− 1/4	2 1/2	3/32	2.4
	6	6 1/4	2 1/2	4 3/4	1	3 3/4	3/32	6.4
	6 1/4	6 3/4	2 1/4	4 1/2	2 1/4	5	3/32	6.4
1980	3 1/4	3 1/2	6 1/4	8	− 1 3/4	− 1/4	1/4	6.4
E-100, 150 ①⑤	3 1/2	3 3/4	5 3/4	7 1/4	− 1 1/2	1/4	1/4	6.4
	3 3/4	4	5	6 3/4	− 1	3/4	1/4	6.4
	4	4 1/4	4 1/2	5 3/4	− 1/2	1 1/4	1/4	6.4
	4 1/4	4 1/2	4	5 1/4	0	1 3/4	1/4	6.4
	4 1/2	4 3/4	3 1/4	4 1/2	1/2	2 1/4	1/4	6.4
	4 3/4	5	2 1/2	4	1	2 3/4	1/4	6.4
	5	5 1/4	2	3 1/4	1 1/2	3 1/4	1/4	6.4
	5 1/4	5 1/2	1 1/2	2 3/4	2	3 3/4	1/4	6.4

Ⓐ Right side height measurement shown; left side height should be 0″ to 7/16″ higher on any one vehicle.
① All vehicles with normal operating attitude.
② Nominal toe setting is 2.5 mm (3/32 inch). Range is 0.8 mm (3/32 inch) out to 5.6 mm (7/32 inch) in.
③ Nominal toe setting is 8 mm (1/32 inch). Range is 2.5 mm (3/32 inch) out to 4 mm (5/32 inch) in.
④ Not Adjustable.
⑤ Toe range is 0″ to 1/4″, 1/8″ nominal.
⑥ Side-to-side variation: Caster 1 1/2°, Camber 23/32°.
⑦ Vehicle height is too high.

FRONT WHEEL ALIGNMENT SPECIFICATIONS
1980 600, 9000 Medium, Heavy and Extra Heavy Trucks

Vehicle Model	Front Axle Capacity	Toe-In	Camber (Degrees)	Caster (Degrees)
F-500, F-600, LN-600 Hydraulic Brakes	5000 5500	3/16″–5/16″ Empty Vehicle	5/8° ± 3/8°	3 1/2° ± 1/2° F-B Series 4 1/2° ± 1/2° LN Series
B500, B-6500, F-C-B-LN-600-700, LT-LNT-800, LT-800-880, F-C-LN-6000, C-7000, L-800-900, LN-800 Hydraulic Brakes	6000 7000	3/16″–5/16″ Empty Vehicle	5/8° ± 3/8°	3 1/2° ± 1/2° F-B Series (Medium) 4 1/2° ± 1/2° LN (Medium) 3 3/4° ± 1/2° L-LN (Heavy) 3° ± 1/2° C Series
F-600-700, 750, B-LN-600-700 LN-F-B-700, LN-7000, F-800, 880 Air Brakes	7000 Medium	5/16″–7/16″ Empty Vehicle	5/8° ± 3/8°	3° ± 1/2° F-B 3°30′ ± 1/2° L
F-C-L-LN-700-7000, LT-800, LN-7000, C-L-LT-LTS-800-900, CT-LN-LNT-800, 880 Hydraulic Brakes	9000	5/16″–7/16″	3/8° ± 3/8° LH C Series – 1/8° ± 3/8° RH C Series 5/8° + 3/8° All Except C Series	4° ± 1/2° All Except C Series 3° ± 1/2° C Series
L-LT-LN-LNT-800, 880, L-LN-LNT-8000, LNT-9000, L-LN-LNT-900, F-LT-LNT-750, 800, C-600-700, 750 C-7000 Air Brakes	7000 Heavy	5/16″–7/16″ Empty Vehicle	5/8° ± 3/8°	3°51′ ± 1/2° C (9.5 Frame) 4°30′ ± 1/2° C (9.76 Frame) 5° ± 1/2° L (Except Drop Frame) 3°30′ ± 1/2° LN-LNT w/Drop Frame
F-LN-700, 750 F-800, LN-7000, Air Brakes	9000 Medium	5/16″–7/16″ Empty Vehicle	5/8° ± 3/8°	3° ± 1/2° F-B 3°30′ ± 1/2° LN
L-LT-LTS-LN-LNT-800-900—8000-9000, LT-LNT-800, C-700-800-880-900-7000-8000, CT-800-900-8000 Air Brakes	9000 Heavy	5/16″–7/16″ Empty Vehicle	5/8° ± 3/8°	5° ± 1/2° All Except Drop Frame 3°30′ ± 1/2° LN-LNT w/Drop Frame 2°51′ ± 1/2° C w/9.5 Frame 4°30′ ± 1/2° C w/9.76 Frame
L-LT-LTS-LN-LNT-C-CT-800-900, L-LT-LTS-LN-LNT-8000-9000, LNT-LT-800, 880 C-8000, CT-8000, W-WT-9000 Air Brakes	12000	3/16″–5/16″ Empty Vehicle	5/8° ± 3/8°	3° ± 1/2° C w/9.5 Frame L-W w/2° Wedge 3°30′ ± 1/2° L w/Drop Frame 4°30′ ± 1/2° C w/9 Frame
C-900, CT-800-900, CT-8000, LT-800-900, LTS-LN-LNT-8000-9000, LNT-LT-800, 900, 8000, 9000 C-800, CT-8000, Air Brakes	16000 18000 20000	5/16–7/16″ Empty Vehicle	5/8° ± 3/8°	3° ± 1/2° C w/16000 Axle 3 1/2° ± 1/2° All w/16-18-20000 lb. Axles Except C

FRONT WHEEL TURN ANGLE SPECIFICATIONS
1981, '82 600-9000 Series Truck

	Turn Angles for Axles											
Models	5500#	6000#7000# Hyd Brakes	7000# Air Brakes	9000# Hyd Brakes	9000# Air Brakes	12000# Hyd Brakes	12000# Air Brakes	12000# Steereze	16000# (G)	16000# (L)	18000#	20000#
F & B	45°	45°	40°	40°	40°	—	—	—	—	—	—	—
L	—	40°	40°	40°	40°	40°	40°	34°	40°	31°	31°	31°
LN	44°①	40°	40°	31°	40°	40°	40°	34°	40°	31°	31°	—
C	—	49°	49°	(P) (M) 37° 40°	(P) (M) 37° 40°	—	40°	34°	40°	34°	31°	—

①34° for 9.00 × 20 tire only
(M) Manual Steering
(P) Power steering
(G) For tire sizes other than 15.00 × 22.5 and 015R × 22.5
(L) For 15.00 × 22.5 and 015R × 22.5

FRONT WHEEL ALIGNMENT SPECIFICATIONS
1981 600-9000 Medium, Heavy and Extra Heavy Trucks

Vehicle Model	Front Axle Capacity	Toe-In ②	Camber (Degrees)	Caster (Degrees)
F-600, LN-600 Hydraulic Brakes	5500	3/16"–5/16" Empty Vehicle	5/8° ± 3/8°	3½° ± ½° F-B Series 4½° ± ½° LN Series
F-C-B-LN-600-700-7000, LT-LNT-800, LT-800, L-800-900, LN-800 Hydraulic Brakes	6000 7000	3/16"–5/16" Empty Vehicle	5/8° ± 3/8°	3½° ± ½° F-B Series (Medium) 4½° ± ½° LN (Medium) 3¾° ± ½° L-LN (Heavy) 3° ± ½° C Series
F-B-LN-700, 7000, F-800 Air Brakes	7000 Medium 7500	3/16"–5/16" Empty Vehicle	5/8° ± 3/8°	3° ± ½° F-B 3°30′ ± ½° L
L-LT-LN-LNT-800, L-LN-LNT-8000, LNT-9000, L-LN-LNT-900, C-600-700, C-7000 Air Brakes	7000 Heavy	3/16"–5/16" Empty Vehicle	5/8° ± 3/8°	2°51′ ± ½° C (9.5 Frame) 4°30′ ± ½° C (9.76 Frame) 5° ± ½° L (Except Drop Frame) 3°30′ ± ½° LN-LNT w/Drop Frame

FRONT WHEEL ALIGNMENT SPECIFICATIONS
1981 600-9000 Medium, Heavy and Extra Heavy Trucks

Vehicle Model	Front Axle Capacity	Toe-In ②	Camber (Degrees)	Caster (Degrees)
FB-LN-700, 7000, F-800 Air Brakes	9000 Medium	3/16"–5/16" Empty Vehicle	5/8° ± 3/8°	3° ± ½° F-B 3°30′ ± ½° LN
C-L-LT-LTS-800-900, CT-LN-LNT-800 Hydraulic Brakes	9000 Heavy	3/16"-5/16" Empty Vehicle	3/8° ± 3/8° LH C Series – 1/8° ± 3/8° RH C Series 5/8° + 3/8° All Except C Series	4° ± ½° All Except C Series 3° ± ½° C Series
L-LT-LTS-LN-LNT-800-900—8000-9000 C-700-800-900—7000-8000, CT-800-900-8000 Air Brakes	9000 Heavy	3/16"–5/16" Empty Vehicle	5/8° ± 3/8°	5° ± ½° All L Except Drop Frame 3°30′ ± ½° LN-LNT w/Drop Frame 2°51′ ± ½° C w/9.5 Frame 4°30′ ± ½° C w/9.76 Frame
L-LT-LTS-LN-LNT-C-CT-800-900, L-LT-LTS-LN-LNT-8000-9000, C-8000, CT-8000, Air Brakes	12000	1/16"–3/16" Empty Vehicle	5/8° ± 3/8°	3° ± ½° C w/9.5 Frame L-W w/2° Wedge 3°30′ ± ½° L w/Drop Frame 4°30′ ± ½° C w/9.76 Frame
C-900, CT-800-900, CT-8000, LT-800-900, LTS-LN-LNT-8000-9000, LNT-LT-800, C-8000 Air Brakes	16000 18000 20000	3/16"–5/16" Empty Vehicle	5/8° ± 3/8°	3° ± ½°C w/16-18000 lb. Axles 3½° ± ½° All w/16-18-20000 lb. Axles-L-Series
CL-9000 CLT-9000	12000	1/16"–3/16" Empty Vehicle	5/8° ± 3/8°	3¼° ± ½°

① The caster specifications shown are with the frame level from front to rear. Measure front to rear frame angle when checking alignment and compensate as follows.
If the front of the frame is lower than the rear, the actual caster angle is obtained by adding the frame angle to the caster angle shown on the checking equipment.
If the front of the frame is higher than the rear, subtract the frame angle from the caster angle shown on the checking equipment.

② Set toe to minimum with radial ply tires.

FRONT WHEEL ALIGNMENT SPECIFICATIONS
1982 600-8000 Medium, Heavy and Extra Heavy Trucks

Vehicle Model	Front Axle Capacity	Toe-In②③	Camber (Degrees)	Caster (Degrees)①
F-600, Hydraulic Brakes	5500	1/16″–3/16″ Empty Vehicle 0″–1/16″ Normally-Loaded Vehicle	5/8° ± 3/8°	3½° ± ½° F-B Series 4½° ± ½° LN Series
F-C-B-600-700 Hydraulic Brakes	6000 7000	1/16″–3/16″ Empty Vehicle 0″–1/16″ Normally-Loaded Vehicle	5/8° ± 3/8°	3½° ± ½° F-B Series (Medium) 4½° ± ½° LN (Medium) 3¾° ± ½° L-LN (Heavy) 3° ± ½° C Series
F-B-700, F-800 Air Brakes	7000 Medium 7500	1/16″–3/16″ Empty Vehicle 0″–1/16″ Normally-Loaded Vehicle	5/8° ± 3/8°	3° ± ½° F-B 3°30′ ± ½° L
C-600-700, C-7000 Air Brakes	7000 Heavy	1/16″–3/16″ Empty Vehicle 0″–1/16″ Normally-Loaded Vehicle	5/8° ± 3/8°	2°51′ ± ½°C (9.5 Frame) 4°30′ ± ½° C (9.76 Frame) 5° ± ½° L (Except Drop Frame) 3°30′ ± ½° LN-LNT w/Drop Frame

FRONT WHEEL ALIGNMENT SPECIFICATIONS
1982 600-8000 Medium, Heavy and Extra Heavy Trucks

Vehicle Model	Front Axle Capacity	Toe-In②③	Camber (Degrees)	Caster (Degrees)①
F-B-700, F-800 Air Brakes	9000 Medium	1/16″–3/16″ Empty Vehicle 0″–1/16″ Normally-Loaded Vehicle	5/8° ± 3/8°	3° ± ½°F-B 3°30′ ± ½° LN
C-800, CT-800 Hydraulic Brakes	9000 Heavy	1/16″–3/16″ Empty Vehicle 0″–1/16″ Normally-Loaded Vehicle	3/8° ± 3/8° LH C Series – 1/8° ± 3/8° RH C Series 5/8° + 3/8° All Except C Series	4° ± ½° All Except C Series 3° ± ½° C Series
C-700-800—7000-8000, CT-800-8000 Air Brakes	9000 Heavy	1/16″–3/16″ Empty Vehicle 0″–1/16″ Normally-Loaded Vehicle	5/8° ± 3/8°	5° ± ½° All L Except Drop Frame 3°30 ± ½° LN-LNT w/Drop Frame 2°51′ ± ½° C w/9.5 Frame 4°30′ ± ½° C w/9.76 Frame
C-CT-800 C-8000, CT-8000, Air Brakes	12000	1/16″–3/16″ Empty Vehicle 0″–1/16″ Normally-Loaded Vehicle	5/8° ± 3/8°	3° ± ½° C w/9.5 Frame L-W w/2° Wedge 3°30′ ± ½° L w/Drop Frame 4°30′ ± ½° C w/9.76 Frame
CT-800, CT-8000, LT-800 C-8000 Air Brakes	16000 18000 20000	1/16″–3/16″ Empty Vehicle 0″–1/16″ Normally-Loaded Vehicle	5/8° ± 3/8°	3° ± ½° C w/16-18000 lb. Axles 3½° ± ½° All w/16-18-20000 lb. Axles-L-Series

① The caster specifications shown are with the frame level from front to rear. Measure front to rear frame angle when checking alignment and compensate as follows. If the front of the frame is lower than the rear, the actual caster angle is obtained by adding the frame angle to the caster angle shown on the checking equipment. If the front of the frame is higher than the rear, subtract the frame angle from the caster angle shown on the checking equipment.

② Set toe to minimum with radial ply tires.

③ The actual toe-in value can vary with front axle load from the empty vehicle condition (as built) to the customer normal operating condition (complete vehicle and normal load).

FRONT WHEEL ALIGNMENT SPECIFICATIONS
Medium and Heavy Duty Vehicles

Vehicle Model	Front Axle Capacity	Toe-In	Camber (Degrees)	Caster (Degrees) ①
F-C-B-600-700 Hydraulic Brakes	6000 7000	1/16"–3/16" Empty Vehicle	5/8° ± 3/8°	3-1/2° ± 1/2° F-B Series (Medium) 3° ± 1/2° C Series
F-B-700, F-800 Air Brakes	7000	1/16"–3/16" Empty Vehicle	5/8° ± 3/8°	3° ± 1/2°
C-600-700, C-7000 Air Brakes	7000	1/16"–3/16" Empty vehicle	5/8° ± 3/8°	2°51′ ± 1/2°C (9.5 Frame) 4°30′ ± 1/2° C Series (9.76 Frame)
F-B-700, F-800 Air Brakes	9000	1/16"–3/16" Empty Vehicle	5/8° ± 3/8°	3° ± 1/2°
C-800, CT-800 Hydraulic Brakes	9000	1/16"–3/16" Empty Vehicle	3/8° ± 3/8° L.H. – 1/8° ± 3/8°R.H.	3° ± 1/2°
C-700-800— 7000-8000, CT-800-800 Air Brakes	9000	1/16"–3/16" Empty Vehicle	5/8° ± 3/8°	2°51′ ± 1/2°C w/9.5 Frame 4°30′ ± 1/2°C w/9.76 Frame
F-FT-800 F-FT-8000 Air & Hydraulic Brakes	9500 12000	1/16"–3/16" Empty Vehicle	3/8° ± 3/8° L.H. – 1/8° ± 3/8° R.H.	5-1/4° ± 1/2° w/9500 lb. Axle 5-1/2° ± 1/2° w/12,000 lb. Axle
C-CT-800 C-8000, CT-8000, Air Brakes	12000	1/16"–3/16" Empty Vehicle	3/8° ± 3/8° L.H. 1/8° ± 3/8° R.H.	3° ± 1/2°C w/9.5 Frame 4°30′ ± 1/2°C w/9.76 Frame
CT-800, CT-8000 C-8000 Air Brakes	16000 18000	1/16"–3/16" Empty Vehicle	5/8° ± 3/8°	3° ± 1/2°C w/16-18000 lb. Axles

① The Caster specifications shown are with the frame level from front to rear. Measure front to rear frame angle when checking alignment and compensate as follows. If the front of the frame is lower than the rear, the actual caster angle is obtained by adding the frame angle to the caster angle shown on the checking equipment. If the front of the frame is higher than the rear, subtract the frame angle from the caster angle shown on the checking equipment.

ENGINE ELECTRICAL

Distributor

Removal and Installation

LIGHT DUTY VEHICLES

NOTE: Certain models are equipped with EEC III or IV. The distributor is locked into position and all timing control is handled by the EEC module. No timing adjustment is required or possible.

1. Remove the air cleaner on V6 and V8 engines. On 4 and 6 cylinder in-line engines, removal of a thermactor (air) pump mounting bolt and drive belt will allow the pump to be moved to the side and permit access to the distributor. If necessary, disconnect the thermactor air filter and lines as well.
2. Remove the distributor cap and position the cap and ignition wires to the side.
3. Disconnect the wire harness plug from the distributor connector. Disconnect and plug the vacuum hoses from the vacuum diaphragm assembly, if equipped.
4. Rotate the engine (in normal direction of rotation) until No. 1 piston is on TDC (Top Dead Center) of the compression stroke. The TDC mark on the crankshaft pulley and the pointer should align. Rotor tip pointing at No. 1 spark plug wire position on distributor cap.
5. On DuraSpark II, turn the engine a slight bit more (if required) to align the stator (pick-up coil) assembly pole with an (the closest) armature pole. On DuraSpark III, the distributor sleeve groove (when looking down from the top) and the cap adaptor alignment slot should align.
6. On DuraSpark II, scribe a mark on the distributor body and engine block to indicate the position of the rotor tip and position of the distributor in the engine. DuraSpark III distributors are equipped with a notched base and will only locate at one position on the engine.
7. Remove the holddown bolt and clamp located at the base of the distributor. (Some DuraSpark distributors are equipped with a special holddown bolt that requires a Torx head wrench for removal). Remove the distributor from the engine. Pay attention to the direction the rotor turns and the position to which the rotor tip points when the drive gear disengages. For reinstallation purposes, the rotor should be at this position to insure proper gear mesh and timing.
8. Avoid turning the engine, if possible, while the distributor is removed. If the engine is turned from TDC position, TDC timing marks will have to be reset before the distributor is installed; Steps 4,and 5.

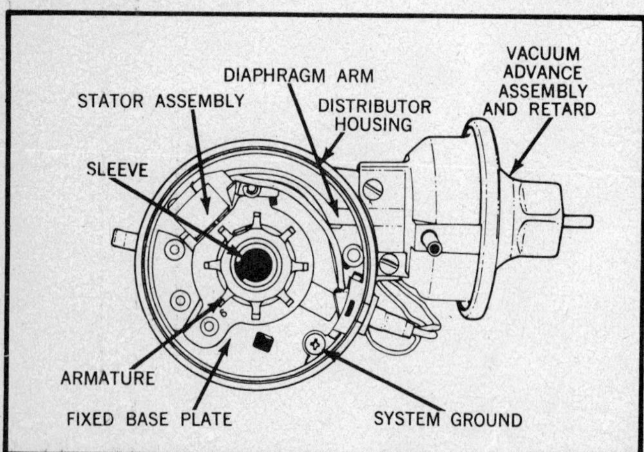

Electronic ignition distributor (© Ford Motor Co.)

9. On DuraSpark II systems; position the distributor in the engine with the rotor aligned to the marks made on the distributor, or to the place the rotor pointed when the distributor was removed. The stator and armature or vane or vane Switch should also be aligned. Engage the oil pump intermediate shaft and insert the distributor until fully seated on the engine, if the distributor does not fully seat, turn the engine slightly to fully engage the intermediate shaft.
10. On DuraSpark III systems, follow the above procedures. Make sure when positioning the distributor that the slot in the distributor base will engage the block tab and the sleeve/adaptor slots are aligned.
11. After the distributor has been fully seated on the block install the hold down bracket and bolt. On DuraSpark III, tighten the mounting bolt. On DuraSpark II, snug the mounting bolt so the distributor can be turned for ignition timing purposes.
12. The rest of the installation is in the reverse order of removal. Check and reset the ignition timing (if necessary) on DuraSpark II systems.

NOTE: A silicone compound is used on rotor tips, distributor cap contacts and on the inside of the connectors on the spark plugs cable and module couplers. Always apply Silicone Dielectric Compound after servicing any component of the ignition system. Various models use a multi-point rotor which do not require the application of dielectric compound.

MEDIUM AND HEAVY DUTY VEHICLES

1. Disconnect the primary wire from the wiring harness.
2. Disconnect the vacuum line(s) at the distributor.
3. Remove the distributor cap.
4. Scribe a mark on the distributor body, indicating the position of the rotor. Scribe another mark on the body and engine

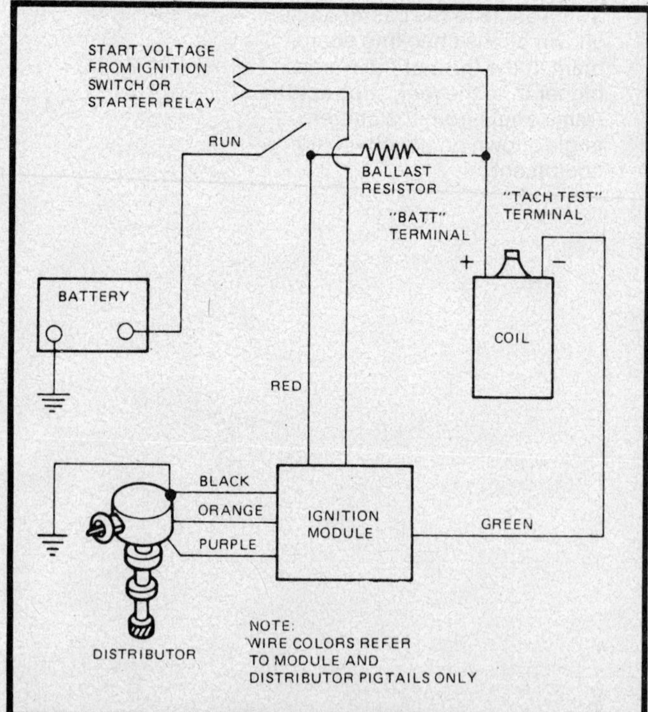

Ignition schematic for Dura Spark II system (© Ford Motor Co.)

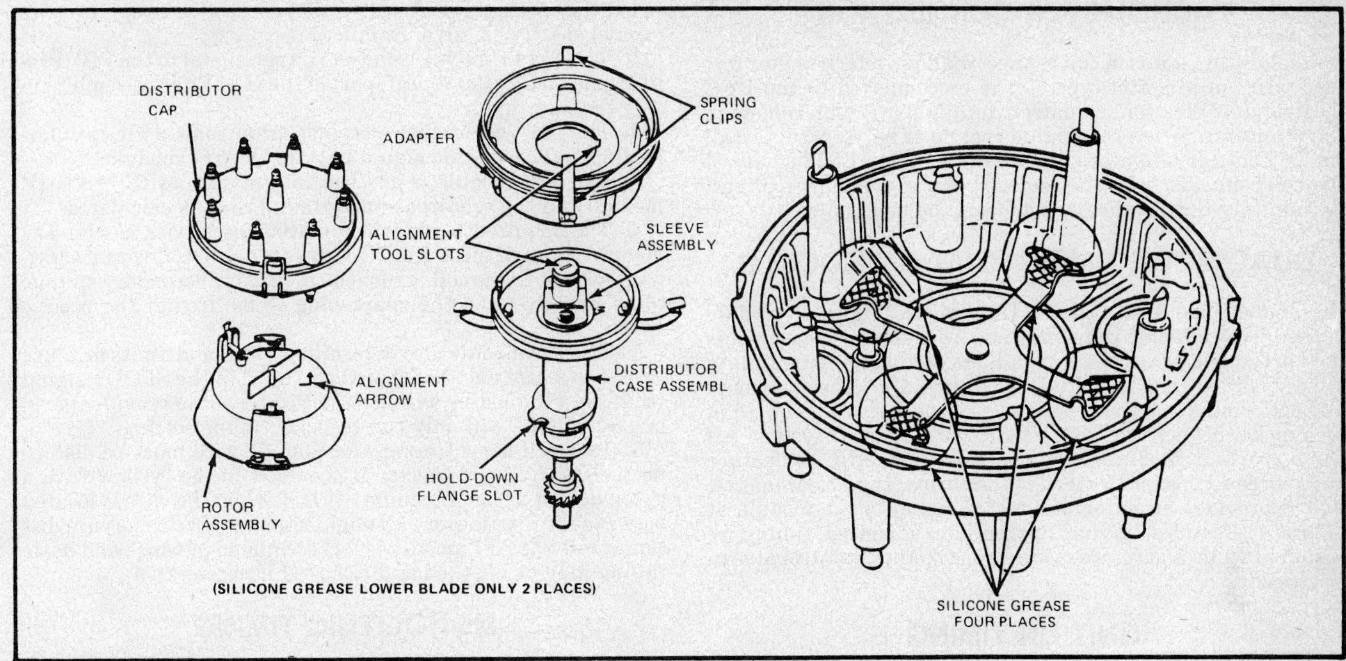

Bi-level distributor cap and rotor—Dura Spark III and EEC system

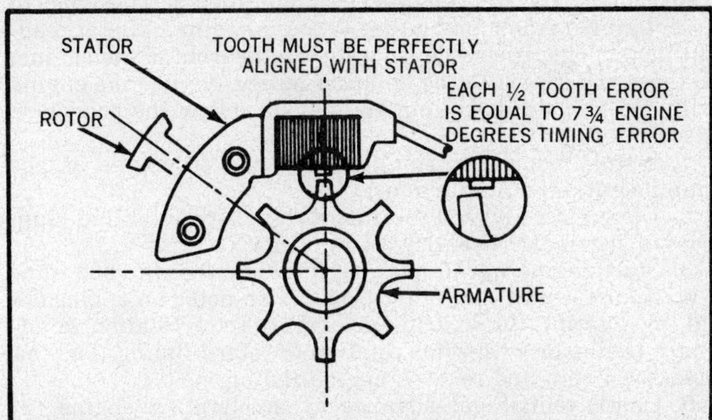

Electronic ignition static timing position (© Ford Motor Co.)

block, indicating the position of the body in the block. These marks will insure that the distributor will be correctly timed when it is reinstalled.

5. Remove hold-down bolt and clamp or retaining bolt and lockwasher and lift the distributor out of the block.

NOTE: Do not rotate the crankshaft while the distributor is removed, or it will be necessary to time the engine.

6. To install, position the distributor in the block with the rotor aligned to the mark previously scribed on the distributor and the marks on the distributor and block aligned.

7. If the crankshaft has been rotated while the distributor was removed, the distributor must be timed with respect to the crankshaft.

8. Rotate the engine until the No. 1 piston is at TDC of the compression stroke. Position the distributor in the block with the rotor in the No. 1 firing position. Rotate the distributor as required.

NOTE: Make sure the oil pump intermediate shaft properly engages the distributor shaft. It may be necessary to crank the engine with the starter after the distributor gear is engaged in order to engage the oil pump intermediate shaft.

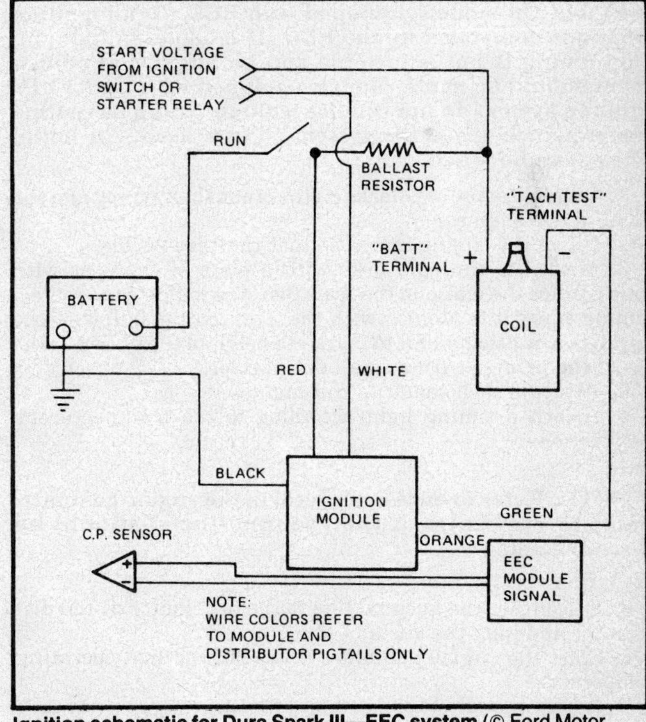

Ignition schematic for Dura Spark III—EEC system (© Ford Motor Co.)

9. Install retaining clamp and bolt or retaining bolt and lockwasher, but do not tighten. Rotate the distributor to advance the timing to the position where the armature tooth is properly aligned.

10. Connect primary wire and install distributor cap.

11. Check and reset ignition timing.

12. Tighten hold-down clamp bolt or retaining bolt. Connect the vacuum hoses as required.

TACHOMETER CONNECTION

The solid state ignition coil connector allows a tachometer test lead with an alligator-type clip to be connected to the DEC (Distributor Electronic Control) terminal without removing the connector. When the engine rpm must be checked, install the tachometer alligator clip into the "TACH TEST" cavity. If the coil connector must be removed, grasp the wires and pull horizontally until it disconnects from the terminals.

DUAL MODE TIMING IGNITION MODULE

On some applications, a special Dura-Spark II ignition module is used with altitude compensation. This special module plus the barometric pressure switch allows the base engine timing to be modified to suit altitude conditions. All other elements and performance characteristics of this module are identical in both modes of operation to the basic Dura-Spark II system. All Dura-Spark II Modules equipped with the altitude feature have three connectors instead of the normal two. A barometric switch provides an automatic retard signal to the module at different altitudes, giving appropriate advanced timing at higher altitude and retard mode for spark knock control at lower altitudes.

IGNITION TIMING

ALL EXCEPT TFI, EEC IV AND MONOLITHIC

NOTE: On models equipped with EEC III, all ignition timing is controlled by the EEC III module. Initial ignition timing is not adjustable and no attempt at adjustment should be made. Models equipped with the TFI IV ignition system do not require ignition timing as routine maintenance, since the system adjusts itself. An initial check can be made.

1. Locate the timing marks on the crankshaft pulley and the front of the engine.
2. Clean the timing marks so that they are visible.
3. Mark the timing marks with a piece of chalk or with paint. Color the mark on the scale that will indicate the correct timing when it is aligned with the mark on the pulley or the pointer. It is also helpful to mark the notch in the pulley or the tip of the pointer with a small dab of color.
4. Attach a tachometer to the engine.
5. Attach a timing light according to the manufacturer's instructions.

NOTE: Refer to emissions decal in the engine compartment to determine if the vacuum line(s) should be disconnected.

6. Disconnect the vacuum line to the distributor at the distributor and plug the vacuum line.
7. Start the engine and allow it to reach normal operating temperature.
8. Adjust the idle to the correct setting.
9. Aim the timing light and check the engine timing. Adjust the ignition timing as required.

EEC IV AND TFI

The connection between the EEC IV microprocessor and the Thick Film Integrated (TFI) ignition module is called the SPOUT circuit. SPOUT simply means "spark out" since a signal carried to the TFI shuts off the coil and produces a spark for firing the spark plugs. A description of the system operation to control spark and advance follows:

1. The TFI IV module sends a voltage signal to the PIP (Profile Ignition Pickup) sensor, part of the Hall Effect assembly inside the distributor.
2. The PIP sensor then provides crankshaft position information and sends this signal back to the TFI module.
3. The TFI module sends the information to the EEC IV module and the required spark timing need is calculated.
4. The required timing information goes back to the TFI module through electrical circuitry (the SPOUT) and the primary circuit to the coil is turned off, causing secondary voltage to be produced and the spark plug to be fired at the precise time.
5. The TFI module also determines dwell and limits primary circuit to a safe value. If there is an open in the SPOUT signal wire, the TFI module will use the PIP sensor to provide spark; but the engine will only run at basic timing setting.
6. To check basic timing, the SPOUT wire must be disconnected. An inline connector is provided on the "yellow with a green dot" or a "black" single SPOUT wire. The wire is located between the distributor and engine harness. With the wire disconnected, the TFI module is locked into no advance and basic timing may be checked and adjusted if necessary.

MONOLITHIC TIMING

The monolithic timing receptacle was made standard on all engines, while still retaining the conventional timing method. The monolithic system employs a timing receptacle designed to accept an electronic probe that is connected to a digital readout meter. The receptacle is located in the front of the engine, so the probe is next to the balancer pulley. To time the engine with the monolithic timing equipment, follow the procedure below.

1. Install monolithic timing equipment to engine as per manufacturerer's instructions.
2. Disconnect all vacuum lines at the distributor and plug. Loosen distributor hold-down bolt.
3. Start engine warm up and reduce idle speed to 600 rpm.
4. Adjust initial timing to specification noted on engine decal, by rotating the distributor against rotor rotation to advance timing or with rotor rotation to retard timing. Tighten hold-down bolt, and recheck engine timing.
5. Check centrifugal advance by accelerating engine (in neutral) to 2500 rpm. If ignition timing advance is noted during acceleration the centrifugal advance mechanism is functional. Refer to the engine decal for this specification. If out of specification remove distributor and make required repairs.
6. To check vacuum advance unplug and reinstall carburetor source vacuum line (removed in Step 2) to outer diaphragm (on dual diaphragm distributors). Accelerate engine to 2500 rpm. Total advance should be greater now than in prior step (centrifugal only) if advance mechanism is functional. Remove distributor and make required repairs if no additional advance is observed and vacuum is noted at the line to the diaphragm.
7. To check vacuum retard operation (dual diaphragm) connect the intake manifold line (removed in Step 2) to the inner diaphragm side of the distributor. With the engine at normal idle, a 6 or 12 degree retard should be noted, depending on shuttle, if the retard mechanism is working properly. If the retard function is not evident, remove distributor and make required repairs.
8. Reconnect all distributor lines properly and check curb idle, reset if necessary.
9. Remove engine tachometer and monolithic timing equipment.

ALTERNATOR

Procedures for diagnosis and repair of the charging system can be found in the "Electrical Section" in the Unit Repair portion of this manual.

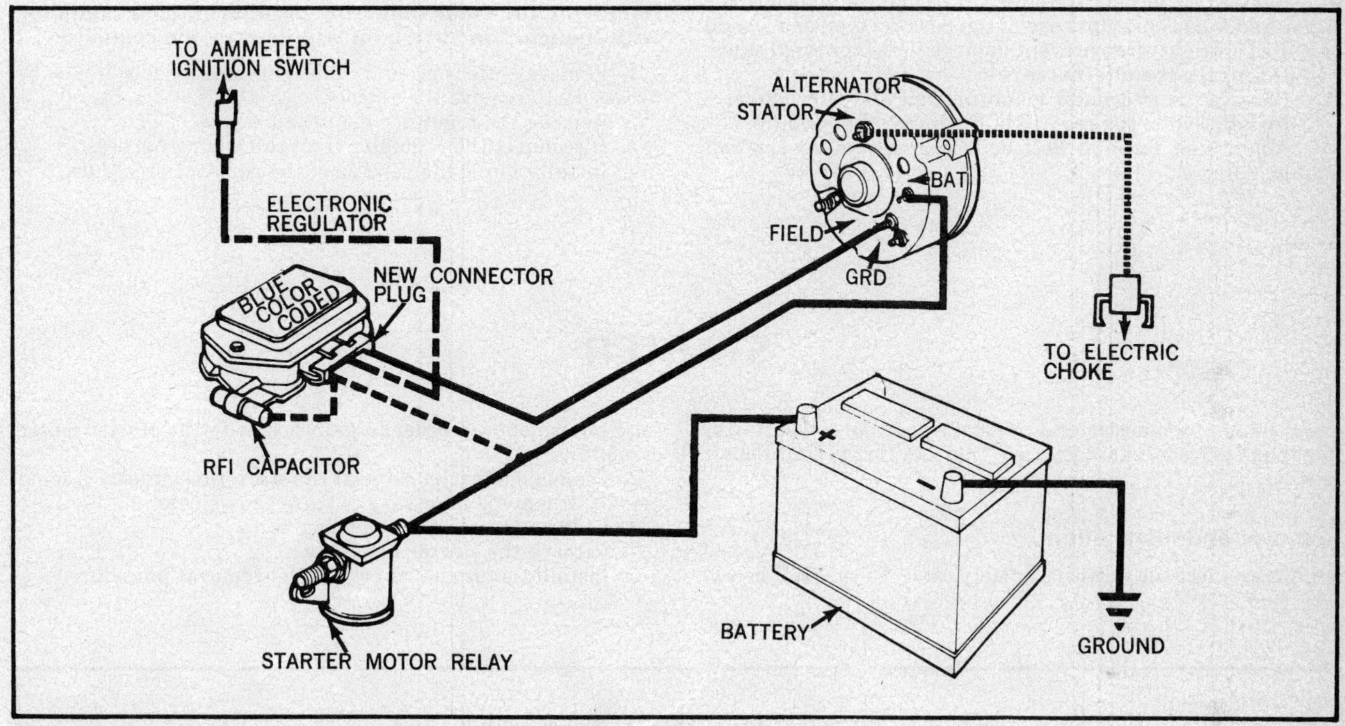

Electronic regulator and ammeter circuitry (© Ford Motor Co.)

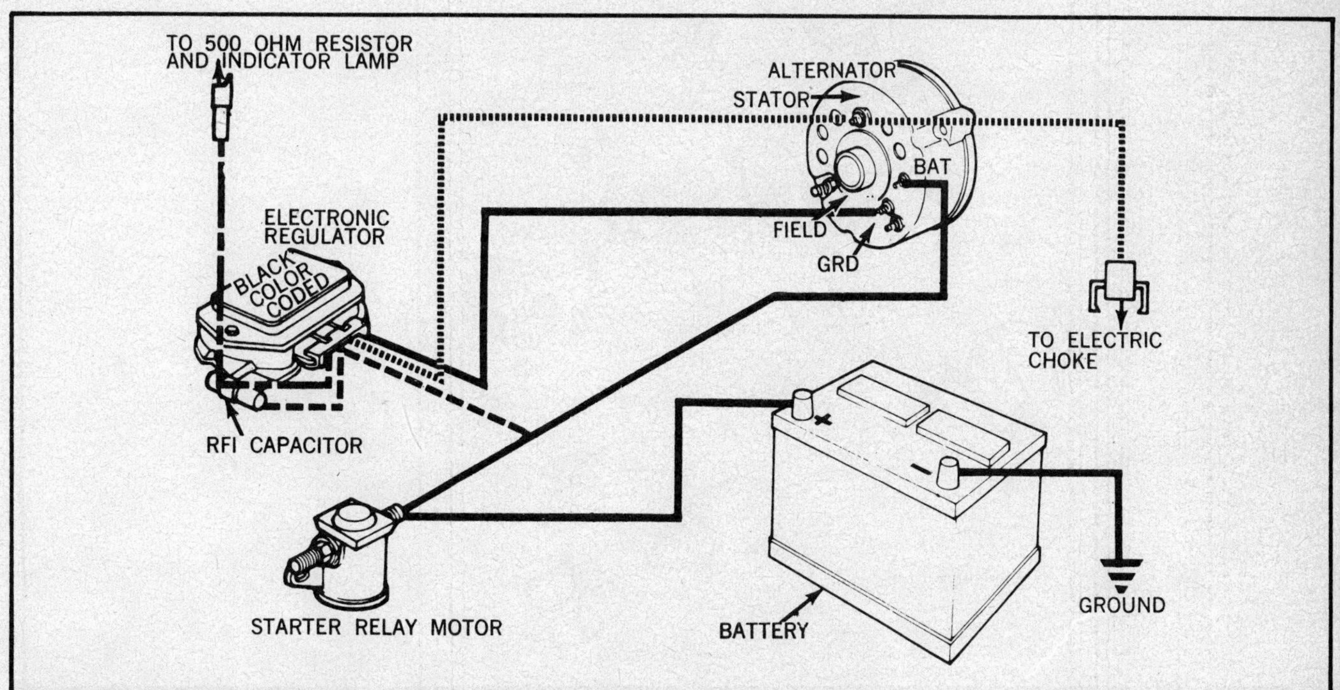

Electronic regulator and warning lamp indicator circuitry (© Ford Motor Co.)

ALTERNATOR

Removal and Installation

1. Disconnect battery ground cable.
2. Loosen the alternator mounting bolts and remove the adjustment arm to alternator attaching bolt.
3. Remove the electrical connectors from the alternator. The stator and field connectors are of the push-on type and should be pulled straight off to prevent damage to the terminal studs.
4. Disengage the alternator belt.
5. Remove the alternator mounting bolt and alternator.
6. Installation is the reverse of the removal procedure.
7. Adjust belt tension. Belt deflection should be approximately ½ in.

REGULATOR

Removal and Installation

NOTE: If vehicle is equipped with an electric choke, be sure to disconnect electric choke wire from starter terminal of the alternator when working on the charging system. Check electric choke wire for a ground condition. Removing the connector from an ungrounded regulator with the ignition switch on will destroy the regulator.

1. Remove battery ground cable. On some models, it may be necessary to remove the battery.
2. Remove the regulator mounting screws.
3. Disconnect the regulator from the wiring harness.
4. Installation is the reverse of the removal procedure.

STARTER

For complete diagnostic and overhaul procedures for starter motor and drive mechanisms, see "Starters" in the Unit Repair Section.

Removal and Installation

1. Disconnect the negative battery cable. Remove all necessary components in order to gain access to the starter motor assembly.
2. Disconnect starter cable at the starter terminal. On some models, it may be necessary to raise the vehicle.
3. Remove the starter mounting bolts.
4. Remove the starter assembly.
5. Installation is the reverse of the removal procedure.

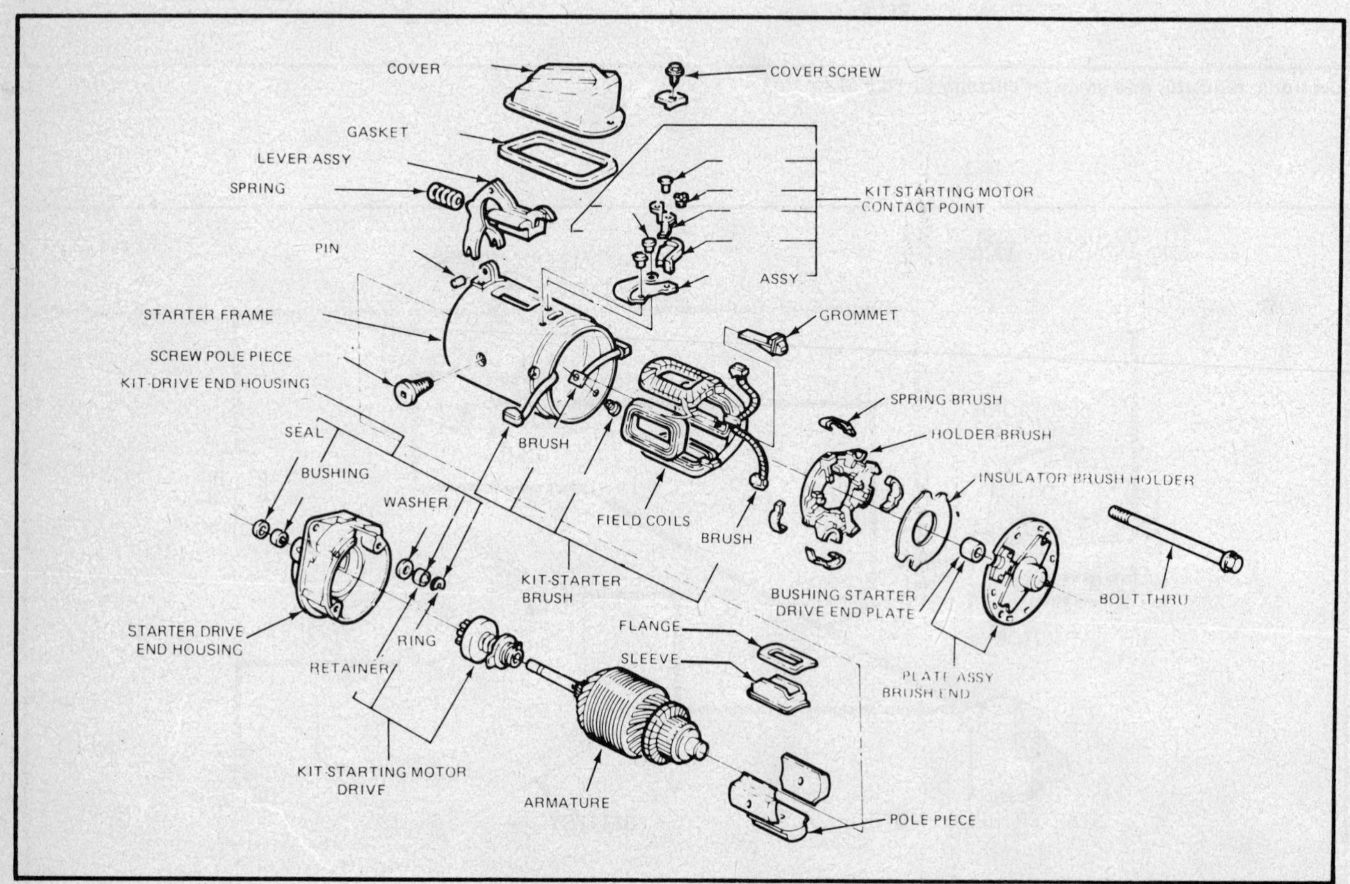

Disassembled view of Autolite starter (© Ford Motor Co.)

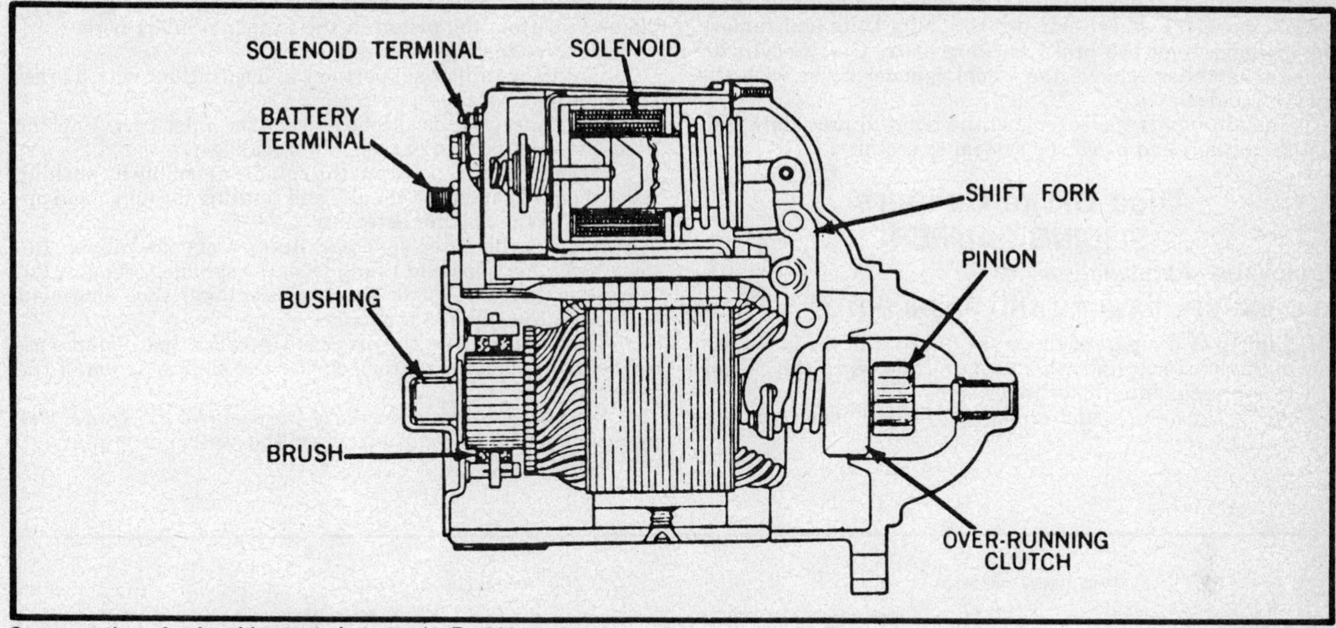

Cross section of solenoid actuated starter (© Ford Motor Co.)

BRAKES

Complete overhaul and service information for hydraulic brake components can be found under the heading of Hydraulic Brake, Power Brake and Disc Brake in the Unit Repair section. All service and overhaul operations for air brake systems are under the heading of Air Brakes in the Unit Repair section.

Master Cylinder

Removal and Installation

1. If stoplight switch is mounted on the master cylinder, disconnect wires.
2. On dash-mounted master cylinders, disconnect the dust boot from the rear of the master cylinder at the dash panel. If the boot is connected to the master cylinder only, leave it in place.
3. Disconnect the hydraulic line(s) from the master cylinder.
4. Disconnect the brake pedal pushrod.
5. Remove the master cylinder retaining bolts. Remove the master cylinder from the vehicle.
6. Installation is the reverse of the removal procedure.

Bleeding

1. Support the master cylinder body in a soft-jawed vise, and fill both reservoirs with extra heavy duty brake fluid.
2. Loosely install plugs in the front and rear outlet ports. Depress the primary piston several times until air bubbles no longer appear in the brake fluid.
3. Tighten the plugs and try to depress the piston. Depressing the piston should be harder after all the air in the brake reservoir is expelled.
4. Remove the plugs. Install the cover and diaphragm assembly, making sure the cover retainer is tightened securely.

Pressure Differential, Metering and Proportioning Valve Assemblies

Different types of pressure differential, proportioning, metering valve assemblies are used on the varied vehicle brake applications. The valve assemblies are normally located on either a bracket or on one of the frame rails.

Removal and Installation

1. Raise the vehicle sufficiently to gain working access to the valve assembly.
2. Disconnect the brake warning light from the pressure differential valve switch, as required.

NOTE: To prevent damage to the brake warning switch wire connector, expand the plastic lugs to allow removal of the shell-wire connector from the switch body.

3. Disconnect the hydraulic brake lines from the valve assembly.
4. Remove the retaining bolts or screws and remove the valve assembly from its mounted position.
5. Differential valves and switches are separate units and are serviced separately. Remove the warning light switch from the valve when replacing either unit.
6. Installation is the reverse of the removal procedure.
7. Bleed the brakes and centralize the pressure differential valve as follows. Turn the ignition switch to ACC or ON position. Loosen the pressure differential valve inlet tube nut on the system opposite the system which was bled last. This will result in unequal pressure in the other direction and allow the valve to center. Slowly depress brake pedal until light goes out. Tighten inlet tube nut. On 500–900 series vehicles, disconnect wires from warning light switch on the differential valve, remove switch. Springs inside valve will center valve. Replace switch and wire.

Wheel Cylinder

Removal and Installation

1. Raise the vehicle and support it safely. Remove the wheel, drum, and brake shoes.
2. Remove the cylinder to shoe connecting links.

3. Disconnect the brake line from the wheel cylinder.
4. Remove the wheel cylinder retaining bolts and remove the cylinder from the brake backing plate. On two-cylinder brake assemblies remove the wheel cylinder cover with the brake cylinder.
5. Installation is the reverse of the removal procedure. Adjust the brakes and bleed the system as required.

Disc Brake Calipers

SLIDING CALIPER

Removal and Installation

ALL, EXCEPT RANGER AND BRONCO II

1. Siphon or dip part of the brake fluid out of the large section of the master cylinder to avoid overflow when the caliper piston is pressed into the cylinder bore.
2. Raise the vehicle and support it safely. Remove the tire and wheel assembly.
3. Position a 8 in. C-clamp on the caliper and tighten the clamp to bottom the piston in the caliper cylinder bore.
4. Remove the key retaining screw.
5. Drive the caliper support key and spring out with a brass rod and light hammer.
6. Disconnect the brake hose from the inlet port. Cap the hose and inlet port to prevent fluid leakage.
7. Remove the caliper from the spindle assembly by pushing it downward against the spindle and rotating the upper end upward out of the spindle assembly.
8. Remove the outer shoe and lining from the caliper. Remove the inner shoe and lining from the spindle assembly. Remove the shoe anti-rattle clip from the lower shoe abutment surface on the spindle assembly.
9. Thoroughly clean the areas of the caliper and spindle assembly that come in contact during the sliding action of the caliper.
10. Installation is the reverse of the removal procedure. Use new components as required. Bleed the system as required.

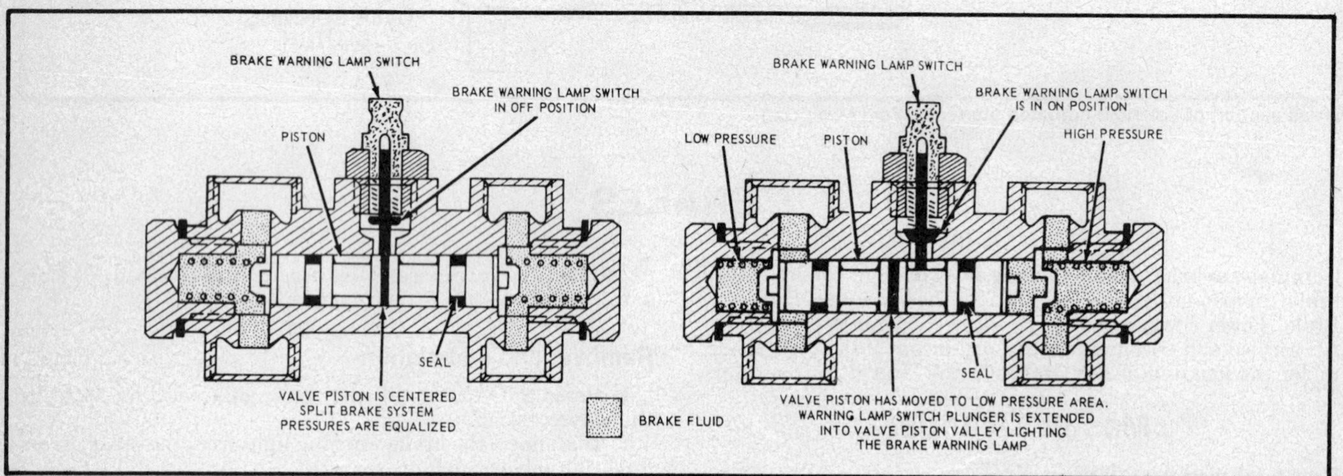

Brake differential valve—500–900 Series w/split hydraulic brakes (© Ford Motor Co.)

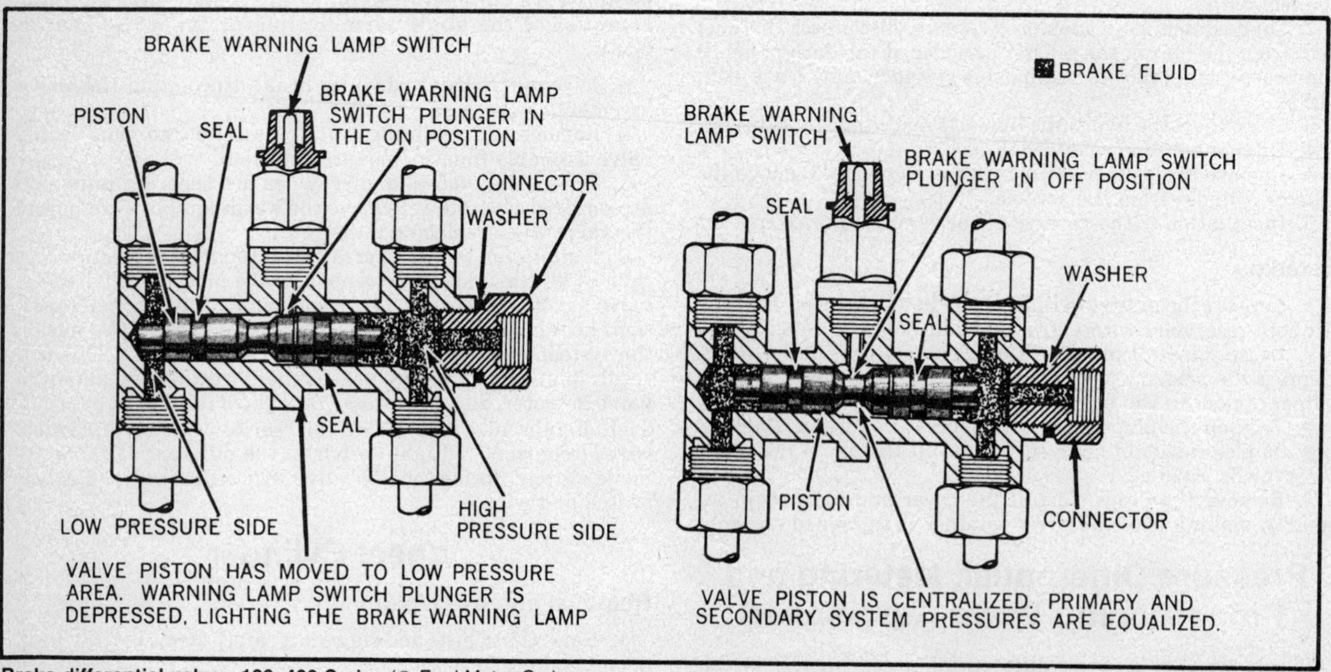

Brake differential valve—100–400 Series (© Ford Motor Co.)

RANGER AND BRONCO II

1. To avoid fluid overflow when the caliper piston is pressed into the caliper cylinder bores, siphon or dip part of the brake fluid out of the larger master cylinder reservoir.
2. Raise the vehicle and support it safely. Remove the front wheel and tire assembly.
3. Place an 8 in. C-clamp on the caliper and tighten the clamp to bottom the caliper piston in the cylinder bore. Remove the clamp.
4. There are three types of caliper pins used: a single tang type, a double tang type and a split-shell type. The pin removal process is dependent upon how the pin is installed (bolt head direction). Remove the upper caliper pin first.
5. On some applications, the pin may be retained by a nut and torx-head bolt (except the split-shell type).
6. If the bolt head is on the outside of the caliper use the following procedure:
   a. From the inner side of the caliper, tap the bolt within the caliper pin until the bolt head on the outer side of the caliper shows a separation between the bolt head and the caliper pin.
   b. Using a hacksaw or bolt cutter, remove the bolt head from the bolt.
   c. Depress the tab on the bolt head end of the upper caliper pin with a suitable tool, while tapping on the pin with a hammer. Continue tapping until the tab is depressed by the v-slot.
   d. Place one end of a punch ($\frac{1}{2}$ in. or smaller) against the end of the caliper pin and drive the caliper pin out of the caliper toward the inside of the vehicle. Do not use a screwdriver or other edged tool to help drive out the caliper pin as the V-grooves may be damaged.
7. If the nut end of the bolt is on the outside of the caliper, use the following procedure:
   a. Remove the nut from the bolt.
   b. Depress the lead tang on the end of the upper caliper pin with a suitable tool while tapping on the pin with a hammer. Continue tapping until the lead tang is depressed by the v-slot. Place one end of a punch ($\frac{1}{2}$ inch or smaller) against the end of the caliper pin and drive the caliper pin out of the caliper toward the inside of the vehicle. Do not use a screwdriver or other edged tool to help drive out the caliper pin as the v-grooves may be damaged.
8. Remove the lower caliper pin per the procedure in Step 4.
9. Remove the caliper from the rotor. If the caliper is to be removed for service, remove the brake hose from the caliper.

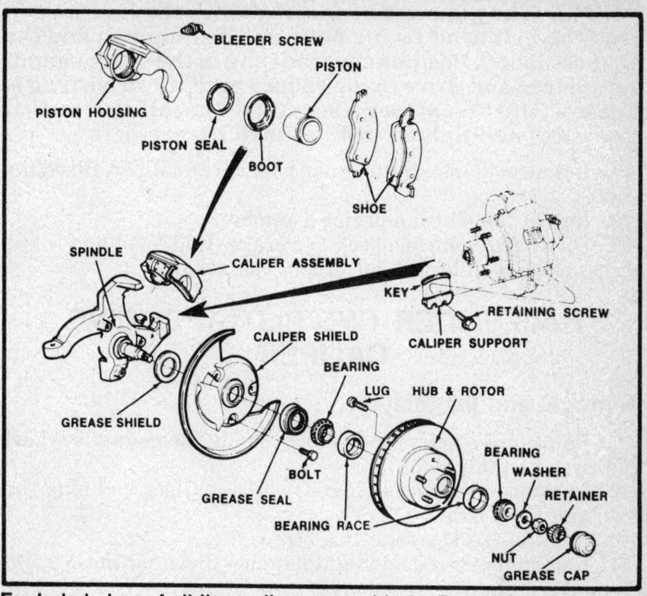

Exploded view of sliding caliper assembly (© Ford Motor Co.)

10. Remove the outer lining. Remove the anti-rattle clips and remove the inner lining.

NOTE: Never reuse caliper pins. Always use new pins whenever a caliper is removed.

11. Place a new anti-rattle clip on the lower end of the inner shoe. Be sure that the tabs of the clip are positioned correctly and that the clip is fully seated.
12. Position the inner shoe and anti-rattle clip in the shoe abutment with the anti-rattle clip tab against the shoe abutment and the loop-type spring away from the rotor. Compress the anti-rattle clip and slide the upper end of the shoe in position. Install the outer shoe, making sure the torque buttons on the shoe spring clip are seated solidly in the matching holes in the caliper.
13. Install the caliper on the spindle, making sure the mounting surfaces are free of dirt and lubricate the caliper grooves with disc brake caliper grease, or equivalent. Install new caliper pins. Make sure that the pins are installed with the tang in the proper position.

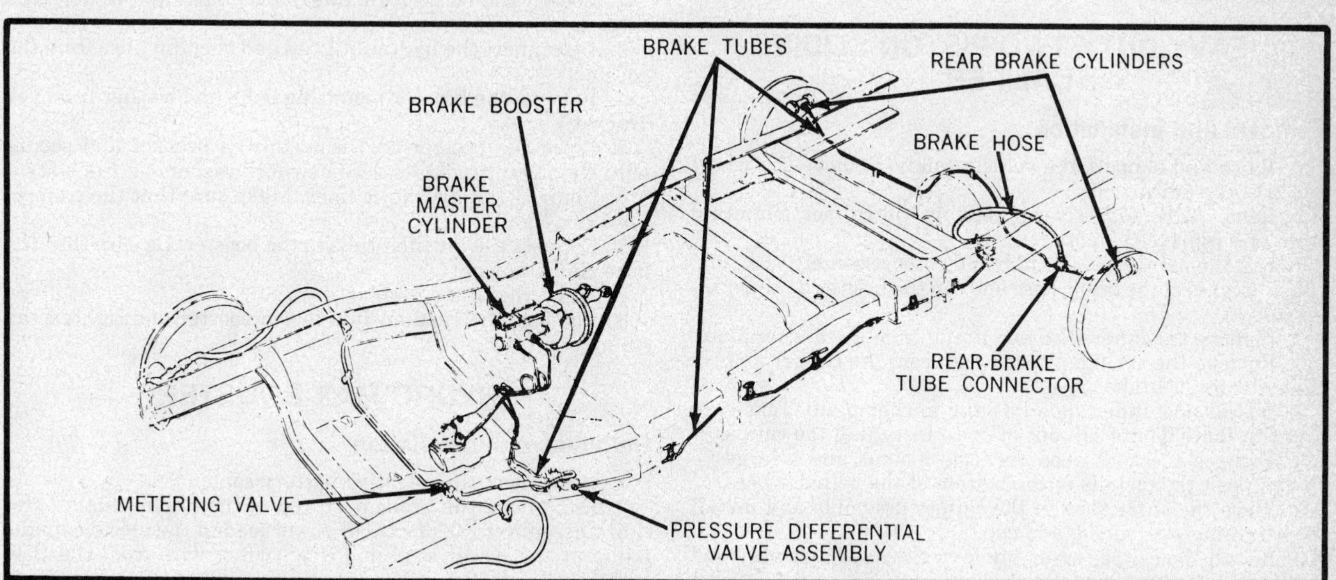

Disc brake system (© Ford Motor Co.)

NOTE: The pin must be installed with the lead tang in first, the bolt head facing outward (if equipped) and the pin positioned. Position the lead tang in the v-slot mounting surface and drive in the caliper until the drive tang is flush with the caliper assembly. Install the nut (if equipped) and tighten to 32–47 inch lbs.

14. If removed, install the brake hose to the caliper. Bleed the brakes.
15. Install the wheel and tire assembly.
16. Lower the vehicle, check the brake fluid level and fill as necessary. Check brakes for proper operation.

RAIL SLIDER TWO PISTON SLIDING CALIPER

Removal and Installation

1. Raise and support the vehicle safely. Remove the wheel and tire assembly.
2. Disconnect the brake hose from the caliper and plug the hose and inlet port.
3. Remove the key retaining screw.
4. Using a brass rod and light hammer drive out the key and spring.
5. Remove the caliper from its support assembly by rotating the key and spring end out and away from the rotor. Slide the opposite end of the caliper clear of the slide in the support end of the rotor.
6. Clean the areas of the caliper and support that come in to contact during the sliding action of the caliper.
7. Clean any brake fluid, grease or grit off the rotor breaking surface.
8. Place the caliper rail into the slide on the support and rotate the caliper into the rotor.
9. Position the key and spring between the caliper and support assembly and start in by hand. Note that the spring is between the key and caliper and that the spring tangs overlap the ends of the key. Use a break adjusting tool to hold up the caliper against the support assembly.
10. Using a hammer, drive the key and spring into position aligning the correct notch with the existing hole in the support.
11. Secure the key to the support with the key retaining screw. Tighten the screw to 20 ft. lbs.
12. Place new copper washer on the brake hose fitting and connect to the caliper inlet port.
13. Bleed the system, lower the vehicle, and refill the master cylinder if necessary.

HEAVY DUTY TWO PISTON SLIDING CALIPER

Removal and Installation

1. Raise and support the vehicle safely. Remove the wheel and tire assembly.
2. Remove the four screws holding the caliper mounting plate and remove the plate.
3. Lift the caliper off the hub and rotor assembly.
4. Disconnect the brake hose and cap the hose and caliper inlet port.
5. Remove the inner shoe and lining from the anchor plate.
6. Remove the spring, pin and cup from the caliper and remove the outer brake shoe.
7. Install new inner shoe into the anchor plate. Take care that the shoes do not fall out prior to installing the caliper.
8. Using a block of wood over the pistons and a large C-clamp, push the pistons to the bottom of the cylinder bore.
9. Place the outer shoe in the caliper assembly and install the retaining pin, spring and cup.
10. Install the caliper assembly over the rotor assembly and position in the anchor plate grooves.
11. Install the caliper hold-down plate and tighten the attaching screws to 40 ft. lbs.
12. Install new copper washer on the brake hose fitting and connect the brake hose to the caliper inlet port.
13. Install the wheel and tire assembly and bleed the system.
14. Lower the vehicle and top off the master cylinder.

Power Boosters

For power booster overhaul procedures see the Unit Repair section.

DASH MOUNTED VACUUM BOOSTER

Removal and Installation

1. Disconnect the negative battery cable. Remove retaining nuts and master cylinder from booster.
2. Loosen hose clamp and remove manifold vacuum hose from booster.
3. From inside the cab, remove the attaching bolt, nut and plastic bushings and disconnect the booster pushrod from the brake pedal.
4. Remove nuts that retain the booster mounting bracket to the dash panel.
5. Remove the booster assembly from engine compartment.
6. To install, mount the booster and bracket assembly to the engine side of the dash panel by sliding the bracket mounting bolts and valve operating rod in through the holes in the dash panel.
7. From inside the cab, install the booster mounting bracket to dash panel retaining nuts.
8. Position the master cylinder to the booster assembly and install the retaining nuts.
9. Connect the manifold vacuum hose to the booster and secure with clamp.
10. From inside the cab connect the booster valve operating rod to the brake pedal with the attaching bolt, nut and plastic bushings.
11. Start engine and check operation of the brake system.

FRAME MOUNTED VACUUM BOOSTER

Removal and Installation

1. Depress the brake pedal several times to remove all vacuum from the system.
2. Loosen the booster air inlet tube clamp and remove the tube.
3. Disconnect the hydraulic lines and vacuum lines from the booster.
4. Remove the booster mounting bolts and booster from the bracket.
5. Place the booster on the mounting bracket and secure with the mounting bolts. Use new lockwashers on the bolts.
6. Connect the hydraulic lines. Make sure that the connections are tight.
7. Connect the air inlet tube to the booster. Be sure that the hose clamp is tight.
8. Bleed the brake system.
9. Connect the vacuum line to the booster and tighten the clamp securely.

HYDRO MAX BOOSTER

Removal and Installation

1. Disconnect the negative battery cable.
2. Disconnect the brake push rod at the brake pedal.
3. Disconnect the electrical power lead to the electric motor pump at the power stud and flow switch wire from the flow switch.

4. Disconnect the hydraulic fluid supply line from the booster inlet port. Cap or plug both the supply line and the inlet port.
5. Remove the hose clamp and disconnect the fluid return line. Cap or plug both the return line and the outlet port.
6. Loosen the four nuts attaching master cylinder to the booster, while supporting the master cylinder.
7. Separate the master cylinder from the booster by pulling it straight apart.
8. Loosen the four bolts attaching the booster to the dash panel. Remove the two bottom bolts and lockwashers and, while supporting the booster, remove the two upper bolts.
9. Pull the booster straight out from the dash panel, and lift it from the engine compartment.
10. Insert the Hydro-Max booster through the dash panel. Be sure that the push rod eye is on the correct side of the brake pedal arm.
11. Install the four bolts with lockwashers, under the bolt head and hand tighten the upper two bolts and then the bottom two bolts. Tighten the bolts to 15–25 ft. lbs., the upper bolts first.
12. Remove the shipping retainer from the outlet end of a new booster, and slide the master cylinder straight onto the booster until the mating surfaces come together.
13. Continue to support the master cylinder and install the upper two nuts, hand tight. Remove the master cylinder support and install the bottom two nuts, hand tight. Tighten each nut to 15–25 ft. lbs. the upper nuts first.
14. Connect the fluid return line and tighten the hose clamp.
15. Carefully start the supply line fitting and tighten to 16–25 ft. lbs. Make sure that the O-ring for the supply line is in place.
16. Connect the brake push rod with bushing to the brake pedal arm.
17. Reconnect the electric power lead to the electric motor pump, and the negative battery cable to the battery.

NOTE: The Hydro-Max booster operates on power steering fluid only. All parts prior to assembly should be clean and free from contamination from any other fluids.

18. To fill the Hydro-Max unit, first prevent the engine from starting by disconnecting the coil wire.
19. Fill the reservoir of the power steering pump supplying the Hydro-Max booster. Use fresh power steering fluid, Dexron®II or equivalent.

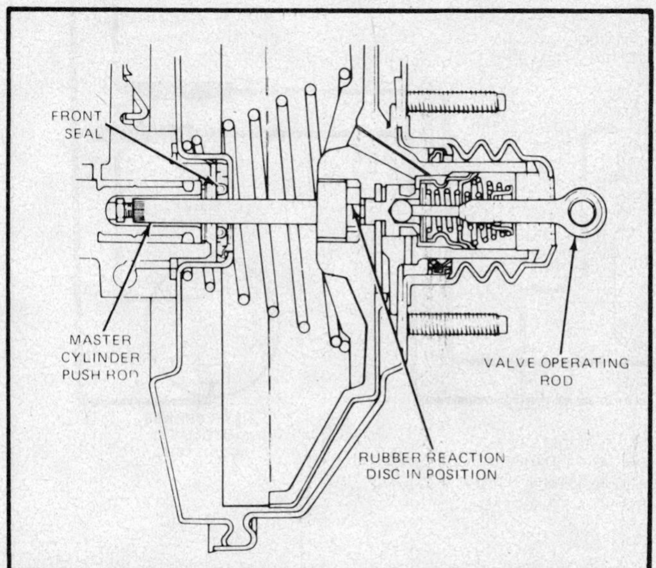

Single diaphragm vacuum booster cross section (© Ford Motor Co.)

20. Crank the engine over several times. Use either remote starter switch or ignition key.
21. Check and refill the reservoir. Crank the engine over several times, again.
22. Refill the reservoir and connect the coil wire. The Hydro-Max, hydraulic lines and the power steering pump should now be filled with fluid.

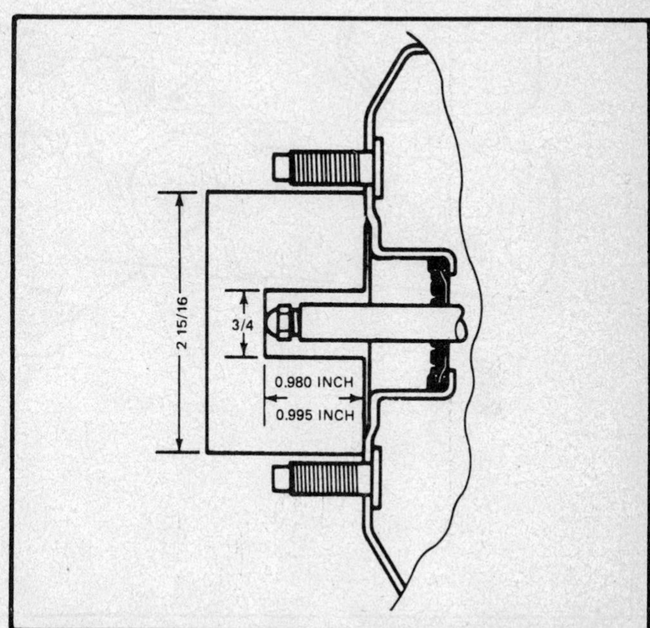

Pushrod (brake pedal) adjustment—Bendix dash mounted brake booster, Midland Ross similar (© Ford Motor Co.)

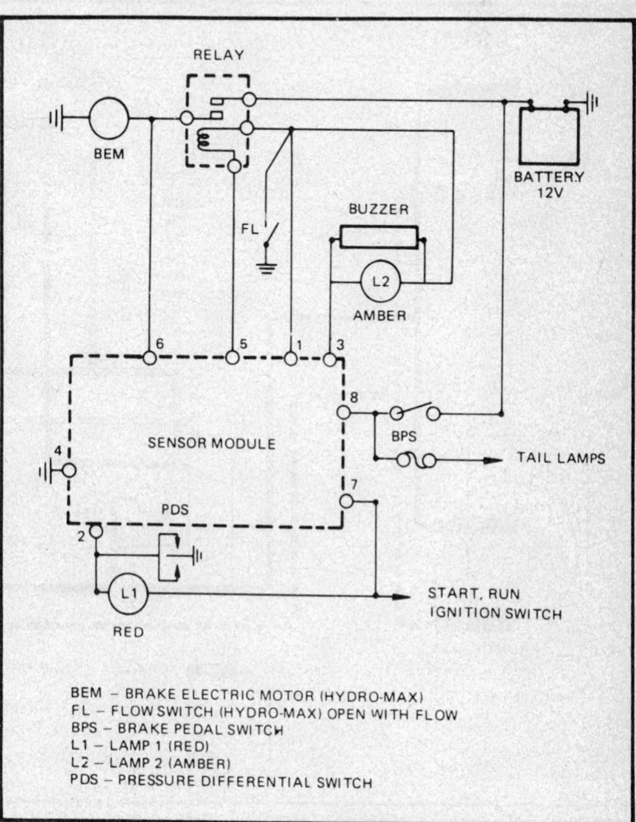

Hydro-Max brake booster wiring schematic (© Ford Motor Co.)

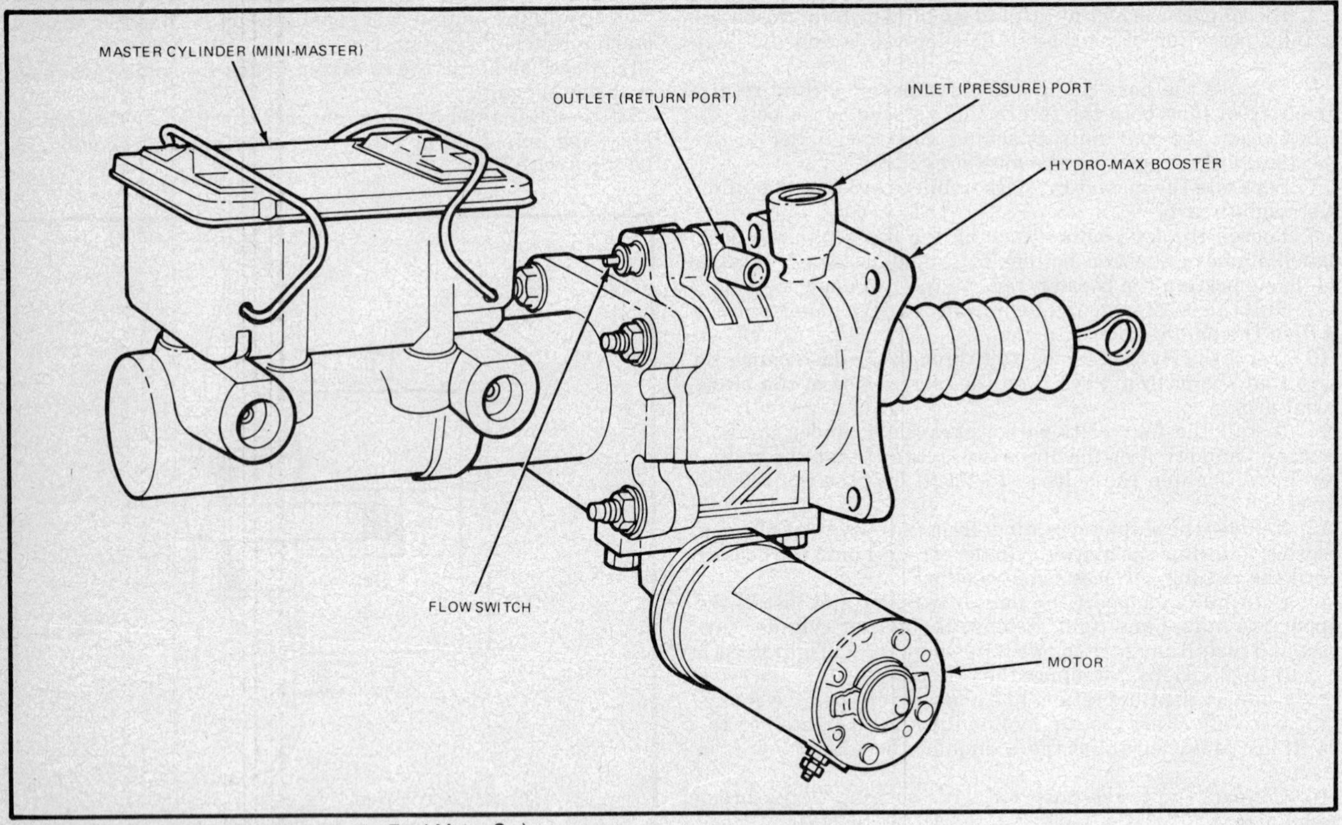

Hydro-Max brake booster assembly (© Ford Motor Co.)

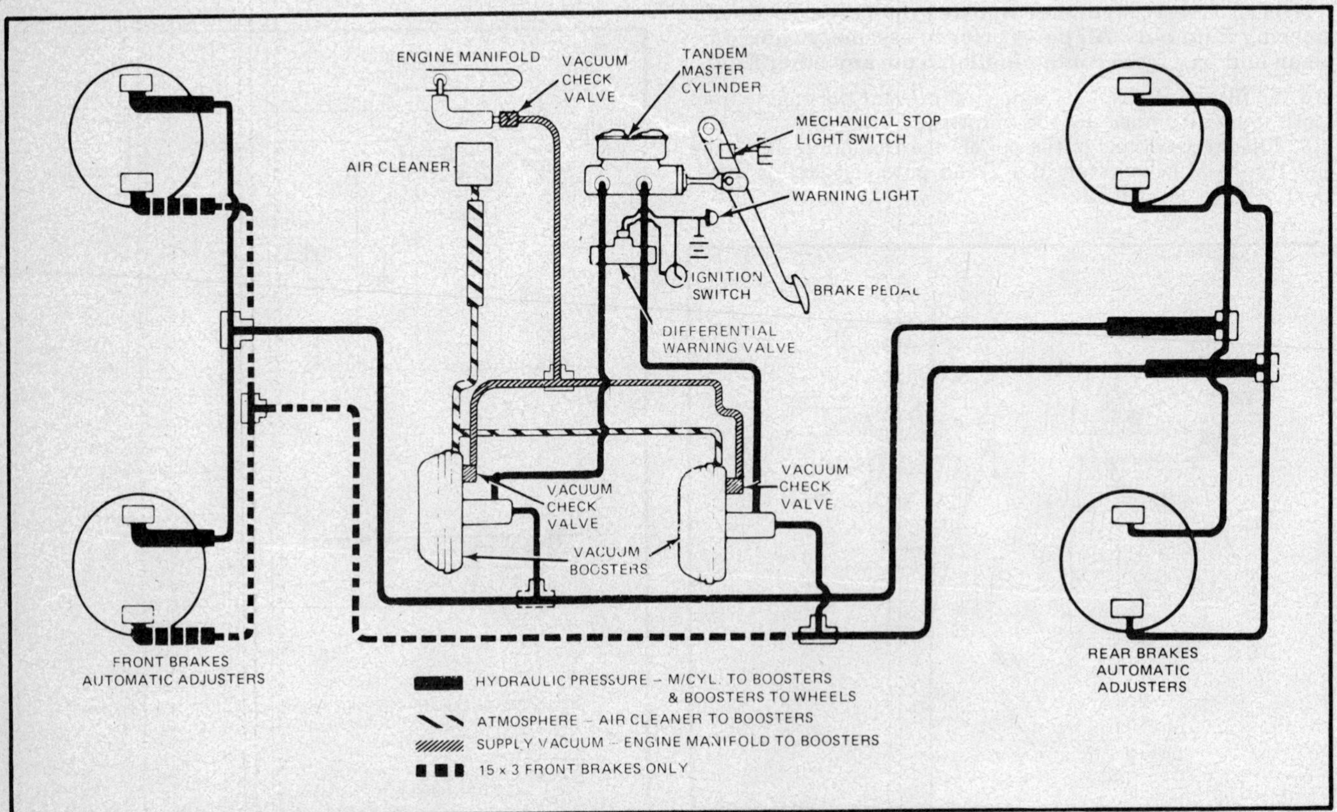

Split hydraulic brake system schematic—typical of medium and heavy duty vehicles (© Ford Motor Co.)

Brake Pedal

Adjustment

DASH MOUNTED BOOSTER

1. Remove the master cylinder.
2. Fabricate a gauge and place it against the master cylinder mounting surface on the booster body.
3. Adjust the push rod screw until the end of the screw just touches the inner edge of the slot in the gauge.
4. Install the master cylinder.

Bleeding System

CONVENTIONAL HYDRAULIC BRAKE SYSTEM

NOTE: On vehicles with frame mounted boosters, engine must be off and all vacuum depleted from the system prior to bleeding.

1. Fill master cylinder reservoir with fluid. Check level of fluid frequently during bleeding procedure.
2. If hydraulic system is equipped with a vacuum booster, bleed the booster before bleeding the rest of the system.
3. If vehicle is equipped with dual slave cylinders, bleed the upper one first. If there are two bleeder screws, bleed the one nearest the power chamber first.
4. Bleed the wheel cylinder with the longest hydraulic line first.
5. Attach bleeder tube to bleeder screw and place other end of tube in a container partially filled with fluid.
6. Loosen bleeder screw, then slowly depress the brake pedal by hand, allowing it to return slowly to the fully-released position. Repeat until all bubbles cease to flow from bleeder tube.
7. Close bleeder screw and remove tube.
8. Repeat this procedure at each wheel until system is completely free of air bubbles.

DUAL HYDRAULIC BRAKE SYSTEMS

The primary and secondary hydraulic brake systems are individual systems that are bled separately. Bleed the longest line first on the individual system being serviced. Be sure to keep reservoir filled during bleeding operation. After bleeding it is necessary to centralize the pressure differential valve. On 500–00 series vehicles, remove the brake warning light switch from the pressure differential valve to prevent damage to the switch assembly.

NOTE: On vehicles with frame mounted boosters, engine must be off and all vacuum depleted from the system prior to bleeding.

1. Bleed master cylinder at the outlet port side of the system being serviced. If there are no bleed screws, loosen the hydraulic line nut. Do not use the secondary piston stop screw located on the bottom of the master cylinder as the stop screw or piston could easily be damaged.
2. Operate pedal slowly until fluid is free of air bubbles, then tighten bleed screw.
3. Follow Steps 1 through 8 of Conventional Bleeding procedure.
4. Centralize the pressure differential valve. Turn the ignition switch to ACC or ON position. Loosen the pressure differential valve inlet tube nut on the system opposite the system which was bled last. This will result in unequal pressure in the other direction and allow the valve to center. Slowly depress brake pedal until light goes out. Tighten inlet tube nut. On 500–900 series vehicles, disconnect wires from warning light switch on the differential valve, remove switch. Springs inside valve will center valve. Replace switch and wire.
5. Check fluid level in reservoir and fill to within ¼ in. of top.

DISC BRAKE HYDRAULIC SYSTEM

To allow brake fluid to reach the caliper assemblies when bleeding disc brake units, the bleeding rod of the metering valve must be pulled forward and held with a special holding tool or its equivalent, on F100, F150, F250 including all 4X4 vehicles, Bronco, E100 and E150 series.

On the F350, E250 and E350 series, the bleeder rod must be pushed inward and held.

The hydraulic system may be bled in the conventional manner, with the following additional steps.

1. First bleed master cylinder, then rear brake cylinders (longest line first).
2. On the front disc brake systems, the bleeder rod on the metering valve must be either pulled or depressed, depending upon the vehicle series, to allow the brake fluid to reach the caliper assemblies. When the bleeding operation is completed, fill the reservoir to within ¼ inch of the top.
3. Centralize the pressure differential valve as described in Bleeding Dual Hydraulic Brake Systems.

Stop Light Switch

PEDAL MOUNTED STOP LAMP SWITCH

Adjustment

Stop light switch should be checked on vehicles with dragging or locking brakes. An improperly positioned stop light switch may restrict the brake pedal from returning to its non applied position and prevent the brake fluid from returning to the master cylinder reservoir which can cause dragging or locked brakes.

Check switch for proper seating by pulling the brake pedal with no more than 25 lbs. force, which will seat the switch properly and may relieve these conditions.

When installing a new stop light switch be sure to insert the switch into the retainer on the brake pedal by pushing the switch rearward until it bottoms in the brake switch bracket. Then manually pull the brake pedal rearward against stop to set switch in proper position.

PEDAL BRACKET MOUNTED STOP LAMP SWITCH

Adjustment

Install the switch into the pedal bracket as far as possible and pull the pedal to its extreme return position to properly set the stop lamp switch assembly.

Air Brakes

Refer to the Brake Unit Repair section for information on Removal and Installation procedures.

Adjustments

GOVERNOR

Before adjusting the pressure settings of the governor, determine the accuracy of the dash gauge by checking the readings against an accurate test gauge. The cut-in cut-out setting is made at the adjusting screw.

1. With the engine running, build up pressure in the system and observe the pressure registered by the dash gauge.
2. If the pressure build-up continues beyond 125 psi before the governor cuts-out, remove the cover from the top of the governor and loosen the locknut. Turn the adjusting screw clock-

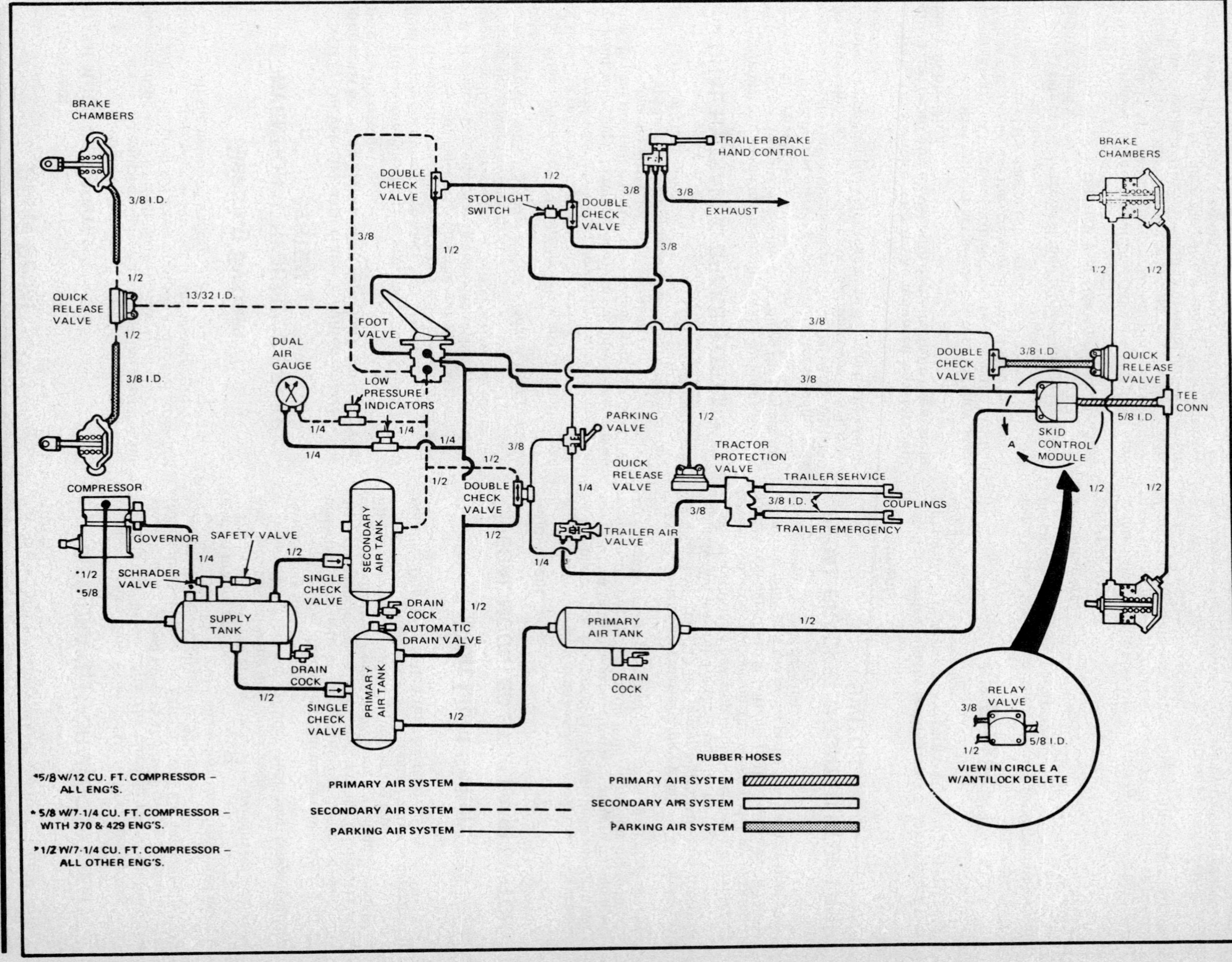

Typical air brake system schematic (with tractor package) (© Ford Motor Co.)

wise to lower the cut-out pressure, and counter clockwise to increase the cut-out pressure. After adjusting the cut-out pressure, tighten the adjusting screw locknut and install the cover.

NOTE: The air pressure range between the cut-out pressure (maximum) and the cut-in pressure (minimum) is fixed at about 20–25 psi and cannot be adjusted.

FOOT CONTROL VALVE

To determine if the brakes are applying properly, proceed as follows:

1. Install a pressure gauge anywhere in the circuit between the control valve and brake chamber, or install the gauge in one of the extra service ports (upper row of ports).
2. Fully depress the brake pedal. The test gauge reading should approximate reservoir pressure as indicated by the dash gauge.
3. Adjust the stop button on the suspended pedal to eliminate free travel.

SLACK ADJUSTER CAM OPERATED BRAKES

Apply the brakes and measure the travel of the brake chamber push rod. If the vehicle is equipped with Maxi brake unit, the minimum air pressure should be 90 psi while measuring the travel.

The travel should be kept to the minimum possible without causing the brakes to drag.

NOTE: Adjustment of the yoke on the brake chamber push rod should not be changed. When new, the yoke is adjusted so that the slack adjuster brake chamber push rod angle is slightly greater than 90° when the brakes are properly adjusted and the brakes are applied. Brake lining wear will not change this angle as long as the slack adjusters are kept adjusted to compensate for lining wear.

Front Brakes: This procedure applies only to vehicles equipped with the S-cam operated brakes. Push rod travel which reaches or exceeds the maximum listed above indicates the need of adjustment. Turn the adjusting screw clockwise until the push for travels $^3/_4$ in. in, going from released to fully applied position. When making the adjustment, turn the screw in quarter turns.

Rear Brakes: This procedure applies to vehicles equipped with either standard or Maxi brake S-cam slack adjusters. Push rod travel which reaches or exceeds the maximum listed above indicates the need of adjustment. Depress the lock sleeve and turn the hex head of the wormshaft clockwise until the push rod travels one inch in, going from released to fully applied position. Be sure that the lock sleeve comes back out of the wormshaft so that the adjustment is locked.

NOTE: When adjusting either the front or rear slack adjuster, raise the wheels and make sure that there is no brake drag.

Stop Light Switch (Air Brake)

If the stop lamp does not operate, connect a jumper wire across the switch terminals. If the lamp lights with the jumper wire connected, remove the wire and replace the switch. If the lamp still does not light, repair or replace the switch lead wires.

Air Compressor

NOTE: Depending on the particular truck model and engine, compressors are mounted in various locations. The procedures for removal and installation differ between vertically mounted units and side mounted units. The following procedures apply generally to liquid cooled compressors, but air cooled installations are similar.

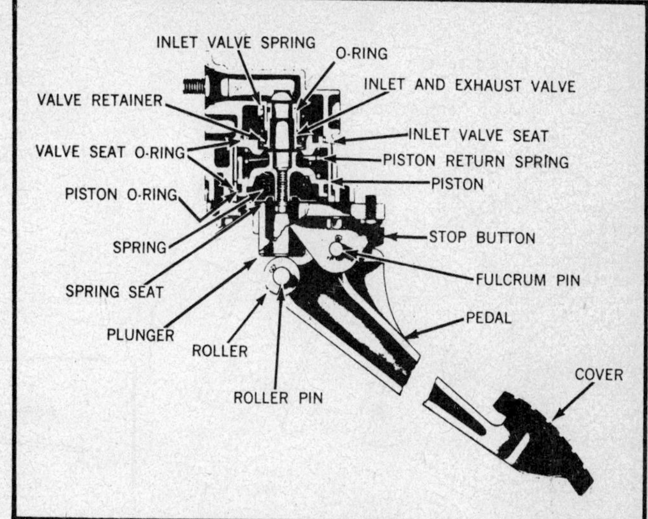

Foot control valve—typical (© Ford Motor Co.)

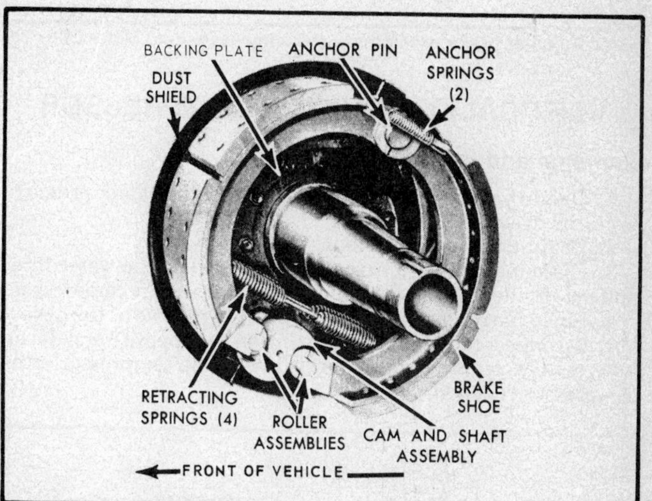

Cam type brake assembly (rear) (© Ford Mutor Co.)

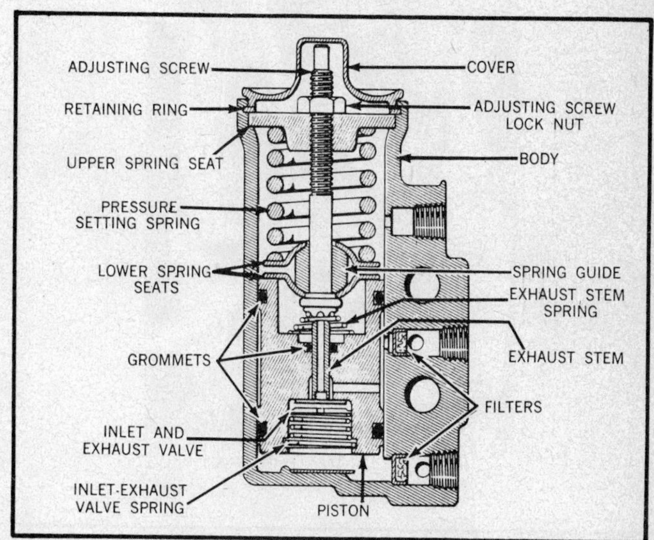

Compressor governor—typical (© Ford Motor Co.)

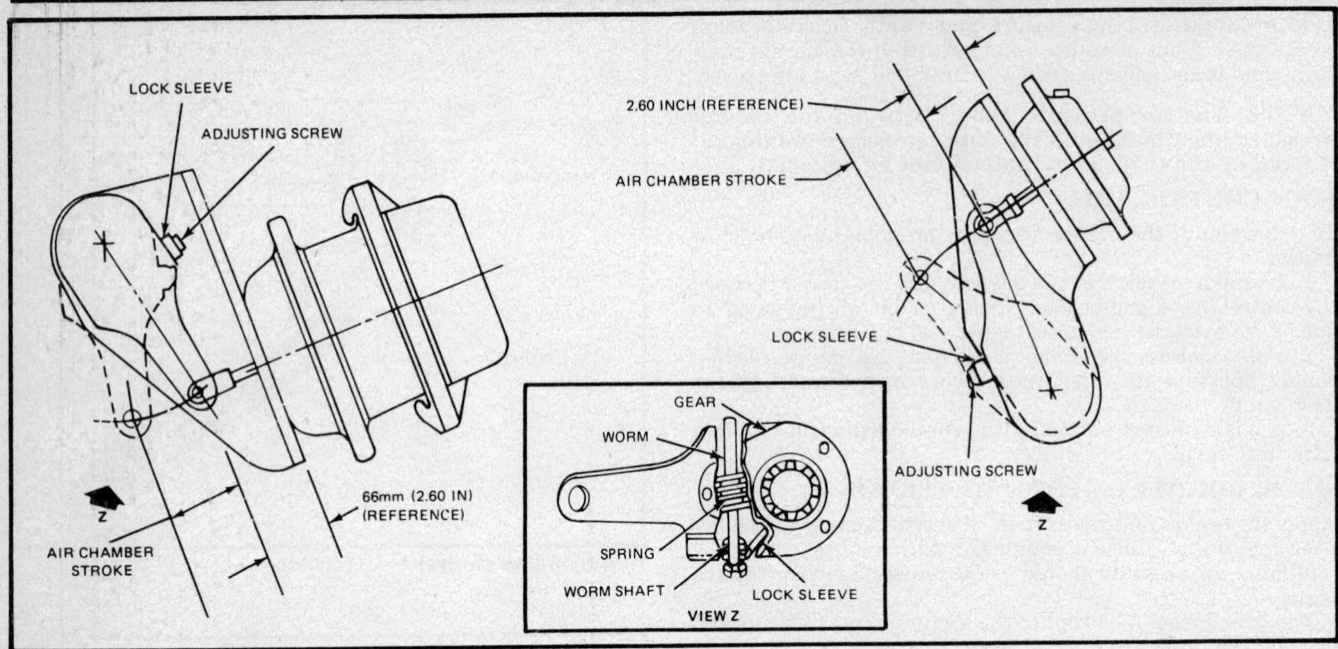

Slack adjuster brake preliminary adjustment (© Ford Motor Co.)

VERTICALLY MOUNTED COMPRESSOR

Removal and Installation

1. Open the reservoir drain cocks to exhaust air pressure from the system.
2. Drain the cooling system.
3. Disconnect the compressor air outlet line, the water inlet and outlet lines, the oil feed and return lines at the compressor.
4. Since the reservoir hose is difficult to remove at the governor, disconnect the hose at the fitting on the opposite end. If the hose is to be replaced, disconnect it from the compressor after compressor removal.

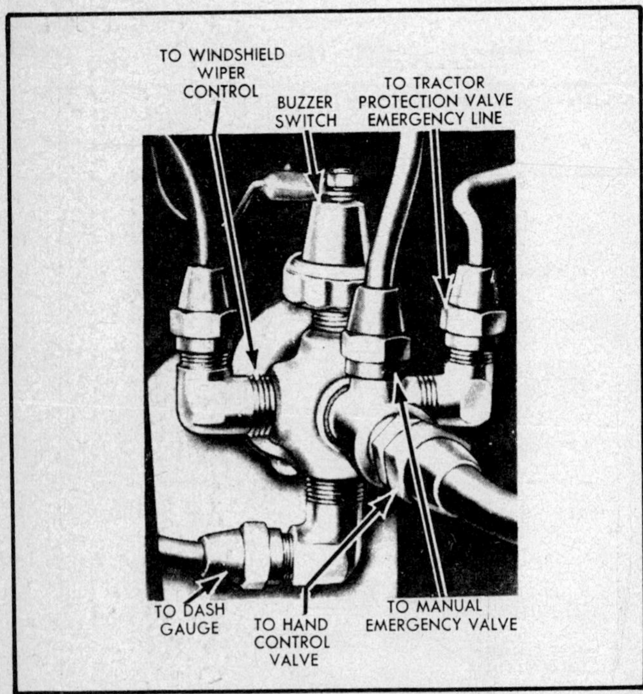

Pressure indicator valve (© Ford Motor Co.)

5. Remove the compressor-to-base plate bolts, then slide the compressor inward on the base plate. Disengage the drive belt and remove the compressor.
6. Transfer the pulley, Woodruff key and attaching nut to the new compressor.
7. Transfer the air outlet elbow and gasket, water outlet fittings, and oil inlet and outlet fittings to the new sealer. Apply sealer to all parts.
8. Transfer the governor and gasket to the new compressor and apply sealer. If the reservoir pressure hose is being replaced, connect it to the governor.
9. Transfer the air inlet filter and gasket to the new compressor and apply sealer.
10. Position the compressor on the base plate and engage the drive belt to the pulley.

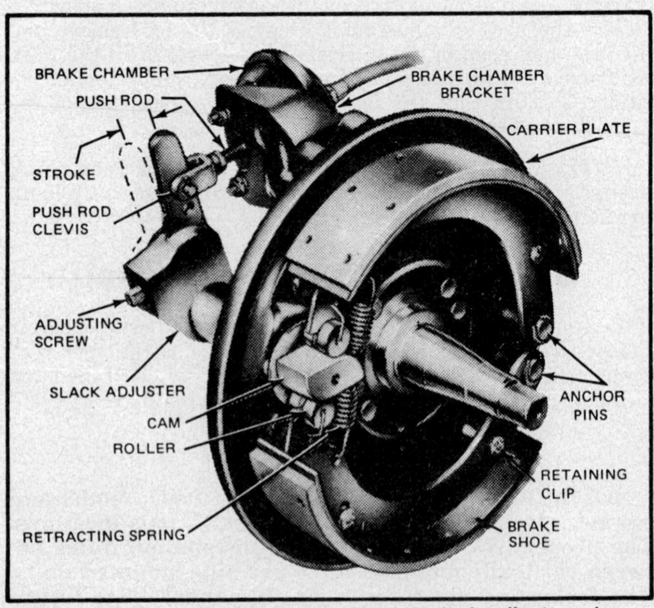

Cam type brake assembly (front) showing slack adjuster adjustment (© Ford Motor Co.)

11. Install the attaching bolts and slide the compressor away from the fan pulley until a ½ inch belt deflection is obtained. Tighten the bolts.
12. Connect the compressor air outlet line, water inlet line, and water outlet line to the compressor.
13. Connect the oil feed and return lines to the compressor.
14. Connect the hose from the governor to the fitting on the reservoir pressure line.
15. Fill the cooling system, close the reservoir drain cocks, start the engine and check for oil, air, or coolant leaks.

SIDE MOUNTED COMPRESSOR

Removal and Installation

1. Drain the cooling system, and open the reservoir drain cocks to exhaust the air pressure from the system.
2. Loosen the idler pivot bolt and adjusting bolt, remove the compressor drive belt.
3. Disconnect all oil, air, and coolant lines from the compressor and the reservoir pressure line from the governor.
4. Remove the bracket bolt at the cylinder head and the bracket bolt and washer at the manifold. Remove the bracket between the exhaust manifold and the cylinder head.
5. On vehicles with power steering, remove the attaching bolt, nut and lockwasher from the clip at the frame side rail. Remove the power steering hose retainer bolt, nut, and lockwasher at the frame crossmember and place the hoses out of the way.
6. Remove the front compressor-to-base attaching bolts.

NOTE: There is very little clearance between the compressor base plate and the engine mount.

7. Remove the remaining bolts.
8. Remove the air compressor from underneath the vehicle in a rearward direction. Discard the base gasket.
9. Remove the compressor pulley cotter pin and Woodruff key, and remove the pulley from the shaft with a suitable puller.
10. On C-series models, install the compressor pulley on the new compressor. On all other models with a side-mounted compressor, install the pulley after the compressor is installed.
11. Transfer all air, water, and oil fittings to the replacement compressor. Coat the threads with sealer.
12. Transfer the air inlet strainer and gasket to the replacement compressor and apply sealer.
13. Transfer the governor and gasket to the new compressor and apply sealer.
14. Clean the compressor base and cylinder block base plate.
15. Apply sealer to both sides of the compressor base gasket.
16. Install pilot studs in the two rear bolt holes of the base plate mounting surface on the cylinder block. Position the base gasket on the base plate over the studs. From underneath the vehicle, install the compressor on the pilot studs and install the three attaching bolts. Remove the pilot studs and install the remaining bolts.
17. On vehicles with power steering, position the power steering hose on the frame rail and secure with the attaching bolt, washer, and nut.
18. Connect the water outlet line to the compressor.
19. Position the steering tube clips on the frame side rail and secure with the attaching nut, bolt, and lockwasher.
20. Connect the water inlet line to the compressor.
21. On all vehicles except C-series, loosen the power steering belt adjustment bolts and loosen the belt to provide clearance for installing the compressor pulley. Install the pulley on the shaft and secure with the nut and cotter pin.
22. Position the power steering belt on the pulleys and adjust the belt tension.
23. Position the air compressor drive belt on the pulleys and adjust the belt tension.
24. Connect the air outlet line to the compressor.
25. Connect the reservoir pressure line at the governor.
26. Fill the cooling system, close the air reservoir drain cocks, and build up pressure in the system. Check for air, oil and coolant leaks.

GOVERNOR

Removal and Installation

1. Exhaust the air from the system.
2. On vertically-mounted compressors, disconnect the governor hose from the fitting in the reservoir pressure line. On side-mounted compressors, disconnect the pressure line at the governor.
3. Remove the attaching bolts and the governor.
4. On vertically-mounted compressors, transfer the hose to the replacement governor.
5. Install the governor, gasket, and the attaching bolts. Apply sealer to the threads.
6. On vertically-mounted compressors, connect the hose to the fitting on the reservoir pressure line. On side-mounted compressors, connect the pressure line to the governor.
7. Test the governor as detailed under Adjustments.

PRESSURE INDICATOR VALVE

Removal and Installation

1. Exhaust the air from the system.
2. Disconnect the wire at the buzzer switch.
3. Disconnect the air lines to the wiper control as required.
4. Unscrew the pressure indicator fitting and remove the assembly.
5. Install the pressure indicator valve assembly.
6. Connect the buzzer switch wire. Turn on the ignition switch to test that the buzzer and light are functioning properly before building up pressure in the system.

FOOT CONTROL VALVE

Removal and Installation

1. Open the reservoir drain cocks to exhaust the air from the system.
2. Disconnect all but one line from the valve ports. Loosen, but do not disconnect, the remaining line. This will prevent the valve from falling when the attaching bolts are removed.
3. Remove the cotter pin and pivot pin that connect the brake treadle to the control valve mounting plate.
4. Remove the control valve attaching bolts.
5. Disconnect the remaining air line from the control valve, and remove the control valve.
6. If the valve is being replaced, transfer all brass fittings and the stop light switch to the new valve. Apply sealer to the threads before installation.
7. Remove the actuating button and rubber seal from the control valve mounting plate to allow installation of the new valve.
8. Position the new valve on the lower dash panel and mounting plate and install the attaching bolts.
9. Install the actuating button in the mounting plate bore, and install the rubber seal to the button and mounting seal.
10. Install the brake treadle on the control valve mounting plate with the pivot pin and cotter pin.
11. Connect the brake service lines to the upper ports of the valve.
12. Start the engine to build up pressure in the system. Check for leaks.

QUICK RELEASE VALVE

Removal and Installation

1. Exhaust the air from the system.

2. Disconnect the air lines at the valve.
3. Remove the valve mounting bolts and the valve.
4. Install the valve and tighten the bolts and nuts.
5. Check the exhaust port to be sure that it is not plugged.
6. Connect the air lines.

RELAY VALVE

Removal and Installation

1. Block the wheels.
2. Exhaust the air from the system.
3. Disconnect the air lines from the relay valve.
4. Remove the valve mounting bolts and remove the valve.
5. Remove the insert (inlet and exhaust valve assembly), by removing the four exhaust cover cap screws and cover. Pull the insert out.
6. Clean and inspect the relay valve air lines. Replace any lines which are damaged or connecting hoses which are deteriorating or show signs of chafing.
7. Mount the relay valve and secure with the attaching bolts.
8. Connect the air lines to the valve.
9. Build up pressure in the system. Test the valve for correct operation and air leaks.

BRAKE SHOES

Removal and installation procedures for brake shoes can be found in the "Air Brake" section in the Unit Repair portion of this manual.

Brake Service Air Chamber

WEDGE TYPE BRAKES

Removal and Installation

1. Exhaust all air from the system.
2. Disconnect the air inlet line from the brake chamber.
3. Using a drift and a light weight hammer, loosen the spanner nut.
4. Unscrew the brake chamber from the wedge housing.
5. Check the position of the wedge in the plunger housing to be sure that the wedge assembly is properly seated.
6. Replace the automatic adjusting identification ring on the brake chamber tube. Thread the spanner nut into the power unit tube.
7. Screw the service chamber into the plunger housing until it bottoms (spanner nut loose).
8. Align the connection ports with the brake lines, if necessary, unscrewing the brake chamber not more than one full turn.
9. Connect the air lines.
10. Make and hold a full pressure brake application. Drive the spanner nut with a drift and hammer until it is tight against the plunger housing. Release the brake pressure.
11. Check for leaks at all connections.

CAM TYPE BRAKES

Removal and Installation

1. Exhaust all air from the system.
2. Disconnect the air line at the brake chamber.
3. Disconnect the push rod clevis pin from the slack adjuster.
4. Remove the attaching nuts, and remove the brake chamber assembly.
5. Check and if necessary, cut the push rod of the new chamber to the same length as on the removed brake chamber.
6. If the chamber is being replaced, transfer the brake line fitting to the new brake chamber.
7. Position the brake chamber assembly on the mounting bracket and install the attaching nuts.
8. Install the clevis and cotter pin.
9. Connect the air line to the brake chamber.
10. Build up pressure in the system and inspect for leaks.
11. Adjust the brakes.

SLACK ADJUSTER CAM TYPE BRAKES

Removal and Installation

1. Remove the clevis pin (on vehicles with a rear wheel spring brake, the spring brake must be released to remove the clevis pin) attaching the slack adjuster to the brake chamber push rod.
2. Remove the lock ring attaching the slack adjuster to the camshaft.
3. Mark the position of the slack adjuster on the camshaft, then slide the slack adjuster off the shaft.
4. Place the slack adjuster on the camshaft, aligning the locating marks. If there is excessive camshaft and play, install an additional spacer at the cam end of the camshaft. Install the lock ring.
5. Connect the brake chamber push rod to the slack adjuster by installing the clevis pin in the upper hole, and installing the cotter pin.
6. Lubricate the slack adjuster. Build up pressure in the system, check operation of brake assembly and for air leaks. Adjust the brakes.

Adjustment

Fully apply the brakes at 689 kPa (100 psi) system pressure and measure the travel of the brake chamber push rod. Maximum travel should not exceed the maximum adjustment specification. Do not change the adjustment of the yoke on the brake chamber push rod. The yoke is factory adjusted so the slack adjuster brake chamber push rod angle is slightly greater than 90 degrees when the brakes are properly adjusted and the brakes are applied. Brake lining wear will not change this angle as long as the slack adjusters are kept adjusted to compensate for lining wear.

Front and Rear Brake Adjustment

The following procedure applies to vehicles equipped with cam operated front and rear brakes.

To adjust the front or rear brakes, raise the tire off the ground and turn the adjusting screw until the wheel is locked. Then loosen the screw to obtain a free rotating wheel.

If the air brake chamber push rod travel reaches or exceeds 38mm (1.50 in.) for type 9, 12 and 16, 44.5mm (1.75 in.) for type 24 or 47.6mm (1.875 in.) for type 30 chambers, proceed as follows: Adjust the slack adjuster travel by depressing the lock sleeve and turning the adjusting screw counter-clockwise for rear cam brakes and clockwise for front cam brakes. Turn the adjusting screw enough clicks to provide air chamber stroke of 28.5 ± 3.1mm (1 1/8 ± 1/8 in.) for type 9–12, and 16 chambers; 38.1 ± 3.1mm (1 1/8 ± 1/8 in.) for type 24 chambers; and 41.2 ± 3.1mm (1 5/8 ± 1/8 in.) for type 30 chamber at 689 ± 34 kPa (100 ± 5 psi) air pressure at the chamber or as indicated by the air gauge in the cab with the engine stopped and the foot pedal fully depressed.

The type of brake chamber is determined by a number stamped on the outer surface.

Air Hydraulic Intensifier

MASTER CYLINDER

Removal and Installation

1. Clean the dirt from around the discharge fitting and the inlet fitting of the master cylinder.

2. Disconnect the inlet (hydraulic reservoir) line from the master cylinder inlet port and plug both the line and port.

3. Disconnect the discharge line and plug the discharge port of the master cylinder. The open brake line should be plugged to prevent contaminants from entering the line or fluid loss.

4. Unscrew the four $^3/_8$ in. screws holding the master cylinder onto the rotochamber. Remove the master cylinder.

5. Bolt the new master cylinder onto the rotochamber. Tighten the cap screws.

6. Remove the plug from the brake line and connect the line to the discharge port on the master cylinder.

7. Remove the plug from the reservoir line and connect it to the master cylinder inlet port.

8. Clean the dirt from around the hydraulic reservoir lid. Unfasten the bail wire from the reservoir lid and remove the lid. Add brake fluid until it is level with the tops of the four vertical ribs in the reservoir.

9. Connect a bleeder bottle to the bleed screw on the master cylinder and allow the unit to gravity bleed. Close the bleed screw when the fluid is flowing freely with no air bubbles.

10. If pressure bleeding is performed on the system, the warning switch on the rotochamber may be tripped and cause the brake light on the instrument panel to come on. After pressure bleeding is complete, manually reset the switch by pushing in the plunger located in the middle of the switch.

11. Fill the fluid reservoir, install the lid and fasten the bail wire in place.

12. Check the installation for leaks as follows:

a. Make sure that system pressure is at least 90 psi.

b. Make a full brake application, hold for 5–10 seconds, then release.

c. Check for fluid leaks around the discharge line and bleeder screw on the master cylinder.

INTENSIFIER UNIT

Removal and Installation

1. Disconnect and cap hydraulic lines. Plug the port in the master cylinder.

2. Discharge the secondary system reservoir and exhaust chamber.

3. Remove the air line and cap to prevent the entry of dirt.

4. Remove the bracket mounting bolts and remove the assembly from the vehicle.

5. Mount the intensifier unit in the vehicle with the bracket attaching bolts and tighten securely.

6. Attach air lines and hydraulic lines, tighten securely.

7. Apply air pressure and hold. Leak test air line connections and intensifier with soap suds.

8. Pressure bleed front brakes at caliper bleed screws.

9. Fill the master cylinder reservoir to $^1/_2$–$^1/_4$ inch below the top of the unit with specified brake fluid.

Parking Brakes

NOTE: For detailed description of Maxi-Brake and MGM Stopgard parking brake refer to the Air Brake section of this manual.

ORSCHELN LEVER

Adjustment

The Orscheln parking brake is the over center locking type. It is adjusted (in the fully released position) by turning the lever knob. When properly adjusted, it pulls over center with a distinct click. No other adjustment is normally required.

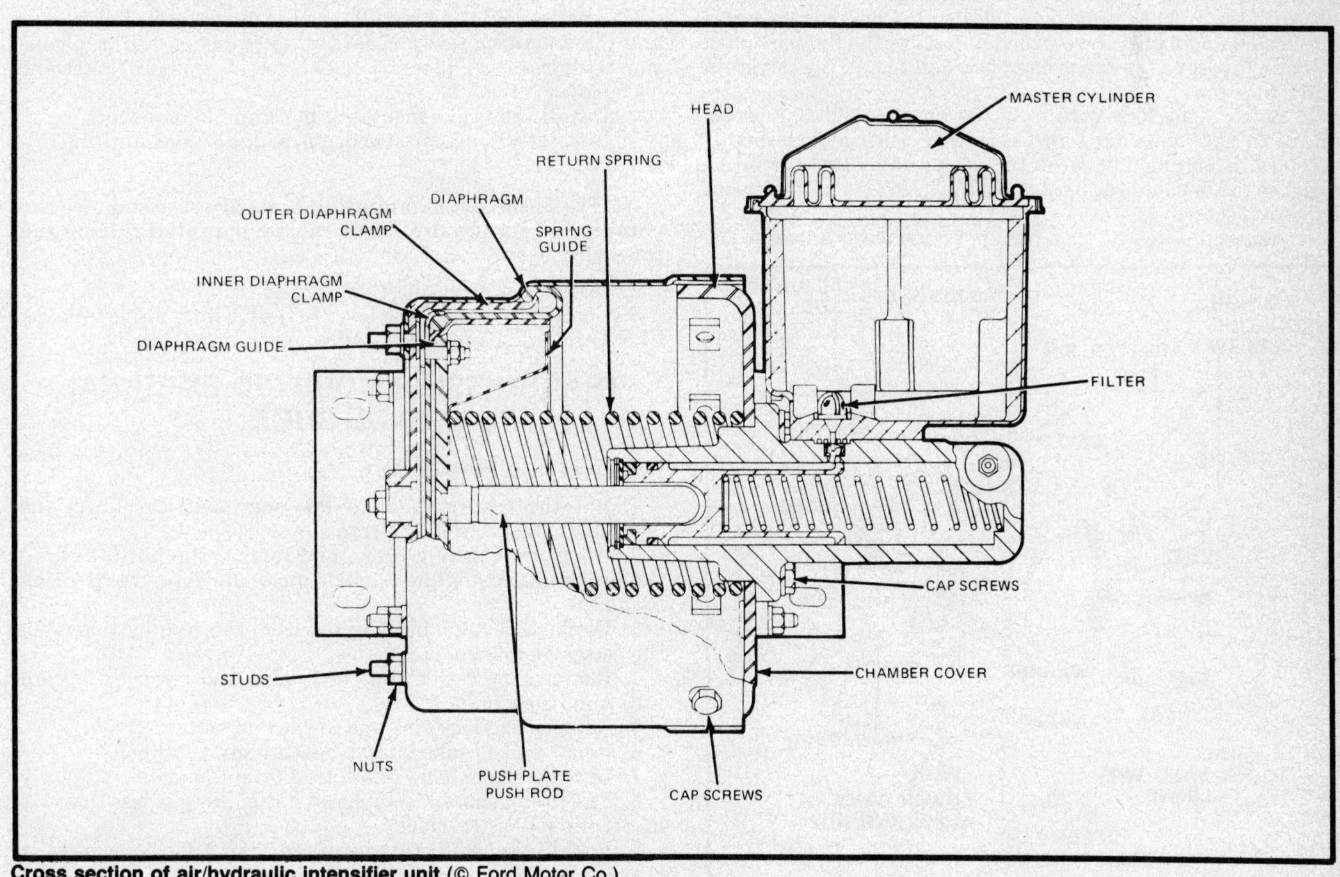

Cross section of air/hydraulic intensifier unit (© Ford Motor Co.)

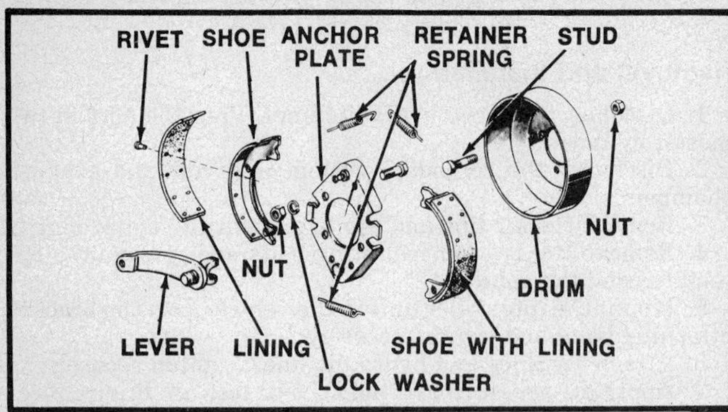

Exploded view of external band type parking brake (© Ford Motor Co.)

CABLE ACTUATED REAR WHEEL TYPE

Adjustment

Adjust service brakes before attempting to adjust the parking brake cables. Place parking brake lever in fully released position, then check for slack in the parking brake two rear cables. Cables are properly adjusted when the rear brake shoes are fully applied when parking brake is applied, and the brake shoes fully release when the parking brake lever is released.

To tighten cables, loosen locknut and tighten adjusting nut on equalizer. Tighten locknut when proper adjustment is obtained.

EXTERNAL BAND TYPE

1. On cable controlled parking brakes, move the parking brake lever to the fully released position. On a vehicle with a rod type linkage, set the lever at the first notch.
2. Check the position of the cam to make sure that the flat portion is resting on the brake band bracket. If the cam is not flat with the bracket, remove the clevis pin from the upper part of the cam and adjust the clevis rod to allow the flat portion of the cam to rest on the brake band bracket. Install the clevis pin and cotter pin.
3. Remove the lock wire from the anchor adjusting screw, and turn the adjusting screw clockwise until a clearance of 0.100 in. is obtained between the brake lining and the brake drum at the anchor bracket. Install the lock wire in the anchor adjusting screw.
4. Adjust the clearance on the upper and lower halves of the band in a similar manner. Adjust for a 0.010 in. clearance between band and drum.

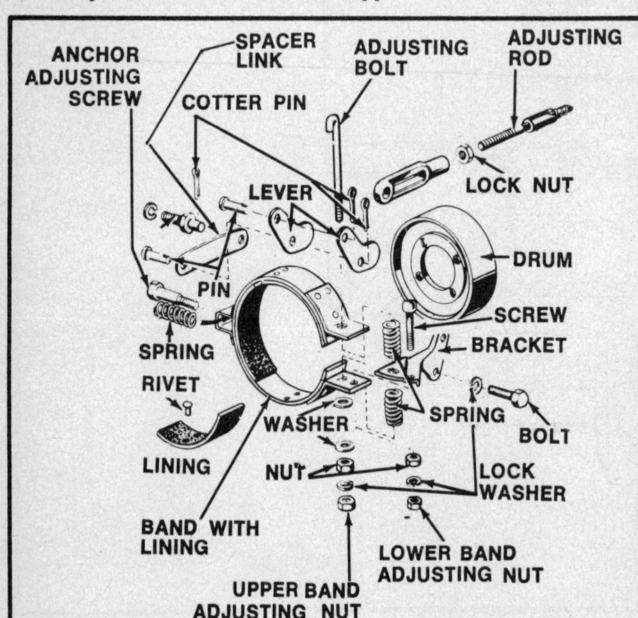

Exploded view of internal shoe type parking brake (© Ford Motor Co.)

INTERNAL SHOE TYPE 9 INCH DRUM

1. Release parking brake lever.
2. Remove cotter pin from the parking brake linkage adjusting clevis pin and remove the clevis pin.
3. Lengthen or shorten adjusting link by turning the clevis. There should be a 0.010 in. clearance between the drum and the band all the way around when the clevis pin is installed.
4. Install a new cotter pin in the clevis pin and check brake operation.

INTERNAL SHOE TYPE 12 INCH DRUM

There is no internal adjustment on this brake. Adjust the linkage as follows:

1. Remove clevis pin, loosen the nuts on the adjusting rod and turn clevis until a $\frac{1}{2}$–$\frac{3}{8}$ in. free-play is obtained at the brake lever with pin installed.
2. Tighten locknuts on adjusting rod and reinstall clevis pin.

INTERNAL SHOE TYPE PARKING BRAKE DRUM AND SHOE

Removal and Installation

1. Remove the drive shaft. Disconnect the parking brake actuating lever from the linkage.
2. Remove the transmission spline flange and drum. Remove the bolts holding the carrier plate to the transmission housing. Slide the plate with the brake shoes and retaining springs off the transmission.
3. Remove the actuating lever, shoe retaining springs, and shoes.
4. Install the brake shoe lower retaining of the shoes.
5. Position the shoes and lower retaining spring on the back of the carrier plate and install the shoe upper retaining springs and the actuating lever. Place the assembly on the transmission with the lever properly positioned at the ball socket and shoe ends.
6. Install the brake mounting bolts and lockwashers.
7. Install the transmission drum, spline flange, nut, and cotter pin.

NOTE: If the drum mounting bolts are pressed into the companion flange the drum can be mounted during the following step.

8. Install the drive shaft and brake drum.
9. Connect the actuating lever to the parking brake linkage. Check the brake operation and adjust if necessary.

TRANSMISSION MOUNTED EXTERNAL BAND SHOE

Removal and Installation

1. Put the transmission in low gear and disconnect the driveshaft flange from the transmission.
2. Apply the parking brake and remove the nut attaching the transmission output shaft flange. Release the parking brake.
3. Disconnect the adjusting rod from the cam by removing the cotter and clevis pins.
4. Remove the cotter and clevis pins and remove the cam link from the cam.
5. Remove the lockwire and anchor adjusting screw.
6. Remove the brake band adjusting nuts and bolts.
7. Lift the brake band and lining from the drum.
8. The lining should be replaced if the lining is less than $\frac{1}{32}$ in. off the top of the rivet.
9. Installation is the reverse of removal. Adjust the parking brake.

FUEL SYSTEM

Information of application and major adjustments can be found in the Carburetor section of this manual.

Idle Mixture Adjustments

Idle Mixture Setting Propane Enrichment Method

1980–82

NOTE: Remove the air cleaner when necessary to perform adjustments.

1. Bring the engine to normal operation temperature and connect a tachometer.

NOTE: If vehicle is equipped with the Dura Spark II ignition system, be sure to use a tachometer rated for this type of ignition system.

2. Disconnect the evaporative emission purge hose from the air cleaner. Disconnect the PCV closure hose from the air cleaner and plug the hose.
3. Adjust the curb idle speed to specifications on engine decal.

NOTE: With the transmission in neutral, run the engine at 2500 rpm for 15 seconds before each speed check. The idle speed must be adjusted with the air cleaner in place.

4. If vehicle is equipped with Thermactor System, revise the dump valve vacuum hoses as follows:
   a. For dump valves with two vacuum fittings, disconnect and plug the hose(s).
   b. For dump valves with one fitting, remove the hose at the dump valve and plug it. Connect a slave hose from the dump valve vacuum fitting to an intake manifold vacuum fitting.
5. Place the special gas tool into the air cleaner evaporative purge nipple. With the engine idling, slowly open the propane valve until the engine speed reaches a maximum and then begins to drop. Note the maximum speed increase. If the speed will not drop, check the bottle gas supply. If necessary, repeat the operation with a new bottle gas supply.
   a. If the speed increase is within specifications, but not zero rpm, proceed to Step 6. If the speed increase is zero and minus specification is zero, proceed to Step 5d.
   b. If the speed increase is higher than specification; enrich the mixture without propane by turning the mixture limiter screws counterclockwise in equal amounts until the rpm increases as necessary. Example: If the increase was 80 rpm and the desired reset is 50 rpm, the mixture screws should be richened to attain a 30 rpm increase. Repeat Steps 3 and 5.
   c. If the speed increase is lower than specifications proceed as follows; lean the mixture without propane by turning the mixture screws clockwise in equal amounts until the rpm decreases as necessary. Example: If the increase was zero rpm and the desired reset increase is 20 rpm, the mixture screws should be leaned to attain a 20 rpm decrease. Repeat Steps 3 and 5.
   d. If the speed increase is zero rpm and the minimum speed gain specification is zero, perform the following speed drop test; Turn the mixture limiters counterclockwise to the maximum rich position. (If the limiters have been removed, do not enrich; assume the mixture screws are already set at the maximum rich position.) Lean the idle fuel mixture by turning the screws clockwise equally as specified. Note the drop in engine rpm.
   e. If the speed drop is equal to or greater than the specified minimum speed drop, return the mixture limiters to the maximum rich position or the mixture screws to the "assumed" maximum rich position. If the engine speed before mixture adjustment was 650 rpm and the speed drop specification is 100 rpm minimum, proceed to Step 6 if the engine speed drops to at least 550 rpm or stalls.
   f. If the speed drop is less than the specified minimum speed drop, leave the mixture limiters or screws in the adjusted position and repeat Steps 3 and 5.
6. If the idle limiters were removed, install new blue service limiters at the maximum rich stop. Check the speed increase after installation of the limiters to be certain that the settings were not disturbed. If the setting is within specification, proceed to Step 7, if not correct as required.
7. Remove the gas tool from the nipple and connect all system components that were removed.
8. Set the curb idle speed to specification if Step 3 required an idle speed adjustment.
9. Turn off the engine and disconnect the tachometer. Every time propane is administered, place the transmission in the range specified on the engine decal. Remove the limiter caps with appropriate tool if required.

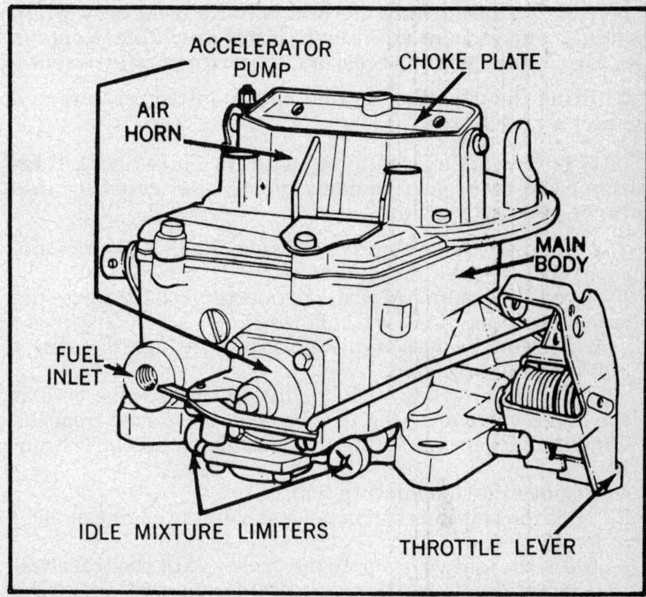

Motorcraft 2100 2 bbl (manual choke) component locations (© Ford Motor Co.)

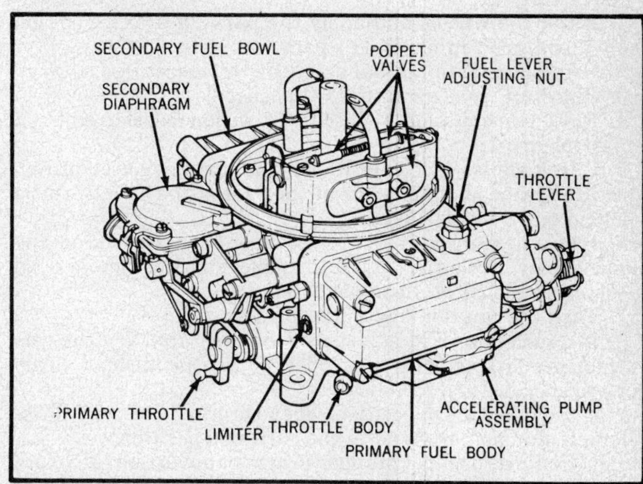

Holley 4 bbl component locations (© Ford Motor Co.)

Idle Fuel Setting Optimum Idle Method

1980–82

NOTE: This alternate method is to be used only when propane enrichment equipment is not available. Remove the air cleaner when necessary to perform adjustments.

1. Bring the engine to normal operation temperature and connect a tachometer.

NOTE: If vehicle is equipped with the Dura Spark II Ignition System, be sure to use a tachometer rated for this type of ignition system.

2. Disconnect the evaorative emission purge hose from the air cleaner.
3. If vehicle is equipped with Thermactor System, revise the dump valve vacuum hoses as follows:
   a. For dump valves with two vacuum fittings, disconnect and plug the hose(s).
   b. For dump valves with one fitting, remove the hose at the dump valve and plug it. Connect a slave hose from the dump valve vacuum fitting to an intake manifold vacuum fitting.
4. Remove the idle mixture limiter.
5. With the transmission in neutral, run the engine at 2500 rpm for 15 seconds.
6. Block the wheels or apply the brake. With the transmission in drive for automatic and neutral for manual, adjust the idle to curb idle rpm plus the optimum idle speed range rpm (if the specified optimum idle speed range is zero rpm, simply adjust to the curb idle rpm).
7. With the transmission in drive for automatic and neutral for manual, adjust the idle mixture screws to the maximum idle rpm, leaving the screws in the leanest position that will maintain this "maximum idle rpm."
8. Repeat Steps 5, 6 and 7 until further adjustment of the idle mixture screws does not increase the idle rpm.
9. If the specified optimum idle speed rpm is zero proceed to Step 11. Otherwise proceed to the next step.
10. With the transmission in drive for automatic and neutral for manual, turn the mixture screws equally in the lean direction until the curb idle rpm is obtained.
11. Install new blue service limiter caps at the maximum rich stops. Check the idle speed to insure that the limiter cap installation did not disturb the setting. Correct if necessary.
12. Turn off the engine, disconnect the tachometer, reinstall the system components, and make sure that the air cleaner attaching nut is tight.

1983 AND LATER 122 CID (2.0L) AND 140 CID (2.3L) ENGINES WITH YFA IV AND YFA IV FB CARBURETORS

1. Block the wheels and apply the parking brake. Position the transmission in neutral or park.
2. Bring engine to normal operating temperature.
3. Place A/C selector in the Off position.
4. Place transmission in specified position as referred to on emissions decal.
5. Check/adjust curb idle RPM. If adjustment is required, turn the hex head adjustment at the rear of the TSP (throttle solenoid positioner) housing.
6. Place the transmission in Neutral or Park. Rev the engine momentarily. Place transmission in specified position and recheck curb idle RPM. Readjust if required.
7. Turn the ignition key to the Off position.
8. If a curb idle RPM adjustment was required and the carburetor is equipped with a dashpot, adjust the dashpot clearance to specification as follows:
   a. Turn key to On position. Open throttle to allow TSP solenoid plunger to extend to the curb idle position.
   b. Collapse dashpot plunger to maximum extent. Measure clearance between tip of plunger and extension pad on throttle vent lever. If required, adjust to specification. Tighten dashpot locknut. Recheck clearance. Turn key to Off position.
9. If curb idle adjustment was required:

Check/adjust the bowl vent setting as follows:
   a. Turn ignition key to the On position to activate the TSP (engine not running). Open throttle to allow the TSP solenoid plunger to extend to the curb idle position.
   b. Secure the choke plate in the wide open position.
   c. Open throttle so that the throttle vent lever does not touch the bowl vent rod. Close the throttle to the idle set position and measure the travel of the fuel bowl vent rod from the open throttle position.
   d. Travel of the bowl vent rod should be within specification (0.100 to 0.150 in.).
   e. If out of specification, bend the throttle vent lever at notch to obtain required travel.

10. Remove all test equipment and reinstall air cleaner assembly. Tighten the holddown bolt to specification.

300 CID (4.4L) ENGINE WITH YFA IV AND YFA IV FB CARBURETOR

1. Block the wheels and apply the parking brake. Position the transmission selector lever in park or neutral.
2. Bring engine to normal operating temperature.
3. Place A/C Heat Selector to Off position.
4. Place transmission in specified gear.
5. Check/adjust curb idle RPM:
   a. TSP-dashpot. Insure that TSP is activated using a $^3/_8$ in. open end wrench, adjust curb idle RPM by rotating the nut directly behind the dashpot housing.
   b. Adjust curb idle RPM by turning the idle RPM speed screw.
   c. Front mounted TSP (Note same as A/C kicker on all other calibrations) insure that TSP is activated. After loosening lock nut, adjust curb idle RPM by rotating TSP solenoid until specified RPM is obtained. Tighten locknut.
6. Check/adjust anti-diesel (TSP-Off). Manually collapse the TSP by rotating the carb throttle shaft lever until the TSP-Off adjusting screw contacts the carburetor body. If adjustment is required, turn the TSP-Off adjusting screw while holding the lever adjustment screw against the stop.
7. Place the transmission in Neutral or Park. Rev the engine momentarily. Place the transmission in specified position and recheck curb idle rpm. Readjust if required.
8. Check/adjust dashpot clearance to 0.120 ± 0.030.
9. If a final curb idle speed adjustment is required, the bowl vent setting must be checked as follows:
   a. Stop the engine and turn the ignition key to the On position, so that the TSP dashpot or TSP is activated but the engine is not running (where applicable). Secure the choke plate in the wide-open position.
   b. Open the throttle, so that the throttle vent lever does not touch the fuel bowl vent rod.
   c. Close the throttle, and measure the travel of the fuel bowl vent rod from the open throttle position. Travel of the fuel bowl vent rod should be within 0.100 to 0.150 in.
   d. If out of specification, bend the throttle vent lever to obtain the required travel.
   e. Remove all test equipment, and tighten the air cleaner holddown bolt to specification.
10. Whenever it is required to adjust engine idle speed by more than 50 rpm, the adjustment screw on the AOD linkage lever at the carburetor should also be readjusted.

173 CID (2.8L), 232 CID (3.8L) & 302 CID (5.0L) ENGINES WITH 2150 2VFB (FEEDBACK) CARBURETOR

1. Set parking brake and block wheels.
2. Put the transmission in Park.
3. Bring the engine to normal operating temperature.

4. Disconnect the electric connector on the EVAP purge solenoid.
5. Disconnect and plug the vacuum hose to the VOTM kicker.
6. Place the transmission in Drive position.
7. Check/adjust curb idle rpm, if adjustment is required:
a. Use the curb idle speed screw.
b. Use the saddle bracket adjusting screw.
8. Place the transmission in Neutral or Park. Rev the engine momentarily. Place the transmission in Drive position and recheck curb idle rpm. Readjust if required.
9. Remove the plug from the vacuum hose to the VOTM kicker and reconnect.
10. Reconnect the electrical connector on the EVAP purge solenoid.

302 CID (5.0L)ENGINE WITH 2150 2V (NON-FEEDBACK) CARBURETOR

1. Set parking brake and block wheels.
2. Place the transmission in Neutral or Park.
3. Bring engine to normal operating temperature.
4. Place A/C Heat selector to Off position.
5. Disconnect and plug vacuum hose to thermactor air bypass valve.
6. Place the transmission in specified gear.
7. Check curb idle rpm. Adjust to specification:
a. Using the curb idle rpm speed screw.
b. Using the saddle bracket adjusting screw.
8. Place the transmission in Neutral or Park. Rev the engine momentarily. Place the transmission in specified position, and recheck curb idle rpm. Readjust if required.
9. Remove plug from vacuum hose to thermactor air bypass valve and reconnect.
10. Whenever it is required to adjust engine idle speed by more than 50 rpm, the adjustment screw on the AOD linkage lever at the carburetor should also be readjusted.

351 CID (5.8L) ENGINE WITH 2150 2V CARBURETOR

1. Block the wheels and apply the parking brake. Position the transmission selector lever in park or neutral.
2. Bring the engine to normal operating temperature.
3. Disconnect purge hose on canister side of evaporator purge solenoid. Check to ensure that purge vacuum is present (solenoid has opened and will require 3- to 5-minute wait after starting engine followed by a short time at part-throttle). Reconnect purge hose.
4. Disconnect and plug the vacuum hose to the VOTM kicker.
5. Place the transmission in specified position.
6. Check/adjust curb idle rpm. If adjustment is required proceed as follows:
a. Use the curb idle speed screw.
b. Use the saddle bracket adjusting screw (ensure curb idle speed screw is not touching throttle shaft lever).
7. Place the transmission in Neutral or Park. Rev the engine momentarily. Place the transmission in specified position and recheck curb idle rpm. Readjust if required.
8. Check/adjust throttle position sensor (TPS).
9. Remove the plug from the vacuum hose to the VOTM kicker and reconnect.
10. Apply a slight pressure on top of the nylon nut located on the accelerator pump to take up the linkage clearance.
11. Turn the nylon nut on the accelerator pump rod clockwise until a 0.010 ± 0.005 clearance is obtained between the top of the accelerator pump and the pump lever.
12. Turn the accelerator pump rod nut one turn counterclockwise to set the lever lash preload.
13. If curb idle adjustment exceeds 50 rpm, adjust automatic transmission TV linkage.

302 CID (5.0L) AND 351 CID (5.8L) ENGINES (CANADA) WITH 2150 2V CARBURETOR

1. Place the transmission in Neutral or Park.
2. Bring engine to normal operating temperature.
3. Place A/C Heat Selector to Off position.
4. Place the transmission in specified gear.
5. Check curb idle rpm. Adjust to specification:
a. Using the curb idle speed screw.
b. Using the hex head on the rear of the solenoid or the saddle bracket adjustment screw.
6. Place the transmission in Neutral or Park. Rev the engine momentarily. Place the transmission in specified position and recheck curb idle rpm. Readjust if required.
7. TSP-Off: With transmission in specified gear, collapse the solenoid plunger, and set specified TSP-Off speed on the speed screw.
8. Disconnect vacuum hose to decel throttle control modulator and plug (if so equipped).
9. Connect a slave vacuum from manifold vacuum to the decel throttle control modulator (if so equipped).
10. Check/adjust decel throttle control rpm. Adjust if necessary.
11. Remove slave vacuum hose.
12. Remove plug from decel throttle control modulator hose and reconnect.

460 CID (7.5L) ENGINE

1. Block the wheels and apply parking brake.
2. Run engine until normal operating temperature is reached.
3. Place the vehicle in Park or Neutral, A/C in Off position, and set parking brake.
4. Remove air cleaner.
5. Disconnect and plug decel throttle control kicker diaphragm vacuum hose.
6. Connect a slave vacuum hose from an engine manifold vacuum source to the decel throttle control kicker.
7. Run engine at approximately 2500 rpm for 15-seconds, then release the throttle.
8. If decel throttle control rpm is not within ± 50 rpm of specification, adjust the kicker.
9. Disconnect the slave vacuum hose and allow engine to return to curb idle.
10. Adjust curb idle, if necessary, using the curb idle adjusting screw.
11. Rev the engine momentarily, recheck curb idle and adjust if necessary.
12. Reconnect the decel throttle control vacuum hose to the diaphragm.
13. Reinstall the air cleaner.

DIESEL ENGINE

NOTE: A special tachometer is required to check engine RPM on a diesel engine.

134 CID (2.2L) ENGINE

1. Block the wheels and apply the parking brake.
2. Start and run engine until the normal operating temperature is reached. Shut off engine.
3. Connect diesel engine tachometer.
4. Start engine and check RPM. Refer to emissions decal for latest specifications. RPM is usually adjusted in Neutral for manual transmissions and Drive for automatic models.
5. The adjustment bolt is located on the bell crank at the top of the injector pump. The upper bolt is for curb idle, the lower for max speed.
6. Loosen the locknut. Turn the adjustment screw clockwise to increase RPM, counter-clockwise to lower the RPM.
7. Tighten the locknut. Increase engine speed several times and recheck idle. Readjust if necessary.

420 CID (6.9L) ENGINE

1. Block the wheels and apply the parking brake.
2. Bring the engine to normal operating temperature. Shut off engine.

3. Connect diesel engine tachometer.

4. Start the engine and check RPM. Refer to the emissions decal for latest specifications. RPM is usually adjusted in Neutral for manual transmissions and Drive for automatic models.

5. Turn the idle speed adjusting screw in the required direction to increase or decrease RPM. The adjusting screw is located on the top of the injector pump above the cold start valve.

6. Place the gear selector in neutral, if automatic, and speed up engine several times. Recheck idle RPM, readjust if necessary.

Carburetor

Removal and Installation

1. Disconnect the negative battery cable. Remove the air cleaner and duct assembly.

2. Remove the throttle cable or rod from the throttle lever. Disconnect the distributor vacuum line, EGR vacuum line, if so equipped, the inline fuel filter and the choke heat tube at the carburetor.

3. Disconnect the choke clean air tube from the air horn. Disconnect the choke actuating cable, if so equipped. Disconnect the electric choke wire at the connector, if so equipped. Disconnect the governor throttle control lines and governor wire connector at the carburetor, if so equipped.

4. Remove the carburetor retaining nuts then remove the carburetor. Remove the carburetor mounting gasket, spacer (if so equipped), and the lower gasket from the intake manifold.

5. Installation is the reverse of the removal procedure. Adjust the carburetor to specification, as required.

Idle Speed Adjustment

1. Start the engine and run it until it reaches operating temperature.

2. If it hasn't already been done, check and adjust the ignition timing. After you have set the timing, turn off the engine.

3. Attach a tachometer to the engine.

4. Turn the headlights on to high beam.

5. On vehicles with manual transmissions, engage the parking brake and place the transmission in Neutral. On vehicles equipped with automatic transmission, engage the parking brake, and place the gear selector in Drive. Block the wheels.

6. Make sure that the choke plate is in the fully open position.

7. Adjust the engine curb idle rpm to the proper specifications. The tachometer reading must be taken with the carburetor air cleaner in place. If it is impossible to make the adjustment with the air cleaner in position, remove it and make the adjustment. Then replace the air cleaner and check the tachometer for the proper rpm reading.

On carburetors equipped with a solenoid throttle positioner, loosen the jam nut on the solenoid at the bracket and rotate the solenoid in or out to obtain the specified curb idle rpm. Disconnect the solenoid lead wire at the connector, set the automatic transmission in Neutral, then adjust the carburetor throttle stop screw to obtain 500 rpm. Connect the solenoid lead wire and open the throttle slightly by hand. The solenoid plunger will follow the throttle lever and remain in the fully extended position as long as the ignition is on and the solenoid energized.

Air Intake Throttle Body

Fuel Injection

Removal and Installation

1. Disconnect the air intake hose.

2. Disconnect the throttle position sensor and air by-pass valve connectors.

3. Remove the four throttle body mounting nuts and carefully separate the air throttle body from the upper intake manifold.

4. Remove and discard the mounting gasket. Clean all mounting surfaces using care not to damage the gasket surfaces of the throttle body and manifold. Do not allow any material to drop into the intake manifold.

5. Install the throttle body in the reverse order of removal. The mounting nuts are tightened to 12–15 ft. lbs.

Fuel Supply Manifold

Removal and Installation

1. Remove the gas tank fill cap. Relieve fuel system pressure by locating and disconnecting the electrical connection to either the fuel pump relay, the inertia switch or the in-line high pressure fuel pump. Crank the engine for about ten seconds. If the engine starts, crank for an additional five seconds after the engine stalls. Reconnect the connector. Disconnect the negative battery cable. Remove the upper intake manifold assembly.

NOTE: Special tool T81P-19623-G or equivalent is necessary to release the garter springs that secure the fuel line/hose connections.

2. Disconnect the fuel crossover hose from the fuel supply manifold. Disconnect the fuel supply and return line connections at the fuel supply manifold.

3. Remove the two fuel supply manifold retaining bolts. Carefully disengage the manifold from the fuel injectors and remove the manifold.

4. When installing: Make sure the injector caps are clean and free of contamination. Place the fuel supply manifold over each injector and seat the injectors into the manifold. Make sure the caps are seated firmly.

5. Torque the fuel supply manifold retaining bolts to 15–22 ft. lbs. Install the remaining components in the reverse order of removal.

NOTE: Fuel injectors may be serviced after the fuel supply manifold is removed. Grasp the injector and pull up on it while gently rocking injector from side to side. Inspect the mounting O-rings and replace any that show deterioration.

Fuel Pump

MECHANICAL FUEL PUMP

Testing

Install a new filter element before making the following tests. Tests are made with the fuel pump installed on the engine, with the engine warmed up to normal operating temperature, and with the engine idling at proper idle speed.

1. Remove air cleaner assembly and disconnect fuel inlet line at the carburetor.

CAUTION

Avoid fuel spillage due to risk of fire.

2. Connect pressure gauge and fitting, flexible hose and restrictor clamp.

3. Operate engine at idle speed. Momentarily open restrictor clamp to bleed system of air.

4. Close restrictor and note reading after pressure has stabilized. See Tune-Up Specifications at the beginning of this section for correct fuel pump pressure. If pressure is below specified value, fuel pump must be replaced or rebuilt.

5. If fuel pump is producing correct pressure, leave engine idling and proceed with volume test.

6. Open restrictor clamp and note time required to expell

one pint into the container. It should take no more than 30 seconds.

7. If it takes more than 30 seconds, check for restriction in the fuel line from the tank by connecting pump to an external fuel source. If the volume test still takes more than 30 seconds per pint, then the fuel pump must be replaced.

ELECTRIC FUEL PUMP

Testing

1. Remove air filter and disconnect the fuel inlet line at the carburetor.
2. Using $^1/_4$ in. pipe fittings (smaller diameter will restrict the flow), connect the pressure gauge, gate valve and flexible hose. Use a suitable container to collect expelled fuel.
3. Operate fuel pump with primer switch.

NOTE: Be sure the battery is fully charged.

Adjust gate valve for a reading of 2 psi, then note time required to expell 1 quart of fuel.

4. If the time required to expell one quart exceeds that specified in the table below, repeat the same test at the outlet at the tank to establish whether or not there is restriction in the fuel line.

Engine	Time (Sec.)
330	40
359/361	37
389/391	34
475	36
477	33
534	30

5. If the fuel pump does not fill the quart container fast enough, the pump must be replaced as a unit.
6. Remove test equipment, connect fuel line and install air cleaner.

MECHANICAL FUEL PUMP

Removal and Installation

1. Disconnect the negative battery cable. Remove all necessary components in order to gain access to the fuel pump mounting bolts.
2. Disconnect inlet and outlet lines from the pump. Remove pump mounting bolts and remove pump and gasket. Discard gasket.
3. To install, clean away all gasket material from mounting pad and pump flange. Apply sealant to new gasket and threads of bolts.
4. Position pump and gasket on the mounting pad, being sure the rocker arm is riding on the cam eccentric. Turn engine over until eccentric is on low side of stroke.
5. Install mounting bolts and tighten securely.
6. Connect fuel lines.
7. Operate engine and check for leaks.

Electric Fuel Pump

Two electric pumps are used on injected models; a low pressure boost pump mounted in the gas tank and a high pressure pump mounted on the vehicle frame. Models equipped with the 7.5L engine use a single low pressure pump mounted in the gas tank. On injected models the low pressure pump is used to provide pressurized fuel to the inlet of the high pressure pump and helps prevent noise and heating problems. The externally

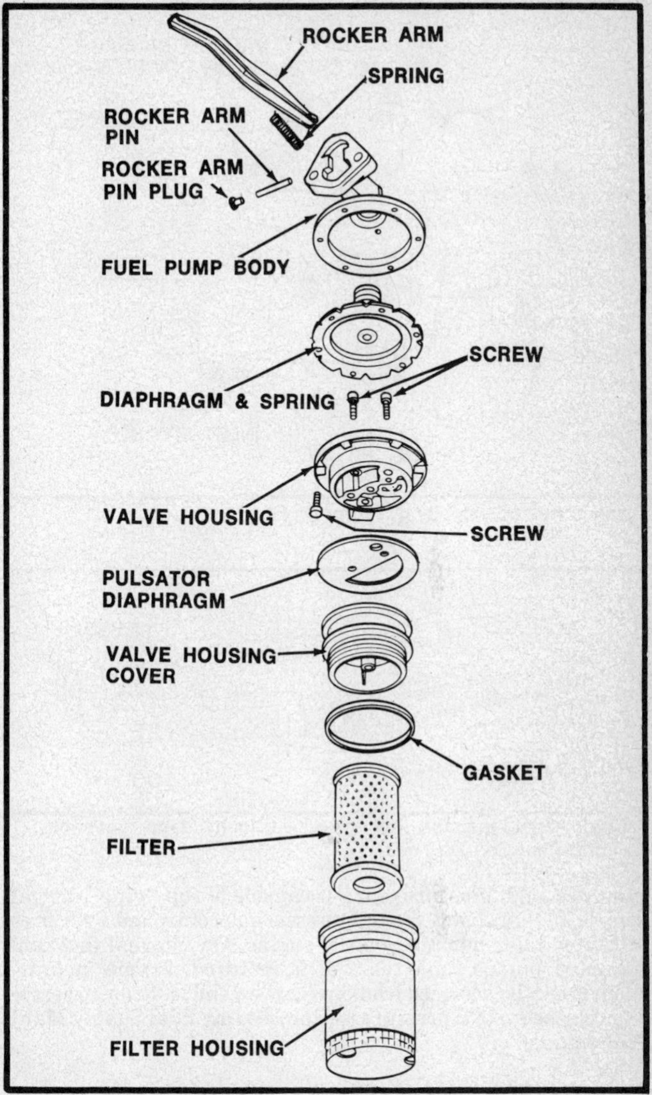

Typical mechanical fuel pump (© Ford Motor Co.)

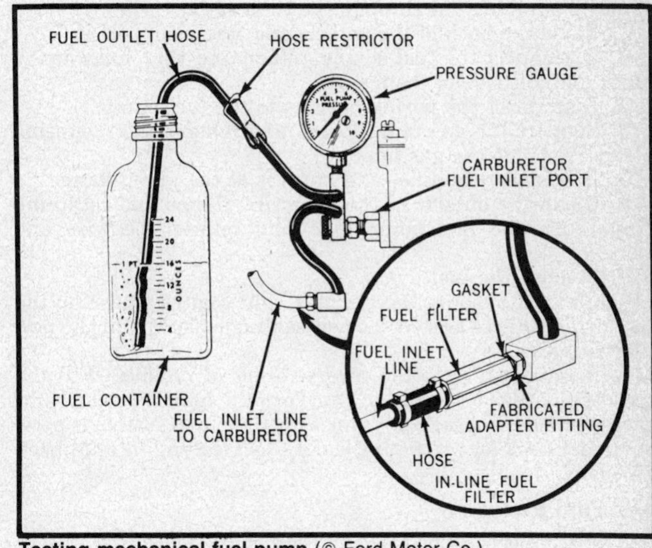

Testing mechanical fuel pump (© Ford Motor Co.)

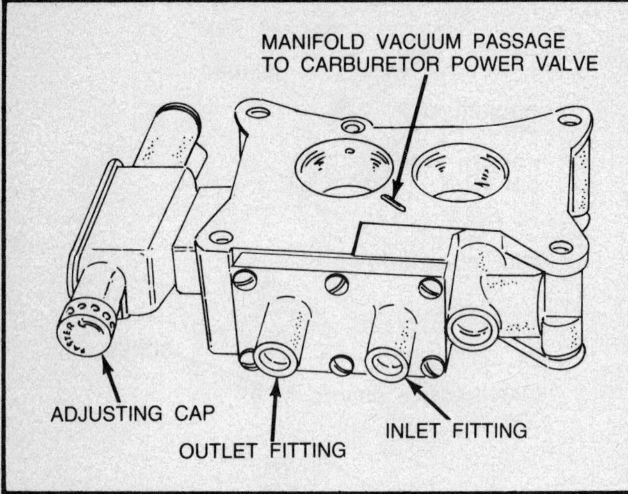

Coolant heated velocity governor (© Ford Motor Co.)

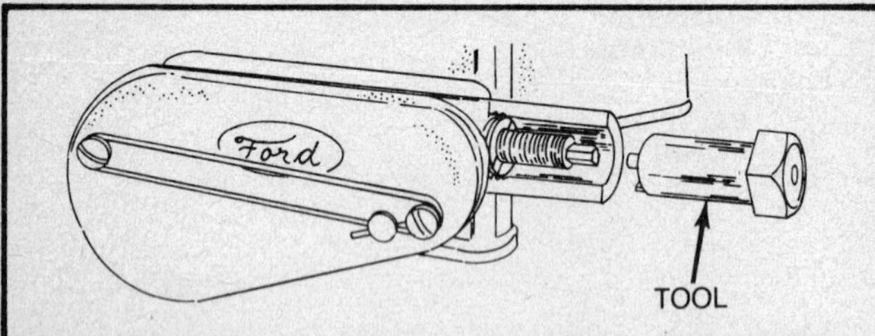

Altitude compensation adjustment—velocity type govenor (© Ford Motor Co.)

mounted high pressure pump is capable of supplying 15.9 gallons of fuel an hour. System pressure is controlled by a pressure regulator mounted on the engine. On internal fuel tank mounted pumps tank removal is required. Frame mounted models can be accessed from under the vehicle. Prior to servicing release system pressure (see proceeding Fuel Supply Manifold details).

Removal and Installation

IN-TANK PUMP

1. Disconnect the negative battery cable.
2. Depressurize the system and drain as much gas from the tank by pumping out through the filler neck.
3. Raise the back of the vehicle and safely support it.
4. Disconnect the fuel supply, return and vent lines at the right and left side of the frame.
5. Disconnect the wiring harness to the fuel pump.
6. Support the gas tank, loosen and remove the mounting straps. Remove the gas tank.
7. Disconnect the lines and harness at the pump flange.
8. Clean the outside of the mounting flange and retaining ring. Turn the fuel pump lock ring counterclockwise and remove.
9. Remove the fuel pump.
10. Clean the mount faces. Put a light coat of grease on the mounting sufaces and on the new sealing ring. Install the new fuel pump.
11. Installation is in the reverse order of removal. Fill the tank with at least 10 gals. of gas. Turn the ignition key ON for three seconds. Repeat 6 or 7 times until the fuel system is pressurized. Check for any fitting leaks. Start the engine and check for leaks.

External Pump

1. Disconnect the negative battery cable.
2. Depressurize the fuel system.
3. Raise and support the rear of the vehicle safely.
4. Disconnect the inlet and outlet fuel lines.
5. Remove the pump from the mounting bracket.
7. Install in reverse order, make sure the pump is indexed correctly in the mounting bracket insulator.

"Quick-Connect" Line Fittings

Removal and Installation

NOTE: "Quick-Connect" (push) type fittings must be disconnected using proper procedures or the fitting may be damaged. Two types of retainers are used on the push connect fittings. Line sizes of $^3/_8$ in. and $^5/_{16}$ in. use a "hairpin" clip retainer. $^1/_4$ line connectors use a "duck bill" clip retainer.

Hairpin Clip

1. Clean all dirt and/or grease from the fitting. Spread the two clip legs about an $^1/_8$ inch each to disengage from the fitting and pull the clip outward from the fitting. Use finger pressure only, do not use any tools.
2. Grasp the fitting and hose assembly and pull away from the steel line. Twist the fitting and hose assembly slightly while pulling, if necessary, when a sticking condition exists.
3. Inspect the hairpin clip for damage, replace the clip if necessary. Reinstall the clip in position on the fitting.
4. Inspect the fitting and inside of the connector to insure freedom of dirt or obstruction. Install fitting into the connector and push together. A click will be heard when the hairpin snaps into proper connection. Pull on the line to insure full engagement.

Duck Bill Clip

1. A special tool is available from Ford for removing the retaining clips (Ford Tool No. T82L-9500-AH). If the tool is not on hand see Step 2. Align the slot on the push connector disconnect tool with either tab on the retaining clip. Pull the line from the connector.
2. If the special clip tool is not available, use a pair of narrow 6 in. channel lock pliers with a jaw width of 0.2 in. or less. Align the jaws of the pliers with the openings of the fitting case and compress the part of the retaining clip that engages the case. Compressing the retaining clip will release the fitting which may be pulled from the connector. Both sides of the clip must be compressed at the same time to disengage.
3. Inspect the retaining clip, fitting end and connector. Replace the clip if any damage is apparent.
4. Push the line into the steel connector until a click is heard, indicting the clip is in place. Pull on the line to check engagement.

Governors

VELOCITY GOVERNORS

Adjustment

1. Connect a tachometer to the engine, warm up the engine then read engine rpm at wide-open throttle. If governed speed is not within the range stamped on the governor plate, adjustment is required.
2. Remove the governor seal.
3. To increase rpm, turn the cap counterclockwise; to decrease the rpm turn it clockwise.
4. If the vehicle is to be operated at a consistent altitude, cut the seal wire and remove the adjusting cap. Do not rotate the cap during removal. Use a mirror and light to observe the position of the slots in the adjusting bushing. Do not disturb the center post or adjusting bushing. If the tool does not engage the

slots easily, remove the tool and realign it. For an increase in the average altitude of operation rotate the inserted tool the amount specified in the table below in the counterclockwise direction.

a. 60° or 1/6 turn rotation is equivalent to one flat of the tool hex head.

5. Remove tool and install cap, but do not turn the adjusting cap.

6. Install a tachometer and check and adjust the no-load setting. It should be 3900 for no-load at altitude and 3600 for load at altitude. Load and no-load speed should be slightly above these speeds if the governor is being adjusted above anticipated operating altitude and slightly below if it is being adjusted below anticipated operating altitude.

7. If load rpm is below 3600 rpm at operating altitude, repeat Step 4 turning the tool counterclockwise. If load governed speed is above 3600 rpm, repeat Step 4 turning the tool clockwise.

8. Seal adjusting cap to the governor body using service governor seal wire.

9. If the engine is to be operated at varying altitudes, adjust the governor for 3800 rpm no-load for sea-level. Using the adjusting cap only, adjust the no-load speed for 4100 rpm at the anticipated altitude by turning the adjustment cap 1/4 turn (clockwise) for each 1000;pr difference between the adjusting and anticipated altitudes. If the maximum operating altitude of the vehicle is lower than the altitude at which the adjustment is being made, adjust the no-load speed to 4100 rpm with the adjusting cap.

Aver. Operating Altitude—Feet	Amount of Tool Rotation
2000	1/3 turn (120°)
3000	1/2 turn (180°)
4000	2/3 turn (240°)
5000	5/6 turn (300°)
6000	1 turn (360°)

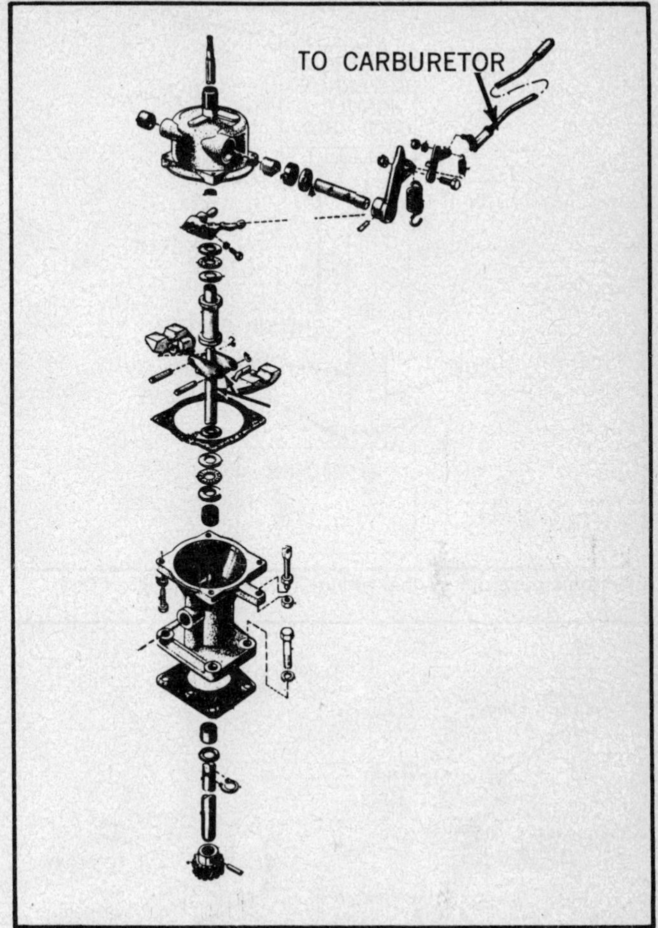

Mechanical governor (© Ford Motor Co.)

VACUUM GOVERNOR

Adjustment

1. Warm up the engine until normal operating temperature is reached, then connect a tachometer.
2. Momentarily operate engine at wide-open throttle (governed speed) and note rpm reading.
3. If governed speed is not at the correct value, turn off the ignition switch and remove adjusting hole cover from the controlling unit (distributor).
4. Crank engine by hand until adjusting nut is aligned with access hole.
5. Turn adjusting nut clockwise to increase speed and counterclockwise to decrease speed. One full turn equals about 150 rpm.
6. Repeat above procedure until proper governed speed is obtained.
7. Install adjusting access hole cover and tighten securely.
8. Install new locking wire and lead seal.

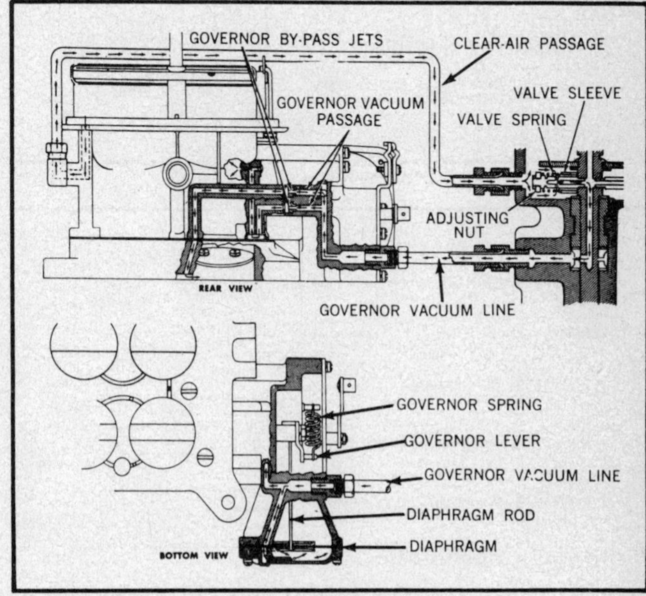

Vacuum governor system (© Ford Motor Co.)

MECHANICAL GOVERNOR

Adjustment

1. Disconnect the throttle control rod at the carburetor.
2. Loosen the top nut on the primary spring adjusting eye bolt.
3. Tighten the bottom nut finger tight, then turn it in two additional turns to pre-load the spring. Tighten the top nut.
4. Move the throttle to the wide open position and connect the governor throttle control rod to the carburetor control arm.
5. Adjust the governor throttle control rod so that the gover-

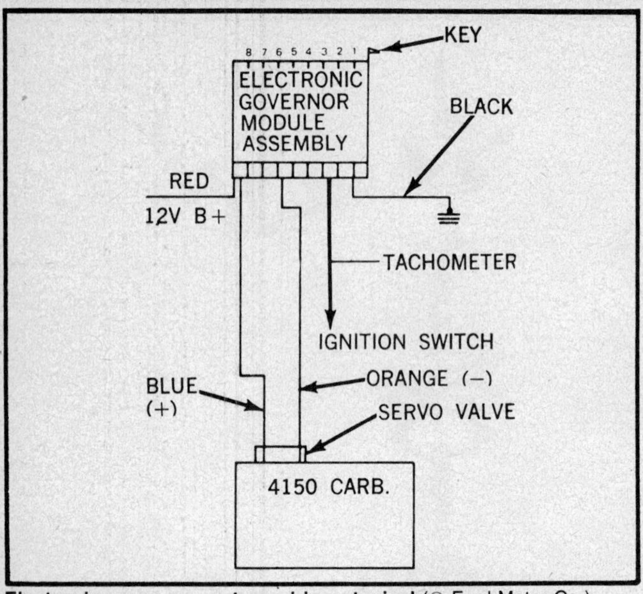

Electronic governor system wiring—typical (© Ford Motor Co.)

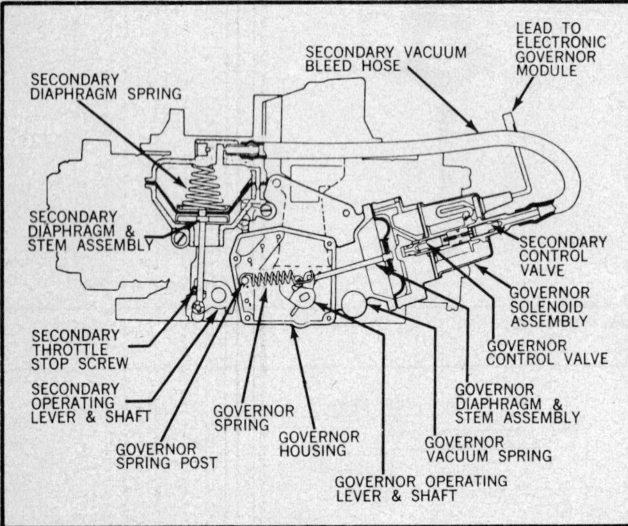

Typical electronic governor system (

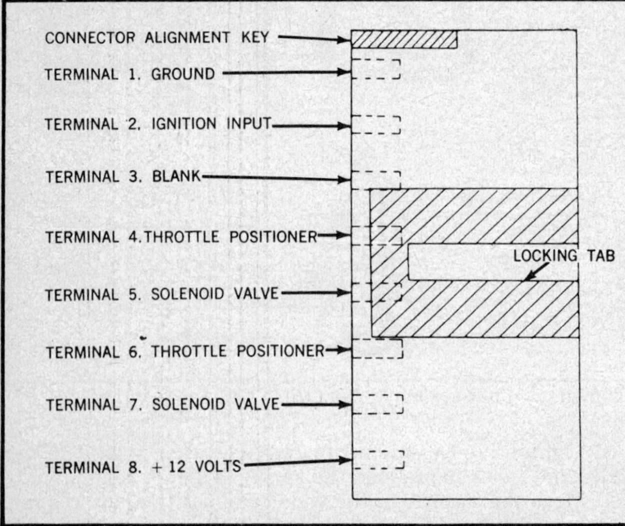

Electronic governor module edge connector (© Ford Motor Co.)

nor throttle control auxiliary lever is full forward, then back off (shorten) the rod one full turn.

6. Check the throttle linkage to be sure that the throttle is wide open when pedal is depressed to the floor. Be sure the rod or cable is attached to the proper hole in the throttle lever.

7. Check operation of choke plate for proper adjustment. On C- and W-Series vehicles the choke plate does not completely close when the dash knob is fully out.

8. To adjust speed, operate the engine (parking brake on) until normal operating temperature is reached. With throttle wide open, adjust main spring (higher tension increases rpm and lower tension decreases rpm). Sensitivity of the governor can be sharpened by installing the governor spring in the hole closest to the lower arm pivot. Adjust governed speed after changing spring position.

ELECTRONIC GOVERNOR CONTROL

The function of the electronic governor control system is to limit engine speed to a predetermined maximum and still allow full power output upon demand close to governed speed. The governor mechanism on the carburetor utilizes engine vacuum to provide the actuating force to modulate throttles, and precise control of the system is achieved by regulating governor and secondary diaphragm vacuum levels with a solenoid valve actuated by an electronic control unit.

The electronic control governor system is composed of an electronic governor module (EGM) and a carburetor control subsystem.

The following checks should be made initially in response to any complaint about governor operation:

NOTE: It is important that the electronic governor module receives 12 volts across pins 1 and 8 of the edge connector. Pin 2 of the edge connector is an ignition input from the negative primary side of the ignition cell. Pins 5 and 7 of the edge connector are a square wave output to the carburetor mounted vacuum solenoid.

1. Check throttle linkage and carburetor primary throttle plates to confirm proper idle position (closed throttles) and proper wide open position.

2. Check carburetor hose from governor solenoid assembly to secondary diaphragm housing for proper attachment and leaks.

3. Check governor solenoid and cover assembly attachment to governor housing (4 screws) for secure assembly.

4. Check secondary operating lever and shaft assembly to ensure that it's properly connected and operating freely.

5. Check electrical connections for breaks or loose wires at harness-to-EGM junction and also at harness-to-carburetor "pigtail" junction.

Diesel Fuel System

INJECTOR TIMING

134 CID (2.2L) Engine

NOTE: Special Tools Ford 14–0303, Static Timing Gauge Adapter and D82L4201A, Metric Dial Indicator, or the equivalents are necessary to set or check the injector timing.

1. Disconnect both battery ground cables. Remove the air inlet hose from the air cleaner and intake manifold.

2. Remove the distributor head plug bolt and washer from the injection pump.

3. Install the Timing Gauge Adapter and Metric Dial Indicator so that the indicator pointer is in contact with the injector pump plunger and gauge reads approximately (0.08 in.).

4. Align the 2° ATDC (after top dead center) on the crankshaft pulley with the indicator on the timing case cover.

5. Slowly turn the engine counterclockwise until the dial indicator pointer stops moving (approximately 30°–50°).
6. Adjust the dial indicator to 0 (Zero). Confirm that the dial indicator does not move from Zero, by rotating the crankshaft slightly right and left.
7. Turn the crankshaft clockwise until the timing mark aligns with the cover indicator. The dial indicator should read 1, plus or minus 0.0008 inch). If the reading is not within specifications, adjust the timing as follows: Loosen the injection pump mounting nuts and bolts. Rotate the injection pump counterclockwise (reverse direction of engine rotation) past the correct timing position, then clockwise until the timing is correct. This procedure will eliminate gear backlash. Repeat Steps 5, 6, and 7 to check that the timing is properly adjusted.
8. Remove the dial indicator and adapter. Install the injector head gasket and plug. Install all removed parts.
9. Run engine, check and adjust idle RPM. Check for fuel leaks.

420 CID (6.9L) Engine

NOTE: Special equipment, a Dynamic Timing Meter, Ford D83T-6002-A or the equivalent is necessary to set or check the "dynamic" injection timing. Both static and dynamic methods follow.

STATIC TIMING

1. Loosen the injection pump to mounting nuts.
2. Rotate the injection pump to bring the mark on the pump into alignment with the mark on pump mounting adapter.
3. Visually recheck the alignment of the timing marks and tighten injection pump mounting nuts.

DYNAMIC TIMING

1. Bring the engine up to normal operating temperature.
2. Stop the engine and install a dynamic timing meter, Rotunda- 78-0100 or equivalent, by placing the magnetic probe pick-up into the probe hole.
3. Remove the No.1 glow plug wire and remove the glow plug, install luminosity probe and tighten to 12 ft. lbs. Install the photocell over the probe.
4. Connect a dynamic timing meter to the battery and adjust the offset of the meter.
5. Set the transmission in neutral and raise the rear wheels off the ground. Using Rotunda- 14-0302, throttle control, set the engine speed to 1400 rpm with no accessory load. Observe the injection timing on the dynamic timing meter.
6. If dynamic timing is not within ± 2° of specification, then injection pump timing will require adjustment.
7. Turn the engine off. Note the timing mark alignment. Loosen the injection pump-to-adapter nuts.
8. Rotate the injection pump clockwise (when viewed from the front of engine) to retard and counter-clockwise to advance timing. Two degrees of dynamic timing is approximately 0.030 inch of timing mark movement.
9. Start the engine and recheck the timing. If the timing is not within ± 1° of specification, repeat Steps 7 through 9.
10. Turn off the engine. Remove the dynamic timing equipment. Lightly coat the glow plug threads with anti-seize compound, install the glow plug and tighten to 12 ft. lbs. Connect the glow plug wires.

Water Separator

Servicing

134 CID (2.2L) ENGINE

Water should be drained from the fuel sedimenter whenever the warning light comes on or every 5,000 miles. More frequent drain intervals may be required depending on fuel quality and vehicle usage.

The instrument panel warning lamp (WATER IN FUEL) will glow when approximately 0.53 quarts of water has accumulated in the sedimenter. When the warning lamp glows, shut off the engine as soon as safely possible. A suitable drain pan or container should be placed under the sedimenter, which is mounted inside the frame rail, underneath the driver's side of the cab. To drain the fuel sedimenter, pull up on the T-handle (located on the cab floor behind the driver's seat) until resistance is felt. Turn the ignition switch to the On position, so the warning lamp glows and hold T-handle up for approximately 45 seconds after lamp goes out.

To stop draining fuel, release T-handle and inspect sedimenter to verify that draining has stopped. Discard drained fluid suitably.

420 CID (6.9L) ENGINE

The 6.9L diesel engine is equipped with a fuel/water separator in the fuel supply line. A "Water in Fuel" indicator light is provided on the instrument panel to alert the operator. The light should glow when the ignition switch is in the START position to indicate proper light and water sensor function. If the light glows continuously while the engine is running, the water must be drained from the separator as soon as practical to prevent damage to the fuel injection system.

F SERIES

1. Stop the vehicle and shut off the engine.

NOTE: Failure to shut off engine prior to draining separator will cause air to enter the fuel system.

2. Unscrew the vent $2\frac{1}{2}$ to 3 turns. The vent is located on the top center of the fuel/water separator unit.
3. Unscrew the water drain located on the bottom of the fuel/water separator $1\frac{1}{2}$ to 2 turns and drain water. Use an appropriate container.
4. After water is completely drained, close the water drain fingertight.
5. Tighten the vent until snug, then turn it an additional $\frac{1}{4}$ turn.
6. Restart the engine and check "Water in Fuel" indicator light. The light should not glow. If it continues to glow, have fuel system checked and repaired.

E SERIES

1. Stop the vehicle and shut Off the engine.
2. Locate the water/fuel separator drain cable knob, attached to the upper cowl flange on the left side of the vehicle, under the hood.
3. Place an approved container under the separator; which is accessible behind the left front wheel.
4. Pull the knob out and hold for 45 seconds.
5. Release knob and remove container.
6. Restart the engine and check "Water in Fuel" indicator lamp. The lamp should not be lit. If it continues to stay lit, have fuel system checked and repaired. The electrical sensor is the only replaceable item on the water/fuel separator. This assembly is threaded into the top of the separator. The remainder of the water/fuel separator is serviced as a complete unit.

NOTE: When draining the water/fuel separator, the water must be drained into an approved container.

INJECTION PUMP

Removal and Installation

134 CID (2.2L) ENGINE

1. Disconnect battery ground cables from both batteries.
2. Remove radiator fan and shroud. Loosen and remove A/C compressor/power steering pump drive belt and idler pulley, if so equipped. Remove injection pump drive gear cover and gasket.
3. Rotate engine until injection pump drive gear keyway is at TDC.

4. Remove large nut and washer attaching drive gear to injection pump.

NOTE: Care should be taken not to drop washer into timing gear case.

5. Disconnect intake hose from air cleaner and intake manifold.
6. Disconnect throttle cable and speed control cable, if so equipped.
7. Disconnect and cap fuel inlet line at injection pump.
8. Disconnect fuel shut-off solenoid lead at injection pump.
9. Disconnect and remove fuel injection lines from nozzles and injection pump. Cap all fuel lines and fittings.
10. Disconnect lower fuel return line from injection pump and fuel hoses. Loosen lower No.3 intake port nut and remove fuel return line.
11. Remove two nuts attaching injection pump to front timing gear cover and one bolt attaching pump to rear support bracket.
12. Install Gear and Hub Remover, Tool T83T-6306-A or equivalent, in drive gear cover and attach to injection pump drive gear. Rotate screw clockwise until injection pump disengages from drive gear. Remove the injection pump.

NOTE: Carefully remove injection pump to avoid dropping key into timing gear case. Disconnect cold start cable before removing injection pump from vehicle. Connect cold start cable to pump before positioning injection pump in timing gear case.

13. Install injection pump in position in timing gear case aligning key with keyway in drive gear in TDC position.

NOTE: Use care to avoid dropping key in timing gear case.

14. Install nuts and washers attaching injection pump to timing gear case and tighten to draw injection pump into position.

NOTE: Do not tighten to specification at this time.

15. Install bolt attaching injection pump to rear support. Install washer and nut attaching injection drive gear to injection pump and tighten.
16. Install injection pump drive gear cover, with new gasket, on timing gear case cover and tighten.
17. Adjust injection timing at this time.
18. Install lower fuel return line to injection pump and intake manifold stud. Tighten Banjo bolt on injection pump and nut on intake manifold. Install connecting fuel hoses and clamps. Install fuel injection lines to injection pump and nozzles and tighten.
19. Connect lead to fuel shut-off solenoid on injection pump. Connect fuel inlet line to injection pump and install hose clamp.
20. Install throttle cable and speed control cable, if so equipped.
21. Air bleed fuel system.
22. Install intake hose on air cleaner and intake manifold.
23. Install A/C compressor/power steering pump drive belt and idler pulley, if so equipped and tighten.
24. Install radiator shroud and radiator fan.
25. Connect battery ground cables to both batteries.
26. Run engine and check for oil and fuel leaks.

420 CID (6.9L) ENGINE

NOTE: Before removing any fuel lines, clean exterior with clean fuel oil or solvent to prevent entry of dirt into engine when fuel lines are removed.

CAUTION

Do not wash or steam clean engine while engine is running. Serious damage to injection pump could occur.

1. Disconnect battery ground cables from both batteries.
2. Remove engine oil filter neck.
3. Remove bolts attaching injection pump to drive gear.
4. Disconnect electrical connectors to injection pump.
5. Disconnect accelerator cable and speed control cable from throttle lever, if so equipped.
6. Remove air cleaner and install intake opening cover.
7. Remove accelerator cable bracket, with cables attached, from intake manifold and position out of the way.

NOTE: All fuel lines and fittings must be capped, to prevent fuel contamination.

8. Remove fuel filter-to-injection pump fuel line and cap fittings.
9. Remove and cap injection pump inlet elbow.
10. Remove and cap injection pump fitting adapter.
11. Remove fuel return line on injection pump, rotate out of the way, and cap all fittings.

NOTE: It is not necessary to remove injection lines from injection pump to remove injection pump. If lines are to be removed, loosen injection line fittings at injection pump before removing it from engine.

12. Remove fuel injection lines from nozzles and cap lines and nozzles.
13. Remove three nuts attaching injection pump to injection pump adapter.
14. If injection pump is to be replaced, loosen injection line retaining clips and injection nozzle fuel lines and cap all fittings. Do not install injection nozzle fuel lines until new pump is installed in engine.
15. Lift injection pump, with nozzle lines attached, up and out of engine compartment.
16. Install new O-ring on drive gear end of injection pump.
17. Move injection pump down and into position.
18. Position alignment dowel on injection pump into alignment hole on drive gear.
19. Install bolts attaching injection pump to drive gear and tighten.
20. Install nuts attaching injection pump to adapter. Align scribe lines on injection pump flange and injection pump adapter and tighten to 14 ft. lbs.
21. If injection nozzle fuel lines were removed from injection pump install at this time.
22. Remove caps from nozzles and fuel lines and install fuel line nuts on nozzles and tighten to 22 ft. lbs.
23. Connect fuel return line to injection pump.
24. Install injection pump fitting adapter with a new O-ring.
25. Clean old sealant from injection pump elbow threads, using clean solvent, and dry thoroughly. Apply a light coating of pipe sealant on elbow threads.
26. Install elbow in injection pump adapter and tighten to a minimum of 6 ft. lbs. Then tighten further, if necessary, to align elbow with injection pump fuel inlet line, but do not exceed 360° of rotation or 10 ft. lbs.
27. Remove caps and connect fuel filter-to-injection pump fuel line.
28. Install accelerator cable bracket to intake manifold.
29. Remove intake manifold cover and install air cleaner.
30. Connect accelerator and speed control cable, if so equipped, to throttle lever.
31. Install electrical connectors on injection pump.
32. Clean injection pump adapter and oil filler neck sealing surfaces.
33. Apply a $\frac{1}{8}$ inch bead of RTV Sealant on adapter housing.
34. Install oil filter neck and tighten.
35. Connect battery ground cables to both batteries. Run engine and check for fuel leaks.
36. If necessary, purge high pressure fuel lines of air by loosening connector one half to one turn and cranking engine until solid fuel, free from bubbles flows from connection.

CAUTION

Keep eyes and hands away from nozzle spray. Fuel spraying from the nozzle under high pressure can penetrate the skin and cause infection. Medical attention should be provided immediately in the event of skin penetration.

37. Check and adjust injection pump timing.

INJECTORS

Removal and Installation

134 CID (2.2L) ENGINE

1. Disconnect battery ground cables from both batteries.
2. Disconnect and remove injection lines from nozzles and injection pump. Cap all lines and fittings.
3. Remove fuel return line and gaskets.
4. Remove bolts attaching fuel line heater clamp to cylinder head and position heater out of the way.
5. Remove nozzles, using a 27mm deepwell socket.
6. Remove nozzle washer (copper) and nozzle gasket (steel), using Tool T71-P-19703-C or equivalent.
7. Clean nozzle assemblies with Nozzle Cleaning Kit, Rotunda 14-0301 or equivalent, and a suitable solvent, and dry thoroughly. Clean nozzle seats in cylinder head with Nozzle Seat Cleaner, T83T-9527-B or equivalant.
8. Position new nozzle washers and gaskets in nozzle seats, install nozzles and tighten.

NOTE: Install nozzle gaskets with blue side face up (toward nozzle).

9. Position fuel line heater clamps, install attaching bolts, and tighten to specification.
10. Install fuel return line with new gaskets on nozzles.
11. Install injection lines on nozzles and injection pump and tighten line nuts.
12. Connect battery ground cables to both batteries. Run engine and check for fuel leaks.

420 CID (6.9L) ENGINE

NOTE: Before removing nozzle assemblies, clean exterior of each nozzle assembly and the surrounding area with clean fuel oil or solvent to prevent entry of dirt into engine when nozzle assemblies are removed. Also, clean fuel inlet and fuel leak-off piping connections. Blow dry with compressed air.

1. Remove fuel line retaining clamp(s) from effected nozzle line(s).
2. Disconnect nozzle fuel inlet (high pressure) and fuel leak-off tees from each nozzle assembly and position out of the way. Cover open ends of fuel inlet lines and nozzles to prevent entry of dirt.
3. Remove injection nozzles by turning counterclockwise. Pull nozzle assembly with copper washer from engine. Be careful not to strike nozzle tip against any hard surface during removal. Cover nozzle assembly fuel inlet opening and nozzle tip with plastic cap to prevent entry of dirt.

NOTE: Remove copper injector nozzle gasket from nozzle bore with Tool T71P-19703-C, or equivalent, if not attached to nozzle tip.

4. Place nozzle assemblies in a fabricated holder as they are removed from the heads. The holder should be marked with numbers corresponding to the cylinder numbering of the engine. Use of this holder permits replacing nozzles in their respective ports in the cylinder heads.
5. Thoroughly clean nozzle bore in cylinder head before reinserting nozzle assembly with nozzle seat cleaner, Tool T83T-9527-A or equivalent. Pay particular attention to seating surface, in order that no small particles of metal or carbon will cause assembly to be cocked or permit blow-by of combustion gases. Blow out particles with compressed air.
6. Remove protective cap and install a new copper gasket on nozzle assembly, with a small dab of grease.

NOTE: Anti-Seize Compound or equivalent should be used on nozzle threads to aid installation and future removal.

7. Install nozzle assembly into cylinder head nozzle bore. Be careful that nozzle tip does not strike against recess wall.
8. Tighten nozzle assembly.
9. Remove protective caps from nozzle assemblies and fuel lines. Install leak-off tees to nozzle assembly.

NOTE: Install two new O-ring seals for each fuel return tee.

10. Connect high pressure fuel line and tighten.
11. Install fuel line retainer clamp(s), and tighten.
12. Start engine.
13. If necessary, purge high pressure fuel lines of air by loosening connector one half to one turn and cranking engine until solid fuel, free from bubbles flows from connection.

CAUTION

Keep eyes and hands away from nozzle spray. Fuel spraying from the nozzle under high pressure can penetrate the skin and cause infection. Medical attention should be provided immediately in the event of skin penetration.

14. Check for fuel leakage at high pressure connections.

Testing

Where ideal conditions of good combustion, specified engine temperature control and absolutely clean fuel prevail, nozzles require little attention. Nozzle trouble is usually indicated by one or more of the following symptoms:

1. Smoky exhaust (black)
2. Loss of power
3. Misfiring
4. Increased fuel consumption
5. Combustion knock
6. Engine overheating

Where faulty nozzle operation is suspected on an engine that is misfiring or puffing black smoke, a simple test can be made to determine which cylinder is causing the difficulty.

With the engine running at a speed that makes the problem most pronounced, momentarily loosen the high pressure fuel inlet line connection on one nozzle assembly sufficiently to "cut-out" the cylinder (one half to one turn) to leak off the fuel charge to the cylinder. Then tighten to specifications.

Check each cylinder in the same manner. If one is found where loosening makes no difference in the irregular operature or causes puffing black smoke to stop, the injection nozzle for the cylinder should be serviced or replaced.

CAUTION

Keep eyes and hands away from nozzle spray. Fuel spraying from the nozzle under high pressure can penetrate the skin and cause infection. Medical attention should be provided immediately in the event of skin penetration.

FUEL CONTROL

On-off fuel control is provided by an electric solenoid located in the diesel injection pump housing cover. Current is supplied to the solenoid when the ignition switch is turned on. If no fuel is supplied with the ignition switch in the on position, check for current at the solenoid terminal before condemning the solenoid.

FUEL CUT OFF SOLENOID

Removal and Installation

1. Disconnect battery ground cables from both batteries.
2. Remove connector from fuel cut-off solenoid.
3. Remove fuel cut-off solenoid assembly.
4. Install fuel cut-off solenoid, with new O-ring and tighten.
5. Install connector on fuel cut-off solenoid.
6. Connect battery ground cables to both batteries. Run engine and check for fuel leaks.

Glow Plug System

134 CID (2.2L) DIESEL ENGINE

The "quick start; afterglow" system is used to enable the engine to start more quickly when the engine is cold. It consists of the flour glow plugs, the control module, two relays, a glow plug resistor assembly, coolant temperature switch, clutch and neutral switches and connecting wiring. Relay power and feedback circuits are protected by fuse links in the wiring harness. The control module is protected by a separate 10A fuse in the fuse panel.

When the ignition switch is turned to the ON position, a Wait-to-Start signal appears near the cold-start knob on the panel. When the signal appears, relay No.1 also closes and full system voltage is applied to the glow plugs. If engine coolant temperature is below 30°C (86°F), relay No.2 also closes at this time. After three seconds, the control module turns off the Wait-to-Start light indicating that the engine is ready for starting. If the ignition switch is left in the ON position about three seconds more without cranking, the control opens relay No.1 and current to the plugs stops to prevent overheating. However, if coolant temperature is below 30°C (86°F) when relay No.1 opens, relay No.2 remains closed to apply reduced voltage to the plugs through the glow plug resistor until the ignition switch is turned off.

When the engine is cranked, the control module cycles relay No.1 intermittently. Thus, glow plug voltage will alternate between 12 and four volts, during cranking, with relay No.2 closed, or between 12 and zero volts with relay No.2 open. After the engine starts, alternator output signals the control module to stop the No.1 relay cycling and the afterglow function takes over.

If the engine coolant temperature is below 30°C (86°F), the No.2 relay remains closed. This applies reduced (4.2 to 5.3) voltage to the glow plugs through the glow plug resistor. When the vehicle is under way (clutch and neutral switches closed), or coolant temperature is above 30°C (86°F), the control module opens relay No.2, cutting off all current to the glow plugs.

Testing the Glow Plugs

1. Disconnect the leads from each glow plug. Connect one lead of the ohmmeter to the glow plug terminal and the other lead to a good ground. Set the ohmmeter on the X1 scale. Test each glow plug in the like manner.
2. If the meter indicates less than one ohm, the problem is not with the glow plug.
3. If the ohmmeter indicates one or more ohms, replace the glow plug and retest.

Removal and Installation

1. Disconnect battery ground cables from both batteries.
2. Disconnect glow plug harness from glow plugs.
3. Using a 12mm deepwell socket, remove glow plugs.
4. Install glow plugs, using a 12mm deepwell socket, and tighten.
5. Install glow plug harness on glow plugs and tighten.
6. Connect battery ground cables to both batteries.

420 CID (6.9L) DIESEL ENGINE

The 6.9L diesel engine utilizes an electric glow plug system to aid in the start of the engine. The function of this system is to pre-heat the combustion chamber to aid ignition of the fuel.

The system consists of eight glow plugs (one for each cylinder), control switch, power relay, after glow relay, wait lamp latching relay, wait lamp and the eight fusible links located between the harness and the glow plug terminal.

On initial start with cold engine, the glow plug system operates as follows: The glow plug control switch energizes the power relay (which is a magnetic switch) and the power relay contacts close. Battery current energizes the glow plugs. Current to the glow plugs and a wait lamp will be shut off when the glow plugs are hot enough. This takes from 2 to 10 seconds after the key is first turned on. When the wait lamp goes off, the engine is ready to start. After the engine is started the glow plugs begin an on-off cycle for about 40 to 90 seconds. This cycle helps to clear start-up smoke. The control switch (the brain of the operation) is threaded into the left cylinder head coolant jacket. The control unit senses engine coolant temperature. Since the control unit senses temperature and glow plug operation the glow plug system will not be activated unless needed. On a restart (warm engine) the glow plug system will not be activated unless the coolant temperature drops below 165°F (91°C).

The fast start system utilizes 6 volt glow plugs in a 12 volt system to achieve rapid heating of the glow plug, a cycling device is required in the circuit.

CAUTION

Never bypass the power relay of the glow plug system. Constant battery current (12 volts) to glow plugs will cause them to overheat and fail.

Testing The Glow Plug

1. Disconnect the leads from the glow plug. Connect one lead of an ohmmeter to the glow plug terminal and the other lead to the metal case of the glow plug. Set the ohmmeter to the X1 scale. Test each glow plug.
2. If the meter indicates less than 2 ohms the problem is not with the glow plug.
3. If the meter indicates 2 ohms or more replace the glow plug and retest.

COOLING SYSTEM

Water Pump

Removal and Installation

122 CID (2.0L) AND 140 CID (2.3L) ENGINES

1. Disconnect the negative battery cable. Drain the cooling system. Loosen and remove the drive belt.
2. Remove the two bolts that retain the fan shroud and position the shroud back over the fan.
3. Remove the four bolts that retain the cooling fan. Remove the fan and shroud.
4. Loosen and remove the power steering and A/C compressor drive belts.
5. Remove the water pump pulley and the vent hose to the emissions canister.

6. Remove the heater hose at the water pump.
7. Remove the cam belt cover. Remove the lower radiator hose from the water pump.
8. Remove the water pump mounting bolts and the water pump. Clean all gasket mounting surfaces.
9. Install the water pump in the reverse order of removal. Coat the threads of the mounting bolts with sealer before installation.

173 CID (2.8L) V6 ENGINE

1. Disconnect the negative battery cable. Drain the cooling system.
2. Loosen and remove drive belts. Remove pump pulley. Disconnect all the water hoses from the water pump and thermostat housing.
3. Remove the radiator shroud (if necessary) and cooling fan and clutch assembly. The fan clutch assembly mounting nut is equipped with a left hand thread, remove by turning clockwise.
4. Remove the mounting bolts and water pump, water inlet and thermostat housing as an assembly.
5. Clean all gasket mounting surfaces. Transfer parts to the new pump.
6. Install the water pump in the reverse order of removal.

232 CID (3.8L) V6 ENGINE

1. Disconnect the negative battery cable. Drain the cooling system.
2. Remove the air cleaner and duct assembly.
3. Remove drive belts and pump pulley. Remove the fan shroud and cooling fan/clutch assembly.
4. Remove the power steering pump with mounting brackets and hoses attached. Position out of the way.
5. Remove the A/C compressor front mounting bracket. Leave the compressor in place.
6. Disconnect the by-pass hose from the water pump. Disconnect the heater and radiator hose at the water pump.
7. Remove the mounting bolts and the water pump.
8. Clean all gasket mounting surfaces. Installation is in the reverse order of removal.

300 CID (4.9L) ENGINE

1. Disconnect the negative battery cable. Drain cooling system.
2. Disconnect radiator lower hose and heater hose at the water pump.
3. Remove fan belt, fan and water pump pulley. Remove the air pump and alternator belts.
4. On vehicles equipped with air compressors, remove the air compressor belt as required.
5. Remove water pump retaining bolts, then remove pump and gasket.
6. To install, clean gasket surfaces of pump body and engine block.
7. If a new water pump is being installed, remove the fittings from the old pump and install them on the new pump.
8. Coat new gasket with water-resistant sealer on both sides and install gasket and pump on engine. Tighten mounting bolts securely.
9. Install water pump pulley, fan and fan belt, adjusting fan belt tension.
10. If so equipped, install air compressor belt.
11. Connect radiator and heater hoses.
12. Fill cooling system and operate engine to bleed air. Check for leaks and recheck coolant level.

255 CID (4.2L), 302 CID (5.0L), 351W CID (5.8L) V8 ENGINES

1. Disconnect the negative battery cable. Drain the cooling system.
2. Remove the bolts securing the fan shroud to the radiator, if so equipped, and position the shroud over the fan.
3. Disconnect the lower radiator hose, heater hose and by-pass hose at the water pump. Remove the drive belts, fan, fan spacer and pulley. Remove the fan shroud, if so equipped.
4. Loosen the alternator pivot bolt and the bolt attaching the alternator adjusting arm to the water pump.
5. Remove the bolts securing the water pump to the timing chain cover and remove the water pump.
6. Install the water pump in the reverse order of removal, using a new gasket.

351M CID (5.8L), 400 CID (6.6L), 460 CID (7.5L) V8 ENGINES

1. Disconnect the negative battery cable. Drain the cooling system and remove the fan shroud attaching bolts.
2. Remove the fan assembly attaching screws and remove the shroud and fan.
3. Loosen the power steering pump attaching bolts.
4. If the vehicle is equipped with air conditioning, loosen the compressor attaching bolts, and remove the air conditioning compressor and power steering pump drive belts.
5. Loosen the alternator pivot bolt. Remove the two attaching bolts and spacer. Remove the drive belt, then rotate the bracket out of the way.
6. Remove the three air conditioning compressor attaching bolts and secure the compressor out of the way.
7. Remove the power steering pump attaching bolts and position the pump to one side.
8. Remove the air conditioner bracket attaching bolts and remove the bracket.
9. Disconnect the lower radiator hose and heater hose from the water pump.
10. Loosen the by-pass hose clamp at the water pump.
11. Remove the remaining water pump attaching bolts and remove the pump from the front cover. Remove the separator plate from the pump. Discard the gaskets.
12. Remove all gasket material from all of the mating surfaces.
13. Install the water pump in the reverse order of removal, using a new gasket and waterproof sealer. When the water pump is first positioned to the front cover of the engine, install only those bolts not used to secure the air conditioner and alternator brackets.

ALL OTHER ENGINES

1. Disconnect the negative battery cable. Drain the cooling system.
2. Loosen and remove the drive belt(s). Disconnect the radiator hose(s), heater hose and water by-pass hose at the water pump.
3. Remove the bolts securing the fan shroud to the radiator, if so equipped.
4. On engines with water-pump mounted fans, remove the fan, spacer and pulley. Let the fan blade rest down in the shroud. On high-fan engines, remove the fan and bracket assembly. On low-fan engines, remove the bolts securing the fan assembly to the crankshaft damper. Remove the fan assembly.
5. On various engines it may be necessary to remove the air brake compressor, if so equipped. Remove the air brake compressor attaching bolts and position the compressor on the frame rail. Remove the air compressor mounting bracket. Loosen air pump and alternator brackets as required.
6. On vehicles with power steering, loosen the power steering pump and position it to one side, leaving the hoses attached.
7. On various engines it may be necessary to remove the air conditioning compressor, if so equipped. Loosen air conditioning compressor top bracket attaching bolts and remove bracket. Remove air conditioner idler arm and bracket assembly.
8. Remove the water pump attaching bolts and remove the water pump.
9. To install, clean all old gasket material from the cylinder front cover and the water pump.
10. Using a new gasket, and sealer, install the water pump.

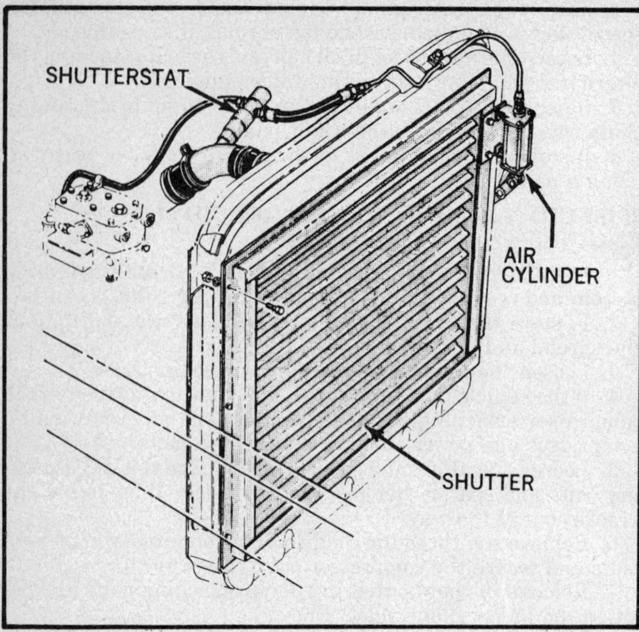

Typical C-Series radiator shutter assembly—air-operated type shown (© Ford Motor Co.)

11. Complete the installation in the reverse order of removal. Fill and bleed the cooling system. Check for leaks.

Radiator Automatic Shutter

The automatic shutter controls engine temperature by regulating air flow through the radiator. It provides faster engine warm-up and less variation in operating temperature.

There are two methods of operating the shutters, a thermostatically operated system, and an air operated system.

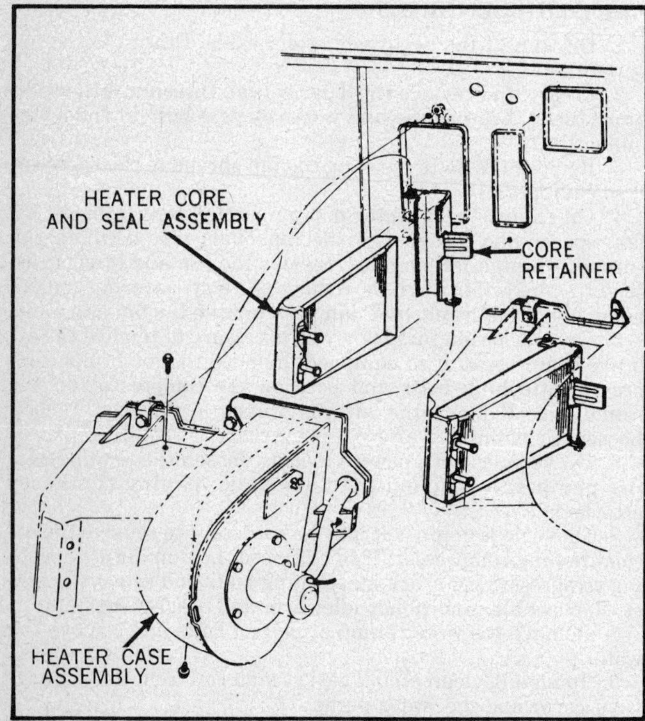

Econoline heater installation—typical (© Ford Motor Co.)

THERMOSTAT OPERATED SYSTEM

The thermostat operated system consists of a shutter control assembly, a shutter control rod or a shutter control cable and a shutter assembly. The shutter control assembly has a power element which works much like a thermostat. When the coolant temperature is below operating temperature, the shutters are closed because of the spring tension at the end of the control rod or cable. As the coolant reaches operating temperature, the power element expands and opens the shutters by working against the spring tension.

AIR OPERATED SYSTEM

The air operated shutter system consists of the shutter assembly, an air cylinder which operates the shutter, and a thermostatically controlled air valve called a shutterstat. With no air pressure on the system, springs in the shutter assembly will hold the shutter blades in the open position. With normal air pressure and the engine below operating temperature, the shutter blades close. As the engine coolant heats to the operating temperature setting of the shutterstat, an air valve in the shutterstat closes, cutting off air to the air cylinder. The air in the air cylinder is then exhausted through the shutterstat and the shutter assembly springs open the shutter blades. Always release the air from the brake system before removing a shutter air line.

Heater Core

Removal and Installation

VANS, WITHOUT AIR CONDITIONING

1. Drain the coolant; remove the battery.
2. Disconnect the resistor wiring harness and the orange blower motor lead. Remove the ground wire screw from the firewall.
3. Detach the heater hoses and the plastic hose retaining strap.
4. Remove the five mounting screws inside the vehicle.
5. Remove the heater assembly.
6. Cut the seal at the top and bottom edge of the core retainer. Remove the two screws and the retainer. Slide the core and seal out of the case.
7. Reverse the procedure for installation.

VANS, WITH AIR CONDITIONING

1. Disconnect the resistor electrical leads on the front of the blower cover inside the vehicle. Detach the vacuum line from the vacuum motor. Remove the blower cover.
2. Remove the nut and push washer from the air door shaft. Remove the control cable from the bracket and the air door shaft.
3. Remove the blower motor housing and the air door housing.
4. Drain the coolant and detach the heater hoses.
5. Remove the heater core retaining brackets. Remove the core and seal assembly.
6. Reverse the procedure for installation.

BRONCO AND PICK-UPS WITH COMFORT VENT HEATERS, WITHOUT AIR CONDITIONING

1. Disconnect the negative battery cable. Disconnect the heater hoses from the heater core tubes and plug the hoses.
2. Remove the glove compartment liner.
3. Remove two spring clips attaching the heater core cover to the plenum along the top edge of the heater core cover.
4. Remove eight screws attaching the heater core cover to the plenum and remove the cover.
5. Remove the heater core from the plenum taking care not to spill coolant from the core.
6. Install the heater core in the plenum.

7. Install the heater core cover screws and spring clips along the top edge of the cover.
8. Install the glove compartment liner.
9. Connect the heater hoses to the heater core. Tighten the hose clamps.
10. Add coolant to raise the coolant level to specification.
11. Check the system for proper operation and for coolant leaks.

BRONCO AND PICK-UPS WITH STANDARD & HIGH OUTPUT HEATERS, WITHOUT AIR CONDITIONING

1. Disconnect the negative battery cable. Disconnect the temperature cable from the temperature blend door and the mounting bracket on top of the heater case.
2. Disconnect the wires from the blower motor resistor and the blower motor.
3. Disconnect the heater hoses from the heater core and plug the hoses.
4. Working under the instrument panel, remove two nuts retaining the left end of the heater case and the right end of the plenum to the dash panel.
5. In the engine compartment, remove one screw attaching the top center of the heater to the dash panel.
6. Remove two screws attaching the right end of the heater case to the dash panel, and remove the heater case from the vehicle.
7. Remove nine screws and one bolt and nut attaching the heater housing plate to the heater case, and remove the heater housing plate.
8. Remove three screws attaching the heater core frame to the heater case and remove the frame.
9. Remove the heater core and seal from the heater case.
10. Position the heater core and seal in the heater case.
11. Install the heater core frame.
12. Position the heater housing plate on the heater case and install the nine screws and one bolt and nut.
13. Position the heater case to the dash panel and install the three attaching screws.
14. Working in the passenger compartment, install two nuts to retain the heater case and plenum right end to the dash panel.
15. Connect the heater hoses to the heater core. Tighten the hose clamps.
16. Connect the wires to the blower motor resistor assembly.
17. Connect the blower motor wires.
18. Position (slide) the self adjusting clip on the temperature cable to a position approximately one inch from the cable end loop.
19. Snap the temperature cable on the cable mounting bracket of the heater case. Then, position the self adjusting clip on the door crank arm.
20. Adjust the temperature cable.
21. Check the system for proper operation.

BRONCO AND PICK-UPS WITH AIR CONDITIONING

1. Disconnect the negative battery cable. Disconnect the heater hoses from the heater core tubes and plug the hoses.
2. Remove the glove compartment liner.
3. Remove eight screws attaching the heater core cover to the plenum and remove the cover.
4. Remove the heater core from the plenum taking care not to spill coolant from the core.
5. Installation is the reverse of removal.

RANGER AND BRONCO II, W OR W/O A/C

1. Disconnect the negative battery cable. Allow the engine to cool down completely. Drain the cooling system to a point that is below the heater hoses.
2. Disconnect the heater hoses from the heater core tubes. Plug the core tubes.
3. From under the dash, remove the screws that attach the access cover to the plenum assembly. Remove the access cover.

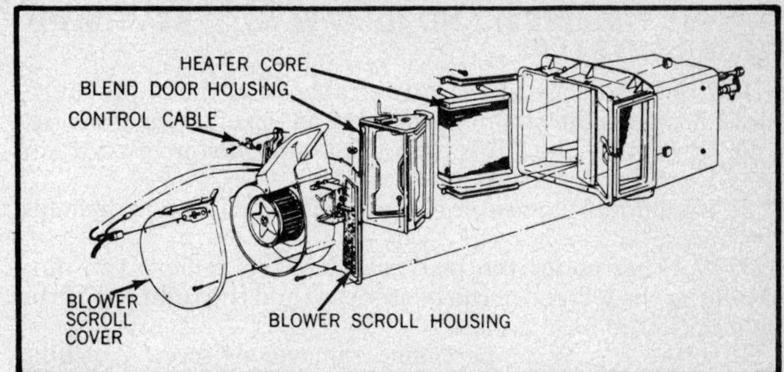

Econoline with A/C-heater core installation—typical (© Ford Motor Co.)

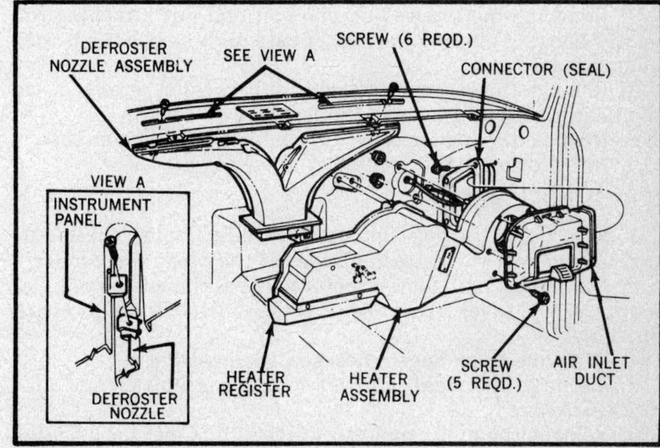

F-100–350 heater installation (© Ford Motor Co.)

4. Pull the core down and out of the plenum assembly.
5. Install in the reverse order. Fill cooling system, start the engine and check for leaks.

F-SERIES (MEDIUM AND HEAVY) WITH COMFORT VENT SYSTEM

1. Disconnect the negative battery cable. Disconnect the heater hoses from the heater core tubes and plug the hoses.
2. Remove the glove compartment liner.
3. Remove two spring clips attaching the heater core cover to the plenum along the top edge of the heater core cover, on vehicles not equipped with air condition.
4. Remove eight screws attaching the heater core cover to the plenum and remove the cover.
5. Remove the heater core from the plenum taking care not to spill coolant from the core.
6. Installation is the reverse of removal.

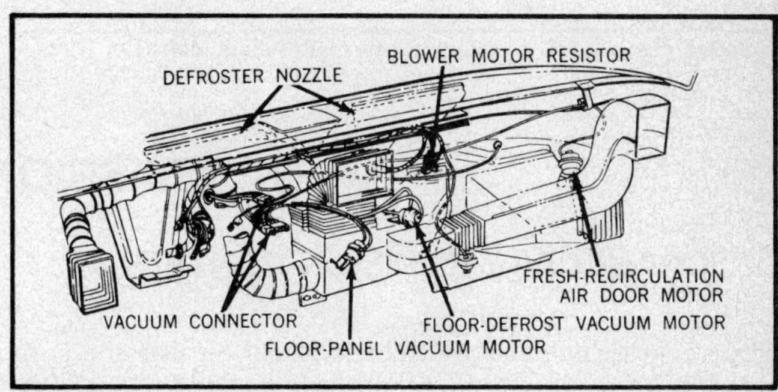

F-100–350 and Bronco heater-A/C installation—typical (© Ford Motor Co.)

F-SERIES (MEDIUM AND HEAVY) WITH STANDARD HEATER SYSTEM

1. Disconnect the temperature cable from the temperature blend door and the mounting bracket on top of the heater case.
2. Disconnect the wires from the blower motor resistor and the blower motor.
3. Disconnect the heater hoses from the heater core and plug the hoses.
4. Working under the instrument panel, remove two nuts retaining the left end of the heater case and the right end of the plenum to the dash panel.
5. In the engine compartment, remove one screw attaching the top center of the heater case to the dash panel.
6. Remove two screws attaching the right end of the heater case to the dash panel and remove the heater case from the vehicle.
7. Remove nine screws and one bolt and nut attaching the heater housing plate to the heater case and remove the heater housing plate.
8. Remove three screws attaching the heater core frame to the heater case and remove the frame.
9. Remove the heater core and seal from the heater case.
10. Installation is the reverse of removal.

C SERIES, L SERIES

1. Disconnect the negative battery cable. Drain the coolant.
2. Disconnect the defroster hoses at the plenum chamber.
3. Disconnect both blower motor wires at the connectors. Remove the side cover trim panel access to the heater motor wire disconnects.
4. Disconnect the heater hoses at the heater core.
5. Remove the heater lower mounting bolts, nuts and lockwashers.
6. Remove the upper mounting screws and move the heater assembly away from the dash. Disconnect the bowden cable from the air inlet door and remove the heater assembly from the vehicle. Remove defroster plenum and motor.
7. Remove the top cover.
8. Remove the heater core mounting screws and remove the core from the housing.
9. Position the new core in the housing, install the mounting screws and install the top cover.
10. Position the heater assembly to the dash and connect and adjust the air door bowden cable. Install defroster plenum and motor.
11. Install the upper mounting screws and the lower mounting bolts, lockwashers and nuts.
12. Connect the heater hoses to the heater.
13. Connect both motor wires, color to color at the disconnects, and install the side cover trim panel.
14. Connect the defroster hoses at the plenum chamber. Install the coolant. Bleed any air from the heater.

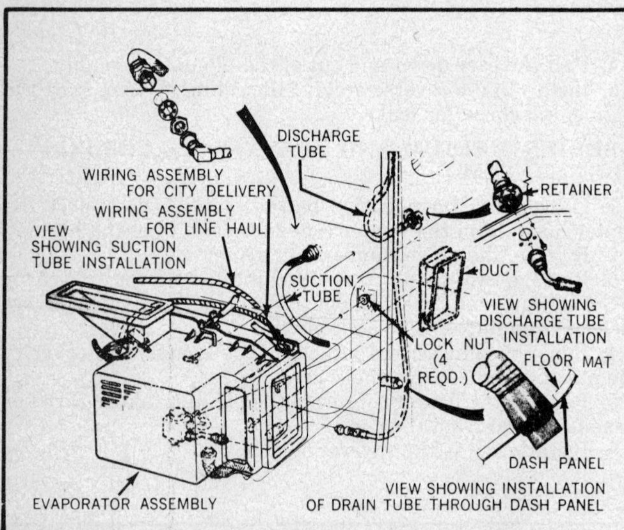

L-Series heater—A/C installation—typical (© Ford Motor Co.)

Auxiliary Heater Case

VANS

Removal and Installation

1. Remove the first bench seat (if so equipped).
2. Remove the auxiliary heater and/or air conditioning cover assembly attaching screws and remove the cover.
3. Position the cover assembly to the body side panel and install the attaching screws.
4. Install the bench seat (if removed) and tighten the retaining bolts 25–45 ft. lbs.

Auxiliary Heater Core and Seal Assembly

VANS

Removal and Installation

1. Remove the first bench seat (if so equipped).
2. Remove auxiliary heater and/or air conditioning cover attaching screws (15) and remove the cover.
3. Partially drain the engine coolant from the coolant system.
4. Remove the heater hoses from the auxiliary heater core assembly (2 clamps).
5. Pull the wiring assembly away from the heater core seal.
6. Slide the heater core and seal assembly out of the housing slot.
7. Slide the heater core and seal assembly into the housing slot (position the wiring to one side).
8. Install the heater hoses to the heater core assembly.
9. Fill the cooling system to specification.
10. Position the cover assembly to the body side panel and install the attaching screws.
11. Install the bench seat (if removed) and tighten the retaining bolts 25–45 ft. lbs.

EMISSION CONTROL

CRANKCASE EMISSION CONTROLS

The crankcase emission control equipment consists of a positive crankcase ventilation (PCV) valve, a crankcase air filter that is vented to the air cleaner, and the hoses that connect the equipment.

When the engine is running, a small amount of the gases formed in the combustion chamber leak by the piston rings and enter the crankcase. The PCV system pulls these gases back into the intake manifold allowing fresh air to flow into the crankcase through the filter and filler cap. For service to the PCV system, refer to the Emission Control in the Unit Repair section.

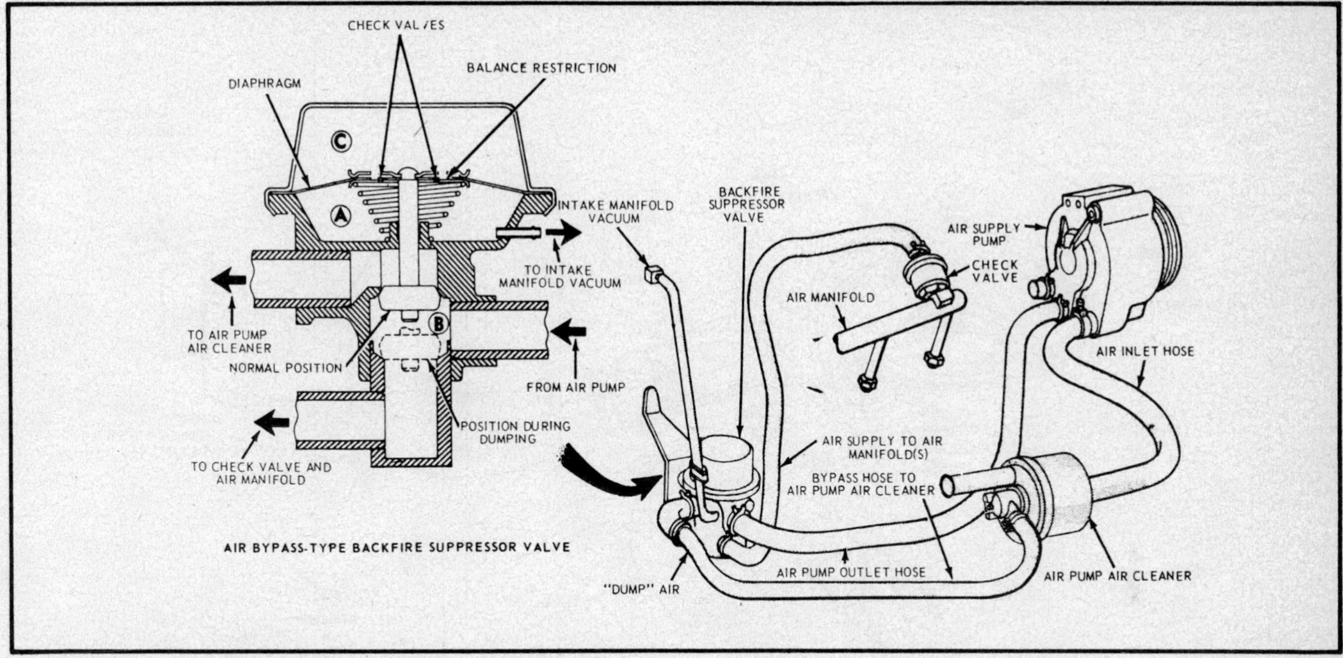

Thermactor exhaust emission control system (© Ford Motor Co.)

EVAPORATIVE EMISSION CONTROL

The evaporative emission control system consists of a sealed fuel tank, a vapor controlling orifice valve located in the top of the fuel tank, a pressure/vacuum relief fuel cap, and a carbon canister. This system is designed to limit the fuel vapors released into the atmosphere.

The open orifice valve is used to control the flow of fuel vapor and to minimize the amount of liquid gasoline entering the fuel vapor delivery line. The delivery line conducts the vapor forward to the carbon canister where the vapor is stored. During normal driving, the engine compartment mounted canister is purged of the fuel vapor by means of a hose connected to the air cleaner assembly. The vapors are drawn into the engine's induction system. The fuel cap is sealed and contains a vacuum and pressure relief valve. The vacuum valve relieves tank vacuum caused by consumption or cooling and the pressure relief valve prevents excessive fuel tank pressurization due to any system component failure or operation extremes.

THERMACTOR AIR INJECTOR SYSTEM

The air injection exhaust emission control system Thermactor consists of a air supply pump, external air manifold or cylinder head/exhaust manifold with internal air passages, air by-pass valve, check valve, and the hoses necessary to connect the components.

The air injection system reduces the carbon monoxide and hydrocarbon content of the exhaust gases by injecting fresh air into the hot exhaust gas stream as it leaves the combustion chamber. A pump supplies the air under pressure to the exhaust port near the exhaust valve by either an external air manifold or through an internal drilled passages in the cylinder head or exhaust manifold. The oxygen in the fresh air plus the heat of the exhaust gases cause further burning which converts the exhaust gases into carbon dioxide and water.

For service on the air injection system, refer to Emission Control in the Unit Repair section.

CATALYTIC CONVERTER

The catalytic converter is a muffler type device installed in the vehicles exhaust system which contains a chemical catalyst. When the hot exhaust gas passes over and through the catalyst, it heats up to a high temperature and the chemical reaction which occurs breaks down the exhaust into harmless elements. For service on the catalytic converter, refer to Emission Control in the Unit Repair section.

THERMOSTATICALLY CONTROLLED AIR CLEANER SYSTEM (TAC)

This system consists of a heat shroud which is integral with the right-side exhaust manifold, a hot air hose and a special air cleaner assembly equipped with a thermal sensor and vacuum motor and air valve assembly.

The purpose of TAC is to get hot air into the carburetor as

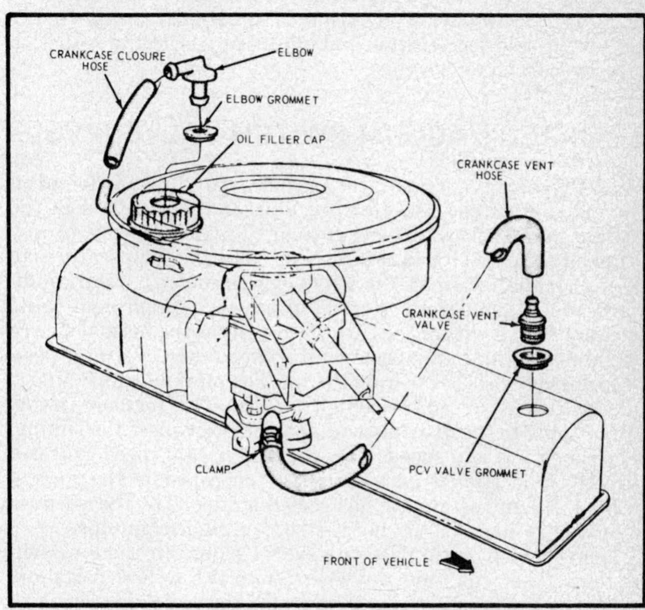

Closed crankcase ventilation system (© Ford Motor Co.)

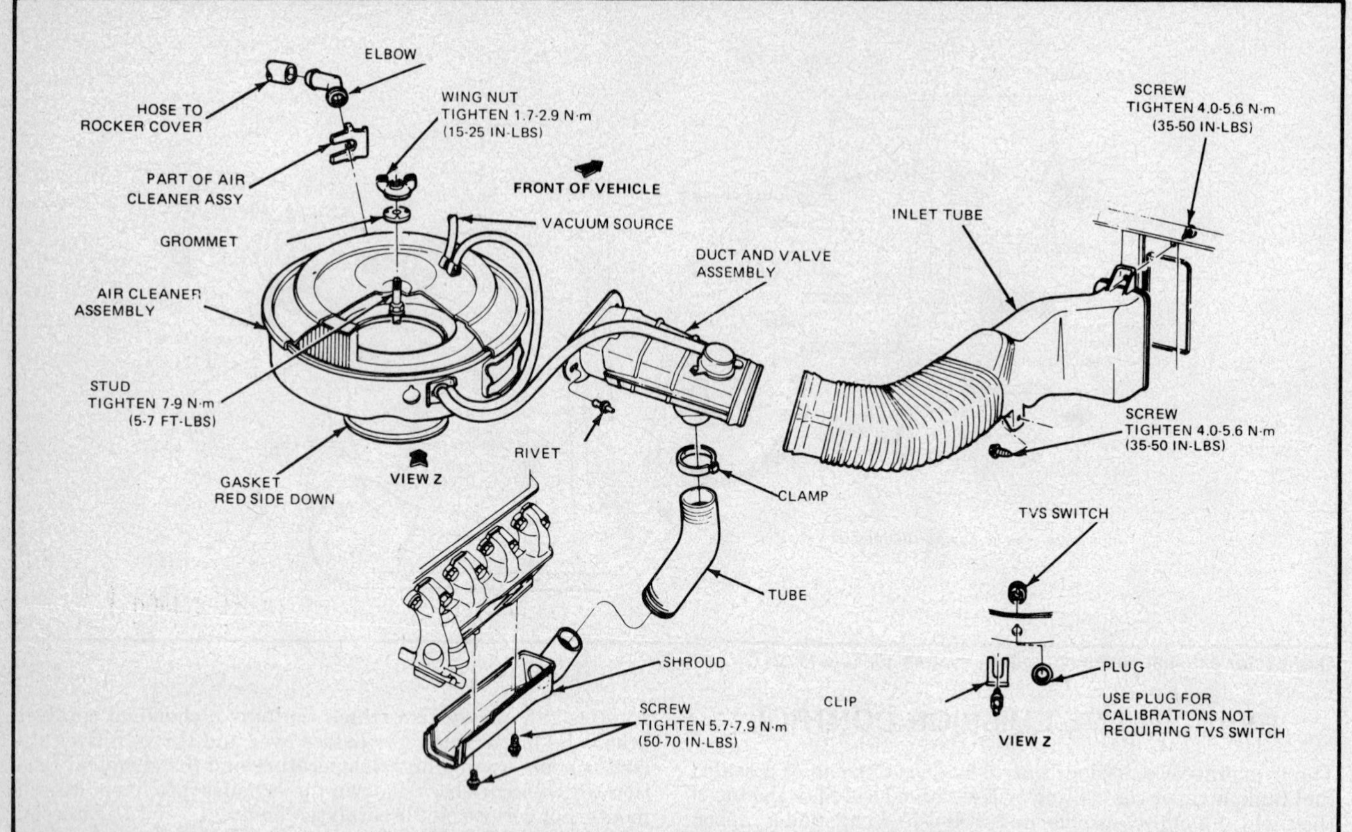

Typical thermostatically controlled air cleaner (TAC) (© Ford Motor Co.)

soon as possible because the engine will emit less pollutants on a lean mixture.

DUAL DIAPHRAGM DISTRIBUTOR

The dual diaphragm distributor has two diaphragms which operate independently. The outer (primary) diaphragm makes use of carburetor vacuum to advance the ignition timing. The inner (secondary) diaphragm uses intake manifold vacuum to provide additional retardation of ignition timing during closed-throttle deceleration and idle, resulting in the reduction of hydrocarbon emissions.

PORTED VACUUM SWITCH VALVE (PVS)

The PVS valve is a temperature sensing valve usually found on the distributor vacuum advance line, and is installed in the coolant outlet elbow. During prolonged periods of idle, or any other situation which causes engine operating temperatures to be higher than normal, the valve, which under normal conditions simply connects the vacuum advance diaphragm to its vacuum source within the carburetor, closes the normal source vacuum port and engages an alternate source vacuum port. This alternate source is from the intake manifold which, under idle conditions, maintains a high vacuum. This increase in vacuum supply to the distributor diaphragm advances the timing, increasing the idle speed. The increase in idle speed causes a directly proportional increase in the operation of the cooling system. When the engine has cooled sufficiently, the vacuum supply is returned to its normal source, the carburetor.

These switches are used in several places in the emission systems. They can have anywhere from two to four ports and can be used to turn vacuum on and off, or to switch between two vacuum sources for a third delivery point.

DECELERATION VALVE

Some engines were equipped with a distributor vacuum advance control valve (deceleration valve) which is used with dual diaphragm distributors to further aid in controlling ignition timing. The deceleration valve is in the vacuum line which runs from the outer (advance) diaphragm to the carburetor, the normal vacuum supply for the distributor. During deceleration, the intake manifold vacuum rises causing the deceleration valve to close off the carburetor vacuum source and connect the intake manifold vacuum source to the distributor advance diaphragm. The increase in vacuum provides maximum ignition timing advance, thus providing more complete fuel combustion and decreasing exhaust system backfire.

EXHAUST GAS RECIRCULATION SYSTEM (EGR)

In this system, a vacuum-operated EGR flow valve is attached to the carburetor spacer (except on the 302 V8). A passage in the carburetor spacer mates with a hole in the mounting face of the EGR valve or the intake manifold. The EGR valve on the 302 V8 is located on the rear of the intake manifold. On all engines except the 302 V8, the system allows exhaust gases to flow from the exhaust crossover, through the control valve and through the spacer into the intake manifold below the carburetor. For those engines where exhaust gases cannot be picked up from the exhaust crossover (6 cylinder) as described above, the gases are picked up from the choke stove located on the exhaust manifold or directly from the exhaust manifold. The exhaust gases are routed to the carburetor spacer through steel tubing.

The vacuum signal which operates the EGR valve originates

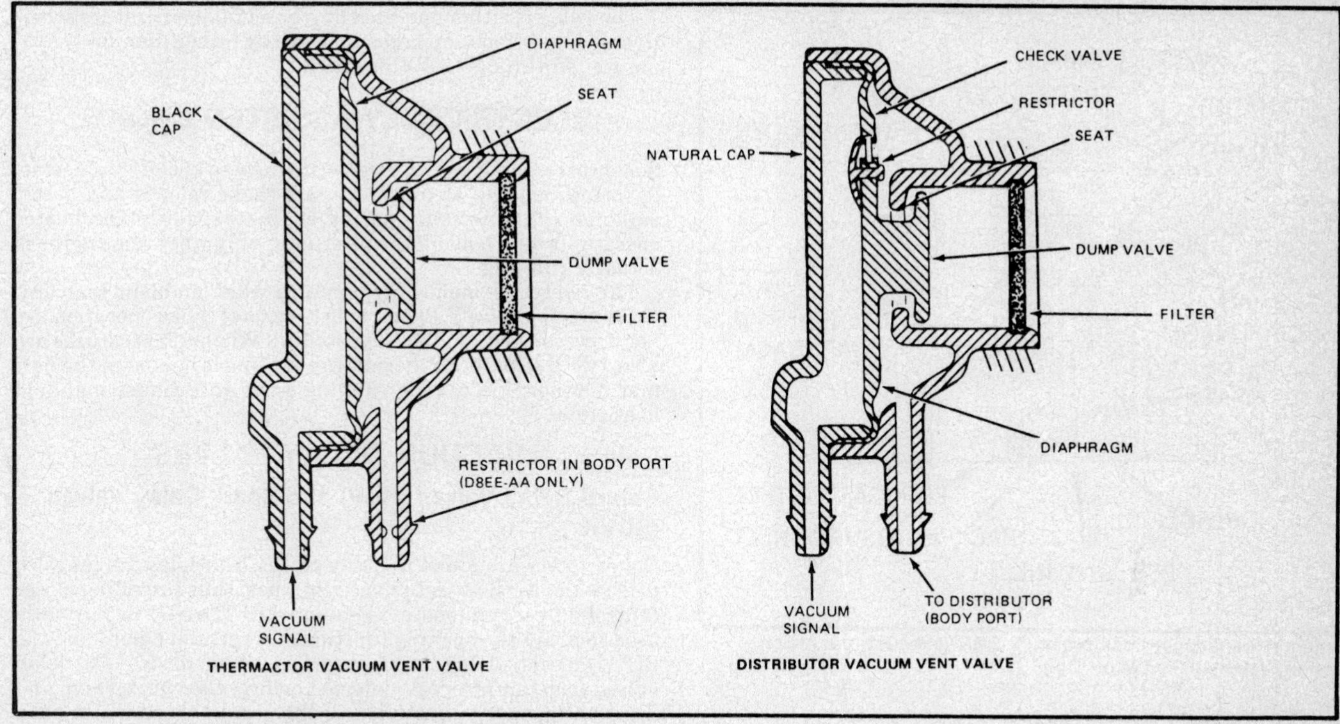

Typical spark delay valves (SDV)—two types illustrated (© Ford Motor Co.)

at the EGR vacuum port in the carburetor. This signal is controlled by at least one, and sometimes, two series of valves.

A water temperature sensing valve (the EGR PVS) which is closed until the water temperature reaches either 60°F or 125°F, depending on application, is always used.

Another system working in conjunction with the EGR system is the EGR/CSC system. This system regulates both the distributor spark advance and operation of the EGR valve according to the temperature of the engine coolant. The system consists of a 95°F EGR valve, a spark delay valve, and a vacuum check valve.

When the engine coolant is below 82°F, the EGR PVS valve admits carburetor EGR port vacuum directly to the distributor advance diaphragm through a one-way check valve. At the same time, the EGR PVS valve shuts off carburetor EGR vacuum to the EGR valve and transmission diaphragm.

When the engine coolant temperature is above 95°F, the EGR PVS valve is actuated and directs carburetor EGR vacuum to the EGR valve and transmission instead of the distributor.

The spark delay valve (SDV) delays carburetor spark advance vacuum to the distributor advance diaphragm by restricting the vacuum through the SDV valve for a predetermined time. During normal acceleration, little or no vacuum is admitted to the distributor advance diaphragm until acceleration is completed, because of the time delay of the SDV valve, and the re-routing of the EGR port vacuum, if the engine coolant temperature is 95°F or higher. The check valve blocks vacuum from the SDV valve to the EGR PVS valve so that carburetor spark vacuum will not be dissipated when the EGR PVS valve is actuated above 95°F. increases and the increase in coolant circulation and fan speed cools the engine.

COLD TEMPERATURE ACTIVATED VACUUM SYSTEM

The cold temperature activated vacuum (CTAV) system was used on 460 CID V8 engines in F-100 vehicles built for sale in California.

The CTAV system more accurately marches spark advance to the engine requirements under cold ambient temperature conditions. The system can select from two vacuum sources for spark advance depending on the ambient temperature: below 45°F for carburetor spark port vacuum, above 65°F for EGR vacuum. In between these two temperature ranges the system will select either source of vacuum, depending on the cycle it is in.

The CTAV system consists of an ambient temperature switch, a three-way vacuum switch, inline vacuum bleed, and a latching relay.

The vacuum from both the spark port of the carburetor and the EGR port is supplied to the three-way solenoid valve. The ambient temperature switch provides the signal that determines which of the sources will be selected. The latching relay provides for only one cycle each time the ignition switch is turned on.

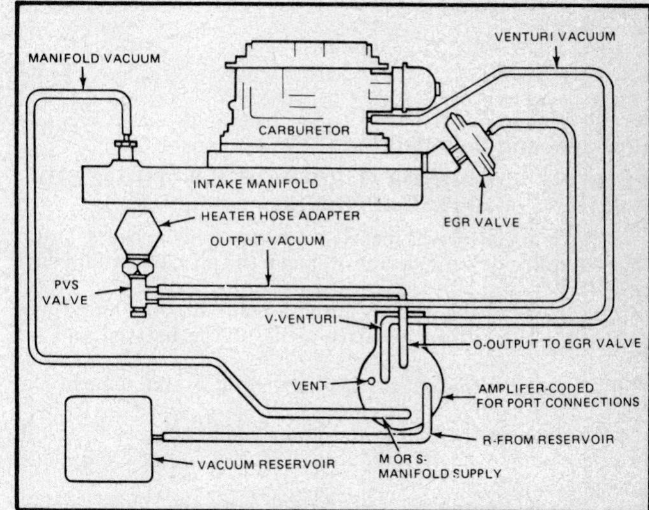

Typical EGR system components (© Ford Motor Co.)

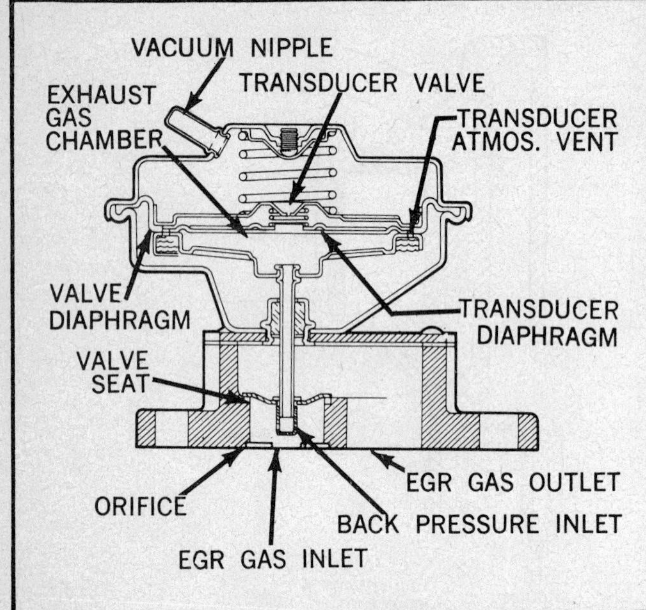

Integral transducer back pressure EGR (exhaust gas recirculation) valve (© Ford Motor Co.)

VACUUM AND SPRING CONTROLLED HEAT CONTROL VALVE

The heat control valve, commonly known as the heat riser, is mounted between the exhaust pipe and the exhaust manifold. The purpose of the device is to provide a quick warm-up of the carburetor and the rest of the induction system.

Fuel will condense on the cold surfaces of the induction system, which causes air/fuel ratios to fluctuate. These variations can cause uneven acceleration and increased emissions. The exhaust control valve, which is thermostatically-controlled, is closed when the engine is cold and routes hot exhaust gases through a passage under the carburetor and over to the opposite exhaust manifold which has no heat control valve and thus no restriction to block the flow of exhaust gases. This quickly warms the air/fuel mixture delivery passages and provides improved mixture control and driveability. As the engine warms up, the valve opens and reduces the flow of exhaust gases through the warm-up passage.

The valve is either operated by a bi-metal temperature sensitive spring or vacuum motor operated by intake manifold vacuum routed through a PVS switch.

ELECTRICALLY-ASSISTED CHOKE

Some carburetors use an electrically heated choke thermostatic spring housing as an aid to fast choke release and better emission characteristics during engine warm-up. The heater operates from a lead off the alternator only when the engine is actually running.

The heater element only operates when ambient temperatures are above 60°F. (when long periods of choke operation are not necessary for engine driveability). When temperatures are below 60°F., the choke thermostatic spring is heated in the normal manner, via a tube running from an exhaust manifold heat stove.

VACUUM DELAY VALVES

Retard Delay Valves (RDV) and Spark Delay Valves (SDV)

Delay valves are found in many places. The delay valves work to slow the air flow in the vacuum lines, thus providing closer control on vacuum operated equipment. The SDV is normally used to delay the opening function of a vacuum device and the RDV is used to delay the closing of a vacuum device. The delay valves have an interval sinterted orifice; the check valve and filter pack must be installed in the correct direction in each system.

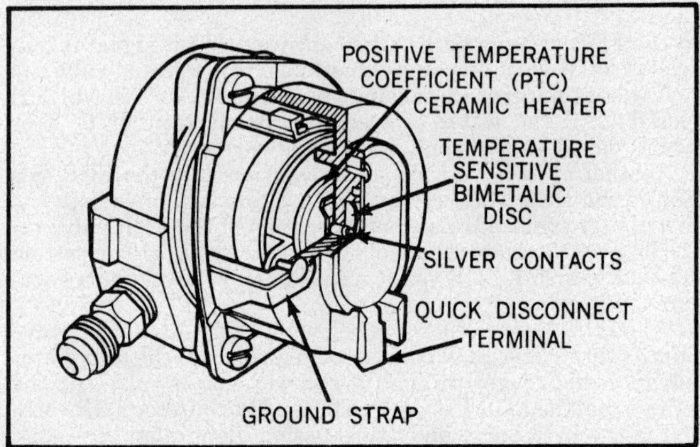

Electric assisted choke (© Ford Motor Co.)

ENGINE

Removal and Installation

PICKUPS AND BRONCO, BRONCO II WITH 122 CID (2.0L) & 140 CID (2.3L) ENGINES

1. Raise the hood and install protective fender covers. Drain the coolant from the radiator. Remove the air cleaner and duct assembly.
2. Disconnect the battery ground cable at the engine and disconnect the battery positive cable at the battery and set aside.
3. Mark the location of the hood hinges and remove the hood.
4. Disconnect the upper and lower radiator hoses from the engine. Remove the radiator shroud screws. Remove the radiator upper supports.
5. Remove engine fan and shroud assembly. Then remove the radiator. Remove the oil fill cap.
6. Disconnect the coil primary wire at the coil. Disconnect the oil pressure and the water temperature sending unit wires from the sending units.
7. Disconnect the alternator wire from the alternator, the starter cable from the starter and the accelerator cable from the carburetor. If so equipped, disconnect the transmission kickdown rod.
8. If so equipped, remove the A/C compressor from the mounting bracket and position it out of the way, leaving the refrigerant lines attached.
9. Disconnect the power brake vacuum hose. Disconnect the chassis fuel line from the fuel pump. Disconnect the heater hoses from the engine.
10. Remove the engine mount nuts. Raise and safely support the vehicle.
11. Drain engine oil from the crankcase. Remove the starter motor.

12. Disconnect the muffler exhaust inlet pipe at the exhaust manifold.

13. Remove the dust cover (manual transmission) or converter inspection plate (automatic transmission).

14. On vehicles with a manual transmission, remove the flywheel housing cover lower attaching bolts. On vehicles with automatic transmissions, remove the converter-to-flywheel bolts, then remove the converter housing lower attaching bolts.

15. Remove clutch slave cylinder (manual transmission). Lower the vehicle.

16. Support the transmission and flywheel or converter housing with a jack.

17. Remove the flywheel housing or converter housing upper attaching bolts.

18. Attach the engine lifting hooks to the existing lifting brackets. Carefully, so as not to damage any components, lift the engine out of the vehicle.

19. To install the engine: If clutch was removed, reinstall. Carefully lower the engine into the engine compartment. On a vehicle with automatic transmission, start the converter pilot into the crankshaft. On a vehicle with a manual transmission, start the transmission main drive gear into the clutch disc. It may be necessary to adjust the position of the transmission in relation to the engine if the input shaft will not enter the clutch disc. If the engine hangs up after the shaft enters, turn the crankshaft in the clockwise direction slowly (transmission in gear), until the shaft splines mesh with the clutch disc splines.

20. Install the flywheel or converter housing upper attaching bolts. Remove the engine lifting hooks from the lifting brackets.

21. Remove the jack from under the transmission. Raise and safely support the vehicle.

22. On a vehicle with a manual transmission, install the flywheel lower housing bolts and tighten to specifications. On a vehicle with an automatic transmission, attach the converter to the flywheel bolts and tighten to specifications. Install the converter housing-to-engine bolts and tighten to specifications.

23. Install clutch slave cylinder.

24. Install the dust cover (manual transmission) or converter inspection plate (automatic transmission). Connect the exhaust inlet pipe to the exhaust manifold.

25. Install the starter motor and connect the starter cables.

26. Lower the vehicle. Install the engine mount nuts and tighten to 65–85 ft. lbs.

27. Connect the heater hoses to the engine. Connect the chassis fuel line to the fuel pump. Connect the power brake vacuum hose.

28. Connect the alternator wire to the alternator, connect the accelerator cable to the carburetor. If so equipped, connect the transmission kickdown rod. If so equipped, install the A/C compressor to the mounting bracket.

29. Connect the coil primary wire at the coil. Connect the oil pressure and water temperature sending unit wires. Install oil fill cap.

30. Install the radiator and secure with upper support brackets. Install the fan and shroud assembly. Connect upper and lower radiator hoses.

31. Install the hood and align.

32. Install the air cleaner assembly. Fill and bleed the cooling system.

33. Fill the crankcase with specified oil. Connect battery ground cable to engine and battery positive cable to battery.

34. Start the engine and check for leaks.

134 CID (2.2L) DIESEL ENGINE

1. Open hood and install protective fender covers. Mark location of hood hinges and remove hood.

2. Disconnect battery ground cables from both batteries. Disconnect battery ground cables at engine.

3. Drain coolant from radiator.

4. Disconnect air intake hose from air cleaner and intake manifold.

5. Disconnect upper and lower radiator hoses from engine. Remove engine cooling fan. Remove radiator shroud screws. Remove radiator upper supports and remove radiator and shroud.

6. Disconnect radio ground strap, if so equipped.

7. Remove No. 2 glow plug relay from dash, with harness attached, and lay on engine.

8. Disconnect engine wiring harness at main connector located on left fender apron. Disconnect starter cable from starter.

9. Disconnect accelerator cable and speed control cable, if so equipped, from injection pump.

10. Remove cold start cable from injection pump.

11. Discharge A/C system and remove A/C refrigerant lines and position out of the way.

12. Remove pressure and return hoses from power steering pump, if so equipped.

13. Disconnect vacuum fitting from vacuum pump and position fitting and vacuum hoses out of the way.

14. Disconnect and cap fuel inlet line at fuel line heater and fuel return line at injection pump.

15. Disconnect heater hoses from engine.

16. Loosen engine insulator nuts. Raise and support the vehicle safely.

17. Drain engine oil from oil pan and remove primary oil filter.

18. Disconnect oil pressure sender hose from oil filter mounting adapter.

19. Disconnect muffler inlet pipe at exhaust manifold.

20. Remove bottom engine insulator nuts. Remove transmission bolts. Lower vehicle. Attach engine lifting sling and chain hoist.

21. Carefully lift engine out of vehicle to avoid damage to components.

22. Install engine on work stand, if necessary.

23. When installing the engine; carefully lower engine into engine compartment to avoid damage to components.

24. Install two top transmission-to-engine attaching bolts. Remove engine lifting sling.

25. Raise and support the vehicle safely.

26. Install engine insulator nuts and tighten to specification.

27. Install remaining transmission to engine attaching bolts and tighten all bolts to specification.

28. Connect muffler inlet pipe to exhaust manifold and tighten to specification.

29. Install oil pressure sender hose and install a new oil filter.

30. Lower vehicle.

31. Tighten upper engine insulator nuts to specification.

32. Connect heater hoses to engine. Connect fuel inlet line to fuel line heater and fuel return line to injection pump. Connect vacuum fitting and hoses to vacuum pump. Connect pressure and return hoses to power steering pump, if so equipped. Check and add power steering fluid.

33. Install A/C refrigerant lines and charge system, if so equipped. Install A/C drive belt, and tighten to specification.

34. Connect cold start cable to injection pump. Connect accelerator cable and speed control cable, if so equipped, to injection pump.

35. Connect engine wiring harness to main wiring harness at left fender apron. Connect radio ground strap, if so equipped.

36. Position radiator in vehicle, install radiator upper support brackets and tighten to specification. Install radiator fan shroud and tighten to specification. Install radiator fan and tighten to specification.

37. Connect upper and lower radiator hoses to engine and tighten clamps to specification. Connect air intake hose to air cleaner and intake manifold.

38. Fill the cooling system.

39. Fill crankcase with specified quantity and quality of oil.

40. Connect battery ground cables to engine. Connect battery

ground cables to both batteries.

41. Run engine and check for oil, fuel and coolant leaks.

173 CID (2.8L) AND 179 CID (2.9L) V6 ENGINES

1. Disconnect the battery ground cable and drain the cooling system.
2. Remove the hood after scribing hinge positions. Remove the air cleaner and intake duct assembly.
3. Remove or disconnect thermactors system parts that will interfere with removal or installation of the engine.
4. Disconnect the radiator upper and lower hoses at the radiator. Remove the fan shroud attaching bolts and position the shroud over the fan. Remove the radiator and shroud.
5. Remove the alternator and bracket. Position the alternator out of the way. Disconnect the alternator ground wire from the cylinder block.
6. Remove A/C compressor and power steering and position out of way, if so equipped.
7. Disconnect the heater hoses at the block and water pump.
8. Remove the ground wires from the cylinder block.
9. Disconnect the fuel tank to fuel pump fuel line at the fuel pump. Plug the fuel tank line.
10. Disconnect the throttle cable linkage at the carburetor and intake manifold.
11. Disconnect the primary wires from the ignition coil. Disconnect the brake booster vacuum hose. Disconnect the wiring from the oil pressure and engine coolant temperature senders.
12. Raise and support the vehicle safely. Disconnect the muffler inlet pipes at the exhaust manifolds.
13. Disconnect the starter cable and remove the starter.
14. Remove the engine front support to crossmember attaching nuts or through bolts.
15. If equipped with automatic transmission, remove the converter inspection cover and disconnect the flywheel from the converter.
16. Remove the kickdown rod. Remove the converter housing to cylinder block bolts and the adapter plate to converter housing bolt.
17. On vehicles equipped with a manual transmission, remove the clutch linkage. Lower the vehicle.
18. Attach engine lifting sling and hoist to lifting brackets at exhaust manifolds.
19. Position a jack under the transmission. Raise the engine slightly and carefully pull it from the transmission. Carefully lift the engine out of the engine compartment so that the rear cover plate is not bent or components damaged.
20. When installing the engine; attach engine lifting sling and hoist to lifting brackets at exhaust manifolds.
21. Lower the engine carefully into the engine compartment. Make sure the exhaust manifolds are properly aligned with the muffler inlet pipes.
22. On a vehicle with a manual transmission, start the transmission main shaft into the clutch disc. It may be necessary to adjust the position of the transmission in relation to the engine if the input shaft will not enter the clutch disc. If the engine hangs up after the shaft enters, turn the crankshaft slowly (transmission in gear) until the shaft splines mesh with the clutch disc splines. On a vehicle with an automatic transmission, start the converter pilot into the crankshaft. Install the clutch housing or converter housing upper bolts, making sure that the dowels in the cylinder block engage the flywheel housing. Remove the jack from under the transmission. Remove the lifting sling.
23. On a vehicle with an automatic transmission, position the kickdown rod on the transmission and engine. Raise the vehicle and secure with safety stands. On a vehicle with an automatic transmission, position the transmission linkage bracket and install the remaining converter housing bolts. Install the adapter plate-to-converter housing bolt. Install the converter-to-flywheel nuts and install the inspection cover. Connect the kickdown rod on the transmission.
24. Install the starter and connect the cable.
25. Connect the muffler inlet pipes at the exhaust manifolds.
26. Install the engine front support nuts and washer attaching it to the crossmember of through bolts. Lower the vehicle.
27. Install the battery ground cable. Connect the ignition coil primary wires, then connect the coolant temperature sending unit and oil pressure sending unit. Connect brake booster vacuum hose. Install the throttle linkage.
28. Connect the fuel tank line at the fuel pump. Connect the ground cable at the cylinder block. Connect the heater hoses to the water pump and cylinder block.
29. Install the alternator and bracket. Connect the alternator ground wire to the cylinder block. Install the drive belt and adjust the belt tension to specifications.
30. Install A/C compressor and power steering pump, if so equipped.
31. Position the fan shroud over the fan. Install the radiator and connect the radiator upper and lower hoses. Install the fan shroud attaching bolts. Fill and bleed the cooling system. Fill the crankcase with the proper grade and quantity of oil. Install thermactor parts removed or disconnected. Reconnect battery ground cable.
32. Charge A/C system if so equipped.
33. Operate the engine at fast idle until it reaches normal operating temperature and check all gaskets and hose connections for leaks. Adjust ignition timing and idle speed.
34. Install the air cleaner and intake duct. Install and adjust the hood.

300 CID (4.9L) ENGINE

1. Drain the cooling system and the crankcase. Remove the hood and the air cleaner. Disconnect the negative battery cable.
2. Disconnect the heater hose from the water pump and coolant outlet housing. Disconnect the flexible fuel line from the fuel pump.
3. Remove the radiator.
4. Remove the fan, water pump pulley, and fan belt.
5. Disconnect the accelerator cable at the carburetor. Remove the throttle return spring. On vehicles equipped with power brakes, disconnect the brake booster vacuum hose at the intake manifold. On vehicles with automatic transmissions, disconnect the transmission kickdown rod at the bellcrank assembly.
6. Disconnect the exhaust pipe from the exhaust manifold.
7. Disconnect the body ground strap and the battery ground cable from the engine.
8. Disconnect the engine wiring harness at the ignition coil, the coolant temperature sending unit, and the oil pressure sending unit. Position the wiring harness out of the way.
9. Remove the alternator mounting bolts and position the alternator out of the way.
10. On a vehicle equipped with power steering, remove the power steering pump from the mounting brackets and move it to one side, leaving the lines attached.
11. Raise and safely support the vehicle. Remove the starter and automatic transmission filler tube bracket, if so equipped. Also, remove the rear engine plate upper right bolt.
12. On manual transmission equipped vehicles, remove the flywheel housing lower attaching bolts and disconnect the clutch return spring.
13. On automatic transmission equipped vehicles, remove the converter housing access cover assembly and remove the flywheel-to-converter attaching nuts. Secure the converter in the housing. Remove the transmission oil cooler lines from the retaining clip at the engine. Remove the lower converter housing-to-engine attaching bolts.
14. Remove the nut from each of the two front engine mounts.
15. Lower the vehicle and position a jack under the transmission and support it. Remove the remaining bellhousing-to-engine attaching bolts.
16. Attach the engine lifting device and raise the engine

slightly and carefully pull it from the transmission. Lift the engine out of the vehicle.

17. To install the engine, place a new gasket on the muffler inlet pipe.

18. Carefully lower the engine into the vehicle. Make sure that the dowels in the engine block engage the holes in the bellhousing.

19. On manual transmission equipped vehicles, start the transmission input shaft into the clutch disc. It may be necessary to adjust the position of the engine or transmission in order for the input shaft to enter the clutch disc. If necessary, turn the crankshaft until the input shaft splines mesh with the clutch disc splines.

20. On automatic transmission equipped vehicles, start the converter pilot into the crankshaft. Unsecure the converter in the housing.

21. Install the bellhousing upper attaching bolts. Remove the jack supporting the transmission.

22. Lower the engine until it rests on the engine mounts. Remove the lifting device.

23. Install the engine mount nuts and tighten them to 45–55 ft. lbs.

24. Install the automatic transmission coil cooler lines bracket, if so equipped.

25. Install the remaining bellhousing attaching bolts.

26. Connect the clutch return spring, if so equipped.

27. Install the starter and connect the starter cable. Attach the automatic transmission fluid filler tube bracket, if so equipped.

28. On vehicles with automatic transmissions, install the transmission oil cooler lines in the bracket at the cylinder block.

29. Connect the exhaust pipe to the exhaust manifold. Tighten the nuts to 25–35 ft. lbs.

30. Connect the engine ground strap and negative battery cable.

31. On vehicles with automatic transmission, connect the kick-down rod to the bellcrank assembly on the intake manifold.

32. Connect the accelerator linkage to the carburetor and install the return spring.

33. On vehicles with power brakes, connect the brake booster vacuum line to the intake manifold.

34. Connect the coil primary wire, oil pressure and coolant temperature sending unit wires, fuel line, heater hoses, and the battery positive cable.

35. Install the alternator to its mounting bracket. Install the power steering pump to its bracket, if so equipped.

36. Install the water pump pulley, spacer, fan, and fan belt. Adjust the belt tension.

37. Install the radiator and connect the upper and lower radiator hoses to the radiator and engine. Connect the automatic transmission oil cooler lines, if so equipped.

38. Install and ajdust the hood.

39. Fill the cooling system. Fill the crankcase.

40. Start the engine and check for leaks. Bleed the cooling system. Adjust the clutch pedal free-play or the automatic transmission control linkage. Install the air cleaner.

232 CID (3.8L) V6 AND V8 ENGINES, EXCEPT 420 CID (6.9L) DIESEL AND 460 CID (7.5L) V8 ENGINES

1. Drain the cooling system and crankcase. Remove the hood.

2. Disconnect the battery, negative cable first, and alternator cables from the cylinder block.

3. Remove the air cleaner and intake duct assembly, plus the crankcase ventilation hose.

4. Disconnect the upper and lower radiator hoses, and, if so equipped, the automatic transmission oil cooler lines.

5. Remove the fan shroud and lay it over the fan. Remove the radiator and fan, shroud, fan, spacer, pulley, and belt.

6. Disconnect the alternator leads and the alternator adjusting bolts. Allow the alternator to swing down out of the way.

7. Disconnect the oil pressure sending unit lead from the sending unit.

8. Disconnect the fuel tank-to-pump fuel line at the fuel pump and plug the line.

9. Disconnect the accelerator linkage at the carburetor. Disconnect the automatic transmission kick-down rod and remove the return spring, if so equipped.

10. Disconnect the heater hoses from the water pump and intake manifold. Disconnect the temperature sending unit wire from the sending unit.

11. Remove the upper bellhousing-to-engine attaching bolts.

12. Disconnect the primary wire from the coil. Remove the wiring harness from the left rocker arm cover and position the wires out of the way. Disconnect the ground strap from the cylinder block.

13. Raise the front of the vehicle and disconnect the starter cable from the starter. Remove the starter.

14. Disconnect the exhaust pipe from the exhaust manifolds.

15. Disconnect the engine mounts from the brackets on the frame.

16. On vehicles with automatic transmissions, remove the converter inspection plate and remove the torque converter-to-flywheel attaching bolts.

17. Remove the remaining bellhousing-to-engine attaching bolts.

18. Lower the vehicle and support the transmission with a jack.

19. Install an engine lifting device.

NOTE: On the V6, the intake manifold is aluminum. If a lifting device is attached to the manifold, all manifold bolts must be installed.

20. Raise the engine slightly and carefully pull it out from the transmission. Lift the engine out of the engine compartment.

21. Install the engine in the reverse order of removal. Make sure that the dowels in the engine block engage the holes in the bellhousing through the rear cover plate. If the engine hangs up after the transmission input shaft enters the clutch disc (manual transmission only), turn the crankshaft with the transmission in gear until the input shaft splines mesh with the clutch disc splines.

22. Tighten the exhaust pipe to exhaust manifold nuts to 25–35 ft. lbs.

460 CID (7.5L) V8 ENGINE

1. Remove the hood.

2. Drain the cooling system, the radiator and the cylinder block.

3. Disconnect the negative battery cable and remove the air cleaner assembly.

4. Disconnect the upper and lower radiator hoses and the transmission oil cooler lines from the radiator.

5. Remove the fan shroud from the radiator and remove the fan from the water pump. Remove the fan and shroud from the engine compartment.

6. Remove the upper support and remove the radiator.

7. If the vehicle is equipped with air conditioning, remove the compressor from the engine and position it out of the way. If the compressor must be removed completely, loosen the air conditioning service valves (disconnect) carefully to discharge the air conditioning system. Remove the compressor.

8. Remove the power steering pump from the engine, if so equipped, and position it to one side. Do not disconnect the fluid lines.

9. Disconnect the fuel pump inlet line from the pump and plug the line.

10. Remove the alternator drive belts and disconnect the alternator from the engine, positioning it aside.

11. Disconnect the ground cable from the right front corner of the engine.

12. Disconnect the heater hoses.

13. Remove the transmission fluid filler tube attaching bolt from the right-side valve cover and position the tube out of the way.
14. Disconnect all vacuum lines at the rear of the intake manifold.
15. Disconnect the speed control cable at the carburetor, if so equipped. Disconnect the accelerator rod and the transmission kickdown rod and secure them out of the way.
16. Disconnect the engine wiring harness at the connector on the fire wall.
17. Raise and support the vehicle safely. Disconnect the exhaust pipes at the exhaust manifolds.
18. Disconnect the starter cable and remove the starter. Bring the starter forward and rotate the solenoid outward to remove the assembly.
19. Remove the access cover from the converter housing and remove the flywheel-to-converter attaching nuts. Remove the lower converter housing-to-engine attaching bolts.
20. Remove the engine mount through-bolts attaching the rubber insulators to the frame brackets.
21. Lower the vehicle and place a jack under the transmission to support it.
22. Remove the converter housing-to-engine block attaching bolts (left-side).
23. Disconnect the coil wire and remove the coil and bracket assembly from the intake manifold.
24. Attach the engine lifting device and carefully lift the engine from the engine compartment.
25. Install the engine in the reverse order of removal.
26. Tighten the alternator pivot bolt to 45–57 ft. lbs. and all the rest of the nuts and bolts as is outlined in the preceding "V8 except 460 Removal and Installation" procedure.

420 CID (6.9L) DIESEL ENGINE

1. Disconnect battery ground cables from both batteries.
2. Scribe alignment marks at hood hinges and remove hood.
3. Drain cooling system.
4. Remove air cleaner and intake duct assembly. Install intake manifold cover over air intake opening.
5. Remove radiator fan shroud halves.
6. Remove fan and clutch assembly. Left-hand thread. Remove by turning nut clockwise.
7. Disconnect radiator upper and lower hoses from radiator.
8. Disconnect automatic transmission oil cooler lines at radiator, if so equipped.
9. Remove radiator.
10. Loosen A/C compressor, if so equipped, and remove drive belt.
11. Remove A/C compressor from its mounting, if so equipped, and position it on radiator upper support.
12. Loosen power steering pump and remove drive belt. Remove power steering pump and position out of the way on left side of engine compartment.
13. Disconnect fuel supply line heater and alternator wires at alternator. Disconnect oil pressure sending unit wire at sending unit. Remove oil pressure sender from dash panel and lay on engine.
14. Disconnect accelerator cable from injection pump. Disconnect speed control cable from injection pump, if so equipped. Remove accelerator cable bracket with cables attached, from intake manifold and position out of the way.
15. Disconnect transmission kick down rod from injection pump, if so equipped. Disconnect main wiring harness connector from right side of engine. Disconnect engine ground strap from rear of engine. Disconnect fuel return hose from left rear of engine.
16. Remove two upper transmission-to-engine attaching bolts.
17. Disconnect heater hoses from water pump and right cylinder head. Disconnect water temperature sender wire from sender on left front of engine block. Disconnect water temperature overheat light switch wire from switch on top of left cylinder head. Position wires out of the way.
18. Raise and safely support the vehicle.
19. Disconnect both battery ground cables from lower front of engine.
20. Disconnect and cap fuel inlet line at fuel supply pump.
21. Disconnect starter cables at starter motor.
22. Disconnect muffler inlet pipe at exhaust manifold.
23. Disconnect engine insulators from No. 1 crossmember. Remove flywheel inspection plate. Remove four converter-to-flywheel attaching nuts, if so equipped. Lower vehicle.
24. Support transmission with a floor jack. Remove four lower transmission to engine attaching bolts.
25. Attach engine lifting sling, and chain hoist. Raise engine high enough to clear number one crossmember and pull forward.
26. Rotate the front of the engine approximately 45 degrees to the left and lift it out of the engine compartment.
27. When installing the engine; lower engine into engine compartment. Use care not to damage windshield wiper motor when installing engine in vehicle.
28. Start transmission main shaft into clutch disc. It may be necessary to adjust position of transmission in relation to engine if main shaft binds or will not enter clutch disc. If engine hangs up after main shaft enters clutch disc, rotate crankshaft slowly (transmission in gear) until mainshaft splines mesh with clutch disc splines. Align convertor to flywheel studs, if so equipped.
29. Lower into engine insulator brackets on number one crossmember.
30. Install four lower transmission to engine attaching bolts and tighten. Remove engine lifting sling. Raise and safely support the vehicle.
31. Install four converter to flywheel attaching nuts, if so equipped. Install flywheel inspection plate.
32. Install engine insulator support to crossmember bracket attaching nuts and washers. Connect muffler inlet pipes to exhaust manifolds. Connect both battery ground cables to the lower front of the engine. Connect starter cables to starter. Install fuel pump inlet line on fuel pump. Lower vehicle.
33. Connect water temperature sender wire to sender on left front of engine block. Connect wire to water temperature overheat light switch on top of left cylinder head. Install heater hoses on right cylinder head and water pump and tighten clamps.
34. Connect engine ground strap at rear of engine. Connect fuel return hose at left rear of engine. Connect transmission kickdown rod, if so equipped.
35. Install accelerator cable bracket on intake manifold. Connect accelerator cable to injection pump. Connect speed control cable, if so equipped, to injection pump.
36. Install oil pressure sender on dash panel. Connect oil pressure gauge sender wire to oil pressure sender.
37. Connect fuel supply line heater and alternator wires to alternator.
38. Install power steering pump and drive belt. Do not adjust belt at this time.
39. Install A/C compressor and drive belt. Adjust A/C compressor and power steering pump drive belts.
40. Install radiator. Connect automatic transmission oil cooler lines at radiator, if so equipped. Connect upper and lower radiator hoses to radiator and tighten hose clamps. Fill and bleed the cooling system.
41. Install fan and clutch assembly. Left hand thread. Turn nut counterclockwise to tighten.
42. Install radiator fan shroud halves.
43. Remove intake manifold cover, and install air cleaner. Install intake duct assembly.
44. Install hood using scribe marks drawn on hood at removal.
45. Connect battery ground cables at both batteries. Check the engine oil level and fill as needed with the specified type

and grade of oil. Run engine and check for fuel, oil and coolant leaks.

VANS WITH 300 CID (4.9L) ENGINE

1. Take off the engine cover, drain the coolant, remove the air cleaner, and disconnect the battery.
2. Remove the bumper, grille, and gravel deflector.
3. Detach the upper radiator hose at the engine. Remove the alternator splash shield and detach the lower hose at the radiator. Remove the radiator and shroud, if equipped.
4. Disconnect the engine heater hoses and the alternator wires. Remove the power steering pump and support.
5. Disconnect and plug the fuel line at the pump.
6. Detach from the engine: distributor and gauge sending unit wires, brake booster hose, accelerator cable and bracket.
7. Disconnect the automatic transmission kickdown linkage at the bellcrank.
8. Remove the exhaust manifold heat deflector and unbolt the pipe from the manifold.
9. Disconnect the automatic transmission vacuum line from the intake manifold and from the junction. Remove the transmission dipstick tube support bolt at the intake manifold.
10. Remove the upper engine-to-transmission bolts.
11. Remove the starter. Remove the flywheel inspection cover. Remove the four automatic transmission torque converter nuts, then remove the front engine support nuts. Remove the oil filter.
12. Remove the rest of the transmission-to-engine fasteners, then lift the engine out from the engine compartment with a floor crane.
13. To replace the engine, lower it into place and start the mounting bolts. Install the upper transmission bolts, the converter nuts, and the lower transmission bolts. Tighten the mounting bolts. Replace all the items removed in the previous steps.

VANS WITH OTHER V8 ENGINES

NOTE: Refer to the proceeding pickup truck section for unit disconnection details on the 6.9L diesel engine.

1. Take off the engine cover, drain the coolant, remove the air cleaner, and disconnect the battery. Remove the bumper, grille, and gravel deflector. Remove the upper grille support bracket, hood lock support, and air conditioning condenser upper mounting brackets.
2. With air conditioning, the system must be discharged to remove the condenser. Disconnect the lines at the compressor.
3. Remove the accelerator cable bracket and the heater hoses. Detach the radiator hoses and the automatic transmission cooler lines, if any. Remove the fan shroud, fan, and radiator.
4. Pivot the alternator in and detach the wires.
5. Remove the air cleaner, duct and valve, exhaust manifold shroud, and flex tube.
6. Disconnect the automatic transmission shift rod.
7. Disconnect the fuel and choke lines, detach the vacuum lines, and remove the carburetor and spacer.
8. Remove the oil filter. Detach the exhaust pipe from the manifold. Unbolt the automatic transmission tube bracket from the cylinder head. Remove the starter.
9. Remove the engine mount bolts. With automatic, remove the converter inspection cover and unbolt the converter from the flex plate.
10. Unbolt the engine ground cable and support the transmission.
11. Remove the power steering front bracket. Detach only one vacuum line at the rear of the intake manifold. Disconnect the engine wiring loom. Remove the speed control servo from the manifold. Detach the compressor clutch wire.
12. Install a lifting bracket and attach a floor crane. Remove the transmission-to-engine bolts, making sure the transmission is supported. Remove the engine.
13. To install the engine, align the converter to the flex plate and the engine dowels to the transmission. With manual transmission, start the transmission shaft into the clutch disc. You may have to turn the crankshaft slowly with the transmission in gear. Install the transmission bolts, then the mounting bolts. Replace all the items removed in the previous steps.

V8 ENGINES, USED IN MEDUIM AND HEAVY DUTY VEHICLES (EXCEPT 370 CID AND 429 CID)

1. On B, F and FT series vehicles, remove engine hood assembly from vehicle; on C and CT vehicles, release cab lock and tilt the cab forward. On N and NT series vehicles, position a suitable support in front of the vehicle to accept the hood and fender assembly when it is fully forward, then raise the hood and fender assembly.
2. Disconnect the ground cable from the battery. On N and NT series, disconnect and remove the battery.
3. Drain cooling system and crankcase.
4. On N and NT series, disconnect the check cable assemblies and let the hood swing forward out of the way, resting on the support. Remove radiator to cowl support rod, disconnect water hoses and unbolt and remove radiator. On C and CT series, remove the heater hoses from the radiator, transmission oil cooler lines (automatic transmission), disconnect upper and lower radiator hoses, disconnect and remove vent line between radiator and supply tank and hose between water outlet housing and supply tank, remove fan (leaving it lay in the shroud), then remove the radiator, shroud and fan as an assembly. Remove radiator supply tank from cab to rear support. On B, F and FT series, disconnect the upper and lower hoses from the engine and water pump, remove the fan, disconnect the transmission oil cooler hoses (if applicable), then unbolt and remove radiator.
5. On a vehicle with power steering, disconnect the power steering pressure line from the pump reservoir and return line from the pump housing. Drain oil, then loosen and remove the power steering drive belt.
6. On N and NT seriess, remove fan.
7. On N, NT, C and CT series, disconnect heater hoses at engine.
8. Remove air cleaner and, if applicable, vent hose from carburetor.
9. Disconnect choke and throttle cables and accelerator linkage.
10. Disconnect tachometer cable (and bracket, is so attached) and position out of the way.
11. Remove ignition coil.
12. On a vehicle with an air compressor, relieve pressure from the system and disconnect main line from the compressor and treadle valve. Remove drive belt if it is still in place.
13. Disconnect fuel line (from tank) at the fuel pump and cap line.
14. Disconnect wires from the alternator and remove wiring harness from engine (or disconnect from junction block).
15. Disconnect cable from starter and remove starter. Remove flywheel lower housing attaching bolts first on L and LT truck. Disconnect engine-to-body ground strap.
16. Unbolt exhaust pipes from right and left exhaust manifolds.
17. Disconnect vacuum lines from intake manifold.
18. Remove clutch return spring and hydraulic clutch slave cylinder attaching bolts on C and CT series.
19. Remove driveshaft center bearing retainer (except on C and CT series) and position a jack under transmission.
20. Remove flywheel housing cover.
21. On B, F and FT series, remove lower clutch housing attaching bolts. Secure lifting apparatus. Remove front engine mount nuts. Remove remaining clutch housing bolts. Raise engine high enough to remove the bolts that attach the engine front mount bracket to the upper insulator. Carefully lift engine away from the transmission and chassis. On C and CT series, remove flywheel housing to engine attaching bolts. Remove nuts and bolts from front engine mount and upper insula-

tor. Attach lifting apparatus and remove engine from chassis. On N and NT series, remove flywheel upper housing to engine attaching bolts. Remove the bolt(s) attaching the front engine mounting plate to the front engine mount. Attach lifting apparatus. Raise engine sufficiently to remove the front support bracket-to-upper insulator bolt and nuts. Remove engine.

22. To install, carefully lower engine into chassis, aligning clutch disc splines with transmission shaft and aligning front engine mount bracket with upper insulator.

23. Install flywheel housing to engine attaching bolts, tightening securely.

24. Install flywheel housing cover.

25. Lower engine and remove jack from under transmission, being careful to keep front engine mounting aligned.

26. Install and tighten front engine mount bolts and nuts. On N and NT series, install front engine mount to mounting plate.

27. Remove lifting apparatus.

28. Install driveshaft center bearing support to frame crossmember.

29. On vehicle with power steering, install power steering unit if it was removed.

30. Install starter motor and starter cable, attaching engine-to-frame ground cable if applicable.

31. Install left and right exhaust pipes to exhaust manifolds, using new gaskets.

32. Connect alternator wires and engine wiring harness wires. Secure engine wiring harness to bracket on engine.

33. On C and CT series, install hydraulic clutch slave cylinder to the flywheel housing and attach the clutch return spring.

34. Secure coil and bracket to cylinder head and connect all leads.

35. Connect vacuum line(s) to intake manifold.

36. Connect fuel line to fuel pump.

37. On C and CT series install radiator supply tank to cab rear support.

38. Connect accelerator linkage, choke and throttle cables and tachometer cable. Adjust linkage and cables if necessary.

39. Connect heater hoses.

40. On vehicles equipped with air system, install and connect all components.

41. Connect engine-to-body ground strap.

42. On N and NT series, install fan. On B, F, FT, C and CT series, place fan in radiator, shroud, then install radiator, shroud and fan (loose) in vehicle. Secure all attaching bolts, insulators and radiator supports. Make sure belts are ready to be installed. Install fan and belts.

43. Connect radiator upper and lower hoses. On C and CT series, connect hoses to radiator supply tank.

44. On vehicle with automatic transmission, connect transmission oil cooler lines to radiator lower tank.

44. On vehicle with automatic transmission, connect transmission oil cooler lines to radiator lower tank.

45. On vehicle with power steering, install and tighten the drive belt and connect power steering pressure line to the pump reservoir and return line to the pump housing.

46. On C and CT series, attach the heater hoses, throttle cable, choke cable and tachometer cable to the radiator.

47. Install air cleaner.

48. Install (if removed) and connect battery cables.

49. Fill crankcase and cooling system.

50. On B, F and FT series, install the hood.

51. On N and NT series, raise hood and connect check cables.

52. Adjust clutch as required.

53. Operate engine and check for lubricant and coolant leaks.

B, F AND LT SERIES WITH 370 CID AND 429 CID V8 ENGINES

1. Drain the cooling system and the engine crankcase. Disconnect the ground cable from the battery. Remove the hood from the vehicle.

2. Disconnect the radiator hoses. Remove the fan. Remove the air cleaner and vent hose from the carburetor.

3. If the vehicle is equipped with automatic transmission, disconnect the oil cooler lines. Remove the radiator.

4. Disconnect the wires from the alternator. Drain the air system and disconnect the air line at the compressor. Disconnect the starter motor cable and remove the starter.

5. Disconnect the muffler inlet pipes from the exhaust manifolds. Disconnect the body-to-engine ground strap from the engine. Disconnect the accelerator linkage at the dash. Disconnect the choke cable (manual choke) and the throttle cable from the carburetor. Disconnect the heater hose from the engine. Disconnect the treadle valve air line.

6. Disconnect and plug the fuel line. Disconnect the wiring harness from the engine. Remove the ignition coil and its mounting bracket.

7. Disconnect the drive shaft center bearing retainer from the cross member to permit raising or lowering of the transmission. Position a jack under the transmission to support it.

8. Remove the cover from the lower end of the clutch housing. Remove the bolts from the lower half of the clutch housing. Remove the nuts that secure the engine support to the upper insulator. Remove the retaining clutch housing attaching bolts.

NOTE: A left and a right lifting bracket are used to remove the engine, the left bracket is placed on the left cylinder head and the right bracket is placed on the right cylinder head. A sling is attached to each bracket to lift out the engine.

9. Secure the lifting sling to the lifting brackets and raise the engine high enough to remove the bolts that attach the engine front support bracket to the upper insulator. Carefully lift the engine away from the transmission and out of the vehicle.

10. To install, lower the engine into the vehicle. Align the clutch hub splines with those on the transmission input shaft. Position the engine in place against the clutch housing and install the attaching bolts. Remove the jack from under the transmission.

11. Lower the engine and align the engine front and rear supports with the upper insulator, and secure. Remove the engine lifting sling and brackets.

12. Secure the drive shaft center bearing support to the frame crossmember. Install the cover on the lower end of the clutch housing. Position a new gasket on each exhaust manifold flange. Secure the muffler inlet pipes to the exhaust manifolds.

13. Install the starter motor and the starter cable. Reconnect the alternator wires to their proper place on the alternator. Secure the coil and its bracket to the left cylinder head. Unplug and connect the fuel line.

14. Connect the accelerator linkage to the dash panel. Connect the treadle valve air line. Connect the choke cable (manual choke) and the throttle cable to the carburetor and adjust both.

15. Connect the engine wiring harness to the respective connectors. Connect the engine-to-body ground strap to the rear of the engine. Connect the heater hoses. Connect the main air line to the compressor.

16. Position the fan in the radiator shroud. Install the radiator. Position the fan on the water pump pulley (or high mount), and secure it in place with the attaching bolts. Connect the radiator hoses. Fill and bleed the cooling system.

17. Fill the engine with the proper grade of oil. Connect the battery cables. Adjust the clutch as required. Start the engine and check for leaks. Install the air cleaner and vent hose. Install the hood.

C AND CT SERIES WITH V8 ENGINES

1. Release the cab lock and tilt the cab forward. Drain the cooling system and the crankcase. Disconnect the battery ground cable.

2. Remove the clamps holding the throttle, choke, and tachometer cables. Remove the clamps securing the heater hoses to the radiator.

3. Remove the air cleaner. Disconnect the accelerator rod, throttle cable and choke cable (manual choke) from the carburetor and position it out of the way. If vehicle is equipped with an air compressor remove the belt.

4. Remove the fan from the crank-shaft damper and lay it inside the fan shroud. If equipped with automatic transmission, disconnect the transmission oil cooler lines at the radiator.

5. Disconnect the radiator hoses. Disconnect and remove the vent line between the radiator and the supply tank and the hose between the water outlet housing and the supply tank.

6. Remove the radiator attaching bolts and insulators from the top brackets and the nuts and insulators from the bottom support rods. Remove the radiator, shroud and fan as an assembly.

7. Disconnect the heater hoses at the water pump and intake manifold and position them out of the way. Remove the ignition coil. Remove the radiator supply tank from the cab rear support.

8. Disconnect and plug the fuel line. Disconnect the windshield wiper and vacuum brake hoses from the intake manifold. If vehicle is equipped with an air compressor, release the air pressure and disconnect the main air line from the compressor.

9. Disconnect the wires from the alternator and the engine wires at the junction block. Remove the clutch return spring. Remove the hydraulic clutch slave cylinder attaching bolts.

10. Remove both muffler inlet pipes from the exhaust manifolds. Disconnect the starter motor cable from the starter and remove the starter. (Ground strap is held by one starter bolt).

11. If equipped with power steering, remove the power steering pump and reservoir and position it out of the way.

12. Position a jack under the transmission. Remove the flywheel housing inspection cover. Remove the flywheel housing-to-engine attaching bolts. Remove the engine front and rear support bolts.

13. Attach the lifting brackets and sling and remove the engine from the vehicle.

NOTE: Left and a right lifting brackets are used to remove the engine. The left bracket is placed on the left cylinder head and the right bracket is placed on the right cylinder head. A sling is attached to each bracket to lift the engine out.

14. To install, position the engine in the vehicle using a floor crane. Engage the clutch hub splines with the transmission input shaft and slide the engine back against the transmission.

15. Install the flywheel housing to engine bolts. Install the flywheel housing inspection cover. Remove the jack from under the transmission.

16. Lower the engine and align the front support bracket with the upper insulator, and install the bolts and nuts. Remove the engine lifting sling and brackets.

17. If so equipped, install the power steering unit. Install the starter and the ground strap. Attach the starter cable to the starter. Install the muffler inlet pipes to the exhaust manifolds, using new gaskets.

18. Install the hydraulic clutch slave cylinder to the flywheel housing, and attach the clutch return spring. Connect the alternator wires to their respective terminals. Connect the engine wiring harness to the junction block. On vehicles equipped with an air compressor, connect the main air line.

19. Connect the brake hose to the intake manifold vacuum connections. Unplug and connect the fuel line. Install the radiator supply tank to the cab rear support. Install the ignition coil to the left cylinder head. Connect the heater hoses to their respective locations.

20. Install the radiator, shroud, and fan (loose inside shroud) in the chassis. Secure the radiator with insulators and nuts to the bottom support rods and insulators and bolts to the top brackets.

21. Connect the radiator to supply tank vent tube. Connect the radiator hoses to their respective locations. Install and connect the water outlet housing-to-supply tank hose.

22. If equipped with automatic transmission, connect the oil cooler lines to the radiator. Install the fan on the crankshaft damper. Install and adjust the air compressor belt, if so equipped.

23. Connect the accelerator rod, throttle cable, and choke cables (manual choke) to the carburetor. Install the air cleaner.

24. Connect the ground cable to the battery. Fill the engine with the proper type oil. Fill the cooling system. Operate the engine at fast idle and check for leaks. Lower the cab and lock it into position.

LN AND LNT SERIES WITH V8 ENGINES

NOTE: Position a suitable support in front of the vehicle to hold the hood and fender assembly when it is fully forward.

1. Raise the hood and fender assembly. Disconnect and remove the battery.

2. Disconnect the check cable assemblies and allow the hood to swing forward, resting on the previously positioned support. Remove the radiator to cowl support rod.

3. If vehicle is equipped with power steering, disconnect the power steering pressure line from the pump reservoir and return line from the pump housing. Drain the power steering fluid.

4. Disconnect the upper radiator hose from the thermostat housing and the lower hose from the water pump. Remove the radiator attaching bolts and insulators from the top radiator support brackets and the nuts and insulators from the bottom support rods. Remove the radiator. Remove the bolts attaching the fan blade to the water pump hub (or high-mount fan hub).

5. If equipped with an air compressor, release the air pressure from the system. Disconnect the main air line from the air compressor. Disconnect the main air line from the treadle value.

6. Remove the air cleaner. Disconnect the heater hoses from the engine. Disconnect and plug the flexible fuel line.

7. Disconnect the choke control cable (manual choke) and the throttle control cable at the carburetor. Disconnect the accelerator linkage.

8. Remove the ignition coil. Disconnect the vacuum line from the intake manifold. Disconnect the wiring harness. Disconnect the wires from the alternator.

9. Remove the flywheel housing cover, and the lower flywheel housing bolts.

10. Disconnect the starter cable from the starter. Remove the starter, dust cover and the engine ground strap.

11. Remove both muffler inlet pipe attaching nuts from the manifold and disengage the inlet pipes.

12. Remove the drive shaft center bearing retainer, to permit raising and lowering of the drive shaft and transmission. Position a jack under the transmission. Remove the flywheel housing-to-engine upper bolts. Remove the bolt(s) attaching the engine front mounting plate to the engine front mount.

13. Attach engine lifting equipment.

NOTE: Left and right lifting brackets are used to remove the engine. The left bracket is placed on the left cylinder head and the right bracket is placed on the right cylinder head. A sling is attached to each bracket to lift out the engine.

14. Raise the engine just enough to remove the front support bracket-to-upper insulator bolts and nuts. Remove the engine from the vehicle.

15. To install, position the engine to align the front support bracket with the upper insulator. Install the bolts and nuts. In-

stall the flywheel housing-to-engine bolts. Lower the engine and remove the transmission jack. Remove the engine lifting brackets.

16. Install the bolt(s) attaching the engine mounting plate to the engine front mount. Install the drive shaft center bearing retainer. Install the flywheel housing cover bolts.

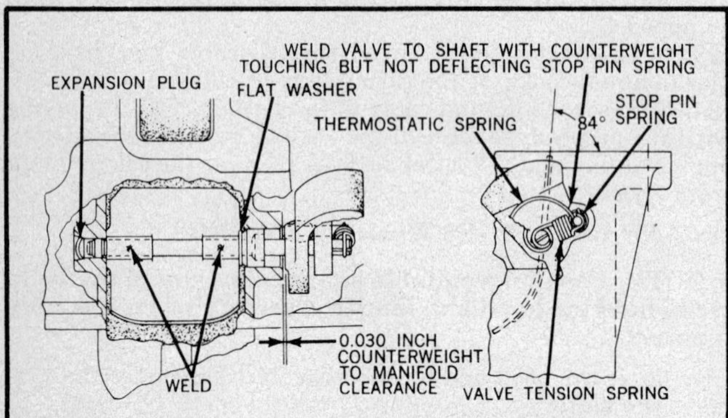

Exhaust valve plate position and counterweight clearance (© Ford Motor Co.)

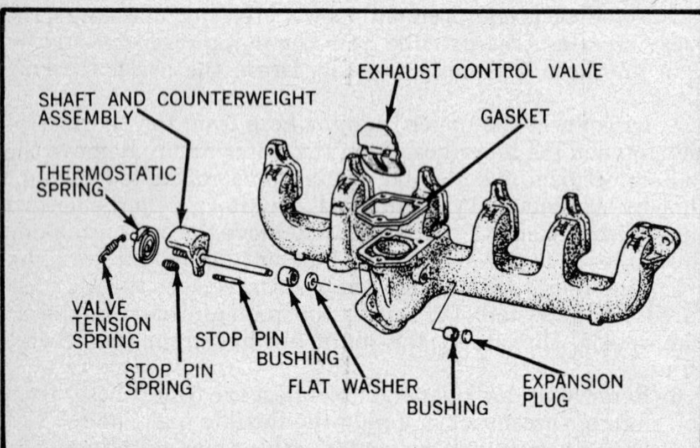

Exhaust control valve assembly—300 engine (© Ford Motor Co.)

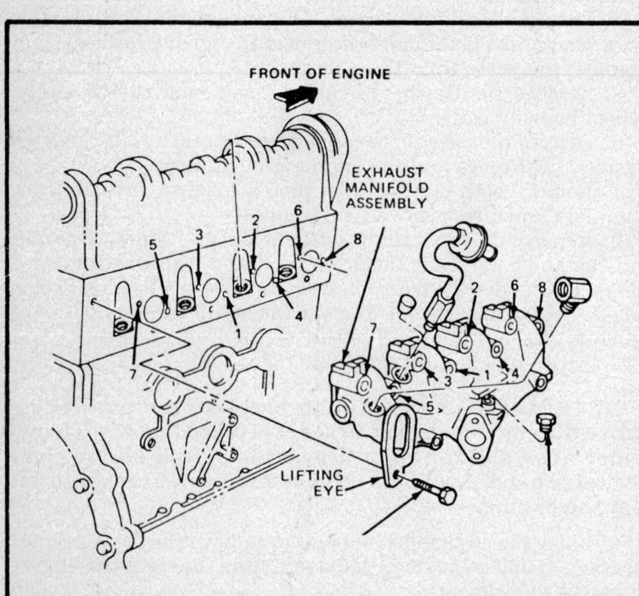

122(2.0L) and 140(2.3L) exhaust manifold bolt tightening sequence (© Ford Motor Co.)

17. Place new gaskets on the end of the muffler inlet pipes and install both exhaust manifolds.

18. Install the starter, engine ground strap and dust cover. Connect the starter cable to the starter. Connect the wires to the alternator and the wiring harness to the engine. Connect the vacuum line to the intake manifold.

19. Position the tachometer cable on the engine, attaching the two clamps, and connect the tachometer cable to the distributor. Install the ignition coil.

20. Connect the choke cable (manual choke) and the throttle cable to the carburetor. Connect the accelerator linkage. Unplug and connect the fuel line. Connect the heater hoses to the engine. Install the air cleaner.

21. If equipped with air brakes, connect the main air line to the compressor and the air line to the treadle valve.

22. Install the fan blade on the hub. Install the radiator. Connect the radiator hoses to their respective locations.

23. If equipped with power steering, install and tighten the drive belt. Connect the power steering pressure line to the pump housing and the return line to the pump reservoir.

24. Install the radiator support rod to the cowl and radiator. Fill the engine with the proper oil. Fill the cooling system.

25. Raise the hood and check cables. Install and connect the battery. Start the engine and check for oil and water leaks.

Exhaust Manifold

Removal and Installation

122 CID (2.0L) AND 140 CID (2.3L) ENGINES

1. Remove the air cleaner and duct assembly. Disconnect the negative battery cable.
2. Remove the EGR line at the exhaust manifold. Loosen the EGR tube. Remove the check valve at the exhaust manifold and disconnect the hose at the end of the air by-pass valve.
3. Remove the bracket attaching the heater hoses to the valve cover. Disconnect the exhaust pipe from the exhaust manifold.
4. Remove the exhaust manifold mounting bolts/nuts and remove the manifold.
5. Install the exhaust manifold in the reverse order.

173 CID (2.8L) V6 AND 179 CID (2.9L) V6 ENGINES

1. Disconnect the negative battery cable. Remove the air cleaner and duct assembly.
2. Remove the left side heat shroud from the exhaust manifold. Remove any thermactor system parts that will interfere with manifold removal. Disconnect the choke heat tube at the carburetor.
3. Disconnect the exhaust pipes from the exhaust manifolds. Remove the mounting nuts from exhaust manifold studs. Remove the exhaust manifolds.
4. Install in the reverse order using new exhaust pipe to manifold gaskets.

300 CID (4.9L) ENGINE

The intake and exhaust manifold on these engines are combination type manifolds and are serviced as a complete unit, see Intake/Exhaust Manifold for the proper removal and installation procedures.

232 CID (3.8L) AND ALL V8 ENGINES

1. Remove the air cleaner if the manifold being removed has the carburetor heat stove attached to it. On 351 and 400 remove the oil filter.
2. Remove the dipstick tube bracket bolt/nut on the 302 V8. On 351 and 400 V8 vehicles with a column mounted automatic transmission lever, disconnect the selector lever cross-shaft for clearance. On 1981 and later models, disconnect the EGO sensor, if equipped.
3. Remove any of the thermactor parts that will interfere with the manifold removal.

4. Disconnect the exhaust pipe or catalytic converter from the exhaust manifold. Remove and discard the donut gasket.
5. Disconnect the EGR downtube. Remove the exhaust manifold attaching screws and remove the manifold from the cylinder head.
6. Install the exhaust manifold in the reverse order of removal. Apply a light coat of graphite grease to the mating surface of the manifold. Install and tighten the attaching bolts, starting from the center and working to both ends alternately. Tighten to the proper specifications.

Intake Manifold

Removal and Installation

122 CID (2.0L) AND 140 CID (2.3L) ENGINES

1. Drain the cooling system. Remove the air cleaner and duct assembly. Disconnect the negative battery cable.
2. Disconnect the accelerator cable, vacuum hoses (as required) and the hot water hose at the manifold fitting. Be sure to identify all vacuum hoses for proper reinstallation.
3. Remove the engine oil dipstick. Disconnect the heat tube at the EGR (exhaust gas recirculation) valve. Disconnect the fuel line at the carburetor fuel fitting.
4. Remove the dipstick retaining bolt from the intake manifold.
5. Disconnect and remove the PCV at the engine and intake manifold.
6. Remove the distributor cap and position the cap and wires out of the way, after removing the plastic plug connector from the valve cover.
7. Remove the intake manifold retaining bolts. Remove the manifold from the engine.
8. Clean all gasket mounting surfaces.

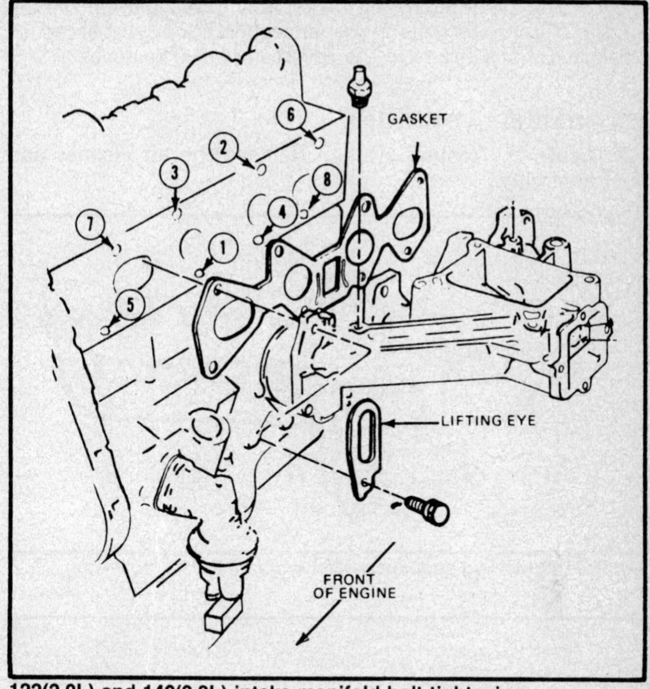

122(2.0L) and 140(2.3L) intake manifold bolt tightening sequence (© Ford Motor Co.)

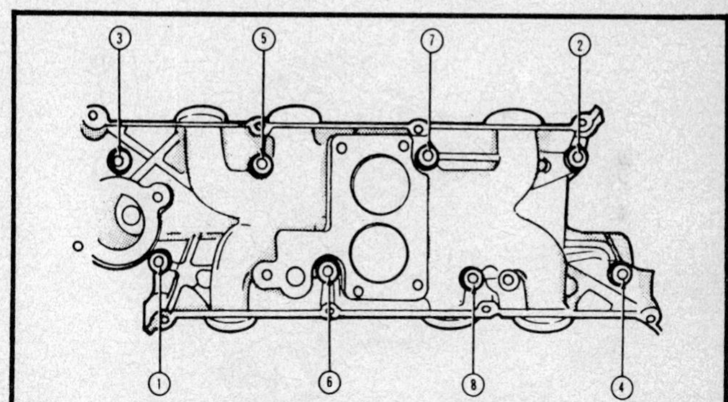

173(2.8L) V6 intake manifold bolt tightening sequence (© Ford Motor Co.)

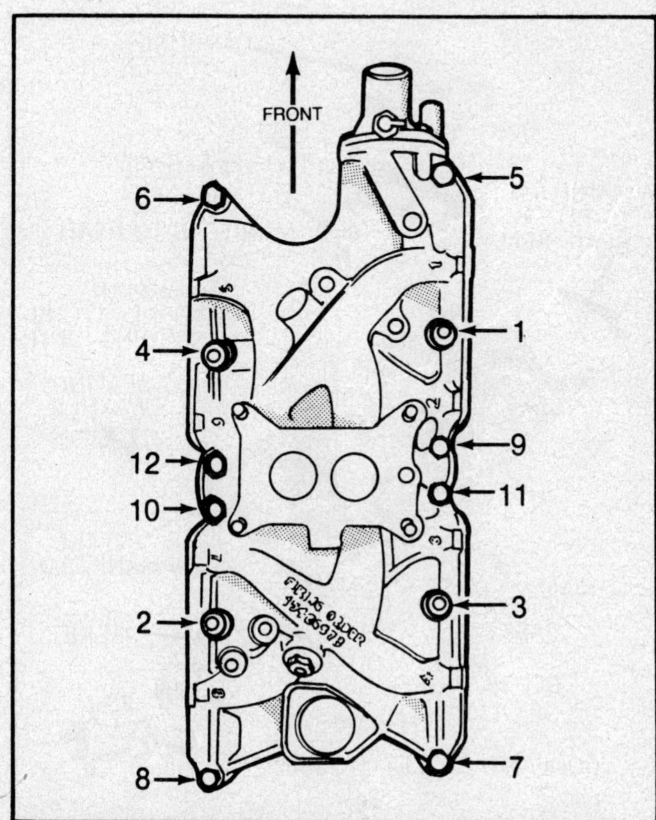

Intake manifold torque sequence—302 V8 (© Ford Motor Co.)

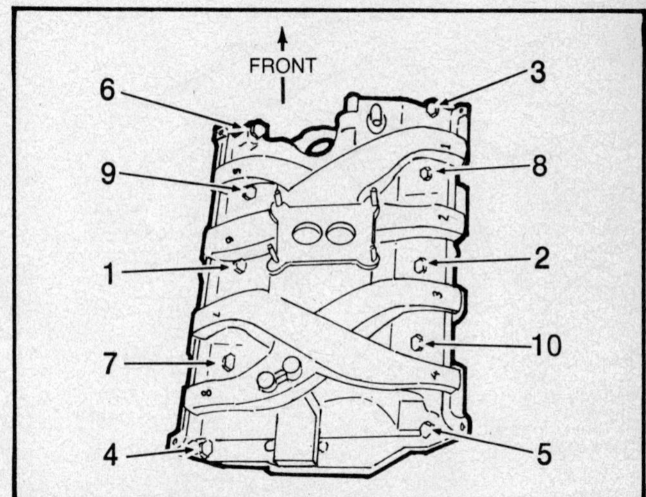

Intake manifold torque sequence—V8 except 302, 351, 370, 429 and 460 (© Ford Motor Co.)

9. Install a new mounting gasket and intake manifold on the engine. Torque the bolts in proper sequence. The rest of the installation procedure is in the reverse order of removal.

173 CID (2.8L) V6 ENGINE

1. Drain the cooling system. Remove the air cleaner and duct assembly.

2. Disconnect the negative battery cable. Disconnect the accelerator cable from the carburetor linkage.

3. Disconnect and remove the upper radiator hose. Disconnect and remove the bypass hose from the intake manifold and thermostat housing.

4. Remove the distributor cap and spark plug wires as an assembly. Turn the engine till No. piston is at TDC (top dead center) on the compression stroke. Remove the distributor.

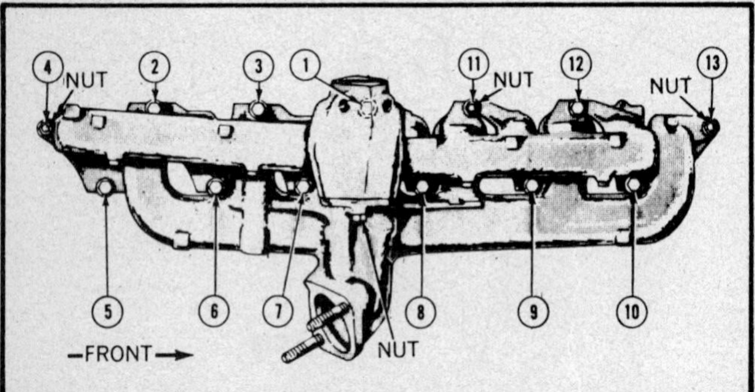

Manifold tightening sequence—300 engine (© Ford Motor Co.)

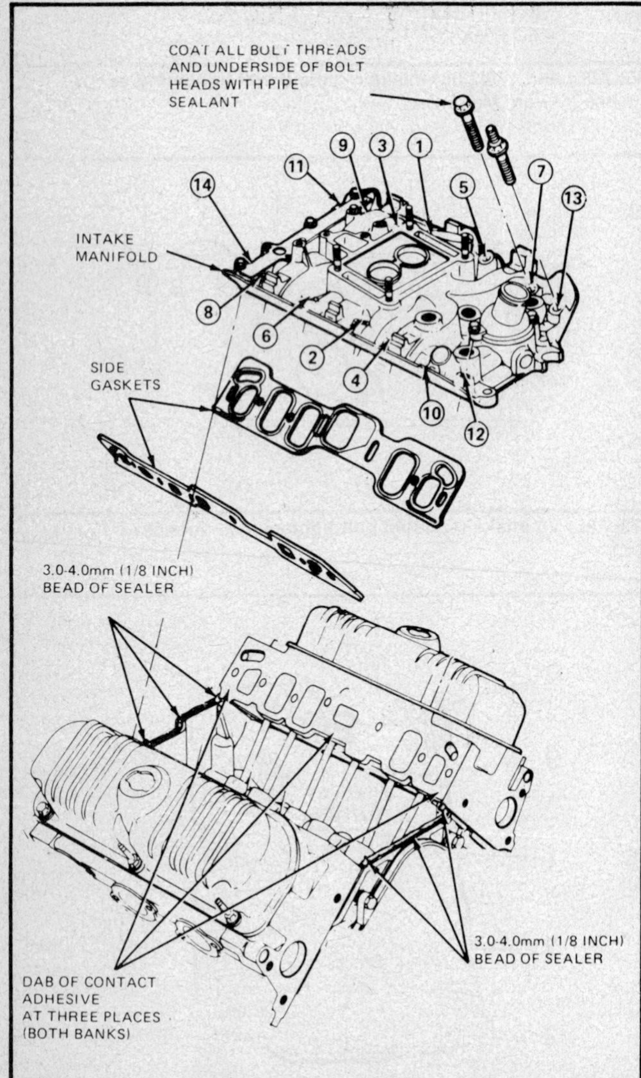

Installation of intake manifold (torque sequence numbered)—232 CID V-6 engine (© Ford Motor Co.)

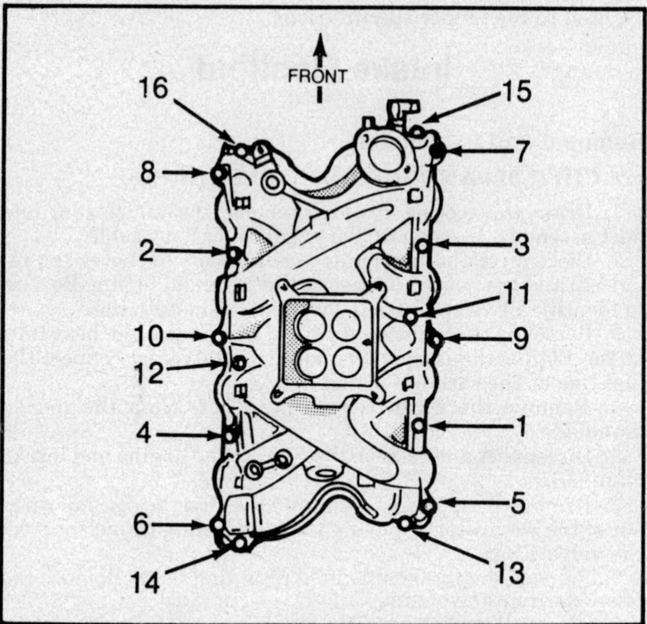

Intake manifold torque sequence—370, 429 and 460 V8 (© Ford Motor Co.)

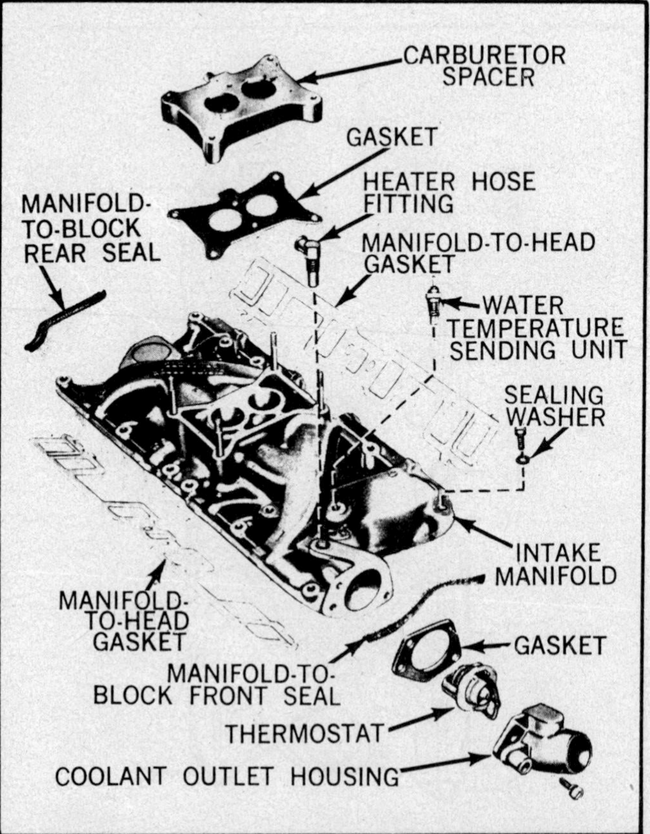

Intake manifold—302 and 351 V8 (© Ford Motor Co.)

5. Remove any vacuum lines and controls that will interfere with the intake manifold removal. Label all hoses for identification.
6. Remove both valve covers. Remove the manifold mounting nuts and bolts. Remove the manifold. Tap the manifold lightly with a plastic mallet (if necessary) to break the gasket seal.
7. Remove all old gasket material and sealing compound from the mounting surfaces.
8. Apply sealing compound to the joining surfaces. Place the intake mounting gasket into position. Make sure that the tab on the right bank head gasket fits into the cutout of the manifold gasket. Apply sealing compound to the intake manifold bolt bosses and install the intake manifold. Tighten the mounting nuts and bolts in the proper torque sequence.
9. Install the distributor and the rest of the removed components in reverse order.
10. Refill the cooling system, start the engine and check for coolant or oil leaks.
11. Check idle RPM and ignition timing. Adjust if necessary.

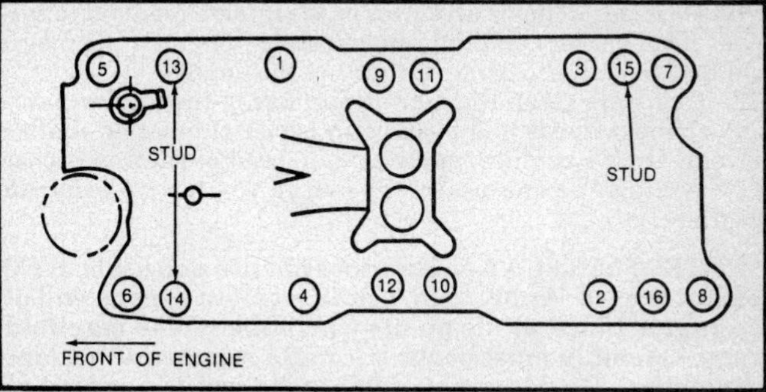

Intake manifold torque sequence—351 V8 (© Ford Motor Co.)

300 CID (4.9L) ENGINE

The intake and exhaust manifolds on these engines are known as combination manifolds and are serviced as a unit.

1. Remove the air cleaner. Disconnect the choke cable at the carburetor. Disconnect the accelerator cable or rod at the carburetor. Remove the accelerator retracting spring.
2. On a vehicle with automatic transmission, remove the kick-down rod-retracting spring. Remove the accelerator rod bellcrank assembly.
3. Disconnect the fuel inlet line and the distributor vacuum line from the carburetor.
4. Disconnect the muffler inlet pipe from the exhaust manifold.
5. Disconnect the power brake vacuum line, if so equipped.
6. Remove the bolts and nuts attaching the manifolds to the cylinder head. Lift the manifold assemblies from the engine. Remove and discard the gaskets.
7. To separate the manifolds, remove the nuts joining the intake and exhaust manifolds.
8. Clean the mating surfaces of the cylinder head and the manifolds.
9. If the intake and exhaust manifolds have been separated, coat the mating surfaces lightly with graphite grease and place the exhaust manifold over the studs on the intake manifold. Install the lockwashers and nuts. Tighten them finger tight.
10. Install a new intake manifold gasket.
11. Coat the mating surfaces lightly with graphite grease. Place the manifold assemblies in position against the cylinder head. Make sure that the gaskets have not become dislodged. Install the attaching washers, bolts and nuts. Tighten the attaching nuts and bolts in the proper sequence to 26 ft. lbs. If the intake and exhaust manifolds were separated, tighten the nuts joining them.

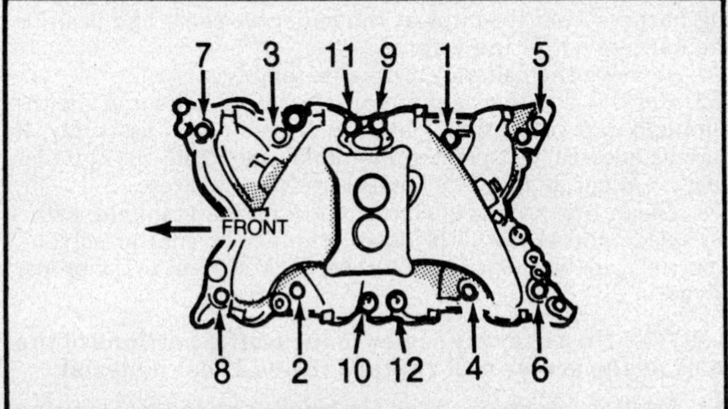

Silicone rubber sealer application on intake manifold seal—351M and 400 V8 engines (© Ford Motor Co.)

12. Position a new gasket on the muffler inlet pipe and connect the inlet pipe to the exhaust manifold.
13. Connect the crankcase vent hose to the intake manifold inlet tube and position the hose clamp.
14. Connect the fuel inlet line and the distributor vacuum line to the carburetor.
15. Connect the accelerator cable to the carburetor and install the retracting spring. Connect the choke cable to the carburetor.
16. On a vehicle with an automatic transmission, install the bellcrank assembly and the kick-down rod retracting spring. Adjust the transmission control linkage.
17. Install the air cleaner.

232 CID (3.8L) V6 AND ALL V8 ENGINES, EXCEPT 460 CID (7.5L), 370 CID (6.1L), 429 CID (7.0L) AND FUEL INJECTED ENGINE MODELS

1. Drain the cooling system, remove the air cleaner and the intake duct assembly.
2. Disconnect the accelerator rod from the carburetor and remove the accelerator retracting spring. Disconnect the automatic transmission kick-down rod at the carburetor, if so equipped.
3. Disconnect the high tension lead and all other wires from the ignition coil.

NOTE: Distributor removal is not necessary on 3.8L V6 engines, disregard steps pretaining to its removal.

4. Disconnect the spark plug wires from the spark plugs by grasping the rubber boots and twisting and pulling at the same time. Remove the wires from the brackets on the rocker covers. Remove the distributor cap and spark plug wire assembly.
5. Remove the carburetor fuel inlet line and the distributor vacuum line from the carburetor.
6. Remove the distributor lockbolt and remove the distributor and vacuum line, as required.
7. Disconnect the upper radiator hose from the coolant outlet housing and the water temperature sending unit wire at the sending unit. Remove the heater hose from the intake manifold.
8. Loosen the clamp on the water pump bypass hose at the coolant outlet housing and slide the hose off the outlet housing.
9. Disconnect the PCV hose at the rocker cover.
10. If the engine is equipped with the Thermactor exhaust emission control system, remove the air pump to cylinder head air hose at the air pump and position it out of the way. Also remove the air hose at the backfire suppressor valve. Remove the air hose bracket from the valve rocker arm cover and position the air hose out of the way. Remove EGR valve tube on V6 models.
11. Remove the intake manifold and carburetor as an assembly. It may be necessary to pry the intake manifold from the

cylinder head. Remove all traces of the intake manifold to cylinder head gaskets and the two end seals from both the manifold and the other mating surfaces of the engine.

12. To install, clean the mating surfaces of the intake manifold, cylinder heads and block with laquer thinner or similar solvent. On V8 engines, apply a $\frac{1}{8}$ in. bead of silicone rubber RTV sealant at the points shown in the accompanying diagram.

NOTE: The 3.8L V6 engine does not use end seals. RTV sealant is used. Apply $\frac{1}{8}$ in. bead of sealant to each end of the engine block at the points where the intake manifold rests. Assembly must occur within 15 minutes of sealant application. Do not apply sealer to the waffle portions of the seals as the sealer will rupture the end seal material.

13. On V8 engines, position new seals on the block and press the seal locating extensions into the holes in the mating surfaces.

14. Apply a $\frac{1}{16}$ in. bead of sealer to the outer end of each manifold seal for the full length of the seal (4 places). As before, do not apply sealer to the waffle portion of the end seals.

NOTE: This sealer sets in about 15 minutes, depending on brand, so work quickly but carefully. Do not drop any sealer into the manifold cavity. It will form and set and plug the oil gallery.

15. Position the manifold gasket onto the block and heads with the alignment notches under the dowels in the heads. Be sure gasket holes align with head holes.

16. Install the manifold and related equipment in reverse order of removal.

FUEL INJECTED ENGINE

NOTE: Discharge fuel system pressure before starting any work that involves disconnecting fuel system lines. See "Fuel Supply Manifold" removal and installation procedures (Gasoline Fuel System section).

1. To remove the upper manifold: Remove the air cleaner. Disconnect the electrical connectors at the air bypass valve, throttle position sensor and EGR position sensor.

2. Disconnect the throttle linkage at the throttle ball and the AOD transmission linkage from the throttle body. Remove the bolts that secure the bracket to the intake and position the bracket and cables out of the way.

3. Disconnect the upper manifold vacuum fitting connections by removing all the vacuum lines at the vacuum tree (label lines for position identification). Remove the vacuum lines to the EGR valve and fuel pressure regulator.

4. Disconnect the PCV system by disconnecting the hose from the fitting at the rear of the upper manifold.

5. Remove the two canister purge lines from the fittings at the throttle body.

6. Disconnect the EGR tube from the EGR valve by loosening the flange nut.

7. Remove the bolt from the upper intake support bracket to upper manifold.
Remove the upper manifold retaining bolts and remove the upper intake manifold and throttle body as an assembly.

8.Clean and inspect all mounting surfaces of the upper and lower intake manifolds.

9.Position a new mounting gasket on the lower intake manifold and install the upper manifold in the reverse order of removal. Mounting bolts are torqued to 12–18 ft. lbs.

10. To remove the lower intake manifold: Upper manifold and throttle body must be removed first.

11. Drain the cooling system. Remove the distributor assembly, cap and wires.

12. Disconnect the electrical connectors at the engine coolant temperature sensor and sending unit, at the air charge temperature sensor and at the knock sensor.

13. Disconnect the injector wiring harness from the main harness assembly. Remove the ground wire from the intake manifold stud. The ground wire must be installed at the same position it was removed from.

14. Disconnect the fuel supply and return lines from the fuel rails.

15. Remove the upper radiator hose from the thermostat housing. Remove the bypass hose. Remove the heater outlet hose at the intake manifold.

16. Remove the air cleaner mounting bracket. Remove the intake manifold mounting bolts and studs. Pay attention to the location of the bolts and studs for reinstallation. Remove the lower intake manifold assembly.

17. Clean and inspect the mounting surfaces of the heads and manifold.

18. Apply a $\frac{1}{16}$ inch bead of RTV sealer to the ends of the manifold seals (at the junction point of the seals and gaskets). Install the end seals and intake gaskets on the cylinder heads. The gaskets must interlock with the seal tabs.

19.
Install locator bolts at opposite ends of each head and carefully lower the intake manifold into position. Install and tighten the mounting bolts and studs to 23–25 ft. lbs. Install the remaining components in the reverse order of removal.

460 CID (7.5L), 370 CID (6.1L), AND 429 CID (7.0L) ENGINES

1. Drain the cooling system and remove the air cleaner assembly.

2. Disconnect the upper radiator hose at the engine.

3. Disconnect the heater hoses at the intake manifold and the water pump. Position them out of the way. Loosen the water pump by-pass hose clamp at the intake manifold.

4. Disconnect the PCV valve and hose at right valve cover. Disconnect all of the vacuum lines at the rear of the intake manifold and tag them for proper reinstallation.

5. Disconnect the wires at the spark plugs, and remove the wires from the brackets on the valve covers. Disconnect the high-tension wire from the coil and remove the distributor cap and wires as an assembly.

6. Disconnect all of the distributor vacuum lines at the carburetor and vacuum control valve and tag them for proper installation. Remove the distributor and vacuum lines as an assembly.

7. Disconnect the accelerator linkage at the carburetor. Remove the speed control linkage bracket, if so equipped, from the manifold and carburetor.

8. Remove the bolts holding the accelerator linkage bellcrank and position the linkage and return springs out of the way.

9. Disconnect the fuel line at the carburetor.

10. Disconnect the wiring harness at the coil battery terminal, engine temperature sending unit, oil pressure sending unit, and other connections as necessary. Disconnect the wiring harness from the clips at the left valve cover and position the harness out of the way.

11. Remove the coil and bracket assembly.

12. Remove the intake manifold attaching bolts and lift the manifold and carburetor from the engine as an assembly. It may be necessary to pry the manifold away from the cylinder heads. Do not damage the gasket sealing surfaces.

13. Clean the mating surfaces of the intake manifold, cylinder heads and block with laquer, thinner or similar solvent. Apply a $\frac{1}{8}$ in. bead of silicone rubber RTV sealant to the proper points.

NOTE: Do not apply sealer to the waffle portions of the seals as the sealer will rupture the end seal material.

14. Position new seals on the block and press the seal locating extensions into the holes in the mating surfaces.

15. Apply a $\frac{1}{16}$ in. bead of sealer to the outer end of each man-

ifold seal for the full length of the seal (4 places). As before, do not apply sealer to the waffle portion of the end seals.

NOTE: This sealer sets in about 15 minutes, depending on brand, so work quickly but carefully. Do not drop any sealer into the manifold cavity. It will form and set and plug the oil gallery.

16. Position the manifold gasket onto the block and heads with the alignment notches under the dowels in the heads. Be sure gasket holes align with head holes.
17. Install the manifold and related equipment in reverse order of removal.

INTAKE/EXHAUST MANIFOLD

Removal and Installation

300 CID (4.9L) ENGINE

1. Remove air cleaner and hot air ducts.
2. Disconnect choke cable and accelerator rod or cable at the carburetor. Remove accelerator retracting spring.
3. On LN series vehicles, disconnect the battery and remove the alternator.
4. On vehicle with an automatic transmission, remove the kickdown rod retracting spring and remove the accelerator rod bellcrank assembly.
5. On C series vehicle, remove the engine oil dipstick and tube.
6. Disconnect fuel inlet line and distributor vacuum line from the carburetor, exhaust pipe from the manifold and, if so equipped, power brake vacuum line.
7. Remove manifold attaching bolts and lift manifolds from engine.
8. To separate manifolds, remove the nuts joining the intake and exhaust manifolds. Discard all gaskets.
9. If the exhaust control valve requires replacement, replace it.
10. To install, clean the mating surfaces of cylinder head and manifolds.
11. If a new manifold is to be used, remove the tube fittings on the old manifold and install them on the new one.
12. Before joining exhaust and intake manifolds, coat the mating surfaces lightly with graphite grease. Use a new gasket and tighten the nuts finger tight.
13. Coat the mating surfaces with graphite grease and install the manifold assembly on the cylinder head. Use a new intake manifold gasket. Tighten the bolts and nuts to 23–28 ft. lbs. torque in the sequence illustrated.
14. Tighten the intake to exhaust manifold stud nuts to 28–33 ft. lbs. torque.
15. Connect exhaust pipe to manifold, tightening nuts to 25–30 ft. lbs. torque.
16. Connect crankcase vent hose to intake manifold inlet tube, fuel inlet line and distributor vacuum line to carburetor, accelerator rod or cable and choke cable to carburetor. Install the accelerator retracting spring.
17. On LN series, install the alternator and belts and connect the battery.
18. On C series, install the dipstick and tube.
19. On a vehicle with an automatic transmission, install the bellcrank assembly and kickdown rod retracting spring. Adjust the transmission control linkage.
20. Install the air cleaner and hot air duct.
21. Adjust idle speed and idle fuel mixture.

EXHAUST CONTROL VALVE

Removal and Installation

300 CID (4.9L) ENGINE

1. Separate intake and exhaust manifolds.
2. Remove valve tension spring, thermostatic spring and stop pin.
3. The valve shaft must be cut with a torch on each side of the valve plate. Remove valve plate and expansion plug.
4. Remove bushings and install new ones. There are two sizes of replacement bushings (OD) so make sure the right ones are used. Ream the ID of bushings to 0.253". The shorter bushing (front) is installed 0.010–0.015" below inside surface of the manifold and the longer bushing (rear) protrudes into the manifold cavity 0.020" (note that beveled end points inward).
5. Slide new shaft into the bushings, flat washer and valve plate. Note that the flat washer is between the valve plate and the long (rearward) bushing. Install a new stop pin spring on the stop pin.
6. Rotate the counterweight and shaft assembly clockwise until the counterweight contacts the stop pin spring, then place a 0.030" feeler gauge between the counterweight and the manifold to maintain the specified clearance. Hold the valve plate at a 84 degree angle to the top surface of the manifold and tack-weld the plate to the shaft, using stainless steel welding rod.
7. Check for free movement of the valve and install expansion plug in the bushing bore.
8. Install the thermostatic spring, positioned so that it will be necessary to wind the spring $\frac{1}{2}$ turn clockwise to hook it over the stop pin.
9. Install a new valve tension spring on the exhaust control valve shaft and the stop pin.

Cylinder Head

Removal and Installation

122 CID (2.0L) AND 140 CID (2.3L) ENGINES

1. Drain the cooling system. Disconnect the negative battery cable.
2. Remove the air cleaner.
3. Remove the valve cover.

NOTE: On models with air conditioning, remove the mounting bolts and the drive belt, and position the compressor, with the hoses attached, out of the way. Remove the compressor upper mounting bracket from the cylinder head.

CAUTION

If the compressor refrigerant lines do not have enough slack to permit repositioning of the compressor without first disconnecting the refrigerant lines, the air conditioning system will have to be evacuated.

4. Remove the intake and exhaust manifolds from the head.
5. Remove the camshaft drive belt cover. Note the location of the belt cover attaching screws that have rubber grommets.
6. Loosen the drive belt tensioner and remove the belt.
7. Remove the water outlet elbow from the cylinder head with the hose attached.
8. Remove the cylinder head attaching bolts.

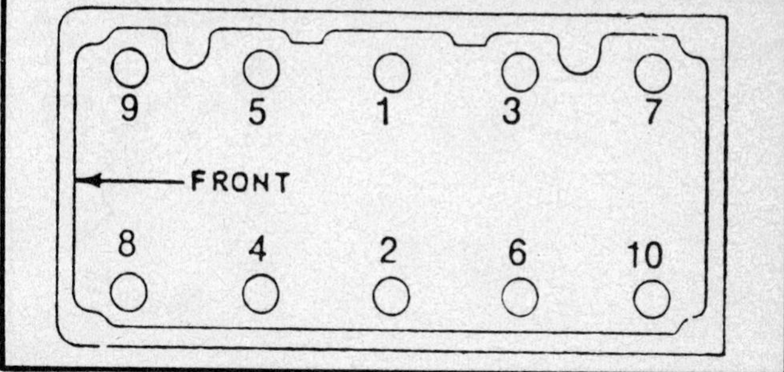

Cylinder head bolt tightening sequence—4 cylinder engines
(© Ford Motor Co.)

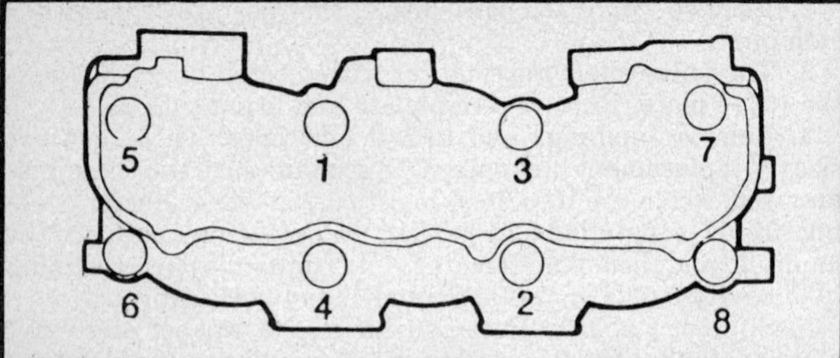

173(2.8L) V6 head bolt tightening sequence (© Ford Motor Co.)

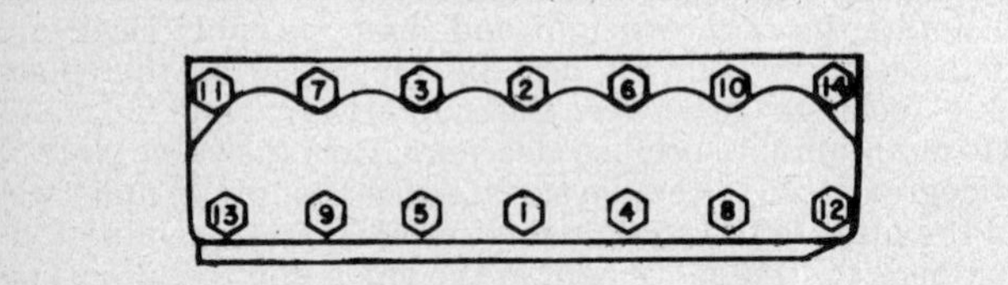

Cylinder head bolt tightening sequence—6-cylinder 300 engine (© Ford Motor Co.)

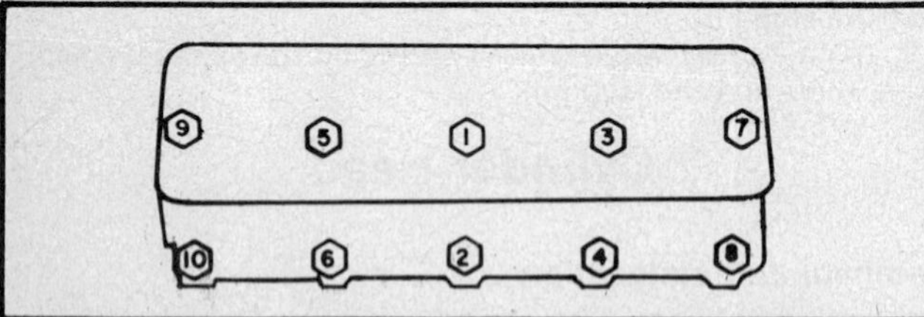

Cylinder head bolt tightening sequence—all V8 engines (© Ford Motor Co.)

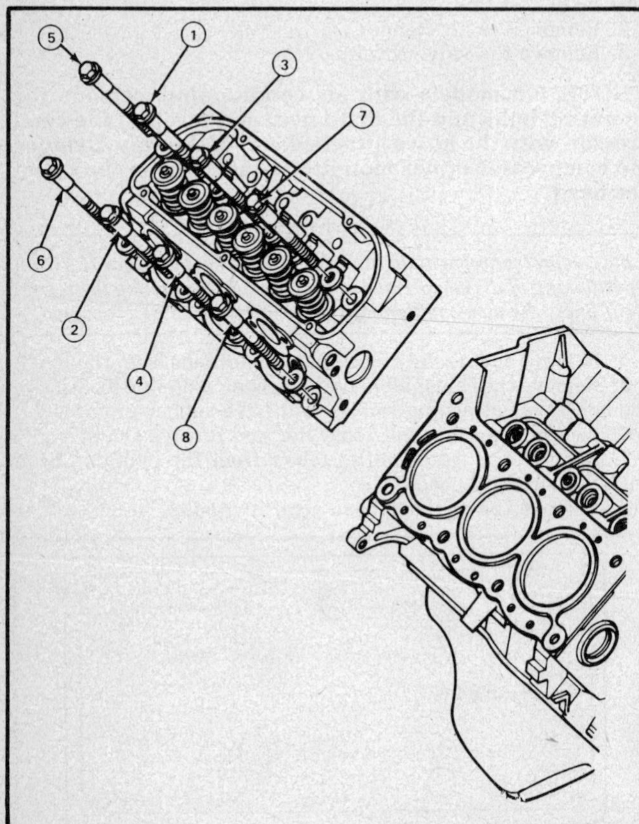

Cylinder head bolt torque sequence (torque sequence numbered)—232 CID V-6 engine (© Ford Motor Co.)

9. Remove the cylinder head from the engine.
10. Clean all gasket material and carbon from the top of the cylinder block and pistons and from the bottom of the cylinder head.
11. Position a new cylinder head gasket on the engine and place the head on the engine.

NOTE: If you encounter difficulty in positioning the cylinder head on the engine block, it may be necessary to install guide studs in the block to correctly align the head and the block. To fabricate guide studs, obtain two new cylinder head bolts and cut their heads off with a hack saw. Then, install the head gasket and head over the bolts. Install the cylinder head attaching bolts, replacing the studs with the original head bolts.

12. Using a torque wrench, tighten the head bolts in the sequence.
13. Install the camshaft drive belt.
14. Install the camshaft drive belt cover and its attaching bolts. Make sure the rubber grommets are installed on the bolts. Tighten the bolts to 6–13 ft. lbs.
15. Install the water outlet elbow and a new gasket on the engine and tighten the attaching bolts to 12–15 ft. lbs.
16. Install the intake and exhaust manifolds.
17. Assemble the rest of the components in reverse order of removal.

173 CID (2.8L) V6 AND 179 CID (2.9L) V6 ENGINES

1. Remove the air cleaner assembly and disconnect the negative battery cable and accelerator linkage. Drain the cooling system.
2. Remove the distributor cap with the spark plug wires attached. Remove the distributor vacuum line and distributor. Remove the hose from the water pump to the water outlet which is on the carburetor.
3. Remove the valve covers, fuel line and filter, carburetor, and the intake manifold.
4. Remove the rocker arm shaft and oil baffles. Remove the pushrods, keeping them in the proper sequence for installation.
5. Remove the exhaust manifold.
6. Remove the cylinder head retaining bolts and remove the cylinder heads and gaskets.
7. Remove all gasket material and carbon from the engine block and cylinder heads and gaskets.
8. Place the head gaskets on the engine block.

NOTE: The left and right gaskets are not interchangeable.

9. Install guide studs in the engine block. Install the cylinder head assemblies on the engine block one at a time. Tighten the cylinder head bolts in sequence.
10. Install the intake and exhaust manifolds.
11. Install the pushrods in the proper sequence. Install the oil baffles and the rocker arm shaft assemblies. Adjust the valve clearances.
12. Install the valve covers with new gaskets.
13. Install the distributor and set the ignition timing.
14. Install the carburetor and the distributor cap with the spark plug wires.
15. Connect the accelerator linkage, fuel line, with fuel filter installed, and distributor vacuum line to the carburetor. Fill the cooling system.

300 CID (4.9L) ENGINE

1. Drain the cooling system. Remove the air cleaner. Remove the oil filler tube. Disconnect the negative battery cable.
2. Disconnect the muffler inlet pipe at the exhaust manifold. Pull the muffler inlet pipe down. Remove the gasket.
3. Disconnect the accelerator rod or cable retracting spring. Disconnect the choke control cable if applicable and the accelerator rod at the carburetor.

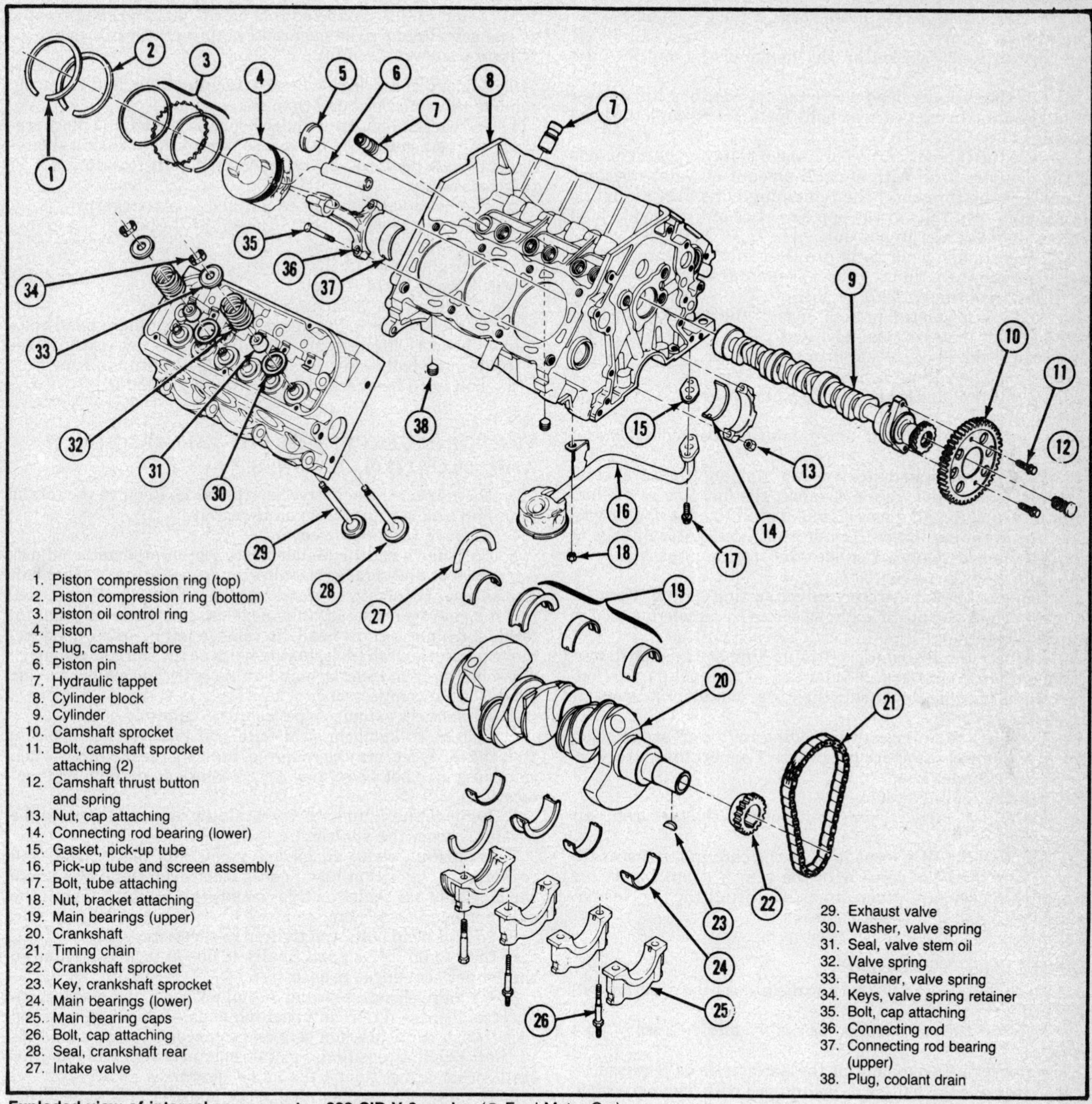

Exploded view of internal components—232 CID V-6 engine (© Ford Motor Co.)

4. Disconnect the transmission kickdown rod. Disconnect the accelerator linkage at the bellcrank assembly.

5. Disconnect the fuel inlet line at the fuel filter hose, and the distributor vacuum line at the carburetor. Disconnect other vacuum lines as necessary for accessibility and identify them for proper connection.

6. Remove the radiator upper hose at the coolant outlet housing.

7. Disconnect the distributor vacuum line at the distributor. Disconnect the carburetor fuel inlet line at the fuel pump. Remove the lines as an assembly.

8. Disconnect the spark plug wires at the spark plugs and the temperature sending unit wire at the sending unit.

9. Grasp the PCV vent hose near the PCV valve and pull the valve out of the grommet in the valve rocker arm cover. Disconnect the PCV vent hose at the hose fitting in the intake manifold spacer and remove the vent hose and PCV valve.

10. Disconnect the carburetor air vent tube and remove the valve rocker arm cover.

11. Remove the valve rocker arm shaft assembly. Remove the pushrods in sequence so that they can be identified and reinstalled in their original positions.

12. Remove the cylinder head bolts and remove the cylinder head. Do not pry between the cylinder head and the block as the gasket surfaces may be damaged.

13. To install the cylinder head: Clean the head and block gasket surfaces. If the cylinder head was removed for a gasket change, check the flatness of the cylinder head and block.

14. Apply sealer to both sides of the new cylinder head gasket, depending on maker of gasket. Refer to gasket manufac-

turers instructions, as required. Position the gasket on the cylinder block.

15. Install a new gasket on the flange of the muffler inlet pipe.

16. Lift the cylinder head above the cylinder block and lower it into position using two head bolts installed through the head as guides.

17. Coat the threads of the No.1 and 6 bolts for the right side of the cylinder head with a small amount of water resistant sealer. Oil the threads of the remaining bolts. Install, but do not tighten, two bolts at the opposite ends of the head to hold the head and gasket in position.

18. The cylinder head bolts are tightened in 3 progressive steps. Torque them (in the proper sequence) to 55 ft. lbs., then 65 ft. lbs., and finally to 75 ft. lbs.

19. Apply Lubriplate® to both ends of the pushrods and install them in their original positions.

20. Install the valve rocker arm shaft assembly.

21. Adjust the valves, as necessary.

22. Install the muffler inlet pipe lockwashers and attaching nuts.

23. Connect the radiator upper hose at the coolant outlet housing.

24. Position the distributor vacuum line and the carburetor fuel inlet line on the engine. Connect the fuel line at the fuel filter hose and install a new clamp. Install the distributor vacuum line at the carburetor. Connect the accelerator linkage at the bellcrank assembly. Connect the transmission kickdown rod.

25. Connect the accelerator rod retracting spring. Connect the choke control cable (if applicable) and the accelerator rod at the carburetor.

26. Connect the distributor vacuum line at the distributor. Connect the carburetor fuel inlet line at the fuel pump. Connect all the vacuum lines using their previous identification for proper connection.

27. Connect the temperature sending unit wire at the sending unit. Connect the spark plug wires. Connect the battery cable at the cylinder head.

28. Fill the cooling system.

29. Install the valve rocker cover. Connect the carburetor air vent tube.

30. Connect the PCV vent hose at the carburetor spacer fitting. Insert the PCV valve with the vent hose attached, into the valve rocker arm cover grommet. Install the air cleaner, start the engine and check for leaks.
fuel mixture.

232 CID (3.8L) V6 ENGINE

1. Drain the cooling system and disconnect the negative battery cable.

2. Remove the air cleaner assembly and necessary duct work.

3. Remove the drive belt for the accessories as required.

4. To remove the left head: If equipped with power steering, remove the pump mounting brackets from the cylinder head and set aside in a position to avoid fluid leakage. Remove and set aside the air conditioner compressor, if equipped.

5. To remove the the right cylinder head: Disconnect the thermactor diverter valve and hose assembly at the by-pass valve and downstream air tube. Remove the assembly. Remove the accessory drive idler. Remove the alternator. Remove the thermactor pump pulley. Remove the thermactor pump. Remove the alternator bracket. Remove the PCV valve.

6. Remove the intake manifold assembly.

7. Remove the rocker arm cover attaching screws and carefully remove the covers.

NOTE: The plastic rocker arm covers will be damaged if excessive force is applied during the removal.

8. Remove the exhaust manifolds.

9. Loosen the rocker arm fulcrum attaching bolts enough to allow the rocker arms to be lifted off the pushrods and rotated to one side. Remove the pushrods, keeping them in order to facilitate easier reassembly.

10. Remove the cylinder head attaching bolts and carefully remove the cylinder head from the engine block.

11. To reassemble the cylinder heads to the engine block, reverse the removal procedures. Use new gaskets during the reassembly, along with new cylinder head bolts to assure a leak tight assembly.

12. The head bolts should be torqued in six stages.
 a. Torque to 47 ft. lbs.
 b. Torque to 55 ft. lbs.
 c. Torque to 63 ft. lbs.
 d. Torque to 74 ft. lbs.
 e. Back off the attaching bolts 2–3 turns.
 f. Repeat Steps a, b, c and d. When the cylinder head bolts have been tightened as outlined, it is not necessary to retighten the bolts after extended engine operation. However, the bolts can be checked for tightness, if desired.

V8 ENGINES, EXCEPT 460 CID (7.5L), 370 CID (6.1L) AND 429 CID (7.0L) ENGINES

1. Disconnect the negative battery cable. Remove the intake manifold and carburetor as an assembly.

2. Remove rocker arm cover.

3. To remove right cylinder head, loosen alternator adjusting arm bolt and remove the alternator mounting bracket bolt and spacer. Swing alternator down out of the way. On some vehicles it may be necessary to remove the coil and air cleaner inlet duct from the right head. To remove left cylinder head, remove accelerator shaft fastening bolts at the front of the head. On some later models, it may be necessary to remove the air conditioning compressor bracket.

4. Disconnect exhaust pipe from the manifold.

5. Loosen rocker arm stud nuts and twist rocker arms so that the pushrods may be removed. Identify the pushrods when removing so that they may be reinstalled in their original locations.

6. Remove the cylinder head retaining bolts and remove the assembly from the vehicle.

7. To install, clean all gasket surfaces of block, head and rocker cover. Position new head gasket over the dowels onto the block (do use sealer on this composition gasket). Install the cylinder head on the engine block.

8. Install head bolts and tighten in three steps: first to 50 ft. lbs., then to 60 ft. lbs., and finally to 65–72 ft. lbs. Tighten in the proper sequence for each step.

9. Clean pushrods, blowing out oil passage, and check them for straightness. Lubricate pushrod ends, valve stem tips and rocker arm cups, fulcrum sets and followers. Install pushrods in their original positions, install exhaust stem caps and install rocker arms. Adjust the valve clearance.

10. Connect the exhaust pipe to the manifold, using new gasket and torque nuts to 25–35 ft. lbs.

11. On right cylinder head, position the alternator and install the attaching bolt and spacer, ignition coil and air cleaner inlet duct. Adjust drive belt tension. On left cylinder head, install accelerator shaft assembly, and air conditioning compressor bracket.

12. Install rocker cover using new gasket and tightening cover bolts to 3–5 ft. lbs.

13. Install intake manifold and carburetor assembly.

14. Install the thermactor air supply assembly where necessary.

370 CID (6.1L), 429 CID (7.0L) AND 460 CID (7.5L) ENGINES

1. Disconnect the negative battery cable. Remove the intake manifold and carburetor as an assembly.

2. Disconnect the exhaust pipe from the exhaust manifold.

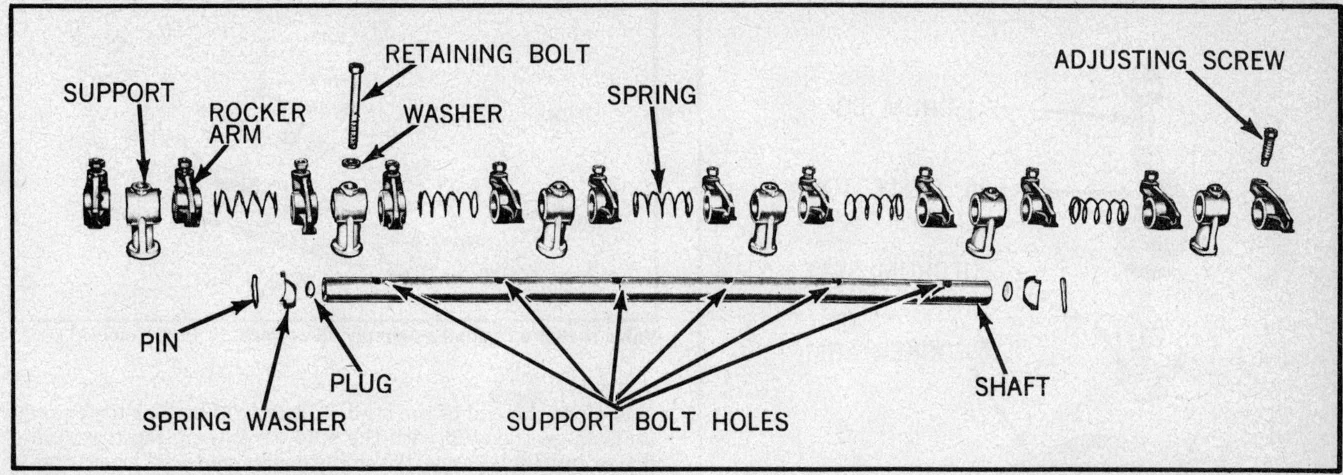

Rocker arm shaft assembly—6-cylinder—typical (© Ford Motor Co.)

Some applications may require the removal of the exhaust manifold at the cylinder heads.

3. Loosen the air conditioning compressor drive belt, if so equipped.
4. Loosen the alternator attaching bolts and remove the bolt attaching the alternator bracket to the right cylinder head.
5. Disconnect the air conditioning compressor from the engine and move it aside, out of the way. Do not discharge the air conditioning system, if possible.
6. Remove the bolts securing the power steering reservoir bracket to the left cylinder head. Position the reservoir and bracket out of the way. Remove air brake and thermactor brackets as necessary.
7. Remove the valve rocker arm covers. Remove the rocker arm bolts, rocker arms, oil deflectors, fulcrums, and pushrods in sequence so that they can be reinstalled in their original positions.
8. Remove the cylinder head bolts and lift the head and exhaust manifold off the engine. If necessary, pry at the forward corners of the cylinder head against the casting bosses provided on the cylinder block. Do not damage the gasket mating surfaces of the cylinder head and block by prying against them.
9. Remove all gasket material from the cylinder head and block. Clean all gasket material from the mating surfaces of the intake manifold. If the exhaust manifold was removed, clean the mating surfaces of the cylinder head exhaust port areas and install the exhaust manifold.
10. Position the two long cylinder head bolts in the two rear lower bolt holes of the left cylinder head. Place a long cylinder head bolt in the rear lower bolt hole of the right cylinder head. Use rubber bands to keep the bolts in position until the cylinder heads are installed on the cylinder block.
11. Position new cylinder head gaskets on the cylinder block dowels. Do not apply sealer to the gaskets, heads, or block.
12. Place the cylinder heads on the block, guiding the exhaust pipe connections. Install the remaining cylinder head bolts. The longer bolts go in the lower row of holes.
13. Tighten all the cylinder head attaching bolts in the proper sequence in three stages: 75 ft. lbs., 105 ft. lbs., and finally, to 135 ft. lbs. When this procedure is used, it is not necessary to retorque the heads after extended use.
14. Connect the exhaust pipes to the exhaust manifolds.
15. Install the intake manifold and carburetor assembly. Tighten the intake manifold attaching bolts in the proper sequence to 25–30 ft. lbs.
16. Install the air conditioning compressor to the engine.
17. Install the power steering reservoir to the engine.
18. Apply oil-resistant sealer to one side of the new valve cover gaskets and lay the cemented side in place in the valve covers. Install the covers.
19. Install the alternator to the right cylinder head and adjust the alternator drive belt tension.
20. Adjust the air conditioning compressor drive belt tension.
21. Fill the radiator with coolant.
22. Start the engine and check for leaks.

Valve Rocker Arm Shaft and Studs

Removal and Installation

122 CID (2.0L) AND 140 CID (2.3L) ENGINES

NOTE: A special tool is required to compress the lash adjuster.

1. Remove the valve cover and associated parts as required.
2. Rotate the camshaft so that the base circle of the cam is against the cam follower you intend to remove.
3. Remove the retaining spring from the cam follower, if so equipped.
4. Using special tool T74P-6565-B or a valve spring compressor tool, collapse the lash adjuster and/or depress the valve spring, as necessary, and slide the cam follower over the lash adjuster and out from under the camshaft.
5. Install the cam follower in the reverse order of removal. Make sure that the lash adjuster is collapsed and released before rotating the cam shaft.

300 CID (4.9L) ENGINE

1. Disconnect the inlet air hose at the oil fill cap. Remove the air cleaner.
2. Disconnect the accelerator cable at the carburetor. Remove the cable retracting spring. Remove the accelerator cable bracket from the cylinder head and position the cable and bracket assembly out of the way.
3. Remove the PCV valve from the valve rocker arm cover. Remove the cover bolts and remove the valve rocker arm cover.
4. Remove the valve rocker arm stud nut, fulcrum seat and rocker arm. Inspect the rocker arm cover bolts for worn or damaged seals under the bolt heads and replace as necessary. If it is necessary to remove a rocker arm stud, Tool T79T-6527-A is available. A 0.006 oversize reamer T62F-6527-B3 or equivalent and a 0.015 inch oversize reamer T62F-6527-B5 or equivalent are available. For 0.010 inch oversize studs, use reamer T66P-6527-B or equivalent. To press in replacement studs, use stud replacer T79T-6527-B or equivalent for 6–300 engines. Rocker arm studs that are broken or have damaged threads may be replaced with standard studs. Loose studs in the head may be replaced with 0.006, 0.010 or 0.015 inch oversize studs which are available for service.

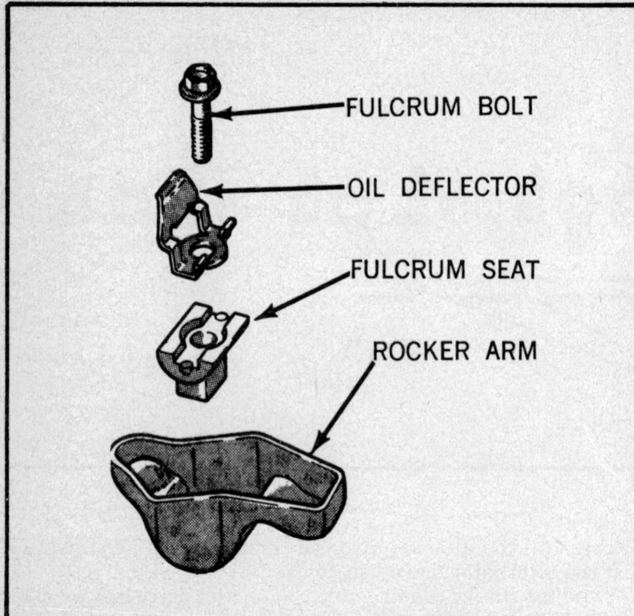

Bolt and fulcrum rocker arm (© Ford Motor Co.)

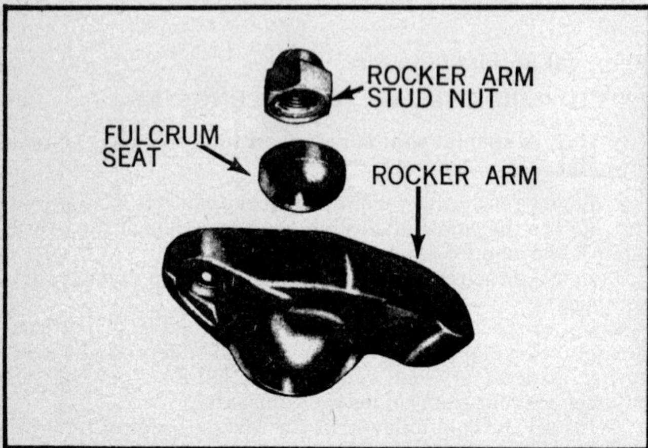

Stud/nut type rocker arm (© Ford Motor Co.)

5. Standard and oversize studs can be identified by measuring the stud diameter within 1 ⅛ in. from the pilot end of the stud. The stud diameters are:
   a. 0.006 oversize — — 0.3774–0.7781
   b. 0.010 oversize — — 0.3814–0.3821
   c. 0.015 oversize — — 0.3864–0.3871

6. When going from a standard size rocker arm stud to a 0.010 or 0.015 inch oversize stud, always use the 0.006 inch oversize reamer before finish reaming with the 0.010 or 0.015 inch oversize reamer.

7. Position the sleeve of the rocker arm stud remover over the stud with the bearing end down. Thread the puller into the sleeve and over the stud until it is fully bottomed. Hold the sleeve with a wrench; then, rotate the puller clockwise to remove the stud. If the rocker arm stud was broken off flush with the stud boss, use an easy-out to remove the broken stud following the instructions of the tool manufacturer.

8. If a loose rocker arm stud is being replaced, ream the stud bore using the proper reamer (or reamers in sequence) for the selected oversize stud. Make sure the metal particles do not enter the valve area.

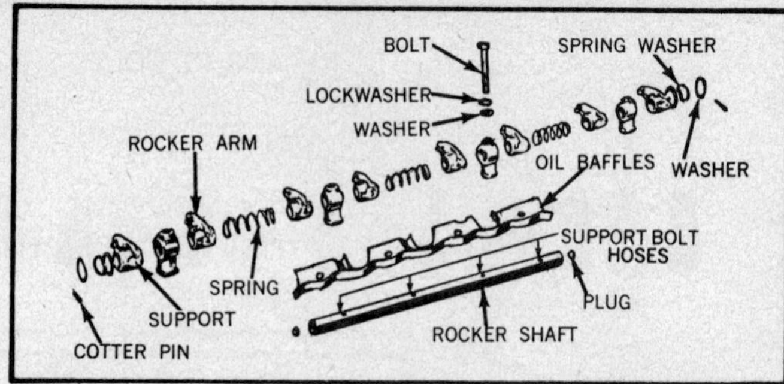

Valve rocker arm shaft assembly V8—typical (© Ford Motor Co.)

9. Coat the end of the stud with Lubriplate® or it's equivalent. Align the stud with the stud bore; then, tap the sliding driver until it bottoms. When the driver contacts the stud boss, the stud is installed to its correct height.

10. Apply Lubriplate® or equivalent to the top of the valve stem and at the push rod guide in the cylinder head.

11 Apply Lubriplate® or equivalent to the rocker arm fulcrum seat and the fulcrum seat socket in the rocker arm. Install the valve rocker arm, fulcrum seat and stud nut.

12. Clean the valve rocker arm cover and the cylinder head gasket surface. Place the new gasket in the cover making sure that the tabs of the gasket engage in the notches provided in the cover.

13. Install the cover on the cylinder head. Make sure the gasket seats evenly all around the head. Partially tighten the cover bolts in sequence, starting at the middle bolts. Then tighten the bolts to 3–5 ft. lb.

14. Install the PCV valve in the rocker arm cover. Install the accelerator cable bracket on the cylinder head and connect the cable to the carburetor.

15. Connect the inlet air hose to the oil fill cap.

16. Install air cleaner.

173 CID (2.8L) V6 ENGINE

1. Remove spark plug wires from the spark plugs.
2. Remove throttle linkage to carburetor if it interferes with removal operation.
3. Remove rocker arm cover attaching screws. Tap rocker arm cover lightly to break gasket seal. Lift off rocker arm cover.
4. Remove rocker arm shaft stand retaining bolts by loosening the bolts two turns at a time, in sequence. Lift off rocker arm and shaft assembly and oil baffle.
5. Loosen the valve lash adjusting screws a few turns.
6. Apply engine oil to the assembly to provide initial lubrication.
7. Install oil baffle and rocker arm shaft assembly to the cylinder block and guide adjusting screws on to push rods.
8. Install and tighten rocker arm stand attaching bolts to specifications, two turns at a time, in sequence.
9. Adjust valve lash to cold specified setting.
10. Clean the valve rocker arm cover and cylinder head gasket surfaces. Coat one side of a new gasket with an oil-resistant sealer and lay cemented side of gasket on the cover. Install the cover, making sure the gasket seats evenly around the head. Tighten the cover attaching bolts.
11. Install all parts removed to gain access to rocker arm and shaft assemblies.
12. Run the engine at fast idle and check for oil leaks.

ALL V8 ENGINES

1. Remove air cleaner, disconnect spark plug leads and remove leads from bracket on the valve rocker cover.
2. Remove crankcase ventilation hose from rocker cover, then remove rocker cover. On left rocker cover the wiring harness must be removed.

3. On right side, start at No. 4 cylinder (rearmost) and loosen the support bolts in sequence, two turns at a time. Remove the shaft assembly and baffle plate after all the bolts have been loosened. The same procedure is followed on the left bank, except that the bolt-loosening sequence starts with the No. 5 cylinder (foremost).

NOTE: The above bolt loosening procedure must be followed to avoid damage to the rocker arm shaft.

4. To install, apply Lubriplate® to the pad end of the rocker arms, to the tip of the valve stems and to both ends of the pushrods.
5. Rotate engine to 45 degrees past No. 1 cylinder TDC.
6. With the pushrods in place, position rocker arm shaft assembly and baffle plate on the cylinder head such that oil holes are on the bottom and identification notch is down and toward the front on the right bank and toward the rear on the left bank. Tighten support bolts finger tight.
7. On the right bank, start at No. 4 cylinder and tighten the support bolts two turns at a time in sequence (4–3–2–1) until the supports are fully in contact with the cylinder head. Then tighten the support bolts to 40–45 ft. lbs. torque. The same procedure is followed on the left valve rocker arm shaft support bolts, starting with the No. 5 cylinder. This procedure allows time for the hydraulic lifter leakdown and thus prevents damage to pushrods, valves and rocker arms.
8. Check valve clearances and adjust if necessary.
9. Install rocker cover, using new gaskets and sealer.
10. Tighten cover retaining bolts to 10–12 ft. lbs., wait two minutes, then tighten to the same torque again.
11. Install crankcase ventilation regulator valve and hose(s), connect spark plug wires and crankcase vent hose, and install air cleaner.

Valve Rocker Arm

Removal and Installation

V8 ENGINES

1. Remove the air cleaner and the intake duct assembly, including the crankcase ventilation hoses.
2. Disconnect all appropriate hoses, wires and equipment necessary to remove the rocker arm valve cover(s).
3. Disconnect the spark plug wires, and remove them from the bracket on the valve rocker arm cover.
4. Remove the valve rocker arm cover. Remove the valve rocker arm stud nut (or bolt), oil deflector (if equipped), fulcrum seat and rocker arm.
5. To install, apply Lubriplate (or equivalent) to the top of the valve stems, rocker arm and fulcrum seats.
6. Install the valve rocker arm and attaching parts. Adjust the valve clearance as outlined in this section.
7. Continue the installation in the reverse order of the removal.
8. Start the engine and check for leaks.

Valve Train

VALVE ARRANGEMENT

173-V6:
RT I-E-I-E-E-I
LT I-E-E-I-E-I

232-V6:
RT I-E-I-E-I-E
LT E-I-E-I-E-I

401, 475, 477, 534-V8:
RT E-I-E-I-I-E-I-E
LT E-I-E-I-I-E-I-E

122/140-4 cy. 8 E-I-E-I-E-I-E-I

300 Six: E-I-E-I-E-I-E-I-E-I-E-I

330, 359, 360, 361, 389, 390, 391-V8:
RT E-I-E-I-E-I-E-I
LT E-I-E-I-E-I-E-I

225, 302, 351, 370, 400, 429, 460-V8:
RT I-E-I-E-I-E-I-E
LT E-I-E-I-E-I-E-I

Preliminary Valve Adjustment

A 0.060 inch shorter push rod or a 0.060 inch longer push rod is available for service to provide a means for compensating for dimensional changes in the valve mechanism.

Valve stem to valve rocker arm clearance should be within specifications with the hydraulic tappet completely collapsed. Repeated valve reconditioning operations (valve and/or valve seat refacing) will decrease the clearance to the point that if it is not compensated for, the lifter will cease to function and the valve will be held open.

To determine whether a shorter or a longer push rod is necessary, refer to the Rocker Arm/Rocker Shaft and Stud section.

VALVE ADJUSTMENT

300 CID (4.9L) ENGINE

1. Crank the engine until the TDC mark on the crankshaft damper is aligned with timing pointer on the cylinder front cover.
2. Scribe a mark on the damper at this point.
3. Scribe two more marks on the damper, each equally spaced from the first mark.
4. With the engine on TDC of the compression stroke, back off the rocker arm adjusting nut until there is end-play in the pushrod. Tighten the adjusting nut until all clearance is removed, then tighten the adjusting nut one additional turn. To determine when all clearance is removed from the rocker arm, turn the pushrod with the fingers. When the pushrod can no longer be turned, all clearance has been removed.
5. Repeat this procedure for each valve, turning the crankshaft ⅓ turn to the next mark each time and following the engine firing order of 1–5–3–6–2–4.

232 CID (3.8L) ENGINE

1. Rotate the crankshaft to place each tappet on the heel (base circle) of the camshaft lobe. As each tappet is located on the base of the lobe, torque the fulcrum attaching bolt to 62–132 inch lbs.

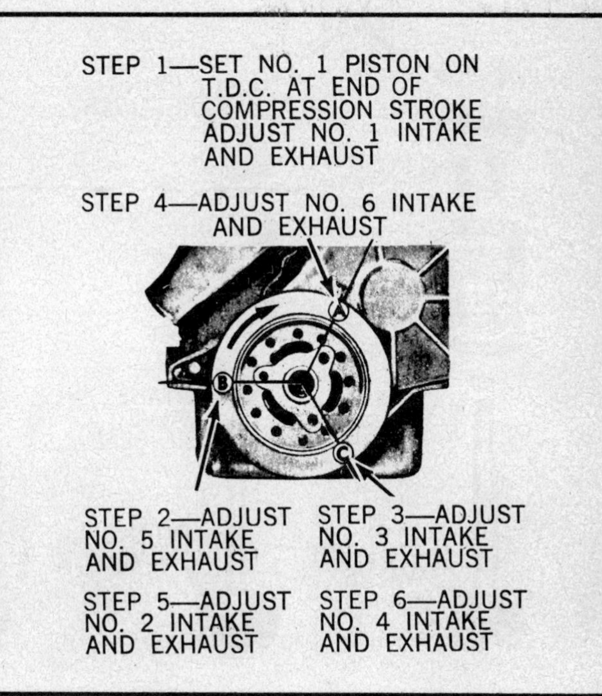
STEP 1—SET NO. 1 PISTON ON T.D.C. AT END OF COMPRESSION STROKE ADJUST NO. 1 INTAKE AND EXHAUST
STEP 4—ADJUST NO. 6 INTAKE AND EXHAUST
A
B
C
STEP 2—ADJUST NO. 5 INTAKE AND EXHAUST
STEP 3—ADJUST NO. 3 INTAKE AND EXHAUST
STEP 5—ADJUST NO. 2 INTAKE AND EXHAUST
STEP 6—ADJUST NO. 4 INTAKE AND EXHAUST
6-cylinder preliminary valve adjustment (© Ford Motor Co.)

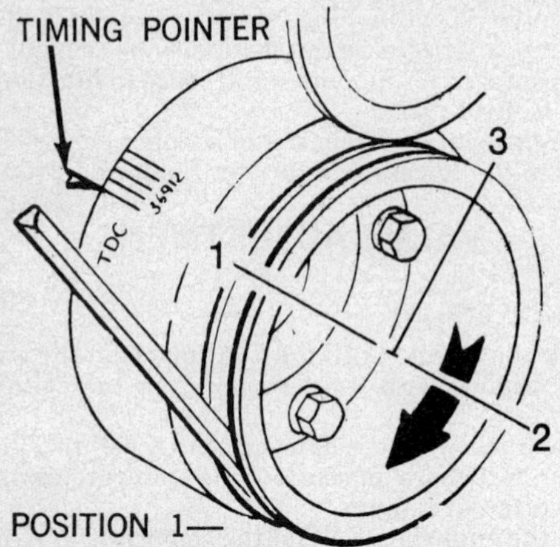
WITH NO. 1 AT TDC AT THE END OF THE COMPRESSION STROKE MAKE A CHALK MARK AT POINTS 2 AND 3 APPROXIMATELY 90 DEGREES APART.
TIMING POINTER
TDC
3
1
2
POSITION 1—
NO. 1 AT TDC AT THE END OF THE COMPRESSION STROKE
POSITION 2—
ROTATE THE CRANKSHAFT 180 DEGREES (ONE HALF REVOLUTION) CLOCKWISE FROM POSITION 1
POSITION 3—
ROTATE THE CRANKSHAFT 270 DEGREES (THREE QUARTER REVOLUTION CLOCKWISE FROM POSITION 2

Position of crankshaft for adjusting valve clearance (© Ford Motor Co.)

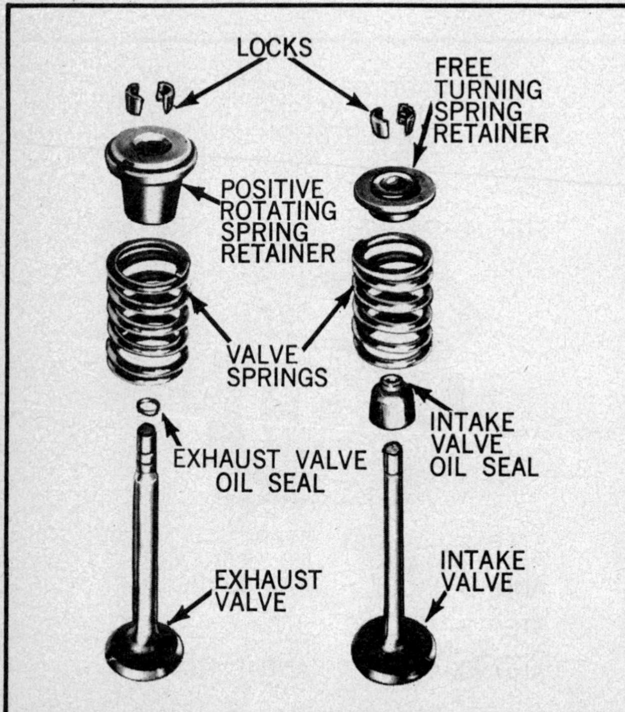
LOCKS
FREE TURNING SPRING RETAINER
POSITIVE ROTATING SPRING RETAINER
VALVE SPRINGS
INTAKE VALVE OIL SEAL
EXHAUST VALVE OIL SEAL
INTAKE VALVE
EXHAUST VALVE

Typical valve layout (© Ford Motor Co.)

NOTE: The fulcrums must be seated in the cylinder head and the pushrods must be seated in the rocker arm sockets, prior to the final tightening.

173 CID (2.8L) ENGINE

1. With engine cold and valve covers removed, place a finger on the adjusting screw of the intake valve rocker arm for cylinder No. 5. Valve arrangement, from front to rear, on the left bank is I(intake)-E(exhaust)I-E-E-I-E-I; on the right it is I-E-I-E-E-I.
2. Use a remote starter switch to bump the engine over until you can just feel the valve begin to open. The cam is now in position to adjust the intake and exhaust valves on the No. 1 cylinder.

Intake valve just opening	Adjust both valves for this cylinder (Intake—0.014 in.; Exhaust—0.016 in.)
5	1
3	4
6	2
1	5
4	3
2	6

3. Adjust the No. 1 intake valve so that a 0.014 in. feeler gauge has a slight drag, while a 0.015 in. feeler gauge is a tight fit. To decrease lash, turn the adjusting screw clockwise; to increase lash, turn the adjusting screw counterclockwise. There are no lockbolts to tighten as the adjusting screws are self-tightening.

CAUTION

Do not use a step-type, "go-no go" feeler gauge. When checking lash, you must insert the feeler gauge and move it parallel with the crankshaft. Do not move it in and out perpendicular with the crankshaft as this will give an erroneous feel which will result in overtightened valves.

11. Adjust the exhaust valve the same way so that an 0.016 in. feeler gauge has a slight drag, while a 0.017 in. gauge is a tight fit.
12. The rest of the valves are adjusted in the same way, in their firing order (1–4–2–5–3–6), by positioning the cam according to the valve adjusting chart.
13. Remove all the old gasket material from the cylinder heads and rocker cover gasket surfaces, and disconnect the negative cable from the battery.
14. Remove the spark plug wires and reinstall the rocker arm covers.
15. Reinstall any hoses and wires which were removed previously.
16. Reinstall the spark plug wires, the alternator drive belt, and the thermactor air by-pass valve and its mounting bracket.
17. Reconnect the battery cable, replace the air cleaner assembly, start the engine, and check for leaks.

V8 ENGINES
ALL EXCEPT 330, 359, 360, 361, 370, 389, 390, 391 AND 429 CID ENGINES

1. Install an auxiliary starter switch. Crank the engine with the ignition switch OFF until No. 1 piston is on TDC after the compression stroke.
2. With the crankshaft in the positions designated in Steps 5, 6 and 7, position a hydraulic tappet compressor tool on the rocker arm.

3. Slowly apply pressure to bleed down the hydraulic tappet until the plunger is completely bottomed. Hold the tappet in this position and check the available clearance between the rocker arm and the valve stem tip with a feeler gauge.

4. If the clearance is less than specification, install a shorter push rod. If clearance is greater than specification, install a longer push rod.

5. With the No. 1 piston on TDC at the end of the compression stroke, Position 1 on the crankshaft pulley, check the following valves:

302 and 460 CID engines

No. 1 intake
No. 1 exhaust
No. 7 intake
No. 5 exhaust
No. 8 intake
No. 4 exhaust

351 and 400 CID engines

No. 1 intake
No. 1 exhaust
No. 4 intake
No. 3 exhaust
No. 8 intake
No. 6 exhaust

6. After these valves have been checked, rotate the crankshaft to Position 2 and check the following valves:

302 and 460 CID engines

No. 5 intake
No. 2 exhaust
No. 4 intake
No. 6 exhaust

351 and 400 CID engines

No. 3 intake
No. 2 exhaust
No. 7 intake
No. 6 exhaust

7. After these valves have been checked, rotate the crankshaft to Position 3 and check the following valves:

302 and 460 CID engines

No. 2 intake
No. 7 exhaust
No. 3 intake
No. 3 exhaust
No. 6 intake
No. 8 exhaust

351 and 400 CID engines

No. 2 intake
No. 4 exhaust
No. 5 intake
No. 5 exhaust
No. 6 intake
No. 8 exhaust

330, 359, 360, 361, 370, 389, 390, 391 AND 429 CID ENGINES:

1. Install an auxiliary starter switch. Crank the engine with the ignition switch OFF until No. 1 piston is on TDC after the compression stroke.

2. With the crankshaft in the positions designated in Steps 5 and 6, position a tappet compressor tool on the rocker arm.

3. Slowly apply pressure to bleed down the hydraulic tappet until the plunger is completely bottomed. Hold the tappet in this position and check the available clearance between the rocker arm and the valve stem tip with a feeler gauge.

4. If the clearance is less than specification, install a shorter push rod. If clearance is greater than specification, install a longer push rod.

5. Rotate the crankshaft until No. 1 piston is on TDC at the end of the compression stroke and check the following valves:

No. 1 intake
No. 1 exhaust
No. 3 intake
No. 4 exhaust
No. 7 intake
No. 5 exhaust
No. 8 intake
No. 8 exhaust

6. After these valves have been checked rotate the crankshaft 360 degrees and check the following valves:

No. 2 intake
No. 2 exhaust
No. 4 intake
No. 3 exhaust
No. 5 intake
No. 6 exhaust
No. 6 intake
No. 7 exhaust

134 CID (2.2L) DIESEL ENGINE

1. Warm the engine until normal operating temperature is reached.

2. Remove the valve cover. Check the head bolt torque in sequence.

3. Turn the engine to bring the No.1 piston to TDC (top dead center) of the compression stroke.

4. Adjust the following valves:

No.1 Intake and Exhaust
No.2 Intake
No.3 Exhaust

5. Rotate the crankshaft 360° and bring No.4 piston to TDC of the compression stroke.

6. Adjust the following valves:

No.2 Exhaust
No.3 Intake
No.4 Intake and Exhaust

7. To adjust the valves, loosen the locknut on the rocker arm. Rotate the adjusting screw clockwise to reduce clearance, counter-clockwise to increase clearance. Clearance is checked with a flat feeler gauge that is passed between the rocker arm and valve stem.

8. After adjustments are made, be sure the locknuts are tight. Be sure mounting surfaces are clean. Install the valve cover and new valve cover gasket.

420 CID (6.9L) Diesel ENGINE

The 6.9L diesel engine is equipped with hydraulic lifters that minimize engine noise and maintain zero lash or tappet clearance. This eliminates the need for periodic adjustment. The hydraulic tappets also incorporate camshaft roller followers for improved camshaft wear characteristics.

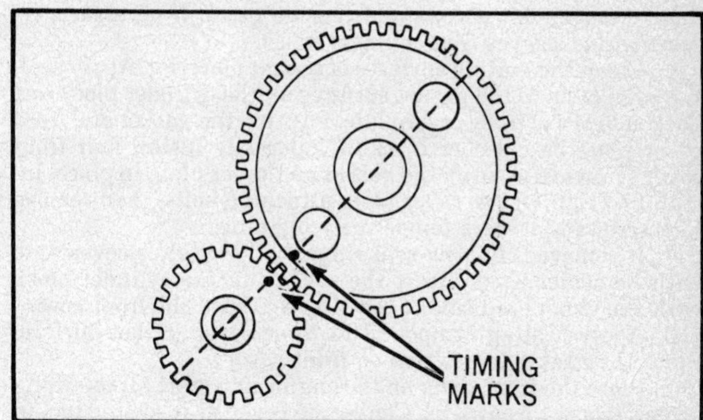

Timing mark alignment—6-cylinder 300 engine (© Ford Motor Co.)

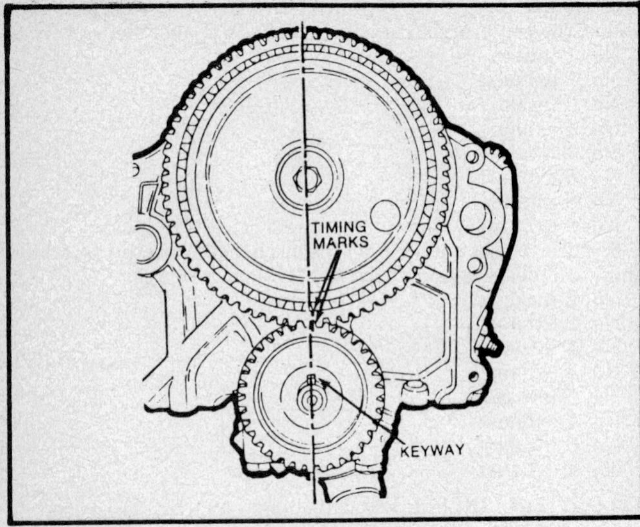

173(2.3L) V6 timing mark alignment (© FOMOCO)

VALVE OVERHAUL

See the General Repair Section for complete valve overhaul procedures. All valves are removed by compressing the spring with a valve spring compressing tool, then removing the keepers from the end of the valve stem. Most models utilized an O-ring or cup type oil seal as illustrated. Valve spring, stem and seal specifications may be found in the Valve Specifications Table at the beginning of this section.

Timing Gears

FRONT COVER

Removal and Installation

173 CID (2.8L) ENGINE

1. Disconnect the negative battery cable. Raise and support the vehicle safely. Remove the oil pan.
2. Drain the coolant. Remove the radiator and any other parts to provide necessary clearance.
3. If equipped with air conditioning, unbolt the compressor and bracket and move them aside. Do not disconnect the A/C lines.
4. Remove alternator, thermactor, and drive belt(s).
5. Remove the fan.
6. Remove the drive pulley from the crankshaft.
7. Remove the front cover retaining bolts. If necessary, tap cover lightly with a plastic hammer to break gasket seal. Remove front cover. If front cover plate gasket needs replacement, remove two screws and remove plate. If necessary, remove guide sleeves from cylinder block.
8. Clean the mating surfaces of gasket material. Apply sealing compound to the gasket surfaces on the cylinder block and back side of the front cover plate. Position the gasket and front cover plate on cylinder block. Temporarily install four front cover screws to position the gasket and cover plate in place. Install and tighten two cover plate attaching bolts, then remove four screws that were temporarily installed.
9. If removed, fit new seal rings to the guide sleeves and, with no sealer used, insert the sleeves in the cylinder block with the chamfered side of the sleeve toward the front cover.
10. Apply sealing compound to front cover gasket surface. Place the gasket in position on front cover.
11. Place the front cover on the engine and start all retaining screws two or three turns. Center the cover by inserting tool in the oil seal.
12. Tighten the front cover attaching screws to specifications.
13. Install the belt drive pulley and tighten the attaching bolt to specifications.
14. Install the oil pan.
15. Install the water pump, water hose, A/C compressor, alternator and drive belt(s). Adjust the drive belt tension to specifications.
16. Fill the cooling system to the proper level with the specified coolant.
17. Operate the engine at fast idle speed and check for coolant and oil leaks.

NOTE: If the guide sleeves were removed, install them with new seal rings but do not use sealing compound.

FRONT COVER SEAL

Removal and Installation

173 CID (2.8L) ENGINE

1. Support the front cover to prevent damage while driving out the seal.
2. Drive out the seal from the front cover.
3. Support the front cover to prevent damage while installing the seal.
4. Coat the new front cover oil seal with a light grease. Install the new seal in the front cover.

TIMING GEARS

Removal and Installation

173 CID (2.8L) ENGINE

1. Drain the cooling system and the crankcase. Remove the oil pan and the radiator.
2. Remove the cylinder front cover and water pump, drive belt, and camshaft.
3. Using a gear puller, remove the crankshaft gear. Remove the key from the crankshaft.
4. Place the spacer and thrust plate on the camshaft.
5. Install the key in the camshaft. Align the keyway in the gear with the key, then slide the gear onto the shaft, making sure that it seats tight against the spacer.
6. Check the camshaft end play. If not within specifications replace the thrust plate.
7. Position the key in the crankshaft. Align the keyway and install the gear.
8. Install the cylinder front cover following the procedures in this section. Replace the oil pan and the radiator.
9. Fill the cooling system and crankcase.
10. Start the engine and adjust the ignition timing. Operate the engine at fast idle and check all hose connections and gaskets for leaks.

Removal and Installation

300 CID (4.9L) ENGINE

1. Bring the engine to No. 1 piston at TDC (top dead center) on the compression stroke. Drain the cooling system. Disconnect negative battery cable.
2. Remove the radiator and shroud.
3. Remove the alternator adjusting arm bolt, loosen the drive belt and swing the alternator arm aside. Remove the fan, drive belts and pulleys.
4. Remove the screw and washer from the end of the crankshaft. Remove the crankshaft damper.
5. Remove the front oil pan and front cover attaching screws.

NOTE: Be careful not to get foreign material in the crankcase during service work, or the crankcase oil will have to be changed.

6. Remove the cylinder front cover and discard the gasket. Replace the crankshaft oil seal when the cylinder front cover is removed.
7. Drive out the crankshaft oil seal with a pin punch. Clean the seal bore in the cover.
8. Remove the camshaft and crankshaft gears using a suitable puller. Install the new gears, camshaft first using Ford tool T65L6306A or the equivalent. Do not hammer on the gears. Install the crankshaft gear over the drive key and install with tool. Verify that the timing marks on both gears are aligned. Install the crankshaft oil slinger.
9. Coat a new crankshaft oil seal with grease and install the seal in the cover. Drive the seal in until it is fully seated in the seal bore.
10. Cut the old front oil pan seal flush at the cylinder block/pan junction and remove the old seal material.
11. Clean all gasket surfaces.
12. Cut and fit a new pan seal flush to the cylinder block pan junction. Use the old seal as a pattern.
13. Coat the gasket surfaces of the block and cover with a resistant sealer. Position a new front cover gasket on the cylinder block.
14. Align the pan seal locating tabs with the pan holes. Pull the seal tabs through until the seal is completely seated. Apply a silicone sealer to the block pan junction.
15. Position the front cover assembly over the end of the crankshaft and against the cylinder block. Start the cover and pan attaching screw. Slide the cover alignment tool over the crank stub and into the seat bore of the cover. Install the alternator adjusting arm, tighten all attaching screws to specification.

NOTE: Tighten the oil pan screws first (compressing the pan seal) to obtain the proper alignment of the cover.

16. Lubricate the crank stub, damper hub I.D. and the seal rubbing surface. Align the damper keyway with the key on the crankshaft and install the damper.
17. Install the washer and the capscrew into the damper and tighten to specification.
18. Install the pulleys, drive belts and the fan.
19. Fill and bleed the cooling system. Operate the engine at fast idle and check for leaks.

Timing Chain and Gears

Removal and Installation

232 CID (3.8L) ENGINE

1. Bring the number one piston to TDC of the compression stroke. Drain the cooling system.
2. Disconnect the cable from the battery negative terminal.
3. Remove the air cleaner assembly and air intake duct.
4. Remove the fan shroud attaching screws. Remove the fan/clutch assembly attaching bolts.
5. Remove the fan/clutch assembly and shroud.
6. Loosen the accessory drive belt idler. Remove the drive belt and water pump pulley.
7. If equipped with power steering, remove the pump mounting brackets' attaching bolts.
8. If equipped with air conditioning, remove the compressor front support bracket. Leave the compressor in place.
9. Disconnect the coolant by-pass hose at the water pump.
10. Disconnect the heater hose at the water pump.
11. Disconnect the radiator upper hose at the thermostat housing.
12. Disconnect the coil wire from the distributor cap and remove the cap with the secondary wires attached.
13. Remove the distributor hold down clamp and lift the distributor out of the front cover.
14. Raise the vehicle and support safely.
15. Remove the crankshaft damper.

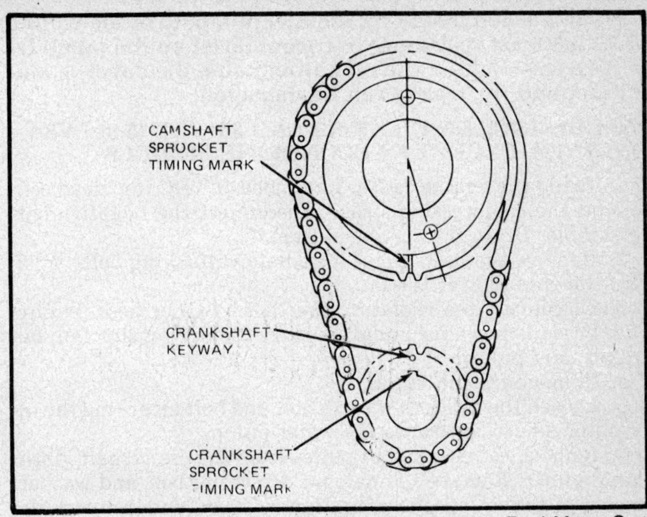

Alignment of timing gears—232 CID V-6 engine (© Ford Motor Co.)

16. Remove the fuel pump crash shield (if so equipped).
17. Disconnect the fuel pump to carburetor fuel line at the fuel pump.
18. Remove the fuel pump attaching bolts. Pull the pump out of the front cover and lay the pump aside with flexible line attached.
19. Remove the oil filter.
20. Disconnect the radiator lower hose at the water pump.
21. Remove the oil pan.

NOTE: The front cover cannot be removed without lowering the oil pan.

22. Lower the vehicle.
23. Remove the front cover attaching bolts. It is not necessary to remove the water pump.

NOTE: Do not overlook the cover attaching bolt located behind the oil filter adapter. The front cover will break if pried upon and all attaching bolts are not removed.

24. Remove the ignition timing indicator.
25. Remove the front cover and water pump as an assembly.
26. Remove the cover gasket and discard.
27. Remove the camshaft thrust button and spring from the end of the camshaft.
28. Remove the camshaft sprocket attaching bolts.
29. Remove the camshaft sprocket, crankshaft sprocket and the timing chain.
30. If not already done, rotate the crankshaft as necessary to position piston No. 1 at TDC and the crankshaft keyway at the twelve o'clock position.
31. Lubricate the timing chain with clean engine oil. Install the camshaft sprocket, crankshaft sprocket and timing chain.
32. Make sure the timing marks on the gears are positioned across from each other. Install the camshaft retaining bolts.
33. Install the camshaft thrust button and spring. Lubricate the thrust button with Polyethylene Grease before installation. The thrust button and spring must be bottomed out in the camshaft seat and must not be allowed to fall out during cover installation.
34. Apply sealer to the gasket mounting surfaces, install a new front cover mounting gasket and the front cover using the two dowels for alignment. Position the timing indicator in place.
35. Apply pipe sealer to the cover mounting bolts before installation. Install bolts and tighten.
36. Install the remaining components in the reverse order of removal.

NOTE: When installing the fuel pump, turn the engine until the least resistance is encountered on the pump lever. Evenly tighten the mounting bolts, the cover is aluminum and the treads can be damaged.

255 CID (4.2L), 302 CID (5.0L) AND 351 CID (5.8L) V8 ENGINES, EXCEPT IN ECONOLINE MODELS

1. Bring the engine to No. 1 cylinder at TDC (top dead center) on the compression stroke. Disconnect the negative battery cable. Drain the cooling system.
2. Remove the fan shroud to radiator attaching bolts. Position the shroud over the fan.
3. Disconnect the radiator lower hose, heater hose and bypass hose at the water pump. Remove the drive belts, fan, fan spacer, and pulley.
4. Remove the fan shroud.
5. Loosen the alternator pivot bolt and bolt attaching the alternator adjusting arm to the water pump.
6. Remove the crankshaft pulley from the crankshaft vibration damper. Remove the damper attaching bolt and washer. Install a puller on the vibration damper and remove the damper.
7. Disconnect the fuel pump outlet line from the fuel pump. Remove the fuel pump to one side with the flexible fuel line still attached:
8. Remove the oil dipstick and the bolt attaching the dipstick to the exhaust manifold.
9. Remove the oil pan to cylinder front cover attaching bolts. Use a knife with a thin blade to cut the oil pan gasket flush with the cylinder block face prior to separating the cover from the cylinder block. Remove the cylinder front cover and water pump as an assembly.
10. Discard the cylinder front cover gasket. Remove the crankshaft front oil slinger.
11. Check the timing chain deflection. The method for checking timing chain deflection is outlined at the end of this section. If the deflection exceeds specification, replace the chain and sprockets as follows:
    a. Crank the engine until the timing marks on the sprockets are correctly aligned.
    b. Remove the camshaft sprocket capscrew, washers, and fuel pump eccentric. Slide both sprockets and the timing chain forward and remove the chain and sprockets as an assembly.
    c. Position the sprockets and timing chain on the camshaft. Be sure that the timing marks are properly aligned.
    d. Install the fuel pump, eccentric, washers, and camshaft sprocket capscrew. Tighten the capscrew to specification.
12. Install the crankshaft front oil slinger.
13. Clean the cylinder front cover, oil pan and block gasket surfaces. Clean the oil pan gasket surface where the oil pan and front cover fasten.
14. Install a new crankshaft front oil seal.
15. Lubricate the timing chain and fuel pump eccentric with a heavy engine oil.
16. Coat the gasket surface of the oil pan with sealer, then cut and position the required sections of a new gasket on the oil pan and apply sealer at the corners. Install the pan seal as required. Coat the gasket surfaces of the block and cover with sealer, and position a new gasket on the block.
17. Position the cylinder front cover on the cylinder block. Use care when installing the cover to avoid seal damage or possible gasket dislocation.
18. Install the cylinder front cover to seal alignment tool.
19. It may be necessary to force the cover downward to slightly compress the pan gasket. This operation can be facilitated by using a suitable tool at the front cover attaching hole locations.
20. Coat the threads of the attaching bolts with a oil-resistant sealer and install the bolts. While pushing in on the alignment tool, tighten the oil pan to cover attaching bolts to specification. Tighten the cover to block attaching bolts to specification. Remove the alignment tool.
21. Apply Lubriplate or equivalent to the oil seal rubbing surface of the vibration damper inner hub to prevent damage to the seal. Apply a white lead and oil mixture to the front of the crankshaft for damper installation.
22. Line up the crankshaft vibration damper keyway with the key on the crankshaft. Install the vibration damper on the crankshaft. Install the capscrew and washer and tighten to specification. Install the crankshaft pulley.
23. Lubricate the fuel pump lever with heavy engine oil and install the pump using a new gasket. Connect the fuel pump outlet pipe.
24. Install the alternator pivot bolt and bolt attaching the alternator adjusting arm to the water pump.
25. Position the fan shroud over the water pump. Install the pulley, spacer and fan. Install and adjust the drive belts and adjust to specified tension. Connect the radiator, heater, and by-pass hoses. Position the fan shroud on the radiator and install the attaching bolts.
26. Fill and bleed the cooling system.
27. Run the engine at fast idle and check for coolant and oil leaks. Check the coolant level. Check and adjust the ignition timing.
28. Install the air cleaner and intake duct assembly including the crankcase ventilation hose.

ECONOLINE WITH 302 CID (5.0L) AND 351W CID (5.8L) V8 ENGINES

1. Bring engine to No. 1 cylinder at TDC (top dead center) on the compression stroke. Disconnect the negative battery cable at the battery. Drain the radiator.
2. Remove the air conditioning idler pulley, bracket and drive belt if equipped.
3. Remove the upper radiator hose. Remove the fan and shroud as an assembly. Raise and support the vehicle safely.
4. Loosen the thermactor and alternator drive belts.
5. Disconnect the lower radiator hose at the water pump. Disconnect the fuel line at the fuel pump and remove the pump. Lower the vehicle.
6. Remove the by-pass hose. Remove the power steering pump drive belt if equipped. Remove the water pump pulley and disconnect the heater hose at the water pump.
7. Remove the air condition compressor upper bracket and the power steering pump mount.
8. Remove the crankshaft pulley. Remove the oil pan to front cover bolts. Remove the front cover.
9. Check timing chain deflection. If the deflection exceeds specification, replace the chain and sprockets as follows:
    a. Crank the engine until the timing marks on the sprockets are correctly aligned.
    b. Remove the camshaft sprocket capscrew, washers, and fuel pump eccentric. Slide both sprockets and the timing chain forward and remove the chain and sprockets as an assembly.
    c. Position the sprockets and timing chain on the camshaft. Be sure that the timing marks are properly aligned.
    d. Install the fuel pump, eccentric, washers, and camshaft sprocket capscrew. Tighten the capscrew to specification.
10. Clean the front cover, fuel pump, and damper. Lubricate the crankshaft front seal. Clean the gasket surface at the pan and trim the gasket. Clean the front cover gasket surface at the block.
11. Replace the oil seal in the front cover. Position the gasket on the front cylinder cover. Apply a silicone sealer to the oil pan and cylinder block junction. Cut the pan gasket and position on pan and front cover.
12. Install the front cover, fuel pump, and crankshaft pulley.
13. Install the power steering pump and water pump by-pass hose. Connect the heater hose at the water pump.
14. Install the air conditioning compressor upper bracket, water pump pulley and power steering drive belt.
15. Install the alternator belt, thermactor belt, and fan/shroud assembly.

16. Adjust the power steering pump drive belt tension to specification.
17. Install the air conditioning drive belt idler pulley and bracket. Install the air conditioning drive belt and tighten to specification.
18. Install the upper radiator hose.
19. Raise and safely support the vehicle. Install the fuel pump with a new gasket and connect the fuel line.
20. Install the lower radiator hose. Adjust the alternator and air injection pump drive belts to specified tension.
21. Drain the crankcase and replace the oil filter. Lower the vehicle.
22. Fill the crankcase and cooling system. Check and adjust ignition timing.
23. Start the engine and run at a fast idle, check for oil and coolant leaks.

351M CID (5.8L) AND 400 CID (6.6L) V8 ENGINES

1. Bring the engine to No. 1 piston at TDC (top dead center) on the compression stroke. Drain the cooling system and disconnect the battery.
2. Remove the fan shroud attaching bolts and move the shroud to the rear.
3. Remove the fan and spacer from the water pump shaft.
4. Remove the air conditioner compressor drive belt lower idler pulley and the compressor mount to water pump bracket.
5. Loosen the alternator and power steering pump and remove the drive belts.
6. Remove the water pump pulley.
7. Remove the alternator and power steering pump brackets from the water pump and position them out of the way.
8. Disconnect the lower radiator and heater hose from the water pump.
9. Remove the crankshaft pulley from the crankshaft vibration damper. Remove the vibration damper attaching screw. Install a puller and remove the damper.
10. Remove the timing pointer.
11. Remove the bolts attaching the front cylinder cover to the cylinder block. Remove the front cover and water pump assembly.
12. Disconnect the fuel pump outlet line from the pump. Remove the fuel pump attaching bolts and lay the pump to one side with the flexible line still attached.
13. Discard the cylinder front cover gasket and oil pan seal.
14. Check the timing chain deflection, as outlined at the end of this section.
15. If the timing chain deflection exceeds specification, proceed as follows:
    a. Crank the engine until the timing marks on the sprockets are aligned.
    b. Remove the camshaft sprocket capscrew, washer, and two piece fuel pump eccentric. Slide both sprockets and the timing chain forward, and remove them as an assembly.
    c. Position the sprockets and timing chain on the camshaft and crankshaft. Be certain that the timing marks on the sprockets are correctly aligned.
    d. Install the two piece fuel pump eccentric, washers, and camshaft sprocket capscrew. Tighten the camshaft capscrew to specification. Make sure that the outer fuel pump eccentric sleeve rotates freely.
16. Coat a new fuel pump gasket with oil resistant sealer and position the fuel pump and gasket on the cylinder block with the fuel pump arm resting on the eccentric outer sleeve. Install the pump attaching bolt and nut and tighten to specification. Connect the fuel pump outlet line.
17. Remove the front crankshaft seal from the front cover. Clean the cylinder front cover and the engine block gasket surfaces.
18. Coat the gasket surfaces of the block and cover with sealer, and position a new gasket on the cylinder block alignment dowels.
19. Position the cylinder front cover and water pump assembly on the cylinder block alignment dowels.
20. Coat the threads of the attaching bolts with an oil resistant sealer and install the timing pointer and attaching bolts. Tighten the bolts to specifications.
21. Install the front cover oil seal into the cylinder front cover.
22. Apply Lubriplate® or its equivalent to the oil seal rubbing surface of the vibration damper inner hub to prevent damage to the seal. Apply a white lead and oil mixture to the front of the crankshaft for damper installation.
23. Line up the crankshaft vibration damper keyway with the key on the crankshaft. Install the vibration damper on the crankshaft by pressing on with appropriate tool. Install the capscrew and washer, tighten to specification. Install the crankshaft pulley.
24. Connect the heater hose and the lower radiator hose to the water pump.
25. Install the air conditioner compressor to water pump bracket and lower idler pulley.
26. Position the alternator bracket and power steering pump bracket on the water pump and install the bolts.
27. Position the water pump pulley on the water pump shaft and install the drive belts.
28. Place the fan shroud over the pulley, and install the fan and spacer.
29. Position the fan shroud over the radiator and install the attaching bolts.
30. Adjust the drive belts to specification.
31. Raise and support the vehicle safely. Remove the oil pan and install new gaskets and seals.
32. Lower the vehicle. Fill the crankcase. Fill and bleed the cooling system. Connect the battery cable.
33. Operate the engine until normal operating temperature has been reached and check for oil or coolant leaks.

ALL OTHER V8 ENGINES, EXCEPT 460 CID (7.5L)

1. Drain the cooling system and the crankcase. Remove the air cleaner. Disconnect the battery ground cable and the distributor vacuum line.
2. Disconnect the upper radiator hose at the thermostat housing and the lower radiator hose at the water pump.
3. Disconnect the transmission oil cooler lines if equipped.
4. Remove the radiator and support as an assembly. If the vehicle is equipped with an automatic radiator shutter, leave it attached to the radiator assembly.
5. Disconnect the heater hose at the water pump. Remove the water pump by-pass hose. On a high fan installation, remove the cooling fan and drive belt.
6. Remove the power steering pump and position it to one side, leaving the hoses attached.
7. If equipped with an air compressor, disconnect the air lines and remove the compressor.
8. Remove the alternator adjusting arm bolt at the alternator. Remove the drive belts. Disconnect the wiring and remove the alternator from the support bracket.
9. Remove the water pump and cooling fan drive belts. Remove the water pump and fan as an assembly. On C-series vehicles, remove the cooling fan from the crankshaft damper.
10. Remove the cap screw and washer from the end of the crankshaft. Install a puller on the crankshaft damper and remove the damper. On some vehicles, it may be necessary to remove the crankshaft pulley bolts.
11. Disconnect the carburetor fuel inlet line at the fuel pump.
12. Remove the fuel pump attaching bolts and lay the fuel pump to one side with the flexible fuel line still attached.
13. Remove the bolts attaching the cylinder front cover to the cylinder block and oil pan. Using a knife with a thin blade, cut the oil pan gasket flush with the cylinder block to oil pan junction prior to separating the cover from the block.
14. Remove the cylinder front cover, alternator support

bracket and adjusting arm, and the engine front support bracket.

15. Discard the cylinder front cover gasket. Remove the oil slinger.

16. Check the timing chain deflection and camshaft end play

17. If the timing chain deflection exceeds specification, proceed as follows:

a. Crank the engine until the timing marks on the sprockets are correctly aligned.

b. Remove the camshaft sprocket capscrew and the fuel pump eccentric.

c. Slide both sprockets and the timing chain forward and remove the sprockets and timing chain as an assembly.

d. Clean the sprockets and chain, replace any worn or damaged parts. Clean the crankshaft damper.

e. Position the sprockets and timing chain of the camshaft and crankshaft. Be sure that the timing marks are in alignment.

f. Install the fuel pump eccentric and the camshaft sprocket cap screw. Tighten the capscrew to specification. If a new thrust plate was installed on the camshaft to bring end play within specifications, check the camshaft end play.

18. Install the crankshaft front oil slinger.

19. Clean all oil pan and cylinder block to front cover gasket surfaces.

20. Coat the gasket surface on the oil pan with sealer. Cut and position the required section of a new gasket on the oil pan. Apply silicone sealer at the corners.

21. Coat the gasket surface of the cylinder block and front cover with sealer and position a new gasket on the cylinder block.

22. Position the cylinder front cover on the cylinder block. Be careful during installation of the cover to avoid dislocation or damage to the gasket.

23. Install the cylinder front cover-to-seal alignment tool in its proper position. It may be necessary to force the cover downward to slightly compress the pan gasket. This operation can be facilitated by using a suitable tool at the cover attaching bolt hole locations in the cylinder block. Position the engine front support bracket and alternator mounting bracket and adjusting arm bracket on the cylinder front cover. Install the attaching bolts.

24. When pushing on the alignment tool, align the oil pan surfaces on the cylinder front cover and cylinder block. Tighten the attaching bolts to specification. Remove the alignment tool.

25. Clean the oil seal rubbing surface on the crankshaft sleeve with solvent and polish with crocus cloth. Examine for grooves, nicks, and burrs which could damage the seal. Lubricate the seal rubbing surface with grease and install the crankshaft sleeve.

26. Lubricate the damper hub and line the damper keyway with the key on the crankshaft. Install the damper on the crankshaft.

27. Install the damper capscrew and washer and tighten the capscrew to specification.

28. Install the power steering pump pulley on the damper and tighten the attaching bolts to specification.

29. Clean the water pump gasket surfaces. Coat the new gaskets with a water resistant sealer and position the gaskets on the cylinder front cover or water pump. Install the water pump and fan assembly. Tighten the attaching bolts to specification. On C-series vehicles, install the cooling fan on the crankshaft damper.

30. Install the alternator and the alternator drive belt. Adjust the alternator and water pump drive belts to the correct tension.

31. Install the power steering pump and drive belt, adjust the drive belt to the correct tension.

32. Install the air compressor and connect the air lines. Install the air compressor drive belt and adjust tension to specification.

33. On a high-fan installation, install the fan and drive belt and adjust the tension to specification.

34. Install the fuel pump using a new gasket.

35. Connect the carburetor fuel inlet line to the fuel pump.

36. Connect the heater hose to the water pump and install the by-pass hose.

37. Install the radiator, radiator support, and shutter assembly (if equipped) as an assembly. Connect the upper and lower radiator hoses.

38. Connect the transmission oil cooler lines and the battery ground cable.

39. If any coolant has entered the oil pan when separating the cylinder front cover from the block, it will be necessary to flush the crankcase.

40. Fill and bleed the cooling system.

41. Fill the crankcase with the correct grade and quality of oil.

42. Install the air cleaner and operate the engine at a fast idle to check for coolant or oil leaks. Adjust the ignition timing and connect the vacuum line to the distributor.

460 CID (7.5L) V8 ENGINE

1. Bring the engine to No. 1 piston at TDC (top dead center) on the compression stroke. Drain the cooling system and crankcase.

2. Remove the radiator shroud and fan.

3. Disconnect the upper and lower radiator hoses, and the automatic transmission oil cooler lines from the radiator.

4. Remove the radiator upper support and remove the radiator.

5. Loosen the alternator attaching bolts and air conditioning compressor idler pulley and remove the drive belts with the water pump pulley. Remove the bolts attaching the compressor support to the water pump and remove the bracket (support), if so equipped.

6. Remove the crankshaft pulley from the vibration damper. Remove the bolt and washer attaching the crankshaft damper and remove the damper with a puller. Remove the Woodruff key from the crankshaft.

7. Loosen the by-pass hose at the water pump, and disconnect the heater return tube at the water pump.

8. Disconnect and plug the fuel inlet and outlet lines at the fuel pump, and remove the fuel pump.

9. Remove the bolts attaching the front cover to the cylinder block. Cut the oil pan seal flush with the cylinder block face with a thin knife blade prior to separating the cover from the cylinder block. Remove the cover and water pump as an assembly. Discard the front cover gasket and oil pan seal.

10. Transfer the water pump if a new cover is going to be installed. Clean all of the gasket sealing surfaces on both the front cover and the cylinder block.

11. Check the timing chain deflection. If timing chain deflection exceeds specification, proceed as follows:

a. Crank the engine until the timing marks on the sprockets are aligned.

b. Remove the camshaft sprocket capscrew, washer, and two piece fuel pump eccentric. Slide both sprockets and the timing chain forward, and remove them as an assembly.

c. Position the sprockets and timing chain on the camshaft and crankshaft. Be certain that the timing marks on the sprockets are correctly aligned.

d. Install the two piece fuel pump eccentric, washers, and camshaft sprocket capscrew. Tighten the camshaft capscrew to specification.

12. Coat the gasket surface of the oil pan with sealer. Cut and position the required sections of a new seal on the oil pan. Apply sealer to the corners.

13. Coat the gasket surfaces of the cylinder block and cover with sealer and position the new gasket on the block.

14. Position the front cover on the cylinder block. Use care not to damage the seal and gasket or mislocate them.

15. Coat the front cover attaching screws with sealer and install them.

NOTE: It may be necessary to force the front cover downward to compress the oil pan seal in order to install the front cover attaching bolts. Use a drift to engage the cover screw holes through the cover and pry downward.

16. Assemble and install the remaining components in the reverse order of removal. Tighten the front cover bolts to 15–20 ft. lbs., the water pump attaching screws to 12–15 ft. lbs., the crankshaft damper to 70–90 ft. lbs., the crankshaft pulley to 35–50 ft. lbs., fuel pump to 19–27 ft. lbs., the oil pan bolts to 9–11 ft. lbs. for the $^5/_{16}$ in. screws and to 7–9 ft. lbs. for the $^1/_4$ in. screws, and the alternator pivot bolt to 45–57 ft. lbs.

TIMING

Timing Cover and Belt

Removal and Installation

122 CID (2.0L) AND 140 CID (2.3L) ENGINES

NOTE: There is an access plug provided in the cam drive belt cover so that the camshaft timing can be checked without removing the drive belt cover.

1. Remove the access plug.
2. Turn the crankshaft until the timing marks on the crankshaft indicate TDC.
3. Make sure that the timing mark on the camshaft drive sprocket is aligned with the pointer on the inner belt cover. Also, the rotor of the distributor must align with the No. 1 cylinder firing position.

NOTE: Never turn the crankshaft of any of the overhead cam engines in the opposite direction of normal rotation. Backward rotation of the crankshaft may cause the timing belt to slip and alter the timing.

4. To replace the timing belt, set the engine to TDC with the No. 1 piston on the compression stroke. The crankshaft and camshaft timing marks should align with their respective pointers and the distributor rotor should point to the no. 1 plug tower.
5. Loosen the adjustment bolts on the alternator and accessories and remove the drive belts. To provide clearance for removing the camshaft belt, remove the fan and pulley.
6. Remove the belt outer cover.
7. Remove the distributor cap from the distributor and position it out of the way.
8. Loosen the belt tensioner adjustment and pivot bolts. Lever the tensioner away from the belt and retighten the adjustment bolt to hold it away.
9. Remove the crankshaft bolt and pulley. Remove the belt guide behind the pulley.
10. Remove the camshaft drive belt.
11. Install the new belt over the crankshaft pulley first, then counterclockwise over the auxiliary shaft sprocket and the camshaft sprocket. Adjust the belt fore and aft so that it is centered on the sprockets.
12. Loosen the tensioner adjustment bolt, allowing it to spring back against the belt.
13. Remove the spark plugs and rotate the crankshaft two complete turns in the normal rotation direction to remove any belt slack. Turn the crankshaft until the timing check marks are lined up. If the timing has slipped, remove the belt and repeat the procedure.
14. Tighten the tensioner adjustment bolt to 14–21 ft. lbs., and the pivot bolt to 28–40 ft. lbs.
15. Replace the belt guide and crankshaft pulley, distributor cap, belt outer cover, fan and pulley, drive belts and accessories. Adjust the accessory drive belt tension. Start the engine and check the ignition timing.

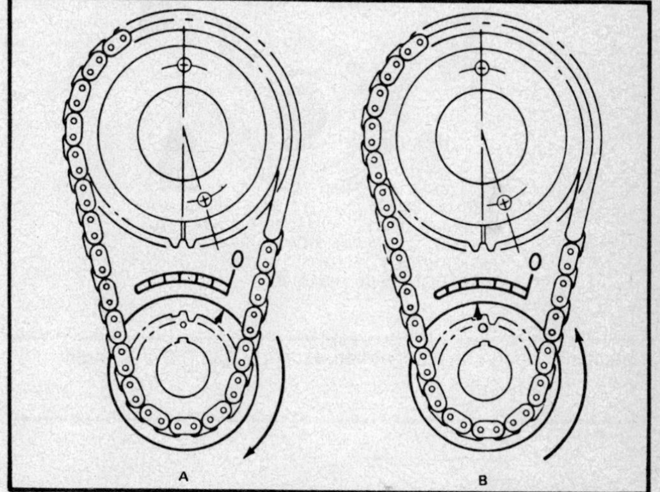

Checking timing chain deflection—232 CID V-6 engine (© Ford Motor Co.)

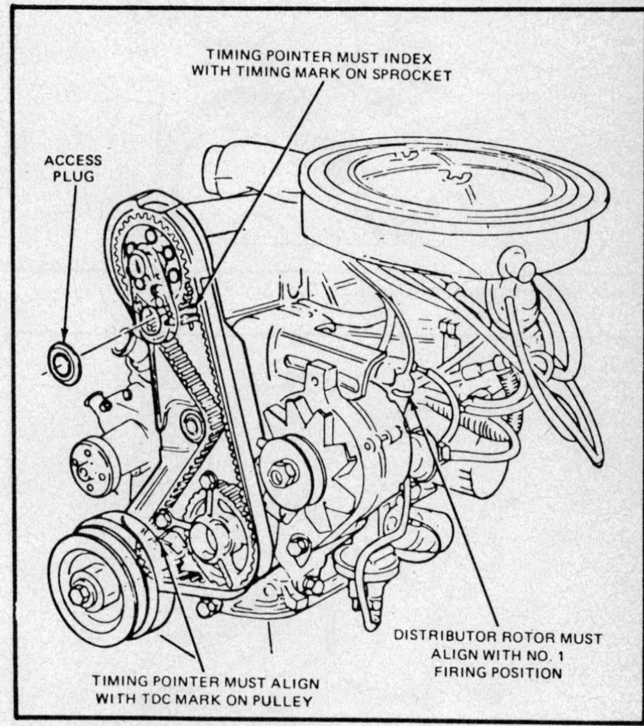

Timing mark alignment—122(2.0L) and 140(2.3L) engines (© Ford Motor Co.)

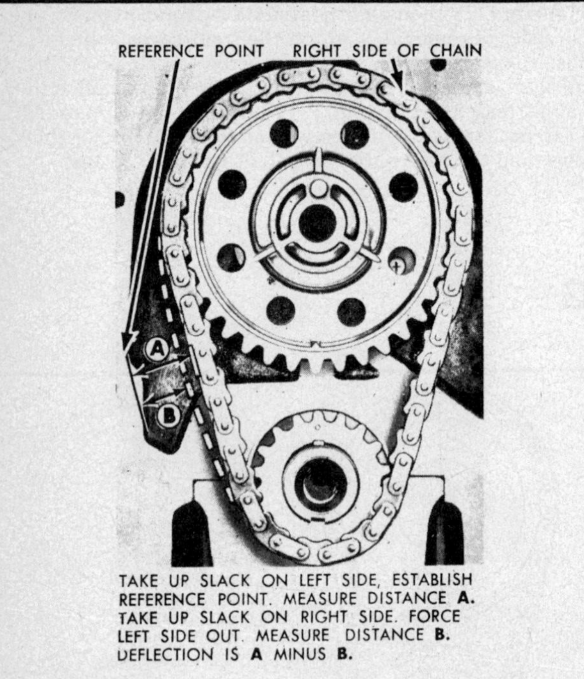

Checking timing chain deflection except —232 CID V-6 engine (© Ford Motor Co.)

Checking timing gear backlash (© Ford Motor Co.)

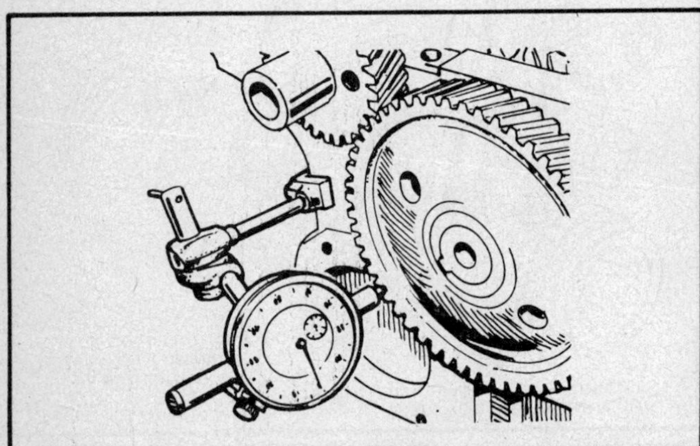

Checking camshaft gear runout (© Ford Motor Co.)

Timing Chain Deflection

EXCEPT 232 CID (3.8L) V6 ENGINE

To measure timing chain deflection, rotate crankshaft clockwise to take up slack on the left side of chain. Choose a reference point and measure distance from this point and the chain. Rotate crankshaft in the opposite direction to take up slack on the right side of the chain. Force the left (slack) side of the chain out and measure the distance to the reference point chosen earlier. The difference between the two measurements is the deflection.

Timing chain should be replaced if deflection measurement exceeds specified limit. On 330, 361, and 391 engines, the deflection measurement should not exceed $^{11}/_{16}$ in., on all other engines the deflection measurement should not exceed $^{1}/_{2}$ in.

232 CID (3.8L) V6 ENGINE

1. Remove the right valve rocker arm cover.
2. Loosen the No. 3 exhaust valve rocker arm and rotate it to one side.
3. Install a dial indicator on the end of the push rod, using proper adapter tools.
4. Turn the crankshaft clockwise until the No. 1 piston is at TDC. The damper mark should point to TDC on the timing degree indicator. This will also take up the slack on the right side of the chain.
5. Zero the dial indicator needle.
6. Turn the crankshaft slowly counterclockwise until the slightest movement is seen on the dial indicator. Stop and observe the damper timing mark for the number of degrees of travel from TDC.
7. If the reading on the timing degree indicator exceeds 6°, replace the timing chain and sprockets.

Camshaft Endplay Measurement

The fiber camshaft gears used on some engines is easily damaged if pried upon while the valve train load is on the camshaft. Loosen rocker arm nuts or rocker arm shaft support bolts before checking camshaft endplay.

Push camshaft toward rear of engine, install and zero a dial indicator, then pry between camshaft gear and block to pull the camshaft forward. If endplay is excessive, check for correct installation of spacer. If spacer is installed correctly, then replace thrust plate.

Measuring Timing Gear Backlash

Use a dial indicator installed on block to measure timing gear backlash. Hold gear firmly against the block while making measurement. If excessive backlash exists, replace both gears.

Camshaft

Removal and Installation

122 CID (2.0L) AND 140 CID (2.3L) ENGINES

NOTE: The following procedure covers camshaft removal and installation with the cylinder head on or off the engine. If the cylinder head has been removed start at Step 9.

1. Drain the cooling system. Remove the air cleaner assembly and disconnect the negative battery cable.
2. Remove the spark plug wires from the plugs, disconnect the retainer from the valve cover and position the wires out of the way. Disconnect rubber vacuum lines as necessary.
3. Remove all drive belts. Remove the alternator mounting bracket-to-cylinder head mounting bolts, position bracket and alternator out of the way.
4. Disconnect and remove the upper radiator hose. Disconnect the radiator shroud.

5. Remove the fan blades and water pump pulley and fan shroud. Remove cam belt and valve covers.
6. Align engine timing marks at TDC. Remove cam drive belt.
7. Raise and support the front of the vehicle safely. Remove the front motor mount bolts. Disconnect the lower radiator hose from the radiator. Disconnect and plug the automatic transmission cooler lines.
8. Position a piece of wood on a floor jack and raise the engine carefully as far as it will go. Place blocks of wood between the engine mounts and crossmember pedestals.
9. Remove the rocker arms.
10. Remove the camshaft drive gear and belt guide using a suitable puller. Remove the front oil seal with a sheet metal screw and slide hammer.
11. Remove the camshaft retainer located on the rear mounting stand by unbolting the two bolts.
12. Remove the camshaft by carefully withdrawing toward the front of the engine. Caution should be used to prevent damage to cam bearings, lobes and journals.
13. Check the camshaft journals and lobes for wear. Inspect the cam bearings, replace as required. The cylinder head must be removed for new bearings to be installed.
14. Cam installation is in the reverse order of removal.

NOTE: Coat the camshaft with heavy SF oil before sliding it into the cylinder head. Install a new front seal. Apply a coat of sealer or teflon tape to the cam drive gear bolt before installation.

CAUTION

After any procedure requiring removal of the rocker arms, each lash adjuster must be fully collapsed after assembly, then released. This must be done before the camshaft is turned.

AUXILIARY SHAFT

Removal and Installation

122 CID (2.0L) AND 140 CID (2.3L) ENGINES

1. Remove the camshaft drive belt cover.
2. Remove the drive belt. Remove the auxiliary shaft sprocket. A puller may be necessary to remove the sprocket.
3. Remove the distributor and fuel pump.
4. Remove the auxiliary shaft cover and thrust plate.
5. Withdraw the auxiliary shaft from the block.

NOTE: The distributor drive gear and the fuel pump eccentric on the auxiliary shaft must not be allowed to touch the auxiliary shaft bearings during removal and installation. Completely coat the shaft with oil before sliding it into place.

6. Slide the auxiliary shaft into the housing and insert the thrust plate to hold the shaft.
7. Install a new gasket and auxiliary shaft cover.

NOTE: The auxiliary shaft cover and cylinder front cover share a gasket. Cut off the old gasket around the cylinder cover and use half of the new gasket on the auxiliary shaft cover.

8. Fit a new gasket into the fuel pump and install the pump.
9. Insert the distributor and install the auxiliary shaft sprocket.
10. Align the timing marks and install the drive belt.
11. Install the drive belt cover.
12. Check the ignition timing.

173 CID (2.8L) V6 ENGINE

1. Disconnect the negative battery cable from the battery. Drain the coolant and remove the radiator, fan, spacer, water pump pulley and the drive belt.

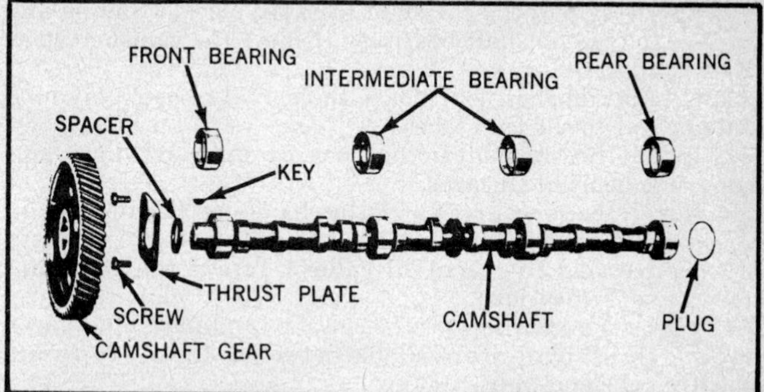

Camshaft 6-cylinder—300 engine (© Ford Motor Co.)

Camshaft thrustplate and spacer—330 engine (© Ford Motor Co.)

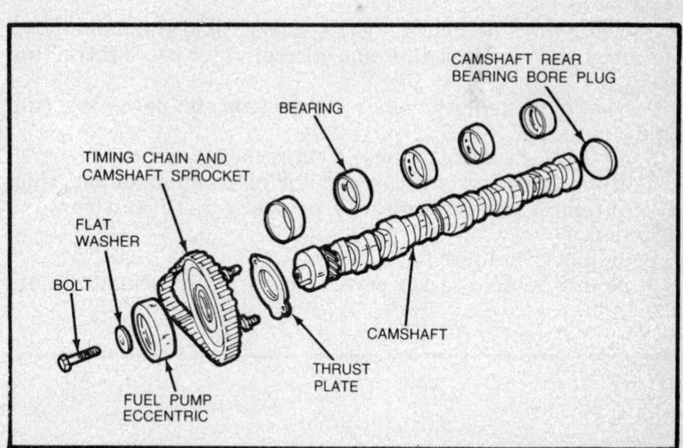

Typical camshaft—V8 engines

2. Remove the distributor cap with spark plug wires as an assembly. Remove the distributor vacuum line, distributor, alternator, thermactor, rocker arm covers, fuel line and filter, carburetor, EGR tube, and intake manifold. Remove the spark plug wire boots.
3. Drain the crankcase. Remove the rocker arm and the shaft assemblies. Lift out the pushrods and place in a marked rack so they can be reinstalled in the same location.
4. Remove the oil pan.
5. Remove the drive sprocket attaching bolt and slide the sprocket off the end of the shaft.
6. Remove the engine front cover and water pump as an assembly.
7. Remove the camshaft gear retaining bolt and slide the gear off the camshaft.
8. Remove the camshaft thrust plate and the screws.
9. Remove the valve lifters.

10. Carefully pull the camshaft from the block, avoiding any damage to the camshaft bearings. Remove the camshaft gear key and spacer ring.
11. Oil the camshaft journals with gear oil or assembly lube and apply it to the cam lobes.
12. Install the camshaft in the block, carefully avoiding damage to the bearing surfaces.
13. Install the spacer ring with the chamfered side toward the camshaft. Insert the camshaft key and install the thrust plate so that it covers the main oil gallery. Torque the attaching screws to specifications.
14. Check the camshaft for the specified end-play. The spacer ring and thrust plate are available in two thicknesses to permit adjusting the end-play.
15. Turn the camshaft and the crankshaft as necessary to align the timing marks and install the camshaft gear. Install the retaining washer and bolt and tighten to specifications.
16. Install the valve lifters to their original locations.
17. Install the engine front cover and water pump as an assembly.
18. Install the belt drive pulley and secure with washer and retaining bolt. Tighten the bolt to specifications.
19. Install the oil pan.
20. Apply a light grease to both ends of the pushrods. Install the valve pushrods in their original locations. Continue the installation in the reverse order of the removal procedure.

300 CID (4.9L) ENGINE

1. Drain the cooling system. Disconnect the negative battery cable. Remove the radiator shroud and radiator. On some models it may be necessary to remove the grille and radiator support for necessary clearance.
2. Remove the front cover.
3. Remove air cleaner and crankcase vent tube at the rocker cover.
4. Disconnect accelerator cable, choke cable and hand throttle cable (if so equipped). Remove accelerator cable retracting spring.
5. If applicable, remove air compressor and power steering belts.
6. Disconnect oil filler hose from rocker cover.
7. Remove distributor cap and wiring as an assembly, then disconnect vacuum line and primary wire and remove distributor.
8. Remove fuel pump.
9. Remove valve rocker cover, loosen rocker arm stud nuts and move rocker arms to one side. Remove push rods, identifying each so that they may be installed in their original locations.
10. Remove push rod cover and valve lifters, identifying the position of each.
11. Turn crankshaft to align timing marks, remove camshaft thrust plate bolts and carefully pull camshaft and gear from block. Metal camshaft gear (300 HD) is bolted onto camshaft and fiber gear (300 LD) is pressed on and must be removed with an arbor press.
12. To install camshaft, oil journals and apply Lubriplate to lobes, then carefully install camshaft, spacer, thrustplate and gear as an assembly, making sure timing marks are aligned, then tightening thrustplate bolts to 19–20 ft. lbs. Do not rotate crankshaft until distributor is installed.
13. Install front cover.
14. Install valve lifters, then the pushrods in their original locations. Apply heavy engine oil to the lifters and Lubriplate to the pushrods.
15. Install in order the following components, if necessary using new gaskets with sealer, pushrod cover, valve rocker cover (adjust valve lash first), distributor (rotor in No. 1 cylinder firing position), fuel pump, distributor cap and wiring assembly, crankcase ventilation valve (in rocker cover), oil filler hose, accelerator cable and retracting spring, choke cable, hand throttle cable, front cylinder cover, water pump pulley, fan, belt, air compressor and power steering belts, radiator, hood latch, grill and air cleaner.
16. Fill crankcase.
17. Fill and bleed cooling system, checking for leaks.
18. Set the ignition timing, then connect distributor vacuum line.
19. Adjust carburetor idle speed and idle fuel mixture.

232 CID (3.8L) V6 AND ALL V8 ENGINES

1. Disconnect the negative battery cable. Remove all required components to gain access to the intake manifold. Remove the intake manifold and valley pan, if so equipped. On Econolines, remove the grill.
2. Remove the rocker covers, and either remove the rocker arm shafts or loosen the rockers on their pivots and remove the push rods. The push rods must be reinstalled in their original positions.
3. Remove the valve lifters in sequence with a magnet. They must be replaced in their original positions.
4. Remove the timing gear cover and timing chain and sprockets.
5. In addition to the radiator and air conditioning condenser, if so equipped, it may be necessary to remove the front grille assembly and the hood lock assembly to gain the necessary clearance to slide the camshaft out the front of the engine.
6. Remove the camshaft thrust plate attaching screws and carefully slide the camshaft out of its bearing bores. Use extra caution not to scratch the bearing journals with the camshaft lobes.
7. Install the camshaft in the reverse order of removal. Coat the camshaft with engine oil liberally before installing it. Slide the camshaft into the engine very carefully so as not to scratch the bearing bores with the camshaft lobes. Install the camshaft thrust plate and tighten the attaching screws to 9–12 ft. lbs. Measure the camshaft end-play. If the end-play is more than 0.009 in., replace the thrust plate. Assemble the remaining components in the reverse order of removal.

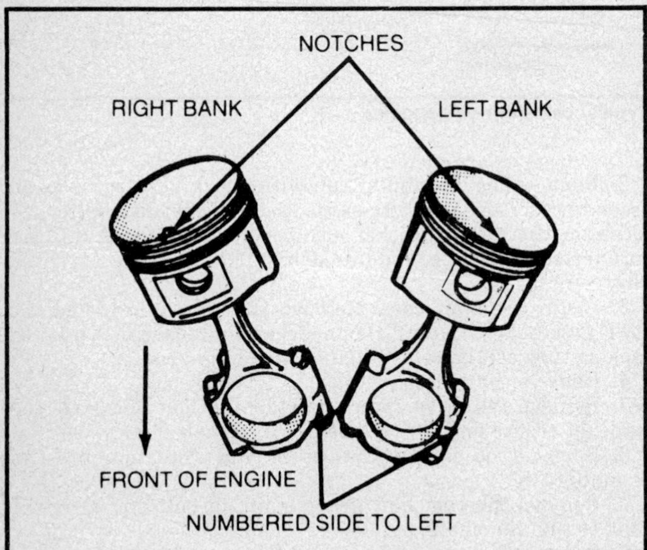

Piston installation—173(2.8L) V6 engine (© FOMOCO)

CAMSHAFT BEARINGS AND VALVE LIFTERS

For detailed procedures for camshaft bearing replacement and hydraulic lifter service see the Unit Repair Section.

Pistons and Connecting Rods

Instructions for fitting of rings and rod bearings, ridge reaming and cylinder honing may be found in the Unit Repair Section.

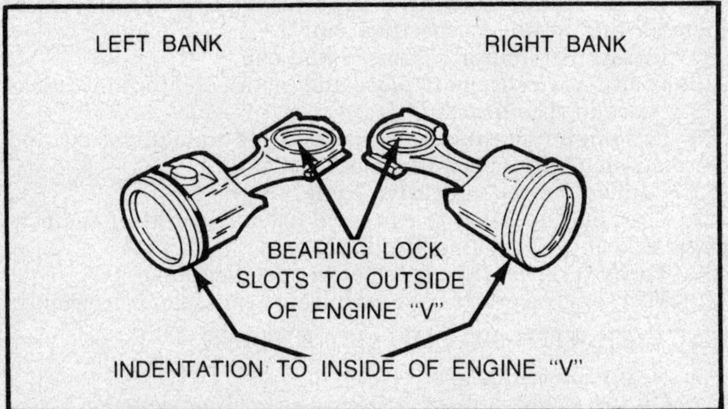

Piston and rod relationship—330, 359, 360, 361, 389, 390 and 391 V8 engines

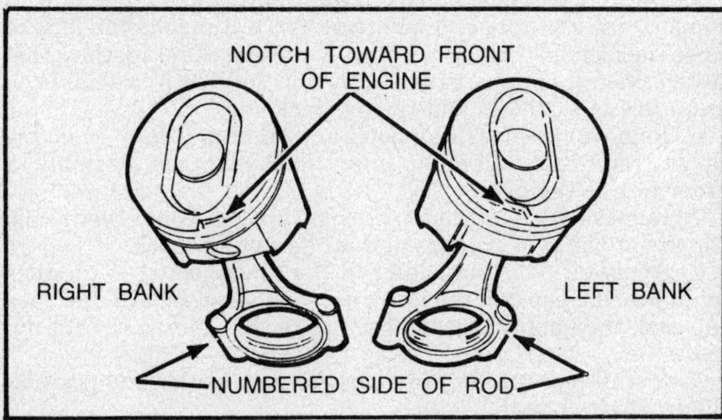

Piston and rod relationship—370, 429 and 460 V8 engines

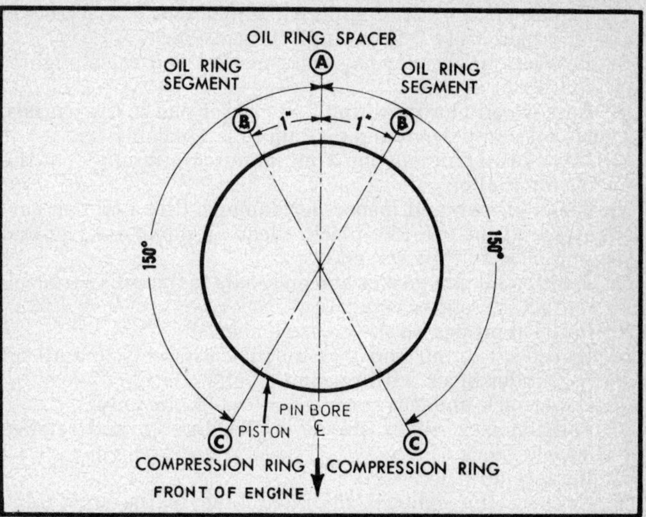

Piston ring gap spacing (© Ford Motor Co.)

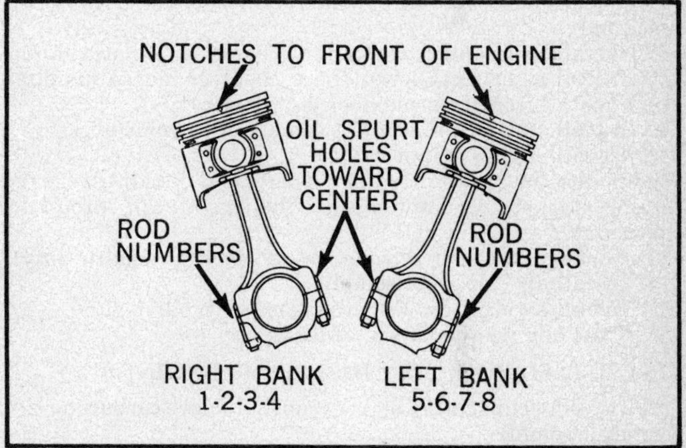

Piston-to-rod relationship—302 and 351M V8, V-6 similar (© Ford Motor Co.)

ENGINE LUBRICATION

Oil Pan

Removal and Installation

122 CID (2.0L) AND 140 CID (2.3L) ENGINES

1. Disconnect the negative battery cable.
2. Remove air cleaner assembly. Remove oil dipstick. Remove engine mount retaining nuts.
3. Remove oil cooler lines at the radiator, if so equipped. Remove (2) bolts retaining the fan shroud to the radiator and remove shroud.
4. Remove radiator retaining bolts (automatic only). Position radiator upward and wire to the hood (automatic only).
5. Raise and safely support the vehicle.
6. Drain oil from crankcase.
7. Remove starter cable from starter and remove starter.
8. Disconnect the exhaust manifold tube to the inlet pipe bracket at the thermactor check valve.
9. Remove transmission mount retaining nuts to the crossmember.
10. Remove bellcrank from converter housing (automatic only).
11. Remove oil cooler lines from retainer at the block (automatic only).
12. Remove front crossmember (automatic only).
13. Disconnect right front lower shock absorber mount (manual only).

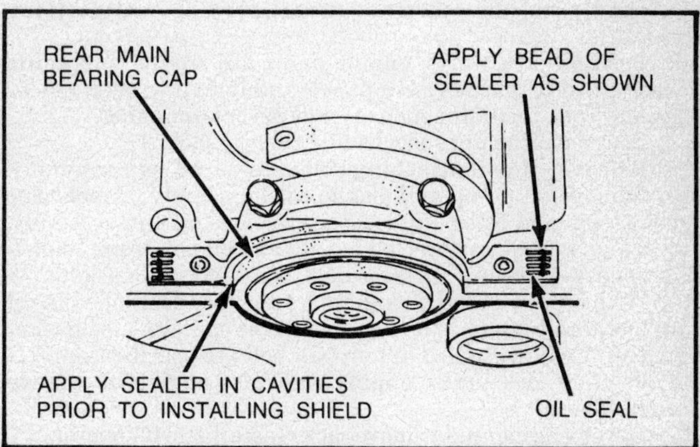

Installing oil pan seal—300 engine

14. Position jack under engine, raise and block with a piece of wood approximately 2 ½ in. high. Remove jack.
15. Position jack under the transmission and raise slightly (automatic only).
16. Remove oil pan retaining bolts, lower pan to the chassis. Remove oil pump drive and pick up tube assembly.
17. Remove oil pan (out the front for automatic only) (out the rear for manual only).
18. Clean oil pan and inspect for damage. Clean oil pan gasket surface at the cylinder block. Clean oil pump exterior and oil pump pick up tube screen.
19. Position oil pan gasket and end seals to the cylinder block (use contact cement to retain).
20. Position oil pan to the crossmember.
21. Install oil pump and pick-up tube assembly. Install oil pan to cylinder block with retaining bolts.
22. Lower jack under transmission (automatic only).
23. Position jack under engine, raise slightly, and remove wood spacer block.
24. Replace oil filter.
25. Connect the exhaust manifold tube to the inlet pipe bracket at the thermactor check valve.
26. Install transmission mount to the crossmember.
27. Install oil cooler lines to the retainer at the block (automatic only).
28. Install bellcrank to converter housing (automatic only).
29. Install right front lower shock absorber mount (manual only). Install front crossmember (automatic only).
30. Install starter and connect cable. Lower vehicle.
31. Install engine mount bolts.
32. Locate the radiator to the supports and install the (2) retaining bracket bolts (automatic only). Install fan shroud on the radiator.
33. Connect oil cooler lines to the radiator (automatic only).
34. Install air cleaner assembly.
35. Install oil dipstick. Fill crankcase with oil.
36. Start engine and check for leaks.

173 CID (2.8L) AND 179 CID (2.9L) V6 ENGINES

1. Disconnect negative battery cable. Remove carburetor air cleaner assembly.
2. Remove fan shroud and position over fan.
3. Remove distributor cap, position forward of dash panel. Remove distributor and cover bore opening.
4. Remove nuts attaching engine front insulators to cross member. Remove engine oil dipstick tube.
5. Raise vehicle and safely support on jackstands.
6. Drain engine crankcase. Remove transmission fluid filler tube and plug pan hole (auto trans. only).
7. Remove engine oil filter element. Disconnect muffler inlet pipe(s).
8. Disconnect oil cooler bracket and lower (if so equipped). Remove starter motor.
9. Position out of way, transmission oil cooler lines (if so equipped). Disconnect front stabilizer bar and position forward.
10. Position jack under engine and raise engine maximum height (until it touches dash panel) and install wooden blocks between front insulator mounts and #2 crossmember.
11. Lower engine onto blocks and remove jack.
12. Remove oil pan attaching bolts. Lower oil pan assembly.
13. Remove oil pump and pickup tube assembly (attached to bearing cap) and lower into oil pan. Remove oil pan assembly.
14. Clean gasket surfaces on engine and oil pan. Apply adhesive to gasket mating surfaces and install oil pan gaskets.
15. With oil pump and pickup tube assembly positioned in oil pan, install oil pump and then install oil pan. Be sure gasket forms an air tight seal. Tighten pan bolts to specification.
16. Position jack under engine and raise engine to remove wooden blocks.
17. Lower engine and remove jack. Install starter motor.
18. Connect muffler inlet pipe(s).
19. Connect front stabilizer bar. Reposition transmission oil cooler lines. Connect cooler bracket (if so equipped).
20. Install new engine oil filter element.
21. Unplug transmission oil pan and install oil filler tube (auto trans. only). Lower vehicle.
22. Install engine oil dipstick tube.
23. Install nuts attaching engine front insulators to crossmember and torque to specification.
24. Install distributor assembly and cap.
25. Position fan shroud in place and install and torque attaching screws to specification.
26. Fill engine crankcase with specified amount of oil and transmission with specified amount of fluid.
27. Connect battery negative cable.
28. Start engine, allow to run until normal operating temperature and check for oil or fluid leaks.
29. Verify ignition timing is set to specification.
30. Turn engine off. Install carburetor air cleaner assembly.

F SERIES WITH 300 CID (4.9L) ENGINE

1. Drain the crankcase.
2. On the F-100–250, also drain the cooling system.
3. Remove radiator from F-100–250 vehicles.
4. Raise and support the vehicle safely. Disconnect and remove the starter.
5. On F-100–250, remove engine front support insulator to support bracket nuts and washers. Use a transmission jack to raise the front of the engine, then install blocks (1 in. thick) between the front support insulators and support brackets. Lower engine onto blocks and remove jack.
6. Remove the attaching bolts and oil pan. It may be necessary to remove the oil pump inlet tube and screen assembly in order to free the pan.
7. Remove the rear main bearing cap and front cover seals. Clean out the seal grooves and all gasket surfaces.
8. Apply oil resistant sealer in the spaces between the rear main bearing cap and the block as illustrated. Install new rear cap seal, then apply a bead of sealer to the tapered ends of the seal.
9. Install new oil pan side gaskets with sealer and position the front cover seal.
10. Clean oil pump pick up assembly and place it in the pan.
11. Position pan under the engine and install pick up assembly.
12. Install pan and attaching bolts, tightening to 10–12 ft. lbs.
13. Raise engine enough with a jack and remove wood blocks. Lower engine and install washers and nuts on the support insulator studs, tightening to 40–60 ft. lbs. on LD trucks and 110–150 ft. lbs. on MD and HD trucks.
14. Install starter and starter cable on F-100–250 trucks.
15. Lower vehicle and install radiator if it was removed.
16. Fill crankcase and cooling system and start engine to check for leaks.

ECONOLINE WITH 300 CID (4.9L) ENGINE

1. Remove the engine cover. Remove the air cleaner and the carburetor.
2. If equipped with air conditioning, discharge the system and remove the compressor.
3. If the vehicle is an E-350, disconnect the thermactor check valve inlet hose and remove the check valve. Remove the EGR valve.
4. Remove the radiator hoses. Unbolt the fan shroud and position on the fan. If equipped with automatic transmission, disconnect the cooler lines and remove the oil filler tube.
5. Remove exhaust inlet pipe to manifold nuts. Raise and support the vehicle safely. Disconnect and plug fuel pump inlet line. Remove the starter. Remove alternator splash shield and front engine support nuts.
6. Remove the power steering return line clip which is located in front of the No. 1 crossmember.

7. Raise the engine and place 3 in. blocks under the engine mounts. Remove the oil pan dipstick tube.
8. Remove the oil pan bolts and remove the oil pan. Remove the pickup tube and screen from the oil pump.
9. Clean the oil pan, tube and screen assembly and the gasket surfaces of the block and oil pan.
10. Install the oil pump and screen assembly, if removed. Cement a new oil pan gasket on the oil pan. Position a new oil pan to cylinder front cover seal on the oil pan. Position the rear seal to the rear bearing cap and apply sealer. Install the oil pan.
11. Install the dipstick tube and lower the engine. Install the support nuts, starter, and connect the fuel line.
12. Install the lower radiator hose. Connect the transmission cooler lines and the transmission fill tube, if equipped.
13. Install the power steering return line clip and position the line.
14. Install the alternator splash shield and lower the hoist. Install the EGR valve and the carburetor. Connect the exhaust.
15. On E-350 models, install the thermactor check valve and connect the inlet hose.
16. Install the fan shroud and the upper radiator hose. Fill the cooling system.
17. Install the air conditioning compressor and charge the system.
18. Replace the oil filter and fill the crankcase. Start the engine and check for leaks. Adjust the carburetor curb idle speed. Install the air cleaner.

232 CID (3.8L) V6 ENGINE

1. Disconnect the cable from the battery negative cable.
2. Remove the air cleaner and duct assembly.
3. Remove the bolts attaching the fan shroud to the radiator and position the shroud over the fan.
4. Remove the engine oil dipstick.
5. Raise and support the vehicle safely. Drain the engine oil and replace the drain plug.
6. Remove the oil filter.
7. Disconnect the muffler inlet pipes from the exhaust manifolds. Remove the clamp attaching inlet pipe to converter pipe and remove inlet pipe from vehicle.
8. Disconnect the transmission shift linkage at the transmission.
9. Disconnect the transmission cooler lines at the radiator if so equipped.
10. Remove the nuts attaching the engine supports to the chassis brackets.
11. Raise the engine as high as possible, and place wood blocks between the engine supports and the chassis brackets. Remove the jack.
12. Remove the oil pan attaching bolts and drop the oil pan. Remove the oil pick-up and tube assembly and let them lay in the oil pan. Remove the oil pan from the vehicle.
13. Clean oil pan and sealing surfaces. Inspect the gasket sealing surfaces for damages and distortion due to overtightening of the bolts. Repair and straighten as required.
14. Trial fit the oil pan to the cylinder block. Make sure enough clearance has been provided to allow the oil pan to be installed without the sealant being scraped off when the pan is positioned under the engine.
15. Remove the oil pan.
16. Lay the oil pick-up and tube assembly and place them in the oil pan.
17. Place the oil pan in position on No. 1 crossmember.
18. Install the oil pick-up and tube assembly using a new gasket. Make sure the support bracket engages the stud on the No. 2 main bearing cap attaching bolt.
19. Tighten the attaching bolts to 15–22 ft. lbs. and the attaching nut to 15–22 ft. lbs.
20. Install a new oil pan rear seal. Using a small screwdriver, work the tabs on each end of the seal into the gap between the rear main cap and cylinder block. With the tabs positioned work the edge of the seal into the seal groove in the rear main cap.
21. Install the oil pan as follows:
   a. Apply a 1/8 in. bead of RTV Sealer to the seam where the front cover and cylinder block join.
   b. Apply a 1/8 in. bead of RTV Sealer to each end of the rear seal where the rear main cap and cylinder block join.
   c. Apply a 1/8 in. bead of RTV Sealer along the oil pan rails on the cylinder block. As the bead crosses the front cover increase the bead width to 1/4 in.
   d. Position oil pan to bottom of engine and secure with bolts. Tighten bolts to 7–8 ft. lbs..
22. Raise the engine and remove the wood blocks. Lower the engine and install the insulator to chassis bracket nuts and washers. Tighten the nuts to 50–70 ft. lbs..
23. Position the inlet pipe to the converter pipe and secure with attaching clamp. Connect inlet pipe to exhaust manifolds and secure with attaching nuts. Tighten to 25–38 ft. lbs..
24. Connect the transmission shift linkage at the transmission.
25. Connect the transmission cooler lines at the radiator if so equipped.
26. Install a new oil filter.
27. Lower the vehicle. Install the air cleaner assembly. Position fan shroud to radiator brace and secure with bolts.
28. Connect the battery negative cable to the battery.
29. Install the engine oil dipstick.
30. Fill crankcase with oil. Run the engine and check for possible leaks.

BRONCO W/302 CID (5.0L) OR 351W CID (5.8L) V8 ENGINES

1. Remove the air cleaner and duct assembly. Remove the oil dipstick tube. Drain the engine oil.
2. Remove the oil pan bolts and remove the oil pan.
3. To install, clean the oil pan and the cylinder block of all old gasket material. Position a new oil pan gasket and end seals to the cylinder block.
4. Clean and install the oil pump pick-up tube and screen assembly, if removed.
5. Install the oil pan to the cylinder block. Install the oil dipstick tube, air cleaner and duct assembly.
6. Fill the crankcase with the proper oil. Start the engine and check for leaks.

F-SERIES

1. Remove the oil dipstick. Remove the bolts attaching the fan shroud to the radiator and position the shroud over the fan.
2. Remove the nuts and lockwashers attaching the engine support insulators to the chassis bracket.
3. Disconnect the oil cooler line at the left side of the radiator, if equipped with automatic transmission.
4. Raise the engine and place wood blocks under the engine supports. Drain the crankcase.
5. Remove the oil pan bolts and lower the oil pan onto the crossmember.
6. Remove the oil pump pick-up tube and screen. Lower this assembly into the oil pan. Remove the oil pan.
7. To install, clean the oil pan, inlet tube and gasket surfaces. Position a new oil pan gasket and seals to the cylinder block.
8. Install the oil pick-up tube and screen to the oil pump, and install the lower attaching bolt and gasket loosely. Place the oil pan on the crossmember. Install the upper pick up tube bolt. Tighten both pick up tube bolts.
9. Install the oil pan. Remove the wood blocks and lower the engine.
10. Install the insulator to chassis bracket nuts and washers.
11. Connect the automatic transmission cooler line, if equipped. Install the fan shroud attaching bolts.
12. Fill the crankcase with oil. Install the oil dipstick. Start the engine and check for leaks.

ECONOLINE

1. Disconnect the battery and remove engine cover. Remove the air cleaner. Drain the cooling system.

2. If equipped with power steering remove the pump and position it out of the way. If so equipped, remove the air conditioning compressor retainer and position the compressor out of the way.

3. Disconnect the radiator hoses. Remove the fan shroud bolts and oil filler tube. Remove the oil dipstick bolt. Raise the vehicle on a hoist.

4. Remove the alternator splash shield. If equipped, disconnect the automatic transmission cooler lines at the radiator.

5. Disconnect and plug the fuel line at the fuel pump. Remove the engine mount nuts. Drain the engine oil. Remove the dipstick tube. Disconnect the muffler inlet pipe from the exhaust manifolds.

6. If equipped, remove the automatic transmission dipstick and tube. Disconnect the manual linkage at the transmission. Remove the center driveshaft support and remove the driveshaft from the transmission.

7. Place a transmission jack under the oil pan and insert a wooden block between the pan and jack.

NOTE: The engine and transmission assembly will pivot around the rear engine mount. The engine assembly must be raised four inches (measured from the front motor mounts). The engine must remain centered in the engine compartment to obtain this much lift.

8. Raise the engine and transmission assembly. Insert wooden blocks to support the engine in its uppermost position.

9. Remove the oil pan bolts and lower the oil pan. Unbolt the oil pump and the oil pick-up tube and lay them in the oil pan. Remove the oil pan from the vehicle. The oil pump must be removed along with the removal of the oil pan.

10. To install, clean the oil pan, oil pick-up tube, oil pump and gasket surfaces. Position new gasket and seals to the engine block.

11. Position the oil pan with the oil pump to vehicle and install the oil pump. Install the oil pan.

12. Continue the installation in the reverse order of removal.

13. Install a new oil filter and fill the crankcase with the proper grade oil. Fill the cooling system. Start the engine and check for oil and water.

351M CID (5.8L) AND 400 CID (6.6L) V8 ENGINES

1. Remove the oil dipstick. Remove the fan shroud bolts and position the shroud over the fan.

2. Raise and support the vehicle safely. Drain the crankcase. Disconnect the starter cable and remove the starter.

3. Place a jack and a wood block under the oil pan and support the engine. Remove the engine front support through bolts.

4. Raise the engine and place wood blocks between the engine supports and the chassis brackets. Remove the jack.

5. If equipped with an automatic transmission, position the oil cooler lines out of the way.

6. Remove the oil pan attaching bolts and remove the oil pan.

7. To install, clean the gasket surfaces of the block, oil pan, oil pick-up tube, and screen. Coat the block surface and the oil pan gasket with sealer. Position the oil pan gasket to the cylinder block.

8. Position the oil pan front seal on the cylinder front cover plate. Position the oil pan rear seal on the rear main bearing cap. Be sure that the tabs on both the front and rear seals are over the oil pan gasket.

9. Position and install the oil pan. Continue the installation in the reverse order of removal.

10. Fill the crankcase. Start the engine and check for oil leaks.

ALL OTHER V8 ENGINES, EXCEPT 460 CID (7.5L)

1. Drain the crankcase and remove the oil dipstick and the dipstick tube.

2. Remove the oil pan bolts and lower the oil pan to the axle. Position the crankshaft so that the counterweight will clear the oil pan.

3. Remove the oil pump and the inlet tube bolts. Place the oil pump, inlet tube screen and intermediate drive shaft into the oil pan. Remove the oil pan and the oil pump.

NOTE: The oil pump must be removed along with the oil pan.

4. To install, clean the oil pan and block gasket surfaces. Position a new gasket on the oil pan.

5. Remove the inlet tube screen from the oil pump. Clean the oil pump and inlet tube screen. Position a new oil pump inlet tube gasket on the oil pump and install the inlet tube.

6. Place the oil pump in the oil pan and position the oil pan on the crossmember. Position a new oil pump gasket on the cylinder block and install the oil pump. Position and install the oil pan. Install the dipstick tube and the dipstick.

7. Replace the engine oil filter element. Fill the crankcase. Start the engine and check for oil leaks.

460 CID (7.5L) V8 ENGINE, EXCEPT IN ECONOLINE MODELS

1. Disconnect the battery ground cable. Disconnect the radiator shroud and position it over the fan.

2. Raise and support the vehicle. Drain the crankcase. Remove the oil filter.

3. Remove the through bolt from each engine support. Place a floor jack under the front edge of the oil pan, with a block of wood between the jack and the oil pan. Raise the engine just high enough to insert 1 ¼ in. blocks of wood between the insulators and the brackets. Remove the floor jack.

4. Remove the oil pan bolts and remove the oil pan. It may be necessary to rotate the crankshaft to provide clearance between the pan and the crankshaft counterweights.

5. To install, clean the gasket surfaces of the block and the oil pan. Coat both surfaces with sealer. Position the oil pan gasket on the cylinder block. Position the oil pan front seal on the cylinder front cover. Position the oil pan rear seal on the rear main bearing cap. Be sure that the tabs on both the front and rear seals are over the oil pan gasket.

6. Position and install the oil pan. Continue the installation in the reverse order of removal.

7. Replace the oil filter and fill the crankcase. Start the engine and check for oil leaks.

ECONOLINE MODELS WITH 460 CID (7.5L) V8 ENGINE

1. Remove the engine cover, disconnect the battery and drain the cooling system.

2. Remove the air cleaner assembly. Disconnect the throttle and transmission linkage at the carburetor. Disconnect the power brake vacuum lines.

3. Disconnect the fuel line, choke lines and remove the carburetor air cleaner adaptor from the carburetor.

4. Disconnect the radiator hoses. If equipped, disconnect the oil cooler lines. Remove the fan assembly and remove the radiator. If equipped, remove the power steering pump and position it aside.

5. Remove the front engine mount attaching bolts. Remove the engine oil dipstick tube from the exhaust manifold. Remove the oil filler tube and bracket.

6. If so equipped, rotate the air conditioning lines (at the rear of the compressor) down to clear the dash (or remove them).

7. Raise and support the vehicle safely. Drain the crankcase and remove the oil filter.

8. Remove the muffler inlet pipe assembly. Disconnect the

manual and kickdown linkage from the transmission. Remove the driveshaft and coupling shaft assembly. Remove the transmission tube assembly.

9. Remove the dipstick and tube from the oil pan. Place a transmission jack under the engine oil pan. Insert a wood block between the jack surface and the oil pan. Jack the engine upward, pivoting on the rear mount until the transmission contacts the floor. Block the engine in position. The engine must remain centralized to obtain the maximum height. The engine must be raised four inches at the mounts to remove the oil pan.

10. Remove the oil pan bolts and lower the oil pan. Remove the oil pump and pick up tube attachments and drop them into the oil pan. Remove the oil pan rearward from the vehicle.

NOTE: The oil pump must be removed when removing the oil pan.

11. To install, clean the oil pan gasket surface at the cylinder block, the oil pan assembly, the oil pump pick up tube, and the screen.

12.Position the oil pan gaskets and end seals to the cylinder block using sealer. Position the oil pan with the oil pump and pick up tube assembly to the chassis and install the oil pump assembly. Position and install the oil pan. Continue the installation in the reverse order of the removal.

13.
Fill the cooling system, replace the oil filter, fill the crankcase and connect the battery. Start the engine and check for oil and water leaks.

Oil Pump

Removal and Installation

ALL ENGINES EXCEPT 232 CID (3.8L) V6 ENGINE

1. Remove the oil pan.
2. Remove the oil pump mounting bolts and remove the oil pump from the cylinder block.
3. To install, prime the pump by filling the inlet port with engine oil. Rotate the pump shaft to distribute oil within the pump body. Install the distributor intermediate shaft in the oil pump rotor shaft.
4. Insert the intermediate shaft into the distributor shaft hex bore. Make certain that the intermediate shaft is properly seated. Do not force the pump into position if it will not seat readily. The intermediate shaft hex may be misaligned with the distributor shaft. To align, rotate the intermediate shaft until it can be seated.
5. Secure the oil pump to the cylinder block and tighten the bolts. Install the oil pan and other related parts.

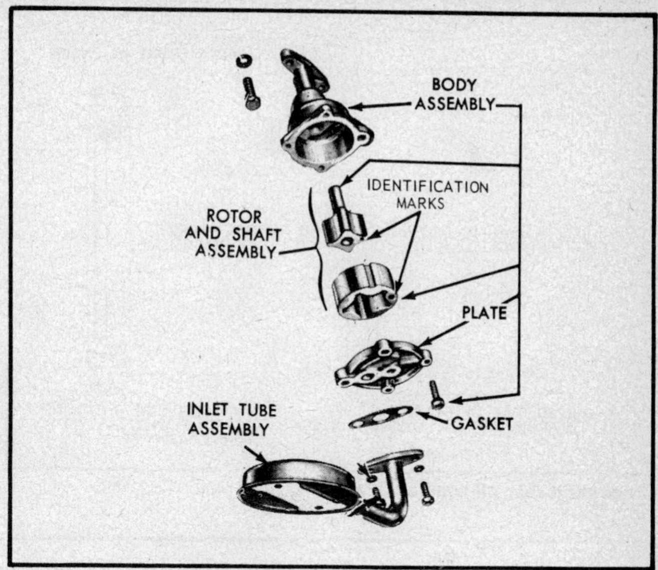

Typical oil pump assembly (© Ford Motor Co.)

232 CID (3.8L) V6 ENGINE

1. If necessary remove the oil filter.
2. Remove the oil pump cover attaching bolts and remove the cover.
3. Lift the pump gears of the pocket in the front cover.
4. Remove the cover gasket. Discard the gasket.
5. If necessary, remove the pump gears from the cover.
6. Pack the gear pocket with petroleum jelly. Do not use chassis lubricant.
7. Install the gears in the cover pocket making sure the petroleum jelly fills all voids between the gears and the pocket.

NOTE: Failure to properly pack the oil pump gears with petroleum jelly may result in failure of the pump to prime when the engine is started.

8. Position the cover gasket and install the pump cover.
9. Tighten the pump cover attaching bolts to 18–22 ft. lbs.

OIL PUMP CLEARANCES

Checking

Thoroughly clean all parts in solvent and dry with compressed air. Check the inside of the pump housing for obvious wear or

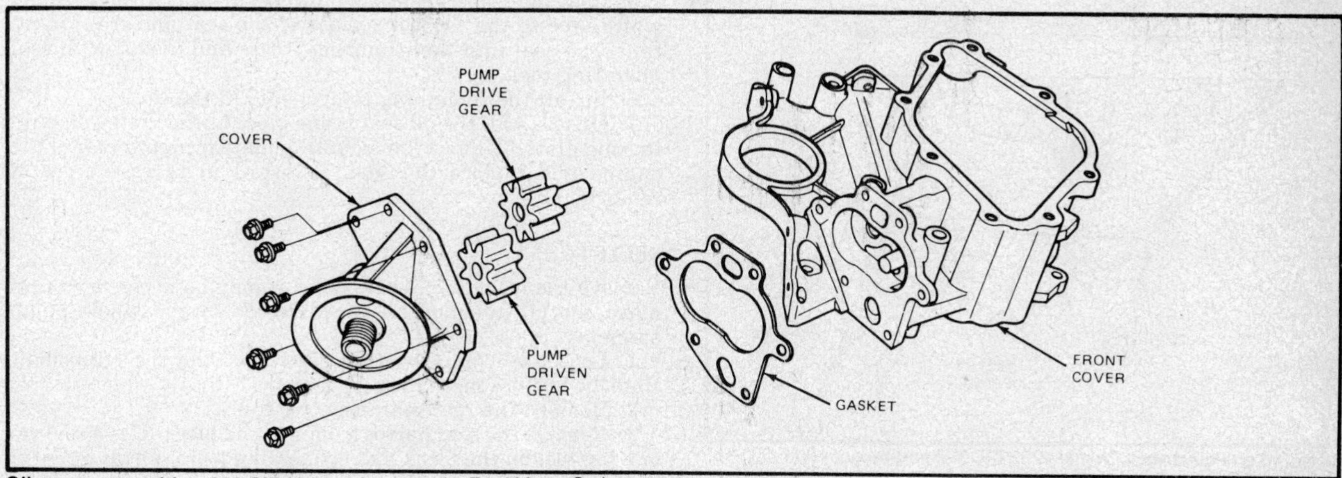

Oil pump assembly—232 CID V-6 engine gear (© Ford Motor Co.)

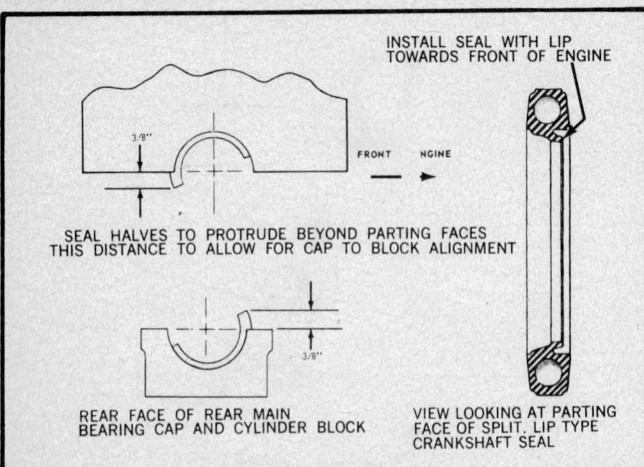

Crankshaft rear oil seal installation (© Ford Motor Co.)

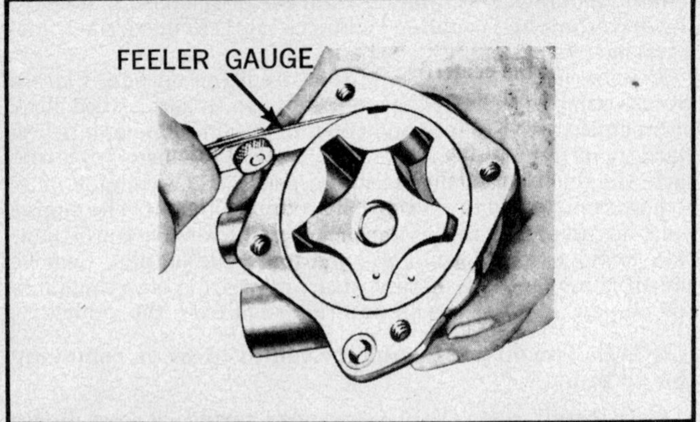

Checking outer race-to-housing clearance (© Ford Motor Co.)

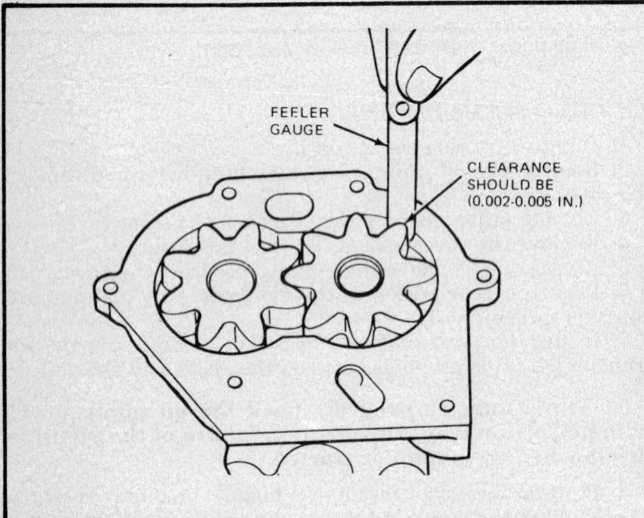

Oil pump side clearance check—232 CID V-6 engine (© Ford Motor Co.)

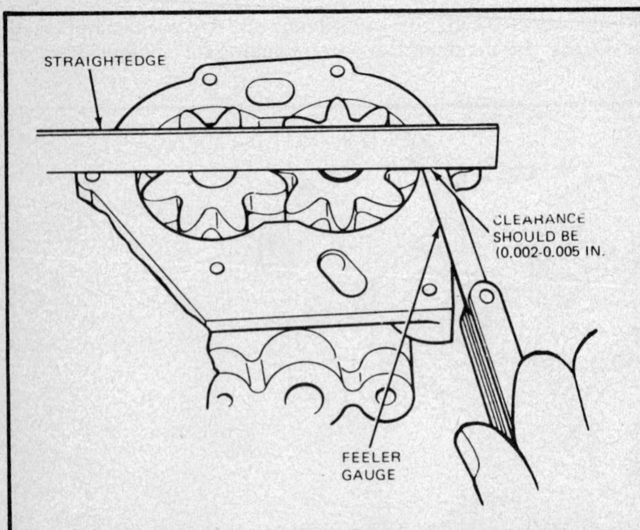

Oil pump end clearance check—232 CID V-6 engine gear (© Ford Motor Co.)

scoring. Check mating surfaces of pump cover and rotors, replace the cover if it is scored or grooved.

Measure outer race to housing clearance and clearance (rotor end-play) between a straightedge and the rotor. The outer race, shaft and rotor are replaceable only as an assembly.

Measure the driveshaft to housing clearance by comparing shaft OD to housing bearing ID.

Inspect relief valve spring for collapsed or worn condition. Check the spring tension. Replace the spring if weak or worn.

Check relief valve piston and bore for scores and free operation.
for leaks.

Rear Main Oil Seal

Removal and Installation

ONE PIECE SEAL

1. Remove the transmission, clutch assembly or converter and flywheel.
2. Lower the oil pan if necessary for working room.
3. On engines except 2.2L, use an awl to punch two small holes on opposite sides of the seal just above the split between the main bearing cap and engine block. Install a sheet metal screw in each hole. Use two small pry bars and pry evenly on both screws using two small blocks of wood as a fulcrum point for the pry bars. Use caution throughout to avoid scratching or damage to the oil seal mounting surfaces.
4. When the seal has been removed, clean the mounting recess.
5. Coat the seal and block mounting surfaces with oil. Apply white lube to the contact surface of the seal and crankshaft. Start the seal into the mounting recess and install with seal mounting tool.
6. Install the remaining components in the reverse.
7. On the 2.2L the oil seal is one piece but mounted on a retaining plate. Remove the mounting plate from the rear of the engine and replace the seal. Reinstall in reverse order of removal.

SPLIT SEAL

Remove the oil pan. In some cases it may be necessary to remove the oil pump pick-up and screen or the whole pump assembly.

1. Loosen all main bearing caps, lowering the crankshaft slightly, but not more than $^{1}/_{32}$ in.
2. Remove the rear main bearing cap.
3. Remove the seal halves from cap and block. Use a seal removing tool on the block half or install a small metal screw in one end so that the seal may be pulled out.

NOTE: Do not damage or scratch the crankshaft seal surfaces.

4. If so equipped, remove the oil seal retaining pin from the bearing cap.
5. Thoroughly clean seal grooves in block and cap with brush and solvent.
6. Dip seal halves in engine oil.
7. Carefully install upper half of seal with the lip facing toward the front of the engine until $^3/_8$ in. is left protruding below parting surface. Be careful not to scrape seal.
8. Tighten all but the rear main bearing caps to specified torque.
9. Install lower seal half in the rear main bearing cap with the lip facing toward the front of the engine. Apply a light coat of oil-resistant sealer to the rear of the top mating surface of the cap. Do not apply sealer to the area forward of the side seal groove.
10. Install rear main bearing cap and tighten bolts to specified torque.
11. Install oil pump and oil pan.
12. Fill crankcase and operate engine to check for leaks.

FRONT SUSPENSION

Solid I Beam

SPRING

Removal and Installation

1980–81 LN 600–700 SERIES

1. Raise the vehicle frame until the weight is off the front springs, with the wheels still touching the floor.
2. Remove the shock absorber.
3. Remove the cotter pin from the support bracket and remove the stud from the front bracket.
4. On vehicles equipped with hydraulic brakes, remove the cotter pin and drive out the spring pin.
5. On vehicles equipped with air brakes, remove the cotter pin and nut from the rear bracket shackle bolt and drive out the bolt.
6. Remove the nuts from the two spring clips (U-bolts) holding the spring on the axle.
7. Position the spring on the spring seat and align the spring eye with the spring bracket.
8. Prior to installation, coat the bushings with lubricant. Drive the stud through the bracket and the eye of the spring.

NOTE: The lubrication opening in the stud should face inward.

9. Install the attaching nut. Tighten the nut to 31–42 ft. lbs. then back it off one castellation. Install a new cotter pin.
10. Install the lubrication fitting.
11. Raise the opposite end of the spring leaf into the spring rear bracket.
12. On vehicles with hydraulic brakes, install the spring pin in the bracket and secure the pin with a new cotter pin.
13. On vehicles with air brakes, install the spring retaining bolt, washer, nut, and new cotter pin.
14. Place the spring clips (U-bolts) in position over the spring clip plate and through the holes in the axle. Make sure that the spring tie bolt is centered in the recess of the axle.
15. Install the nuts on the spring clips. Lower the vehicle to the floor and tighten the spring clip nuts. Lubricate the front pin.

F AND B SERIES, EXCEPT 1983 AND LATER F SERIES WITH 9500 AND 12000 lb. FRONT AXLES

1. Raise the vehicle frame until the weight is off the front spring with the front wheel still touching the floor.
2. Support the front axle with jacks, to remove the weight from the spring U-bolts.
3. Disconnect the shock absorber from the leaf spring.
4. Remove the nut and bolt that retains the spring to the front bracket.
5. Remove the nut and bolt that retains the spring to the rear bracket.
6. Remove the four U-bolt nuts and washers and the two U-bolts. Remove the spring.
7. Position the spring at the spring seat and align the spring eye with the front spring bracket.
8. Prior to installation coat the bushing with Multi-Purpose Lubricant or equivalent. Gently slide the bolt through the bracket and spring eye.
9. Install the washer and nut. Tighten the nut to 220–300 ft. lbs. Install the cotter pin.
10. Raise rear end of spring into the bracket.
11. Install the through bolt and nut and tighten nut to 75–105 ft. lbs. Install cotter pin.
12. Place the U-bolts in position over the spring and through the holes in the axle. Make sure that the spring tie bolt is centered in the recess of the axle. Install the nut and washers on the U-bolts. Lower the vehicle to the floor and tighten the U-bolt nuts to specification. Install the shock absorber. Remove the jack.

1983 AND LATER F SERIES WITH 9500 AND 12000 FRONT AXLES

1. Raise the vehicle until the weight is off the front springs, with the wheels still touching the floor. Remove the shock absorber, if so equipped.
2. Remove the bolts that secure the pin in the front bracket.
3. Remove the retaining pin from the front bracket.
4. Remove the four through bolts and then the two shackle pins securing the shackle assembly. Remove the shackle from the spring and rear bracket.

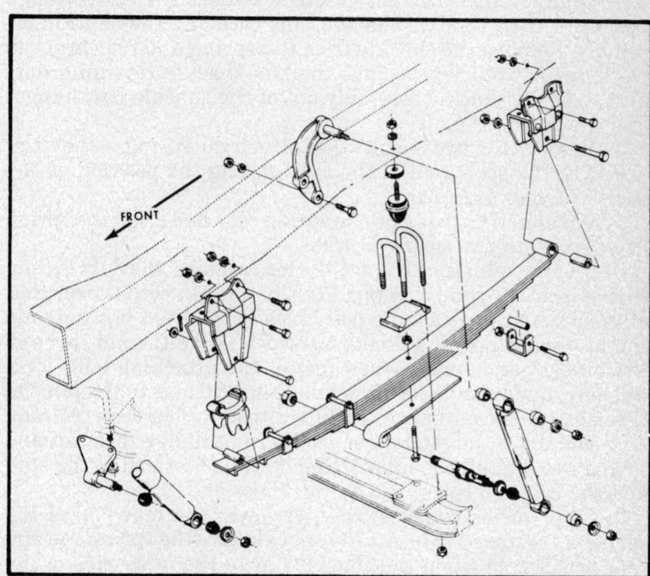

Front spring installation—F-B 600–750 (© Ford Motor Co.)

5. Remove the two U-bolts that attach the spring to the axle.
6. Lift the spring from the axle noting the position of any caster wedges or spacer.
7. To install, position the spring on the spring seat and align the spring front eye with the spring bracket.
8. Remove the zerk fitting from the retaining pin. Position the pin with the notches aligned with the attaching bolt holes in the front bracket and the lubricator opening facing outward. Drive the pin through the bracket and spring, then install the attaching bolts, washers, and lock nuts. Install the zerk fitting in the pin.
9. Align the shackle assembly upper holes with the rear bracket holes and the shackle lower holes with the spring eye. Drive one shackle pin through the upper hole and bracket and the other pin through the lower hole and spring eye. Be sure that the notches in the shackle pins are aligned with the attaching (pinch) bolt holes in the shackle and that the lube openings face outward.
10. Install the pinch bolts and nuts and tighten to specification.
11. On vehicles equipped with a spacer, place it on the axle.
12. On vehicles equipped with a caster wedge, place it on the axle with the thick edge in the same position as it was originally.
13. Position the U-bolts over the spacer and spring and through the holes in the axle. Make sure the spring tie bolt is centered in the recess of the axle, spacer or caster wedge.
14. Install the shock absorber lower bracket to the underside of the axle with the U-bolt ends entering the holes in the bracket. Install the flat washers and locknuts on the U-bolts.
15. Lower the vehicle to the floor and tighten the spring U-bolt nuts to specifications as listed at toe end of this Section. Lubricate all pins with Multi-Purpose Lubricant, or equivalent.

1980–81 L, LT, LN, LNT, 600, 900, 8000 AND 9000 C AND CT SERIES

1. Raise the vehicle until the weight is off the front springs, with the wheels still touching the floor. Remove the shock absorber, if equipped.
2. On all vehicles except the C-series, remove the bolt securing the spring pin in the front bracket.
3. Remove the retaining pin from the bracket. On C-series vehicles, remove the cotter pin and nut from the spring stud and drive the stud out of the front hanger bracket and spring eye.
4. On all vehicles except C-series, remove the four through bolts and then the two shackle pins securing the shackle assembly. Remove the shackle from the spring and rear bracket. On C-series vehicles, remove the two shackle retaining nuts and slide the shackle assembly out of the shackle bar, hanger and the spring eye.
5. Remove the two U-bolts that attach the spring to the axle.
6. Lift the spring off of the axle, noting the position of any caster wedges or spacers.
7. Position the spring on the spring seat and align the spring front eye with the spring bracket.
8. On all vehicles except C-series, remove the lubricating fitting from the retaining pin. Position the pin with the notches aligned with the attaching bolt holes in the front bracket, and the lubricator opening facing outward. Drive the pin through the bracket and spring, then install the attaching bolt, lockwashers, and nuts. Install the lubricator fittings in the pin. On C-series vehicles, remove the lube fittings from the retaining stud and drive the stud through the front hanger bracket and spring eye. Install the lube fitting on the outer end of the stud and the nut and cotter pin on the inner end.
9. On C-series vehicles, raise or lower the rear end of the spring as required to insert the shackle into the spring eye and rear bracket. Position the shackle bar to the inner side of the rear bracket, and drive the shackle assembly pins through the hanger bracket, spring eye and shackle bar. Install the two shackle retaining nuts and cotter pins.
10. On all vehicles except C-series, align the shackle assembly upper holes with the rear bracket holes and the shackle lower holes with the spring eye. Drive one shackle pin through the upper hole and bracket and the other pin through the lower hole and spring eye.

NOTE: Be sure that the notches in the shackle pins are aligned with the attaching (pinch) bolt holes in the shackle and that the lube openings face outward.

11. Install the pinch bolts and nuts, tighten.
12. On vehicles equipped with a spacer, place it on the axle.
13. On vehicles equipped with caster wedge, place it on the axle in the same position as removed.
14. Position the U-bolts over the spacer and through the holes in the axle.

NOTE: Make sure that the spring tie bolt is centered in the recess of the axle, spacer or caster wedge.

15. Install the shock absorber lower bracket to the underside of the axle, except C-series vehicles, with the spring clip (U-bolt) ends entering the holes in the bracket. Install the flat washers and lock nuts on the spring clip.
16. Lower the vehicle to the floor and tighten the clip nuts. Lubricate the shackle bolts.

1982 AND LATER C AND CT SERIES

1. Raise the vehicle until the weight is off the front springs, with the wheels still touching the floor. Support the front axles with jacks to remove weight from U-bolts. Remove the shock absorber, if so equipped.
2. Remove the cotter pin and nut from the spring stud and drive the stud out of the front hanger bracket and spring eye.
3. Remove the two shackle retaining nuts and slide the shackle assembly out of the shackle bar, the rear hanger bracket and the spring.
4. Remove the two U-bolts that attach the spring to the axle.
5. Lift the spring from the axle noting the position of any caster wedges or spacer.
6. Position the spring on the spring seat and align the spring front eye with the spring bracket.
7. Remove the zerk fitting from the retaining stud and insert the stud through the front hanger bracket and spring eye. Install the zerk fitting on the outer end of the stud and the nut and cotter pin on the inner end.
8. Raise or lower the rear end of spring as required to insert the shackle into the spring eye and rear bracket. Position the shackle bar to the inner side of the rear bracket, and drive the shackle assembly pins through the hanger bracket, spring eye and shackle bar. Install the two shackle retaining nuts and cotter pins.
9. On vehicles equipped with a spacer, place it on the axle.
10. On vehicles equipped with a caster wedge, place it on the axle with the thick edge in the same position as it was originally.
11. Position the U-bolts over the spring and spacer and through the holes in the axle. Make sure the spring tie bolt is centered in the recess of the axle, spacer or caster wedge.
12. Install the shock absorber lower bracket to the underside of the axle, with the U-bolts ends entering the holes in the bracket. Install the flat washers and lock nuts on the U-bolts.
13. Lower the vehicle to the floor and tighten the U-bolt nuts to specifications as listed at the end of this Section. Lubricate the shackle bolts with Multi-Purpose Lubricant, or equivalent.

Spindle

Removal and Installation

1. Loosen the front wheel hub bolt nuts. Raise the front of the vehicle and remove the wheel.

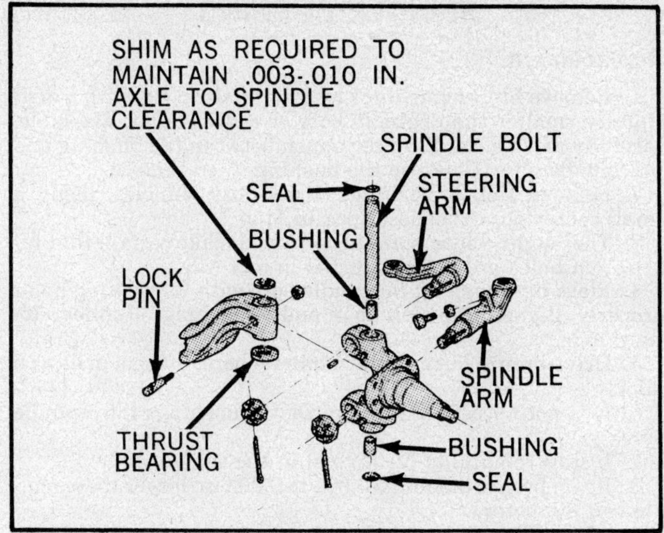

Spindle installation—6000–7000 lb. axles (© Ford Motor Co.)

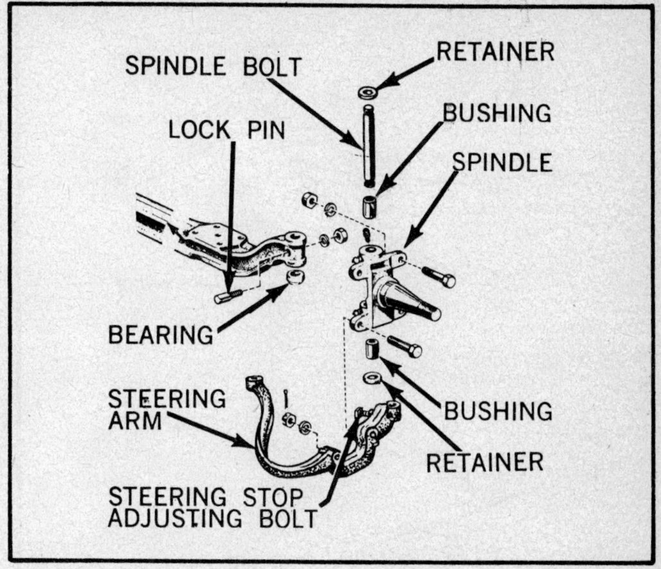

Spindle installation—P-Series (© Ford Motor Co.)

2. Remove the hub and drum and the wheel bearing from the spindle.
3. If the brake backing plate is bolted to the spindle, remove the plate from the spindle. To prevent damage to the brake hose, hang the backing plate from the frame.
4. Disconnect the spindle arms from the spindle.
5. On 5000,5500, 6000 and 7000 lb axles with hydraulic brakes, remove the seal (O-ring) from the top of the spindle pin. Remove the nut from the spindle bolt lock pin and drive the lock pin out of the axle. Drive the spindle bolt out from the top of the axle with a suitable drift.
6. On 7000 (with air brakes), 8000, 9000, 9500, 12000, 16000 and 18000 lb axles, three separate spindle top mountings are used. Vehicles equipped with either a 7000, 8000, 9000, 9500 or 12000 lb axle utilizes a three-bolt cap/zerk fitting with a gasket. The 16000 and 18000 lb axles have a combination brake hose/zerk cap (Fig. 8). After removing the appropriate cap and gasket, the lower spindle pin seal should be removed on 7000 lb. (with air brake), on 7000, 8000 and 9000 lb. remove the snap ring and expansion plug from the bottom of the spindle bolt. On 9500, 12000, 16,000 and 18,000 lb axles, remove the three bolts, cap, zerk fitting and gasket. Drive out the threaded lock pins with a bronze drift; then, drive out the spindle pin from the top of the axle with a bronze drift.
7. Remove the spindle assembly from the axle.
8. To assemble, place the spindle in position on the axle. Insert the spindle bolt thrust bearing between the bottom of the axle and the spindle. Pack the thrust bearing and coat all mating surfaces of spindle and axle parts with Multi-Purpose Lubricant, or equivalent prior to assembly. On all axles, the thrust bearing must be installed with the retainer lip facing down. The shim (or shims) is placed between the top of the axle and the spindle. A 0.003–0.010 inch axle to spindle clearance must be maintained on all axles.
9. On 6000, 7000 and 8000 lb axles and some 9000 lb. axles, line up the notch in the spindle pin with the spindle pin hole in the axle. The spindle pin must be installed with the end marked T facing upward. Drive the spindle pin with a bronze drift through the axle until the notch and hole are in line. Install a new lock pin from either side of the I-Beam. Seat the lock pin by striking it with a hammer and punch, and then install the nut on the lock pin (certain axles will have two lock pin holes on each side of axle. Do not install both lock pins from the same side of the axle). Install a new seal (O-ring) in the groove at each end (or spindle cap and gasket on top and expansion plug and lock ring on the bottom depending on axle) of the spindle pin.
10. On all other front axles with air or hydraulic brakes, line up the notches in the spindle pin with the lockpin holes in the axle. Drive the spindle pin through the axle, with a drift until the notches and holes are in line. Install the lower (longer) lockpin first and seat by striking prior to installing nut. Install the upper (shorter) lockpin first and seat by striking prior to installing nut. Tighten nuts to 50–70 ft. lbs. Do not install both lockpins from same side of axle.
11. Install the brake backing plate on the spindle. On 6000 lb and larger axles, installing the spindle arms before installing the brake backing plate.
12. Lubricate the spindle bushings until lubricant is visible at the spindle to axle area.
13. Install the hub and drum assembly and the wheel. Adjust the wheel bearings.
14. Check and adjust the toe-in.

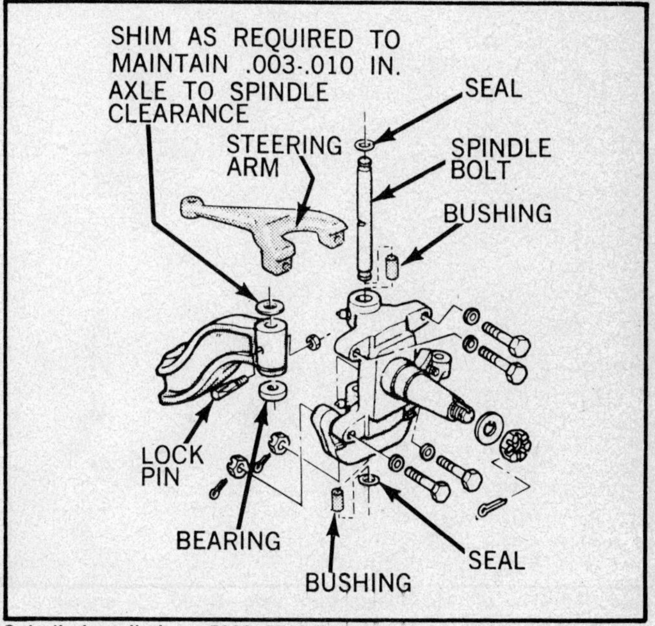

Spindle installation—5000–5500 lb. axles (© Ford Motor Co.)

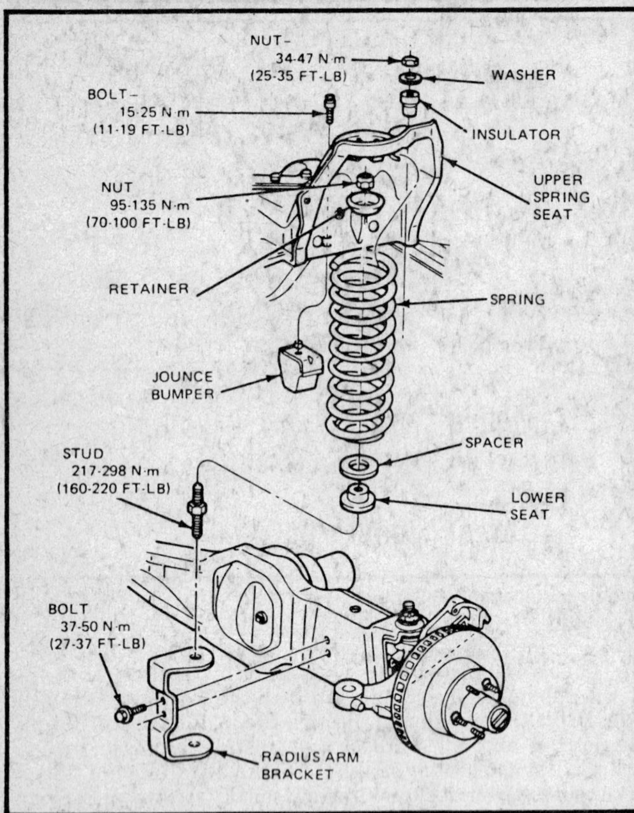

Coil spring and related components—Ranger and Bronco II
(© Ford Motor Co.)

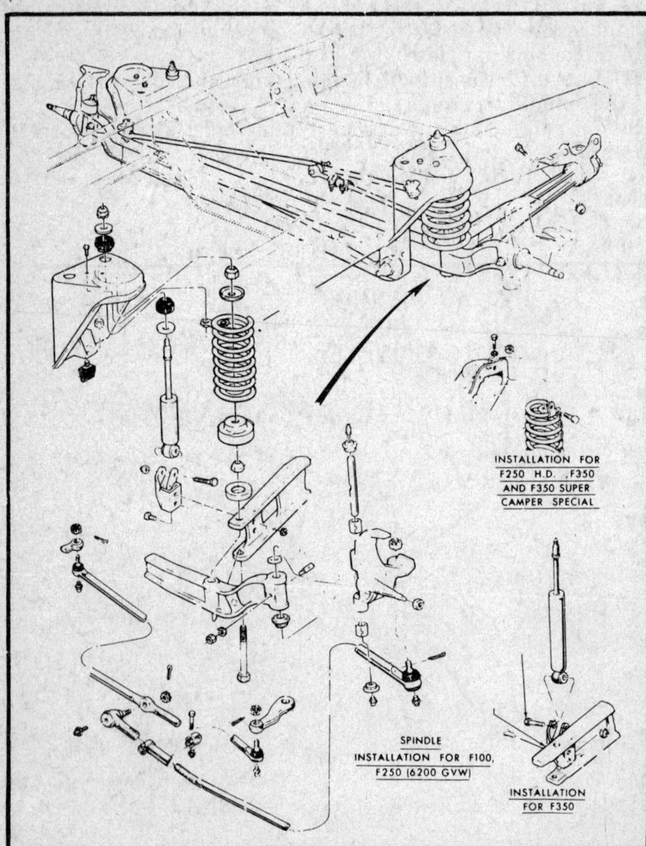

Exploded view of twin I-beam front axle—F-100–350 shown
(© Ford Motor Co.)

SPINDLE BUSHING

Replacement

1. Remove bronze bushings by driving them out with a drift slightly smaller than spindle bore. If a drift is not available, carefully drive a small center punch between the bushing and the spindle bore. Collapse the bushing, then remove.
2. Remove Delrin bushings, light duty vehicles, using a small center punch as described in Step 1.
3. Thoroughly clean spindle bores and make certain that lubrication holes are not obstructed in any way.
4. Place new bushing in spindle bore with lubricating holes properly aligned. Position open end of bushing oil groove toward axle.
5. Drive bronze bushing into spindle bore, using a drift as a pilot.
6. It is not necessary to drive Delrin bushings into spindle bores.
7. Install remaining bushing(s) in the same manner.
8. Ream bronze bushings 0.001 to 0.003 in. larger than spindle bolt diameter.
9. DO NOT ream Delrin bushings.
10. After reaming bronze bushings, clean out spindle bore to remove metal shavings.
11. Apply a light coat of oil to all bushings before spindle assembly and installation.

Twin I Beam

SPRING

Removal and Installation

2WD

1. Raise the front of the vehicle and place jackstands under the frame and a jack under the axle. Remove wheel and tire assemblies. Remove caliper and suspend with wire so that there is no tension on the brake hose.
2. Disconnect the shock absorber from the lower bracket.
3. Remove the rebound bracket. On Ranger and Bronco II, remove the lower spring retainer.
4. On all models except Ranger and Bronco II, remove the two spring upper retainer attaching bolts from the top of the spring upper seat and remove the retainer.
5. Remove the nut attaching the spring lower retainer to the lower seat and axle and remove the retainer.
6. Lower the axle and remove the spring. Some downward pressure using a prybar may be required.
7. Place the spring in position and raise the front axle.
8. Position the spring lower retainer over the stud and lower seat, and install the two attaching bolts.
9. Position the upper retainer over the spring coil and against the spring upper seat, and install the two attaching bolts.
10. Tighten the upper and lower retainer attaching nuts and bolts to 15–25 ft. lbs.
11. Connect the shock absorber to the lower bracket and install the rebound bracket.
12. Remove the jack and safety stands.

4WD BRONCO, F-150

1. Raise the vehicle on a hoist and support it safely. Remove the shock absorber lower attaching bolt and nut.
2. Remove the spring lower retainer nuts from inside of the spring coil.
3. Remove the upper spring retainer by removing the attaching screw.
4. Raise and support the vehicle safely. Position safety stands under the frame side rails and lower the axle enough to relieve tension from the spring.

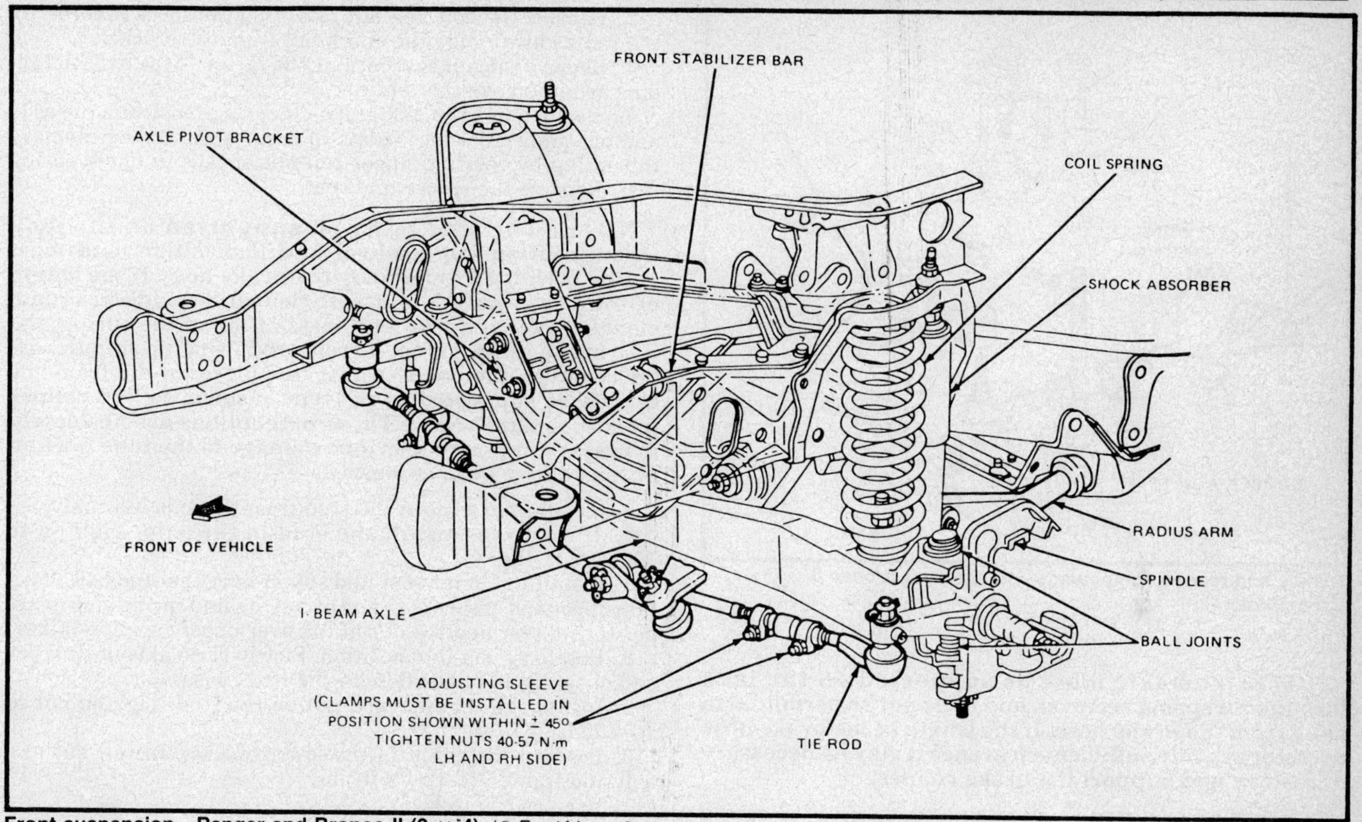

Front suspension—Ranger and Bronco II (2 × 4) (© Ford Motor Co.)

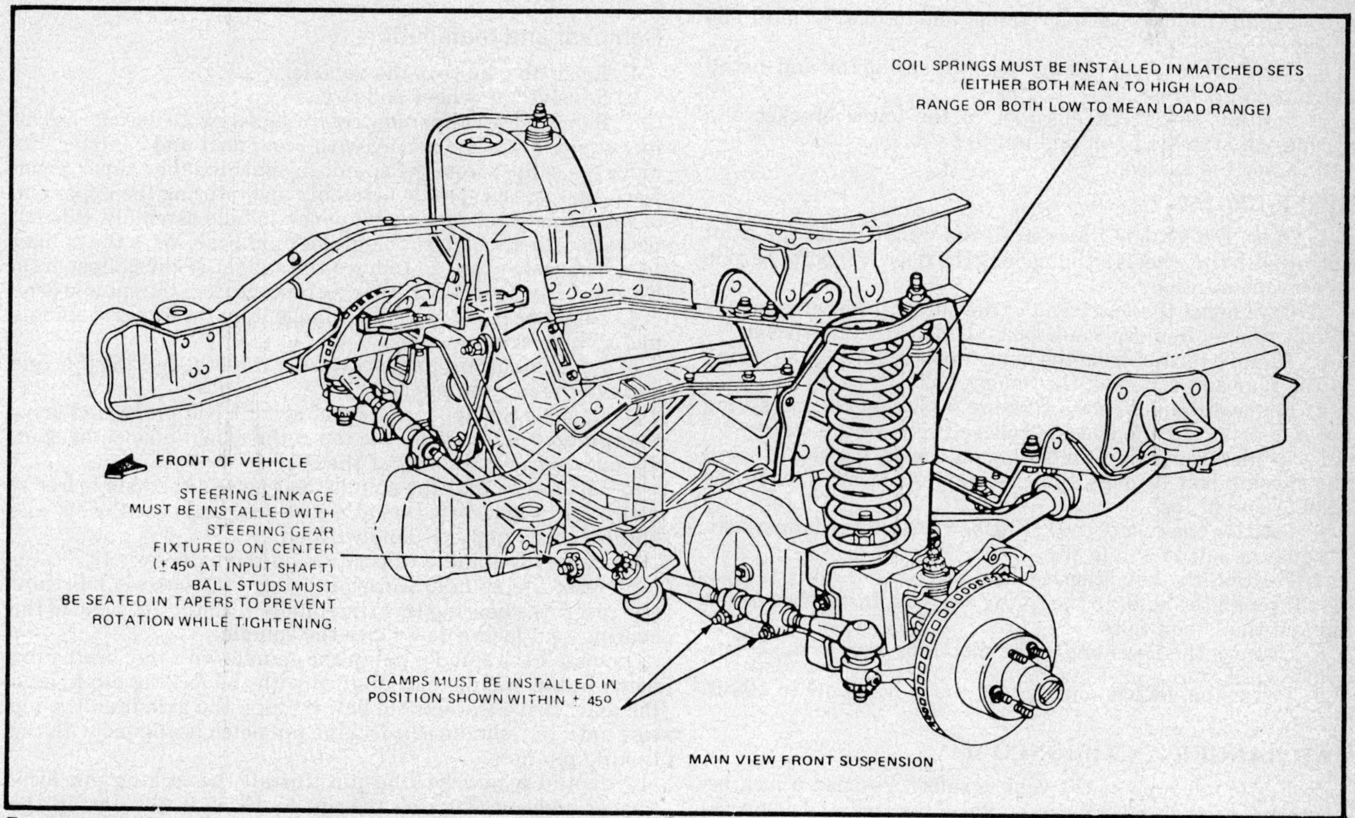

Front suspension—Ranger and Bronco II (4 × 4) (© Ford Motor Co.)

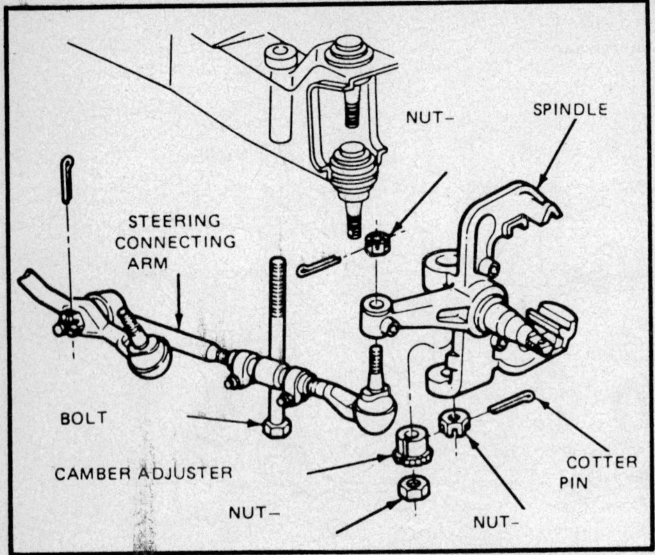

Spindle and related components—Ranger and Bronco II
(© Ford Motor Co.)

NOTE: The axle must be supported on the jack throughout spring removal, and must not be permitted to hang from the brake hose. If the length of the brake hose does not provide sufficient clearance it may be necessary to remove and support the brake caliper.

5. Remove the spring lower retainer and lower the spring from the vehicle.
6. To install place the spring in position and slowly raise the front axle. Make sure the springs are positioned correctly in the upper spring seats.
7. Install the lower spring retainer and torque the nut to 50 ft. lbs.
8. Position the upper retainer over the spring coil and install the attaching screws.
9. Position the shock absorber to the lower bracket and torque the attaching bolt and nut to 53 ft. lbs.
10. lower the vehicle.

4WD F-250–350

1. Raise the vehicle frame until the weight is off the front spring with the wheels still touching the floor. Support the axle to prevent rotation.
2. Disconnect the lower end of the shock absorber from the U-bolt spacer. Remove the U-bolts. U-bolt cap and spacer.
3. Remove the nut from the hanger bolt retaining the spring at the rear and drive out the hanger bolt.
4. Remove the nut connecting the front shackle and spring eye and drive out the shackle bolt and remove the spring.
5. To install position the spring on the spring seat. Install the shackle bolt through the shackle and spring. Torque the nuts to 135 ft. lbs.
6. Position the rear of the spring and install the hanger bolt. Torque the nut to 175 ft. lbs.
7. Position the U-bolt spacer and place the U-bolts to position through the holes in the spring seat cap. Install but do not tighten the U-bolt nuts.
8. Connect the lower end of the shock absorber to the U-bolt spacer.
9. Lower the vehicle and tighten the U-bolt nuts to 100 ft. lbs.

4WD RANGER AND BRONCO II

1. Raise and support the vehicle safely. Position a jack beneath the spring under the axle. Raise the jack and compress the spring.
2. Remove the bolt and nut retaining the shock absorber to the radius arm. Slide the shock out from the bracket.
3. Remove the nut that retains the spring to the axle and radius arm. Remove the retainer.
4. Slowly lower the axle until all spring tension is released and adequate clearance exists to remove the spring. Remove the spring by rotating upper coil out of tabs in upper spring seat. Remove the spacer and seat.

NOTE: The axle must be supported on the jack throughout spring removal and installation, and must not be permitted to hang by the brake hose. If the length of the brake hose is not sufficient to provide adequate clearance for removal and installation of the spring, the disc brake caliper must be removed from the spindle. After removal, the caliper must be placed on the frame or otherwise supported to prevent suspending the caliper from the caliper hose. These precautions are absolutely necessary to prevent serious damage to the tube portion of the caliper hose assembly.

5. If required, remove the stud from the axle assembly.
6. If removed, install the stud in the axle. Tighten to 160–220 ft. lbs.
7. Install the lower seat and spacer over the stud/bolt. Position upper end of spring so end of coil fits into spring stop in upper spring seat and top of coil fits over upper spring retainer.
8. Rotate spring into position. Slowly raise axle until lower end of spring is in position on the lower insulator.
9. Install the retainer and nut on the stud. Tighten nut to 70–100 ft. lbs.
10. Position the shock in the lower bracket. Install nut and bolt and tighten to 42–72 ft. lbs.
11. Remove the jack.

Front Wheel Spindle and King Pin

Removal and Installation

1. Raise and support the vehicle safely.
2. Remove the wheel and tire.
3. Remove the caliper key retaining screw. Drive out the caliper support key and spring with brass drift and hammer. Remove the caliper from the spindle by pushing the caliper downward against the spindle assembly and rotating the upper end of the caliper upward and out of the spindle assembly. It is not necessary to disconnect the brake fluid hose. Wire the caliper to a suspension part to remove the weight of the caliper from the hose. Disconnect the steering linkage from the spindle arm.
4. Disconnect the steering linkage from the integral spindle and spindle arm.
5. Remove the nut and lockwasher from the locking pin, and remove the locking pin.
6. Remove the upper and lower spindle bolt plugs, and drive the spindle bolt out from the top of the axle. Remove the spindle and bearing. Knock out the seal
7. Make sure that the spindle bolt hole in the axle is free of nicks, burrs and dirt. Install a new seal and coat the spindle bolt bushings and bolt hole with oil.
8. Place the spindle in position on the axle.
9. Pack the spindle thrust bearing with chassis lubricant and insert the bearing into the spindle with the open end of the bearing seal facing down into the spindle.
10. Install the spindle pin in the spindle with the locking pin notch in the spindle bolt aligned with the locking pin hole in the axle. Drive the spindle bolt through the axle from the top side until the spindle bolt locking pin notch is aligned with the locking pin hole.
11. Install a new locking pin. Install the locking pin lockwasher and nut. Tighten the nut to 40–55 ft. lbs. Install the spindle bolt plugs at the top and bottom of the spindle bolt.

12. Position the caliper on the spindle assembly. Be careful to prevent tearing or cutting of the piston boot as the caliper is slipped over the inner brake pad. Use a suitable tool to hold the upper machined surface of the caliper against the surface of the spindle. Install the caliper support spring and key. Drive the key and spring into position with a soft hammer. Install the key retaining screw and tighten the nut to 50–70 ft. lbs. advancing the nut as necessary to install the cotter pin.
13. Install the wheel.
14. Grease the spindle assembly with a grease gun.
15. Check and adjust, if necessary, the toe-in adjustment.

Front Wheel Spindle with Stamped I Beam with Balljoints

Removal and Installation

1. Raise and support the vehicle safely. Remove the tire and wheel assembly.
2. Remove the caliper assembly from the rotor and hold it out of the way with wire.
3. Remove the dust cap, cotter pin, nut retainer, nut washer, and outer bearing, and remove the rotor from the spindle.
4. Remove inner bearing cone and seal. Discard the seal. Remove brake dust shield.
5. Disconnect the steering linkage from the integral spindle and spindle arm by removing the cotter pin and nut and then removing the tie rod end from the spindle arm.
6. Remove the cotter pins from the upper and lower ball joint studs. Remove the nuts from the upper and lower ball joint stud.
7. Strike the inside area of the spindle to pop the ball joints loose from the spindle.

NOTE: Do not use a pickle fork to separate the ball joint from the spindle as this will damage the seal and the ball joint socket.

8. Remove the spindle.
9. Prior to assembly, make sure the upper and lower ball joint seals are in place. Place the spindle over the ball joints.
10. Install the nut on the lower ball joint stud and partially tighten to 30 ft. lbs. Advance the castellated nut as required and install the cotter pin. If the lower ball stud turns while the nut is being tightened, push the spindle up against the ball stud. The lower must not be tightened first.
11. Install the camber adapter in the upper spindle over the upper ball joint stud. Be sure the adapter is aligned properly.
12. Install the nut on the upper ball joint stud. Hold the camber adaptor with a wrench to keep the ball stud from turning. If the ball stud turns, tap the adapter deeper into the spindle. Tighten the nut to 85–100 ft. lbs and contine tightening the castellated nut until it lines up with the hole in the stud. Install the cotter pin.
13. Retighten lower nut. Install the dust shield.
14. Pack the inner and outer bearing cone with C1AZ-19590-B (ESA-M1C75-B) Equivalent bearing grease. Use a bearing packer. If a bearing packer is unavailable, pack the bearing cone by hand working the grease through the cage behind the rollers.
15. Install the inner bearing cone and seal. Install the hub and rotor on the spindle.
16. Install the outer bearing cone, washer, and nut. Adjust bearing end play and install the nut retainer, cotter pin and dust cap.
17. Install the caliper.
18. Connect the steering linkage to the spindle. Tighten the nut to 52–73 ft. lbs and advance the nut as required for installation of the cotter pin.
19. Install the wheel and tire assembly. Lower the vehicle.
20. Check and, if necessary adjust the toe setting.

Camber Adjuster

Removal and Installation

1. Remove the cotter pin and the nut from the upper ball joint stud.
2. Strike the inside of the spindle to pop the upper ball joint from the spindle.
3. If the upper ball joint does not pop loose, remove the cotter pin and back the lower ball joint nut about half way down the lower ball joint stud, and strike the side of the lower spindle.
4. Remove the camber adapter (camber adjustment sleeve) using Ball Joint Removing Tool (D81T-3010-B) or equivalent.
5. Install the correct adaptor in the spindle. On the right spindle the adaptor slot must point forward to make a positive camber change or rearward for a negative camber change. On the left spindle, the adaptor slot must point rearward for a positive camber change and forward for a negative change.
6. If both nuts were loosened, completely remove the spindle, and reinstall. Be sure the lower ball joint stud nut is always tightened before the upper nut. Apply Locktite or equivalent to stud threads before installing nut.
7. If only the upper ball joint stud nut was removed, install the nut and tighten to 85–110 ft. lbs and continue tightening the castellated nut until it lines up with the hole in the upper stud. Install the cotter pin.

Ball Joints

Removal and Installation

1. Raise and support the vehicle safely. Remove the spindle.
2. Remove the snap ring from the ball joints. Assemble the C-frame puller and adapters on the upper ball joint. Turn the forcing screw clockwise until the ball joint is removed from the axle.
3. Assemble the C-frame assembly and receiver cup on the lower ball joint and turn the forcing screw clockwise until the ball joint is removed.
4. Always remove the upper ball joint first. Do not heat the ball joint or the axle to aid in the removal.
5. Installation is the reverse of removal. The lower ball joint must be installed first.

Front Wheel Spindle

Removal and Installtion

4WD

NOTE: This procedure also includes bearing and seal replacement and repacking

1. Raise and support the vehicle safely.
2. If equipped with manual locking hubs as follows:
   a. Remove the six socket head bolts from the cap assembly and separate the cap assembly and separate the cap assembly from the body.
   b. Remove the snap-ring from the end of the axle shaft.
   c. Remove the lock ring seated in the groove of the wheel hub and slide the body assembly out of the wheel hub.
3. If equipped with automatic locking hubs remove the hubs as follows:
   a. Remove the bolts and remove the hub cap assembly from the spindle.
   b. Remove the bolt from the end of the shaft.
   c. Remove the lock ring seated in the groove of the wheel hub.
   d. Remove the body assembly from tne spindle. Use a puller if necessary.
   e. Unscrew all three set screws in the spindle locknut until the heads are flush with the edge of the locknut.

4. Remove the outer spindle locknut with tool T80T-4000V, automatic hub locknut wrench. Remove the front hub grease cap and driving hub snap-ring.
5. Remove the splined driving hub and the pressure spring. Slightly pry off if necessary.
6. Remove the wheel bearing locknut, lock ring and adjusting nut using special tool T59T-1197-B or equivalent.
7. Remove the hub and disc assembly. The outer wheel bearing and spring retainer will slide out as the hub is removed.
8. Remove the spindle nuts and remove the spindle, splash shield and axle shaft assembly.

NOTE: It may be necessary to break the spindle loose with a plastic hammer.

9. Clean all old grease from the needle bearings and wipe clean the spindle face that mates with the spindle bore seal.
10. Remove the spindle bore seal, V-seal, and thrust washer from the outer axle shaft. Clean and replace if necessary.
11. Using Multi-Purpose Lubricant Ford ESA-M1C75-B or equivalent, thoroughly lubricate the needle bearing and pack the spindle face that mates with the spindle bore seal.
12. Position the V-seal in the spindle bore next to the needle bearing. Assemble the spindle bore seal on the axle shaft.
13. Assemble the spindle with the axle shaft on the knuckle studs and tighten the retaining nuts to 75 ft. lbs.
14. Carefully drive the inner bearing cone and grease seal out of the hub using tool T77F-1102-A or equivalent.
15. Inspect the inner bearing cups and if necessary remove with a drift.

NOTE: If new cups are installed, install new bearings.

16. Lubricate the bearings with the lubricant specified earlier and clean all old grease from the hub. Pack the cones and rollers with lubricant. Try to pack as much as possible between the rollers and the cages.
17. Position the inner bearing cone and roller in the inner cup and install the grease retainer.
18. Install the hub and disc assembly on the spindle.
19. Install the outer bearing cone and roller, and the adjusting nut.
20. Using tool T59T-1197-B or equivalent and a torque wrench tighten the bearing adjusting nut to 50 ft. lbs. while rotating the wheel back and forth. Back off the adjusting nut no more than 90 degrees.
21. Assemble the lock ring by turning the nut to the nearest hole and inserting the dowel pin.

NOTE: The dowel pin must seat in the lock ring hole for proper bearing adjustment and wheel retention.

22. Install the outer lock nut and tighten to 65 ft. lbs. Final end play on the wheel and spindle should be 0.001–0.006 inch.
23. Adjust the brake if necessary and lower the vehicle.

Knuckle and Ball Joint

Replacement

4WD

NOTE: A combination ball joint puller/press and a special spanner wrench are needed for this job.

1. Follow the procedures under axle shaft removal.
2. Disconnect the connecting rod end from the knuckle.
3. Remove the cotter pin from the upper ball socket and loosen the upper and lower ball socket nuts. Discard the nut from the lower ball socket after the knuckle breaks loose from the yoke.
4. Remove the knuckle from the yoke. If the upper socket remains in the yoke, remove it by hitting the top of the stud with a soft-faced hammer. Discard the socket and adjusting sleeve.
5. Remove the bottom socket with a ball joint puller, after first removing the snap ring.
6. To install, place the knuckle in a vise and assemble the bottom socket. Place the new socket into the knuckle making sure it isn't cocked, place the driver over the socket, place the forcing screw into the socket and force the socket into the knuckle.
7. Make sure that the socket shoulder is seated against the knuckle. Use a 0.0015 in. feeler gauge between the socket seat and the knuckle.
8. The gauge should not enter the area of minimum contact. Install the snap ring.
9. Assemble the top socket into the knuckle. Assemble the holding plate onto the backing plate screw. Tighten the nuts snugly. Place a new socket into the knuckle. Be sure it is not cocked. Place a driver over the socket and force the socket assembly into the knuckle. Using a 0.0015 in. gauge, check the fit at the shoulder. The gauge should not enter the area of minimum wrench.
10. Install a new adjusting sleeve into the top of the yoke leaving about two threads exposed.
11. Assemble the knuckle and yoke. Install a new nut on the bottom socket and make it finger tight.
12. Place a wrench and step plate over the adjusting sleeve and install the puller so that it grasps the step plate. Tighten the forcing screw to pull the knuckle assembly into the yoke. With torque still applied, tighten the nut to 70–90 ft. lbs. If the bottom stud should turn with the nut, add more torque to the puller forcing screw. Remove the puller, step plate and holding plate.
13. Tighten the adjusting sleeve to 40 ft. lbs. and remove the wrench.
14. Install the top socket nut and torque it to 100 ft. lbs. Line up the cotter pin hole by tightening, not loosening, the nut. Install the cotter pin and test the steering effort with a spring scale attached to the knuckle. Pull should not exceed 26 ft. lbs. If it does, the ball joints will have to be replaced.
15. Connect the steering linkage to the knuckle. Torque it to 40 ft. lbs.
16. Install the axle shaft.

Radius Arm

Removal and Installation

ALL, EXCEPT BRONCO, F-150 WITH 4WD, RANGER AND BRONCO II

1. Raise and support the vehicle safely. Place safety stands under the frame and a jack under the wheel or axle.
2. Disconnect the shock absorber from the radius arm bracket.
3. Remove the two spring upper retainer attaching bolts from the top of the spring upper seat and remove the retainer.
4. Remove the nut which attaches the spring lower retainer to the lower seat and axle and remove the retainer.
5. Lower the axle and remove the spring.
6. Disconnect the steering rod from the spindle arm.
7. Remove the spring lower seat and shim from the radius arm. Then, remove the bolt and nut which attach the radius arm to the axle.
8. Remove the cotter pin, nut and washer from the radius arm rear attachment .
9. Remove the bushing from the radius arm and remove the radius arm from the vehicle.
10. Remove the inner bushing from the radius arm.
11. Position the radius arm to the axle and install the bolt and nut finger-tight.
12. Install the inner bushing on the radius arm and position the arm to the cotter pin.

13. Install the bushing, washer, and attaching nut. Tighten the nut and install the cotter pin.
14. Connect the steering rod to the spindle arm and install the attaching nut. Tighten the radius arm to axle attaching bolt and nut.

F-150 4WD

1. Raise the vehicle and position safety stands under the frame side rails.
2. Remove the shock absorber lower attaching bolt and nut and pull the shock absorber free of the radius arm.
3. Remove the lower spring retaining bolt from the inside of the radius arm.
4. Remove the nut attaching the radius arm to the frame bracket and remove the radius arm rear insulator. Lower the axle and allow the axle to move forward.

NOTE: The axle must be supported on the jack throughout spring removal, and must not be permitted to hang from the brake hose. If the length of the brake hose does not provide sufficient clearance it may be necessary to remove and support the brake caliper.

5. Remove the bolt and stud attaching the radius arm to the axle.
6. Move the axle forward and remove the radius arm from the axle. Then, pull the radius arm from the frame bracket.
7. Installation is the reverse of the removal. Install new bolts and the stud type bolt which attach the radius arm to the axle and tighten to 210 ft. lbs. Tighten the radius arm rear attaching nut to 100 ft. lbs.

BRONCO

1. Raise the vehicle and position safety stands under the frame side rails.
2. Remove the shock absorber to lower bracket attaching bolt and nut and pull the shock absorber free of the radius arm.
3. Remove spring lower retainer attaching bolt from inside of the spring coil.
4. Remove the nut attaching the radius arm to the frame bracket and remove the radius arm rear insulator. Lower the axle and allow axle to move forward

NOTE: The axle must be supported on the jack throughout spring removal and installation, and must not be permitted to hang by the brake hose. If the length of the brake hose is not sufficient to provide adequate clearance for the removal and installation of the spring, the disc brake caliper must be removed from the spindle. After removal, the caliper must be placed on the frame or otherwise supported to prevent suspending the caliper from the caliper hose. Thses precautions are absolutely necessary to prevent serious damage to the tube portion of the caliper hose assembly.

5. Remove the bolt and stud attaching radius arm to axle.
6. Move the axle forward and remove the radius arm from the axle. Then, pull the radius arm from the frame bracket.
7. Position the washer and insulator on the rear of the radius arm and insert the radius arm into the frame bracket.
8. Position the rear insulator and washer on the radius arm and loosely install the attaching nut.
9. Position the radius arm to the axle.
10. Install new bolts and study type bolt attaching radius arm to axle. Tighten to 180–240 ft. lbs.
11. Position the spring lower seat, spring insulator and retainer to the spring and axle. Install the two attaching bolts. Tighten the nuts to 30–70 ft. lbs.
12. Tighten the radius rod rear attaching nut to 80–120 ft. lbs.
13. Position the shock absorber to the lower bracket and install the attaching bolt and nut. Tighten the nut to 40–60 ft. lbs. Remove safety stands and lower the vehicle.

RANGER AND BRONCO II

1. Raise the front of the vehicle and place safety stands under the frame. Place a jack under the axle.

NOTE: The axle must be supported on the jack throughout spring removal and installation, and must not be permitted to hang by the brake hose. If the length of the brake hose is not sufficient to provide adequate clearance for removal and installation of the spring, the disc brake caliper must be removed from the spindle. After removal, the caliper must be placed on the frame or otherwise supported to prevent suspending the caliper from the caliper hose. These precautions are absolutely necessary to prevent serious damage to the tube portion of the caliper hose assembly.

2. Disconnect the lower end of the shock absorber from the shock lower bracket (bolt and nut).
3. Remove the front spring. Loosen the axle pivot bolt.
4. Remove the spring lower seat and stud from the radius arm, and then remove the bolts that attach the radius arm to the axle and front bracket.
5. Remove the nut, rear washer and insulator from the rear side of the radius arm rear bracket.
6. Remove the radius arm from the vehicle, and remove the inner insulator and retainer from the radius arm stud.
7. Installation is the reverse of removal.

Stabilizer Bar

Removal and Installation

BRONCO AND 4WD PICKUPS

1. Remove nuts, bolts and washers connecting the stabilizer bar to connecting links. Remove nuts and bolts of the stabilizer bar retainer.
2. Remove stabilizer bar insulator assembly.
3. To remove the stabilizer bar mounting bracket, the coil spring must be removed as described above under spring removal. Remove the lower spring seat. The bracket attaching stud and bracket can now be removed.
4. To install the stabilizer bar mounting brackets, locate the brackets so that the locating tang is positioned in the radius arm notch (or quad shock bracket notch if vehicle has quad shocks). Install a new stud. Torque to 180–220 ft. lbs. A new stud is required because of the adhesive on the threads. Reposition the spring lower seat and reinstall the spring and retainers.
5. To reinstall the stabilizer bar insulator assembly, assemble all nuts, bolts and washers to the bar, brackets, retainers and links loosely. With the bar positioned correctly, torque retainer nuts to 32–35 ft. lbs. with retainer around the insulator. Then torque all remaining nuts at the link assemblies to 41–50 ft. lbs.

RANGER AND BRONCO II

1. Remove the nuts and U-bolts retaining the lower shock bracket/stabilizer bar bushing to radius arm.
2. Remove retainers and remove the stabilizer bar and bushing.
3. Place stabilizer bar in position on the radius arm and bracket.
4. Install retainers and U-bolts. Tighten retainer bolts to 35–50 ft. lbs. Tighten U-bolts to 48–64 ft. lbs.

FRONT DRIVE AXLE

Axle Shaft

Removal and Installation

F SERIES

1. Remove the axle shaft assembly.
2. Remove the stub assembly by removing the three bolts attaching the retainer plate to the carrier housing.
3. Place the axle shaft in a vise and drill a ½ in. hole in the outside of the bearing retaining ring to a depth of ¾ of the thickness of the ring.
4. Place a chisel across the hole and strike sharply with a hammer to remove the retaining ring. Replace the bearing retaining ring upon assembly.
5. Press the bearing from the axle shaft using an axle bearing remover tool.
6. Remove the steal and retainer plate from the stub shaft.
7. To install place the new seal and retainer plate on the shaft.
8. Place the bearing on the shaft with the large radius on the inner race facing the yoke end of the shaft.
9. Press the bearing onto the shaft using an axle bearing replacer and a pinion bearing cone remover. A 0.0015 in. feeler gauge should not fit between the bearing seat and the bearing.
10. Using the same special tools in Step 9 press the bearing retainer ring onto the stub shaft. A 0.0015 in. feeler gauge should not fit between the ring and the bearing. There must be one point between the bearing and the ring where the feeler

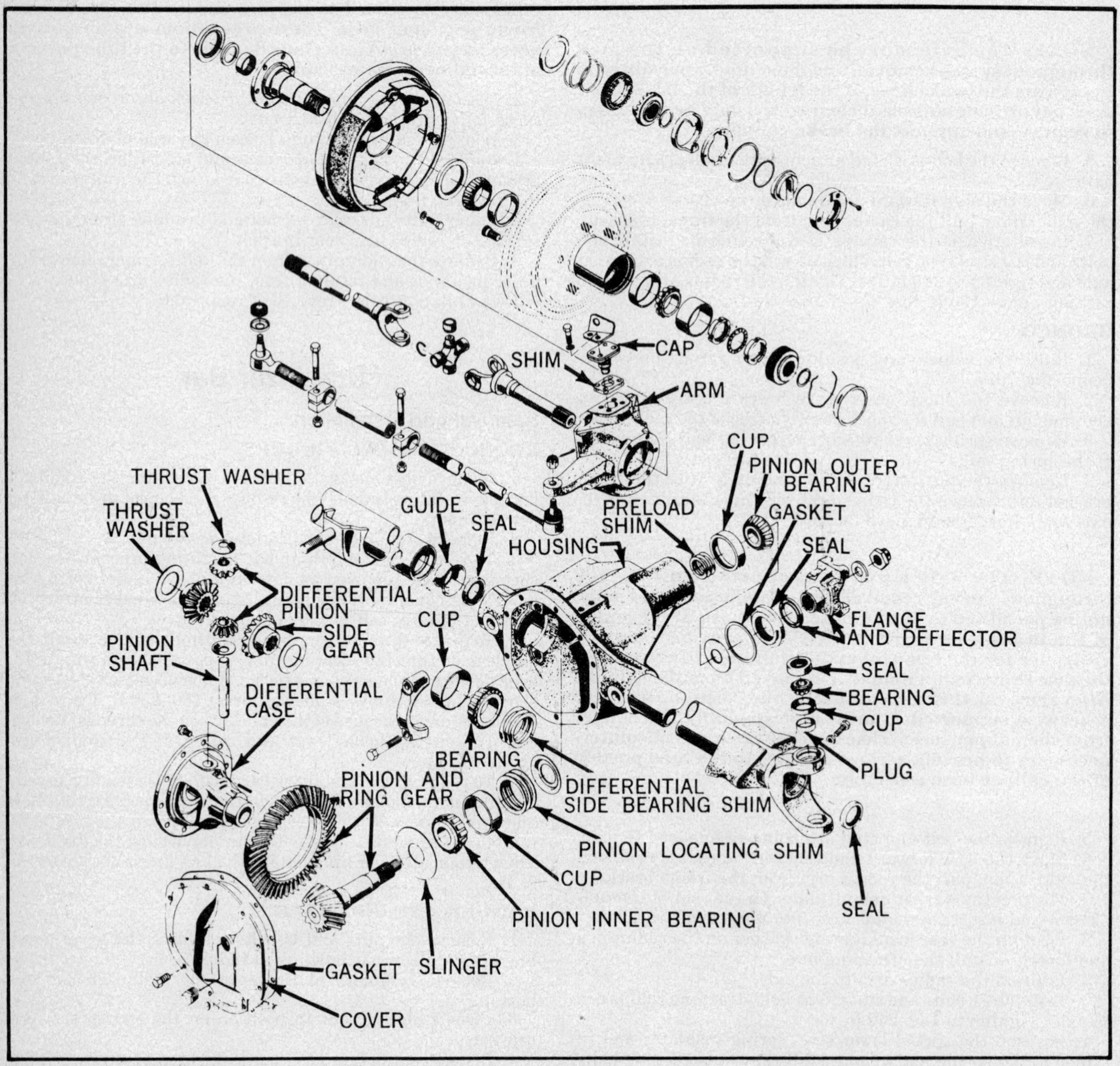

Front drive axle—F-100 and F-150 (© Ford Motor Co.)

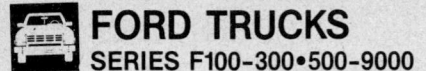

gauge cannot enter. If the feeler gauge enters completely around the circumference press the retainer further onto the shaft.

11. Push the seal and retainer plate away from the bearing to form a space between the seal and the bearing. Fill the space with the proper bearing grease and wrap tape around the space.

12. Pull the seal towards the bearing until it contacts the inner race and forces the grease between the rollers and cup. Remove the tape.

13. Install the stub shaft in the carrier and install the three retainer bolts. Tighten to 35 ft. lbs.

14. Install the right hand axle shaft assembly into the slip yoke.

15. Install the spindle.

BRONCO

1. Remove spindle nuts and remove spindle. It may be necessary to tap the spindle with a rawhide or plastic hammer to break the spindle loose. Remove spindle, splash shield and axle shaft assembly.

2. Place the spindle in a vise with a shop towel around the spindle to protect the spindle from damage. Using a slide hammer and a seal remover tool remove the axle shaft seal and then the needle bearing from the spindle bar.

3. If the tie rod has not been removed, then remove cotter key from the tie rod nut and then remove nut. Tap on the tie rod stud to free it from the steering arm.

4. Remove the cotter pin from the top ball joint stud. Loosen the nut on the top stud and the bottom nut inside the knuckle. Remove the top nut.

5. Sharply hit the top stud with a plastic or rawhide hammer to free the knuckle from the tube yoke. Remove and discard bottom nut. Use new nut upon assembly.

6. Remove camber adjuster with a pitman arm puller.

7. Place knuckle in vise and remove snap ring from bottom ball joint socket if so equipped.

8. Press the bottom ball joint socket from the knuckle with the special removal tools. Remove the top ball joint in the same manner.

NOTE: Always remove bottom ball joint first.

9. Pull out the seal with the appropriate puller tool. Remove and discard seal.

10. Install a new seal on the differential, with the differential seal replacer tool.

11. Slide the seal and tool into the carrier housing bore. Seat the seal with a plastic or rawhide hammer.

12. Place lower ball joint (stud does not have a cotter key hole in stud) in knuckle and press into position using ball joint installation.

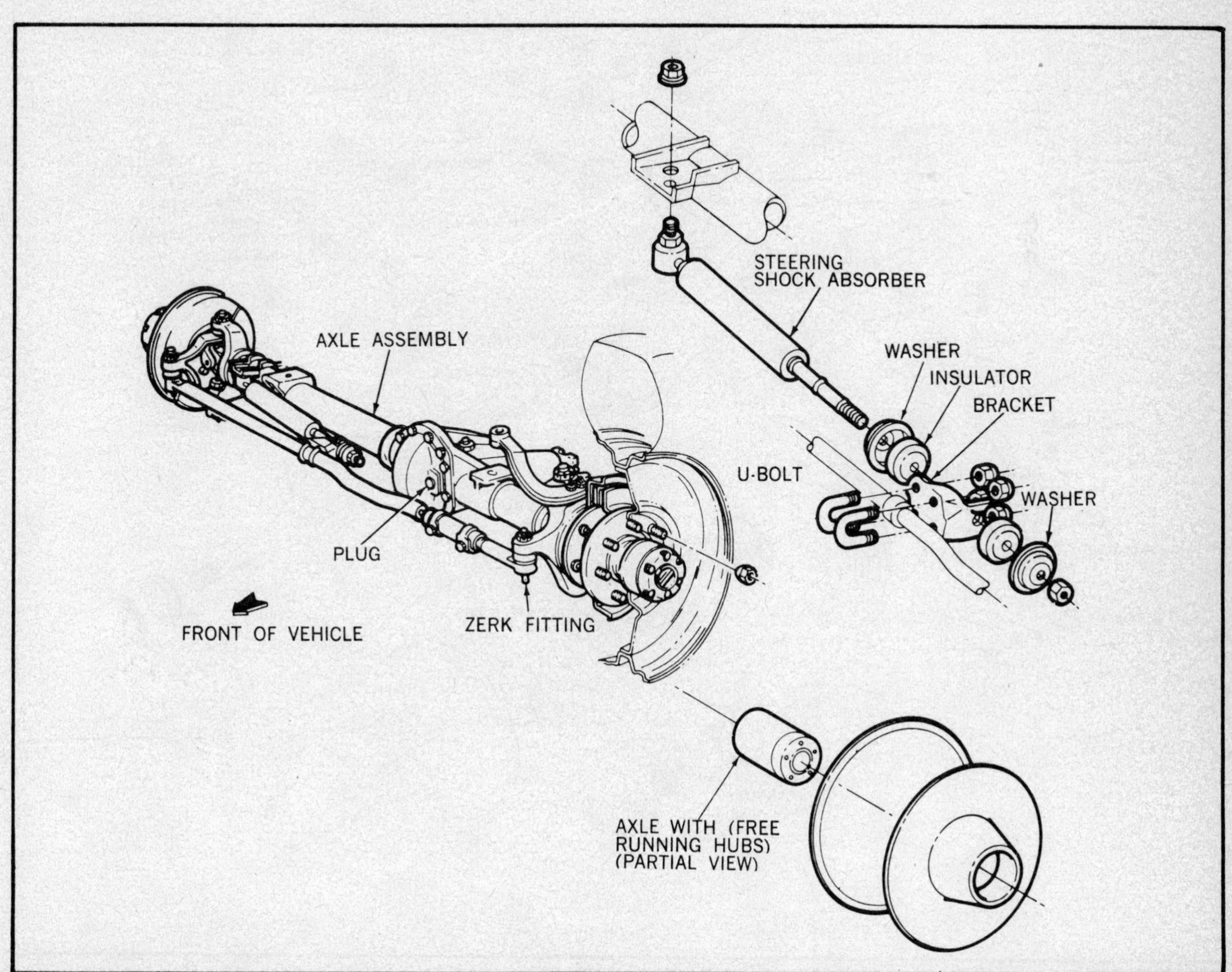

Front axle assembly—F-250 (4 × 4)—typical (© Ford Motor Co.)

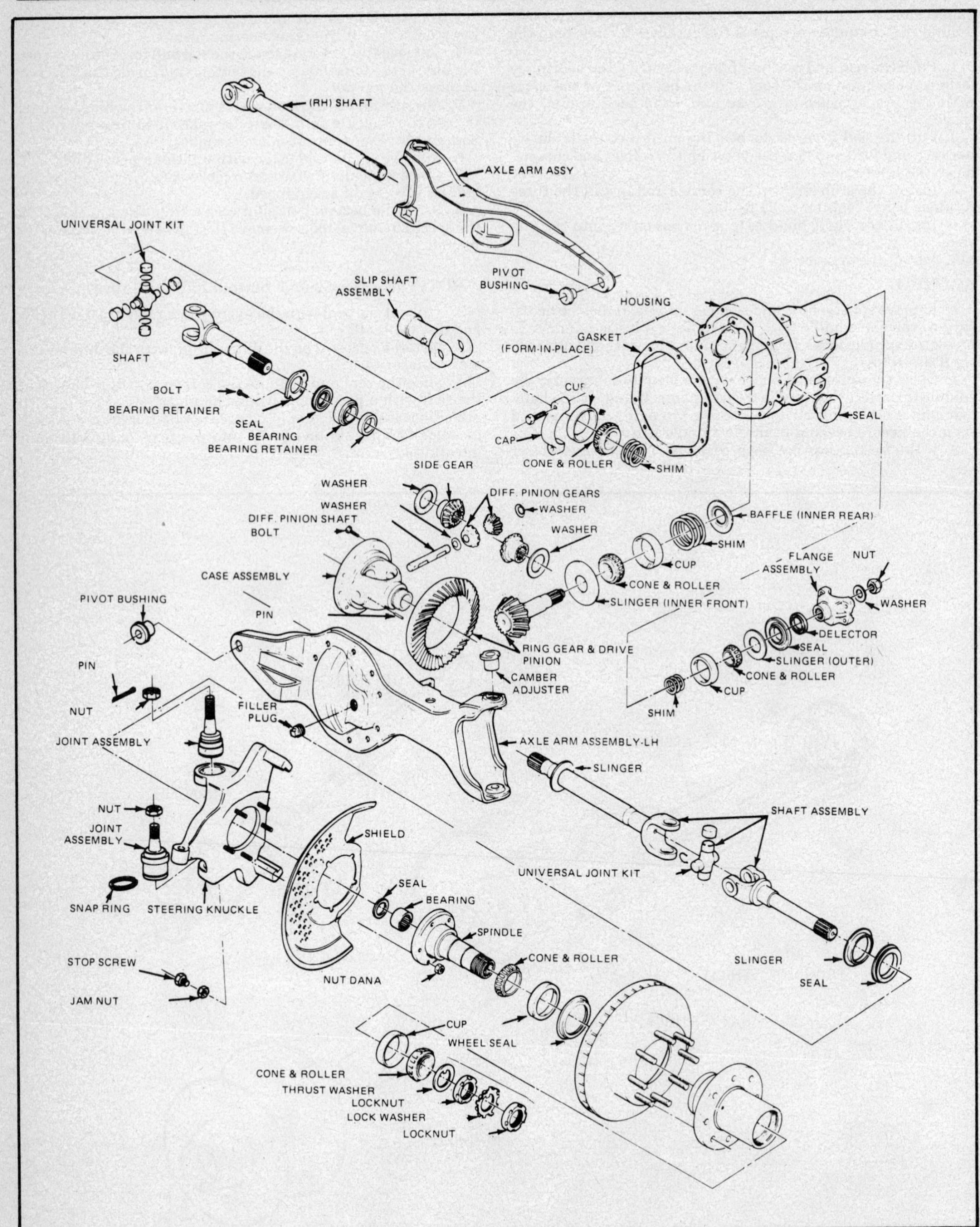

Exploded view of Dana 50 IFS front driving axle—typical of 44 IFS and H/D models (© Ford Motor Co.)

SEAL
RIGHT AXLE ARM
KEYSTONE CLAMP
SLIP YOKE AND
STUB SHAFT
RIGHT SHAFT AND
JOINT ASSEMBLY
RUBBER BOOT
LEFT AXLE ARM

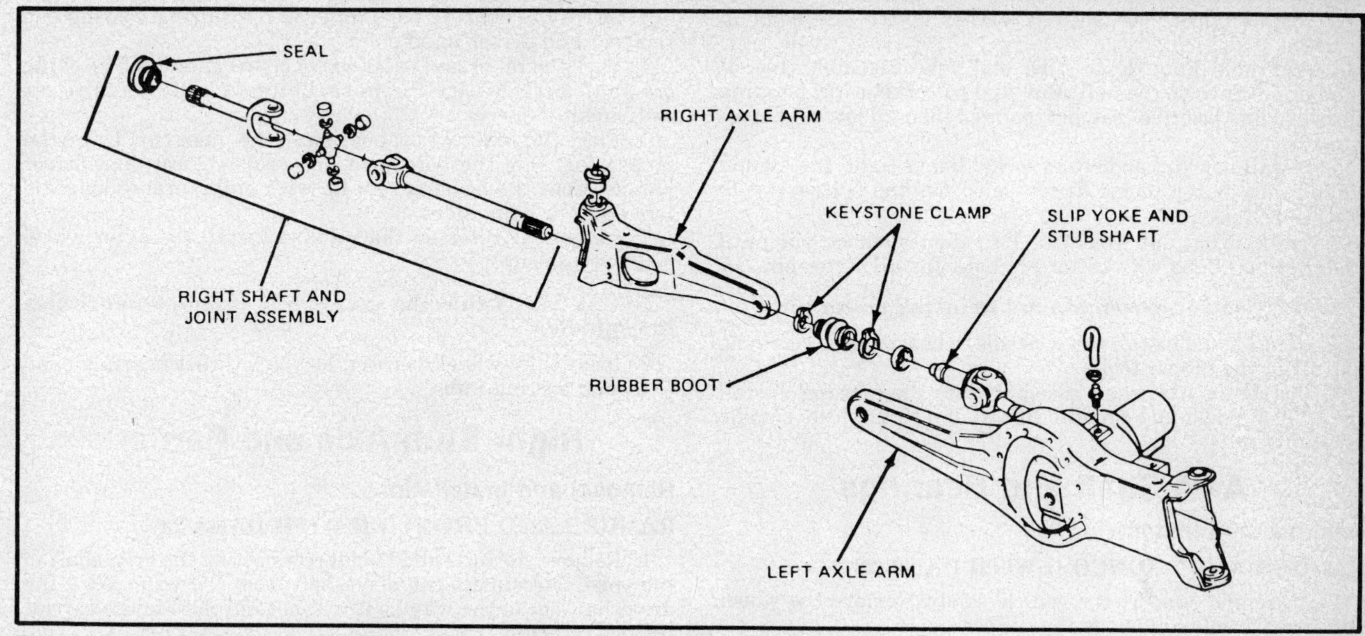

Right axle and joint assembly—Ranger and Bronco II (4 × 4) (© Ford Motor Co.)

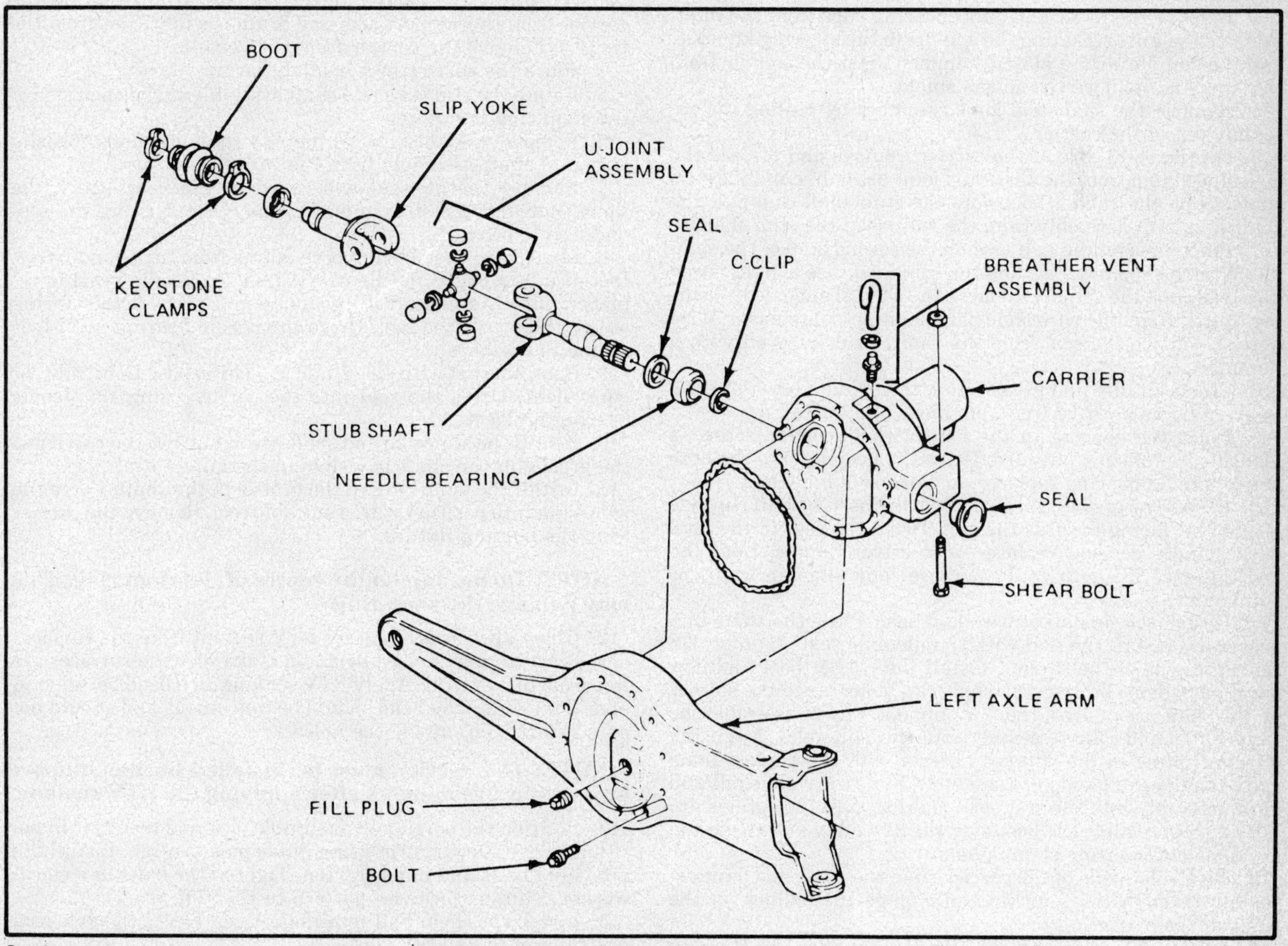

BOOT
SLIP YOKE
U-JOINT
ASSEMBLY
SEAL
C-CLIP
BREATHER VENT
ASSEMBLY
KEYSTONE
CLAMPS
CARRIER
STUB SHAFT
NEEDLE BEARING
SEAL
SHEAR BOLT
LEFT AXLE ARM
FILL PLUG
BOLT

Carrier assembly and related components—Ranger and Bronco II (© Ford Motor Co.)

13. Install upper ball joint (stud has cotter key hole) in knuckle.
14. Assemble knuckle to tube and yoke assembly. Install camber adjuster on top ball joint stud with the arrow pointing outboard for "positive" camber, pointed inboard for "negative" camber.
15. Install new nut on bottom socket finger tight. Install and tighten nut on top socket finger tight. Tighten bottom nut to 90–110 ft. lbs.
16. Tighten top nut to 100 ft. lbs., then advance nut until castellation aligns with cotter pin hole. Install cotter pin.

NOTE: Do not loosen top nut to install cotter pin.

17. Remove and install a new needle to bearing in the spindle bar using the proper tool.
18. Install the axle shaft assembly into the housing. Install the splash shield and spindle. Install and tighten the spindle attaching nuts.

Axle Shaft and Bearings

Removal and Installation

RANGER AND BRONCO II WITH DANA 28

1. Raise and support the vehicle safely. Remove the wheel and tire assembly. Remove the caliper.
2. Remove hub locks, wheel bearings, and lock nuts.
3. Remove the hub and rotor. Remove the outer wheel bearing cone. Remove the grease seal from the rotor. Remove the inner wheel bearing.
4. Remove the inner and outer bearing cups from the rotor. Remove the nuts retaining the spindle to the steering knuckle. Tap the spindle with a plastic hammer to jar the spindle from the knuckle. Remove the splash shield.
5. Remove the shaft and joint assembly by pulling the assembly out of the carrier.
6. On the right side of the carrier, remove and discard the keystone clamp from the shaft and joint assembly and the stub shaft. Slide the rubber boot onto the stub shaft and pull the shaft and joint assembly from the splines of the stub shaft.
7. Place the spindle in a vise on the second step of the spindle. Wrap a shop towel around the spindle or use a brass jawed vise to protect the spindle. Remove the oil seal and needle bearing from the spindle with slide hammer and soal remover. If required, remove the seal from the shaft, by driving off with a hammer.
8. Clean all dirt and grease from the spindle bearing bore. Bearing bores must be free from nicks and burrs.
9. Place the bearing in the bore with the manufacturer's identification facing outward. Drive the bearing into the bore using spindle bearing replacer, and driver handle tool.
10. Install the grease seal in the bearing bore with the lip side of the seal facing towards the tool. Drive the seal in the bore with spindle bearing replacer, and driver handle. Coat the bearing seal lip with multi-purpose long life lubricant, or equivalent.
11. If removed, install a new shaft seal. Place the shaft in a press, and install the seal with spindle/axle seal installer. On the right side of the carrier, install the rubber boot and new keystone clamps on the stub shaft slip yoke. Since the splines on the shaft are phased, there is only one way to assemble the right shaft and joint assembly into the slip yoke. Align the missing spline in the slip.yoke barrel with the gapless male spline on the shaft and joint assembly. Slide the right shaft and joint assembly into the slip yoke making sure the splines are fully engaged. Slide the boot over the assembly and crimp the keystone clamp using clamp pliers.
12. On the left side of the carrier slide the shaft and joint assembly through the knuckle and engage the splines on the shaft in the carrier.
13. Install the splash shield and spindle onto the steering knuckle. Install and tighten the spindle nuts to 35–45 ft. lbs.
14. Drive the bearing cups into the rotor using bearing cup replacer and driver handle.
15. Pack the inner and outer wheel bearings and the lip of the oil seal with Multi-Purpose Long-Life Lubricant, or equivalent.
16. Place the inner wheel bearing in the inner cup. Drive the grease seal into the bore with hub seal replacer, and driver handle. Coat the bearing seal lip with multipurpose long life lubricant, or equivalent.
17. Install the rotor on the spindle. Install the outer wheel bearing into cup.

NOTE: Verify that the grease seal lip totally encircles the spindle.

18. Install the wheel bearing, locknut, thrust bearing, snap ring, and locking hubs.

Right Stub Axle and Carrier

Removal and Installation

RANGER AND BRONCO II WITH DANA 28

1. Remove the nuts and U-bolts connecting the driveshaft to the yoke. Disconnect the driveshaft from the yoke. Wire the driveshaft out of the way, so it will not interfere in the carrier removal process.
2. Remove both spindles and the left and right shaft and U-joint assemblies.
3. Support the carrier with a suitable jack and remove the bolts retaining the carrier to the support arm. Separate the carrier from the support arm and drain the lubricant from the carrier. Remove the carrier from the vehicle.
4. Place the carrier in a holding fixture.
5. Rotate the slip yoke and shaft assembly so the open side of the snap ring is exposed.
6. Remove the snap ring from the shaft. Remove the slip yoke and shaft assembly from the carrier.
7. Remove the oil seal and caged needle bearings at the same time, using a slide hammer, and collet. Discard the seal and needle bearing.
8. Make sure the bearing bore is free from nicks and burrs. Install a new caged needle bearing on the needle bearing replacer, with the manufacturer name and part number facing outward towards the tool. Drive the needle bearing until it is seated in the bore.
9. Coat the seal with Long-Life Multi-Purpose Lubricant, or equivalent. Drive the seal into the carrier using the needle bearing replacer.
10. Install the slip yoke and shaft assembly into the carrier so the groove in the shaft is visible in the differential case.
11. Install the snap ring in the groove in the shaft. Force the snap ring into position with a suitable tool. Remove the carrier from the holding fixture.

NOTE: Do not tap on the center of the snap ring. This may damage the snap ring.

12. Clean all traces of gasket RTV sealant from the surfaces of the carrier and support arm and make sure the surfaces are free from dirt and oil. Apply RTV sealant, in a bead between $\frac{1}{4}$ and $\frac{3}{8}$ in. wide. The bead should be continuous and should not pass through or outside the holes.

NOTE: The carrier must be installed on the support arm within five minutes after applying the RTV sealant.

13. Position the carrier on a suitable jack and install it in position on the support arm using guide pins to align. Install the attaching bolts and hand tighten. Tighten the bolts in a clockwise or counter-clockwise pattern to 40–50 ft. lbs.
14. Install the shear bolt retaining the carrier to the axle arm and tighten to 75–95 ft. lbs.
15. Install both spindles and the left and right shaft and joint

assemblies as described in the removal and installation portion of this section. Connect the driveshaft to the yoke. Install the nuts and U-bolts and tighten to 8–15 ft. lbs.

Axle Shaft Bearing

Removal and Installation

1980–81 MODELS WITH DANA 44IFS, 44IFS-HD or 50IFS AXLES

1. Remove the axle shaft assembly.
2. Remove the stub assembly by removing 3 bolts attaching retainer plate to carrier housing.
3. Place the axle shaft in a vise and drill a $\frac{1}{4}$ in. hole in the outside of the bearing retaining ring to a depth $\frac{3}{4}$ in. the thickness of the ring.

NOTE: Do not drill through the ring because this will damage the axle shaft.

4. With a chisel placed across the hole, strike sharply with a hammer to remove the retaining ring. Replace bearing retaining ring upon assembly.
5. Press the bearing from the axle shaft with the axle bearing remover and sleeve.

NOTE: Do not use a torch to aid in bearing removal or the stub shaft will be damaged.

6. Remove the seal and retainer plate from the stub shaft. Discard seal and replace with new seal upon assembly.
7. Inspect the retainer plate and stub shaft for distortion, nicks or burns. Replace if necessary.
8. Install retainer plate and new seal on shaft. Coat oil seal with ESA-M175B or equivalent.
9. Place the bearing on the shaft. The large radius on the inner race must face the yoke end of the shaft.
10. Use axle bearing replacer and pinion bearing cone remover to press the bearing onto the shaft until completely seated. A 0.0015 in. feeler gauge should not fit between the bearing seat and bearing.
11. Use the axle bearing replacer and pinion bearing cone remover to press the bearing retainer ring onto the stub shaft. Press the bearing retainer ring until completely seated. A 0.015 in. feeler gauge should not fit between the ring and bearing. There must be one point between the bearing and ring where the feeler gauge cannot enter. If feeler gauge enters completely around the circumference press the retainer further onto the shaft.
12. Push the seal and retainer plate away from the bearing to form a space between the seal and bearing. Fill the space with wheel bearing grease.
13. With the space filled with grease, wrap tape around the space.
14. Pull the seal towards the bearing until it contacts the inner race. This will force grease between the rollers and cup. Remove tape.

NOTE: If grease is not visible on the small end of the rollers, repeat Steps 6 through 8 until grease is visible. Install the slip yoke and U-joint to stub shaft.

15. Install the stub shaft in the carrier and install 3 retainer bolts. Torque to 30–40 ft. lbs. Install right hand axle shaft assembly into slip yoke.
16. Install splash shield and spindle.

Pinion Seal

Removal and Installation

LIGHT DUTY VEHICLES

NOTE: A torque wrench capable of at least 225 ft. lbs. is required for pinion seal installation.

CAUTION

Some vehicles use a collapsible spacer to set pinion depth and preload. When replacing the pinion seal always install a new spacer. Never tighten the pinion nut more than 225 ft. lbs. or the spacer will be compressed too far.

1. Raise and support the vehicle safely. Position jackstands under the frame rails. Allow the axle to drop to rebound position for working clearance.
2. Mark the companion flanges and U-joints for correct reinstallation position.
3. Remove the drive shaft. Use a suitable tool to hold the companion flange. Remove the pinion nut and companion flange.
4. Use a slide hammer and hook or sheet metal screw to remove the oil seal.
5. If the vehicle uses a collapsible spacer, install new spacer. Install a new pinion seal after lubricating the sealing surfaces. Use a suitable seal driver. Install the companion flange and pinion nut. On models using a spacer, tighten the nut to 225 ft. lbs. On other models, pinion nut torque is 200–220 ft. lbs.

Front Drive Axle Housing

SOLID AXLE HOUSING WITH COIL SPRINGS

Removal and Installation

1. Raise the vehicle and support safely. Remove the wheels from the axle hubs.
2. The hubs, drums or rotors, axle shafts and other components can be removed in the conventional manner.
3. Remove the hydraulic brake line brackets from each end of the axle without breaking the hydraulic connection. Disengage the hydraulic lines from the axle clips. Tie the lines to the frame.
4. Disconnect the steering tie rod at the spindle connecting rod ends. Disconnect the axle stabilizer bar.
5. Disconnect the front drive shaft at the pinion companion flange and universal joint. Secure the drive shaft out of the working area.
6. Lower the vehicle onto the safety stands and place a jack under the axle to support it while disconnecting it from the radius arms.
7. Each radius arm and cap is marked, since they are manufactured as matched pairs. Remove the bolts attaching the radius to the radius arm caps. Remove the rubber insulators and roll the axle from under the vehicle.
8. To install, position the front drive axle under the vehicle, using a floor jack, and install the radius arms, insulators and caps to the axle. Numbers on radius arm and cap should be matched. Torque the attaching bolts to specifications, tightening them diagonally in pairs.
9. Raise the vehicle to working height and install the drive shaft to the pinion companion flange at the universal joint. Torque the universal joint U-bolt nuts to specifications.
10. Connect the axle stabilizer bar. Connect the steering tie rod to the spindle arms by means of the steering connecting rod ends. Torque the attaching nuts to specifications, then install the cotter pins.
11. Install the axle shafts, spindles and brake backing plates.
12. Position the hydraulic brake lines and brackets, then install the retaining clips.
13. Install the hubs, drums or rotors, axle shafts and other components that may have been removed during the removal of the unit from the vehicle.
14. Fill the unit to its proper level with lubricant and lower the vehicle.

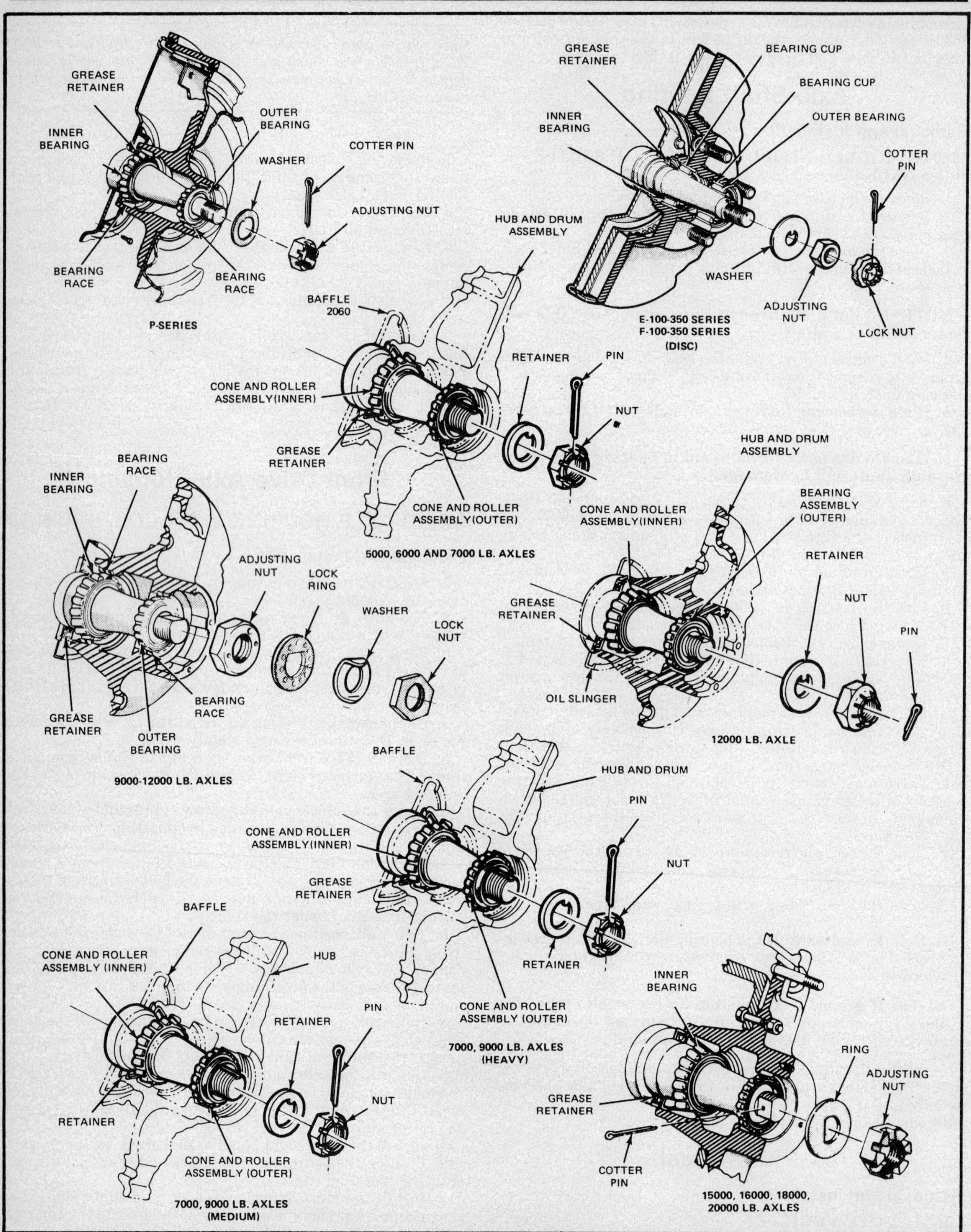

Front hubs, bearings and locking components—varied axles (© Ford Motor Co.)

SOLID AXLE HOUSING WITH LEAF SPRINGS

Removal and Installation

1. Raise the vehicle and support safely. Remove the wheel assemblies from the hubs.
2. The hubs, rotors, axle shafts and other components can be removed in the conventional manner.
3. Disconnect both front axle shock absorbers at their lower ends.
4. Disconnect the front axle drive shaft at the pinion flange.
5. Support the front axle on a transmission jack, then remove the spring clip (U-bolt) nuts and the spring seats.
6. Lower the axle assembly and roll it from under the vehicle.
7. Installation is the reverse of removal.

Front Wheel Bearings

Removal and Installation

LIGHT DUTY VEHICLES WITH 2WD

1. Raise and support the vehicle safely.
2. Remove the lug nuts and remove wheel/tire assembly from the hub. Remove the caliper assembly from the rotor and caliper support. Hang the caliper with a length of heavy wire above the hub.
3. Remove the grease cap with a suitable tool.
4. Remove the cotter pin and discard it.
5. Remove the nut lock, adjusting nut, and washer from the spindle.
6. Wiggle the hub so that the outer wheel bearing comes loose and can be removed. Remove the outer bearing.
7. Remove the hub from the spindle.
8. Place a block of wood or drift pin through the spindle hole and tap out the inner grease seal and bearing.
9. Place all of the bearings, nuts, nut locks, washers and grease caps in a container of solvent. Use a light soft brush to throughly clean each part.
10. Clean the inside of the hub, including the bearing races, and the spindle. Remove all traces of old lubricant from these components.
11. Inspect the bearings for pitting, flat spots, rust, and rough areas. Check the races in the hub and the spindle for the same defects and rub them clean with a cloth that has been soaked in solvent. If the races show hair line cracks or worn shiny areas, they must be replaced.
12. Pack the bearings with the proper grade and type wheel bearing grease.

NOTE: Sodium based grease is not compatible with lithium based grease. Be careful not to mix the two types. The best way to prevent this is to completely clean all of the old grease from the hub and spindle before installing any new grease.

13. Turn the hub assembly over so that the inner side faces up, making sure that the race and inner are are clean, and drop the inner wheel bearing into place. Using a hammer and a block of wood, tap the new grease seal in place.
14. Slide the hub assembly onto the spindle. Keep the hub centered on the spindle to prevent damage to the grease seal and the spindle threads.
15. Place the outer wheel bearing in place over the spindle. Place the washer on the spindle after the bearing. Screw on the spindle nut and turn it down until a slight binding is felt.
16. With a torque wrench, tighten the bearings. Install the nut lock over the nut so that the cotter pin hole in the spindle is aligned with a slot in the nut lock. Back off the adjusting nut and the nut lock two slots of the nut lock and install the cotter pin.

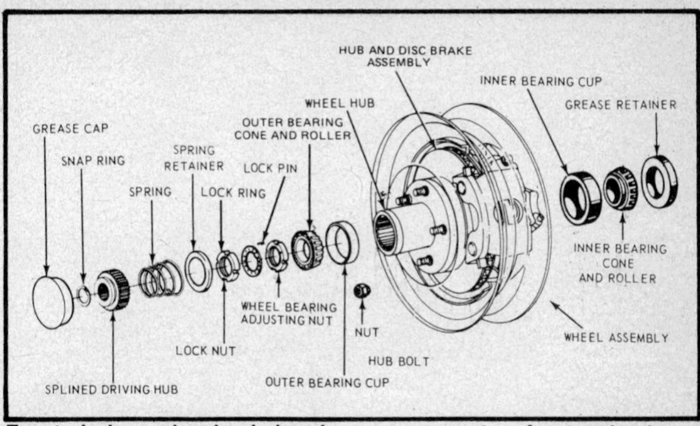

Front hub and wheel bearing components, front wheel drive—typical (© Ford Motor Co.)

17. Bend the longer of the two ends opposite the looped end out and over the end of the spindle. Trim both ends of the cotter pin just enough so that the grease cap will fit, leaving the bent end shaped over the end of the spindle.
18. Install the grease cap, brake caliper if so equipped, and the wheel/tire assembly. The wheel should rotate freely with no noise or noticeable end-play.

4WD FRONT WITHOUT FREE-RUNNING HUBS EXCEPT RANGER AND BRONCO II

NOTE: Sodium based grease is not compatible with lithium based grease. Be careful not to mix the two types. The best way to prevent this is to completely clean all of the old grease from the hub assembly before installing any new grease.

1. Raise and support the vehicle safely.
2. Remove the front hub grease cap and driving hub snap-ring.
3. Remove the splined driving hub and the pressure spring. This may require slight prying with a suitable tool.
4. Remove the wheel bearing locknut, lockring, and adjusting nut.
5. Remove the caliper assembly.
6. Carefully drive out the inner bearing cone and grease seal from the hub.
7. Inspect the bearing cups (races) for cracks and pits. If the cups are excessively worn or there are pits or cracks visible, replace them along with the cones. The cups are removed from the hub by driving them out with a drift pin. They are installed in the same manner.
8. If it is determined that the cups are in satisfactory condition and are to remain in the hub, clean and inspect the cones (bearings). Refer to the bearing diagnosis chart. Replace the bearings if necessary. If it is necessary to replace either the cone or the cup, both parts should be replaced as a unit.
9. Thoroughly clean all components in a suitable solvent and blow them dry with compressed air or allow them to dry while resting on clean paper.

NOTE: Do not spin the bearings with compressed air while drying them.

10. Cover the spindle with a cloth and brush all loose dust and dirt from the brake assembly. Remove the cloth and thoroughly clean the inside of the hub and the spindle.
11. Pack the inside of the hub with wheel bearing grease. Add grease to the hub until the grease is flush with the inside diameter of the bearing cup.
12. Pack the bearing cone and roller assemblies with wheel bearing grease.
13. Position the inner bearing into the inner bearing cup and install the new grease seal.

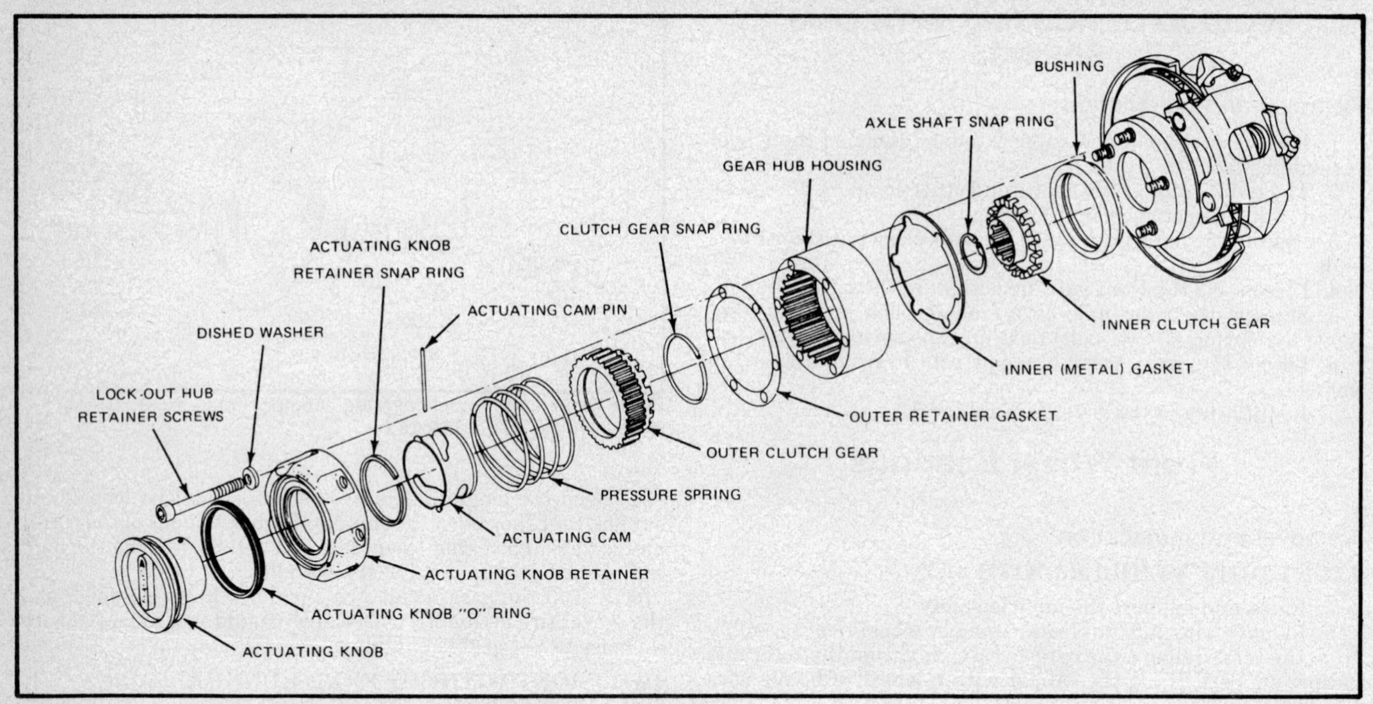

Exploded view of external lock-out hub (© Ford Motor Co.)

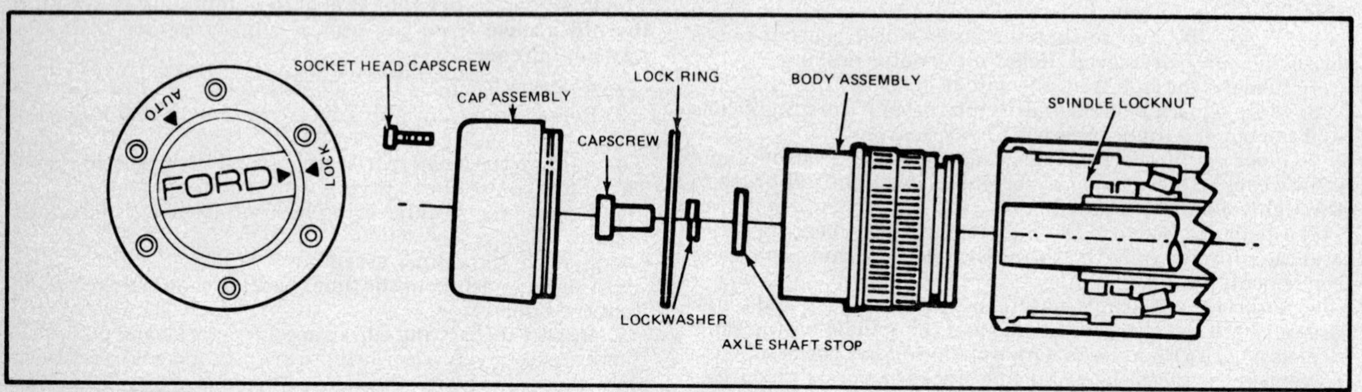

Automatic locking hub control (© Ford Motor Co.)

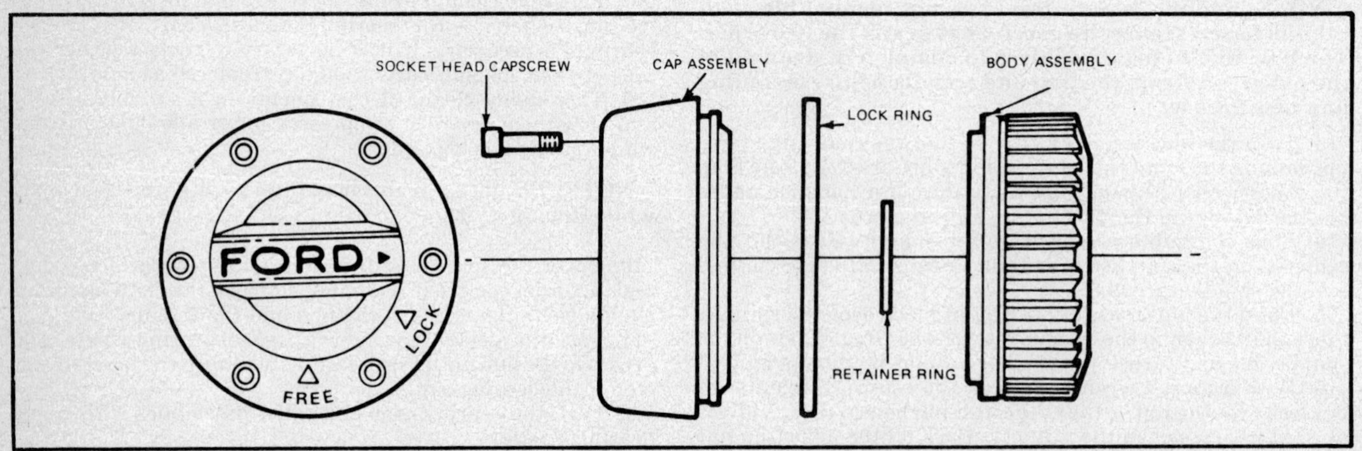

Manual locking hub control (© Ford Motor Co.)

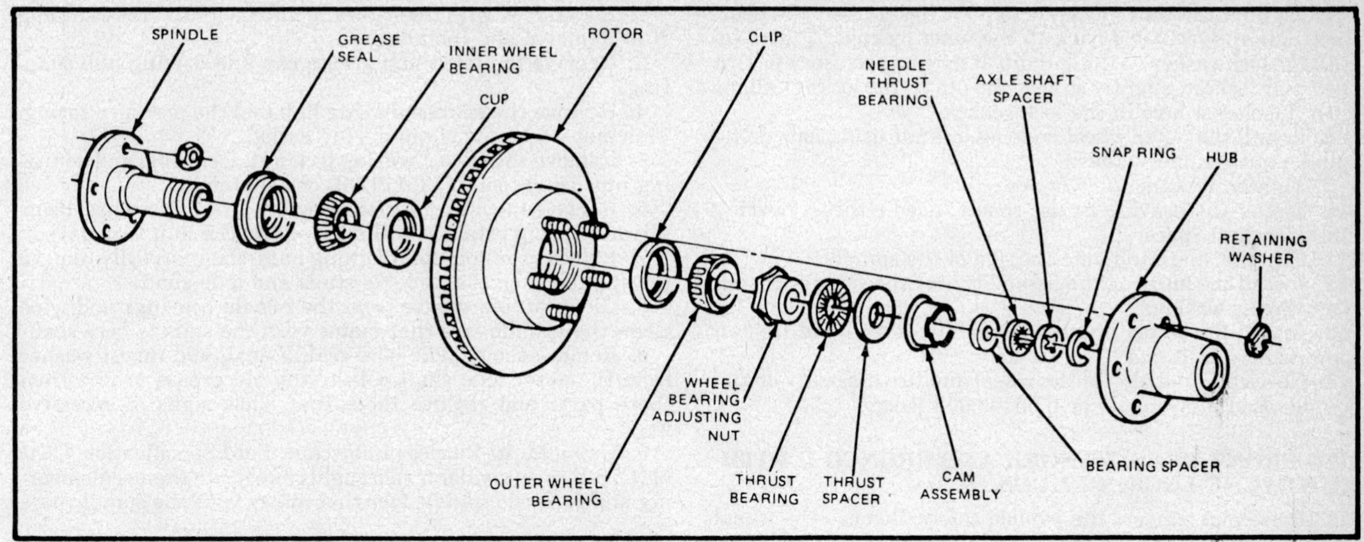

Automatic locking hubs—Ranger and Bronco II (© Ford Motor Co.)

14. Carefully position the hub assembly onto the spindle. Be careful not to damage the new seal. Install the caliper.
15. Place the outer bearing into position on the spindle and into the bearing cup.
16. Install the bearing adjusting nut and tighten it to 50 ft. lbs. while rotating the hub back and forth to seat the bearings.
17. Back off the adjusting nut about 90°.
18. Assemble the lockring by turning the nut to the nearest notch where the dowel pin will enter.
19. Install the outer locknut and torque to 80–100 ft. lbs. The final end-play of the wheel on the spindle should be 0.001–0.010 in.
20. Install the grease cap and adjust the brakes, if they were backed off to remove the hub assembly. Lower the vehicle.

4WD FRONT WITH FREE-RUNNING HUB EXCEPT RANGER AND BRONCO II

1. Raise the vehicle and support it safely. Remove the tire and wheel assembly.
2. To remove hub, first separate cap assembly from body assembly by removing the six (6) socket head capscrews from the cap assembly and slip apart.
3. Remove snap-ring (retainer ring) from the end of the axle shaft.
4. Remove the lock ring seated in the groove of the wheel hub. The body assembly will now slide out of the wheel hub. If necessary, use an appropriate puller to remove the body assembly.
5. Install hub in reverse order of removal. Torque socket head capscrews to 30–35 inch lbs

AUTOMATIC LOCKING HUBS, EXCEPT RANGER AND BRONCO II

1. Raise the vehicle and support it safely. Remove the wheel and tire.
2. Remove capscrews and remove hub cap assembly from spindle. Remove capscrew from end of axle shaft.
3. Remove lock ring seated in the groove of the wheel hub with a knife blade or with a small sharp awl with the tip bent in a hook.
4. Remove body assembly from spindle. If body assembly does not slide out easily, use an appropriate puller.
5. Unscrew all three sets in the spindle locknut until the heads are flush with the edge of the locknut. Remove outer spindle locknut with automatic hub lock nut wrench.
6. Reinstall in reverse order of removal. Tighten the outer spindle locknut to 15–20 ft. lbs. with automatic hub lock nut wrench. Tighten down all three set screws. Firmly push in body assembly until the friction shoes are on top of the spindle outer locknut.
7. Install capscrew into the axle shaft and tighten to 35–50 ft. lbs.
8. Place cap on spindle and install capscrews. Tighten to 35–50 inch lbs Turn dial firmly from stop to stop, causing the dialing mechanism to engage the body spline.

NOTE: Be sure both hub dials are in the same position; "AUTO" or "LOCK."

4WD FRONT HUBS, RANGER AND BRONCO II, EXCEPT WITH AUTOMATIC LOCKING HUBS

1. Raise and support the vehicle safely.
2. Remove the wheel lug nuts and remove the wheel and tire assembly.
3. Remove the retainer washers from the lug nut studs and remove the manual locking hub assembly. To remove the interal hub lock assembly from the outer body assembly, remove the outer lock ring seated in the hub body groove. The internal assembly, spring and clutch gear will now slide out of the hub body.

NOTE: Do not remove the screw from the plastic dial.

4. Rebuild the hub assembly in the reverse order of disassembly.
5. Install the manual locking hub assembly over the spindle and place the retainer washers on the lug nut studs.
6. Install the wheel and tire assembly. Install the lug nuts and tighten to 85–115 ft. lb.

Manual Hub Adjustment

ALL MODELS SO EQUIPPED

1. Raise and support the vehicle safely. Remove the wheel lug nuts and remove the wheel and tire assembly.
2. Remove the retainer washers from the lug nut studs and remove the manual locking hub assembly from the spindle.
3. Remove the snap ring from the end of the spindle shaft.
4. Remove the axle shaft spacer, needle thrust bearing and the bearing spacer.
5. Remove the outer wheel bearing locknut from the spindle using a four-prong spindle nut spanner wrench. Make sure the tabs on the tool engage the slots in the locknut. Remove the locknut washer from the spindle.
6. Loosen the inner wheel bearing locknut using four prong spindle nut spanner wrench. Make sure that the tabs on the tool engage the slots in the locknut and that the slot in the tool is over the pin on the locknut.

7. Tighten the inner locknut to 35 ft. lbs. to seat the bearings. Spin the rotor and back off the inner locknut 1/4 turn. Install the lockwasher on the spindle. It may be necessary to turn the inner locknut slightly so that the pin on the locknut aligns with the closest hole in the lockwasher.
8. Install the outer wheel bearing locknut using four prong spindle nut spanner wrench.
9. Tighten locknut to 15 ft. lbs.
10. Install the bearing thrust spacer, needle thrust bearing and axle shaft spacer.
11. Clip the snap ring onto the end of the spindle.
12. Install the manual hub assembly over the spindle. Install the retainer washers.
13. Install the wheel and tire assembly. Install and tighten lugnuts 85–115 ft. lbs.
14. Check the end play of the wheel and tire assembly on the spindle. End play should be 0.001–0.003 inch.

4WD FRONT HUBS, RANGER AND BRONCO II WITH AUTOMATIC LOCKING HUBS.

1. Raise and support the vehicle safely. Remove the wheel lug nuts and remove the wheel and tire assembly.
2. Remove the retainer washers from the lug nut studs and remove the automatic locking hub assembly from the spindle.
3. Remove the snap ring from the end of the spindle shaft.
4. Remove the axle shaft spacer, needle thrust bearing and the bearing spacer. Being careful not to damage the plastic moving cam, pull the cam assembly off the wheel bearing adjusting nut and remove the thrust washer and needle thrust bearing from the adjusting nut.
5. Loosen the wheel bearing adjusting nut from the spindle using a 2 3/8 inch hex socket tool.
6. While rotating the hub and rotor assembly, tighten the wheel bearing adjusting nut to 35 ft. lbs. to seat the bearings, then back off the nut 1/4 turn (90°).
7. Retighten the adjusting nut to 16 in. lb. using a torque wrench. Align the closest hole in the wheel bearing adjusting nut with the center of the spindle keyway slot. Advance the nut to the next hole if required.
8. Install the locknut needle bearing and thrust washer in the order of removal and push or press the cam assembly onto the locknut by lining up the key in the fixed cam with the spindle keyway.
9. Install the bearing thrust washer, needle thrust bearing and axle shaft spacer. Clip the snap ring onto the end of the spindle.
10. Install the automatic locking hub assembly over the spindle by lining up the three legs in the hub assembly with three pockets in the cam assembly. Install the retainer washers.
11. Install the wheel and tire assembly. Install and tighten lugnuts to 85–115 ft. lbs.
12. Final end play of the wheel on the spindle should be 0.001–0.003 in.

BEARING REPLACEMENT OR REPACKING

1. Raise the vehicle and support on safety stands.
2. If equipped with free-running hubs refer to Free-Running Hub Removal and Installation.
3. Remove the front hub grease cap and driving hub snapring.
4. Remove the splined driving hub and the pressure spring. This may require a slight prying assist.
5. Remove the wheel bearing lock nut, lock ring, and adjusting nut using tool T59T-1197-B, or equivalent.
6. Remove the hub and disc assembly. The outer wheel bearing and spring retainer will slide out as the hub is removed.
7. Remove the spindle retaining nuts, then carefully remove the spindle from the knuckle studs and axle shaft.
8. Clean all old grease from the needle bearings and wipe clean the spindle face that mates with the spindle bore seal.
9. Remove the spindle bore seal, V-seal, and thrust washer from the outer axle shaft. Clean any old grease or dirt from these parts and replace those that show signs of excessive wear.
10. Using Multi-Purpose Lubricant, Ford Specification ESA-M1C75-B or equivalent, thoroughly lubricate the needle bearing and pack the spindle face that mates with the spindle bore seal.
11. Assemble the V-seal in the spindle bore next to the needle bearing. Assemble the spindle bore seal on the axle shaft.
12. Assemble the spindle with the axle shaft on the knuckle studs. Adjust the retaining nuts to 50–60 ft. lbs.
13. Carefully drive the inner bearing cone and grease seal out of the hub using Tool T69L-1102-A.
14. Inspect the bearing cups for pits or cracks. If necessary, remove them with a drift. If new cups are installed, install new bearings.
15. Lubricate the bearings with Multi-Purpose Lubricant Ford Specification, ESA-M1C7-B or equivalent. Clean all old grease from the hub. Pack the cones and rollers. If a bearing packer is not available, work as much lubricant as possible between the rollers and the cages.
16. Position the inner bearing cone and roller in the inner cup and install the grease retainer.
17. Carefully position the hub and disc assembly on the spindle.
18. Install the outer bearing cone and roller, and the adjusting nut.
19. Using a torque wrench, tighten the bearing adjusting nut to 50 ft. lbs., while rotating the wheel back and forth to seat the bearings.
20. Back off the adjusting nut approximately 90 degrees.
21. Assemble the lock ring by turning the nut to the nearest hole and inserting the dowel pin. The dowel pin must seat in a lock ring hole for proper bearing adjustment and wheel retention.
22. Install the outer lock nut and tighten to 50–80 ft. lbs. Final end play of the wheel on the spindle should be 0.001 to 0.010 in.
23. Install the pressure spring and driving hub snap-ring.
24. Apply non-hardening sealer to the seating edge of the grease cap, and install the grease cap.
25. Adjust the brake if it was backed off.
26. Lower the vehicle.

MANUAL STEERING GEAR

MANUAL STEERING GEAR

For manual steering overhaul procedures refer to the Unit Repair section.

Removal and Installation

E SERIES

1. Raise and support the vehicle safely.
2. Disconnect the flex coupling from the steering shaft flange by removing the two attaching nuts.
3. Disconnect the drag link from the sector shaft arm.
4. Support the steering gear and remove the bolts and washers that attach the steering gear assembly to the frame side rail. Lower the steering gear from the vehicle.
5. Remove the coupling to gear attaching bolt from the lower half of the flex coupling and remove the coupling from the steering gear assembly.

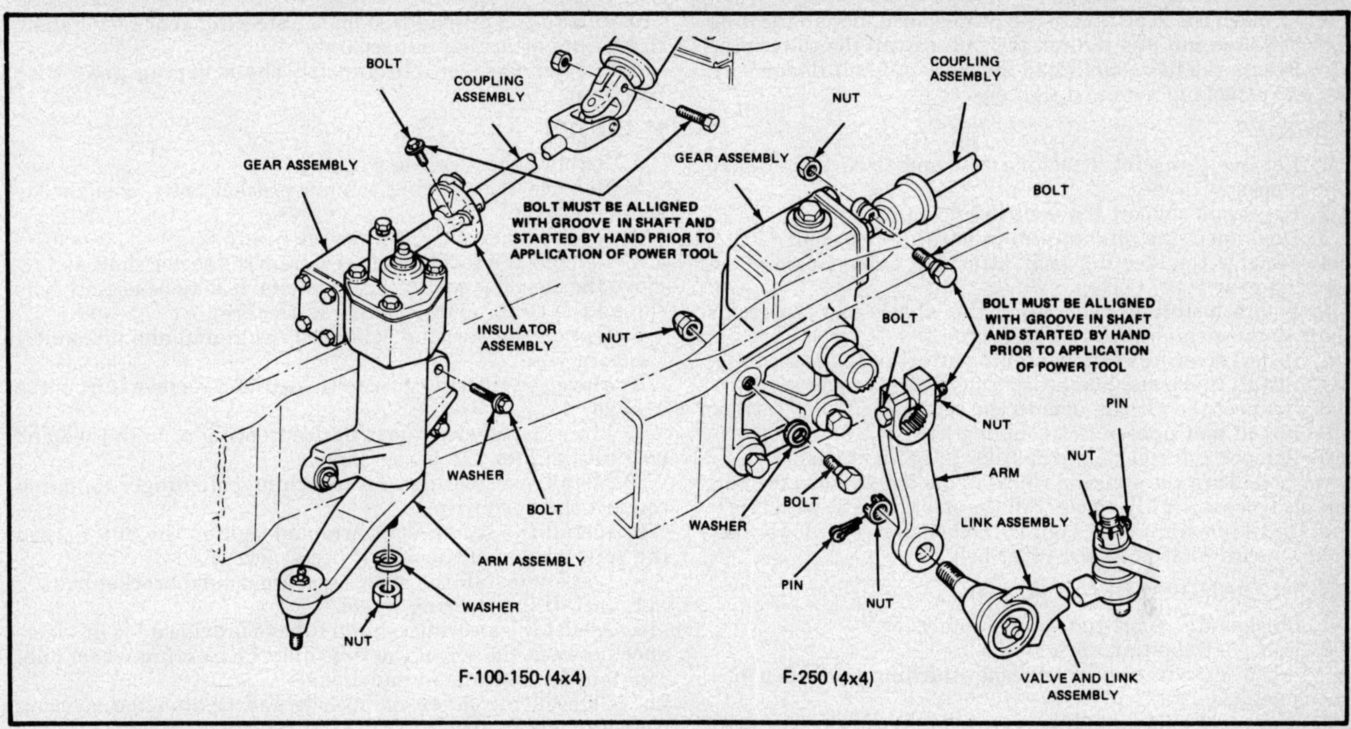

F-100, F-150 and F-250 manual steering gear installation (© Ford Motor Co.)

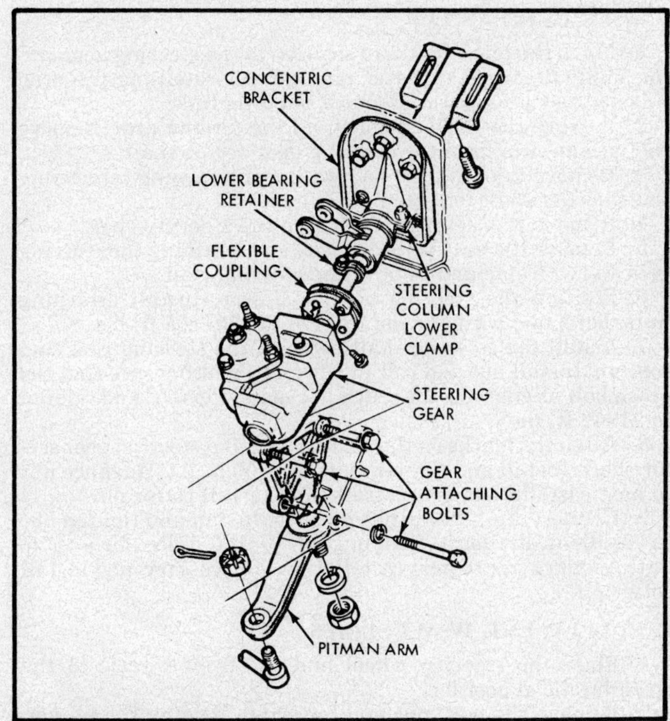

Steering gear installation—F-100, 250 and 350 (4 × 2) (© Ford Motor Co.)

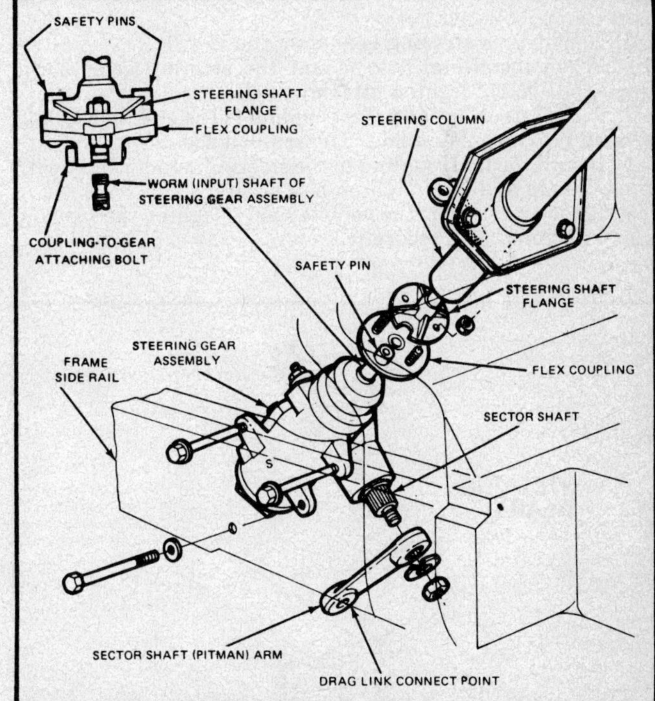

Econoline manual steering gear installation (© Ford Motor Co.)

6. Remove the pitman arm to sector shaft attaching nut and washer. Remove the pitman arm from the sector shaft.
7. Install the flex coupling on the worm shaft of the gear assembly. Install a new coupling-to-gear attaching bolt and tighten.
8. Center the input shaft. The center position is approximately three turns from either stop.
9. Assemble the pitman arm on the sector shaft pointing downward. Install the attaching nuts and washers. Tighten the nuts.
10. Position the steering gear assembly so that the stud bolts on the flex coupling enter the bolt holes in the steering shaft flange, and the holes in the mounting bosses of the gear match the bolt holes in the frame side rail.
11. While supporting the gear in the proper position, install the gear to frame side rail attaching bolts and washers, tighten.

12. Connect the drag link to the pitman arm. Install the drag link ball stud nut and tighten the nut. Install the cotter pin.
13. Secure the flex coupling to the steering shaft flange with the two attaching nuts and tighten.

F SERIES

1. Remove flex joint attaching bolt and remove the brake line bracket.
2. Raise and support the vehicle safely.
3. Disconnect the pitman arm from the sector shaft.
4. Remove the steering gear attaching bolts. Remove the steering gear.
5. Before installing gear, align the wheels and the sector shaft to the straight-forward position.
6. Install steering gear, tightening attaching bolts securely.
7. Install the brake line bracket to the gear cover studs.
8. Connect the pitman arm to the sector shaft.
9. Install and tighten flex coupling bolt.
10. Remove the steering gear filler plug and housing lower cover bolt. Turn the steering wheel to the left to move the ball nut away from the filler hole. Fill the steering gear with lubricant (until lubricant comes out of the housing cover lower bolt hole). Install filler plug and cover bolt.

BRONCO AND F SERIES (4 × 4)

1. Raise and support the vehicle safely.
2. Remove the pitman arm.
3. Remove the three gear to frame attaching bolts, then lower the vehicle.
4. Remove the flex coupling clamp bolt at the steering gear input shaft and loosen the other clamp bolt (steering column). Remove the coupling from the steering gear input shaft. Discard clamp, bolt and nut.
5. Remove the steering gear from the vehicle.
6. When installing, first mount the steering gear to the frame, but do not tighten attaching bolts.
7. Install steering shaft flex coupling to the gear input shaft using a new clamp and bolt. Tighten bolt securely.
8. Install the flex coupling to the steering column shaft with a new clamp and bolt. Tighten bolt securely.
9. Raise and support the vehicle safely. Tighten the steering gear attaching bolts securely.

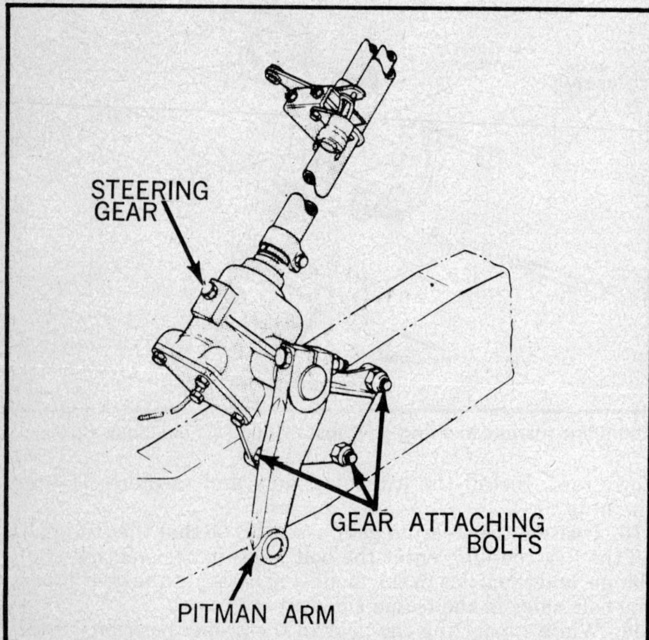

P-Series manual steering gear installation (© Ford Motor Co.)

10. Install the pitman arm on the steering gear sector shaft, tightening attaching nut securely.
11. Lower the vehicle and fill the steering gear with lubricant.

P SERIES

1. Remove the steering wheel.
2. Remove the steering column bracket bolts from the instrument panel.
3. Raise and support the vehicle safely.
4. Remove the sector shaft arm from the sector shaft and remove the steering gear attaching bolts. It may be necessary to spread the sector shaft opening in the arm.
5. Loosen the steering column lower clamp and disconnect the horn wire.
6. Move the steering gear to the left and remove it from the vehicle.
7. Place the steering gear in the steering column tube and partially tighten the lower clamp.
8. Install the steering gear attaching bolts finger tight and connect the horn wire.
9. Install the sector shaft arm and tighten the nut. Spread the split portion of the arm if necessary.
10. Loosely install the steering column tube bracket bolts.
11. Install the steering wheel.
12. Adjust the steering column tube to provide a $\frac{1}{16}$ in. clearance between the top of the tube and the steering wheel hub. Tighten the instrument panel bolts.
13. Tighten the lower clamp bolt and tighten the steering gear attaching bolts.
14. Lower the vehicle.

F B SERIES 500 AND UP

1. Mark the pitman arm in relation to the steering gear sector shaft. Remove the cotter pin and nut retaining the drag link to the Pitman arm. Remove the drag link.
2. Remove the nut and bolt from the pitman arm. Remove the pitman arm from the steering gear sector shaft.
3. Remove the nut, bolt and washer in the joing connecting the steering shaft to steering column.
4. Remove the steering shaft from the steering gear.
5. Remove the nuts bolts and washers retaining the steering gear to the frame and remove the steering gear.
6. Position the steering gear on frame. Install attaching nuts, bolts and washers and tighten to 150–205 ft. lbs.
7. Install the steering shaft between the steering gear and column. Install nut and bolt in slip joint, making sure that the pinch bolt aligns with the notch in the input shaft, and tighten to 31–42 ft. lbs.
8. Align the marks on the pitman arm and steering gear sector shaft. Install and tighten nut 220–300 ft. lbs. Advance nut to next castellation, if necessary, and install cotter pin.
9. Connect drag link to pitman arm. Install and tighten nut to 75–105 ft. lbs. for a $\frac{3}{4}$ in. nut or 110–150 ft. lbs. for a $\frac{7}{8}$ in. nut. Advance nut to next castellation, if necessary, and install cotter pin.

L, N, L, LT, LNT, W, WT SERIES

1. Place the steering wheel and the front wheels in the straight ahead position.
2. Remove the bolt, nut and cotter pin holding the pitman arm to the sector shaft. Remove the pitman arm from the shaft.
3. Mark the steering gear input shaft and the U-joint yoke for alignment.
4. Remove the cotter pin, bolt and nut holding the U-joint to the steering gear input shaft, and slide the joint up and off the input shaft.
5. Remove the bolts, nuts, cotter pin, and strap retainers holding the steering gear or steering gear bracket to the frame side rail.
6. Remove the steering gear.
7. Place the gear (or gear and bracket) on the side rail. In-

stall the bolts, nuts and strap retainers and tighten. Advance the nut to the next castellation if necessary and install the cotter pins.

8. Align the marks on the input shaft and U-joint yoke and place the steering shaft U-joint on the steering gear input shaft and install a new nut and bolt. Tighten the nuts. Advance to the next castellation if necessary and install the cotter pin.

NOTE: Be sure the bolt engages in the slot on the steering gear input shaft.

9. Place the pitman arm on the steering shaft and install the bolt and nut. On W and L series vehicles, align the slash marks on the pitman arm with the serrations on the sector shaft. Tighten the bolts. Advance the nut to the castellation if necessary and install the cotter pin.

C SERIES

1. Tilt the cab up and remove the horn wire brush from the steering column just below the instrument panel bracket.
2. Remove the bolt that attaches the U-joint to the steering gear.
3. Turn the wheels all the way to the right. Remove the sector arm attaching nut and bolt. Pry the sector arm off the sector shaft. Spread the sector shaft opening in the arm if necessary.
4. Remove the steering gear housing attaching bolts and remove the gear.
5. Place the steering gear housing on the frame side rail and install the attaching bolts. Tighten the nuts and install the cotter pins.
6. Center the steering gear input shaft. Turn the steering wheel to position the lower spoke in a vertical position.
7. With a helper, push the steering shaft down until the U-joint is in position on the steering gear input shaft. Install and tighten the U-joint attaching bolt and nut.
8. Install the sector shaft arm on the sector shaft. Make sure it is in line with the lock bolt slot in the sector shaft. Install and tighten the bolt and nut. Spread the sector shaft opening in the arm if necessary.
9. Connect the hornwire. Road test the vehicle in check for proper steering operation.

WORM BEARING PRELOAD

Adjustment

F SERIES

Always check and adjust worm and roller mesh after check checking and adjusting worm bearing preload.

1. Remove the pitman arm from sector shaft and the horn button and spring from the steering wheel. Disconnect the horn wire at the relay.
2. Turn steering wheel to end of travel.
3. Use a torque wrench on the steering wheel nut and measure the lowest torque required to move the wheel at a constant speed. This torque is the worm bearing preload.
4. If the preload is not 4–5 inch lbs. (manual) or 3–4 inch lbs (power assist), adjust the preload as follows: loosen the steering shaft bearing adjuster locknut and turn adjuster to set the preload.
5. Tighten bearing adjuster locknut, install the pitman arm and horn components.

BRONCO, BRONCO II AND RANGER

Remove the gear from the vehicle, if required to gain access to adjusting screws. Loosen locknut and back off the mesh and roller adjusting nut. Check the torque required to rotate the input shaft 1 $\frac{1}{2}$ turns either side of center. If bearing preload is not 5–10 inch lbs., 9–10 inch lbs. On the Ranger and Bronco II,

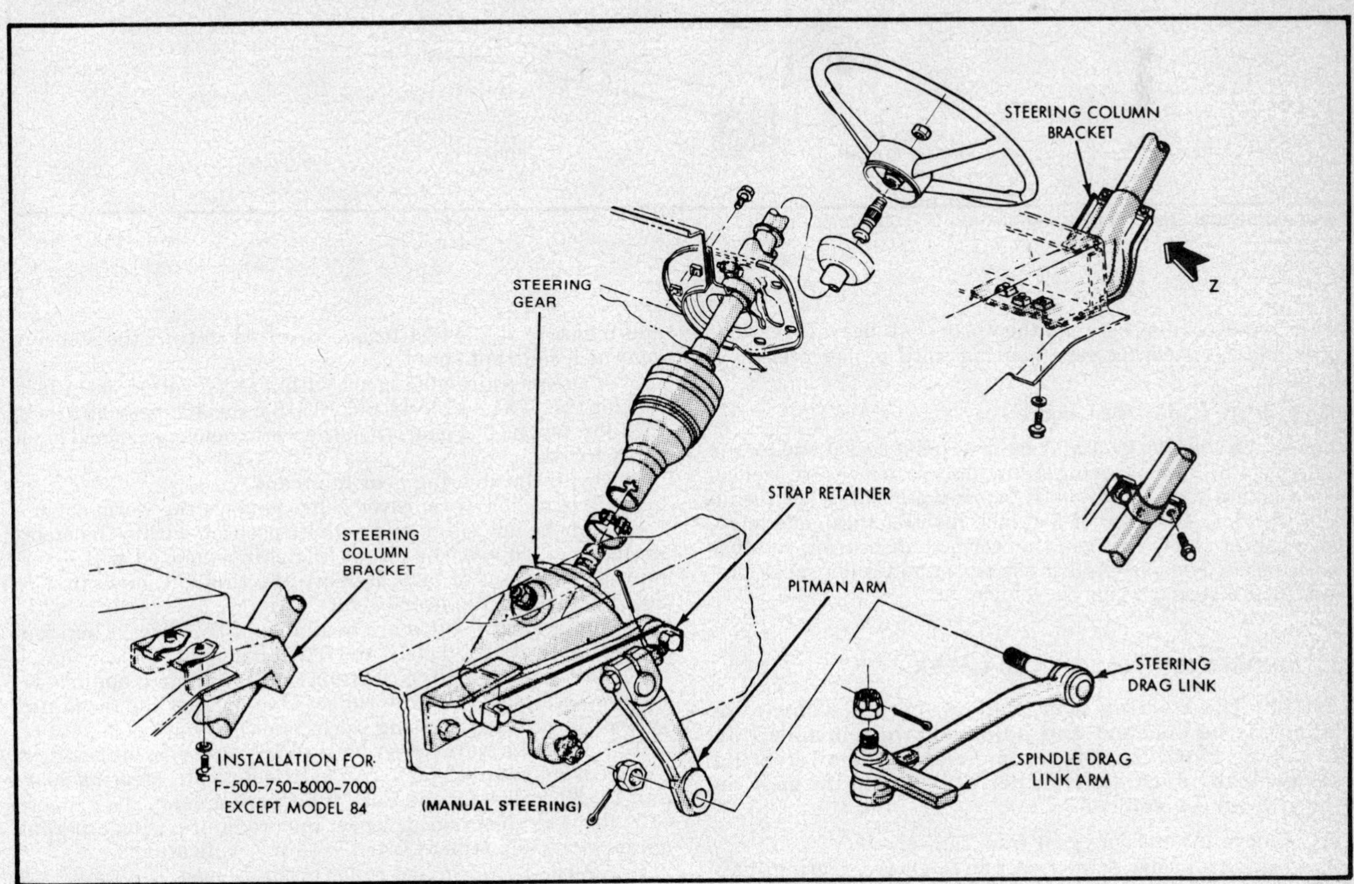

F-B 500–750 manual steering gear installation (© Ford Motor Co.)

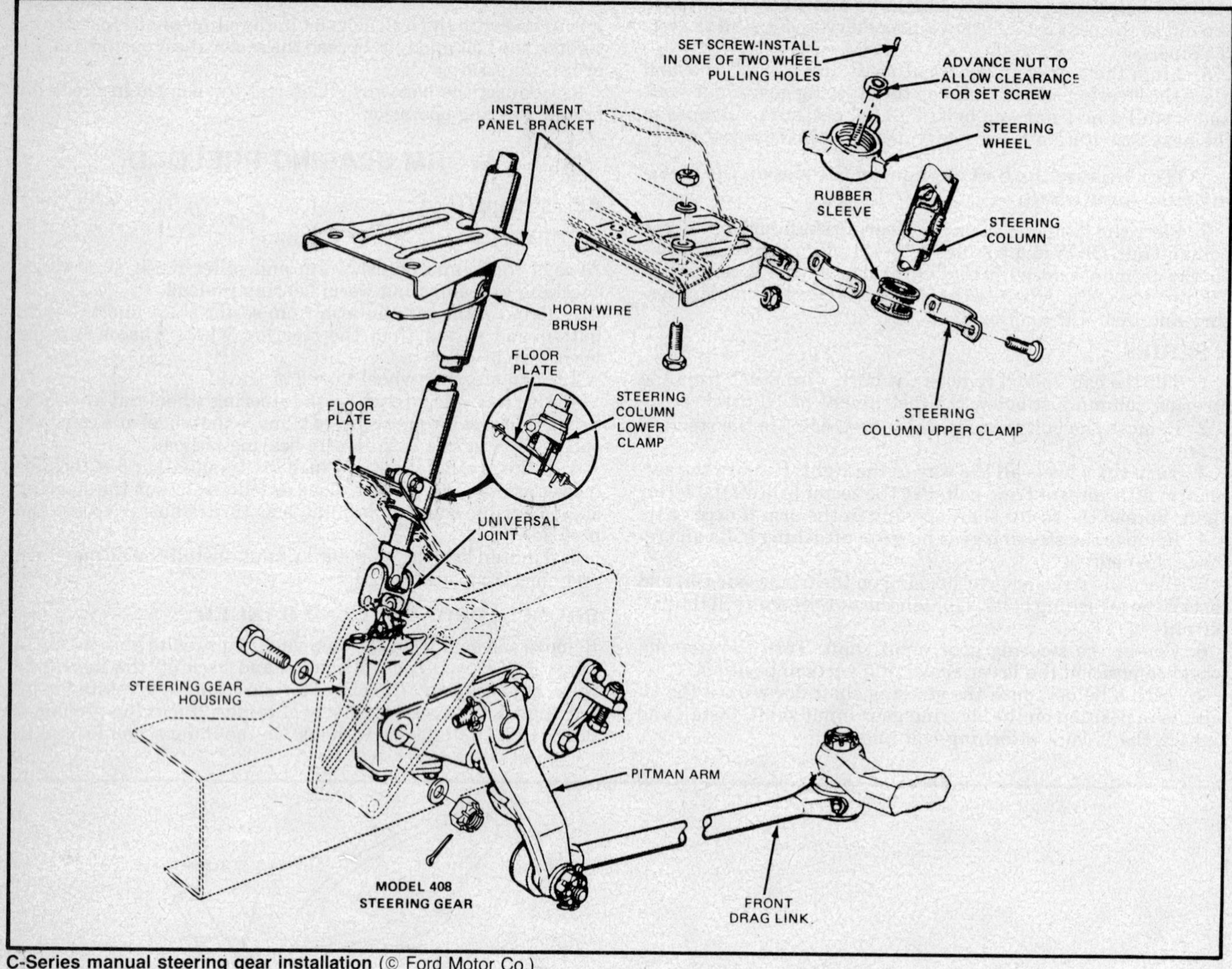

C-Series manual steering gear installation (© Ford Motor Co.)

add or remove shims between the worm shaft bearing retainer cover and the steering gear housing until proper preload is obtained.

1980 F, B, L, C, 600–9000 models

Remove the steering gear and use a 12-point socket and torque wrench on the lower steering serrated shaft to measure preload at a constant speed rotation. If bearing preload is not within 9–11 inch lbs. (C-series) or 5–9 inch lbs. (F-series), add or remove gasket shims between the worm shaft bearing retainer and the gear housing. Adjust the worm and roller mesh preload. Install steering gear in vehicle.

ALL MODELS 600–8000 1981 AND LATER

NOTE: The steering gear, may on certain vehicle installations be checked and adjusted while installed on the vehicle. However, it is recommended that all steering gear preload adjustments be performed with the gear removed from the vehicle.

1. Remove the steering gear from the vehicle.
2. Position a twelve point socket on the lower steering shaft serrations. Install an inch pound torque wrench to the socket and measure the lowest torque required to turn the steering gear at a constant speed.
3. If the measurement is not within specification, 6–11 inch lbs. for the 378 gear, 9–14 inch lbs. for the 408 gear and 9–16 inch lbs. for the 504 gear, then the worm bearing preload must be adjusted.
4. Drain the steering gear lubricant.
5. Remove the worm cover bolts. Remove the worm cover.
6. Remove one shim, and note its position within the steering gear assembly. The size of the shim removed will determine the amount of lash. Remove the thinner shims first to avoid brinelling the bearing raceways.
7. Replacement shims are available in five sizes. They are; 0.002, 0.003, 0.005, 0.0075 and 0.010 inch.
8. When reassembling the unit rubber shims, if applicable, must be installed with the rubber side against the machined surface in the gear housing worm cover.
9. Torque the worm cover bolts to 18–22 ft. lbs. for the Ross 378 steering gear, 45–55 ft. lbs. for the Ross 504 steering gear, and 24–35 ft. lbs. for the Ross 408 steering gear.
10. Recheck the preload, repeat the procedure using different shims if the adjustment is not within specification.
11. Adjust the worm and roller mesh preload.
12. Install the steering gear.

WORM AND ROLLER MESH

Adjustment

Always check and adjust worm bearing preload before making the mesh adjustment.

1. Remove the steering gear from the vehicle if required to gain access to the adjusting screws.
2. Measure the torque required to move the gear through middle (straight-ahead) position with a torque wrench on the input shaft. The highest reading is used. If it is not 24–29 inch lbs. (C-series), 14–22 inch lbs. (F-500–750) or 12–21 inch lbs. (Bronco), loosen locknut and turn adjusting screw until correct mesh load is obtained. Tighten locknut.
3. Recheck mesh load, install steering gear in vehicle and fill gear with lubricant.

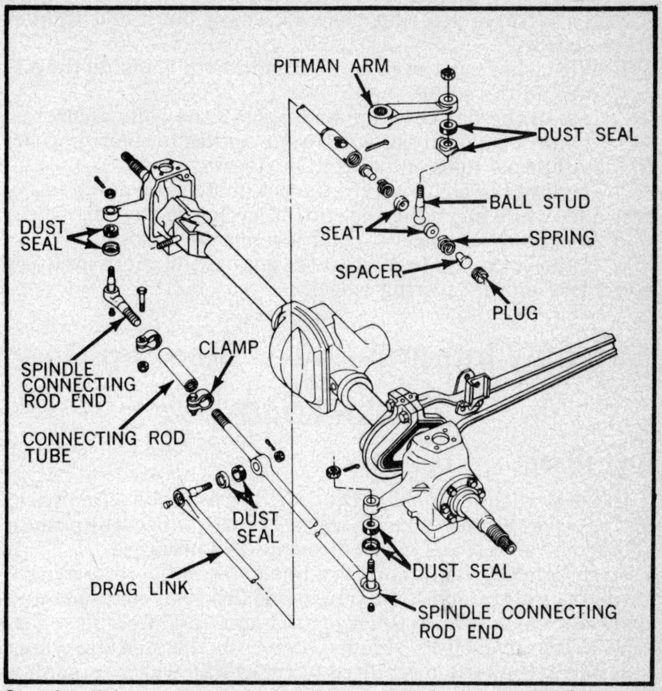

STEERING WORM AND SECTOR

Adjustment

1. Remove the steering gear from the vehicle, if required to gain access to the adjusting screws.
2. Tighten the worm bearing adjuster plug until all end play is removed. Loosen it $1/4$ turn.
3. Using a socket on an in. lb. torque wrench, turn the worm shaft full right and back $1/2$ turn.
4. Tighten the adjuster plug until 5–8 inch lbs. is reached. Tighten the locknut to 85 ft. lbs.
5. Turn the worm shaft from stop to stop, counting the number of turns. Turn the shaft back exactly half the number of turns to the center position.
6. Turn the sector shaft adjuster screw clockwise to remove all lash between the ball nut and sector teeth. Tighten the locknut.

Steering linkage—F-100 and (4 × 4) Bronco (© Ford Motor Co.)

7. Using a socket and inch lb. torque wrench, note the highest reading required to rotate the gear through the center position, which should be 16 inch lb.
8. If necessary, adjust the sector shaft adjuster screw to obtain the proper torque and recheck it.
9. Install steering gear, if removed.

POWER STEERING GEAR

For power steering gear overhaul procedures, see the General Repair Section.

Ford Integral Power Steering Gear

STEERING GEAR MESHLOAD

Adjustment

1. Make sure that the steering column is correctly aligned.
2. Disconnect the steering linkage from the pitman arm on the steering gear. Remove the horn pad.
3. Disconnect the fluid reservoir return line and cap the reservoir return line tube. Place the end of the return line in a clean container and turn the steering wheel back and forth several times to empty the steering gear.
4. Turn the steering wheel nut with an inch pound torque wrench slowly. Find the torque required at $1/2$ turn off right and left stops, $1/2$ turn off center both right and left, and over-center (full turn). The over-center torque should be 4–6 inch lbs. more than the end readings, but the total over-center torque must not exceed 14 inch lbs.
5. To correct, back off the pitman shaft adjuster all the way, then back in $1/2$ turn. Recheck the over-center torque. Loosen the locknut and tighten the sector shaft adjusting screw until the over-center torque reads 4–6 inch lbs. higher, but doesn't exceed 14 inch lbs. Tighten the adjusting screw locknut and recheck.
6. Refill the system with the fluid specified. Bleed the system of air by turning the steering wheel all the way to the right and left several times with the engine warmed up. Do not hold the steering against the stops or pump damage will result.

Removal and Installation

1. Disconnect pressure and return lines from the steering gear, being sure to tag them for identification. Plug lines and ports.
2. Remove brake lines attached to bracket on the steering gear.
3. Remove the two bolts that secure the flex coupling to the steering gear and to the column steering shaft assembly.
4. Raise and support the vehicle safely.
5. Remove the pitman arm from the sector shaft, using a puller if necessary.
6. If vehicle has a standard transmission, remove the clutch release lever retracting spring.
7. Remove the steering gear attaching bolts and steering gear, working the steering gear free of the flex coupling.
8. To install, slide the flex coupling into place on the bottom of the steering shaft.
9. Set the steering wheel so that the spokes are horizontal and center the steering gear input shaft.
10. Slide the steering gear input shaft into the flex coupling.

Install the three steering gear attaching bolts and tighten them securely.

11. With wheels in the straight ahead position, install the pitman arm on the sector shaft.
12. Install the flex coupling and tighten the bolts securely.
13. Connect fluid pressure and return lines to steering gear. Reinstall brake lines on bracket on steering gear.
14. Remove the coil wire, fill the power steering pump reservoir and, while engaging the starter, cycle the steering wheel to distribute the fluid. Add fluid if reservoir is not full.
15. Connect the coil wire, start the engine and check for leaks while cycling the steering wheel.

Saginaw Integral Power Steering Gear

MESH LOAD

Adjustment

1. On Econolines, remove the drag link from the pitman arm and remove the horn pad. On all others, disconnect the pitman arm from the sector shaft and remove the horn pad.
2. Disconnect the fluid return line and cap the reservoir return line. Put the end of the return line in a clear container and cycle the wheel several times to discharge fluid from the gear.
3. Using an inch lb. torque wrench on the steering wheel nut, check the torque required to rotate the wheel through a 180° arc on each side of center. The new gear over center torque should be 4–8 inch lbs. greater than the end readings but the total should not exceed 18 inch lbs. Used gears should be 4–5 inch lbs. greater than the end reading, but should not exceed 14 inch lbs.
4. To adjust, make sure the pitman shaft over center adjusting screw is backed all the way out. Turn it in ½ turn.
5. Rotate the shaft from one stop to the other. Count the number of turns and locate the center position. Check the combined preload on the ball and thrust bearing by rotating the shaft through the center of travel. Note the highest reading.
6. Tighten the adjusting screw until the torque wrench reads 3–6 inch lbs., higher than the reading in Step 5. The total should not exceed 14 inch lbs.
7. Hold the adjusting screw and tighten the locknut to 35 ft. lbs.

Removal and Installation

ALL, EXCEPT ECONOLINE

1. Disconnect the pressure and return lines and plug the lines and ports.
2. Raise and support the vehicle safely.
3. Disconnect and remove the pitman arm.
4. Unbolt the gear from the frame rails and lower the vehicle.
5. Remove the pinch-bolt from the flange and insulator.
6. Unbolt the horn and hold it outward.
7. Remove the attaching bolts and remove the gear from the vehicle, with the shaft and joint assemblies as a unit.
8. Remove the pinch-bolt from the shaft and joint.
9. Remove the shaft and joint from the gear.
10. Installation is the reverse of removal.
11. Remove the coil wire, fill the power steering pump reservoir and, while engaging the starter, cycle the steering wheel to distribute the fluid. Add fluid if reservoir is not full.
12. Connect the coil wire, start the engine and check for leaks while cycling the steering wheel.

ECONOLINE

1. Disconnect the pressure and return lines and plug the ports.

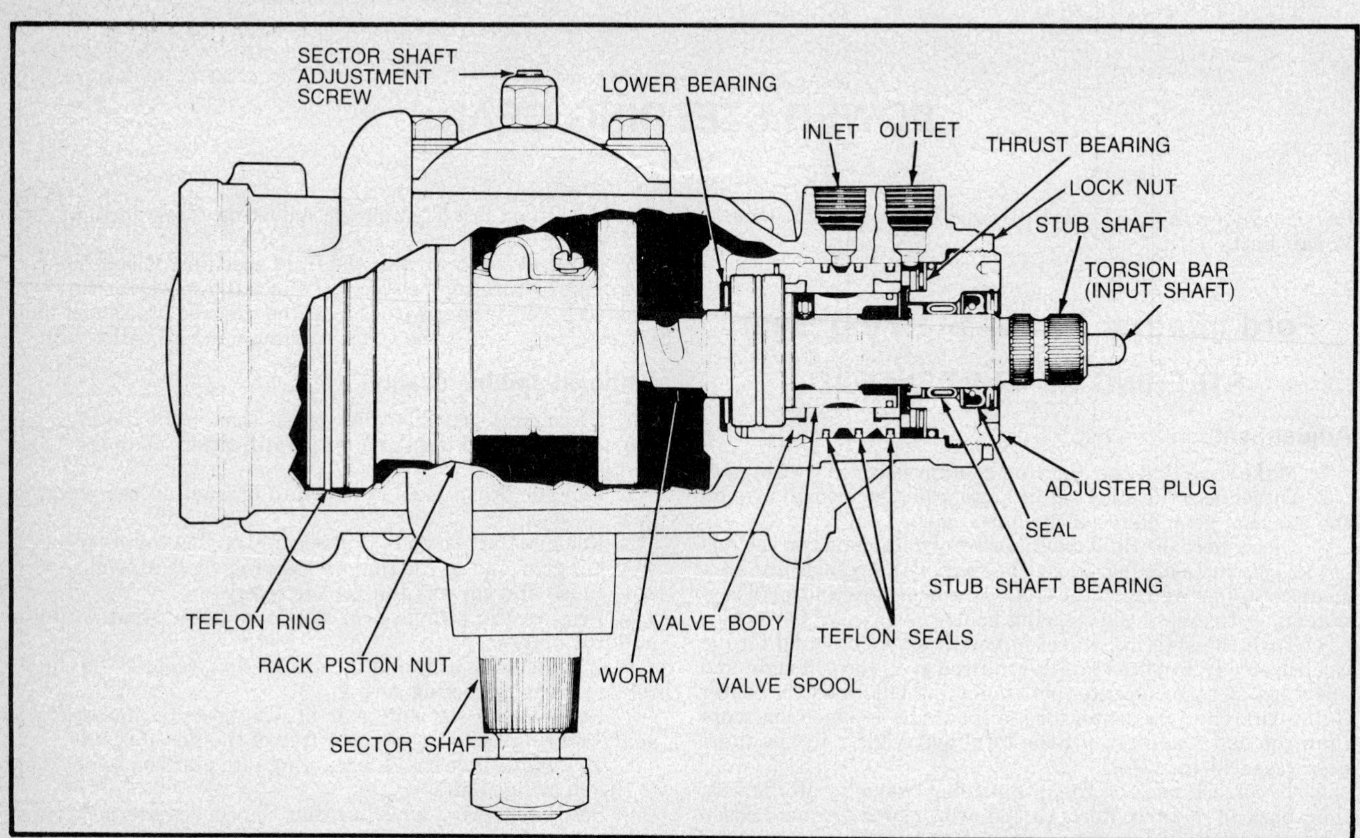

Ford integral power steering gear (© Ford Motor Co.)

2. Raise and support the vehicle safely. Remove the drag link from the pitman arm.
3. Unbolt the flex coupling from the steering shaft.
4. Support the gear and remove the attaching bolts.
5. Remove the pinch bolt from the flex coupling and remove the coupling from the gear.
6. Remove the pitman arm from the sector shaft.
7. Installation is the reverse of removal.
8. Remove the coil wire, fill the power steering pump reservoir and, while engaging the starter, cycle the steering wheel to distribute the fluid. Add fluid if reservoir is not full.
9. Connect the coil wire, start the engine and check for leaks while cycling the steering wheel.

Ross HF-54, HF-64 and HFB-64 Integral Power Steering Gears

Removal and Installation

1. Position a drain pan under the steering gear and disconnect the pressure line from the gear, the return line from the gear and the turning hoses if so equipped. Mark all lines for identification.
2. Remove the pitman arm from the sector shaft.
3. Disconnect the universal joint from the input shaft of the gear, sliding it up and off the shaft.
4. Remove the steering gear attaching bolts and remove the gear.

NOTE: ON some vehicles equipped with manual transmission, it may be necessary that the front engine mount must be loosened. Remove the exhaust pipes shields and loosen the exhaust pipes. Remove the clutch spring bracket, from under the left side pipe. Unbolt the transmission mount and jack the transmission. Remove the mounting pads. Unbolt the clutch bracket from the steering gear. Unbolt the gear from the frame. Remove the floor board covering the gearshift and brake levers. Move the engine and transmission to the right and remove the gear.

5. To install, first position gear in vehicle and install and tighten attaching bolts.
6. Connect universal joint to the steering gear input shaft.
7. Install pitman arm on the sector shaft.
8. Connect all hydraulic lines in their original locations.
9. Fill power steering hydraulic system, start engine and check for leaks.

Ross HFB-52 Integral Power Steering Gear

Removal and Installation

1. Place a drain pan under the steering gear. Disconnect the power steering pressure line at the gear and the return line at the gear. If equipped, disconnect the turning hoses.
2. Remove the cotter pin, bolt and nut (or castellated nut and cotter pin) holding the pitman arm to the sector shaft, and remove the pitman arm from the sector shaft.
3. Remove the U-joint yoke and input shaft bolt and nut (or castellated nut and cotter pin). Mark for re-installation.
4. Remove the bolts and nuts holding the steering gear or the steering gear bracket to the frame side rail. Remove the unit from the vehicle.
5. To install, place the gear (or gear and bracket) on the side rail. Install the bolts, nuts and lock straps (if equipped). Advance the nuts to the next castellation, if necessary, and install the cotter pins.
6. Continue the installation in the reverse order of the removal.

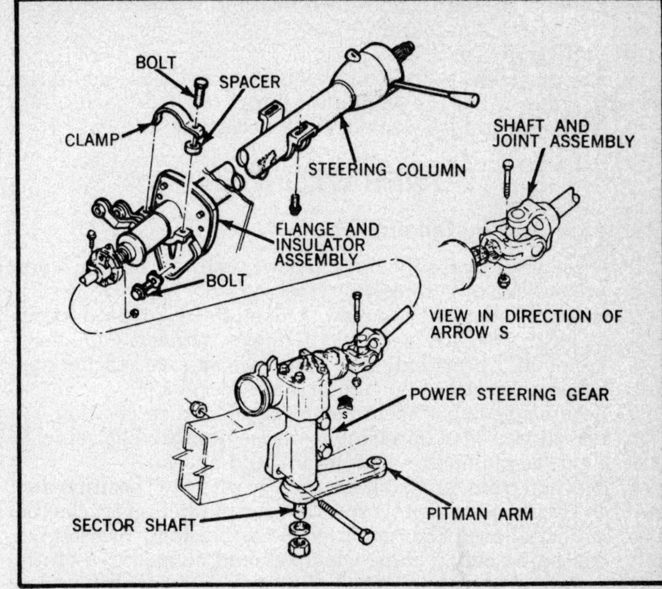

Bronco power steering gear installation (© Ford Motor Co.)

7. Fill the power steering pump reservoir with fluid. Start the engine, turn the steering wheel from left to right, and check for fluid leaks.

LINKAGE ASSIST

Removal and Installation

NOTE: See Power Steering in the Unit Repair section for control valve overhaul and service procedures.

1. Disconnect pressure and return hoses at valve assembly.
2. Cap hoses and connections at valve assembly. Fasten hoses so that ends are above fluid level in reservoir and tag them for reinstallation identification.
3. Disconnect ball ends at steering arm and steering knuckle arm and remove control valve and drag link assembly.
4. To install, connect control valve sliding sleeve end at steering arm and install nut and cotter pin.
5. Connect drag link end to steering knuckle arm and install nut and cotter pin.

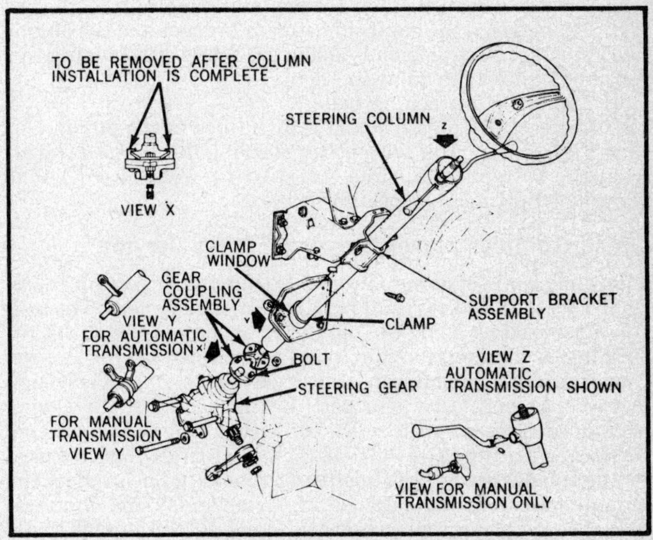

Econoline power steering gear installation (© Ford Motor Co.)

6. Connect pressure and return hydraulic lines at valve assembly, tightening securely.
7. Refill pump reservoir.
8. Bleed system by turning steering wheel back and forth several times while the engine is idling.
9. Recheck fluid level and refill if necessary.

POWER CYLINDER

Removal And Installation

1. Disconnect hydraulic lines at power cylinder and cap ends and connections at cylinder.
2. Remove cotter pin and nut at ball studs (and tie rod clamp U-bolts on lightweight vehicles). Remove cylinder.
3. To install, insert ball stud into place on axle bracket and install nut and cotter pin, tighten nut securely.
4. Rotate steering wheel to extreme right turn position.
5. Install tie rod clamp loosely (on medium weight vehicles loosen tie rod clamp and install ball stud and nut).
6. Position cylinder piston rod in fully retracted position and tighten U-bolt clamps on tie rod. On medium weight trucks the ball stud will have to be connected to tie rod clamp bracket before tightening clamp bolts. Clamp should be mounted on tie rod at a 20° angle to the vertical. Nuts on U-bolts are torqued to 40 ft. lbs.
7. Connect hydraulic lines to power cylinder in their original position.
8. Bleed system by turning the steering wheel back and forth several times with the engine idling.

Power Steering Pump

Removal and Installation

LIGHT DUTY VEHICLES, ALL EXCEPT CII PUMP

1. Disconnect the pressure and return lines from the pump and plug them to prevent loss of fluid or entrance of dirt into the system.
2. Loosen the belt tension adjusting bolt all the way.
3. Remove the bolts attaching the pump mounting bracket to the air conditioning bracket (if equipped).
4. Remove the pump, mounting bracket, and pulley asssembly.
5. Install the pump, bracket and pulley assembly and loosely attach the bolts that secure the pump mounting bracket to the air conditioning bracket (if equipped).
6. Install the drive belts on the pulley.
7. Loosely install the belt tension adjusting nut.
8. Pry between the pump adjustment bracket and the engine block until correct tension is achieved. While still holding this tension, tighten the adjusting bolt.
9. Tighten all attaching bolts.
10. Connect the pressure and return lines to the pump.
11. Fill the reservoir with power steering fluid. Bleed the air from the system by turning the steering wheel from left to right several times. Inspect for leaks.

Quick Connect Power Steering Fitting Service

The quick connect power steering fitting, under certain conditions may leak and/or result in improper engagement. The leak can be caused by a cut O-ring, imperfections in the outlet fitting inside diameter, or improperly machined O-ring groove. Improper engagement can be caused by an improperly machined tube end, tube gear port. If a leak occurs, the O-ring should be replaced with quick connect O-rings (3/8 tube end: 388749-S; 5/16 tube end; 388748-S). The O-rings that are used on the tube-O power steering fitting should not be used on the quick connect fitting because of dimensional and material changes. If O-ring replacement does not solve the leak problem, outlet fitting replacement and, lastly, hose replacement should be made. If improper engagement occurs due to a missing or bent snap ring, or improperly machined tube nut, it may be repaired with a service snap ring kit (kit includes a new tube nut). The system should then be properly filled, the engine started, and the steering wheel cycled from lock-to-lock to test for positive engagement. If the hose assembly still does not engage, replace the entire hose assembly. Quick connect hose assemblies for service have tube nuts, snap rings, and O-rings already attached. When the quick connect tube nut is tightened or loosened, a tube nut wrench, not an open end wrench, is recommended. An open end wrench may result in tube nut deformation under excessive torque conditions. Care must be taken not to overtighten the tube nut. Tighten to 10–15 ft. lbs. Swivel and/or end play of the quick connect fittings is normal, and does not indicate an undertightened fitting.

CII PUMP

NOTE: The CII pump is equipped with a fiberglas reservoir and can be identified by the reservoir. Never pry against the fiberglas, as damage will occur. The 3.8L V-6 with a serpentine belt driving driving the power steering pump uses a separate idler pulley on a slider-type bracket for belt tension adjustment. To adjust or remove the belt tension, loosen the bolts in the slider slots and tighten the adjusting belt as required to obtain the correct belt tension.

1. To remove the power steering fluid from the pump reservoir, disconnect the fluid return hose at the reservoir and drain the fluid into a container. Remove the pressure hose from the pump.
2. Remove the bolts from the pump adjustment bracket. Loosen the pump sufficiently to remove the belt off the pulley. Remove the pump (still attached to the adjustment bracket) from the support bracket.
3. Remove the pulley from the pump if required.
4. Remove the bolts attaching the adjustment bracket to the pump and remove the pump.
5. Place the adjustment bracket on the pump. Install and tighten the bolts to specification.
6. Install the pulley on the pump if removed.
7. Place the pump with adjustment bracket and pulley on the support bracket. Install the bolts connecting the support bracket to the adjustment bracket.
8. Place the belt on the pulley and adjust belt tension. Tighten bolts on adjustment bracket.
9. Install the pressure hose to the pump fitting.
10. Connect the return hose to the pump, and tighten the clamp.
11. Fill the reservoir with specified power steering fluid, start the engine and turn the steering wheel from stop to stop to remove air from the system.
12. Check for leaks and recheck the fluid level. Add fluid if necessary.

MEDIUM AND HEAVY DUTY VEHICLES

1. Disconnect the negative battery cable.
2. Drain as much fluid from the pump as possible, using a suction gun.
3. Disconnect all hoses from the power steering pump. Plug the openings to prevent dirt from entering the system and fluid from leaking out.
4. On C series vehicles, remove the pump from the engine and rest it on the frame before disconnecting the hoses.
5. On 8.2 liter diesel engine equipped vehicles, loosen the adjusting bracket bolt and the pivot bolt to remove the belts from the pump pulley. Remove the adjusting and pivot bolts, and remove the complete pump assembly.
6. On gasoline engine equipped vehicles, loosen the four nuts attaching the pump bracket to the engine bracket. Loosen the nut on the adjusting stud and remove the belts from the

pump pulley. Remove four nuts and remove the complete pump assembly.

7. On Cat 3208 engine equipped C series vehicles, loosen the three bolts at the bracket attachment to the engine. Pivot the pump to loosen the belts from the pump pulley. Remove the three bolts from the engine and remove the complete pump assembly.

8. On Cat 3208 engine equipped F and B series vehicles, loosen the three bolts at the bracket adjusting slots, and loosen the adjusting bolt to remove the belts from the pump pulley. Remove the three bolts at the adjusting slots and remove the complete pump assembly.

9. Installation is the reverse of removal. Adjust the pump belt tension to 110–140 ft. lbs. on new belts and 90–120 ft. lbs. for a used belt.

10. Connect all hoses. Fill the reservoir with the proper fluid. Bleed the system and check for leaks.

Bleeding System

1. Check the power steering reservoir fluid level and fill as necessary.

2. Run the engine until it reaches normal operating temperature.

3. Turn the steering wheel all the way to the left and right several times. Do not hold the wheel in the far left or right position for more than five seconds as damage to the pump may occur.

4. On models with automatic bleeding, run the engine at idle while loosening the manual bleed screw at the gear. Loosen the screw one turn. Rotate the steering wheel to the full left and right stops until clear clean fluid is discharged at the bleed screw. Tighten the bleed screw.

5. Stop the engine. Recheck the fluid level and adjust as required.

Steering Linkage Connecting Rods

VANS AND 2WD PICKUPS

Removal and Installation

Replace the drag link if a ball stud is excessively loose or if the drag link is bent. Do not attempt to straighten a drag link. Replace the connecting rod if the ball stud is excessively loose, if the connecting rod is bent or if the threads are stripped. Do not attempt to straighten connecting rod. After installing a connecting rod or adjusting toe-in check to insure that the adjustment sleeve clamps are correctly positioned on the F and E100 and F and E150 and to insure that the clamp stop is correctly installed on the F and E250 and F and E350.

1. Remove the cotter pins and nuts from the drag link, ball studs and from the right connecting rod ball stud.

2. Remove the right connecting rod ball stud from the drag link.

3. Remove the drag link ball studs from the spindle and the Pitman arm.

4. Position the new drag link, ball studs in the spindle, and Pitman arm and install nuts.

5. Position the right connecting rod ball stud in the drag link and install nut.

6. Tighten the nuts to 50–75 ft. lbs. and install the cotter pins.

7. Pemove the cotter pin and nut from the connecting rod.

8. Kemove the ball stud from the mating part.

9. Loosen the clamp bolt and turn the rod out of the adjustment sleeve. Count the number of turns for approximate position when installing.

10. Lubricate the threads of the new connecting rod, and turn it into the adjustment sleeve to about the same distance the old rods were installed. This will provide an approximate toe-in setting. Position the connecting rod ball studs in the spindle arms.

11. Install the nuts on to the connecting rod ball studs, tighten the nut to 50–75 ft. lbs. and install the cotter pin.

12. Check the toe-in and adjust, if necessary. After checking or adjusting toe-in, center the adjustment sleeve clamps between the locating nibs, position the clamps and tighten the nuts to 29–41 ft. lbs.

4WD PICKUPS

Removal abd Installation

1. Raise and support the vehicle safely. Disconnect the drag link from the spindle connecting rod end.

2. Disconnect the right spindle connecting rod end from the right spindle arm.

3. Disconnect the left spindle connecting rod ends from the left spindle arm and remove the spindle connecting rod ends from the vehicle.

4. Place the connecting rod ends in a vise and loosen the connecting rod tube clamps.

5. Remove the short (right) rod end from the connecting rod tube and remove the tube from the long (left) connecting rod end.

6. Clean and oil the threads on all the parts to be reused.

7. Install the connecting rod tube and clamps on the left spindle connecting rod end. Don't tighten the clamps yet.

8. Install the right connecting rod end in the tube and remove the assembly from the vise.

9. Install new dust seals on the left spindle connecting rod end and position the end on the left spindle arm.

10. Install the connecting rod end attaching nut, tighten it, and install the cotter pin.

11. Install new dust seals on the right spindle connecting rod end and position the end on the right spindle arm. Install the attaching nut, tighten it, and install the cotter pin.

12. Install new seals on the drag link ball stud and position the drag link on the spindle connecting rod end. Install the attaching nut, tighten it, and install the cotter pin.

13. Lubricate the spindle connecting rod ends and drag link.

14. Lower the vehicle and check and adjust the toe-in setting. Tighten the connecting rod clamps after adjusting the toe-in.

BRONCO

Removal and Installation

1. Remove the cotter pins and nuts from the drag link, ball studs and from the right connecting rod ball studs.

2. Remove the right connecting rod ball stud from the right spindle assembly and pitman arm.

3. Remove the drag link ball studs from the spindle and the connecting rod assembly.

4. Loosen the clamp bolt and turn the rod out of the adjustment sleeve.

5. Lubricate the threads of the new connecting rod, and turn it into the adjustment sleeve to about the same distance the old rods were installed. This will provide an approximate toe-in setting. Position the connecting rod ball studs in the spindle arms.

6. Position the new drag link, ball studs in the spindle, and connecting rod assembly and install nuts.

7. Position the right connecting rod ball stud in the drag link and install nut.

8. Tighten all the nuts to 50–75 ft. lbs. and install the cotter pins.

9. Remove the cotter pin and nut from the left connecting rod.

10. Install the nuts on the connecting rod ball studs, tighten the nut to 50–75 ft. lbs. and install the cotter pin.

11. Check the toe-in and adjust, if necessary. After checking or adjusting toe-in, center the adjustment sleeve clamps between the locating nibbs, position the clamps and tighten the nuts to 29–41 ft. lbs.

CLUTCH

9.37 IN., 10 IN., 11 IN., 11.5 IN., 12 IN. AND 13 IN. SINGLE DISC CLUTCH ASSEMBLIES

Removal and Installation

1. Disconnect the release lever retracting spring and push-rod at the lever.
2. If so equipped, remove the slave cylinder attaching bolts.
3. Remove the transmission.
4. If there is no dust cover on the flywheel housing remove the starter. Remove the release lever and bearing and remove the housing.
5. If the flywheel housing has a dust cover, remove it with the housing. Remove the release lever and bearing from the clutch housing. Mark the pressure plate and cover assembly and the flywheel, so that the parts can be reinstalled in the same position.
6. Loosen the pressure plate attaching bolts evenly until the springs are loose then remove the bolts, pressure plate assembly and clutch disc. Do not remove the pilot bushing unless it is to be replaced.
7. To install, position the disc on the flywheel and install a pilot tool or spare transmission spline shaft.
8. Install the pressure plate assembly over the aligning tool and align the marks made during removal. Install the retaining bolts, tightening securely.
9. Remove pilot tool and apply a light coat of lithium-base grease to the hub splines of the clutch disc.
10. Apply lithium-base grease to the sides of the driving lugs.
11. Position throwout bearing and bearing hub on the release lever and install release lever on the trunnion in the flywheel housing.

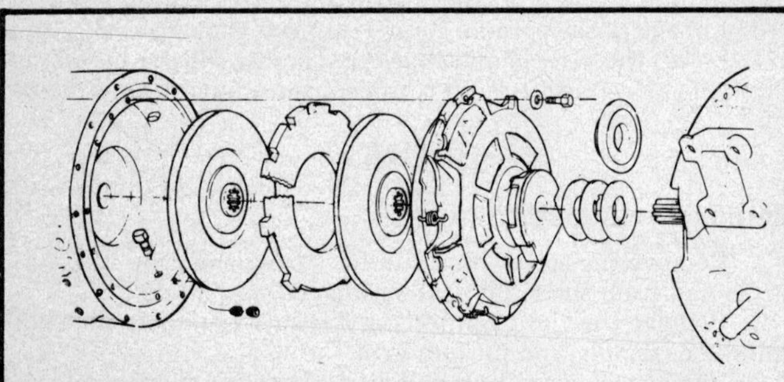

Exploded view of 14 and 15½ double disc clutch, typical installation (© Ford Motor Co.)

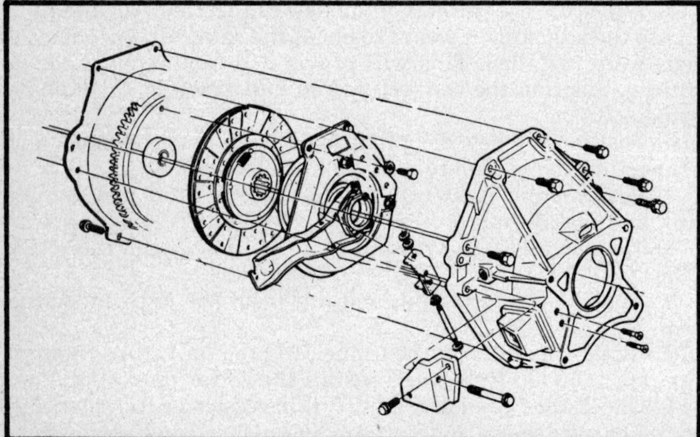

Exploded view of typical single plate clutch installation (© Ford Motor Co.)

12. Apply a light film of lithium-base grease to the release lever fingers and to the lever trunnion or fulcrum. Fill the angular groove of the release bearing hub with grease.
13. If removed, install the flywheel housing, tightening bolts securely.
14. Install the starter motor if it was removed.
15. Apply a light film of lithium-base grease to the transmission front bearing retainer and install the transmission assembly on the clutch housing, tightening attaching bolts securely.
16. Install the slave cylinder, if applicable.
17. Adjust the clutch linkage and install the clutch housing dust cover.

14 IN. SINGLE PLATE CLUTCH ASSEMBLY

Removal and Installation

1. Disconnect the clutch pedal assist spring, removing the left-hand exhaust pipe from the manifold if necessary.
2. Disconnect the release lever retracting spring and remove the slave cylinder attaching bolts, if applicable.
3. Remove the transmission.
4. Insert two $^3/_4$ in. wood blocks between the throwout bearing housing and the rear surface of the pressure plate assembly.
5. Remove the clutch to flywheel bolts and remove the flywheel ring and pressure plate assembly. Remove the clutch disc.
6. To install, position the clutch disc and pressure plate assembly on the flywheel and start the bolts.

NOTE: The long hub of the clutch disc faces the rear.

7. Insert a spare transmission splined shaft or a disc aligning tool through the disc and into the pilot bushing. Tighten pressure plate bolts evenly and securely.
8. Remove the wood blocks and aligning tool or shaft.
9. Install the transmission.
10. Install the clutch slave cylinder.
11. Connect the release lever retracting spring and exhaust pipe.
12. Connect the clutch pedal assist spring.
13. Check internal clutch adjustment, linkage adjustment and correct if necessary.

14 IN. SINGLE CERAMIC DISC

Removal and Installation

1. Disconnect the clutch pedal assist spring. If necessary, remove the left-hand muffler pipe.
2. Disconnect the release lever retracting spring. If so equipped, remove the bolts that attach the slave cylinder to the clutch housing, and remove the slave cylinder.
3. Remove the transmission. Pull the transmission straight out until it is clear of the clutch assembly. An unsupported, partially removed or installed transmission can spring or distort the clutch disc.
4. Remove the two clutch brake discs and one washer from the transmission input shaft.
5. Insert two $^3/_4$ in. wood blocks between the release bearing housing and the rear surface of the pressure plate assembly.
6. Remove the clutch-to-flywheel bolts and remove the pressure plate assembly.
7. Remove the clutch disc.
8. To install, place the clutch disc and the pressure plate assembly in position on the flywheel and start but do not tighten the bolts. Make sure the clutch disc is installed with the marking "flywheel side" to the front of the vehicle. Insert the clutch alignment tool, through the disc and into the pilot bearing.

Tighten the pressure plate bolts alternately and evenly to 35–42 ft. lbs.

NOTE: On Dana clutches install the pressure plate with the adjusting ring lock at the bottom for possible readjustment after assembly.

9. Remove the two wood blocks from the release bearing and aligning tool.
10. Position a clutch brake disc, a washer and a clutch brake disc on the transmission input shaft. Make sure the discs and washer are splined to the input shaft.
11. Install the transmission.
12. If so equipped, connect the slave cylinder to the clutch housing.
13. Connect the release lever retracting spring. If removed, connect the left hand muffler pipe.
14. Connect the clutch pedal assist spring. Check the internal clutch adjustment and linkage adjustment and make necessary corrections.

14 IN. DOUBLE CERAMIC DISC

Removal and Installation

1. Disconnect the clutch pedal assist spring. If necessary, remove the left-hand muffler inlet pipe.
2. Disconnect the release lever retracting spring.
3. Remove the transmission. Pull the transmission straight out until it clears the clutch assembly. An unsupported, partially removed or installed transmission can spring or distort the clutch disc.
4. Remove the two clutch brake discs and one washer from the transmission input shaft.
5. Insert two $^3/_4$ in. wood blocks between the release bearing housing and rear surface of the pressure plate assembly.
6. Remove the cover plate to flywheel bolts and remove the cover.
7. Remove the rear clutch disc.
8. On Lipe clutches, remove the clutch plate, front clutch disc and adapter ring.
9. On Dana clutches, remove the mounting straps from the adaptor rings, and remove the clutch plate, front clutch disc and adapter ring.
10. To install, position the adapter ring on the flywheel. Install the two headless bolts 180° apart from each other in a mounting boss next to the cover plate slot in the adapter ring. The two headless bolts will act as a guide during installation.
11. Position the front clutch disc in the adapter ring. Make sure the markings 'Flywheel Side' are facing the front of the vehicle.
12. Install the clutch plate, making sure the drive lugs are engaged in the slots in the adapter ring.
13. Position the rear clutch disc against the clutch plate. Make sure the makings 'Pressure Plate Side' face the rear of the vehicle.
14. Insert clutch alignment tool, through the two clutch discs and drive plate into the pilot bearing.
15. On Dana clutches, install the mounting straps. Make sure the straps retain the drive plate lugs to the adapter ring.
16. Install the cover over the alignment tool and in position on the headless bolt guides. Remove the headless bolts and install but do not tighten the bolts retaining the cover to the flywheel. Tighten the bolts alternately and evenly to 35–42 ft. lbs.

NOTE: On Dana clutches, install the cover with the adjusting ring lock at the bottom for possible readjustment after assembly.

17. Remove the two wood blocks from the release bearing housing and cover. Remove the clutch alignment tool.
18. Install a clutch brake disc, a washer and a clutch brake disc on the transmission input shaft. Make sure the discs and washer are splined to the input shaft.
19. Install the transmission.
20. Connect the release lever retracting spring. If removed, connect the left-hand muffler inlet pipe.
21. Connect the clutch pedal assist spring. Check the internal clutch adjustments and linkage adjustment and make necessary adjustments.

13 IN. DOUBLE DISC CLUTCH

Removal and Installation

1. Disconnect the clutch pedal reacting spring.
2. Remove the muffler inlet pipe if necessary.
3. Remove the bolts that attach the slave cylinder to the clutch housing.
4. Disconnect the slave cylinder push rod at the release lever. Disconnect the release lever retaining spring.
5. Remove the transmission.
6. Remove the dust cover from the clutch housing.
7. Remove the clutch release bearing and hub from the release lever.
8. Mark the center drive plate, pressure plate, cover assembly, and flywheel so that the parts may be installed in the same relative position.
9. Loosen the pressure plate and cover attaching bolts evenly until the pressure plate springs are expanded. Remove the bolts.
10. Remove the pressure plate and cover, the discs, and the intermediate pressure plate through the opening in the bottom of the clutch housing.
11. Remove the pilot bearing only if replacement is necessary.
12. Install the pilot bearing if it was removed.
13. Position the discs and second pressure plate on the flywheel so that the pilot tool can enter the clutch pilot bushing. When installing the original pressure plate and cover assembly, align the assembly and flywheel according to the match marks made during the removal operations. The long end of the clutch disc hub must face the rear of the transmission. The front (flywheel) side of the center drive plate is stamped "flywheel side" on one of the lugs.
14. Position the clutch discs, center drive plate, pressure plate and cover assembly on the flywheel and install the retaining bolts that fasten the assembly to the flywheel. Tighten the bolts to specification. Remove the clutch pilot tool.
15. Position the clutch release bearing and hub on the release lever.
16. Install the transmission assembly on the clutch housing.
17. Install the slave cylinder and tighten the bolts.
18. Adjust the slave cylinder push rod. Connect the release lever reacting spring and (if removed) install the muffler left inlet pipe. Connect the clutch pedal reacting spring.
19. Lubricate the release bearing through the grease fitting with $^1/_2$ oz. of the specified lubricant.
20. Install the clutch housing dust cover.

14 IN. AND 15.5 IN. DOUBLE DISC

Removal and Installation

1. Disconnect the clutch pedal assist spring. If necessary, remove the left muffler inlet pipe.
2. Disconnect the release lever reacting spring. Remove the bolts that attach the slave cylinder. Remove the slave cylinder.
3. Remove the transmission.
4. Insert two $^3/_4$ in. wood blocks between the release bearing housing and the rear surface of the pressure plate assembly.
5. Remove the clutch-to-flywheel bolts and remove the flywheel ring and pressure plate assembly.
6. Remove the rear disc, intermediate plate, and the front disc from the engine. If necessary, remove the clutch drive pin retaining set screw and remove the four intermediate pressure plate drive pins.

7. Install the pressure plate drive pins in the flywheel if they were removed. Make sure they are a press fit. Oversize pins are available for service. Install the intermediate pressure plate and check the clearance between the pin heads and slots in the pressure plate. A clearance of 0.006–0.010 in. is required, measured on the same side of all pins. Replace the pins or plate if necessary. Remove the intermediate plate, and using an adjustable square to maintain pin head alignment, install the pin set screws.

8. Place the front driven disc (shorter hub than rear disc) in the flywheel with the hub facing the rear. Set the intermediate pressure plate in the flywheel, aligning the slots with the pins. The side marked FRONT should face the engine. Position the read driven plate in the flywheel with the long end of the splined hub toward the rear. Insert the clutch disc aligning tool through the two discs and into the pilot bushing. Place the main (rear) pressure plate and flywheel ring assembly in position and start the bolts. Tighten the pressure plate bolts evenly and tighten them to specification.

9. Remove the wood blocks from the release bearing housing and pressure plate. Remove the spline aligning tool.

10. Install the transmission.

11. If the vehicle is equipped with a slave cylinder, install the slave cylinder on the clutch housing. Connect the release lever reacting spring and the left-hand muffler inlet pipe if it was removed.

12. Connect the clutch pedal assist spring. Check the internal clutch adjustment, and make necessary correction.

Mechanical Clutch Linkage

Adjustment

The clutch pedal free travel is the distance between the clutch pedal in the fully released position and the pedal position at which the clutch release fingers contact the clutch release bearing (this can be felt).

The clutch pedal total travel is the distance between the floor pan and the top of the pedal when the clutch is in the fully released position.

Only the clutch pedal free travel is adjusted. If the pedal free travel is not within $^{11}/_{16}$ in. to 1 $^1/_8$ in., adjust the clutch release rod until correct free travel is obtained.

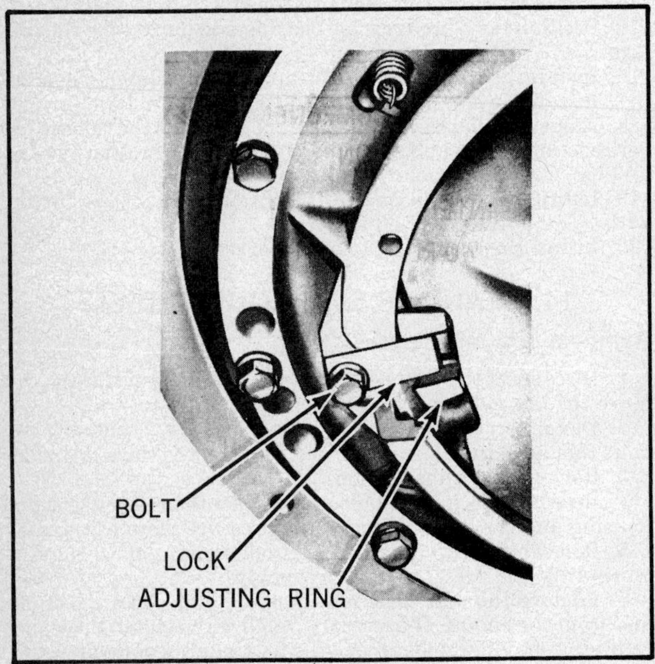

Internal clutch adjustment (© Ford Motor Co.)

ECONOLINE

First the clutch pedal total travel is adjusted. It should be between 7 $^1/_2$ in. and 7 $^3/_4$ in. Adjustment is made by loosening the locknut on the pedal stop eccentric bolt and turning the eccentric bolt until correct total travel is obtained. Tighten locknut.

Check the clutch pedal free travel. It should be 1 $^1/_8$ in. to 1$^3/_8$ in. Adjustment is made at the clutch release rod turnbuckle.

BRONCO, BRONCO II AND RANGER

If the clutch pedal total travel is not within 6 $^{11}/_{16}$ in. or 6 $^3/_4$ in. to 7 in., move the clutch pedal bumper and bracket up or down to obtain required free travel.

Check and adjust pedal free travel. It should be $^3/_4$ in. to 1 $^1/_2$ in. Adjustment is made at the clutch release rod turnbuckle.

F AND N SERIES

Total pedal travel is adjusted at the pedal bumper stop. Pedal free travel is made at the clutch release rod.

F SERIES

1. Measure the clutch pedal free-play by depressing the pedal slowly until the free-play between the release bearing assembly and the pressure plate is removed. Note this measurement. The difference between this measurement and when the pedal is not depressed is the free-play measurement.

2. If the free-play measurement is less than $^3/_4$ in., the clutch linkage must be adjusted.

3. Loosen the two jam nuts on the release rod under the vehicle and back off both nuts several turns.

4. Loosen or tighten the first jam nut (nearest the release lever) against the bullet (rod extension) until a free-play measurement of $^3/_4$ in. to 1 $^1/_2$ in. is obtained. A free-play measurement closer to 1 $^1/_2$ in. is more desirable.

5. When the correct free-play measurement is obtained, hold the first jam nut in position and securely tighten the other nut against the first.

6. Recheck the free-play adjustment.

NOTE: Total pedal travel is fixed and is not adjustable.

HYDRAULIC ACTUATED CLUTCH

NOTE: Before adjusting hydraulic clutch, check the level of fluid in the master cylinder reservoir, filling to within $^1/_2$ in. of the top if necessary. Bleed the hydraulic system as required.

Bleeding

1. Attach a funnel to the bleeder screw of the slave cylinder by means of a transparent bleeder hose. The funnel must be higher than the master cylinder.

2. Pour fluid into the funnel as the system is filling, being careful not to cause bubbles in the fluid. Bleeder screw must be open.

3. Close the bleeder screw when master cylinder reservoir is full.

4. Check the slave cylinder pushrod total travel which should be 1 $^1/_8$ in.

5. The clutch master cylinder relief port must be open in order to bleed the system. Clutch master cylinder pushrod lash of $^1/_4$ in. is required on the P-500 and 5000 series vehicles to permit the conventional type master cylinder piston to return to the piston stop ring and open the relief port. The clutch master cylinder cannot be adjusted on the P-350, 400, 3500 and 4000 series vehicles. In the case of tilt-cab (C-series) master cylinder, the O-ring seal on the end of the pushrod must not seat against the piston. Uncovering of the piston port is accomplished by adjustment of the pushrod to a piston lash of $^1/_4$ in. Forcing the clutch pedal to compress the pedal bumper more than normal by jamming a suitable tool between the pedal pad and the floor insures a complete uncovering of the relief port.

External Adjustment

There are two adjustments for obtaining clutch pedal free travel. The initial pedal free travel should be $^1/_4$ in. for all models. On F, N, NT, and T series vehicles the pedal height is first adjusted to 8 $^1/_{16}$ in. to 8 $^3/_{16}$ in. at the pedal stop. Turn eccentric bolt on pedal to obtain an initial pedal free travel of $^3/_{16}$ in. to $^3/_8$ in. Remove retracting spring, push slave cylinder pushrod as far forward as possible and release lever back until it contacts the release fingers. Adjust the nut on the pushrod for a clearance of $^1/_4$ in. between pushrod adjusting nut and release lever. A total pedal travel of at least 2 in. should result.

On P and C Series vehicles, the initial pedal free travel is that distance of pedal travel before the master cylinder pushrod contacts the piston. On C Series vehicles this adjustment is made with the eccentric bolt and on P Series it is made by rotating the master cylinder pushrod. Obtain an initial pedal free travel of $^1/_4$ in. With the retracting spring removed, the slave cylinder pushrod held completely forward and the release lever held in contact with the release fingers, turn adjusting nut on the slave cylinder pushrod to obtain a final pedal free travel of approximately 2 in.

Internal Adjustment

1. Remove inspection cover from the bottom of the clutch housing.
2. Disconnect the retracting spring and hold the release lever against the throwout bearing. Measure the distance between the throwout bearing and the clutch spring hub (synchromatic transmission) or clutch brake (non-synchromatic transmission). On vehicles with the 14 in. single plate clutch, this distance should be $^{11}/_{32}$ in. to $^{13}/_{32}$ in. On all Spicer clutches, also adjust the adjusting ring to obtain a $^1/_4$ in. clearance between release yoke fingers and the throwout bearing.

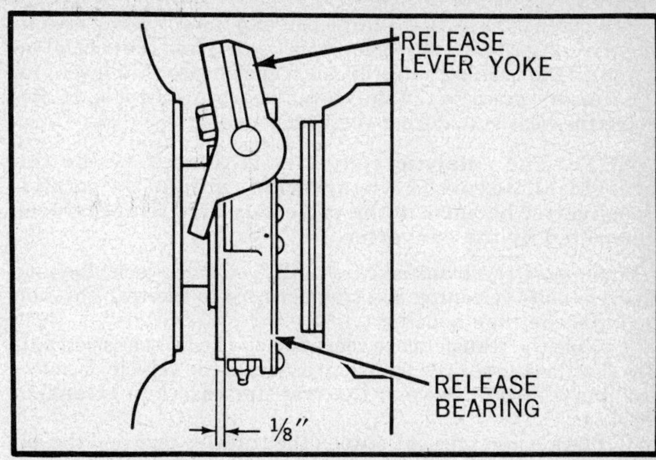

Spicer clutch adjustment (© Ford Motor Co.)

3. If adjustment is necessary, rotate the clutch assembly to get at the adjusting lockring and bolt. Remove the bolt and lockring.
4. With clutch pedal held or blocked in the released position, rotate the adjusting ring (use a pry bar) clockwise to move the throwout bearing toward the flywheel or counterclockwise to move the throwout bearing away from the flywheel. Rotating the adjusting ring one lug position moves the throwout bearing about $^1/_{32}$ in.
5. Let clutch pedal return to engage the clutch, then recheck clearance.
6. Install lock and bolt.
7. Adjust clutch linkage.
8. Connect the retracting spring and replace the clutch housing cover.

TRANSFER CASE

For transfer case overhaul procedures, see the Unit Repair section.

Removal and Installation

BRONCO (DANA 20)

1. Shift the transfer case into neutral and remove the fan shroud. Raise and support the vehicle safely. Support transfer case shield, then remove shield.
2. Drain the transmission and transfer case lubricant then disconnect driveshafts from transfer case.
3. Disconnect speedometer cable and shift rods.
4. A special tool must be placed in the transmission shift levers to keep the input shaft roller bearings from falling out.
5. Remove the frame crossmember from side frame and transfer case, first raising transmission and removing adapter insulators.
6. Disconnect the shift rod from the transfer case shift lever bracket.
7. Remove the shift lever bracket to transfer case adapter bolt and let the assembly hang.
8. Position a transmission jack under the transfer case, remove the transfer case to transmission attaching bolts, then pull the transfer case back until it clears the transmission output shaft.
9. To install, place the transfer case in position and install the attaching bolts, tightening securely.
10. Install the shift lever to transfer case adapter. Connect the shift rod to the shift lever bracket.
11. Raise the transmission and transfer case high enough to provide clearance for installing the crossmember. Position the upper insulators on the crossmember, install the crossmember, then lower the transmission and install the bolts, tightening securely.
12. Remove fabricated tool from shift levers and install the shift rods.
13. Connect the speedometer cable.
14. Install the forward and rear driveshafts.
15. Fill the transmission and transfer case with lubricant.
16. Install transfer case shield.

RANGER AND BRONCO II (BW 13-50)

1. Raise and safely support the vehicle. Remove the skid plate from the frame.
2. Place a drain pan under transfer case, remove the drain plug and drain fluid from the transfer case.
3. Disconnect the four-wheel drive indicator switch wire connector at the transfer case.
4. Disconnect the front driveshaft from the axle input yoke.
5. Loosen the clamp retaining the front driveshaft boot to the transfer case, and pull the driveshaft and front boot assembly out of the transfer case front output shaft.
6. Disconnect the rear driveshaft from the transfer case output shaft yoke.
7. Disconnect the speedometer driven gear from the transfer case rear cover. Disconnect the vent hose from the control lever.

8. Loosen or remove the large bolt and the small bolt retaining the shifter to the extension housing. Pull on the control lever until the bushing slides off the transfer case shift lever pin. If necessary, unscrew the shift lever from the control lever. Remove the heat shield from the transfer case.

NOTE: The catalytic converter is located beside the heat shield. Be careful when working around the catalytic converter because of the extremely high temperatures generated by the converter.

9. Support the transfer case with a suitable jack. Remove the five bolts retaining the transfer case to the transmission and the extension housing.
10. Slide the transfer case rearward off the transmission output shaft and lower the transfer case from the vehicle. Remove the gasket from between the transfer case and extension housing.
11. Place a new gasket between the transfer case and the extension housing.
12. Raise the transfer case with a suitable jack so that the transmission output shaft aligns with the splined transfer case input shaft. Slide the transfer case forward onto the transmission output shaft and onto the dowel pin. Install the five bolts retaining the transfer case to the extension housing. Tighten bolts to 23–35 ft. lbs.
13. Remove the transmission jack from the transfer case.
14. Install the heat shield on the transfer case. Tighten the bolts to 27–37 ft. lbs.
15. Move the control lever until the bushing is in position over the transfer case shift lever pin. Install and hand start the attaching bolts. First, tighten the large bolt retaining the shifter to the extension housing to 70–90 ft. lbs., then the small bolt to 31–42 ft. lbs.

NOTE: Always tighten the large bolt retaining the shifter to the extension housing before tightening the small bolt.

16. Install the vent assembly so the white marking on the hose is in position in the notch in the shifter.

NOTE: The upper end of the vent hose should be two inches above the top of the shifter and positioned inside of the shift lever boot.

17. Connect the speedometer driven gear to the transfer case rear cover. Tighten the screw to 20–25 inch lbs.
18. Connect the rear driveshaft to the transfer case output shaft yoke. Tighten the bolts to 12–15 ft. lbs.
19. Clean the transfer case front output shaft female splines. Apply 5–8 grams of multi-purpose long-life lubricant, or equivalent to the splines. Insert the front driveshaft male spline.
20. Connect the front driveshaft to the axle input yoke. Tighten the bolts to 12–15 ft. lbs.
21. Push the driveshaft boot to engage the external groove on the transfer case front output shaft. Secure with a clamp.
22. Connect the four-wheel drive indicator switch wire connector at the transfer case.
23. Install the drain plug and tighten to 14–22 ft. lbs. Remove the fill plug and install 3 pints of DEXRON®-II, automatic transmission fluid, or equivalent. Install fill plug and tighten to 14–22 ft. lbs.
24. Install the skid plate to frame. Tighten nuts and bolts to 22–30 ft. lbs.
25. Lower the vehicle.

F-100, 150 (4 × 4) (DANA 21)

1. Raise and support the vehicle safely. Disconnect the front and rear driveshafts.
2. Disconnect the shift rod from transfer case shift lever.
3. Remove transmission extension housing to transfer case attaching bolts and remove the transfer case.
4. To install, position transfer case and new gasket to extension housing and install attaching bolts.
5. Connect shift rod to shift lever.
6. Connect the front and rear driveshafts.
7. Lower vehicle and check for proper operation.

F-250 (4 × 4) (DANA 24)

1. Raise and support the vehicle safely. Drain the transfer case lubricant.
2. Disconnect front and rear driveshafts, speedometer cable and shift rods.
3. Position a transmission jack under the transfer case and remove mounting bolts. Remove transfer case.
4. To install, raise transfer case on the jack and install nuts on mounting studs.
5. Connect shift rod, speedometer cable and driveshafts.
6. Fill transfer case to filler plug with lubricant.

NEW PROCESS MODEL 205

1. Drain the transfer case and remove the rear driveshaft.
2. On F-250 models remove the front driveshaft from the transfer case. On F-100 models remove the front driveshaft and remove the transmission adapter to transfer case bolts.
3. Disconnect the shift rod and speedometer cable. Disconnect the reaction bar.
4. Support the transfer case with a jack and remove the transfer case mounting bolts.
5. Remove the transfer case from the vehicle.
6. To install reverse the removal procedures. Fill transfer case to the filler plug with the proper lubricant.

ROCKWELL

1. Drain transfer case and disconnect speedometer cable.
2. Disconnect front and rear driveshafts and secure with wire or rope so that they do not hang.
3. Disconnect parking brake at the bellcrank and secure rod out of the way.
4. Disconnect the clutch and shift rods.
5. Support the transfer case with a transmission jack and remove the support bracket bolts. Remove transfer case.
6. Install with the use of a transmission jack. Install and tighten mounting bolts.
7. Connect and adjust parking brake rod at the bellcrank.
8. Connect the clutch and shift rods.
9. Connect front and rear driveshafts.
10. Connect speedometer.
11. Fill transfer case with lubricant.

NEW PROCESS MODEL 203

1. Drain the transfer case by removing the power take-off lower bolts and the front output rear cover lower bolts.
2. Disconnect the front axle driveshaft from the flange at the transfer case.
3. Disconnect the shift rods from the transfer case.
4. Disconnect the speedometer cable and lockout light switch wire from the transfer case rear output shaft housing.
5. Remove the transfer case-to-transmission adapter attaching bolts. Disconnect the rear axle driveshaft at the transfer case flange.
6. Position a transmission jack under the transfer case and secure it with a chain.
7. Remove the transfer case mounting bolts and remove the unit from the vehicle.
8. Install the transfer case in the reverse order of removal. Fill the transfer case to the filler plug with the proper lubricant.

NEW PROCESS MODEL 208

1. Raise the vehicle and support it safely. Drain the fluid from the transfer case.
2. Disconnect the four wheel drive indicator switch wire connector at the transfer case.

3. Disconnect the speedometer driven gear from the transfer case rear bearing retainer.
4. Remove the nut retaining the transmission shift lever assembly to the transfer case.
5. Remove the skid plate from the frame, if so equipped.
6. Remove the heat shield from the frame.
7. Support the transfer case with a transmission jack or equivalent.
8. Disconnect the front driveshaft from the front output shaft yoke.
9. Disconnect the rear driveshaft from the rear output shaft yoke.
10. Remove the bolts retaining the transfer case to the transmission adapter.
11. Lower the transfer case from the vehicle.
12. When installing place a new gasket between the transfer case and the adapter.
13. Raise the transfer case with a transmission jack so the transmission output shaft aligns with the splined transfer case input shaft.
14. Install the bolts retaining the case to the adapter.
15. Connect the rear driveshaft to the rear output shaft yoke.
16. Connect the front driveshaft to the front output yoke.
17. Remove the transmission jack from the transfer case.
18. Position the heat shield to the frame crossmember and mounting lug to the transfer case and install and tighten the bolts and screw.
19. Install the skid plate to the frame.
20. Install the shift lever to the transfer case and tighten the retaining nut.
21. Install the speedometer driven gear to the transfer case.
22. Connect the four wheel drive indicator switch wire to the transfer case.
23. Install the drain plug. Remove the filler plug and install six pints of Dexron® II or equivalent type transmission fluid.
24. Lower the vehicle.

BORG WARNER MODEL 1345

1. Raise the vehicle and support it safely.
2. Drain the fluid from the transfer case.
3. Disconnect the four wheel drive indicator switch wire connector at the transfer case.
4. Remove the skid plate from the frame, if so equipped.
5. Disconnect the front driveshaft from the front output yoke.
6. Disconnect the rear driveshaft from the rear output shaft yoke.
7. Disconnect the speedometer driven gear from the transfer case rear bearing retainer.
8. Remove the retaining rings and shift rod from the transfer case shift lever.
9. Disconnect the vent hose from the transfer case.
10. Remove the heat shield from the frame.
11. Support the transfer case with a transmission jack.
12. Remove the bolts retaining the transfer case to the transmission adapter.
13. Lower the transfer case from the vehicle.
14. When installing place a new gasket between the transfer case and the adapter.
15. Raise the transfer case with the transmission jack so that the transmission output shaft aligns with the splined transfer case input shaft. Install the bolts retaining the transfer case to the adapter.
16. Remove the transmission jack from the transfer case.
17. Connect the rear driveshaft to the rear output shaft yoke.
18. Install the shift lever to the transfer case and install the retaining nut.
19. Connect the speedometer driven gear to the transfer case.
20. Connect the four wheel drive indicator switch wire connector at the transfer case.
21. Connect the front driveshaft to the front output yoke.

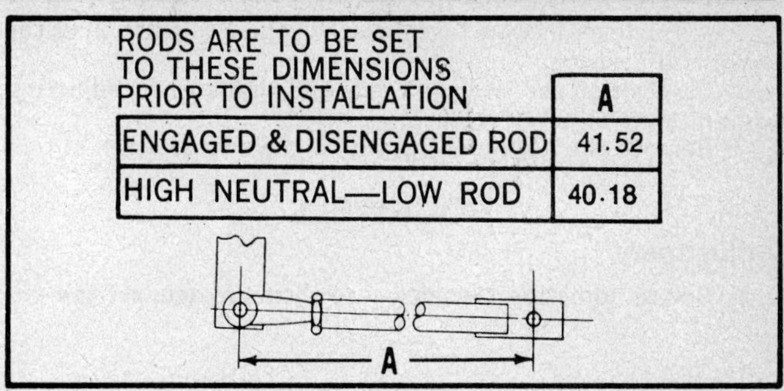

RODS ARE TO BE SET
TO THESE DIMENSIONS
PRIOR TO INSTALLATION
A
ENGAGED & DISENGAGED ROD
41.52
HIGH NEUTRAL—LOW ROD
40.18
A

Rockwell transfer case rod adjustments (© Ford Motor Co.)

22. Position the heat shield to the frame crossmember and the mounting lug on the transfer case. Install and tighten the retaining bolts.
23. Install the skid plate to the frame.
24. Install the drain plug. Remove the filler plug and install six pints of Dexron® II type transmission fluid or equivalent.
25. Lower the vehicle.

Transfer Case Shift Linkage

NEW PROCESS MODEL 205

Adjustment

MANUAL TRANSMISSION

Adjust the length of the shift rod between the transfer case and the shift lever with the lever in 4WD-Low so that the distance between the rear face of the transmission and the shift lever-to-rod clevis pin is 3.94 in to 3.82 in.

AUTOMATIC TRANSMISSION

Adjust the length of the shift rod between the transfer case and the shift lever with the lever in 4WD-Low so that the distance between the upper surface of the automatic transmission extension housing and the upper horizontal edge of the shift lever is 0.640 in. to 0.600 in.

NEW PROCESS 203 FULL TIME 4WD

Adjustment

1. Place the shifter lever in neutral. Remove the two adjusting nut studs.
2. Install 0.25 in. diameter alignment pin (1.25 in. long) through the shifter assembly.
3. Align as follows:
   a. Bottom lever, (lock lever) rotate clockwise to the forward position.

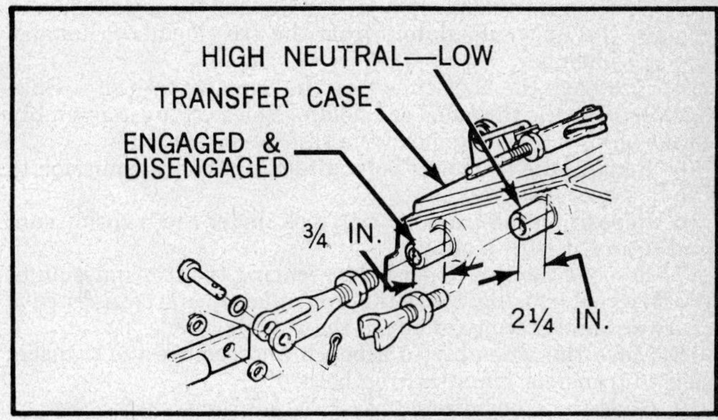

Transfer case control lever rod and shift lever rod (© Ford Motor Co.)

b. Top lever, (range lever) place in the mid-position or the neutral position.

4. Re-position the two shift rods and tighten new adjusting stud nuts to 15–20 ft. lbs.

5. Remove the alignment pin from the shifter assembly.

ROCKWELL

Adjustment

1. Before adjusting transfer case shift linkage, set the engaged and disengaged rod to 41.52 in. (dimension A) and the high-neutral-low rod to 40.18 inch. (dimension A).

2. Run the jamnut on each clevis to full thread. Install clevises in transfer case so they bottom in shift rails.

3. Back off clevises (not over 90 degrees) so clevis pins are horizontal to the ground. Tighten the jamnuts.

4. When adjusting the control and shift lever rods the levers should be $^3/_4$ in. from the seat cushion frame with the seat in full forward position. The shift rails in the transfer case should be located in detent disengage and low position.

MANUAL TRANSMISSION

For complete manual transmission overhaul procedures, see the Unit Repair section.

FORD 3.03 THREE SPEED

Removal and Installation

BRONCO

1. Shift the transfer case into Neutral.
2. Remove the bolts attaching the fan shroud to the radiator support, if so equipped.
3. Raise and support the vehicle safely.
4. Support the transfer case shield with a jack and remove the bolts that attach the shield to the frame side rails. Remove the shield.
5. Drain the transmission and transfer case lubricant. To drain the transmission lubricant, remove the lower extension housing-to-transmission bolt.
6. Disconnect the front and rear driveshafts at the transfer case.
7. Disconnect the speedometer cable at the transfer case.
8. Disconnect the T.R.S. switch, if so equipped.
9. Disconnect the shift rods from the transmission shift levers. Place the First-Reverse gear shift lever into the first gear position and insert the fabricated tool. The tool consists of a length of rod, the same diameter as the holes in the shift levers, which is bent in such a way to fit in the holes in the two shift levers and hold them in the position stated above. More important, this tool will prevent the input shaft roller bearings from dropping into the transmission and output shaft. This tool is a must when perfprming this operation.
10. Support the engine with a jack.
11. Remove the two cotter pins, bolts, washers, plate and insulators that secure the crossmember to the transfer case adapter.
12. Remove the crossmember-to-frame side support attaching bolts.
13. Position a transmission jack under the transfer case and remove the upper insulators from the crossmember. Remove the crossmember.
14. Roll back the boot enclosing the transfer case shift linkage. Remove the threaded cap holding the shift lever assembly to the shift bracket. Remove the shift lever assembly.
15. Remove the two lower bolts attaching the transmission to the flywheel housing.
16. Reposition the transmission jack under the transmission and secure it with a chain.
17. Remove the two upper bolts securing the transmission to the flywheel housing. Move the transmission and transfer case rearward and downward out of the vehicle.
18. Move the assembly to a bench and remove the transfer case-to-transmission attaching bolts.
19. Slide the transmission assembly off the transfer case.
20. To install, position the transfer case to the transmission. Apply an oil-resistant sealer to the bolt threads and install the attaching bolts. Tighten to 42–50 ft. lbs.
21. Position the transmission and transfer case on a transmission jack and secure them with a chain.
22. Raise the transmission and transfer case assembly into position and install the transmission case to the flywheel housing.
23. Install the two upper and two lower transmission attaching bolts and torque them to 37–42 ft. lbs.
24. Position the transfer case shift lever and install the threaded cap to the shift bracket. Reposition the rubber boot.
25. Raise the transmission and transfer case high enough to provide clearance for installing the crossmember. Position the upper insulators to the crossmember and install the crossmember-to-frame side support attaching bolts.
26. Align the bolt holes in the transfer case adapter with those in the crossmember, then lower the transmission and remove the jack.
27. Install the crossmember-to-transfer case adapter bolts, nuts, insulators, plates and washers. Tighten the nuts and secure them with cotter pins.
28. Remove the engine jack.
29. Remove the fabricated tool and connect each shift rod to its respective lever on the transmission. Adjust the linkage.
30. Connect the speedometer cable.
31. Connect the T.R.S. switch, if so equipped.
32. Install the front and rear driveshafts to the transfer case.
33. Fill the transmission and transfer case to the bottom of the filler hole with the recommended lubricant.
34. Position the transfer case shield to the frame side rails and install the attaching bolts.
35. Lower the vehicle.
36. Install the fan shroud, if so equipped.
37. Check the operation of the transfer case and the transmission shift linkage.

E SERIES

1. Raise and support the vehicle safely. Drain the lubricant from the transmission by removing the drain plug if the vehicle is so equipped. For models without drain plugs, remove the lower extension housing-to-transmission bolt.
2. Disconnect the driveshaft from the flange at the transmission. Secure the front end of the driveshaft out of the way with lock wire.
3. Disconnect the speedometer cable from the extension housing and disconnect the gear shift rods from the transmission shift levers. Remove the wire to the TCS switch if so equipped.
4. Position a transmission jack under the transmission. Secure the transmission to the jack.
5. Raise the transmission slightly and remove the four bolts retaining the transmission support crossmember to the frame side rails. Remove the bolt retaining the transmission extension housing to the crossmember.

6. Remove the four transmission-to-flywheel housing bolts.
7. Position engine support bar (tool T65E-6000-J) to the frame.
8. Lower the transmission.
9. To install, make certain that the machined surfaces of the transmission case and the flywheel housing are free of dirt, paint and burrs.
10. Install a guide pin in each lower mounting bolt hole.
11. Start the input shaft through the release bearing. Align the splines on the input shaft with the splines in the clutch disc. Move the transmission forward on the guide pins until the input shaft pilot enters the bearing or bushing in the crankshaft. If the transmission front bearing retainer binds up on the clutch release bearing hub, work the release bearing lever until the hub slides onto the transmission front bearing retainer. Install the two transmission-to-flywheel housing upper mounting bolts and lockwashers. Remove the two guide pins and install the lower mounting bolts and lockwashers.
12. Raise the jack slightly and remove the engine support bar.
13. Position the support crossmember on the frame side rails and install the retaining bolts. Install the extension housing-to-crossmember retaining bolt.
14. Connect the gear shift rods and the speedometer cable.
15. Install the driveshaft and torque the attaching bolts to specification.
16. Fill the transmission to the bottom of the filler hole with the recommended lubricant.
17. Adjust the clutch pedal free travel and shift linkage as required.

F SERIES

1. Raise and support the vehicle safely. Support the engine with a jack and wood block placed under the oil pan.
2. Drain the transmission lubricant by removing the drain plug if the vehicle is so equipped. For models without drain plugs, remove the lower extension housing-to-transmission bolt.
3. Position a transmission jack under the transmission.
4. Disconnect the gear shift linkage at the transmission.
5. If the vehicle has a four-wheel drive, remove the transfer case shift lever bracket from the transmission.
6. On the Warner T-85N model, disconnect the solenoid and governor wires at the connectors near the solenoid. Remove the overdrive wiring harness from its clip on the transmission. Disconnect the overdrive cable.
7. Disconnect the speedometer cable. Disconnect the driveshaft from the transmission.
8. Remove the transmission-to-clutch housing attaching bolts.
9. Move transmission to the rear until the input shaft clears the clutch housing and lower the transmission. Do not depress the clutch pedal while the transmission is removed.
10. Before installing the transmission, apply a light film of lubricant to the clutch disc splines, release bearing inner hub surfaces, release lever fulcrum and fork and the transmission front bearing retainer. Exercise care to avoid contaminating the clutch disc with excessive grease.
11. Place the transmission on a transmission jack. Raise the transmission until the input shaft splines are in line with the clutch disc splines. The clutch release bearing and hub must be properly positioned in the release lever fork.
12. Install a guide stud in each lower clutch housing-to-transmission case mounting bolt and align the splines on the input shaft with the splines on the clutch disc.
13. Slide the transmission forward on the guide studs until it contacts the clutch housing.
14. Install the two transmission to flywheel housing upper mounting bolts and nuts. Remove the two guide studs and install the lower mounting bolts.
15. Connect the speedometer cable and the driven gear.
16. Install the driveshaft.
17. Connect each shift rod to its respective lever on the transmission.
18. If the vehicle is equipped with four-wheel drive, install the four-wheel drive shaft bracket.
19. Fill the transmission to the proper level with an approved lubricant.
20. Adjust the clutch pedal free travel and shift linkage as required.

Warner T 18 and T 19 Four Speed

Removal and Installation

EXCEPT 4 × 4 WITH T 18 TRANSMISSION AND 4 × 2 WITH T 19B

1. Disconnect the back-up light switch located at the rear of the gearshift housing cover.
2. Remove the rubber boot, floor mat, and the body floor pan cover, and remove the transmission shift lever. Remove the weather pad and pad retainer.
3. Raise and support the vehicle safely. Position a transmission jack under the transmission, and disconnect the speedometer cable.
4. If the vehicle is equipped with band-type parking brake, disconnect the brake cable clevis at the cam. Remove the brake cable conduit clamp.
5. Remove the front U-joint flange attaching bolts. Remove the bolts that attach the coupling shaft center support to the crossmember and wire the coupling shaft and driveshaft to one side. Remove the transmission rear support, as required.
6. Remove the transmission attaching bolts.
7. Move the transmission to the rear until the input shaft clears the clutch housing, and lower the transmission.

NOTE: Before installing the transmission, apply a light film of lubricant to the clutch disc splines, release bearing inner hub surfaces, release lever fulcrum and fork, and the transmission front bearing retainer. Care must be exercised to avoid excessive grease from contaminating the clutch disc.

8. Place the transmission on a transmission jack, and raise the transmission until the input shaft splines are aligned with the clutch disc splines. The clutch release bearing and hub must be properly positioned in the release lever fork.
9. Install guide studs in the clutch housing and slide the transmission forward on the guide studs until it is in position on the clutch housing. Install the attaching bolts and nuts. Remove the guide studs and install the two lower attaching bolts.
10. Connect the speedometer cable and driven gear and parking brake clevis. Install the brake cable conduit clamp, and shift linkage.
11. Install the bolts attaching the coupling shaft center support to the crossmember.
12. Install the bolts attaching the front U-joint flange to the transmission output shaft flange. Install the transmission rear support, if removed.
13. Connect the back-up light switch.
14. Install the shift lever and lubricate the spherical ball seat with lubricant.
15. Install the weather pad and pad retainer. Install the floor pan cover, floor mat and boot.

4 × 4 (WITH T 18 TRANSMISSION)

1. Open the door and cover seat. Remove the shift knobs. Remove the transmission shift lever boot assembly.
2. Remove the screws holding the floor mat. Remove the screws holding the access cover to the floor pan. Place the shift lever in reverse and remove the cover.
3. Remove the insulator and the dust cover. Remove the transfer case shift lever. Remove the bolts holding the shift cover and the gasket.

4. Cover the shift cover opening to protect the transmission from dirt during the removal procedure.
5. Raise and support the vehicle safely. Drain the transmission.
6. Disconnect the front and the rear driveshaft from the transfer case and wire them out of the way. Remove the cotter pin that holds the shift link in place and remove the shift link.
7. Remove the speedometer cable from the transfer case. Position a transmission jack under the transfer case. Remove the bolts holding the transfer case to the transmission and remove the transfer case from the vehicle.
8. Remove the bolts that hold the rear support bracket to the transmission.
9. Position a transmission jack under the transmission and remove the rear support bracket and brace. Remove the bolts that hold the transmission to the bell housing and remove the transmission.
10. To install, place the transmission on a transmission jack and install it in the vehicle. Install two guide pins in the bell housing top holes, to guide the transmission in place.
11. Install the two lower bolts, remove the guide pins and install the upper two bolts.
12. Continue the installation in the reverse order of the removal. Fill the transfer case and the transmission with lubricant. Lower the vehicle.

4 × 2 (WITH T 19B TRANSMISSION)

1. Remove the floor mat, and the body floor pan cover, and remove the gearshift lever shift ball and boot as an assembly. Remove the weather pad.
2. Raise and support the vehicle safely. Position a suitable jack under the transmission, and disconnect the speedometer cable.
3. Disconnect the back-up lamp switch located at the rear of the gear shift housing cover.
4. Disconnect the drive shaft or coupling shaft and clutch linkage from the transmission and wire it to one side.
5. Remove the transmission rear insulator and lower retainer. Remove the crossmember. Remove the transmission attaching bolts.
6. Move the transmission to the rear until the in shaft clears the clutch housing. Lower transmission.
7. Place the transmission on a suitable jack install guide studs in the clutch housing and raise the transmission until the input shaft splines are aligned with the clutch disc splines. The clutch release bearing and hub must be properly positioned in the release lever fork.
8. Slide the transmission forward on the guide stud until it is in position on the clutch housing. Install the attaching bolts and tighten them to 45–50 ft. lbs. Remove the guide studs and install the lower attaching bolts.
9. Install the crossmember. Position the insulator and retainer between the transmission and crossmember. Install bolts and tighten to 45–60 ft. lbs. Install the nut retaining the insulator and retainer to crossmember. Tighten to 50–70 ft. lbs.
10. Connect the speedometer cable and driven gear and clutch linkage.
11. Install the bolts attaching the front U-joint of the coupling shaft to the transmission output shaft flange. Install the transmission rear support and upper and lower absorbers. Connect the back-up lamp switch.
12. Install the shift lever, boot and shift ball as and assembly and lubricate the spherical ball seat with Multi-Purpose Long-Life Lubricant C1AZ-1959 (ESA-M1C75-B) or equivalent.
13. Install the weather pad. Install the floor pan cover and floor mat.

Four Speed Overdrive Transmission

Removal and Installation

1. Raise and support the vehicle safely. Mark the driveshaft so that it may be installed in the same position. Disconnect the driveshaft from the U-joint flange. Slide the driveshaft off the transmission output shaft and install the extension housing seal installation tool into the extension housing to prevent the transmission lubricant from leaking out.
2. Disconnect the speedometer cable at the extension housing. Remove the retaining clips, flat washers, and spring washers that secure the shift rods to the shift levers. Remove the bolts connecting the shift control to the transmission extension housing. Remove the nut connecting the shift control to the transmission case.

NOTE: A '6' or '8' is stamped on the transmission extension housing by the shift control plate bolt holes. The '6' and '8' refer to either a 6 or 8 cylinder engine application. The shift control plate bolts must be placed in the right holes for proper plate positioning dependent upon the engine used in the vehicle.

3. Remove the rear transmission support connecting bolts attaching the support on the crossmember to the transmission extension housing. Support the engine with a transmission jack and remove the extension housing-to-engine rear support attaching bolts.
4. Raise the rear of the engine high enough to relieve the weight from the crossmember. Remove the bolts retaining the crossmember to the frame side supports and remove the crossmember.
5. Support the transmission on a jack and remove the transmission-to-flywheel housing bolts. Move the transmission and the jack rearward until the transmission input shaft clears the flywheel housing. Lower the engine enough to obtain clearance for transmission removal and remove the unit.

NOTE: Do not depress the clutch pedal while the transmission is removed.

6. To install, make sure that the mounting surfaces of the transmission and the flywheel housing are free of dirt, paint, and burrs. Install two guide pins in the flywheel housing lower mounting bolt holes. Move the transmission forward on the guide pins until the input shaft splines enter the clutch hub splines and the case is positioned against the flywheel housing.
7. Install the two upper transmission mounting bolts, remove the guide pins and install the lower mounting bolts.
8. Continue the installation in the reverse order of the removal.
9. Fill the transmission to the proper level with lubricant. Lower the vehicle. Check the shift and crossover motion for full shift engagement and smooth crossover operation.

Four Speed Transmission

Removal and Installation

RANGER AND BRONCO II

1. Place the gearshift lever in neutral. Remove the boot retainer screws. Remove the bolts attaching the retainer cover to the gearshift lever retainer. Disconnect the clutch master cylinder push rod from the clutch pedal.
2. Pull the gearshift lever assembly, shim and bushing straight up and away from the gearshift lever retainer. Cover the shift tower opening in the extension housing with a cloth.
3. Disconnect the clutch hydraulic system master clyinder push rod from the clutch pedal.

4. Open the hood and disconnect the negative battery cable from the battery terminal.

5. Raise and safely support the vehicle. Disconnect the driveshaft at the rear axle. Pull the driveshaft rearward and disconnect from the transmission. Install a suitable plug in the extension housing to prevent lubricant leakage.

6. Remove the clutch housing dust shield and slave cylinder and secure it at one side.

7. Remove the speedometer cable from the extension housing or from the speed control sensor, if so equipped.

8. Disconnect the starter motor and back-up lamp switch wires. Place a jack under the engine, protecting the oil pan with a wood block.

NOTE: If the vehicle is equipped with four wheel drive, remove the transfer case.

9. Remove the starter. Position a suitable jack under the transmission assembly. Remove the bolts attaching the transmission to the engine rear plate. Remove the nuts and bolts attaching the transmission mount and damper to the crossmember.

10. Remove the nuts attaching the crossmember to the frame side rails and remove the crossmember.

11. Lower the engine jack. Work the clutch housing off the locating dowels and slide the transmission rearward until the input shaft spline clears the clutch disc. Remove the transmission from the vehicle.

13. Make sure that the machined mating surfaces and the locating dowels on the engine rear plate are free of burrs, dirt or paint. Check the mating face of the clutch housing and the locating dowel holes for burrs, dirt or paint. Mount the transmission on a suitable jack. Position it under the vehicle and start the input shaft into the clutch disc. Align the splines on the input shaft with the splines in the clutch disc. Move the transmission forward and carefully seat the clutch housing on the locating dowels of the engine rear plate. The engine plate dowels must not shave or burr the clutch housing dowel holes.

14. Install the bolts that attach the clutch housing to the engine rear plate. Remove the transmission jack.

15. Install the starter motor.

16. Raise the engine and install the rear crossmember and attaching nuts and washers.

17. Install the bolts, nuts and washers attaching the transmission mount and damper to the crossmember. Remove the engine jack.

NOTE: On four wheel drive units install the transfer case.

18. Insert the driveshaft into the transmission extension housing and install the center bearing attaching nuts, washers and lockwashers.

19. Connect the driveshaft to the rear axle drive flange.

20. Connect the starter and back-up lamp switch wires. Install the clutch slave cylinder and dust shield on the clutch housing. Install the speedometer cable.

21. Check the transmission fluid level at the fill plug. Fill with specified lubricant if necessary. Lower the vehicle.

22. Open the hood and connect the negative battery cable to the battery terminal.

23. Re-connect the clutch master cylinder push rod to the clutch pedal.

24. Remove the cloth from the shift tower opening in the extension housing. Avoid getting dirt inside the transmission.

25. Position the gearshift lever assembly straight up above the gearshift lever retainer, then insert the gearshift in the retainer. Install the bolts attaching the retainer cover to the gearshift lever retainer.

26. Install the cover boot with the retainer screws.

Five Speed Overdrive and Five Speed Transmission

Removal and Inspection

RANGER AND BRONCO II

1. Place the gearshift lever in neutral. Remove the boot retainer screws. Remove the bolts attaching the retainer cover to the gearshift lever retainer. Disconnect the clutch master cylinder push rod from the clutch pedal.

2. Pull the gearshift lever assembly, shim and bushing straight up and away from the gearshift lever retainer. Cover the shift tower opening in the extension housing with a cloth.

3. Disconnect the clutch hydraulic system master cylinder push rod from the clutch pedal.

4. Open the hood and disconnect the negative battery cable from the battery terminal.

5. Raise and safely support the vehicle. Disconnect the driveshaft at the rear. Pull the driveshaft rearward and disconnect from the transmission. Install a suitable plug in the extension housing to prevent lubricant leakage.

6. Remove the clutch housing dust shield and slave cylinder and secure it at one side.

7. Remove the speedometer cable from the extension housing.

8. Disconnect the starter motor and back-up lamp switch wires.

9. Place a jack under the engine, protecting the oil pan with a wood block.

NOTE: If vehicle is four wheel drive, remove the transfer case.

10. Remove the starter motor. Position a suitable jack under the transmission.

11. Remove the bolts, lockwashers and flat washers attaching the transmission to the engine rear plate.

12. Remove the nuts and bolts attaching the transmission mount and damper to the crossmember.

13. Remove the nuts attaching the crossmember to the frame side rails and remove the crossmember.

14. Lower the engine jack. Work the clutch housing off the locating dowels and slide the transmission rearward until the input shaft spline clears the clutch disc. Remove the transmission from the vehicle.

15. Installation is the reverse of removal.

NEW PROCESS 435 FOUR SPEED

Removal and Installation

1. If equipped, remove the rubber boot and floor mat.

2. If necessary, remove the floor pan transmission cover plate. It may be necessary first to remove the seat assembly.

3. Disconnect the back-up light switch located in the rear of the gearshift housing cover.

4. Raise and support the vehicle safely. Position a transmission jack under the transmission, and disconnect the speedometer cable.

5. Disconnect the parking brake lever from its linkage, and remove the gearshift housing. On a C-Series, disconnect parking brake cable and bracket at the transmission.

6. Disconnect the driveshaft. Remove the bolts that attach the coupling shaft center support to the cross-member and wire the coupling shaft and driveshaft to one side. If equipped, remove the transfer case. Remove the transmission rear support as required.

7. Remove the two transmission upper mounting nuts at the clutch housing.

8. Remove the transmission attaching bolts at the clutch housing, and remove the transmission.

9. Before installing the transmission, apply a light film of lubricant to the clutch disc splines, release bearing inner hub surfaces, release lever fulcrum and fork, and the transmission front bearing retainer. Care must be exercised to avoid excessive grease from contaminating the clutch disc.

10. Place the transmission on a transmission jack, and raise the transmission until the input shaft splines are aligned with the clutch disc splines. The clutch release bearing and hub must be properly positioned in the release lever fork.

11. Install guide studs in the clutch housing and slide the transmission forward on the guide studs until it is in position on the clutch housing. Install the attaching bolts and nuts. Remove the guide studs and install the two lower attaching bolts.

12. Install the bolts attaching the coupling shaft center support to the crossmember.

13. Connect the driveshaft and the speedometer cable. Install transmission rear support, if removed. Install transfer case, if removed.

14. Connect the parking brake to the transmission.

15. Connect the back-up light switch.

16. If equipped, install the weather pad, the pad retainer and the transmission cover plate. Install the seat assembly if it was removed.

NEW PROCESS 542 FIVE SPEED TRANSMISSION

Removal and Installation

1. Remove the floor mat and the floor plate. Loosen the two nuts that secure the top of the transmission to the clutch housing studs. If the vehicle is not raised on a hoist, it may be necessary to remove the parking brake lever before the transmission can be removed.

2. Remove the shift lever and drain the transmission.

3. Disconnect the driveshaft or coupling shaft at the parking brake drum. If the vehicle is equipped with a coupling shaft support, disconnect the support bracket and remove the coupling shaft.

4. Disconnect the parking brake adjusting rod and the speedometer cable.

5. Remove the dust cover from the bottom of the clutch housing. Position a transmission jack under the transmission. Remove the top nuts, and the bottom bolts and lockwashers that hold the transmission to the clutch housing.

6. Remove the transmission rearward until the input shaft splines clear the clutch housing. Be careful that the clutch release bearing and hub do not drop out of the release lever fork. Lower the transmission to the floor.

7. Place the transmission on the transmission jack and raise the transmission until the input shaft splines are aligned with the clutch disc splines. The clutch release bearing and hub must be properly positioned in the release lever fork. Slide the transmission forward until it is in position on the clutch housing.

8. Install the lockwashers and the top nuts and the bottom bolts and tighten to specification.

9. Install the dust cover on the bottom of the clutch housing. Connect the speedometer cable.

10. Connect the parking brake adjusting rod.

11. Install the coupling shaft in the support bracket and connect the support bracket to the support plate. Connect the coupling shaft or driveshaft at the transmission. Install the shift lever.

12. Lower the vehicle to the floor and install the floor plate and the floor mat. Fill the transmission to the correct level with the correct lubricant.

13. Check the clutch pedal free travel and adjust if necessary.

CLARK, FULLER, AND SPICER 5 SPEED TRANSMISSIONS

Removal and Installation

1. Remove the floor mat and floor plate. On spicer transmissions, remove the 1st-reverse lockout plunger retainer, spring and plunger. Remove the gear shift lever housing and disconnect the parking brake lever (if so equipped). Cover the case opening to prevent foreign material from entering the case.

2. On C-series vehicles, shift the transmission into neutral, release the lock and tilt the cab forward. Remove the rear cross-shaft housing bolts. Tie the housing so that it does not fall. If necessary, raise the rear of the vehicle and install safety stands to provide room for the removal of the transmission. On some vehicles, it may be necessary to block the wheels and remove the cross shaft housing bolts and tie the housing out of the way.

3. Drain the transmission. Disconnect the driveshaft or coupling shaft at the parking brake drum. If the vehicle is equipped with a coupling shaft support, disconnect the support bracket and remove the coupling shaft.

4. Disconnect the parking brake rod (if so equipped) and the speedometer cable. Remove the speedometer driven gear. Check the speedometer driven gear bushing in the mainshaft rear bearing cap on Spicer transmissions.

5. Disconnect the clutch linkage at the release arm. If the vehicle is equipped with a slave cylinder, disconnect the slave cylinder return spring, remove the slave mounting bolts, and set the slave cylinder out of the way.

6. Remove the dust cover from the bottom of the clutch housing.

7. Clark and Spicer transmissions: Position a transmission jack under the transmission. Remove the top nuts and the bottom bolts and lockwashers that attach the transmission to the clutch housing.
UF9
Fuller transmissions: Position a jack under the transmission and raise it slightly to relieve the pressure at the side rail mounting brackets. Remove the side rail bracket stud nuts, insulators and reinforcements. Remove the side rail brackets and the bolts that attach the clutch housing to the engine.

8.On some vehicles, it may be necessary to remove the bolts and lockwashers that attach the transmission support to the frame side rail brackets. Mark the washers so that they can be re-installed in their original position. Remove the lock wire and the transmission support-to-transmission case bracket bolts, washers, and insulators. Remove the support the attach a chain hoist to the transmission. Remove the bolts that attach the clutch housing to the engine.

9.Move the transmission to the rear until it is clear and remove it from the vehicle.

10. Install the t [illegible]smission in the reverse order of removal.

NOTE: On Cl[illegible]k and Fuller transmissions, when installing the gear shift lever housing, always lower it straight down onto the gear shift housing.

FULLER AND SPICER TRANSMISSIONS, 6 SPEED AND UP

Removal and Installation

1. Bleed the air reservoir and disconnect the air line at the rear of the transmission. Drain the transmission lubricant.

2. Disconnect the driveshaft at the transmission companion flange.

3. Disconnect the speedometer cable at the transmission.

4. Clean the area around the cross shaft housing. Remove the housing and tie it out of the way. Cover the opening in the gear shaft housing to prevent foreign material from entering.

5. Remove the shift control cable. Remove the retaining clamps for the speedometer and fuel line.

6. Disconnect the nylon cables at the air valve and shift cyl-

inder. Tie the air cables next to the chassis frame to prevent damage to the cables when the transmission is removed.

7. Disconnect the clutch linkage at the clutch release arm. Remove all but two of the clutch attaching bolts at the engine. Remove the clutch housing dust cover.

8. Place a jack under the transmission and raise slightly to relieve the pressure at the side rail mounting brackets. Remove the bolts attaching the transmission support to the frame side rail brackets. After removing the lockwire, remove the transmission support-to-transmission case bolts, washers, insulators, and spacers. Remove the support.

9. Remove the remaining clutch housing attaching bolts. Pull the transmission rearward to clear the input shaft.

10. Raise the rear of the vehicle and support with safety stands. Remove the transmission from the vehicle.

11. Install the transmission in the reverse order of removal. If the pilot bearing was removed, the new bearing must be pressed approximately $^{1}/_{16}$ in. beyond the flush position.

12. When installing the air lines to the cab control valve, relative to the piston air valve, keep the air lines with the protective cover at least four inches from the exhaust manifold. Heat will melt the protective cover and the air lines. Sharp bends in the air lines will restrict the required air pressure of 50–55 psi.

Gearshift Linkage

FORD 3.03 THREE SPEED, EXCEPT VANS

Adjustment

1. Place the shifter in the Neutral position and insert a gauge pin ($^{3}/_{16}$ in. diameter) through the steering column shift levers and the locating hole in the spacer.

2. If the shift rods at the transmission are equipped with threaded sleeves, adjust the sleeves so that they enter the shift levers on the transmission easily with the shift levers in the Neutral position. Now lengthen the rods seven turns of the sleeves and insert them into the shift levers.

3. If the shift rods, are slotted, loosen the attaching nut, make sure that the transmission shift levers are in the Neutral position, then retighten the attaching nuts.

4. Remove the gauge pin and check the operation of the shift linkage.

FOUR SPEED OVERDRIVE W/EXTERNAL LINKAGE, EXCEPT VANS

Adjustment

1. Attach the shift rods to the levers.
2. Rotate the output shaft to determine that the transmission is in neutral.
3. Insert an alignment pin into the shift control assembly alignment hole.
4. Attach the slotted end of the shift rods over the flats of the studs in the shift control assembly.
5. Install the locknuts and remove the alignment pin.

VANS WITH FORD 3.03 THREE SPEED TRANSMISSION

Adjustment

1. Place the gearshift lever in the Neutral position.
2. Loosen the adjustment nuts on the transmission shift levers sufficiently to allow the shift rods to slide freely on the transmission shift levers.
3. Insert a $^{3}/_{16}$ in. rod through the pilot hole in the shift tube mounting bracket until it enters the adjustment hole of both the upper and lower shift lever.
4. Place the transmission shift levers in the Neutral position and tighten the adjustment nuts on the transmission shift levers.
5. Remove the $^{1}/_{4}$ in. rod from the pilot hole, and check the operation of the gearshift lever in all gear positions.

VANS WITH FOUR SPEED OVERDRIVE TRANSMISSION W/EXTERNAL LINKAGE

Adjustment

1. Disconnect the 3 shift rods from the shifter assembly.
2. Insert a 0.25 in. diameter pin through the alignment hole in the shifter assembly. Make sure the levers are in the neutral position.
3. Align the 3 transmission levers as follows: forward lever (3rd–4th lever) in the mid-position (neutral), rearward lever (1st–2nd lever) in the mid-position (neutral), and middle lever (reverse lever) rotate counterclockwise to the neutral position.
4. Rotate the output shaft to assure that the transmission is in neutral.
5. Attach the slotted end of the shift rods over the slots of the studs in the shifter assembly. Install and tighten the locknuts to 15–20 ft. lbs.
6. Remove the alignment pin. Check for proper operation.

Auxiliary Transmission

Removal and Installation

1. Position the vehicle so that the auxiliary transmission can be easily reached. Drain the lubricant.
2. Remove the cotter pins and the clevis pins from the auxiliary transmission shift rods as follows:
   a. Move each shift rod into the forward position.
   b. Remove the pins and push each shaft to the neutral position.
3. Disconnect the U-joint at the front of the auxiliary transmission. Disconnect the U-joint at the rear of the auxiliary transmission and position the driveshaft out of the way.
4. Disconnect the speedometer cable from the transmission. If the speedometer cable cannot be readily disconnected, remove the parking brake drum and linkage, then disconnect the speedometer cable.
5. Remove the parking brake adjusting rod clevis pin and disconnect the parking brake lever to cam connector.
6. Position a transmission jack under the transmission and fasten the transmission to the jack with a safety chain.
7. Remove the transmission mounting stud (or bolt), insulator nut, cotter pins and nuts.

NOTE: When studs are used, do not disturb the stud-to-mounting bracket nuts.

8. Lower and remove the auxiliary transmission from the vehicle.
9. To install, position the insulators and reinforcements, if used, on the transmission mounting brackets and raise the transmission into place. Install the remaining insulators, retaining nuts and washers.
10. Adjust the auxiliary transmission so that it is parallelled to the main transmission within plus or minus $^{1}/_{2}$ degree. The coupling shaft between the two transmissions must be parallel to the transmissions from zero degree to one degree up at the auxiliary transmission end.

NOTE: The front two adjusting bolts and the rear two adjusting bolts must have final adjusting dimensions within $^{1}/_{8}$ in. of each other respectively.

11. Install the speedometer cable. If the parking brake drum has been removed, install the drum and the linkage. Attach the parking brake connector to the adjusting rod with a clevis pin.
12. Position the driveshaft and connect the rear U-joint. Connect the gear shift connecting rods to the transmission shift rods with clevis pins and new cotter pins. Connect the U-joint at the front of the auxiliary transmission.
13. Fill the transmission with the proper lubricant. Adjust the parking brake and shift linkage if required.

AUTOMATIC TRANSMISSION

For complete automatic transmission overhaul procedures, see the Unit Repair section.

C4 AND C5 AUTOMATIC TRANSMISSION

Removal and Installation

F SERIES

1. Raise and support the vehicle safely. Disconnect the transmission fluid filler tube from the pan. Drain the transmission fluid.
2. At the front lower edge of the converter housing, remove the cover attaching bolts and remove the dust cover. Remove the splash shield at the control levers.
3. Remove the drive shaft or coupling shaft. Remove the converter drain plug. Allow the converter to drain and install the drain plug.
4. Disconnect the oil cooler lines from the transmission.
5. Disconnect the manual and downshift linkage rods from the transmission control levers.
6. Remove the speedometer gear from the extension housing.
7. Remove the four converter to flywheel attaching nuts. Disconnect the starter cable. Remove the three starter to converter housing attaching bolts. Remove the starter.
8. Disconnect the vacuum line from the diaphragm unit and the vacuum line retaining clip.
9. Position the transmission jack to support the transmission. Install the safety chain to hold the transmission on the jack.
10. Remove the two engine rear support crossmember-to-frame attaching bolts.
11. Remove the two engine rear support-to-extension housing attaching bolts.
12. Raise the transmission and remove the rear support. Remove the six converter housing-to-engine attaching bolts.
13. Move the transmission away from the engine. Lower the transmission and remove it from under the vehicle.
14. To install, secure the transmission on a transmission jack. Align the transmission with the engine and move it into place, using care not to damage the flywheel and the converter pilot.

NOTE: The converter must rest squarely against the flywheel. This indicates that the converter pilot is not binding in the crankshaft.

15. Install the six converter housing-to-engine attaching bolts. Install the converter-to-flywheel attaching nuts.
16. Install the rear support. Install the rear support-to-extension housing attaching bolts.
17. Position the starter into the converter housing and install the three attaching bolts. Install the starter cable.
18. Remove the transmission jack.
19. Connect the transmission filler tube to the transmission pan. Connect the oil coolers lines to the transmission.
20. Install the speedometer driven gear in the extension housing.
21. Connect the transmission linkage rods to the transmission control levers.

NOTE: When making transmission control attachments, new retaining rings and grommets should be used.

22. Install the driveshaft or coupling shaft.
23. Install the vacuum line in the retaining clip. Connect the vacuum line to the diaphragm unit.
24. At the front lower area of the converter housing, install the lower cover and the control lever dust shield. Install the attaching bolts.
25. Secure the fluid filler tube to the pan.
26. Lower the vehicle.
27. Fill the transmission to the proper level.
28. Raise the vehicle and check for transmission fluid leakage. Lower the vehicle and adjust the throttle and manual linkage.

E SERIES

1. Working from inside the vehicle, remove the engine compartment cover.
2. Disconnect the neutral start switch wires at the plug connector.
3. If the vehicle is equipped with a V8 engine, remove the flex hose from the air cleaner heat tube.
4. Remove the upper converter housing-to-engine attaching bolts.
5. On V8 egnines, remove the upper muffler inlet pipe-to-exhaust manifold flange nut (right side of engine).
6. Raise the vehicle and support it safely.
7. On V8 engines, remove the three remaining muffler inlet pipe-to-exhaust manifold flange nuts and allow the exhaust pipe to hang.
8. Disconnect the transmission filler tube at the pan and drain the transmission fluid.
9. At the front lower edge of the converter housing, remove the dust cover attaching bolts and remove the cover.
10. Remove the converter-to-flywheel attaching nuts. As the flywheel is being rotated, remove the converter drain plug and drain the fluid from the converter.
11. Disconnect the driveshaft from the transmission companion flange and position it out of the way.
12. Remove the bolt retaining the fluid filler tube to the engine and remove the tube.
13. Disconnect the starter cable at the starter. Remove the starter-to-converter housing attaching bolts and remove the starter.
14. Position an engine support bar to the side rail and engine oil pan flanges.
15. Disconnect the cooler lines from the transmission. Disconnect the vacuum line from the vacuum disphragm unit.
16. Remove the speedometer driven gear from the extension housing.
17. Disconnect the manual and downshift linkage rods from the transmission control levers.
18. Install the converter drain plug. If the converter is not going to be cleaned, torque the drain plug to specification.
19. Position a transmission jack to support the transmission. Install the safety chain to hold the transmission on the jack.
20. Remove the bolt and nut securing the rear mount to the crossmember. Remove tbe four bolts retaining the crossmember to the side rails. Then, with the transmission jack, raise the transmission and remove the crossmember.
21. Remove the remaining converter housing-to-engine attaching bolts. Lower the transmission and remove it from under the vehicle.
22. Position the transmission on the jack and secure the transmission and converter to the jack with the safety chain.
23. Raise the transmission and guide the transmission and converter into position. The converter-to-flywheel retaining studs must line up with the holes in the flywheel. The converter hub must enter the end of the crankshaft.
24. Install the converter engine attaching bolts. Install the converter-to-flywheel attaching nuts.
25. Install the crossmember. Install the rear mount-to-crossmember attaching bolt and nut.

26. Remove the safety chain and remove the jack from under the vehicle. Remove the engine support bar.
27. Connect the cooler lines to the transmission. Connect the vacuum line to the vacuum diaphragm unit.
28. Install the speedometer driven gear into the extension housing.
29. Connect the transmission linkage rods to the transmission control levels.
30. Connect the transmission filler tube to the transmission pan. Secure the tube to the engine with the attaching bolt.
31. Install the converter dust cover.
32. Position the starter into the converter housing and install the attaching bolts. Install the starter cable.
33. Install the driveshaft.
34. If equipped with a V8 engine, install the muffler inlet pipe on the exhaust manifolds and install and torque the three retaining nuts.
35. Lower the vehicle.
36. On V8 engines, install and torque the upper muffler inlet pipe-to-exhaust manifold flange nut.
37. Install the upper converter housing-to-engine attaching bolts.
38. On V8 engines, install the flex hose to the air cleaner heat tube.
39. Connect the neutral start switch wires at the plug connector.
40. Fill the transmission to the proper level with the specified fluid.
41. Check for transmission fluid leakage. Lower the vehicle and adjust the throttle and manual linkage.
42. Install the engine compartment cover.

BRONCO

1. Working from the engine compartment, remove the screws retaining the fan shroud to the radiator.
2. Raise the vehicle and support it safely. Remove the transfer case shield, if equipped. Drain the transfer case.
3. Remove the fluid filler tube from the transmission oil pan and drain the transmission fluid.
4. Remove the converter drain plug access cover.
5. Remove the converter-to-flywheel nuts. Place a wrench on the crankshaft pulley bolt to turn the converter to gain access to the nuts.
6. With the wrench on the crankshaft pulley bolt, turn the converter to gain access to the drain plug. Drain the fluid and replace the drain plug.
7. Disconnect the rear driveshaft at the transfer case and move it out of the way. Disconnect and remove the front driveshaft.
8. Disconnect the complete exhaust system. Remove the speedometer gear from the transfer case. Disconnect the oil cooler lines from the transmission.
9. Disconnect the manual and downshift linkage rods from the transmission control levers.
10. Disconnect the neutral safety switch wires from the retaining clamps and connectors.
11. Disconnect the starter cable. Remove the starter-to-converter housing bolts. Remove the starter.
12. Remove the vacuum hoses from the transmission vacuum unit. Disconnect the vacuum lines from the retaining clip.
13. Remove the bolts, washers, plates and insulators that secure the crossmember to the transfer case adapter.
14. Remove the crossmember-to-frame side support bolts. Position a transmission jack to support the transmission and the transfer case.
15. Raise the transmission and the transfer case assembly and remove the bolts securing the left side support bracket to the frame. Remove the side support bracket, crossmember and upper crossmember insulators from the vehicle.
16. Raise the transmission and the transfer case slightly and disconnect the shift rod from the transfer shift lever bracket.
17. Remove the shift lever bracket-to-transfer case adapter bolts and allow the assembly to hang by the shift lever.
18. Secure the transmission and the transfer case assembly to a transmission jack and remove the converter housing-to-engine bolts.
19. Move the transmission and the transfer case assembly away from the engine. Lower the assembly and remove it from the vehicle.
20. To install, position the converter to the transmission making sure the converter drive flats are fully engaged in the pump gear.
21. With the converter properly installed, position the transmission and the transfer case assembly on a transmission jack and secure the assembly in place.
22. Rotate the converter until the studs and the drain plug are in alignment with their holes in the flywheel.
23. With the transmission and the transfer case mounted on a transmission jack, move the assembly forward into position, using care not to damage the flywheel and the converter pilot.

NOTE: The converter must rest squarely against the flywheel. This indicates that the converter pilot is not binding in the engine crankshaft.

24. Continue the installation in the reverse order of the removal. When the transmission linkage rods are connected to the transmission control levers, always install new retaining rings and grommets.
25. Fill the transfer case with lubricant. Fill the transmission to the proper level with the specified fluid. Adjust the manual and downshift linkage as required.

C6 AUTOMATIC TRANSMISSION

Removal and Installation

F SERIES AND BRONCO

1. Raise and support the vehicle safely.
2. Remove the two upper converter housing-to-engine bolts.
3. Remove the bolt securing the fluid filler tube to the engine cylinder head.
4. Drain the fluid from the transmission and converter.
5. Disconnect the coupling shaft or driveshaft from the transmission companion flange and position it out of the way.
6. Disconnect the speedometer cable from the bearing retainer.
7. Disconnect the throttle and manual linkage rods from the levers at the transmission.
8. Disconnect the oil cooler lines from the transmission.
9. Remove the vacuum hose from the vacuum unit. Remove the vacuum line retaining clip.
10. Disconnect the cable from the terminal on the starter motor. Remove the three attaching bolts and remove the starter motor.
11. Remove the four flywheel attaching nuts. Place a wrench on the crankshaft pulley attaching bolt to turn the converter to gain access to the nuts.
12. On F-150–F-250 (4 × 4) and Bronco remove the transfer case, if equipped.
13. Remove the two engine rear support crossmember-to-frame attaching bolts.
14. Remove the two engine rear support-to-extension housing attaching bolts.
15. Remove the eight bolts securing the No. 2 crossmember to the frame side rails.
16. Raise the transmission with a transmission jack and remove both crossmembers.
17. Secure the transmission to the jack with the safety chain.
18. Remove the remaining converter housing-to-engine attaching bolts.
19. Move the transmission away from the engine. Lower the transmission and remove it from under the vehicle.

20. To install, tighten the converter drain plug. Position the converter on the transmission making sure the converter drive flats are fully engaged in the pump gear.
21. With the converter properly installed, place the transmission on the jack. Secure the unit to the jack with a chain.
22. Rotate the converter so that studs and drain plug are in alignment with those in the flywheel.
23. Move the transmission toward the cylinder block until they are in contact.

NOTE: The converter must rest squarely against the flywheel. This indicates that the converter pilot is not binding in the engine crankshaft.

24. Install the converter housing-to-engine bolts.
25. Remove the transmission jack safety chain from around the transmission.
26. Position the No. 2 crossmember to the frame side rails. Install the attaching bolts.
27. If equipped, install the transfer case.
28. Position the engine rear support crossmember to the frame side rails. Install the rear support to extension housing mounting bolts.
29. Lower the transmission and remove the jack.
30. Secure the engine rear support crossmember to the frame side rails with the attaching bolts.
31. Connect the vacuum line to the vacuum diaphragm making sure that the metal tube is secured in the retaining clip.
32. Connect the oil cooler lines to the transmission.
33. Connect the throttle and manual linkage rods to their respective levers on the transmission.
34. Connect the speedometer cable to the bearing retainer.
35. Secure the starter motor in place with the attaching bolts. Connect the cable to the terminal on the starter.
36. Install a new O-ring on the lower end of the transmission filler tube and insert the tube in the case.
37. Secure the converter-to-flywheel attaching nuts. Use a wrench on the crankshaft pulley attaching nut to rotate the flywheel. Do not use a wrench on the converter attaching nuts to rotate it.
38. Install the converter housing dust shield and secure it with the attaching bolts.
39. Connect the coupling shaft driveshaft.
40. Adjust the shift linkage.
41. Lower the vehicle. Then install the two upper converter housing-to-engine bolts.
42. Position the transmission fluid filler tube to the cylinder head and secure with the attaching bolt.
43. Fill the transmission to the correct level with the specified lubricant. Start the engine and shift the transmission through all ranges, then re-check the fluid level.

E SERIES

The removal and installation procedure for Econolines equipped with the C-6 automatic transmission is the same as Econolines equipped with the C-4 automatic transmission.

Refer to the C-4 automatic transmission section for the removal and installation procedures.

600-SERIES

1. Remove the six floor covering molding retaining screws from the left side of the vehicle and remove the molding.
2. Remove the three body bolt cover retaining screws and remove the cover. Remove the body bolt and nut.
3. Remove the two rear body bolt covers and loosen the body bolts.
4. Raise the left side of the body with a jack and place a 1 $^5/_8$ in. piece of wood between the frame and the body mounting surfaces. Lower the jack.
5. Connect a remote control starter button to the solenoid.
6. Remove the rear support-to-crossmember bolts.
7. With a transmission jack positioned at the rear of the engine, raise the engine and transmission high enough to remove the rear supports.
8. Drain the automatic transmission fluid.
9. Remove the converter drain plug access cover bolts from the lower end of the converter housing.
10. Remove the converter-to-flywheel nuts. Crank the engine to turn the converter to gain access to the nuts.
11. Crank the engine to gain access to the converter drain plug. Drain the fluid and replace the drain plug.
12. Disconnect the starter cable from the starter. Remove the starter retaining bolts. Remove the starter.
13. Disconnect the driveshaft at the transmission and move it aside.
14. Disconnect the speedometer cable. Disconnect the parking brake linkage. Disconnect the shift cable from the manual lever at the transmission.
15. Remove the bolts that secure the shift cable bracket to the converter housing and move the cable and bracket aside.
16. Disconnect the downshift rod from the transmission downshift lever.
17. Disconnect the vacuum hose from the vacuum diaphragm at the rear of the transmission. Remove the vacuum line from the retaining clip at the transmission.
18. Disconnect the oil cooler lines at the transmission case. Remove the transmission filler tube and dipstick.
19. Position a transmission jack under the transmission and secure the transmission to the jack with a safety chain.
20. Remove the converter housing-to-engine bolts.
21. Move the transmission assembly away from the engine. Tilt the assembly forward, and with the jack guide it over the crossmember. Lower the jack and remove the assembly from the vehicle.
22. To install, tighten the converter drain plug. Position the converter to the transmission making sure the converter drive flats are fully engaged in the pump gear.
23. With the converter properly installed, place the transmission on the jack. Secure the transmission to the jack with a safety chain.
24. Rotate the converter until the studs and the drain plug are in alignment with their holes in the flywheel.
25. Raise the transmission and position it over the crossmember to the engine.

NOTE: Be careful not to damage the flywheel and converter pilot. The converter must rest squarely against the flywheel. This indicates that the converter pilot is not binding in the engine crankshaft.

26. Continue the installation in the reverse order of the removal. When replacing the transmission filler tube be sure to use a new O-ring.
27. Fill the transmission to the correct level with the proper fluid. Adjust the transmission control linkage, as required. Check the transmission, converter and oil cooler lines for leaks.

C3 AUTOMATIC TRANSMISSION

Removal and Installation

RANGER AND BRONCO II

1. Raise and support the vehicle safely. Place a drain pan under the transmission fluid pan. Starting at the rear of the pan and working toward the front, loosen the attaching bolts and allow the fluid to drain. Then remove all of the pan attaching bolts except two at the front, to allow the fluid to further drain. After all the fluid has drained, install two bolts on the rear side of the pan to temporarily hold it in place.
2. Remove the converter drain plug access cover and adapter plate bolts from the lower end of the converter housing.

3. Remove the four flywheel to converter attaching nuts. Crank the engine to turn the converter to gain access to the nuts, using a wrench on the crankshaft pulley attaching bolt. On belt driven overhead camshaft engines, never turn the engine backwards.

4. Crank the engine until the converter drain plug is accessible and remove the plug. Place a drain pan under the converter to catch the fluid. After all the fluid has been drained from the converter, reinstall the plug and tighten to 20–30 ft. lbs. Remove the driveshaft. Install cover, plastic bag etc. over end of extension housing.

5. Remove the speedometer cable from the extension housing. Disconnect the shift rod at the transmission manual lever. Disconnect the downshift rod at the transmission downshift lever.

6. Remove the starter-to-converter housing attaching bolts and position the starter out of the way.

7. Disconnect the neutral start switch wires from the switch. Remove the vacuum line from the transmission vacuum modulator.

8. Position a suitable jack under the transmission and raise it slightly.

9. Remove the engine rear support-to-crossmember bolts. Remove the crossmember-to-frame side support attaching bolts and remove the crossmember insulator and support and damper.

10. Lower the jack under the transmission and allow the transmission to hang.

11. Position a jack to the front of the engine and raise the engine to gain access to the two upper converter housing-to-engine attaching bolts.

12. Disconnect the oil cooler lines at the transmission. Plug all openings to keep out dirt.

13. Remove the lower converter housing-to-engine attaching bolts. Remove the transmission filler tube.

14. Secure the transmission to the jack with a safety chain.

15. Remove the two upper converter housing-to-engine attaching bolts. Move the transmission to the rear and down to remove it from under the vehicle.

16. Position the converter to the transmission making sure the converter hub is fully engaged in the pump. With the converter properly installed, place the transmission on the jack and secure with safety chain.

17. Rotate the converter so the drive studs and drain plug are in alignment with their holes in the flywheel. With the transmission mounted on a transmission jack, move the converter and transmission assembly forward into position being careful not to damage the flywheel and the converter pilot.

18. Install the two upper converter housing-to-engine attaching bolts and tighten to 28–38 ft. lbs.

19. Remove the safety chain from the transmission. Insert the filler tube in the stub tube and secure it to the cylinder block with the attaching bolt. Tighten the bolt to 28–38 ft. lbs. If the stub tube is loosened or dislodged, it should be replaced. Install the oil cooler lines in the retaining clip at the cylinder block. Connect the lines to the transmission case.

20. Remove the jack supporting the front of the engine. Raise the transmission. Position the crossmember, insulator and support and damper to the frame side supports and install the attaching bolts. Tighten the bolts to 20–30 ft. lbs.

21. Lower the transmission and install the rear engine support-to-crossmember nut. Tighten the bolt to 60–80 ft. lbs.

22. Remove the transmission jack. Install the vacuum hose on the transmission vacuum unit. Install the vacuum line into the retaining clip.

23. Connect the neutral start switch plug to the switch. Install the starter and tighten the attaching bolts to 15–20 ft. lbs.

24. Install the four flywheel-to-converter attaching nuts.

25. Install the converter drain plug access cover and adaptor plate bolts. Tighten the bolts to 12–16 ft. lbs.

26. Connect the muffler inlet pipe to the exhaust manifold.

27. Connect the transmission shift rod to the manual lever. Connect the downshift rod to the downshift lever.

28. Connect the speedometer cable to the extension housing. Install the driveshaft. Tighten the companion flange U-bolt attaching nuts to 70–95 ft. lbs.

29. Adjust the manual and downshift linkage as required.

30. Lower the vehicle. Fill the transmission to the proper level with the specified fluid.

C5 Automatic Transmission

RANGER AND BRONCO II, EXCEPT 4 × 4 MODELS

1. Raise the vehicle and safely support it. Place the drain pan under the transmission fluid pan. Starting at the rear of the pan and working toward the front, loosen the attaching bolts and allow the fluid to drain. Finally remove all of the pan attaching bolts except two at the front, to allow the fluid to further drain. With fluid drained, install two bolts on the rear side of the pan to temporarily hold it in place.

2. Remove the converter drain plug access cover from the lower end of the converter housing.

3. Remove the converter-to-flywheel attaching nuts. Place a wrench on the crankshaft pulley attaching bolt to turn the converter to gain access to the nuts.

4. Place a drain pan under the converter to catch the fluid. With the wrench on the crankshaft pulley attaching bolt, turn the converter to gain access to the converter drain plug and remove the plug. After the fluid has been drained, reinstall the plug.

5. Disconnect the driveshaft from the rear axle and slide shaft rearward from the transmission. Install a suitable cover in the extension housing to prevent fluid leakage. Mark the rear driveshaft yoke and axle flange so they can be installed in their original position.

6. Disconnect the cable from the terminal on the starter motor. Remove the three attaching bolts and remove the starter motor. Disconnect the neutral start switch wires at the plug connector.

7. Remove the rear mount-to-crossmember attaching nuts and the two crossmember-to-frame attaching bolts. Remove the right and left gusset.

8. Remove the two engine rear insulator-to-extension housing attaching bolts.

9. Disconnect the TV linkage rod from the transmission TV lever. Disconnect the manual rod from the transmission manual lever at the transmission.

10. Remove the two bolts securing the bellcrank bracket to the converter housing.

11. Raise the transmission with a suitable jack to provide clearance to remove the crossmember. Remove the rear mount from the crossmember and remove the crossmember from the side supports. Lower the transmission to gain access to the oil cooler lines. Disconnect each oil line from the fittings on the transmission.

12. Disconnect the speedometer cable from the extension housing.

13. Remove the bolt that secures the transmission fluid filler tube to the cylinder block. Lift the filler tube and the dipstick from the transmission.

14. Secure the transmission to the jack with the chain. Remove the converter housing-to-cylinder block attaching bolts.

15. Carefully move the transmission and converter assembly away from the engine and, at the same time, lower the jack to clear the underside of the vehicle.

16. Tighten the converter drain plug to specifications. Position the converter on the transmission, making sure the converter drive flats are fully engaged in the pump gear by rotating the converter.

17. With the converter properly installed, place the transmission on the jack. Secure the transmission to the jack with a chain.

18. Rotate the converter until the studs and drain plug are in alignment with the holes in the flywheel. Move the converter and transmission assembly forward into position, using care not to damage the flywheel and the converter pilot. The converter must rest squarely against the flywheel. This indicates that the converter pilot is not binding in the engine crankshaft.
19. Install and tighten the converter housing-to-engine attaching bolts to specification.
20. Remove the safety chain from around the transmission.
21. Install the new O-ring on the lower end of the transmission filler tube. Insert the tube in the transmission case and secure the tube to the engine with the attaching bolt.
22. Connect the speedometer cable to the extension housing.
23. Connect the oil cooler lines to the right side of transmission case.
24. Secure the engine rear support to the extension housing and tighten the bolts to specification.
25. Position the crossmember on the side supports. Lower the transmission and remove the jack. Secure the crossmember to the side supports with the attaching bolts.
26. Position the damper assembly over the engine rear support studs. (The painted face of the damper is facing forward when installed in the vehicle.) Secure the rear engine support to the crossmember.
27. Position the bellcrank to the converter housing and install the two attaching bolts.
28. Connect the TV linkage rod to the transmission TV lever. Connect the manual linkage rod to the manual lever at the transmission.
29. Secure the converter-to-flywheel attaching nuts and tighten them to specification.
30. Install the converter housing access cover and secure it with the attaching bolts.
31. Secure the starter motor in place with the attaching bolts. Connect the cable to the terminal on the starter. Connect the neutral start switch wires at the plug connector.
32. Connect the driveshaft to the rear axle so the index marks on the companion flange and the rear yoke are aligned. Lubricate the slip yoke with grease. Adjust the shift linkage as required.
33. Adjust throttle linkage.
34. Lower the vehicle. Fill the transmission to the correct level with the specified fluid. Start the engine and shift the transmission to all ranges, then recheck the fluid level.

RANGER AND BRONCO II 4×4

1. Remove the bolt securing the fluid filler tube to the engine valve cover bracket. Raise the vehicle and safely support it.
2. Place a drain pan under the transmission fluid pan. Starting at the rear of the pan and working towards the front, loosen the attaching bolts and allow the fluid to drain. Finally, remove all of the pan attaching bolts except two at the front, to allow the fluid to drain further. With fluid drained, install two bolts on the rear side of the pan to temporarily hold it in place.
3. Remove the converter drain plug access cover from the lower end of the converter housing. Remove the converter-to-flywheel attaching nuts. Place a wrench on the crankshaft pulley attaching bolt to turn the converter to gain access to the nuts.
4. Place a drain pan under the converter to catch the fluid. With the wrench on the crankshaft pulley attaching bolt, turn the converter to gain access to the converter drain plug and remove the plug. After the fluid has been drained, reinstall the plug.
5. Disconnect the cable from the terminal at the starter motor. Remove the three attaching bolts and remove the starter motor. Disconnect the neutral start switch wires at the plug connector.
6. Remove the rear mount-to-crossmember attaching nuts and the two crossmember-to-frame attaching bolts. Remove the right and left gusset.
7. Remove the two engine rear insulator-to-extension housing attaching bolts.
8. Disconnect the TV linkage rod from the transmission TV lever. Disconnect the manual rod from the transmission manual lever at the transmission. Disconnect the downshift and manual linkage rods from the levers on the transmission.
9. Remove the vacuum hose from the vacuum diaphragm unit. Remove the vacuum line from the retaining clip.
10. Remove the two bolts securing the bellcrank bracket to the converter housing.
11. Remove the transfer case.
12. Raise the transmission with a transmission jack to provide clearance to remove the crossmember. Remove the rear mount from the crossmember and remove the crossmember from the side supports.
13. Lower the transmission to gain access to the oil cooler lines.
14. Disconnect each oil line from the fittings on the transmission.
15. Disconnect the speedometer cable from the extension housing.
16. Secure the transmission to the jack with the chain. Remove the converter housing-to-cylinder block attaching bolts.
17. Carefully move the transmission and converter assembly away from the engine and, at the same time, lower the jack to clear the underside of the vehicle.
18. Position the converter on the transmission, making sure the converter drive flats are fully engaged in the pump gear by rotating the converter.
19. With the converter properly installed, place the transmission on the jack. Secure the transmission to the jack with a chain.
20. Rotate the converter until the studs and drain plug are in alignment with the holes in the flywheel.
21. Move the converter and transmission assembly forward into position, using care not to damage the flywheel and the converter pilot. The converter must rest squarely against the flywheel. This indicates that the converter pilot is not binding in the engine crankshaft.
22. Install and tighten the converter housing-to-engine attaching bolts.
23. Remove the safely chain from around the transmission.
24. Install a new O-ring on the lower end of the transmission filler tube. Insert the tube in the transmission case.
25. Connect the speedometer cable to the extension housing.
26. Connect the oil cooler lines to the right of the transmission case.
27. Position the crossmember on the side supports. Position the rear mount insulator on the crossmember and install the attaching bolts and nuts.
28. Install the transfer case.
29. Secure the engine rear support to the extension housing. Lower the transmission and remove the jack.
30. Secure the crossmember to the side supports with the attaching bolts and tighten to specification.
31. Position the bellcrank to the converter housing and install the two attaching bolts.
32. Connect the downshift and manual linkage rods to their respective levers on the transmission.
33. Connect the vacuum line to the vacuum diaphragm making sure that the line is in the retaining clip.
34. Secure the converter-to-flywheel attaching nuts. Install the converter housing access cover and secure it with the attaching bolts.
35. Secure the starter motor in place with the attaching bolts. Connect the cable to the terminal on the starter. Connect the neutral start switch wires at the plug connector.
36. Adjust the shift linkage as required. Lower the vehicle.
37. Position the transmission fluid filler tube to the valve cover bracket and secure with the attaching bolt. Fill the transmission to the correct level. Start the engine and shift the transmission to all ranges, then recheck the fluid level.

AUTOMATIC OVERDRIVE

Removal and Installation

1. Raise the vehicle and support it safely.
2. Place the drain pan under the transmission fluid pan. Starting at the rear of the pan and working toward the front, loosen the attaching bolts and allow the fluid to drain. Finally remove all of the pan attaching bolts except two at the front, to allow the fluid to further drain. With fluid drained, install two bolts on the rear side of the pan to temporarily hold it in place.
3. Remove the converter drain plug access cover from the lower end of the converter housing.
4. Remove the converter-to-flywheel attaching nuts. Place a wrench on the crankshaft pulley attaching bolt to turn the converter to gain access to the nuts.
5. Place a drain pan under the converter to catch the fluid. With the wrench on the crankshaft pulley attaching bolt, turn the converter to gain access to the converter drain plug and remove the plug. After the fluid has been drained, reinstall the plug.
6. Disconnect the driveshaft from the rear axle and slide shaft rearward from the transmission. Install a seal installation tool in the extension housing to prevent fluid leakage.
7. Disconnect the cable from the terminal on the starter motor. Remove the three attaching bolts and remove the starter motor. Disconnect the neutral start switch wires at the plug connector.
8. Remove the rear mount-to-crossmember attaching bolts and the two crossmember-to-frame attaching bolts.
9. Remove the two engine rear support-to-extension housing attaching bolts.
10. Disconnect the TV linkage rod from the transmission TV lever. Disconnect the manual rod from the transmission manual lever at the transmission.
11. Remove the two bolts securing the bellcrank bracket to the converter housing.
12. Raise the transmission with a transmission jack to provide clearance to remove the crossmember. Remove the rear mount from the crossmember and remove the crossmember from the side supports.
13. Lower the transmission to gain access to the oil cooler lines.
14. Disconnect each oil line from the fittings on the transmission.
15. Disconnect the speedometer cable from the extension housing.
16. Remove the bolt that secures the transmission fluid filler tube to the cylinder block. Lift the filler tube and the dipstick from the transmission.
17. Secure the transmission to the jack with the chain.
18. Remove the converter housing-to-cylinder block attaching bolts.
19. Carefully move the transmission and converter assembly away from the engine and, at the same time, lower the jack to clear the underside of the vehicle.
20. Remove the converter and mount the transmission in a holding fixture.
21. Tighten the converter drain plug.
22. Position the converter on the transmission, making sure the converter drive flats are fully engaged in the pump gear by rotating the converter.
23. With the converter properly installed, place the transmission on the jack. Secure the transmission to the jack with a chain.
24. Rotate the converter until the studs and drain plug are in alignment with the holes in the flywheel.
25. Move the converter and transmission assembly forward into position, using care not to damage the flywheel and the converter pilot. The converter must rest squarely against the flywheel. This indicates that the converter pilot is not binding in the engine crankshaft.
26. Install and tighten the converter housing-to-engine attaching bolts to 40–50 ft. lbs.
27. Remove the safety chain from around the transmission.
28. Install a new O-ring on the lower end of the transmission filler tube. Insert the tube in the transmission case and secure the tube to the engine with the attaching bolt.
29. Connect the speedometer cable to the extension housing.
30. Connect the oil cooler lines to the right side of transmission case.
31. Position the crossmember on the side supports. Position the rear mount on the crossmember and install the attaching bolt and nut.
32. Secure the engine rear support to the extension housing and tighten the bolts to 16–20 ft. lbs.
33. Lower the transmission and remove the jack.

ALLISON AT SERIES AUTOMATIC TRANSMISSION MODELS

Removal and Installation

1. Remove the right and left door sill scuff plates. Move the floor mat out of the way. Remove the bolts securing the transmission access cover to the floor pan and remove the cover.
2. On a one-piece driveshaft, disconnect the shaft from the yoke at the parking brake drum. On vehicles with a two-piece driveshaft, disconnect the coupling shaft from the yoke at the parking brake drum. Remove the center support bearing bracket. Move the forward end of the driveshaft out of the way.
3. Disconnect the parking brake linkage and remove the parking brake drum from the output shaft flange.
4. Remove the parking brake handle and brackets from the transmission case.
5. Place a drain pan under the transmission and drain the fluid.
6. Disconnect the speedometer cable from the rear of the transmission.
7. Disconnect the oil cooler lines at the transmission.
8. Disconnect the vacuum line from the vacuum modulator.
9. Remove the vacuum modulator retainer bolt and remove the retainer. Remove the vacuum modulator valve actuating rod from the case.
10. Disconnect the shift cable from the manual selector lever at the transmission.
11. Remove the two bolts holding the shift cable bracket to the transmission and position the cable and bracket out of the way.
12. Remove the inspection cover from the bottom front side of the flywheel housing.
13. Remove the six converter to flywheel attaching bolts. It may be necessary to turn the engine over manually.
14. Remove the four upper and two lower converter housing to flywheel attaching bolts.
15. Remove the bolts and nuts securing the two rear engine supports to the cross member. Remove the lower insulators and flat washers.
16. Loosen the front engine support bolts.
17. Position a transmission jack under the transmission and secure the transmission to the jack with a chain.
18. Place a jack under the engine. Raise both jacks to relieve the pressure on the cross member.
19. Remove the two upper engine rear support insulators from the crossmember.
20. Remove the bolts securing the engine rear support brackets to the transmission and remove the brackets.
21. With both jacks supporting the engine and transmission, remove the remaining converter housing to flywheel attaching bolts.
22. Pull the transmission rearward until the converter housing touches the body sheet metal. Then, tilt the rear of the transmission upward until the bottom of the converter housing clears the crossmember. Lower the transmission assembly and

remove it from the underside of the vehicle. If necessary, raise the rear of the vehicle to permit the transmission to clear the chassis.

NOTE: Prior to installing the transmission, it is mandatory that the flexplate be checked for runout. The maximum T.I.R. should be 0.020 in. for AT-540 and 0.030 in. for AT 545. In addition, the flywheel housing transmission mounting face alignment inspection should be made on the engine flywheel housing transmission surface. The face and bore runout should not exceed 0.008 in. T.I.R.

23. Position the torque converter on the transmission, engaging the turbine shaft with the stator and the hub with the oil pump drive gear.
24. Place the transmission on a jack and secure with a chain.
25. Raise the converter and transmission of the jack and move the transmission assembly into position over the cross member. Align the holes in the converter with the holes in the flywheel.
26. Install six converter housing-to-flywheel attaching bolts, three on each side. Tighten the bolts to specification.
27. Lower the engine jack and remove it from the vehicle.
28. Position the engine rear support brackets on the side of the transmission and secure with the attaching bolts.
29. Position the two upper engine rear support insulators on the crossmember. Position the lower insulators and flat washers on the cross member and install the rear support-to-cross member bolts and nuts. Tighten the bolts to specification.
30. Lower the transmission jack and remove it from the vehicle.
31. Install the four upper and two lower converter housing-to-flywheel attaching bolts.
32. Tighten the front engine support bolts to specification.
33. Install the six converter to flywheel attaching bolts. Tighten the bolts to specification.
34. Install the inspection cover on the bottom front side of the flywheel housing.
35. Position the shift cable bracket on the transmission and install the attaching bolts.
36. Connect the shift cable to the manual lever on the transmission.
37. Install the vacuum modulator actuating rod and vacuum modulator into the case. Install the vacuum modulator retainer and secure with the attaching bolt.
38. Connect the vacuum line to the vacuum modulator.
39. Connect the oil cooler lines to the transmission.
40. Connect the speedometer cable.
41. Install the fluid filler tube on the oil pan.
42. Position the parking brake handle and bracket on the transmission and secure with the attaching bolts.
43. Install the parking brake drum and connect the parking brake linkage.
44. Install the driveshaft, center support bearing bracket and the coupling shaft. Connect the coupling shaft to the parking brake drum and tighten all bolts.
45. Position the transmission access cover on the floor pan and secure with the attaching screws.
46. Add enough automatic transmission fluid to the transmission to bring the fluid level to the full mark on the transmission.
47. Check the transmission for leaks. Road test the unit.

ALLISON MT SERIES AUTOMATIC TRANSMISSION MODELS

Removal and Installation

NOTE: Nothing fastens the torque converter to the transmission. A retaining strap must be used for handling. The torque converter and the transmission must be removed from and installed in the vehicle as the unit. The transmission cannot be removed from or installed on the converter in the vehicle.

1. Remove the filler tube from the oil pan and drain the oil from the transmission.
2. Install a protective plug in the drain hole.
3. On vehicles with a one piece drive line, disconnect the shaft from the pinion shaft flange and from the yoke at the parking brake drum. Do not remove the bolt that attaches the flange to the transmission output shaft. On vehicles with two piece driveshafts, disconnect the coupling shaft from the yoke at the parking brake drum, and then remove the center support bearing bracket. Move the forward end of the driveshaft out of the way.
4. Disconnect the speedometer cable from the rear of the transmission.
5. Disconnect the throttle control rod and the selector lever cable from the levers on the left side of the transmission housing. Remove the cable clamp bracket from the transmission.
6. Disconnect the parking brake linkage.
7. Disconnect the oil cooler lines from the fittings on the retarder valve body, then remove the forward fitting. Plug the lines and valve body openings. If desired, the lines and valve body can be drained, but they should be plugged before removing the transmission assembly from the vehicle.
8. Remove the dust shield from the bottom front side of the flywheel housing.
9. Remove the nuts and flat washers that hold the converter pump cover to the engine flywheel. The nuts and washers can be reached through an opening in the lower right side of the flywheel housing. The flywheel must be turned to remove all the nuts and washers.
10. Cut the lock wires and remove the two bolts and nuts that hold the converter housing to the frame crossmember.
11. Cut the lock wire and remove the two bolts, washers, and insulators from the top of the transmission rear support and crossmember.
12. Place an engine support under the rear of the engine, then raise the engine to take the weight off the crossmember.
13. Support the transmission with a 1000 pound transmission jack. The jack should be placed so that the oil pan does not support the entire weight of the transmission. Fasten a safety chain over the top of the transmission and to both sides of the jack.
14. Remove the two bolts from each end of the transmission rear support crossmember, and remove the crossmember.
15. Remove the bolts and lockwashers that attach the converter housing to flywheel housing.
16. Move the transmission assembly away from the engine until the converter clears the crossmember. If necessary raise the floor pan slightly to permit the converter housing to clear the crossmember.

NOTE: If the engine, flywheel housing has been replaced, check the housing alignment and flywheel shim adjustment before installing the torque converter and transmission. The flywheel housing transmision mounting face alignment inspection should be made on the engine flywheel housing transmission surface. The face bore runout should not exceed 0.008 in. T.I.R.

17. Raise the transmission assembly on the jack, then move the unit into position over the crossmember that supports the converter. Align the studs in the converter with the holes in the flywheel. Install the two guide studs in the flywheel housing, then push the unit forward so that the converter studs enter the holes in the flywheel.
18. Install the bolts, except the fluid filler tube support bracket bolt, and lockwashers that attach the converter housing to the flywheel housing. Torque the bolts to 23–28 ft. lbs.

19. Install six new self-locking nuts and flat washers to attach the converter to the engine flywheel. Torque the nuts to 34–40 ft. lbs.
20. Install the dust shield on the bottom front side of the flywheel housing.
21. Install the transmission rear support crossmember on top of the frame brackets, then install the bolts on the cross member and tighten to 40–45 ft. lbs. torque.
22. Lower the jack, and remove it from under the vehicle. Remove the engine support.
23. Install the nuts and bolts that hold the converter housing to the frame crossmember and tighten the bolts to 70–91 ft. lbs. torque. Install the lock wire.
24. Install the bolts, washers, and insulators at the transmission rear 60 ft. lbs. torque and install the support. Tighten the bolts to 40 ft. lbs. install lock wire.
25. Install the oil cooler lines.
26. Install the selector lever cable bracket on the left side of the transmission and tighten the attaching screws to 8–10 ft. lbs. torque.
27. Connect the selector lever cable to the lever on the left side of the housing.
28. Connect the selector lever cable to the lever on the left side of the housing.
28. Connect the fluid filler tube to the oil pan, then install the tube support bracket bolt.
29. Push the breather hose across the top of the transmission and connect the hose to the fitting above the left PTO plate. Tighten the hose clamp.
30. Connect the parking brake linkage.
31. If the exhaust system was removed or disconnected during transmission removal, install and connect the parts.
32. Install the driveshaft, center bearing support bracket, and the coupling shaft. Connect the coupling shaft to the parking brake drum. Tighten all nuts and bolts.
33. Connect the speedometer cable to the rear of the transmission.
34. Adjust the selector lever linkage.
35. Check all fluid line connections for tightness, and lower the vehicle to the floor.
36. Add enough automatic transmission fluid to the converter and transmission to bring the fluid level up to the full mark on the dipstick.

SHIFT LINKAGE

Adjustment

BRONCO, ECONOLINE AND F SERIES

1. With the engine stopped, place the transmission selector lever at the steering column in the D position and hold against the "D" stop.
2. Loosen the shift rod adjusting nut at the transmission lever.
3. Shift the manual lever at the transmission to the D position, two detents from the rear. On an F-100 with 4WD, move the bellcrank lever.
4. With the selector lever and transmission manual lever in the D position, tighten the adjusting nut to 12–18 ft. lbs. Do not allow the rod or shift lever to move while tightening the nut.
5. Check the operation of the shift linkage.

F-600 SERIES

1. With the engine stopped, position the transmission selector lever in the D position.
2. Disconnect the shift cable clevis at the transmission manual level. Move the transmission manual lever to the D position.
3. With the transmission manual lever in the D position, adjust clevis until it freely enters into the hole of the manual lever.

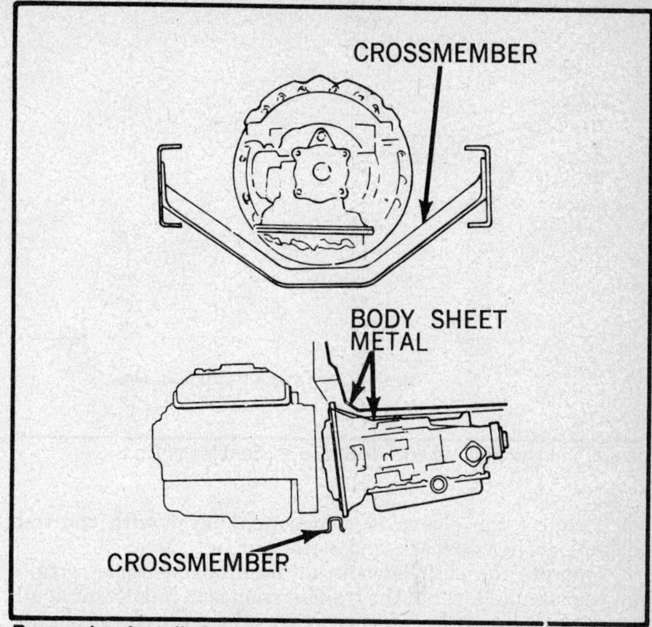

Removal or installation of Allison AT-540 transmission (© Ford Motor Co.)

4. Connect the clevis to the manual lever and secure it with the flat washers, spring washer and cotter pin.
5. Operate the shift lever in all positions. It may be necesary to re-adjust the clevis slightly to obtain the detent position in all drive ranges.

ALLISON AUTOMATIC TRANSMISSION

1. With the engine off, position the selector in the "R" position.
2. Disconnect the shift level cable sleeve at the transmission manual shift lever.
3. Shift the transmission manual lever to "R" (all the way forward and upward).
4. With the manual lever in the "R" position, adjust the sleeve until it freely enters into the hole in the manual lever.

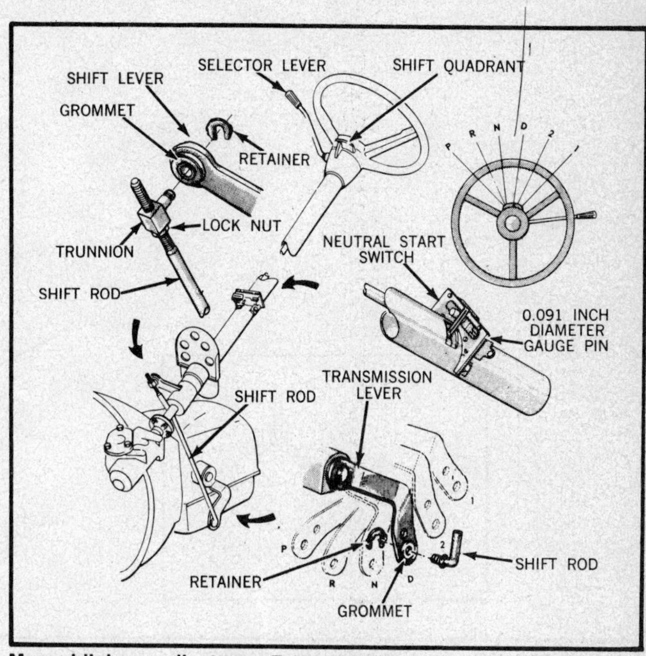

Manual linkage adjustment F-100-250-350 (© Ford Motor Co.)

TRUNNION
NEUTRAL
STARTER SWITCH
SHIFT
LEVER
SHIFT ROD
TRANSMISSION LEVER
P
R
N D 2 1

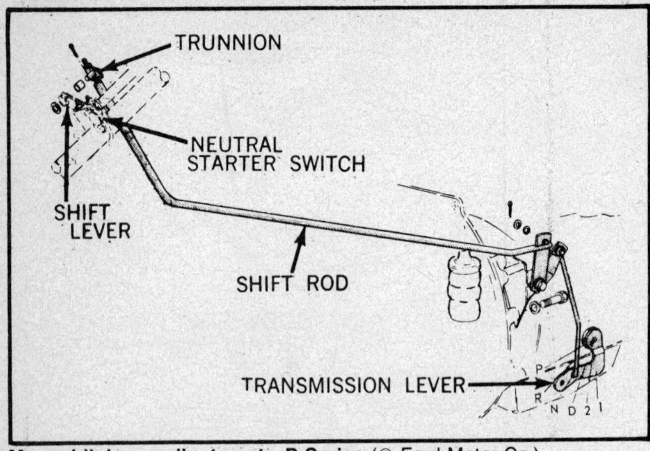

Manual linkage adjustment—P-Series (© Ford Motor Co.)

5. Connect the sleeve to the manual lever with the flat washers, spring washers, and cotter pin.

6. Operate the shift lever in all positions to make certain that the manual lever at the transmission is in full detent at all gear ranges. It may be necessary to re-adjust the sleeve slightly to obtain the detent position in all drive ranges.

Throttle Valve Linkage

Adjustment At The Carburetor W/Rod

AUTOMATIC OVERDRIVE

The TV control linkage may be adjusted at the carburetor using the following procedure:

1. Check that engine idle speed is set at specification.
2. De-cam the fast idle cam on the carburetor so that the throttle lever is at its idle stop. Place shift lever in N (neutral), set park brake (engine off).
3. Backout linkage lever adjusting screw all the way (screw end is flush with lever face).
4. Turn in adjusting screw until a thin shim (0.005 inch max.) or piece of writing paper fits snugly between end of screw and throttle lever. To eliminate effect of friction, push linkage lever forward (tending to close gap) and release before checking clearance between end of screw and throttle lever. Do not apply any load on levers with tools or hands while checking gap.
5. Turn in adjusting screw an additional four turns (Four turns are preferred. Two turns minimum is permissible if screw travel is limited).
6. If it is not possible to turn in adjusting screw at least two additional turns or if there was insufficient screw adjusting capacity to obtain an initial gap in Step 2 above, refer to Linkage Adjustment at Transmission. Whenever it is required to adjust

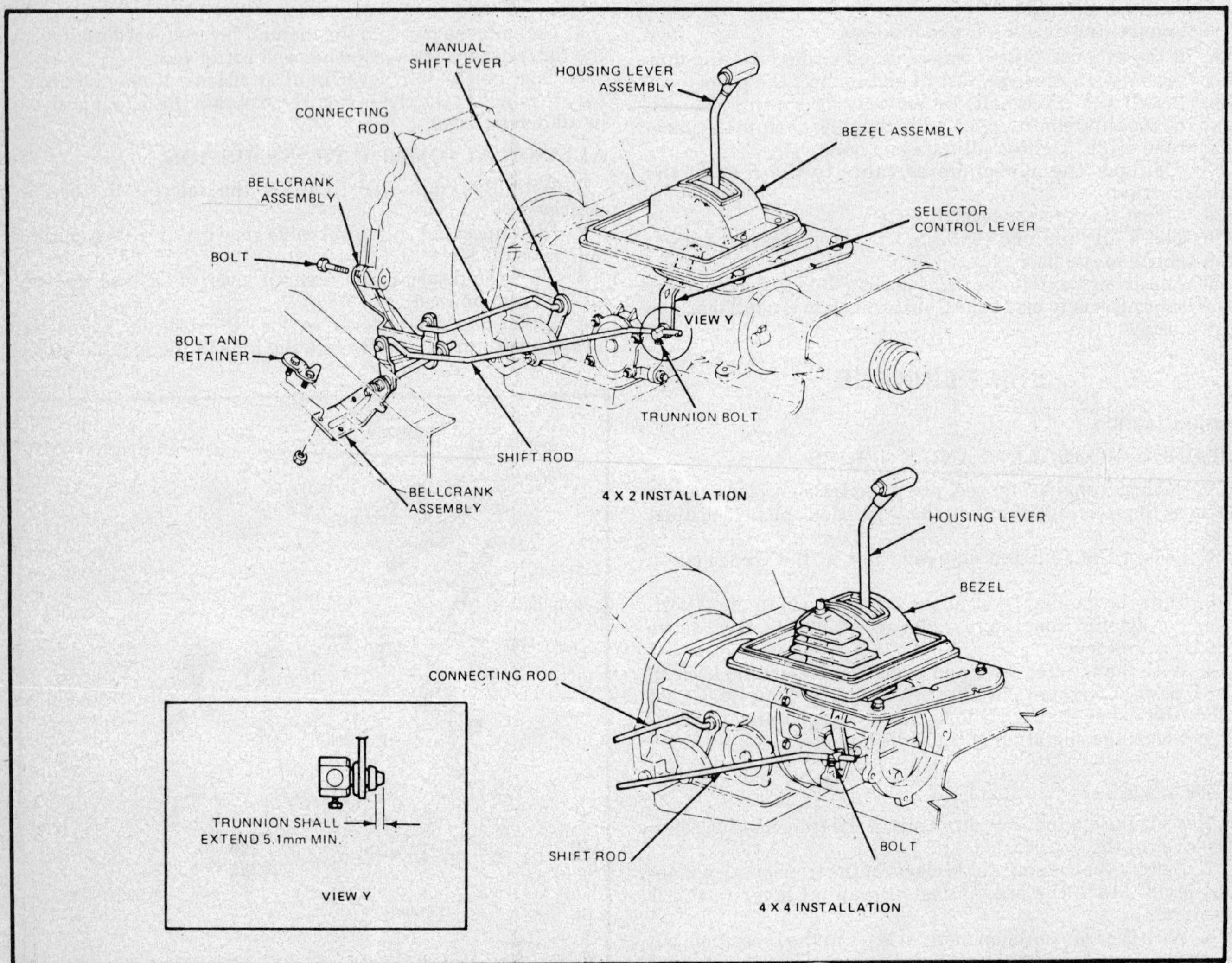

MANUAL
SHIFT LEVER
HOUSING LEVER
ASSEMBLY
CONNECTING
ROD
BEZEL ASSEMBLY
BELLCRANK
ASSEMBLY
SELECTOR
CONTROL LEVER
BOLT
VIEW Y
BOLT AND
RETAINER
TRUNNION BOLT
SHIFT ROD
BELLCRANK
ASSEMBLY
4 X 2 INSTALLATION
HOUSING LEVER
BEZEL
CONNECTING ROD
TRUNNION SHALL
EXTEND 5.1mm MIN.
SHIFT ROD
BOLT
VIEW Y
4 X 4 INSTALLATION

Floor shift controls—C5 automatic transmission (© FOMOCO) idle speed by more than 50 rpm, the adjustment screw on the linkage lever at the carburetor should also be readjusted. After making any idle speed adjustments, always verify the linkage lever and throttle lever are in contact with the throttle lever at its idle stop and the shift lever is in N (neutral).

Adjustment At Transmission

The linkage lever adjustment screw has limited adjustment capability. If it is not possible to adjust the TV linkage using this screw, the length of the TV control rod assembly must be readjusted using the following procedure. This procedure must also be followed whenever a new TV control rod assembly is installed.

1. Raise and support the vehicle safely. Set the engine curb idle speed to specification.
2. With engine off de-cam the fast idle cam on the carburetor so that the throttle lever is against the idle stop. Place shift lever in Neutral and set park brake (engine off).
3. Set the linkage lever adjustment screw at its approximately mid-range.
4. If a new TV control rod assembly is being installed. Connect the rod to the linkage lever at the carburetor.
5. Using a 13 mm box end wrench, loosen the bolt on the sliding trunnion block on the TV control rod assembly.
6. Remove any corrosion from the control rod and freeup the trunnion block so that it slides freely on the control rod. Insert pin into transmission lever grommet.
7. Push up on the lower end of the control rod to insure that the linkage lever at carburetor is firmly against the throttle lever. Release force on rod. Rod must stay up.
8. Push the TV control lever on the transmission up against its internal stop with a firm force (approximately 5 pounds) and tighten the bolt on the trunnion block. Do not relax force on lever until it is tightened.
9. Lower the vehicle and verify that the throttle lever is still against the idle stop. If not, repeat Steps 2 through 9.

Adjustment W/Cable

Whenever it is required to adjust the idle speed by more than 150 RPM, the TV control cable should be readjusted. Failure to do so may result in the symptoms due to a "to short" cable if the idle speed was increased or a "too long" cable if the idle speed was reduced.

Idle Speed Change	Turns on linkage lever adjuster screw
Less than 50 rpm	No change required
50 to 100 rpm increase	1½ turns out
50 to 100 rpm decrease	1½ turns in
100 to 150 rpm increase	2½ turns out
100 to 150 rpm decrease	2½ turns in

1. Check and set, if necessary, engine idle speed to specification with and without TSP activated.
2. Shut engine off. Remove air cleaner. Set parking brake block wheels and put selector in "N". (Do not put selector in "P").
3. Verify that the cable routing is free of sharp bends or pressure points and that the cable operates freely. Lubricate the TV lever ball stud. Check for damage to cable or rubber boot.
4. Unlock the locking tab at the carburetor end by pushing up from below, and prying up the rest of the way to free the cable.
5. A retention spring must be installed on the TV control lever, to hold it in the idle position (as far to rear as the lever will travel) with about ten pounds of force. If a suitable single spring is not available, two V8 TV return springs may be used. Attach retention spring(s) to the transmission TV lever hook rear end of spring to the transmission case.
6. De-cam the carburetor. The carburetor throttle lever must be in the anti-diesel idle position. Verify that the take-up spring (carburetor end of the cable properly tensions the cable. If the spring is loose or bottomed out, check for bent brackets.
7. Push down the locking tab until flush.
8. Remove the detent springs from the transmission lever.

Band Adjustments

C4, C5 AND C6 AUTOMATIC TRANSMISSION

Intermediate Band Adjustment

1. Raise and support the vehicle safely. Clean adjusting screw, apply penetrating lubricant and remove and discard locknut.
2. Install a new locknut (loosely) and torque adjusting screw to 10 ft. lbs., then back off 1 $^3/_4$ turns.
3. Hold adjusting screw and tighten locknut.

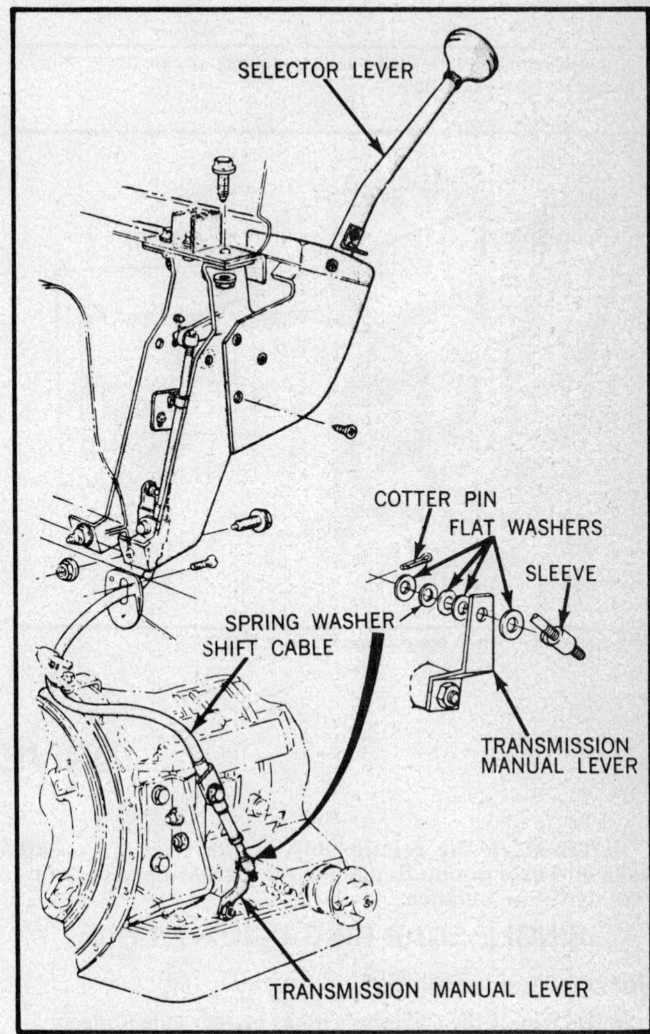

Typical Allison AT-540 automatic transmission selector lever linkage (© Ford Motor Co.)

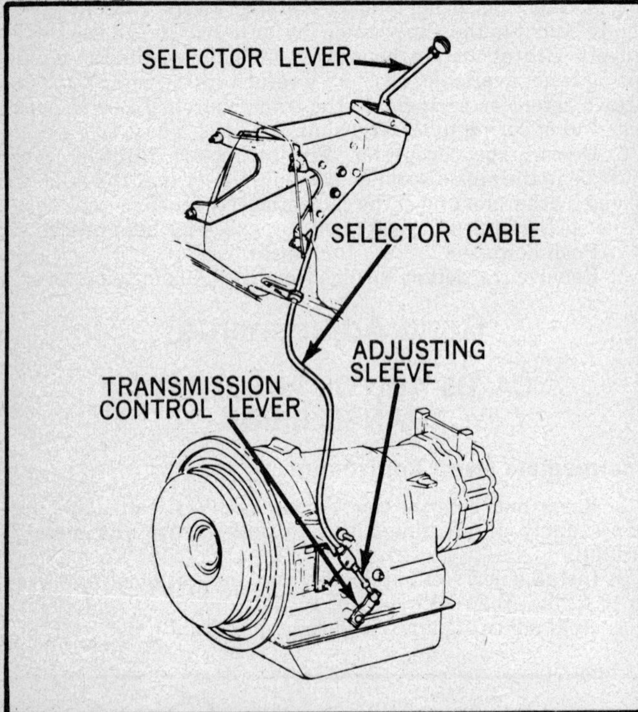

Typical Allison MT-Series automatic transmission selector lever linkage (© Ford Motor Co.)

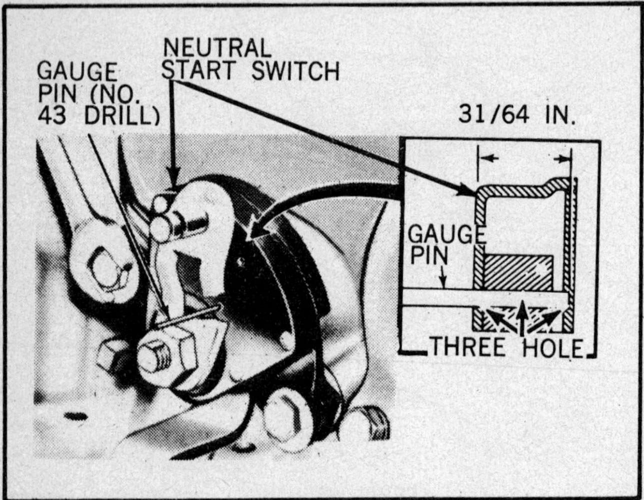

Neutral safety switch adjustment (© Ford Motor Co.)

C4 and C5 Low-Reverse Band Adjustment

1. Raise and support the vehicle safely. Clean all dirt from around the band adjusting screw and remove and discard the locknut.
2. Install a new locknut on the adjusting screw. Using a torque wrench, tighten the adjusting screw to 10 ft. lbs.
3. Back off the adjusting screw exactly 3 full turns.
4. Hold the adjusting screw steady and tighten the locknut to 35–45 ft. lbs.

C3 AUTOMATIC TRANSMISSION

Front Band Adjustment

1. Remove the downshift rod from the transmission downshift lever. Clean all of the dirt away from the band adjusting nut and screw area. Remove and discard the locknut.
2. Tighten the adjusting screw to 10 ft. lbs. Back off the adjusting screw exactly two turns.
3. Install a new locknut, hold the adjusting screw in position and tighten the locknut to 35–45 ft. lbs. Install the downshift rod.

Neutral Safety Switch

Adjustment

ALL EXCEPT F-500–600 AND ALLISON

1. Hold the steering column transmission selector lever against the Neutral stop.
2. Move the sliding block assembly on the neutral switch to the neutral position and insert a 0.091 in. gauge pin or $^3/_{32}$ inch drill in the alignment hole on the terminal side of the switch.
3. Move the switch assembly housing so that the sliding block contacts the actuating pin lever. Secure the switch to the outer tube of the steering column and remove the gauge pin.
4. Check the operation of the switch. The engine should only start in Neutral and Park.

F-500-600

1. Check the starter at all selector lever positions. The circuit must be open at all positions except "N" (neutral).
2. To adjust, loosen the neutral switch to bracket attaching screws.
3. Position the switch so that the starter circuit is closed when the selector lever is in the "N" (neutral) position.

ALLISON

1. Check the starter circuit at all selector positions. The circuit must be open in all positions except the "N" (neutral) position.
2. Loosen the switch-to-bracket attaching screws.
3. Position the switch so that the starter circuit is closed when the selector lever is at "N".

DRIVESHAFT

NOTE: Mark the relationship of the rear driveshaft yoke and axle pinion flange before disassembly, to maintain driveline balance.

SINGLE SNAP RING U-JOINT TYPE

Removal and Installation

1. Disconnect the driveshaft from the rear axle flange.
2. If vehicle has a coupling shaft, slide the driveshaft off the coupling splines.
3. Working from the center support nearest to the rear of the vehicle, remove the two attaching bolts and support the bearing.
4. On a vehicle with more than one coupling shaft, disconnect the rear shaft from the front one.
5. Remove the remaining center support attaching bolts and support the bearing.
6. Remove the transmission coupling shaft flange attaching nuts and remove the shaft and center bearing(s) as an assembly.

7. Thoroughly clean all driveshaft components before installing.
8. To install, connect the front flange or joint to the transmission flange.
9. Secure the center bearing to the frame bracket, tightening the bracket attaching bolts securely.
10. If vehicle has more than one coupling shaft, connect the rear shaft to the forward one, then install the remaining center support.
11. Connect the rear universal to the rear axle flange, tightening nuts or bolts securely.
12. Be sure all driveshaft and coupling shaft yokes are in phase.

CENTER BEARING

Removal and Installation

1. Remove the driveshafts.
2. Remove the two center support bearing attaching bolts and remove the assembly from the vehicle.
3. Do not immerse the sealed bearing in any type of cleaning fluid. Wipe the bearing and cushion clean with a cloth dampened with cleaning fluid.
4. Check the bearing for wear or rough action by rotating the inner race while holding the outer race. If wear or roughness is evident, replace the bearing. Examine the rubber cushion for evidence of hardening, cracking, or deterioration. Replace it if it is damaged in any way.

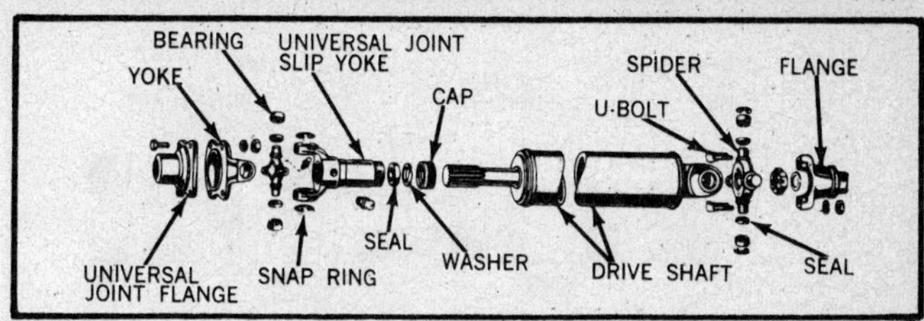

Drive shaft components—115" wheelbase (© Ford Motor Co.)

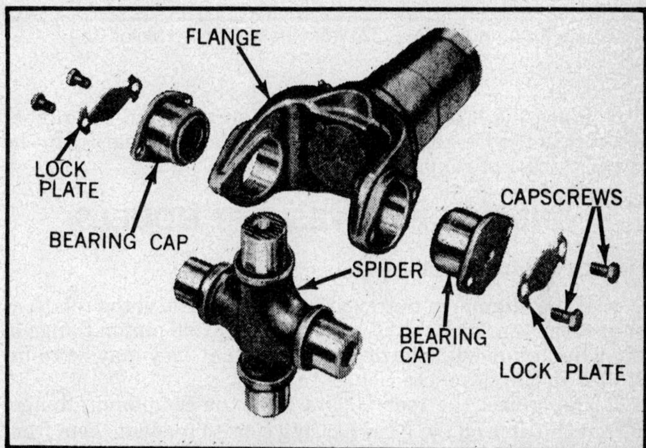

Exploded view of bolted end cap type U-joint (© Ford Motor Co.)

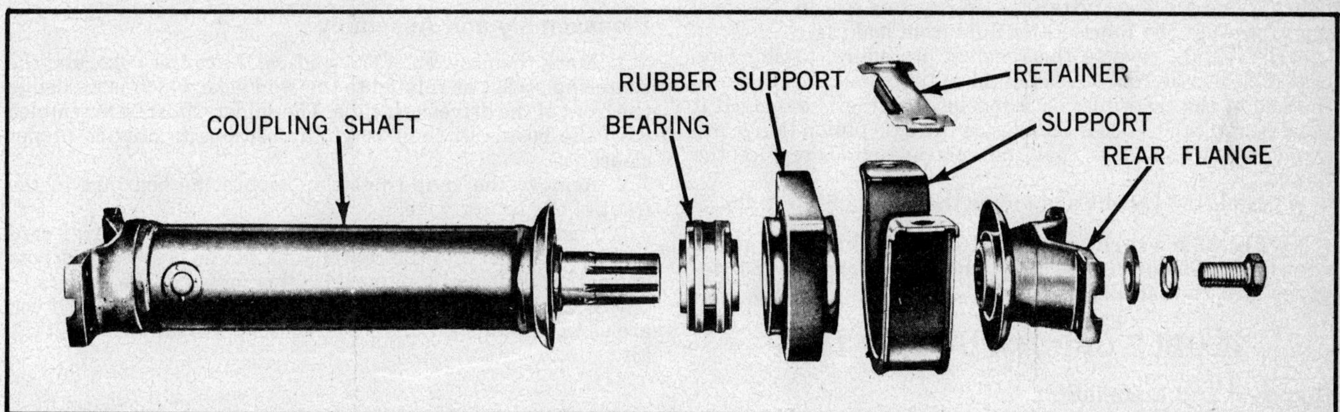

Coupling shaft and center support bearings (© Ford Motor Co.)

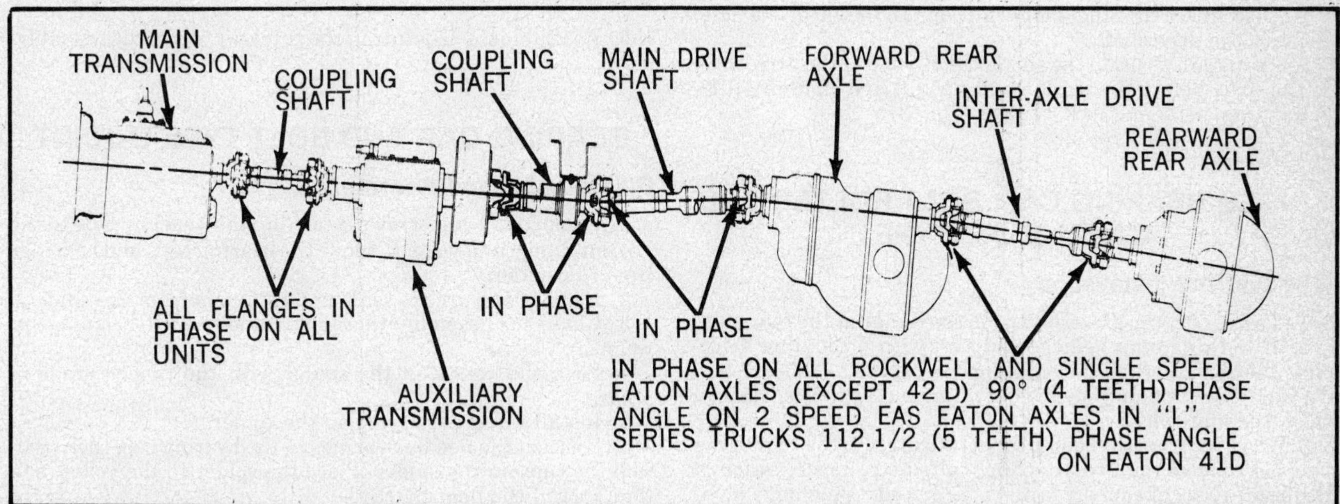

Typical tandem axle drive shaft (© Ford Motor Co.)

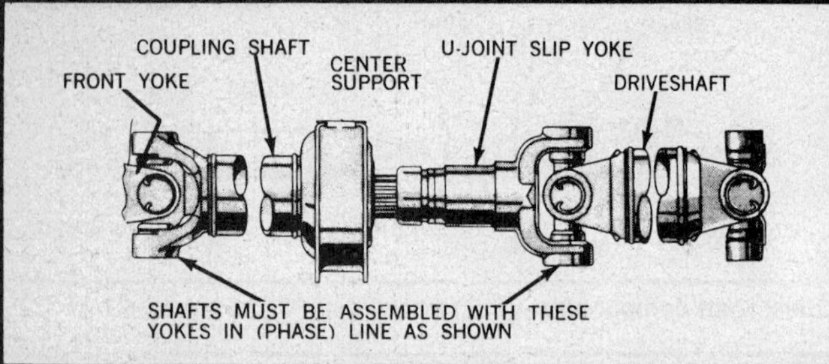

Drive shaft components—132" wheelbase (© Ford Motor Co.)

5. Place the bearing in the rubber support and the rubber support in the U-shaped support and install the bearing in the reverse order of removal.

ONE PIECE DRIVESHAFT MODELS

Removal and Installation

1. If the alignment marks are not visible, mark the relationship of the rear drive shaft yoke and the drive pinion flange of the axle in line with the drive shaft so that they may be re-installed in the same position.
2. Disconnect the rear U-joint from the companion flange. Wrap tape around the loose bearing caps to prevent them from falling off the spider. Pull the driveshaft toward the rear of the vehicle until the slip yoke clears the transmission extension housing and the seal. Install the appropriate tool in the housing to prevent the lubricant or fluid from leaking.
3. To install, reverse the removal procedure, taking note that if either the rubber seal on the output shaft or the seal in the end of the transmission extension housing is damaged it must be replaced. Also if the lugs on the axle pinion flange are shaved or distorted so that the bearings slide, replace the flange.
4. Install the U-bolts and torque the nuts to 8–15 ft. lbs.

NOTE: If a vibration should exist, the driveshaft should be disconnected from the axle, rotated 180 degrees and re-installed.

DOUBLE CARDAN U-JOINT TYPE

Removal and Installation

1. To remove the front or rear driveshaft, disconnect the double cardan joint from the flange at the transfer case.
2. Disconnect the single U-joint from the flange at the axle. Remove the driveshaft.
3. To install, position the single U-joint end of the driveshaft to the axle, before the cardan end. Install and tighten all U-bolts, nuts, bolts and lockwashers.

SINGLE BEARING CAP, BOLT/BOLTED END CAP U-JOINT TYPE

Removal and Installation

1. Disconnect the driveshaft from the flange at the rear axle.
2. If working on a vehicle equipped with a coupling shaft, slide the driveshaft off the coupling shaft splines. On some Mechanics, Rockwell, and heavy duty Spicer assemblies, remove the attaching bolts.
3. Working from the center support nearest to the rear of the vehicle, remove the two attaching bolts and support bearing. Different types of support brackets are used. Some have elongated mounting holes. This permits close adjustment.
4. If working on a vehicle equipped with more than one coupling shaft, disconnect the rear shaft from the front one.
5. Remove the remaining center support attaching bolts and support the bearing.
6. Remove the nuts that attach the coupling shaft flange to the transmission, and remove the shaft and center bearing assembly.
7. Thoroughly clean all driveshaft components before installation.
8. Connect the front flange or joint of the driveshaft or coupling shaft to the flange on the transmission.
9. Secure the center bearing to the frame bracket with the center support and attaching bolts. Note that L-series vehicles are adjustable with two-piece center support brackets. Tighten all bolts.
10. If working on a vehicle with more than one coupling shaft, connect the rear shaft to the forward one, then install the remaining center support. Make sure all splines are properly lubricated.
11. Connect the U-joint to the rear axle flange and tighten the nuts or bolts.
12. Make sure that all driveshaft and coupling shaft yokes are properly in phase.

U-Joints

SINGLE SNAP RING TYPE U-JOINT AND DOUBLE CARDAN TYPE U-JOINT

Disassembly and Assembly

1. Mark the position of the spiders, the center yoke, and the centering socket as related to the stud yoke which is welded to the front of the driveshaft tube. The spiders must be assembled with the bosses in their original positions to provide proper clearance.
2. Remove the snap-rings that secure the bearings in the front of the center yoke.
3. Position the driveshaft in a vise so that the bearing caps that are pressed into the center yoke can be pressed or driven out with a drift and hammer. Do this for all of the spiders.
4. Clean all the serviceable parts in cleaning solvent. If you are using a repair kit, install all of the parts supplied with the kit.

NOTE: If the driveshaft is damaged in any way, replace the complete driveshaft to insure a balanced assembly.

5. Assemble the U-joints in the reverse order of disassembly.

BEARING CAP AND BOLT TYPE U-JOINT

Disassembly and Assembly

1. Remove the cap screws attaching the bearing caps to the U-joint flange and yoke. Remove the bearing caps and bearings from the spider.
2. Remove the grease seals and retainers from the spider.
3. Clean the assembly thoroughly and check for damage or wear.
4. Pack the recess in the spider with the proper grade of grease.
5. Install the grease seals on the spider.
6. Position the needle bearings in the bearing cap, then position the caps on the spider. Place the spider in the yokes, and then install the bearing caps.
7. Lubricate the U-joints with the proper grade of grease.

BOLTED END CAP TYPE U-JOINT

Disassembly and Assembly

1. Bend the tangs on the lock plates away from the capscrews.
2. Remove the capscrews and lock plates holding the bearing caps to the U-joint flange. Remove the bearing caps and bearings from the flange and spider.
3. If the bearing caps are integral, tap the bearing cap lightly clockwise and, using a screw driver, pry under first one end of the bearing cap and then the other until the bearing comes out of the yoke. Turn the joint over, and remove the opposite bearing in the same way.
4. If the bearing cap and bearing are separate, the bearing cap will come off with a light tap. Remove the bearings by first tapping with a round soft drift on the exposed face of one bearing until the opposite bearing comes out. Turn the joint over and tap the exposed end of the journal cross pin until the opposite bearing is free.
5. Remove the spider. All burrs on the bearing cap or yoke must be removed before replacing the spider in the yoke.
6. Clean all parts thoroughly and inspect for damage or wear.
7. Before assembling, fill the journal passages with a long life lubricant of the proper grade.
8. Position the needle bearings in the bearing caps.
9. Position the spider in the flange and install the bearing caps through the yoke and onto the spider. Press or tap the bearing caps into place with a soft drift.
10. Position the lock plates on the bearing caps and secure with the capscrews. Bend the tabs of the lock up against the capscrews.
11. Lubricate the U-joint with a long life grease of the proper grade.

REAR AXLE

See the Unit Repair section for overhaul procedures for rear axles.

Integral Carrier Axle (Dana)

Removal and Installation

1. Loosen the wheel stud nuts and the axle shaft retaining bolts.
2. Disconnect the rear shock absorbers from the spring seat caps. Then raise the rear end of the vehicle frame until the weight is off the rear springs. Place safety stands under the frame in this position.
3. Disconnect the flexible hydraulic line at the frame and disconnect the axle vent hose at the axle connection.
4. Disconnect the parking brake cable (if so equipped) at the equalizer, and remove the cables from the cable support brackets.
5. Disconnect the driveshaft from the rear U-joint flange.
6. Remove the nuts from the spring clips (U-bolts), and remove the spring seat caps.
7. Roll the axle from under the vehicle, and drain the lubri-

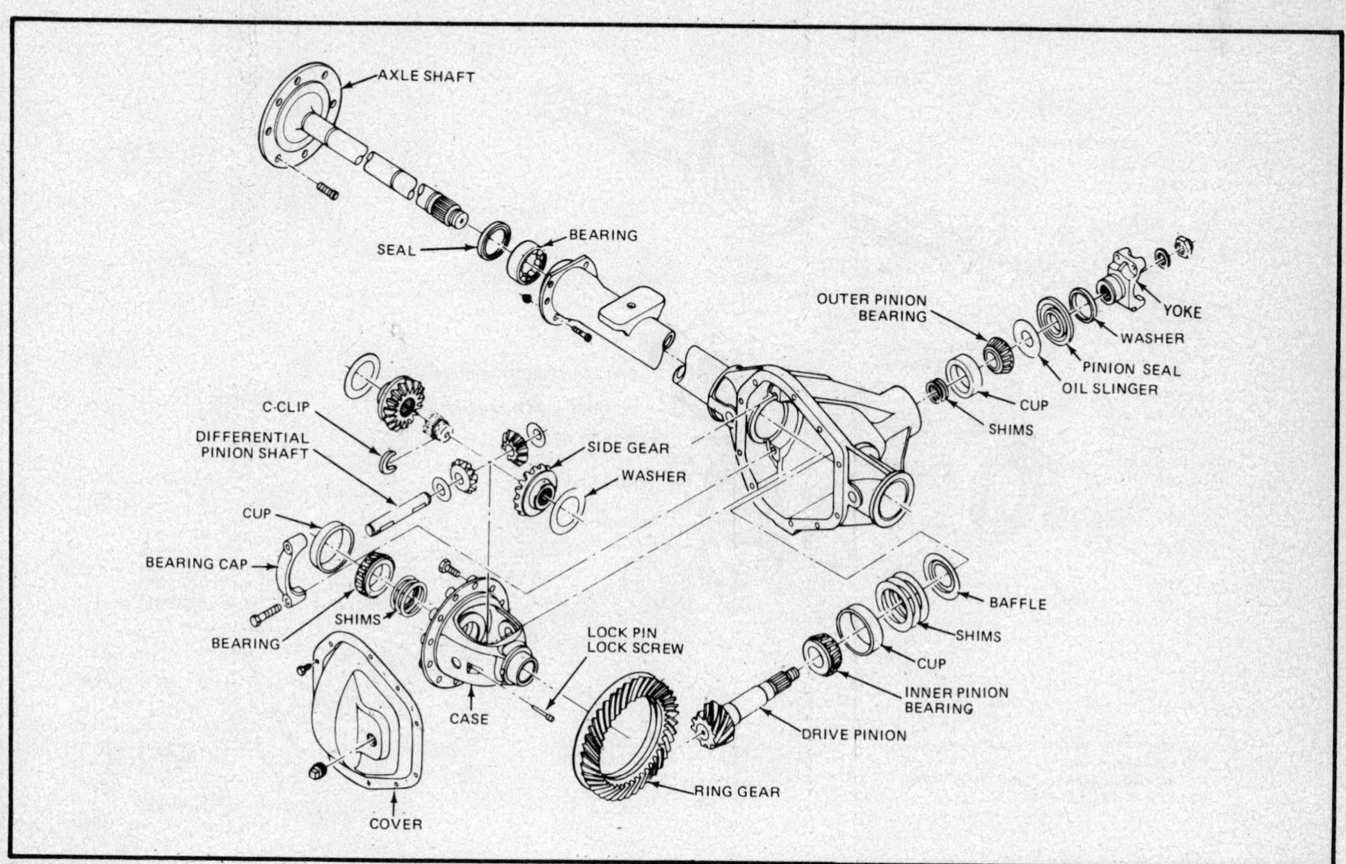

Ford integral carrier differential (© Ford Motor Co.)

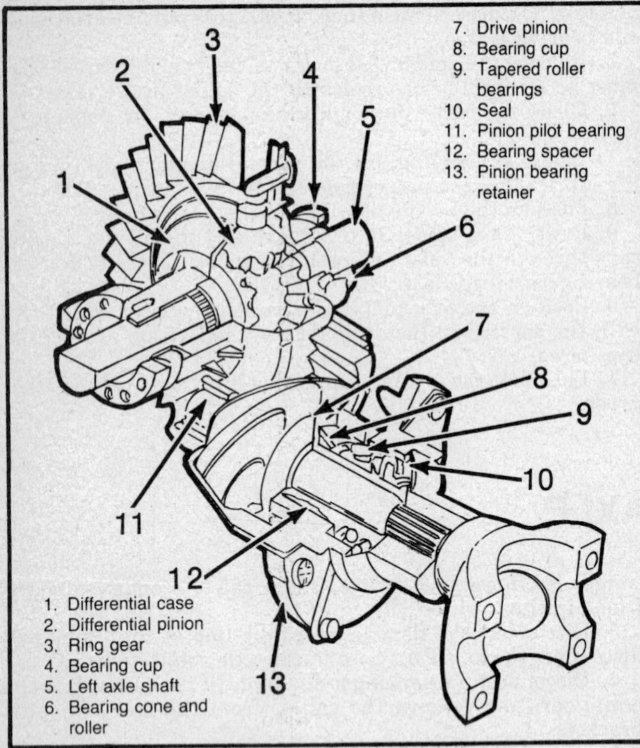

Ford banjo (removable carrier) type differential

cant. Remove the wheels. Mount the axle in a work stand.

8. Replace the hub inner grease seal. Install the axle shafts through the housing ends so that they will spline to the differential side gears. Install the shaft retaining bolts and lock washers.

9. After installing rear wheels, roll the axle assembly under the vehicle.

10. Install the spring clips (U-bolts) and spring seat caps. Torque the nuts to 165–185 ft. lbs.

11. Connect the rear shock absorbers.

12. Lower the vehicle to the floor. Connect the driveshaft to the rear universal joint flange.

13. Connect and adjust the parking brake cables (if so equipped).

14. Connect the hydraulic brake hose and bleed the brakes. Also connect the axle vent hose to the axle fitting.

15. Fill the axle with the proper grade and amount of lubricant.

Ford Removable Carrier Axle

CARRIER ASSEMBLY

Removal and Installation

1. Raise the vehicle and support it safely. Remove the two rear wheel and tire assemblies.

2. Remove the two brake drums (3 Tinnerman nuts at each drum) from the axle shaft flange studs. If difficulty is experienced in removing the drums, back off the brake shoes.

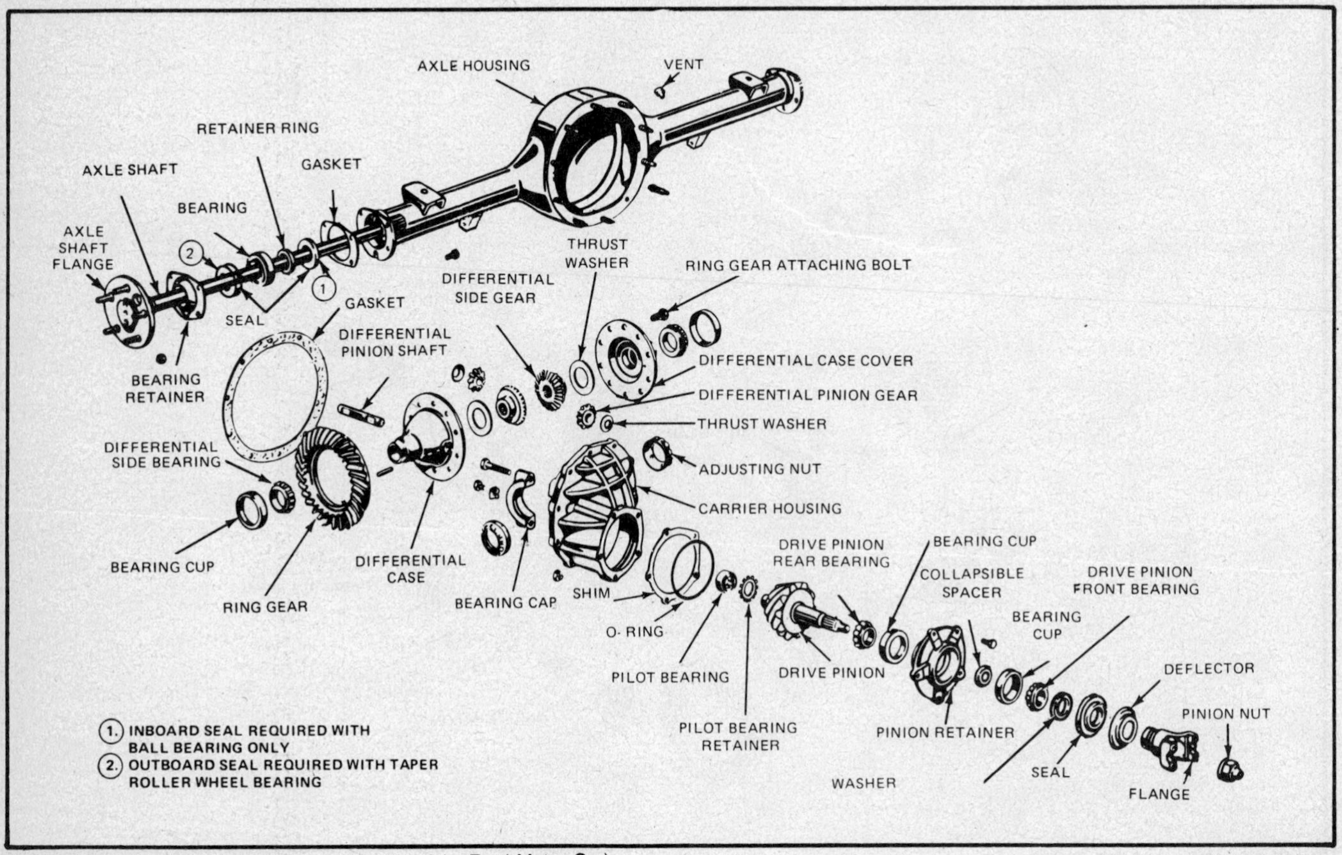

Exploded view of Ford banjo type differential (© Ford Motor Co.)

3. Working through the hole provided in each axle shaft flange, remove the nuts that secure the rear wheel bearing retainer plate. Pull each axle shaft assembly out of the axle housing using axle shaft remover, Tool 4235-C. Care must be exercised to prevent damage to oil seal, if so equipped. Any roughing or cutting of the seal element during removal or installation can result in early seal failure. Install a nut on one of the brake carrier plate attaching bolts to hold the plate to the axle housing after the shaft has been removed. Whenever a rear axle shaft is replaced, the wheel bearing oil seals must be replaced. Remove the seals with tool 1175-AB.

4. Make scribe marks on the driveshaft end yoke and the axle U-joint flange to insure proper position at assembly. Disconnect the driveshaft at the rear axle U-joint, remove the driveshaft from the transmission extension housing. Install oil seal replacer tool T57P-7657-A in the housing to prevent transmission leakage.

5. Place a drain pan under the carrier and housing, remove the carrier attaching nuts, and drain the axle. Remove the carrier assembly from the axle housing.

6. Synthetic wheel bearing seals must not be cleaned, soaked or washed in cleaning solvent. Clean the axle housing and shafts using kerosene and swabs. To avoid contamination of the grease in the sealed ball bearings, do not allow any quantity of solvent directly on the wheel bearings. Clean the matting surfaces of the axle housing and carrier.

7. Position the differential carrier on the studs in the axle housing using a new gasket between carrier and housing. Install the carrier-to-housing attaching nuts.

8. Remove the oil seal replacer tool from the transmission extension housing. Position the driveshaft so that the front U-joint slip yoke splines to the transmission output shaft.

9. Connect the driveshaft to the axle U-joint flange, aligning the scribe marks made on the driveshaft end yoke and the axle U-joint flange during the removal procedure. Install the U-bolts and nuts and torque to specifications.

10. Wipe a small amount of an oil-resistant sealer on the outer edge of each seal before it is installed. Do not put any of the sealer on the sealing lip. Install the oil seals in the ends of the rear axle housing with the special tool.

11. Install the two axle shaft assemblies in the axle housing. Care must be exercised to prevent damage to the oil seals. The shorter shaft goes into the left side of the housing. When installing an axle shaft, place a new gasket between the housing flange and the brake backing plate, and carefully slide the axle shaft into the housing so that the rough forging of the shaft will not damage the oil seal. Start the axle splines into the differential side gear, and push the shaft in until the bearing bottoms in the housing.

12. Install the bearing retainer plates on the attaching bolts on the axle housing flanges. Install and tighten the nuts on the bolts.

13. Install the two rear brake drums and the drum attaching nuts.

14. Install the rear wheel and tire assemblies.

15. If the rear brake shoes were backed off, adjust the brakes.

16. Fill the rear axle with lubricant.

AXLE HOUSING

Removal and Installation

1. Remove the carrier assembly from the axle housing.

2. Position safety stands under the rear frame members, and support the axle housing with either a floor jack or hoist.

3. Disengage the brake line from the clips that retain the line to the axle housing.

4. Disconnect the vent tube from the rear axle housing.

5. Remove the brake backing plate assemblies from the axle housing, and support them with wire. Do not disconnect the brake line.

6. Disconnect each rear shock absorber from the mounting bracket stud on the axle housing.

7. Lower the rear axle slightly to reduce some of the spring tension. At each rear spring, remove the spring clip (U-bolt) nuts, spring clips, and spring seat caps.

8. Remove the rear axle housing from under the vehicle. If the axle housing is new, install a new vent. The hose attaching portion must face toward the front of the vehicle.

9. Install new rear wheel bearing oil seals in the ends of the rear axle housing. If leather type wheel bearing service seals are to be installed, soak the new rear wheel bearing oil seals in SAE 10 oil for $\frac{1}{2}$ hour before installation.

10. Position the rear axle housing under the rear springs. Install the spring clips (U-bolts), spring seat caps, and nuts. Torque the spring clip nuts evenly.

11. If a new axle housing is being installed, remove the bolts that attach the carrier plate and bearing retainer from the old housing flanges. Position the bolts in the new housing flanges to hold the brake backing plates in position. Install the backing plates with new gaskets between the housing flange and the brake backing plate.

12. Connect the vent tube to the axle housing.

13. Position the brake line to the axle housing, and secure with the retaining clips.

14. Raise the rear axle housing and springs enough to allow connecting the rear shock absorbers to the mounting bracket studs on the axle housing.

15. Install the carrier assembly and the two axle shaft assemblies in the axle housing as outlined in this section.

Single-Speed, Single Reduction Axles

DIFFERENTIAL CARRIER

Removal and Installation

1. Drain the axle lubricant.

2. Remove the axle shaft and the stud nuts and lockwasher. If tapered dowels are installed in the axle shaft flange, hold a short drift firmly in the center of the flange, and then strike it sharply to loosen the dowels. Remove the dowels and then remove the axle shaft.

3. Tapered dowels are not used at the axle shaft flange on most of the larger vehicles, on these flanges, two threads are provided. Use one or both puller threads to remove the axle shafts.

4. Disconnect the driveshaft at the rear U-joint pinion flange.

5. Support the carrier assembly with a roller jack, then remove the carrier-to-housing stud nuts or bolts, and lock washers.

6. Tighten the puller screws, when provided in the carrier, until the carrier is loosened from the housing, and then back off the puller screws. Remove and discard the gasket.

7. Place the carrier on a transmission stand.

8. Position a new gasket on the axle housing.

NOTE: A dry gasket will prevent creeping between the carrier and housing under heavy loads.

9. Place the differential carrier assembly on a roller jack, and roll the carrier into position. Start the carrier into the housing with four capscrews (or stud nuts) equally spaced.

10. Tighten the capscrews (or nuts) alternately to draw the carrier square into the housing. Install the remaining carrier-to-housing lockwashers and capscrews (or nut), then tighten.

11. Install new gaskets on the wheel hubs, then install the axle shafts. Install the dowels, lockwashers, and stud nuts.

12. Connect the driveshaft at the rear U-joint flange.

13. Fill the axle with the proper grade of lubricant.

REAR AXLE HOUSING

Removal and Installation

1. Disconnect the driveshaft and remove the axle shafts and differential carrier.
2. Disconnect the rear shock absorbers from the spring seal caps or shock absorber brackets. Raise the rear of the vehicle frame until the weight is off the rear springs. Place safety stands under the frame.
3. Disconnect the flexible hydraulic brake hose or air lines at the frame or frame cross member.
4. Remove the nuts from the spring clips (U-bolts), and remove the spring seat caps and shock absorber brackets.
5. Roll the axle housing and rear wheels from underneath the vehicle.
6. Remove the wheels from the axle housing.
7. Install the axle housing in the reverse order of removal.

Two Speed, Double Reduction Axles

DIFFERENTIAL CARRIER

Removal and Installation

1. Shift the axle into the low range.
2. Drain and discard the lubricant. On Spicer units remove the shift unit from the carrier housing.
3. Remove the axle shafts, stud nuts and lockwashers. Strike the center of each axle flange with a hammer and drift to loosen the tapered dowels, when used. Remove the axle shafts from the housing.
4. Remove the electric shift unit from the carrier housing. Disconnect the driveshaft at the rear U-joint flange.
5. Support the carrier on a roller jack. Remove the carrier-to-housing bolts and lockwashers or stud nuts.
6. Remove the carrier from the axle housing. Remove and discard the carrier-to-housing gasket.
7. Install guide studs in the axle housing. Place a new gasket over the guide studs.
8. Install the carrier in the axle housing. As the carrier-to-housing bolts are installed, remove the guide studs. Tighten the nuts and/or bolts.
9. Install the axle shafts through the housing ends so that they will spline to the differential side gears. Install the tapered dowels, when used, lockwashers, and axle shaft flange stud nuts.
10. Install the electric shift unit. Connect the driveshaft at the rear U-joint flange.
11. Fill the axle with the proper grade lubricant up to the bottom of the filler hole in the rear cover, then add one pint of axle lubricant at the lubricant channel filler plug.
12. Road test the vehicle.

REAR AXLE HOUSING

Removal and Installation

1. Disconnect the driveshaft and remove the axle shafts and differential carrier.
2. Disconnect the rear shock absorbers from the spring seal caps of shock absorber brackets. Raise the rear of the vehicle frame until the weight is off the rear springs. Place safety stands under the frame.
3. Disconnect the flexible hydraulic brake hose or air lines at the frame or frame crossmember.
4. Remove the nuts from the spring clips (U-bolts), and remove the spring seat caps and shock absorber brackets.
5. Roll the axle housing and rear wheels from underneath the vehicle.
6. Remove the wheels from the axle housing.
7. Install the axle housing in the reverse order of removal.

Eaton Tandem Axles

POWER DIVIDER AND CARRIER

Removal and Installation

1. Block the wheels.
2. Drain the power divider and axle housing.
3. Remove the vacuum or air shift components as equipped. Remove the lockout cylinder and mounting bracket from the power divider.
4. Disconnect the driveshaft at the input shaft.
5. Remove the air brake line from the right-hand forward axle brake chamber and the connector on the axle housing.
6. Remove both axle shafts.
7. Position a roller jack, with cradle, beneath the power divider and carrier. Fasten the assembly to the cradle.
8. Remove the axle carrier to housing stud nuts.
9. Disconnect the inter-axle driveshaft at the power divider output shaft flange.
10. Hold the output shaft flange, and remove the flange nut. Pull the flange out.
11. Carefully remove the power divider and carrier from the housing. As the power divider and carrier are moved out of the housing, the output shaft and roller bearing inner race must slide out of the straight rollers in the axle housing cover.
12. Remove the power divider and carrier from under the vehicle.
13. Clean the inside of the axle housing.
14. Remove the power divider output shaft flange seal from the axle housing rear cover. Remove the flange spacer and the roller bearing from the cover.
15. Mount the power divider and carrier in a roller jack.
16. Place a new gasket on the axle housing. Install the gasket dry to prevent leakage due to creeping caused by sealing compound.
17. Start the carrier housing on the axle housing studs and pull it into position with the stud nuts. Tighten the nuts.
18. Install the roller bearing outer race and cage in the housing cover. Place the spacer next to the bearing.
19. Install a new seal in the housing cover for the output shaft flange.
20. Start the flange on the output shaft. Hold the flange and pull it into position with the flange nut and flat washer. Tighten the nut and install a new cotter pin.
21. Connect the inner-axle drive shaft. Connect the drive shaft at the input shaft flange.
22. Install and connect the power divider lockout unit. Install the air line to the brake chamber.
23. Place new gaskets on the wheel hub studs and install the axle shafts. Tighten the stud nuts.
24. Fill the power divider and axle housing with the proper grade lubricant.

REAR AXLE CARRIER

Removal and Installation

For removal and installation of the rear axle carrier, follow the procedure outlined in the Single-Speed, Single-Reduction Axle or Two-Speed, Double Reduction Axle.

FORWARD CARRIER 1983 AND LATER

Removal and Installation

NOTE: The output shaft rear bearing retaining washer is frequently lost when the differential carrier assembly is removed. It may adhere to the yoke, to the face of the output shaft bearing, fall on the floor or into the housing.

Locate this washer before continuing! If it is not reinstalled, the end of the yoke will wear the output shaft bearing very quickly. If it is left in the housing, it can be picked up by the ring gear motion and cause premature axle failure.

1. Drain the axle lubricant. Disconnect the inner axle driveline.
2. Remove the output shaft nut, flat washer and yoke. Disconnect the differential lockout air line. Disconnect main driveline. Loosen input shaft yoke nut but do not remove. Remove stud nuts and axle shafts. (If used, remove lockwashers and taper dowels). If necessary, loosen dowels by holding a brass drift in the center of the shaft head and striking drift a sharp blow with a hammer.

NOTE: Do not strike the shaft head with a hammer. Do not use chisels or wedges to loosen shaft or dowels.

5. Do not lie under the carrier after the fasteners have been removed. Use a transmission jack to support the carrier assembly during removal.
6. Remove nuts, cap screws, and lockwashers fastening carrier to axle housing. Remove differential carrier assembly.

NOTE: When installing differential carrier assembly, it is important to follow correct procedures to assure useful life. Failure to correctly install rear bearing and retaining washer could result in premature axle failure.

7. Apply gasket compound. Install differential carrier assembly in axle housing. Install nuts, cap screws and lockwashers. Tighten to specifications.
8. Install output shaft rear bearing. Tap the outer race (with a sleeve or drift) until it is seated firmly in the machined pocket of the cover. Secure with snap ring.
9. Lubricant and install the rear bearing sleeve on the output shaft. Make certain it fits snugly against the shoulder at the forward edge of the shaft splines.
10. Install a new output shaft seal in the axle housing cover and lubricate the seal inner diameter to prevent damage during yoke installation.
11. Slide the rear bearing retaining washer over the splines of the outer shaft until it seats flush against the output shaft bearing.
12. Install output yoke, flat whaser and self-locking nut. Tighten to specifications.
13. Install axle shafts and stud nuts. (If used, also install lock-washers and taper dowels).
14. Connect the main and inner axle drivelines. Fill the axle with lubricant. Connect the differential lockout air line.

POWER DIVIDER

Removal and Installation

1983 AND LATER

NOTE: The power divider can be replaced with the axle housing in or out of the chassis and with the differential carrier assembled to the axle housing. During the removal and installation, the power divider assembly must be supported. If the unit is not supported properly, the inner-axle differential may fall from the carrier.

1. If the power divider is removed with the axle installed in the chassis, use a transmission jack to support the assembly.
2. Disconnect the main driveline. Loosen, but do not remove the input yoke unit. Disconnect the lockout air line.
3. Position a drain pan under the power divider assembly.
4. To remove power divider assembly, remove cover cap screws and lockwashers. Support power divider assembly. Then, tap backface of input yoke to dislodge cover from differential carrier. If cover does not dislodge easily, strike the sides of the cover near the dowel pin locations. Drain the axle lubricant.
5. Pull the power divider assembly forward until it is free from the carrier. Remove the assembly.
6. Installation is the reverse of removal.
7. With power divider assembled to differential carrier, check end play with dial indicator. End play should be 0.003–0.007 inch. If necessary, adjust end play.
8. Connect drivelines. Connect lockout air line. Fill the assembly with the proper grade and type lubricant.

REAR CARRIER

Removal and Installation

1983 AND LATER

1. Drain lubricant.
2. Disconnect inter-axle driveline.

NOTE: For easier disassembly, the drive pinion nut can be loosened after driveline is disconnected.

3. Remove stud nuts and axle shafts. (If used, remove lockwashers and taper dowels.) If necessary, loosen dowels by holding a brass drift in the center of the shaft head and striking it a sharp blow with a hammer.

NOTE: Do not strike the shaft head with a hammer. Do not use chisels or wedges to loosen shaft or dowels.

4. Do not lie under carrier after fasteners are removed. Use transmission jack to support and remove differential carrier assembly. Remove nuts, cap screws and lockwashers fastening carrier to axle housing. Remove differential carrier assembly.
5. Installation is the reverse of removal.

Rockwell Tandem Axles

INTER AXLE DIFFERENTIAL AND FORWARD CARRIER

Removal and Installation

1. Disconnect the forward drive shaft at the inter-axle differential input shaft flange.
2. Disconnect the rear drive shaft at the through shaft flange.
3. Remove the plug from the bottom of the axle housing and drain the lubricant. Drain the lubricant from the inter-axle differential cover by removing the bottom plug.
4. Remove the axle shaft, stud nuts and lockwashers. If tapered dowels are installed in the axle shaft flange, hold a short drift firmly in the center of the axle shaft flange, and then strike it sharply to loosen the dowels and remove the axle shaft. Tapered dowels are not used at the axle shaft flange on most of the larger trucks. On these flanges, two puller threads are provided. Use one or both puller threads to remove the axle shafts.
5. Remove the attaching screws and lockwashers, and remove the shift housing assembly.
6. Remove the shift lever attaching nut, and lift out the button, shift lever, cap, and spring.
7. Remove the through-shaft, cage and flange assembly. To free the through-shaft cage from the housing bore, it may be necessary to tap the yoke with a soft mallet. While the through-shaft assembly is being drawn out from the rear of the housing, work the sliding clutch splines by hand at the shift lever opening. When the through-shaft clears the opening, lift out the clutch.
8. Remove all the carrier-to-housing nuts except the two nuts, which should be loosened but left on the studs to prevent the carrier from falling. Break the carrier loose with a rawhide mallet.

9. Place a roller jack under the carrier, and remove the two top nuts. Work the carrier free. A small pinch bar may be used to straighten the carrier in the housing bore, but the end of the bar should be rounded to prevent indenting the carrier flange.

10. Clean the inside of the axle housing and install a new gasket over the housing studs.

11. Mount the inter-axle differential and carrier assembly on a roller jack and move the assembly into position. Start the carrier into the housing with nuts and flat washers, equally spaced on the housing. Tighten the nuts enough to draw the carrier into the housing.

12. Remove the nuts and flat washers, install the lockwashers and stud nuts. Tighten the nuts.

13. Insert the through-shaft and cage, with a new gasket, into the cage bore in the rear of the axle. Move the through-shaft in until the forward end of the shaft is even with the shift lever opening.

14. Slide the splined clutch collar over the forward end of the shaft, through the shift opening, and ease the shaft through and into the forward side gear of the inter-axle differential. At the same time, pass the splined clutch collar through and onto the through-shaft clutch splines.

15. Install the through-shaft cage retaining screws and lockwashers, tighten the screws.

16. Install the shift lever spring, cup, and lever over the shift lever bolt. Properly locate the lever inner yoke in the clutch groove at this time.

17. Install the shift lever button and nut. Tighten the nut and install a new cotter pin.

18. Position the shift shaft housing with a new gasket, on the carrier. Be sure that the shift lever outer yoke is properly located in the shift shaft collar groove.

19. Install the shift housing capscrews and tighten.

20. Install the axle shafts and the retaining nuts and lockwashers.

21. Remove the fill plugs on the axle housing and inter-axle differential cover and fill the assembly with the proper grade of lubricant. Install the plugs.

22. Connect the rear drive shaft at the through shaft flange.

23. Connect the forward drive shaft at the inter-axle differential input shaft flange.

REAR AXLE CARRIER

Removal and Installation

For removal and installation of the rear axle carrier, follow the procedures outlined in Single-Speed, Single-Reduction Axle Removal and Installation.

Axle Shaft

FORD REMOVABLE CARRIER

Removal and Installation

1. Raise and support the vehicle and remove the wheel/tire assembly from the brake drum.

2. Remove the nuts which secure the brake drum to the axle flange, then remove the drum from the flange.

3. Working through the hole provided in each axle shaft flange, remove the nuts which secure the wheel bearing retainer plate.

4. Using an axle puller, pull the axle shaft assembly out of the axle housing.

NOTE: The brake backing plate must not be dislodged. Install one nut to hold the plate in place after the axle shaft is removed.

5. If the axle has ball bearings: Loosen the bearing retainer ring by nicking it in several places with a cold chisel, then slide it off the axle shaft. On models equipped with a thick retaining ring, drill a $\frac{1}{4}$ in. to $\frac{1}{2}$ in. hole part way through the ring, then break it with a cold chisel. A hydraulic press is needed to press the bearing off and to press the new one on. Press the new bearing and the new retainer ring on separately. Use a slide hammer to pull the old seal out of the axle housing. Carefully drive the new seal evenly into the axle housing, preferably with a seal driver tool.

6. If the axle has tapered roller bearings, use a slide hammer to remove the bearing cup from the axle housing. Drill a $\frac{1}{4}$–$\frac{1}{2}$ in. hole part way through the bearing retainer ring, then break it with a cold chisel. A hydraulic press is needed to press the bearing off and remove the seal. Press on the new seal and bearing, then the new retainer ring. Do not press the bearing and ring on together. Put the cup on the bearing, not in the housing, and lubricate the outer diameter of the cup and seal.

7. With ball bearings: Place a new gasket between the housing flange and backing plate. Carefully slide the axle shaft into place. Turn the shaft to start the splines into the side gear and push it in.

8. With tapered roller bearing: Move the seal out toward the axle shaft flange so there is at least $\frac{3}{32}$ in. between the edge of the outer seal and the bearing cup, to prevent snagging on installation. Carefully slide the axle shaft into place. Turn the shaft to start the splines into the side gear and push it in.

9. Install the bearing retainer plate.

10. Replace the brake drum and the wheel and tire.

DANA INTEGRAL CARRIER

Removal and Installation

1. Remove the lockbolts and lockwashers which hold the axle flange to the hub and and drum assembly.

NOTE: It is not necessary to raise the vehicle to remove the axle shafts.

2. Carefully slide the axle shaft out of the axle housing.

3. Clean the mating surfaces of the axle flange and the hub and drum assembly.

4. Position a new gasket on the axle flange and carefully slide the axle shaft into the axle housing. When the splined end of the axle shaft reaches the side gear, gently rotate the shaft until it is inserted into the side gear.

5. Position the gasket between the axle flange and the hub and drum and install the lockbolts and lockwashers.

6 ¾ INCH INTEGRAL TYPE

Removal and Installation

NOTE: This carrier assembly is used in some Ranger and Bronco II vehicles. Refer to the Removable Carrier section for the proper procedures.

"C" LOCK TYPE INTEGRAL CARRIER

Removal and Installation

1. Raise the vehicle and support it safely.

2. Remove the wheels and tires from the brake drums.

3. Place a drain pan under the housing and drain the lubricant by loosening the housing cover.

4. Remove the locks securing the brake drums to the axle shaft flanges and remove the drums.

5. Remove the housing cover and gasket, if used.

7. Working through the opening in the differential case, remove the side gear pinion shaft lockbolt and the side gear pinion shaft.

8. Push the axle shafts inward and remove the C-locks from the inner end of the axle shafts. Temporarily replace the shaft and lockbolt to retain the differential gears in position.

9. Remove the axle shafts with a slide hammer. Be sure the seal is not damaged by the splines on the axle shaft.

10. Remove the bearing and oil seal from the housing. Both the seal and bearing can be removed with a slide hammer. Two types of bearings are used on some axles, one requiring a press fit and the other a loose fit. A loose fitting bearing does not necessarily indicate excessive wear.

11. Inspect the axle shaft housing and axle shafts for burrs or other irregularities. Replace any work or damaged parts. A light yellow color on the bearing journal of the axle shaft is normal, and does not require replacement of the axle shaft. Slight pitting and wear is also normal.

12. Lightly coat the wheel bearing rollers with axle lubricant. Install the bearings in the axle housing until the bearing seats firmly against the shoulder.

13. Wipe all lubricant from the oil seal bore, before installing the seal.

14. Inspect the original seals for wear. If necessary, these may be replaced with new seals, which are prepacked with lubricant and do not require soaking.

15. Install the oil seal.

16. Remove the lockbolt and pinion shaft. Carefully slide the axle shafts into place. Be careful that you do not damage the seal with the splined end of the axle shaft. Engage the splined end of the shaft with the differential side gears.

17. Install the axle shaft C-locks on the inner end of the axle shafts and seat the C-locks in the counterbore of the differential side gears.

18. Rotate the differential pinion gears until the differential pinion shaft can be installed. Install the differential pinion shaft lockbolt. Tighten to 15–22 ft. lbs.

19. Install the brake drum on the axle shaft flange.

20. Install the wheel and tire on the brake drum and tighten the attaching nuts.

Axle Shaft Bearing

Removal and Installation (Axle Out)

NOTE: Whenever an axle shaft is removed, the oil seal should be replaced. Remove the axle oil seal with a suitable axle seal removing tool. Inspect the machine surfaces of the axle shaft and the axle housing for rough spots or other irregularities which could affect the bearing action of the oil seal.

1. Drill a $^1/_4$ to $^1/_2$ in. hole in the outside diameter of the inner retainer to a depth of approximately $^3/_4$ in. the thickness of the retainer ring.

NOTE: Do not drill all the way through the retainer ring as the drill could damage the axle shaft.

2. After drilling the retainer ring, use a chisel positioned across the drilled hole and strike sharply to split the retainer ring. Discard the retainer, as it is not reusable.

3. Press the bearing off the axle shaft with a suitable tool.

4. To install, coat the wheel bearing bores with axle lubricant. Place the bearing retainer plate on the axle shaft, if removed.

5. Press the new wheel bearing on the axle shaft with a suitable tool. Press the bearing inner retainer ring on the axle shaft under the retainer seats firmly against the bearing.

NOTE: Do not attempt to press both the bearing and the inner retainer ring on the axle shaft at the same time.

Pinion Seal

Removal and Installation

LIGHT DUTY VEHICLES

NOTE: The drive pinion oil seal can be replaced without removing the differential carrier assembly from the housing.

1. Raise the vehicle and support it safely. Remove both rear wheels and brake drums.

2. Match mark the drive shaft end yoke and the axle U-joint flange to insure proper positioning at re-installation. Disconnect the drive shaft from the axle U-joint flange. Do not drop the loose U-joint bearing cups. Mark the cups so that they will be in their original position in relation to the flange when they are reassembled.

3. Remove the drive shaft from the transmission extension housing. Install an oil seal replacer tool in the housing to prevent the transmission fluid from leaking out.

4. Position an inch lb. torque wrench on the pinion nut. Record the torque required to maintain rotation of the pinion shaft through several revolutions.

5. Scribe the pinion shaft and the U-joint flange inner surface for assembly re-alignment. Hold the flange with the pinion yoke holding tool and remove the integral pinion nut and washer.

6. Clean the front drive pinion bearing retainer around the oil seal. Place a drain pan under the seal, or raise the front of the vehicle higher than the rear.

7. Using the pinion yoke holding tool remove the U-joint flange.

8. Using an oil seal removal tool, remove the drive pinion oil seal. Clean the oil seal seat.

9. To install, position the new seal in the retainer, using the applicable tool.

10. Check the splines on the drive pinion shaft to be sure that they are free of burrs. If they are not remove them by using a fine crocus cloth, working in a rotational motion. Apply a small amount of lubricant to the U-joint flange and the pinion shaft.

11. Install the U-joint flange. Install a new integral nut and washer on the pinion shaft (hold the shaft with the pinion yoke holding tool while tightening the nut).

12. Tighten the pinion shaft nut, rotating the pinion occasionally to insure proper bearing seating, and to take frequent preload readings. If the recorded preload is less than specification, (8–14 inch lbs. for the old bearing, 17–27 inch lbs. for the new bearing) tighten to specification. If the preload is higher than specification, tighten to the original reading.

NOTE: Under no circumstances should the pinion nut be backed off to lessen the preload. If this is done, a new collapsible spacer must be installed.

13. Remove the oil seal replacer tool from the transmission extension housing and install the front end of the drive shaft on the transmission output shaft.

14. Connect the rear end of the drive shaft to the axle U-joint flange, aligning the scribe marks made on the drive shaft end yoke and the axle U-joint flange.

15. Check the lubricant level.

NOTE: Make sure that the axle is in the running position. Add whatever amount of the proper lubricant is necessary to reach the lower edge of the filler plug hole.

16. Install the brake drum and attaching nuts. Install the wheels and tires. Lower the vehicle.

MEDIUM AND HEAVY DUTY VEHICLES

NOTE: The drive pinion oil seal can be replaced without removing the differential carrier assembly from the rear axle or the rear axle from the vehicle.

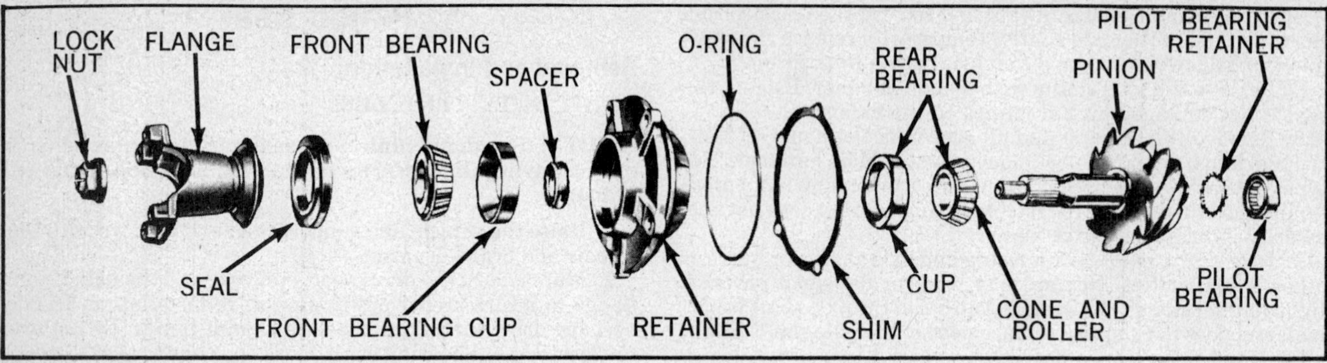

Pinion and bearing retainer components—typical (© Ford Motor Co.)

1. Disconnect the drive shaft from the rear U-joint pinion flange.
2. With a pinion yoke holding tool installed on the U-joint flange, remove the cotter pin, nut and washer from the drive pinion shaft. Remove the flange.
3. Remove the bolts that attach the oil seal retainer and the pinion bearing retainer to the carrier. Remove the oil seal retainer and gasket.
4. Using an oil seal removal tool, remove the oil seal from the retainer.
5. To install, coat the outside edge of the new oil seal with an oil-resistant sealer and press it into the oil seal retainer, using the proper oil seal replacer tool. Apply a light coat of lubriplate to the contact areas of the seal and the drive pinion shaft.
6. Position the oil seal retainer and a new gasket against the pinion bearing retainer. Install and tighten the bolts that attach the oil seal retainer and the pinion bearing retainer to the differential carrier assembly.
7. Install and tighten the U-joint flange, nut, washer and cotter pin. Connect the drive shaft to the rear U-joint flange.
8. Check the lubricant level and fill as necessary.

REAR WHEEL BEARINGS

F250–350, E250–350 MODELS

The wheel bearings on the full floating rear axle are packed with wheel bearing grease. Axle lubricant can also flow into the wheel hubs and bearings, however, wheel bearing grease is the primary lubricant. The wheel bearing grease provides lubrication until the axle lubricant reaches the bearings during normal operation.

1. Set the parking brake and loosen the axle shaft bolts.
2. Raise the rear wheels off the floor and place jackstands under the rear axle housing so that the axle is parallel with the floor.
3. Remove the axle shaft bolts.
4. Remove the axle shaft and gaskets.
5. With the axle shaft removed, remove the gasket from the axle shaft flange studs.
6. Bend the lockwasher tab away from the locknut, and then remove the locknut, lockwasher, and the adjusting nut.
7. Remove the outer bearing cone and pull the wheel straight off the axle.
8. With a piece of hardwood which will just clear the outer bearing cup, drive the inner bearing cone and inner seal out of the wheel hub.
9. Wash all the old grease or axle lubricant out of the wheel hub, using a suitable solvent.
10. Wash the bearing cups and rollers and inspect them for pitting, galling, and uneven wear patterns. Inspect the roller for end wear.
11. If the bearing cups are to be replaced, drive them out with a drift. Install the new cups with a block of wood and hammer or press them in.
12. If the bearing cups are properly seated, a 0.0015 in. feeler gauge will not fit between the cup and the wheel hub.
13. Pack each bearing cone and roller with a bearing packer or in the manner previously outlined for the front wheel bearings on 2WD trucks.
14. Place the inner bearing cone and roller assembly in the wheel hub. Install a new inner seal in the hub.
15. Install the wheel.
16. Install and tighten the bearing adjusting nut to 50–80 ft. lbs. while rotating the wheel.
17. Back off (loosen) the adjusting nut $^3/_8$ of a turn.
18. Apply axle lube to a new lockwasher and install it with the smooth side out.
19. Install the locknut and tighten it to 90–110 ft. lbs. The wheel must rotate freely after the locknut is tightened. The wheel end-play should be within 0.001–0.010 in.
20. Bend two lockwasher tabs inward over an adjusting nut flat and two lockwasher tabs outward over the locknut flat.
21. Install the axle shaft, gasket, lockbolts, and washers. Tighten the bolts to 40–50 ft. lbs.
22. Adjust the brakes, if necessary.

REAR SUSPENSION

REAR SPRING (SINGLE AXLE)

Removal and Installation

E SERIES

1. Raise the rear end of the vehicle and support the chassis with safety stands. Support the rear axle with a floor jack or hoist.
2. Disconnect the lower end of the shock absorber from the bracket on the axle housing.
3. Remove the two spring clips (U-bolts) and the spring clip cap.
4. Lower the axle and remove the spring front bolt from the hanger.
5. Remove the two attaching bolts from the rear of the spring. Remove the spring and the shackle.
6. Assemble the upper end of the shackle to the spring with the attaching bolt.
7. Connect the front of the spring to the front bracket with the attaching bolt.
8. Assemble the spring and shackle to the rear bracket with the attaching bolt.
9. Place the spring clip plate over the head of the center bolt.

10. Raise the axle with a jack and guiding it so that the center bolt enters the pilot hole in the pad on the axle housing.
11. Install the spring clips, cap and attaching nuts. Tighten the nuts snugly.
12. Connect the lower end of the shock absorber to the lower bracket.
13. Tighten the spring front mounting bolt and nut, the rear shackle nuts and spring clip nuts.
14. Remove the safety stands and lower the vehicle.

F SERIES 2WD AND RANGER/BRONCO II

1. Raise the vehicle frame, until the weight is off the rear spring, with the tires still touching the floor.
2. Remove the nuts from the spring U-bolts and drive the U-bolts from the U-bolt plate. If so equipped, remove the auxiliary spring and the spacer.
3. Remove the spring-to-bracket nut and bolt at the front of the spring.
4. Remove the shackle upper and lower nuts and bolts at the rear of the spring. Remove the spring and shackle assembly from the rear shackle bracket.
5. If the bushings in the spring or shackle are worn or damaged, replace them.
6. To install, position the spring in the shackle, and install the upper shackle-to-spring bolt and nut with the bolt head facing outboard.
7. Position the front end of the spring in the bracket and install. Position the shackle in the rear bracket and install.
8. Position the spring on top of the axle with the spring tie bolt centered in the hole provided in the seat. If equipped, install the auxiliary spring and spacer.
9. Install the spring U-bolt plate and nuts. Lower the vehicle. Tighten the spring U-bolt nuts. Tighten the front spring bolt and nut and the rear shackle bolts and nuts.

BRONCO

1. Raise the vehicle by the axles and install safety stands under the frame.
2. Disconnect the shock absorber from the axle.
3. Remove the U-bolt attaching nuts and remove the two U-bolts and the spring clip plate.
4. Lower the axle to relieve spring tension and remove the nut from the spring front attaching bolt.
5. Remove the spring front attaching bolt from the spring and hanger with a drift.
6. Remove the nut from the shackle to hanger attaching bolt and drive the bolt from the shackle and hanger with a drift and remove the spring from the vehicle.
7. Remove the nut from the spring rear attaching bolt. Drive the bolt out of the spring and shackle with a drift.
8. Position the shackle (closed section facing toward front of vehicle) to the spring rear eye and install the bolt and nut.
9. Position the spring front eye and bushing to the spring front hanger, and install the attaching bolt and nut.
10. Position the spring rear eye and bushing to the shackle, and install the attaching bolt and nut.
11. Raise the axle to the spring and install the U-bolts (when an axle cap is not used, the U-bolt shank should contact the leaf edges) and spring clip plate. Align the spring leaves.
12. Tighten the U-bolt nuts and the spring front and rear attaching bolt nuts. The U-bolts should contact the spring assembly edges or axle seat.
13. Connect the shock absorber to the axle and tighten the nut.
14. Remove the safety stands and lower the vehicle.

F SERIES 4WD

1. Raise the vehicle frame until the weight is off the rear springs with the wheels still touching the floor.
2. Remove the nuts from the spring U-bolts.
3. Drive the U-bolts out of the shock absorber lower bracket and the spring cap and remove the U-bolts.
4. Remove the spacer from the top of the spring.

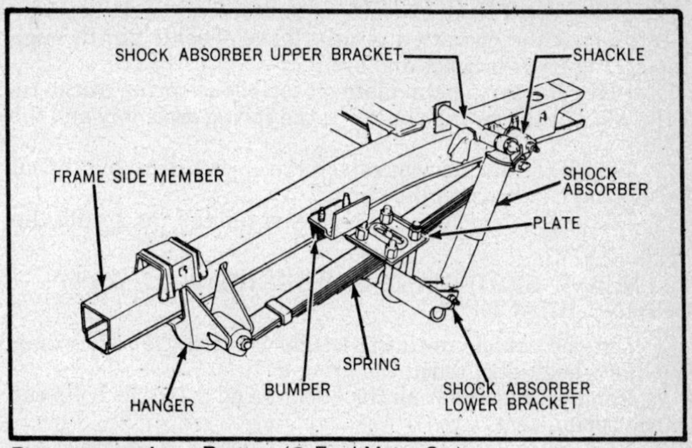

Rear suspension—Bronco (© Ford Motor Co.)

5. If equipped with auxiliary springs, remove the auxiliary spring and spacer.
6. Remove the shackle to bracket bolt and nut from the rear of the spring.
7. Remove the spring-to-hanger bolt and nut from the front of the spring and remove the spring.
8. Remove the shackle-to-spring bolt and nut and remove the shackle from the spring.
9. Position the shackle to the spring and install the attaching bolt and nut. The bolt must be installed so the nut is away from the frame.
10. Position the spring to the spring front hanger and install the attaching bolt and nut.
11. Position the shackle to the bracket and install the attaching bolt and nut.
12. Align the spring toe bolt with the pilot hole in the axle spring seat and, if so equipped, install the auxiliary spring and spacer.
13. Position the spacer on top of the spring and install the U-bolts over the spacer, spring and axle.
14. Position the spring cap and shock lower bracket to the axle and U-bolts. Install the U-bolt attaching nuts.
15. Lower the vehicle and tighten the front spring bracket bolt and nut and the rear shackle bolts and nuts.

C SERIES

1. Raise the vehicle frame until the weight is off the rear springs with the wheels still touching the floor.
2. Remove the nuts from the spring clips (U-bolts) and drive the clips out of the spring seat cap. If so equipped, remove the auxiliary spring and spacer.
3. Remove the shackle pin locking bolts from each spring bracket.
4. A hole is provided in the frame opposite each spring bracket for removing the shackle pin. Insert a drift from the inside of the frame through these holes and drive the shackle pin out of each bracket.
5. Remove the spring and shackle assembly from the truck. Separate the spring from the shackle by removing the locking bolt and driving out the shackle lower pin from the shackle and spring eye.
6. Remove the lubricating fittings from the shackle pins.
7. Align the upper bore of the shackle with the holes in the rear bracket. Drive the shackle upper pin through the shackle and bracket with the pin lubricator hole facing outward.
8. Line up the shackle pin groove with the locking bolt hole in the bracket and install the locking bolt, washer and nut.
9. Install the spring seat and the wedge (if so equipped) between the axle and the spring. Position the spring on the axle, being sure that the spring tie bolt is in the hole provided in the axle or spring seats. If so equipped, install the auxiliary spring and spacer.
10. Drive the shackle lower pin through the shackle and

spring rear eye. Install the locking bolt, washer and nut as before. Repeat the operation to install the shackle pin through the spring front bracket and eye.

11. Place the spring clip plate on top of the spring at the tie bolt, and put the spring clips over the spring assembly and the axle.

12. Install the spring seat cap on the spring clips and install the spring clip nuts on the clips.

13. Lower the vehicle to the floor and tighten the spring clip nuts.

L, LN, B, W SERIES AND B–F SERIES WITH CAST SPRING BRACKETS

1. Lift the vehicle until the weight is off of the rear spring but the wheels still touch the ground.

2. Remove the nuts from the U-bolts and drive the bolts out of the spring seat caps.

3. Remove the auxiliary spring and spacer, if equipped.

4. Support the spring and remove the front shackle pins. The lower pin is held in place by a lock bolt and the upper is held by a cotter pin.

5. Remove the cotter pin in the rear shackle pin and remove the pin. Remove the spring from the vehicle.

6. To install place the spring in the rear shackle bracket and install the shackle pin and cotter pin.

7. With a jack or C-clamp press the front eye of the spring up into the bracket until the eye is lined up with the hole in the bracket. Install the shackle pins in the spring and secure them in place with the lock bolt or the cotter pin.

8. Install the spring seat and the wedge (if so equipped) between the axle and spring and install the U-bolts over the axle and install the nuts on the bolts after installing the spring seat cap.

9. Lower the vehicle and tighten the nuts on the U-bolts securely.

F AND B SERIES WITH STAMPED SPRING BRACKETS

1. Raise the vehicle frame until the weight is off the rear springs with the wheels still touching the floor.

2. Remove the nuts and washers from the spring U-bolts (clips) and drive the U-bolts out of the spring cap. Remove the auxiliary spring and spacer, if equipped.

3. Support the spring and remove the front spring bolts and rebound pins. The spring bolts is held in place by a slot nut and cotter pin, and the lower rebound pin is held in place by a self-locking pin and washer.

4. Remove the rear rebound pin which is held in place by a self-locking pin and washer, and remove the spring.

5. Position the spring in the rear bracket and install the rebound pin, self-locking pin and washer.

6. Position the spring in the front bracket. Install the rebound pin, and secure with a self-locking pin and washer.

7. Using a C-clamp or jack, force the front eye of the spring up into the bracket until the eye is aligned with the holes in the bracket. Install the lower spring bolt through the front bracket and spring eye. Install the slot nut and washer. Align the slot opening of the slot nut with the hole on the spring bolt in a tightening direction and secure with a cotter pin.

8. Position the spring seat and wedge (if so equipped) between the axle and spring. If so equipped, install the auxiliary spring and spacer. Place the U-bolt pad on the top of the spring at the tie bolt, and put the spring U-bolt over the spring assembly and axle.

9. Install the spring cap on the spring U-bolt and install the spring U-bolt nuts and washers on the U-bolts.

10. Lower the vehicle to the floor and tighten the spring U-bolt nuts.

REAR SPRING (Hendrickson Tandems)

Removal and Installation

1. Raise the rear of the vehicle and position the blocks under the frame behind the rear axle.

2. Remove the wheels, hub, and drum from the forward rear axle.

3. Remove the support beam bar saddle caps from the lower side of the support beam.

4. Position a jack under the front end of the support beam.

5. Remove the shackle pin lock pin from the spring front bracket and remove the shackle pin.

6. Lower the support beam and spring. Remove the spring from the support beam.

7. RV, RVE, VA and VEA suspension: Remove the U-bolt nuts and remove the saddle and U-bolts from the spring. RT, RTA and RTEA suspension: Remove the spring plate-to-support beam saddle attaching bolts and nuts. Remove the saddle and spring plate from the spring.

8. RV, RVE, VA and VEA suspension: Position the saddle on the spring and install the U-bolts and nuts. Tap the U-bolts with a hammer while tightening the nuts. RT, RTA and RTEA suspension: Position the spring plate and saddle on the spring. Snug up, but do not tighten, the saddle nuts. Tighten the spring plate set screw and lock down, then tighten the saddle nuts.

9. Position the spring and saddle on the support beam and spring rear bracket.

10. Raise the support beam and spring, and position the spring on the front spring bracket.

11. Align the spring with the front bracket and install the shackle pin.

12. Install the shackle pin lock pin and tighten the lock pin nut.

13. Install the hub, drum, and wheel on the forward rear axle.

14. Remove the jack from the support beam and the blocks from the rear of the frame. Lower the saddle on the support beam bar center insulator bushing and install the saddle caps.

15. Install the saddle caps and tighten.

NOTE: The weight of the vehicle must be on the suspension when the saddle cap attaching nuts are tightened.

SHOCK ABSORBER

Removal and Installation

ECONOLINE AND BRONCO

1. Raise the vehicle and support it safely.

2. Remove the shock absorber lower attaching nut and bolt, and swing the lower end free of the mounting bracket on the axle housing.

3. Remove the attaching nut from the upper mounting stud, and remove the shock absorber.

4. To install, position the shock absorber with the rubber bushings and steel washers to the upper mounting bolt.

5. Swing the lower end of the shock absorber into the mounting bracket on the axle housing. Install the attaching washers, mounting bolt, and self-locking nut.

6. Install the self-locking nut on the upper mounting bolt.

7. Lower the vehicle.

ALL OTHERS

1. Remove the self-locking nut, steel washer, and rubber bushings at the upper and lower ends of the shock absorber.

2. Remove the unit from the vehicle.

3. To install, position the shock absorber on the mounting brackets with the large diameter at the top.

4. Install the rubber bushing, steel washer, and self-locking nut.

INDEX

BEFORE SERVICING, SEE THE SAFETY NOTICE AT THE FRONT OF THE BOOK

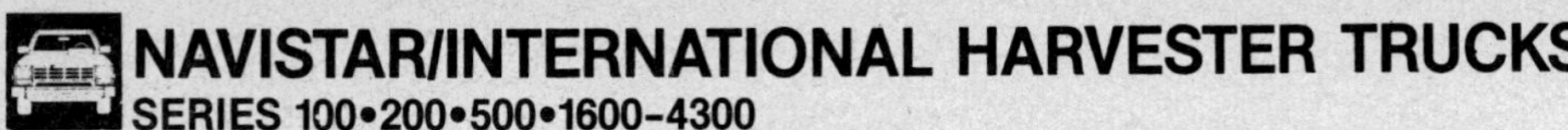

ENGINE APPLICATIONS

Series	Axles	Engines—HP Rating
Scout Series (with or without top):		
Scout II	4 × 2	G 86-158
Scout II	4 × 4	G 86-158
Multi-Stop Series:		
MS-1210	4 × 2	G 158–163
MS-1510	4 × 2	G 158–163
Pickup Models:		
150 Bonus Load, Regular	4 × 2	G 140–163
200 Bonus Load, Regular	4 × 2	G 140–163
150 Bonus Load, Regular	4 × 4	G 140–163
200 Bonus Load, Regular	4 × 4	G 140–163
Travel all:		
150	4 × 2	G 187–196
200	4 × 2	G 187–196
150	4 × 4	G 187–196
200	4 × 4	G 187–196
Light-Duty Series:		
150	4 × 2	G 140–196
200	4 × 2	G 140–196
500	4 × 2	G 140–196
150	4 × 4	G 140–196
200	4 × 4	G 140–196
Loadstar Series—S1600–2100:		
1600	4 × 2	G 157
1700	4 × 2	G 190
1750	4 × 2	D 150–175
1800	4 × 2	G 205–235
1850	4 × 2	D 170–210
1600	4 × 4	G 147
1700	4 × 4	G 157
F-1800	6 × 4	G 205–235
F-1850	6 × 4	D 170–210
S-1600	4 × 2	G 345–158
S-1700	4 × 2	G 345–158
S-1700	4 × 2	D 170–150
S-1800	4 × 2	G 345–158
S-1800	4 × 4	G 345–158
S-1800	4 × 4	D 190–170
S-1900	6 × 4	G 404–188
S-1900	6 × 6	G 404–188
S-1900	6 × 6	G 404–188
S-1900	6 × 4	D 190–170

Series	Axles	Engines—HP Rating
S-1900	6 × 6	D 190–170
S-2100	6 × 4	G 537–208
S-2100	6 × 4	D DT466–180
Fleetstar A Series—S2200–2600:		
2010A	4 × 2	D 209–227
2050A	4 × 2	D 170–216
2070A	4 × 2	D 228–290
F-2010A	6 × 4	G 209–227
F-2050A	6 × 4	D 170–216
F-2070A	6 × 4	D 228–290
S-2200	4 × 2	D 426–228
S-2500	6 × 4	G 537–208
S-2500	6 × 4	D 426–228
S-2600	6 × 4	G 537–208
S-2600	6 × 4	D 426–228
Transtar Series:		
4270	4 × 2	D 260–350
4370	4 × 2	D 290–350
F-4270	6 × 4	D 260–430
F-4370	6 × 4	D 290–450
Paystar Series:		
5050	4 × 4	D 190–210
5070	4 × 4	D 228–304
F-5050	6 × 4	D 190–210
F-5070	6 × 4	D 228–400
F-5050	6 × 6	D 190–210
F-5070	6 × 6	D 228–400
Cargostar Series:		
CO-1610B	4 × 2	G 157
CO-1710B	4 × 2	G 205
CO-1810B	4 × 2	G 205–235
CO-1850B	4 × 2	D 170–190
CO-1910B	4 × 2	G 209–227
CO-1950B	4 × 2	D 170–210
COF-1810B	6 × 4	G 205–235
COF-1910B	6 × 4	G 209–227
COF-1950B	6 × 4	D 170–210
CO Transtar II Series:		
CO-4070B	4 × 2	D 290–350
COF-4070B	6 × 4	D 290–450

GENERAL ENGINE SPECIFICATIONS

Cyl. CID	Year	Bore × Stroke	Firing Order	Horsepower @ rpm	Torque @ rpm	Comp. Ratio	Carbu-retor	Valve Lifter	Oil Pressure (psi)
4-196	1980	4.125 × 3.656	1-3-4-2	111 @ 4400	153 @ 2000	8.2	1V	Hyd.	40–50
8-304	1980	3.825 × 3.219	1-8-4-3-6-5-7-2	147 @ 3900	226 @ 2000	8.2	2V	Hyd.	40–50
8-345	1980–86	3.875 × 3.656	1-8-4-3-6-5-7-2	157 @ 3800	265 @ 2000	8.1	2V	Hyd.	40–50
8-392	1980–84	4.125 × 3.656	1-8-4-3-6-5-7-2	194 @ 3600	302 @ 2800	8.0	4V	Hyd.	40–50
8-404	1980–82	4.125 × 3.740	1-2-7-3-4-5-6-8	189 @ 3600	326 @ 2200	8.0	2V	Hyd.	44–50
8-404	1980–82	4.125 × 3.740	1-2-7-3-4-5-6-8	210 @ 3600	336 @ 2800	8.1	4V	Hyd.	44–50
8-446	1980–82	4.125 × 4.180	1-2-7-3-4-5-6-8	235 @ 2600	385 @ 2600	8.1	4V	Hyd.	44–50
8-537	1980–82	4.625 × 3.750	1-8-7-3-6-5-4-2	208 @ 3200	415 @ 2000	7.5	2V	Hyd.	45–55
8-537	1980–82	4.625 × 3.750	1-8-7-3-6-5-4-2	236 @ 3600	429 @ 2200	7.5	4V	Hyd.	45–55
8-605	1980–82	4.625 × 4.50	1-8-7-3-6-5-4-2	227 @ 3200	446 @ 2000	7.5	4V	Hyd.	45–55

TUNE-UP SPECIFICATIONS

Cyl. CID	Year	Spark Plug Gap (in.)	Distributor Point Dwell (deg.)	Distributor Point Gap (in.)	Ignition Timing (deg.)	Cranking Compression (psi)	Valve Clearance In	Valve Clearance Exh	Governor No Load RPM	Fuel Press. (psi)	Idle Speed (rpm) Std	Idle Speed (rpm) Auto
4-196	1980	0.035	24–34	①	0④	143	0	0	4000⑤	5	700	700N
8-304	1980	0.035	30	①	10B②	145	0	0	3900⑤	5	700	650N
8-345	1980–86	0.035	30	①	5B②	143	0	0	3800	5	700	700N
8-392	1980–84	0.035	30	①	OTDC②	140	0	0	3600	5	700	600D
8-404	1980–82	0.035	24–34	①	9B③	140	0	0	3600	5	575	657
8-446	1980–82	0.035	24–34	①	5B⑥	145	0	0	3600	5	575	675
8-537	1980–82	0.035	24–34	①	7B	140	0	0	3400	5	550	650
8-605	1980–82	0.035	24–34	①	7B	140	0	0	3400	5	550	650

B-Before top dead center
TDC-Top dead center
① Conventional Point Gap—0.016–0.020 in.
Cam Angle—28–32°
Breakerless Air Gap—0.008 in.
Cam Angle—24–34°
② Timed at number 8 cylinder, located on the right bank, rear of the engine.
LPG—345 engine timing goes to 10° before top dead center.
③ 5° before top dead center
④ 5° before top dead center on automatic transmission models
⑤ Maximum recommended rpm
⑥ 10° before top dead center on California models

NOTE: The underhood specifications sticker often reflects tune-up specifications changes made in production. The sticker figures must be used if they disagree with those in this chart.

FIRING ORDER

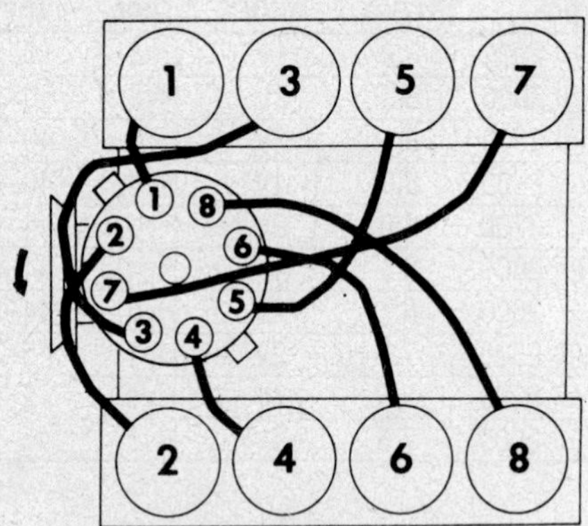

MV 404 and 446 1-2-7-3-4-5-6-8
(© International Harvester Co.)

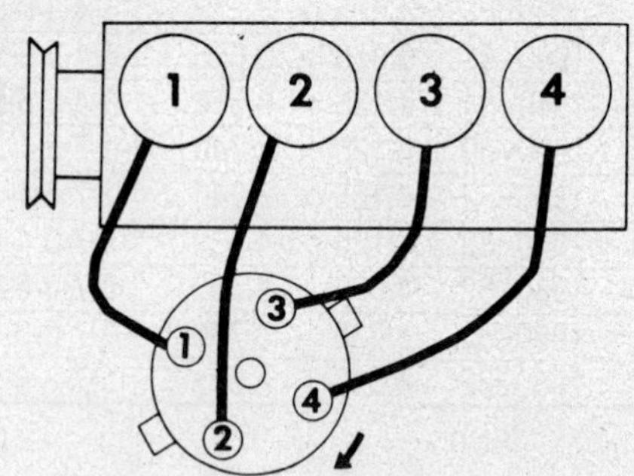

4 cylinder 4-196 1-3-4-2
(© International Harvester Co.)

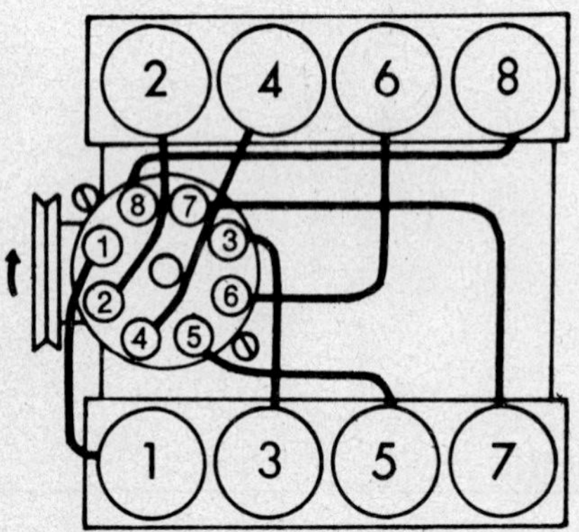

8 cylinder 478 and 549 1-8-7-3-6-5-4-2
(© International Harvester Co.)

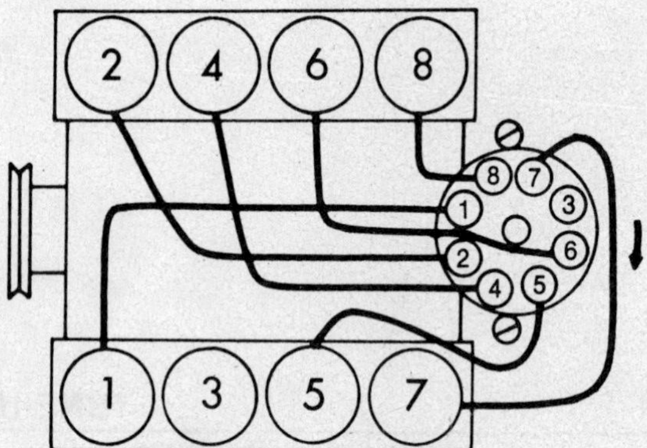

8 cylinder V 537 and 605 1-8-7-3-6-5-4-2
(© International Harvester Co.)

CRANKSHAFT SPECIFICATIONS

(All measurements in inches)

	Mean Bearing Journals				Connecting Rod Journals		
Cyl. CID	Journal Diameter	Oil Clearance	Shaft End-Play	Thrust on No.	Journal Diameter	Oil Clearance	Rod Side Clearance
4-196	2.7484–2.7494	.001–.004	.003–.008	3	2.373–2.374	.0011–.0036	.004–.011
8-304	2.7484–2.7494	.001–.004	.003–.008	3	2.373–2.374	.0011–.0036	.004–.011
8-345	2.7484–2.7494	.0010–.0040	.0030–.0080	3	2.4995–2.500	.0011–.0036	.0080–.0160
8-392	2.7484–2.7494	.0010–.0040	.0030–.0080	3	2.4995–2.5000	.0011–.0036	.0080–.0160
8-404	3.1228–3.1236	.0010–.0036	.0025–.0085	3	2.4980–2.4990	.0011–.0036	.008–.020
8-446	3.1228–3.1236	.0010–.0036	.0025–.0085	3	2.4980–2.4990	.0011–.0036	.008–.020
8-537	3.1235–3.1245	.0015–.0035	.0060–.0120	3	2.6230–2.6240	.0011–.0036	.008–.018
8-605	3.1235–3.1245	.0015–.0035	.0060–.0120	3	2.6230–2.6240	.0011–.0036	.008–.018

VALVE SPECIFICATIONS

Cyl. CID	Angle (deg.) Face	Angle (deg.) Seat	Stem Dia. (in.) In	Stem Dia. (in.) Ex	Stem-to-Guide Clearance (in.) In	Stem-to-Guide Clearance (in.) Ex	Valve Lift In.	Valve Spring Tension Lbs @ Inches	Spring Free Length
4-196	④	④	.372	.415	.001–.0035	.0015–.004	①	188 @ 1.428	2.065
8-304	45	45	.372	.371	.001–.0035	.0015–.004	①	180–195 @ 1.429	2.065
8-345	45	45	.372	.371	.001–.0035	.0015–.004	①	180–195 @ 1.429	2.065
8-392	④	④	.372	.414	.001–.0035	.0015–.004	①	180–195 @ 1.429	2.065
8-404	45	45	.372	.372	.0012–.0028	.0017–.0024	.435	188 @ 1.429	2.065
8-446	45	45	.372	.372	.0012–.0028	.0017–.0024	.435	188 @ 1.429	2.065
8-537	②	②	.435	.434	.0016–.0034	.002–.0037	.465	200 @ 1.397	2.075
8-549	③	③	.435	.434	.0015–.0035	.0015–.0045	.426	113–121 @ 1.663⑧	2.562⑤
8-605	②	②	.435	.434	.0016–.0034	.002–.0037	.465	200 @ 1.397	2.075

① Intake .440; Exh. 395
② Intake 15; Exh. 45
③ Intake 15; Exh. 45
④ Intake 30; Exh. 45
⑤ Inner 2.281
⑥ Not used
⑦ Not used
⑧ Inner 79–87 @ 1.538

PISTON RING SPECIFICATIONS

(All measurements in inches)

Cyl. CID	Ring Gap Compression	Ring Gap Oil Control	Ring Clearance Compression	Ring Clearance Oil Control
4-196	.013–.023	.013–.028	.0015–.003	.002–.0035
8-304	.010–.020	.015–.055①	.0015–.003	.000–.0084
8-345	.010–.020	.015–.055①	.0015–.003	.000–.0084
8-392	.013–.023	.013–.028	.0015–.003	.002–.0035
8-404	.013–.023	.013–.023	.002–.004	.002–.004
8-446	.013–.023	.013–.023	.002–.004	.002–.004
8-537	.012–.022②	.012–.022	.002–.004	.002–.004
8-549	.013–.025	.013–.028	.0035–.005	.001–.003
8-605	.012–.022②	.012–.022	.002–.004	.002–.004

① Spring spacer or steel rails—no gap at joint
② 2nd compression—.014–.024

STANDARD TORQUE SPECIFICATIONS AND CAPSCREW MARKINGS

SAE Grade Number	U.S. BOLTS 1 or 2			5			6 or 7			8		
Capscrew Head Markings Manufacturer's marks may vary. Three-line markings on heads below indicate SAE Grade 5. 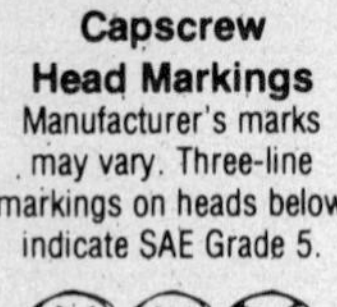	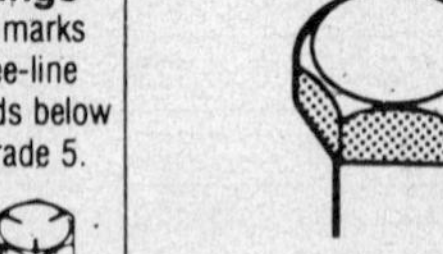						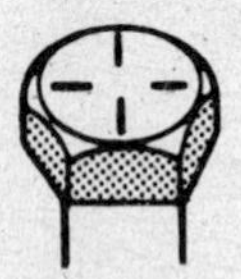			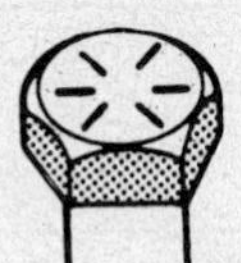		
Usage	Used Frequently			Used Frequently			Used at Times			Used at Times		
Quality of Material	Indeterminate			Minimum Commercial			Medium Commercial			Best Commercial		
Capacity Body Size	**Torque**			**Torque**			**Torque**			**Torque**		
(inches)-(thread)	Ft-Lb	kgm	Nm	Ft-Lb	kgm	Nm	Ft-Lb	kgm	Nm	Ft-Lb	kgm	Nm
1/4-20	5	0.6915	6.7791	8	1.1064	10.8465	10	1.3630	13.5582	12	1.6596	16.2698
-28	6	0.8298	8.1349	10	1.3830	13.5582				14	1.9362	18.9815
5/16-18	11	1.5213	14.9140	17	2.3511	23.0489	19	2.6277	25.7605	24	3.3192	32.5396
-24	13	1.7979	17.6256	19	2.6277	25.7605				27	3.7341	36.6071
3/8-16	18	2.4894	24.4047	31	4.2873	42.0304	34	4.7022	46.0978	44	6.0852	59.6560
-24	20	2.7660	27.1164	35	4.8405	47.4536				49	6.7767	66.4351
7/16-14	28	3.8132	37.9629	49	6.7767	66.4351	55	7.6065	74.5700	70	9.6810	94.9073
-20	30	4.1490	40.6745	55	7.6065	74.5700				78	10.7874	105.7538
1/2-13	39	5.3937	52.8769	75	10.3725	101.6863	85	11.7555	115.2445	105	14.5215	142.3609
-20	41	5.6703	55.5885	85	11.7555	115.2445				120	16.5860	162.6960
9/16-12	51	7.0533	69.1467	110	15.2130	149.1380	120	16.5960	162.6960	155	21.4365	210.1490
-18	55	7.6065	74.5700	120	16.5960	162.6960				170	23.5110	230.4860
5/8-11	83	11.4789	112.5329	150	20.7450	203.3700	167	23.0961	226.4186	210	29.0430	284.7180
-18	95	13.1385	128.8027	170	23.5110	230.4860				240	33.1920	325.3920
3/4-10	105	14.5215	142.3609	270	37.3410	366.0660	280	38.7240	379.6240	375	51.8625	508.4250
-16	115	15.9045	155.9170	295	40.7985	399.9610				420	58.0860	568.4360
7/8-9	160	22.1280	216.9280	395	54.6285	535.5410	440	60.8520	596.5520	605	83.6715	820.2590
-14	175	24.2025	237.2650	435	60.1605	589.7730				675	93.3525	915.1650
1-8	236	32.5005	318.6130	590	81.5970	799.9220	660	91.2780	894.8280	910	125.8530	1233.7780
-14	250	34.5750	338.9500	660	91.2780	849.8280				990	136.9170	1342.2420

TORQUE SPECIFICATIONS

(All measurements in ft. lbs.)

Cyl. CID	Head Bolts	Rod Cap Bolts	Main Cap Bolts	Crankshaft Balancer Bolt	Flywheel Bolts	Manifolds In.	Manifolds Ex.
4-196	100–110	40–45	75–85	100–110	45–55	25–30	14–16
8-304	100–110	40–45	75–85	100–110	45–55	40–45	40–45
8-345	100–110	40–45	75–85	100–110	45–55	40–45	40–45
8-392	100–110	40–45	75–85	100–110	45–55	40–45	40–45
8-404	100–110	38–44	90–100	80–100	40–45	38–44	15–21
8-446	100–110	38–44	90–100	80–100	40–45	38–44	15–21
8-537	80–90	65–70	125–135	260–290	110–120	30–38	30–38
8-605	80–90	65–70	125–135	260–290	110–120	30–38	30–38

FRONT END ALIGNMENT SPECIFICATIONS

Axle	Caster Level Frame	Camber	Toe-in	King Pin Inclination
FA-1	2° ± 1° (Not Metro) 2° ± ½° (Metro)	1½° ± ½°	1⁄16 ± 1⁄16	4°
FA-3	0°	1°	3⁄16	8½°
FA-10	3° ± ½°	1½° ± ½°	1⁄16 ± 1⁄16	4°
FA-13	0°	1°	3⁄16	8½°
FA-12	2° ± 1° (Not Motor Home) 4° ± ½° (Motor Home)	½° ± ½°	1⁄16 ± 1⁄16	4°
FA-28	1° ± 1° (Not Motor Home or Metro) 4° ± ½° (Motor Home) 3° ± ½° (Metro)	½° ± ½°	1⁄16 ± 1⁄16	4°
FA-44	0°	1°	3⁄16	8½°
FA-48	2° ± 1° (Not Motor Home) 4° ± ½° (Motor Home)	½° ± ½°	1⁄16 ± 1⁄16	4°
FA-54	1	0°	1⁄16	8°
FA-57	0° ± 2	2°	0-3⁄8	0°
FA-59	0° ± 2	2°	0-3⁄8	0°
FA-68	2° ± 1°	½° ± ½°	1⁄16 ± 1⁄16	4°
FA-69	3° ± ½° (Cargostar Manual Strg.) 4½° ± ½° (Cargostar Power Strg.)	½° ± ½° ½° ± ½°	⅛ ± 1⁄16 ⅛ ± 1⁄16	4° 4°
FA-71	2° ± ½°	½° ± ½°	1⁄16 ± 1⁄16	LT 4¼° RT 4½°
FA-72	2° ± ½°	½° ± ½°		4°
FA-73	2° ± ½°	½° ± ½°	1⁄16 ± 1⁄16	LT 4¼° RT 4½°
FA-74	3° ± ½° (Manual Strg.) 4½° ± ½ (Power Strg.)	½° ± ½°	⅛ ± 1⁄16	LT 4¼° RT 4½°
FA-78	0 ± 2	2°	0-3⁄8	0°
FA-91	2° ± 1° (Not CO-190) 2° ± ½° (CO-190)	½° ± ½°	1⁄16 ± 1⁄16	4°
FA-98	2° ± 0° (Not Fleetstar A) 2° ± ½° (Fleetstar A 4 × 2) 4° ± ½° (Fleetstar A 4 × 4)	½° ± ½°	1⁄16 ± 1⁄16	4°
FA-99	3° ± ½° (Cargostar Manual Strg.) 4½° ± ½° (Cargostar Power Strg.)	½° ± ½°	⅛ ± 1⁄16	4°
FA-101	2° ± ½° (Not Fleestar 6 × 4) 4° ± ½° (Fleetstar 6 × 4)	½° ± ½° ½° ± ½°	1⁄16 ± 1⁄16 1⁄16 ± 1⁄16	LT 4¼° RT 4½° LT 4¼° RT 4½°
FA-103	3° ± ½° (Manual Strg.) 4½° ± ½° (Power Strg.)	½° ± ½°	⅛ ± 1⁄16	LT 4¼° RT 4½°
FA-109	Lt. ¼ + ½ Rt. 0 + ½	1°	1⁄16	4½ R.H. 4¼ L.H.
FA-112	3½	0°	1⁄16	1°
FA-136	4	0°	1⁄16	5½°
FA-139	Lt. ¼ ± ½ Rt. 0 ± ½	1°	1⁄16	4½ R.H. 4¼ L.H.

FRONT END ALIGNMENT SPECIFICATIONS

Axle	Caster Level Frame	Camber	Toe-in	King Pin Inclination
FA-182	4	0°	1/16	5½°
FA-228	4	0°	1/16	5½°
FA-309	Lt. ¼ ± ½ Rt. 0 ± ½	1°	1/16	4½ R.H. 4¼ L.H.
FA-329	3	Lt. ¼ + ½ Rt. 0 + ½	1/16	4½ R.H. 4¼ L.H.
FA-339	3	Lt. ¼ + ½ Rt. 0 + ½	1/16	4½ R.H. 4¼ L.H.

ELECTRICAL SYSTEM

Distributor

Removal and Installation

1. Remove distributor cap along with the high tension wires.
2. Disconnect the distributor leads from the positive and negative terminals of the ignition coil.
3. Disconnect the deceleration throttle modulator lead wire (white) at the connector and disconnect the tachometer drive cable, if so equipped.
4. Scribe a mark on the distributor housing in line with the tip of the rotor.
5. Mark position of distributor body on the engine block or mounting bracket.
4. If so equipped, remove vacuum advance line and the governor lines.
5. Loosen clamp screw or hold-down bolt and remove distributor from engine.
6. To install, reverse the above procedure, making sure to align marks which position rotor and distributor body.
7. If the engine has been disturbed (crankshaft position unknown), rotate engine until engine is in no. 1 firing position (no. 8 on V-304, 345, and 392 engines). Compression stroke may be felt by placing finger tightly over spark plug hole as engine is rotating. Holding distributor shaft so that rotor is in no. 1 (or no. 8 on V-304, 345, 392) firing position, insert distributor, rotating slightly until it drops into keyed position.
8. Adjust ignition timing before tightening clamp screw or hold-down bolt.

BREAKER POINTS

NOTE: Some of these models may still be using the conventional breaker point system. The models not equipped with breaker points are equipped with an electronic breakerless (Prestolite) ignition system.

Replacement

1. Unsnap and remove distributor cap.
2. Remove rotor and dust cover if so equipped.
3. Loosen nut retaining primary and condenser leads and remove leads.
4. Remove breaker assembly mounting screws.
5. Remove breaker assembly, carefully freeing conductor spring. Do not lose eccentric screw which may fall out.
6. To install, follow the above procedure in reverse order, being sure to include eccentric screw.
7. Lightly lubricate cam with distributor cam grease.
8. Set breaker gap and ignition timing.

Adjustment

INTERNAL ADJUSTMENT TYPE

1. Remove distributor cap.
2. Loosen distributor housing clamp screw or hold-down bolt.
3. Rotate distributor until cam positions breaker points at maximum gap.
4. Inspect alignment of breaker points and, if necessary, gently bend the stationary contact support (never bend arm) with needle-nose pliers.
5. Loosen lock screws which mount breaker assembly and adjust gap using a small screwdriver in slots of contact bracket and upper plate. On models without slots and with eccentric adjusting screw instead, rotate adjusting screw until proper gap is obtained.
6. Replace cap and set ignition timing.

EXTERNAL ADJUSTMENT TYPE

1. With engine idling, raise window in distributor cap and insert proper "hex" wrench into adjustment screw.
2. Turn wrench clockwise until engine begins to miss, then back off ½ turn, or until dwell meter reads specified dwell angle.

NOTE: To remove distributor cap, press down in slot of latch head with a screwdriver and twist.

ELECTRONIC IGNITION SYSTEM

The I.H. electronic ignition system contains three major components, a breakerless distributor, a standard ignition coil, and an electronic ignition control unit. The conventional cam, ignition points, and condensor are replaced by the sensor and trigger wheel, which signals the control box when to open and close the primary circuit to induce the high voltage in the ignition coil secondary circuit. This high voltage is directed in the conventional manner, to the rotor, distributor cap, spark plug cables, and to the spark plugs.

Dwell angle is determined by the angle between the adjacent teeth of the trigger wheel and by the air gap between the ends of the trigger wheel teeth and the center line of the sensor. Since no wearing surfaces exist on the trigger wheel and the sensor, dwell remains constant and no adjustment is required,

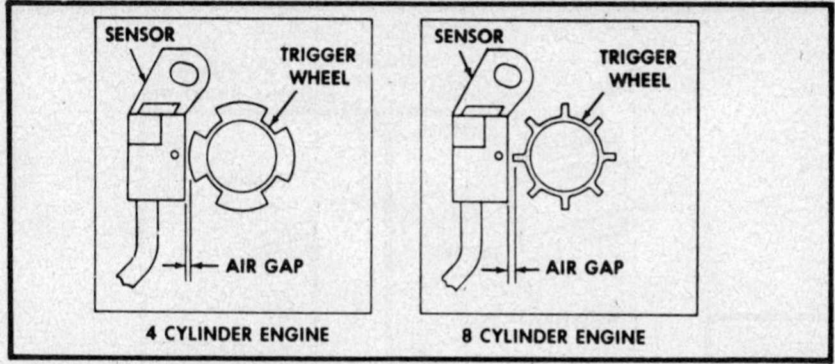

Air gap location, trigger wheel to sensor
(© International Har vester Co.)

after the initial sensor air gap is made.

To obtain the proper dwell reading, the air gap should be adjusted with the use of a brass feeler gauge, placed between the center line of the sensor and an aligned tooth of the trigger wheel. Attach a modified dwell meter to the distributor circuitry in a conventional manner, and operate the engine at curb idle. If the dwell is within specifications, the trigger wheel to sensor gap is satisfactory. If the dwell is out of specifications, stop the engine and move the sensor toward the trigger wheel to decrease dwell, and move the sensor away from the trigger wheel to increase dwell.

NOTE: Dwell is affected approximately ½ degree per each 0.001 inch of sensor movement.

In the event of engine misfire or surging, other possible sources of trouble should be checked first, such as carburetion and fuel supply. Then check for breaks in the wiring and for corroded or loose connections.

The timing may be set in the conventional way: rotate the distributor housing while the timing marks are viewed with a timing strobe light.

If the engine will not run at all, remove a lead from one of the spark plugs and hold ½" from the engine block while cranking engine. If there is no spark, check wiring and connections.

CAUTION

Never disconnect the high voltage lead between the coil and distributor and never disconnect more than three spark plugs at a time unless the ignition switch is off.

To make compression checks, disconnect the harness plug at the control box or disconnect the lead at the negative terminal of the coil.

ADJUSTING AIR GAP

The air gap should be adjusted with the use of a brass (non-metallic) feeler gauge, placed between the center line of the sensor and a aligned tooth of the trigger wheel. Loosen the sensor hold down screw and move the sensor until the gauge will pass through with a slight drag. Tighten the hold down screw. Dwell angle is determined by the angle between the adjacent teeth of the trigger wheel and by the air gap between the ends of the wheel teeth and the center line of the sensor. Since no wearing surfaces exist on the trigger wheel and sensor, dwell remains constant and no adjustment is required after the initial sensor air gap is made. Gap should be 00.008.

NOTE: For electronic ignition troubleshooting, refer to the Electrical section in Unit Repair.

IGNITION TIMING

See Tune-up Specification table at the beginning of this section for timing settings. Timing light is connected to the no. 1 spark

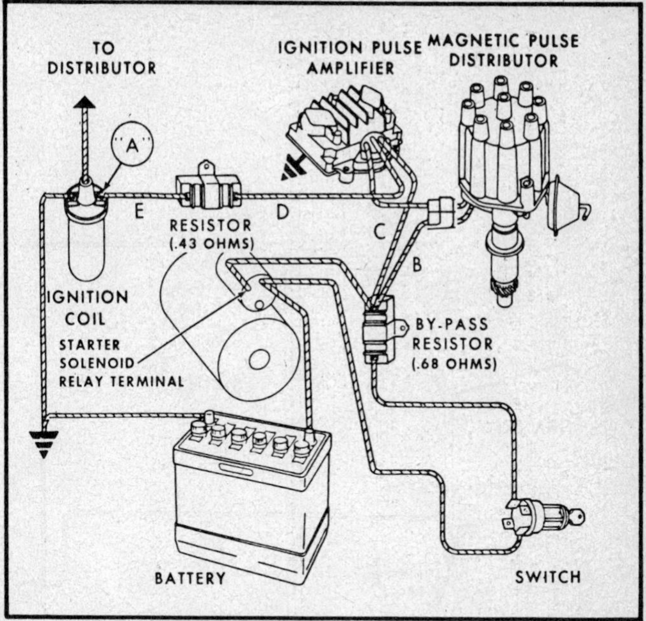

Typical transistor ignition wiring (© International Harvester Co.)

plug lead (no. 8 on V-304, 345, 392).

1. Remove and plug the vacuum line(s) from the distributor advance/retard mechanism. Be sure there is no vacuum leak at the line(s).
2. Connect the timing light.
3. Mark the crank pulley and timing quadrant lines with chalk or paint to make them easier to see.
4. Start the engine and aim the timing light at the timing quadrant.
5. The timing is adjusted by loosening the distributor hold-down nut and turning the distributor either clockwise or counterclockwise as required until the mark on the pulley aligns with the correct degree marking on the quadrant.
6. Tighten the hold-down nut and recheck the timing, readjust if necessary.
7. Stop the engine, remove the timing light and reconnect the vacuum line(s).

Alternators

PRECAUTIONS

Rectifiers and regulators in alternator systems are easily damaged by incorrect polarity. Observe the following precautions when wiring and testing circuits:

1. Always be certain of battery polarity.
2. Always connect booster battery negative to negative and positive to positive.
3. Never ground alternator output terminal.
4. When adjusting voltage regulator, be careful not to short adjusting tool.
5. Before making any tests, turn off ignition switch and disconnect battery ground.
6. Never use a fast charge with the battery connected unless charging unit is equipped with a special alternator protector.
7. Never try to polarize the alternator regulator, this will cause severe damage to the regulator and alternator.

Removal and Installation

1. Disconnect the negative battery cable.
2. Remove the wire terminals from the rear of the alternator.

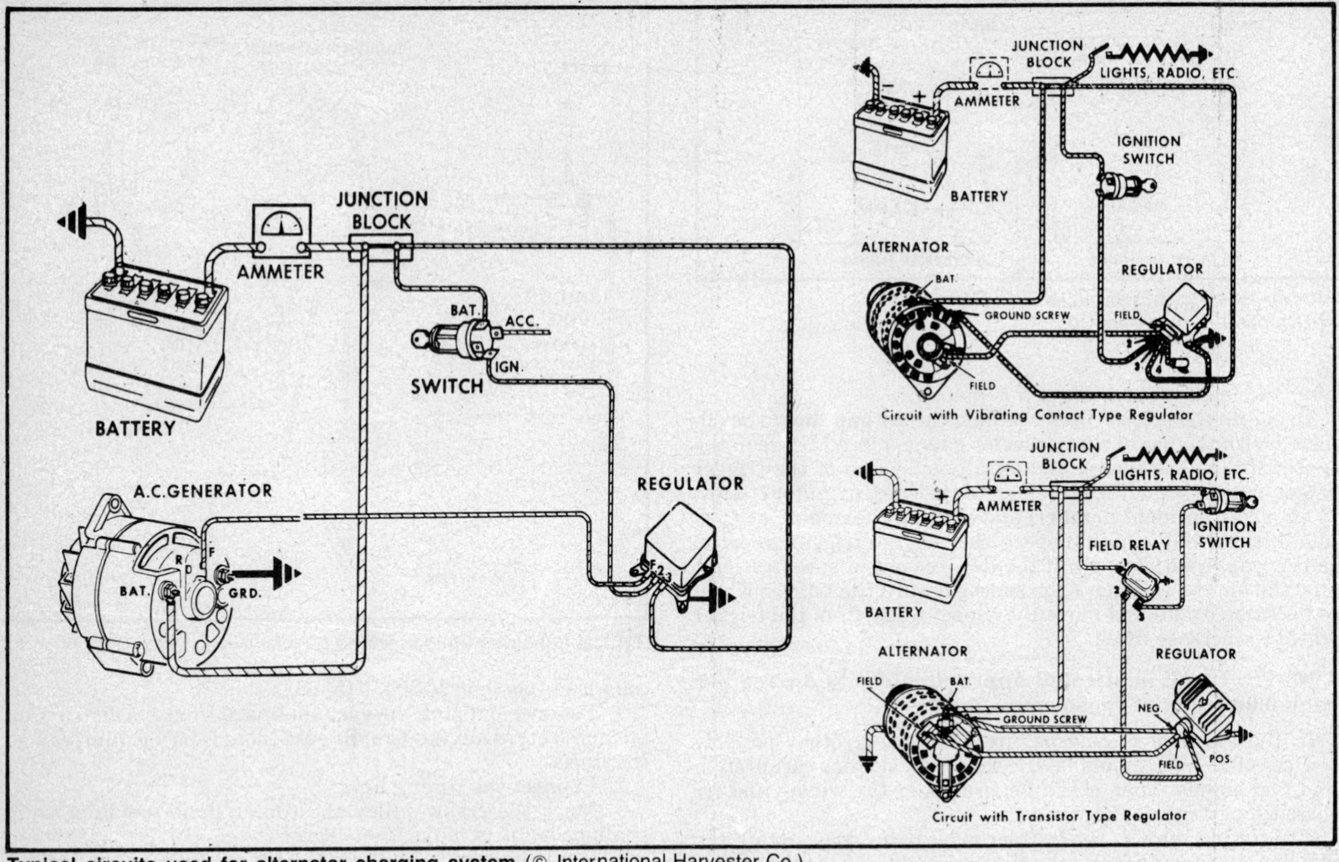

Typical circuits used for alternator charging system (© International Harvester Co.)

3. Loosen the adjusting strap and pivot bolts. Push inward on the alternator to loosen the belt and slip it off the pulley.
4. Remove the adjusting strap and pivot bolts, and remove the alternator from the engine.
5. Installation is in the reverse of the removal. Adjust the belt to have no more than ½ inch deflection on the longest span of the belt.

Voltage Regulators

Two types of voltage regulators are used to control the output of the alternators. One type is the internal unit, mounted within the alternator, and the second is an external type, normally mounted on the inner fender panel or the firewall.

EXTERNAL TYPE

Removal and Installation

1. Disconnect clamp lead at the negative terminal of battery.
2. Disconnect the wiring harness connector at regulator terminals.
3. Remove mounting screws and regulator unit from vehicle.
4. To install, reverse the above procedure.
5. Reconnect cable clamp to battery terminal, checking polarity first.

INTERNAL TYPE

Adjustment

1. Remove the alternator as outlined.
2. Mark and separate the front housing from the rear housing.
3. Remove the diode trio screws and nuts, and remove the trio assembly.
4. Remove the two remaining screws in the regulator, and remove the brush holder and the regulator from the rear housing.
5. Installation is the reverse order of the removal, assuring that the insulated sleeves are installed on the proper screws, during installation.

NOTE: Refer to the Unit Repair Section for more repair information.

Starter

For servicing and overhauling starter motors, see Electrical Diagnosis Section of Unit Section.

ELECTRIC

Removal and Installation

1. Disconnect cable clamp from negative terminal of battery.
2. Disconnect cable and wire leads from terminals of solenoid assembly, identifying leads with tags. If the solenoid is not mounted directly on the starter motor, disconnect the cable from the solenoid to the motor at the motor terminal.
3. Remove starter motor mounting bolts or stud nuts.
4. Pull starter assembly forward to clear housing and remove starter.
5. To install, reverse the above procedure, installing new tang lockwashers where removed.

BRAKES

Hydraulic Brakes

Late model trucks are equipped with a dual hydraulic brake system in which there are separate hydraulic systems for the front and rear brakes. In this dual system a warning light switch operates a warning light on the dashboard when there is a pressure failure in either the front or rear system. A power system may be employed to reduce the effort applied to the brake pedal. See General Repair Section for hydraulic brake service and overhaul.

MASTER CYLINDER

Removal and Installation

1. Disconnect hydraulic lines from master cylinder.
2. Disconnect master cylinder pushrod at brake pedal and remove nuts securing cylinder to dash panel.
3. If master cylinder is mounted on power unit, remove nuts securing master cylinder to power unit and remove cylinder from vehicle.
4. Installation is the reverse of the above procedure.
5. Bleed system.

WARNING LIGHT SWITCH

Resetting

Once a difference of 85 ± 150 psi. pressure between the front and rear systems has activated the warning light switch, it will not go off by itself and must be manually reset.

1. Clean switch and disconnect wire from terminal.
2. Unscrew and completely remove switch from body. This will allow the pistons to center and hold the switch in "off" position.
3. Screw switch back into body and reconnect wire to terminal.
4. If fluid is in the switch cavity, press brake pedal to see if piston O-ring seals are leaking. If there is leakage, the O-rings must be replaced.
5. Warning light switch should be checked periodically for proper function and the presence of foreign matter and dirt.

BRAKE SHOES

NOTE: Refer to the brake section in the unit repair section of this manual for information, on the medium and heavy duty truck brake systems.

Adjustment

1. Remove rubber dust cover from access hole.
2. Using an adjusting tool or screwdriver, turn star screw until shoes drag on the drum.
3. Rotate star screw back from drag position until drag is completely eliminated.
4. On brakes equipped with automatic adjusters it will be necessary to hold the adjusting lever away from the star wheel with a screwdriver while the adjustment is made.

Bleeding System

1. Before bleeding the brake system, disconnect electrical wire from warning light switch and remove any foreign material or dirt accumulation around warning light switch. Then remove the switch from body. The switch must be removed to prevent shearing of the end of the pin due to unequal pressures created between front and rear systems while bleeding.
2. Fill master cylinder reservoir (s) with clean brake fluid.

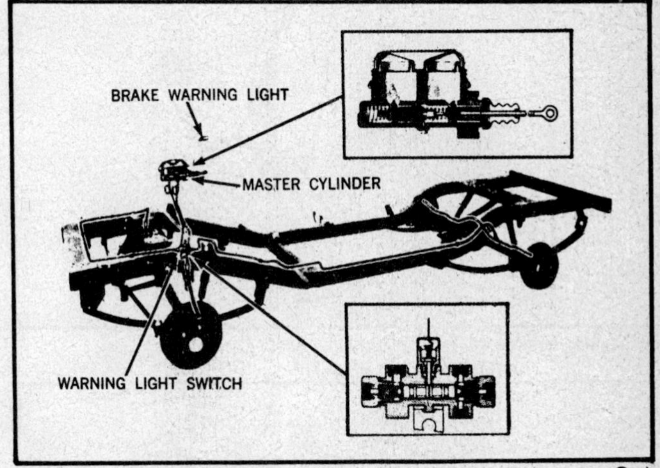

Typical standard dual brake system (© International Harvester Co.)

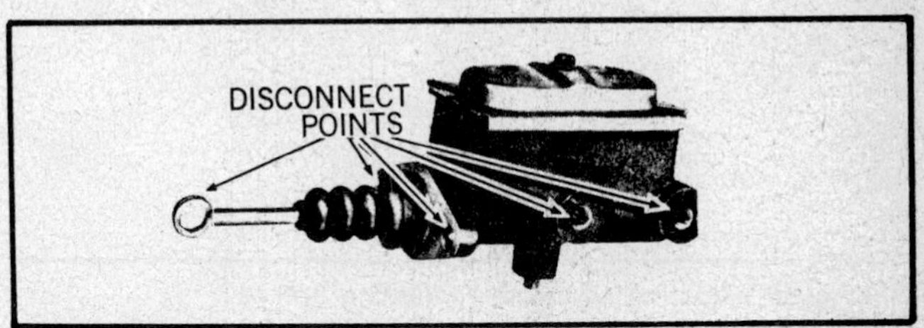

Tandem master cylinder disconnect points (© International Har vester Co.)

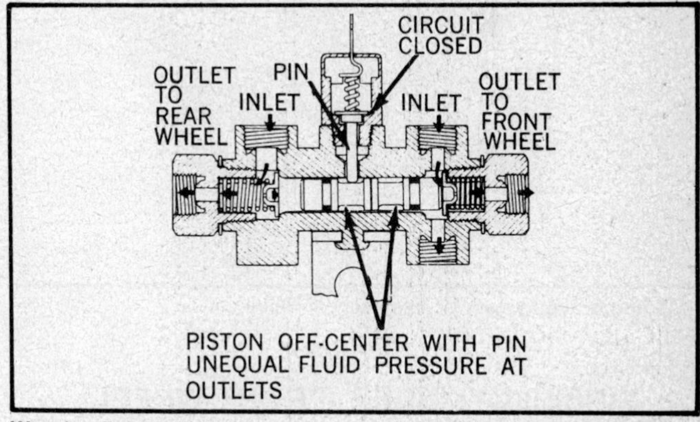

Warning light switch circuit closed (© International Harvester Co.)

3. Attach bleeder hose to bleeder valve on wheel cylinder and place free end of bleeder hose in a jar partially filled with fluid. On some models it may be necessary to take the wheel off to get at the bleeder valve.
4. While the brake pedal is being pressed steadily, open the bleeder valve until the fluid coming from the hose is clean and free of air bubbles, then close bleeder valve and release brake pedal.
5. If the brake pedal goes to the floorboard before the bleeding becomes clean, more fluid will have to be added to the reservoir and the above process repeated.
6. Repeat the above procedure for each wheel cylinder, making sure to check the level of fluid in the reservoir frequently.

NOTE: On models equipped with power boosters, the booster must be bled first.

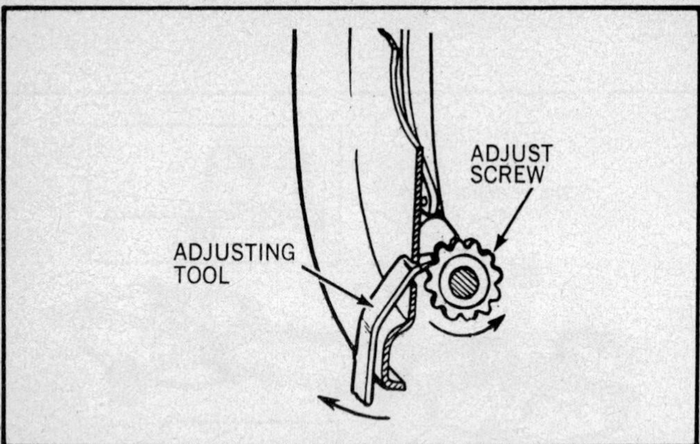

Adjusting brakes (© International Harvester Co.)

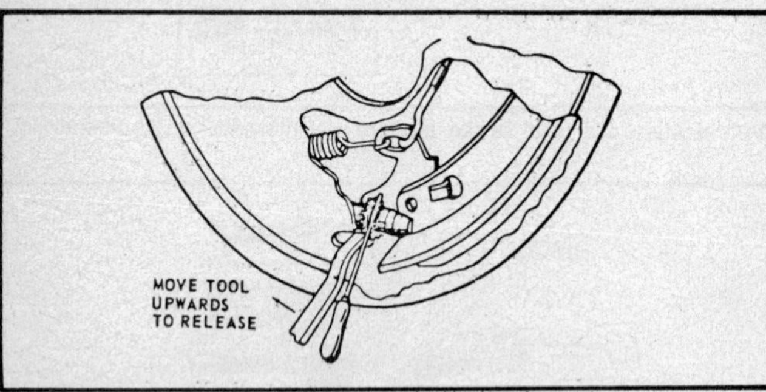

Backing off adjusting screw self-adjusting brakes (© International Harvester Co.)

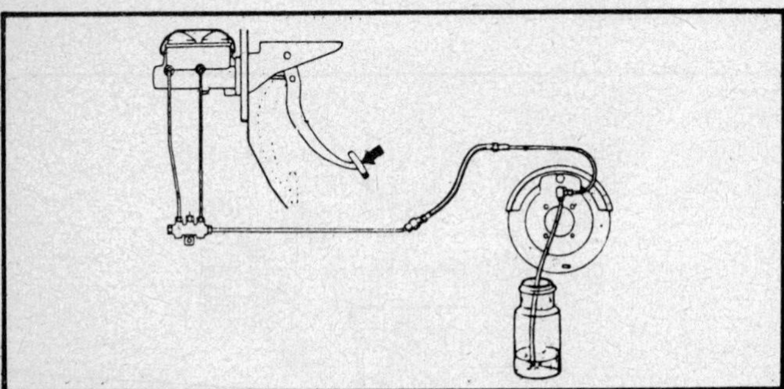

Bleeding brake system (© International Harvester Co.)

WHEEL CYLINDER (FRONT WHEEL)

Removal

1. Raise the front of the vehicle and support it safely.
2. Remove the front wheel assembly, including the drum, to expose the brake shoes.
3. Remove the brake shoes from the brake support plate.
4. Loosen or remove the hydraulic brake line. Remove the wheel cylinder from the brake support plate.

NOTE: The brake hose can be loosened at the cylinder and removed when the cylinder is loose from the support plate, or can be removed from the pipe and fitting at the frame rail, and withdrawn with the wheel cylinder from the brake support plate, to be separated later.

Installation

1. Connect the brake hose to the wheel cylinder and install the wheel cylinder to the brake support plate.
2. Install the brake lining and secure.
3. Install the drum and wheel assembly.
4. Adjust the wheel bearings and brakes.
5. Bleed the hydraulic system. Refill the master cylinder.

NOTE: The warning switch should be disconnected and removed from its seat in the switch until after the bleeding operation is completed.

WHEEL CYLINDER (REAR WHEEL)

Removal

1. Raise the rear of the vehicle and support it safely.
2. Remove the axle shaft (if full floating), and the rear wheel assembly.
3. If necessary, remove the drum separately.
4. Remove the brake lining from the brake support plate.
5. Remove the hydraulic line from the wheel cylinder.
6. Remove the wheel cylinder attaching bolts and remove the cylinder.

Installation

1. Install the wheel cylinder on the brake support plate.
2. Install the hydraulic line to the wheel cylinder.
3. Install the brake shoes on the brake support plate.
4. Install the drum, if removed separately.
5. Install the wheel assembly and the axle shaft (if removed).
6. Bleed the system and refill the master cylinder. Refer to the *NOTE* under the front cylinder installation concerning the warning switch removal during bleeding.

Disc Brakes

The disc brakes are the sliding caliper, single piston type, and are used on the front wheels in combination with drum type brakes on the rear.

Removal

1. Raise the front of the vehicle and support it safely.
2. Remove the front wheels from the hub.
3. Remove approximately a third of the fluid from the large reservoir of the master cylinder, to avoid leakage of fluid when the pistons are forced back into the calipers.
4. Position a large "C" clamp over the caliper and engage the rear of the caliper with the shoe of the clamp, and place the screw on the outboard disc pad. Tightening the screw will cause the piston to be forced deeper in the bore by the movement of the caliper.
5. Remove the key retaining screw and drive the support key and support spring from the caliper and support, using a brass drift and a light hammer.
6. Remove the caliper from the support bracket and support the assembly on a wire.

CAUTION

Do not support the assembly by the brake hose.

NOTE: It is not necessary to remove the brake hose from the caliper when only replacing the disc pads, and therefore it would not be necessary to bleed the caliper when reinstalled.

7. Remove the disc pads from the calipers.

Installation

1. Position the new disc pads into the calipers, using a new anti-rattle spring clip, and position it on the inboard pad.

2. Place the caliper assembly over the rotor and engage the anchor bracket.
3. Position the caliper support spring and support key between the bottom edge of the caliper and the anchor bracket.
4. With the use of a brass drift and hammer, drive the key and spring assembly into position and install the key retaining screw.
5. Refill the master cylinder as needed, apply the brakes several times to seat the pads, and recheck the master cylinder fluid level.
6. Install the wheels and lower the vehicle.

BRAKE PEDAL HEIGHT

Adjustment

There are no provisions available for the adjustment of the brake pedal height. However, it should be checked to determine if sufficient height exists. Corrections can only be made by replacement of parts, alignment, or straightening of the affected parts. To determine if sufficient pedal height exists, open a wheel cylinder bleed valve to simulate a failed system, and depress the brake pedal. The pedal should not contact the floor board during this test.

NOTE: Close the bleeder valve before releasing the brake pedal. The brake warning light switch will have to be reset after the test is completed.

STOPLIGHT SWITCH

Adjustment

No stoplight switch adjustments are provided. If the stop lamps are inoperative, a defective switch, defective bulbs, loose or broken connections, or an improper positioned switch would be indicated. A mechanical type switch is located on the brake pedal, at the pushrod bolt location, while the hydraulic type switch is located on or near the master cylinder, and operated by hydraulic pressure.

The air brake system on the straight truck models, utilizes two air operated switches. One switch is used on the primary brake system, and the second switch is used on the secondary brake system, to provide stop lamps in case of a failure in one of the systems. The tractor type models use a single switch, but it is mounted on a double check valve, and is operated by air being passed through from both the primary and secondary brake systems.

VACUUM POWER BRAKES

The vacuum power cylinder used with the single and dual hydraulic brake systems assists braking differently than a power booster in that its activation results directly from the foot pedal and not from the master cylinder. There are single and tandem dual types. Both types are mounted on the engine side of the firewall.

VACUUM POWER BRAKE CYLINDER

Removal and Installation

1. Disconnect vacuum hose from check valve.
2. Disconnect hydraulic lines from master cylinder.
3. Disconnect pedal link from pedal from inside the cab.
4. Remove bolts which mount the bracket to the firewall.
5. To install reverse the above procedure.
6. Bleed master cylinder output ports while connecting tube nuts which secure lines to ports.
7. Bleed hydraulic brake system.

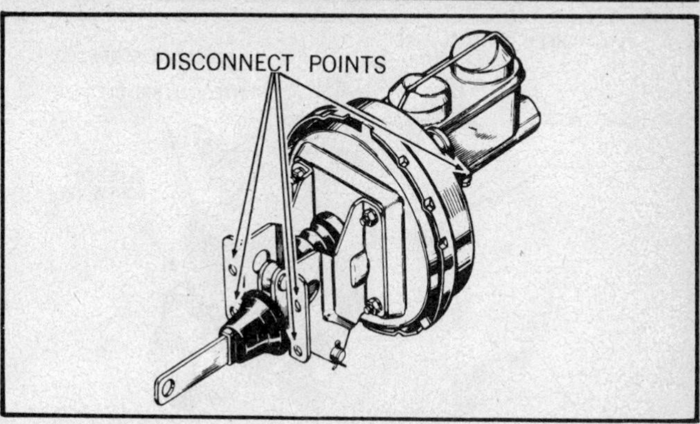

Power cylinder disconnect points (© International Harvester Co.)

VACUUM BRAKE BOOSTERS

Vacuum boosters add pressure to the hydraulic brake system. The activation and amount of pressure is controlled by a hydraulic line from the master cylinder. Disassembly and service procedures for vacuum boosters may be found in the General Repair Section.

Removal and Installation

1. On units lacking integral air filter, remove air inlet hose (from engine air cleaner).
2. Disconnect vacuum inlet tube (coming from engine manifold).
3. Disconnect hydraulic line from master cylinder and hydraulic line going to wheel cylinders.
4. Remove mounting bolts and lift out vacuum unit.
5. To install, reverse the above procedure.
6. Bleed complete hydraulic system, starting with cylinder on vacuum unit as described below.

VACUUM BOOSTER SYSTEM

Bleeding

1. The booster must be bled before proceeding to wheel cylinders.
2. All vacuum boosters have a bleed valve on the control valve as indicated in the figures by the number "1". This valve must always be bled first.
3. On boosters having an additional bleeder valve on the hydraulic cylinder indicated by the number "2", bleed this cylinder after control valve.
4. Bleed wheel cylinders as described in preceding section.

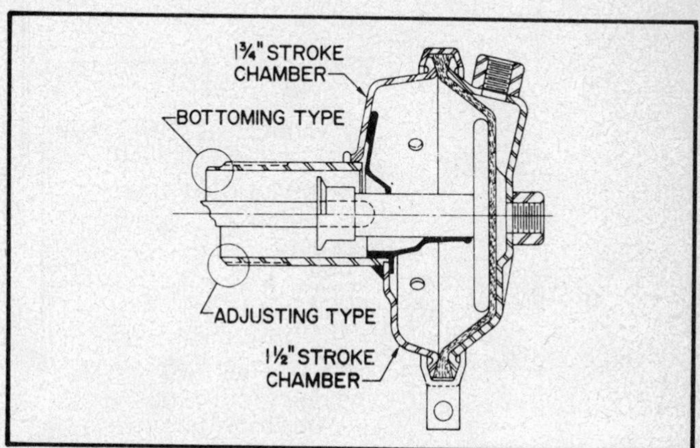

Power brake air chamber (© International Harvester Co.)

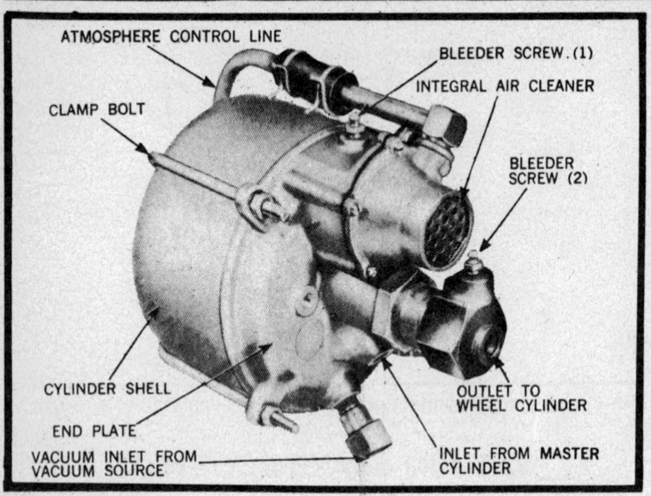

Power cylinder with integral air cleaner (© International Harvester Co.)

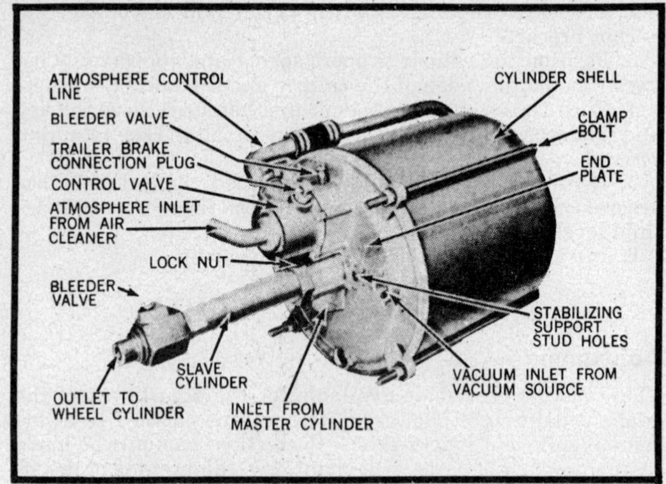

Typical single cylinder booster (© International Harvester Co.)

TRAILER BRAKE HAND CONTROL

Adjustment

The advance control valve is used in conjunction with the Hydrovac and trailer brake system to vary the initial braking of the trailer.

1. Place advance plate in full released position (rotate counterclockwise).
2. While coasting on smooth road at 20 mph, apply valve by rotating clockwise until a slight drag is felt from the trailer brakes.
3. Rotate advance plate to where it just touches the valve operating handle. This releases the brakes on the trailer but sets the advance effect.
4. Leaving advance valve controls as set above, gently apply tractor brakes to check the "advance" of the trailer brakes.

Parking Brake

Adjustment

REAR BRAKE TYPE

1. Loosen locknut on the equalizer rod and turn front nut forward several turns.
2. Turn the locknut (rear) forward just enough to remove any slack but not so much that the brake shoes lift off their anchors.
3. Tighten both nuts against the equalizer.

DRIVE SHAFT BAND TYPE

1. Leaving parking brake lever in the extreme release position, check that the cam lever is resting squarely on upper brake band bracket. This is adjusted by removing the clevis pin

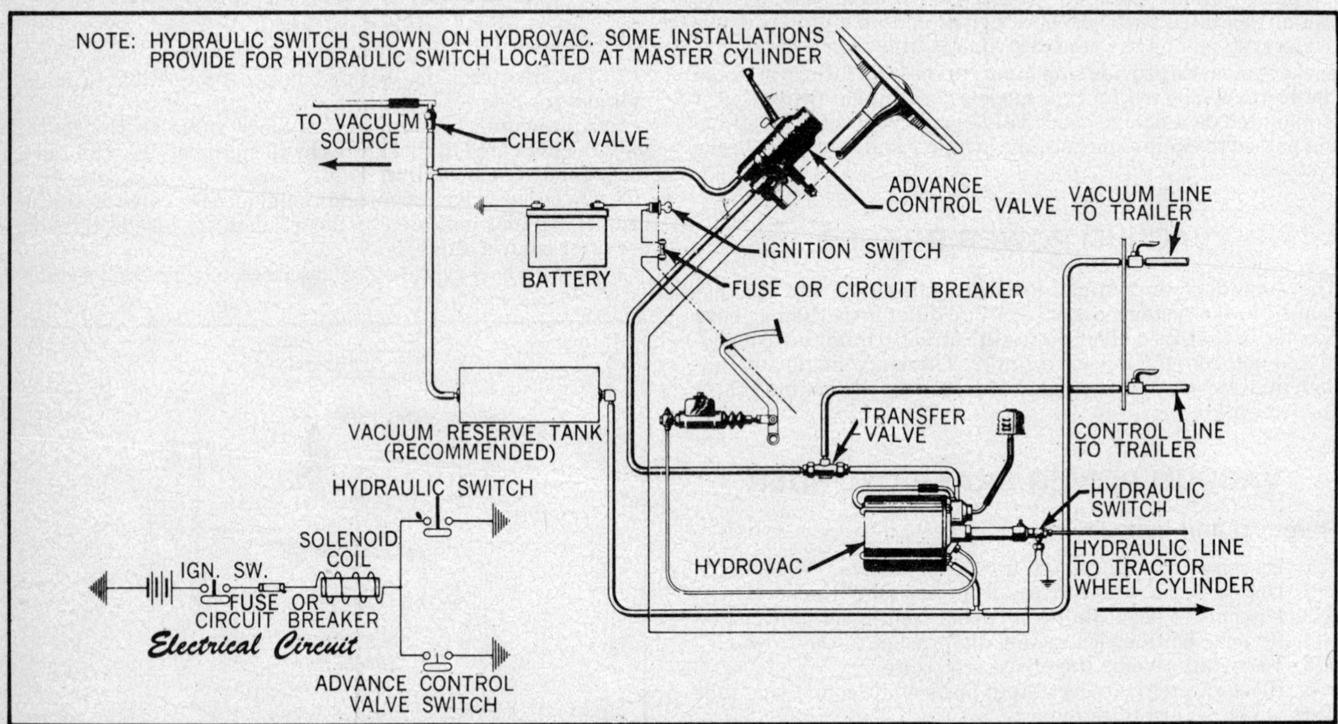

Typical advance trailer brake control valve installation (© International Harvester Co.)

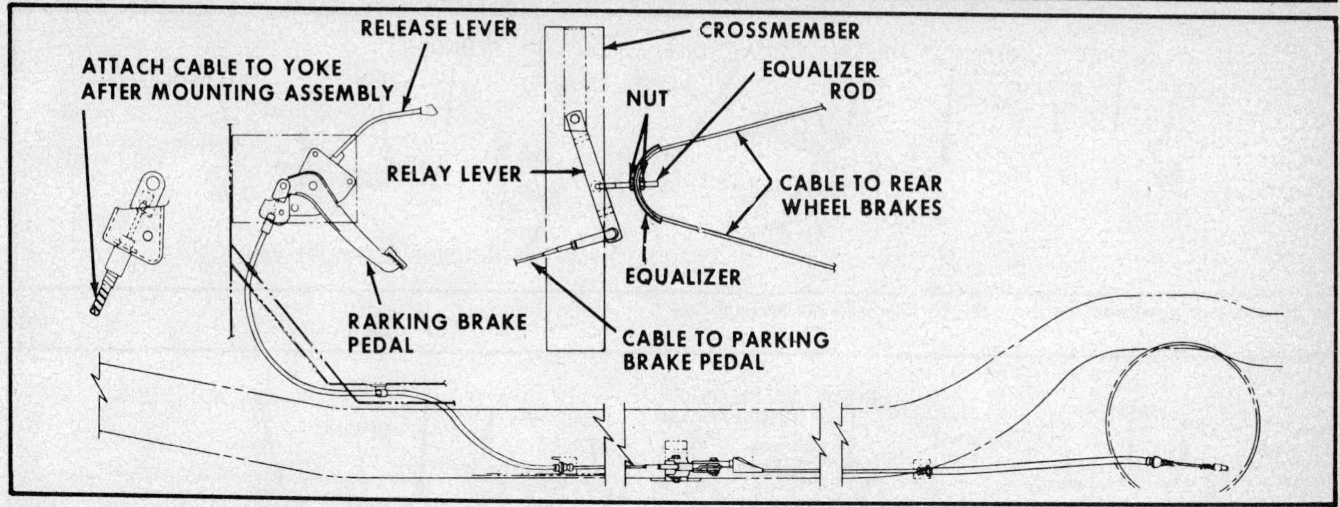

Parking brake cable adjustment (© International Harvester Co.)

and readjusting yoke.

2. Adjust screw nut (1) until a clearance of 00.020 to00.030" is reached.

3. Adjusting nuts (4) on bolt (5), obtain 00.020 to 00.030" clearance on lower half of lining and drum.

4. Adjust nuts (2) on bolt (3) for a clearance of 00.020 to 00.030" clearance on top half of lining.

5. Lock all adjustments with lock nuts.

ENCLOSED DRUM TYPE

1. Block the vehicle wheels.

2. Disconnect the clevis pin from the bellcrank and clevis at the brake assembly.

3. Move the hand brake control lever approximately $^1/_4$ to $^3/_8$ inch in the apply direction to compensate for the allowable freeplay.

4. Move the bellcrank lever in the apply direction until contact is made with the brake cam, without any brake shoe movement.

5. Adjust the clevis until the hole in the clevis aligns with the mating hole in the positioned bellcrank lever.

6. Assemble the clevis and bellcrank lever. Tighten the clevis locknut.

7. Recheck the freeplay and lever adjustment.

NOTE: If the vehicle is equipped with the Orschelm type parking brake lever, (over-center type), rotate the adjusting knob on the end of the lever, while in the released position, to attain a force of 90 lbs. to apply the parking brake. When properly adjusted, a distinct click will be heard when pulled over center.

SPRING ACTUATED TANDEM TYPE AIR CONTROLLED

This unit is a spring actuated type parking brake consisting of a tandem-type cylinder, connected to the brake shoes, through the air brake slack adjuster and brake camshaft. The cylinder assembly is divided into two sections. One section is the regu-

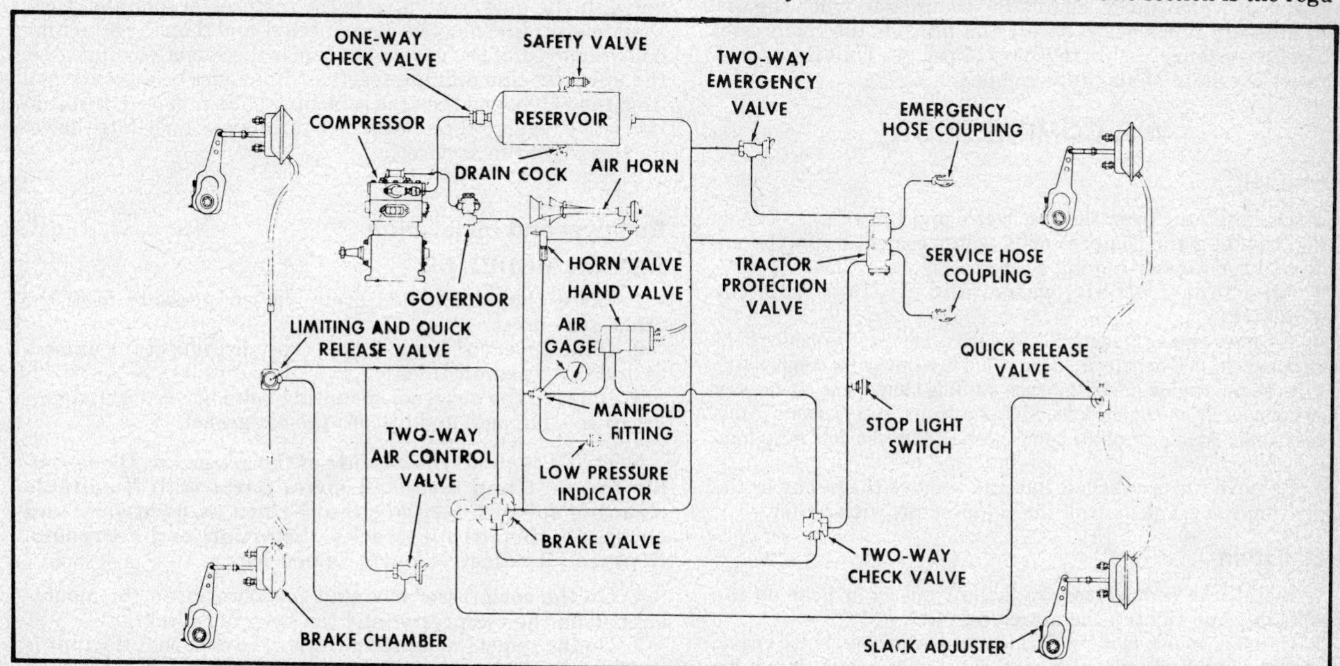

Typical air brake system (© International Harvester Co.)

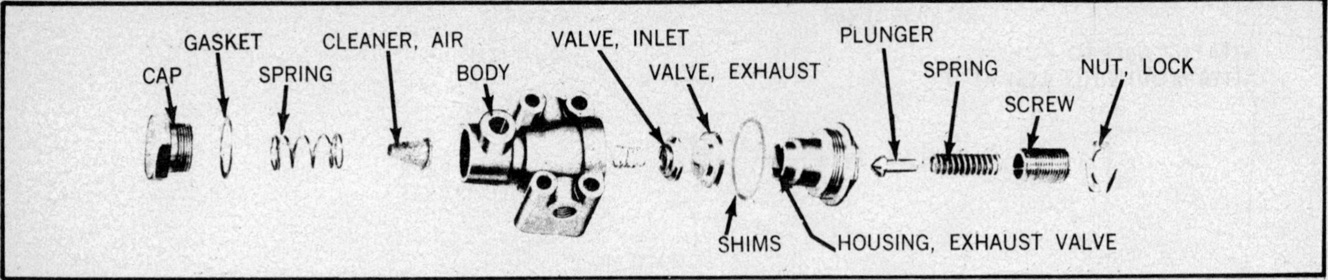

Air compressor governor—early models (© International Harvester Co.)

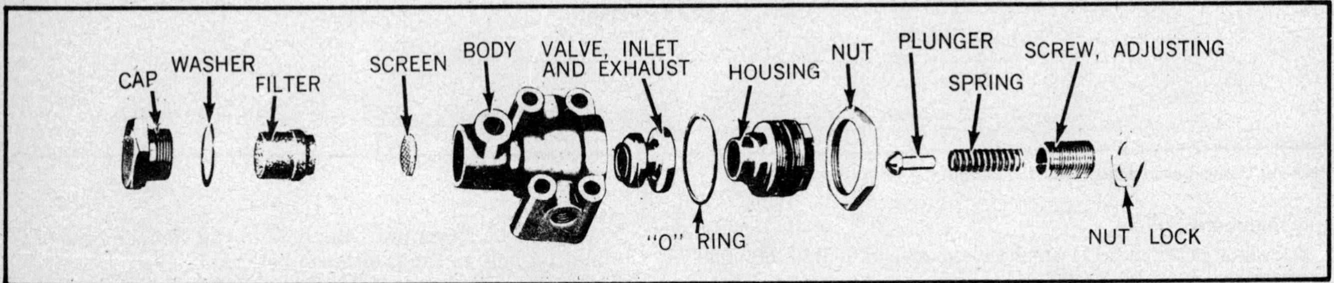

Air compressor governor—late models (© International Harvester Co.)

lar air brake chamber, and the second is the spring actuated chamber, containing a powerful spring, compressed by air pressure and applied by the operator with the use of a control valve. The brake adjustment is controlled by the adjustment of the slack adjuster for the regular brakes.

Air Brake System

Air brake systems are composed of a compressor, a reservoir, brake actuating chambers and a network of lines and valves which control operation. The piston-type air compressor is belt driven directly from the engine and is dependent upon the engine for its lubrication. Pressure in the system is regulated by a governor which starts loading the compressor when the system pressure drops below 95 psi and unloads the compressor when the system pressure reaches 110 psi. See Unit Repair section for overhaul of air brake components.

AIR COMPRESSOR

Removal

1. Drain all air from the reservoirs and lines.
2. Providing the compressor is water cooled, drain the engine and compressor cooling system.
3. Disconnect all air, water, and oil lines from the compressor.
4. **Gasoline engine models:** Remove the compressor mounting bolts and remove the belt or belts from the pulleys. Remove the compressor.
   a. **Diesel engine models:** Attach a lifting sling to the compressor and remove the mounting bolts. Slide the compressor rearward to disengage the drive gear of the compressor and lift the unit away from the engine.
5. Remove the crankshaft nut and remove the pulley or the gear from the crankshaft of the compressor, with puller.

Installation

1. Install the compressor crankshaft pulley or gear on the crankshaft and tighten the attaching nut.
2. **Gasoline engine models:** Position the compressor on the engine bracket and install the mounting bolts, but do not tighten. Install the belts on the pulleys and adjust. Tighten the mounting bolts.
   a. **Diesel engine models:** Mount the compressor in a sling and lift it to the rear of its mounting position. Slide the compressor forward and engage the drive gear with the idler timing gear. Install the mounting bolts and tighten.
3. Attach the air, water, and oil lines to the compressor.
4. Operate the compressor and inspect for oil, water or air leaks.

COMPRESSOR GOVERNOR VALVE

The compressor governor valve can be either the remote-mounted or compressor-mounted type. The air system must be drained before any attempt is made to remove either type valve. If the governor valve is the compressor-mounted type, the reservoir line must be disconnected, and then the attaching bolts removed. If the governor valve is the remote-mount type, the unloader line and the reservoir line must be disconnected from the valve, and then the attaching bolts removed. Installation is the reverse of removal. Test the air system before the vehicle is placed in service.

Removal and Installation

BENDIX MODEL D-2

1. Block the wheels and drain the air pressure from the brake system.
2. If the governor is the remote type, disconnect the unloader and the reservoir lines.
3. Remove the governor mounting bolts, governor and gasket (if so equipped) and discard the old gasket.

NOTE: Clean off the outside of the governor. Disassemble the unit and clean all metal parts with a suitable cleaning solvent. Replace the O-rings as necessary and check all springs for cracks, distortion and corrosion. Replace all defective parts as necessary.

4. On the compressor mounted govenors, clean the mounting pad on the compressor and the governor block.
5. On the remote mounted governor, be sure that the unit is positioned with the exhaust ports pointed down. This unit should be mounted higher than the compressor so that the con-

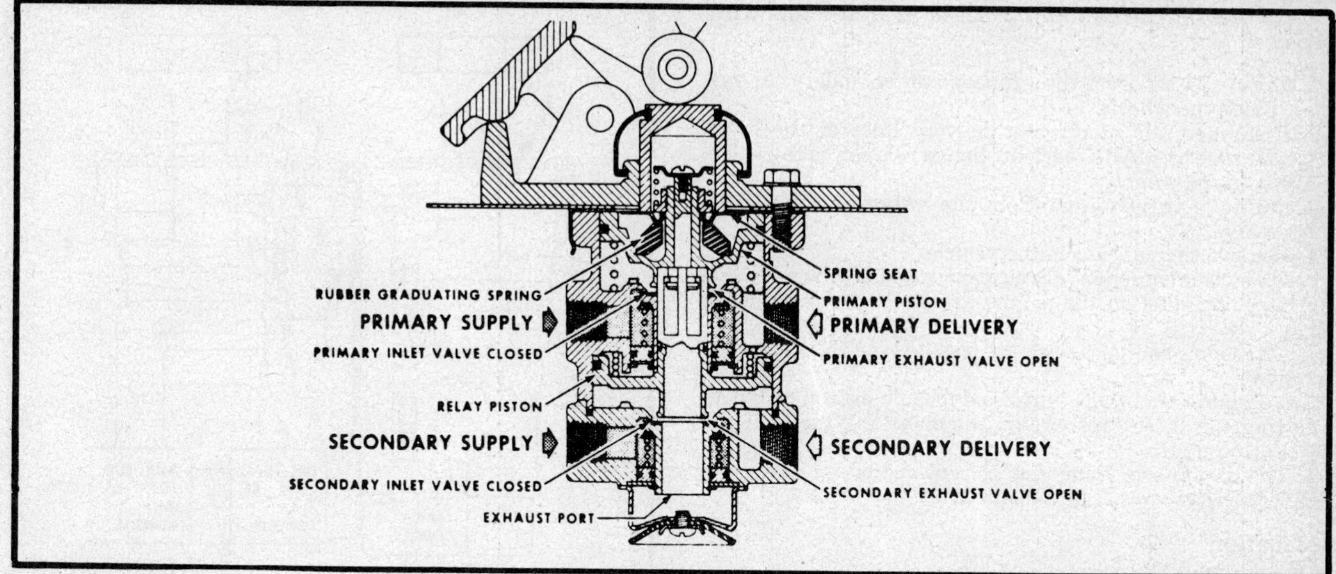

Typical brake (foot) valve

necting lines will drain away from the governor.

6. Install the governor with a new mounting gasket (if so equipped). Connect all the air lines to the governor, including the unloader and the reservoir lines. Test the governor and adjust as necessary.

MIDLAND ROSS MODELS

1. Block the wheels and drain the air pressure from the brake system.
2. Drain the air pressure from the brake system and disconnect the air lines at the governor and unloader.
3. Remove the nuts and or bolts holding the governor to the compressor bracket.
4. Remove the governor and discard the old gasket.

NOTE: Clean off the outside of the governor. Disassemble the unit and clean all metal parts with a suitable cleaning solvent. Replace the O-rings as necessary and check all springs for cracks, distortion and corrosion. Replace all defective parts as necessary.

5. Place the governor in position with the new gasket. Install the mount bolts and or nuts and tighten to specifications.
6. Build up the air pressure in the brake system. Check the governor for air leaks and proper operation, adjust as necessary.

RESERVOIR

Removal

1. Drain the air from the reservoir and lines.
2. Remove the air lines to the reservoir.
3. Loosen and remove the attaching straps holding the reservoir to the frame or crossmember.
4. Remove the reservoir assembly.

Installation

1. Install the reservoir and secure it with the attaching straps.
2. Attach the air lines to the reservoir.
3. Close the drain cock and build up air pressure to test air holding ability.

NOTE: The combined volume of all reservoirs and supply reservoirs must be twelve times the combined volume

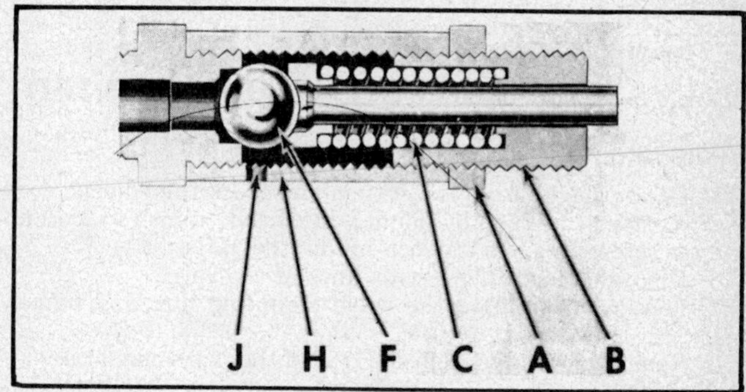

Safety valve (© International Harvester Co.)

of all service brake chambers at maximum travel, and should never be altered.

CONTROL AND CHECK VALVES

Removal and Installation

NOTE: Before any valve, line, or fitting is loosened or removed, all air must be drained from the system. Personal injury can result if these precautions are not adhered to.

The safety valve, pressure gauge or gauges, low pressure indicator, stop light switch, automatic reservoir drain valve, check valves, inversion valve, and quick release valves are located in the lines and may be bolted to the frame or crossmember. To remove or install the above mentioned valves, is simply a matter of disconnecting and connecting the lines from the valve, and removing or installing any attaching bolts, and repairing or replacing the affected valve. The lines must be maintained in their proper order so as not to interchange the primary and secondary air systems.

BRAKE VALVE

Removal

NOTE: On tilt cab models, remove the brake pedal from the brake (foot) valve and the brake valve retaining

bolts. Then tilt the cab and proceed as in the following steps.

1. Drain the air from the primary and secondary air systems. Block the wheels.
2. Disconnect all supply and delivery lines at the brake valve. Be sure to 'MARK' each air line in relation to the valve, to assist in reassembly.
3. Remove the fittings from the valve and mark for reassembly.
4. Remove the valve from the vehicle.
5. On models equipped with suspended pedal valves, remove the attaching nuts on the engine fire wall side and remove valve.
6. On models equipped with the treadle type valve, proceed as follows.
   a. Remove the brake valve and treadle assembly, by removing the three capsrews on the outer bolt circle of the mounting plate.
2. The basic valve alone may be removed by removing the three capscrews on the inner bolt circle.

Installation

1. The installation of the brake valve is the reverse of removal. Connect all fittings and lines in their proper order, and test the brake operation before vehicle movement.

SPRING BRAKE TWO-WAY CONTROL VALVE PUSH AND PULL—DASH MOUNTED

Removal

1. Drain the air from the system and block the wheels.
2. Remove the knob by using a hex head wrench to loosen the set screw. Remove the lock nut on the valve.
3. Disconnect and tag the air lines at the valve.
4. Loosen and remove the valve mounting nut, and name plate.
5. Remove the valve from the rear of the instrument panel.

Installation

1. The installation is in the reverse order of the removal. Test the system before vehicle operation.

FLIP SWITCH—DASH MOUNTED

Removal

1. Drain air from the system.
2. Remove the air lines from the valve.

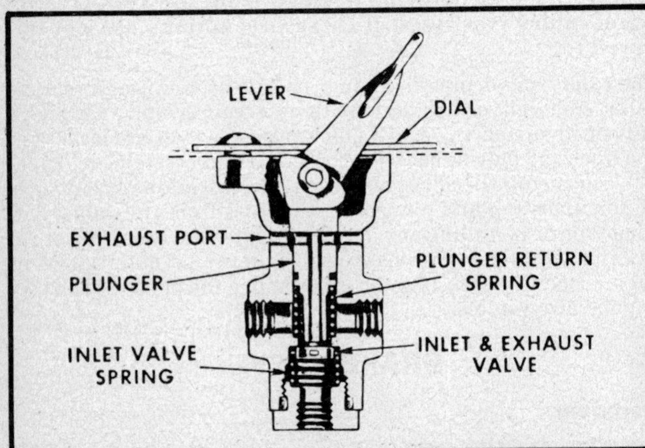

Exploded view of the dash mounted flip switch

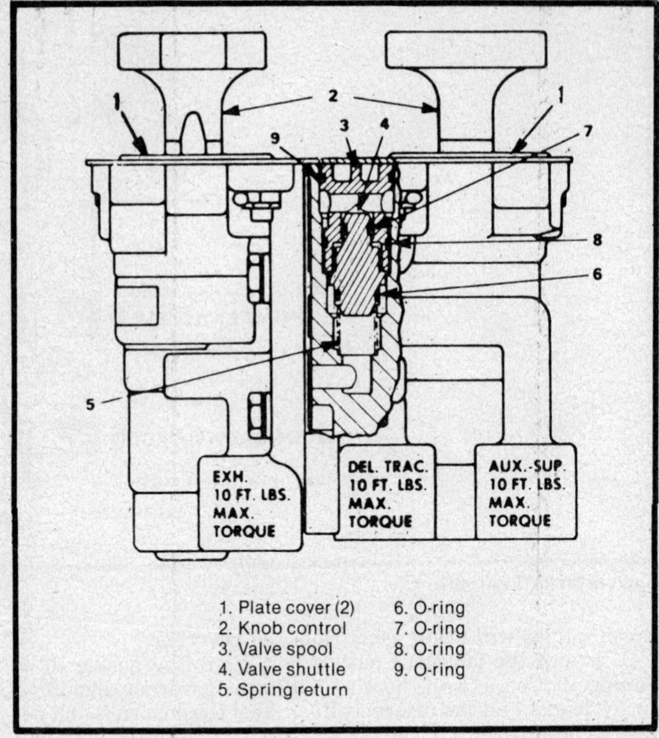

Cross section of a modular control valve

3. Remove the machine screw securing the valve to the instrument panel and remove the valve.

Installation

1. Installation is the reverse of removal. Test the system before vehicle operation.

MODULAR CONTROL VALVE

NOTE: The modular valve is located in the dash panel and it is a three valve assembly. It controls the tractor brakes, supplies air to the trailer and controls the trailer brakes.

Removal

1. Block the wheels and drain the air pressure from the brake system.
2. Remove the bezel (dash) panel and remove the instrument panel access cover. This will expose the valve body cover plates.
3. Tag all the air lines going in to the valve and remove the air lines from the valve.
4. Remove the knobs for the valve and remove the valve lock nuts. Remove the valve from the rear of the instrument panel.
5. Remove all fittings from the rear of the valve. Be sure to take notice to the direction of all the fittings.

Installation

1. Installation is the reverse order of the removal procedure Be sure apply a non-hardening sealing compound to the fittings. Do not apply more than 10 ft. lbs. of torque to the fittings.

AIR COMPRESSOR GOVERNOR

Adjustment

1. Check governor filter and supply line for any restriction.
2. Loosen adjusting screw locknut and exhaust valve housing locknut.
3. Unscrew adjusting screw four turns.
4. Screw in exhaust valve housing until it bottoms. Do not tighten; seats are easily ruined.
5. Back off exhaust valve housing $^3/_4$ turn.
6. While holding exhaust valve housing, turn in adjusting screw three turns after it has made contact with the spring. A slight resistance should be felt when contact is made. If this contact cannot be felt, turn adjusting screw until it sticks out $^3/_8$" from exhaust valve housing.
7. Start engine and build up air pressure to 115 psi and shut off engine. If governor cuts out before 115 psi, turn adjusting screw out one turn and repeat this step.
8. With pressure holding at 115 psi, turn in adjusting screw until governor cuts out (dull pop).
9. Start truck engine and bleed pressure down until governor cuts in. Cut-in pressure should be 93–98 psi.
10. If cut-in pressure is below 93 psi, hold adjusting screw and turn out exhaust valve housing ($^1/_{16}$ turn equals 5 psi).
11. If cut-in pressure is above 98 psi, hold adjusting screw and turn in exhaust valve housing.
12. Repeat steps until proper cut-in pressure is reached.
13. Check cut-out pressure and adjust if necessary.
14. Tighten adjusting screw locknut and exhaust valve housing locknut.

AIR RESERVOIR SAFETY VALVE

Adjustment

1. Connect an accurate air pressure gauge to the emergency line at the rear of the truck and open emergency line valve. With truck engine running, turn air supply valve to the air supply position to bypass governor. Let pressure rise in reservoir until 150 psi is reached then quickly shut off air supply valve.
2. If the safety valve did not blow off at 150 psi or blew off before that pressure, loosen locknut (A) and turn adjusting screw (B) either in for higher pressure setting or out for lower pressure setting.

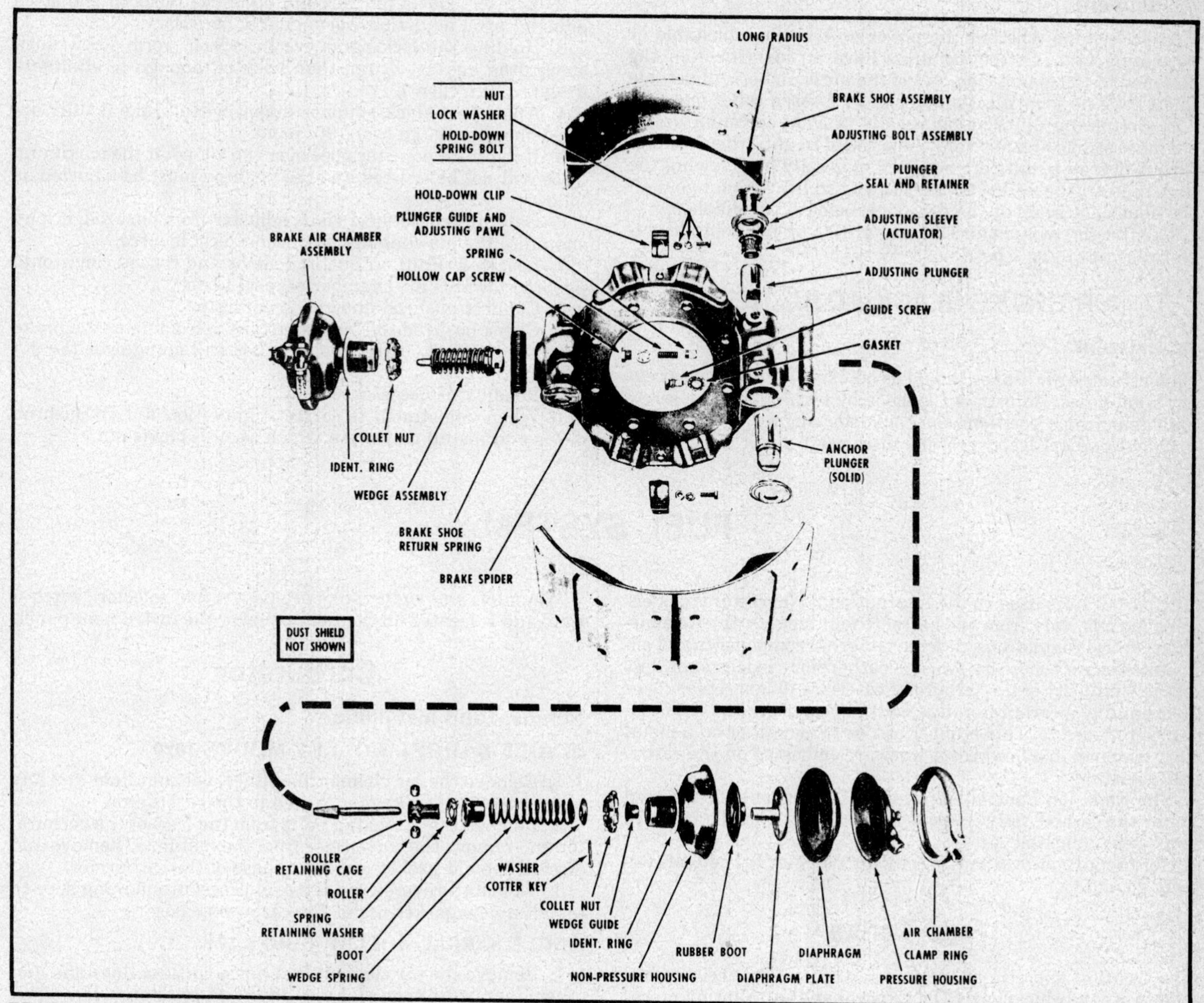

RDA brake with integral plunger housings (© International Harvester Co.)

3. When adjustment is complete, tighten locknut and reduce pressure in system to normal 100 psi by applying and releasing brakes.

PLUNGER ACTUATED BRAKE

Adjustment

1. Jack or hoist wheels free of ground.
2. Remove dust cover from adjusting slot (two places on each brake).
3. Turn the star wheel until heavy drag on drum is developed.
4. Back off bolt barely past light drag.
5. Replace dust covers in adjusting slots.
6. Repeat for other brakes.
7. If brakes are equipped with automatic adjusters, check drum to lining clearance. If it is more than 0.060", adjust brakes manually until they can be serviced. See Unit Repair section for servicing air brakes.

AIR POWER UNIT

Adjustment

1. Determine whether the power unit is the adjustable or bottoming type. Bottoming units have an identification tag fastened to the clamp ring bolt of the air chamber. Adjustable units have no identification markings. Loosen collet nut.
2. Bottoming units automatically provide optimum useful chamber stroke and need only be screwed in until they bottom.
3. Adjustable units are adjusted manually by screwing the unit in until the wedge is just starting to lift the plungers off the abutment seats at the first movement of the diaphragm.
4. After screwing in air chamber unit to proper depth, tighten collet nut to lock position.

AIR BRAKE SLACK ADJUSTERS

Adjustment

Cam actuated air brakes should be adjusted for lining wear every 2000 miles. Adjustment is made by turning a worm screw on a gear which positions slack adjuster angle.

1. With wheel free to rotate, disconnect pushrod from the slack adjuster to determine whether or not it is in fully released position.

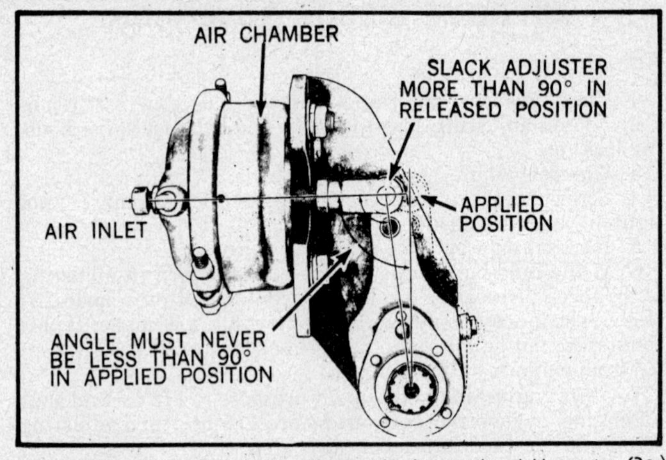

Foundation air brake slack adjuster (© International Harvester Co.)

2. Reinsert clevis pin through bottomed pushrod and slack adjuster arm, adjusting worm gear if necessary.
3. Holding the locking sleeve in, adjust worm screw until shoes drag against drum, then back off enough to eliminate drag ($\frac{1}{4}$ of a turn).
4. Angle that slack adjuster makes when brake is fully applied should not "go over" 90° point.
5. If the slack adjuster goes over the 90° point the maximum force will not be exerted and the pushrod must be adjusted as follows:
6. Carefully disconnect slack adjuster from pushrod, it may snap into the air chamber with considerable force.
7. Loosen locknut on pushrod clevis and thread clevis onto pushrod towards air chamber several turns.
8. Connect pushrod and clevis with pin.
9. Check pushrod-to-slack adjuster angle again as the brake is applied to make sure that it is not still going over the 90° point.
10. Readjust if necessary.
11. When adjustment is correct tighten locknut on pushrod clevis and install cotter pin which secures clevis pin.

FUEL SYSTEM

The carburetors used on the International Harvester truck engine models, vary from one barrel to four barrels. Due to emission control regulations, different internal components and adjustments are necessary for each carburetor model, regardless of the similarity of the carburetor exteriors. When replacing or overhauling a carburetor, it is most important the model number is referred to. This number can be found either on a metal tag, fastened to a bowl cover screw, or embossed on the carburetor casting.

The Emission Control Information Label should be referred to for the correct specifications necessary for the idle mixture and speed adjustments.

For carburetor overhaul specifications, refer to the Unit Repair Section.

Fuel Tanks

The location and size of the fuel tanks vary as the requirements of the vehicle vary. The removal and installation procedure will depend upon the location and size of the tanks.

When left and right tanks are used a fuel selector switch is used and is located on the floor panel or the instrument panel.

Carburetor

Removal and Installation

SINGLE-BARREL HOLLEY MODEL 1920

1. Remove the air cleaner, fuel lines, vacuum lines and any other hoses and linkage attached to the carburetor.
2. Remove the attaching bolts from the base of the carburetor and remove the carburetor from the manifold. Remove and discard the old gasket under the base of the carburetor.
3. To install reverse the removal procedure making sure to install a new gasket under the carburetor base.

SINGLE-BARREL HOLLEY MODEL 1940

1. Remove the air cleaner, fuel lines, vacuum lines and any other lines or linkage attached to the carburetor.
2. Remove the attaching bolts from the base of the carbure-

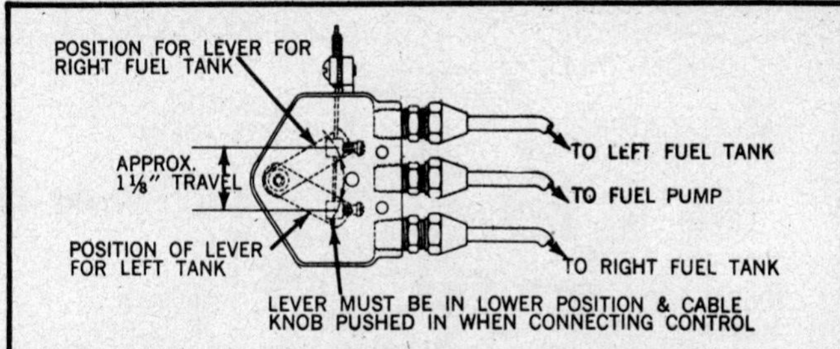

Fuel tank selector valve cable positions (© International Harvester Co.)

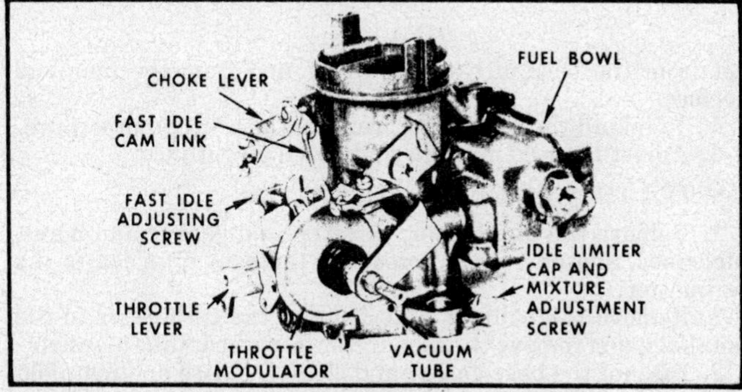

Model 1920 carburetor (© International Harvester Co.)

tor and remove the carburetor from the manifold. Remove and discard the old gasket from under the carburetor.

3. To install reverse the removal procedure making sure to install a new gasket under the carburetor base.

TWO-BARREL HOLLEY MODELS 2100 AND MODEL 2210-C

1. Remove air cleaner, throttle linkage and choke cable.
2. Disconnect fuel line and distributor and governor vacuum lines.
3. Remove bolts from mounting studs and lift off carburetor.
4. To install, clean manifold mating surface and install a new flange gasket.
5. Install carburetor but do not tighten down stud nuts.
6. Connect fuel line and vacuum lines.
7. Tighten nuts on mounting studs in an alternating fashion so that flange gasket compresses evenly for a good seal.
8. Connect throttle linkage and choke cable, making sure that choke plates are fully open when the choke knob is pushed in.
9. Check throttle for complete travel.
10. Install air cleaner.
11. Adjust carburetor as described.

TWO-BARREL HOLLEY MODELS 2300 AND 2300G

1. Remove air filter and disconnect fuel line, distributor and governor vacuum lines and throttle and choke linkages.
2. Remove mounting stud nuts and lift off carburetor.
3. Remove flange gasket and discard.
4. To install, clean manifold mating surface and install a new flange gasket.
5. Operate choke and throttle levers to be sure they are functioning properly.
6. Install carburetor and mounting stud nuts, but do not tighten nuts.
7. Connect fuel line, vacuum lines and throttle and choke linkage.
8. Tighten down mounting stud nuts in an alternating criss-cross pattern to make sure that flange gasket is compressed evenly.
9. Check to see that choke plate is fully open and dashboard knob is in when connecting choke.

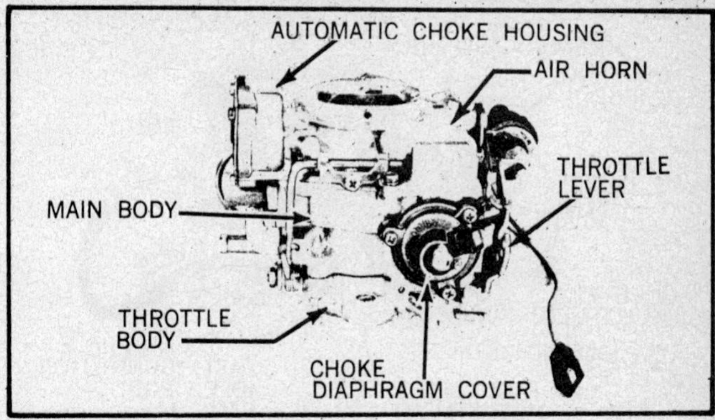

Model 1940 carburetor (© International Harvester Co.)

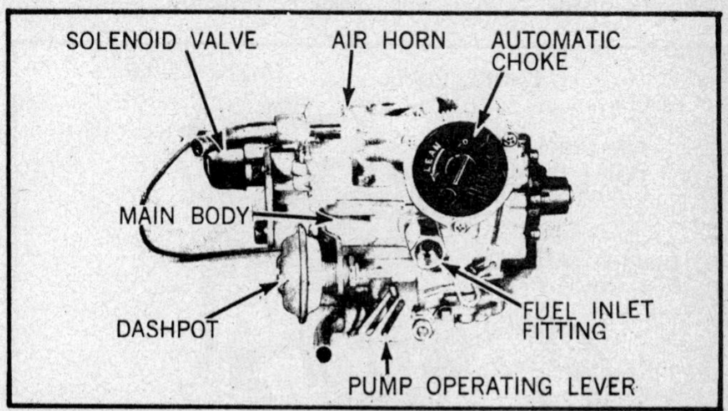

Model 1940 Holley carburetor with dashpot (© International Harvester Co.)

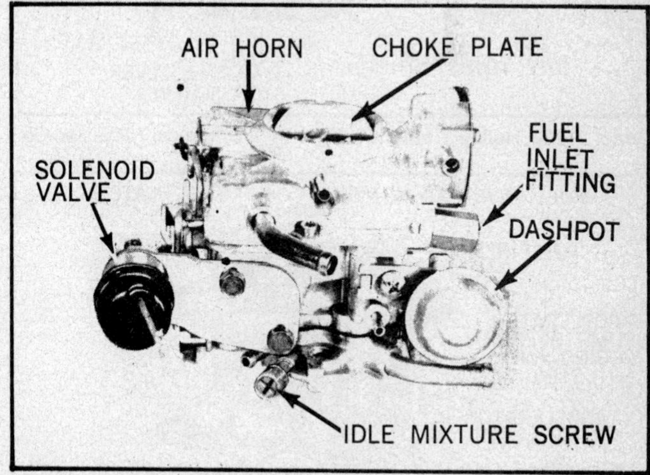

Carburetor model 1940 (© International Harvester Co.)

10. Make all adjustments described in text.
11. Install air cleaner.

FOUR-BARREL HOLLEY MODEL 2140G AND 2140SG

1. Remove the air cleaner, throttle linkage, vacuum lines, fuel lines, choke control cable, and other hoses and linkages attached to the carburetor.
2. Remove the attaching bolts or nuts from the base of the carburetor, and remove the carburetor from the manifold.
3. Discard the base gasket and clean the base and manifold surfaces of gasket particles.
4. To reinstall the carburetor, reverse the removal procedure, using a new base gasket.

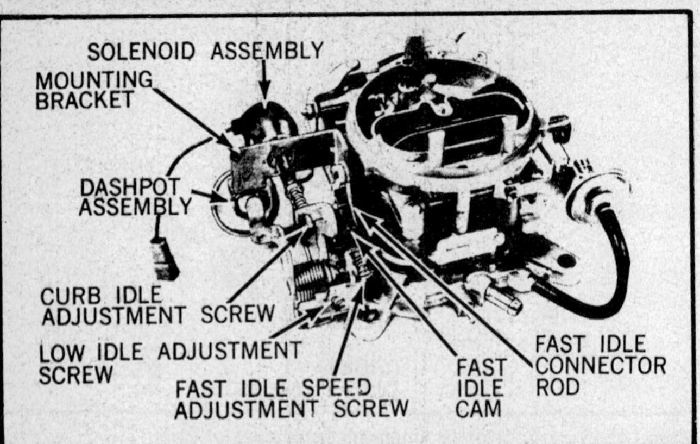

Carburetor model 2210C (© International Harvester Co.)

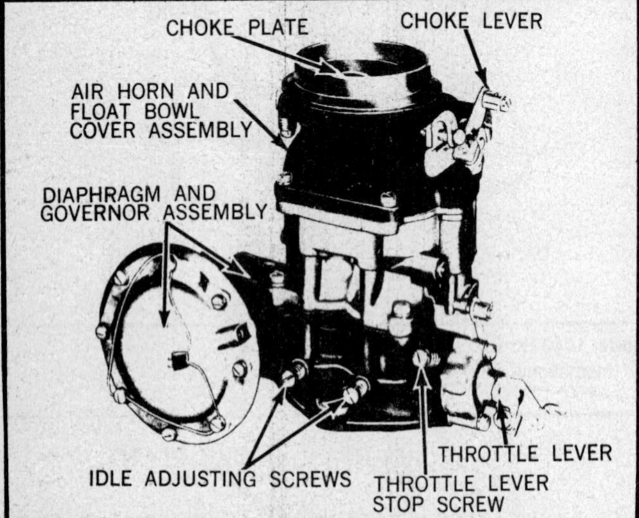

Model 2110G Holley 2 bbl carburetor (© International Harvester Co.)

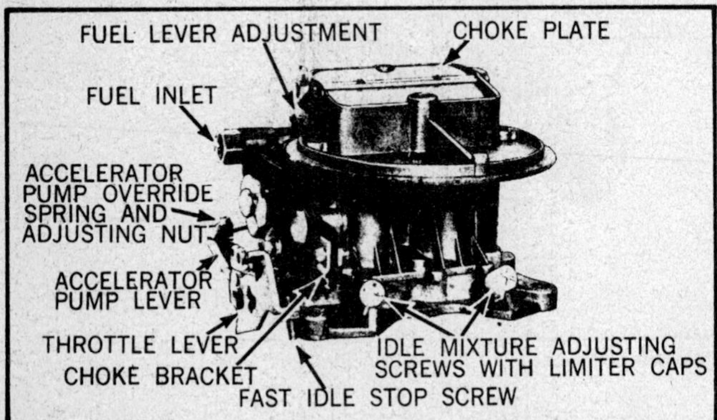

Carburetor model 2300 (© International Harvester Co.)

5. Adjust the carburetor as outlined.

FOUR-BARREL HOLLEY MODEL 4150, 4150C, 4150G and 4150EG

1. Remove the air cleaner, throttle linkage and choke linkage, fuel lines, vacuum lines, and other hoses and linkages attached to the carburetor.
2. Remove the nuts or bolts holding the carburetor to the intake manifold.
3. Lift the carburetor from the manifold and remove the gasket from the base of the carburetor and from the manifold surface.
4. To install the carburetor, reverse the removal procedure.
5. Adjust the idle mixture and speed as outlined.

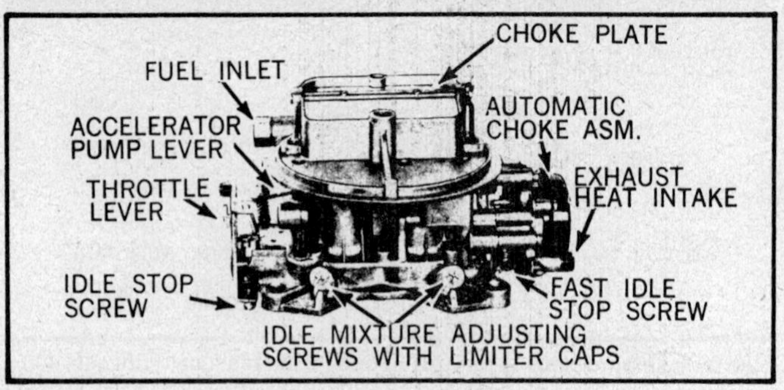

Carburetor model 2300G (© International Harvester Co.)

CARTER THERMO-QUAD CARBURETOR

1. Remove the air cleaner, throttle linkage, vacuum hoses, fuel lines, and any other hoses and linkages attached to the carburetor.
2. Remove the bolts or nuts holding the carburetor to the manifold, and remove the carburetor from the intake manifold.
3. Discard the base gasket and clean the base and manifold surface of gasket particles.
4. To install the carburetor, reverse the removal procedure, using a new base gasket.
5. Adjust the idle speed and air mixture as outlined.

IDLE MIXTURE AND SPEED

Adjustment

To comply with the mandated emission control requirements, certain procedures must be followed when adjusting the air/fuel mixture and speed. The engine must be at normal operating temperature, choke open, air cleaner installed, dwell and ignition timing correct, and the parking brake applied. The following procedures apply to all carburetors, with minor deviations possible, depending upon the carburetor used.

CAUTION

Observe the following precautions when adjusting the idle mixture and speed.

1. Do not idle the engine for longer than three minutes at a time.
2. After each three minute interval, increase the engine speed to 2000 rpm for one minute.
3. Continue with the idle adjustment and repeat step 2 as necessary.

Preliminary Idle Setting

AFTER CARBURETOR OVERHAUL

1. Connect a calibrated tachometer to the engine.
2. Connect a test vacuum gauge to the engine intake manifold.
3. Operate the engine at a fast idle speed to bring the operating temperature to normal.
4. Adjust the carburetor to the specified idle speed. Refer to the chart at the beginning of this section.
5. Adjust the idle mixture screw(s) and idle speed screw to obtain lean best idle at the specified speed.

NOTE: Lean best idle is the point at which intake manifold vacuum starts to drop due to leanness.

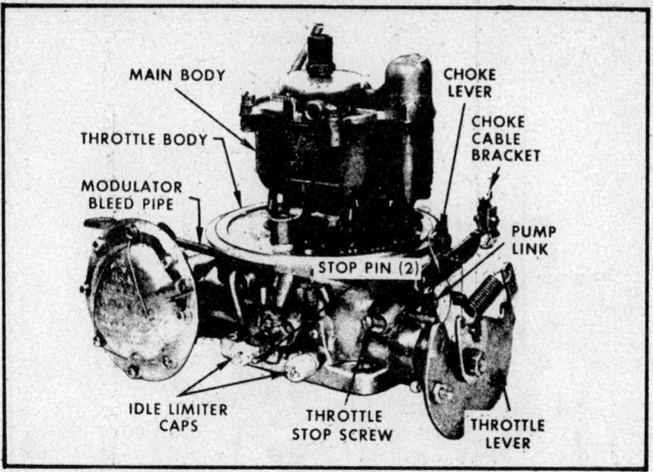

Carburetor model 2140G (© International Harvester Co.)

6. Install the colored (service) plastic cap (s) with the tab fully turned counterclockwise against the stop.
7. Adjust the idle speed to specifications.
8. Make final idle adjustments to obtain the recommended idle setting.

Idle Adjustment

LEAN DROP METHOD

1. Connect a calibrated tachometer to the engine.
2. Rotate the idle adjusting screw(s) counterclockwise against the stops.
3. Adjust the idle speed to give an engine speed 25 rpm higher than the specified idle speed.
4. Rotate the idle mixture screw(s) clockwise slowly and equally (if two) until the specified speed is obtained.
5. If the engine is rough or the specified idle speed cannot be attained, remove the limiter cap(s) and continue the adjustment as outlined in step 4, until the specified rpm is attained and the engine is smooth.
6. Install new plastic limiter cap(s) with the tab fully counterclockwise against the stop.
7. Readjust as necessary to maintain the specified rpm.

EXHAUST ANALYZER METHOD

When exhaust analyzer equipment is used, the following procedure is recommended to be used to adjust the idle mixture and speed. The test equipment must give accurate readings in the 0–5% carbon monoxide (CO) range.

1. Connect a calibrated tachometer to the engine and insert the exhaust analyzer into the exhaust pipe.

NOTE: Refer to the manufacturers instructions for complete connection procedures.

2. Operate the engine for fifteen minutes at fast idle speed (approximately 1000–1200 rpm), to bring engine to normal operating temperature and to stabilize the temperature of the exhaust analyzer.
3. Calibrate the test equipment as per the manufacturers instructions.

NOTE: If the combustion analyzer does not respond to changes in the mixture quality, check for leaks or restrictions in the sample lines. The thermal conductivity instruments used in the analyzer are both temperature and pressure sensitive, and require a definite sample flow. Refer to the manufacturer's instructions as necessary.

4. Adjust the idle mixture screw (s) counterclockwise against the tab stop.

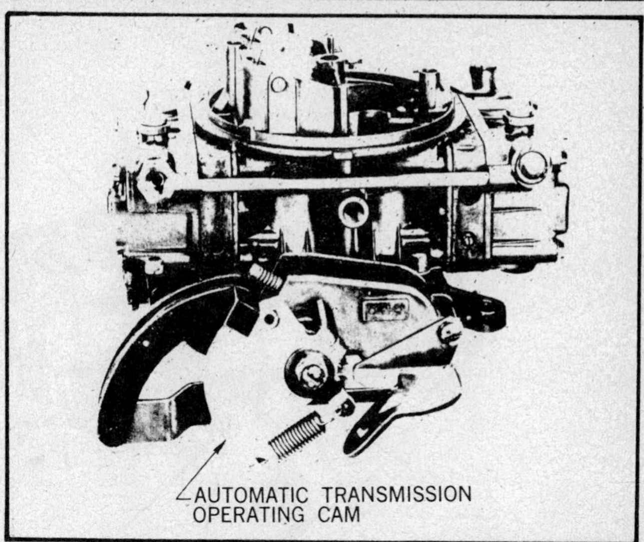

Model 4150G carburetor with automatic transmission operating cam (© International Harvester Co.)

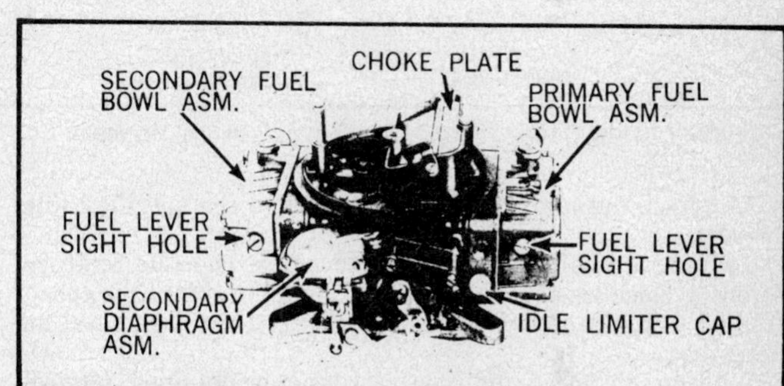

Carburetor model 4150G (© International Harvester Co.)

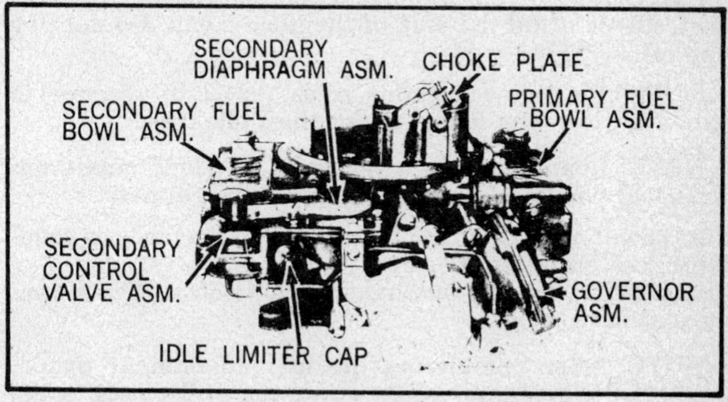

Carburetor model 4150 (© International Harvester Co.)

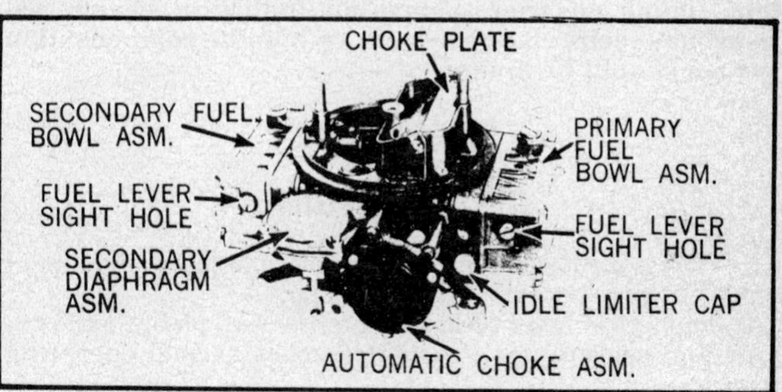

Carburetor model 4150C (© International Harvester Co.)

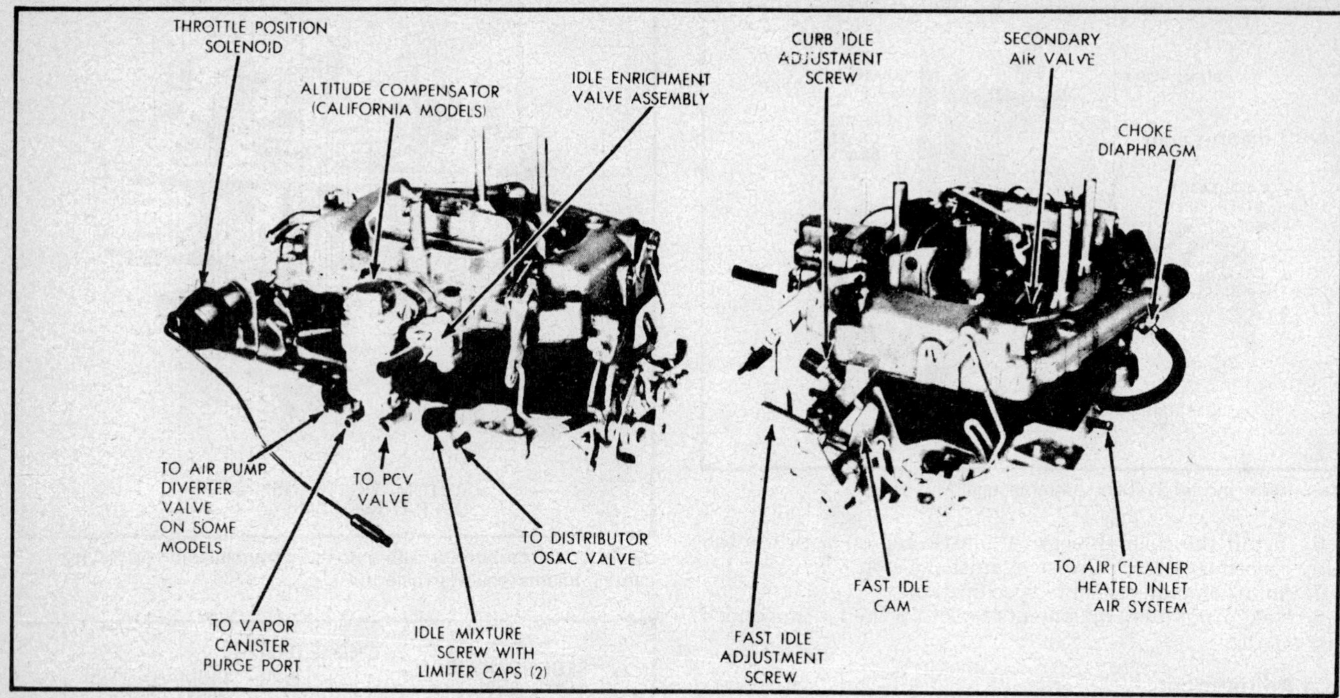

Carburetor model Carter Thermo-Quad (© International Harvester Co.)

5. Adjust the idle speed screw to obtain the specified idle speed.
6. Observe the analyzer dial and adjust the idle mixture screw (s) clockwise by $^1/_{16}$ turn increments to obtain the specified idle mixture seting and readjust the idle speed as necessary.
7. If the idle speed and mixture cannot be obtained, remove the idle limiter cap (s).

NOTE: To prevent damage to the mixture screw(s) or seat, file or grind the side of the plastic cap. Do not pry cap off.

8. With the engine operating, adjust the mixture screw(s) to obtain the lean best idle at the specified idle speed.

NOTE: Lean best idle is the point at which maximum manifold vacuum begins to drop due to leanness.

9. Install new plastic limiter cap(s) with the tab fully counterclockwise against the stop.
10. Readjust the idle mixture screw(s) to obtain the recommended CO setting.

NOTE: After completing the idle adjustment procedure, if unsatisfactory idle operation still exists, a recheck of the ignition system, crankcase ventilation system, timing advance system, air induction system, exhaust gas recirculation system, or hot idle compensation system should be made.

Idle Speed

DIESEL ENGINE

1. Adjust the low idle speed at the low idle speed adjustment screw at the rear of the injection pump.
2. Connect a diesel tachometer to the engine. Start the engine and operate until coolant reaches normal operating temperature.
3. Allow the engine to idle and note the idle speed shown on the tachometer. If the low idle speed is not within specifications (700–750 rpm) adjust as required.
4. Loosen the buffer locknut. Back off the buffer screw adjustment. Loosen the locknut on the idle speed adjustment screw. Turn the idle screw to obtain the correct idle speed. Tighten the locknut.
5. Turn the buffer screw in until it touches or increases idle. Increase the idle speed by 10–25 rpm. Back off the buffer screw one full turn. Tighten locknut.

Fuel Pumps

The fuel pumps used on the gasoline engines are of two types.
1. **Mechanical type:** This type is mounted on the engine block and is operated by a special eccentric on the camshaft.
2. **Electric type:** This type is mounted in the fuel tank and is supported by an adjustable hanger assembly, therefore, making it adaptable to all I.H. fuel tank depths. A spring loaded latch is normally used to permit easy motor replacement.

MECHANICAL FUEL PUMP

Removal

1. Remove the fuel inlet pipe or hose and the outlet fuel pipe to the carburetor from the fuel pump fittings.
2. Remove the attaching bolts from the fuel pump housing to engine block and remove the fuel pump.
3. Clean the gasket surfaces of all gasket particles.

Installation

1. Install new gasket on the fuel pump mounting flange and install the fuel pump operating arm into the hole in the block, and into contact with the eccentric lobe on the camshaft.
2. Install the attaching bolts and tighten the pump to the block securely.
3. Install the inlet hose or pipe, and the outlet pipe to the fuel pump and tighten securely to avoid air leaks.

NOTE: An additional hose may be used from the fuel

filter to the fuel pump. Install to the proper fitting if so equipped.

ELECTRIC FUEL PUMP

Removal

1. Remove the electrical connections, the outlet pipe or hose, and the retaining screws holding the assembly to the tank.
2. Withdraw the pump/support assembly from the tank, being careful not to allow dirt to enter the tank hole.
3. With the unit out of the tank, remove the pump from the support assembly.
4. Remove the gasket and any particles from the gasket surfaces.

Installation

1. Install the pump assembly into the support arms and retain it securely.
2. Using a new gasket, insert the pump/support assembly into the tank and secure it with the attaching screws. Tighten securely to avoid air or gasoline leaks.
3. Install the outlet pipe or hose and the electrical connections to the assembly.

Fuel Pump Pressure Test

1. Disconnect fuel line at carburetor inlet and attach pressure gauge between the inlet and disconnected line.
2. Start engine and take reading. Consult Tune-up Specifications at the beginning of this section for correct pump pressure.
3. When engine is stopped, the pressure should remain constant or very slowly return to zero.

Fuel Pump Capacity Test

1. Disconnect fuel line from the fuel pump.
2. Connect a piece of hose to the line so that fuel can be directed into a measuring container.
3. Start engine and note time it takes to fill a pint container. Pump should fill one pint within 20–30 seconds.

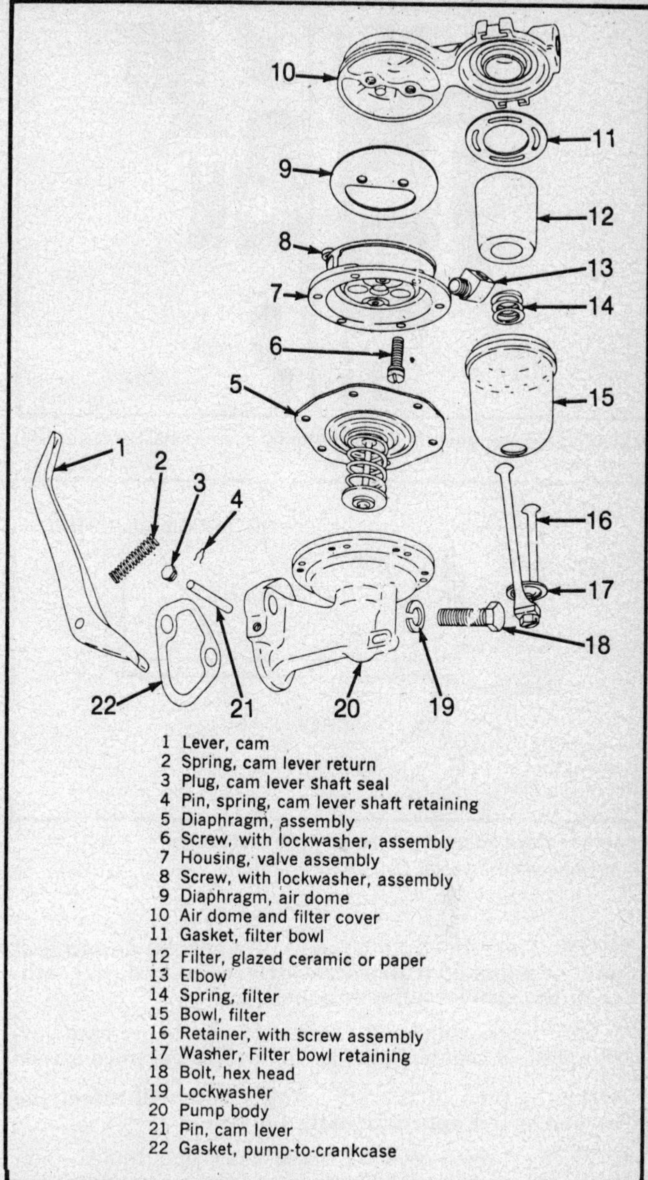

Exploded view of mechanical fuel pump—typical (© International Harvester Co.)

Governor Speed

Adjustments

Excessive engine rpm causes rapid wear and strains on the internal engine parts, and for this reason, many engines are governed at predetermined rpm. The recommended no-load governed rpm for each engine is found in the specification charts at the beginning of the chapter and should be referred to when determining the need for governed rpm changes.

Adjustment of the governed speed is made at the governor spinner valve, located in the distributor housing for the V8 engines.

Adjustment Procedure

V8 ENGINE GOVERNOR

1. Connect a calibrated tachometer to the engine.
2. Accelerate the engine and observe the governed speed at no-load. Refer to the specification charts at the beginning of this chapter.
3. If necessary, adjust the governor by removing the seal wire, governor clamp and gasket from the distributor housing.
4. With the ignition off, rotate the engine until the adjusting screw hole appears in the opening of the distributor housing.
5. With a $\frac{1}{8}$ Allen wrench, remove the adjusting hole plug from the governor.
6. With the use of a special tool (IH SE-2072-2) inserted through the governor adjusting hole, engage the adjusting screw tang.

Cutaway view of in-tank fuel pump mounted with adjustable supports (© International Harvester Co.)

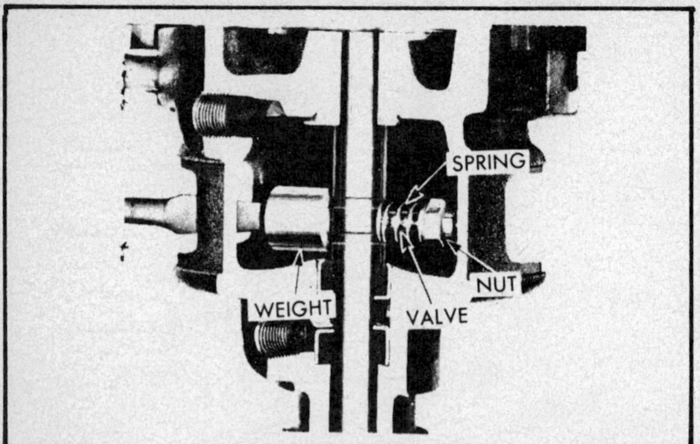

Adjusting spinner governor distributor (© International Harvester Co.)

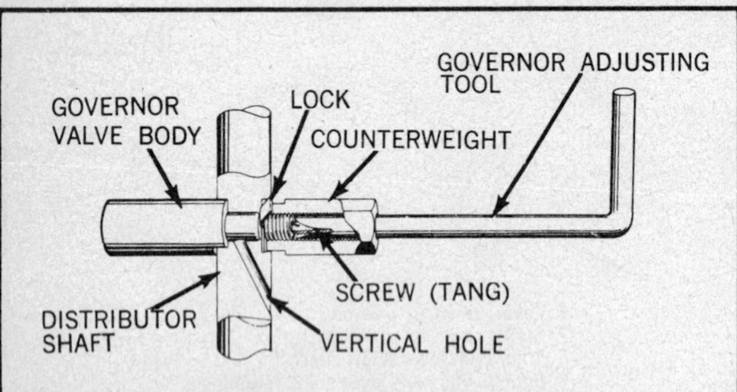

Governor valve adjustment model 1530 distributor. (© International Harvester Co.)

NOTE: The adjusting screw is of a special design and cannot be adjusted with a screwdriver or any device, other than the special adjusting tool.

7. Turning the adjusting screw clockwise to decrease governed speed, or counterclockwise to increase governed speed.

NOTE: $^1/_4$ turn of the adjusting screw will affect the governed speed approximately 100 rpm.

8. When specified governed speed has been attained, reinstall the plug in the adjusting hole and tighten securely.
9. Reinstall governor clamp and gasket on the distributor housing and install a new seal wire.

LPG (PROPANE-BUTANE)

Carburetor Adjustment

V304, 345, AND 549 ENGINES

Setting the idle fuel adjustment automatically gives the correct mixture for part and full throttle operation.

CAUTION

Liquefied petroleum gas is extremely flammable. Observe all safety precautions regardless of the nature of work being performed. No work is to be done on fuel tanks except by qualified concerns who normally service such containers.

1. Set throttle for fast idle by turning throttle stop screw in from closed position 3 or 4 turns.
2. Start engine and adjust idle adjusting screw in drag link (either end) until engine runs smoothly. Turning screw in (clockwise) enriches mixture.
3. Adjust throttle stop screw for idle of 600 rpm.
4. Readjust idle adjusting screw in drag link for maximum engine speed. If engine speed starts to go above 900 rpm, set back speed with throttle stop screw to 600 rpm and continue adjusting drag link screw for maximum engine speed.
5. Adjust idle to 400 rpm and replace cotter pin in drag link adjusting screw to lock adjustment.

Carburetor Diagnosis Service

The following diagnosis and troubleshooting chart can be used as a general guide to determine the causes of carburetor related problems. When the problem has been isolated to a particular component and more information is needed, refer to the related chapter within this section, or to the Unit Repair Section.

ROUGH IDLE OR STALLING – ENGINE HOT OR COLD

1. Binding linkage, choke valve, or choke piston.
2. Disconnected or broken choke control cable.
3. Incorrect choke thermostat adjustment.
4. Fast idle linkage and cam not properly adjusted.
5. Idle mixture screw(s) out of adjustment.
6. Idle speed screw out of adjustment.
7. Air cleaner air flow restricted.
8. Hot idle compensator valve stuck.
9. Secondary throttle plates open (4V carburetors).
10. Clogged air bleed or idle passages.
11. Vacuum leakage.
12. Improper float level.
13. Electrical or emission control systems malfunction.

POOR LOW SPEED OPERATION

1. Clogged idle transfer slots.
2. Clogged air bleed or idle passages.
3. Air cleaner air flow restricted.
4. Improper float level.
5. Faulty automatic choke operation.
6. Improper use of hand controlled choke.
7. Vacuum leakage.
8. Electrical or emission control system malfunction.

POOR ENGINE ACCELERATION

1. Improper acceleration pump stroke.
2. Inoperative or missing pump discharge check valve, ball, or needle.
3. Damaged or worn pump diaphragm or piston.
4. Leaking gaskets.
5. Defective fuel pump.
6. Clogged discharge jets.
7. Electrical or emission control systems malfunction.

POOR HIGH SPEED OPERATION

1. Defective fuel pump or clogged fuel filter.
2. Clogged vacuum passages.
3. Power valve stuck.
4. Metering rods stuck.
5. Improper size or obstructions in the main jets.
6. Restricted air supply to air cleaner.
7. Improper float level.
8. Electrical or emission control system malfunction.

SURGING – CRUISING SPEEDS

1. Clogged main jets.
2. Undersize main jets.
3. Low fuel level.
4. Defective fuel pump or clogged fuel filter.
5. Blocked air bleeds.
6. Restricted air supply to air cleaner.
7. Vacuum leakage.
8. Metering rods out of adjustment.
9. Power valve sticking.

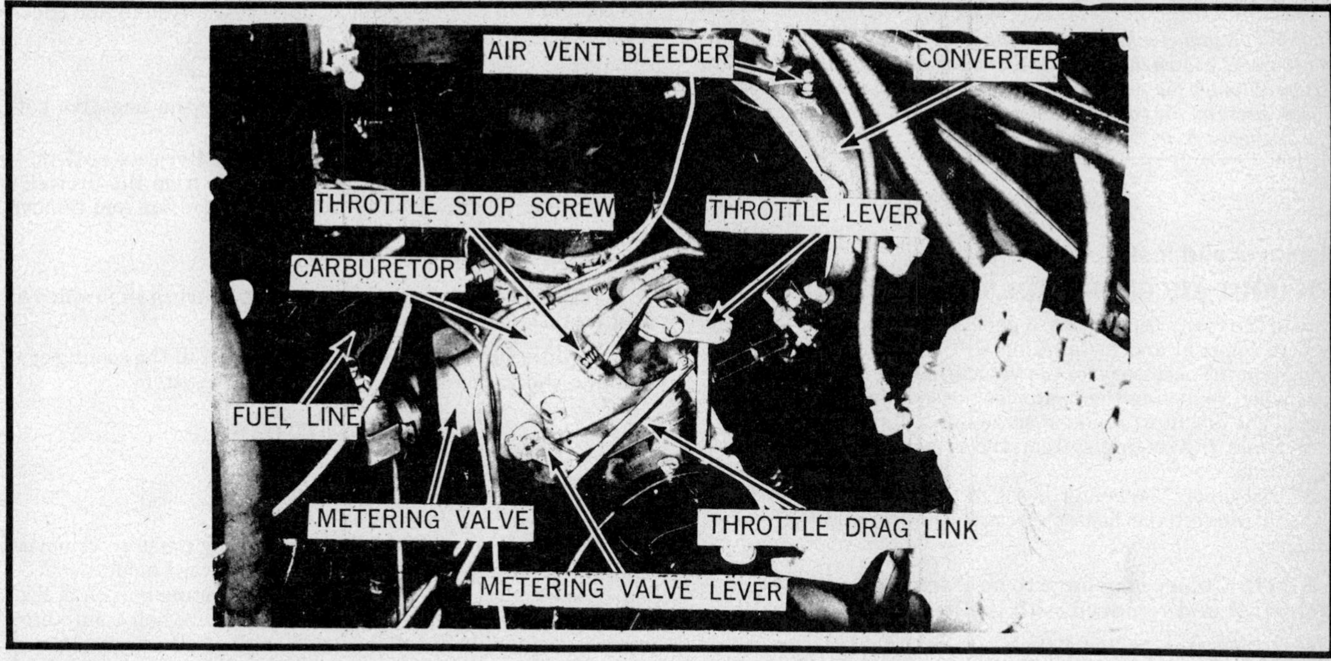

LPG carburetion (© International Harvester Co.)

10. Electrical or emission control system malfunction.

STALLING WHEN THE ACCELERATOR IS CLOSED QUICKLY

1. Improperly adjusted or defective throttle modulator or dash pot.
2. Clogged air bleed or idle passages.
3. Vacuum leakage.
4. Throttle plates not closing.

GOVERNOR NOT OPERATING—NO ENGINE SPEED CONTROL

1. Seal broken - Governor maladjusted.
2. Vacuum leakage or lines broken.
3. Modulator diaphragm leaking or broken.
4. Sticking governor spinner valve.

GOVERNOR CUTS OFF AT LOW SPEEDS—ERRATIC OPERATION

1. Clogged distributor governor filter.
2. Restricted vacuum lines.
3. Sticking governor spinner valve.
4. Restrictions in the spinner shaft or housing.

ENGINE SURGES AT AND BELOW GOVERNED SPEED

1. Vacuum leakage or restriction.
2. Carburetor jets or air bleeds clogged.
3. Spinner valve sticking.
4. Electrical or emission control systems malfunction.

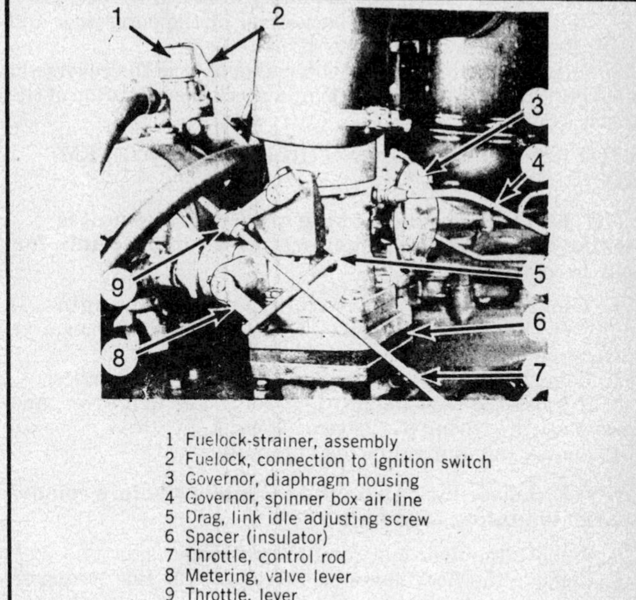

1 Fuelock-strainer, assembly
2 Fuelock, connection to ignition switch
3 Governor, diaphragm housing
4 Governor, spinner box air line
5 Drag, link idle adjusting screw
6 Spacer (insulator)
7 Throttle, control rod
8 Metering, valve lever
9 Throttle, lever

LPG carburetor (© International Harvester Co.)

COOLING SYSTEM

The cooling system is a closed type, utilizing a two valve pressure cap. One valve is used to relieve excessive pressure from the system, and the second valve is used to allow atmospheric air to enter the system during the cooling down period. The engine temperature is controlled in two ways. One method is by a thermostat, located on the front of the engine block or cylinder head. The second method is by a shutter assembly, mounted on the grille of the vehicle, and controlled by heat sensitive switches mounted on the engine and radiator. The coolant is forced through the engine and radiator by the water pump, located on the front of the engine, which is belt driven by the crankshaft pulley.

CAUTION

To avoid personnel injury, remove the pressure cap from the radiator in two steps. Loosen the cap to its first notch and allow the pressure to escape through the overflow pipe. After the pressure has been released, press on the cap and continue to turn until the prongs on the cap disengage from the radiator neck.

Heater Core

Removal and Installation

WITHOUT AIR CONDITIONING EXCEPT SCOUT

Due to the many body styles, a general description of the heater core removal and installation will be outlined. Utilize the operations as necessary for the vehicle being serviced. Use caution when removing the heater box assembly, to avoid breakage to the box due to hidden screws or bolts.

1. Drain the cooling system and remove the negative battery cable.
2. Disconnect the heater hoses at the heater core tubes.
3. Disconnect the heater electrical wiring and the control cables.

NOTE: Cables may have to be disconnected at the control panel and removed with the heater box.

4. Remove the heater distribution manifold at the heater box.
5. Remove the heater box attaching bolts or nuts from the cab side and from the engine side of the firewall.
6. Remove the heater box assembly from the vehicle.
7. Remove the heater box back cover or the outer door and shaft. Remove the heater core.
8. The installation of the heater assembly is the reverse of removal. Fill the cooling system and check the operation of the heater system.

WITH AIR CONDITIONING (BLEND AIR SYSTEM) EXCEPT SCOUT

NOTE: This air conditioning/heater system unit is located under the passenger seat as a compact unit, for ease in servicing.

1. Close the heater hose shutoff valves at engine, if equipped, or drain the cooling system. Disconnect the negative battery cable.
2. Remove the heater hoses from the heater core tubes.
3. Remove the floor mounted blower motor well cover, and disconnect the wiring at the connectors.
4. Loosen the unit mounting stud nuts.

NOTE: Lower the cab on the CO models before removing the mounting stud nuts.

5. Remove the floor mat from the passenger side.
6. Remove the floor panel on the passenger side to expose the air duct.
7. Remove the rubber seals from the fresh air duct and treated air duct.
8. Remove the hose connecting the bunk duct to the blower housing (if equipped).
9. Remove the thumb screws securing the passenger seat and heater cover plate assembly. Remove the seat and cover assembly.
10. Disconnect the control cables at the heater assembly.
11. Disconnect the electrical wiring from the heater assembly.
12. Remove the unit mounting stud nuts and washers. Remove the heater assembly from the cab.
13. Remove the sponge rubber seals on the heater tubes and set aside for later installation.
14. The installation is in the reverse of the removal. Replace the coolant lost during removal, operate the system and check for leakage.

SCOUT

1. Drain the cooling system and remove the negative battery cable.
2. Remove the heater hoses from the heater core outlets.
3. Remove the windshield washer bottle from the firewall.
4. Remove the cover plate from the heater box and remove the heater core from the housing.
5. Remove the core end cover.

NOTE: Do not damage the core fins during the removal and installation procedure.

6. Installation is the reverse of removal. Fill the cooling system and check the operation of the heater system.

WATER PUMP

Removal

1. Drain cooling system.
2. If radiator shrouds hinder access they must be removed before proceeding (large V-8's and cab-forward models).
3. Loosen alternator pivot bolts and adjusting bolt on bracket to relieve tension on the fan belt and remove belt from water pump pulley. On V(S) 549, 537, 605 engines all accessories are driven by belts from the water pump pulley and are removed by loosening the alternator and power steering pump adjusting brackets and pivots. The idler pulley on the belts between the crankshaft and water pump pulleys is then loosened so that these belts may be removed.
4. On 549, 537 and 605 engines the fan blades and pulley are removed.
5. Remove all pipes and hoses connected to the water pump.
6. Remove mounting bolts or stud nuts and water pump. On all models except 4–196 and V-304, 345 and 392, only the front half of the pump housing is removed for water pump servicing.
7. Installation is the reverse of the above procedure. Be sure to install new gaskets and, if applicable, new O-rings on pipe end fittings.

Service

ENGINE MODELS 404, 446, V537 AND V605

This water pump is nonadjustable, has a packless seal and must be serviced as a complete unit: in the event of malfunction the whole assembly is replaced.

1. Remove pump as described in the preceding section.
2. Clean impeller cavity before installing new pump.
3. Spin shaft on new pump to be sure it rotates freely.
4. Install as described in preceding section, using a new gasket.

Disassembly

ENGINE MODELS 4–196 AND 4–196E

1. Separate the housing from the pump body.

NOTE: The housing holds the impeller and shaft assembly.

2. Unless special tools, number SE 1950 and SE 1950–1 installers or their equivalents are used, the following measurements should be taken and recorded for the reassembly of the pump.
    a. Measure the distance from the pump hub to the end of the shaft and record the measurement.
    b. Measure the distance from the impeller hub to the end of the shaft and record the measurement.
3. Remove the snap-ring from the groove in front of the shaft bearing assembly.

4. Press the shaft and bearing assembly from the housing and from the impeller.

NOTE: The bearing and shaft assembly are replaced as an assembly only.

5. Remove the seal from the rear of the housing with the aid of a drift and hammer.

Assembly

1. Press a new seal into the housing bore.
2. Install new slinger on the bearing shaft, if not equipped, 1½ inch from the rear end of the shaft to the forward edge of the slinger.
3. Press the bearing and shaft assembly into the housing and install the snap-ring.
4. Using special tool SE 1950 or equivalent, or by using the measurement taken before removal, press the impeller in place on the shaft.
5. Using special tool SE 1950–1 or equivalent, or by using the measurement taken during the removal, press the pulley hub in position on the shaft.
6. Using a new gasket, install the pump housing to the pump body and secure with the attaching bolts.

ENGINE MODELS 549 SERIES, V304, 345 AND 392

1. Remove the pump housing from the pump body on engine models V 304, 345 and 392.
2. Remove the pulley from the shaft, and the bearing and shaft snap-ring.
3. Remove the impeller from the bearing shaft and the shaft from the housing by the use of a press.
4. Using a drift and hammer, remove the seal and discard.
5. Remove the impeller seat and bushing from the housing and discard.

Installation

1. Install new bushing and seat into the housing bore.
2. Install a new seal into the housing.
3. Press the bearing and shaft assembly into the housing until the bearing bottoms into the counterbore.

NOTE: Due to variations in the pump housing, bearings and shaft assembly, and the impeller, the impeller cannot be pressed to the correct location on the shaft during the first press application. The following procedure must be used to achieve the correct location of the impeller.

4. With the use of SE 2086 special tool kit or its equivalent, select a 0.060 shim stop and place it on the impeller end of the shaft and press the impeller on the shaft until the press ram bottoms on the shim.

NOTE: The purpose of the shim stop is to limit the travel of the pump shaft in the impeller, so that an interference will exist between the impeller and the pump housing.

5. Place the pump assembly on the front cover of the engine and install two bolts finger tight.
6. With the use of a feeler gauge, determine the clearance between the housing flange and the front cover.
7. Record the clearance and add to the specification of 0.015 inch running clearance. Subtract the total of the two from the original 0.060 shim thickness and record.
8. From the special tool kit SE 2086 or its equivalent, select the shims to provide the thickness of the above recorded figure, and place the shims on the shaft end. Press the impeller further onto the shaft until the ram bottoms on the shim stop. This operation should provide the proper operating clearance for the impeller.

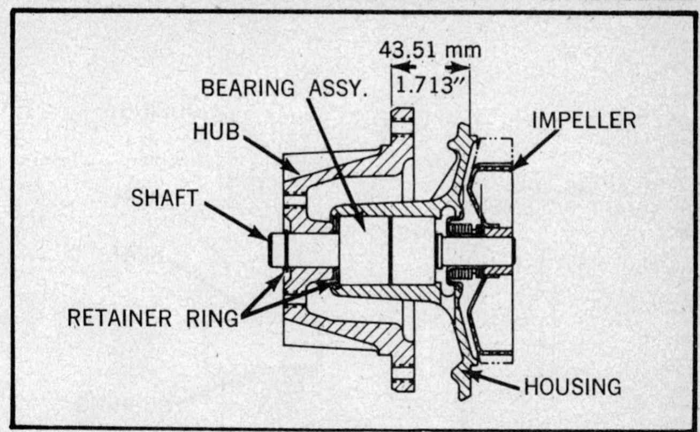

Sectional view of water pump—V537 and 605 engines
(© Inter national Harvester Co.)

Water pump location—MV404 and 446 engines
(© International Harvester Co.)

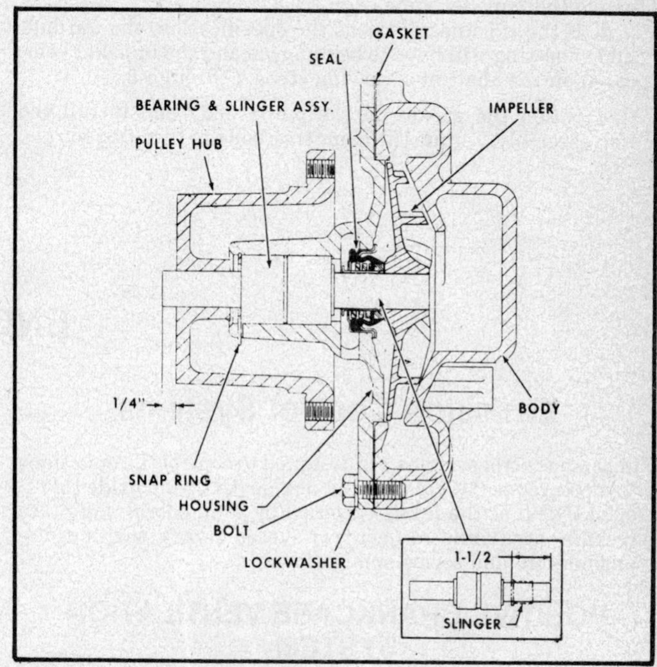

Sectional view of water pump—4-196 engine
(© International Harvester Co.

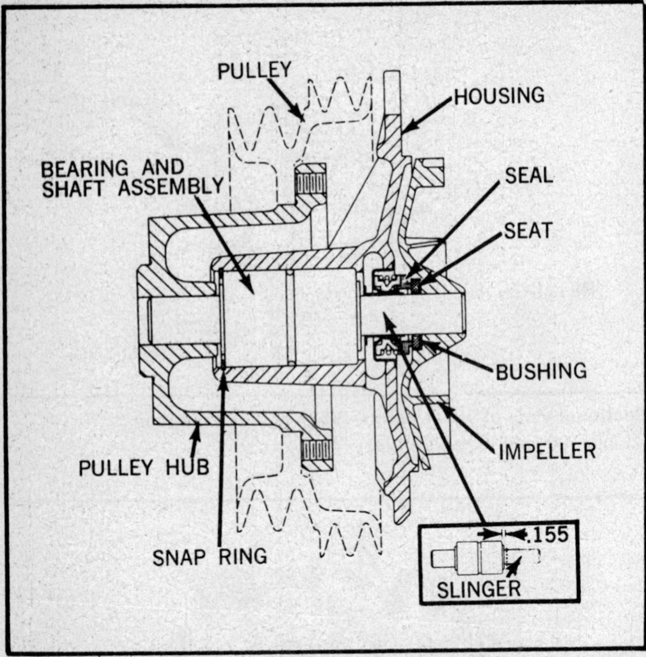

Sectional view of water pump—478 and 549 engines (© International Harvester Co.)

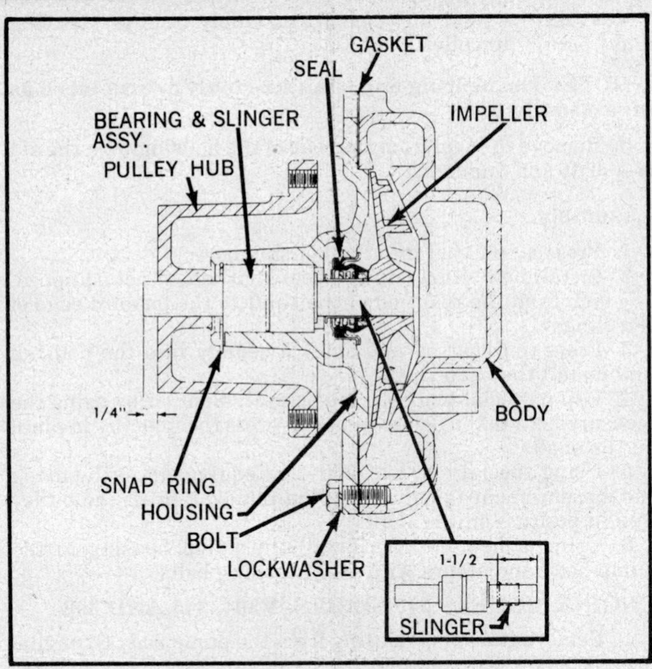

Water pump—V266, 304, 345 and 392 engines (© International Harvester Co.)

NOTE: If no clearance exists between the housing flange and the front cover, and the impeller turns free, check the impeller running clearance by the following method.

a. Use molding clay and place on the edges of two of the impeller vanes.

b. Install the pump and torque the mounting bolts. Do not rotate the impeller.

c. Remove the pump and measure the thickness of the moulding clay on the vanes. The thickness should be 0.015 above the impeller vane edge.

d. If the thickness exceeds the specification, the fan hub and snap-ring will have to be removed and the impeller relocated on the shaft by following steps 4 through 8.

9. Position the gasket on the pump body and install the pump assembly. Torque the mounting bolts to specified torque.

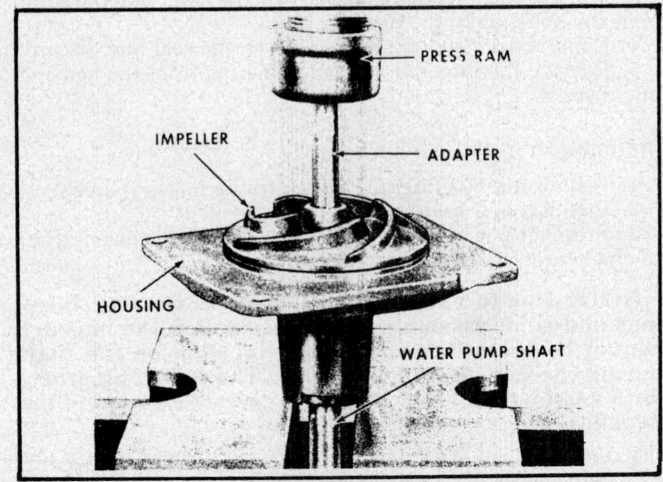

Removal of water pump shaft and bearing assembly from the pump housing (© International Harvester Co.)

ENGINE

Emission Control Systems

Emission control systems are designed to control the emissions of hydrocarbons (HC), carbon monoxide (CO), and oxides of nitrogen (NOx) at the levels specified by the Federal and State governments. Emission control systems vary with engine transmission, and series applications.

POSITIVE CRANKCASE VENTILATION SYSTEM

The positive crankcase ventilation system draws the crankcase vapors into the intake manifold to be burned along with the air-fuel mixture. This is normally a closed system so that the crankcase vapors are not emitted into the atmosphere. The system consists of a valve and hose routings mounted to and operated by engine vacuum from the intake manifold.

THERMOSTATICALLY CONTROLLED AIR CLEANER SYSTEM

The air cleaner snorkel incorporates a thermostatically controlled valve, which directs air from the exhaust manifold area and from the engine compartment, depending upon the

underhood temperature, to insure the carburetor induction air is warm before entry into the engine.

AIR GUARD SYSTEM

This system is used to inject air into the exhaust ports to mix with the hot unburned gases, and to further burn the combustion mixture and reduce the emissions of hydrocarbons and carbon monoxide into the atmosphere. The system includes an air pump, a diverter valve, hose routings, and air injector manifolds and tubes.

EXHAUST GAS RECIRCULATION SYSTEM

This system is used to meter exhaust gases into the combustion chambers to dilute the intake charge, thereby reducing the peak temperature of the gases and limit the formation of the oxides of nitrogen that form as the result of the high temperature during the combustion process. The system consists of an exhaust gas recirculating valve which connects the intake manifold to the exhaust manifold, and is operated by vacuum and temperature.

FUEL TANK VAPOR EMISSION CONTROL SYSTEM

A closed fuel tank vent system is used to prevent fuel vapors from entering the atmosphere. The system consists of a two-way relief valve filler cap, which is closed to the atmosphere under normal operating conditions and opens when pressure exceeds 0.75 to 1.50 PSI, or vacuum exceeds 15 to 25 in.. A liquid check valve is used to route the vapors and collect any liquid before they are drawn into the fuel vapor storage cannister. The vapors are then drawn into the intake manifold through the air cleaner assembly. The amount of vapor drawn from the cannister is relative to the air velocity through the air cleaner snorkel.

VACUUM THROTTLE MODULATING SYSTEM

This system is used to reduce the emissions of hydrocarbons during rapid throttle closure at high speeds. It consists of a deceleration valve and a throttle modulating diaphragm located on the carburetor base to allow the throttle to remain slightly open and admit more air into the combustion chambers to lean out the overrich mixture. The decel valve and the modulator diaphragm are operated by engine vacuum signals.

ELECTRIC CHOKE

This system is used to assist in maintaining an open choke butterfly during cruising conditions, when vacuum may not be sufficient to draw enough heated air from the manifold to the choke assembly. When the engine cylinder head temperature is below 130 degrees, the electric choke is inoperative and the choke operates in the normal manner. Above the stated temperature, the electric choke is in operation.

Engine Assembly

Removal and Installation

The following is an outline of general engine removal. Removal procedure will vary from truck to truck due to the variety of body models and accessory equipment. Before lifting out engine be certain that everything has been disconnected. Remove anything that might be in the way of the actual lifting.

1. Drain water from radiator and engine block.

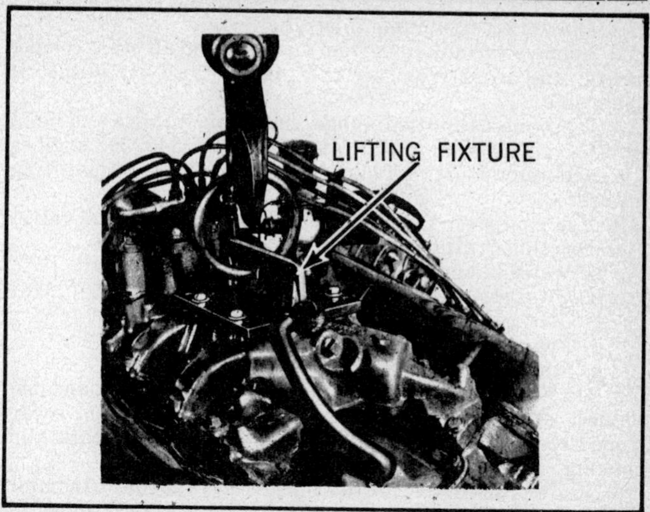

Engine lifting sling—V8 engines (© International Harvester Co.)

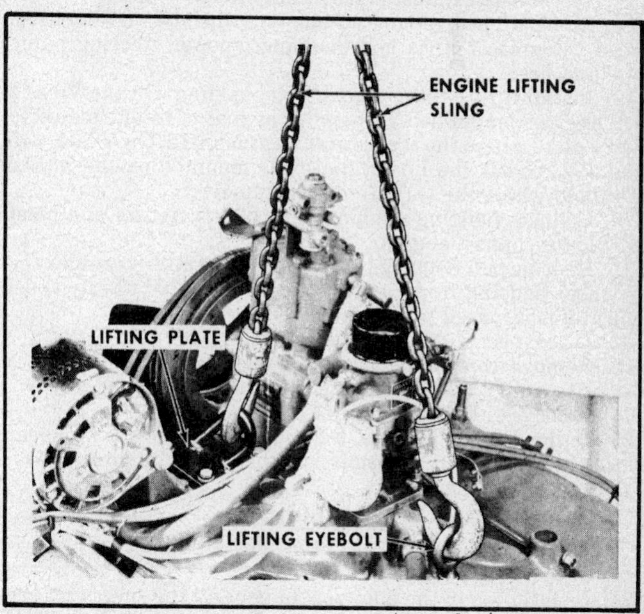

Engine removal using lifting sling (© International Harvester Co.)

2. Drain crankcase oil.
3. Disconnect battery ground cable and remove cable clamp from hot terminal of battery.
4. Remove all water hoses to radiator and heater.
5. Remove fan blades and fan shroud.
6. Remove any radiator cross-brace rods or brackets.
7. Remove radiator mounting bolts and lift out radiator.

CAUTION

On vehicles with LPG fuel systems observe all safety precautions. Be sure shop procedures are in compliance with local fire regulations. Close all tank valves and exhaust fuel from lines before working on fuel system.

8. On conventional chassis, remove hood hinge bracket mounting bolts and remove hood assembly. On CO models, tilt cab forward and prop securely. On cab-forward models, remove all front end sheet metal: bumper, fenders, radiator shell and disconnect any wiring that goes to these parts.
9. Disconnect and remove air filter from engine. Remove breather hose from air cleaner, if applicable.

10. Disconnect fuel pump inlet line.
11. Remove vacuum lines from manifold and all other components, and lines from air compressor and air pump, if applicable.
12. Disconnect throttle linkage, choke control wire and hand throttle control wire, if applicable. On V304, 345, 392 engines the carburetor must be removed for the fitting of the lifting fixture.
13. If so equipped, disconnect wire from heater control valve.
14. Disconnect all wiring from engine.
    a. Water temperature gauge sender.
    b. Oil pressure gauge sender.
    c. Generator wires.
    d. Primary ignition wire to resistor.
    e. Starter solenoid wires and battery cable.
15. On V478 and 549 engines, loosen alternator belts and disconnect alternator strap bracket to swing alternator away from thermostat housing. Then remove thermostats and housing.
16., If so equipped, remove tachometer drive at the distributor on the small V8 or at the rear of the block on the big V8.
17. Disconnect exhaust pipes at manifolds.
18. If so equipped, remove automatic transmission filler tube, freon compressor lines and disconnect power steering pump line and hose.
19. Install lifting fixtures and suitable sling. On the V8 and 549 engines an eye bolt is installed at rear of intake manifold and a plate where the thermostat was mounted. On V-304, 345 and 392 models the lifting fixture is mounted on the intake manifold where the carburetor was removed.
20. Connect hoisting equipment to lifting fixture and hoist enough to support engine.
21. Remove bell housing mounting bolts. On V-8 engines the flywheel housing front cover is removed before the flywheel housing is removed from crankcase.
22. Disconnect clutch linkage.
23. Remove front engine mounting bolts. On some models it is easier to unbolt the mount from the frame crossmember.
24. Remove side engine mount bolts.
25. In hoisting out engine, first pull engine forward to clear clutch assembly from transmission, then tilt front up and carefully out of the chassis.

CAUTION

Avoid damaging clutch driven disc.

26. Installation of the engine is in general the reverse of the above described procedure. Be careful when installing that wires are not pinched between engine and frame. Lower the engine until transmission main drive gear spline can be aligned with the clutch driven disc. The weight of the engine must remain supported until the bell housing is secured to flywheel housing. After engine has been secured to chassis, remove hoisting equipment and lifting fixtures.

Manifolds

INTAKE MANIFOLD

Removal and Installation

4 CYLINDER AND V8 ENGINES

1. If engine is in vehicle, remove air cleaner and, if applicable, governor vacuum line.
2. Disconnect throttle linkage, choke cable and fuel line.
3. Remove carburetor.
4. On V304, 345 and 392 engines, disconnect hose from thermostat housing and bracket for spark plug wires.
5. On 4 cylinder models, remove coil, coil mounting bracket and ignition resistor from intake manifold.

Intake manifold removal—V8 engines (© International Harvester Co.)

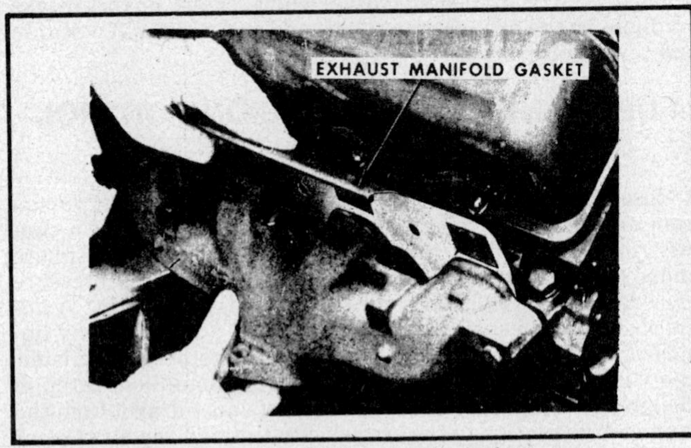

Exhaust manifold removal—OHV4 and V8 engines (© International Harvester Co.)

6. Remove positive crankcase ventilation pipe and vacuum line.
7. Remove mounting bolts, manifold and gasket.
8. Installation is the reverse of the above procedure. Install new gaskets and tighten the mounting bolts from the center out, torquing to 40–45 ft. lbs.

EXHAUST MANIFOLD

Removal and Installation

4 CYLINDER AND V8 ENGINES

1. Disconnect exhaust pipe from manifold.
2. Unbolt exhaust manifold from head.
3. Remove manifold.
4. Installation is the reverse of the above procedure. Install new manifold-to-head gasket and new manifold-to-pipe gasket.
5. Torque manifold-to-head bolts to 25–30 ft. lbs.

Cylinder Head

Removal and Installation

V8 AND 4 CYLINDER ENGINES

1. Remove intake and exhaust manifolds as described in preceding section. On V8's, this may entail removal of the air compressor and air compressor mounting bracket.
2. Head removal is facilitated by the use of a lifting sling which is attached with bolts in the intake manifold mounting bolt holes.

3. Remove cylinder head covers and gaskets.
4. Loosen rocker arm shaft bracket bolts and remove the rocker arm assembly.

NOTE: Be sure to remove and keep track of the two dowel sleeves on the end brackets of the rocker arm assembly.

5. Remove pushrods, marking them so that they may be installed in their same locations.
6. Remove spark plug wires.
7. Remove cylinder head bolts.
8. When lifting off cylinder, do not lose the two locating dowel sleeves.
9. Installation is basically the reverse of the above procedure, with the exception of the following additional steps.
10. Be sure to use a new head gasket and to reinstall dowel sleeves when positioning the head and mounting the rocker assembly. Reinstall pushrods in their original locations.
11. On 4–196 and V-304, 345 and 392, turn engine crankshaft until leading edge of balance weight on crankshaft pulley is aligned with the zero degree mark on the timing indicator before installing rocker arm assembly.
12. On 4–196 engines, be sure to install rocker assembly so that the oil feed shaft bracket is third from the rear.
13. On V304 and 345 engines, install rocker arm assembly so that the notches at the end of the shaft are facing upward. Oil feed brackets are third from the rear on the right (even numbers) bank and third from the front on the left (odd numbers) bank.
14. On the 549 engines, rocker arm assembly mounting bolts serve as head bolts and are tightened in the head bolt torque sequence. Torque head bolts in the sequence pattern illustrated to 80–90 ft. lbs. torque.

CAUTION

Do not use a power wrench on heads of engines with hydraulic lifters. Torque head bolts slowly so that the leakdown of the lifters may relieve strain from the valve train.

15. On 4–196 and V-304, 345 and 392 engines, tighten the head bolts in the sequence illustrated to 90–100 ft. lbs.
16. Retorque head bolts to the specified torque after 1000 miles of operation.
17. Install rocker covers and any other equipment removed for head work. Replace rocker cover gasket if necessary.

Cylinder head dowel sleeve location—OHV-4 and V8 engines
(© International Harvester Co.)

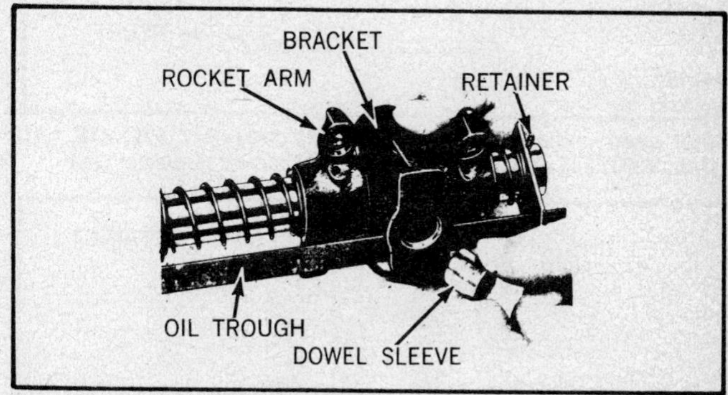

Rocker arm shaft dowel sleeve—OHV-4 and V8 engines
(© International Harvester Co.)

Valves

VALVE ROTATORS

4 CYLINDER AND V8 ENGINES

Rotators are used between the valve springs and the cylinder heads on both the intake and exhaust valves on the VS478, VS 549, V 537 and V 605 engines. On the 4–196, MV-404, MV-446, V-304, V-345 and V-392 engines, rotators are used between the valve spring and the cylinder head on the exhaust valve only.

NOTE: Keep the valves and their related parts together so they may be reinstalled in their respective positions.

VALVE TRAIN SERVICE

The 4–196 and V8 engines utilized hydraulic lifters for which there is no lash adjustment. Excess noise in the valve train of these engines indicates that service is required. Instructions for servicing hydraulic lifters may be found in the Unit Repair section.

Valve removal, service, and installation procedures may be found in the Engine Rebuilding section. See specifications table at the beginning of this section for valve spring and valve seat angle specifications.

4–196 Engine:
E E E E
I I I I

MV 404, 446, V 537, 605, V-304, 345 and 392 Engines:
I E I E I E I E
E I E I E I E I

549 Engines:
E I I E E I I E
E I I E E I I E

ROCKER ARM

Removal and Installation

1. Remove rocker cover and gasket.
2. Remove rocker arm assembly mounting bolts and flat washers.
3. Remove rocker assembly.
4. If applicable, remove clip-ring and retainer to disassemble rocker components. Be sure to keep all parts in order so that they may be replaced in their original positions.
5. Clean all parts thoroughly, making sure that oil passages are clear. If necessary to remove plugs from ends of shaft, drill a hole in one plug, knock out the other with a steel rod, then knock out the drilled plug.
6. Inspect shaft for wear and warpage. Replace bent or worn shaft.
7. On engines without hydraulic lifters, inspect rocker arm adjusting screws for wear at the contact surface and for damaged threads. Replace any that are defective.
8. Inspect rocker arm shaft bushings for wear. On 549 and early V-304, 345 engines the rocker arm bushings may be pressed out and new bushings pressed in. On all other engines the bushing is integral with the rocker arm, and if the bushing is worn, the whole rocker arm must be replaced.
9. Inspect valve stem contact pad surfaces of rocker arm and

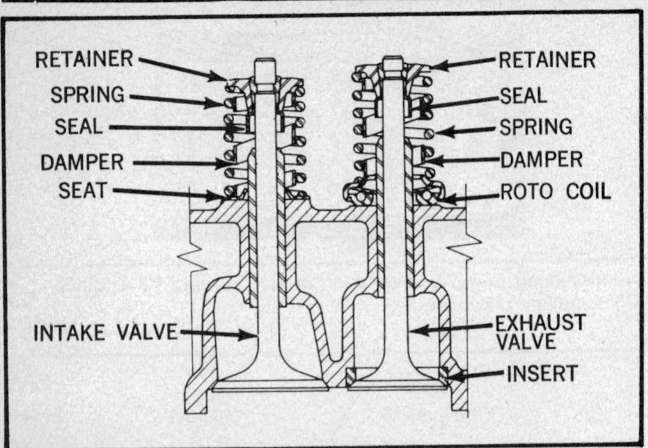

Rotor used under exhaust valve spring only—MV 404, 446, 4-196, V304, 345 and 392 engines (© International Harvester Co.)

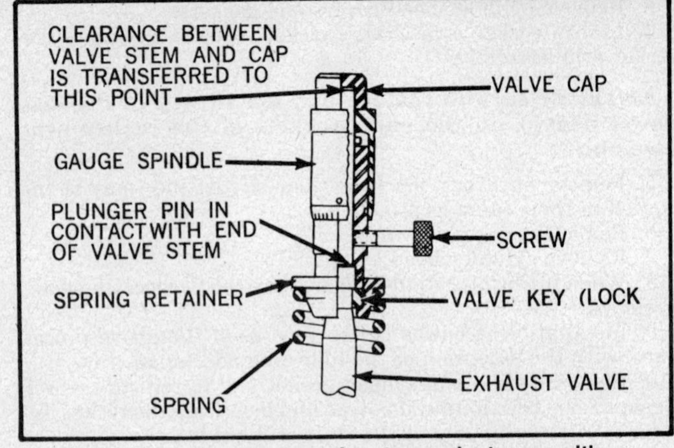

Measuring clearance between valve stem and rotor cap with micrometer (© International Harvester Co.)

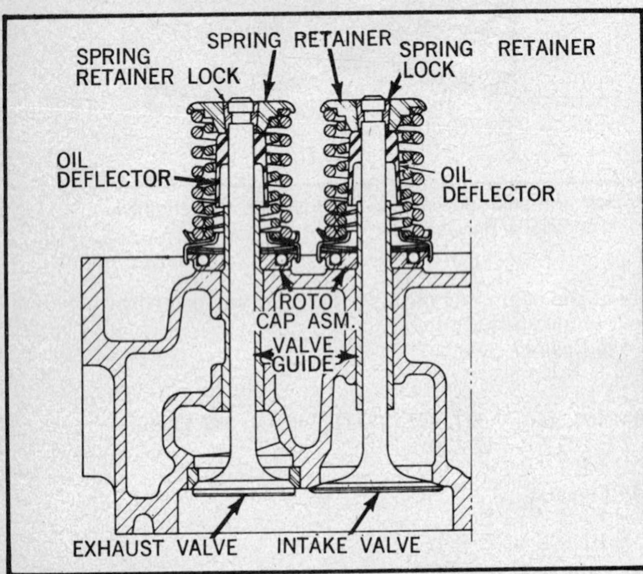

Rotors used under valve springs on intake and exhaust valve—478 and 549 engines (© International Harvester Co.)

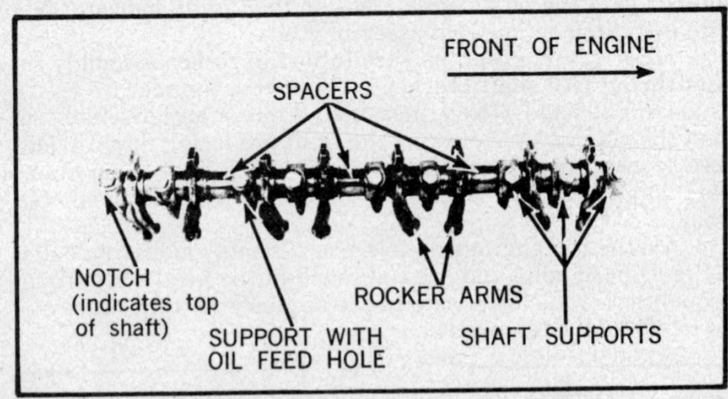

Rocker arm assembly—4-196 (© International Harvester Co.)

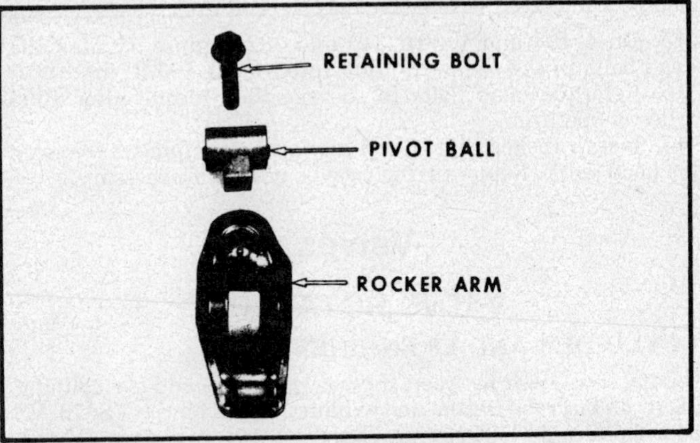

Rocker arm assembly—MV404 and 446 engines
(© International Harvester Co.)

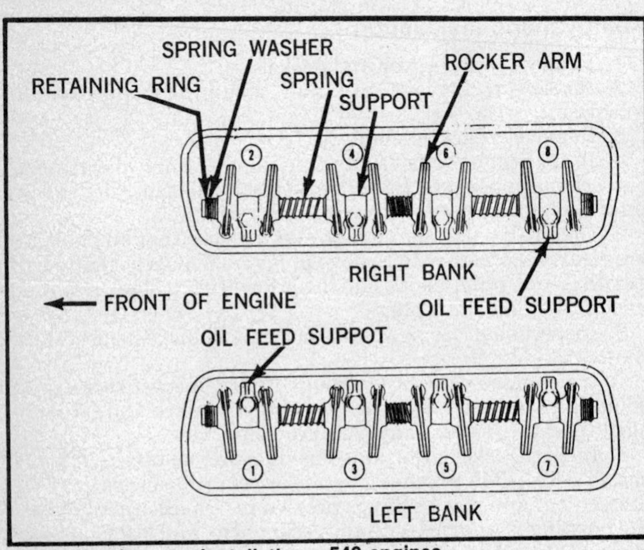

Correct rocker arm installation— 549 engines
(© Inter national Harvester Co.)

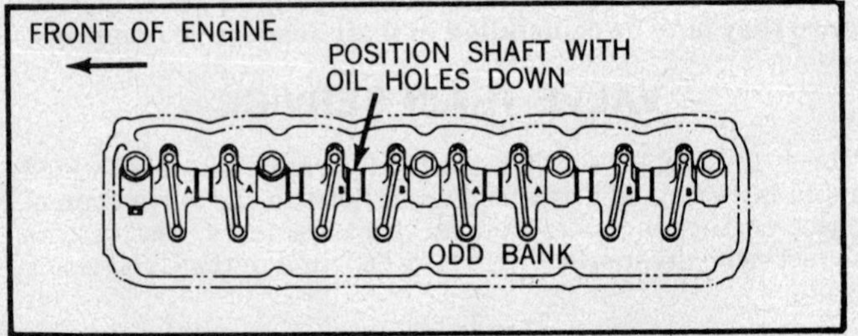

Correct rocker arm positioning—V537 and 605 engines
(© International Harvester Co.)

resurface if wear is excessive. Do not remove more than 0.010" of material when resurfacing.

10. If applicable, replace any defective tension springs.

11. Remove and inspect push rods one by one (to insure original position). Roll them on a flat surface to check for straightness. Replace any pushrods that are bent, have loose ends or are worn.

12. Reassemble all rocker arm assembly components in their original order.

13. Install rocker arm assembly, making sure that the oil feed bracket is in the proper position and that dowel sleeves are in place. On 4–196 and V-304, 345 and 392 engines turn the crankshaft until leading edge of balance weight on crankshaft pulley is aligned with the zero degree mark on the timing indicator before installing rocker arm assembly.

14. Tighten mounting bolts.

15. Adjust rocker arm to valve stem clearance as described above.

16. Install rocker cover, replacing gasket if necessary.

NOTE: Later MV 404 and 446 engines use the individual type rocker arms. Inspect the bearing surface of the pivot ball and bridge to determine the extent of wear and need for replacement.

Timing Case and Gears

CRANKSHAFT PULLEY

Removal and Installation

Accessibility of the crankcase pulley and front (timing) cover will vary according to the model. On some vehicles the timing case will be accessible only if the engine is completely removed. The following instructions are general and apply to most front cover repairs and service.

1. Drain cooling system.
2. Disconnect radiator hoses and remove radiator. In some cases the radiator shroud and truck hood must be removed.
3. Loosen front engine mounts and jack up engine enough to provide access to the crankshaft pulley with a puller.
4. Loosen and remove fan belts and remove fan blades.
5. Remove crankshaft pulley retaining bolt. On 478 and 549 engines, scribe a line alongside the timing indicator and remove the indicator from front cover. The line is for reassembly purposes.
6. Using a suitable puller, remove the pulley from the crankshaft. On some models the pulley is in two pieces and the pulley must be unbolted from its hub before the hub is removed with a puller.

FRONT OIL SEAL

Removal and Installation

1. Remove crankshaft pulley as described in steps 1 through 6 above.
2. Remove seal. It is preferable to use an appropriate seal puller. Use a new gasket when installing front cover and be sure to align cover before tightening.
3. Install a new seal using a suitable seal installing tool if possible. Lubricate first and be careful not to damage seal or seating surface of cover.
4. Install crankshaft pulley, fan belt and fan blades.
5. Lower engine and tighten mounting bolts.
6. Install radiator, shroud, hoses and whatever else was removed.
7. Fill cooling sytem.

TIMING GEAR

Removal and Installation

Timing gears can be removed without disassembling the engine. In some cases, however, the engine must be removed.

1. Remove crankcase pulley as described in steps 1 through 6 above.
2. Remove engine front cover.
3. Rotate engine to align timing marks on crankshaft gear and camshaft gear.

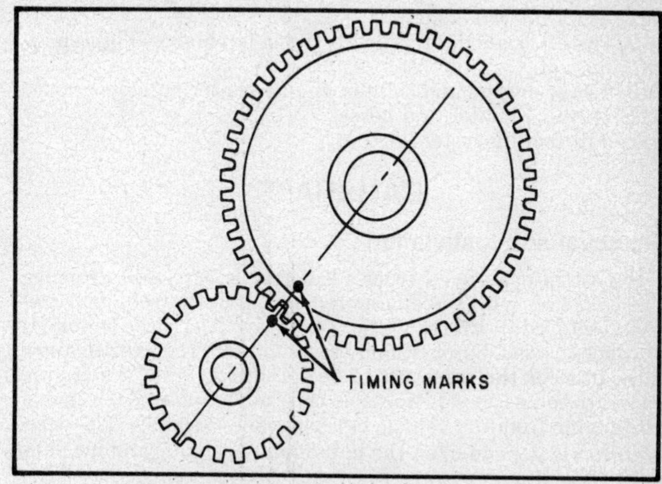

Timing gear alignment marks (© International Harvester Co.)

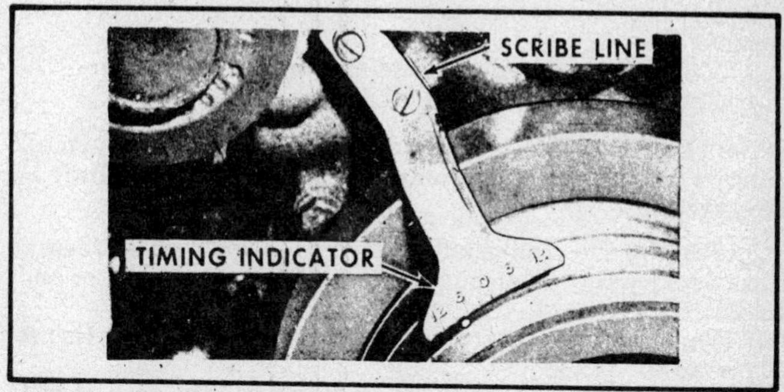

Marking exact position of timing indicator—V8 engines (© International Harvester Co.)

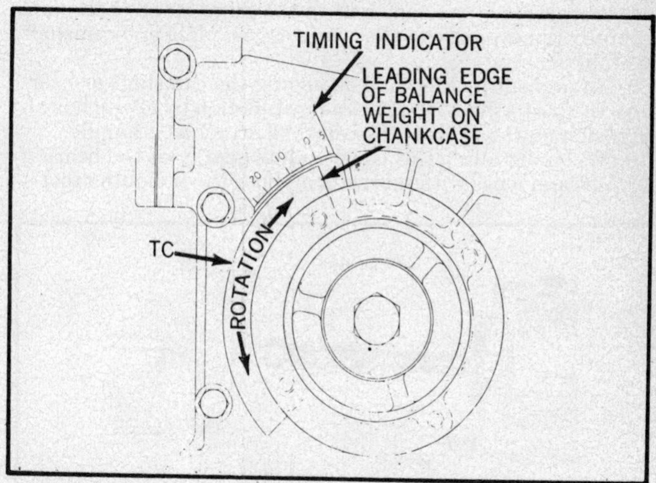

Correct pulley location for installing pushrods—OHV-4 and small V8 engines (© International Harvester Co.)

4. To remove either gear, remove bolt and washer. Use a suitable puller.
5. Use a suitable installing tool to install gears. Lubricate with engine oil and insert key in shaft to align gear. Align timing marks as illustrated. Be careful not to damage threads on shaft. Install and tighten retaining bolt.
6. Rotate engine to check that gears are not binding.
7. Check gear backlash with a dial indicator. It should be within 0.0005–0.0045" on OHV4 and V8 engines.
8. Use a new gasket when installing front cover and be sure to align cover before tightening. On some models there is an oil slinger on the crankshaft.
9. Install crankshaft pulley, belt and fan blades. Tighten retaining bolt.
10. Lower engine and tighten engine mounting bolts.
11. Install radiator and hoses.
12. Fill cooling system.

CAMSHAFT

Removal and Installation

On most International truck models, it is possible to remove the camshaft with the engine remaining in the vehicle. However, the body grille work, radiator, A/C condensor (if equipped), hood, bumper, and braces must be removed to allow clearance for the camshaft to be withdrawn from the engine block. In some cases, it would be more advantageous to remove the engine from the vehicle to replace the camshaft. The decision would depend upon the individual mechanic and his shop facilities.

1. Remove the intake manifolds on the V8 engines, and the rocker covers on all engines.
2. Remove the rocker arms or assemblies, pushrods and tappets.
3. Remove the distributor and mechanical fuel pump.
4. Remove the oil pan and oil pump, if necessary.

NOTE: RD series, 549 engines have camshaft driven oil pumps which must be removed before the camshaft is removed.

5. Remove the crankshaft pulley as previously described.
6. Remove the water pump, front timing cover, gasket and seal.
7. Remove the two screws securing the camshaft thrust flange to the block.
8. Remove the fuel pump cam, distributor drive gear, thrust plate, camshaft gear and camshaft as an assembly, by pulling forward on the camshaft on the 404, 446 and 537 engines. On all other, remove the camshaft thrust plate mount bolts and carefully remove the camshaft gear, thrust plate and camshaft as an assembly.
9. To prevent nicking and damaging the camshaft or bearings, use a camshaft removal and installation tool, which is an extension on the front of the camshaft to act as a handle.
10. When installing the camshaft and gear, coat the bearing surfaces and lobes with lubricant and use the installing tool if possible, to aid in the installation of the camshaft. Make sure the gear timing marks align properly.

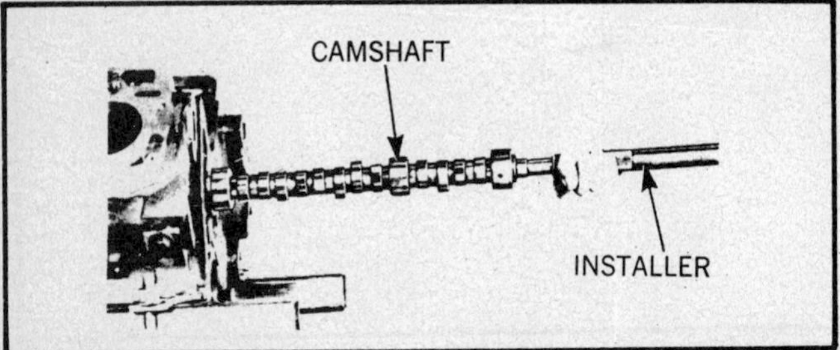

Use of a camshaft remover and installer (© International Harvester Co.)

NOTE: FTVS 549 engines should have the camshaft gear retarded one tooth from normal position.

11. Working through the two large holes in the camshaft gear, install the two thrust flange screws and tighten to proper torque specifications.
12. Check timing gear backlash. If the end play exceeds the allowable limits, replace the thrust flange.
13. Place the oil slinger over the end of the crankshaft.
14. Install the front cover, using a new seal and gasket. Align the cover before tightening the bolts to the specified torque.
15. Install the crankshaft pulley, tightening to the proper torque.
16. Install the cylinder head, if removed, the intake manifold, tappets, pushrods, and rocker arms. Torque all bolts to the specified torque.
17. Install the fan pulley, blades and belts.
18. Install the distributor and fuel pump.
19. Install the oil pump and oil pan.
20. If the engine was raised, lower and tighten the engine mounts.
21. Complete the assembly as necessary for the removed body parts.
22. Start the engine, time it to specifications, and check for proper operation.

Pistons and Connecting Rods

For piston and connecting rod overhaul procedures see Engine Rebuilding section.

PISTON

Removal and Installation

1. Remove oil pan and oil pump. On some models this may require loosening the engine mounts and jacking up the engine until spacer blocks can be installed. When removing oil pump on big V8's turn crank until counter weight is out of the way.
2. Remove cylinder head. See Cylinder Head Removal and Installation.
3. Using a ridge reamer, remove the ridge from the top of the cylinders.
4. Rotate the crankshaft until journal is in lowermost position for removal of connecting rod assemblies. Remove the cap and push the connecting rod and piston up through the cylinder bore. Replace the cap and bearing inserts on the rods so the numbered sides match. The numbers indicate position.
5. To install pistons and connecting rods, rotate crankshaft until No. 1 crankpin is at the bottom of its stroke. Correctly seat rod bearing insert in rod then dip piston assembly in clean oil to lubricate rings. Using a ring compressor, install piston and rod in cylinder. Push piston in, do not strike. On 4–196 and all V8 engines, the piston assembly is installed with the word "UP" toward the top (camshaft) side of the engine block.
6. Place lower half of bearing insert in rod cap and lubricate with oil. Assemble bearing cap to connecting rod with the number side of cap on the same side as the number on the connecting rod. Lubricate threads of bolts with engine oil and install bolts, tightening to the correct torque (see Specifications at the beginning of this section.
7. Rotate crankshaft and repeat installation procedure with the rest of the pistons and connecting rods.
8. Install oil pump and oil pan, using a new pan gasket if necessary.
9. Install cylinder head as described in Cylinder Head Removal and Installation.
10. If engine was raised, remove spacers and lower engine.

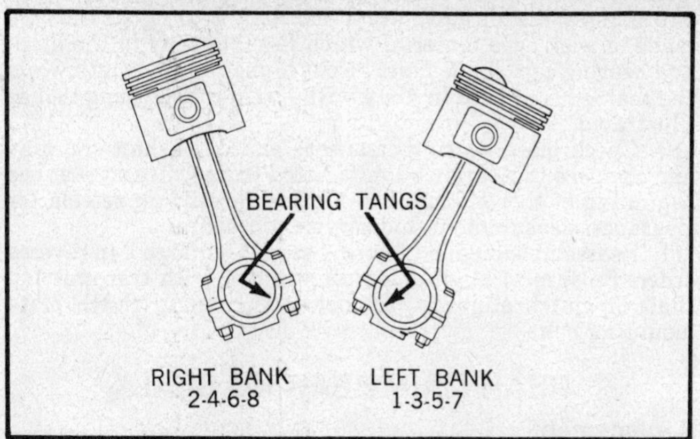

Correct assembly of pistons and rods—V8 engines (© International Harvester Co.)

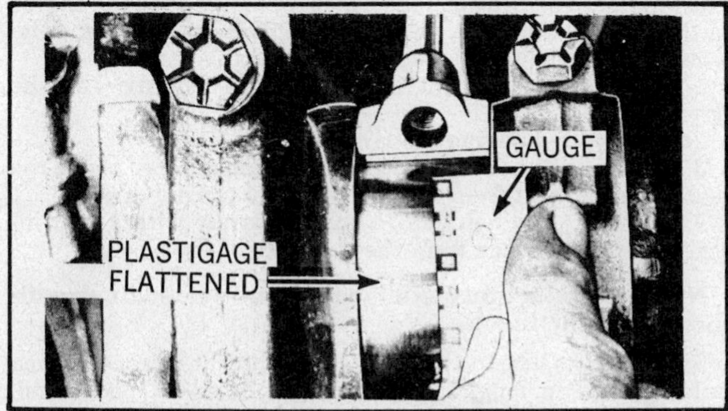

Piston installation (© International Harvester Co.)

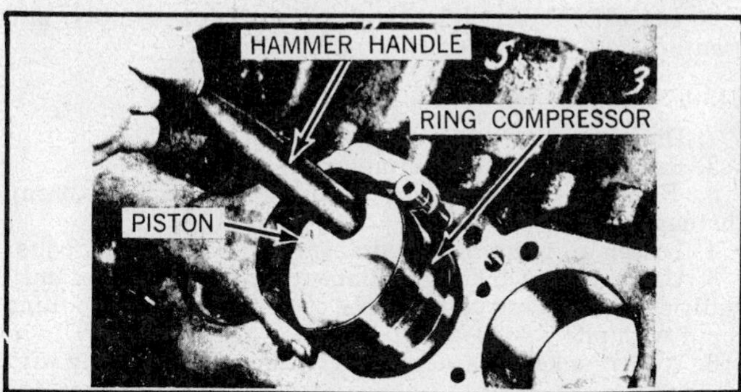

Checking connecting rod bearing clearance with plastigage—typical (© International Harvester Co.)

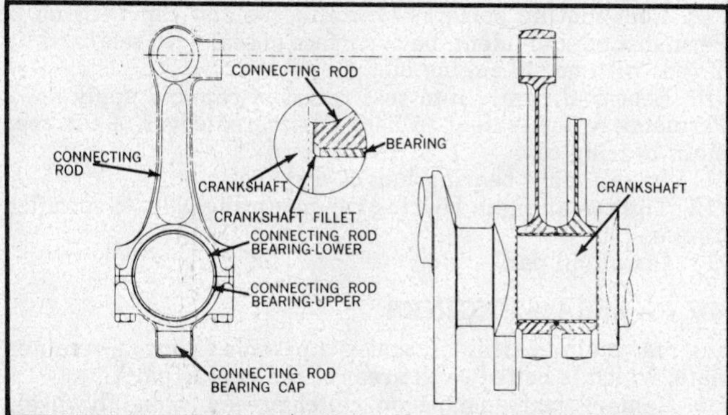

Proper installation of connecting rods to crankshaft (© International Harvester Co.)

Tighten engine mount bolts.

PISTON RING

Replacement

1. Remove pistons as described above.
2. Remove both compression rings and three-piece oil ring.
3. Using rings which correspond to the piston size (standard or oversize), check rings for gap clearance and ring-to-groove side clearance.
4. Install rings on piston with a suitable ring expander tool.
5. Install piston assembly as described above.

Engine Lubrication

OIL PAN

Removal and Installation

The engine and mounts may have to be loosened from the crossmember and lifted, and spacer blocks installed between the mounts and crossmember, to gain clearance to remove the oil pan from the engine. Other engine applications may only require the removal of steering linkage to gain sufficient clearance. Be sure to clean all old gasket material from the oil pan and the block before installing the oil pan and new gasket.

MAIN BEARING

Replacement

On most models it is possible to replace main bearings without removing the engine from the vehicle. However, it is easier to do a better job with the engine removed and, if facilities are available for pulling the engine, this is the preferable method. See "Engine R&R" above. For detailed procedures on main bearing, rod bearing and crankshaft servicing see General Repair Section.

1. Remove crankshaft pulley and front (timing) cover.
2. Remove cylinder head(s) and piston assemblies.
3. If the bell housing and transmission were not removed during engine removal, remove them now.
4. On many engines the clutch plate may be compressed by installing three cap screws ($^3/_8$"–16 × 2$^1/_2$" for 478 and 549 engines and three capscrews $^3/_8$"–16 × 2" for V-304, 345, 392 engines). If the clutch plate cannot be compressed in this way, cut three $^1/_2$" × 1" × 3" wood blocks and insert them between the clutch fingers and back plate. Loosen backing plate mounting bolts slightly if it is difficult to insert wood blocks. A third alternative procedure for compressing the clutch plate is to insert three retaining clips as illustrated. The clutch plate is compressed during removal and installation of the clutch to prevent warpage.
5. Remove the backing plate mounting bolts and clutch assembly.
6. Remove flywheel bolts and pull off flywheel.
7. Remove main bearing caps. On OHV4, V-304, 345 and 392 engines use a rear main bearing cap puller to remove rear main bearing cap.
8. When installing new main bearings make sure that the oil holes are properly aligned and that bearing tangs are fitted into tang recesses. Thoroughly clean all surfaces and coat lightly with oil. Be sure to align timing marks when positioning crankshaft. On the OHV4 and V304, 345 and 392 engines the numbered sides of the main bearing caps face the left side of the engine. On 549, 537 and 605 engines the bearing caps are installed with the numbered side facing to the right side of the engine. When tightening main bearing caps, first tap them lightly into place, then tighten bolts in an alternating manner

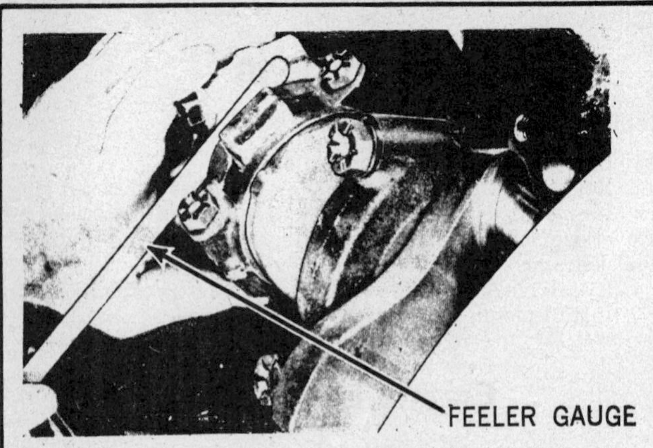

Checking connecting rod end clearance—typical (© International Harvester Co.)

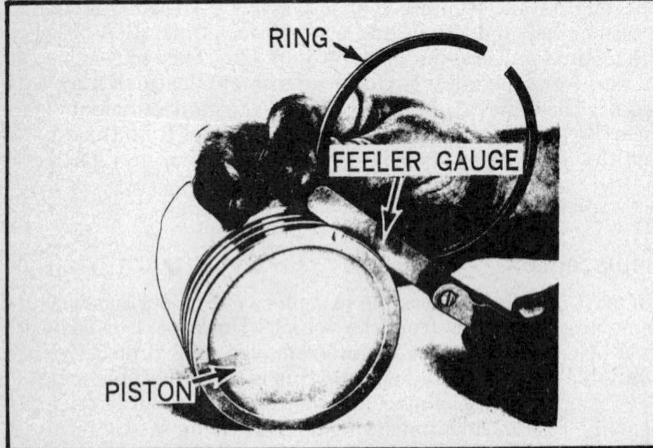

Checking ring groove clearance (© International Harvester Co.)

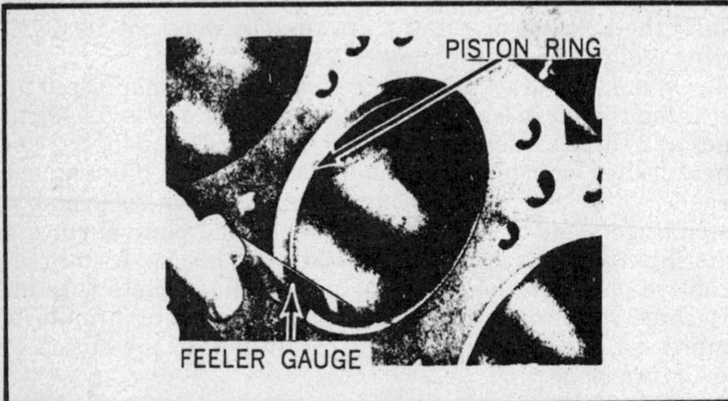

Checking ring groove clearance (© International Harvester Co.)

until the specified torque is reached. See specifications for correct torque.

9. Install a new rear main bearing oil seal. On OHV4 and V-304, 345 and 392 engines the round seal is pressed in after the rear main bearing cap is installed. Rear main bearing cap side oil seals are installed on these engines with an installer tool made from a piece of ⅛" welding rod. Puddle a ball on the end of the rod and file the ball to approximately 5.32" diameter. On RD engines the rear upper seal and retainer are installed before the crankshaft and the lower main bearing lower oil seal is installed after the rear main bearing cap, using new gaskets on each side of the lower seal retainer. On 549 engines the rear main bearing cap side seals are marked for right and left side. 549 engines, the top and bottom rear main bearing oil seals are made of wick type material which fits into slots in the block and bearing cap. These must be cut to the correct length while the seal is being held in place with a seal compressing tool as illustrated.

10. Check main bearing clearance and crankshaft end play and compare to clearance limits listed in Specifications at the beginning of this section. See Engine Rebuilding section for clearance measurement and service procedures.

11. Reassemble engine following steps 1 through 7 in reverse order. Be sure to align clutch driven disc with transmission shaft or clutch aligning tool before tightening clutch plate mounting bolts.

REAR MAIN BEARING SEAL

Replacement

OHV 4, V 304, 345, 392, 536, and 605 ENGINES

The rear main bearing cap seal can be replaced with the engine in the chassis, but the transmission, clutch assembly, and flywheel must be removed to gain access to the seal.

1. Remove the transmission, clutch assembly, and the flywheel.
2. Remove the engine oil pan.
3. With a slide hammer with a screw end adapter pierce the seal and remove it from the recess in the cap and block.
4. Lubricate the new seal, seat it squarely with a seal installer tool 0.085 inch from the rear face of the block.

NOTE: Production installed seals are seated flush with the rear of the block.

5. Install the bearing cap side seals with the use of a ⅛ inch welding rod, 8 in. long, with a $^{5}/_{32}$ inch puddled ball on the end. Cut off any excess side seal, flush with the oil pan block surface.
6. Install the oil pan, flywheel, clutch assembly, and transmission.

549 ENGINES

1. Drain crankcase and remove oil pan.
2. Remove rear main bearing cap.
3. Remove oil seal from bearing cap and clean cap thoroughly.
4. Loosen all remaining main bearing cap mounting bolts.
5. Using a brass drift and hammer, tap the upper seal until sufficient seal is protruding on the other side to permit pulling it out with pliers.
6. Wipe crankshaft seal surface clean and coat lightly with oil.
7. Coat crankcase surface of upper seal with soap and the lip of seal with No. 40 engine oil.
8. Install upper seal with lip toward front of engine.
9. Coat mating surfaces of crankcase and cap with no. 2 Permatex or equivalent, back surface of seal with soap and lip of seal with no. 40 engine oil.
10. Seat seal firmly into seal recess of cap and apply no. 2 Permatex or equivalent to both chamfered edges of the rear main bearing cap.
11. Install main bearing halves and cap.
12. Tighten all main bearing cap mounting bolts to specified torque.
13. Install oil pan.

MV 404 and 446 ENGINES

The rear main bearing oil seal is a pressed fit into a retainer plate, which is bolted to the rear of the engine block.

1. Remove the transmission, clutch assembly, and flywheel.
2. Remove the capscrews holding the retainer to the engine block, and remove the retainer.

Installation of rear main bearing cap side seals—V304, 345 and 392 engines (© International Harvester Co.)

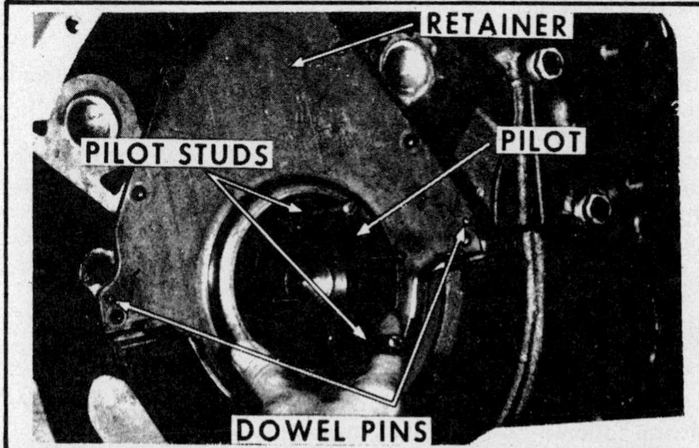

Rear main bearing oil seal installation—MV404 and 406 engines (© International Harvester Co.)

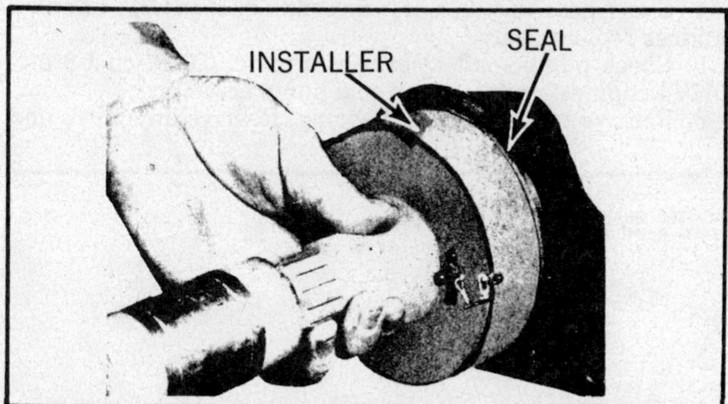

Installing rear main oil seal (© International Harvester Co.)

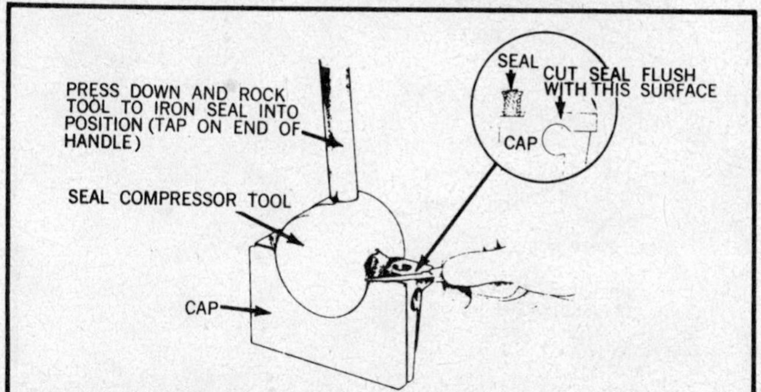

Installation of oil seal into rear main bearing cap (© International Harvester Co.)

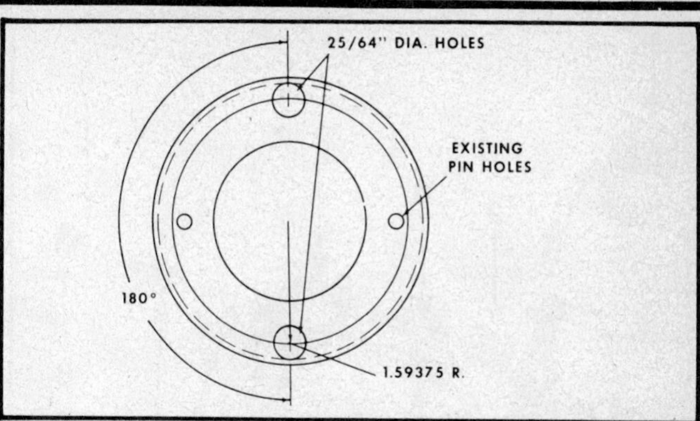

Rework of pilot tool SE1942-2 for MV404 and 446 engine rear main bearing oil seal installation (© International Harvester Co.)

3. Press out the old seal from the retainer, clean the retainer seal pocket, and press the new seal in place on the retainer.

NOTE: The seal must be installed from the crankcase side of the retainer, flush with the seal bore inner surface.

4. With the use of tool SE-1942–2 pilot, or its equivalent, install the rear oil seal and retainer with gaskets on the engine block.

NOTE: When using the SE-1942–2 pilot tool to install the seal with the engine in the vehicle, drill two $^{25}/_{64}$ inch diameter holes in the pilot, 180 degrees apart, 90 degrees from each existing hole. This will allow the use of two $^{3}/_{8}$ × 4 inch pilot studs to serve as a safety measure to retain the pilot on the crankshaft.

5. Replace the flywheel, clutch assembly, and transmission.

OIL FILTER

Replacement

On all models, the oil filter unit is on the left side of the engine block. All engines except the 478 and 549 series, use a spin-on type oil filter, which is replaced as a complete unit, using a strap wrench to remove it from the engine. Follow the instructions printed on the filter assembly to install.

The VS series use a paper type filter, inserted in the filter shell, with the shell bolted to the filter base. To replace the filter, follow this procedure.

1. Remove drain plug from bottom of filter body, drain oil and replace drain plug.
2. Loosen filter body retaining bolt and remove filter body and element. Check condition of body to base gasket and replace if necessary.
3. Wash filter body with cleaning solvent, being sure to remove all sediment.
4. Install new filter element onto filter base with seal end away from base. Be sure element is fully seated onto base.
5. Install oil filter body and bolt with spring, making sure body seats evenly on gasket. Tighten filter body retaining bolt to 30–35 ft. lbs. torque on all engines.
6. Start engine and run for at least 5 minutes until oil is warm and check for leaks.
7. Check crankcase oil level. Lubricant capacity of oil filter is about one quart.

OIL PUMP

Removal and Installation

1. Drain crankcase and remove oil pan.
2. Remove oil pump mounting bolts and pull straight down on pump to remove.
3. When installing oil pump, guide pump shaft into position

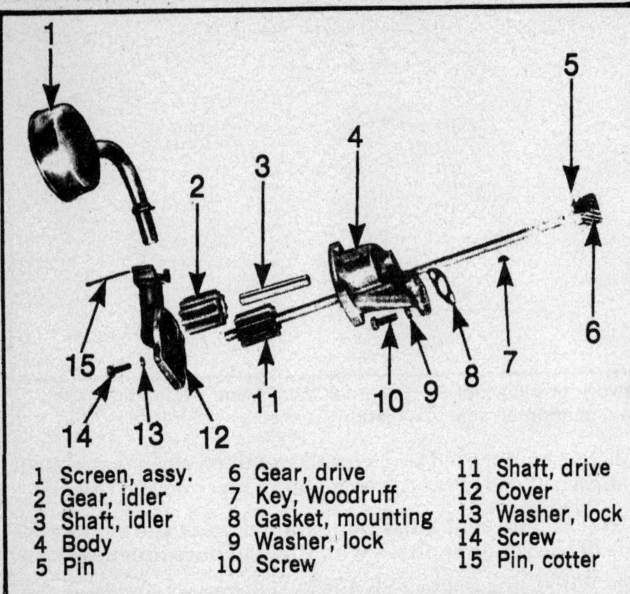

Typical gear type oil pump (© International Harvester Co.)

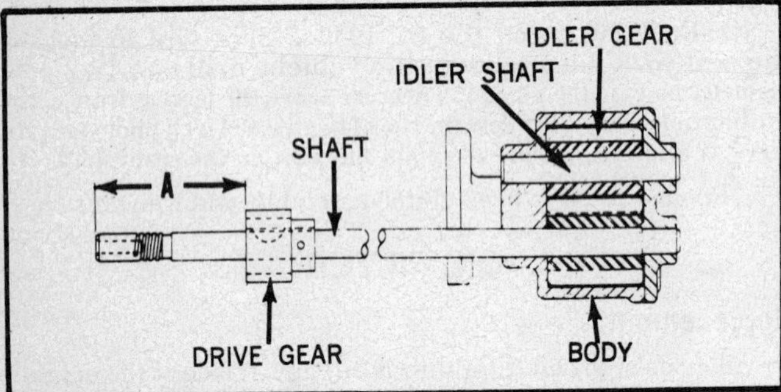

Oil pump drive gear installation—478 and 548 engines 2⅞" front mounted distributor "A" 1$^{15}/_{16}$" rear mounted distributor (© International Harvester Co.)

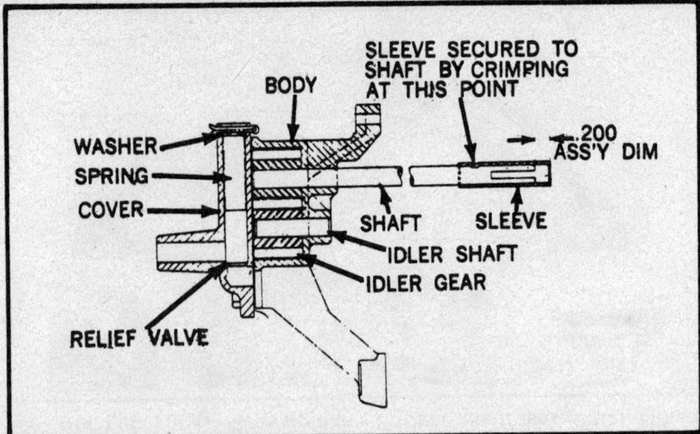

Oil pump shaft sleeve installation—OHV4, 304, 345 and 392 engines (© International Harvester Co.)

and rotate shaft until tang of drive gear is engaged. On 478 and 549 engines use a new oil pump gasket when installing. On RD engines the oil pump shaft drives the distributor shaft and must be installed so that it is correctly timed to the crankshaft. Rotate the crankshaft until No. 1 cylinder is in firing position. On RD engines the oil pump is installed so that the slot in the top of the shaft is at a 60–degree angle to the side of the engine.

4. Tighten oil pump mounting bolts to 25–30 ft. lbs. for all.
5. Install oil pan and fill crankcase.

Service and Overhaul

1. Thoroughly clean oil pump. Do not disturb or remove pickup tube unless absolutely necessary.
2. Remove pump cover bolts and pump cover.
3. Check gear to body clearance. 0.0007–0.0027" on the OHV4 and V8 engines, obtain new parts.
4. Check gear backlash. If it exceeds 0.011" on OHV4 and V8 engines replace gears.
5. Check pump shaft clearance in bore. 0.003" on V8 and OHV4 engines, replace the whole pump assembly.
6. Remove relief valve and spring. Remove any burrs and

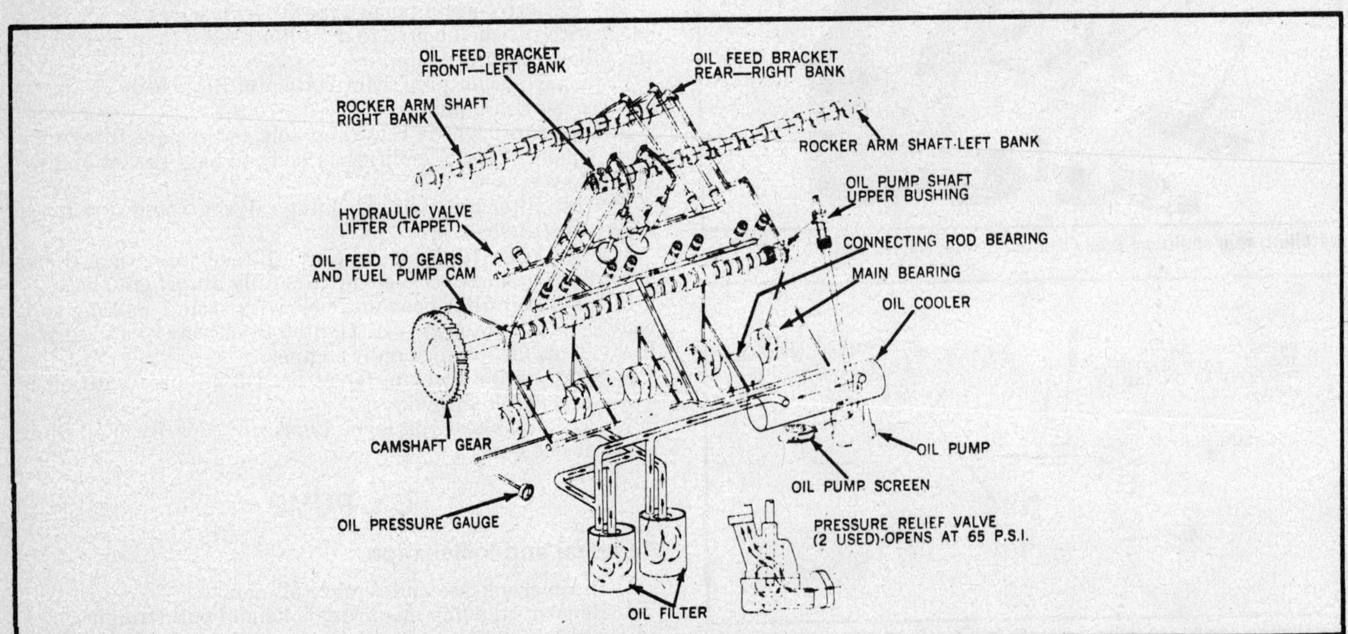

Lubricating system circuits—V537 and 605 engines (© International Harvester Co.)

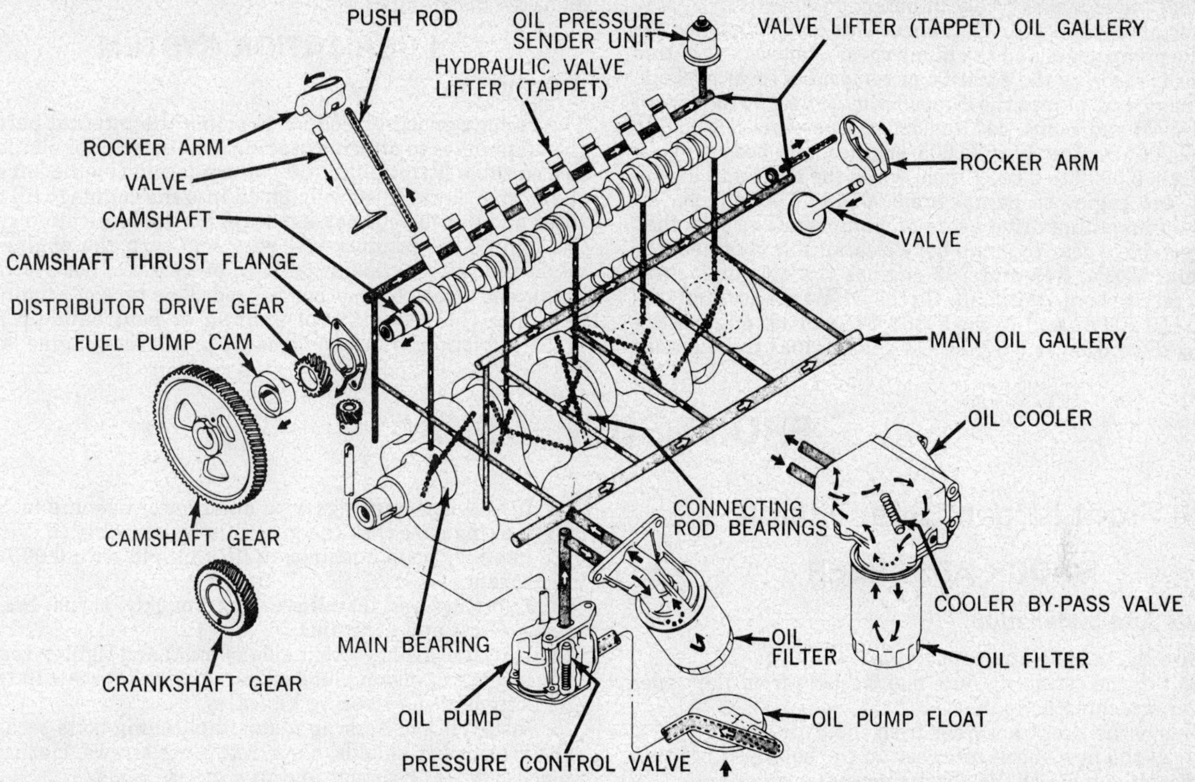

Lubricating system circuits—MV404 and 466 engines (© International Harvester Co.)

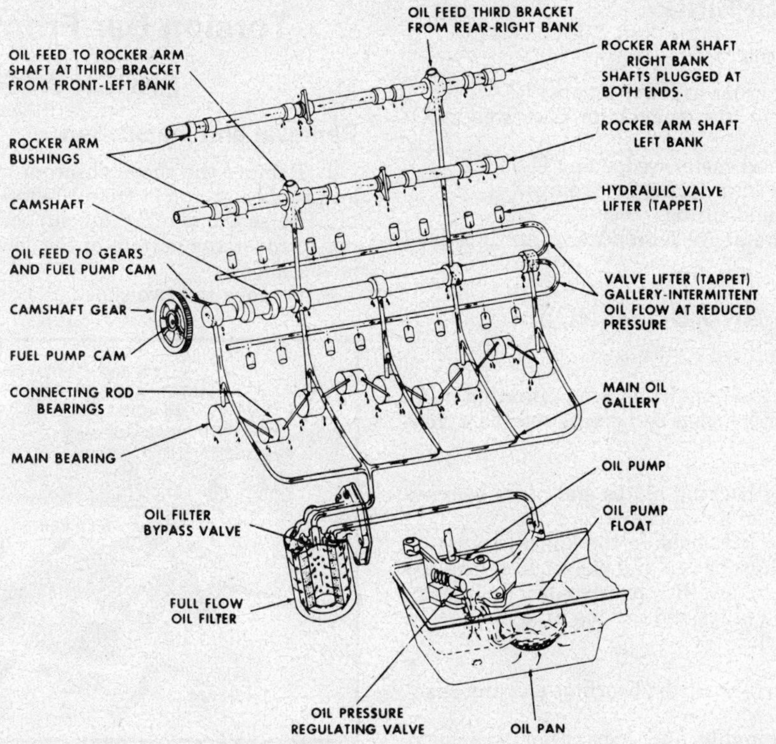

Lubricating system circuits—V304, 345 and 392 engines (© International Harvester Co.)

clean. Be sure to install with bevelled or pointed end in seat. Check that valve moves freely in bore.

7. Check body and gear clearance. This is the distance between the pump gears and the pump cover. Adjustment of this clearance is made by the addition or removal of cover gaskets. On 549 engine oil pumps the clearance must be 0.0015–0.009". On the OHV4 and Y-304, 345 and 392 engines, the clearance is 0.0015–0.006".On the V 537, 605 engines, the body to gear clearance is 0.0007 to 0.0027 inch, while the clearance on the MV 404, 446 engine oil pumps are 0.0014 to 0.0054 inch.

8. When installing drive gears on pump shaft be sure that the correct drive gear to pump body clearance is obtained. On OHV4 and V-304, 345 and 392 engines the oil pump shaft sleeve is crimped onto the shaft. On the OHV4 the assembly dimension is 0.200 in. and on the V-304, 345 and 392 engines the assembly dimension is 0.375in. On 549 engines the distance "A" is 2 $^{7}/_{8}$" for front-mounted distributors, 1 $^{15}/_{16}$ " for rear-mounted distributors.

LUBRICATION SYSTEM

Priming

The recommended procedure to prime the internal parts and the oil pump is to attach a bearing leak detector or similar tool to a suitable fitting on the oil gallery, located on the left side of the engine block. Inject enough oil into the engine to fill the oil filter and the various passage ways for the lubrication system. Disconnect the primary coil wire and turn the engine over, while the priming operation is in process. Do not overfill the crankcase when this method is used. This type of priming will minimize the possibility of scuffing or heat build-up in the areas of friction, which could cause premature engine failure.

FRONT SUSPENSION

Front I-Beam Suspension

SHOCK ABSORBER

Removal And Installation

1. Raise the vehicle and support safely.
2. Remove the retaining nuts and washers from the upper and lower attaching bolts.
3. Remove the shock absorber from the bolts.
4. Install the new shock absorber on the bolts and position the rubber grommets at the shock absorber eyes.
5. Install the retaining nuts and washers on the upper and lower attaching bolts and tighten securely.
6. Lower the vehicle.

SPRING

Removal and Installation

1. Disconnect shock absorber at lower mount.
2. Raise front of vehicle just enough to take weight off spring.
3. Unbolt U-bolts, tapered caster wedge and U-bolt.
4. Remove lube fittings from spring mountings.
5. Remove spring pins and spring.
6. To install, reverse the above procedure, mounting fixed end of spring first.

KING PIN AND BUSHINGS

Replacement

1. Remove spindle nuts and spindle bearing retaining nuts.
2. Remove wheels, inner bearings and grease retainers from spindles.
3. Remove dirt shields.
4. Remove bolts holding backing plates and place backing plate assemblies over ends of axle I-beam.
5. Remove tapered draw keys holding the knuckle pins.
6. Remove expansion plugs or cap and gasket from the top and bottom of steering knuckles. (Remove expansion plugs by drilling a hole in one of the plugs and driving king pin with a punch to remove the other).
7. Drive out king pin.
8. Remove steering knuckles, thrust bearings and any spacer shims present.
9. Clean all parts thoroughly and inspect for wear and damage.
10. Remove old bushings with an arbor or drift.
11. Install new bushings with an arbor or bushing installing tool, making sure that the grease holes are aligned.
12. Ream or hone bushings to fit king pin with 0.001–0.002 in. clearance.
13. Lubricate and install steering knuckle, thrust bearings, spacer shims and king pins.
14. Install draw key (front side of axle) and tighten securely.
15. Insert expansion plugs or cap and gasket seals in the top and bottom of the steering knuckles.
16. Install brake backing plates, tightening bolts securely.
17. Install dirt shields, their retaining screws, cleaned and repacked wheel bearings and new grease seals.
18. Install wheel and spindle nuts, rotating wheel while tightening nut until slight drag is felt. Back off to the first castellation and install new cotter pin.
19. Lubricate and check and align front wheels if necessary.

Torsion Bar Front Suspension

SHOCK ABSORBER

Removal and Installation

1. Remove the shock absorber upper retaining nut, washer, and rubber grommet from the top of the upper control arm.
2. Raise the vehicle and support it in such a manner so as not to cover the bottom of the lower arm with a floor jack or jack stands.
3. Remove the two shock absorber retaining bolts from the

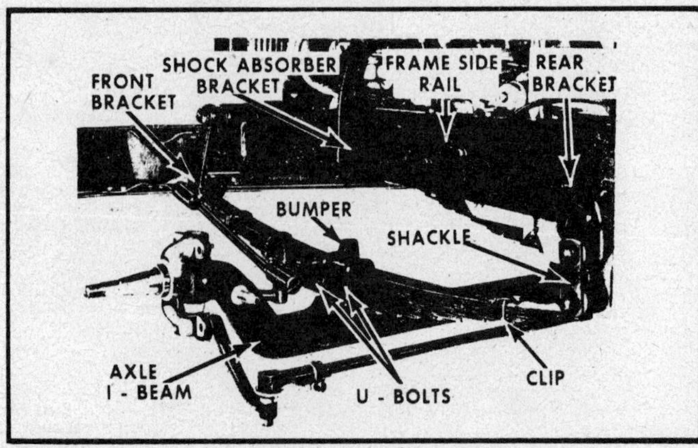

Typical front spring installation (medium only) (© International Harvester Co.)

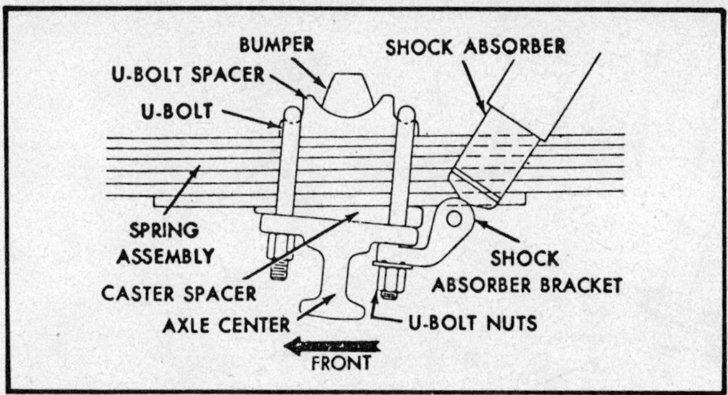

Typical front axle mounting (© International Harvester Co.)

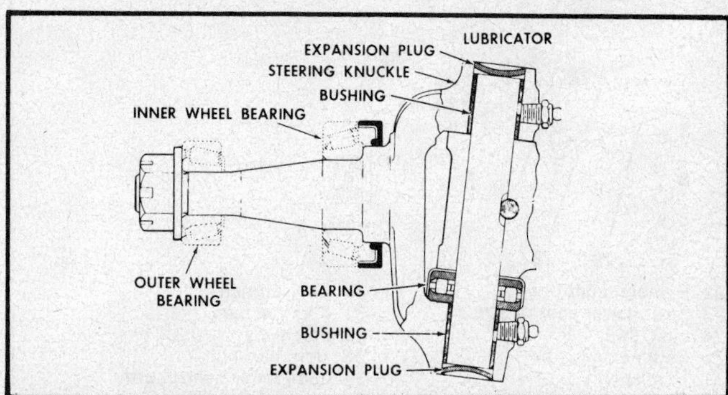

Typical steering knuckle expansion type seal plugs (© International Harvester Co.)

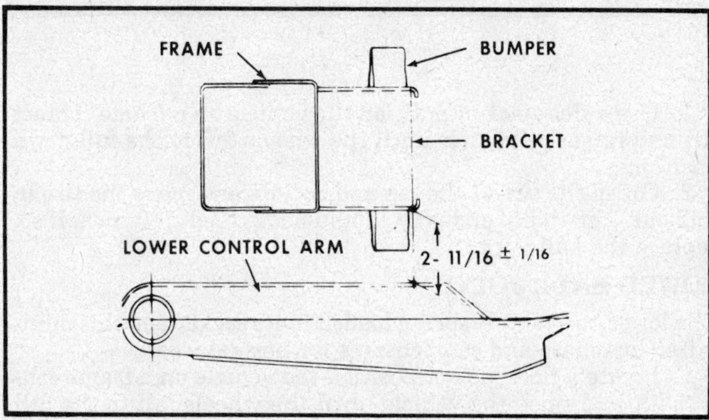

Checking front suspension height (© International Harvester Co.)

bottom of the lower control arm and withdraw the shock absorber.

4. To install new shock absorber, position the washer and rubber grommet on the extended shock absorber rod, and position the shock absorber up through the lower control arm, and engage the hole in the upper control arm with the extended rod.

5. Install the two bottom retaining bolts and tighten the shock absorber securely to the lower control arm.

6. Carefully lower the vehicle, so as not to lose the shock absorber rod from the upper control arm hole.

7. Install the upper rubber grommet, washer, and nut on the rod and tighten until the rubber grommet squeezes out slightly.

NOTE: Follow the manufacturers recommendation concerning the installation of lock nuts or self-locking nuts.

TORSION BAR

Removal and Installation

Right and left torsion bars are not interchangeable. The bars are marked with an "L" or "R" on one end and the bars should always be installed with the marked end towards the rear of the vehicle. There is an arrow indicating the direction of wind-up on the end of the bar.

1. Jack up the vehicle by the frame crossmember and release the load from the torsion bar by loosening the retainer lever adjusting bolt.

2. Remove retainer lever adjusting bolt and slide retainer lever from end of torsion bar.

3. Remove torsion bar by sliding it rearward.

CAUTION

Do not nick or scratch torsion bars—this may create a fracture.

4. To install torsion bar, position torsion bar in upper control arm, observing right and left side and rearward direction as indicated above.

5. Install retainer lever on end of torsion bar and position bar nut in bracket on frame so that torsion bar adjusting bolt may be installed.

6. Insert bolt in bar washer, then through retainer lever and bracket and thread into bar nut.

7. Adjust height by lowering vehicle to ground (check for correct tire pressure), bouncing front end up and down, then turning bolt on torsion bar adjusting lever until correct height is achieved. Measure height between top and lower control arm and lower edge of rubber bumper frame bracket (vehicle unloaded).

UPPER CONTROL ARM

Removal and Installation

1. Jack up vehicle by front frame crossmember until front wheels are off the ground.
2. Remove wheel and torsion bar (see preceding section).
3. Disconnect top mount of shock absorber.
4. Remove cotter pin, nut and dust seal (cut away seal) from lower ball joint.
5. Drive out lower ball joint stud (do not damage threads) or use special ball stud remover and nut.
6. Remove fender splash panel front shield.
7. Remove nut and washers from front end of upper control arm spindle and carefully drive out spindle with hammer.
8. Remove upper control arm.
9. To install, position upper control arm and install spindle through arm and bracket from rear.
10. Install flat washer, lock washer and nut. Tighten securely.
11. Install fender splash panel front shield.
12. Install new dust seal on ball stud, then line up shock absorber with hole in control arm and position ball stud into steering knuckle. Use jack to raise lower control arm until ball stud is well into steering knuckle.
13. Install nut on ball stud. Tighten securely.
14. Install top mounting of shock absorber, tightening just enough to squash rubber cushion slightly.
15. Install torsion bar on upper control arm as described in preceding section.
16. Mount front wheel.
17. Check alignment (see Unit Repair section) of steering.

LOWER CONTROL ARM

Removal and Installation

1. Raise vehicle by jacking frame crossmember. Remove wheel.

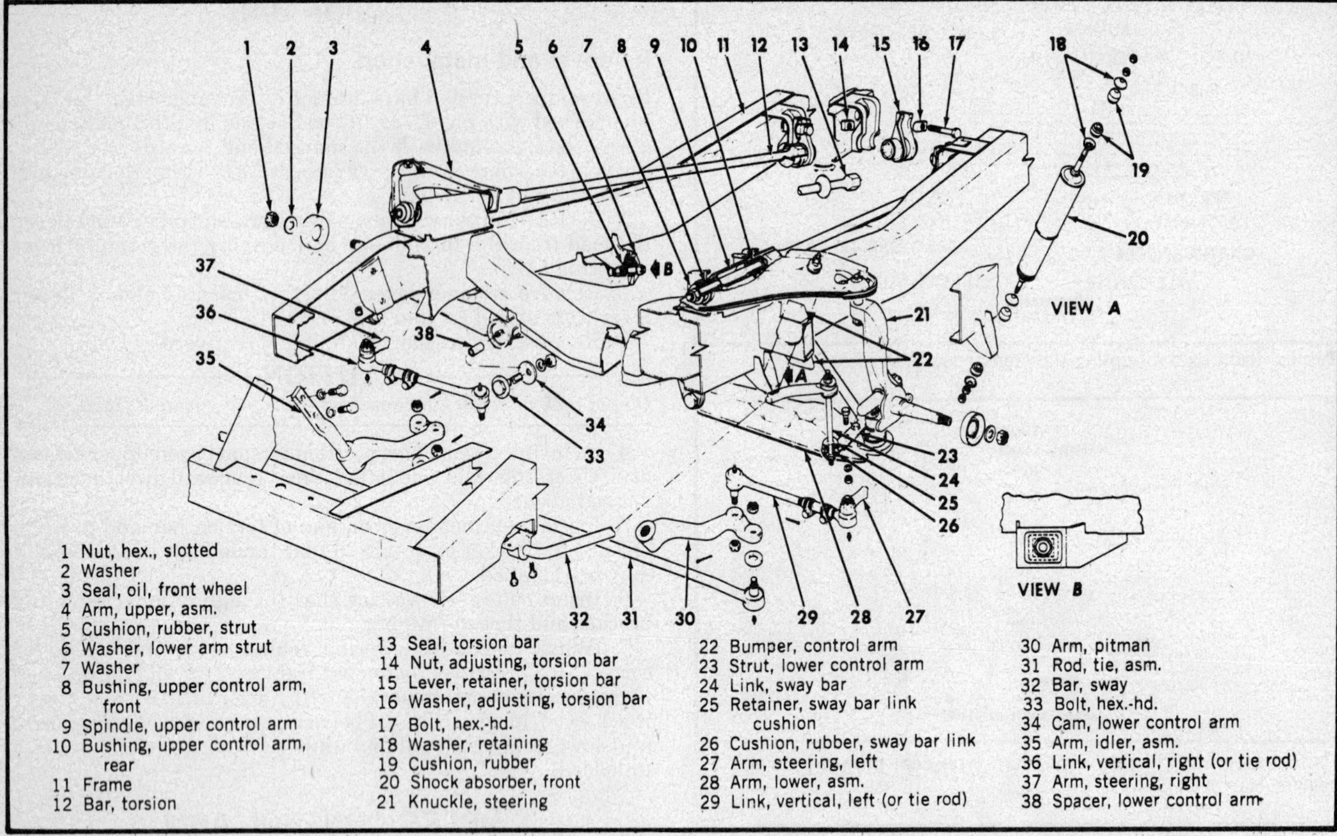

Torsion bar front wheel suspension (© International Harvester Co.)

2. Disconnect sway bar link from strut and remove two bolts which secure strut to lower control arm.
3. Cut away dust seal from lower ball stud and remove cotter pin and nut from lower ball stud.
4. Either drive out ball stud with a soft hammer while supporting control arm or use special ball stud remover and nut.
5. Disconnect tie rod end from either side of vehicle.
6. Remove nut, lockwasher, cam and bolt from lower control arm and frame bracket.
7. Remove control arm and spacer in bushing.
8. To install, place new dust seal on ball stud and position ball stud into steering knuckle.
9. Tighten nut on ball stud and install cotter pin.
10. Position spacer in bushing and, while holding control arm in position, install bolt from front. Install cam, lockwasher, and nut, tightening to 81–135 ft. lbs. torque.
11. Mount strut to lower control arm tightening bolts securely.
12. Connect tie rod end.
13. Position cushion and retainer on sway bar link into strut with cushion, retainer and nut. Tighten nut until cushion is slightly squashed. Insert cotter pin.
14. Mount front wheel.
15. Check alignment (see Unit Repair section) and tighten nut on strut to 120–150 ft. lbs. torque and camber adjusting bolt nut to 81–135 ft. lbs. torque.

BALL JOINT

Inspection

UPPER BALL JOINT

The upper ball joint is a loose fit when not connected to the steering knuckle.

1. Use a floor jack or position the vehicle on a frame contact lift and raise the vehicle until the wheels fall to the full down position.
2. Grasp the tire at the top and bottom and move the tire in and out. The radial end play should not exceed .180 inch. If so, replace the ball joint.

LOWER BALL JOINT

The lower ball joint is spring loaded in its socket and this minimizes looseness and compensates for normal wear.

1. Locate a floor jack or position the vehicle on a frame contact lift and raise the vehicle until the wheels fall to the full down position.
2. Grasp the tire at the top and bottom and move the tire in and out. Any movement at the ball joint socket and stud indicates wear and the loss of preload, and the ball joint should be replaced.

Removal and Installation

Refer to Independent Front Suspension-Coil Spring, for the procedures necessary to remove and install the ball joints.

Independent Front Suspension – Coil Spring

SHOCK ABSORBER

Removal and Installation

1. Remove the shock absorber upper retaining nut, washer, and rubber grommet from the top of the upper control arm.
2. Raise the vehicle and support it in such a manner so as

not to cover the bottom of the lower arm with a floor jack or jack stands.

3. Remove the two shock absorber retaining bolts from the bottom of the lower control arm and withdraw the shock absorber.

4. To install new shock absorber, position the washer and rubber grommet on the extended shock absorber rod, and position the shock absorber up through the lower control arm, and engage the hole in the upper control arm with the extended rod.

5. Install the two bottom retaining bolts and tighten the shock absorber securely to the lower control arm.

6. Carefully lower the vehicle, so as not to lose the shock absorber rod from the upper control arm hole.

7. Install the upper rubber grommet, washer, and nut on the rod and tighten until the rubber grommet squeezes out slightly.

NOTE: Follow the manufacturers recommendation concerning the installation of lock nuts or self-locking nuts.

BALL JOINT

Inspection

UPPER BALL JOINT

The upper ball joint stud is spring loaded in its socket and this minimizes looseness and compensates for normal wear.

1. Locate a floor jack under the lower control arm on the outboard side and raise the vehicle so that the wheels clear the floor.

2. Grasp the tire at the top and bottom and move the tire in and out. If any perceptible lateral or vertical movement is noted, the ball joint should be replaced.

LOWER BALL JOINT

The lower ball joints are a loose fit when not connected to the steering knuckle.

1. Locate a floor jack under the lower control arm on the outboard side and raise the vehicle until the wheels clear the floor.

2. Grasp the tire at the top and bottom and move the tire in and out. The radial play should not exceed .250 inch. If so, the ball joint should be replaced.

COIL SPRING

Removal and Installation

1. Raise the front of the vehicle and support safely on floor stands.
2. Remove the wheels and tires.
3. Remove the caliper from the rotor assembly and support to avoid damage to the brake hose.
4. Remove the hub assembly from the steering knuckle.
5. Remove the brake shield from the knuckle.
6. Disconnect the sway bar link, if equipped.
7. Remove the axle bumper and wheel stop bracket from the lower control arm.

NOTE: This also disconnects the lower control arm rod assembly from the control arm.

8. Remove the shock absorber.
9. Position the spring compressor screw into the shock absorber upper mounting hole in the crossmember. Position the puller hooks under the lower second spring coil and turn the spring compressor screw until coil spring unseats from the lower control arm.
10. Remove the cotter pins from the upper and lower ball joint studs, and loosen the lower nut approximately two turns.

NOTE: The cotter pin is removed from the upper ball joint stud to allow a special tool to be placed over the upper stud and nut.

11. With the aid of special tool SE-2493 (ball joint stud remover) or its equivalent, and by placing it over the upper stud at its hex end, extend the screw to contact the lower ball joint stud.
12. Apply pressure by turning the screw out from the tool. Tap the steering knuckle lightly to loosen the stud from the knuckle.
13. Remove the tool and remove the nut from the lower ball joint stud. Separate the ball joint stud from the knuckle.
14. Loosen the spring compressor and relieve the spring of all tension. Remove the spring from the vehicle.
15. Position new spring into the crossmember and the lower control arm.

NOTE: Turn the coil spring to line up the bottom coil with the seal groove in the lower control arm.

16. Install the hooks of the spring compressor under the second coil of the spring. Tighten the compressor until the lower ball joint stud can be installed into the steering knuckle.
17. Position a hydraulic jack under the lower control arm and raise the arm until the bottom ball joint stud will enter the steering knuckle. Install the nut and torque to specifications.
18. Install the cotter pins in both the upper and lower ball joint studs. Confirm the position of the spring in the lower arm.
19. Remove the spring compressor tool and install the shock absorber.
20. Install the lower control arm rod assembly and axle bumper and wheel stop bracket to the lower control arm.
21. Install the brake shield on the steering knuckle.
22. Install the rotor-hub assembly.
23. Install the caliper on the rotor assembly.
24. Install the wheel and tire assembly.
25. Remove the floor stands and lower the vehicle to the floor.
26. Depress the brake pedal to force the disc pads against the rotor.

UPPER CONTROL ARM AND BALL JOINT

Removal and Installation

Follow the procedure outlined under Coil Spring Removal And Installation, except that the special tool SE-2493 or its equivalent, is used to apply pressure to the upper ball joint stud after loosening the nut approximately two turns. Follow the procedure as outlined.

1. After removing the ball joint stud from the steering knuckle, remove the upper control arm from the frame rail.
2. Place the upper control arm in a vise and with a ball joint remover socket, remove the ball joint from the upper arm.
3. Lubricate the threads in the arm and place the new ball joint into the arm.
4. With the use of the ball joint socket, tighten the ball joint to specifications in the upper arm.
5. Inner upper arm bushings may be replaced by pressing the old bushings out and pressing the new bushings into the upper arm.
6. Install the upper arm onto the frame rail and tighten securely.
7. Follow the procedure outlined under the Coil Spring Removal and Installation to complete the operation.

LOWER CONTROL ARM AND BALL JOINT

Removal and Installation

Follow the procedure outlined under Coil Spring Removal and Installation to remove the coil spring from the suspension. After the coil spring is removed, follow this procedure to remove the lower control arm and ball joint.

1. After removing the lower ball joint stud from the steering knuckle, remove the lower control arm from the frame bracket.
2. Place the lower control arm in a vise.
3. Remove the ball joint from the lower control arm with the aid of tool SE-2494–2 ball joint remover and installer, or an equivalent tool.
4. Lubricate the threads in the arm and place a new ball joint into the control arm.
5. With the use of tool SE-2494–2 or equivalent, tighten the ball joint into the arm.
6. Inner lower arm bushings may be replaced by pressing the old bushings out and pressing the new bushings into place.
7. Install the lower arm onto the frame rail bracket and tighten securely.
8. Follow the procedure outlined under "Coil Spring Removal and Installation" to complete the operation.

FRONT WHEEL BEARING

Adjustment

ALL NON-DRIVING AXLES

1. While rotating the wheel and hub assembly, adjust the spindle nut to 30 ft.lbs (50 ft. lbs. on Loadstar and Cargostar), then back off nut $^1/_4$ turn.
2. **Series 100 and 200:** Finger tighten and insert lock so that cotter pin can be inserted with out backing off nut.

Loadstar and Cargostar: If the lock or cotter pin can be installed at this position, do so, if not, tighten to the nearest locking position and insert the cotter pin or lock.

NOTE: Bent type lockwashers must have one tab bent over the adjusting nut. With double locknuts, tighten jam nut to 100–200 ft. lbs. and bend one tab of the lockwasher over the jam nut.

All other series: Finger tighten and if possible, insert cotter pin. If not able to install cotter pin, back off the nut to the nearest hole and insert the cotter pin.

NOTE: When using the cotter pin as a lock, the long tang should be bent over the spindle end. Clip the remaining tang, leaving enough stock to bend down against the side of the nut.

Front Drive Axle

For Service on Transfer Case and Differential, see Unit Repair Section.

The front drive axles incorporate hypoid gears and use both spherical and ball joint wheel-end steering knuckles. The axle shaft assemblies are full floating and may be removed without disassembling the steering knuckles. Two types of axle shafts are used, one, a drive flange arrangement, bolted to the hub, and a second, mated to an internally splined gear, which in turn is splined and mated to the wheel hub, to transmit the driving torque to the front wheels.

LEAF SPRING

Removal and Installation

1. Raise the vehicle and support on the frame rails behind the front springs with floor stands.
2. Remove the shock absorber from the spring.
3. Remove the U-bolts, spring bumpers and retainer, or the U-bolt seat.
4. Remove the lubricators, if used.
5. Remove the nuts from the shackles and bracket pins.
6. Slide the spring off the bracket and shackle pins.
7. Remove the spring from the vehicle.
8. Installation is the reverse of removal. Tighten all nuts and bolts securely.

FRONT DRIVE AXLE

Removal and Installation

1. Jack up truck until load is removed from springs and block up frame to safely hold weight.
2. Drain lubricant from main housing and, if applicable, from wheel end housings.
3. Disconnect brakes.
4. Disconnect drag link from ball stud bracket.
5. Disconnect drive shaft from pinion shaft yoke.
6. Supporting axle with a portable floor jack, remove spring U-bolts.
7. Roll axle assembly out from under truck.
8. To install, reverse the above procedure.

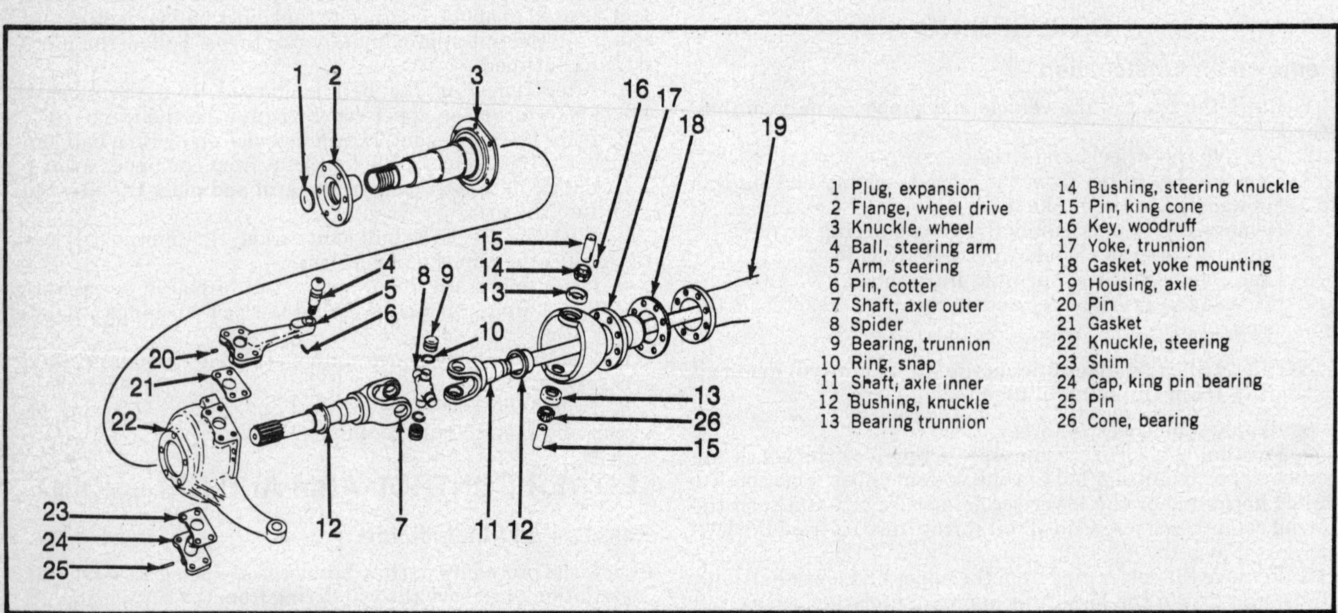

Front drive axle (© International Harvester Co.)

Adjustments

Preload on the knuckle bearings of these front axles must be maintained at all times. Check for looseness each time knuckle is lubricated.

1. Jack up front end of truck until off-center weight of the wheel is relieved (wheel just barely touching ground).
2. Remove wheel and wheel adapter from hub.
3. Disconnect tie rod and drag link.
4. Remove axle shaft.
5. To remove play (check for play by pushing and pulling on top and bottom of knuckle) and increase preload drag, turn adjusting bolt into back of knuckle. Preload should read (spring scale hooked into end of steering arm) 12 lbs.

FRONT WHEEL BEARING

Adjustment

1. Remove wheel and adapter from hub.
2. Remove axle shaft or internal gear, and adjusting nut lock plate.
3. Tighten nut until just against bearing.
4. Rotate the wheel forward and backward until a slight drag can be felt. Turn nut back to the first lock hole to obtain about a $1/2$ hole relief.
5. Bearing adjustment is correct when no play can be felt when pushing and pull at top and bottom of wheel.

Reference for overhaul procedures see International Single Reduction Rear Axle in The Unit Repair section.

AXLE SHAFT AND UNIVERSAL JOINT

Removal

AXLES HAVING DRIVE FLANGE

1. Raise vehicle, support with floor stands and remove wheel from vehicle.
2. Remove grease cap and snap-ring from end of axle shaft.
3. Remove drive flange capscrews, lockwasher, flange and gasket. If equipped with locking hubs, bend up locking tab, take out capscrews and remove clutch body. Remove hub body. Loosen setscrew and unscrew drag shoe from spindle.

NOTE: Lift off clutch body holding it erect so as not to let drive pins fall out of body. If they do fall out, be certain to install them during reassembly.

4. Remove brake drum countersunk setscrews, where applicable and remove drum.
5. Bend the lip on the wheel bearing lockwasher away from the outer wheel bearing nut and remove the nut and lockwasher. Remove wheel bearing adjusting nut (inner) and bearing lockwasher.
6. Remove the wheel hub with wheel bearing.
7. Remove backing plate and wheel spindle retaining bolts and lockwashers. Support backing plate to prevent damage to brake hose if hose is not disconnected.
8. Remove wheel bearing spindle with bushing. If spindle bushing requires replacing, press out bushing using an adapter of correct size. An alternate method of bushing removal is the use of a cape chisel or punch to collapse the bushing.
9. Pull axle shaft and universal joint assembly out of axle housing.

Installation

1. Insert axle shaft and universal joint assembly into axle housing. Position splined end of axle shaft into differential pinion gear and push into place.
2. If wheel bearing spindle bushing was removed, press new bushing into spindle using an installer tool or adapter of proper size. Lubricate ID of bushing with chassis lube when installed to provide initial lubrication. Bushing should be pressed in until bushing flange is seated against shoulder in spindle. Assemble wheel spindle and backing plate to steering knuckle. Secure with six (6) bolts and lockwashers and tighten to specifications. Connect hydraulic brake fluid line if disconnected.
3. Pack wheel bearings using a pressure lubricator or by carefully working lubricant into bearing cones by hand. Slide lubricated inner wheel bearing on spindle until it stops against spindle shoulder.
4. Apply thin coating of lubricant specified for wheel bearings to seal lip and install seal into wheel hub using an adapter of correct diameter. Lip of seal should extend towards wheel (away from backing plate assembly).
5. Assemble wheel hub on spindle. Install lubricated outer wheel bearing cone on spindle. Push cone on spindle until it rests against bearing cup.
6. Install wheel bearing lockwasher and adjusting (inner) nut. Tighten adjusting nut until there is a slight drag on the bearings when the hub is turned; then back-off approximately one-sixth turn.
7. Install tang-type lockwasher and lock nut (outer). Tighten nut and bend lockwasher tang over lock nut. If axle is equipped with locking hubs, install drag shoe on spindle and tighten setscrew.
8. Align splines of drive flange with those of axle shaft and secure drive flange and new gasket to wheel hub with capscrews and lockwashers. Tighten capscrews securely. If equipped with locking hubs, lightly lubricate hub body and clutch using a light grade chassis lubricant and install new gasket, hub body, snap-ring and hub clutch. Be certain that all drive pins are positioned in locking hub clutch when clutch is installed. Secure hub clutch to wheel hub with capscrews and lock. Tighten to specifications and bend tang over head of capscrew.
9. Install snap-ring and grease cup if not equipped with locking hubs.
10. Assemble brake drum and wheels to wheel hub. Bleed and adjust brakes.

CAUTION

Be certain that master cylinder is full of brake fluid after completing bleeding operation.

Removal

AXLES HAVING DRIVE GEAR

1. Raise and support vehicle with floor stands placed under frame rails. Remove wheel from vehicle.
2. Lightly tap alternately around edge of hub cap with hammer and screwdriver or similar tool until hub cap is removed.
3. If axle is equipped with locking hubs, remove the eight (8) socket-head setscrews securing hub clutch assembly to wheel hub assembly.

NOTE: Drive pins may fall out of hub clutch when separated from wheel hub assembly. Be certain to replace them during installation.

4. Remove retaining ring from wheel hub if equipped with locking hubs.
5. Remove snap-ring from axle shaft.
6. Pull drive gear out of wheel hub. If difficulty is encountered in removing drive gear, obtain a screwdriver or similar tool having the end bent approximately 90° with the handle. Insert end of tool into groove in drive gear and withdraw gear. If necessary, move wheel alternately backward and forward to aid removal of gear.
7. Remove retaining ring and locking hub body, if so equipped.
8. Using Wheel Bearing Adjusting Nut Wrench, remove

wheel bearing outer nut and slide lock ring off of axle shaft. Again using wrench, remove wheel bearing inner nut.

9. Pull drive gear spacer out of wheel hub.

10. Remove brake drum from wheel hub and slide wheel hub assembly off of spindle.

NOTE: Do not allow tapered roller bearings to drop on floor as bearings may be damaged.

11. Remove screws retaining grease guard to backing plate. Take off grease guard and gasket.

12. Remove the six (6) bolts securing wheel spindle and backing plate to steering knuckle. Pull spindle with bushing off of axle shaft. If spindle bushing requires replacing, press or drive out bushing using an adapter of correct size. An alternate method of bushing removal is the use of a cape chisel or punch to collapse the bushing.

13. Pull axle shaft and universal joint assembly out of axle housing.

Installation

1. Proceed with steps 1 through 5 of Axle Shaft and Universal Joint Installation (axles having drive flange).

2. Insert drive gear spacer over spindle and against outer wheel bearing cup.

3. Position wheel bearing inner adjusting nut wheel bearing adjusting nut wrench with pin in nut extending toward handle

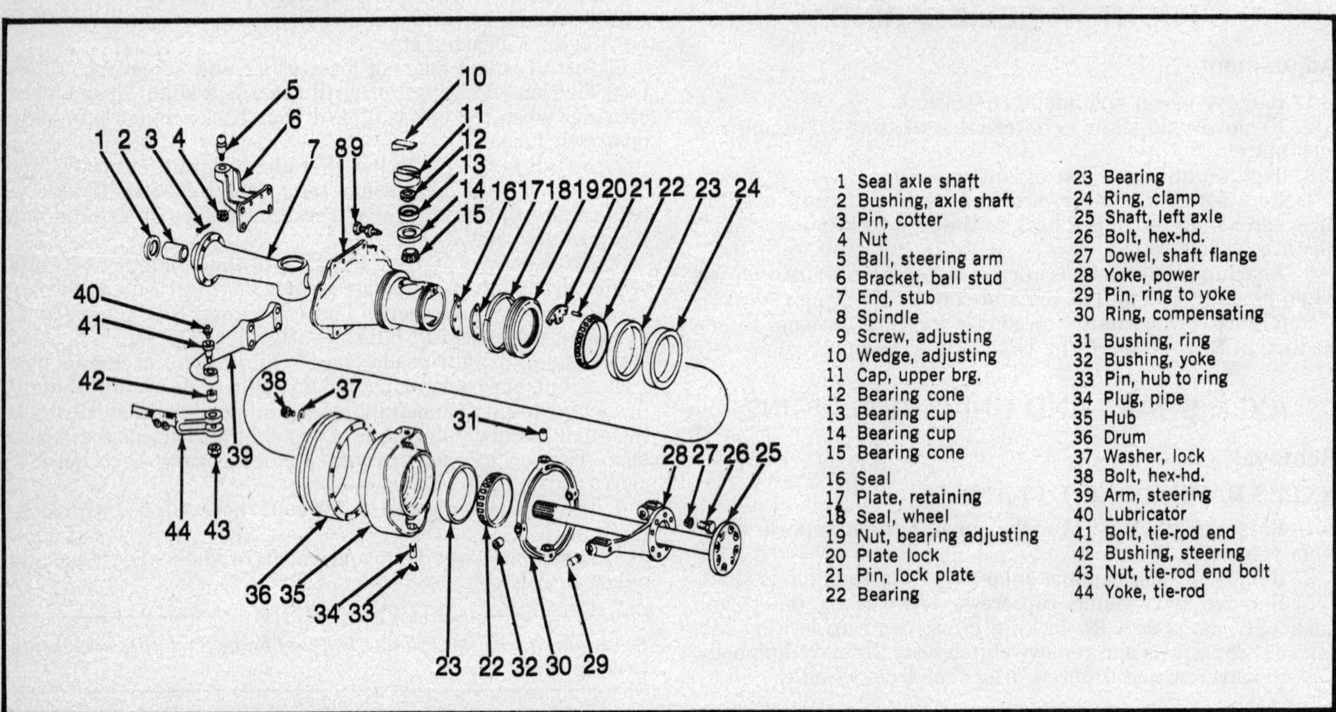

Front drive axle (drive gear type) (© International Harvester Co.)

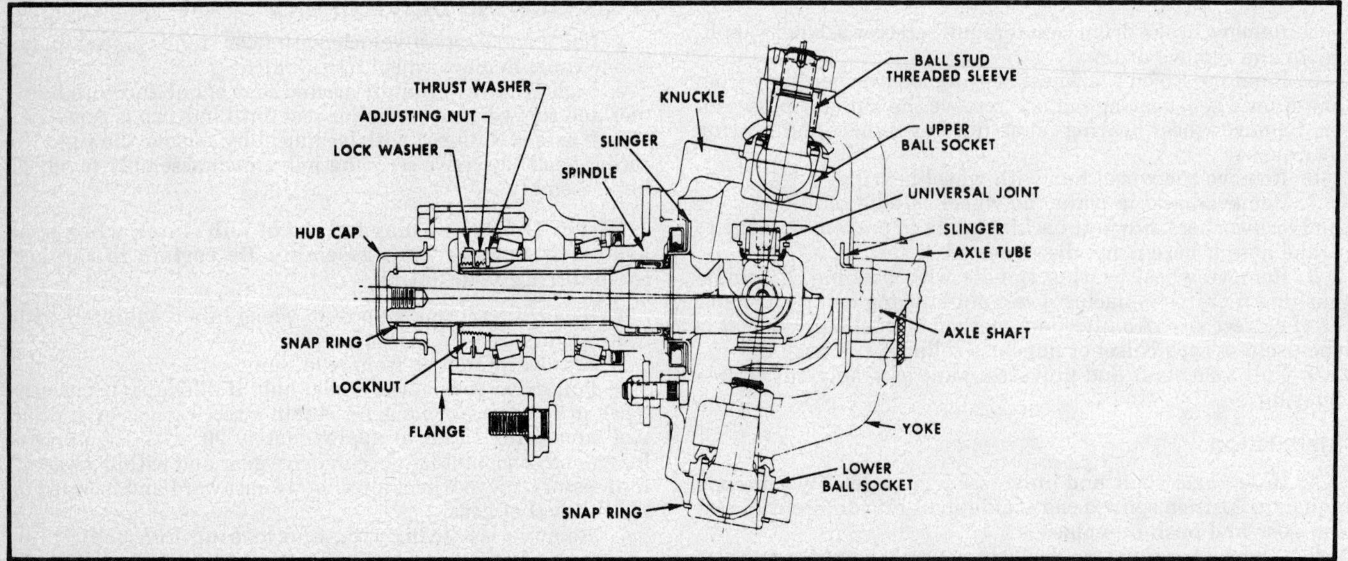

Front drive axle with 40° steer (© International Harvester Co.)

end of wrench. Install nut on spindle and tighten until it is snug against outer wheel bearing; then loosen adjusting nut $1/4$ turn. Align tang on adjusting nut lock ring with groove in wheel spindle. Slide ring on spindle and index pin on adjusting nut with hole in lock ring. If pin will not index with hole in lock ring, turn adjusting nut to the left (Loosen) until it will index.

NOTE: When attempting to index pin with hole in lock ring, turn nut very slightly since adjusting nut should be locked with first hole in lock ring past $1/4$ turn lose. Position wheel bearing outer nut in adjusting nut wrench and install on spindle. Tighten nut securely.

4. Align splines on axle shaft and splines in wheel hub with those of drive gear. Insert drive gear on axle shaft. Push gear into hub until it rests against drive gear spacer.

NOTE: Groove on side of gear must be toward hub cap.

5. If axle is equipped with locking hubs, lightly lubricate locking hub body using a light grade chassis lubricant. Align splines and insert hub body into wheel hub.
6. Install snap-ring on end of axle shaft.
7. Place retaining ring in groove in wheel hub, if equipped with locking hub.
8. If applicable, lightly grease hub clutch assembly using a light grade chassis lubricant. Be sure that all eight drive pins are positioned in the locking hub clutch. Assemble hub clutch to hub body and secure with eight socket head setscrews.
9. Position hub cap on wheel hub and lightly tap alternately around cap until flange is against edge of hub.
10. Assemble brake drum and wheel to wheel hub. Bleed and adjust brakes.

CAUTION

Be certain that the master cylinder is full of brake fluid after bleeding operation.

STEERING KNUCKLE (SPHERICAL)

Removal

1. Remove drag link at steering arm and tie-rod at steering knuckle.
2. Remove oil seal retaining bolts from inner flange of steering knuckle and remove oil seals.
3. Remove bolts and lockwashers securing king pin lower bearing cap. Remove bearing cap and shim pack. Retain shim pack for use during reassembly.
4. Remove capscrews or self-locking nuts, which ever is applicable, securing steering arm or upper bearing cap to steering knuckle.
5. Lift steering arm assembly and knuckle until bronze bearing cone will clear ball yoke. Separate steering knuckle from ball yoke.

NOTE: Do not allow lower tapered roller bearing cone to drop on floor during removal of steering knuckle.

6. Support steering knuckle and with a long brass drift, drive or press king pin out of bronze bearing cone.

NOTE: Be careful not to damage end of king pin during removal of cone.

Installation

1. Assemble steering arm to knuckle using original shim pack. Install self-locking nuts or capscrews and tighten securely.
2. Coat king pin and bronze bearing cone ID and OD with chassis lubricant to prevent galling. Align serrations of new bronze bearing cone with serrations of king pin and press cone on king pin.

NOTE: Make sure the cone is pressed all the way on or against the shoulder.

3. With bronze cone and tapered roller bearing pre-lubricated, place tapered roller bearing cone into cup at lower end of ball yoke. While retaining lower bearing cone in position, assemble steering knuckle to ball yoke. Seat bronze cone into cup at upper end of ball yoke.
4. Lubricate lower king pin with chassis lubricant and using original shim pack, install lower bearing cap to knuckle securing with bolts and lockwasher. Tighten bearing cap bolts securely.
5. Assemble opposite knuckle proceeding with instructions similar to those outlined above.
6. Individually check knuckle bearing preload by placing a torque wrench on any one (1) of the steering arm or bearing cap bolts or nuts. Read the starting torque (not rotating torque). Remove or add shims at the lower bearing cap until the specified preload is obtained. Knuckle bearing preload should be checked without ball joint oil seal, drag link or tie-rod installed.
7. Assemble the knuckle oil seals with the split on top. Knuckle retainer plate must be adjacent to ball yoke; followed by rubber seal, felt seal and metal retainer. Install seal retainer bolts and tighten securely.
8. Connect tie-rod to steering knuckle and tighten nut. Connect drag link to steering arm ball. Install cotter keys.

Cleaning, Inspection

All parts of the wheel end assembly should be thoroughly cleaned and dried with compressed air or a lint-free clean cloth.
Inspect all parts for wear, cracks or other damage. Replace all oil seals, felts and gaskets to prevent lubricant leakage.

STEERING KNUCKLE (BALL JOINT)

Removal

1. With the vehicle safely supported, remove the wheel and brake drum.
2. Remove the backing plate and the spindle from the knuckle.

NOTE: If necessary, tap the spindle lightly with a soft hammer to loosen it from the knuckle bolts. The spindle oil seal, needle bearings and bronze spacer can be removed and replaced at this time.

3. Remove the axle from the housing.

NOTE: The slingers can be removed from the axle by using pullers or tapping the axle through the slingers.

4. Disconnect and remove the tie rod from the steering arm.
5. Remove the cotter pin from the upper ball socket stud and remove the nut.
6. Remove the nut from the lower ball socket stud and discard.

NOTE: This nut is of a special torque design and should only be used one time.

7. Remove the lower ball socket snap-ring (used on 4 × 4 applications only), and unseat the upper and lower ball socket studs with a lead hammer or with a puller tool arrangement, to separate the knuckle from the yoke.

NOTE: If the upper ball socket stud remains in the yoke flange, remove it by striking it on the stud with a soft hammer.

8. With the aid of puller tools or a press and ram, remove the bottom ball socket.
9. Reverse the knuckle and remove the upper ball socket.

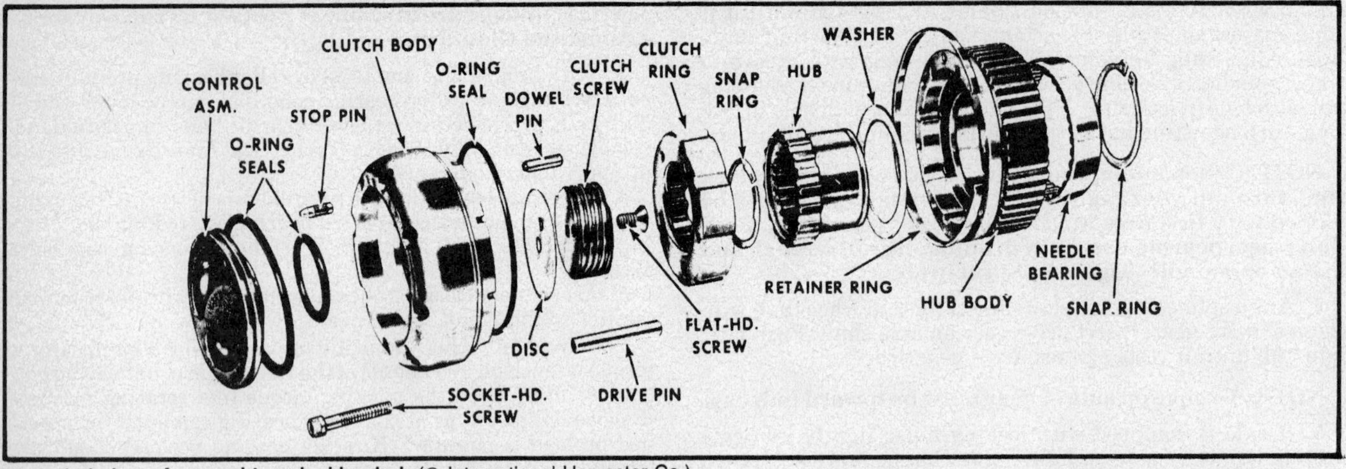

Exploded view of manual type locking hub (© International Harvester Co.)

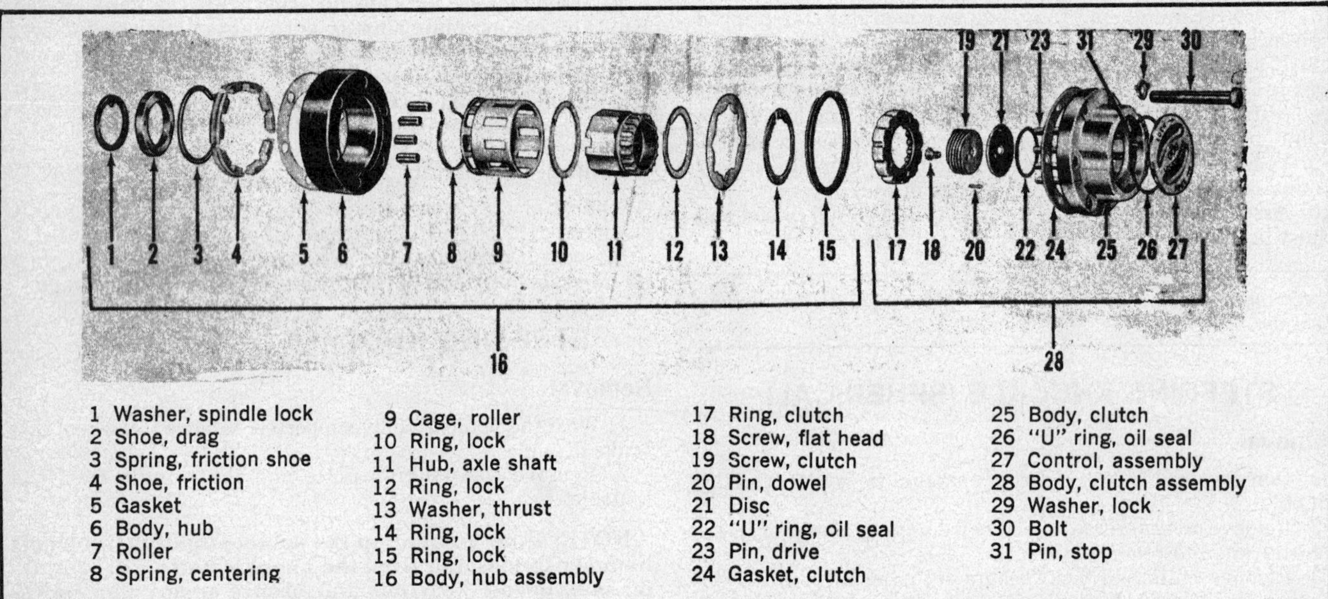

1 Washer, spindle lock
2 Shoe, drag
3 Spring, friction shoe
4 Shoe, friction
5 Gasket
6 Body, hub
7 Roller
8 Spring, centering
9 Cage, roller
10 Ring, lock
11 Hub, axle shaft
12 Ring, lock
13 Washer, thrust
14 Ring, lock
15 Ring, lock
16 Body, hub assembly
17 Ring, clutch
18 Screw, flat head
19 Screw, clutch
20 Pin, dowel
21 Disc
22 "U" ring, oil seal
23 Pin, drive
24 Gasket, clutch
25 Body, clutch
26 "U" ring, oil seal
27 Control, assembly
28 Body, clutch assembly
29 Washer, lock
30 Bolt
31 Pin, stop

Exploded view of lock-o-matic hub (© International Harvester Co.)

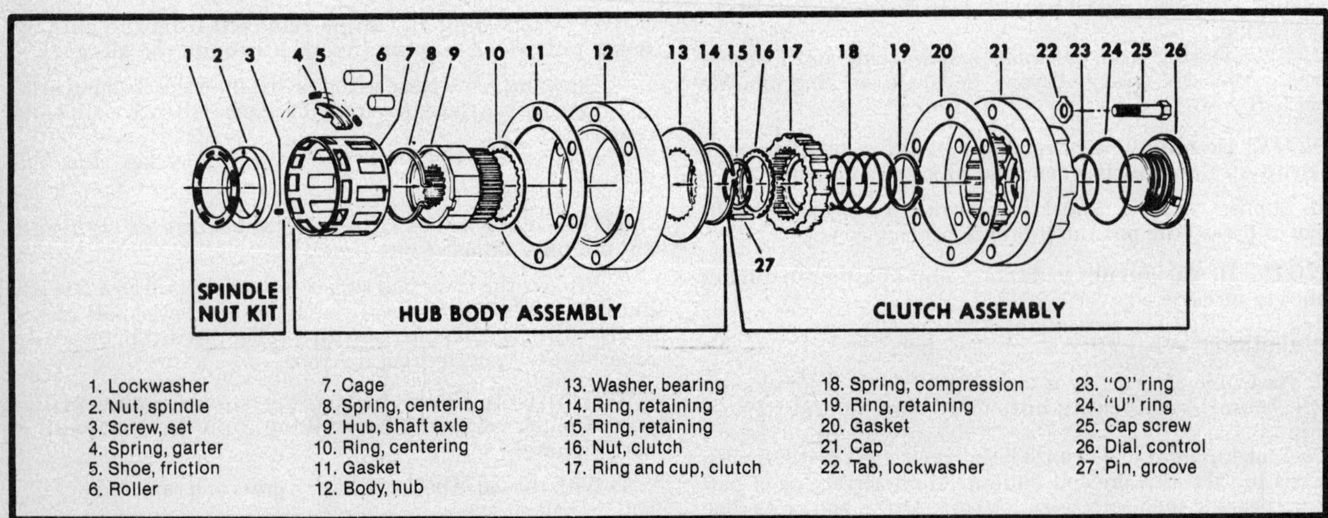

1. Lockwasher
2. Nut, spindle
3. Screw, set
4. Spring, garter
5. Shoe, friction
6. Roller
7. Cage
8. Spring, centering
9. Hub, shaft axle
10. Ring, centering
11. Gasket
12. Body, hub
13. Washer, bearing
14. Ring, retaining
15. Ring, retaining
16. Nut, clutch
17. Ring and cup, clutch
18. Spring, compression
19. Ring, retaining
20. Gasket
21. Cap
22. Tab, lockwasher
23. "O" ring
24. "U" ring
25. Cap screw
26. Dial, control
27. Pin, groove

Exploded view of the Warn automatic locking hub

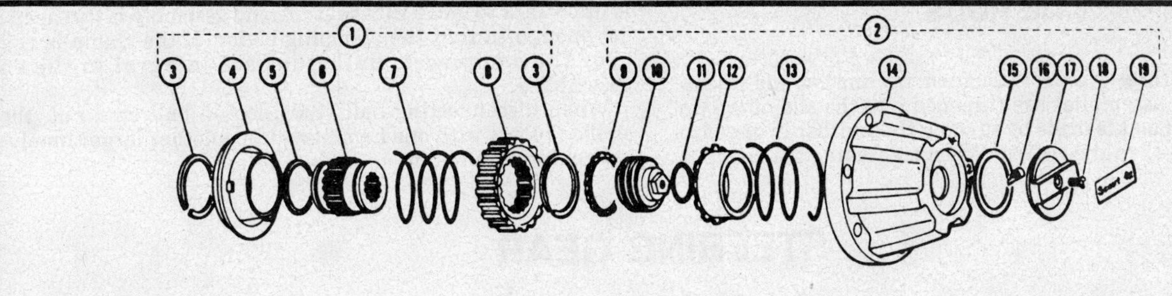

Exploded view of the Warn manual locking hub

10. With the aid of a special socket, remove the threaded sleeve in the top flange of the yoke.

Installation

1. Assemble the lower ball socket into the knuckle with a press and ram or a puller tool arrangement, making sure that the ball socket is firmly seated against the knuckle. Install the snap-ring on the 4 × 4 application.
2. Assemble the upper ball socket into the knuckle with a press and ram or a puller type tool arrangement, making sure that the ball socket is firmly seated against the knuckle.

NOTE: Use a 0.0015 inch feeler gauge blade between the socket and knuckle. The blade should not enter at the minimum area of contact.

3. Install new threaded sleeve into the top flange of the yoke, leaving approximately two threads exposed.
4. Install the knuckle assembly to the yoke, using a new nut on the lower ball socket stud. Torque the lower nut to 80 ft. lbs.
5. With the use of a special socket, torque the threaded sleeve to 50 ft. lbs. in the upper yoke flange.
6. Install the top ball socket stud nut and torque to 100 ft. lbs. Align the cotterpin holes between the stud and the castellated nut. Do not loosen nut to align the holes. Install the cotter pin.
7. Assemble the tie rod to the steering arm.
8. Assure that slingers are properly installed on the axle shaft and install the shaft into the housing.
9. Position the spindle over the axle end with the bronze bushing in place.
10. Install the backing plate and torque the nuts to 30 ft. lbs.
11. Install the hub and wheel assembly, and lower the vehicle.

CHECKING BALL SOCKETS FOR LOOSENESS

To check the ball sockets for excessive looseness, raise the vehicle and attach a dial indicator to the lower yoke or axle tube and set the indicator against the knuckle or lower ball socket, with a loaded pressure so as to read in both directions. Grasp the wheel at the top and bottom and move the wheel inward and outward. If the total indicator reading exceeds 0.020 inch, both the upper and lower ball sockets should be replaced.

FRONT DRIVE LOCKING HUBS

Two types of locking hubs are used: manual and Lock-O-Matic. Manual locking hubs are either engaged or disengaged, depending on how they are set. Lock-O-Matic hubs, when in "free" position, automatically engaged axle and wheel when forward torque is applied by the axle shaft. Thus, whenever front wheel drive is disengaged at the transmission, the wheels free wheel. "Lock" position is required only when engine braking control on the front wheel is desired.

Removal and Installation

1. Bend up tabs on mounting bolt lock washers.
2. Remove six (eight) mounting bolts using a thin-walled socket or appropriate hex wrench (externally splined type).
3. When clutch body is lifted off, immediately tilt it up so that the drive pins do not fall out.
4. Remove lock ring holding hub body onto axle shaft and pull off hub body.
5. Remove drag shoe (Lock-O-Matic only) from axle spindle by loosening hex-head set screw and unscrew drag shoe.
6. To install, reverse the above procedure.

Steering Linkage

See Unit Repair section for steering alignment procedures. See specifications at the beginning of this section for steering alignment specifications.

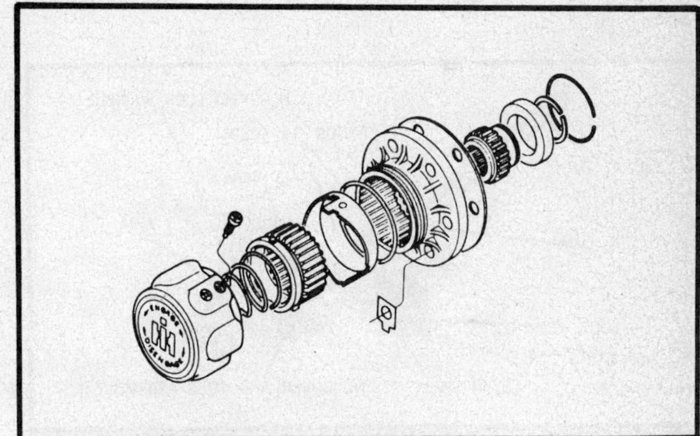

Exploded view of the Dualmatic locking hub

TIE RODS

Tie rods are of three-piece construction: rod and two end assemblies. The end assemblies are threaded into the end of the tie rod and adjustment is made by turning them either in or out to shorten or lengthen the tie rod. When tightening the clamp it is important to make sure that the end assembly is threaded in far enough so that the clamping action of the clamp is right over the end pieces. Ball studs are integral in the end assemblies.

When disconnecting ball studs, loosen ball stud nut, then strike the nut with one hammer while another larger hammer is backing up the nut.

STEERING GEAR

Manual Steering Gear

For manual steering gear overhaul, see the Unit Repair section.

Removal and Installation

1. Loosen collar clamp at bottom of steering wheel column.
2. Remove nut or loosen clamp bolt which secures steering arm to lever shaft, removing steering arm from lever shaft using a suitable puller if necessary.
3. Remove mounting bolts and steering gear assembly.
4. To install, reverse the above procedure, taking special care not to bind steering column if there is no universal joint.

TWIN STUD LEVERSHAFT TYPE

Adjustment

1. Free steering gear of all load by disconnecting drag link from steering arm and loosening bracket clamp on steering gear jacket tube.
2. To adjust end-play on cam (ball thrust bearings), loosen lock nut and adjusting screw, then unscrew four upper cover (steering column) bolts.
3. Remove (cut) or add shims, replacing and tightening down upper cover to test drag. Drag should be just slight enough so that steering wheel can be moved from lock to lock with one finger.
4. To adjust lever shaft cams for backlash, place steering wheel in middle (straight-forward) position and turn adjusting screw until very slight drag is felt through mid-position range.
5. Tighten lock nut and give final test for drag.
6. Install drag link onto levershaft and tighten clamp on steering gear jacket tube.

Triple Roller Steering Gear

1. To check cam preload, disconnect linkage from steering arm and turn steering wheel through entire range, noting lash area.

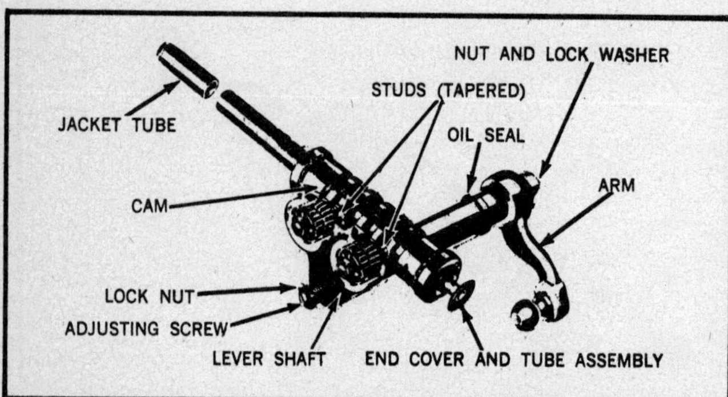

Twin stud levershaft steering gear (© International Harvester Co.)

2. Check the preload in lash area. It should be 7–13 in. lbs.
3. If adjustment is necessary, drain lubricant and remove four lower cover bolts.
4. Remove top shim with a knife, being careful not to mutilate remaining shims.
5. Replace lower cover and tighten bolts to 13–22 ft. lbs. torque.
6. Recheck preload and repeat above procedure if necessary.
7. Refill with SAE multi-purpose type gear lubricant.
8. To adjust levershaft, raise the vehicle and centralize the steering.
9. Rotate the steering 180° through center and check preload:
   S–161:2–3$^3/_8$ lbs.
   S–108 and S–165: 1$^{11}/_{16}$–3$^1/_4$ lbs.
   S–109: 2$^5/_8$–3$^7/_8$ lbs.
10. To adjust:
    a. Loosen lock nut.
    b. Turn slotted adjusting screw clockwise to increase preload; counterclockwise to decrease.
    c. When preload is within specifications, hold adjusting screw and tighten lock nut to 16–20 ft. lbs.

CAM (WORM) AND ROLLER TYPE

1. Disconnect linkage from pitman arm and drain lubricant.
2. Loosen locknut (1) at housing side cover, then turn adjusting screw (6) counterclockwise one turn to assure release of levershaft preload.
3. Turn steering wheel tube to about center of travel and check bearing preload (should register $^9/_{16}$ to 1$^1/_8$ ft. lbs. @ 9" radius).
4. If preload needs adjustment, drain lubricant and remove four housing cover bolts and housing.
5. Remove one shim.
6. Replace housing cover and bolts, torquing bolts to 18–22 ft. lbs.
7. Check preload and repeat the above procedure if necessary.
8. Adjust levershaft preload by turning adjusting screw (6). Correct levershaft preload is $^3/_4$ to 1$^1/_4$ ft. lbs. @ 9" radius (over cam preload).
9. Refill with SAE-90 SP type lubricant.

RECIRCULATING BALL TYPE

Worm Bearing Adjustment

1. Raise the vehicle and disconnect the linkage from the pitman arm.
2. Loosen the adjuster lock nut and turn the worm bearing adjuster plug clockwise.
3. Using a spring scale attached to the steering wheel, pull at a right angle to the wheel spoke, and measure the pull required to keep the wheel moving.
4. Turn the adjuster plug until a pull of 14–18 inch lbs is obtained on the spring scale.

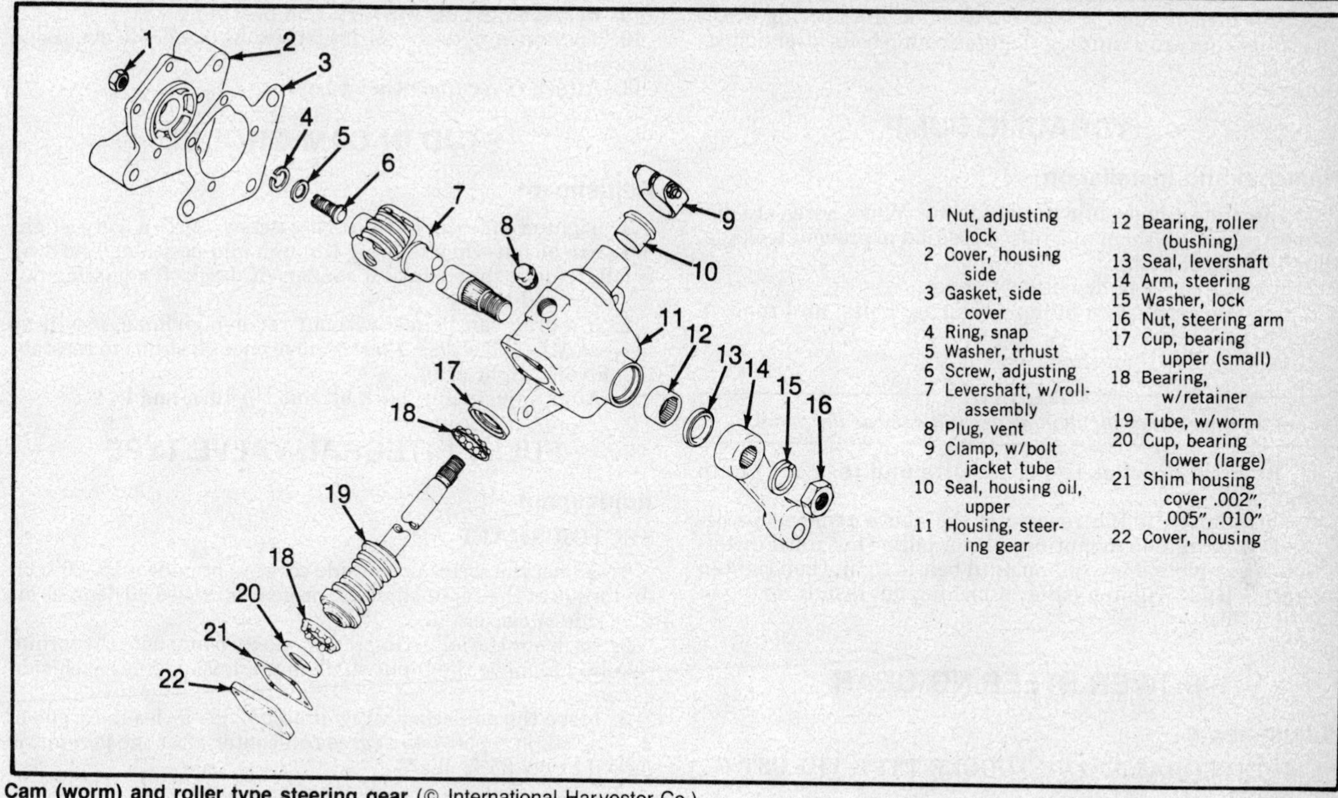

Cam (worm) and roller type steering gear (© International Harvester Co.)

5. Tighten the adjuster plug lock nut and recheck worm bearing preload. Readjust if necessary.

Pitman Shaft Preload Adjustment

1. Center the steering wheel by turning wheel from the extreme right to the extreme left position, counting the exact number of turns.
2. Return the steering wheel to the exact half-way position and mark the wheel.
3. Loosen the preload adjuster lock nut and turn the adjuster clockwise until all lash between the gears is removed.
4. Tighten the locknut and as outlined previously, with the aid of a spring scale, pull the steering wheel through the center position. The pull pressure should be 24–30 inch lbs
5. After all adjustments have been made, reconnect the steering linkage to the pitman arm. Lower the vehicle.

Steering Wheel Alignment

1. Set front wheels in a straight-ahead position. This can be checked by driving the vehicle a short distance on a flat surface to determine steering wheel position when vehicle is following a straight path.
2. Raise vehicle and check number of turns required from center point to extreme right and left. The number of turns should be the same in each direction.
3. If step 2 moves wheels off of straight-ahead, loosen adjusting sleeve clamps on both left and right-hand tie rods, then turn both sleeves an equal number of turns in the same direction to bring gear back on high point.

Power Steering Gear

For overhaul of power steering systems, see the Unit Repair Section.

IN-LINE BOOSTER

Removal and Installation

1. Disconnect and plug hydraulic lines from valve and cylinder unit.
2. Loosen clamp bolts and disconnect cylinder link from cylinder.
3. Remove nut and lockwasher from piston rod and remove rod from frame bracket.
4. Loosen clamp bolt and unscrew cylinder assembly from pivot on relay.
5. Installation is the reverse of the above procedure. Be sure to center steering wheel and wheels before tightening clamp bolts of cylinder link. Bleed hydraulic system.

HYDRAULIC CYLINDER

Removal

1. Disconnect hydraulic lines from cylinder and plug lines.
2. Unbolt piston rod from frame bracket, noting approximate position of clamp.
3. Disconnect cylinder assembly from steering linkage.
4. Installation is the reverse of the above procedure. Approximate original position of clamp on piston rod, center adjusting steering wheel if necessary.

SEPARATE CONTROL VALVE

Removal

1. Disconnect and plug hydraulic lines from control valve.
2. Loosen clamp bolts at each end of control valve and remove valve.
3. Installation is the reverse of removal. Since the control valve in this type of power steering system serves, in a sense,

as a relay arm, it must be adjusted to center the steering wheel for straight-forward running. Tighten clamp bolts after adjustment is made.

HYDRAULIC PUMP

Removal and Installation

1. Disconnect hydraulic lines at pump. When hoses are disconnected, secure them in a raised position to prevent leakage. Plug fittings of pump.
2. Remove drive pulley attaching nut.
3. Loosen bracket-to-pump mounting bolts, and remove pump belt.
4. Slide pulley from shaft.

CAUTION

Do not hammer pulley off shaft as this will damage the pump.

5. Remove bracket-to-pump bolts and take off pump assembly.
6. Installation is the reverse of the above removal procedure. Do not tighten mounting bolts or pulley nut until installation is complete. Move pump until belt is tight, then tighten mounting bolts. Tighten pulley attaching nut last, torquing to 35–45 ft. lbs.

POWER STEERING GEAR

Adjustments

SEMI-INTEGRAL VALVE TOGGLE TYPE THRUST BEARING ADJUSTMENT

1. Free steering gear of load by disconnecting drag link.
2. Turn gear off center to free stud in the cam groove.
3. Remove yoke and joint assembly from stub shaft.
4. Remove key from stub shaft.
5. Remove upper cover.
6. Reassemble actuator housing screws with a $^{3}/_{8}''$ thick spacer under each head to hold actuator and cam assembly in the gear.
7. Remove the adjusting nut, lockwasher, thrust washer and thrust housing.
8. Clean threads on nut and camshaft so that nut can be run freely by hand.
9. Reassemble nut, washers, and bearing.
10. Tighten nut to 10 ft. lbs., then back off 10–20°. Bend locknut.
11. Attach cover and other parts.

STUD IN CAM GROOVE

Adjustment

1. Tighten side cover adjusting screw until a very slight drag can be felt when turning through mid-position. If no drag is felt, remove shims until it can be felt. Back off adjusting nut $^{1}/_{16}$ turn and lock.
2. If a drag can be felt without removing shims, it will be necessary to add shims, then remove enough shims to reestablish a very slight drag.
3. After adjustment, back off nut $^{1}/_{16}$ turn and lock.

FULLY INTEGRAL VALVE TYPE

Adjustment

SECTOR SHAFT

1. Adjust the screw in the side cover to provide a 15–20 inch lbs torque at the input shaft as the gear is moved 90 degrees either side of center.
2. Back out the adjusting screw one turn and note the torque required to move the input shaft through 90 degrees each side of center.
3. Move the adjusting screw in to provide a rise in torque of 2–4 in. lbs. at a point 45 degrees off center after the jam nut is locked at 20–25 ft. lbs.

NOTE: Input torque of the completely assembled gear unit less oil, should not exceed 15 in. lbs. over full travel of 95 degrees at the output shaft.

VALVE THRUST BEARINGS

NOTE: The upper housing must be removed for this adjustment procedure.

1. Tighten the adjusting nut until all play is removed from the bearings and zero preload exists.
2. Back off the nut approximately 20 degrees and bend one tang of the lock washer into a matching slot in the adjusting nut.

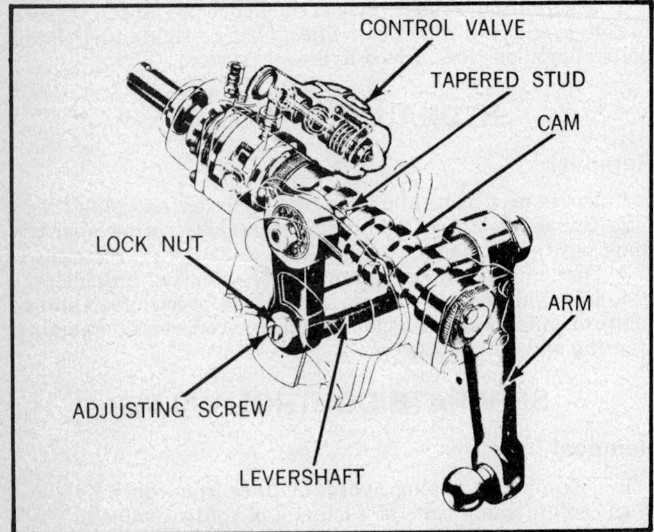

Power steering gear with toggle type integral valve (© International Harvester Co.)

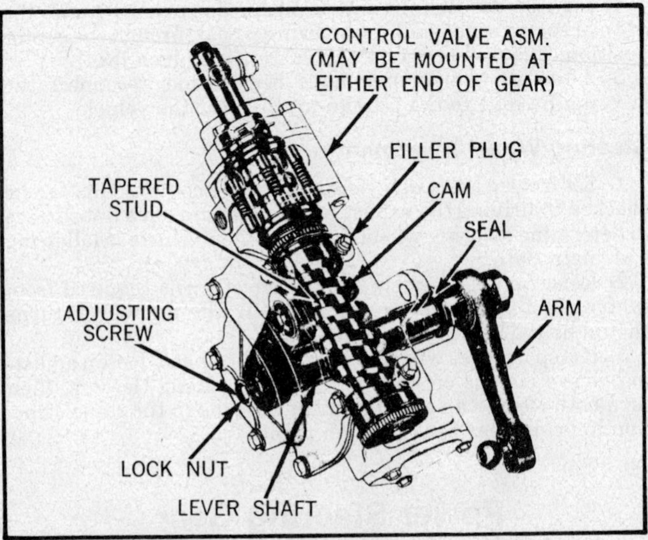

Model S36 power steering gear with integral concentric valve (© International Harvester Co.)

3. Check for free rotation of the valve on the shaft and for any perceptible end-play. The assembly should rotate at 3–5 in. lbs.

PRESSURE RELIEF VALVE

1. Install a suitable pressure gauge in the line between the pump and the steering valve pressure port.
2. Actuate the steering to provide full travel to the wheel stops and note the pressure reading on the gauge.
3. Adjust the pressure relief screw in a clockwise direction to provide a pressure of at 400 psi below the maximum operating pressure.

NOTE: Care should be exercised not to hold the pressure for more than 15 seconds, while the adjustment is being made or damage to the pump from excess heat can result.

4. Repeat the above procedure for the other direction of steering.

Full and Semi-Integral Steering Gear

Removal and Installation

1. Remove horn button from steering wheel. Unscrew retaining screws and remove base plate assembly. Remove steering wheel nut.
2. Using a suitable puller, remove steering wheel. Loosen nut on steering column shaft collar and remove steering column shaft from gear. Retain woodruff key.

NOTE: Where the steering column is the jointed type, the steering column and wheel need not be removed.

3. Using suitable puller, remove pitman arm from levershaft.
4. Identify hydraulic connecting lines by tagging and marking the valve ports to which they are connected. Disconnect hydraulic lines from valve. Plug all openings.
5. Remove mounting flange bolts and remove gear from chassis.
6. To install, mount steering gear in chassis and fasten securely.
7. Place woodruff key in stud end of steering gear and install collar of steering column shaft. Secure with bolt and nut.
8. Center steering gear. Center steering wheel. Set front wheels straight ahead.
9. Connect drag link to ball on steering arm.
10. Install steering arm on levershaft of gear. If arm does not line up with splines of shaft, turn steering wheel to the right of left $\frac{1}{4}$ turn until it does.
11. Secure arm to levershaft with lockwasher and nut. Tighten nut to 250 ft. lbs.
12. Install hydraulic lines to control valve.
13. Fill the steering gear housing with the specified lubricant on the semi-integral power steering units.
14. Fill the Power steering reservoir with the recommended fluid and bleed the system.

OUTPUT SHAFT PRELOAD

Adjustment

INTEGRAL ROTARY VALVE TYPE

1. Position steering in the straight-ahead position. Check for lash by moving steering wheel. If there is steering wheel movement without moving the steering arm, over-center adjustment must be made.
2. Disconnect steering arm and remove horn ring.
3. Position steering wheel at center of travel, then turn $\frac{1}{2}$ turn off center.

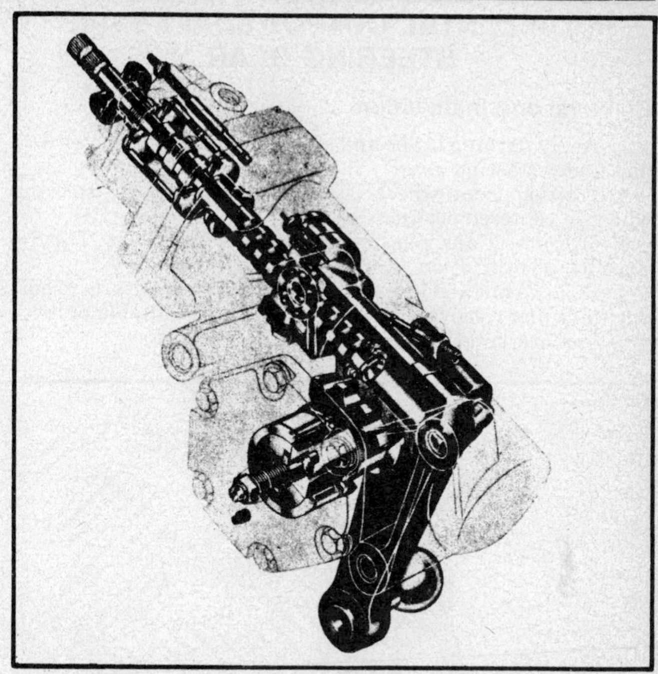

Types S261, 277, 301, 302, 320, 322, 323 and 325 integral power steering gear (© International Harvester Co.)

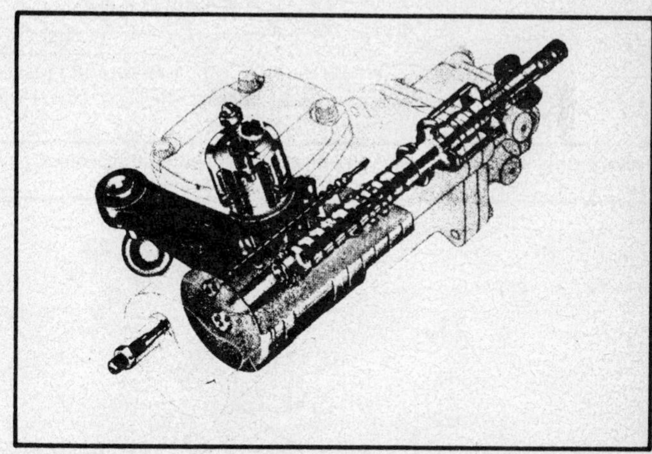

Types S276 and 299 integral power steering gear (© International Harvester Co.)

4. Using an inch pound torque wrench and socket on the steering wheel retaining nut, determine the torque required to rotate the shaft slowly through a 20–degree arc. Turn gear to center and take a second reading. If second torque reading is 4–8 in. lbs. in excess of first reading, no preload adjustment is necessary.
5. If adjustment is required, loosen adjuster screw locknut and turn screw until second reading exceeds first reading by 4–8 in. lbs.
6. Tighten locknut while holding adjusting screw in place to 27–37 ft. lbs. torque.
7. Recheck torque reading after adjustment is made.
8. Install steering arm, tightening nut to 120–125 ft. lbs. torque.
9. Install horn ring.

HORIZONTAL OUTPUT SHAFT TYPE STEERING GEAR

Removal and Installation

1. Apply parking brake and raise front of vehicle. Place drip pan under steering gear.
2. Position front wheels straight ahead and tie steering wheel in centered position.
3. Disconnect and plug hydraulic lines from gear. Tag the lines for identification.
4. Remove nut and lockwasher securing steering arm to output shaft and remove arm from shaft with a suitable puller.
5. Remove lower flexible coupling clamp bolt.
6. Remove steering gear mounting bolts and remove gear from chassis.
7. To install, set gear assembly on center and position gear in chassis.
8. Insert gear stub shaft into lower flexible coupling and install and tighten gear mounting bolts to 55–60 ft. lbs. torque.
9. Install and tighten lower flexible coupling bolt clamp to 30–35 ft. lbs. torque.
10. With steering wheel centered and front wheels straight ahead, place steering arm on output shaft by matching master serrations of arm with shaft. Secure arm to shaft with lockwasher and nut, tightening nut to 120–125 ft. lbs. torque. Untie steering wheel.
11. Remove plugs and connect hydraulic lines to proper ports,

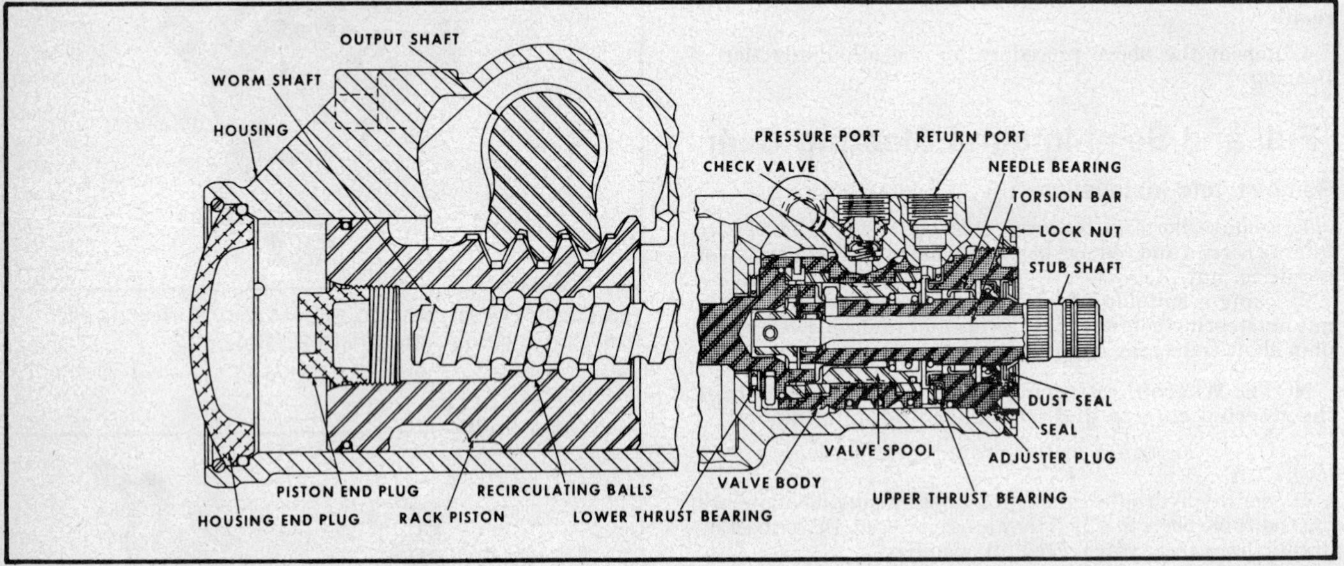

Rotary valve type power steering gear (© International Harvester Co.)

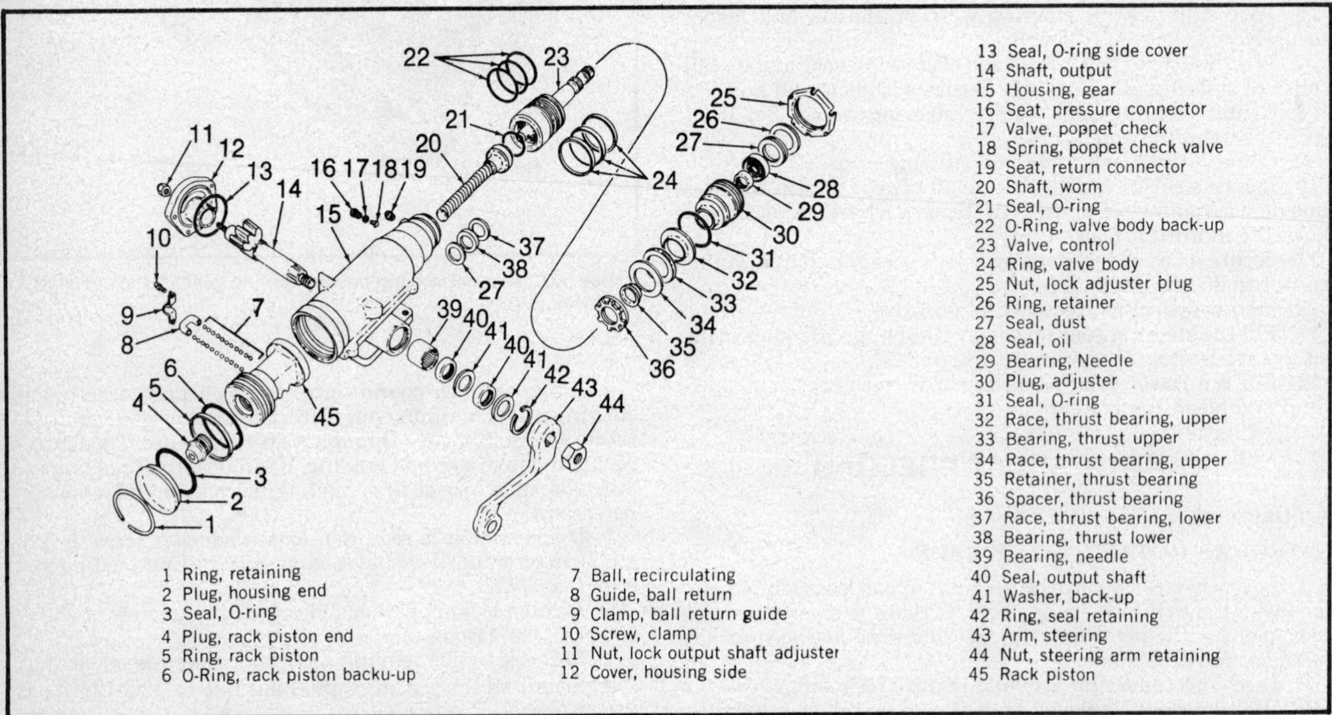

Integral rotary type power steering gear (© International Harvester Co.)

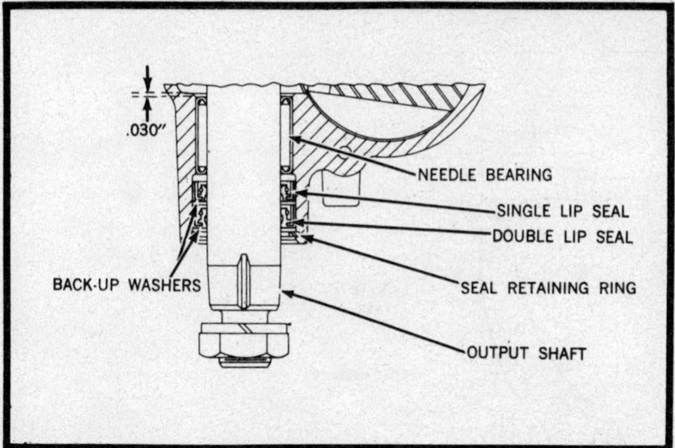

Correct installation of output shaft seal and bearing S281 and 282 (© International Harvester Co.)

tightening connections to 20–30 ft. lbs. torque.

12. Fill power steering system with fluid and start engine. Bleed system.
13. Check system for operation and leaks.
14. Remove drip pan and lower vehicle.

VERTICAL OUTPUT SHAFT TYPE STEERING GEAR

Removal and Installation

1. Follow steps 1 through 6 of the horizontal shaft gear removal above, leaving out step 2 (centering and tying steering wheel). Disconnect battery cables, remove battery and battery box from chassis to permit gear removal.
2. To install, follow steps 7 through 11 of horizontal output shaft gear installation described above.
3. Install battery box, battery and cables.
4. Follow steps 12 through 14 of horizontal output shaft installation described above.

POWER SYSTEM

Bleeding

1. Fill pump reservoir to correct level with fluid.
2. Start engine and turn steering wheel through entire travel two or three times. This will permit air to escape and be replaced with fluid.
3. Check fluid level and refill if necessary.

NOTE: A bleeder screw has been added to the power steering gear housing (Ross HFB – 64) on the CO9670 vehicles equipped with power steering. This manual bleeder screw, is located at the top of the steering hear housing. The following procedure are for bleeding the air from this power steering system.

1. Fill the power steering reservoir until it is almost full. Crank the engine for 10 seconds without letting it start. If the engine does start, shut the engine down immediately. Check and refill the reservoir, repeat this step at least three times and each time checking and refilling the reservoir.

NOTE: Do not allow the fluid to drop significantly or run low in the reservoir, as this will induce air into the system.

2. Start the engine and let it idle for two minutes. Shut the engine off and check the fluid level in the reservoir. With the engine idling, steer the gear from full left turn to full right turn several times.
3. Now with the steering gear in the straight ahead position, loosen the manual bleeder screw using a $^5/_{16}$ socket. Loosen the screw about one turn.
4. Allow air and aerated fluid to bleed out around the bleeder screw until only clear fluid is discharged. Close the bleeder screw and check the reservoir.

NOTE: Do not turn the steering wheel while the bleeder screw is open, as this will induce air into the system.

5. Repeat step 2 three or four times, starting the steering maneuver with the bleeder screw closed, until only clear fluid is discharged when the bleeder screw is opened. Torque the bleeder screw to 27 to 33 ft. lbs. check and refill the reservoir, as necessary.

CLUTCH

NOTE: Due to the various medium and heavy duty truck models and different power combinations used, the clutch operating clearances and specifications are given in the owner-operator manual, accompanying each truck. The clutch release bearing may be actuated by mechanical, hydraulic, or a combination of air over hydraulic means, and for this reason the owner-operator manual should be referred to regarding the free travel and pedal height measurement for the particular model being serviced.

Hydraulic Clutch

Adjustment

LIGHT DUTY VEHICLES

1. Check clutch pedal height. If it is not approximately $7^3/_4$ in. from the floorboard (measured at right angles from floorboard), loosen two bolts on the clutch pedal stop bracket and move bracket either way until proper pedal height is achieved. Tighten bracket mounting bolts.
2. Clutch pedal push rod to master cylinder piston clearance is adjusted by loosening the locknut on the pushrod and turning the rod either in or out until $^3/_{16}$ in. is obtained before the clutch pedal push rod contacts the master cylinder. Tighten locknut on pushrod and recheck pedal stroke.
3. Release bearing to clutch lever (finger) clearance is adjusted at the slave cylinder pushrod. Measure stroke of clutch pedal required to produce contact of clutch release bearing to clutch release levers. If it is not $1^7/_8$" ± $^1/_8$", loosen locknut on slave cylinder pushrod and rotate pushrod either in or out until proper pedal travel is obtained. Tighten locknut on pushrod and recheck pedal free travel.

MEDIUM AND HEAVY DUTY VEHICLES

1. Clutch pedal pushrod stroke adjustment is made by disconnecting clutch pedal from pushrod (remove yoke pin). Holding master cylinder pushrod out snugly against the stop in the end of the cylinder and making sure that the spring is holding the clutch pedal against its stop, adjust yoke on pushrod until

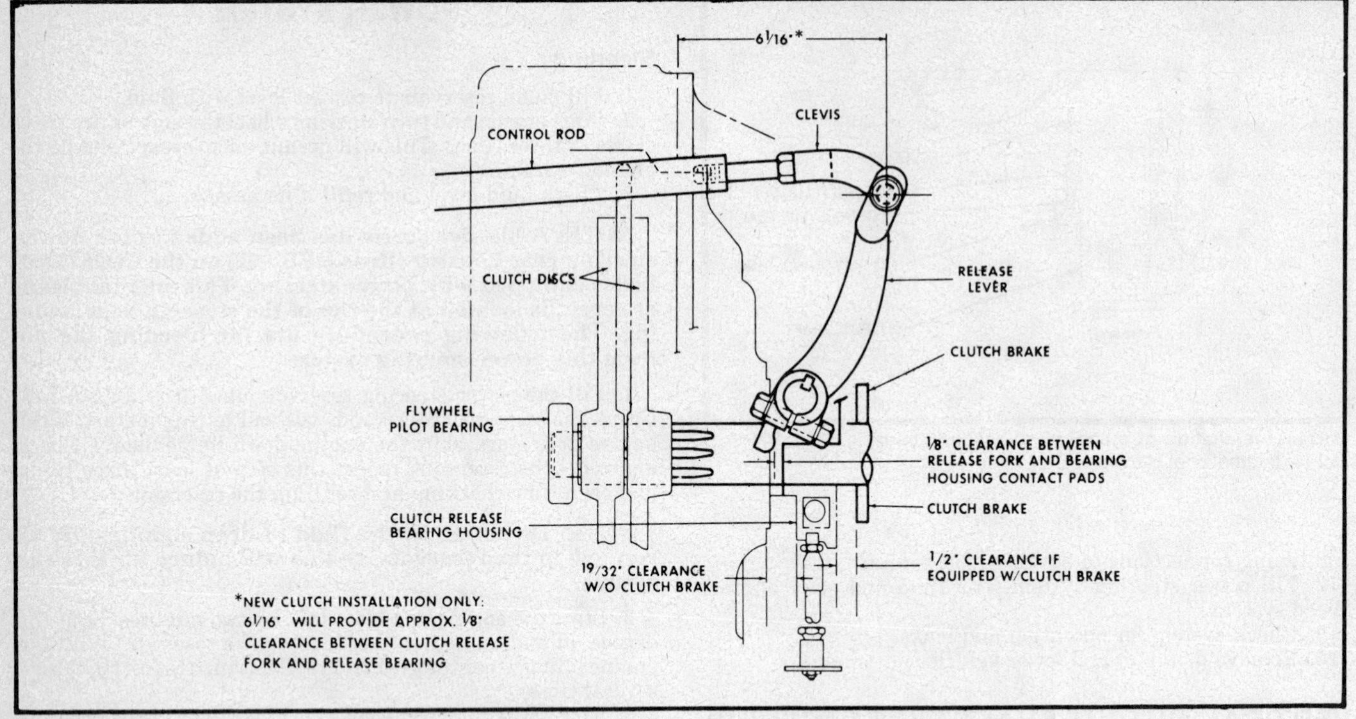

Clutch clearance—heavy duty vehicles with two clutch discs (© International Harvester Co.)

yoke can be connected to pedal. Install yoke pin and cotter pin. Tighten locknut on yoke. A clutch pedal free travel of $^5/_{16}$" should result.

2. Clutch finger to bearing clearance is adjusted at the slave cylinder pushrod. Clutch pedal should travel $1^1/_2$" before clutch bearing makes contact with release fingers. Loosen locknut on slave cylinder pushrod and turn pushrod to obtain correct pedal travel. Tighten locknut and recheck pedal travel.

SLAVE CYLINDER

Adjustment

PUSH TYPE CLUTCH

1. First make sure that the clutch pedal is properly adjusted. If it is not, adjust as necessary.
2. Remove the slave cylinder return spring, loosen the adjusting yoke locknut and disconnect yoke from the release shaft lever.
3. Adjust the slave cylinder push rod by turning the adjusting yoke until the clutch release bearing contacts the pressure plate and the slave cylinder piston is bottomed out, with the adjusting yoke pin installed.
4. Shorten the slave cylinder push rod, turning the adjusting yoke five turns from the position established in the next step, to obtain the proper release bearing clearance.
5. Install the yoke pin and retainer, then tighten the adjusting yoke locknut. Reinstall the slave cylinder return spring. Road test the vehicle to check for proper clutch operation.

PULL TYPE CLUTCH

1. First make sure that the clutch pedal is properly adjusted. If it is not, adjust as necessary.
2. Disconnect the slave cylinder adjusting yoke. Adjust the slave cylinder push rod as necessary to obtain $^1/_8$ in. clearance between the release shaft fork and release bearing housing, with the yoke pin installed and the slave cylinder bottom out in the housing.

MECHANICALLY CONTROLLED LINKAGE OR CABLE

Adjustment

LIGHT DUTY VEHICLES

1. Measure and correct the clutch pedal height to approximately 9 in.

NOTE: On some models it may be necessary to increase the clutch pedal height setting slightly over the amount specified, in order to obtain complete clutch release.

2. Disconnect the return spring on release fork.
3. Loosen the nut on the cable or linkage rod.
4. Hold the pedal assembly against the pedal stop and lengthen or shorten the rod or cable to obtain zero clearance at the release bearing face and the pressure plate fingers.
5. After obtaining zero clearance, lengthen or shorten cable or linkage to obtain $^3/_{32}$ in. between the bearing face and the fingers of the pressure plate.
6. Tighten nut on the cable or linkage rod.
7. Reconnect the return spring.

MEDIUM AND HEAVY DUTY VEHICLES

EXTERNAL ADJUSTMENT

NOTE: Refer to the owner-operator manual for the correct free travel and pedal height for the particular model being serviced.

1. In general, the mechanically controlled clutch should have $1^1/_2$ inch of free travel before the clutch begins to disengage.
2. Pedal clearance or free travel in the linkage must be sufficient to prevent the clutch from being partially disengaged. A clearance of $^1/_8$ inch should be maintained between the yoke fingers and the release bearing wear pads.

3. Slave cylinder air assist units must have an average of $\frac{1}{2}$ inch clutch release bearing travel for proper release.

INTERNAL ADJUSTMENT

1. Remove the clutch housing inspection cover.
2. Inspect the running clearance between the release fork and the bearing housing for $\frac{1}{8}$ inch clearance.
3. Inspect the clearance between the release bearing and the clutch brake (if equipped with a clutch brake), or the clearance between the clutch cover hub and the release bearing housing (if not equipped with a clutch brake).

NOTE: Gauges of proper thickness can be fabricated locally.

a. Vehicles with clutch brake - Weld $\frac{1}{2}$ inch stock material to a handle to check the gap between the release bearing and the clutch brake assembly and use a $\frac{1}{8}$ inch wire rod to check the release bearing to release lever clearance.

b. Vehicles with out clutch brake - Weld a $\frac{19}{32}$ in. stock material to a handle to check the gap between the release bearing and the clutch cover hub. The same $\frac{1}{8}$ inch rod as used above, can be used to check the clearance between the release bearing and the release lever.

4. If the clearances are more or less than specified, readjust as follows:

a. Rotate the engine flywheel until the adjusting ring lock is exposed. Remove the lock bolt and pry the lock free of the adjuster ring.

CAUTION

Lock is spring loaded.

b. Release clutch by blocking the pedal in the depressed position.

c. Turn the clutch adjusting ring counterclockwise to move the release bearing housing towards the flywheel and clockwise to move the bearing housing away from the flywheel.

NOTE: Rotation of one lug position will move the release bearing housing approximately $\frac{1}{32}$ inch.

d. Re-engage the clutch and check clearance. Readjust as necessary.

e. Install the lock plate, bolt and washer and install the clutch housing cover plate.

CLUTCH MASTER CYLINDER

Removal and Installation

1. Remove hydraulic line from master cylinder and remove yoke pins connecting pedal to master cylinder pushrod. On models with dual cylinders (brake/clutch integral unit), disconnect brake hydraulic line, stoplight switch wire and brake pedal. If the fluid reservoir is separate from the cylinder unit, disconnect reservoir fluid line.
2. Remove cylinder assembly mounting bolts and remove cylinder.
3. To install, first mount the cylinder unit, then connect hydraulic lines.
4. Adjust clutch pedal as described above.
5. Bleed hydraulic clutch system.

SLAVE CYLINDER

Removal and Installation

1. Disconnect slave cylinder pushrod from clutch release lever.
2. Disconnect hydraulic line.
3. Unbolt and remove slave cylinder unit.

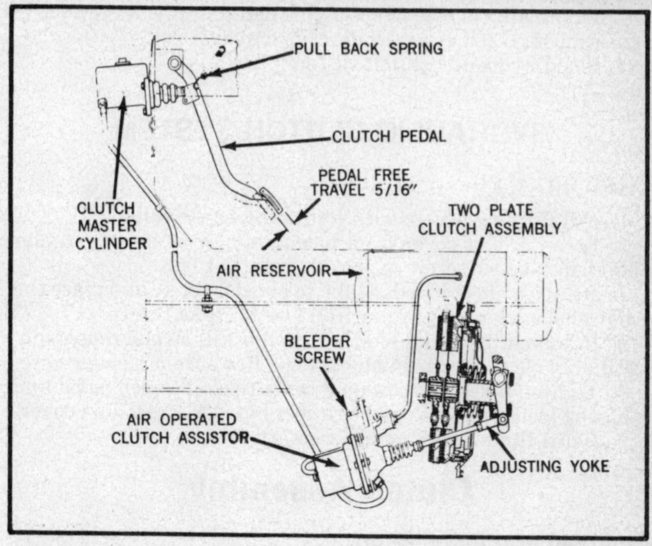

Clutch control diagram—combination air-hydraulic (© International Harvester Co.)

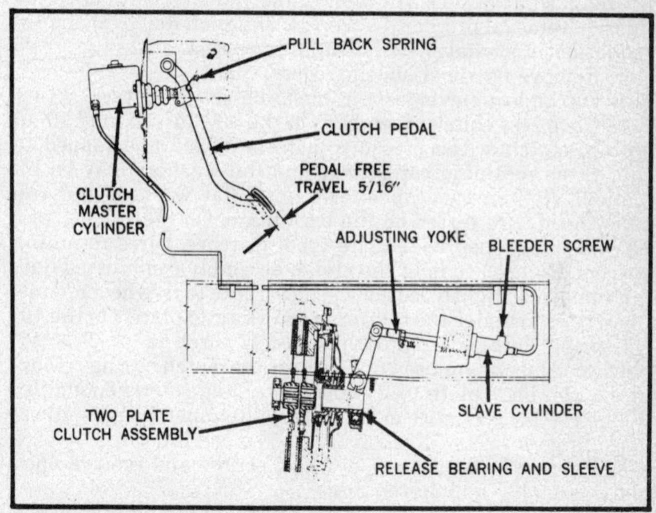

Clutch control diagram—hydraulic (© International Harvester Co.)

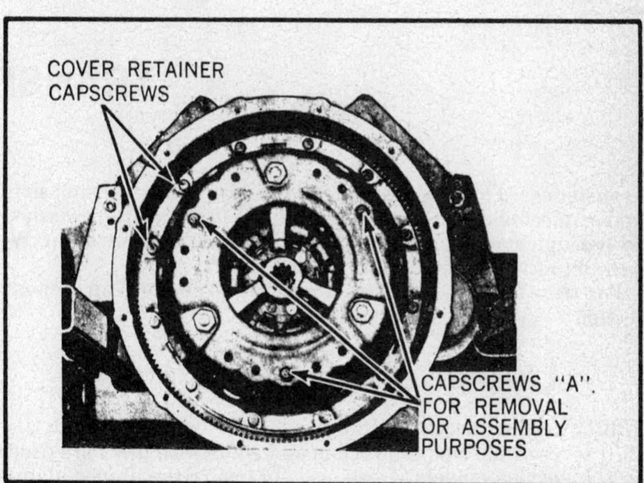

Clutch compression cap screws (© International Harvester Co.)

4. To install, reverse Steps 1 through 3.
5. Adjust clutch pedal as described above.
6. Bleed hydraulic clutch system.

HYDRAULIC CLUTCH SYSTEM

Bleeding

1. Fill fluid reservoir with hydraulic brake fluid.
2. Remove dust cover from bleeder screw on slave cylinder and open bleeder screw approximately $^3/_4$ turn.
3. Attach a short bleeder tube to bleeder screw and place the other end in clear container filled with brake fluid.
4. Pump clutch pedal slowly through full stroke repeatedly until only clear (no air bubbles) fluid flows from bleeder hose.
5. Tighten bleeder screw on down stroke of clutch pedal and remove bleeder tube. Replace rubber bleeder screw dust cover.
6. Refill fluid reservoir if necessary.

Clutch Assembly

Removal and Installation

1. Remove transmission. Extreme care should be taken to support the transmission until it is completely removed so that the main shaft splines will clear the driven member. For transmission removal procedures see Transmission Removal and Installation immediately following this section.
2. Remove flywheel housing cover.
3. Disconnect clevis yoke from clutch release lever.
4. Compress clutch assembly. On the 13", 14", 15" and 10" (9 spring) clutches, the pressure plate is drilled and tapped so that three retaining cap screws and flat washers may be installed. Tighten the cap screws until flat washers and cap screw heads are seated on the back plate. On the 11", 12" and 10" (6 spring, open back plate type) clutches, three retaining spacers are used to hold the clutch assembly compressed during removal. Slightly loosen the back plate to flywheel mounting screws to wedge the retaining spacers into place. On the 10" six spring (full back plate type) clutch, three $^5/_8$" × 3" × $^1/_4$" hardwood blocks are used to compress the clutch during removal. Loosen back plate to flywheel retaining screws enough to wedge the blocks between the back plate inner flange and release fingers.
5. Remove back plate to flywheel screws and remove back plate assembly and driven disc.
6. When removing the clutch assembly, observe that the balance mark (spot of white paint) on the back plate flange is located as near as possible to the balance mark ("L") stamped on the flywheel face. These balance marks should be located in the same relative position at clutch installation. If there are no marks, scribe a line to indicate correct position.
7. To install clutch, position the clutch driven member so that the long portion of the hub is toward the rear (all except the 10" 6 spring open back plate type, which may be fitted either way). Clutch must be compressed for correct installation.
8. Place clutch assembly over the driven member on the flywheel so that the balance mark (spot of white paint) is as near as possible to the flywheel balance mark ("L"). Loosely install two or three back plate to flywheel mounting screws.
9. Using a clutch aligning arbor or transmission main drive gear shaft to hold the driven member in place, complete installation of the remaining back plate to flywheel mounting screws and lockwashers. Tighten capscrews alternately and evenly.
10. Remove retaining capscrews, wood blocks or retaining spacers which were used to hold the clutch compressed.
11. Install transmission as described in Transmission Removal and Installation.
12. Connect linkage to clutch release lever.
13. Install flywheel housing cover.
14. If the vehicle is equipped with a hydraulic system, bleed the system and refill the reservoir with hydraulic fluid.
15. If the vehicle is equipped with the manual type linkage or cable, adjust as outlined.

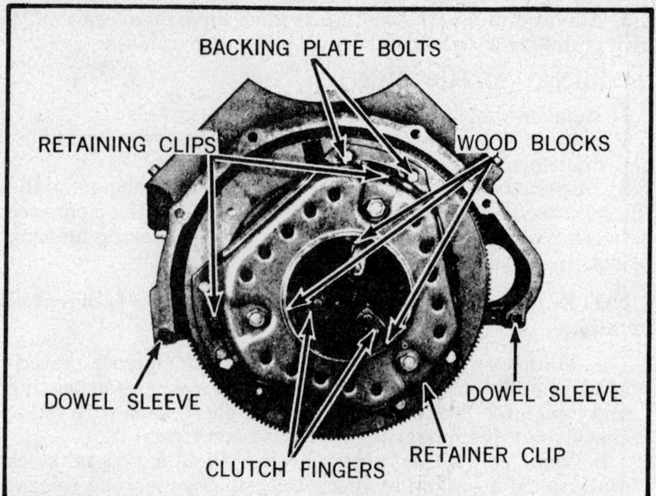

Using wood blocks to compress clutch fingers (© International Harvester Co.)

TRANSFER CASE

Transfer cases may be mounted to the rear of the transmission and connected directly to the output shaft of the transmission by a coupler, or may be mounted to a crossmember and connected to the transmission by a driveshaft.

For transfer case overhaul procedures, see the Unit Repair section.

Linkage and Cable Controls

Shifter rods connect the shift arms of the transfer case to the shift lever arms. Non-adjustable and adjustable links are used on the various models of vehicles. To insure the proper alignment of the rods to the arms, use the following procedure.

Linkage Adjustment

1. Place the shift lever in the neutral position.
2. Remove the shift control rod at the transfer case.
3. Assure that the shift arm of the transfer case is in the center or neutral position.
4. If the control rod is adjustable, position the trunnion or clevis to align with the hole in the shift arm of the transfer case.
5. If the control rod is non-adjustable and the rod does not line up with the hole in the shift arm of the transfer case, replacement or bending will be necessary for the control rod.
6. Reconnect the control rod to the transfer case shift arm and check for proper operation.

Cable Adjustment

A pull on the cable will engage the gears. To disengage, merely push the control cable in. To adjust, follow this procedure.

1. Pull the control cable knob out approximately two in. and block in this position.
2. Loosen the cable mounting housing jam nut.
3. Remove the two cable mounting housing bolts.
4. Unscrew the cable mounting housing away from the transfer case housing.
5. Confirm the inner clevis is positioned in the engaged position.
6. Turn the cable housing down the cable jacket to a snug fit against the gasket on the transfer case mounting boss. Install the two retaining screws.
7. Turn the jam nut down the cable jacket and secure against the cable mounting housing.
8. Remove the control cable knob block and operate the cable assembly to check the shifter operation.

CABLE ASSEMBLY

Removal

1. Leave the control knob pushed in.
2. Loosen the cable jam nut at the cable mounting housing on the transfer case and turn it back to the end of the threads.
3. Remove the two bolts holding the cable mounting housing to the transfer case.
4. Unscrew the housing all the way to the jam nut.
5. Pull the cable mounting housing forward until the inner cable jaw nut is clear.
6. Loosen the inner cable jam nut at the shift clevis and unhook the cable end pin from the clevis.
7. Position the shift cable to obtain working clearance.

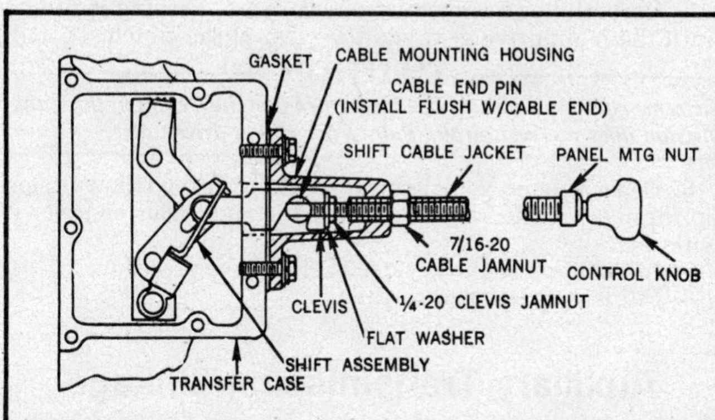

Exploded view of shift cable control (© International Harvester Co.)

Installation

1. Turn the jam nut and the cable mounting housing to the bottom of the thread end.
2. With the transfer case shifter assembly in the fully engaged position, install the cable mounting housing gasket to the case.

NOTE: The clevis is pulled out to engage.

3. Connect the cable end pin to the shifter assembly and secure with the jam nut.

NOTE: Confirm that the pin is installed flush with the cable end.

4. Block the control knob out approximately two in..
5. Turn the cable mounting housing down the cable jacket to a snug fit against the gasket on the transfer case mounting boss.
6. Secure the cable mounting housing with the two mounting bolts to the transfer case.
7. Turn the jam nut down the cable jacket and lock against the cable mounting housing.
8. Remove the block from the shift control cable knob and operate the cable to check the shifter operation.

TRANSFER CASE

Removal and Installation

FRAME MOUNTED

1. Drain the transfer case and disconnect the rear axle drive shaft at the transfer case.
2. Disconnect the front drive shaft at the transfer case.

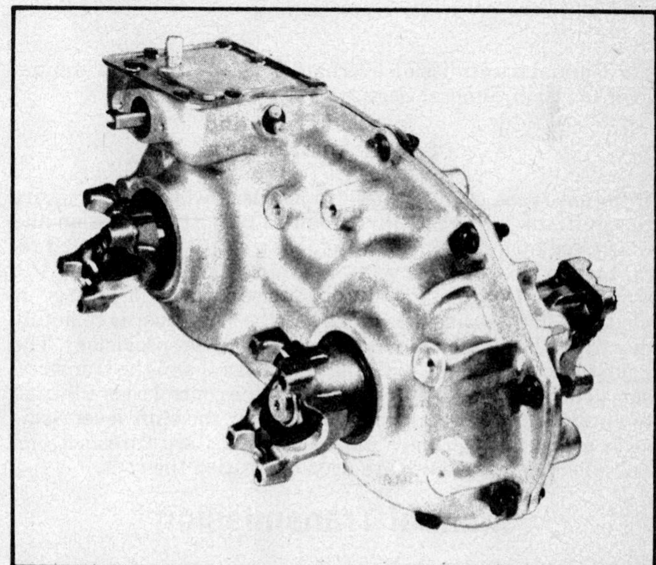

Frame mounted transfer case—typical (© International Harvester Co.)

Transmission mounted transfer case—typical (© International Harvester Co.)

3. Disconnect the speedometer cable, and indicator light switch wire, if equipped.
4. Disconnect the shift linkage. If equipped with a shift cable, refer to the cable removal and installation outlined previously.
5. Place a transmission jack under the transfer case and remove the mounting bolts from the frame to case. On the two speed models, remove the transfer case flange to transmission attaching bolts and then remove the transfer case.
6. Remove the transfer case from the vehicle.
7. The installation of the transfer case is the reverse of removal.

TRANSMISSION MOUNTED

1. Disconnect the rear driveshaft at the transfer case and drain the case assembly.
2. Disconnect the front driveshaft at the transfer case.
3. Disconnect the speedometer cable and the indicator light switch wire, if equipped.
4. Disconnect the shift linkage or cable. If equipped with a shift cable, refer to the removal and installation of the cable outlined previously.
5. Place a transmission jack under the transfer case and remove the flange bolts holding the transfer case to the transmission.
6. Pull the transfer case rearward to disengage the transmission output shaft from the coupler.
7. Lower the transfer case and remove from the vehicle.
8. The installation of the transfer case is the reverse of removal.

MANUAL TRANSMISSION

For manual transmission overhaul procedures see the Manual Transmission General Section.

Shift Linkage

Different types of transmissions are used which may require the shift linkage to be either mounted in the transmission and controlled by a shift lever, or to have a shift lever mounted remotely with linkage rods connecting the lever to the tramission. No adjustment is provided when the linkage is mounted in the transmission. When the shift lever is remotely mounted, the connecting rods have adjustment provisions. The adjustments are made with the shift control and the transmission arms in the neutral position, and the control rods adjusted to enter either the transmission arms or the shift lever arms with a free fit. Normally the control rods are threaded and trunnions and jam nuts are used to position the rods.

Manual Transmission

Removal and Installation

Removal and installation of manual transmissions will vary in detail, depending on which vehicle is being serviced. The following general procedure includes the basic steps common to all models.

1. Access to the transmission may be improved by removing cab floor panels.
2. Raise vehicle on a hoist or jack up and support with jack stands.
3. Drain the transmission lubricant.
4. Disconnect drive shaft at the transmission. If the vehicle is equipped with a transfer case which is not mounted directly to the transmission, disconnect the shaft between the transfer case and transmission at the yoke. If the vehicle is equipped with a transfer case which is mounted directly to the transmission, it must be removed with the transmission as a unit and the forward and rear drive shafts must be disconnected. Secure shaft out of the way with wire.
5. Disconnect shift linkage from transmission shift levers. If the vehicle is equipped with a transfer case which is mounted directly to the transmission, disconnect the shift linkage from the transfer case shift levers.
6. If the vehicle is equipped with a transmission mounted handbrake, disconnect the handbrake cable at the relay lever.
7. Disconnect speedometer cable from the transmission.
8. Remove the clutch slave cylinder from its mount. Do not disconnect the hydraulic line from the slave cylinder. Secure the push rod to the slave cylinder to avoid ejection of the internal components. Keeping the hydraulic system sealed eliminates the necessity of bleeding.
9. On some models it may be necessary to remove the starter motor.
10. Support the rear of engine by means of a hydraulic jack.
11. Remove the transmission mounting bolts and insulators at the engine rear crossmember. If possible, remove the rear engine crossmember. Remove gear shift lever and housing from top of transmission if applicable.
12. Attach suitable hoisting equipment or jack to transmission and raise enough to support the transmission assembly.
13. Remove top transmission to clutch housing bolts and install transmission guide pins.
14. Remove remaining transmission to clutch housing bolts.
15. Carefully pull transmission rearward, keeping it in line until the main drive gear shaft is clear of the clutch.

CAUTION

Extreme care must be exercised to insure that the weight of the transmission does not rest on the hub of the clutch driven disc.

16. Depending on vehicle model, either lift the transmission up through the floorboard and out the right door or lower it with a jack.
17. Installation is the reverse of the above procedure.
18. Fill transmission with fluid.

Auxiliary Transmission Linkage

Adjustment

1. Disconnect the shift rods at the lever assembly.
2. Position the transmission shafts in neutral.
3. Position the shift control lever so that the slots in the rails are exactly opposite each other with the lever inclined to the rear.
4. Adjust each rod clevis until the pins enter the shift control rail and clevis easily.
5. Install the clevis pins and retainers.
6. Check the shift operation.

Auxiliary Transmission

Removal and Installation

1. Drain the lubricant from the auxiliary transmission.
2. Remove the pins and retainers from the shift rods and remove the rods from the rails.

3. Disconnect the front drive shaft universal joint and tie out of the way.
4. Disconnect the rear drive shaft universal joint and tie the shaft out of the way.
5. Remove the speedometer cable, if equipped.
6. Remove the parking brake linkage from the output shaft parking brake drum.
7. Place a transmission jack under the auxiliary transmission, remove the mounting bolts, and remove the unit from the vehicle.
8. Installation is the reverse of removal.

AUTOMATIC TRANSMISSION

Identification

Two types of automatic transmissions are used in the I. H. vehicles. The model T-409 use a cast iron case with a removable aluminum converter housing. The transmission model T-407 uses a complete aluminum case and converter housing, cast as a unit. The rear extension housings may differ from one transmission to another, due to the vehicle application of engine and drive train. Some models may use a parking brake mounted on the rear extension housing. All transmissions use a parking pawl type lock, controlled by the shift linkage. The selector lever may be mounted on the floor or on the steering column, along with an indicator quadrant for the gear position.

For automatic transmission overhaul procedures, see the Automatic Transmission section in the Unit Repair section.

Transmission Model T-409

Removal and Installation

1. Raise the vehicle with a hoist.
2. Disconnect the fluid filler tube at the pan, and drain the fluid. Loosening the tube clip capscrew at the extension on the starting motor will permit rotating filler tube for transmission removal.
3. Disconnect the vacuum line at vacuum unit located at rear of transmission.
4. Disconnect the speedometer cable at speedometer adapter on transmission.
5. Disconnect the hand brake cable at drive shaft brake if chassis is so equipped.
6. Disconnect the shift linkage at manual shift lever on transmission.
7. Disconnect the two oil cooler lines on right side of transmission if chassis is so equipped.
8. Disconnect the drive shaft at transmission companion flange.

NOTE: Wire the end of the drive shaft to the frame to permit transmission removal.

9. Place the hydraulic hoist with a suitable transmission lift cradle in position under the transmission oil pan. Adjust the hoist to align the cradle to the transmission oil pan flnage so that the weight of the transmission case is supported by the hoist.
10. Remove the transmission case to converter housing upper capscrews and install two pilot studs into the capscrew holes.
11. Remove the transmission case to converter lower capscrews.
12. With the hydraulic hoist and cradle adjusted so the transmission case is in alignment with the converter housing, pull the transmission rearward with the hydraulic hoist to disengage the transmission from the converter housing and converter assembly. Lower transmission and remove from the vehicle.
13. To install, place two transmission pilot studs in the upper transmission to converter housing mounting screw holes.
14. Mount the transmission on a jack and position it under vehicle.

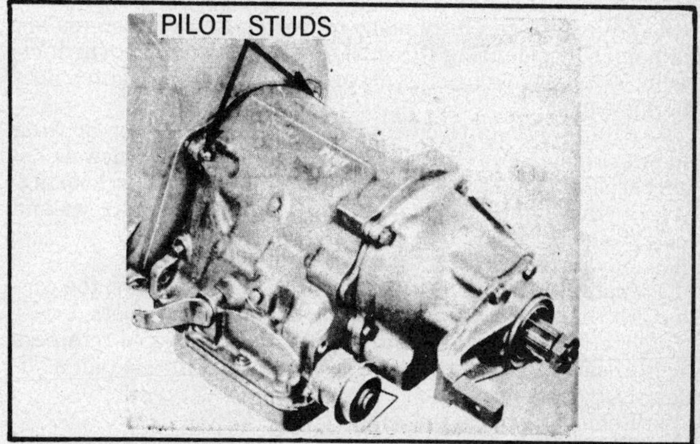

Pilot stud location automatic transmission (© International Harvester Co.)

15. Rotate engine until the front pump drive lugs on the converter are in a vertical position.
16. Rotate the front pump until the slots in the pump drive gear are in a vertical position.
17. Apply lubricant similar to lubriplate to seal the surface of converter impeller cover hub.
18. Being extremely careful to align the turbine shaft splines with the turbine hub splines and the converter impeller lugs with the slots in the front pump drive gear, raise transmission and move it forward into the converter housing and converter.
19. Install the transmission to converter housing lower mounting screws. Remove two pilot studs and install upper mounting screws. Tighten all mounting screws securely.
20. Install oil cooler lines on the right side of the transmission if so equipped.
21. Connect the shift linkage at the manual shift lever on the transmission.
22. Connect the hand brake cable to the drive shaft brake if so equipped.
23. Connect the speedometer cable to the transmission.
24. Connect the vacuum line to the vacuum unit located at the rear of transmission.
25. Connect the fluid filler tube to the oil pan, tightening securely. Also tighten tube clip capscrews at the extension on the starter motor.
26. Connect the drive shaft to the transmission companion flange. Tighten mounting screws securely and lock with lock plates.
27. Lower vehicle to floor and fill transmission with type "A" automatic transmission fluid.
28. Road test vehicle to check performance and shift points.

TORQUE CONVERTER

Removal and Installation

1. Remove transmission as described above.

2. Disconnect and remove starter motor.
3. If vehicle has conventional chassis, remove floormat and transmission floor opening cover.
4. Install a rear engine support or support the rear weight of the engine with a jack.
5. Remove converter housing to crossmember mounting bolts, lower insulators and retainers.
6. Unbolt and remove rear engine crossmember.
7. Remove eight capscrews and lockwashers which attach converter housing to crankcase adapter and remove converter housing. On some models it may be necessary to lower the engine to provide clearance for converter removal.
8. Remove six nuts which attach the converter assembly to the flywheel assembly and remove converter.
9. To install, carefully place converter into position (do not damage bolt mounting threads) and install six nuts which attach converter to converter drive plate, but do not tighten nuts at this time.
10. After thoroughly cleaning crankcase converter housing adapter, install converter housing and engage the dowels being careful not to damage the dowels or the converter housing.
11. Install eight converter housing mounting capscrews and lock washers.
12. Install rear engine crossmember.
13. Install upper and lower insulators and retainers, the converter to crossmember mounting bolts and lockwashers. Lower converter housing and engine. With insulators and retainers firmly seated, hand tighten bolts, then give bolts one-half additional turn and lock.
14. Remove rear engine support or jack.
15. If vehicle has conventional chassis, install floormat and transmission floor opening cover.
16. Install starter motor and wiring.
17. Install transmission as described above.
18. Rotate engine and converter assembly through two complete revolutions to center converter (to rotate, remove spark plugs and pry on drive plate ring gear).
19. Tighten converter to the converter drive plate attaching nuts.
20. Install converter housing adapter cover.

TRANSMISSION FLUID

Replacement

1. Transmission fluid should be changed and bands adjusted every 15,000 miles.
2. Remote converter housing front plate.
3. Remove one of the converter drain plugs, then rotate converter 180 degrees and remove other converter drain plug.
4. Disconnect fluid filler tube at the transmission pan.
5. Drain fluid and remove pan. Clean pan.
6. Connect filler tube to pan and tighten securely.
7. Install drain plugs in converter cover and tighten them to 7–10 ft. lbs. torque.
8. Install converter housing front plate.
9. Add five quarts of Dexron II® automatic transmission fluid through filler tube.
10. Run engine at idle (do not race) for about two minutes, then add five more quarts of fluid. Let engine idle until it reaches normal operating temperature.
11. Move selector lever through all positions, then place it in "P" (park). Check fluid level and add enough fluid to bring level up to the "F" (full) mark on indicator.

FRONT BAND

Adjustment

1. Drain fluid from transmission and remove pan (disconnect filler tube from pan).

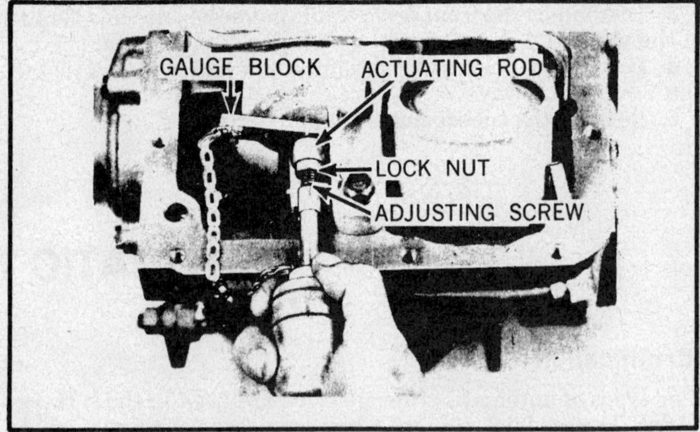

Adjusting front band (© International Harvester Co.)

2. Loosen front servo adjusting screw locknut two full turns and check the adjusting screw for free rotation.
3. Pull back on the actuating rod and insert gauge block of the front band adjusting tool (SE-1910) between the servo piston stem and adjusting screw. Tighten adjusting screw until adjusting tool handle overruns. Holding adjusting screw stationary, tighten locknut to 20–25 ft. lbs. torque. Remove gauge block.
4. Install fluid screen and pan, using a new gasket. Connect filler tube to pan.
5. Refill transmission as described above, adding new fluid if necessary.

REAR BAND

Adjustment

1. If vehicle is conventional model, remove floor mat and transmission cover plate from floor board.
2. Clean adjusting screw threads thoroughly and oil threads.
3. Loosen rear band adjusting locknut.
4. Using tool SE-1909, tighten adjusting screw until wrench overruns, at 10 ft. lbs. torque.

NOTE: If adjusting screw is tighter than overrun of wrench, loosen screw and retighten.

5. Back off adjusting screw one and one-half turns, then hold adjusting screw stationary and tighten locknut to 25–40 ft. lbs. torque.

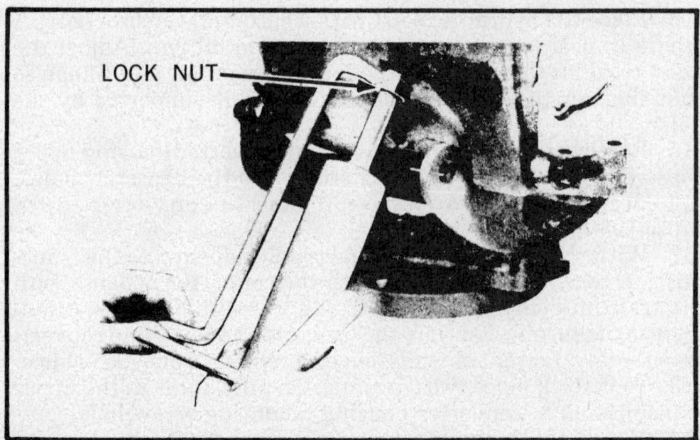

Adjusting rear band (© International Harvester Co.)

CAUTION

Severe damage may result if the adjusting screw is not backed off exactly one and one-half turns.

6. Install transmission cover plate and floor mat to floor board.

SHIFT LINKAGE

Adjustment

1. With engine off, disconnect the manual shift rod from the selector lever on the steering column and the transmission lever on the conventional chassis, or bellcrank on the Metro chassis.
2. Position selector lever in "D" and place transmission manual lever in the "D" detent (second from the top of the transmission).
3. Position the manual shift rod into the ball joint on the steering column. The opposite end of the rod should be installed in the transmission shift lever on the conventional chassis and secured with a washer and cotter pin. On the Metro chassis, the rod yoke should be positioned on the bellcrank and secured with the clevis pin, washer and cotter pin.
4. Tighten ball joint nut at the steering column lever.
5. Move the selector lever through all positions, checking the alignment of the pointer in all positions.

KICKDOWN SWITCH

Adjustment

1. On the conventional chassis the kickdown switch is located in the toeboard under the throttle pedal. On the Metro chassis it is mounted on a bracket under the toeboard and operated by a pad welded to one of the throttle linkage rods.
2. Loosen two mounting nuts and turn them either direction until a clearance of $\frac{1}{4}$ in. is obtained between switch and throttle pedal on the conventional chassis and between switch and throttle linkage pad on the Metro chassis.

VACUUM CONTROL

Adjustment

1. Connect a tachometer to the engine.
2. Remove the $\frac{1}{8}$ in. pipe plug located on the left front of the transmission case. Install a pressure gauge line connection at this point, then connect a pressure gauge to the line and place gauge in cab.
3. Start engine and move selector lever to "D" (drive) position. Apply hand brake and accelerate engine until 1000 rpm is reached. Pressure reading on gauge should be 82–88 psi.
4. If correct pressure is not obtained, loosen locknut on vacuum control unit (located at rear of transmission) and turn vacuum unit clockwise to increase pressure or counterclockwise to decrease pressure. Adjust for proper pressure, then tighten locknut.

CAUTION

Do not operate engine over 10 seconds at any one time while performing the above.

NEUTRAL SAFETY SWITCH

Adjustment

1. Place the selector lever in the "N" position and loosen the two capscrews securing the switch to the steering jacket tube.
2. Using a $\frac{3}{32}$ in. punch as an aligning tool, insert the pin into the hole on the face of the switch.

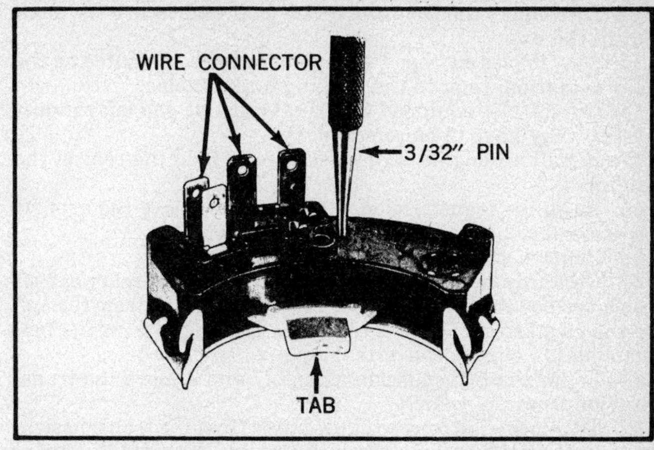

Using a 3/32" pin punch to adjust safety starter switch (© International Harvester Co.)

NOTE: If necessary, rotate the switch until the pin enters freely into the hole in the switch.

3. Secure the two capscrews holding the switch to the steering jacket tube and remove the pin punch.
4. Attempt to start the vehicle in all positions. If the engine will start in the "P" and the "N" positions and not in any of the others, the switch is correctly adjusted.

CAUTION

Block the wheels before testing the switch adjustment.

Transmission Model T-407

Removal

NOTE: The transmission and converter must be removed as a unit assembly. Damage can result to the converter drive plate, pump bushing, or to the pump seal, if the converter is allowed to remain on the converter drive plate.

1. Connect a remote switch to the starter solenoid so that the engine can be rotated from under the vehicle.
2. Disconnect the coil high tension cable.
3. Raise the vehicle and support safely.
4. Remove the engine rear crossmember on 4 × 4 vehicles, if necessary.
5. Remove the cover plate from the front of the converter housing to provide access to the converter drain plug and mounting bolts.
6. Rotate the engine to bring the drain plug to the six o'clock position. Drain the converter and loosen the pan bolts to drain the transmission.
7. Mark the converter and drive plate to aid in the assembly. Rotate the engine to locate the converter-to-drive plate bolts and remove the bolts.
8. Disconnect the negative battery cable and remove the starter motor assembly.
9. Disconnect the wires from the back-up light and neutral start switch.
10. Disconnect the gearshift cable or rod and bellcrank from the transmission.
11. Disconnect the throttle rod from the left side of the transmission.
12. Disconnect the cooler lines at the transmission and remove the filler tube.
13. Disconnect the speedometer cable, and move cable away from the transmission.

14. Disconnect the front universal joint and secure the shaft out of the way.
15. On vehicles equipped with parking brake mounted on the rear extension, remove the parking brake cable.
16. On vehicles equipped with dual exhaust, the left exhaust system may have to be removed.
17. Install an engine support fixture to hold the rear of the engine.
18. Raise the transmission slightly, and remove the support crossmember holding the rear mount assembly.
19. Remove all bell housing bolts.
20. Carefully move the transmission assembly rearward off the block dowels and disengage the converter hub from the end of the crankshaft. Place a converter holding tool on the bell housing to hold the converter in place.
21. Lower the transmission assembly and remove the transmission from the vehicle.
22. To remove the converter assembly from the transmission, remove the holding tool and carefully slide the converter out of the transmission.

Installation

1. Rotate the pump rotors with tool SE-2402 or its equivalent, so that the lugs on the pump inner rotor are vertical.
2. Position the converter so that the impeller shaft slots are vertical and carefully slide the converter assembly over the input shaft and reaction shaft. Make sure that the converter slots fully engage the pump inner rotor lugs.

NOTE: The surface of the converter front cover lug should be at least $^1/_2$ inch to the rear of a straightedge, placed on the face of the bell housing, when the converter is pushed all the way into the transmission.

3. Install the converter holding tool to hold the converter in place.
4. Position the transmission on a jack assembly and move the unit under the vehicle.
5. Rotate the converter to align the previously made marks on the drive plate and converter.
6. Raise the transmission and align with the engine. Install a pilot stud to aid in the alignment of the converter to the drive plate. Carefully work the transmission assembly forward over the engine block dowels with the converter hub entering the crankshaft opening.
7. Install the converter housing bolts and tighten to specified torque.
8. Install the crossmember and mount at the rear of the transmission. Remove the engine support fixture.
9. Install the oil filler tube and speedometer cable.
10. Connect the throttle rod and the gear shift rod to the transmission levers.
11. Connect the wires to the neutral start and back-up light switch.
12. Install the drive shaft and front universal joint.
13. Install the starter motor assembly.
14. Remove the pilot stud from the converter and install the bolts to the converter-drive plate assembly.
15. Install the cooler lines to the transmission.
16. Install the converter access plate on the front of the converter housing.
17. If the left exhaust system was removed, replace the pipes and brackets.
18. Install the parking brake cable and adjust, if equipped with the extension housing parking brake assembly.
19. Adjust the shift and throttle linkage.
20. Fill the transmission and connect the negative battery cable, if not done, and start the engine. Recheck the fluid level and refill as necessary.

TRANSMISSION FLUID

Drain and Refill

1. Raise the vehicle on a jack or hoist. Support safely.
2. Place a large drain container under the tranmission oil pan.
3. Loosen the pan bolts and tap one corner of the pan to break it loose, allowing the fluid to drain.
4. Remove the access plate from the front of the converter housing. Remove the converter drain plug and allow the fluid to drain.
5. Remove and clean the pan, remove the fluid filter and discard.
6. Install a new filter assembly on the valve body and tighten the screws securely.
7. Using a new pan gasket, install the pan and tighten the bolts securely.
8. Install and tighten the converter drain plug.
9. Install the converter housing access plate.
10. Install six quarts of transmission fluid into the transmission. Start the engine and allow to run for two minutes. Check the fluid level and add enough oil to bring the level to the "ADD ONE PINT" mark.
11. Recheck the level after moving the selector lever through all the gear positions and after the transmission has reached normal operating temperature. The level should be between the "FULL" mark and the "ADD ONE PINT" mark.

KICKDOWN BAND

Adjustment

NOTE: The kickdown band is located on the left side of the transmission case near the throttle lever shaft.

1. Loosen the locknut and back off approximately five turns. Turn the adjusting screw and check for binding, if the screw does bind, lubricated the screw as necessary.
2. Tighten the adjusting screw to 6 ft. lbs. and back off the adjusting screw 2 $^3/_4$ on the 4 cylinder vehicles and 2 $^1/_4$ on the six and eight cylinder vehicles.
3. While holding the adjusting screw in position, torque the lock nut to 29 ft. lbs.

LOW AND REVERSE BAND

Adjustment

1. Raise the vehicle, support safely, drain the transmission fluid, and remove the pan.
2. Loosen the lock nut on the adjusting screw.
3. Tighten the adjusting screw to 6 ft. lbs. Back off the adjusting screw 2 $^1/_4$ turns.
4. While holding the adjusting screw ,torque the lock nut to 30 ft. lbs.
5. Install the pan using a new pan gasket.
6. Fill the transmission with fluid, start the engine and recheck the level. Add as necessary.

BACK-UP LIGHT AND NEUTRAL START SWITCH

Adjustment and Replacement

No provisions are made for any adjustments of the back-up light and neutral start switch. The neutral start circuit is controlled by the inner terminal and the back-up light circuits are controlled by the two outside terminals.

The replacement of the switch is accomplished by unscrewing the switch from the transmission case, and screwing a new switch into the case. Since fluid leakage will occur when removing the switch, fluid must be added after the new switch is installed.

SHIFT LINKAGE

Adjustment

ADJUSTABLE CABLE CONTROL

1. Install cable conduit anchor clamps at both ends.
2. Install swivel on the control lever so that a distance of .55 inch exists from the end of the cable to the opposite side of the trunnion. Tighten the jam nut securely.
3. With the control in PARK position and transmission lever in the full rearward position (PARK detent), adjust the yoke so that the rod end pin installs freely and secure the yoke nut and install the cotter pin.

COLUMN SHIFT

1. Assemble all linkage parts, but leave the upper control rod bolt loose.
2. Place the selector lever in DRIVE position.
3. Move the shift control lever on the transmission to the DRIVE position.
4. Tighten the upper bolt on the control rod to 14–16 ft. lbs.
5. Check the adjustment as follows.
   a. Shift effort must be free and detents feel crisp. All gate stops must be positive.
   b. Key start must only occur in the PARK or NEUTRAL positions.
   c. Detent positions must be in proper relationship to the transmission lever positions.

THROTTLE VALVE LINKAGE

Adjustment

1. With the engine off and an assistant holding the accelerator pedal to the floor, check for full carburetor throttle plate opening.
2. If necessary, adjust the throttle cable and pdeal floor stop to obtain wide open throttle.
3. If necessary, adjust the idle speed of the engine with the use of a tachometer and with the engine at normal operating temperature and the carburetor off the fast idle cam. Adjust the curb idle speed, (throttle stop solenoid activated) with the transmission in neutral and the air conditioning in the OFF position.

NOTE: Be sure that carburetor is not being held open by a deceleration valve dashpot, solenoid valve, or a vacuum throttle modulator valve.

CAUTION

All components in the throttle control and transmission linkage system must operate freely with absolutely no sticking, excessive friction, or interference from other chassis components.

THROTTLE LINKAGE

V-304, V-345 and V-392 and Engines With 2210, 2300 and 4150 Holley Carburetors

Two types of throttle linkages are used on these carburetors to transmissions. They are designated as first release and modified type linkages. The differences are:

a. **First release:** has both the throttle push rod and the throttle valve control rod piloted by guide holes in the throttle valve rod bracket. The throttle push rod is capped by a lock nut and acorn nut.

b. **Modified type:** has only the throttle valve control rod piloted in the throttle valve rod bracket. The throttle push rod is piloted in the spring clip plate which is welded to the throttle valve control rod.

FIRST RELEASE ADJUSTMENT

1. On the first release type throttle valve linkage, loosen the jam nut of the acorn adjusting nut and turn the acorn nut clockwise until clearance between the acorn nut and the spring clip is obtained.
2. Move the throttle valve linkage control rod to its forward most position. Adjust the acorn nut so it just rides against the spring clip on the throttle valve control rod and tighten the jam nut.
3. Check the throttle linkage for freedom of movement by pushing the linkage to its full rearward position and making sure its complete return to the full forward position.

MODIFIED LINKAGE ADJUSTMENT

1. Loosen the jam nut and turn the adjusting nut clockwise until clearance between adjusting nut and spring clip is obtained.
2. Move the control rod to its forward most position. Adjust the nut so it just rides against the spring clip on the throttle valve control rod and tighten the jam nut.
3. Check the throttle linkage for freedom of movement by pushing the linkage to its full rearward position and making sure of its complete return to the full forward position.

V-345 and V-392 Engines With Carter Thermo-Quad Carburetor

NOTE: Two types of throttle linkages are used as with the V-304, V-345 and V-392 carburetors.

FIRST RELEASE ADJUSTMENT

This procedure is the same as for the V-304, V-345 and V-392.

MODIFIED LINKAGE ADJUSTMENT

1. Loosen the jam nut and turn the adjusting nut clockwise until the adjusting nut just contacts the spring clip.
2. Move the control rod to its forward most position. Adjust the nut so it just rides against the spring clip on the throttle valve control rod and tighten the jam nut.
3. Check the throttle linkage for freedom of movement and return to its full forward position when moved.

DRIVESHAFT AND U JOINTS

Driveshaft Assembly

It is imperative that all components of the drive train be tight to insure balance. Check companion flanges at the axles and transmission, center bearing mounts and engine mounts.

When assembling drive train, lubricate slip joint (splined) assemblies and universal joint bearings. Make sure that universal joints are kept on parallel planes by observing the arrows stamped on the shaft end and slip yoke.

Removal and Installation

1. Beginning at the front or the rear of the shaft, bend the lock strip tabs, if equipped, away from the bolts in the trunnion

flanges of the universal joints. Mark the shaft, universal joint, and yoke for proper reassembly.

2. Remove the bolts from the trunnion flange to yoke and support the ends of the shaft.

3. If equipped with a center bearing assembly, use a floor jack or other means to support the shaft assembly and center bearing during removal. Remove the bolts from the center bearing to crossmember and lower the shaft assembly.

NOTE: Some drive shafts will have a slip joint or universal joint near the center bearing assembly. Separating the shaft at these points will lighten the weight and control awkwardness of handling the complete shaft assembly during the disassembly and assembly.

4. The installation of the shaft is in the reverse of the removal procedure. Make sure all indexing marks are properly aligned.

Universal Joints

To remove universal joints, bend down tabs on bearing bolt lock plate and remove four bolts at each universal joint. Joint and shaft assembly must be removed as a unit to service "R" type trunnion bearings. Do not disassemble drive shaft from slip yoke unless these parts are to be replaced. On vehicles equipped with "CL" type trunnion bearings, the universal joint may be unbolted from both the drive shaft and the companion flange and the whole shaft assembly does not have to be removed to service one joint.

When replacing trunnion bearings, remove retaining clips then carefully drive out one, then the other, bearing. Use new packing washers (seals) when reassembling.

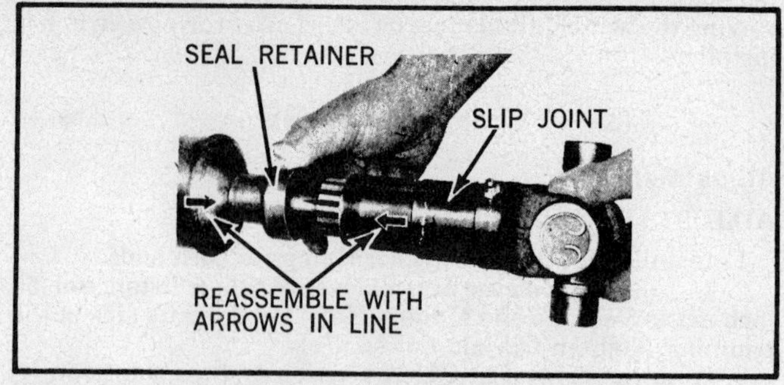

Correct slip joint assembly (© International Harvester Co.)

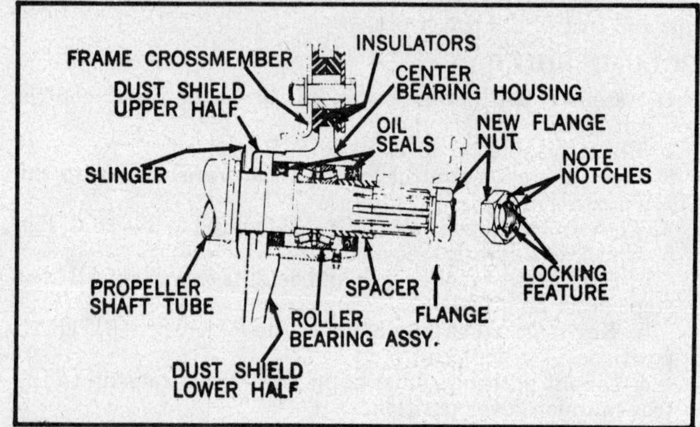

Silent spin type center drive shaft bearing (© International Harvester Co.)

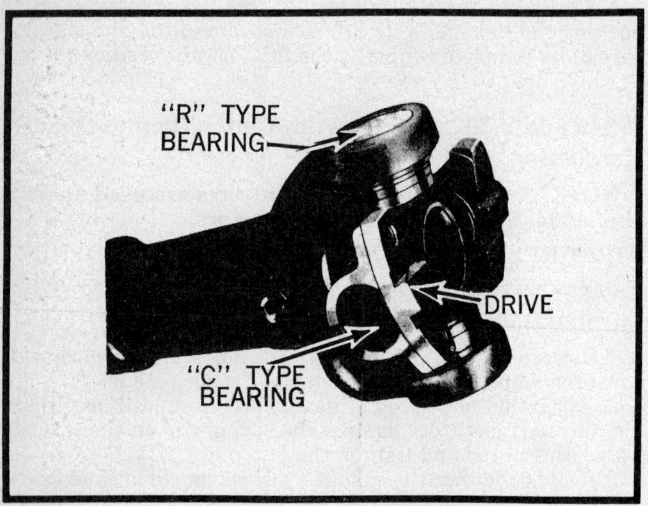

CR type universal joint (© International Harvester Co.)

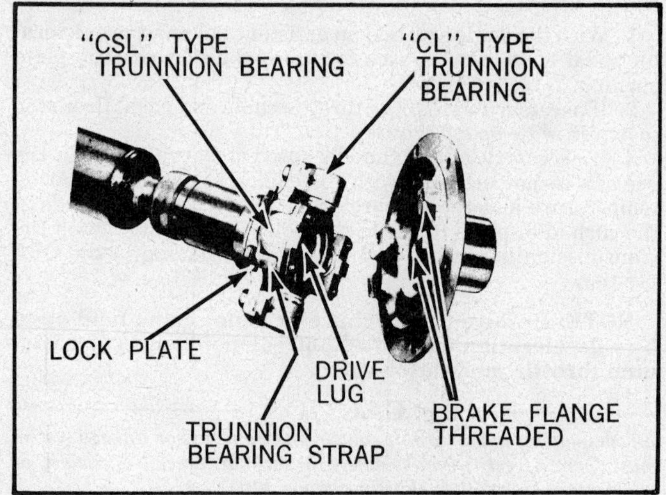

CL type universal joint (© International Harvester Co.)

DRIVE AXLE

For overhaul procedures and out of truck adjustments see Rear Axle section.

Rear Axle Assembly

Removal and Installation

LIGHT DUTY TRUCKS

1. Raise the rear of the vehicle and support it safely, with suitable jack stands at the frame in front of the rear springs.
2. Remove the rear tire and wheel assemblies. Disconnect the drive shaft from the axle ans place it out of the way.
3. Disconnect the brake hose from the housing and the parking brake cable from the backing plates. Disconnect the shock absorbers from the lower mounting and positoned them out of the way.
4. Using a floor jack or equivalent, support the the axle assembly. Remove the U-bolt nuts holding the the axle assembly to the leaf springs, then remove the spring plates.
5. Remove the lower spring shackle mounting bolt nut and the bolt. lower the vehicle and slide the axle assembly out from underneath the vehicle.
6. Installation is the reverse order of the removal procedure.

MEDIUM AND HEAVY DUTY TRUCKS

1. Jack and block up truck until load is removed from springs and rear wheels are clear of the ground.
2. Drain differential housing.
3. Disconnect brake lines and parking brake cables (where used).
4. On two speed differentials, disconnect control wires or air hoses from the shift mechanism.
5. Disconnect driveshaft at rear axle companion flange.
6. Support differential on portable floor jack and take off U-bolts at springs.
7. Roll out axle from under truck.
8. Installation is the reverse of the above procedure. Be sure to bleed hydraulic brake systems. Remove axle housing breather valve and clean thoroughly with solvent.

TANDEM AXLE

1. Jack and block up truck until load is removed from springs and rear wheels are clear of the ground.

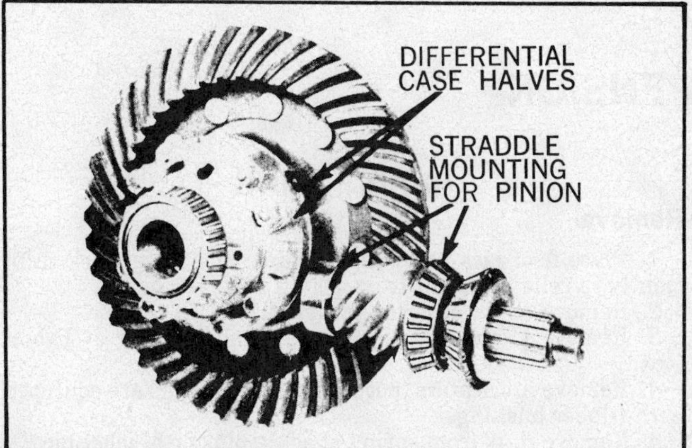

Single reduction type final axle drive (© International Harvester Co.)

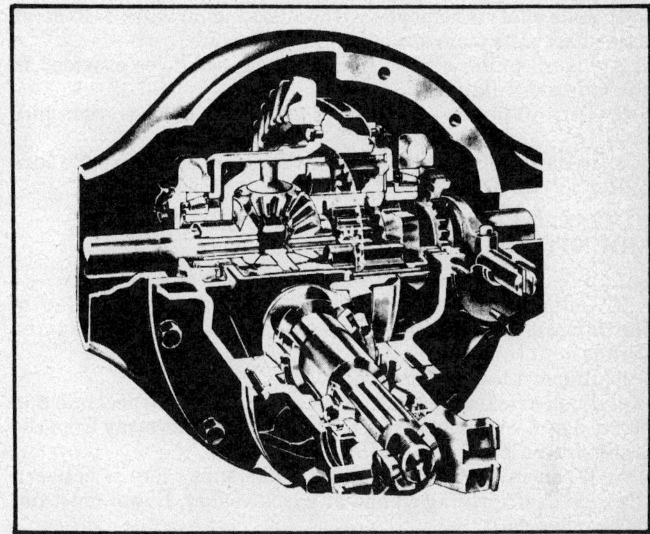

Two speed planetary gear type final axle drive (© International Harvester Co.)

2. Drain the differential housing into a suitable drain pan.
3. Remove the output shaft and yoke. Disconnect the differential lockout air line and main drive line.
4. Loosen the input shaft yoke nut, but do not remove. Remove the wheel assemblies and axle shafts.
5. Support differential carrier with a floor jack or a chain fall. Remove nuts and lock washers and separate differential from the axle housing.
6. Remove the differential from the vehicle. This procedure is for the removal of the front differential. The rear differential removal procedure is simliar to the front removal and installation.
7. Installation is the reverse order of the removal procedure.

Rear Axle Shaft

Removal and Installation

SEMI-FLOATING TYPE

1. Remove wheel and nut from axle shaft end.
2. Remove hub and drum assembly with a suitable puller.
3. Unbolt and remove brake backing plate and bearing retainer.
4. Pull axle shaft and bearing using suitable puller. Bearings are pressed on.
5. When installing axle shaft assembly, use new oil seals and be careful not to damage seals.
6. Lightly tap bearing cap into axle housing.
7. Install shims on end of axle housing flange and insert backing plate bolts to retain shims.
8. Install backing plate, bearing retainer and seal retainer. Tighten nuts to specified torque.
9. Install wheel hub. Grasp wheel hub and pull outward to be sure that axle shaft is withdrawn as far as possible.
10. Check axle shaft end-play as follows: Mount dial indicator on stationary location at right-hand side of axle assembly. Position indicator against end of axle shaft and check shaft end-play. If end play is not within 0.006″, shims must be added or removed between backing plate and axle housing flange.

11. Place key in axle shaft and install hub and drum assembly on shaft, securing with washer and nut. Tighten nut and install cotter pin.

FULL-FLOATING TYPE

1. Axle shaft is removed without taking off wheels. Remove axle shaft nuts from studs in the wheel hub.
2. Install puller screws in the two tapped holes provided in the axle shaft flange.
3. Turn in puller screws until axle shaft is loose, then pull axle.
4. Installation is the reverse of the above procedure. Be sure puller screws are removed.

FULL-FLOATING TYPE WITH TAPERED DOWEL MOUNTING

1. Remove flange nuts from studs of wheel hub.
2. Using a heavy hammer, strike sharply on the center of the flange of the axle shaft. This will unseat and loosen tapered dowels.
3. Remove tapered dowels.
4. Push axle flange back into position against wheel hub and strike again with a hammer to spring axle shaft away from the wheel hub. Do not pry on flange.
5. When installing axle shaft, make sure there is between the axle shaft driving flange and lockwasher. Dowel must not be "sunken in."

AXLE SHAFT BEARING AND OIL SEAL

Removal and Installation

The only axle type that has a bearing mounted on the shaft is the semifloating axle. Follow the procedure outlined under the Axle Shaft Removal to expose the seals and bearings for replacement.

1. The bearing must be pressed from the axle shaft and a new one pressed back on the shaft to seat against the bearing shoulder on the axle.
2. Lubricate the bearing with wheel bearing grease and fill the roller cavities completely.
3. Remove the axle tube inner seal by the use of a seal puller or by engaging the lip of the seal with the end of the axle shaft and prying outward on the seal.
4. Using a seal installer or its equivalent, seat the seal against the shoulder within the axle tube.
5. During assembly of the brake support plate, install the outer seal.

NOTE: Lubricate the lips of the seals during installation.

OIL SEAL AND WHEEL BEARING

Installation and Adjustment

FULL FLOATING AXLE

1. Raise the rear of the vehicle and support safely. Keep both rear wheels parallel with the floor surface.
2. Remove the axle as outlined under Rear Axle Shaft Removal.
3. Remove the wheel bearing locknut by bending the lock tab away from the locknut shoulders. Remove the locknut and lock.
4. Place a dolly under the rear wheels and maneuver the truck height so that the wheels are neither hanging nor supporting the truck.
5. Remove the adjusting nut and outer wheel bearing. Pull the wheel assembly outward and off the housing tube.
6. Remove the oil seal and inner wheel bearing from the truck side of the hub assembly.
7. Clean the hub of any old grease and replace the bearings and races as necessary. Repack the bearings if they are to be used again. Pack wheel bearing grease in the hub cavity between the inner and outer bearings.
8. Install the wheel hub oil seal and clean the hub and drum of any grease droppings.
9. Install the wheel assembly on the housing tube, keeping the hub assembly parallel with the housing tube.
10. Install the outer bearing and adjuster nut. Raise the vehicle and wheel assembly upward to clear the dolly.
11. Tighten the adjusting nut to 50 ft. lbs. while rotating the wheels to seat the bearings.
12. Back off the adjusting nut $\frac{1}{4}$ turn and install the lockwasher and locknut. Tighten the locknut to 150 ft. lbs. and bend the lock tabs to secure the nut.

NOTE: Assemblies using doweled adjusting nuts and pierced wheel bearing locknut, require 200–300 ft. lbs. torque on the outer nut.

13. Install the axle shaft and bolt to the wheel assembly.
14. Lower the vehicle and check the level of lubricant in the differential.

Locking Differentials

For overhaul procedures of differentials with "NoSPIN" and "PowrLok" locking units see Rear Axle portion of Unit Repair section.

REAR SUSPENSION

The rear springs used on the IH vehicles are classified as leaf, air, and rubber block types. The heavier the vehicle load requirement, the heavier the spring assemblies would be to carry the load. Care should be exercised in the removal and installation of the spring assemblies so that personal injury can be avoided. The suspensions using shock absorbers will normally be found on the light and medium duty vehicles. The removal and installation of the shock absorbers require only the removal and installation of the retaining nuts or bolts, with the possibility of raising the vehicle for working clearance.

The following procedure can be used as a general outline for the removal and installation of leaf springs. The air and rubber block suspension, along with the tandem leaf springs, are outlined in this section.

REAR SPRING

Removal

1. Place floor jack under truck frame and raise truck sufficiently to relieve weight from spring to be removed.
2. Remove shock absorbers where used.
3. Remove U-bolts, spring bumper and retainer or U-bolt seat.
4. Remove lubricators (not used where springs are equipped with rubber bushings).
5. Remove nuts from spring shackle pins or bracket pins.
6. Slide ring off bracket pin and shackle pin.
7. If spring is rubber bushed, bushing halves may be removed from each side of spring and shackle eye.

Installation

1. Install pivot end of spring first. Align shackle end to other frame bracket. When installing nuts on spring pins which are welded or pressed in, be sure that washer is tightened against shoulder of pin. Spring pins which are driven in must be installed so that slot for lock bolt is aligned. Spring pins which are threaded in must be installed so that the lubrication hole is facing up. Tighten pin into bracket, then back off one-half turn. Install locknut tightly and install cotter pin. Turn pin out to permit installation of cotter pin.
2. Install lubricators.
3. Install U-bolt seat or retainer and U-bolts. Install U-bolt nuts, but do not tighten.
4. Install shock absorber where used.
5. Lower vehicle.
6. Tighten U-bolt nuts securely.

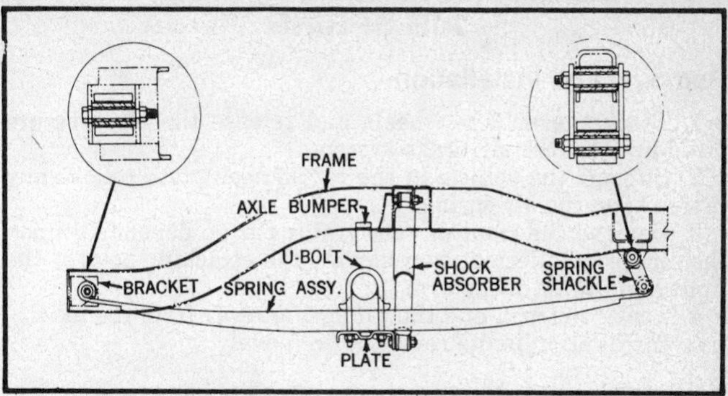

Rear spring installation diagram light and medium duty vehicles (© International Harvester Co.)

Air Suspension

The air suspension system was developed to improve the ride characteristics of highway transport vehicles. The major components, whether used on single or tandem axles, are as follows: trailing arms, frame hanger brackets, shock absorbers, track bars, air springs, axle connections, air leveling valve.

SPRING HEIGHT

Adjustment

1. Start engine, and wait until the air pressure indicates near maximum pressure of 85–90 lbs.
2. Measure the distance from the top of the trailing arm to the bottom of the frame at the rear of the air spring on one side only.
3. If the distance is greater than $12^1/_4$ in., ($\pm ^3/_8$ inch), shorten the linkage from the height control valve arm to the axle, wait 15 seconds and remeasure. Repeat the procedure if necessary.
4. If the distance is less than $12^1/_4$ in., ($\pm ^3/_8$), lengthen the linkage from the height control valve arm to the axle, wait 15 seconds and remeasure. Repeat the procedure if necessary.
5. Repeat the adjustment procedure on the opposite side of vehicle.

AIR SPRING PRESSURE BALANCE

Air spring pressure imbalance on an unloaded IH air suspension system is a normal condition and causes no harm to the suspension components so long as chassis remains unloaded. If, however, the imbalance continues after the chassis is loaded, do not operate the vehicle until the cause is located and corrected. These causes can be incorrect spring height adjustment, air leaks, plugged or pinched air lines, defective leveling control valve, or loose or broken parts.

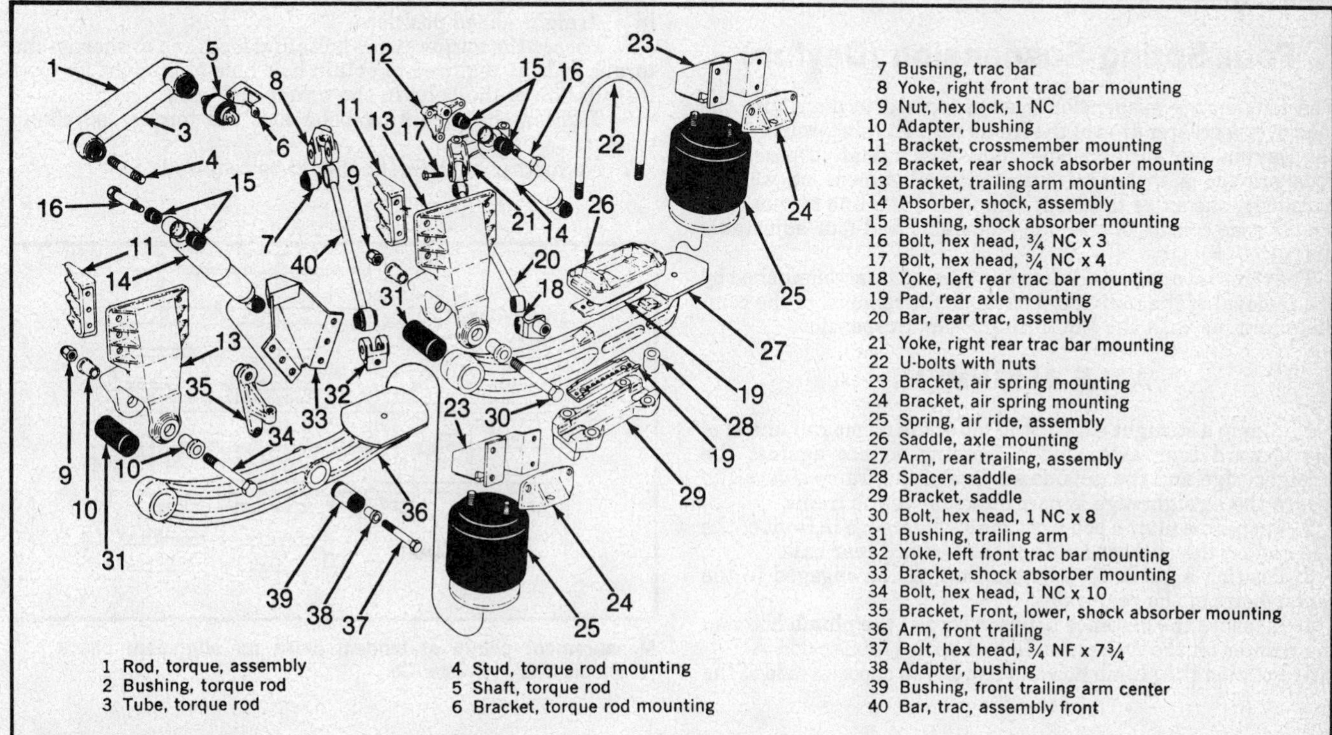

Exploded view of air suspension—typical (© International Harvester Co.)

AIR SPRING

Removal and Installation

1. Block the vehicle wheels and release the air pressure build-up from the air brake system.
2. Support the vehicle in the raised position to relieve any pressure on the air spring.
3. Remove the front or rear trailing arm, depending upon the air spring affected, by removing the attaching bolts at the front and center of the arm.
4. Lower the arm and the air spring away from the axle.
5. Installation is the reverse of removal.

Equalizing Beam Suspension (Hendrickson)

Tandem drive axles require a special suspension which permits flexibility between the axles, the equalizing beam suspension. Semi-elliptic springs are used mounted on saddle assemblies above the equalizer beams and pivoted at the front end on spring pins and brackets. The rear end of the springs have no rigid attachment to the spring brackets, but are free to move forward and backward to compensate for spring deflection.

NOTE: As options, airspring assemblies and four point rubber mounted suspensions are available in place of the leaf spring type.

There are two approaches to servicing the suspension system. One is the removal and installation of individual parts. Removal and overhaul of the entire unit can also be done.

CAUTION

When complete removal is performed, be careful when disconnecting the torque rods, springs, or rubber cushions from the frame since the axle assemblies will be free to roll or pivot at the equalizer beam ends. Use jacks and other equipment and block the vehicle securely to prevent injury to personnel and damage to the unit.

Four Spring Suspension (Dayton)

The four spring suspension system is used to distribute the load over a greater area of the frame rail. The six torque rods of the Dayton four spring suspension serve a dual purpose. The rods provide a means of suspension alignment as well as permiting the axles to accept complete drive line torque. The torque rods consist of two non-adjustable and four adjustable units.

The removal and installation of parts can be accomplished by the removal of the individual parts or the removal of the complete unit, as with the Equalizing Beam Suspension.

AXLE ALIGNMENT

1. Clamp a straight edge to the top of the frame rail ahead of the forward rear axle. Use a framing square against the straight-edge and the outside surface of the frame siderail to insure the straightedge is perpendicular to the frame.
2. Suspend a plumb bob from the straightedge in front of the tire and on the outboard side of the forward rear axle.
3. Position a bar with pointers that can be engaged in the center holes of the rear axles.
4. Measure the distance between cord of the plumb bob and the pointer on the forward axle and record (dimension A).
5. Position the plumb bob and bar on the opposite side of the vehicle and measure as outlined in paragraph 4. Record the result.
6. Any difference in dimensions from side to side must be equalized if the difference exceeds 0.0625 inch.
7. Equalize the dimensions by loosening the clamp bolts on the lower adjustable torque rod on the forward rear axle and adjusting the length of the torque rod. Tighten the clamp bolts.

NOTE: Remove one end of the left and right upper torque rods on the forward rear axle to relieve any stresses which may be present due to an improperly adjusted torque rod, before adjusting the lower torque rods.

8. Reposition the bar pointers to the axle centers on each side. If any differences exist in the center to center measurement, (dimension B), after the forward rear axle has been squared to the frame, the rear rear axle must also be aligned.
9. To align the rear axle, loosen the clamp bolts on the lower adjustable torque rod and adjust to equalize the center to center distance between the axle ends. Tighten the clamp bolts.
10. Reinstall the upper torque rod ends that were removed in step 7. Tighten the mounting bolts.

AXLE LOAD DISTRIBUTION

The Dayton four spring suspension provides for equal load distribution through the adjustment of the upper torque rod lengths. To adjust, follow this procedure.

1. Disconnect the forward and rear upper torque rods at the frame crossmembers.
2. If the vehicle is equipped with an adjustable fifth wheel, position it in the normal operating location.
3. Apply the maximum rated load on the suspension assembly to obtain the full deflection of the leaf springs when adjusting the torque rods.
4. To settle the suspension to normal operating position, move the vehicle to a level area and bring the vehicle to an easy stop, using the trailer brake, if equipped. Keep the vehicle in a straight ahead position.
5. Loosen the torque clamp bolts and lengthen or shorten the torque rods as required to obtain bolt hole alignment for easy installation of the bolts in the torque rod ends.
6. Tighten the mounting bolts and the torque rod clamp bolts.
7. No further adjustment should be required.

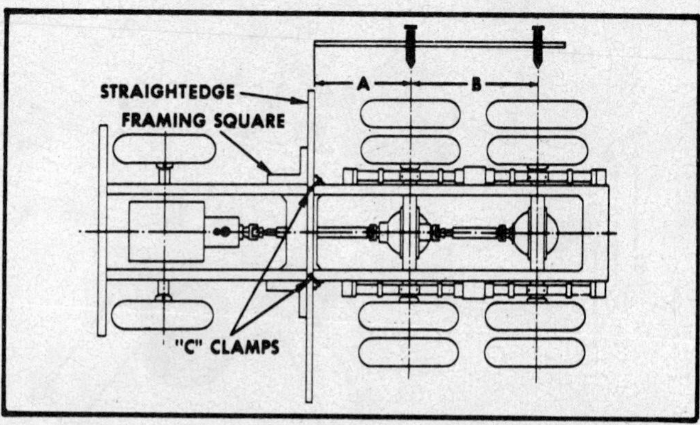

Measurement points of tandem axles for alignment check
(© International Harvester Co.)

INDEX

BEFORE SERVICING, SEE THE SAFETY NOTICE AT THE FRONT OF THE BOOK

GENERAL ENGINE SPECIFICATIONS

Year	Engine No. Cyl. Displacement (cu. in.)	Carburetor Type	Horsepower @ rpm①	Torque @ rpm (ft lbs)①	Bore and Stroke (in.)	Advertised Compression Ratio	Oil Pressure @ 30 mph (psi)
'80	6-258	2 bbl	110 @ 3200	210 @ 1800	3.750 × 3.895	8.0:1	37
	8-304	2 bbl	125 @ 3200	220 @ 2400	3.750 × 3.440	8.40:1	37
	8-360	2 bbl	175 @ 4000	285 @ 2900	4.080 × 3.440	8.25:1	37
'81	4-151	2 bbl	87 @ 4400	128 @ 2400	4.00 × 3.00	8.3:1	36–41
	6-258	2 bbl	110 @ 3200	210 @ 1800	3.750 × 3.895	8.0:1	37
	8-304	2 bbl	125 @ 3200	220 @ 2400	3.750 × 3.440	8.40:1	37
	8-360	2 bbl	175 @ 4000	285 @ 2900	4.080 × 3.440	8.25:1	37
'82	4-151	2 bbl	87 @ 4400	128 @ 2400	4.00 × 3.00	8.3:1	36–41
	6-258	2 bbl	110 @ 3200	210 @ 1800	3.750 × 3.895	8.0:1	37
	8-360	2 bbl	175 @ 4000	285 @ 2900	4.080 × 3.440	8.25:1	37
'83	4-150	1 bbl	83 @ 4200	116 @ 2600	3.876 × 3.188	9.2:1	40
	4-151	2 bbl	87 @ 4400	128 @ 2400	4.00 × 3.00	8.3:1	36–41
	6-258	2 bbl	110 @ 3200	210 @ 1800	3.750 × 3.895	8.0:1	37
	8-360	2 bbl	175 @ 4000	285 @ 2900	4.080 × 3.440	8.25:1	37
'84	4-150	1 bbl	83 @ 4200	116 @ 2600	3.876 × 3.188	9.2:1	40
	6-173	2 bbl	110 @ 4800	148 @ 2000	3.50 × 2.99	8.5:1	45
	6-258	2 bbl	110 @ 3200	210 @ 1800	3.750 × 3.895	8.0:1	37
	8-360	2 bbl	175 @ 4000	285 @ 2900	4.080 × 3.440	8.25:1	37
'85–'86	4-150	1 bbl②	83 @ 4200	116 @ 2600	3.876 × 3.188	9.2:1	40
	4-126	Diesel	N/A	N/A	3.358 × 3.503	21.5:1	11.6③
	6-173	2 bbl	110 @ 4800	148 @ 2000	3.50 × 2.99	8.5:1	45
	6-258	2 bbl	110 @ 3200	210 @ 1800	3.750 × 3.895	8.0:1	37
	8-360	2 bbl	175 @ 4000	285 @ 2900	4.080 × 3.440	8.25:1	37

① Horsepower and torque are SAE net figures. They are measured at the rear of the transmission with all accessories installed and operating. Since the figures vary when a given engine is installed in different models, some are representative rather than exact.

② Some vehicles are equipped with fuel injection.

③ 11.6 at Idle
45.5 at 3000 RPM

TUNE-UP SPECIFICATIONS

Year	Engine No. Cyl Displacement (cu. in.)	hp	Spark Plugs Type	Spark Plugs Gap (in.)	Distributor Point Dwell (deg)	Ignition Timing (deg)⑯	Valves Intake Opens⑰ (deg)	Fuel Pump Pressure (psi)	Idle speed Man Trans	Idle speed Auto Trans
'80	6–258	110	N-13L	.035	Electronic	8B	14½	4–5	700	600
	8–304	125	N-12Y	.035	Electronic	8B⑤	14¾	5–6½	700(500)	600
	8–360	175	N-12Y	.035	Electronic	8B	14¾	5–6½	800	600
'81	4–151	87	RBL13Y6	.060	Electronic	14⑳	33	4–5¾	500	650
	6–258	110	N-13L	.035	Electronic	8B	14½	4–5	700	600
	8–304	125	N-12Y	.035	Electronic	8B⑤	14¾	5–6½	700	600
	8–360	175	N-12Y	.035	Electronic	8B	14¾	5–6½	800	600
'82	4–151	87	RBL13Y6	.060	Electronic	14⑳	33	4–5¾	500	650
	6–258	110	N-13L	.035	Electronic	8B	14½	4–5	700	600
	8–360	175	N-12Y	.035	Electronic	8B	14¾	5–6½	800	600

TUNE-UP SPECIFICATIONS

Year	Engine No. Cyl Displacement (cu. in.)	hp	Spark Plugs Type	Spark Plugs Gap (in.)	Distributor Point Dwell (deg)	Ignition Timing (deg)⑯	Valves Intake Opens⑰ (deg)	Fuel Pump Pressure (psi)	Idle speed Man Trans	Idle speed Auto Trans
'83	4–150	—	RFN14LY	.035	Electronic	12B	27	6½–8	750	750
	4–151	87	R44T5X	.060	Electronic	10B㉑	33	6½–8	900	700
	6–173	110	RUT2YC	.041	Electronic	10B	21	5–7	750	750
	6–258	110	RFN14LY	.035	Electronic	8B㉒	14½	4–5	700	600
	8–360	175	RN12Y	.035	Electronic	8B	14¾	5–6	800	600
'84	4–150	—	RFN14LY	.035	Electronic	12B	27	6½–8	750	750
	6–173	110	RUT2YC	.041	Electronic	10B	21	5–7	750	750
	6–258	110	RFN14LY	.035	Electronic	8B㉒	14½	4–5	700	600
	8–360	175	RN12Y	.035	Electronic	8B	14¾	5–6	800	600
'85–'86	4–150	—	RFN14LY	.035	Electronic	12B	27	6½–8	750	750
	4-126	—	NONE		NONE	—	—	N/A	750–850	750–850
	6–173	110	RUT2YC	.041	Electronic	10B	21	5–7	750	750
	6–258	110	RFN14LY	.035	Electronic	8B㉒	14½	4–5	700	600
	8–360	175	RN12Y	.035	Electronic	8B	14¾	5–6	800	600

NOTE: If the information given in this chart disagrees with the information on the engine tune-up decal, use the specifications on the decal.
NOTE: Figures in parentheses are for California engines
B-Before top dead center (BTDC)
⑤ w/manual trans.—5B CJ model only
⑯ With vacuum advance disconnected
⑰ All figures before TDC
⑳ Both manual and automatic transmissions
㉑ w/auto. trans; 12B
㉒ Calif. CJ w/man. trans; 6B

FIRING ORDERS

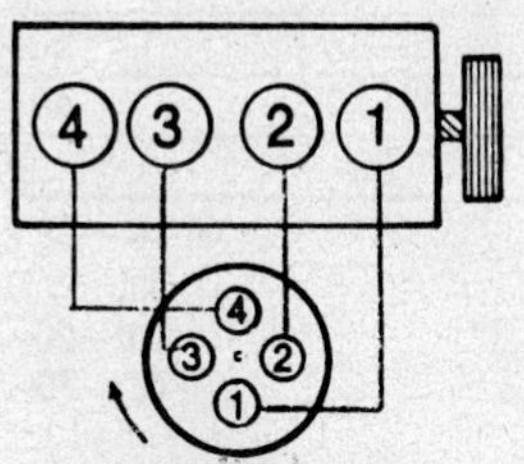

AMC 150 4cyl
Engine firing order 1-3-4-2
Distributor rotation—Clockwise

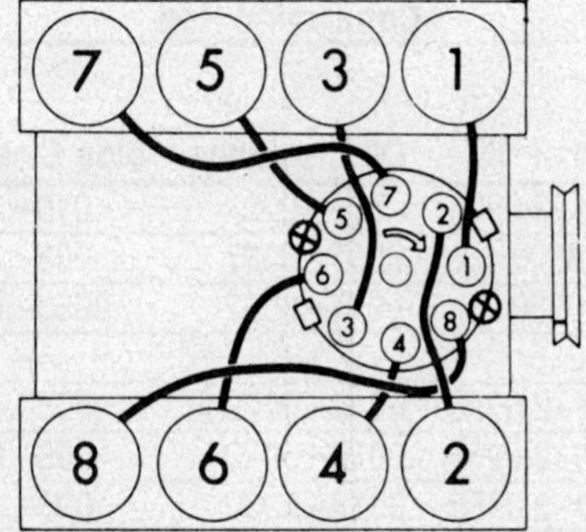

V8 engines
Firing order: 1-8-4-3-6-5-7-2

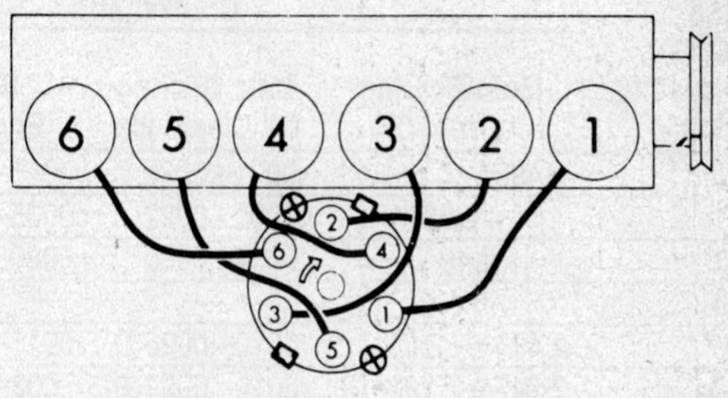

6 cylinder engines
Firing order: 1-5-3-6-2-4

FIRING ORDERS

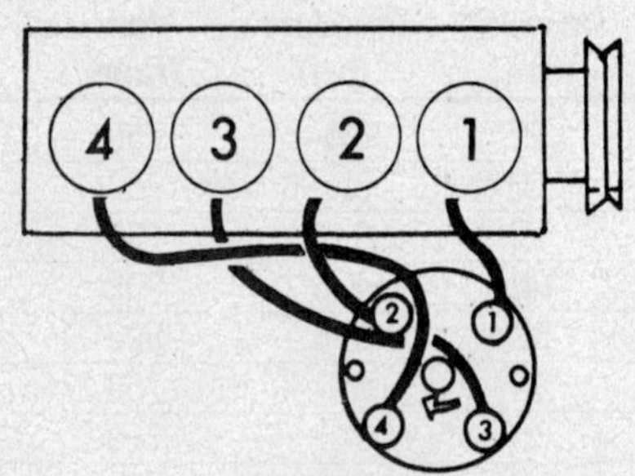

AMC 151 CID 4-cyl.
Engine firing order: 1-3-4-2
Distributor rotation: clockwise

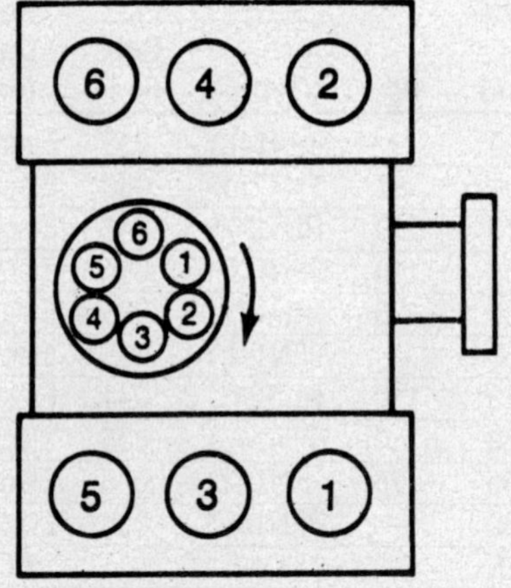

173 V6 (2.8 L)
Engine firing order: 1-2-3-4-5-6
Distributor rotation: clockwise

TORQUE SPECIFICATIONS

(All readings in ft. lbs.)

Engine No. cyl Displacement (cu in.)	Cylinder Head Bolts	Rod Bearing Bolts	Main Bearing Bolts	Crankshaft Balancer Bolt	Flywheel-to-Crankshaft Bolts	Manifold Intake	Manifold Exhaust
4-150	85	33	80	20	65	23	23
4-151	95	30	65	160	55	40	40
6-173	70	37	70	75	50	23	25
6-258	95–115	26–30①	75–85	50–64	95–120	37–47	20–30②
8-304,360	100–120	26–30①	90–105	48–64	95–120	37–47	20–30③
4-126	④	48	69	96	44	N/A	N/A

N/A - Not Appicable
① 30–35 for '80
② 18–20 for '80
③ 20–30, center two bolts; 12–18, outer four bolts for '80
④ 1st—22 ft. lbs.
2nd—37 ft. lbs.
3rd—20–77 ft. lbs.
4th—70–77 ft. lbs.

CRANKSHAFT AND CONNECTING ROD SPECIFICATIONS

(All measurements given in inches)

Engine No. Cyl. Displacement (cu. in.)	Crankshaft: Main Bearing Journal Dia	Crankshaft: Main Bearing Oil Clearance	Crankshaft: Shaft End Play	Crankshaft: Thrust on No.	Connecting Rod: Journal Dia	Connecting Rod: Oil Clearance	Connecting Rod: Side Clearance
4-150	2.4996–2.5001	.0001–.0025	.0015–.0065	2	2.0934–2.0955	.001–.003	.010–.019
4-151	2.2988	.0005–.0022	.0035–.0085	5	1.8690	.0007–.0027	.006–.022
6-173	2.4940	.0017–.0030	.0020–.0067	3	1.9980	.0014–.0032	.0063–.0173
4-126	2.475	—	—	—	2.216	—	—
6-258	2.4986–2.5001	.0010–.0020①	.0015–.0065⑤	3	2.0934–2.0955	.0010–.0020②	.005–.014
V8-304	2.7474–2.7489③	.0010–.0020④	.003–.008⑥	3	2.0934–2.0955	.0010–.0020	.006–.018
V8-360	2.7474–2.7489③	.0010–.0020④	.003–.008	3	2.0934–2.0955	.0010–.0030	.006–.018

② '80–'82: .0010–.0025 (.0015–.0020 preferred)
③ #5: 2.7464–2.7479
④ #5: .0020–.0030
⑤ '81–'82: #1: .005–.0026
2,3,4,5,6: .0005–.0030
7: .0011–.0035
⑥ '81–'82: .0010–.0030 #5: .0020–.0040

VALVE SPECIFICATIONS

Engine No. Cyl. Displacement (cu. in.)	Seat Angle ① (deg)	Face Angle ② (deg)	Spring Test Pressure (lbs @ in.)	Spring Installed Height (in.)	Stem-to-Guide Clearance (in.) Intake	Stem-to-Guide Clearance (in.) Exhaust	Stem Diameter (in.) Intake	Stem Diameter (in.) Exhaust
4-150	—	44	212 @ 1.20	1.82	.0010–.0030	.0010–.0030	.3412	.3412
4-151	46	45	82 @ 1.66④	1 21/32 ③ ④	.0010–.0027	.0010–.0027	.3422	.3422
6-173	46⑤	45⑤	195 @ 1.18	1.57	.0010–.0027	.0010–.0027	.3416	.3416
6-258	44½	44	100 @ 1 13/16 ④	2 15/64 ③ ④	.0010–.0030	.0010–.0030	.3720	.3720
8-304	44½	44	84 @ 1 13/16 ④	2 15/64 ③ ④	.0010–.0030	.0010–.0030	.3720	.3720
8-360	44½	44	84 @ 1 13/16 ④	2 15/64 ③ ④	.0010–.0030	.0010–.0030	.3720	.3720
4-126		45	51 @ 1.54	1.779	—	—	.3140	.3140

① Exhaust valve seat angle given; all intake valve seat angles are 30° unless otherwise noted
② Exhaust valve face angle given; all intake valve face angles are 29° unless otherwise noted
③ '80–2"
④ Without rotaters
⑤ Intake or Exhaust V6 only

PISTON RING SPECIFICATIONS

All measurements given in inches

Engine No. Cyl. Displacment (cu. in)	Ring Gap: Top Compression	Ring Gap: Bottom Compression	Ring Gap: Oil Control	Ring Side Clearance: Top Compression	Ring Side Clearance: Bottom Compression	Ring Side Clearance: Oil Control	Piston to Bore Clearance
4-150	.010–.020	.010–.020	.010–.025	.0017–.0032	.0017–.0032	.001–.008	.0009–.0017
4-151	.010–.020	.010–.020	.010–.020	.0025–.0033	.0025–.0033	.0025–.0033	.0025–.0033
6-173	.010–.020	.010–.020	.020–.055	.0012–.0028	.0016–.0037	.0078 max.	.0017–.0027
6-258	.010–.020	.010–.020	.010–.025	.0015–.003	.0015–.003	.001–.008	.0009–.0017
8-304	.010–.020	.010–.020	.010–.025	.0015–.0035	.0015–.003	.0011–.008	.0010–.0018
8-360	.010–.020	.010–.020	.015–.045	.0015–.0035	.0015–.0035	.000–.007	.0012–.0020
4-126	—	—	—	—	—	—	—

ENGINE ELECTRICAL

Distributor

Removal and Installation

1. Disconnect the negative battery cable. Remove all necessary components in order to gain access to the distributor assembly.
2. Remove the distributor cap and wires. Remove all electrical connections and vacuum lines as required.
3. Note the position of the rotor in relation to the base. Scribe a mark on the base of the distributor and on the engine block to facilitate reinstallation. Align the marks with the direction the metal tip of the rotor is pointing.
4. Remove the bolt that holds the distributor to the engine.
5. Lift the distributor assembly from the engine.
6. Installation is the reverse of the removal procedure.

NOTE: Some distributors have a gear on the end of the distributor shaft and a gear on the end of the oil pump drive, these gears have to mesh with the same teeth as originally installed when the distributor is inserted into the engine. If the distributor shaft gear and the oil pump drive gear are one tooth off from what they are supposed to be, the engine will not run correctly.

If the engine has been turned while the distributor has been removed, or if the marks were not drawn, it will be necessary to initially time the engine. Follow the procedure below:

1. It is necessary to place the No. 1 cylinder in the firing position to correctly install the distributor. To locate this position, some engines have marks placed on the flywheel while other engines have marks placed on the timing gear covers and crankshaft pulleys. The flywheel marks may be viewed

through a covered opening directly in back of the starting motor by loosening the hole cover and sliding it to one side.

2. Remove the No. 1 cylinder spark plug. Turn the engine until the piston in No. 1 cylinder is moving up on the compression stroke. This can be determined by placing your thumb over the spark plug hole and feeling the air being forced out of the cylinder.

3. Oil the distributor housing lightly where the distributor bears on the cylinder block.

4. When the distributor shaft has reached the bottom of the hole, move the rotor back and forth slightly until the drive gears of the distributor and cam mesh and until the distributor assembly slides down into place.

5. Install the spark plug into the No. 1 spark plug hole. Install the distributor.

IGNITION TIMING

ALL ENGINES, EXCEPT DIESEL

1. Locate the timing marks on the crankshaft pulley and the front of the timing case cover.

2. Clean off the timing marks.

3. Use chalk or white paint to color the mark on the scale that will indicate the correct timing, when aligned with the mark on the pulley or the pointer.

4. Attach a tachometer to the engine.

5. Attach a timing light to the engine.

6. Disconnect and plug the vacuum lines to the distributor, if equipped. Loosen the distributor lockbolt just enough so that the distributor can be turned with a little resistance.

7. Adjust the idle to the correct specification.

8. With the timing light aimed at the pulley and the marks on the engine, turn the distributor in the direction of rotor rotation to retard the spark, and in the opposite direction of rotor rotation to advance the spark. Align the marks on the pulley and the engine with the flashes of the timing light.

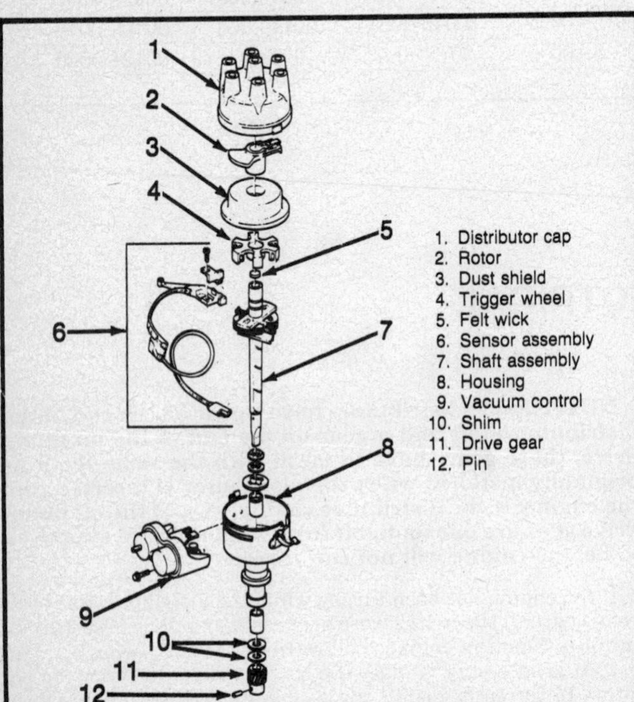

Typical electronic ignition distributor—exploded view
(© Jeep Corp.)

DIESEL ENGINE

The injection pump static timing must be adjusted manually, without the aid of electronic meters, for proper engine operation and to conform to the manufacturer recommended timing procedures for emission control.

NOTE: Special dial indicator tools must be used for the static timing procedure. If the tools are not available, do not attempt this procedure.

1. Remove the screw plug and gasket, located between the four (4) high pressure fuel outlets at the rear of the fuel injection pump.

2. Install the dial indicator support tool in place of the screw plug. Insert the stem of the dial indicator into the support tool.

3. Loosen the retaining screw, move the levers back slightly and turn the control cable clevis pin $^1/_4$ of a turn to disengage the cold start system.

4. Rotate the crankshaft clockwise (viewed from the front of the engine) 1 and $^1/_2$ turns. The dial indicator pointer will stop moving when the injection pump piston is at Bottom Dead Center (BDC).

5. Zero the dial indicator pointer with the injection pump piston at Bottom Dead Center (BDC).

6. Remove the Top Dead Center (TDC) slot access hole screw plug from the cylinder block and insert the TDC rod from the dial indicator set, into the access hole.

7. Manually rotate the crankshaft slowly clockwise, as viewed from the front of the engine, until the TDC rod can be inserted into the TDC slot in the crankshaft countershaft.

8. At TDC, the dial indicator pointer should indicate a piston lift travel distance of 0.82 ± 0.02mm (0.032 ± 0.001 in.).

9. If the fuel injection pump piston lift travel distance is not within tolerance, the pump position must be adjusted. To adjust the pump position, observe the dial indicator as the pump is rotated towards the engine and then away. This will increase the pump lift. To decrease the pump lift, rotate the pump away from the engine. Tighten the injection pump retaining bolts.

NOTE: Always adjust the pump piston lift by rotating the pump away from the engine. This is the normal direction of the pump rotation. When increasing the piston lift, rotate the pump towards the engine until the piston lift is greater than the specified tolerance and then rotate the pump away from the engine until the correct piston lift is indicated on the dial indicator.

10. Remove the TDC rod from the crankshaft counterweight TDC slot.

11. Observe the dial indicator and rotate the crankshaft clockwise two (2) complete revolutions until the TDC rod can be inserted into the crankshaft countershaft TDC slot.

12. The dial indicator pointer should return to zero and then move to 0.82 ± 0.02mm (0.032 ± 0.001 in.). This will indicate that the fuel injection pump static timing is correct.

13. Remove the TDC rod from the crankshaft counterweight TDC slot and install the screw plug into the cylinder block access hole.

14. Remove the dial indicator and support tool from the injection pump and install the replacement washer and screw plug into the injection pump.

15. Compress the timing control lever and install the clevis pin in its initial position on the cable clamp. With the lever against the clevis, tighten the screw.

MAGNETIC TIMING PROBE EXCEPT DIESEL

A bracket and hole are cast into the timing case cover for the use of a magnetic timing probe, connected to a special electronic timing meter for precise ignition timing. The probe is inserted into the hole of the bracket until the vibration damper is touched. When the engine is started, the probe is automatically

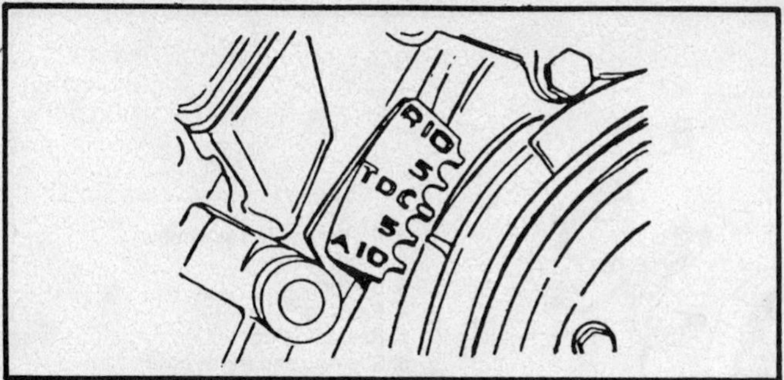

Timing mark location—8 cyl. engines (© Jeep Corp)

BEFORE
16
12
8
4
BTDC
ATDC
NOTCH

Timing mark location—6 cyl. engines (© Jeep Corp)

spaced away from the damper by the damper's eccentricity, or being slightly out of center. The probe senses a milled slot on the damper and compensating for the bracket's ATDC position, registers the reading on the timing meter. Any necessary corrections can then be made to the ignition timing.

NOTE: Do not use the probe bracket and hole to check the ignition timing when using a conventional timing light.

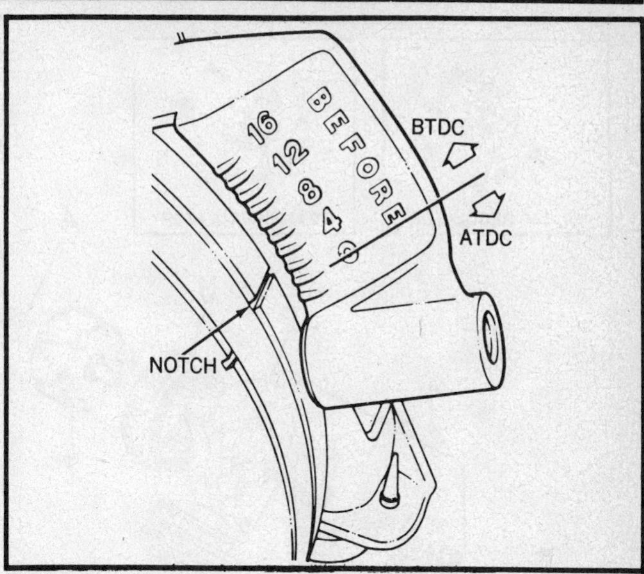

ALTERNATOR

Refer to the Electrical Unit Repair section for detailed alternator test and overhaul procedures.

Removal and Installation

1. Disconnect the negative battery cable from the battery. Remove all necessary components in order to gain access to the alternator assembly.

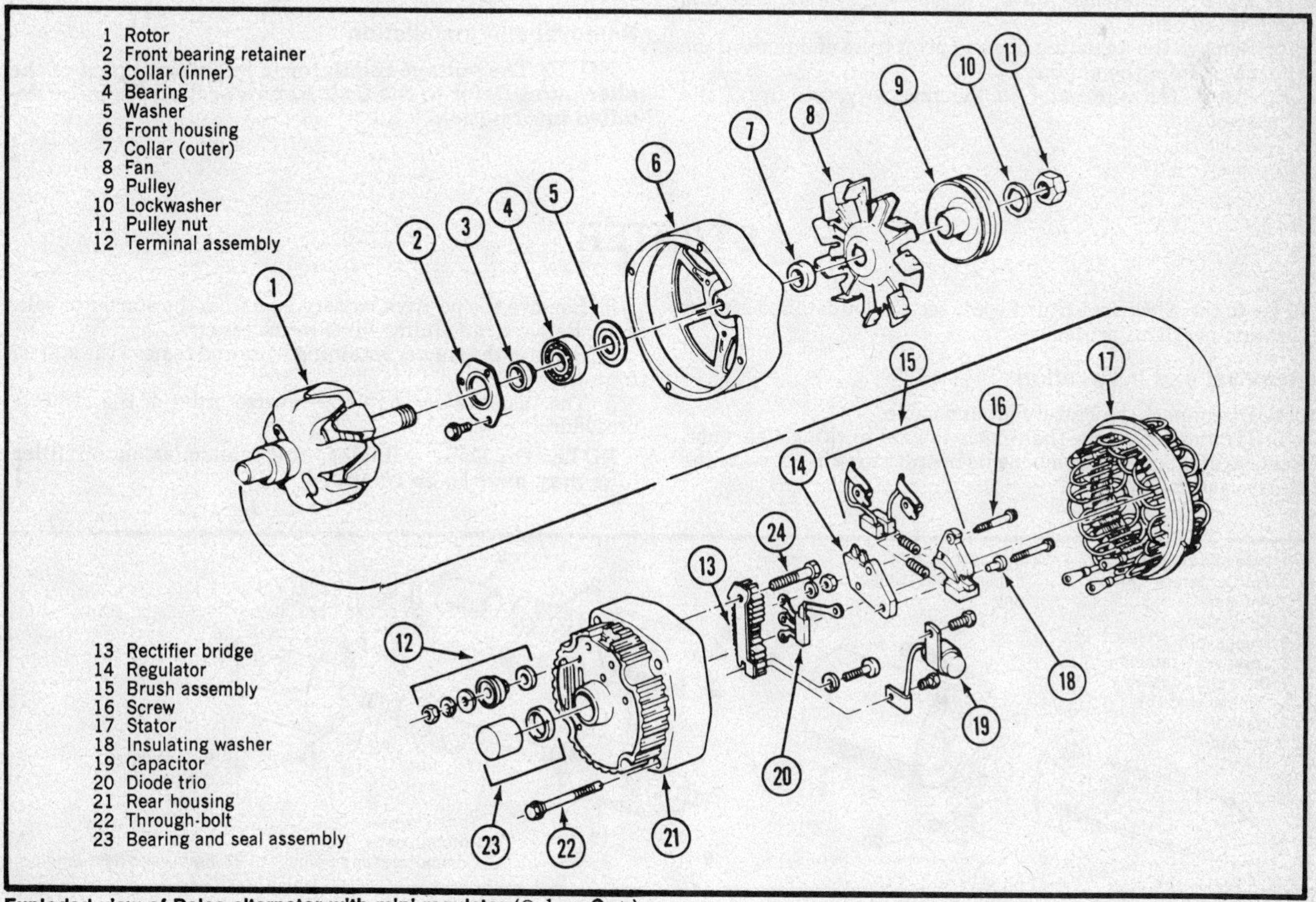

1 Rotor
2 Front bearing retainer
3 Collar (inner)
4 Bearing
5 Washer
6 Front housing
7 Collar (outer)
8 Fan
9 Pulley
10 Lockwasher
11 Pulley nut
12 Terminal assembly
13 Rectifier bridge
14 Regulator
15 Brush assembly
16 Screw
17 Stator
18 Insulating washer
19 Capacitor
20 Diode trio
21 Rear housing
22 Through-bolt
23 Bearing and seal assembly

Exploded view of Delco alternator with mini regulator (© Jeep Corp)

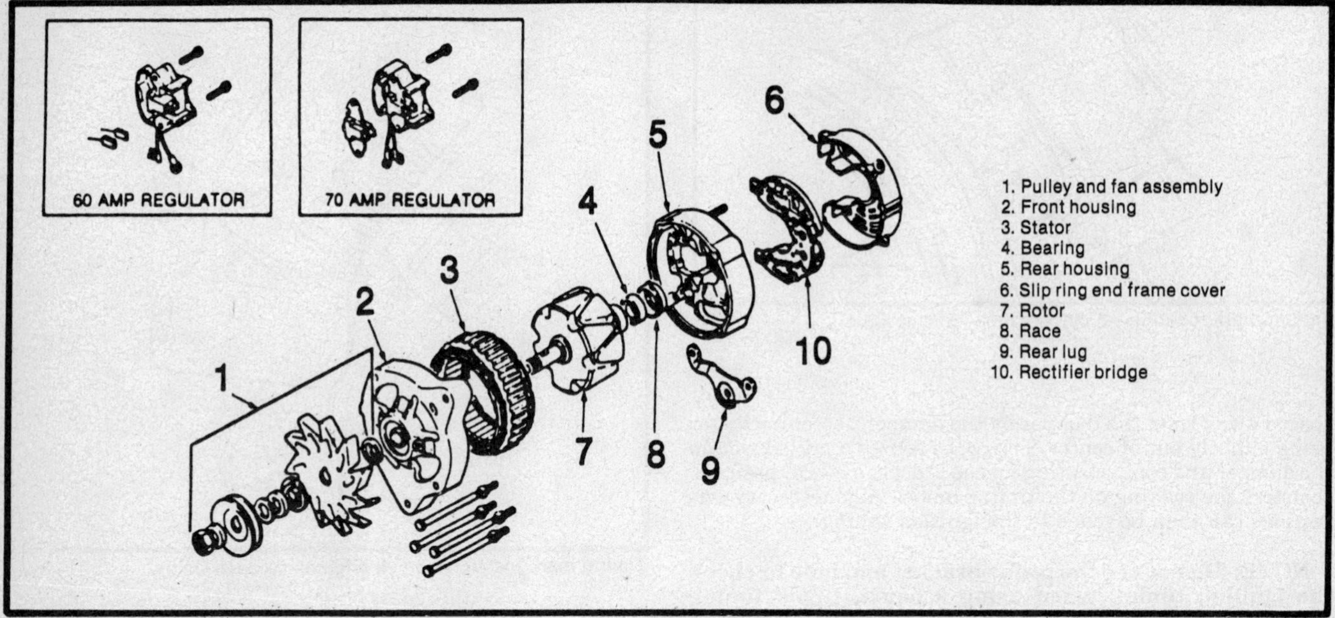

Exploded view of Paris-Rhone alternator (© Jeep Corp.)

2. Remove the wire terminals attached to the rear of the alternator.
3. Loosen the bolt holding the adjusting bar and the pivot bolt at the opposite side of the alternator.
4. Move the alternator inward to relieve the belt tension and remove the belt.
5. Remove the adjusting bar and pivot bolts and remove the alternator from the engine.
6. Install the alternator in the reverse procedure of the disassembly.
7. When installing the belt, adjust to allow ½ in. play on the longest run between the pulleys.

Voltage Regulator

Removal and Installation

NOTE: The voltage regulator is an integral part of the alternator. Refer to the Unit Repair section for more detailed information.

STARTER

Refer to the Electrical Unit Repair section for detailed starter test and overhaul procedures.

Removal and Installation

1. Disconnect the battery ground cable.
2. If necessary, raise the vehicle to gain working clearance. Remove all necessary components in order to gain access to the starter assembly.
3. Remove the positive battery lead from the starter or solenoid. Remove remaining wires as necessary.
4. Remove the starter retaining bolts and remove the starter from the vehicle.
5. The installation is in the reverse order of the removal procedure.

NOTE: On some vehicles, the transmission oil filler tube may have to be removed.

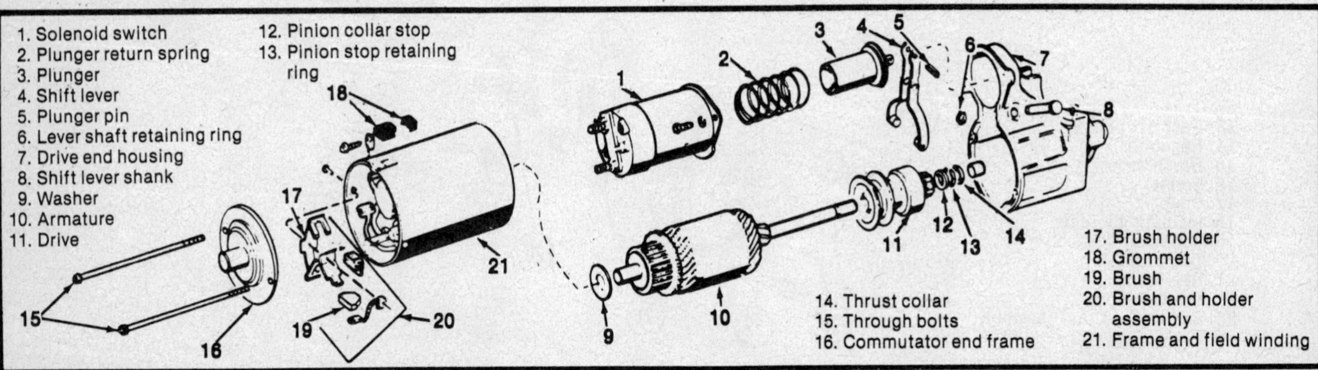

Delco starter motor—exploded view (© Jeep Corp.)

1. Bushing
2. Screw
3. Shield
4. Solenoid switch
5. Retainer
6. Stop ring
7. Bushing
8. Overrunnig clutch drive
9. Fork
10. Bearing pedestal
11. Sealing rubber
12. Planetary gear system
13. Armature
14. Stator Frame
15. Bush holder
16. Gasket
17. Commutator end shield
18. Bushing
19. Seal ring
20. Shim
21. Shim
22. Retaining washer
23. Closure cap
24. Hexagon-screw
25. Screw

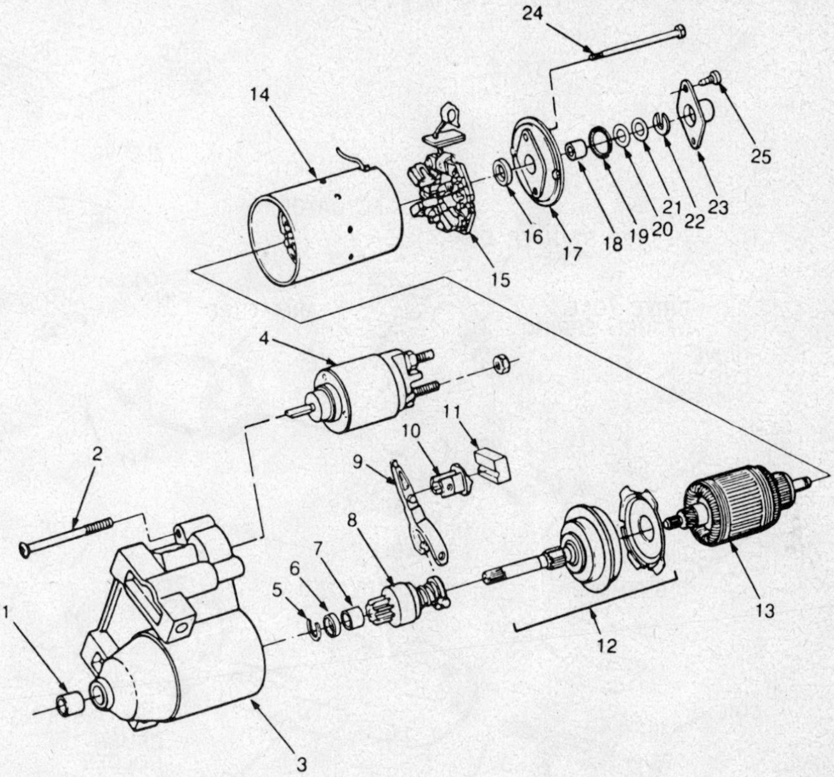

Bosch starter motor—exploded view (© Jeep Corp.)

1. End housing bushing
2. Drive-end housing
3. Spacer
4. Pad
5. Solenoid plate
6. Solenoid
7. Pinion shift yoke
8. Support plate
9. Support plate bushing
10. Field winding and pole shoe sets (4)
11. Pole shoe screw (4)
12. Armature housing
13. Grommet
14. Brush set (4) 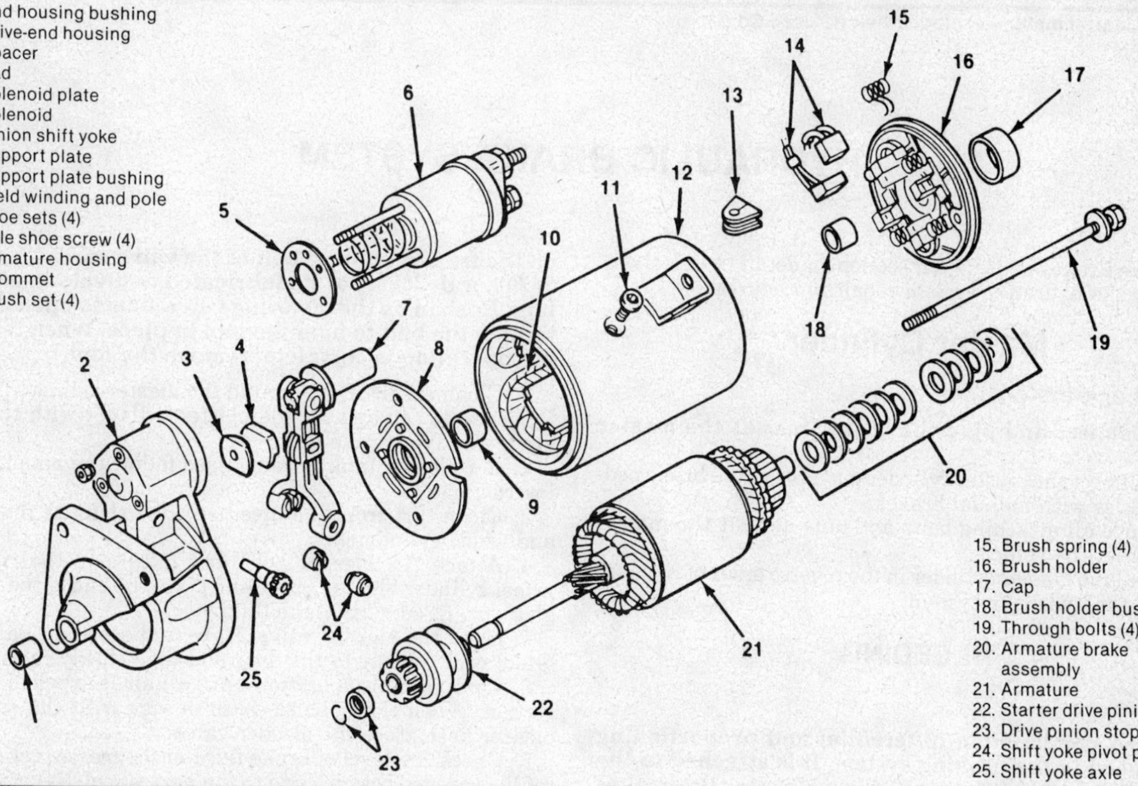
15. Brush spring (4)
16. Brush holder
17. Cap
18. Brush holder bushing
19. Through bolts (4)
20. Armature brake assembly
21. Armature
22. Starter drive pinion
23. Drive pinion stop
24. Shift yoke pivot pins
25. Shift yoke axle

Paris-Rhone starter motor—exploded view (© Jeep Corp.)

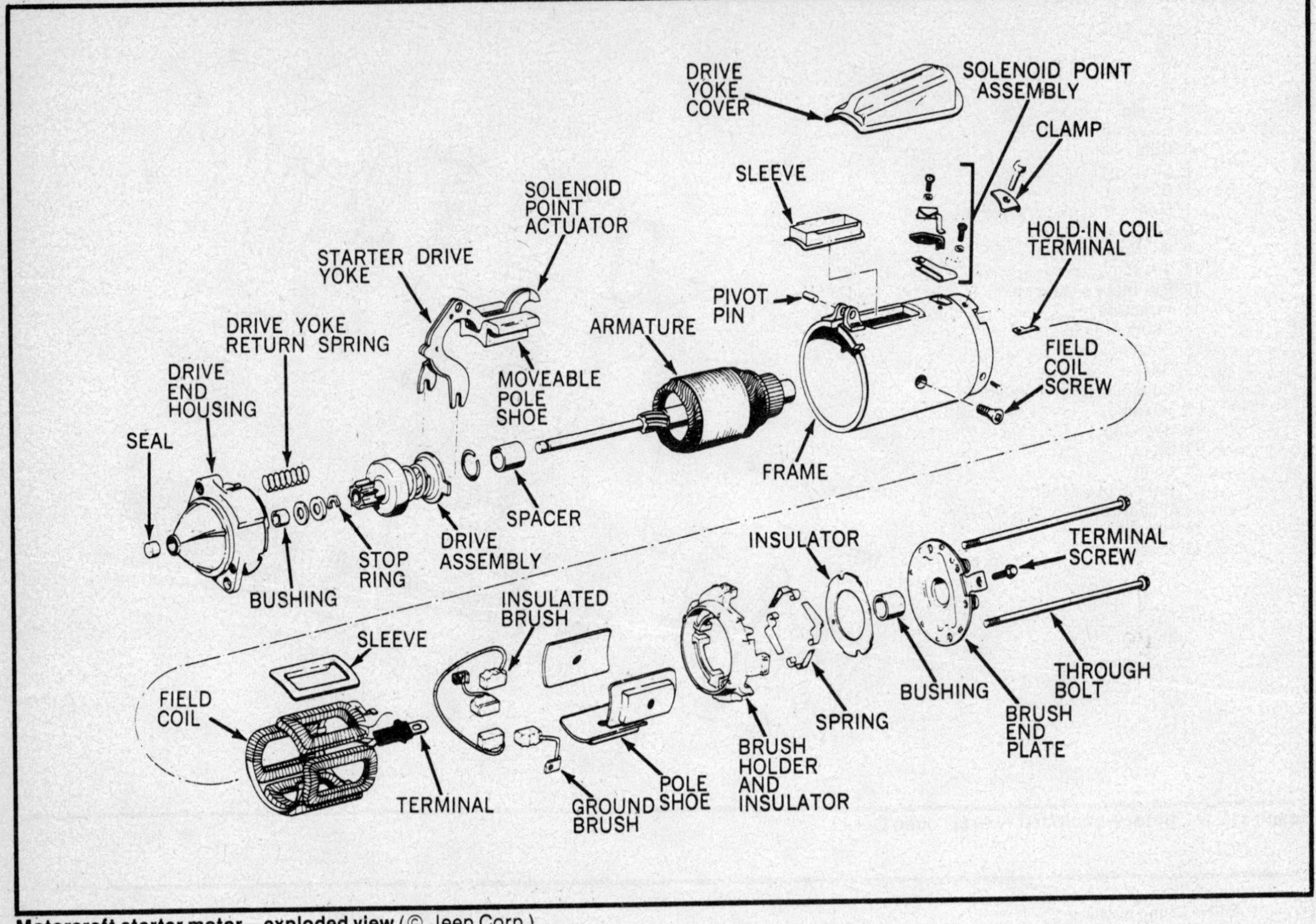

Motorcraft starter motor—exploded view (© Jeep Corp.)

HYDRAULIC BRAKE SYSTEM

Refer to the Brakes Unit Repair section for detail troubleshooting and brake hydraulic system repair procedures.

Master Cylinder

Removal and Installation

1. Disconnect and plug the brake lines at the master cylinder.
2. Disconnect the master cylinder push rod at the brake pedal on vehicles with manual brakes.
3. Remove all attaching bolts and nuts and lift the master cylinder from the vehicle.
4. Install the master cylinder in the reverse order of removal and bleed the hydraulic system.

BLEEDING

Procedure

NOTE: A combination differential and proportioning valve is used in the braking system. It is attached to the inner side of the left frame rail. When bleeding the brakes the metering section of the valve must be held open. Loosen the front mounting bolt of the valve and insert tool J–23709 or J–26869, or its fabricated equivalent, under the bolt. Push in on the metering valve stem to open it and retighten the bolt to hold the tool in place. When the bleeding operation is complete, remove the tool.

1. Clean all dirt from around the master cylinder filler cap. Remove the cap and fill the master cylinder with the proper grade and type brake fluid.
2. If a bleeder tank is being used follow the manufacturers instructions.
3. Clean dirt from the bleeder connections at the calipers and wheel cylinders.
4. Attach the bleeder hose and fixture to the right rear wheel cylinder bleeder screw and place the end of the tube in a glass jar, filled with brake fluid.
5. Open the bleeder valve. Have and assistant depress the brake pedal slowly to the floor and then slowly release it.
6. Continue this operation until all air is expelled from the system. When the bubbles cease to appear at the end of the bleeder hose, close the bleeder valve.
7. Check the level of brake fluid in the master cylinder and refill as needed before going to the next wheel. Never reuse old brake fluid.

8. Repeat Steps 4–7 on the left rear wheel than the right front wheel and finally the left front wheel.

Wheel Cylinder

Removal and Installation

1. Raise and support the vehicle and remove the brake drums and brake shoes.
2. Disconnect the brake line. Do not bend the line away from the wheel cylinder. When the cylinder is removed from the support plate, the line will separate from the wheel cylinder easily.
3. Remove the wheel cylinder mounting bolts and remove the wheel cylinder from the brake backing plate.
4. Clean the wheel cylinder mounting surface on the brake support plate. Clean the brake line fitting and threads.
5. Start the brake line fitting into the wheel cylinder and attach the wheel cylinder to the support plate and tighten the brake line fitting. Tighten the wheel cylinder mounting bolts to 18 ft. lbs.

Disc Brakes

Removal and Installation

1. Remove the wheel and tire assembly.
2. Remove approximately ⅔ of the brake fluid from the front section of the master cylinder.
3. Using a C-clamp, bottom the piston in its bore by placing the solid end of the clamp on the back of the caliper and the screw end contacting the metal part of the out board shoe, and tighten the clamp screw.

NOTE: This procedure backs the brake shoes off the rotor surface, easing the lining replacement.

4. Remove both allen head mounting screws from the caliper to support, and lift the caliper off the rotor.

NOTE: Hang the caliper by a wire hook or tie it to the frame, to avoid allowing the brake hose to support the weight of the caliper assembly.

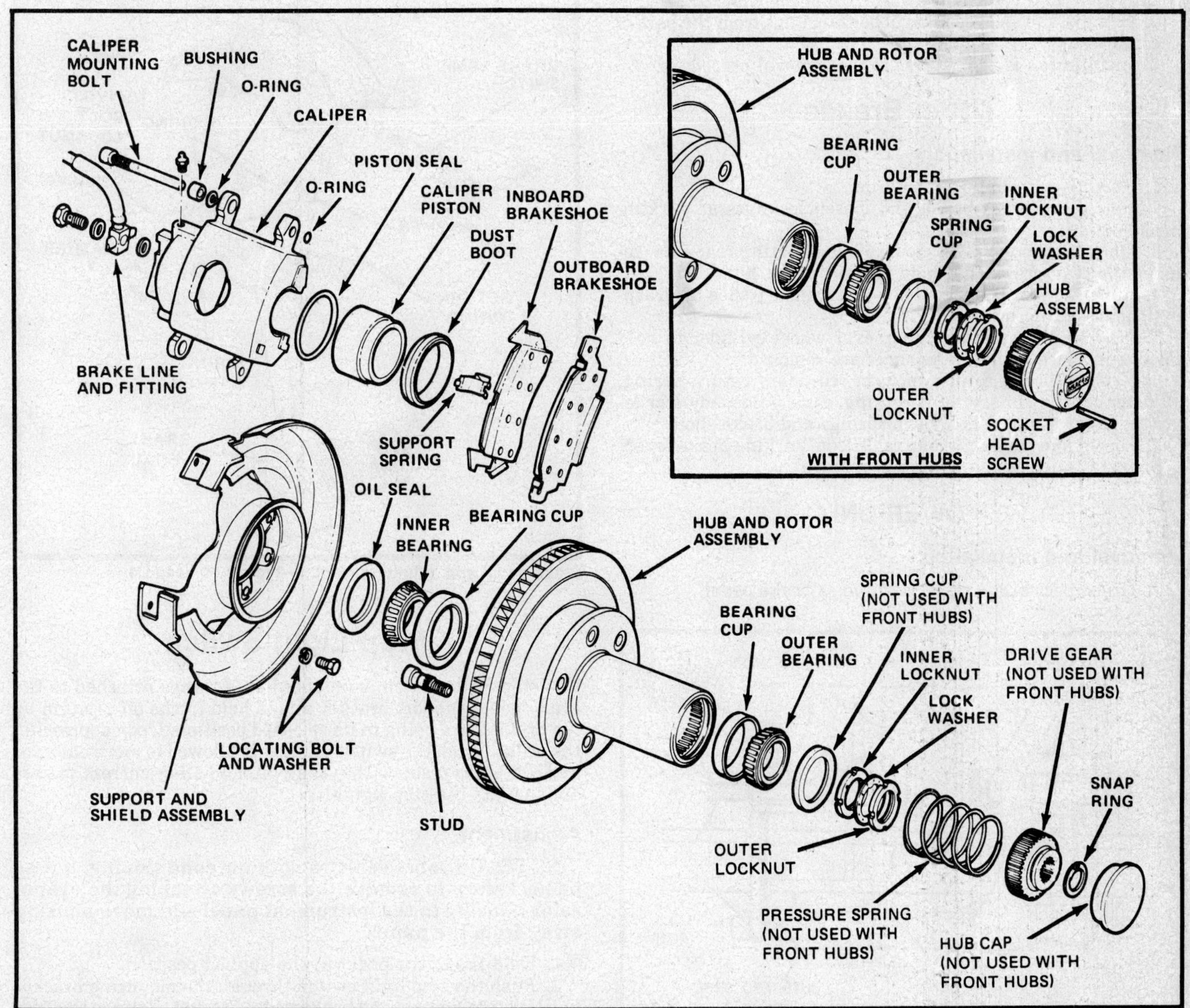

Typical disc brake assembly (© Jeep Corp)

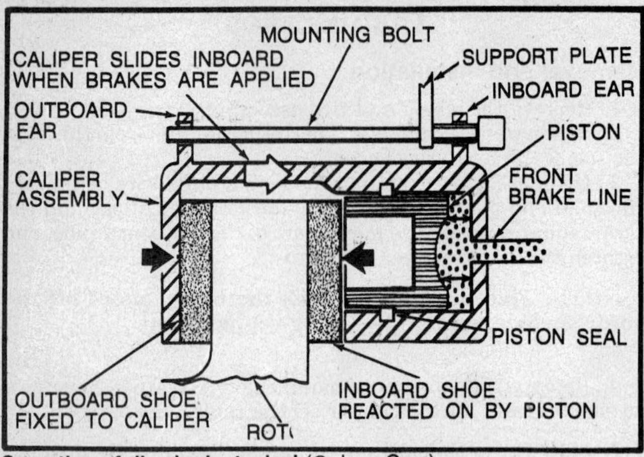

Operation of disc brake typical (© Jeep Corp)

5. Remove both disc brake shoes from the caliper, and note the position of the support spring on the inboard shoe for later installation, and remove the spring from the shoe.
6. Remove the sleeves and rubber bushings from the ears of the calipers.
7. Installation is the reverse of the removal procedure.

Drum Brakes

Removal and Installation

1. Remove wheel and brake drum.
2. Release parking brake and loosen locknuts at parking brake equalizer.
3. On truck models with model 60 full-floating rear axle, remove the two screws that hold rear drums on hubs.
4. Remove lever tang from hole in secondary shoe by grasping the adjusting lever with a pliers.
5. Place brake cylinder clamp over wheel cylinder to hold pistons in place while brake shoes are removed.
6. Remove brake return springs, secondary return spring, adjuster cable, primary return spring, cable guide, adjuster lever, adjuster springs, holddown springs and brake shoes.
7. Disengage parking brake cable from parking brake lever.
8. Installation is the reverse of removal.

POWER UNIT

Removal and Installation

1. Disconnect brake pedal pushrod at brake pedal.

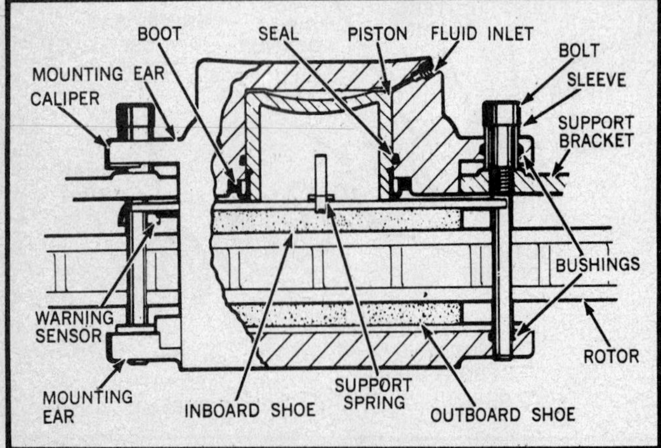

Exploded view of single piston caliper (© Jeep Corp)

2. Disconnect vacuum hose from booster check valve.
3. Remove attaching nuts and separate master cylinder from brake booster. Do not disconnect brake lines at master cylinder.
4. If equipped, remove the bolts holding power unit bellcrank to dash panel and remove power unit and bellcrank as one assembly. Remove the bellcrank from the original power unit and lubricate the pivot pins with chassis lubricant before installing it on the replacement unit.
5. Remove the bolts retaining the power unit to the dash panel and remove the unit.
6. Installation is the reverse of removal.

NOTE: When replacing the power brake unit, use the pushrod that is supplied with the new unit, as it has been correctly gauged and preset to the new unit.

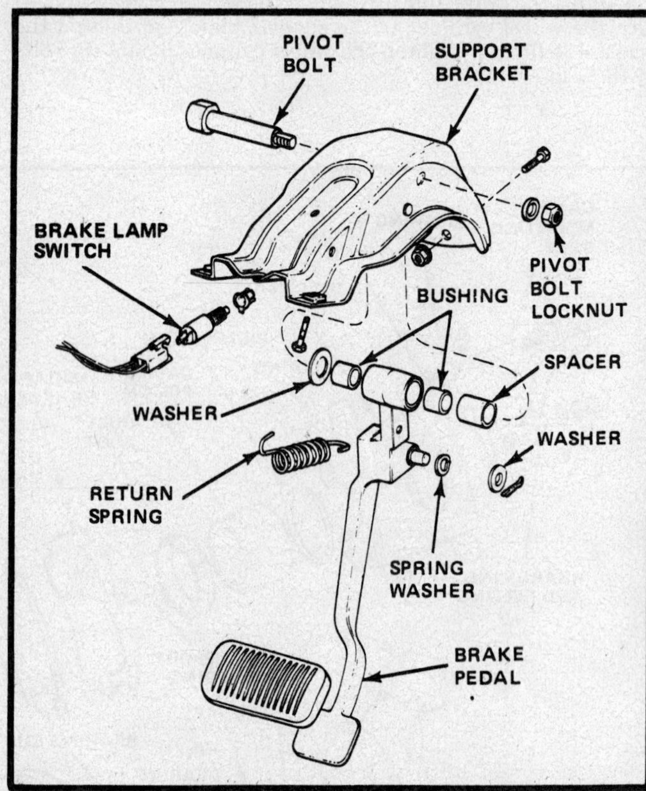

Brake pedal and adjusting switch—typical (© Jeep Corp)

Stop Light Switch

The stop light switch is mounted on a flange attached to the brake pedal support bracket and is held in the off position by the brake pedal being in its released position. Upon depressing the brake pedal, the switch plunger is allowed to move outward and contact is made within the switch to allow current to pass and operate the stop lights.

Adjustment

NOTE: On some vehicles with air conditioning, it may be necessary to remove the screws attaching the evaporator housing to the instrument panel and move housing away from the panel.

1. Hold the brake pedal in the applied position.
2. Push the stop light switch through the mounting bracket until it stops against the brake pedal bracket. Release the pedal to set the switch in the proper position.

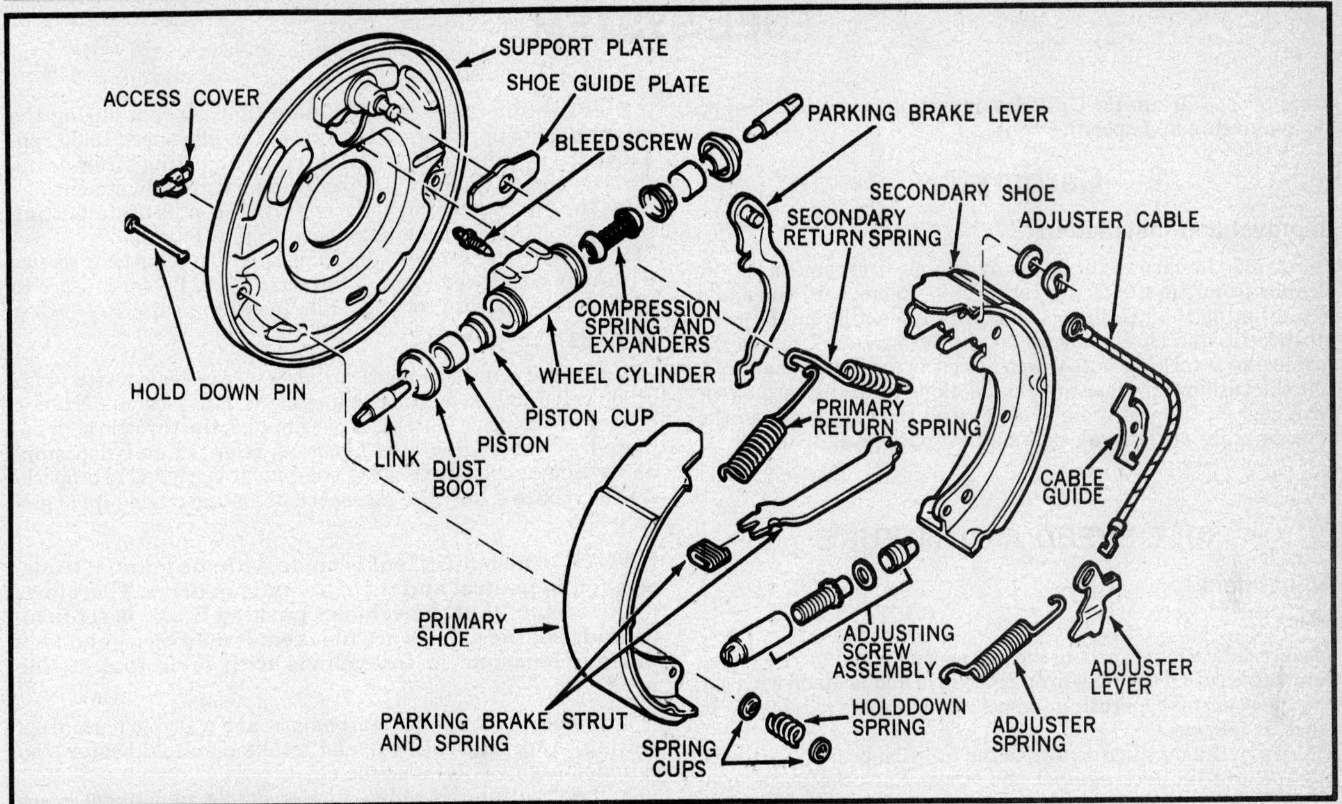

Drum brake assembly—CJ models (© Jeep Corp)

3. Check the position of the switch. The switch plunger should be in the ON position and activate the brake lights after a brake pedal travel of $^3/_8$ to $^5/_8$ in.

Parking Brake

Adjustment

CJ, SCRAMBLER, GRAND WAGONEER AND TRUCK

1. Make sure that the hydraulic brakes are in satisfactory adjustment.
2. Raise the rear wheels off the ground and disengage the parking brake pedal.
3. Loosen the locknut on the brake cable adjusting rod, located directly behind the frame center crossmember.
4. Spin the wheels and tighten the adjustment until the rear wheels drag slightly. Loosen the adjustment until there is no drag and the wheels spin freely.
5. Tighten the locknut to lock the adjusting nut.

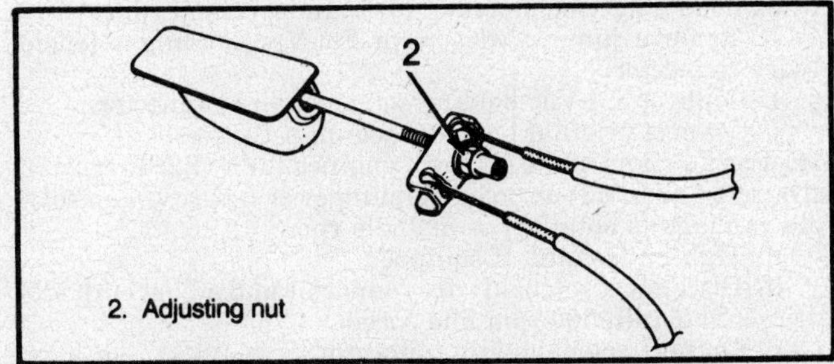

Wagoneer, Cherokee and Comanche parking brake adjusting nut (© Jeep Corp.)

CHEROKEE, WAGONEER AND COMANCHE

1. Make sure that the hydraulic brakes are in satisfactory adjustment.
2. Position the parking brake lever in the fifth notch.
3. Raise and support the vehicle safely. Using adjustment gauge J-34651 apply 55 inch lbs. torque . Adjust the nut on the equalizer so that the gauge pointer is in the blue band.
4. Fully apply and release the parking brake lever five times. Recheck the adjustment.

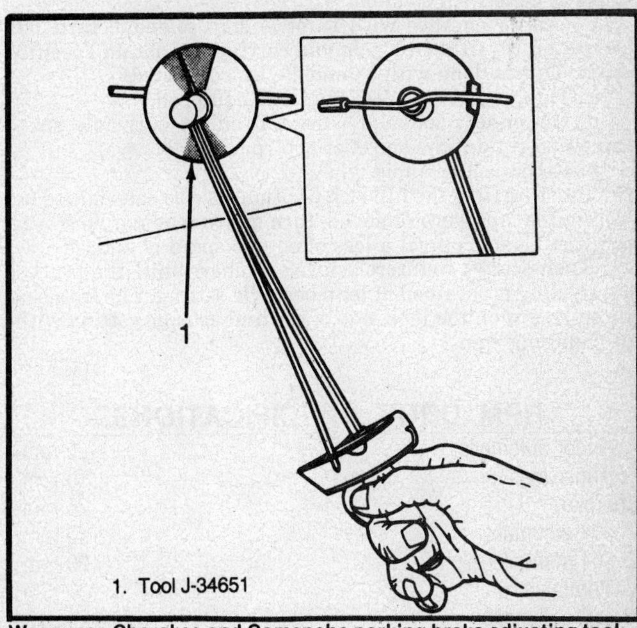

Wagoneer, Cherokee and Comanche parking brake adjusting tool (© Jeep Corp.)

FUEL SYSTEM

Refer to the Carburetor Unit Repair section for exploded views of carburetors and specifications.

Carburetor

Removal and Installation

To remove the carburetor from any engine, first remove the air cleaner from the top of the carburetor. Remove all lines and hoses, noting their positions to facilitate installation. Remove all throttle and choke linkage at the carburetor. Remove the carburetor attaching nuts which hold it to the intake manifold. Lift the carburetor from the engine along with the carburetor base gasket. Discard the gasket. Install the carburetor in the reverse order of removal, using a new base gasket.

IDLE SPEED AND MIXTURE

Adjustment

1980

The procedure for adjusting the idle speed and mixture on Jeep vehicles is called the lean drop procedure and is made with the engine at normal operating temperature and the air cleaner in place as follows:

1. Turn the mixture screws to the full rich position with the tabs on the limiters against the stops. Note the position of screw head slot inside limiter cap slots.
2. Remove idler limiter caps.
3. Remove limiter caps by threading a sheet metal screw in center of cap and turning clockwise. Discard limiter caps.
4. Reset adjustment screws to same position noted before limiter caps were removed.
5. Start engine and allow it to reach normal operating temperature.
6. Adjust idle speed to 30 rpm above the specified rpm in the Tune-Up Specifications.
   a. On 6 cylinder engines with throttle stop solenoid, turn nut on solenoid plunger in or out to obtain specified rpm. This is done with solenoid wire connected.
   b. On V8 engines with throttle stop solenoid, turn hex screw on throttle stop solenoid carriage to obtain specified rpm. This is done with solenoid wire connected.
   c. Tighten solenoid locknut, if so equipped.
   d. Disconnect solenoid wire and adjust curb idle speed screw to obtain idle speed of 500 rpm.
   e. Reconnect solenoid wire.
7. Starting from the full rich position, as was determined before limiter caps were removed, turn mixture adjusting screws clockwise (leaner) until a loss of engine speed is noticed.
8. Turn screws counterclockwise (richer) until the highest rpm reading is obtained at lean best idle setting. The lean best idle setting is on the lean side of the highest rpm setting without changing rpm.

RPM DROP SPECIFICATIONS

6 cylinder automatic	25 rpm
6 cylinder manual	50 rpm
(Cherokee)	25 rpm
V8 304 automatic	40 rpm
V8 304 manual	20 rpm
(California)	100 rpm
V8 360 automatic	20 rpm
V8 360 manual	50 rpm

9. If the idle speed changed more than 30 rpm during the mixture adjustment procedure, reset the idle speed to 30 rpm above the specified rpm with idle speed adjusting screw or the throttle stop solenoid and repeat the mixture adjustment.
10. The final adjustment is to turn the mixture adjusting screws clockwise until engine rpm drop as follows:
11. Install new limiter caps over mixture adjusting screws with tabs positioned against full rich stops. Be careful not to disturb idle mixture setting while installing caps.

1981–82

Idle mixture screws on these carburetors are sealed with plugs or dowel pins. A mixture adjustment must be undertaken ONLY when the carburetor is overhauled, the throttle body replaced, or the engine does not meet required emission standards. Since expensive testing equipment is needed to properly set the mixture, only the idle speed adjusting procedure is given below.

NOTE: The adjustment is made with the manual transmission in neutral and the automatic in drive. Therefore, make certain that the vehicles parking brake is set firmly, and that the wheels are blocked. It may be a good idea to have someone in the vehicle with their foot on the brake.

1. Connect tachometer, start engine and warm to normal operating temperature. Choke and intake manifold heater (six-cylinder engine only) must be off.
2. If not within OK range, turn curb idle adjustment screw to obtain specified curb idle rpm.
3. For six cylinder engine (BBD carburetor):
   a. Disconnect vacuum hose from vacuum actuator and holding solenoid wire connector. Adjust curb (slow) idle speed adjustment screw to obtain specified curb (slow) idle rpm if not within OK range. Refer to Emission Control Information label, and Tune-Up Specifications.
   b. Apply direct source of vacuum to vacuum actuator.
   c. Turn vacuum actuator adjustment screw on throttle lever until specified rpm is obtained (900 rpm for manual transmissions, and 800 rpm for automatic transmissions).
   d. Disconnect manifold vacuum source from vacuum actuator.
   e. With jumper wire apply battery voltage (12V) to energize holding solenoid. Turn A/C on, if equipped.

NOTE: Throttle must be opened manually to allow Sol-Vac throttle positioner to be extended. With Sol-Vac throttle positioner extended, idle speed should be 650 rpm for automatic transmission equipped vehicles and 750 rpm for manual transmission equipped vehicles.

   g. If idle speed is not within tolerance, adjust Sol-Vac (hex-head adjustment screw) to obtain specified rpm.
   h. Remove jumper wire from Sol-Vac holding solenoid wire connector.
   i. Connect Sol-Vac holding solenoid wire connector.
   j. Connect original hose to vacuum actuator.
4. For four and eight cylinder engines (2SE, E2SE or 2150 carburetor, turn nut on solenoid plunger or hex screw on solenoid carriage to obtain specified idle rpm:
   a. Tighten locknut, if equipped.
   b. Disconnect solenoid wire connector and adjust curb idle screw to obtain 500 rpm idle speed.
   c. Connect solenoid wire connector.
   d. If model 2150 carburetor (eight-cylinder engine, is equipped with dashpot. With throttle at curb idle position,

fully depress dashpot stem and measure clearance between stem and throttle lever. Clearance should be 0.032 in. (0.813mm). Adjust by loosening locknut and turning dashpot.

4-CYLINDER ENGINE IDLE ADJUSTMENT (2.5L)

1983–84

1. Fully warm-up the engine.
2. Choke Fast Idle Adjustment.
   a. Disconnect and plug the EGR valve vacuum hose.
   b. Position the fast idle adjustment screw on the second step of the fast idle cam with the transmission in neutral.
   c. Adjust fast idle speed to: 2000 rpm – Man. Trans./2300 rpm – Auto. Trans.
   d. Allow the throttle to return to normal curb idle and reconnect the EGR vacuum hose.
3. Sole-Vac Vacuum Actuator Adjustment
   a. Remove the vacuum hose to the vacuum actuator and plug the hose. Connect an external vacuum source to the actuator and apply 10–15 inches Hg. of vacuum to the actuator.
   b. Shift transmission to Neutral.
   c. Adjust idle speed to the following rpm using the vacuum actuator adjustment screw on the throttle lever: 850 rpm – Auto. Trans./950 rpm – Man. Trans.
   The adjustment is made with all accessories turned off.

NOTE: The curb idle should always be adjusted after vacuum actuator adjustment.

4. Curb Idle adjustment.
   a. Remove the vacuum hose to the sole-vac vacuum actuator and plug the hose.
   b. Shift transmission into Neutral.
   c. Adjust the curb idle using the $1/4$ in. hex-head adjustment screw on the end of the sole-vac unit. Set speed to: 750 rpm – Man. Trans./700 rpm – Auto. Trans.

NOTE: Engine speed will vary 10–30 rpm during this mode due to closed loop fuel control.

Reconnect the vacuum hose to the vacuum actuator.

5. TRC Adjustment (Anti-Diesel)

The TRC screw is preset at the factory and should not require adjustment. However, to check adjustment, the screw should be $3/4$ turn from closed throttle position.

SIX-CYLINDER ENGINE IDLE ADJUSTMENT (4.2L)

1. Sole-Vac Vacuum Actuator Adjustment
   a. Disconnect and plug the vacuum hose to the sole-vac vacuum actuator.
   b. Disconnect the sole-vac electrical connector.
   c. Connect an external vacuum source to the vacuum actuator and apply 10–15 inches (Hg.) of vacuum.
   d. Open throttle for *at least 3.0 seconds* (1200 rpm); then close throttle.
   e. Set the speed using the vacuum actuator adjustment screw on the throttle lever to obtain specified rpm.
   f. Disconnect the external vacuum source.
   g. Reconnect the sole-vac vacuum hose and electrical connector.
2. Sole-Vac Holding Solenoid Adjustment

NOTE: The sole-vac vacuum actuator adjustment should always precede the sole-vac solenoid adjustment.

   a. Disconnect and plug the vacuum hose to the sole-vac vacuum actuator.
   b. Disconnect the sole-vac electrical connector.
   c. Energize the sole-vac holding solenoid with either of the two following methods: Apply battery voltage (+ 12V) to the solenoid, or reconnect the sole-vac electrical connector and turn on the rear window defogger or turn on the air conditioner with the compressor disconnected.
   d. Open throttle for *at least 3.0 seconds* (1200 rpm) to allow the sole-vac holding solenoid to fully extend.
   e. Set the speed using the $1/4$ in. hex-head adjustment screw on the end of the sole-vac unit to obtain the specified rpm.
   f. Reopen the throttle above 1200 rpm to insure the correct holding position and reset speed if necessary.
   g. Reconnect the vacuum hose to the sole-vac actuator.
   h. Reconnect the sole-vac electrical connector if disconnected.

Idle Speed

Adjustment

1985–86 4–150 CID ENGINE WITH YFA CARBURETOR, TRC (ANTI DIESEL) AND CEC SYSTEM

The TRC (anti-diesel) adjustment screw is statically set at $3/4$ of turn from the throttle valve closed position during the factory assembly and does not normally require readjustment. Should this adjustment be required, turn the adjustment screw counterclockwise to the throttle plate closed position and then turn the screw clockwise $3/4$ turn.

SOLE-VAC VACUUM ACTUATOR

Adjustment

1. Connect a tachometer to the ignition coil TACH wire connector.
2. Place the transmission in the NEUTRAL position and lock the parking brake.
3. Start the engine and allow it to reach normal operating temperature.
4. Connect an external vacuum source to the SOLE-VAC vacuum actuator and apply 10–15 in. Hg. of vacuum. Plug the engine vacuum hose.
5. Adjust the vacuum actuator until an engine speed of approximately 1000 rpm is achieved.

NOTE: Refer to the Vehicle Emission Control Information Label for the latest specifications for the particular engine being adjusted.

6. Remove the vacuum source from the vacuum actuator and retain the plug in the vacuum hose from the engine.
7. Turn the hex-head curb idle speed adjustment screw until the speed of 500 rpm is obtained.

NOTE: Refer to the Vehicle Emission Control Label for the latest specifications for the particular engine being adjusted.

8. Stop the engine and connect the engine vacuum hose to the vacuum actuator.
9. Remove the tachometer from the engine.

IDLE MIXTURE

Adjustment

4–150 CID ENGINE WITH YFA CARBURETOR AND CEC SYSTEM

The idle mixture is preset at the time of manufacture and should normally not require re-adjustment. To prevent easy access to the idle mixture screw, a tamper resistant plug is set into the carburetor assembly to cover the screw. Should adjustment be required due to system diagnosis, contamination, replacement of components or tampering, the following procedure may be used to bring the adjustment into compliance with specifications.

1. Connect a tachometer to the TACH terminal of the ignition coil wire connector and a dwell meter to the mixture sole-

noid test terminals in the diagnosis connector (D2–14 and D2–7) and adjust the dwell meter to the 6 cylinder scale.

2. If the idle mixture screw tamper resistant plug has not been removed, the carburetor must be removed from the engine for access to the plug. With the carburetor off the engine, invert the carburetor and place it in a suitable holding device and remove the plug by drilling a $\frac{1}{8}$ in. hole in the center, installing a self-tapping screw and pulling the plug from the carburetor.

3. Reinstall the carburetor on the engine, connect all lines and wires.

4. Place the transmission in the NEUTRAL position and apply the parking brake.

5. Disconnect and plug the canister purge vacuum hose at the charcoal canister.

6. Start the engine and operate at fast idle speed to bring the engine and coolant to normal operating temperature, thus allowing the CEC (feedback) system to operate in the CLOSED LOOP mode of operation.

7. Return the engine to idle speed and adjust the carburetor for an idle speed 700 rpm for A/T equipped vehicles in DRIVE and 750 rpm in NEUTRAL for M/T equipped vehicles.

8. Adjust the idle mixture screw to obtain an average dwell reading of between 25 and 35 degrees, with 30 degrees preferred.

9. If the dwell is too low, turn the idle mixture screw counterclockwise (out). If the dwell is too high, turn the idle mixture screw clockwise (in).

NOTE: Allow time for the system to react and stabilize after each movement of the adjusting screw. The feedback system is very sensitive to adjustments.

10. Observe the final dwell indication with the adjusting tool removed. If the specified dwell cannot be obtained by adjustment, inspect the carburetor idle circuits for air leaks, restrictions and etc. Do any necessary repairs.

11. When the adjustment is complete, connect the canister purge hose and adjust the idle speed to specifications.

12. Stop the engine and remove the tachometer and dwell meter.

13. Plug the idle mixture adjusting screw opening with RTV sealant.

14. Install the gasket and the air cleaner assembly on the carburetor.

IDLE SPEED

Adjustment

6–258 CID ENGINE WITH MODEL BBD CARBURETOR AND CEC SYSTEM

NOTE: The carburetor choke and intake manifold heater must be off. This occurs when the engine coolant heats to approximately 160 degrees F.

1. Have the engine at normal operating temperature. Connect a tachometer to the ignition coil negative (TACH) terminal.

2. Remove the vacuum hose to the SOLE-VAC vacuum actuator unit. Plug the vacuum hose. Disconnect the holding solenoid wire connector.

3. Adjust the curb (slow) idle speed screw to obtain the correct curb idle speed. Refer to the specifications under Idle Speed or refer to the Emission Information label, under the hood, for the correct curb idle engine rpm.

4. Apply a direct source of vacuum to the vacuum actuator, using a hand vacuum pump or its equivalent. When the SOLE-VAC throttle positioner is fully extended, turn the vacuum actuator adjustment screw on the throttler lever until the specified engine rpm is obtained. Disconnect the vacuum source from the vacuum actuator.

5. With a jumper wire, apply battery voltage (12 volts) to energize the holding solenoid.

NOTE: The holding wire connector can be installed and either the rear window defroster or the air conditioner (with the compressor clutch wire disconnected) can be turned on to energize the holding solenoid.

6. Hold the throttle open manually to allow the throttle positioner to fully extend.

NOTE: Without the vacuum actuator, the throttle must be opened manually to allow the SOLE-VAC throttle positioner to fully extend.

7. If the holding solenoid idle speed is not within specifications, adjust the idle using the $\frac{1}{4}$ in. hex-headed adjustment screw on the end of the SOLE-VAC unit. Adjust to specifications.

8. Disconnect the jumper wire from the SOLE-VAC holding solenoid wire connector, if used. Connect the wire connector to the SOLE-VAC unit, if not connected. Install the original vacuum hose to the vacuum actuator.

9. Remove the tachometer and if disconnected, connect the compressor clutch wire. Install any other component that was previously removed.

IDLE FUEL MIXTURE

Adjustment

6–258 CID ENGINE WITH BBD CARBURETOR AND CEC SYSTEM

CAUTION

The idle mixture adjustment should only be performed if the adjustment screws were removed during a carburetor overhaul procedure.

NOTE: When the carburetor is mounted to the engine, it must be removed to gain access to the dowel pin locations, whose removal must be accomplished before any adjustment of the mixture screws can be made.

1. Connect a tachometer and warm the engine to normal operating temperature.

2. Set the parking brake firmly and chock the wheels. Position the gear selector in the neutral position for manual transmission equipped vehicles and in the 'D' position for automatic transmission equipped vehicles.

3. Adjust the idle speed as previously outlined.

4. Adjust the idle mixture screws clockwise (lean) until a loss of engine rpm is noted. (Idle drop specification is 50 rpm for both automatic and manual transmission equipped vehicles).

5. Turn the idle mixture screws counterclockwise (rich) until the highest engine rpm indication is obtained.

NOTE: Do not turn the screws any further than the point at which the highest engine rpm is first obtained. This is referred to as 'best lean mixture'. The engine idle speed will increase above the curb idle speed by an amount that corresponds approximately to the idle drop specifications listed on the Emission Information Label.

6. As the final adjustment. turn the mixture screws clockwise (lean) to obtain the specified drop in engine rpm. Turn both mixture screws in small, equal amounts until the specified idle drop is achieved.

NOTE: If the final engine rpm differs more than 30 rpm plus or minus from the original curb idle rpm, adjust the curb idle speed to specifications and repeat the mixture adjustment procedure.

7. Install the dowel pins after completing the idle mixture adjustment. Use care not to disturb the mixture screw positions.

NOTE: It is necessary to remove the carburetor to gain access to the dowel pin locations. After the carburetor has been re-installed, again check the idle speed specifications and correct as required.

IDLE SPEED

Adjustment

V8-360 CID ENGINE WITH MODEL 2150 CARBURETOR

NOTE: If the vehicle is equipped with automatic transmission, lock the parking brake, chock the wheels and place the selector lever in DRIVE position before adjusting the idle speed.

1. Connect a tachometer to the ignition coil negative terminal.
2. Start the engine and allow it to reach normal operating temperature.
3. Turn the hex-head adjustment screw on the solenoid carriage to obtain the correct engine speed of 600 rpm. (Verify from Emission Control label, located under the engine hood).
4. Disconnect the solenoid wire connector and adjust the curb idle speed screw to obtain 500 rpm. (Verify from Emission Control label, located under the engine hood).
5. Re-connect the solenoid wire connector and stop the engine.
6. If equipped with a dashpot, position the throttle at the curb idle position and depress the dashpot stem.
7. Measure the clearance between the stem and the throttle lever. A clearance of 0.032 in. should exist.
8. Adjust the clearance as required by loosening the locknut and turning the dashpot until the correct clearance is obtained. Tighten the dashpot locknut.

IDLE MIXTURE

Adjustment

V8-360 CID ENGINE WITH MODEL 2150 CARBURETOR

NOTE: The idle mixture adjustment screws are concealed by tamper resistant caps. The idle mixture should be adjusted only if the mixture adjustment screws were removed or altered during major carburetor overhaul or tampering.

1. Connect a tachometer to the ignition coil negative terminal.
2. Start the engine and allow it to reach normal operating temperature.
3. Set the parking brake and chock the wheels. Position the automatic transmission in the DRIVE detent.
4. Be sure choke is completely off and the idle speed is set to specifications.
5. Turn the idle mixture adjusting screws clockwise (leaner) until a perceptible loss of engine speed (rpm) is noted on the tachometer.
6. Turn the idle mixture adjusting screws counterclockwise (richer) until the highest engine speed (rpm) is obtained.
7. This position of the idle mixture adjusting screws is referred to as the LEAN BEST IDLE.
8. For the final adjustment, turn both idle mixture adjusting screws clockwise in small, equal amounts until the specified idle speed drop is noted on the tachometer.

IDLE SPEED

Adjustment

V6-173 CID ENGINE WITH MODELS 2SE and E2SE CARBURETOR

NOTE: Some California vehicles using the V6 engine, are equipped with a 2200 hour engine timer. The timer activates a solenoid to control operation of the carburetor secondary vacuum brake after 2200 hours of vehicle operation. The timer is not a serviceable component and must not be disassembled. In the event of a timer malfunction, the complete engine wiring harness must be replaced

IDLE SPEED

Adjustment

Model 2SE CARBURETOR (49 STATES AND CANADA)

1. Connect a tachometer to the ignition coil negative terminal or to the pigtail wire connector above the heater blower motor.
2. Disconnect the plug the vacuum hose at the distributor vacuum advance.
3. If necessary, adjust the ignition timing with the engine speed at or below specifications.
4. Reconnect the vacuum hose to the distributor vacuum advance unit.
5. Disconnect the deceleration valve hose and canister purge hose. Plug the hose and remove the air cleaner assembly.
6. If equipped with air conditioning, turn the control switch to the ON position and open the throttle momentarily to insure the solenoid armature is fully extended. Adjust the solenoid idle speed adjusting screw to obtain the specified engine curb idle speed rpm. Turn the A/C control switch to the OFF position.
7. If not equipped with A/C, adjust the engine idle speed rpm with the solenoid idle speed adjusting screw. Disconnect the solenoid wire and adjust the curb idle.
8. Install the air cleaner assembly. Connect all hoses and other connections.

MODEL E2SE CARBURETOR (CALIFORNIA)

1. Connect a tachometer to the ignition system. Start the engine and operate to normal operating temperature.
2. Turn off all accessories including the A/C system.
3. Put the manual transmission equipped vehicles in NEUTRAL and the A/T equipped vehicles in DRIVE with the parking brake locked and the wheels chocked.
4. Adjust the curb idle speed adjusting screw to obtain the specified rpm of 700 for both manual and automatic transmission equipped vehicles.
5. Disconnect the vacuum hose from the idle kick actuator and connect an outside vacuum source to the actuator. Apply 15 in. Hg. of vacuum to the actuator.
6. Adjust the actuator hex-head adjustment screw for the specified rpm of 1200 with both types of transmissions in the NEUTRAL position.
7. Stop the engine, remove the tachometer and vacuum pump. Install the vacuum hose to the actuator.

IDLE MIXTURE

Adjustment

MODEL 2SE CARBURETOR WITH PROPANE

NOTE: The idle mixture screws have been adjusted at the time of manufacture and are sealed. Only after major carburetor overhaul, throttle body replacement or if high

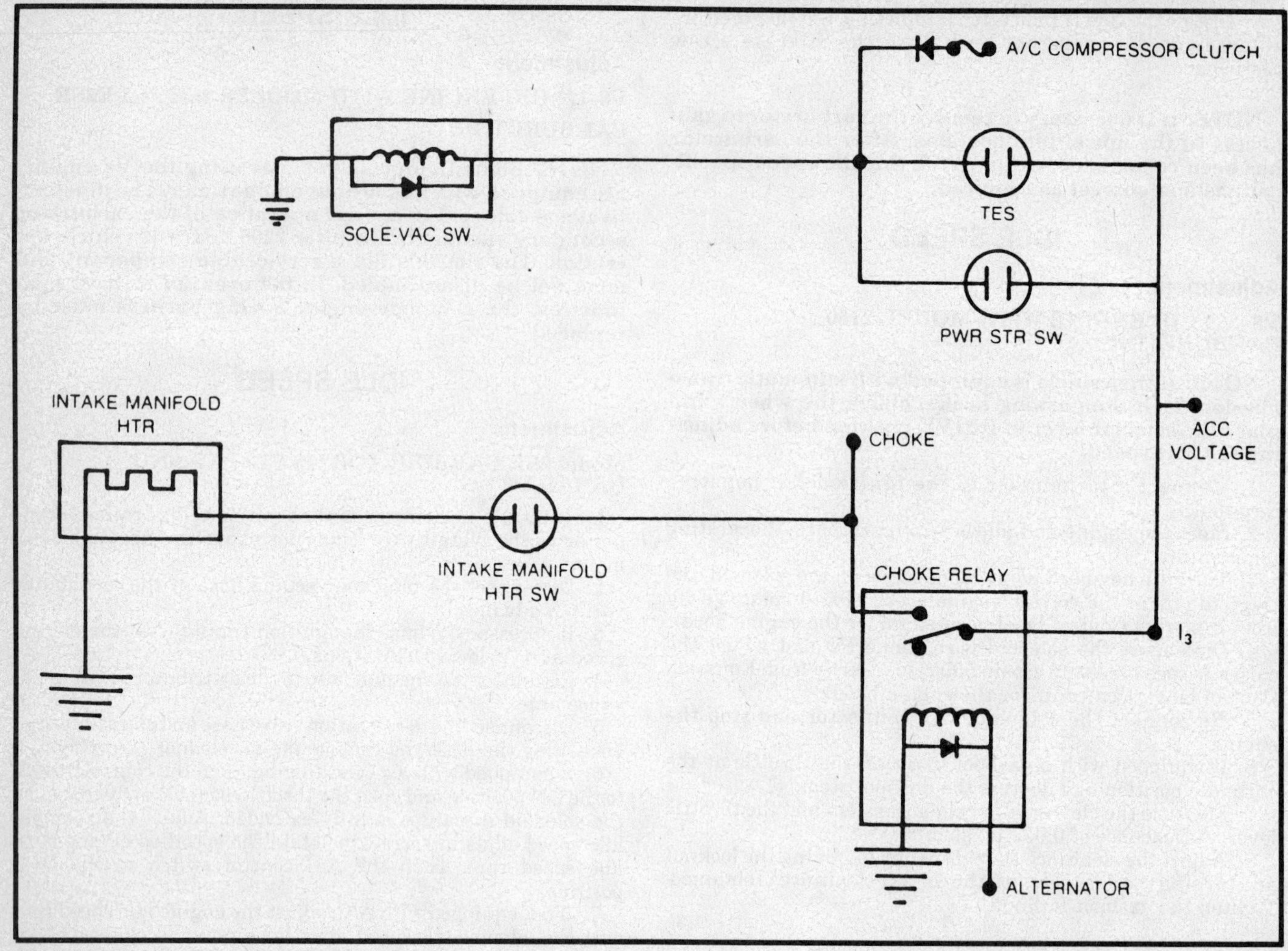

SOLE-VAC wiring schematic (© Jeep Corp.)

emissions are occurring, should any attempt be made to adjust the mixture screws.

1. Set the parking brake and block the wheels. Attach a calibrated tachometer to the engine.
2. Disconnect and plug the canister purge line to the carburetor.
3. Disconnect the vacuum advance hose and plug it. Adjust the ignition, timing, if necessary.
4. Adjust the carburetor idle speed to specifications. Disconnect the crankcase ventilation hose from the air cleaner.
5. Insert the hose with the rubber stopper from the propane valve and special adapter tool, into the air cleaner crankcase ventilation hose hole.

NOTE: The propane cylinder must be vertical during the adjustment procedure.

6. With the engine at normal operating temperature and running, the A/T equipped vehicles in the DRIVE position and the M/T equipped vehicles in the NEUTRAL position, slowly open the propane cylinder control valve to allow propane to enter the carburetor.
7. Continue to add propane until the idle speed increases to the maximum enriched idle rpm and then, because of over richness, will drop. Note the maximum enriched idle rpm.

NOTE: If a rich rpm cannot be obtained, check for an empty propane cylinder or propane system leaks.

8. The propane enrichment is the difference between curb idle speed and the maximum enrichment idle rpm.
9. The maximum enrichment idle rpm is the curb idle rpm plus the propane enrichment rpm.
10. If the maximum enrichment idle rpm is within the specifications, the idle mixture is correct. If so, remove the propane tube and install the crankcase ventilation tube in the air cleaner assembly.
11. If the maximum enriched idle rpm is not within the specifications, remove the carburetor from the engine to gain access to the tamper resistant plugs covering the idle mixture screw.

NOTE: A portion of the throttle base must be cut and the plugs crushed in order to expose the idle mixture adjusting screws. Remove the screws, a special tool (Kent Moore J–29030–B or equivalent) is used to attach to the heads of the screws to gain access for movement of the screws. Re-install the carburetor on the engine and connect all components.

12. Modify special Kent Moore tool J–29030–B by grinding $^1/_8$ in. off the rear and $^1/_4$ in. off the front of the tool.
13. Install the propane cylinder kit to the air cleaner assembly. Snug the idle mixture screw to its seat and back it out three (3) turns.
14. Start the engine, bring to normal operating temperature, set the parking brake, chock the wheels and place the

transmission in the DRIVE (Auto) or the NEUTRAL (manual) position.

15. Back the idle mixture screws out (richer, 1/8th turn at a time) until the maximum idle speed is obtained. The adjust the idle speed to the maximum enriched idle rpm.

16. Turn the mixture screws in clockwise (1/8th turn at a time) until the idle speed attains the specified curb idle speed.

17. Check the maximum enriched rpm with the propane too. If not within specifications, refer to Step 5 and repeat the procedure.

18. When the mixture and idle speed have been properly adjusted, stop the engine, remove the propane cylinder and hose from the air cleaner.

19. Remove the carburetor, remove the special tool (K/M J–29030–B or equivalent) , seal the idle mixture screw access hole with RTV sealant and re-install the carburetor.

20. Install the air cleaner, connect the crankcase ventilation hose and any vacuum hoses that were previously removed. Adjust the idle speed as required.

IDLE DROP PROCEDURE

MODEL 2SE CARBURETOR

1. The carburetor must be removed from the vehicle and the tamper resistant plugs removed from the throttle body as noted under the idle mixture adjustment with propane outline.

2. Connect a tachometer to the ignition system, have the engine at normal operating temperature, apply the parking brakes securely, chock the wheels and position the A/T gear selector in DRIVE and the M/T in NEUTRAL.

3. Adjust the idle speed to specifications.

4. Turn the idle mixture adjusting screw clockwise (lean) until a perceptible loss of rpm is noted.

5. Turn the idle mixture adjusting screw counterclockwise (rich) until the highest engine rpm is attained, Do not turn the screw any further than the point at which the highest engine rpm is first attained. This is referred to a LEAN BEST IDLE.

NOTE: The engine speed will increase above curb idle speed an amount that corresponds approximately to the lean drop specifications of 20 rpm.

6. As a final adjustment, turn the idle mixture screw clockwise in increments until the specified drop (20 rpm) is attained.

NOTE: If the final rpm differs more than ± 30 rpm from the original set curb idle speed, adjust the curb idle speed to the specified engine rpm and repeat the above steps.

7. Remove the air cleaner, remove the carburetor and the modified special tool or its equivalent. Install RTV sealer in the idle mixture screw access hole.

8. Install the carburetor and air cleaner assembly. Adjust the engine idle speed to specifications as required.

IDLE MIXTURE

Adjustment

MODEL E2SE CARBURETOR (FEEDBACK TYPE)

NOTE: Each carburetor has been calibrated at the factory and should not normally need adjustment in the field. However, should a diagnosis indicate the need for adjustment due to emission failure or replacement of critical components, the idle mixture can be adjusted using the following procedure.

1. Remove the carburetor from the engine and remove the tamper resistant plug in order to gain access to the idle mixture adjusting screw.

2. Modify special Kent Moore tool J–29030–B or its equivalent, by grinding 1/8 in. off the rear and 1/4 in. off the front of the tool. Place the modified tool onto the idle mixture adjusting screw.

3. Turn the idle mixture screw in until it is lightly seated and back out four (4) turns.

NOTE: If the seal in the air horn concealing the idle air bleed has been removed, replace the air horn. If the seal is still in place, do not remove the seal.

4. Remove the vent stack screen assembly to gain access to the lean mixture screw.

5. Turn the lean mixture screw in until lightly bottomed and then back out 2 and 1/2 turns

NOTE: Some resistance should be felt. If not, remove the screw and inspect for the presence of the spring.

6. Install the carburetor on the engine with the modified tool installed on the mixture adjusting screw. Do not install the air cleaner and gasket.

7. Disconnect the bowl vent line at the carburetor, disconnect the EGR valve hose and the canister purge hose at the carburetor. Cap the carburetor ports.

8. Refer to the Vehicle Emission Control Information label diagram, located under the vehicle hood, and locate the hose from port D on the carburetor to the temperature sensor and the secondary vacuum break thermal vacuum switch.

9. Disconnect the hose at the temperature sensor on the air cleanser and plug the hose.

10. Connect a dwell meter positive probe to the mixture control solenoid dwell test wire with a green connection.

11. Connect the negative probe to ground and set the meter at the 6 cylinder scale position.

12. Connect a tachometer to the ignition system, set the parking brake and chock the wheels.

13. Place the transmission in PARK (auto) or NEUTRAL (manual).

14. Start and operate the engine until normal operating temperature is reached and the Electronic Engine Control System is in the closed loop mode of operation.

15. Operate the engine at 3000 rpm and adjust the lean mixture screw slowly in small increments, allowing time for the dwell to stabilize after turning the screw to obtain an average dwell of 35 degrees.

16. If the dwell is too low, back the screw out and if too high, turn the screw in. If unable to adjust to specifications, inspect the main metering system for leaks, restriction, etc.

17. Return the engine to idle speed. Allow the engine to stabilize before the dwell is recorded.

NOTE: The mixture control (MC) solenoid dwell is an indication of the ratio of ON to OFF time. The dwell of the MC solenoid is used to determine the calibration and is sensitive to changes in the fuel mixture caused by heat, air leaks, etc. While the engine is idling, it is normal for the dwell to increase and decrease fairly constant over a relativity narrow range, such as 5 degrees. However, it may occasionally vary as much as 10–15 degrees momentarily because of temporary mixture changes. The dwell specified is the average of the most consistant variations. The engine must be allowed to stabilize its self for a few minutes after returning the engine to idle in order to obtain a correct average.

18. Adjust the idle mixture screw with the modified tool J–29030–A or its equivalent, to obtain an average dwell of 25 degrees. If the dwell is too high, turn the screw in and if the dwell is too low, back the screw out. Allow time for the dwell to stabilize after each adjustment, because the adjustment is very sensitive. If unable to adjust to specifications, check for idle system air or vacuum leaks and restrictions.

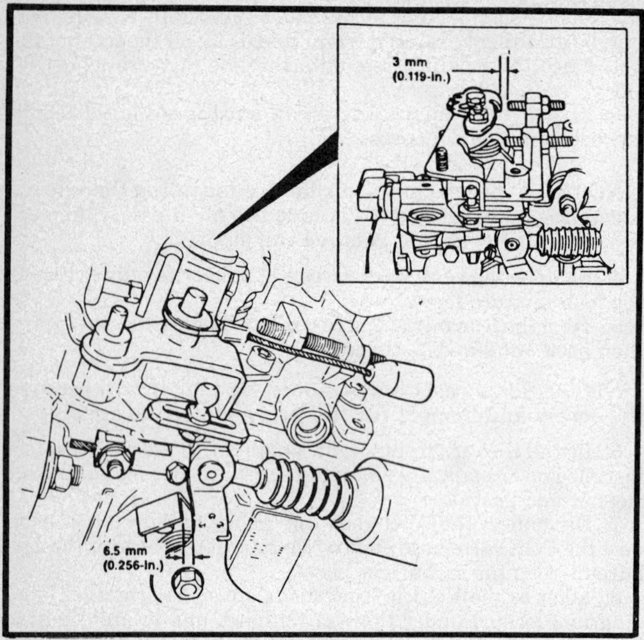

Diesel engine injection pump idle adjustment (© Jeep Corp.)

19. Disconnect the mixture control solenoid and check for and engine speed change of at least 50 rpm. If the rpm does not change enough, inspect the idle air bleed circuit for restrictions, leaks, etc.

20. Increase the engine speed to 3000 rpm and operate for a few minutes. Note the dwell which should be varying with an average indications of 35 degrees.

21. If the average dwell is not at 25 degrees, adjust the lean mixture screw.

22. After adjusting the lean mixture screw, adjust the idle mixture screw to obtain 25 degrees dwell.

23. If at an average dwell of 25 degrees, remove the carburetor from the engine, remove the modified tool J–29030–A or equivalent from the idle mixture screw and seal the access hole with RTV sealant.

24. Install the carburetor, connect all disconnected components and install the vent screen. Verify the idle speed is within specifications.

IDLE SPEED

Adjustment

MODEL 4-126 CID DIESEL ENGINE WITH TURBOCHARGER

1. The idle speed is adjusted on the injection pump linkage.
2. Loosen the screw locknut, adjust the idle speed to 800 ± 50 rpm with the adjusting screw and tighten the locknut.

Fuel Pump

MECHANICAL

Removal and Installation

1. Remove all the necessary components in order to gain access to the fuel pump. Disconnect the fuel lines.
2. Remove the two attaching bolts that hold the fuel pump to the engine and lift the fuel pump off of the engine.
3. Before installing the fuel pump, make sure that all of the mating surfaces are clean.
4. Cement a new gasket to the mating surface of the fuel pump.
5. Position the fuel pump on the cylinder block so that the cam lever of the pump rests on the camshaft.
6. Secure the pump to the engine with the two bolts and lock washers.
7. Connect the fuel lines to the fuel pump.

ELECTRIC

Removal and Installation

1. Disconnect the negative battery cable. Remove all necessary components in order to gain access to the fuel tank sending unit.
2. Drain the fuel from the fuel tank. Raise and support the vehicle safely.
3. Remove the fuel inlet and outlet hoses from the sending unit. Remove the sending unit wires.
4. Remove the sending unit retaining lock ring. Remove the sending unit, which incorporates the electric fuel pump, along with the O-ring seal from the fuel tank.
5. Installation is the reverse of the removal procedure. Be sure to use a new O-ring seal.

Fuel Injection Pump

DIESEL ENGINE

Removal and Installation

1. Disconnect the negative battery cable. Remove the timing belt cover.
2. Install sprocket holding tool MOT–854. Remove the camshaft sprocket retaining bolt. Remove the special tool.
3. Loosen the tensioner bolts and move the timing belt tensioner away from the timing belt. Tighten the tensioner bolts.
4. Remove the timing belt from the injection pump sprocket.
5. Disconnect all the fuel pipe fittings from the injectors. Plug the injectors to prevent dirt from entering the fuel system.
6. Disconnect the fuel pipe fittings from the fuel injection pump. Plug the fittings to prevent dirt from entering the system.
7. Remove the fuel line fittings from the vehicle. Remove all hoses and connectors from the injection pump assembly.
8. Remove the fuel injection pump retaining bolts. Remove the fuel injection pump and bracket from the engine as an assembly.
9. To install, attach the pump mounting brackets and the pump to the cylinder head using the retaining bolts.
10. Position the camshaft sprocket timing mark at the 12 o'clock position. Position the fuel injection pump sprocket at the 12 o'clock position
11. Install the timing belt. Continue the installation in the reverse order of the removal procedure. Adjust the timing as required.

Injection Pump Static Timing Adjustment

1. Loosen the injection pump adjustment screw. Turn the control cable clevis pin about one-quarter of a turn in order to disengage the cold start system control.
2. Rotate the crankshaft two revolutions counterclockwise and align the camshaft and the injection pump sprocket timing marks with the marks on the timing mark cover.
3. Install special tool MOT–861 in the crankshaft counterweight top dead center slot.
4. Remove the screw plug which is located between the four high pressure fuel outlets at the rear of the fuel injection pump.
5. Remove the cooper washer from the screw plug.

6. Install dial indicator support, tool MOT–856 or equivalent in place of the screw plug. Insert the stem of the dial indicator into the support tool.
7. Remove the top dead center rod, tool MOT–861, from the crankshaft counterweight TDC slot.
8. Slowly turn the crankshaft counterclockwise until the dial indicator pointer stops moving. Zero the dial indicator pointer.
9. Slowly turn the crankshaft clockwise until the top dead center rod, tool MOT–861, can be inserted into the TDC slot in the crankshaft counterweight.
10. At TDC the dial indicator pointer should indicate a piston lift travel distance of 0.031–0.033 in..
11. If the pump piston travel lift distance is not within specification, the pump position must be adjusted.
12. Loosen the pump adjusting bolts. Observe the dial indicator gauge. To increase the piston lift, rotate the pump toward the engine and then away from the engine. To decrease the piston lift, rotate the pump away from the engine.

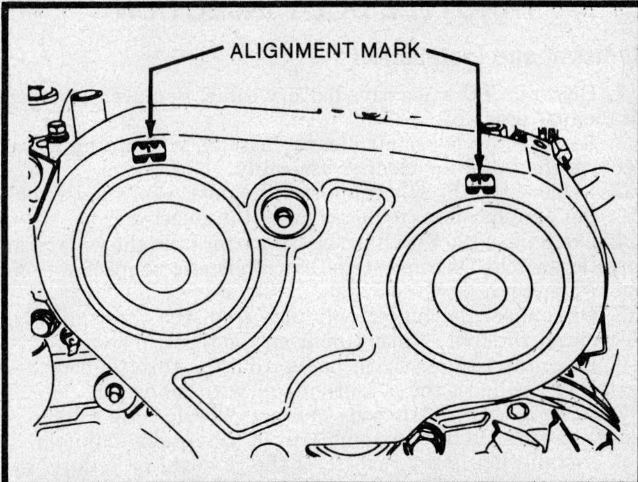

Diesel engine injection pump timing cover locating marks
(© Jeep Corp.)

NOTE: Adjust the piston lift by rotating the pump away from the engine. This is the normal direction of pump rotation. When increasing the piston lift, rotate the pump toward the engine until the piston lift is greater than the specification, then rotate the pump away from the engine until the correct piston lift is indicated on the dial indicator gauge.

13. Tighten the injection pump adjustment bolts. Remove the top dead center rod, tool MOT–861, from the crankshaft counterweight.
14. Observe the dial indicator gauge. Rotate the crankshaft two complete revolutions until the top dead center rod can be inserted into the crankshaft counterweight TDC slot.
15. The dial indicator pointer should return to the correct injection pump timing specification, this will indicate that the injection pump timing is correct.
16. Remove the tool and reinstall all components that were removed.

Fuel Injectors

DIESEL ENGINE

Removal and Installation

1. Disconnect the negative battery cable. Remove all the necessary components in order to gain access to the fuel injectors.

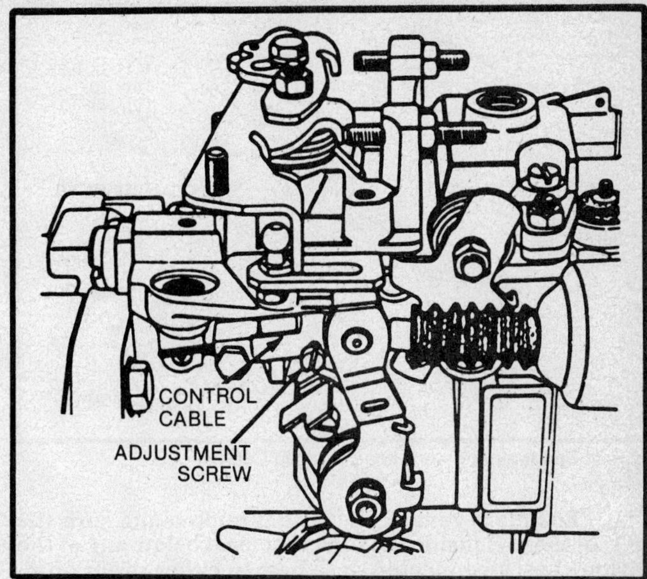

Diesel engine injection pump adjusting screw location
(© Jeep Corp.)

2. Remove the fuel injector lines.
3. Remove the fuel injectors from their mountings in the cylinder head.
4. Installation is the reverse of the removal procedure. Be sure to use new cooper washers and heat shields. Be sure to reinstall the injectors in their original bores.

Fuel Tank

Removal and Installation

ALL MODELS EXCEPT 1984 AND LATER WAGONEER, CHEROKEE AND COMANCHE

The fuel tank is attached to the frame by brackets and bolts. The brackets are attached to the tank at the seam flange.

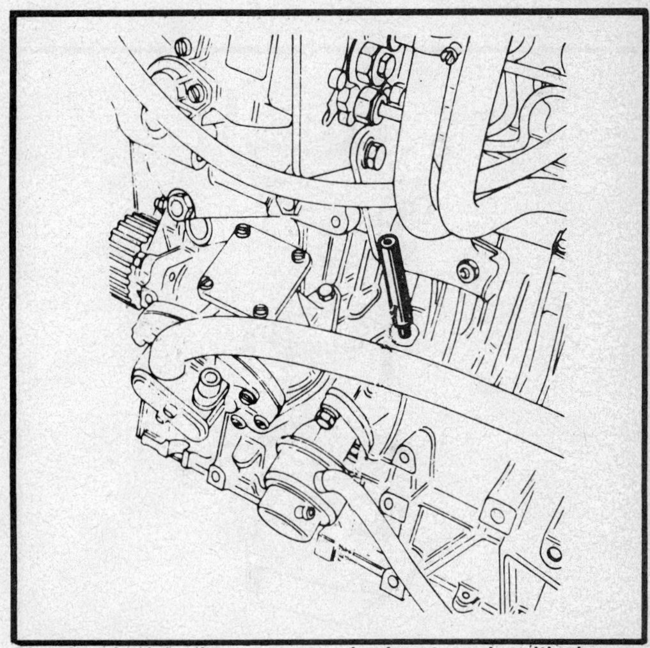
Diesel engine injection pump—top dead center rod positioning
(© Jeep Corp.)

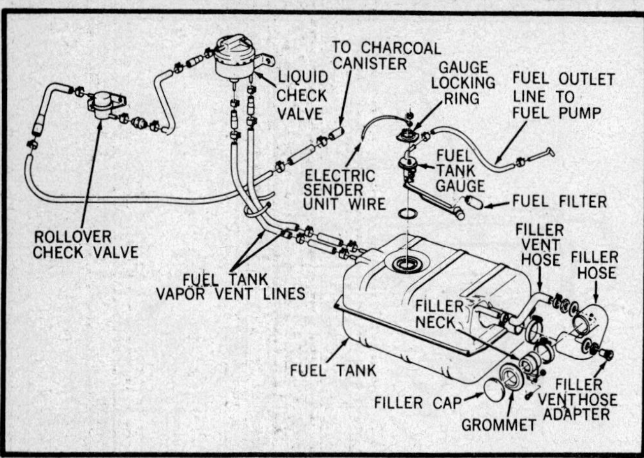

Typical fuel tank and vent lines (© Jeep Corp)

NOTE: Before removing the fuel tank, make sure the level of the fuel inside the tank is at least below any of the various hoses connected. It is best to either drain or siphon the majority of fuel out of the tank to make it easier to handle while removing it.

To remove the tank, loosen all of the clamps retaining the hoses to the tank and disconnect the hoses from the tank. It may be necessary to remove the fuel tank-to-mounting bracket screws and lower the tank slightly to gain access to some of the connecting hoses. Disconnect the tank from the mounting brackets, if not already done, and lower the tank from under the vehicle. Be careful not to spill any fuel in the tank while removing it.

NOTE: On some vehicles, it may be necessary to remove the parking brake cable guide clips and skid-plate, if equipped, and to disconnect one brake cable at connector.

Install the fuel tank in the reverse order of removal.

1984 AND LATER WAGONEER AND CHEROKEE

1. Drain the fuel tank. Place a jack under the skid plate and remove the strap nuts.

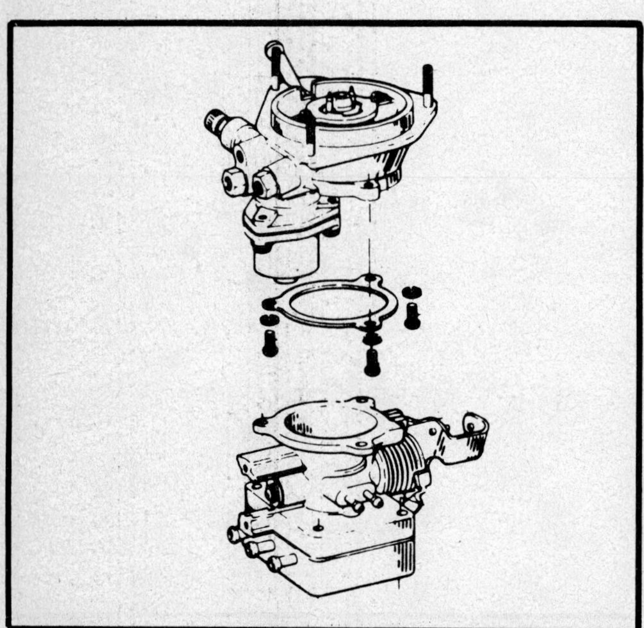
Fuel body assembly—exploded view (© Jeep Corp.)

2. Disconnect all hoses and wires connected to the tank.
3. Partially lower the tank and disconnect the tank vapor vent hoses.
4. Remove the tank.
5. Installation is the reverse of the removal procedure.

COMANCHE

1. Disconnect the negative battery cable. Raise and support the vehicle safely.
2. Remove the rear propeller shaft.
3. If equipped, remove the skid plate.
4. Disconnect the fuel inlet and outlet lines at the sending unit. Disconnect the electrical wires from the sending unit.
5. Remove the protective shield. Loosen and remove the fuel tank retaining straps.
6. Lower the fuel tank from the vehicle.
7. Installation is the reverse of the removal procedure.

Fuel Injection

THROTTLE BODY INJECTION

Removal and Installation

1. Disconnect the negative battery cable. Remove the upper air cleaner assembly.
2. Remove the lower air cleaner assembly retaining bolts. Remove the lower air cleaner assembly.
3. Remove the throttle cable and the return spring. Disconnect the wire harness connector from the injector.
4. Disconnect the wire harness connector from the wide open throttle switch. Disconnect the wire harness connector from the ISC motor.
5. Disconnect the fuel supply pipe from the throttle body. Disconnect the fuel return pipe from the throttle body.
6. Disconnect the vacuum hoses from the throttle body assembly. Disconnect the potentiometer wire connector.
7. Remove the throttle body to manifold retaining bolts. Remove the throttle body assembly from the intake manifold.
8. Installation is the reverse of the removal procedure. Be sure to use a new gasket between the throttle body assembly and the intake manifold.

FUEL BODY ASSEMBLY

Removal and Installation

1. Remove the throttle body assembly from the vehicle.
2. Remove the torx head screws that retain the fuel body to the throttle body. Remove and discard the gasket.
3. Installation is the reverse of the removal procedure. Be sure to use a new gasket.

FUEL PRESSURE REGULATOR

Removal and Installation

1. Remove the throttle body assembly from the vehicle.
2. Remove the three retaining screws that hold the pressure regulator to the fuel body.
3. Remove the pressure regulator assembly. Note the location of the components for reassembly. Discard the gasket.
4. Installation is the reverse of the removal procedure. Be sure to use a new gasket.

FUEL INJECTOR

Removal and installation

1. Remove the air cleaner and hose assembly.
2. Remove the fuel injector wire. Remove the fuel injector retainer clip screws. Remove the fuel injector retainer clip.

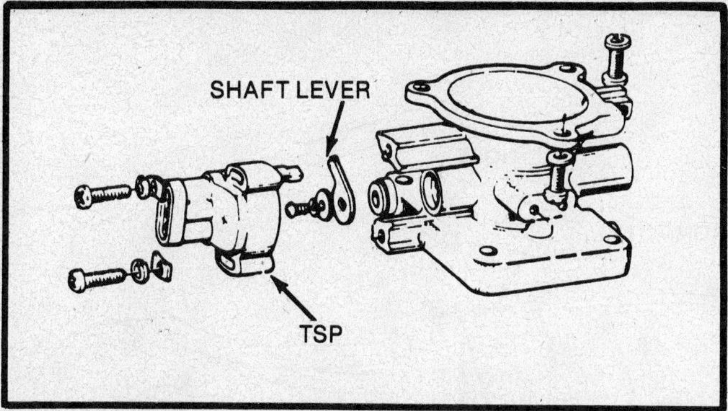

Throttle position sensor assembly (© Jeep Corp.)

3. Using a small pair of pliers, gently grasp the center collar of the injector, between the electrical terminals, and carefully remove the injector using a lifting-twisting motion.
4. Discard the upper and lower O-rings. Note that the back up ring fits over the upper O-ring.
5. Installation is the reverse of the removal procedure. Lubricate both O-rings with light oil before installation.

THROTTLE POSITION SENSOR

Removal and Installation

1. Remove the upper and lower air cleaner assemblies.
2. Remove the throttle body assembly from the vehicle.
3. Remove the two torx head retaining screws holding the TPS assembly to the throttle body.
4. Remove the throttle position sensor from the throttle shaft lever.
5. Installation is the reverse of the removal procedure.

IDLE SPEED ACTUATOR MOTOR

Removal and Installation

NOTE: The closed throttle switch is integral with the motor.

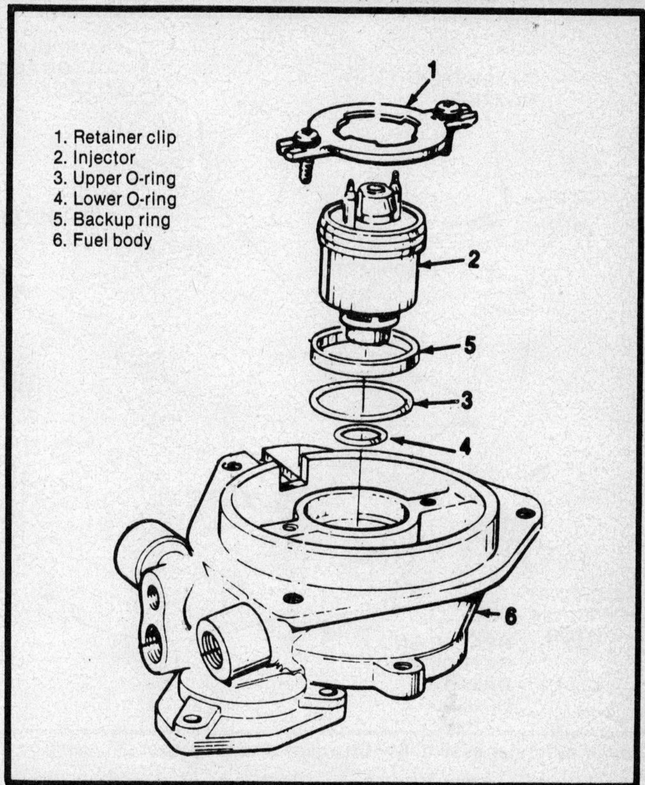

Fuel injector and related components (© Jeep Corp.)

1. Disconnect the throttle return spring. Disconnect the wire harness connector from the motor.
2. Remove the motor to bracket retaining nuts. Be sure to use a back up wrench as not to remove the motor studs which hold the motor together.
3. Remove the motor from the bracket.
4. Installation is the reverse of the removal procedure.

COOLING SYSTEM

Water Pump

Removal and Installation

NOTE: Some four cylinder engines with air condition are equipped with a serpentine drive belt and have a reverse rotating water pump coupled with a viscous fan drive assembly. The components are identified by the words REVERSE stamped on the cover of the viscous drive and on the inner side of the fan. The word REV is also cast into the body of the water pump.

4–151 CID ENGINE

1. Disconnect the battery cable and drain the coolant.
2. Loosen the alternator and remove the fan belt.
3. Remove the power steering and air conditioning belts, if so equipped.
4. Remove the fan, spacer, and water pump pulley.
5. Remove the heater hose and the lower radiator hose at the pump.
6. Remove the water pump retaining bolts and the pump.
7. Installation is the reverse of the removal procedure.

150 FOUR CYLINDER AND 258 SIX CYLINDER ENGINES

1. Drain the cooling system.
2. Disconnect the radiator and heater hoses from the water pump.
3. Loosen the alternator adjustment strap screw, upper pivot bolt and remove the drive belt.
4. If the vehicle is equipped with a radiator shroud, separate the shroud from the radiator to facilitate removal and installation of the cooling fan and hub.
5. Remove the cooling fan and hub assembly.
6. Remove air conditioning intermediate idler pulley and mounting bracket, if so equipped.
7. Remove the power steering pump front mounting bracket, if so equipped.
8. Remove the water pump and gasket from the engine.
9. Clean all the old gasket material from the gasket surface of the engine.
10. Install the new water pump and assemble the engine in the reverse order of removal, tightening the water pump retaining bolts to 13 ft. lbs.

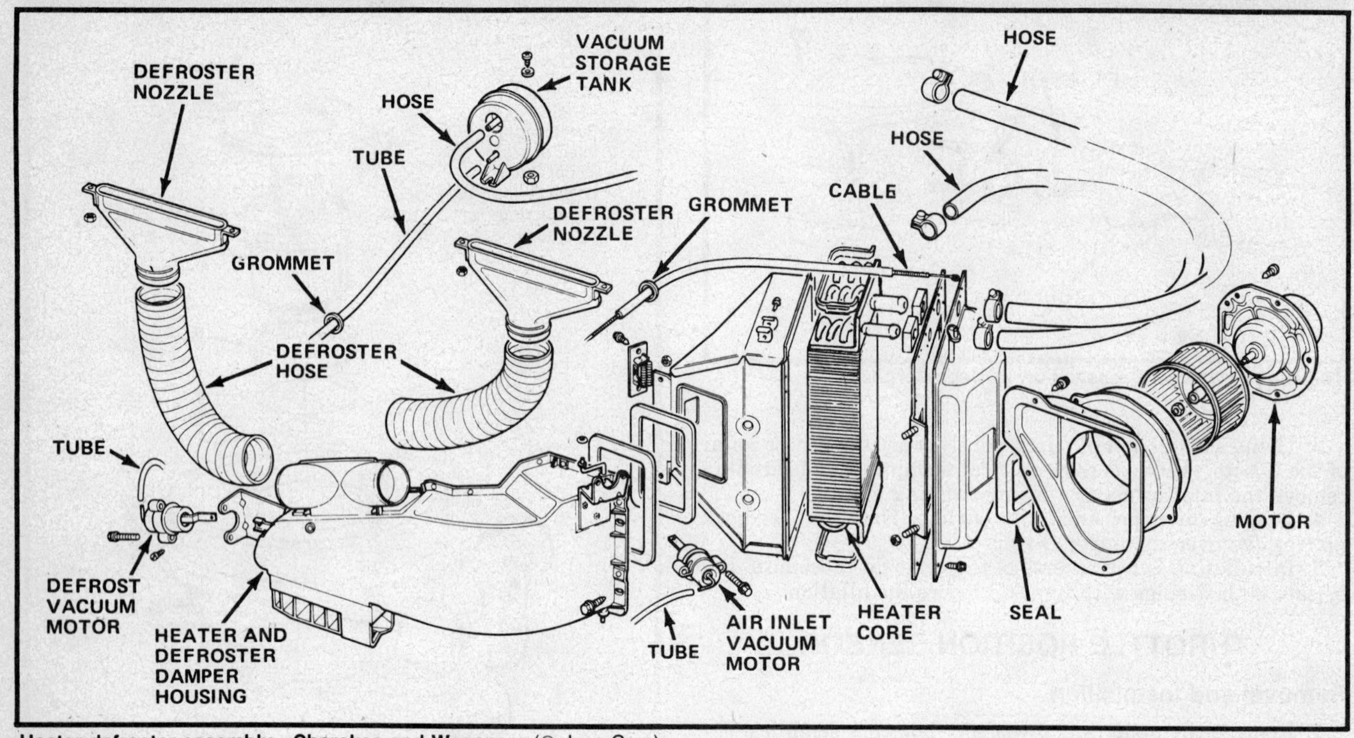

Heater defroster assembly—Cherokee and Wagoneer (© Jeep Corp)

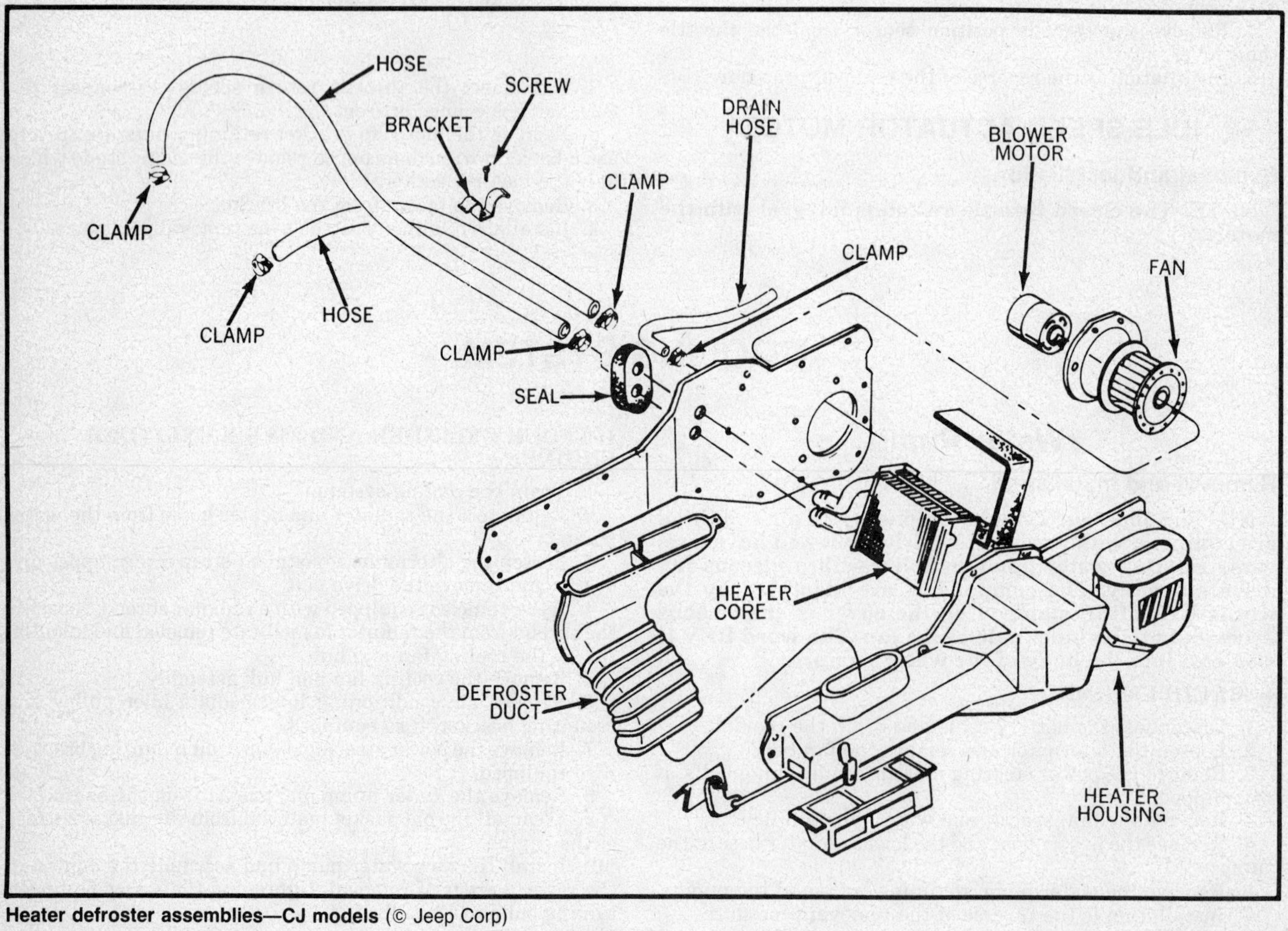

HOSE
SCREW
BRACKET
DRAIN
HOSE
BLOWER
MOTOR
CLAMP
CLAMP
CLAMP
FAN
CLAMP
HOSE
CLAMP
CLAMP
SEAL
HEATER
CORE
DEFROSTER
DUCT
HEATER
HOUSING

Heater defroster assemblies—CJ models (© Jeep Corp)

V6 AND V8 ENGINES

1. Disconnect the negative battery cable.
2. Drain the radiator and disconnect the upper radiator hose at the radiator.
3. Loosen all the drive belts.
4. Remove the fan and hub assembly.
5. Separate the radiator shroud from the radiator, if so equipped.
6. If the vehicle is equipped with a viscous fan, remove the fan assembly and shroud all at the same time. Do not unbolt the fan blades.

NOTE: The studs in the water pump may back out of the water pump while removing the nuts, preventing the fan assembly from clearing the water pump. If this happens, install a double nut on the stud(s) and remove the studs.

7. On some vehicles equipped with air conditioning, install a double nut on the air conditioning compressor bracket to water pump stud and remove the stud. Removal of this stud eliminates removing the compressor mounting bracket.
8. Remove the alternator and mounting bracket assembly and place it aside. Do not disconnect the alternator wires.
9. Remove the two nuts attaching the power steering pump to the rear half of the pump mounting bracket, if so equipped.
10. Remove the two bolts attaching the front half of the bracket to the rear half.
11. Remove the remaining upper bolt from the inner air pump support brace, loosen the lower bolt and drop the brace away from the power steering front bracket.
12. Remove the front half of the power steering bracket from the water pump mounting stud.
13. Disconnect the heater hose, by-pass hose, and lower radiator hose at the water pump.
14. Remove the water pump and gasket from the timing chain cover and clean all old gasket material from the gasket surface of the timing chain cover.
15. Install the new water pump and assemble the remaining components in the reverse order of removal, tightening the water pump-to-engine block screws to 25 ft. lbs. and the water pump-to-timing case cover screws to 4 ft. lbs. (48 inch lbs.)

DIESEL ENGINE

1. Disconnect the negative battery cable. Drain the engine coolant.
2. Remove all necessary components in order to gain access to the water pump assembly.
3. Remove the coolant hose from the water pump. Remove the drive belts. Remove the fan and hub assembly.
4. It is not necessary to remove the timing belt tensioner. Use a long strap and clip in order to retain the timing belt tensioner plunger in place.
5. Remove the water pump retaining bolts. Remove the water pump assembly from the vehicle.
6. Installation is the reverse of the removal procedure. Be sure to use a new water pump gasket.

Heater Core

Removal and Installation

CJ AND SCRAMBLER

1. Remove the battery, drain the cooling system, and disconnect the heater hoses.
2. Disconnect the damper door control cable.
3. Disconnect the blower motor wire harness and ground wire at the switch and instrument panel.
4. Remove the defroster duct hose. On some vehicles it may be necessary to first remove the glove box.
5. If equipped,disconnect the heater to air deflector duct at the heater housing.
6. Remove the nuts from the heater housing studs, protruding into the engine compartment.
7. Remove the heater housing assembly from the vehicle and remove the core from the housing.
8. Installation is the reverse of the removal procedure.

Removal and Installation

1980-83 CHEROKEE, 1980 AND LATER GRAND WAGONEER AND TRUCK

1. Remove the negative battery cable and drain the cooling system.
2. Disconnect the temperature control cable from the blend air door.
3. Remove the heater hoses and blower motor resistor wires.
4. Remove the heater core housing to dash panel attaching screws or nuts, projecting into the engine compartment.
5. Remove the heater housing assembly from the vehicle.
6. Separate the halves of the housing, after scribing a mark on the two halves. Remove the core retaining screws and remove the heater core.
7. Installation is the reverse of the removal procedure.

Removal and Installation

1984 AND LATER CHEROKEE, WAGONEER AND COMANCHE

1. Disconnect the negative battery cable.Drain the cooling system.
2. Disconnect the hoses at the core tubes.
3. Disconnect the battery ground cable.
4. Discharge the refrigerant from the A/C system.
5. Disconnect the refrigerant lines at the expansion valve.
6. Disconnect the blower motor wires and vent tube.
7. If equipped, Remove the console.
8. Remove the lower instrument panel section.
9. Disconnect all wires and hoses at the case.
10. Cut the plastic retaining strap which holds the evaporator/ blower housing to the heater core housing.
11. Disconnect the heater control cables.
12. Remove the clip at the rear of the blower housing flange and remove the retaining screws.
13. Remove the housing attaching nuts from the studs on the engine compartment side of the firewall. Remove the evaporator drain tube.
14. Remove the right kick panel and the instrument panel support bolt.
15. From the right side, gently pull the housing down and toward the rear. Remove the housing from the vehicle.
16. Remove the left kick panel and remove the instrument panel retaining bolt. Remove the right and left "A" pillar trim.
17. Remove the defroster bezel attaching screws. Remove the bezel and panel screws.
18. Lower the steering column.
19. Pull the instrument panel about 3 inches outward.
20. Unscrew and remove the defroster ducts. Disconnect the hoses.
21. Disconnect the vacuum hoses at the core housing.
22. Remove the two heater housing retaining nuts in the engine compartment and remove the core housing.
23. Installation is the reverse of removal.
24. Evacuate, charge and leak test the A/C system.

EMISSION CONTROLS

Emission Control Systems

Emission control systems are designed to control the emissions of hydrocarbons (HC), carbon monoxide (CO), and oxides of nitrogen (NOx), at the levels specified by Federal and State governments. Emission control systems vary in their usage, in relationship to engine, transmission, and series applications.

Overhaul of the units are covered in the Unit Repair Section.

EXHAUST GAS RECIRCULATION SYSTEM (EGR)

The Exhaust Gas Recirculation System is designed to lower the temperature of the burning air/fuel mixture in the combustion chamber by having metered amounts of exhaust gas redirected into the combustion chamber to dilute the air/fuel mixture. The EGR system consists of a diaphragm-activated exhaust flow control valve (EGR valve), Coolant temperature override (CTO) valve, thermal vacuum switch (TVS) and connecting hoses.

NOTE: Do not disconnect the vacuum hose or cause the EGR valve to become inoperative for an extended period of time because the resulting pre-ignition could cause piston burning and scuffing to occur.

EGR SYSTEM COOLANT TEMPERATURE OVERRIDE (CTO) VALVE

If equipped, the EGR System CTO valve is located in the coolant passage at the left side of the intake manifold and is also used for distributor vacuum advance control. When the coolant temperature is below the calibrated rating of the CTO valve, there is no vacuum applied to the EGR valve. The valve starts to open at approximately 115 degrees F.

EGR SYSTEM THERMAL VACUUM SWITCH (TVS)

If equipped, the thermal vacuum switch (TVS) is located in the air cleaner and functions as an off-on switch, controlled by air cleaner intake air temperature. It purpose is to control the vacuum between the EGR system CTO valve and the EGR valve.

At air temperature below 40–55 degrees F., the TVS prevents vacuum from opening the EGR valve, thus preventing EGR valve operation and improving cold engine driveability.

NOTE: A TVS valve is used for other engine related systems to control operations that require air cleaner intake air to be at the proper temperature before system operation is activated.

CATALYTIC CONVERTER

A catalytic converter is used as part of the exhaust system to have the exhaust gases pass through and undergo a chemical reaction which changes the hydrocarbons and carbon monoxide into harmless carbon dioxide and water before it is emitted into the atmosphere. Beads of Alumina, covered with Platinum and Palladium are used as the catalyst. Unleaded gasoline must be used, as leaded fuel poisons or spoils the catalyst used in the converter.On late model vehicles a dual bed monolithic-type or COC pellet type catalytic converters are used. The monolithic type is not serviceable, but the pellets can be replaced in the pellet type. The stainless steel converter body is designed to last the life of the automobile, but excessive heat can cause premature converter failure. Although the excessive heat would be contained in the converter, the cause of the overheating would not be the fault of the converter, but from an outside source. A defective fuel system, air injection system or ignition system malfunction that permits unburned fuel to enter the converter will usually be the cause. If the converter is heat damaged, the cause must be located and repaired before a new converter is installed.

POSITIVE CRANKCASE VENTILATION SYSTEM (PCV)

The PCV System functions to prevent crankcase vapors from entering the atmosphere. Filtered air is routed to the crankcase, the vapors drawn out and routed into the intake manifold to be burned along with the air/fuel mixture. Should the crankcase vapors (blowby) exceed the flow capacity of the PCV valve, the air flow in the system reverses and the vapors are drawn through the air cleaner element and into the carburetor to be burned along with the air/fuel mixture.All late model 4–150 CID and 6–258 CID engines are equipped with the Computerized Emission Control (CEC) Fuel Feedback system, a PCV valve solenoid is installed in the PCV hose to close the crankcase ventilation system when the engine is operating at idle speed. The anti-dieseling relay system is used on the 4–150 CID engine to momentarily energize the PCV solenoid when the ignition key is turned off, to prevent air from entering the intake manifold below the throttle plates of the carburetor, thus preventing engine dieseling.

THERMOSTATICALLY CONTROLLED AIR CLEANER SYSTEM (TAC)

The thermostatically controlled air cleaner system operates to avoid the induction of cold air into the carburetor and intake manifold before the engine reaches normal operating temperature. When the engine is first started, a thermostatically controlled valve in the air cleaner snorkel closes to outside air and exhaust manifold heater air is directed into the air cleaner assembly, carburetor, and intake manifold. As the engine warms, and the surrounding air temperature increases, the valve in the air cleaner snorkel opens and admits air from the engine compartment, while closing off the heated manifold air.

FUEL TANK VAPOR EMISSION CONTROL SYSTEM

A closed fuel tank vent system is used to prevent fuel vapors from entering the atmosphere. The raw vapors are routed into the intake system and burned along with the fuel-air mixture.

The system consists of a two-way relief valve filler cap, which is closed to the atmospheric pressure under normal operating conditions and opens when pressure exceeds 0.75 to 1.50 psi, or a vacuum of 15 to 25 inches. A liquid check valve is used to route the vapors and collect any liquid before the vapors are drawn into and stored in the fuel vapor storage canister, until they are drawn into the intake manifold through the carburetor air cleaner assembly. The amount of vapors drawn from the canister is relative to the air velocity passing through the air cleaner snorkel.

FUEL EVAPORATION EMISSION CONTROL SYSTEM

Fuel Vapor Control System and Components

The fuel vapor control system prevents fuel vapors from escaping into the atmosphere. Fuel vapors from the fuel tank and the carburetor bowl are collected in a storage canister and are metered into the intake manifold to be burned along with the air/fuel mixture, when the engine is started and operated.

Fuel Vapor Storage Canister

The fuel vapor canister is filled with activated charcoal granules, which absorb the fuel vapors that enter the canister. When the engine is started, the fuel vapors are metered into the induction system, along with the air/fuel mixture.

Fuel Tank Vent Rollover Check Valve

In the event of an automobile rollover, the rollover check valve prevents the loss of fuel through the vent hose or pipe.

Carburetor External Bowl Fuel Vapor Vent

The carburetor external bowl fuel vapor vent provides an outlet for the fuel vapors when the engine is not in the operating mode, to prevent the vapors from entering the atmosphere.

Pressure/Vacuum Fuel Tank Cap

The filler cap incorporates a two-way (pressure and Vacuum) relief valve that is closed during normal operation. The valve is calibrated to open when the pressure is in excess of 0.8 psi or a vacuum in excess of 0.1 in. Hg. develops in the fuel tank. As the pressure or vacuum is relieved, the valve returns to its normally closed position. In the event of a vehicle rollover, the fuel filler cap provides additional protection from spilled fuel.

Fuel Return System

To reduce the possibility of high temperature fuel vapor problems, certain 6–258 CID engine applications may be equipped with the fuel return system. This system consists of a hose connecting the fuel filter to the fuel tank, through a third nipple on the filter. The fuel filter must be positioned with the third nipple on the top of the filter during its installation. During normal operation, a small amount of fuel returns to the tank, rather than entering the carburetor bowl. A one-way check valve is positioned in the return line, at the filter or the hose, to prevent fuel from returning to the carburetor through the fuel return line.

VACUUM THROTTLE MODULATING SYSTEM (VTM)

The VTM system is used to reduce the emission of hydrocarbons during rapid throttle closure at high speeds and consists of a deceleration valve and a throttle modulating diaphragm located on the carburetor base to allow the throttle to remain slightly open and admit more air into the combustion chambers to lean out the overrich mixture, during the rapid throttle release. The decel valve and modulator diaphragm are operated by engine vacuum signals.

TRANSMISSION CONTROLLED SPARK SYSTEM (TCS)

The TCS system is used to reduce the emission of oxides of nitrogen by lowering the peak combustion temperatures during the power stroke by not allowing vacuum to be routed to the distributor vacuum advance unit during low speed operation, thereby not allowing the advance unit to operate. This system is controlled by switches located and operated by the transmission gear selector, or oil pressure, directed to a switch, at a predetermined speed.

SPARK COOLANT TEMPERATURE OVERRIDE SWITCH (SPARK CTO)

This system is used to override the TCS system to improve driveability during the warmup period by providing full distributor vacuum advance operation until the temperature reaches 160°F within the cooling system. The system then reverts to the transmission controlled spark system.

PULSE AIR SYSTEM

The Pulse Air Injection System utilizes the alternating positive and negative exhaust pressure pulsations instead of an air pump to inject air into the exhaust system and produce exhaust gas oxidation. The air enters through the filtered side of the air cleaner to the air control valve. When opened by the air switch, the air control valve allows the air to continue to and through the air injection check valve. The air enters the exhaust system, either upstream or downstream from the check valve, air is injected either into the front exhaust pipe (upstream) or into the catalytic converter (downstream), depending upon the engine operating conditions. The CEC system micro computer unit (MCU) controls the switching operation.

AIR INJECTION CHECK VALVE

The air injection check valve is a one-way reed valve that is opened and closed by the negative and positive exhaust pressure pulsations. During the negative exhaust pulse (low Pressure), atmospheric pressure opens the check valve and forces air into the exhaust system. Being a one-way valve, the valve reed prevents exhaust from being forced back through the valve during the positive exhaust pressure pulsations (high pressure).

AIR CONTROL VALVE

The air control valve controls the supply of filtered air routed to the air injection check valve. The valve is opened and closed by the air switch solenoid.

AIR SWITCH SOLENOID

The air switch solenoid controls the air control valve by switching the vacuum on and off. The solenoid is controlled by the micro computer unit (MCU).

VACUUM STORAGE TANK

Engine vacuum is stored in a reservoir tank until released by the air switch solenoid.

MICRO COMPUTER UNIT (MCU)

The MCU switches air either upstream or downstream, depending upon the engine operating conditions, by energizing and de-energizing the air switch solenoids.

AIR PUMP AIR INJECTION SYSTEM

The air pump air injection system incorporates a belt driven air pump, a vacuum controlled diverter (bypass) valve, two air injection manifolds with check valves and the necessary connecting hoses. This system provides for air injection into the exhaust manifold and into the air cleaner assembly.

AIR PUMP

The air pump is designed for long life and is serviced only by replacement. Do not disassemble the air pump for any reason since the internal components are not servicable.

DIVERTER (BYPASS) VALVE

The diverter valve has two outlets, one for each air injection manifold. The valve momentarily diverts air pump output from the manifolds and vents it to the atmosphere during rapid engine deceleration. The valve also functions as a pressure release valve for excessive air pump output. California vehicles use a combination electrical diverter valve and a vacuum switching valve. The diverter valve solenoid is controlled directly by the electronic control module (ECM) so that air is diverted to the air cleaner when the solenoid is de-energized at the following specified times.

a. Engine not operating (electrical control).
b. First five (5) seconds of any start up of the engine (electrical control).
c. High electrical load on the engine control system.
d. Closed throttle deceleration (vacuum control).

AIR INJECTION MANIFOLDS

The air injection manifolds distribute the air via the diverter valve , to each of the exhaust manifold inlet ports. A check valve , incorporating a stainless steel spring plunger and an asbestos seat, is integral with each air injection manifold. The function of the check valve is to prevent the reverse flow of exhaust gases to the air pump during the pump or drive belt failure, or diverter valve bypass (vent) operation. The air injection tubes are mounted to the exhaust manifold and route the airflow into the inlet ports.

COMPUTERIZED EMISSION CONTROL (CEC) SYSTEM

Some vehicles are equipped with the Computerized Emission Control (CEC) System which is an electronically controlled fuel feedback system that controls undesirable emissions to the atmosphere and maintains the ideal air/fuel ratio to provide an optimum balance between the emissions and engine performance. The system uses a micro computer unit (MCU), numerous signal input sensors and several output components. Based on the engine operating conditions, relayed to the MCU by input sensor signals, the MCU generates output signals to provide the proper air/fuel mixture, proper ignition timing and engine idle speed.

The system operates in either of two modes, the closed loop mode or the open loop mode. Closed loop is when the air/fuel ratio is varied, according to the oxygen content tin the exhaust gases. In the open loop mode, the air/fuel ratio is predetermined by the MCU for a number of engine operating conditions, such as engine start-up, cold engine operation, or wide open throttle (WOT) position. When the engine is started, the MCU then determines in which mode of operation , (closed or open loop), the engine should be operating. The MCU determines this by monitoring the input signals from the various input components, such as the air and coolant temperature information, engine rpm information and vacuum levels.

The MCU operates the system in the open loop mode based on a priority rating for the various predetermined engine operating conditions. It continues to operate the system and the MCU output components in the open loop mode until such time as a closed loop mode of operation is indicated. At this time, the MCU shifts the operation to the closed loop mode. Based on the oxygen content in the exhaust gases, and other inputs, it continues to operate the system in the closed loop mode, constantly varying the air/fuel ratio to maintain the optimum 14.7:1 ratio.

The engine operating conditions are constantly being monitored by the MCU and any changes that occur during the engine operation are quickly detected by the MCU, which places the system back in the appropriate open mode of operation.

CEC SYSTEM COMPONENTS

1. Micro computer unit (MCU)
2. Oxygen sensor
3. Thermal electric switch (TES)
4. Coolant temperature switch (CTS)
5. Four inch vacuum switch
6. Ten inch vacuum switch
7. Wide open throttle switch
8. Engine rpm (TACH) voltage
9. Stepper motor (in carburetor)
10. Dual bed catalytic converter
11. Altitude jumper wire
12. Knock sensor
13. Electronic control unit to advance or retard ignition timing
14. Idle relay
15. SOLE-VAC Throttle positioner
16. Idle solenoid
17. Upstream and downstream air switch solenoids
18. PCV valve shut-off solenoid
19. Bowl vent solenoid
20. Intake manifold heater switch.

The CEC system controls the air/fuel ratio with movable air metering pins, visible from the top of the carburetor air horn, that are driven by an MCU controlled stepper motor. The stepper motor moves the metering pins in increments or small steps via electrical impulses generated by the MCU. The MCU causes the stepper motor to drive the metering pins to a richer or leaner position in reaction to voltage input from the oxygen sensor, located in the exhaust manifold. The oxygen sensor voltage varies in reaction to changes in the exhaust gas content of oxygen. Because the content of oxygen in the exhaust gas indicates the completeness of the combustion process, it is a reliable indicator of the air/fuel mixture that is entering the combustion chamber.

Because the oxygen sensor only reacts to oxygen, any air leak or malfunction between the carburetor and the sensor may cause the sensor top provide erroneous voltage output. This could be caused by a manifold air leak or malfunctioning secondary air checks valve.

The engine operation characteristics never quite permit the MCU to compute a single metering pin position that constantly provides the optimum air/fuel mixture. Therefore, closed loop operation is characterized by constant movement of the metering pins because the MCU is forced constantly to make small corrections in the air/fuel mixture, in an attempt to create the optimum air/fuel mixture ratio of 14.7:1.

COMPUTER COMAND CONTROL (CCC OR C3) SYSTEM

Late model Jeep Vehicles equipped with a V6 cylinder engine and a California emissions package, have a self-diagnostic system with a CHECK ENGINE light mounted in the instrument panel cluster.

DIAGNOSTIC PROCEDURES

The self-diagnostic system detects the troubles most likely to occur. The diagnostic system illuminates the CHECK ENGINE light when a trouble is detected. When a jumper wire is connected between trouble code TEST terminals 6 and 7 of the 15 terminal diagnostic connector, the CHECK ENGINE light will flash a trouble code or codes that indicate the trouble area.

For a bulb and system check, the CHECK ENGINE light will illuminate when the ignition switch is turned ON and the engine not started. If the test terminals are then grounded, the light will flash a code 12 that indicates the self- diagnostic system is operational. A code 12 consists of one (1) flash, followed by a short pause, then two (2) flashes in quick succession. After a longer pause, the code will repeat its self two (2) more times.

When the engine is started, the CHECK ENGINE light will remain on momentarily and then will go off. If the CHECK ENGINE light remains on, the self-diagnostic system has detected a trouble in the operational components. If the test terminals are then grounded, the trouble code will be flashed three (3) times. If more than one trouble has been detected, each trouble code will be flashed three (3) times. The trouble codes will flash in numeric order (lowest number code first). The trouble code series will repeat as long as the test terminals are grounded.

A trouble code indicates a trouble in a particular circuit or component. Trouble code 14, for example, indicates a trouble in the coolant sensor circuit, which includes the coolant sensor, connector, harness and the ECM. The procedure for locating trouble is in accompanying chart 14. Similar diagnostic charts are provided for each code.

The absence of a code does not mean a system is trouble free, because the self-diagnostic system does not detect all possible troubles. To determine if their is a system problem, a System Performance Test is necessary. This test is made when the CHECK ENGINE light and the self-diagnostic system do not indicate a problem, but the system is suspected because no other reason can be found for the complaint.

TROUBLE CODE MEMORY

When a problem develops in the feedback system, the CHECK ENGINE light will illuminate and a trouble code will be stored in the ECM memory. If the fault is intermittent, the CHECK ENGINE light will be turned off after ten (10) seconds when the problem ceases. However, the trouble code will be retained in the ECM memory until the battery voltage to the ECM is removed. To accomplish this, remove the negative battery cable for at least ten (10) seconds to erase all stored trouble codes.

SYSTEM PERFORMANCE

The system should be considered as a possible source of trouble for engine performance, fuel economy and exhaust emission complaints, ONLY AFTER normal engine diagnosis has been completed. In many cases, the feedback system has been blamed for engine performance problems, when only simple, basic engine problems have been the cause.

The system performance test verifies the system is functioning correctly and each step should be followed completely. Do not skip steps in order to short cut the tests.

TROUBLE CODE IDENTIFICATION

NOTE: The trouble code will be flashed on the CHECK ENGINE light only if a trouble exist that pertains to the following codes. Any codes stored in the ECM from a problem that has ceased to exist, will be erased from the ECM memory after fifty (50) engine starts.

1. Trouble Code 12 – No distributor reference pulses to the ECM. This code is not stored in memory and will only flash while the trouble exists. This is a normal code with the ignition ON and the engine not operating.
2. Trouble Code 13 – Refers to oxygen sensor circuit. The engine must operate up to five (5) minutes at part throttle , under road load, before this code will appear.
3. Trouble Code 14 – Coolant sensor circuit has short circuit. The engine must operate up to five (5) minutes before this code will appear.
4. Trouble Code 15 – Coolant sensor circuit has open circuit. The engine must operate up to five (5) minutes before this code will appear.
5. Trouble Code 21 – Throttle positioner sensor circuit problem. The engine must operate up to twenty five (25) seconds at specified curb idle speed before this code will appear.
6. Trouble Code 23 – The Mixture control solenoid has a short circuit to ground or an open circuit.
7. Trouble Code 34 – Vacuum sensor circuit problem. The engine must operate up to five (5) minutes at the specified curb idle speed before this code will appear.
8. Trouble Code 41 – No distributor reference pulses to the ECM at the specified engine manifold vacuum. This code will be stored in the ECM memory.
9. Trouble Code 42 – Electronic Spark Timing (EST) bypass circuit or EST circuit has short circuit to ground or an open circuit.
10. Trouble Code 44 – Lean exhaust indication. The engine must operate up to five (5) minutes, be in closed loop operation mode and at part throttle before this code will appear.
11. Trouble Code 44 and 45 at the same time – Indicates a faulty oxygen sensor.
12. Trouble Code 45 – Rich exhaust indication. The engine must operate up to five (5) minutes, be in closed loop and at part throttle before this code will appear.
13. Trouble Code 51 – Faulty calibration unit (PROM) or installed improperly. It requires up to thirty (30) seconds before this code will appear.
14. Trouble Code 54 – Mixture Control solenoid circuit has a short circuit and/or a faulty ECM.
15. Trouble Code 55 – Voltage reference has short circuit to ground (terminal 21), a faulty oxygen sensor or ECM.

ENGINE

Refer to the Engine General Repair Section for troubleshooting and rebuilding Engine

Removal and Installation

150 FOUR CYLINDER ENGINE

1. Disconnect the battery cable.
2. Remove the air cleaner.
3. Remove the hood. Discharge the A/C system using the proper precautions.
4. Drain the radiator.
5. Remove the lower radiator hose.
6. Remove the upper radiator hose and coolant recovery hose.
7. Remove the fan shroud. If equipped, disconnect the transmission fluid cooler lines.
8. Remove the radiator. If equipped, remove the A/C condenser.
9. Remove the fan assembly and install a $^5/_{16} \times ^1/_2$ in. SAE capscrew through the fan pulley into the water pump flange to maintain the pulley and water pump in alignment when the crankshaft is rotated.
10. Disconnect the heater hoses.

11. Disconnect the throttle linkages, cruise control cable (if equipped) and throttle valve rod.
12. Disconnect the wires from the starter motor solenoid and disconnect CEC System wire harness connector. If equipped with fuel injection, disconnect all fuel injection harness connectors. Disconnect the fuel line from the fuel pump.
13. If equipped with fuel injection, disconnect the quick connect fuel lines at the inner fender panel by squeezing the two retaining tabs against the fuel tube. Pull the fuel tube and the retainer from the quick connect fitting. Disconnect the TDC sensor wire connection. Disconnect the fuel line from the fuel pump.
14. If equipped with air conditioning, remove the service valves and cap the compressor ports.
15. Disconnect the fuel return hose from the fuel filter.
16. Remove the power brake vacuum check valve from the booster, if equipped.
17. If equipped with power steering, disconnect the hoses, drain the pump and cap the fittings in order to prevent dirt from entering the system.
18. Identify, tag and disconnect all necessary wire connectors and vacuum hoses.
19. Raise the vehicle and support it safely.
20. Remove the starter.
21. Disconnect the exhaust pipe from the manifold.
22. Remove the flywheel housing access cover. On models with automatic transmission, mark the converter and drive plate location and remove the converter-to-drive plate bolts.
23. Remove the upper flywheel housing bolts and loosen the bottom bolts.
24. Remove the engine mount cushion-to-engine compartment bracket bolts.
25. Lower the vehicle. Attach a lifting device to the engine.
26. Raise the engine off the front supports.
27. Place a support stand under the converter (or flywheel) housing.
28. Remove the remaining converter (or flywheel) housing bolts.
29. Lift the engine out of the engine compartment.
30. Installation is the reverse of removal.

151 FOUR CYLINDER ENGINE

1. Disconnect the negative battery cable. Remove the hood. Remove the air cleaner.
2. Drain the coolant. Disconnect the radiator hoses. Disconnect the automatic transmission lines from the radiator. If there is a radiator shroud, remove it, then remove the radiator.
3. Remove the fan and spacer.
4. Remove and set aside the power steering pump and belt. Do not disconnect any of the hydraulic lines.
5. Bleed the compressor refrigerant charge, observe all safety precautions. Remove the condenser and receiver assembly.
6. Noting their positions, disconnect all wires, lines, linkages, and hoses from the engine.
7. Drain the oil and remove the filter.
8. Remove both engine front support cushion to frame retaining nuts.
9. Disconnect the exhaust pipe at the support bracket and the manifold.
10. Support the engine with lifting equipment.
11. Remove the front support cushion and bracket assemblies from the engine.
12. Remove the transfer case lever boot, the floor mat and the transmission access cover.
13. In automatic transmissions, remove the upper bolts holding the bellhousing to the engine adapter plate. On manual transmissions, remove the upper bolts holding the clutch housing to the engine.
14. Remove the starter.
15. On automatics, remove the two adapter plate inspection covers. Mark the relationship of the converter to the flex plate and remove the converter-to-flex plate bolts. Remove the rest of the bolts holding the bellhousing to the adapter plate. On manual transmissions, remove the clutch housing lower cover and the rest of the bolts holding the clutch housing to the engine.
16. Support the transmission with a floor jack and remove the engine by pulling it forward and upward.
17. Installation is the reverse of the removal procedure.

173 SIX CYLINDER ENGINE

1. Disconnect the battery cable.
2. Remove the air cleaner.
3. Remove the hood. Discharge the A/C system using the proper safety precautions.
4. Drain the radiator.
5. Remove the lower radiator hose.
6. Remove the upper radiator hose and coolant recovery hose.
7. Remove the fan shroud.
8. If equipped, disconnect the transmission fluid cooler lines.
9. Remove the radiator. If equipped with A/C remove the condenser.
10. Remove the fan assembly.
11. Remove the heater hoses.
12. Disconnect the throttle linkage, including the cruise control cable and automatic transmission throttle valve cable.
13. Remove the power brake booster hose.
14. Identify, mark and disconnect the necessary wire connectors and vacuum hoses.
15. Remove the power steering pump assembly and lay aside.
16. Disconnect the fuel line at the fuel pump.
17. Disconnect the hoses from the A/C compressor.
18. Raise and support the vehicle.
19. Remove the exhaust pipes from the exhaust manifold.
20. Disconnect the exhaust pipe at the catalytic converter flange and allow the exhaust pipe to drop out of the way.
21. Remove the flywheel/converter housing access cover.
22. Remove the torque converter bolts.
23. Disconnect the wires at the starter.
24. Remove the flywheel/converter housing bolts.
25. Lower the vehicle.
26. Place a support under the transmission.
27. Remove the air pump and hose from the bracket.
28. Attach an engine lifting device to the engine.
29. Remove the engine mount through bolts.
30. Disconnect the ground strap at the rear of the left cylinder head.
31. Remove the engine from the engine compartment.
32. Installation is the reverse of removal.

258 SIX CYLINDER ENGINE

1. Remove the hood after marking the hinge locations.
2. Disconnect the negative battery cable. Remove the air cleaner.
3. Drain the coolant. Disconnect the radiator hoses. Disconnect automatic transmission cooler lines from the radiator. If there is a radiator shroud, remove it, then remove the radiator.
4. Remove the fan assembly and install a $^5/_{16} \times ^1/_2$ in. SAE capscrew through the fan pulley into the water pump flange to maintain the pulley and water pump in alignment when the crankshaft is rotated.
5. Remove and set aside the power steering pump and belt. Do not disconnect the hydraulic lines. If equipped, remove the power brake vacuum check valve from the booster.
6. Bleed the compressor refrigerant charge. Be sure to observe all safety precautions. Remove the condenser and receiver assembly.
7. Disconnect all wires, lines, linkage, and hoses from the engine.
8. Raise and support the vehicle safely. Drain the oil and remove the filter. Remove the starter. Remove the engine ground strap.

9. Remove both engine front support cushion-to-frame retaining nuts.
10. Disconnect the exhaust pipe at the support bracket and the manifold.
11. Support the engine with the lifting equipment.
12. Remove the front support cushion and bracket assemblies from the engine.
13. Remove the flywheel housing access cover. On models with automatic transmission, mark the converter and drive plate location and remove the converter-to-drive plate bolts.
14. Remove the upper flywheel housing bolts and loosen the bottom bolts.
15. Remove the engine mount cushion-to-engine compartment bracket bolts.
16. Lower the vehicle. Attach a lifting device to the engine.
17. Raise the engine off the front supports.
18. Place a support stand under the converter (or flywheel) housing.
19. Remove the remaining converter (or flywheel) housing bolts.
20. Lift the engine out of the engine compartment.
21. Installation is the reverse of removal.

DIESEL ENGINE

1. Disconnect the battery cables and remove the battery. Remove the hood.
2. If equipped, remove the skid plate.
3. Drain the radiator. Remove the air cleaner assembly.
4. If equipped, discharge the A/C compressor. Be sure to observe all safety precautions.
5. Disconnect the radiator hoses and remove the "E" clip from the bottom of the radiator.
6. Raise and support the vehicle safely. If the vehicle is equipped with automatic transmission disconnect the oil cooler lines at the radiator.
7. Remove the splash shield from the oil pan. Lower the vehicle.
8. Loosen the radiator shroud and remove the radiator fan assembly. Remove the shroud and the splash shield.
9. Remove the radiator and the condenser assembly from the vehicle. Remove the inner cooler.
10. Remove the exhaust shield from the manifold. Disconnect the hoses at the remote oil filter. Remove the oil filter.
11. Tag and disconnect all vacuum hoses and electrical connections. Disconnect and plug the fuel inlet and outlet lines at the fuel pump. If equipped with automatic transmission, remove the left motor mount through bolt retaining nut.
12. Remove the motor mount retaining bolts. Disconnect the accelerator cable. Raise and support the vehicle safely.
13. Disconnect and drain the power steering hoses at the power steering pump.
14. Disconnect the exhaust pipe at the exhaust manifold. Remove the motor mount retaining nuts.
15. Support the engine. Remove the left motor mount bolts, automatic transmission equipped vehicles, remove the left motor mount.
16. Remove the starter.
17. If the vehicle is equipped with automatic transmission, mark and remove the converter to drive plate bolts through the starter opening. Install the left motor mount and retaining bolts finger tight. Install the motor mount cushion through bolt. Remove the engine support.
18. Remove the transmission to engine retaining bolts.
19. Lower the vehicle. Remove the remaining engine to transmission retaining bolts.
20. Remove the power steering pump from the engine. Remove the oil separator and disconnect the hoses. Disconnect the heater hoses.
21. Remove the remaining engine to transmission retaining bolt.
22. Remove the reference pressure regulator from the dash panel. Install the engine lifting device and position a jack under the transmission.
23. Remove the engine from the vehicle.
24. Installation is the reverse of the removal procedure.

V8 ENGINES

1. Disconnect the negative battery cable. Remove the hood.
2. Remove the air cleaner assembly.
3. Drain the radiator. Remove the upper and lower radiator hoses. If equipped with automatic transmission, disconnect the cooler lines.
4. Remove the radiator from the vehicle.
5. Remove the fan assembly.
6. If equipped with power steering remove the pump and lay it aside. Do not disconnect the hoses from the pump.
7. If the vehicle is equipped with A/C discharge the system . Observe all the required safety precautions. Remove the condenser and the receiver.
8. Remove the battery and the battery tray from the vehicle.
9. Remove the heater core housing and charcoal canister from the firewall as required.
10. If equipped, remove cruise command vacuum servo bellows and mounting bracket as a complete assembly.
11. On some CJ models it may be necessary to remove the left front support cushion and bracket from cylinder block.
12. Disconnect all wires, lines linkage, and hoses which are connected to the engine.
13. If equipped with automatic transmission, disconnect the transmission filler tube bracket from the right cylinder head. Do not remove the filler tube from the transmission.
14. Remove both engine front support cushion-to-frame retaining nuts.
15. Support the weight of the engine with a lifting device.
16. On some vehicles, it will be necessary to remove the transfer case shift lever boot, floor (if so equipped), and transmission access cover.
17. Remove the upper bolts which secure the transmission bellhousing to the engine adapter plate on vehicles equipped with automatic transmission. If equipped with manual transmission, remove the upper bolts which secure the clutch housing to the engine.
18. Disconnect the exhaust pipes at the exhaust manifolds and support bracket.
19. Remove the starter motor.
20. Support the transmission with a floor jack.
21. If equipped with automatic transmission, remove the two engine adapter plate inspection covers. Mark the assembled position of the converter and flex plate and remove the converter-to-flex plate cap screws. Remove the remaining bolts which secure the transmission bellhousing to the engine adapter plate.
22. If equipped with manual transmission, remove the clutch housing lower cover and the remaining bolts which secure the clutch housing to the engine.
23. Remove the engine by pulling upward and forward.

NOTE: If equipped with power brakes, care must be taken to avoid damaging the power unit while removing the engine.

24. Installation is the reverse of the removal procedure.

Manifolds

INTAKE MANIFOLD

Removal and Installation

150 FOUR CYLINDER ENGINE

NOTE: It may be necessary to remove the carburetor or the throttle body from the intake manifold before the manifold is removed.

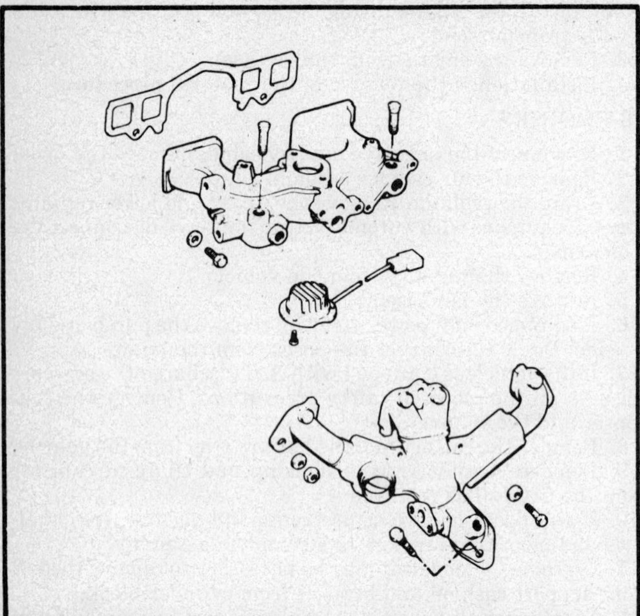

4-150 intake/exhaust manifold with electric fuel heater
(© Jeep Corp.)

1. Disconnect the negative battery cable. Drain the radiator.
2. Remove the air cleaner. Disconnect the fuel pipe. Remove the carburetor or the throttle body, as required.
3. Disconnect the coolant hoses from the intake manifold.
4. Disconnect the throttle cable from the bellcrank.
5. Disconnect the PCV valve vacuum hose from the intake manifold.
6. If equipped, remove the vacuum advance CTO valve vacuum hoses.
7. Disconnect the system coolant temperature sender wire connector (located on the intake manifold). Disconnect the air temperature sensor wire, if equipped.
8. Disconnect the vacuum hose from the EGR valve.
9. On vehicles equipped with power steering remove the power steering pump and its mounting bracket. Do not detach the power steering pump hoses.
10. Disconnect the intake manifold electric heater wire connector, as required.
11. Disconnect the throttle valve linkage, if equipped with automatic transmission.
12. Disconnect the EGR valve tube from the intake manifold.
13. Remove the intake manifold attaching screws, nuts and clamps. Remove the intake manifold. Discard the gasket.
14. Clean the mating surfaces of the manifold and cylinder head.

NOTE: If the manifold is being replaced, ensure all fittings, etc. are transferred to the replacement manifold.

15. Installation is the reverse of removal. Torque manifold bolts to 23 ft. lbs.

151 FOUR CYLINDER ENGINE

1. Disconnect the negative battery cable.
2. Remove air cleaner and PCV valve hose.
3. Drain cooling system.
4. Tag and remove vacuum hoses (ensure distributor vacuum advance hose is removed).
5. Disconnect fuel pipe and electrical wire connections from carburetor.
6. Disconnect carburetor throttle linkage. Remove carburetor and carburetor spacer.
7. Remove bellcrank and throttle linkage brackets and move to one side for clearance.
8. Remove heater hose at intake manifold.
9. Remove alternator. Note position of spacers for installation.
10. Remove manifold-to-cylinder head bolts and remove manifold.
11. Position replacement gasket and install replacement manifold on cylinder head. Start all bolts.
12. Tighten manifold-to-cylinder head bolts using sequence. Tighten all bolts with 37 ft. lbs. (50 Nm) torque.
13. Connect heater hose to intake manifold.
14. Install bellcrank and throttle linkage brackets.
15. Connect carburetor throttle linkage to brackets and bellcrank.
16. Install carburetor spacer and tighten bolts with 15 ft. lbs. (20 Nm) torque.
17. Install carburetor and gasket. Tighten nuts with 15 ft. lbs. (20 Nm) torque.
18. Install fuel pipe and electrical wire connections. Install vacuum hoses.
19. Connect the negative battery cable.
20. Refill cooling system. Start engine and inspect for leaks.
21. Install air cleaner and PCV valve hose.

173 SIX CYLINDER ENGINE

NOTE: It may be necessary to remove the carburetor from the intake manifold before the manifold is removed.

1. Disconnect the negative battery cable. Remove the rocker covers. Drain the radiator.
2. If equipped with A/C disconnect the compressor and move it to on side. Disconnect the spark plugs wires at the spark plugs. Disconnect the wires at the ignition coil.
3. If equipped, remove the air pump and bracket.
4. Remove the distributor cap. Mark the position of the ignition rotor in relation to the distributor body, and remove the distributor. Do not crank the engine with the distributor removed.
5. Remove the EGR valve. Remove the air hose. Disconnect the charcoal canister hoses. Remove the pipe bracket from the left cylinder head, if equipped.
6. Remove the diverter valve. Remove the power brake vacuum hose. Remove the heater and radiator hoses from the intake manifold.
7. Disconnect and label the vacuum hoses. If equipped, remove the EFE pipe from the rear of the manifold. Disconnect the coolant temperature switches.
8. Remove the carburetor linkage. Disconnect and plug the fuel line.
9. Remove the manifold retaining bolts and nuts.
10. Remove the intake manifold. Remove and discard the gaskets, and scrape off the old silicone seal from the front and rear ridges.
11. The gaskets are marked for right and left side installation; do not interchange them. Clean the sealing surface of the engine block, and apply a $^{3}/_{16}$ in. bead of silicone sealer to each ridge.
12. Install the new gaskets onto the heads. The gaskets will have to be cut slightly to fit past the center pushrods. Do not cut any more material than necessary. Hold the gaskets in place by extending the ridge bead of sealer $^{1}/_{4}$ in. onto the gasket ends.
13. Install the intake manifold. The area between the ridges and the manifold should be completely sealed.
14. Install the retaining bolts and nuts, and tighten in sequence to 23 ft. lbs. Do not overtighten; the manifold is made from aluminum, and can be warped or cracked with excessive force.
15. The rest of installation is the reverse of removal. Adjust the ignition timing after installation, and check the coolant level after the engine has warmed up.

258 SIX CYLINDER ENGINE

NOTE: The intake and exhaust manifold are mounted externally on the left side of the engine and are attached to the cylinder head. They are removed as a unit.

1. Disconnect the negative battery cable. Remove the air cleaner and carburetor.
2. Disconnect the accelerator cable from the accelerator bellcrank.
3. Disconnect the PCV vacuum hose from the intake manifold. Remove the vacuum advance CTO valve vacuum hoses as required.
4. Disconnect the distributor vacuum hose and electrical wires at the TCS solenoid vacuum valves. If equipped, disconnect the CEC system coolant temperature sender wire connector on the intake manifold.
5. Remove the TCS solenoid vacuum valve and bracket from the intake manifold. In some cases it might not be necessary to remove the TCS unit.
6. Disconnect the EGR valve and back pressure sensor hoses. If equipped, disconnect the electric heater wire connector. Remove the carburetor from the vehicle.
7. Remove the power steering mounting bracket and pump and set it aside without disconnecting the hoses. Remove air pump, if equipped.
8. Remove the EGR valve and backpressure sensor. If equipped, remove air conditioning drive belt idler assembly from cylinder head.
9. Disconnect the exhaust pipe from the manifold flange. If equipped with automatic transmission disconnect the throttle valve linkage.
10. Remove the manifold attaching bolts, nuts and clamps.
11. Separate the intake manifold and exhaust manifold from the engine as an assembly, and discard the gasket.
12. If either manifold is to be replaced, they should be separated at the heat riser area.
13. Clean the mating surface of the manifolds and the cylinder head before replacing the manifolds. Replace them in reverse order of the above procedure with new gasket. Tighten the bolts and nuts to the specified torque in the proper sequence.

DIESEL ENGINE

1. Disconnect the negative battery cable. Disconnect the air inlet hose at the intake manifold.
2. Remove all necessary components in order to gain access to the intake manifold retaining bolts.
3. Tag and remove all vacuum hoses and electrical connections that are attached to the intake manifold.
4. Remove the intake manifold retaining bolts. Remove the assembly from the vehicle. Discard the intake manifold gaskets.
5. Installation is the reverse of the removal procedure.

V8 ENGINES

1. Disconnect the negative battery cable. Drain the coolant from the radiator.
2. Remove the air cleaner assembly.
3. Disconnect the spark plug wires.
4. Disconnect the upper radiator hose and the by-pass hose from the intake manifold. Disconnect the heater hose from the rear of the manifold.
5. Disconnect the ignition coil bracket and lay the coil aside.
6. If equipped, Disconnect the TCS solenoid vacuum valve from the right side valve cover.
7. Disconnect all lines, hoses, linkages and wires from the carburetor and intake manifold and TCS components as required. Remove carburetor.
8. Disconnect the air delivery hoses at the air distribution manifolds.

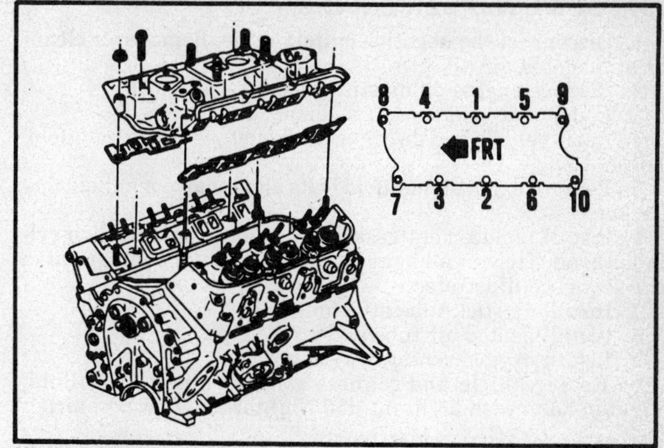

V6-173 intake manifold and torque sequence for attaching bolts (© Jeep Corp.)

9. Disconnect the air pump diverter valve and lay the valve and the bracket assembly, including the hoses, forward of the engine.
10. Remove the intake manifold after removing the cap bolts that hold it in place. Remove and discard the side gaskets and the end seals.
11. Clean the mating surfaces of the intake manifold and the cylinder head before replacing the intake manifold. Use new gaskets and tighten the cap bolts to the correct torque. Install in reverse order of the above procedure.

EXHAUST MANIFOLD

Removal and Installation

150 FOUR CYLINDER ENGINE

1. Disconnect the negative battery cable. Remove the intake manifold.
2. Disconnect the EGR valve tube.
3. Disconnect the exhaust pipe from the exhaust manifold.
4. Disconnect the oxygen sensor wire connector.
5. Remove the sensor from the manifold if a replacement manifold is to be installed.
6. Remove the nuts from the end studs. Remove the exhaust manifold.
7. Installation is the reverse of removal. Torque manifold nuts 23 ft. lbs., oxygen sensor 35 ft. lbs.

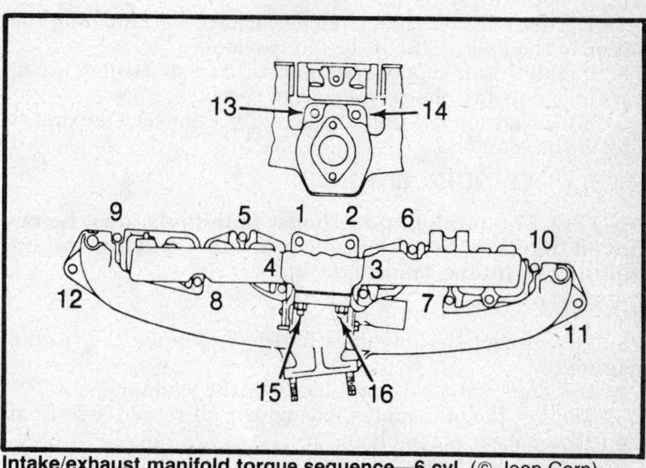

Intake/exhaust manifold torque sequence—6 cyl. (© Jeep Corp)

151 FOUR CYLINDER ENGINE

1. Disconnect the negative battery cable. Remove air cleaner and heated air tube.
2. Remove engine oil dipstick tube attaching bolt.
3. Remove oxygen sensor, if equipped.
4. Raise vehicle and disconnect exhaust pipe from manifold. Lower vehicle.
5. Remove exhaust manifold bolts and remove manifold and gasket.
6. Install replacement gasket and exhaust manifold on cylinder head. Tighten all bolts with 39 ft. lbs. (52 Nm) torque in the sequence illustrated.
7. Install dipstick tube attaching bolt.
8. Install heated air tube and air cleaner.
9. Install oxygen sensor, if removed.
10. Raise vehicle and connect exhaust pipe to manifold. Tighten bolts with 35 ft. lbs. (50 Nm) torque. Lower vehicle.

173 SIX CYLINDER ENGINE

LEFT SIDE

1. Disconnect the negative battery cable. Remove the air cleaner. Remove the carburetor heat stove pipe.
2. Remove the air supply plumbing from the exhaust manifold.
3. Raise and support the vehicle safely. Unbolt and remove the exhaust pipe at the manifold.
4. Unbolt and remove the manifold.
5. Clean the mating surfaces of the cylinder head and manifold. Install the manifold onto the head, and install the retaining bolts finger tight.
6. Tighten the manifold bolts in a circular pattern, working from the center to the ends, to 25 ft. lbs. in two stages.
7. Connect the exhaust pipe to the manifold.
8. The remainder of installation is the reverse of removal.

RIGHT SIDE

1. Disconnect the negative battery cable. Raise and support the vehicle safely.
2. Disconnect the exhaust pipe from the exhaust manifold.
3. Lower the vehicle. Remove the spark plug wires from the plugs. Number them first if they are not already labeled. Remove the cruise control servo from the right inner fender panel, if equipped.
4. Remove the air supply pipes from the manifold. Remove the pulsair bracket bolt from the rocker cover, on models so equipped, then remove the pipe assembly.
5. Remove the manifold retaining bolts and remove the manifold.
6. Clean the mating surfaces of the cylinder head and manifold. Position the manifold against the head and install the retaining bolts finger tight.
7. Tighten the bolts in a circular pattern, working from the center to the ends, to 25 ft. lbs. in two stages.
8. Install the air supply system.Install the spark plug wires. If equipped install the cruise control servo.
9. Raise and support the vehicle safely. Connect the exhaust pipe to the manifold.

258 SIX CYLINDER ENGINE

NOTE: The intake and exhaust manifolds must be removed together. See the procedure for removing and installing the intake manifold.

DIESEL ENGINE

1. Disconnect the negative battery. Remove the intake manifold.
2. Disconnect the exhaust pipe from the adapter.
3. Remove the oil supply pipe and the oil return hose from the turbocharger assembly.
4. Disconnect the turbocharger air inlet and outlet hoses.
5. Remove the turbocharger retaining bolts. Remove the turbocharger from the vehicle.
6. Remove the exhaust manifold retaining bolts. Remove the exhaust manifold and gasket. Discard the gasket.
7. Installation is the reverse of the removal procedure.

V8 ENGINES

1. Disconnect the negative battery cable. Disconnect the spark plug wires.
2. Disconnect the air delivery hose at the distribution manifold.
3. Remove the air distribution manifold and the injection tubes.
4. Disconnect the exhaust pipe at the manifold.
5. Remove the exhaust manifold attaching bolts and washers along with the spark plug shields.
6. Separate the exhaust manifold from the cylinder head.
7. Install in reverse order of the above procedure. Clean the matting surfaces and tighten the attaching bolts to the correct torque.

Turbocharger

DIESEL ENGINE

Removal and Installation

1. Disconnect the negative battery cable.
2. Remove all the necessary components in order to gain access to the turbocharger retaining bolts.
3. Disconnect the exhaust pipe flange. Remove the oil supply pipe. Remove the oil return hose.
4. Remove the turbocharger retaining bolts. Remove the turbocharger from the vehicle.
5. Installation is the reverse of the removal procedure.

Engine Mounts

Removal and Installation

ALL ENGINES

Resilient rubber mounting cushions support the engine and transmission at three points. A cushion is located at each side on the center line of the engine, with the rear supported by a cushion between the transmission extension housing and the rear engine support crossmember.

Replacement of the cushion may be accomplished by supporting the weight of the engine or transmission at the area of the cushion.

Cylinder Head

Removal and Installation

150 FOUR CYLINDER ENGINE

1. Disconnect the battery cable.
2. Drain the coolant and disconnect the hoses at the thermostat housing.
3. Remove the air cleaner.
4. Remove the valve cover.
5. Remove the rocker arms, bridge and pivot assemblies. Remove the push rods.

NOTE: Retain the push rods, bridge, pivot and rocker arms in the same order as removed to facilitate installation in the original positions.

6. Disconnect the power steering pump bracket. Set the pump and bracket aside. Do not disconnect the hoses.
7. Remove the intake and exhaust manifolds from the cylinder head.

8. If equipped with air conditioning, perform the following:
a. remove the air conditioner compressor drive belt.
b. loosen the alternator drive belt.
c. remove the A/C compressor/alternator bracket-to-cylinder head mounting screw.

NOTE: The serpentine drive belt tension is released by loosening the alternator.

9. Remove the bolts from the A/C compressor (if equipped) and alternator mounting bracket and set the compressor aside.
10. Disconnect the ignition wires and remove the spark plugs.
11. Disconnect the temperature sending unit wire connector.
12. Remove the cylinder head bolts, cylinder head and gasket.
13. Thoroughly clean the machined surfaces of the cylinder head and block. Remove all gasket material and cement.
14. Installation is the reverse of removal, with the following recommendations.
15. Apply an even coat of sealing compound, or equivalent, to both sides of the replacement cylinder head gasket and position the gasket on the cylinder block with the word TOP facing upward.
16. Coat the threads of the stud bolt in the number eight sequence position with Permatex sealant or equivalent. Torque to 75 ft. lbs.

NOTE: Do not apply sealing compound to the cylinder head and block machined surfaces. Do not allow the sealing compound to enter the cylinder bores.

17. Torque the head bolts to 85 ft. lbs. in the proper sequence.

151 FOUR CYLINDER ENGINE

1. Disconnect the negative battery cable. Drain the cooling system and disconnect the hoses at the thermostat housing.
2. Remove the cylinder head cover (valve cover), the gasket, the rocker arm assembly, and the pushrods.

NOTE: The pushrods and rockers must be replaced in their original positions.

3. Remove the intake and exhaust manifold from the cylinder head.
4. Disconnect the spark plug wires and remove the spark plugs to avoid damaging them.
5. Remove air conditioning drive belt idler bracket from cylinder head. Loosen alternator belt and remove bracket-to-head mounting screw. Remove compressor mounting bracket and set the unit aside.
6. Disconnect the temperature sending unit wire, ignition coil and bracket assembly and battery ground cable from the engine.
7. Remove the cylinder head bolts, the cylinder head and gasket from the block.
8. To install, reverse the above procedure. Tighten the cylinder head bolts to the specified torque, in the proper sequence.

173 SIX CYLINDER ENGINE

LEFT SIDE

1. Disconnect the negative battery cable. Raise and support the vehicle safely. Disconnect the exhaust pipe from the exhaust manifold.
2. Drain the coolant from the block and lower the vehicle.
3. Remove the intake manifold.
4. Remove the exhaust manifold.
5. If equipped, remove the powewr steering pump and bracket.
6. Remove the dipstick tube.
7. Loosen the rocker arm bolts and remove the pushrods. Keep the pushrods in the same order as removed.
8. Remove the cylinder head bolts in stages and in the reverse order of the tightening sequence.

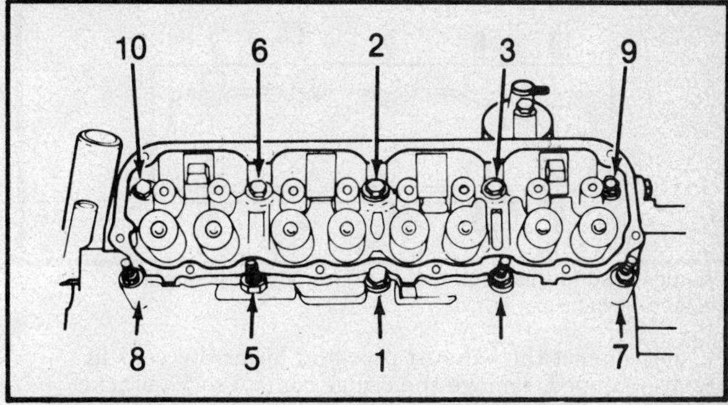

4–150 cylinder head torque sequence (© Jeep Corp)

9. Remove the cylinder head. Do not pry on the head to loosen it.
10. Installation is the reverse of removal.

NOTE: The words "This side Up" on the new cylinder head gasket should face upward. Coat the cylinder head bolts with sealer and torque to specifications.

RIGHT SIDE

1. Disconnect the negative battery cable. Raise and support the vehicle safely. Drain the coolant from the block.

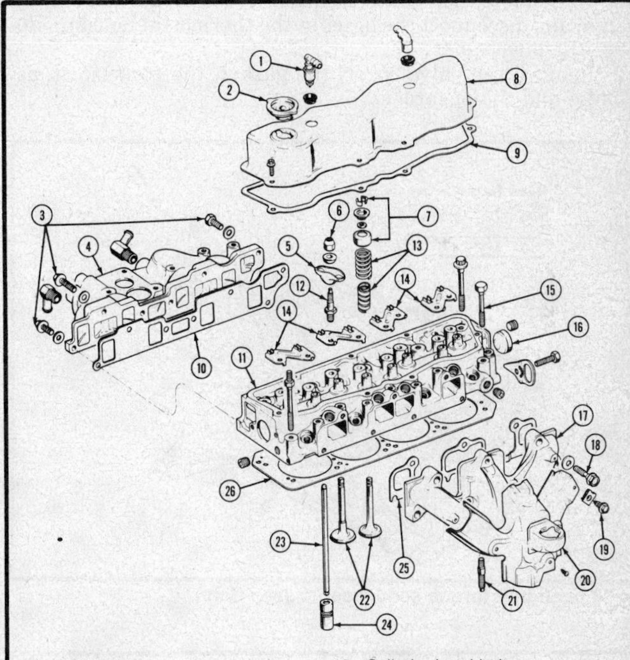

Exploded view of the cylinder head assembly-151 four cylinder (© AMC Corp)

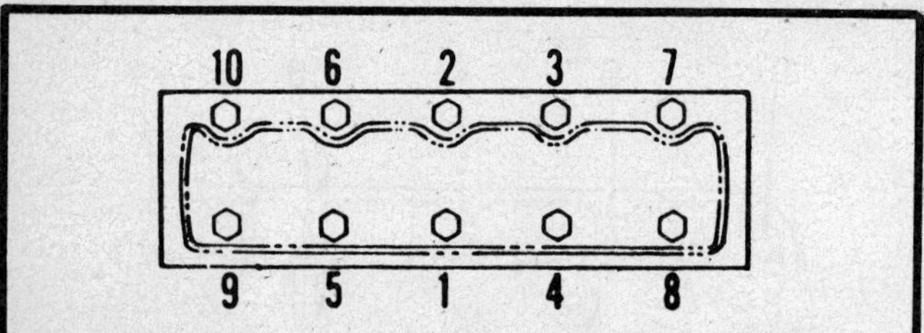

Cylinder head torque sequence—151 four cylinder engine (© Jeep Corp.)

2. Disconnect the exhaust pipe and lower the vehicle.
3. If equipped, remove the cruise control servo bracket.
4. Remove the alternator and air pump bracket assembly.
5. Remove the intake manifold.
6. Loosen the rocker arm nuts and remove the pushrods. Keep the pushrods in the order in which they were removed.
7. Remove the cylinder head bolts in stages and in the reverse order of the tightening sequence.
8. Remove the cylinder head. Do not pry on the cylinder head to loosen it.
9. Installation is the reverse of removal. The words "This side Up" on the new cylinder head gasket should face upwards. Coat the cylinder head bolts with sealer and tighten them to specification.

258 SIX CYLINDER ENGINE

1. Disconnect the negative battery cable. Drain the cooling system and disconnect the hoses at the thermostat housing. Remove the air cleaner.
2. Remove the valve cover, the gasket, the rocker arm assembly, and the pushrods.

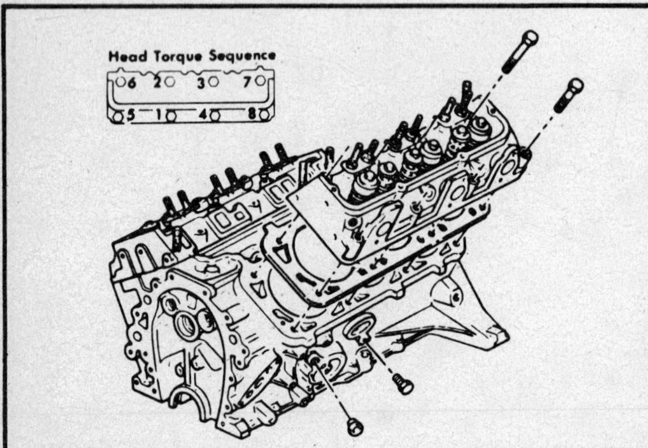

6–173 head bolt torque sequence (© Jeep Corp)

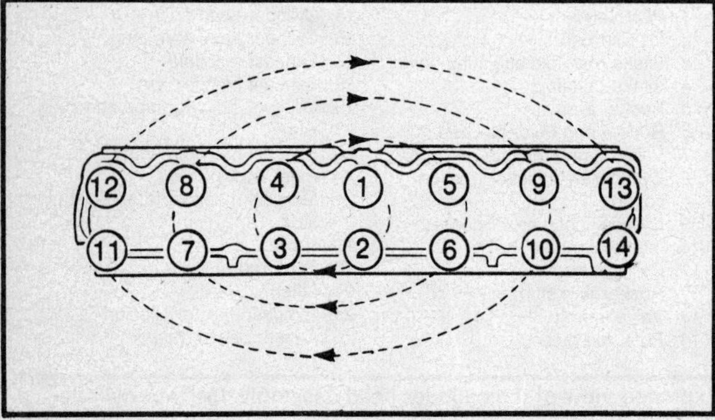

Cylinder head bolt tighting sequence—6 cyl. (© Jeep Corp)

NOTE: The pushrods and rockers must be replaced in their original positions.

3. Disconnect the power steering pump and bracket from the cylinder head. Lay the assembly aside and do not disconnect the power steering pump hoses. Remove the intake and exhaust manifold from the cylinder head.
4. Disconnect the spark plug wires and remove the spark plugs to avoid damaging them.
5. Remove air conditioning drive belt idler bracket from cylinder head. Loosen alternator belt and remove bracket-to-head mounting screw. Remove compressor mounting bracket and set the unit aside.

NOTE: On vehicles so equipped, the serpentine drive belt tension is released by loosening the alternator.

6. Disconnect the temperature sending unit wire, ignition coil and bracket assembly and battery ground cable from the engine.
7. Remove the cylinder head bolts, the cylinder head and gasket from the block.
8. To install, reverse the above procedure. Tighten the cylinder head bolts to the specified torque, in the proper sequence.

DIESEL ENGINE

1. Disconnect the negative battery cable.
2. Remove the intake manifold. Remove the exhaust manifold.
3. Remove the valve cover. Drain the engine coolant. Remove the timing belt cover.
4. Install sprocket holding tool MOT–854 or equivalent and remove the camshaft sprocket retaining bolt. Remove the special tool.
5. Loosen the bolts and move the tensioner away from the timing belt. Retighten the tensioner bolts.
6. Remove the timing belt from the sprockets.

NOTE: If it is necessary to remove the fuel injection pump sprocket, use special tool BVI–28–01 or BVI–859 to accomplish this procedure.

7. Disconnect the fuel pipe fittings from the injectors. Plug them in order to prevent dirt from entering the system.
8. Disconnect the fuel pipe fittings from the fuel injection pump. Plug them in order to prevent dirt from entering the system.
9. Remove the fuel pipes from there mountings on the engine. Remove all hoses and connectors from the fuel injection pump.
10. Remove the injection pump retaining bolts. Remove the fuel injection pump and its mounting brackets, as an assembly, from the vehicle.
11. Remove the the retaining bolts (F) and nuts (G) from the cylinder head. Loosen pivot bolt (H) but do not remove it. Remove the remaining cylinder head bolts.
12. Place a block of wood against the cylinder head and tap it with a hammer in order to loosen the cylinder head gasket. The pivot movement will be minimal due to the small clearance between the studs and the cylinder head. Remove the pivot bolt (H) from the cylinder head.
13. Remove the retaining bolts and the rocker arm shaft assembly from the cylinder head.

NOTE: Do not lift the cylinder head from the cylinder block until the gasket is completely loosened from the cylinder liners. Otherwise, the inner seals could be broken.

14. Remove the cylinder head and the gasket from the engine block.
15. Installation is the reverse of the removal procedure. Be sure that the new cylinder head gasket is positioned properly on the cylinder head and that it is the correct thickness for piston protrusion.

16. Torque the cylinder head retaining bolts to 22 ft. lbs., then to 37 ft. lbs, then to 70–77 ft. lbs. Once all the bolts are tightened recheck the torque.

NOTE: The cylinder head bolts must be retightened after the cylinder head is installed in the vehicle. Operate the engine for a minimum of twenty minutes. Allow the engine to cool for a minimum of two and one half hours. Loosen each cylinder head bolt in sequence about one-half turn. Then retighten in the proper sequence and torque to 70–77 ft. lbs. For the final tightening, tighten the bolts again in sequence without loosening them to 70–77 ft. lbs.

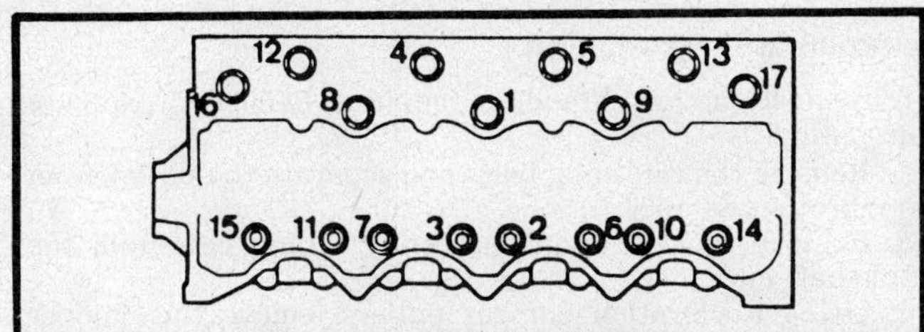

Cylinder head torque sequence—diesel engine (© Jeep Corp.)

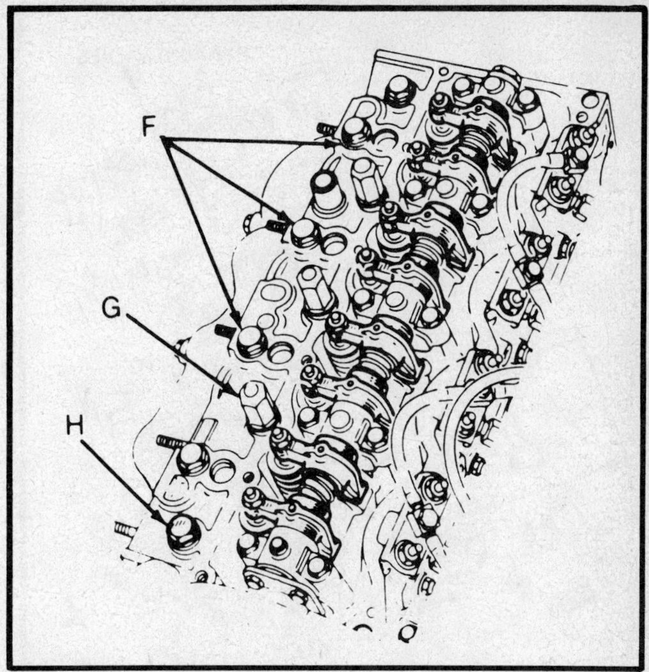

Head bolt removal procedure—diesel engine (© Jeep Corp.)

V8 ENGINES

1. Disconnect the negative battery cable. Drain the cooling system and the cylinder block.
2. When removing the right cylinder head, it may be necessary to remove the heater core housing from the firewall.
3. Remove the valve cover(s) and gasket(s).
4. Remove the rocker arm assemblies and push rods.

NOTE: The valve train components must be replaced in their original positions.

5. Remove the spark plugs to avoid damaging them.
6. Remove the intake manifold with the carburetor still attached.
7. Remove the exhaust pipes at the flange of the exhaust manifold. When replacing the exhaust pipes, it is advisable to install new gaskets at the flange.
8. Loosen all of the drive belts.
9. Disconnect negative battery cable at cylinder head. Remove air conditioning compressor mount bracket and alternator support brace from cylinder head.
10. Disconnect the air pump and power steering pump brackets from the cylinder head.
11. Remove the cylinder head bolts and lift the head(s) from the cylinder block.
12. Remove the cylinder head gasket(s) from the head(s) or the block.
13. To install, reverse the above procedure.

NOTE: Apply an even coat of sealing compound to both sides of the new head gasket only. Wire brush the cylinder head bolts, then lightly oil them prior to installation. First, tighten all bolts to 80 ft. lbs., then tighten them to the specified torque. Follow the correct tightening sequence.

Rocker Arm Assemblies

Removal and Installation

150 FOUR CYLINDER AND 258 SIX CYLINDER ENGINES

1. Disconnect the negative battery cable. Remove the valve cover.
2. Remove the two capscrews at each bridge and pivot assembly.
3. Remove the bridges, pivots and rocker arms. Keep them in order as they must be installed in the same position as they were removed.
4. Installation is the reverse of the removal procedure. Torque the capscrews to 19 ft. lbs. Be sure to use new gaskets as required.

151 FOUR CYLINDER AND 173 SIX CYLINDER ENGINES

1. Disconnect the negative battery cable. Remove the valve cover and gasket.
2. Remove the rocker arm nut and ball.
3. Lift the rocker arm off the rocker arm stud, always keep the rocker arm, nut and ball together and always assemble them on the same stud.
4. Remove the pushrod from its bore. Make sure the pushrods are always returned to the same bore with the same end in the block.
5. Reverse the above procedure for installation. Tighten the rocker arm nut to 20 ft. lbs.

NOTE: On the six cylinder engine tighten the rocker arm nut until it just touches the valve stem. Rotate the engine until number one piston is at TDC of the compression stroke. The "0" on the timing scale should be aligned with the timing pointer and the rotor should be at the

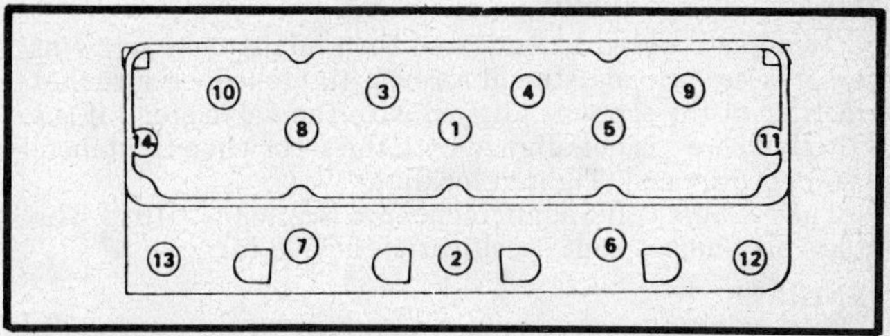

Cylinder head torque sequence—V8 engine (© Jeep Corp.)

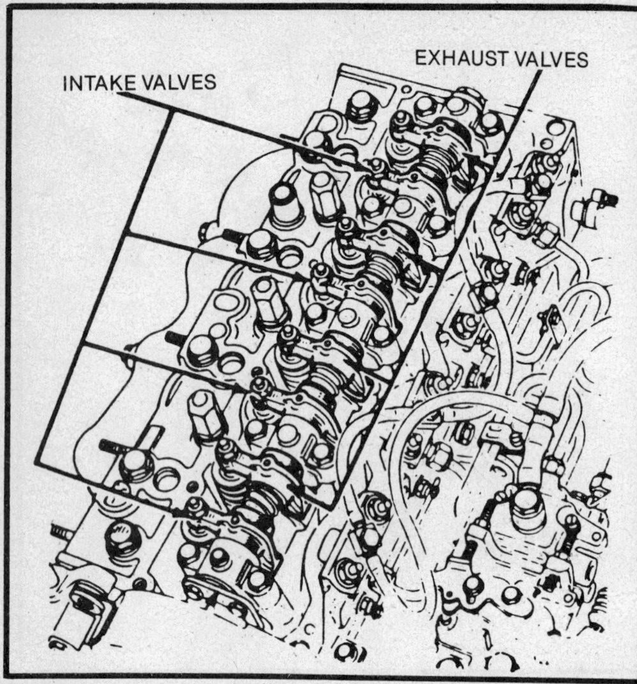

Diesel engine valve adjustment sequence (© Jeep Corp.)

number one spark plug tower of the distributor cap. The following valves can now be adjusted. Exhaust valves–1–2–3, Intake valves–1–5–6. Turn the adjusting nut until it backs off the stem slightly, then tighten until it just touches the stem. Then turn the nut one and one-half turns more to center the tappet plunger. Rotate the engine one complete revolution more. This will bring number four piston to TDC on the compression stroke. At this point the following valves should be adjusted. Exhaust valves–4–5–6, Intake valves–2–3–4.

DIESEL ENGINE

1. Disconnect the negative battery cable. Remove the cylinder head cover and gasket.
2. Remove the valve cover.
3. Remove the rocker shaft retaining bolts. Remove the rocker arm shaft assembly from the vehicle.
4. Installation is the reverse of the removal procedure. Be sure to use new gaskets and adjust the valves as required.
5. Be sure that the engine is cold before adjusting the valves.
6. Set number one cylinder to TDC on the compression stroke and check the valve clearance of number one and number two intake and number one and number three exhaust valves. Adjust as required.
7. Rotate the crankshaft 360 degrees and check the clearance of the number three and number four intake and number two and number four exhaust valves. Adjust as required.

NOTE: The number one cylinder is located at the flywheel end of the engine.

8. To adjust, loosen locknut and turn adjustment screw as necessary. As each adjustment screw is tightened, be sure that the bottom of the screw is aligned with the valve stem. If the adjustment screw is not aligned with the stem when tightened, the stem could bend. Tighten locknut.
9. The exhaust valve adjustment specification is .010 in. The intake valve adjustment specification is .008 in.

V8 ENGINES

1. Remove the cylinder head cover and gasket.
2. Loosen the bridged pivot capscrews a turn at a time, so as not to break the bridge.
3. Remove the rocker arm and bridge assembly from the cylinder head.
4. Install the rocker arms and bridge assembly on the cylinder head, and align the pushrods.
5. Install the capscrews and tighten each one a turn at a time to avoid breaking the bridge. Tighten the capscrews to 19 ft. lbs. torque.
6. Install the cylinder head cover with a new gasket and torque the cover bolts to 50 inch lbs.

Crankshaft Pulley Assembly (Vibration Damper)

Removal and Installation

1. Remove the fan shroud, as required. Remove drive belts from pulley.
2. Remove the retaining bolts and separate the pulley from the vibration damper.
3. Remove the vibration damper retaining bolt from the crankshaft end.
4. Using a vibration damper puller, remove the damper from the crankshaft.
5. Upon installation, align the key slot of the pulley hub to the crankshaft key. Complete the assembly in the reverse order of removal. Torque the retaining bolts to specifications.

Timing Gear Cover and Oil Seal

Removal and Installation

150 FOUR CYLINDER ENGINE

1. Disconnect the negative battery cable. Remove the radiator fan shroud, if equipped.
2. Remove the vibration pulley and damper assembly. Remove the fan and hub assembly.
3. If equipped, remove the A/C compressor. Remove the alternator bracket assembly from the cylinder head and position it aside.
4. Remove the oil pan to timing case cover retaining bolts, and the cover to cylinder block bolts.
5. Remove the timing case cover, front seal and gasket from the engine block.
6. Upon installation, cut off the oil pan side gasket end tabs and the oil pan front seal tabs flush with the front face of the cylinder block and remove the gasket tabs.
7. Using new gaskets as required complete the installation in the reverse order of the removal procedure.

151 FOUR CYLINDER ENGINE

1. Raise the hood.
2. Disconnect the negative battery cable.
3. Remove the fan and spacer.
4. Loosen the two lower cover retaining screws.
5. Remove the top cover retaining screw and nut and remove the cover, lifting it until the slots clear the lower screws.
6. To install, position the cover, lowering it until the slots are over the lower screws. Tighten the lower screws finger tight.
7. Install the upper screw and nut, then tighten all four screws to 50 inch lbs.
8. Install the spacer and fan, tightening the bolts to 20 ft. lbs.
9. Connect the battery cable.

173 SIX CYLINDER ENGINE

1. Disconnect the negative battery cable. Remove the drive belts.

2. Remove the radiator fan shroud. Remove the fan and pulley assembly.
3. If the vehicle is equipped with A/C, remove the compressor from the mounting bracket. Remove the mounting bracket.
4. Drain the cooling system. Remove the water pump. Remove the vibration damper.

NOTE: On some vehicles the outer ring (weight) of the harmonic balancer is bonded to the hub with rubber. The balancer must be removed with a puller which acts on the inner hub only. Pulling on the outer portion of the balancer will break the rubber bond or destroy the tuning of the torsional damper.

5. Disconnect the lower radiator hose and heater hose.
6. Remove timing gear cover attaching screws, and cover and gasket.
7. Clean all the gasket mounting surfaces on the front cover and block. Apply a continuous $^3/_{32}$ in. bead of sealer to front cover sealing surface and around coolant passage ports and central bolt holes.
8. Apply a bead of silicone sealer to the oil pan-to-cylinder block joint.
9. Install a centering tool in the crankcase snout hole in the front cover and install the cover.
10. Install the front cover bolts finger tight, remove the centering tool and tighten the cover bolts. Install the harmonic balancer, pulley, water pump, belts, and all other parts.

NOTE: Breakage may occur if the balancer is hammered back onto the crankshaft. A press or special installation tool is necessary.

258 SIX CYLINDER ENGINE

1. Disconnect the negative battery cable. Remove the drive belts, engine fan and hub assembly, the accessory pulley and vibration damper. Remove the A/C compressor and alternator bracket assembly.
2. Remove the oil pan to timing chain cover screws and the screws that attach the cover to the block.
3. Raise the timing chain cover just high enough to detach the retaining nibs of the oil pan neoprene seal from the bottom side of the cover. This must be done to prevent pulling the seal end tabs away from the tongues of the oil pan gaskets which would cause a leak.
4. Remove the timing chain cover and gasket from the engine.
5. Using the proper tool cut off the oil pan seal end tabs flush with the front face of the cylinder block and remove the seal. Clean the timing chain cover, oil pan, and cylinder block surfaces.
6. Remove the crankshaft oil seal from the timing chain cover.
7. Install in reverse order of the above procedure. It will be necessary to cut the same amount from the end tabs of a new oil pan seal as was cut from the original seal, before installing the new gasket. Be sure to use gasket sealer on both sides of the timing cover gasket.

DIESEL ENGINE

1. Disconnect the negative battery cable.
2. Remove all necessary components in order to gain access to the timing belt cover bolts.
3. Remove the timing belt cover retaining bolts. Remove the timing belt cover from the engine.
4. Installation is the reverse of the removal procedure.

V8 ENGINE

1. Remove the negative battery cable.
2. Drain the cooling system and disconnect the radiator hoses and by-pass hose.

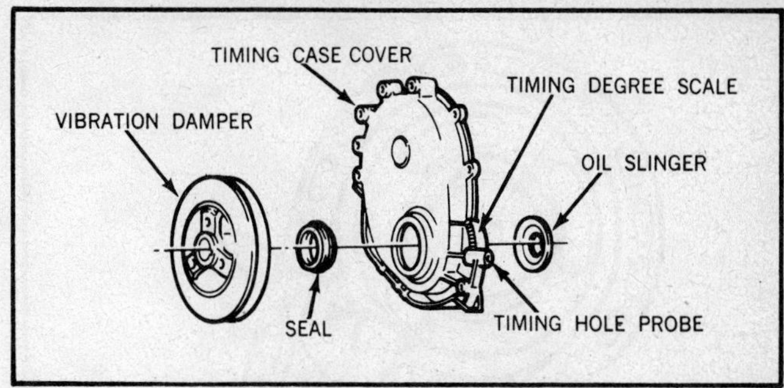

Timing case cover—6 cyl. engine (© Jeep Corp)

3. Remove all of the drive belts and the fan and spacer assembly. Remove air conditioning compressor and bracket assembly from the engine, if equipped. Do not disconnect air conditioning hoses.
4. Remove the alternator and the front portion of the alternator bracket as an assembly.
5. Disconnect the heater hose.
6. Remove the power steering pump, and/or the air pump, and the mounting bracket as an assembly. Do not disconnect the power steering hoses.
7. Remove the distributor cap and note the position of the rotor. Remove the distributor.
8. Remove the fuel pump.
9. Remove the vibration damper and pulley.
10. Remove the two front oil pan bolts and the bolts which secure the timing chain cover to the engine block.

NOTE: The timing gear cover retaining bolts vary in length and must be installed in the same locations from which they were removed.

11. Remove the cover by pulling forward until it is free of the locating dowel pins. Remove the oil slinger.
12. Clean the gasket surface of the cover and the engine block.
13. Pry out the original seal from inside the timing chain cover and clean the seal bore.
14. Drive the new seal into place from the inside with a block of wood until it contacts the outer flange of the cover.
15. Apply a light film of motor oil to the lips of the new seal.
16. Before reinstalling the timing gear cover, remove the lower locating dowel pin from the engine block. The pin is required for correct alignment of the cover and must either be reused or a replacement dowel pin installed after the cover is in position.
17. Cut both sides of the oil pan gasket flush with the engine block with a razor blade.
18. Trim a new gasket to correspond to the amount cut off at the oil pan.
19. Apply seal to both sides of the new gasket and install the gasket on the timing case cover.
20. Install the new front oil pan seal.
21. Align the tongues of the new oil pan gasket pieces with the oil pan seal and cement them into place on the cover.
22. Apply a bead of sealer to the cutoff edges of the original oil pan gaskets.
23. Place the timing case cover into position and install the front oil pan bolts. Tighten the bolts slowly and evenly until the cover aligns with the upper locating dowel.
24. Install the lower dowel through the cover and drive it into the corresponding hole in the engine block.
25. Install the cover retaining bolts in the same locations from which they were removed, tightened to 25 ft. lbs.
26. Assemble the remaining components in the reverse order of removal.

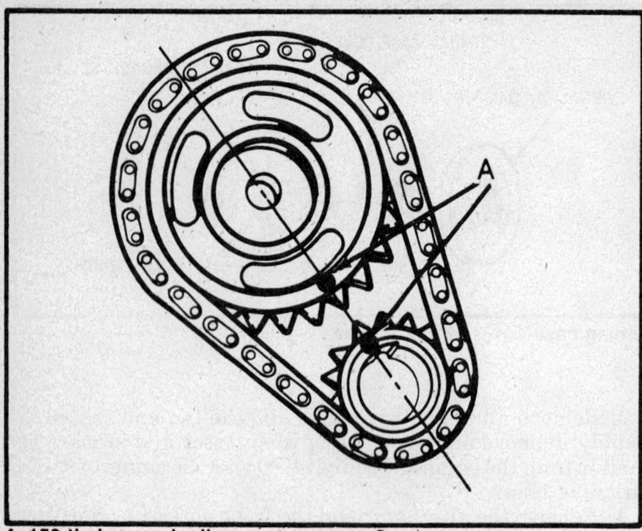

4–150 timing mark alignment (© Jeep Corp)

Timing Chain, Gears or Belt

Removal and Installation

150 FOUR CYLINDER ENGINE

1. Disconnect the negative battery cable. Remove the timing case cover.
2. Rotate the crankshaft until the zero timing mark on the crankshaft sprocket is closest to and on center line with the mark on the cam sprocket.
3. Remove the oil slinger from the crankshaft.
4. Remove the camshaft retaining bolt and remove the sprockets and chain as an assembly.
5. Installation is the reverse of removal, with the following recommendations:
    a. Turn the tensioner lever to the unlock (down) position.
    b. Pull the tensioner block toward the tensioner lever to compress the spring. Hold the block and turn the tensioner lever to the lock (up) position.
    c. Torque the camshaft sprocket retaining bolt to 50. ft. lbs

151 FOUR CYLINDER ENGINE

1. Raise the hood and install a bolt in the hood hold open link.
2. Disconnect the negative battery cable.
3. Remove the air conditioning and alternator belts.

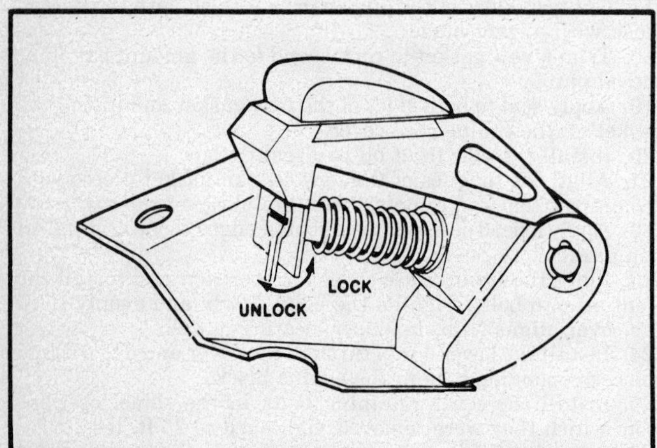

4–150 timing chain tensioner (© Jeep Corp)

4. Remove the crankshaft pulley and the four pulley-to-sprocket bolts. Remove the pulley and damper or washer as applicable.

NOTE: It is not necessary to remove the pulley if only the camshaft sprocket is being removed.

5. Drain the engine coolant and loosen the water pump bolts to relieve tension on the timing belt.
6. Remove the timing belt lower cover.
7. Remove the timing belt.
8. Align one of the holes in the camshaft sprocket with the bolt behind the sprocket. Using a socket on the bolt to keep the sprocket from rotating, remove the sprocket retaining bolt and washer.
9. Remove the camshaft sprocket.
10. The crankshaft sprocket may be removed with a puller.
11. Press the crankshaft sprocket back on. Make sure that the timing mark is facing out and that the key is installed.
12. To install the camshaft sprocket, align the dowel in the camshaft with the locating hole in the end of the camshaft sprocket.
13. Install the sprocket retaining bolt, tightening to 80 ft. lbs.
14. Align the timing mark on the camshaft sprocket with the notch on the timing belt upper cover and the crankshaft timing mark with the cast rib on the oil pump cover.
15. Install the timing belt on the crankshaft sprocket, then with the back of the belt positioned in the water pump track, install the belt on the camshaft sprocket. Make sure the sprockets maintain their indexed positions.
16. Install the lower timing belt cover, using anti-sieze compound on the threads of the bolts and torquing them 50 inch lbs.
17. Adjust the timing belt tension.
18. Fill the cooling system.
19. Install the accessory drive pulley to the crankshaft sprocket, aligning the tang on the pulley with the keyway on the crankshaft. Install the damper locating dowel in the locating hole of the sprocket.
20. Loosely install the four sprocket bolts, then install the crankshaft (center) bolt. Tighten the crankshaft bolt to 80 ft. lbs. and the four sprocket bolts to 15 ft. lbs.
21. Install the alternator and air conditioning belts and tighten to proper adjustment.
22. Install the engine front cover, fan and fan spacer.
23. Connect the battery cable.

173 SIX CYLINDER ENGINE

1. Disconnect the negative battery cable. Remove the timing cover. Crank the engine until the marks punched on both sprockets are closest to one another and in line between the shaft centers.
2. Remove the three bolts that hold the camshaft sprocket to the camshaft. This sprocket is a light press fit on the camshaft and is located by a dowel. The chain comes off with the camshaft sprocket. A gear puller may be required to remove the camshaft sprocket.
3. Without disturbing the position of the engine, mount the new crank sprocket on the shaft, then mount the chain over the camshaft sprocket. Arrange the camshaft sprocket in such a way that the timing marks will line up between the shaft centers and the camshaft locating dowel will enter the dowel hole in the cam sprocket.
4. Place the cam sprocket, with its chain mounted over it, in position on the front of the camshaft and pull up with the three bolts that hold it to the camshaft.
5. After the sprockets are in place, turn the engine two full revolutions to make certain that the timing marks are in correct alignment between the shaft centers.
6. Continue the installation in the reverse order of the removal procedure.

258 SIX CYLINDER ENGINE

1. Disconnect the negative battery cable. Remove the drive belts, engine fan and hub assembly, accessory pulley, vibration damper and timing chain cover.
2. Remove the oil seal from the timing chain cover.
3. Remove the camshaft sprocket retaining bolt and washer.
4. Rotate the crankshaft until the timing mark on the crankshaft sprocket is closest to and in a center line with the timing pointer of the camshaft sprocket.
5. Remove the crankshaft sprocket, camshaft sprocket and timing chain as an assembly. Disassemble the chain and sprockets.
6. Assemble the timing chain, crankshaft sprocket and camshaft sprocket with the timing marks aligned.
7. Install the assembly to the crankshaft and the camshaft.
8. Install the camshaft sprocket retaining bolt and washer and tighten to 45–55 ft. lbs.
9. Install the timing chain cover and a new oil seal.
10. Install the vibration damper, torque the retaining bolt to 80 ft. lbs., accessory pulley, engine fan and hub assembly and drive belts. Tighten the belts to the proper tension.

DIESEL ENGINE

1. Disconnect the negative battery cable.
2. Remove the timing belt cover.

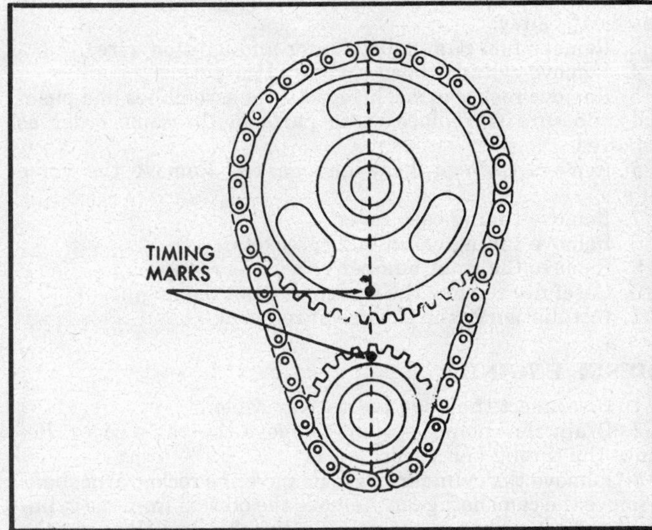

Alignment of timing chain sprockets—6 cyl. (© Jeep Corp)

3. Install sprocket holding tool MOT–854 or equivalent and remove the camshaft sprocket retaining bolt. Remove the special tool.
4. Loosen the bolts and move the chain tensioner away from the timing belt. Tighten the tensioner bolts.
5. Remove the timing belt from the sprockets.
6. If it is necessary to remove the fuel injection pump sprocket, use tools BVI–28–01 and BVI–859, or equivalent.
7. Installation is the reverse of the removal procedure.

V8 ENGINE

1. Disconnect the negative battery cable. Remove the timing chain cover and gasket.
2. Remove the crankshaft oil slinger.
3. Remove the camshaft sprocket retaining bolt and washer, distributor drive gear and fuel pump eccentric.
4. Rotate the crankshaft until the timing mark on the crankshaft sprocket is adjacent to, and on a center line with, the timing mark on the camshaft sprocket.

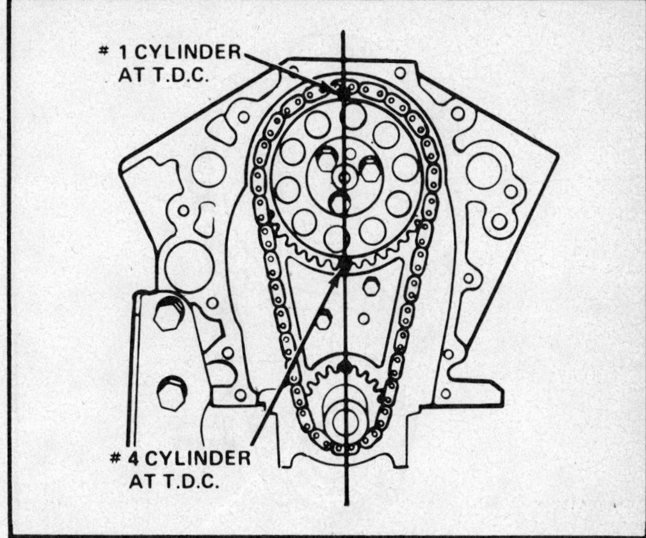

6–173 timing mark alignment (© Jeep Corp)

5. Remove the crankshaft sprocket, camshaft sprocket and timing chain as an assembly. Disassemble the chain and sprockets.
6. Assemble the timing chain, crankshaft sprocket and camshaft sprocket with the timing marks on both sprockets aligned.
7. Install the assembly to the crankshaft and the camshaft.
8. Install the fuel pump eccentric, distributor drive gear, washer and retaining bolt. Tighten the bolt to 25–35 ft. lbs.

NOTE: The fuel pump eccentric must be installed with the stamped word "REAR" facing the camshaft sprocket.

9. Install the crankshaft oil slinger.
10. Install the timing chain cover using a new gasket and oil seal.

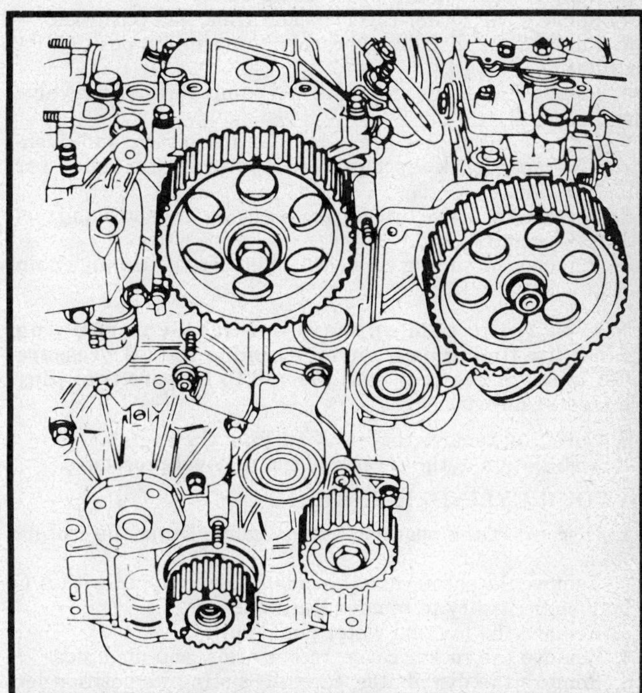
Alignment of timing belt sprockets—diesel engine (© Jeep Corp.)

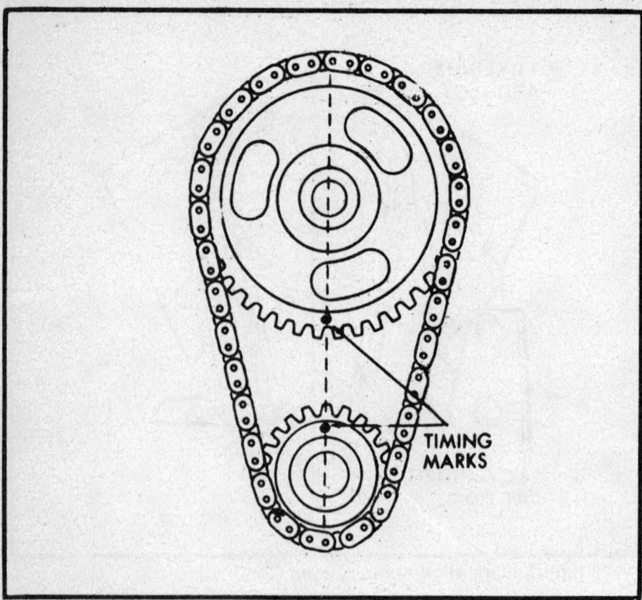

Alignment of timing chain sprockets—V8 (© Jeep Corp)

Camshaft

NOTE: Caution must be taken when performing this procedure. Camshaft bearings are coated with babbit material, which can be damaged by scraping the cam lobes across the bearing.

Removal and Installation

150 FOUR CYLINDER ENGINE

1. Disconnect the negative battery cable. Drain the cooling system.
2. Remove the shroud and the radiator. If equipped with A/C remove the condenser.
3. Remove the fan and water pump pulley.
4. Remove the rocker cover, rocker arms, and pushrods.
5. Remove the distributor, carefully noting its position for installation.
6. Remove the spark plugs and fuel pump. Remove the valve cover.
7. Remove the rocker arms, bridges and pivots, and pushrods. Be sure to keep these components in order for reinstallation.
8. Remove the valve lifters from the cylinder head using tool J–21884 or equivalent.
9. Remove the timing case cover. Remove the timing chain and sprockets.

NOTE: If the cam appears to have been rubbing against the timing case cover, examine the oil pressure relief holes in the rear cam journal to be sure that they are free of debris.

10. Carefully remove the camshaft from the engine.
11. Installation is the reverse of the removal procedure.

151 FOUR CYLINDER ENGINE

1. Disconnect the negative battery cable. Drain the cooling system.
2. Remove the shroud and the radiator. If equipped with A/C it may be necessary to remove the condenser.
3. Remove the fan and water pump pulley.
4. Remove the rocker cover, rocker arms, and pushrods.
5. Remove the distributor, carefully noting its position for installation.
6. Remove the spark plugs and fuel pump.
7. Remove the pushrod cover and gasket, then remove the lifters.
8. Remove the crankshaft hub and timing gear cover.
9. Remove the two camshaft thrust plate screws by working through the holes in the gear.
10. Remove the camshaft and gear assembly by pulling it through the front of the block.
11. Install in reverse order, make sure camshaft surfaces are dust free and lubed with oil. Torque the thrust plate screws to 75 inch lbs.

173 SIX CYLINDER ENGINE

1. Disconnect the negative battery cable. Drain the cooling system.
2. Remove the radiator. If equipped with A/C remove the condenser. Remove the intake manifold and valve lifters. Remove fuel pump and pump pushrod.
3. Remove the timing cover. Remove camshaft sprocket bolts, sprocket and timing chain. A light blow to the lower edge of a tight sprocket should free it (use a plastic mallet).
4. Install two bolts in cam bolt holes and pull cam from block.
5. Installation is the reverse of the removal procedure.

258 SIX CYLINDER ENGINE

1. Disconnect the negative battery cable. Drain and remove radiator.
2. If equipped, remove air conditioning condenser and receiver assembly.
3. Remove fuel pump, distributor and ignition wires.
4. Remove cylinder head cover and gasket.
5. Remove rocker arms, bridged pivot assemblies and pushrods. Be sure to replace these parts in the same order as removed.
6. Remove cylinder head and gasket. Remove the valve lifters.
7. Remove timing case cover.
8. Remove timing chain and sprockets.
9. Remove the front bumper or grill as required.
10. Carefully remove the camshaft from the engine.
11. Installation is the reverse of removal.

DIESEL ENGINE

1. Disconnect the negative battery cable.
2. Drain the cooling system. Remove the valve cover. Remove the timing belt cover.
3. Remove the cylinder head. Remove the rocker arm shaft. Remove the camshaft gear. Remove the oil seal from the cylinder head by prying it out using a suitable tool. Remove the camshaft from the cylinder head.
4. Installation is the reverse of the removal procedure.

V8 ENGINE

1. Disconnect the negative battery cable. Drain and remove radiator.
2. If equipped, remove air conditioning condenser and receiver assembly as a charged unit.
3. Remove fuel pump, distributor and ignition wires.
4. Remove cylinder head cover and gasket.
5. Remove drive belts, fan, and hub assembly.
6. Remove intake manifold.
7. Remove rocker arms, bridged pivot assemblies and pushrods. Be sure to replace these parts in the same order as removed.
8. Remove the valve lifters.
9. Remove timing case cover.
10. Remove distributor drive gear and fuel pump eccentric from the camshaft.

NOTE: The fuel pump eccentric must be installed with the word "REAR" facing the camshaft sprocket.

11. Remove timing chain and sprockets.
12. Remove the front bumper or grill, and hood latch support bracket as required.
13. Carefully remove the camshaft from the engine.
14. Installation is the reverse of removal.

Pistons and Connecting Rods

IDENTIFICATION

NOTE: If there is a notch on the top of the piston or an "F" mark anywhere on the piston, it must face the front of the engine.

4–151 Engine

The letter "F" or the notches in the edge of the piston, goes toward the front of the engine. On the 151 four cylinder engine the notch on the connecting rod should be opposite the notch on the piston.

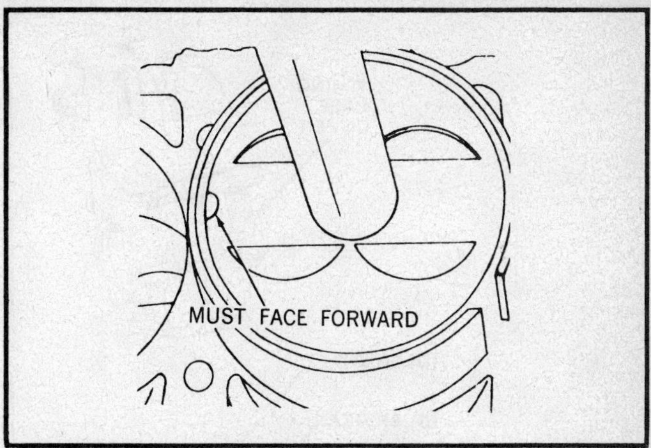

Piston installation—all engines (© Jeep Corp)

150, 258 and V8 Engines

The connecting rod caps are stamped with the number of the cylinder to which they belong. Replace them in there original positions. The numbered sides and squirt hole must face the camshaft when assembled in the six cylinder engine. The numbered sides must face out on the V8 engines when assembled.

V6 Engine

There is a machined hole or a cast notch "E" in the top of all pistons to indicate proper installation. The piston assemblies should always be installed with the hole or notch toward the front of the engine.

Diesel Engine

Mark the connecting rods and rod bearing caps on the intermediate shaft side of the cylinder block with the number of the corresponding cylinder. Number one cylinder is located at the flywheel/drive plate end of the engine block. When removing, remove each connecting rod, cylinder liner and piston as a complete assembly. Each piston and cylinder liner are matched as a set be sure that they are marked properly for installation. Install the assembly according to the marks made during the removal stage of the overhaul.

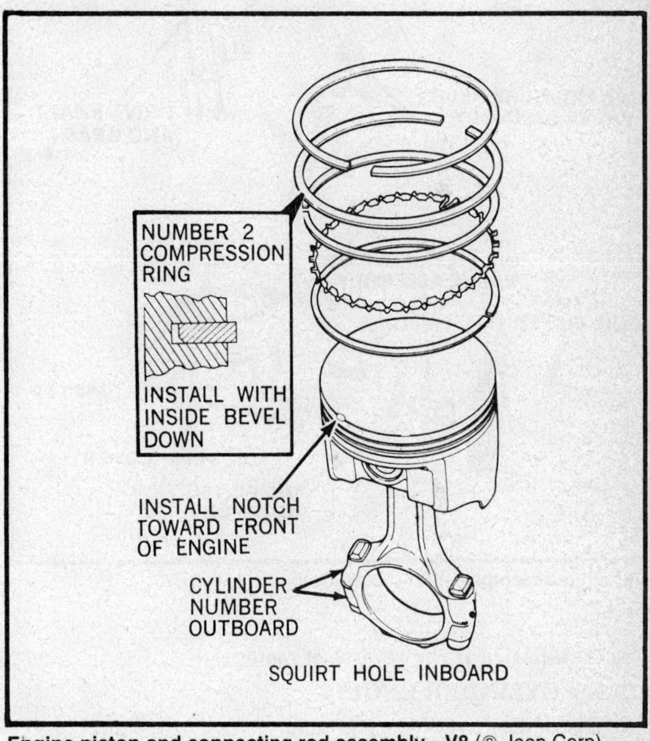

Engine piston and connecting rod assembly—V8 (© Jeep Corp)

ENGINE OILING SYSTEM

Oil Pan

Removal and Installation

150 FOUR CYLINDER ENGINE

1. Disconnect the negative battery cable. Raise and support the vehicle safely. Drain the engine oil.
2. Disconnect the exhaust pipe at the exhaust manifold. Disconnect the exhaust hanger at the catalytic converter. Lower the pipe.
3. Remove the starter. Remove the torque converter housing access cover.
4. Remove the oil pan retaining bolts. Remove the oil pan from the vehicle.
5. Installation is the reverse of the removal procedure.

151 FOUR CYLINDER ENGINE

1. Disconnect the negative battery cable. Raise and support the vehicle safely. Drain engine oil, and remove starter.
2. On CJ models: place jack under transmission bellhousing. Disconnect right engine support cushion bracket from block and raise engine to allow clearance for the oil pan.
3. Remove oil pan, also remove the front and rear neoprene seals and side gaskets.

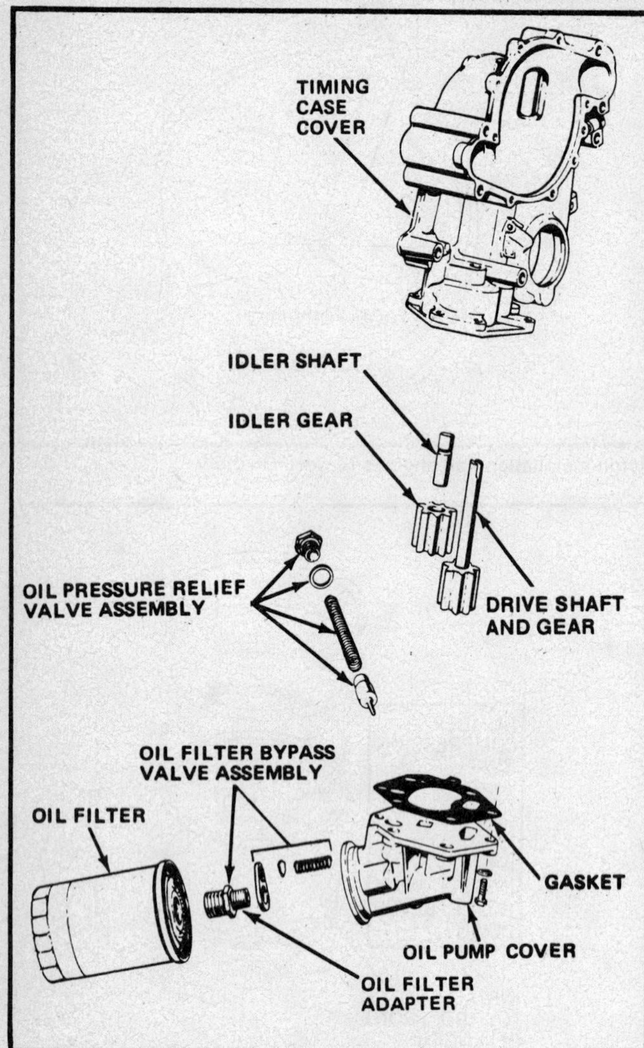

Oil pump assembly—V8 (© Jeep Corp)

4. Installation is the reverse of removal.

173 SIX CYLINDER ENGINE

1. Disconnect the battery ground.
2. Disconnect the right exhaust pipe at the manifold.
3. Raise and support the vehicle safely.
4. Disconnect the left exhaust pipe at the manifold.
5. Remove the starter.
6. Remove the flywheel access cover.
7. Disconnect the exhaust pipe at the converter and lower it so that the Y portion rests on the upper control arms.
8. Unbolt and remove the oil pan.
9. Clean all RTV gasket material from the mating surfaces.
10. Installation is the reverse of removal. Apply RTV in a $^1/_8$ in. bead on the pan lip.

258 SIX CYLINDER ENGINE

1. Disconnect the negative battery cable. Raise and support the vehicle safely. Drain engine oil, and remove starter. Remove the flywheel cover access housing.
2. On some vehicles it may be necessary to place a jack under the transmission bellhousing. Disconnect right engine support cushion bracket from block and raise engine to allow clearance for the oil pan.
3. Remove oil pan, also remove the front and rear neoprene seals and side gaskets.
4. Installation is the reverse of removal.

DIESEL ENGINE

1. Disconnect the negative battery cable. Raise and support the vehicle safely. Remove the converter housing shield, as required.
2. Drain the engine oil . This engine has two oil drain plugs, both must be opened.
3. Remove all the necessary components in order to gain access to the oil pan retaining bolts.
4. Remove the oil pan retaining bolts. Remove the oil pan from the engine.
5. Installation is the reverse of the removal procedure.

V8 ENGINE

1. Disconnect the negative batttery cable. Raise and support the vehicle safely. Drain engine oil and remove starter. Remove the converter housing access cover.
2. On some vehicles it may be necessary to remove the frame cross bar and automatic transmission lines.
3. If required, cut the corner of engine mount on right side to provide clearance for pan removal.
4. If equipped with manual transmission, bend tabs down on dust shield.
5. Remove oil pan bolts and pan.
6. Remove oil pan front and rear neoprene oil seals.
7. Installation is the reverse of removal.

Oil Pump

Removal and Installation

ALL EXCEPT V8 AND DIESEL ENGINES

1. Disconnect the negative battery cable. Raise and support the vehicle safely. Drain the engine oil. Remove the oil pan. Drain the engine oil and remove the oil pan.
2. Remove the oil pump retaining screws, oil pump, and gasket from the engine block.
3. Remove the cover retaining screws, cover, and gasket from the pump body.
4. Measure the gear end clearance between the gears and the face of the oil pump body.
5. Measure the gear lobe clearance to the pump body sides.
6. Remove the gears and shaft from the body.
7. Remove the cotter pin, spring retainer, spring, and oil pressure relief valve from the pump body.
8. Repair or replace defective components as required.
9. Installation is the reverse of the removal procedure. Be sure to use new gaskets and seals as required.

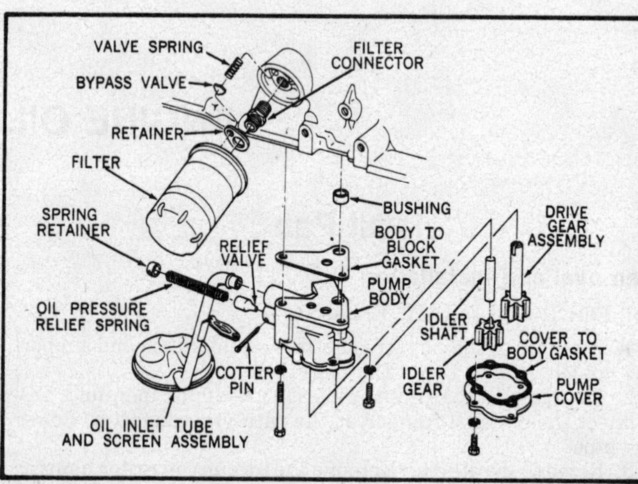

Oil pump assembly—6 cyl. (© Jeep Corp)

NOTE: Fill the pump gear cavity with petroleum jelly prior to the installation of the pump cover, to insure self priming.

V8 ENGINES

1. Disconnect the negative battery cable. Drain the engine oil. Remove the engine oil filter.
2. Remove the engine oil pump cover from the timing chain cover. Remove the oil pump gears and shaft.
3. Remove the oil pressure relief valve from the body.
4. Inspect the gears for abnormal wear, chips, looseness on the shafts, galling, and scoring.
5. Inspect the cover and cavity for breaks, cracks, distortion, and abnormal wear.
6. Install the gears into the pump cavity, and with the use of a straight edge and feeler gauge, check the gear to housing clearance.
7. If the clearances measure out of the allowable span, the timing chain cover and gears should be replaced.
8. Installation is the reverse of the removal procedure. be sure to use new gaskets and seals as required.

NOTE: Fill the pump gear cavity with petroleum jelly prior to the installation of the pump cover, to insure self priming.

DIESEL ENGINE

1. Disconnect the negative battery cable.
2. Remove the vacuum pump along with the oil pump drive gear.
3. Remove the timing belt cover. Loosen the intermediate shaft drive sprocket using tool MOT–855 or equivalent.
4. Remove the intermediate shaft bolt, sprocket, cover, clamp plate and intermediate shaft.
5. Raise and support the vehicle safely. Drain the engine oil. Remove the oil pan.
6. Remove the piston skirt cooling oil jet assembly to oil pump pipe.
7. Remove the oil pump retaining bolts. Remove the oil pump.
8. Be sure that the oil pump locating dowels are in place on the pump.
9. Inspect the gears for abnormal wear, chips, looseness on the shafts, galling, and scoring.
10. Inspect the cover and cavity for breaks, cracks, distortion, and abnormal wear.
11. Install the gears into the pump cavity, and with the use of a straight edge and feeler gauge, check the gear to housing clearance.
12. Repair or replace defective components as required.

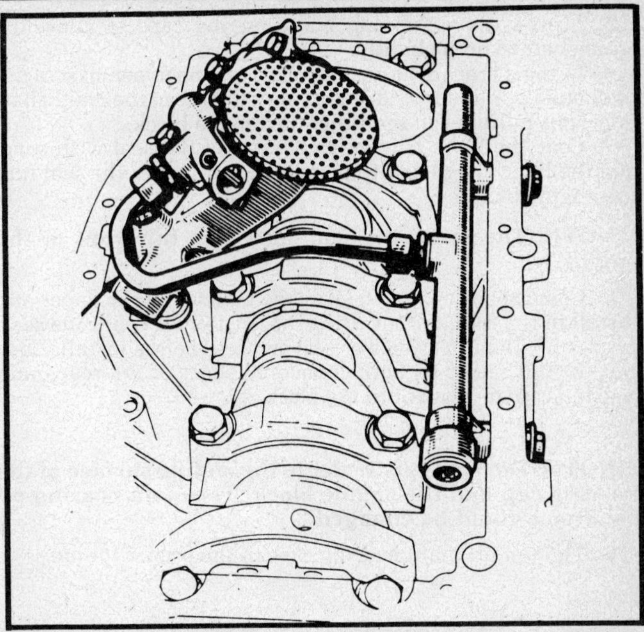

Oil pump location—diesel engine (© Jeep Corp.)

13. Installation is the reverse of the removal procedure. Be sure to use new gaskets and seals as required.

Rear Main Bearing Oil Seal

Removal and Installation

1. Disconnect the negative battery cable. Raise the vehicle and support it safely.
2. Drain the engine oil. Remove the oil pan.
3. Remove the oil pan gaskets and neoprene seals. Clean all sealing surfaces.
4. Remove the rear main bearing cap and discard the bottom oil seal.

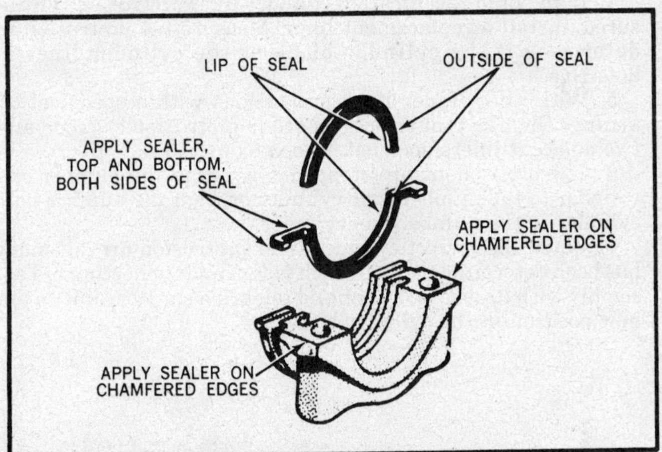

Rear main seal installation—all engines (© Jeep Corp)

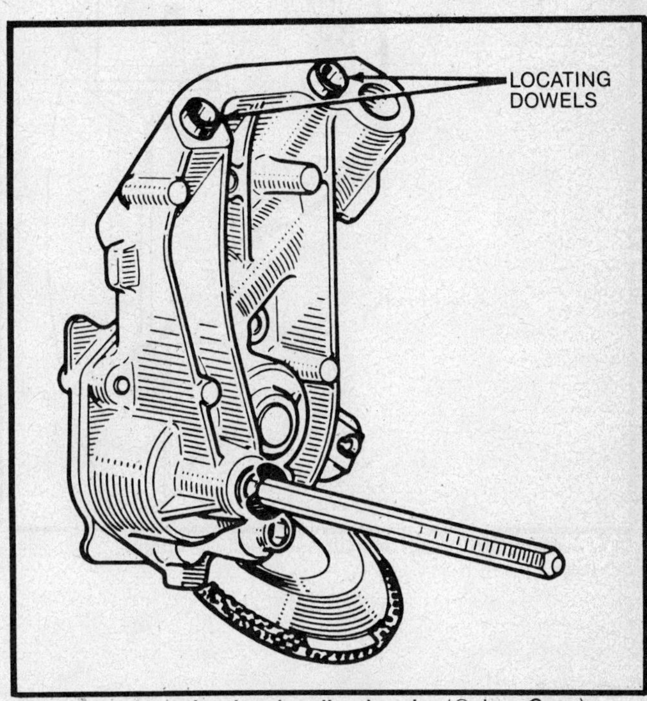

Oil pump and locating dowels—diesel engine (© Jeep Corp.)

5. Loosen the remaining main bearing caps to allow the crankshaft to drop slightly.

6. Using a brass drift and hammer, tap the upper oil seal until enough seal is exposed on the opposite side of the crankshaft to permit pulling the seal from the engine block.

7. Coat the block contacting surface of the seal with soap, and the lip of the seal with engine oil and install the seal into the engine block.

NOTE: The lip of the seal must face the front of the engine.

8. Coat the lower seal in the same manner as the upper and install in the rear main bearing cap. Install RTV silicone sealer or equivalent to the lower seal end tabs before installation.

9. Install sealer on both chamfered edges of the rear main bearing cap and install to the block.

NOTE: Do not apply sealer to the mating surface of the bearing cap and the engine block. The main bearing oil clearance could be changed.

10. Tighten all main bearing caps to the proper torque.

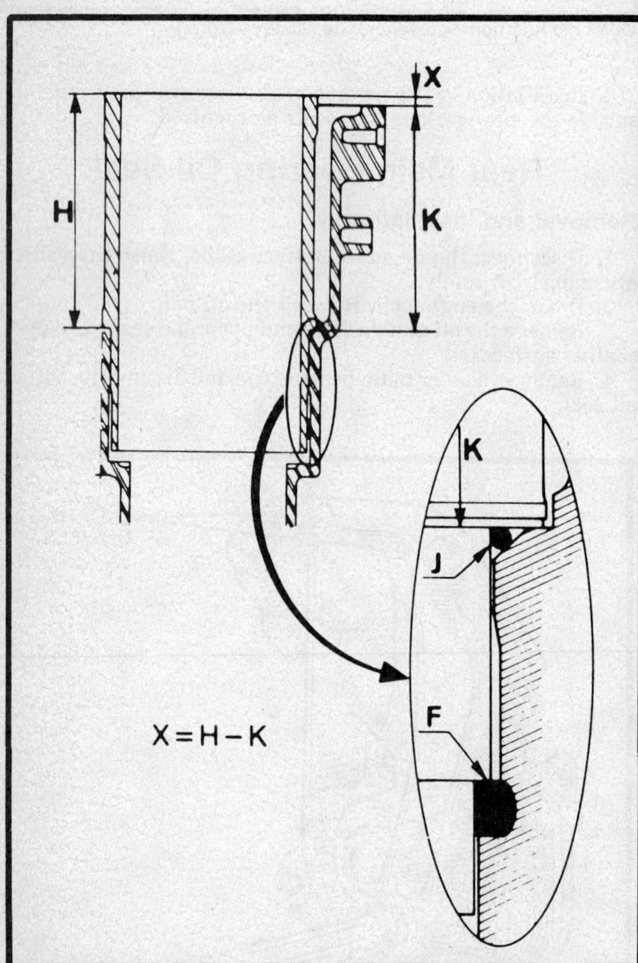

Cylinder liner protrusion measurement—diesel engine
(© Jeep Corp.)

11. Install the oil pan using new gaskets and seals. Add the necessary oil to the oil pan, lower the vehicle, start the engine and inspect for oil leaks.

Wet Cylinder Liners

DIESEL ENGINE

Removal and Installation

1. Remove the engine from the vehicle.
2. Remove the cylinder head.
3. Remove the oil pan.
4. Remove the cylinder liner along with the piston and connecting rod assembly.
5. Separate the piston assembly from the cylinder liner. Remove the O-ing seal and the plastic ring from the cylinder liner.
6. If the liner is going to be replaced, be sure to also replace the piston assembly, as they are a matched set.
7. Upon installation, install the piston assembly into the cylinder liner with tool MOT–851 or equivalent.

NOTE: The cylinder liners require a rubber O-ring seal and a plastic ring to provide a seal between the liner and the cylinder block, as each liner is supported by the cylinder block. The correct liner protrusion "X" which is above the cylinder block is achieved by close matching tolerances when the cylinder liner and block are manufactured. If replacement liners are required, the liner protrusions above the cylinder block must be measured and all the cylinder liners rearranged according to the results of the measurements.

Cylinder Liner Protursion Measurement

1. Insert each reusable cylinder liner in its original position in the cylinder block. If applicable, insert the replacement liner in the cylinder block.
2. Install tool MOT–LM and MOT–251–01 or equivalent, on the engine block and tighten the screw clamp. Position tool MOT–252–01 or equivalent, across each cylinder liner, in turn, and secure it with tool MOT–853 or equivalent. Tighten the tool retaining bolts gradually and torque them to 37 ft. lbs. This will assure that each cylinder liner will be firmly in contact with the cylinder block
3. Measure the protrusion "X" of each cylinder liner above the cylinder block using the dial indicator and block gauge. The correct specification is 0.0019–0.0047 in..
4. If an out of specification cylinder liner protrusion is measured, install a replacement liner. Measure the protrusion to determine if the cylinder block or the cylinder liner is defective.
5. With all cylinder liner protrusions within specification arrange them so that the difference in protrusion between any two adjacent liners does not exceed 0.0016 in..
6. The protrusions are stepped down from the number one cylinder to the number four cylinder or from the number four cylinder to the number one cylinder.
7. When the correct cylinder liner protrusion arrangement has been determined, match each piston and connecting rod assembly with its original liner and remark each according to the new position in the cylinder block.

FRONT AXLE AND SUSPENSION

Refer to the Drive Axles Unit General Repair for application, troubleshooting overhaul, and specifications.

Front Axle Assembly

Removal and Installation

EXCEPT 1984 AND LATER WAGONEER, CHEROKEE AND COMANCHE

1. Raise and support the vehicle safely. Remove the wheel covers and wheels.
2. Index the propeller shaft to the differential yoke for the proper alignment upon installation. Disconnect the propeller shaft at the axle yoke and secure the shaft to the frame rail.
3. Disconnect the steering linkage from the steering knuckles. Disconnect the shock absorbers at the axle housing.
4. If the vehicle is equipped with a stabilizer bar, remove the nuts attaching the stabilizer bar connecting links to the spring tie plates.
5. On vehicles equipped with sway bar, remove nuts attaching sway bar connecting links to spring tie plates.
6. Disconnect the breather tube from the axle housing. Disconnect the stabilizer bar link bolts at the spring clips.
7. Remove the brake calipers, hub and rotor, and the brake shield.
8. Remove the U-bolts and the tie plates.
9. Support the assembly on a jack and loosen the nuts securing the rear shackles, but do not remove the bolts.
10. Remove the front spring shackle bolts. Lower the springs to the floor.
11. Pull the jack and axle housing from underneath the vehicle.
12. Installation is the reverse of the removal procedure. Check the front end alignment, as required.

1984 AND LATER WAGONEER, CHEROKEE AND COMANCHE

1. Raise and support the vehicle safely.
2. Remove the wheels, calipers and rotors.
3. Disconnect all vacuum hoses at the axle.
4. Mark the relation between the front driveshaft and yoke.
5. Disconnect the stabilizer bar, rod and center link, front driveshaft, shock absorbers, steering damper, track bar.
6. Place a floor jack under the axle to take up the weight.
7. Disconnect the upper and lower control arms at the axle and lower the axle from the truck.
8. Installation is the reverse of the removal procedure.

NOTE: Discard the U-joint straps new replacement straps must be used whenever the straps are removed.

Shock Absorbers

The upper ends of the shock absorbers are attached to the frame side rails with mounting brackets and pins. The lower ends are attached to the axle or to the spring by mounting.

Front Leaf Spring

Removal and Installation

1. Raise the vehicle and support it safely.
2. Position a jack under the axle. Raise the axle to relieve the springs of the axle weight.
3. If equipped, disconnect the stabilizer bar. Remove the spring U-bolts and tie plates.
4. Remove the bolt attaching the spring front eye to the shackle.
5. Remove the bolt attaching the spring rear eye to the shackle.
6. Remove the spring from its mounting.
7. Installation is the reverse of the removal procedure.

Front Coil Spring

Removal and Installation

1. Raise the vehicle and support it safely.
2. Remove the wheels.
3. Match-mark and disconnect the front driveshaft.
4. Disconnect the lower control arm at the axle.
5. Disconnect the track bar at the frame. Place a floor jack under the axle.
6. Disconnect the stabilizer bar and shock absorbers.
7. Disconnect the center link at the pitman arm.
8. Lower the axle with a floor jack, loosen the spring retainer and remove the spring.
9. Installation is the reverse of removal.

Selective Drive Hubs

Front drive hubs are serviced as either a complete assembly or a sub assembly, such as the hub body or hub clutch assembly. Do not attempt to disassemble these units. If the entire hub assembly or subassembly has to be replaced it must be replaced as a complete unit.

CJ MODELS

Removal and Installation

1. Remove the bolts and the tabbed lockwashers that attach the hub body to the axle hub. Save the bolts and the washer.
2. Remove the hub body and gasket. Discard the gasket.
3. Do not turn the hub control dial once the hub body has been removed.
4. Remove the retaining ring from the axle shaft. Remove the hub clutch and bearing assembly.
5. Clean and inspect the components for wear and damage. Replace defective components as required.
6. Installation is the reverse of the removal procedure.
7. Turn the control hub dials to the 4X2 position and rotate the wheels. They should rotate freely, if not check the hub installation. Be sure that the controls are in the fully engaged position.

CHEROKEE, GRAND WAGONEER AND TRUCK

Removal And Installation

1. Remove the socket head screws from the hub body assembly.

2. Remove the large retaining ring from the axle hub. Remove the small retaining ring from the axle shaft.
3. Remove the hub and clutch assembly.
4. Clean and inspect the components for wear and damage. Replace defective components as required.
5. Installation is the reverse of the removal procedure.
6. Turn both controls to the FREE position and rotate the wheels. They must rotate freely, if they drag check the hub installation. Be sure that the control dials are in the fully engaged position.

Axle Shaft

Removal and Installation

CJ AND SCRAMBLER

1. Raise and support the vehicle safely. Remove the tire and wheel. Remove the disc brake caliper.
2. Remove the bolts attaching the front hub to the axle and remove the hub body and gasket.
3. Remove the retaining ring from the axle shaft. Remove the hub clutch and bearing assembly from the axle.
4. Straighten the lip of the lock washer. Remove the outer lock nut, lock washer, inner locknut and tabbed washer. Use tool J–25103, or equivalent, in order to remove the locknut.
5. Remove the outer bearing and remove the disc brake rotor. Remove the disc brake caliper adapter and splash shield. Remove the axle spindle.

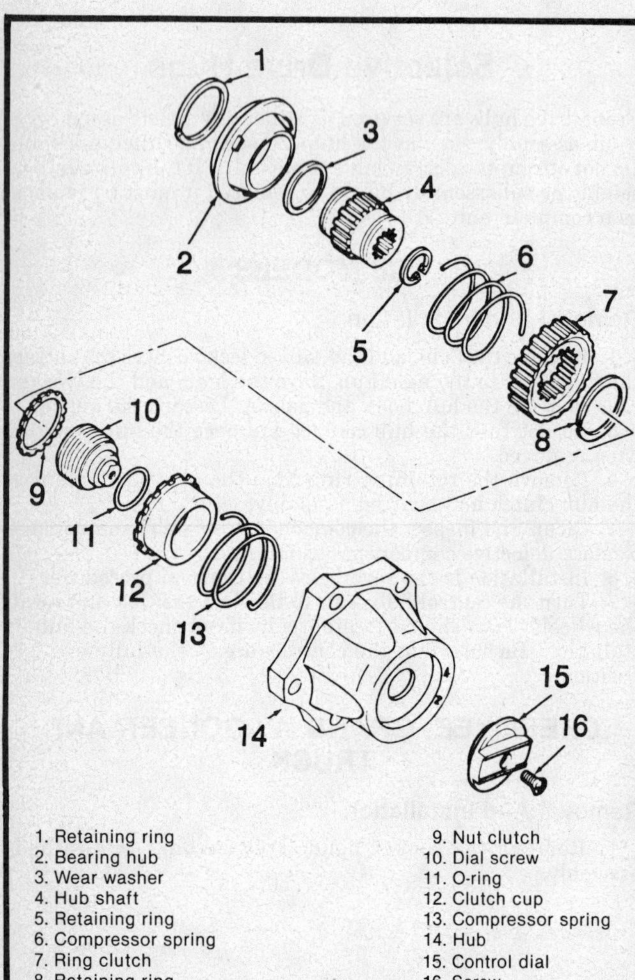

Front drive hubs—CJ and Scrambler (© Jeep Corp.)

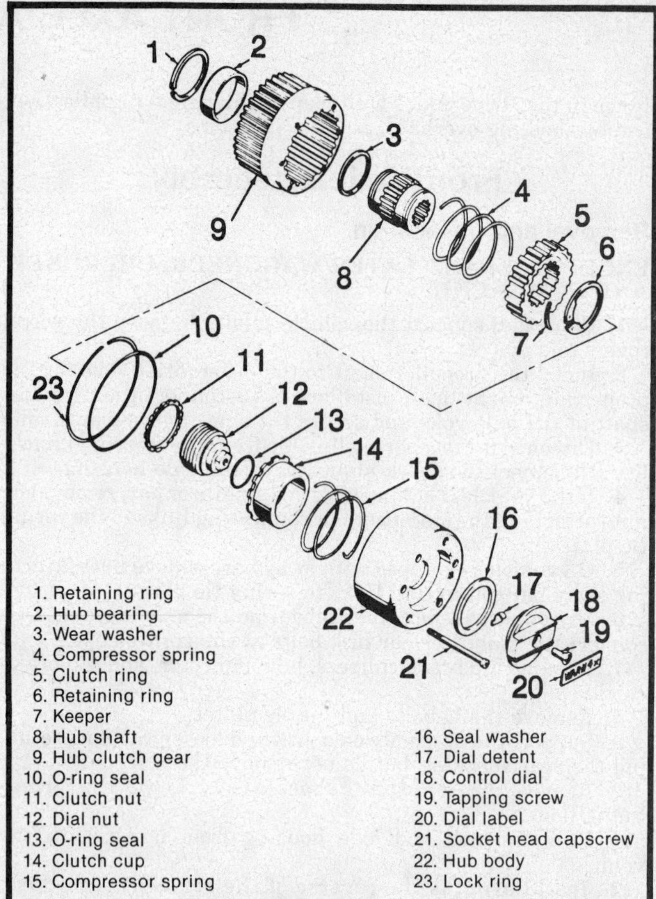

Front drive hubs—Grand Wagoneer and Truck (© Jeep Corp.)

6. Remove the axle shaft and universal joint assembly.
7. Installation is the reverse of the removal procedure.

CHEROKEE, GRAND WAGONEER AND TRUCK

1. Raise and support the vehicle safely. Remove the disc brake caliper.
2. On vehicles without front hubs, remove the rotor hub cap. Remove the axle shaft snap ring, drive gear, pressure spring and spring retainer.
3. On models with front hubs, remove the socket head screws from the hub body. Remove the hub body and the large retaining ring. Remove the small retaining ring from the axle shaft. Remove the hub clutch assembly from the axle.
4. Remove the outer locknut ,washer and inner locknut using tool J–6893–03 or equivalent.
5. Remove the rotor. The spring retainer and the outer bearing are removed with the rotor.
6. Remove the nuts and bolts attaching the spindle and support shield. Remove the spindle and the support shield.
7. Remove the axle shaft.
8. Installation is the reverse of the removal procedure.

1984 AND LATER WAGONEER, CHEROKEE AND COMANCHE

1. Raise and support the vehicle safely.
2. Remove the wheels, calipers and rotors.
3. Remove the cotter pin, locknut and axle hub nut.
4. Remove the hub-to-knuckle attaching bolts.
5. Remove the hub and splash shield from the steering knuckle.

To remove the left shaft:
6. Remove the axle shaft from the housing.
To remove the right shaft:
7. Disconnect the vacuum harness from the shift motor.
8. Remove the shift motor from the housing.
9. Remove the axle shaft from the housing.
10. To install the right axle shaft first be sure that the shift collar is in position on the intermediate shaft and that the axle shaft is fully engaged in the intermediate shaft end.
11. Install the shift motor, making sure that the fork engages with the collar. Tighten the bolts to 8 ft. lb.
12. On the left side, install the axle shaft in the housing.
13. Partially fill the hub cavity of the knuckle with chassis lube and install the hub and splash shield.
14. Tighten the hub bolts to 75 ft. lb.
15. Install the hub washer and nut. Torque the nut to 175 ft. lb. Install the locknut. Install a new cotter pin.
16. Install the rotor, caliper and wheel.

Steering Knuckle Service

STEERING KNUCKLE

Removal and Installation

EXCEPT 1984 AND LATER CHEROKEE, WAGONEER AND COMANCHE

1. Remove the axle assmebly from the vehicle.
2. Disconnect the tie rod end at the steering knuckle arm.
3. Remove and discard the lower ball stud jamnut.
4. Remove the cotter pin from the upper ball stud. Loosen the stud nut until the top edge of the nut is flush with the top of the stud.
5. Unseat the upper and lower ball studs using a hammer. Remove the upper ball stud nut and the steering knuckle.
6. Remove the upper ball stud split ring seat using tool J-23447 or tool J-25158.
7. Installation is the reverse of the removal procedure.

1984 WAGONEER, CHEROKEE AND COMANCHE

1. Remove the outer axle shaft.
2. Remove the caliper anchor plate from the knuckle.
3. Remove the knuckle-to-ball joint cotter pins and nuts.
4. Drive the knuckle out with a brass hammer.

NOTE: A split ring seat (3) is located in the bottom of the knuckle. During installation, this ring seat must be set to a depth of 5.23mm (.206). Measure the depth to the top of the ring seat (4).

5. Installation is the reverse of removal. Tighten the knckle retaining nuts to 75 ft. lb. and the caliper anchor bolts to 77 ft. lb.

BALL JOINTS

CJ, SCRAMBLER, CHEROKEE, GRAND WAGONEER AND TRUCK

Removal and Installation

LOWER BALL STUD

1. Remove the steering knuckle from the vehicle. Position the assembly in a suitable holding fixture with the upper ball stud pointing downward.
2. Attach tool J-2511-1, or equivalent to the spindle mating surface of the knuckle assembly. Position tool J-25211-3 on the lower ball stud.
3. Assemble and install the puller on the steering knuckle. Hook one arm of the puller in the plate of tool J-25211-1 and the opposite arm of the tool in the steering knuckle.

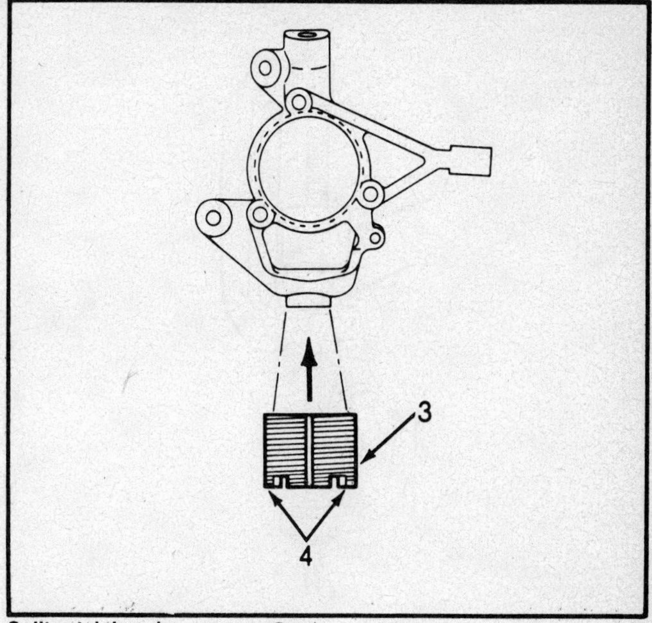

Split retaining ring (© Jeep Corp)

4. Tighten the puller screw to press the lower stud out of the knuckle.
5. Remove the tools from the knuckle.
6. Installation is the reverse of the removal procedure.

UPPER BALL STUD – CJ AND SCRAMBLER

1. Remove the steering knuckle from the vehicle. Position the assembly in a suitable holding fixture with the upper ball stud pointing downward.
2. Remove both arms from tool J-25215. Place button J-25211-3 on the upper ball stud.
3. Install adapter tool J-25211-4 on the nut end of the puller screw so that the adapter shoulder faces the nut end of the screw.
4. Insert the nut end of the puller screw through the upper ball stud hole in the knuckle. Hold the adapter and the frame against the knuckle.
5. Remove the lower ball stud from the knuckle.
6. Installation is the reverse of the removal procedure.

UPPER BALL STUD – CHEROKEE, GRAND WAGONEER AND TRUCK

1. Remove the steering knuckle from the vehicle. Position the assembly in a suitable holding fixture with the upper ball stud pointing downward.
2. Remove both arms from tool J-25215. Place button J-25211-3 on the upper ball stud.
3. Thread the puller frame halfway onto the puller screw. Insert the nut end of the screw through the lower ball stud hole in the steering knuckle. Position the puller frame against the knuckle and the puller screw against tool J-25211-3.
4. Tighten the puller screw and press the upper ball stud out of the steering knuckle.
5. Installation is the reverse of the removal procedure.

1984 AND LATER WAGONEER, CHEROKEE AND COMANCHE

Removal and Installation

UPPER BALL JOINT

1. Remove the steering knuckle from the vehicle.
2. Position the receiver tool (1) over the top of the ball joint.

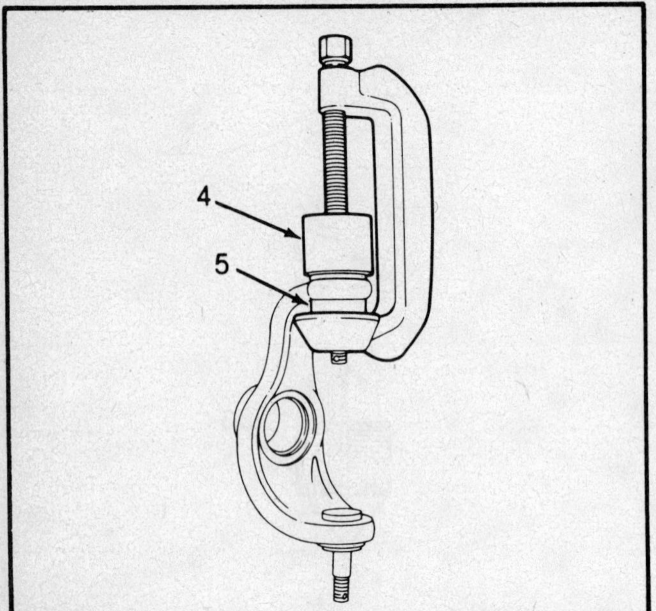

Upper ball joint removal (© Jeep Corp)

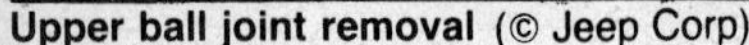

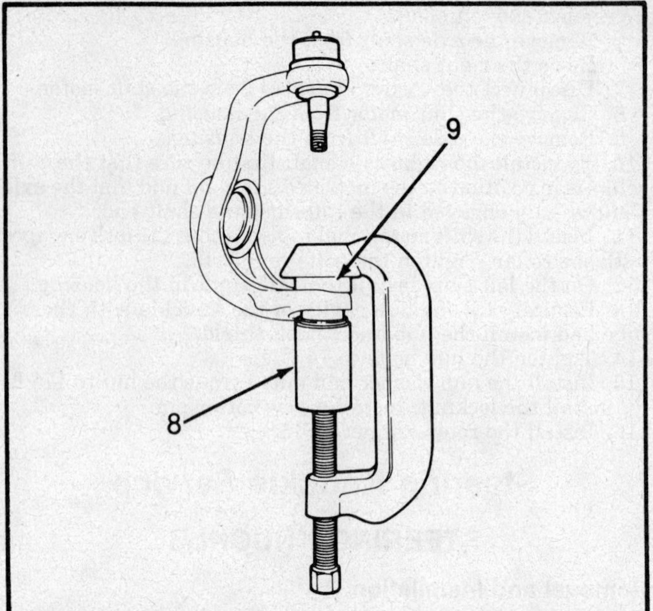

Lower ball joint installation (© Jeep Corp)

Set the adapter tool (2) in a C-clamp (3) and position the clamp so that tightening the clamp screw will remove the ball joint.

3. To install, use the same C-clamp, with adapter tool as illustrated.

LOWER BALL JOINT

1. With the knuckle removed from the vehicle, use a Cclamp, with receiver tool (6) and adapter tool (7) as illustrated, to force out the ball joint.
2. To install, use the same C-clamp, with adapter tools (8 and 9), as illustrated.

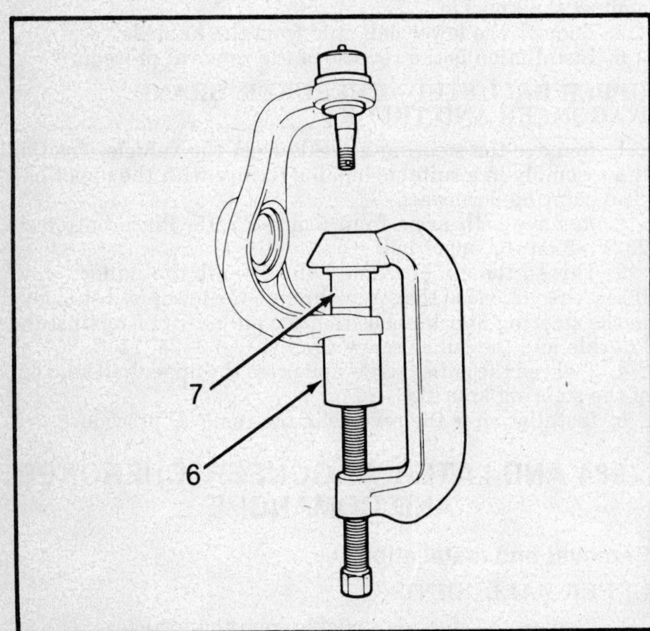

Lower ball joint removal (© Jeep Corp)

Upper Ball Joint Adjustment

Adjustment of the upper ball joint is necessary only when there is excessive play in the steering, persistent loosening of the steering linkage, or abnormal wear of the tires.

Adjustment Procedure

EXCEPT 1984 AND LATER WAGONEER, CHEROKEE AND COMANCHE

1. Raise and support the vehicle safely. Remove the front tires.
2. If the vehicle is equipped with a steering damper, disconnect it at the tie rod and move it aside.
3. Unlock the steering column. Disconnect the steering connecting rod. Disconnect the connecting rod at the right side of the tie rod.
4. Remove the cotter pin and the retaining nut attaching the tie rod to the right side steering knuckle.
5. Rotate both steering knuckles through a complete arc several times. Work from the right side of the vehicle when rotating the knuckles.
6. Install a torque wrench on the tie rod retaining nut and check the torque. The torque wrench must be positioned at a ninety degree angle to the steering knuckle arm in order to obtain a correct reading.
7. Rotate the steering knuckles slowly through a complete arc and measure the torque required to rotate the knuckles.
8. If the reading is less than 25 ft. lbs. turning effort is within specification. If not then procede as follows.
9. Disconnect the tie rod from both steering knuckles. Install a one half by one inch bolt, flat washer and nut in the tie rod stud mounting hole in one of the steering knuckles. Tighten the bolt and nut.
10. Install the torque wrench according to Step six.
11 Rotate the steering knuckles slowly through a complete arc and measure the torque required to rotate the knuckles.
12 If the reading is less than 10 ft. lbs. turning effort is within specification and the defect is not related to the knuckle ball studs.
13. Install components that were removed to accomplish this procedure.
14. Lower the vehicle.

FRONT WHEEL BEARING

Adjustment

CJ AND SCRAMBLER

1. Raise and support the vehicle safely.
2. Remove the bolts attaching the front hub to the hub rotor. Remove the hub body and gasket.
3. Remove the snap ring from the axle shaft and remove the hub clutch assembly.
4. Straighten the lip of the outer lock nut tabbed washer. Remove the outer locknut and tabbed washer.
5. Loosen and then tighten the inner locknut to 50 ft. lbs. Rotate the wheel while tightening the nut to seat the bearing properly.
6. Back off the inner locknut about one-sixth of a turn as you are turning the wheel. The wheel must rotate freely.
7. Install the tabbed washer and the outer locknut.
8. Torque the outer locknut to 50 ft. lbs.
9. Recheck the bearing adjustment. The wheel must rotate freely. Correct as required.
10. Install components as they were removed.

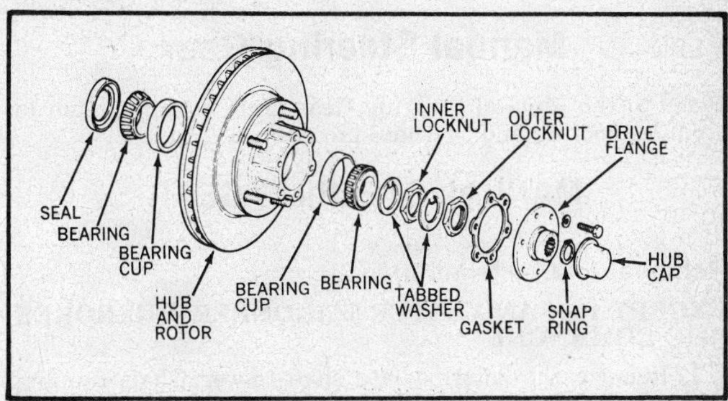

Front wheel attaching parts—CJ model—disc brakes (© Jeep Corp)

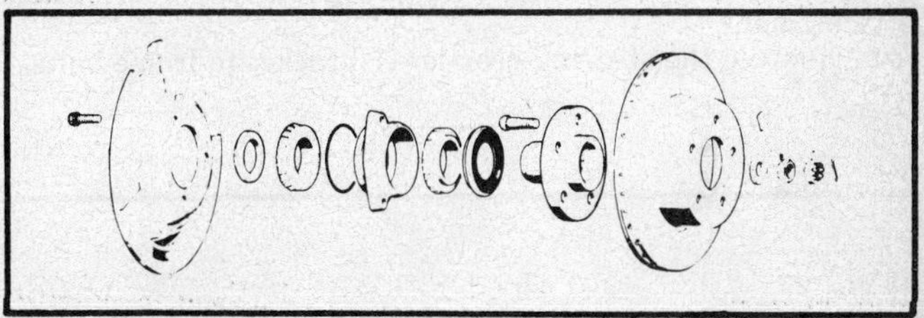

1984 CJ-7, Scrambler, Wagoneer and Cherokee front wheel bearing (© Jeep Corp)

CHEROKEE, WAGONEER, AND TRUCK

1. Raise and support the vehicle safely.
2. If the vehicle is not equipped with front hubs, Remove the wheel cover and hubcap. Remove the drive gear snap ring. Remove the drive gear, pressure spring and spring cup.
3. If the vehicle is equipped with front hubs, Remove the socket head screws from the hub body and remove the body from the hub clutch assembly. Remove the large retaining ring from the hub. Remove the small retaining ring from the axle shaft. Remove the hub and clutch assembly. Remove the outer locknut and lock washer.
4. Seat the bearings by loosening and then tightening them to 50 ft. lbs. Back off the inner locknut about one-sixth of a turn while rotating the wheel.
5. Install the lock washer. Align one of the lock washer holes with the peg on the inner locknut and install the washer on the nut.
6. Install and torque the outer locknut to 50 ft. lbs. Recheck the bearing adjustment. Correct as required.
7. On vehicles without front hubs, The spring cup must be installed so the recessed side faces the bearing and the flat side faces the pressure spring. The pressure spring should contact the flat side of the cup only.
8. Install the spring cup and the pressure spring. Install the drive gear and the drive gear snap ring.
9. If the vehicle is equipped with front hubs, Install the clutch assembly. Install the small retaining ring on the axle shaft. Install the large retaining ring on the hub.
10. Install the hub body on the hub clutch. Install the socket head screws in the hub and torque them to 30 inch lbs.
11. Lower the vehicle.

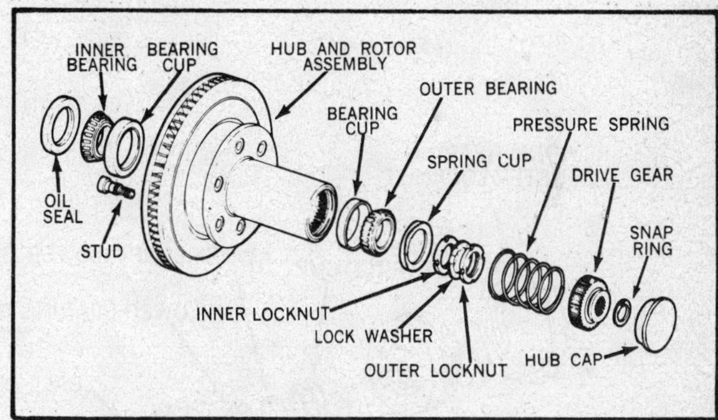

Front wheel attaching parts—Cherokee and Wagoneer (© Jeep Corp)

1984 AND LATER CHEROKEE, WAGONEER AND COMANCHE – TYPE ONE

1. Raise and support the vehicle safely. Remove the wheel. Remove the disc brake caliper as required. Remove the cotter pin, locknut and axle hub nut.
2. Tighten the hub bolts to 75 ft. lbs.
3. Install the hub washer and nut and tighten the hub nut to 175 ft. lbs. Install the locknut and new cotter pins.
4. Install the caliper, if removed. Install the wheel. Lower the vehicle.

1984 and LATER CHEROKEE, WAGONEER AND COMANCHE – TYPE TWO

1. Raise and support the vehicle safely. Remove the wheel. Remove the caliper, as required.
2. Remove the grease cap, cotter pin and nut retainer.
3. Tighten the spindle nut to 25 ft. lbs. while rotating the rotor.
4. Loosen the spindle nut about one half turn while rotating the wheel. Torque the nut to 19 ft. lbs.
5. Install removed components.

STEERING GEAR

Manual Steering Gear

Refer to the Manual Steering Gear Unit Repair section for trouble-shooting and overhaul procedures.

MANUAL STEERING GEAR

Removal and Installation

EXCEPT 1984 AND LATER WAGONEER, CHEROKEE AND COMANCHE

1. Remove the intermediate shaft-to-wormshaft coupling clamp bolt and disconnect the intermediate shaft.
2. Remove the pitman arm nut and lockwasher.
3. Using a puller, remove the pitman arm from the shaft.
4. On some vehicles, raise the left side of the vehicle slightly to relieve tension on the left front spring and rest the frame on a jackstand.
5. Remove the steering gear lower bracket-to-frame bolts.
6. Remove the bolts attaching the steering gear upper bracket to the crossmember. One of these bolts is a Torx® head bolt. This bolt, and some others may be removed with the aid of a 9 in. extension. Remove the gear.

NOTE: Loctite 271® or similar material must be applied to all attaching bolt threads prior to installation.

7. Position the tie plate upper and lower mounting brackets on the gear and install the bolts. Torque the bracket-to-gear bolts to 70 ft. lbs. and the bracket-to-tie plate bolt to 55 ft. lbs.
8. Align and engage the intermediate shaft coupling with the steering gear wormshaft splines.
9. Position the steering gear on the frame and install the mounting bolts. Torque the bolts to 55 ft. lbs. Install the pitman arm and torque the nut to 185 ft. lbs.

NOTE: The steering gear may produce a slight roughness which can be eliminated by turning the steering wheel full left and right 10–15 times.

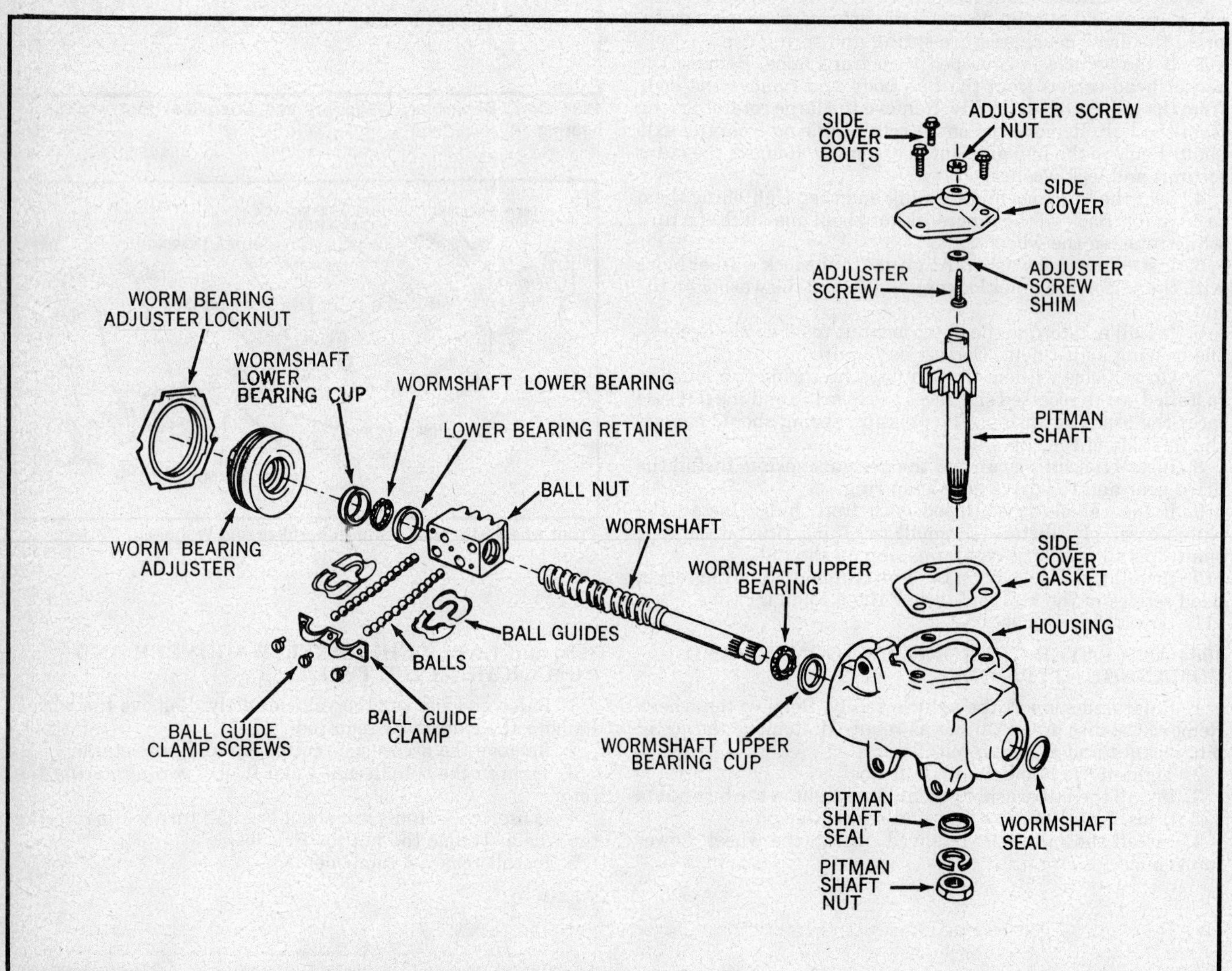

Manual steering gear—typical (© Jeep Corp)

1984 AND LATER WAGONEER, CHEROKEE AND COMANCHE

1. Disconnnect the steering shaft from the gear.
2. Raise and support the vehicle safely.
3. Disconnect the center link from the pitman arm.
4. Remove the front stabilizer bar.
5. Remove the pitman arm nut, mark the relation between the arm and shaft, and using a puller, pull the pitman arm from the shaft.
6. Remove the gear attaching bolts and remove the gear.
7. Installation is the reverse of removal. Observe the following torques:
   a. Center link-to-pitman arm: 35 ft. lb.
   b. Stabilizer bar-to-link: 27 ft. lb.
   c. Pitman arm-to-gear: 185 ft. lb.
   d. Steering gear-to-frame: 65 ft. lb.

STEERING GEAR CLEARANCE

Adjustment

1. Loosen the locknut and turn the adjusting screw on the side cover, counterclockwise until the worm gear shaft turns freely through its entire range of travel.
2. Count the number of turns necessary to rotate the worm gear shaft through its travel.
3. Turn the shaft to center point.
4. Rotate the shaft back and forth over center, and tighten the adjusting screw until the shaft binds slightly at the center point.
5. Adjust the screw to obtain a rolling torque of 7–12 inch lbs. through the center.
6. Hold the adjusting screw and tighten the locknut to 16–20 ft. lbs.

WORM BEARING PRELOAD

Adjustment

1. Tighten the worm bearing adjuster until it bottoms, then back it off ¼ turn.
2. Install a torque wrench and socket J-7754 or its equivalent on the splined end of the wormshaft.
3. Rotate the wormshaft clockwise until it hits the stop, then back it off ½ turn.
4. Tighten the wormshaft bearing adjuster until the torque required to rotate the shaft is 5–8 inch lbs.

NOTE: The adjustment must be made with the wormshaft no more than ½ turn from the stop.

5. Tighten the worm bearing adjuster locknut. Check rotating torque. Check and record the worm bearing preload reading.

PITMAN SHAFT OVERCENTER

Adjustment

1. Rotate the wormshaft from stop-to-stop and count the number of turns.
2. Rotate the wormshaft back from the stop, ½ the total number of turns.
3. Install a torque wrench and socket J–7754 on the splined end of the wormshaft.
4. Tighten the pitman shaft adjuster screw, while rotating the shaft back and forth over center, until the torque equals the worm bearing preload setting of 5–8 inch lbs. previously recorded.
5. Rotate the shaft over center and continue tightening the adjuster until the drag torque is increased by an additional 4–10 inch lbs., but do not exceed 16 inch lbs. combined total.

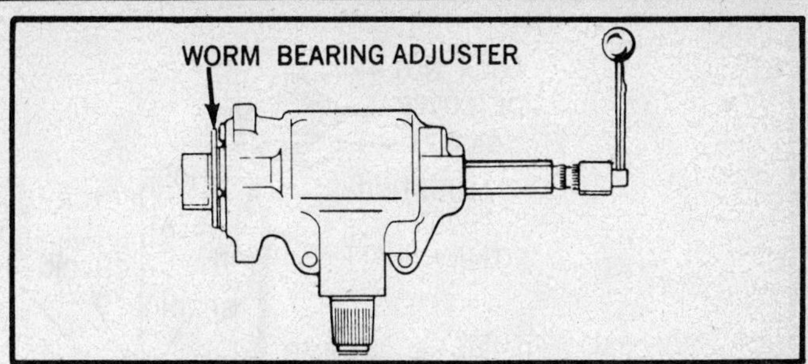

Adjusting worm bearing preload (© Jeep Corp)

6. Hold the adjuster screw and tighten the locknut to 23 ft. lbs. Do not allow the adjuster to turn, or the adjustment will have to be made over again.

POWER STEERING GEAR

Removal and Installation

ALL, EXCEPT 1984 AND LATER WAGONEER, CHEROKEE AND COMANCHE

1. Disconnect the hoses at the gear and raise them above the pump to prevent fluid loss.
2. Remove the clamp bolt and nut attaching the intermediate shaft coupling to the steering gear stub shaft and disconnect the intermediate shaft.
3. Mark the pitman shaft and arm for alignment. Remove the pitman nut and lockwasher and remove the pitman arm with a puller.
4. On some vehicles it will be necessary to raise the left side of the vehicle slightly to relieve tension from the spring. Support with a jack stand under the frame.
5. Remove the three lower steering gear mounting bracket-to-frame bolts.
6. Remove the two steering gear-to-crossmember upper bolts. Remove the gear and brackets as an assembly.
7. Remove the brackets from the gear.

NOTE: Prior to installation, all bolts must be coated with Loctite 271® or its equivalent.

8. Position the mounting brackets on the gear and torque the bolts to 70 ft. lbs.

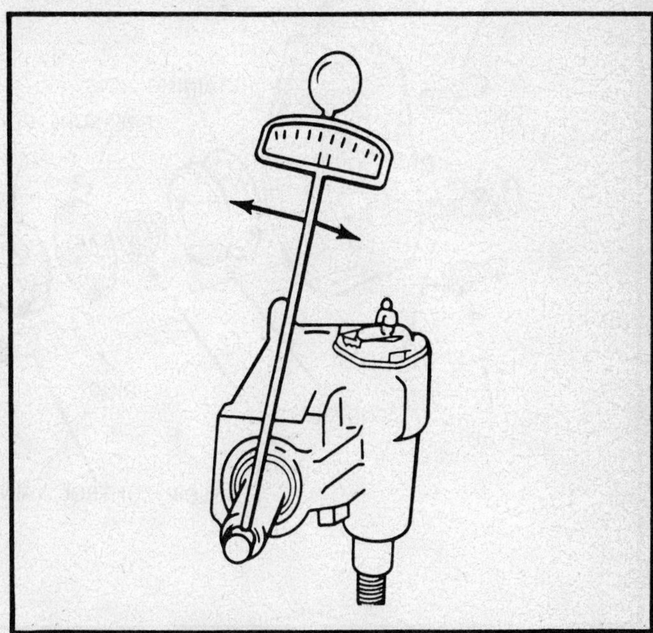
Adjusting pitman shaft overcenter drag (© Jeep Corp)

LOCK NUT
SIDE COVER
GASKET
ADJUSTING SCREW
PITMAN SHAFT
HOSE CONNECTOR SEAT
POPPET CHECK VALVE
HOSE CONNECTOR SEAT
STUB SHAFT
SEAL RINGS (3)
DAMPER O-RING
ADJUSTER PLUG LOCK NUT
SPOOL VALVE
BACKUP O-RING (3)
VALVE BODY
WORM SHAFT
SPRING
BALL RETURN GUIDE HALVES
CLAMP
RACK PISTON
RETAINING RING
HOUSING END PLUG
RACE
O-RING
THRUST BEARING
RACE
BEARING
RACES
BEARING RETAINER
RETAINING RING
SPACER
DUST SEAL
BALL BEARINGS (24)
GEAR HOUSING
THRUST BEARING
BACKUP O-RING
O-RING
OIL SEAL
RACK PISTON SEAL RING
O RING
ADJUSTER PLUG
RACK PISTON END PLUG
OIL SEALS
NEEDLE BEARING
WASHERS
RETAINING RING
PITMAN ARM NUT

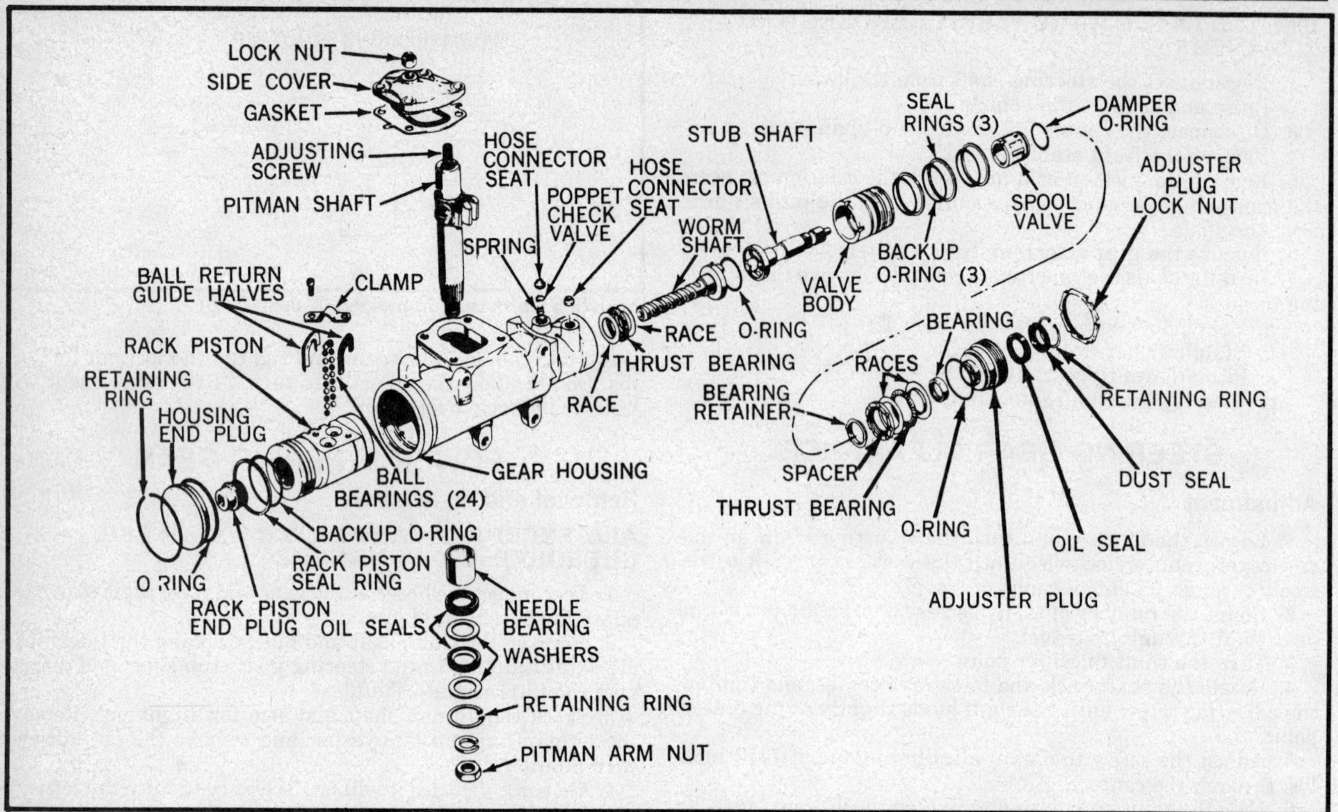

Power steering gear assembly—typical (© Jeep Corp)

CAP
MOUNTING STUD
RESERVOIR
RETAINING RING
RETAINING RING
UNION FITTING
PRESSURE PLATE
PUMP RING
VANE
DOWEL PIN(2)
MOUNTING STUD O-RING
THRUST PLATE
SEAL
PUMP BODY
PUMP SHAFT SEAL
O-RING
O-RING
MOUNTING STUD
END PLATE
SPRING
VALVE SPRING
PUMP SHAFT
FLOW CONTROL VALVE
MOUNTING STUD O-RING

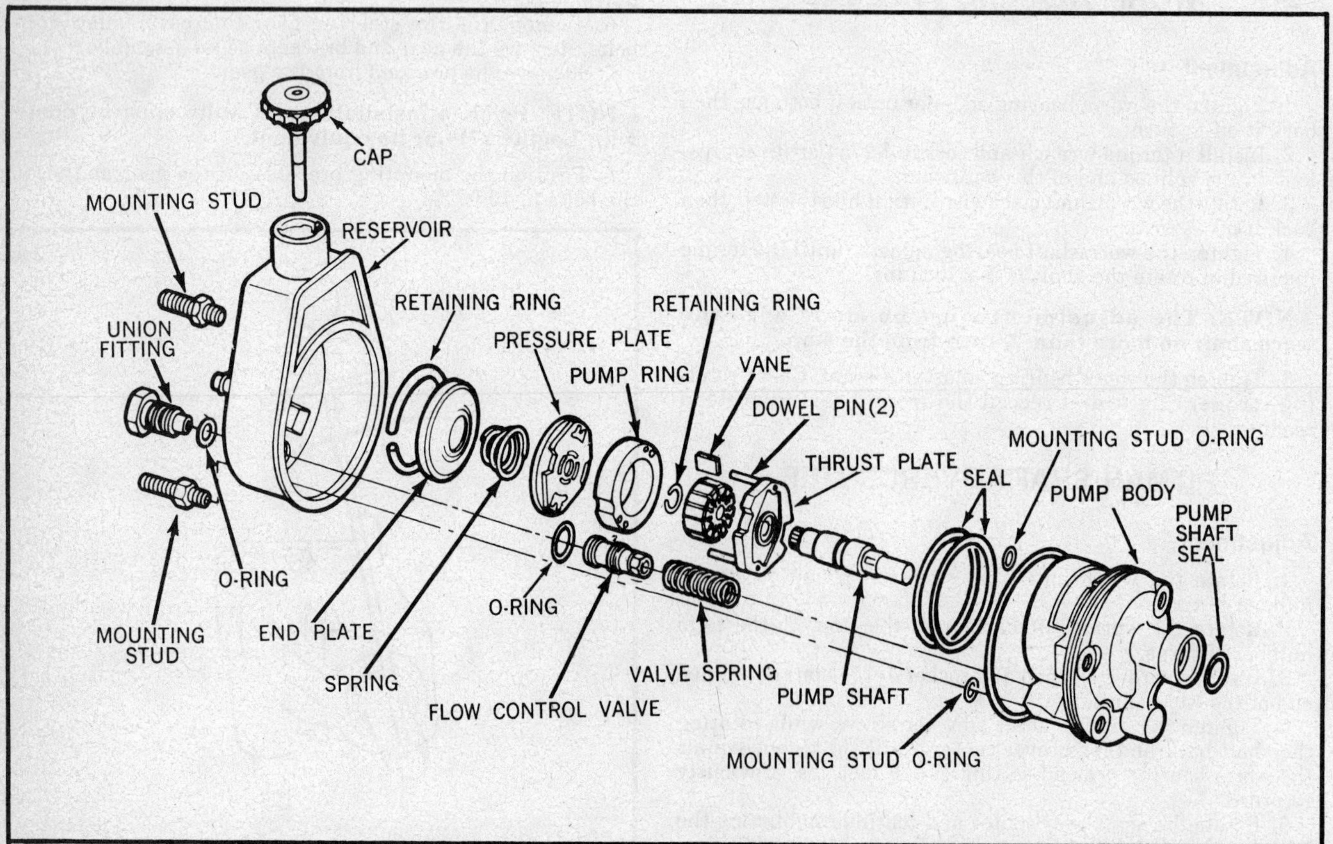

Power steering pump typical (© Jeep Corp)

9. Align and connect the intermediate shaft coupling to the steering gear stub shaft.
10. Position the steering gear on the frame and crossmember. Install and tighten the bolts to 55 ft. lbs.
11. Lower the vehicle.
12. Install the intermediate shaft coupling-to-steering gear stub shaft clamp bolt and nut. Tighten the nut to 45 ft. lbs.
13. Align and install the Pitman arm, nut and lockwasher. Torque the nut to 185 ft. lbs. Stake the nut in two places.
14. Connect the hoses. Torque the hose connections to 25 ft. lbs.

1984 AND LATER WAGONEER, CHEROKEE AND COMANCHE

1. Place the wheels in a straight ahead position.
2. Position a drain pan under the gear.
3. Disconnect the hoses at the gear and raise and secure the hose ends to prevent draining. Cap the hose ends.
4. Disconnect the intermediate shaft from the stub shaft.
5. Raise and support the front of the vehicle safely. Mark the relation between the pitman arm and shaft.
6. Disconnect the center link from the pitman arm and remove the stabilizer bar.
7. Using a puller, remove the pitman arm.
8. Unbolt and remove the gear.
9. Installation is the reverse of removal. Observe the following torques:
   a. Steering gear-to-frame: 65 ft. lb.
   b. Pitman arm-to-shaft: 185 ft. lb.
   c. Stabilizer bar-to-frame: 55 ft. lb.
   d. Stabilizer bar-to-link: 27 ft. lb.
   e. Center link-to-pitman arm: 35 ft. lb.

ADJUSTMENTS

NOTE: The gear must be adjusted off the vehicle. All adjustments must be made in the sequence described below. Worm bearing preload is always adjusted first!

WORM BEARING PRELOAD

Adjustment

1. Mount the gear assembly in a vise.
2. Torque the adjuster plug to 20 ft. lbs.
3. Mark the gear housing in line with one of the adjuster plug holes.
4. Measure counterclockwise $^3/_{16}$–$^1/_4$ in from the first mark on all models except Wagoneer, Cheroke and Comanche and $^1/_2$ in. from the first mark on Wagoneer, Cherokee and Comanche, and remark the housing.
5. Turn the adjuster plug counterclockwise to align the hole with the second mark.
6. Hold the adjuster plug and torque the locknut to 85 ft. lbs. Do not allow the adjuster to turn.
7. Turn the stubshaft clockwise to its stop, then back $^1/_4$ turn.
8. Using a torque wrench of no more than 50 in. lb. capacity and a 12 point deep socket, check the rotating torque at the splined end of the stub shaft at or near a vertical position. Torque should be 4–10 inch lbs.
9. If the torque cannot be adjusted within these limits, the gear will have to be rebuilt.

PITMAN SHAFT OVERCENTER

Adjustment

1. Loosen the adjuster screw locknut.
2. Turn the adjuster screw counterclockwise until the screw is fully extended. Turn the screw back in one full turn.
3. Count the number of turns to rotate the stubshaft from stop-to-stop.
4. Turn the shaft back $^1/_2$ the number of turns. At this point the flat surface of the stubshaft should be upward and the master spline on the Pitman shaft should be aligned with the adjuster screw.
5. Install a 50 inch lbs. torque wrench and deep 12 point socket on the splined end of the stub shaft. Place the torque wrench in a vertical position.
6. Rotate the torque wrench 45° to each side and record the highest torque at or near center. Record this reading.
7. Adjust the torque by turning the adjuster screw clockwise. Adjustment is: the recorded reading plus 4–8 inch lbs. for new gears, but not exceeding 14 inch lbs. total; the previously recorded reading plus 4–5 inch lbs. for used gears, but not exceeding 14 inch lbs. combined total.
8. Tighten the adjuster screw locknut to 20 ft. lbs. while holding the adjuster screw.
9. Install the gear.

POWER STEERING PUMP

Removal and Installation

1. Disconnect the negative battery cable. Remove all the necessary components in order to gain access to the power steering retaining bolts.
2. Remove the pump drive belt tension adjusting bolt. Disconnect the belt from the pump.
3. Disconnect the return and pressure hoses from the pump. Cover the hose connector and union on the pump and open ends of the hoses to avoid the entrance of dirt.
4. On some V8 engines, it will be necessary to, remove the front bracket from the engine. Remove the two nuts which secure the rear of the pump to the bracket, and the two bolts which secure the front of the pump to the bracket and remove the pump.
5. To install, position the pump in the bracket and install the rear attaching screws. Install the front bracket, as required.
6. Connect the hydraulic hoses. Adjust the drive belt tension.
7. Fill the pump reservoir to the correct level.
8. Start the engine and wait for at least three minutes before turning the steering wheel. Check the level frequently during this time.
9. Slowly turn the steering wheel through its entire range a few times with the engine running. Recheck the level and inspect for possible leaks.

NOTE: If air becomes trapped in the fluid, the pump may become noisy until all of the air is out. This may take some time since trapped air does not bleed out rapidly.

TIE ROD END

Removal and Installation

1. Remove the cotter pins and retaining nuts at both ends of the tie rod and from the end of the connecting rod where it attaches to the tie rod.
2. Remove the nut attaching the steering damper push rod to the tie rod bracket and move the damper aside.
3. Remove the tie rod ends from the steering arms and connecting rod. It may be necessary to use a puller on some vehicles.
4. Count the number of threads showing on the tie rod before removing the ends, as a guide to installation.
5. Loosen the adjusting tube clamp bolts and unthread the ends.
6. Installation is the reverse of removal. Torque the connecting rod-to-tie rod nut to 70 ft. lbs.
7. Adjust toe-in, if necessary.

CLUTCH

Removal and Installation

4–151 ENGINE

1. Disconnect the negative battery cable. Remove the shift lever boot.
2. Remove the shift lever assembly.
3. Raise the vehicle and support it on jack stands.
4. Remove the transmission and transfer case.
5. Remove the slave cylinder-to-clutch housing bolts.
6. Disengage the slave cylinder pushrod from the throwout lever and move the cylinder out of the way.
7. Remove the starter.
8. Remove the throwout bearing.
9. Unbolt and remove the clutch housing.
10. Mark the position of the clutch pressure plate and remove the pressure plate bolts evenly, a little at a time in rotation.
11. Remove the pilot bushing lubricating wick from its bore in the crankshaft and soak the wick in clean engine oil.
12. Installation is the reverse of removal. Torque the pressure plate bolts to 23 ft. lbs., tightening them evenly, a little at a time in rotation. Torque the clutch housing to 54 ft. lbs.; the transmission-to-clutch housing bolts to 54 ft. lbs.; the transfer case-to-transmission bolts to 30 ft. lbs.

4–150, V6–173 AND DIESEL ENGINE

1. Disconnect the negative battery cable. Remove the transmission/transfer case assembly.
2. Mark the position of the clutch pressure plate in relation to the flywheel for installation.
3. Loosen the pressure plate bolts evenly, a little at a time each! Failure to loosen the bolts evenly, in rotation, will cause warping of the pressure plate.
4. When all spring tension is relieved from the pressure plate, back out the bolts and remove the pressure plate and driven plate.
5. If the pilot bushing is equipped with a lubricating wick, remove it and soak it in clean engine oil.
6. Installation is the reverse of removal. Tighten the pressure plate bolts evenly, in rotation in three or four different steps, to:
   a. 4–150: 23 ft. lb.
   b. 6–173: 16 ft. lb.

6–258, V8 ENGINES

1. Disconnect the negative battery cable. Remove the transmission.
2. Remove the starter.
3. Remove the throwout bearing and sleeve assembly.
4. Remove the bell housing.

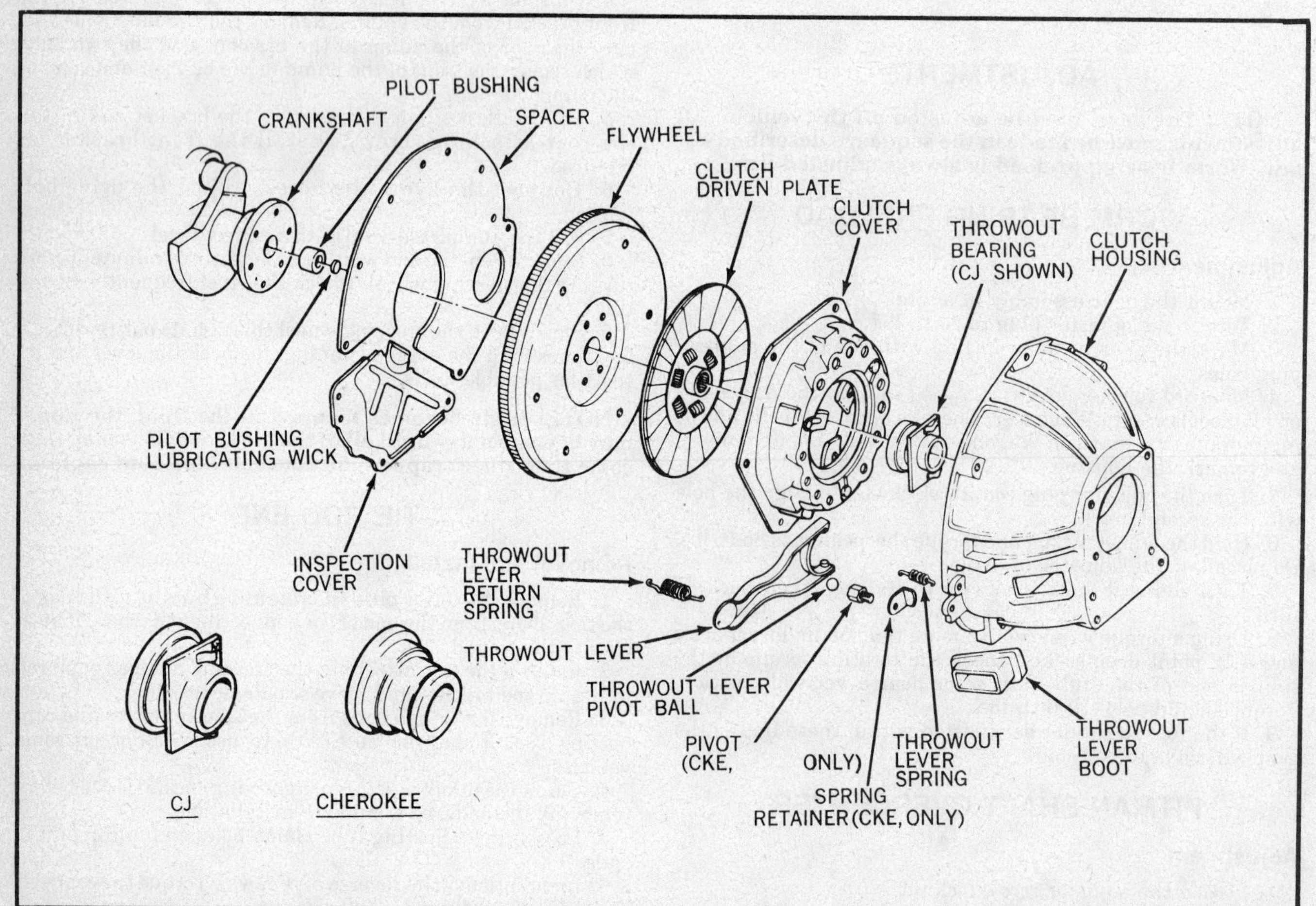

Clutch assembly and throw out bearing—typical (© Jeep Corp)

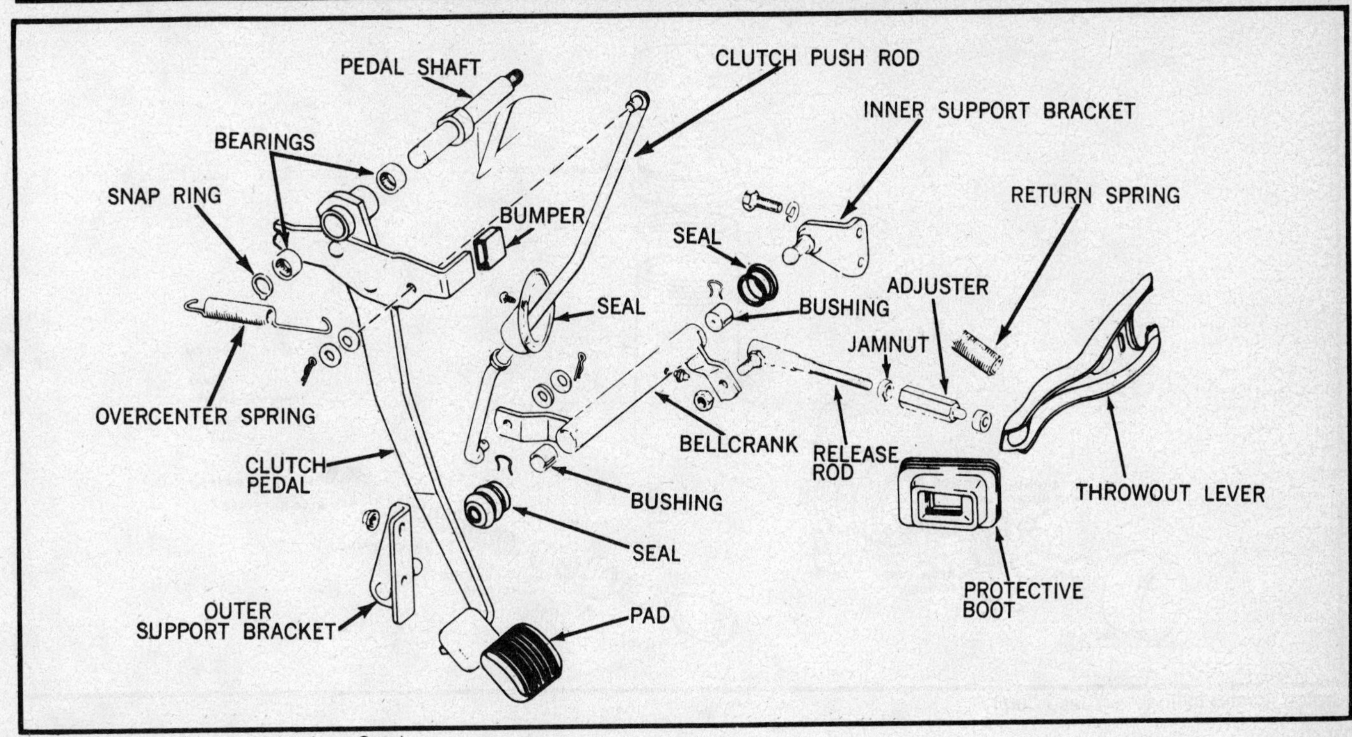

PEDAL SHAFT
CLUTCH PUSH ROD
BEARINGS
INNER SUPPORT BRACKET
SNAP RING
BUMPER
RETURN SPRING
SEAL
SEAL
BUSHING
ADJUSTER
JAMNUT
OVERCENTER SPRING
BELLCRANK
RELEASE ROD
CLUTCH PEDAL
THROWOUT LEVER
BUSHING
SEAL
PROTECTIVE BOOT
OUTER SUPPORT BRACKET
PAD
Clutch linkage—CJ model (© Jeep Corp)

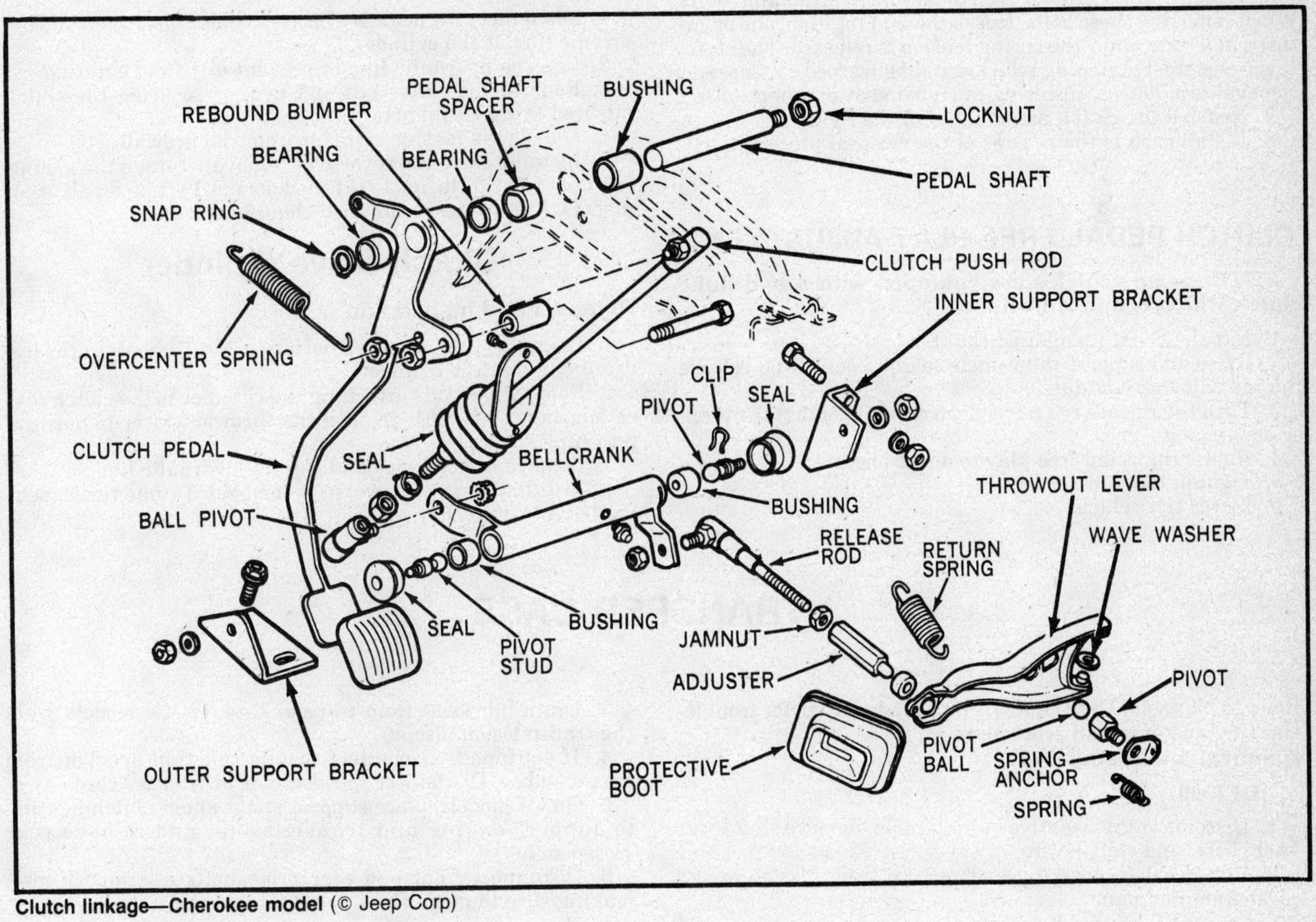

PEDAL SHAFT SPACER
BUSHING
REBOUND BUMPER
LOCKNUT
BEARING
BEARING
PEDAL SHAFT
SNAP RING
CLUTCH PUSH ROD
INNER SUPPORT BRACKET
OVERCENTER SPRING
CLIP
PIVOT
SEAL
CLUTCH PEDAL
SEAL
BELLCRANK
THROWOUT LEVER
BUSHING
BALL PIVOT
RELEASE ROD
RETURN SPRING
WAVE WASHER
SEAL
BUSHING
JAMNUT
PIVOT STUD
ADJUSTER
PIVOT
PIVOT BALL
SPRING ANCHOR
OUTER SUPPORT BRACKET
PROTECTIVE BOOT
SPRING
Clutch linkage—Cherokee model (© Jeep Corp)

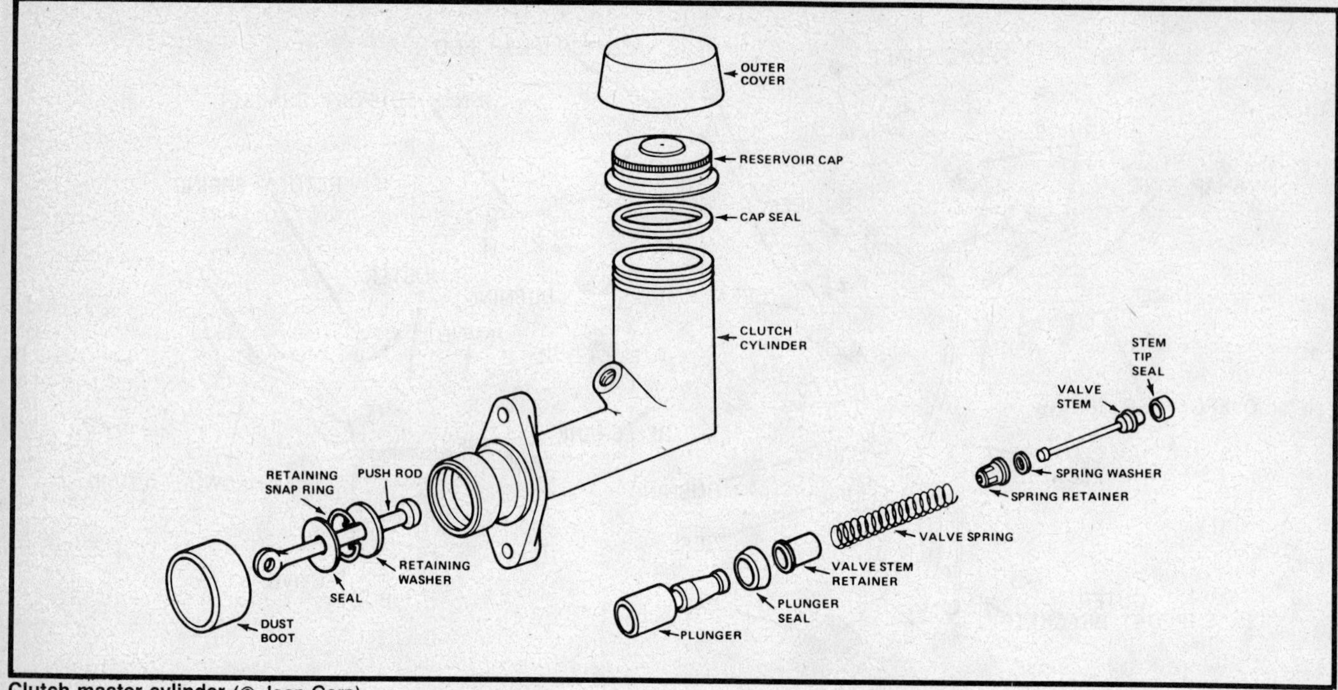

Clutch master cylinder (© Jeep Corp)

5. Mark the clutch cover, pressure plate and the flywheel with a center punch so that these parts can be later installed in the same position.
6. Remove the clutch cover-to-flywheel attaching bolts. When removing these bolts, loosen them in rotation, one or two turns at a time, until the spring tension is released. The clutch cover is a steel stamping which could be warped by improper removal procedures, resulting in clutch chatter when reused.
7. Remove the clutch assembly from the flywheel.
8. Installation is the reverse of the removal procedure.

CLUTCH PEDAL FREE-PLAY ADJUSTMENT

NOTE: Some vehicles are equipped with a hydraulic clutch which is non–adjustable.

1. Lift the pedal up against the stop.
2. Raise and support the vehicle safely. Loosen and release the rod adjuster jam nut.
3. Turn the release rod adjuster in or out to obtain the proper adjustment.
4. Adjust the pedal free-play to about one in..
5. Tighten the jam nut.
6. Lower the vehicle.

Clutch Master Cylinder

Removal and Installation

1. Disconnect the negative battery cable. Disconnect the hydraulic line at the cylinder.
2. Cap the hydraulic line to prevent dirt from entering.
3. Remove the cotter pin and washer securing the clutch pushrod to the pedal arm.
4. Unbolt the master cylinder from the firewall.
5. Installation is the reverse of removal. Torque the mounting nuts to 11 ft. lb. on 4–151 models and 19 ft. lb on all other models. Fill the reservoir with clean brake fluid.

Clutch Slave Cylinder

Removal and Installation

1. Disconnect the negative battery cable. Disconnect the hydraulic line at the cylinder.
2. Remove the bolts attaching the cylinder to the clutch cover housing. On 4–151, remove the throwout lever-to-pushrod retaining spring.
3. Remove the cylinder and cap the hydraulic line.
4. Installation is the reverse of removal. Torque the attaching bolts to 16 ft. lb.

TRANSFER CASE

Refer to "Transfer Case" in the Unit Repair section for troubleshooting and overhaul procedures.

Removal and Installation

MODEL 20

1. Disconnect the negative battery cable. Remove shift lever knob, boot, and shift lever.
2. Remove floor covering and remove transmission access cover from floorpan.
3. Drain lubricant from transfer case. On CJ models drain the transmission also.
4. If equipped, disconnect torque reaction bracket from crossmember. Disconnect speedometer at transfer case.
5. On CJ models, place support stand under clutch housing to support engine and transmission, and remove rear crossmember.
6. Disconnect front and rear driveshafts at transfer case, making sure to mark shaft yokes for assembly.

7. On Cherokee and Truck models, disconnect parking brake cable at equalizer and exhaust pipe support bracket at transfer case.
8. Remove bolts attaching transfer case to transmission and remove transfer case.

NOTE: One transfer case attaching bolt must be removed from front end of the case. This bolt is located at the bottom right corner of the transmission.

9. Install a new gasket on the transmission.
10. Shift the transfer case into 4WD low and install the case assembly on the guide bolts.
11. Rotate the transfer case output shaft until the transmission main shaft gear engages the rear output shaft gear of the transfer case.
12. Slide the transfer case forward until the two units mate flush.
13. Install one upper bolt, remove the dowel guide bolts and install the remaining bolts. Torque to 30 ft. lbs.
14. Connect the speedometer cable and parking brake cable.
15. Install the propeller shafts after aligning the indexing marks.
16. Fill the unit with gear lube, and lower the vehicle.
17. Install the transfer case shift lever, boot, and knob.

MODEL 207

1. Shift the unit into 4–High. Disconnect the negative battery cable.
2. Raise and support the vehicle safely.
3. Drain the lubricant from the case.
4. Mark the rear axle yoke and drive shaft for reference.
5. Remove the rear driveshaft.
6. Disconnect the speedometer cable, vacuum hoses and vent hose from the case.
7. Raise the transmission and transfer case slightly, and remove the crossmember attaching bolts.
8. Remove the crossmember.
9. Mark the front driveshaft and transfer case flange for reference.
10. Disconnect the front driveshaft from the transfer case.
11. Disconnect the shift lever linkage at the case.
12. Remove the shift lever bracket bolts.
13. Support the transfer case safely. Remove the attaching bolts and lower the case from the vehicle.
14. Installation is the reverse of removal. Observe the following torques:
    a. Shift lever nut: 18 ft. lb.
    b. Transfer case-to-Transmission adapter nut: 26 ft. lb.
    c. Transfer case mounting bolt: 22 ft. lb.

MODEL 208

1. Disconnect the negative battery cable. Raise and safely support the vehicle safely.
2. Drain the lubricant from the transfer case.
3. Disconnect the speedometer cable and indicator switch wires. Disconnect the transfer case shift lever link at the operating lever.
4. Support the rear of the transmission and remove the rear crossmember.
5. Mark the transfer case front and rear output shaft yokes and driveshafts for assembly alignment reference.
6. Disconnect the front and rear driveshafts at the transfer case yokes. Secure the shafts to the frame rails with wires to keep them out of the way.
7. Disconnect the parking brake cable guide from the pivot located on the right frame rail, if necessary.
8. Remove the bolts that attach the exhaust pipe support bracket to transfer case, if necessary.
9. Remove the bolts that attach the transfer case to the transmission.
10. Move the transfer case assembly rearward until it is free of the transmission output shaft. Remove and lower the transfer case.
11. Installation is in the reverse order of removal. Torque the transfer case mounting bolts to 40 ft. lbs.

MODEL 219

1. Disconnect the negative battery cable. Raise and support the vehicle safely.
2. Remove reduction unit on Cherokee, Wagoneer, and Truck models, if equipped.
3. Index the marks on the front and rear yokes and propeller shafts for proper alignment during assembly.
4. Disconnect both the front and rear propeller shafts. On CJ–7 models, place support stand under transmission and remove crossmember.
5. Mark the vacuum diaphragm control for identification during the assembly, and then disconnect the vacuum hoses, wiring, and speedometer cable.
6. Disconnect the parking brake cable guide from the pivot on the right frame side.
7. Remove the two front side transfer case to transmission bolts, and install a guide bolt into the upper hole.
8. Remove the two rear side bolts, holding the transfer case to the transmission, and install a guide bolt into the upper hole.
9. Move the transfer case rearward until the unit is free of the transmission output shaft and guide pins. Lower the assembly to the floor.
10. Remove all gasket material from the rear of the transmission.
11. Install a new gasket on the rear of the transmission.
12. Install the guide bolts in the upper transmission adapter and transfer case, if they were removed.
13. Raise the transfer case, engage the guide bolts, and move the case assembly forward to the transmission. Make sure a flush fit is achieved.
14. If necessary, rotate the transfer case rear output shaft yoke until the drive hub splines align with the transmission output shaft.
15. Install front and rear attaching bolts, and remove the guide bolts during this operation.
16. Attach the exhaust pipe bracket support, if removed.
17. Align the propeller shaft and indexing marks on the yokes and attach the propeller shafts.
18. Connect the speedometer cable, wiring, and vacuum hoses.
19. Connect the parking brake cable guide to the pivot bracket on the right frame side.
20. Install the specified lubricant, and lower the vehicle.

MODEL 228 AND 229

1. Disconnect the negative battery cable. Raise and support the vehicle safely.
2. Drain the lubricant from the transfer case.
3. Disconnect the speedometer cable and vent hose. Disconnect the transfer case shift lever link at the operating lever.
4. Support the weight of the transmission safely. Remove the rear crossmember.
5. Mark the relation of the front and rear driveshafts with their yokes for reference.
6. Disconnect the front and rear driveshafts at the yokes.
7. Disconnect the shift motor vacuum hoses.
8. Disconnect the transfer case shift linkage.
9. Support the transfer case with a jack and remove the transfer case-to-transmission bolts.
10. Move the transfer case rearward and lower it from the vehicle.
11. Installation is the reverse of removal. Don't install any mounting bolts until all parts are aligned. Make sure that all splined shafts mesh properly before tightening bolts. Torque

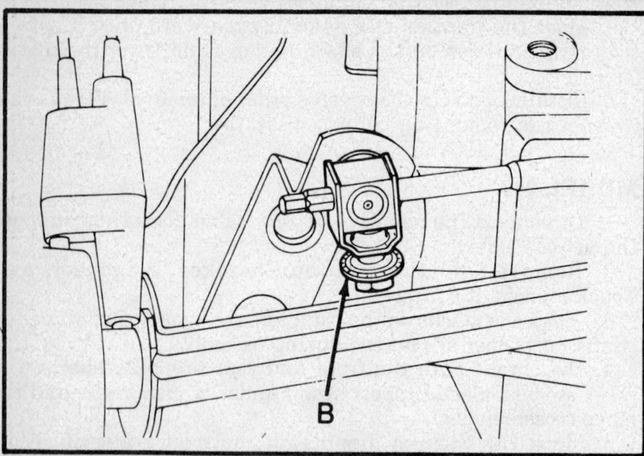

B is the adjusting point on the 229 (© Jeep Corp)

the transfer case-to-transmission bolts to 40 ft. lb. and the driveshaft yoke nuts to 10 ft. lb. (120 in. lb.)

MODEL 300

1. Disconnect the negative battery cable.
2. On models with a manual transmission; remove the shift lever knob, trim ring and boot from the transmission and transfer case shift levers.
3. Remove the floor covering and remove the transmission access cover from the floorpan.
4. Raise and safely support the vehicle. Drain the lubricant from the transfer case.
5. Support the engine and transmission under the clutch bell housing and remove the rear crossmember.
6. Mark the transfer case front and rear yokes and driveshafts for assembly alignment reference.
7. Disconnect the front and rear driveshafts at the transfer case. Secure the shafts out of the way.

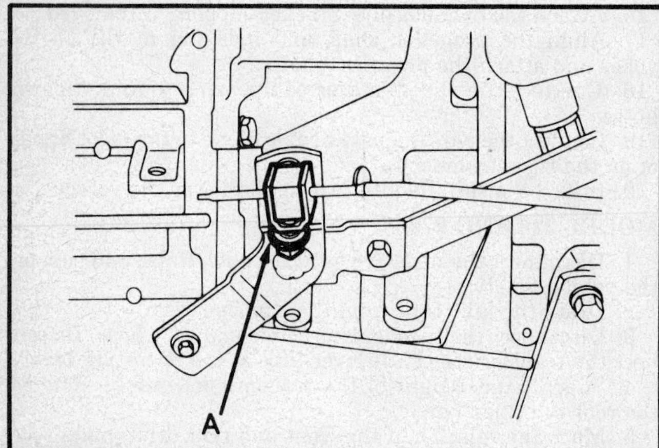

A is the adjusting point on the 207 (© Jeep Corp)

8. Disconnect the speedometer cable at the transfer case. Disconnect the parking brake cable at the equalizer and the exhaust pipe support bracket at the transfer case to gain any needed clearance.
9. Remove the bolts mounting the transfer case to the transmission. Remove the transfer case.
10. Installation is in the reverse order of removal. The transfer case should be shifted into the 4L position before installation. Rotate the output shaft yoke until the transmission output shaft gear engages the transfer case input shaft. Torque the mounting bolts to 30 ft. lbs.

Linkage Adjustments

The Shifter rails of the transfer case lever assembly connect to the shifter rails of the transfer case either directly or through non-adjustable links on vehicles with manual transmissions. An adjustable trunnion is provided on the lower shift rod to provide desired adjustment on automatic transmission equipped models. The linkage should be lubricated periodically.

QUADRA-TRAC®

Since the Quadra-Trac® system is a "full time 4WD" system, and is constantly engaged in 4WD, there is no "shift linkage" as such. There are two features which can be operated manually concerning the transfer case: the "Lock-Out" feature and the engagement of the optional "Low Range Reduction Unit."

Since the "Lock-Out" feature is a vacuum actuated unit, there are no external adjustments that can be made other than making sure that all vacuum lines are in place, connected and not damaged in any way.

The reduction unit is actuated by a shift cable and can be adjusted in the following manner:

1. Loosen the nut which clamps the cable to the shift lever pivot. Be sure that the cable can move freely in the pivot.
2. Move the reduction shift lever to the most rearward detent position (Hi-Range position).
3. Push the Low Range lever inward until it stops. Pull the Low Range lever out slightly, no more than $^{1}/_{16}$ in.
4. Tighten the cable clamp nut at the reduction unit shift lever.

NOTE: This procedure only applies to the Quadra-Trac transfer case equipped with a reduction unit.

MODEL 207 AND 229 RANGE CONTROL LINKAGE ADJUSTMENT

1. Place the range control lever in the 2WD position (high range position for model 229).
2. Insert a $^{1}/_{8}$ in. spacer between the shift gate and the lever.
3. Hold the lever in this position and place the transfer case lever in 2WD (high range position for model 229).
4. Adjust the link at the block, A (207) or B (229), to provide a free pin at the case outer lever.

MANUAL TRANSMISSION

Refer to "Manual Transmission Overhaul" in the Unit Repair section for application, troubleshooting and overhaul.

Transmission

Removal and Installation

ALL EXCEPT CHEROKEE, WAGONEER AND COMANCHE

1. Disconnect the negative battery cable. Remove the shift level knobs, trim rings, and bolts.
2. If the vehicle is equipped with the T4 or T5 transmission, Remove the bolts attaching the transmission shift lever housing to the transmission. Remove the lever and the housing.
3. If the vehicle is equipped with the T176 transmission press and turn the transmission shift lever retainer counterclockwise to release the lever. Remove the lever, boot, spring and seat as an assembly.
4. Raise the vehicle and support it safely.
5. Mark the rear propeller shaft and the transfer case yoke for reassembly. Disconnect the rear propeller shaft at the transfer case yoke. Move the shaft aside and secure it out of the way
6. Support the rear of the engine by placing a support under the clutch housing.
7. Remove the nuts and bolts attaching the rear crossmember to the frame rails and rear support cushion. Remove the rear crossmember from the vehicle.
8. Disconnect the speedometer cable, back-up light switch, four wheel drive indicator switch wire and the transfer case vent hose at the transfer case assembly.
9. Mark the front propeller shaft and the transfer case yoke for reassembly. Disconnect the front propeller shaft from the transfer case yoke. Move the shaft to the side and position it out of the way.
10. On T4, T5 and T176 transmissions except the T176 transmission in the Grand Wagoneer and truck, remove the transfer case shift lever as follows. Remove the shift lever retaining nut. Remove the cotter pins that retain the shift control link pins in the shift rods and remove the pins. Remove the shifter shaft and disengage the shift lever from the shift control links. Slide the lever upward in the boot in order to move the lever out of the way.
11. If the vehicle is a Grand Wagoneer or truck equipped with the T176 transmission, remove the cotter pin and washers that connect the link to the shift lever and disconnect the link from the shift lever.
12. Support the transmission and transfer case assembly.
13. Remove the bolts attaching to the clutch housing. Remove the transmission and transfer case assembly. Remove the bolts attaching the transfer case to the transmission and remove the transmission.
14. Installation is the reverse of the removal procedure.

CHEROKEE, WAGONEER AND COMANCHE

1. Disconnect the negative battery cable. Raise the shift lever boot and remove the upper part of the console.
2. Remove the lower part of the console.
3. Remove the inner boot.
4. Remove the shift lever using tool J–34635.
5. Raise and support the vehicle safely. Drain the transmission and transfer case, if equipped. Mark the relation between the rear driveshaft and the transmission output yoke. Remove the driveshaft.
6. If the vehicle is equipped with a transfer case,position a support stand under the transfer case in order to support the weight of both the transmission and the transfer case assembly.
7. If the vehicle is not equipped with a transfer case, position a support under the transmission assemblt in order to support the weight of the transmission.
8. Remove the nuts and bolts attaching the rear crossmember to the frame rails and rear support cushion. Remove the rear crossmember. Disconnect the speedometer cable, backup light switch. If equipped,disconnect the transfer case vent hose.
9. Disconnect the transfer case vacuum hoses and linkage. Remove the clutch slave cylinder.
10. If equipped, mark the front propeller shaft and transfer case yoke for reinstallation. Move the shaft aside and secure it out of the way.
11. Properly support the transmission and the transfer case as required.
12. Remove the transmission-to-engine mounting bolts, move the assembly rearward and lower it from the vehicle.
13. If the vehicle is equipped with a transfer case remove the transfer case to transmission retaining bolts.
14. Installation is the reverse of removal. Make sure that the shaft splines mesh before tightening the mounting bolts. Observe the following torques:
    a. Crossmember-to-body: 30 ft. lb.
    b. Crossmember-to-transmission: 33 ft. lb.
    c. Transmission-to-engine: 28 ft. lb.
    d. Transfer case-to-transmission adapter: 26 ft. lb.
    e. U-joints-to-yokes: 170 in. lb.

LINKAGE ADJUSTMENTS

The shift lever is connected to the transfer case shift rails through rods and nonadjustable links, therefore external adjustments are not possible.

AUTOMATIC TRANSMISSION

Removal and Installation

1980 AND LATER EXCEPT 1984 AND LATER CHEROKEE, WAGONEER AND COMANCHE

1. Disconnect the negative battery cable.
2. Disconnect the fan shroud, if equipped.
3. Disconnect the transmission oil fill tube top bracket.
4. Raise the vehicle and support it safely.
5. Remove the inspection cover from the lower part of the converter housing.
6. Remove the oil filler tube and dipstick.
7. Remove the starter.
8. Mark the driveshafts and yokes for position. Disconnect the driveshafts from the transfer case yokes. Secure the shafts to the frame with wire so they are out of the way.
9. On eight cylinder models, disconnect the exhaust pipes at the exhaust manifolds and remove, if necessary, to gain clearance.
10. Drain the transfer case lubricant and transmission fluid.
11. Disconnect the speedometer cable, gearshift linkage,

throttle linkage and the wires to the neutral safety switch.
12. Mark the converter drive plate and converter for location reference.
13. Remove the bolts that attach the converter to the drive plate.
14. Support the transmission-transfer case assembly on a suitable jack. Be sure the transmission assembly is firmly chained or secured for removal.
15. Remove the rear crossmember. Lower the transmission slightly and disconnect the oil cooler lines.
16. Remove the bolts that mount the transmission to the engine.
17. Move the transmission and converter back and away from the engine. Make sure the converter breaks loose from the drive plate and is firmly mounted on the transmission.
18. Hold the converter in position and lower the transmission assembly until the converter housing clears the engine.
19. Remove the transmission and transfer case assembly from under the vehicle.
20. Remove the transfer case.
21. Installation is in the reverse order of removal. Be sure to line up the marks on the converter and drive plate when reinstalling. Transmission mounting bolts are torqued to 28 ft.

1984 AND LATER CHEROKEE, WAGONEER AND COMANCHE

TWO WHEEL DRIVE

1. Disconnect the negative battery cable. Raise and support the vehicle safely.
2. Mark the rear propeller shaft and yoke for reassembly. Disconnect and remove the rear propeller shaft.
3. Remove the torque converter inspection cover. Mark the converter drive plate and converter assembly for reassembly.
4. Remove the bolts attaching the torque converter to the flex plate. Properly support the transmission assembly.
5. Remove the bolts attaching the rear crossmember to the transmission side rail. Disconnect the exhaust pipe at the catalytic converter.
6. Lower the transmission slightly in order to disconnect the fluid cooler lines.
7. Disconnect the backup light switch wire and the speedometer cable. Disconnect the transmission linkage.
8. Remove the bolts attaching the transmission assembly to the engine. Move the transmission assembly and the torque converter rearward to clear the crankshaft.
9. Carefully lower the transmission assembly from the vehicle.
10. Installation is the reverse of the removal procedure.

FOUR WHEEL DRIVE

1. Disconnect the negative battery cable. Raise and support the vehicle safely.
2. Mark the rear propeller shaft and yoke for reassembly. Disconnect and remove the rear propeller shaft.
3. Remove the torque converter inspection cover. Mark the converter drive plate and converter assembly for reassembly.
4. Remove the bolts attaching the torque converter to the flex plate. Properly support the transmission assembly.

NOTE: If the vehicle is equipped with a diesel engine, remove the left motor mount and starter in order to gain access to the torque converter drive plate bolts through the starter opening.

5. Remove the bolts attaching the rear crossmember to the transmission side rail. Disconnect the exhaust pipe at the catalytic converter.
6. Lower the transmission slightly in order to disconnect the fluid cooler lines. Mark the front propeller shaft assembly for reinstallation. Disconnect the propeller shaft at the transfer case and secure the assembly out of the way.
7. Disconnect the backup light switch wire and the speedometer cable. Disconnect the transfer case and the transmission linkage. Disconnect the vacuum lines and the vent hose.
8. Remove the bolts attaching the transmission assembly to the engine. Move the transmission assembly and the torque converter rearward to clear the crankshaft.
9. Carefully lower the transmission assembly from the vehicle. Remove the transfer case retaining bolts from the transmission assembly.
10. Installation is the reverse of the removal procedure.

LINKAGE ADJUSTMENT

1. Raise and safely support the vehicle.
2. Loosen the shift rod trunnion jamnuts.
3. Remove the lockpin that retains the shift rod trunnion to the bell crank. Disengage the trunnion and shift rod at the bell crank.
4. Place the gear shift lever in the Park position and lock the steering column.
5. Move the transmission lever rearward into the Park detent. Be sure the lever is as far rearward as it will go.
6. Check the engagement of the Park detent by trying to rotate the driveshaft (rear wheels must be off of the ground). The shaft will not rotate if the Park detent is engaged.
7. Adjust the trunnion until it will fit in the bell crank arm freely. Tighten the jamnuts. Install the lock pin.
8. Check engine starting in Park and Neutral, be sure it will not start in any other gear.

FRONT BAND

Adjustment

The front band adjusting screw is located on the left side of the transmission case just above the manual valve and throttle control levers.

1. Raise and safely support the vehicle.
2. Loosen the adjusting screw locknut and back if off five turns.
3. Check the adjusting screw to make sure it turns freely, lubricate it if necessary.
4. Tighten the adjusting screw to 36 inch lbs.
5. Back of the adjusting screw two turns. Tighten the locknut. Do not allow the adjusting screw to turn when tightening the locknut.

REAR BAND

Adjustment

NOTE: The transmission oil pan must be removed to gain access to the adjusting screw.

1. Raise and safely support the vehicle.
2. Drain the transmission fluid and remove the oil pan.
3. The adjusting screw is located on the right rear side above the rear side edge of the filter.
4. Loosen the locknut. Tighten the adjusting screw to 41 inch lbs. Back off the adjusting screw four turns on models 904 through 1983 and 7 turns on 904 in 1984 and later vehicles, four turns on 999, and two turns on model 727. Hold the adjusting screw so that it will not turn and tighten the locknut.
5. Install the oil pan and new gasket.
6. Lower the vehicle and fill the transmission to the correct level.

NEUTRAL SWITCH

Adjustment

The neutral safety switch is located on the side of the transmission by the manual linkage. It is an electrical switch that is thread mounted. The neutral starting section of the switch is contained in the center terminal of the three terminal switch. The other terminals control the backup lights.

Test and Replacement

1. Raise and support the vehicle safely. Remove the wiring connector from the switch. Test for continuity between the center terminal pin and the transmission case. Continuity should exist only when the transmission control is in Park or Neutral.
2. If test shows that the switch is defective, check the gearshift linkage adjustment before replacing the switch.
3. Remove the switch from the transmission. A certain amount of fluid will leak out when the switch is removed, have a container ready to catch the fluid.
4. Move the gearshift lever to Park and neutral positions. Inspect the switch operating lever fingers and manual lever and shaft for proper alignment with the switch opening in the transmission case.
5. Install a new switch and seal into the transmission case. Tighten to 24 ft. lbs. Test for continuity.
6. Lower the vehicle and correct the transmission fluid level.

Transmission Oil Pan and Filter

Removal and Installation

1. Raise the vehicle and support safely.
2. Position a drain pan under the transmission and remove the oil pan bolts, except the four corner ones.
3. Loosen the corner bolts and pry the oil pan loose from the transmission case.
4. Allow the oil to drain from the corners of the oil pan, while tilting the pan to remove as much oil as possible.
5. Carefully remove the corner bolts and the oil pan from the transmission case.
6. Remove the oil filter, oil pan gasket.
7. Installation is the reverse of the removal procedure. Lower the vehicle and fill the transmission to the proper level with automatic transmission fluid.

THROTTLE LINKAGE

Adjustment

4–151 ENGINE

1. Remove the air cleaner.
2. Remove the spark plug wire holder from the throttle cable bracket and move the holder and wires aside.
3. Raise and support the vehicle safely.
4. Hold the throttle control lever rearward against its stop. Hook one end of a spare spring to the lever and hook the oposite end to any convenient point. This will hold the lever in position.
5. Lower the vehicle.
6. Block the choke open and move the carburetor linkage completely off the fast idle cam.
7. On vehicles without air conditioning, turn the ignition to ON to energize the solenoid.
8. Unlock the throttle control cable by releasing the T shaped adjuster clamp on the cable by lifting it upward with a small screwdriver.
9. Grasp the outer sheath of the cable and move the cable and sheath forward to remove any load on the cable bell crank.
10. Adjust the cable by removing the cable and sheath rearward until there is no play at all between the plastic cable and the bell crank ball.
11. When play has been eliminated, lock the cable by pressing the T shaped clamp downward until it snaps into place.
12. Turn the ignition off. Install all parts and remove the spare spring.

4–150 ENGINE WITH CARBURETOR

1. Disconnect the throttle control rod spring at the carburetor.
2. Raise and support the vehicle safely.
3. Use the throttle control rod spring to hold the transmission throttle control lever forward against its stop.
4. Hook one end of a spring on the throttle control lever and the other end of the spring on the throttle linkage bellcrank bracket, which is attached to the torque converter housing.
5. Lower the vehicle. Block the choke in the open position. Set the carburetor throttle off the fast idle cam.
6. Turn the ignition key to the "ON" position in order to energize the solenoid.
7. Open the throttle halfway to allow the solenoid to lock. Return the carburetor to the idle position.
8. Loosen the retaining bolt on the throttle control adjusting link. Do not remove the spring clip and nylon washer.
9. Pull the end of the link to eliminate lash. Tighten the retaining bolt. Turn the ignition to the "OFF" position.
10. Raise and support the vehicle safely. Remove the throttle control rod spring from the linkage. Lower the vehicle. Install the spring on the throttle control rod.

4–151 ENGINE WITH FUEL INJECTION

NOTE: An idle speed assembly exerciser box is required in order to make this adjustment. The purpose of this special tool is to by-pass the idle speed motor.

1. Be sure that the vehicle ignition key is in the "OFF" position. Raise and support the vehicle safely.
2. Hook one end of a spring on the throttle control lever and the other end of the spring on the throttle linkage bellcrank bracket, which is attached to the torque converter housing. Lower the vehicle.
3. Disconnect the idle speed actuator motor wire harness and connect the idle speed assembly exerciser box. Upon connection, the adjustment light should turn off and the ready light should turn on.
4. Loosen the retaining bolt on the throttle control adjusting link. Pull the end of the link in order to eliminate lash and tighten the link retaining bolt.
5. Press the extend button on the idle speed assembly exerciser box until the idle speed actuator motor ratchets.
6. Disconnect the idle speed assembly exerciser box and reconnect the idle speed actuator motor wiring harness.
7. Raise and safely support the vehicle. Remove the spring from the linkage. Lower the vehicle.

DIESEL ENGINE

NOTE: Special tool J–35514, throttle valve lever and cable adjusting tool, will be required in order to complete this procedure.

1. Disconnect the throttle valve cable from the pin on the throttle valve lever.
2. Disconnect the cable from the transmission throttle lever. Remove and discard the cable.
3. Set the injection pump automatic advance lever at the curb idle position. Loosen the screw and turn the cable clevis one-quater of a turn. The lever should be seated against the stop in the curb idle position.

4. Install the throttle valve lever and cable adjusting tool. Loosen the tool thumbscrew and move the sliding legs rearward. Position the notched leg on the cable bracket. Rest the legs on the lever. Move the legs forward until the rear leg lightly touches the cable attaching pin. Retighten the thumbscrew.

5. Check the throttle valve lever travel by moving the lever to the wide open throttle position. The cable attaching pin should now lightly touch the forward leg of the sliding legs on the special tool.

6. If the pin does not touch the forward leg of the tool, or if the pin tends to move the tool too much the throttle lever travel must be adjusted.

7. To adjust the throttle lever travel, hold the lever in the wide open throttle position. Loosen the lever screws and move the lever in or out in order to adjust the travel. The pin should lightly touch the forward leg of the tool when the lever travel is adjusted properly at wide open throttle. Tighten the screws to 66 inch lbs. Return the lever to the curb idle position and verify that the pin is again lightly touching the forward leg of the tool.

NOTE: If the pin does not lightly touch the rear leg at the curb idle position, loosen the thumbscrew. Re set the rear sliding leg of the tool so that it touches the pin. Repeat the above steps until correct lever travel is obtained.

8. Install a new throttle valve cable.

6–173 ENGINE

1. Remove the air cleaner assembly. Raise and support the vehicle safely.

2. Hold the throttle control lever rearward against its stop. Use a spring to hold the lever. Hook one end of the spring to the lever and the other end to a convenient mounting point.

3. Lower the vehicle. Block the choke open and set the carburetor linkage off of the fast idle cam.

4. Unlock the throttle control cable by releasing the T-shaped cable adjuster clamp. Release the clamp by lifting it upward using a suitable tool.

5. Grasp the cable outer sheath and move the cable and sheath forward, this will remove any cable load on the throttle cable bellcrank.

6. Adjust the cable by moving the cable and sheath rearward until there is zero lash between the plastic cable end and the bellcrank ball.

7. When this has been accomplished, lock the cable by pressing the T-shaped adjuster clamp downward.

8. Install the air cleaner assembly. Raise and support the vehicle safely. Remove the spring from its mounting. Lower the vehicle.

6–258 ENGINE

1. Disconnect the throttle control rod spring at the carburetor.

2. Raise and support the vehicle safely.

3. Use the throttle control rod spring to hold the throttle control lever forward against its stop, by hooking one end of the spring on the throttle control lever and the other end on the throttle linkage bell crank bracket which is attached to the transmission housing.

4. Block the choke plate open and move the throttle linkage off the fast idle cam.

5. On carburetors equipped with a throttle operated solenoid valve, turn the ignition ON to energize the solenoid, then open the throttle halfway to allow the solenoid to lock and return the carburetor to the idle position.

6. Loosen the retaining bolt on the throttle control adjusting link. Do not remove the spring clip and nylon washer.

7. Pull on the end of the link to eliminate play and tighten the retaining bolt.

8. Remove the throttle control rod spring and install it on the control rod from where it came.

9. Lower the vehicle.

V8 ENGINE

1. Disconnect the throttle control rod spring at the carburetor.

2. Raise and support the vehicle safely.

3. Use the throttle control rod spring to hold the transmission throttle valve control lever against its stop.

4. Block the choke plate open and make sure the throttle linkage is off the fast idle cam.

NOTE: On carburetors equipped with a throttle operated solenoid valve, turn the ignition to ON to energize the solenoid. Then turn the throttle halfway to allow the solenoid to lock and return the carburetor to idle.

5. Loosen the retaining bolt on the throttle control rod adjuster link. Remove the spring clip and move the nylon washer to the rear of the link.

6. Push on the end of the link to eliminate play and tighten the link retaining bolt.

7. Install the nylon washer and spring clip.

8. Remove the throttle control rod spring and install it in its intended position.

9. Lower the vehicle.

U-JOINTS AND DRIVE LINE

Drive Shaft

Removal and Installation

In order to remove the front and rear driveshafts, unscrew the attaching nuts from the universal joint's U-bolts, remove the U-bolts and slide the shaft forward or backward toward the slip-joint. The shaft can then be removed from the end yokes and removed from under the vehicle. Install the driveshaft in the reverse order.

NOTE: Some driveshafts are marked at the slip-joints with arrows on the spline and sleeve yoke. When installing the driveshaft, align the arrows to have the yokes at the front and rear of the shaft in the same parallel plane.

U-Joint Overhaul

SNAP-RING TYPE

Disassembly and Assembly

1. Remove the snap-rings.

2. Press on the end of one bearing until the opposite bearing is pushed from the yoke arm.

3. Turn the joint over. Press the first bearing back out of the arm by pressing on the exposed end of the journal shaft. Repeat this operation for the other two bearings, then lift out the journal assembly by sliding it to one side.

4. Wash all parts in solvent and inspect for wear. Replace all worn parts.

5. Install new gaskets on the journal assembly. Make certain that the grease channel in each journal trunnion is open.
6. Pack the bearing cones one-third full of grease and install the rollers.
7. Assemble in the reverse order of disassembly. If the joint binds when assembled, tap the arms lightly to relieve any pressure on the bearings at the end of the journal.

U-BOLT TYPE

Disassembly and Assembly

Remove the attaching U-bolts to release one set of bearing races. Slide the driveshaft into the yoke flange to remove the races. The rest of the disassembly and repair procedure is the same as that given above for the snap-ring type of cross and roller joint. The correct U-bolt torque is 15–20 ft. lbs.

BALL AND TRUNNION

Disassembly and Assembly

1. Clamp the shaft firmly in a vise.
2. Bend the grease cover lugs away from the universal joint body. Remove the cover and gasket.
3. Remove the two clamps from the dust cover. Push the joint body toward the driveshaft tube. Remove two each; centering buttons, spring washers, ball and roller bearings, and thrust washers, from the trunnion pin.
4. Press the trunnion pin from ballhead.
5. If the ballhead is bent out of alignment or if the trunnion pin bore is worn or damaged, replace the driveshaft.
6. To reassemble: secure the larger end of the dust cover to the joint body with the larger of two clamps. Install the smaller clamp. Fit the cover over the ballhead shaft.
7. Push the universal joint cover toward the driveshaft tube. Press the trunnion pin into the centered position. If the trunnion pin is not centered, imbalance will result.
8. Install the thrust washers, ball and roller bearings, spring washer, and centering buttons on the trunnion pin. Compress the centering buttons. Move the joint body to hold the buttons in place.
9. Insert the breather between the dust cover and the ballhead shaft, along the length of the shaft. The breather must extend no more than ½ in. beyond the dust cover. Tighten the clamp screw to secure the cover to the shaft. Cut away any portion of dust cover protruding under the clamps.
10. Pack the raceways around the ball and roller bearings with about 2 oz. of universal joint grease.
11. Position the gasket and grease cover on the body. Bend the lugs of the cover into the notches of the body. Move the body back and forth to distribute grease in the raceways.

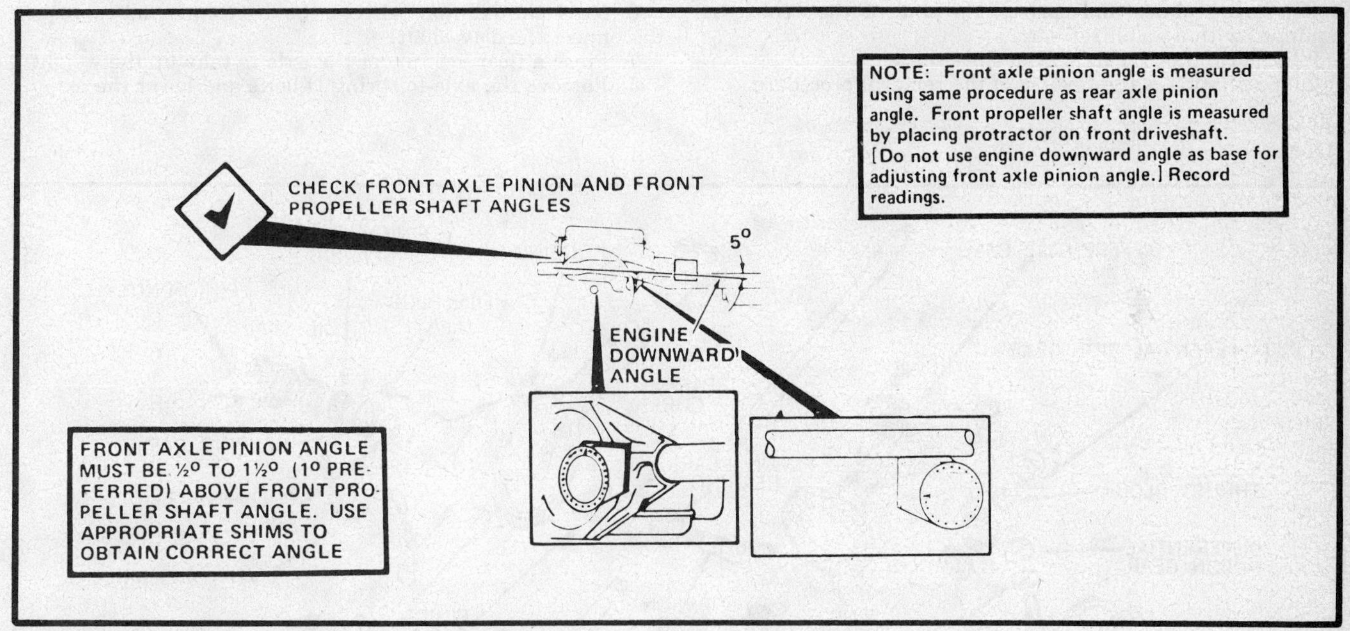

Checking drive shaft angle and alignment (© Jeep Corp.)

DRIVE AXLES (REAR)

Refer to the Drive Axle Unit Repair section for application, troubleshooting, and overhaul procedures.

Rear Axle Assembly

Removal and Installation

CJ AND SCRAMBLER

1. Remove the cotter pins from the axle shaft nuts. Remove the axle shaft nuts. Raise the vehicle and support it safely.
2. Remove the rear wheels. Remove the brake drum retaining screws. Remove the brake drums.
3. Remove the axle hub using tool J–25109–01 or equivalent. Disconnect the brake lines at the wheel cylinders. Remove the support plates, oil seals and retainers and the end play shims.
4. Axle shaft end play shims are installed on the left side of the axle only.
5. Remove the axle shafts using tool J–2498 or equivalent.

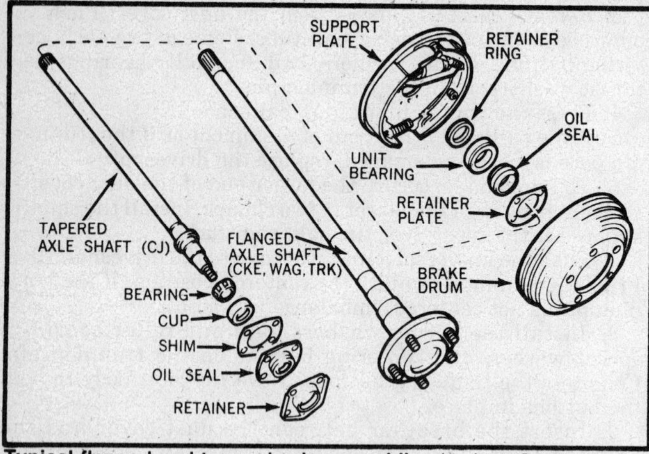

Typical flanged and tapered axle assemblies (© Jeep Corp)

Drain the lubricant and remove the axle housing cover.

6. Disconnect the parking brake cables at the equalizer. Mark the propeller shaft for reinstallation. Disconnect the shaft at the axle yoke.
7. Disconnect the flexible brake hose at the body floorpan bracket. Disconnect the vent hose at the axle tube.
8. Support the rear axle assembly. Remove the spring U-bolts, spring plates and spring clip plate if the vehicle is equipped with a stabilizer bar.
9. Remove the rear axle from the vehicle.
10. Installation is the reverse of the removal procedure.

CHEROKEE, GRAND WAGONEER AND TRUCK

1. Raise the vehicle and support it safely.
2. Remove the rear wheels.
3. Place an indexing mark on the rear yoke and propeller shaft, and disconnect the shaft.
4. Disconnect the shock absorbers from the axle tubes.
5. Disconnect the brake hose from the tee fitting on the axle housing.
6. Disconnect the parking brake cable at the frame mounting.
7. Remove U-bolts. On vehicles with spring mounted above axle, disconnect spring at rear shackle.
8. Support the axle on a jack, remove the spring clips, and remove the axle assembly from under the vehicle.
9. Installation is the reverse of removal.

NOTE: Bleed and adjust brakes accordingly.

1984 AND LATER CHEROKEE, WAGONEER AND COMANCHE

1. Raise and support the vehicle safely.
2. Remove the wheels and brake drums.
3. Disconnect the shock absorbers.
4. Disconnect the brake hose at the frame rail.
5. Disconnect the parking brake cables at the equalizer.
6. Mark the relation between the driveshaft and yoke, and disconnect the driveshaft.
7. Place a floor jack under the axle to take up the weight.
8. Remove the axle-to-spring U-bolts and lower the axle.

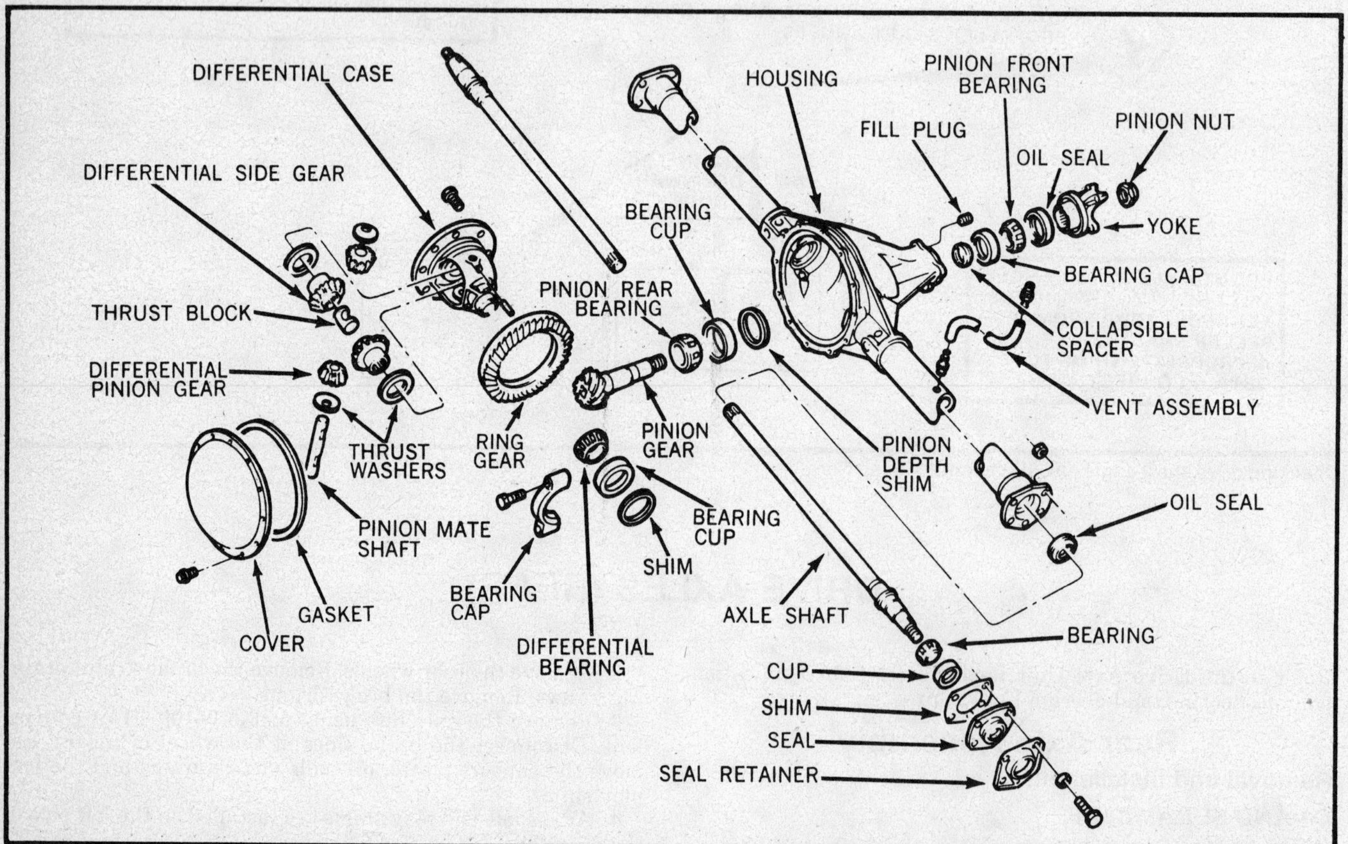

Tapered shaft axle assembly—CJ model (© Jeep Corp)

9. Installation is the reverse of removal. Observe the following torques:
   a. U-joint strap bolts: 170 in. lb.
   b. Shock absorber-to-axle: 44 ft. lb.
   c. Spring-to-axle U-bolts: 52 ft. lb.
10. Bleed the brakes. Road test the truck.

Axle Shaft

CJ AND SCRAMBLER

Removal and Installation

1. Remove the cotter pins from the axle shaft nuts. Remove the axle shaft nuts. Raise the vehicle and support it safely.
2. Remove the rear wheels. Remove the brake drum retaining screws. Remove the brake drums.
3. Remove the axle hub using tool J–25109–01 or equivalent. Disconnect the brake lines at the wheel cylinders. Remove the support plates, oil seals and retainers and the end play shims.
4. Axle shaft end play shims are installed on the left side of the axle only.
5. Remove the axle shafts using tool J–2498 or equivalent.
6. Installation is the reverse of the removal procedure.

NOTE: On vehicles equipped with a Trac Loc differential, do not rotate the differential gears unless both axles are in position. If one shaft is removed and the other shaft rotated, the side gear splines will become misaligned and prevent installation of the replacement shaft.

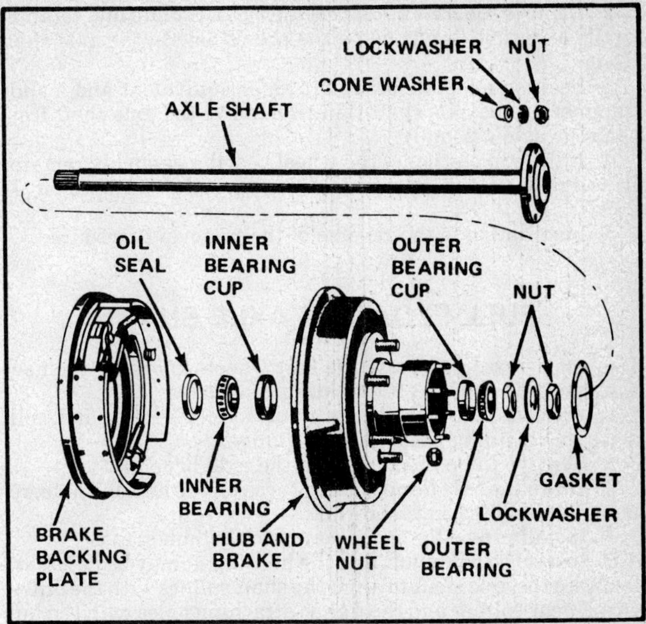

Axle shaft and wheel attaching parts—full floating axle (© Jeep Corp)

CHEROKEE, GRAND WAGONEER AND COMANCHE

Removal and Installation

1. Raise and support the vehicle safely. Remove the wheels. Remove the brake drum.

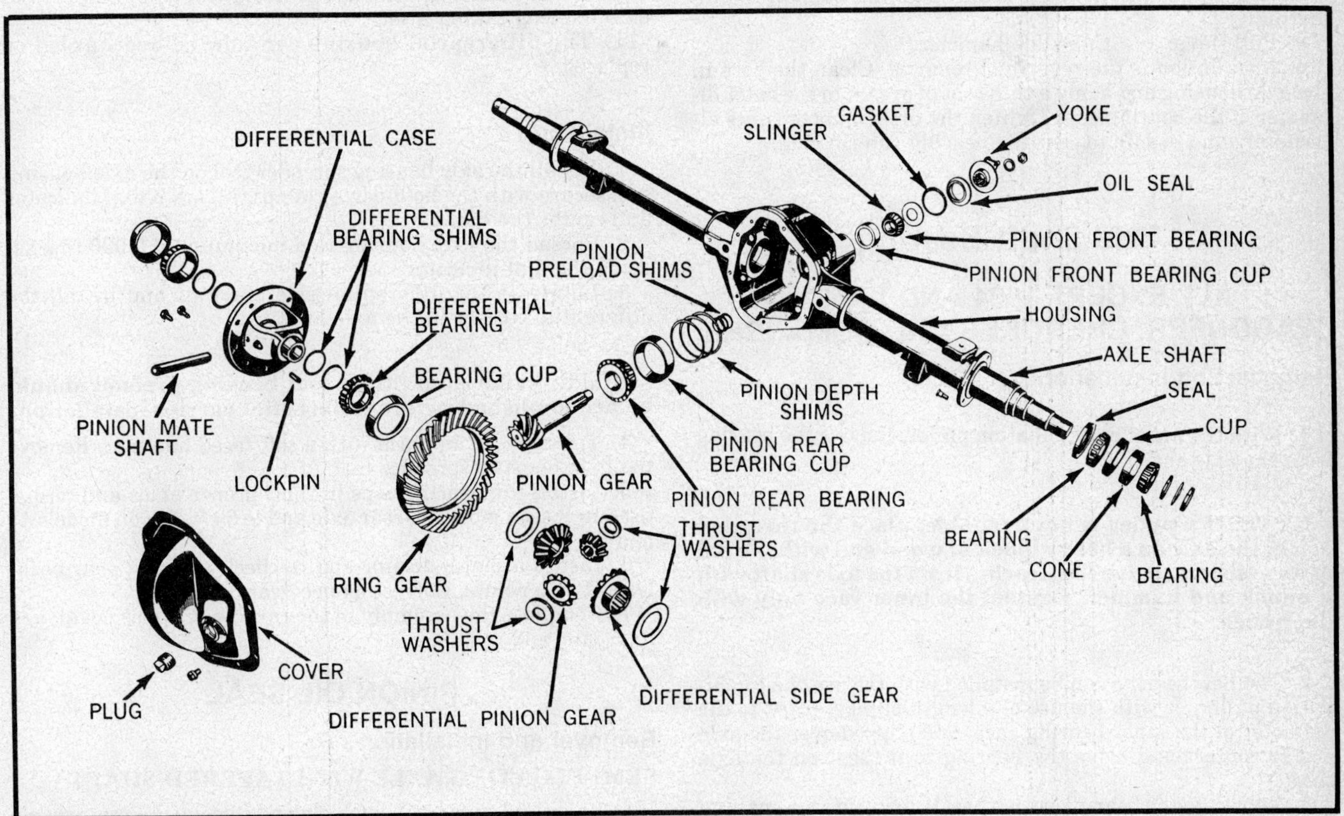

Full Floating rear axle assembly (© Jeep Corp)

2. Remove the nuts attaching the support plate and retainer to the axle tube flange using the access hole in the axle shaft flange.

3. Position adapter tool J-21579, or equivalent and a slide hammer on the axle shaft flange. Remove the axle shaft from the rear axle assembly.

4. If the cup portion of the wheel bearing assembly remains in the axle assembly, remove it using tool J-2619-01 or J-26941.

5. Installation is the reverse of the removal procedure.

FULL FLOATING AXLE SHAFT

It is not necessary to raise the rear wheels in order to remove the rear axle shaft on full-floating rear axles.

1. Remove the axle flange nuts, lock washers, and split washers retaining the axle shaft flange.
2. Remove the axle shaft from the axle housing.
3. Clean the axle flange mating area on the hub and axle, removing all old gasket material.
4. Install a new flange gasket onto the hub studs.
5. Insert the axle shaft into the housing. It may be necessary to rotate the axle shaft to align the shaft splines with the differential gear splines and the flange attaching holes with the hub studs.
6. Install the split washers, lockwashers, and flange nuts. Tighten the nuts securely.

1984 AND LATER WAGONEER, CHEROKEE AND COMANCHE

Removal and Installation

1. Raise and support the vehicle safely.
2. Remove the wheel, brake drum and brake support retaining nuts.
3. Pull the axle with a slide hammer.
4. Installation is the reverse of removal. Clean the bore in the axle housing and apply a thin coat of grease to the outer diameter of the bearing cup. Tighten the brake support nuts alternately and evenly to seat the bearing cup rib ring.

Axle Shaft Bearing

ALL EXCEPT 1984 AND LATER WAGONEER, CHEROKEE AND COMANCHE

Removal and Installation

1. With the aid of a combination puller, remove the bearing from the axle shaft.

NOTE: If a puller is not available, place the threaded end of the axle on a heavy block of wood and with the aid of an assistant, drive the bearing from the axle shaft with a punch and hammer. Contact the inner race only with the punch.

2. The new bearing can be installed with the use of a combination puller, or with the use of a length of pipe, fitted to the diameter of the inner bearing race, and slipped over the axle end to contact and drive the bearing to its seat on the axle shaft.
3. Lubricate the bearing with wheel bearing grease, making sure the grease fills the cavities between the bearing rollers.

1984 AND LATER WAGONEER, CHEROKEE AND COMANCHE

Removal and Installation

1. Position the axle shaft in a vise.
2. Remove the retaining ring by drilling a ¼ in. hole about ¾ of the way through the ring, then using a cold chisel over the hole, split the ring.
3. Remove the bearing with an arbor press, discard the seal and remove the retainer plate.
4. Installation is the reverse of removal. The new bearing must be pressed on. Make sure it is squarely seated.

Differential Assembly

Removal

1. Raise the vehicle and support safely. Remove the wheels, drums and axle shafts.
2. Drain the axle housing lubricant and remove the axle housing cover.
3. Mark the differential bearing caps for alignment during the assembly.
4. Loosen the bearing cap bolts, but do not remove.
5. Install an axle housing spreader tool on the axle housing and secure with the hold-down clamps.
6. Mount a dial indicator on the axle housing to measure the amount of spread. Zero the indicator dial.
7. Spread the axle housing no more than 0.020 in..
8. Remove the differential bearing caps and the dial indicator from the housing.
9. Using two pry bars, remove the differential carrier from the axle housing.
10. Remove the spreader tool from the housing as soon as the differential carrier is removed to avoid the possibility of the axle housing taking a set.
11. The differential housing can now be overhauled or replaced.

Installation

1. Install the axle housing spreader tool on the axle housing and secure with the hold-down clamps. Install a dial indicator and center the dial.
2. Spread the axle housing to a maximum of 0.020 in.. Remove the dial indicator.
3. Lubricate the differential side bearings and install the differential carrier in the axle housing.

NOTE: Prior shim fitting and bearing preload should be accomplished before differential carrier installation.

4. Tap the unit in place with a soft faced hammer. Remove the axle housing spreader tool.
5. Install the bearing caps in their proper place and torque to 40 ft. lbs. on model 30 rear axle and to 80 ft. lbs. on models 44 and 60.
6. Install a dial indicator and re-check the ring gear backlash at two points. Correct as necessary.
7. Complete the assembly in the reverse of the removal, add lubricant and road test.

PINION OIL SEAL

Removal and Installation

SEMI-FLOATING AXLE WITH TAPERED SHAFT

1. Raise and support the vehicle and remove the rear wheels and brake drums.

2. Mark the driveshaft and yoke for reassembly and disconnect the driveshaft from the rear yoke.
3. With a socket on the pinion nut and an in. lb. torque wrench, rotate the drive pinion several revolutions. Check and record the torque required to turn the drive pinion.
4. Remove the pinion nut. Use a flange holding tool to hold the flange while removing the pinion nut. Discard the pinion nut.
5. Mark the yoke and the drive pinion shaft for reassembly reference.
6. Remove the rear yoke with a puller.
7. Inspect the seal surface of the yoke and replace it with a new one if the seal surface is pitted, grooved, or otherwise damaged.
8. Remove the pinion oil seal.
9. Before installing the new seal, coat the lip of the seal with rear axle lubricant.
10. Install the seal, driving it into place with the proper driving tool.
11. Install the yoke on the pinion shaft. Align the marks made on the pinion shaft and yoke during disassembly.
12. Install a new pinion nut. Tighten nut until end-play is removed from the pinion bearing. Do not overtighten.
13. Check the torque required to turn the drive pinion. The pinion must be turned several revolutions to obatin an accurate reading.
14. Tighten the pinion nut to obtain the torque reading observed during disassembly (Step 3) plus 5 inch lbs. Tighten the nut minutely each time, to avoid overtightening. Do not loosen and then retighten the nut.

NOTE: If the desired torque is exceeded, a new collapsible pinion spacer sleeve must be installed and the pinion gear preload reset. Refer to the Unit Repair section and Overhaul procedures for this operation.

15. Install the driveshaft, aligning the index marks made during disassembly. Install the rear brake drums and wheels.

SEMI-FLOATING AND FULL-FLOATING AXLES WITH FLANGE SHAFT

1. Raise and support the vehicle.
2. Mark the driveshaft and yoke for reference during assembly and disconnect the driveshaft at the yoke.
3. Remove the pinion shaft nut and washer.
4. Remove the yoke from the pinion shaft, using a puller.
5. Remove the pinion shaft oil seal.
6. Install the new seal with a suitable driver.
7. Install the pinion shaft washer and nut. Tighten the nut to 210 ft. lbs. on the semi-floating axles and 260 ft. lbs. on the full-floating axles.
8. Align the index marks on the driveshaft and yoke and install the driveshaft. Tighten the attaching bolts or nuts to 16 ft. lbs.
9. Remove the supports and lower the vehicle.

WHEEL BEARING

Adjustment

FULL FLOATING AXLE

1. Raise the vehicle so that the wheel can be rotated. Support the vehicle safely.
2. Remove the axle shaft.
3. Straighten the lip of the lockwasher and remove the lockwasher and lock nut.
4. Tighten the adjusting nut and rotate the wheel until binding exists. Back off the adjusting nut $\frac{1}{6}$ turn until the wheel rotates freely without any lateral shake.
5. Replace the lockwasher and tighten the lock nut, bending the lip of the lockwasher over the lock nut.
6. Install the axle with a new gasket and tighten the axle nuts securely.

REAR SUSPENSION

Spring

Removal and Installation

MOUNTED BELOW THE AXLE

1. Raise the vehicle and support the axle.
2. Disconnect the shock absorber and stabilizer bar, if so equipped.
3. Remove the U-bolts and tie plates.
4. Disconnect the front and rear ends of the spring and remove the spring.
5. The spring can be disassembled by removing the spring rebound clips and the center bolt.
6. Installation is the reverse of the removal procedure.

MOUNTED ABOVE THE AXLE

1. Raise the vehicle and support the frame ahead of the axle.
2. If the left side spring is being removed, remove the fuel tank skid plate.
3. Remove the wheel.
4. Disconnect the shock absorber.
5. Remove the tie plate U-bolts and the tie plate. Remove the bolt attaching the spring rear eye to the spring shackle.
6. Remove the bolt attaching the spring front eye to the spring hanger on the frame rail.
7. Remove the spring from the vehicle.
8. Installation is the reverse of the removal procedure.

1984 AND LATER WAGONEER, CHEROKEE AND COMANCHE

1. Raise and support the vehicle safely.
2. Raise the axle assembly to relieve the weight.
3. Remove the wheel. Remove the shock absorber at the axle.
4. If equipped, disconnect the stabilizer bar links and the spring tie plate.
5. Remove the spring tie plate U-bolt and the spring tie plate. Remove the rear eye to spring shackle bolt and the front eye to bracket bolt.
6. Lower the spring from the vehicle.
7. Installation is the reverse of the removal procedure.

Shock Absorber

Removal and Installation

1. Raise the vehicle for working clearance and support safely.
2. Place a jack under the axle assembly and raise to relieve the springs of axle weight and to place the shock absorber in its mid stroke.
3. Remove the retaining nuts or bolts and remove the shock absorber from the vehicle.
4. Install the new shock absorber and tighten the attaching nuts or bolts.
5. Lower the vehicle to the ground.

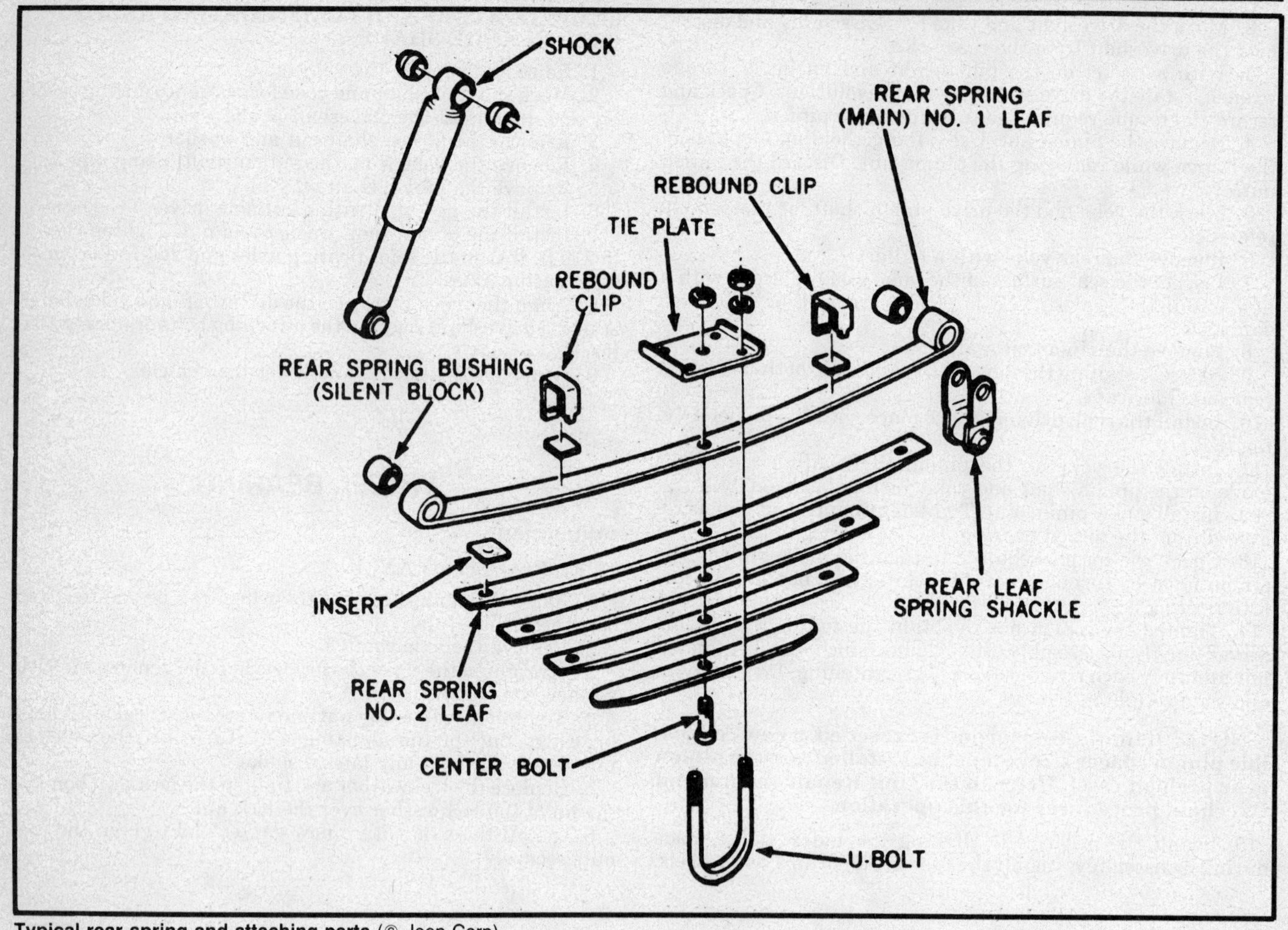

Typical rear spring and attaching parts (© Jeep Corp)

INDEX

BEFORE SERVICING, SEE THE SAFETY NOTICE AT THE FRONT OF THE BOOK

MACK

NOTE: The procedures in this section can be applied to the Mack Mid–Liner, however any special Mid–Liner procedure will be covered separately in this section and will be listed under Mid–Liner.

GENERAL ENGINE AND TUNE-UP SPECIFICATIONS

Engine Model	Bore × Stroke (inches)	Piston Displ. Cu. In.	Horsepower @ rpm	Torque @ rpm	Firing Order	Governor Speed No Load	Idle Speed rpm	Injection Pump Timing (deg.)
E6-315	4.875 × 6.0	672	315 @ 1900	1050 @ 1450	1-5-3-6-2-4	2225②	①	25°B
EC6-330	4.875 × 6.0	672	330 @ 1950	1065 @ 1400	1-5-3-6-2-4	2150	525–575	16°B
E6-350	4.875 × 6.0	672	350 @ 1950	1132 @ 1400	1-5-3-6-2-4	2150	525–575	22°–23°B
ENDT(B)865	5.25 × 5.0	866	322 @ 2400	1100 @ 1350	1-5-4-8-6-3-7-2	2650	600–650	25°B
ENDT(B)866	5.25 × 5.0	866	375 @ 2200	1040 @ 1600	1-5-4-8-6-3-7-2	2500	600–650	25°B
EM9-400	5.375 × 5.50	998	392 @ 2100	1520 @ 1230	1-5-4-8-6-3-7-2	2420	600–650	17°B
EM9-400R	5.375 × 5.50	998	400 @ 1700	1520 @ 1230	1-5-4-8-6-3-7-2	1970	600–650	17°B
EMC9-400	5.375 × 5.50	998	392 @ 2100	1520 @ 1230	1-5-4-8-6-3-7-2	2420	600–650	13°B
EMC9-400R	5.375 × 5.50	998	400 @ 1700	1520 @ 1230	1-5-4-8-6-3-7-2	1970	600–650	13°B
EM6-225	4.875 × 6.0	672	225 @ 2100	844 @ 1260	1-5-3-6-2-4	2325	525–575	25°B
EM6-250R	4.875 × 6.0	672	250 @ 1700	940 @ 1260	1-5-3-6-2-4	1950	600–650	④
EM6-275	4.875 × 6.0	672	275 @ 2100	1038 @ 1260	1-5-3-6-2-4	2315	525–575	25°B
EM6-275L	4.875 × 6.0	672	275 @ 1700	1275 @ 1020	1-5-3-6-2-4	1900	525–575	22°B
EM6-275R	4.875 × 6.0	672	275 @ 1605	1038 @ 1260	1-5-3-6-2-4	1790	525–575	23°B
EMC6-285	4.875 × 6.0	672	283 @ 2100	1080 @ 1200	1-5-3-6-2-4	2290	525–575	14°B
EMC6-285R	4.875 × 6.0	672	285 @ 2100	1080 @ 1200	1-5-3-6-2-4	2050	525–575	14°B
EM6-300	4.875 × 6.0	672	300 @ 2100	1125 @ 1260	1-5-3-6-2-4	2330	525–575	24°B
EM6-300R	4.875 × 6.0	672	300 @ 1700	1125 @ 1260	1-5-3-6-2-4	2150	525–575	24°B
ER-315R	4.875 × 6.0	672	315 @ 1800	1050 @ 1405	1-5-3-6-2-4	2225	600–650	25°B
ER-325	4.875 × 6.0	672	325 @ 1950	1050 @ 1400	1-5-3-6-2-4	2150	525–575	24°B
ER-325R	4.875 × 6.0	672	325 @ 1950	1050 @ 1400	1-5-3-6-2-4	2030	525–575	24°B
E6-350R	4.875 × 6.0	672	350 @ 1800	1131 @ 1400	1-5-3-6-2-4	2050	525–575	22°–23°B
EC6-350	4.875 × 6.0	672	350 @ 1950	1131 @ 1400	1-5-3-6-2-4	2200	525–575	17°B
EM9-400R	5.375 × 5.50	998	400 @ 1900	1520 @ 1530	1-5-4-8-6-3-7-2	2175	600–650	—
EMC9-400R	5.375 × 5.50	998	400 @ 1900	1520 @ 1230	1-5-4-8-6-3-7-2	2175	600–650	—
E9-440	5.375 × 5.50	998	440 @ 1800	1495 @ 1350	1-5-4-8-6-3-7-2	2100	600–650	—
06.20.30J⑤	4.724 × 5.1	538	210 @ 2400	516 @ 1500	1-5-3-6-2-4	2690	600	19°B⑥
06.20.30K⑤	4.724 × 5.1	538	210 @ 2300	516 @ 1500	1-5-3-6-2-4	2620	600	19°B⑥
06.02.12A⑤	4.016 × 4.5	335	175 @ 2800	376 @ 1800	1-5-3-6-2-4	3130	600	20°B⑥
06.02.12B⑤	4.016 × 4.5	335	175 @ 2800	376 @ 1800	1-5-3-6-2-4	3130	600	21°B⑥
06.02.12C⑤	4.016 × 4.5	335	175 @ 2800	376 @ 1800	1-5-3-6-2-4	2980	600	21°B⑥
06.02.12E⑤	4.016 × 4.5	335	164 @ 2800	358 @ 1800	1-5-3-6-2-4	3130	600	16°B⑥

NOTE: The line setting ticket often reflects specification changes made in production, the specifications on the line ticket must be used if they disagree with the specifications in this chart. All rpm specifications on the Mack Mid-Liner are ±30 rpm.

① American Bosch pump-525–575 rpm
Robert Bosch pump-600–650 rpm
② American Bosch pump-2100 rpm
③ United Technologies Diesel Systems pump-21°B
Robert Bosch pump-20°B
④ United Technologies Diesel Systems pump-22°B
Robert Bosch-25°B
B-Before top dead center
⑤ Mid-Liner
⑥ ±30 inches before top dead center

TRUCK MODELS AND ENGINE APPLICATION

Series	Diesel Engine HP Rating
R SERIES	
R487P, R492P	190–210
R487T, R492T	190–210
R600T Models	180–285
R700T Models	325–375
R600ST Models	237–285
R700ST Models	290–325
R700S Models	325–375
R400P	175–210
R600T	200–285
R600ST	237–350
R700S	290–350
R700ST	270–435
RM SERIES	
RM4874X	210
RM6004X	237-350
RM6006X	237-350
RM6006SX	285-350
RM4874X Models	190
RM6004X Models	180–285
RM6006S Models	237-285
RM6006SX Models	237-285
RL & RS SERIES (Mack Western)	
RL & RS400L Models	195–225
RL & RS600L Models	237-304
RL & RS700L Models	237-304
RL & RS700LT Models	237-304
RL & RS400LS, RL & RS600LS Models	195-304
RL & RS700LS Models	237-375
RL & RS700LST Models	237-375
RL & RS400LS Mixer Chassis	195–225
RL 685LS Mixer Chassis	237
RL600LS	237-315
RL & RS600L	237-335
RL & RS600LS	237-335
RWL & RWS700L	237-525
RWL & RWS700LS	237-525
U SERIES	
U487T, U492T	190–210
U600T Models	237-285
U600ST Models	237-285
U700ST	325-375
U600T	200–350
U600TS	237-350
U700ST	250-435
DM & DMM SERIES (Dump-Mixer)	
DM487S, DM492S	190–210
DM607X	180
DM600S Models	180–285
DM600SX Models	180–285
DMM6006S	237-285

TRUCK MODELS AND ENGINE APPLICATION

Series	Diesel Engine HP Rating
DM & DMM SERIES (Dump-Mixer)	
DMM6006SX	237–285
DM800ST Models	325–400
DM800SX Models	237–400
DM400S	210
DM625X	237–350
DM600S	200–350
DM600SX	237–350
DM800SX	237–450
DM800ST	350–450
DM600S	237–350
DMM6006S	237–350
DMM6006SX	237–350
HMM SERIES	
HMM6856S	237
MB SERIES	
MB487P, MB492P	175–210
MB487T, MB492T	175–210
MB600T Models	180–210
MB487S, BM492S	180–240
MB600S Models	180–240
MC & MR SERIES	
MC400P	175–210
MC400S	210
MC600P	200–285
MC600S	200–285
MR400P	175–210
MR400S	210
MR600P	200–285
MR600S	200–285
F SERIES	
F700T Models	237–350
F700ST Models	260–290
F700T	237–350
F700ST	237–435
FL & FS SERIES (Mack Western)	
FL & FS700L Models	237–425
FL & FS700LT Models	237–425
FL & FS700LS Models	237–375
FL & FS700LST Models	237–375
MS SERIES	
MS200P	175–210
MS300P	210
MS300T	210
WL & WS SERIES	
WL & WS700L (regular cab)	237–525
WL & WS700LS (sleeper cab)	237–525
Wl & WS700L (sleeper cab)	237–450
WL & WS700LS (regular cab)	237–450
WL & WS700LS (sleeper cab)	237–450

WHEEL ALIGNMENT SPECIFICATIONS

Toe-in setting for Mack FA300 through FA1000 series axles—1/16 to 3/16 inch
Toe-in setting for Rockwell-standard axles—0 to 1/8 inch
All settings are for empty vehicle
Axle model number is located at right front, between spring pad and knuckle

Front Axle Model FA-	Caster, Degrees		Camber Degrees	Kingpin Angle Degrees
	Manual Steering	Power Steering		
"CF" MODELS				
FW537C,D	1 to 3	Ross 1–3	½ to 1	7
FW537C,D	1 to 3	Sheppard 4–6	½ to 1	7
616C,D	1 to 3	4 to 6	½ to 1	5½
W616D	1 to 3	4 to 6	½ to 1	5½
"DM" MODELS				
532	1 to 3	4 to 6	½ to 1	7
W532	1 to 3	4 to 6	½ to 1	7
5321	1 to 3	4 to 6	½ to 1	7
534	1 to 3	4 to 6	½ to 1	8
5341	1 to 3	4 to 6	½ to 1	8
535	1 to 3	4 to 6	½ to 1	7
5351	1 to 3	4 to 6	½ to 1	7
W536	1 to 3	4 to 6	½ to 1	7
W537	1 to 3	4 to 6	½ to 1	7
600	1 to 3	4 to 6	½ to 1	3½
601	1 to 3	4 to 6	½ to 1	3½
6001	1 to 3	4 to 6	½ to 1	3½
6011	1 to 3	4 to 6	½ to 1	3½
604	1 to 3	4 to 6	½ to 1	5½
6041	1 to 3	4 to 6	½ to 1	5½
6042	1 to 3	4 to 6	½ to 1	5½
6043	1 to 3	4 to 6	½ to 1	5½
S605	—	7 to 9	0 to ⅛	0
612	1 to 3	4 to 6	½ to 1	3½
W612	1 to 3	4 to 6	½ to 1	3½
701	1 to 3	4 to 6	½ to 1	3½
702	1 to 3	4 to 6	½ to 1	3½
703	1 to 3	4 to 6	½ to 1	3½
W538C	1 to 3	4 to 6	½ to 1	7
616D	1 to 3	4 to 6	½ to 1	5½
W616D	1 to 3	4 to 6	½ to 1	5½
617D	1 to 3	4 to 6	½ to 1	5½
W617D	1 to 3	4 to 6	½ to 1	5½
618W	1 to 3	4 to 6	Left ¼ to ¾ Right – ¼ to + ¼	LH 5¾ RH 6¼
W618W	1 to 3	4 to 6	Left ¼ to ¾ Right – ¼ to + ¼	LH 5¾ RH6¼
619W	1 to 3	4 to 6	Left ¼ to ¾ Right – ¼ to + ¼	LH 5¾ RH 6¼

Front Axle Model FA-	Caster, Degrees		Camber Degrees	Kingpin Angle Degrees
	Manual Steering	Power Steering		
"DM" MODELS				
W619W	1 to 3	4 to 6	Left ¼ to ¾ Right – ¼ to + ¼	LH 5¾ RH 6¼
"DML" AND "DMM" MODELS				
616C,D	1 to 3	4 to 6	½ to 1	5½
617C	1 to 3	4 to 6	½ to 1	5½
W617C	1 to 3	4 to 6	½ to 1	5½
703C	1 to 3	4 to 6	½ to 1	3½
"F" MODELS				
511	0 to 2	4 to 6	½ to 1	8
5111	0 to 2	4 to 6	½ to 1	8
512	0 to 2	4 to 6	½ to 1	7
514	0 to 2	4 to 6	½ to 1	7
5141	0 to 2	4 to 6	½ to 1	7
532	1 to 3	4 to 6	½ to 1	7
L532	1 to 3	4 to 6	½ to 1	7
W532	1 to 3	4 to 6	½ to 1	7
5321	1 to 3	4 to 6	½ to 1	7
534	1 to 3	4 to 6	½ to 1	8
5341	1 to 3	4 to 6	½ to 1	8
535	1 to 3	4 to 6	½ to 1	7
L535	1 to 3	4 to 6	½ to 1	7
5351	1 to 3	4 to 6	½ to 1	7
W536	1 to 3	4 to 6	½ to 1	7
W537	1 to 3	4 to 6	½ to 1	7
703	1 to 3	4 to 6	½ to 1	3½
705	1 to 3	4 to 6	½ to 1	3½
604	1 to 3	4 to 6	½ to 1	5½
535N	1 to 3	4 to 6	½ to 1	7
W538C	1 to 3	4 to 6	½ to 1	7
616C,D	1 to 3	4 to 6	½ to 1	5½
W616D	1 to 3	4 to 6	½ to 1	5½
W619W	1 to 3	4 to 6	Left ¼ to ¾ Right – ¼ to + ¼	LH 5¾ RH 6¼
"FL" AND "FS" MODELS				
FF931	—	Ross 2	—	5¾
FL931	—	Ross 2	—	LH 5¾ RH 6¼
W536,W537	—	Ross 3	½ to 1	7

WHEEL ALIGNMENT SPECIFICATIONS

Toe-in setting for Mack FA300 through FA1000 series axles—1⁄16 to 3⁄16 inch
Toe-in setting for Rockwell-standard axles—0 to 1⁄8 inch
All settings are for empty vehicle
Axle model number is located at right front, between spring pad and knuckle

Front Axle Model FA-	Caster, Degrees Manual Steering	Caster, Degrees Power Steering	Camber Degrees	Kingpin Angle Degrees
"FM" MODELS				
W538C	1 to 3	4 to 6	½ to 1	7
616C,D	1 to 3	4 to 6	½ to 1	5½
"MB" MODELS				
511	0 to 2	4 to 6	½ to 1	8
514	0 to 2	4 to 6	½ to 1	7
532	1 to 3	4 to 6	½ to 1	7
W532	1 to 3	4 to 6	½ to 1	7
5321	1 to 3	4 to 6	½ to 1	7
5341	1 to 3	4 to 6	½ to 1	8
534	1 to 3	4 to 6	½ to 1	8
535	1 to 3	4 to 6	½ to 1	7
W536	1 to 3	4 to 6	½ to 1	7
W537	1 to 3	4 to 6	½ to 1	7
604	1 to 3	4 to 6	½ to 1	5½
W612	1 to 3	4 to 6	½ to 1	3½
FW537C,D	1 to 3	Ross 1 to 3	½ to 1	7
FW537C,D	1 to 3	Sheppard 4 to 6	½ to 1	7
616C,D	1 to 3	4 to 6	½ to 1	5½
W616D	1 to 3	4 to 6	½ to 1	5½
W619W	1 to 3	4 to 6	Left ¼ to ¾ Right − ¼ to + ¼	LH 5¾ RH 6¼
"MC" and "MR" MODELS				
W536C,D,N, W	1 to 3	4 to 6	½ to 1	7
FW537C,D	1 to 3	Ross 1 to 3	½ to 1	7
FW537C,D	1 to 3	Sheppard 4 to 6	½ to 1	7
W537C,D,N, W	1 to 3	4 to 6	½ to 1	7
616C,D	1 to 3	4 to 6	½ to 1	5½
W616D	1 to 3	4 to 6	½ to 1	5½
617C,D	1 to 3	4 to 6	½ to 1	5½
W617C,D	1 to 3	4 to 6	½ to 1	5½
"MCE" AND "MRE" MODELS				
W537C,D,N, W	1 to 3	4 to 6	½ to 1	7
W538C	1 to 3	4 to 6	½ to 1	7
616C,D	1 to 3	4 to 6	½ to 1	5½

Front Axle Model FA-	Caster, Degrees Manual Steering	Caster, Degrees Power Steering	Camber Degrees	Kingpin Angle Degrees
"MCE" AND "MRE" MODELS				
W617C,D	1 to 3	4 to 6	½ to 1	5½
"R" AND "U" MODELS				
511	0 to 2	4 to 6	½ to 1	8
5111	0 to 2	4 to 6	½ to 1	8
512	0 to 2	4 to 6	½ to 1	7
514	0 to 2	4 to 6	½ to 1	7
5141	0 to 2	4 to 6	½ to 1	7
532	1 to 3	4 to 6	½ to 1	7
L532	1 to 3	4 to 6	½ to 1	7
5321	1 to 3	4 to 6	½ to 1	7
534	1 to 3	4 to 6	½ to 1	8
5341	1 to 3	4 to 6	½ to 1	8
535	1 to 3	4 to 6	½ to 1	7
L535	1 to 3	4 to 6	½ to 1	7
5351	1 to 3	4 to 6	½ to 1	7
W532	1 to 3	4 to 6	½ to 1	7
W536	1 to 3	4 to 6	½ to 1	7
W537	1 to 3	4 to 6	½ to 1	7
601	1 to 3	4 to 6	½ to 1	3½
6011	1 to 3	4 to 6	½ to 1	3½
604	1 to 3	4 to 6	½ to 1	5½
612	1 to 3	4 to 6	½ to 1	3½
W612	1 to 3	4 to 6	½ to 1	3½
616C,D	1 to 3	4 to 6	½ to 1	5½
W616D	1 to 3	4 to 6	½ to 1	5½
W617C,D	1 to 3	4 to 6	½ to 1	5½
"RL", and "RM" and "RS" MODELS				
511	0 to 2	4 to 6	½ to 1	8
5111	0 to 2	4 to 6	½ to 1	8
514	0 to 2	4 to 6	½ to 1	7
5141	0 to 2	4 to 6	½ to 1	7
532	1 to 3	4 to 6	½ to 1	7
L532	1 to 3	4 to 6	½ to 1	7
5321	1 to 3	4 to 6	½ to 1	7
534	1 to 3	4 to 6	½ to 1	8
5341	1 to 3	4 to 6	½ to 1	8
535	1 to 3	4 to 6	½ to 1	7
L535	1 to 3	4 to 6	½ to 1	7

WHEEL ALIGNMENT SPECIFICATIONS

Front Axle Model FA-	Caster, Degrees Manual Steering	Caster, Degrees Power Steering	Camber Degrees	Kingpin Angle Degrees
	"RL", and "RM" and "RS" MODELS			
535N	1 to 3	4 to 6	½ to 1	7
5351	1 to 3	4 to 6	½ to 1	7
600	1 to 3	4 to 6	½ to 1	3½
6001	1 to 3	4 to 6	½ to 1	3½
W536C,D,N, W	1 to 3	4 to 6	½ to 1	7
W537C,D,N, W	1 to 3	4 to 6	½ to 1	7
616C,D	1 to 3	4 to 6	½ to 1	5½
W617C,D	1 to 3	4 to 6	½ to 1	5½
703C	1 to 3	4 to 6	½ to 1	3½
FF931	1 to 3	—	—	5¾
FA618	—	Ross 3	—	LH 5¾ RH 6¼

Front Axle Model FA-	Caster, Degrees Manual Steering	Caster, Degrees Power Steering	Camber Degrees	Kingpin Angle Degrees
	"RL", and "RM" and "RS" MODELS			
FA618	—	Garrison 6	—	LH 5¾ RH 6¼
W536, W537	3	Garrison 6	½ to 1	7
	"WL" AND "WS" MODELS			
FF931	3	—	—	5¾
FF931	—	Sheppard 5	—	5¾
FF931	—	Ross 3	—	5¾
FAW618	—	Sheppard 5	—	LH 5¾ RH 6¼
W536, W537	—	Ross 2	½ to 1	7
W536, W537	—	Sheppard 5	½ to 1	7

MINIMUM COMPRESSION PRESSURE PSI

Engine Series	Altitude Feet 0	2,000	4,000	6,000	8,000	10,000	12,000	14,000
Non-turbocharged six cylinder	530	500	460	430	390	360	340	310
Turbocharged/charged air cooling six cylinder	475	445	415	385	355	325	295	275
V8—866 cu. in. 14.95:1①	485	455	425	385	355	335	305	285
V8—866 cu. in. 15.7:1①	540	410	480	440	410	380	350	330
V8—400 series②	585	555	525	495	465	435	405	375

①Compression ratio ②998 Cubic inches

TORQUE SPECIFICATIONS
Mack Mid-Liner

(All specifications in ft. lb.)

Engine	Cylinder Head Bolts	Connecting Rod Bearing Bolts	Main Bearing Bolts	Crank Pulley Bolt	Flywheel Bolts	Manifold Intake	Manifold Exhaust
06.20.30J	133①	155	243	81②	126	35	44
06.20.30K	133①	155	243	81②	125	35	44
06.02.12A	129–136③	74–81	118–133	83–94	148	31–35	31–35
06.02.12B	129–136③	74–81	118–133	83–94	148	31–35	31–35
06.02.12C	129–136③	74–81	118–133	83–94	148	31–35	31–35
06.02.12E	129–136③	74–81	118–133	83–94	148	31–35	31–35

① 14mm cylinder head bolts 133 ft. lbs.
18mm cylinder head bolts 266 ft. lbs.
② Class 100 81 ft. lbs.
Class 80 59 ft. lbs.
③ Cylinder head stud nuts

CHASSIS STANDARD TORQUE VALUES CHART

	National Fine (NF) Formerly SAE			NATIONAL COARSE (NC) Formerly USS		
Dia.	No. of Threads	Grade 5①	Grade 8②	No. of Threads	Grade 5①	Grade 8②
¼	28	7.5-8.5	—	20	7-7.5	—
5/16	24	15-17	—	18	14-15.5	—
⅜	24	28-31	—	16	25-28	—
7/16	20	45-50	—	14	40-44	—
½	20	69-76	138-152	13	61-68	122-136
9/16	18	99-103	196-216	12	96-108	192-212
⅝	18	134-148	268-296	11	122-135	244-270
¾	16	238-264	476-528	10	216-238	432-476
⅞	14	377-416	745-832	9	346-372	692-744
1	14	576-637	1152-1274	8	520-575	1040-1150
1⅛	12	820-905	1640-1810	7	735-815	1470-1630
1¼	12	1125-1245	2250-2490	7	1035-1140	2070-2280
1½	12	1990-2200	3980-4400	6	1800-2180	3600-4360

NOTE: This table is to be used only for those chassis nuts, bolts or screws where no special torque value is given.
① - Plated or lubricated with mixture of SAE 30 oil & white lead ② - Dry threads

NORMAL COMPRESSION SPECIFICATIONS

Engine Series	Normal Compression (psi)
END475	540
ENDT475	470
ET477	470
END(B)673E	530
ENDT(B)673	575
ENDT(B)673C	460
ET(B)673	460
ET(B)673E	460
ETY(B)673E	635
ETAY(B)673A	460
ETAZ(B)673	460
ETAZ(B)673A	460
ETAZ(B)673C	460
ENDT(B)675	460
ETY(B)675	585
ENDT(B)676	460
ETA(B)676B	460
ETAY(B)676	460
ETAY(B)676D	460
END707	530
END711	530

FRONT OF ENGINE

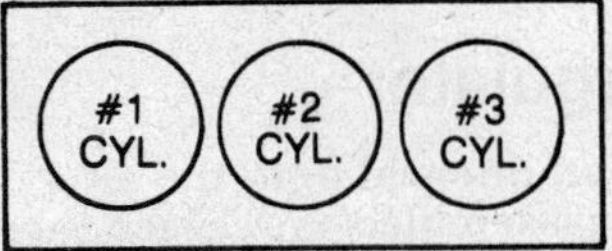

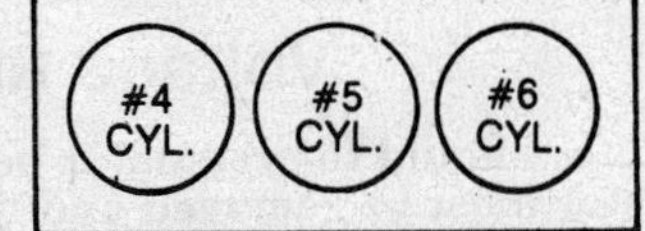

All 6 cylinder engines— 1, 5, 3, 6, 2, 4

VALVE CLEARANCE SPECIFICATIONS

Engine Series	Cold Static	
	Intake	Exhaust
END475	0.014	0.018
ENDT475	0.014	0.028
ET477	0.014	0.028
0.6.20.30J①	0.014	0.018
0.6.20.30K①	0.014	0.018
0.6.02.12A①	0.010	0.018
0.6.02.12B①	0.010	0.018
0.6.02.12C①	0.010	0.018
0.6.02.12E①	0.010	0.018
6-Cyl	0.016	0.024
All V8	0.016	0.026

① Mid-Liner

DIESEL FIRING ORDER

FRONT OF ENGINE

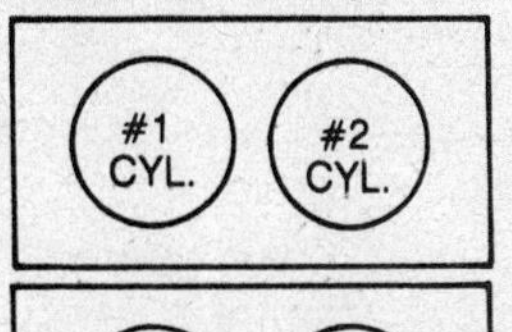

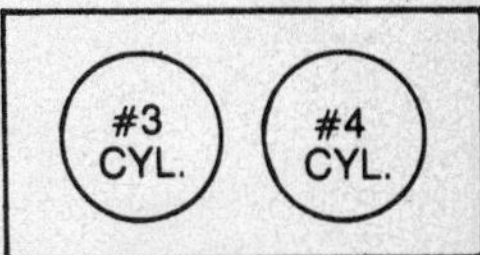

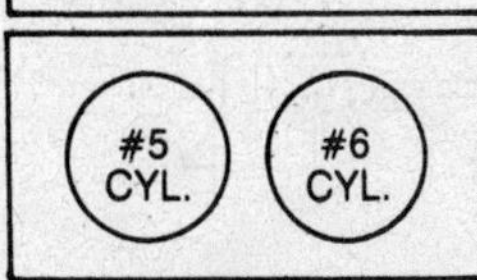

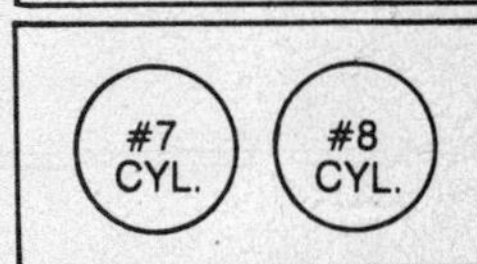

All V8 engines— 1, 5, 4, 8, 6, 3, 7, 2

ELECTRICAL SYSTEM

The electrical system is either a 12 or 24 volt system, usually using a positive ground. A negative ground may be used on some model applications. Both AC and DC type generators are used with the electrical output controlled by a standard or transistorized regulator.

CAUTION

Note the polarity of the battery and charging system before servicing.

Electrical Starting System

Removal

1. Remove the ground battery cable.
2. Remove the wires and cable from the starter terminals.
3. Remove the starter mounting bolts and remove the starter from the engine.

Installation

1. Place the starter in position on the engine and install the mounting bolts and tighten securely.
2. Install the cable and wires to the starter terminals.
3. Attach the ground battery cable to the battery post.

Air Starting System

The air starter motor is a five-vaned air motor with gear reduction which turns the engine through a conventional type Bendix drive. An air starting reservoir provides air for the cranking motor only. Connection is through a flexible hose with a quick acting valve to permit operation of the motor. Air pressure adjustment, delivered, is 95–120 psi., maximum. A check valve is attached to the reservoir.

Operation

1. Engine start button must be in starting or running position.
2. Disengage the clutch completely and press accelerator pedal half way down.
3. Push the air starter control lever ball down QUICKLY and release as soon as the engine fires.
4. Build up air to maximum pressure on regular air pressure gauge before shutting down and parking for the night.

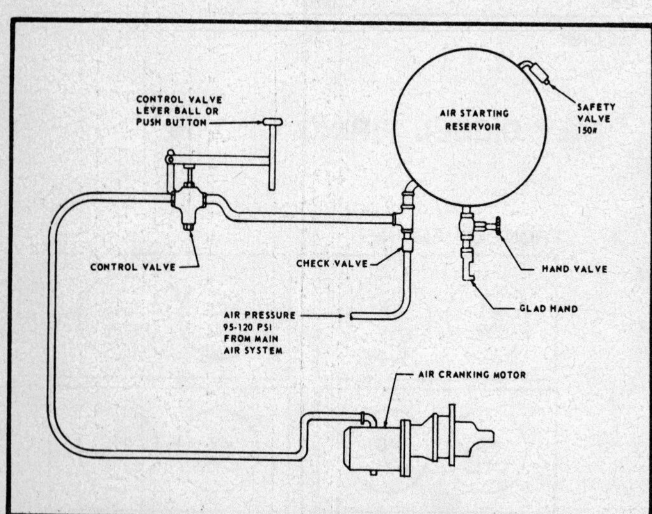

Typical air starting system (© Mack Trucks, Inc.)

Starter Motor

Removal

1. Drain air at reservoir.
2. Disconnect air line at cranking motor.
3. Remove cranking motor mounting bolts and disengage assembly from flywheel housing.

Installation

1. Position starter motor assembly to flywheel housing and install mounting bolts and nuts. Torque to 45–55 ft. lbs.
2. Connect air line to starter.
3. Charge system to maximum pressure and test.

Alternator

Removal

1. Remove the ground battery cable from the battery.
2. Disconnect and mark the wires, unless a quick disconnect connector is used.
3. Remove the braces and bolts from the alternator to the engine.
4. Loosen the adjusting strap and remove the drive belts.

CAUTION

When the alternator automatic adjuster is used without a stop nut on the adjusting link, the two adjusting nuts must be loosened before removing the capscrew that holds the top adjusting link to the alternator. The adjusting link will fly out with considerable force if this procedure is not followed.

5. Remove the bolt(s) from the mounting bracket and remove the alternator.

NOTE: On single bolt models, it may be necessary to remove the complete alternator mounting bracket to obtain clearance for the bolt removal.

Installation

1. Place the alternator on the mounting bracket and install the bolt(s) through the mounting bracket and alternator lugs.

NOTE: If the bracket was removed from the engine with the alternator attached, install the assembly.

2. Place the belts over the pulleys and connect the adjusting strap.
3. Install the braces and bolts, but do not tighten.
4. Adjust the belts to proper tension and tighten the adjusting strap bolts. Tighten the brace bolts and the alternator lug bolts.
5. If the automatic adjuster is used, adjust the length of the spring to 3.85 in. and then tighten the mounting bolts and the adjusting link screw. Belt tension should be 80 pounds.
6. Connect the wires to the alternator, as marked.
7. Reconnect the ground battery cable. (Refer to the Electrical Section for the overhaul of the electric starter and alternator).

Voltage Regulator

Note: Should the regulator be an integral unit, the alternator must be removed and disassembled to replace the regulator unit.

Removal

1. Remove the ground battery cable.
2. Disconnect the wire leads to the regulator and mark them for reinstallation.
3. Remove the capscrews holding the regulator to the firewall or the inner fender panel. Remove the regulator.

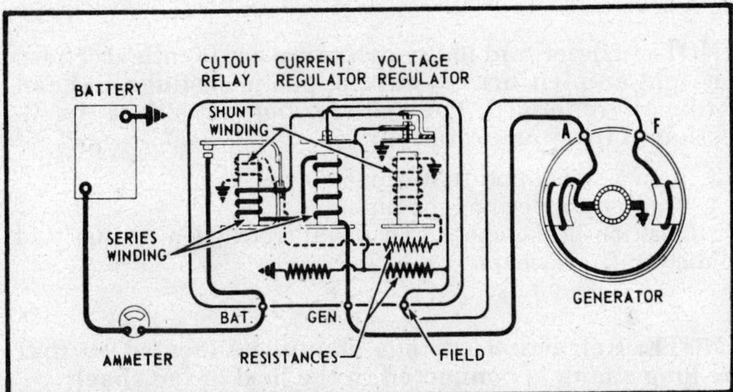

Typical 12 or 24 volt regulator wiring schematic (© Mack Trucks, Inc.)

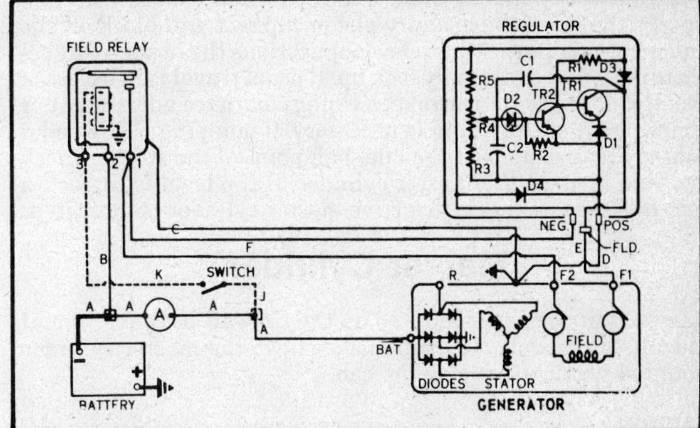

Typical wiring schematic—full transistorized regulator (© Mack Trucks, Inc.)

Installation

1. Install the regulator to the firewall or the inner fender panel with the capscrews.
2. Attach the wires to the terminals of the regulator.
3. Connect the ground battery cable to the battery post.
4. Start the engine and observe the charging rate.

BRAKE SYSTEM

The Mack truck brake system utilizes both drum and disc brakes, actuated by a vacuum assisted hydraulic system, an air assisted hydraulic system, or by an air only system.

The unit overhaul procedures are outlined in the General Brake section.

Vacuum–Hydraulic Brakes

Pedal effort is dependent on the maintenance of a proper fluid level in the master cylinder. This compensates for brake lining wear and also insures proper free play to allow complete return

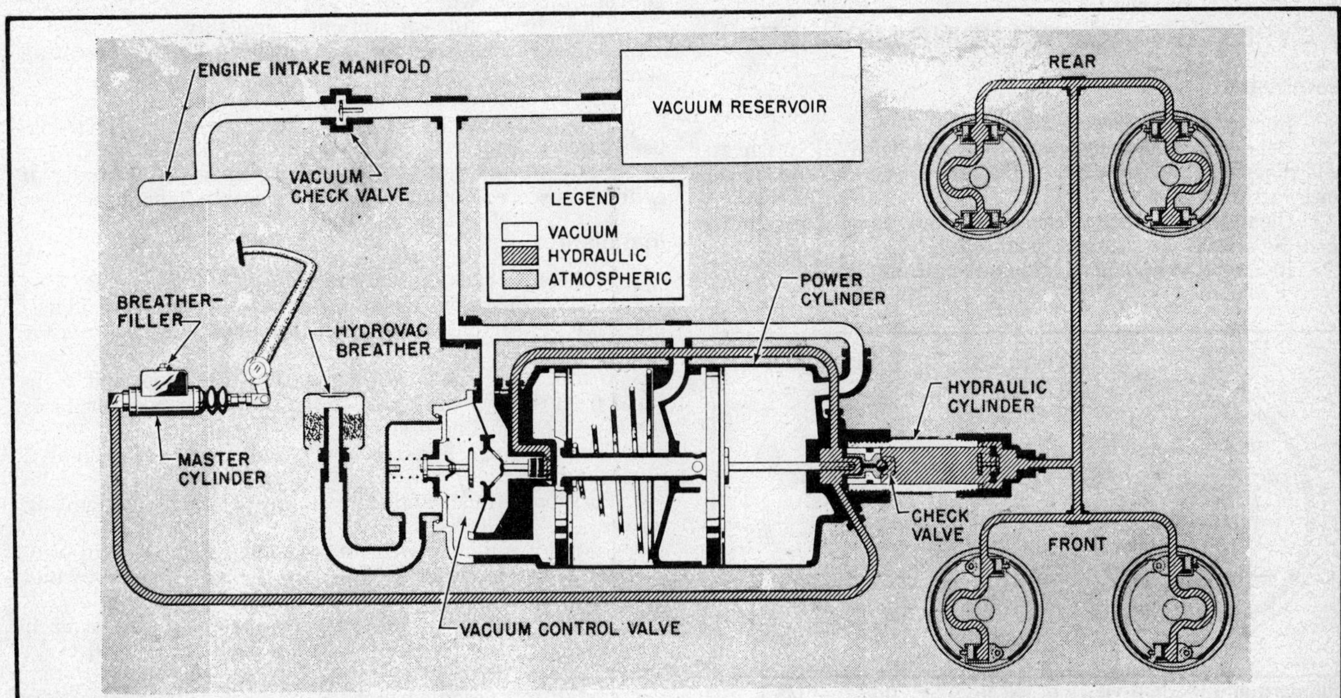

Typical vacuum-hydraulic brake system (© Mack Trucks, Inc.)

of the master cylinder piston. If the piston does not return completely, the lip of the primary piston cup seal will block off the compensating port. After a few applications the brakes will begin to drag and eventually lock up. If pedal travel is in excess of two–thirds of the total stroke, a lining clearance adjustment or replacement of the lining is necessary. If pumping of the pedal fails to bring it up past the one–half point of the stroke, check the fluid level in the master cylinder. If the level is correct, a leak in the system or a defective master cylinder is indicated.

Master Cylinder

Master cylinders are mounted on the firewall in conventional and tilt cab models. Tilt cab models have the master cylinder mounted vertically inside the cab.

Removal

NOTE: Clean all fittings before proceeding.

1. Loosen locknut and remove push rod.
2. Remove the stoplight switch from the tee on the pressure side of the master cylinder.
3. On tilt cap models, remove the floor mat to protect from brake fluid.
4. Disconnect brake fluid lines.
5. Remove mounting bracket bolts and remove the unit.
6. Wipe all fittings with a clean, dry cloth.

Installation

1. Install new gasket and push rod boot.
2. Install cylinder with bracket.
3. Insert push rod and adjust locknut to provide a $\frac{1}{16}$ in. clearance between push rod and plunger.
4. Install stoplight switch in tee on pressure side of cylinder.
5. Wipe clean and reconnect fluid lines.

CAUTION

Do not over–tighten fittings.

Wheel Cylinders

TYPE F BRAKE, INCLUDING MID–LINER

Removal

1. Remove front wheels and drums.
2. Remove retraction springs and hold down "C" washers. Lift shoes off the back plate. Take care not to lose the spring anti–rattle washers.
3. Clean line connection thoroughly and remove the connector tube nuts from the wheel cylinder.
4. Remove the anchor bolts and mounting screws.

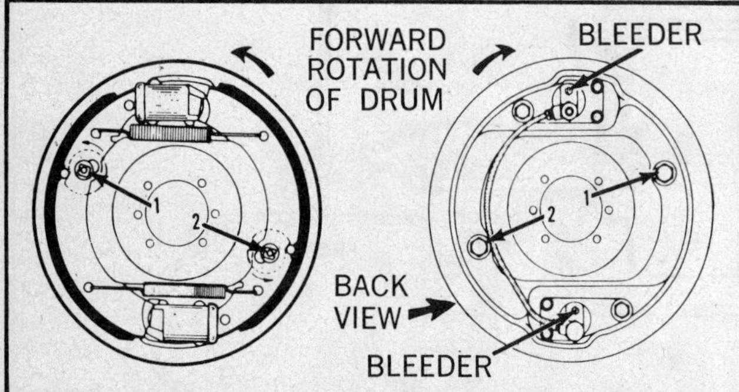

Outboard and inboard views of left front "F" brake (© Mack Trucks, Inc.)

5. Mark the connector tube ports on each wheel for reference.
6. Insert a clean rubber or wood plug in the end of tubing.
7. Protect brake linings from fluid and remove the cylinder. If a cylinder is scored, a replacement is preferable to rebuilding.

Installation

1. Clean all fittings.
2. Position wheel cylinder and tighten all bolts and mounting screws.

NOTE: Upper and lower cylinders are identical. Those for right and left brakes have opposite castings and can not be interchanged. The cylinder bore must face the direction of foreward rotation.

3. Remove plug and refit connector tubes.
4. Tighten connector tube nuts.
5. Position brake shoes and install retraction springs and hold down C–washers.

NOTE: Retraction springs should be located so that the long shank is connected to the heel of the shoe.

6. Install drums and wheels; bleed the system.

TYPE FR–2 BRAKE

Removal

1. Remove rear wheels and drums. It may be necessary to back off the adjusters.
2. Remove retraction springs by sliding looped ends off pins.
3. Remove hold down lock wires, castle nuts and plain washers. Lift off shoes.
4. Remove shoe heel anchor pins.
5. Remove adjuster wheel lock springs by removing the attaching screws from each spring.
6. Thread each adjusting screw out from the shoe side of its support. Lift star wheel out of slot.
7. Clean brake line connections thoroughly.
8. Remove connector tube nuts, anchor bolts and mounting screws.
9. Mark connector tube ports for reference.
10. Remove connector tubes and plug ends with a clean rubber or wood plug.
11. Protect brake linings from fluid and remove cylinder. If cylinder is scored, replacement is preferable to honing.

Installation

1. Make sure backing plate is tight on axle flange.
2. Insert adjuster wheel in anchor support, thread in adjusting screw and install star wheel lock spring in each anchor support.
3. Install each wheel cylinder so that the longer end, measured from the hydraulic port to the end of the cylinder, faces the shoe toe adjustment slot.
4. Clean fittings and reconnect connector tubes. Tighten tube nuts.
5. Position cylinder and tighten anchor bolts and mounting screws.
6. Install each shoe with its toe–identified by a cutaway portion of the web–positioned next to the adjusting screw and adjuster wheel.
7. Install hold down plain washer and castle nut at each shoe. Tighten each finger tight, then back each off $\frac{1}{4}$ to $\frac{1}{3}$ turn.
8. Install retraction springs.
9. Install drums and wheels; bleed system.

TYPE FR BRAKE

Removal

1. Remove rear wheels and drums. It may be necessary to back off the adjusters.
2. Remove retraction springs.
3. Remove hold down nut, lockwasher and plain washer at each end of shoe and remove shoe.
4. On each side, rotate the adjusting worm forward until the adjusting screw is free of the worm wheel and shoe. Pry out the worm retainer snap–ring to free the remaining parts: throughst washers, sleeve, worm, and worm wheel.
5. Clean all fittings.
6. Mark connector tubes for reference.
7. Disconnect hydraulic tube nut and loosen anchor block nuts.
8. Disconnect connector tubes and plug with clean rubber or wood plugs.
9. Remove anchor bolts and mounting screws and remove cylinders.
10. Be careful not to lose spring washers installed on the two locating lugs on each cylinder.

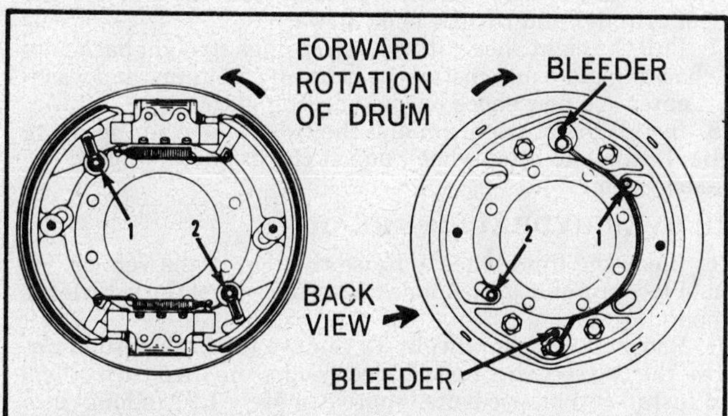

Outboard and inboard views of left rear "FR" brake (© Mack Trucks, Inc.)

Installation

1. Make sure backing plates are tight on the axle flanges.
2. Clean all fittings.
3. Connect connector tubes and tighten tube nuts.
4. Position wheel cylinders making sure a spring washer is located on each locating lug between the cylinder and the cover strap. Each cylinder should be positioned so that the long stroke side faces the adjusting slot in the backing plate and shoe toe.
5. Assemble cover and anchor block to cylinder.
6. Tighten anchor bolts and adjusting screw.

NOTE: Anchor block bolts should be tightened as follows:
$^5/_8$ × 18 – 105–130 ft. lbs., $^3/_4$ × 16 – 175–220 ft. lbs.

7. Place an adjuster worm in its sleeve on each shoe and install adjuster parts in each shoe web, one throughst washer at each end of the worm, and the retainer snap–ring on the opposite side of the web from the backing plate. Start the adjuster screw into the worm wheel and rotate the worm wheel to thread the screw into the shoe web.
8. Install shoes so that the adusting worm in the shoe toe is accessible through the adjusting slot.
9. Install and tighten hold down bolts, washers and nuts and connect retraction springs.
10. Install drums and wheels.
11. Lubricate and adjust wheel bearings.

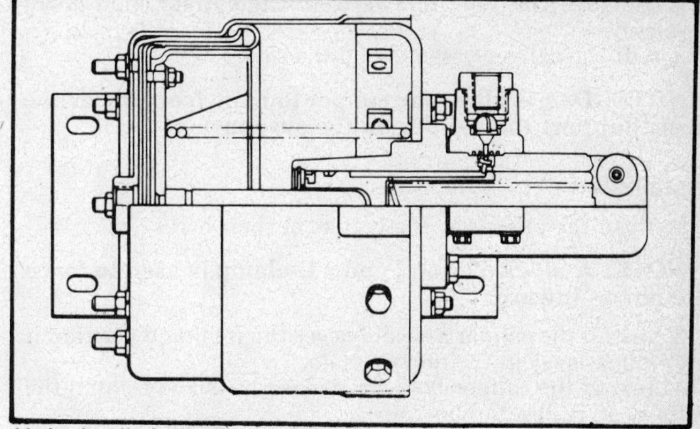

Air-hydraulic intensifier (© Mack Trucks, Inc.)

Air Hydraulic Brakes

DISC BRAKES

Disc brakes are used on various front axle applications, and are of the sliding caliper, dual piston design. The pistons are actuated by hydraulic pressure which is multiplied through the use of air over hydraulic fluid intensifier. The master cylinder includes both the air and hydraulic systems. Each is considered a separate system, although both systems operate together. No manual adjustment is required for disc brakes, as they adjust automatically during the braking operation. The wedge or cam type brakes are used on the rear wheels, in conjunction with the disc brakes, and adjusted either manually or automatically.

Disc Brake Caliper

Removal

1. Remove approximately $^2/_3$ of the brake fluid from the master cylinder disc brake reservoir.
2. Raise the vehicle and safely support the front of the vehicle.
3. Remove the front wheels.

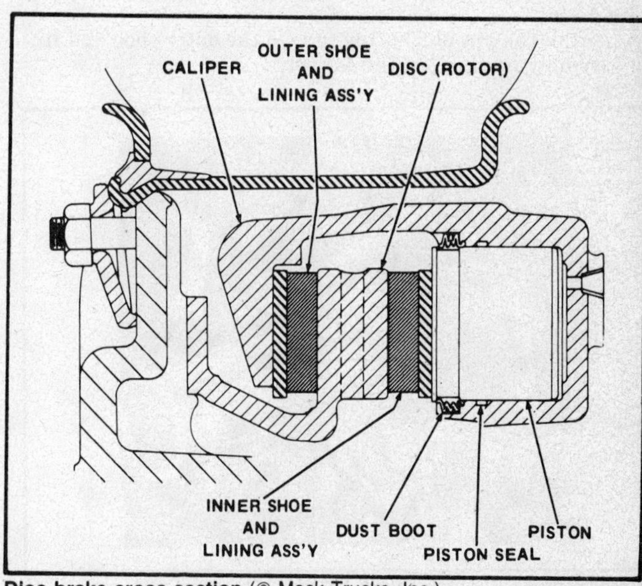

Disc brake cross section (© Mack Trucks, Inc.)

4. Remove the four screws from the caliper hold down assembly.
5. Lift the caliper assembly off the rotor.

NOTE: Do not allow the caliper to hang from the brake hose. Support the caliper on the suspension.

Installation

1. Push the pistons to the bottom of their bores.

NOTE: A block of wood and a C-clamp is used to force the piston inward.

2. Install the caliper assembly over the rotor and position it into the grooves in the anchor plate.
3. Install the caliper hold-down assemblies and tighten the bolts to 40 ft. lbs. torque.
4. Add fluid to the master cylinder reservoir $^1/_4$ in. from the reservoir top.
5. Bleed the hydraulic system, if any lines have been disconnected.
6. Pump the brake pedal several times to assure that the lining is against the rotor.
7. Install the wheels and lower the vehicle.

Shoe and Lining (Caliper Removed)

Removal

1. Remove the inner shoe and lining assembly from the anchor plate.
2. Remove the shoe and lining hold-down spring, pin and cup.
3. Remove the outer shoe and lining assembly from the caliper.

NOTE: For caliper overhaul procedures, refer to the General Brake Repair Section.

Installation

1. Install the new inner shoe and lining assembly into the anchor plate.
2. Push the pistons to the bottom of their bores.

NOTE: A block of wood and a C-clamp is used to force the piston inward.

3. Install the outer shoe and lining assembly into the caliper.
4. Install the pin and spring to hold the outer shoe and lining assembly in place on the caliper.

Cam type brake (© Mack Trucks, Inc.)

Shoe And Lining, Mid–liner Models MS–200, MS–300

Removal

AIR OVER HYDRAULIC BRAKES–FRONT

1. Block the rear wheels. Raise the front of the vehicle and place suitable jack stands under the front of the vehicle for support.
2. Place a wheel jack or dolly under the front wheel.
3. Remove the front wheel. To remove the brake drum, unscrew the two securing bolts (directly opposite from each other) and install two metric bolts (approxitmately 1.97 in.long) into the threaded holes in order to extract the brake drum.
4. Unscrew the nut holding the screw that secures the (right) brake shoe to the backing plate. Free the brake shoe from the wheel cylinder, tilt the brake shoe forward to release the return springs. Remove the brake shoe and return springs. Do the same to the left brake shoe.
5. Apply to the shoe supports, Molykote G or equivalent on each cylinder and on the side of the holding cups.
6. Install the new left brake shoe and retaining bolt, nut and washer. Insert the right brake shoe with the return springs hooked in the left shoe and the right shoe, into the groove of the wheel cylinder and tilt the shoe forward.
7. Pull the right shoe with return springs straight back onto the backing plate and install the retaining bolt, nut and washer. Center the new shoes on the backing plate.
8. Install the brake drum and the two brake drum securing bolts. Install the front wheel, adjust the brakes and bleed the brake system.

AIR OVER HYDRAULIC–REAR

1. Block the front wheels. Raise the rear of the vehicle.
2. Place suitable jack stands under the rear of the vehicle for support.
3. Remove the rear wheels. To remove the brake drum, unscrew the two securing bolts (directly opposite from each other) and install two metric bolts (approxitmately 1.97 in.long) into the threaded holes in order to extract the brake drum.
4. Unscrew the nut holding the screw that secures the upper brake shoe to the backing plate. Free the brake shoe from the wheel cylinder, tilt the brake shoe outward to release the return springs. Remove the brake shoe and return springs. Do the same to the lower brake shoe.
5. Apply to the shoe supports, Molykote G or equivalent on each cylinder and on the side of the holding cups.
6. Install the new lower brake shoe and retaining bolt, nut and washer. Insert the upper brake shoe with the return springs hooked into the lower shoe and the upper shoe, into the groove of the wheel cylinder and tilt the shoe outward.
7. Pull the upper shoe with return springs straight up and back onto the backing plate and install the retaining bolt, nut and washer. Center the new shoes on the backing plate.
8. Install the brake drum and the two brake drum securing bolts. Install the rear wheels, adjust the brakes and bleed the brake system.

Cam Brakes

The cam type brakes has the cam located between the "live" or free ends of the brake shoes. The slack adjuster, activated by an air chamber, rotates the cam and camshaft, forcing the shoes against the drum. Although the cam displaces both shoes equally, one shoe (primary) tends to self energize its-self into the drum during the drum's rotation, while the remaining shoe (secondary) is repelled by the rotation. Because of this braking action, different composition linings are used on the primary and secondary shoes and should not be interchanged. To locate the primary shoe, follow the rotation of the drum and the first shoe after passing the cam is the primary shoe.

Removal

1. Raise the rear of the vehicle and support it safely.
2. Remove the wheel and drum assemblies.
3. Remove the shoe return springs.
4. Remove the lock rings, retainers and felts from the brake shoe anchor pins.
5. Cut the anchor pin lock wire and remove the pins.
6. Remove the retaining clip and the brake shoe roller.
7. Remove the slack adjuster lock ring and spacing washer.
8. Remove the camshaft, washer and felt seal.
9. Remove the nylon bushings, if necessary.

NOTE: Where lip type seals are used and the nylon bushings are replaced, the seals will have to be replaced.

Installation

1. Install the nylon bushings, if necessary.
2. Install the brake shoe rollers and retainers.
3. Install the camshaft, washer and felt seals.
4. Place the brake shoe assembly over the spider and tap the anchor pin into position.
5. Install the lock screws and thread with the lock wire. Secure the wire.
6. Position the felts, retainers and lock rings on the anchor pins.
7. Using new springs, install the brake shoe return springs.
8. Assemble the slack adjuster on the splined end of the camshaft, using spacers and washers on each side of the adjuster to obtain 0.030–0.060 end-play.

Adjustment

The brake to drum adjustment is covered under the slack adjuster outline.

Maintenance

Periodic adjustment of the manual slack adjusters should be done monthly or every 8,000 miles.

Wedge Brakes

These double actuated brakes are used in straight air or air-over-hy-draulic systems. Mountings are either spider or backing plate, with air chambers or hydraulic units serving as actuators.

Wedge actuated brakes differ from conventional types in that they do not utilize slack adjusters and brake camshafts for application of linings to drums. Air or hydraulic pressure forces a wedge between plungers, causing the plungers to spread and push the brake shoes against the brake drums. Adjustment, either manual or automatic is made at one of the plungers, termed the adjusting plunger. There is one adjusting plunger for each brake wedge.

MAINTENANCE

EVERY TWO MONTHS OR 25,000 MILES

1. Check lining wear to determine replacement.
2. With automatic adjusters, check the lining-to-drum clearance. If clearance is less than 0.06 in., adjusters are adequate.
3. Check service air system and spring brake air system, where used, by cycling respective application valves.

EVERY YEAR OR 100,000 MILES

CAUTION

If the brakes are equipped with auxiliary spring power units, compress the power springs before starting any disassembly or removal of wheels and drums. This is done by turning the power spring compressor bolt 18 times clockwise.

1. Inspect plunger seals.
2. If seals are cut, torn, or leaking, overhaul actuating components.
3. Check upper adjusting plunger and seal.

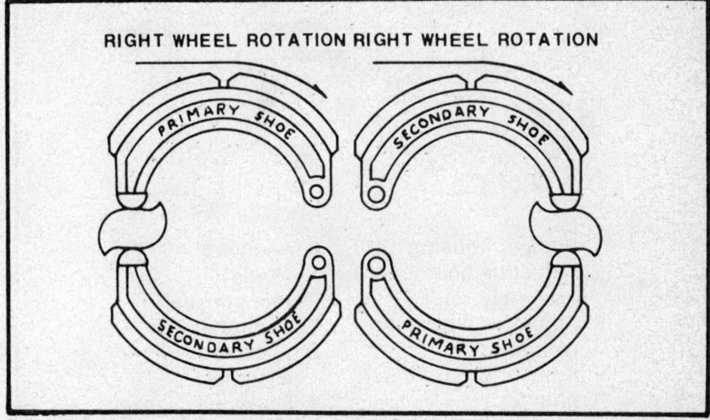

Locating primary shoe (© Mack Trucks, Inc.)

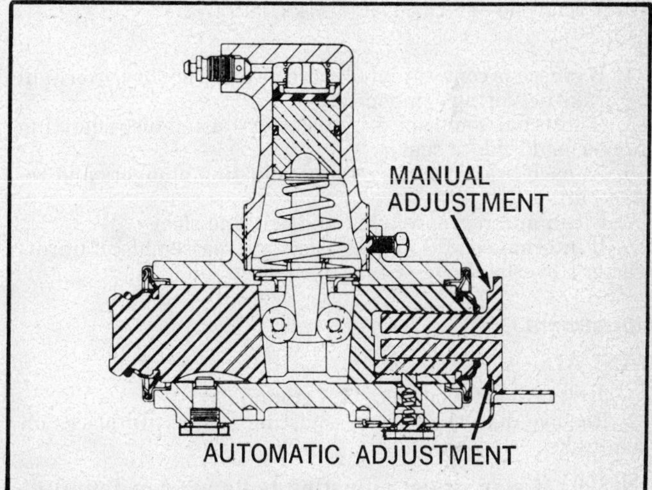

Wedge actuation—hydraulic cylinder (© Mack Trucks, Inc.)

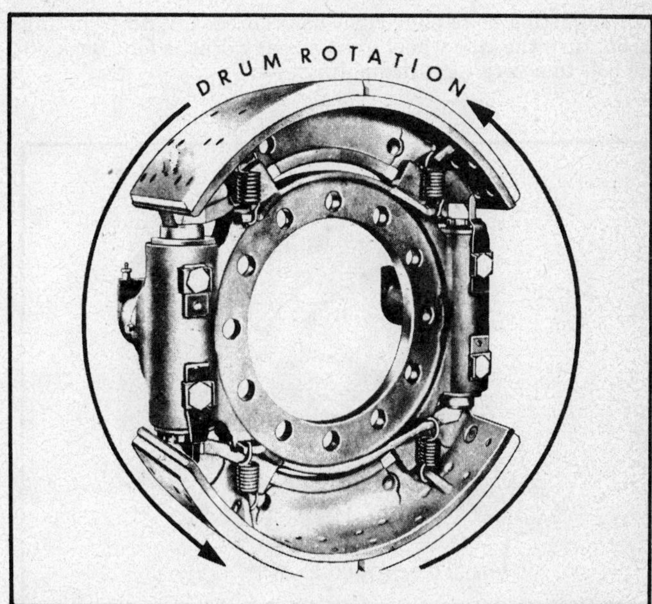

Wedge type brake (© Mack Trucks, Inc.)

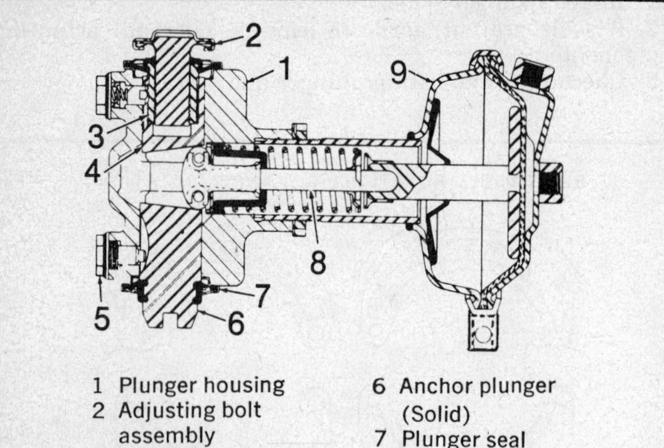

Wedge actuation—air chamber (© Mack Trucks, Inc.)

4. If grease is contaminated, hard or parts are dry, overhaul the brake actuating components.
5. If internal condition is satisfactory, assemble, adjusting plunger and replace seal.
6. At each brake reline, remove adjusting plungers and related parts.
7. Clean and regrease adjusting bolt and sleeve.
8. If internal condition is satisfactory, reassemble; if unsatisfactory, overhaul.

Adjustment

MANUAL

1. Jack or hoist wheels free of ground.
2. Remove dust cover from adjusting slot at two places on each brake.

NOTE: If star wheel adjusting bolts are not found at these positions, the brakes have been assembled on the wrong wheels.

3. Adjusting bolts have right hand threads. With adjusting spoon, turn the star wheel until a heavy drag is felt. Back off the bolt to a very light drum drag.

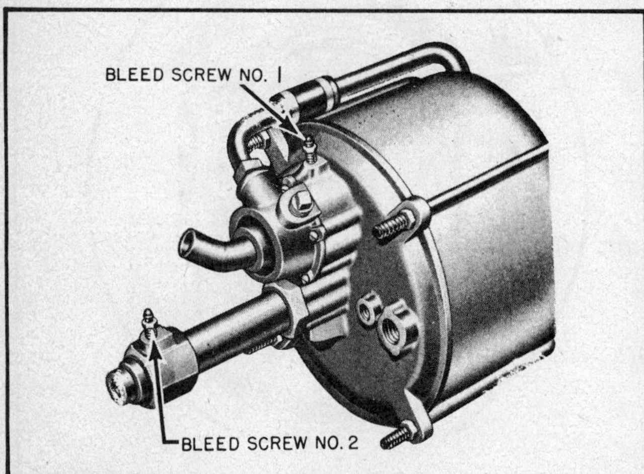

Hydrovac bleeder locations (© Mack Trucks, Inc.)

4. Repeat for other shoes.
5. Replace dust covers.

AUTOMATIC

Check the drum-to-lining clearance with a feeler gauge. If the clearance is more than 0.06 in., adjust the brake manually until the lining can be serviced.

Hydraulic System Bleeding

CAUTION

Before bleeding, make sure the engine is shut down and there is no air in the system.

PRESSURE BLEEDING

NOTE: A full pressure bleeder tank with a constant capacity of 25–35 psi is necessary. Pressure should not drop below 15 psi. Fill master cylinder from tank before beginning operation, making sure that fluid is free from air bubbles.

1. With master cylinder pressurized, bleed Hydrovac first, starting with bleeder screw no. 1 on the control valve.
2. Immerse loose end of bleeder hose in small quantity of fluid in a clean quart jar held beneath the bleeder screw level.
3. When a solid stream of fluid is seen, close the bleeder screw.
4. Repeat with no. 2 screw.
5. Bleed the wheel cylinders in the same manner. Where two cylinders are used on the same wheel, bleed the one first in line, first.

MANUAL BLEEDING

1. Shut down engine, drain vacuum from reservoir. Keep master cylinder at least half full. Use bleeder hose and container as described above.
2. Open no. 1 bleeder screw on Hydrovac.
3. Pump pedal slowly until bubble-free fluid is seen.
4. Depress pedal to floorboard and close bleeder screw.
5. Release pedal.

NOTE: When pedal is at floor of each stroke, bleeder screw must be closed and reopened at the top of the stroke.

LUBRICATION OF HYDROVAC

1. With the engine off, pump the brakes to release the vacuum and lubricate the unit with the brakes released. DO NOT OVER-LUBRICATE.
2. Where a lubrication plug is provided, remove the plug.
3. Inject two ounces of recommended vacuum cylinder oil through the port.
4. Replace and tighten lube plug.
5. If no plug is furnished, loosen hose clamps and slide hose on the control tube away from the control valve.
6. Use a gun type oiler to inject two ounces of the recommended vacuum cylinder oil into the unit. Insert the spout of the oiler well down into the tube to be sure that all the oil enters the vacuum cylinder.

Hydrovac Unit

Removal

NOTE: Before servicing, wipe all fittings clean and dry.

1. Disconnect push rod clevis at pedal.
2. Remove vacuum hose from unit.
3. Disconnect hydraulic lines.
4. Remove any stoplight wires.
5. Remove retaining bolts and lift out unit and bracket.

Installation

1. Mount unit in place and tighten bolts to a loose hanging position.
2. Secure push rod to pedal and check free play.
3. Tighten mounting nuts and hydraulic lines.
4. Install vacuum lines.
5. Connect stoplight wires.
6. Bleed brakes.

AIR BRAKE SYSTEM

A dual circuit air brake system has been incorporated to comply with the emergency braking requirements of the Federal Motor Vehicle Safety Standards (FMVSS-121).

This dual system consists of two completely separate circuits; a primary air circuit supplying the rear brakes, and a secondary air circuit supplying the front brakes. The system operates through a dual delivery treadle valve, and check valves protect each circuit in case of air loss from one of the systems. A dual air gauge is mounted on the dash to monitor the air pressure in both systems and has a visible red light and an audible buzzer to warn the operator of low air pressure in the systems.

The air brake systems are supplied with compressed air from a belt or gear driven air compressor, mounted on the engine. A governor regulates the amount of air pressure build-up by the compressor.

The air brake system should be tested and maintained at regular intervals.

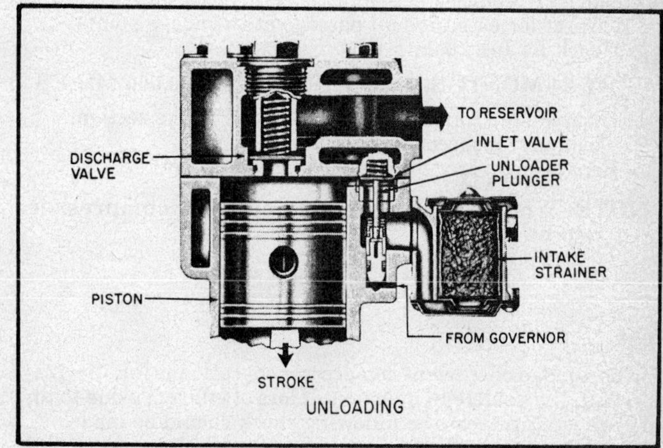

Compressor unloading operation (© Mack Trucks, Inc.)

Tests

1. Drain reservoirs daily: with system charged, open all drain cocks until filters and reservoir have been drained.
2. Check stoplight switch: with system drained, start engine and depress pedal slowly. Lamps should light before 10 psi.
3. Check low pressure indicator: indicator should light or buzzer should operate up to 70 psi.
4. Pressure build-up test: at fast idle, a pressure of 50–90 psi. should be attained within 5 minutes.

Refer to the General Brake section for specific unit overhaul.

Compressor

Compressors in general use are single stage, reciprocating piston type units. Those in use on Mack Trucks have rated capacities of $7\frac{1}{4}$–$14\frac{1}{2}$ cubic feet per minute at 1250 rpm. All units have automatic type inlet valves. Unloading mechanism is located in the cylinder block and there are no external moving parts.

The compressor is constantly engaged while the engine is running. Actual compression of air is controlled by a governor. The governor starts and stops the compression of air by loading or unloading the compressor according to the air pressure in the lines.

UNLOADED OPERATION

When air pressure in the reservoir reaches maximum, the compressed air passes through the governor into the cavity below the unloading pistons in the compressor cylinder block. This pressure lifts the pistons which, in turn, lift the inlet valves off their seats. With the inlet valves off their seats, air during the upstroke is forced through the inlet cavity to the other cylinder which forces a downstroke of the piston. When reservoir pressure reaches minimum, air beneath the pistons is unloaded and the compressing cycle begins.

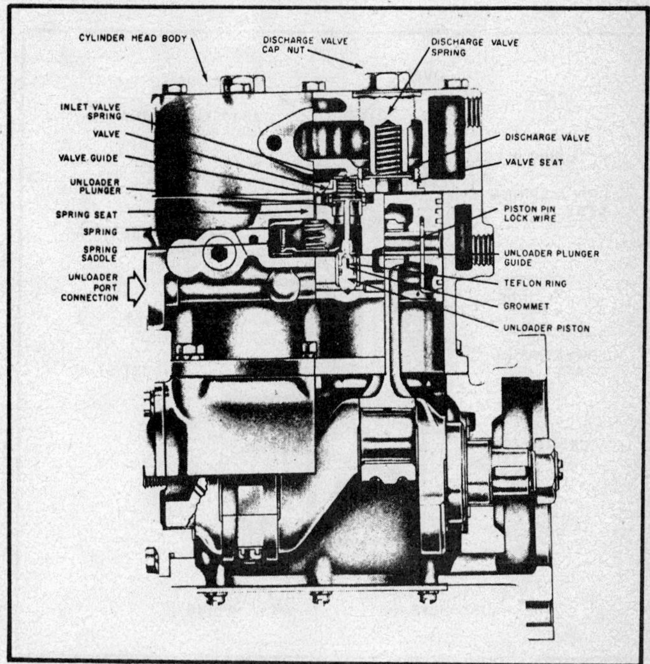

Air compressor (© Mack Trucks, Inc.)

PREVENTIVE MAINTENANCE

EVERY 90 DAYS, 500 HOURS, OR 16,000 MILES

1. Remove the air strainer.
   a. If paper, replace.
   b. If washable, clean in solvent or soapy water, oil and reinstall.
2. On models without the air strainer, inspect the hoses and adapter connections for tightness and condition, from the main engine air intake air cleaner to the compressor.
3. Check the compressor drive alignment and mounting bolts.

EVERY 6 MONTHS, 1,800 HOURS, OR 50,000 MILES

1. Remove discharge valve cap nuts and check for carbon deposits.
2. Check discharge line for carbon.
3. If excess carbon is found, the head or discharge line must be cleaned or replaced.
4. Inspect for excessive oil passage at the above points.
5. Check for full coolant flow.

EVERY 24 MONTHS, 7,200 HOURS, OR 200,000 MILES

1. Disassemble compressor. See General Brake section.
2. Clean and inspect all parts thoroughly.
3. Repair or replace all damaged or worn parts.

NOTE: When draining engine coolant, compressor must also be drained.

AIR LEAKAGE

Test

The best judge of efficient compressor operation is familiarization with the vehicle in question. If loss of efficiency due to an air leak is suspected, the following check should be made:

1. Apply outside compressed air to the discharge port and listen for air escaping past the discharge valves.
2. Build up pressure with the compressor until the governor cuts out. Stop the engine and listen for air escaping at the intake.
3. If leakage is detected, pinpoint the leak with soapy water around the unloading pistons.
4. If no leaks are found at the pistons, the discharge valves are at fault.

Removal

1. Block or hold vehicle by means other than the air brakes.
2. Drain air from system.
3. Drain coolant from engine block.
4. Disconnect all air, oil, and water lines.
5. Remove nuts and washers from mounting studs and pull compressor back off studs.

Installation

1. Run engine briefly to clear and check oil supply lines.
2. Check oil return lines and passages.
3. Check coolant supply lines.
4. Inspect drive gears and couplings.
5. Clean mating surfaces of compressor and housing. Place new gasket on studs.
6. Install drive coupling on hub and position compressor on mounting studs. Guide compressor into mesh with driven disc making sure coupling teeth engage disc.
7. Install nuts and washers and torque to 60–65 ft. lbs.
8. Connect water, air and oil lines and fill cooling system.
9. Run engine and check compressor for noise, leaks and output. Check build-up time and governor action.

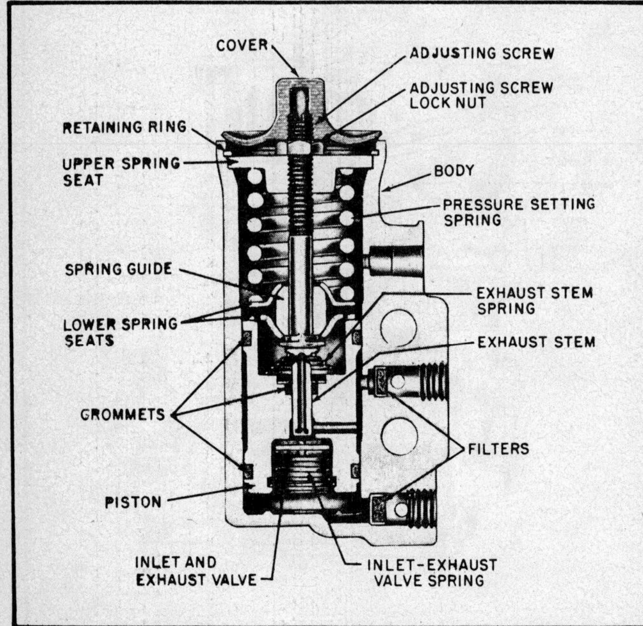

Governor (© Mack Trucks, Inc.)

MID-LINER AIR COMPRESSOR

Removal

1. Disconnect the negative battery cables, tilt the cab over making sure to lock the cab safety hinges in place.
2. Drain the air system and drain the cooling system through the drain plugs in the radiator and the metal water pump tube.
3. Remove the air compressor inlet air hoses and remove the turbocharger air inlet pipe. Disconnect the compressor air discharge pipe.
4. Remove the two clamps on the connecting sleeve of the compressor coolant discharge line. Slide the sleeve onto the compressor coolant discharge pipe, so as to disconnect it from the air compressor.
5. Remove the air compressor lubrication feed line. Remove the air compressor mounting nuts and bolts, remove the air compressor from the vehicle.

Installation

1. Clean the gasket faces on the engine and air compressor. Install a new gasket using sealing compound # 5166-52414 or equivalent.
2. Installation of the air compressor is the reverse order of the removal procedure.
3. After installation check the cooling system and the air system for leaks.

Governor

The governor automatically controls the air pressure in the air brake system. Air pressure acts on the governor piston to overcome the pressure setting spring. This controls the inlet and exhaust valves. Air is either admitted or exhausted from the compressor unloading mechanism.

PREVENTIVE MAINTENANCE

EVERY 900 HOURS OR 25,000 MILES

1. Clean filters without removing from body by washing in solvent.
2. If filters are removed, they must be replaced.

EVERY 3,600 HOURS OR 100,000 MILES

1. Disassemble governor.
2. Clean and inspect all parts.

Running Inspection

1. Start engine and build up pressure.
2. Note pressure at cut out: 120 psi. is preferred.
3. With engine still running apply brake several times and note cut in pressure: 100 psi. is preferred.

Pressure Changes

If pressure settings noted above are not met:

1. Remove top cover of governor.
2. Loosen adjusting screw locknut.
3. Turn adjusting screw counterclockwise to raise, clockwise to lower pressure.

NOTE: Set cut-out only.

4. Tighten adjusting screw locknut.
5. Replace cover.

Leakage Tests

1. Set governor in cut out position.
2. Check exhaust port for leakage at exhaust valve seat, or stem grommet, also at the upper piston grommet.
3. Set governor at cut in position and check exhaust port for inlet valve leakage by applying soap solution at the port.
4. Check the bottom piston grommet.
5. If excessive leakage at any of the above is found, the governor should be returned to the factory for a rebuilt unit.

Removal

1. Block or hold vehicle by means other than the air brakes.
2. Drain air system.
3. Thoroughly clean all fittings and lines.
4. Remove mounting bolts.
5. Remove governor unit.

Installation

1. Make certain both air lines to governor are clean.
2. Position governor with exhaust port towards ground.
3. Tighten bolts finger tight.
4. Start fittings, tighten mounting bolts, tighten fittings.
5. Test governor, check for leaks.

Slack Adjusters

The slack adjusters serve as mechanical leverage for brake application. Air pressure exerted against a diaphragm in the brake chamber or power cylinder moves a rod linked to the slack adjuster. The brake camshaft, splined to the slack adjuster, rotates with slack adjuster movement. The integral constant lift cam spreads the shoes against the drum. Brake adjustment is provided at the slack adjuster.

The two manual types of slack adjusters differ primarily in the adjustment screw locking device. Type 1 uses a lock ball and detent adjustment lock, while type 2 uses a sliding sleeve lock.

Two types of automatic slack adjusters are used. Type 1 has an internal rack and pinion linkage which rotates a worm shaft and wheel to maintain the proper lining to drum clear-

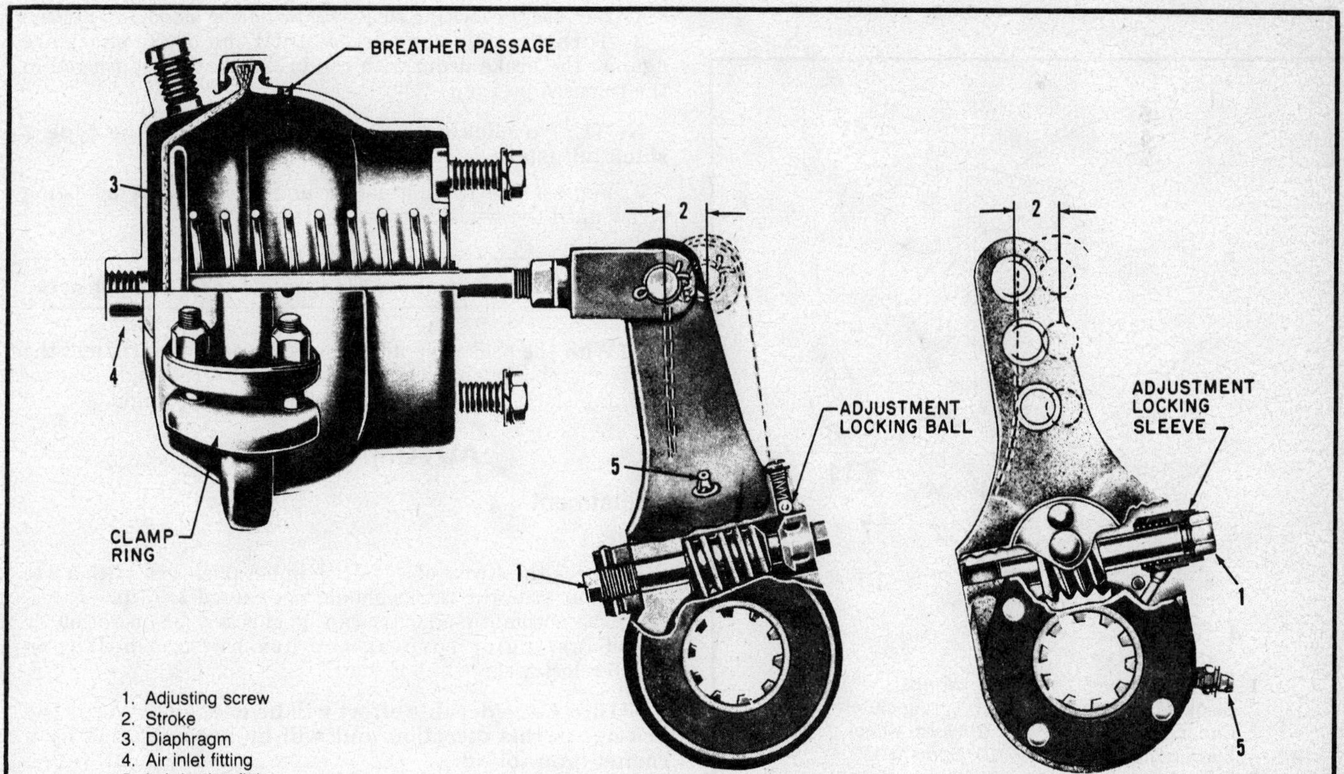

Manual slack adjusters (© Mack Trucks, Inc.)

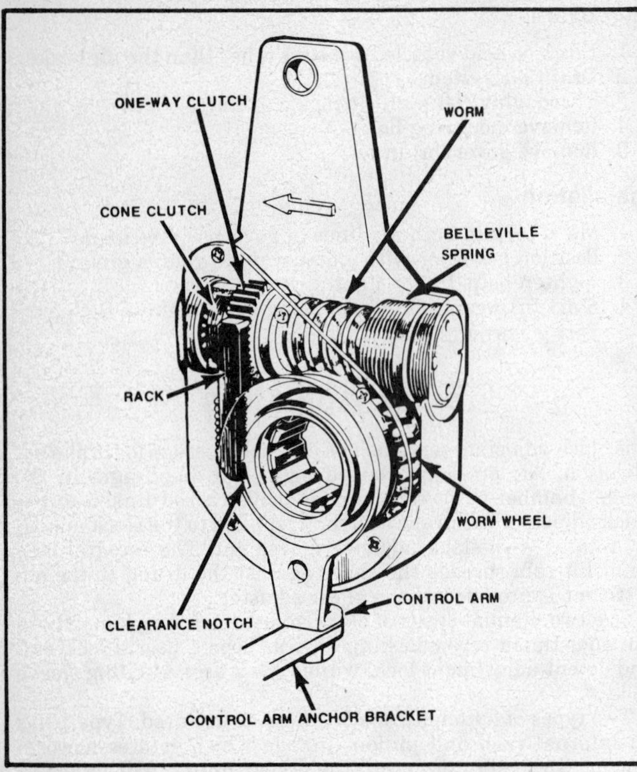

Type 1 automatic slack adjuster (© Mack Trucks, Inc.)

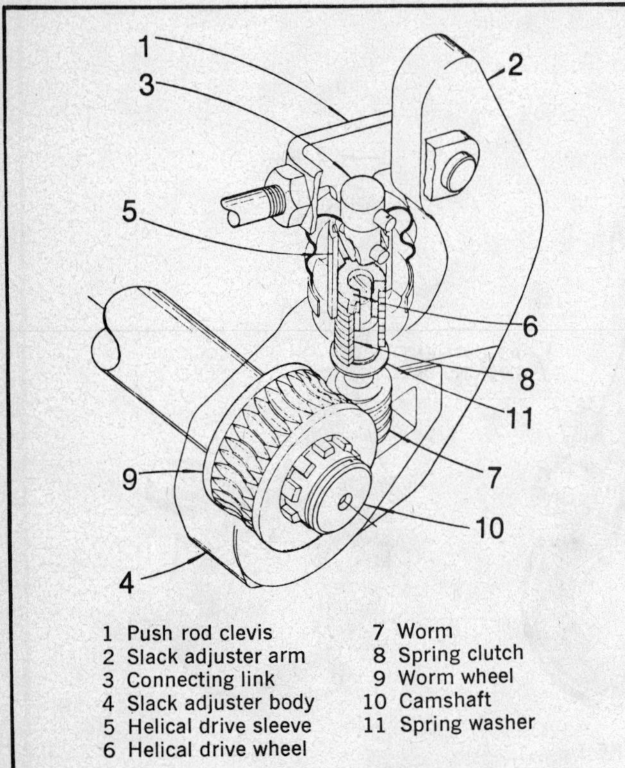

Type 2 automatic slack adjuster (© Mack Trucks, Inc.)

ance. Type 2 has a special push rod clevis which pushes an external link towards the body of the slack adjuster, actuating a helical drive sleeve, which rotates a worm gear to maintain the desired lining to drum clearance.

NOTE: The automatic slack adjusters are interchangeable with the manual types.

CAUTION

If an automatic slack adjuster is found to be inoperative, do not attempt to repair as special tools are required. Replace the defective adjuster with a new unit.

MANUAL TYPE

Adjustment

TYPE 1

1. Turn the adjusting screw until the brake shoes are against the brake drum with the brake chamber push rod in the released position.

NOTE: A distinct click will be heard each time the spring loaded ball seats in the adjusting screw indent.

2. Back off the adjusting screw to four full notches.

NOTE: Make sure that the locking ball is seated in the notch.

3. Be assured of no brake dragging with the brakes released.

NOTE: With the brakes applied, the slack adjuster arm and the brake chamber push rod should form an approximate angle of 90 degrees. All slack adjusters on the vehicle should be at the same angle.

TYPE 2

1. Depress the locking sleeve *before* turning the adjusting screw.
2. Turn the adjusting screw until the brake shoes are against the brake drum with the brake chamber push rod in the released position.

NOTE: No clicking noise will occur with the type 2 slack adjusters.

3. Depress the locking sleeve and back off the adjusting screw until the wheel is free to rotate.

CAUTION

Return the locking sleeve to its locked position on the adjusting screw.

4. With the brakes applied, the slack adjuster arm and the brake chamber push rod should form a 90 degree angle. The remaining slack adjusters should be at the same angle.

AUTOMATIC TYPE

Adjustment

TYPE 1

1. Check the stroke of the air chamber push rod. With a 6 to 7 in. lever arm, the stroke should not exceed 1 $^{3}/_{4}$ in.
2. The automatic adjuster can be checked for operation by re-ad-justing or turning the hex-nut one-half turn counterclockwise.

NOTE: Considerable effort will be needed to rotate the hex-nut in this direction and will be accompanied by a rachet type sound.

3. Apply full pressure brake applications and observe the rotation of the hex-nut during the return of each stroke.
4. When the hex-nut rotation is stopped, the adjustment is completed.

TYPE 2

1. Check the stroke of the air chamber push rod. With a 6 to 7 in. lever arm, the stroke should not exceed 1 $^1/_2$ in.
2. To check the automatic adjuster for operation, remove the $^1/_4$ in. pipe plug from the automatic slack adjuster housing.
3. Using a $^1/_4$ in. male hex wrench, turn the worm shaft counter-clockwise approximately one turn.
4. Measure the stroke of the air chamber push rod in the applied and released positions.
5. Apply the brakes under full air pressure for a number of times and remeasure the stroke of the air chamber push rod. The distance should diminish if the automatic adjuster is working properly.
6. Reinstall the $^1/_4$ in. pipe plug in the automatic slack adjuster housing.

Inspection

1. Apply brakes and check that slack adjusters rotate freely.
2. Release brakes and check that slack adjusters return to the released position freely and without binding.
3. Release brakes and check that the angle formed by the slack adjuster arm and the brake chamber push rod is greater than 90°.
4. Apply the brake and check that the above angle is still greater than 90°.

Removal

1. Remove clevis pin at lever.
2. Remove lock ring and washer on splined camshaft.
3. Slide adjuster off splined shaft.

Installation

1. Make sure spacer washers are in place if used.
2. Slide slack adjuster on splined camshaft, lock in place with snap-ring and washer.
3. Connect yoke clevis pin. Make certain angle is greater than 90°.
4. Lubricate adjuster.

Brake Chambers

The brake chambers, like the slack adjusters, convert applied pressure into mechanical force and motion, thereby applying the brakes.

PREVENTIVE MAINTENANCE

EVERY MONTH OR 2,000 MILES

1. Check brake chamber push rod travel. Travel should be kept as close as possible without excessive dragging.
2. Check push rod to slack adjuster alignment in applied and released positions. Action should not bind.
3. Check angle formed by slack adjuster arm and push rod for required in excess of 90°.

EVERY 3,600 HOURS OR 100,000 MILES

1. Disassemble the air chamber and clean all parts.
2. Replace the diaphragm, spring and all other rubber parts.
3. Replace all corresponding parts in the opposite air chamber on the same axle.

Inspection

1. Apply brakes and check that push rod does not bind.
2. Release brakes and check push rod return.
3. Check push rod travel for minimum play.
4. With chamber pressurized, check for leakage.

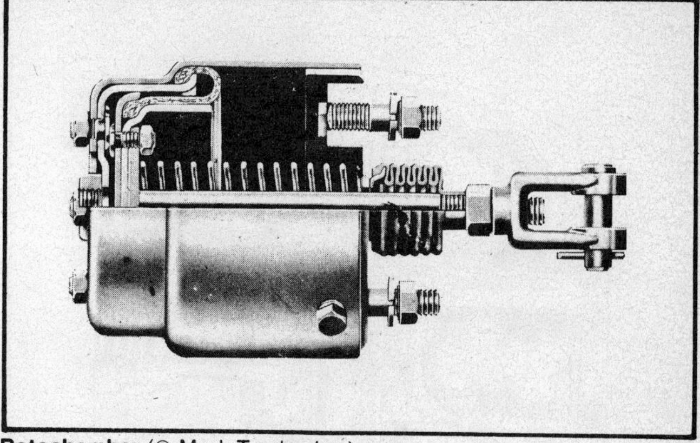

Rotochamber (© Mack Trucks, Inc.)

CAM TYPE

Removal

1. Disconnect air hose from chamber.
2. Remove clevis pin from yoke.
3. Remove nuts and washers from mounting studs.
4. Remove chamber.

Installation

1. Place chamber on mounting bracket and secure with stud nuts and lockwashers.
2. Connect air hose.
3. Install slack adjuster yoke clevis pin after adjusting for minimum travel.
4. Check that angle made by rod and slack adjuster is not less than 90°.
5. Check for leaks and shoe adjustment.

WEDGE BRAKE TYPE

Removal

1. Block or hold vehicle by means other than air brakes.
2. Disconnect air hose from chamber.
3. Remove lockwasher tangs from notches in spanner nut and spider housing.
4. Loosen spanner nut and unscrew chamber from housing.

Installation

1. Screw air chamber in spider housing until it bottoms.
2. Back off until air port aligns with air hose no more than one turn.

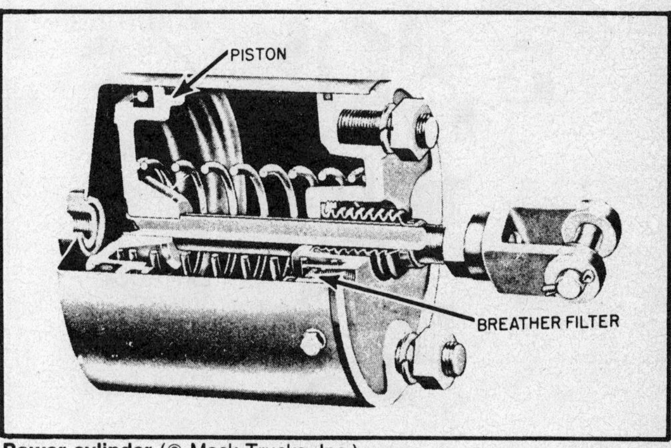

Power cylinder (© Mack Trucks, Inc.)

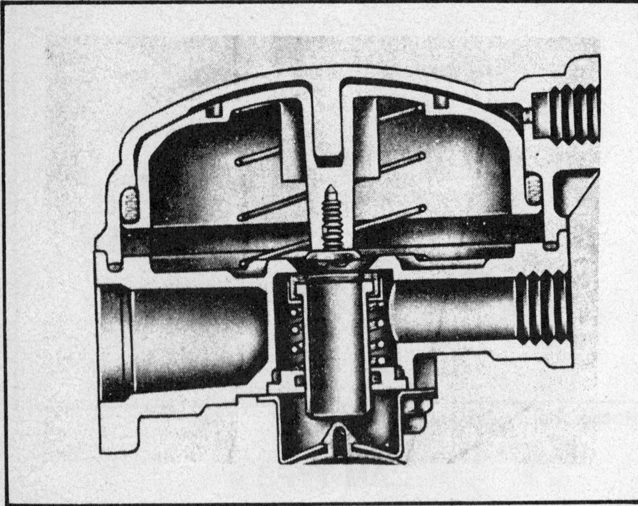
Relay valve (© Mack Trucks, Inc.)

3. Lock chamber in position with spanner nut and lockwasher.
4. Start engine, charge system, and check for leaks.
5. Pump brakes to allow adjusters to adjust brakes.

CAUTION

When brakes are equipped with auxiliary spring brake power units, compress the power springs before removing wheels and drums.

Brake Application Valve

This valve controls the air pressure being delivered to the brake actuators. The amount of air pressure delivered to the brake chambers is determined by the position of the application valve treadle.

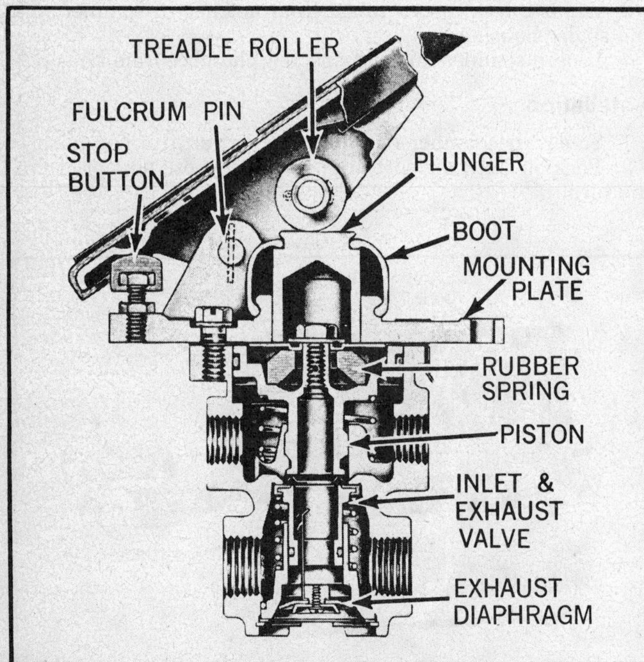

Brake application valve (© Mack Trucks, Inc.)

PREVENTIVE MAINTENANCE

EVERY 3 MONTHS, 300 HOURS OR 20,000 MILES

1. Lube treadle roller, roller pin and hinge pin with engine oil.
2. Lift boot away from plunger or mounting plate and put a few drops of light oil between the plunger and mounting plate.
3. Clean the exhaust valve.

EVERY YEAR, 3,600 HOURS OR 100,000 MILES

1. Replace inlet and exhaust valves, exhaust diaphragm, grommets, and rubber graduating spring, if worn.

EVERY 2 YEARS, 7,200 HOURS OR 200,000 MILES

1. Disassemble, clean and inspect all parts.
2. Replace any worn parts.

Inspection

Check delivery pressure of brake valve with a test gauge at various treadle positions. Fully applied pressure should be equal to reservoir pressure. Pressure should drop to zero when pedal is released.

Leakage Tests

1. Release valve fully; check exhaust port for leakage.
2. Make and hold high pressure.
3. Coat the exhaust port and top of valve with soapy water. No leaks are permissible.

Removal

1. Block or hold vehicle by means other than air brakes.
2. Drain air system.
3. Remove all lines and wires.
4. Remove fulcrum pin and pedal.
5. Remove mounting bolts and valve.

Installation

1. Mount valve in position. Install bolts loosely.
2. Start all fittings.

NOTE: Keep sealant off first two threads of fittings.

3. Tighten mounting bolts and all fittings.
4. Replace pedal.
5. Run engine and charge air system.
6. Depress pedal and check all fittings with soapy water.
7. Check and adjust pedal free play.
8. Check valve action.

Relay Valve

This valve is used to operate brakes on the rear axle of multi-axle tractors or trucks and tractors with long wheel bases. It is operated by the brake valve and maintains the same pressure to the brake actuators as is being delivered to it by the brake valve.

PREVENTIVE MAINTENANCE

Each year the relay valve should be disassembled and cleaned. Replace all rubber parts, if worn or damaged.

Inspection

Fully charge the system, make several applications and check for prompt response at each wheel.

Leakage Tests

1. Fully release the valve.
2. Coat exhaust port of relay valve with soapy water.

3. Maximum leakage of a one in. soap bubble every three seconds is permissible.
4. Make and hold a brake application and coat the exhaust port of the relay valve with soapy water. A maximum leakage of a one in. soap bubble is not less than two seconds is permissible.

Low Pressure Indicator

This unit is composed of a body and cover between which is clamped a spring-loaded rubber diaphragm. Electrical contacts and terminals are located in the assembly. Its function is to warn the operator of low pressure in the system. Since it is a sealed unit, it requires no maintenance other than periodic cleaning of the external terminals.

Inspection

Reduce reservoir pressure. Indicator should sound between 54 and 66 psi.

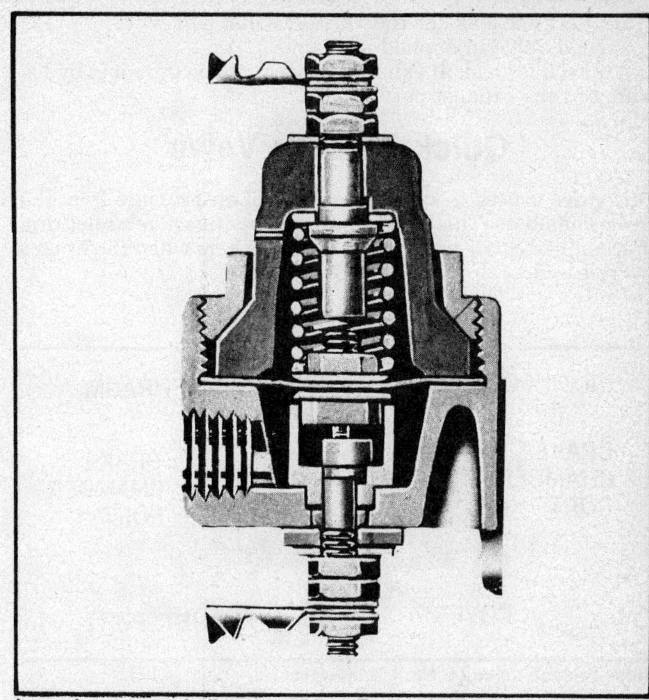

Low air pressure indicator (© Mack Trucks, Inc.)

Stoplight Switch

This unit is operated by the brake valve. Its function is to activate the rear lamps during brake application.

PREVENTIVE MAINTENANCE

EVERY 300 HOURS OR 8,000 MILES

1. Check electrical connections.

EVERY 3,600 HOURS OR 100,000 MILES

1. Disassemble unit and clean all parts.
2. Replace the diaphragm.

Inspection

Apply and release brakes. Note operation of rear lamps.

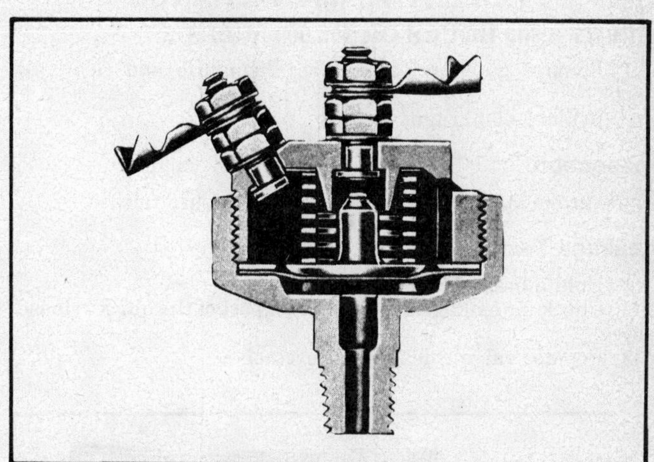

Stoplight switch (© Mack Trucks, Inc.)

Safety Valve

The unit is a spring-loaded ball check type valve which protects the system against excessive air pressure. Normal setting is 150 psi.

PREVENTIVE MAINTENANCE

EVERY YEAR OR 50,000 MILES

1. Safety valve should be removed and thoroughly cleaned.

Inspection

Pull end of valve stem to remove load from ball. Safety valve should blow off. If not, the ball is stuck in its seat.

Leakage Test

Leakage at the exhaust port in the spring cage should not exceed a three in. soap bubble in three seconds.

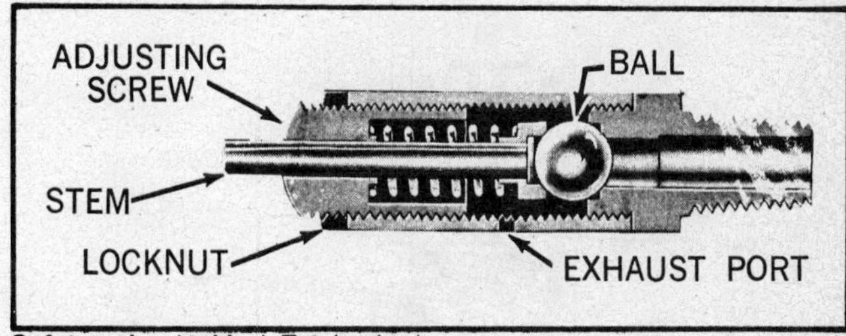

Safety valve (© Mack Trucks, Inc.)

Hand Control Valve

This valve controls the trailer brakes independently of the tractor brakes, and is mounted on the right side of the steering column. The valve is manually controlled and has positions for "Apply", "Hold", and "Release".

PREVENTIVE MAINTENANCE

EVERY 3,600 HOURS OR 100,000 MILES

1. Check valve for proper operation.
2. Inspect all sections of valve for lubrication.

Inspection

Check delivered pressure with a test gauge. Fully applied pressure should be 75–85 psi.

Leakage Tests

1. Hold valve in released position.

2. Check for leaks at the valve exhaust port.
3. Hold valve in applied position.
4. Check for leak at exhaust valve or piston grommet by listening at the exhaust port.

Quick Release Valve

This valve is used to speed up release of air pressure from the brake chambers. This is accomplished by the valve's releasing of accumulated air pressure in the chambers when the brakes are released.

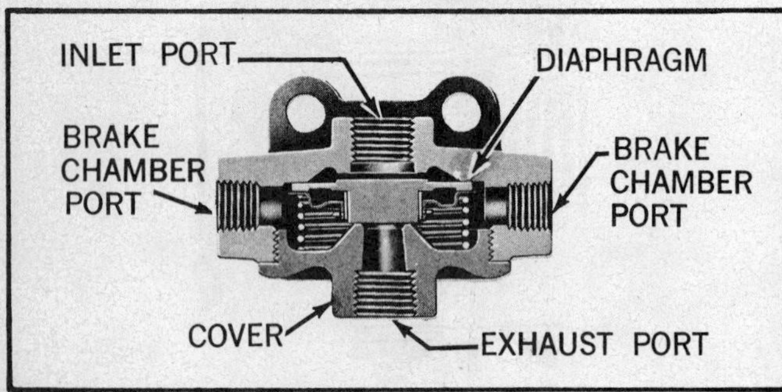

Quick release valve (© Mack Trucks, Inc.)

PREVENTIVE MAINTENANCE

EVERY 3,600 HOURS OR 100,000 MILES

1. Remove quick release valve, dismantle and clean all parts.
2. Replace diaphragm if worn.

Inspection

Make brake application and check for pressure release.

Leakage Test

1. Hold a brake application.
2. Check for leakage at the exhaust port of the quick release valve.
3. Replace valve if leakage is excessive.

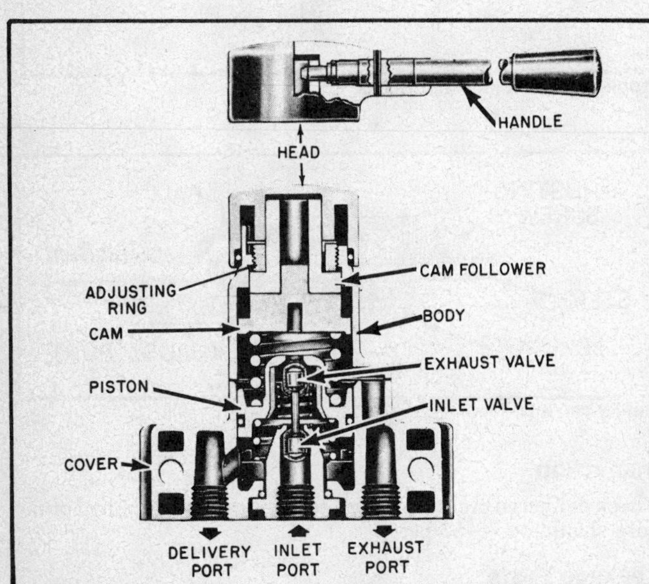

Hand control valve (© Mack Trucks, Inc.)

Air Hose Coupling

The coupling is a simple but precision made aluminum mating part which is utilized anywhere the main air supply must be tapped for trailer or accessories. The aluminum housing encloses a steel strip cast in the body to prevent wear at the mating point.

PREVENTIVE MAINTENANCE

EVERY MONTH OR 2,000 MILES

1. Check packing for cuts, brittleness or other sealing defects.

Leakage Test

1. Replace packing ring if leakage at joint exceeds a one in. soap bubble per second.
2. Replace coupling if leakage appears elsewhere.

Double Check Valves

These are used where it is necessary to direct air flow from two lines to a single line automatically. There are two types: shuttle and disc.

The shuttle type uses a cast body and two end caps. Inside the valve are two rubber seal gaskets and a brass shuttle.

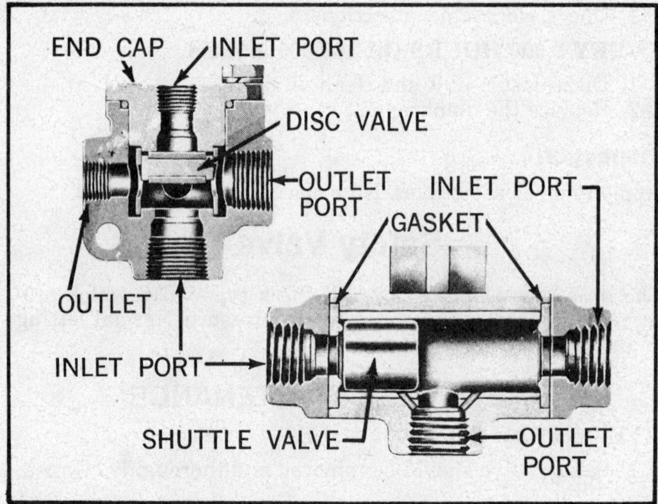

Double check valves (© Mack Trucks, Inc.)

The disc type uses a cast body and end caps. Inside the valve is a rubber disc and disc guide. One end cap serves as a seat for the disc; the other end is tapped for the air connection.

PREVENTIVE MAINTENANCE

EVERY 3,600 HOURS OR 100,000 MILES

The valve should be dismantled and thoroughly cleaned. With a shuttle valve unit, replace the rubber seats; with a disc unit, replace the rubber disc.

Inspection

1. Apply foot brake and check braking action.
2. Release foot brake and note proper brake release.
3. Apply hand brake and note that brakes on trailer apply.
4. Release hand brake and note that trailer brakes release.

Leakage Test

1. Apply foot brake and check for leakage at exhaust port of hand brake valve.
2. Apply hand brake and check for leakage at exhaust port of foot brake valve. Leakage of a three in. soap bubble in three seconds is permissible in either of the above tests. Excessive leakage means replacement of either the rubber seals or rubber disc.

Limiting and Quick Release Valve with Two Way Control Valve

The limiting and quick release valve is used in combination with a two way control valve in some air brake systems. Under normal driving conditions, it functions as a quick release valve. In adverse weather conditions, the driver can reduce the braking action of the front brakes by 50% by operating the handle of the two way valve.

The two way valve is usually an on-off valve mounted on the instrument panel. The dial is marked "Dry Road"–"Slippery Road".

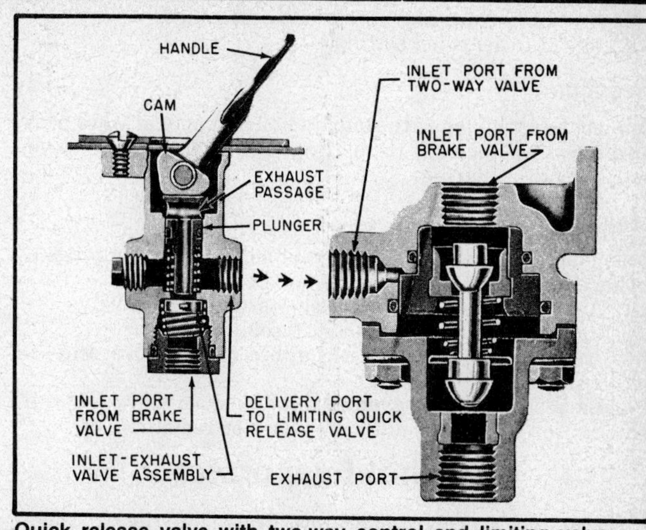

Quick release valve with two-way control and limiting valve (© Mack Trucks, Inc.)

PREVENTIVE MAINTENANCE

EVERY YEAR OR 50,000 MILES

The valve should be disassembled and cleaned. Inlet and exhaust valve boots and piston grommets should be checked and replaced as necessary.

Inspection

1. Disconnect one front brake chamber line.
2. Remove the plug from the unused brake chamber port.
3. Install test gauge in this port.
4. Install another test gauge in the foot brake delivery line.
5. Place the handle of the two way valve in the "Dry Road" position.
6. Make a foot valve application. Both gauges should read the same.
7. Release the foot valve. Both gauges should immediately drop to zero.
8. Place handle of the two way valve in the "Slippery Road" position.
9. Make a foot valve application. The test gauge at the brake chamber should read about one half that of the gauge in the delivery line.

Leakage Test

1. Place two way handle in the "Dry Road" position, make and hold a brake application. Check the exhausts of both the two way and limiting and quick release valves for leakage.
2. Place the handle of the two way valve in the "Slippery Road" position. Make a foot brake application and check the exhaust of the two way valve for leakage.

If valves do not function properly, they must be replaced.

Pressure Regulating Valve

This valve controls the pressure of a volume of compressed air. It remains closed until its setting is reached. At this point it opens, and excess air escapes through its exhaust port, maintaining a constant pressure.

At the present time, its chief use is in protected air brake systems to control the amount of air taken from the air brake system for auxiliary devices. The valve is connected between the air brake reservoir and the auxiliary equipment reservoir. The usual setting is 60 psi.

PREVENTIVE MAINTENANCE

EVERY MONTH OR 2,000 MILES

1. Check mounting bolts and pressure adjusting screw for tightness.
2. Check for leakage at the small vent hole in the spring cage.

EVERY 6 MONTHS OR 25,000 MILES

1. Connect a test gauge to the supply lines.
2. Observe the point at which the valve opens.
3. If pressure setting is off by 5 lbs. either way, adjust the setting.
4. Tighten the locknut after adjustment.

EVERY YEAR OR 50,000 MILES

1. Disassemble regulating valve and clean all parts.
2. Replace diaphragm.

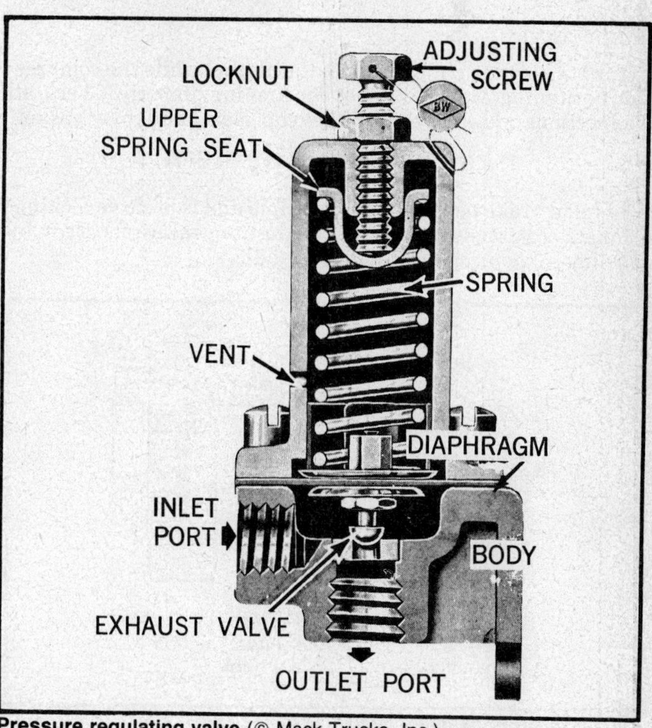

Pressure regulating valve (© Mack Trucks, Inc.)

3. Assemble valve and check with test gauge.
4. Adjust to specified setting.

Inspection

Connect a test gauge to the supply line and note at what pressure the valve opens. If the setting is more than 5 lbs. either way, adjust the setting.

Leakage Test

No leakage is permissible at the vent hole in the spring cage. If leakage occurs, the diaphragm must be replaced.

1. Apply pressure at 10 lbs. below setting to the valve.
2. Coat the outlet port with soap solution.
3. Leakage of a three in. bubble in three seconds is permissible.
4. Excessive leakage denotes dirty or worn valve seats, in which case the unit should be repaired or replaced.

Alcohol Evaporator

This unit allows alcohol vapors to be drawn into the air system to prevent system freezing in sub-freezing weather. The assembly consists of an evaporator body, an integral mounting bracket and a container for the alcohol. The unit is connected to the compressor intake where vacuum draws in the vapors through a strainer.

PREVENTIVE MAINTENANCE

EVERY 1,000 MILES

1. Check the alcohol level and refill with 188 proof methyl alcohol. If the alcohol isn't evaporating, the unit should be inspected.

EVERY 1,800 HOURS OR 50,000 MILES

1. Remove the strainer in the bottom of the evaporator body.

EVERY 3,600 HOURS OR 100,000 MILES

1. Disassemble evaporator unit and clean thoroughly.
2. Inspect all parts for cracks.
3. Check evaporator tube for clogging.
4. Replace all gaskets.

Inspection

If air bubbles are not present in the alcohol while the compressor is running, the unit is not functioning properly. Check all connections and condition of filler cap gasket and cover gasket.

Hand Brake System

The hand brake uses a toggle principle and is positive locking. Linkage adjustment can be made to compensate for wear by turning a knob cap on the lever handle.

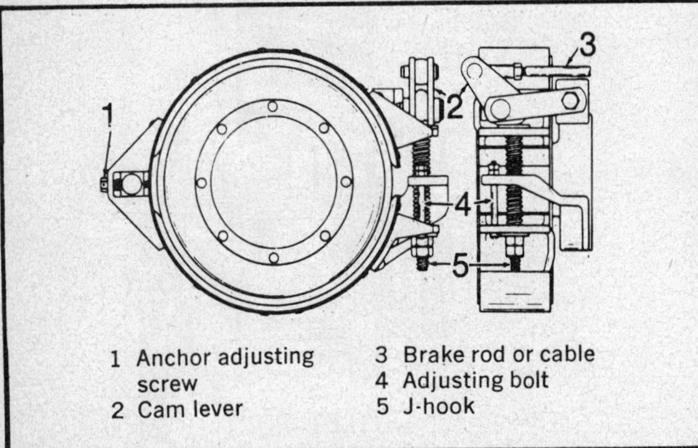

Typical external clamping band type hand brake (© Mack Trucks, Inc.)

Lever Adjustment

1. Set hand brake lever in full release position.
2. Turn knob clockwise until the lever pull becomes hard over the center point and a distinctive click is heard. This indicates the lining is tight against the drum.

When hand adjustment can no longer be made:

1. Set hand brake lever in full released position.
2. Turn knob counterclockwise until the clevis pin bottoms.
3. If the hand brake lining is serviceable, adjust to proper clearance. See section on Hand Brake Lining Assembly.
4. If the lever will not pull over center or the bellcrank does not stop against the bracket pin, adjust the length of pull rod or cable.

FRICTION LOCK ADJUSTMENT

The function of the friction lock is to apply effort required to turn the adjusting knob. Knobs are preset to a medium effort.

There are two types: a spring and ball type and a neoprene O-ring type.

Adjusting the Friction Knob Tension

1. Place lever in full released position.
2. Rotate the knob counterclockwise as far as it will go.
3. Grasp upper and lower half of the adjusting knob with two vise-grip pliers. Turn the upper half counterclockwise to unlock for adjustment.
4. Turning the lower half clockwise will increase the tension, counterclockwise will decrease the tension.
5. When tension has been set tighten the upper half against the lower.
6. Readjust hand brake lever.

HAND BRAKE LINING ASSEMBLY—SHOE TYPE

Adjustment

1. Jack up rear wheels clear of floor.
2. Place brake lever in full release position.
3. Set adjustment knob so that clevis pin bottoms.
4. Turn eccentric adjuster located near top of support plate in the direction of the drum rotation until drag occurs.
5. Back off eccentric until .010 in. free clearance is attained.
6. Turn drum so that adjusting hole in drum lines up with adjusting screw.
7. Insert adjusting tool in adjusting hole and turn star wheel to adjust shoe to drum.
8. Remove clevis pin and check brake cable or rod.
9. Back off star wheel until drag is released–about 10 notches.
10. Lower vehicle and remove jack.

HAND BRAKE LINING ASSEMBLY—BAND TYPE

Adjustment

1. Set hand brake in full released position.
2. Set adjustment knob so that clevis pin bottoms.
3. Adjust screw on anchor bracket for 0.015 in. clearance between drum and lining at the bracket.
4. Turn adjusting bolt for 0.015 in. clearance along the lower half of band.
5. Adjust J-hook bolt for 0.015 in. clearance along upper half of band.
6. Note position of cam lever. Cams should lift J-hook bolt when rod or cable moves upward. Adjust as necessary.
7. Recheck for 0.015 in. clearance all around.

FUEL SYSTEM

For information on the diesel fuel and diesel injection systems, refer to the Mack Diesel Engine section of this book.

Low Idle Adjustment

NOTE: All adjusting devices on Mack fuel injection pumps and governors, except the low idle adjusting screw, are wired and lead sealed. While the vehicle is under warranty, unauthorized removal of seals will void governor, injection pump and engine warranties.

Attach Mack special tool (J28559) Digistrobe to the engine.

1. Locate and mark the TDC indicator on the vibration damper.
2. Flash the Digistrobe at the recommended low idle speed.
3. Start the engine and direct the Digistrobe flash at the vibration damper. The mark on the vibration damper should be aligned and the Digistrobe should read out at the correct rpm. If the low idle speed is not correct, adjust it.
4. Locate the low idle adjusting screw on the top of the throttle housing cover. Loosen the low idle screw locknut.
5. Turn the idle screw until the correct rpm is showing on the Digistrobe. Hold the idle screw and tighten the locknut.

COOLING SYSTEM

Thermostat

The thermostat regulates the flow of coolant through the radiator and is the primary control of engine operating temperature. Engine life and engine performance are directly dependent upon proper thermostat operation. If the thermostat has been removed check the bellows for rupture or distortion. If the valve can be pulled or pushed off its seat with little effort when the thermostat is cold, or it does not seat properly, the unit is probably defective.

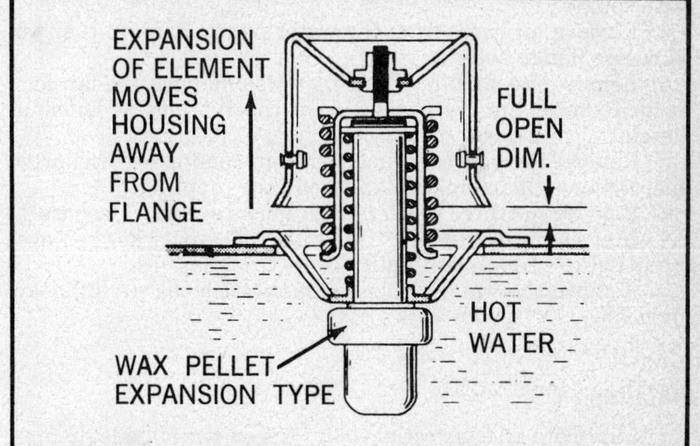

Wax pellet type thermostat (© Mack Trucks, Inc.)

Radiator Shutter System

When the cooling system incorporates a radiator shutter system and the engine is below operating temperature, a control valve directs air to the shutter cylinder to close the shutter. Since the shutter is closed air cannot be drawn through the radiator and the engine temperature rises rapidly. When the operating temperature of the control valve is reached, air is allowed to exhaust from the shutter cylinder and the springs open the shutter.

Failure of the shutter to close completely may be caused by a leaky cylinder, or by misalignment of the shutter frame side member. Dirty linkage may also cause a binding condition which will result in faulty engine temperature control.

When lubrication of the shutter linkage is necessary use a lightweight oil sparingly to each movable joint. Excessive lubrication will only increase the rate of dirt accumulation.

NOTE: When replacing a thermostat or shutterstat be sure to install with the correct part to maintain the designed operating temperature for each engine.

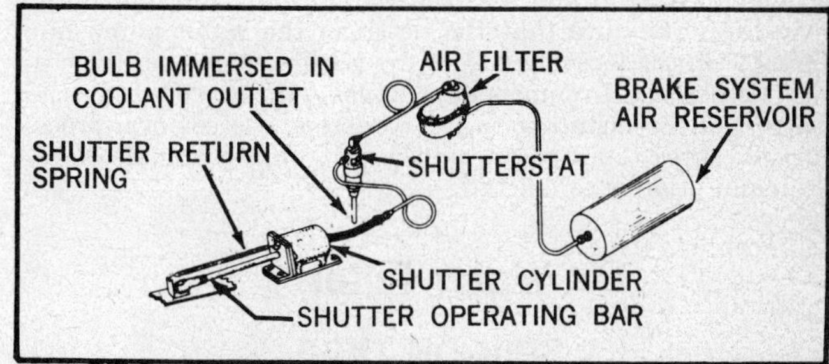

Shutter control layout—non-current production models (© Mack Trucks, Inc.)

Water Pump

Removal

1. Disconnect the ground battery cable.
2. Drain the radiator.
3. Break loose the fan pulley bolts.
4. Loosen the generator at the bolt on the adjusting bracket and remove the bolts.
5. Remove the fan blade and pulley.

NOTE: The fan assembly must not be bent or damaged to assure proper balance during operation.

6. Loosen the clamps and disconnect all hoses from the water pump.
7. Remove the water pump to block retaining bolts and remove the pump.

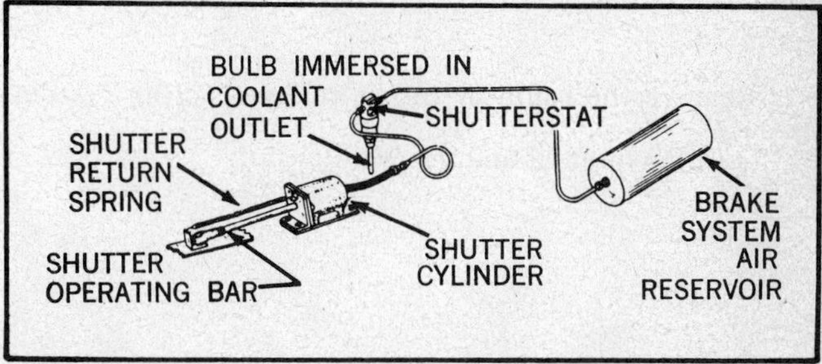

Shutter control layout—current production models (© Mack Trucks, Inc.)

Installation

1. Install the pump to the cylinder block using a new sealer coated pump to block gasket.
2. Install the fan blade and pulley to the water pump.
3. Connect all hoses to the water pump and tighten the clamps.
4. Install the fan belts and tighten the generator.
5. Fill the system with coolant and add anti-freeze if necessary.
6. Connect the ground battery cable.
7. Start the engine and check for leaks.

MID – LINER

Removal

1. Disconnect the negative battery cables, and tilt the cab over. Be sure that the cab tilt saftey catches are locked in place.
2. Drain the coolant from the cooling system, by removing the the drain plug from the metal coolant tube ruuning to the water pump.
3. Remove all hoses from the water pump. Remove the two oil cooler flange bolts.
4. Remove the six fan mounting nuts and push the fan forward. Remove the two screws from the thermostat housing flange.
5. Remove the pipe coupling of the air compressor discharge line. Remove the metal coolant feed tube coupling.
6. Remove the three water pump casing cap screws, separate the water pump casing from the timing gear cover and remove the impeller from underneath.
7. Remove the water pump assembly from the timing gear cover.

Installation

1. Lubricate and install new O-rings on the outside diameter of the pump hub. Now line up the notch in the water pump hub with the locating lug on the engine timing gear cover.
2. Using installer # J29419 with driver handle # J8092 or equivalent, install and seat the water pump into the timing gear cover. Be sure that the notch in the water pump hub mates with the locating lug on the timing gear cover.
3. Reinstall all components flanges with new O-rings and the rest of the installion is the reverse of the removal procedure. Be sure to start engine and check for any coolant leaks after installation is completed.

Water Filter

SPIN-ON TYPE

The spin-on type water filter is compatible with both water and anti-freeze and provides maximum protection as both a filter and a corrosion inhibitor.

Removal

1. Remove the radiator cap to relieve cooling system pressure.
2. Turn the filter off and remove.

Installation

1. Clean the mounting surface on the bracket and apply a light film of oil on the face of the gasket.
2. Position the filter and turn one full turn after the gasket contacts the base.
3. Replace the radiator cap and start the engine to check for leaks.
4. Turn the engine off and tighten the filter slightly.

ELEMENT TYPE

Removal

1. If present close the inlet and outlet line shut-off valves.
2. If shut-off valves are not present in this system, drain the radiator.
3. Remove the two filter cover retaining bolts and disconnect the hose from the cover.
4. Remove the upper plate and filter element.
5. Remove the lower corrosion resistor plate.
   a. If the plate is discolored, clean with a wire brush.
   b. Replace the plate if it becomes thin and pliable or develops large jagged holes.
6. Clean the cylindrical spring or replace if necessary.
7. Remove the body housing sump plug, clean out the housing, then replace the plug.

Installation

1. Place the cylindrical spring, the lower corrosion resistor plate, the new element and top plate into the body housing.
2. Clean the cover gasket and housing surfaces and replace the cover with the two retaining bolts.
3. Open the inlet and outlet shut-off valves if applicable, or refill the coolant system if it was drained.

TYPE SERVICE	NEW INSTALLATION	REPEAT SERVICE
HIGHWAY OR LONG HAUL	2500-3000 MILES	7500-10,000 MILES
LOCAL DELIVERY AND LOW MILEAGE	2500-3000 MILES	2500-3000 MILES OR 100-150 HOURS

Water filter service interval chart (© Mack Trucks, Inc.)

4. Start the engine and let it idle.
5. Check the inlet line condition indicator to see that the water flow is toward the filter.
6. Feel the filter housing for a temperature increase and if the system is air locked, bleed the air from the system by disconnecting the outlet hose at the filter until coolant escapes, then connect and tighten the hose.

NOTE: When anti-freeze is used in the system, the (chromate) standard filter element must be replaced with a PAF type filter element.

ENGINE

Mid – Liner

ALL MODELS

Removal

NOTE: For information on the other diesel engines that are used in Mack trucks, refer to the Mack Diesel Engine section of this book. There may be small differences in the removal of the 06.20.30 series engine and the removal of the 06.02.12 series engine.

1. Disconnect the negative battery cables, drain the air system, engine oil and cooling system.
2. Tilt the cab and remove the cab supporting cross beam as follows:
   a. Loosen the clamps and remove the three hoses from the coolant expansion tank. Remove the cylinder head gas relief line, radiator gas relief line and the feed line from the coolant expansion tank to the water pump suction sides.
   b. Remove the air inlet pipe bracket, the engine oil lube gauge and disconnect the sheath.
   c. Remove the engine oil filter hose and on the tractor models, disconnect the control pipes of the trailer service brake.
   d. Remove the right hand fender and on the tractor models, disconnect the feed pipes of the trailer brake system. Remove the two bottom mounting bolts of the left hand fender.
   e. Suspend the crossbeam with slings and remove the mounting bolts at the right and left of the frame. Release and remove the crossbeam assembly from the vehicle.
3. Remove the exhaust pipe by removing the four bolts from the pipe flange and separate the bottom exhaust pipe.
4. Remove the air induction piping as follows:
   a. Remove the air compressor inlet line, the turbo charger inlet pipe and loosen the three air induction piping brackets.
   b. Loosen the two clamps and remove the air induction pipe connecting sleeve.
5. Disconnect the tachometer drive cable and disengage it by removing the mounting brackets.
6. Remove the the engine oil dipstick sheath. Tag and disconnect the plug from the pressure sending unit and the plug from the engine oil circuit pressure switch.
7. Remove the two power steering hydraulic pump mounting bolts and remove the pump and secure against the frame.

NOTE: Do not disconnect the lines to the steering pump, it would only cause unneccesary drainage of the power steering hydraulic circuit.

8. Tag and disconnect the fuel supply and return lines to and from the fuel tank and plug the pipe orfices.
9. Disconnect the throttle linkage at the injection pump governor for the throttle lever and stop lever controls.
10. Disconnect the air discharge line from the air compressor.
11. Tag and disconnect the power supply cables and exciter wire to the alternator. Secure wiring harness out the way along the frame.
12. Tag and disconnect the power cables and solenoid wire to the starter and disconnect the grounding braid strap. Refer to the transmission portion of this section for for the removal of the transmission.
13. Connect a engine hoist to the front eyes of the lifting bracket on the engine and to the fixed lifting rings located on the rear engine supports.
14. Remove the engine mounting bolts. Mark the locations of mounting pad insulators. Also mark the alignment position of the right insulator for re-installation purposes.

NOTE: When raising and removing the engine from the vehicle, be sure to protect the water filter on the right hand side (or remove it) and the alternator on the left hand side (or remove it).

15. Raise the engine a little to move the engine forward to clear the flywheel housing on the starter side from the left rear engine support on the frame. Now raise the engine and remove it from the vehicle, placing it on a suitable engine stand.

Installation

1. Before installing the engine, check the condition of the water and air hoses, hydraulic lines and check out the overall condition of the basic engine components.
2. Place the engine support insulators in there place according to the alignment markings made during the removal procedure.
3. Installation is the reverse order of the removal procedure.
4. Torque the front engine mounting bolts to 70 ft. lbs. and the rear engine mounting bolts to 206 ft. lbs. on the 06.20.30 series engines. Torque the front engine mounting bolts to 22 to 26 ft. lbs. and the rear engine mounting bolts to 148 ft. lbs. on the 06.02.12 series engines.
5. Refill the engine lubricating system and the cooling system. Start the engine, check it for leaks and road test the vehicle.

FRONT AXLE SUSPENSION

Front axle used on highway trucks and tractors are of I beam, reverse-Elliott construction. Steering is a knuckle pin and ball and roller type with front eliptical leaf springs.

Front Spring

Removal

EYE AND RUBBER MOUNTING TYPE

1. With jack or overhead crane, remove chassis weight from springs.
2. Remove spring U-bolts and nuts and disconnect shock absorbers.
3. Cut lockwire on fixed pin retaining bolt and remove bolt.
4. Remove rubber shock insulator cap retaining bolts and remove cap.
5. Raise chassis so that rubber insulators may be removed.

NOTE: Mark position of caster plate for assembly.

6. Remove spring from axle.

Installation

1. With chassis suspended, place spring on front axle.

NOTE: Position caster plate as per marks.

2. Be sure main leaf bushing is in proper position and install fixed pin.

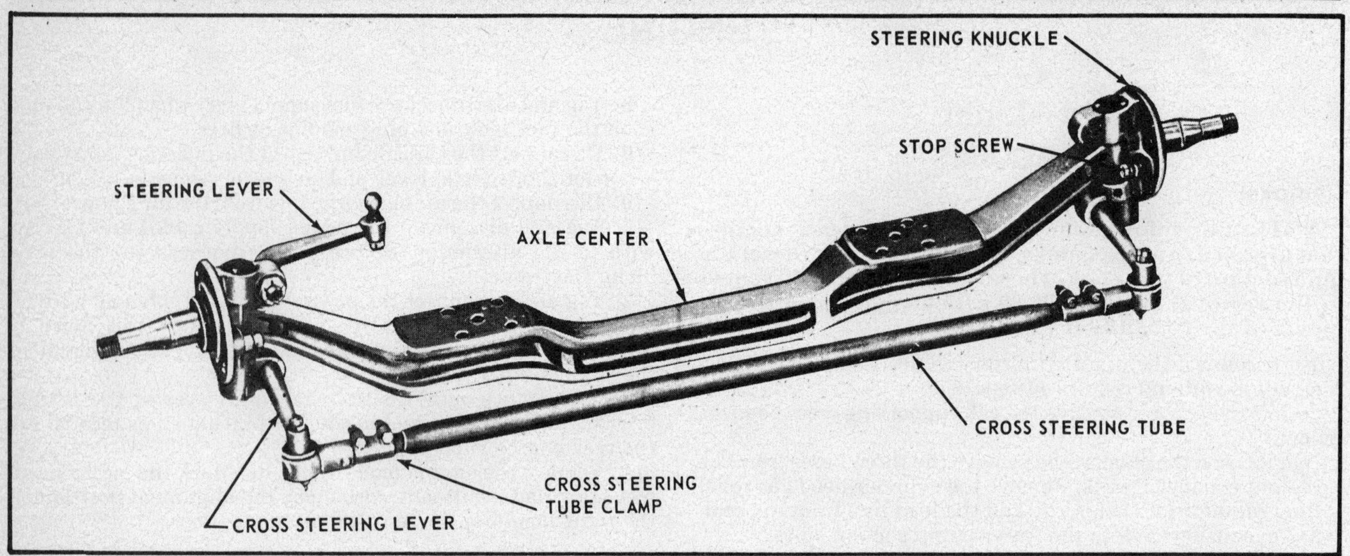

Typical front axle (© Mack Trucks, Inc.)

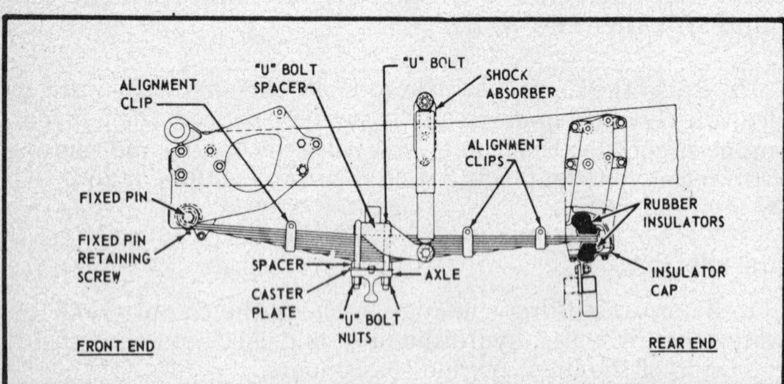

Typical front spring eye and rubber mounting (© Mack Trucks, Inc.)

3. Install fixed pin retaining cap-screw, torque and safety wire.
4. Install rubber shock insulator over the end of the spring and make certain that the rubber fits properly in the cup riveted to the spring. Push spring up into the shock insulator housing and install cap.

NOTE: Do not grease or oil insulators. Ordinary dishwashing liquid is sufficient lubricant.

5. Lower chassis to position spring.
6. Position spring U-bolt spacer on top of spring and install U-bolts.
7. Position shock absorber bracket and towing eye and install U-bolts and retaining nuts.

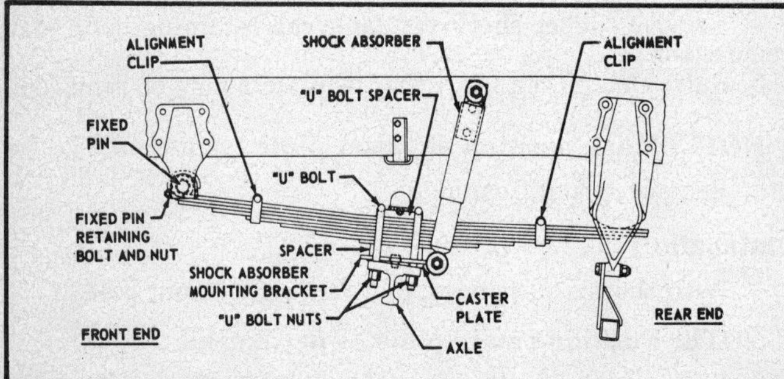

Typical front spring eye and slipper mounting (© Mack Trucks, Inc.)

8. Torque U-bolts.
9. Reconnect shock absorber.

EYE AND SLIPPER TYPE

Removal

1. With a jack or shop crane, take chassis weight from springs by lifting at frame.
2. Remove spring U-bolts and nuts and disconnect shock absorbers.
3. Remove fixed pin retaining bolt and nut and remove fixed pin.

NOTE: Check the caster plate and mark for assembly.

4. Raise chassis slightly and remove spring.

Installation

1. With chassis suspended, position spring in place on front axle.

NOTE: Position caster plate as per marks.

2. Be sure main leaf bushing is in position and install fixed pin, pin retaining bolt and nut.
3. ower chassis to position spring.
4. Position U-bolt spacer on top of spring and install U-bolts.
5. Position shock absorber bracket and towing eye and install U-bolt retaining nuts.
6. Tighten U-bolt nuts to recommended torque.
7. Reconnect shock absorber.

Steering Knuckle

TYPE I KNUCKLE

Removal

1. Jack vehicle and remove wheel and hub assembly. Always use stands when removing wheels.
2. Disconnect drag link from steering lever and cross steering tube from cross steering levers.
3. Remove brake mechanism assembly complete with anchor plate or spider assembly.

NOTE: Wire anchor plate or spider assembly to chassis.

4. Remove oil seal and retainer from upper knuckle boss. Remove expansion plug from lower boss.
5. Remove draw pin.
6. Drive knuckle pin out of knuckle.
7. Remove knuckle and throughst bearing.

Installation

1. If bushings were removed, press new bushings into place and line ream to size. Align lubricant holes.
2. Lubricate knuckle pin and bushings and install knuckle and throughst bearing on axle.
3. Install knuckle pin and hold knuckle with throughst bearing against axle center. Check dimension A. Dimension A should be 0.037–0.057 in. If excessive, replace bearing.
4. Install draw pin.
5. Drive new expansion plug into lower knuckle boss.
6. Install oil seal retainer and new oil seal in upper boss.
7. Install brake mechanism assembly with anchor plate or spider assembly.
8. Reconnect drag link and cross steering tube and install wheel and hub assembly.
9. Lubricate knuckle pin bushings with proper grease.
10. Remove jacks and stands.

TYPE II KNUCKLE

Removal

1. Jack vehicle, place stands and remove wheel and hub assembly.
2. Disconnect drag link from steering lever and cross steering tube from cross steering levers.
3. Remove brake mechanism assembly complete with anchor plate or spider. Wire anchor plate to chassis.
4. Remove top and bottom knuckle covers.
5. Remove locknut cotter pin, locknut, lockwasher, taper nut washer, taper nut and throughst bearing.
6. Place piece of wood on top of pin to protect pin and drive pin out through bottom of knuckle. Lift knuckle off axle.

Installation

1. If bushings were removed, press new bushings into place and line ream to size. Align lubricant holes in bushings.
2. Lubricate bushings and install knuckle and pin on axle. Tap bottom of knuckle pin with soft mallet to position pin in axle center.
3. Install throughst bearing, taper nut and related parts. Adjust axle center to knuckle clearance.
4. Reinstall brakes, steering linkage and wheels.
5. Lubricate knuckle pin bushings.
6. Remove jacks and stands.

TYPE III

Removal

1. Jack vehicle, place stands and remove wheel and hub assembly.
2. Disconnect drag link from steering lever and cross steering tube from cross steering levers.
3. Remove brake mechanism assembly complete with anchor plate or spider assembly. Wire anchor plate to chassis.
4. Remove knuckle cap or expansion plug, throughst bearing adjusting screw and throughst bearing.
5. With a brass drift, drive knuckle pin out through bottom of knuckle. Lift knuckle off axle.

Installation

1. If bushings were removed press in new ones and align tube holes. Bushings for needle bearing knuckle are assembled with groove run-out towards bottom.

NOTE: Bushings used in needle bearing knuckles do not require reaming.

2. If knuckle is type with expansion plug, install it at this time, using the following procedure:
   a. Insert plug in knuckle bore with concave side facing out.

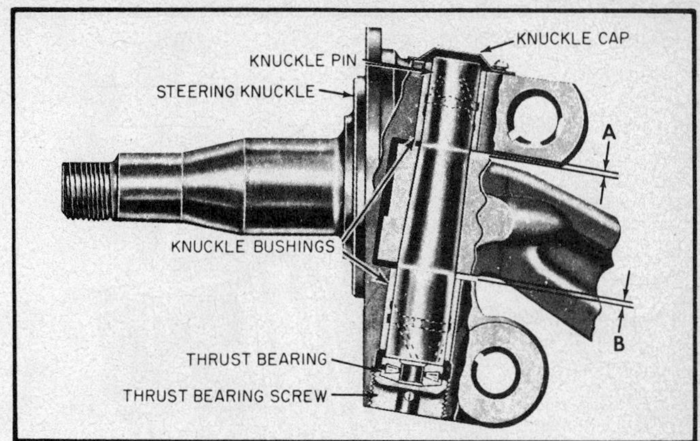

Type I steering knuckle (© Mack Trucks, Inc.)

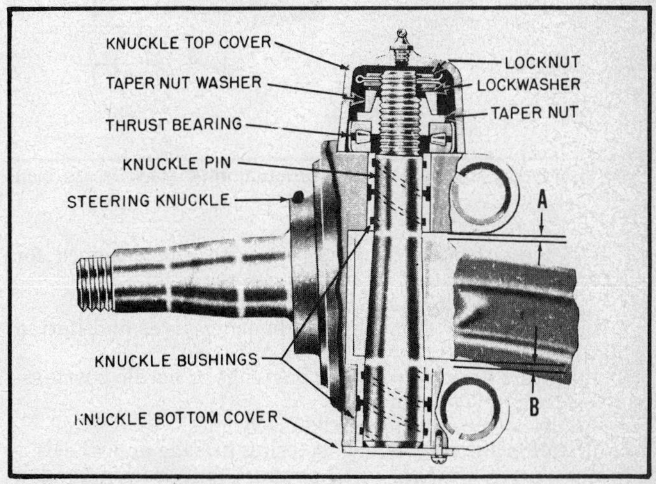

Type II steering knuckle (© Mack Trucks, Inc.)

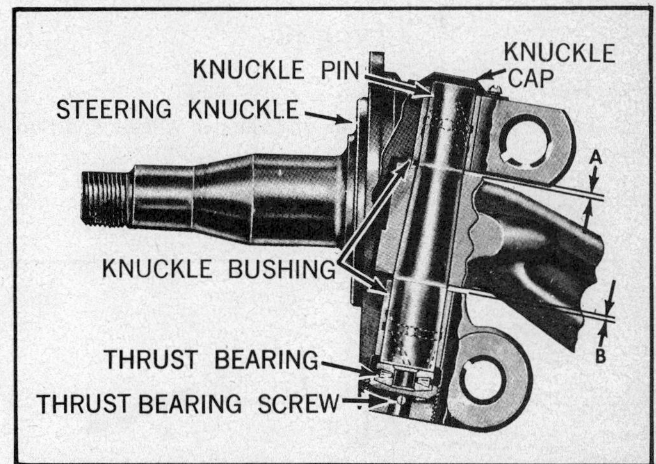

Type III steering knuckle without needle bearing (© Mack Trucks, Inc.)

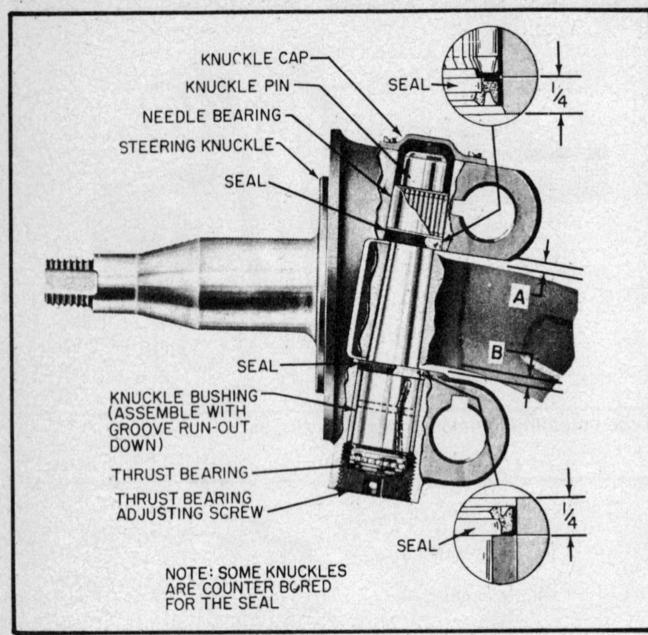

Type III steering knuckle—current production (© Mack Trucks, Inc.)

b. Set anvil on a firm support with end designed for knuckle service facing up.

c. Place knuckle on anvil fully and squarely.

d. Insert driver through both housing bores and flatten plug against anvil.

3. Lubricate knuckle pins and bushings or needle bearings, and assemble knuckle on axle.
4. Adjust axle center-to-knuckle clearance.
5. Install brake mechanism, steering linkage and wheels.
6. Lubricate knuckle pin bushings with recommended grease.
7. Remove jacks and stands.

TYPE IV

Removal

1. Jack vehicle, place stands and remove wheels and hub assembly.
2. Disconnect cross steering tube from cross steering lever and drag link from steering lever.

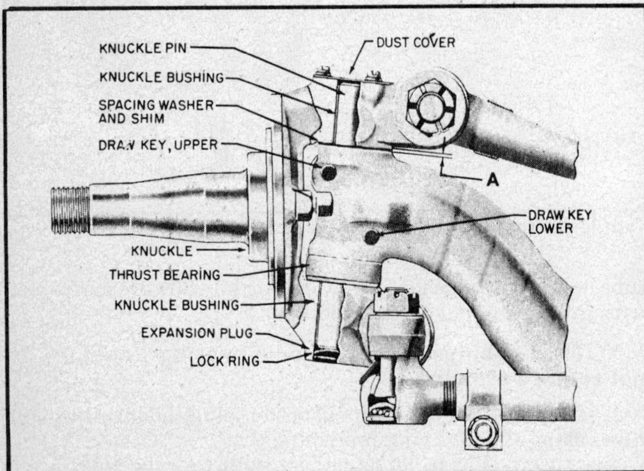

Type IV steering knuckle (© Mack Trucks, Inc.)

3. Remove any brake parts that interfere with removal of knuckle pin.
4. Remove lock ring and expansion plug from bottom of knuckle.
5. Remove capscrews, dust cover and gasket from top of knuckle.
6. Drive out draw keys, using a drift against the small end.
7. Drive knuckle pin out of knuckle, using a brass drift and lift knuckle off axle.

Installation

1. Using a driver with a pilot .010 in. less than the I.D. of the bushing, and $^1/_2$ in. long, press new bushing into place. Press in three stages to facilitate alignment. Bushing should press flush with inner face of boss.
2. Ream metallic, not plastic, bushing to size.
3. Position knuckle on axle with throughst bearing between axle and lower boss of knuckle. Install retainer lip down.
4. Align holes in knuckle and axle then jack knuckle so that no clearance remains between lower knuckle boss, throughst bearing and axle. Do not install knuckle pin.
5. Check clearance between upper knuckle boss and axle. Clearance should not exceed 0.015 in. Adjust with shims.
6. Align flats on knuckle pin with draw key holes in knuckle and drive knuckle pin into place.
7. Install draw keys. Be sure flat lines up with corresponding flat on knuckle pin.

NOTE: Install one key from each side of axle center. Do not install both keys from the same side. Secure keys by center punching edge of hole.

8. Install expansion plug and lock ring in bottom boss.
9. Install dust cover and gasket on top boss.
10. Reassemble all brake and steering parts and mount wheels.
11. Lubricate knuckle pin bushings.
12. Remove jacks and stands.

Wheel Bearing

Adjustment

1. Raise the vehicle and support safely.
2. Remove the hub cap, cut the adjusting nut lock wire, remove the cotter pin or straighten the D-washer and remove the locknut as required.
3. Be assured that the brake shoes do not cause a dragging condition while rotating the wheel.

NOTE: Disc brake pads may have to be forced away from the rotor to allow freedom of wheel rotation.

4. Tighten the bearing adjusting nut while rotating the wheel, alternately in both directions, until a slight drag is felt.
5. Back off the adjusting nut or castle nut $^1/_6$ to $^1/_3$ of a turn to align with the nearest locking hole, if applicable.
6. The bearing end play should be 0.003 to 0.008 in..
7. Secure the locks as required to the spindle.
8. Install the hub cap and lower the vehicle to the floor.

NOTE: On the Mid–Liner, torque the wheel bearing lock nut to 74 ft. lbs. and then loosen the nut a $^1/_4$ of a turn to ensure normal bearing play and to permit the installation of the cotter pin through the castle nut slots.

Front Driving Axle

Removal and Installation

1. Raise the vehicle and support safely so that the weight of the chassis is off the springs.
2. Remove the wheels and drum assemblies.

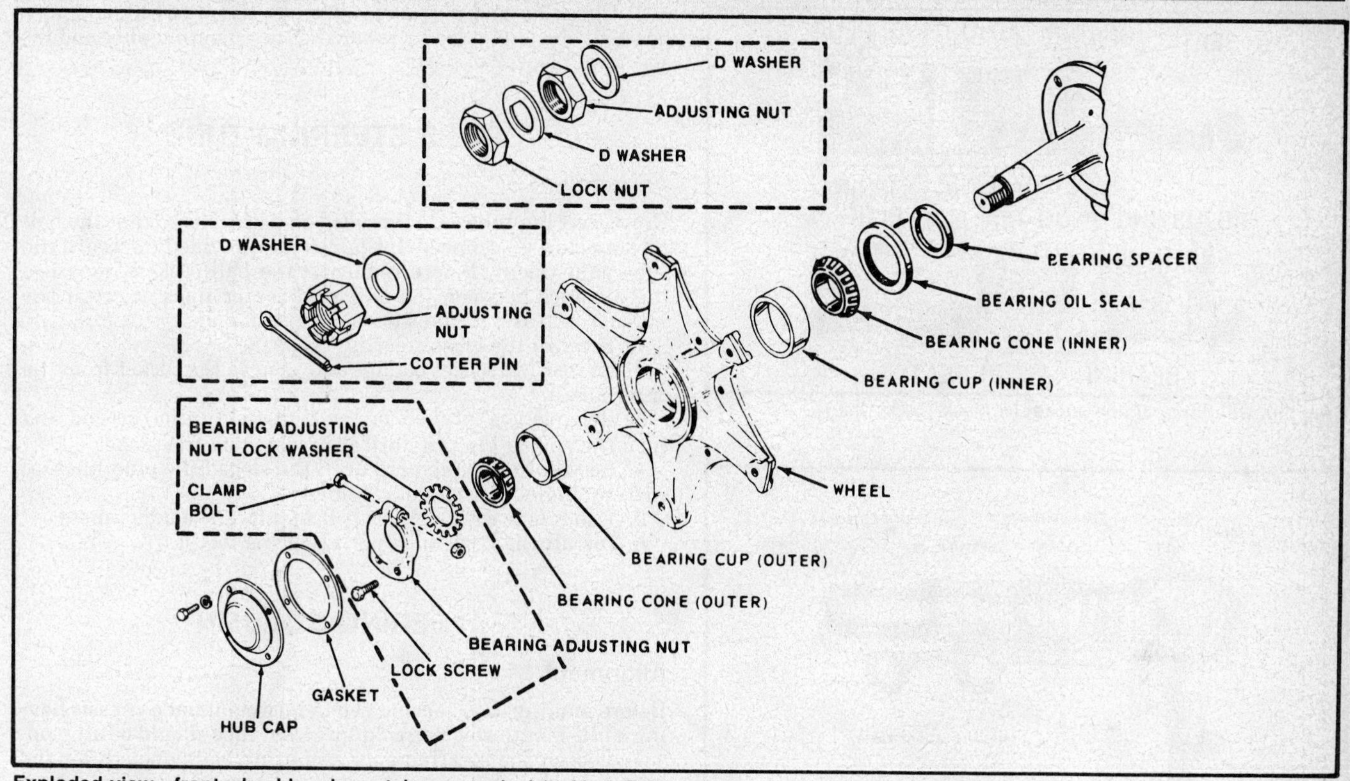

Exploded view—front wheel bearing retainers—typical (© Mack Trucks, Inc.)

3. Match-mark the driveshaft flange to the yoke and disconnect the driveshaft.
4. Disconnect the shock absorbers, air lines and steering linkage.
5. Match-mark the caster plate, if used, and remove the spring clip nuts while supporting the drive axle housing.
6. Remove the drive axle housing from under the vehicle.
7. The installation is the reverse of the removal procedure.
8. Tighten all bolts and nuts to specified torque.

MID – LINER

Removal and Installation

NOTE: This procedure deals with one side of the vehicle, so just repeat this procedure for both sides of the vehicle.

1. Block the rear wheels. Raise the vehicle and support safely so that the weight of the chassis is off the springs.
2. Remove the wheels and drum assemblies.
3. Remove the cotter pin from drag link ball joint and using a suitable tool uncouple the drag link. Remove the shock absorber.
4. Remove the retaining clip from the flexible tube of the brake line and disconnect and cap the brake line and place away from the work area.
5. Disconnect and cap the air line from the air cylinder. Place a floor jack or equivalent under the front axle, remove the nuts from the spring clips (U-bolts) and lower the front axle. Remove the front axle.
6. Installation is the reverse order of the removal procedure. Be sure to bleed the brake system. The following torque chart should be used on the installation procedure:
   a. Front shock absorber lower pin nut—148 ft. lbs.
   b. Front shock absorber upper pin nut—22 ft. lbs.
   c. Spring pin pinch bolt—30 ft. lbs.
   d. Spring U-bolts—266 ft. lbs.
   e. Front spring rear retaining screw—44 ft. lbs.
   f. Drag link ball joint nut—133 ft. lbs.

STEERING LINKAGE

The steering linkage consists of the drag link, cross steering tube and the various steering levers to which they are attached. There are two different types of drag links. One type has both the ball socket retainer integral with the link and can be adjusted. The other type uses an integral ball socket retainer at one end and a removable ball socket assembly at the opposite end. This type must be replaced when worn.

DRAG LINK

Adjustment

1. Remove the cotter pin and turn the adjusting plug in until solid resistance is felt. This means that the bearing has contacted the spring plug or seat and seating will occur at 50 to 60 ft. lbs. torque.

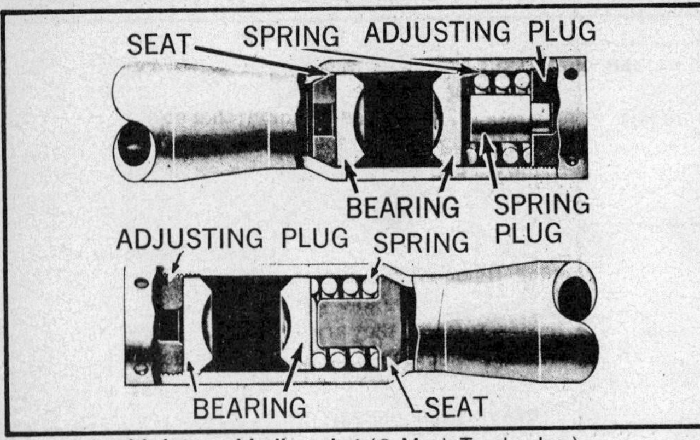

Drag link with integral ball socket (© Mack Trucks, Inc.)

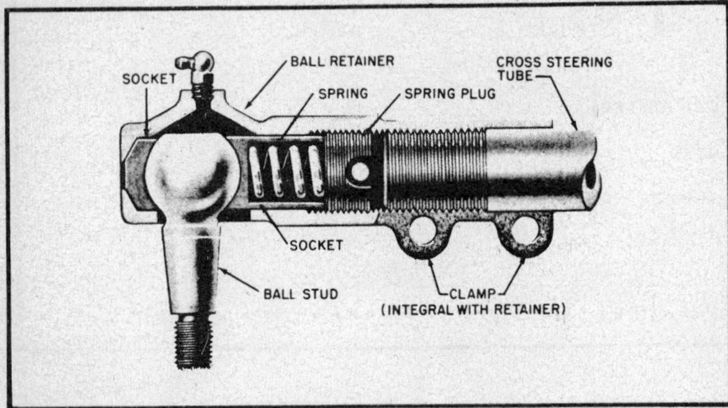

Cross steering socket retainer (© Mack Trucks, Inc.)

2. Back the adjusting plug out to the first position in which the cotter pin hole in the drag link lines up with the slot in the adjusting plug. Lock the adjustment with a cotter pin.

3. Check for end-play and if present, the drag link end may be easily disassembled by removing the adjusting plug and inspecting for broken parts.

CROSS STEERING TUBE

Adjustment

Cross steering tubes are threaded on both ends so that the ball sockets may be connected. Clamps are provided to secure the tube adjustment. Before removing the ball sockets, measure the distance between the ball stud center lines or count the number of turns it takes to remove each end.

1. Remove the cross steering tube.
2. Loosen the socket clamps and remove the socket from the cross tube.
3. Remove the lockbolt or the cotter pin from the end and turn the spring plug in until it is seated on the socket.
4. Loosen the spring plug until the slot in the plug lines up with the holes in the ball retainer.
5. Use a new cotter pin or bolt and lock the adjustment.
6. Install the cross tube and reset the toe-in.

STEERING COLUMN

Alignment

Before making any steering gear adjustments, the chassis having a full-length steering column jacket tube should be aligned.

1. Loosen the steering gear mounting bolts enough for the gear to shift.
2. Line up the jacket tube assembly with the angle determined by the column support bracket and tighten the mounting bolts.
3. Loosen the steering column support bracket screws.
4. Allow the bracket to shift and align itself with the jacket tube.
5. Tighten the support bracket screws.

MANUAL STEERING GEAR

Good steering performance is dependent on the steering gear being in its center position when the front road wheels are in a straight ahead position. The steering gears are designed to have less lash in the straight ahead position than at either turn position. In a correctly adjusted steering gear, the low lash area or high "spot" can be felt by the operator.

Steering Gear–Models 25, 26, 251 and 261

NOTE: The steering gear model number is stamped on the steering gear housing.

WORM BEARING PRE-LOAD

Checking

1. Jack the front wheels off the floor.
2. Turn the steering wheel two turns to the right from the straight-ahead position and secure at that point. There is now clearance between the worm and roller.
3. Grip the jacket tube firmly just below the steering wheel hub and slightly rest the side of a finger on the wheel hub. Have an assistant shake the road wheels sideways. If end-play can be felt at the steering hub the worn bearings must be adjusted.

NOTE: If the steering shaft is the type that incorporates universal joints, use the following procedure.

4. Disconnect the drag link from the steering gear lever.
5. Turn the steering wheel to the end of travel both ways to determine that lash exists between the worm and roller.
6. Rotate the steering column approximately one quarter turn and note the torque required. Torque can be determined with a torque wrench or observing pounds of pull required at a point nine in. from the center of the steering wheel. See the specification chart.

Adjustment

Adjusting shims can be removed to increase pre-load and added to reduce pre-load.

1. Drain the lubricant (except those gears with shims at the upper end).
2. Remove the worm cover screws and cover.
3. When it is necessary to remove a shim, separate the shims

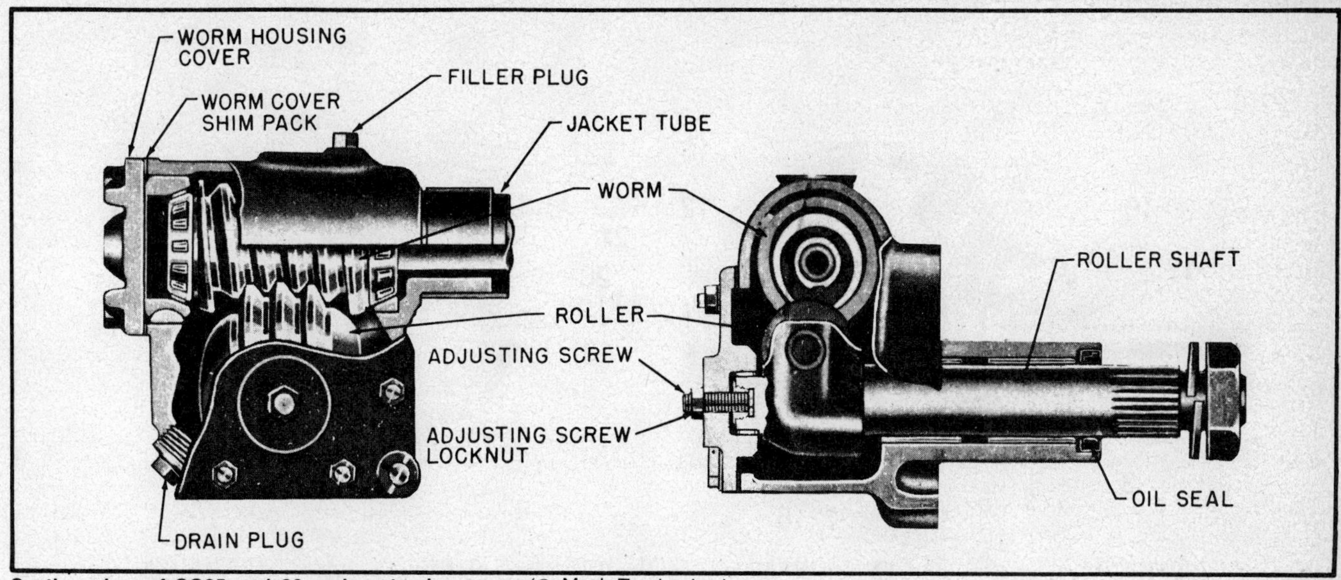

Section view of SG25 and 26 series steering gears (© Mack Trucks, Inc.)

in the gear with a knife and remove one thin shim. Be careful not to damage the remaining shims.

4. Replace the worm cover and tighten the screws to the specified torque.
5. Check the pre-load and repeat the procedure if necessary.

ROLLER SHAFT

Adjustment

NOTE: The following operation must be done after the worm bearing pre-load is established.

1. Center the steering gear by counting the number of turns required to travel from full right to the full left position then turning back from one extreme one-half the total number of turns.
2. Measure the torque it takes to rotate the gear through the center using the method described under checking worm bearing pre-load.

NOTE: The total pre-load, which includes the worm shaft plus the roller shaft, should be a minimum of $^3/_4$ pounds pull or 6 $^3/_4$ in. lbs.

3. If adjustment is necessary, loosen the roller shaft adjusting screw locknut and turn the adjusting screw clockwise to increase pre-load or counterclockwise to reduce pre-load.
4. Check the pre-load and repeat the adjustment if necessary.
5. When the adjustment is correct, hold the roller shaft adjusting screw and tighten the locknut to the specified torque.

Steering Gear – Model SG-46

NOTE: The steering gear model number is stamped on the steering gear housing. Always check the worm bearing adjustment first before making the sector lash adjustment.

WORM BEARING PRE-LOAD

Checking

1. Disconnect the drag link from the steering gear lever. Note the position for reassembly.
2. Loosen the locknut, and turn the lash adjuster a few turns counterclockwise.
3. Tighten all the side cover bolts.
4. Turn the steering wheel gently in one direction until it is stopped by the gear "stops" or by reaching the extreme end; then back off one full turn.

NOTE: Do not turn the wheel hard against the "stops" when the drag link is disconnected.

5. Attach a spring scale at the rim of the wheel.
6. Pull on the scale in a line at a right angle to the wheel spoke and measure the amount of pull that is needed to keep the wheel moving. Refer to the specification chart.
7. If the pull is not within the limits, adjust the worm bearings. See worm bearing pre-load adjustment procedure.

Adjustment

1. Loosen the locknut and turn the worm bearing adjuster screw clockwise until all the end play is gone.
2. Using the spring scale, check the steering wheel rim pull and turn the adjuster screw until the correct adjustment is obtained.
3. Tighten the locknut.
4. The sector shaft lash adjustment must be made following the worm bearing adjustment.

SECTOR SHAFT LASH

Adjustment

1. Make sure the steering gear side cover bolts are tight.
2. Center the steering gear by turning the steering wheel gently from the extreme right to the extreme left positions and counting the exact number of turns. Rotate the steering wheel exactly half-way; then mark the position on the top or bottom with a piece of tape.
3. Turn the lash adjuster screw clockwise to remove all backlash between the gear teeth. The amount of backlash can be felt by pushing backward or forward on the lower end of the steering gear lever.
4. Tighten the lash adjuster locknut to the specified torque when all backlash has been removed.
5. Using a spring scale measure the steering wheel rim pull through the center position. See the specifications chart.

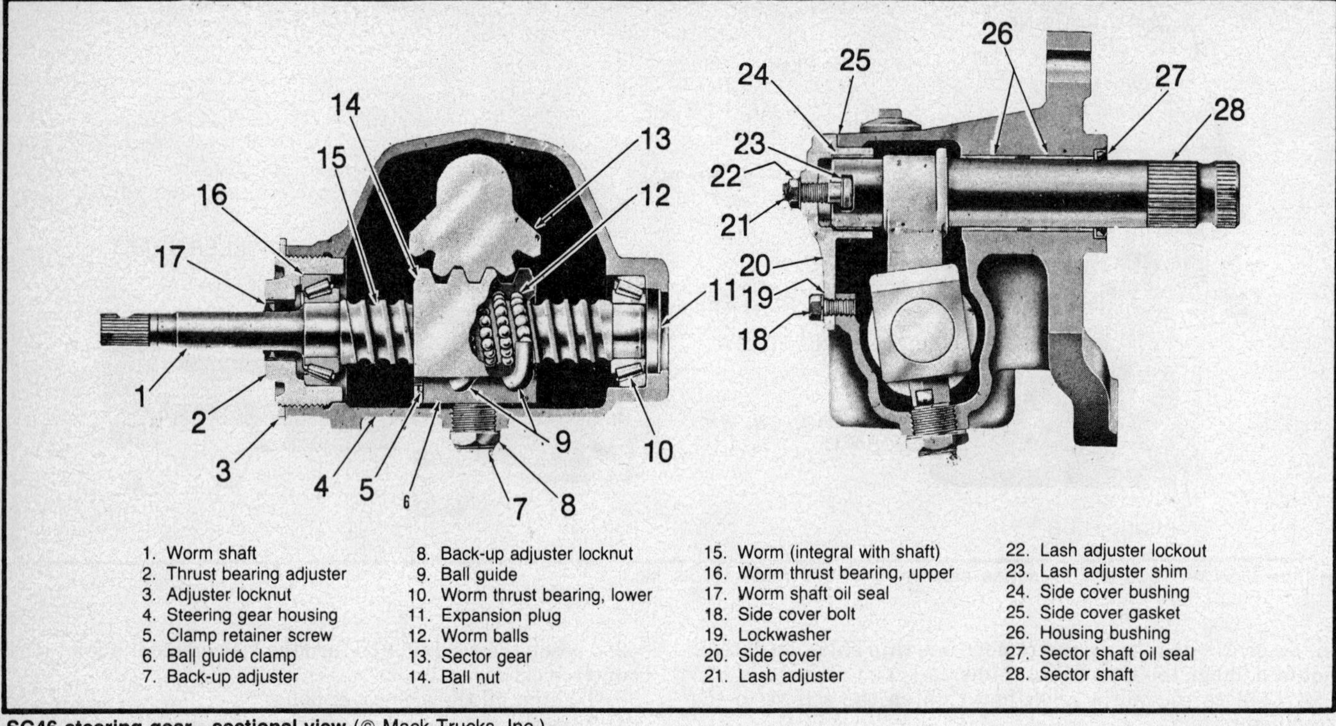

SG46 steering gear—sectional view (© Mack Trucks, Inc.)

6. If the rim pull is not within the specified limits, loosen the locknut and turn the adjuster screw to obtain limits.
7. Tighten the locknut and recheck.
8. After all other adjustments have been made, adjust the back-up adjuster.
   a. Turn the adjuster all the way, then back off $^1/_8$ to $^1/_4$ turn.

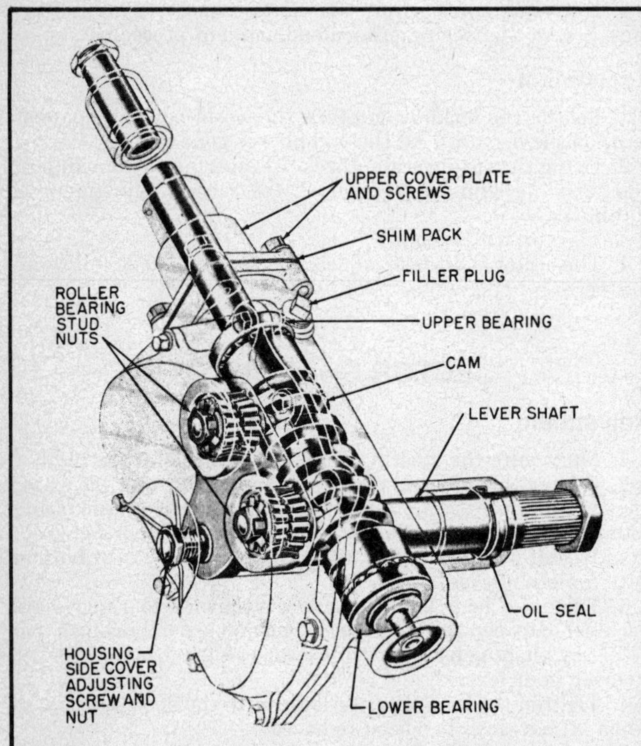

SG42 steering gear—phantom view (© Mack Trucks, Inc.)

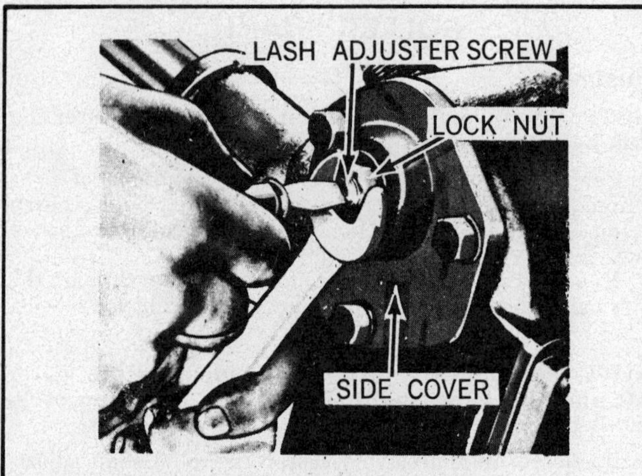

Adjusting sector gear lash (© Mack Trucks, Inc.)

   b. Tighten the locknut.
9. Connect the drag link to the steering gear lever.

Steering Gear – Model-SG42

NOTE: The steering gear model number is stamped on the steering gear housing.

CAM BEARING PRE-LOAD

Checking

1. Disconnect the drag link from the steering gear lever.
2. Loosen the lever shaft adjusting screw locknut and back out several turns.

3. Rotate the steering gear. There will be a slight drag if the adjustment is correct.
4. If the gear binds or turns freely without a slight drag, the cam bearing needs adjustment.

Adjustment

1. Remove the upper cover to expose the shims.
2. Using a knife remove one of the shims, without damaging the others, to increase pre-load.
3. If less pre-load is desired, add shims.
4. Replace the cover and tighten the attaching screws.
5. Recheck and repeat if necessary.
6. When the correct cam bearing pre-load is obtained adjust the stud mesh.

STUD MESH

Adjustment

1. Disconnect the steering linkage.
2. Center the steering gear.
   a. Turn the steering wheel from full right to full left and count the number of turns required.
   b. Turn the steering wheel back exactly one-half as many turns.
3. A slight drag will be felt when the steering gear is turned through its mid position if the mesh adjustment is correct.
4. To correct adjustment, loosen the adjusting screw locknut and turn the adjusting screw clockwise to reduce backlash or counterclockwise to increase it.
5. Tighten the locknut and connect the steering linkage.

POWER STEERING

Garrison and Ross Linkage System—Separate Cylinder Valve

CONTROL VALVE

Disassembly

1. Remove the dust seal.
2. Straighten the lock rings and unlock the end cover and the reducer end cover.
3. Remove the end cover and reducer end cover retaining screws.
4. Remove the lock rings from both ends of the valve body.
5. Remove the O-ring retainer and the O-ring from the spools threaded end.
6. Before removing the valve spool, note the position of the threaded end in relation to the valve body ports so the spoon end will not be reversed during assembly.
7. Remove the valve spool from the valve body.
8. Remove the glands, spring and reaction rings from the valve body and spool.
9. Remove the O-rings from each gland.
10. All the parts of the relief valve should not require servicing unless a leaking condition is evident.

NOTE: To disassemble the relief valve assembly, remove the plug.

CAUTION

Do not damage any surfaces or edges during disassembly.

Assembly

1. Install the ball into the relief valve hole in the valve body.
2. Slide the spring in the valve body.
3. Install the O-ring and plug flush with the outside surface of the valve body.
4. Slide one reaction ring and spring on the unthreaded end of the spool.
5. Install an O-ring on a gland and slide it on the unthreaded end of the spool.
6. Install the small O-ring in the short counterbore of the gland and install the O-ring retainer.
7. Install the C-washer.
8. Insert the spool assembly all the way in the valve body.
9. Install the lock ring with the legs toward the valve body and screw the reducer end cover on tight.

NOTE: Position the tab over the relief valve plug to retain the plug.

10. Install the reaction ring and the second spring over the threaded end of the spool.
11. Install the O-ring over on the outside of the gland and slide the gland onto the threaded end of the spool.
12. Install the small O-ring seal in the short counterbore of the gland. When sliding the gland over the threaded end of the spool, be careful of the seal.
13. Install the O-ring retainer.
14. Install the lock ring with the legs toward the valve body and screw on the end cover tightly.
15. Place the lock rings into the notches in the end covers.

POWER CYLINDER

Disassembly

1. Move the cylinder piston rod in and out until the oil is drained from the cylinder assembly.
2. Remove the end cover.
3. Push the bearing into the cylinder barrel about a half in. and remove the retaining ring from the groove in the cylinder.

CAUTION

Do not slide the bearing off the outer end of the piston rod as yet, in order to prevent damage by the threads.

4. Pull the piston rod and internal parts from the cylinder barrel as a unit.
5. Hold the piston rod by two wrench flats just above the thread end and remove the piston retaining nut.

CAUTION

Be careful not to damage the threads or finish of the rod.

6. Slide the piston off and remove the piston rings.
7. Slide the bearing off the piston end of the rod. Remove the O-ring and back-up ring.
8. Remove the seal and O-ring.

Assembly

1. Use all new seals and O-rings and lubricate with a light oil before assembly.
2. Install the O-ring seal in the bearing.
3. Install the back-up ring and O-ring to the bearing.
4. Slide the bearing onto the piston rod starting from the piston end.
5. Install the piston rings on the piston. The rings should move freely in the piston grooves.
6. Install the piston and tighten the retaining nut to 60–65 ft. lbs.

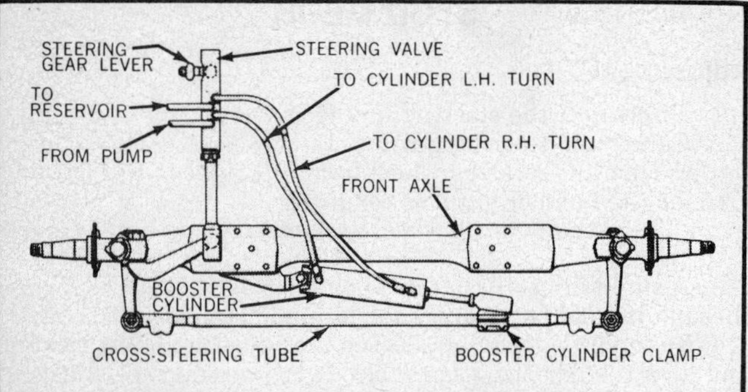

Garrison hydraulic steering linkage (© Mack Trucks, Inc.)

CAUTION

If a torque wrench is not being used be careful not to over tighten.

7. Slide the piston about halfway into the cylinder barrel. Be careful not to damage the O-ring when sliding past the porthole.
8. Install the piston retaining ring.
9. Install the seal with the lip toward the outside of the bearing.
10. Move the rod back and forth to see if it moves freely and install the end cover.

Ross Linkage System – In Line Booster

CYLINDER AND VALVE

Disassembly

1. Move the cylinder piston rod in and out until the oil is drained from the cylinder assembly.
2. Remove the nut from the threaded end of the piston rod then remove the cushion retainers and cushions.
3. Remove the three end plate retaining screws and remove the end plate.
4. Remove the retaining ring.
   a. Push the gland into the cylinder assembly about $^1/_4$ in.

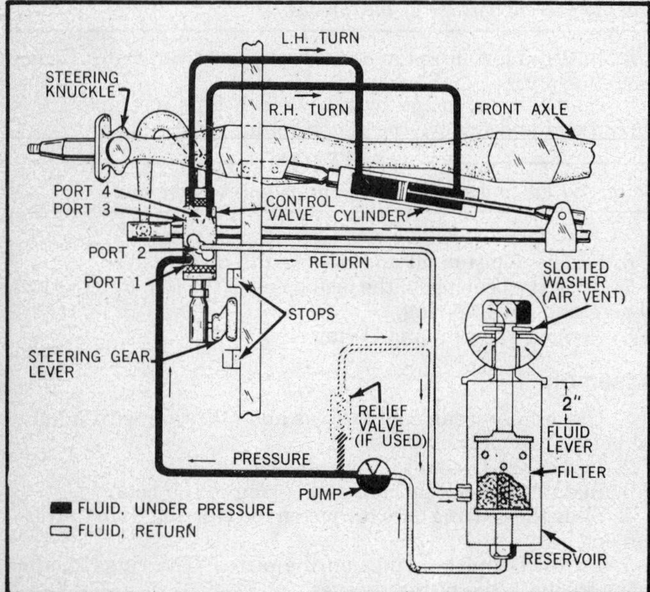

Hydraulic steering layout, Ross separate cylinder and valve (© Mack Trucks, Inc.)

   b. Using a punch through the knock-out hole of the cylinder barrel, compress and remove the retaining ring.
5. Pull on the piston rod and remove the cylinder internal parts.
6. Remove the gland from the rod.
7. Remove the sealing parts in the gland.
   a. Remove the lock ring.
   b. Remove the retaining washers, oil seal, spacer washer, leather back-up ring and O-ring.
   c. Remove the O-ring and back-up ring from the outside of the gland.
8. Hold the piston rod by two wrench flats just above the threaded end and remove the piston retaining nut.

CAUTION

Be careful not to damage the threads or finish of the rod.

9. Slide the piston assembly off the rod and remove the piston rings and seal.

NOTE: Check the poppet valves in the piston for leakage and if defective, replace the piston assembly.

10. Remove the slotted nut from the ball stud and remove the dust seal cover and dust seal.
11. Straighten the one staked place in the end cap and remove the cap.
12. Remove the lockpin and unscrew the adjusting plug.
13. Remove the washer and spring from inside the plug.
14. Remove the outer ball seat and the ball stud.
15. Remove the lubrication fitting.
16. Pull out the ball socket housing and remove the two steel balls.
17. Pull out the valve body spool assembly without damaging the threads in the outer end of the valve housing.

NOTE: After removing the valve body spool assembly, the four small O-rings may not remain in the end of the valve body and should be found on the face of the cylinder.

18. Disassemble the flexure rod, socket shell and valve body and spool.
   a. To keep the flexure rod from turning when unscrewing the elastic nut, reassemble the ball stud against the inner ball seat and install the outer ball seat in the socket shell then screw in the adjusting plug.
   b. Unscrew the elastic nut.
   c. Remove the ball stud, seats, and adjusting plug from the socket shell.
   d. Remove the washers, spring, socket shell and flexure rod.
   e. Push out from the opposite end of the four O-ring counterbores and remove the spool.
19. Remove the plug assembly, spring and ball.

Assembly

1. Use all new seals and O-rings and lubricate with a light oil before assembly.
2. Install the sealing parts in the gland.
   a. Install the inside O-ring, the leather back-up ring, brass spacing washer and the steel retaining washer.
   b. Install the oil seal with the lip of the seal toward the outside.
   c. Install the second steel retaining washer and retain all the oil seal parts with the lock ring.
3. Install the back-up ring, then the O-ring on the outside of the gland.

NOTE: The O-ring should be on the pressure side.

4. Slide the gland onto the piston rod starting from the piston end of the rod.

5. Install the seal in the piston ring groove and the piston rings over the seal.
6. Install the piston and tighten the retaining nut to 60–65 ft. lbs.
7. Slide the piston about halfway into the cylinder barrel. Be careful not to damage the O-ring when sliding the piston past the retaining ring groove in the cylinder.
8. Install the gland retaining ring in the cylinder groove.
9. Move the rod back and forth to see if it moves freely and install the end plate. Tighten to 8–10 ft. lbs.
10. Install the inner cushion retainer with the cup side out.
11. Install the inner rubber cushion, outer rubber cushion, then the outer cushion retainer with the cup side in.
12. Secure the assembly until it is ready for installation on the chassis with the nut at the end of the piston rod.
13. Install the O-ring in the groove on the spool and insert the spool in the valve body.

NOTE: Insert the spool from the opposite end of the four small O-ring seats to prevent the spool O-ring from being damaged by the sharp inner edges of the body.

14. If the plug assembly spring and ball has been removed, stand the body on end and drop the ball into the hole. Put a new O-ring on the plug and place the spring over the plug stem. Insert the plug into the hole until it is even with the end face of the valve body.
15. Install the flexure rod to the socket shell.
16. Install the inner ball seat, ball stud, outer ball seat and adjusting plug to the socket shell and tighten securely.
17. Carefully place this assembly in a vise holding the threaded end of the shell.
18. Slide the valve body and spool assembly over the flexure rod.
19. Install the centering washer spring, centering washer, seal, second centering washer and the heavy washer.
20. Press the washer down carefully and start the elastic nut on the end of the flexure rod.
21. Use a box wrench and push down on top of the heavy washer, rotating the valve body back and forth until the seal and outer centering washer enter the valve body completely.
22. Make sure the parts are seated properly and tighten the nut to 10–12 ft. lbs.

NOTE: Hold the valve body in one hand and press the threaded end of the flexure rod against a solid object to see if the spool moves freely.

23. Remove the ball stud, seats and adjusting plug from the socket shell, then remove the flexure rod and socket shell from the valve assembly.
24. Install the four O-rings to the end of the valve body.
25. Slide the valve body with the flexure rod into the cylinder housing assembly and make sure roll pin in the valve body fits in the hole on the face of the cylinder head.
26. Install the socket housing over the socket shell and align the slotted opening in the socket housing with the rectangular opening in the cylinder housing assembly.
27. Install the inner ball seat.
28. Apply a small amount of heavy grease into the two small holes in the socket shell and insert the balls.
29. Insert the ball stud into the socket shell through the rectangular opening in the cylinder housing and ball socket housing.

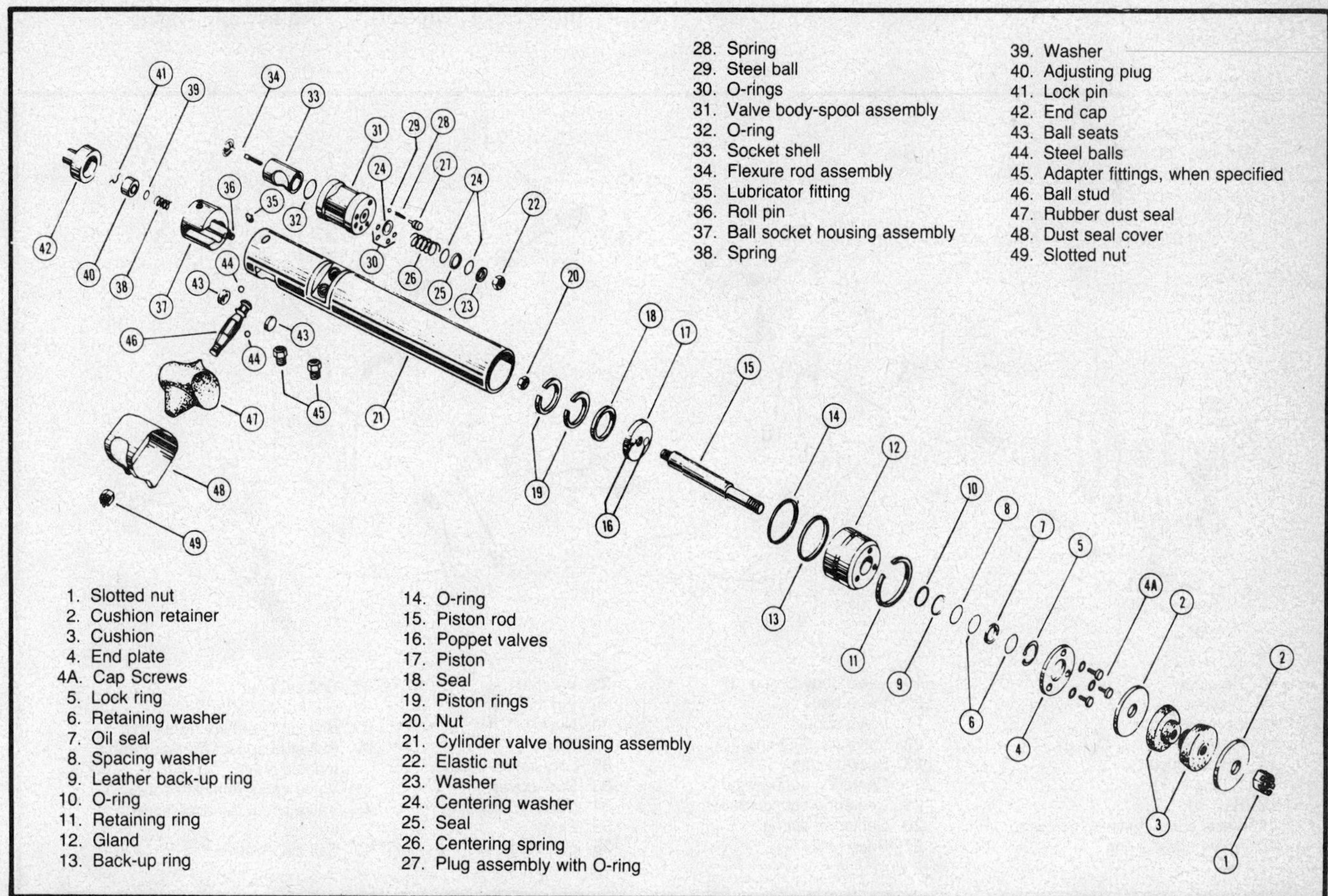

Exploded view of Ross inline booster (© Mack Trucks, Inc.)

NOTE: Care must be taken to make sure that the balls remain in position in the groove in the ball stud when it rests against the inner ball seat.

30. Install the outer ball seat.
31. Install the washer and spring into the opening of the adjusting plug.
32. Screw the adjusting plug into the threaded end of the socket shell.
    a. Tighten the plug hand tight, then back off to the nearest aligning hole.
    b. Insert the lockpin and snap into place.
33. Install the end cap and tighten to 50–60 ft. lbs., and crimp the cylinder housing at the place provided.
34. Install the lubrication fitting.
35. Install the rubber dust seal then the metal dust seal cover.
36. Install the slotted nut to the end of the ball stud.

Vickers Linkage System

CYLINDER AND VALVE

Disassembly

CAUTION

Before removing the assembly or parts of the assembly, be certain the unit is not subjected to hydraulic pressure.

1. Remove the four nuts which attach the control ball stud housing and valve body assembly to the cylinder.
2. Remove the housing and valve assembly from the cylinder.
3. Remove the three O-rings from the recesses in the valve body.
4. Lightly clamp the valve body in a vise and remove the snap-ring washer, and pin.
5. Remove the plug.
6. Remove the ball stud, ball stud seats, spring washer and spacer.

NOTE: Current production ball stud sleeves use an integral spacer. When the new style sleeve is used the ball stud spacer is not needed.

7. Remove the self locking nut from the capscrew.
8. Remove the capscrew, washer, and control ball stud sleeve.
9. Lift the two centering spring washers, centering spring, and spacer from the valve body.
10. Remove the valve spool from the control ball stud end of the body.
11. Remove the back-up ring if there, and the O-ring from the spool.

NOTE: A new improved Teflon back-up ring is used on the current assemblies and is included in the seal kits. This ring may be used on the units not originally equipped with one.

12. Remove and inspect the check valve retaining plug and the valve body cylinder locating pin.

NOTE: The cylinder assembly is a sealed unit. Overhaul procedures consist of replacing the sealing parts on the rod end only.

13. Remove the nut, bolt and lockwasher and unscrew the ball stud assembly.
14. Using snap-ring pliers, remove the retainer snap-ring.
15. Rotate the rod and pull it far enough from the cylinder to expose the scraper, wiper ring, retainer and washer.

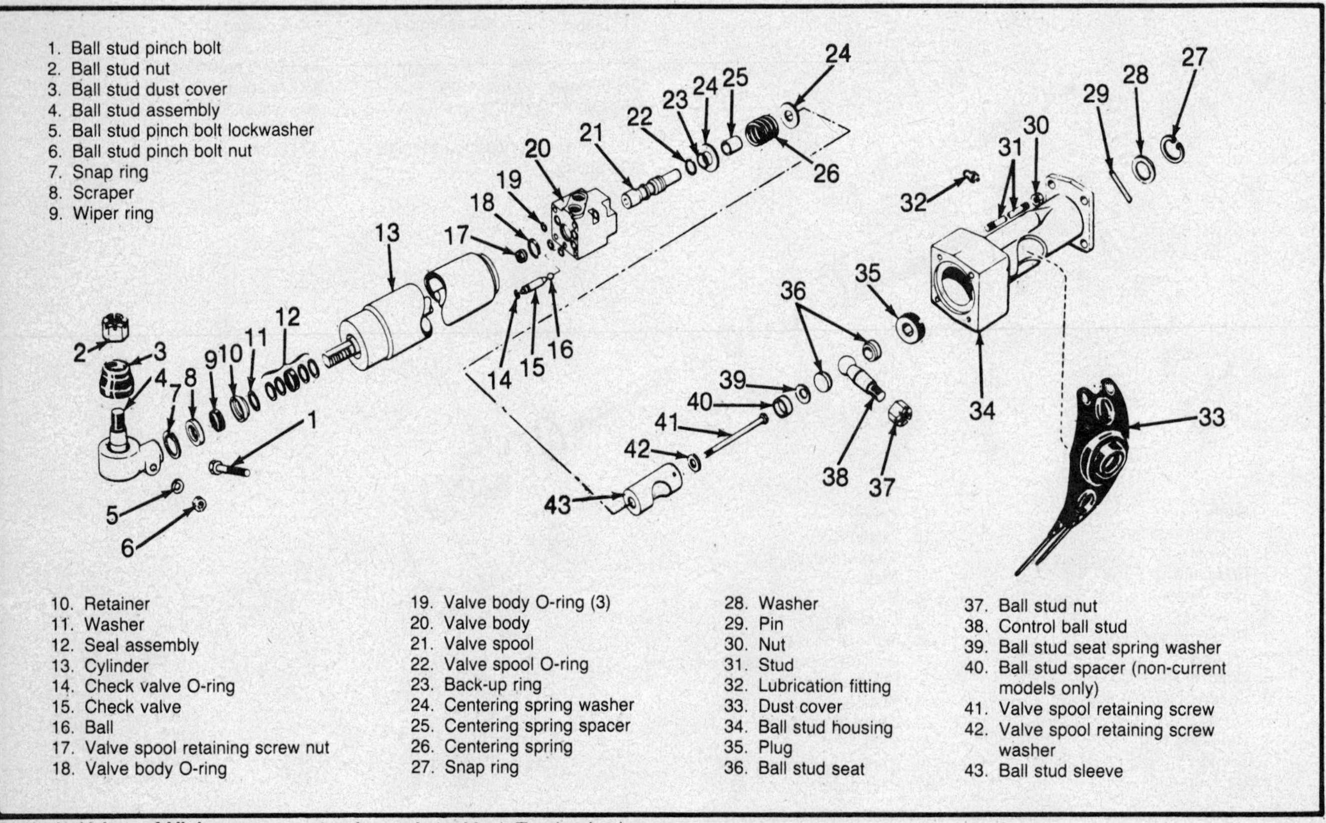

Exploded view of Vickers power steering unit (© Mack Trucks, Inc.)

16. The shaft seal assembly may be removed with a hooked scriber.

Assembly

1. Replace all seals with new ones and coat with liberal amounts of grease or petroleum jelly.
2. Check all parts for wear, cracks or pitting and replace if necessary.
3. Clean all parts and immerse in clean hydraulic fluid before reassembly.
4. Install new O-rings in the cylinder end of the valve body and on the control ball stud end of the valve spool.
5. Install the back-up ring.
6. Install the spool from the control ball stud end of the bore to avoid damage to the O-ring during installation.
7. Install the washer spacer, centering spring, washer, control ball stud sleeve and the capscrew washer. Coat the capscrew with a small amount of sealer and install.
   a. Install a new self-locking nut and while tightening until all play is gone between the two retaining washers, make sure that the centering spring remains aligned between the two retaining washers.
   b. Back the nut off one flat $^1/_6$ turn or sixty degrees.

NOTE: The current production valve assemblies have the spool valve retaining nut and screw drilled at assembly so that a cotter pin may be used. It is recommended that the units not having this modification be changed when being rebuilt. To do so draw the nut up tight and back off $^1/_3$ of a turn. Drill a $^5/_{64}$ hole through the nut screw. Drill through the tapered portion of the nut and not the hex. Insert a cotter pin and bend the ends around the nut.

8. Start the control ball stud sleeve plug into the control ball stud sleeve.
9. Slide the control ball stud housing over the control ball stud sleeve.
10. If removed install the studs which attach the valve and ball stud housing to the cylinder.
11. Install three new O-rings in the recesses in the valve body.
12. Connect the cylinder to the valve body and make sure the locating pin on the check valve fits in the recessed hole on the cylinder face.
13. Position the ball stud housing and install the stud-nuts while holding the valve and control assembly to prevent misalignment of O-rings. Tighten the nuts to 30–40 ft. lbs.
14. Install the control ball stud spacer on the non-current models.
15. Install the ball stud seat spring washer with it raised side facing the ball stud.
16. Install the ball stud seats and the control ball stud.
17. Center the stud in the sleeve and tighten the ball stud plug until it is snug against the ball stud seat.
   a. Back the plug out until the first slot lines up with the hole in the sleeve.
   b. Insert the lock-pin, washer and snap-ring.
18. Grease the control housing, under low pressure through the grease fitting.
19. Install the rod seal assembly parts.
   a. Coat the seal parts with a petroleum jelly.
   b. Install the two back-up rings over the rod and in the cylinder cap bore. Stagger the split ends.
   c. Install the seal ring and the two outer back-up rings and stagger the split ends.
20. Install the washer, retainer, wiper and scraper on the rod, then the snap-ring.
21. Screw the ball stud assembly on the rod and install the ball stud pinch bolt, lockwasher and nut.
   a. Tighten the pinch bolt to 40–45 ft. lbs. when using a grade eight bolt or 20–30 ft. lbs. when using a grade five bolt.

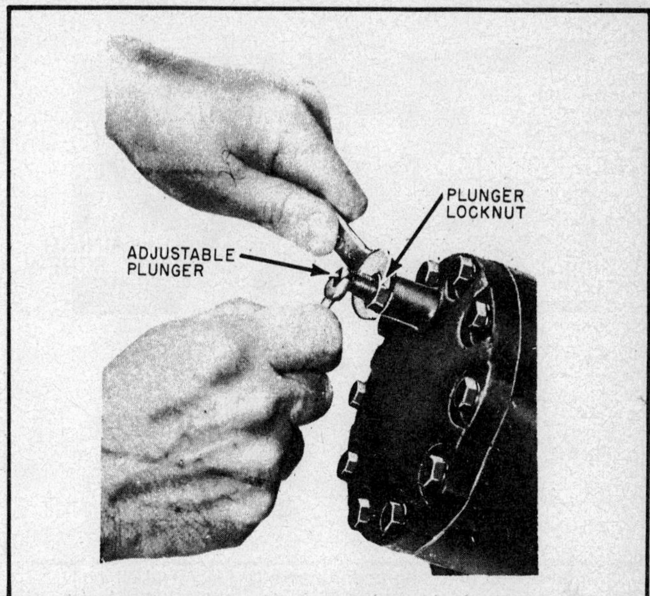

Removing relief valve plunger (© Mack Trucks, Inc.)

Sheppard Integral Type System

STEERING GEAR WITHOUT MITER GEARBOX

Disassembly

1. Loosen the plunger locknut and remove the relief valve plungers.
2. Remove the housing cover bolts and tap on the end of the output shaft to loosen the cover.
3. Remove the output shaft and gear assembly from the housing.
   a. Before moving, check the scribe marks on the rack and gear for alignment purposes during reassembly.
   b. If the marks can not be seen make your own so that the parts can be easily timed during reassembly.

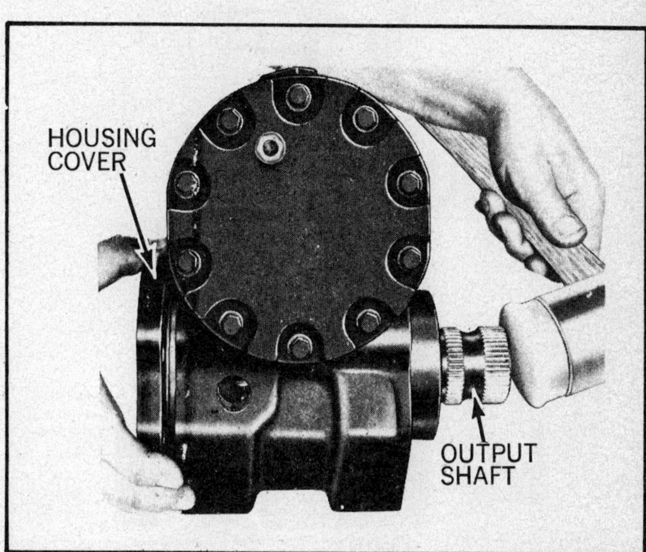

Removing output shaft (© Mack Trucks, Inc.)

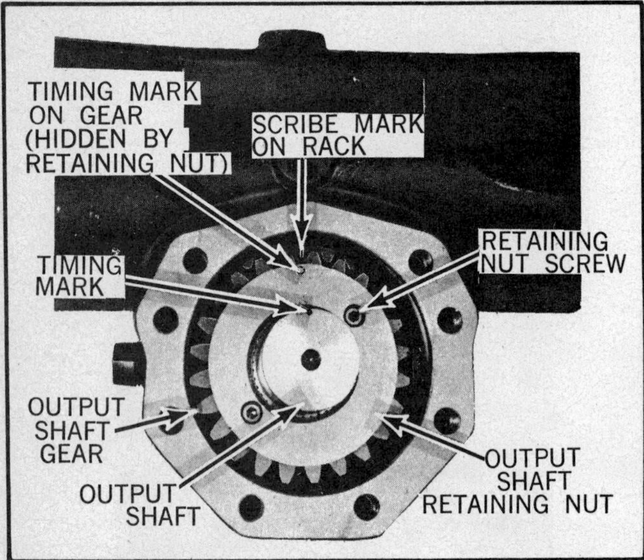

Output shaft and gear alignment marks (© Mack Trucks, Inc.)

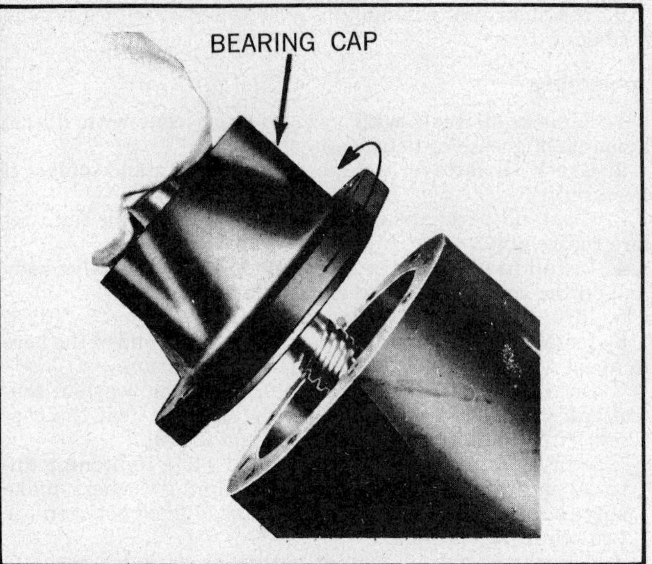

Removing bearing cap and actuating shaft (© Mack Trucks, Inc.)

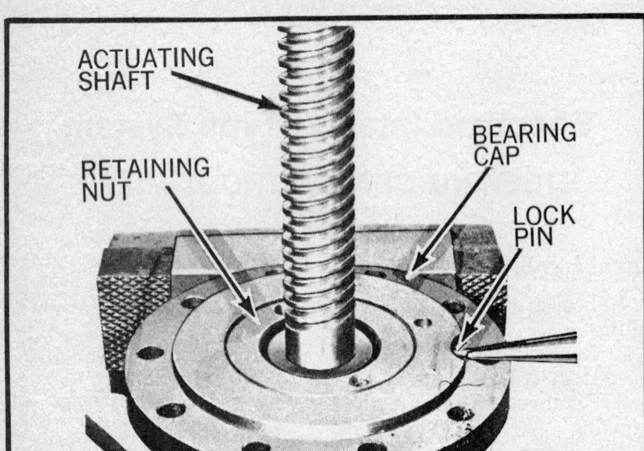

Disassembling bearing cap and actuating shaft (© Mack Trucks, Inc.)

4. Leave the gear on the output shaft unless replacement is necessary.
   a. To disassemble the output shaft and gear, remove the screws which secure the gear retaining nut.
   b. Turn the retaining nut counterclockwise and remove the nut.
   c. Press the output shaft out of the gear.
5. Mark the cylinder head and housing for reassembly and remove the cylinder head and gasket.
6. Mark the bearing cap and housing for reassembly and remove the bearing cap attaching bolts.
7. Turn the bearing cap and actuating shaft out of the actuating valve.
8. Disassemble the bearing and actuating shaft only if a defect is suspected.
   a. To disassemble, remove the lock-pin from the retaining nut.
   b. Use a spanner wrench and remove the retaining nut.
   c. Tap or press the actuating shaft out of the bearing cap.

NOTE: The bearing and actuating shaft is serviced as a unit and should not be disassembled after removing from the bearing cap.

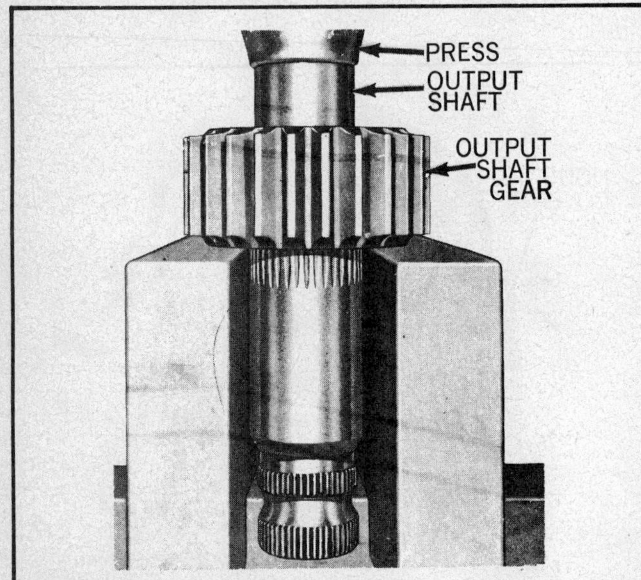

Removing output gear from shaft (© Mack Trucks, Inc.)

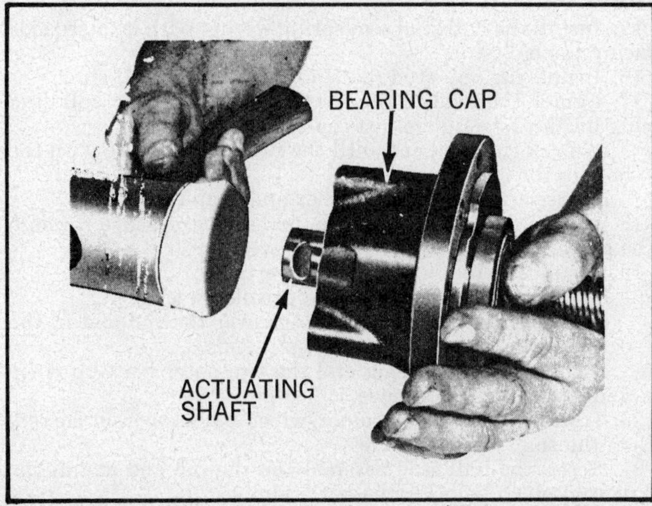

Removing actuating shaft and bearing assembly from bearing cap (© Mack Trucks, Inc.)

Removing dirt seal from bearing cap (© Mack Trucks, Inc.)

d. Pry the dirt seal from the bearing cap.
e. Drive the oil seal from the bearing cap.

9. Pull the piston assembly out of the housing.
10. Mark the piston and valve adjusting nut for reassembly. Remove the lockpin from the nut, then remove the nut.
11. Remove the reversing spring and without forcing, remove the actuator valve from the piston.
12. Remove the valve positioning pin.
13. Remove the second reversing spring from the piston.
14. Remove the piston rings.
15. Remove the valve seats, balls and spring from the piston.

CAUTION

Be careful when removing the valve seats as the balls are spring loaded.

16. Remove the output shaft seal.
17. If it is necessary to replace the output shaft bushings in either the housing or cover, use a puller.

Assembly

1. Clean all parts individually in a solvent and replace any parts that are worn or broken.
2. If removed, press new cover or housing bushings flush with the inside face.

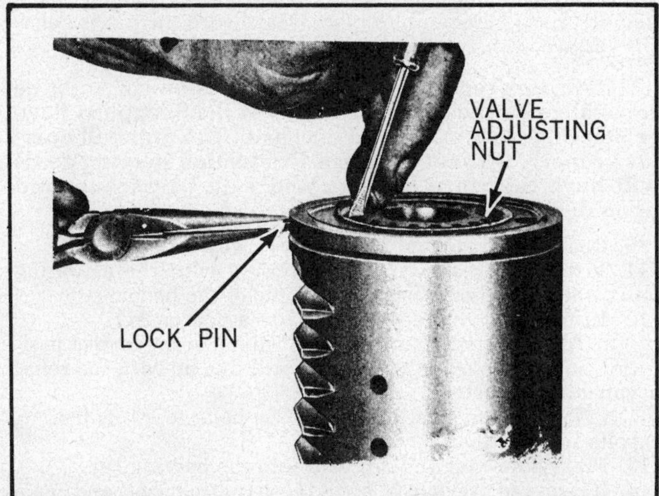

Removing valve positioning pin (© Mack Trucks, Inc.)

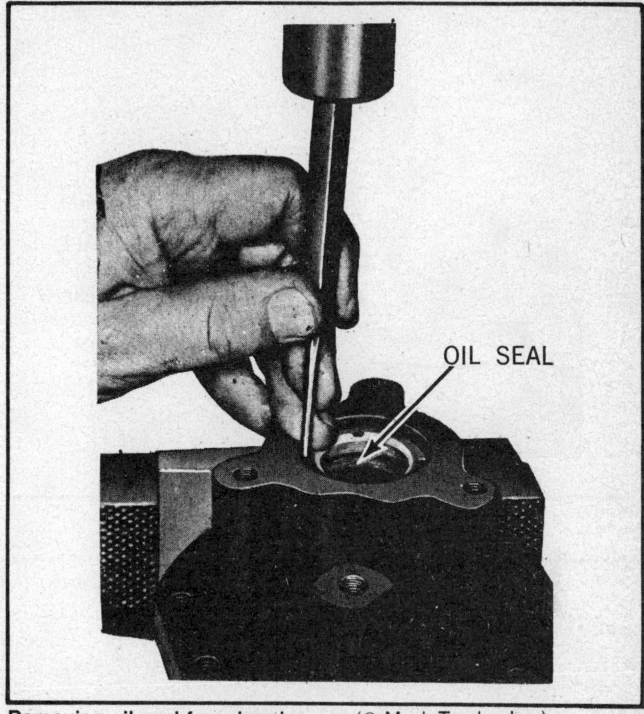

Removing oil seal from bearing cap (© Mack Trucks, Inc.)

Removing piston assembly from housing (© Mack Trucks, Inc.)

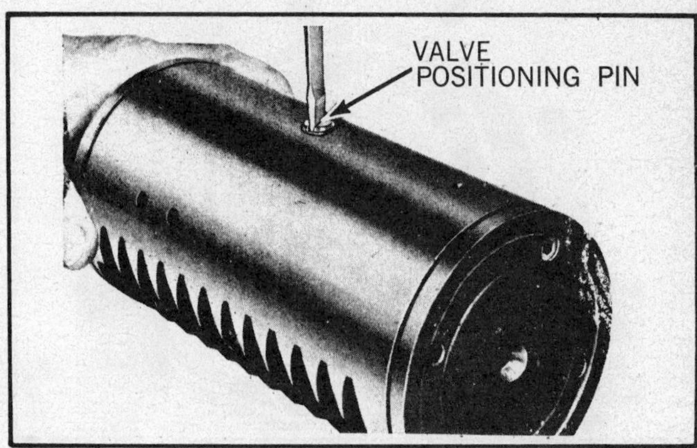

Removing valve adjusting nut lockpin (© Mack Trucks, Inc.)

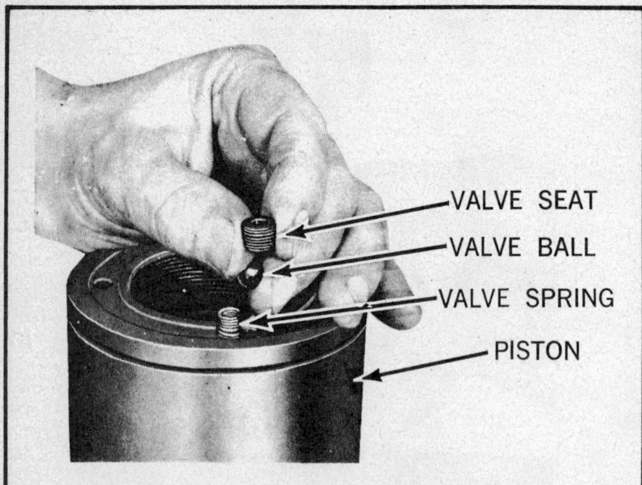

Removing relief valve from piston (© Mack Trucks, Inc.)

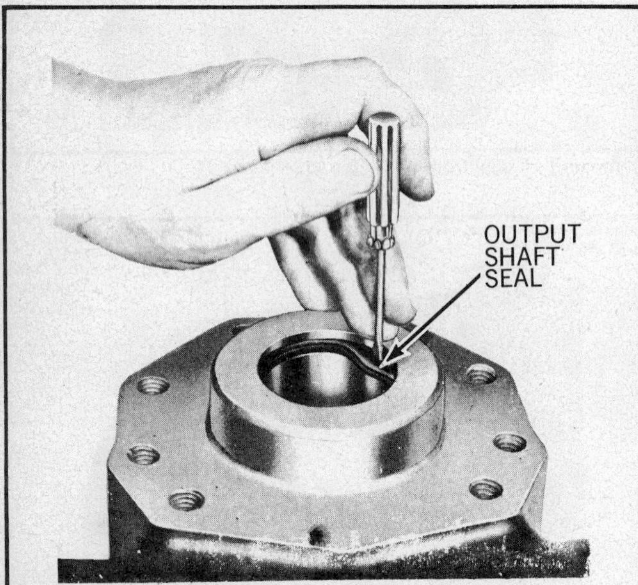

Removing output shaft seal (© Mack Trucks, Inc.)

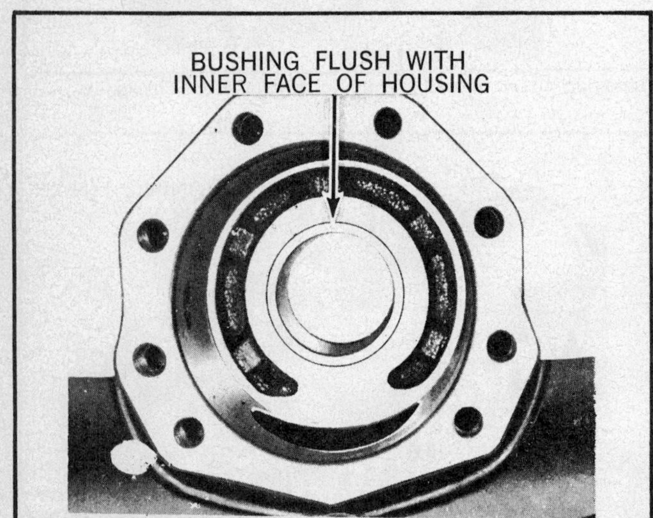

Installing housing bushing (© Mack Trucks, Inc.)

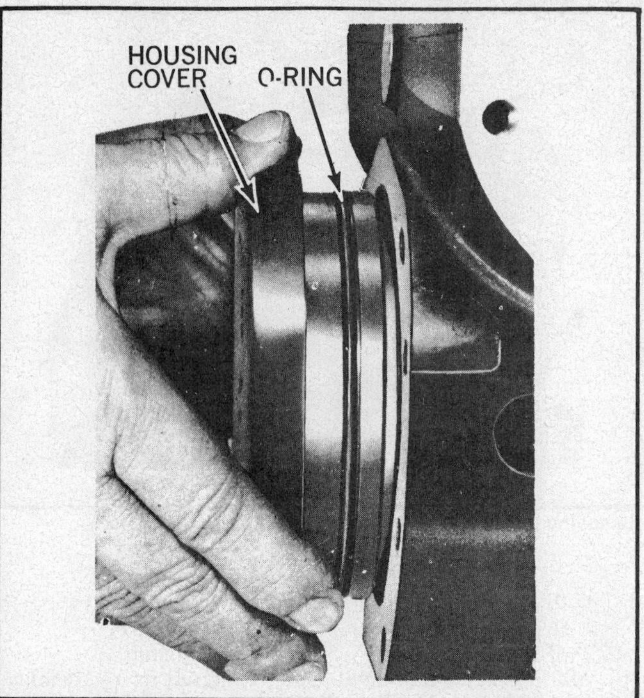

Installing housing cover (© Mack Trucks, Inc.)

3. Install a new output shaft seal.
4. Insert a valve spring, ball and seat into each bore.

NOTE: Be sure the valve seats are flush with or below the surface of the piston.

5. Place one of the reversing springs on the bottom of the actuating valve bore and center so the actuating valve end will enter into the spring.
6. Install the valve positioning pin in the piston.
   a. Turn the pin into the piston until it protrudes $^1/_4$ in. into the actuating valve bore.
   b. Make sure the flats on the pin are parallel to the axis of the piston so the pin will enter the slot.
7. Insert the actuating valve into the piston with the slot for the positioning pin first. Place the second reversing spring on the valve.
8. Install the valve adjusting nut into the piston and turn it clockwise until it makes contact with the reversing spring.
9. Align the marks previously made on the nut and piston and drive the lock-pin into place. Make sure the pin is below the surface of the piston.

NOTE: It is recommended that the piston rings not be reinstalled on the piston assembly of the Sheppard Power Steering Gear during an overhaul. The unit will operate properly without the rings. Production steering gears will have the rings omitted, and may be encountered upon disassembly of the steering gear.

10. Coat the piston and housing bore with oil.
11. Install the piston into the housing with the actuating valve end towards the bearing cap end of the housing.
12. Install the cylinder head and use a new gasket.
    a. Align the marks so the head will be in the correct position and the relief valve plunger will line up with the relief valve in the piston.
    b. Torque the attaching bolt. ($^5/_{16}$ bolts to 20 ft. lbs., $^3/_8$ bolts to 33 ft. lbs.)
13. Press a new oil and dirt seal into the bearing cap.
14. If removed previously, press the actuating shaft and bearing assembly into the bearing cap.

15. Install the actuating shaft bearing retaining nut and insert the locking pin.

NOTE: When using a new retaining nut the hole for the lockpin must be drilled after the nut is seated. Use a $^{3}/_{32}$ in. drill and drill the nut $^{3}/_{16}$ in. deep through the hole in the bearing cap.

16. Thread the actuating shaft into the actuating valve and install the bearing cap with a new gasket.
   a. Align the marks on the cap and housing to insure the plunger lining up with the relief valve.
   b. Hold the bearing cap in the proper position and turn the actuating shaft until the bearing cap is seated.
   c. Torque the attaching bolts ($^{5}/_{16}$ bolts to 20 ft. lbs. $^{3}/_{8}$ bolts to 33 ft. lbs.).
17. Install the output shaft on the gear if it was previously disassembled.
Align the marks on the output shaft and the gear and press the gear on the shaft.
18. Insert the output shaft and gear assembly into the gear housing and make sure the timing mark on the gear is aligned with the mark on the rack.

NOTE: It may be necessary to make another scribe mark on the rack if the original mark is difficult to see when the output shaft gear is in place. It is important that the rack and gear are correctly timed.

19. Install the output shaft gear retaining nut and tighten against the gear while aligning the holes in the nut and the gear.
Install and tighten the two retaining nut screws.
20. Place a new O-ring in the groove and install the housing cover.
   a. Tap the cover with a soft hammer to seat it properly.
   b. Install the attaching bolts and tighten ($^{7}/_{16}$ bolts to 20–36 ft. lbs., $^{5}/_{8}$ bolts to 100 ft. lbs.).
21. Use new O-rings and install the relief valve plungers. Turn into the bearing cap or cylinder head approximately six turns.
22. Install the gear in the vehicle and make the final relief valve plunger adjustments.
See the "Relief Valve Plunger Adjustment" for procedures.

STEERING GEAR WITH MITER GEARBOX

Disassembly

1. Loosen the locknut and remove the relief valve plunger in the cylinder head.
2. Remove the housing cover bolts and tap on the end of the output shaft to loosen the cover.
3. Remove the output shaft and gear assembly from the housing.
   a. Before removing, check the scribe marks on the rack and gear for alignment purposes during reassembly.
   b. If the marks cannot be seen, make your own so that the parts can be easily timed during reassembly.
4. Leave the gear on the output shaft unless replacement is necessary.
   a. To disassemble the output shaft and gear, remove the screws which secure the gear retaining nut.
   b. Turn the retaining nut counterclockwise and remove the nut.
   c. Press the output shaft out of the gear.
5. Mark the cylinder head and housing for reassembly and remove the cylinder head and gasket.
6. Mark the bearing cap and housing for reassembly and remove the bearing cap attaching bolts.
7. Turn the bearing cap and actuating shaft out of the actuating valve.

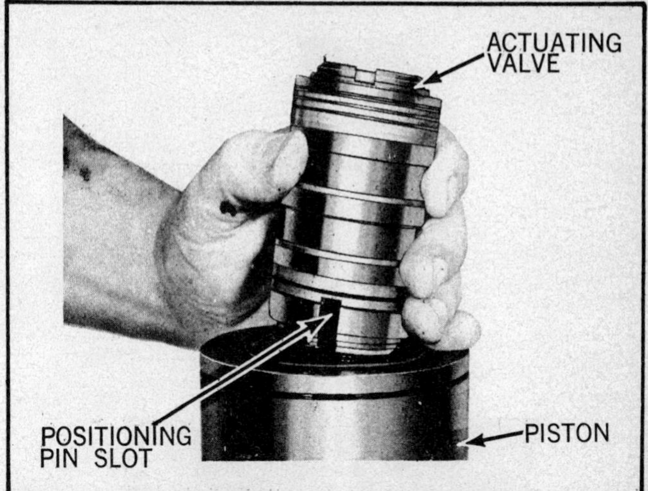

Installing actuating valve (© Mack Trucks, Inc.)

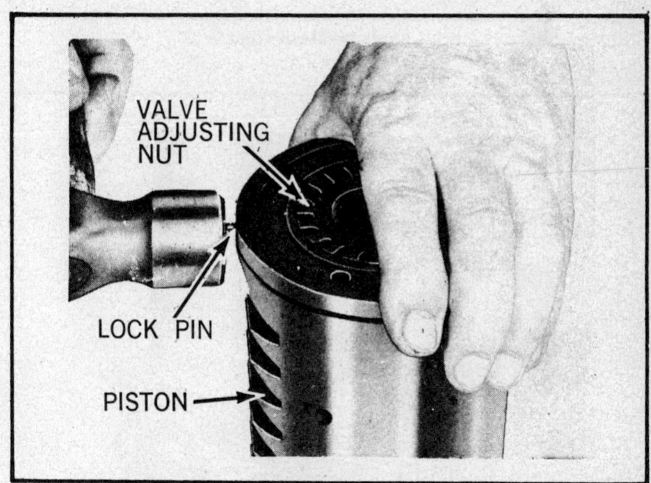

Installing valve adjusting nut and lock pin (© Mack Trucks, Inc.)

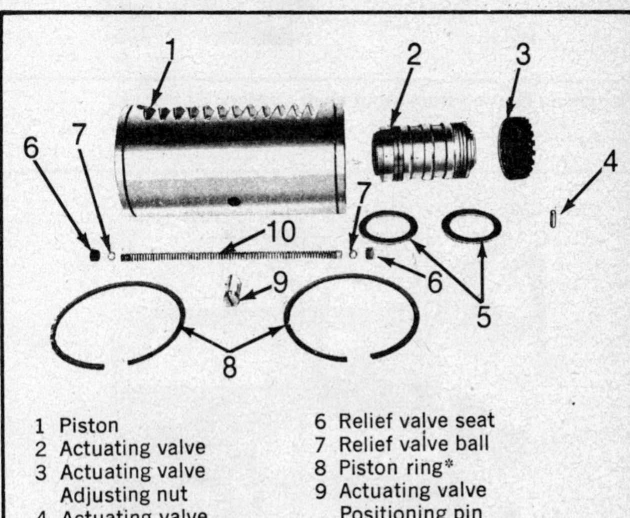

Exploded view of piston assembly (© Mack Trucks, Inc.)

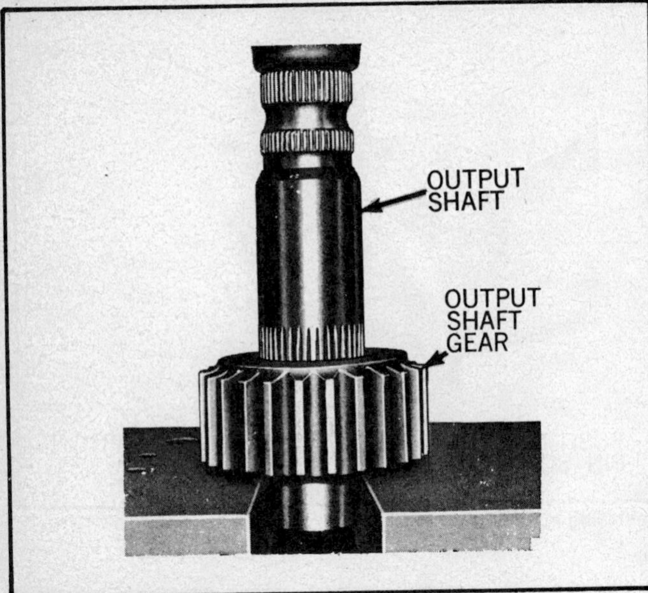

Pressing gear on output shaft (© Mack Trucks, Inc.)

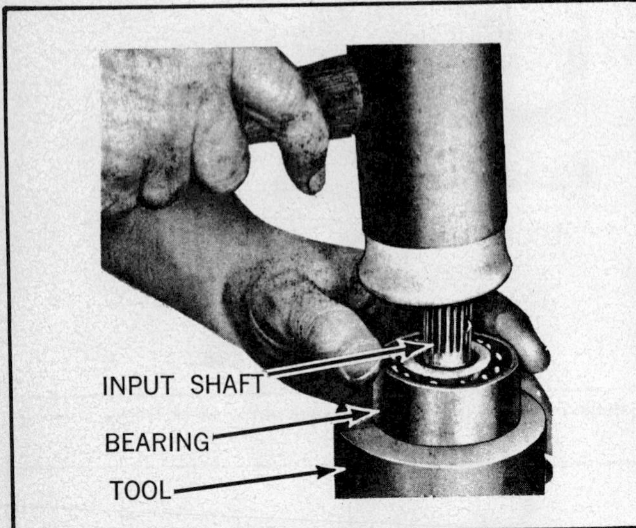

Removing bearing from input shaft (© Mack Trucks, Inc.)

Removing bearing retaining nut lockpin (© Mack Trucks, Inc.)

8. Remove the cover attaching bolts and remove the cover with the input shaft and bearing assembly. Check for the shaft and gear timing marks.
9. Remove the input gear by driving out the retaining pin.
10. Pull the bearing retaining nut lock-pin from the gear box cover.
11. Use a spanner wrench and turn the bearing retainer nut counterclockwise and remove it from the gearbox cover.
12. Remove the bearing and input shaft assembly from the cover using a soft hammer.
13. If necessary, the shaft can be driven or pressed out of the bearing.
14. Remove the seal from the cover.
15. Remove the bolts, including the one hidden inside the housing, that attaches the gearbox housing to the bearing cap. Tap the gearbox with a soft hammer to loosen it, then lift it from the bearing cap.
16. Remove the bearing cap O-ring.
17. Remove the gear retaining nut and washer from the shaft and pull the gear off the shaft.
18. Mark the bearing retaining nut at the pin hole location for reassembly.
19. Remove the lockpin from the bearing cap and remove the bearing retaining nut.
20. Remove the shims located next to the bearing and save for reassembly.
21. Remove the bearing cap to housing screws.
22. Note the timing marks on the actuating shaft and valve for reassembly then turn and unscrew the bearing cap and shaft assembly out of the valve.
23. Remove the actuating shaft and bearing from the bearing cap by tapping easily with a soft hammer.
24. If necessary, remove the fixed plunger from the bearing cap. Pry the plunger lock-pin out far enough from the cap to be gripped with pliers then withdraw the pin completely.

NOTE: Do not remove the fixed plunger unless damaged.

25. Remove the oil seal from the bearing cap.
    a. On non-current models pry the seal from the bearing cap.
    b. On current models, holes in the cap are provided so that the seal may be driven out with a punch.

Assembly

1. Clean all parts individually in a solvent and replace any parts that are worn or broken.
2. Position a new seal in the bearing cap so that the lip faces the piston side and press into place.
3. If the fixed plunger was removed insert it in the bearing cap and install the retaining pin. Make sure the pin is below the surface of the bearing cap.
4. Press the bearing on the actuating shaft.
5. Press the shaft and bearing assembly into the bearing cap without damaging the seal.
6. Screw the actuating shaft into the actuating valve and align the timing marks.
7. Install the bearing cap attaching bolts and tighten. ($^5/_{16}$ bolts to 20 ft. lbs., $^3/_8$ bolts to 33 ft. lbs.)
8. Place the shims over the bearing and install the bearing retaining nut.
    a. Tighten the nut against the bearing while aligning the mark on the nut with the lock-pin hole.
    b. Install the lock-pin.
9. Position the gear on the actuating shaft and install the washer and nut.
10. Install a new O-ring in the groove in the bearing cap.
11. Position the gearbox housing on the bearing cap and tap into place using a soft hammer.
12. Install the gearbox housing to bearing cap retaining bolts and washers including the bolt inside the housing.

13. Install a new cover seal.
14. Press or drive the input shaft into the bearing.
15. Install the bearing and shaft assembly into the cover.
16. Install the bearing retaining nut and turn clockwise into the cover.
17. Install the bearing retaining nut lock-pin.
18. Install the miter gear on the input shaft and align the timing marks.
19. Install the retaining pin.
20. Install the cover assembly and shim on the gearbox housing.
21. Fill the gearbox housing with the correct grade of grease through the grease fitting.

RELIEF VALVE PLUNGER

Adjustment

This adjustment should be made periodically and any time the gears, springs, axle, etc. are disturbed. The adjustment is important because it protects the pump, steering gear, and steering linkage from overloading when the wheels are at full turn. Steering gears using the miter gearbox do not have an adjustable plunger at the gearbox end.

WITH MITER GEARBOX

1. With the power off check the right and left steering angles (See the steering angle procedures in the General Repair Section.)
2. Turn the adjustable plunger in the cylinder head inward until it bottoms.
3. Return the wheels to the straight forward position and start the engine to operate the power steering.
4. For the right turn adjustment, proceed as follows:
   a. Slowly turn the steering wheel to the right until the hydraulic assist is stopped (resistance in the wheel is felt). The wheel should not be forced beyond this point.
   b. Hold the wheel at this position and measure the clearance between the axle turn circle stop-screw and boss or stop-nut on the back of the knuckle.
   c. Set clearance by adjusting the drag link.
   d. Loosen the drag link clamp and lengthen the link to decrease clearance and shorten the length to increase the clearance.
   e. After the adjustment has been made, measure the clearance again.
5. For left turn adjustment, proceed as follows:
   a. Slowly turn the steering wheel to the left until the hydraulic assist is stopped (resistance in the wheel is felt). The wheel should not be forced beyond this point.

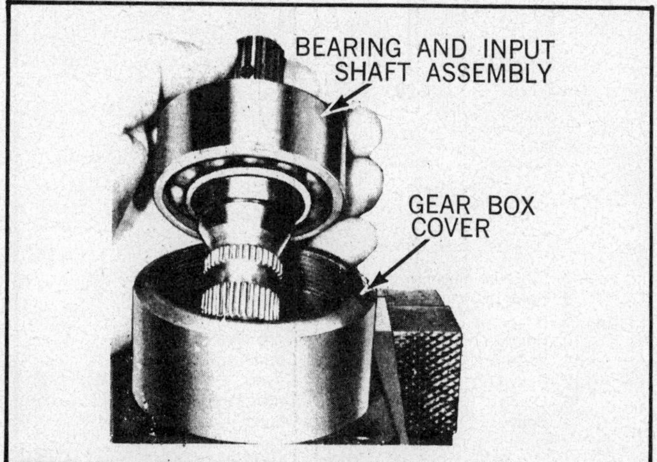

Removing bearing and input shaft assembly (© Mack Trucks, Inc.)

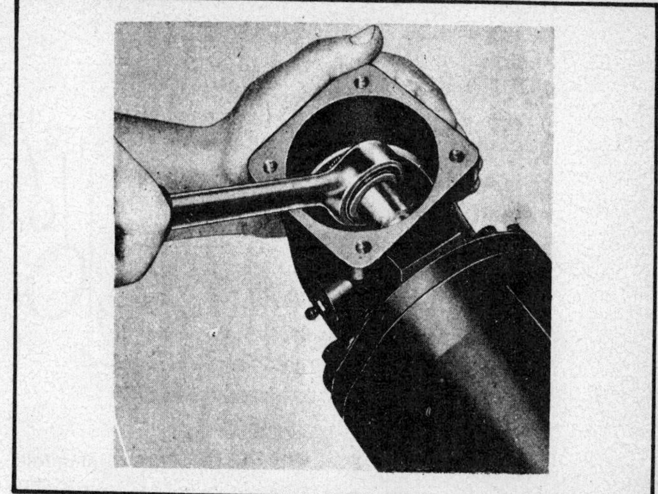

Removing hidden capscrew holding gearbox (© Mack Trucks, Inc.)

   b. Hold the wheel at this position and measure the clearance between the axle turn circle stop-screw and boss or stop-nut.
   c. The clearance should be $^1/_8$ in.. If the clearance is incorrect, adjust the relief valve plunger at the lower end of the cylinder.
   d. Turn the valve in to increase clearance and out to decrease clearance.

NOTE: If it is impossible to obtain accurate adjustments in the previous steps, check to see that the arrow stamped on the output shaft is indexed with the notched mark on the steering lever. The spline groove marked with a zero is not the index point.

6. Tighten all clamps and lock-nuts and shut down the engine.

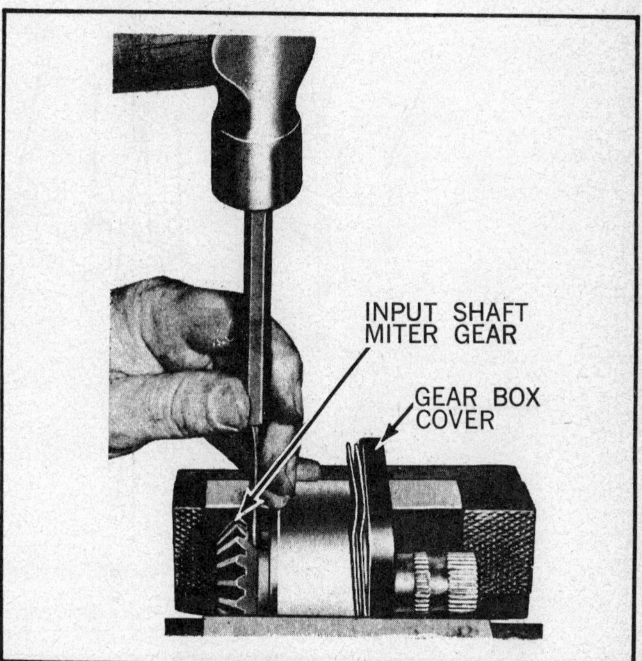

Removing miter gear retaining pin (© Mack Trucks, Inc.)

1 Manifold assembly
2 Manifold retaining screw
3 Manifold retaining screw washer
4 O-ring
5 O-ring
6 Pressure plate spring
7 Pressure plate
8 Rotor ring pin
9 Ring
10 Rotor
11 Vane
12 Body O-ring
13 O-ring
14 Body
15 Key
16 Oil seal
17 Shaft outer bearing
18 Shaft
19 Thrust spacer
20 Shaft inner bearing
21 Control valve plug
22 O-ring
23 Control valve assembly
24 Control valve spring
25 Cover
26 Cover screw
27 Control valve retaining pin

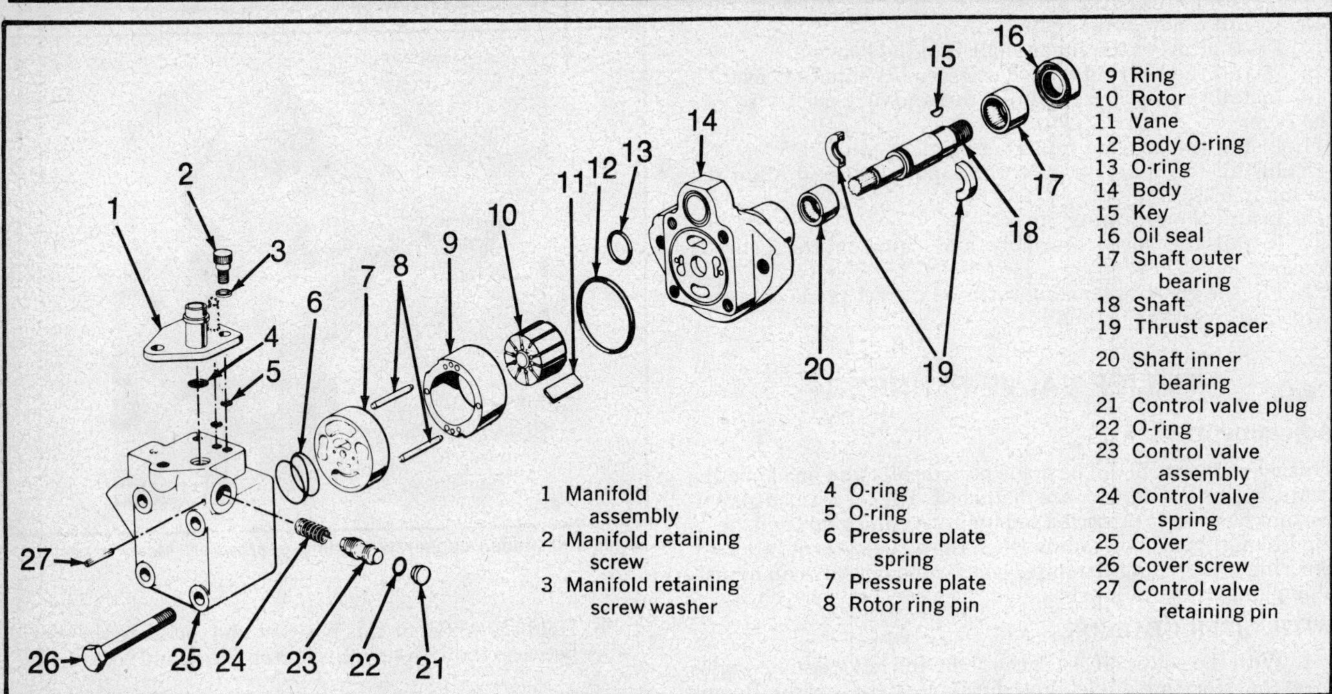

Vickers VTM27 series pump—non-current model (© Mack Trucks, Inc.)

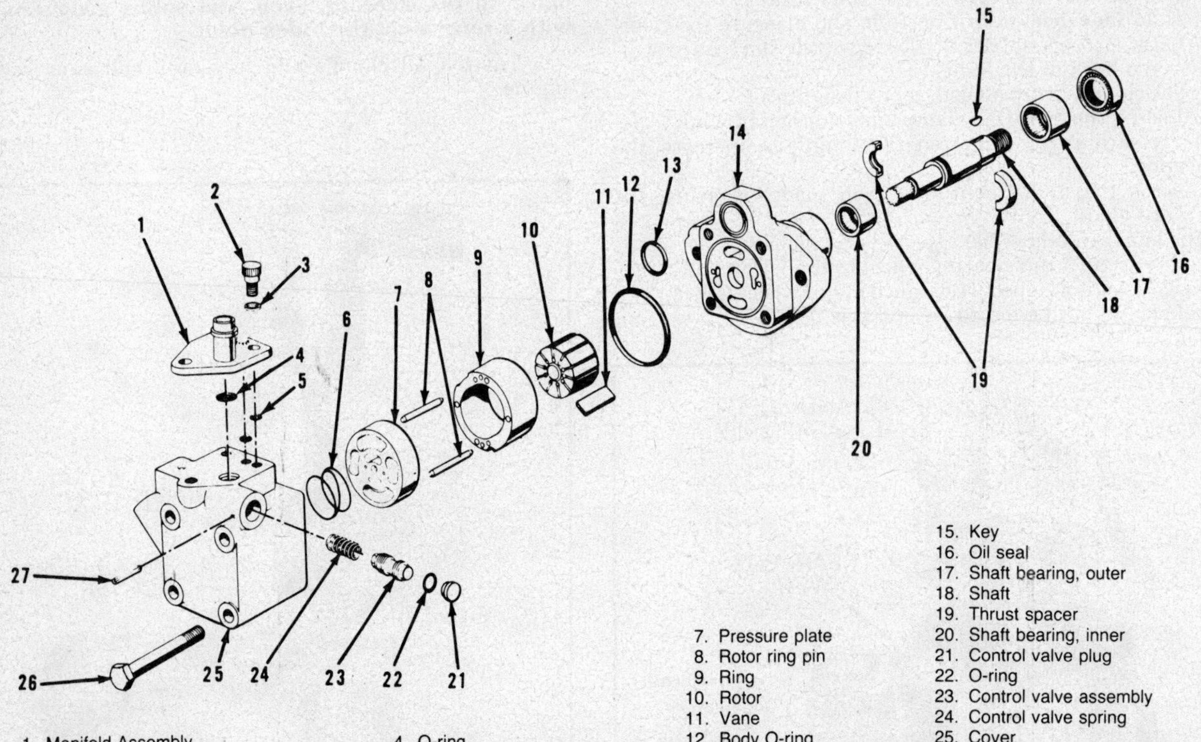

1. Manifold Assembly
2. Manifold retaining screw
3. Manifold retaining screw washer
4. O-ring
5. O-ring
6. Pressure plate spring
7. Pressure plate
8. Rotor ring pin
9. Ring
10. Rotor
11. Vane
12. Body O-ring
13. O-ring
14. Body
15. Key
16. Oil seal
17. Shaft bearing, outer
18. Shaft
19. Thrust spacer
20. Shaft bearing, inner
21. Control valve plug
22. O-ring
23. Control valve assembly
24. Control valve spring
25. Cover
26. Cover screw
27. Control valve retaining pin

Vickers V200 series pumps (© Mack Trucks, Inc.)

WITHOUT MITER GEARBOX

1. With the power off, check the right and left steering angles (see the steering angle procedures in the General Repair Section).
2. Turn the adjustable plungers all the way in.
3. Start the engine and run at a fast idle so the power steering operates.
4. For the left turn adjustment, proceed as follows:
   a. Turn the steering wheel to the left until the relief valve contacts the plunger. This can be felt by an increased steering effort.
   b. Hold the wheel at this position and do not force the wheel beyond this point.
   c. Check the clearance between the axle stop-screw and the boss.
   d. Turn the bearing cap upper plunger outward until the clearance is $^1/_8$ in. between the stop-screw and boss.
   e. Tighten the lock-nut.
5. For the right turn adjustment, proceed as follows:
   a. Turn the steering wheel to the right until an increased steering effort is felt.
   b. Hold the wheel at this position and do not force the wheel beyond this point.
   c. Turn the cylinder head plunger outward until there is a clearance of $^1/_8$ in. between the stop-screw and boss.
   d. Tighten the locknut.

Vickers Power Steering Pump

V-200 SERIES

Disassembly

1. Clamp pump in vise with cover end up and remove cover screws. Lift off cover and remove O-ring.
2. If pump is equipped with flow control valve, remove plug spring and valve subassembly.
3. Remove pressure plate and spring.
4. Mark position of ring and remove it along with locating pin.
5. Separate vanes from rotor and slide rotor from shaft.
6. Turn pump body over and remove shaft key and outer bearing snap-ring. Tap on splined end of shaft with a soft hammer to force it out of housing.
7. If bearing is to be removed, support the inner race and press shaft out of bearing.
8. Pull shaft seal out of body.
9. Press inner bearing out of body.

Assembly

1. Coat all parts with hydraulic fluid before assembly.
2. If flow control valve is used, assemble components into cover. If cover has a blind bore, install spring first, then valve. Install snap-ring and plug. Install screen and retaining plug.
3. Press shaft into outer bearing while supporting inner race. Press inner bearing into body using a driver on the outer race.
4. Install seal. Seals should be assembled with holes facing the shaft end of the pump. Lube lip with petroleum jelly.
5. Slide driveshaft in place until outer bearing is sealed. Install bearing retaining snap-ring in body.
6. Install new O-ring in body. Insert ring locating pins in body and assemble ring so that arrow points in direction of rotation.
7. Install rotor on shaft and insert vanes in rotor slots. Be sure radiused edge of vanes is toward the ring.
8. Place pressure plate over locating pins and flat against ring.
9. Insert pressure plate spring in pressure plate recess, then install cover using new O-ring. Be sure outlet port in cover is in correct position with respect to inlet port in body. Tighten attaching bolts to specified torque. Check binding.

VTM 27 AND VTM 42 SERIES

Disassembly

NOTE: Two versions of the VTM 27 are in use. The non-current production pump uses needle bearings on the shaft; the current models use ball bearings and dispense with the throughst spacers.

1. If the pump has an attached reservoir, remove it before working by removing wing nut, washer, cover and gasket. Lift washer, filter retainer, spring and filter element from stud. Remove reservoir stud and nut, two reservoir retaining screws, baffle and reinforcing plate. Separate reservoir from pump. Discard O-rings.
2. If pump has manifold instead of reservoir, remove it along with attaching capscrews, copper washer and O-rings.
3. Clamp pump mounting flange in a vise with soft jaws. Remove cover attaching bolts and separate cover from body.
4. Remove pressure plate spring and pressure plate.
5. Remove ring, locating pins and rotor and vane assembly. Remove and discard O-rings found between body and cover.
6. Mount cover in a vise and drive relief valve retaining pin out. Do not allow relief valve plug and subassembly to fall from bore. Remove plug, valve and spring from bore.
7. Non-current VTM 27: support shaft outer end of pump body on a two in. pipe coupling and using an arbor press, remove the shaft assembly, shaft throughst spacers, outer needle bearing and shaft seal.
8. Current VTM 27 and all VTM 42: remove large snap-ring retaining ball bearing in body. Press shaft and bearing assembly from body. Remove snap-ring that retains bearing on shaft and remove bearing if unserviceable.
9. Inner bearing, if used, and seal in current production pumps, can be driven from body using a pin punch.

Assembly

NOTE: Lubricate all parts in hydraulic fluid before assembly. For non-current production VTM 27 pump, use steps 1 through 4 and steps 9 through 15. For current production VTM 27 and 42 pumps, use steps 5–15.

1. Install inner bearing by pressing into body with an arbor press.
2. Assemble throughst spacers on shaft and install shaft in pump body.
3. Press outer needle bearing over shaft and into pump body to $^1/_{64}$ in. past seal shoulder. This gives 0.010–0.015 in. end play.
4. Position seal on body and press into place until it contacts locating shoulder.
5. Press inner bearing into body.
6. Press seal into body.
7. Press ball bearing on shaft and secure with snap ring.
8. Install shaft and bearing assembly into body. Install snap-ring.
9. Install locating pins in pump body. Install ring over pins according to direction of rotation.
10. Install rotor with chamfered edge towards inner ring contour.
11. Install vanes with radiused edge towards inner ring contour.
12. Install pressure plate.
13. Insert O-ring in body, then install pressure plate spring and cover. Tighten cover screws to torque.
14. Place spring and valve assembly in relief bore. Position valve with hex towards spring. Insert plug, with O-ring, in bore and hold in place while driving in new retaining pin.

15. Install reservoir or manifold as required. Place new O-rings over reservoir outlet tube and use copper washer on screw which enters oil passage if manifold is used. Assemble reservoir.

Mack-Scania Pump

Disassembly

1. Remove cover retaining capscrews.
2. Tap cover with soft mallet to separate from housing.
3. Remove housing O-ring from groove in pump housing.

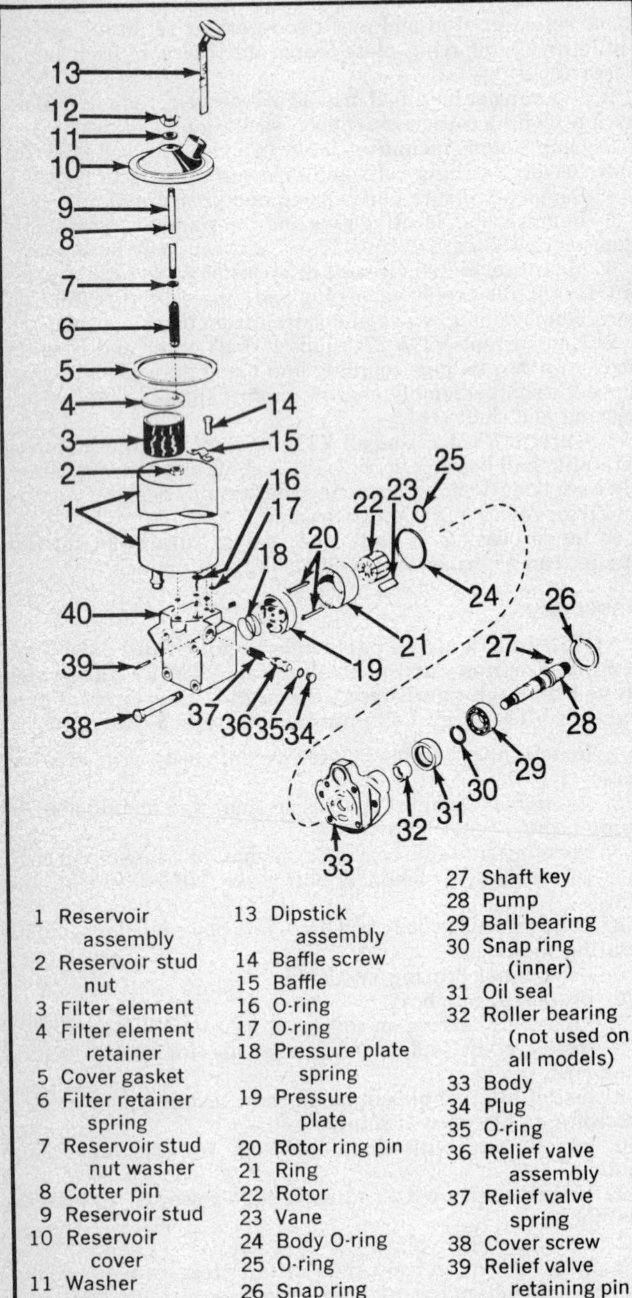

Vickers current VTM27 and VTM42 pumps (© Mack Trucks, Inc.)

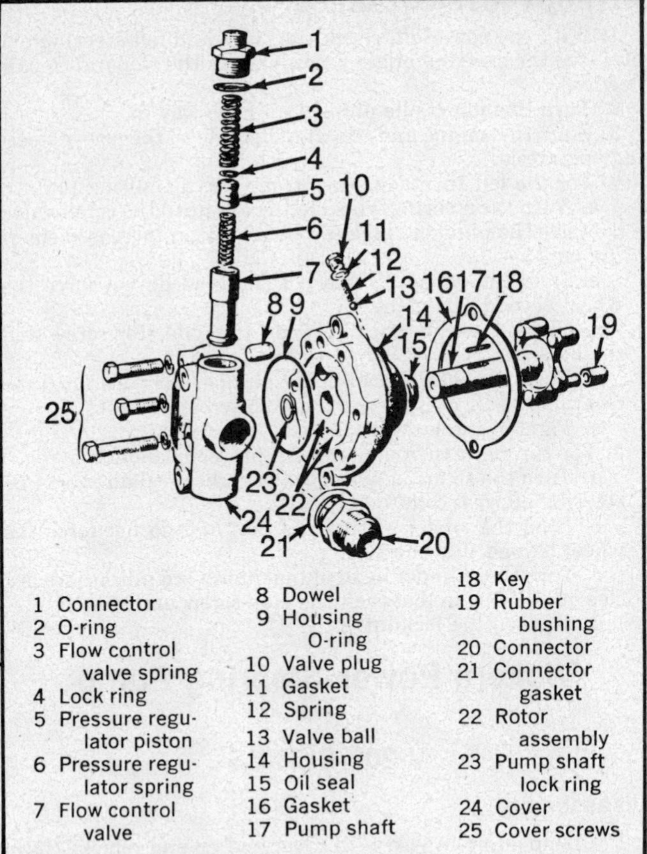

Exploded view of Mack-Scania pump (© Mack Trucks, Inc.)

4. Remove lock ring from shaft and lift rotor assembly out of housing.
5. Remove key from shaft and tap shaft out of housing.
6. Remove oil seal.
7. Remove connector from valve body.

CAUTION

Take care when removing connector as it compresses the flow control spring and could cause injury if not restrained when unscrewed.

8. Remove flow control spring.
9. Turn cover assembly over and tap lightly to remove valve assembly.
10. Use suitable pliers and remove snap-ring.
11. Remove piston and spring from valve body.

Assembly

1. Install spring and piston in flow control valve body and secure with snap-ring.
2. Position valve body into pump cover and install spring.
3. Position new O-ring on connector and install in cover.
4. Install new oil seal in housing.
5. Position rotor assembly in housing and install shaft, aligning keyway in shaft with key slot in rotor.
6. Install key in shaft and rotor.
7. Install lockring on shaft and position new O-ring on housing.
8. Install cover-to-housing aligning dowelpins.
9. Install cover.
10. Turn shaft to be sure pump rotates freely with no binding.

Eaton Pump

Disassembly

1. Remove coupling assembly from pump shaft.
2. Place pumps in soft jawed vise and remove cover attaching screws. Separate cover from body.
3. Remove cover and O-ring seal. Do not lose O-ring retainer.
4. Mark rotors for reference. Remove pump shaft, key, snap-ring and inner rotor from pump body.
5. Remove outer rotor by turning body over and tapping on a soft surface.
6. Slide rotor and key off pump shaft.
7. Remove oil seal from body.
8. Disassemble flow control relief valve by:
   a. Remove connector, O-ring and flow control valve spring.
   b. Tap cover on soft surface to dislodge valve assembly.
   c. Remove relief valve by pushing valve into flow control valve and removing snap-ring. Remove valve and spring.

Assembly

NOTE: Lubricate all parts before assembly.

1. Install new oil seal in pump body. Press seal in place using a driver on outer edge of seal.
2. Install inner rotor and key on shaft and insert shaft and rotor assembly into body, coupling end front.
3. Place outer rotor in body. Be sure rotors are aligned according to marks made during disassembly.
4. Locate O-rings in body and insert throughst washer in cover. Place cover in position on body and tighten to torque.
5. Reassemble flow control relief valve by:
   a. Insert spring and relief valve into flow control valve, small end first.
   b. Push relief valve into flow control valve far enough to allow installation of snap-ring.
   c. Install valve assembly into pump body, narrow land first, insert spring and install connector using new O-ring.
6. Install coupling assembly on shaft. Torque bolts.

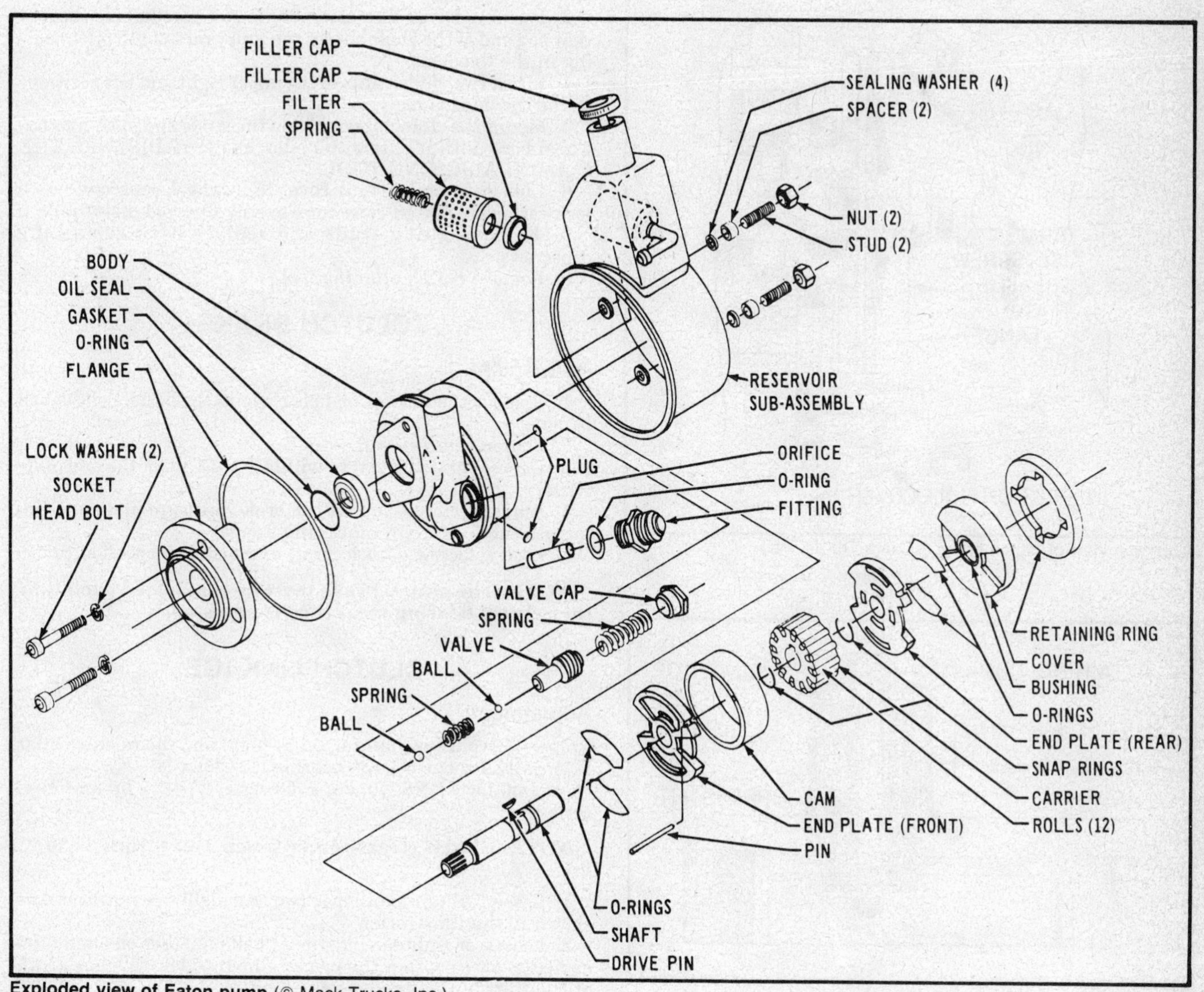

Exploded view of Eaton pump (© Mack Trucks, Inc.)

CLUTCH

The clutch used in current production vehicles is classified by series to identify basic functions. Service instructions for a specific series apply to all variations within that series. The following procedure is a general clutch removal and installation procedure.

Removal

NOTE: Always mark clutch and flywheel, preferably with a center punch, before removing to facilitate installation.

1. Use spring retention tools or retaining cups as shown when removing a clutch assembly from the flywheel.
2. To use spring retention tool, bottom screws in tapped holes in pressure plate. Tighten tool nuts snugly against tool bracket. Tighten nuts evenly to relieve spring tension on pressure plate.

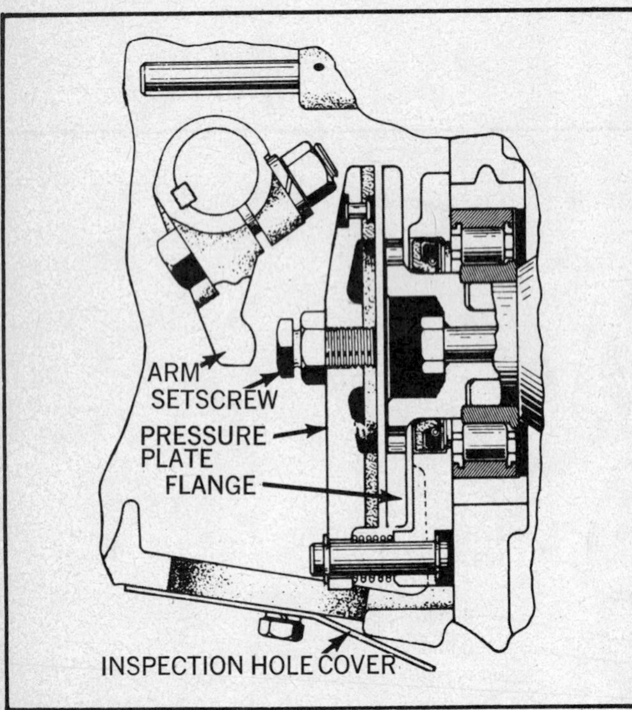

Sectional view of clutch brake (© Mack Trucks, Inc.)

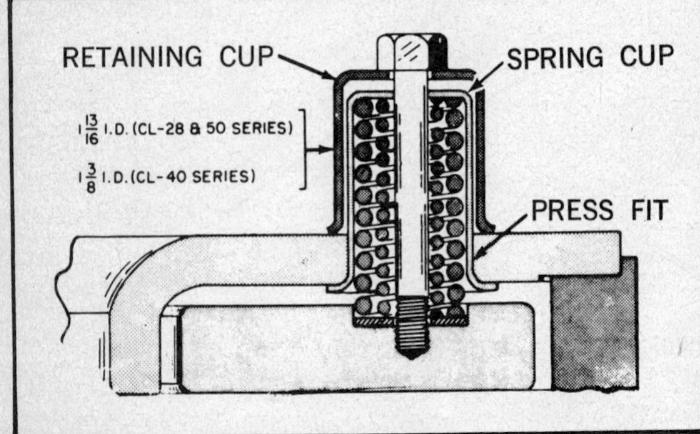

Retaining cups (© Mack Trucks, Inc.)

NOTE: These are not used on CL-58 series.

3. Remove the two clutch-to-flywheel capscrews with lockwashers at the upper right and left positions of the flywheel.
4. Install two headless guide studs long enough to support the clutch assembly during removal of the remaining capscrews.
5. Carefully remove clutch and disc assembly from flywheel and place on bench.
6. Remove guide studs from flywheel.

CAUTION

Driven disc is free when removed. Take care not to drop it.

Installation

1. Use spring retention tools or spring retaining cups to hold new clutch assembly together during installation.

CAUTION

Be sure to remove retaining cups after installation.

2. Insert clutch aligning tool through driven disc from rear of long hub side.
3. Position driven disc assembly in countersunk flywheel so that peg end of the shaft enters the inner race of the pilot bearing in the flywheel.
4. Insert two guide studs in the upper right and left positions in the flywheel rim.
5. Mount the clutch assembly on the studs and push into flywheel bore until it enters the pilot. DO NOT DISTURB THE CLUTCH ALIGNING TOOL.
6. Lubricate and install cover-to-flywheel capscrews with lockwashers. Tighten capscrews evenly to avoid distortion.
7. Remove guide studs and replace with remaining capscrews.
8. Remove clutch aligning tool.

CLUTCH BRAKE

Adjustment

1. Remove the inspection hole cover in the bottom of the bell housing.
2. Loosen setscrew nut.
3. Depress clutch pedal to within $^1/_2$ to 1 in. of the end of its travel.
4. Adjust setscrew so that the brake pressure plate and lining assembly firmly contacts the flange.
5. Lock setscrew with locknut and install inspection cover.

NOTE: The clutch brake must be readjusted each time the release bearing clearance is adjusted.

CLUTCH LINKAGE

Adjustment

Proper clearance is maintained by adjusting the release collar externally. Proper release bearing clearance is: $^1/_8$–$^3/_{16}$ in. for CL-28, 40, 50, & 58 series $^1/_{16}$–$^3/_{16}$ in. for CL-47 series.

NOTE: Clutch release lever pinch bolt torque is 30 ft. lbs.

1. Loosen jam nuts number two and eight, all nut locations shown in the illustration.
2. Loosen or tighten adjustment bolts number one and nine as necessary to obtain the proper clutch pedal travel as given at the start of this procedure.

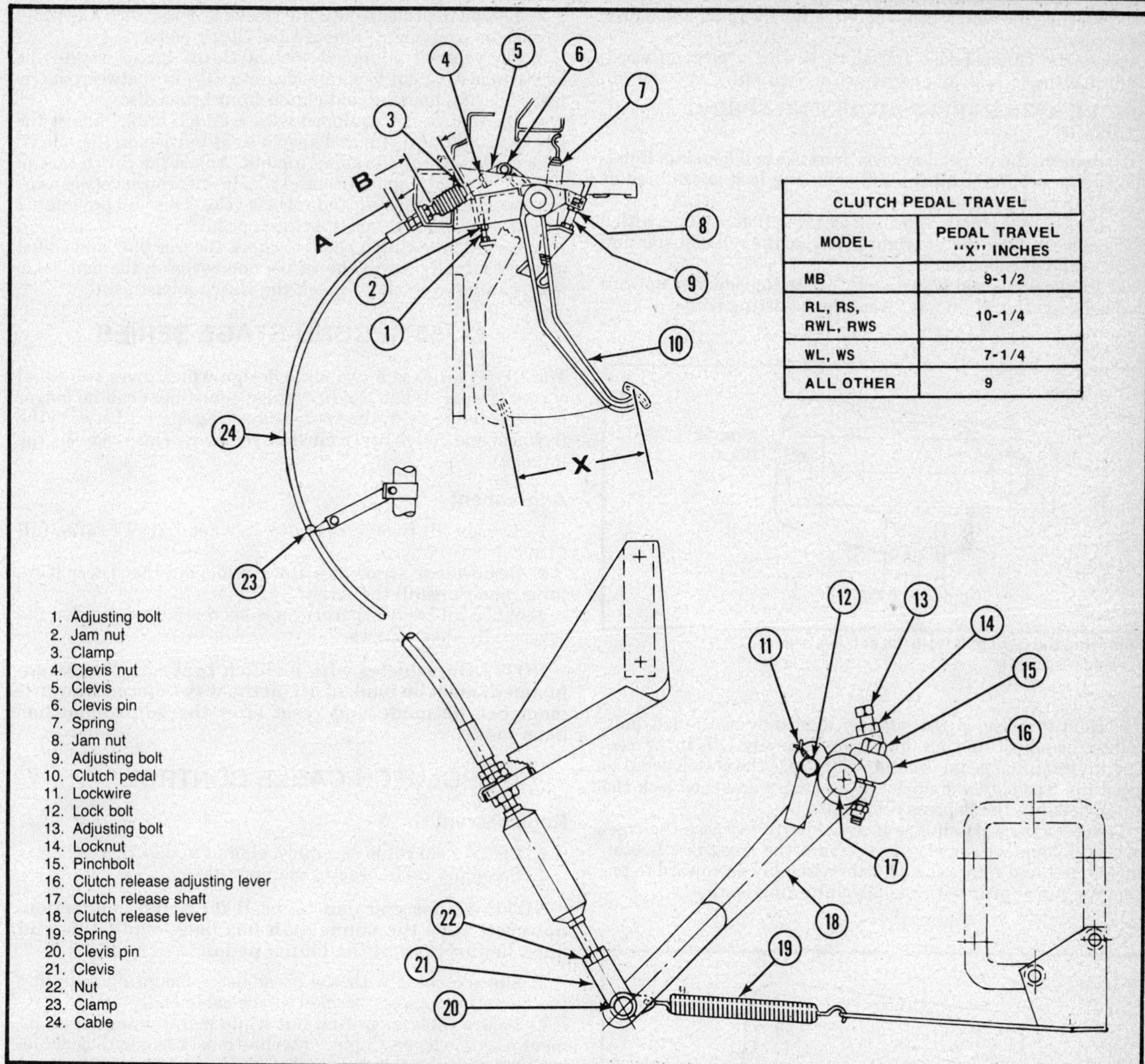

Clutch control adjustment chart—MB models (© Mack Trucks, Inc.)

3. Be sure that the clutch pedal has approximately 1 $^1/_2$ in. of free-play. If this free play can not be obtained through the external clutch linkage, the clutch will have to be adjusted internally.

MID-LINER

1. Loosen the jam nut, move the clutch fork to bring the throwout bearing into contact with the clutch mechanism.
2. Loosen or tighten the yoke to adjust the clutch pedal clearance. The clearance at the throwout bearing should be 0.012 in. for the MS300 model and 0.00 in. (no clearance) for the MS200 model.

Internal Clutch Adjustments

NOTE: It is important to find out what clutch application is installed into the truck before starting any clutch adjustments.

SPICER ANGLE-SPRING CLUTCH

1. Remove the inspection cover from the bell housing. Bump the engine around until the adjusting lock is centered at the bell housing opening.
2. Depress the clutch pedal and lock it in that position with a block of wood. Remove the adjusting lock and lock strap from the clutch.
3. Using a suitable tool turn the adjusting ring, each notch in the adjusting ring is approxitmately 0.020 in. So if the ring has been turned three notches, it has made the released bearing move approximately $^1/_{16}$ in. Rotate the ring clockwise to increase the free play and counterclockwise to decrease the free-play.
4. Visually check to see if there is appproxitmately $^1/_2$ in. clearance between the the face of the release bearing housing and the clutch brake. For the proper release, the release bearing must move approxitmately $^1/_2$ between the end of the free-play travel and clutch brake actuation point.

5. Release the clutch pedal to check the free play and adjust as necessary.
Depress the clutch pedal and block it with a piece of wood. Reinsatll the lock strap and adjusting lock nut.

SPICER ANGLE – SELF ADJUSTING SPRING CLUTCH

1. Remove the inspection cover from the bell housing. Bump the engine around until the self adjusting lock is centered at the bell housing opening.
2. Depress the clutch pedal and lock it in that position with a block of wood. Remove the right bolt from the self adjuster and loosen the left adjuster.
3. To allow manual adjustment, rotate the adjuster upward to disengage the worm gear from the adjusting ring.

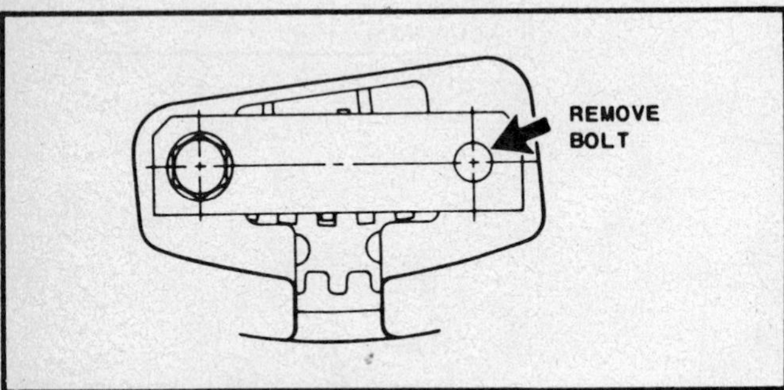

Removing the right bolt from the self adjuster
(© Mack Trucks, Inc.)

4. Hold the disengaged adjuster amd tighten the left bolt. Rotate the adjusting ring until approximately 1 $^1/_2$ in. of free-play in the clutch pedal is obtained (release the clutch pedal to check the free play and adjust as necessary and then lock the clutch pedal in the depress position).
5. Rotate the adjusting ring clockwise to increase the free-play and counterclockwise to decrease the free-play. Loosen the left bolt and rotate the adjuster assembly downward to engage the worm gear with the adjusting ring teeth.

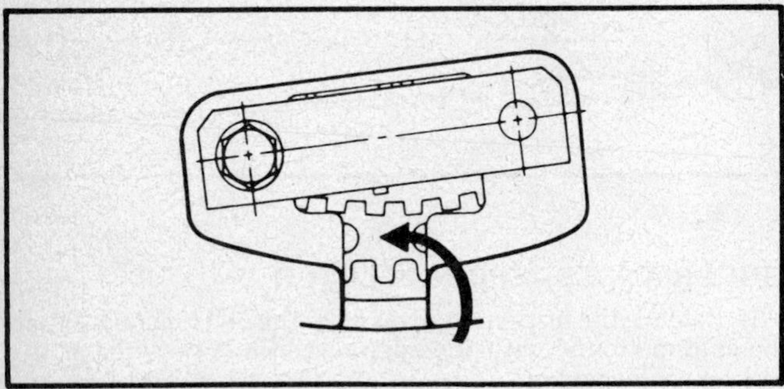

Turning the adjusting ring (© Mack Trucks, Inc.)

6. Install the right bolt and tighten both bolts. Check to see that the actuator arm is inserted into the release sleeve retainer. If the adjusting assembly has been installed correctly, the adjuster assembly spring will move back and forth with the pedal stroke.
7. Reinstall the inspection cover on the bell housing. Road test vehicle to check the clutch adjustment.

LIPE CLUTCH

1. Remove the inspection cover from the bell housing. Depress the clutch pedal and lock it in that position with a block of wood.
2. Loosen the release bearing sleeve lock nut with a spanner wrench or equivalent. Release the clutch pedal.
3. On vehicles equipped with a clutch brake, rotate the sleeve adjusting nut to obtain clearance ($^1/_2$ in.) between the release bearing housing and clutch front brake disc.
4. On vehicle not equipped with a clutch brake, adjust the sleeve to obtain $^9/_{16}$ in. and keep a light tension on the release yoke while turning the adjusting nut. Adjust the clutch control linkage to obtain approxitmately $^1/_8$ in. clearance between the release bearing housing and release yoke. This will provide a 1 $^1/_2$ of free-play travel at the clutch pedal.
5. Release the clutch pedal to check the free play and adjust as necessary. Reinstall the inspection cover on the bell housing, road test vehicle to check the clutch adjustment.

CL-50 SECOND STAGE SERIES

The CL-50 series is a two plate design which gives two equal stages of wear. When the first stage adjustment can no longer be made due to wear, the twelve adjusting spacers between the flywheel and clutch cover must be removed. This readjusts the linkage.

Adjustment

1. Loosen all twelve cover-to-flywheel screws three full turns.
2. Remove one screw at a time, removing the spacer it retains, and reinstall the screw.
3. When all twelve spacers have been removed, tighten the cover-to-flywheel screws.

NOTE: On vehicles with a clutch brake, the brake adjustment must be backed off all the way before an adjustment can be made and reset after the adjustment has been made.

CLUTCH CABLE CONTROL

Replacement

1. Remove old cable assembly, clamps and fasteners.
2. Preadjust cable bracket clamp nuts.

NOTE: Either end can be used for pedal connection, however, once the connection has been made, this end must be installed at the clutch pedal.

3. Slip the cable with the preadjusted mounting nuts into the mounting support bracket at the cable end.
4. Secure cable mounting nut while maintaining an alignment with the lever. Cable centerline must align with pedal lever so clevis pin slides in freely.
5. Route cable along original path so that all exhaust components are avoided. All bends must have a radius greater than 8 in.
6. Screw cable on clevis end fitting.
7. Adjust boot overall length with clevis pin installed and pedal in the fully engaged position.
8. Tighten clevis nut.
9. At clutch end, follow steps 3–5 except:
   a. Use all effective threads on cable end fitting when attaching clevis.
   b. Install cable retainer or shield and bolt in place
10. Check installation for clearances and bends.
11. Position boots in recesses provided.
12. Adjust clutch for bearing clearance.

DYNAMAX CLUTCH

CL-72 & CL-721 SERIES

This type clutch is a four plate, push-type wet clutch secured to the flywheel in the normal manner. It is made up of a drive

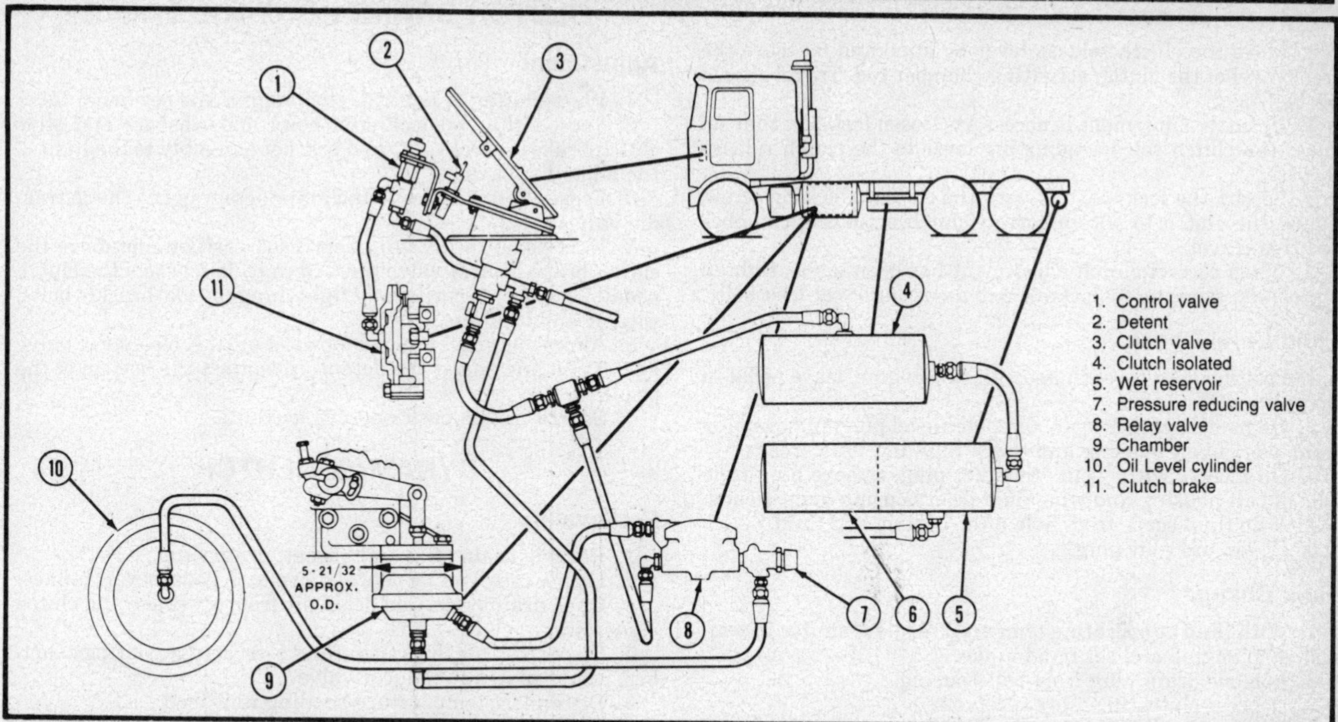

Dynamax clutch air control system (© Mack Trucks, Inc.)

ring, cover and spring loaded pressure plate. Engagement occurs when the disc pack is clamped to the flywheel by the pressure plate. Drive is transmitted through the disc pack and center hub assembly which is splined to the mainshaft. Release is conventional. Lubrication is accomplished in the normal wet-type manner with engaged pressure at 80 psi and disengaged pressure at 90–95 psi. at 1200 rpm.

CLUTCH CONTROL

Clutch operation is activated by air piped from the truck's main air supply to the clutch air reservoir and then to the treadle air valve. The system is quite similar to the air brake system. When the treadle is depressed air is simultaneously supplied to the clutch engagement cylinder and through a reducer to the fluid reservoir, thus raising the level in the bell housing.

CLUTCH BRAKE

The clutch brake is air operated at the bottom $1/10$ in. of the clutch valve stroke and serves the same purpose as a standard clutch brake.

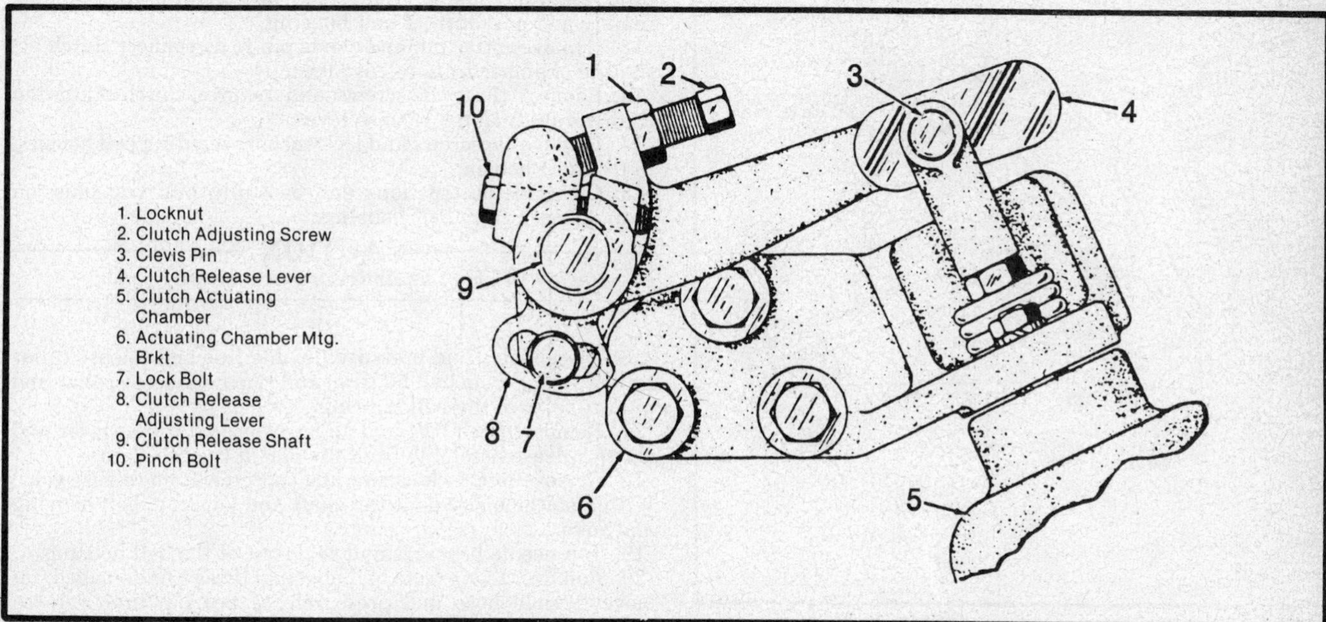

Making the clutch adjustment on a Dynamax clutch (© Mack Trucks, Inc.)

Clutch Adjustment

1. Move the clutch release lever by hand and measure the free travel of the clutch actuating chamber rod. Travel should be $^3/_8$–$^3/_{16}$ in.
2. If clutch adjustment is necessary, loosen lock bolt that secures the clutch release adjusting lever to the clutch release lever.
3. Loosen the locknut, and with the clutch adjusting screw, adjust the clutch to obtain correct clutch actuating chamber rod free travel.
4. When correct clutch adjustment has been made, tighten clutch adjusting screw locknut and adjusting lever lock bolt.

Fluid Level Check

1. Position shift lever in neutral, stop engine, leave pedal in up position.
2. On models with 1 $^1/_2$ in. diameter level plug, remove plug from side of bell housing and check fluid level at threads.
3. On models with $^1/_4$ in. diameter plug, remove plug from side of bell housing and wipe fluid from housing and threads.
4. If no fluid seeps from hole after wiping, add fluid.
5. Clean and refit plug.

Fluid Change

1. With fluid at operating temperature, place shifter in neutral, stop engine and set hand brake.
2. Remove drain plug from bell housing.
3. Depress clutch to empty reservoir.
4. Release pedal and reinstall plug.
5. Remove level plug and fill with Dexron® or equivalent fluid.
6. Install level plug.
7. Depress clutch pedal slowly several times to activate reservoir chamber and expel any air.
8. Remove level plug and check. If necessary, add fluid.
9. Replace level plug.

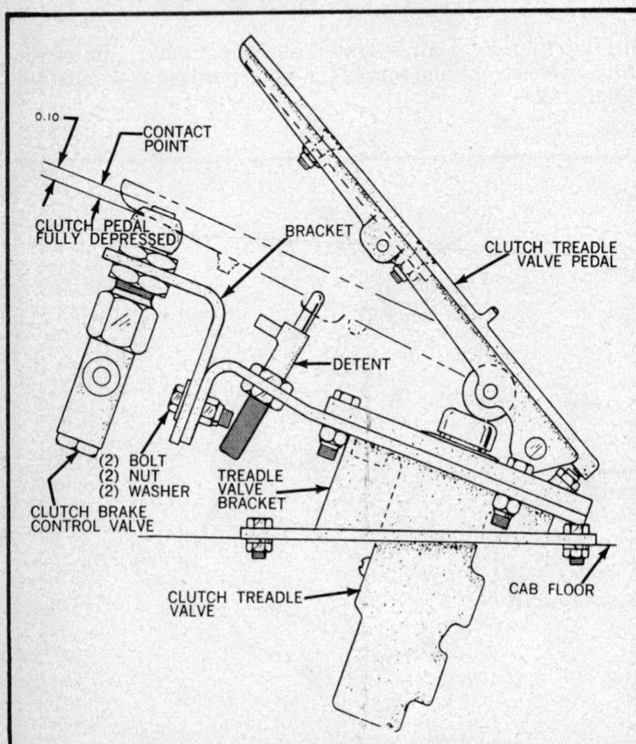

Clutch brake control valve adjustment (© Mack Trucks, Inc.)

CLUTCH BRAKE CONTROL VALVE

Adjustment

1. Place shifter in neutral, stop engine and set handbrake.
2. Loosen the two locknuts, bolts and washers and slide clutch brake control valve and bracket assembly to the limit of the adjusting slots.
3. Loosen detent locknut and lower detent in the clutch treadle valve bracket.
4. Hold pedal in the fully depressed position and move the clutch brake control valve upward until it contacts the clutch pedal. Lock in this position by tightening the two bracket bolts, washer and locknuts.
5. Allow the pedal to move upward until it clears the valve by 0.03 in. and adjust the detent up against the bottom of the pedal.
6. Secure in this position with locknuts.

DYNAMAX CLUTCH

Removal

1. Remove drain plug and gasket; drain fluid.
2. Empty reservoir by depressing clutch pedal several times.
3. Open drain cocks and drain air from air brake and clutch reservoir.
4. Disconnect air lines from fluid reservoir, actuating chamber, relay valve and reducer valve.
5. Disconnect temperature sending unit lead.
6. Remove fluid pressure line from top of bell housing.
7. On R, U, and DM models, remove the cab floorboard.
8. Remove capscrews and lift off hand hole cover from bell housing.
9. Position hand inside bell housing to hold pitot tube clamp and remove the two capscrews and lockwashers. Extract pitot tube clamp from bell housing.
10. Work pitot tube free of collector ring and clutch drive ring and pull it back into the bell housing.

CAUTION

To avoid damage to the pitot tube, it must be disconnected from the bell housing before the transmission is removed.

11. Remove capscrews and remove bell housing sump cover, fluid reservoir chamber, relay valve and pressure regulator assembly and gasket from bell housing.
12. Remove cotter pin and clevis pin to disconnect clutch actuating chamber from release lever.
13. Remove three capscrews and remove clutch actuating chamber from clutch release lever.
14. Remove capscrews and lockwashers securing bell housing to flywheel housing.
15. Clear all obstructions and carefully pull transmission straight back from bell housing.

CAUTION

Do not allow weight of transmission to rest on drive pinion.

16. Disconnect fluid pressure flexible line and release collar return spring from bell housing and remove release collar and pitot tube from the bell housing.
17. Remove pinch bolt and slide release adjusting lever and clutch release assembly from the clutch release shaft.
18. Remove nut, lockwasher and capscrew from release yoke. With a suitable size drift tap shaft and key from bell housing and yoke.
19. Tap needle bearings and seals out of the bell housing.
20. Remove O-ring from bell housing. If worn or damaged, remove flexible hose and press release bearing from release collar.

21. Install three $^3/_8$–16 × 2 $^1/_4$ in. capscrews and flat washers into the tapped holes in the pressure plate to release spring pressure from the center hub and disc pack assembly.
22. Remove upper right and left capscrews and lockwashers from the clutch cover and install two guide studs.
23. Remove the remaining clutch cover-to-flywheel capscrews and lockwashers. Remove clutch cover and center hub and disc pack assembly from the drive ring.

NOTE: If drive ring replacement is necessary, tap the three countersunk holes and use a puller to remove.

Installation

1. Install pilot bearing into the flywheel and secure collector ring to the flywheel with its mounting bolts.
2. Install long guide studs into the upper right and left holes of the flywheel.
3. Slide drive ring onto the guide studs and tap the drive ring into its pilot in the flywheel.
4. Install the center hub and disc pack assembly into the drive ring.
5. Install a clutch aligning tool through the center hub and disc pack assembly into the pilot bearing.
6. Slide the clutch cover assembly onto the guide studs and up to the drive ring. Align the "A" on the cover with the "A" on the ring.
7. Secure the assembly to the flywheel with capscrews and lockwashers.
8. Tighten capscrews evenly to avoid distortion.
9. Remove the guide studs and install capscrews and lockwashers.
10. Remove the three shipping screws and flat washers one turn at a time to relieve clutch spring tension evenly.
11. Remove clutch aligning tool.
12. Install needle bearings and oil seals in the bell housing for the release shaft.
13. Position release yoke and key into bell housing and install clutch release shaft through bell housing yoke and key.
14. Secure yoke on the clutch release shaft with capscrew lockwasher and nut.
15. Press release bearing on the release collar and install flexible hose in the release collar.
16. Install straight connector and pitot tube to the flexible hose.
17. Slide the release collar assembly on the drive pinion cover and release collar.
18. Secure the fluid pressure flexible line in the bell housing.
19. Lubricate the O-ring with petroleum jelly and install in its groove in the bell housing.
20. Guide the transmission assembly into the flywheel housing being sure the main drive pinion indexes properly with the center hub and disc pack.
21. Secure the bell housing to the flywheel housing with capscrews and lockwashers.
22. Position new pitot tube clamp in the bell housing and secure finger tight with the two capscrews and lockwashers.
23. Rotate and slide the pitot tube in the clamp as necessary to center the open end of the pitot tube in the collector ring at approximately the 270° position.
24. Push the pitot tube forward as far as it will go.
25. Mark the tube where it is clamped to the bell housing.
26. Carefully pull the pitot tube back until it contacts the collector ring.
27. Again mark the tube where it contacts the bell housing.
28. Put a third mark in the center of the other two and position the tube so it is centered where it clamps to the bell housing.
29. Without sliding the pitot tube, rotate it until the open end just contacts the collector ring.
30. Hold the tube in this position and tighten the two clamp capscrews sufficiently to crimp the tube.

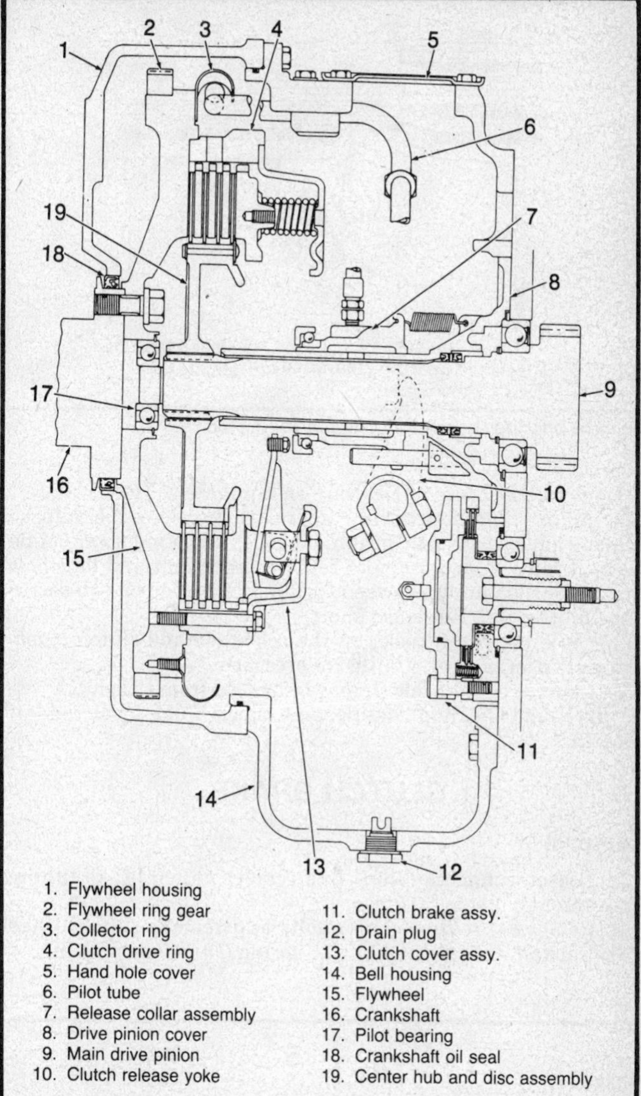

Sectional view of Dynamax clutch (© Mack Trucks, Inc.)

31. Position the hand hole cover to the bell housing and secure with six bolts.
32. Slide clutch release lever and clutch release adjusting lever assembly on the end of the clutch release shaft and secure with a pinch bolt.
33. Position the clutch actuating chamber to the clutch release lever and secure with a clevis pin and cotter pin.
34. Secure actuating chamber mounting bracket to the bell housing with the three mounting bolts.
35. Apply a thin coat of self vulcanizing elastomer both sides of the fluid reservoir mounting gasket and secure to sump cover with two mounting nuts and washers.
36. Apply a thin coat of self vulcanizing elastomer to both sides of the sump cover gasket and secure the assembly to the bell housing with the eight mounting bolts.
37. Install breather, temperature sending unit and gasket, and drain plug in bell housing.
38. Connect electrical lead to the sending unit.
39. Connect the air lines to the fluid reservoir chamber, clutch actuating chamber, relay valve and reducing valve. Connect the fluid pressure line at the top of the bell housing.
40. Install ear engine supports, connect drive line and reinstall any items removed or disconnected.

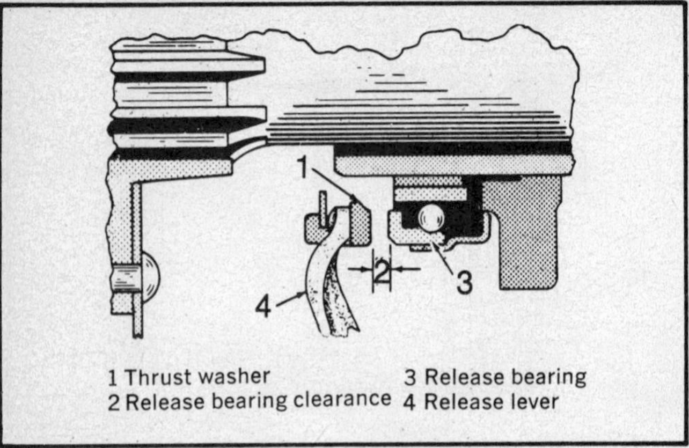

Release bearing clearance (© Mack Trucks, Inc.)

41. Install 14 pints of Dexron® or Equivalent Fluid.

42. Adjust clutch according to instructions in the release bearing adjustment paragraph. If proper adjustment cannot be made it may be necessary to remove pinch bolt and lock bolt and move the clutch release adjusting lever one or two serrations on the clutch release shaft.

43. Close the drain cocks on the air brake and clutch reservoirs, start engine and build up pressure.

44. Depress pedal a few times to expel air from the clutch reservoir chamber. Stop engine and check fluid level; add if necessary.

CLUTCH BRAKE

Removal

1. Loosen connection nuts and remove clutch brake tubing from the two elbow fittings.

2. Remove three mounting bolts and remove clutch brake cover, piston, three clutch brake springs, and disc retainer.

Installing bearing cover and brake sleeve (© Mack Trucks, Inc.)

3. Slide the two internal and two external friction discs from the clutch brake sleeve.

4. Remove clutch brake sleeve screw and clutch brake sleeve.

5. Remove four bearing cover retaining screws and remove bearing cover and O-ring.

Installation

1. Apply a thin coat of white grease on the oil seal contact area of the clutch brake sleeve and on the oil seal lips.

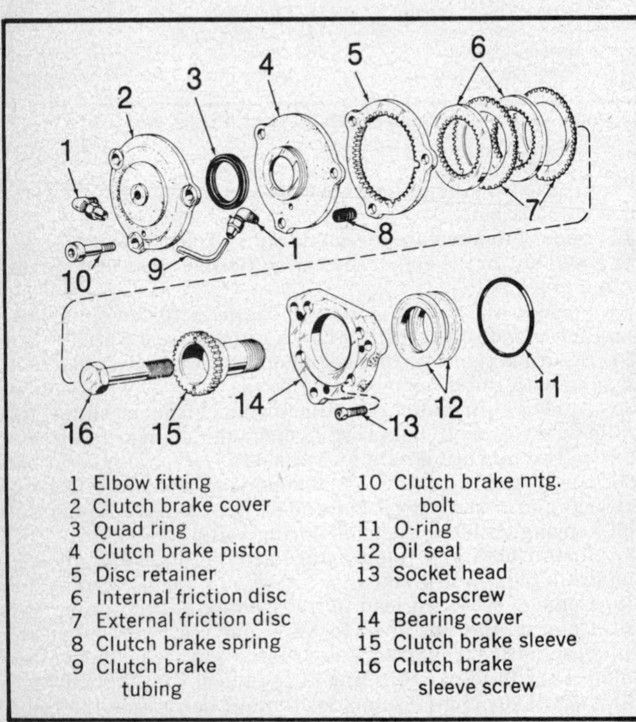

Exploded view of clutch brake (© Mack Trucks, Inc.)

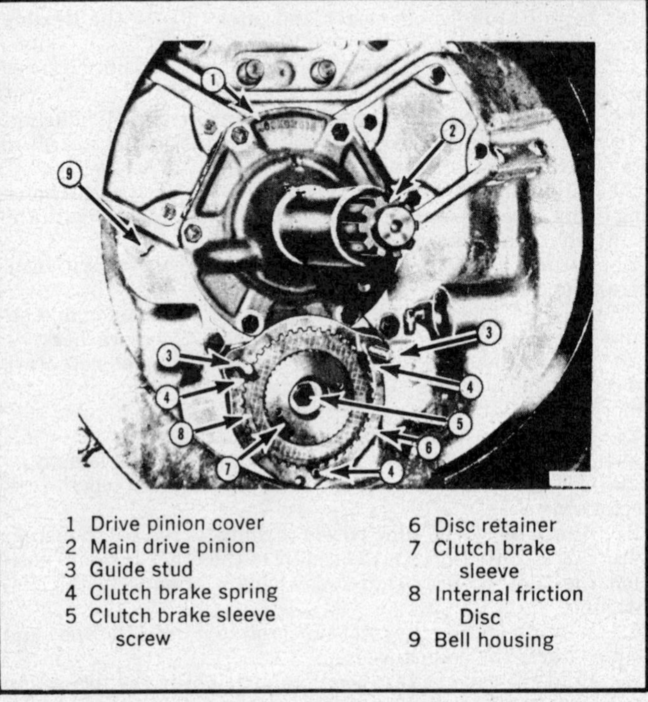

Clutch brake disc retainer and disc installation (© Mack Trucks, Inc.)

2. Guide sleeve into cover and oil seal assembly.
3. Install two guide studs into the two housing cover upper mounting holes of the bell housing.
4. Install O-ring into the recess in the rear of the bearing cover and carefully guide bearing cover and sleeve assembly onto the two guide studs and into the bell housing.
5. Using the appropriate tool, tighten the clutch brake sleeve onto the transmission lower countershaft.
6. Install the two lower socket-head capscrews and secure the bearing cover to the transmission.
7. Remove the two guide studs and install the two upper socket-head capscrews.
8. Install the clutch brake sleeve screw into the clutch brake and lower countershaft.
9. Thread the two guide studs into the upper tapped holes of the bearing cover.
10. Install disc retainer onto the two guide studs.
11. Install an external disc, internal disc, external disc, internal disc in that order into the disc retainer.
12. Install three clutch brake springs into the clutch brake retainer.
13. Coat quad ring with white grease and install on brake piston.
14. Assemble clutch brake cover on piston without distorting the quad ring.
15. Guide the cover and piston assembly onto the two guide studs and three clutch brake springs.
16. Install the bottom clutch brake mounting bolt.
17. Remove the two guide studs and install the two remaining mounting bolts.
18. If removed, install the elbow fittings into the bell housing and clutch brake cover.
19. Secure the clutch brake tubing to the two elbow fittings with the two connector nuts.

TRANSMISSION

The Mack transmission models are available in five, ten and fifteen forward speeds, with one, two, three and five reverse speeds. The transmissions are of the heavy duty design for use both off the road and over the road applications.

Removal

ALL, EXCEPT WITH DYNAMAX

1. Place transmission in neutral.
2. Secure vehicle other than with air brakes and drain air system.
3. Drain Transmission.
4. Remove U-bolts from propeller shaft and collapse slip joint. Be sure to catch bearings.
5. Remove shaft and joints as assembly by taking out flange bolts.
6. Disconnect batteries.
7. With conventional cabs, remove floor boards.
8. Disconnect speedometer cable where applicable.
9. Remove shift lever assembly.
10. Remove auxiliary shift levers where applicable.
11. Disconnect linkages.
12. Remove parking brake lever.
13. Disconnect auxiliary shafts, PTO shafts and control lever or shaft.
14. On models with Eaton Road Ranger transmission, disconnect air lines.
15. Carefully displace, all fuel, air and electric lines where braced to transmission.
16. Drain hydraulic system where applicable.
17. Position transmission jack under transmission and chain transmission to jack, be sure of alignment.
18. Disconnect clutch linkage and tube lines from throw out bearing.
19. Loosen and remove transmission to bell housing bolts.
20. Pull transmission straight back and lower to floor level.
21. Pull transmission back to intermediate axle, turn sideways, raise chassis and remove.
22. Place chain on rear companion flange and front housing for hoist from jack.

NOTE: Pilot bearing should be replaced.

NOTE: COE models: Transmission is removed with shop crane. Brace cab in addition to locking devices. Disconnect and remove U-shaped rear cab support and lock.

Installation

1. Secure transmission to jack, raise chassis and position transmission for insertion.
2. Insert headless dowel pins as guide studs in the upper left and right flywheel housing to bell housing bolt holes.
3. Raise transmission and using guide studs, slowly and carefully slide transmission into position.

CAUTION

Make certain mainshaft splines mesh with clutch assembly. Care should be taken to avoid damage to new pilot bearing.

4. With guide studs in position, insert bolts and snug-up. Remove guide studs, insert remaining two bolts and torque to specifications.
5. Connect clutch linkage and tube line to throw-out bearing.
6. Remove chains and transmission jack.
7. Rebracket all displaced lines.
8. Reconnect all air and hydraulic lines.
9. Connect auxiliary shafts, P.T.O. shafts, and control lever or shaft.
10. Reinstall parking brake lever and adjust.
11. Reconnect linkages and adjust.
12. Reinstall auxiliary shift levers.
13. Reinstall shift lever assembly.
14. Reconnect speedometer cable.
15. Replace floor boards.
16. Reconnect batteries.
17. Replace propellor shaft.
18. Refill and bleed hydraulic system.
19. Refill transmission.
20. Start engine and charge air system.
21. Check all adjustments.

NOTE: For transmission removal with Dynamax, see Clutch section.

MID-LINER

Removal

5-SPEED TRANSMISSION

1. Disconnect the negative battery cables. Block the wheels, raise and support vehicle safely, using suitable jack stands.

2. Disconnect and mark all electrical connectors. Disconnect the speedometer drive. Remove the gear shift lever.
3. Remove the drive shaft bolts and drive shaft. Remove the clutch slave cylinder plate.
4. Remove the shaft bolt and shaft. Remove the four clutch slave cylinder mounting bolts.
5. Position a suitable transmission jack under the transmission and remove the transmission case mounting bolts.
6. Remove the ground strap and pull the jack back until the clutch housing is behind the cross member.
7. Lower the transmission jack and remove the transmission from underneath the vehicle.
8. Installation is the reverse order of the removal procedure. Torque the drive shaft bolts to 25 ft. lbs., the clutch slave cylinder mounting bolts to 15 ft. lbs., The gear shift control joint nut to 26 ft. lbs. and the transmission case bolts to 33 ft. lbs. Road test the vehicle to check the operation of the transmission.

NOTE: Some Mid-Liners will be equipped with Allison Automatic Transmissions. The removal and installtion procedures for this transmission are not available at the time of this publication.

Power Take-Off

MACK FLYWHEEL P.T.O.

The P.T.O. is mounted between the engine and transmission bell housing and operates independently of the main clutch and transmission. The P.T.O. drive is continuous as long as the engine is operating and is not interrupted when declutching. A "safety-fuse" clutch on the output shaft permits momentary shaft slippage under extreme shock loads to protect the gearing and shafts.

Removal

1. Remove the driven shaft from the P.T.O. clutch drive flange.
2. Remove the clutch drive flange from the clutch drive disc by removing the capscrews.
3. Remove the cotter pin and nut from the P.T.O. driveshaft.
4. Remove the drain plugs and drain the oil from the unit.
5. Match-mark and disconnect the transmission driveshaft.
6. Support the weight of the transmission and remove the transmission to P.T.O. flange bolts.
7. Carefully move the transmission rearward, away from the P.T.O. housing.

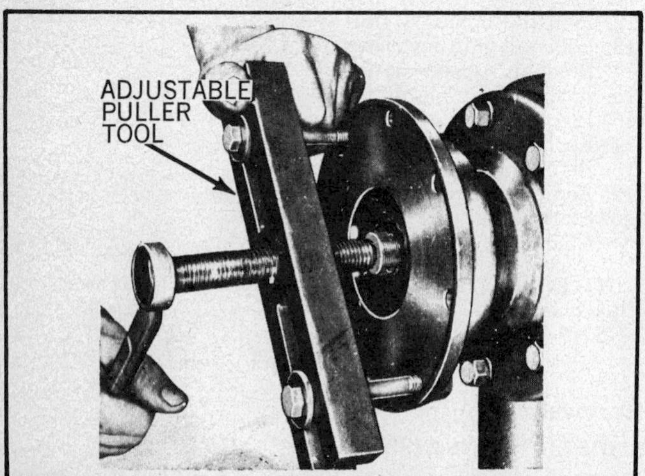

Removing drive flange (© Mack Trucks, Inc.)

CAUTION

Do not pull the clutch release bearing off the end of the transmission collar.

NOTE: Vehicle models with CL82-83 clutches; Remove the inspection plate on the transmission before removal and remove the release bearing snap-ring and bearing assembly.

8. Remove the P.T.O. assembly from the flywheel housing.

Installation

1. Position the P.T.O. assembly to the flywheel housing and index the drive gear teeth with the drive sleeve and install the flange bolts.

NOTE: For Spicer clutch models, install the clutch bearing and snap-ring.

2. Carefully install the transmission input shaft into the P.T.O. and throw-out bearing, and install the flange bolts around the flywheel housing.
3. Align the match-marks and install the driveshaft.
4. Torque the P.T.O. driveshaft nut to 100–110 ft. lbs. and install the cotter pin.

CAUTION

The torque value of the driveshaft nut is very important. Insufficient torque value may allow the "safety-fuse" clutch to slip while overtorque value will eliminate the safety feature of the clutch.

5. Position the clutch drive flange to the clutch disc and install the socket headed capscrews.
6. Connect the drive unit to the clutch drive flange and install 5 pints of the recommended oil to the P.T.O. unit.

LOWER COUNTERSHAFT WITH EIGHT HOLE P.T.O.

Removal

1. Drain lubricant.
2. Remove lower countershaft rear bearing cover with O-ring.
3. Remove left hand power take-off (8 bolts).
4. Slide countershaft rearward slightly and note timing marks on front and rear countershaft splines. If marks are not visible, mark the shaft for reference.
5. Slide countershaft partially from rear bearing opening.
6. Remove oil slinger.
7. Remove front snap-ring. Slide snap-ring and oil aligner from shaft leaving rear snap-ring in place.

Installation

1. Install power take-off gear, with retaining snap-ring, on shaft.
2. Align timing marks on front and rear countershafts.
3. Slide shaft forward until rear bearing positioning ring seats against case.
4. Position power take-off gear on countershaft splines.
5. Install gear front snap-ring in groove.
6. Install O-ring in countershaft rear bearing cover.
7. Install cover with washers and capscrews; torque to 30–40 ft. lbs.
8. Install power take-off assembly.
9. Fill transmission.

RIGHT COUNTERSHAFT WITH SIX HOLE P.T.O.

Removal

1. Drain lubricant.

2. Remove lower and right countershaft rear bearing covers with O-rings.
3. Remove left and right P.T.O. covers.
4. Slide lower rear countershaft rearward slightly and note timing marks on front and rear countershaft splines. If timing marks are not visible mark each shaft for reference.
5. Remove lower rear countershaft from case through rear bearing opening.
6. Slide right rear countershaft rearward slightly and note timing marks on front and rear countershaft splines. If marks are not visible, mark shafts for reference.
7. Slide right rear countershaft partially from rear bearing opening.
8. Remove front snap-ring from oil slinger.
9. Slide spring and oil slinger from shaft. Leave rear snap-ring in place.

Installation

1. Insert P.T.O. gear through left power take-off opening. Work gear across transmission and install on right countershaft.
2. Install power take-off gear retaining front snap-ring on shaft.
3. Align right rear countershaft timing mark with timing mark on front countershaft.
4. Slide shaft forward until countershaft rear bearing snap-ring seats against case.
5. Position power take-off gear on countershaft splines.
6. Install gear front snap-ring in groove.
7. Align lower rear countershaft timing mark with mark on front countershaft. Slide shaft forward until rear bearing snap-ring seats against case.
8. Install left power take-off cover with washers and capscrews.
9. Install O-rings in countershaft rear bearing covers.
10. Install covers with washers and capscrew; torque to 30–40 ft. lbs.
11. Install P.T.O. assembly.
12. Fill transmission.

TRANSFER CASE

Hi-Lo shift is provided and controlled by the operator. A planetary gear type center differential is used to maintain four wheel drive at all times, without requiring the operators attention. However, an operator controlled air operated differential lock-out is provided for extreme traction conditions.

Removal and Installation

1. Match-mark the driveshafts and yokes and disconnect the drive-shafts.
2. Disconnect the shift control rod.
3. Disconnect the air lines to the lock-out and the power take off units.
4. Remove any other attachments that may be connected to the transfer case.
5. Position a jack under the transfer case and chain the case to the jack.
6. Relieve the weight of the transfer case by the jack and remove the side mounting bolts.
7. Lower the transfer case and remove from under the vehicle.
8. The installation is the reverse of the removal.

Side view of transfer case (© Mack Trucks, Inc.)

REAR AXLE

Mack provides rear axles in three capacity classifications which are medium-duty, heavy-duty and extra heavy-duty. The axles are available in single-reduction, dual-reduction and two-speed dual-reduction gearing. The Mack Inter-Axle Power Divider third differential is available for tandem carriers, with or without a driver controlled lockout. Full floating axle shafts are used and may be removed without disturbing the rear wheels.

CARRIER ASSEMBLY

Removal

1. Steam clean carrier and adjacent components.
2. Position drain pan and drain lubricant.
3. Remove axle driveshaft flange bolts.
4. Hit axle shaft flange sharply with soft mallet to loosen and free dowels.
5. Disconnect universal at carrier pinion and secure shaft up and out of the way.

NOTE: With electric shift, mark and remove red and black wires. Tape ends.

6. Loosen, but do not remove, two top bolts to prevent carrier from falling.
7. Remove remaining carrier-to-housing bolts and install two guide studs in the upper left and right positions.
8. For top mounted carriers, remove level gear compartment cover and remove the two (3 in CRD-95) capscrews in side carrier housing.

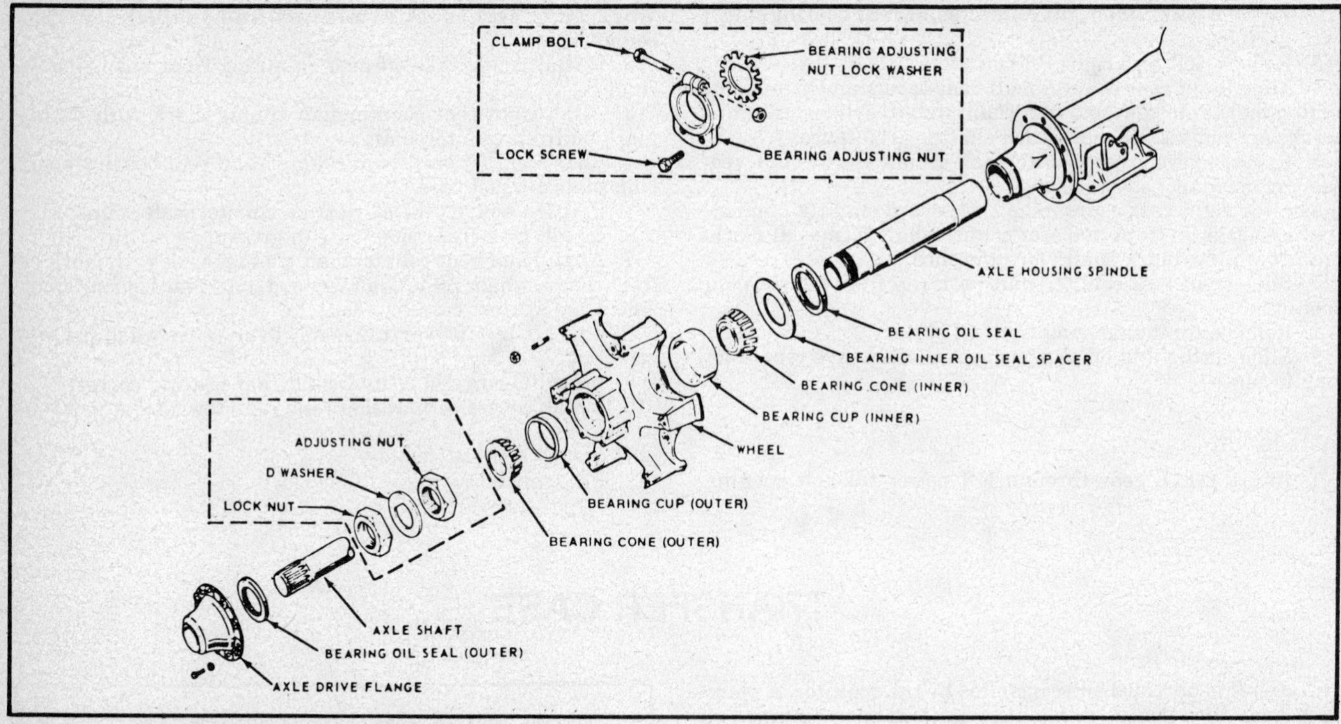

Splined type rear axle shaft components (© Mack Trucks, Inc.)

CAUTION

Before releasing carrier, position floor jack and secure to carrier.

9. Remove the two top fasteners.
10. Work carrier free using jack screws and a pry bar.
11. Lower jack with carrier.

Installation

1. Clean all gasket surfaces.
2. Clean and dry interior of housing.
3. With Rockwell-Standard carriers install new gasket on carrier-to-axle housing studs. For Mack carriers with closed differentials, fill differential with one pint of oil before assembly. With Mack open differentials, no priming is needed.

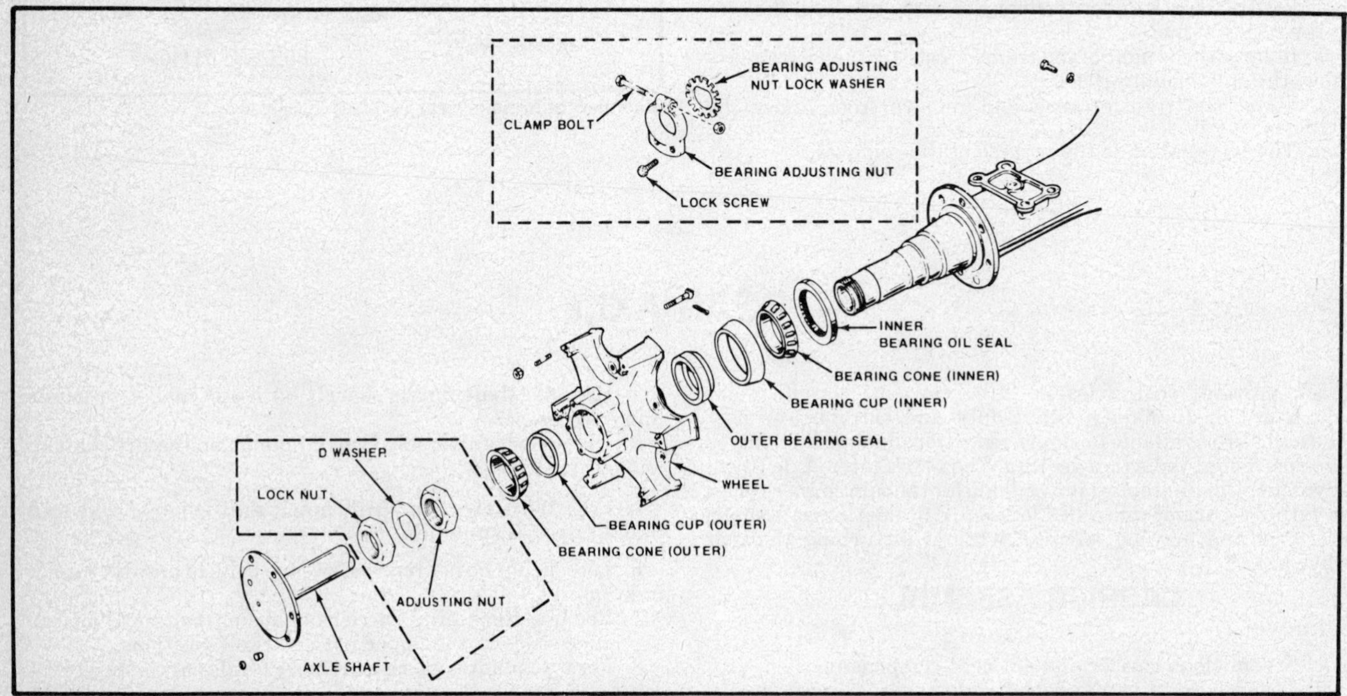

Flange type rear axle shaft components (© Mack Trucks, Inc.)

4. Install two guide studs at the upper left and right positions and apply a coating of non-hardening gasket sealer to mating face of axle housing.
5. Roll carrier into position. Engage carrier with guide studs and draw into housing with four equally spaced bolts.

CAUTION

Do not drive in with hammer.

NOTE: For Rockwell-Standard carriers, install lockwashers and stud nuts under housing off sets on any studs before carrier is drawn into housing.

6. For Mack carriers, remove guide studs. Install remaining capscrews and lockwashers and alternately draw carrier squarely into axle housing. Be certain to install and torque the two (3 in CRD-95) capscrews inside bevel gear compartment on top mounted type.
7. Torque all bolts.
8. Remove jack.
9. Reconnect propeller shaft.
10. Reinstall wires.
11. On Rockwell-Standard axles, install new axle flange gasket over each wheel hub mounting stud.
12. Lubricate splines and insert shafts into housing to engage shaft splines with side gear splines.
13. Rotate shaft until splines engage side gear splines and flange holes align with studs or threaded holes in wheel hubs.
14. Install tapered dowels in flange tapered holes.
15. Install lockwashers and stud nuts or capscrews alternately and evenly on each axle.
16. Fill axle housing.
17. Lubricate universal joint.
18. Jack up both rear wheels and operate in high transmission gear at approximately 25–30 mph for five minutes.

MID – LINER

Removal

1. Drain the gear oil from the axle and remove the center plug from the rear wheel hub.
2. Remove the snap ring and install axle remover # J29407 or equivalent. With the tool installed in the end of the shaft, remove the axle shaft.
3. Remove the drive shaft at the carrier input flange and tie it off against the chassis out of the way.
4. Remove the carrier bolts, but leave two of them in for safety purposes. Remove the brake line support brackets from the brake lines.
5. Using a suitable transmission jack with a differential adapter, slightly lift the assembly up and remove the two remaining carrier bolts. Slowly pull back on the jack until the carrier assembly clears its housing and lower the jack. Remove the carrier from the vehicle.

Installation

1. Installation is the reverse order of the removal procedure, always replace the O-ring located between the axle housing and the carrier.
2. Coat the carrier bolt threads with a suitable sealant and torque them to 60 ft. lbs. Torque the drive shaft to carrier flange bolts to 100 to 110 ft. lbs. and torque the axle drive flange plug to 590 ft. lbs.

DIFFERENTIAL AND GEAR ASSEMBLY

Removal

TYPE RAS-307 REAR AXLE

1. Mark one differential carrier leg and bearing cup for reference.

Removing differential and gear assembly from bearing pedes- (© Mack Trucks, Inc.)

2. Cut lock wire and remove adjusting nut lock and capscrews. Remove bearing cap stud, nuts or capscrews, bearing caps and adjusting nuts.
3. Lift out differential and gear assembly.

PINION BEARING AND PINION ASSEMBLY

Removal

1. Hold flange or yoke with suitable tool and remove yoke or flange nut and washer.
2. Remove drive flange or yoke with a suitable puller.
3. Remove pinion bearing cover stud nuts or capscrews then remove bearing cover and oil seal assembly.
4. Remove pinion bearing retainer using jackscrews in holes provided.
5. Wire adjustment shims together for use at reassembly.

Removing pinion bearing retainer (© Mack Trucks, Inc.)

Aligning punch mark on bearing pedestal and cup (© Mack Trucks, Inc.)

Adjusting differential bearing preload (© Mack Trucks, Inc.)

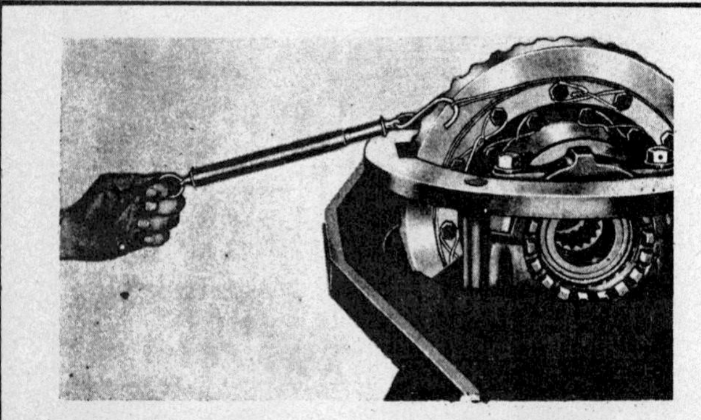

Measuring rolling-drag or preload differential bearing (© Mack Trucks, Inc.)

PINION AND BEARING RETAINER ASSEMBLY

Installation

1. Install proper shim pack with thin shims on both sides for maximum sealing.
2. Position pinion and cage assembly over studs and tap into position with soft mallet.
3. Install lockwasher and stud nuts or capscrews. Torque to specifications.

DIFFERENTIAL AND GEAR ASSEMBLY

Installation

1. After checking related parts, coat the differential bearing cones and cups with lubricant.
2. Place bearing cups over the assembled cones and position assembly in carrier.
3. Insert bearing adjusting nuts and turn hand tight against bearing cups.
4. Install bearing caps in the correct location as marked and tap lightly into position.

CAUTION

Do not cross thread adjusting nuts.

5. Install flat washers and stud nuts or capscrews. Torque.

DIFFERENTIAL BEARING PRELOAD

Adjustment

1. With dial indicator at backface of bearing, loosen bearing adjusting nut outside opposite gear only sufficient to notice end-play on indicator.
2. Tighten adjusting nut to obtain zero end-play.
3. Check gear for runout. Runout should not exceed .008 in.
4. Tighten adjusting nuts one notch each from zero end-play to preload differential bearings.

DIFFERENTIAL AND GEAR ASSEMBLY

Removal

CRS-84, 840, RAS-301, 507, 508, 509 AND 512 SINGLE REDUCTION AXLES

1. Loosen jam nut and remove bevel gear adjustable throughst screw and jam nut from left side of carrier housing.
2. Position carrier in stand with pinion pointing toward the floor. Mark one bearing cap and pedestal leg for proper remating.
3. Cut lock wires on adjusting nut lock capscrews and pedestal capscrews. Remove differential bearing adjusting nut lock capscrews and lock. Remove differential pedestal bearing cap, capscrew, bearing caps and adjusting nuts.
4. Lift out differential and gear assembly with the bearing cups and place on clean bench.
5. Remove bevel gear bronze throughst shoe from inside of carrier housing.

DRIVE PINION ASSEMBLY

Removal

1. Remove drive flange or yoke nut cotter pin.
2. Attach a suitable flange or yoke holding device and remove flange nut.
3. With a puller, remove flange or yoke from pinion shaft splines.
4. Cut and remove lock wire from hypoid pinion bearing cover capscrews. Remove bearing cover capscrews and washers.

Typical Mack single-reduction rear axle (© Mack Trucks, Inc.)

Remove bearing cover and flange or yoke spacer from pinion shaft. Remove oil seal from bearing cover.

5. Install two $^5/_8$ X 11 jack screws in holes provided in bearing retainer flange and remove pinion, bearing and bearing retainer from carrier housing. Apply pressure evenly with these screws. Wire shim pack together.

DIFFERENTIAL GEAR ASSEMBLY

Installation

1. Remove assembly from bench vise and place bearing cups on differential bearing cones, then position entire differential assembly in carrier housing pedestals.
2. Install bearing adjusting nuts and bearing pedestal cups. Install pedestal bearing capscrews and tighten slightly just so the adjusting nuts can be moved.

CAUTION

Do not cross thread adjusting nuts.

3. Install differential bearing adjustment fixture so that it engages the integral bearing support lugs provided on the bearing pedestal caps with the fixture positioning legs resting on the carrier bolting flange. Lubricate with SAE 30 oil.
4. Wrap string around outside diameter of left half casing flange several times in back of the hypoid gear.
5. Attach spring scale to looped end of string, pull horizontally to test bearing drag. Proper drag is 4–6 lb. max.
6. Using a dial indicator at the backface of the gear check hypoid gear for runout. If runout exceeds 0.004 in., find and correct cause.
7. Remove differential assembly from housing.

HYPOID PINION ASSEMBLY

Installation

1. Install pinion assembly and shim pack on carrier housing.
2. Install differential assembly keeping adjusting nut marks in relation to bearing cap. This will maintain preload.

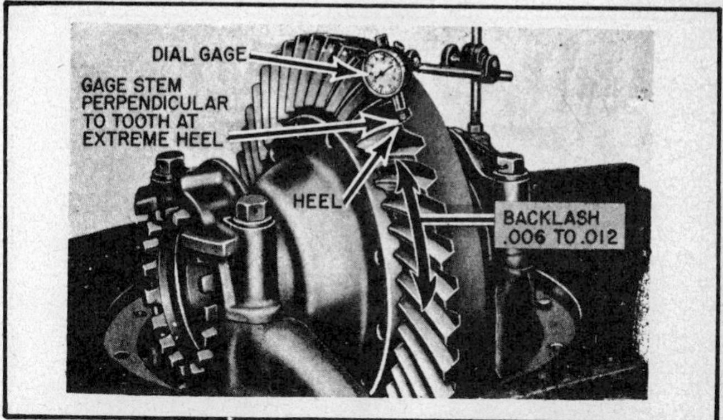

Checking backlash of hypoid gear set (© Mack Trucks, Inc.)

3. Check torque of pedestal bearing cap capscrews as shown also hypoid pinion bearing retainer capscrews.
4. Check gear tooth contact pattern for correct bearing.
5. Turn carrier on right side, place hypoid gear and rotate gear until blind hole in shoe is opposite throughst shoe adjusting screw hole.

Check run-out of hypoid gear (© Mack Trucks, Inc.)

6. Install adjusting screw in carrier housing so that pilot end of screw engages hole provided in throughst shoe then tighten finger tight.

7. Install screw locknut and with a screwdriver wrench, back off adjusting screw $^1/_4$ turn to provide 0.010–0.020 in. clearance between shoe and gear. Hold screw in this position and tighten locknut to 350–400 ft. lbs. Recheck clearance.

8. After all rechecks, install adjusting nut locks with capscrews and lock in place by bending washer up against capscrew head flat on one side and bending washer down on the other side.

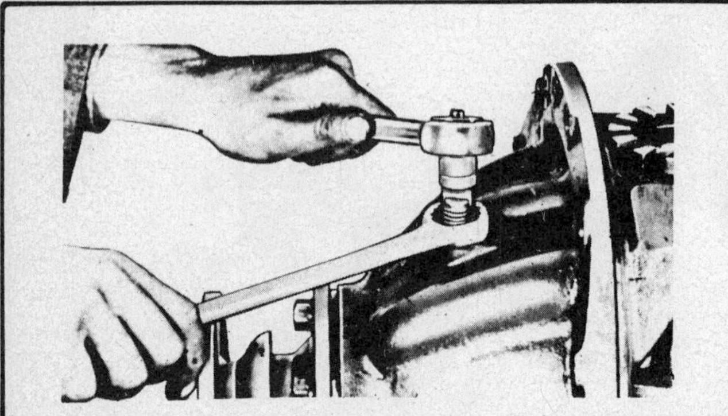

Locking adjusting screw in position (© Mack Trucks, Inc.)

Bearing cup eccentric lockwasher engaged in slot (© Mack Trucks, Inc.)

Torquing differential bearing cap capscrews (© Mack Trucks, Inc.)

Front Mounted Dual Reduction Rear Axles

The following apply generally to all front mounted dual reduction rear axle carriers.

DRIVE PINION ASSEMBLY

Removal

1. Thoroughly clean carrier externally.
2. Mount unit in overhaul stand.
3. Remove flange or yoke cotter pin.
4. Install holding tool on drive flange or yoke and remove unit.
5. Remove pinion bearing cover capscrews, and pinion to carrier housing capscrews.
6. Install two jackscrews in tapped holes provided and remove bevel pinion housing assembly from carrier housing. Apply pressure to jackscrews evenly.

DIFFERENTIAL AND BULL GEAR ASSEMBLY

Removal

1. With carrier in overhaul stand, position with pinion opening toward floor. Mark one bearing cap and pedestal leg for reference.
2. Remove differential pedestal bearing capscrews.

With CRD-117, 116, 78, and 62 series carriers:

a. Cut lock wires retaining adjusting nut lock capscrews and pedestal capscrews.

b. Remove differential bearing adjusting nut lock capscrews and locks.

c. Remove differential pedestal bearing cap capscrews and bearing caps.

With CRD-118, 119 and 62 series carriers:

a. Remove cotter pin from adjusting nut lock pin in right pedestal bearing cap.

b. Remove lock pin and back off bearing adjusting nut.

c. Cut safety wire and remove pedestal bearing cap capscrews or cotter pins and bearing stud nuts.

d. Remove pedestal bearing caps.

3. Remove differential and bull gear assembly with bearing cups and adjusting nuts.
4. Place on a clean bench.

NOTE: These carriers use eccentric washer type locks in the bearing pedestals to prevent rotation of the bearing cups.

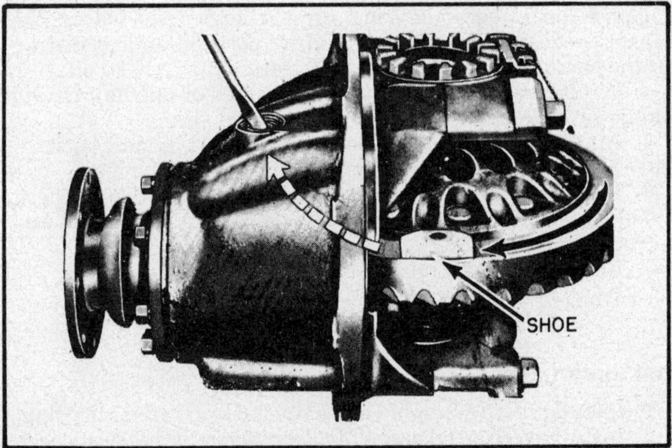

Positioning hypoid gear bronze thrust shoe (© Mack Trucks, Inc.)

HELICAL PINION AND GEAR ASSEMBLY

Removal

TYPE CRD-117, 1171, 116, 1161, 78 AND 94 REAR AXLE (HEAVY DUTY)

1. Remove pinion shaft bearing cup retainer and cover assembly capscrews.
2. Insert three jackscrews in tapped holes provided and remove cup retainer assembly from carrier housing. Apply pressure evenly to jackscrews.
3. Remove pinion and gear assembly from carrier. Save shims.

PINION BEARING

Replacement

1. Clamp bearing cup retainer in large vise. Remove cup from each of the retainers.
2. Place helical pinion and gear assembly in vise equipped with soft metal jaws. Cut safety wire and remove right bearing clamp plate capscrews and clamp plate from pinion shaft.

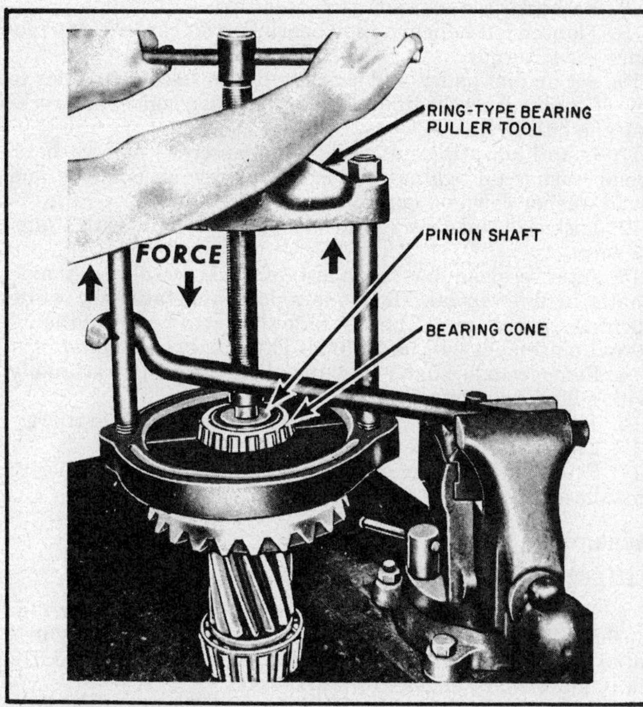

Removing pinion shaft bearing cones (© Mack Trucks, Inc.)

3. Using a segmented puller, remove helical pinion shaft bearing cones.
4. Position assembly in hydraulic press and press helical pinion shaft out of spiral bevel gear.
5. Remove gear key from pinion shaft and gear spacer, if one is provided.

HELICAL PINION AND GEAR ASSEMBLY

Removal

TYPE CRD-118, 1181, 119, 1191 AND 62 REAR AXLE (EXTRA HEAVY DUTY)

1. Remove helical pinion shaft bearing cover capscrews. Save shims. Remove bearing covers.

Removing helical pinion bearing retainer assembly (© Mack Trucks, Inc.)

2. Remove bearing cap from carrier housing.
3. Place helical pinion and gear assembly in soft jawed vise. Cut safety wire and remove right bearing clamp plate capscrews and clamp plate from pinion shaft.
4. With a segmented puller, remove helical pinion shaft bearing cones.
5. Position assembly in a hydraulic press and press helical pinion shaft out of spiral bevel gear.
6. Remove gear key from pinion shaft and gear spacer.

Pressing pinion shaft out of bevel gear hub (© Mack Trucks, Inc.)

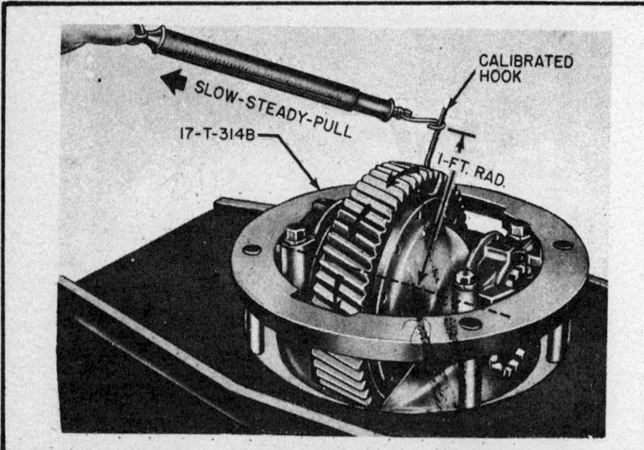

Checking rolling-drag of preloaded differential bearing (© Mack Trucks, Inc.)

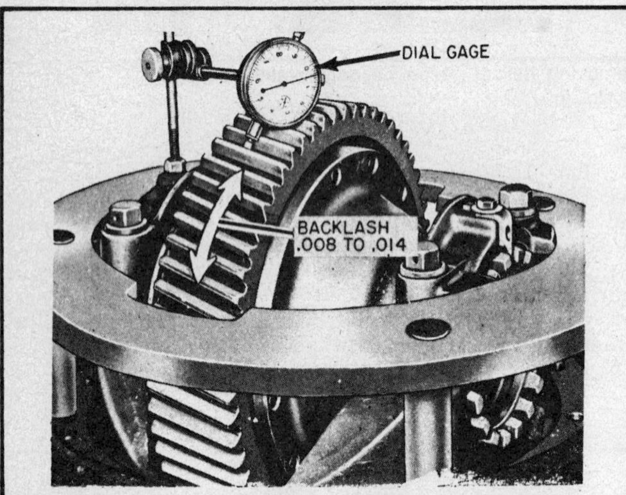

Measuring backlash of helical gear set (© Mack Trucks, Inc.)

Torquing differential bearing pedestal cap capscrews (© Mack Trucks, Inc.)

Assembly

CRD-117, 1171, 116, 1161, 78 & 94 CARRIER

1. Place bearing caps on differential bearing cones and, with jack, carefully position differential assembly in carrier housing differential bearing pedestal so that bearing cups are seated properly.
2. Install bearing adjusting nuts in threaded bearing pedestal.
3. Install bearing caps and capscrews so that threaded portion engages adjusting nut threads squarely. Tap caps in place and tighten bearing cap capscrews finger tight.

NOTE: Do not crossthread adjusting nuts.

4. Install differential bearing adjusting fixture on carrier so that it engages the integral bearing support lugs provided on the bearing pedestal caps. Position fixture leg on the carrier housing bolt flange.
5. Lubricate bearings with SAE 80 oil and torque capscrews.
6. Attach spring scale to a calibrated lever on the bull gear 90° to the center hub. Make reading with a slow steady pull. A pull of 2–3 lbs. is required. Adjust if necessary.
7. Torque differential bearing pedestal capscrews: $^3/_4$ X 10 Grade 8, dry 365–395 ft. lbs.; oiled 265–295 ft. lb.
8. Recheck drag and adjust if necessary.
9. Tighten left helical pinion bearing cover capscrews to recommended torque.
10. Set up dial gauge and check bull gear backlash. Refer to specification chart for limits. Hold the pinion rigid while rocking the bull gear.
11. Install adjusting nut locks with capscrews and washers. Bend washer up against nut lock capscrew on one side and bend washer down on opposite side of both locks.
12. Lock pedestal capscrew head together in pairs with a safety wire.
13. After preload has been established, install both axle shafts in differential. Hold one axle shaft stationary while turning the bull gear. The free axle shaft will turn and the internal movement will be audible. The should be no binding.
14. Remove axle shafts and install drive pinion assembly with adjusting shims.
15. Tighten all nuts and bolts as specified on torque chart.
16. Check entire system for free movement of parts.
17. Prime unit with one pint of axle lubricant just prior to installation.

Assembly

CRD-62 DIFFERENTIAL GEAR

1. Press new undersized bushing in differential casing. Bushing must be flush at both ends. Center the assembly in a lathe and bore out bushing inside diameter from 3.311 to 3.312 in. Remove sharp edges, chips and burrs.
2. Press new bushing in each of the three bevel pinion gears and in a lathe bore out the new bushings from 1.4425 to 1.4440 in. Remove sharp edges, chips and burrs.
3. Start pinion studs in holes provided in differential casing.
4. Lubricate each bevel pinion and throughst washer with axle lubricant and position in differential casing. Align with pinion stud.
5. Push each stud through throughst washer and pinion gear until it bottoms.
6. Align marked spline of bull gear with marked splines of differential casing and engage. Install 15 short bolts and run nuts down finger tight.
7. Press right differential bearing cone on hub of right differential casing cover.
8. Press left differential bearing cone on hub of left differential casing cover.
9. Stand left casing cover on its hub end. Lubricate side gear and throughst washer with axle lubricant. Place these parts in a machined portion in cover.

10. Position assembled differential casing and bull gear on side gear so that gear hub enters casing bushing and bevel pinion gears mesh with side gear.
11. Dip remaining side gear and throughst washer in axle lubricant and mesh gear with assembled pinion gears.
12. Position throughst washer in counterbore provided in right casing cover and install cover on the differential casing. Align casing and cover bolt holes and install six long through bolts. Finger tighten nuts on bolts.

NOTE: Three of these long bolts engage a groove in the three pinion studs.

13. Place differential and bull gear in upright position on bench, clamp and tighten bolts to specifications; 15 short bolts: dry 110–130 ft. lbs., oiled 80–100 ft. lbs. 6 long bolts: dry 225–255 ft. lbs., oiled 165–195 ft. lbs.
14. Check free movement of gears. No bind should exist.
15. Place the left differential bearing cup on left bearing cone.
16. Start bearing adjusting nut on threaded portion of right differential bearing cup for about two turns and place on right differential bearing cone.
17. Using a jack, position entire assembly in carrier housing differential bearing pedestals. Each cup has an extended slot to receive a lockwasher.
18. Position bearing cups in the pedestals so that slots line up with the bearing cap parting surface on each pedestal.
19. Position bearing cup.
20. Position cup lock on top stud of each pedestal.
21. Engage lock with slot in each bearing cup.
22. Turn lock so that the widest part of the eccentric engages the bearing cap slot. Install bearing caps according to marks made at disassembly.

Differential bearing adjusting lock nut (© Mack Trucks, Inc.)

NOTE: Counter-bored leg of bearing caps should register with the eccentric cup locks.

23. Install four $^{7}/_{8}$ in. castled nuts to secure the caps snugly but do not tighten.
24. Tap parts with soft mallet to make sure these parts are seated firmly. Tighten bearing adjusting nut against pedestal.
25. Install bearing adjustment fixture on carrier so that it engages the integral bearing support lugs provided on the bearing pedestal cups with the fixture positioning legs resting on the carrier housing bolt flange. Lubricate the bearings with SAE 30 oil.

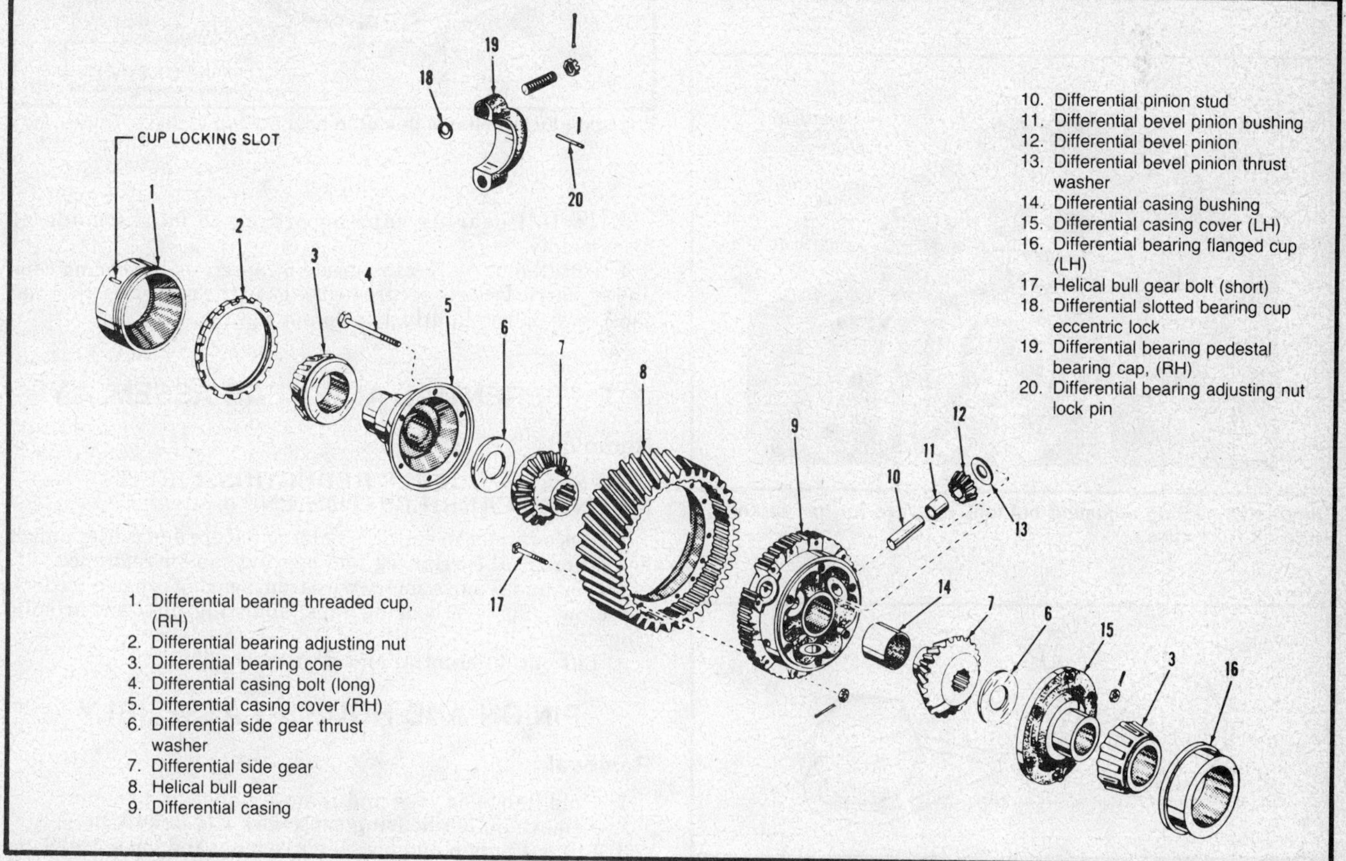

CUP LOCKING SLOT

1. Differential bearing threaded cup, (RH)
2. Differential bearing adjusting nut
3. Differential bearing cone
4. Differential casing bolt (long)
5. Differential casing cover (RH)
6. Differential side gear thrust washer
7. Differential side gear
8. Helical bull gear
9. Differential casing
10. Differential pinion stud
11. Differential bevel pinion bushing
12. Differential bevel pinion
13. Differential bevel pinion thrust washer
14. Differential casing bushing
15. Differential casing cover (LH)
16. Differential bearing flanged cup (LH)
17. Helical bull gear bolt (short)
18. Differential slotted bearing cup eccentric lock
19. Differential bearing pedestal bearing cap, (RH)
20. Differential bearing adjusting nut lock pin

Non-current production CRD-62 differential gear assembly (© Mack Trucks, Inc.)

26. Torque bearing capscrews.
27. Attach a spring scale to a calibrated lever hooked on the bull gear so that scale pulls at 90° to hub. A pull of 2–3 lbs. is required. Adjust if necessary.
28. Check alignment of lock pin hole in right hand bearing cap and bearing adjusting nut slot. Adjust if necessary.
29. Torque differential bearing pedestal capscrews or nuts as applicable. Refer to bearing adjustment and torque chart.
30. Recheck preload. Adjust if necessary.
31. Insert adjusting nut lock pin in right bearing cap until it engages slot in adjusting nut. Lock pedestal capscrew heads together in pairs with safety wire.

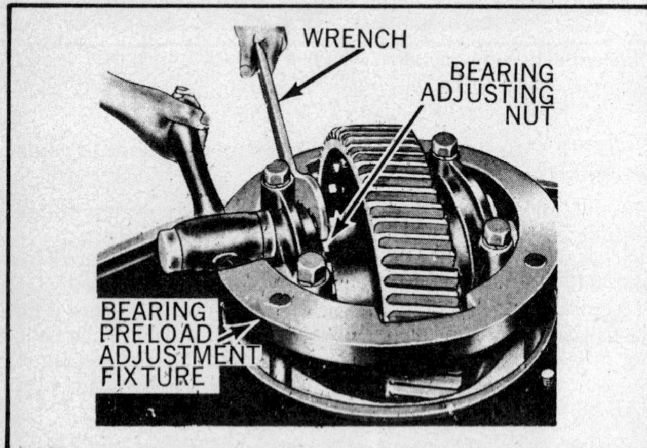

Adjusting differential bearings (© Mack Trucks, Inc.)

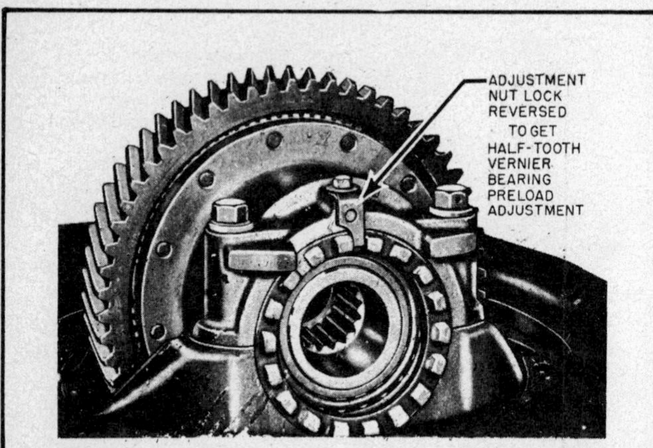

Differential bearing adjusting nut lock reversed for half tooth (© Mack Trucks, Inc.)

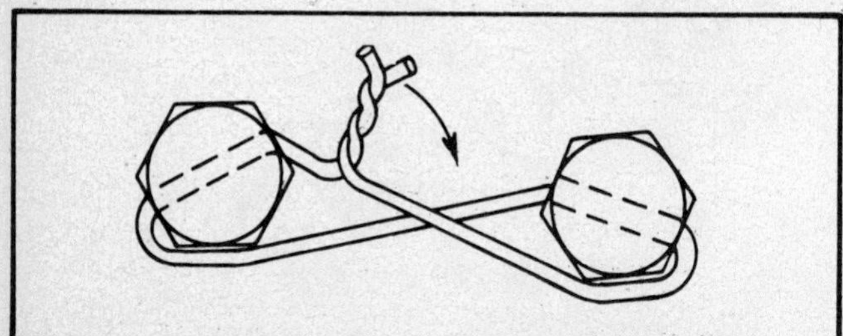

Correct method of installing lock wire (© Mack Trucks, Inc.)

32. After establishing preload, install both axle shafts in differential. Hold one axle shaft stationary while turning the bull gear. There should be no binding. Internal parts should be heard moving.
33. Remove axle shafts and install drive pinion assembly with adjusting shims.
34. Tighten all nuts and bolts as specified.
35. Check entire unit for free movement of parts. Install carrier housing inspection plugs. Prime with one pint of lubricant until ready for installation.

Assembly

CRD-118, 1181, 119, 1191 CARRIER

See CRD-62 assembly step 15–35 skipping steps 19–23. In place of steps 19–23, do the following:

1. Engage cup eccentric lock with slot provided in each bearing cup.
2. Turn locks so that widest part of the eccentric engages the bearing cap slot.

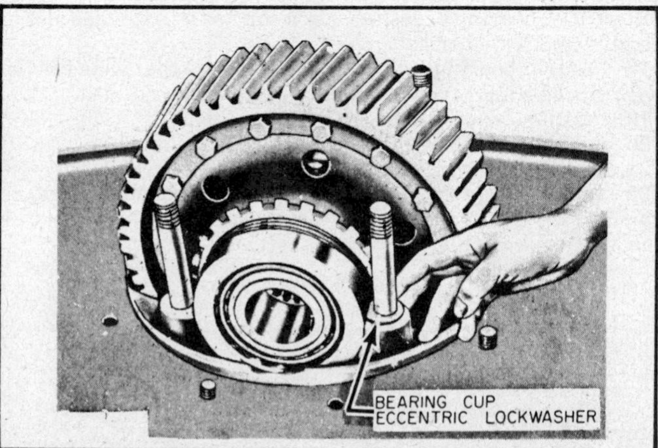

Engaging lockwasher with slot in bearing cup (© Mack Trucks, Inc.)

3. Install bearing caps according to marks made at disassembly.
4. Install four $^{7}/_{8}$ X 9 in., grade 6 capscrews in bearing caps and eccentric locks to secure bearings in the pedestals. Run the capscrews down slightly, but do not tighten.

DIFFERENTIAL AND GEAR ASSEMBLY

Removal

TWO SPEED, DOUBLE REDUCTION, FRONT MOUNTED CARRIERS (TIMKEN)

1. Place carrier in suitable holding fixture and center punch one differential carrier leg and bearing cap for reference.
2. Clip and remove safety wire from bearing cap and nutlock capscrews. Remove bearing caps, adjusting nuts and/or split rings.
3. Lift out differential and gear assembly.

PINION AND HOUSING ASSEMBLY

Removal

1. Hold flange or yoke and remove flange or yoke nut.
2. Remove pinion housing capscrews and lockwashers.
3. Lift out pinion and housing assembly and lay aside. Save shims.

CROSS SHAFT ASSEMBLY

Removal

1. Remove capscrews and lockwashers from cross shaft left bearing retainer.
2. Force out bearing retainer with a pry bar between the back of the hypoid gear and carrier housing.
3. Wire shim pack together.
4. Thread out cross shaft assembly.

With high speed carriers on some models:

5. Raise cross shaft assembly through bearing retainer bore.
6. Clip lockwires and remove capscrews and bearing cone clamp plate.
7. Using suitable cone puller, remove cross shaft left bearing cone.
8. Remove high speed helical pinion from cross shaft.
9. Lift out and remove cross shaft assembly from carrier housing.

ELECTRIC SHIFT UNIT (SIDE-MOUNTED TYPE WITH SOLID PUSH ROD)

Removal

1. Clip and remove lockwire at fork locking screws.
2. Loosen locknut on shift for lockscrew and remove screw and nut.
3. Remove the two mounting stud nuts and lockwashers.
4. Withdraw electric shift unit and push rod assembly from carrier and fork hub, then remove fork.
5. Tap push rod guide sleeve from carrier with a plastic mallet.
6. Wire guide sleeve shim pack together.

CROSS SHAFT ASSEMBLY (WIDE RANGE CARRIERS WITH HIGH SPEED PINION)

Assembly

1. Lubricate cross shaft bearings and cups with light machine oil.
2. Install cross shaft assembly minus high speed helical pinion into carrier with bearing cover of hypoid side removed.
3. Install high speed helical pinion and set up in a press so that the bearing retaining clamp plate at the hypoid side of the cross shaft may be rested on a support at the cover opening.
4. Press bearing cone opposite hypoid gear onto cross shaft. Install bearing retaining clamp plate and capscrews. Tighten all capscrews to specified torque and install safety wire.
5. Install bearing cup in case bore and bearing pack on hypoid side of carrier.
6. Replace capscrews and lockwashers. Torque to specifications.

With Carriers permitting complete assembly of cross shaft before threading into carrier housing:

7. Lubricate cross shaft bearings and cups with light machine oil.
8. Install bearing cup in housing bore.
9. Install bearing cover using the correct shim pack.
10. Tighten capscrews to proper torque.
11. Thread cross shaft assembly past differential bearing supports and position in the bearing cup on the hypoid gear side.

The following apply to both types:

12. Press bearing cup into left bearing retainer.
13. Place original shim pack on pilot of bearing retainer so that all bolt holes in these parts are aligned.
14. Start bearing retainer and cup assembly and shim pack into carrier housing bore.
15. Tap bearing retainer into position with a soft mallet. Install capscrews and lockwashers and tighten to proper torque.
16. Rotate cross shaft and gear assembly several times before checking preload to assure normal bearing contact.
17. Lock low speed helical pinion and cross shaft with the shift collar. Wrap a strong cord around the helical pinion and pull on a horizontal line with a pound scale.
18. Read rotating pull. Preload torque should be between 5–15 in. lbs. Adjust with shims under retainer to decrease load; remove shims to increase load.

PINION AND HOUSING ASSEMBLY

Installation

1. Install pinion housing assembly using corrected shim pack or original shim pack.
2. Install capscrews and lockwashers; tighten to proper torques.

ELECTRIC SHIFT UNIT

Installation

1. Align mounting flange stud holes with mounting studs in carrier housing and shift fork push rod sleeve into bore provided in carrier housing.
2. Install original shim pack between sleeve flange and carrier housing, then tap sleeve all the way in.
3. Hold shift fork in position. Align threaded lockscrew hole in fork hub with blind drill hole in push rods and slide push rod in fork hub until holes align.
4. Install nut on shift fork setscrew and install assembly in fork hub. Tighten screw in hub and make sure end of screw engages blind hole in push rod, then tighten nut to 30–35 ft. lbs. to lockscrew in position. Wire drilled head of fork setscrew to fork with soft iron wire.
5. If electric shift unit is fully assembled, remove front cover and hand turn drive screw until nut is positioned. This step is necessary to prevent damage to the drive nut contact bumper.
6. Pull out torsion spring winding, lever pivot shaft, and torsion spring and spring winding lever assembly.
7. Place gasket on shift unit mounting flange pilot.
8. Align electric shift until mounting flange stud holes align with mounting studs and, allowing protruding push rod to enter unit, start unit on mounting studs.
9. Start nuts with lockwashers on studs for a few turns each. Engage vee ends of winding lever drive yoke legs with trunnions on each side of drive nut. Swing torsion spring and winding lever assembly inside shift unit housing.
10. Raise assembly so that extended torsion spring ends straddle fixed drive pin in end of slotted push rod.
11. Install pivot shaft through winding lever hub and into blind mounting hole provided in the motor housing to position and support lever and spring.
12. Hand turn drive screw to the UP position then tighten unit mounting stud nuts 25–35 ft. lbs.
13. Using a 12 volt battery with two test leads, touch one wire to the electric shift unit housing and the other to the red motor wire. The motor wire will wind the torsion spring which will move the shift collar into engagement with the *High Range* pinion clutching teeth.
14. Check clearance of shift fork pads in shift collar groove with feeler gauge. The clearance should not be less than .010 in. minimum on each side of fork in both the *High and Low Range* positions.

NOTE: When checking shift fork clearance in shift collar groove the shift collar must be flush with the end face of the helical pinion in both the High and Low Range.

15. If shift fork clearances are not correct, add or remove shims from pack under push rod sleeve as required to obtain correct adjustment.

16. Shift unit several times electrically and recheck clearances. If correct, install front cover with its gasket on electric shift unit. Do not lubricate until carrier is mounted in vehicle axle, then follow instructions cast on the cover.

DIFFERENTIAL AND HELICAL GEAR ASSEMBLY

Installation

1. Lubricate bearing cones and cups.
2. Place bearing cups over assembled differential bearing cones, then position differential assembly in carrier.

TYPE I: threaded adjusting ring

3. Insert bearing adjusting rings and turn them hand tight against bearing cups.
4. Position differential bearing caps in place making sure they are properly aligned.

TYPE II: combination of one threaded adjusting ring and one split ring

5. Position split ring in groove of carrier leg and insert threaded adjusting ring on opposite side. Turn threaded ring hand tight against bearing cup.
6. Position differential bearing caps in place making sure they are properly aligned.

TYPE III: split ring

7. Insert one split ring in carrier leg groove.
8. Move differential assembly over so that face of bearing cup is held tightly against inserted ring.
9. Install opposite split ring by tapping it into the groove by use of a blunt end drift.
10. Position differential bearing cups in place making sure they are properly aligned.

For all above.

11. Install pedestal bearing cap capscrews and tighten to specified torque.

CARRIER, DIFFERENTIAL AND GEAR ASSEMBLY

Disassembly

MODELS 95, 951, 96, 961 REAR AXLE DOUBLE REDUCTION, TOP MOUNTED CARRIERS WITH LOCKOUT

1. Mount the carrier assembly in a suitable holder.
2. Match-mark the bearing caps, remove the lock wire, bearing cap bolts, and the caps. Remove the differential and gear assembly from the carrier housing.

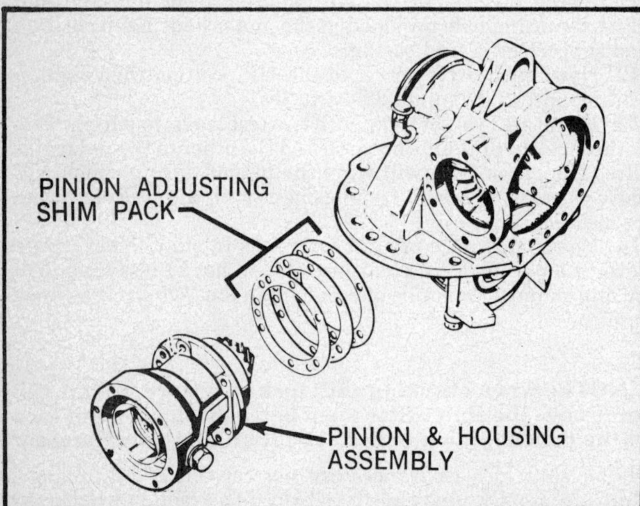

Drive pinion assembly and shim pack (© Mack Trucks, Inc.)

3. Remove all the covers from the carrier housing. Remove the lock wire and remove the lockout shifter fork screw.
4. Remove the air shift cylinder and withdraw the piston shaft from the shifter fork.
5. Remove the cage drive yoke nut or bolts by engaging the teeth of the sliding clutch to the teeth of the outer cam and by jamming the teeth of the bevel gear set with a soft iron rod.

NOTE: On carriers without the lockout device, use a holding bar tool to permit the removal of the yoke nuts or bolts.

6. Remove the lockout to power divider housing, fork, clutch, driving cage, wedges and inner cam assembly.
7. Remove the through-shaft and attaching parts from the carrier housing.
8. Remove the through-shaft bearing retainer from the carrier with the aid of jackscrews.
9. Remove the nut from the driven pinion shank with the aid of the soft iron rod still in mesh with the bevel gear set.
10. Remove the nuts or clamp plate bolts from the helical pinion bevel gear and the right hand bearing ends.
11. Install two jack screws in the threaded holes provided in the helical pinion bearing retainer mounting flange and remove the retainer assembly from the carrier assembly.

NOTE: This operation will also remove the R.H. bearing cone from the helical pinion shaft.

12. Remove the helical pinion and bevel gear assembly from the carrier housing through the bevel gear compartment opening.
13. Remove the bearing cup from the carrier housing bulkhead.
14. Disassemble the individual assemblies on the bench as required. Maintain the shims in the packs as removed.

FOR CARRIERS WITHOUT THE LOCKOUT DEVICE ONLY

1. Remove the case bearing cover to pinion housing capscrews. Slowly rotate the cover until two diagonally opposed cover capscrew holes uncover and register with two threaded holes in the bearing retainer flange, which is between the cover and the pinion housing.
2. Install two jack screws in the threaded holes provided and withdraw the cage assembly, bearing and yoke assembly from the bevel pinion housing.

NOTE: A press must be used to disassemble the cage, bearing and yoke.

3. Remove the bevel pinion housing to carrier housing capscrews.
4. Install two jack screws into the threaded holes provided in the mounting flange and withdraw the pinion housing assembly from the carrier housing.
5. Keep all the shims together as a pack for use in the reassembly.

Unit Disassembly

The unit disassembly of the individual units should be accomplished on the bench. Match-marks should be made on the components being separated, to aid in the assembly. Shim packs should remain with the units, from which they were removed, to aid in the determination of the thicknesses needed, during the assembly.

New bearing cones and cups would normally be replaced during an overhaul, and the preloading of the bearings are most important. The preload of used or run-in tapered bearings should be adjusted to one half the value specified for the new bearings.

A press will be needed to assist in the removal of the various bearings and retainers, during the disassembly of the carrier assembly components.

The procedures outlined will cover the assembly of the component units.

BEVEL PINION

Assembly

1. Press bearing cups in the pinion housing.
2. Press the rear bearing cone on the pinion shank.
3. Install the pinion into the housing and install the selective washer and the pinion front bearing cone over the pinion shank.
4. Place the assembled unit in a press and apply the recommended load to the front bearing inner race.
5. Check the rolling drag. If not within the prescribed limits, change to a thinner or a thicker selective washer until the desired reading is obtained.
6. Remove the unit from the press and assemble the pinion bearing cover and seal assembly on the conventional type pinion housing assembly. Install the yoke and nut, tighten to the specified torque and install the cotter pin.
7. Install the outer cam, washer and nut into the power divider type pinion housing. Tighten the nut to the specified torque and install the cotter pin.
8. Install the adjustment shims, removed during the disassembly, on the pinion housing pilot, align all mating capscrew holes and install the pinion assembly into the carrier housing. Tighten the capscrews to the specified torque.
9. Install a pinion setting gauge into the carrier housing and establish the correct pinion depth.
10. When the correct pinion depth is obtained by changing the necessary shims, remove the pinion assembly and shims from the carrier housing temporarily.

HELICAL PINION

Assembly

1. Install new bearing cups into the bearing retainer as necessary.
2. Assemble the helical pinion shaft with the right and left bearings assembled on the shaft and installed into the bearing retainer.
3. Place the assembly into a press and check the rolling drag of the preloaded bearings. If not within the prescribed limits, change the shims to a thicker or thinner shim until the desired limits are reached.
4. Remove the assembly from the press and tap the right hand bearing from the pinion shaft.
5. Install the gear key in the keyway provided in the pinion shaft left hand end. Align with the beveled gear hub and press the helical pinion shaft into the gear hub.
6. Install the lock pin in the inner end of the bearing retainer, if previously removed.
7. Install the original shim pack over the retainer body and start the retainer into the right hand side of the carrier housing.
8. Align the matching capscrew holes of the retainer mounting flange and original shim pack with the threaded holes in the carrier housing and tap the housing retainer into the housing with a soft headed hammer.
9. Temporarily, use shorter screws and install in the retainer to the housing. Tighten to specifications.
10. Install the left hand bearing cup through the bevel gear compartment in the carrier bore. Assure that the slot on the thick end of the cup straddles the lock pin in the end of the bearing retainer.
11. Install the right hand bearing cone spacer on the pinion shaft end.
12. Install the helical pinion and gear assembly in the carrier housing through the bevel gear compartment opening and while holding the assembly in position, install the right hand bearing cone on the pinion end.
13. Install the bearing cone fasteners provided and tighten as noted on the torque chart.

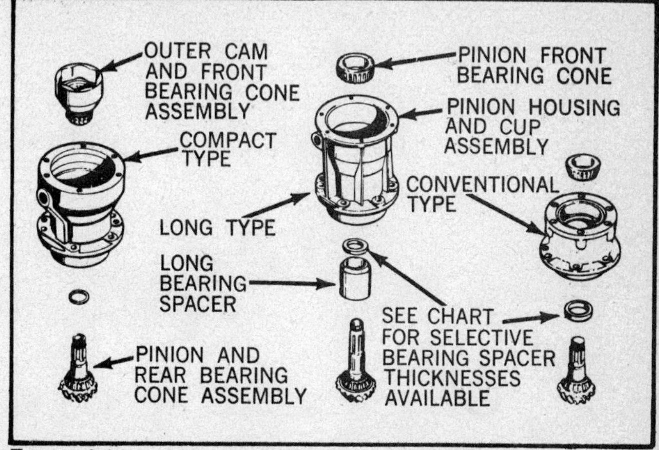

Types of drive pinion assemblies used (© Mack Trucks, Inc.)

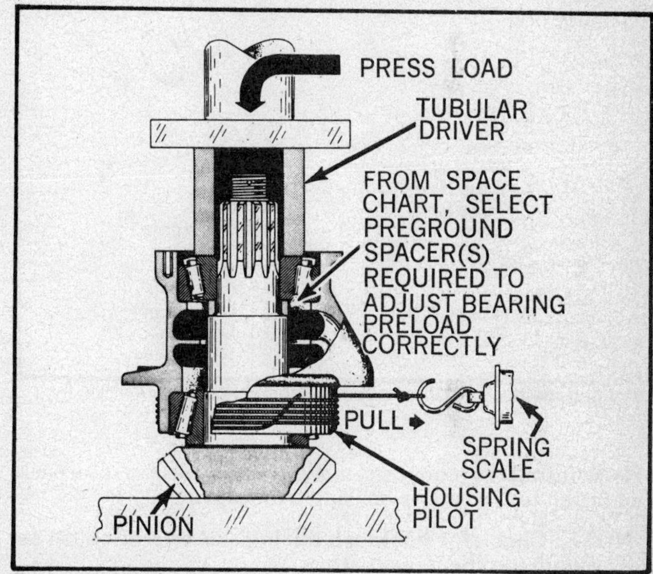

Typical method of checking pinion bearing preload (© Mack Trucks, Inc.)

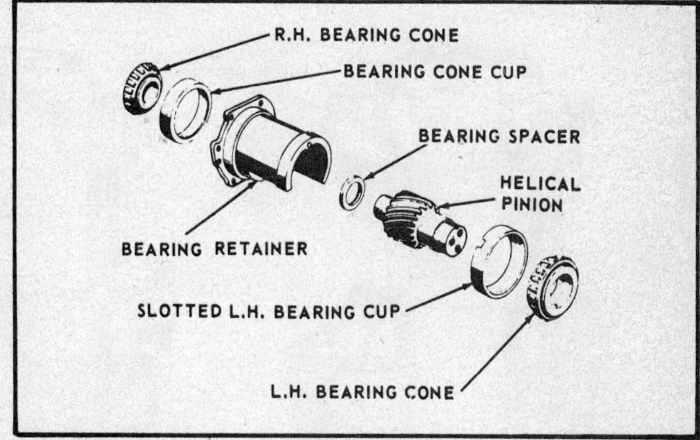

Helical pinion shaft, bearings and bearing retainers (© Mack Trucks, Inc.)

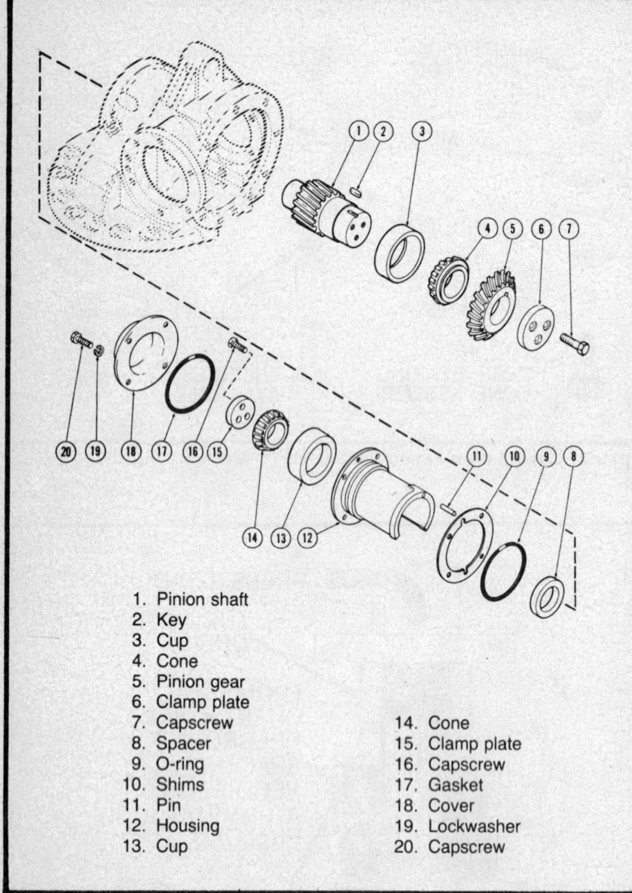

Retaining methods—helical pinion assembly (© Mack Trucks, Inc.)

14. Reinstall the pinion assembly with the selected shim pack and fasten to the carrier housing with capscrew.

NOTE: Check for backlash during this operation, so as not to damage the gear teeth.

15. Adjust the gear set for correct teeth contact and adjust the backlash to 0.006–0.012 in..
16. After the correct gear mesh adjustments have been made, remove the pinion assembly from the carrier housing.
17. Loosen the right hand bearing cone nut or plate capscrews. Rap the nut or capscrews sharply with a rawhide hammer to relieve the bearing preload.

NOTE: The helical pinion bearing preload is relieved to allow the preloading of the differential bearings during the assembly of the differential assembly into the carrier housing. This method avoids the need to remove the helical pinion from the assembly. The bearings will again be preloaded after the differential assembly bearing preload is completed.

DIFFERENTIAL CASE

Assembly

1. Press the bearing cone on the left side of differential case hub.

NOTE: This cone has long, thin rollers and is paired to a fixed flanged cup.

2. Press the bearing cone onto the right side differential case hub.

NOTE: This cone has shorter rollers than the left cone, and mates with the adjustable externally threaded cup.

3. With the left hand differential case standing on its hub, lubricate and install the spider, throughst washers, bevel gears, and side gears. Be sure that the locking tube of the throughst washers engage the blind drilled holes provided in the casing halves.
4. Locate the driving spline indexing marks and engage the bull gear internal splines with the mating splines on the right hand casing.
5. Install the bull gear self locking capscrews finger tight and clamp the bull gear in a vise and tighten the capscrews to the proper torque.
6. Check the differential gears for freedom of movement.

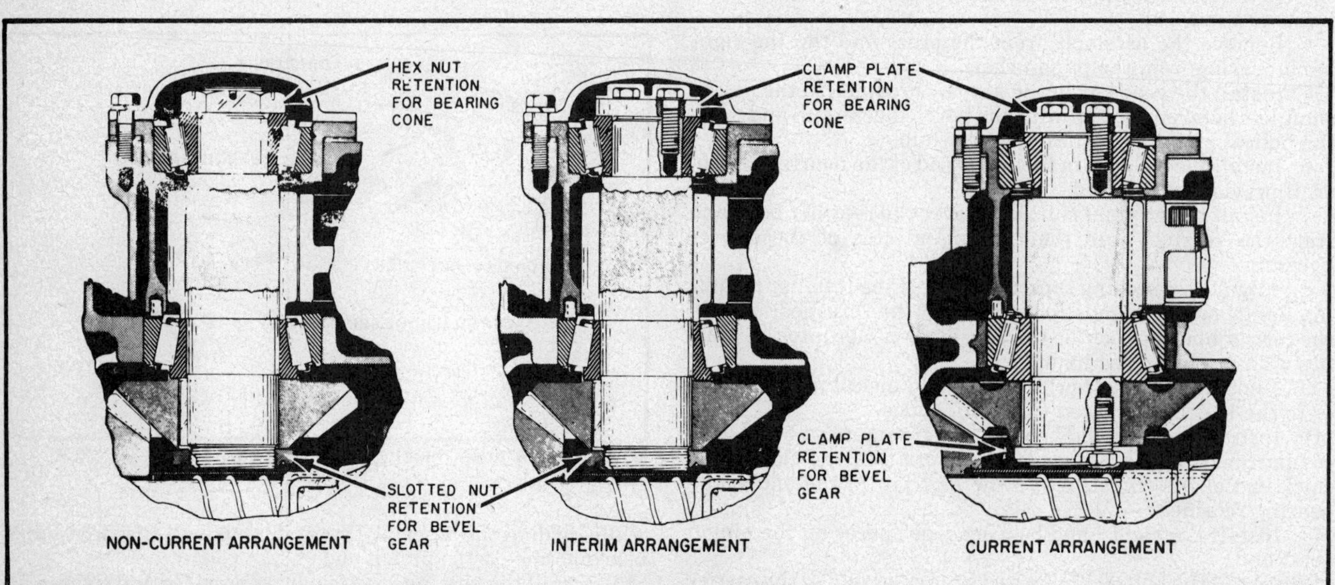

Methods of retaining helical pinion gear and bearings (© Mack Trucks, Inc.)

POWER DIVIDER DIFFERENTIAL

Assembly

1. Press a new bushing into the power divider driving cage hub until it bottoms.

CAUTION

Do not over-drive the bushing.

2. Press the left hand bearing cone on the hub of the power divider differential casing and put aside, temporarily.
3. Press the right hand bearing cone on the hub of the power divider driving cage.
4. Install the power divider driving cage outer retaining ring in the groove provided between the cage wedge holes.
5. Install the twenty-four wedges from the inside of the cage so that the word "OUT" on each wedge is outside the cage.

NOTE: Make sure all the wedges are pushed outward as far as they will go, so that the land of each contacts the retaining ring.

6. Lubricate the inner cam and install in the cage. Press all the driving wedges inward so that all contact the inner cam tracks.
7. Install the axle shaft spacer in the counterbore provided in the inner cam, if the axle shafts used are free-splined at both ends.

NOTE: This spacer prevents the loss of splined engagement of the free-floating axle shafts with the driving cams in the differential and the axle drive flange at the wheels. Integral flange type axles do not require a spacer.

8. Install the outer cam down over the assembled wedges. The cam will drop into place when all the wedges contact the inner cam tracks.
9. Align the spline indexing marks on the bull gear (two "O" marks), and the outer cam (one "O" mark). If the indexing marks have been properly engaged, the capscrew through holes will be in perfect alignment.
10. Install the bull gear mounting capscrews from the cage side and tighten finger tight.
11. Clamp the bull gear in a vise and torque the capscrews to proper specifications.
12. Install the lock wire and tighten.
13. Lubricate the entire assembly with a recommended gear oil.

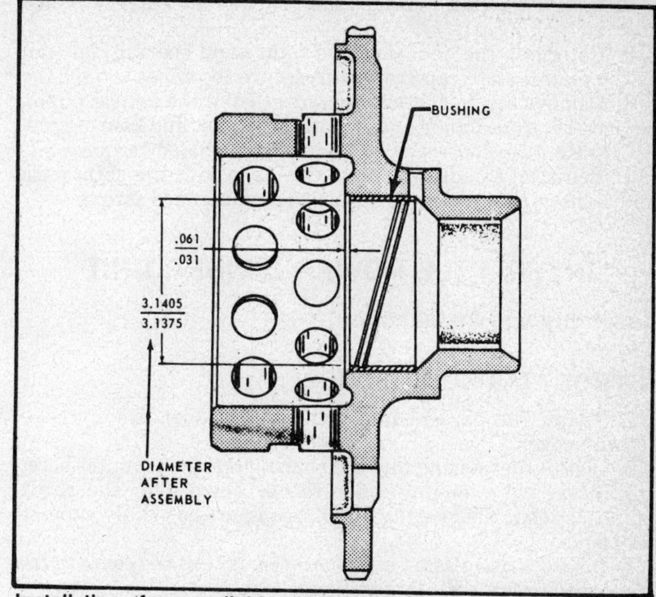

Installation of power divider driving cage (© Mack Trucks, Inc.)

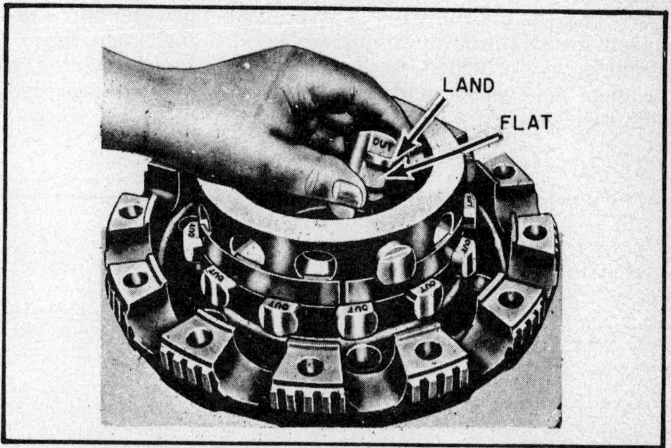

Installation of driving wedges, showing milled flats, separating land and the word "OUT" (© Mack Trucks, Inc.).

DIFFERENTIAL ASSEMBLY

Installation

1. Install the adjusting nut onto the threaded bearing cup approximately two turns, and place the assembly on the right hand bearing cone.
2. Place the flanged bearing cup on the left bearing cone.

NOTE: The left hand bearing cup has a flanged area which engages the machined surface on the inner side of the left hand bearing pedestal and cap when installed. This positions the differential and bull gear so that only the differential bearing preload can be made. The bull gear position can not be varied.

3. Position the entire differential assembly into the carrier housing differential bearing pedestals and install the bearing caps with the capscrews. Tighten finger tight while tapping on the bearing caps for perfect seating.
4. Install the differential bearing adjustment fixture on the carrier so that it engages the integral bearing support lugs provided on the bearing pedestal caps with the fixture positioning legs resting on the carrier housing bolting flange.
5. While turning the differential assembly, adjust the slotted bearing nut with a spanner wrench to slightly preload the bearings.
6. Attach a spring scale to a calibrated lever, hooked on the bull gear, so that the scale pulls at a radius of one foot from the centerline of the differential.
7. Rotate the assembly with a slow, steady pull and observe the pounds pull necessary to maintain the rotation.
8. With a spanner wrench, tighten or loosen the right hand bearing adjusting nut until a pull of two to three pounds is necessary to maintain the rotation.

NOTE: There are two unequally spaced lock pin holes in the right hand bearing cap to provide half-tooth adjustment of the nut. This provides accurate preloading facilities. If both holes are blocked after reaching a minimum of two pounds pull, tighten the nut until one or the other is unblocked by the nut teeth. Install the lock pin.

9. Tighten the capscrews for the bearing caps to their recommended torque.
10. Recheck the rolling drag. There should not be any binding of the differential assembly.

11. Install the lock wire on the bearing cap capscrews and secure.
12. Retighten the helical pinion right hand bearing cone nut or the clamp plate capscrews and secure to proper torque.
13. Remove the temporary capscrews from the helical pinion bearing retainer flange and install the gasket and bearing cover. Tighten the capscrews to their recommended torque.
14. Reinstall the drive pinion assembly with the shim pack and tighten the capscrews to their recommended torque.

INTER-AXLE POWER DIVIDER UNIT

Assembly and Installation

WITHOUT LOCKOUT DEVICE

1. Install the oil seal into the power divider driving cage bearing cover.
2. Install the bearing into the bearing retainer counter bore.
3. Press the bearing and retainer down over the shaft splines, so that the bearing inner race is seated solidly against the cage.
4. Install a new gasket and the cover. Install the cover to retainer capscrews and tighten finger tight.
5. If used, slide the rubber dust shield onto the drive yoke hub, lubricate the yoke on the shaft splines of the cage shaft. Install the nut, but tighten later.
6. Place the assembly in the up position (open end up). If removed, install the outer driving wedge retaining ring in the external groove provided between the wedge holes. Install the complete matched set of driving wedges in the holes provided from inside the cage.

NOTE: The flats of one row of wedges must face the flats of the other row of wedges.

7. Push the wedges outward and install the inner retaining ring in the groove provided between the wedge rows.

NOTE: New wedges and inner cams have a coating of dry lubricant bonded to the parts. Do not attempt to remove.

8. Lubricate the inner cam and place inside the cage and wedge assembly. Push all the wedges inward until the inner wedge ends engage the inner cam lobes.
9. Install a new gasket on the pinion housing. Center the cage and wedge assembly over the outer cam and lower into place.

CAUTION

The cage assembly must be in perfect alignment and centered over the outer cam, otherwise wedge hangup at the outer cam will occur.

10. Align the capscrew holes of the bearing retainer with the threaded holes in the pinion housing and install the capscrews. Draw the assembly together and torque the capscrews to specifications.
11. Install a holding bar on the cage drive yoke and tighten the yoke self-locking nut or bolt to torque specifications.

POWER DIVIDER UNITS

WITH LOCKOUT DEVICE

These units are assembled in the same manner as the units without the lockout device. The lockout device mechanism is placed between the drive yoke and the power divider. All units

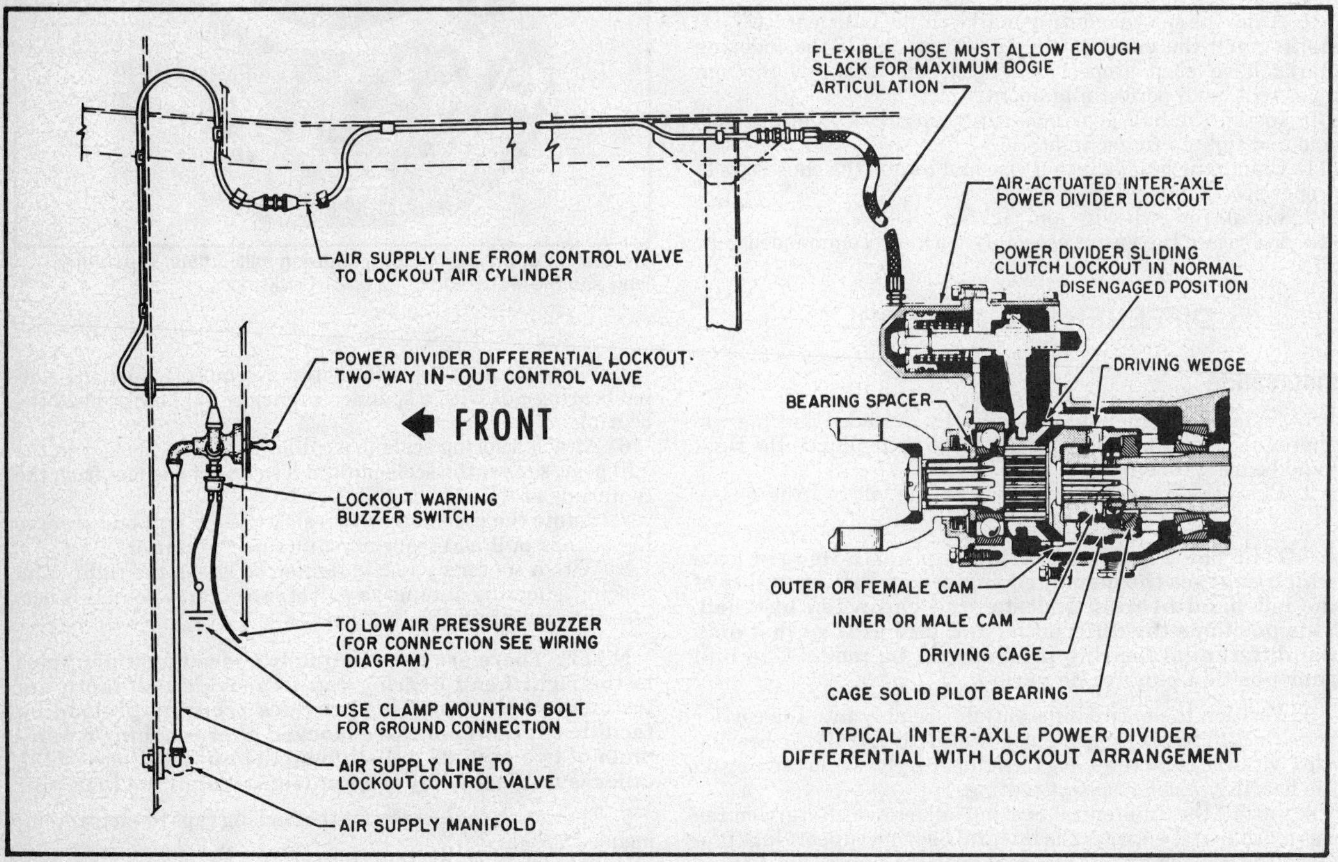

Inter-axle power divided control system (© Mack Trucks, Inc.)

have a left handed nut to position the solid pilot bearing on the driving cage shaft, and should be tightened to 800 to 1200 ft. lbs. torque. Stake the lip of the nut in two places into the slots provided on the shaft.

Reassemble the lockout device in the reverse order of the disassembly.

INTER-AXLE THROUGH-SHAFT

Assembly and Installation

1. Press a new oil seal into the bearing cover.
2. Slide the rear bearing oil slinger on the rear end of the through-shaft.
3. Position the rear bearing with the filler notches pointing away from the slinger and press the bearing onto the rear end of the through-shaft.
4. Position the rear bearing retainer and oil tube assembly in a press, lower the through-shaft and bearing assembly into position and press the bearing into the retainer counterbore.

NOTE: Temporarily install the rear bearing cover over the bearing and apply a light press pressure to the cover so that the pilot contacts the bearing outer race firmly. Measure the gap between the bearing cover and the retainer flange with a feeler gauge. To this figure, add .005 to .010 in. to compensate for the gasket. This will provide a leakproof joint and a clamping force on the outer race of the rear bearing to prevent the race from rotating in the retainer.

5. Remove the bearing cover from the rear bearing retainer and install the necessary gaskets between the two units.
6. Press the bearing cover to mate with the holes in the retainer and install yoke hub onto the through-shaft splines.

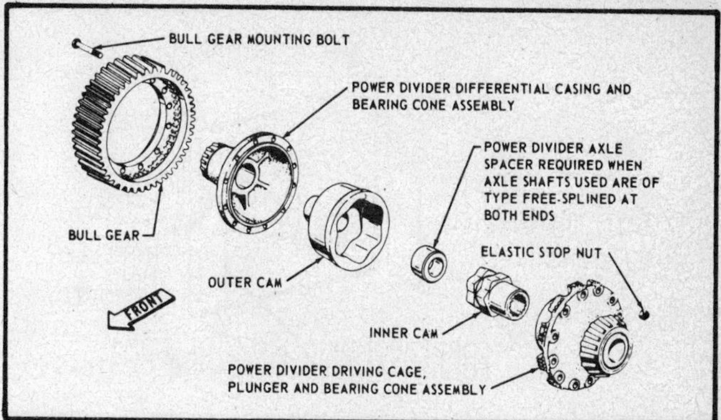

Exploded view of power divider differential—typical (© Mack Trucks, Inc.)

NOTE: Carefully press the yoke through the mounted oil seal until the end of the yoke firmly engages the bearing inner race.

7. Lubricate the splined end of the through-shaft and carefully star the entire through-shaft and bearing assembly into the carrier.
8. Engage the through-shaft splines with the mating splines of the inner cam of the Inter-Axle Power Divider. Align and install the capscrews into the mating threaded holes of the carrier assembly, so that the pump oil inlet opening in the bearing retainer will be on top when the unit is mounted in the vehicle. Tap into position with a soft faced hammer.
9. Install the capscrews and tighten to specifications.
10. Using a holding bar on the yoke, tighten the yoke nut or bolt to 480–520 ft. lbs. and install the cotter pin.
11. Install all compartment covers tighten the capscrews to specifications.

PROPELLER SHAFT AND U-JOINTS

Lubrication

SLIDING SPLINES

1. A uniform coating of grease on both the circumference and length of the female spline is necessary to avoid contamination.
2. The spline should be relubed at each removal and reassembly.

JOURNAL CROSS ASSEMBLIES

1. Lubricate needle bearings with MG-A multipurpose grease.
2. Apply grease under pressure of at least 80 psi.

Inspection

Worn or misaligned parts can usually be determined by sight, shaking, or road test. Check for worn slip splines and proper alignment. Total propeller shaft tube runout should not exceed .015 in. Slip stub shaft must not exceed .005 in.

Removal and Installation

1. Remove U-bolts and collapse slip joint. Be sure to catch bearings.
2. Remove shaft and joints as an assembly by taking out flange bolts.
3. Where fixed or swing type center bearing is used inspect for loose mountings and deteriorated rubber bushings.
4. For installation, reverse the above.

U-JOINT

Disassembly and Assembly

1. Remove caps or snap-rings as applicable.
2. Using suitable drift or press, drive against one bearing to force the opposite bearing from the yoke.
3. Drive exposed end to force out opposite bearing.
4. Remove cross.
5. For reassembly reverse the above using all new seals.

NOTE: Lube fitting faces shaft.

Yoke Alignment

1. Remove the propeller shaft joint bearings and cross.

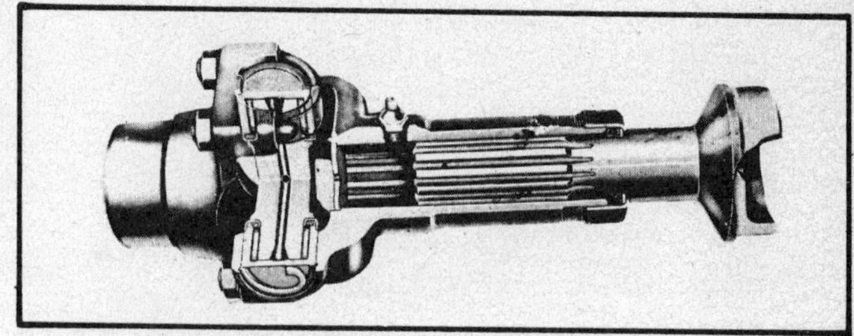

U-bolt joint universal (© Mack Trucks, Inc.)

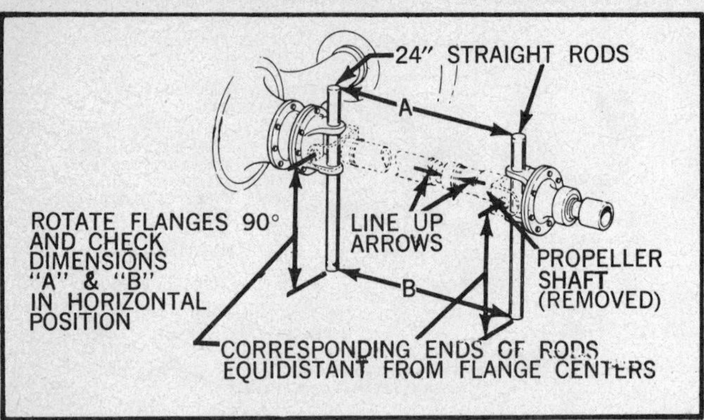

Measuring flange alignment (© Mack Trucks, Inc.)

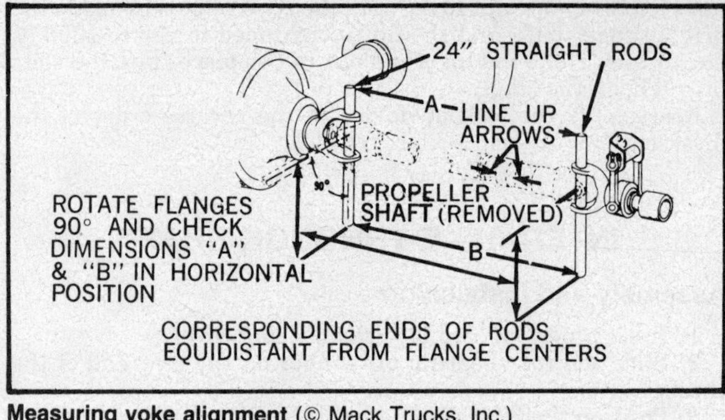

Measuring yoke alignment (© Mack Trucks, Inc.)

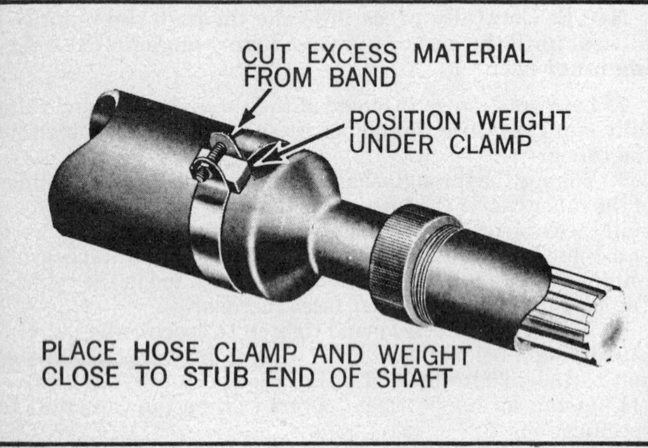

Method of balancing drive shaft (© Mack Trucks, Inc.)

2. Using a 24 in. bar of round stock secured in the joined cross bar of each end yoke, measure the distance between the bars accurately.
3. Flange yokes may be aligned in a similar manner.

Correcting Misalignment

1. Driving and driver flanges: check for 0.004 in. maximum eccentricity and 0.005 in. maximum runout.
2. Midship transmission flange: shim front and rear mounts as necessary.
3. Rear axle pinion flange (4-wheel truck): install wedge plates between spring pads and springs. Wedges should be $^1/_{16}$ in. at thin edge.
4. Rear axle pinion flange (6-wheel truck): adjust torque rods.

Propeller Shaft Balancing

If due to part replacement balancing needed:
1. Uncouple rear shaft and rotate 180 degrees, if vibration persists.
2. Using an adjustable hose clamp and small rectangular lead weight secure the weight to the drive shaft at the yoke end.
3. More weight around shaft until minimum vibration is noted. Mark that spot.
4. Remove clamp and weight and weld a steel weight equal to the combined weight of the clamp and lead weight.

REAR SUSPENSION

Rear Spring

EYE AND SLIPPER MOUNTING TYPE

Removal

1. Using either a jack or shop crane, remove chassis weight from springs by lifting at frame.

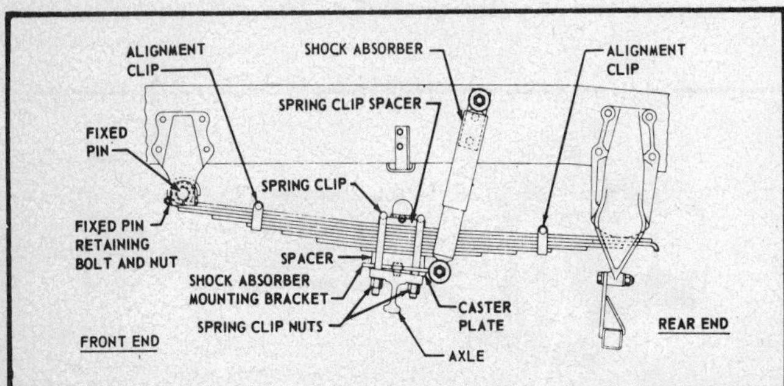

Typical rear spring eye and slipper mounting (© Mack Trucks, Inc.)

2. Remove spring U-bolt nuts and remove U-bolts and any shock absorber linkage.
3. Remove fixed pin retaining bolt and nut.
4. Remove fixed pin.
5. Remove rebound pin cotter pins and rebound pins.
6. Raise chassis so that spring can be removed.

NOTE: Mark caster plate for assembly.

7. Remove spring.

Installation

1. Lower chassis into alignment with spring and position spring on rear axle.

NOTE: Position caster plate as per marks.

2. Install fixed pin and secure with bolt and nut.
3. Install rebound pin and any insulators and secure with cotter pin.
4. Lower chassis so that weight of vehicle is on spring.
5. Install spring U-bolt spacer on top of spring and install U-bolt.

6. Install spring and clamping plate saddle as applicable and secure with nuts.
7. Tighten U-bolt nuts to recommended torque.
8. Reconnect any shock absorbers.

VARIABLE RATE AND RADIUS ROD MOUNTING TYPE

Removal

1. Suspend frame with jack or shop crane.
2. Remove spring U-bolt nuts and remove U-bolts and any shock absorber linkage.
3. Remove radius rod fixed pin retaining bolt and nut.
4. Using a "C" clamp around the radius rod arm and over the main spring leaf, if applicable, clamp together until the load is off the radius rod pin and remove radius rod pin.
5. Remove rebound cotter pins and remove rebound pins and insulators.
6. Raise chassis slightly so spring may be removed.

NOTE: Mark caster plate for assembly.

7. Remove spring.

Installation

1. With the chassis suspended, position the spring in place on the rear axle.

NOTE: Align caster as per marks.

2. Install radius rod fixed pin and secure with nut and bolt.
3. Install rebound pins and insulators and secure with cotter pins.
4. Lower chassis so that weight of vehicle is on springs.
5. Install spring U-bolt spacer or clamping plate, as applicable, on top of spring and install U-bolts.
6. Install spring lower spacer and saddle as applicable, and secure with nuts.
7. Tighten U-bolt nuts to recommended torque.
8. Reconnect shock absorber if applicable.

Bogie Spring

CAMEL BACK LEAF SPRING TYPE

Removal

1. Jack up both axles and remove wheels from proper side.
2. Remove chassis weight from spring with jack and support.
3. Remove rubber shock insulators caps and lower rubber insulators.
4. Remove spring rear U-bolt retaining nuts and remove U-bolt.
5. Install two bolts and nuts to hold upper and lower sections of trunnion together when the other U-bolt is removed.
6. Remove spring front U-bolt retaining nuts and remove U-bolt.
7. Raise both rear axles until the top rubber shock insulators or spring loaded buttons and saddles can be removed.
8. Remove spring from trunnion housing using shop crane.

Installation

1. With chassis supported on heavy duty axle stands and both rear axles jacked up, position spring on trunnion support with portable crane.
2. Install front U-bolt and secure with nuts.
3. Remove two bolts installed to hold the upper and lower section of the trunnion together.
4. Install spring rear U-bolt and secure with nuts.

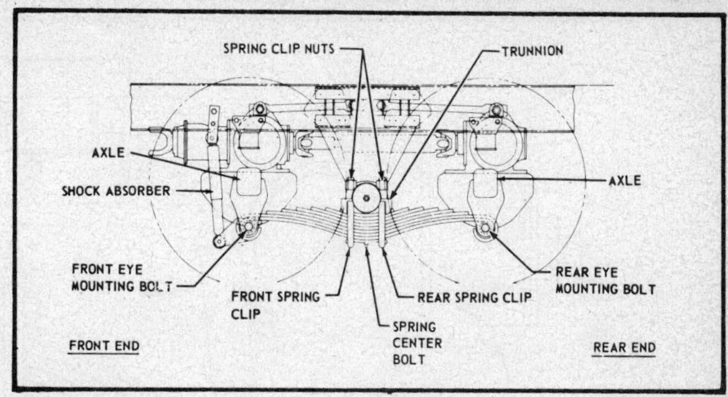

Typical inverted camel back leaf spring mounting (© Mack Trucks, Inc.)

5. Position top rubber insulators or spring loaded buttons and saddles as applicable, on top of spring. Lower both axles.
6. Install lower rubber insulators in caps and install caps on end of springs.
7. Install insulators cap retaining capscrews or bolts and nuts. Tighten to specified torque.
8. Install wheels on axles.
9. Remove stands from under chassis and jacks from under axles.

INVERTED CAMEL BACK LEAF TYPE

Removal

1. Jack up both axles and remove the wheels from the side to be worked.
2. Jack up chassis to remove weight from springs. Support chassis.
3. Support spring and remove spring front and rear eye mounting bolts nuts and remove bolts.
4. Remove spring rear U-bolt retaining nuts and remove U-bolt.
5. Install two suitable bolts and nuts to hold upper and lower trunnion mount together when the other U-bolt is removed.
6. Remove spring front U-bolt retaining nuts and remove U-bolt.
7. Remove spring from chassis using portable crane.

Installation

1. With chassis supported on heavy stands and rear axles jacked up, position spring and install front and rear eye mounting bolts and nuts. Torque to specifications.
2. Raise axles to position spring on trunnion. Position center bolt.
3. Install spring front U-bolt and secure with nuts.
4. Remove the two bolts and nuts installed to hold the upper and lower section of the trunnion together.
5. Install spring rear U-bolt and secure with nuts. Tighten to specified torque.
6. Install wheels on axles.
7. Remove stands and jacks.

WALKING BEAM AND LEAF TYPE

Removal

1. Jack up both axles and remove the wheels from worked side.
2. Jack up chassis to remove weight from springs. Support chassis.
3. Support spring and remove front and rear eye mounting nuts and bolts.
4. Remove U-bolt nuts and remove spring and lower support.

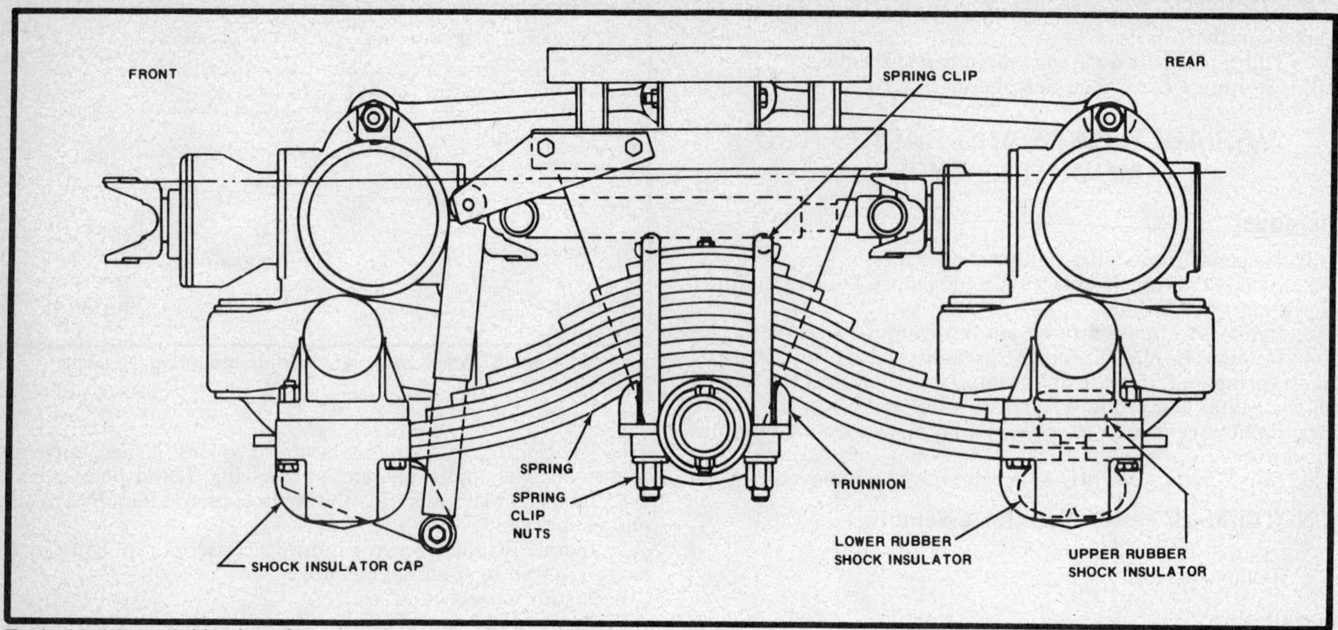

Typical bogie camel back spring mounting (© Mack Trucks, Inc.)

Installation

1. With chassis and axles supported, position spring and install front and rear retaining bolts and nuts.
2. Place chassis weight on springs.
3. Install U-bolts and lower support. Secure with nuts. Tighten nuts to recommended torque.
4. Install wheels on axles.
5. Remove stands from under chassis and jacks from under axles.

MID–LINER

Removal and Installation

1. Block the front wheels and raise the rear of the vehicleusing a floor jack or equivalent under the differential housing. Place a pair of suitable jack stands under the chassis at the front section of the rear axle.
2. With the jack still under the differential housing, remove the U-bolts from the springs. Lower the rear axle, so as to disengage the spring center bolt from the rear axle spring pad.
3. Support the spring with a suitable floor jack and a support plate. The spring center bolt will be positioned in a hole of the supporet plate.
4. Remove the spring pin pinch bolt and remove the grease fitting from the spring pin. Install spring pin extractor # J29441 or equivalent into the threaded hole of the spring pin (grease fitting hole) and remove the spring pin. The pin can also be removed with a strong pin punch and a hammer using extreme care.
5. Using the jack and support plate, remove the spring from the rear of the vehicle.
6. Installation is the reverse of the removal procedure, be sure to use a suitable chassis grease on the spring pins before installing them. Use the following torque chart during the installation procedure.
   a. U-bolts— —332 ± 22 ft. lbs.
   b. Rear spring rear bracket— —45 ft. lbs.
   c. Spring pin pinch bolt— —30 ft. lbs.

Tightening Sequence

When tightening U-bolt nuts on either front or rear springs use the following order:

1. Two rear U-bolt nuts to snug.
2. Two front U-bolt nuts to snug.
3. Two rear U-bolt nuts to torque.
4. Two front U-bolt nuts to torque.

When tightening rubber shock insulator bolts or nuts; all should be snugged down, then torqued at diagonal corners.

Wheel Bearing Adjustment

NOTE: If the brakes are tight on the drums a false bearing adjustment will result.

1. Tighten the bearing adjusting nut, while rotating the wheel alternately in both directions. Stop tightening the adjusting nut when the wheel starts to bind slightly as it is rotated.
2. Back-off the bearing adjusting nut $^1/_{12}$ to $^1/_3$ of a turn and align the lock screw with the nearest locking hole (if equipped with a locking type nut).
3. Use a dial indicator to check the bearing/wheel end play. The end play should be 0.003 in. to 0.008 in.. Secure the wheel and axle assembly as required.

MID–LINER

Adjustment

HUBS WITHOUT HUB REDUCTION GEARS

1. Tighten the wheel bearing lock nut with a torque wrench to 258 ft. lbs., while rotating the hub in both directions.
2. Back off the lock nut a $^1/_4$ of a turn and lock it in place by bending the lockplate in a slot.

HUBS WITH HUB REDUCTION GEARS

1. Tighten the wheel bearing lock nut with a torque wrench to 258 ft. lbs., while rotating the hub in both directions.
2. Back off the lock nut a $^1/_2$ of a turn, rotate the hub in both directions and re-torque the lock nut to 110 ft. lbs. Lock the nut in ti place by bending the lockplate in a slot.

INDEX

ALTERNATORS AND REGULATORS

ELECTRONIC IGNITION SYSTEMS

STARTER MOTORS

ELECTRICAL DIAGNOSIS

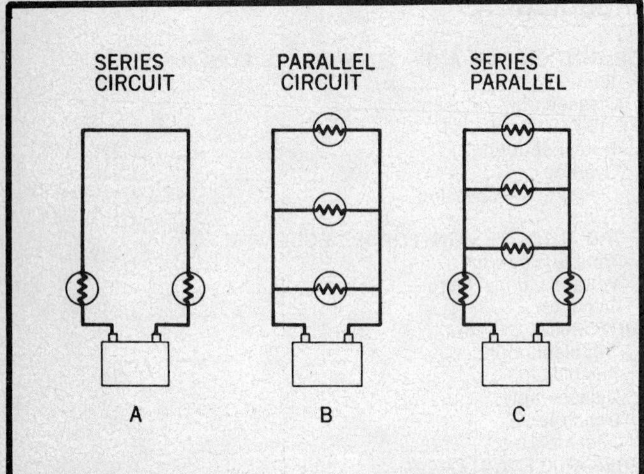

Basic electrical circuits

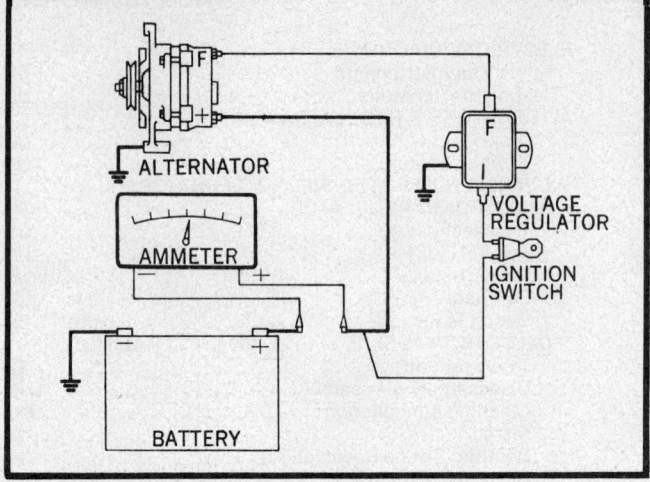

Ammeter connected in series circuits

To satisfy the growing trend toward organized engine diagnosis and tune-up, the following gauge and meter hook-ups, as well as diagnosis procedures are covered. The most sophisticated tune-up and diagnostic facilities are no more than a complex of the basic gauges and meters in common, everyday use. Therefore, to understand gauge and meter hook-ups, their applications and procedure, is to be equipped with the know how to perform the most exacting diagnosis.

KNOW YOUR INSTRUMENTS

Ohmmeter

An ohmmeter is used to measure electrical resistance in a unit or circuit. The ohmmeter has a self-contained power supply. In use, it is connected across (or in parallel with) the terminals of the unit being tested.

Ammeter

An ammeter is used to measure current (amount of electricity) flowing through a unit, or circuit. Ammeters are always connected in the line (in series) with the unit or circuit being tested.

Voltmeter

A voltmeter is used to measure voltage (electrical pressure) pushing the current through a unit, or circuit. The meter is connected across the terminals of the unit being tested.

Testing the Starter Motor

TESTING THE STARTER CIRCUIT

The starter circuit should be divided and tested in four separate tests. These tests are cranking voltage check, amperage draw, voltage drop (grounded side) and voltage drop (battery side). The battery must be in good condition for this test to have significance. To accurately check battery condition, use equipment designed to measure its capacity under a load. Instructions accompanying the equipment should be followed.

Cranking Voltage

Connect voltmeter leads to prods tapped into the battery posts (observe polarity and reverse meter leads if necessary). Remove the high tension wire from the distributor cap and ground it to prevent starting. With electronic ignition, disconnect the control box harness from the distributor. Now, turn the key. Observe both voltmeter reading and cranking speed. The cranking speed should be even, and at satisfactory rate of speed, with a voltmeter reading of at least 9.6 volts for 12 volt systems.

Amperage Draw

The amount of current the starter motor draws is usually (but not always) associated with the mechanical problem involved in cranking the engine. (Mechanical trouble in the engine, frozen or worn starter parts, misaligned starter or starter components, etc.) Because starter motor amperage draw is directly influenced by anything restricting the free turning of the engine, or starter, it is important that the engine and all components be at operating temperatures. To measure starter current draw, remove the high tension wire from the center of the distributor cap and ground it. With electronic ignition, disconnect the control box harness from the distributor. A very simple and inexpensive starter current indicator is available in auto stores. This indicator is an induction type gauge and shows, without disconnecting any wires, starter current draw. Place the yoke of the meter directly over the insulated starter supply cable (cable must be straight for a minimum of 2 in.). Close the starter switch for about 20 seconds, watch the meter dial and record the average reading. If the indicator swings in the wrong direction, reverse the position of the meter. The cranking amperage draw can vary from 150–400 amperes, depending on the engine size, engine compression, and starter type.

NOTE: When starter specifications are not available, average starter draw amperage can be derived from testing a like starter unit, known to be operating satisfactorily.

More accurate but complex equipment is available from many manufacturers. This equipment consists of a combination voltmeter, ammeter and carbon pile rheostat. When using this equipment, follow the equipment manufacturer's proce-

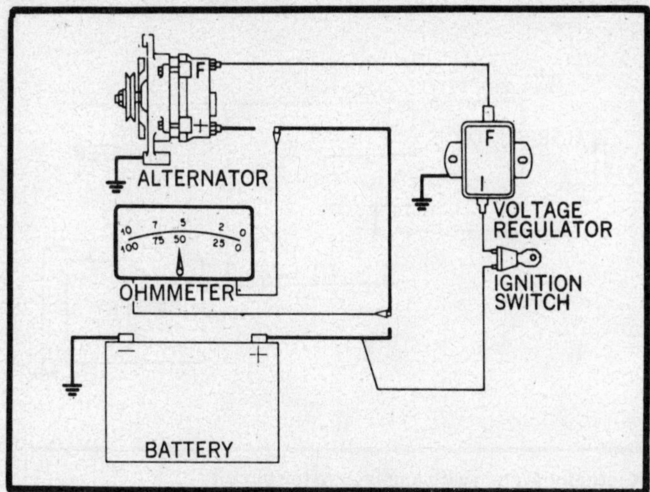

Ohmeter connected to test wire resistance

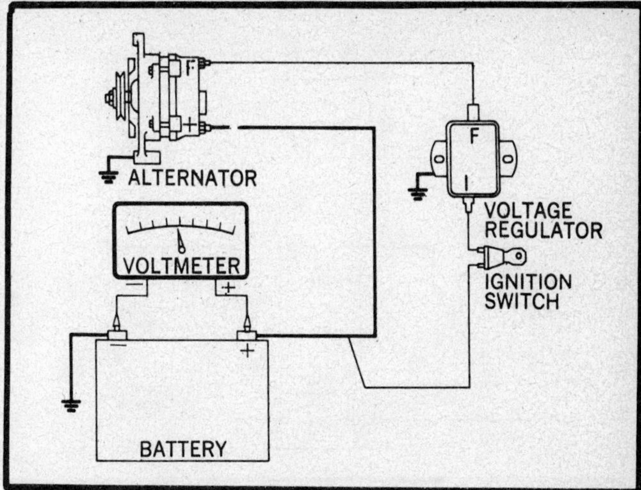

Voltmeter connected in parallel circuits

dures and recommendations. High amperage and lazy performance would suggest an excessively tight engine, friction in the starter or starter drive, grounded starter field or armature. Normal amperage and lazy performance suggest high resistance, or possibly poor connections somewhere in the starter circuit. Low amperage or lazy or no performance suggest battery condition poor, bad cables or connections along the line.

Voltage Drop (Grounded Side)

With a voltmeter on the 3 volt scale, without disconnecting any wires, connect negative test lead of the voltmeter to a prod secured in the grounded battery post. The positive test lead is connected to a cleaned, bare metal portion of the starter motor housing. Close the starter switch and note the voltmeter reading. If the reading is the same as battery reading, the ground circuit is open somewhere between the battery and the starter. In many cases the reading will be very small. the reading shown will indicate voltage drop (loss) between battery ground post and starter housing. The drop should not exceed 0.2 volt. If the voltage drop is above the specified amount, the next step is to isolate the correct cause. It can be a bad cable or connection anywhere in the battery to starter ground circuit. A check of this type should progress along the various points of possible trouble, between the battery ground post and the starter motor housing, until the trouble spot has been located.

Voltage Drop (Battery Side)

Bad starter cranking may result from poor connections or faulty components of the battery or hot phase of the starter motor circuit. To check this phase of the circuit, without disconnecting any wires, connect one lead of a voltmeter to a prod secured in the hot post of the battery and the other voltmeter lead to the field terminal of the starting motor. The meter should be set to the 16-20 volt scale. Before closing the starter switch, the voltmeter reading will be that of the battery. After closing the starter switch, change the selector on the voltmeter to the 3 volt scale. With a jumper wire between the relay battery terminal and the relay starter switch terminal, crank the engine. If the starter motor cranks the engine the relay (solenoid) is operating. While the engine is being cranked, watch the voltmeter. It should not register more than 0.5 volt. If more than this, check each part of the circuit for voltage drop to isolate the trouble, (high resistance), and crank the engine. The voltmeter should show no more than 0.1 volt. If this reading is correct, move the same voltmeter lead to the starting motor terminal of the relay (solenoid). While the engine is being cranked, the voltmeter should show no more than 0.3 volt. If it does, the

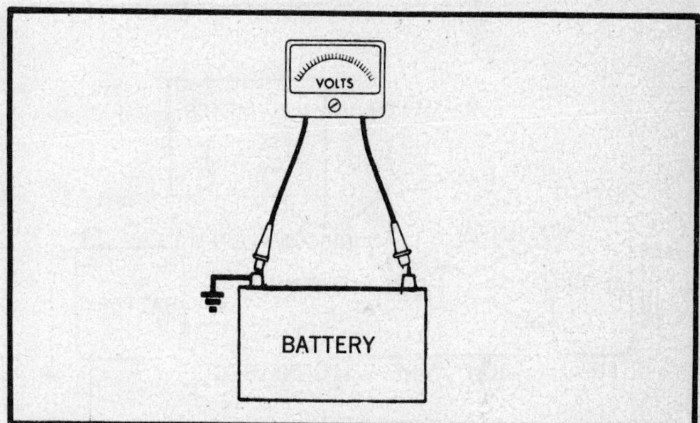

Voltmeter attached to battery for cranking voltage test

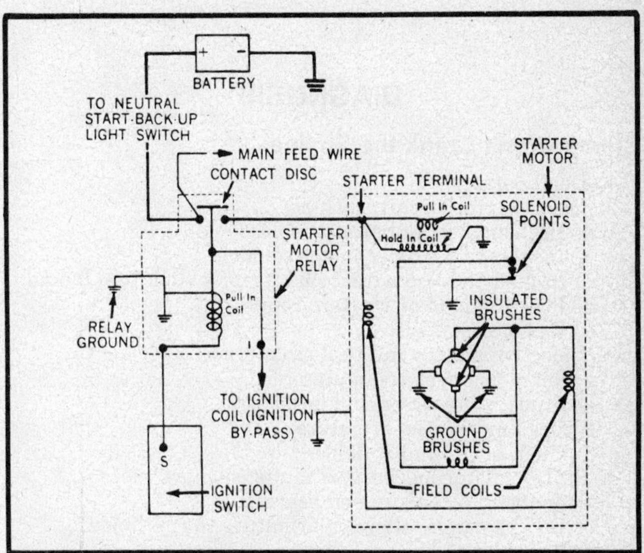

Positive engagement starter circuits (© Jeep Corp.)

trouble lies in the relay. If the reading is correct, the trouble is in the cable or connections between the relay and the starter motor.

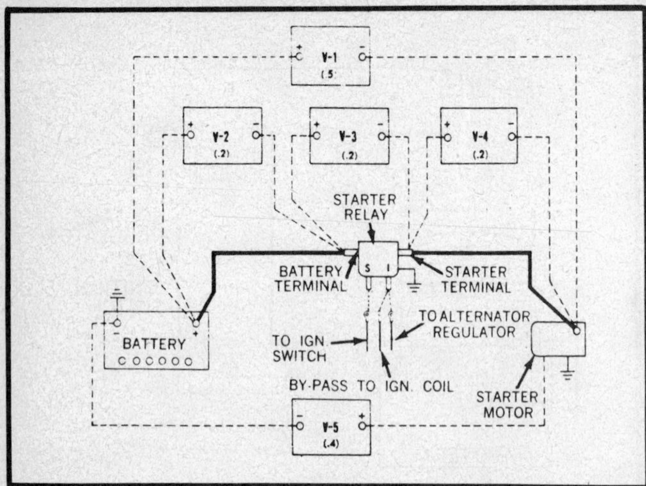

Starter cable resistance tests—typical (© Jeep Corp.)

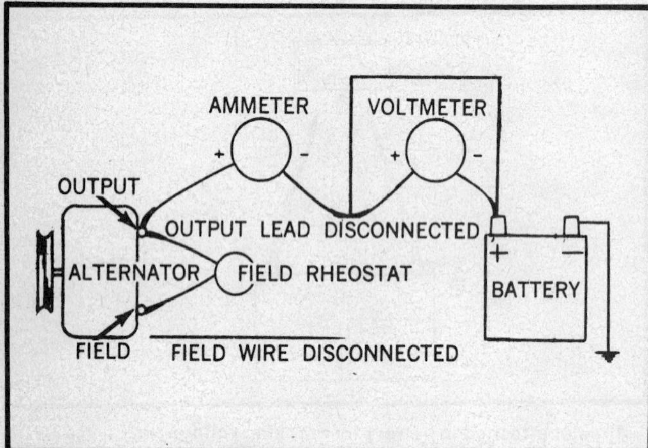

Checking charging system resistance—typical

DIAGNOSIS

Starter Won't Crank the Engine

1. Dead battery.
2. Open starter circuit, such as:
   a. Broken or loose battery cables.
   b. Inoperative starter motor solenoid.
   c. Broken or loose wire from starter switch to solenoid.
   d. Poor solenoid or starter ground.
   e. Bad starter switch.
3. Defective starter internal circuit, such as:
   a. Dirty or burnt commutator.
   b. Stuck, worn or broken brushes.
   c. Open or shorted armature.
   d. Open or grounded fields.
4. Starter motor mechanical faults, such as:
   a. Jammed armature end bearings.
   b. Bad bearings, allowing armature to rub fields.
   c. Bent shaft.
   d. Broken starter housing.
   e. Bad starter worm or drive mechanism.
   f. Bad starter drive or flywheel driven gear.
5. Engine hard or impossible to crank such as:
   a. Hydrostatic lock, water in combustion chamber.

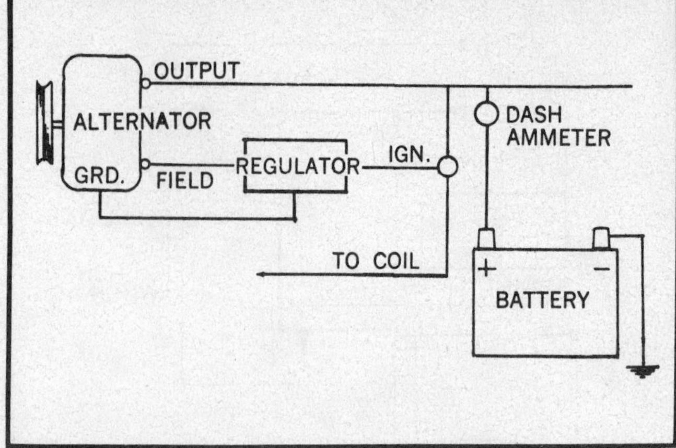

Alternator system with ammeter in the circuit

   b. Crankshaft seizing in bearings.
   c. Piston or ring seizing.
   d. Bent or broken connecting rod.
   e. Seizing of connecting rod bearing.
   f. Flywheel jammed or broken.
6. Starter spins free, won't engage such as:
   a. Sticking or broken drive mechanism.

Alternators and Regulators

IS IT THE ALTERNATOR OR THE VOLTAGE REGULATOR?

The first step in diagnosing troubles of the charging system, is to identify the source of failure. Does the fault lie in the alternator or the regulator? The next move depends upon preference or necessity; either repair or replace the offending unit.

It is just as easy to separate an alternator, electrically, from the AC regulator as it is to separate its counterpart, the DC generator from its regular.

AC generator output is controlled by the amount of current supplied to the field circuit of the system.

Unlike the DC generator, an AC generator is capable of producing substantial current at idle speed. Higher maximum output is also a possibility. This presents a potential danger when testing. As a precaution, a field rheostat should be used in the field circuit when making the following isolation test. The field rheostat permits positive control of the amount of current allowed to pass through the field circuit during the isolation test. Unregulated alternator capacity could ruin the unit.

NOTE: Most manufacturers of precision gauges offer special test connectors, in sets, that will adapt to the leads and connections of any AC charging system.

ALTERNATOR TEST PLANS

The following is a procedure pattern for testing the various alternators and their control systems. There are certain precautionary measures that apply to alternator tests in general. These items are listed in detail to avoid repetition when testing each make of alternator and to encourage a habit of good test procedure.

1. Check alternator drive belt for condition and tension.
2. Disconnect battery cables, check physical, chemical, and electrical condition of battery.
3. Be absolutely sure of polarity before connecting any battery for starting.

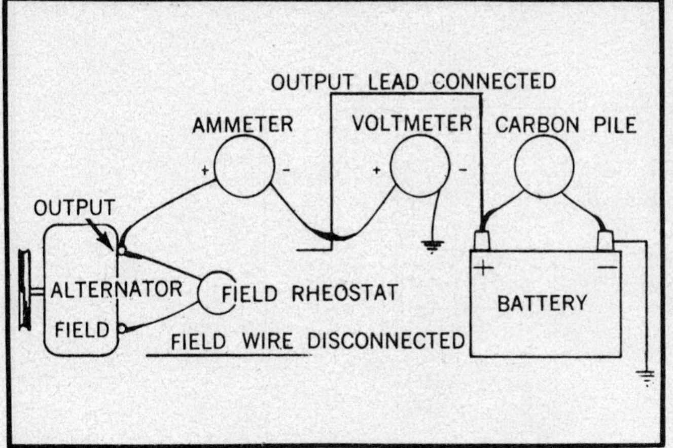

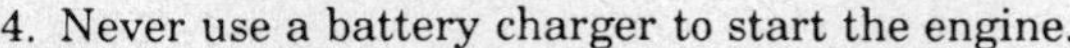

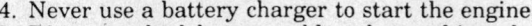

Checking current output of the charging system—typical

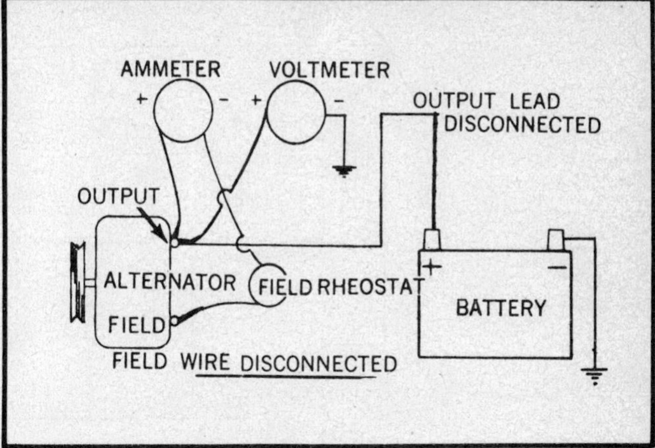

Checking current field draw—typical

4. Never use a battery charger to start the engine.
5. Disconnect both battery cables when making a battery recharge hook-up.
6. Be sure of polarity hook-up when using a booster battery for starting.
7. Never ground the alternator output or battery terminal.
8. Never ground the field circuit between alternator and regulator.
9. Never run any alternator on an open circuit with the field energized.
10. Never try to polarize an alternator, unless directed by the alternator manufacturer.
11. Do not attempt to "motor" an alternator.
12. The regulator cover must be in place when taking voltage limiter readings.
13. The ignition switch must be in off position when removing or installing the regulator cover.
14. Use insulated tools only to make adjustments to the regulator.
15. When making engine idle speed adjustments, always consider potential load factors that influence engine rpm. To compensate for electrical load, switch on the lights, radio, heater, air conditioner, etc.

Diagnosis

1. Low or no charging such as:
   a. Blown fuse.
   b. Broken or loose fan belt.
   c. Voltage regulator not working.
   d. Brushes sticking.
   e. Slip ring dirty.
   f. Open circuit.
   g. Bad wiring connections.
   h. Bad diode rectifier.
   i. High resistance in charging circuit.
   j. Voltage regulator needs adjusting.
   k. Grounded stator.
   l. May be open rectifiers (check all three phases.).
   m. If rectifiers are found blown or open, check capacitor.
2. Noisy unit, such as:
   a. Damaged rotor bearing.
   b. Poor alignment of unit.
   c. Broken or loose belt.
   d. Open diode rectifiers.
3. Regulator points burnt or stuck, such as:
   a. Regulator set too high.
   b. Poor ground connections.
   c. Shorted generator field.
   d. Regulator air gap incorrect.

Chrysler Isolated Field Alternator (Electronic Regulator)

The Chrysler isolated field alternator derives its name from its construction. Both of the brushes are insulated from ground and there is no heat sink connection, thereby isolating the internal field.

TROUBLESHOOTING

Fusible Links

Chrysler Corporation trucks have a single fusible link which is connected between the starter relay and the junction block. Failure of this link will cause all electrical systems to stop functioning.

Charging System Operation

NOTE: If the current indicator is to give an accurate reading, the battery cables must be of the same gauge and length as the original equipment.

1. With the engine running and all electrical systems off, place a current indicator over the positive battery cable.
2. If a charge of about 5 amps is recorded, the charging system is working. If a draw of about 5 amps is recorded the system is not working. The needle moves toward the battery when a charge condition is indicated and away from the battery when a draw condition is indicated. If a draw is indicated, proceed to the next testing procedure. If an overcharge of 10–15 amps is indicated, check for faulty regulator.

Ignition Switch to Regulator Circuit Check

1. Disconnect the regulator wires at the regulator.
2. Turn the key on but do not start the engine.
3. Using a voltmeter or test light, check for voltage across the I and F terminals. If there is current present, the circuit is good. If there is no current, check for bad connections, a bad ballast resistor, a bad ammeter, broken wires, or bad ground at the alternator or voltage regulator. Also, check for voltage from the I wire to ground; current should be present. Check for voltage from the F terminal to ground; current should not be present.

Isolation Test

1. Disconnect, at the alternator, the wire that runs between one of the alternator field connections and the voltage regulator.

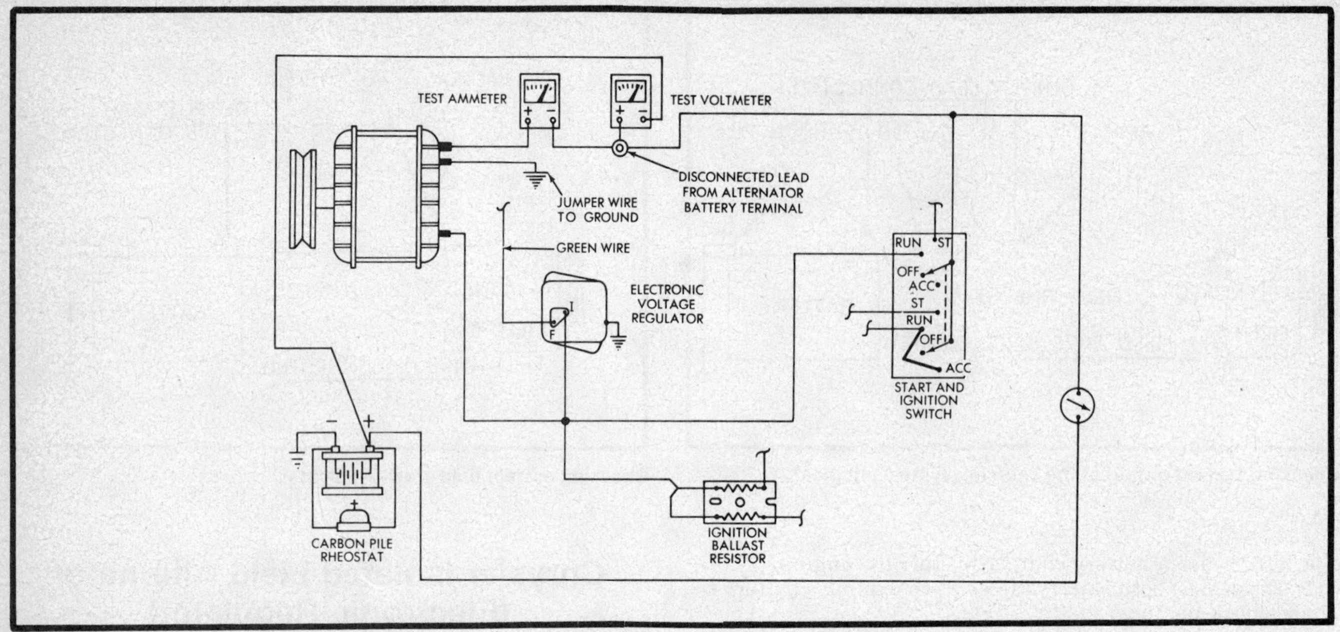

Charging circuit resistance test (© Chrysler Corp.)

2. Run a jumper wire from the disconnected alternator terminal to ground.

3. Connect a voltmeter to the battery. The positive voltmeter lead connects to the positive battery terminal, and the negative lead goes to the negative terminal. Record the reading.

4. Make sure that all electrical systems are turned off. Start the engine. Do not race the engine.

5. Gradually raise engine speed to 1500-2000. There should be an increase of one or two volts on the voltmeter. If this is true, the alternator is good and the voltage regulator should be repaired. If there is no voltage increase, the alternator is faulty.

Charging Circuit Resistance Test

The purpose of this test is to determine the amount of "voltage drop" between the alternator output terminal wire and the battery.

1. Disconnect the battery ground cable at the "BAT" lead at the alternator output terminal.
2. Connect an ammeter with a scale to 10 amps in series between the alternator "BAT" terminal and the disconnected "BAT" wire.
3. Connect the positive lead of a voltmeter to the disconnected "BAT" wire. Connect the negative lead of the voltmeter to the negative post of the battery.
4. Disconnect the green colored regulator field wire from the alternator. Connect a jumper lead from the alternator field terminal to ground.
5. Connect a tachometer to the engine and reconnect the battery ground cable.
6. Connect a variable carbon pile rheostat to the battery cables. Be sure the carbon pile is in the "OPEN" or "OFF" position before connecting the leads to the battery terminals.
7. Start the engine and operate at an idle.
8. Adjust the engine speed and carbon pile to maintain a flow of 20 amperes in the circuit. Observe the voltmeter reading which should not exceed 0.7 volts.
9. If a higher voltage reading is indicated, inspect, clean and tighten all connections in the charging system.
10. If necessary, a voltage drop test can be done at each connection until the excessive resistance is located.
11. If the charging system resistance is within specifications, reduce the engine speed, turn off the carbon pile rheostat and stop the engine. Remove battery ground cable.
12. Remove the test instruments from the electrical system and reconnect the charging system wiring. Reconnect the battery ground cable.

Current Output Test

This test determines if the alternator is capable of delivering its rated current output.

1. Disconnect the battery ground cable and the "BAT" lead wire at the alternator output terminal.

2. Connect an ammeter in series between the alternator output terminal and the disconnected "BAT" lead wire.

NOTE: The ammeter must have a scale of 100 amps.

3. Connect the positive lead of a voltmeter to the output terminal of the alternator and the negative lead to a good ground.

4. Disconnect the green colored wire at the voltage regulator and connect a jumper wire from the alternator field terminal to ground.

5. Connect a tachometer to the engine and reconnect the battery ground wire.

6. Connect a variable carbon pile rheostat between the positive and negative battery cables.

NOTE: Be sure the rheostat control is in the "OPEN" or "OFF" position before connecting the leads to the battery cables.

7. Start the engine and operate at idle. Adjust the carbon pile rheostat control and the engine speed in increments until the voltmeter reading is 15 volts (13 volts for the 100 and 117 amp alternators) and the engine speed is 1250 rpm (900 rpm for the 100 and 117 amp alternators). Do not allow the voltage to rise to 16 volts.

8. The ammeter readings must be within specification.

NOTE: If measured at the battery, current output will be approximately 5 amperes lower than specified.

9. If the readings are less than specified, the alternator should be removed and checked during a bench test.

10. After the current output test is completed, reduce the en-

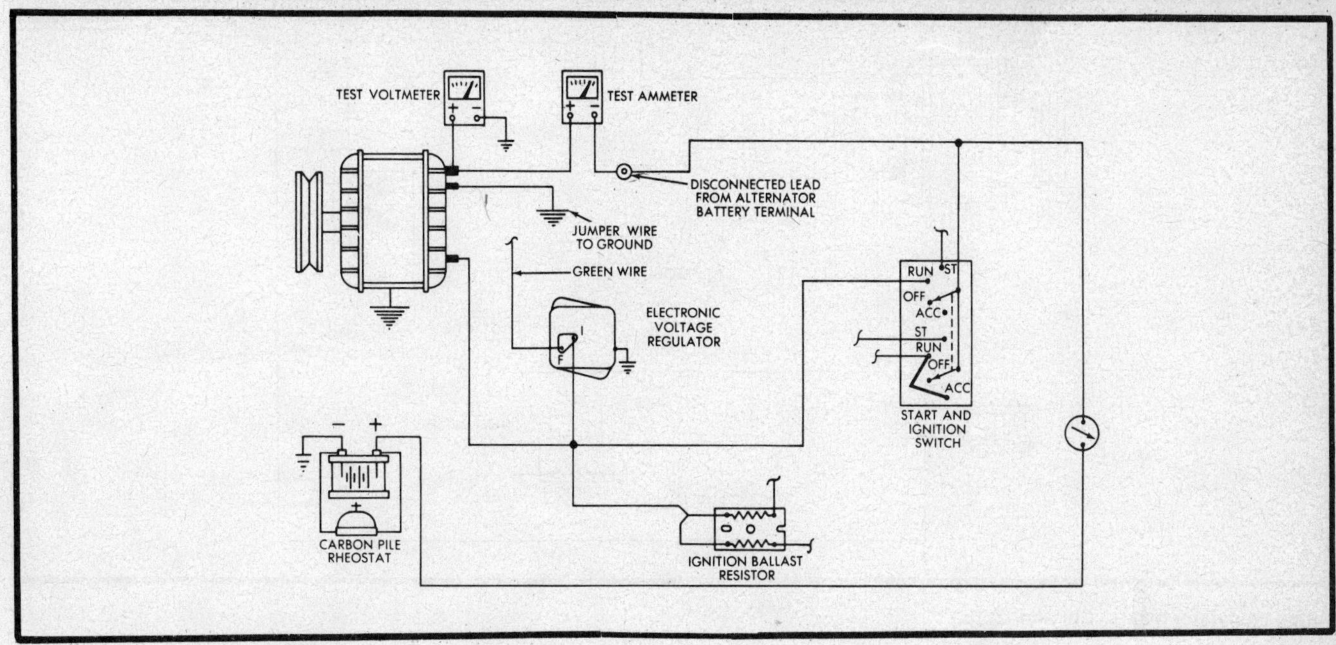

Current output test (© Chrysler Corp.)

gine speed, turn the carbon pile rheostat off and then stop the engine.

11. Disconnect the battery ground cable, remove the ammeter, voltmeter and carbon pile. Remove the jumper wire from the field terminal and reconnect the green colored wire to the alternator field terminal.

12. Reconnect the battery cable, if no further testing is to be done to the charging circuit.

Current Rating	Identification	Current Output
41 amp	Red or violet tag	40 amps min.
60 amp	Blue, natural or yellow	57 amps min.
100, 117 amp	Yellow	72 amps min.

Rotor Field Coil Draw Test

1. If on the vehicle, remove the drive belt and wiring connections from the alternator.
2. Connect a jumper wire from the negative terminal of the battery to one of the field terminals of the alternator.
3. Connect the test ammeter positive lead to the other field terminal of the alternator and the negative ammeter lead to the positive battery terminal.
4. Connect a jumper wire between the alternator end shield and the battery negative terminal.
5. Slowly rotate the alternator pulley by hand and observe the ammeter reading.
6. The field coil draw should be 4.5 to 6.5 amperes at 12 volts (4.75 to 6.0 amperes at 12 volts if vehicle is equipped with a 100 or 117 amp alternator).
7. A low rotor coil draw is an indication of high resistance in the field coil draw indicates an open rotor or defective brushes.
8. Remove the test equipment and jumper leads.

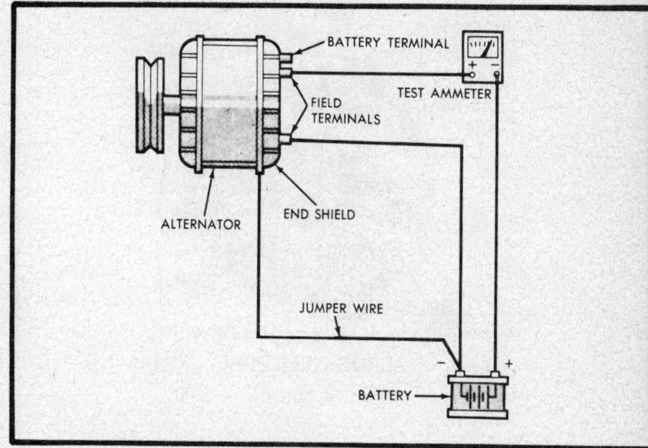

Rotor field coil current draw test (© Chrysler Corp.)

Electronic Voltage Regulator Test

1. Make sure battery terminals are clean and battery is charged.
2. Connect the positive lead of a test voltmeter to ignition Terminal No. 1 of the ballast resistor.
3. Connect the negative voltmeter lead to a good body ground.
4. Start engine and allow it to idle at 1250 rpm, all lights and accessories turned off. Voltage should be within specification.
5. If the voltage regulator is below specification, check the following:

a. Voltage regulator; ground check voltage drop between regulator cover and ground.

b. Harness wiring; disconnect regulator plug (ign. switch off), then turn on ign. switch and check for battery voltage at the terminals having the red and green leads. Wiring harness must be disconnected from the regulator when checking individual leads. If no voltage is present in either lead, the problem is in the truck wiring or alternator field.

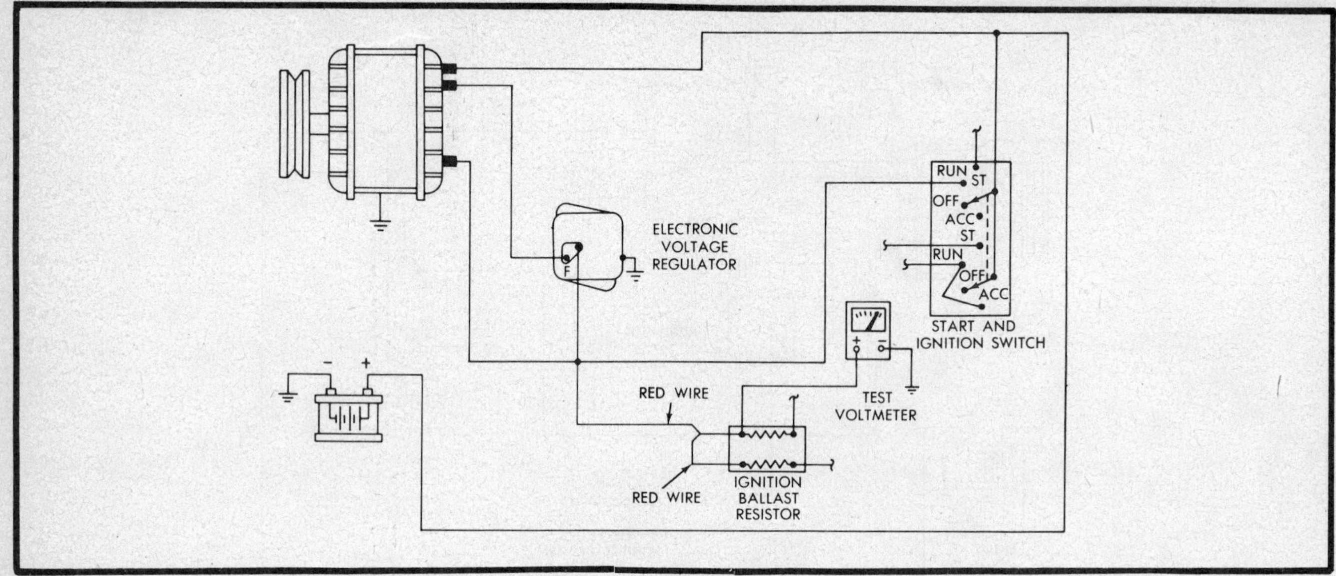

Voltage regulator test (© Chrysler Corp.)

Ambient Temp. ¼ in. from Regulator	Voltage
20°F.	14.9 to 15.9
80°F.	13.9 to 14.6
140°F.	13.3 to 13.9
Above 140°F.	Less Than 13.6

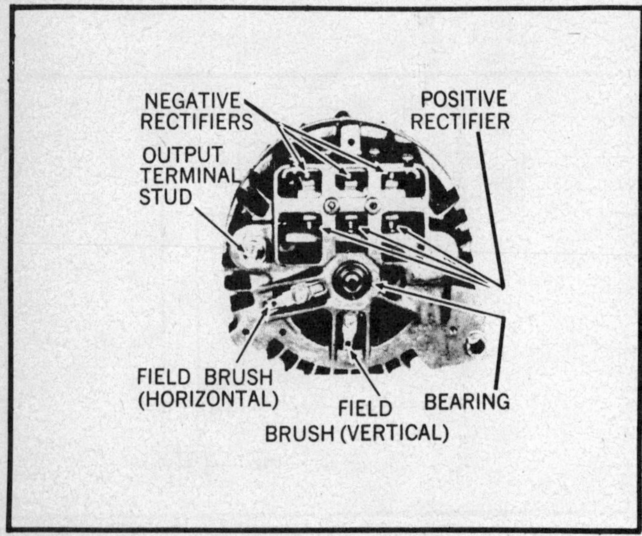

View of rear housing—except 100 amp alternator
(© Chrysler Corp.)

6. If Step 5 tests showed no malfunctions, install a new regulator and repeat Step 4.
7. If voltage is above specifications (Step 4), or fluctuates, check the following:
   a. Ground between regulator and body, and between body and engine.
   b. Ignition switch circuit between switch and regulator.
8. If voltage is still more than ½ volt above specifications, install a new regulator and repeat Step 4.

Chrysler Overhaul and Internal Testing

Alternator disassembly, repair and assembly procedures are basically the same for all Chrysler alternators. Certain variations in design, or production modifications, could require slightly different procedures that should be obvious upon inspection of the unit being serviced.

Disassembly

NOTE: To prevent damage to the brush assemblies (100 and 117 amp), they should be removed before proceeding with the disassembly of the alternator. The brushes are mounted in a plastic holder that positions the brushes vertically against the slip rings.

1. Remove the retaining screw, flat washer, nylon washer and field terminal and carefully lift the plastic holder containing the spring and brush assembly from the end housing.
2. The ground brush (40 and 60 amp) is positioned horizontally against the slip ring and is retained in the holder that is integral with the end housing. Remove the retaining screw and lift the clip, spring and brush assembly from the end housing. The stator is laminated, don't burr the stator or end housings.
3. Remove the through bolts and pry between the stator and drive end housing with a suitable tool. Carefully separate the drive end housing, pulley and rotor assembly from the stator and rectifier housing assembly.
4. The pulley is an interference fit on the rotor shaft. Remove with a puller and special adapters.
5. Remove the three nuts and washers and, while supporting the end frame, tap the rotor shaft with a plastic hammer and separate the rotor and end housing.
6. The drive end ball bearing is an interference fit with the rotor shaft. Remove the baring with puller and adapters.

NOTE: Further dismantling of the rotor is not advisable, as the remainder of the rotor assembly is not serviced separately.

7. Remove the DC output terminal nuts and washers and re-

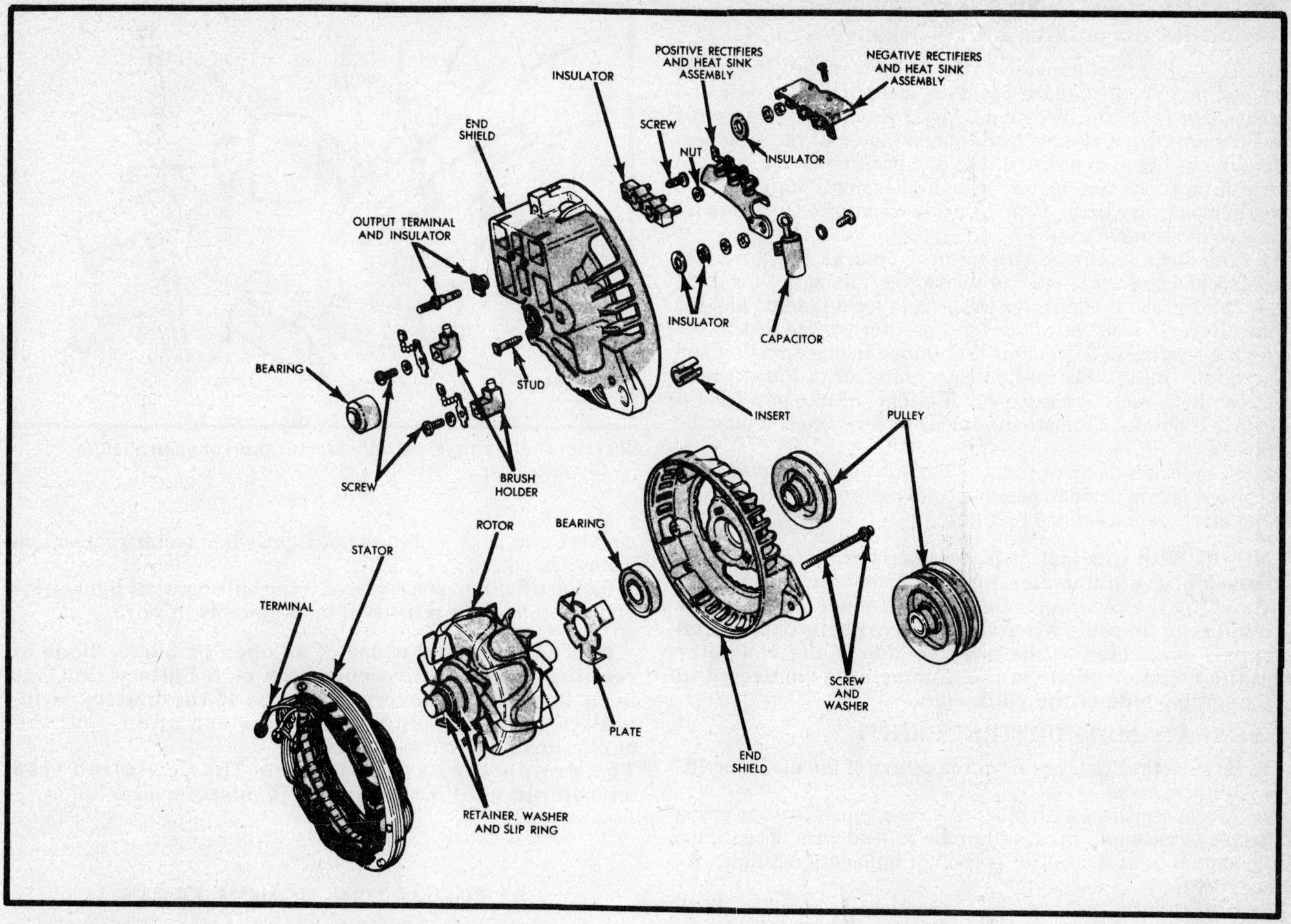

Typical Chrysler alternator—exploded view (© Chrysler Corp.)

move terminal screw and inside capacitor (on units so equipped).

8. Remove the insulator.

NOTE: Positive rectifiers are pressed into the heat sink and negative rectifiers in the end housing. When removing the rectifiers, it is necessary to support the end housing and/or heat sink to prevent damage to these castings. Another caution is in order relative to diode rectifiers. Don't subject them to unnecessary jolting. Heavy vibration or shock may ruin them.

9. Cut rectifier wire at point of crimp. Support rectifier housing. The factory tool is cut away and slotted to fit over the wires and around the bosses in the housing. Be sure that the bore of the tool completely surrounds the rectifier, then press the rectifier out of the housing.

NOTE: The roller bearing in the rectifier end frame is a press fit. To protect the end housing it is necessary to support the housing with a tool when pressing out the bearing.

BENCH TESTS

Testing Silicone Diode Rectifiers With Ohmmeter

PREFERRED METHOD (RECTIFIERS OPEN IN ALL THREE PHASES)

1. Disassembly the alternator and separate the wires at the Y-connection of the stator.

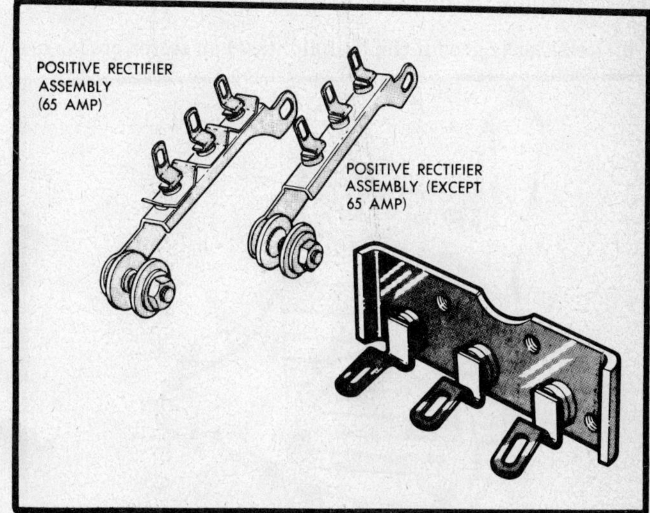

Chrysler charging system positive and negative rectifier identification (© Chrysler Corp.)

2. There are six doide rectifiers mounted in the back of the alternator (40 and 60 amp). Three of them are marked with a plus (+), and three are marked with a minus (-). These marks indicate diode case polarity.

NOTE: The 100 and 117 amp alternator has twelve silicone diodes. Six positive and six negative.

3. To test, set ohmmeter to its lowest range. If case is marked positive (+), place positives meter probe to case and negative probe to the diode lead. Meter should read between 4 and 10 ohms. Now, reverse leads of ohmmeter, connecting negative meter probe to positive case and positive meter probe to wire of rectifier. Set meter on a high range. Meter needle should move very little, if any (infinite reading). Do this to all positive diode rectifiers.

4. The diode rectifiers with minus (-) marks on their cases are checked the same way as above. Only now the negative ohmmeter probe is connected to the case for a reading of 4–10 ohms. Reverse leads as above for the other part to test.

5. If a reading of 4–10 ohms is obtained in one direction and no reading (infinity) is read on the ohmmeter in the other direction, diode rectifiers are good. If either infinity or a low resistance is obtained in both directions on a rectifier, it must be replaced.

6. If meter reads more than 10 ohms when ohmmeter positive probe is connected to positive on diode, and negative probe to negative, replace diode rectifier.

NOTE: With this test, it is necessary to determine the polarity of the ohmmeter probes. This can be done by connecting the ohmmeter to a DC voltmeter. The voltmeter will read up-scale when the positive probe of the ohmmeter is connected to the positive side of the voltmeter and the negative probe of the ohmmeter is connected to the negative side of the voltmeter.

ALTERNATE METHOD (TEST LIGHT)

1. Be sure that the lead from the center of the diode rectifiers is disconnected.

2. To test rectifiers with plus (+ — case, touch positive probe of tester to case and minus (-) probe to lead wire of rectifier. Bulb should light if rectifier is good. If bulb does not light, replace rectifier.

3. Now reserve tester probe connections to rectifier. Bulb should not light. If bulb does light, replace rectifier.

4. For testing minus (-) marked cases, follow above procedure, except that now bulb should light with negative probe of tester touching rectifier case and positive probe touching lead wire.

5. Rectifier is good if the bulb lights when tester probes are

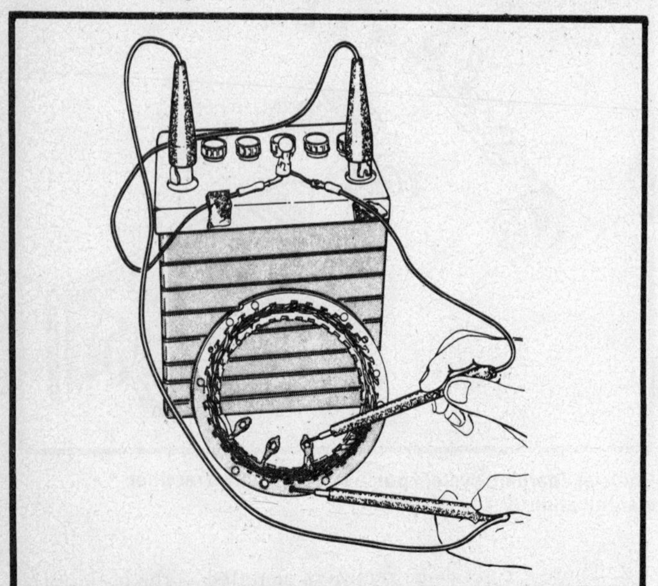

Chrysler charging system stator test for ground
(© Chrysler Corp.)

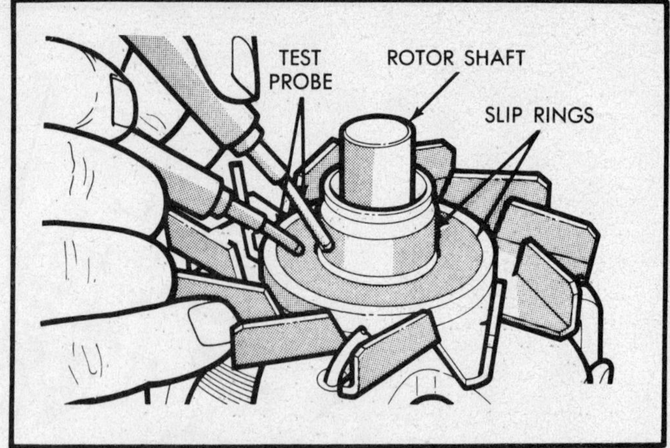

Chrysler charging system rotor test for short or open circuits
(© Chrysler Corp.)

connect one way, and does not light when tester connections are reversed.

6. Rectifier must be replaced if the bulb does not light either way. Also, replace rectifier if bulb lights both ways.

NOTE: The usual cause of an open or blown diode or rectifier is a defective capacitor or a battery that has been installed in reverse polarity. If the battery is installed properly and the diodes are open, test the capacitor.
The capacitor capacities are: Int. installed (158 microfarad min). Ext. installed (5 microfarad min).

ALTERNATOR BENCH TESTS

Field Coil Draw

1. Connect a jumper between one FLD terminal and the positive terminal of a fully charged 12 volt battery.

2. Connect the positive lead of a test ammeter to the other field (FLD) terminal and the negative test lead to the negative battery terminal.

3. Slowly rotate the rotor by hand and observe the ammeter. The proper field coil draw is 2.3 to 2.7 amps at 12 volts.

NOTE: Field coil draw for the 100 and 117 ampere alternators should be 4.75 amperes to 6.0 amperes at 12 volts.

Field Circuit Ground Test

1. Touch one test lead of a 110 volt AC test bulb to one of the alternator brush (field) terminals and the other test lead to the end shield.

2. If the lamp lights, remove the field brush assemblies and separate the end housing by removing the three through bolts.

3. Place one test lead on a slip ring and the other on the end shield.

4. If the lamp lights, the rotor assembly is grounded internally and must be replaced.

5. If the lamp does not light, the cause of the problem was a grounded brush.

Grounded Stator

1. Disconnect the diode rectifiers from the stator leads.

2. Test from stator leads to stator core, using a 110 volt test lamp. Test lamp should not light. If it does, stator is grounded and must be replaced.

Low Output

1. Perform Steps 1, 2 and 3 (rectifier open in all three phases). If the rectifiers are found to be within specifications, replace the stator assembly.

Current Output Too High (No Control) Caused by Open Rectifier or Open Phase

1. Perform Steps 1, 2 and 3 (rectifier open in all three phases). If the rectifier tests satisfactorily, inspect the stator connections before replacing the stator.

Assembly

1. Support the heat sink or rectifier end housing or circular plate.
2. Check rectifier identification to be sure the correct rectifier is being used. The part numbers are stamped on the case of the rectifier. They are also marked, red for positive and black for negative.
3. Start the new rectifier into the casting and press it in squarely.

NOTE: Do not start rectifier with a hammer or it will be ruined.

4. Crimp the new rectifier wire to the wires disconnected at removal, or solder (using a heat sink with rosin core solder).
5. Support the end housing on tool so that the notch in the support tool will clear the raised section of the heat sink, then press the bearing into position with tool SP-3381, or equivalent. New bearings are pre lubricated, additional lubrication is not required.
6. Insert the drive end bearing in the drive end housing and install the bearing plate, washers and nuts to hold the bearing in place.
7. Position the bearing and drive end housing on the rotor shaft and, while supporting the base of the rotor shaft, press the bearing and housing in position on the rotor shaft with an arbor press and arbor tool. Be careful that there is no cocking of the bearing at installation, or damage will result. Press the bearing on the rotor shaft until the bearing contacts the shoulder on the rotor shaft.
8. Install pulley on rotor shaft. Shaft of rotor must be supported so that all pressing force is on the pulley hub and rotor shaft.

NOTE: Do not exceed 6,800 lbs. pressure. Pulley hub should just contact bearing inner race.

9. Some alternators will be found to have the capacitor mounted internally. Be sure the heat sink insulator is in place.
10. Install the output terminal screw with the capacitor attached through the heat sink and end housing.
11. Install insulating washers, lockwashers and locknuts.
12. Make sure the heat sink and insulator are in place and tighten the locknut.
13. Position the stator on the rectifier end housing. Be sure that all of the rectifier connectors and phase leads are free of interference with the rotor fan blades and that the capacitor (internally mounted) lead has clearance.
14. Position the rotor assembly in the rectifier end housing. Align the through bolt holes in the stator with both end housings.
15. Enter stator shaft in the rectifier end housing bearing, compress stator and both end housings manually and install through bolts, washers and nuts.
16. Install the insulated brush and terminal attaching screw.
17. Install the ground screw and attaching screw.
18. Rotate pulley slowly to be sure the rotor fan blades do not hit the rectifier and stator connectors.

Delcotron 10-S1, 15-S1, Type 100 (General Motors Corp.)

NOTE: The internal alternator wiring is identical between the 10-S1, 15-S1 and the 27-S1 units, except the 10-S1 uses a Wye stator winding while a Delta stator winding is used in the 15-S1 and 27-S1 alternators. The disassembly and assembly of the units remain basically the same.

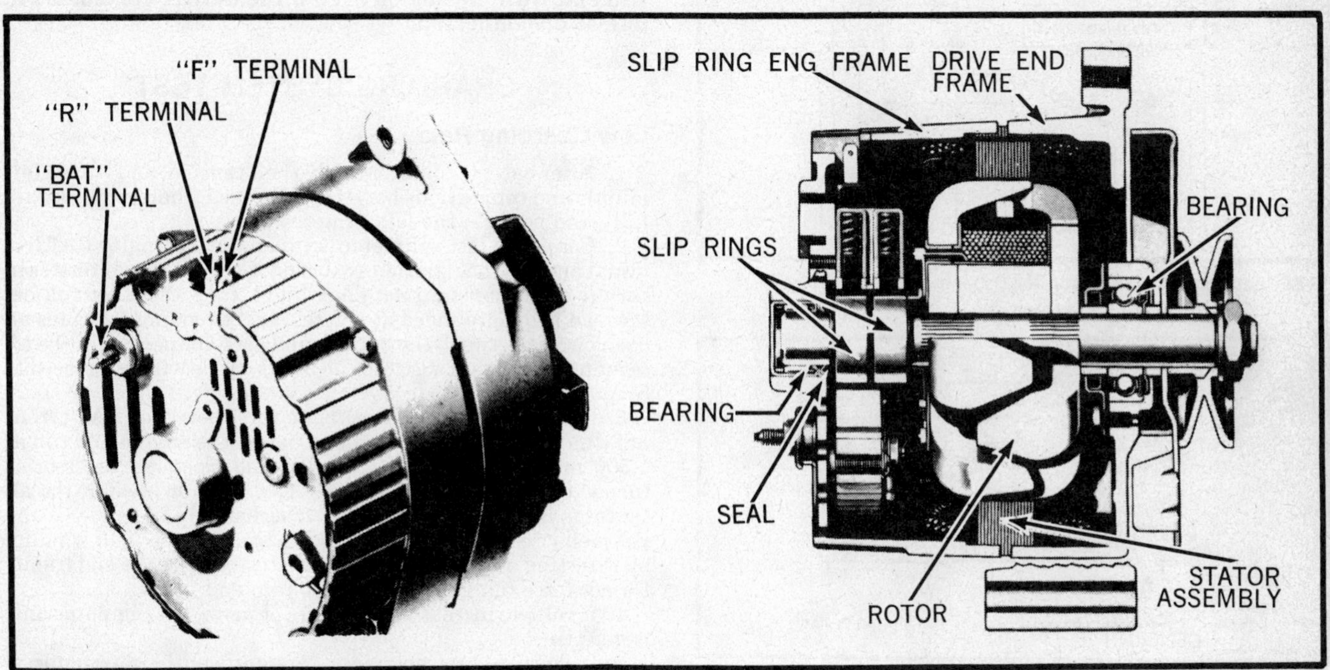

10-SI delcotron (c General Motors Corp.)

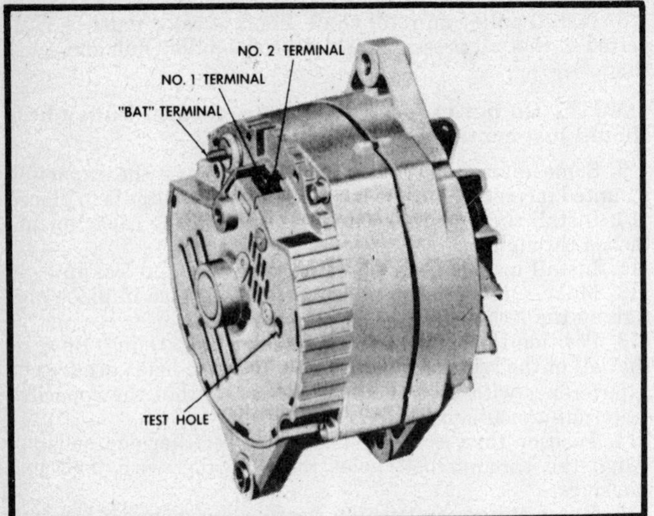

27-SI Type 100 delcotron (© General Motors Corp.)

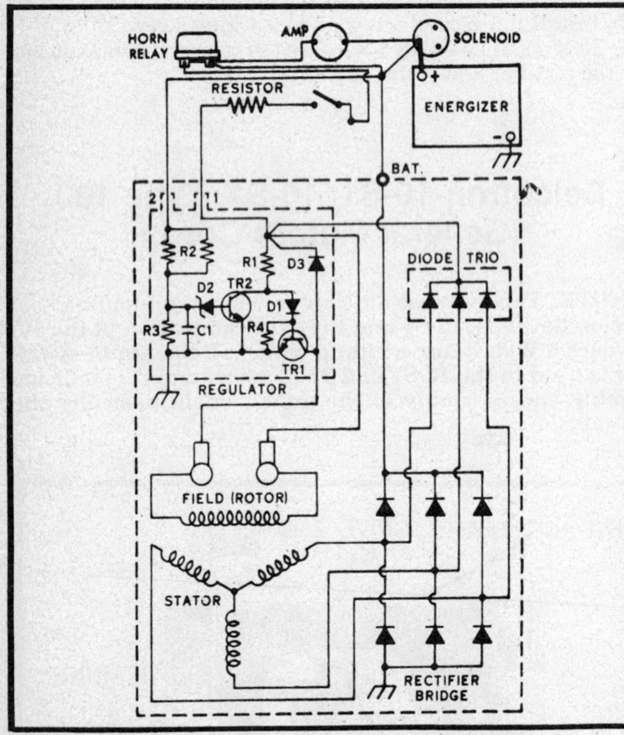

10-SI Charging circuit schematic (© General Motors Corp.)

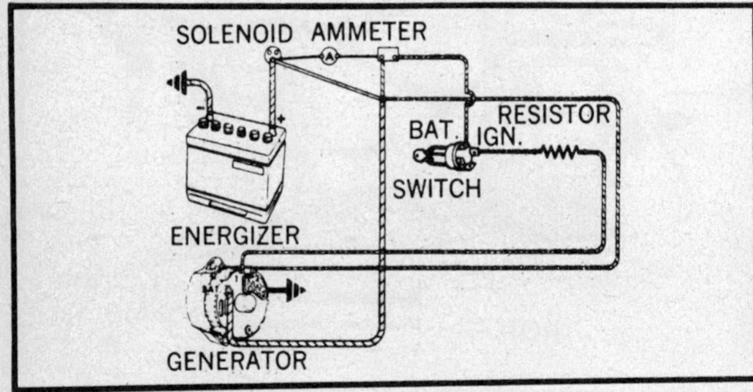

10-SI basic wiring diagram (© General Motors Corp.)

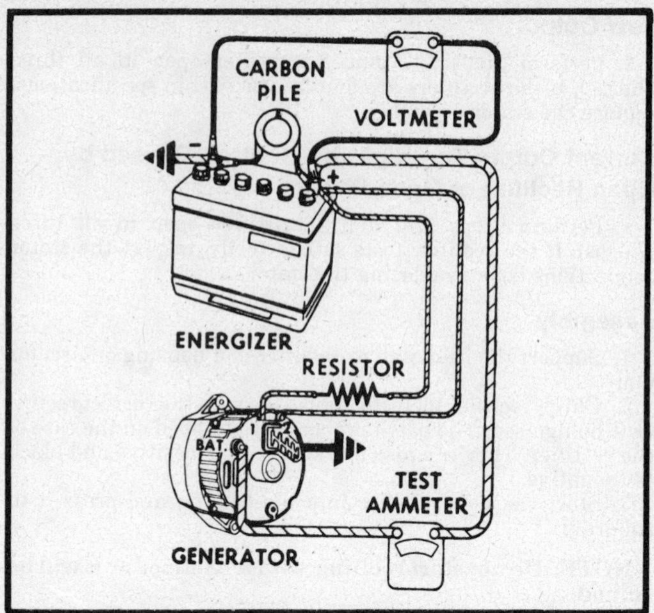

10-SI output test connections (© General Motors Corp.)

DELCOTRON 10-S1 AND 15-S1

This system is an integrated AC generating system containing a built in voltage regulator. Removal and replacement is essentially the same as for the standard AC generator. The regulator is mounted inside the slip ring end frame. All regulator components are enclosed in an epoxy molding, and the regulator cannot be adjusted.

TROUBLESHOOTING

NOTE: See the "Alternator Test Plans" section before proceeding further. Make sure that the continuous running blower, if equipped, is disconnected. This blower will run with the key on even if the blower control is off, unless disconnected.

CHARGING SYSTEM TEST

Low Charging Rate

1. After battery condition, drive belt tension, and wiring terminals and connections have been checked, charge the battery fully and perform the following test.
2. Connect a test voltmeter between the alternator BAT terminal and ground, ignition switch on. Connect the voltmeter in turn to alternator terminals No. 1 and No. 2, the other voltmeter lead being grounded as before. A zero reading indicates an open circuit between the battery and each connection at the alternator. If this test discloses no faults in the wiring, proceed to Step 3.
3. Connect the test voltmeter to the alternator BAT terminal (the other test lead to ground), start the engine and run at 1,500 to 2,000 rpm with all lights and electrical accessories turned on. If the voltmeter reads 12.8 volts or greater, the alternator is good and no further checks need be made. If the voltmeter reads less than 12.8 volts, ground the field winding by inserting a suitable tool into the test hole in the end frame. Do not force tab more than $^3/_4$ in. into end frame.
4. If voltage increases to 13 volts or more, the regulator unit is defective.
5. If voltage does not increase significantly, alternator is defective.

Alternator Output Test

1. Connect a test voltmeter, ammeter and a 10 ohm, 6 watt resistor into the charging circuit. Do not connect the carbon pile to the battery posts at this time.
2. Increase alternator speed and observe voltmeter if voltage is uncontrolled with speed and increases to 15.5 volts or more, check for a grounded brush lead clip as covered previously. If brush lead clip is not grounded, the voltage regulator is faulty and must be replaced.
3. Connect the carbon pile load to the battery terminals.
4. Operate the alternator at moderate speed and adjust the carbon pile to obtain maximum alternator output as indicted on the ammeter. If output is within 10 amperes of rated output as stamped on the alternator frame, alternator is ok. If output is not within specifications, ground the alternator field by inserting a suitable tool into the test hole in the end frame. If output now is within 10 amperes of rating, replace the voltage regulator; if still not within specifications, check field winding, diode trio, rectifier bridge and stator, as described later.

Disassembly and Assembly

1. Hold generator in a vice, clamping the mounting flange lengthwise.
2. Make a scribe mark to help locate frame end parts in the same position during assembly.
3. Remove 4 through bolts and separate the slip ring end frame from the drive end frame and rotor assembly.
4. Remove 2 stator lead attaching nuts and separate stator from end frame.
5. Remove insulated screws and ground screw from brush holder. Remove diode trio, resistor, brush holder, and regulator from end frame.
6. Remove screws attaching capacitor to end frame and diode bridge. Remove capacitor.
7. 10-S1 Series alternators, remove ground screw and battery terminal stud nut from rectifier bridge. Remove rectifier bridge, terminal stud, and insulating washer from end frame. On 27-S1 Series alternators, remove 2 ground screws, a connector strap screw, and the battery terminal stud nut. Remove rectifier bridge, connector, terminal stud, and insulating washers from end frame.
8. Press bearing from end frame using a tube slightly smaller OD than the bearing. Support the end frame from inside and press bearing from outside toward the inside.

NOTE: Some models may have a seal separate and in front of bearing. Discard the seal when replacing the bearing as the new bearing has an integral seal.

9. To separate the drive end frame from rotor place the rotor in a vise and tighten only enough to permit pulley nut removal. Rotor may be distorted if vise is over tightened. Remove pulley nut, washer, pulley, fan, and collar from rotor shaft. Remove drive end frame from rotor shaft and remove rotor from vise.
10. Press bearing from drive end frame after removing bearing retainer plate. Remove screws attaching bearing seal and retainer assembly to housing. Support end frame from inside the housing on a metal tube with a slightly larger ID than the OD of the bearing. Press bearing and grease slinger (or flat washer used on some models) from end frame using a metal tube or collar against the grease slinger.
11. To assemble, reverse the order of the disassembly procedure. Torque the pulley nut to 50 ft. lbs.

NOTE: During the assembly, do not interchange the ground screw (without insulator) for an insulated screw as this would cause uncontrolled or no alternator output.

Cleaning and Inspection

1. Clean all metal parts, except stator and rotor assemblies, in solvent.

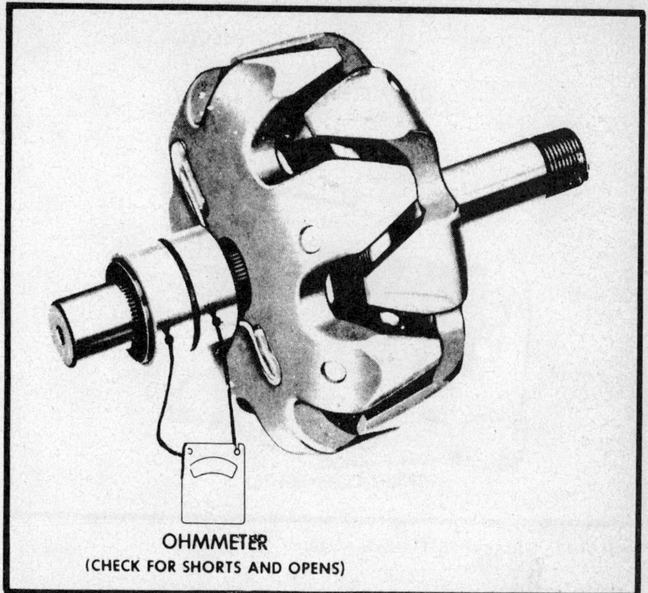

GM charging system checking rotor for grounds or open circuits (© General Motors Corp.)

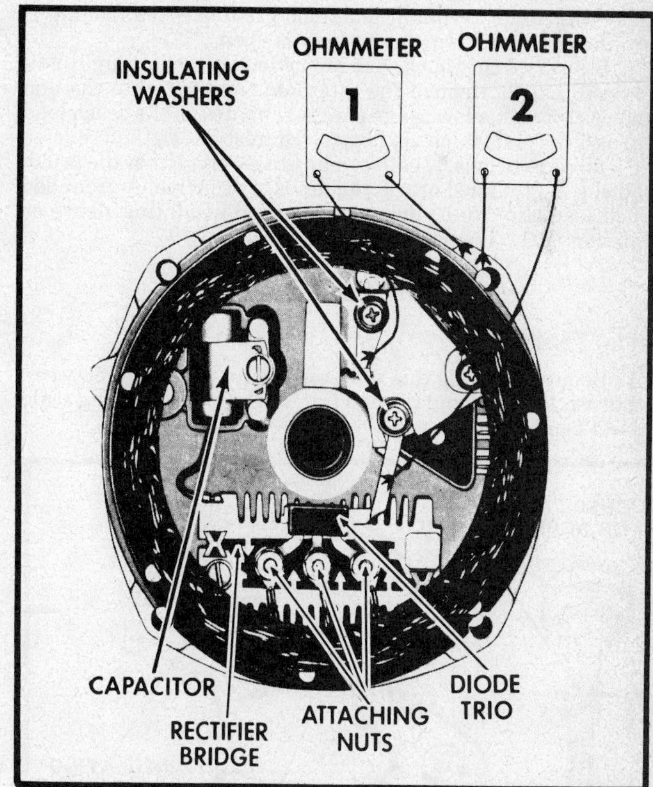

10-SI brush lead clip ground test (© General Motors Corp.)

2. Wipe off bearings and inspect them for pitting or roughness.
3. Inspect rotor slip-rings for scoring. They may be cleaned with 400 grit sandpaper (not emery), rotating the rotor to make the rings concentric. Maximum out of true is 0.001 in. If slip rings are deeply scored, the entire rotor must be replaced as a unit.
4. Inspect brushes for wear minimum length is $\frac{1}{4}$ in.

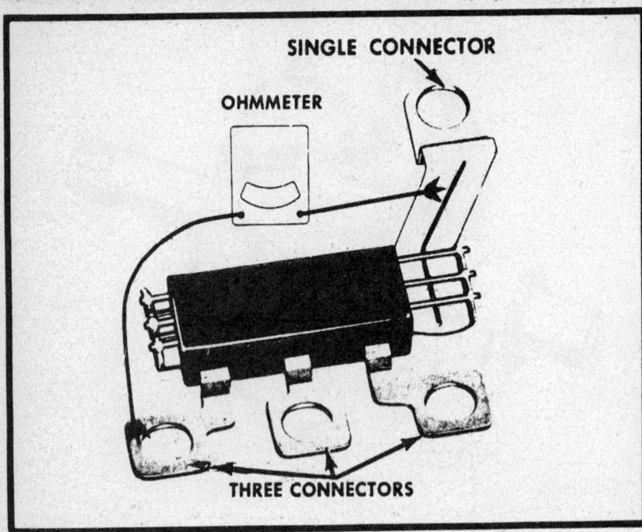

10-SI diode trio test (© General Motors Corp.)

CHARGING SYSTEM TEST

High Charging Rate

1. With the battery fully charged, connect a voltmeter between alternator terminal no. 2 and ground. If the reading is zero, no. 2 circuit from the battery is open.

2. If no. 2 circuit is ok, but an obvious overcharging condition still exists, remove the alternator and separate the end frames. Connect a low range ohmmeter between the brush lead clip and the end frame, as illustrated (test no. 1), then reverse the lead connections. If both readings are zero, either the brush lead clip is grounded or the regulator is defective. A grounded brush lead clip can be due to a damaged insulating sleeve or omission of the insulating washer.

DIODE TRIO

Initial Testing

1. Before removing this unit, connect an ohmmeter between the brush lead clip and the end frame. The lowest reading scale should be used for this test.

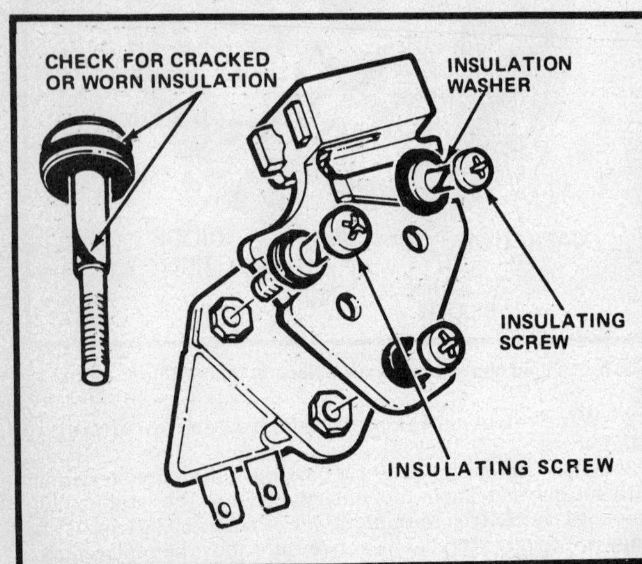

10-SI brush holder (© General Motors Corp.)

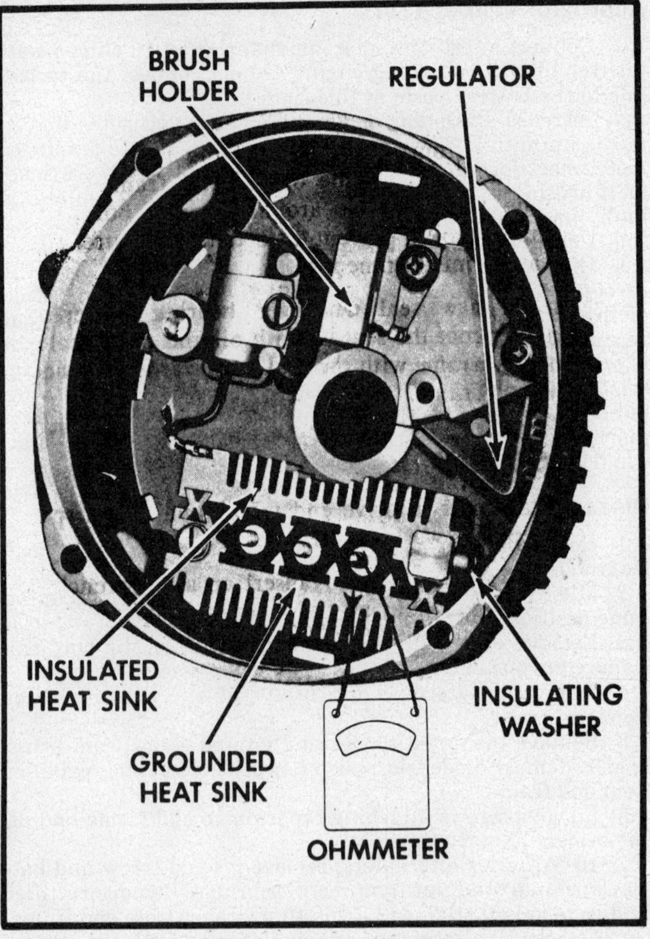

10-SI rectifier bridge testing (© General Motors Corp.)

2. After taking a reading, reverse the lead connections. If the meter reads zero, the brush lead clip is probably grounded, due to omission of the insulating sleeve or insulating washer.

Removal

1. Remove the three nuts which secure the stator.
2. Remove stator.
3. Remove the screw which secures the diode trio lead clip, then remove diode trio.

NOTE: The position of the insulating washer on the screw is critical; make sure it is returned to the same position on reassembly.

Testing

1. Connect an ohmmeter, on lowest range, between the single brush connector and one stator lead connector.

2. Observe the reading, then reverse the meter leads. Repeat this test with each of the other two stator lead connectors. The readings on each of these tests should not be identical, there should be one low and one high reading for each test. If this is not the case, replace the diode trio. Do not use high voltage on the diode trio.

RECTIFIER BRIDGE

Testing

1. Connect an ohmmeter between the heat sink (ground) and the base of one of the three terminals. Then, reverse the

meter leads and take a reading. If both readings are identical, the bridge is defective and must be replaced.

2. Repeat this test with the remaining two terminals, then between the insulated heat sink (as opposed to the grounded heat sink in previous test) and each of the three terminals. As before, if any two readings are identical, on reversing the meter leads, the rectifier bridge must be replaced.

Removal

1. Remove the attaching screw and the BAT. terminal screw.
2. Disconnect the condenser lead.
3. Remove the rectifier bridge. The insulator between the insulated heat sink and the end frame is extremely important to the operation of the unit. It must be replaced in exactly the same position on reassembly.

BRUSH AND/OR VOLTAGE REGULATOR

Assembly and Disassembly

1. Remove two brush holder screws and stator lead to strap nut and washer, brush holder screws and one of the diode trio lead strap attaching screws.

NOTE: The insulating washers must be replaced in the same position on reassembly.

2. Remove brush holder and brushes. The voltage regulator may also be removed at this time, if desired.
3. Brushes and brush spring must be free of corrosion and must be undamaged and completely free of oil or grease.
4. Insert spring and brushes into holder, noting whether they slide freely without binding. Insert wooden or plastic toothpick into bottom hole in holder to retain brushes.

NOTE: The brush holder is serviced as a unit; individual parts are not available.

5. Reassemble in reverse order of disassembly.

Delotron 27-S1 Series, Type 200

The 27-S1 Series, type 200 alternator features a solid state voltage regulator that is mounted inside the slip ring end frame. The regulated voltage can be adjusted externally by repositioning a voltage adjustment cap located on the slip ring end frame. Two brushes carry current through the two slip rings to the field coil, mounted on the rotor. The stator windings are assembled on the inside of a laminated core that forms part of the frame. A rectifier bridge connected to the stator windings contains six diodes, their main function is to change the stator A.C. current to a D.C. current which is present at the output terminal. Field current is supplied through residual magnetism and a diode trio, which is also connected to the stator windings. A capacitor (or condensor) is mounted in the end frame to protect the rectifier bridge and diode trio from high voltages and also suppresses radio noise. An "R" terminal is provided to operate auxiliary equipment in some circuit.

ALTERNATOR OUTPUT TEST

To test the output of the alternator in a bench test stand, have a fully charged battery and connect an ammeter between the battery positive post (on negative grounded units) and the battery terminal of the alternator. Connect a voltmeter to the positive and negative posts of the battery. Ground the battery negative post to the alternator frame or to a common ground.

NOTE: Rotor magnetism must be present in this alternator to perform properly. If the alternator has been disassembled for service, it may be necessary to induce magnetism back into the rotor to provide voltage build up when the engine is started. To magnetize the rotor, connect the integral charging system to the battery in a normal manner, then momentarily connect a jumper lead from the battery positive post to the integral charging system relay terminal. This procedure will restore normal residual magnetism in the rotor.

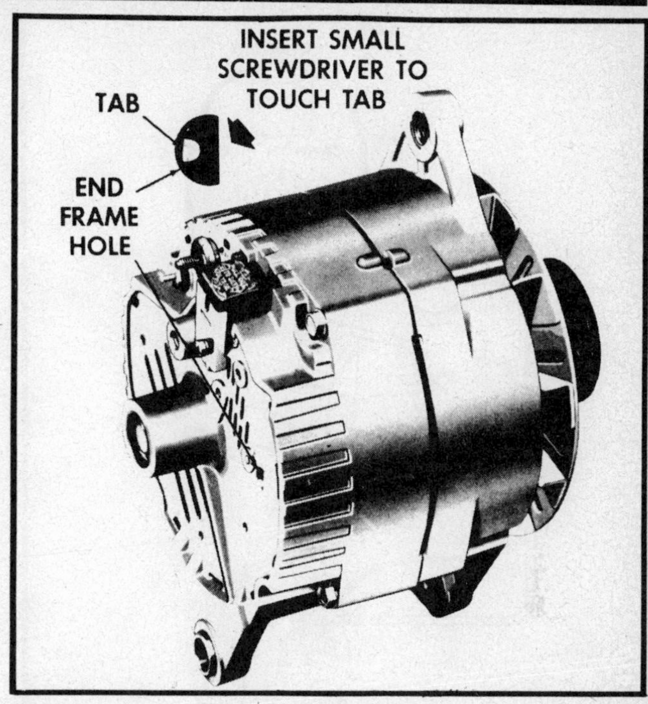

27-SI type 200 field tab location (© General Motors Corp.)

1. After making the required meter connections between the alternator and the battery on the test stand, proceed as follows.
2. Slowly increase the alternator speed and observe the voltage.
3. If the voltage is uncontrolled with speed and increases over 15.5 volts on a 12 volt system, test the regulator. The regulator can be tested on a commercial tester. If a tester is not available, replace the voltage regulator.
4. If the voltage is below 15.5 volts on a 12 volt system, connect a carbon pile rheostat to the battery. Operate the alternator at a moderate speed and adjust the rheostat as required to obtain the maximum current output.
5. If the output is within 10 amperes of the rated output as stamped on the alternator frame, the alternator is good.
6. If the output is not within 10 amperes of the rated output, keep the battery loaded with the carbon pile and ground the tab in the end frame hole. The tab is within $^3/_4$ in. of the casting surface. Do not force the probe tool deeper than one inch into the end frame.
7. Operate the alternator at moderate speed and adjust the carbon pile rheostat as required to obtain maximum output, with the tab pushed in to ground.
8. If the output is not within 10 amperes of the rated output, check the field winding, diode trio, rectifier bridge and stator.
9. Stop the unit and disconnect the various test meters from the alternator and make necessary repairs or tests.

ELECTRICAL TESTS

NOTE: The electrical tests are made in the same manner as the tests for the 10-S1 and 27-S1, type 100 alternators with the exception of the following.

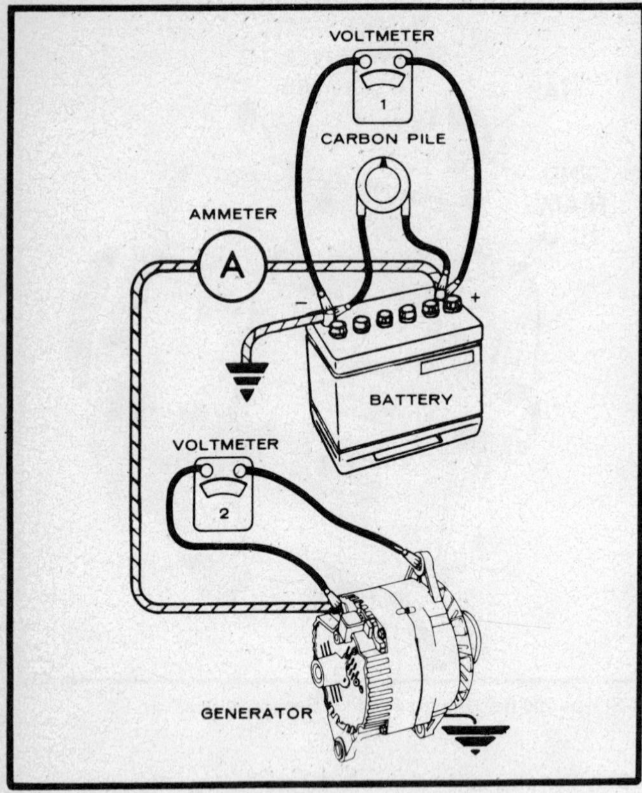

27-SI type 200 bench test connections for checking alternator output (© General Motors Corp.)

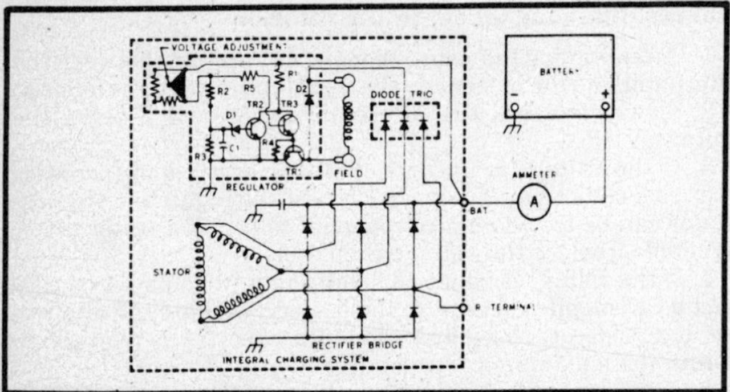

27-SI type 200 wiring schematic (© General Motors Corp.)

1. The Delta windings of the stator cannot be checked for open circuits.

2. The regulator can be checked with a commercial tester and the connector cap can be checked with an ohmmeter. Check the connector body with the ohmmeter in the middle range scale. Connect the ohmmeter to each adjacent pair of terminals, making four checks in all. If any one check is infinite, replace the connector body.

VOLTAGE ADJUSTMENT

A four positioned cap (connector body), is used to regulate the desired increase or decrease of voltage by removing the cap from its seat and rotating in 90 degree increments. Reposition the cap in its seat and align the proper marking on the cap with the indicator arrow on the alternator housing. The cap is marked "LO", "2", "3" and "HI".

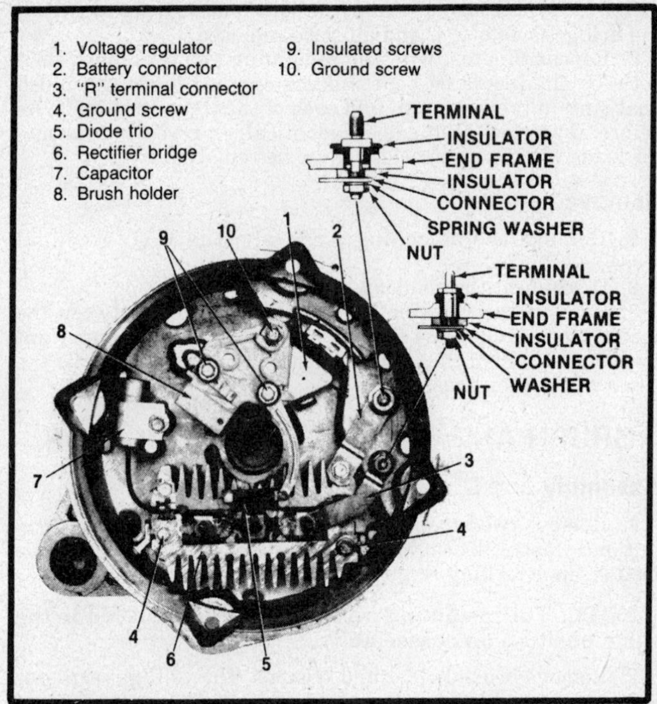

End frame components type 205 shown others typical
(© General Motors Corp.)

Disassembly and Assembly

1. Hold generator in a vice, clamping the mounting flange lengthwise.
2. Make a scribe mark to help locate frame end parts in the same position during assembly.
3. Remove 4 through bolts and separate the slip ring end frame from the drive end frame and rotor assembly.
4. Remove 3 stator lead attaching nuts and separate stator from end frame.
5. Remove 3 screws from brush holder and disconnect regulator lead from regulator. Remove diode trio and brush holder. Then lift regulator and unplug it from the voltage adjustment connector body.
6. Remove screw and clip attaching the connector body to the end frame. Pull connector body from end frame.
7. Remove screws attaching capacitor to end frame and diode rectifier bridge.
8. Remove 2 ground screws attaching diode bridge to end frame. Then disconnect the "R" terminal and battery terminal connectors from the bridge and end frame. Remove rectifier bridge from end frame.
9. Press bearing from end frame using a tube with a slightly smaller OD than the bearing. Support the end frame from inside and press bearing from outside toward the inside. Some models have a seal separate and in front of bearing. Discard the seal when replacing the bearing as the new bearing has an integral seal.
10. Separate drive end frame from rotor by placing the rotor in a vise and tighten only enough to permit pulley nut removal. Rotor may be distorted if vise is over tightened. Remove pulley nut, washer, pulley, fan, and slinger collar from rotor shaft. Remove drive end frame and rear collar from rotor shaft and remove rotor from vise.
11. Press bearing from drive end frame after removing bearing retainer plate. Remove screws attaching bearing seal and retainer assembly to housing. Support end frame from inside the housing on a metal tube slightly larger ID than the OD of

the bearing. Press bearing from end frame using a metal tube or collar against the bearing inner race.

12. The assembly is in the reverse order of the disassembly. Tighten the pulley nut to 75 ft. lbs. Do not interchange the ground screw (without insulator) for an insulated screw as this may cause uncontrolled or no alternator output.

Delcotron 27-S1 Series, Type 205

The type 205, 27-S1 series is basically the same as the type 200, but with internal wiring changes. A recognizable feature of this alternator from the outside is the splined rotor shaft extending from the rear of the end housing. The regulator voltage setting is not adjustable and the rotor field windings do not rely on residual magnetism to excite the field circuit to begin the charging cycle. The initial field current is supplied through an indicator light circuit with connectors engaging their respective terminals at the end frame housing. The 27S1-205 generators are used with the Deutz air-cooled diesel. Both 65A and 80A models are similar to those used on gas engine vehicles except for the inclusion of a vacuum pump.

TEST SPECIFICATIONS

	Field Current	Output Amps @ rpm
65A	4.4–4.9	55 @ 2000
		68 @ 7000
80A	4.4–4.9	52 @ 2000
		72 @ 5000

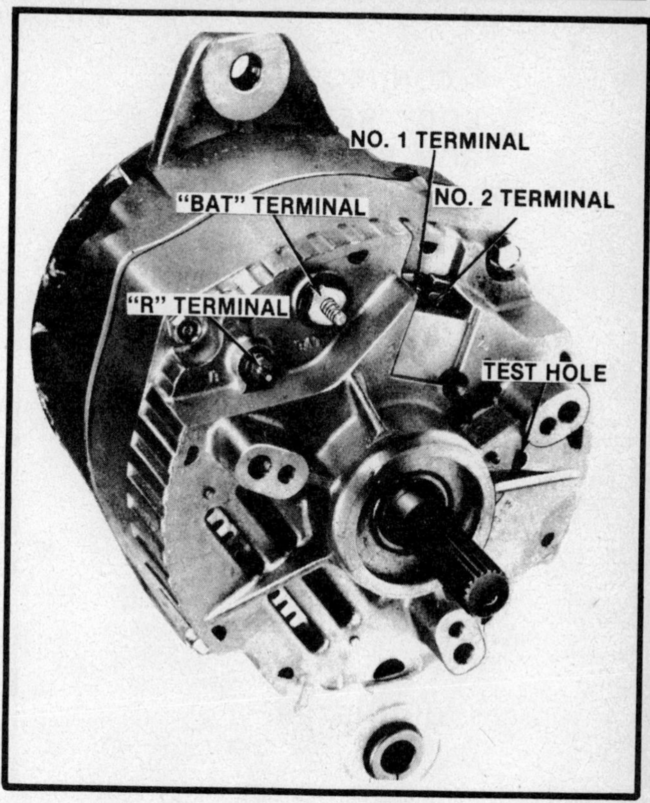

27-SI type 205 wiring terminal position on end frame (© General Motors Corp.)

ELECTRICAL TESTS

The electrical tests of the internal components are basically the same as the tests performed on the type 200 components.

Disassembly and Assembly

The disassembly and assembly is typical of the 27-S1 series.

Delcotron 40-S1 Series, Type 150

The alternator features a fully adjustable built in, solid state voltage regulator and six silicone diodes mounted in heat sinks, to convert the alternating current, produced in the Delta wound stator, to direct current. The unit uses a capacitor to assist in suppressing transient voltage which could effect diode operation. A diode trio is used to supply field current to the rotor.

TROUBLESHOOTING

NOTE: Refer to the "Alternator test plans" section before proceeding with any alternator tests. Because of the high output of amperage that can be produced, extreme care must be exercised in the testing and handling of these units.

CHARGING SYSTEM TESTS

High and Low Rated Output

1. After checking the battery condition drive belt tension, and wiring terminals, charge the battery fully and perform the following tests.

2. Disconnect the negative battery cable and connect an am-

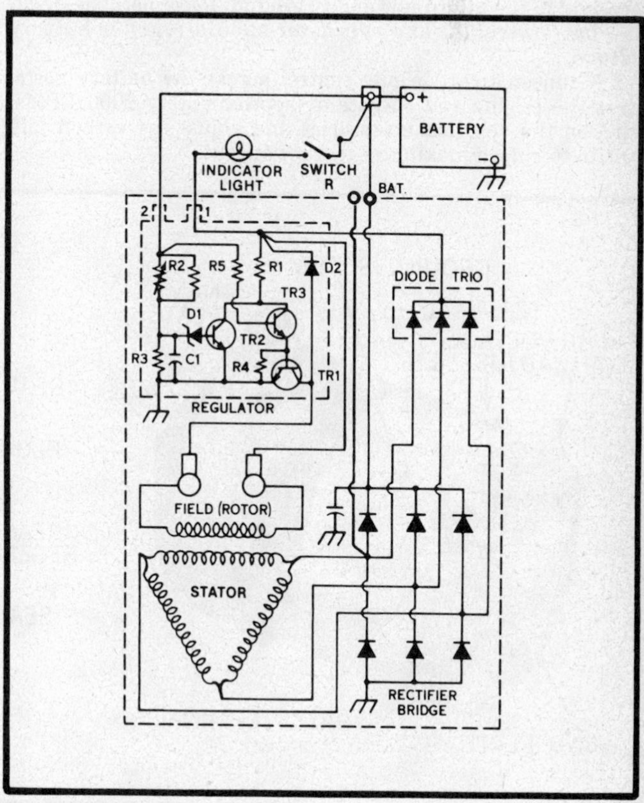

27-SI type 205 wiring schematic (© General Motors Corp.)

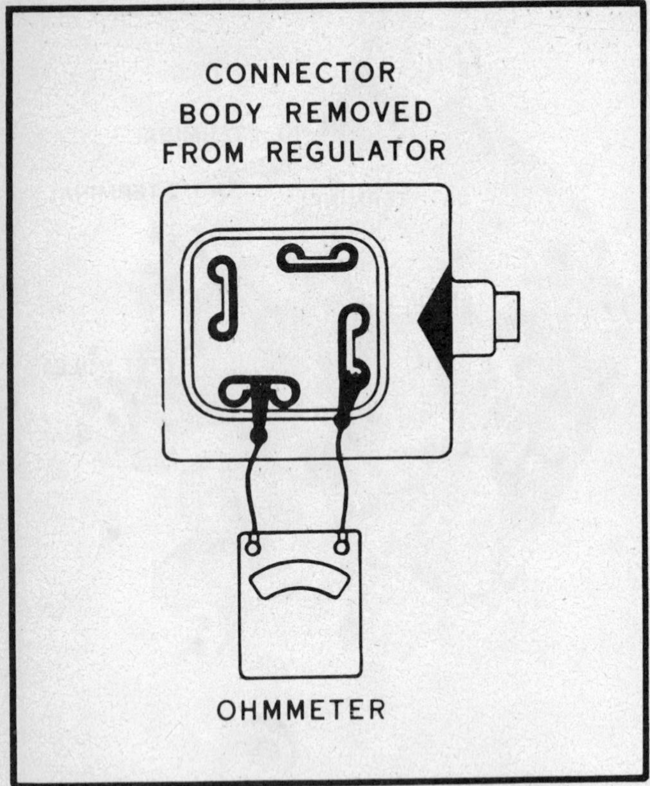

Checking connector body with ohmeter—typical
(© General Motors Corp.)

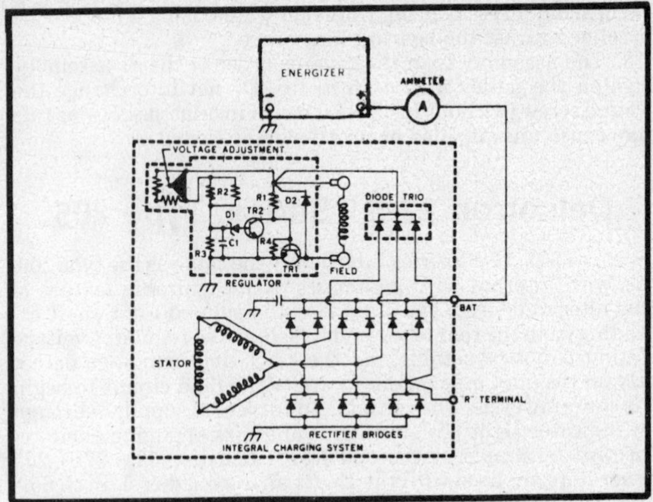

40-SI Charging circuit (© General Motors Corp.)

meter between the positive battery post and the battery terminal of the alternator. Connect a voltmeter between the battery terminal of the alternator and to ground. Reconnect the negative battery cable. The voltmeter should register battery voltage.

3. Connect a carbon pile control across the battery posts. Start the engine and operate at approximately 2000 RPMs. Turn on the vehicles' accessories and adjust the carbon pile control to obtain maximum current output.

4. If the amperage reading is within 10% of the rated output, the alternator is not defective. If the amperage is not within the 10% range, the alternator should be removed for testing and repairs.

NOTE: With the carbon pile control in the off position, and the engine operating at 2000 RPMs, the voltage reading should increase to 15 volts. If needed, the voltage can be adjusted up or down scale by raising the voltage regulator cap and relocating it in one of the new positions, which are indicated by; LO(low), 2(med.low), 3(med.high), and HI(high). Recheck the voltage reading after movement of the cap.

Disassembly

1. Remove the cover plate from the rear housing.
2. Remove the pulley nut, pulley, fan, slinger, and spacer collar.
3. Remove the four through bolts. Separate the rear housing from the stator and drive end frame by inserting a suitable tool

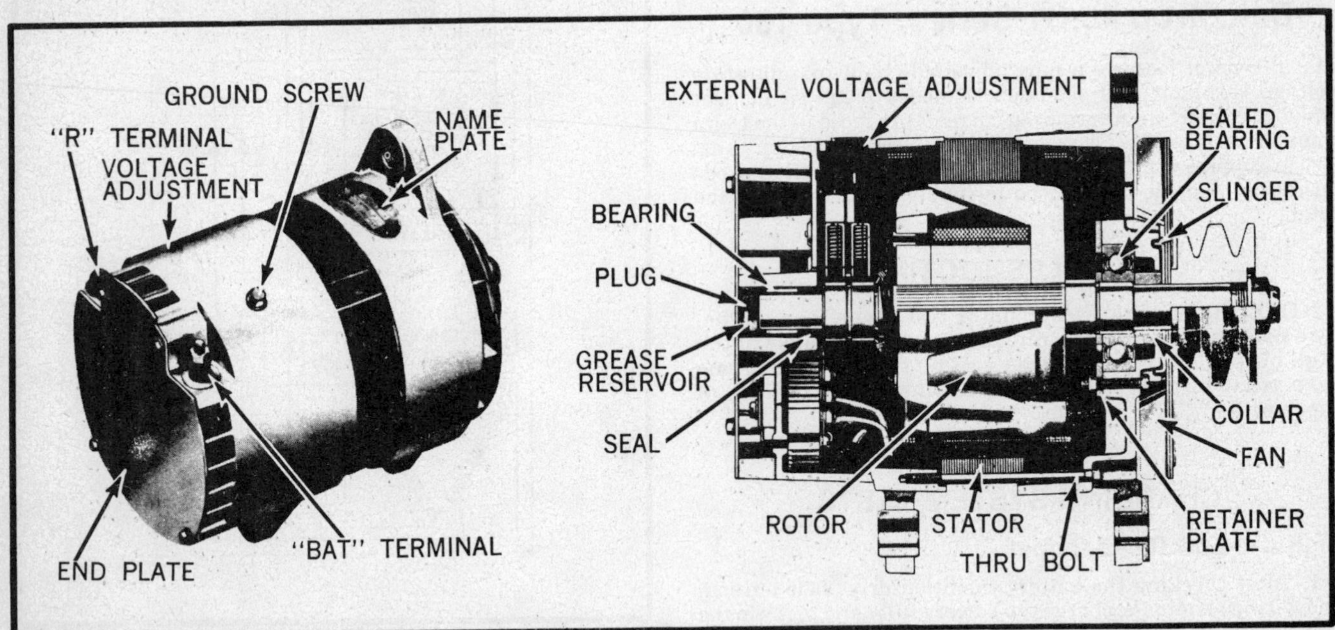

40-SI typical 100 amp alternator (© General Motors Corp.)

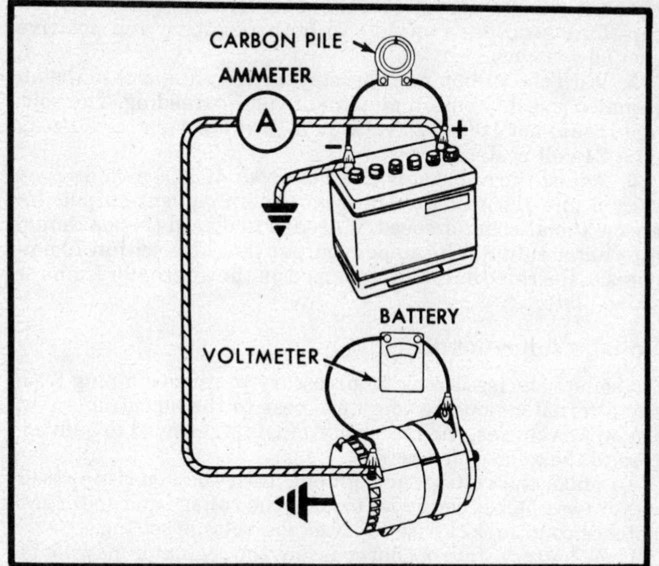

40-SI test connections (© General Motors Corp.)

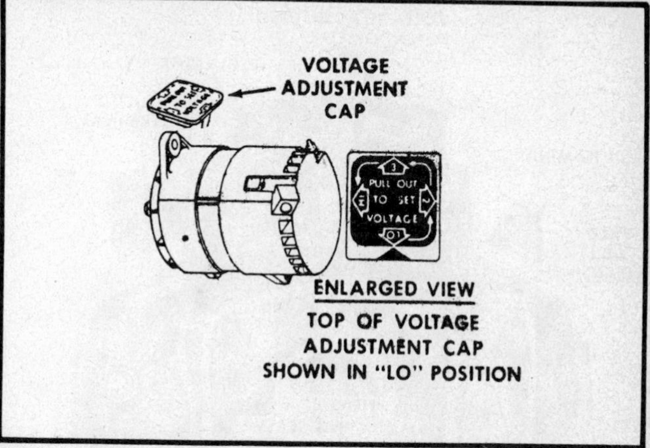

40-SI voltage adjustment cap (© General Motors Corp.)

in the stator slots. Expect the brushes to fall from their holders. Do not break them.

4. Disconnect the stator leads from the rectifier bridge and remove the stator from the frame.

Testing

Follow the procedure for testing the diode trio, rectifiers, stator, and rotor as outlined under the 10SL alternator section. The field current specifications are 4.0 to 4.5 amperes at 12 volts.

Assembly

1. Install brushes into their holders and insert a wire to hold them in place.
2. Assemble the three stator wire leads to the rectifier bridges.
3. Assemble the drive end frame and rotor into the stator and rectifier end frame assembly carefully so as not to damage the seal. Install the four through bolts and tighten.
4. Assemble the collar spacer, slinger, fan, and pulley. While holding the rotor shaft, torque the pulley nut to 72 ft. lbs.
5. Release the brushes by removing the wire from the holder. Install the end plate cover. Rotate the rotor assembly to insure that no windings or wires contact the rotor surface.

Delcotron 25-S1 Series, Type 400

The 25-S1 series is a 12 volt, self rectifying, brushless unit, equipped with a built in voltage regulator. The only movable part is the rotor, which is mounted on roller and ball bearings. All the current carrying conductors are stationary, which includes the field windings, the stator windings, the six rectifying diodes and the regulator circuit components. The regulator and rectifying diodes are enclosed in a common sealed compartment.

The unit can be used with either negative or positive grounded circuits. The specially designed output terminals are color coded and used as follows. The red output terminal is used for the positive battery wire when used with a negative grounded system. The black output terminal is used for the negative battery wire when used with a positive grounded system. An "R" terminal is provided for use to operate auxiliary equipment as required.

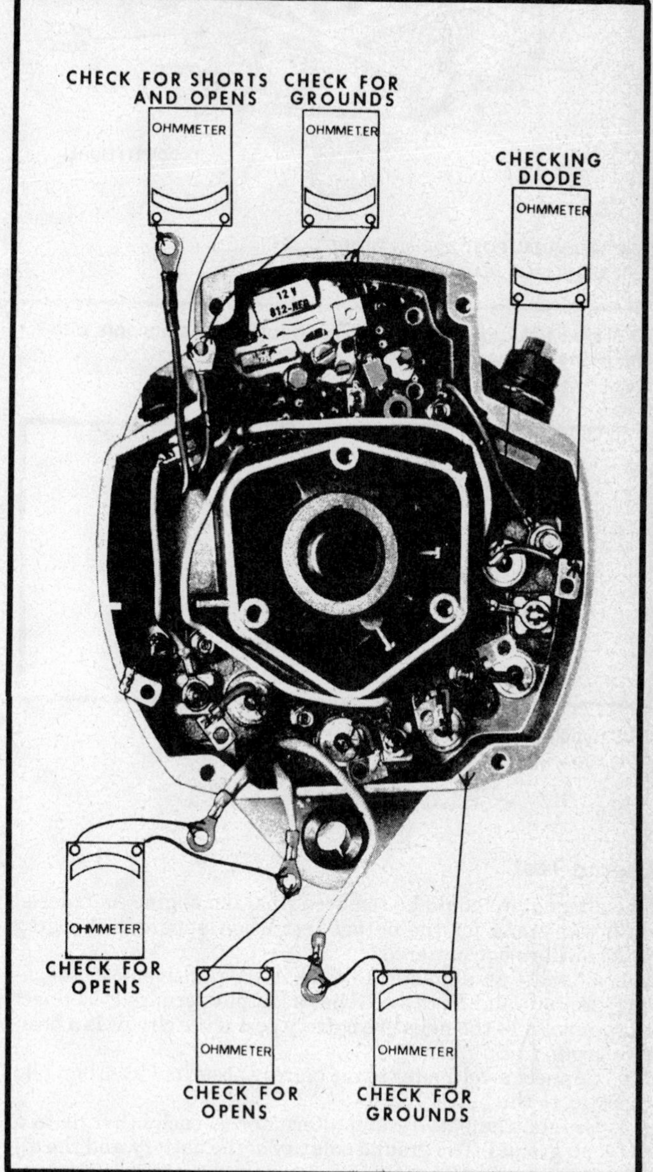

25-SI type 400 electrical test connections using an ohmmeter (© General Motors Corp.)

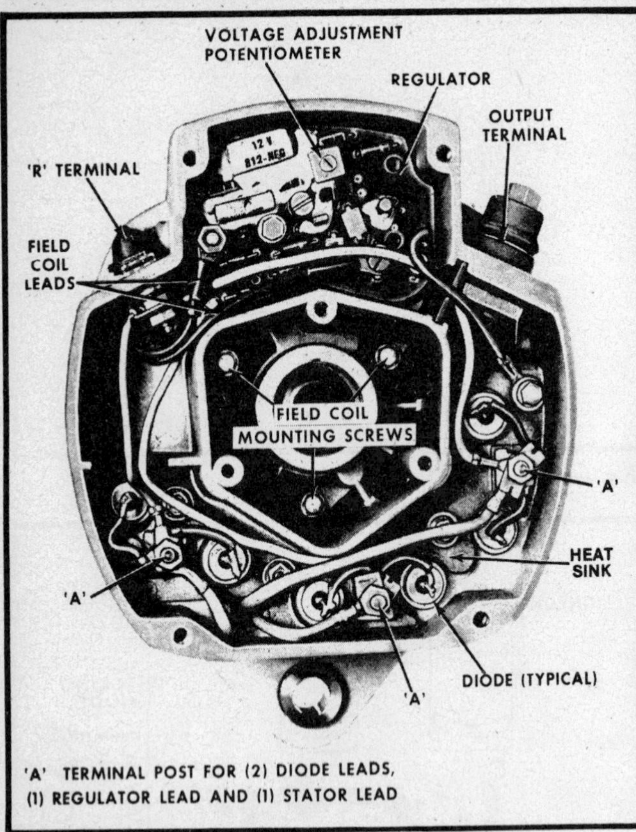

25-SI type 400 location of wiring and electrical components with end frame removed (© General Motors Corp.)

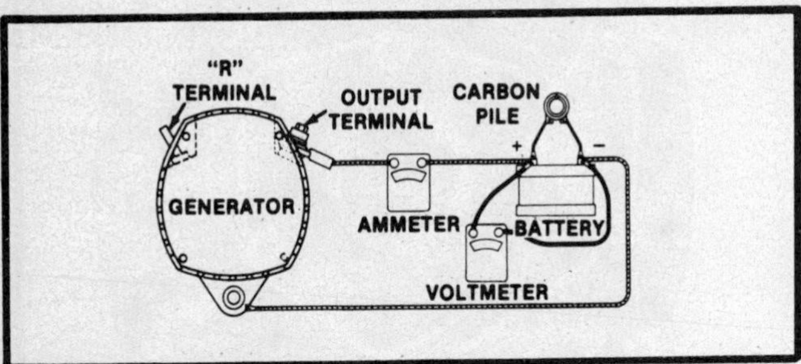

25-SI type 400 test connections for output test (© General Motors Corp.)

ELECTRICAL TESTS

Output Test

The alternator should be removed from the engine and placed on a test stand for the output test when apparent charging problems are encountered.

1. Connect an ammeter to the battery positive post, (negative ground) and to the alternator output terminal. Connect the ammeter to the negative battery post if the circuit is a positive ground.
2. Connect a voltmeter to the battery posts and a carbon pile rheostat to the battery posts.
3. Ground the battery and alternator to each other or to a common ground. The ground polarity of the battery and the alternator must be the same.
4. To restore the normal residual magnetism in the rotor, momentarily connect a jumper lead from the battery connected alternator output terminal to the relay terminal of the alternator. This procedure applies to both negative and positive ground systems.
5. With the carbon pile rheostat turned off, increase the alternator speed to obtain maximum voltage reading. The voltage should not exceed 15 volts on a 12 volt system, or 30 volts on a 24 volt system.
6. Adjust the alternator speed to about 4000 rpm and adjust carbon pile rheostat to obtain maximum current output. Increase the alternator speed, if needed to obtain the maximum alternator output. The ampere output should be within 10 amperes of the rated output as stamped on the alternator frame or name plate.

Voltage Adjustment

On some vehicles it may be necessary to remove a plug from the alternator housing to gain access to the adjusting screw. On other vehicles, the rear cover must be removed to gain access to the adjusting screw.

To make the voltage adjustment, turn the adjusting screw one or two notches clockwise to raise the voltage and one or two notches counterclockwise to lower the voltage setting.

If the battery state of charge is low, the regulator may not be limiting the voltage and turning the adjusting screw will show no change on the voltmeter. However, turning the adjusting screw will change the voltage setting to a new value, which will be indicated by the voltmeter as the battery state of charge increases.

Component Test

Before proceeding with the following tests, remove the rectifier end frame plate, cover and gasket. Disconnect the field coil leads from the regulator and the diode and stator leads from the heat sink terminal posts.

Field Coil

To check for ground, connect a test lamp, or an ohmmeter to one field coil lead and to the end frame. If the lamp lights, or if ohmmeter reading is low, the field coil is grounded.

To check for opens, connect a test lamp, or an ohmmeter to the two field coil leads as shown. If the lamp fails to light, or if ohmmeter reading is high (infinite), the field coil is open.

The winding is checked for short circuits by connecting a battery and ammeter in series with the field coil. Note the ammeter reading. An ammeter reading above the specified value indicates shorted windings. An alternate method is to check the resistance of the field by connecting an ohmmeter to the field coil. If the resistance reading is below the specified value, the winding is shorted. The specified resistance value can be determined by dividing the voltage by the current.

Stator

The stator windings may be checked with a 110 volt test lamp or an ohmmeter. If the lamp lights, or if the meter reading is low when connected from any stator lead to the frame, the windings are grounded.

If the lamp fails to light, or if the meter reading is high when successively connected between each pair of stator leads, the windings are open. A short circuit in the stator windings is difficult to locate without laboratory test equipment due to the low resistance of the windings. However, if all other electrical checks are normal and the generator fails to supply rated output, shorted stator windings are indicated.

To replace the stator, separate drive end frame from rectifier end frame, and pull leads and grommet through hole. Place grease on grommet and pull into hole during assembly.

Rectifier Diodes

Check each of the six diodes by connecting an ohmmeter using the lowest range scale to the diode lead and case. Then reverse

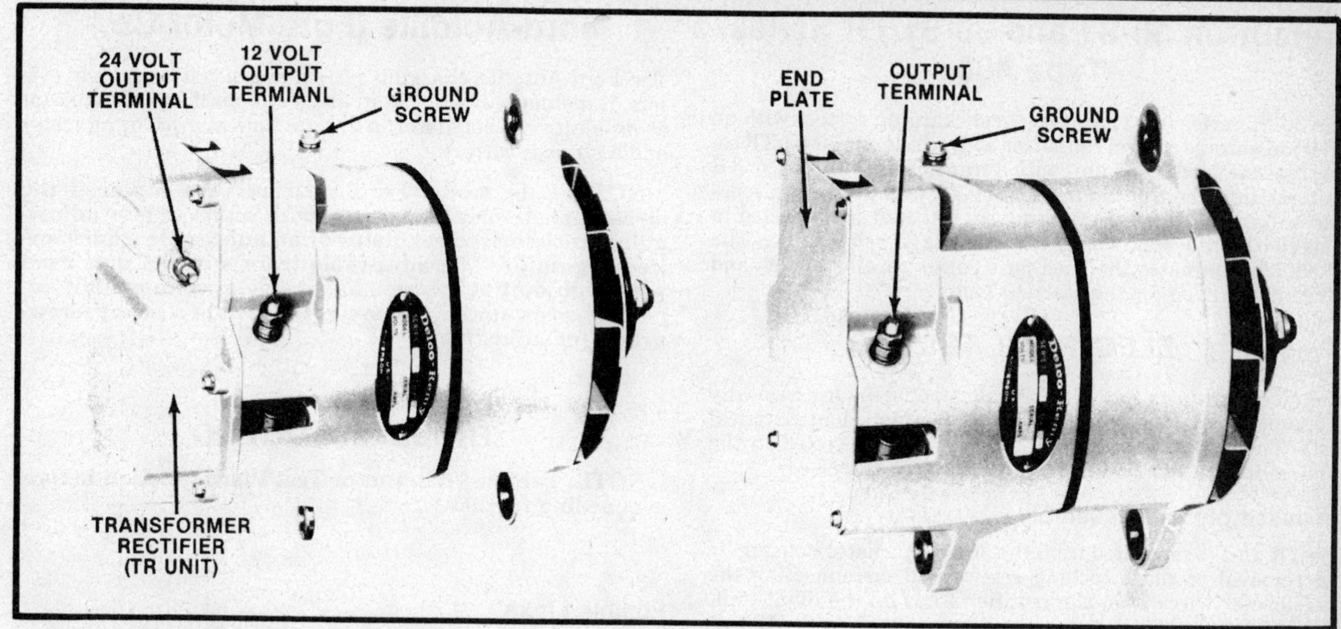

Side views of the 30-SI and the 30-SI/TR alternators (© General Motors Corp.)

the ohmmeter lead connections to the diode lead and case. If both readings are the same, replace the diode. A good diode will give one high and one low reading. Do not use high voltage such as 110 volt test lamps, to check diodes. This could damage the diodes.

Voltage Regulator Checks and Repairs

Two different voltage regulator boards are used on the early and the later model alternators. Seven components of the boards are serviceable and replacement parts should be available for them. However, should difficulty be encountered in obtaining the parts, the entire board should be replaced.

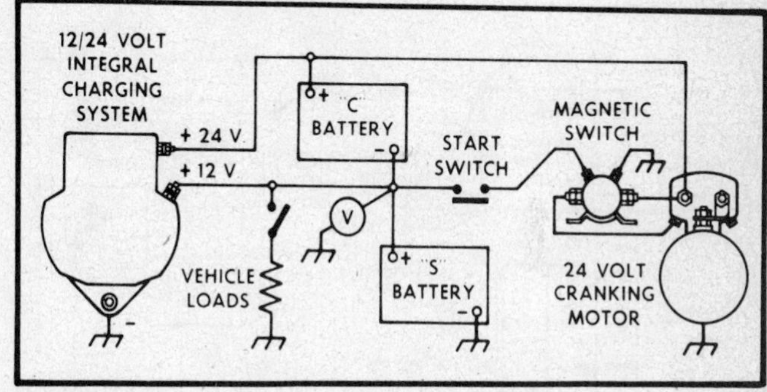

30-SI/TR wiring schematic (© General Motors Corp.)

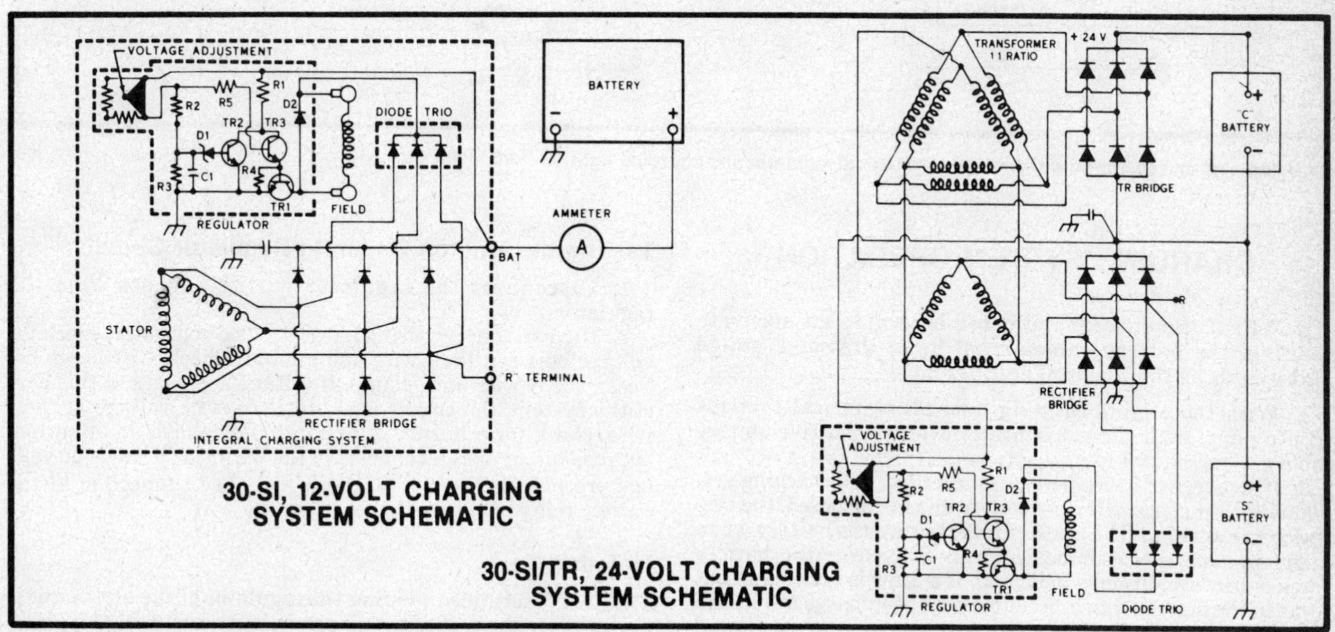

30-SI and 30-SI/TR wiring schematics (© General Motors Corp.)

Delcotron 30-S1 and 30-S1/TR Series, Type 400

The 30-S1 series is a 12 volt integral charging system with an external voltage control connector body, while the 30-S1/TR series is a standard 30-S1 unit with a transformer rectifier, or TR unit, mounted on the end frame. The TR unit provides a separate voltage to charge a cranking battery that is connected in series with the system's battery to provide 24 volt starting. The 30-S1/TR eliminates the need for a series parallel switch and associated wiring for the starting motor.

ELECTRICAL TESTS

The electrical tests for the internal components are basically the same as the Delcotron 27-SI, type 200 component electrical tests. The TR unit's rectifier bridge diodes are tested in the same manner as the 30-SI series alternator diodes.

Disassembly and Assembly

The TR unit is separated from the 30-SI alternator housing by the removal of the attaching screws and disconnecting the transformer wires from the rectifier studs on the 30-SI unit. The TR rectifier bridge connection is removed from the 12 volt heat sink on the 30-SI rectifier bridge. The assembly of the TR unit is in the reverse of the removal procedure.

Ford-Autolite (Ford Motor Co.)

The Ford-Autolite charging system is a negative ground system. It includes an alternator, an electro mechanical regulator or an electronic regulator, a charge indicator or an ammeter and a storage battery.

NOTE: Late model Ford systems have replaced the electro mechanical regulator with either a non adjustable transistorized regulator or an adjustable transistorized regulator. The adjustable transistorized unit used with high output systems has a single, voltage limit adjusting screw under the cover. Do not use a metal screwdriver for adjustment.

TROUBLESHOOTING

NOTE: See the "Alternator Test Plans" section before proceeding further.

Fusible Links

Check the fusible link located between the starter relay and the alternator. Replace the link if it is burned or open.

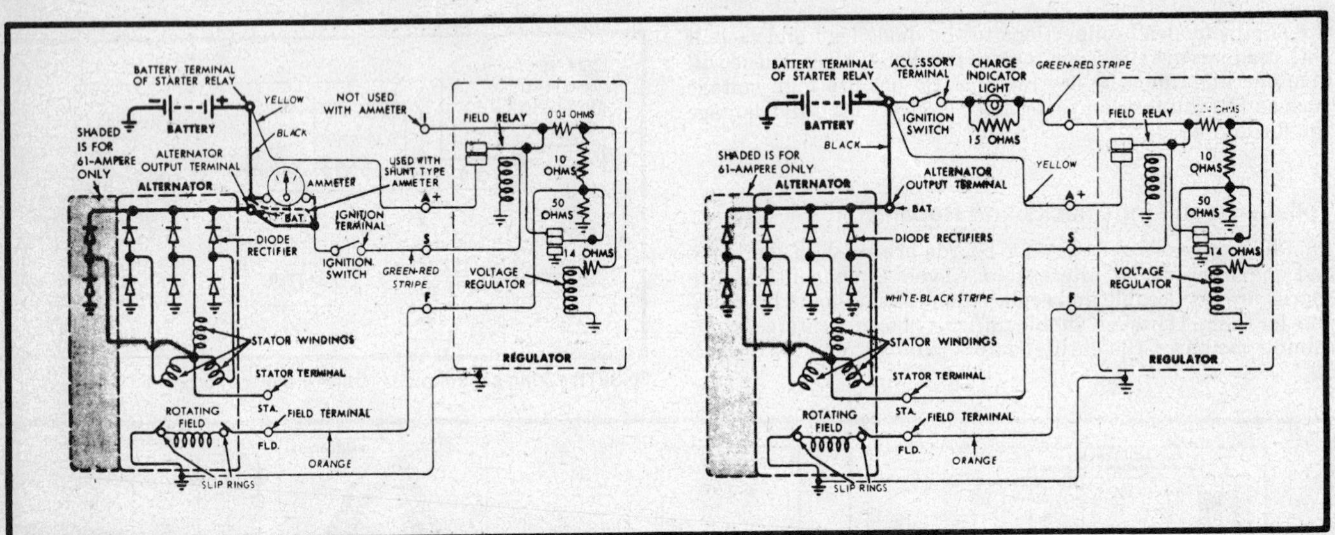

Charging system schematic with electro mechanical regulator and charging light (© Ford Motor Co.)

CHARGING SYSTEM OPERATION

NOTE: If the current indicator is to give an accurate reading, the battery cables must be of the same gauge and length as the original equipment.

1. With the engine running, and all electrical systems turned off, place a current indicator over the positive battery cable.
2. If a charge of about 5 amps is recorded, the charging system is working. If a draw of about 5 amps is recorded, the system is not working. The needle moves toward the battery when a charge condition is indicated, and away from the battery when a draw condition is indicated. If a draw is indicated, continue to the next testing procedure. If an overcharge of 10 to 15 amps is indicated, check for a faulty regulator or a bad ground at the regulator or the alternator.

Testing the Ignition Switch to Regulator Circuit

1. Disconnect the regulator wiring harness from the regulator.
2. Turn on the key. Using a test light or voltmeter, check for voltage between the I wire and ground. Check for voltage between the A wire and ground. If voltage is present at this part of the system, the circuit is ok. If there is no voltage at the I wire, check for a burned out charge indicator bulb, a burned out resistor, or a break or short in the wiring. If there is no voltage present at the A wire, check for a bad connection at the starter relay or a break or short in the wire.

Isolation Test

This test determines whether the regulator or the alternator is faulty, after the rest of the circuit is found to be in good working order.

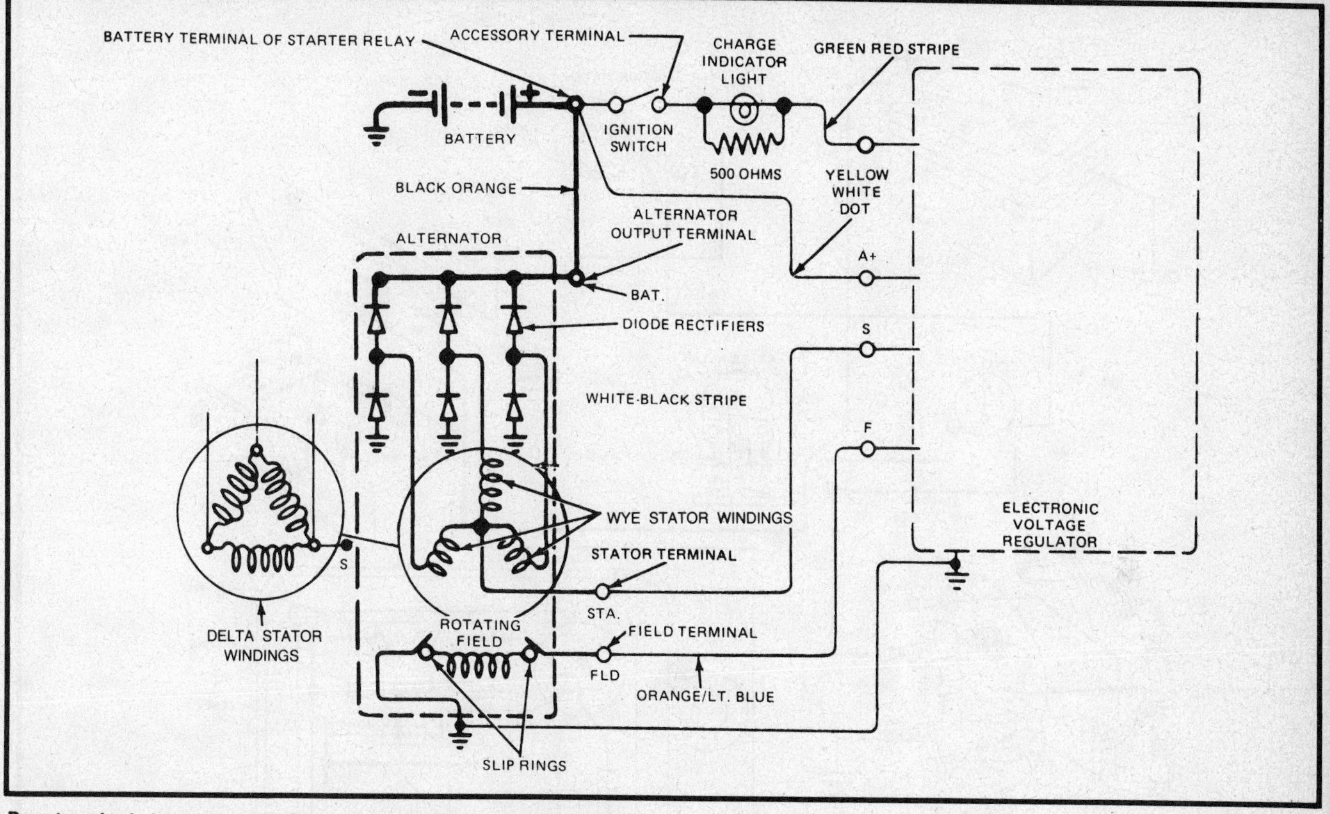

Rear terminal alternator charging system schematic with indicator light—typical of side terminal alternators (© Ford Motor Co.)

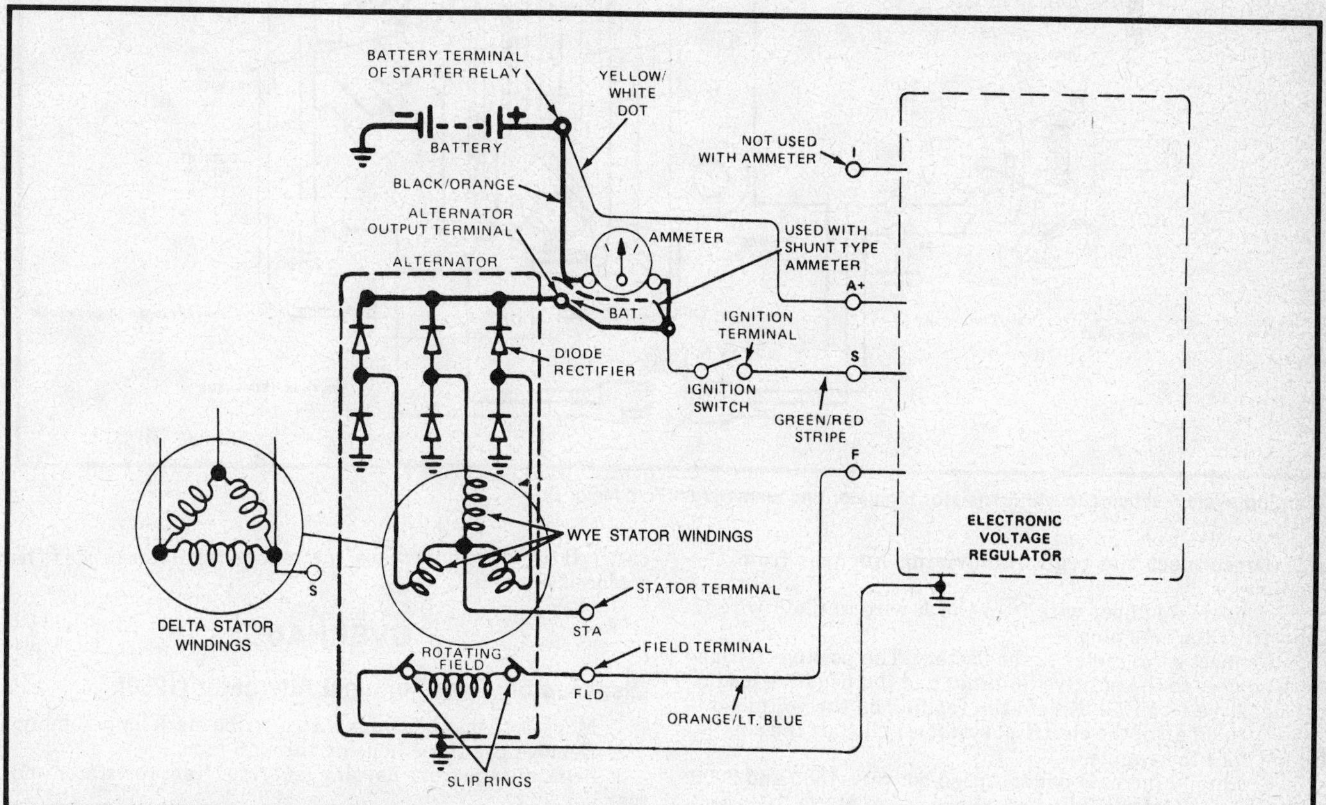

Rear terminal alternator charging system schematic with ammeter—typical of side terminal alternators

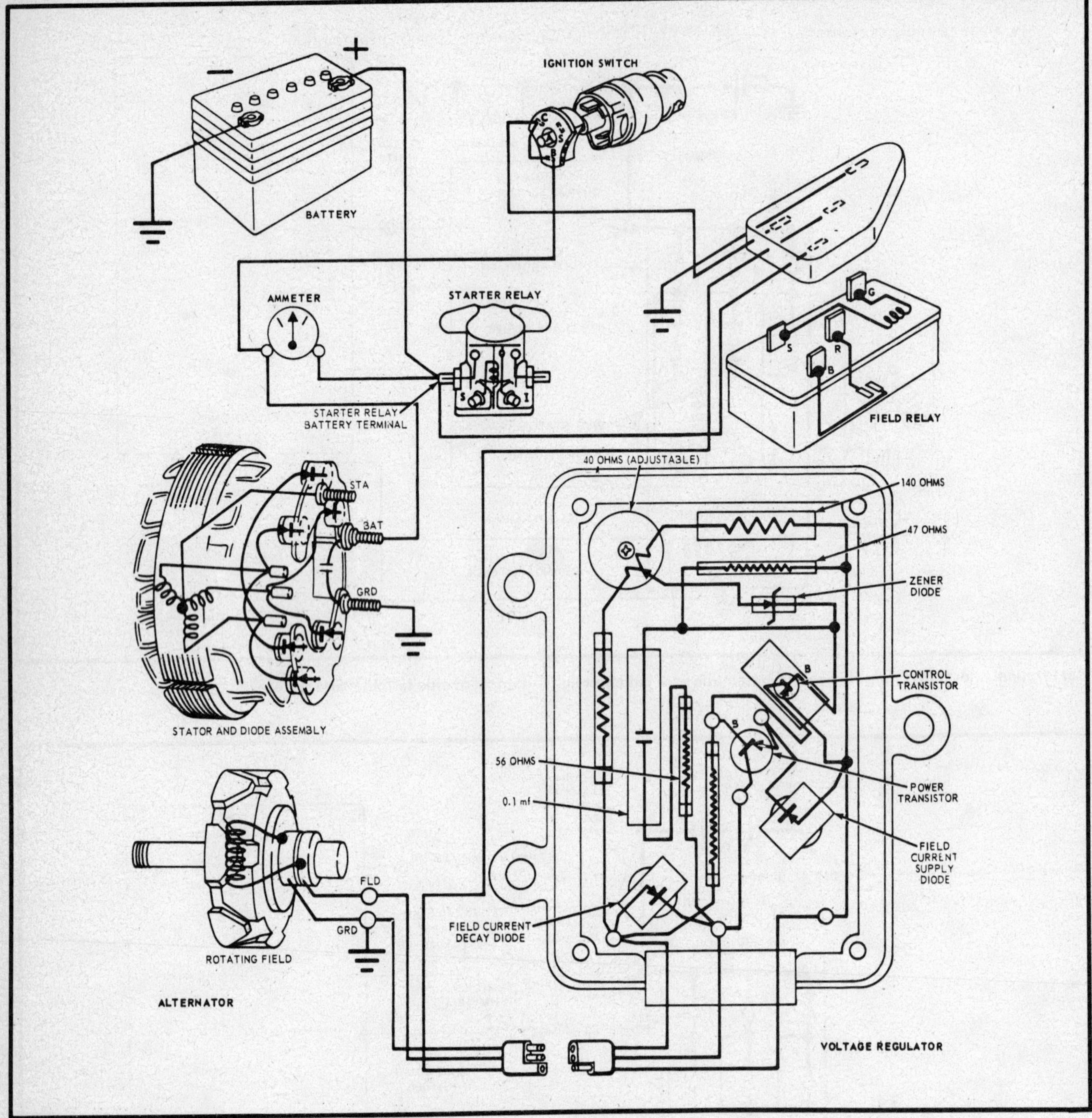

Charging system schematic with transistor regulator and ammeter (© Ford Motor Co.)

1. Disconnect the regulator wiring harness from the regulator.
2. Connect a jumper wire from the A wire to the F wire in the wiring harness plug.
3. Connect a voltmeter to the battery. The positive voltmeter lead goes to the positive terminal and the negative lead to the negative terminal. Record the reading on the voltmeter.
4. Turn off all of the electrical systems and start the engine. Do not race the engine.
5. Gradually increase engine speed between 1500 and 2000 rpm. The voltmeter reading should increase above the previously recorded battery voltage reading by at least one to two volts. If there is no increase, the alternator is not working correctly. If there is an increase, the voltage regulator needs to be replaced.

OVERHAUL

Disassembly Rear Terminal Alternator (1980)

1. Mark both end housings with a scribe mark for assembly.
2. Remove the three housing through bolts.
3. Separate the front housing and rotor from the stator and rear housing.
4. Remove the nuts from the rectifier to rear housing mounting studs, and remove the rear housing.

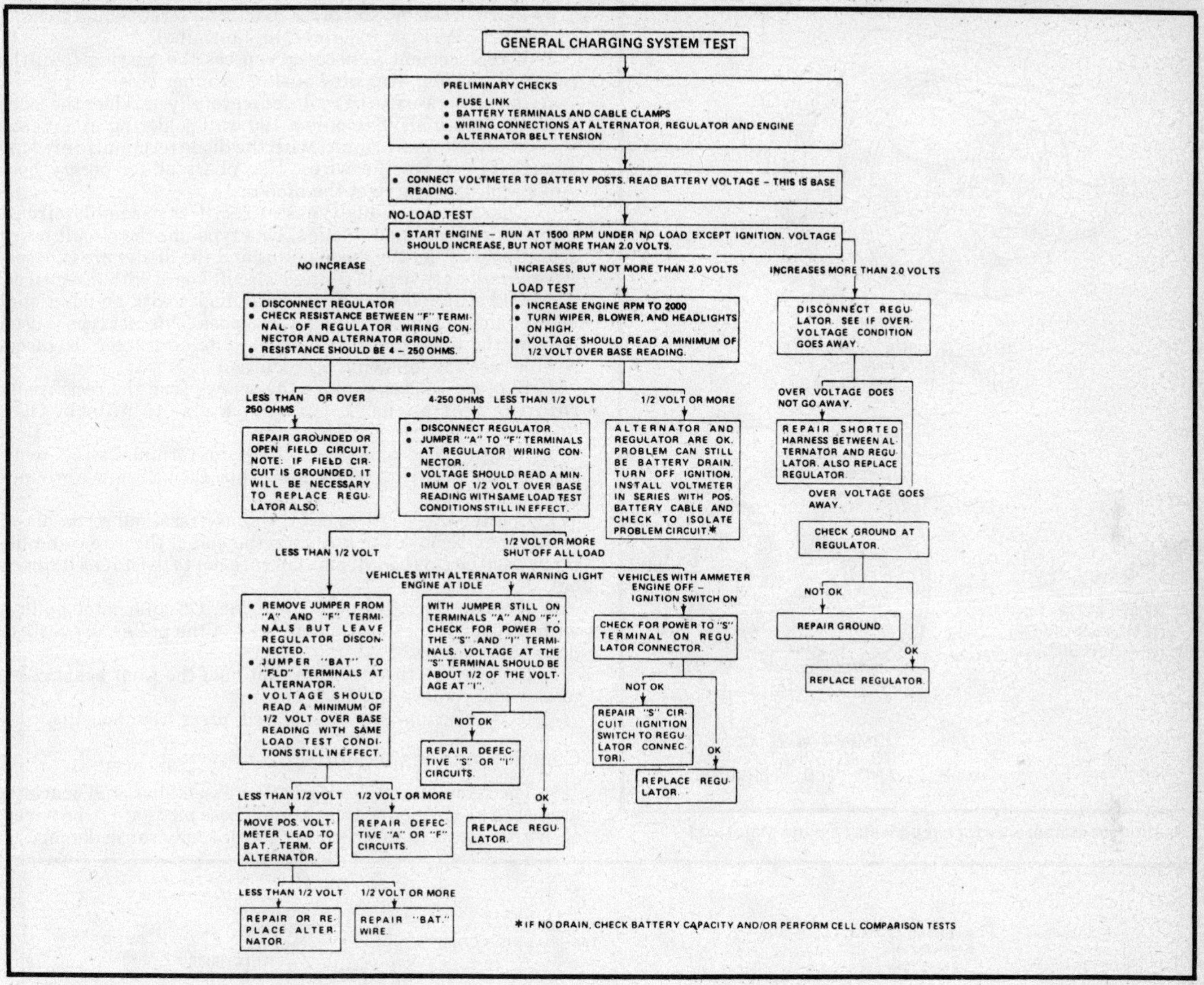

GENERAL CHARGING SYSTEM TEST

PRELIMINARY CHECKS
- FUSE LINK
- BATTERY TERMINALS AND CABLE CLAMPS
- WIRING CONNECTIONS AT ALTERNATOR, REGULATOR AND ENGINE
- ALTERNATOR BELT TENSION

- CONNECT VOLTMETER TO BATTERY POSTS. READ BATTERY VOLTAGE – THIS IS BASE READING.

NO-LOAD TEST
- START ENGINE – RUN AT 1500 RPM UNDER NO LOAD EXCEPT IGNITION. VOLTAGE SHOULD INCREASE, BUT NOT MORE THAN 2.0 VOLTS.

NO INCREASE
- DISCONNECT REGULATOR
- CHECK RESISTANCE BETWEEN "F" TERMINAL OF REGULATOR WIRING CONNECTOR AND ALTERNATOR GROUND.
- RESISTANCE SHOULD BE 4 – 250 OHMS.

LESS THAN OR OVER 250 OHMS

REPAIR GROUNDED OR OPEN FIELD CIRCUIT. NOTE: IF FIELD CIRCUIT IS GROUNDED, IT WILL BE NECESSARY TO REPLACE REGULATOR ALSO.

4-250 OHMS

- DISCONNECT REGULATOR.
- JUMPER "A" TO "F" TERMINALS AT REGULATOR WIRING CONNECTOR.
- VOLTAGE SHOULD READ A MINIMUM OF 1/2 VOLT OVER BASE READING WITH SAME LOAD TEST CONDITIONS STILL IN EFFECT.

LESS THAN 1/2 VOLT

- REMOVE JUMPER FROM "A" AND "F" TERMINALS BUT LEAVE REGULATOR DISCONNECTED.
- JUMPER "BAT" TO "FLD" TERMINALS AT ALTERNATOR.
- VOLTAGE SHOULD READ A MINIMUM OF 1/2 VOLT OVER BASE READING WITH SAME LOAD TEST CONDITIONS STILL IN EFFECT.

LESS THAN 1/2 VOLT

MOVE POS. VOLTMETER LEAD TO BAT. TERM. OF ALTERNATOR.

LESS THAN 1/2 VOLT

REPAIR OR REPLACE ALTERNATOR.

1/2 VOLT OR MORE

REPAIR "BAT." WIRE.

1/2 VOLT OR MORE

REPAIR DEFECTIVE "A" OR "F" CIRCUITS.

1/2 VOLT OR MORE
SHUT OFF ALL LOAD

VEHICLES WITH ALTERNATOR WARNING LIGHT ENGINE AT IDLE

WITH JUMPER STILL ON TERMINALS "A" AND "F", CHECK FOR POWER TO THE "S" AND "I" TERMINALS. VOLTAGE AT THE "S" TERMINAL SHOULD BE ABOUT 1/2 OF THE VOLTAGE AT "I".

NOT OK

REPAIR DEFECTIVE "S" OR "I" CIRCUITS.

OK

REPLACE REGULATOR.

VEHICLES WITH AMMETER ENGINE OFF – IGNITION SWITCH ON

CHECK FOR POWER TO "S" TERMINAL ON REGULATOR CONNECTOR.

NOT OK

REPAIR "S" CIRCUIT (IGNITION SWITCH TO REGULATOR CONNECTOR).

OK

REPLACE REGULATOR.

INCREASES, BUT NOT MORE THAN 2.0 VOLTS

LOAD TEST
- INCREASE ENGINE RPM TO 2000
- TURN WIPER, BLOWER, AND HEADLIGHTS ON HIGH.
- VOLTAGE SHOULD READ A MINIMUM OF 1/2 VOLT OVER BASE READING.

LESS THAN 1/2 VOLT (see 4-250 OHMS branch above)

1/2 VOLT OR MORE

ALTERNATOR AND REGULATOR ARE OK. PROBLEM CAN STILL BE BATTERY DRAIN. TURN OFF IGNITION. INSTALL VOLTMETER IN SERIES WITH POS. BATTERY CABLE AND CHECK TO ISOLATE PROBLEM CIRCUIT*

INCREASES MORE THAN 2.0 VOLTS

DISCONNECT REGULATOR. SEE IF OVERVOLTAGE CONDITION GOES AWAY.

OVER VOLTAGE DOES NOT GO AWAY.

REPAIR SHORTED HARNESS BETWEEN ALTERNATOR AND REGULATOR. ALSO REPLACE REGULATOR.

OVER VOLTAGE GOES AWAY.

CHECK GROUND AT REGULATOR.

NOT OK

REPAIR GROUND.

OK

REPLACE REGULATOR.

*IF NO DRAIN, CHECK BATTERY CAPACITY AND/OR PERFORM CELL COMPARISON TESTS

Charging system tests using ohmmeter and voltmeter (© Ford Motor Co.)

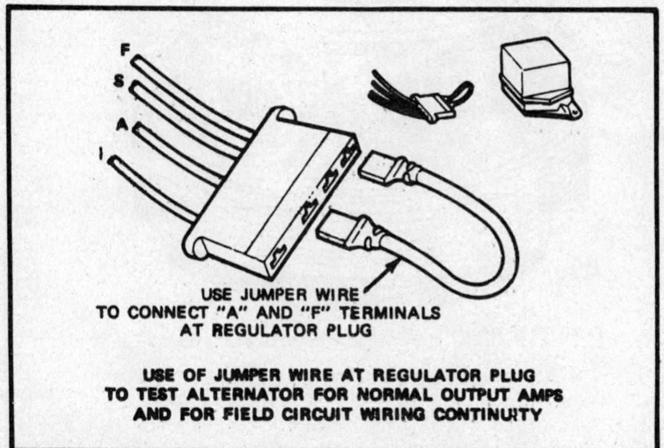

F
S
A
I
USE JUMPER WIRE
TO CONNECT "A" AND "F" TERMINALS
AT REGULATOR PLUG
USE OF JUMPER WIRE AT REGULATOR PLUG
TO TEST ALTERNATOR FOR NORMAL OUTPUT AMPS
AND FOR FIELD CIRCUIT WIRING CONTINUITY

Isolation test jumper wire (© Ford Motor Co.)

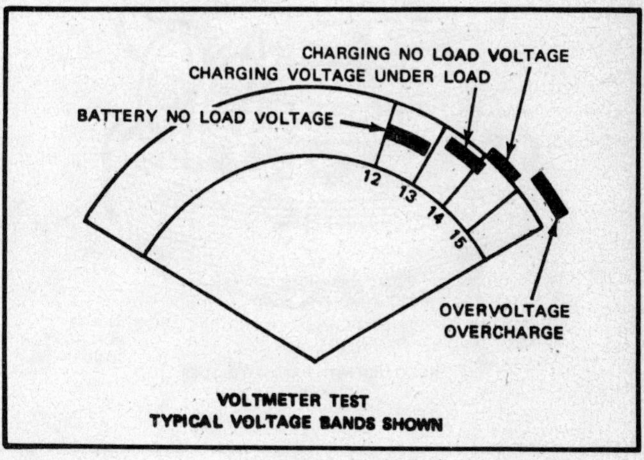

Voltmeter reading during isolation test (© Ford Motor Co.)

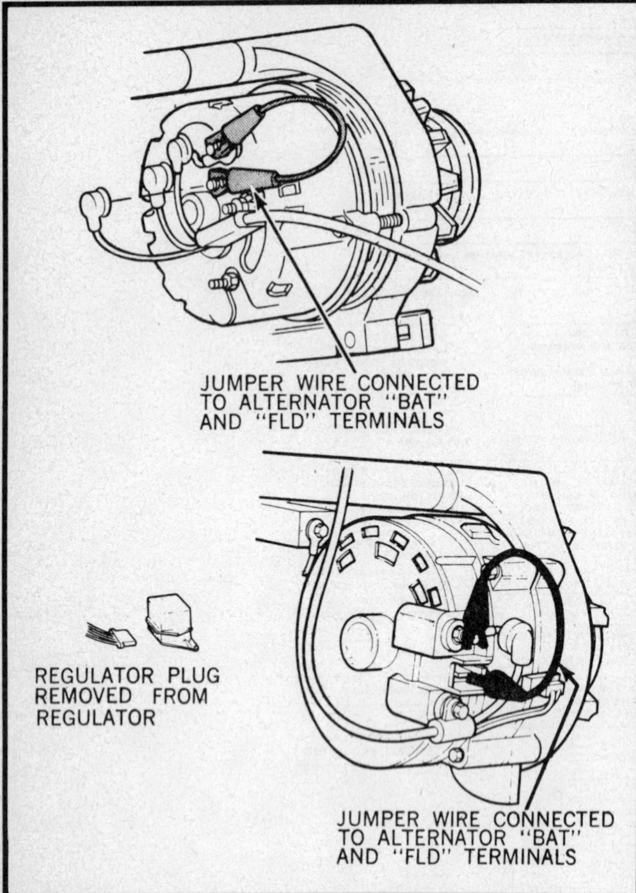

Location for jumper wire for circuit tests (© Ford Motor Co.)

5. Remove the brush holder mounting screws and the holder, brushes, springs, insulator, and terminal.

6. If replacement is necessary, press the bearing from the rear end housing, support housing on inner boss.

7. If rectifiers are to be replaced, carefully unsolder the leads from the terminals. Use only a 100 watt soldering iron. Leave the soldering iron in contact with the diode terminals only long enough to remove the wires. Use pliers as temporary heat sinks in order to protect the diodes.

8. There are various types of rectifier assembly circuit boards installed in production. One type has the circuit board spaced away from the diode plates and the diodes are exposed. Another type consists of a single circuit board with integral diodes; and still another has integral diodes with an additional booster diode plate containing two diodes. This last type is used only on the eight diode 61 amp autolite alternator. To disassemble, use the following procedures.

9. Exposed Diodes, remove the screws from the rectifier by rotating bolt heads ¼ turn clockwise to unlock, then unscrewing.

10. Integral Diodes,press out the stator terminal screw, making sure not to twist it while doing this. Do not remove grounded screw.

11. Booster Diodes,press out the stator terminal screw about ¼ in., then remove the nut from the end of the screw and lift screw from circuit board, making sure not to twist it as it comes out.

12. Remove the drive pulley and fan. On alternator pulleys with threaded holes in the outer end of the pulley, use a standard puller for removal.

13. Remove the three screws that hold the front bearing retainer, and remove the front housing.

14. If the bearing is to be replaced, press from housing.

Cleaning and Inspection

1. The rotor, stator, diode rectifier assemblies, and bearings are not to be cleaned with solvent. These parts are to be wiped off with a clean cloth. Cleaning solvent may cause damage to

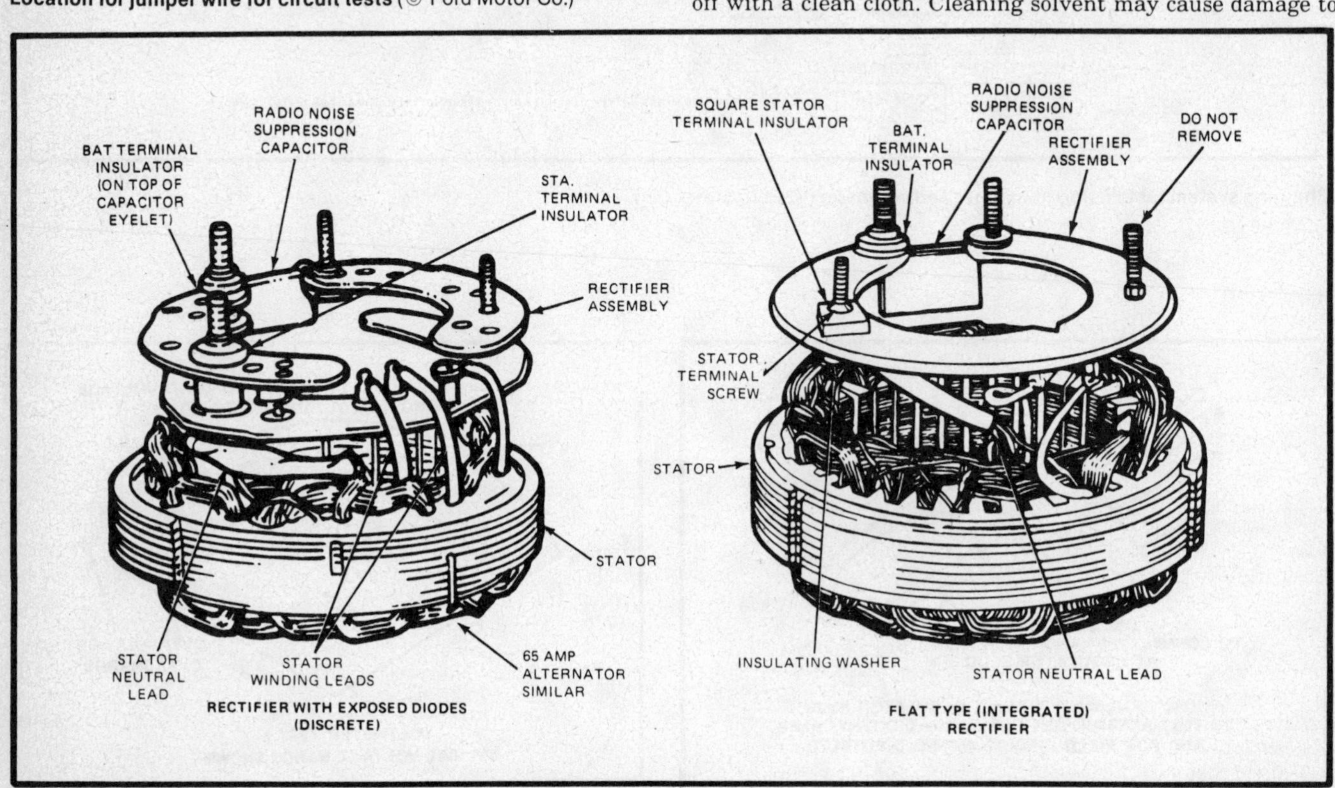

Typical stator and rectifier assemblies (© Ford Motor Co.)

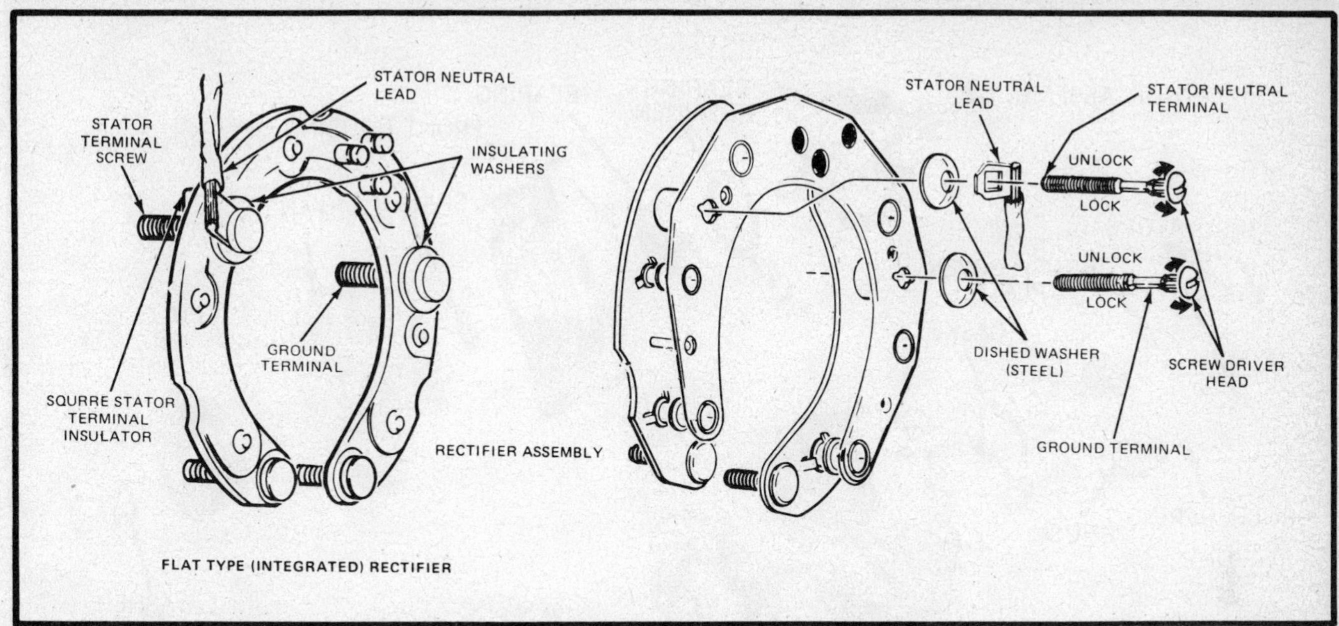

Typical rectifier assemblies (© Ford Motor Co.)

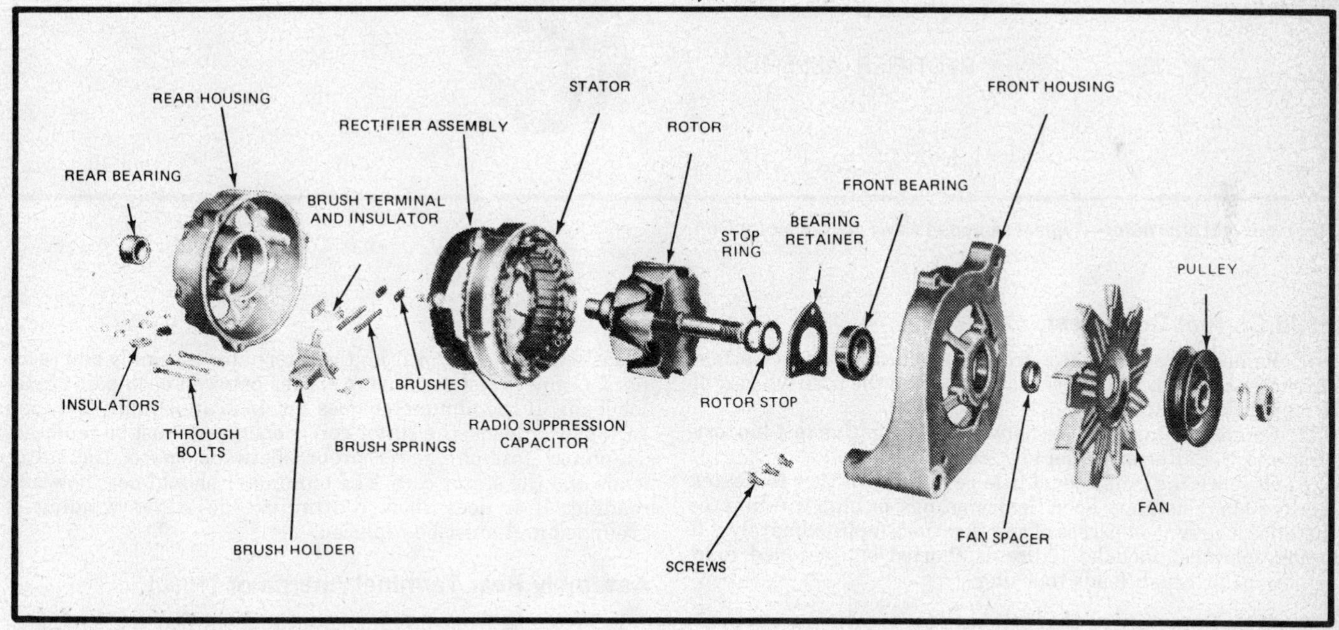

Exploded view of a rear terminal alternator (© Ford Motor Co.)

the electrical parts or contaminate the bearing internal lubricant. Wash all other parts in solvent and dry them.

2. Rotate the front bearing on the driveshaft. Check for any scraping noise, looseness or roughness that indicates that the bearing is excessively worn. As the bearing is being rotated, look for excessive lubricant leakage. If any of these conditions exist, replace the bearing. Check rear bearing and rotor shaft.

3. Place the rear end housing on the slip ring end of the shaft and rotate the bearing on the shaft. Make a similar check for noise, looseness or roughness. Inspect the rollers and cage for damage. Replace the bearing if these conditions exist, or if the lubricant is missing or contaminated.

4. Check both the front and rear housings for cracks.

5. Check all wire leads on both the stator and rotor assemblies for loose soldered connections, and for burned insulation. Solder all poor connections. Replace parts that show burned insulation.

6. Check the slip rings for damaged insulation and runout. If the slip rings are more than 0.0005 in. out of round, take a light cut (minimum diameter limit 1.22 in.) from the face of the rings to true them. If the slip rings are badly damaged, the entire rotor will have to be replaced, as they are serviced as a complete assembly.

7. Replace any parts that are burned or cracked. Replace brushes that are worn to less than $^5/_{16}$ in. in length. Replace the brush spring if it had less than 7 to 12 oz. tension.

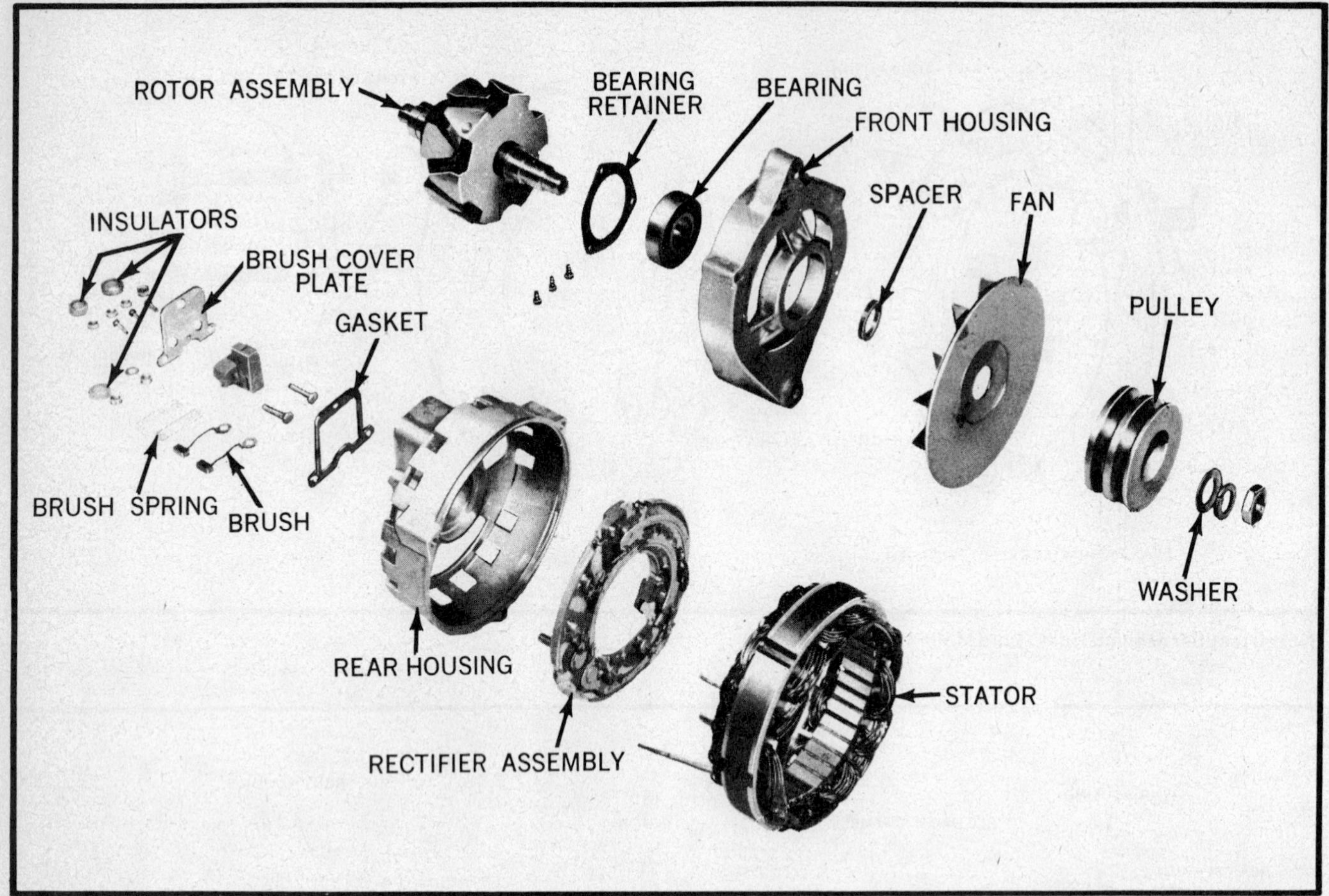

Rear terminal alternator—typical exploded view (© Ford Motor Co.)

Field Current Draw Test

1. Remove the alternator from the vehicle. Connect a test ammeter between the alternator frame and the positive post of a 12 volt test battery.
2. Connect a jumper wire between the negative test battery post and the alternator field terminal.
3. Observe the ammeter. Little or no current flow indicates high brush resistance, open field windings, or high winding resistance. Current in excess of specifications (approximately 2.9 amps. for most models) indicates shorted or grounded field windings, or brush leads touching.

NOTE: Sometimes the alternator produces current output at low engine speeds, but ceases to put out at higher speeds. This can be caused by centrifugal force expanding the rotor windings to the point where they short to ground. Place in a test stand and check field current draw while spinning alternator.

Diode Tests

Disassemble the alternator. Disconnect diode assembly from stator and make tests. To test one set of diodes, contact one ohmmeter probe to the diode plate and contact each of the three stator lead terminals with the other probe. Reverse the probes and repeat the test. All six tests (eight for 61 amp autolite eight diode models) should show a reading of about 60 ohms in one direction and infinite ohms in the other. If two high readings, or two low readings, are obtained after reversing probes the diode is faulty and must be replaced.

Stator Tests

Disassemble the stator from the alternator assembly and rectifiers. Connect test ohmmeter probes between each pair of stator leads. If the ohmmeter does not indicate equally between each pair of leads, the stator coil is open and must be replaced.

Connect test ohmmeter probes between one of the stator leads and the stator core. The ohmmeter should not show any reading. If it does show continuity, the stator winding is grounded and must be replaced.

Assembly Rear Terminal Alternator (1980)

1. Press the front bearing into the front housing boss, putting pressure on outer race only. Install bearing retainer.
2. If the stop ring on the driveshaft was damaged, install a new stop ring. Push the new ring onto the shaft and into the groove.
3. Position the front bearing spacer on the driveshaft against the stop ring.
4. Place the front housing over the shaft, with the bearing positioned in the front housing cavity.
5. Install fan spacer, fan, pulley, lockwasher and retaining nut and tighten nut to 60–100 ft. lbs. holding the drive shaft with an Allen key.
6. If rear bearing was removed, press a new one into rear housing.
7. Assemble brushes, springs, terminal and insulator in the brush holder, retract the brushes and insert a short length of $\frac{1}{8}$ in. rod or stiff wire through the hole in the holder to hold the brushes in the retracted position.

8. Position the brush holder assembly in the rear housing and install mounting screws. Position brush leads to prevent shorting.
9. Wrap the three stator winding leads around the circuit board terminals and solder them using only rosin core solder and a 100 watt iron. Position the stator neutral lead eyelet on the stator terminal screw and install the screw in the rectifier assembly.
10. Exposed Diodes, insert the special screws through the wire lug, dished washers and circuit board. Turn $^1/_4$ turn counterclockwise to lock in place.
11. Integral Diodes, insert the screws straight through the holes. The dished washers are to be used on the molded circuit boards only. Using these washers on a fiber board will result in a serious short circuit, as only a flat insulating washer between the stator terminal and the board is used on fiber circuit boards.
12. Booster Diodes, position the stator wire terminal on the stator terminal screws, then position screw on rectifier. Position square insulator over the screw and into the square hole in the rectifier, rotate terminal screw until it locks, then press it in fingertight. Position the stator wire, then press the terminal screw into the rectifier and insulator with a vise.
13. Place the radio noise suppression condenser on the rectifier terminals. With molded circuit board, install the STA and BAT terminal insulators. With fiber circuit board, place the square stator terminal insulator in the square hole in the rectifier assembly, then position BAT terminal insulator.
14. Position the stator and rectifier assembly in the rear housing, making sure that all terminal insulators are seated properly in the recesses. Position STA, BAT and FLD insulators on terminal bolts; install nuts.
15. Clean the rear bearing surface of the rotor shaft with a rag, then position rear housing and stator assembly over rotor. Align matchmarks made during disassembly and install through bolts. Remove brush retracting wire and place a dab of silicone sealer over the hole.

Disassembly Rear Terminal Alternators (1981 and Later)

1. Scribe the end housings and stator frame for alignment during reassembly, and then remove the three housing through bolts.
2. Separate the front housing and rotor assembly from the stator and rear housing. If there is resistance in pulling the front housing free, tap the front housing lightly with a plastic tipped hammer to break it loose.
3. Remove the brush springs from the brush holder, located in the rear housing.
4. Note the colors and locations of nuts, washers, and insulators on the back of the rear housing for reconnection. Then, remove all of them.
5. Remove the stator and rectifier assembly from the rear housing.
6. Remove the screws attaching the brush holder to the rear housing; then remove the brush holder, brushes, and brush terminal insulator.
7. Press the bearing out of the rear housing with an arbor press. Make sure the housing is supported as close as possible to the bearing boss to prevent damage to it.
8. Clamp the front housing in a vise equipped with protective jaws. Remove the drive pulley retaining nut. This requires a $^5/_{16}$ in. socket and $^3/_4$ in. wrench to drive it, and a special tool that passes through the center of the socket wrench, and locks onto the rotor shaft, and prevents it from turning as the nut is removed. Then, remove the lockwasher, drive pulley, fan, and fan spacer.
9. Remove the rotor from the front housing and remove the housing from the vise.
10. Remove the front bearing spacer from the rotor shaft, but leave the stop ring in place unless it is damaged.
11. Remove the screws that attach the front bearing retainer to the front housing and remove the retainer. Then remove the bearing from the housing by sliding it out, or, if there is resistance, using an arbor press. If a press is needed, make sure to support the housing close to the bearing boss to prevent damage.
12. Remove the battery terminal insulator and radio suppression capacitor from the rectifier assembly.
13. Use a 100 watt soldering iron to unsolder the stator leads where they connect to the rectifier. Make sure the iron is hot before starting and work quickly to avoid damaging the rectifier. Do this by using needle nose pliers to pull upwards on the stator lead terminals where they connect to the rectifier assembly. Once each connector comes loose, shake the molten solder from it.
14. Disconnect the stator neutral lead from the rectifier of each type as follows. Flat, integrated type rectifier, press the stator terminal screw straight out of the rectifier. Do not turn the screw during removal or the serrations holding it in place will be damaged. Exposed diode, separate type rectifier, turn the stator terminal screw $^1/_4$ turn to unlock it and remove it.
20. If it is necessary to remove the ground terminal, follow the appropriate procedure above.

Cleaning and Inspection

NOTE: These alternators come equipped with either standard or high temperature rectifier assemblies and bearings. High temperature alternators must use high temperature parts or failure will occur.

1. Wipe the rotor, stator and bearings with a clean cloth. Do not use solvent.
2. Rotate the front bearing on the drive end of the rotor shaft, checking for noise, looseness, roughness, or lubricant leakage. Replace the bearing if any of these defects are noted.
3. Inspect the rear bearing surface of the rotor shaft for roughness or severe chatter marks; replace the rotor assembly if the shaft is not smooth. Then, place the rear bearing onto the slip ring end of the shaft and rotate it. Inspect as for the front bearing, checking additionally for damaged rollers or cage. Replace the bearing if there are any of these conditions present or if the lubricant has been lost or contaminated.
4. Check the pulley and fan for looseness on the rotor shaft or distortion, and replace if either condition exists.
5. Inspect both halves of the housing for cracks, especially in webbed areas, and replace as necessary.
6. Check all leads on the stator and rotor for loose or broken soldered connections and for burned insulation. Resolder poor connections and replace parts with burned insulation.
7. Check the slip rings for nicks and surface roughness. Turn the rings to as small as 1.22 in. diameter, if necessary. If they are badly damaged, the rotor must be replaced.
8. Inspect the brushes for wear beyond $^1/_4$ in. and replace as necessary.

Assembly Rear Terminal Alternators (1981 and Later)

1. Install the front bearing in its housing, pressing on the outer race only. Then, position the bearing retainer on the front housing and install the attaching screws, torquing screws 25 to 40 inch lbs.
2. If the stop ring was removed from the rotor shaft, install a new one. Slide it over the end of the shaft and into the groove without opening it with snap ring pliers, or permanent deformation will result.
3. Install the bearing spacer onto the rotor shaft with the recessed side against the stop ring.
4. Install the rotor into the front housing. Clamp the housing in a vise.
5. Install the fan spacer, fan, drive pulley, lockwasher, and nut onto the rotor shaft. Torque the nut 60 to 100 ft. lbs. using the special tool used in removal.

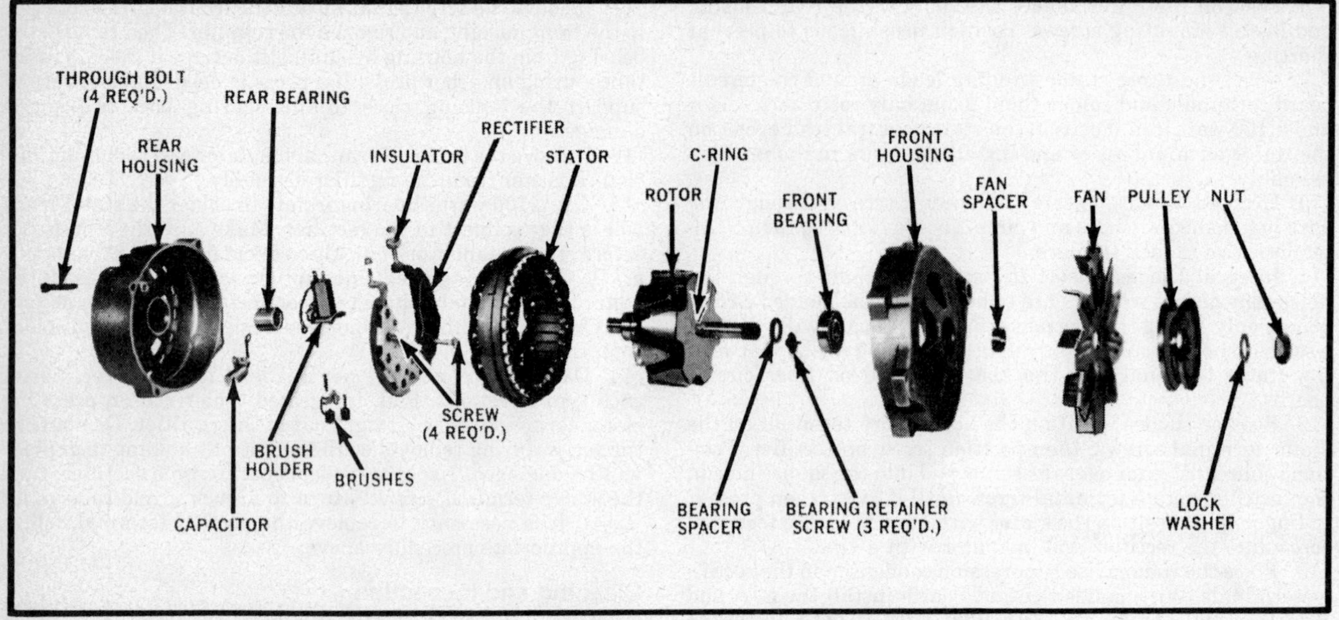

Side terminal alternator—typical exploded view (© Ford Motor Co.)

6. Install the rear bearing with an arbor press and supporting the housing close to the bearing boss. Make sure the bearing is flush with the surface of the housing.

7. Position the brush wiring eyelet over the brush terminal and install the terminal insulator.

8. Install the springs and brushes into the brush holder and then insert a piece of stiff wire through the brush holder to hold them in position against spring tension. Then position the brush holder in the rear housing. Install the brush holder mounting screws, making sure the ground brush wiring eyelet is positioned under the left hand mounting screw. Then, holding the brush holder firmly against the housing, torque the retaining screws 17 to 25 inch lbs.

9. Connect the stator neutral lead to the rectifier of each type as follows. Flat, integrated type rectifier, position the stator terminal insulator and the stator neutral lead on the rectifier assembly. Insert the terminal screw and press it into position. Make sure it is pressed in far enough to keep the neutral lead terminal from moving. Exposed diode, separate type rectifier, position the stator neutral lead and dished washer on the rectifier assembly. Insert the terminal screw and lock it into place by rotating it ¼ turn.

10. If the ground terminal was removed from the rectifier assembly, install it pressing or turning it as outlined above for the appropriate type of rectifier.

11. Make sure the insulator sleeves are in place. Then, wrap the stator winding leads around the terminals of the rectifier assembly and solder them with a 100 watt iron and rosin core electrical solder. Work quickly to make sure you do not overheat the rectifier.

12. Install the radio suppression capacitor and battery terminal insulator to the rectifier assembly. Then, install the insulator onto the stator terminal screw. Finally, align the terminal screws on the rectifier assembly with the holes on the back of the rear housing and install the stator rectifier assembly in to the rear housing. Make sure the terminal insulators are seated in their recesses.

13. Install the external insulators, washers, and nuts onto the terminals, following the color code. Black on "STA" terminal, Red on "BAT" terminal and Orange on "FLD" terminal. Torque the nut for the red lead 30 to 55 inch lbs., and the others 25 to 35 inch lbs.

14. Wipe the rear end bearing surface of the rotor shaft with a clean, lint-free rag. Then, remove the rotor and front housing assembly from the vise. Finally, position the rear housing and stator assembly over the rotor and align the scribe marks made during disassembly. Make sure the machined portion of the stator core is seated in the stop in both end housings. Install the through bolts.

15. Remove the wire holding the brushes in a retracted position.

Disassembly Side Terminal Alternator

1. Mark the front and rear housings and the stator for reassembly in the same positions. Then, remove the four housing through bolts. Without separating the rear housing and stator, pull the front housing and rotor from the assembly. Slots are provided in the front housing to help you pry it away from the stator.

2. Remove the drive pulley nut with a $^{5}/_{16}$ in. socket and ¾ in. wrench to drive it and a special tool that passes through the center of the socket to hold the shaft in place. Remove the lockwasher, pulley, fan, and fan spacer from the rotor shaft. Finally, pull the rotor and shaft from the front housing and remove the rotor shaft spacer.

3. Remove the three screws retaining the bearing to the front housing. If the bearing shows either wear or loss of lubricant, press it out of the housing, being sure to support the housing close to the bearing boss to prevent damage to it.

4. Unsolder and disengage the three stator leads from the rectifier. Use a hot iron and work quickly to avoid overheating it. Then, lift the stator from the rear housing.

5. Quickly unsolder and disengage the brush holder lead from the rectifier.

6. Remove the screw attaching the capacitor lead to the rectifier. Then, remove the four screws attaching the rectifier to the rear housing. Finally, remove the two terminal nuts and insulator from the outside of the housing and remove the rectifier.

7. Remove the two screws attaching the brush holder to the housing and remove the brushes and holder. Remove the two rectifier insulators from the housing bosses.

8. Remove any sealing compound from the rear housing and brush holder.

9. Remove the screw attaching the capacitor to the rear housing and remove the capacitor.

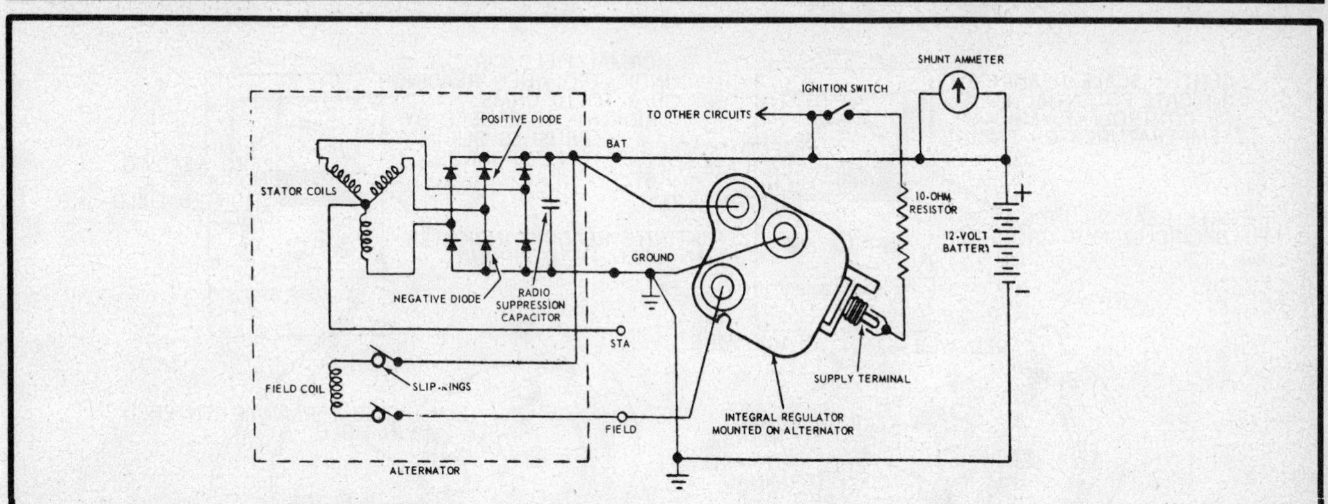

Charging system schematic with integral regulator (© Ford Motor Co.)

10. Inspect the rear bearing for excessive wear, damage, or loss of lubricant and, if necessary press it out, supporting the housing close to the bearing boss to prevent damage to it.

Cleaning and Inspection

See the procedures for cleaning and inspection of the 1981 and later rear terminal alternator above, which are identical.

Assembly Side Terminal Alternators

1. If the front bearing is being replaced, first press the new bearing into the housing, putting pressure on the outer race only. Then, install the bearing retaining screws and torque them to 25–40 inch lbs.
2. Place the inner spacer on to the rotor shaft and insert the rotor shaft into the center of the front bearing.
3. Install the fan spacer, fan, pulley, lockwasher, and nut onto the rotor shaft, in that order. Then, tighten the nut using the socket, open end wrench, and special tool used in removal.
4. If the rear bearing is being replaced, press a new one in by the outer face only until the rear face is flush with the outer surface of the bearing boss.
5. Position the brush terminal on the brush holder. Then, install the springs and brushes in the holder, and insert a piece of stiff wire across in front of the brushes to retain them in a retracted position for assembly.
6. Position the brush holder in the rear housing and start the attaching screws. Make sure the wire retaining the brushes sticks out far enough for you to pull it from the housing after the alternator is assembled. Poke any sealer that may be present out of the pin hole in the housing. Then, hold the brush holder firmly toward the brush enclosure opening while tightening the attaching screws. Finally, reseal the crack between the brush holder and the brush cavity in the rear housing with a body sealer. Don't use a silicone sealant.
7. Position the capacitor in the rear housing and start install the attaching screw.
8. Place the two rectifier bosses in the housing.
9. Place the insulator on the larger ("BAT") terminal of the rectifier and position the rectifier in the rear housing. Place the outside insulator on the "BAT" terminal. Install the nuts on both "BAT" and "GRD" terminals finger tight.
10. Start the four rectifier attaching screws. Then, tighten the "BAT" terminal nut to 35–50 inch lbs. and the "GRD" nut to 25–30 inch lbs. These nuts are located on the outside of the housing. Finally, tighten the four rectifier attaching screws to 40–50 inch lbs.

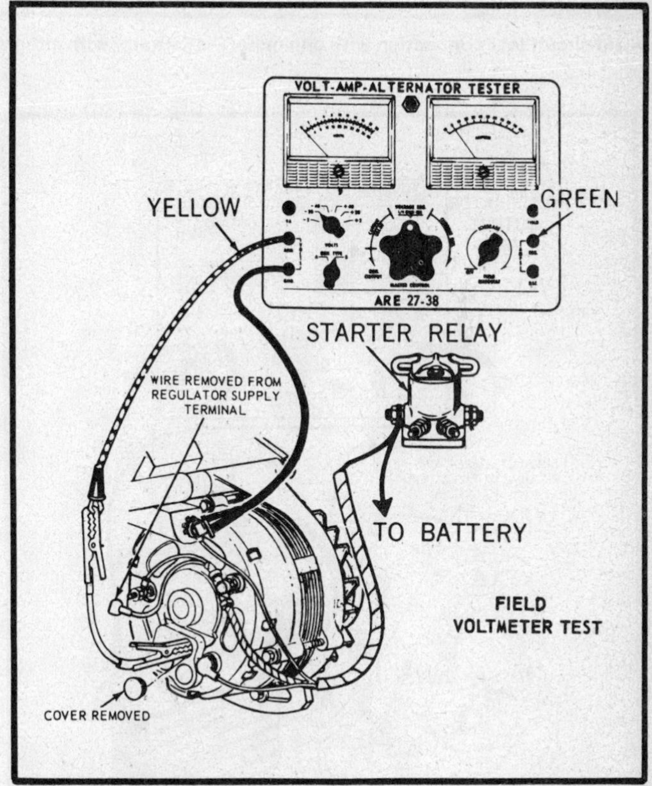

Output test connection—alternator with integral regulator (© Ford Motor Co.)

11. Connect the capacitor lead to the rectifier with the attaching screw.
12. Press the brush holder lead onto the rectifier pin and solder it securely. Use a hot iron and work quickly so the rectifier does not overheat.
13. Position the stator in the rear housing, aligning the scribe marks made at the beginning of disassembly. Press the three stator leads onto the rectifier pins and solder securely. Again, work quickly to protect components.
14. Position the rotor and front housing into/onto the stator and rear housing. Align the marks made in disassembly, and

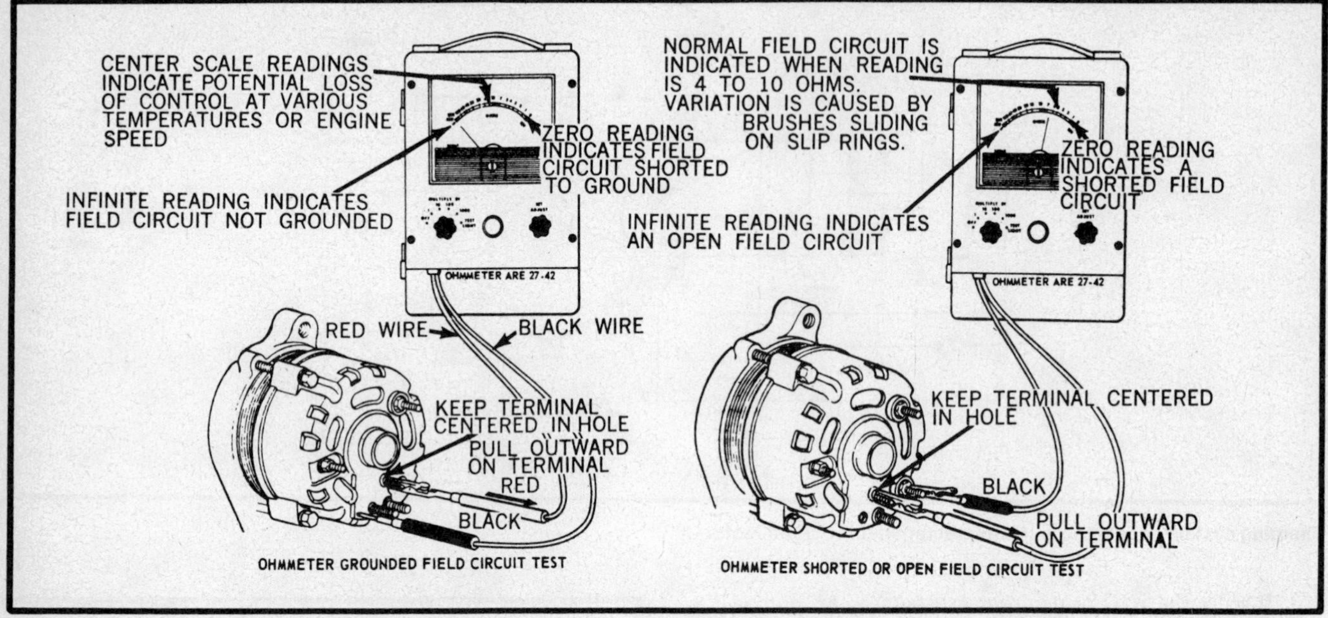

Field circuit test connection with ohmmeter—alternator with integral regulator (© Ford Motor Co.)

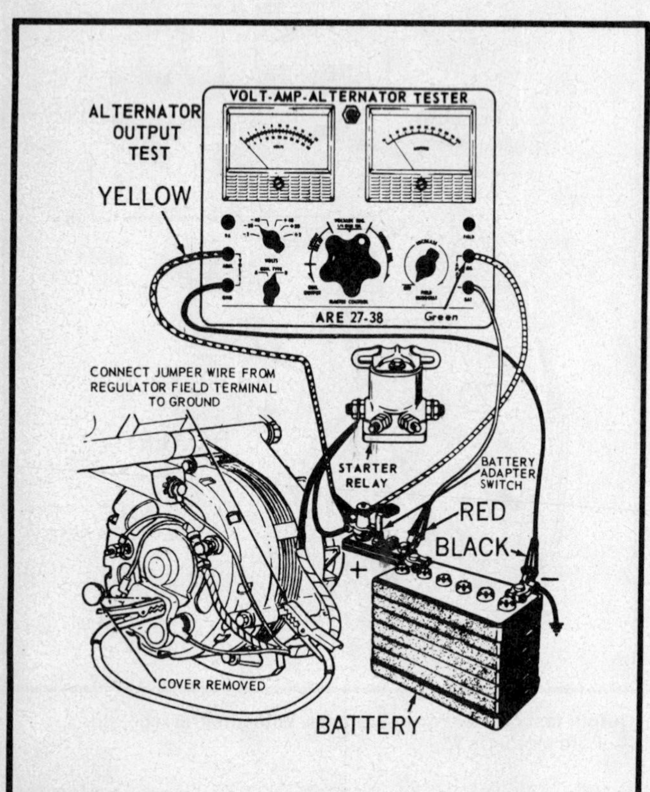

Voltmeter test connection—alternator with integral regulator (© Ford Motor Co.)

then install the through bolts. Tighten two opposing bolts first; then, tighten the other two opposing bolts.

15. Test the unit for binding by spinning the fan. Remove the wire retracting the brushes and seal the hole with waterproof cement. Do not use a silicone sealer.

Autolite Alternator with Integral Regulator

Some vehicles are equipped with an Autolite alternator having an integral regulator mounted to the rear end housing. The regulator is a hybrid unit featuring use of solid state integrated circuits. These circuits may consist of transistors, diodes and resistors. The unusual feature of this type of micro-electronic circuit is that the entire circuit is within a silicone crystal approximately $\frac{1}{8}$ in. square. Because of the small size of the circuit, it is not repairable or adjustable and must be replaced as a unit if found to be defective. It should be noted that the size of the regulator housing is dictated only by the fact that some means of connecting the regulator to the alternator is necessary. Overhaul is the same as for other Autolite alternators.

TROUBLESHOOTING

NOTE: See the "Alternator Test Plans" section before proceeding further.

Fusible Links

Check the fusible link located between the starter relay and the alternator. Replace the link if it is burned or open.

Output Test

1. Place transmission in Neutral or Park.
2. Remove the positive battery cable and install a battery adapter switch in the line.
3. Attach one lead of a test voltmeter to the negative battery post and the other test lead to the circuit side of the adapter switch.
4. Connect a test ammeter to each side of the adapter switch, so that charging current will go through the ammeter when the switch is opened.
5. Connect a jumper wire between the alternator frame and the integral regulator field terminal (cover plug removed).
6. Close adapter switch, start engine and open adapter switch.
7. Running engine at 2000 rpm, observe voltmeter and ammeter. At 15 volts indicated, the ammeter should read 50 to 57

amps. If so, and there is still a no-charge condition, the regulator is probably faulty and must be replaced. An output 2 to 8 amps. below 50 amps. usually indicates an open diode rectifier, while an output 10 to 15 amps. below minimum specifications usually indicates a shorted diode. An alternator with a shorted diode usually will whine at idle speed.

Field Test (Voltmeter)

1. Turn ignition switch to OFF position.
2. Remove wire from regulator supply terminal.
3. Remove cover plug from regulator field terminal and connect one test voltmeter lead to this terminal. A $\frac{1}{4}$ ohm resistor should be in the circuit.
4. Connect the other test voltmeter lead to a good engine ground.
5. The voltmeter should read 12 volts. If no voltage is present, the field circuit is open or grounded.
6. If voltmeter reads more than I volt, but still less than battery voltage, there is probably a partial ground in the alternator field circuit and the circuit should be checked with an ohmmeter.

Field Test (Ohmmeter)

1. Disconnect battery ground cable, remove alternator from the vehicle.
2. Remove the regulator from the alternator.
3. Perform the ohmmeter test. If any of the tests indicate a field circuit problem, disassemble the alternator to further isolate the trouble. Connect each ohmmeter probe to a slip ring. Resistance should be 4 to 5 ohms. A higher reading indicates a damaged slip ring soldered connection or a broken wire. A lower reading indicates a shorted wire or slip ring assembly.
4. Connect one ohmmeter probe to a slip ring and the other probe to the rotor shaft. Any reading other than infinite ohms indicates a short to ground. If neither of these tests (A and B) isolates the trouble, the brushes or brush assembly are the probable cause.

Voltage Limiter Test

1. Check the battery specific gravity. If it is not at least 1230, charge the battery or install a charged battery for the test.
2. Make sure all lights and accessories are turned off, including such items as dome lights.
3. Make the test connections.
4. Place transmission in Neutral or Park, close battery adapter switch and start the engine.
5. Open the battery adapter switch and operate engine at 2000 rpm for 5 minutes. The voltmeter should read 13.3 to 15.3 volts.
6. If voltage does not rise above 12 volts, perform a regulator supply voltage test to determine whether or not the regulator is getting voltage from the battery. Before replacing a regulator, check the wiring of the entire charging system for shorts, opens, or high resistance connections.

Regulator Supply Voltage Test

The regulator is "turned on" by the application of battery voltage through a 10 ohm resistor wire. If the supply circuit is defective, the regulator will not function and the alternator will not put out current.

1. Connect a 12 volt test light or voltmeter between the regulator supply lead and ground.
2. Turn on the ignition switch. The test light should glow or the voltmeter indicate. If not, the supply circuit should be checked back to the battery, especially the resistance wire.

Overhaul

The overhaul procedures for the alternator are the same as for the Ford Autolite electro mechanical alternator.

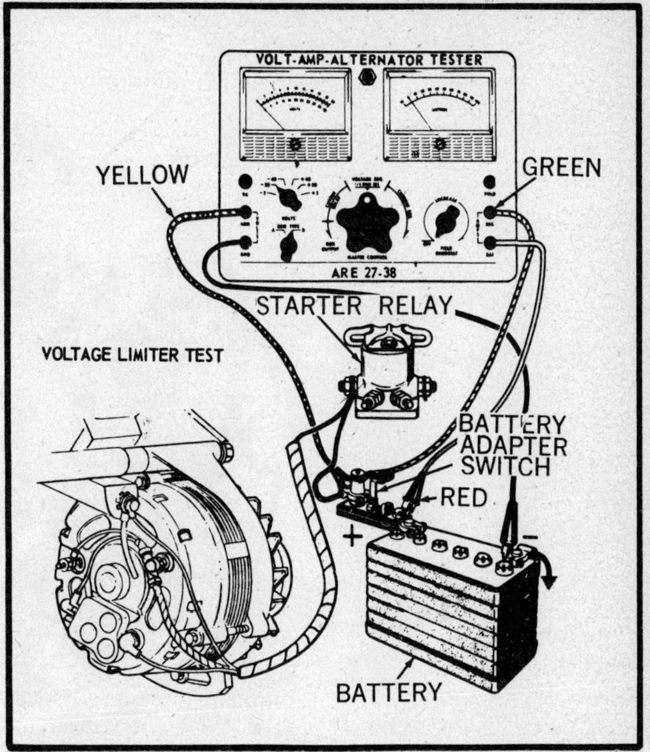

Voltage limiter test connections—alternator with integral regulator (© Ford Motor Co.)

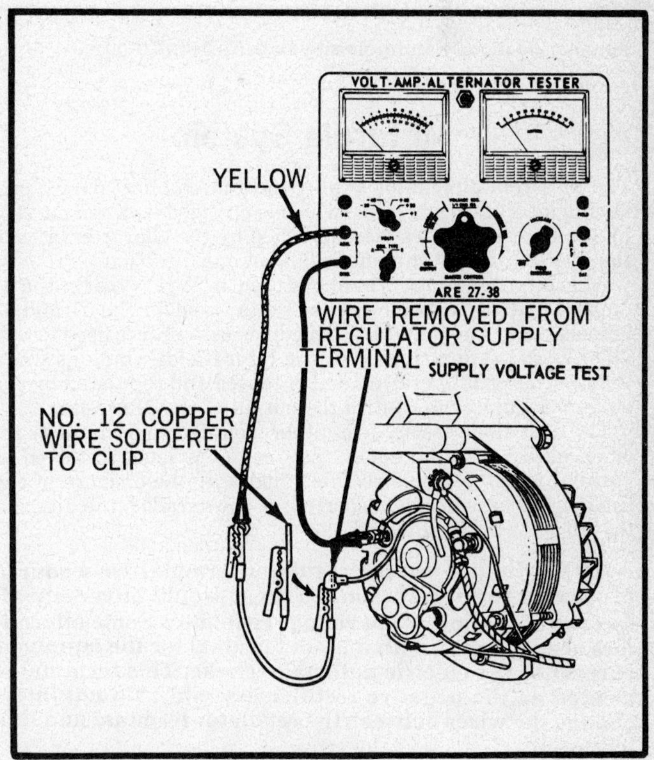

Supply voltage test connections—alternator with integral regulator (© Ford Motor Co.)

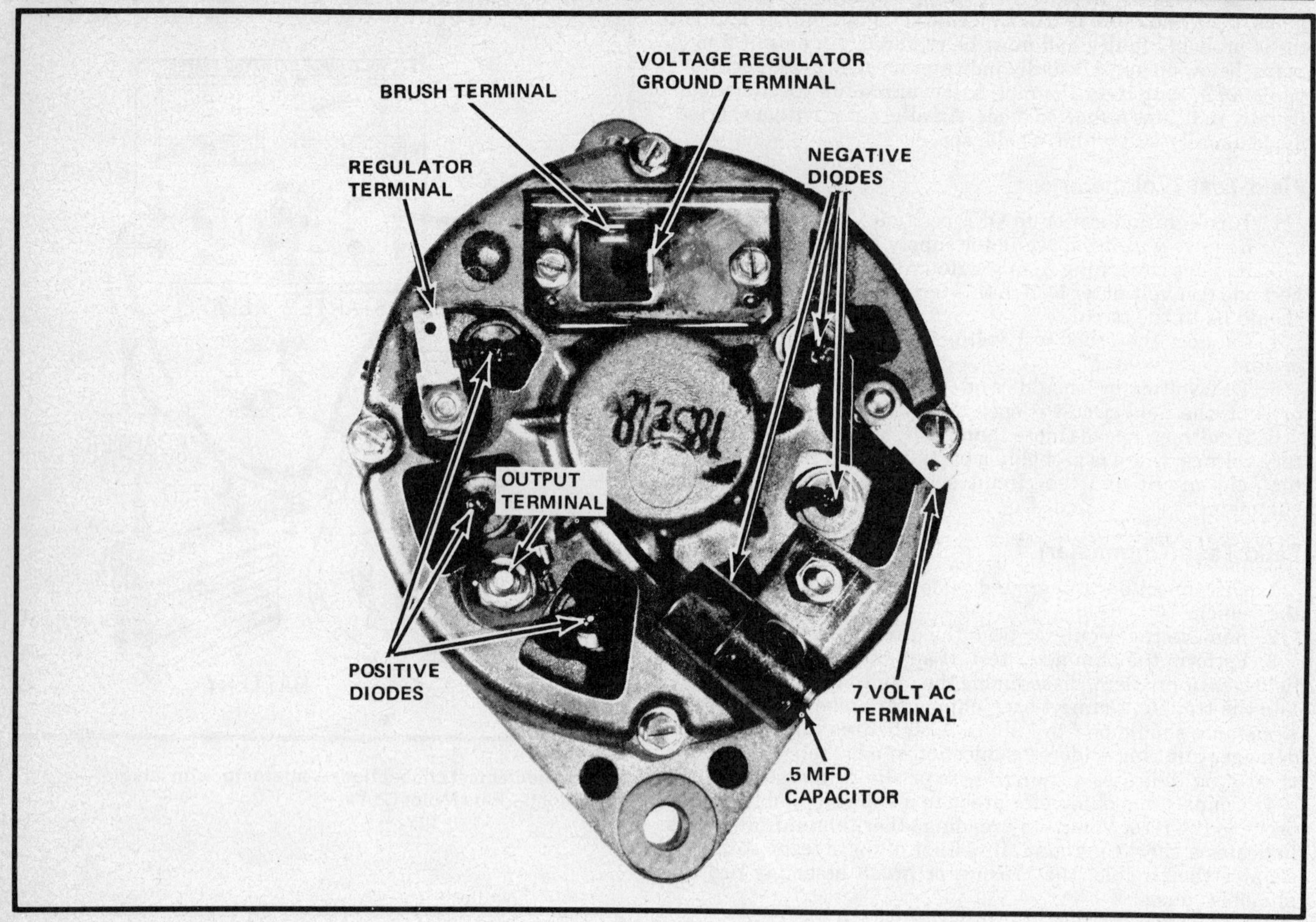

Terminal locations—Motorola alternator (© Jeep Corp.)

Motorola System

The Motorola alternator is an electro mechanical device producing alternating current, which is changed to direct current by the rectifier diodes, accomplished by the characteristics of the diodes to allow current to flow in one direction

A three phase stator winding is used, a "Wye" type for the 37 ampere rated alternator, and a "Delta" type for the 51 and 55 ampere rated alternators. A field diode assembly is used to provide the excitation current to the rotor (field) windings when the alternator is operating and is sensed and regulated by the voltage regulator to control the output of the alternator.

The field diode assembly is either mounted on a circuit board or encased within an epoxy "pot" with the leads attached in parallel to the positive rectifier diodes. If one or more of the field diodes become open, shorted, or downgraded, the alternator out put will be affected.

NOTE: Do not use the regulator terminal for a source of current for any reason. To do so would adversely affect the operation of the voltage regulator. Some alternators are equipped with a 7 volt terminal for the supply of current to the electric automatic choke. This terminal is located on the negative rectifier assembly. Do not interchange the wires between the regulator terminal and this terminal.

The voltage regulator is a sealed unit and requires no adjustment. Replacement of the unit is required if the regulator becomes defective.

TROUBLESHOOTING

NOTE: See the "Alternator Test Plans" section before proceeding further.

Fusible Link Test

There are many fuse links in the truck however the fuse link located in the wiring between the battery terminal of the horn relay to the main wire harness is the only one that concerns the charging system. This link protects the entire wiring harness. If it fails, all the electrical systems will fail to function.

Testing the Ignition Switch to Regulator Circuit

1. Disconnect the regulator wires from the regulator.
2. Turn on the key. Using a test light or voltmeter, check for current between the voltage supply wire and ground. This wire is usually orange and has another wire connected to it, usually blue or orange with a tracer.
3. If current is present, this part of the system is ok. If not voltage is present, check for broken or shorted wiring, a bad indicator bulb, a bad fuse in the fuse panel, or a bad connection at the ignition switch or on the battery side of the starter relay.

ALTERNATOR TESTS (IN VEHICLE)

NOTE: Various types of charging system testers are available to perform the tests necessary to determine if the system or components are defective. Follow the manufacturers instructions for the tester being used, as the following charging system tests are generalized.

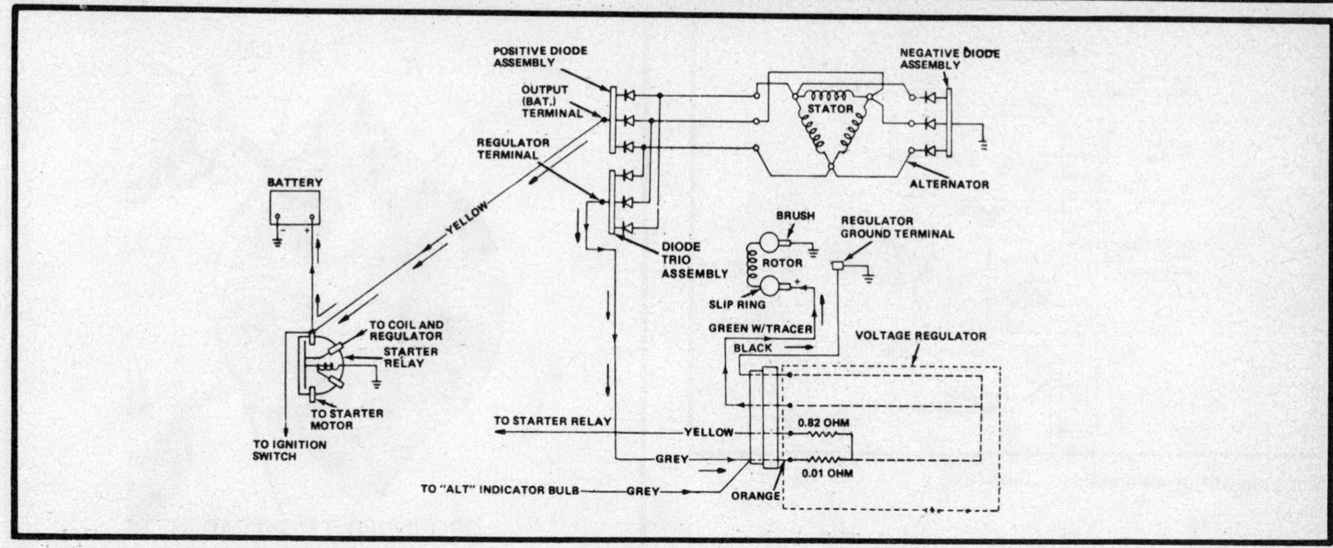

Motorola charging system schematic (© Jeep Corp.)

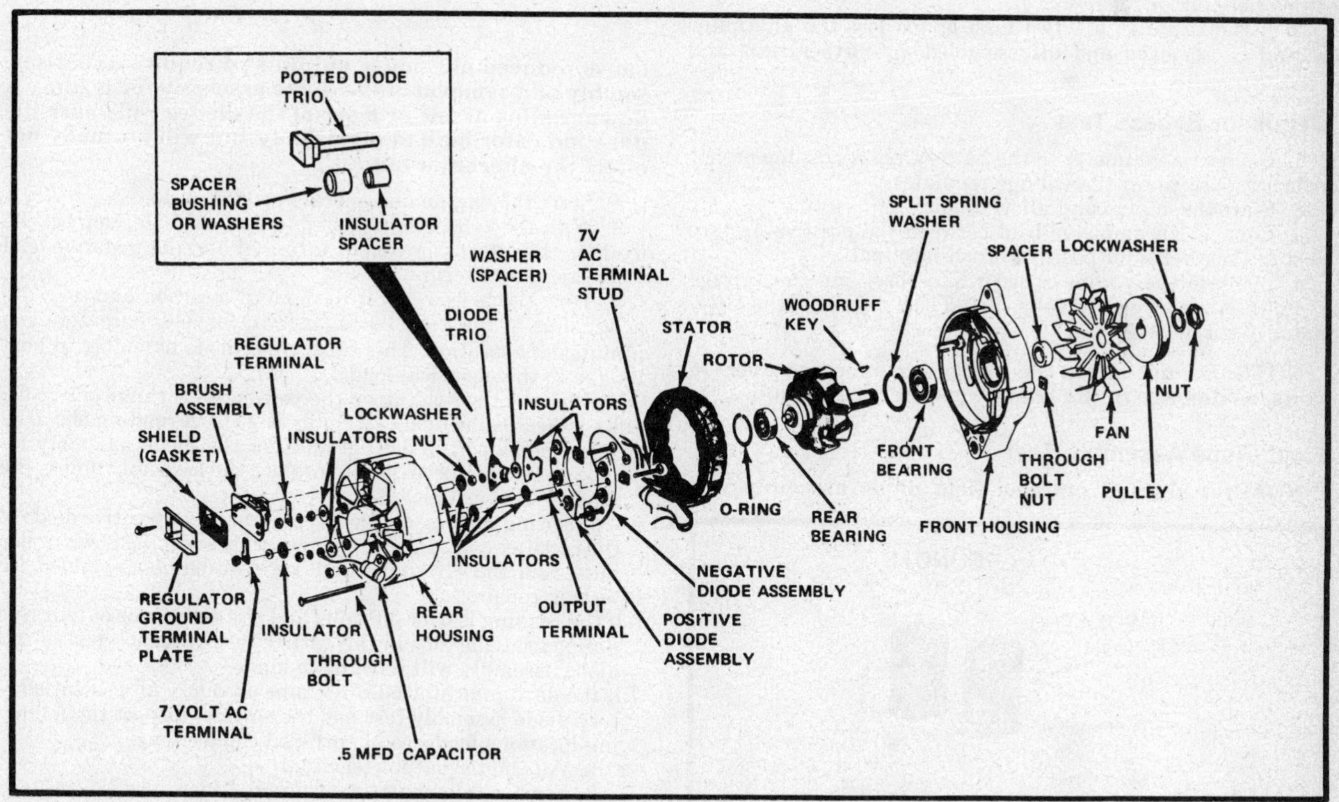

Motorola alternator—exploded view (© Jeep Corp.)

CAUTION

Do not disconnect the output lead or the voltage regulator, other than as directed, while the alternator is being operated. Do not ground the field terminal. Severe charging system damage could result.

Alternator Output Test

1. Connect voltmeter to battery, observing proper polarity.
2. Start the engine and operate at 1000 RPMs for two minutes with the headlamps on low beam.
3. Observe the voltage reading. If the voltage remains above 13 volts and below 15 volts, the alternator and the regulator are working satisfactorily.
4. If the voltage is registering out of the above range, further testing will have to be done.

Field Draw Test

1. Loosen the alternator belt so that the rotor can be turned by hand.
2. Connect ammeter leads between the positive battery post and the positive brush post on the alternator.

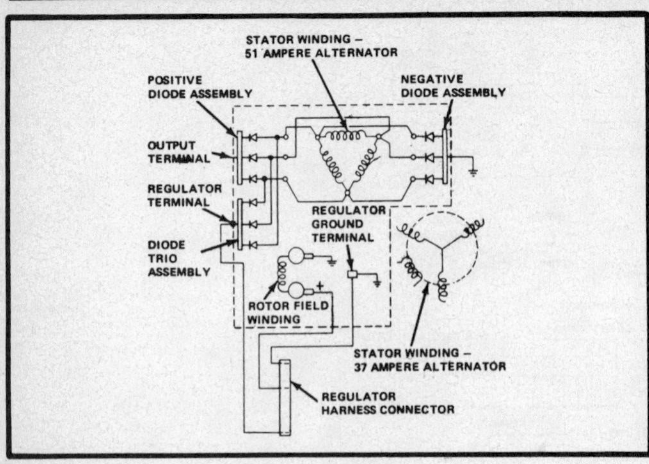

Motorola wiring schematic (© Jeep Corp.)

3. The ammeter should register a reading within a range of 1 ½ to 3 amperes and if by turning the rotor by hand, the reading varies within the scale, the brushes and the slip rings require cleaning or repairs.

4. If the readings are two high or too low, the alternator should be removed and disassembled for further tests and repairs.

Regulator Bypass Test

1. Connect a voltmeter to the battery, observing the proper polarity. Disconnect the voltage regulator.
2. Start the engine and allow to idle.
3. Connect an ammeter lead between the positive battery post to the alternator positive brush terminal.
4. Increase the engine speed while observing the voltage reading. A reading of 16 volts should be obtained, if the alternator is not defective.

NOTE: Do not allow the voltage to increase over 16 volts, as damage to the charging system can result.

Field Diode Assembly Test

NOTE: A shorted or open field diode assembly will cause reduced alternator output and require unit disassembly and removal of the diode assembly for testing. A downgrading of one or more of the diodes will cause the dash indicator bulb to glow dimly, but will normally not effect the alternator output.

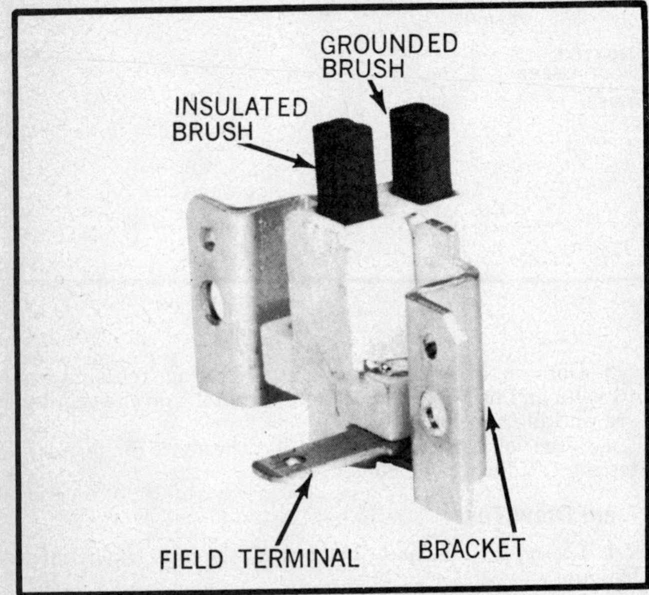

Motorola brush terminal—typical (© Jeep Corp.)

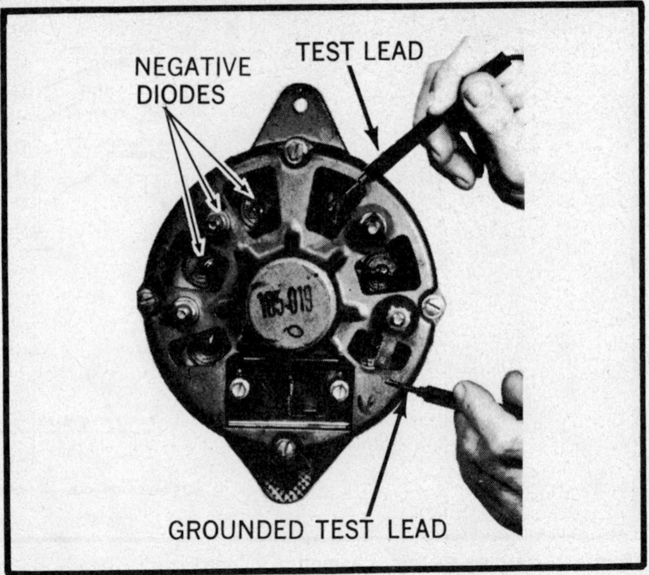

Motorola stator circuit test (© Jeep Corp.)

1. Start the engine and operate at idle speed.
2. With the voltmeter adjusted to the low scale, connect the leads to the alternator output terminal and the negative lead to the regulator terminal.
3. Turn the blower motor to the high position and turn the headlamps to the high beam position for approximately two minutes of operation. This causes the diode assembly to heat up due to the electrical load.
4. Observe the reading on the voltmeter. A range of 0 to 0.2 volts indicates the diode assembly is good. A reading above 02 volts indicates the downgrading of the diode assembly although it is not necessary to replace the assembly unless the reading is over 0.6 volts.
5. A pulsating reading on the meter indicates a positive diode of the rectifier or a soldered connection is breaking down under heat, and the alternator will have to be disassembled for testing repairs.
6. If the reading is over 0.6 volts and the alternator output was deemed satisfactory in the earlier tests, a bench test of the diode assembly will have to be made.
7. If the dash indicator bulb remains on dimly after a satisfactory diode assembly test has been made, inspect the following locations for loose or corroded connections.
   a. Alternator output terminal
   b. Starter relay battery terminal
   c. Ignition switch
   d. Fuse panel
   e. Instrument harness connections
   f. Instrument cluster printed circuits
   g. Indicator bulb socket
   h. Main wiring harness connectors

ALTERNATOR

Disassembly

1. Remove the two self tapping screws and the cover. Pull the brush assembly straight up to clear the locating pins, then lift out the brush assembly.

2. Scribe a matchmark across the front housing, stator, and rear housing. Remove the four through bolts and nuts, then carefully separate the rear housing and stator from the front housing using the proper tools, which are positioned in the slots provided. Do not insert the proper tools deeper than $^1/_{16}$ in., to avoid damaging stator winding.

3. Remove the four locknuts and insulating washers that hold the stator and diode assembly, then separate the assembly from the rear housing. Avoid bending the stator wires, do not unsolder the wires without using pliers as a heat sink.

4. There is no reason to remove the rotor from the front housing unless there is a defect in the field coil or front bearing. Front and rear bearings are lubricated for life and sealed, and as a rule, do not go bad unless the drive belt has been adjusted with too much tension. If the rotor must be removed, use a puller to remove the front drive pulley, then unseat the split ring washer using long nose pliers through the front housing to compress the washer while pulling on the rotor. Tap the rotor shaft lightly to remove the rotor and front bearing, then reach in and remove the split ring washer. Bearings must be removed using a puller and new bearings must be pressed into place.

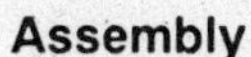

Assembly

1. Clean the bearing and the inside of the bearing hub in the front housing, then gently seat the bearing using a socket of appropriate size and a small hammer.

2. Insert the split-ring washer into the hub of the front housing and seat the washer in its groove. Be extremely careful doing this, because the bearing seal is easily damaged.

3. The front bearing now must be seated against the shoulder on the rotor shaft. Install the fan and pulley spacer, then the Woodruff key, fan and pulley. Using a $^7/_{16}$ in. socket or equivalent tool to fit inside the rear bearing race, apply pressure to drive the bearing against the shoulder of the rotor shaft.

4. Assemble the front and rear housing assemblies by hand, making certain that the rear bearing is properly sealed in the rear housing hub and that the diode wires are not touching the rotor at any point.

5. Align the matchmarks made during disassembly, then spin the rotor to make sure sufficient clearance exists between it and the diode wires. Install the through-bolts and tighten them evenly, using only a hand wrench. Continue assembly in reverse of disassembly.

STATOR

In-Circuit Test

NOTE: When making the in-circuit test, consideration must be given to the rectifier diodes, which are connected to the stator windings. When properly polarized, the diode will conduct current in one direction only. A shorted diode would make the stator appear to be shorted also, so if during this test, a defect is noted, the stator windings and the rectifier diodes must be tested individually. Do not use a 120 volt test lamp as the diodes will be damaged.

1. With the use of a diode continuity light tool or a DC test lamp, connect one test lead to a diode and the second lead to ground. Observe the test lamp and reverse the test leads.

2. The test lamp should light in one direction and not in the other with the leads reversed. If the test lamp lights in both directions, the stator windings are shorted or one of the negative diodes are shorted. Disassemble, unsolder, and test. If the test lamp does not light in either direction, all three rectifiers in the negative assembly are indicated to be open. Disassemble, unsolder, and test.

Out of Circuit Tests

To prepare for out of circuit tests, the stator and diode assembly must be removed from the rear housing. Unsolder the stator leads from the diode stems. Upon reassembly, be certain that the same leads are soldered to the diodes in the same location as removed.

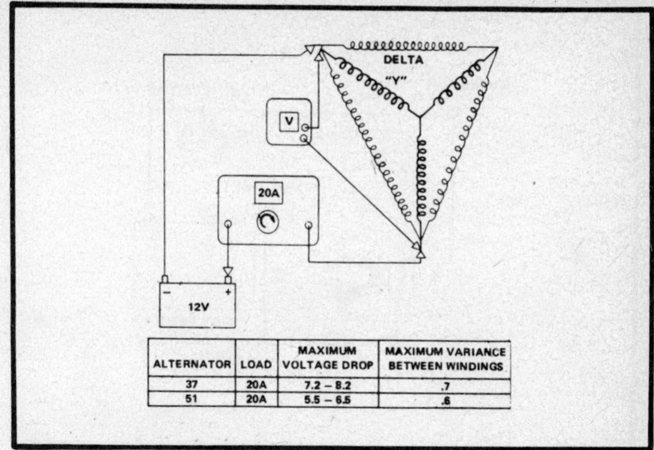

ALTERNATOR	LOAD	MAXIMUM VOLTAGE DROP	MAXIMUM VARIANCE BETWEEN WINDINGS
37	20A	7.2 – 8.2	.7
51	20A	5.5 – 6.5	.6

Motorola stator load test (© Jeep Corp.)

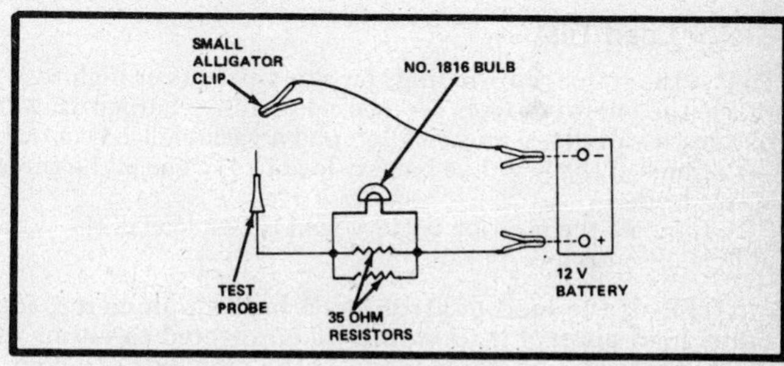

Rectifier diode tester (© Jeep Corp.)

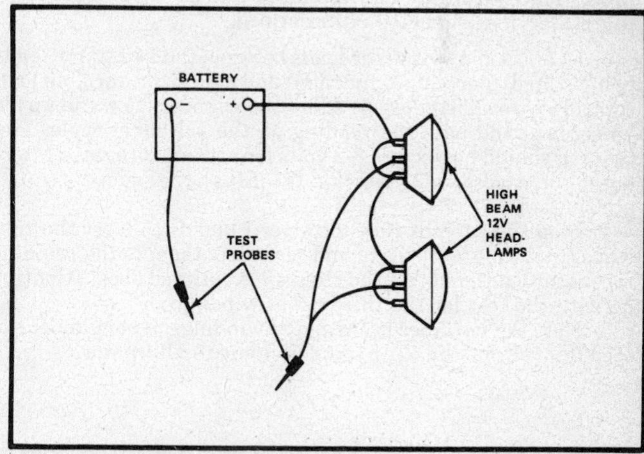

Field diode tester (© Jeep Corp.)

Stator Short Test

1. With the use of a test lamp or ohmmeter, test the windings of the stator by attaching one lead to the stator core and probing the stator leads with the other test lead.

2. The test lamp will light and the ohmmeter will register if a short circuit exists between the windings and the core. The short circuit must be found or the stator unit be replaced.

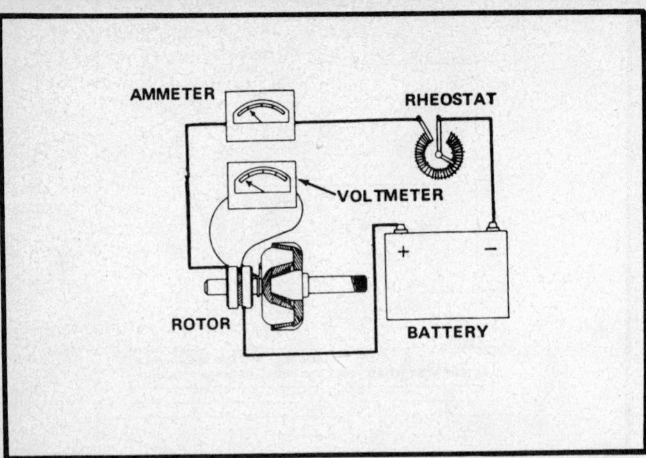

Motorola rotor winding test (© Jeep Corp.)

Stator Load Test

To test the stator coil windings for short circuits or high resistance, the following tools are needed. A fully charged 12 volt battery, a voltmeter, an ammeter, and a variable load control.

1. Connect the negative battery lead to any one of the three stator leads.
2. Connect the positive battery lead to one lead of the variable load control.

NOTE: If the load control has a built in ammeter, the other load control lead would be connected to either of the two remaining stator leads. If the ammeter is a separate unit, the remaining load control lead would be connected to the positive ammeter lead and the negative ammeter lead would be connected to one of the two remaining stator leads (series connection).

3. Connect the voltmeter leads between the two stator leads being tested, (parallel connection) and adjust the variable load control to draw 20 amperes. Allow the windings to warm up for 15 seconds and note the reading on the voltmeter scale. The reading should not exceed 8.2 volts for a 37 ampere rated alternator, or exceed 6.5 volts for the 51 and 55 ampere rated alternators.
4. Stop the current flow to the coil and disconnect the test leads from the stator leads and reconnect them to the remaining stator leads and test the circuits as outlined above. Continue with the test for the third set of windings.
5. Note the variance between the windings. It should not exceed 0.7 volt for the 37, 51 and 55 ampere alternator.

Rectifier Diode Test

1. With diodes unsoldered, use a commercial type tester and follow the manufacturer's test procedure or make up a heavy load tester.

NOTE: A 15 ampere load is necessary to properly test the rectifier diodes for heat related defects.

2. With the use of the heavy load tester probes, connect them to the diode so the test bulb is lighted.
3. Maintain the test load on the diode for 1 to 3 minutes. If the light flickers or goes out, the diode is defective.
4. If the light remains on after three minutes, immediately reverse the test leads. If the test bulb lights, the diode is defective.
5. Test the remaining diodes in the same manner. The diodes are normally not replaced separately, but are replaced as a positive or negative rectifier bridge assembly.

NOTE: When soldering the stator wires to the diodes, it is advisable to use a set of needle nose pliers attached to the diode stem, to act as a heat sink to avoid heat damage to the diodes.

Field Diode Assembly (Diode Trio)

Two types of diode assemblies are used. The board and the potted type and both are tested with the same procedure.

1. With the diode assembly removed, use a commercial type tester and follow the manufacturer's test procedures or make a load tester.
2. Connect the test leads to one of the diodes so that the test bulb is lighted.

NOTE: A one ampere load is needed to properly test the field diode assembly for heat related defects.

3. Maintain a load on the diode for approximately one minute to detect any heat failure.
4. Reverse the test leads and if the test bulb would light, the diode is defective. Test the remaining diodes.

Rotor Winding Tests

With the rotor removed, use a test probe connected in series with a 110 volt test lamp. Place one probe on a slip ring and the other probe on the rotor core. The rotor is shorted if the test bulb lights.

To test for shorted windings, use a fully charged 12 volt battery, an ammeter, a voltmeter, a variable rheostat, and test probes. With the use of the test probe leads, place the rheostat and ammeter in series with the battery. Connect one test probe to one slip ring and the other test probe to the other slip ring. Place the voltmeter in parallel with the slip rings.

Slowly reduce the resistance of the rheostat to zero and with

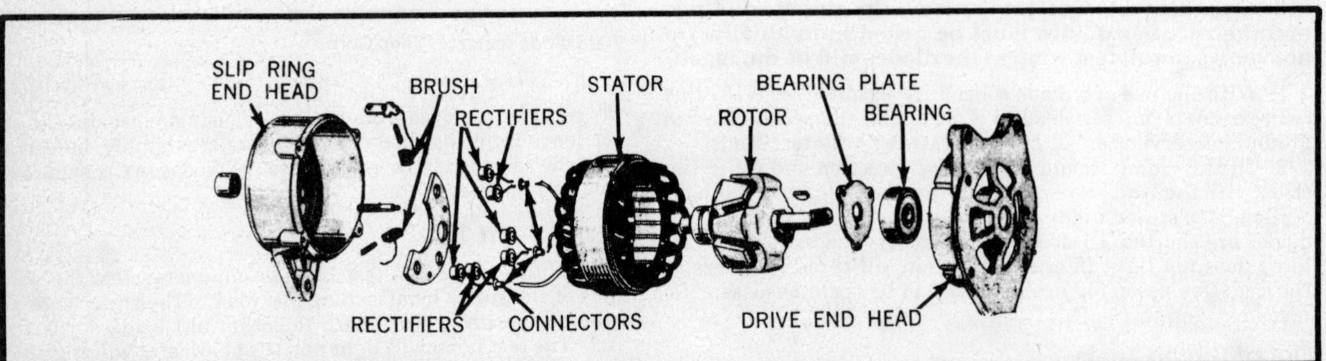

Prestolite alternator—exploded view (© Prestolite Corp.)

full battery voltage, (12.6 ± 0.2 volt), applied to the rotor coil, the field current should register between 1.8 to 2.5 amperes. Excessive ampere draw would indicate shorted windings and low ampere draw would indicate open windings of the rotor.

The Prestolite System

Pretolite alternators incorporate an isolation diode, mounted as a component part of the internal positive heat sink assembly. Such alternators are almost identical to late model Motorola units in operation. Test procedures for the Motorola alternator also apply to the diode equipped Prestolite.

TROUBLESHOOTING

NOTE: See the "Alternator Test Plans" section before proceeding further.

Fusible Link Test

See the Motorola system section for the fuse link test.

Charging System Operation

See the Motorola system section for the "Charging System Operation" tests.

Testing the Ignition Switch to Regulator Circuit

1. Disconnect the regulator wires from the regulator.
2. Turn on the key. Using a test light or voltmeter, check for current between the I terminal and ground and the L terminal ground. If voltage is present, this part of the system is ok. If no voltage is present, check for broken or shorted wires, a bad indicator bulb, a bad ammeter (if so equipped), or bad connections.

Alternator Disassembly

1. Remove the two brush mounting screws and cover, then tip the brush assembly away from the alternator and remove.
2. Matchmark the rear housing, stator and drive end housing, then remove the four retaining screws. The stator and rear housing are removed as a unit by tapping lightly with a fiber hammer to separate them from the front housing.
3. The rotor should not be removed unless it or the front bearing is defective. To remove the rotor under these conditions, first remove the pulley nut and pulley (using a two jaw puller), then remove the fan, Woodruff key and spacer. The rotor is removed from the front housing using a three-paw puller.
4. The front bearing is easily removed, after taking out the retaining ring, by pressing it out in a large vise using sockets to support the housing from the rear.

Stator Coil Test (Diode Type)

1. Using a No. 57 bulb, connected in series with a 12 volt battery, as a test light, touch one test lead to the connection of the three stator windings and the other test lead to each stator lead that is connected to the diodes. If the bulb does not light, the winding is open.
2. To test for a grounded stator, use a 110 volt test lamp. First disconnect the diodes from the stator leads, then touch one test lead to the stator core and the other test lead to each of the three stator leads. If the test lamp lights, the winding is grounded.

NOTE: If all other components are ok. and alternator still does not work, it can be assumed that the stator windings are internally shorted. This type of short is impossible to detect by using the previous test. Diode tests are the same as for the Motorola alternator.

Alternator Assembly

1. Press the front bearing into the front housing, making sure the dust seal faces the rotor. Install the bearing retaining snap ring, then press the shoulder of the shaft against the inner bearing race using a tool that fits over the shaft and against the race. Install the spacer, Woodruff key, fan and pulley, then install lockwasher and pulley nut.
2. Install the diode heat sink, negative diodes and stator. Solder any stator to diode connections that were unsoldered, using pliers as a heat sink to prevent overheating.
3. Install the rotor and front drive housing to stator and rear housing, aligning matchmarks made during disassembly. Install the four retaining screws, then the brush holder assembly and retaining screws.
4. Make sure the stator leads and brush holder assembly clear the rotor and that the rotor can be spun by hand without binding.

The Leece-Neville System

2600 SERIES, JB TYPE (105 AMPS) AND 2700 SERIES, JB TYPE (130 AMPS)

The Leece-Neville charging systems use varied types of alternator housings and controls. The types most commonly encountered on medium and heavy trucks will be described as follows.

105 AMPERE ALTERNATOR (EARLY TYPE)

With the use of an adjustable carbon pile load control, field rheostat control, and volt/amp tester, the rated ampere output and field current draw can be tested with the alternator mounted on the engine. If any indication of malfunction is determined, the alternator should be removed and the internal circuits tested.

Upon disassembly, the testing procedure for the internal circuits follows the outline described in the Autolite (Ford) type alternator section.

Rated Output Test

1. With battery disconnected, ignition switch in off position, and the wire disconnected at the alternator B+ terminal, hook an ammeter between the alternator B+ terminal and the wire that was just disconnected from this terminal.
2. Disconnect wire from the alternator F terminal.
3. With the field rheostat adjusted to open position, connect its leads to the alternator F terminal and the alternator B+ terminal.
4. Hook up a voltmeter between the alternator B+ terminal and ground.
5. Reconnect battery cables.
6. Connect a carbon pile load control between the battery posts.
7. With a tachometer connected to the engine, start the engine and set its speed at the recommended rpm.
8. While watching both ammeter and voltmeter, adjust the carbon pile load control to maintain 15 volts. When field rheostat control is fully closed, note voltmeter and ammeter readings.
9. Adjust field rheostat to open position and carbon pile control to off.
10. Compare readings with specifications. Readings should be at least equal to rated output specified by the manufacturer. If output complies with specifications, proceed to the voltage regulator test. If readings are below rated output, it indicates possible internal troubles.

Field Current Draw Test

1. Disconnect battery ground cable.
2. Disconnect carbon pile, voltmeter, ammeter and field rheostat from the previous check.

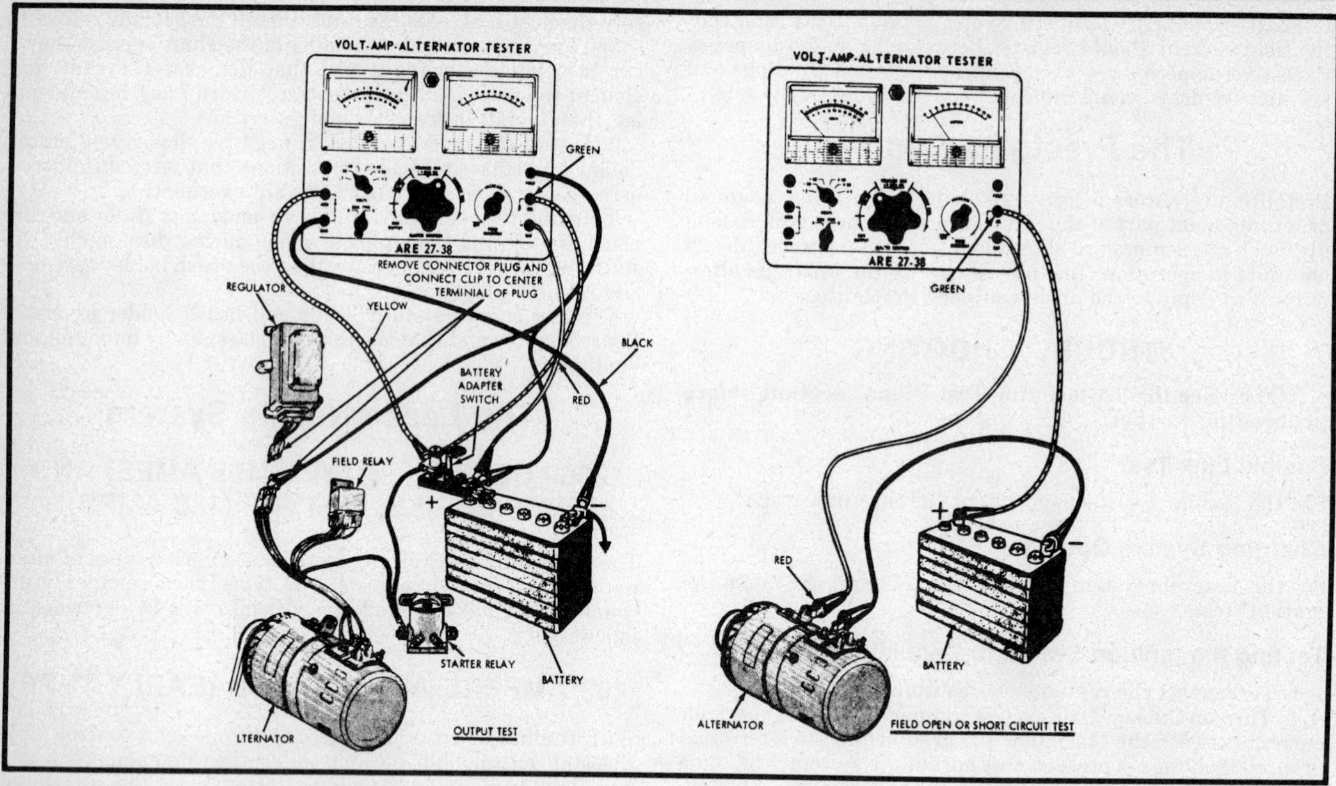

105 amp alternator test (© Ford Motor Co.)

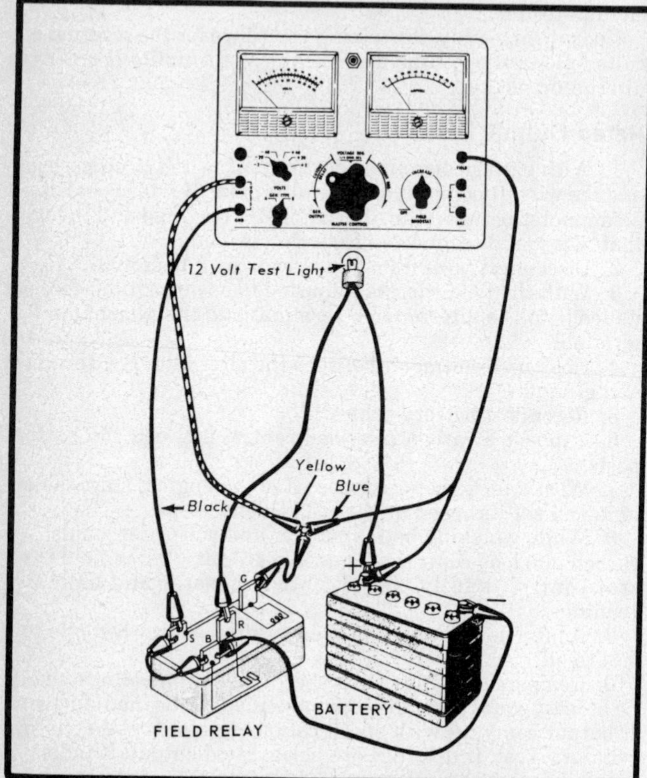

Leece-Neville system—field relay test (© Ford Motor Co.)

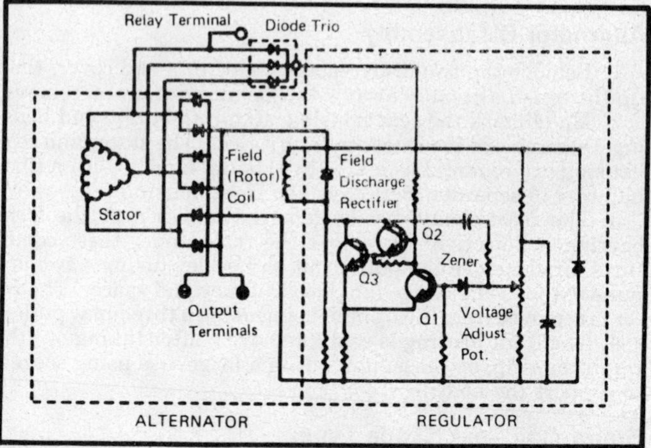

JB series wiring schematic—typical (© GM Corp.)

3. Reconnect the regular circuit wire to the alternator B+ terminal.
4. With the field rheostat adjusted to the open position, connect one of its leads to the alternator B+ terminal and the other lead to a test ammeter lead.
5. Connect the remaining ammeter lead to the alternator F terminal.
6. Connect one voltmeter lead to the alternator F terminal and the remaining voltmeter lead to ground.
7. Reconnect battery ground cable, start the engine, and run it at about 1,000 rpm.
8. With field rheostat in closed position, read the ammeter and voltmeter for a very brief period.
9. Compare these readings with specifications.
10. If readings are low, it indicates trouble in slip rings or brushes.
11. If readings are too high, it indicates trouble in the rotor field windings.

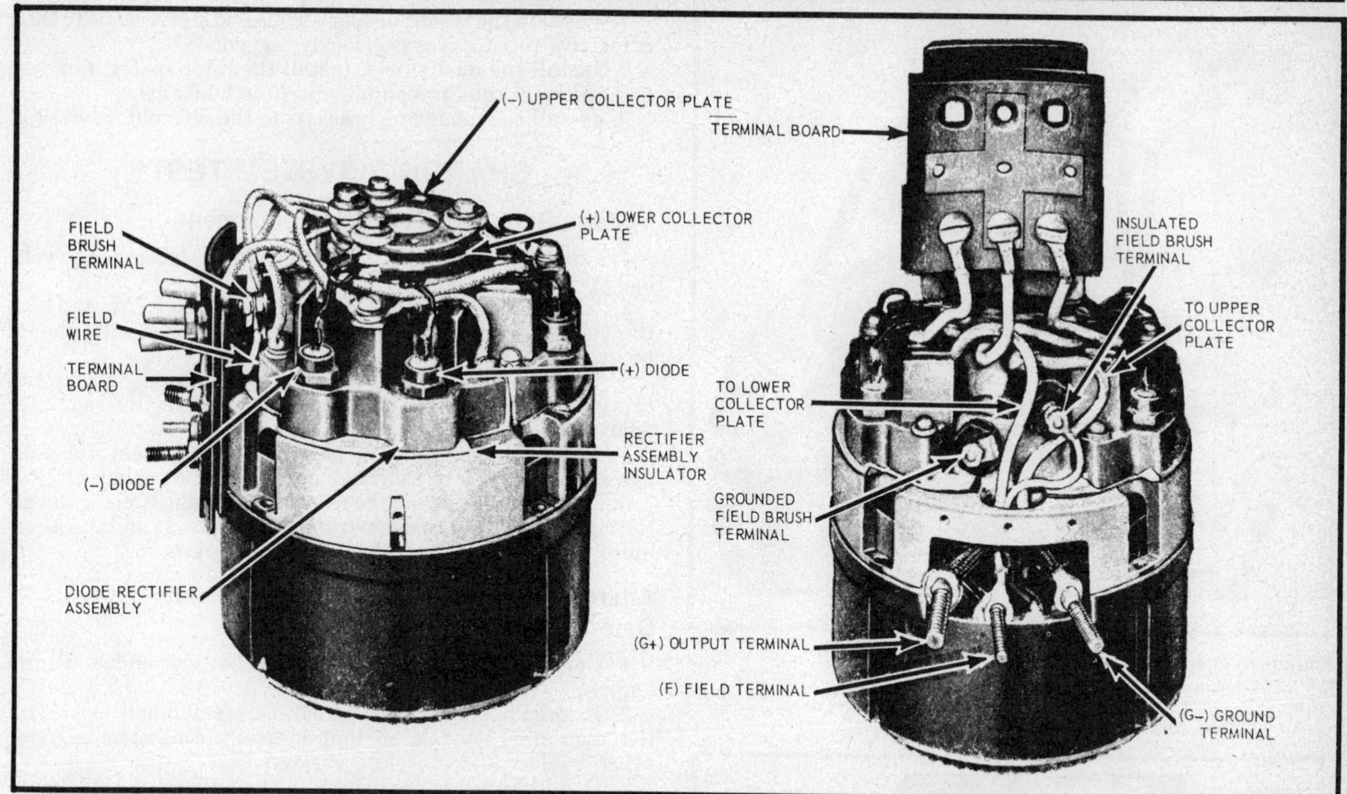

Leece-Neville 105 amp collector plates and wire lead assembly (© Ford Motor Co.)

12. If readings are as specified on an alternator which did not deliver its rated output, look for trouble in the stator or diodes.

Disassembly

1. Remove the mounting brackets. Remove the pulley nut, pulley, fan, key, and spacer from rotor shaft.
2. Remove the dust shield. Remove three screws holding the six stator and terminal board wire leads to the rectifier assemblies.
3. Remove the three screws holding the terminal board to the brush end housing.
4. Remove the field lead from the brush holder and remove the brush assembly from the housing.
5. Remove the four through bolts and separate the drive end housing and rotor from the stator and brush end housing. Remove the stator from the brush end housing.
6. The bearings can be pressed from the rotor shaft and replaced. The slip rings can be pressed from the rotor after removal of the field wire.
7. Remove the two circular copper collector plates from the brush end housing.

NOTE: The retaining screws hold the diode lead wires and terminal board output leads. Tag the wires for identification during assembly.

8. Remove the terminal board and the rectifier assemblies from the brush end housing.
9. Testing of the internal circuits can now be accomplished.

Assembly

1. Replace any necessary parts and assemble the terminal board and wires.
2. Position the two stator winding insulators in the brush end housing.
3. Install the rectifier assemblies and insulators into the brush end housing.

Removal of diode trio (© General Motors Corp.)

4. Position the terminal board and wire assembly, the two circular collector plates, insulators, and washers into the brush end housing and install the retaining screws with the diode leads and output leads in their respective locations as previously tagged.
5. Position the stator to the brush end housing and connect the assembly to the rotor and drive end housing. Install the four through bolts and tighten.
6. Install the brushes, springs, and brush holders into the housing and connect the field wire to the brush holder.

Voltage regulator adjustment (© General Motors Corp.)

Brush and spring positioning (© General Motors Corp.)

7. Position the terminal board leads and stator leads to their respective rectifiers as previously tagged.
8. Install the dust shield. Install the rotor spacer, fan, key, and pulley. Torque the pulley nut 70 to 80 ft. lbs.
9. Install the mounting brackets to the alternator housing.

CHARGING SYSTEM TESTS

Voltage Regulator Test and Adjustment

1. Connect a voltmeter across the battery. Observe the voltage and start the engine.
2. Increase the engine speed to 1000 to 1500 RPMs and note the voltage reading. An increase to 13.6 to 14.2 volts should occur.
3. If the voltage reading is out of specifications, attempt to bring the voltage within the ok range by rotating the regulator adjusting screw back and forth.
4. If the voltage cannot be lowered by adjustment, the voltage regulator may be defective and should be replaced.
5. If the voltage cannot be raised by the adjustment, the alternator, regulator, or diode trio may be at fault and the alternator must be removed for testing and repairs.

Alternator, Regulator or Diode Trio Fault Determination

1. Connect a voltmeter across the battery and start the engine.
2. Insert a paper clip type wire into the small hole located on the regulator housing, so that it firmly contacts the outer brush holder.
3. Connect a jumper wire from the negative output terminal to the stiff wire inserted in the regulator housing.
4. With the engine operating between 1500 to 2000 RPMs the voltmeter reading should rise above battery voltage. This indicates the alternator is good and the fault lies with the voltage regulator and/or the diode trio.
5. If the voltage reading does not increase above battery voltage, the alternator must be removed for testing and repairs.

Checking Output (Alternate Method)

An alternate method used to check current output from each phase is to construct a test lamp from a two filament sealed beam bulb, connected in such a manner that the two filaments are in parallel.

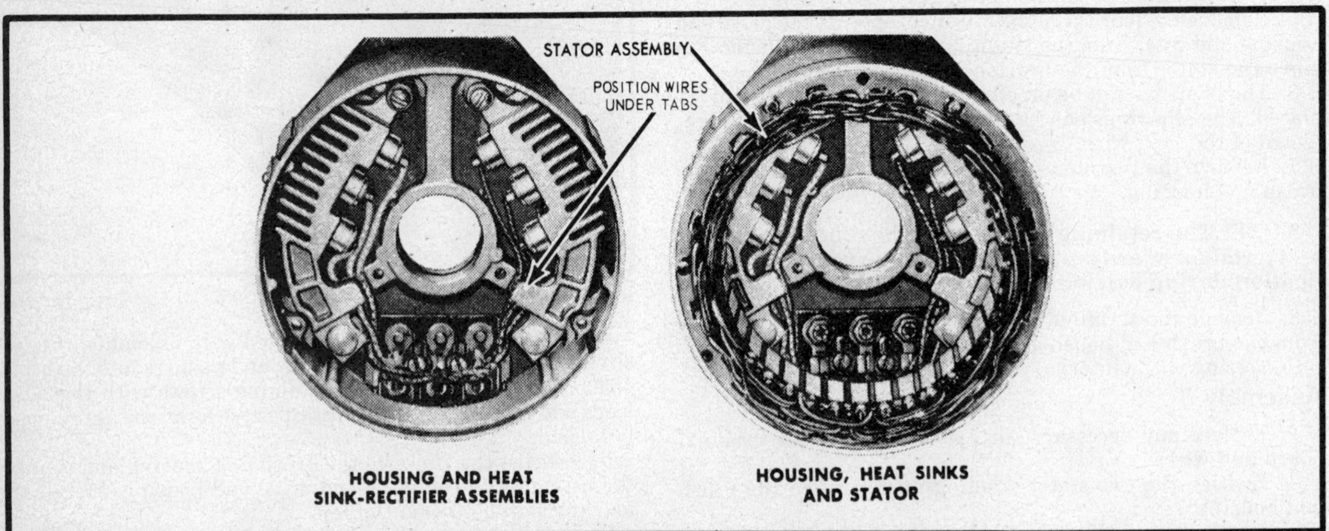

Brush end housing, rectifier and stator assembly—Leece-Neville (© Ford Motor Co.)

Testing alternator using jumper wire (© General Motors Corp.)

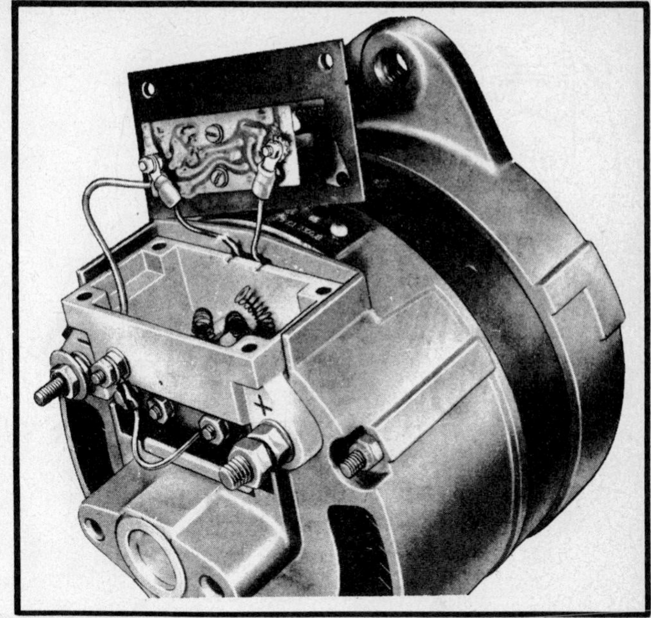

Voltage regulator panel (© General Motors Corp.)

The lamp should light with equal brilliancy when each phase is tested. If a dimmer light is observed between two phases, a defective diode, stator, or power diode is indicated and further testing would have to be done. Point to point resistance checks with an ohmmeter on the circuit board of the voltage regulator can be misleading and inconclusive, due to the circuitry in parallel of the capacitors, resistors, diodes and transistors. To check a regulator, it is advisable to install it on an alternator known to be good, if possible. If in doubt, replace the regulator with a new unit.

Testing

Follow the procedure for testing the diode trio, rectifiers, stator, and rotor as outlined under the 10 SI alternator section. The field current specifications are 2.8 amperes at 12 volts for the 2600 JB alternator and 5.0 to 6.0 amperes at 12 volts for the 2700 JB alternator.

TRANSFORMER/RECTIFIER UNIT (TR UNIT)

The TR unit is installed on the slip ring end frame of the 2600 JB alternator units, as required by the vehicle application. The TR unit is used for charging the cranking battery on 12 volt systems where a 24 volt starting system is used. This type of system utilizes two sets of 12 volt batteries, in series, to provide 24 volts for cranking. The vehicle system's 12 volt battery is charged in the conventional manner by the alternator and provides power for the 12 volt vehicle loads, such as lights, heater, etc. The cranking battery is charged by the TR unit and since the load demand on this battery is for starting only, the 15 amps available from the TR unit is normally sufficient to recharge the battery. As the cranking battery becomes charged up, the TR unit output current will gradually drop to about one amp when the terminal voltage of the battery reaches 13.8 volts.

When the TR unit is used with the alternator, the available 12 volt alternator output will be reduced proportionally and should be recognized when the alternator may not have sufficient capacity to recharge the batteries during periods of high frequency startings and extra power needed during the starting procedure.

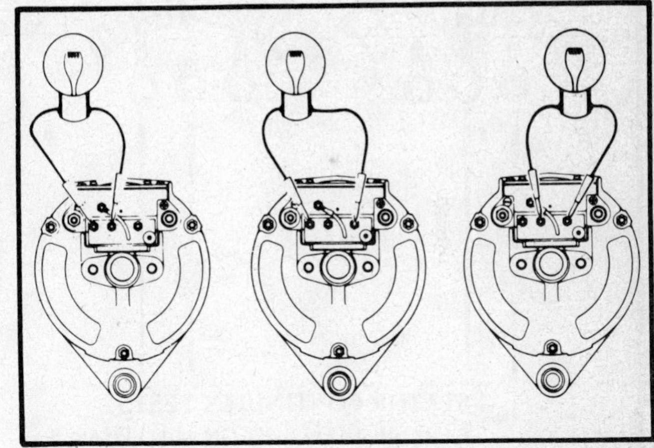

Alternate method of testing alternator output using a test lamp (© General Motors Corp.)

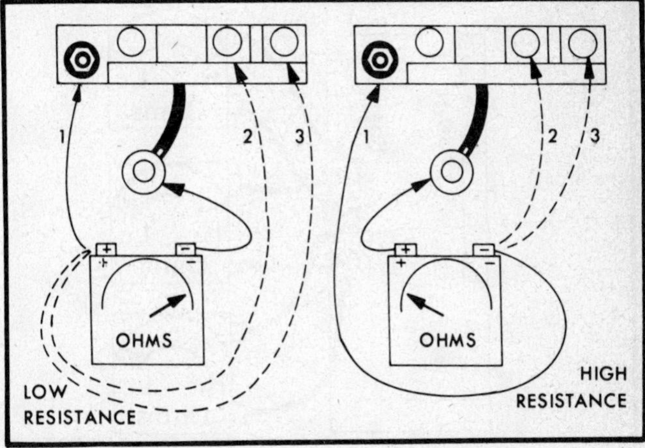

Method of testing diode trio (© General Motors Corp.)

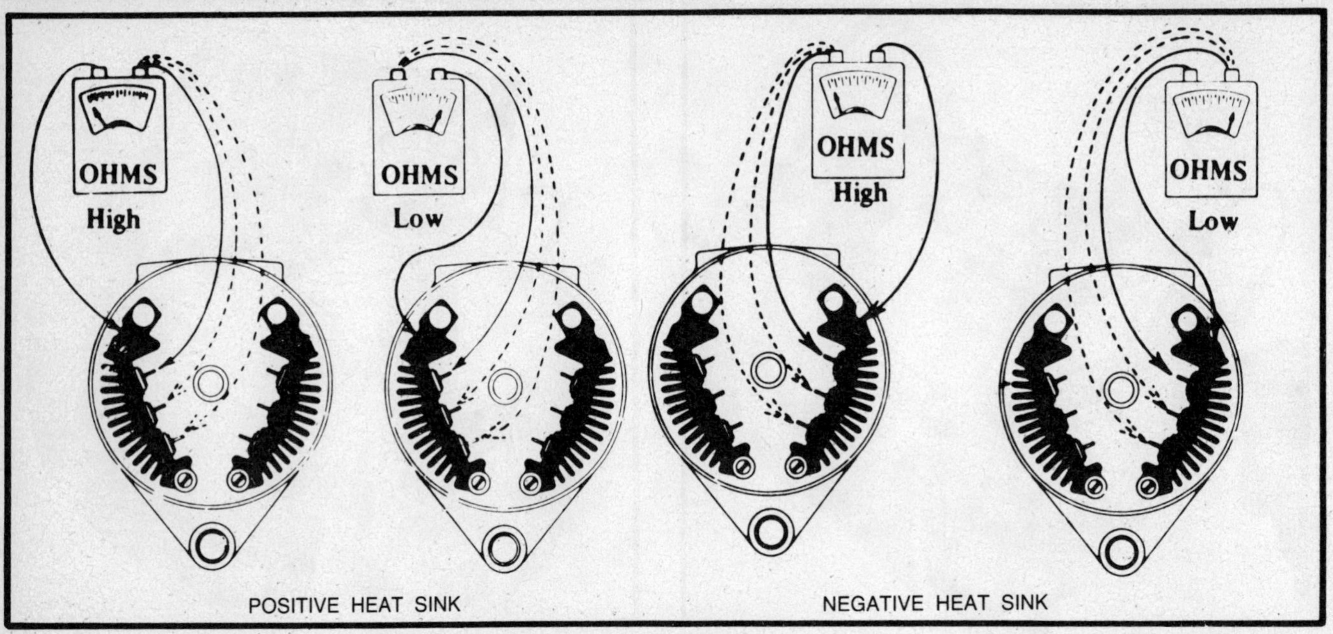

Testing the positive and negative heat sinks—Leece-Neville (© General Motors Corp.)

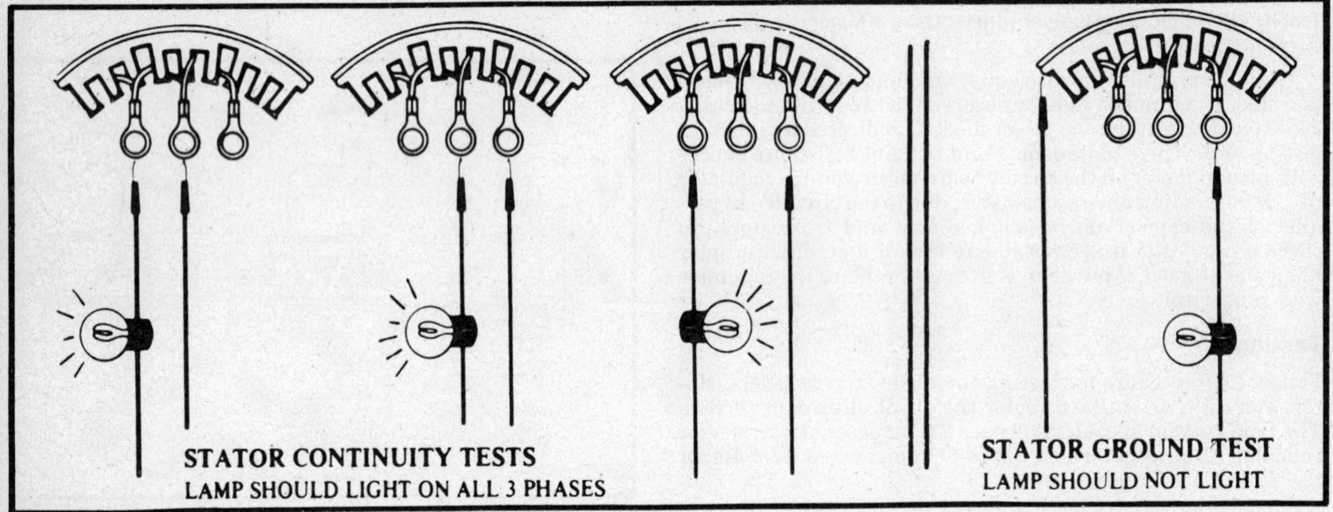

Stator test—Leece-Neville (© General Motors Corp.)

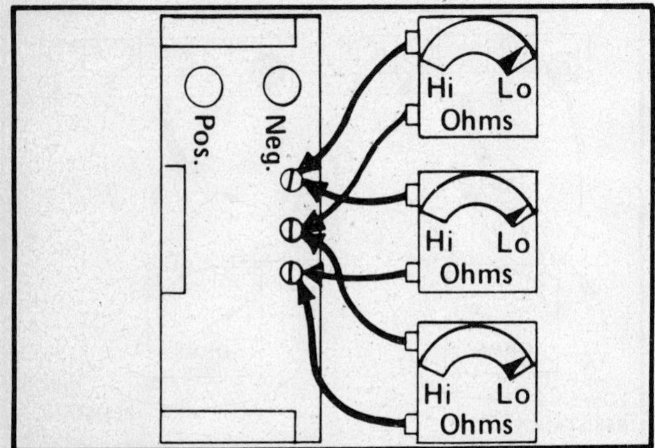

Transformer primary continuity test using an ohmmeter (© General Motors Corp.)

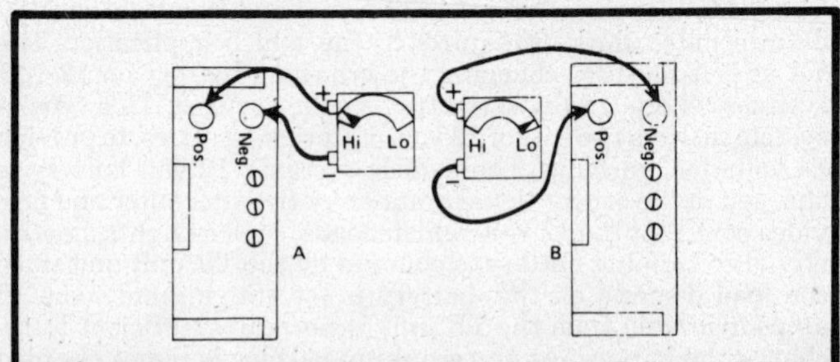

Rectifier test on the transformer/rectifier unit using an ohmmeter (© GM Corp.)

3425 Series, JA Type (Leece-Neville)

The alternator is a self oad limiting unit with a fully adjustable solid state internal regulator. The alternator unit is driven by a coupler from the engine accessory drive gear. The diodes are mounted in heat sinks and convert the alternating current

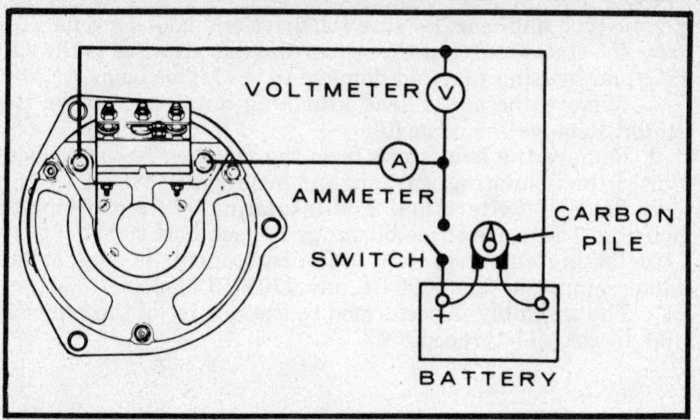

2600-JB series test connections·(© General Motors Corp.)

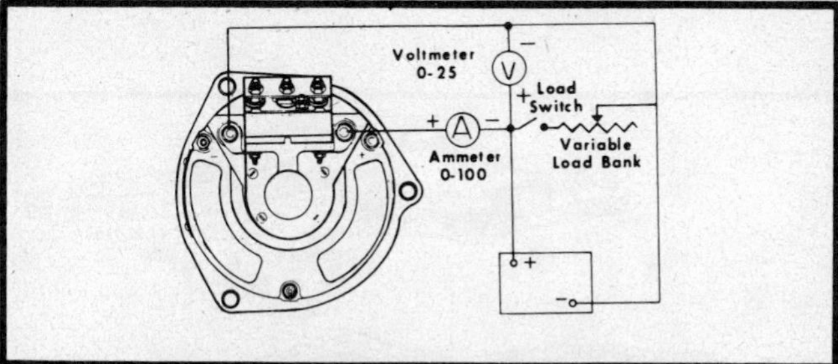

Connections for alternator output test—3425-JA
(© General Motors Corp.)

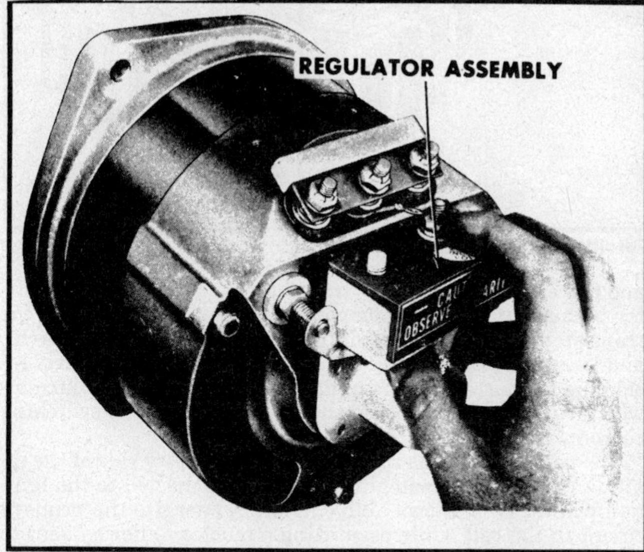

Removal or installation of brush holder and voltage regulator—3425-JA (© General Motors Corp.)

from a delta wound stator, to direct current. A capacitor is used to assist in suppressing transient voltage which could damage the diodes. The brushes and voltage regulator are mounted in a water proof housing, located at the rear of the alternator, that can be removed for replacement or inspection without disassembling the entire unit.

ELECTRICAL TESTING

The electrical testing of the internal components are done in the same manner as the 2600 JB and 2700 JB models.

Disassembly and Assembly

1. Remove the rotor shaft nut and pull the keyed coupling

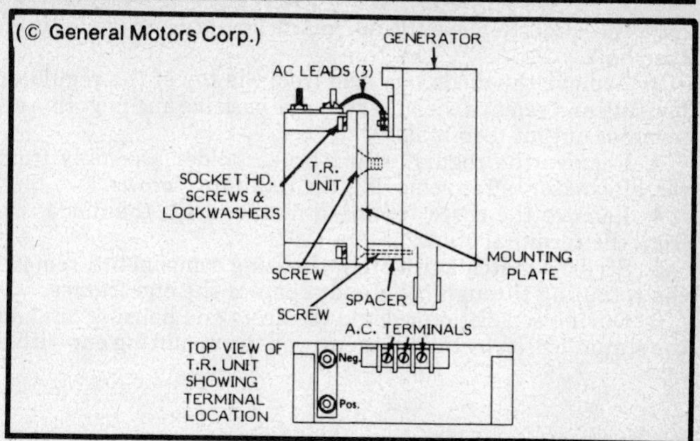

TR unit connected to 2600-JB series alternator

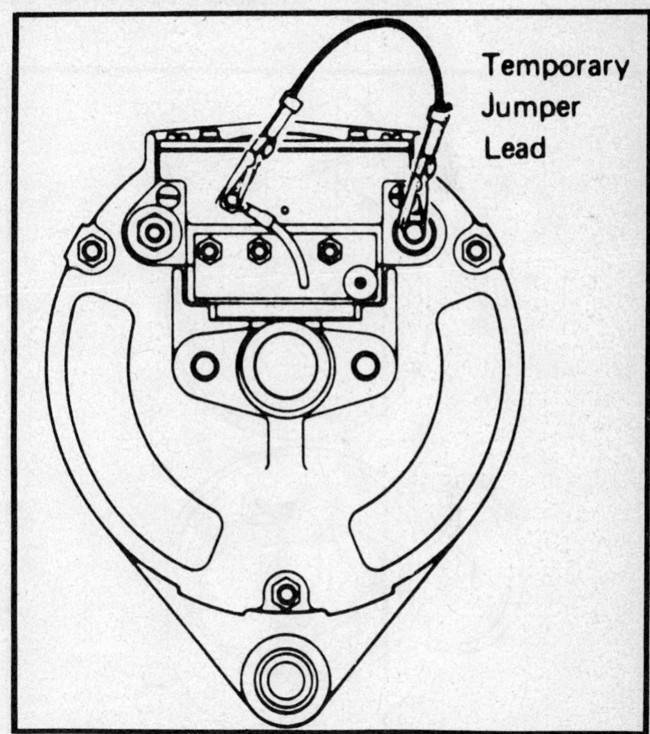

Reestablishing magnetism with jumper lead(© General Motors Corp.)

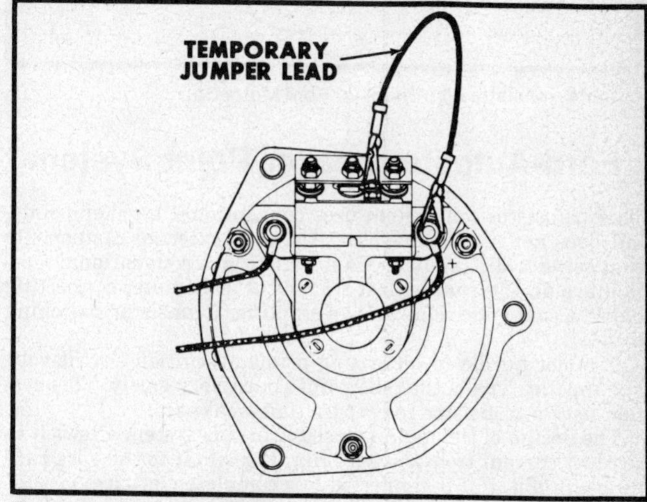

Temporary jumper lead positioned to magnetize the rotor—3425-JA (© General Motors Corp.)

from the shaft. Remove the fan guard, key, fan and spacer from the shaft.

2. Remove the diode trio lead from the top of the regulator housing and remove the nuts from the positive and negative alternator output terminals.

3. Remove the regulator and brush holder assembly from the alternator, after removing the retaining screws.

4. Remove the three retaining nuts and lift the diode trio from the terminal studs.

5. Scribe a match mark on the housing components, remove the retaining through bolts and separate the end frames.

6. During separation, should the drive end housing bind on the stator, loosen by tapping gently on the mounting ear with a plastic type hammer. Be sure the drive end housing separates from the stator and that the stator remains attached to the slip ring end housing to avoid damage to the stator leads.

7. Remove the stator lead attaching nuts and remove the stator. Remove the capacitor.

8. Remove the heat sinks from the housing. Note the location of the insulating washers and bushings.

9. Remove the terminal stud insulating bushings from the housing. There are three bushings in each hole.

10. Testing and inspection of the components is done in the same manner as the 2600 JB and 2700 JB models.

11. The assembly is performed in the reverse of the removal and disassembly procedure.

ELECTRONIC IGNITION SYSTEM

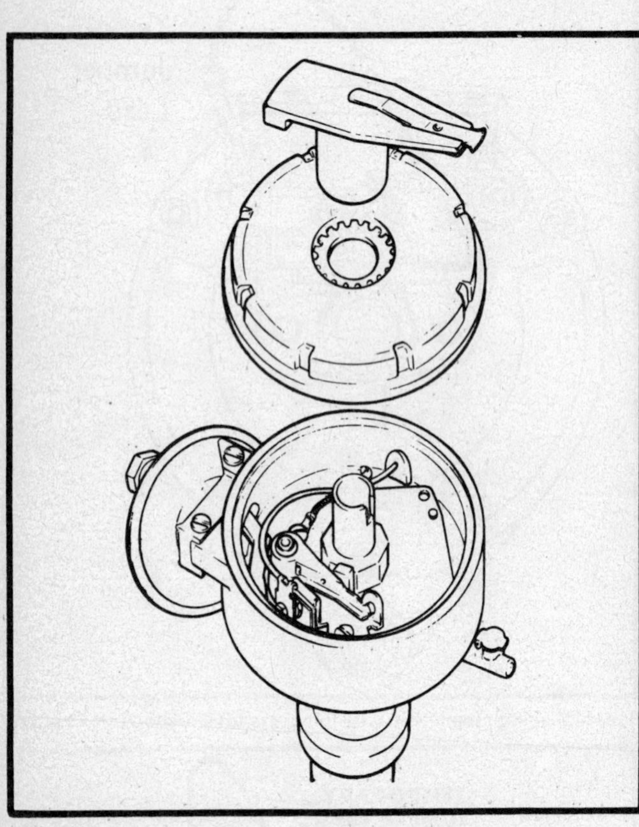

Autolite transistor distributor (© Ford Motor Co.)

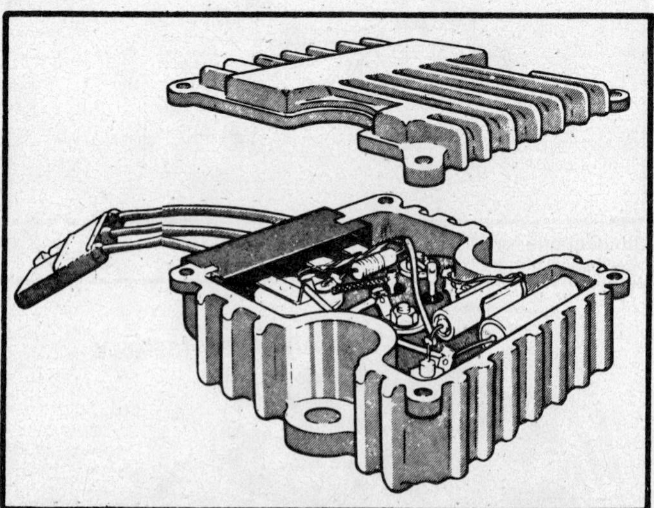

Autolite amplifier assembly (© Ford Motor Co.)

Ford-Autolite Breaker Point System

This transistorized system uses conventional breaker points, but does not use a condenser. The only external components that serve to distinguish this system from a conventional ignition are an external ballast resistor, a tachometer connecting block, a cold-start relay and an amplifier (transistor switching device).

The major hurdle to increasing primary ignition circuit voltage inpoint-type is that the points burn very easily. This system uses a transistor to by-pass that weakness.

The design of the main transistor in this system allows it to conduct current from the wire running into it to the wire running out of it, if it is connected to a complete electrical circuit. However, as the current passes through the transistor, it breaks that current down into two paths, one of high voltage and one of low voltage. This transistor is called a PNP transistor because of its three component parts. The top part of the transistor is called a collector (C), the middle part the base (B), and lower part the emitter (E). The two currents that form inside the transistor are the high current one, or power current, which runs from E to C and the low current, or the switching current, which runs from B to E.

The power current is connected to the primary side of the ignition coil and the switching current is connected to the ignition points. This allows high current to energize the primary circuit in the coil while permitting a much smaller current to pass through the points.

In order for the transistor to pass current, both the power circuit and the switching circuit must make a complete circuit. This has made adaptation of this transistor system to an automotive ignition system relatively simple. When the ignition key is turned on and the breaker points are closed, current passes from the battery, through the ignition switch, to the amplifier which contains the PNP transistor. As the current from the battery passes through the transistor, the two transistor circuits are connected as follows: the power current is connected to the coil, and the switching current is connected to the points. Since the points are closed, both transistor circuits are complete and the primary side of the ignition coil builds up a magnetic field. When the ignition points open, the switching circuit in the transistor (B to E) opens causing the transistor to stop passing current. When the transistor stops passing current, the primary ignition circuit breaks down, and the induction of the magnetic field from the primary circuit in the coil

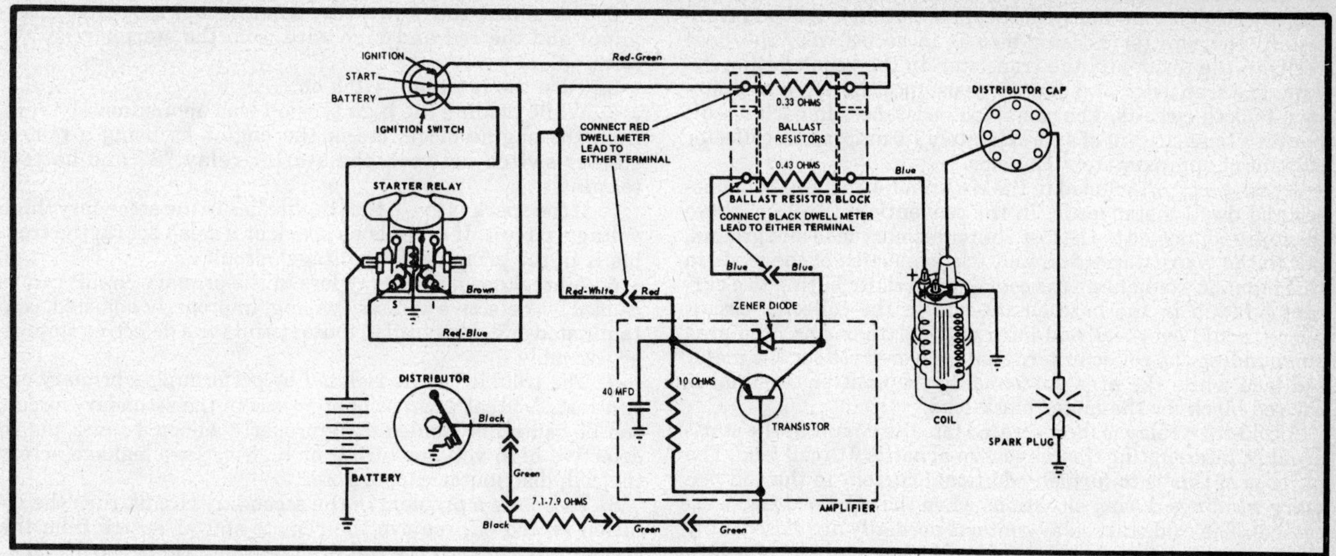

Transistor ignition circuit (© Ford Motor Co.)

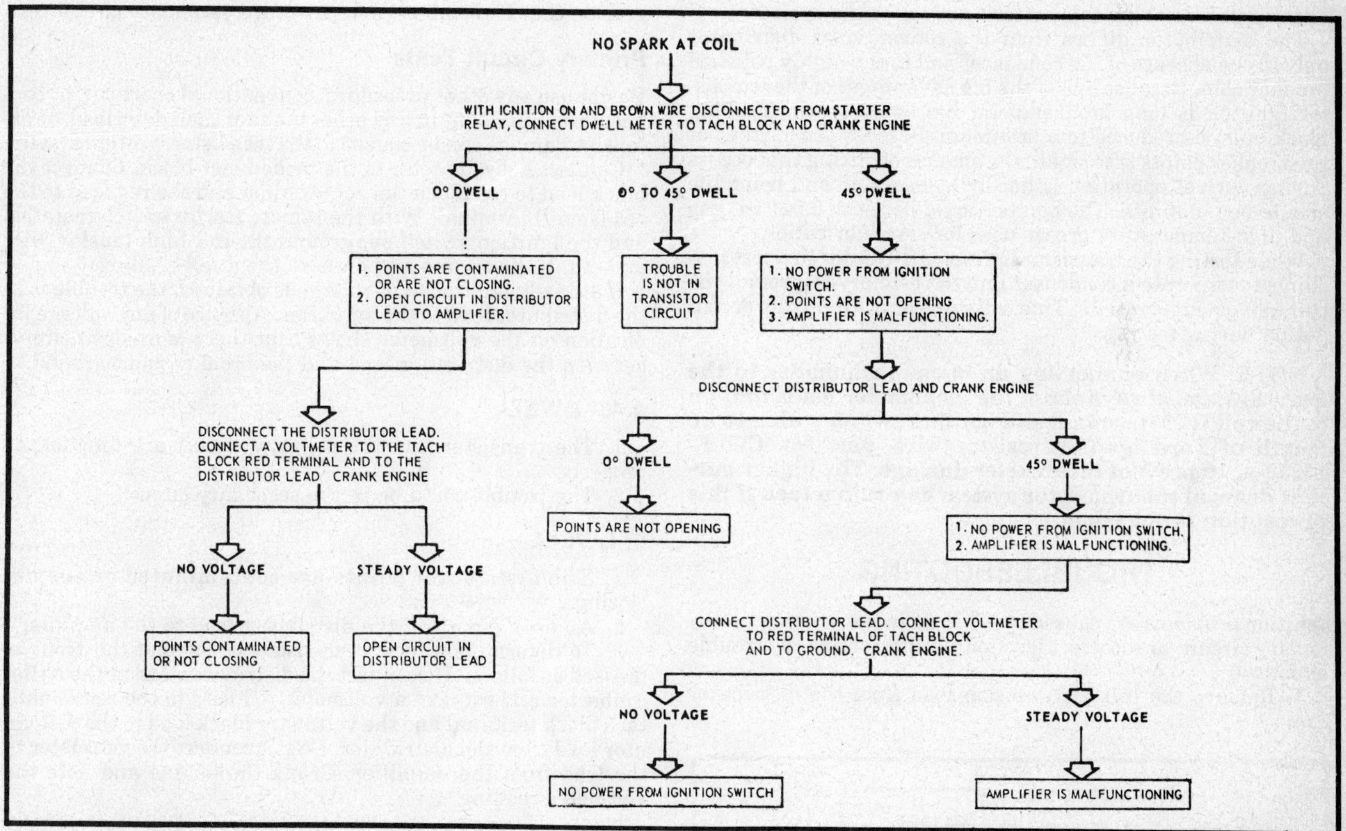

NO SPARK AT COIL

WITH IGNITION ON AND BROWN WIRE DISCONNECTED FROM STARTER RELAY, CONNECT DWELL METER TO TACH BLOCK AND CRANK ENGINE

- 0° DWELL
  1. POINTS ARE CONTAMINATED OR ARE NOT CLOSING.
  2. OPEN CIRCUIT IN DISTRIBUTOR LEAD TO AMPLIFIER.

  DISCONNECT THE DISTRIBUTOR LEAD. CONNECT A VOLTMETER TO THE TACH BLOCK RED TERMINAL AND TO THE DISTRIBUTOR LEAD CRANK ENGINE
  - NO VOLTAGE → POINTS CONTAMINATED OR NOT CLOSING
  - STEADY VOLTAGE → OPEN CIRCUIT IN DISTRIBUTOR LEAD
- 0° TO 45° DWELL
  - TROUBLE IS NOT IN TRANSISTOR CIRCUIT
- 45° DWELL
  1. NO POWER FROM IGNITION SWITCH.
  2. POINTS ARE NOT OPENING
  3. AMPLIFIER IS MALFUNCTIONING.

  DISCONNECT DISTRIBUTOR LEAD AND CRANK ENGINE
  - 0° DWELL → POINTS ARE NOT OPENING
  - 45° DWELL
    1. NO POWER FROM IGNITION SWITCH.
    2. AMPLIFIER IS MALFUNCTIONING.

    CONNECT DISTRIBUTOR LEAD. CONNECT VOLTMETER TO RED TERMINAL OF TACH BLOCK AND TO GROUND. CRANK ENGINE.
    - NO VOLTAGE → NO POWER FROM IGNITION SWITCH
    - STEADY VOLTAGE → AMPLIFIER IS MALFUNCTIONING

Autolite transistor ignition troubleshooting chart (© Ford Motor Co.)

into the secondary circuit in the coil takes place. However, since the initial voltage in the primary circuit in the coil was much higher than in a conventional system, the voltage build-up in the coil will be much quicker and will rise to a higher level than in a conventional ignition system.

The other components of the system, all of which are contained in the amplifier housing with the PNP transistor, are a condenser, a zener diode, a toroid, a base to emitter resistor, and a collector resistor.

The base resistor is similar to the conventional ignition resistor wire and is located between the distributor and the transistor (heat sink). It provides an 9.0 ohm resistance which is necessary for current limitation and it should not be replaced with any other wire, resistance or otherwise. To do so would result in immediate transistor destruction.

The collector and emitter resistors both are located in a ballast resistor block made of white ceramic for electrical and thermal insulation. Both resistors serve the same purpose limiting system current and control of voltages within their respective circuits. The two resistors are in series in the collector-emitter circuit, together with the ignition coil, toroid and transistor. The emitter resistor also is in series with the base resistor, the torid, and the transistor, in the base-emitter circuit. The transistor and emitter resistance therefore are common to both circuits. The combined resistances in each circuit permit a base current of approximately 1.0 amp. and a collector current of approximately 12 amps.

A tach block is included in the circuit for attaching tachometer and dwell meter leads. In the conventional system, these leads are connected to the distributor primary lead and ground, but in the transistorized circuit, the connection of the leads in this manner would jump the contact gap, contributing to a current buildup in the base circuit and in the collector circuit which would overheat and burn out the transistor. The area surrounding the collector terminal is colored red for the meter red lead while the area surrounding the emitter terminal is colored black for the meter black lead.

A cold start relay is incorporated into the circuit at the starter relay, interrupting the conventional battery to coil lead. The purpose of this is to furnish additional current to the coil primary windings during situations when the starter draw is excessive. The cold start relay contacts normally are closed; only opening during the cranking cycle. However, when the available battery voltage drops below a predetermined value during the cranking cycle, they again close, bypassing the ignition resistor and furnishing full battery current to the system.

The distributor differs from the conventional distributor only in the absence of the condenser and in the highly polished breaker cam. Because one of the big advantages of the transistor ignition is long breaker point life, wear on the rubbing block must be reduced to a minimum. Because the current at the breaker points is so small, the amount of pitting that occurs during normal operation is hardly measurable and point life should be indefinite. The points should be set to 0.020 in. gap and high-temperature grease used for cam lubrication.

When testing the transistor ignition distributor in a test machine, incorporate a condenser into the primary-to-ground circuit using a jumper wire. This will prevent point pitting or oxidation during testing.

NOTE: When connecting an in-car tachometer to the Ford System, always shunt the tachometer leads that go to the coil IIGN terminal and ignition switch with a 10 in. length of Ford ignition resistor wire, part No. COLF-12250-A, to prevent tachometer damage. The higher current draw of the transistor system can ruin a tach if this precaution is not taken.

TROUBLESHOOTING

Ignition problems are caused by a failure in the primary or secondary circuit, or incorrect ignition timing. Isolate the trouble as follows.

1. Remove the coil high tension lead from the distributor cap.

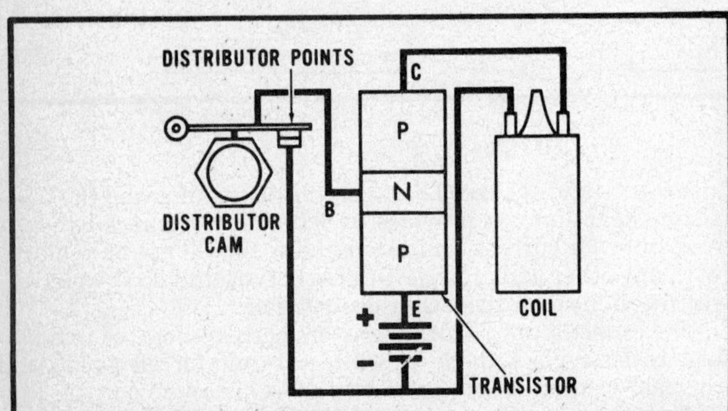

Primary circuit connected to PNP transistor (© Ford Motor Co.)

2. Disconnect the brown wire from the starter relay "I" terminal and the red and blue wire from the starter relay "S" terminal.
3. Turn the ignition switch on.
4. While holding the high tension lead approximately $1/4$ in. from the engine block, crank the engine by using a remote starter switch between the starter relay "S" and battery terminals.
5. If the spark is good, the trouble lies in the secondary (high voltage) circuit. If there is no spark or a weak spark, the trouble is in the primary (low voltage) circuit.
6. A breakdown or energy loss in the primary circuit can be caused by, defective primary wiring, improperly adjusted, contaminated or defective distributor points or a defective amplifier assembly.
7. The trouble can be isolated by performing a primary circuit test. A breakdown or energy loss in the secondary circuit can be caused by, fouled or improperly adjusted spark plugs, defective high voltage wiring or high voltage leakage across the coil, distributor cap, or rotor.
8. To isolate a problem in the secondary circuit, turn the ignition switch off, remove the remote starter switch from the starter relay, install the coil high tension lead in the distributor cap, the red and blue wire to the starter relay (this goes on the "S" terminal) and the brown wire to the starter relay (this goes on the "I" terminal) and perform a secondary circuit test.

Primary Circuit Tests

Do not use any other procedure, conventional short-cut, or connect test equipment in any other manner than described, or extensive damage can be caused to the transistor ignition system.

Connect a dwell meter to the tachometer block. Connect the black lead to the black (large) terminal and the red lead to the red (small) terminal. With the remote starter switch installed and the ignition switch on, ground the coil high tension wire and crank the engine and observe the dwell reading.

If a steady indication of voltage is obtained, the trouble is in the distributor lead to the amplifier. Absence of any voltage indication on the voltmeter shows that there is an open circuit between the distributor lead and the breaker point ground.

0-45° DWELL

1. The transistor and the primary circuit are functioning properly.
2. The trouble could be in the secondary circuit.

0° DWELL

1. The distributor points are contaminated or are not closing.
2. An open circuit in the distributor lead to the amplifier.
3. To determine which item listed is causing the trouble, proceed as follows. Disconnect the distributor lead at the bullet connector and connect a voltmeter red lead to the red (small) tach block terminal and the voltmeter black lead to the distributor lead from the distributor. Do not connect the voltmeter to the lead from the amplifier. Crank the engine and note the voltmeter reading.

45° DWELL

1. No power from the ignition switch.
2. The distributor points are closed and not opening.
3. Defective amplifier assembly. To determine which of the three items listed is causing the trouble, proceed as follows. Disconnect the distributor lead at the bullet connector, and crank the engine. If the dwell meter indicates 0° dwell, the distributor points are not opening. If 45° dwell is indicated, the amplifier is malfunctioning or there is no power from the ignition switch.
4. Use a voltmeter or test light to determine if the transistor (amplifier assembly) is at fault. Connect the voltmeter to the

red-green lead terminal of the ballast resistor and to ground. Crank the engine.

5. Absence of any voltage indication on the voltmeter shows there is an open circuit, or no power between the ignition switch and the amplifier. The ballast resistor could be defective. Replace it with a good ballast resistor, and repeat the test.

6. A steady indication of voltage on the voltmeter indicates either a defective amplifier or the coil to amplifier lead is defective or improperly connected to the ballast resistor. Disconnect the amplifier at the quick disconnect. Connect an ohmmeter across the outside terminals of the amplifier side of the quick disconnect. Reverse the ohmmeter leads.

7. If a very high resistance is obtained one way and a very low or zero resistance is obtained the other way, the amplifier is not defective. Check the coil to amplifier wiring for a loose connection or defective wiring.

8. After a repair has been made, run through the test again to check for any other malfunctions.

Ford-Motorcraft Solid State Ignition System (SSI)

The Ford-Motorcraft Solid State Ignition System is a pulse triggered, breakerless, transistor controlled ignition system. The system utilizes most of the standard ignition components, but substitutes an amplifier module and magnetic pickup assembly for the conventional ignition contact points.

OPERATION

With the ignition switch "on", the primary circuit is on and the ignition coil is energized. When the armature "spokes" approach the magnetic pick-up coil assembly, they induce a voltage which tells the amplifier to turn the coil primary current off. A timing circuit in the amplifier module will turn the current on again after the coil field has collapsed. When the current is "on", it flows from the battery through the ignition switch, the primary windings of the ignition coil, and through the amplifier module circuits to ground. When the current is off, the magnetic field built up in the ignition coil is allowed to collapse, inducing a high voltage into the secondary windings of the coil. High voltage is produced each time the field is thus built up and collapsed.

The high voltage flows through the coil high tension lead to the distributor cap where the rotor distributes it to one of the spark plug terminals in the distributor cap. This process is repeated for every power stroke of the engine.

Ignition system troubles are caused by a failure in the primary and/or the secondary circuit; incorrect ignition timing; or incorrect distributor advance. Circuit failures may be caused by shorts, corroded or dirty terminals, loose connections, defective wire insulation, cracked distributor cap or rotor, defective pick-up coil assembly or amplifier module, defective distributor points, fouled spark plugs, or by improper dwell angle.

If an engine starting or operating trouble is attributed to the ignition system, start the engine and verify the complaint. On engines that will not start, be sure that there is gasoline in the fuel tank and that fuel is reaching the carburetor. Then locate the ignition system problem by an oscilloscope test or by a spark intensity test.

PRIMARY CIRCUIT TESTING

A breakdown or energy loss in the primary circuit can be caused by: defective primary wiring, loose or corroded connections, inoperative or defective magnetic pick-up coil assembly, or defective amplifier module.

A complete test of the primary circuit consists of checking the circuits in the ignition coil, the magnetic pick-up coil assembly and the amplifier module. Wiring harness checks will be included as a part of basic component circuit tests. Always inspect connectors for dirt, corrosion or poor fit before assuming you have spotted a possible problem.

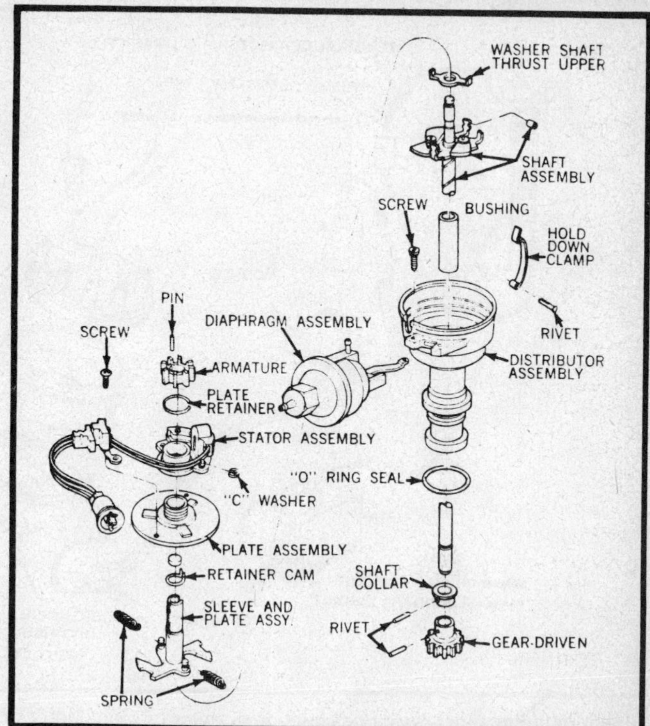

Eight cylinder breakerless distributor—exploded view
(© Ford Motor Co.)

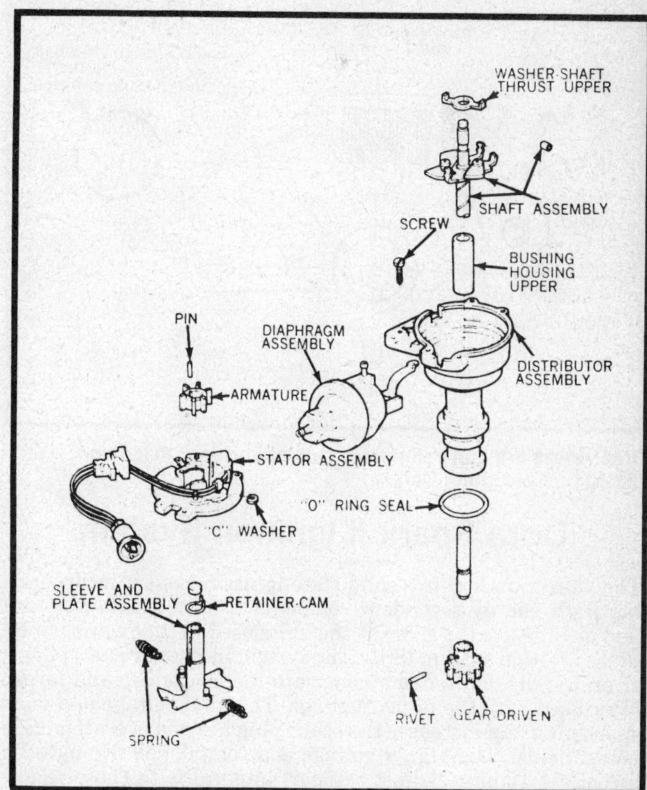

Six cylinder breakerless distributor—exploded view
(© Ford Motor Co.)

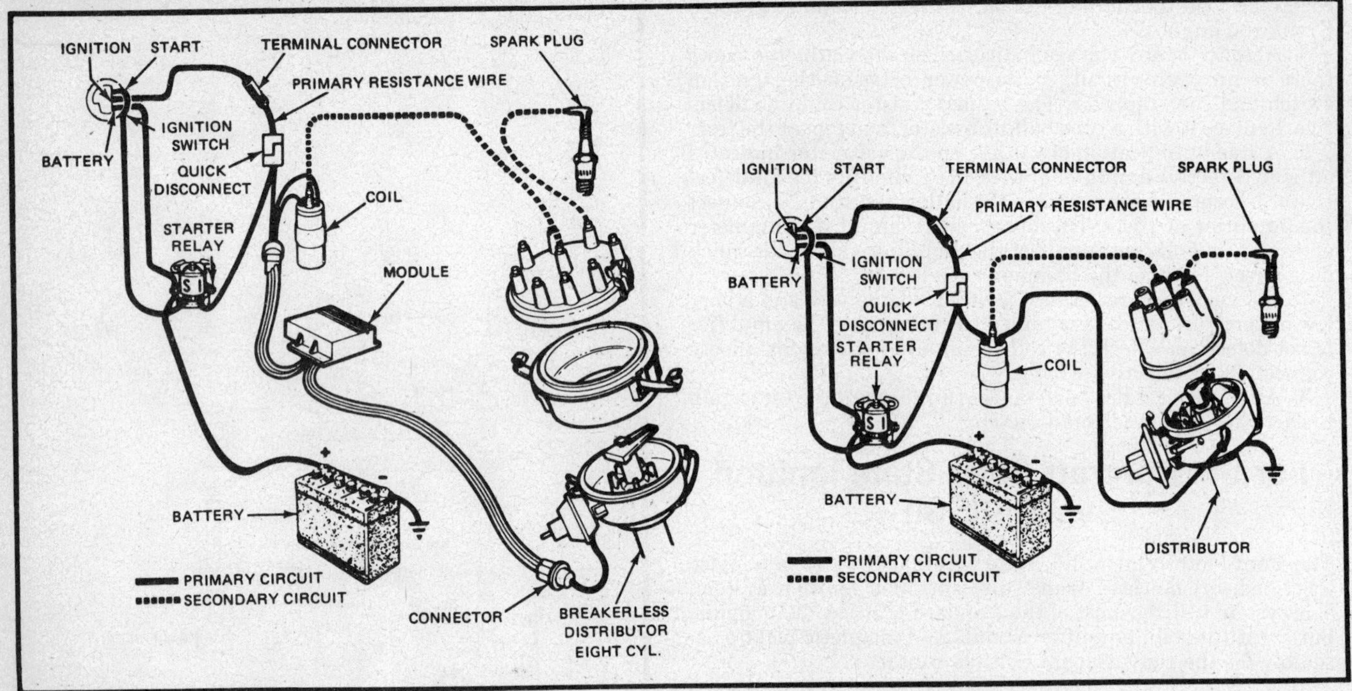

Circuit roundings for breakerless ignition systems (© Ford Motor Co.)

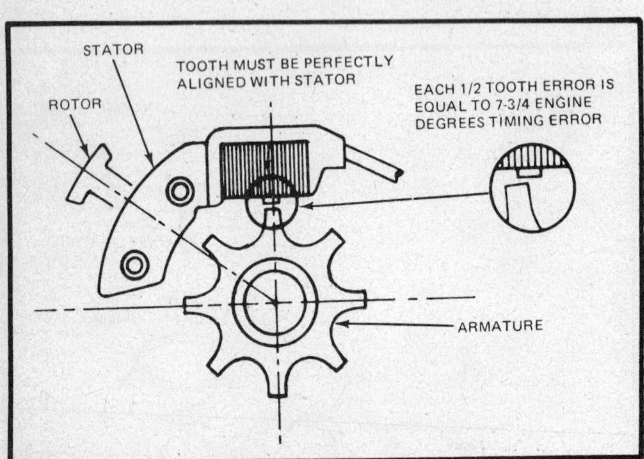

Breakerless armature alignment in relationship with ignition timing (© Ford Motor Corp.)

Dura Spark II Ignition System

The Dura Spark II is a solid state ignition system incorporating high energy secondary components. The distributor, coil and module are the same as the units used in the regular Solid State Ignition system (SSI). The system incorporates an adapter on the distributor to accomodate the larger cap and larger rotor used with the higher voltage. The high voltage and wide spark plug gap increases the spark plug life and overall engine performance. The higher voltage is accomplished through the use of a 1.10 ohm ballast resistor, integral with the primary wire harness, which increases the energy input to the coil and in turn, the secondary energy level. The system is easily identified by the large blue adapter and distributor cap.

DUAL MODE TIMING IGNITION MODULE

On some applications, a special Dura Spark II ignition module is used with altitude compensation. This special module plus the barometric pressure switch, allows the base engine timing to be modified to suit altitude conditions. All other elements and performance characteristics of this module are identical in both modes of operation to the basic Dura Spark II system. All Dura Spark II modules equipped with altitude features, have three connectors instead of the normal two. A barometric switch provides an automatic retard signal to the module at different altitudes, giving appropriate advanced timing at higher altitude and retard mode for spark knock control at lower altitudes.

DISTRIBUTOR

The distributors are equipped with both vacuum and centrifugal spark advances which operate the same regardless of the type of ignition system used. A dual vacuum advance is used on certain engines to provide ignition retard during engine closed throttle operation, to help control engine exhaust emissions.

CIRCUIT OPERATION

All systems consist of a primary (low voltage) and a secondary (high voltage) circuit. The components involved in the primary circuit are, the battery, the ignition switch, the primary circuit resistance wire (integral wire in the SSI and Dura Spark II systems), the primary windings of the ignition coil, the magnetic pickup coil assembly in the distributor and the ignition module. The components of the secondary circuit are, secondary windings of the ignition coil, distributor rotor, cap and adapter (Dura Spark II), secondary spark plug wires and spark plugs.

Operation

With the ignition in the "ON" position, the primary circuit is energized and the magnetic field is built up by the current flowing through the primary windings of the ignition coil. When the armature spokes align with the center of the magnetic pickup coil, the module turns off the coil primary current and the high voltage is produced in the secondary circuit by the

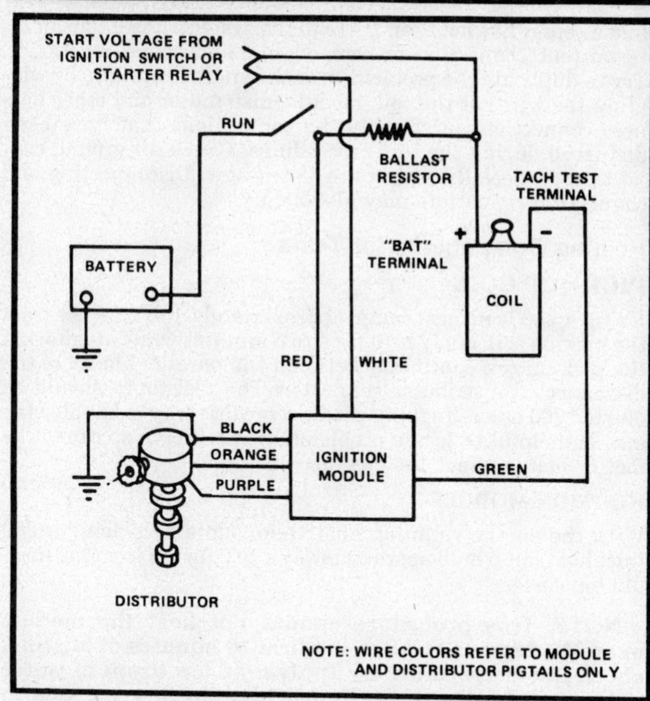

Schematic of the dura spark II and solid state ignitions
(© Ford Motor Co.)

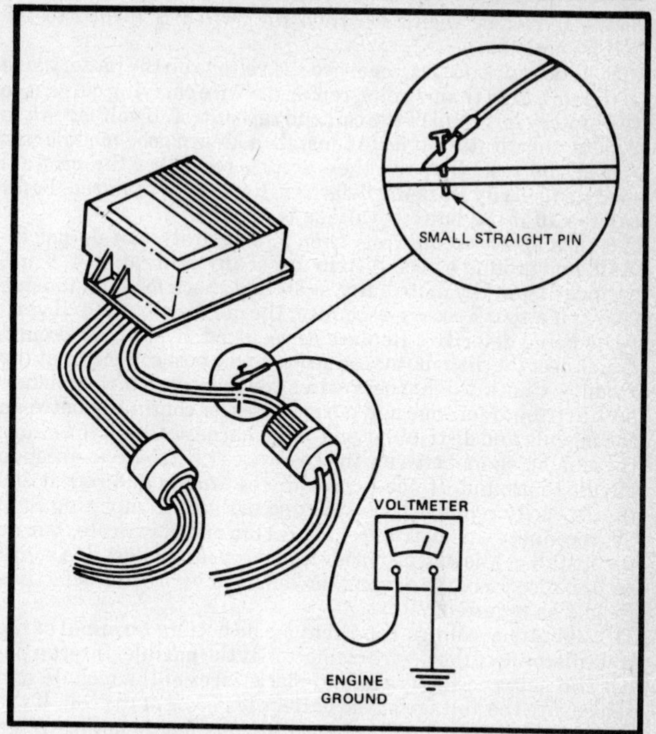

Measuring battery voltage using a straight pin (© Ford Motor Co.)

collapsing magnetic field. High voltage is produced each time the magnetic field is caused to collapse due to a timing circuit in the module, which starts and stops the primary circuit through the coil. The high voltage flows through the coil secondary lead to the distributor cap, where the rotor distributes the spark to the proper spark plug terminal in the distributor cap. The secondary current then flows through the secondary wire to the spark plug.

System Adjustments

No adjustments are made to the Dura Spark II ignition system except the initial timing and spark plug gap.

SECONDARY WIRE USAGE

Dura Spark II

Spark plug wires that are used with the Dura Spark II system are 8mm in size, to contain the higher output voltage. Two types of wires are used in this system and some engines will have both types. It is important to identify the type of wire to a cylinder before a replacement is obtained and installed. Both types are blue in color and have silicone jacketing. The insulation material underneath the jacketing can be a EPDM or have another silicone layer, separated by glass braid. EPDM wires are used where the engine temperatures are cooler and are identified by the letters "SE". The silicone jacket type are used where the engine temperatures are high and are identified by the letters "SS".

NOTE: Whenever a Dura Spark II high tension wire is removed for any purpose from a spark plug, coil or distributor cap, silicone grease must be applied to the boot before it is reconnected.

The spark plug wires are marked with the cylinder number, model year and date of cable manufacture (quarter and year). Service replacement wires do not have this information.

Solid State Ignition System (SSI)

The SSI system used 7mm secondary wires and should not be interchanged with the Dura Spark II secondary wires.

Dura Spark II Solid State Ignition (SSI)

To properly diagnose the ignition system, a starting place must be established and an order of inspection followed until the fault is found and repaired. A recheck should be made, again in its order of inspection, to verify the repairs and to assure trouble free operation.

Run Mode Test

1. If no spark is available at the spark plug, remove the coil high tension lead at the distributor and either place it $\frac{1}{4}$ inch from the engine block or place a modified spark plug into the coil wire and ground the spark plug body.
2. Turn the ignition switch to the "RUN" position and tap the distributor body with a suitable tool. Check for spark while tapping.
3. If spark is available, crank the engine with the starter and check for spark. If spark occurs, the primary ignition system is ok.
4. If no spark occurs, turn the key to the "OFF" position and crank the engine to align the engine timing pointer with the initial timing degree line on the damper pulley. Turn the key to the "RUN" position and again tap the distributor and check for spark.
5. If no spark occurs, measure battery voltage and measure the battery voltage on the module's red wire without disconnecting any connectors. The voltage in the red wire should equal battery voltage.
6. If battery voltage is not present in the module red wire, repair the circuit between the battery and the module connector. Recheck the voltage supply.
7. With the voltage present in the module's red wire, cycle the ignition switch between the "RUN" and "OFF" position. A

spark should be seen each time the switch is turned to the "OFF" position.

8. If no spark occurs, measure the voltage on the battery side of the coil. Less than 6 volts, repair the wire carrying current to the battery terminal of the coil and repeat test. If voltage is 6 to 8 volts, substitute, but do not install, a known good module and repeat the test. If spark then occurs, reconnect the original module to verify its being defective. Replace as required. Refer to Step 10 if the battery voltage is present.

9. If a spark occurs from Step 7, substitute, but do not install, and ground a good distributor of any calibration 4, 6 or 8 cylinder. Spin the distributor shaft and check for high tension spark. If a spark occurs, reconnect the old distributor and verify its being defective. Replace as required. If no spark occurs, disconnect the distributor connector and 4 post connector at the module. Check the harness wires that mate with the module and distributor orange and purple wires for continuity between the module and distributor end of the harness. Check to be sure there is no short between the two wires and there is an open circuit to ground. If not ok, repair the wiring and repeat the test to verify repairs. If no spark occurs after completing Step 9b, reconnect the distributor connector and substitute, but do not install, a known good module and repeat the test. If a spark occurs, reconnect the original module and verify it is defective. Repair as required.

10. If battery voltage is present at the battery terminal of the coil. Disconnect the 4 wire connector at the module. Insert a paper clip between the green and black wires of the module and remeasure the voltage at the battery terminal of the coil. If the voltage is between 6 to 8 volts, substitute, but do not install, a known good module and repeat the tests. If spark occurs, reconnect the old module and verify its being defective. Replace as required. If battery voltage is still present at the battery terminal of the coil, be sure the coil connector remains in place on the coil and ground the negative terminal of the coil. Remeasure the voltage on the coil battery terminal. If battery voltage still is present, remove the paper clip from the 4 wire connector and reconnect the module. Substitute, but do not install, a known good coil and repeat the test. If a spark does not occur, connect the original coil and substitute a known good module, but do not install, and repeat the test. If a spark occurs, replace the module as required. If 4 to 7 volts is measured at the coil positive terminal, remove the ground from the coil negative terminal and ground the paper clip connector in the 4 wire connector. Remeasure the voltage at the coil battery terminal. The voltage should be 4 to 7 volts. If the 4 to 7 volts are present, repair the ground circuit mating with the module black wire. Remove the paper clip from the 4 wire connector and reconnect the module. Repeat the test. If no voltage is present, repair the module to coil wire that mates with the module green wire. Remove the paper clip from the connector and reconnect the module. Repeat the test.

Cranking Test

1. Measure the voltage at the battery terminal of the ignition coil while cranking the engine. The reading should be within 1.0 volt of battery voltage. If not within specifications, repair the wire or circuit to the coil terminal.
2. While cranking the engine, check for spark from the high tension leads.
3. If no spark occurs, check the battery voltage on the white wire, while cranking the engine without disconnecting the module's two wire connectors. The voltage should be within 1.0 volt of battery voltage. If not, repair the white feed wire to the module.
4. Substitute, but do not install, a known good module and repeat the test. If a spark occurs, reconnect the original module and verify its being defective. Replace as required.

INTERMITTENT OPERATION DIAGNOSIS

Should the ignition system become operative during the tests and a repair has not been made to the system, it is likely an intermittent connection or component has become functional. Try to duplicate the problem with the engine running, by wiggling the wires at the coil, module, distributor and other harness connections, preferably the connections that have been disturbed during the test proceedings. Check all ground connections, especially within the distributor. Disconnecting and connecting connectors may also help.

Heating Components for Tests

PICK–UP COIL

Using a 250 watt heat lamp, approximately 1 to 2 inches from the pick-up coil, apply heat for 4 to 6 minutes while monitoring the pick-up coil continuity between the parallel blades of the disconnected distributor connector. The resistance should be 400 to 1000 ohms. Tapping with a screwdriver type handle may also be helpful to locate problems. If specifications cannot be met or held, replace the pick-up coil.

IGNITION MODULE

With the engine running, heat the module by placing a 250 watt heat lamp bulb approximately 1 to 2 inches from the module top surface.

NOTE: This procedure should not heat the module over 212 degrees F. After the first 10 minutes of heating, check the temperature by applying a few drops of water on the module housing. Repeat the check every one to two minutes until the water droplets boil.

Tapping the module may be helpful, but do not tap hard enough to damage or distort the housing. If this procedure results in an ignition malfunction, substitute, but do not install, a known good module. If the ignition malfunction is corrected by the substitution, reinstall the original module and recheck. Replace the module as required.

Dura Spark III Ignition System

This system is used in conjunction with EEC III (an Electronic Engine Control System) that controls spark advance in response to various engine sensors. On 3.8 litre V6 engines, the distributor is only slightly modified from the Dura Spark II model. The distributor stator provides the signal that, on Dura Spark II systems, caused the ignition module to interrupt the primary circuit; on this system, however, the EEC microprocessor determines the actual instant at which spark occurs. This means that the centrifugal and vacuum advance systems on the distributor are disabled and the microprocessor determines vacuum and centrifugal advance curves.

On V8 engines, the distributor stator assembly is replaced by a crankshaft position sensor; thus, the distributor consists only of the mechanical shaft and housing and the high tension cap and rotor. On these engines, the distributor has a fixed position in relation to the engine and it is the rotor position, rather than distributor position that is adjustable. In all other respects, the system resembles the Dura Spark II.

Rotor Alignment V8 Engines with Dura Spark III

1. Remove the distributor cap, noting the approximate location of the high tension wire going to No. 1 cylinder. Rotate the engine until No. 1 cylinder firing position is being approached by the rotor and the engine nears 0 degrees TDC. Remove the rotor and position a distributor alignment tool so that when the alignment slots reach an aligned position, the tool will slip into place.
2. Turn the engine very slowly until the tool just slips into the alignment slots, and then stop rotating the engine. Read the position of the timing mark on the vibration damper. If it is between 4 degrees Before Top Center and 4 degrees After Top Center, the rotor alignment meets specification. In this case, remove the tool, and reposition the rotor and cap. If the timing

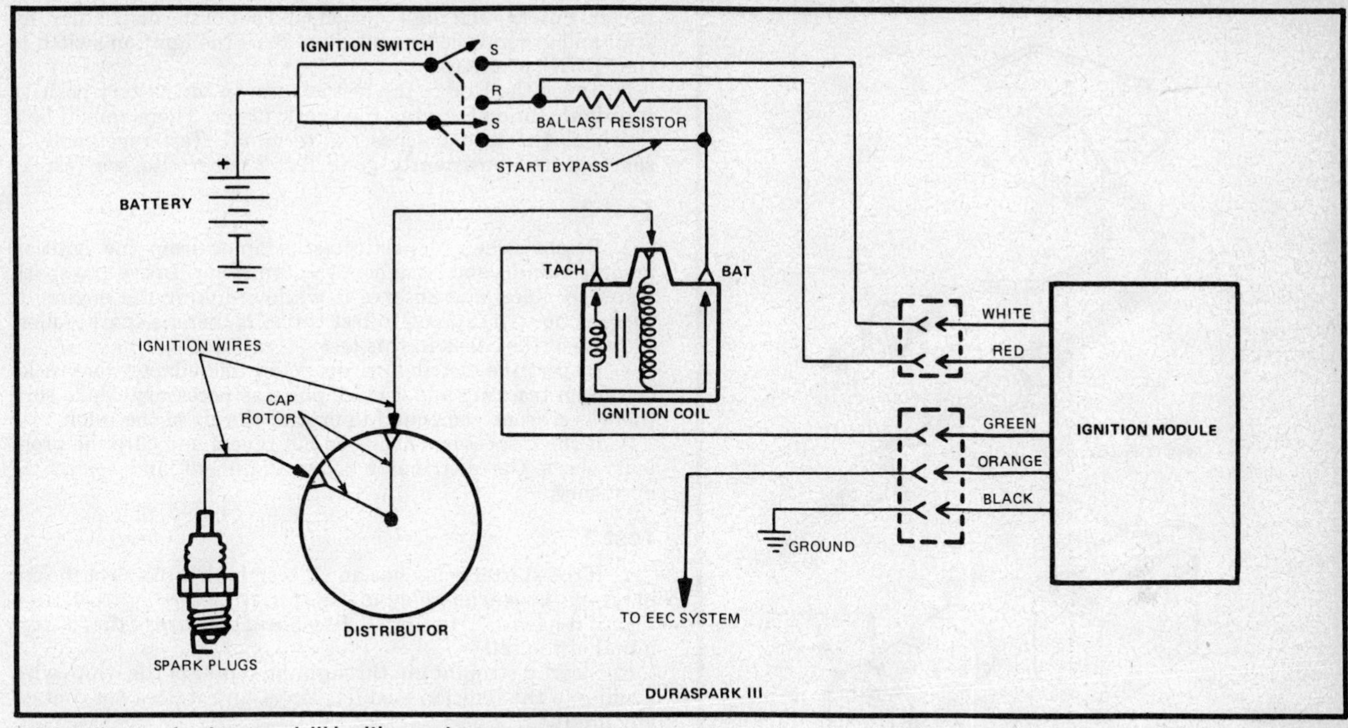

Wiring diagram for dura spark III ignition system (© Ford Motor Co.)

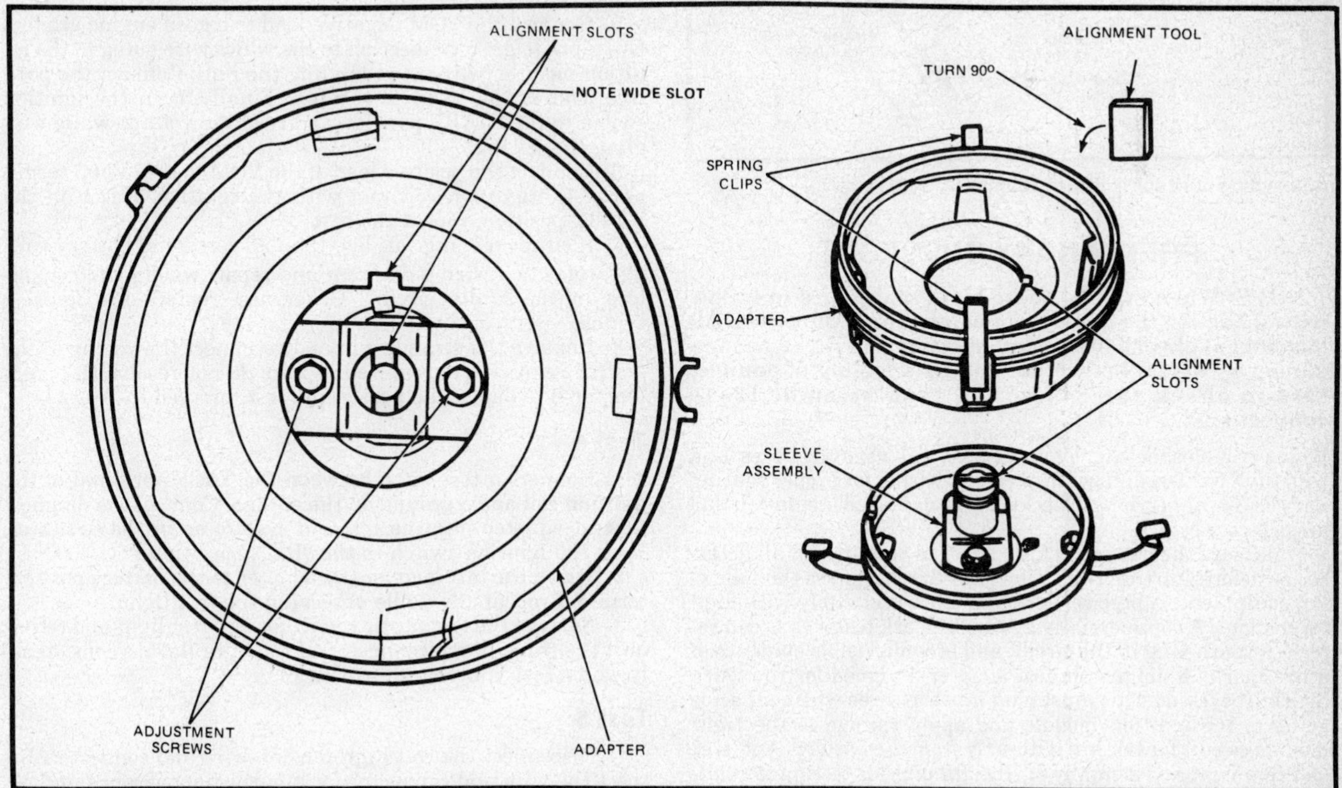

Rotor alignment—dura spark III (© Ford Motor Co.)

mark is outside these limits, proceed with the Steps that follow.

3. Remove the alignment tool. Rotate the engine until the timing marks align at 0 degrees, TDC.

4. Loosen the two sleeve assembly adjustment screws. Then, rotate the sleeve assembly until the alignment tool can be inserted. With the tool in position, tighten the adjusting screws. Then, remove the tool, and install the rotor and cap.

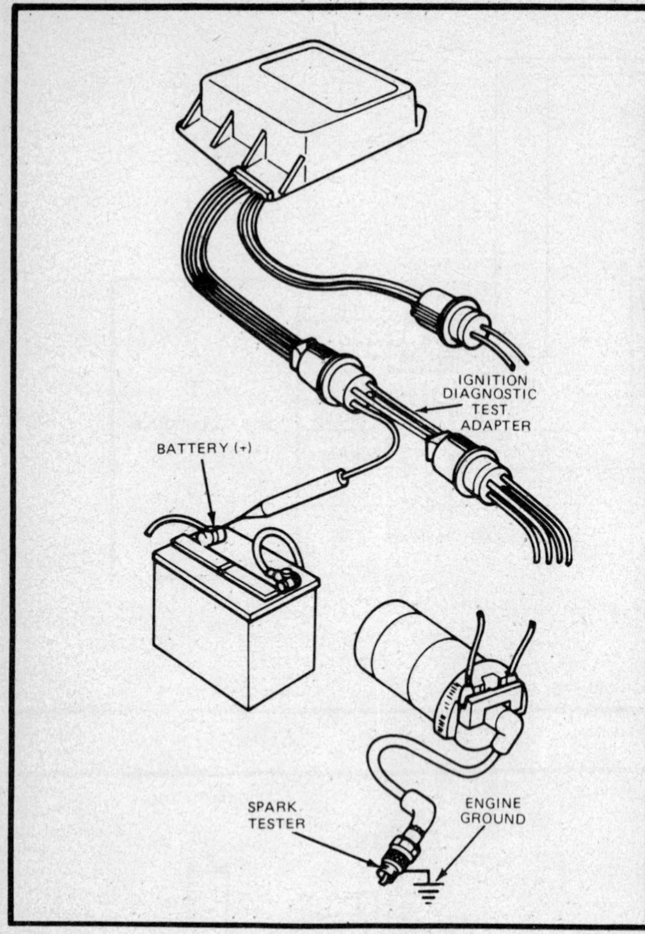

Connecting dura spark III test adapter (© Ford Motor Co)

PRELIMINARY CHECKOUT

NOTE: When making these tests, make sure to follow wiring back to the module for color coding purposes. All instrument checks for wiring integrity should be accompanied by visual inspection and by wiggling of connectors to check for either bad insulation or loose connections.

Begin troubleshooting by inspecting all vacuum hoses and both high tension and wiring harness wiring for proper routing and secure connections. Check also for damaged insulation and burned connectors.

Make sure the battery is fully charged and turn off all accessories before starting tests. The procedure requires the following equipment. A precise volt/ohmmeter, preferably with digital readout. A commercially available spark tester that can replace a spark plug in the circuit and provide visible evidence of a hot spark. A diagnostic test adapter designed for the Dura Spark III system. This must plug into the three wire connector going to the ignition module and apply voltage to the right module circuit for testing it directly from the battery. And a 12 volt test light and a supply of straight pins for testing for voltage and resistance in the wiring.

Test 1

1. Disconnect the three-wire ignition module connector. Inspect the connector for damage, dirt, or corrosion. If none are present, proceed with Step 2 otherwise, make repairs as necessary.
2. Install the test adapter between the two halves of the connector. Pull the coil high tension lead out of the distributor, install and ground the spark tester. Turn the ignition switch to the "RUN" position.
3. Touch the lead to the test adapter to the battery positive terminal while observing the spark tester. There should be a spark as the lead touches the terminal. Test repeatedly. If spark occurs consistently, go to Test 2.Otherwise, see Test 4.

Test 2

1. Remove the diagnostic test adapter from the ignition module circuit, and reconnect the connector. Leave the spark tester in place, and observe it while cranking the engine. If there is no spark, go on to test three. If there is spark, follow the rest of the Steps in this test.
2. Inspect the distributor cap, rotor, and adapter for cracks or carbon tracking and replace parts as necessary. Make sure there is silicone compound to protect the tip of the rotor.
3. If the inspections above do not reveal and cure the problem, check the distributor rotor alignment and correct as necessary.

Test 3

1. If the starter relay has an "I" terminal, disconnect the cable from the starter relay to the starter motor.
2. If it has no "I" terminal, disconnect the wire to the "S" terminal of the relay.
3. Insert a straight pin through the center of the white wire leading to the ignition module. Make sure it does not contact any ground.
4. Measure the voltage existing between the positive and negative battery terminals.
5. Connect the VOM negative lead to a good engine ground. Use a pin to get a connection to the white wire going to the ignition module (without grounding the pin). Connect the positive lead to the VOM to the pin. Finally, turn the ignition switch to the START position and read the voltage while wiggling the wiring.
6. Connect the positive lead of the VOM to the "Batt" terminal of the ignition coil and with the ignition switch in the START position, repeat the test.
7. If either reading was less than 90 percent of battery voltage, refer to a wiring diagram and repair wiring and connectors in the faulty circuit. Otherwise, replace the ignition switch.
8. Remove the straight pin and reconnect the wiring to the starter relay. If the required repairs do not resolve the problem, or if both circuits passed the test, proceed to Test 4.

Test 4

1. Connect a test lamp between the TACH terminal of the ignition coil and a ground on the engine. Connect the diagnostic test adapter into the ignition system as in the first test. Turn the ignition switch to the "RUN" position.
2. Touch the test lead for the adapter to the battery positive terminal repeatedly while observing the test light.
3. Remove the diagnostic connector and test light and reconnect the three-prong connector. If the light flashes consistently, go to Test 5; if not, go to Test 6.

Test 5

1. Disconnect the coil high tension wire and connector. Inspect the wire and connector for a burned appearance and replace parts as necessary. Inspect the coil for cracks or carbon tracking in the high tension connector, and replace it if necessary.
2. Test the high tension lead with an ohmmeter by removing it and connecting the meter to either end. Resistance should be 5,000 ohms per inch or less. If resistance is too high, replace the wire.
3. Measure the coil secondary circuit resistance by connect-

ing the ohmmeter between the coil BATT terminal and the high voltage connector. Resistance must be between 7700 ohms and 10500 ohms. If resistance is either above or below this range, replace the coil.

4. Replace or reconnect parts as necessary.

Test 6

1. If the starter relay has an "I" terminal, disconnect the cable from the relay to the starter motor. If there is no "I" terminal on the relay, disconnect the wire to the "S" terminal of the relay. Insert straight pins into the centers of the red and white module wires. DO NOT GROUND. Measure the exact voltage by connecting the voltmeter between the positive and negative battery terminals.

2. Connect the voltmeter negative lead between the base of the distributor and the pin passing through the red lead. Turn the ignition switch to the "RUN" position. Measure the voltage while wiggling the wiring.

3. Connect the voltmeter positive lead over to the pin running through the white wire. Turn the ignition switch tot he START position and read the voltage while wiggling the wiring.

4. Repeat the step above, but with the positive lead attached to the BATT terminal on the ignition coil to test the ballast resistor bypass. Turn the ignition switch off, remove the straight pins, and reconnect the starter wiring.

5. If the voltage was more than 90 percent of battery voltage, inspect the wiring harness for faulty circuits and repair as necessary. Replace the ignition switch, or replace the radio interference capacitor on the coil as necessary until the system can pass the test.

Test 7

1. Attach the negative lead of the voltmeter to an engine ground, and the positive lead to the BATT terminal on the coil.

2. With the ignition switch in the RUN position, measure the voltage.

3. Turn the ignition switch off and remove the voltmeter leads. If the voltage is 6 to 8 volts, proceed to Test 8; if it is less than 6 volts or greater than 8 volts, proceed to Test 9.

Test 8

1. Disconnect the ignition module three wire connector and the connector at the coil for the wire from the ignition module. Repair or replace bad connectors as necessary.

2. Connect an ohmmeter between an engine ground (-) and the TACH terminal of the coil. Reconnect module and coil connectors. If resistance is greater than one ohm, replace the module. If it is one ohm or less, just inspect the wiring harness between the module and coil to make sure there are no wiring problems.

Test 9

1. Disconnect the ignition coil primary connectors. Measure coil primary resistance by connecting an ohmmeter between the BATT and TACH terminals. Disconnect the ohmmeter and reconnect connectors.

2. If resistance is between .8 and 1.6 ohms, proceed to Test 10. If resistance is less than or greater than specification, replace the coil.

Test 10

1. Insert a straight pin into the green wire at the module without grounding it.

2. Attach the negative lead of the voltmeter to an engine ground. Then, turn the ignition switch on and measure the voltage, first at the straight pin in the green wire and then at the TACH terminal of the ignition coil. If the difference in voltage is more than 5 volts, inspect and repair the green module to coil wire as necessary. If it is less than 0.5 volts, but more than 1.5, proceed to Test 12. If it is 1.5 volts or less, proceed to the test of the ballast resitor, Test 11.

3. Turn the ignition off and remove the leads and straight pin.

Test 11

1. Disconnect the two wire connector to the ignition module. Repair any defects in the connectors. Disconnect the coil primary connector.

2. Use an ohmmeter to measure resistance of the circuit between the BATT terminal of the ignition coil connector and the wiring harness connector mating with the red wire from the module. In both cases, measure on the wiring harness side, not at the coil or at the wire leading to the module.

3. If the resistance is 0.8 to 1.6 ohms, replace the ignition module. If it is less than 0.8 or greater than 1.6 ohms, replace the ballast resistor.

4. Remove the ohmmeter and reconnect connectors as necessary.

Test 12

1. Insert a straight pin into the black wire at the ignition module without grounding it.

2. Connect a voltmeter between the pin and an engine ground, with the positive lead at the pin. Turn the ignition switch to RUN position.

3. If the voltage read is less than 0.5 volt, replace the ignition module. If it is greater than 5 volts, proceed to the final test for further diagnosis of problems in the ground circuit.

4. Turn the ignition switch off, remove the voltmeter connectors and remove the straight pin.

Test 13

1. Disconnect the threewire connector to the module. Connect an ohmmeter between an engine ground and the harness side terminal mating with the black wire from the module. Read the resistance while wiggling the harness.

2. If resistance is less than one ohm, look for a problem in the wiring harness connectors and the module black wire. The problem is either intermittent or not in the ignition system. If resistance is greater than one ohm, inspect the harness and connectors between the module and ground connection. Repair wiring as necessary, disconnect the ohmmeter, and reconnect the connector.

Thick Film Integrated (TFI) Ignition System

1983 AND LATER RANGER, 1984 AND LATER BRONCO II W/2.8L V6 ENGINE

The 2.8L V6 engine used in the Range and Bronco II uses a new universal distributor design which is gear driven and has a die cast base that incorporates an integrally mounted TFI-IV ignition module. The distributor also uses a "Hall Effect" vane switch stator assembly and has a provision for fixed octane adjustment. The new design eliminates the conventional centrifugal and vacuum advance mechanisms.

DISTRIBUTOR IDENTIFICATION

The 2.8L distributor assembly can be identified by the part number information printed on a decal attached to the side of the distributor base.

NOTE: No distributor calibration is required and it is not normally necessary to adjust initial timing.

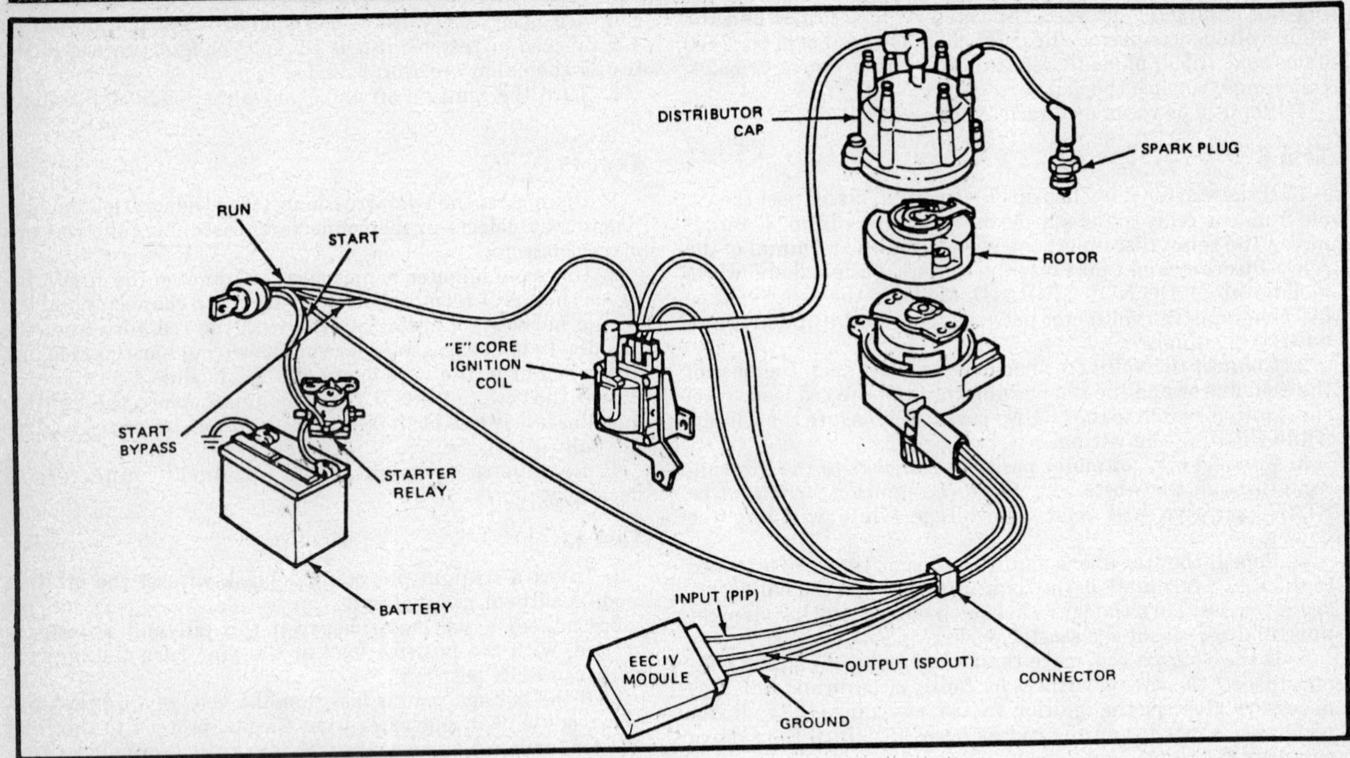

TFI ignition system (© Ford Motor Co.)

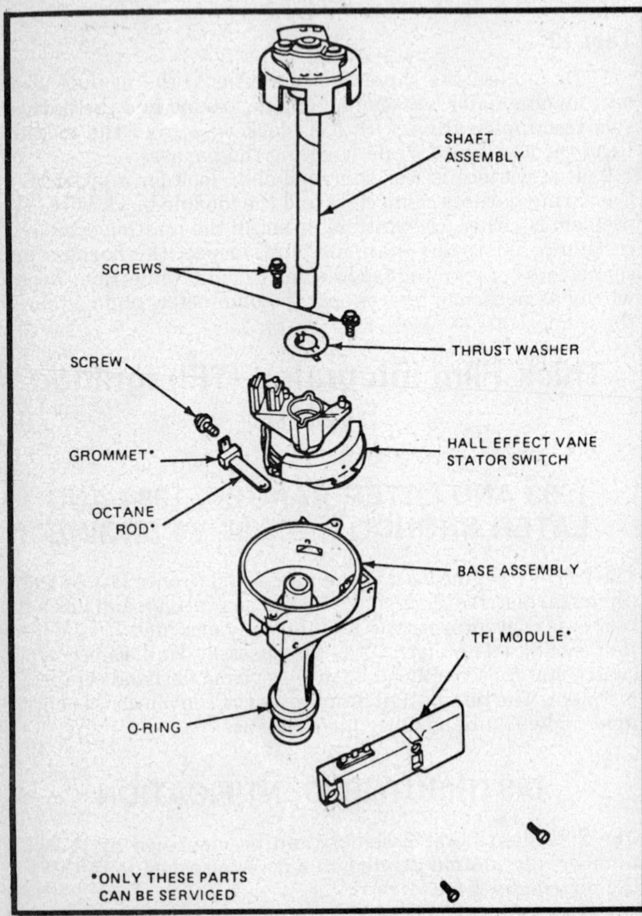

Exploded view of the universal distributor used with TFI ignition systems (© Ford Motor Co.)

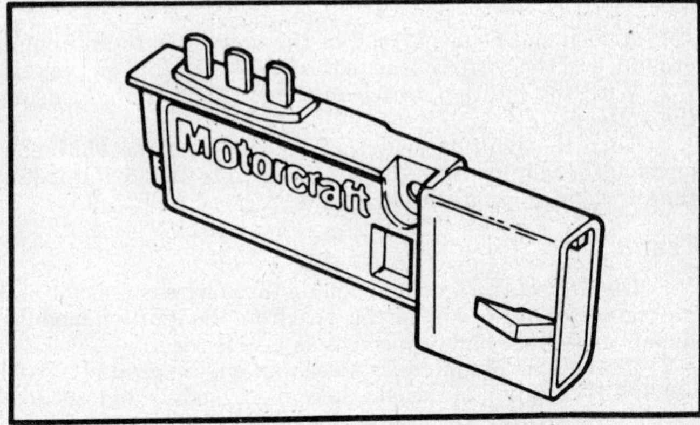

TFI ignition module—type IV (© Ford Motor Co.)

1.The new cap, adapter and rotor are designed for use with the new universal distributor.
2.The spark plug is a 14mm standard reach, tapered seat design.
3.The ignition module is a Thick Film Integrated design. The module is contained in moulded thermo plastic and is mounted on the distributor base. The TFI-IV module features a "push start" mode. This will allow "push starting" of the vehicle if it becomes necessary.
4.The TFI-IV system uses an "E-Core" ignition coil, which replaces the oil-filled design used with previous ignition systems.

Adjustments

Provisions have been incorporated into the Universal Distributor to allow fixed adjustment capability for octane needs. The adjustment is accomplished by replacing the standard 0° rod located in the distributor bowl with either a 3° or a 6° retard rod, which is released for service only through prior factory authorization.

NOTE: Except for the cap, adapter, rotor, TFI module, O-ring and octane rod, no other distributor assembly parts are replaceable. There is no calibration required with the universal distributor.

DISTRIBUTOR CAP, ADAPTER AND ROTOR

Removal

1. Remove the secondary wires.
2. Unclip the distributor cap and lift straight off the distributor.
3. Loosen the adapter attaching screws and remove the adapter.
4. Loosen the screw attaching the rotor to the distributor and remove the cap, if necessary.

Installation

1. If previously removed, position the distributor rotor with the square and round locator pins matched to the rotor mounting plate. Tighten the screws 2.1 to 2.9 ft. lbs.
2. Install adapter in position and tighten attaching screws 2.1 to 2.9 ft. lbs.
3. Install the cap, noting the square alignment locator, and fasten the clips.
4. Install secondary wires, noting correct locations on the distributor cap.

TFI IGNITION MODULE

Removal

1. Remove distributor cap and adapter. Position it and the attached wires aside so as not to interfere with the work area.
2. Remove TFI harness connector.
3. Remove distributor from engine using security type distributor hold down bolt Tool T82L-12270-A, or equivalent.
4. Place removed distributor on work bench. Remove the two TFI module attachment screws.
5. Pull right side of module down the distributor mounting flange and then back up to disengage module terminals for connector in distributor base. The module may then be pulled toward flange and away from the distributor.

NOTE: Do not attempt to lift module from mounting surface prior to moving entire TFI module toward distributor flange as the pins at the distributor/module connector will break.

Installation

1. Coat the metal base plate of the TFI ignition module with silicone compound, approximately $\frac{1}{32}$ in. thick. Use D7AZ-19A331-A or equivalent grease.
2. Place TFI module on distributor base mounting flange.
3. Carefully position TFI module assembly toward distributor bowl and engage securely the three distributor connector pins.
4. Install the two TFI module mounting screws and tighten them 9 to 16 inch lbs.
5. Install distributor on engine.
6. Install distributor cap and adapter and tighten adapter mounting screws.
7. Install TFI harness connector.
8. Using an induction timing lamp, verify engine timing per engine decal.

OCTANE ROD

Removal

1. Remove cap, adapter and rotor.
2. Remove the octane rod 4mm retaining screw.
3. Slide the octane rod grommet out to a point where the rod can be disengaged from the stator retaining post and remove the octane rod. Retain the grommet for use with the new octane rod.

Installation

1. Install the grommet on the new octane rod.
2. Install the octane rod into the distributor, making sure it engages the stator retaining post.
3. Install the retaining screw and tighten to 15–35 inch lbs.
4. Install the rotor, adapter and cap. Tighten rotor and adapter attaching screws.

HIGH TENSION WIRES

Whenever a high tension wire is removed for any reason from a spark plug, coil or distributor cap or a new high tension wire is installed, silicone dielectric compound D1AZ-19A331-A or equivalent must be applied to the boot before it is reconnected. Using a small clean tool, coat the entire interior surface of the boot with Motorcraft silicone dielectric compound D7AZ-19A331-A or equivalent.

Insert each wire on the proper terminal of the distributor cap. Be sure the wires are all the way down over their terminals. The No. 1 terminal is identified on the cap. Install the wires starting with No. 1. The firing order is 1-4-2-5-3-6 clockwise.

Remove the wire retaining brackets from the old high tension wire set and install them on the new set in the same relative position. Install the wires in the brackets on the valve rocker arm covers. Connect the wires to the proper spark plugs. Install the coil wire.

TACHOMETER CONNECTION

The ignition coil connector allows a tachometer connection using an alligator clip without removing the coil connector.

Delco Remy High Energy Ignition (HEI) System

COMPONENTS

The Delco Remy High Energy Ignition (HEI) System is a breakerless, pulse triggered, transistor controlled, inductive discharge ignition system. There are only nine external electrical connections; the ignition switch feed wire, and the eight spark plug leads. On V8 engines, the ignition coil is located within the distributor cap, connecting directly to the rotor.

OPERATION

The magnetic pick up assembly located inside the distributor contains a permanent magnet, a pole piece with internal teeth, and a pick-up coil. When the teeth of the rotating timer core and pole piece align, an induced voltage in the pick-up coil signals the electronic module to open the coil primary circuit. As the primary current decreases, a high voltage is induced in the secondary windings of the ignition coil, directing a spark through the rotor and high voltage leads to fire the spark plugs. The dwell period is automatically controlled by the electronic module and is increased with increasing engine rpm. The HEI System features a longer spark duration which is instrumental in firing lean and EGR diluted fuel/air mixtures. The condenser (capacitor) located within the HEI distributor is provided for noise (static) suppression purposes only and is not a regularly replaced ignition system component.

Some 1983 and later engines use an Electronic Spark Timing (EST) distributor. This unit replaces vacuum and centrifugal

HEI DIAGNOSIS CHART 1983 AND LATER
Engine Cranks, But Will Not Start

PRELIMINARY

NOTE: Perform Diagnostic Circuit Check before using this procedure.
If a tachometer is connected to the tachometer terminal, disconnect it before proceeding with the test.
Intermittent no start may be caused by wrong pick-up or ignition coil.

1. Check spark at plug with ST-125 while cranking (if no spark on one wire, check a second wire). *

- Spark → Check fuel, spark plugs, etc.
- No Spark → Disconnect 4 term. EST connector and see if engine will run.
  - Runs → See Code 42 chart.
  - Doesn't run →

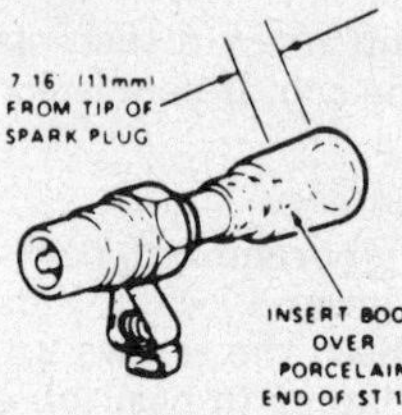

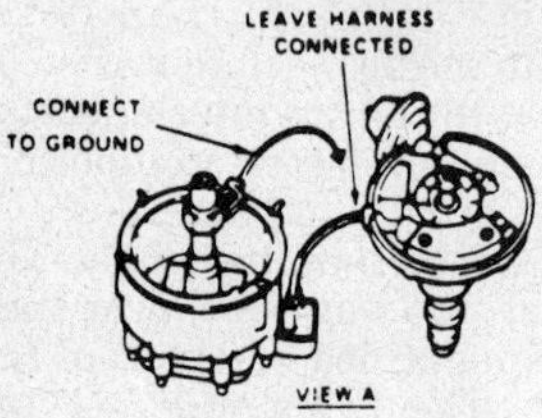

2. Check voltage at distributor "bat" terminal while cranking

- Under 7 volts → Repair primary circuit to ignition switch.
- 7 volts or more →

3. With ignition "on," check "tach" terminal voltage.

- Under 1 Volt → It is faulty ign. coil connection or coil
- 1 to 10 Volts → Replace module and check for spark from coil as in Step 6.
  - Spark → System OK
  - No Spark → Replace ign. coil. It, too, is faulty.
- 10 Volts or More →

4. Check for spark at coil output terminal with ST-125 while cranking. (View A)

- Spark → Check color match of pick-up coil connector and ign. coil lead. ** Inspect cap for water, cracks, etc. If OK replace rotor.
- No Spark →

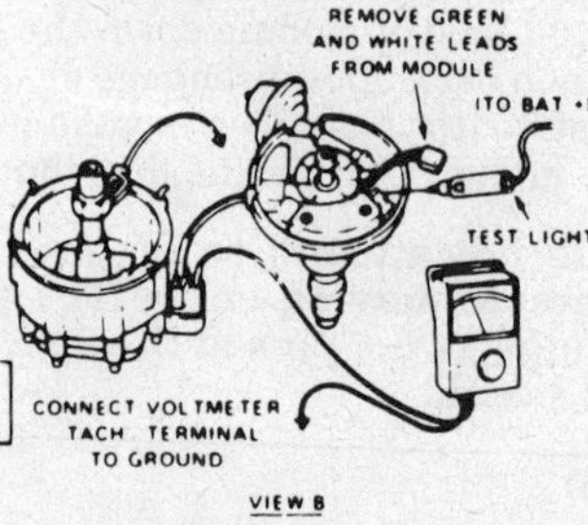

5. Remove pick-up coil leads from module Check tach. term. voltage with "ign" "on." Watch voltmeter as test light is momentarily connected from bat. + to module terminal "P". (View B) Not more than 5 seconds

- No Drop In Voltage → Check module grnd. and for open in wires from cap to distributor. If OK, replace mod.
- Voltage Drops →

6. Check for spark from coil with ST-125 as test light is removed from module terminal.

- Spark → It is pick-up coil or connections. Coil resistance should be 500-1500 ohms and not grounded.
- No Spark →
  - If module tester is available, test module
    - OK → Check ign. coil ground. If OK, replace ign. coil.
    - Bad → Replace module
  - If no module tester is available →

7. Check ign. coil ground circuit. If OK, replace ign. coil and repeat Step 6.

- Spark → System OK
- No Spark → Coil removed is OK, reinstall original coil and replace module.

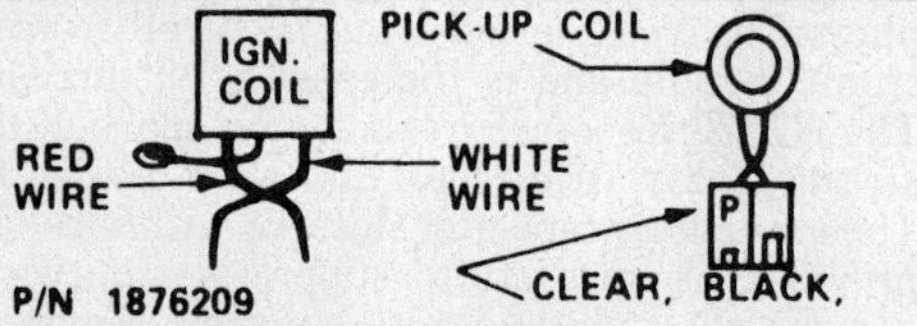

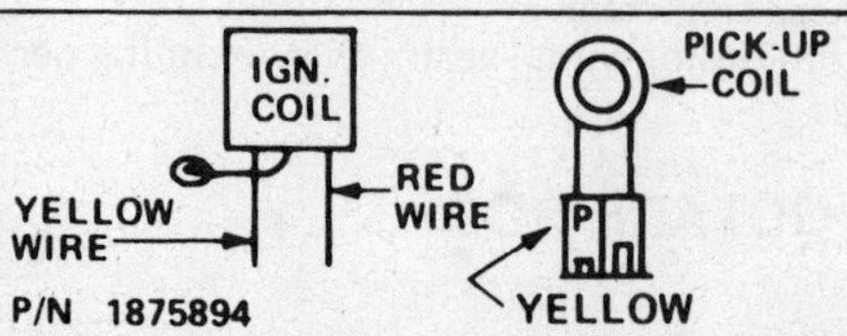

* A few sparks and then nothing, is considered no spark.

HEI DIAGNOSIS CHART 1983 AND LATER
Continued

TROUBLE CODE 42
BYPASS OR EST PROBLEM

If vehicle will not start and run, check for grounded EST wire to ECM terminal "12." (Grounded and open EST circuit on 5.0L VIN "Y".)

A 1981 HEI module can cause a Code 42.

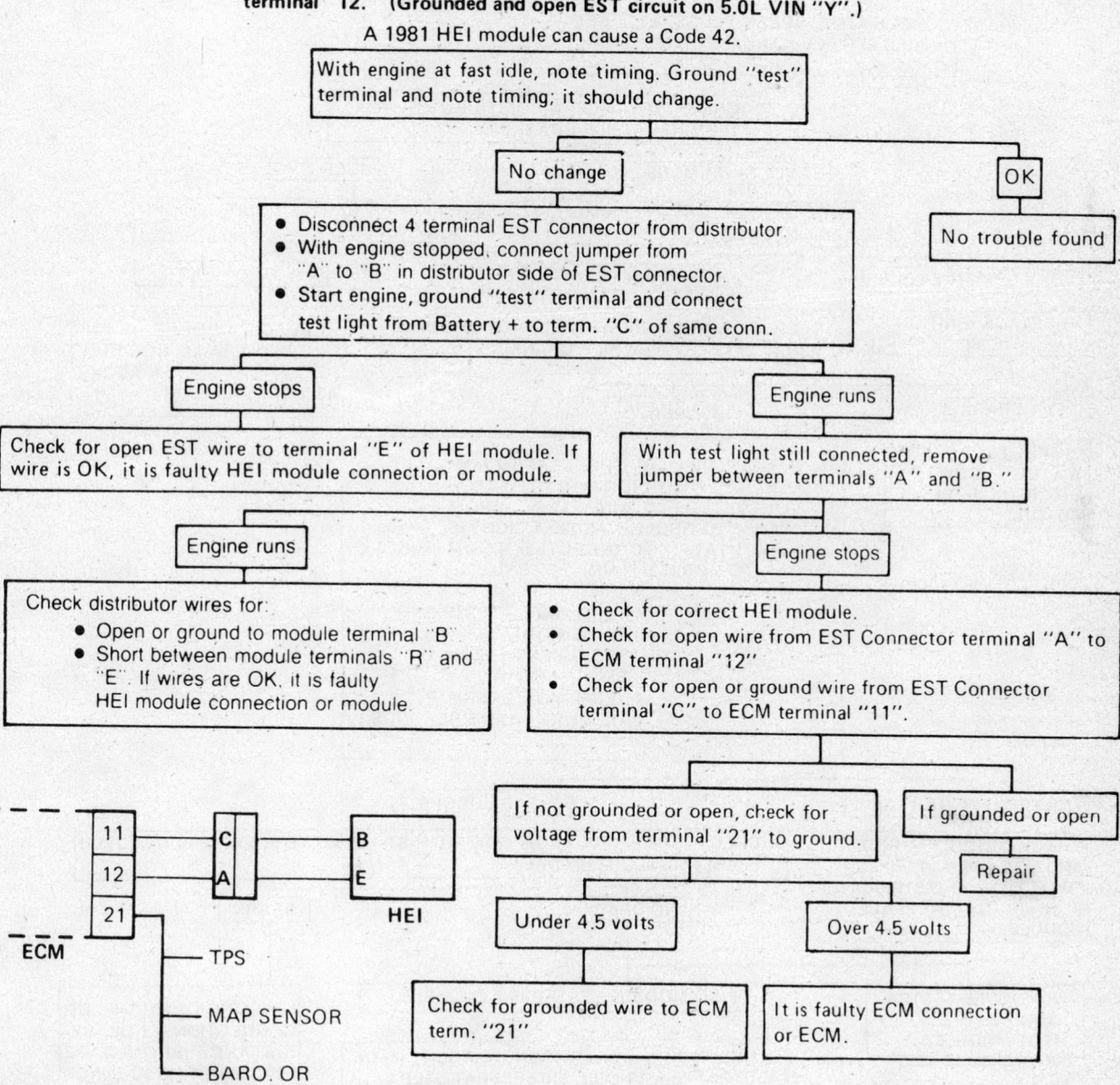

With engine at fast idle, note timing. Ground "test" terminal and note timing; it should change.

- **No change**
  - Disconnect 4 terminal EST connector from distributor.
  - With engine stopped, connect jumper from "A" to "B" in distributor side of EST connector.
  - Start engine, ground "test" terminal and connect test light from Battery + to term. "C" of same conn.
    - **Engine stops** → Check for open EST wire to terminal "E" of HEI module. If wire is OK, it is faulty HEI module connection or module.
    - **Engine runs** → With test light still connected, remove jumper between terminals "A" and "B."
      - **Engine runs** → Check distributor wires for:
        - Open or ground to module terminal "B".
        - Short between module terminals "B" and "E". If wires are OK, it is faulty HEI module connection or module.
      - **Engine stops**
        - Check for correct HEI module.
        - Check for open wire from EST Connector terminal "A" to ECM terminal "12"
        - Check for open or ground wire from EST Connector terminal "C" to ECM terminal "11".
          - **If not grounded or open, check for voltage from terminal "21" to ground.**
            - **Under 4.5 volts** → Check for grounded wire to ECM term. "21"
            - **Over 4.5 volts** → It is faulty ECM connection or ECM.
          - **If grounded or open** → Repair
- **OK** → No trouble found

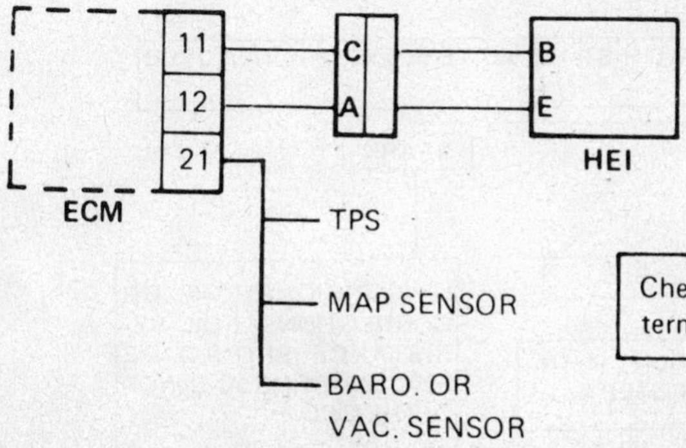

HEI DIAGNOSIS CHART
Engine Cranks But Will Not Start

(If a tachometer is connected to the tachometer terminal, disconnect it before proceeding with the test.)

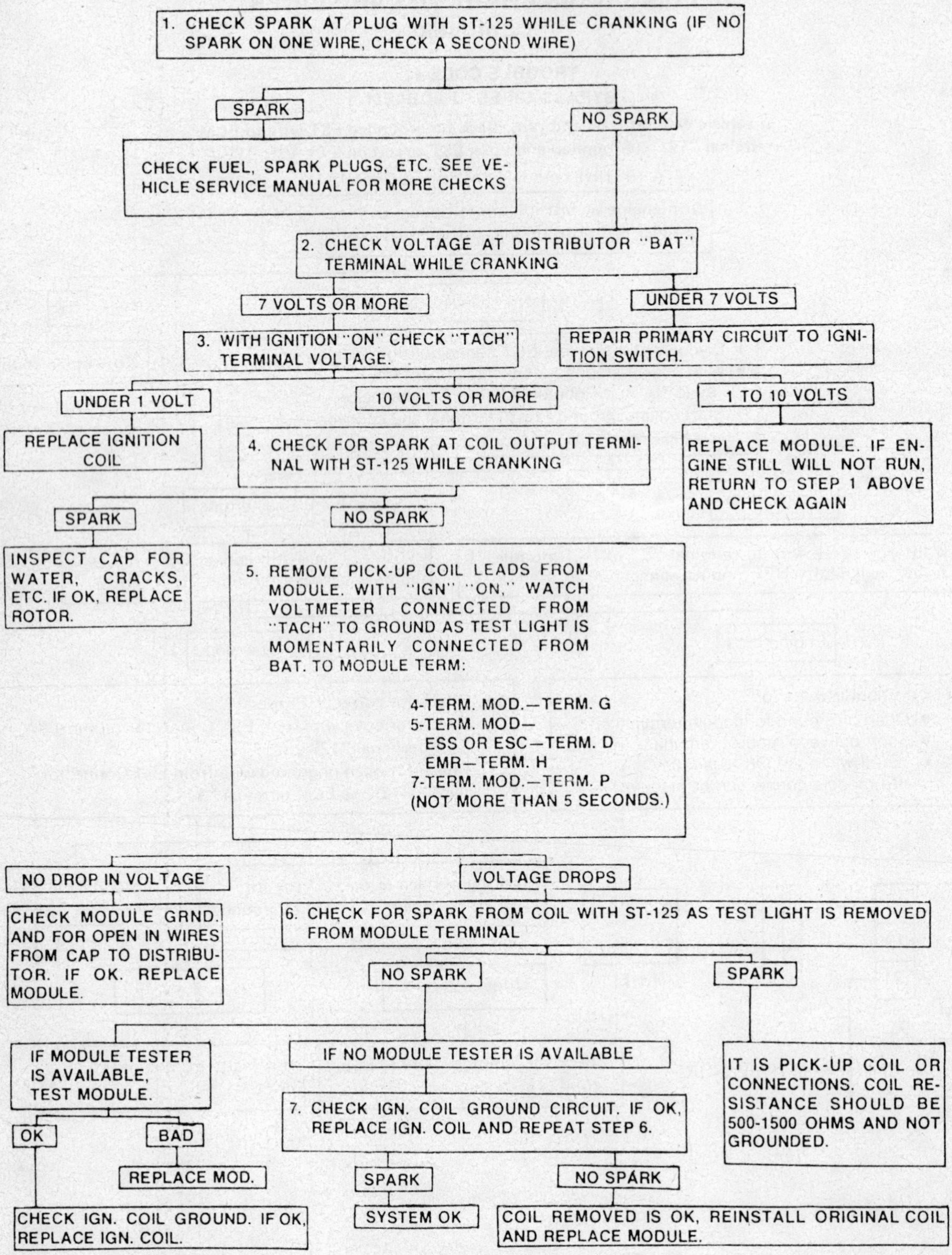

1. CHECK SPARK AT PLUG WITH ST-125 WHILE CRANKING (IF NO SPARK ON ONE WIRE, CHECK A SECOND WIRE)

- SPARK → CHECK FUEL, SPARK PLUGS, ETC. SEE VEHICLE SERVICE MANUAL FOR MORE CHECKS
- NO SPARK → 2.

2. CHECK VOLTAGE AT DISTRIBUTOR "BAT" TERMINAL WHILE CRANKING

- 7 VOLTS OR MORE → 3.
- UNDER 7 VOLTS → REPAIR PRIMARY CIRCUIT TO IGNITION SWITCH.

3. WITH IGNITION "ON" CHECK "TACH" TERMINAL VOLTAGE.

- UNDER 1 VOLT → REPLACE IGNITION COIL
- 10 VOLTS OR MORE → 4.
- 1 TO 10 VOLTS → REPLACE MODULE. IF ENGINE STILL WILL NOT RUN, RETURN TO STEP 1 ABOVE AND CHECK AGAIN

4. CHECK FOR SPARK AT COIL OUTPUT TERMINAL WITH ST-125 WHILE CRANKING

- SPARK → INSPECT CAP FOR WATER, CRACKS, ETC. IF OK, REPLACE ROTOR.
- NO SPARK → 5.

5. REMOVE PICK-UP COIL LEADS FROM MODULE. WITH "IGN" "ON," WATCH VOLTMETER CONNECTED FROM "TACH" TO GROUND AS TEST LIGHT IS MOMENTARILY CONNECTED FROM BAT. TO MODULE TERM:

4-TERM. MOD.—TERM. G
5-TERM. MOD—
ESS OR ESC—TERM. D
EMR—TERM. H
7-TERM. MOD.—TERM. P
(NOT MORE THAN 5 SECONDS.)

- NO DROP IN VOLTAGE → CHECK MODULE GRND. AND FOR OPEN IN WIRES FROM CAP TO DISTRIBUTOR. IF OK. REPLACE MODULE.
- VOLTAGE DROPS → 6.

6. CHECK FOR SPARK FROM COIL WITH ST-125 AS TEST LIGHT IS REMOVED FROM MODULE TERMINAL

- NO SPARK →
  - IF MODULE TESTER IS AVAILABLE, TEST MODULE.
    - OK → CHECK IGN. COIL GROUND. IF OK, REPLACE IGN. COIL.
    - BAD → REPLACE MOD.
  - IF NO MODULE TESTER IS AVAILABLE → 7.
- SPARK → IT IS PICK-UP COIL OR CONNECTIONS. COIL RESISTANCE SHOULD BE 500-1500 OHMS AND NOT GROUNDED.

7. CHECK IGN. COIL GROUND CIRCUIT. IF OK, REPLACE IGN. COIL AND REPEAT STEP 6.

- SPARK → SYSTEM OK
- NO SPARK → COIL REMOVED IS OK, REINSTALL ORIGINAL COIL AND REPLACE MODULE.

ESC SYSTEMS DIAGNOSIS

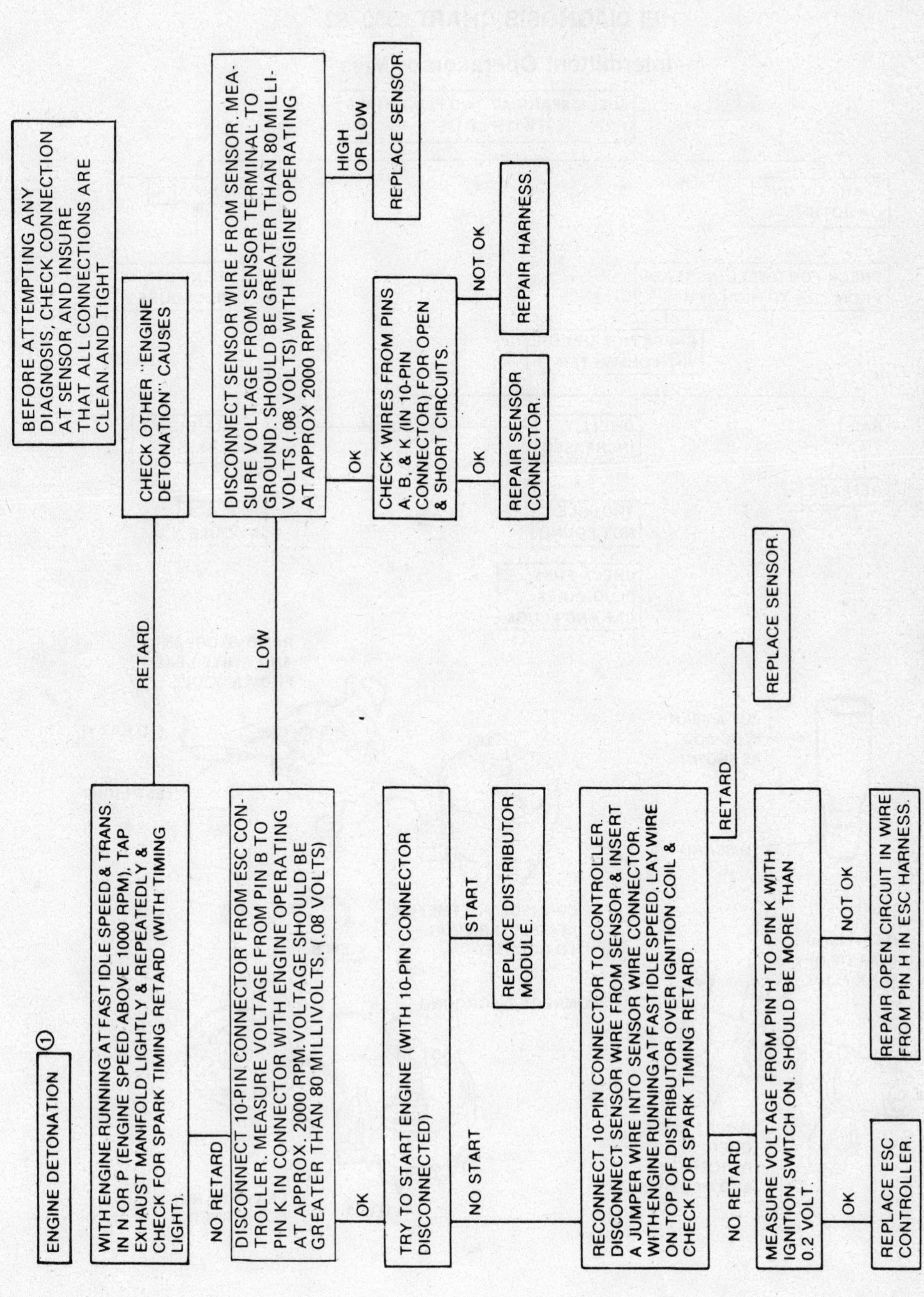

ENGINE DETONATION ①
BEFORE ATTEMPTING ANY DIAGNOSIS, CHECK CONNECTION AT SENSOR AND INSURE THAT ALL CONNECTIONS ARE CLEAN AND TIGHT
WITH ENGINE RUNNING AT FAST IDLE SPEED & TRANS. IN N OR P (ENGINE SPEED ABOVE 1000 RPM), TAP EXHAUST MANIFOLD LIGHTLY & REPEATEDLY & CHECK FOR SPARK TIMING RETARD (WITH TIMING LIGHT).
RETARD
CHECK OTHER "ENGINE DETONATION" CAUSES
NO RETARD
DISCONNECT 10-PIN CONNECTOR FROM ESC CONTROLLER. MEASURE VOLTAGE FROM PIN B TO PIN K IN CONNECTOR WITH ENGINE OPERATING AT APPROX. 2000 RPM. VOLTAGE SHOULD BE GREATER THAN 80 MILLIVOLTS. (.08 VOLTS)
LOW
DISCONNECT SENSOR WIRE FROM SENSOR. MEASURE VOLTAGE FROM SENSOR TERMINAL TO GROUND. SHOULD BE GREATER THAN 80 MILLIVOLTS (.08 VOLTS) WITH ENGINE OPERATING AT APPROX 2000 RPM.
HIGH OR LOW
REPLACE SENSOR.
OK
CHECK WIRES FROM PINS A, B, & K (IN 10-PIN CONNECTOR) FOR OPEN & SHORT CIRCUITS.
NOT OK
REPAIR HARNESS.
OK
REPAIR SENSOR CONNECTOR.
OK
TRY TO START ENGINE (WITH 10-PIN CONNECTOR DISCONNECTED)
START
REPLACE DISTRIBUTOR MODULE.
NO START
RECONNECT 10-PIN CONNECTOR TO CONTROLLER. DISCONNECT SENSOR WIRE FROM SENSOR & INSERT A JUMPER WIRE INTO SENSOR WIRE CONNECTOR. WITH ENGINE RUNNING AT FAST IDLE SPEED, LAY WIRE ON TOP OF DISTRIBUTOR OVER IGNITION COIL & CHECK FOR SPARK TIMING RETARD.
RETARD
REPLACE SENSOR.
NO RETARD
MEASURE VOLTAGE FROM PIN H TO PIN K WITH IGNITION SWITCH ON. SHOULD BE MORE THAN 0.2 VOLT.
NOT OK
REPAIR OPEN CIRCUIT IN WIRE FROM PIN H IN ESC HARNESS.
OK
REPLACE ESC CONTROLLER.
① SOME OCCASIONAL TRACE-TO-LIGHT DETONATION IS ACCEPTABLE.

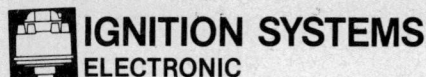

HEI DIAGNOSIS CHART 1980-82

Intermittent Operation or Miss

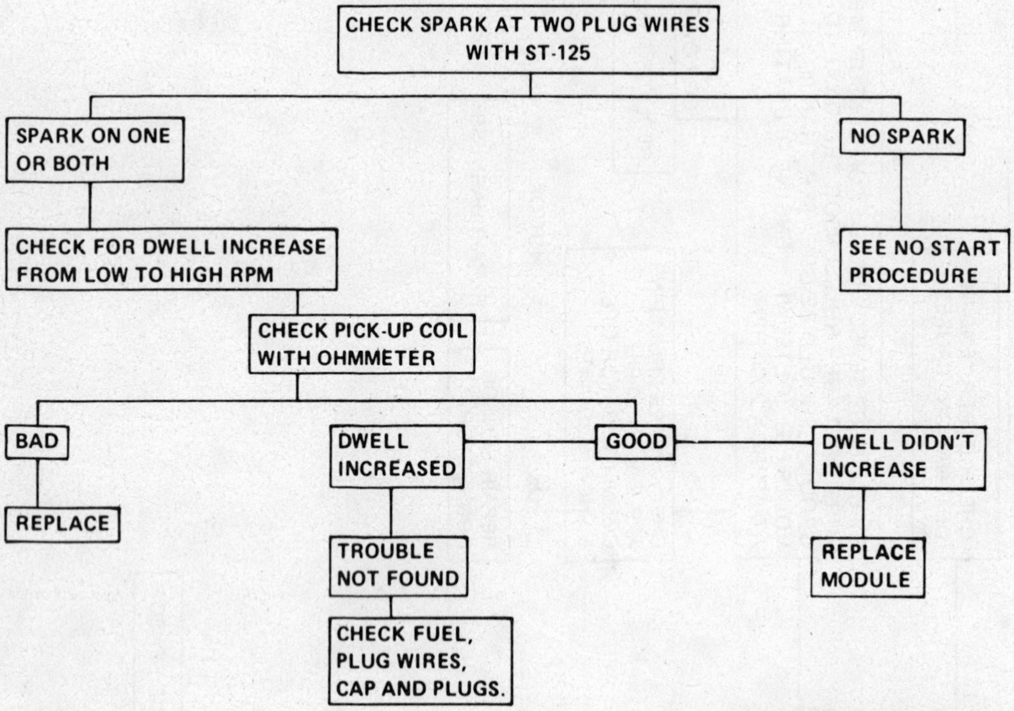

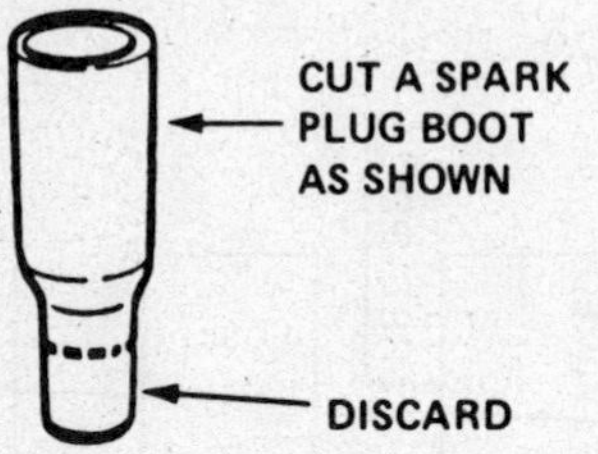

- CHECK SPARK AT TWO PLUG WIRES WITH ST-125
  - SPARK ON ONE OR BOTH
    - CHECK FOR DWELL INCREASE FROM LOW TO HIGH RPM
      - CHECK PICK-UP COIL WITH OHMMETER
        - BAD
          - REPLACE
        - GOOD
          - DWELL INCREASED
            - TROUBLE NOT FOUND
              - CHECK FUEL, PLUG WIRES, CAP AND PLUGS.
          - DWELL DIDN'T INCREASE
            - REPLACE MODULE
  - NO SPARK
    - SEE NO START PROCEDURE

CUT A SPARK PLUG BOOT AS SHOWN

DISCARD

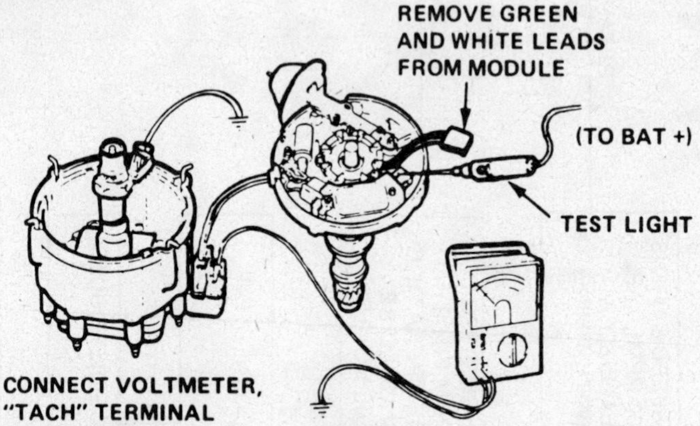

7/16" (11mm) FROM TIP OF SPARK PLUG

INSERT BOOT OVER PORCELAIN END OF ST-125

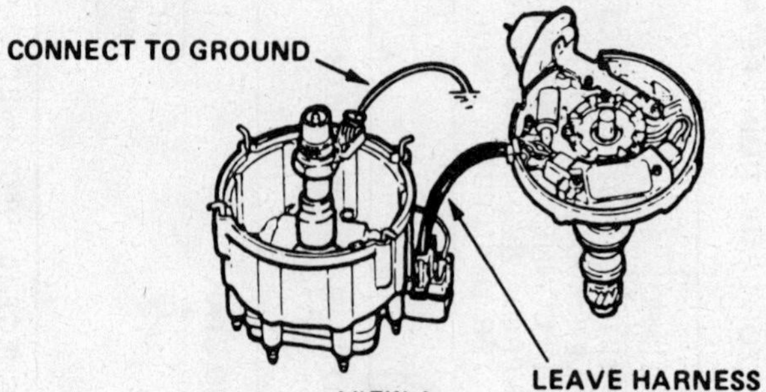

REMOVE GREEN AND WHITE LEADS FROM MODULE

(TO BAT +)

TEST LIGHT

CONNECT VOLTMETER, "TACH" TERMINAL TO GROUND

VIEW B

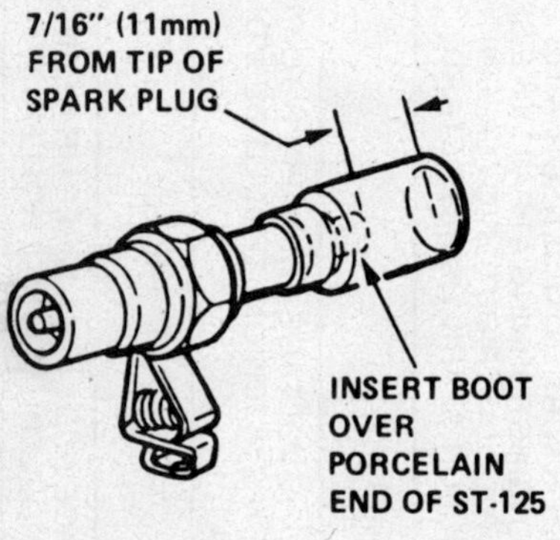

CONNECT TO GROUND

LEAVE HARNESS CONNECTED

VIEW A

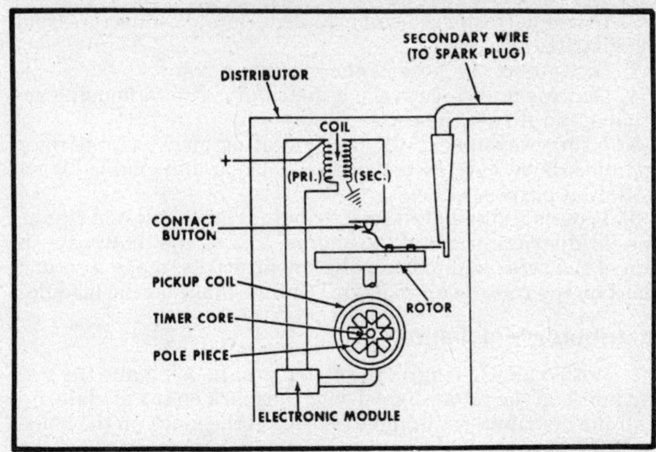

HEI schematic (© General Motors Corp.)

advance units with an electronic actuator. A vacuum sensor provides manifold vacuum information, and a reference pulse is generated by a pulse generator located near the engine vibration damper. These signals are fed to an Electronic Control Module which, in turn, sends a signal to the EST distributor for ignition timing determination.

Some 1983 and later 5.0 liter V8 engines also use an Electronic Spark Control (ESC) which responds to engine detonation with retardation of ignition timing. An engine block mounted sensor detects the presence of vibration generated by detonation and signals the ESC controller to process the signal and adjust the timing via the actuator on the distributor. The system gradually retards the spark until detonation has disappeared. A failed sensor would produce occasional detonation.

These ESC equipped engines also have a "tip in" vacuum switch. When the throttle is suddenly opened and manifold vacuum is suddenly decreased, the switch contacts close to send a signal to the ESC controller to arbitrarily retard the spark to prevent knock. Thus, if the engine knocks for a very short time after a rapid opening of the throttle, this switch may be at fault.

MAJOR REPAIR OPERATIONS (DISTRIBUTOR IN ENGINE)

Ignition Coil Replacement V8 Engines

1. Disconnect the feed and module wire terminal connectors from the distributor cap.
2. Remove the ignition set retainer.
3. Remove the 4 coil cover to distributor cap screws and the coil cover.
4. Remove the 4 coil to distributor cap screws.
5. Using a blunt drift, press the coil wire spade terminals up out of distributor cap.
6. Lift the coil up out of the distributor cap.
7. Remove and clean the coil spring, rubber seal washer and coil cavity of the distributor cap.
8. Reverse the above procedures to install.

Ignition Coil Replacement Six Cylinder Engines

On 6 cylinder engines, a separate ignition coil is used. To remove and install it, proceed as follows.

1. Remove the ignition switch to coil lead from the coil.
2. Unfasten the distributor leads from the coil.
3. Remove the screws which secure the coil to the engine and lift it off.
4. Installation is the reverse of removal.

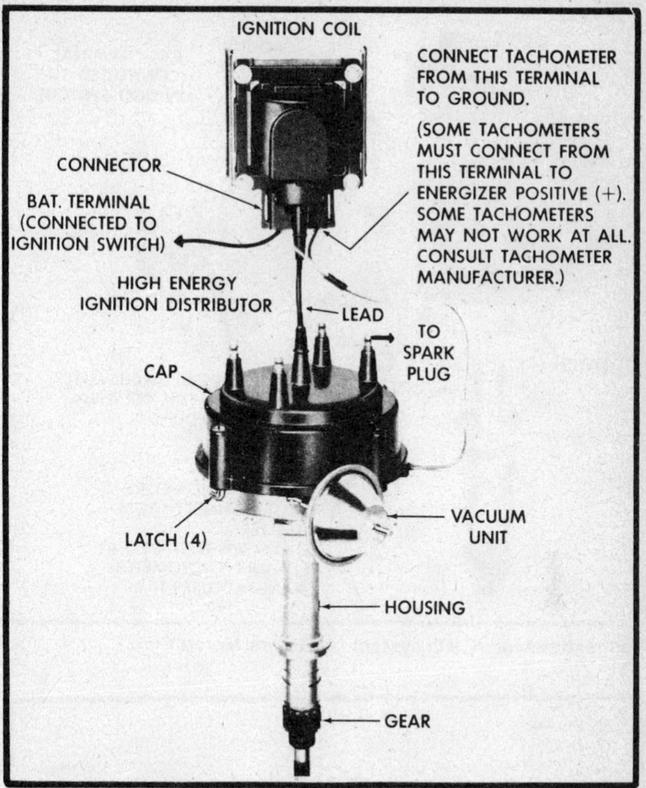

Connections for inline six cylinder HEI system (© General Motors Corp.)

Distributor Cap Replacement

1. Remove the feed and module wire terminal connectors from the distributor cap.
2. Remove the retainer and spark plug wires from the cap.
3. Depress and release the 4 distributor cap to housing retainers and lift off the cap assembly.
4. Remove the 4 coil cover screws and cover (V8 only).
5. Using a finger or a blunt drift, push the spade terminals up out of the distributor cap (V8 only).
6. Remove all 4 coil screws and lift the coil, coil spring and rubber seal washer out of the cap coil cavity (V8 only).
7. Using a new distributor cap, reverse the above procedures to assemble.

Rotor Replacement

1. Disconnect the feed and module wire connectors from the distributor.
2. Depress and release the 4 distributor cap to housing retainers and lift off the cap assembly.
3. Remove the two rotor attaching screws and rotor.
4. Reverse the above procedure to install.

Vacuum Advance Unit Replacement

1. Remove the distributor cap and rotor as previously described.
2. Disconnect the vacuum hose from the vacuum advance unit. Remove the module.
3. Remove the two vacuum advance retaining screws, pull the advance unit outward, rotate and disengage the operating rod from its tang.
4. Reverse the above procedure to install.

Module Replacement

1. Remove the distributor cap and rotor.

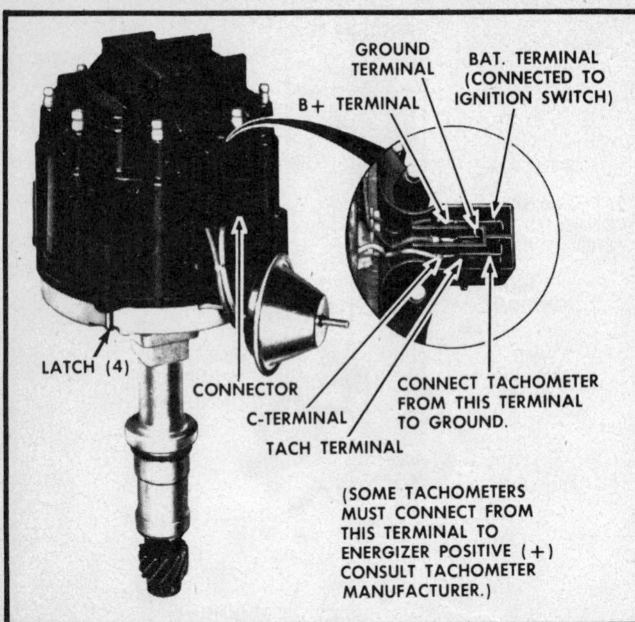

Connections for V8 HEI system (© General Motors Corp.)

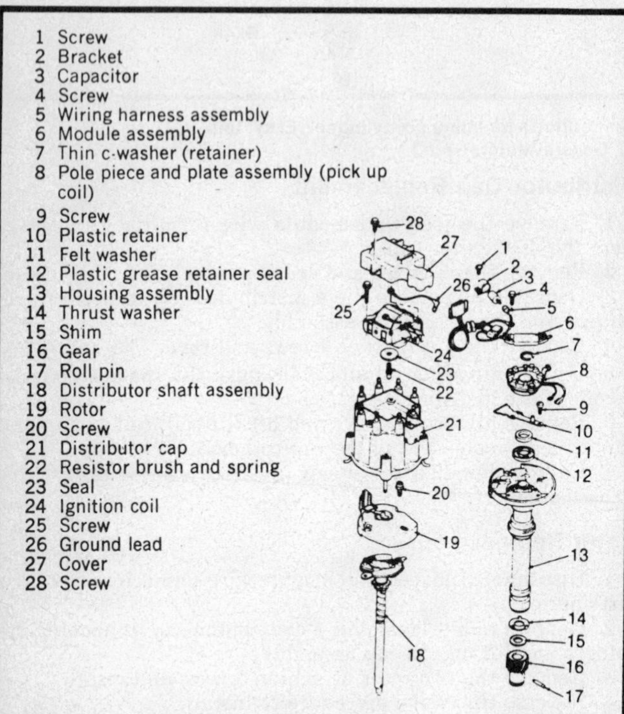

HEI distributor—exploded view eight cylinder (© General Motors Corp.)

2. Disconnect the harness connector and pick-up coil spade connectors from the module (note their positions).

3. Remove the two screws and module from the distributor housing.

4. Coat the bottom of the new module with dielectric lubricant. Reverse the above procedure to install. Be sure that the leads are installed correctly.

Distributor Removal

1. Disconnect the ground cable from the battery.

2. Disconnect the feed and module terminal connectors from the distributor cap.

3. Disconnect the hose at the vacuum advance.

4. Depress and release the 4 distributor cap to housing retainers and lift off the cap assembly.

5. Using crayon or chalk, make locating marks on the rotor and module and on the distributor housing and engine for installation purposes.

6. Loosen and remove the distributor clamp bolt and clamp, and lift distributor out of the engine. Noting the relative position of the rotor and module alignment marks, make a second mark on the rotor to align it with the one mark on the module.

Distributor Installation

1. With a new O-ring on the distributor housing and the second mark on the rotor aligned with the mark on the module, install the distributor, taking care to align the mark on the housing with the one on the engine. It may be necessary to lift the distributor and turn the rotor slightly to align the gears and the oil pump driveshaft.

2. With the respective marks aligned, install the clamp and bolt finger tight.

3. Install and secure the distributor cap.

4. Connect the feed and module connectors to the distributor cap.

5. Connect a timing light to the engine and plug the vacuum hose.

6. Connect the ground cable to the battery.

7. Start the engine and set the timing.

8. Turn the engine off and tighten the distributor clamp bolt. Disconnect the timing light and unplug and connect the hose to the vacuum advance.

SERVICE PROCEDURES (DISTRIBUTOR REMOVED)

Driven Gear Replacement

1. With the distributor removed, use a $1/8$ in. pin punch and tap out the driven gear roll pin.

2. Hold the rotor end of shaft and rotate the driven gear to shear any burrs in the roll pin hole.

3. Remove the driven gear from the shaft.

4. Reverse the above procedure to install.

Mainshaft Replacement

1. With the driven gear and rotor removed, gently pull the mainshaft out of the housing.

2. Remove the advance springs, weights and slide the weight base plate off the mainshaft.

3. Reverse the above procedure to install.

Pole Piece, Magnet or Pick Up Coil Replacement

1. With the mainshaft out of its housing, remove the 3 retaining screws, pole piece and magnet and/or pick up coil.

2. Reverse the removal procedure to install making sure that the pole piece teeth do not contact the timer core teeth by installing and rotating the mainshaft. Loosen the 3 screws and realign the pole piece as necessary.

ESC SERVICE PROCEDURES

Diagnosis

Before attempting to find an electrical or electronic problem with the Electronic Spark Control or Computer Command Control System, check that all electrical and vacuum connectors are securely connected. Otherwise, needless diagnostic or repair time may be expended. If no bad electrical or vacuum connections are found, refer to the accompanying charts.

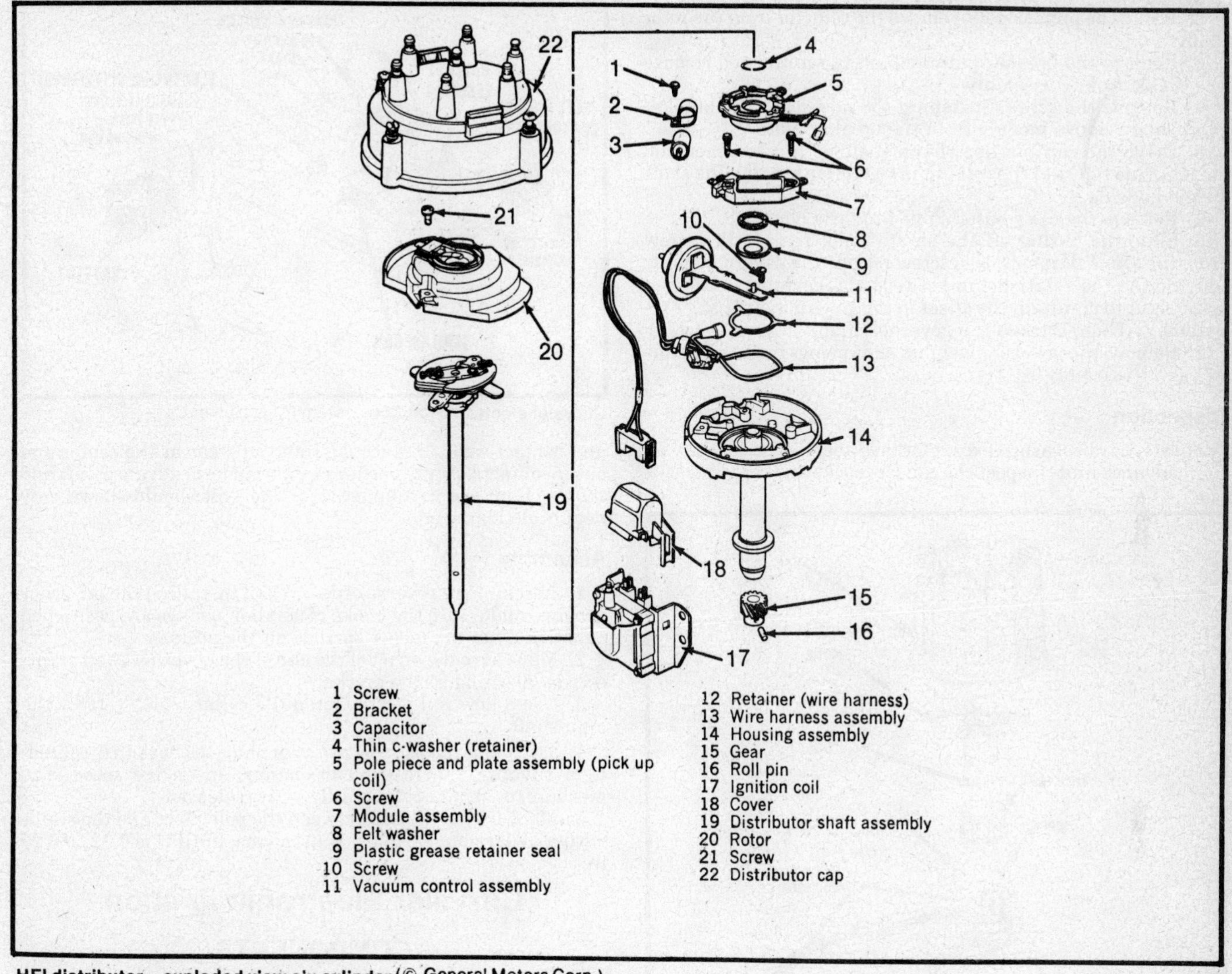

HEI distributor—exploded view six cylinder (© General Motors Corp.)

Detonation Sensor Replacement

The detonation sensor is located on the lower portion of the block on the right side, just in front of the starter. To replace it, first unlatch and then pull off the connector. Apply a wrench to the flats and unscrew the sensor. Screw the new sensor in place and tighten with the wrench. Reconnect the connector and try to gently pull the connector from the sensor with slight force to make sure it is latched in place. Finally, push it back on with about 10 lb. of force to make sure it's seated.

ESC Controller Replacement

The ESC Controller is located on the mounting bracket for the brake pedal, just to the right of the steering column. To replace it, first release and disconnect the wiring connector from underneath. Remove the screw fastening the top of the brace which runs from the brake pedal bracket to the lower controller mounting bracket. This is the screw nearest the firewall accessible from inside the brake pedal bracket.

Remove the two screws holding the lower controller mounting bracket and lower brace in place, and remove the lower bracket, brace and controller.

To install, first position the controller with the connection at the bottom and tabs facing away from the steering column. Slide the controller unit up under the tab at the top of its mounting bracket. Put the lower controller mounting bracket in position and install its rear screw. Position the brace so that its lower screw hole lines up with the open screw hole in the lower mounting bracket and its upper screw hole lines up with that in the brake pedal bracket. Install the screw which fastens the lower controller bracket and brace. Install the screw fastening the upper brace to the pedal mounting bracket. Finally, connect the electrical connector, checking that it locks securely.

DISTRIBUTOR

Disassembly

4 CYL. OHC ENGINE, CHEVY S-15

1. Remove the cap, rotor, and the packing which seals the cap at the bottom.
2. Remove the reluctor cover by squeezing together the fastening tangs and pulling it out.
3. Remove the vacuum advance unit's mounting screws and remove the unit from the distributor.
4. Remove the screw which attaches the wiring harness clip to the side of the distributor and remove the clip. Disconnect the two connectors from the breaker plate. Slide the harness sealing grommet up and out of the side of the distributor and remove the harness.

5. Using the proper toole, remove the reluctor from the rotor shaft.
6. Remove the breaker plate mounting screws, and remove the breaker plate assembly.
7. Remove the screws fastening the module to the breaker plate, and remove module from the breaker plate.
8. Drive the roll pin out of the shaft with a hammer and punch. This refers to the roll pin in the collar keeping the shaft in the housing.
9. Remove the distributor shaft from the housing.
10. Slide the O-ring off the shaft. Then, remove the screw from the top of the shaft, this screw retains the governor shaft.
11. Scribe the relationship between the governor shaft and rotor shaft to maintain the offset in the governor shaft after reassembly. Then, remove the governor shaft.
12. Remove the governor weights and springs from the governor shaft assembly.

Inspection

All parts may be washed except for the inner surface of the vacuum advance unit. Inspect the cap for cracks and carbon tracks and contact wear. Inspect the rotor for wear at the center and outer contacts. Apply vacuum to the vacuum advance unit and then seal off the vacuum source. The unit should shown only negligible leakage.

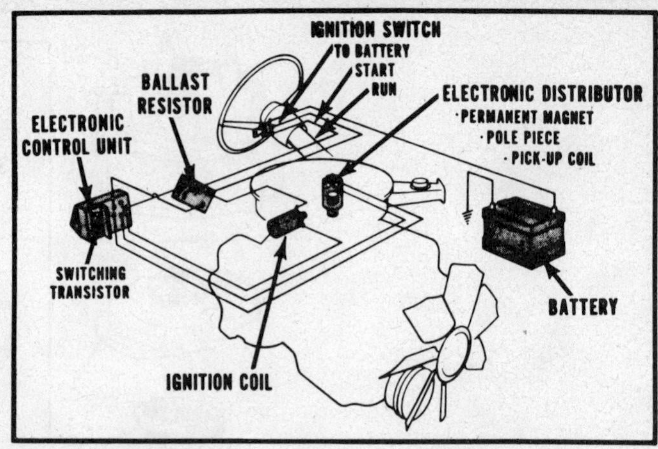

Chrysler electronic ignition system (© Chrysler Corp.)

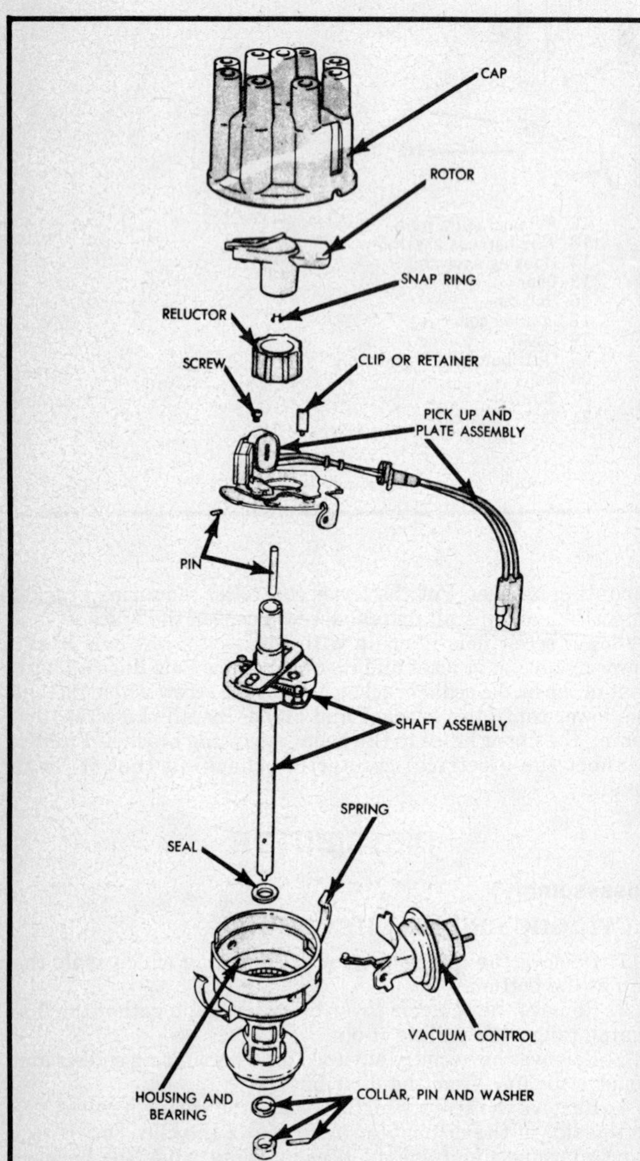

Exploded view of V8 electronic distributor (© Chrysler Corp.)

Assembly

1. Assemble in reverse order. When installing the governor springs, make sure the hooks of smaller springs are positioned below those of the larger springs on the posts.
2. Make sure the offset of the end of the governor shaft is correct by aligning scribe marks.
3. Use a new roll pin to fasten the collar which retains the mainshaft.
4. Twist and release the governor shaft to check that centrifugal advance will respond to changes in engine speed. The mechanism should return fully when released.
5. Measure the air gap between the pole piece and the stator with a feeler gauge. Adjust if necessary until it is 0.12 to 0.20 in.

Chrysler Electronic Ignition

COMPONENTS

This system consists of a special pulse sending distributor, an electronic control unit, a two element ballast resistor, and a special ignition coil. The distributor does not contain breaker points or a condenser, these parts being replaced by a distributor reluctor and a pick up unit.

OPERATION

The ignition primary circuit is connected from the battery, through the ignition switch, through the primary side of the ignition coil, to the control unit where it is grounded. The secondary circuit is the same as in conventional ignition systems; the secondary side of the coil, the coil wire to the distributor, the rotor, the spark plug wires, and the spark plugs.

The magnetic pulse distributor is also connected to the control unit. As the distributor shaft rotates, the distributor reluctor turns past the pick-up unit. As the reluctor turns past the pick up unit, each of the eight teeth on the reluctor pass near the pick up unit once during each distributor revolution (two crankshaft revolutions since the distributor runs at one half crankshaft speed). As the reluctor teeth move close to the pick up unit, the magnetic rotating reluctor induces voltage into the magnetic pick up unit. This voltage pulse is sent to the ignition control unit from the magnetic pick up unit. When the pulse enters the control unit, it signals the control unit to interrupt the ignition primary circuit. This causes the primary circuit to collapse and begins the induction of the magnetic lines of force from the primary side of the coil into the second-

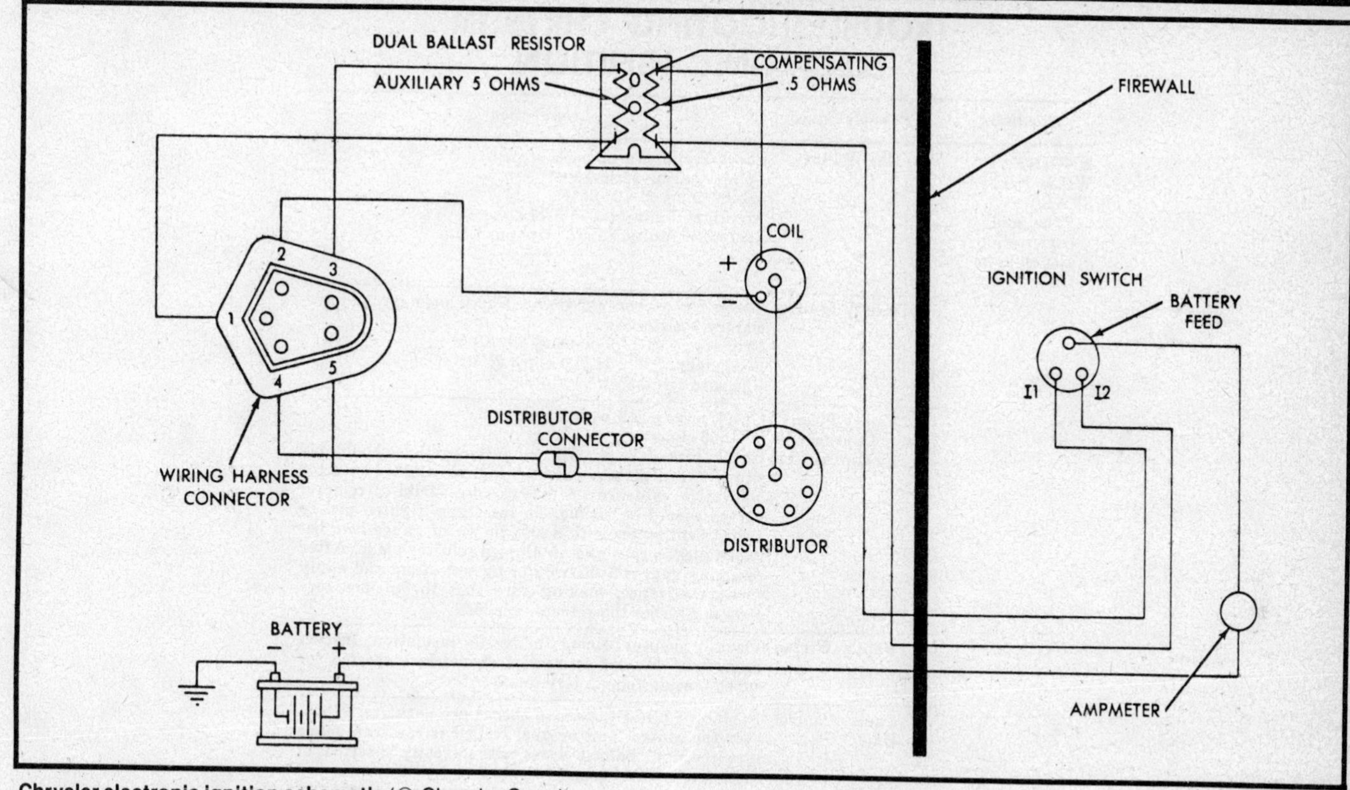

Chrysler electronic ignition schematic (© Chrysler Corp.)

ary side of the coil. This induction provides the required voltage to fire the spark plugs.

The advantages of this system are that the transistors in the control unit can make and break the primary ignition circuit much faster than conventional ignition points can, and higher primary voltage can be utilized, since this system can be made to handle higher voltage without adverse effects, whereas ignition breaker points cannot. The quicker switching time of this system allows longer coil primary circuit saturation time and longer induction time when the primary circuit collapses. This increased time allows the primary circuit to build up more current and the secondary circuit to discharge more current.

PICK UP COIL

Replacement

1. Remove the distributor from the engine.
2. Using the proper tool, pry the reluctor off the shaft from the bottom. Be careful not to damage the teeth on the reluctor.
3. Unfasten the vacuum advance to distributor housing screws. Remove the vacuum unit, after disconnecting the arm from the upper plate.
4. Unfasten the pickup coil wires from the distributor housing.
5. Unfasten the two screws which secure the lower plate to the distributor housing. Lift out the lower plate together with the upper plate and pickup coil.
6. Separate the upper and lower plates by depressing the retaining clip on the underside of the plate and slide it away from the stud. The pickup coil will come off with the upper plate as they cannot be separated. They must be serviced as an assembly.
7. Installation is the reverse of removal. Place a small amount of distributor grease on the support pins on the lower plate.

Air Gap Adjustment

1. Align one reluctor tooth with the pickup coil tooth.
2. Loosen the pickup coil hold down screw.
3. Insert a 0.008 in. nonmagnetic feeler gauge between the reluctor tooth and the pickup coil tooth.
4. Adjust the air gap so that contact is made between the reluctor tooth, the feeler gauge, and the pick-up coil tooth.
5. Tighten the hold down screw.
6. Remove the feeler gauge. No force should be required in removing the feeler gauge.
7. Check the air gap with a 0.008 in. feeler gauge. A 0.008 in. feeler gauge should not fit into the air gap. A 0.008 in. feeler gauge can be forced into the air gap. Do not force the gauge into the air gap.
8. Apply vacuum to the vacuum unit and rotate the governor shaft. The pickup pole should not hit the reluctor teeth. The gap was not properly adjusted if any hitting occurs. If hitting occurs on only one side of the reluctor, the distributor shaft is probably bent, and the governor and shaft assembly should be replaced.

TROUBLESHOOTING ELECTRONIC IGNITION SYSTEM

Chrysler Corporation has an Electronic Ignition System Tester to be used when checking the system. However, many shops are not able to obtain this equipment, so an alternate method has been developed. The system may be tested using a voltmeter with a scale of 20 volts and an ohmmeter with a scale of 20000 ohms. When the ignition system is suspected of malfunctions, the following procedure should be used.

1. Inspect the secondary wires for cracks and tightness.
2. Check all primary wires and connections at the components for tightness.

TROUBLESHOOTING CHRYSLER ELECTRONIC IGNITION

Condition	Possible Cause	Correction
ENGINE WILL NOT START (Fuel and carburetion known to be OK)	a) Dual Ballast	Check resistance of each section: Compensating resistance: .50-.60 ohms @ 70°-80°F Auxiliary Ballast: 4.75-5.75 ohms Replace if faulty. Check wire positions.
	b) Faulty Ignition Coil	Check for carbonized tower. Check primary and secondary resistances: Primary: 1.41-1.79 ohms @ 70°-80°F Secondary: 9,200-11,700 ohms @ 70°-80°F Check in coil tester.
	c) Faulty Pickup or Improper Pickup Air Gap	Check pickup coil resistance: 400-600 ohms Check pickup gap: .010 in. feeler gauge should not slip between pickup coil core and an aligned reluctor blade. No evidence of pickup core striking reluctor blades should be visible. To reset gap, tighten pickup adjustment screw with a .008 in. feeler gauge held between pickup core and an aligned reluctor blade. After resetting gap, run distributor on test stand and apply vacuum advance, making sure that the pickup core does not strike the reluctor blades.
	d) Faulty Wiring	Visually inspect wiring for brittle insulation. Inspect connectors. Molded connectors should be inspected for rubber inside female terminals.
	e) Faulty Control Unit	Replace if all of the above checks are negative. Whenever the control unit or dual ballast is replaced, make sure the dual ballast wires are correctly inserted in the keyed molded connector.
ENGINE SURGES	a) Wiring	Inspect for loose connection and/or broken conductors in harness.
SEVERELY (Not Lean	b) Faulty Pickup Leads	Disconnect vacuum advance. If surging stops, replace pickup.
Carburetor)	c) Ignition Coil	Check for intermittent primary.
ENGINE MISSES (Carburetion OK)	a) Spark Plugs	Check plugs. Clean and regap if necessary.
	b) Secondary Cable	Check cables with an ohmmeter, or observe secondary circuit performance with an oscilloscope.
	c) Ignition Coil	Check for cabonized tower. Check in coil tester.
	d) Wiring	Check for loose or dirty connections.
	e) Faulty Pickup Lead	Disconnect vacuum advance. If miss stops, replace pickup.
	f) Control Unit	Replace if the above checks are negative.

3. Check and note the battery voltage.

4. Be sure the ignition switch is in the "OFF" position and remove the multi-wiring connector from the control unit.

5. Turn the ignition switch to the "ON" position and connect the negative lead of the voltmeter to a good ground.

6. Connect the positive lead of the voltmeter to the number 1 terminal of the wiring harness connector. The voltage should be within 1 volt of battery voltage. If more than 1 volt, the circuit must be checked for high resistance.

7. Connect the positive lead of the voltmeter to the wiring harness connector number 2 terminal. Available voltage should be within 1 volt of battery voltage. If more than 1 volt, the circuit should be checked for high resistance.

8. Connect the positive lead of the voltmeter to the wiring harness connector terminal number 3. Available voltage should be within 1 volt of battery voltage. If more than 1 volt, the circuit must be checked for high resistance.

9. Turn the ignition switch to the "OFF" position.

10. Connect an ohmmeter to the wiring harness connector terminal numbers 4 and 5. This checks the distributor pickup coil. The ohmmeter resistance reading should be between 150 and 900 ohms. If the readings are higher or lower than specified, disconnect the dual lead connector coming from the distributor. Using the ohmmeter leads, check the resistance at the dual lead connector. If the reading is not between 150 and 900 ohms, replace the pickup coil assembly in the distributor. If the reading is within specifications at the dual lead connector, check the wiring harness between the control unit and the dual lead connector.

11. Connect one ohmmeter lead to a good ground and the other lead to either connector of the distributor. The ohmmeter should show an open circuit. If the ohmmeter shows a reading, the pickup coil in the distributor must be replaced.

12. When checking the electronic control unit, connect one ohmmeter lead to a good ground and the other lead to the control unit connector pin number 5. The ohmmeter should show continuity between the ground and the connector pin. If continuity does not exist, tighten the bolts holding the control unit to the vehicle panel and recheck. If continuity does not exist, the control unit must be replaced.

13. Reconnect the wiring harness at the control unit and distributor. Whenever removing or replacing the wiring harness connector to the control unit or the distributor, the ignition switch must be in the "OFF" position.

14. Check the reluctor tooth and pickup coil air gaps, specifications of 0.008 in.

15. To check the secondary ignition system, remove the high voltage cable from the center tower of the distributor cap and hold approximately $^{3}/_{16}$ in. from the engine block and crank the engine with the ignition switch in the "START" position.

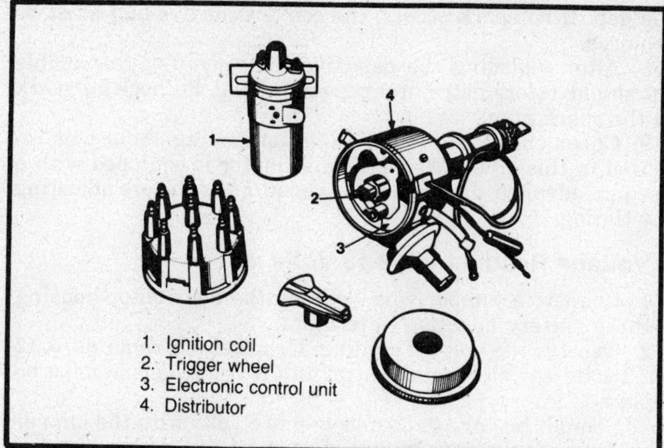

Major components in breakerless electronic ignition system (© IH Co.)

16. If arcing does not occur, replace the control unit. Recheck by cranking the engine. If arcing still does not occur, replace the ignition coil.

Breakerless Integral Electronic Ignition System

PRESTOLITE IDN-4000 SERIES

The Breakerless Integral Electronic Ignition system is available for both the four cylinder and V8 engines. The system consists of two major components, the ignition coil and the distributor. The electronic control unit, consisting of a circuit board and sensor, is located within the distributor and is replaced as a complete unit, should service be required. Either a four or eight toothed trigger wheel is located on the distributor shaft, depending upon the engine in which it is to be used.

The distributor is easily identified by the male type terminal on the distributor cap secondary system. The distributor incorporates a mechanical (centrifugal) spark advance system. Most distributors will have a vacuum operated advance system to automatically provide the correct spark advance timing for the various engine speed and load conditions.

The sensor mounting plate configuration and vacuum advance unit location varies between distributors with clockwise and counterclockwise rotation.

Disassembly

The disassembly and overhaul of the distributor is similar to that of the conventional point type distributor. Certain specifications should be adhered to during the overhaul of the distributor. The distributor shaft side play should be between 0.002 and 0.004 inch with a maximum of 0.006 inch. The distributor shaft end play should be 0.035 to 0.040 inch, except distributors with left hand (counterclockwise) rotation, which should be 0.004 to 0.018 inch. The distributor dwell should be 26 to 32 degrees, except distributors numbered IDN-4002R, IDN-4001, IDN-4010 and IDN-4001A, which have a dwell of 28 to 34 degrees.

All distributors should have an air gap between the end of the trigger wheel tooth and the sensor of 0.008 inch.

Sensor to Trigger Wheel Air Gap Adjustment

1. Rotate the distributor shaft until one tooth of the trigger wheel is aligned with the center of the sensor. The trigger wheel tooth should be perpendicular to the flat surface of the sensor when properly aligned.

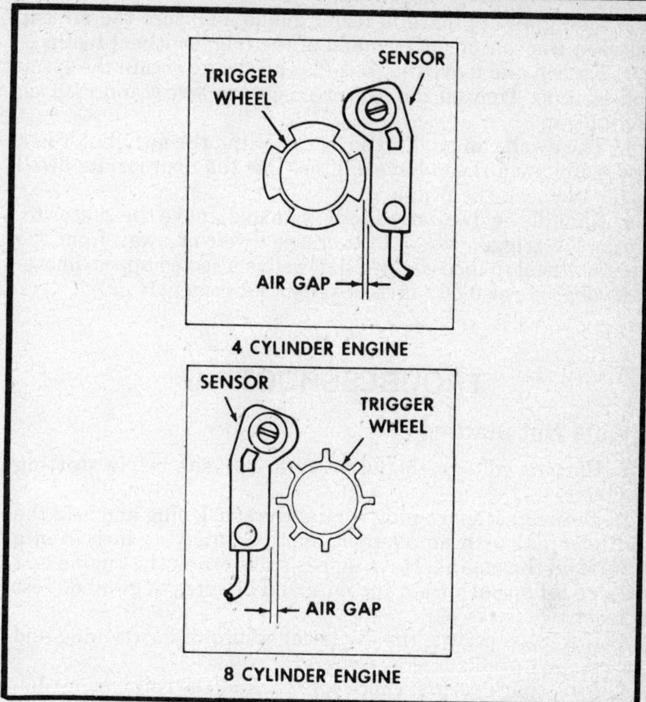

Checking air gap (© IH Co.)

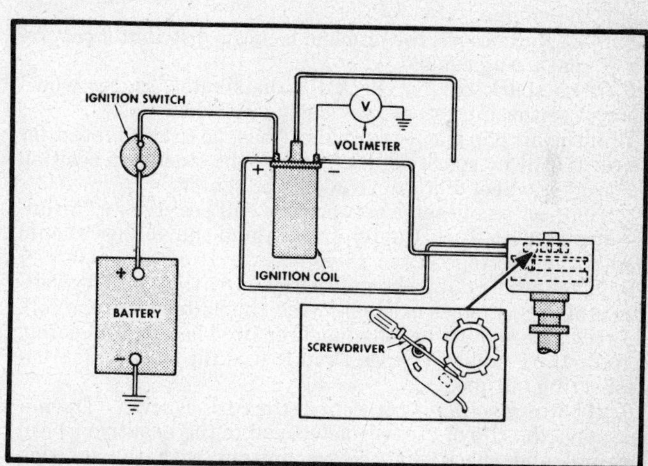

Testing electronic control unit (© IH Co.)

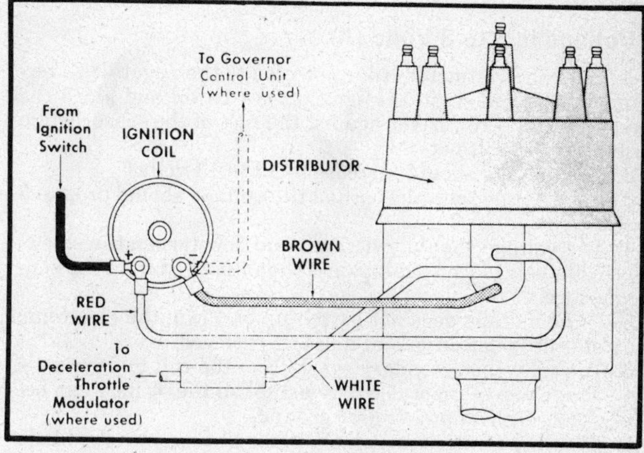

Primary wiring—breakerless distributor (© IH Co.)

2. Using an appropriate feeler gauge, measure the air gap between the sensor and the end of the trigger wheel tooth.

3. Loosen and move the sensor as needed to obtain the specified air gap. Tighten the sensor mounting screw and recheck the air gap.

4. The dwell can be checked by installing the distributor in a test stand or in the vehicle engine. Use the appropriate dwell meter to check the dwell.

5. Should the dwell need to be changed, move the sensor towards the trigger wheel to decrease dwell or away from the trigger wheel to increase dwell. Dwell is affected approximately ½ degree per 0.001 inch of sensor movement.

TROUBLESHOOTING

Engine Not Starting

1. Battery voltage should be 12 to 13 volts before starting the tests.

2. Disconnect spark plug wire at the spark plug and hold the end terminal with an adapter, approximately ½ inch from a ground on the engine. Have an assistant crank the engine and observe for a spark from the wire and adapter to ground. Test at least two wires.

3. If a spark occurs, the electrical system is functioning and the no start problem is elsewhere.

4. If no spark occurs, check for spark at the coil lead by disconnecting it from the distributor cap and holding it approximately ½ inch from a ground and again, have an assistant crank the engine.

5. If a spark occurs, the problem is in the distributor cap, rotor or spark plug cables.

6. If no spark occurs, check the distributor trigger wheel tooth to sensor air gap as previously outlined.

7. If the air gap is out of specifications, adjust and retest for spark. If still no spark occurs, "bump" the starter to position two trigger wheel teeth to straddle the sensor.

8. Connect a voltmeter between the coil positive (+) terminal and ground. Turn the ignition on and the voltage should read battery voltage (12 to 13 volts).

9. Should the voltage be noticeably lower than battery voltage, a high resistance exists between the battery and the coil. This resistance must be found and repaired before proceeding. Refer to the Primary Voltage Drop Test at the end of this troubleshooting outline.

10. If battery voltage is present at the coil positive (+) terminal, move the clip of the voltmeter lead to the negative (-) coil terminal and check the voltage present with the ignition switch on. The voltage obtained will be one of the following. Normal voltage 5 to 8 volts, problem voltage 12 to 13 volts or 0 to 5 volts.

If Voltage is 5 to 8 Volts (A)

1. With the voltmeter still connected to the negative (-) terminal of the coil, turn the ignition switch on and place the blade of a flat screwdriver against the face of the sensor while observing the voltmeter.

2. The voltage should increase to 12 to 13 volts.

3. Remove the screwdriver and the voltage should drop to 5 to 8 volts.

4. The voltage should switch up and down when the screwdriver blade is placed against and then removed from the sensor surface.

5. If the voltage does not switch up or down, the electronic control unit is defective and must be replaced.

6. To verify the secondary spark from the coil to ground as the voltage moves up or down, re-establish the ½ inch gap between the coil lead and engine ground.

7. With the ignition switch on, place the screwdriver blade against the face of the sensor and a spark should occur across the gap. If no spark occurs, the coil is defective and must be replaced.

8. After replacing the defective component(s), reassemble the shield, rotor, distributor cap and wiring. Recheck for spark at the spark plugs.

9. Check the dwell and the ignition timing. Adjust as required in this order. When the distributor is equipped with a vacuum advance, disconnect the vacuum hose before adjusting the timing.

If Voltage Reading Is 12-13 Volts (B)

1. Connect a jumper wire between the distributor housing and the battery negative (-) terminal.

2. Observe the voltage reading. If the voltage remains at 12 to 13 volts, the electronic control unit is defective and must be replaced.

3. Should the voltage change to 5 to 8 volts with the jumper wire connected, a poor ground circuit exists between the distributor and the battery. All grounding straps should be examined, cleaned and tightened as required.

If The Voltage Is Between 0-5 Volts (C)

1. Disconnect the voltmeter lead from the coil and disconnect the brown wire from the coil negative (-) terminal, with the other voltmeter lead still connected to a ground.

2. With the ignition switch on, observe the voltage reading. If the voltage is still 0 to 5 volts, the coil is faulty and must be replaced.

3. If the voltage increases to 12 to 13 volts, the electronic control unit is defective and must be replaced.

4. After the necessary repairs are made, be sure to reconnect the brown wire to the coil negative (-) terminal.

PRIMARY VOLTAGE DROP TEST

1. Remove the distributor cap, rotor and shield. "Bump" the starter to position two teeth of the trigger wheel, straddling the sensor.

2. Connect the voltmeter positive (+) lead to the battery positive (+) post and connect the voltmeter negative (-) lead to the coil positive (+) terminal.

3. Turn the ignition on and observe the voltmeter reading. A reading of less than one volt should be obtained.

4. If a voltage reading higher than one volt exists, move the following components while observing the voltmeter scale, battery cables, starter solenoid battery terminal, dash panel connector at the firewall (if used), ammeter terminals and the ignition switch connectors.

5. If a fluctuation or upswing of the voltmeter is noted while flexing the connectors and cables, a poor connection or defective cable exists and must be corrected.

SWITCHES AND SOLENOIDS

Magnetic Switches

Magnetic switches serve only to make contact for the starter motor. Usually, such switches are located on the inner fender panel, although they are found mounted on the starter in a few cases.

Magnetic Switches with Two Control Terminals

On this type of magnetic switch current is supplied from the ignition switch or transmission neutral button to one of the magnetic switch control terminals. The other control terminal is connected to the transmission neutral safety switch (on the transmission) where it is grounded.

Magnetic Switches with Ignition Resistor ByPass Terminals

All normally use a magnetic switch with a single control terminal. The second terminal is an ignition resistor by-pass terminal.

SOLENOIDS WITHOUT RELAYS

This type of starter solenoid is always mounted on the starter. Makes electrical contact for the starter and pulls the starter and drive clutch into mesh with the flywheel. The Chrysler reduction gear starter has this solenoid embodied in the starter housing. There is only one control terminal on the solenoid. The ignition by-pass terminal is usually marked R or IGN, if it is used.

SOLENOIDS WITH SEPARATE RELAYS

The solenoid itself is always mounted on the starter. In addition to making contact for the starter, it also pulls the starter drive clutch gear into mesh with the flywheel. A single control terminal is used on the solenoid itself. The relay is usually found mounted to the inner fender panel or on the firewall.

SOLENOIDS WITH BUILT IN RELAYS

These units are always mounted on the starter and are connected, through linkage, to the starter drive clutch. The relay portion is a square box built into and integral with the front end of the solenoid assembly.

NEUTRAL SAFETY SWITCHES

The purpose of the neutral safety switch is to prevent the starter from cranking the engine except when the transmission is in neutral or park. On some trucks the neutral safety switch is located on the transmission. It serves to ground the solenoid or magnetic switch, whichever is used. On other trucks the neutral safety switch is located either at the bottom of the steering column, where it contacts the shift mechanism, on the steering column, underneath the dash, or on the shift linkage (console). Some manual transmission models have a clutch linkage safety switch to prevent starter operation unless the clutch pedal is depressed. On most trucks the neutral safety switch and the backup light switch are combined into a single switch mechanism.

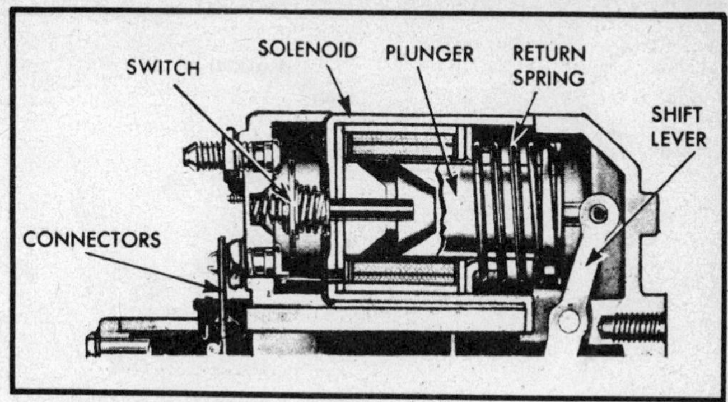

Starter solenoid mounted on starter motor

Troubleshooting Neutral Safety Switches (Quick Test)

If the starter fails to function and the neutral safety switch is to be checked, a jumper can be placed across its terminals. If the starter then functions the safety switch is defective.

In the case of neutral safety switches with one wire, this wire must be grounded for testing purposes. If the starter works with the wire grounded, the switch is defective.

Neutral Safety Switch (Back Up Light Switch)

When the neutral safety switch is built in combination with the back-up light switch, the easiest way to tell which terminals are for the back-up lights is to take a jumper and cross every pair of wires. The pair of wires which light the back-up lamps should be ignored when testing the neutral safety switch. Once the back-up light wires have been located, jump the other pair of wires to test the neutral safety switch. If the starter functions only when the jumper is placed across these two wires, the neutral safety switch is defective or requires adjustment.

STARTING SYSTEMS

Reduction Gear Starter Motor

CHRYSLER CORPORATION

The housing is die cast aluminum. A 3.5 to 1 reduction, combined with the starter to ring gear ratio, results in a total gear reduction of about 45 to 1.

NOTE: The high pitched sound is caused by the higher starter speed.

The positive shift solenoid is enclosed in the starter housing and is energized through the ignition switch. When ignition switch is turned to start, the solenoid plunger engages drive gear through a shifting fork. At the completion of travel, the plunger closes a switch to revolve the starter.

The tension of the spring type shifting prevents a butt tooth lock up and motor will not start before total shift. An overrunning clutch prevents motor damage if key is held on after engine starts. No lubrication is required due to Oilite bearings.

Disassembly

1. Support assembly in a vise equipped with soft jaws. Do not clamp. Care must be used not to distort or damage the die cast aluminum.
2. Remove the through olts and the end housing.
3. Carefully pull the armature up and out of the gear housing, and the starter frame and field assembly. Remove the steel and fiber thrust washer.

NOTE: On eight cylinder engines the starting motors have the wire of the shunt field coil soldered to the brush terminal. Six cylinder engines have the four coils in series and do not have a wire soldered to the brush terminal. One pair of brushes is connected to this terminal. The other pair of brushes is attached to the series field coils by means of a terminal screw. Carefully pull the frame and field assembly up just enough to expose the terminal screw and the solder connection of the shunt field at the brush terminal. Place two wood blocks between the

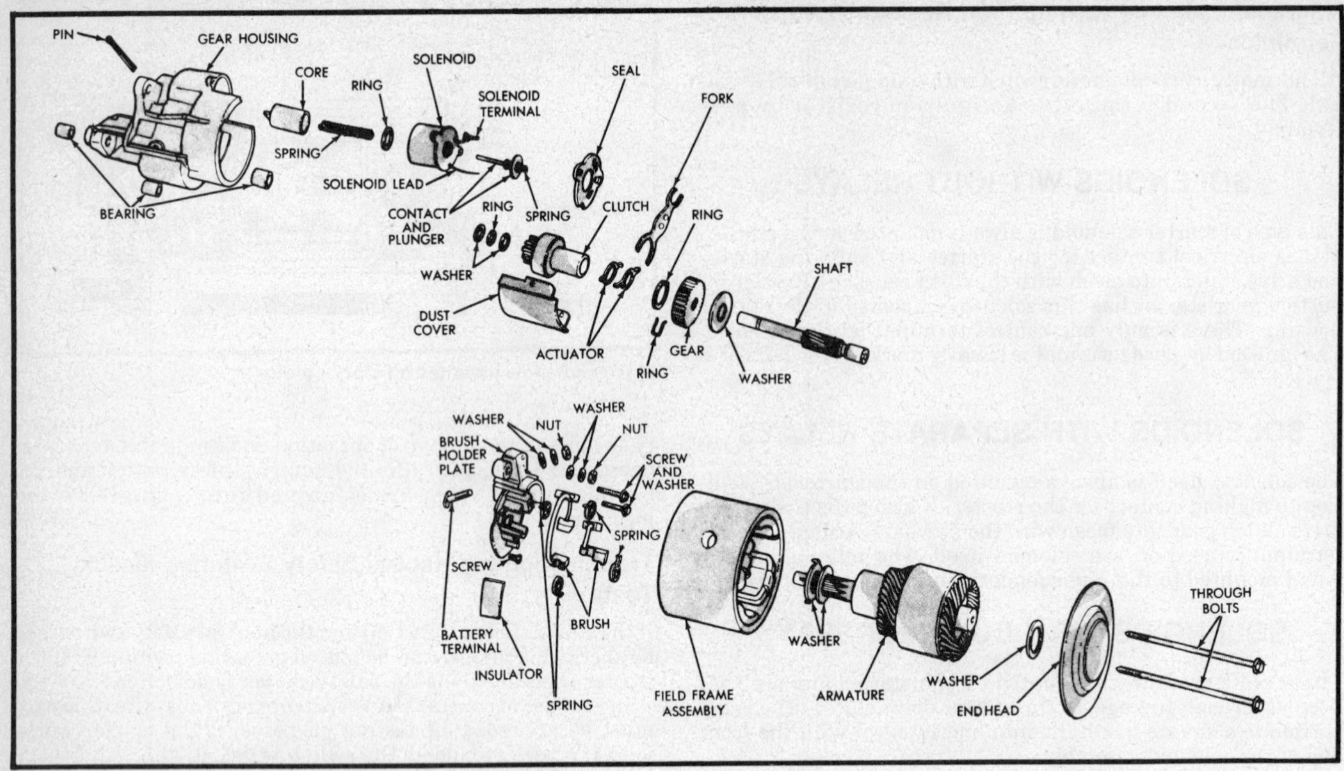

Reduction gear starter—exploded view (© Chrysler Corp.)

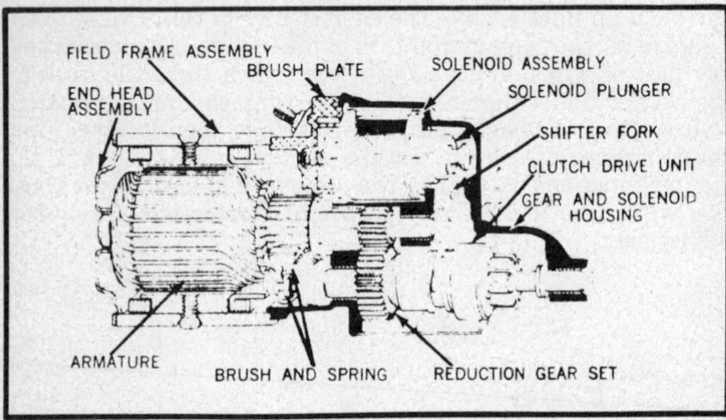

Reduction gear starter—cross section (© Chrysler Corp.)

starter frame and starter gear housing to facilitate removal of the terminal screw and unsoldering of the shunt field wire at the brush terminal.

4. Support the brush terminal with a finger behind terminal and remove screw.
5. On eight cylinder engine starters unsolder the shunt field coil lead from the brush terminal and housing.
6. The brush holder plate with terminal, contact and brushes is serviced as an assembly.
7. Clean all old sealer from around plate and housing.
8. Remove the brush holder attaching screw.
9. On the shunt type, unsolder the solenoid winding from the brush terminal.
10. Remove $^{11}/_{32}$ in. nut, washer and insulator from solenoid terminal.
11. Remove brush holder plate with brushes as an assembly.
12. Remove gear housing ground screw.
13. The solenoid assembly can be removed from the well.
14. Remove nut, washer and seal from starter battery terminal and remove terminal from plate.
15. Remove solenoid contact and plunger from solenoid and remove the coil sleeve.
16. Remove the solenoid return spring, coil retaining washer, retainer and the dust cover from the gear housing.
17. Release the snap-ring that locates the driven gear on pinion shaft.
18. Release front retaining ring.
19. Push pinion shaft toward the rear and remove snap-ring, thrust washers, clutch and pinion, and two shift fork nylon actuators.
20. Remove driven gear and friction washer.
21. Pull shifting fork forward and remove moving core.
22. Remove fork retainer pin and shifting fork assembly. The gear housing with bushings is serviced as an assembly.

Replacement of Brushes

1. Brushes that are worn more than one-half the length of new brushes, or are oil soaked, should be replaced.
2. When resoldering the shunt field and solenoid lead, make a strong, low-resistance connection using a high temperature solder and resin flux. Do not use acid or acid core solder. Do not break the shunt field wire units when removing and installing the brushes.

Starter Clutch and Pinion Gear Inspection

1. Do not immerse the starter clutch unit in a cleaning solvent. The outside of the clutch and pinion must be cleaned with a cloth so as not to wash the lubricant from the inside of the clutch.
2. Rotate the pinion. The pinion gear should rotate smoothly and in one direction only. If the starter clutch unit does not function properly, or if the pinion is worn, chipped, or burred, replace the starter clutch unit.

Commutator Inspection

1. Inspect the commutator and the surface contacted by the

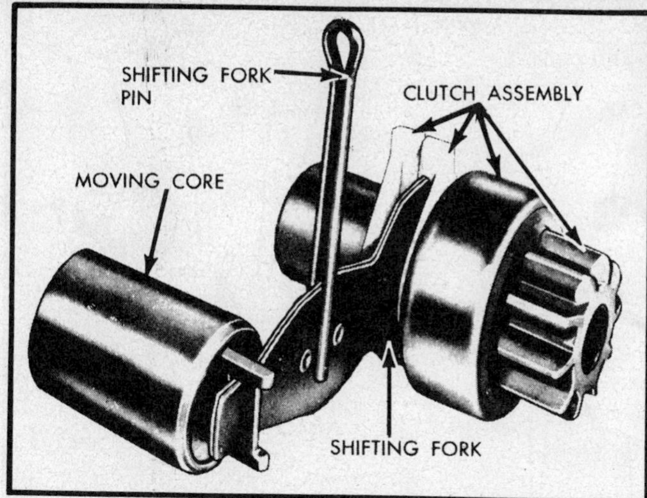

Shift fork and clutch arrangement (© Chrysler Corp.)

brushes when the starter is assembled, for flat spots, out of roundness, or excessive wear.

2. Reface the commutator if necessary, removing only a sufficient amount of metal to provide a smooth, even surface.

3. Using light pressure, clean the grooves of the face of the commutator with a pointed tool. Neither remove any metal or widen the grooves.

Assembly

1. The shifter fork consists of two spring steel plates held together by two rivets. Before assembling the starter, check the plates for side movement. After lubricating between the plates with a small amount of SAE 10 engine oil, they should have about $^1/_{16}$ in. side movement to insure proper pinion gear engagement.

2. Position the shift fork in the drive housing and install the shifting fork retainer pin. One tip of the pin should be straight and the other bent at a 15 degree angle away from the housing. The fork and retainer pin should operate freely after bending the tip of the pin.

3. Install the solenoid moving core and engage the shifting fork.

4. Place the pinion shaft into the drive housing and install the friction washer and drive gear.

5. Install the clutch and pinion assembly, thrust washer, and retaining washer.

6. Engage the shifting fork with the clutch actuators. The friction washer must be positioned on the shoulder of the splines of the pinion shaft before the driven gear is positioned.

7. Install the driven gear snap ring.

8. Install the pinion shaft retaining ring.

9. The starter solenoid return spring can now be inserted in the moveable core.

10. Install the solenoid contact plunger assembly into the solenoid and reform the double wires so they can be curved around the contactor. This will allow the terminal stud to enter the brush holder properly. The contactor must not touch these double wires after assembly is complete.

11. Assemble the battery terminal stud in the brush holder.

12. Position the seal on the brush holder plate.

13. Run the solenoid lead wire through the hole in the brush holder and attach the solenoid stud, insulating washers, flat washer, and nut.

14. Wrap the solenoid lead wire tightly around the brush terminal post and solder it.

15. Fix the brush holder to the solenoid attaching screws.

16. Gently lower the solenoid coil and brush plate into the gear housing.

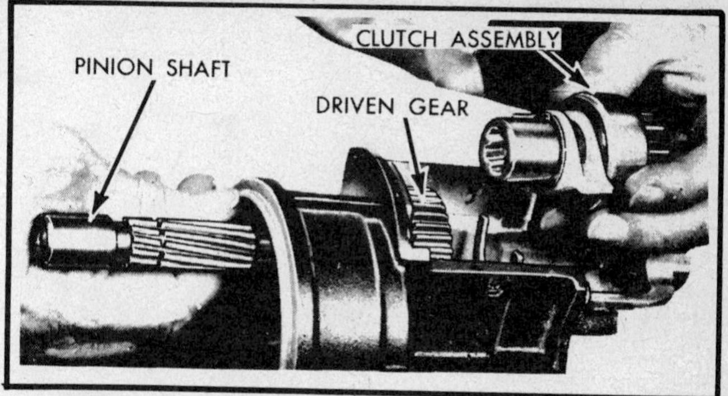

Removing clutch assembly (© Chrysler Corp.)

17. Position the brush plate assembly into the starter gear housing, install the nuts, and tighten.

18. Solder the shunt coil lead wire to the starter brush terminal.

19. Install the brush terminal screw.

20. Position the field frame on the gear housing and start the armature into the housing, carefully engaging the splines on the shaft with the reduction gear by rotating the armature.

21. Install the fiber thrust washer and the steel washer on the armature shaft.

22. Replace the starter end housing and starter throughbolts; tighten securely.

Direct Drive Starter Motor

CHRYSLER CORPORATION

This starter can be identified by the externally mounted solenoid bolted to the case.

Disassembly

1. Remove through bolts and tap commutator end head from frame.

2. Remove thrust washers from armature shaft.

3. Lift brush holder springs and remove brushes from holders.

4. Remove brush holder plate.

5. Disconnect the field coil wires at the solenoid connector, and remove the solenoid screws.

6. Remove solenoid and boot.

7. Drive out shift fork pivot pin.

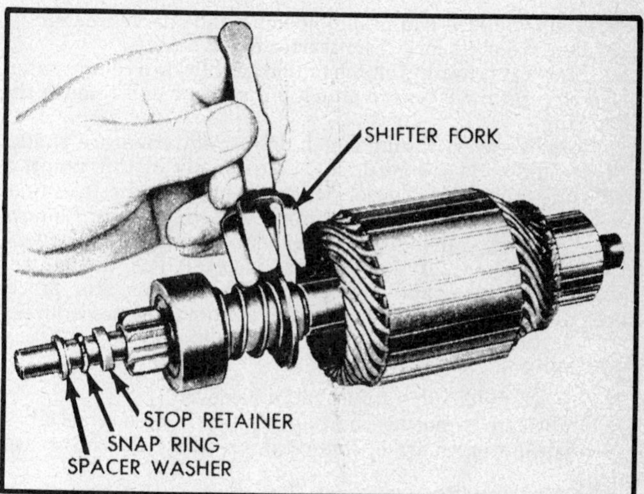

Removing shift fork (© Chrysler Corp.)

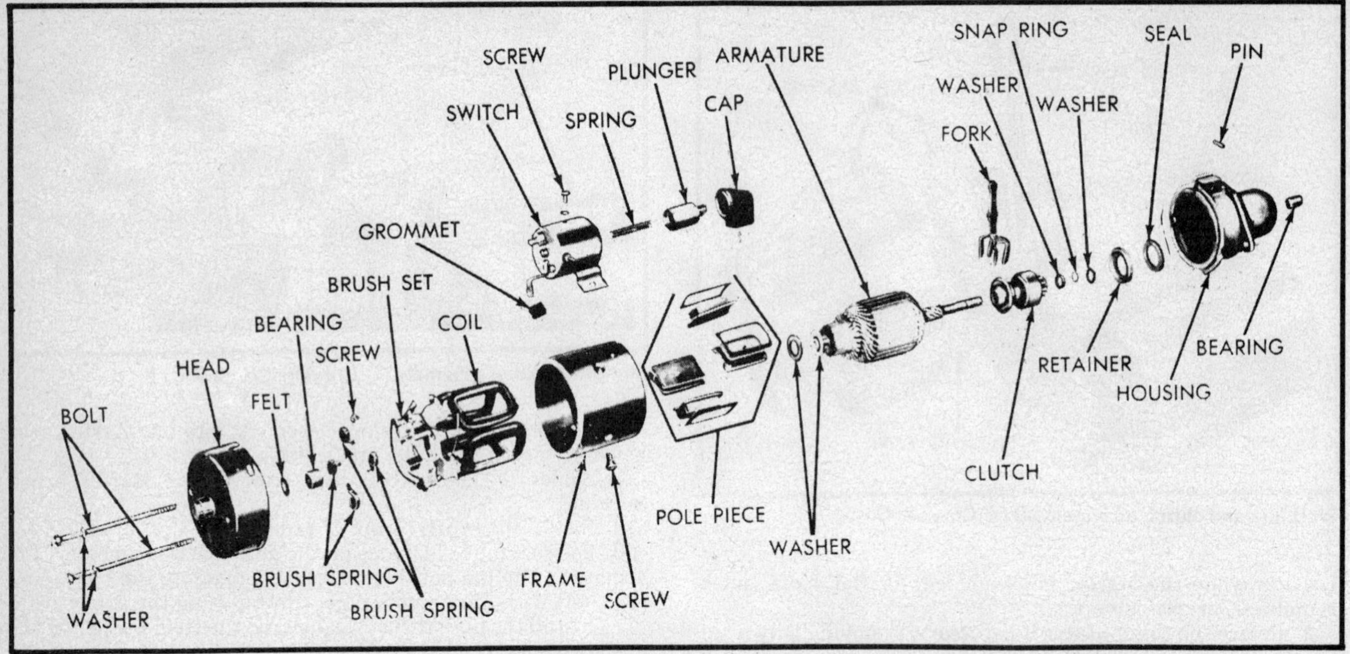

Chrysler direct drive starter—exploded view (© Chrysler Corp.)

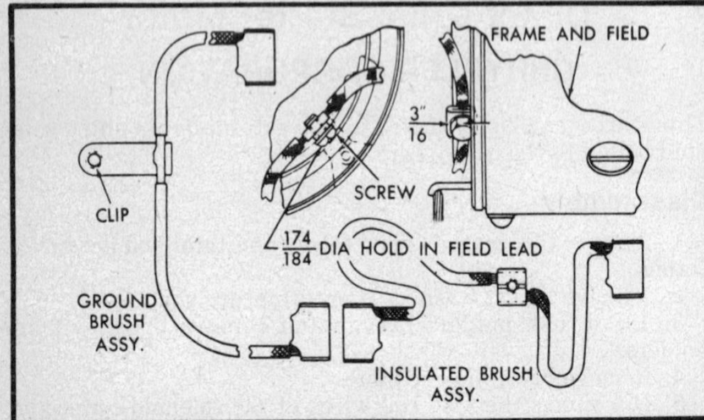

Brush lead arrangement—Chrysler direct drive starter (© Chrysler Corp.)

8. Remove drive end pinion housing and spacer washer.
9. Remove shift fork from starter drive.
10. Slide overrunning clutch pinion gear toward commutator, drive stop retainer toward clutch pinion gear and remove the snap ring.
11. Remove overrunning clutch drive from armature shaft.
12. If field coils are good, stop disassembly at this point. If field coils must be replaced, remove ground brushes terminal screw and remove brushes, terminal and shunt wire. Remove pole shoe screws, using the proper tools. Remove field coils.
13. Replacement of the brushes, inspection of the starter clutch and pinion, and inspection of the commutator procedures are the same as the reduction gear starter procedures.

Assembly

1. Install field coils into frame, if removed.
2. Lubricate armature shaft and splines with engine oil.
3. Install starter drive, stop retainer, lock ring and spacer washer.
4. Install shift fork, with narrow leg of fork toward commutator.
5. Install pinion housing onto armature shaft, indexing shift fork with slot in housing.
6. Install shift fork pivot pin.
7. With clutch drive, shift fork, and pinion housing assembled onto the armature, slide armature into frame until pinion housing indexes with slot.
8. Install solenoid and boot, tightening bolts to 60-70 in. lbs.
9. Connect field coil wires to solenoid connector, making sure they do not touch frame.
10. Install brush holder plate, indexing tang in frame hole.
11. Place brushes in holders, making sure field coil wires do not interfere.
12. Install thrust washers on commutator end of armature shaft to obtain a maximum of 0.010 in. end play.
13. Install commutator end head and through-bolts. Tighten bolts 40 to 50 in. lbs.
14. Measure drive gear pinion clearance; it should be $^1/_8$ in. Adjust by moving solenoid fore and aft as required.

Motorcraft Positive Engagement Starter Motor

FORD MOTOR CO.

This starting motor is a series parallel wound, four pole, four brush unit. It is equipped with an overrunning clutch drive pinion, which is engaged with the flywheel ring gear by an actuating lever, operated by a movable pole piece. This pole piece is hinged to the starter frame and can drop into position through an opening in the frame.

Three conventional field coils are located at three pole piece positions. The fourth field coil is designed to serve also as an engaging coil and a hold in coil for the operation of the drive pinion.

When the ignition switch is turned to the start position, the starter relay is energized and current flows from the battery to the starter motor terminal. This prime surge of current first flows through the starter engaging coil, creating a very strong magnetic field. This magnetism draws the movable pole piece

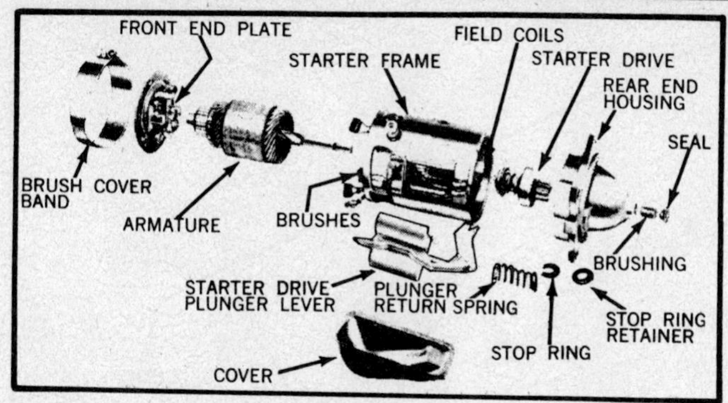

Starter motor—exploded view (© Ford Motor Co.)

down toward the starter frame, which then causes the lever attached to it to move the starter pinion into engagement with the flywheel ring gear.

When the movable pole shoe is fully seated, it opens the field coil, grounding contacts, and the starter is then in normal operation. A holding coil is used to hold the movable pole shoe in the fully seated position during the engine cranking operation.

Vehicles equipped with automatic transmissions have a starter neutral switch circuit control. This is to prevent operation of the starter if the selector lever is not in Neutral or Park.

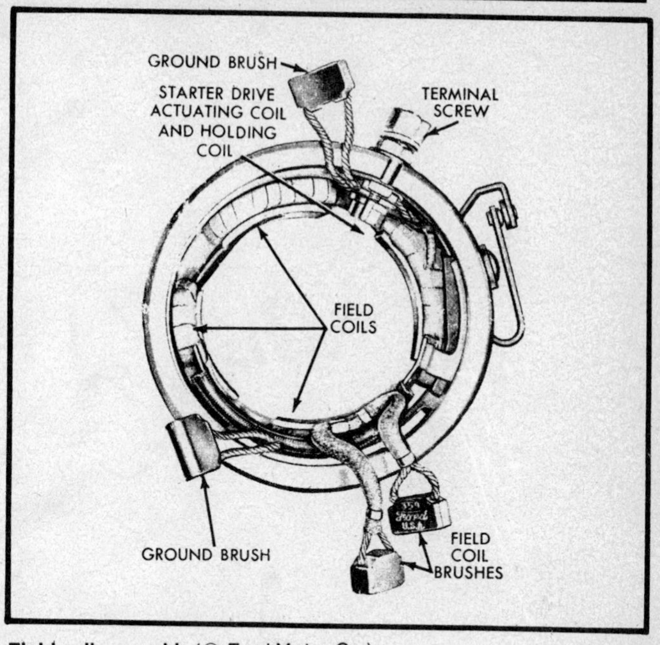

Field coil assembly (© Ford Motor Co.)

Disassembly

1. Remove brush cover band and starter drive gear actuating lever cover. Observe the brush lead locations for reassembly, then remove the brushes from their holders. Factory brush length is $\frac{1}{2}$ in., wear limit is $\frac{1}{4}$ in.
2. Remove the through bolts, starter drive gear housing and the drive gear actuating lever return spring.
3. Remove the pivot pin retaining the starter gear actuating lever and remove the lever and the armature.
4. Remove the stop ring retainer. Remove and discard the stop ring holding the drive gear to the armature shaft; then remove the drive gear assembly.
5. Remove the brush end plate.
6. Remove the two screws holding the ground brushes to the frame.
7. On the field coil that operates the starter drive gear actuating lever, bend the tab up on the field retainer and remove the field coil retainer.
8. Remove the three coil retaining screws. Unsolder the field

Starter cranks engine slowly

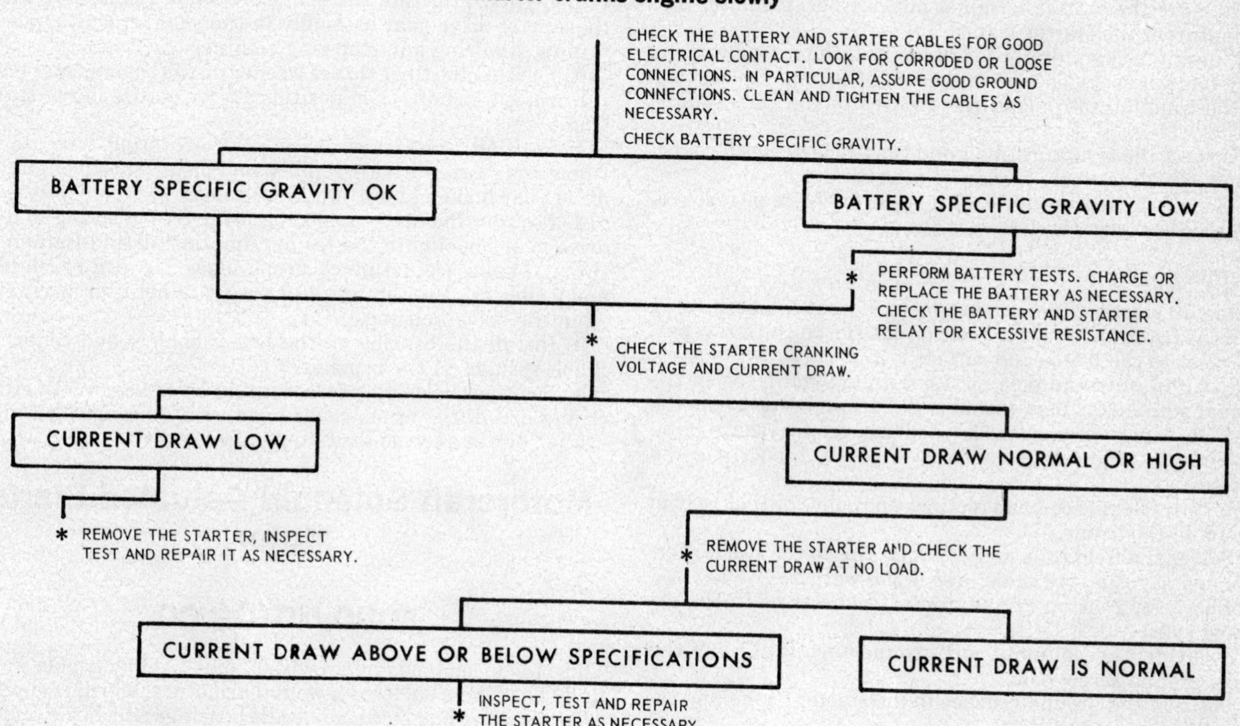

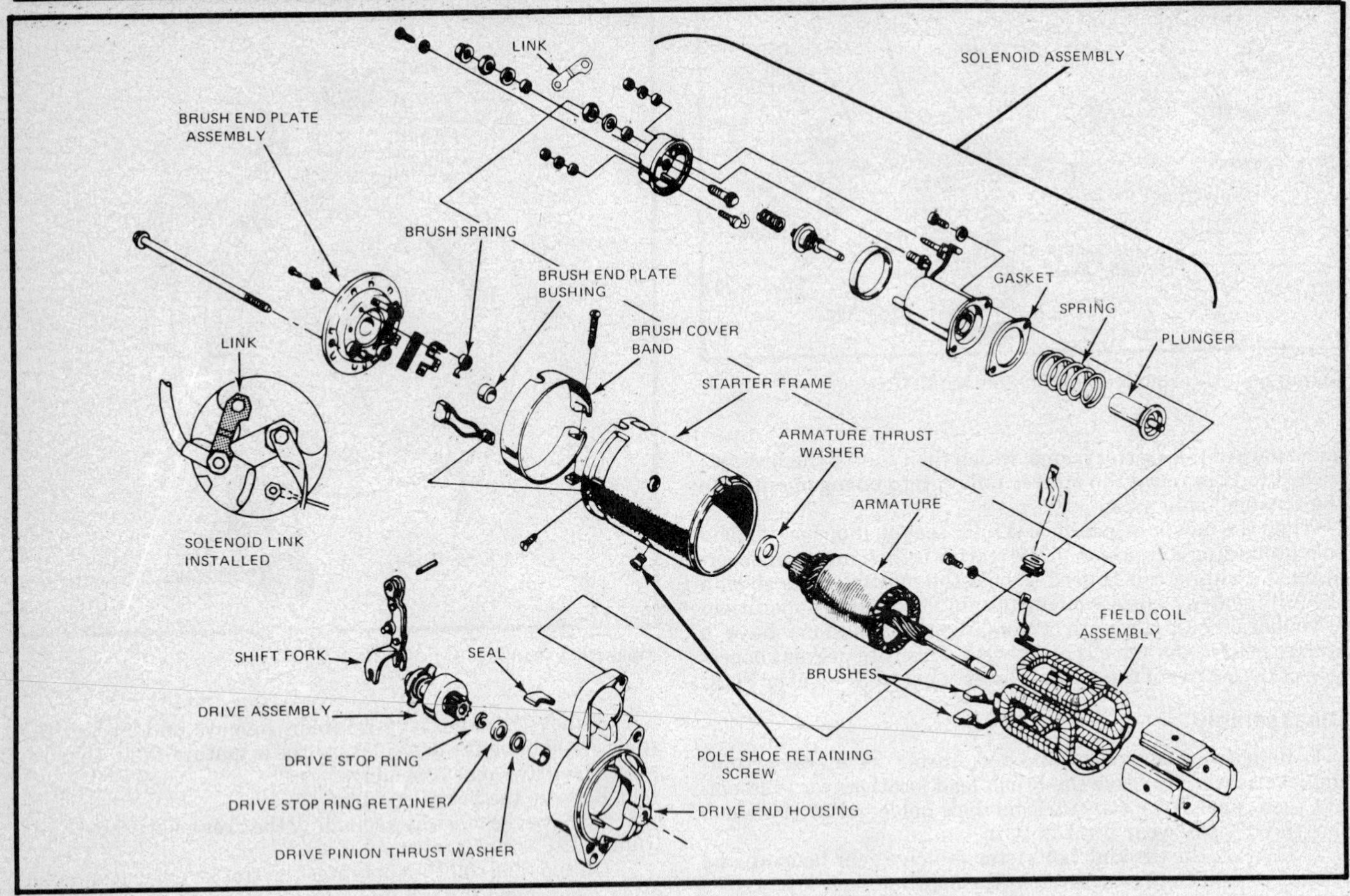

Ford Solenoid starter motor (© Ford Motor Co.)

coil leads from the terminal screw, then remove the pole shoes and coils from the frame (use a 300 watt iron).

9. Remove the starter terminal nut, washer, insulator and terminal from the starter frame.

10. Check the commutator for runnout. If the commutator is rough, has flat spots, or is more then 0.005 in. out of round, reface the commutator. Clean the grooves in the commutator face.

11. Inspect the armature shaft and the two bearings for scoring and excessive wear. Replace if necessary.

12. Inspect the starter drive. If the gear teeth are pitted, broken, or excessively worn, replace the starter drive.

Assembly

1. Install starter terminal, insulator, washers and retaining nut in the frame. (Be sure to position the slot in the screw perpendicular to the frame end surface.)

2. Position coils and pole pieces, with the coil leads in the terminal screw slot, then install the retaining screws. As the pole screws are tightened, strike the frame several sharp hammer blows to align the pole shoes. Tighten, then stake the screws.

3. Install solenoid coil and retainer and bend the tabs to hold the coils to the frame.

4. Solder the field coils and solenoid wire to the starter terminal, using rosin core solder and a 300 watt iron.

5. Check for continuity and ground connections in the assembled coils.

6. Position the solenoid coil ground terminal over the nearest ground screw hole.

7. Position the ground brushes to the starter frame and install retaining screws.

8. Position the brush end plate to the frame, with the end plate boss in the frame slot.

9. Lightly lubricate the armature shaft splines and install the starter drive gear assembly in the shaft. Install a new retaining stop ring and stop ring retainer.

10. Position the fiber thrust washer on the commutator end of the armature shaft, then position the armature in the starter frame.

11. Position the starter drive gear actuating lever to the frame and starter drive assembly, and install the pivot pin. Fill drive gear housing bore $\frac{1}{4}$ full of grease.

12. Position the drive actuating lever return spring and the drive gear housing to the frame, then install and tighten the through bolts. Do not pinch brush leads between brush plate and frame. Be sure that the stop ring retainer is properly seated in the drive housing.

13. Install the brushes in the brush holders and center the brush springs on the brushes.

14. Position the drive gear actuating lever cover on the starter and install the brush cover band with a new gasket.

15. Check starter no load amperage draw.

Motorcraft Solenoid Actuated Starter Motor

FORD MOTOR CO.

This starter motor is a four brush, four field, four pole wound unit. The frame encloses a wound armature, which is supported at the drive end by caged needle bearings and at the commu-

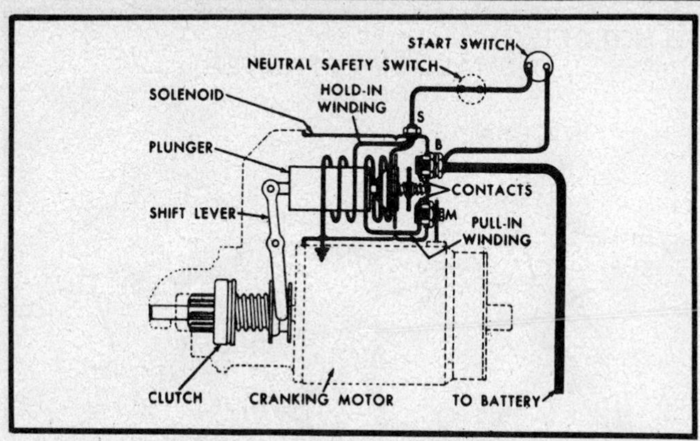

Delco solenoid windings (© General Motors Corp.)

tator end by a sintered copper bushing. The four pole shoes are retained to the frame by one pole screw apiece, and on each pole shoe is wound a ribbon type field coil connected in series parallel.

The solenoid is mounted to a flange on the starter drive housing, which encloses the entire shift mechanism and solenoid plunger. The solenoid utilizes two windings, a pull in winding and a hold in winding.

Disassembly

1. Disconnect the copper strap from the solenoid starter terminal, remove the remaining screws and remove the solenoid.
2. Loosen the retaining screw and slide the brush cover band back far enough to gain access to the brushes.
3. Remove the brushes from their holders, then remove the through-bolts and separate the drive end housing from the frame and brush end plate. Factory brush length is $^1/_2$ in., wear limit $^1/_4$ in.
4. Remove the solenoid plunger and shift fork. These two items can be separated from each other by removing the roll pin.
5. Remove the armature and drive assembly from the frame. Remove the drive stop ring and slide the drive off the armature shaft.
6. Remove the drive stop ring retainer from the drive housing.
7. Inspection of the commutator, armature and bearings, and pinion gear procedures is the same as the positive engagement starter procedures.

Assembly

1. Lubricate the armature shaft splines with Lubriplate, then install drive assembly and a new stop ring.
2. Lubricate shift lever pivot pin with Lubriplate, then position solenoid plunger and shift lever assembly in the drive housing.
3. Place a new retainer in the drive housing. Apply a small amount of Lubriplate to the drive end of the armature shaft, then place armature and drive assembly into the drive housing, indexing the shift lever tangs with the drive assembly.
4. Apply a small amount of Lubriplate to the commutator end of the armature shaft, then position the frame and field assembly to the drive housing.
5. Position the brush plate assembly to the frame, making sure it properly indexes. Install through bolts and tighten 45 to 85 inch lbs.
6. Install brushes into their holders and make sure leads are not touching any interior starter components.

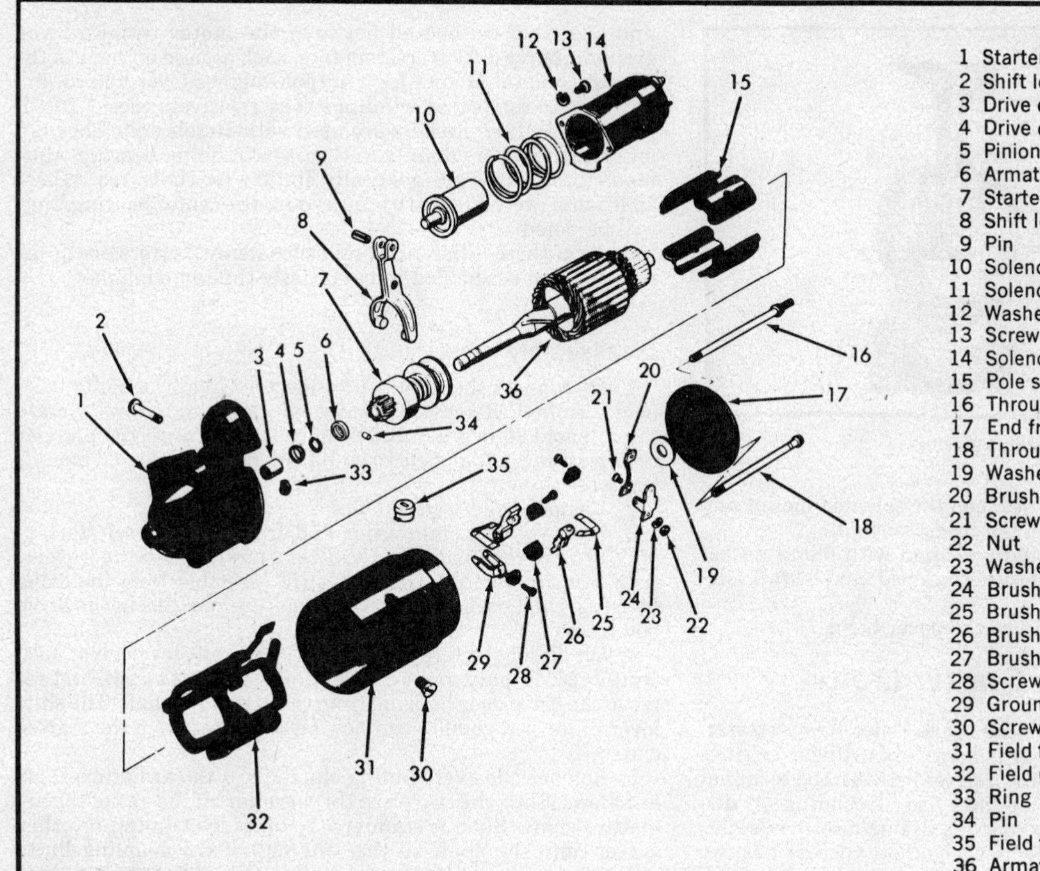

Delco starter—exploded view (© General Motors Corp.)

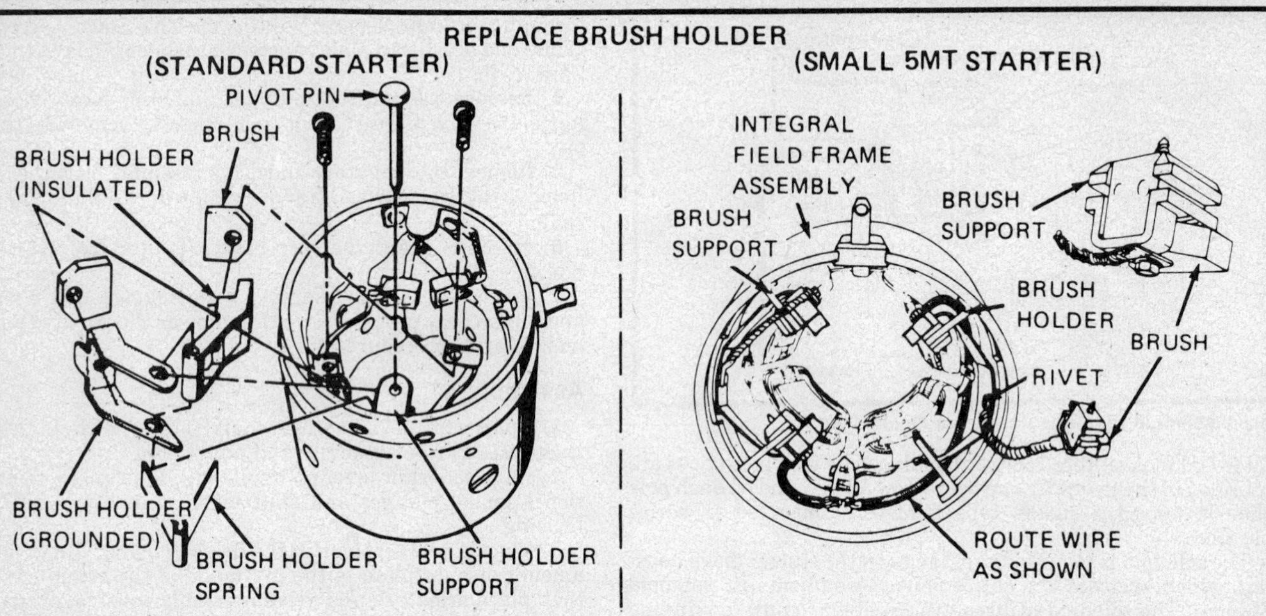

REPLACE BRUSH HOLDER

(STANDARD STARTER)

PIVOT PIN
BRUSH
BRUSH HOLDER (INSULATED)
BRUSH HOLDER (GROUNDED)
BRUSH HOLDER SPRING
BRUSH HOLDER SUPPORT

14. If necessary to replace brush holder parts, proceed as follows:

a. Remove brush holder pivot pin which positions one insulated and one grounded brush.

b. Remove brush spring.

c. Replace brushes as necessary.

(SMALL 5MT STARTER)

INTEGRAL FIELD FRAME ASSEMBLY
BRUSH SUPPORT
BRUSH SUPPORT
BRUSH HOLDER
BRUSH
RIVET
ROUTE WIRE AS SHOWN

a. Remove brush holder from brush support.

b. Remove screw from brush holder and separate brush and holder.

c. Inspect brush holder for wear or damage.

d. Replace brushes and/or holders as necessary.

Brush holder removal procedure—delco starters (© General Motors Corp.)

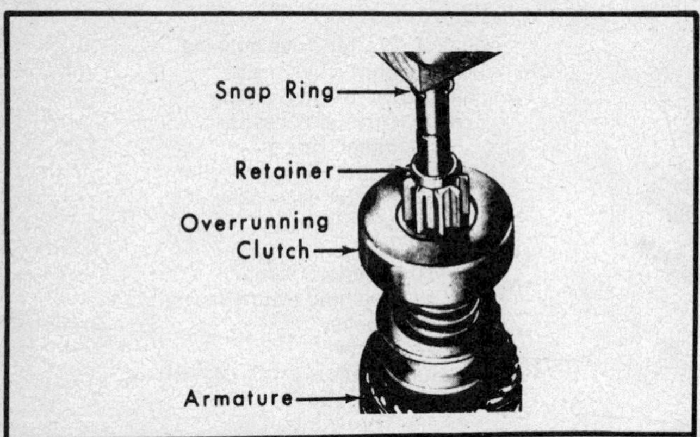

Removing armature snap ring—delco starter
(© General Motors Corp.)

7. Place the rubber gasket between the solenoid mount and the frame solenoid mount and the frame surface.

8. Place the starter solenoid in position with metal gasket and spring, install heat shield (if so equipped) and install solenoid screws.

9. Connect copper strap and install cover band.

Delco Remy Starter Motor

There are many different versions of the Delco Remy starter, depending upon application. In general, six cylinder engines use a unit having four field coils in series between the terminal and armature. Standard V8 engines use, depending on displacement, one of three types: one has two field coils in series with the armature and parallel to each other; another has two field coils in parallel between the field terminal and ground, and another has three field coils in series with the armature and one field connected between the motor terminal and ground. Heavy duty starter motors, such as used on some of the largest General Motors high output engines (over 400 cu. in.) have series compound windings. The relatively recent 20MT, 25MT, and 27MT starters are used with diesels only. They differ from the others mainly in the use of a center bearing. Most repair procedures are generally similar for them, too. Where additional procedures are required for the center bearing, they will be noted.

In spite of these differences, all Delco Remy starters are disassembled and assembled in essentially the same manner.

Disassembly

1. Disconnect the field coil connectors from the motor solenoid terminal. Remove the solenoid mounting screws. Rotate the solenoid 90 degrees and remove it along with the plunger return spring. On models so equipped, remove solenoid mounting screws.

2. Remove the through bolts.

3. Remove the commutator end frame. On diesel starters only, remove the insulator. On all starters, remove the washer, field frame assembly, and armature assembly from the drive housing. On diesel starters, the armature remains in the drive end frame.

4. On diesel starters only, remove the shift lever pivot bolt. On the 25MT only, remove the center bearing screws and remove the drive gear housing from the armature shaft. The shift lever/plunger assembly can now be separated from the starter clutch.

5. Remove the overrunning clutch from the armature shaft as follows. Slide the two piece thrust collar off the end of the armature shaft. Slide a standard $\frac{1}{2}$ in. pipe coupling or other spacer onto the shaft so that the end of the coupling butts against the edge of the retainer. Tap the end of the coupling with a hammer, driving retainer towards armature end of snap

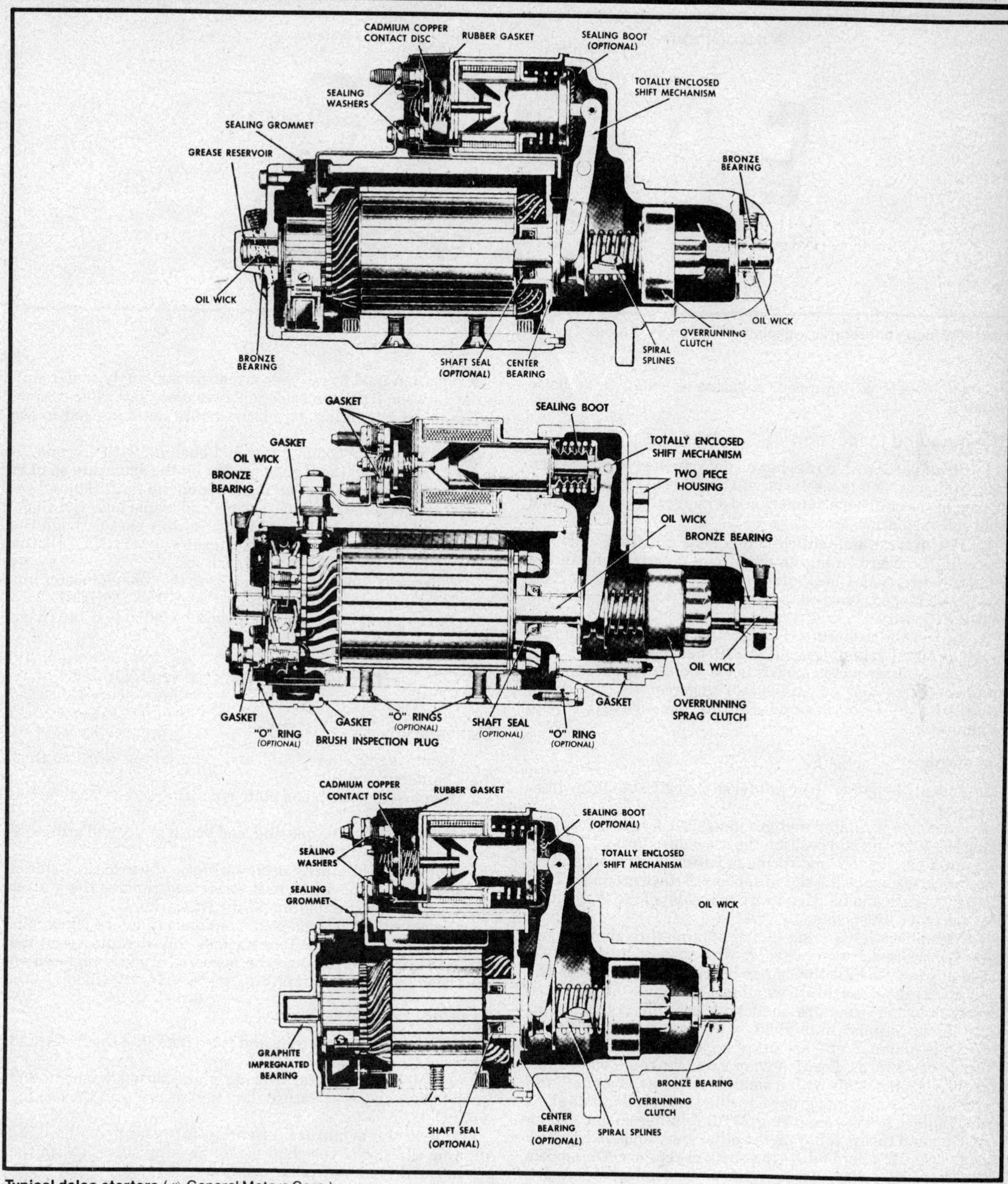

Typical delco starters (© General Motors Corp.)

ring. Remove snap ring from its groove in the shaft using pliers. Slide retainer and clutch from armature shaft. On diesel starters, also remove the fiber washer and center bearing.

6. On 1980 starters, disconnect the brush assembly from the field frame by releasing the V-spring and removing the support pin. Pull the brush holders, brushes, and springs out as a unit and disconnect leads. On 1981 and later starters (except 5MT), remove the pivot pin which holds the brush holder and one insulated and one grounded brush in place. Remove the brush spring. On the 5MT starter, remove the brush holder from the brush support. Remove the screw from the brush holder and separate the brush and holder.

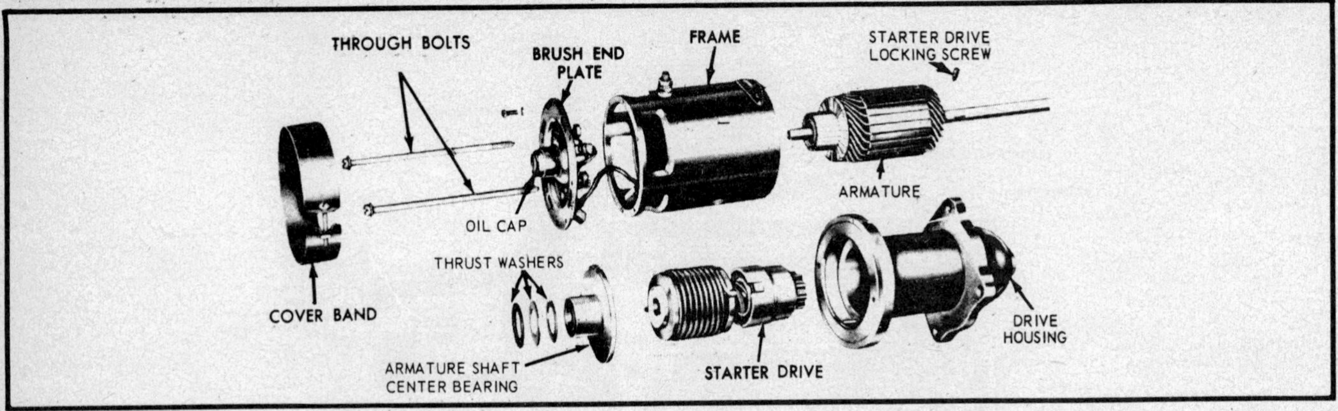

Prestolite heavy duty starter—exploded view (© Ford Motor Co.)

7. On models so equipped, separate solenoid from lever housing.

Cleaning and Inspection

1. Clean parts with a rag, but do not immerse the parts in a solvent. Immersion in a solvent will dissolve the grease that is packed in the clutch mechanism and damage the armature and field coil insulation.
2. Test overrunning clutch action. The pinion should turn freely in the overrunning direction and must not slip in the cranking direction. Check pinion teeth to see that they have not been chipped, cracked, or excessively worn. Replace the unit if necessary.
3. Inspect the armature commutator. If the commutator is rough or out of round, it should be turned down.
4. Some starter motor models use a molded armature commutator design and no attempt to undercut the insulation should be made or serious damage may result to the commutator.

Assembly

1. Install brushes into holders. Install solenoid, if so equipped.
2. Assemble insulated and grounded brush holder together using the V-spring and position the assembled unit on the support pin. Push holders and spring to bottom of support and rotate spring to engage the slot in support. Attach ground wire to grounded brush and field lead wire to insulated brush, then repeat for other brush sets.
3. Assemble overrunning clutch to armature shaft as follows. Lubricate drive end of shaft with silicone lubricant. On diesel starters, install the center bearing assembly with the bearing facing the armature winding. Then, slide the clutch assembly onto the armature shaft with the pinion facing outward. Slide retainer onto shaft with cupped surface facing away from pinion. Stand armature up on a wood surface, commutator downwards. Position snap ring on upper end of shaft and drive it onto shaft with a small block of wood and a hammer. Slide snap ring into groove. Install thrust collar onto shaft with shoulder next to snap ring. With retainer on one side of snap ring and thrust collar on the other side, squeeze together with two sets of pliers until ring seats in retainer. On models without thrust collar, use a washer. Remember to remove washer before continuing.
4. Lubricate drive end bushing with silicone lubricant, then slide armature and clutch assembly into place, at the same time engaging shift lever with clutch. On 1981 and later non-diesel starters, the shift lever may be installed in the drive gear housing first. On the 25MT diesel starter only, install the center bearing screws and the shift lever pivot bolt. Tighten all securely.
5. Position field frame over armature and apply sealer (silicone) between frame and solenoid case. Position frame against drive housing, making sure brushes are not damaged in the process.
6. Lubricate the commutator end bushing with silicone lubricant. Place a leather brake washer on the armature shaft of gas engine starters. Place an insulator on the shaft of diesel engine starters. Slide the commutator end frame onto the shaft. Install the through bolts, making sure they pass through the bolt holes in the insulator on diesel starters. Install the through bolts and tighten to 65 inch lbs.
7. Reconnect field coil connector(s) to the solenoid motor terminal. Install solenoid mounting screws, if so equipped.
8. Check pinion clearance; it should be 0.010 to 0.140 in. on all models.

Prestolite Starter Motor

Disassembly

1. Remove the cover band and remove the brushes from their holders.
2. Remove the brush end plate mounting screws and the two through bolts.
3. Remove the drive housing, end brush plate, and armature from the starter frame.
4. Compress the starter drive spring on the armature side of the shaft and remove the lock screw and remove the starter drive, center bearing plate and thrust washers.
5. Remove the four field pole shoes and remove the field coils from the frame. The positive brushes can be replaced on the field coils by soldering, and the negative brushes replaced on the brush end plate by riveting.

Assembly

1. Assemble the field coils and pole shoes into the frame and secure with screws.
2. Assemble the center bearing plate, thrust washers, and starter drive on the armature shaft and secure with the locking screw.
3. Place the armature assembly into the drive housing aligning the slot in the shaft center bearing support with the pin in the drive housing.
4. Install the end frame to the frame housing and install the six mounting screws.
5. Position the armature assembly into the frame housing and engage the frame dowel with the bolt of the drive frame. Install the two through bolts and secure.
6. Install the brushes into the holders. Center the brush springs on the brushes and locate the insulated brush leads clear of the armature. Install the cover band.

Brakes

INDEX

HYDRAULIC BRAKE SYSTEM TROUBLE DIAGNOSIS

Condition	Possible Cause	Correction
Insufficient brakes	1. Improper brake adjustment. 2. Worn lining. 3. Sticking brakes. 4. Brake valve pressure low. 5. Slack adjuster to diaphragm rod not adjusted properly. 6. Master cylinder low on brake fluid.	1. Adjust brakes. 2. Replace brake lining and adjust brakes. 3. Lubricate brake pivots and support platforms. 4. Inspect for leaks and obstructed brake lines. 5. Adjust slack adjuster. 6. Fill master cylinder and inspect for leaks.
Brakes apply slowly	1. Improper brake adjustment or lack of lubrication. 2. Low air pressure. 3. Brake valve delivery pressure low. 4. Excessive leakage with brakes applied. 5. Restriction in brake line or hose.	1. Adjust brakes and lubricate linkage. 2. Check belt tension and compressor for output. Adjust as necessary. 3. Check valve pressure and clean or replace as necessary. 4. Inspect all fittings and lines for leaks and repair as necessary. 5. Clean or replace brake line or hose.
Spongy pedal	1. Air in hydraulic system. 2. Swollen rubber parts due to contaminated brake fluid. 3. Improper brake shoe adjustment. 4. Brake fluid with low boiling point. 5. Brake drums ground excessively.	1. Fill and bleed hydraulic system. 2. Clean hydraulic system and recondition wheel cylinders and master cylinder. 3. Adjust brakes. 4. Flush hydraulic system and refill with proper brake fluid. 5. Replace brake drums.
Erratic brakes	1. Linings soaked with grease or brake fluid. 2. Primary and secondary shoes mounted in wrong position.	1. Correct the leak and replace brake lining. 2. Match the primary and secondary shoes and mount in proper position.
Chattering brakes	1. Improper adjustment of brake shoes. 2. Loose front wheel bearings. 3. Hard spots in brake drums. 4. Out-of-round brake drums. 5. Grease or brake fluid on lining.	1. Adjust brakes. 2. Clean, pack and adjust wheel bearings. 3. Grind or replace brake drums. 4. Grind or replace brake drums. 5. Correct leak and replace brake lining.
Squealing brakes	1. Incorrect lining. 2. Distorted brakedrum. 3. Bent brake support plate. 4. Bent brake shoes. 5. Foreign material embedded in brake lining. 6. Dust or dirt in brake drum. 7. Shoes dragging on support plate. 8. Loose support plate. 9. Loose anchor bolts. 10. Loose lining on brake shoes or improperly ground lining.	1. Install correct lining. 2. Grind or replace brake drum. 3. Replace brake support plate. 4. Replace brake shoes. 5. Replace brake shoes. 6. Use compressed air and blow out drums and support plate and shoes. 7. Sand support plate platforms and lubricate. 8. Tighten support plate attaching nuts. 9. Tighten anchor bolts. 10. Replace brake shoes and cam-grind lining.
Brakes fading	1. Improper brake adjustment. 2. Improper brake lining. 3. Improper type of brake fluid. 4. Brake drums ground excessively.	1. Adjust brakes correctly. 2. Replace brake lining. 3. Drain, flush and refill hydraulic system. 4. Replace brake drums.
Dragging brakes	1. Improper brake adjustment. 2. Distorted cylinder cups. 3. Brake shoe seized on anchor bolt. 4. Broken brake shoe return spring. 5. Loose anchor bolt. 6. Distorted brake shoe. 7. Loose wheel bearings.	1. Correct adjust brakes. 2. Recondition or replace cylinder. 3. Clean and lubricate anchor bolt. 4. Replace brake shoe return spring. 5. Adjust and tighten anchor bolt. 6. Replace defective brake shoes. 7. Lubricate and adjust wheel bearings.

HYDRAULIC BRAKE SYSTEM TROUBLE DIAGNOSIS

Condition	Possible Cause	Correction
Dragging brakes	8. Obstruction in brake line. 9. Swollen cups in wheel cylinder or master cylinder. 10. Master cylinder linkage improperly adjusted.	8. Clean or replace brake line. 9. Recondition wheel or master cylinder. 10. Correctly adjust master cylinder linkage.
Hard pedal	1. Incorrect brake lining. 2. Incorrect brake adjustment. 3. Frozen brake pedal linkage. 4. Restricted brake line or hose.	1. Install matched brake lining. 2. Adjust brakes and check fluid. 3. Free up and lubricate brake linkage. 4. Clean out or replace brake line hose.
Wheel locks	1. Loose or torn brake lining. 2. Incorrect wheel bearing adjustment. 3. Wheel cylinder cups sticking. 4. Saturated brake lining.	1. Replace brake lining. 2. Clean, pack and adjust wheel bearings. 3. Recondition or replace the wheel cylinder. 4. Reline front, rear or all four brakes.
Brakes fade (high speed)	1. Improper brake adjustment. 2. Distorted or out of round brake drums. 3. Overheated brake drums. 4. Incorrect brake fluid (low boiling temperature). 5. Saturated brake lining.	1. Adjust brakes and check fluid. 2. Grind or replace the drums. 3. Inspect for dragging brakes. 4. Drain flush and refill and bleed the hydraulic brake system. 5. Reline brakes as necessary.

HYDRAULIC SYSTEM SERVICE

Basic Hydraulic System

The hydraulic system controls the braking operation and consists of a master cylinder, hydraulic lines and hoses, control valves and calipers and/or wheel cylinders. When the brake pedal is depressed, the master cylinder forces brake fluid to the calipers and/or cylinders, via lines and hoses. Sliding rubber seals contain the fluid and prevent leakage.

Return springs in the master cylinder help the brake pedal return to the original unapplied position. Check valves (in most cases) regulate the return flow of the fluid to the master cylinder. Other valves, such as the metering valve, proportioning valve, or combination valve, regulate the flow of fluid to the caliper/wheel cylinder, to achieve efficient braking.

Single Braking Systems

On single brake systems, the master cylinder has only one piston which operates all of the wheel cylinders. The single brake system is confined to over the road vehicles above 10000 lbs. GVW, industrial and construction equipment.

Dual Braking Systems

The "dual"system differs from the "single" system by employing a "tandem" master cylinder, essentially two master cylinders (usually) formed by aligning two separate pistons and fluid reservoirs into one cylinder bore. Dual brake lines "split" the calipers and/or wheel cylinders into two groups, each actuated by a separate master cylinder piston. In event of failure of one of the "dual" systems, the other should provide enough braking power to safely stop the vehicle. The dual system usually includes a red warning light on the instrument panel which is activated by a pressure differential valve. The valve is sensitive to any loss of hydraulic pressure that might result from a braking failure on either side of the system.

Light trucks are equipped with either a front/rear wheel "split" or a diagonally "split" system. On front/rear systems, the front wheels are connected to one circuit while the rear wheels are connected to the other circuit. Diagonally split systems have diagonally opposite wheels connected to each circuit. Medium and heavy trucks may use the front/rear split or, if equipped with two wheel cylinders per wheel, each circuit will operate one cylinder per wheel.

General Information

Servicing the hydraulic brake system is chiefly a matter of adjustments, replacement of worn or damaged parts and correcting the damage caused by grit, dirt or contaminated brake fluid. Always make sure the brake system is clean and tightly sealed when a brake job is completed and that only approved heavy duty brake fluid is used.

The approved heavy duty type brake fluid retains the correct consistency throughout the widest range of temperature variation, will not affect rubber cups, helps protect the metal parts of the brake system against failure and assures long trouble free brake operation.

Never use brake fluid from a container that has been used for any other liquid. Mineral oil, alcohol, antifreeze, or cleaning solvents, even in very small quantities, will contaminate brake fluid. Contaminated brake fluid will cause piston cups and the valve(s) in the master cylinder to swell or deteriorate.

Brake adjustment is required after installation of new or relined brake shoes. Adjustment is also necessary whenever excessive travel of pedal is needed to start braking action.

LOW PEDAL

Normal brake lining wear reduces pedal reserve. Low pedal reserve may also be caused by the lack of brake fluid in the master cylinder. The wear condition may be compensated for by a minor brake adjustment. Check fluid level in master cylinder and add as required.

FLUID LOSS

If the master cylinder requires constant addition of hydraulic fluid, fluid may be leaking past the piston cups in the master cylinder or brake cylinders, the hydraulic lines; hoses or connections may be loose or broken. Loose connections should be tightened, or other necessary repairs or parts replacement made and the hydraulic brake system bled.

FLUID CONTAMINATION

To determine if contamination exists in the brake fluid, as indicated by swollen, deteriorated rubber cups, the following tests can be made.

Place a small amount of the drained brake fluid into a small clear glass bottle. Separation of the fluid into distinct layers will indicate mineral oil content. Be safe and discard old brake fluid that has been bled from the system. Fluid drained from the bleeding operation may contain dirt particles or other contamination and should not be reused.

BRAKE ADJUSTMENT

Self adjusting brakes usually do not require manual adjustment but in the event of a brake reline it may be advisable to make the initial adjustment manually to speed up adjusting time.

AUTOMATIC ADJUSTER CHECK

Raise and safely support the vehicle, have a helper in the driver's seat to apply brakes. Remove the plug from the adjustment slot to observe adjuster star wheel. Then, to exclude possibility of maximum adjustment which is, the adjuster refuses to operate because the closest possible adjustment has been reached; the star wheel should be backed off approximately 30 notches. It will be necessary to hold adjuster lever away from star wheel to allow backing off of the adjustment.

Spin the wheel and brake drum in reverse direction and apply brakes vigorously. This will provide the necessary inertia to cause the secondary brake shoe to leave the anchor. The wrap up effect will move the secondary shoe, and a cable or link will pull the adjuster lever away from the starwheel teeth. Upon release of brake pedal, the lever should snap back in position, turning star wheel. Thus, a definite rotation of adjuster star wheel can be observed if automatic adjuster is working properly. If by the described procedure one or more automatic adjusters do not function properly, the respective drum must be removed for adjuster servicing.

HYDRAULIC LINE REPAIR

Steel tubing is used in the hydraulic lines between the master cylinder and the front brake tube connector, and between the rear brake tube connector and the rear brake cylinders. Flexible hoses connect the brake tube to the front brake cylinders or calipers and to the rear brake tube connector.

When replacing hydraulic brake tubing, hoses, or connectors, tighten all connections securely. After replacement, bleed the brake system at the wheel cylinders or calipers and at the booster, if equipped with a bleeder screw.

BRAKE TUBE

If a section of the brake tube becomes damaged, the entire section should be replaced with tubing of the same type, size, shape, and length. Copper tubing should not be used in the hydraulic system. When bending brake tubing to fit the frame or rearaxle contours, be careful not to kink or crack the tube.

All brake tubing should be double flared to provide good leak proof connections. Always clean the inside of a new brake tube with clean isopropyl alcohol.

BRAKE HOSE

A flexible brake hose should be replaced if it shows signs of softening, cracking, or other damage.

When installing a new brake hose, position the hose to avoid contact with other vehicle components.

Hydraulic Control Valves

PRESSURE DIFFERENTIAL VALVE

Also known as a "warning valve", "dash-lamp valve" or "system effectiveness indicator". The valve activates a panel warning lamp in event of pressure loss failure. As pressure fails in one "split" system, the other system's normal pressure causes a piston in the switch to compress a spring and move until an electrical circuit is completed lighting the dash lamp. On some vehicles the spring balanced piston automatically recenters when the brake pedal is released, thus flashing the warning lamp only during brake application. On other vehicles the lamp will stay on until the cause of pressure loss is corrected.

Valves (pressure differential, metering or proportioning) may be located separately, but are usually part of a combination valve. On some brake systems the valve and switch are part of the master cylinder.

Resetting Valves

The pressure differential valve on many vehicles (equipped with a combination valve) will re-center automatically upon brake application after repairs to the system are completed. Other systems require manual resetting. Repair system as required, open a bleeder screw in the half of the system that did not fail. Turn on the ignition to light the warning lamp and slowly depress the brake pedal until the lamp goes out. If too much pressure is applied the piston will go to the other side and the procedure will have to be reversed by opening a bleeder screw in the opposite half of the system.

METERING VALVE

Often used on vehicles equipped with front disc and rear drum brakes, the metering valve improves braking balance during light brake applications by preventing application of the front disc brakes until pressure is built-up in the hydraulic system. The built up hydraulic pressure overcomes the tension of the rear brake shoe return springs. Thus, when the front brake pads contact the rotor the rear brakes shoes move outward to contact the brake drum at the same time.

The metering valve should be inspected whenever the brakes are serviced. A slight amount of moisture inside the boot does not indicate a defective valve, however a great deal of fluid indicates a worn valve and replacement is indicated. Make sure to install the brake lines in the correct ports when installing a new valve, crossed lines will cause the rear brakes to drag.

If a pressure bleeder is used to bleed a hydraulic system that includes a metering valve, the valve stem (inside the boot on some valves) must either be pushed in or pulled out, depending upon the type of valve. Never apply excessive pressure that might damage the valve. Never use a solid block or clamp to force the valve open. If the valve must be blocked, rig the stem with a yieldable spring load and take care not to exert more than normal pressure.

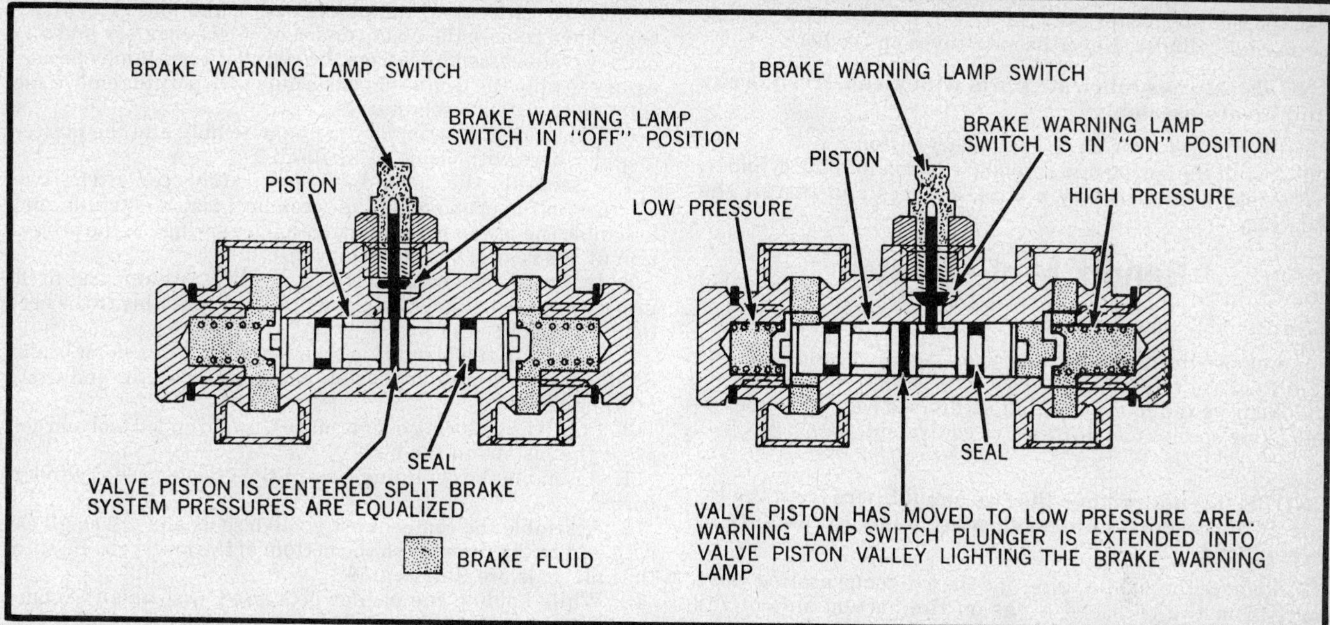

Differential valve system with split hydraulic brakes (© Ford Motor Co.)

If the brakes are to be bled manually using the brake pedal, the pressure developed is sufficient to overcome the metering valve and the stem need not be pushed in or pulled out.

PROPORTIONING VALVE

Used on vehicles equipped with front disc and rear drum brakes, the proportioning valve is installed in the line(s) to the rear drum brakes, and in a split system, below the pressure differential valve. By reducing pressure to the rear drum brakes, the valve helps to prevent premature lock-up during severe brake application and provides better braking balance.

Whenever the brakes are serviced, the valve should be inspected. To check valve operation, install hydraulic gauges ahead and behind the valve and determine that it has an operative transition point above which rear brake pressure is proportioned. If the valve is leaking replacement is required. Make sure the valve port marked "R" is connected to the rear brake line(s).

COMBINATION VALVE

A valve combining two or three functions (metering, proportioning, and/or brake warning) may be used. The combination valve is usually mounted under the hood close to the master cylinder, where the brake lines can be easily routed to the front and rear wheels. The combination valve is a non-serviceable unit, and if found to be malfunctioning, must be replaced as a unit.

Master Cylinder Service

CLEANING AND INSPECTION

Thoroughly clean the master cylinder and any other parts to be reused in clean alcohol. DO NOT USE PETROLEUM PRODUCTS FOR CLEANING. If the bore is not badly scored, rusted or corroded, it is possible to rebuild the master cylinder in some cases. A slight bit of honing is permissible to clean up and smooth out the bore. A master cylinder rebuilding kit and fresh fluid should be used. If the cylinder bore is badly pitted or corroded, or if it has been rebuilt before, the master cylinder should be replaced with a new one. Do not hone or repair a scratched or pitted bore of an aluminum master cylinder. Replace the master cylinder. Be sure to note the relative positions of all the parts, paying particular attention to the way the rubber cups are facing. Lubricate all new rubber parts with brake fluid or brake system assembly lubricant.

Cast Iron Bore Cleanup

Crocus cloth or an approved cylinder hone should be used to remove lightly pitted, scored, or corroded areas from the bore. Brake fluid can be used as a lubricant while honing lightly. The master cylinder should be replaced if it cannot be cleaned up readily. After using the crocus cloth or a hone, the master cylinder should be thoroughly washed in clean alcohol or brake fluid to remove all dust and grit. If alcohol is used, dry parts thoroughly before reinstalling. Other solvents should not be used. Check the clearance between the bore wall and the piston (primary piston of a dual system master cylinder) it should be as follows. If a narrow $\frac{1}{8}$ in. to $\frac{1}{4}$ in. wide. If a 0.006 in. feeler gauge can be inserted between the wall and a new piston, the clearance is excessive, and the master cylinder should be replaced. The maximum clearance allowed for units containing pistons without replenishing holes is 0.009 in.

Aluminum Bore Cleanup

Inspect the bore for scoring, corrosion and pitting. If the bore is scored or badly pitted and corroded the assembly should be replaced. Under no conditions should the bore be cleaned with an abrasive material. This will remove the wear and corrosion resistant anodized surface. Clean the bore with a clean piece of cloth around a wooden dowel and wash thoroughly with alcohol. Do not confuse bore discoloration or staining with corrosion.

Quick Take Up (GMC)

Disassembly and Assembly

1. Depress the primary piston and remove the snapring.
2. Remove the primary and secondary pistons and return springs from the cylinder bore.
3. Disassemble the secondary piston.

4. Inspect the master cylinder bore. If it is corroded, replace the master cylinder. Never use abrasives on the bore.

NOTE: Always lubricate parts with clean, fresh brake fluid before assembly.

5. Install new seals on the secondary piston.
6. Install the spring and secondary piston into the cylinder.
7. Install the primary piston, depress and install the snapring.

Bendix Mini – Master

Disassembly and Assembly

1. Remove the reservoir cover and diaphragm, and drain the fluid from the reservoir.
2. Remove the four bolts that secure the body to the reservoir using special tool J–25085 or equivalent.

NOTE: Do not remove the two small filters from the inside of the reservoir unless they are damaged and are to be replaced.

3. Remove the small O-ring and the two compensating valve seals from the recessed areas on the bottom side of the reservoir.
4. Depress the primary piston using a tool with a smooth round end. Then remove the compensating valve poppets and the compensating valve springs from the compensating valve ports in the master cylinder body.
5. Remove the snapring at the end of the master cylinder bore. Then release the piston and remove the primary and secondary piston assemblies from the cylinder bore. It may be necessary to plug the front compensating valve port to remove the secondary piston assembly.
6. Lubricate the secondary piston assembly and the master cylinder bore with clean brake fluid.
7. Assemble the secondary spring (shorter of the two springs) in the open end of the secondary piston actuator, and assemble the piston return spring (longer spring) on the projection at the rear of the secondary piston.
8. Insert the secondary piston assembly, actuator end first, into the master cylinder bore and press the assembly to the bottom of the bore.
9. Lubricate the primary piston assembly with clean brake fluid. Insert the primary piston assembly, actuator end first, into the bore.
10. Place the snapring over a smooth round ended tool and depress the pistons in the bore.
11. Assemble the retaining ring in the groove in the cylinder bore.
12. Assemble the compensating valve seals and the small O-ring seal in the recesses on the bottom of the reservoir. Be sure that all seals are fully seated.
13. While holding the pistons depressed, assemble the compensating valve springs and the compensating valve poppets in the compensating valve ports.
14. Holding the pistons compressed, position the reservoir on the master cylinder body and secure it with the four mounting bolts. Torque the bolts 12 to 15 ft. lbs.

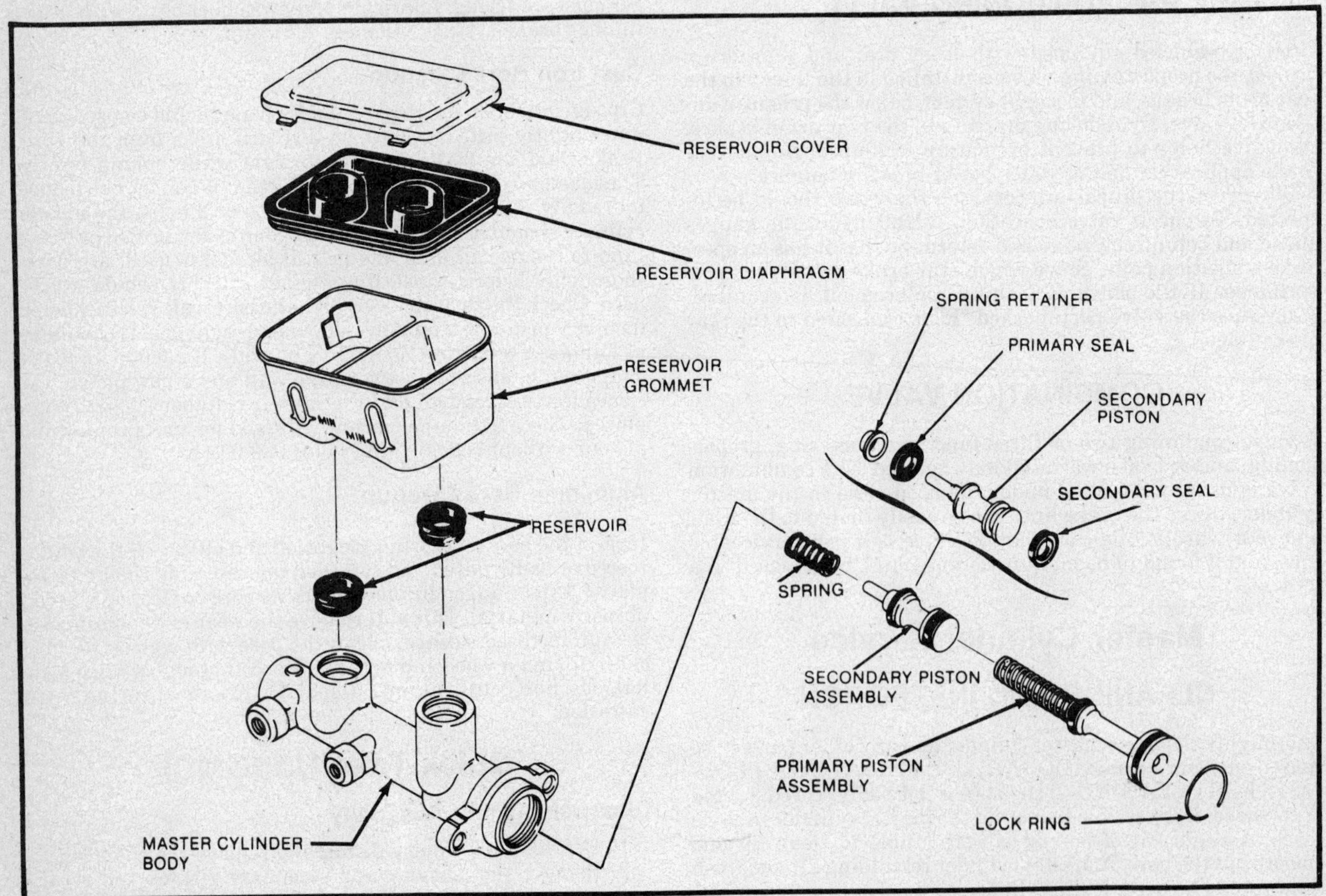

Quick take up master cylinder (© GM Corp.)

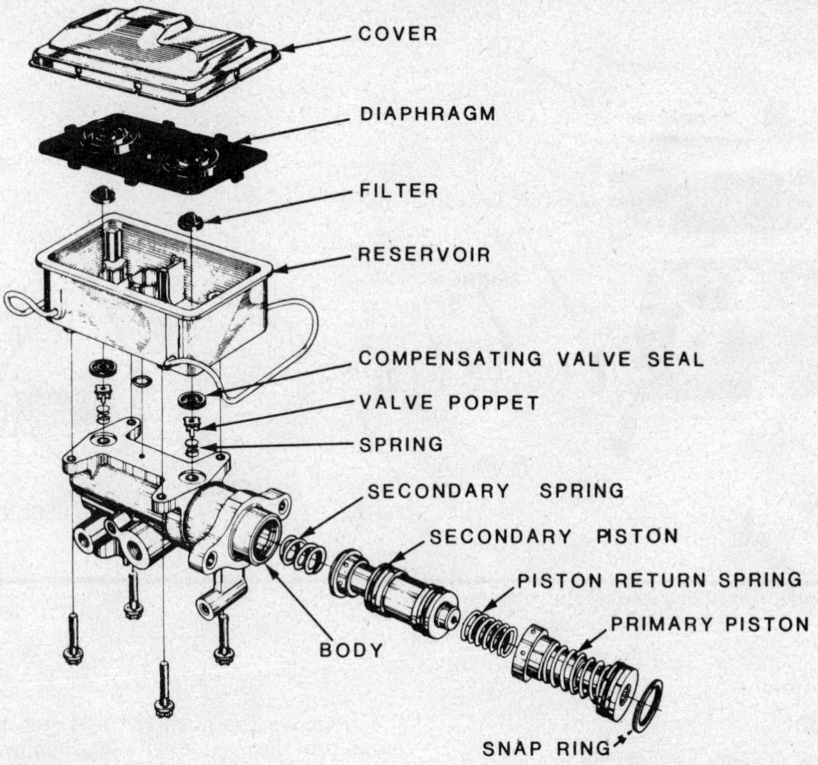

Bendix mini master cylinder—exploded view (© GM Corp.)

Bendix Tandem

Disassembly

1. Clean the outside of the master cylinder assembly. Remove the residual pressure valves.
2. Remove the tube seats by installing easy outs firmly into the seats. Tap lightly with a hammer to loosen, remove seats.
3. Slide clamp off master cylinder cover and remove the cover and its gasket. Drain the brake fluid from the master cylinder.
4. Remove the snapring from the open end of the cylinder with snap ring pliers. Remove the washer from cylinder bore.
5. Remove the front piston retaining screw. Carefully remove the rear piston assembly.
6. Remove the front piston assembly.

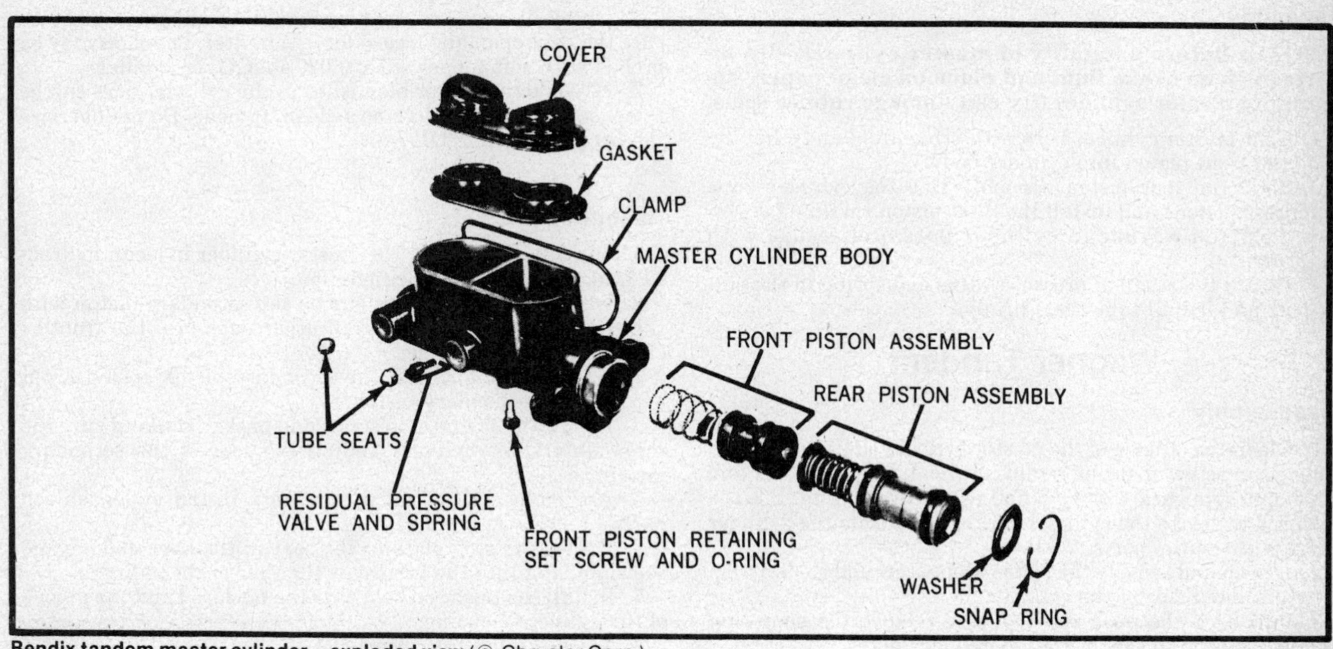

Bendix tandem master cylinder—exploded view (© Chrysler Corp.)

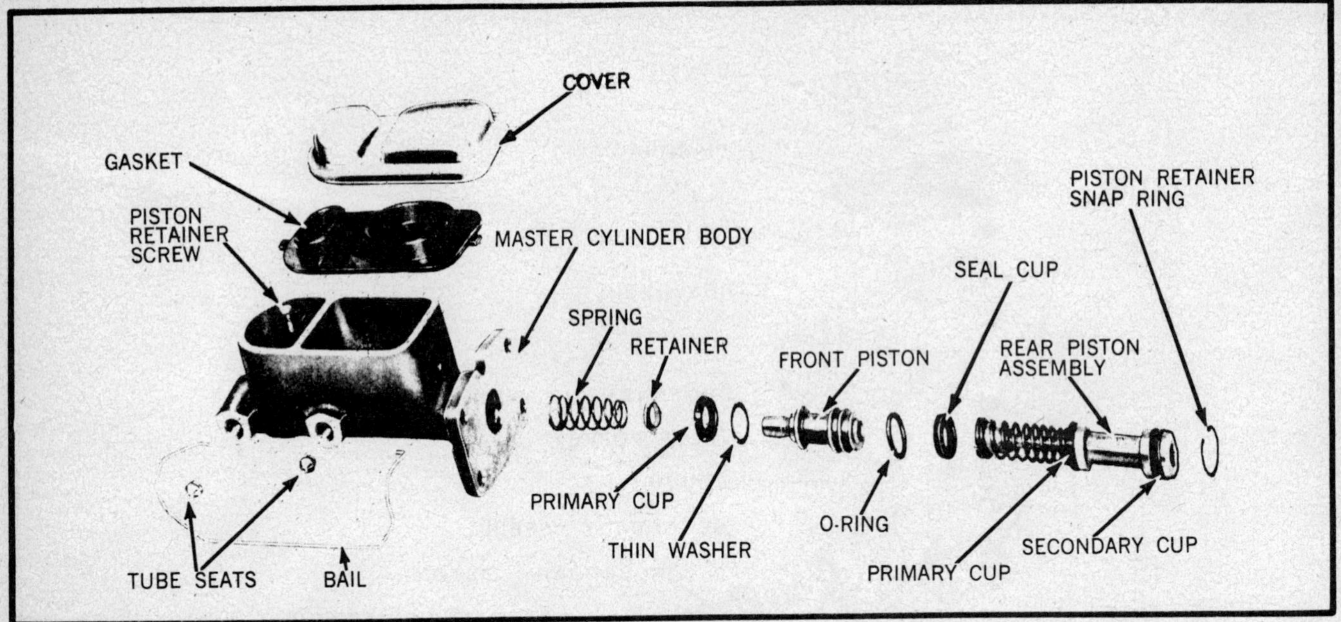

Chrysler tandem master cylinder—exploded view (© Chrysler Corp.)

Cleaning and Inspection

1. Clean all parts with a suitable solvent and dry with filtered compressed air. Wash cylinder bore with clean brake fluid and check for damage or wear.
2. If cylinder bore is lightly scratched or shows slight corrosion it can be cleaned with crocus cloth. Heavier scratches or corrosion can be removed by honing, providing that diameter of cylinder bore is not increased by more than 0.002 in. If master cylinder bore does not clean up at 0.002 in. when honed, the master cylinder should be replaced.
3. If master cylinder pistons are badly scored or corroded, replace them with new ones. All caps and seals should be replaced when rebuilding a master cylinder.

Assembly

NOTE: Before assembly of master cylinder, dip all parts in clean brake fluid and place on clean paper. Assembling master cylinder dry can damage rubber seals.

1. Coat master cylinder bore with brake fluid and carefully slide the front piston into cylinder body.
2. Slide the rear piston assembly into the cylinder bore. Compress pistons and install the front piston retaining screw.
3. Position washer in cylinder bore and secure with snapring.
4. Install the residual pressure valve and spring in the outlet port and install tube seats firmly.

Wagner Tandem

Disassembly

1. Clean the outside of the master cylinder. Remove the cylinder cover screw or spring retaining clip. Lift off the cover and the diaphragm gasket and pour off excess brake fluid. Use the push rod to stroke the cylinder forcing fluid from the cylinder through the outlet ports.
2. Loosen and remove the piston stop screw and gasket from the right hand side of the cylinder.
3. Pull back the push rod boot and remove the snap-ring from the groove in the end of the cylinder bore.
4. Remove the push rod and stop plate from the internal parts from the master cylinder. Remove the internal parts from the master cylinder. If the parts will not slide out apply air pressure at the secondary outlet port. If after applying air, parts still do not move easily, check bore carefully for extensive damage which may eliminate possibility of rebuilding master cylinder.

Inspection and Repair

1. Clean all parts in clean brake fluid. Inspect the parts for chipping, excessive wear or damage. Replace them as required. When using a master cylinder repair kit, install all the parts supplied.
2. Check all recesses, openings and internal passages to be sure they are open and free of foreign matter. Passages may be probed with soft copper wire, 0.020 in. OD, or smaller.
3. Minor scratches or blemishes in the cylinder bore can be removed with crocus cloth or a clean up hone. Do not oversize the bore more than 0.007 in.

Assembly

1. Dip all parts except the master cylinder in clean hydraulic brake fluid of the specified type.
2. Install the rear rubber cup on the secondary piston with the cup lip facing the rear. All other cups face the front or closed end of the cylinder.
3. Assemble and install the secondary piston spring, front cup, and the secondary piston.
4. Install the piston stop screw and gasket, making sure the screw enters the cylinder behind the rear of the secondary piston.
5. Assemble and install the primary piston and push rod parts.
6. Locate the stop plate in the seat in the bore and engage the snap ring into the groove at the rear of the cylinder.
7. Install the push rod boot onto the push rod and the groove of the cylinder housing.
8. Bleed the master cylinder.

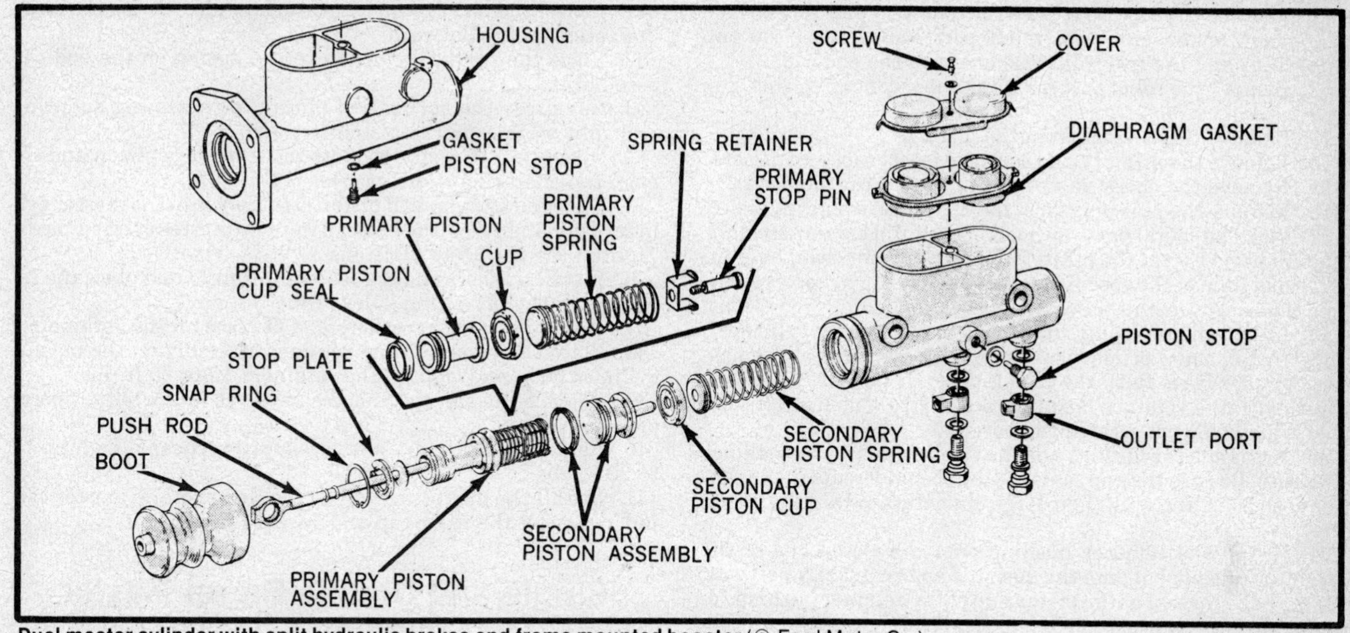

Dual master cylinder with split hydraulic brakes and frame mounted booster (© Ford Motor Co.)

Midland–Ross Tandem (Removable Reservoirs Type)

Disassembly and Assembly

1. Clean the outside of the cylinder and remove the filler cap and gasket (diaphragm). Pour out any brake fluid that may remain the reservoir. Stroke the push rod serveral times to remove fluid from the cylinder bore.
2. Remove the reservoir retainers, washers, and reservoir from the master cylinder body.
3. Remove the two rubber washers from the reservoir and the two O-rings from the reservoir retainers.
4. Remove the snapring, spring retainer and push rod spring.
5. Unscrew the retainer bushing counterclockwise and remove the push rod, retainer bushing, seal retainer and primary piston from the master cylinder.
6. Remove the primary piston from the push rod and discard it.
7. Remove the seal retainer, and retainer bushing from the push rod. Remove the two lip seals and two O-rings from the retainer bushing.
8. Unscrew the end cap counterclockwise and remove the end cap and secondary piston assembly from the master cylinder.
9. Remove the snapring from the secondary piston and remove the piston and return spring from the end cap and stop rod assembly.
10. Remove the two lip seals from the piston.

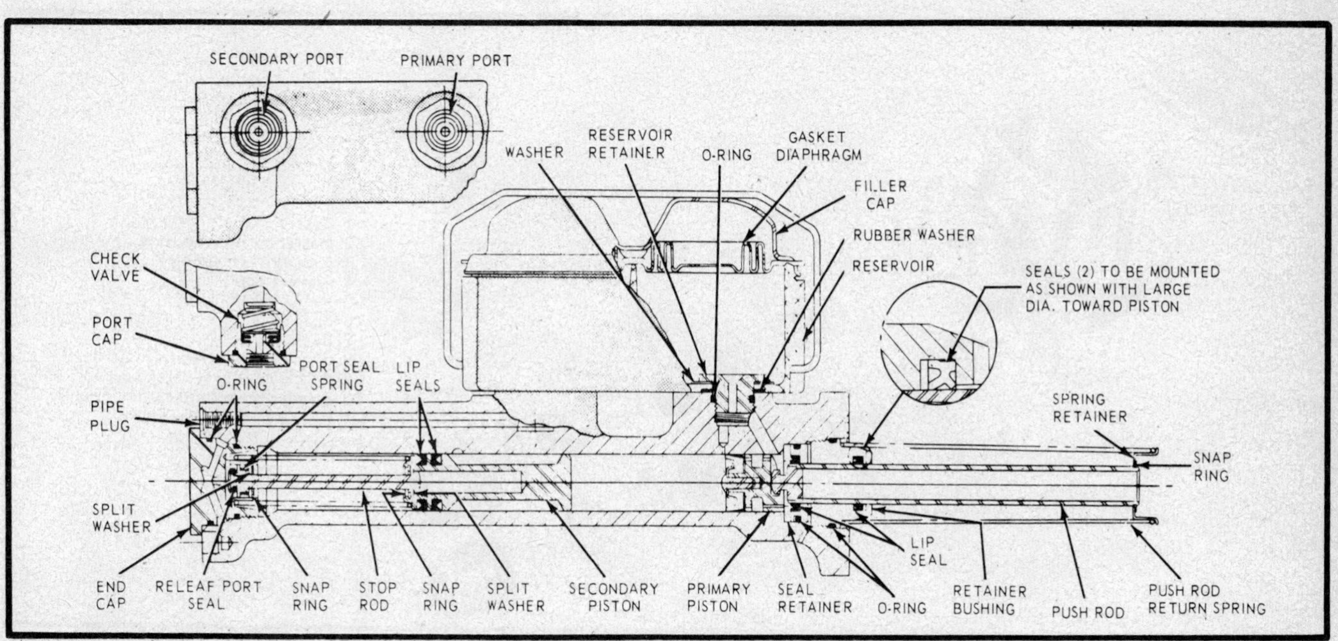

Dual master cylinder with Midland Ross dash mounted booster (© Ford Motor Co.)

11. Remove the snapring from the end cap and remove the secondary piston stop rod, relief port seal spring, the two snaprings and the two split washers from the end cap.
12. Remove the relief port seal from the secondary piston stop rod.
13. Remove the O-rings from the end cap.
14. Remove the primary and secondary port caps and discard.
15. Remove the check valves and springs from the ports.
16. Remove the pipe plug from the end of the master cylinder.
17. Wash all metal parts in clean brake fluid before assembly. Dip all parts except the master cylinder body in clean hydraulic brake fluid of the specified type. When using a master cylinder repair kit, install all of the parts supplied.
18. Install the pipe plug in the end of the master cylinder.
19. Install a new primary piston into the front end of the master cylinder bore. Push the piston through the bore until it is flush with the retainer bushing recess. Use a nonmetallic object which will not scratch the bore.
20. Assemble the O-rings and the two lip seals on the retainer bushing. Be sure the slip seals fit into the undercuts in the center of the bushing with their large diameters toward the piston end.
21. Install the retainer bushing onto the closed end of the push rod and push it onto the push rod approximately half way. Be sure the lip seal at the piston end of the retainer bushing remains in the undercut portion of the retainer bushing.
22. Install the seal retainer onto the closed end of the push rod with the raised lip toward the retainer bushing.
23. Insert the push rod into the master cylinder bore and hook the push rod onto the primary piston.
24. Slide the seal retainer into the recess in the master cylinder bore.
25. Screw the retainer bushing into the master cylinder body and tighten 15 to 20 ft. lbs.
26. Install the push spring with the large end toward the master cylinder and install the spring retainer and snapring.
27. Install the O-rings on the end can.
28. Install the relief port seal on the secondary piston stop rod.
29. Place the port seal spring, split washer (largest of two), and snapring (largest of two) on the piston stop rod.
30. Slide the assembly into the end cap and engage the snapring into its groove.
31. Install the lip seals on the secondary piston with the large diameters facing outward.
32. Place the secondary piston return spring on the end cap assembly.
33. Compress the spring and place the remaining snapring and split washer on the piston stop rod.
34. Slide the piston stop rod into the secondary piston and engage the snap-ring in its groove.
35. Slide the end cap and piston assembly into the master cylinder bore and screw the end cap into the master cylinder body. Tighten the cap 15 to 20 ft. lbs.
36. Install washers on the reservoir retainer and place the retainers in the mounting holes of the reservoir.
37. Place the rubber washers and O-rings on the retainers.
38. Place the reservoir and retainer assembly on the master cylinder body and tighten the retainers 15 to 20 ft. lbs.
39. Replace the springs and check valves in the output ports of the cylinder.
40. Replace the primary and secondary port caps. Tighten 15 to 20 ft. lbs.
41. Install the mounting seal on the flange of the master cylinder. Install the filler cap and gasket (diaphragm).

Single and Double Barrel Master Cylinders (GMC)

Disassembly and Assembly

1. Clean the outside of the master cylinder.
2. Remove the snapring from the groove in the cylinder bore.
3. Remove the washer (stop plate) from the clutch bore.
4. Remove the piston assembly, primary cup, return spring and retainer assembly, check valve, and the check valve seat from the brake cylinder bore.
5. Remove the piston assembly, primary cup, and return spring and retainer assembly from the clutch cylinder bore.
6. Remove the cover and the bleeder screw valve from the housing.
7. Thoroughly clean all parts with brake fluid.
8. Check the clearance between the piston and the cylinder wall. It should be within 0.001 in. to 0.005 in.
9. Coat all internal parts with brake fluid.

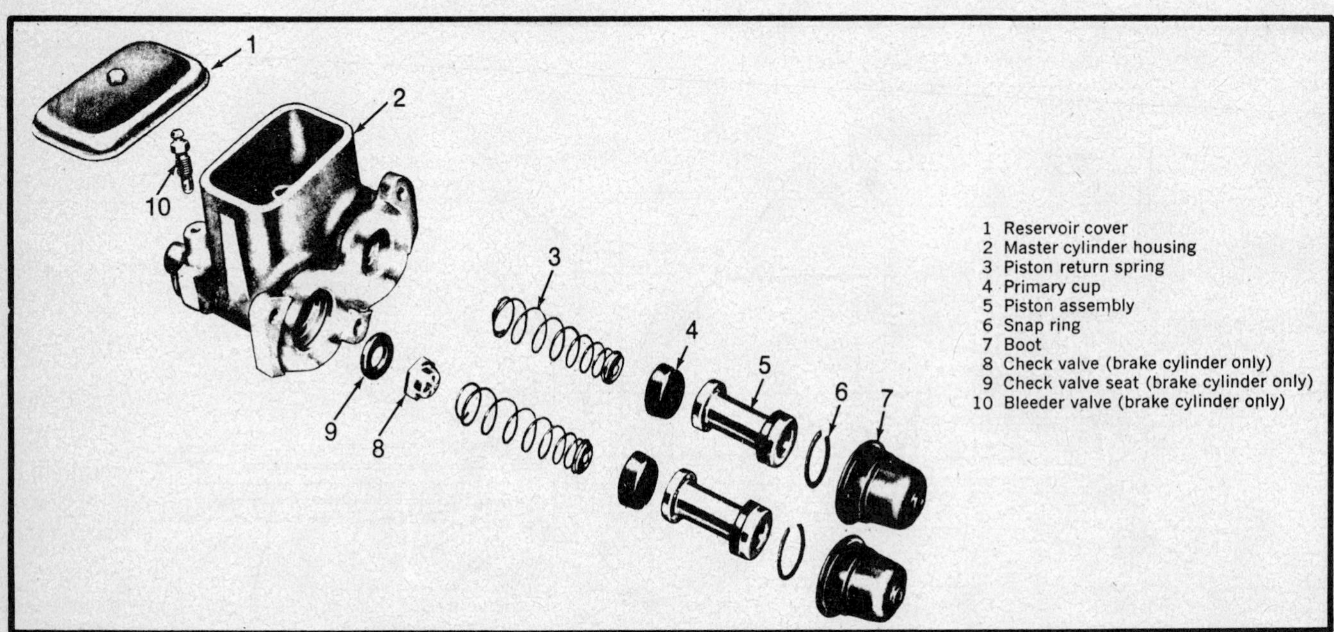

Dual reservoir master cylinder (© GM Corp.)

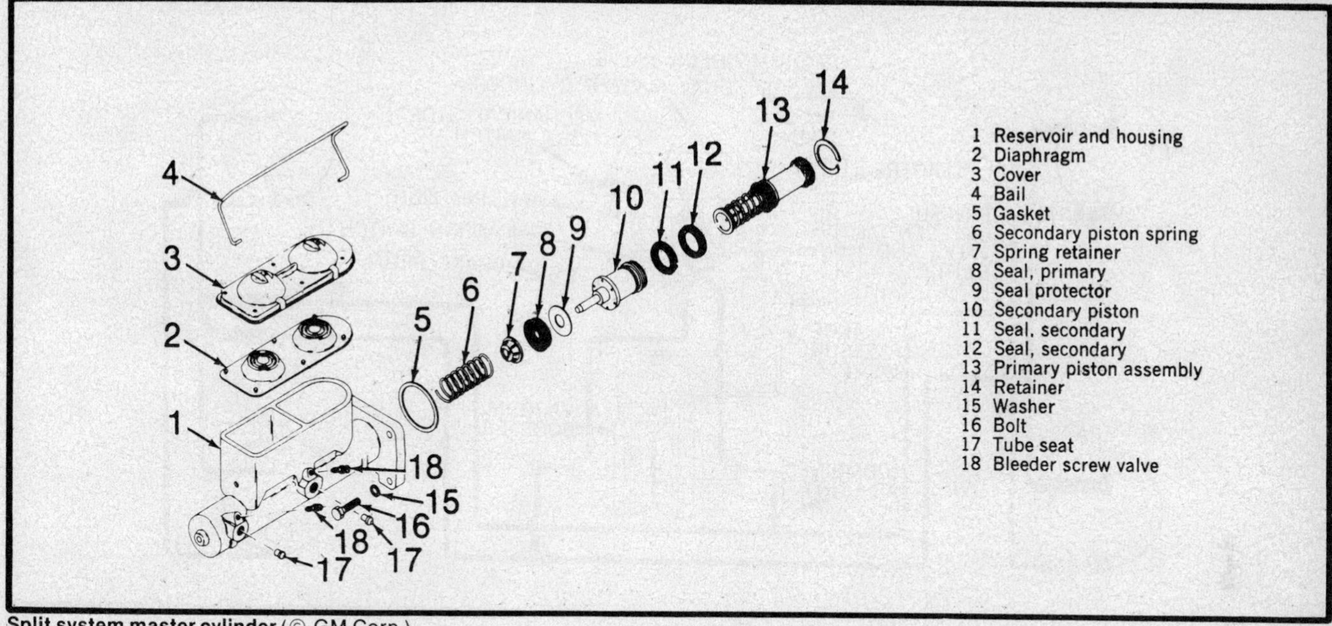

Split system master cylinder (© GM Corp.)

10. Install the parts in the brake cylinder bore. Install the check valve seat and then the check valve in the cylinder bore. Install the short return spring in the bore with the large diameter end of the spring over the check valve.

11. Install the primary cup in the cylinder bore with the lip of the cup toward the outlet end. Make sure the end of the return spring seats inside the cup.

12. Insert the piston and secondary cup assembly into the cylinder bore with the open end of the piston toward the open end of the cylinder bore.

14. Press all parts into the cylinder bore and install the washer (stop plate) if used and the snapring.

15. Install the parts in the clutch cylinder bore. Install the long return spring with the large diameter end first in the cylinder bore. Install the primary cup with the lip of the cup toward the outlet end.

16. Insert the piston and secondary cup into the cylinder bore, with the open end of the piston toward the open end of the cylinder. Press all parts into the cylinder bore and install the washer (stop plate) if used and the snapring.

17. Install the cover and the bleeder screw.

Split System Tandem (GMC)

Disassembly and Assembly

1. Remove the cover and reservoir seal.
2. Remove the retaining ring from the groove in the end of the cylinder of the cylinder bore.
3. Remove all parts from the cylinder bore.
4. Remove the bleeder screw valves.
5. Clean all parts in clean brake fluid.
6. Leave a coating of brake fluid on all internal parts and install parts in the cylinder bore using new rubber seals.
7. Install retainer ring and bleeder screws.

Bleeding Brakes

BENCH BLEEDING PROCEDURES

Bench bleed the master cylinder before installation. In order to expel air trapped in the cylinder, tandem master cylinders must be bench bled before they are installed on the vehicle. Bench bleeding reduces the possibility of air getting in the brake lines. Follow this simple procedure for bench bleeding:

1. Route two shortened brake lines from the outlet connection(s) into the fluid reservoir(s), below the normal fluid level.
2. Fill the reservoir(s) with fresh brake fluid and pump the cylinder until air bubbles no longer appear in the reservoir. If the cylinder does not have a check valve at the outlet port, use a clean piece of rubber or plastic, or the end of your finger to close off the end of the tubing during the back stroke. Otherwise, the fluid will merely pump back and forth in the tubing.
3. When all air has been purged from the master cylinder, bend the tubes up out of the fluid, and remove them. Refill the cylinder and securely install the master cylinder cap.
4. Install the master cylinder on the vehicle. Attach the lines, but do not tighten the tube connection.

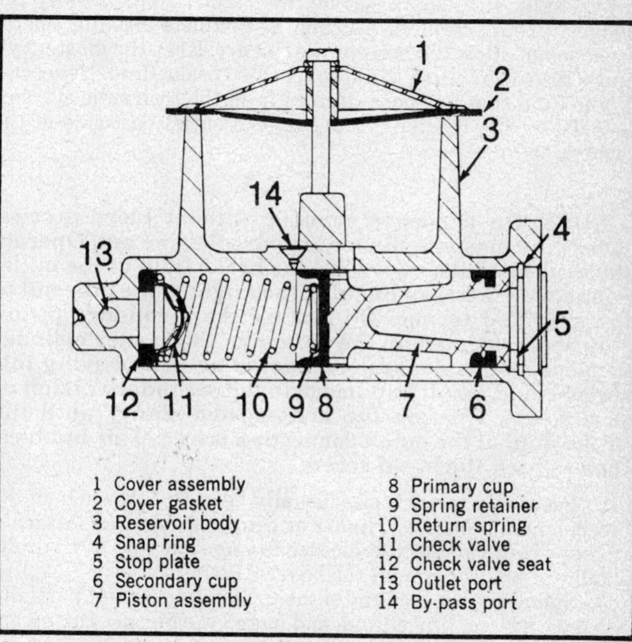

Single reservoir master cylinder (© GM Corp.)

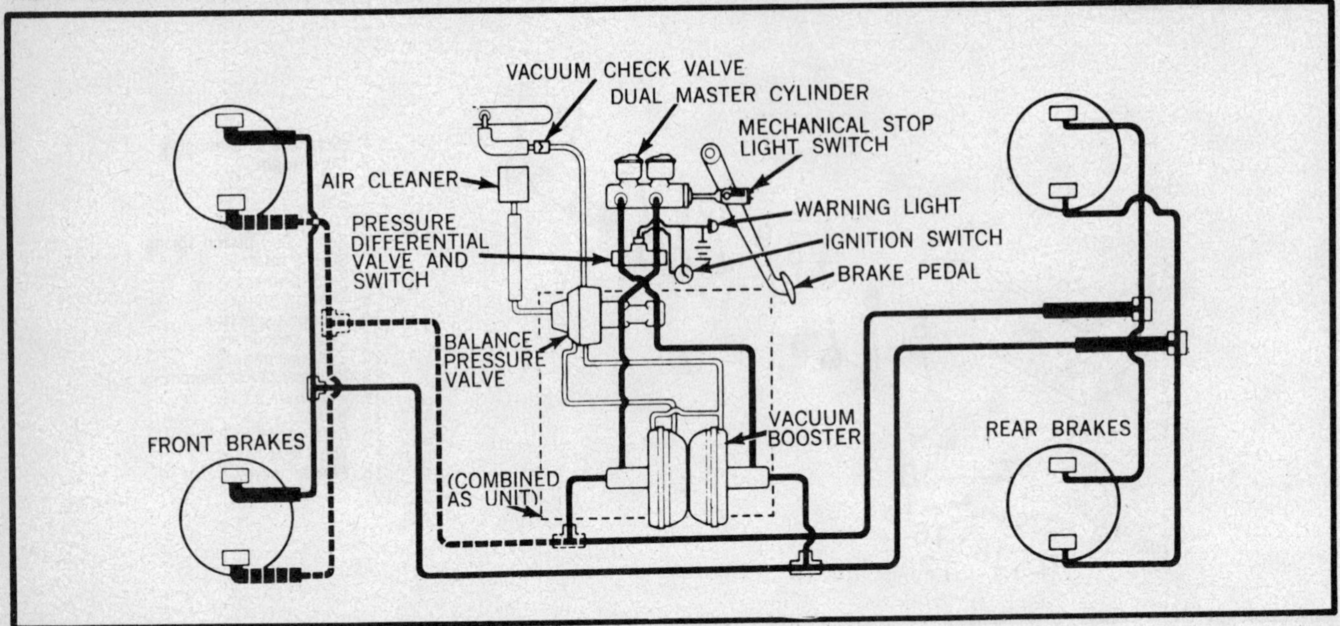

Split hydraulic brake system with frame mounted booster (© For Motor Co.)

5. Force out any air that might have been trapped in the connection by slowly depressing the pedal several times. Tighten the nut slightly before releasing pedal, and loosen before depressing each time. Catch the fluid in a rag to avoid damaging car finish. DO NOT BOTTOM THE PISTON. Tighten the connections when air bubbles are no longer present in the fluid. Make sure the master cylinder is adequately filled with brake fluid.

MANUAL BLEEDING

NOTE: See below for GM "Quick Take-Up" cylinder bleeding sequence

Bleed the longest line first on the individual system (i.e. front/rear split or diagonally front wheel, opposite side rear wheel split. If a single system, the right rear is usually the longest.) being serviced. During the complete bleeding operation, do not allow the reservoir to run dry. Keep the master cylinder reservoirs filled with the specified brake fluid. Never use brake fluid that has been drained from the hydraulic system.

1. Bleed the master cylinder at the outlet port side of the system being serviced.

NOTE: On a master cylinder without bleed screws, loosen the master cylinder to hydraulic line nut. Operate the brake pedal slowly until the brake fluid at the outlet connection is free of bubbles, then tighten the tube nut to the specified torque. Do not use the secondary piston stop screw located on the bottom of the master cylinder to bleed the brake system. Loosening or removing this screw could result in damage to the secondary piston or stop screw. Operate the brake pedal slowly until the brake fluid at the outlet connection is free of air bubbles, then tighten the bleed screw.

2. Position a suitable size (usually $^3/_8$ in.) box wrench on the bleeder fitting on the cylinder or caliper to be bled. Attach a rubber drain tube to the bleeder fitting. The end of the tube should fit snugly around the bleeder fitting.
3. Submerge the free end of the tube in a container partially filled with clean brake fluid, and loosen the bleeder fitting approximately $^3/_4$ turn.
4. Push the brake pedal down slowly thru its full travel. Close the bleeder fitting, then return the pedal to the full released position. Repeat this operation until air bubbles cease to appear at the submerged end of the bleeder tube.
5. When the fluid is completely free of air bubbles, close the bleeder fitting and remove the bleeder tube.
6. Repeat this procedure at the brake cylinder or caliper on the other side of the split system. Refill the master cylinder reservoir after each cylinder or caliper is bled. When the bleeding is complete, the master cylinder fluid level should be filled to within $^1/_4$ in. from the top of the reservoirs.
7. Centralize the pressure differential valve.

GM QUICK TAKE UP MASTER CYLINDER

Special procedures are required to manually bleed the quick take-up brake system used on some General Motors vehicles. Bleed the master cylinder first. Disconnect the left front brake line at the master cylinder, and fill the master cylinder until fluid flows from the port. Catch fluid in a rag and don't allow fluid or rag to contact car finish. Connect the line and tighten fitting.

Depress the brake pedal one time slowly and hold. Loosen same brake line fitting to purge air from the system. Retighten the fitting and release the brake pedal slowly. Wait 15 seconds. Then repeat the sequence, including the 15 second wait until all air is removed. Next bleed the right front connection in the same way as the left front.

Bleed the wheel cylinders and calipers only after you are sure that all the air has been removed from the master cylinder. Follow the specified RR, LF, LR, RF sequence and depress the brake pedal slowly one time before opening bleeder screw to release air. Tighten screw, slowly release pedal, and wait 15 seconds. Repeat all steps, including the 15 second delay until all air has been removed from the system. Rapid pumping of this system moves the secondary master cylinder piston down the bore in a manner that makes it difficult to bleed the left front/right rear part of the system.

SURGE BLEEDING

This method includes both manual and pressure bleeding, and

deliberately creates a churning (higher pressure) turbulence in wheel cylinders so that any remaining air can be drawn off in the form of aerated fluid. It is important to remove all possible air before surging, this method is never used unless the routine manual or pressure bleeding method proves inadequate.

1. Bleed the brakes at all wheels in a usual manner.
2. At each wheel cylinder, in turn, open the bleeder screw and press the brake pedal down sharply several times. Close the bleeder screw. The action creates a turbulence in each cylinder, forcing out practically all of the remaining trapped air.

NOTE: After bleeding the brake system, road test to insure proper operation of the braking system.

BLEEDING THE POWER BRAKE UNIT

On power booster equipped vehicles, the engine should be turned off and the power system purged of vacuum or compressed air by depressing the brake pedal several times. After bleeding the master cylinder, bleed the power brake unit (if equipped with a bleeder screw).

Pressure multiplying type power units often have bleeder screws to remove the air trapped within the unit. If the unit has more that one bleeder screw, bleed the one at the pressure (main) cylinder first and the control valve second. When bleeding, manually close the bleeder screw before the pedal is allowed to back stroke each time.

Wheel Cylinders and Calipers

DRUM BRAKE WHEEL CYLINDER

The wheel cylinder performs in response to the master cylinder. It receives fluid from the hydraulic hose through its inlet port. As the pressure increases the wheel cylinder cups and pistons are forced apart. As a result, the hydraulic pressure is converted into mechanical force acting on the brake shoes. The wheel cylinder size may vary from front to rear. The variation in wheel cylinder size (diameter) is one of the factors controlling the distribution of braking force in a vehicle. Larger diameter wheel cylinders are normally specified for the front brakes of front engine passenger cars equipped with drum brakes. Bleeder screws are provided to remove air or vapor trapped in the system.

Three types of wheel cylinders are normally used with drum brakes.

Single Piston or "Single-end" Type

A single piston wheel cylinder has only one cup, piston, and dust boot and spring. It may also contain a cup filler or cup expander.

Double Piston or "Double-end" Straight Bore Type

The double piston, straight bore type is most commonly used. This type carries two opposed pistons, two cups and two boots.

Double Piston or "Double-end" Step Bore Type

This type is used on some of the non-servo brakes and has the same components as the straight bore type. Two different sized dust boots, cups, and pistons are used. Opposed pistons of different diameters exert different amounts of force.

SERVICE PROCEDURES

Wheel cylinders may need reconditioning or replacement whenever the brake shoes are replaced or when required to correct a leak condition. On many designs, the wheel cylinders can be diassembled without removing them from the backing plate. On some designs, however, the cylinder is mounted in an indention in the backing plate or a cylinder piston stop is welded to the backing plate. When servicing brakes of this type, the cylinder must be removed from the backing plate before being disassembled.

Diagnostic Inspection and Cleaning

Leaks which coat the boot and the cylinder with fluid, or result in a dropped reservoir fluid level, or dampen and stain the brake linings are dangerous. Such leaks can cause the brakes to "grab" or fail and should be immediately corrected. A leakage, not immediately apparent, can be detected by pulling back the cylinder boot. A small amount of fluid seepage dampening the interior of the boot is normal, however a dripping boot is not. Unless other conditions causing a brake to pull, grab, or drag becomes obvious, the wheel cylinder is a suspect and should be included in general reconditioning.

Cylinder binding may be caused by rust, deposits, grime, or swollen cups due to fluid contamination, or by a cup wedged into an excessive piston clearance. If the clearance between the pistons and the bore wall exceeds allowable values, a condition called "heel drag" may exist. It can result in rapid cup wear and can cause the pistons to retract very slowly when the brakes are released.

A ring of a hard, crystal like substance is sometimes noticed in the cylinder bore where the piston stops after the brakes are released.

Some front wheel cylinders have a baffle located between the opposed pistons. The baffle contains a small hole which causes the cylinder to act as a fluid shock absorber damping servo brake shoes as they become energized. These cylinders cannot be honed and should be replaced if the bore is pitted or corroded.

Hydraulic system parts should not be allowed to come in contact with oil or grease, neither should those be handled with greasy hands. Even a trace of any petroleum based product is sufficient to cause damage to the rubber parts.

RECONDITIONING DRUM BRAKE WHEEL CYLINDERS

It is a common practice to recondition a drum brake wheel cylinder without dismounting it, however some brakes are equipped with external piston stops which prevent disassembly unless the cylinder is removed. In order to dismount, remove the shoe springs and spread the shoes apart, disconnect the brake line, remove the mounting bolts or retaining clips, and pull the cylinder free.

Most wheel cylinders are attached to the backing plate with bolts and are easily removed for service or replacement. In recent years, some GM vehicles use a retaining clip for this purpose. To remove this type cylinder, use a special service tool, or insert $1/8$ in. diameter or less awls or pins into the slots between wheel cylinder pilot and retainer locking tabs. Bend both tabs away at the same time until tabs spring over the shoulder, releasing cylinder. Discard the old retainer.

To replace the wheel cylinder, use a new retainer and the following procedure.

1. Hold wheel cylinder against backing plate by inserting a block between the wheel cylinder and axle shaft flange.
2. Position wheel cylinder retainer clip so the tabs will be away from and in horizontal position with the backing plate when installing.
3. Press new retaining clip over wheel cylinder abutment and into position using 1 $1/8$ in. 12 point socket. The retainer is in place when the tabs are snapped under the retainer abutment. Examine closely to be sure both retainer tabs are properly engaged.

Another variation of retainer clip is used on some imported vehicles. The retainer usually consists of two or three separate pieces which when slid together will lock themselves and the

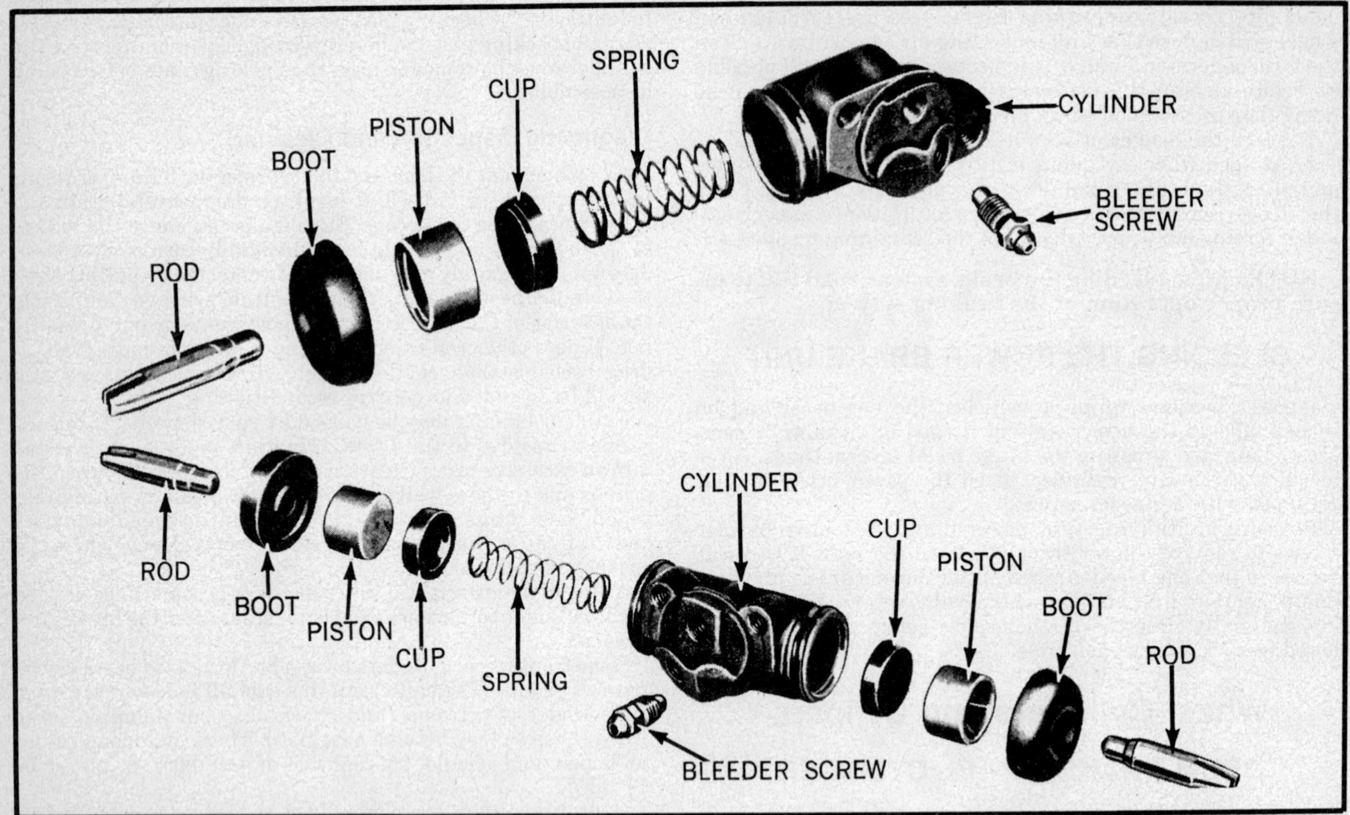

Typical wheel cylinder—exploded view (© Chrysler Corp.)

wheel cylinder in place. The retainers can be carefully removed without incurring damage which allows them to be reused. If they are damaged or corroded, however, they must be replaced.

Pull the protective dust boots off the cylinder. Internal parts should slide out, or be picked out easily. Parts can be driven out with a wooden dowel, or blown out at low pressure by applying compressed air to the fluid inlet port. Parts which cannot be removed easily indicate they are damaged beyond repair and the cylinder should be replaced.

Clean the cylinder and the parts in alcohol and/or brake fluid. (Do not use gasoline or other petroleum based products.) Use only lint free wiping cloths. Crocus cloth can be used to clean minute scratches, signs of rust, corrosion or discoloration from the cylinder bore and pistons. Slide the cloth in a circular rather than a lengthwise motion. A clean up hone may be used. After a cylinder has been honed, inspect it for excessive piston clearance and remove any burrs formed on the edge of fluid intake or bleeder screw ports.

NOTE: Do not rebuild aluminum cylinders. A cylinder that does not clean up at 0.002 in. should be discarded and a new cylinder installed. (Black stains on the cylinder walls are caused by the piston cups and will do no harm.)

Assemble the cylinder with the internal parts, making sure that the cylinder wall is wet with brake fluid. Insert the cups and pistons from each end of a double end cylinder; do not slide them through the cylinder. Cup lips should always face inward.

Disc Brake Caliper

An integral part of the caliper, the caliper bore(s) contains the piston(s) that direct thrust against the brake pads supported within the caliper. Since all braking forces (pad application force) are applied on each side of the rotor with no self energization, the cylinder and piston are large in comparison to a drum brake wheel cylinder.

FIXED CALIPER TYPE

A fixed type caliper is mounted solidly to the spindle bracket.

Pistons are located on both sides of the rotor, in inboard and outboard caliper halves. Fluid passes between caliper halves through an external crossover tube or through internal passages. A bleeder screw is located in the inboard caliper half. A dust boot protecting each cylinder fits in a circumferential groove on the piston.

FLOATING CALIPER TYPE

Floating or sliding calipers are free to move in a fixed bracket or support.

The piston is located only on the inboard side of the caliper housing, which straddles the rotor. The cylinder piston applies the inboard brake shoe directly, and simultaneously hydraulic pressure slides the caliper in a clamping action which forces the caliper to apply the outboard brake shoe.

The actual applying movement is small. The unit merely grips during application, relaxes upon release, and the shoes do not retract an appreciable distance from the rotor. The fluid inlet port and the bleeder screw are located n the inboard side of the caliper. A dust boot is fitted into a circumferential groove on the piston and into a recess at or near the outer end of the cylinder bore.

HYDRAULIC SEAL ARRANGEMENTS

Seal arrangements at the caliper pistons vary depending upon the brake manufacturer. Three makes of fixed caliper brakes,

Bendix, Budd, and Delco-Moraine, use a ring seal which fits in a circumferential groove on the piston.

A fixed seal is now commonly used in brake calipers. During the very small applying movement of the piston, the elasticity of the fixed seal permits some deflection in the cylinder groove. The seal deflects as the brakes are applied and relaxes as the brakes are released, retracting the piston a small amount. Some GM types have a rolling seal that retracts the piston slightly further to reduce pad rubbing friction.

A scratched piston, nicked seal, or a sludge or varnish deposit which lifts the sealing edge away from the piston will cause a fluid leak. A serious leak could develop if calipers are not reconditioned when new pads are installed. Then dust and road grime, gradually accumulating behind the dust boot, could be carried into the seal when the piston is shoved inward to accommodate new thick linings. Old seals may have taken a "set," thus preventing proper seating in the retainer groove and on the piston. Therefore, when reconditioning calipers, new seals should be installed.

Service Procedures

Before servicing, syphon or syringe about $^2/_3$ of the fluid from the master cylinder reservoir do not allow the, fluid level to fall below the cylinder intake port. To prevent a gravity loss of fluid, plug the brake line after disconnecting from the caliper. To recondition, remove the caliper from the vehicle, allow the unit to drain, and remove the brake shoes. For benchwork, clamp the caliper housing in a soft jaw vice. On fixed-caliper types, remove the bridge bolts and separate the caliper into halves. Remove the sealing O-rings at cross-over points, if the unit has internal fluid passages across the halves.

Whenever required, use special tools to remove pistons, dust boots, and seals. If compressed air is used, apply it gradually, gently ease the pistons from the cylinders, and trap them in a clean cloth; do not allow them to pop out. Take care to avoid pinching hands or fingers.

While removing stroking type seals and boots, work lip of boot from the groove in the caliper. After the boot is free, pull the piston, and strip the seal and boot from the piston.

While removing fixed position (rectangular ring) seals and boots, pull the piston through the boot. Do not use a metal tool which would scratch the piston. Use a small pointed wooden or plastic tool to lift the boots and seals from the grooves in the cylinder bore.

Cleaning, Inspection, and Installation

Use only alcohol and/or brake fluid and a lint free wiping cloth to clean the caliper and parts. Other solvents should not be used. Blow out passages with compressed air. Always wear eye protection when using compressed air or cleaning calipers.

To correct minor imperfections in the cylinder bore, polish with a fine grade of crocus cloth working in a circular rather than a lengthwise motion. Do not use any form of abrasive on a plated piston. Discard a piston which is pitted or has signs of plating wear.

Inspect the new seal. It should lie flat and be round. If it has suffered a distorted "set" during its shelf life, do not use it. Lubricate the cylinder wall and parts with brake fluid.

While installing stroking type seals and boots, stretch the boot and the seal over the piston and seat them in position.

Use special alignment tools for inserting lip cup seals. Be sure the seal does not twist or roll.

Where the boot lip is retained inside the cylinder bore the following method works well.

1. Lubricate bottom inside edge of piston and brake seal in caliper with brake fluid.
2. Pull boot over bottom end of piston so that boot is positioned on bottom of piston with lip about $^1/_4$ in. up from bottom end.
3. Hold piston suspended over bore.
4. Insert back boot lip into groove in caliper.
5. Then tuck the sides of boot into groove and work forward until only one bulge remains.
6. Tuck the final bulge into front of the groove.
7. Then push the piston carefully through the seal and boot to the bottom of the bore. The inside of the boot should slide on the piston and come to rest in the boot groove.
8. If the boot lip is retained outside the cylinder bore, first stretch boot over the piston and seat it in its groove, then press the piston through the seal. Fully depress the piston. You'll need 50 to 100 pounds force to fasten the boot lip in place. On some designs, it is necessary to use a wooden drift or a special tool to seat the metal boot in the caliper counterbore below the face of the caliper.

INSTALLING FIXED CALIPER BRIDGE BOLTS

If the caliper contains internal fluid cross-over passages, be sure to install the new O-ring seals at joints. Install high tensile strength bridge bolts on the mated caliper halves. Never replace the bridge bolts with ordinary standard hardware bolts.

Brake Disc (Rotor)

ROTOR RUNOUT

Manufacturers differ widely on permissible runout, but too much can sometimes be felt as a pulsation at the brake pedal. A wobble pump effect is created when a rotor is not perfectly smooth and the pad hits the high spots forcing fluid back into the master cylinder. This alternating pressure causes a pulsating feeling which can be felt at the pedal when the brakes are applied. This excessive runout also causes the brakes to be out of adjustment because disc brakes are self adjusting, they are designed so that the pads drag on the rotor at all times and therefore automatically compensate for wear. To check the actual runout of the rotor, first tighten the wheel spindle nut to a snug bearing adjustment, end play removed. Fasten a dial indicator on the suspension at a convenient place so that the indicator stylus contacts the rotor face approximately one in. from its outer edge. Set the dial at zero. Check the total indictor reading while turning the rotor one full revolution. If the rotor is warped beyond the runout specification, it is likely that it can be successfully remachined.

Lateral Runout: A wobbly movement of the rotor from side to side at it rotates. Excessive lateral runout causes the rotor faces to knock bac the disc pads and can result in chatter, excessive pedal travel, pumping or fighting pedal and vibration during the breaking action.

Parallelism (lack of): Refers to the amount of variation in the thickness of the rotor. Excessive variation can cause pedal vibration or fight, front end vibrations and possible "grab" during the braking action; a condition comparable to an "out-of-round brake drum." Check parallelism with a micrometer, "mike" the thickness at eight or more equally spaced points, equally distant from the outer edge of the rotor, preferrably at mid-points of the braking surface. Parallelism then is the amount of variation between maximum and minimum measurements.

Surface of Micro-inch finish, flatness, smoothness: Different from parallelism, these terms refer to the degree of perfection of the flat surface on each side of the rotor, that is, the minute hills, valleys and swirls inherent in machining the surface. In a visual inspection, the remachined surface should have a fine ground polish with, at most, only a faint trace of nondirectional swirls.

Disc Brake Surface Refinishing

To meet mandated brake system performance requirements, semi-metallic brake linings have been used for several years in some vehicle applications. In order to maintain the proper performance, it is important to correctly service these semi-metallic brake components as outlined in the following procedures.

Service Recommendations

1. Semi-metallic linings should be replaced with semi-metallic service linings, equal to the original equipment specifications.
2. Routine replacement of the disc pads does not require rotor refinishing, unless damage or extreme wear to the rotor has occurred.
3. Rotor refinishing should only be required if non-parallelism, excessive runout, rotor damage or scoring of the rotor surface has occurred.
4. If refinishing is necessary, the semi-metallic brake pads require a micro- inch surface refinish like new vehicle rotor specifications (10 to 50 micro-inches with non-directional swirl patterns).
5. The recommended procedure for obtaining this finish is outlined in the following chart.

ROTOR REFINISHING

Procedure	Rough Cut	Finish Cut
Spindle Speed	150 RPM	150 RPM
Depth of Cut Per Side	.005″	.002″
Tool Cross Feed Per Rev.	.006″.010″	.002″ Max.
Vibration Dampener	Yes	Yes
Swirl Pattern-120 GRIT	No	Yes

6. When refinishing brake rotors for semi-metallic linings, the following is important;
   a. The brake lathe must be in good working order and have the capability to produce the intended surface finish.
   b. Use the correct tool feed and arbor speeds. Too fast a speed or too deep a cut can result in a rough finish.
   c. Cutting tools must be sharp.
   d. Adapters must be clean and free of nicks.
   e. Lathe finish cuts should be further improved and made non-directional by dressing the rotor surface with a sanding disc power tool, such as AMMCO model 8350 Safe Swirl Disc Rotor Grinder or its equivalaent.
   f. Rotor surfaces are to be refinished to 10 to 50 micro-inches.
7. To become familiar with the required surface finish, drag the fingernail over the surface of a new rotor from parts stock or on a new vehicle. If your brake equipment cannot produce this smooth-a-finish when correctly used, contact the equipment manufacturer for corrective instructions.
8. When installing new rotors from service stock, do not refinish the surface as these parts are to the recommended finish. It also is not required to refinish a rotor on a vehicle which has a smooth finish.

Drum Brake Service

Basic Service

CAUTION

Do not blow the brake dust out of the drums with compressed air or lung power; always use a damp cloth, a vacuum unit and soft brush to gather the dust particles into a container for disposal. Use a nose/mouth protective cover Brake linings contain asbestos, a known cancer causing substance. Dispose of the residue safely.

NOTE: Never work on a vehicle supported only by a jack. Use a hydraulic lift and/or jack stands to support the vehicle safely.

Check For Leaks

Press the brake pedal to ensure that there are no leaks in the hydraulic system. If the pedal does not remain hard and drops to the end of its pedal travel, an internal or external fluid leakage is indicated in the master cylinder, hoses, wheel cylinders, or brake calipers. When performing this test, the engine should be running, if equipped with power brakes. With power brakes, it is normal for the pedal to drop slightly when the engine starts. If the pedal continues to drop, a leak in the system is indicated.

Drum Inspection

Check the drums for any cracks, scores, grooves, or out-of-round conditions. Slight scores can be removed with fine emery cloth, while extensive scoring requires machining the drum on a suitable drum lathe.

If the friction surface of the brake drum is scored or otherwise damaged beyond the allowable machining specification, it will require replacement. After machining, the drum diameter must not exceed the diameter specification cast on the drum or 0.060 in. (1.5mm) over the original nominal diameter. Carefully look for signs of grease, oil or brake fluid on the drum assembly and repair as required.

Rebuild the Wheel Cylinders

It is always a good practice to rebuild or replace the wheel cylinder when relining the brakes. This helps to assure a properly operating brake system and to prevent premature leakage of brake fluid past the cups and piston seals.

Clean and Lubricate

With the brake parts off, clean the backing plate with a damp cloth to avoid raising any asbestos dust and dispose of the rag after use. Clean any rust with a wire brush. File smooth any ridges or rough edges on the contact points of the backing plate. Lubricate the contact points with an approved brake lubricant. Clean and lightly lubricate the adjuster threads and screw the adjuster all the way together to facilitate reassembly of the brake components. If the wheel bearings are available, wash in solvent and repack with lubricant. Check the backing plate retaining bolts for tightness.

Reassemble And Install The Brake Shoes

Reassemble the brake shoes in the reverse order of their removal. Make sure all parts are in their proper position and that both brake shoes are properly positioned at either end of the adjuster assembly. Also, both brake shoes should correctly engage the wheel cylinder push rod and parking brake links, if equipped. With the brake shoes and components in position, measure the inside of the drum diameter and adjust the brake shoes to match the diameter with a brake shoe pre-set measuring tool. Install the brake drum and make final brake adjustment, as required. Install the remaining components and torque to specifications.

BLEED AND ROAD TEST

Bleed the air from the hydraulic system to insure a high, hard pedal and road test the vehicle. Self-adjusting mechanisms are activated by the application of the brake pedal when the vehicle is driven in reverse, driven forward or when the parking brake is applied. Be sure the road test course includes enough stops, enough traveling in reverse, and the use of the parking brake assembly, to allow the self adjusters to perform the proper adjustment on all wheels.

DRUM BRAKE SERVICE

Wagner

TWIN ACTION TYPE

Twin-action brake is a four-anchor type. Brake shoes are self-centering in operation, and both shoes are self-energizing in both forward and reverse.

Two wheel cylinders are mounted on opposite sides of the backing plate. One brake shoe is mounted above wheel cylinders and one below. Sliding pivot type anchor is used at front end of upper shoe and at rear end of lower shoe. Adjustable anchor is used at front end of lower shoe and at rear end of upper shoe. Four shoe return springs hold shoe ends firmly against anchors when brakes are released.

Anchor brackets are steel forgings, attached to flange on axle housing in conjunction with the backing plate. At adjustable anchor end of each shoe, shoe web bears against flat head of adjusting screw which threads into anchor bracket. The adjusting screw heads are notched and are rotated for brake adjustment through access holes in backing plate. A lock spring which fits over anchor bracket holds adjusting screw in position.

The brake backing plate has six machined bearing surfaces, three for each shoe, against which the inner edge of each shoe bears. Two brake shoe guide bolts are riveted to backing plate and extend through holes in center of brake shoe web. Shoes are retained on guide bolts by flat washers, nuts, and cotter pins.

Wheel cylinder push rods make contact between wheel cylinder pistons and brake shoes.

Inner edge of brake drum has a groove which fits over a flange on the edge of backing plate, forming a seal against the entrance of dirt and mud.

TWIN—ACTION TYPE REAR BRAKE

Brake Shoe Removal

1. Remove brake drums.

NOTE: If brake drums are worn severely, it may be necessary to retract the adjusting screws.

2. Remove the brake shoe pull back springs.

NOTE: Since wheel cylinder piston stops are incorporated in the anchor brackets, it is not necessary to install wheel cylinder clamps when the brake shoes are removed.

3. Loosen the adjusting lever cam cap screw, and while holding the star wheel end of the adjusting lever past the star wheel, remove the cap screw and cam.
4. Remove the brake shoe hold down springs and pins by compressing the spring and, at the same time, pushing the pin back through the flange plate toward the tool. Then, keeping the spring compressed, remove the lock (C-washer) from the pin with a magnet.
5. Lift off the brake shoe and self-adjuster lever as an assembly.
6. The self-adjuster lever can now be removed from the brake shoe by removing the hold-down spring and pin. Remove lever return spring also.

NOTE: The adjusting lever, override spring and pivot are an assembly. It is not recommended that they be disassembled for service purposes unless they are broken. It is much easier to assemble and disassemble the brake leaving them intact.

7. Thread the adjusting screw out of the brake shoe anchor and remove and discard the friction spring.
8. Clean all dirt out of brake drum. Inspect drums for roughness, scoring or out-of-round. Replace or recondition drums as necessary.
9. Carefully pull lower edges of wheel cylinder boots away from cylinders. If brake fluid flows out, overhaul of the wheel cylinders is necessary.

NOTE: A slight amount of fluid is nearly always present and acts as a lubricant for the piston.

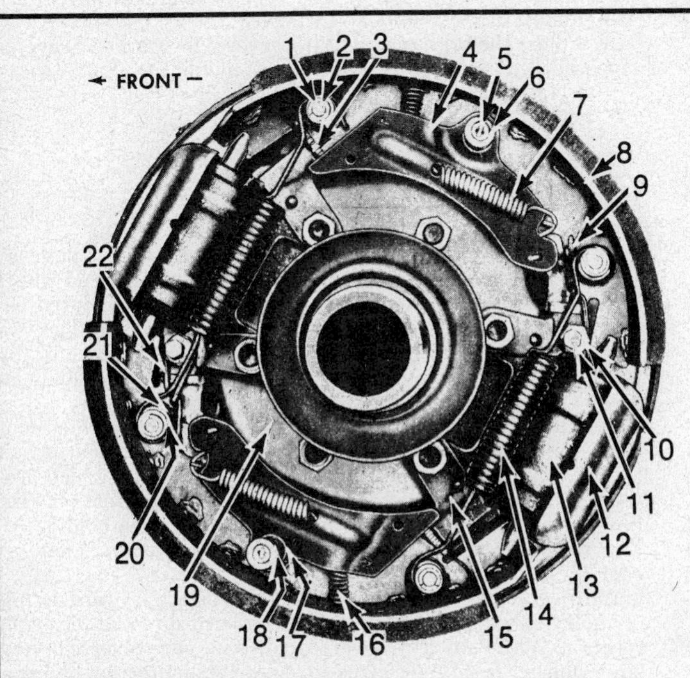

1. Hold-down pin spring lock
2. Hold-down pin
3. Adjusting screw
4. Adjusting lever
5. Adjuting lever pin spring
6. Hold-down spring cup
7. Lever override spring
8. Brake shoe and lining
9. Adjusting lever pivot
10. Adjusting lever cam
11. Adjusting lever bolt
12. Wheel cylinder shield
13. Wheel cylinder
14. Brake shoe return spring
15. Brake shoe anchor
16. Lever return spring
17. Adjusting lever pin sleeve
18. Hold-down spring
19. Brake backing plate
20. Hold-down pin retainer
21. Hold-down pin spring
22. Adjusting lever link

Twin action self adjusting brakes (© GM Corp.)

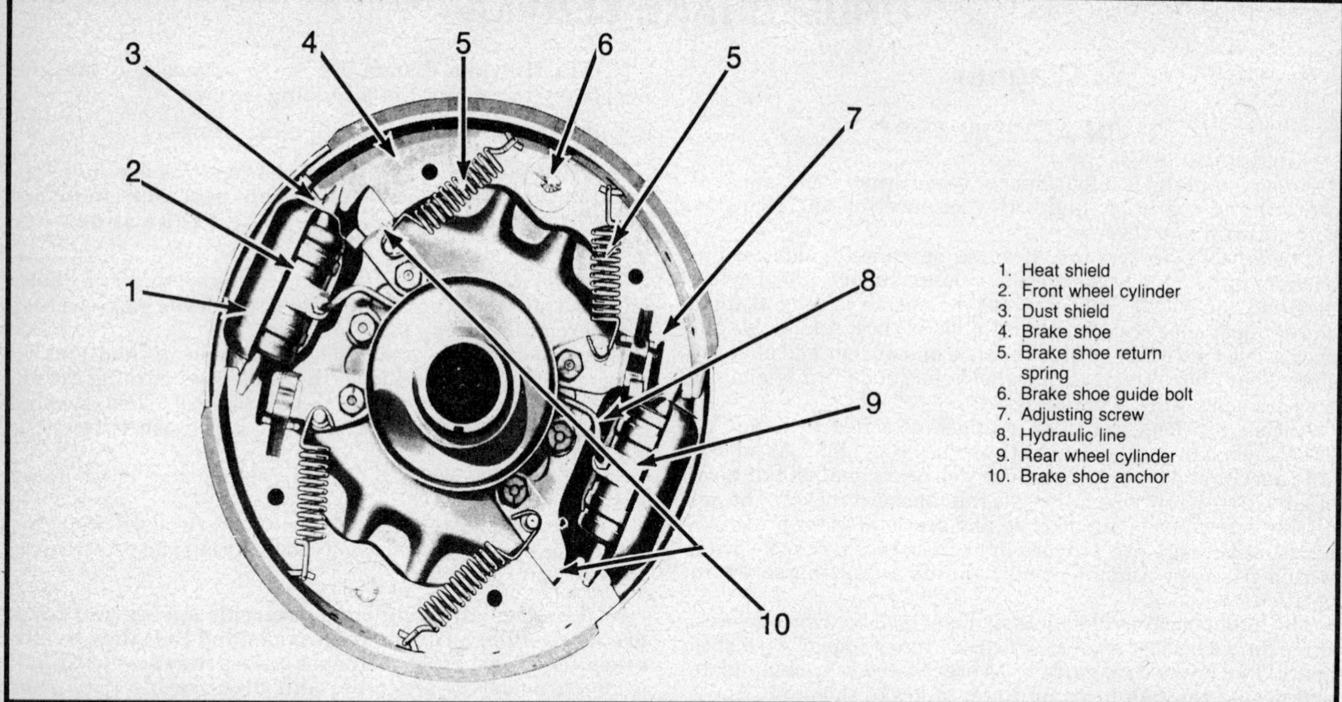

Twin action type brake installed (© GM Corp.)

10. Inspect flange plate for oil leakage past axle shaft oil seals. Install seals if necessary.

Brake Shoe Installation

1. Put a light film of lubricant on shoe bearing surfaces of brake flange plate and on threads of adjusting screw.
2. Thread adjusting screw completely into anchor without friction spring to be sure threads are clean and screw turns easily. Then remove screws, position a new friction spring on screw and reinstall in anchor.
3. Assemble self-adjuster assembly and lever return spring to brake shoe and position adjusting lever link on adjusting lever pivot.
4. Position hold-down pins in flange plate.
5. Install brake shoe and self-adjuster assemblies onto hold down pins. Insert ends of shoes in wheel cylinder push rods and legs of friction springs.

NOTE: Make sure the toe of the shoe is against the adjusting screw.

6. Install cup, spring and retainer on end of hold-down pin. With spring compressed, push the hold-down pin back through the flange plate toward the tool and install the lock on the pin.
7. Install brake shoe return springs.
8. Holding the star wheel end of the adjusting lever as far as possible past the star wheel, position the adjusting lever cam into the adjusting lever link and assemble with cap screw.
9. Check the brake shoes for being centered by measuring the distance from the lining surface to the edge of the flange plate. To center the shoes, tap the upper or lower end of the shoes with a plastic mallet until the distances at each end become equal.
10. Locate the adjusting lever 0.020 to 0.039 in. above the outside diameter of the adjusting screw thread by loosening the cap screw and turning the adjusting cam.

NOTE: To determine 0.020 to 0.039 in., turn the adjusting screw 2 full turns out from the fully retracted position. Hold a 0.060 in. wire gauge at a 90° angle with the star wheel edge of the adjusting lever. Turn the adjusting cam until the adjusting lever and threaded area on the adjusting screw just touch the wire.

11. Secure the adjusting cam cap screw and retract the adjusting screw.
12. Install brake drums and wheels.
13. Adjust the brakes by making several forward and reverse stops until a satisfactory brake pedal height results.

Wagner

TYPE F

Two identical brake shoes are arranged on backing plate so that their toes are diagonally opposite. Two single-end wheel cylinders are arranged so that each cylinder is mounted between the toe of one shoe and the heel of the other. The two wheel cylinder pistons apply an equal amount of force to the toe of each shoe. Each cylinder casting is shaped to provide an anchor block for the brake shoe heel.

Each shoe is adjusted by means of an eccentric cam which contacts a pin pressed into brake shoe web. Each cam is attached to the backing plate by a cam and shoe guide stud which protrudes through a slot in the shoe web and, in conjunction with flat washers and C-washers, also serves as a shoe hold-down. Two return springs are connected between the shoes, one at each toe and heel.

With vehicle moving forward, both shoes are forward acting (primary shoes), self-energizing in forward direction of drum rotation. With vehicle in reverse, both shoes are reverse acting since neither is self-energized in the reverse direction of drum rotation.

Brake Shoe Removal

1. Remove both brake shoe return springs, using brake spring pliers.
2. Remove C-washer and flat washer from each adjusting cam and hold-down stud. Lift shoes off backing plate.

Cleaning and Inspection

1. Clean all dirt out of brake drum. Inspect drum for roughness, scoring, or out-of-round. Replace or recondition brake drum as necessary.
2. Inspect wheel bearings and oil seals.
3. Check backing plate attaching bolts to make sure they are tight. Clean all dirt off backing plate.
4. Inspect brake shoe return springs. If broken, cracked, or weakened, replace with new springs.
5. Check cam and shoe guide stud and friction spring on backing plate for corrosion or binding. Cam stud should turn easily with a wrench but should not be loose. If frozen, lubricate with kerosene or penetrating oil and work free.
6. Examine brake shoe linings for wear. Lining should be replaced if worn down close to rivet heads.

Brake Shoe Installation

1. Install anti-rattle spring washer on each cam and shoe guide stud, pronged side facing adjusting cam.
2. Place shoe assembly on backing plate with cam and shoe guide stud inserted through hole in shoe web; locate shoe toe in wheel cylinder piston shoe guide and position shoe heel in slot in anchor block.
3. Install flat washer and C-washer on cam and shoe guide stud. Crimp ends of C-washer together.
4. After installing both shoes, install brake shoe return springs. To install each spring, place spring end with short hook in toe of shoe, then using brake spring pliers, stretch spring and secure long hook end in heel of opposite shoe.
5. Install hub and brake drum assembly.
6. Adjust brake.
7. After checking pedal operation, road test vehicle.

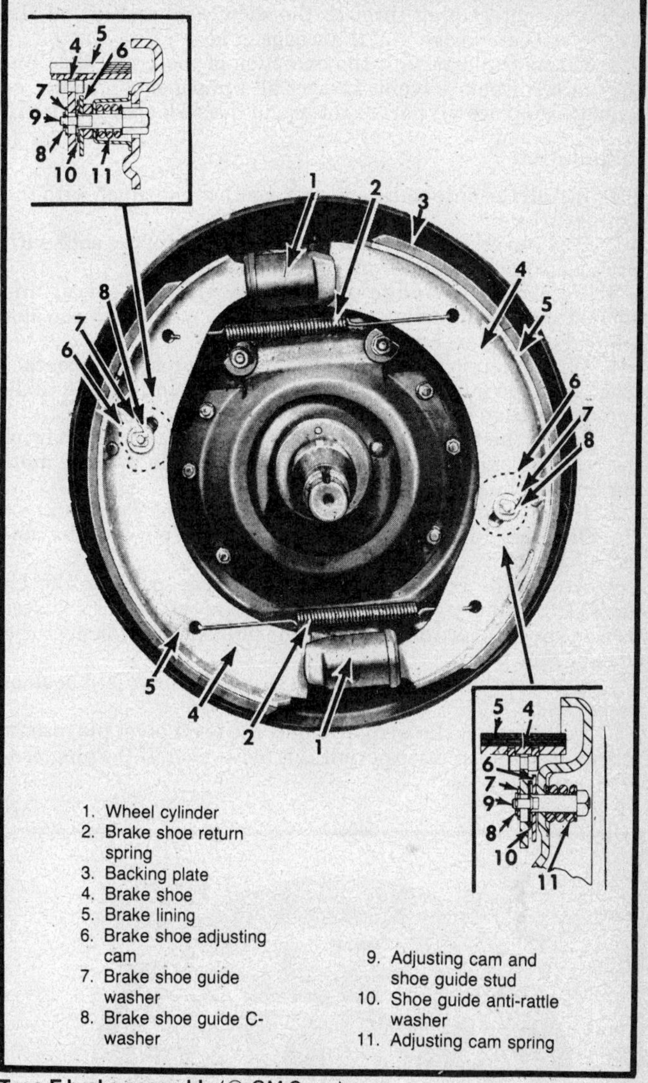

Type F brake assembly (© GM Corp.)

Wagner Type FA

BRAKE SHOES

Removal

1. Block brake pedal in up position. Raise vehicle off ground and support.
2. Remove the brake drums. Disconnect the shoe retaining springs and hold down clips and lift off shoes.
3. Unhook the wedge actuating coil spring from the wedge.
4. Unhook the lever actuating spring from the shoe web, work the spring coil off the lever pivot pin and slide the spring "U" hook off the contact plug-lever pin.

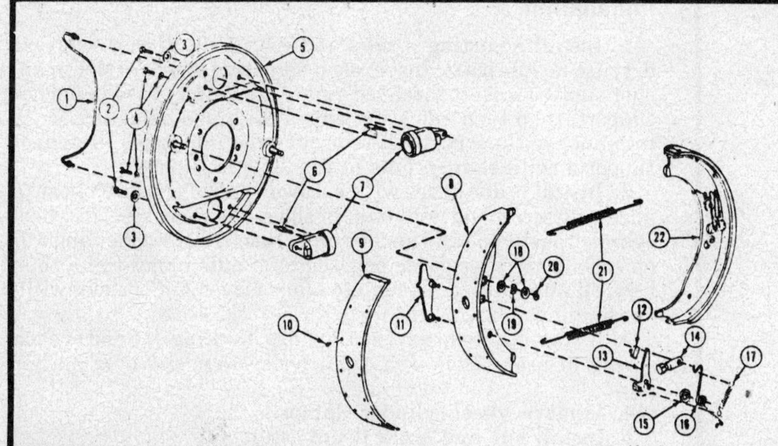

Exploded view of Wagner type FA brake assembly (© Chrysler Corp.)

5. Pull the adjuster lever from the opposite side of the shoe web, the contact plug through the shoe table and lift off the wedge washer, wedge and the wedge guide.
6. Clean all parts with the exception of the brake shoe linings in a suitable solvent. Inspect all components for wear or damage. Replace all parts that are in questionable condition.

Installation

1. Install the automatic adjuster, contact plug flush with the lining surface.
2. Position the wedge guide on the back side of the shoe with serrations facing away from the shoe table.
3. Position the wedge on the shoe with the serrations against matching serrations on the wedge guide with the slot aligned on the lever pivot pin hole.
4. Working from the drum side of the shoe, insert the contact plug, with the guide shank through the hole in the shoe table and over wedge guide and wedge.
5. Insert the adjuster lever pins through the shoe web from the opposite side, guiding actuating (center) pin into the mating hole of the contact plug shank.
6. Install the wedge washer over the shoulder of the pivot pin. Slide the U-hook of adjuster spring on the pin over the contact plug shank.
7. Attach the end of the wedge actuating spring to the U-hook of the adjusting spring. Position the coil of the adjuster torsion spring over the pivot pin and pull spring hook over the edge of shoe web.
8. Connect the wedge actuating spring on the raised hook of wedge fork.
9. Fully retract the wedge against the lever pivot pin, pressing upon contact plug to permit this movement. If the plug protrudes more than 0.005 in. above lining, clamp shoe in vise so that jaws press against adjuster lever. With a file, press down on the plug until it is even with the brake lining. Exercise caution when filing so as not to create a flat spot on the brake lining. If the fully extended plug is more than 0.005 in. below the surface of the lining, replace with a new contact plug.
10. Locate the shoe on hold-downs. Install the retracting springs, long ends of springs are at the ends of shoes.

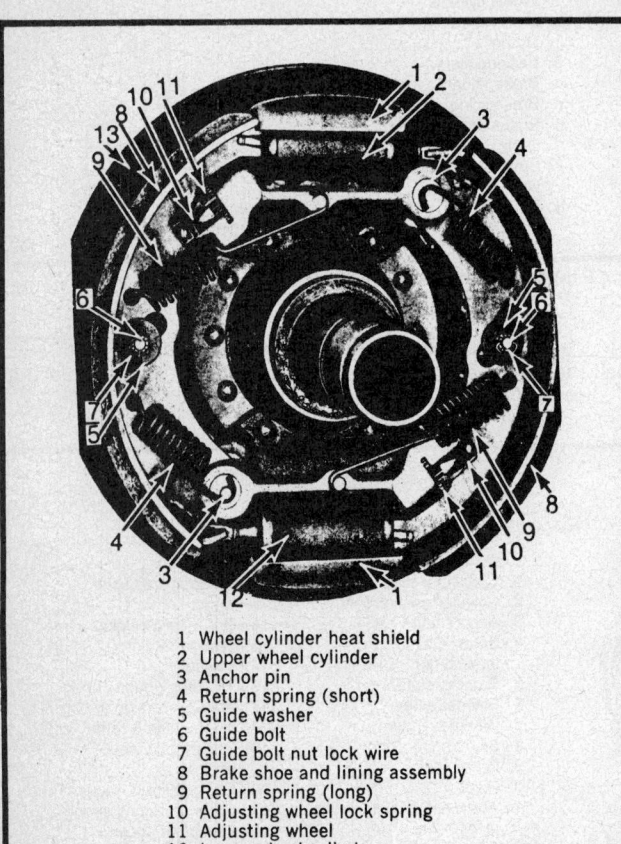

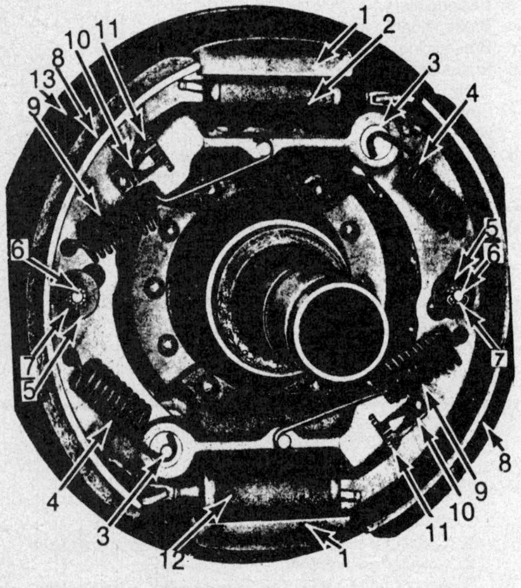

1 Wheel cylinder heat shield
2 Upper wheel cylinder
3 Anchor pin
4 Return spring (short)
5 Guide washer
6 Guide bolt
7 Guide bolt nut lock wire
8 Brake shoe and lining assembly
9 Return spring (long)
10 Adjusting wheel lock spring
11 Adjusting wheel
12 Lower wheel cylinder
13 Backing plate

Type FR3 brake assembly (© GM Corp.)

Initial Adjustment

1. Fully release the manual cams.
2. Center each shoe by sliding up or down on its anchor slot until the leading and trailing edges of the lining are equal distant from the inner curl of the support plate.
3. Install the wheel and drum.
4. Rotate the manual adjuster cam in the direction of forward drum rotation, while rotating the drum in the same direction, until the shoe slightly drags on the brake drum. Back off adjuster until drag is just relieved. Use only sufficient adjustment torque to obtain drag that will just allow turning the wheel by hand (approximately 120 to 130 inch lbs.) as excessive torque may damage the adjuster mechanism.
5. Adjust other manual adjuster in the same manner, forward to tighten, and reverse to relieve drag.
6. Lower vehicle and road test. Automatic adjusters should operate from this point and additional manual adjustment should not be necessary.

Wagner Type FR–3

Each brake is equipped with two double-end wheel cylinders which apply hydraulic pressure to both the toe and the heel of two identical, self-centering shoes. The shoes anchor at either toe or heel, depending upon the direction of rotation. Each adjusting screw is threaded into or out of its support by means of an adjusting wheel. Adjusting wheels are accessible through adjusting slots in the backing plate.

BRAKE SHOES

Removal

1. Remove hub and brake drum assembly.
2. Install wheel cylinder clamps to hold pistons in cylinders.
3. Remove brake shoe return springs.
4. Remove lock wires, nuts, and washers from brake shoe guide bolts, then remove brake shoe assemblies.
5. Remove screws attaching adjusting wheel lock springs to anchor supports. Thread each adjusting screw from the shoe side of its anchor support by turning adjusting wheels, then lift adjusting wheels out of slots in anchor supports.

Installation

1. Install adjusting screws and wheels in anchor supports dry; use no lubricant. Insert each adjusting wheel in slot in anchor support, insert threaded end of adjusting screw in anchor support, then turn adjusting wheel to thread adjusting screw into anchor support. Insert anchor pins into holes in anchor supports, with slots in pins facing slots in supports.
2. Install brake shoes with cutaway end of shoe web next to adjusting screw and with ends of shoes engaging slots in wheel cylinder push rods and anchor pins. Install flat washer and nut on each brake shoe guide bolt. Tighten nuts finger-tight, then back off nuts only far enough to allow movement of shoes without binding.
3. Install brake shoe return springs, hooking one end of each spring in brake shoe web, then hook other end over anchor pins.
4. Remove wheel cylinder clamps.
5. Install hub and brake drum assembly.
6. Adjust brakes.

7. After checking pedal operation, road test vehicle.

Wagner Type FR–3A and FR–5A

The FR–3A brake system is basically the same as the FR–3 except in that the FR–3A employs a self-adjuster assembly and the FR–3 does not. Each shoe is individually adjusted to compensate for wear by a link-crank system. This serves to maintain a high, firm brake pedal at all times.

BRAKE SHOES

Removal

1. Remove the hub and brake drum assemblies.
2. Remove the two springs for the automatic adjusters.
3. Remove the two long crank links from the adjuster assemblies by turning back the star wheel cranks until their slots align with the crank link U-hooks. Lift out the links and then slide the S-hooks out of the adjuster cranks.
4. Remove the short crank links by rotating the adjuster cranks until the link U-hooks clear the eccentrics on the brake shoe webs, then remove the small U-hooks from the adjuster cranks.
5. Spread the C-washers for the adjuster cranks and remove the cranks.
6. Remove the hold down bolt which holds the star wheel crank to the anchor support and remove the crank.
7. Remove the adjuster eccentric screw and eccentric from the brake shoe.
8. Remove the two long and the two short brake shoe return springs.

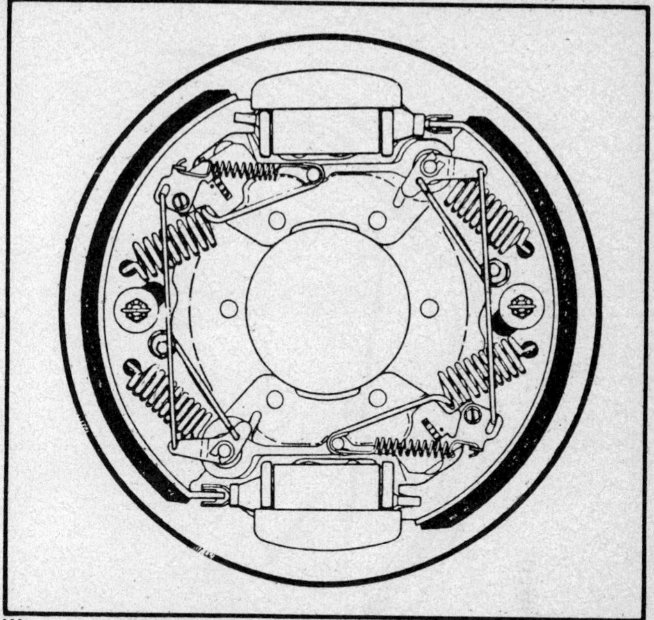

Wagner type FR-3A and FR-5A brake assembly (© Chrysler Corp.)

9. Remove the lock wires, hold-down nuts and washers from the hold down bolt and remove the brake shoes from the backing plate.
10. Thread each star wheel screw out of the anchor support

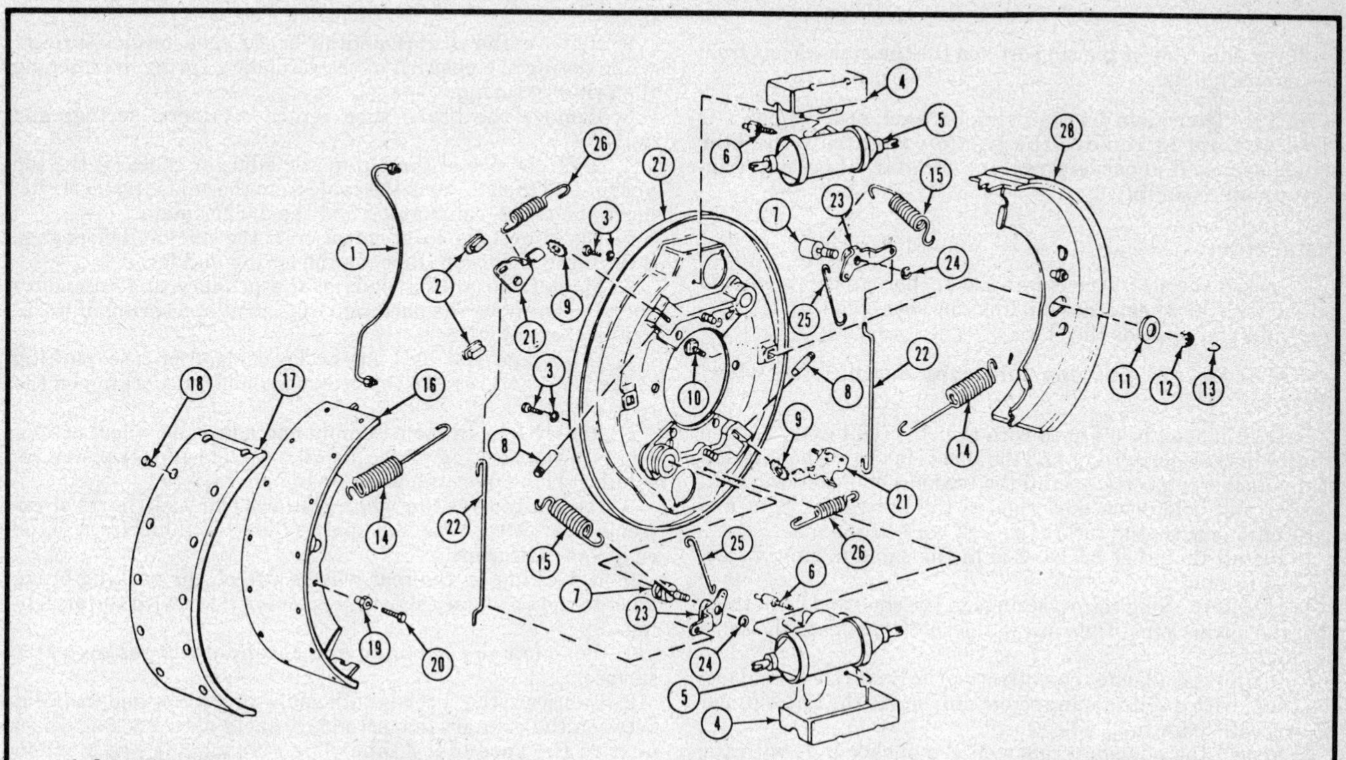

1 Connector tube
2 Adjuster slot cover
3 Screw and lockwasher
4 Wheel cylinder cover
5 Wheel cylinders
6 Bleeder screws
7 Forward-acting anchor pin
8 Starwheel adjuster screw
9 Shoe adjuster starwheel
10 Shoe hold-down carriage bolt
11 Shoe hold-down washer
12 Shoe hold-down castellated nut
13 Hold-down nut lockwire
14 Long shoe retracting spring
15 Short shoe retracting spring
16 Brake shoe
17 Brake lining
18 Rivet
19 Automatic adjuster hex eccentric
20 Eccentric self-tapping screw
21 Starwheel crank assembly
22 Long starwheel crank link
23 Automatic adjuster anchor crank
24 Anchor crank 'C' washer
25 Short anchor crank link
26 Automatic adjuster spring
27 Support plate
28 Complete shoe assembly

Wagner type Fr-3A and FR-5A brake assembly—exploded view (© Chrysler Corp.)

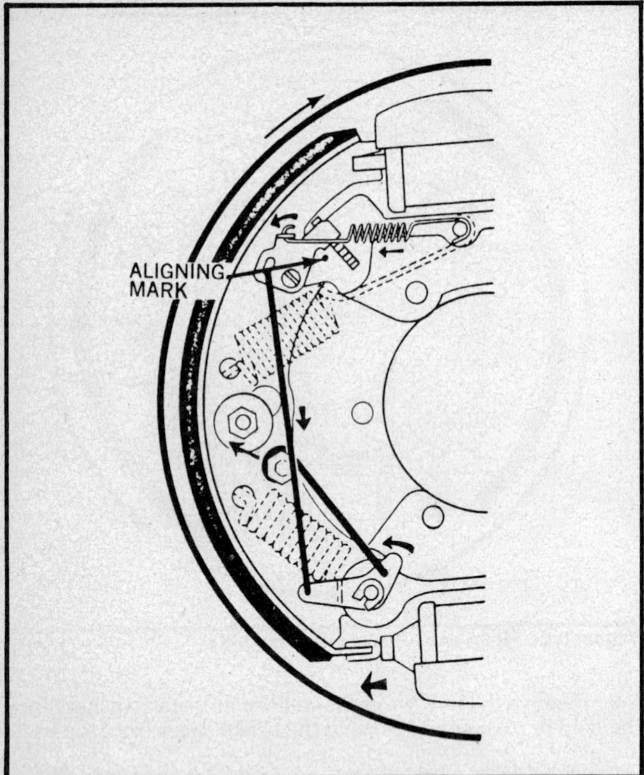

Wagner type FR-3A and FR-5A alignment marks (© Chrysler Corp.)

from the shoe side of the support and lift the star wheels from the support slots.

NOTE: There is a friction ring on each star wheel. DO NOT attempt to remove the friction ring from the star wheel screw. If necessary replace the star wheel and friction as an assembly.

Installation

1. Install the star wheels into the anchor support slots and thread the star wheel screws in from the shoe side with the friction ring end towards the shoe.

NOTE: Do not put any lubricant on the star wheel screws.

2. Position one brake shoe with the "toe" (cut away portion of web) in the adjuster slot and the "heel" in the anchor pin slot of the anchor supports. Install the brake shoe hold down bolt, washer and hold down nut. Tighten the nut finger tight and back off one turn and insert the lock wire in the nut.
3. Install the other brake shoe in the same manner as described in Step 2.
4. Install the long return springs in the shoe and hook them over the anchor pins. Then install the short springs in the same manner.
5. Install the adjuster eccentrics on the brake shoes and fasten them with a self-tapping screw, only make the screw finger tight to allow for final adjustment.
6. Install the adjuster cranks on the anchor pins with the long arm towards the shoe and the bushing towards the backing plate so that they rotate easily while resting against the return springs hooks.
7. Install the C-washer for the adjuster crank and crimp in place.
8. On the anchor support place the star wheel and fasten with the crank bolt.
9. On each adjuster crank assembly install the short links small hook into the short arm of the crank from the lower side and hook the other end of the link around the eccentric on the shoe web.
10. Install the long link S-hook into the long arm of the adjuster crank from the upper side. Then rotate the star wheel crank so the slot lines up with the U-hook on the long link. Insert the hook and rotate the crank back to its adjusting position.
11. Install the adjuster springs with the short hooks on the star wheel crank fingers and the long hook on the outer groove of the anchor pin on the wheel cylinder side.
12. Adjust the brakes in the following manner:
    a. Center the shoes on the backing plate.
    b. On the shoe web, rotate the eccentrics until the linkage aligns the star wheel crank pawl with the center line of the star wheel screw.
    c. When they are aligned, tighten the self-tapping screw to 19 ft. lbs. torque.
    d. Install hub and drum assembly and remove the plugs from the slots in the backing plate.
    e. Adjust the brakes in the normal manner to achieve the required amount of drag on each wheel.
13. Road test the vehicle to check for proper braking action.

Bendix Duo Servo Type

BRAKE SHOES

Removal and Installation

1. With the vehicle raised and supported safely, loosen the parking brake equlizer nut, if working on the rear wheel brakes.
2. Remove the drums andthe brake shoe return springs, while noting the position of the secondary spring overlapping the primary spring.
3. Remove the brake shoe return retainers, springs and nails.
4. Slide the eye of the automatic adjuster cable off the top anchor and then unhook the cable from the adjusting lever. Remove the cable, cable guide and the anchor plate.
5. Disconnect the lever spring from the lever and disengage it from the shoe web. Remove the spring and lever.
6. Spread the anchor ends of the primary and secondary shoes and remove the parking brake strut and spring, if working on the rear wheels.
7. Disengage the parking brake cable from the parking brake lever and remove the brake assembly, if working on the rear wheels.
8. Remove the brake assembly and adjusting wheel assembly from the backing plate. Install a wheel cylinder piston retaining spring over the wheel cylinder.
9. Inspect the backing plate platforms for nick, burrs or extreme wear. After cleaning, apply a thin coat of lubricant to the suypport platforms.
10. If working on the rear wheels, attach the parking brake lever to the secondary shoe and retain in place with the attaching clip.
11. Position the primary and secondary shoes on a flat surface.
12. Lubricate the threads of the adjusting screw and install it between the primary and secondary shoes with the star wheel next to the secondary shoe. The star wheels are marked "R"(right side) and "L" (left side) and indicate their location on the vehicle.
13. Overlap anchor ends of the primary and secondary brake shoes and install the adjusting spring and lever.
14. Hold the brake shoes in their relative position on the backing plate and if working with the rear brake shoes, engage the parking brake cable into the parking brake lever.

15. Retain the brake shoes with the retainer nails, springs and retainer, while installing the rear wheels parking brake strut and spring in position between the two shoes, if working on the rear wheels.
16. Complete the installation of the shoes to the backing plate and install the anchor pin plate.
17. Install the eye of the adjusting cable over the anchor pin and install the return spring between the primary shoe and the anchor spring.
18. Install the cable guide in the secondary shoe. Then install the secondary return spring, being sure the the secondary spring overlaps the primary spring.
19. Place the adjusting cable in the groove of the cable guide and engage the hook of the cable into the adjusting lever.
20. Be sure the adjuster operates satisfactorily and adjust the brake shoes to match the drum diameter.
21. Install the brake drum and retaining clips, make final brake shoe adjustments and prepare for road test.

Two—Piston Single Cylinder Hydraulically Actuated Type

Both shoes pivot on anchor pins at the bottom of the support plate. The shoes are actuated by one wheel cylinder which is of the double piston type. Specifications for heel and toe clearance of the shoes should be strictly followed to obtain efficient brake operation.

BRAKE SHOES

Removal And Installation

1. Back off the adjusting cam and remove the wheel and drum assembly.
2. Remove the brake shoe return spring
3. Install wheel cylinder piston clamp to prevent the pistons from being forced from the cylinder.
4. Remove the C-washer and retainer, guide spring retainer and guide spring from the anchor bolts to remove the brake shoes.
5. To install the brake shoes, reverse the removal procedure.

ADJUSTMENTS

Since tapered brake lining is thicker at the center than at the ends, the adjustment procedures outlined must be performed in order to assure maximum braking efficiency.

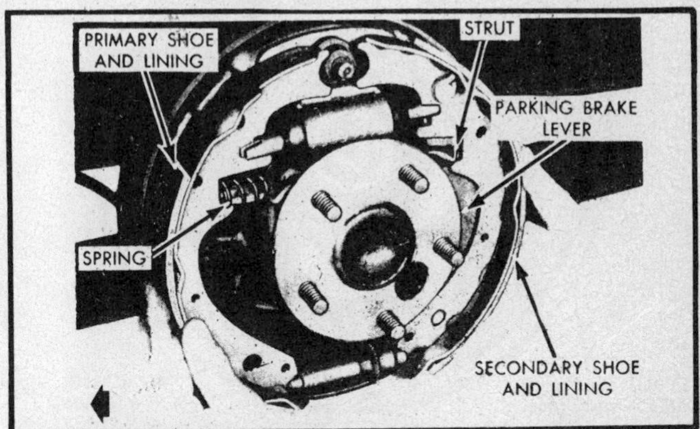

Installing brake shoes (© Chrysler Corp.)

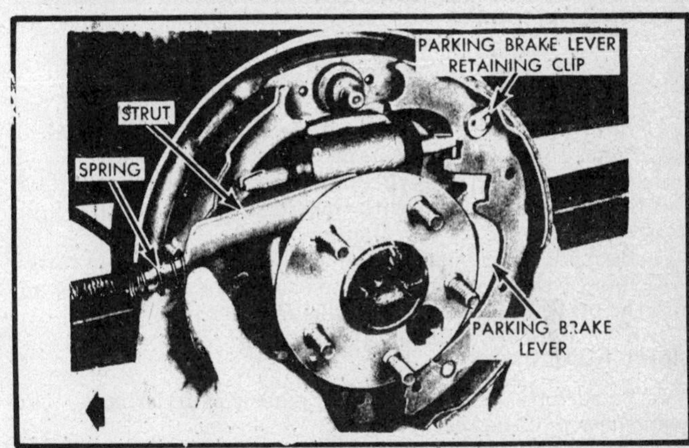

Removing or installing parking brake strut and spring—rear (© Chrysler Corp.)

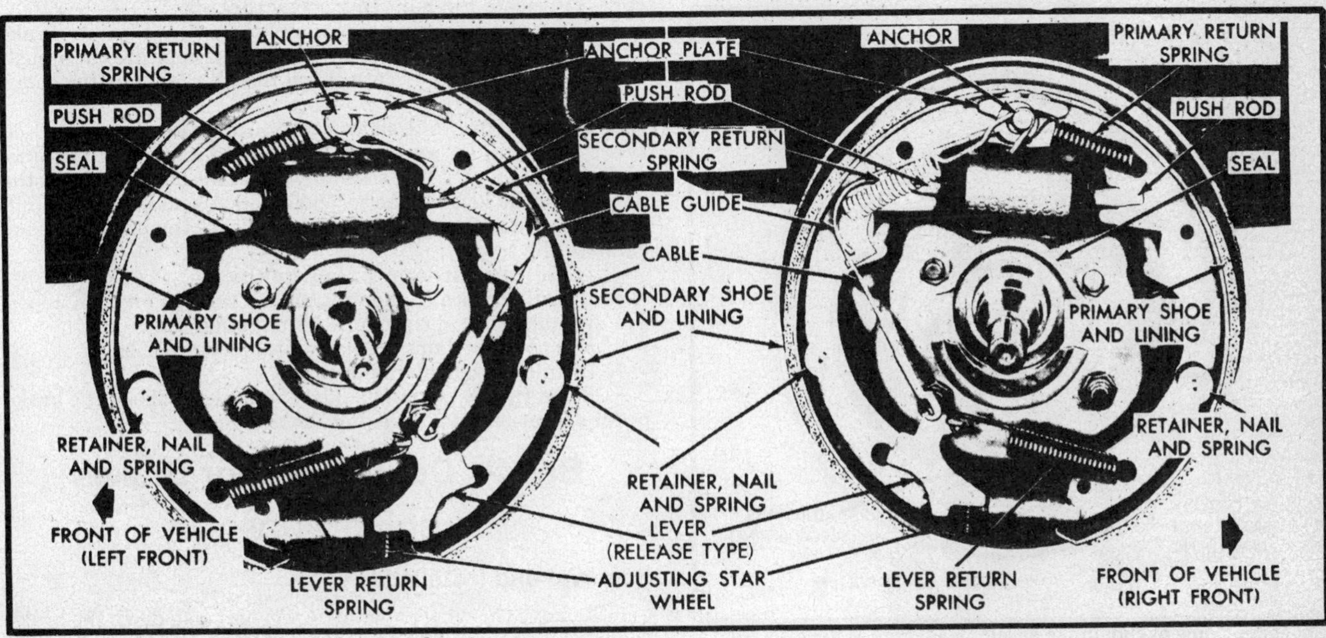

Chrysler front brake assembly (© Chrysler Corp.)

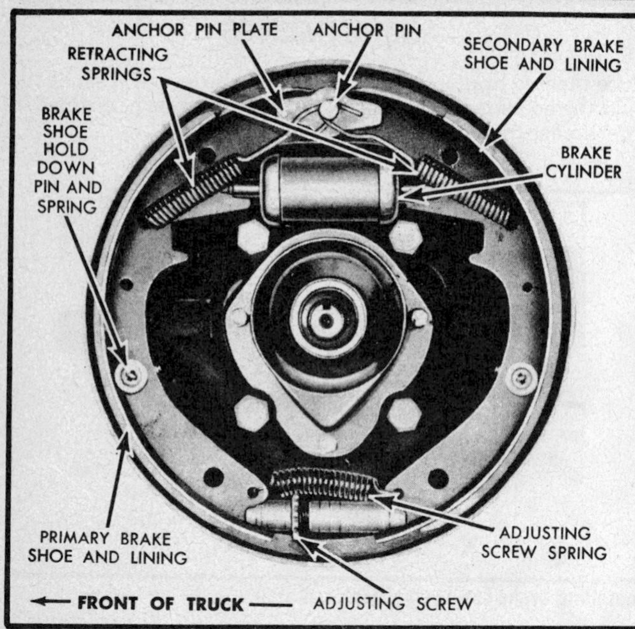

Duo-servo single anchor assembly (© Ford Motor Co.)

Minor Adjustment

1. Raise the vehicle and support safely so that the wheels of the brakes to be adjusted can be rotated freely.
2. While rotating the wheel forward and backward. adjust the shoe out to the drum with the adjusting cam until a light drag is obtained.
3. Back off the adjustment until the wheel is free to turn.
4. Repeat this operation on the other shoe. Continue to adjust the other brake shoes in a like manner.

Major Adjustment

1. Be sure the fluid level in the master cylinder is $^3/_8$–$^1/_2$in. from the top of the reservoir.
2. Loosen the locknuts and turn the brake shoe anchor bolts to the fully released position.

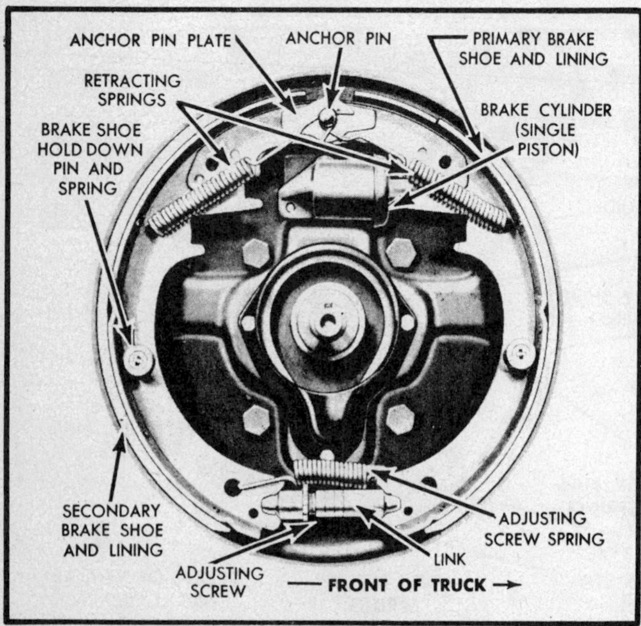

Uni-servo single anchor brake assembly (© Ford Motor Co.)

3. Adjust the anchor bolt and cam, the minor anchor bolt and the minor adjustment cam at the top of the brake shoe to give equal clearance at the toe and heel of the brake shoes. Make sure that sufficient center contact is maintained to produce a slight drag.
4. Lock the anchor adjusting nut. After adjusting the clearance on one shoe, repeat the procedure on the other shoe, then apply the brakes a couple of times to make sure the adjustment is to specifications.

NOTE: Whenever cams are adjusted, check the brakes by applying pressure on the brake pedal several times so as to make sure wheel drag has not increased, since the spring loaded cams may cause shoe adjustment to change by shifting position. Wheels should have a slight drag at room temperature.

Bendix Single Anchor Brakes

BRAKE SHOES

Removal

1. Remove the wheel and drum. Do not push down the brake pedal after the brake drum has been removed. On a truck equipped with a vacuum or air booster, be sure the engine is stopped and there is no vacuum or air pressure in the system before disconnecting the hydraulic lines.
2. Clamp the brake cylinder boots against the ends of the cylinder, and remove the brake shoe retracting springs from both shoes.
3. Remove the anchor pin plate.
4. Remove the hold-down spring cups and springs from the shoes, and remove the shoes and the adjusting screw parts from the carrier plate. Do not let oil or grease touch the brake linings. If the shoes on a rear brake assembly are being removed, remove the parking brake lever, link, and spring with the shoes. Unhook the parking brake cable from the lever as the shoes are being removed.
5. If the shoes are from a rear brake assembly, remove the parking brake lever from the secondary shoe.

Installation

1. Coat all points of contact between the brake shoes and the other brake assembly parts with Lubriplate® or a similar lubricant. Lubricate the adjusting screw threads.
2. Place the adjusting screw, socket, and nut on the brake shoes so that the star wheel on the screw is opposite the adjusting hole in the carrier plate. Then install the adjusting screw spring.
3. Position the brake shoes and the adjusting screw parts on the carrier plate, and install the hold-down spring pins, springs, and cups. When assemblying a rear brake, connect the parking brake lever to the secondary shoe, and install the link and spring with the shoes. Be sure to hook the parking brake cable to the lever.
4. Install the anchor pin plate on the pin.
5. Install the brake shoe retracting springs on both shoes. The primary shoe spring must be installed first.
6. Remove the clamp from the brake cylinder boots.
7. Install the wheel and drum.
8. Bleed the system and adjust the brakes. Check the brake pedal operation after bleeding the system.

Bendix Double Anchor Brakes

BRAKE SHOES

Removal and Installation

1. Remove the wheel and drum. Do not push down the brake pedal after the brake drum has been removed. On trucks

equipped with vacuum boosters, be sure the engine is stopped and there is no vacuum in the system before disconnecting the hydraulic lines.

2. Clamp the brake cylinder boots against the ends of the cylinder, and remove the brake shoe retracting springs from both shoes.

3. At each shoe, remove the 2 brake shoe retainers and washers from the hold-down pins and remove the spring and pin from the carrier plate. Remove the anchor pin retainers and remove the shoes from the anchor pins. Do not allow grease or oil to touch the linings.

4. Clean all brake assembly parts. If the adjusting cams do not operate freely apply a small quantity of lubricating oil to points where the shaft of the cam enters the carrier plate. Wipe dirt and corrosion off the plate.

5. Clean the ledges on the carrier plate with sandpaper. Coat all points of contact between the brake shoes and the other brake assembly parts with high temperature grease.

6. Position the brake shoes on the carrier plate with the heel (lower) end of the shoes over the anchor pins and the toe (upper) end of the shoes engaged in the brake cylinder link. Install the hold-down spring pins, spring, washers and retainers.

7. Install the anchor pin retainers and then install the brake shoe return spring.

8. Turn the brake shoe adjusting cams to obtain maximum clearance for brake drum installation.

9. Install the wheel and drum assembly.

10. Bleed the brake system and adjust the brakes.

11. Check brake pedal operation and road test.

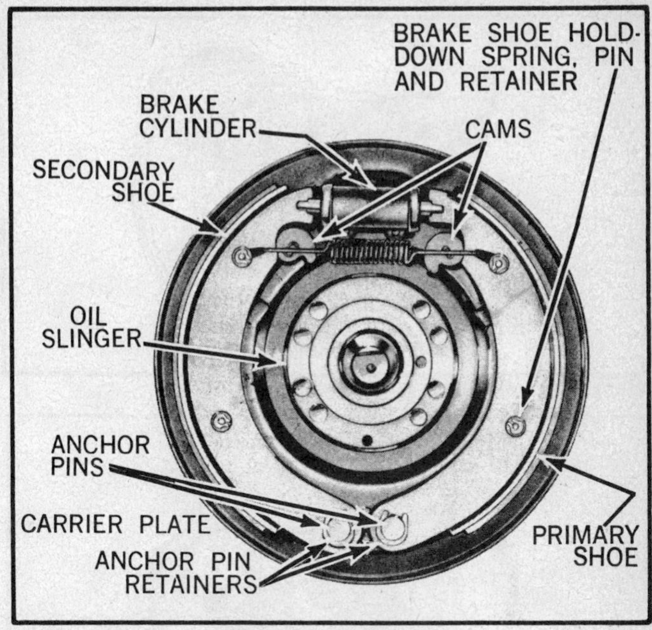

Double anchor brake assembly (© Ford Motor Co.)

Bendix Two Cylinder Brakes

BRAKE SHOE

Removal

1. Remove the wheel, and then remove the drum or the hub and drum assembly. Mark the hub and drum to aid assembly in the same position. On trucks equipped with vacuum or air boosters, be sure the engine is stopped and there is no vacuum or air pressure in the system before disconnecting the hydraulic lines.

2. Clamp the brake cylinder boots against the ends of the cylinder and remove the four brake shoe retracting springs.

3. Remove the brake shoe guide bolt cotter pin, nut, washer, and bolt from both shoes, and remove the shoes from the carrier plate.

4. Remove the clamp-type adjusting wheel lock from the anchor pin support, and unthread the adjusting screw and wheel assembly from the anchor pin support.

Installation

1. Clean the carrier plate ledges with sandpaper. Coat all points of contact between the brake shoes and other brake assembly parts with high temperature grease.

2. Thread the adjusting screw and wheel assembly into the anchor pin support and install the clamp-type adjusting wheel lock. Thread the adjusting wheel into the support so that the brake shoe will rest against the adjusting wheel end.

3. Place the brake shoe over the two brake shoe anchor pins, insert the ends in the brake cylinder links, and install the shoe guide bolt, washer, and nut. Finger tighten the nut, then back off one full turn, and install the cotter pin.

4. Install the four retracting springs.

5. Remove the cylinder clamps, install the drum or the hub and drum assembly, then install the wheel assembly. Align the marks on the hub and drum during installation.

6. Bleed and adjust the brakes.

7. Check pedal operation and road test.

BENDIX BRAKE SHOES

ADJUSTMENT

The brake drums should be at normal room temperature, when the brake shoes are adjusted. If the shoes are adjusted when the shoes are hot and expanded, the shoes may drag as the drums cool and contract.

A minor brake adjustment re-establishes the brake lining-to-drum clearance and compensates for normal lining wear.

A major brake adjustment includes the adjustment of the brake shoe anchor pins as well as the brake shoes. Adjustment of the anchor pin permits the centering of the brake shoes in the drum.

Adjustment procedures for each type of brake assembly are given under the applicable heading.

Minor Adjustment

The brake shoe adjustment procedures for the uniservo single anchor brake assembly are the same as those for the duo-servo single anchor type.

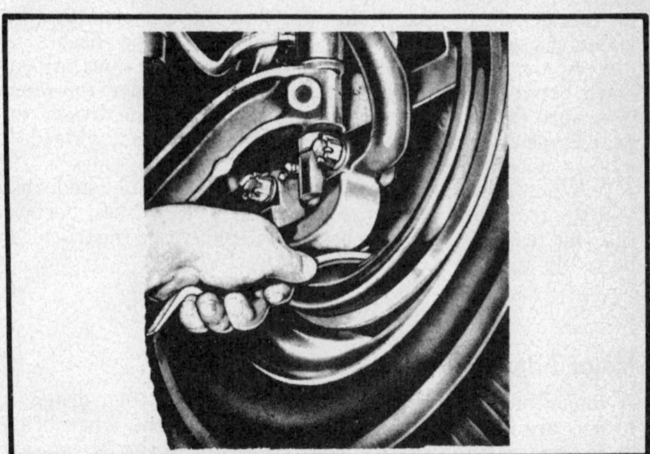
Duo-servo brake adjustment (© Ford Motor Co.)

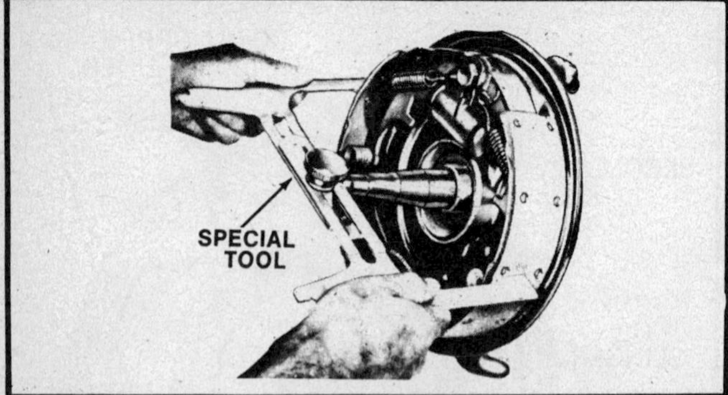

Measuring brake shoes (© Ford Motor Co.)

Measuring brake drum (© Ford Motor Co.)

A major brake adjustment should be performed when dragging brakes are not corrected by a minor adjustment, when brake shoes are relined or replaced, or when brake drums are machined.

Duo—Servo Single Anchor Brake

The duo-servo single-anchor brake is adjusted by turning an adjusting screw located between the lower ends of the shoes.

1. Raise the truck until the wheels clear the floor.
2. Remove the cover from the adjusting hole at the bottom of the brake carrier plate, and turn the adjusting screw inside the hole to expand the brake shoes until they drag against the brake drum.
3. When the shoes are against the drum, back off the adjusting screw 10 or 12 notches so that the drum rotates freely without drag.
4. Install the adjusting hole cover on the brake carrier plate.
5. Check and adjust the other three brake assemblies. When adjusting the rear brake shoes, check the parking brake cables for proper adjustment. Make sure that there is clearance between the ends of the parking brake link and the shoes.
6. Apply the brakes. If the pedal travels more than halfway down between the released position and the floor, too much clearance exists between the brake shoes and the drums. Repeat Steps 2 and 3 above. Internal inspection and/or bleeding may be necessary.
7. When all brake shoes have been properly adjusted, road test the truck and check the operation of the brakes. Perform the road test only when the brakes will apply and the truck can be safely stopped.

SINGLE ANCHOR PIN

Major Adjustment

A major brake adjustment should be made when dragging brakes are not corrected by a minor adjustment, when brake shoes are relined or replaced, or when brake drums are machined.

1. Raise the truck until the wheel clears the floor.
2. Rotate the drum until the feeler slot is opposite the lower end of the secondary (rear) brake shoe.
3. Insert a 0.010 in. feeler gauge through the slot in the drum. Move the feeler up along the secondary shoe unit it is wedged between the secondary shoe and the drum.
4. Turn the adjusting screw (star wheel) to expand the brake shoes until a heavy drag is felt against the drum. Back off the adjusting screw just enough to establish a clearance of 0.010 in. between the shoe and the drum at a point 1 $\frac{1}{2}$ in. from each end of the secondary shoe. This adjustment will provide correct operating clearance for both the primary and secondary shoes. If the 0.010" clearance cannot be obtained at both ends of the secondary shoe, the anchor pin must be adjusted.
5. To adjust the anchor pin setting, loosen the anchor pin nut just enough to permit moving the pin up or down by tapping the nut with a soft hammer. Do not back the nut off too far or the shoes will move out of position when the nut is tightened. Tap the anchor pin in a direction that will allow the shoes to center in the drum and provide an operating clearance of 0.010 in.. Torque the anchor pin nut to 80–100 ft. lbs. Recheck the secondary shoe clearance at both the heel and toe ends of the shoe.
6. When all brake shoes and anchor pins have been properly adjusted, road test the truck and check the operation of the brakes. Perform the road test only when the brakes will apply and the truck can be safely stopped.

Double Anchor Pin

Major Adjustment

1. Raise the truck until the wheels clear the floor.
2. Rotate the drum until the feeler slot is opposite the lower (heel) end of the secondary (rear) brake shoe.
3. Insert a 0.007 in. feeler gauge through the slot in the drum. Move the feeler up along the secondary shoe until it is wedged between the shoe and the drum.
4. Loosen the secondary shoe anchor pin nut. Turn the secondary shoe anchor pin until the brake shoe-to-drum clearance at a point 1 $\frac{1}{2}$ in. from the heel end of the shoe is 0.007 in. Remove the feeler gauge.
5. Rotate the drum until the feeler slot is opposite the upper (toe) end of the secondary brake shoe.
6. Insert a 0.010 in. feeler gauge through the slot in the drum. Move the feeler gauge down along the secondary shoe until it is wedged between the shoe and the drum. Turn the adjusting cam, to expand the brake shoe, until a heavy drag is felt against the drum.
7. Turn the anchor pin until the brake shoe-to-drum clearance at a point 1 $\frac{1}{2}$ in. from the toe end of the shoe is 0.010 in.. Remove the feeler gauge.
8. Torque the anchor pin nut to 80–100 ft. lbs. Recheck the heel and toe clearances.
9. Using the preceding secondary brake shoe adjustment procedure as a guide, adjust the primary brake shoe-to-drum clearance.
10. Road test the truck and check the operation of the brakes.

NOTE: Perform the road test only when the brakes will apply and the truck can be safely stopped.

Kelsey Hayes

FRONT BRAKE SHOES

Removal

1. Raise the vehicle until the wheel clears the floor. Remove the wheel, drum and hub assembly.
2. Clamp the wheel cylinder boots against the ends of the cylinder.

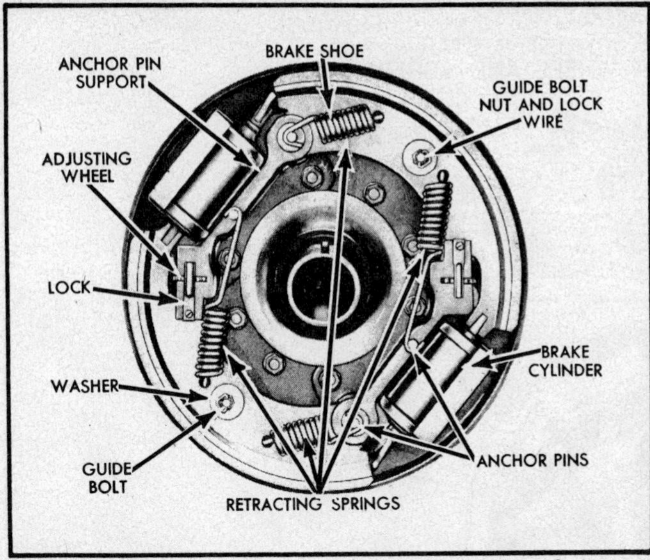

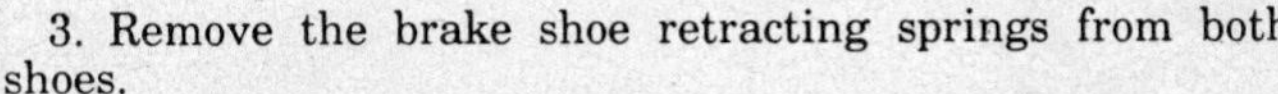
Two cylinder brake—equal length springs (© Ford Motor Co.)

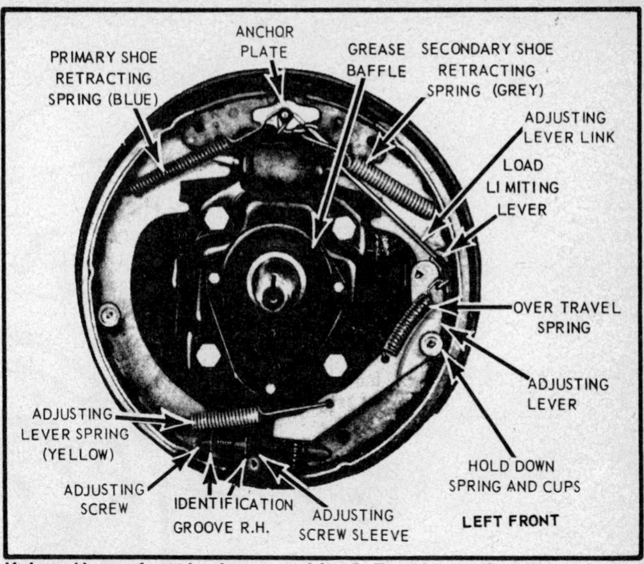

Kelsey-Hayes front brake assembly (© Ford Motor Co.)

3. Remove the brake shoe retracting springs from both shoes.
4. Remove the adjusting lever link, anchor plate and the adjusting lever spring.
5. Remove the hold down spring cups, springs and the adjusting lever.
6. Remove the brake shoes and adjuster screw assembly from the backing plate.

Installation

1. Clean all brake dust from the brake assembly parts with a clean dry rag.
2. Coat all points of contact between the shoes and other brake parts with high temperature grease.
3. Coat the adjuster screw with high temperature grease before assembly. Thread the adjuster screw into the adjuster screw sleeve.
4. Position the brake shoes on the backing plate and install the adjusting lever, hold down pins, springs and cups.
5. Position the adjuster screw assembly on the brake shoes so that the star wheel is opposite the adjusting slot in the backing plate. Install the adjusting lever spring.
6. Install the anchor plate and adjusting lever link.
7. Install the secondary brake shoe retracting spring.
8. Install the primary brake shoe retracting spring.
9. Remove the clamp from the wheel cylinder boots.
10. Install the wheel, drum and hub assembly.
11. Adjust the brakes. Subsequent adjustment will be automatic.

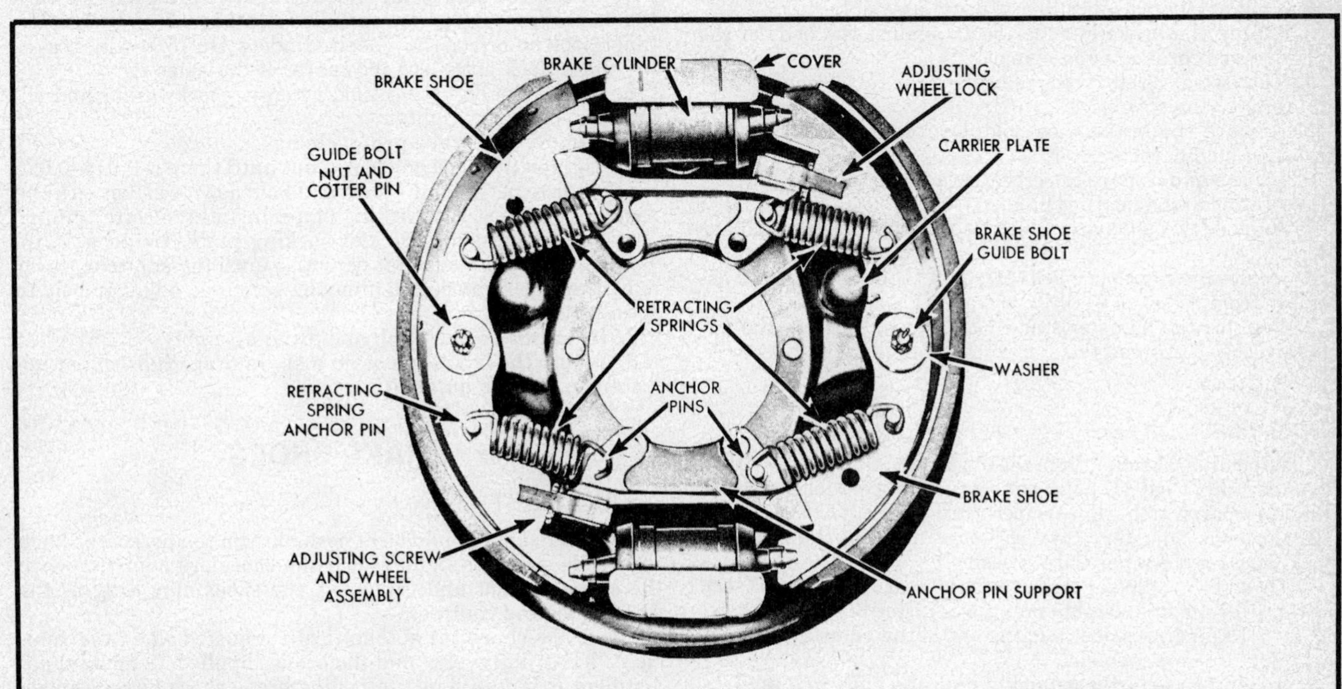

Two cylinder brake—unequal length springs (© Ford Motor Co.)

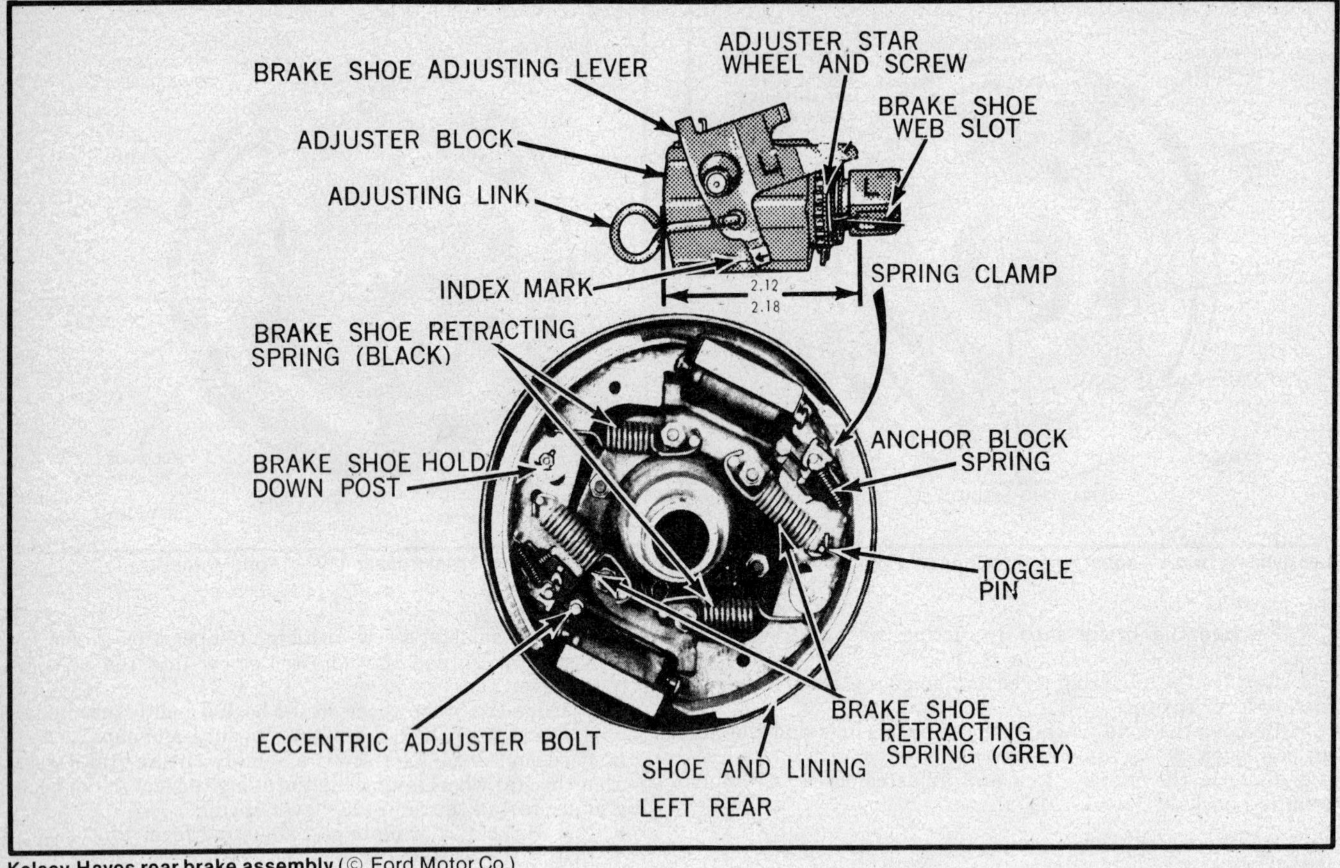

Kelsey-Hayes rear brake assembly (© Ford Motor Co.)

REAR BRAKE SHOES

Removal

1. Raise the truck until the wheel clears the floor.
2. Remove the wheel, hub and drum assembly.
3. Clamp the brake cylinder boots against the ends of the cylinder with brake piston clamps.
4. The two different types of brake shoe retracting springs and remove the springs.
5. Remove the brake shoe hold down post cotter key, nut, and shoe hold down washer.
6. Loosen and remove the eccentric adjuster bolt, lock washer, eccentric and adjusting link.
7. Remove the shoe and lining assembly from the backing plate.
8. Remove the anchor block spring and slide the adjuster assembly from the shoe web.
9. Remove the adjuster star wheel and screw from the adjuster block. Unthread the star wheel from the adjuster screw.

Installation

1. Wipe all brake dust from the brake assembly parts with a clean dry rag. Coat all points of contact between brake shoes and other parts with high temperature grease.
2. Coat the adjuster screw and the inside of the adjuster block with high temperature grease.
3. Thread the adjuster screw onto the star wheel and insert the adjuster screw assembly into the adjuster block. Maintain a 2.12–2.18 in. dimension from the end of the adjuster block to the adjuster screw web slot.
4. Install the adjuster assembly onto the shoe web and attach the anchor block spring.
5. Place the brake shoe over the retracting spring toggle pin and insert the ends of the shoe in the wheel cylinder links.
6. Install the shoe hold down washer and nut. Do not install the cotter pin.
7. Install the four brake shoe retracting springs. Make sure the retracting springs are installed. On 15 × 5 in. brakes the inner hook ends face the wheel cylinders. On 15 × 4 in. brakes the inner hook ends face the center of the axle.
8. Install the adjusting link, eccentric, lockwasher and adjuster bolt. Do not tighten.
9. Remove the brake piston clamps.
10. Tighten the shoe hold down nut until there is 0.015–0.025 in. clearance between the shoe and hold down washer with the shoe held against the backing plate. Install the cotter pin.
11. Center the shoes on the backing plate. Using a $\frac{1}{2}$ in. wrench, rotate the adjuster eccentric until the adjusting lever is at the index mark. Tighten the eccentric adjuster bolt to specification.
12. Install the wheel, hub and drum assembly.
13. Adjust the brake to obtain a slight drag. Subsequent adjustments will be automatic.

BRAKE SHOES

ADJUSTMENT

The brake drums should be at normal room temperature, when the brake shoes are adjusted. If the shoes are adjusted when the shoes are hot and expanded, the shoes may drag as the drums cool and contract.

The brake shoes are automatically adjusted when the vehicle is driven in reverse and the brakes applied. A manual adjustment is required only after the brake shoes have been relined or replaced. The manual adjustment is performed while the drums are removed, using the tool and the procedure detailed below.

When adjusting the rear brake shoes, check the parking brake cables for proper adjustment. Make sure that the equalizer operates freely.

Adjustment of Brake Shoes:

1. Use special drum diameter to lining gauge and adjust the lining to the inside diameter of the drum braking surface.
2. Reverse the gauge and adjust the brake shoes to touch the gauge. The gauge contact points on the shoes must be parallel to the vehicle with the center line through the center of the axle. Hold the automatic adjusting lever out of engagement while rotating the adjusting screw, to prevent burring the screw slots. Make sure the adjusting screw rotates freely.
3. Apply a small quantity of high temperature grease to the points where the shoes contact the carrier plate, being careful not to get the lubricant on the linings.
4. Install the drums. Install the retaining nuts and tighten securely.
5. Install the wheels on the drums and tighten the mounting nuts to specification.
6. Complete the adjustment by applying the brakes several times while backing the vehicle.
7. After the brake shoes have been properly adjusted, check the operation of the brakes by making several stops while operating in a forward direction.

KELSEY HAYES SELF ADJUSTING BRAKES

Adjustment

TWO CYLINDER FRONT BRAKES

Two cylinder front brakes are adjusted by means of exposed, hex-head, self-locking cam adjusters. The brakes are to be manually adjusted initially. Subsequent adjustment is automatic.

Adjustment of Brakes

1. Raise the vehicle and check the front brakes for drag by rotating the wheels.
2. Adjust one shoe by rotating the wheel backward and forward while turning the cam hex-head with a wrench. Bring the shoe out to the drum until a light drag is felt. Do not apply excessive force on the hex head cam, as automatic adjuster parts can be damaged. Back off the adjustment until the wheel turns freely. Adjust the other cam on the same wheel in the same manner.
3. Adjust the other front wheel brake using the procedure above.
4. Apply the brakes and recheck the adjustment.

KELSEY HAYES SELF ADJUSTING BRAKES

Adjustment

Rear Brakes

The brake shoes are automatically adjusted when the vehicle is driven in reverse and the brakes applied. A manual adjustment is required only after the brake shoes have been relined or replaced.

The two-cylinder brake assembly brake shoes are adjusted by turning adjusting wheels reached through slots in the backing plate.

Two types of two-cylinder brake assemblies are used on truck rear wheels. The assemblies differ primarily in the retracting spring hookup, and in the design of the adjusting screws and locks. However, the service procedures are the same for both assemblies.

The brake adjustment is made with the vehicle raised. Check the brake drag by rotating the drum in the direction of forward rotation as the adjustment is made.

1. Remove the adjusting slot covers from the backing plate.
2. Turn the rear (secondary shoe) adjusting screw inside the hole to expand the brake shoe until a slight drag is felt against the brake drum.
3. Repeat the above procedure on the front (primary) brake shoe.
4. Replace the adjusting hole covers.
5. Complete the adjustment by applying the brakes several times while backing the vehicle.
6. After the brake shoes have been properly adjusted, check the operation of the brakes by making several stops while operating in a forward direction.

Rear Brake Assembly Used With Hydro-Max Power Booster

1984 AND LATER

The rear drum brakes are a completely new simplified design incorporating many air brake type features. Shoe and lining removal requires only removal of the two shoe retractor springs. The automatic adjusting mechanisms are part of the wheel cylinder pistons and are submerged in the brake fluid protected from any road contaminants. Automatic adjustment will take place in either forward or reverse direction. The lining blocks, four per wheel, are tapered from $^3/_4$ in. thick in the center to $^5/_8$ in. thick at the ends. There are two lining inspection holes in the backing plate with removable rubber plugs. The lining blocks have a wear limit groove in the edge of the material visible through the inspection holes.The shoes can be backed off manually through two 'adj' access holes in the backing plate for drum removal.

MANUAL ADJUSTMENT AND DE – ADJUSTMENT

Manual adjustment should not be considered as an alternative to the auto-adjuster. It has two functions:

1. To initially set shoe to drum clearance with automatic adjusting brakes, it is important to set the shoe to drum clearance prior to driving the vehicle. To adjust, using the backing plate as a fulcrum, turn the manual override wheel in a counterclockwise direction as viewed when looking down the piston.
2. To de-adjust the brake shoes (where there is a lipped drum condition), remove the plugs from the adjustment holes marked 'ADJ' in the backing plate. Insert a brake adjustment tool or a flat-bladed screwdriver until it engages a slot in the manual override wheel. Use the backing plate as a fulcrum to turn the manual override wheel in a clockwise direction (as viewed when looking down the piston) until the lining clears the drum. Repeat with the other shoe and remove the drum.

BRAKE SHOE AND LINING

Removal

NOTE: Always replace brake shoes and linings in axle sets. When replacing shoes, always replace the return springs to insure proper operation of the auto-adjuster.

1. Raise the vehicle and install safety stands. Remove the wheel and tire assembly.
2. Remove the adjuster plugs from the slots in the backing plate marked 'ADJ'. Remove the adjuster sight hole plugs.
3. Insert a brake adjustment tool or a flat-bladed screwdriver into the adjustment slot until the blade engages the slots in the adjustment wheel. Turn the wheel in a clockwise direction (when viewed looking down the piston) until the shoe and lining clears the drum. Remove the drum.

4. In order for de-adjustment to take place, there must be a load applied to the wheel cylinder pistons. For this reason, fully de-adjust both wheel cylinders before removing the shoes.

NOTE: To avoid locking the auto-adjust mechanism in the fully de-adjusted position, wind out each wheel cylinder piston one complete turn after fully de-adjusting the pistons.

5. Remove the springs, with a removal tool.
6. Insert the removal tool in the loop on the return spring. Rest the fulcrum of the tool against the wheel cylinder body. Unhook the spring from the shoe web. Support the lower shoe and repeat procedure for other spring. Remove the shoes. Remove and discard the springs.

NOTE: Make sure the fulcrum of the tool does not rest on the adjusting wheel or the dust boot.

CAUTION

Do not use an air gun to remove dust from the backing plate. Remove dust with Brake Service Vacuum. Dust may also be removed with a damp rag.

7. Inspect the wheel cylinder/adjuster for leaks by removing the tappet head assembly. Lift the dust boot from the piston. If fluid escapes, rebuild or replace the wheel cylinder/adjuster.
8. Inspect the wheel cylinder/parking brake expander by removing the dust boot and inspecting for leaks. If leaks are present, rebuild or replace the wheel cylinder/expander.
9. If leakage is not evident, install the dust boot and tappet head assembly on the wheel cylinder. Temporarily place an elastic band around the cylinders to keep the pistons in place. Use a wire brush to remove any corrosion from the backing plate, taking care not to damage the wheel cylinder and boots.

Installation

1. Remove the elastic band from the wheel cylinders.
2. Lightly smear the abutment ends of the new shoes and the tips of the steady posts with high temperature grease. Keep the grease away from all hydraulic components and the shoe linings. The replacement brake shoes must be installed correctly to the brake, i.e. the linings are symmetrical on platform, although there is a taper on the shoe, the only way to correct installation is via the web profile.
3. Use the correct color of new shoe return springs. The RED colored springs with one coil is used on wheel cylinder/parking brake expander side of the backing plate on the right and left side. The GREEN colored shoe return spring with two coils is used on the wheel cylinder/adjuster side of the LEFT brake assembly. The YELLOW colored spring with two coils is used on the wheel cylinder/adjuster on the RIGHT brake assembly.

NOTE: After a spring is removed, it must be discarded and replaced with a new spring to insure proper operation of the auto-adjuster.

4. Install the springs on the shoes into position. Insert the end of the spring opposite the loop in the shoe. Use the spring removal-installation tool by placing it in the loop of the spring. Rest the fulcrum of the tool on the wheel cylinder body. Use the tool as a lever to lift up the spring and insert it into the hole in the shoe.

CAUTION

Make sure the fulcrum of the tool does not rest on the manual override wheel or dust boot of the wheel cylinder.

5. Install the drum or spider/drum assembly.
6. Manually adjust the wheel cylinders through the backing plate adjusting holes until the shoe to drum clearance is less than 1.8 mm (0.070 in.). Apply the brake pedal to centralize the shoes and release the brake pedal.
7. Check the shoe to drum clearance by using a feeler gauge placed through the lining inspection holes in the backing plate. If the reading is not 0.51–0.76mm (0.020–0.030 in.), manually adjust the wheel cylinder through the manual override wheel until the specified dimensions are obtained.
8. Bleed the brakes.
9. Install the wheel and tire. Install the lug nuts and tighten.
10. Insert the plugs in the inspection, adjuster slot and adjustment slots in the backing plate.
11. Check the brake fluid level in the master cylinder.

NOTE: The service brake system uses Ford Heavy Duty Brake Fluid, C6AZ–19542–A or –B (ESA–M6C25–A) or equivalent and is filled at the Hydro-Max master cylinder. The parking brake system uses Ford Automatic Transmission Fluid, ESP–M2C138–CJ, DEXRON® II or equivalent and is filled at the brake pump reservoir. DO NOT MIX FLUIDS.

12. Road test vehicle and check brake operation.

WHEEL CYLINDER/PARKING BRAKE EXPANDER

Removal

NOTE: If both the wheel cylinder/adjuster and the wheel cylinder/parking brake expander are to be serviced, the complete backing plate assembly may be removed by disconnecting the fluid lines (service and parking) and removing the bolts retaining the wheel cylinder assemblies and backing plate to the axle flange. Removal of the assemblies can then take place on the bench. IF THE BACKING PLATE ASSEMBLY IS TO BE REMOVED, PRESSURE MUST BE RELEASED BY CAGING THE SPRING IN THE PARKING BRAKE CHAMBER.

1. Attach a tube to the bleeder screw on the wheel cylinder/parking brake expander. Place the other end of the tube in a container. Unscrew the bleeder screw one-half turn. Pump the brake pedal to remove all brake fluid from the rear brake system. Discard the brake fluid.
2. Remove the shoe and lining.
3. Remove the parking brake chamber from the wheel cylinder/parking brake expander.
4. Remove the bolt retaining the bridge tube retainer to the backing plate and remove the retainer. Disconnect the bridge tube from the cylinders and remove the bridge tube.
5. Insert an Allen-head wrench into the bolts in the rear of the backing plate and remove the bolts retaining the wheel cylinder/parking brake expander to the backing plate.
6. Remove the three 9/16–18 in. bolts, nuts and washers retaining the wheel cylinder/parking brake expander and backing plate to the axle flange. Remove the wheel cylinder/parking brake expander and gasket from the backing plate.
7. Remove any rust or corrosion from the backing plate with a wire brush.

Installation

1. Install a new gasket on the wheel cylinder/parking brake expander. Position the assembly on the backing plate.
2. Install the three 9/16–18 in. bolts, nuts and washers retaining wheel cylinder/parking brake expander and backing plate to the axle flange. Tighten the bolts.
3. Install the Allen-head head bolts in the rear of the backing plate retaining the assembly to the plate.
4. Install the parking brake chamber.
5. Connect the bridge tube to the wheel cylinders. Install the bridge tube retainer and tighten the bolt.

6. Install the shoe and lining and adjust the lining-to-drum clearance.
7. Fill the Hydro-Max master cylinder reservoir with clean Heavy Duty Brake Fluid. Bleed the service brakes.
8. If required, bleed the parking brakes. Check the brake pump reservoir with the parking brake applied and if required, fill to the specified level with DEXRON®II or equivalent.

NOTE: The service brake system uses Ford Heavy Duty Brake Fluid, C6AZ–19542–A or –B (ESA–M6C25–A) or equivalent and is filled at the Hydro-Max master cylinder. The parking brake system uses Ford Automatic Transmission Fluid, ESP–M2C138–CJ, DEXRON® II or equivalent and is filled at the brake pump reservoir. DO NOT MIX THE FLUIDS.

9. Apply the brakes and check for leaks. Road test the vehicle and check for proper operation.

WHEEL CYLINDER/ADJUSTER

Removal

NOTE: If both the wheel cylinder/adjuster and the wheel cylinder/parking brake expander are to be serviced, the complete backing plate assembly may be removed by disconnecting the fluid lines (service and parking) and removing the bolts retaining the wheel cylinder assemblies and backing plate to the axle flange. Removal of the assemblies can then take place on the bench. IF THE BACKING PLATE ASSEMBLY IS TO BE REMOVED, PRESSURE MUST BE RELEASED BY CAGING THE SPRING IN THE PARKING BRAKE CHAMBER.

1. Attach a tube to the bleeder screw on the wheel cylinder/parking brake expander. Place the other end of the tube in a container. Unscrew the bleeder screw one half turn. Pump the brake pedal to remove all brake fluid from the rear brake system. Discard the brake fluid.
2. Remove the brake shoe and lining.
3. Disconnect the hydraulic brake line from the fitting on the wheel cylinder/adjuster.
4. Remove the bolt retaining the bridge tube retainer to the backing plate and remove the retainer. Disconnect the bridge tube from the wheel cylinders and remove the bridge tube.
5. Insert an Allen-head wrench into the bolts in the rear of the backing plate and remove the bolts retaining the wheel cylinder/adjuster to the backing plate.
6. Remove the three 9/16–18 in. bolts, nuts and washers retaining the wheel cylinder/adjuster and backing plate to the axle flange. Remove the wheel cylinder/adjuster and gasket from the backing plate.
7. Remove any rust or corrosion from the backing plate with a wire brush.

Installation

1. Install a new gasket on the wheel cylinder/adjuster. Position the assembly on the backing plate.
2. Install the three 9/16–18 in. bolts, nuts and washers retaining the wheel cylinder/adjuster and backing plate to the axle flange. Tighten the bolts.
3. Install and tighten the Allen-head bolts in the rear of the backing plate that retain the assembly to the plate.
4. Connect the bridge tube to the wheel cylinders. Install the bridge tube retainer and tighten the bolt.
5. Connect the hydraulic brake line to the wheel cylinder/adjuster.
6. Install the shoe and lining and adjust the lining-to-drum clearance. Tighten the bleeder screw.
7. Fill the Hydro-Max master cylinder reservoir to the specified level with clean Heavy Duty Brake Fluid. Bleed the service brake system.

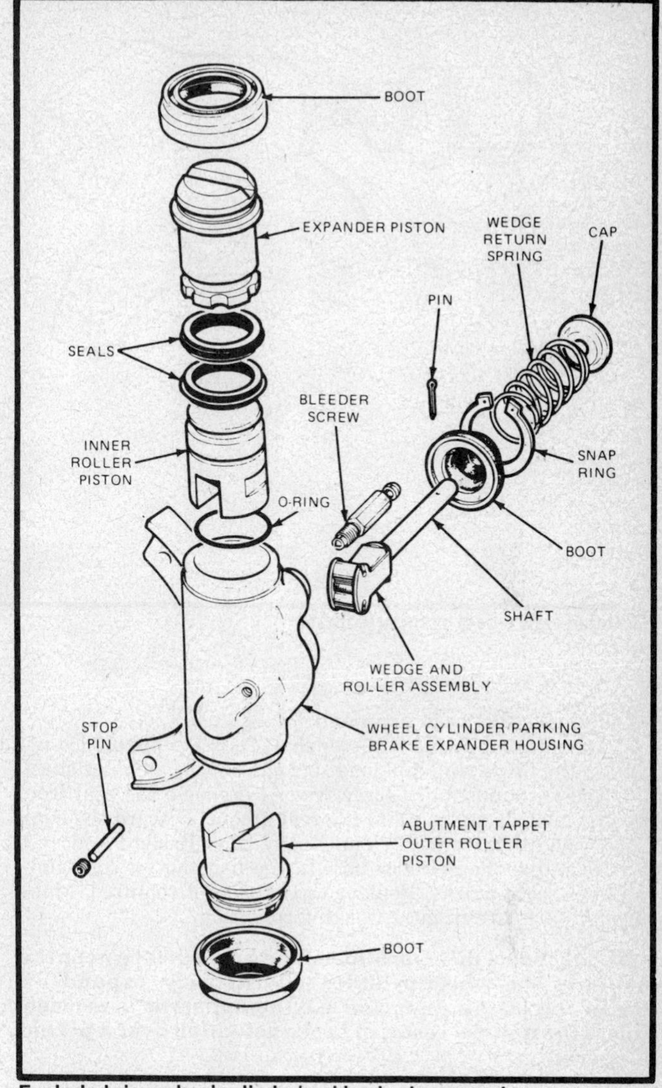

Exploded view wheel cylinder/parking brake expander

NOTE: The service brake system uses Ford Heavy Duty Brake Fluid, C6AZ–19542–A or –B (ESA–M6C25–A) or equivalent and is filled at the Hydro-Max master cylinder. The parking brake system uses Ford Automatic Transmission Fluid, ESP–M2C138–CJ, DEXRON® II or equivalent and is filled at the brake pump reservior. DO NOT MIX THESE FLUIDS.

8. Apply the brakes and check for leaks. Road test the vehicle and check for proper operation.

WHEEL CYLINDER/ADJUSTER

Disassembly

NOTE: Use only clean Heavy Duty Brake Fluid to clean the parts. The same brake fluid is also required for lubrication purposes upon assembly.

1. Make sure cylinder, work bench, tools and hands are clean before proceeding with disassembly.
2. Remove the tappet head and manual adjuster assembly. Slip the dust boot off the housing.
3. Use air pressure to remove both piston and adjuster assemblies from housing. Use care when applying air pressure and removing the piston.

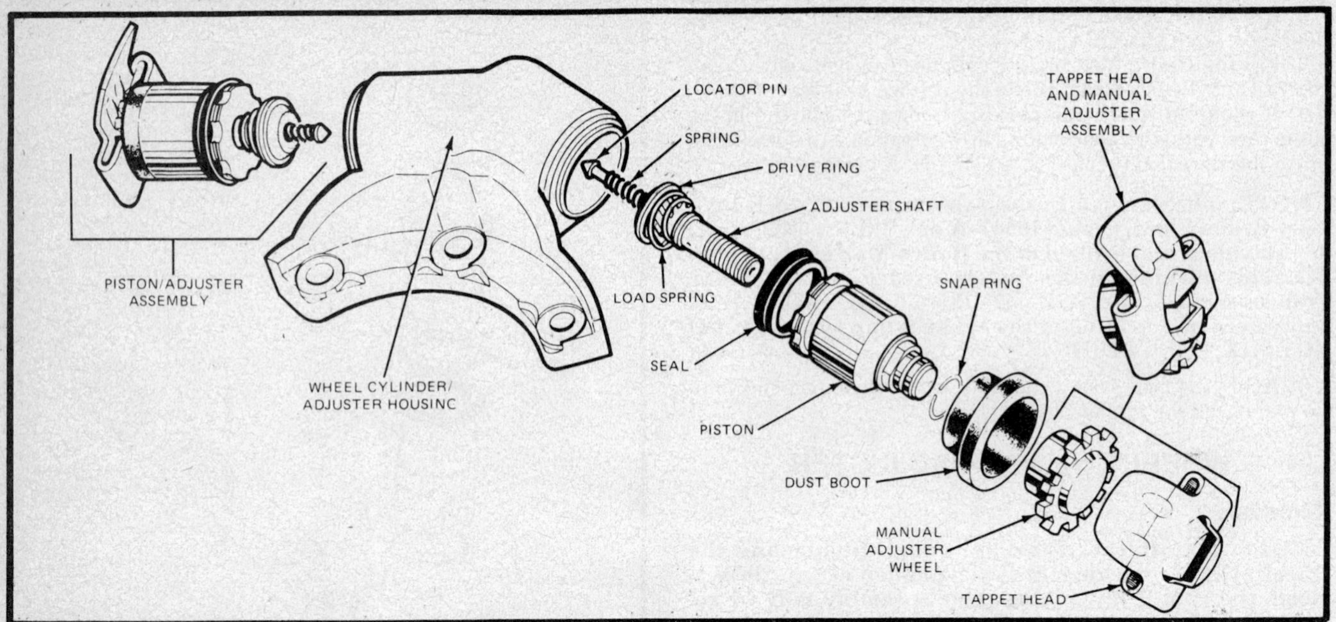

Exploded view wheel cylinder/adjuster

4. Remove the locator pin and spring.
5. Do not remove the adjuster shaft from the piston. Do not remove the drive ring and load spring from the adjuster shaft.
6. Use a round-tipped screwdriver to remove the seal from the piston so as not to score the seal groove. Discard the seal.
7. Wash all parts with clean Heavy Duty Brake Fluid.
8. Examine the cylinder bore in the housing for corrosion, ridges or score marks. Replace the housing if required. Make sure all parts are in good working condition.

NOTE: Some discoloration of the bore surface near the mouth of the wheel cylinder (alternatively 'expander'), and of the piston diameter may be apparent in service. This is the natural result of brake actuation over a peroid of operation.

Assembly

1. Install a new seal in the groove on the piston.
2. Turn the adjuster shaft until it bottoms in the piston and then unscrew the shaft one full turn.

NOTE: It is essential that the adjuster shaft rotates freely in the piston to allow for the initial self-adjuster movement to take place. If the shaft does not rotate freely in the piston or binds, replace the piston and adjuster shaft.

3. Install the spring and locator pin in the adjuster shaft.
4. Lubricate the piston with clean Heavy Duty Brake Fluid. Install the piston assembly in the housing cylinder bore.
5. Install the dust boot onto the wheel cylinder.
6. Install the tappet head and manual adjuster assembly.

NOTE: Do not turn the manual adjuster wheel.

WHEEL CYLINDER/PARKING BRAKE EXPANDER

Disassembly

1. Place the wheel cylinder/parking brake expander in a soft jawed vise.
2. Press down on the shaft and return spring and remove the pin from the shaft. Slowly release wedge return, spring and remove the cap and return spring from the shaft.
3. Remove the snap ring that retains the shaft and boot in the housing. Remove and discard the dust boot.
4. Remove stop pin from the housing.
5. Remove and discard the dust boots from the housing.
6. Remove the abutment tappet outer roller piston.
7. Remove the wedge and roller assembly.
8. Remove the bleed screw.
9. Push the expander piston and the inner roller piston out of the opposite side of the housing.
10. Remove and discard the O-rings and wiper seals from the pistons.
11. Wash all parts in clean Heavy Duty Brake Fluid.
12. Inspect the cylinder bore and pistons for evidence of corrosion, ridges or scoring. Replace, if required.

Assembly

CAUTION

Care must be taken when assembling the wheel cylinder/parking brake expander. Both Ford Heavy Duty Brake Fluid, C6AZ–19542–A or –B (ESA–M6C25–A) or equivalent and a synthetic based grease are used within the housing (BATCO 5–86–B Grease or equivalent or Castrol G 148 or equivalent) because they are compatible with each other. THE USE OF ANY MINERAL BASED GREASE WILL CAUSE CONTAMINATION OF THE SEALS AND MAY RESULT IN BRAKE FAILURE. Use only the specified lubricants.

1. Thoroughly smear the wedge, cage and roller with the grease supplied. Fit the wedge seal to the stem as close to the cage as possible. Insert the assembly into the housing and retain with a new circlip.
2. Coat the outside diameter and the ramp on the abutment tappet outer roller piston with BATCO S–86–B grease or equivalent or Castrol G 148 or equivalent. Install the outer roller piston in the bore so the ramp engages the wedge and roller assembly. Install a new dust boot over the outer roller piston on the housing.
3. Coat the inner roller piston ramp and O-ring with or equivalent and install the O-ring on the piston.

4. Coat the wiper seals with clean Heavy Duty Brake Fluid, or equivalent. Install the wiper seals on the piston so seal lips face the wedge and roller assembly.

5. Install the inner roller piston so the ramp engages the wedge and roller.

6. Install the expander piston in the bore. Install a new dust boot over the expander piston on the housing.

7. Push down on each tappet until the cage and roller is engaged and install the stop pin. Tighten to 21 Nm (16 ft. lbs).

8. Install the return spring and cap over the shaft. Compress the spring with the cap and install the cotter pin. Slowly releasethe spring and cap into position.

NOTE: If the parking brake cable is replaced, prestretch it by applying the parking brake hard about three times before attempting adjustment.

DISC BRAKE SERVICE

Floating Caliper Disc Brakes

This disc brake is a floating caliper design with one or two pistons on one side of the rotor. It is a two piece unit consisting of the caliper and cylinder housing. The caliper is mounted to the anchor plate on two mounting pins which travel in bushings in the anchor plate. The bushings and pins are protected by toot type seals.

Two brake shoe and lining assemblies are used in each caliper, one on each side of the rotor. The shoes are identical and are attached to the caliper with two mounting pins.

The cylinder housing contains the two pistons. The pistons are fitted with an insulator on the front and a seal on the back lip. A friction ring is attached to the back of the piston with a shouldered cap screw. The pistons and cylinder bores are protected by boot seals which are fitted to a groove in the piston and attached to the cylinder housing with retainers. The cylinder assembly is attached to the caliper with two cap screws and washers.

The anchor plate is bolted directly to the spindle. It positions the caliper assembly over the rotor forward of the spindle.

DISC BRAKE SHOE ADJUSTMENT

The front disc brake assembly is designed so that it is inherently self-adjusting and requires no manual adjustment.

DISC BRAKES—TROUBLE DIAGNOSIS

Cause	Correction
1. Master cylinder fluid level low.	1. Fill to proper level with approved fluid. (Fluid level drops as disc brake linings wear.)
2. Poor quality brake fluid (low boiling point) in system.	2. Drain hydraulic system and fill with approved.
3. Air in hydraulic system.	3. Bleed hydraulic system and refill with approved fluid.
4. Hoses soft or weak (expanding under pressure).	4. Replace defective hoses. Combination valve and all cups and seals in complete brakes.
1. Power brake malfunctioning.	1. Check and repair power unit.
2. Linings soiled with brake fluid, oil or grease.	2. Replace shoes and linings.
3. Lines, hoses or connections dented, kinked, collapsed, clogged or disconnected.	3. Repair or replace defective parts.
4. Master cylinder cups swollen.	4. Drain hydraulic system, flush system with brake fluid and replace combination valve and all cups and seals in complete brake system.
5. Master cylinder bore corroded or rough.	5. Repair or replace master cylinder.
6. Caliper pistons frozen or seized.	6. Disassemble caliper and free pistons (replace if necessary).
7. Caliper cylinder bores corroded or rough.	7. Disassemble caliper and remove corrosion or roughness, or replace caliper.
8. Pedal push rod and linkage binding.	8. Free and lubricate.
9. Metering valve not working.	9. Replace combination valve.
GRABBING OR PULLING (Severe Reaction To Pedal Pressure and Out of Line Stops)	
1. Linings soiled with brake fluid, oil or grease.	1. Replace shoes and linings.
2. Caliper loose.	2. Tighten caliper mounting bolts to specified torque.
3. Lines, hoses or connection dented, kinked, collapsed or clogged.	3. Repair or replace defective parts.
4. Master cylinder bore corroded or rough.	4. Repair or replace master cylinder.
5. Caliper pistons frozen or seized.	5. Disassemble caliper and free pistons (replace if necessary).
6. Caliper cylinder seals soft or swollen.	6. Drain hydraulic system, flush system with brake fluid and replace all cups and seals in complete brake system.
7. Caliper cylinder bores corroded or rough.	7. Disassemble caliper and remove corrosion or roughness, or replace caliper.

DISC BRAKES—TROUBLE DIAGNOSIS

Cause	Correction
8. Pedal linkage binding (and suddenly releasing).	8. Free and lubricate linkage.
9. Metering valve not functioning properly.	9. Replace combination valve.
FADING PEDAL (Pedal Falling Away Under Steady Pressure)	
1. Poor quality brake fluid (low boiling point) in system.	1. Drain hydraulic system and fill with approved fluid.
2. Hydraulic connections loose; lines or hoses ruptured (causing leakage).	2. Tighten or replace defective parts.
3. Master cylinder cup worn or damaged. (primary, secondary or both).	3. Repair master cylinder.
4. Master cylinder bore corroded, worn or scored.	4. Repair or replace master cylinder.
5. Caliper cylinder seals worn or damaged.	5. Replace seals.
6. Caliper cylinder bores corroded, worn or scored.	6. Disassemble caliper and remove corrosion or scoring, or replace caliper.
7. Bleed screw open.	7. Close bleed screw and bleed hydraulic system.
NOISE AND CHATTER (May Be Accompanied By Brake Roughness and Pedal Pumping)	
1. Disc has excessive lateral runout.	1. Replace or machine disc.
2. Disc has excessive thickness variations (out of parallel).	2. Replace or machine disc.
3. Disc has casting imperfections.	3. Replace disc.
4. Car creeping or moving slowly with brakes applied (may produce groan or crunching noise).	4. Increase or decrease pedal effort slightly.
5. Squeal, during application.	5. A small amount of high-pitched squeal is inherent in disc brake design and must be considered normal. Some relief may be obtained with service package backing.
DRAGGING BRAKES (Slow or Incomplete Release of Brakes)	
1. Lines, hoses or connections dented, kinked, collapsed or clogged.	1. Repair or replace defective parts.
2. Master cylinder compensating port restricted by swollen primary cup.	2. Drain hydraulic system, flush system with brake fluid and replace combination valve and all cups and seals in complete brake system.
3. Residual pressure check valve in lines to front wheels.	3. Remove check valve.
4. Caliper pistons frozen or seized.	4. Disassemble caliper and free pistons (replace if necessary).
5. Caliper cylinder seals swollen.	5. Drain hydraulic system, flush system with clean brake fluid and replace combination valve and all cups and seals in complete brake system.
6. Caliper cylinder bores corroded or rough.	6. Disassemble caliper and remove corrosion or roughness, or replace caliper.
7. Hydraulic push rod on power brake out of adjustment or binding (causing primary cup to restrict master cylinder compensating port).	7. Adjust or free and lubricate.

Automatic adjustment for lining wear is achieved by the piston and friction ring sliding outward in the cylinder bore. The piston assumes a new position in the cylinder and maintains the correct adjustment.

FRONT DISC BRAKE SHOE AND LINING

NOTE: Refer to following section for caliper and pad service for the Ford Ranger and Bronco II.

Replace shoe and lining assemblies when lining is worn to a minimum of $\frac{1}{16}$" in thickness (combined thickness of shoe and lining $\frac{1}{4}$ in. minimum).

Removal

1. Remove the shoe and lining mounting pins, anti-rattle springs and old shoe and lining assemblies.

Installation

1. Remove the master cylinder cover.
2. Loosen the piston housing-to-caliper mounting bolts sufficiently to permit the installation of new shoe and lining assemblies. Do not move pistons.
3. Install new shoe and lining assemblies. Install the brake shoe mounting pins and anti-rattle springs. Be sure that the spring tangs are located in the holes provided in the shoe plates.
4. Torque the brake shoe mounting pins to 17–23 ft. lbs.
5. Reset the pistons to the correct location in the cylinders by placing shims or feeler gauges of 0.023–0.035 in. thickness between the shoe plate of the outboard shoe and lining assembly and the caliper; then, retighten the piston housing-to-caliper mounting bolts. Keep the cylinder housing square with the caliper.

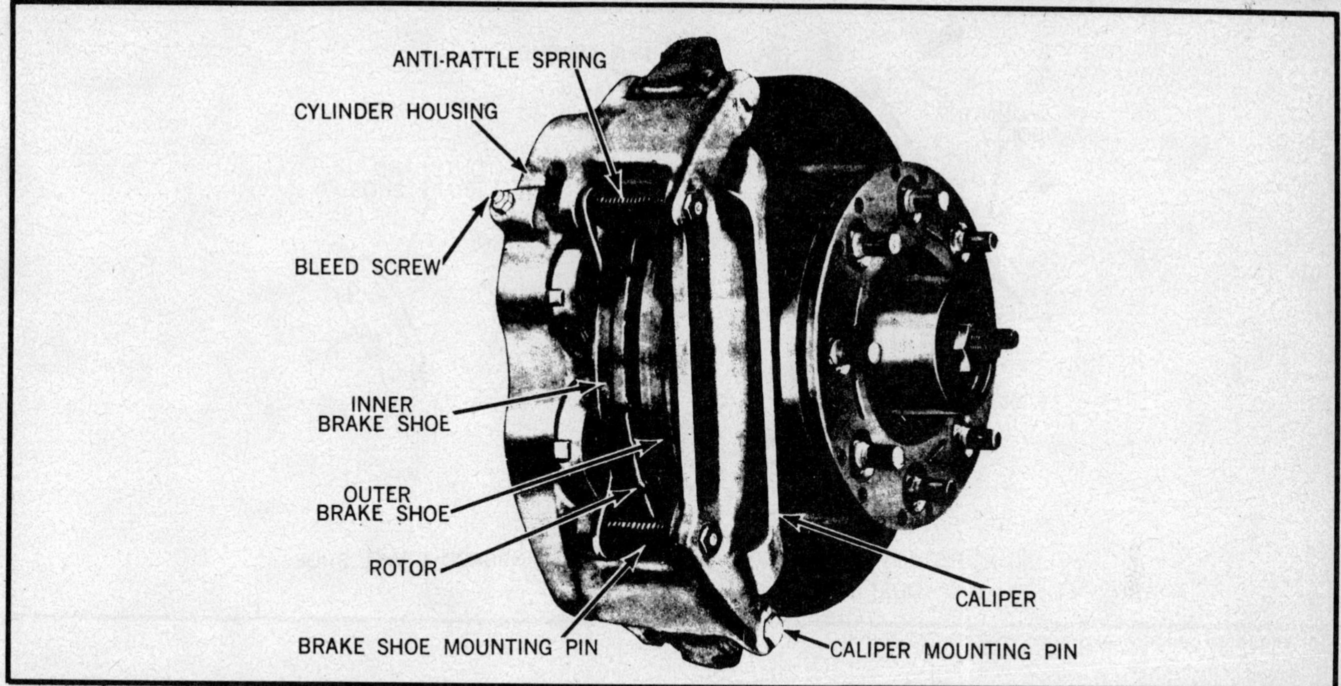

Floating disc brake caliper (© Ford Motor Co.)

6. Loosen the piston housing-to-caliper mounting bolts and remove the shims.
7. Torque the piston housing-to-caliper mounting bolts to 155–185 ft. lbs.
8. Check the master cylinder reservoirs.
9. Install the master cylinder cover.

DISC BRAKE CALIPER

Removal

1. Remove the wheel and tire assembly.
2. Remove the pins and nuts retaining the caliper assembly to the anchor plate.
3. Disconnect the brake hose from the caliper and remove the caliper.

Installation

1. Connect the brake hose to the caliper.
2. Position the caliper assembly to the anchor plate and install the retaining pins and nuts. Torque the nuts to specifications.
3. Install drum and wheel and bleed brake system.

NOTE: If the caliper assembly is leaking, the piston assemblies must be removed from the piston housing and replaced. If the cylinder bores are scored, corroded or ex-

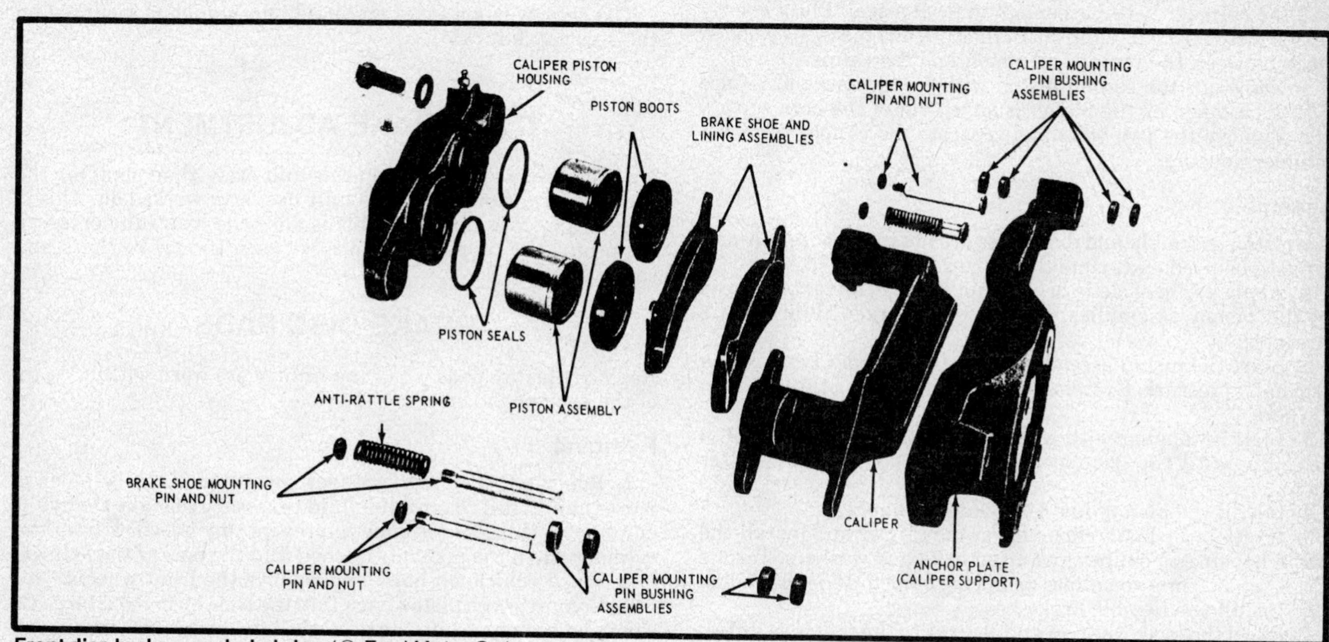

Front disc brake—exploded view (© Ford Motor Co.)

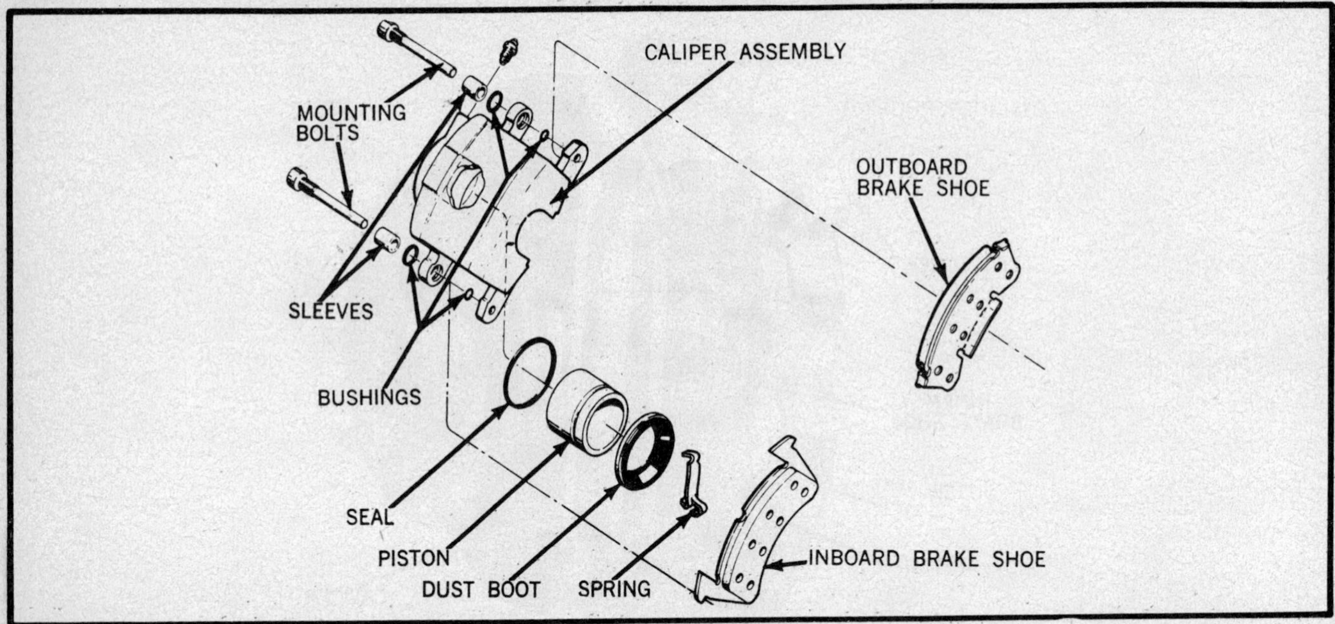

Bolt mounted caliper—exploded view (© GM Corp.)

cessive wear is evident, the piston housing must be replaced. Do not hone the cylinder bores. Piston assemblies are not available for oversize bores. The piston housing must be removed from the caliper for replacement.

Disassembly

1. Remove the two pins and nuts retaining the caliper to the support. Disconnect the flexible brake hose and plug the end to prevent brake fluid leakage.
2. Remove the boot retainers and remove the dust boots from the pistons and cylinder housing.
3. Position the caliper assembly in a vise.
4. Place a block of wood between the caliper and the cylinders, and apply low pressure air to the brake hose inlet. One piston will be forced out.
5. Reverse the piston and install it by hand pressure back into the cylinder bore far enough to form a seal. Block the reversed piston from moving out of the bore and place the wooden block between the remaining piston and the caliper.
6. Force out the second piston with low pressure air. Care should be taken as the piston is forced out of the bore.
7. Remove the two bolts and separate the caliper from the cylinder housing.

Assembly

The piston assembly and dust boots are not to be reused. A new set is to be used each time the caliper is assembled.

1. Apply a film of clean brake fluid in the cylinder bores and on the piston assemblies. Do not apply brake fluid on the insulators.
2. Start the piston assemblies into the cylinder bores using firm hand pressure. Exercise care to avoid cocking the piston in the bore.
3. Lightly tapping with a rawhide mallet, seat each piston assembly until the friction ring bottoms out in the cylinder bore.
4. Install the piston dust boots and retainers.
5. Position the piston housing on the caliper and install the piston housing-to-caliper mounting bolts and washers. Torque the piston housing-to-caliper mounting bolts to 155–185 ft. lbs.
6. Install the flexible brake hose.
7. Bleed the brake system and centralize the pressure differential valve.

NOTE: Do not move the vehicle after working on the disc brakes until a firm brake pedal is obtained.

Sliding Caliper Disc Brakes—Single Piston

CHRYSLER CORP. AND GENERAL MOTORS CORP. TYPES

This caliper is a one piece type with a single piston on the inboard side. The piston is made of steel and is plated to resist wear and corrosion. The piston has a square cut seal which provides for a seal between the piston and the caliper cylinder wall. A rubber dust boot located in a groove in the cylinder helps keep contamination from the piston and cylinder wall.

The caliper is mounted on an adapter which is mounted on the steering knuckle.

DISC BRAKE ADJUSTMENT

No adjustment is required on this unit other than applying the pedal several times after the unit has been worked on. This is to seat the shoes and after this is done the hydraulic pressure maintains the proper clearance between the brake shoes and the rotor.

BRAKE DISC PADS

Replace the disc pads when the linings are worn within $^1/_{16}$ in. of the shoe or the rivets.

Removal

1. Remove the master cylinder cover and if the cylinder is more than $^1/_3$ full remove the fluid necessary to make the cylinder only $^1/_3$ full. This is done to prevent any overflow from the cylinder when the piston is pushed into the bore of the caliper.
2. Raise vehicle on hoist and remove the front wheels.
3. Compress the piston back into the bore by using a large C-clamp and compressing the unit until the piston bottoms in the bore.

4. Remove the two retaining bolts that hold the caliper into the support. If the caliper has retaining clips remove the retaining clips and anti-rattle springs. If the caliper has key type retainers, remove the key retaining screws, and using a hammer and drift, punch drive the key out of the caliper.

5. Slide the caliper off the rotor disc. Be careful not to damage the dust boot on the piston when removing the caliper.

NOTE: Do not let the caliper hang with the brake hose supporting the weight. This can cause damage to the hose which could result in a loss of brakes. Set the caliper on the front suspension arm or tie rod.

6. Remove the outer shoe from the caliper. It may be necessary to tap the shoe to loosen it from the caliper. Remove the inner shoe from the caliper or spindle assembly depending on where the shoe stays.

7. Remove the shoe support spring from the piston.

Cleaning and Inspection

Clean the sliding surfaces of the caliper and clean any dirt from the mounting bolts, clips or keys.

Inspect the boot on the piston for signs of cracks, cuts or other damage. Check to see if there is signs of fluid leaking around the seal on the piston. This will show up in the boot. If there is an indication of a fluid leak, the entire caliper has to be disassembled and the seal replaced.

Installation

1. Make sure that the piston is fully bottomed in the cylinder bore and install the outboard shoe in the recess of the caliper.

NOTE: On shoes with anti-rattle springs be sure to install the spring before installing the shoe in the caliper.

2. Place the outer shoe on the caliper and press it into place with finger pressure.

3. Position the caliper on the rotor and carefully slide it down into position over the rotor.

4. Install the caliper mounting bolts and torque them to 35 ft. lbs. On models with retaining clips install the anti-rattle springs and the retaining clips and torque the retaining screws to 200 inch lbs. On models with key type retainers press down the caliper and install the key in its slot and drive it in place with a hammer and drift. Install the retaining screw and torque to 12–18 ft. lbs.

5. Install the wheels and lower the vehicle. Check the master cylinder fluid level and add any fluid necessary to bring it up to the proper level.

6. Pump the brake pedal several times until a firm brake pedal is established. Road test the vehicle to check for proper operation.

DISC CALIPER

Removal

1. Remove the cover on the master cylinder and check if the fluid level is 1/3 full. If it is more than 1/3 full remove the necessary amount to bring the level down. This step is necessary to avoid overflow from the master cylinder when the piston is compressed into the cylinder bore.

2. Raise the vehicle and remove the wheel.

3. Compress the piston into the caliper bore and remove the brake hose from the caliper. Tape the end of the hose to prevent dirt from entering the line.

4. Remove the caliper retaining bolts, clips or wedges and remove the caliper from the vehicle.

Disassembly

1. Clean the outside of the caliper with clean brake fluid and drain any fluid from the caliper.

2. Remove the piston from the caliper by connecting the hydraulic line to the caliper and gently stroking the brake pedal. This will push the piston from the caliper bore.

3. With care remove the boot from the caliper piston bore.

4. Remove the piston seal from the caliper bore using a piece of wood or plastic.

NOTE: DO NOT use a metal tool to remove the seal. This can damage the bore or burr the edges of the seal groove.

5. Remove the bleeder valve.

Cleaning and Inspection

1. Clean all the parts with clean brake fluid and blow out all the passages in the caliper.

NOTE: When ever the caliper is disassembled, discard the boot and piston seal. These parts must not be reused.

2. Inspect the outside of the piston for signs of wear, corrosion, scores or any other defects. If any defects are detected replace the piston.

3. Check the caliper bore for the same defects as the piston. However, the bore can be cleaned up to a point with crocus cloth. If there are any marks that will not clean up with the cloth the caliper must be replaced.

Assembly and Installation

1. Lube the caliper bore and the piston with clean brake fluid and position the seal for the piston in the cylinder bore groove.

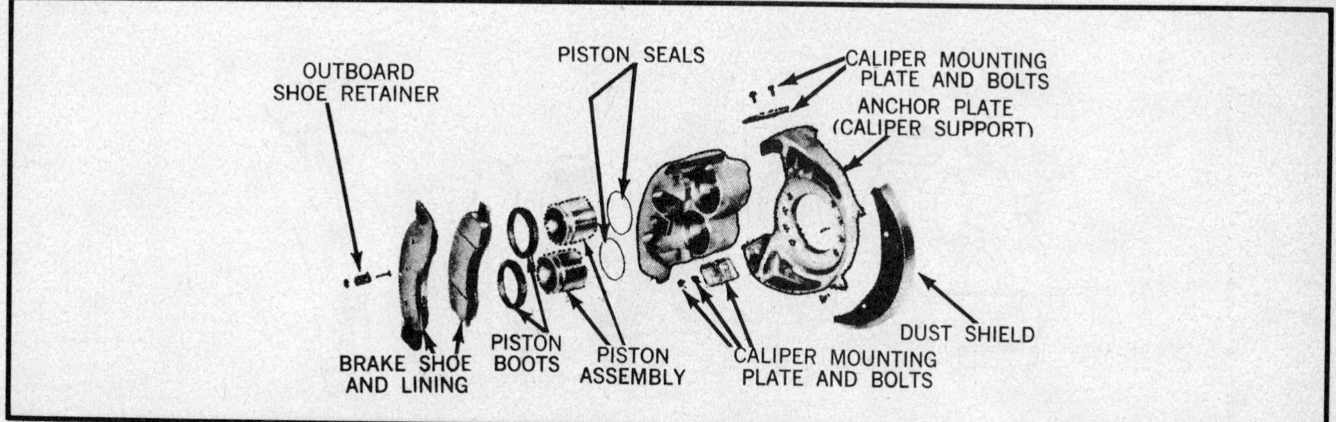

Sliding caliper disc brakes—bouble piston (© Ford Motor Co.)

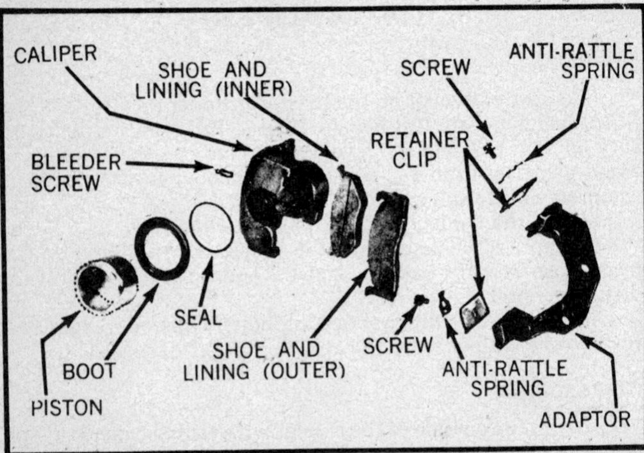

Caliper assembly retaining clip (© Chrysler Corp.)

2. Install the dust boot into the groove in the piston with the fold faces toward the open end of the piston.
3. Install the piston in the bore being careful not to unseat the piston seal in the bore.
4. With the piston bottomed in the cylinder position the boot in the groove in the caliper. Make sure that the retaining ring in the seal is pressed down evenly around the cylinder.

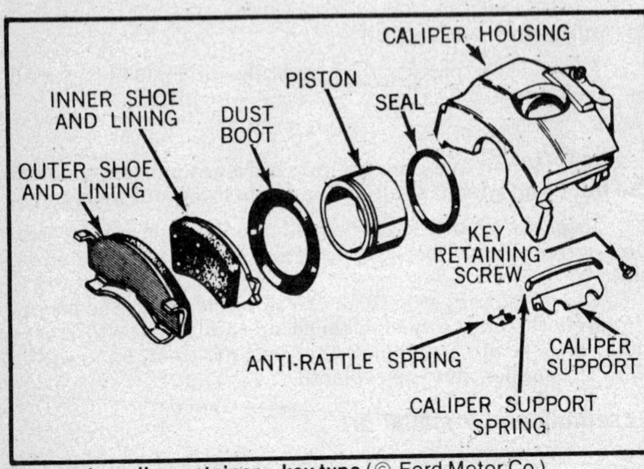

Disc brake caliper retainer—key type (© Ford Motor Co.)

5. Install the bleeder screw in the caliper and install the caliper back on the vehicle.
6. Connect the brake hoses and bleed the calipers of air. When bleeding is done pump the pedal several times to develop a firm brake pedal.

Sliding Caliper Disc Brakes (Double Piston)

BRAKE SHOE AND CALIPER

Removal

1. Drain about $^2/_3$ of the total brake fluid from the reservoir.
2. Jack up the vehicle and remove the front wheels.
3. Remove the four screws and remove the caliper hold-down assembly.
4. Lift the caliper off the hub and rotor. If the caliper is to be removed, disconnect the hydraulic line; if not, lay the caliper on the susp^nsion or support with a length of wire.
5. Remove the inner and outer shoe and lining.

Disassembly

1. Drain the brake fluid from the caliper and clean the exterior with clean brake fluid.
2. Place a small block of wood under the caliper pistons and place a protective pad over the exterior. Remove the pistons by directing compressed air into the caliper fluid outlet.
3. Remove and discard piston boots.
4. Remove the piston seals from the groove in the caliper bore.

Assembly

1. Clean all parts in clean brake fluid and blow dry.
2. Dip the new piston seal in clean brake fluid and install it into the cylinder groove.

NOTE: Be sure that the seal is not rolled or twisted in the groove.

3. Install the dust boot in the cylinder groove.
4. Coat the outside diameter of the piston with clean brake fluid. Use something plastic or wood and gradually work the dust boot around the piston.
5. Press the piston straight into the caliper bore until it bottoms. Position the boot in the piston groove.

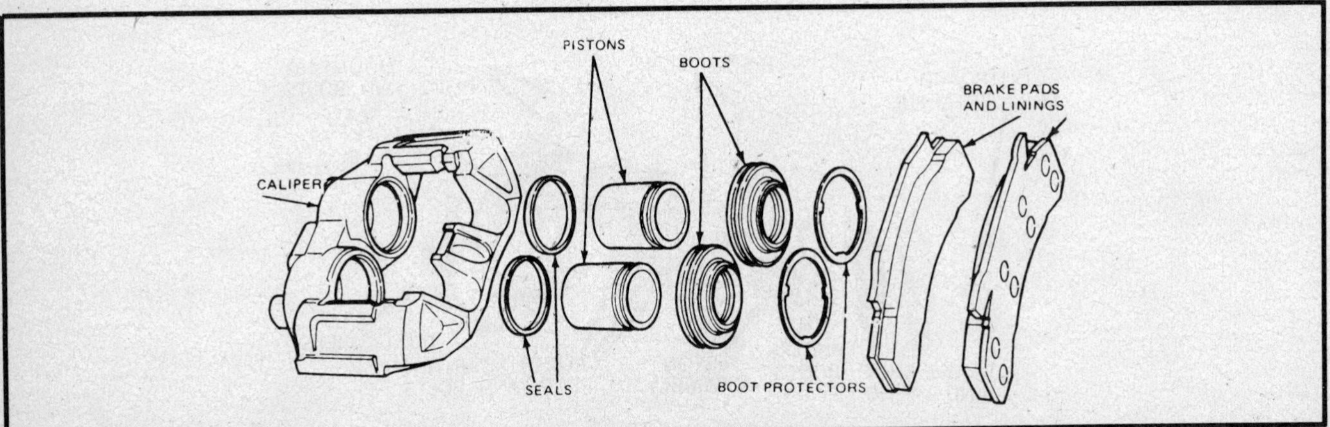

Rail slider caliper—6000 and 7000 pound front axle

Installation

1. Install a new shoe and lining assembly into the anchor plate.
2. Push the pistons to the bottom of the piston bore. Place a small block of wood over both pistons and boots. Push the pistons to the bottom of the bores with a C-clamp.
3. Install the outer shoe and lining onto the caliper and install the shoe hold-down spring and pin.
4. Install the caliper assembly over the hub, rotor and inner shoe, and position into the inner grooves in the anchor plate.
5. Install the caliper hold-down parts and tighten to 40 ft. lbs.
6. Add extra heavy duty brake fluid to bring the level to $^1/_4$ in. from the top of the reservoir.
7. Bleed the system and add fluid as necessary.

DISC BRAKES

Ford Ranger and Bronco II

INSPECTION

Replace the front pads when the pad thickness is at the minimum thickness recommended by Ford Motor Co. ($^1/_{32}$ in.), or at the minimum allowed by the applicable state or local motor vehicle inspection code. Pad thickness may be checked by removing the wheel and looking through the inspection port in the caliper assembly.

FRONT CALIPER AND DISC BRAKE PADS

Removal & Installation

NOTE: Always replace all disc pad assemblies on an axle. Never service one wheel only.

1. To avoid fluid overflow when the caliper piston is pressed into the caliper cylinder bores, siphon or dip part of the brake fluid out of the larger master cylinder reservoir (connected to the front disc brakes). Discard the removed fluid.
2. Raise the vehicle and install jack stands. Remove a front wheel and tire assembly.
3. Place an eight in. C-clamp on the caliper and tighten the clamp to bottom the caliper piston in the cylinder bore. Remove the clamp.

NOTE: Do not use a screwdriver or similar tool to pry piston away from the rotor.

4. There are three types of caliper pins used: a single tang type, a double tang type and a split-shell type. The pin removal process is dependent upon how the pin is installed (bolt head direction). Remove the upper caliper pin first.

NOTE: On some applications, the pin may be retained by a nut and torx-head bolt (except the split-shell type).

5. If the bolt head is on the outside of the caliper, use the following procedure:
   a. From the inner side of the caliper, tap the bolt within the caliper pin until the bolt head on the outer side of the caliper shows a separation between the bolt head and the caliper pin.
   b. Using a hacksaw or bolt cutter, remove the bolt head from the bolt.
   c. Depress the tab on the bolt head end of the upper caliper pin with a screwdriver, while tapping on the pin with a hammer. Continue tapping until the tab is depressed by the v-slot.
   d. Place one end of a punch ($^1/_2$ in. or smaller) against the end of the caliper pin and drive the caliper pin out of the caliper toward the inside of the vehicle. Do not use a screwdriver or other edged tool to help drive out the caliper pin as the v-grooves may be damaged.

CAUTION

Never reuse caliper pins. Always install new pins whenever a caliper is removed.

6. If the nut end of the bolt is on the outside of the caliper, use the following procedure:
   a. Remove the nut from the bolt.
   b. Depress the lead tang on the end of the upper caliper pin with a screwdriver while tapping on the pin with a hammer. Continue tapping until the lead tang is depressed by the v-slot.
   c. Place one end of a punch ($^1/_2$ in. or smaller) against the end of the caliper pin and drive the caliper pin out of the caliper toward the inside of the vehicle. Do not use a screwdriver or other edged tool to help drive out the caliper pin as the v-grooves may be damaged.
7. Repeat the procedure in Step 4 for the lower caliper pin.
8. Remove the caliper from the rotor. If the caliper is to be removed for service, remove the brake hose from the caliper.
9. Remove the outer pad. Remove the anti-rattle clips and remove the inner pad.
10. To install, place a new anti-rattle clip on the lower end of the inner pad. Be sure the tabs on the clip are positioned properly and the clip is fully seated.
11. Position the inner pad and anti-rattle clip in the pad abutment with the anti-rattle clip tab against the pad abutment and the loop-type spring away from the rotor. Compress the anti-rattle clip and slide the upper end of the pad in position.
12. Install the outer pad, making sure the torque buttons on the pad spring clip are seated solidly in the matching holes in the caliper.
13. Install the caliper on the spindle, making sure the mounting surfaces are free of dirt and lubricate the caliper grooves with Disc Brake Caliper Grease. Install new caliper pins, making sure the pins are installed with the tang in position.
14. The pin must be installed with the lead tang in first, the bolt head facing outward (if equipped) and the pin properly positioned. Position the lead tang in the v-slot mounting surface and drive in the caliper until the drive tang is flush with the caliper assembly. Install the nut (if equipped) and tighten to 32–47 inch lbs.

CAUTION

Never reuse caliper pins. Always install new pins whenever a caliper is removed.

15. If removed, install the brake hose to the caliper.
16. Bleed the brakes as described earlier in this chapter.
17. Install the wheel and tire assembly. Torque the lug nuts to 85–115 ft. lbs.
18. Remove the jack stands and lower the vehicle. Check the brake fluid level and fill as necessary. Check the brakes for proper operation.

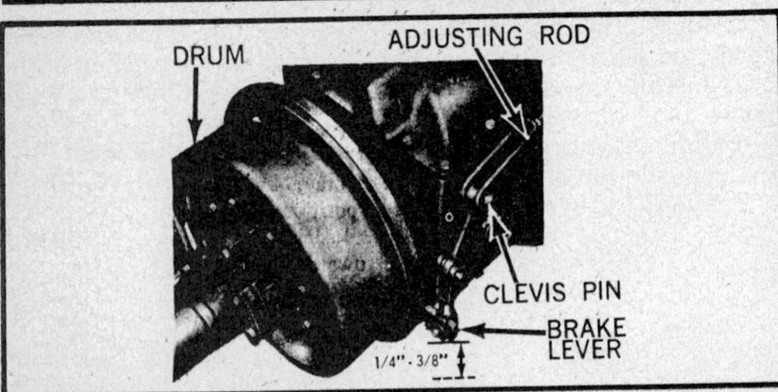

Shoe type parking brake (© Ford Motor Co.)

Parking Brakes

INTERNAL SHOE TYPE

Adjustment

NINE INCH DIAMETER DRUM

1. Release the parking brake lever in the cab.
2. From under the truck, remove the cotter pin from the parking brake linkage adjusting clevis pin. Remove the clevis pin.
3. Lengthen the parking brake adjusting link by turning the clevis. Continue to lengthen the adjusting link until the shoes seat against the drum when the clevis pin is installed.
4. Remove the clevis pin and shorten the linkage adjustment until there is 0.010 in. clearance between the shoes and the drum. The measurement should be taken at all points around the drum with the clevis pin installed.
5. Install a new cotter pin in the clevis retaining pin and check the brake operation.

Twelve Inch Diameter Drum

There is no internal adjustment on this brake. Adjustment is made on the linkage. Remove the clevis pin, loosen the nuts on the adjusting rod, and turn the clevis on the rod until a $\frac{1}{4}$–$\frac{3}{8}$ in. free play is obtained at the brake lever. Tighten the nuts, and connect the clevis to the bellcrank with the clevis pin.

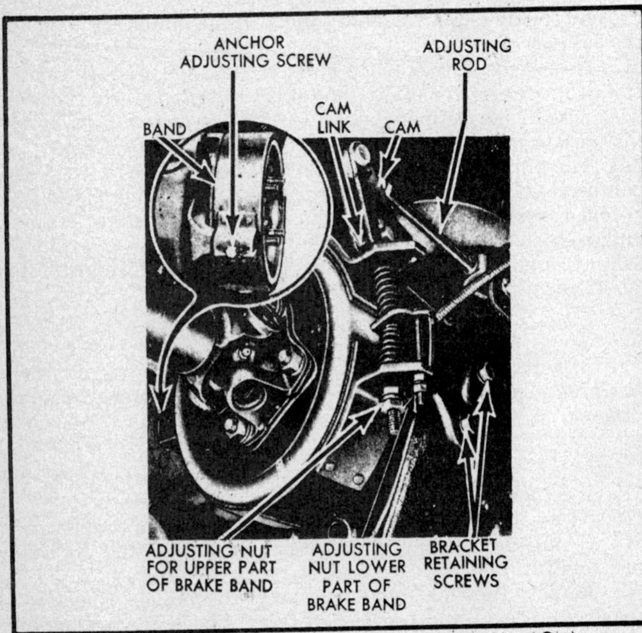

Typical external band type parking brake (© Ford Motor Co.)

EXTERNAL BAND TYPE

Adjustment

1. On cable-controlled parking brakes, move the parking brake lever to the fully released position. On a vehicle with a rod-type linkage, set the lever at the first notch.
2. Check the position of the cam to make sure the flat portion is resting on the brake band bracket. If the cam is not flat with the bracket, remove the clevis pin from the upper part of the cam, and adjust the clevis rod to allow the flat portion of the cam to rest on the brake band bracket. Install the clevis pin and cotter pin.
3. Remove the lock wire from the anchor adjusting screw, and turn the adjusting screw clockwise until a clearance of 0.010 in. is established between the brake lining and the brake drum at the anchor bracket. Install the lock wire in the anchor adjusting screw.
4. Loosen the lock nut on the adjusting screw for the lower half of the brake band, and adjust the screw to establish a 0.010 in. clearance between the lining and the brake drum at the lower half of the brake band. Tighten the lock nut.
5. Turn the upper band adjusting rod nut until a 0.010 in. clearance is established between the upper half of the band and the drum.
6. Apply and release brake several times to insure full release.

PARKING BRAKE INCLUDED WITH REAR BRAKES

Before attempting parking brake adjustment, make sure that the rear brakes are fully adjusted.

1. Raise and support the rear axle. Release the parking brake.
2. Apply the pedal or handle one to four clicks.
3. Adjust the cable equalizer nut under the truck until a moderate drag can be felt when the rear wheels are turned forward.
4. Release the parking brake and check that there is no drag when the wheels are turned forward.

NOTE: If the parking brake cable is replaced, prestretch it by applying the parking brake hard about three times before attempting adjustment.

Parking Brake Assembly Used With Hydro—Max Power Booster

1984 AND LATER

The parking brake is actuated by a spring/ramp assembly. The spring is compressed by Hydro-Max pump hydraulic pressure of 110 PSI minimum. The parking brakes are set by the release of this hydraulic pressure. The unit is sealed and full of fluid to prevent road contamination. As long as there is pump pressure, the parking brake can be released with a parking brake control in the cab. If the parking brake is set and no pump pressure is available, the spring can be caged by turning the nut, pinned to the stud, clockwise until the distance between the nut and spring can is 2 ± $\frac{1}{4}$ in.. This cages the spring in the spring chamber, releasing the parking brake.

WHEEL CYLINDER/PARKING BRAKE EXPANDER

Removal

NOTE: If both the wheel cylinder/adjuster and wheel cylinder/parking brake expander are to be serviced, the complete backing plate assembly may be removed by disconnecting the fluid lines (service and parking) and re-

moving the bolts retaining the wheel cylinder assemblies and backing plate to the axle flange. Removal of the wheel cylinder assemblies can then take place on the bench. IF THE BACKING PLATE ASSEMBLY IS TO BE REMOVED, PRESSURE MUST BE RELEASED BY CAGING THE SPRING IN THE PARKING BRAKE CHAMBER.

1. Attach a tube to the bleeder screw on the wheel cylinder/parking brake expander. Place the other end of the tube in a container. Unscrew the bleeder screw one-half turn. Pump the brake pedal to remove all brake fluid from the rear brake system. Discard the brake fluid.
2. Remove the shoe and lining.
3. Remove the parking brake chamber from the wheel cylinder/parking brake expander.
4. Remove the bolt retaining the bridge tube retainer to the backing plate and remove the retainer. Disconnect the bridge tube from the cylinders and remove the bridge tube.
5. Insert an Allen-head wrench into the bolts in the rear of the backing plate and remove the bolts retaining the wheel cylinder/parking brake expander to the backing plate.
6. Remove the three 9/16–18 in. bolts, nuts and washers retaining the wheel cylinder/parking brake expander and backing plate to the axle flange. Remove the wheel cylinder/parking brake expander and gasket from the backing plate.
7. Remove any rust or corrosion from the backing plate with a wire brush.

Installation

1. Install a new gasket on the wheel cylinder/parking brake expander. Position the assembly on the backing plate.
2. Install the three 9/16–18 in. bolts, nuts and washers retaining wheel cylinder/parking brake expander and backing plate to the axle flange. Tighten the bolts.
3. Install the Allen-head head bolts in the rear of the backing plate retaining the assembly to the plate.

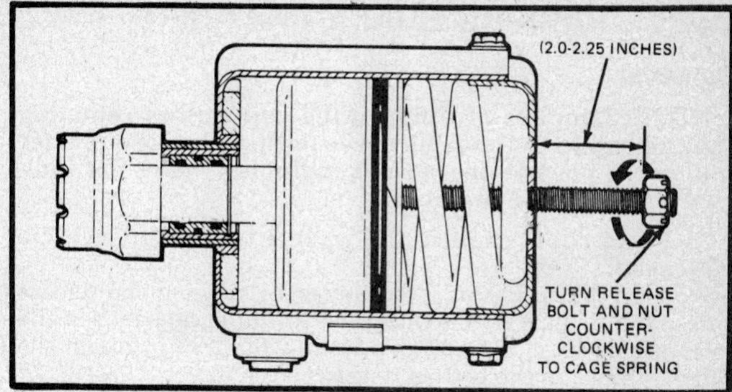

Parking brake chamber caging spring

4. Install the parking brake chamber.
5. Connect the bridge tube to the wheel cylinders. Install the bridge tube retainer and tighten the bolt.
6. Install the shoe and lining and adjust the lining-to-drum clearance.
7. Fill the Hydro-Max master cylinder reservoir with clean Heavy Duty Brake Fluid. Bleed the service brakes.
8. If required, bleed the parking brakes. Check the brake pump reservoir with the parking brake applied and if required, fill to the specified level with DEXRON®II or equivalent.

NOTE: The service brake system uses Ford Heavy Duty Brake Fluid, C6AZ–19542–A or –B (ESA–M6C25–A) or equivalent and is filled at the Hydro-Max master cylinder. The parking brake system uses Ford Automatic Transmission Fluid, ESP–M2C138–CJ, DEXRON®II or equivalent and is filled at the brake pump reservoir. DO NOT MIX THE FLUIDS.

9. Apply the brakes and check for leaks. Road test the vehicle and check for proper operation.

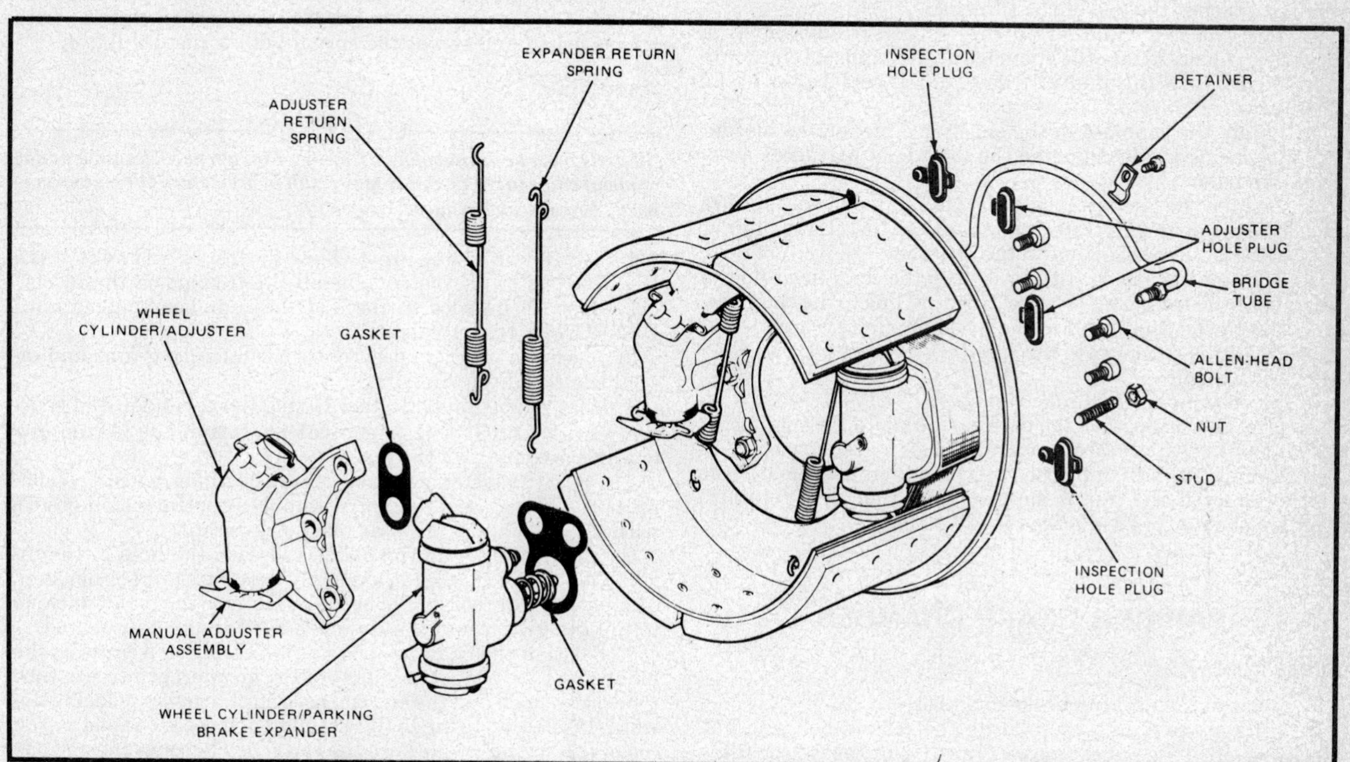

Drum brake system and related components

PARKING BRAKE CHAMBER

Removal

NOTE: Droplets of fluid on the cap screws retaining the end cap to the housing of the parking brake chamber indicate a normal operating condition. It does not indicate a leak in the chamber.

1. Place chocks under the wheels to prevent vehicle movement.
2. Cage the spring in the chamber by turning the release bolt and nut counterclockwise. The spring is caged when the release bolt extends 50.80–57.15mm (2.00–2.25 in.) from the filter retainer to the bottom of the release nut.

CAUTION

Do not use an impact wrench to cage the spring. Air tools can damage the piston and prevent proper spring caging.

3. Remove the system pressure by opening the bleeder valve.
4. Disconnect the fluid line from the fitting and cap the line. Remove the inlet fitting and bleeder screw from the chamber.
5. Loosen the jam nut that retains the chamber to the wheel cylinder/parking brake expander. Rotate the chamber counterclockwise until the fluid inlet port points downward and the fluid drains out. Discard the fluid.
6. Rotate the chamber counterclockwise and remove the chamber from the wheel cylinder/parking brake expander. Cap the fluid inlet fitting to prevent the entry of contaminants into the chamber.

Installation

1. Prior to installing the chamber, make sure the spring is caged. The spring is caged when the release bolt extends 50.80 ± 6.35mm (2.0 ± $^1/_4$ in.) from the filter retainer to the bottom of the release nut.
2. If removed, install the jam nut on the mounting tube until the nut reaches the end of the threads.
3. Position the chamber on the wheel cylinder/parking brake expander. Rotate the chamber until it stops in the cylinder. Make sure the jam nut does not interfere with the chamber.
4. Rotate the chamber in the opposite direction the bleeder screw is facing straight up and the fluid inlet port faces away from the axle.
5. Tighten the jam nut to 203 Nm (150 ft. lbs.), making sure the chamber does not rotate out of position. Install the bleeder screw and fluid inlet fitting in the chamber.
6. Tighten the bleeder fitting. Uncap the fluid line and the chamber fluid inlet port. Connect the fluid line to the chamber.
7. Check the fluid level in the brake pump reservoir. If required, fill the reservoir to the specified level with DEXRON® II or equivalent.
8. Bleed the parking brake chambers.
9. Check for leaks with the parking brakes in the applied position and in the released position. Repair as required.
10. Uncage the spring by turning the nut on the release bolt clockwise until the nut is snug against the filter retainer. Tighten the nut to 28–40 Nm (20–30 ft. lbs.).

PARKING BRAKE CHAMBER

Disassembly

1. Remove the parking brake chamber.
2. Uncage the spring by rotating the release bolt and nut clockwise until the nut extends 3.17mm ($^1/_8$ in.) above the filter retainer.

NOTE: To facilitate the spring uncaging procedure, apply 120 psi of air pressure to the fluid inlet port. Remove air pressure when the spring is uncaged.

CAUTION

Do not use an impact wrench to uncage the spring. The piston may be damaged and prevent proper spring caging.

3. Drive the roll pin from the release bolt and nut. Unscrew the nut and remove the filter retainer and filter.
4. In the end of the release bolt, cut a slot 1.587mm ($^1/_{16}$ in.) wide and 3.175mm ($^1/_8$ in.) deep. Insert a screwdrier in the slot and rotate the release bolt clockwise until the bolt is completely beneath the end cap and all threads are disengaged.
5. Place the chamber assembly in a press with the mounting tube supported by tube-type press stock and the end cap assembly facing the press ram. Bring the press ram down firmly on the end cap and make sure the press ram is centered on the end cap.

NOTE: The press must have a minimum capacity of 2500 lbs. and a minimum press ram travel of 6 in.

6. Remove the six cap screws retaining the end cap to the chamber assembly.
7. Slowly relax the pressure on the press ram and allow the spring to expand until it raises the end cap six in. above the chamber housing. Remove the spring and end cap from the chamber housing.
8. Drive the piston from the chamber housing with a brass drift and mallet.
9. With the piston supported, drive out the release bolt and socket by striking the release bolt with a hammer. Remove and discard all the O-rings from the rod socket. Discard the release bolt.
10. Remove the retaining ring from inside the chamber housing.
11. Position a brass drift through the mounting tube so it rests against the insert and drive out the insert. Remove and discard all the O-rings on the insert.
12. Inspect all parts for wear or damage and replace as required. If the spring shows signs of rust or corrosion, clean with a wire brush and recoat the spring with a rust inhibitor.

Assembly

CAUTION

All parts must be clean before assembly. Foreign particles such as dirt or metal chips in the chamber may result in premature O-ring replacement, leakage and reduced service life.

1. Coat the three new O-rings for the insert with DEXRON®II or equivalent. Install the O-rings on the insert.
2. Coat all interior surfaces of the chamber housing with DEXRON®II or equivalent.
3. Place the insert in position in the mounting tube and install the retaining ring.
4. Coat the piston and a new O-ring (large) and piston bearing with DEXRON® II or equivalent. Install the O-ring and bearing assembly on the piston.
5. Place the piston assembly in the chamber housing. Compress the O-ring and bearing assembly into the piston groove with a suitable tool (such as plastic tie wrap).
6. Carefully line up the piston rod with the hole in the insert. Gently tap the piston assembly into the chamber housing. The compressor tool should be loose. Remove the tool. Continue to tap the piston into the chamber until completely seated.
7. Position the chamber housing assembly in a press so the mounting tube portion is supported by an appropriate size tube type press stock and the end cap portion of housing is facing upward. Insert the spring in the chamber and place the end cap on top of the spring. Make sure the cap screw holes in the end cap are aligned with the holes in the housing. Slowly and carefully

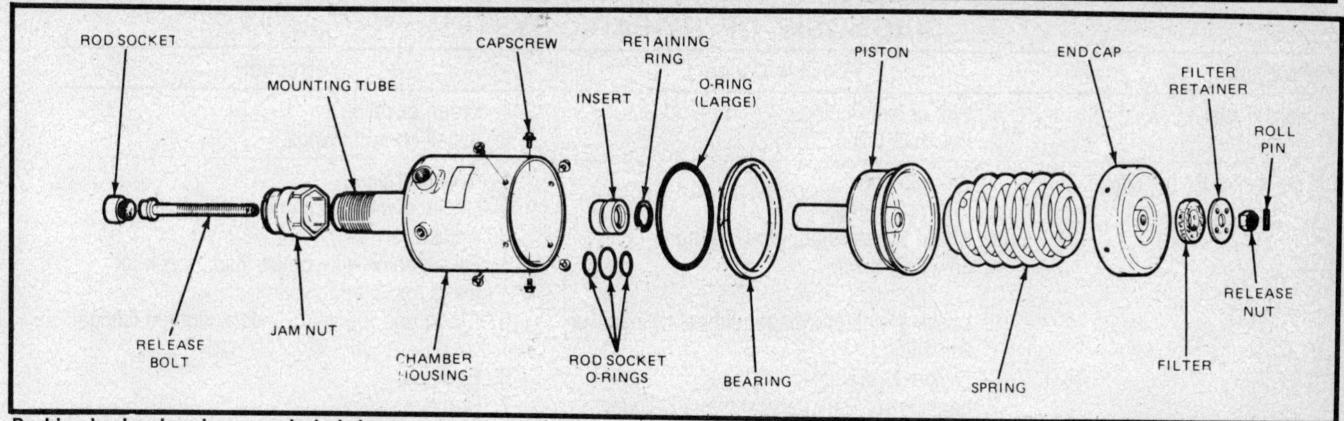

Parking brake chamber—exploded view

bring the press ram down to compress the end cap and spring. Make sure the press ram is centered on the end cap and the end cap is in alignment with the housing. Compress the spring until the holes in the end cap and housing are aligned. DO NOT RELEASE PRESSURE.

CAUTION

The press must have a minimum capacity of 2500 lbs. and a minimum travel of six in.

8. Install the six cap screws retaining the end cap to the chamber. Tighten the cap screws alternately and evenly to 55–81 Nm (40–60 ft. lbs.).
9. Install a new release bolt through the mounting tube and piston. Insert a $^5/_{16}$ in. hex driver and rotate the bolt through the end cap. Tighten the bolt by hand until the bolt protrudes through the end cap and is snug.
10. Install a new filter and the filter retainer over the release bolt. Screw on the release nut until the nut slots align with bolt hole. Install the roll pin.
11. Cage the spring by rotating the release bolt and nut counterclockwise until the bolt and nut projects 50.80–57.15mm (2.0–2.25 in.) from the bottom of the nut to the top of the filter retainer.

NOTE: To facilitate spring caging, apply 120 psi of air pressure to the fluid inlet. Release air pressure after the spring is caged.

CAUTION

Do use an impact wrench to cage the spring. Air tools may damage the piston and prevent proper spring caging.

12. Place the chamber assembly in a press so the end cap rests on the press bed. Position the rod socket into the end of the piston rod.
13. Press the rod socket securely in place.
14. Check that the rod socket is properly installed by measuring the distance between the top of the rod socket and the top of the mounting tube. The distance should be 81.28 ± 1.52mm (3.20 ± 0.06 in.).
15. Install the chamber.

BLEEDING PARKING BRAKES

1. Check the fluid level in the brake pump reservoir with the parking brakes applied. If required, fill the reservoir to the specified level with Ford Automatic Transmission Fluid, ESP–M2C138–CJ, DEXRON®II or equivalent.
2. Place chocks under the wheels to prevent vehicle movement.
3. Start the engine and run at normal curb idle speeds. Run the engine for at least two minutes to purge all air from the lines in the system before the Parking Brake Unitized Valve.
4. Place a wrench on the parking brake chamber bleeder fitting of the right rear chamber. (On tandem axles, start bleeding on right rear/rear axle chamber.) Attach a rubber drain tube to the bleeder fitting making sure the end of the tube fits snugly around the fitting.
5. Submerge the free end of the tube in a container partially filled with Ford Automatic Transmission Fluid, ESP–M2C138–CJ, DEXRON®II or equivalent. Loosen the bleeder fitting three-quarters of a turn.
6. Apply the parking brake. Close the bleeder fitting and release the parking brake. Repeat this operation until air bubbles no longer apperar in the submerged end of the bleeder tube.
7. When the fluid is completely free of air bubbles, tighten the bleeder fitting and remove the bleeder tube.
8. Repeat this procedure on the left rear parking brake chamber. (On tandem axles, bleed the chamber on the left side of the rear/rear axle, then bleed the chamber on the right side of the forward/rear axle and finally, bleed the chamber on the left side of the forward/rear axle).
9. Check Fluid level and refill as required.

CAGING PARKING BRAKE CHAMBER SPRING

Cage the spring by rotating the release bolt and nut counterclockwise until the bolt and nut projects 50.80–57.15mm (2.0–2.25 in.) from the bottom of the nut to the top of the filter retainer.

CAUTION

Do use an impact wrench to cage the spring. Air tools may damage the piston and prevent proper spring caging.

UNCAGING PARKING BRAKE CHAMBER SPRING

Uncage the spring by rotating the release bolt and nut clockwise until the nut extends 3.17mm ($^1/_8$ in.) above the filter retainer.

CAUTION

Do not use an impact wrench to uncage the spring. The piston may be damaged and prevent proper spring caging.

DIAGNOSIS OF HY-PARK SYSTEM

Problem	Possible Cause	Correction
Hard Pedal	1. Wet or worn linings. 2. Incorrect lining.	1. Clean or reline. 2. Install correct linings.
Excessive Pedal Travel	1. Worn Linings. 2. Incorrect lining. 3. Slack adjusters out of adjustment. 4. Low fluid level. 5. Leaking master cylinder, wheel cylinder, or line fittings. 6. Broken hydraulic line. 7. Leaking Hy-Park service brake cylinder seal. 8. Front brakes out of adjustment. 9. Air in system. 10. Improper brake fluid. 11. Master cylinder internal leaks.	1. Reline brakes. 2. Replace with recommended lining. 3. Adjust. 4. Fill reservoir with brake fluid; check for leaks and bleed system. 5. Clean and rebuild cylinders; tighten fittings. 6. Replace. 7. Replace. 8. Bleed system. 9. Bleed system. 10. Flush system and refill with recommended brake fluid. 11. Clean and rebuild.
Park brake self applies when engine is stopped	1. Leaking lines or connections. 2. Hy-Park valves leaking. 3. Check valve leaking internally. 4. Hy-Park chamber diaphragm leak. 5. Hy-Park chamber front housing seal leak.	1. Tighten or replace. 2. Repair or replace. 3. Repair or replace. 4. Replace. 5. Replace.
Park brake applied; will not release	1. Leaking lines or connections. 2. Hy-Park chamber diaphragm leak. 3. Hy-Park chamber front housing seal leak. 4. Hy-Park valves leaking. 5. Hy-Park valves malfunction.	1. Tighten or replace. 2. Replace. 3. Replace. 4. Repair or replace. 5. Repair or replace.
Slow park brake application	1. Return line to reservoir is restricted. 2. Relay valve not functioning properly. 3. Hand control valve malfunction. 4. Restricted pilot line; control valve to relay. 5. Wrong size park brake lines to Hy-Park chambers.	1. Check for kinks, pinched line. 2. Repair or replace. 3. Repair or replace. 4. Check for kinks, pinched line. 5. Replace.
Slow park brake release	1. Hydraulic pump drive belt broken. 2. Restricted lines. 3. Leaking lines or connections. 4. Air in system. 5. Hy-Park valves malfunction.	1. Replace. 2. Check line from diverter valve to control valve and relay; park brake line to Hy-Park chambers. 3. Tighten or replace. 4. Bleed system. 5. Repair or replace.
Slow service brake release	1. Restricted lines. 2. Brake pedal binding. 3. Slack adjusters out of adjustment. 4. Binding cam or camshaft. 5. Weak shoe return springs.	1. Check for kinks, pinched line. 2. Free pedal lubricate. Check master cylinder operation. 3. Adjust. 4. Lubricate; replace if not effective. 5. Replace springs.
Park brake does not hold	1. Incorrect slack adjuster and push rod angle. 2. Hy-Park actuator rod not extending. 3. Excessive lining and/or drum wear. 4. Grease or fluid soaked lining.	1. Adjust. 2. Check Hy-Park actuator rod travel. Repair or replace. 3. Replace. 4. Replace.
Hy-Park system pressure over 120 PSI	1. diverter valve malfunction. 2. Restricted diverter valve pilot line.	1. Repair or replace. 2. Check for kinks, pinched, or plugged line.
Relief valve "blows off"	1. Relief valve malfunction. 2. System pressure above normal (120 psi).	1. Repair or replace. 2. Refer to previous problem.

DIAGNOSIS OF HYDRAULIC PUMP

Problem	Possible Cause	Correction
Pump noise	1. Loose Belt. 2. Line touching other parts of vehicle. 3. Low fluid level. 4. Air in the fluid. 5. Excessive back pressure caused by lines, booster head, or steering gear. 6. Internal damage to pump.	1. Tighten belt. 2. Adjust line position. 3. Fill reservoir 4. Locate source of air leak and correct. 5. Locate restriction and correct. Bleed system. 6. Repair or overhaul pump.
Leaks at top of reservoir	1. Reservoir too full. 2. Air in the fluid.	1. Fill to proper level. 2. Locate source of air leak and correct. Bleed system.
Leaks at the reservoir	1. Ring seal cut. 2. O-ring improperly installed.	1. Replace O-ring seal. 2. Install seal properly.
Leaks at the pressure fitting or mounting stud	1. Not tighten sufficiently. 2. Cross threaded or damaged seat. 3. Defective seat on hose end. 4. Damaged seals.	1. Torque to 30–40 ft. lbs. 2. Replace damaged part. 3. Replace hose. 4. Replace seals.
Leaks at the shaft seal	1. Defective seal. 2. Damaged shaft.	1. Replace seal. 2. Replace shaft.
Leaks in metal parts	1. Poor casting.	1. Replace defective parts.
Pump inoperative, poor, or no assist	1. Loose drive belt. 2. Low fluid level. 3. Air in the fluid. 4. Defective lines, booster head or steering gear. 5. Internal damage to pump.	1. Tighten belt. 2. Fill reservoir to proper level. 3. Locate source of air leak and correct. 4. Correct. 5. Repair or overhaul pump.

Hy–Park System

The Hy-Park brake system is comprised basically of a hydraulic service brake system in conjunction with a hydraulically released, spring applied parking brake.

Hydraulic brake fluid from the master cylinder is used to actuate the rear S-cam service brakes. A hydraulic pump (power steering pump on medium duty trucks) delivers power steering fluid, under pressure, to compress the power spring in the Hy-Park actuator (chamber). Application and release of the parking brake is controlled by a hand valve, which is located in the cab. The rear brake is a conventional S-cam brake such as the type found on vehicles equipped with air brakes.

When the engine is running, the hydraulic pump directs fluid, under pressure, through the steering gear (and the Hy-power booster when used). From the steering gear, the fluid flows to the Hy-Park system through the diverter valve. A pilot line, located downstream from the check valve, attaches directly to the diverter valve, enabling the valve to sense low pressure in the system.

When the parking brakes are set, the pressure in the system will drop, causing the diverter valve to close. When this happens, the fluid from the closed diverter valve will then flow to the relay valve and to the hand control valve, but with the brakes, applied, flow is stopped at these points.

NOTE: The check valve, located between the diverter valve and the relay valve, is designed to retain the power steering fluid in the system units at a minimum pressure of 100 psi (operational level).

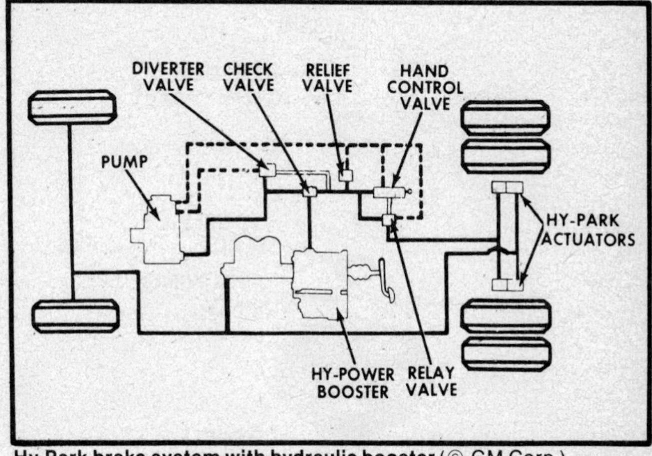

Hy-Park brake system with hydraulic booster (© GM Corp.)

When the pressure in the system is approximately 100 psi, the diverter valve will open, redirecting fluid flow to the pump reservoir.

When the hand control valve is moved to the "release" position, the fluid in the system (at operational pressure) will be directed to the relay valve diaphragm. This will cause the relay valve to switch, which will allow fluid to flow through the line from the diverter valve to the actuator. As the fluid begins to flow to the actuators, the pressure in the system will drop. A

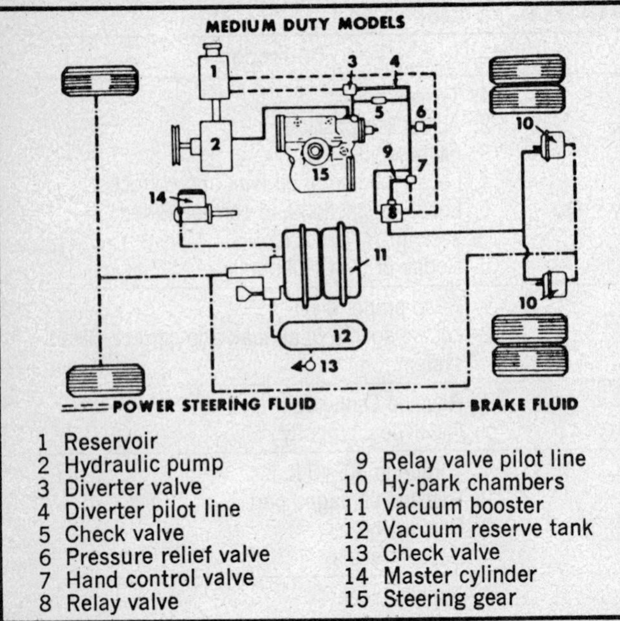

Hy-Park brake system with vacuum booster and power steering (© GM Corp.)

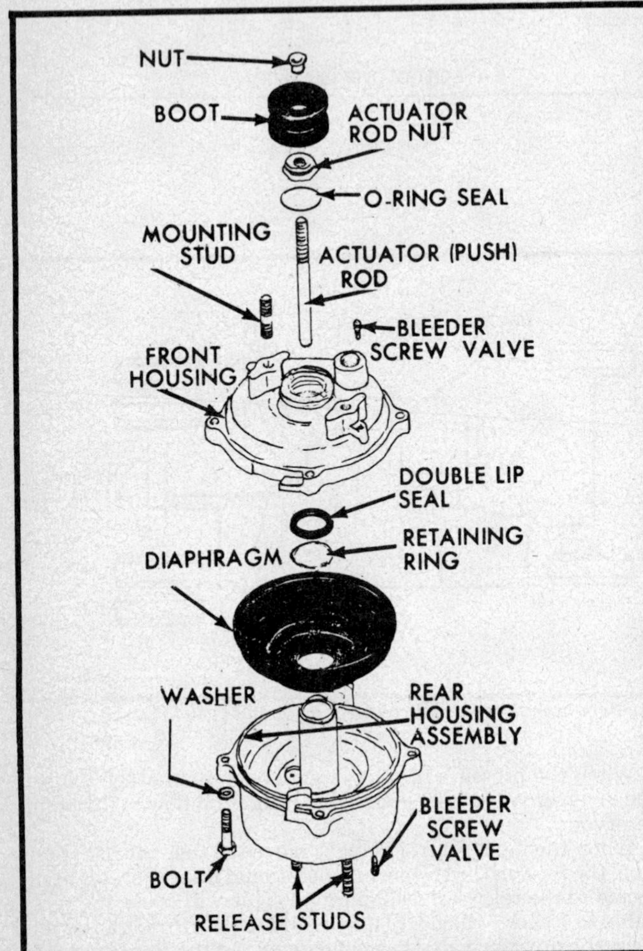

Hy-Park chamber—disassembled (© GM Corp.)

drop in pressure will be sensed by the diverter valve, allowing more fluid to be admitted to the system.

Fluid, delivered to the actuators under pressure, will compress the apply springs and release the parking brakes. The fluid will continue to flow until the springs are compressed to their release position. As the springs are being compressed, fluid pressure will continue to increase. The increased fluid pressure will be sensed by the diverter valve, which will open and direct fluid flow back to the pump reservoir. The system will continue to function in this manner until the hand control valve is moved to the "brake apply" position.

When the hand control valve is moved to the "brake apply" position, the pressure stored in the relay valve line is directed to the return line. A loss of pilot pressure will cause the relay valve to switch, which will cause fluid to flow from the actuators and into the return line. Pressure in the actuators will drop as the fluid returns to the reservoir, and the power springs will expand, which will force fluid back through the relay valve and return line, causing the parking brakes to be applied.

NOTE: With the engine OFF, a leak in a pressurized line at any point between the check valve and the actuators will cause the parking brakes to apply.

HY–PARK ACTUATOR CHAMBER OPERATION

The Hy-Park chamber is essentially two brake units combined in one assembly. It houses the parking brake power apply spring, diaphragm, and the spring sleeve/diaphragm support assembly. It also houses the service brake apply piston, acutator rod, and return spring.

The actuator rod is connected through a clevis and slack adjuster to an S-cam wheel brake assembly. When the brake pedal is depressed, hydraulic brake fluid pressure moves the brake apply piston forward against the actuator rod, which applies the service brakes. When the pedal is released, the return spring moves the brake apply piston back until it bottoms in the apply piston housing.

The parking brake components operate over the brake apply piston housing and within the main chamber housing. When in operation, power steering fluid, which is delivered to the actuator under pressure fills the area of the chamber between the chamber housing and the diaphragm. As the chamber fills with fluid, the pressure acts against the diaphragm, which in turn acts against the diaphragm support, thereby compressing the power spring. By compressing the power spring the parking brake is released. When the fluid is discharged from the actuator, the power spring expands, forcing the apply piston housing forward against the actuator rod nut, which moves the actuator rod forward, thereby applying the brakes.

Disassembly

CAUTION

The Hy-Park actuator houses two types of hydraulic fluid: brake fluid and power steering fluid. These two very different types of hydraulic fluid are not compatible, and should not be allowed to come into contact with one another, nor should they be allowed to come into contact with components of the system for which they are not intended. If, at any time during disassembly or assembly, either fluid contacts a rubber sealing component of the wrong system, i.e., should power steering fluid contaminate the apply piston double lip seal, or, if brake fluid should contaminate the actuator diaphragm or boot, then the affected seal(s) should be discarded, as the fluid will attack the seal and cause it to deteriorate. If care is not exercised during the overhaul procedure, to isolate these two fluids, then inevitable deterioration will result, causing leakage at the seals and eventual system malfunction.

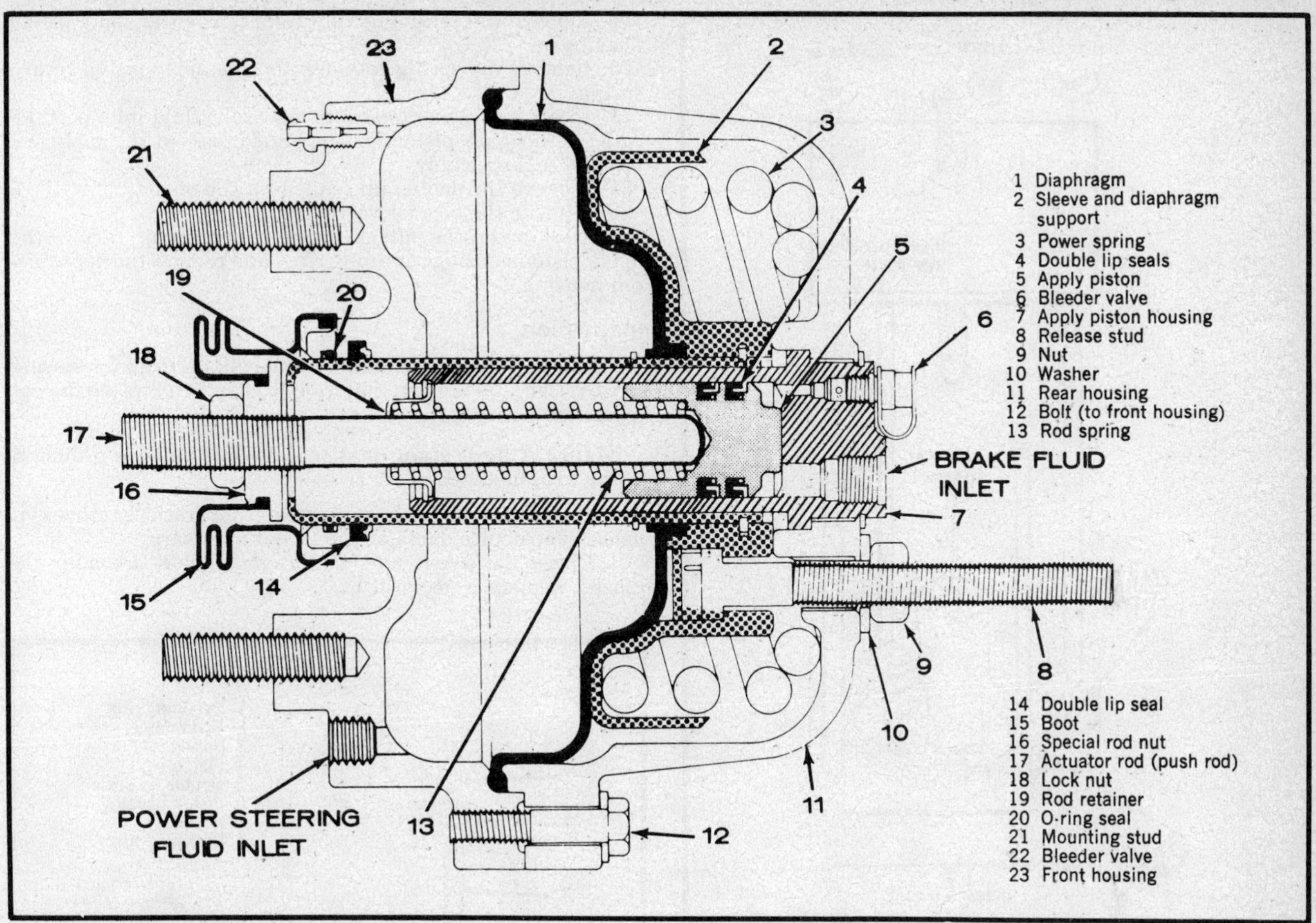

1 Diaphragm
2 Sleeve and diaphragm support
3 Power spring
4 Double lip seals
5 Apply piston
6 Bleeder valve
7 Apply piston housing
8 Release stud
9 Nut
10 Washer
11 Rear housing
12 Bolt (to front housing)
13 Rod spring
14 Double lip seal
15 Boot
16 Special rod nut
17 Actuator rod (push rod)
18 Lock nut
19 Rod retainer
20 O-ring seal
21 Mounting stud
22 Bleeder valve
23 Front housing

BRAKE FLUID INLET
POWER STEERING FLUID INLET

Hy-Park actuator components (© GM Corp.)

NOTE: Before attempting to remove or disassemble the parking brake chamber, it will be necessary to "cage" (compress) the power spring in the rear chamber housing. Failure to properly cage the spring before removal or disassembly could result in serious personal injury, as the load on the compressed power spring is approximately 2,000 pounds. Refer to the Chevrolet Truck section of this manual for caging and removal/installation instructions.

1. Position the chamber unit in a vise with the front housing up, by clamping across the release screws.

NOTE: In order to prevent damaging the threads of the release screws, line the jaws of the vise with strips of wood or soft metal, or thread extra nuts onto the release screws and clamp across the flat area of the nuts.

2. Lift up on the acutator rod, while separating the boot from the groove in the front cover, and remove the actuator rod, boot, actuator rod nut, and lock nut.
3. Separate the boot from the groove in the actuator rod nut, and remove the actuator rod nut and lock nut from the actuator rod if these parts are to be replaced.
4. Remove the bleeder screw valve.
5. Remove the four housing attaching bolts, and separate the front and rear housing.
6. Firmly grasp the front housing, and turn it in a counterclockwise direction to detach the locking tabs on the front housing from the locking arms on the rear housing. Remove the front housing.
7. Remove the O-ring and double lip seal from their respective grooves in the front housing.
8. Remove the retaining ring which secures the diaphragm to the sleeve and diaphragm support assembly.
9. Lift off the diaphragm by pulling it up and over the sleeve.
10. Place the rear housing assembly in a special tool fixture J–28570 or an equivalent holding fixture.

NOTE: The special tool fixture J–28570 is equipped with an extended tubular support, which can be installed on a transmission holding fixture base J–3289–2 or its equivalent.

11. Position adapter J–28570–5 on the support sleeve.

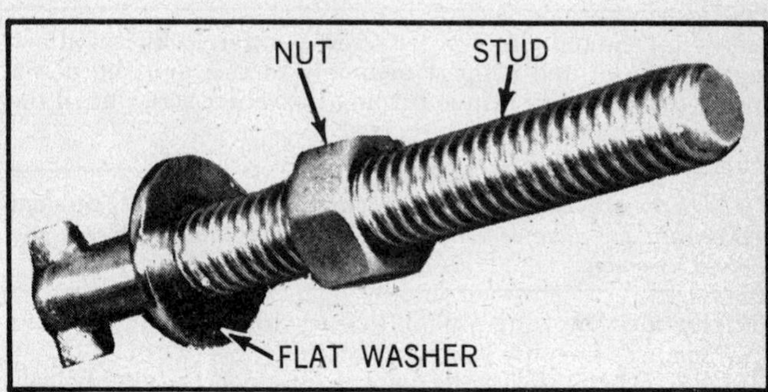

Release stud, nut and washer (© GM Corp.)

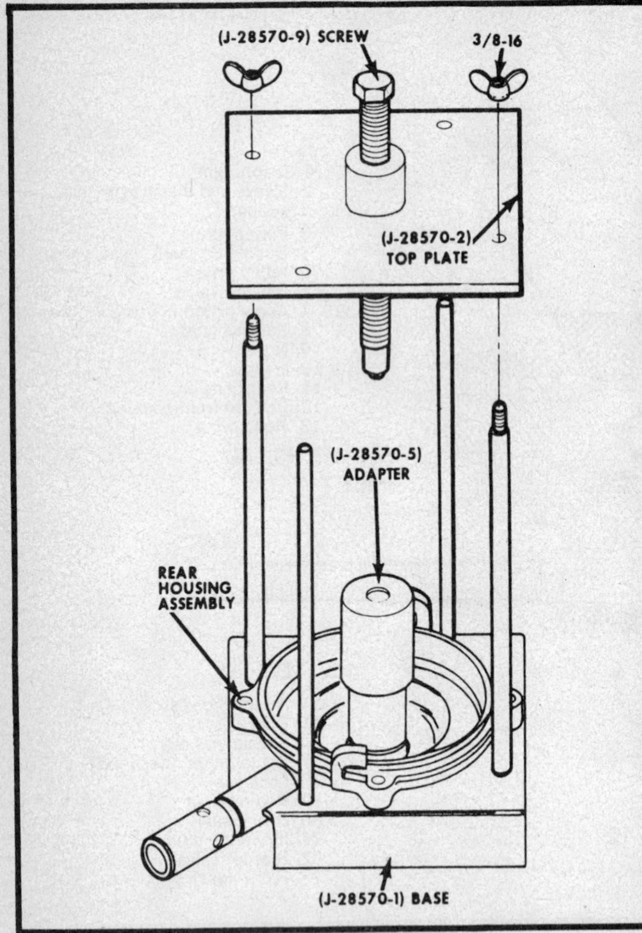

Rear housing holding fixture (© GM Corp.)

12. Install the top plate J–28570–2 over the upright rods, and secure in place with wing nuts.
13. Thread the screw J–28570–9 down through the center of the top plate until the ball end of the screw seats in the adapter.
14. Take all the slack out of the assembly by tightening the screw against the adapter.
15. Working from the other side of the fixture, loosen the two release stud nuts a few turns. Press on the release screws (toward the chamber) and turn the release screws 90 degrees counterclockwise to the stops. Withdraw the release studs.

CAUTION

At this stage of the procedure, DO NOT remove the wing nuts which secure the fixture top plate in place until the power spring is completely relaxed, or serious personal injury could result.

16. Turn the top plate center screw counterclockwise, allowing the sleeve and support assembly to rise and the power spring to expand. Continue turning the center screw until the power spring is completely relaxed.

CAUTION

DO NOT remove the fixture wing nuts until clearance (slack) develops between the top plate center screw, the adapter, and the sleeve and support assembly.

17. Remove the wing nuts, lift off the top plate, and remove the housing assembly from the fixture.
18. Remove the sleeve and diaphragm support assembly from the rear housing. Remove the power spring.
19. Remove the retaining ring from inside the apply piston housing.
20. Remove the spring retainer and the apply piston return spring.
21. Insert a wooden dowel into the brake fluid inlet port, located in the apply piston housing, and press out the apply piston and seal assembly.
22. Remove the double lip seals from the piston.
23. Remove the bleeder valve.
24. Working on the outside of the rear housing, remove the apply piston housing retaining ring, and remove the apply piston housing.

Inspection

1. Check the apply piston housing cylinder bore for scoring or corrosion. If a scoring condition exists, then replace the apply piston housing.

NOTE: A light stain or discoloration may be polished using crocus cloth.

2. Check the front and rear housings for cracks or other evidence of structure damage. Replace if necessary.
3. Check the sleeve and diaphragm support assembly for cracks. Replace if necessary.

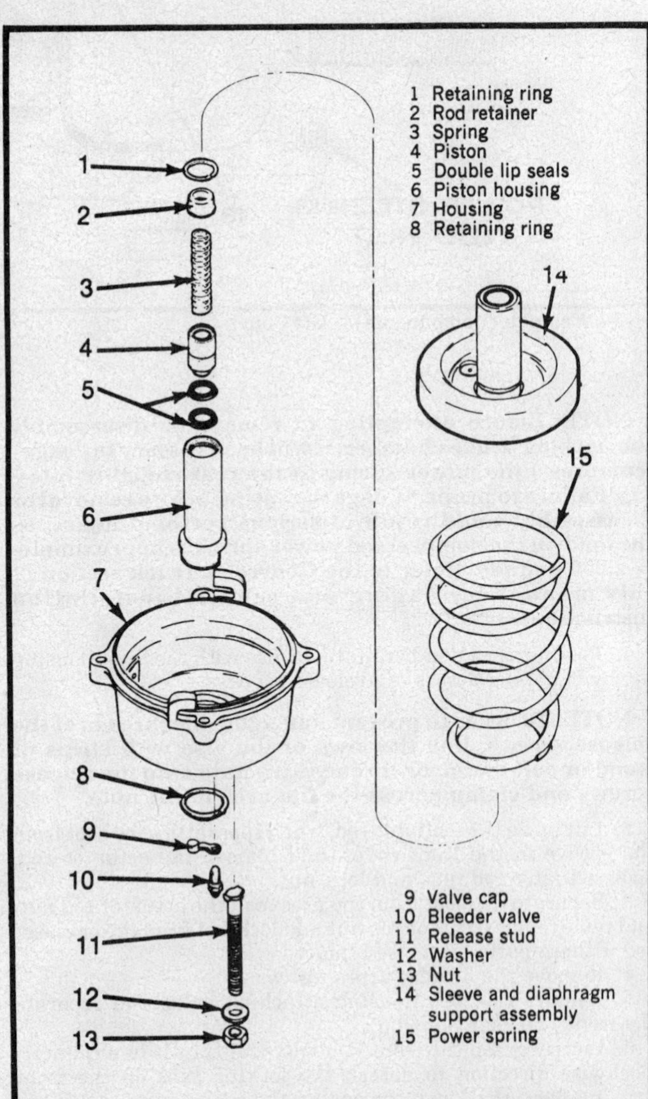

Hy-Park rear housing and related components (© GM Corp.)

4. Check the O-ring and seal groove lands for nicks or burrs. Repair or replace as necessary.

5. Check the area of the sleeve and support assembly, which contacts the diaphragm, for burrs. Repair or replace as necessary.

6. Check the outside edge of the sleeve for nicks or burrs. Repair or replace as necessary.

Assembly

NOTE: Before reassembling the actuator, clean all parts to be reused with denatured alcohol.

1. Lubricate the new double lip seals with brake fluid, and install in the grooves of the piston, with the lips facing the closed end of the piston housing.

2. Install the piston and seal assembly into the apply piston housing, and seat the piston to the bottom of the housing.

3. Install the return spring, actuator rod retainer, and the retaining ring in the apply piston housing.

4. Position the rear housing, with the newly installed parts, into the fixture base.

5. Install the power spring, tapered end down, in the rear housing. Position the spring so that the end of the spring butts against the stop in the housing.

6. Hold the sleeve and diaphragm support assembly with the edge of the sleeve facing up. Install the release studs in the diaphragm support assembly with the edge of the sleeve facing up. Install the release studs in the diaphragm support slots. Turn the release studs 90 degrees clockwise to the stop, then allow the studs to drop down. Make sure the release studs are properly engaged by turning them while pulling down. The studs should not turn in either direction, and should be hanging straight down.

7. Place the sleeve and diaphragm support assembly, with the release studs, directly over the power spring. Turn the diaphragm support assembly so that the release studs are positioned directly over their corresponding holes in the rear housing, then rotate the diaphragm support assembly a few degrees counterclockwise.

NOTE: As the power spring is being compressed, it will force the diaphragm support assembly to turn in a clockwise direction. When this happens, the release studs will not properly align with the holes in the rear housing. In order to compensate for the additional turning of the diaphragm support assembly, it will be necessary to rotate the diaphragm support assembly a few degrees counterclockwise.

8. Place the adapter over the end of the sleeve and diaphragm support assembly, and install the top plate and wing nuts.

CAUTION

Make certain that the wing nuts are securely tightened. Do NOT remove the wing nuts until the power spring is caged with the release studs, or serious personal injury could result.

9. Thread the center screw down through the top plate until it seats in the adapter. Continue turning the screw, and compress the power spring until the ends of the release studs are about to enter the holes in the rear housing. Make sure that the studs are aligned with the holes in the rear housing. If not, then back off the center screw, and begin again by repositioning the diaphragm support assembly. Again, compress the power spring until the studs are aligned with the holes in the rear housing.

10. Using a suitable tool, guide the release studs into the rear housing holes. If the studs enter at an angle and bind in the rear housing, then it will be necessary to release the fixture, and reposition the parts.

11. Continue compressing the power spring until the sleeve and diaphragm support assembly bottoms in the rear housing.

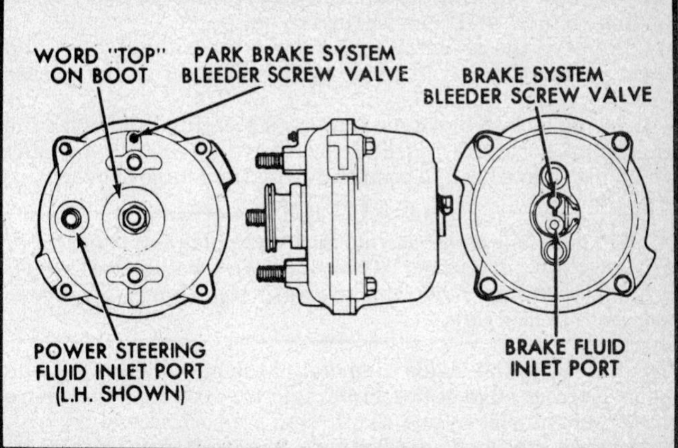

Front and rear housing alignment (© GM Corp.)

Install the nuts and washers on the release studs. Hand tighten the nuts and washers until they bottom against the rear housing.

12. Carefully, back off the center screw, until clearance develops between the center screw, adapter, and the sleeve and diaphragm support assembly.

CAUTION

Be certain that there is slack (clearance) between the center screw and the adapter, as this is an indication that the power spring is caged by the release studs. DO NOT proceed until the slack condition is achieved.

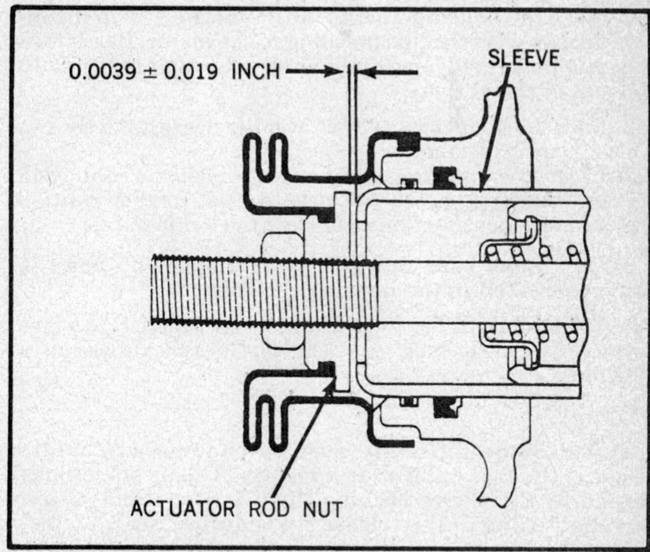

Rod nut to sleeve clearance (© GM Corp.)

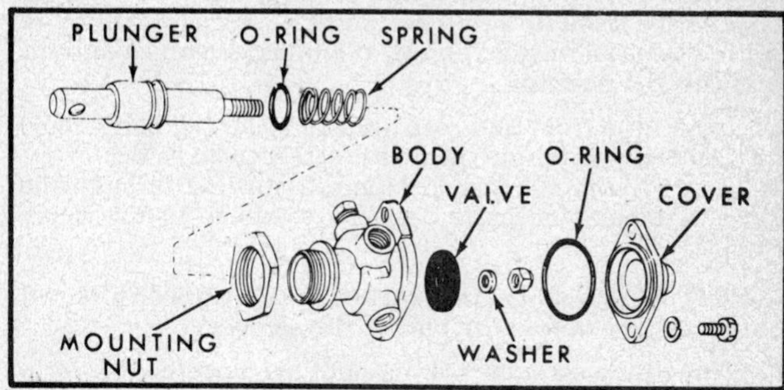

Hand control valve (© GM Corp.)

13. Remove the wing nuts, which secure the top plate to the holding fixture, and remove the top plate.
14. Remove the actuator rear housing from the fixture, and again, secure the unit in a vise by clamping across the release screws.
15. Using a cloth moistened in power steering fluid, wipe the interior of both housing and the sleeve to remove any dirt which may have been deposited during the course of overhaul.

CAUTION

DO NOT allow any power steering fluid to enter the hole in the end of the sleeve. Also, as a matter of procedure, the manufacturer specifically advises that the diaphragm, double lip seal, O-ring, and boot be replaced with new parts.

16. Lubricate the inside diameter of the new diaphragm (the inside circular edge of the diaphragm that contacts the sleeve portion of the sleeve and diaphragm support assembly) with fresh power steering fluid before installing it over the sleeve.
17. Install the diaphragm over the sleeve. The lower inside diameter of the diaphragm must be fully seated in the groove in the sleeve and diaphragm support assembly.
18. Position the outside edge of the diaphragm in the recess area of the rear housing.
19. Install the diaphragm retaining ring in the groove provided in the sleeve, which is located directly above the lower inside diameter of the diaphragm.
20. Install the bleeder valve in the front housing.
21. Using fresh power steering fluid, lubricate the double lip seal and the O-ring, and install them in their respective grooves in the front housing.

NOTE: Install the O-ring in the groove closest to the outside of the housing. Install the double lip seal in the inside groove with the lips pointing to the inside. Be certain that NO power steering fluid enters through the hole in the end of the sleeve.

22. Slide the front housing down over the sleeve, until the two housings come together.
23. Locate the front housing at an angle of approximately 45 degrees counterclockwise from the normal contact position with the rear housing. This will clear the locking arms.

NOTE: Make sure that the outer diaphragm bead is properly seated in the housing recesses.

24. Turn the front housing clockwise until the locking tabs engage under the locking arms. The bolt holes should now be in alignment.

NOTE: Some difficulty may be encountered while aligning the front and rear housings. This is sometimes caused by the sleeve cocking slightly, as a result of uneven tightening of the release studs during the "caging" operation. If this happens, it may be necessary to move one of the release stud nuts, only slightly, to correct the condition. It is important that the angular relationship between the front and rear housings be correct. When the unit is installed in the vehicle, the bleeder valves should be in the UP position.

25. Install the front and rear housing attaching bolts (four) and washers, and torque them alternately to 20 ft. lbs.
26. Insert the rounded end of the actuator rod through the sleeve, retainer, and spring, until it bottoms in the apply piston.

NOTE: At this stage, the start of the threads on the rod should be just below the end of the sleeve.

27. Thread the actuator rod nut onto the actuator rod, for a distance of just a few threads.
28. Apply Loctite®601, or an equivalent adhesive chemical, to the threads of the actuator rod just above where they enter the sleeve and upwards for a distance of approximately one half in..
29. While pressing against the end of the actuator rod to be sure that it is firmly seated in the apply piston, thread the actuator rod nut down the actuator rod until the clearance between the actuator rod nut and the end of the sleeve is 0.039 ± 0.019 in.

NOTE: It will be necessary to allow the assembly to stand undisturbed, for approximately five minutes, until the Loctite® cures.

30. After the adhesive has cured, remove the rod from the actuator, and install the lock nut.
31. Secure the inner (inside diameter) bead of the boot into the groove on the actuator rod nut.
32. Install the actuator rod assembly in the Hy-Park actuator, positioning the boot so that the side marked TOP is at the top of the unit.

NOTE: When the boot is properly positioned, a tab inside the boot along the beaded edge will fit in a notch in the front housing.

33. Cover the power steering fluid inlet port to prevent dirt from entering the Hy-Park assembly, and remove the assembly from the vise.

HAND CONTROL VALVE

Disassembly

1. Remove the two, valve body-to-cover, attaching screws, and separate the valve body from the cover.
2. Remove the O-ring, and discard.
3. Unscrew the nut from the plunger, and remove the washer and the valve.
4. Remove the plunger, O-ring, and spring.
5. Check all metal component parts for excessive wear or defects.

Assembly

NOTE: Prior to assembly, all metal must be thoroughly cleaned and inspected. Apply a thin film of silicone lubricant to the valve body bores, plunger, valve and the O-rings.

1. Position the plunger spring in the valve body.
2. Install a new O-ring on the plunger, and install the plunger in the valve body.
3. Install a new O-ring in the valve body.
4. Position a new valve and washer over the end of the plunger, and install the nut.
5. Install the two, valve body-to-cover attaching screws.

DIVERTER VALVE

Disassembly

1. Remove the retaining ring.
2. Remove the cap and the cap O-ring.
3. Remove the spring, pin, and shim.
4. Remove the piston and O-ring.

NOTE: Examine metal parts for excessive wear. The piston should be replaced if the valve surface is hardened or deteriorated. If any part is excessively worn, it should be replaced.

Assembly

NOTE: Discard all O-rings, and replace them with new parts. Discard the spring, and replace with a new spring.

1. Apply a thin film of silicone lubricant to the valve and valve body bore.
2. Install a new O-ring on the piston, and install the piston in the valve body.
3. Position the shim on the piston, and install the pin and a new spring.
4. Install a new O-ring on the cap. Center the cap over the pin, and install the cap in the valve body bore.
5. Install the retaining ring.

NOTE: Use shims on the end of the pin to obtain 60 psi valve closing 95 psi opening pressures.

PRESSURE RELIEF VALVE

Disassembly

1. Remove the four, cover, retaining screws.
2. Remove the springs and shims from the cover.
3. Remove the piston assembly from the valve body bore.
4. Examine all parts for excessive wear.

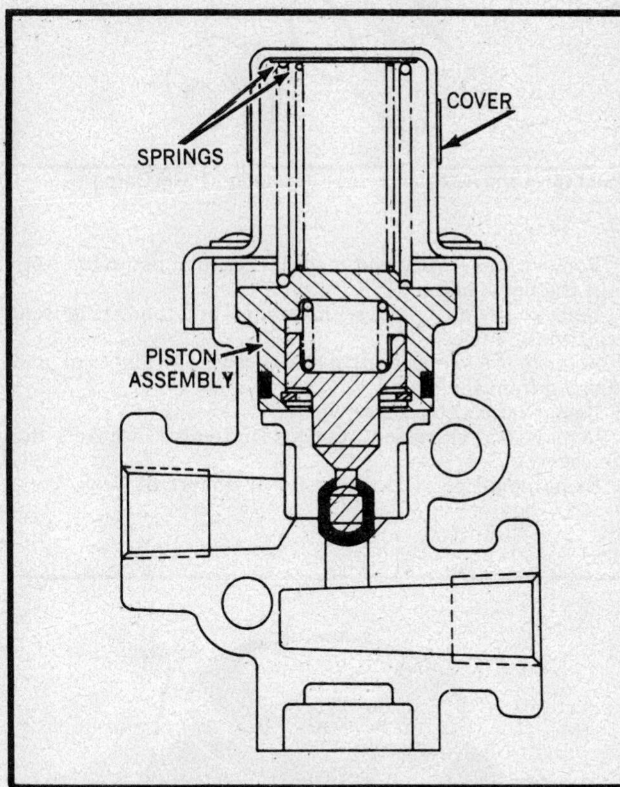

Pressure refile valve (© GM Corp.)

Assembly

NOTE: All parts must be thoroughly cleaned prior to assembly.

1. Apply a thin film of silicone lubricant to the piston assembly and the valve body bore.
2. Install a new piston assembly in the valve body bore.
3. Position the springs over the piston.
4. Place the shims in the cover, and install the cover and shims over the springs.
5. Install the four, cover, retaining screws.

NOTE: Add or remove shims as necessary to obtain approximately 130 psi nominal opening pressure.

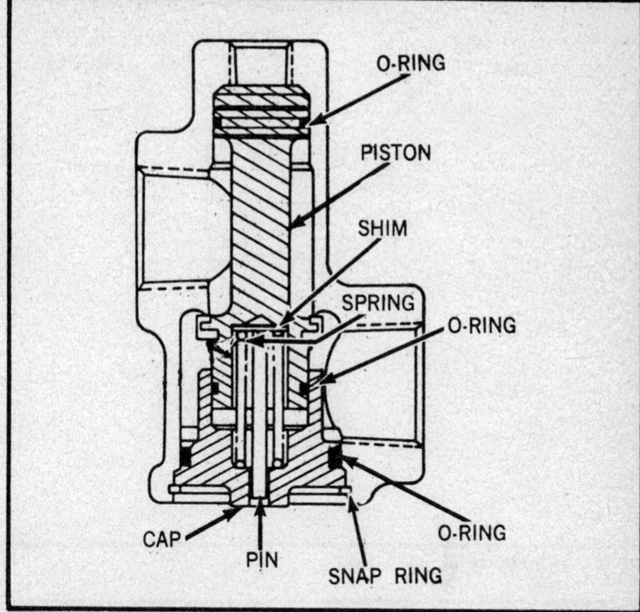

Diverter valve (© GM Corp.)

CHECK VALVE

Disassembly

1. Remove the cap from the body.
2. Remove the gasket.
3. Remove the spring and seal assembly.
4. Check seal assembly for deterioration or hardening.
5. Check spring for rust, or cracked or weakened coils.
6. Check the cap and valve body bore for excessive wear.

Assembly

NOTE: All parts must be thoroughly cleaned prior to assembly.

1. Apply a thin film of silicone lubricant to the seal assembly and the valve body bore.
2. Place the spring in the valve body with the small diameter facing outward.
3. Position the seal assembly in the valve body, over the spring.
4. Install a new gasket on the end cap.
5. Install the end cap in the valve body, and tighten securely.

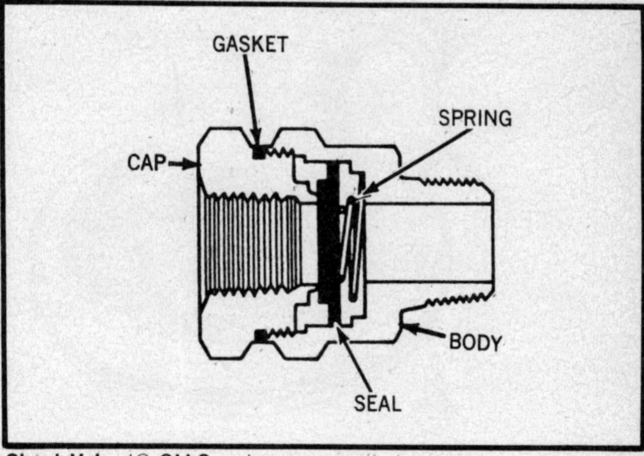

Check Valve (© GM Corp.)

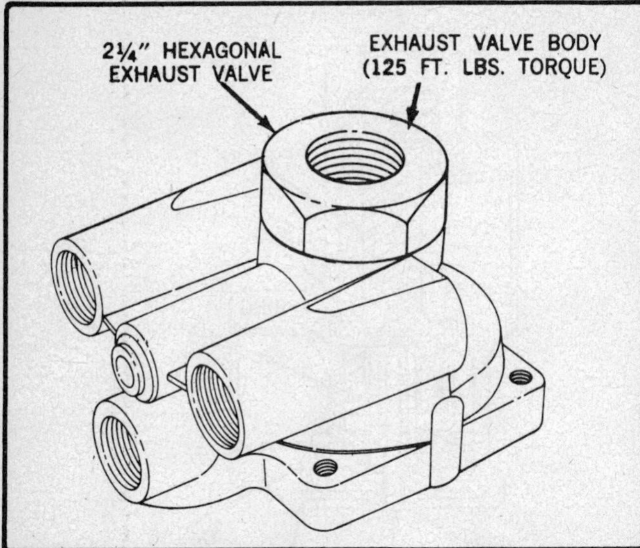

Exhaust valve body (© GM Corp.)

RELAY VALVE

Disassembly

NOTE: Visually inspect the casting of the valve for excessive cracks of fractures. If the valve appears excessively damaged, replace it with a new valve.

1. Scribe the outside valve cover, mounting bracket (if equipped), and body to ensure proper part alignment during assembly.
2. Remove the four cover screws.
3. Remove the valve cover and piston assembly.
4. Remove the 2 ¼ in. hexagonal exhaust valve.
5. Remove the exhaust valve O-ring.

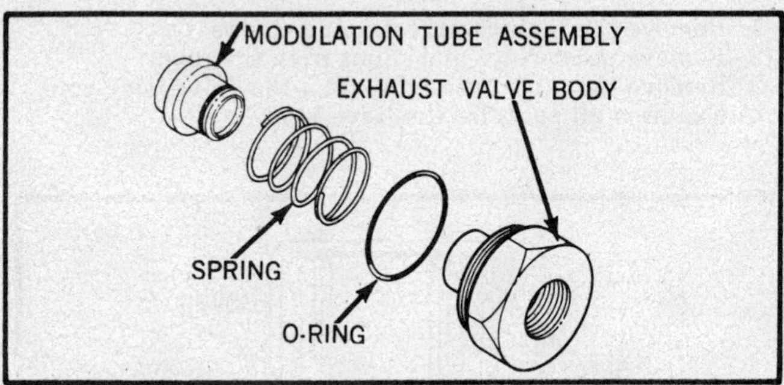

Exhaust valve and modulation tube assembly (© GM Corp.)

6. Remove the spring and modulation tube assembly from within the valve body.
7. Remove the inlet seal, seal retainer, and the O-ring from the modulation tube.
8. Remove the exhaust valve seal screw, the valve seal, and the O-ring from the piston.
9. Remove the valve cover O-ring.
10. Remove the valve seat, O-ring, and valve disc from the valve cover.
11. Examine all parts for excessive or abnormal wear.

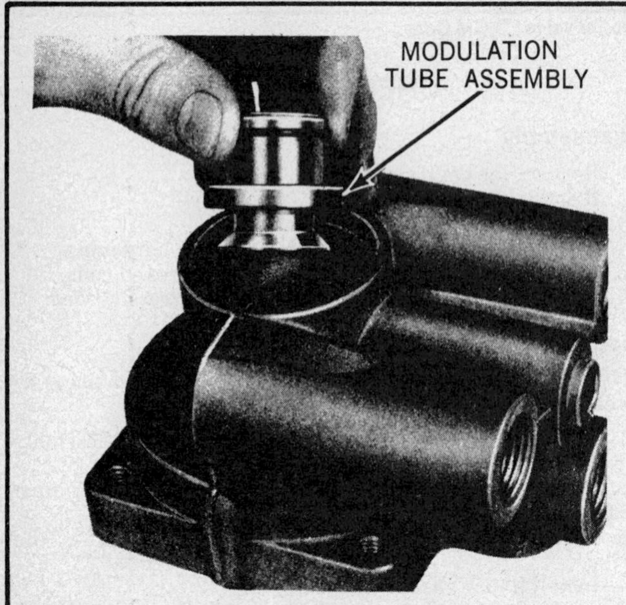

Installing modulation tube assembly (© GM Corp.)

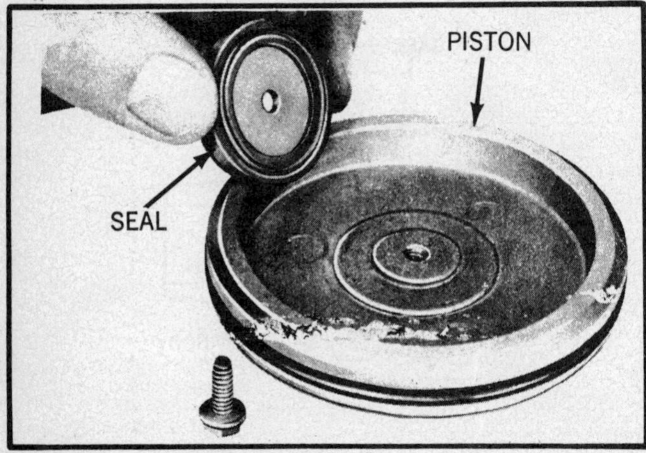

Exhaust valve seal and piston (© GM Corp.)

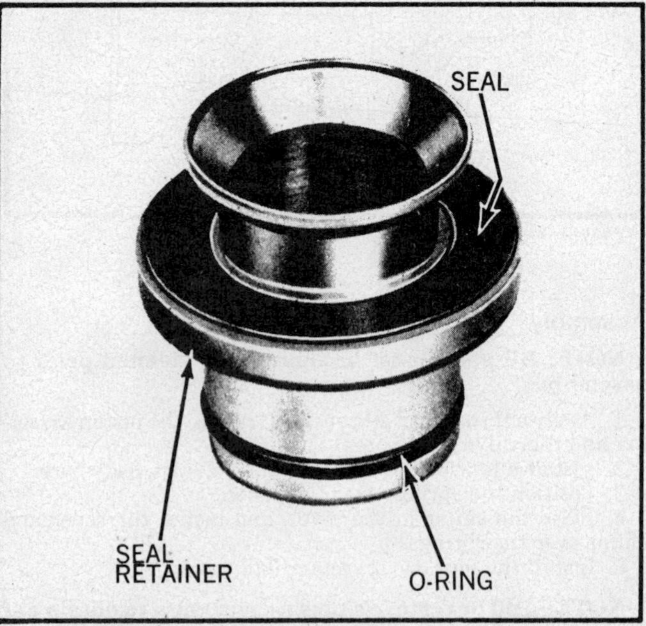

Modulation tube assembly (© GM Corp.)

NOTE: The inlet valve seal (positioned around the modulation tube) and the valve disc (located under the valve seat in the end of the relay valve assembly opposite the exhaust valve body) must be smooth on the valve face area. The exhaust valve seal face (the seal which is attached to the piston by a retaining screw) must be flat and smooth in the area contacting the modulation tube seat. Any part(s) which appears defective or worn should be replaced.

Assembly

1. Apply a light coat of silicone lubricant to the O-rings, O-ring sealing surfaces, the valve body, the modulation tube, and the outer edges of the piston.
2. Install the inlet valve seal and a new O-ring on the modulation tube.
3. Install the seal retainer over the modulation tube and around the valve seal.
4. Insert the modulation tube assembly into the valve body until the valve seal comes to rest against the valve body seat.
5. Install the spring over the modulation tube assembly so that it rests on the seal retainer.
6. Install a new O-ring on the exhaust valve body.
7. Thread the exhaust valve into the main valve body being careful to align the exhaust valve with the spring which now rests on the seal retainer. Torque the exhaust valve body to 125 ft. lbs.
8. Position the exhaust valve on the piston with the raised circular ring of the valve seal resting against the piston, and install the exhaust valve seal screw. Torque the screw to 48 inch lbs.
9. Install a new O-ring on the piston.
10. Install a new O-ring on the valve cover.
11. Install the piston into the cover.
12. Install a new O-ring seal onto the valve seat.
13. Install the valve disc (if so equipped) and valve seat into the valve cover.
14. Install the piston and cover assembly into the valve body.
15. Position the mounting bracket onto the cover (if so equipped), and install the four cover screws. Torque the screws to 135 inch lbs.

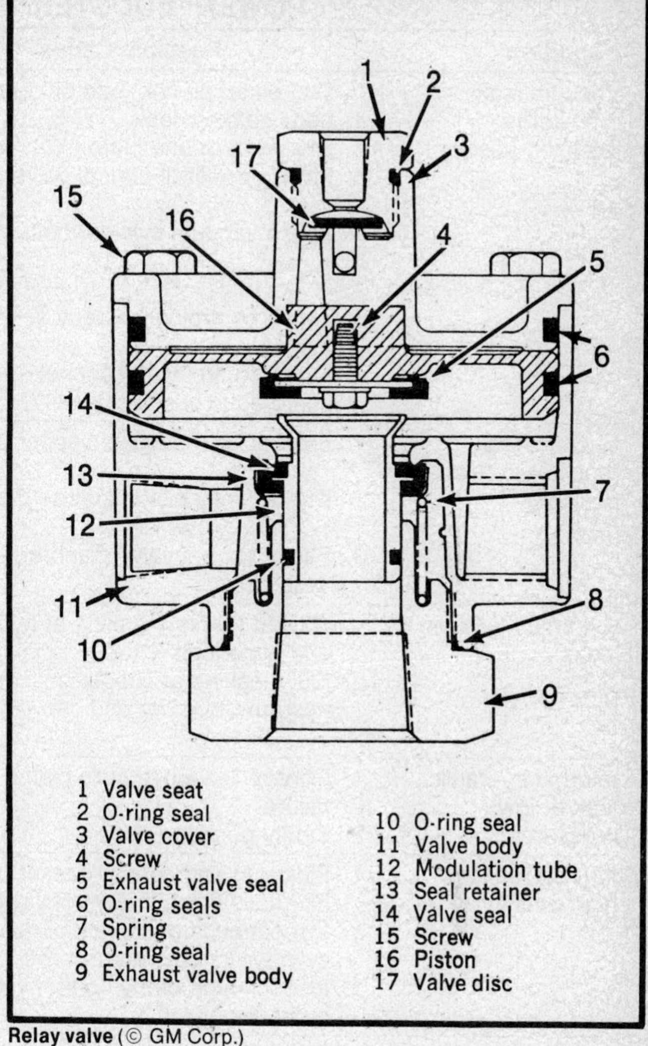

Relay valve (© GM Corp.)

DISC TYPE

This type of parking brake is used only on models equipped with auxiliary transmissions. A ventilated disc is mounted between the drive shaft and the auxiliary transmission shaft flange. The brake shoes are mounted on opposite sides of the disc. The brake is applied through use of mechanical linkage which forces the brake shoes against the disc.

Adjustment

1. Disconnect the brake cable or the rod clevis from the brake lever.
2. Tighten the adjusting nut until the spring pressure pushes the brake lever against the front lever arm.
3. Insert a $\frac{1}{32}$ in. shim between the rear shoe and the disc.
4. Tighten the adjusting screw so that the front shoe is firmly against the disc, yet still allowing removal of the shim.
5. Remove the shim and adjust the parallel adjusting screws so that both linings are parallel to the disc. This should provide $\frac{1}{64}$ in. clearance between the shoes and disc.
6. Making sure the brake lever in the cab is fully released, adjust the clevis on the brake cable as much as necessary to allow installation of clevis pin through the clevis and brake lever without changing position of the lever. Install the pin and cotter pin.
7. Make sure all lock nuts and adjusting screws are tightened securely.

POWER BOOSTER TROUBLE DIAGNOSIS

Condition	Possible Cause	Correction
Vacuum leak (booster in released position)	1. End plate, center plate or control valve body gaskets leak.	1. Recondition booster unit.
	2. Distortion of end plate.	2. Replace end plate.
	3. Misalignment of control valve poppet.	3. Disassemble, clean and correctly reassemble.
	4. Loose vacuum cylinder bolts.	4. Coat vacuum cylinder bolts lightly with a suitable sealing compound and tighten to specified torque.
	5. Loose control valve body screws.	5. Tighten control valve body screws to specified torque.
	6. Large control valve poppet spring not centered in spring retainer.	6. Disassemble unit and correctly reassemble.
Vacuum leak (booster in applied position)	1. Leak at control valve poppet and seat.	1. Clean and inspect poppet and seat for damage and repair as necessary.
	2. Dry or faulty piston leather packing.	2. Clean and lubricate piston leather or replace.
	3. Faulty control valve disphragm assembly.	3. Replace faulty parts.
External hydraulic leaks	1. Gasket (O-ring) leaking at hydraulic end plate joint.	1. Disassemble clean and replace (O-ring) gasket and reassemble.
	2. Fluid leaking at copper gasket under hydraulic cylinder end cap.	2. Remove end cap and inspect copper gasket and seat install new copper gasket.
Internal hydraulic leak at low pressures	1. Control valve hydraulic piston cup failure.	1. Recondition control valve unit.
	2. Faulty push rod seal.	2. Replace push rod seal.
Internal leaks at high pressure	1. Fluid passing copper gasket under hydraulic fitting in control valve.	1. Clean and inspect gasket and fitting, replace if faulty.
	2. Inspect cups and seals of master cylinder for cuts and scores.	2. Hone master cylinder and replace cups and seals.
	3. Inspect cups of the control valve hydraulic piston.	3. Replace faulty cups.
Hydraulic pressure buildup (without added input)	1. Check hydraulic piston check valve and slot for foreign material under valve.	1. Clean or replace valve and seats as condition indicates.
Failure to release	1. Weak vacuum cylinder piston return spring.	1. Replace vacuum cylinder piston return spring.
	2. Dry vacuum piston leather packing.	2. Lubricate vacuum piston leather packing.
	3. Swollen rubber cups due to inferior or contaminated brake fluid.	3. Flush hydraulic system and recondition or replace all cylinders.
	4. Damaged or dented vacuum cylinder shell.	4. Replace vacuum cylinder shell.
	5. Dirty or sticky control valve piston.	5. Recondition control valve assembly.
Failure of booster to operate within specified pressures	1. Rusty, dirty or distorted vacuum cylinder shell.	1. Clean or replace vacuum cylinder shell.
	2. Dry or worn vacuum cylinder leather packing.	2. Recondition and lubricate the vacuum booster.
	3. Swollen rubber cups due to inferior brake fluid.	3. Recondition the master cylinder. Replace brake fluid.
	4. Worn or scored hydraulic cups.	4. Recondition the master cylinder.
	5. Dirt, rust or foreign matter in any component of the system.	5. Recondition and lubricate the brake booster assembly.

POWER BOOSTER TROUBLE DIAGNOSIS

Condition	Possible Cause	Correction
Loss of fluid	1. Fluid leaking past cup in master cylinder.	1. Recondition master cylinder or replace.
	2. Brake wheel cylinders leaking.	2. Recondition or replace wheel cylinders.
	3. Loose hydraulic hose connectors.	3. Inspect and tighten all hydraulic connections.
	4. Leaking stop light switch.	4. Replace stop light switch.
Presence of brake fluid on hy-power vacuum cylinder	1. Piston cup or push rod seal leaking.	1. Recondition master cylinder.
Pedal kicks back against foot when brakes are applied	1. Vacuum leakage.	1. Inspect and correct vacuum leak.
	2. Dirt under control valve or damaged seat.	2. Clean and recondition booster assembly.
	3. Weak or broken spring.	3. Replace spring.
Brakes are slow to release ①	1. Incorrect pedal linkage adjustment.	1. Adjust and lubricate pedal linkage.
	2. Compensating port of master cylinder plugged.	2. Clean master cylinder with compressed air.
	3. Brake shoes sticking.	3. Free up and lubricate brake shoes.
	4. Weak brake shoe return spring.	4. Replace brake shoe return spring.
	5. Booster control valve piston sticking.	5. Clean booster control valve piston and lubricate.
	6. Booster air filter clogged.	6. Clean air filter in mineral spirits.
	7. Control valve diaphragm return spring missing.	7. Install new control valve return spring.
	8. Defective check valve in slave cylinder piston.	8. Recondition slave cylinder pistons.
	9. Dirt under atmospheric valve disc.	9. Clean atmospheric valve.
Engine runs unevenly at idle with brakes released	1. Vacuum leakage.	1. Inspect and tighten all vacuum fittings.
	2. Dirt under control valve disc or damaged seat.	2. Clean control valve or replace.
	3. Defective spring.	3. Replace defective spring.
Engine runs evenly and pedal is hard with brakes applied	1. Control valve piston assembly not seating on vacuum disc.	1. Clean or replace control valve piston assembly.
	2. Defective control valve plate and diaphragm.	2. Replace control valve plate and diaphragm.
	3. Defective pressure plate and diaphragm.	3. Replace pressure plate and diaphragm.
Brake pedal is hard at different intervals	1. Defective manifold check valve.	1. Clean or replace manifold check valve.
	2. Slave cylinder piston sticking due to dirt or inferior brake fluid.	2. Clean and recondition slave cylinder.
	3. Brake booster air cleaner clogged.	3. Clean air cleaner in mineral spirits and blow dry with compressed air.

①Jack up truck and determine whether or not the brakes are dragging before further testing is done.

POWER BRAKE BOOSTER SERVICE

Brake System Preliminary Checks

Always check the fluid level in the brake master cylinder reservoir(s) before performing the test procedures. If the fluid level is not within $\frac{1}{4}$ in. of the top of the master cylinder reservoirs, add the specified brake fluid.

Push the brake pedal down as far as it will go. If the pedal travels more than halfway between the released position and the floor, adjust the brakes. If the vehicle is equipped with automatic brake adjusters, serveral sharp brake applications while backing up may be necessary to adjust the brakes.

Road test the vehicle and apply the brakes at a speed of about 20 mph to see if the vehicle stops evenly. If not, the brakes should be adjusted. Perform the road test only when the brakes will apply and the vehicle can be safely stopped.

DUAL BRAKE WARNING LIGHT SYSTEM TESTS

1. Turn the ignition switch to the ACC or ON position. If the light on the brake warning lamp remains on, the condition may be caused by a shorted or broken switch, grounded switch wires or the differential pressure valve is not centered. Centralize the differential pressure valve. If the warning light remains on, check the switch connector and wire for a grounded condition and repair or replace the wire assembly. If the condition of the wire is good, replace the brake warning lamp switch.
2. Turn the ignition switch to the start position. If the brake warning lamp does not light, check the light and wiring and replace or repair wiring as necessary. When both brake systems are functioning normally, the equal pressure at the pressure differential valve during brake pedal application keeps the valve centered. The brake warning light will be on only when the ignition key is in the start position.
3. If the brake warning lamp does not light when a pressure differential condition exists in the brake system, the warning lamp may be burned out, the warning lamp switch is inoperative or the switch to lamp wiring has an open circuit. Check the bulb and replace it, if required. Check the switch to lamp wires for an open circuit and repair or replace them, if required. If the warning lamp still does not light, replace the switch.

POWER BRAKE FUNCTION

Testing

With the engine stopped, eliminate all vacuum from the system by pumping the brake pedal several times. Then push the pedal down as far as it will go, and note the effort required to hold it in this position. If the pedal gradually moves downward under this pressure, the hydraulic system is leaking and should be checked by a hydraulic pressure test.

With the brake pedal still pushed down, start the engine. If the vacuum system is operating properly, the pedal will move downward. If the pedal position does not change, the vacuum system is not operating properly and should be checked by a vacuum test.

VACUUM BOOSTER CHECK VALVE

Testing

Disconnect the line from the bottom of the vacuum check valve, and connect a vacuum gauge to the valve. Start the engine, run it at idle speed, and check the reading on the vacuum gauge.

The gauge should register 17–19 in. Hg. with standard transmission and 14–15 in. Hg. in Drive range if equipped with an automatic transmission. Stop the engine and note the rate of vacuum drop. If the vacuum drops more than one in. Hg. in 15 seconds, the check valve is leaking. If the vacuum reading does not reach 18 in. Hg. or is unsteady, an engine tuneup is needed.

Remove the gauge and reconnect the vacuum line to the check valve.

BENDIX PISTON TYPE VACUUM BOOSTER

Testing

Disconnect the vacuum line from the booster end plate. Install a tee fitting in the end plate, and connect a vacuum gauge (no. 1) and vacuum line to the fitting. Install a second vacuum gauge (no. 2) in place of the pipe plug in the booster control valve body.

Start the engine, and note the vacuum reading on both gauges. If both gauges do not register manifold vacuum, air is leaking into the vacuum system. If both gauges register manifold vacuum, stop the engine and note the rate of vacuum drop on both gauges. If the drop exceeds one in. Hg. in 15 seconds on either gauge, air is leaking into the vacuum system. Tighten all vacuum connections and repeat the test. If leakage still exists, the leak may be localized as follows:

1. Disconnect the vacuum line and gauge no. 1 from the booster.
2. Connect vacuum gauge no. 1 directly to the vacuum line. Start the engine and note the gauge reading. Stop the engine and check the rate of vacuum drop. If gauge no. 1 does not register manifold vacuum, or if the vacuum drop exceeds 1 in. Hg. in 15 seconds, the leak is in the vacuum line or check valve connections.
3. Reconnect vacuum gauge no. 1 and the vacuum line to the tee fitting. Start the engine, and run it at idle speed for one minute. Depress the brake pedal sufficiently to cause vacuum gauge no. 2 to read from zero to 1 in. Hg. Gauge no. 1 should register manifold vacuum of 17–19 in. Hg. with standard transmission and 14–16 in. Hg. in Drive range if equipped with an automatic transmission. If the drop of vacuum on gauge no. 2 is slow, the air cleaner, or air cleaner line, may be plugged. Inspect and if necessary, clean the air cleaner.
4. Release the brake pedal and observe the action of gauge no. 2. Upon releasing the pedal, the vacuum gauge must register increasing vacuum until manifold vacuum is reached. The rate of increase must be smooth, with no lag or slowness in the return to manifold vacuum. If the gauge readings are not as outlined, the booster is not operating properly and should be removed and overhauled.

DIAGRAGM TYPE VACUUM BOOSTER

Testing

This procedure can be used to test all diaphragm boosters which are equipped with a pipe thread outlet on the atmosphere portion of the diaphragm chamber.

Remove the pipe plug from the rear half of the booster chamber, and install a vacuum gauge. Start the engine and run it at idle speed. The gauge should register 18–21 in. Hg.

1. With the engine running, depress the brake pedal with enough pressure to show a zero reading on the vacuum gauge. Hold the pedal in the applied position for one minute. Any downward movement of the pedal during this time indicates a brake fluid leak. Any kickback (upward movement) of the pedal indicates brake fluid is leaking past the hydraulic piston check valve.
2. With the engine running, push down on the brake pedal with sufficient pressure to show a zero reading on the vacuum gauge. Hold the pedal down, and shut the engine off. Maintain

pedal position for one minute. A kickback of the pedal indicates a vacuum leak in the vacuum check valve, in the vacuum line connections, or in the booster.

VACUUM–HYDRAULIC BOOSTER SYSTEMS

Bleeding

1. Eliminate vacuum in the booster by depressing the brake pedal several times while the engine is not running.
2. On trucks not equipped with reservoir tanks, disconnect the manifold tube at the booster side of the manifold check valve (engine not running).
3. Alternately loosen the brake tube at each unit until all air is expelled. Booster slave-cylinder is bled first.

CAUTION

Where air pressure brake bleeding equipment is used to bleed brakes, do not use more than 25–30 psi.

NOTE: A piston stop is provided in the slave cylinder to eliminate the possibility of damaging the return spring while bleeding the system. This damage occurs only when bleeding the brakes with a vacuum present in the booster system.

Hydraulic Tandem Brake Unit

Disassembly

1. Disconnect hydraulic and vacuum by-pass tube from valve body.
2. Remove control valve air inlet fitting from control valve body.
3. Remove control valve body and valve parts from end plate.
4. Make a special tool.

NOTE: If this is to be a regular service this tool is recommended. For one time or emergency, a vise, "C" clamps, and a guide tube 10 in. long may be used.

5. Insert tool through end plate opening, and force vacuum cylinder piston forward.
6. Attach flange of tool to end plate with three valve body cover screws.
7. Loosen slave cylinder check nut, and remove slave cylinder.
8. Compress push rod pin retaining spring, remove retainer pin, then remove hydraulic piston from push rod.
9. Hold end cap in a vise, and remove hydraulic cylinder from cap.
10. Loosen vacuum hose clamps, then slide both hoses on the vacuum tube toward center plate.
11. Remove hydraulic by-pass tube from rear end plate, then remove return spring compression tool from end plate.
12. Remove the nuts and studs from power cylinder, then disassemble end plates, cylinder shells and center plate assembly.
13. Force center plate and vacuum piston together, and insert a rod through hole in piston rod to hold piston return spring in the compressed position.
14. Place assembly ring over piston, then remove piston assembly, but keep piston parts assembled in assembly ring. After vacuum tubes and tee fittings have been removed from center plate, position plate on a flat surface.
15. Remove fast application valve cover.
16. To disassemble the diaphragm assembly, hold valve shaft with a screwdriver, and remove nut.
17. Lift retainer and diaphragm off valve shaft.
18. Turn center plate upside down, then remove valve seat plate screws and plate, gasket, valve, and spring from center plate.

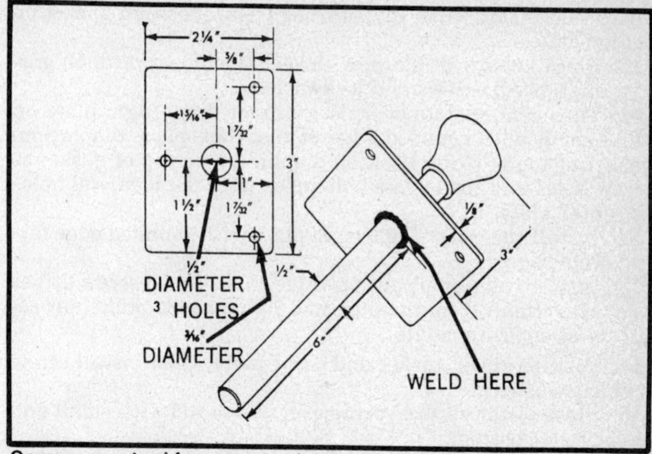

Compressor tool for vacuum piston return spring
(© Chrysler Corp.)

19. Position front end plate assembly on a flat surface with flat side down.
20. Remove the O-ring seal, snap-ring and retainer washer, push rod seal spring and flange washer, push rod rubber cup seal, and guide washer from end plate.
21. Drive push rod leather seal out of end plate.
22. Position end plate in a holding fixture, then remove hydraulic valve fitting with a 1 ⅞ in. socket wrench.
23. Push hydraulic piston out of valve fitting, and remove gasket from fittings.

NOTE: Clean all metal parts in a suitable cleaning fluid. After cleaning, wash all the hydraulic system parts in alcohol. Examine the bore of the cylinder shells for rust and corrosion, and polish with fine steel wool or crocus cloth if necessary. If the cylinders are badly pitted or scored, install new cylinders. If felt type wicks are worn, replace them with cotton type wicks.

CAUTION

Use overhaul kit and install ALL parts contained. Do not gamble on ANY old parts that the kit replaces.

Assembly

1. Install nut on piston rod with flat side of nut upward.
2. Position larger diameter piston plate on piston rod with chamfered side of hole at top. Guide rubber seal ring over threads of piston rod.
3. Place assembly ring on a flat surface, then install leather packing, with lip side upward; and smaller diameter piston plate with chamfered side of hole downward in the ring.
4. Cut a new piece of wick to the required length, then place it against inner face of leather packing lip.
5. Assemble expander ring against wick with gripper points upward, and hook notched end of spring under the clip near opposite end of spring. Position cut of retainer plate over loop of the spring.
6. Hold piston parts in the assembly ring, assemble them on end of piston rod, then install nut on tip of piston assembly. Tighten nut until it is flush with end of rod. Stake nuts securely at two places.
7. Clamp staked nut firmly in a vise, and tighten nut on opposite side of piston plate solidly against piston plate.
8. Press the fast application valve stem and push rod seals into center plate. The application valve seal must be flush with bottom of hole. The push rod seal should rest against the shoulder of center plate. Position center plate. Then place valve spring on top of seal with the small end at top.
9. Install the bullet-nosed tool at threaded end of valve

shaft, and insert valve shaft through seal. Position gasket on center plate.

10. Place valve seat plate, with seat side downward, on gasket, and install screws and lockwashers.

11. Turn center plate over. Place lower diaphragm plate on valve shaft with rounded edge at top, then place diaphragm gasket at top of plate. Position diaphragm on top of gasket so screw holes and the bypass hole index with the identical holes in center plate.

12. Install the other diaphragm plate with rounded edge facing diaphragm.

13. Install valve shaft nut on valve shaft. Use a screw driver to prevent shaft from turning, and tighten nut. Stake nut securely at opposite points.

14. Position cover gasket and cover plate, then install screw and lockwashers.

15. Place piston return spring over piston rod with small end of spring at bottom.

16. Carefully guide piston rod through leather seal in center plate, with piston stop flanges of center plate facing upward. Press center plate down against spring, and insert a rod in piston rod. Thread piston rod nut on piston rod, with flat side of nut upward to limit of threads.

17. If forward piston was disassembled to replace leather piston packing, cotton wicking, or other parts, assemble the piston parts in the ring and turn assembly ring over.

18. Remove larger piston plate and O-ring seal.

19. With assembly ring still in place, guide the remaining piston parts over end of push rod and against piston nut. Carefully install O-ring seal over threads of piston rod.

20. Place the larger diameter piston plate on piston rod with chamfered side of hole toward O-ring seal.

21. Assemble large end of push rod in end of piston rod and install retainer pin. Install piston rod nut on end of piston rod with flat side downward. Tighten nut until it is flush with face of piston rod, then stake nut securely at opposite points.

22. Hold piston rod nut in a vise or with a wrench, and tighten inner nut securely against piston. Care must be exercised when tightening inner nut to prevent expander spring retainer plate from shifting.

23. Remove assembly ring, then remove rod holding return spring compressed. Install a new copper gasket in end cap.

24. The hydraulic cylinder must be assembled with milled flats next to end cap. Tighten hydraulic cylinder solidly in end cap, then thread check nut on hydraulic cylinder up to the limit of the threads.

25. Install check nut seal (if used) in groove or cylinder tube. Install bleeder screw in cap.

26. Press push rod leather seal into hydraulic cylinder bore of front end plate from inner side of plate with lip of seal toward outer end of the plate. Install push rod seal parts.

27. The chamfered side of stop washer is down, lip of cup is up, flat side of washer is next to cup, and small end of spring is down. Place washer against spring. Install snap-ring in inner groove of end plate.

28. Install stop washer with flat side in control valve hydraulic fitting. Install stop washer retaining ring.

29. Dip hydraulic piston cups in brake fluid, and assemble them on the hydraulic piston with lips of cups positioned away from each other. Insert piston into the fitting with open end of piston toward stop washer.

30. Install a new gasket on the hydraulic fitting (copper gasket on fitting without the groove, and a rubber seal gasket on fitting with the groove). Install the hydraulic fitting in end plate with a 1 $^7/_8$ in. socket wrench. Tighten fitting equipped with a rubber gasket firmly, and fitting equipped with a copper gasket to 324–330 ft. lbs.

31. Assemble vacuum control parts in control body. Install a new lead washer.

32. Hold slave cylinder end cap in a vise, and thread cylinder into end plate. Install T-fitting and tubes on center plate.

33. Position an end plate gasket on the plate, place cylinder shell on end plate, and coat interior of cylinder with vacuum cylinder oil.

34. Dip cylinder piston on packing in vacuum cylinder oil and allow the excess oil to drain off the wickings.

35. Position a gasket on ledge of center plate, then carefully guide push rod through seal in front end plate. At the same time, align the vacuum tube in end plate with vacuum tube on center plate. Slide hose in place to contact the two vacuum tubes.

36. Position a new gasket at center plate ledge.

37. Coat the interior of cylinder shell with vacuum cylinder oil, then tip cylinder at a 45 degree angle to prevent damage to the piston leather packing.

38. Carefully push the cylinder over piston and onto center plate.

39. Place a new gasket on ledge of end plate, then install end plate on cylinder, aligning end plate vacuum tube and center plate tube. Install cylinder studs and tighten nuts evenly.

40. To assemble the hydraulic piston parts, place large end of spring in retainer cup, then install check ball in piston body behind spring.

41. Dip piston cup in brake fluid, then install it on piston with lip of cup toward check ball.

42. Position the vacuum hoses on tubes, and tighten hose clamps firmly.

43. Connect hydraulic by-pass tube to front and rear end plate.

44. Remove slave cylinder from end plates, then insert and attach return spring compressing tool.

45. Assemble hydraulic piston on push rod.

46. Make certain lock ring is positioned over the retainer pin. Install hydraulic gasket in the plate. Carefully guide the hydraulic cylinder over piston cup, and thread cylinder into end plate.

47. Adjust cylinder 7 $^3/_4$ in., measuring between points shown in illustration.

48. Align bleeder screw in end cap with bleeder screw in control valve.

49. Remove spring compressing tool. After cylinder length adjustment is completed, tighten cylinder check nut solidly.

50. Install guide pins, made from 8–32 × 2 $^1/_2$ in. machine screws with the heads cut off, in end plate.

51. Install diaphragm with diaphragm stem inserted into hydraulic control piston hole. Place diaphragm return spring and control valve body on top of diaphragm.

52. Remove guide pins, one at a time, and replace each guide pin with an attaching screw and a new lock washer. Tighten screws progressively and firmly.

53. Install air inlet fitting in control body, then install retainer.

54. Install vacuum by-pass tube.

55. Inspect assembly to see that all bolts, nut, screws, washers and plugs are in place, and that all tubes, clamps, and fittings are firmly tightened.

Installation

1. Position assembly on mounting brackets, and install attaching bolts.
2. Tighten bolts firmly.
3. Connect stop light wires and hydraulic lines to stop light switch.
4. Attach vacuum hose to booster.
5. Connect master cylinder hydraulic line to booster control valve.
6. Connect wheel cylinder hydraulic line to booster end cap.
7. Attach air inlet hose to control valve air inlet fitting, then check and tighten connections.
8. Remove lubricating plugs from end and center plates.
9. Add vacuum cylinder oil to level of filler holes, install plugs, then bleed hydraulic system.

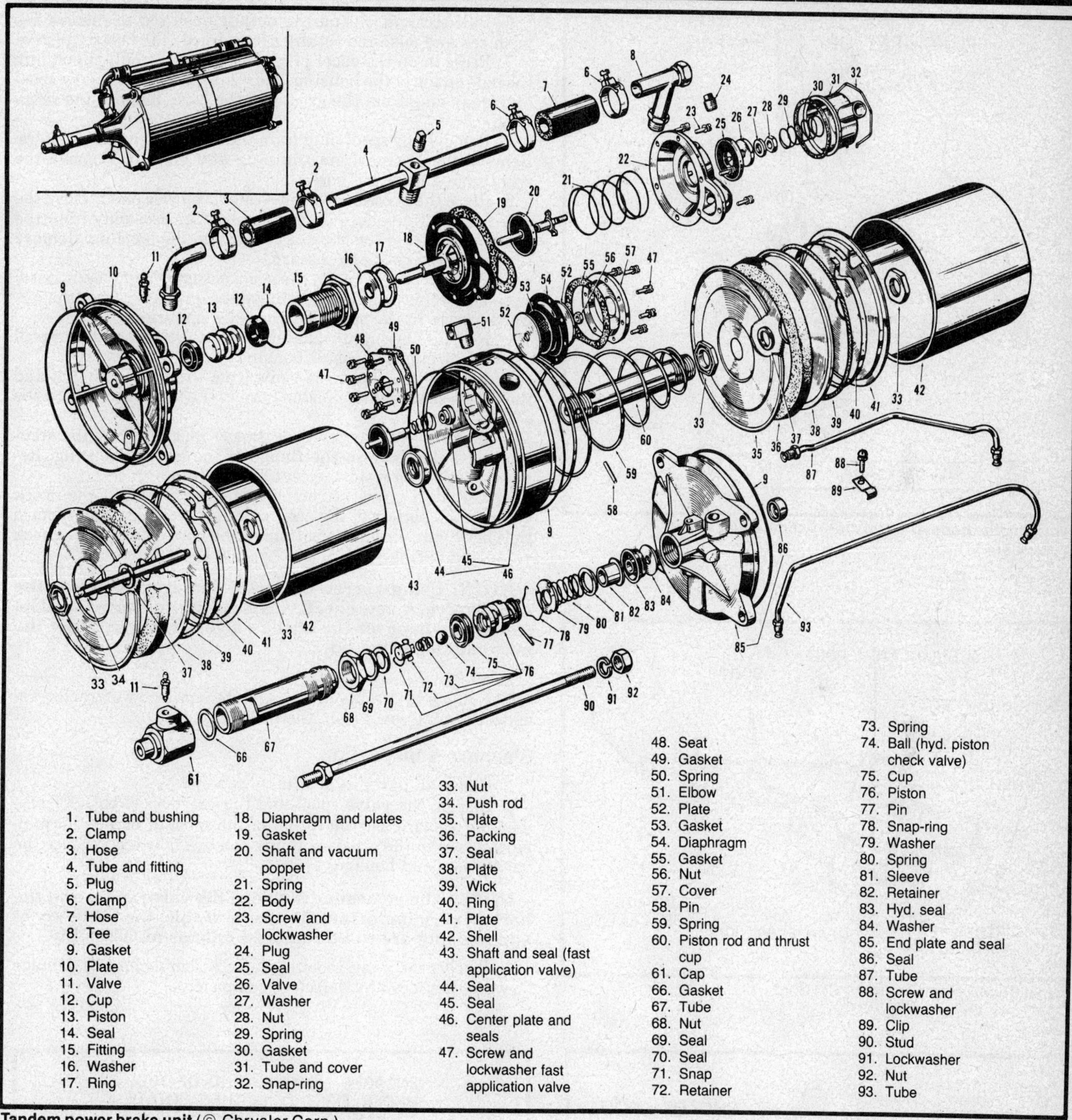

Tandem power brake unit (© Chrysler Corp.)

Bendix Hydro – Boost

The Bendix Hydro-Boost uses the hydraulic pressure supplied by the power steering pump to provide a power assist to brake application.

Disassembly

1. Place the booster in a vise with the bracket end up. Using a hammer and chisel, cut the bracket nut that holds the linkage bracket to the booster assembly. The nut should be cut at the open slot in the booster cover threads. Care must be exercised to avoid damage to the threads. Spread the nut and remove the bracket.
2. Remove the pedal boot by pulling if off over the pedal rod eyelet.
3. Position pedal rod removing tool around the pedal rod. The tool should be resting on the booster cover. Insert a punch through the pedal rod from the lower side of the special tool. Push the punch through until it rests on the higher side of the tool. Push up on the punch to shear the pedal rod retainer; remove the pedal rod.
4. Remove the grommet from the groove near the end of the pedal rod and from the groove in the input rod.
5. Disengage the tabs of the spring retainer from the ledge inside the opening near the master cylinder mounting flange of the booster. Remove the retainer and piston return spring from the opening.

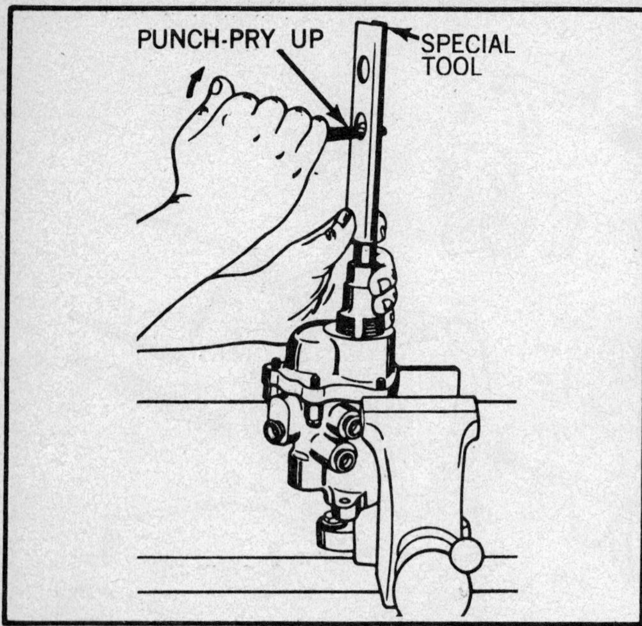

Removing the booster pedal rod—Bendix hydro boost (© GM Corp.)

6. Pull straight out on the output push rod to remove the push rod and push rod retainer from inside the booster piston.

7. Press in on the spool plug, and insert a small punch into the hole on top of the housing. This unseats one side of the spool plug snap-ring from the groove in the bore. Remove the snap-ring.

8. Remove the spool plug from the bore with a pair of pliers. Remove the O-ring from the plug and discard. Remove the spool spring from the bore.

9. Place the booster cover in a soft-faced vise and remove the cover retaining bolts. Remove the booster assembly from the vise and separate the booster cover from the housing. Remove the large seal ring and discard.

10. Press in on the end of the spool assembly, and use a spiral snap-ring removing tool to remove the snap-ring from the forward groove in the spool. Discard the snap-ring.

11. Remove the input rod and piston assembly, and the spool assembly from the booster housing.

12. Remove the input rod seals from the input rod end, and the piston seal from the piston bore in the housing. Discard the seals.

13. Remove the plunger, seat, spacer and ball from the accumulator valve bore in the flange of the booster housing. Remove the O-ring from the seat and discard.

14. Thread a screw extractor into the opening in the check valve in the bottom of the accumulator valve bore, and remove the check valve from the bottom of the bore. Discard the check valve and O-ring.

NOTE: Using a screw extractor damages the seat in the check valve. A new check valve, O-ring and valve must be installed whenever the check valve is removed from the accumulator valve bore.

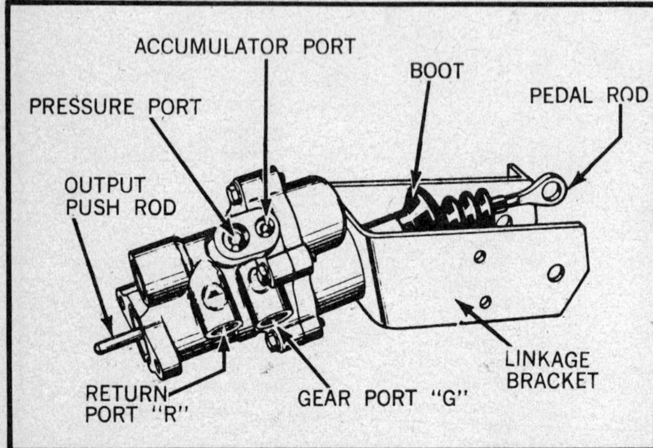

Typical Bendix hydro boost (© GM Corp.)

15. Using a $\frac{1}{4}$ or a $\frac{5}{16}$ in. spiral flute type screw extractor, remove the tube seats from the booster ports.

Cleaning & Inspection

1. Clean all parts in a suitable solvent.

2. Inspect the valve spool and the valve spool bore for any damage or ware. Discoloration of the spool or bore is normal, particulary in the grooves. If any damage is noted, replace the valve spool and housing.

NOTE: The clearance between the valve spool and the bore is very important. Because of this, the valve spool and housing are to be replaced only as an assembly.

3. Inspect the input rod and piston assembly for any damage or ware. Replace any defective components.

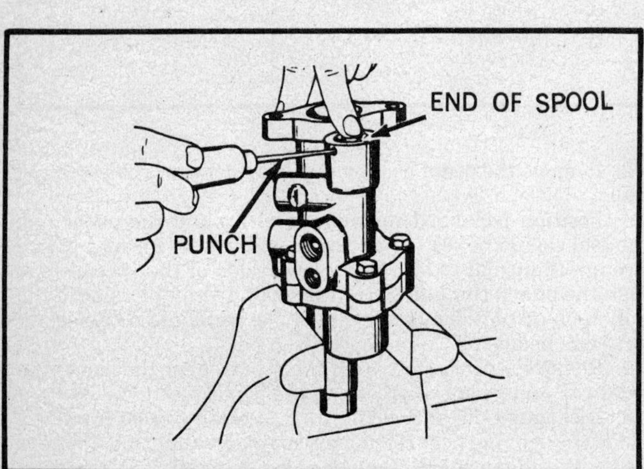

Removing the spool plug from Bendix hydro boost (© GM Corp.)

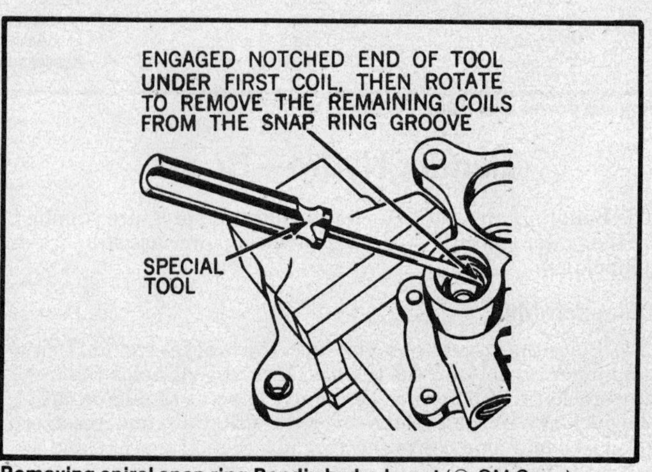

Removing spiral snap ring Bendix hydro boost (© GM Corp.)

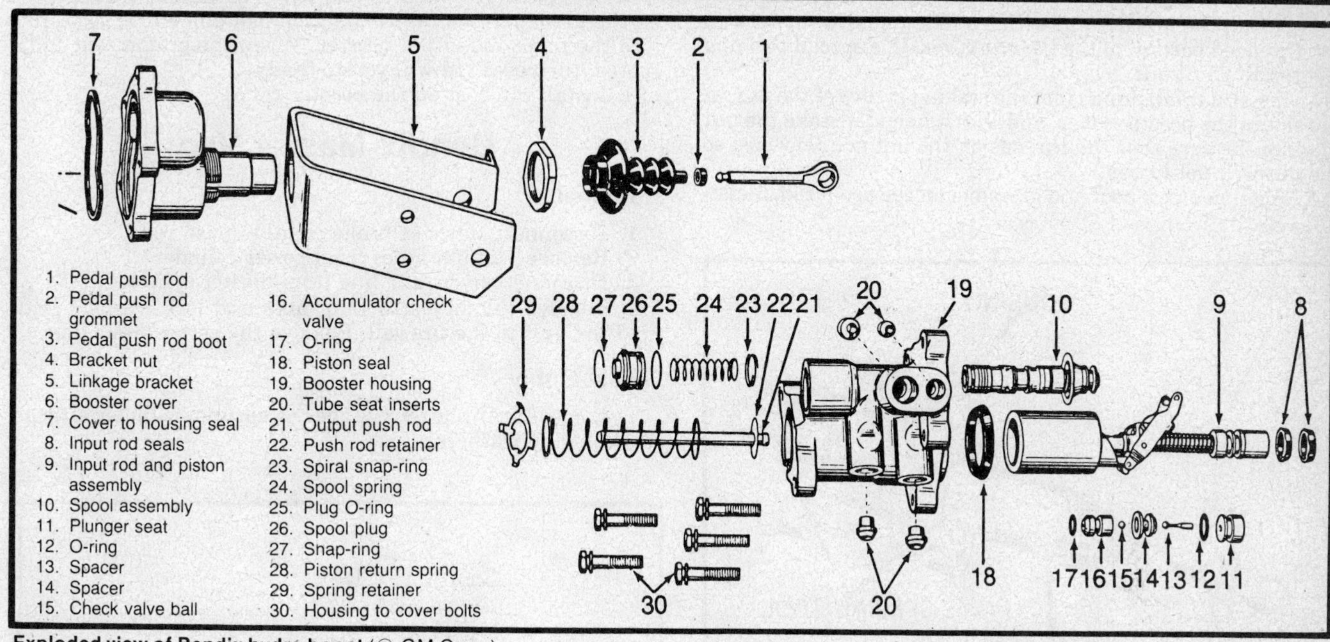

Exploded view of Bendix hydro boost (© GM Corp.)

4. Inspect the piston bore in the housing for any damage or ware. If defective, replace the booster housing and spool valve assembly.

Assembly

CAUTION

Parts must be kept VERY clean. If there is any reason to doubt the cleanliness of the components, re-wash before assembly.

Lubricate all seals and metal friction points with power steering fluid before assembly. Whenever the booster is disassembled, be sure that seals, tube inserts, spiral snap-ring, check valve and ball are replaced.

1. Position a tube seat in each booster port and screw a spare tube nut in each port to press the seat down into the port. Do not tighten the tube nuts in the port as this may deface the seats. Remove the spare tube nuts and check for aluminium chips in the ports. Be sure that there is no foreign matter in the ports.
2. Coat the piston bore and piston seal with clean power steering fluid. Assemble the seal in the piston bore. The lip of the seal must be towards the rear (away from the master cylinder mounting flange). Be sure that the seal is fully seated in the housing.
3. Lubricate the input rod end, input rod seals and the seal installer tool with clean power steering fluid. Slide the seals on the tool with the lip of the cups towards the open end of the tool. Slide the tool over the input rod end end down to the second groove; then slide the forward seal off the tool and into the groove. Assemble the other seal in the first groove. Be sure, that both seals are fully seated.
4. Lubricate the piston and piston installing tool with clean power steering fluid. Insert the large end of the tool into the piston and the tool and piston into the piston bore, through the seal.
5. Position the O-ring on the accumulator check valve and coat the assembly with clean power steering fluid. Insert the check valve in the accumulator valve recess in the housing flange. Place the ball and spacer in the same recess.
6. Place the O-ring on the changing valve plunger seat and insert the plunger into the seat. Dip the assembly in clean power steering fluid and insert it into the changing valve recess.
7. Coat the spool assembly with clean power steering fluid and insert in the spool bore. Be sure that the pivot pins on the upper end of the input rod lever assembly are engaged in the groove in the sleeve. Remove piston installing tool.
8. Separate the two components of the snap-ring installation tool and place the spiral snap-ring on the tool. Insert the rounded end of the installer into the spool bore. While pressing on the rear of the spool, slide the snap-ring off the tool and into the groove near the forward end of the spool by pressing in on the tool sleeve. Check to be sure that the retaining ring is fully seated.
9. Place the housing seal in the groove in the housing cover. Join the booster housing and cover and secure with five attaching bolts. Tighten the bolts to 18–26 ft. lbs.

CAUTION

It is very important that the same cover attaching bolts are used as they are designed for the booster only. If they are damaged replace with the same part numbers.

10. Place an O-ring on the spool plug. Insert the spool spring and the spool plug in the forward end of the spool bore. Press in on the plug and position the snap-ring in its groove in the spool valve bore.
11. Place the linkage bracket on the booster assembly. The tab on the inside of the large hole in the bracket should fit into the slot in the threaded portion of the booster cover.

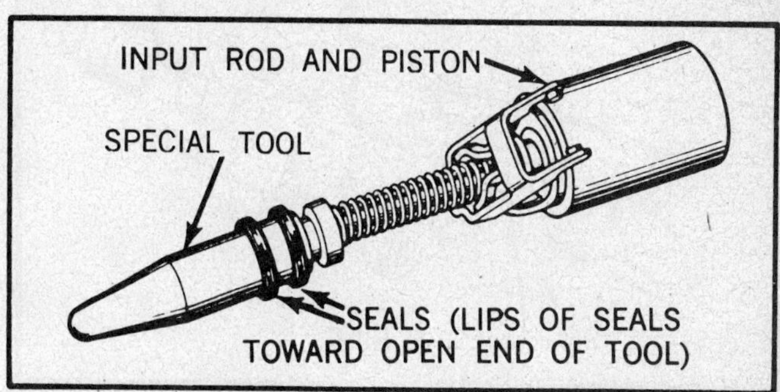

Installing input rod seals Bendix hydro boost (© GM Corp.)

12. Install the bracket nut with a staking groove outward on the threaded portion to the booster cover. Use special tool and tighten to 95–120 ft. lbs.

13. Insert a small punch into the staking groove of the nut, at the slot in the booster cover, and with a hammer stake the nut in place. Be sure that the threads on the nut are deformed so the nut will not loosen.

14. Position a new boot and grommet on the pedal rod. Moisten the grommet and insert the grommet end of the pedal rod into the input rod of the booster. When the grommet is fully seated, the pedal rod will rotate freely.

15. Install the boot on the booster cover.

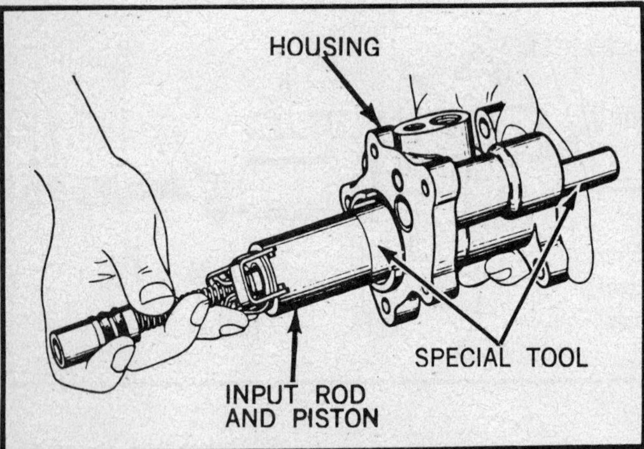

Installing input rod and piston assembly in Bendix hydro boost (© GM Corp.)

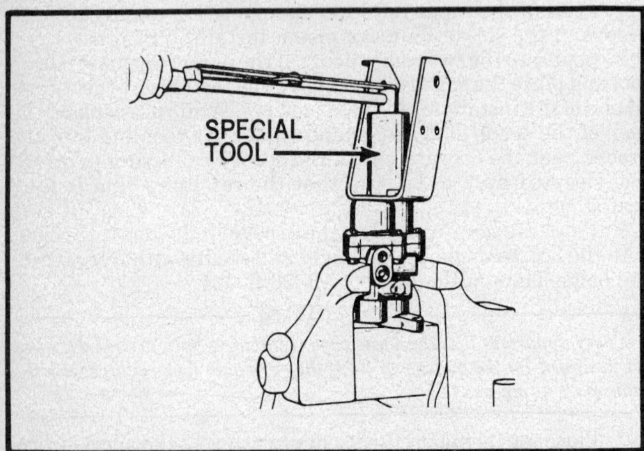

Installing linkage bracket nut Bendix hydro boost—typical (© GM Corp.)

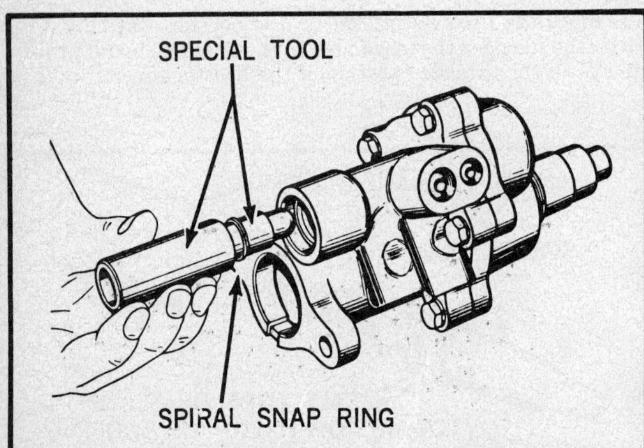

Installing spiral snap ring Bendix hydro boost (© GM Corp.)

Bendix Master Vac

Removal

1. Disconnect clevis at brake pedal to push rod.
2. Remove vacuum hoses from power cylinder.
3. Disconnect hydraulic line from master cylinder.
4. Remove the four attaching nuts and lock washers that hold the unit to the firewall. Remove the power brake unit.

Disassembly

1. Remove four master cylinder to vacuum cylinder attaching nuts and washers.

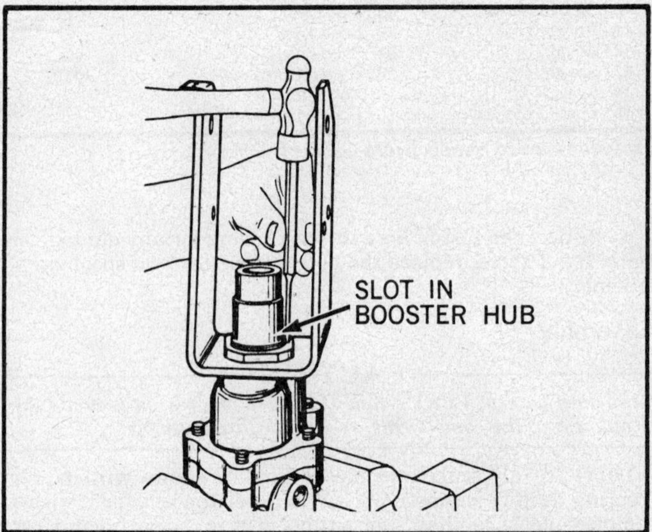

Staking linkage bracket nut Bendix hydro boost (© GM Corp.)

2. Separate master cylinder from vacuum cylinder, then remove the rubber seal from the outer groove at end of master cylinder.
3. Remove the push rod from the power section. (Do not disturb adjusting screw.)
4. Remove push rod boot and valve operating rod.
5. Scribe alignment marks across the rear shell and vacuum cylinder. Remove all but two of the end plate attaching screws (opposite each other). Hold down on the rear shell while removing the two remaining screws to prevent the piston return spring from expanding.
6. Scribe a mark across the face of the piston, to index the mark on the rear shell, and remove rear shell with vacuum piston and piston return spring.
7. Remove vacuum hose from vacuum piston and from vacuum tube on inside of rear shell. Separate rear shell from vacuum piston.
8. Remove air cleaner and vacuum tube assembly, and air filter from the rear shell.
9. Spring the felt retaining ring enough to disengage ring from grooves in bosses on rear piston plate.
10. Remove piston felt and expander ring from piston assembly.
11. Remove six piston plate attaching screws and separate front piston plate and piston packing from piston plate.
12. Remove valve return spring, floating control valve and diaphragm assembly, valve spring and diaphragm plate. Sepa-

rate floating control valve spring-retainer and control valve diaphragm from control valve.

13. Remove rubber reaction disc and shim (if present) from front piston plate.

NOTE: Do not remove the valve operating rod and valve plunger from the rear piston plate unless it is necessary to replace defective parts. Normally, the next two Steps can be omitted.

14. When it is necessary to replace the valve operating rod or valve plunger, remove valve rod seal from groove in piston plate and pull seal over end of rod.

15. Hold piston with valve plunger side down and inject alcohol into valve plunger through opening around valve rod. This will wet the rubber lock in the plunger. Then drive or pry valve plunger off the valve rod.

NOTE: If master cylinder is not to be rebuilt, omit Steps 16–19.

16. Remove snap-ring from groove in base at end of master cylinder.

17. Remove piston assembly, primary cup, retainer spring, and check-valve from master cylinder.

18. Remove filler cap and gasket from master cylinder body.

19. Remove secondary cup from master cylinder piston.

Cleaning Note

After disassembly, cleaning of all metal parts in satisfactory commercial cleaner solvent is recommended. Use only alcohol or Declene on rubber parts or parts containing rubber. After cleaning and drying, metal parts should be rewashed in clean alcohol or Declene before assembly.

Assembly

Steps 1–5 apply to a completely disassembled master cylinder. Otherwise, omit Steps 1–5.

1. Coat bore of master cylinder with brake fluid.
2. Dip secondary cup in brake fluid and install on master cylinder piston.
3. Dip other piston parts in brake fluid and assemble the piston. Install piston.
4. Install snap-ring into groove of cylinder.
5. Use new gasket and install filler cap.
6. Assemble valve rod seal on rod and insert valve rod through the piston. Dip valve plunger in alcohol and assemble to ball end of valve rod. Be sure ball end of rod is locked in place in plunger.
7. Assemble floating control valve diaphragm over end of floating control valve. Be sure disphragm is in recess of floating control valve. Press control valve spring retainer over end of control valve and diaphragm.
8. Clamp valve operating rod in a vise with rear piston plate up. Lay leather piston packing on rear piston plate with lip of leather over edge of piston plate.
9. Install floating control valve return spring over end of valve plunger.
10. Assemble diaphragm plate to diaphragm and assemble floating control valve with diaphragm in recess of rear piston plate.
11. Install floating control valve spring over retainer. Align and assemble front piston plate with rear piston plate. Center the floating control valve spring on front piston plate and center valve plunger stem in hole of piston.
12. Holding front and rear piston plates together, loosely install six piston plate cap screws.
13. Install shim and rubber reaction disc in recess at center of front piston plate.

NOTE: A piston assembling ring is handy in assembling the piston.

14. Place the assembling tool over piston packing, turn piston assembly upside down and assemble the expander ring against inside lip of leather packing. Saturate felt with vacuum cylinder oil or shock absorber fluid, type A. Then assemble in expander ring. Assemble retainer ring over bosses on rear piston plate. Be sure retainer is anchored in grooves of piston plate.
15. Assemble air cleaner filter over vacuum tube of air cleaner and attach air cleaner shell in position with screws.
16. Slide vacuum hose onto vacuum inlet tube of piston and align hose to lay flat against piston.
17. Wipe a coat of vacuum cylinder oil on bore of cylinder. Remove assembling ring from vacuum piston and coat leather piston packing with vacuum cylinder oil.
18. Install rear shell over end of valve operating rod and attach vacuum hose to tube end on each side of end plate.

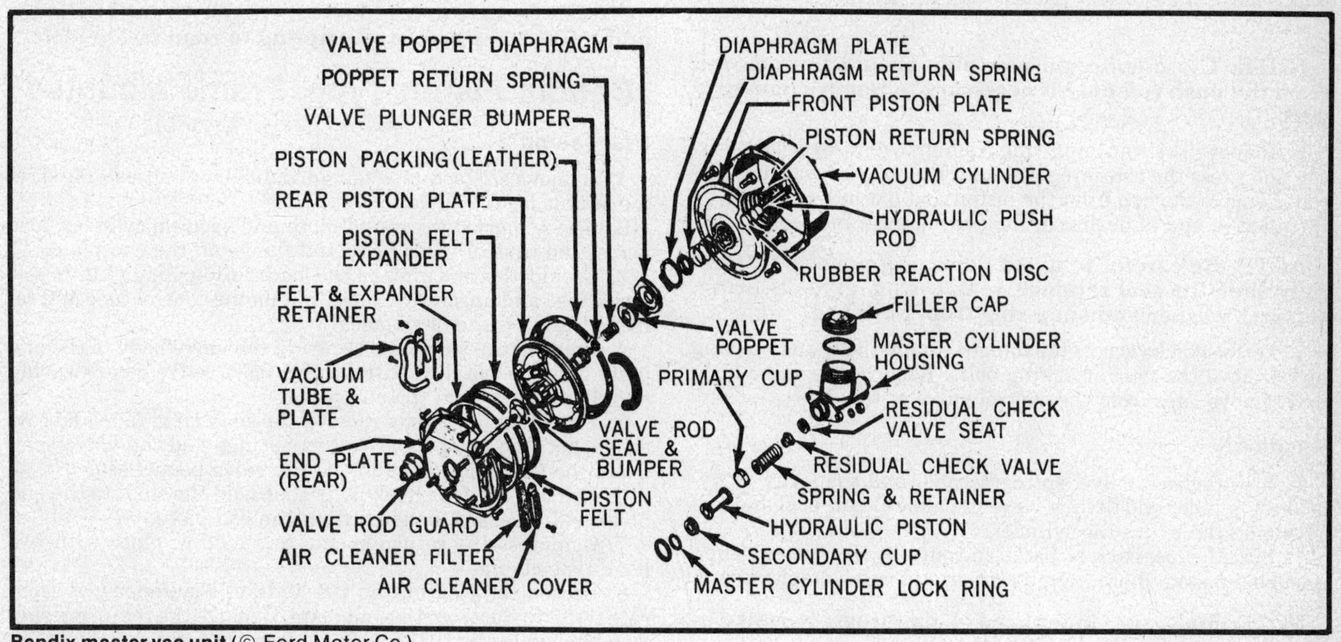

Bendix master vac unit (© Ford Motor Co.)

19. Center small diameter end of piston return spring in vacuum cylinder. Center large diameter of spring on piston. Check alignment mark on piston with marks on vacuum cylinder and rear shell, compress spring and install two attaching screws at opposite sides to hold rear shell and cylinder together. Now, install balance of screws and tighten evenly.
20. Dip small end of pushrod boot in alcohol and assemble guard over end of valve operating rod and over flange of shell.
21. Insert large end of pushrod through hole in end of vacuum cylinder and guide into hole of front piston plate.

NOTE: Before going on with assembly, check the distance from the outer end of the pushrod to the master cylinder mounting surface on the vacuum cylinder. This measurement should be 1.195–1.200 in.

22. After pushrod adjustment is correct, replace rubber seal in groove on master cylinder body.
23. Assemble master cylinder to the vacuum cylinder at four studs. Replace lock washers and nut and securely tighten.

Bendix Single Diaphragm Type Frame Mounted

Disassembly

1. Remove the booster unit and hydraulic cylinder from frame mounting bracket.
2. Scribe marks across front and rear shells and across flange of hydraulic cylinder. Disconnect the control tube nut from the control valve seat and remove the seal from the tube.
3. Remove the clamp band from the booster unit and disassemble the rear shell.

NOTE: The plug in the rear shell should be removed only if it is damaged.

4. Roll the bead of the diaphragm back from the front shell flange and compress the return spring for the diaphragm slightly. Remove the snap-ring from groove near the end of the hydraulic cylinder. Remove the hydraulic parts, push rod and diaphragm as an assembly.
5. Remove diaphragm return spring from piston end of push rod. Remove bolts securing hydraulic cylinder to front shell and remove the cylinder gasket from the shell.

NOTE: The diaphragm assembly should be removed from the push rod only if necessary to remove damaged parts.

6. Remove the retaining ring from groove in hydraulic piston and press the retaining pin from hole in push rod and piston. Remove the cup from the piston and if a new seal is to be installed in end of push rod, remove old push rod seal.

NOTE: Be careful to avoid damaging push rod. Carefully slide the seal retainer, seal, O-ring, guide bearing, retainer washer and snap-ring from push rod.

7. Scribe marks across the flanges of valve body and housing and remove the four attaching bolts. Remove the valve body and remove cups from the control valve piston.

Assembly

1. Install check valve, spring, washer and snap-ring in hydraulic cylinder end fitting. Next assemble O-ring seal and end fitting on the hydraulic cylinder.
2. Install cups, back to back, on control valve piston. Then assemble piston, diaphragm retainer and valve diaphragm.

NOTE: Make sure inner bead of diaphragm is seated in the piston groove.

3. Install the spring retainer, with the flange down, on the spring in the valve body. Install the piston and diaphragm assembly on the retainer and press the outer bead of the diaphragm into the groove in the valve body.
4. Coat the valve piston with clean brake fluid and assemble the piston in the control valve cylinder bore. Align the scribe marks on the valve cylinder body and housing and attach with bolts. Torque bolts to 40–60 inch lbs.
5. If installing new seal on push rod, place new seal on clean block of wood, with the rubber side down. Place the push rod vertically on the seal stem and strike the threaded end with a soft mallet to seat the seal stem in the push rod.

NOTE: Make sure the shoulders of the push rod and seal are in contact.

6. Slide snap-ring, retaining washer, guide bearing with O-ring seal in outer groove of guide, seal cup and seal retainer on push rod.
7. Attach the piston to the push rod with retaining ring and pin. Dip the piston cup in the clean brake fluid and install on piston.
8. Install new gasket in groove at flange end of hydraulic cylinder and install cylinder on front shell with the hold down bolts.
9. Install the diaphragm return spring, with the large coil first, against the diaphragm plate. Lubricate the cylinder bore with clean brake fluid and carefully insert the piston, cups and seals into cylinder bore. Roll back the edge of the diaphragm and press against the diaphragm to compress the return slightly. When push rod and parts are installed all the way into the cylinder bore, install the retaining snap-ring.

NOTE: Be sure the snap-ring is seated properly before releasing pressure on the spring.

10. Coat both sides of the diaphragm lightly with talcum powder or silicone lubricant. Align scribe marks made on front and rear shells and press the rear shell flange and diaphragm bead into position against the front shell flange.
11. Install the clamp band on the shells and secure with bolt. Install a new seal on the control vacuum tube and assemble the tube and hose onto the rear shell tube and tighten nut.
12. Reinstall on vehicle and check for vacuum leaks and road test to check for proper operation.

NOTE: Be sure to bleed all air from hydraulic cylinder and brake lines before attempting to road test vehicle.

Bendix Piston Type, Frame Mounted

Disassembly

1. Remove all vacuum and hydraulic lines to booster and remove unit from vehicle.
2. Scribe marks across end plate and vacuum cylinder, also across the control valve body and flange on the end plate.
3. Clamp the end nut of the hydraulic cylinder in a soft jawed vise and unscrew the lock nut on the control tube and remove the tube and O-ring seal.
4. Remove the four bolts securing the valve body to the end plate and remove the control valve body, valve return spring and diaphragm from the end plate.
5. From the valve body remove the snap-ring, tube and cover, gasket, the two poppet return springs and the valve seal. From the valve housing remove the valve poppet seal.
6. Remove the four hook bolts that hold the shell to the end plate and separate the shell from the end plate.
7. Compress the return spring and hold in place with two hook type clamps.
8. Loosen the lock nut on the hydraulic cylinder and separate the cylinder from the end plate. Remove the retaining ring from the hydraulic piston and press out the retaining pin in the

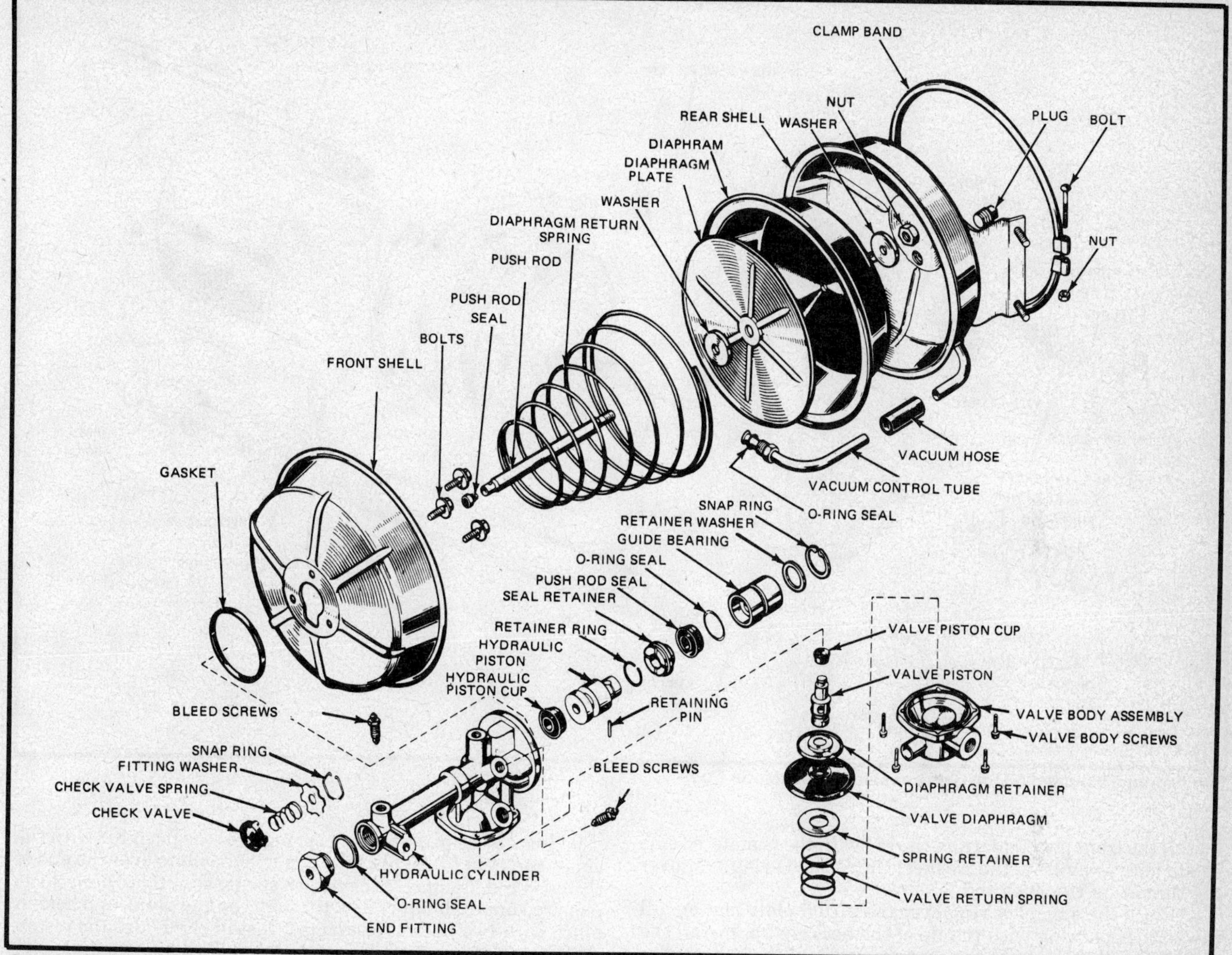

Bendix single diaphragm frame mounted booster (© Ford Motor Co.)

piston. Remove the piston from the push rod and remove the piston cup from the piston.

9. Compress the piston return spring and remove the hook clamps. Separate the piston and push rod assembly from the end plate, and remove the return spring from the push rod.

10. From the end plate remove the seal O-ring, stop washer, snap-ring, spring, sleeve, retainer, seal cup, push rod washer and small seal O-ring. On the opposite of the end plate remove the large seal O-ring.

11. From the control valve opening in the end plate, remove the retaining snap-ring, piston stop washer and valve fitting. Remove the O-ring seal from the valve fitting.

12. Remove the hydraulic piston from the valve fitting and remove the piston cups from the piston.

13. To prevent damaging the push rod when disassembling the vacuum power piston, clamp the push rod in a soft jawed vise. Next remove the nut, piston felt retainer, packing ring, packing wick, rear plate, packing, front plate and washer from the push rod.

14. To remove the end cap on hydraulic cylinder, loosen the lock nut on the cylinder and remove the cap. Remove the seal O-ring, snap-ring, check valve spring and residual pressure check valve from the end cap.

Assembly

1. Assemble the residual pressure check valve, check valve spring, snap-ring and seal O-ring in the end cap. Screw the end cap on the cylinder tube until the tube bottoms in the cap and lock in place with the lock nut.

2. Make a vacuum piston assembly ring by cutting a one in. wide section from an old cylinder shell of the proper size. Install the flat washer over the threaded end of the push rod, then

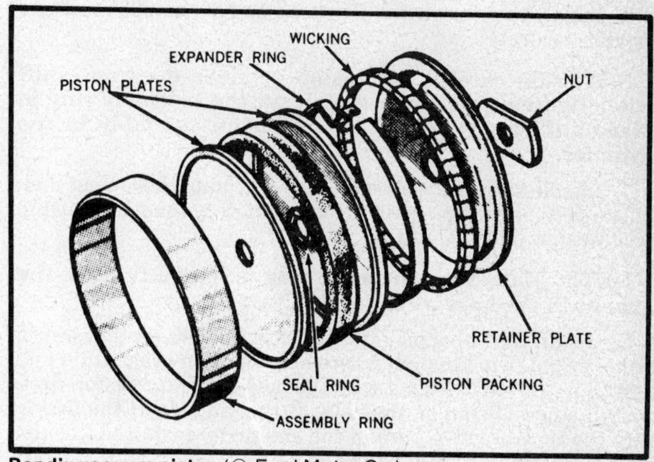

Bendix vacuum piston (© Ford Motor Co.)

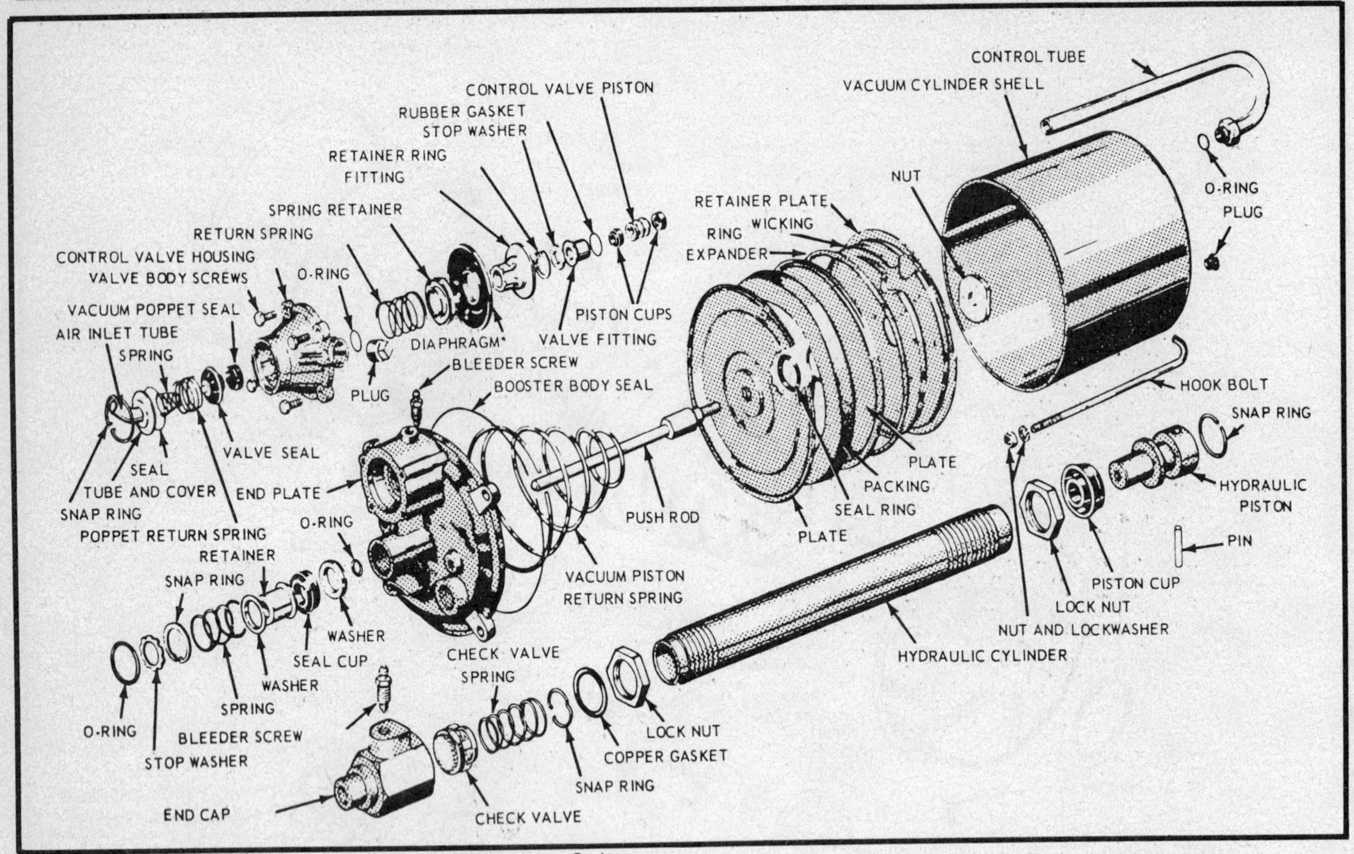

Bendix frame mounted piston type booster (© Ford Motor Co.)

install the front piston plate on the rod with the chamfered side of the hole away from the washer. Guide the O-ring seal over the threads of the push rod.

3. Place the assembly ring over the piston plate and install the leather packing with the lip of the packing up. Install the rear piston plate keeping the chamfered side of the hole next to the seal.

4. Cut the packing wick to the required length and saturate with a good quality oil. Install the wick against the inner lip of the leather packing.

5. Install the packing expander ring inside the wick with the gripping point up. Put the notch, at the loop end of the ring, under the clip on the opposite end of the ring. Install the piston retainer with the cut < chout portion over the loop of the expander ring.

6. Install the nut on the threaded end of the push rod and tighten securely.

NOTE: Be careful the piston retainer does not shift when tightening the nut. Also leave the assembly ring in place until ready to install the piston assembly in the cylinder.

7. Install in the center bore of the end plate the O-ring seal, push rod washer, cup retainer, sleeve, spring, snap-ring, piston stop washer and seal O-ring.

NOTE: Make sure the snap-ring is seated fully, in the groove in the bore of the end plate.

8. Install the valve piston cups, back to back, on the control valve piston. Dip the piston assembly in clean brake fluid and install in the valve fitting with the hole end of the piston first. Install a new O-ring on the valve fitting and insert the fitting into the control valve bore in the end plate. Install the piston stop washer and snap-ring in the bore.

9. Install the piston return spring over the push rod with the small end next to the piston. Slide the end plate over the end of the push rod. Compress the return spring slightly to project the push rod approximately 2 in. through the end plate, and hold in place with two hook type clamps. Install the hydraulic piston on the end of the push rod and attach with the retainer pin. Slide the snap-ring into its groove to hold the pin in place.

10. Dip the piston cup in clean brake fluid and install the cup on the piston with the lip away from the end plate. Next dip the piston assembly in clean brake fluid and coat the inside of the hydraulic cylinder with fluid. Guide the hydraulic cylinder over the piston being careful not to turn the lip of the seal cup backwards when installing.

11. Screw the hydraulic cylinder into the end plate until the cylinder bottoms. Then back off the cylinder until the bleeder screw in the end cap aligns with the bleeder screw in the end plate and tighten the lock nut. Compress the return spring and remove the hook clamps.

12. In the groove in the end plate install the large O-ring seal. Coat the inside of the vacuum cylinder with a good quality oil. Remove the assembly ring from the piston and insert the piston into the cylinder.

NOTE: Tip the piston 45 degrees or more when sliding it into the cylinder. This will make it easier to install the piston. Align the scribe marks on the end plate and cylinder shell and install the hook bolts, lock washers and nuts. Tighten the nuts a little at a time to avoid warping the end plate or the cylinder shell.

13. Install the valve diaphragm and spring retainer on the diaphragm plate. Install the valve poppet seal over the end of the valve seal and place the assembly in the valve body.

14. Install the poppet return springs with the small end of the small spring over the button on the valve seal. In the recess in

the valve body, install the O-ring seal and attach the tube and cover with the snap-ring.

15. In the groove in the control vacuum port of the valve body install the small O-ring seal.

16. Install the valve diaphragm and spring retainer assembly on the end plate flange and position the control valve return spring on the retainer. Position the control valve housing on the spring and secure with the four hold down bolts.

NOTE: Be sure to align the scribe marks made on the housing and end plate before assembling the housing to the end plate.

17. Install the O-ring seal on the end of the vacuum tube and install the tube with one end in the control valve body and the other end secured to the rear of the shell with the tube nut.

18. Install the unit on the vehicle and check for vacuum leaks and road test for proper operation of unit.

NOTE: Be sure to bleed all air from the hydraulic cylinder and brake lines before road testing the vehicle.

Bendix Dual Diaphragm Type

This unit features a direct pedal connection to a vacuum unit mounted on the firewall, with the master cylinder directly mounted to booster.

The booster chamber contains two diaphragms and is under constant engine vacuum. When brakes are applied, the control valve is opened to allow atmospheric pressure behind both diaphragms. This provides the power boost to the master cylinder.

This vacuum-suspended system provides reserve against fade. Pedal linkages are eliminated, no additional vacuum storage tanks are needed.

NOTE: Do not attempt to diasassemble the booster. It is serviced only by the dealer.

Bendix Tandem Diaphragm Type Frame Mounted

Disassembly

1. Remove all hydraulic and vacuum lines attached to booster and hydraulic cylinder. Then remove the unit from frame brackets and remove from vehicle.
2. Scribe marks across both clamp rings onto the shell surfaces, also across top of hydraulic cylinder flange onto the front shell. Scribe marks across control valve body and housing below hydraulic cylinder.
3. Disconnect the control tube and nut from control valve port and remove the three hose clamps and tee. Remove the seal ring from the control tube.
4. Remove the rear clamping ring and remove the rear shell.
5. Remove the front clamping ring and separate the front, center and rear shells and remove the diaphragm assemblies.
6. Clamp the hydraulic cylinder in a soft jawed vice being careful to avoid damaging cylinder.
7. Press on the spring retainer to compress the diaphragm return spring and remove the three bolts that hold the hydraulic cylinder to the front shell and support plate. Then carefully release the pressure on the return spring and pull the push rod and hydraulic piston from the cylinder.
8. Remove the return spring from the piston end of the push rod.

NOTE: Do not remove the spring retainer except to replace damaged parts.

9. Remove the snap-ring from the groove in the piston and press plunger pin from the hole in the piston and push rod.
10. Remove the piston, snap-ring, seal retainer, push rod cup, push rod bearing and support plate and piston stop from the push rod.
11. Remove the cup from the piston and the O-ring from the groove in the push rod bearing.
12. Remove the end fitting from the hydraulic cylinder and remove the snap-ring from the end cap. Disassemble the residual pressure check valve.
13. Remove the end fitting seal from the push rod being careful not to damage the push rod.
14. Clamp the nut, on the push rod seat end of the rear shaft, in a vise and remove by unscrewing the shaft. Remove the assembly from the vise and remove the front diaphragm and diaphragm plate from the shaft.
15. Slide center shells off the shaft and remove the O-ring seal from its groove in the hub of the center shells.
16. Clamp the nut on the rear shaft and remove by unscrewing the shaft. Remove the nut, washer, rear diaphragm, diaphragm plate and washer from the shaft.
17. Remove the valve body and control valve from the valve housing.
18. Remove the cups from the control valve piston and slide the control valve diaphragm and retainer off the opposite end of the piston.

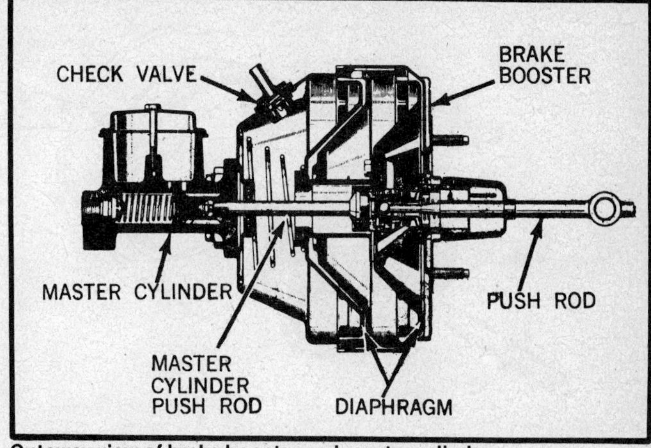

Cutaway view of brake booster and master cylinder
(© Chrysler Corp.)

Cleaning and Inspection

Clean all metal parts in clean metal parts cleaner. Discard any old parts that are to be replaced with new ones. Clean all hydraulic parts in clean brake fluid. Check the diaphragms for cracks, tears and kinks and replace any diaphragms that are questionable. Inspect all metal and plastic parts for nicks, cracks, scores or burrs and replace any damaged parts. Check the shells for cracked or broken welds, dents or cracks. DO NOT attempt to disassemble the center shell assembly. Inspect the hydraulic cylinder bore and valve body bore for any surface damage. Remove deposits, pitted areas or light scores with crocus cloth. Replace the part if it can not be cleaned up with crocus cloth.

Assembly

1. Install the valve piston cups back to back in the grooves on the control valve piston.
2. Slide the valve diaphragm retainer, with the flange side first, onto the other end of the piston. Wet the inside of the valve diaphragm with alcohol and slide it over the end of the piston and seat it against the retainer. Install the spring retainer on the hub of the valve diaphragm with the flange side away from the diaphragm.
3. Install the control valve piston and diaphragm assembly on the return spring. Position the spring around the vacuum

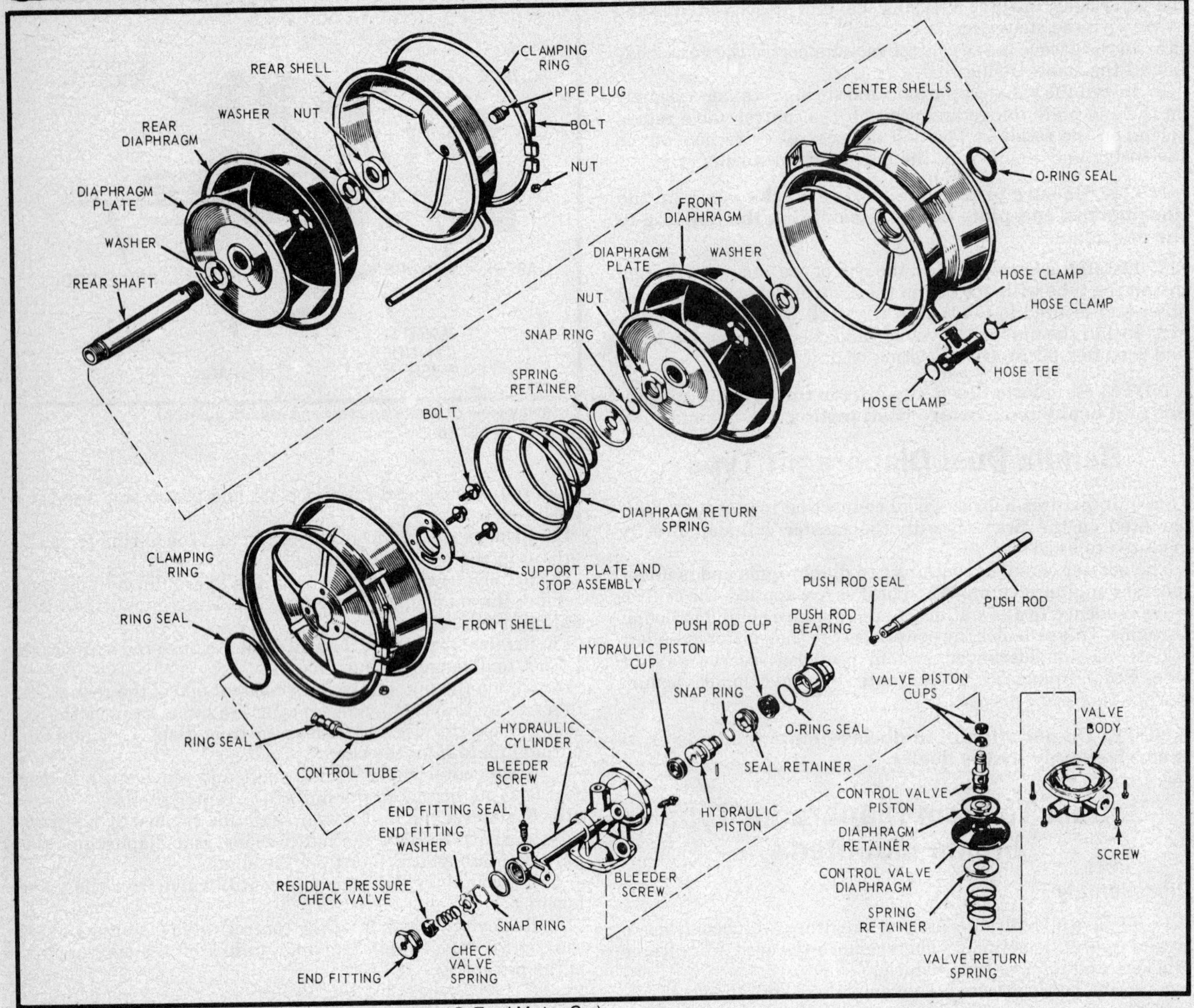

Bendix tandem diaphragm frame mounted booster (© Ford Motor Co.)

poppet guides in the valve body and press the bead of the diaphragm firmly into the groove on the flange of the valve body.

4. Dip the control valve piston and cups into clean brake fluid and install them into the control valve bore in the hydraulic cylinder. Align the scribe marks on the valve body and housing and attach with four bolts. Tighten the bolts to 40–60 inch lbs.

5. Assemble the washer, rear diaphragm plate, diaphragm and washer onto the rear shaft with the holes in the shaft towards the diaphragm.

6. Install the nut on the end of the shaft and tighten to 10–15 ft. lbs. Stake the nut in two places to prevent any movement.

7. Install the O-ring seal in its groove inside the hub of the center shells. With a silicone lubricant, coat the seal and bearing and the outer surface of the rear shaft.

8. Insert the front end of the rear shaft through the middle of the center shells.

9. Install the washer, front diaphragm and diaphragm plate on the end of the shaft. Screw on retaining nut and tighten to 10–15 ft. lbs. Stake the nut in two places to prevent any movement.

10. To install a new push rod seal, in end of push rod, place new seal face down on a clean block of wood. Place the push rod uptight on the seal stem and strike end of rod with a soft mallet to seat the seal.

NOTE: Be sure that the shoulders of the seal and push rod are in contact.

11. Dip all hydraulic parts, push rod and push rod bearing in clean brake fluid. Install the support plate and piston stop assembly, push rod bearing, with O-ring in its groove, push rod cup and seal retainer on the push rod.

12. Install the snap-ring on the piston but not in its groove. Attach the piston to the push rod with the plunger pin and then slide the snap-ring into its groove in the piston.

13. Dip the piston cup in brake fluid and install on the piston with the open flared end away from the piston.

14. Install the residual pressure check valve in the end fitting, then install the check valve spring and washer in the end fitting and secure with the snap-ring.

15. Install the gasket onto the end fitting and screw into the hydraulic cylinder and tighten to 50–85 ft. lbs.

16. Install the O-ring seal in groove around the hydraulic cylinder flange.

17. Slide the small end of the diaphragm return spring over the piston end of the push rod. Lubricate the piston and cylinder bore with clean brake fluid.

18. Bottom the small end of the return spring against the spring retainer on the push rod and place the large coil of the

spring in the front shell with the piston through the hole in the shell.

19. With the return slightly compressed, guide the piston, seal retainer, push rod cup, and push rod bearing into the cylinder bore. Seat the cylinder flange against the front shell, make sure the O-ring is in place. Place the support plate and stop plate on the opposite side of the shell and secure the stop assembly and front shell to the cylinder with the three securing bolts. Release the pressure on the spring.

20. On the front and rear diaphragm beads put a light coat of talcum powder or silicone lubricant.

21. Guide the rear shaft onto the push rod and align the scribe marks made on the front shell flanges. Press the shells together and seat the bead of the diaphragm all the way around in the shell flanges.

22. Install the clamp ring on the shell falnges and align the scribe marks. Tighten the clamp screw to 30–40 inch lbs.

23. Align the scribe marks on the rear shells and press them together making sure the diaphragm bead is in the shell flange all the way around. Install the clamp ring, aligning the marks, and tighten the clamp bolt to 30–40 inch lbs.

24. Install the hose tee to the control tube on the rear shell and to hose nipple on the center shell.

25. Install the seal ring on the end of the control tube and nut assembly and attach the tube to the hose tee with a hose clamp. Screw the nut onto the control valve port and tighten to 80–120 inch lbs.

26. Install unit on vehicle and test for vacuum leaks and road test for proper operation.

NOTE: Be sure to bleed hydraulic cylinder of all air before attempting to road test vehicle.

Bendix Single Diaphragm Booster

Disassembly

1. Scribe a line across the front and rear housings for reassembly.
2. Pull the piston rod from the front housing and remove the seal.
3. Attach a holding fixture to the front housing and clamp the base in a vise with the power section up.
4. Loosen the locknut and remove the pushrod device and locknut.
5. Remove the mounting bracket from the rear housing.
6. Remove the dust boot retainer, dust boot and silencer from the diaphragm plate extension.
7. The edge of the rear housing contains twelve lances. Four of these lances (one in each quadrant) are deeper than the other lances. The metal that forms the four deep lances must be partially straightened so that the lances will clear the cutouts in the front housing.

NOTE: If the metal tabs that form the deep lances crack or break during straightening, the housing must be replaced.

8. Place a spanner wrench over the studs on the rear housing and attach with nuts and washers.
9. Press down on the spanner wrench and rotate the rear housing clockwise to separate the two housings.

NOTE: It may be necessary to tap the rear housing lightly with a plastic hammer to loosen.

10. Lift the rear housing assembly from the unit.
11. Use a small screwdriver and carefully remove the air filter element from the diaphragm plate extension.
12. Separate the diaphragm plate assembly from the rear housing and disassemble the plate assembly.
13. Remove the rolling diaphragm from the groove in the diaphragm plate hub.

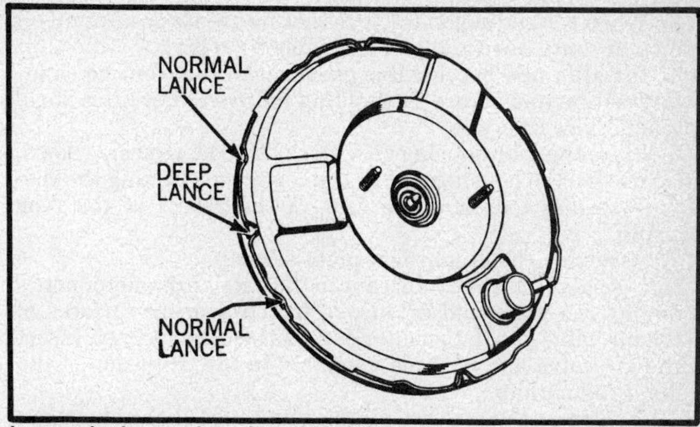

Lances in the rear housing (© GM Corp.)

NOTE: Protect the diaphragm from oil, and nicks.

14. Hold the diaphragm plate in a horizontal position and depress the push rod approximately $^1/_{16}$ in. and rotate the piston so the air valve lock will fall from its location. Remove the air valve pushrod assembly and the reaction disc.
15. If a new seal is needed, support the outer surface of the rear housing and drive out the seal with a suitable tool.

NOTE: Do not reuse old seal once it has been removed.

16. Remove the check valve and grommet from the front housing and discard.
18. Remove the front housing from the holding fixture.

Assembly

1. Use clean brake fluid and thoroughly clean all reusable brake parts.
2. Inspect all rubber parts and replace if nicked, cut or damaged.

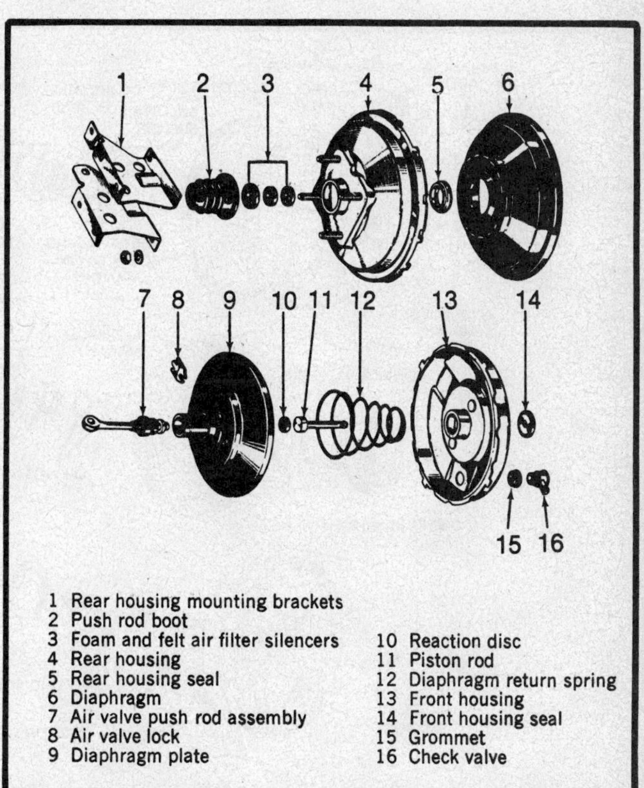

Bendix single diaphragm booster (© GM Corp.)

3. When rebuilding, make sure that no grease or mineral oil comes in contact with any of the rubber parts.
4. Install a new check valve grommet in the front housing.
5. Position and secure the holding fixture to the front housing and place in a vise.
6. Place the rear housing on a block of wood, stud side down, and position the housing seal in the center hole. Using the special installing tool seat the seal in the recess of the rear housing.
7. Assemble the diaphragm plate assembly:
   a. Apply a silicone lubricant to the outside diameter of the diaphragm plate and extension, to the bearing surfaces of the air valve and to the outer edge of the valve poppet. Insert the air valve and pushrod assembly in the extension of the diaphragm plate.
   b. Depress the pushrod slightly and install the air valve. Make sure the lock indexes and retains the air valve.
   c. Install the rolling diaphragm in the groove of the diaphragm plate.
   d. Apply silicone lubricant to the surface of the reaction disc and position the disc in the center bore of the diaphragm plate. Use the piston rod to seat the disc in the bore.

NOTE: It is important that the disc be fully seated before removing the piston rod.

8. Apply silicone lubricant to the inside diameter of the rear housing seal and the diaphragm bead contact surface of the rear housing. Install the diaphragm plate assembly in the rear housing.
9. Position the air filter element over the pushrod and into the diaphragm plate extension. Install the air filter retainer.
10. Attach the base of the holding fixture to the front housing and clamp the base in a vise with the power section up.
11. Place a spanner wrench over the studs on the rear housing.
12. Place a diaphragm plate return spring in the front housing and position the rear housing assembly on the front housing with the small end of the spring downward. Align the scribe marks and lock in place.
13. Press down on the spanner wrench and rotate the rear housing counterclockwise to assemble the two housings.

NOTE: Bend the lances in on the rear housing. If the tangs crack or break, it will be necessary to replace that half of the housing.

14. Remove the spanner wrench from the rear shell.
15. Install the air silencer over the push rod end, then the boot retainer.
16. On vehicles with a clevis type push rod, install the locknut and clevis.
17. Install the mounting bracket to the rear shell, if so equipped.
18. Remove the cylinder from the vise and remove the holding fixture.
19. Apply silicone lubricant to the piston rod and guide the rod into the center bore of the diaphragm plate until it is fully seated.

NOTE: Keep the lubricant away from the rounded end of the rod.

20. Press the seal into the front housing until it is bottomed in the recess of the housing.

Midland Ross Diaphragm Type

The self-contained booster assembly is mounted on the engine side of the firewall. It is connected directly to the brake pedal. This booster is not equipped with a separate vacuum tank.

The master cylinder is attached to the forward side of the booster. The balance of the hydraulic brake system is identical to other standard service brakes.

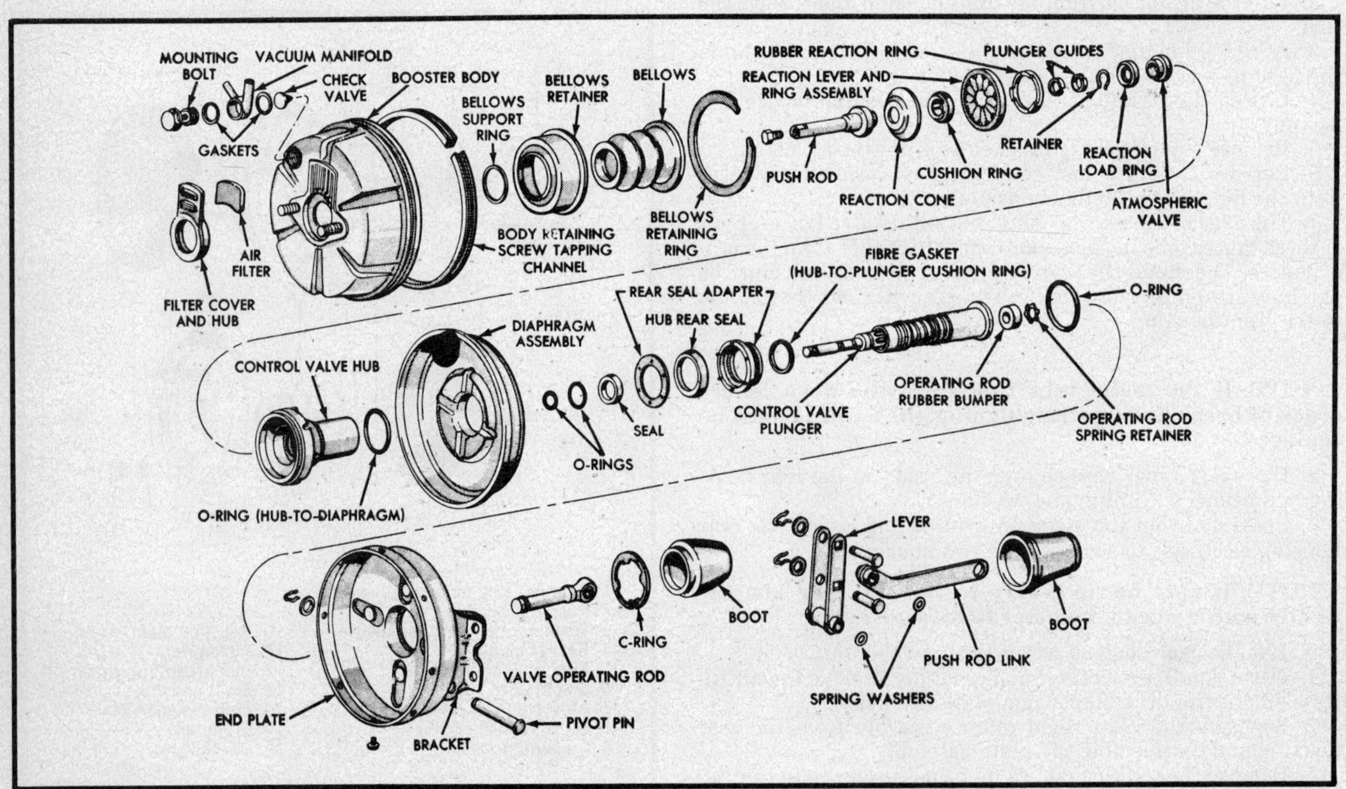

Disassembled view of booster (© Ford Motor Co.)

Booster Repairs

1. Separate master cylinder from booster body.
2. Remove air filter cover and hub and the filter from the booster body.
3. Remove the vacuum manifold mounting bolt, manifold, gaskets and vacuum check valve from the booster body.
4. Disconnect the valve operating rod from the lever by removing its retaining clip, washers, and pivot pin.
5. Disconnect the lever from the booster end plate brackets by removing its retaining clip, washers, and pivot pin.
6. Remove two brackets from the end plate.
7. Remove the rubber boot from the valve operating rod.
8. To remove the bellows, control valve, and diaphragm assemblies, remove large C-ring that holds the rear seal adapter assembly to the booster end plate.
9. Scribe matching lines on the booster body and the end plate. Then remove the ten retaining screws. Tap the outside of the plate with a soft hammer and separate the plate from the booster body.
10. Push the bellows assembly into the vacuum chamber and remove the bellows, control valve, and diaphragm as an assembly from the booster body.
11. Remove the outer O-ring from the control valve hub.
12. To disassemble the bellows, pushrod, and control valve assemblies, remove the large bellows retaining ring, bellows, bellows retainer, and support ring from the diaphragm and valve assembly.
13. Remove the retainer and support ring from the bellows.
14. Remove pushrod assembly, the reaction lever and ring assembly, and the rubber reaction ring from the control valve hub.
15. Remove the reaction cone and cushion ring from the pushrod assembly. Then disassemble the reaction levers from the ring.
16. Remove the two plastic plunger guides from the control valve plunger. Then remove the retainer that holds the reaction load ring and atmospheric valve on the control valve hub.
17. Slide the reaction load ring and atmospheric valve from the control valve hub.
18. Separate the control valve hub and the plunger assembly from the diaphragm by sliding the plunger and rear seal adapter from the rear of the hub. Then remove the hub outer O-ring from the front side of the diaphragm.
19. To disassemble the control valve plunger, remove the hub rear seal adapter from the valve plunger assembly, and remove the seal from the adapter.
20. Remove the O-rings, the seal, and the fiber gaskets from the plunger.
21. If the plunger assembly needs to be replaced, hold the plunger and pull out the valve operating rod with pliers. Do not separate the operating rod and plunger unless the plunger is to be replaced.

Assembly

1. If valve operating rod was removed for replacement of plunger, install a new rubber bumper and spring retainer on the rod before installing it on the replacement plunger. Then push the rod firmly until it bottoms in the plunger.
2. Install fiber gaskets, plunger seal, and the two O-rings on the plunger assembly.
3. Install the valve hub rear seal in the adapter assembly with the sealing lip toward the rear. Then slide the adapter assembly onto the plunger with the small diameter end of the hub toward the rear.
4. To assemble the control valve, pushrod, and bellows assemblies, install the hub outer O-ring. Then install the plunger with the seal adapter and the hub on the diaphragm. To do this, hold the hub on the front side of the diaphragm and insert the plunger assembly in the hub from the rear side of the diaphragm.
5. Install atmospheric valve and then the reaction load ring onto the plunger and hub. Compress the valve spring, and install the load ring retainer into the groove of the plunger.
6. Install two plastic plunger guides into their grooves on the plunger.
7. Install rubber reaction ring into the valve hub so that the ring locating knob indexes in the notch in the hub, with the ring tips toward the front.
8. Assemble the reaction lever and ring assembly, and install the assembly into the valve hub.
9. Install the reaction cone and cushion ring on the pushrod. Then install the pushrod assembly on the valve hub so that the plunger indexes in the rod.
10. Assemble the bellows, retainer, and support ring. The ring should be positioned on the middle fold of the bellows.
11. Position the bellows assembly on the diaphragm, and secure it with the retaining ring. Make sure the retaining ring is fully seated.
12. Install the bellows, control valve, and diaphragm assemblies with a screwdriver, moving the booster body retaining screw tapping channel just enough to provide a new surface for the self-tapping attaching screws.
13. Install the diaphragm, the control valve components, and the bellows as an assembly into the booster body. (Be sure the lip of the diaphragm is evenly positioned on the retaining radius of the booster body.) Pull the front lip of the bellows through the booster body, and position it around the outer groove of the body.
14. Install O-ring in the front side of the end plate, and locate the plate on the booster body. Align the scribed lines, compress the two assemblies together with a clamp. Then install all ten self-tapping attaching screws.
15. Install the large C-ring onto the rear seal adapter at the rear side of the end plate.

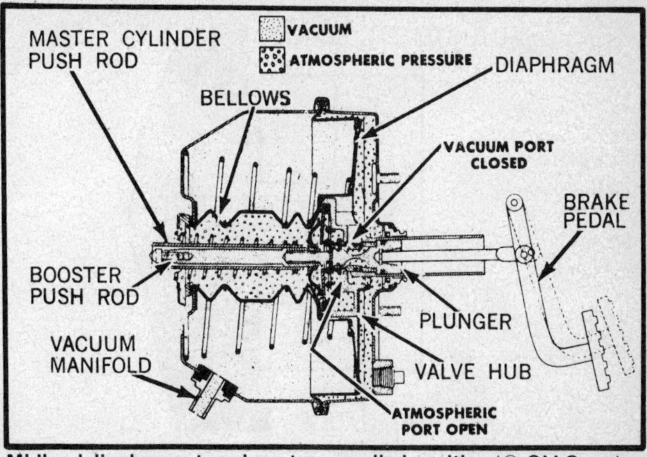

Midland diaphragm type booster—applied position (© GM Corp.)

Pushrod Adjustment

The pushrod has an adjusting screw to maintain the correct relationship between the control valve plunger and the master cylinder piston after the booster is completely assembled. If this screw is not properly adjusted, the brakes may drag.

To check adjustment of the screw, make a gauge to the dimensions shown. Place this gauge against the master cylinder mounting surface of the booster body. The pushrod screw should be adjusted so that the end of the screw just touches the inner edge of the slot in the gauge.

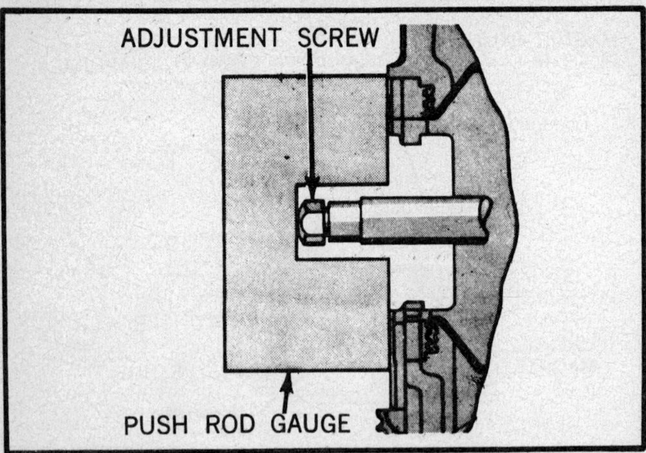

Checking pushrod screw with gauge (© Ford Motor Co.)

Booster Installation

1. Install rubber boot on the valve operating rod.
2. Position the two mounting brackets on the end plate, and install on retaining nuts.
3. Connect the lever assembly to the lower end of the mounting brackets with its pivot pin. Then install the spring washer and retaining clip.
4. Connect the valve operating rod to the upper end of the lever with its pivot pin, washer, and retaining clip.
5. Install the vacuum check valve, the vacuum manifold, the two gaskets, and the mounting bolt. Torque the mounting bolt to 8–10 ft. lbs.

Midland Diaphragm Type Frame Mounted

The Midland frame mounted booster is a remote type, without mechanical operation, utilizing vacuum to boost the hydraulic pressure between master and wheel cylinder.

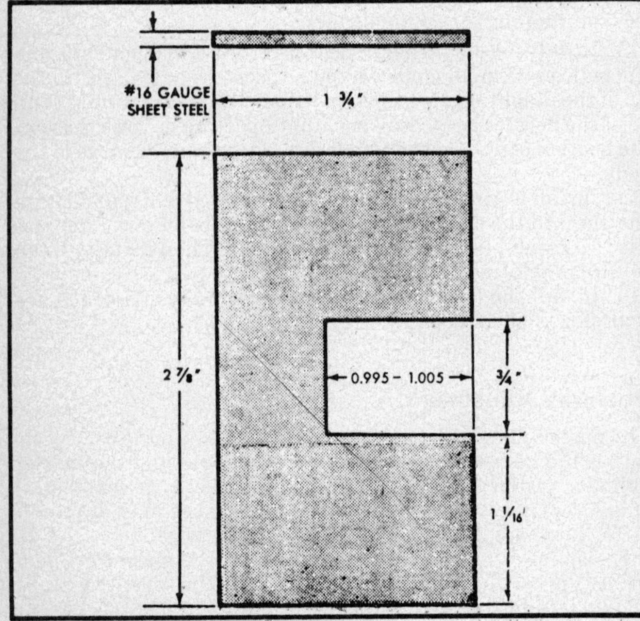

Pushrod gauge (© Ford Motor Co.)

Removal

1. Remove all hydraulic lines from the booster unit hydraulic cylinder.
2. Remove all vacuum lines from the booster unit and remove the support bracket bolts.
3. Remove the unit from the vehicle and place on a clean work bench.

Disassembly

1. Remove the control tube from the control valve body and the rear body.
2. Scribe marks across the diaphragm body and across the flanges of the slave cylinder body and the control valve body.
3. Remove the body clamp carefully, and remove the rear body and diaphragm with the return spring.
4. Remove the push rod, spring retainer and collar from the return spring.
5. Scribe a line across the valve body cover and the valve body, and remove the valve body cover and gasket.
6. Remove the valve body, spring, and the piston and diaphragm assembly from the slave cylinder.
7. From the end of the slave cylinder remove the end plug, copper gasket, spring, spring seat and spring retainer.
8. Remove the piston cup and piston assembly from the cylinder.

NOTE: If the assembly does not fall free from the cylinder it may be pushed out by inserting the push rod through the bushing.

9. From the hydraulic piston remove the check valve, check valve retainer and the return spring.
10. Hold the cylinder in a soft jawed vise and remove the push rod bushing, lockwasher and front body.
11. Remove the gasket, rubber seal and transfer bushing from the slave cylinder body. From the bushing remove the two push rod bushing snap-rings, and remove the washer and two seals. From the outside of the push rod bushing remove the O-ring seal.
12. From the lower end of the control valve piston remove the seal, also remove the seal from the piston boss.
13. Remove the retaining nut from the piston boss and remove the diaphragm plate and control valve diaphragm.
14. Remove the screw, lockwasher, spacer, spring, disc., and the seal from the control valve body.

Assembly

1. Install new spring in the control valve body and assemble the spring and spacer in the valve body. Secure with the screw and locknut.
2. Secure the control valve diaphragm and plate in place with the attaching nut.
3. On the control valve piston install the piston seal.
4. In the hydraulic piston install the check valve spring, check valve and retainer, making sure that the valve floats free in the bore and does not bind.
5. On the front end of the slave cylinder body, install the transfer bushing, seal and gasket.
6. In the push rod bushing install the push rod seals, washer and snap-rings.

NOTE: Install the push rod seals with the open end of the seal towards the slave cylinder body. Install the lockwasher over the end of the rod bushing and install the bushing seal.

7. With the slave cylinder mounted in a vise, position the front body over the end of the cylinder, inserting the transfer bushing in the front body.
8. Thread push rod bushing in place and tighten securely, making sure the front body seats squarely on the slave cylinder body.

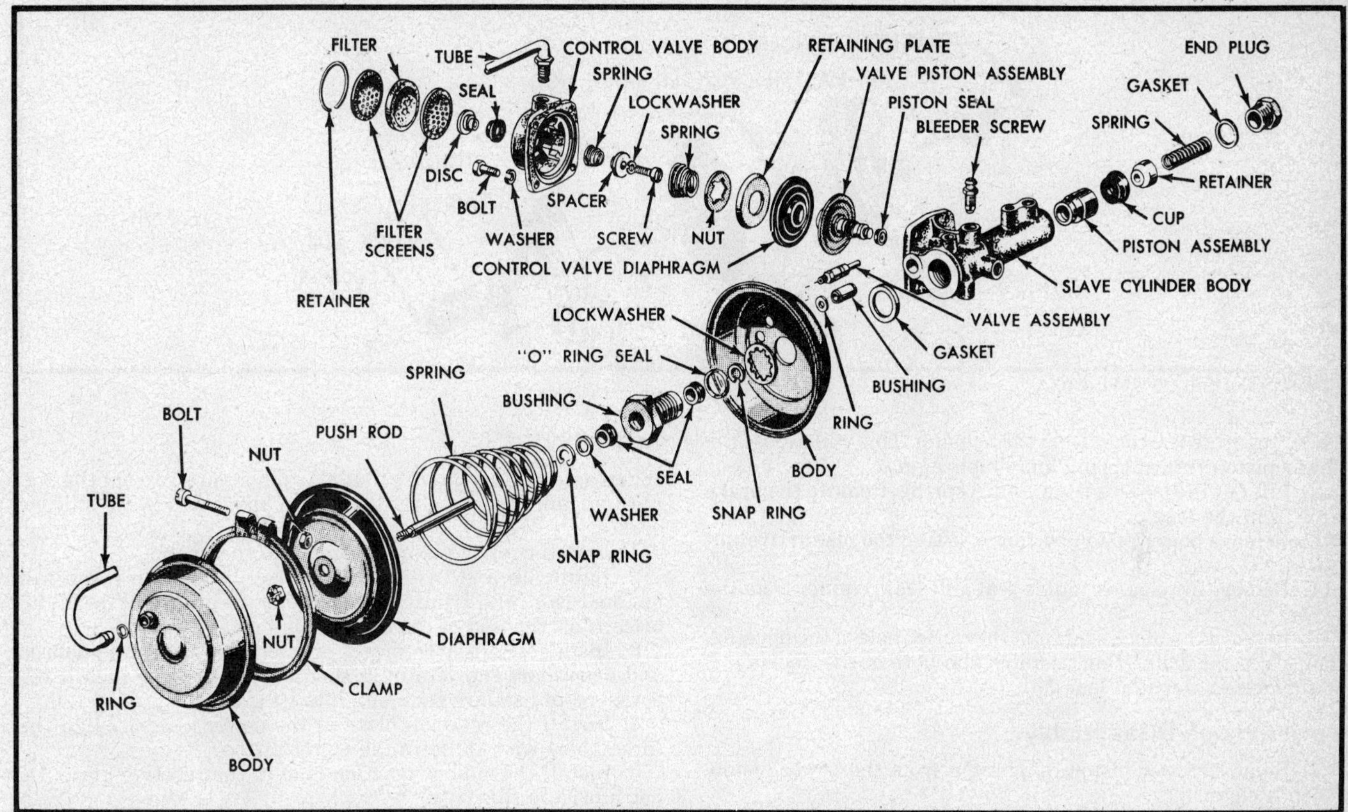

Midland vacuum booster (© Ford Motor Co.)

9. Coat the piston bore of the slave cylinder with brake fluid, also the hydraulic piston, seals, spring retainer and spring.
10. With the recessed end towards the push rod bushing, install the hydraulic piston in the slave cylinder bore. On top of the piston, install the piston cup, large spring retainer and spring. Install the spring seat in the spring coils.
11. Install a new copper gasket on the end plug and screw the plug into the cylinder tightening securely.
12. Dip the control valve piston and diaphragm in brake fluid and position the control valve spring on the diaphragm, making sure that the small end of the spring is over the piston boss.
13. With the control valve body positioned over the spring, and with the scribe marks aligned, secure the valve body to the slave cylinder with the four attaching bolts.
14. Install a new gasket on the valve body cover and secure the cover to the valve body with the four attaching bolts.
15. Install the collar over the threaded end of the push rod and position the retainer on the spring. Insert the rod and collar through the coils of the spring and the retainer. Install the diaphragm over the threaded end of the push rod and secure in place with the push rod nut. Coat the push rod with brake fluid.
16. Install the return spring assembly over the push rod bushing.
17. Install the rear body on the diaphragm aligning the scribe marks on the front and rear shells. Making sure the bead of the diaphragm is properly placed between the body halves, compress the return spring and install and tighten the ring clamp band.
18. Install the by-pass tube and install the unit on the vehicle.
19. Check the unit for vacuum leaks and road test the vehicle for proper operation of the unit.

NOTE: Bleed all air from the hydraulic cylinder and lines before road testing the vehicle.

Kelsey – Hayes Diaphragm Type

IDENTIFICATION

The Kelsey-Hayes power brake unit can be identified by the twistlock method of locking the housing and cover together, plus the white-colored vacuum check valve assembly.

Removal

1. With engine off, apply brakes several times to equalize internal brake pressure.
2. Disconnect hydraulic line from master cylinder.
3. Disconnect vacuum hose from power brake check valve.
4. Disconnect power brake from brake pedal (under instrument panel).
5. Disconnect power brake unit from dash panel.
6. Remove power brake and master cylinder assembly from the vehicle.

Disassembly

1. Separate master cylinder from power brake unit.
2. Remove master cylinder pushrod and air cleaner plate.
3. Mount the power unit in a vise with the master cylinder attaching studs up.
4. Scribe an index line across the housing and cover for reassembly reference.
5. Pry out the housing lock. Do not damage the lock, as it must be used at assembly.
6. Remove check valve from cover by prying out of rubber grommet.
7. Place parking brake flange holding tool over the master cylinder mounting studs.
8. Rotate the tool and cover in a counterclockwise direction.

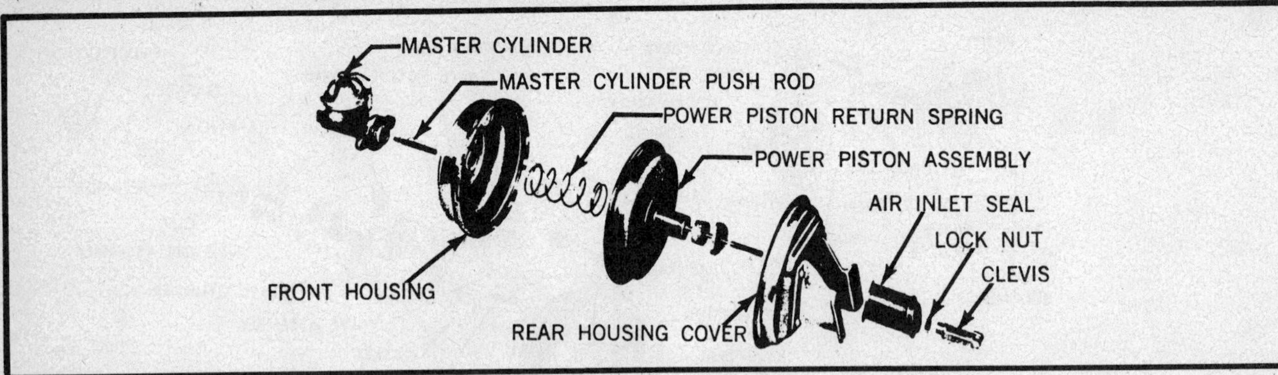

Power brake unit (© GM Corp.)

Then, separate the cover from the housing. This will expose the power piston return spring and diaphragm.

9. Lift out the power piston return spring. Remove the brake unit from the vise.
10. Remove power piston by slowly lifting the piston straight up.
11. Remove air cleaner, guide seal and seal retainer from the cover.
12. Remove the block seal from the center hole of the housing, using a blunt drift. (Don't scratch the bore of the housing, it could cause a vacuum leak.)

Power Piston Disassembly

1. Remove power piston diaphragm from the power piston. Keep it clean.
2. Remove screws that attach the plastic guide to the power piston. Remove guide and place to one side.
3. Remove the power piston square seal ring, reaction ring insert, reaction ring and reaction plate.
4. Depress operating rod slightly, then remove the Truarc snap-ring.
5. Remove control piston by pulling the operating rod.
6. Remove the O-ring seal from the end of the control piston.
7. Remove the filter elements and dust felt from the control piston rod.

Cleaning and Inspection

Thoroughly wash all metal parts in a suitable solvent and dry with compressed air. The power diaphragm, plastic power piston and guide should be washed in a mild soap and water solution. Blow dust and all cleaning material out of internal passages. All rubber parts should be replaced, regardless of condition. Install new air filters at assembly. Inspect all parts for scoring, pits, dents or nicks. Small imperfections can be smoothed out with crocus cloth. Replace all badly damaged parts.

Assembly

When assembling, be sure that all rubber parts, except the diaphragm and the reaction ring are lubricated with silicone grease.

1. Install control piston O-ring onto the piston.
2. Lubricate and install the control piston into the power piston. Install the Truarc snap-ring into its groove. Wipe all lubricant off the end of the control piston.
3. Install air filter elements and felt seal over the pushrod and down past the retaining shoulder on the rod. Install the power piston square seal ring into its groove.
4. Install the reaction plate in the power piston. Align the three holes with those in the power piston.
5. Install the rubber reaction ring in the reaction plate. Do not lubricate this ring.
6. Lubricate outer diameter of the reaction insert and install in the reaction ring.
7. Install reaction insert bumper into the guide.
8. Place guide on the power piston, align the holes with the aligning points on the power piston. Install retaining screws and torque to 80–100 inch lbs.
9. Install diaphragm on power piston; be sure that the diaphragm is correctly seated in the power piston groove.
10. With the housing blocked to prevent damage, install the block seal in the housing.
11. Install a new cover seal on the retainer and lubricate thoroughly, inside and out, with silicone grease, then install in the cover bore. Install new air filter.
12. Lubricate check valve grommet and install the vacuum check valve.
13. Mount the power unit in a vise, with master cylinder attaching studs up.
14. Apply a light coating of silicone grease to the bead, outer edge only, of the power piston diaphragm.
15. Install the power piston assembly in the housing with the operating rod down.

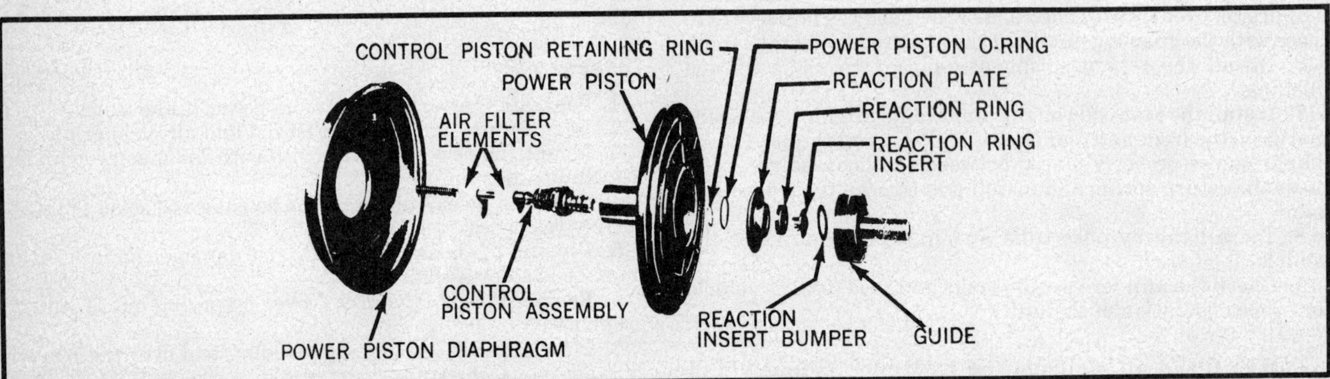

Power piston assembly (© GM Corp.)

16. Install the power piston return spring into the flange of the guide.
17. Place the cover over the return spring and press down on the cover. At the same time, pilot the guide through the seal.
18. Rotate the cover to lock it to the housing. Be sure the scribe lines are in correct index and that the diaphragm is not pinched during assembly.
19. Install the housing lock on one of the long tangs of the housing.
20. Remove the power unit from the vise.
21. Install the master cylinder push-rod and air cleaner plate, then install the master cylinder on the studs. Install attaching nuts and washers. Torque to 200 inch lbs.

Installation

1. Install the power brake seal to the firewall.
2. Install power brake unit onto firewall and torque the attaching nuts to 200 inch lbs.
3. Install pushrod to brake pedal attaching bolt. Torque to 30 ft. lbs.
4. Install vacuum hose onto the power brake unit.
5. Attach the hydraulic tube and fill the master cylinder. Bleed hydraulic system.
6. Adjust stop light switch if necessary.

Delco Single Diaphragm Booster

Disassembly

1. Scribe a mark on the bottom center of front and rear housings for reassembly.
2. Attach a base tool to the front housing and clamp the base in a vise with the power section up.
3. Separate the front and rear housings by securing a spanner wrench to the bracket. Press down on the wrench and rotate rear housing counterclockwise to the unlocked position. Loosen the housing carefully as it is spring loaded.
4. Remove the spanner wrench, then lift the rear housing and power piston assembly from the unit. Remove the return spring.
5. Remove the silencer by removing the retaining ring on the push rod.
6. Remove the seal, vacuum check valve and grommet from the front housing.
7. Remove the power piston assembly from the rear housing.
8. Remove the silencer from the neck of the power piston tube.
9. Remove the lock ring from the power piston.
10. Remove the reaction retainer, piston, plate, levers, bumper and spring.
11. Place a power piston wrench in a vise and position the assembly so that the three lugs on the tool fit into the three notches in the piston.
12. Press down on the support plate and rotate it counterclockwise until it separates from the power piston.
13. Remove the diaphragm from the support plate.
14. Position the power piston, tube down, in a tool fabricated from a piece of wood 2 × 4 × 8 in. long with a 1 $^3/_8$ in. hole in the center clamped in a vise.
15. Remove the snap-ring on the air valve.
16. Using the power pump and press plate insert the power piston, tube down, in a press plate and remove the air valve assembly using a $^3/_8$ in. drive extension as a remover.
17. Remove the floating control valve assembly from the push rod. Use a new one when rebuilding.
18. Push the master cylinder push rod from the center of the reaction retainer.
19. Remove the O-ring from the groove in the master cylinder piston rod.

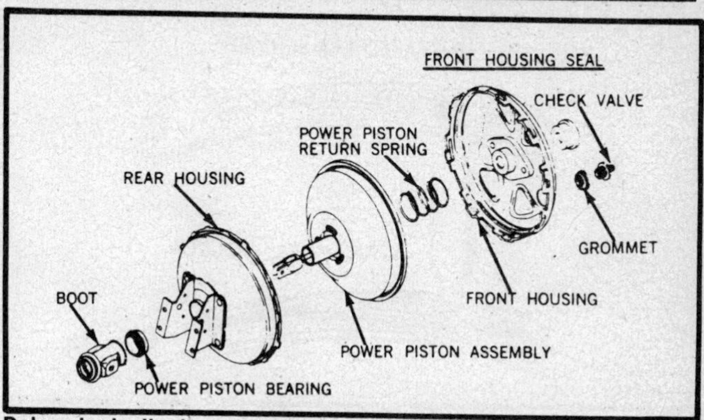

Delco single diaphragm booster (© GM Corp.)

Assembly

1. Use clean brake fluid and thoroughly clean all resuable brake parts.
2. Inspect all rubber parts and replace if nicked, cut or damaged.
3. When rebuilding make sure that no grease or mineral oil comes in contact with any of the rubber parts.
4. Install a new vacuum check valve using a new grommet.
5. Position a new front housing seal so that the flat surface of the cup lies against the bottom depression in the housing.
6. Place a new O-ring in the groove on the master cylinder piston rod, wipe a thin film of silicone lubricant on the O-ring.
7. Insert the master cylinder piston rod through the reaction retainer so the round end protrudes from the end of the tube on the reaction retainer.
8. Place the power piston wrench in a vise and position the power piston on the wrench so that the three lugs fit into the notches.
9. Position a new O-ring on the air valve on the second groove from the push rod end.
10. Place a new floating control valve on the push rod-air valve assembly so that the flat face of the valve will seat against the valve seat on the air valve.

NOTE: The old floating control valve assembly must be replaced with a new one since the force required to remove it distorts component parts.

11. Wipe a thin film of silicone lubricant on the control valve and the O-ring on the air valve.
12. Push the air valve push rod assembly, air valve first, onto its seat in the tube of the power piston.
13. Place the control valve retainer over the push rod so that the flat side seats on the floating control valve.
14. Press the floating control valve and its retainer onto the power piston tube by use of an installer tool and pushing down by hand.
15. After the floating control valve is seated, position the push rod limiter washer over the push rod and down onto the valve.
16. Stretch the air filter element over the end of the push rod and press it into the power piston tube.
17. Assemble the power piston diaphragm to the support plate. The raised flange of the diaphragm is pressed through the hole in the center of the support plate.

NOTE: Be sure that the edge of the center hole fits into the groove in the flange of the diaphragm.

18. Pull the diaphragm away from the outside diameter of the support plate so that the support plate can be gripped with both hands.
19. With the power piston still positioned on the holding tool in a vise, coat the bead of the diaphragm that contacts the power piston with silicone lubricant.

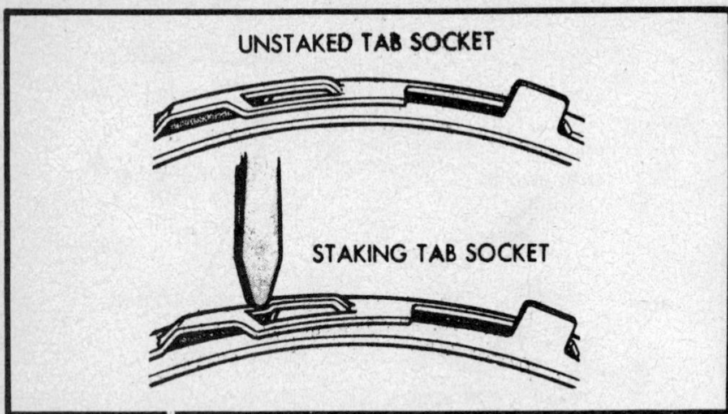

Staking housing tabs (© GM Corp.)

20. Place the support plate and diaphragm assembly over the tube of the power piston with the locking tangs facing downward.

NOTE: The flange of the power piston will fit into the groove on the power piston.

21. Press down and rotate the support plate clockwise, until the lugs on the power piston come against the stops on the support plate.
22. Turn the assembly over and place tube down in a tool, fabricated from a piece of wood 2 × 4 × 8 in. long with a 1 ³⁄₈ in. hole in the center, clamped into a vise.
23. Replace the snap-ring into the groove of the air valve.

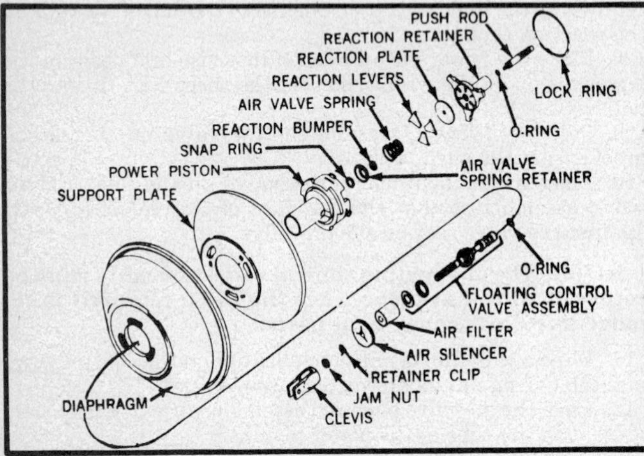

Power piston assembly (© GM Corp.)

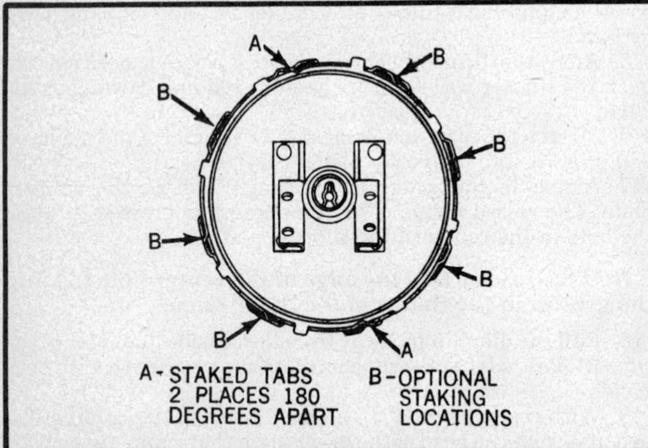

Housing locking tabs (© GM Corp.)

24. Place the air valve spring retainer on the snap-ring and assemble the reaction bumper into the groove in the end of the air valve.
25. Position the air valve return spring, large end down, on the spring retainer.
26. Place the three reaction levers into position with the wide ends in the slots of the power piston and the narrow ends resting on top of the air valve return springs.
27. Position the reaction plate (with the numbered side up) on top of the reaction levers. Press down on the plate until the large ends of the reaction levers pop up so the plate rests flat on the levers and is centered.
28. With the round end of the master cylinder piston rod up, and with the reaction retainer held toward the top of the piston rod, place the small end of the piston rod in the hole in the center of the reaction plate. Line up the ears on the reaction retainer with the notches in the power piston and push the reaction retainer down until the ears seat in the notches.
29. With pressure on the reaction retainer, position the large lock ring down over the master cylinder push rod.
30. There is a lug on the power piston which has a raised divider in the center. One end of the lock ring goes under the lug and on one side of the divider.
31. As you work your way around the power piston, the lockring goes over the ear of the reaction retainer and under a lug on the power piston until the other end of the lock ring is seated under the lug with the raised divider.

NOTE: Make certain both ends of the lock ring are securely under the large lug.

32. Place a new power piston bearing in the center of the rear housing so the flange on the center hole of the housing fits into the groove of the power piston bearing. The large flange on the power piston bearing will be on the stud side of the housing. Coat the inside of the bearing with silicone lubricant.
33. Place the air silencer over the holes on the tube of the power piston. Wipe the tube with silicone lubricant.
34. Attach the holding fixture to the front housing and clamp the base in a vise.
35. Place the power piston return spring over the insert in the front housing.
36. Lubricate the inside diameter of the support plate seal, the reaction retainer tube, and the beaded edge of the diaphragm with silicone lubricant.
37. Place the rear housing assembly over the front housing assembly and align the scribe marks of the two housings so they will match when in the locked position.
38. Place a spanner wrench on the rear housing and tighten the nuts and washers to the bolts.
39. Press down on the spanner wrench and twist the rear housing clockwise until fully locked.

NOTE: Do not break the studs loose in the rear housing or put pressure on the power piston tube when locking the housings.

40. Remove the spanner wrench and the holding fixture from the front housing.
41. Push the felt silencer over the pushrod and seat it against the end of the power piston tube.
42. Push the plastic boot and seat it against the rear housing. The raised tabs on the side of the boot will locate in the holes in the center of the brackets.
43. Stake the front and rear housing in two places: 180° apart.

NOTE: The interlock tabs should not be used for staking a second time. When all tabs have been staked once, the housing must be replaced.

Delco Tandem Dual Diaphragm Type

Disassembly

1. Scribe a line across the front and rear housing for reassembly.
2. Attach the base of a special holding fixture or equivalent to the front housing with nuts and washers and draw down tight to eliminate damage to the studs. Clamp the base in a vise with the power section up.
3. On vehicles with a straight mounting bracket place a spanner wrench over the studs on the rear housing and attach with nuts and washers.
4. On vehicles with a tilted mounting bracket there is a special tool placed inside the mounting bracket with the spanner wrench placed on top.
5. Press down on the spanner wrench and rotate the rear housing counterclockwise to separate the two housings. Remove the special tools.
6. Remove the power piston return spring, and remove and discard the vacuum check valve and grommet from the front housing.
7. Remove the front housing seal.
8. Remove the boot retainer and boot from the rear housing and remove the felt silencer from inside the boot.
9. Remove the power piston group from the rear housing and remove the primary power piston bearing from the center opening of the rear housing.
10. Remove piston rod retainer and piston rod from the secondary piston.
11. Mount a special double ended tool with the large diameter end up in a vise. Position the secondary power piston so that the two radial slots in the piston fit over the ears of the tool.

NOTE: Due to an optional construction design on the primary and secondary power pistons the special tool used in Step 11 will have to be reworked.

12. Fold back the primary diaphragm from the outside diameter of the primary support plate. Grip the edge of the support plate and rotate it counterclockwise to unscrew the primary power piston from the secondary power piston.
13. Remove the housing divider from the secondary power piston bearing from the housing divider.
14. The secondary power piston should still be positioned on the special double ended tool. Fold back the secondary diaphragm from the outside diameter of the secondary support plate. Rotate the support plate clockwise to unlock the secondary power piston.
15. Remove the secondary diaphragm from the secondary support plate.
16. Remove the reaction piston and disc from the center of the secondary power piston by pushing down on the end of the piston.
17. Remove the air valve spring from the end of the valve, if not removed earlier.
18. Remove the primary diaphragm and piston using the same procedure as the secondary with the exception of turning the support plate counterclockwise to unlock it.
19. Remove the air filter from the tubular section of the primary power piston.
20. Remove the power head silencer from the neck of the power piston tube.
21. Remove the rubber reaction bumper from the end of the air valve.
22. Using snap-ring pliers, remove the retaining ring from the air valve.
23. Remove the air valve push rod assembly.
    a. The recommended method would be to place the primary power piston in an arbor press and press the air valve push rod assembly out the bottom of the power piston tube using a rod not larger than ½ in. in diameter.

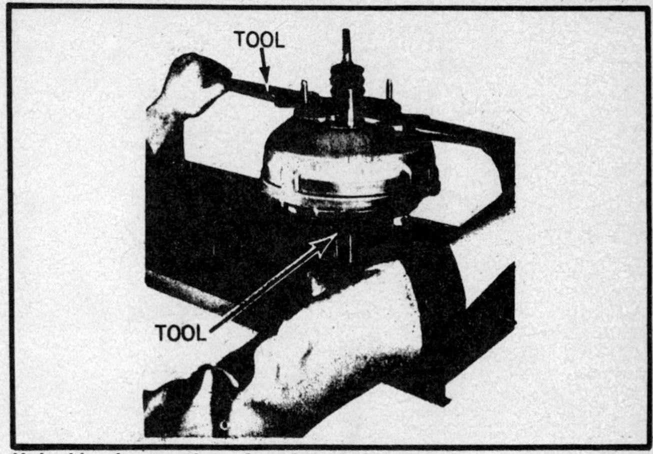

Unlocking front and rear housing (© GM Corp.)

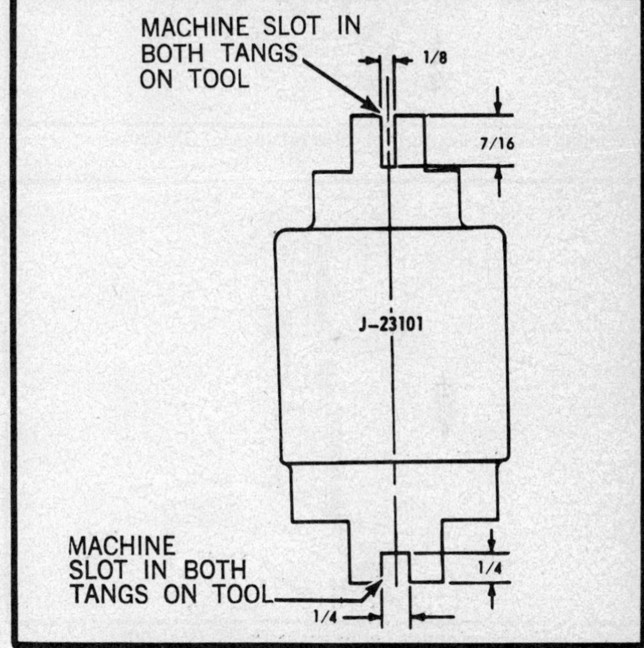

Reworking of tool for optional power piston design (© GM Corp.)

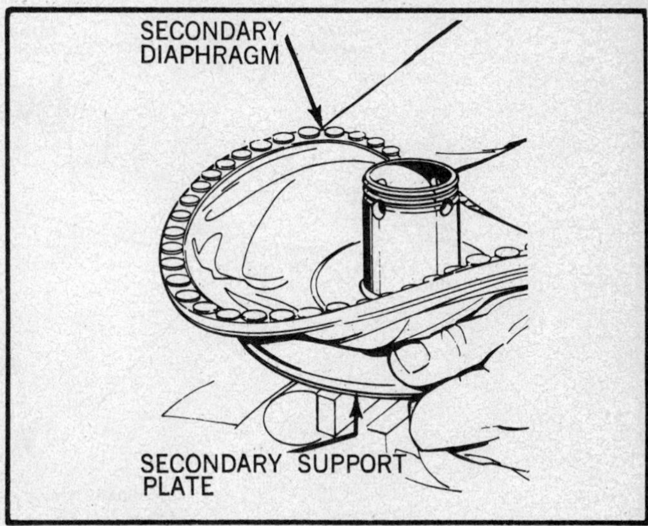

Locking or unlocking the secondary support plate and power piston (© GM Corp.)

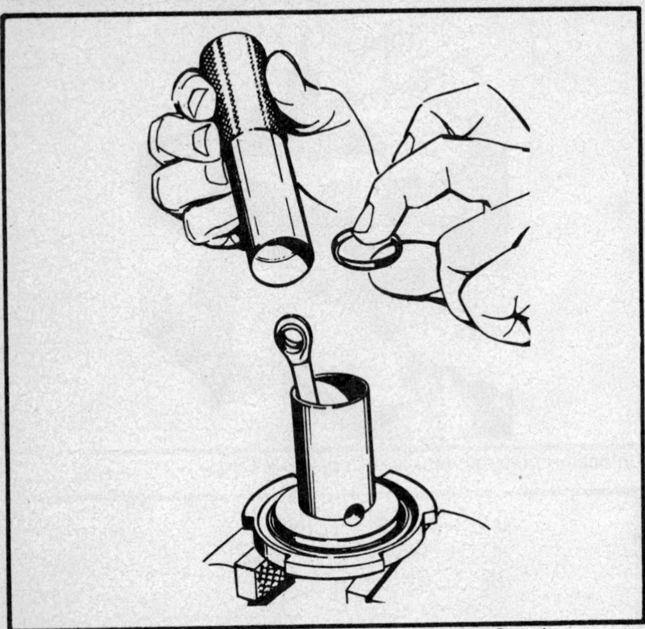

Installing the floating control valve retainer (© GM Corp.)

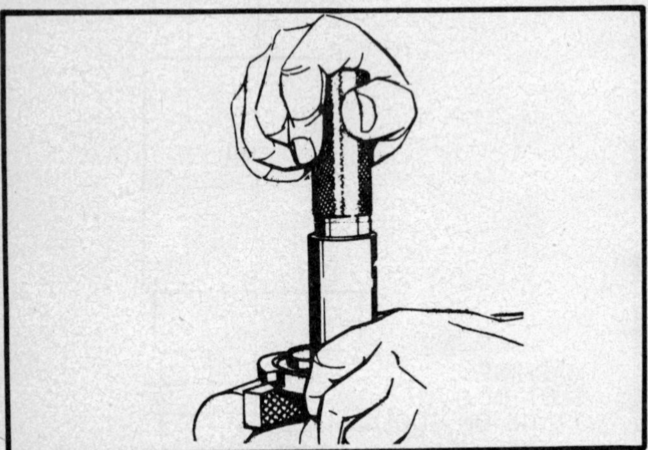

Seating the floating control valve assembly (© GM Corp.)

b. An alternate method would be to insert a heavy, round shanked screwdriver on both sides of the pushrod and pull the air valve push rod assembly straight out.

24. Remove the O-ring seal from the air valve.

Assembly

1. Use clean brake fluid and thoroughly clean all reusable brake parts.

2. Inspect all rubber parts and replace if nicked, cut or damaged.

3. When rebuilding, make sure that no grease or mineral oil comes in contact with any of the rubber parts.

4. Install a new vacuum check valve and a new grommet in the front housing.

5. Place a new seal in the front housing so that the flat surface lies against the bottom of the depression in the housing.

6. Reassemble the power piston group.

7. Lubricate the inside and outside diameter of the O-ring seal with silicone lubricant and place on the air valve.

8. Wipe a thin film of silicone lubricant on the large and small outside diameter of the floating control valve. If the floating control valve needs replacement, it will be necessary to replace the complete air valve-push rod assembly.

9. Place the air valve end of the air valve push rod assembly into the tube of the primary power piston. Manually press the air valve push rod assembly so that the floating control valve bottoms on the tube section of the primary power piston.

10. Place the inside diameter of the floating control valve retainer on the outside diameter of the special installer. Place it over the pushrod so that the closed side of the retainer seats on the floating control valve. Using the installer manually press the retainer and floating control valve to seat in the tube.

11. Stretch the filter element over the pushrod and press it into the piston tube.

12. Place the retaining ring into the groove in the air valve using snap-ring pliers.

13. Position the rubber reaction bumper on the end of the air valve.

14. Determine the correct reaction piston and apply a light coat of silicone lubricant to the outside diameter of the rubber reaction disc.

15. Place the rubber reaction disc in the large cavity of the secondary power piston and push the disc down to seat on the reaction piston.

16. Unlock the secondary power piston from the primary power piston.

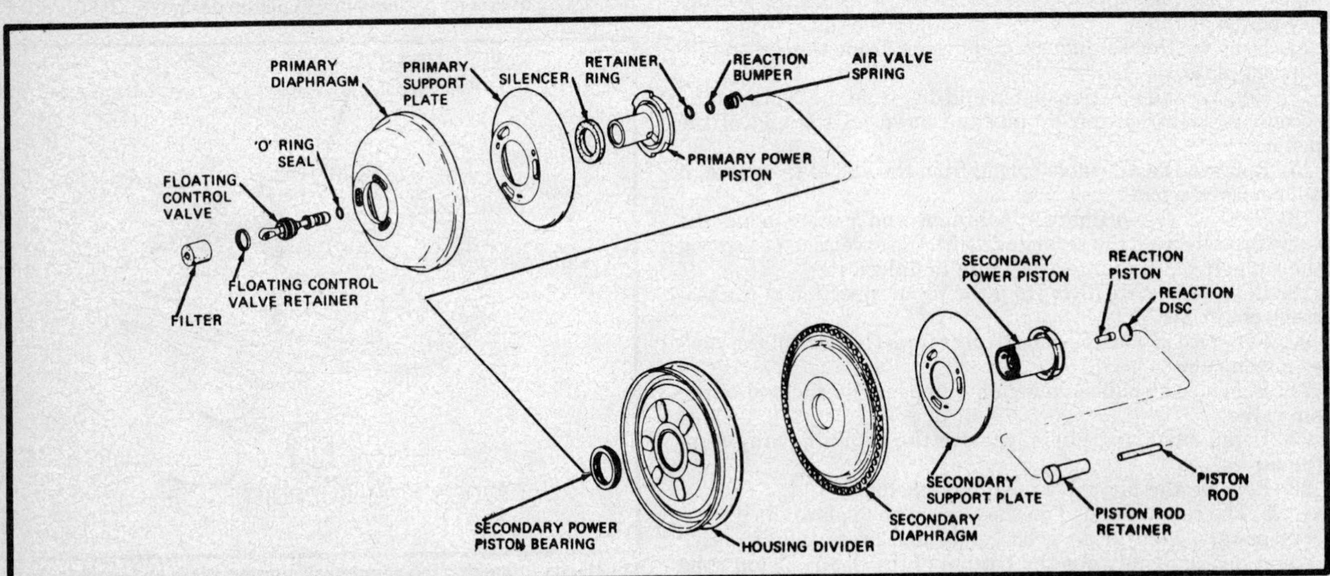

Power piston group (© GM Corp.)

17. Assemble the primary diaphragm to the primary support plate opposite the locking tangs. Press the raised flange on the inside diameter of the diaphragm through the center hole of the support plate. Be sure that the edge of the support plate center hole fits into the groove of the flange.

NOTE: Lubricate the inside diameter of the diaphragm and the raised surface of the flange with a light coat of silicone lubricant.

18. Mount the special tool used in Step 11 of the disassembly procedures in a vise with the small end up. Position the primary power piston so that the two radial slots in the piston fit over the ears (tangs) of the tool.
19. Fold the primary diaphragm away from the outside diameter of the primary support plate.
20. Place the primary support plate and diaphragm assembly over the tube of the primary piston. Make sure the locking tangs are facing down.
21. Press down and rotate the support plate clockwise until the tabs on the piston contact the stops.
22. Place the power head silencer on the tube of the piston so that the holes at the base of the tube are covered.
23. Coat the outside of the tube with silicone lubricant.
24. Remove the primary piston assembly from the special tool and lay it aside.
25. Assemble the secondary diaphragm to the secondary support plate following the same steps for assembling the primary support plate except mount the special tool with the large diameter up, and press down and turn the plate counterclockwise until the piston contacts the stops.
26. Leave the secondary power piston on the tool and in the vise.
27. Apply a light coat of talcum powder or silicone lubricant to the bead on the outside diameter of the secondary diaphragm. This will make it easier for reassembly of the front and rear housing.
28. Place the secondary bearing in the inside diameter of the housing divider so that the extended lip of the bearing faces up.
29. Lubricate the inside diameter of the bearing with silicone lubricant.
30. Using a special protector tool or equivalent, position the secondary bearing on the threaded end of the secondary power piston.
31. Hold the housing divider so that the six oblong protrusions on the middle of the divider are facing up. Press the divider down over the tool and onto the piston tube so it rests against the support ring. Remove the bearing protector tool.
32. Pick up the primary power piston assembly and fold the primary diaphragm away from the outside diameter of the support plate.
33. Place the small end of the air valve return spring on the air valve so that it contacts the air valve retaining ring.
34. Position the primary power piston. Make sure that the air valve return spring seats down over the raised center section of the secondary piston.
35. Rotate the secondary power piston clockwise into the threaded portion of the primary piston. Tighten to 5–15 ft. lbs.
36. Fold the primary diaphragm back into position.
37. Cover the outside diameter of the piston rod retainer with a light coat of silicone lubricant.
38. Insert the master cylinder piston rod retainer into the secondary power piston so that the flat end bottoms against the rubber reaction disc.
39. Place the new primary piston bearing in the rear housing center hole. The thin lip of the bearing will protrude to the outside of the housing. Coat the inside diameter of the bearing with silicone lubricant.
40. Mount the holding fixture in a vise and position the front housing so that the housing studs fit in the holes provided in the tool.
41. Place the power piston return spring over the inset in the front housing.
42. Assemble the power piston assembly to the rear housing by pressing the tube of the primary piston through the rear housing bearing until the housing divider seats in the rear housing and the primary piston bottoms against the housing.
43. Hold the rear housing with the mounting studs up and position it so that the tangs on the edge of the front housing are locked in the slots on the edge of the rear housing. The scribe marks on the top of the housings will be in line.
44. Lower the rear housing assembly onto the front housing.

NOTE: The power piston spring must seat in the depression in the face of the secondary power piston. Check that the bead on the outside diameter of the secondary diaphragm is positioned between the edges of the housing.

45. Assemble the front and rear housings with the spanner wrench.
46. Replace the silencer and boot.

Hydro – Max Electro Hydraulic Brake Booster

OPERATION

TO 1983

Beneath the booster a vane type pump is attached and is integral with a 12 volt DC electric motor. If the vehicle engine was not operating or a hose or belt was broken the pump and motor would serve as a reserve power source to provide boost pressure. The electric pump draws fluid from the low pressure side of the booster piston and delivers it to the high pressure side. The electric pump provides one-half of the primary system pressure.

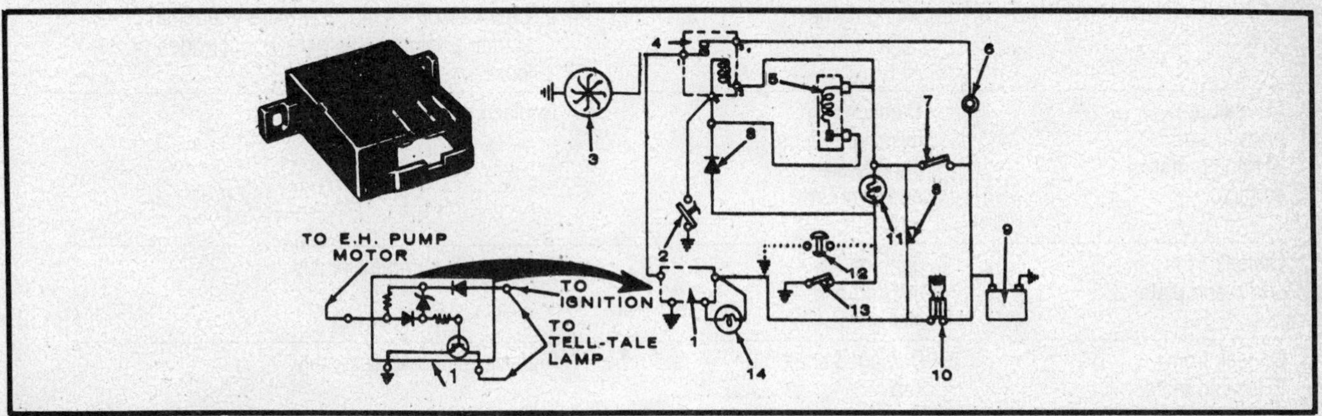

Hydraulic booster electrical diaghram (© GM Corp.)

Electro-Hydraulic Pump Diagnosis

Mode	Tell-Tale #1①	Tell-Tale #2②	Buzzer
Engine off—ignition off			
No brake apply	off	off	off
Brake apply	on	off	on
Engine off—ignition on with or without brake apply—(bulb check)	on	on	on
Engine off—ignition on start with or without brake apply	on	on	on
Engine on with or without brake apply	off	off	off
Engine on—primary boost interrupted with or without brake apply	on	on	on
Engine on—open circuit in EH pump motor with or without brake apply	off	on	off

①Brake ②Brake Elect. Hyd. Boost

DIAGNOSIS OF EH PUMP

Problem	Possible Cause	Correction
Excessive Pump Noise (gurgle, chatter, etc.)	Trapped air in pump.	Depress brake pedal lightly with the engine off for thirty seconds and release. Recheck and should the problem persist, repeat above procedure after a three minute waiting period.①
Inoperative pump	Non-functioning motor.	1. Check electrical connection between motor lead wire and wiring harness. If loose, corroded, or disconnected, clean and secure connection. 2. Check grounding of pump housing to booster. The pump housing must be securely bolted to the booster to properly ground the motor. 3. Replace EH Pump
	Low or no voltage at motor connection of wiring harness.	1. Check condition of battery and battery terminals.Correct an abnormally low battery condition and/or clean battery terminals if necessary. 2. Check electrical leads at battery terminal of starter or ignition bus bar—not corroded or loose.
Oil leak at booster and EH pump mating surface.	Damaged or missing O-rings at pressure and/or return port.	Replace two O-rings.
Oil leak from pump end plate	damaged or missing end plate seal.	Replace EH pump assembly.
Oil leak from EH pump motor	Damaged shaft seal.	Replace EH pump assembly.

①This noise will diminish upon continued use of the brakes under normal driving conditions.

ELECTRICAL CONTROL CIRCUITS

The electric pump operation is controlled by a relay which is operated by a flow switch located in the booster outlet to sense the fluid flow. A pedal switch also controls the electric pump operation whenever the brake pedal is depressed and the engine is not operating. The system is monitored by two dash mounted tell-tale lamps and a buzzer. The two lamps will be marked to:

1. Warn of failure of the primary system.
2. Warn of failure of the reserve system.
3. To make the driver aware that the reserve is in operation, the dash lamp will light and the buzzer will sound. The monitoring system is controlled by a solid state module, and two in line diodes. The plug in module is not repairable and must be replaced as a unit.

WARNING MODES

The function of the system warning devices, tell-tales and alarm buzzer, under different vehicle operational modes are indicated in the Electro-Hydraulic Pump Diagnosis Chart.

ELECTRO – HYDRAULIC PUMP

Diagnosis

1. The pump and tell-tale light does not come on when the brake pedal is depressed with the engine off:
   a. Check the brake pedal switch.
   b. Check for electrical continuity through the pump flow switch.
   c. Check for voltage to the ignition side of the relay coil.
   d. Check for voltage at the battery connection to the relay coil.
   d. Check for voltage at the battery connection to the relay.
   e. Check for an open at the ignition diode.
   f. Check for voltage at the pump terminal at the relay.
2. The engine is off and the pump is operating but the light is not on when the brake pedal is depressed.
   a. Check the voltage at the warning light bulb.
   b. Replace the bulb.
3. The engine and the pump are off, but when the brake pedal is depressed, the light is on.
   a. Check the voltage at the pump motor.
   b. Replace pump.
4. The accessories, radio, heater, wipers etc. operate when the brake pedal is depressed and the engine off.
   a. Check the ignition diode for a short.
5. The pump and warning light stay on after the engine is started.
   a. Check for air in the boost systems.
   b. Check to see if the flow switch is shorted or in the stuck position.
   c. Check to see if the relay is in the closed position.

Hydro–Max

1984 AND LATER

The main features of the new style Hydro-Max system are as follows;

1. All front brakes are dual piston, disc brakes of the Dayton/Walther design.
2. The parking brake is actuated by a spring/ramp assembly, located on the rear wheel backing plate and controlled by hydraulic pressure from the Hydro-Max pump, through a parking brake control in the cab of the vehicle.
3. The hydraulic brake system is a vertically split system, with the front disc brakes as one system and the rear brakes as the other system, except on tandem equipped vehicles.
4. The tandem vehicle brakes are split with the front disc and one of the wheel cylinders of the forward axle as one system and the second wheel cylinder of the forward axle and the total rear axle as the second system.
5. The hydraulic brake pump and reservoir is completely separate from the power steering system and uses Dexron®II A/T fluid for operation of the in-wheel parking brake system. Brake fluid is used in the two brake systems.
6. Seals are located between the master cylinder and the booster, along with spacing, making it impossible for the two fluids to mix. A vent is provided between the two units to for normal fluid "weepage".

DAYTON/WALTHER DISC BRAKES

The Dayton/Walther disc brakes are dual piston, sliding caliper units, using semi-metallic, asbestos-free disc pads, interchangable from right to left and from outer to inner. One common caliper is used on both the right and left sides with the bleed screw port located at the top of each caliper.

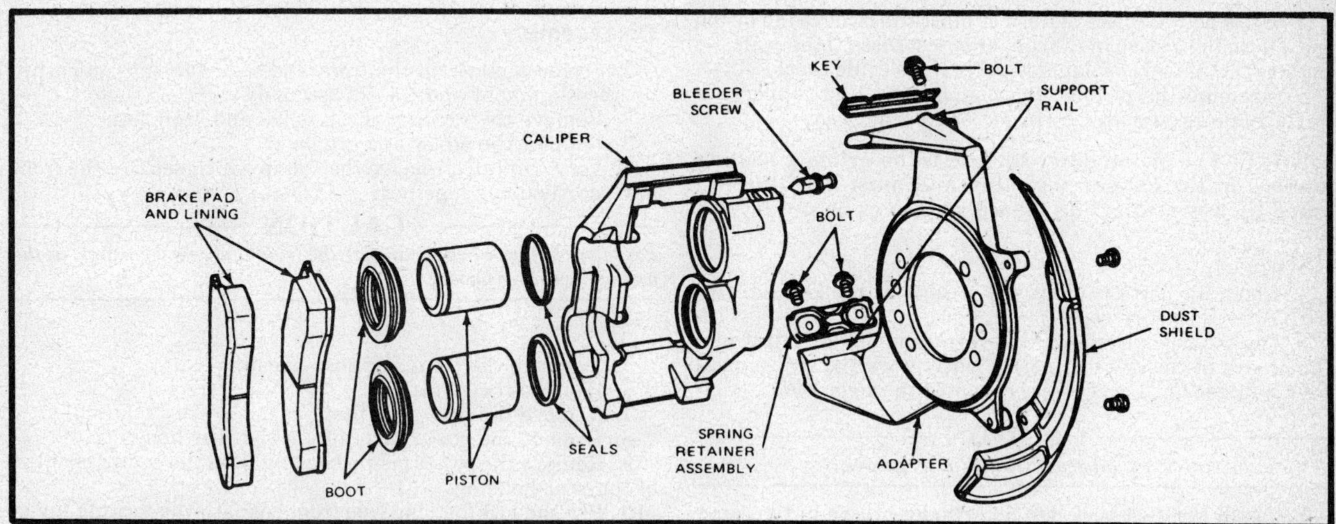

Sliding caliper—8000, 9000, 9500, and 12000 pound front axle

Removal

NOTE: Disc pads should be replaced when the lining is worn to a minimum thickness of 0.032 in. (0.794mm) above the pad plate, unless state or local vehicle inspection codes dictates otherwise.

1. Remove approximately $\frac{2}{3}$ of the brake fluid from the reservoir of the master cylinder for the front brake system.
2. Raise the vehicle and support safely. Remove the wheel assembly to expose the caliper.
3. Remove the two bolts and the spring retainer from the bottom end of the caliper.
4. Remove the bolt at the top end of the caliper support and remove the key from between the caliper and the support rails by sliding it from, the assembly.
5. With the caliper resting on the lower rail, rotate the upper end up and away from the upper rail and lift the assembly from the rotor.
6. Do not allow the caliper to hang by the jounce hydraulic iine. Either disconnect the line or hang the caliper from the frame with a piece of wire.
7. Remove the lining from the caliper, starting with the pad farthest from the pistons.
8. If the disc pads are to be replaced only, use a block of wood and a C-clamp to push the pistons back into the calipers.
9. Install the disc pads and calipers in the reverse order of the removal procedure.

CALIPERS

Disassembly

1. With the caliper removed from the vehicle and the hose removed, clean the assembly with isopropyl alcohol or brake fluid.

CAUTION

Do not use mineral based cleaning solvents to clean the assembly. Damage to the new rubber parts can occur due to the solvent not being completely cleaned from the assembly.

2. Place a shop towel covered wooden block under the caliper pistons and direct compressed air into the fluid port to slowly push the pistons from their bores in the caliper.

CAUTION

Do not place fingers on the front of the pistons to catch or protect them during the removal. Personal injury could occur when thee pistons are blown from the caliper bores.

3. Remove and discard the piston boots.
4. Use a pointed piece of wood or plastic to remove the piston seals from the groove in the caliper bores. Discard the seals. Do not use metal tools as damage to the bore could occur.
5. Examine the pistons, the piston bores and calipers for damage, nicks, scoring , corrosion or extreme wear.

NOTE: The piston outer surface is the primary sealing surface in the caliper assembly and must not be refinished by any means nor should abrasives be used.

Assembly

1. Clean all parts in isopropyl alcohol or brake fluid. Dry with filtered compressed air.
2. Dip the new piston seal in brake fluid and install it into the groove in the cylinder bore. Gently work the seal around with a finger until it is properly seated in the groove.

CAUTION

Be sure the seal is not twisted or rolled in its groove.

3. Install the dust boot into its cylinder groove in the same manner as the piston seal was installed.
4. Coat or dip the piston in brake fluid and using a small flat plastic or wooden tool, gradually work the dust boot around the piston.
5. Press the piston straight into the caliper bore until it bottoms. The boot internal diameter should slide up the piston as the piston is pushed into the caliper bore and slide into position in the boot groove of the piston.
6. Install the second piston in the same manner as the first piston was installed.
7. Upon completion, the caliper is ready to be re-installed on the axle, along with the disc pads.

SPIDER, HUB AND ROTOR ASSEMBLY

The spider, hub and rotor assembly can be inspected for damages, scores or abnormal wear and replaced as required.

Dual Power Brake System (G.M.)

The Dual Power Brake System (DPB) is a system which utilizes two power boosting units in series to provide the power assist necessary to stop the vehicle. This is accomplished by combining a vacuum operated booster with a hydraulically operated booster in tandem arrangement with a standard dual master cylinder. Assist power generated by the vacuum booster is transmitted forward to the hydraulic booster, where the apply power is, again, assisted or augmented by the hydraulic booster. Doubly assisted power available at the hydraulic booster is transmitted to the master cylinder, thereby developing hydraulic pressure up to a maximum of approximately 600 psi. Refer to the Chevrolet or G.M.C. sections of this manual for removal and installation instructions, as they pertain to components of the dual power booster.

CAUTION

The Dual Power Brake System is comprised of two separate hydraulic systems, and should be treated as such. One system operates with hydraulic brake fluid, and the other system operates with power steering fluid. These two very different types of hydraulic fluid are not compatible, and should not be allowed to come into contact with one another, nor should they be allowed to come into contact with components of the system for which they are not intended. DO NOT mix these fluids together. DO NOT reuse the old fluid. If care is not exercised to isolate these two fluids during the overhaul procedure, then inevitable deterioration will result, causing leakage at the seals and eventual system malfunction.

VACUUM BOOSTER

Disassembly

1. Scribe a mark on the front and rear housings to ensure proper alignment and ease of assembly.
2. Remove the vacuum check valve and grommet.
3. Remove the elbow and grommet.
4. Very carefully, remove the clamp which secures the front and rear housing together.

CAUTION

Exercise caution when separating the front and rear housings, as the booster is spring loaded.

5. Separate the front and rear housings.
6. Remove the clevis.
7. Remove the boot and filter.
8. Remove the power piston from the rear housing.
9. Remove the power piston bearing from the center opening of the rear housing.
10. Pry the locking ring free from beneath the locking lug of the power piston, and remove the locking ring.

DUAL POWER BRAKE OPERATIONAL CHECKS

	Vacuum Light & Buzzer	Brake Light	Parking Brake Light
Warning system check (Buzzer and warning lights):			
1. Ignition off, engine off.	Off	Off	Off
2. Ignition on, engine off.	On below 9″ Vac Off above 12″ Vac	On	On with park brake applied Off with park brake released
3. Ignition on, cranking engine.	Same as 2	Off	Off
4. Ignition on, engine running.	Same as 2	Off if both booster pump and brake system is normal. On if either system is malfunctioning	Same as 2

Vacuum system check: With vacuum gage at 15 inches and ignition off, make a single brake application, observe vacuum gauge, and feel brake pedal resistance.	Satisfactory vacuum boost should show vacuum drop on brake application, and further drop on brake release. In addition, pedal should move freely and smoothly with light pedal pressure before becoming firm. No gauge movement indicates faulty vacuum gauge. Continuing vacuum drop with brake applied indicates a leaking internal air valve. Vacuum drop with brakes released indicates leaking check valve.
Hydraulic system boost check: Make full brake application, depress clutch and turn key to start engine.	Satisfactory hydraulic boost is indicated by brake pedal traveling further to floor when engine starts. No further travel indicates no hydraulic boost.
Dual system check: With engine continuing to run, check vacuum gauge for 15″ vacuum minimum. Make a slow application. First travel is vacuum boost only, further travel causes supplementary hydraulic boost.	15″ minimum on instrument panel gauge. First travel should have no brake apply noise; further travel should have hydraulic throttling noise. Immediate noise indicates faulty vacuum system, no noise indicates faulty hydraulic booster system.
Master cylinder check: With engine continuing to run, make a full brake application and hold for one minute.	Pedal should remain solid indicating master cylinder seals are good and holding. Spongy pedal indicates air in brake apply system. Slowly sinking pedal followed by brake light coming on indicates faulty master or wheel cylinder.
Brake adjustment check: Brake adjustment on vehicles with the DPB is automatic. With booster system operational and engine running, brake pedal travel will give an indication of brake adjustment.	Pedal travel of approximately 4 inches indicates normal brake adjustment. With pedal travel over 6½ inches, brake adjustment should be checked.

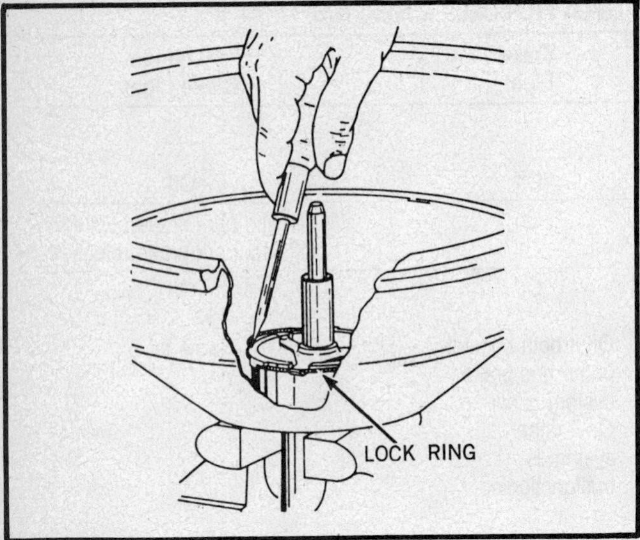

Removal of lock ring (© GM Corp.)

11. Remove the reaction retainer, the control valve, the reaction plate, the two reaction levers, the air valve spring, and the spring retainer.
12. Separate the control valve sleeve from the control valve. Remove the two double lip seals from the control valve.
13. Secure the square end of special tool J–21524, or its equivalent, in a vise. Position the diaphragm support plate and power piston over the raised lugs with the tubular end of the power piston facing upwards.
14. While gripping the steel support plate, press down on it, rotating it counterclockwise until the support plate separates from the power piston.
15. Remove the diaphragm support plate and the diaphragm.
16. Separate the diaphragm from the support plate.
17. Remove the silencer from the tubular end of the power piston.
18. Surround the lugged end of the power piston (the end of the power piston opposite the tubular end) with shop towels or a material of similar consistency, and secure the power piston in a vise with the tubular end facing downward.

NOTE: DO NOT tighten the vise directly on the tube, as the tube acts as a bearing surface. Tighten the vise only enough to hold the power piston in place. Excessive tightening may crack or distort the tube.

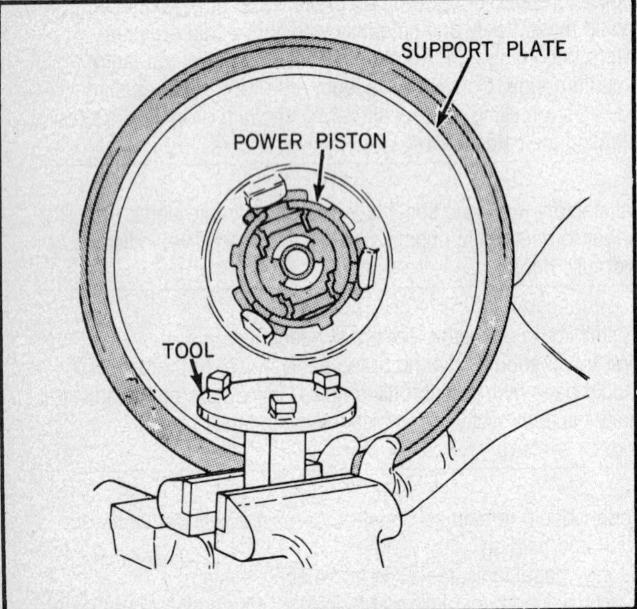

Power piston and support plate separating tool (© GM Corp.)

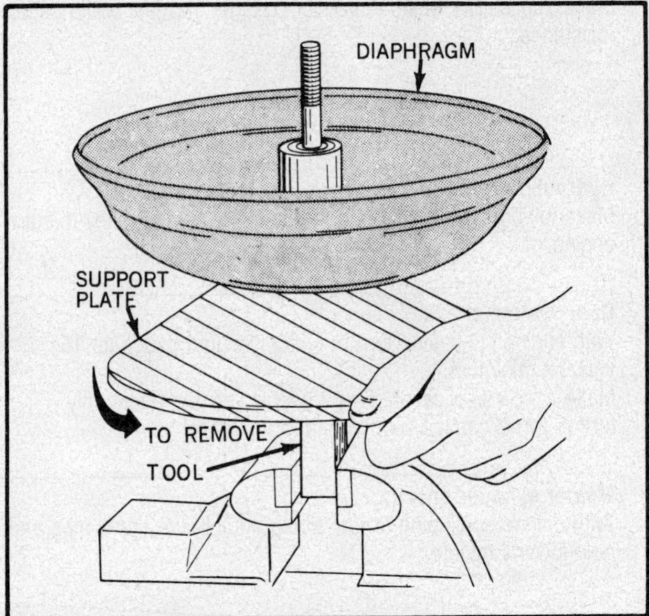

Removing support plate and diaphragm (© GM Corp.)

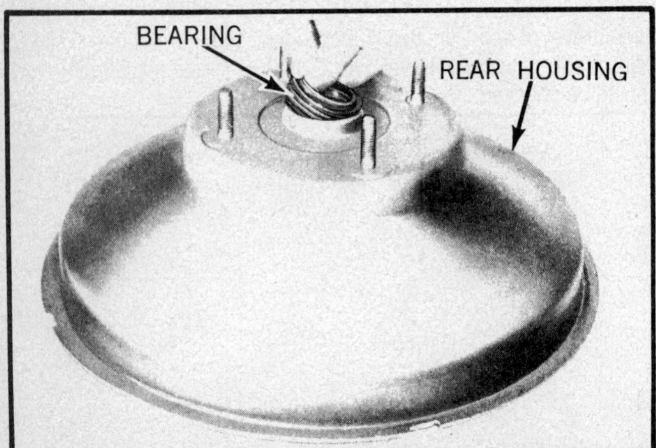

Power bearing removal (© GM Corp.)

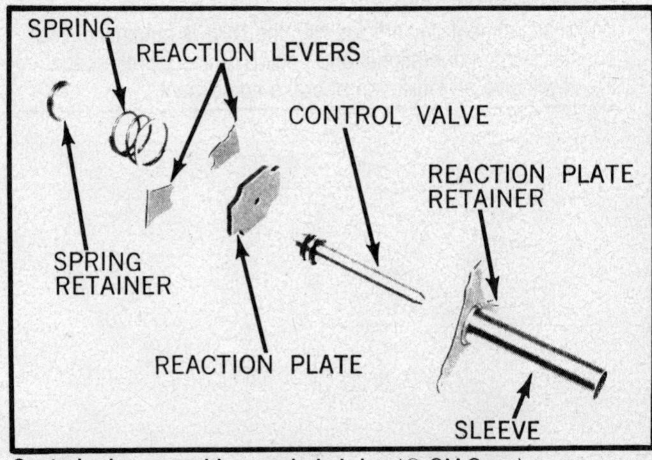

Control valve assembly—exploded view (© GM Corp.)

19. Working at the lugged end of the power piston, remove the retaining ring from the air valve.
20. Working at the tubular end of the power piston, thread the clevis onto the air valve. Insert the blade of a screwdriver through the hole in the clevis, and use it to pull the valve out of the power piston. Remove the clevis.
21. Remove the air valve O-ring, floating control valve retainer, spring, retainer, spring, spring seat, and the floating control valve.
22. Clean all parts in denatured alcohol, and dry with filtered, compressed air.
23. Check all parts for damage or excessive wear.

NOTE: The manufacturer states specifically that internal parts or surfaces are NOT to be remachined. DO NOT use abrasive to remove surface defects. Replace worn or damaged parts and rubber sealing components.

Assembly

1. Apply a thin film of lubricant on the air valve O-ring and on the surface of the air valve.
2. Install the O-ring in the second groove of the air valve.
3. Secure the square end of special tool J–21524, or its equivalent, in a vise.
4. Insert the valve end of the air valve into the tube of the power piston. Push the valve all the way in, until it stops against its seat.
5. Lubricate the outside diameter of the new floating control valve assembly.
6. Assemble the spring seat, floating control valve spring (small end of the spring first), and spring retainer to the floating control valve assembly.
7. Install the floating control valve assembly over the push rod end of the air valve and into the tube of the power piston (floating control valve first).
8. Install the floating control valve retainer over the end of the air valve push rod and onto the floating control valve assembly. Position special tool J–23175A or its equivalent over the retainer, and manually press the floating control valve assembly and retainer to seat in the tube of the power piston. If the power piston is to be replaced, it will be necessary to gauge the power piston-to-air valve clearance in order to select the proper control valve. To gauge, complete the following procedure;
   a. Install the retaining ring into the top groove in the air valve.
   b. Pull back lightly on the air valve push rod, and slowly return the air valve to its normal position.
   c. Position special tool J–28673, or its equivalent, over the air valve at the lugged end of the power piston, aligning the lugs of the tool with the three cut-out lands on the large diameter of the power piston. Twist the floating pin, located in the center of the tool, a minimum of ½ turn to relieve tension on the O-ring in the tool.
   d. Insert a feeler gauge between the floating pin and the main body of the gauge tool. The clearance measured in in. or millimeters will determine which control valve will be installed during final assembly.
   e. Select a control valve from the Control Valve Chart that comes closest to the clearance measured by the feeler gauge. Control valves are identified by grooves near the seal end of the valve. (see Control Valve Chart).

CONTROL VALVE CHART

Inches	Millimeters	Id Grooves
0.040–0.051	1.016–1.295	1
0.028–0.039	0.711–0.991	2
0.015–0.027	0.381–0.686	3

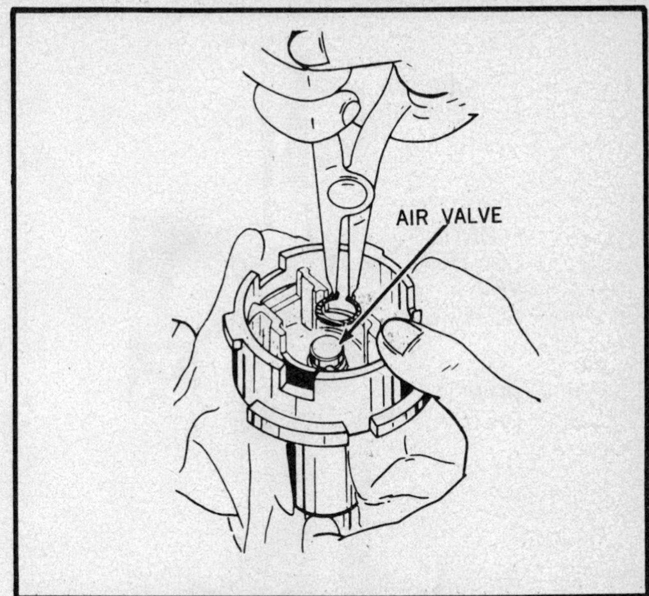

Air valve snapring removal (© GM Corp.)

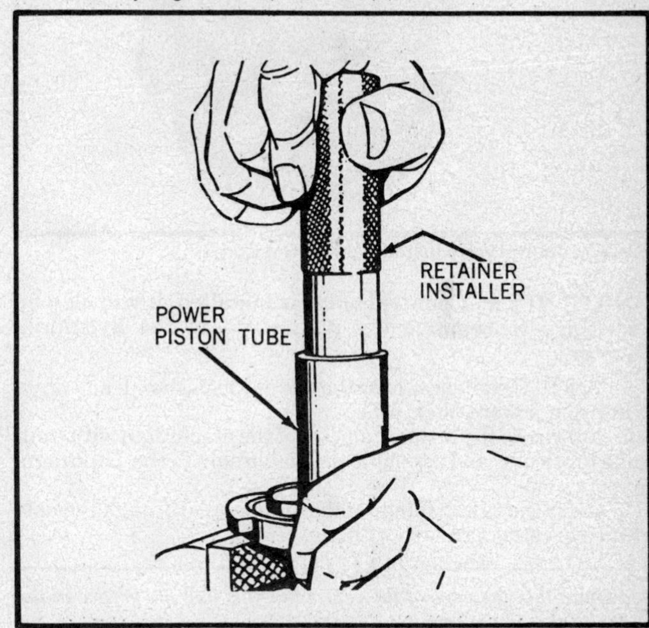

Pressing floating control assembly and retainer (© GM Corp.)

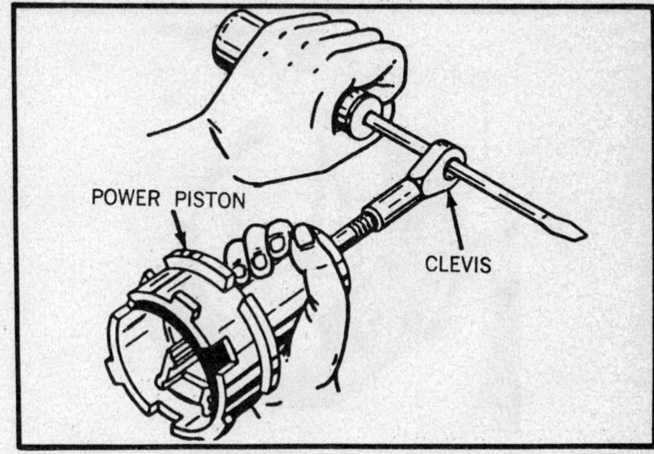

Air valve removal (© GM Corp.)

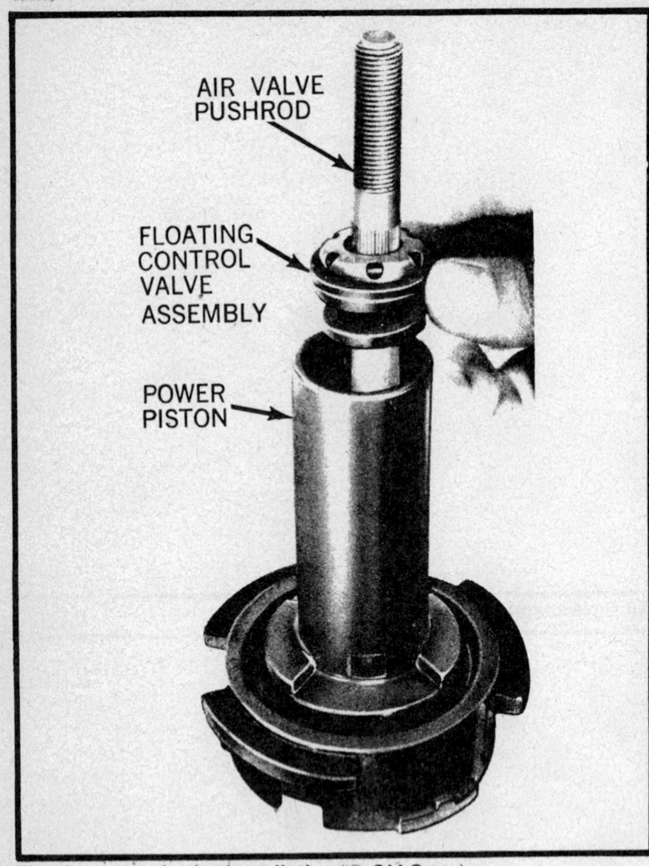

Floating control valve installation (© GM Corp.)

NOTE: If a new control valve is installed, it will also be necessary to regauge the piston rod of the hydraulic booster.

9. Install the silencer over the end of the push rod, and press it into the power piston tube.

10. Lubricate the inside diameter of the diaphragm with a silicone lubricant, and assemble the diaphragm to the diaphragm support plate.

11. Press the raised flange of the diaphragm through the hole in the center of the support plate.

CAUTION

Be certain that the edge of the center hole fits into the groove in the flange of the diaphragm.

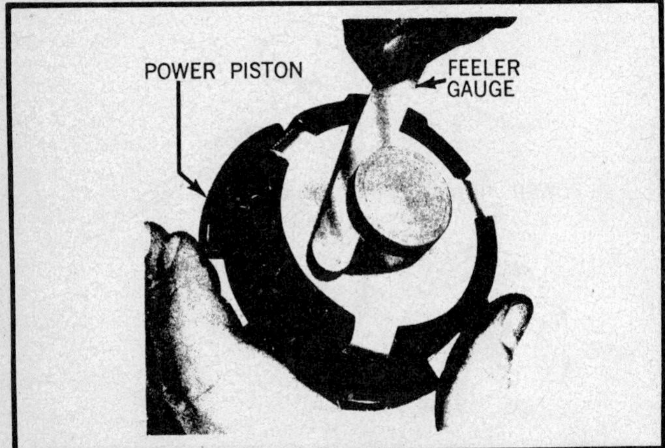

Gauging air valve clearance (© GM Corp.)

12. Lubricate the section of the diaphragm that contacts the power piston with a power brake silicone lubricant.

13. Position the support plate and the diaphragm over the power piston tube. While pressing down on the support plate, turn the support plate until the locking lugs on the power piston come against the stops on the support plate.

14. Invert the piston and diaphragm assembly. Surround the lugged end of the power piston (the end of the power piston opposite the tubular end) with shop towels or a material of similar consistency, and secure the power piston in a vise with the tubular end facing downward.

CAUTION

DO NOT tighten the vise directly on the tube, as the tube acts as a bearing surface. Tighten the vise only enough to hold the power piston in place. Excessive tightening may crack or distort the tube.

15. Install the air valve spring retainer to seat on the retaining ring.

CAUTION

Check the position of the reaction plate in the power piston before placing reaction levers and spring in position. Note that the reaction plate is designed so that it will fit only one way in the power piston. DO NOT force the plate as the power piston may become damaged.

16. Place the air valve return spring, small end down, on the spring retainer.

17. Place the two reaction levers into position, aligning the tabs on the wide end with the slots provided for them.

18. Install two new seals in the grooves on the control valve with the lips of the seals facing toward the chamfered end. Make sure the seals are lubricated.

19. Assemble the control valve, valve sleeve, and the reaction retainer.

20. Install the reaction plate on top of the reaction levers.

21. Holding the chamfered end of the control valve in an upright position, and with the reaction retainer positioned toward the top of the assembly, insert the small end of the control valve in the hole in the center of the reaction plate. Seat the ears of the reaction retainer in the notches of the power piston.

NOTE: A special tool J-24433 or its equivalent may be used to hold the control valve components in place. Another way of installing the control valve components is to fabricate a tool, the inside diameter of which is $1^3/_4$ in., and the overall length of which is approximately 5–7 in. The outside diameter of the tool should not exceed $1\,^7/_8$ in. Place the locking ring around the tool before pushing components down.

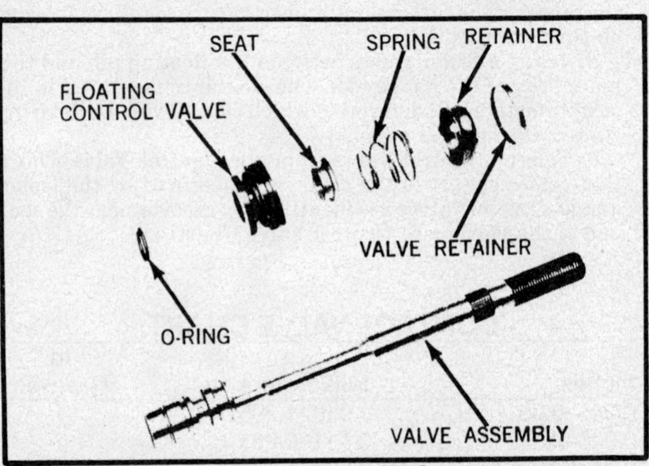

Air valve assembly—exploded view (© GM Corp.)

22. Make sure that the reaction plate is flat on the reaction levers and that the ears on the reaction retainer are fully seated in the piston notches.
23. Locate the one lug on power piston which has a raised divider in the center. Position one end of the locking ring under the lug and to one side of the divider.
24. Working your way around the power piston, fit the locking ring over the ears of the reaction retainer and under the lugs of the power piston, until the other end of the locking ring is seated under the lug with the raised divider.
25. Be certain that both ends of the locking ring are under the large lug of the power piston, and that the ends of the locking ring are against the divider.
26. Install two new grommets in the front housing.
27. Install the new vacuum check valve and elbow.
28. Install the power piston bearing in the rear housing. The formed flange on the housing center hole must fit into the groove in the bearing. Also, the flange and thin lip on the bearing must project out the stud side of the rear housing.
29. Apply a thin coat of lubricant to the inside diameter of the power piston bearing.
30. Lay the front housing on a flat clean surface.
31. Position the power piston return spring on the front housing, and center it.
32. Apply a thin film of lubricant on the tube of the power piston. Assemble the power piston to the rear housing by pressing the tube of the piston through the rear housing bearing, until the piston bottoms against the housing.
33. Hold the rear housing and power piston assembly so that the mounting studs are facing up.
34. Position the assembly over the front housing, aligning the scribe marks made prior to disassembly.

NOTE: Vacuum may be applied to the vacuum check valve to facilitate assembly. The other vacuum tube must be plugged.

35. Assemble the rear housing to the front housing.

CAUTION

Be certain that the return spring seats around the power piston, and that the bead on the outside diameter of the diaphragm is properly seated.

36. Install the clamp, and torque to 60 inch lbs.
37. Disconnect the vacuum source from the vacuum check valve, if used, and unplug the other tube.
38. Invert the assembly, and position it over a cylindrical device of sufficient diameter and length in order to clear the studs and accept the air valve push rod.
39. Assemble the hydraulic booster to the vacuum booster.
40. Gauge the output push rod (piston rod) of the hydraulic booster.
41. Install the filter in the boot. Install the boot assembly over the power piston tube.

Hydraulic Booster (Dual Power)

Disassembly

1. Pull the piston rod out with a twisting motion.

NOTE: It is advised that this be done over a large open container as the fluid must be drained from the booster.

2. Secure the booster in a vise by clamping across the body flange (flow switch up).
3. Remove the flow switch and the flow switch O-ring seal.
4. Insert a suitable pry tool under the lip of the cap, and pry the cap free. Be careful not to bend or distort the cap.

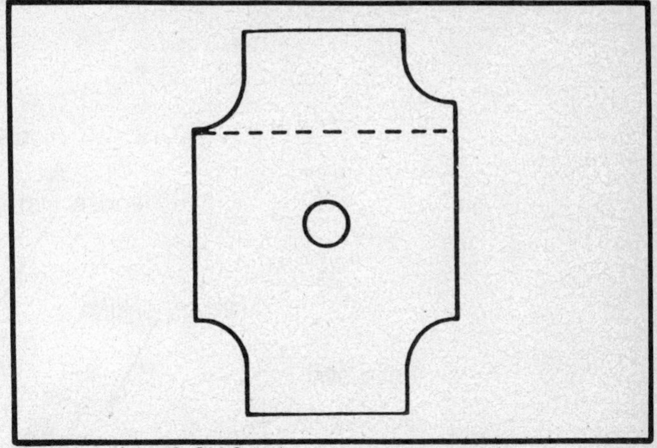

Reaction plate (© GM Corp.)

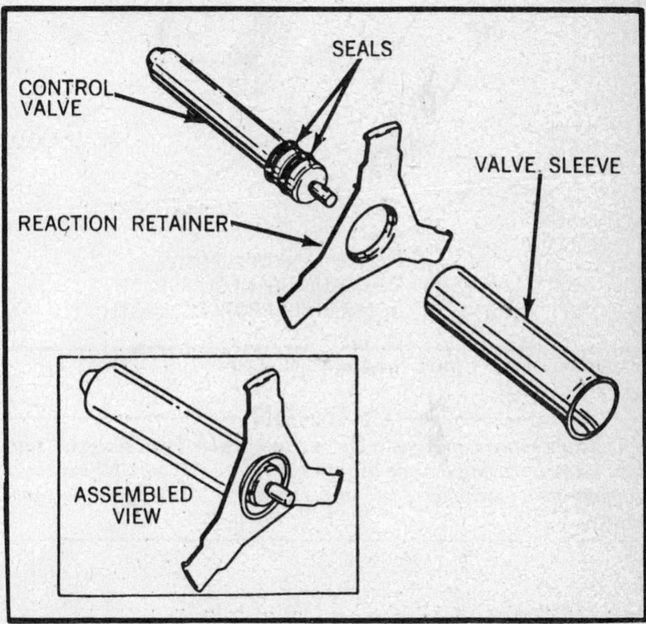

Assembled view of control valve and related components (© GM Corp.)

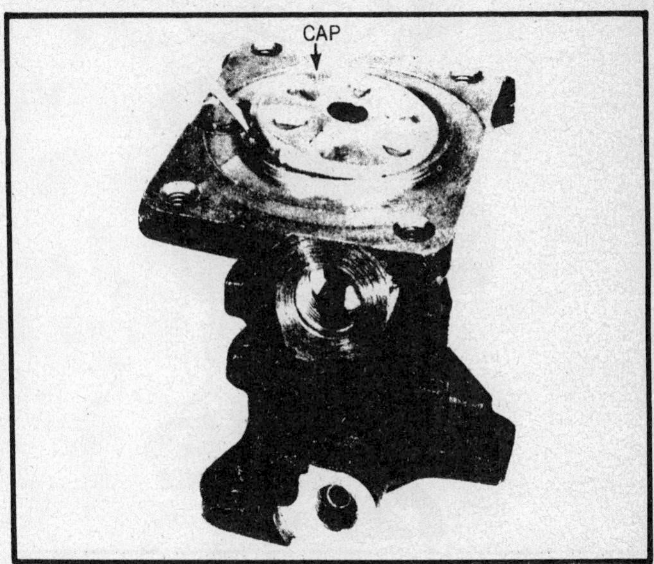

Removing booster cap (© GM Corp.)

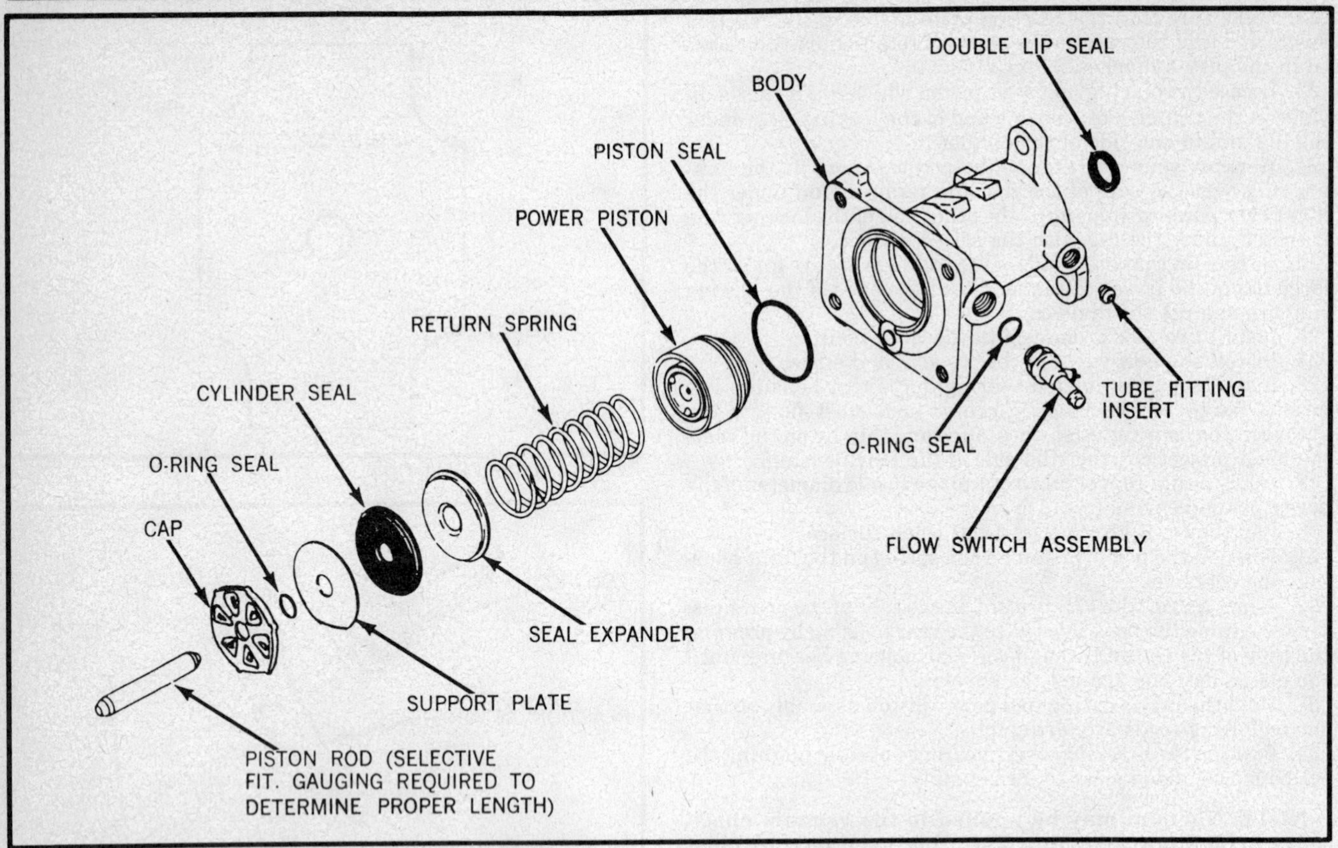

DOUBLE LIP SEAL
BODY
PISTON SEAL
POWER PISTON
RETURN SPRING
CYLINDER SEAL
O-RING SEAL
CAP
TUBE FITTING INSERT
O-RING SEAL
FLOW SWITCH ASSEMBLY
SEAL EXPANDER
SUPPORT PLATE
PISTON ROD (SELECTIVE FIT. GAUGING REQUIRED TO DETERMINE PROPER LENGTH)

Exploded view of hydraulic booster (dual power) (© GM Corp.)

CAUTION

The piston return spring is under a considerable load. Exercise caution when removing the cap as spring pressure may forcibly expel the support plate, cylinder seal, and expander, resulting in personal injury.

5. Remove the O-ring from the cap.
6. Remove the support plate, cylinder seal, and seal expander.
7. Remove the return spring and the piston.
8. Remove the double lip seal from the narrow end of the booster body.

Power piston installation (© GM Corp.)

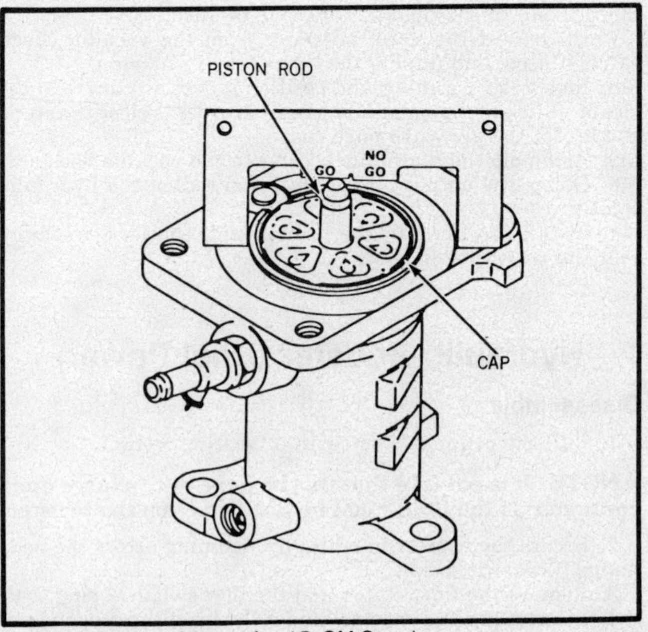

Gauging piston rod extension (© GM Corp.)

9. Remove the seal from the power piston.
10. Clean all parts, thoroughly, and check for excessive wear or damage. Replace parts as necessary.

NOTE: The manufacturer states specifically that internal parts of surfaces are NOT to be remachined. DO NOT use abrasives to remove surface defects.

Assembly

1. Secure the booster in a vise with the large bore up.
2. Lubricate the piston seal, and install it on the power piston.
3. Install the piston in the booster body bore. Press the piston to bottom in the bore. Be careful not to roll the seal.
4. Install the return spring.
5. Lubricate the inside and outside diameters of the cylinder seal.
6. Assemble the O-ring seal, support plate, cylinder seal, and seal expander against the cap in the order in which they are to be installed.
7. Position this assembly over the booster and on the return spring.
8. Push the cap down until the extensions on the cap contact the booster casting, and tap into place using a rubber or plastic mallet.

NOTE: Make sure that the cap is flush with the casting.

9. Install the flow switch with a new O-ring.

NOTE: If the original flow switch shows signs of leakage, discard it and replace it with a new switch.

10. Install the piston rod and gauge the length of the rod.

NOTE: It is advised that the gauging procedure be performed after any hard parts have been replaced, or if any components of the vacuum booster have been replaced.

Gauging the Piston Rod

1. Press down on the piston to be sure that all internal parts are bottomed in the booster.
2. Using special tool J-28675 or any suitable push rod height gauge, check the extended length of the piston rod to determine whether, or not, it falls within limits.
3. If it has been determined that the extended length of the piston push rod does not fall within limits, then select a rod of suitable length from among the six rods available, each of a differnt length. (See Piston Rod Chart).

REPLACEMENT PISTON RODS

Inches	Millimeters
4.018–4.024	102.05–102.21
4.041–4.047	102.63–102.79
4.063–4.070	103.21–103.37
4.086–4.093	103.79–103.95
4.109–4.115	104.37–104.53
4.132–4.139	104.96–105.12

4. Repeat the gauging procedure for each piston rod which is used in selecting one of proper length.

Air Hydraulic Intensifier

DESCRIPTION

The intensifier is used to convert air pressure into mechanical force on the hydraulic system which operates the disc brakes. Air pressure is applied to a diaphragm in the roto-chamber. The diaphragm, through a push rod, activates a master cylinder. The master cylinder transmits hydraulic pressure to the brake caliper pistons. The air hydraulic intensifier is used in conjunction with the sliding caliper (double piston) disc brake system used on some heavy duty models.

Disassembly

NOTE: Soak chamber in solvent for 24 hours if there are signs of rust accumulation.

1. Remove the master cylinder cap and separate the master cylinder from the chamber cover.

NOTE: Do not get cleaning solvent on master cylinder seals.

2. Remove the chamber cover cap screws and cover. Remove the spring and spring guides if so equipped.
3. Remove the nuts at the air inlet end that secure the diaphragm outer clamp to the body.
4. Grasp the push rod and pull the diaphragm and clamp assembly out of the body.
5. Unroll the diaphragm.
6. Remove the outer clamp.
7. Remove the nuts from the inside of the guide.
8. Separate the inner clamp, diaphragm, push plate and rod assembly and guide.

Assembly

1. Clean and inspect all parts.
2. Drain the master cylinder and inspect for wear. Do not repair. Install a new master cylinder if necessary.
3. Place the small diameter end of the diaphragm in the inner diaphragm clamp.
4. Install the diaphragm guide through the diaphragm and over the clamp studs and against the diaphragm bead.
5. Install the push rod plate and rod assembly against the guide and over the studs. Then install the nuts and washers.
6. Place the assembly inside of the outer clamp and roll the outer bead of the diaphragm back and over the end of the outer clamp.
7. Lubricate the inside wall of the body and the diaphragm surface with a silicone lubricant or equivalent.
8. Slide the assembled parts into the body so that the diaphragm outer bead fits snugly against the shoulder in the body and the outer clamp studs are through the holes in the body.
9. Install the nuts and lockwashers.
10. Install the spring and guides, if used.
11. Install the cover and screws.
12. Attach the master cylinder and reservoir and fill with the specified brake fluid.

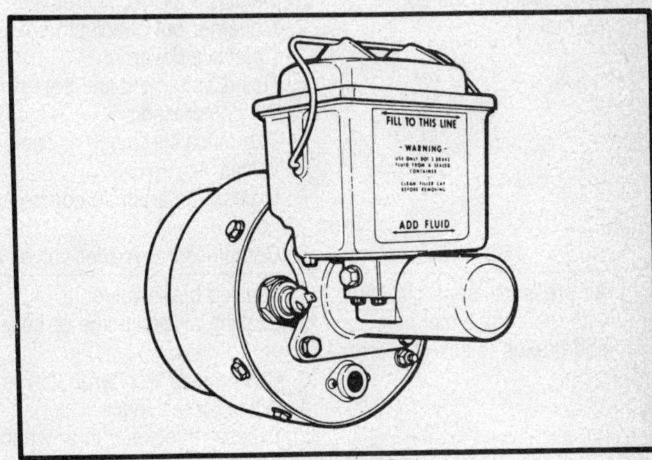

Air hydraulic intensifier (© Ford Motor Co.)

AIR BRAKES TROUBLE DIAGNOSIS

Condition	Possible Cause	Correction
Insufficient brakes	1. Brakes need adjusting. 2. Low air pressure (below 80 pounds). 3. Brake valve delivery pressure below normal.	1. Adjust brakes. 2. Inspect air compressor and inspect all fittings and lines for leaks. 3. Inspect air compressor and repair or replace.
Brakes apply too slowly	1. Brakes need adjusting or lubricating. 2. Low air pressure (below 80 pounds). 3. Brake valve delivery pressure below normal. 4. Excessive leakage with brakes applied. 5. Restricted tubing or hose.	1. Adjust brakes and lubricate brake anchors and brake support platforms. 2. Inspect compressor and air lines, repair as necessary. 3. Inspect pressure and air lines, repair as necessary. 4. Inspect all lines and fittings and repair as necessary. 5. Clean or replace tubing or hose.
Brakes do not apply	1. No air pressure in brake system. 2. Restricted or broken tubing or hose. 3. Defective brake valve.	1. Inspect air compressor and drive belt. 2. Clean out air system or replace broken hose. 3. Replace brake valve.
Brakes do not release	1. Brake shoes binding. 2. Brake valve not in fully released position. 3. Defective brake valve. 4. Restriction in air lines or hose.	1. Clean and lubricate all brake shoe anchors. 2. Align and adjust valve. 3. Replace brake valve. 4. Clean out all air lines or hoses.
Air pressure will not raise to normal	1. Defective air gauge (registering incorrectly.) 2. Excessive leakage. 3. Air reservoir drain cock open. 4. Governor out of adjustment. 5. No clearance at compressor. 6. Slipping compresor drive belt. 7. Defective or worn compressor.	1. Replace the air gauge. 2. Inspect all joints with soapy water and correct as necessary. 3. Close reservoir drain cock. 4. Inspect and adjust governor. 5. Check and adjust compressor unloading valves. 6. Adjust compressor drive belt. 7. Replace air compressor.
Air pressure raises slowly to normal	1. Excess leakage. 2. Clogged compressor air filter. 3. No clearance at compressor unloading valves. 4. Compressor discharge valves caking. 5. Slipping compressor drive belt. 6. Worn compressor. 7. Excessive carbon in compressor cylinder head or discharge line.	1. Inspect all lines and fittings, then repair as necessary. 2. Clean and air dry the compressor air filter. 3. Clean, reseat and adjust the compressor valves. 4. Clean the carbon and reseat the valves. 5. Tighten or replace the compressor drive belt. 6. Replace the air compressor. 7. Clean the carbon and reseat the valves.
Air pressure rises above normal	1. Defective air gauge (registering incorrectly. 2. Governor out of adjustment. 3. Defective governor. 4. Restriction in the line between governor and the compressor. 5. Too much clearance at compressor unloader valves. 6. Excessive carbon in compressor cylinder head. 7. Compressor unloader valves stuck closed.	1. Replace the air gauge. 2. Clean and adjust governor. 3. Replace governor. 4. Clean all air lines and recheck fittings for leaks. 5. Adjust unloader valves. 6. Clean the carbon and reseat the valves. 7. Clean and seat the valves.
Air pressure drops quickly with the engine stopped and brakes released	1. Leaking brake valve. 2. Leaking air brake line or hose. 3. Compressor discharge valves leaking. 4. Governor leaking. 5. Excessive leakage in any part of the air brake system.	1. Clean, reseat or replace the brake valve. 2. Test all air brake joints with soap suds and repair as necessary. 3. Reseat or replace the discharge valve. 4. Reseat or replace the governor 5. Test the air brake joints with soap suds and repair as necessary.

AIR BRAKES TROUBLE DIAGNOSIS

Condition	Possible Cause	Correction
Air pressure drops quickly with engine stopped and brakes fully applied	1. Brake chamber diaphragm leaking. 2. Brake valve leaking. 3. Leakage elsewhere in the system.	1. Recondition or replace the brake booster. 2. Rebuild or replace the brake valve. 3. Repair as necessary.
Compressor knock	1. Drive pulley loose. 2. Back lash in drive gears or drive coupling. 3. Bearings worn or burned out. 4. Excessive carbon in compressor cylinder head.	1. Tighten pulley nut, or install a new pulley if inner diameter of the hub is worn. 2. If drive gears or coupling show back lash replace as necessary. 3. Replace compressor. 4. Clean carbon from cylinder head.
Safety valve blows off	1. Safety valve out of adjustment. 2. Pressure in air system above normal. 3. Governor out of adjustment.	1. Adjust safety valve. Turn adjusting screw clockwise to raise blow-off pressure and counterclockwise to lower blow-off pressure. Adjust blow-off pressure to 150 pounds. 2. Refer to "Air Pressure Rises Above Normal." 3. Adjust governor to maintain pressure at 80 to 85 pounds and compression at 100 to 150 pounds.
Excessive oil or water in air brake system	1. Reservoir too full of oil or water. 2. Compressor passing excessive amount of oil. 3. Compressor air strainer is dirty.	1. Drain reservoir more frequently. 2. If condition exists, compressor is worn. Replace the compressor. 3. Wash air cleaner in mineral spirits and dry with compressed air.

AIR BRAKES

Air Supply System

The air supply system is used with the full air brake system. In the full air system, air pressure is applied directly to the shoes through a diaphragm and mechanical linkage.

If the brake system is not operating properly, the air supply system should be checked first.

OPERATING TESTS

Before performing any of the following tests, operate the engine until the air pressure builds up to 90 psi. With the air brake system charged, open the drain cocks in each reservoir. Close the drain cocks after all moisture is drained from the reservoirs. Some models have automatic moisture ejector valves and do not require manual draining.

LOW PRESSURE INDICATOR

Exhaust the brake system pressure and observe the pressure at which the warning buzzer sounds. The contacts in the indicator should close the circuit to the buzzer, when reservoir pressure is between 58 psi minimum and 65 psi maximum. If the buzzer does not start to sound within this pressure range during discharge, or if a sounding buzzer does not stop within this pressure range during the pressure buildup, the electrical connections are loose or the indicator valve is not operating properly.

RESERVOIR SAFETY VALVE

To determine if the safety valve is operative, pull the exposed end of the valve stem. If the safety valve does not blow off when the stem is pulled, the valve ball is probably stuck in its seat. In such a case, remove and disassemble the valve for cleaning.

AUTOMATIC MOISTURE EJECTOR VALVE

With the system charged, make several foot valve applications and note each time an application is made if an exhaust of air occurs at the exhaust port of drain valve. If no air comes out, push the wire stem. If no air comes out, the filter is plugged and the valve should be removed and cleaned.

NOTE: Because the automatic moisture ejector valve functions as reservoir pressure is reduced, excessive leakage in the system will cause constant exhausting of the valve.

GOVERNOR

With the engine running, build up air pressure in the system, and observe at what pressure reading on the dash gauge the pressure stops climbing. This is the point of governor cutout which should be between 118 and 125 lbs.

With the engine still running, slowly reduce the air pressure in the system by applying and releasing the brakes. Observe the pressure reading on the dash gauge at the point where the pressure starts to build up again. This is the point of governor cut-in which should be between 98 and 104 lbs.

If the governor does not cut the compressor in and out according to these specifications, adjust the governor pressure settings. Before adjusting the governor, check the accuracy of the dash gauge with a test gauge.

CHECK PRESSURE BUILD–UP

With the engine running at fast idle speed, observe the time required to raise system pressure from 50 to 90 lbs. If more than five minutes is required, perform the leak tests as outlined in the following paragraphs.

Also check for low engine idle speed, a slipping compressor drive belt, excessive carbon in the compressor cylinder head, or a worn out air compressor.

CHECK STOP LIGHT SWITCH

With all air pressure exhausted from the air brake system, start the engine and move the brake valve to the applied position. Stop lights should light before the dash gauge registers 5 psi. Release the brakes.

QUICK RELEASE VALVE AND RELAY VALVE

With the air brake system fully charged, apply the brakes. Inspect the brake action on the wheels controlled by the quick release valve or relay valve in question. The brakes should apply promptly. Release the brakes and inspect to be sure that the air pressure is exhausted rapidly from the exhaust port. Be sure the exhaust port is not restricted.

LEAK TESTS

With the engine stopped and the brakes fully applied, watch the rate of drop in air pressure as registered by the dash gauge. With the engine stopped and the reservoirs charged to the governor cutout pressure (118–125 psi), the rate of drop should not exceed 2 psi per minute. The rate of drop should also not exceed 3 psi per minute after the initial drop with brakes fully applied. If the pressure drops faster than specified, check the items outlined in the following paragraphs.

COMPRESSOR

With the engine stopped, discharge valve leakage can be detected by carefully listening at the compressor for the sound of escaping air. With air pressure applied to the unloader cavity (with governor cut-off), remove the air filter or the air pick up tube and check for air leaks by squirting oil around the unloader plunger and stem. If excessive air leaks are found, replace the unloader mechanism.

GOVERNOR

With the governor in the cutout position, test for leakage at the exhaust valve by applying soap suds to the exhaust vent in the body.

With the governor in the cut-in position, test for leakage of the inlet valve by applying soap suds to the exhaust vent in the body.

In either of the foregoing tests, leakage in excess of 1 in. soap bubble in three seconds indicates the governor should be replaced.

RESERVOIR SAFETY VALVE

Coat the end of the safety valve with soap suds. Leaks causing not more than a 3 in. soap bubble in three seconds are permissible.

AUTOMATIC MOISTURE EJECTOR VALVE

With the system charged and pressure stabilized in the system, there should be no leaks at the drain valve exhaust. A constant slight exhaust of air at the drain valve exhaust could be caused by excessive leakage in the air brake system.

BRAKE CONTROL VALVE

With the pedal fully released, coat the exhaust port with soap suds to check for leaks. With the pedal fully applied, coat the exhaust port with soap suds and check for leaks. Leaks causing not more than a three" soap bubble in three seconds are permissable.

BRAKE CHAMBERS

With the brakes fully applied, coat the clamp ring and bolt flanges holding the diaphragm in place with soap suds. No leaks are permissable.

QUICK RELEASE VALVE

With brakes applied, coat the exhaust port with soap suds to detect leakage. Leakage in excess of a 3 in. soap bubble in three seconds is not permissible.

RELAY VALVE

With the brakes released, coat the exhaust port with soap suds and observe the leakage.

With the brakes fully applied, coat the exhaust port with soap suds and observe the leakage.

Leakage in either of the foregoing tests should not exceed a 3 in. soap bubble in three seconds.

Rockwell Wedge Type

SERVICE AIR CHAMBER

Removal

NOTE: Exhaust all air pressure from the system before attempting repair work.

1. Disconnect the air inlet line.
2. Using a drift and a light hammer, loosen the spanner nut.
3. Unscrew the service chamber assembly from the wedge housing.

Installation

1. Check position of the wedge in plunger housing to make certain wedge assembly is properly seated. Be sure to replace automatic adjusting identification ring on service chamber tube. Thread spanner nut onto power unit tube.
2. Screw the service chamber into the plunger housing until it bottoms (spanner nut loose).
3. Align connection ports with brake lines, if necessary, by unscrewing service chamber not more than one full turn.
4. Connect brake lines.
5. Make the hold a full pressure brake application. Drive spanner nut with a drift and hammer until it is tight against the plunger housing. Release the brake pressure.
6. Check for leaks at all connections.

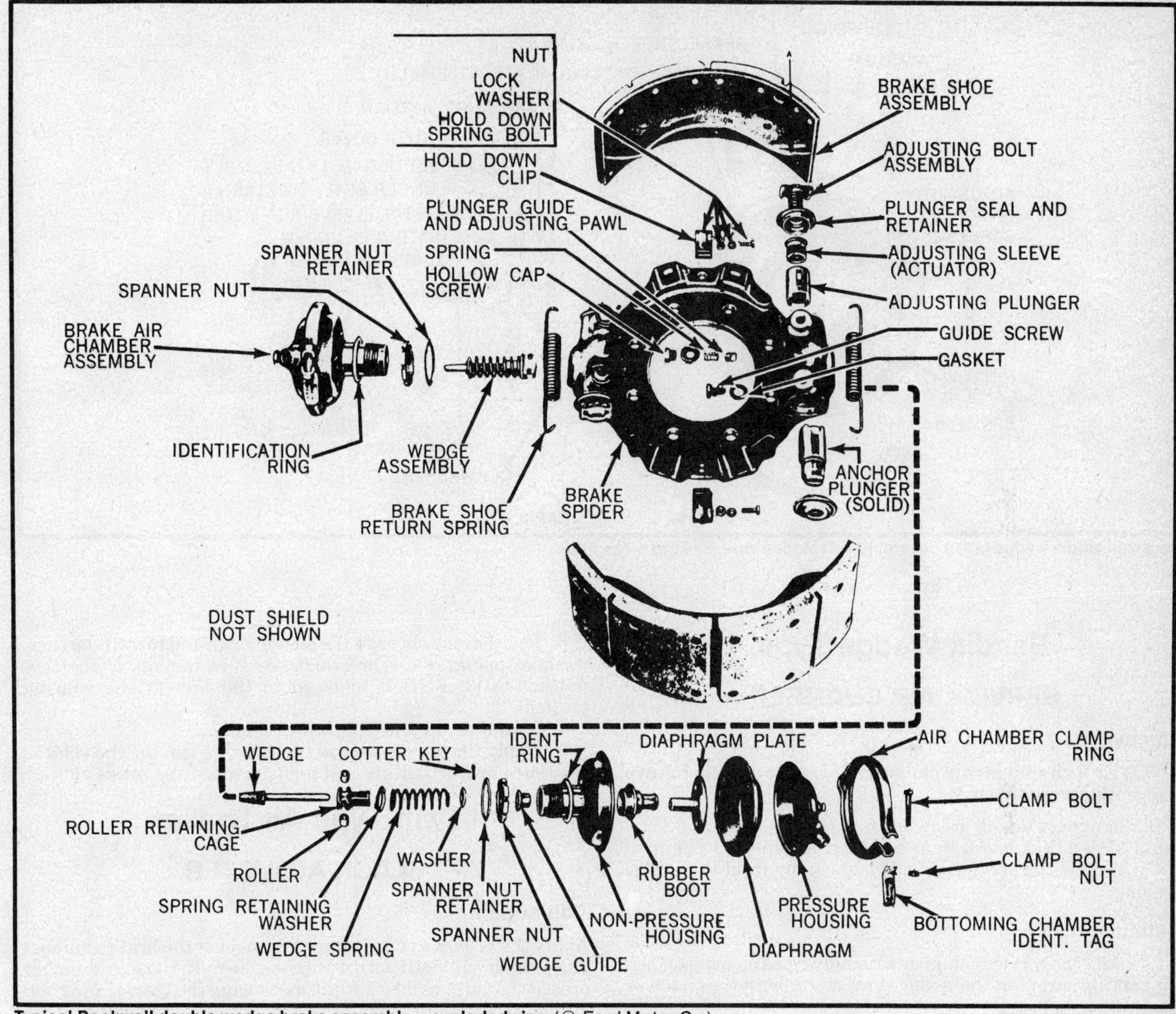

Typical Rockwell double wedge brake assembly—exploded view (© Ford Motor Co.)

BRAKE SHOE

Removal

1. Remove the wheel, hub and drum assembly.

NOTE: If equipped with Fail-Safe units, be sure that the brakes are released (actuating spring compressed by turning the release bolt approximately 18 to 21 turns clockwise.) Do not force.

2. Remove the brake shoe retracting springs.
3. Remove the shoe hold-down springs on single wedge brakes.
4. Remove the shoes.

Installation

1. Clean, inspect and lubricate the brake actuator and adjuster assemblies.
2. Apply a film of high temperature grease at all shoe contact points.
3. Mount the ends of the brake shoes in the grooves in the actuating plungers. When installing shoes on double wedge brake assemblies, make certain that the end, marked is mounted on a plunger having an adjusting or star wheel. Install the shoe hold-down springs on single wedge brakes.
4. Install new shoe retracting springs.
5. Install the wheel, hub, and drum assembly.

NOTE: If equipped with Fail-Safe Units, turn the release bolt counterclockwise until the stop is reached (approximately 18 to 21 turns) to release the manual compression of the actuating spring. Do not force the release bolt.

Adjustment

The wedge type air brakes are self adjusting.

A preliminary adjustment can be made by rotating the wheels forward and applying air to the brake chambers 25 or 30 times.

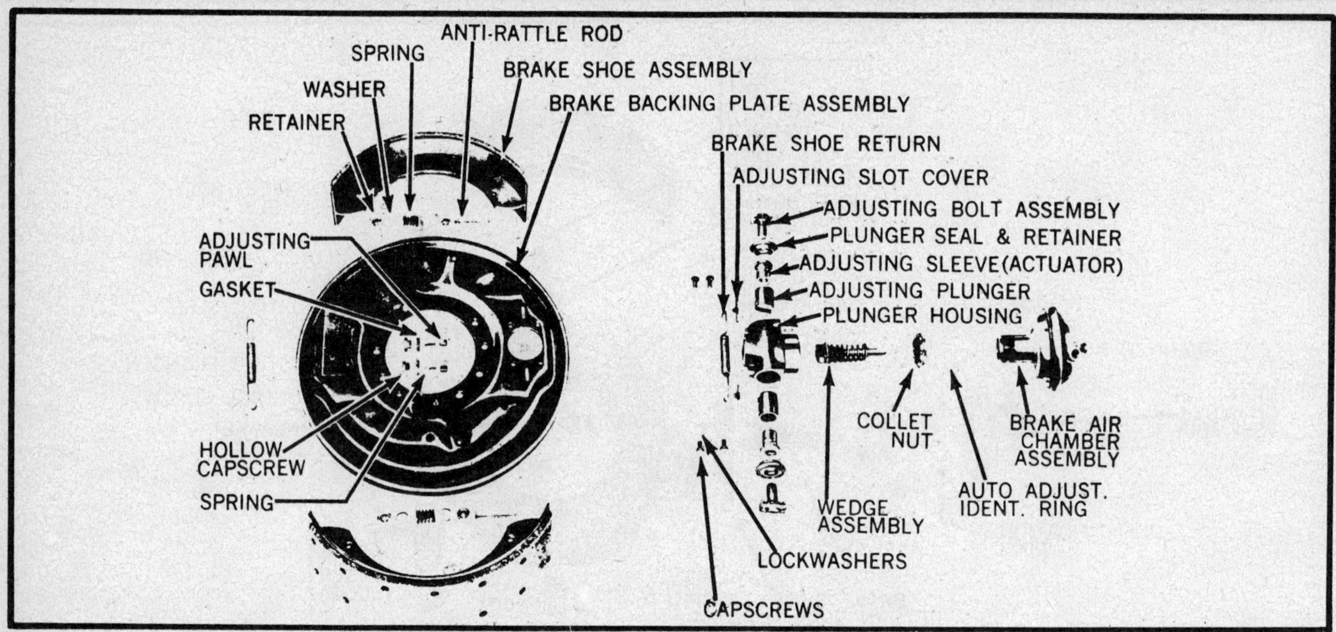

Rockwell single wedge brake assembly—exploded view (© Ford Motor Co.)

Bendix Wedge Type

SERVICE AIR CHAMBER

Removal

NOTE: Exhaust all air pressure from the system before attempting repair work.

1. Disconnect the air inlet line.
2. Using a drift and a light hammer, loosen the locknut.
3. Unscrew the service chamber assembly from the wedge housing.

Installation

1. Insert the service chamber assembly into the wedge housing making sure that the wedge shaft mates with the piston or diaphragm shaft seat.
2. Screw the service chamber assembly into the wedge housing until it bottoms, then back out less than one turn to align the unit with the air inlet line.
3. Tighten the locknut, using a drift and hammer.
4. Connect the air inlet line and restore system air pressure. Check for operation.

BRAKE SHOE

Removal

All brake shoes, front and rear, are constructed with an adjusting end and an anchor end. When installing the shoes, make certain that the end marked ADJ. END is mounted correctly in the adjusting plunger link. To remove the brake shoes, follow this procedure:

1. Unhook the two shoe-to-shoe springs.
2. Remove the brake shoes.

Installation

1. Coat the shoe slots in the anchoring plungers with Lubriplate* or equivalent lubricant..
2. Clean the shoe guide bosses and the steady rests on the torque spider and coat the rubbing surfaces with the lubricant.
3. Position the shoes in the steady rests and install the shoe-to-shoe springs. On rear brakes, be sure the end of the shoe marked ADJ. END is engaged in the link at the adjuster plunger.
4. Install drum and hub, wheel and tire.
5. Apply the brakes several times before moving the vehicle, to assure proper seating and adjustment of the brake shoes.

Cam Type Air Brakes

SLACK ADJUSTER

Adjustment

Apply the brakes and measure the travel of the brake chamber push rod. If equipped with a Maxi-brake unit, the minimum air pressure should be 90 psi while measuring the travel. The travel should be kept to the minimum possible without causing the brakes to drag. Adjustment of the yoke on the brake chamber push rod should not be changed. When new, the yoke is adjusted so that the slack adjuster brake chamber push rod angle is slightly greater than 90 degrees when the brakes are applied. Brake lining wear will not change this angle as long as the slack adjusters are kept adjusted to compensate for lining wear.

FRONT

This procedure applies only to trucks equipped with S-cam operated brakes.

A push rod travel, that reaches or exceeds the maximum indicates need of adjustment. Turn the adjusting screw clockwise until the push rod travels $^3/_4$" in going from released to fully applied position. When making the adjustment, turn the screw in quarter turns.

REAR

This procedure applies to vehicles equipped with either standard or maxi-brake S-cam type slack adjusters.

A push rod travel, that reaches or exceeds the maximum indicates need of adjustment. Depress the lock sleeve and turn the hexagon head of the wormshaft clockwise until the push rod travels one in. in going from released to fully applied posi-

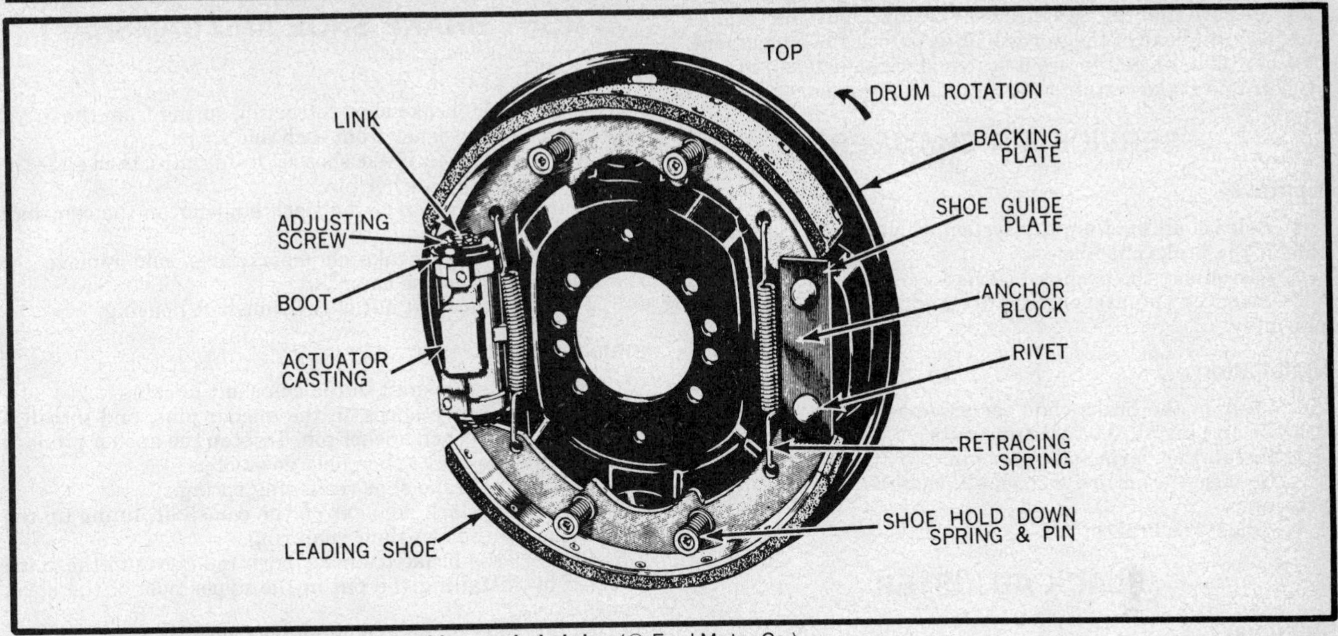

Front non servo Bendix wedge brake assembly—exploded view (© Ford Motor Co.)

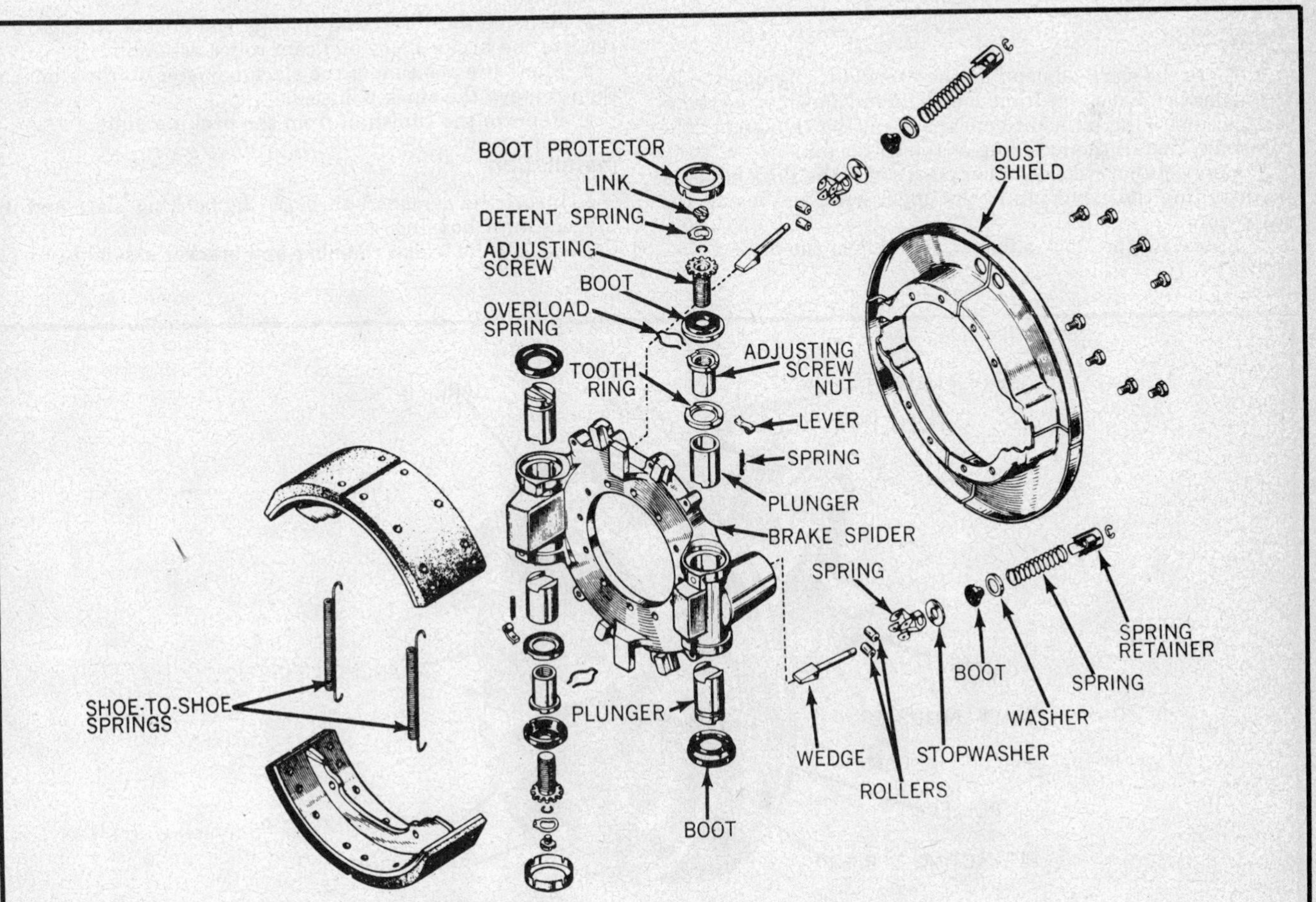

Bendix wedge brake assembly—exploded view (© Ford Motor Co.)

tion. Be sure that the lock sleeve comes back out and engages the hexagon head of the wormshaft as to lock the adjustment.

When adjusting either front or rear slack adjusters, raise the wheels and make certain that there is no brake drag.

SERVICE AIR CHAMBER

Removal

1. Release all air from the system, then disconnect the air line at the brake chamber.
2. Disconnect the push rod clevis from the slack adjuster.
3. Remove the attaching nuts and the brake chamber assembly.

Installation

1. Position the brake chamber assembly on the mounting bracket and install the attaching nuts.
2. Install the clevis and cotter pin.
3. Connect the air line to the brake chamber and build up air pressure.
4. Adjust the brakes.

SLACK ADJUSTER

Removal

1. Remove the clevis pin attaching the slack adjuster to the brake chamber push rod.
2. Remove the lock ring (front) or cotter pin (rear) attaching the slack adjuster to the camshaft.
3. Mark the position of the slack adjuster on the camshaft, then slide the slack adjuster off the shaft.

Installation

1. Place the slack adjuster on the camshaft, aligning the locating marks. Excessive front camshaft end play may be remedied by installing an additional spacer at the cam end of the camshaft. Install the lock ring or the cotter pin.
2. Connect the brake chamber push rod to the slack adjuster by installing the clevis pin in the upper hole, and install the cotter pin.
3. Lubricate the slack adjuster, and adjust the brakes.

FRONT BRAKE SHOE AND CAMSHAFT

Removal

1. Remove the brake shoe retracting spring from the brake shoes and the C-washer from each anchor pin.
2. Remove the four brake shoe retaining clips, then slide the brake shoes off the anchor pin.
3. Mark the position of the slack adjuster on the camshaft housing.
4. Disconnect the brake chamber clevis, and remove the slack adjuster from the camshaft.
5. Pull the camshaft out of the camshaft housing.

Installation

1. Install the camshaft in the camshaft housing.
2. Slide the brake shoes on the anchor pins, and install a new C-washer on each anchor pin. Tighten the anchor pin lock nuts. Install the brake shoe hold down clips.
3. Install the brake shoe retracting spring.
4. Install the slack adjuster on the camshaft, lining up the marks. Install the camshaft snap ring.
5. Connect the brake chamber push rod clevis to the slack adjuster by installing the pin in the upper hole of the slack adjuster.
6. Install the hub and drum and wheel.

EATON REAR BRAKES—S CAM TYPE

Removal

1. Remove the axle shaft, wheels, and hub and drum assembly.
2. Remove the retracting springs and anchor springs, then remove the brake shoes and cam roller assemblies.
3. Mark the position of the slack adjuster on the camshaft, then remove the slack adjuster.
4. Remove the camshaft from the backing plate.

Installation

1. Insert the camshaft through the backing plate and into the camshaft housing.
2. Install the brake chamber and bracket assembly.

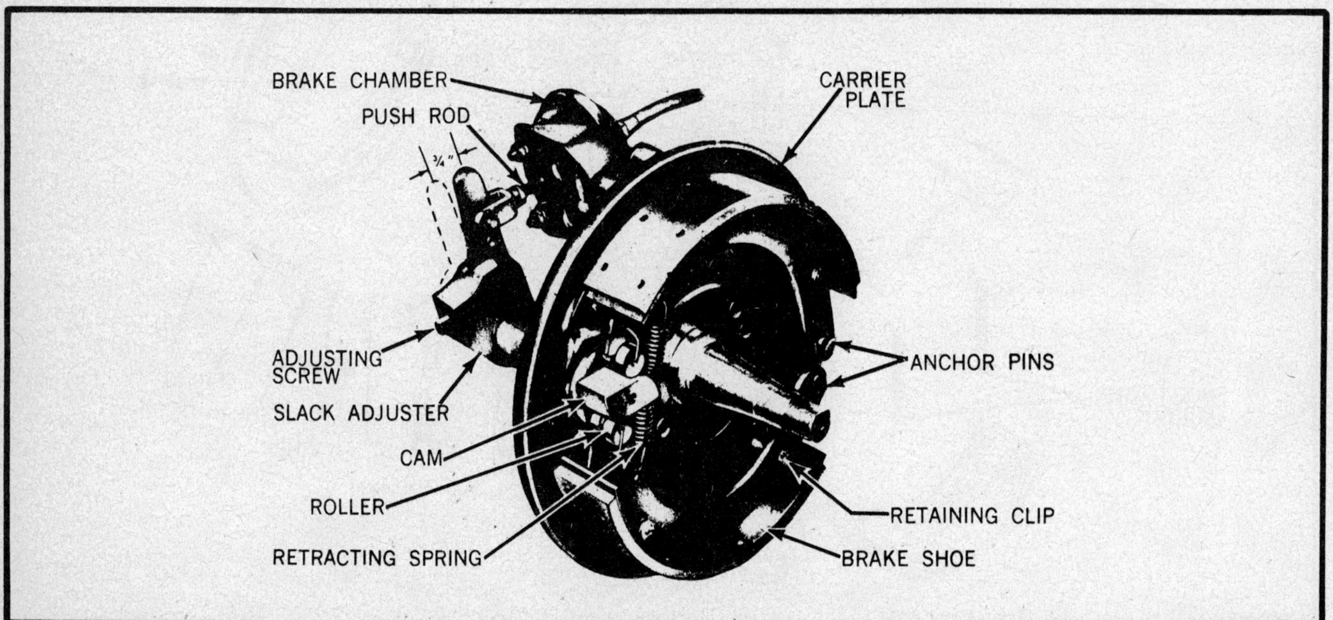

Typical S-cam type brake assembly (© Ford Motor Co.)

3. Install the slack adjuster on the camshaft, aligning the locating marks, and install the cotter pin.
4. Lubricate the camshaft, rollers, and pins with Lubriplate. Do not lubricate the cam face.
5. Position the cam rollers and pins in the brake shoes in position on the anchor pin and cam.
6. Install the retracting springs and anchor springs.
7. Install the hub, wheels, and axle shaft.
8. Adjust the brakes and slack adjuster.

Brake Chambers

The brake chamber assembly is used at each wheel and converts the energy of compressed air into mechanical force and motion required to apply the brakes. There are two basic types of brake chambers, one is a standard chamber and the other incorporates an emergency back-up system on top of a service brake chamber.

The emergency system uses a large power spring to apply the brakes when the air pressure falls below a certain level. The spring mechanically applies the brakes.

CAUTION

In the following paragraphs are the repair procedures for several types of brake chambers. Take extreme caution in disassembling the units which have spring applied emergency systems. The power spring is very powerful and one can be severely injured if some of the repair steps are not followed carefully. On some of the chambers it is necessary to use a hydraulic press to help remove the power spring. If a press is not available DO NOT attempt to disassemble the unit.

STOP MASTER BRAKE CHAMBERS

Removal

1. Drain all air from the system and disconnect the air lines from the chamber.
2. Using a punch or small chisel, drive the tabs of the lockwasher from the notches in the spanner nut which secures the brake chamber to the spider housing.
3. Using a punch and hammer or a wrench, loosen the spanner nut and remove the brake chamber from the brake housing.

Disassembly

1. Remove the clamping ring nut and bolt.
2. Scribe a mark across the pressure and non-pressure housing to assure proper assembly of the unit.
3. Remove the diaphragm, plate rod, rubber boot and plastic guide from the housing.

Cleaning and Inspection

1. Clean all the metal parts with a good cleaning solvent and wipe dry with a cloth or blow dry with air.

CAUTION

Do not use any solvent on the diaphragm.

2. Inspect the diaphragm for any sign of wear or deterioration and replace the diaphragm if necessary.
3. Examine all other parts for wear, cracks, obstructed passageways or dirt. Replace parts as necessary.

Assembly

1. In the non-pressure housing, install the boot, rod, guide and diaphragm.
2. Align the scribe marks on the pressure and non-pressure housings and secure the clamp ring in place with the nut and bolt.
3. Thread the chamber into the brake housing until it bottoms, then back the chamber out, not more than one turn, so the chamber ports are in line with the air lines. Lock the chamber in place by tightening the spanner nut and lock in place by staking the lockwasher tabs in place on the nut and housings.
4. Connect the air lines and check the unit for any air leaks.

STOP MASTER FAIL–SAFE BRAKE CHAMBERS

Removal and Disassembly

CAUTION

Before attempting to remove the brake chamber, block the wheels securely because the parking brake will not be applied.

1. With the air pressure up to normal and the brake released, loosen the release bolt lock and set to one side. Compress the power spring by turning the release bolt clockwise as far as it will go (approx. 18 turns).
2. Drain the air from the system and disconnect the air lines from the brake chambers.
3. Scribe marks across the pressure and non-pressure housings and loosen the clamping ring. Slide the ring forward and hang on the non-pressure plate tube.
4. Remove the entire cap and spring assembly, pressure housing and diaphragm. The diaphragm plate rod and boot will stay in the non-pressure housing.
5. Hold the pressure housing in a soft jawed vise.

NOTE: Do not tighten the vise too tightly for this could distort the housing.

6. Remove the washer and the O-ring seal from the pressure housing.
7. Remove the piston assembly from the cap by pulling the piston straight out from the cap.

NOTE: Sometimes when the spring is fully compressed, it will cock slightly making it necessary to loosen the release bolt a few turns so the piston may be removed easily.

8. Rivets hold together the piston, retainer plate, seal and expander. If any part in this assembly is defective the entire assembly must be replaced. The parts in this assembly are not serviced separately.
9. The cap and spring assembly is also serviced as an assembly. If any part in this unit is defective, the entire unit must be replaced.

NOTE: DO NOT attempt to disassemble the cap and spring assembly.

Cleaning and Inspection

1. Clean all metal parts with a good parts cleaner and wipe dry with a clean cloth or blow dry with air.
2. Inspect all parts for signs of wear, scratches, pitting, scores, deterioration, dirt or obstructions, and replace any parts as necessary.

NOTE: Unless the cap and spring assembly is in bad condition, it should not be replaced. If replacement is necessary, see the procedure in Step 9 of the removal section.

3. Discard the old O-ring seal and rubber washer in the housing.

Assembly

1. In the groove in the pressure housing, install a new O-ring seal.
2. Install the piston in the pressure housing.

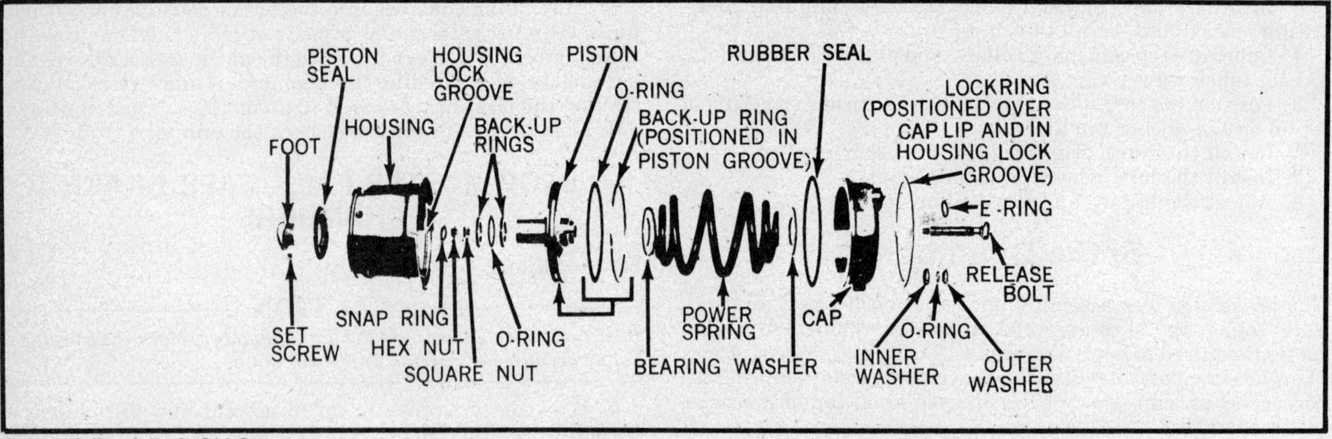

Super "fail safe" (© GM Corp.)

3. At the bottom of the internal threads in the pressure housing install a new rubber washer. Thread the cap and spring assembly into the pressure housing and tighten securely.

4. Position the piston diaphragm over the plate rod in the nonpressure housing. Install the pressure housing over the assembly, aligning the scribe marks on the housings to ensure alignment of the air lines.

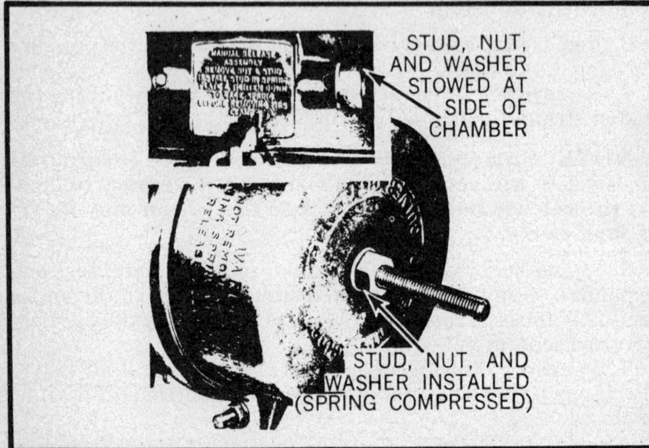

Spring compressing assembly (© GM Corp.)

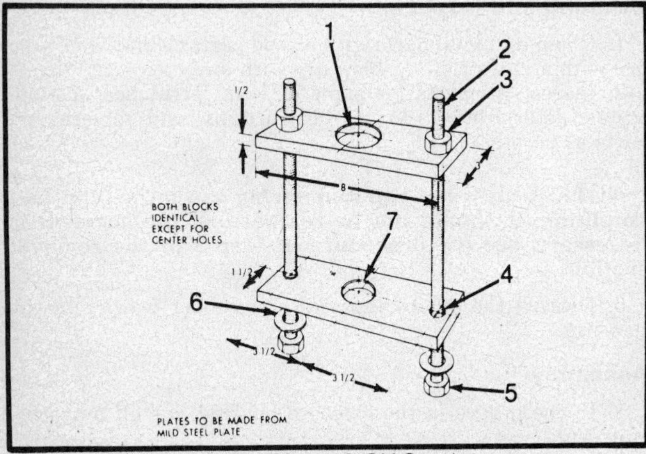

Power spring compressing fixture (© GM Corp.)

5. Install the clamping ring over the pressure and non-pressure housings and tighten with the nut and bolt.

6. Install the air lines and build up air pressure to the normal level. Push the parking brake knob in to allow air to enter the outer brake chamber.

7. Turn the release bolt counterclockwise as far as it will go to release the spring pressure.

8. Check for air leaks and road test the vehicle to check for proper operation of the unit.

STOP MASTER SUPER FAIL—SAFE BRAKE CHAMBERS

Removal and Disassembly

NOTE: Before attempting to remove the brake chamber, block the wheels firmly because the parking brake will not be applied when the chamber is removed.

1. With the air pressure up to a normal level, cage the power spring by turning the release bolt 18 to 21 turns clockwise. Do not force the bolt beyond the stop point.

2. Remove the clamp ring on the pressure and non-pressure housings and remove the pressure housings.

3. Release the foot set screw and remove the foot from the piston.

4. Remove the piston seal from the back of the housing. Also remove the sealing compound found at the joint between the cap and housing.

5. Remove the lock ring from the housing and separate the cap and the spring piston assembly from the housing.

6. Remove the back-up rings and the O-ring seal from the housing groove.

7. Remove the snap ring and hex nut from the release bolt.

8. Secure the cap and the spring and piston assembly in a spring compressing fixture.

NOTE: This fixture is necessary to hold the power spring compressed during disassembly. Without this device it is not possible to disassemble the unit safely. If one of these fixtures is not available or can not be made, DO NOT attempt to disassemble the unit any further. If a fixture is available proceed with the following steps:

9. With the unit firmly secured in the compressing fixture, turn the release bolt until the square nut falls free.

10. Release pressure on the fixture until the spring is unloaded and remove the unit from the fixture.

11. Separate the spring and piston from the cap. Remove the backup ring and O-ring seal from the piston.

12. Remove the two spring bearing washers and remove the E-ring from the release bolt.
13. Remove the flat washer from the release bolt and remove the bolt from the cap.
14. Remove the O-ring seal and second flat washer from the release bolt.

Cleaning and Inspection

1. Clean and inspect all parts for signs of wear and deterioration.
2. Use clean solvent on all metal parts but DO NOT use any on the rubber back-up rings or O-ring seals.

NOTE: The sealing compound on the cap locking ring must be replaced to prevent contamination from the outside.

Assembly

1. Install the outer flat washer and O-ring seal on the release bolt.
2. Install the release bolt in the hole in the cap, with the head of the bolt towards the outside of the cap.
3. Install the inner flat washer and E-ring on the release bolt.
4. Take the two spring bearing washers and install one on the piston and the other in the cap.
5. On the piston, install the back-up ring and the O-ring seal.
6. Install the spring and piston in the cap assembly. Install the assembly in the compressing fixture and compress the spring.
7. Install the square nut on the release bolt and tighten enough to hold the spring securely. Remove the assembly from the fixture.
8. Install the hex nut and snap ring on the release bolt.
9. Install the back-up rings and the O-ring seal in the groove in the housing.
10. Install the cap, spring and piston assembly in the housing, with the rubber seal between the cap and housing.
11. Install the lock ring in the housing and seal the joint between the cap and housing with sealing compound.
12. Install the piston in the housing and thread the foot, through the housing, into the piston.
13. Lock the foot in place with the set screw and lock the set screw in place with sealer.
14. Assemble the pressure housing to the non-pressure housing and secure the two housings together with the clamping ring.
15. Connect the air lines and build air pressure up to a normal level and uncage the release spring by turning the release bolt counterclockwise as far as it will go.
16. Check unit for air leaks and road test vehicle for proper operation.

ANCHORLOK BRAKE CHAMBERS

NOTE: Before removing the brake chamber, make sure that the wheels of the vehicle are securely blocked against movement. When the chamber is removed the parking brake will not be applied.

Removal and Disassembly

1. Release all air from the system and disconnect the air lines from the brake chamber.
2. Remove the release stud from the carrying pocket in the housing. Remove the plug in the end of the housing and insert the release stud through the hole in the housing and the spring pressure plate. Turn the stud $\frac{1}{4}$ turn to engage the tangs on the release stud with the slots in the pressure plate. Install the nut on the stud and tighten with a wrench to compress the spring. Tighten the nut until the spring is completely caged.

NOTE: Make sure the tangs on the stud stay engaged with the slot in the plate. DO NOT remove the nut and stud unless the chamber is installed and securely clamped.

3. Disconnect the push rod yoke from the slack adjuster.
4. Remove the securing bolts from the brake chamber and remove the chamber from the vehicle.
5. Remove the parking brake housing-to-adapter clamping ring.
6. Remove the parking brake housing, spring and pressure plate as an assembly.

NOTE: The spring, housing and pressure plate are serviced as an assembly and should not be taken apart.

7. Remove the parking brake diaphragm and remove the adapter-to-service chamber clamping ring.
8. Remove the adapter and service brake diaphragm.

Cleaning and Inspection

1. Clean all metal parts with clean solvent and inspect all parts for signs of wear and deterioration. Replace all parts necessary.

NOTE: Do not disassemble the spring, housing and pressure plate assembly. This is to be serviced only as a complete unit.

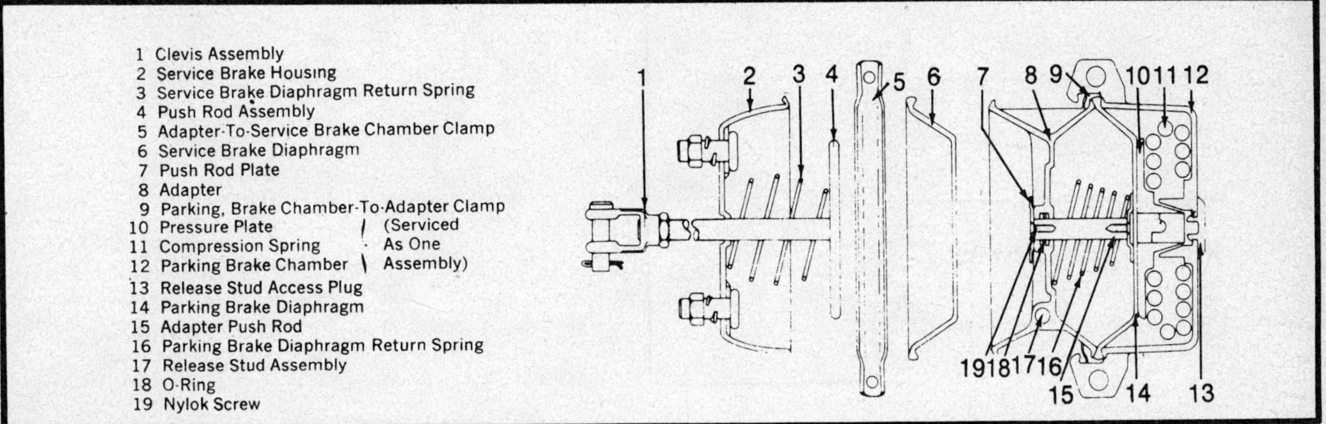

Anchorlok brake assembly—exploded view (© Ford Motor Co.)

Assembly

1. Install a new service brake diaphragm on the service brake body. Position the adapter assembly on the service brake body and install the chamber clamping ring and tighten securely.
2. Install a new parking brake diaphragm on the adapter housing. Install the parking brake housing, spring and pressure plate assembly on the adapter housing and secure in place with the clamping ring, tightening the bolt firmly.
3. Install the assembly on the mounting bracket and secure with the attaching nuts.
4. Connect the push rod yoke to the slack adjuster.
5. Connect the air lines to the chamber and build up air pressure to a normal level. Remove the brake release stud from the back of the chamber and replace it in the storage compartment on the chamber. Install the access plug in the hole in the back of the chamber.
6. Check the unit for air leaks and road test vehicle for proper operation of the unit.

MAXIBRAKE BRAKE CHAMBERS

Removal and Disassembly

1. Release all air from the system and disconnect the air lines from the brake chamber.

NOTE: Before releasing all air from the system block the wheels securely to guard against movement of the vehicle.

2. Install a Schrader valve in the spring brake chamber and charge the chamber with approximately 100 lbs. of air pressure. This holds the parking brake spring compressed.
3. Disconnect the push rod yoke from the slack adjuster. Remove the mounting nuts from the support bracket and remove the chamber from the vehicle.
4. Scribe marks across the clamp ring, pressure plate and cylinder assembly so they can be reassembled in their proper places.
5. Mount the cylinder assembly in a vise using one of the mounting studs with the nut installed to hold on to.

NOTE: Be sure to release the air pressure in the unit before disassembly.

6. Remove the clamping ring and remove the pressure plate and the service brake diaphragm from the cylinder assembly.
7. From the push rod, remove the clevis yoke. Push inward on the face plate of the push rod and remove the flanged nut from the back of the push rod shaft. Remove the push rod, spring retainer and return spring from the cylinder.
8. Using a spring compressing tool, insert the end through the neck of the piston from the back, and remove the push rod bushings.
9. Install the spring compressing tool through the cylinder assembly and loosely install the spacer and nut on the threaded end. The tool is used to compress the parking brake spring so the unit can be safely disassembled.
10. Tighten the nut on the tool shaft until the flat part of the tool is resting firmly against the spring support.
11. Remove the eight screws that hold the support plate in place. Slowly back off the nut on the compressing tool until all the pressure is off the spring. Remove the tool and the spring from the cylinder.
12. With air, blow any loose dirt from the cylinder and wipe the walls of the cylinder clean. Drive the piston, for the parking brake, from the cylinder by using a drift or socket of the

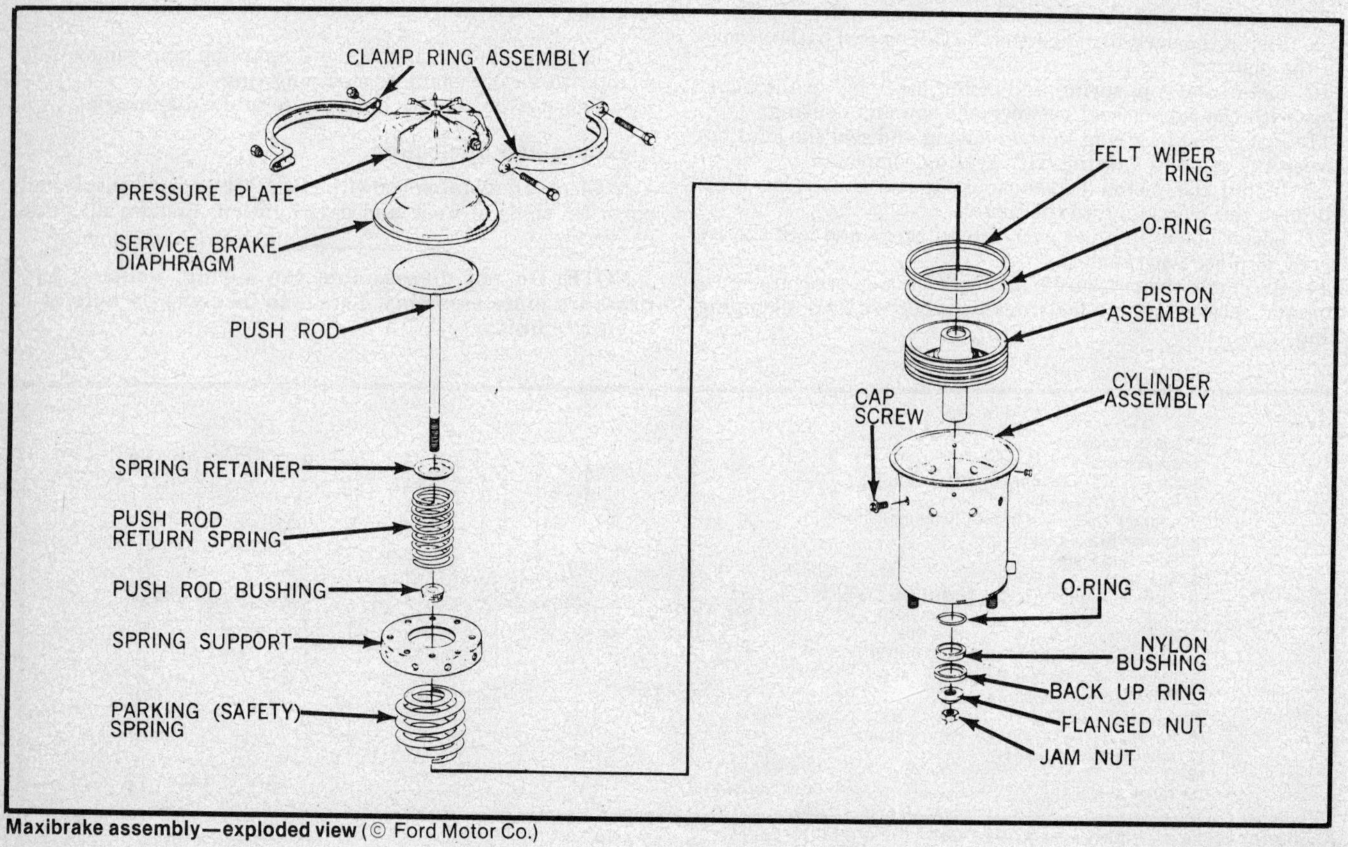

Maxibrake assembly—exploded view (© Ford Motor Co.)

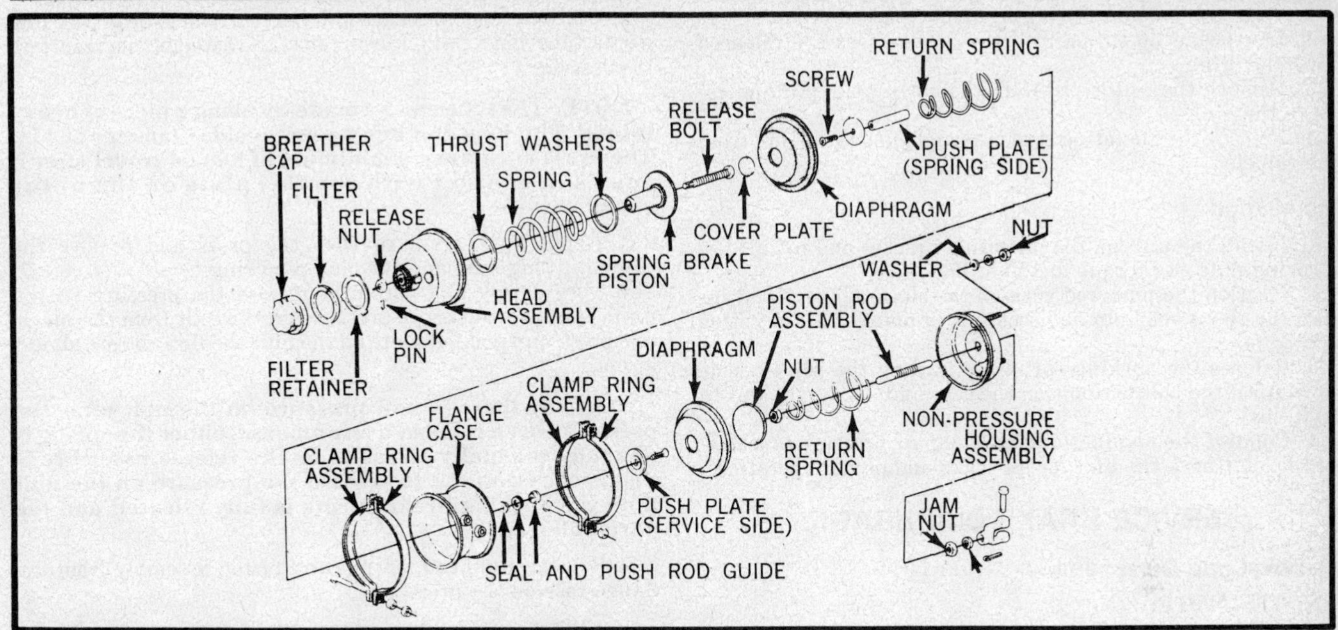

MGP stopgard brake assembly—exploded view (© Ford Motor Co.)

proper size. Remove the O-ring and wiper ring from the piston grooves.

13. Remove the O-ring, nylon bushing and back-up ring from the cylinder center boss.

Cleaning and Inspection

1. Clean all metal parts in clean solvent and inspect them for signs of wear. Check the diaphragms for signs of deterioration or cracks and replace them as necessary. Replace any seals or parts that may come with a rebuilding kit.

2. Coat the groove inside the center boss with a good quality grease and fill the piston O-ring groove half full. Lightly coat the inside of the cylinder with grease. With a rust inhibitor compound coat the piston safety spring.

Assembly

1. In the groove in the cylinder boss install the back-up ring and then install the nylon bushing.

NOTE: The bushing must be installed with the beveled side facing the inside of the cylinder.

2. In the bottom groove of the piston, install the large O-ring seal, saturate the felt wiper ring with a good oil and install it in the top groove of the piston.

3. Install the piston assembly in the cylinder holding the felt ring in place. If it is necessary, use a block of wood and a light hammer to bottom the piston in the cylinder.

4. Install the piston spring on the piston in the cylinder and place the spring support on top of the spring. Install the spring compressing tool through spring and cylinder. Tighten the nut on the tool slightly while centering the spring on the piston hub. Then tighten the nut securely until the holes in the spring support and cylinder are in alignment.

5. Install the eight screws that hold the support plate in place and tighten them securely.

6. Remove the spring compressing tool from the cylinder.

7. Into the piston install the push rod bushing and tap the bushing slightly to make sure it is seated.

8. Install the push rod spring retainer and spring on the push rod and install the assembly in the cylinder. Secure the push rod in place with the flanged nut.

9. Install the service brake diaphragm on the pressure plate, with the crown surface facing the pressure plate.

10. Install the pressure plate and diaphragm on the cylinder assembly making sure that the scribe marks are in alignment. Press on the top of the pressure plate to compress the service return spring and install the clamping ring. Torque the bolt on the clamping ring to 150–175 inch lbs.

11. With a Schrader® valve installed in the safety chamber air inlet, apply enough air pressure to compress the safety spring and piston assembly.

12. Tighten the flanged nut on the push rod shaft until there is $^1/_{16}$ in. clearance between the flange of the nut and neck of the piston tube. Lock the nut in place with the jam nut.

13. Install the clevis yoke on the push rod maintaining a clearance of 2 $^{15}/_{16}$ in. between the centerline of the clevis pin holes and the mounting flanges of the cylinder assembly, on type 24 or 30 units. On type 36 units the clearance should be 3 $^1/_4$ in.

14. Pressurize the unit with air and check for air leaks. After checking, leave the chamber charged with air and install the brake chamber assembly on the mounting brackets on the vehicle. Install the attaching nuts and torque them to 110–150 ft. lbs.

15. Connect the push rod yoke to the slack adjuster and release the air from the unit through the Schrader valve and remove the valve.

16. Connect the air lines to the chamber and build air pressure up to a normal level.

17. Check the unit for leaks again and road test the vehicle to check for proper operation.

MGM STOPGARD BRAKE CHAMBER

Removal

COMPLETE UNIT

1. Release all air from the system and remove the air lines from the brake chamber.

NOTE: Block the wheels securely against movement, when the chamber is removed there will be no parking brake.

2. Cage the parking spring by removing the breather cap and unscrewing 30 turns until the brake shoes are released from the drum.
3. Remove the cotter pin from the clevis yoke pin and remove the pin.
4. Remove the mounting stud nuts and remove the unit from the vehicle.

Installation

1. Install the unit on the mounting bracket and install the securing nuts and torque to 150 ft. lbs.
2. Position the push rod yoke on the slack adjuster and install the clevis yoke pin and secure it in place with the cotter pin.
3. Release the parking spring by turning the release bolt down until the bolt bottoms on the case and torque the nut to 50 ft. lbs.
4. Connect the air lines and build up air pressure to a normal level. Check the unit for air leaks and proper operation.

SERVICE BRAKE DIAPHRAGM

Removal and Disassembly

NOTE: NOTE:

Before working on vehicle block the wheels against movement. The parking brake will not be applied when the brake chamber is removed.

1. Cage the parking spring as described in Step number 2 of the complete unit removal procedures.
2. Release all the air from the system and remove the air lines from the brake chamber.
3. Supporting the chamber with one hand, loosen the retaining bolt on the clamping ring for the service brake chamber and remove the ring. Lift the spring brake chamber away from the service brake chamber and set aside.
4. Remove the service brake diaphragm and inspect it for cracks, signs of wear or signs of deterioration. Inspect the return spring, service piston and the inside of the exposed chambers for signs of wear and replace any parts necessary.

Assembly

1. Install the diaphragm over the service piston and spring and check the alignment of the spring to the chamber and piston while installing.
2. Install the spring brake chamber on the diaphragm in the same position it was removed in and install the clamping ring. Tighten the nuts on the clamp to 25–35 ft. lbs. Check around the ring when assembling to make sure of proper alignment and clamp seating. Tap around the clamp ring with a soft hammer to help seat the clamp and retorque the nuts.
3. Release the parking spring following the procedure described in Step number 3 of the Complete Unit Installation section.
4. Connect the air lines to the chamber and build up air pressure to a normal level. Operate the brake several times to check the operation of the unit.
5. With pressure in the chambers, check the unit for leaks with soapy water. Release the air in the service brake section only and retorque the clamping ring to 25–35 ft. lbs.

PARKING BRAKE DIAPHRAGM

Removal and Disassembly

NOTE: Before working on the vehicle block the wheels against any movement. The parking brake will not be applied when the brake chamber is removed.

1. To remove the chamber, follow Steps 1 through 3 in the Service Brake Diaphragm Removal section.
2. Place the spring brake chamber in a hydraulic press using a split tube and a flat plate on top of the assembly for a surface to press on.

NOTE: The tube can be made by using a piece of heavy tubing, 5 in. long and having an outside diameter of 4 in. The press must have a minimum of 8 in. of travel after it comes in contact with the flat plate on top of the chamber.

3. Apply light pressure with the press and remove the clamping ring nuts and the clamping ring.
4. Very slowly and carefully release the pressure on the unit. There should be no pressure on the unit from the inside and press ram and flat plate on the unit should separate almost at once.

NOTE: If there is still pressure on the unit after the press has been relaxed a fair amount, either the spring is not fully manually released or the release assembly is damaged. Continue to release the pressure on the unit until the parking brake spring is fully released and the parts fall free.

5. Remove the head, spring and piston assembly from the flange case on the press.

CAUTION

Be very careful with the head assembly because the parking spring is caged by the release bolt between the head and the piston.

6. Remove the parking brake diaphragm and inspect the inside of the flange case for wear or damage. If any parts are damaged, see the Parking Brake Air Chamber Disassembly procedures to repair.

NOTE: Make sure that the screw holding the push rod is tightened securely.

Assembly

1. Install the diaphragm on the flange case and place the parking brake spring and piston assembly on the diaphragm.
2. Check all the parts for proper alignment and place the unit in the press with the split tube and flat plate in place.
3. With the press, apply light pressure to the assembly and install the clamping ring and tighten the bolts to 25–35 ft. lbs. Tap around the outside edge of the clamping ring with a soft hammer and retorque the clamp to 25–35 ft. lbs.
4. Leave the assembly in the press and attach an air line with 100–125 psi of pressure to the spring brake inlet and check the unit for leaks. If any leaks are discovered disassemble the unit and reposition the parts and reassemble. After the unit passes the leak test retorque and clamp nuts to 25–35 ft. lbs. again.
5. Install the unit on the vehicle following Steps 2 through 5 in the Service Brake Diaphragm Assembly section.

SPRING BRAKE AIR CHAMBER

Removal and Disassembly

1. Remove the spring brake section from the vehicle as described in Steps 1 through 3 in the Service Brake Diaphragm Removal section.

NOTE: If the power spring is broken, it can usually be confirmed by unscrewing the retaining bolt and shaking the unit. If there is a noticeable rattle from the head end of the unit this usually means that the spring is broken. Further indication of a broken spring is light resistance when the release bolt is screwed into the unit.

CAUTION

Even if the spring is broken it is necessary to manually cage the spring before disassembling the unit.

2. From the release bolt remove the lock pin with a small punch.
3. Remove the head, spring and piston assembly from the flange case as described in Steps 1 through 5 in the Parking Brake Diaphragm Removal section.
4. Install the head, spring and piston assembly in a hydraulic press using two split tubes.

NOTE: A tube 4 in. in diameter and 3 in. long must be placed under the unit supporting the piston and another 4 in. in diameter and 6 in. long must be placed on top of the assembly between the press ram and the head. A flat metal plate must be placed on top of the top tube to provide a flat surface for the press to press on. Also the press must be able to travel away from the assembly a minimum of 8 in. or the spring will not release completely.

CAUTION

Without the press and tube assembly the unit can not be disassembled safely. If a press is not available, DO NOT attempt to disassemble the unit.

5. Make sure that the assembly is straight in the press and apply light pressure on the unit with the press.
6. Pop the center plug out of the bottom of the piston with a screwdriver, and using a long, broad bladed screwdriver, unscrew the release bolt until it falls free. If the bolt binds, apply a little more pressure to the assembly with the press.
7. When the release bolt is removed, very slowly release the pressure on the head until the press ram separates from the head.
8. Remove the head assembly and remove the spring, thrust washers, and piston from the press. Clean all the parts and inspect for any signs of damage and wear and replace the parts as necessary.

Assembly

1. Before assembling the head, spring and piston, grease the inside of the head assembly, the outside of the piston shank, the inside of the piston shank and the threads of the release bolt.
2. Position the split tube on the press and install the following parts on top of it: piston, thrust washer (late models use a spring shield cup instead of the washer), spring, thrust washer and head. On top of the head install the second split tube with the flat plate on top of it.
3. Check the parts to make sure they are in alignment straight up and down and slowly apply pressure to the assembly while checking constantly for any misalignment that might occur.

CAUTION

Stand to the side of the press when compressing the spring. If misalignment occurs, release the pressure on the unit and start to compress the spring again.

4. When the piston spring is fully compressed and the piston bottoms against the head, install the release bolt through the bottom of the piston and screw the bolt in until approximately 3 in. of the bolt extend through the top of the head.
5. Relax pressure on the press slowly until the press ram separates from the split tube and flat plate.
6. Remove the head assembly from the press and install the release nut on the release bolt and lock it in place with the lock pin.
7. Install the piston plug until it bottoms against the head, by tapping it with a light hammer.
8. Follow Steps 1 through 5 in the Parking Brake Diaphragm Assembly section to install the unit back on the vehicle.

MGM Shortstop Brake Chamber

Removal

COMPLETE UNIT

1. Drain all air from the system and disconnect the air lines from the unit.

NOTE: Block the wheels of the vehicle securely. When the brake chamber is removed the parking brake will not be applied.

2. Remove the breather cap and filter and unscrew the release bolt as far as it will go.
3. On the service brake chamber tube, loosen the lock nut with a drift punch and hammer.
4. From the wedge housing unscrew the entire shortstop and service brake chamber assembly and remove from the vehicle.

Installation

1. Make sure that the release bolt is unscrewed completely and screw the entire unit into the wedge housing until it bottoms against the housing.
2. Back the unit out less than one turn to align the hose connections.
3. Tighten the lock nut securely on the brake chamber tube and connect the air lines to the unit.
4. Charge the unit with air and tighten the release bolt into the unit. Install the cap and filter on the unit.
6. Check the unit for leaks and road test the vehicle for proper operation of the unit.

SHORTSTOP UNIT ONLY

Removal

1. Drain the air from the system and disconnect the air lines from the unit.

NOTE: Block the wheels of the vehicle securely. When the brake chamber is removed the parking brake will not be applied.

2. Remove the breather cap and filter and unscrew the release bolt as far as it will go.
3. Remove the clamping ring on the brake chamber and shortstop unit and remove shortstop unit from the vehicle.

Installation

1. Making sure that the release bolt is unscrewed completely, install the unit on the brake chamber and install the clamping ring. Tighten the bolts securely.
2. Connect the air lines and charge the chamber with air. Screw the release bolt into the unit tightly. Install the cap and filter assembly and check the unit for leaks and road test the vehicle for proper operation of the unit.

Disassembly

1. Remove the shortstop unit only from the vehicle and using a sharp, thin bladed knife, remove the soft sealer from the head of the Phillips head screw in the case assembly.
2. Remove the Phillips head screw and the plate under it.
3. From the top of the head remove the release bolt and washer and insert a screw driver through the release bolt hole. Hold the screwdriver against the top of the push rod and charge the spring air chamber with air (minimum 70 psi).

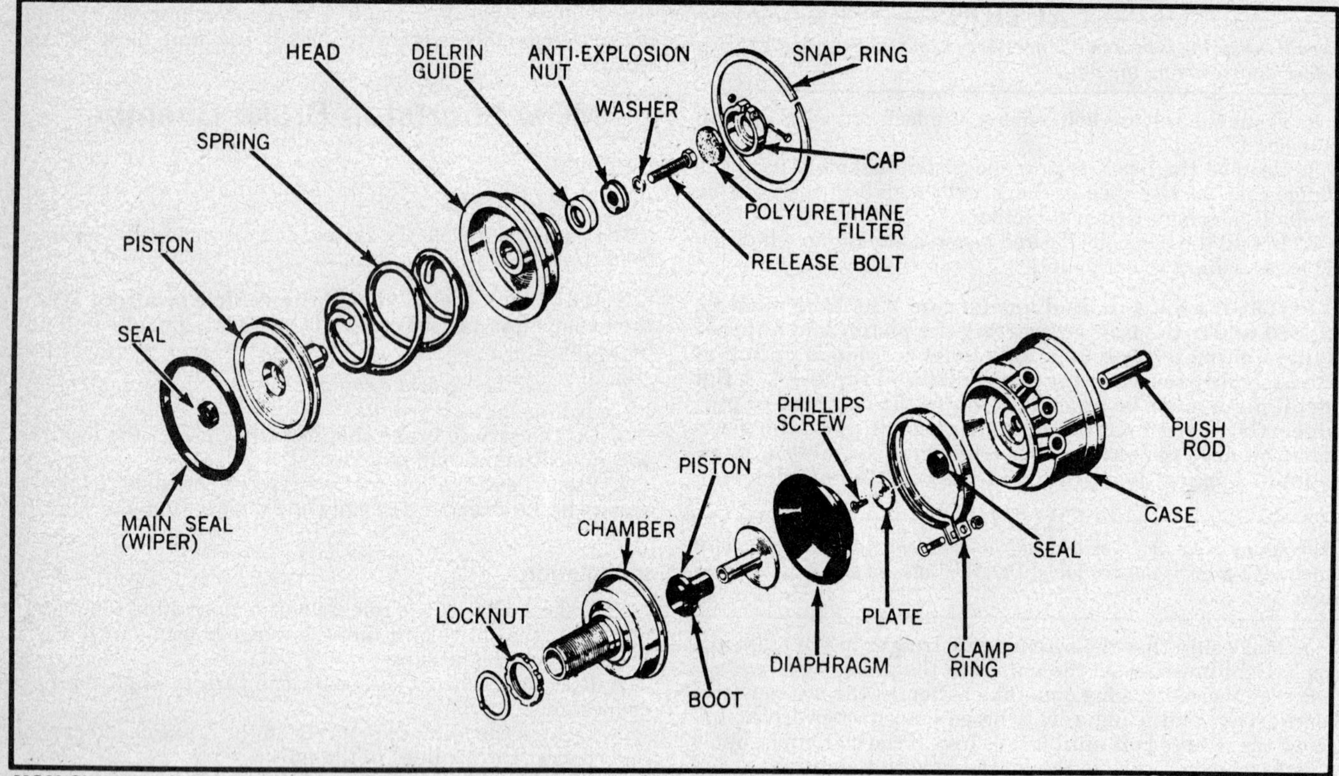

MGM Shortstop brake (© Ford Motor Co.)

4. Remove the screwdriver and using a drift punch and hammer remove the anti-explosion nut and Delrin washer from the top of the head.
5. Release the air in the chamber and remove the sealer in the groove for the snap ring in the head.
6. Install the assembly in a press with the case side down. The press must have a minimum of 6 in. of travel away from the unit or the head cannot be disassembled safely.
7. Apply a little pressure to the head with the press.

NOTE: Do not attempt to press the head into the case assembly too far or the case assembly will be damaged.

8. Remove the snap-ring from the groove in the head with a pry bar. Relax the pressure of the press very slowly. The spring will push the head out of the case.

NOTE: If the assembly has a broken spring use a cage or screen for protection when disassembling.

9. When the pressure is off of the head, remove the assembly from the press. Remove the head and spring from the case. Hold the piston by the hub and remove it from the case by pulling straight out.
10. Clean all parts and inspect them for signs of wear and damage. Replace all parts necessary.

Assembly

1. Lubricate the inside of the case assembly with a low temperature moly-type grease. Also lubricate the seal groove of the piston, the collar seal and the push rod seal.
2. Install the seal on the piston if removed and install the piston in the case by tilting the piston to one side and inserting it in the case and slowly bringing it to a straight position in the case bore.
3. Install the push rod in the seal in the piston. Install the spring on the piston and install the head on top of the spring.
4. Place the assembly in the press and using care start to compress the spring into the case.

NOTE: Make sure that the spring and head assembly goes into the case straight, if it does not, stop, release the press and start to compress the assembly again.

5. Continue to press the head into the case until the head bottoms against the shoulder in the case. Install the snap ring in the groove in the case and tap the ends of the snap ring to make sure that it is seated properly.
6. Release the pressure on the press and remove the assembly from the press.
7. Insert a screwdriver through the release bolt hole and press down firmly on the push rod. Charge the cylinder with air (minimum 70 psi).
8. Remove the screwdriver and install the Delrin guide washer and the anti-explosion washer and tighten to 30 ft. lbs.
9. Install the release bolt and washer in the assembly. Install the plate and Phillips head screw in the push rod and tighten.
10. Release pressure on the unit and apply sealer to the groove over the snap-ring.
11. Install the unit back on the vehicle and check for leaks and road test for proper operation.

AIR DISC BRAKES

Design configurations of air disc brakes differ, but basic operation is similar. Clamping force is generated by the powershaft and powershaft nut. When the brakes are applied, the air chamber pushes the slack adjuster (either manual or automatic adjuster) and in turn the powershaft is rotated within the nut. When this action takes place, the powershaft moves the piston outward pressing the inboard lining against the disc rotor. As the braking action continues, the caliper is drawn inward and brings the outboard lining into contact with the disc rotor. The inward movement of the caliper allows equal clamping force on both sides of the disc rotor. The clamping force is directly related to the powershaft input torque.

Most calipers have a "window" built-in to allow visual inspection of the disc pad lining. Others, have lining wear indicators to advise when lining replacement is necessary.

PAD REPLACEMENT

NOTE: Because of the various designs and installation recommendations, it is suggested that the manufacturer's technical information be refered to for service procedures.

ROCKWELL DURA-MASTER

1. Jack up and support the axle to be serviced.
2. Remove the tire and wheel assembly. If the vehicle employs a parking/emergency air system with spring type chambers, be sure to mechanically cage each chamber to the off position.
3. Fully back off the slack adjuster by first removing the pressure relief capscrew, spring and pawl assembly from the side of the slack adjuster. Use the proper size wrench and turn the manual adjusting nut end of the worm clockwise until the brake piston assembly is fully backed away from the disc roter. Do not force the manual adjusting nut past normal stop.

CAUTION

Do not turn the manual adjusting nut clockwise without removing the pressure relief capscrew. Damage will occur to the pawl spring and adjusting pawl.

4. Remove the pad anti-rattle clip from the caliper. Squeeze the sides of the clip together and pivot the clip up and out of the caliper.
5. Loosen the nut at the top caliper slide pin retainer in the torque plate upper arm.
6. Depress the caliper slide pin retainer while carefully pulling out the slide pin from the inboard boss. The retainer must be depressed enough to disengage the slide pin groove. Leave the slide pin seated partially in the torque plate arm to support the caliper.
7. Support the caliper at the air chamber and pull the slide pin from the torque plate arm and caliper outboard boss. Disconnect the air lines if necessary, do not allow the caliper to be supported with the air lines.
8. Remove the pads from the caliper assembly. Inspect and replace, if necessary, slide pin, torque plate bushings and caliper bushings.
9. Push the piston fully into the caliper.
10. Install the inboard pad first, than the outboard pad.
11. Coat the slide pin with anti-seize compound. Hold the inboard and outboard pads apart. Raise the caliper and position over the disc rotor so that the pads are on opposite sides of the rotor.
12. Continue to raise the caliper until the bores in the caliper and torque plate arm are aligned. Hold the caliper in position and install the slide pin.
13. Depress the slide pin retainer and install.
14. Remove and lubricate the lower slide pin, make sure the caliper does not swing. Install lower slide pin.
15. Uncage chamber, lubricate components. Adjust brakes.

BENDIX

The need for relining can be determined by checking the caliper position in the anchor plate. Shoe suspension bolts are released and pads are removed and installed through the "window" in the caliper.

KELSEY HAYES

1. Raise and support axle. Remove the tire and wheel assembly. Cage chambers.
2. Remove the caliper. Replace the inboard pad.
3. Install the outboard pad in the caliper. Install the caliper and reverse the remainder of the removal process.

EATON

Pad replacement is achieved by removing the twin retaining nuts and bolts. Caliper removal is not required.

B.F. GOODRICH

1. Remove the tire and wheel assembly after safely raising and supporting the axle.
2. Cage chambers. Remove the four caliper support bracket nuts and lift the caliper clear of the rotor.
3. Remove the old pads by sliding the support bracket from the caliper. Retract the piston.
4. Mount the new pads in the support bracket and reinstall on the caliper. Install caliper.

SLACK ADJUSTERS

The slack adjuster is the final link between the pneumatic (air) system and the foundation brake in an S cam type system. The arm of the slack adjuster is fastened to the push rod of the air chamber with a yoke, and the spline end is installed on the brake cam shaft.

The slack adjuster is a lever converting the lineal force of the chamber push rod into a torque which turns the brake cam shaft and applies the brake.

Two types of slack adjusters are in use: the manual adjuster, which requires periodic manual adjustment; and the automatic slack adjuster which will automatically adjust during normal service brake applications. Most slack adjusters utilize the worm and gear principle and fundamentally differ only in their torque specification.

Manual Slack Adjusters

Manual slack adjusters contain four basic components: the body, worm, gear and adjusting screw. The adjusting mechanism consists of an external screw or nut. Turning the screw or nut rotates the worm gear which turns the slack adjuster gear.

The adjustment causes the slack adjuster gear, brake cam shaft and brake cam to spread the brake shoes compensating for lining wear. A spring loaded locking sleeve or a lock ball indent is utilized to prevent the adjusting screw from backing off on light to medium rated slack adjusters. Heavier rated adjusters use a lock ball or plunger and worm shaft indent adjustment lock. The lock ball or plunger must engage the indent on the worm shaft after the adjustment is made. An audible metallic click can be heard when the indent is engaged.

Automatic Slack Adjusters

Design configurations of automatic slack adjusters differ, but basic operation is similar. When the brakes are applied, the chamber push rod causes the slack adjuster to rotate, and the adjusting linkage which is connected to the yoke actuates the adjusting crank. The adjusting crank rotates a drive sleeve through the clutch spring until the drive sleeve engages spline teeth on the worm shaft. If, by this time, the brake shoes have not contacted the brake drum, the worm shaft will be rotated by the drive sleeve. The worm shaft then turns the worm, rotating the gear and cam shaft, adjusting the brakes.

After the brake shoes contact the brake drum, the torque required to turn the worm and gear exceeds the capacity of the clutch spring and the spring slips. This action prevents over adjustment of the brakes.

During brake release, the adjusting crank rotates in the opposite direction and the drive clutch spring slips on the drive sleeve. An anti-reverse spring holds the worm shaft and prevents any backward rotation of the worm shaft during brake release, thus preventing brake unadjustment.

Removal & Installation

MANUAL ADJUSTERS

CAUTION

Before attempting to remove slack adjusters, proper precautions should be taken so that the automatic application of the chambers does not occur while removing or installing slack adjusters, causing possible injury. Depending on the type of chamber, it may be necessary to drain all air reservoirs or mechanically cage spring loaded chambers. Always block the wheels or mechanically secure the vehicle.

1. Remove the chamber push rod pin.
2. Remove the retaining mechanism from the end of the brake cam shaft.
3. Remove the slack adjuster from the spline end of the brake cam shaft.
4. Provide clearance so the slack adjuster can be rotated to the maximum stroke of the chamber.
5. Install the slack adjuster on the cam shaft so the adjustment screw and grease fitting (if equipped) are accessible for servicing.
6. Check to be sure that the angle formed by the slack adjuster arm and chamber push rod is greater than 90°.
7. Align the slack adjuster arm with the center of the push rod yoke. Use spacers, if necessary to obtain 0.030–0.060 in. end play.
8. Install the slack adjuster retaining mechanism on the end of the brake cam shaft.
9. Install the yoke pin and secure with a new cotter pin.

Automatic Adjusters

Because of the various designs and installation recommendations, it is suggested by the truck manufacturers that the slack adjuster manufacturer's technical information be referred to for service procedures.

ADJUSTMENT PROCEDURE

Manual Adjuster

NOTE: All adjustments should be made with cold drums and brakes fully released.

1. Jack and support wheel off of the ground. Make sure that the wheel will turn freely.
2. **Slack adjuster with positive lock mechanism:** Thoroughly clean the adjusting screw nut and locking sleeve area. Position a wrench or socket over the adjusting screw and disengage the locking sleeve by depressing. Make the necessary adjustment by turning the adjusting screw with the locking sleeve depressed until the brakes begin to drag. Adjustment should be backed off so that the wheel will turn freely. The actuator stroke should be as short as possible without the brakes dragging. When the adjustment is completed, the adjusting screw should be positioned so that the locking sleeve engages the adjusting screw nut, thereby locking the adjusting screw in place. Do not attempt to turn the adjusting screw without fully depressing the lock sleeve.
3. **Slack adjuster with ball indent lock mechanism:** Back-off (counter-clockwise) the worm shaft lock screw (if equipped). Make necessary adjustment by turning the adjusting screw. Make certain that the lock ball or plunger engages the indent on the plunger shaft. After proper adjustment, apply the brakes and hold application. The angle formed by the slack adjuster arm and the actuator push rod should be slightly greater than 90° in both the applied and released position. All slack adjusters on the vehicle should be at the same angle.

MAXIMUM CHAMBER STROKE BEFORE ADJUSTMENT

Chamber Type	Stroke
GENERAL MOTORS CORPORATION ①	
9	1½″ (38.1 mm)
12	1½″ (38.1 mm)
16	1¾″ (44.5 mm)
20	1¾″ (44.5 mm)
24	1¾″ (44.5 mm)
30	2.0″ (50.8 mm)
36	2½″ (63.5 mm)
FORD MOTOR COMPANY ②	
12, 16	1⅜″ (38 mm)
24	1¾ (44.5 mm)
30	2.0″ (47.6 mm)

① —@ 80 psi
② —@ 100 psi

Automatic Adjuster

After installation, an automatic adjuster should be manually adjusted as required. Consult the manufacturer's product literature for proper adjustment procedures which is not supplied by the truck manufacturers.

PREVENTIVE MAINTENANCE

Manual Adjuster

1. Every month, 8,000 miles or 300 operating hours; check the chamber push rod travel. The stroke should be as short as possible without the brakes dragging or chamber rod binding. Adjust if necessary.
2. Every 6 months, 50,000 miles or 1800 operating hours, lubricate with chassis lube.

SERVICEABILITY TESTING

1. Apply the brakes and check to be sure the slack adjusters rotate freely and without binding.
2. Release the brakes and check to be sure the slack adjusters return to the fully released position without binding.
3. With the brakes released, check to be sure that the angle formed by the slack adjuster arm and chamber push rod is still slightly greater than 90°. All slack adjusters should be set at this same angle.

Automatic Adjuster

While the various automatic slack adjuster designs vary in the manner in which they are installed and operate, all are designed to automatically maintain a pre-determined brake chamber stroke, thereby eliminating the need for periodic manual adjustment. Some designs adjust upon application, while others adjust upon release. For specific information on operation, lubrication and preventive maintenance refer to the manufacturer's service information.

REPLACEMENT TIPS

When replacing a slack adjuster, be sure the replacement is the same size as original equipment. Check the following key dimensions:

1. Arm length (center of spline to center of arm hole to be used).
2. Type and width of spline.
3. Yoke pin diameter.
4. If offset, determine offset dimension.
5. After installation, make sure adequate clearance in both fully applied and fully released positions is present.

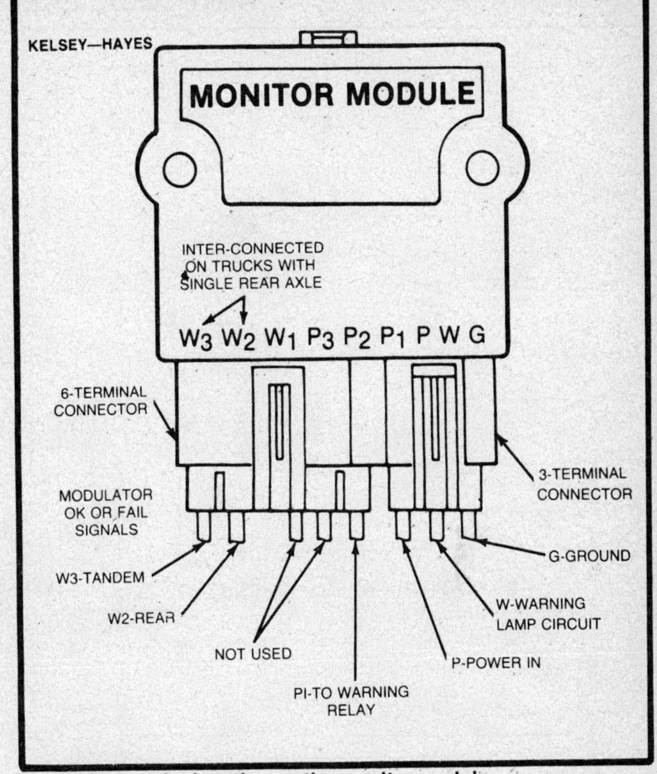

Monitor test point location on the monitor module (© Ford Motor Co.)

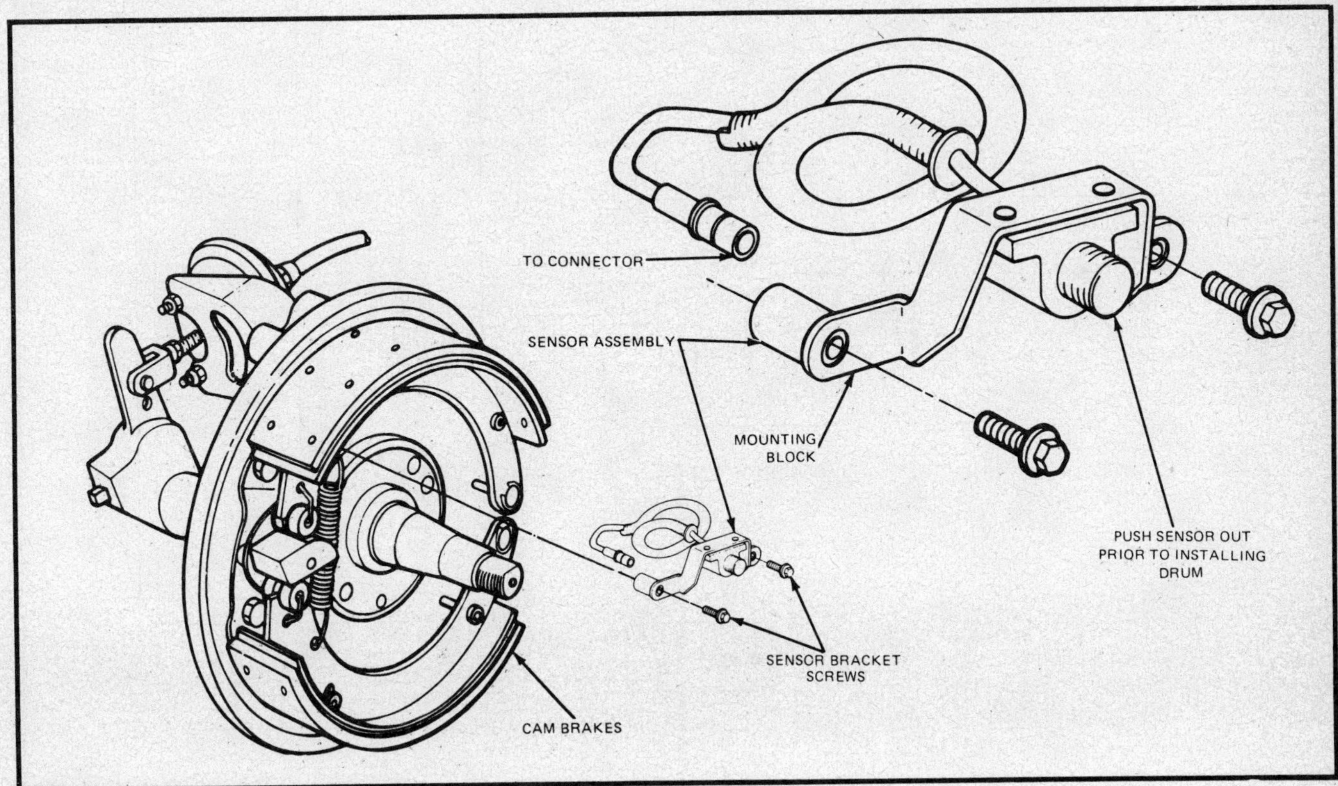

Sensor assembly and location on brake backing plate (© Ford Motor Co.)

ANTI-LOCK ELECTRICAL SCHEMATIC

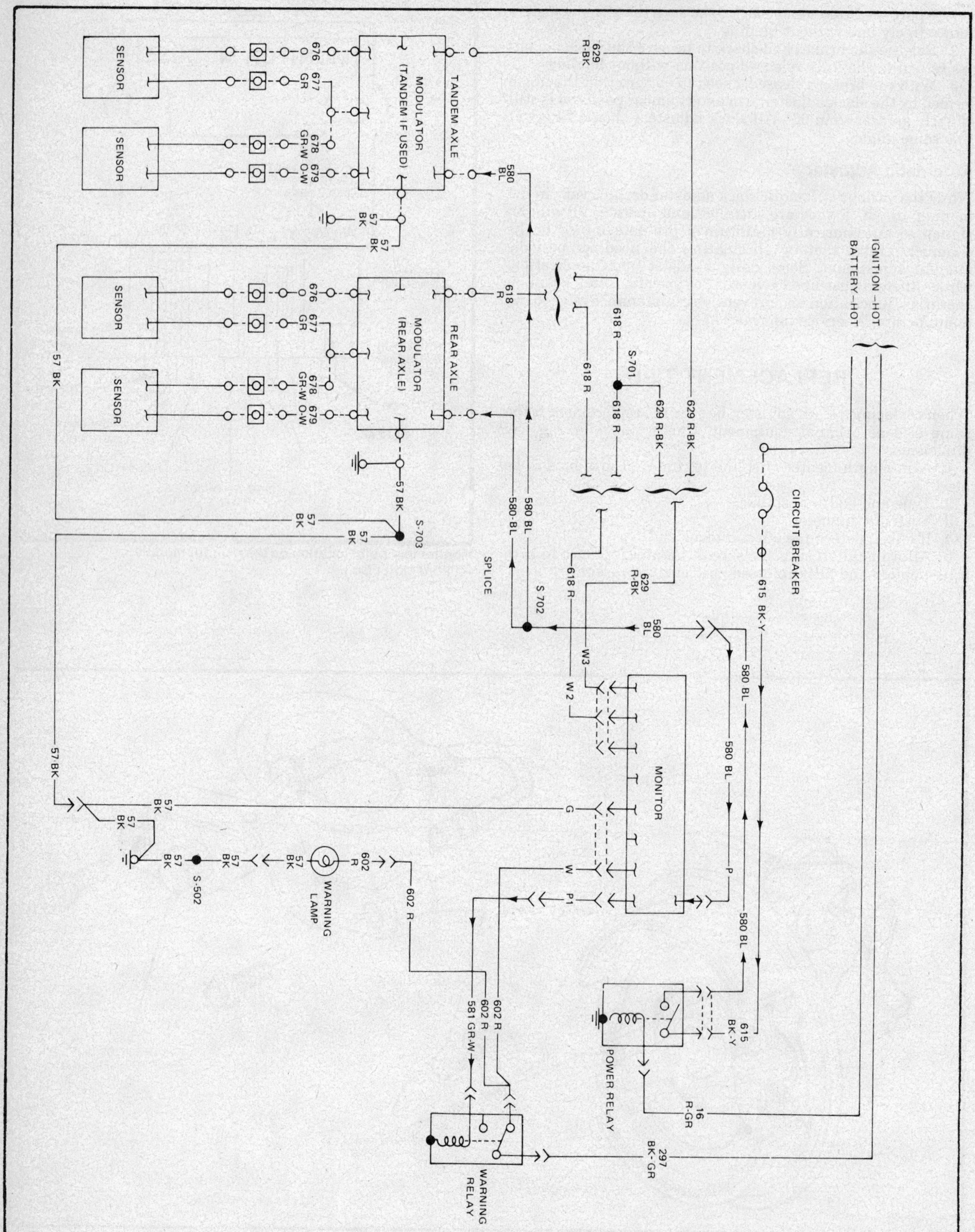

ANTI-LOCK SYSTEM DIAGNOSIS

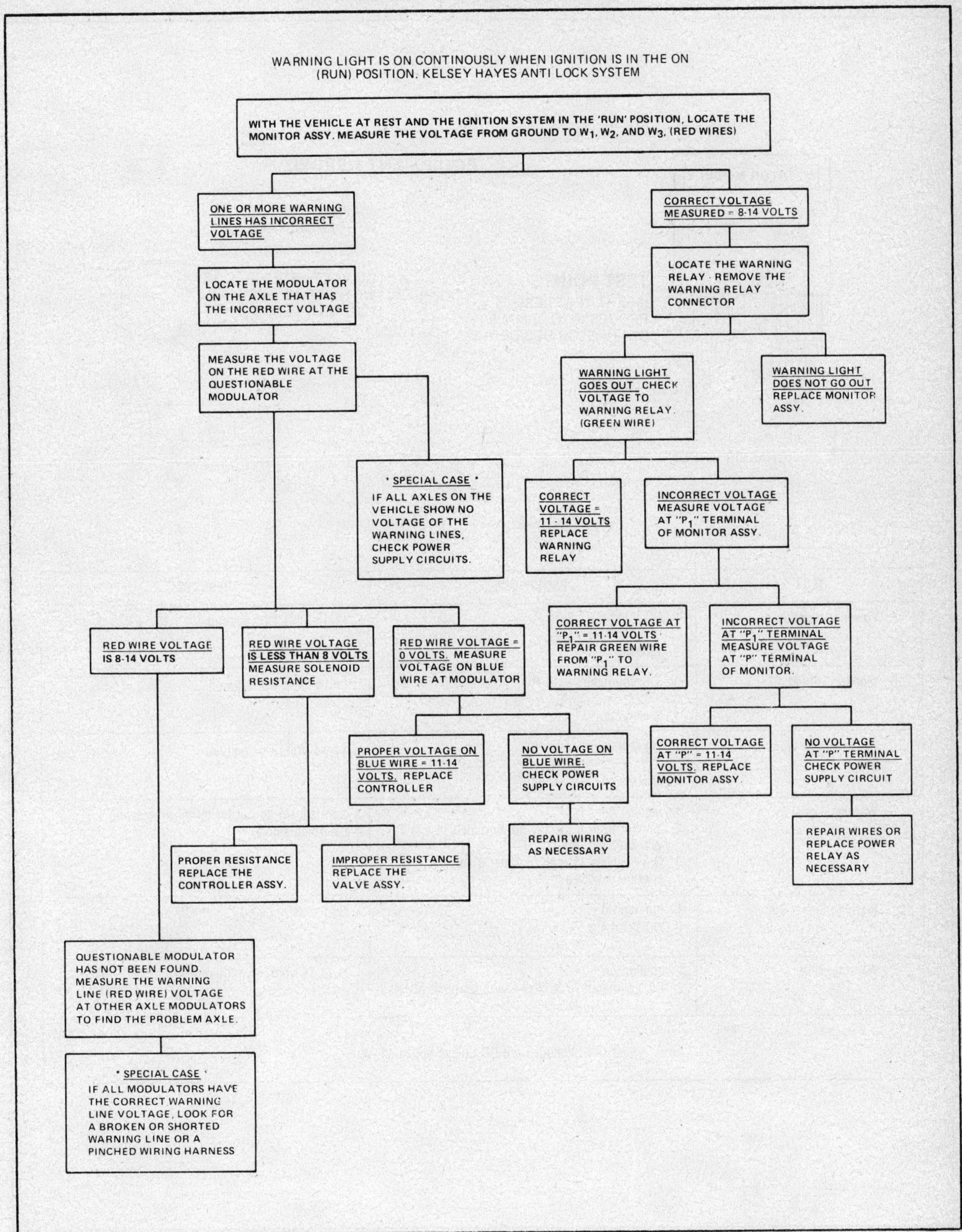
WARNING LIGHT IS ON CONTINOUSLY WHEN IGNITION IS IN THE ON (RUN) POSITION. KELSEY HAYES ANTI LOCK SYSTEM
WITH THE VEHICLE AT REST AND THE IGNITION SYSTEM IN THE 'RUN' POSITION, LOCATE THE MONITOR ASSY. MEASURE THE VOLTAGE FROM GROUND TO W_1, W_2, AND W_3. (RED WIRES)
ONE OR MORE WARNING LINES HAS INCORRECT VOLTAGE
CORRECT VOLTAGE MEASURED = 8-14 VOLTS
LOCATE THE MODULATOR ON THE AXLE THAT HAS THE INCORRECT VOLTAGE
LOCATE THE WARNING RELAY · REMOVE THE WARNING RELAY CONNECTOR
MEASURE THE VOLTAGE ON THE RED WIRE AT THE QUESTIONABLE MODULATOR
WARNING LIGHT GOES OUT CHECK VOLTAGE TO WARNING RELAY. (GREEN WIRE)
WARNING LIGHT DOES NOT GO OUT REPLACE MONITOR ASSY.
* SPECIAL CASE * IF ALL AXLES ON THE VEHICLE SHOW NO VOLTAGE OF THE WARNING LINES, CHECK POWER SUPPLY CIRCUITS.
CORRECT VOLTAGE = 11 - 14 VOLTS REPLACE WARNING RELAY
INCORRECT VOLTAGE MEASURE VOLTAGE AT "P_1" TERMINAL OF MONITOR ASSY.
RED WIRE VOLTAGE IS 8-14 VOLTS
RED WIRE VOLTAGE IS LESS THAN 8 VOLTS MEASURE SOLENOID RESISTANCE
RED WIRE VOLTAGE = 0 VOLTS. MEASURE VOLTAGE ON BLUE WIRE AT MODULATOR
CORRECT VOLTAGE AT "P_1" = 11-14 VOLTS REPAIR GREEN WIRE FROM "P_1" TO WARNING RELAY.
INCORRECT VOLTAGE AT "P_1" TERMINAL MEASURE VOLTAGE AT "P" TERMINAL OF MONITOR.
PROPER VOLTAGE ON BLUE WIRE = 11-14 VOLTS. REPLACE CONTROLLER
NO VOLTAGE ON BLUE WIRE. CHECK POWER SUPPLY CIRCUITS
CORRECT VOLTAGE AT "P" = 11-14 VOLTS. REPLACE MONITOR ASSY.
NO VOLTAGE AT "P" TERMINAL CHECK POWER SUPPLY CIRCUIT
REPAIR WIRING AS NECESSARY
REPAIR WIRES OR REPLACE POWER RELAY AS NECESSARY
PROPER RESISTANCE REPLACE THE CONTROLLER ASSY.
IMPROPER RESISTANCE REPLACE THE VALVE ASSY.
QUESTIONABLE MODULATOR HAS NOT BEEN FOUND. MEASURE THE WARNING LINE (RED WIRE) VOLTAGE AT OTHER AXLE MODULATORS TO FIND THE PROBLEM AXLE.
* SPECIAL CASE * IF ALL MODULATORS HAVE THE CORRECT WARNING LINE VOLTAGE, LOOK FOR A BROKEN OR SHORTED WARNING LINE OR A PINCHED WIRING HARNESS

KELSEY-HAYES MONITOR DIAGNOSIS TESTS

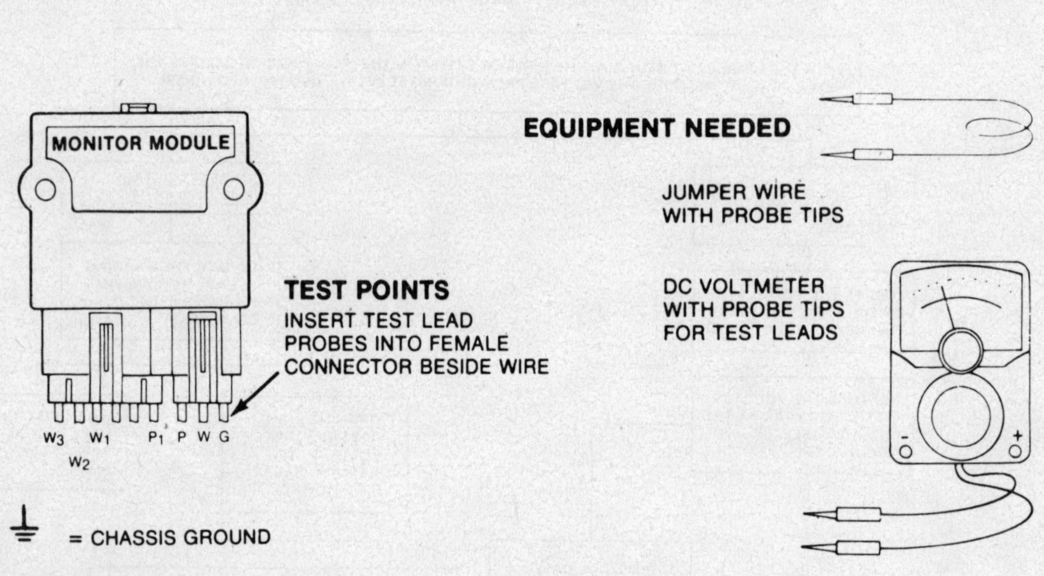

TEST	PROCEDURE	RESULTS
A. Power to Monitor	1. DC Voltmeter: + to P – to ⏚ 2. Ignition on	11-14 volts DC required
B. Monitor Ground	1. DC Voltmeter: + to P – to G 2. Ignition on	11-14 volts DC required
C. Power Out to Warning Relay	1. DC Voltmeter: + to P_1 – to ⏚ 2. Ignition on	11-14 Volts DC required
D. Warning Signal In	1. Ingition on 2. Jumper from P (or any hot terminal) to W1, W2, W3 in turn. 3. Drive vehicle 15 mph or faster if vehicle speed is involved	Light should go out for terminal receiving a warning signal
D1. Warning Signal Out	1. Ignition on 2. DC Voltmeter: + to W – to ⏚	Zero volts required
E. Warning Relay	1. Ignition on 2. DC Voltmeter: + to green wire terminal of relay – to ⏚	11 to 14 volts DC required

NOTE: Voltages are DC unless specified AC.

Engine Rebuilding

INDEX

GENERAL INFORMATION

This section describes in detail, the procedures involved in rebuilding a typical gasoline engine. A rebuilt engine can be expected to give many miles of dependable service only if the proper reconditioning procedures are performed and clearances are kept within the manufacturer's recommended specifications.

The following systems of the gasoline engine should be checked to determine to what degree the rebuilding should be accomplished.

Engine Oil Pressure

The engine oil pressure developed should be compared to the manufacturer's recommended pressure, which is necessary to provide lubricating oil to the engine oil circuits. If the pressure is below specifications, the cause must be located and repaired.

The following wear points should be considered during this determination.

Oil Pump – Check Gear clearances (a new oil pump is a good investment).

Main Bearings and Journals – Check clearances, taper and roundness.

Connecting Rod Bearings and Journals – Check clearances, taper and roundness.

Camshaft and Bearings – Check clearances, taper and roundness.

Rocker Arms, Rocker Arm Shafts – Check arm and shaft wear, ball and seat wear.

Tappets – Check clearances between tappet and bore and for excessive leakdown of hydraulic tappets.

Leakage of oil pressure along external or internal oil galleries or gaskets.

Dilution of the oil by gasoline leakage through failures of the carburetor or mechanical fuel pump.

External damage to the oil pan, causing blockage or movement of the oil pick-up tube, resulting in loss of oil pick-up to the pump.

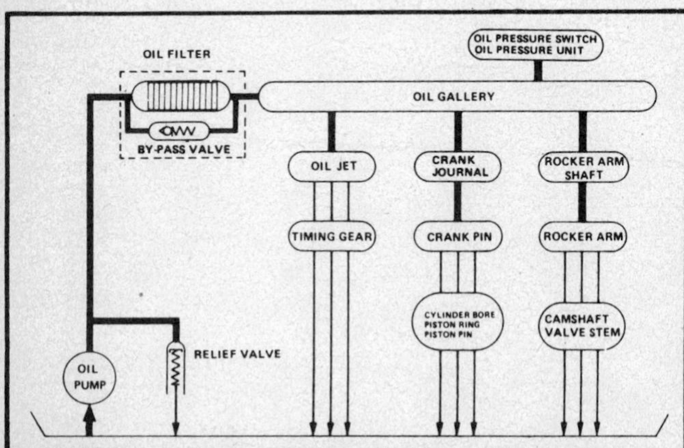

Engine oil flow diagram—typical

Compression

Compression in an engine is determined by the correct fit and sealing efficiency of the piston and rings against the cylinder walls, the quality of the seal between the valve and its seat and the seal between the cylinder head, head gasket and block. Here are some important check points.

Valve, seat and face – Machine face and seat to original specifications.

Valve guides – The reconditioned seat and face won't hold up long if the valve stem clearance isn't within specifications.

Valve seals – Oil reaching the valve seat will become a solid when it combines with the heat in the combustion chamber. This solid (carbon) will build up and eventually keep the valve from seating.

Cylinder walls – Check for taper, out-of-round and hone to proper cross hatch pattern.

Pistons – Check all dimensions. A poorly fitted piston will shorten the life of the new rings.

COMPRESSION PRESSURE COMPARISON CHART

Minimum pressure is 75% of maximum pressure

Maximum PSI	Minimum PSI	Maximum PSI	Minimum PSI	Maximum PSI	Minimum PSI
134	101	174	131	214	160
136	102	176	132	216	162
138	104	178	133	218	163
140	105	180	135	220	165
142	107	182	136	222	166
144	108	184	138	224	168
146	110	186	140	226	169
148	111	188	141	228	171
150	113	190	142	230	172
152	114	192	144	232	174
154	115	194	145	234	175
156	117	196	147	236	177
158	118	198	148	238	178
160	120	200	150	240	180
162	121	202	151	242	181
164	123	204	153	244	183
166	124	206	154	246	184
168	126	208	156	248	186
170	127	210	157	250	187
172	129	212	158		

NOTE: To Determine if the engine compression is satisfactory, most engine manufacturers require that a complete compression test be done, with the lowest cylinder pressure reading not being less than 75% of the highest reading. Look for uniformity of compression between cylinders, rather than specific compression pressures of an engine.

Cooling System

Maintaining engine temperatures within the specified range is critical to the life of a rebuilt engine. Until new parts mate properly with each other, excessive heat can cause permanent damage or substantially reduce the service life of the reconditioned engine. If the engine is operated at temperatures below normal, the oil may not properly lubricate all of the parts. Some parts that should be checked during the rebuilding process are:

Coolant passages – Should be free of rust and corrosion deposits.

Core plugs – All plugs should be replaced during the rebuilding process.

Hoses – Should be free of cracks, hard spots and oil softened spots.

Thermostat – Check for opening and closing at the specified temperature.

Radiator – Check for leaks and rust or corrosion deposits.

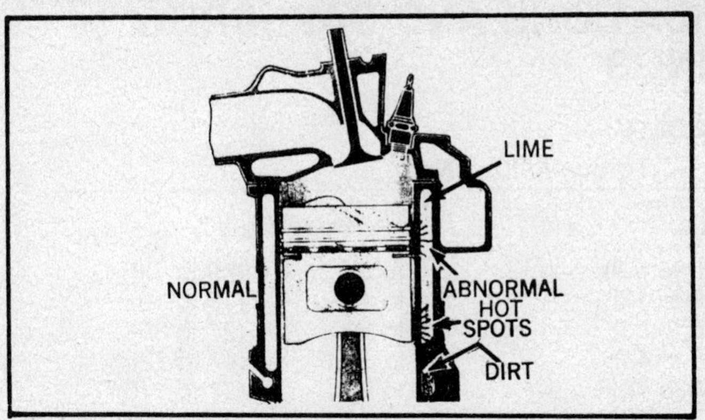

Illustration of cooling system passages being restricted, causing internal engine problems

Pressure cap – Should hold specified pressure, also check the gasket and vent valve operation.

Engine Noises

Engine noises are not only annoying, but indicate conditions inside the engine that can limit the service life of the engine or shut it down completely. Generally, noises are caused by too much clearance between parts or loss of oil supply. Engine noises can be caused by any of the following parts.

Main bearings
Connecting rod bearings
Piston and/or rings

STANDARD TORQUE SPECIFICATIONS AND CAPSCREW MARKINGS

Newton-Meter has been designated as the world standard for measuring torque and will gradually replace the foot-pound and kilogram-meter torque measuring standard. Torquing tools are still being manufactured with foot-pounds and kilogram-meter scales, along with the new Newton-Meter standard. To assist the repairman, foot-pounds, kilogram-meter and Newton-Meter are listed in the following charts and should be followed as applicable.

U.S. BOLTS

SAE Grade Number	1 or 2			5			6 or 7			8		
Capscrew Head Markings Manufacturer's marks may vary. Three-line markings on heads below indicate SAE Grade 5.												
Usage	Used Frequently			Used Frequently			Used at Times			Used at Times		
Quality of Material	Indeterminate			Minimum Commercial			Medium Commercial			Best Commercial		
Capacity Body Size	**Torque**			**Torque**			**Torque**			**Torque**		
(inches) – (thread)	Ft-Lb	kgm	Nm	Ft-Lb	kgm	Nm	Ft-Lb	kgm	Nm	Ft-Lb	kgm	Nm
1/4–20	5	0.6915	6.7791	8	1.1064	10.8465	10	1.3630	13.5582	12	1.6596	16.2698
–28	6	0.8298	8.1349	10	1.3830	13.5582				14	1.9362	18.9815
5/16–18	11	1.5213	14.9140	17	2.3511	23.0489	19	2.6277	25.7605	24	3.3192	32.5396
–24	13	1.7979	17.6256	19	2.6277	25.7605				27	3.7341	36.6071
3/8–16	18	2.4894	24.4047	31	4.2873	42.0304	34	4.7022	46.0978	44	6.0852	59.6560
–24	20	2.7660	27.1164	35	4.8405	47.4536				49	6.7767	66.4351
7/16–14	28	3.8132	37.9629	49	6.7767	66.4351	55	7.6065	74.5700	70	9.6810	94.9073
–20	30	4.1490	40.6745	55	7.6065	74.5700				78	10.7874	105.7538
1/2–13	39	5.3937	52.8769	75	10.3725	101.6863	85	11.7555	115.2445	105	14.5215	142.3609
–20	41	5.6703	55.5885	85	11.7555	115.2445				120	16.5860	162.6960
9/16–12	51	7.0533	69.1467	110	15.2130	149.1380	120	16.5960	162.6960	155	21.4365	210.1490
–18	55	7.6065	74.5700	120	16.5960	162.6960				170	23.5110	230.4860
5/8–11	83	11.4789	112.5329	150	20.7450	203.3700	167	23.0961	226.4186	210	29.0430	284.7180
–18	95	13.1385	128.8027	170	23.5110	230.4860				240	33.1920	325.3920
3/4–10	105	14.5215	142.3609	270	37.3410	366.0660	280	38.7240	379.6240	375	51.8625	508.4250
–16	115	15.9045	155.9170	295	40.7985	399.9610				420	58.0860	568.4360
7/8–9	160	22.1280	216.9280	395	54.6285	535.5410	440	60.8520	596.5520	605	83.6715	820.2590
–14	175	24.2025	237.2650	435	60.1605	589.7730				675	93.3525	915.1650
1–8	236	32.5005	318.6130	590	81.5970	799.9220	660	91.2780	894.8280	910	125.8530	1233.7780
–14	250	34.5750	338.9500	660	91.2780	849.8280				990	136.9170	1342.2420

STANDARD TORQUE SPECIFICATIONS AND CAPSCREW MARKINGS

METRIC BOLTS

Description	Torque ft-lbs. (Nm)			
Thread for general purposes (size x pitch (mm)	Head Mark 4		Head Mark 7	
6 x 1.0	2.2 to 2.9	(3.0 to 3.9)	3.6 to 5.8	(4.9 to 7.8)
8 x 1.25	5.8 to 8.7	(7.9 to 12)	9.4 to 14	(13 to 19)
10 x 1.25	12 to 17	(16 to 23)	20 to 29	(27 to 39)
12 x 1.25	21 to 32	(29 to 43)	35 to 53	(47 to 72)
14 x 1.5	35 to 52	(48 to 70)	57 to 85	(77 to 110)
16 x 1.5	51 to 77	(67 to 100)	90 to 120	(130 to 160)
18 x 1.5	74 to 110	(100 to 150)	130 to 170	(180 to 230)
20 x 1.5	110 to 140	(150 to 190)	190 to 240	(160 to 320)
22 x 1.5	150 to 190	(200 to 260)	250 to 320	(340 to 430)
24 x 1.5	190 to 240	(260 to 320)	310 to 410	(420 to 550)

CAUTION: Bolts threaded into aluminum require much less torque.

Tools

The tools required for the basic rebuilding procedure should, with minor exception, be those included in a mechanic's tool kit. Accurate torque wrench, micrometers and dial indicators should readily be available to the repairman. Special tools are available from the major tool suppliers. The services of a competent automotive machine shop must also be available.

Precautions

When assembling the engine, any parts that will be in frictional contact must be pre-lubricated, to provide protection on initial start-up.

Any product specifically formulated for this purpose may be used. Where semipermanent locked but removable installation of bolts or nuts is desired, threads should be cleaned and coated with a liquid locking compound. Studs may be permanently installed using a stud mounting compound. Bolts and nuts with no torque specification should be tightened according to size (see chart).

Aluminum has become increasingly popular for use in engines, due to its low weight and excellent heat transfer characteristics. The following precautions should be observed when handling aluminum engine parts.

Never hot-tank aluminum parts.

Remove all aluminum parts (identification tags, etc.) from engine parts before hot-tanking (otherwise they will be removed during the process).

Always coat threads lightly with engine oil or anti-seize compounds before installation, to prevent seizure.

Heli-coil

Never over-torque bolts or spark plugs in aluminum threads. Should stripping occur, threads can be restored according to the following procedure, using Heli-Coil thread inserts.

Tap drill the hole with the stripped threads to the specified size, using the Specified tap.

NOTE: Heli-Coil tap sizes refer to the size thread being replaced, rather than the actual tap size.

Tap the hole for the Heli-Coil. Place the insert on the proper installation tool (see Heli-Coil chart with kit). Apply pressure on the insert while winding it clockwise into the hole, until the top of the insert is one turn below the surface. Remove the installation tool and break the installation tang from the bottom of the insert by moving it up and down. If the Heli-Coil must be removed, tap the removal tool firmly into the hole, so that it engages the top thread and turn the tool counterclockwise to extract the insert.

Broken Bolts or Studs

Snapped bolts or studs may be removed, using a stud extractor (unthreaded) or locking pliers (threaded). Penetrating oil will often aid in breaking frozen threads. In cases where the stud or bolt is flush with, or below the surface, proceed as follows.

Drill a hole in the broken stud or bolt, approximately 1/2 its diameter. Select a screw extractor of the proper size and tap it into the stud or bolt. Turn the extractor counterclockwise to remove the stud or bolt.

Locating Metal Flaws and Cracks

Magnaflux and Zyglo are inspection techniques used to locate material flaws, such as stress cracks. Magnafluxing coats the part with fine magnetic particles and subjects the part to a magnetic field. Cracks cause breaks in the magnetic field,

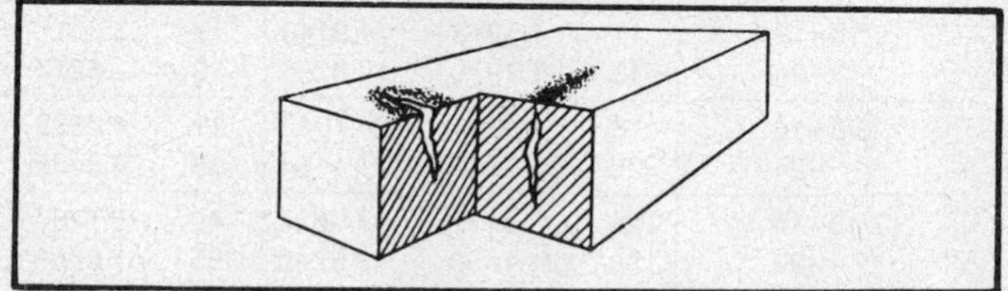

Magnaflux® indication of cracks

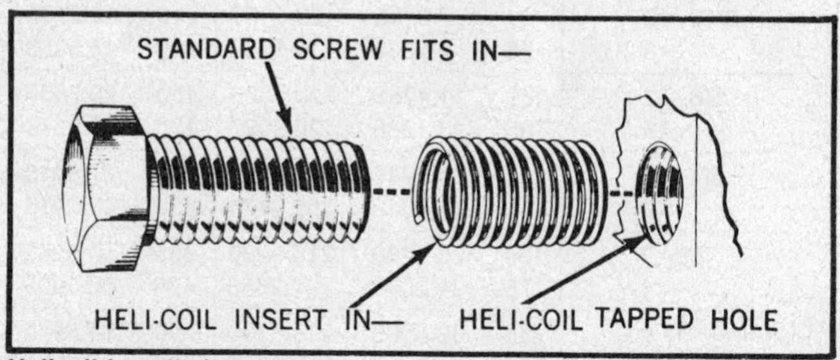

Helicoil installation

which are outlined by the particles. Since Magnaflux is a magnetic process, it is applicable only to ferrous materials. The Zyglo process coats the material with a fluorescent dye penetrant and then subjects it to blacklight inspection, under which cracks glow brightly. Parts made of any material may be tested using Zyglo. While Magnaflux and Zyglo are excellent for general inspection and locating hidden defects, specific checks of suspected cracks may be made at lower cost and more readily using spot check dye. The dye is sprayed onto the suspected area, wiped off and the area is then sprayed with a developer. Cracks then will show up brightly. Spot check dyes will only indicate surface cracks; therefore, structural cracks below the surface may escape detection. When questionable, the part should be tested using Magnaflux, Zyglo or their equivalent.

REBUILDING GASOLINE ENGINES

The section is divided into two parts. The first, Cylinder Head Reconditioning, assumes that the cylinder head is removed from the engine, all manifolds are removed and the cylinder head is on a workbench. The camshaft should be removed from overhead cam cylinder heads. The second section, Cylinder Block Reconditioning, covers the block, pistons, connecting rods and crankshaft. It is assumed that the engine is mounted on a work stand and the cylinder head and all accessories are removed.

In many cases, a choice of methods is provided. The choice of method for a procedure is at the discretion of the user.

Many makes and types of special tools are available to the rebuilder for the express purpose of making a specific rebuilding operation easier and quicker. It is the choice of the rebuilder as to the tool desired and obtained.

Cylinder Head Reconditioning

IDENTIFY THE VALVES

Invert the cylinder head and clean the carbon from the valve heads. Number the valve heads from front to rear with touch-up paint or a felt tip marking pencil. Upon removal of the valves from the cylinder head, place them in a holder, made from cardboard, wood or metal, in their respective order.

REMOVE THE ROCKER ARMS

Remove the rocker arms and shaft or balls and nuts, if not done during the cylinder head removal. Wire the sets of rockers, balls and nuts together and identify according to the corresponding valve.

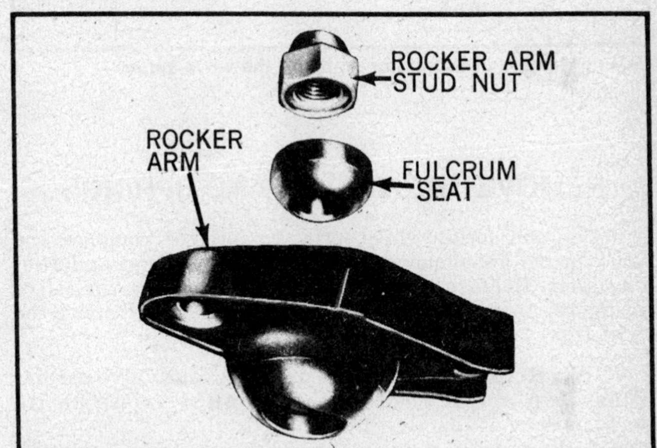

Individual rocker arm assembly

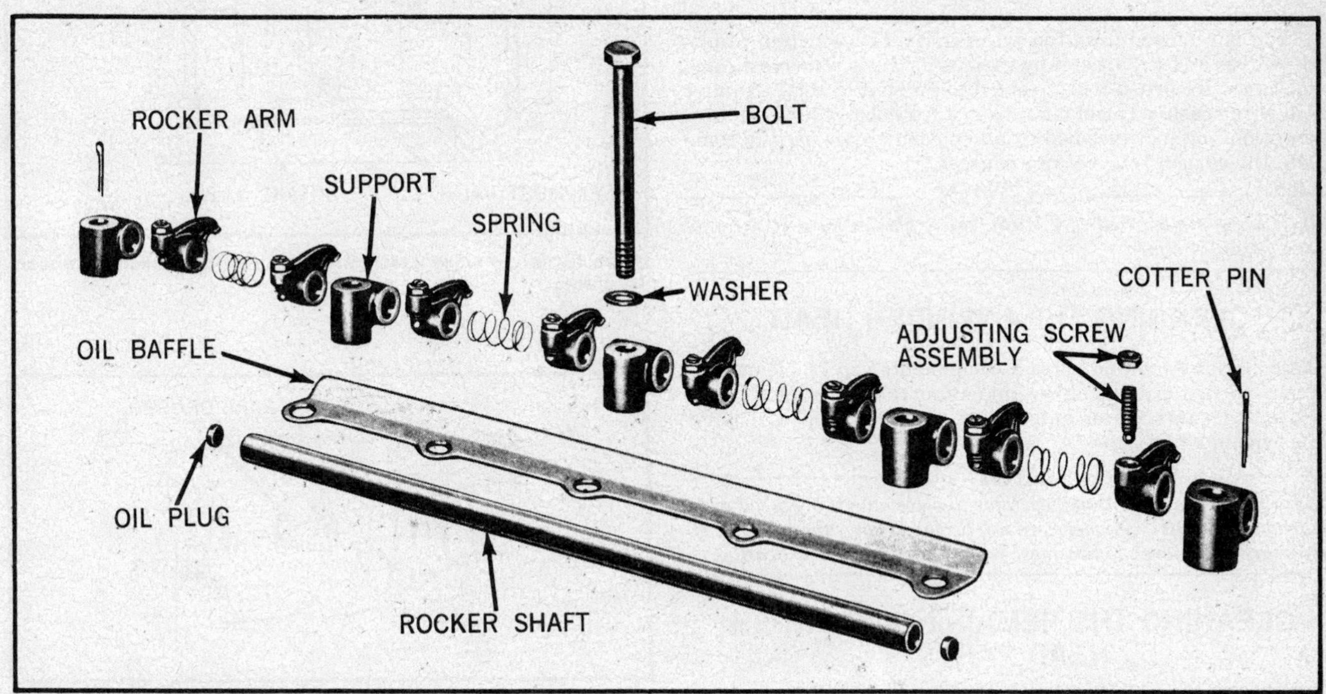

Rocker arm and shaft assembly—typical

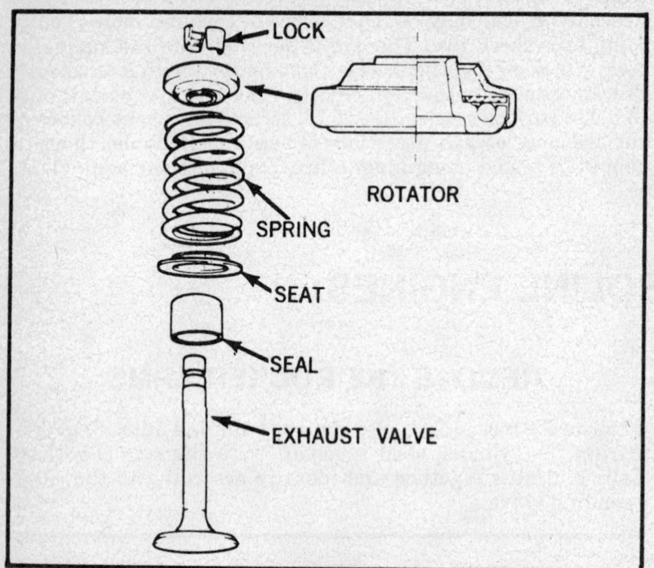

Valve assembly using rotator on top of the valve spring

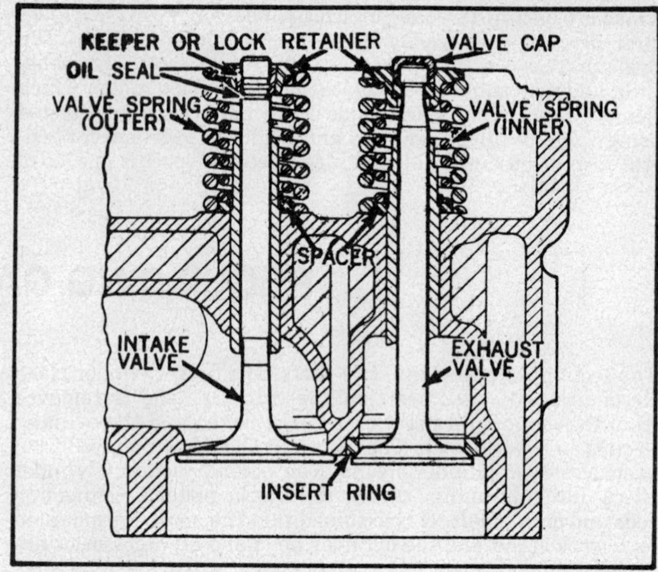

Cross section of valve assemblies with valve rotor cap on exhaust valve stem

REMOVE THE VALVES AND SPRINGS

Using an appropriate valve spring compressor, compress the valve springs and remove the keepers with needlenose pliers or a magnet. Release the compressor and remove the valve spring, retainer and oil seal from the valve stem. Remove the valve from the cylinder head and keep in order.

NOTE: Rotor units are used on numerous valve assemblies. Replace the rotor if any doubt exists on its performance.

DE-CARBON THE CYLINDER HEAD AND VALVES

Carbon is removed from the cylinder head combustion chamber, valves and valve ports by various methods. The most common is a wire brush tool, chucked to an electric drill. A hand held wire brush, a chisel made from hard wood or a special carbon removing tool supplied by a tool company is used to complete the carbon removal procedure.

CAUTION

When using a motorized wire brush, safety glasses must be worn to avoid personal injury.

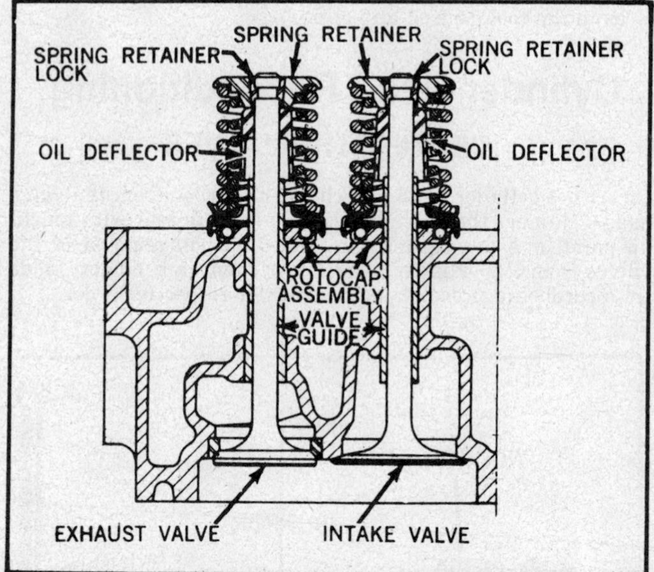

Cross section of valve assemblies with roto-cap assembly under the spring

CLEANING THE CYLINDER HEAD

The cylinder head and certain components can be cleaned of grease, corrosion and scale by immersing them in a "Hot Tank" solution. Generally, an automotive machine shop will have this type of equipment.

CAUTION

Consult with the "Hot Tank" operator to determine if overhead cam bearings of an OHC cylinder head will be damaged by the solution. If necessary to remove the bearings, replace them with new bearings.

CLEANING THE REMAINING CYLINDER HEAD PARTS

Using solvent, clean the rocker arm assemblies, (or rocker

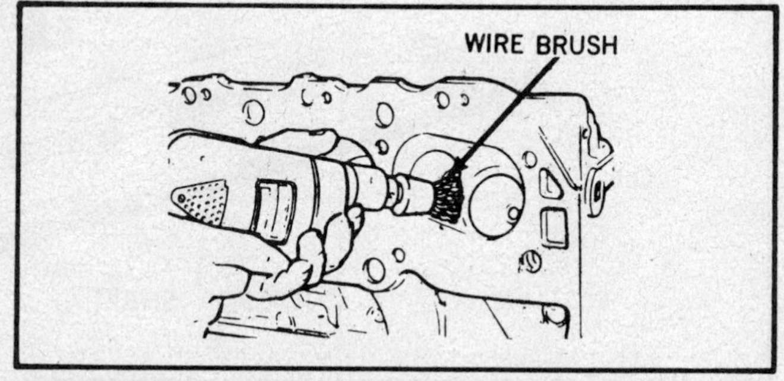

Removing carbon from the cylinder head

balls and nuts) springs, spring retainers, keepers, all bolts and nuts, push rods and rocker arm cover.

CHECK THE CYLINDER HEAD FOR WARPAGE

Place a straightedge across the gasket surface of the cylinder head. Using feeler gauges, determine the clearance at the center of the straightedge. Measure across both diagonals, along the longitudinal centerline and across the cylinder head at several points. If warpage exceeds 0.003 in. in a 6 in. span, or 0.006 in. over the total length, the cylinder head must be resurfaced.

NOTE: If warpage exceeds the manufacturer's maximum tolerance for material removal, the cylinder head must be replaced.

When milling the cylinder heads of V-type engines, the intake manifold mounting position is altered and must be corrected by milling the manifold flange a proportionate amount.

CHECK THE VALVE STEM TO GUIDE CLEARANCE

Clean the valve stem with a solvent to remove all gum and varnish. Clean the valve guides with a solvent and/or a wire type expanding valve guide cleaner tool. Insert the proper valve into its guide and hold the valve head to the valve seat tightly. Mount a dial indicator on the spring side of the cylinder head so that the dial indicator foot is against the valve stem, protruding from the guide, at a 90° angle. Move the valve off its seat and measure the valve guide to stem clearance by moving the stem back and forth to actuate the dial indicator. Measure the

Cleaning valve guides with wire type cleaner

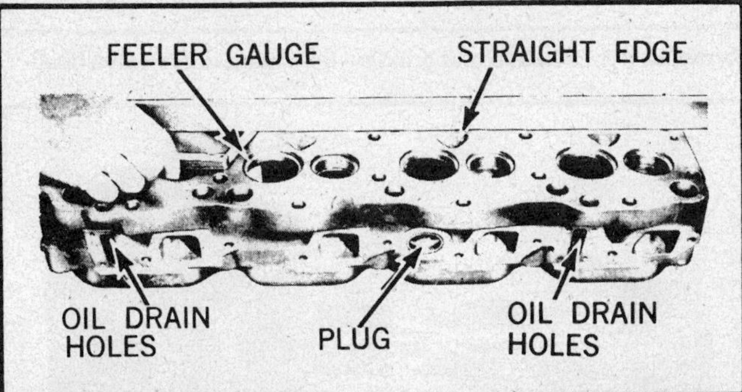

Checking cylinder head surface for flatness with feeler gauge and straight edge

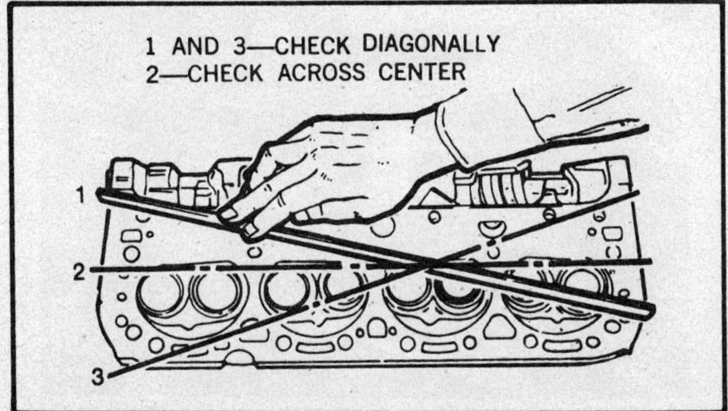

Location of straight edge to check cylinder head surface for flatness

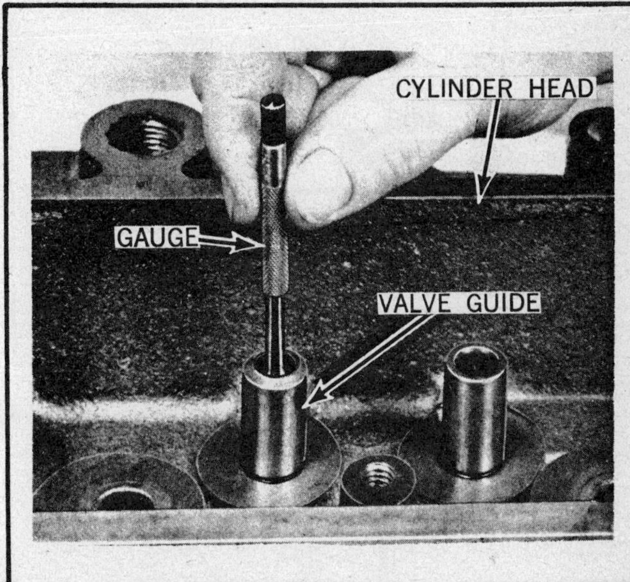

Measuring valve guide with small hole gauge

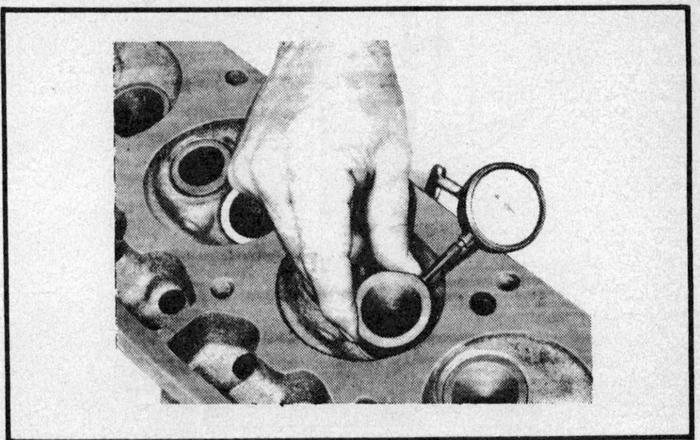

Measuring valve guide wear at valve stem

valve stems using a micrometer and compare to specifications to determine if the valve stem or valve guide is responsible for the excessive wear clearance.

An alternate method of checking the valve stem to guide clearance is to mount a dial indicator on the combustion side of the cylinder head, with the foot of the indicator to contact the side of the valve head. The valve head is moved away from its seat a predetermined distance, either by a special collar tool, placed on the valve stem between the head of the valve and the guide, or by measuring the height of the valve head above the seat with the use of a scale. The valve head is moved back and forth to actuate the dial indicator. Measure the valve stems, using a micrometer and compare to specifications.

Determination of wear from either the valve guide or valve stem can be made. Other types of measuring methods are available to the rebuilder. Go and No-Go gauge, inside caliper type small hole gauges or shim stock can be used to determine the wear of the guides.

Careful inspection will detect bellmouthing or elliptical wear of the guides, normally at the port end of the guide.

REPLACING VALVE SEAT INSERTS

Most exhaust and some intake valve seats are of the insert type and can be replaced if found to be loose, burned or cracked.

The valve seat insert can be removed by either pulling it from its counterbore with a puller, or by drilling a small hole into the seat insert on two sides and cracking it with a chisel. Care must be exercised to avoid drilling into the cylinder head. The insert counterbore in the cylinder head, should be machined prior to the insert installation, with special emphasis on having the bottom of the counterbore square to insure proper seating of the valve insert. Most inserts are supplied in standard, 0.015 in. and 0.030 in. oversizes.

After installation of the valve seat insert, grinding by a refacing machine should be made to insure the seat is angled to specification and in proper relationship to the valve guide.

REPLACING VALVE GUIDES

INTEGRAL GUIDE TYPE

These types of cylinder heads do not have removable guides but

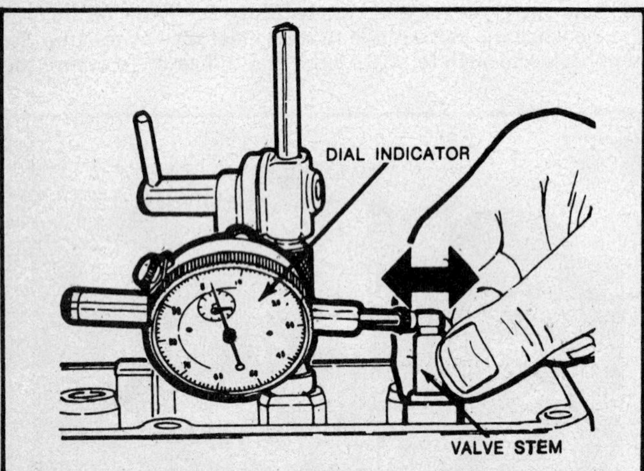

Measuring valve guide wear at valve stem

Correct seal installation and grinding in relation to the valve head

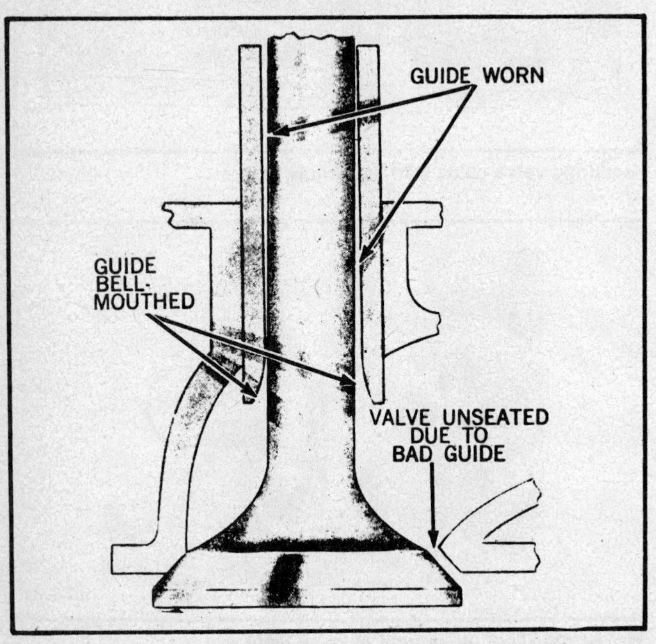

Effects of worn and bellmouthed guides on valve head seating

Machining cylinder head for valve seat insert installation—typical

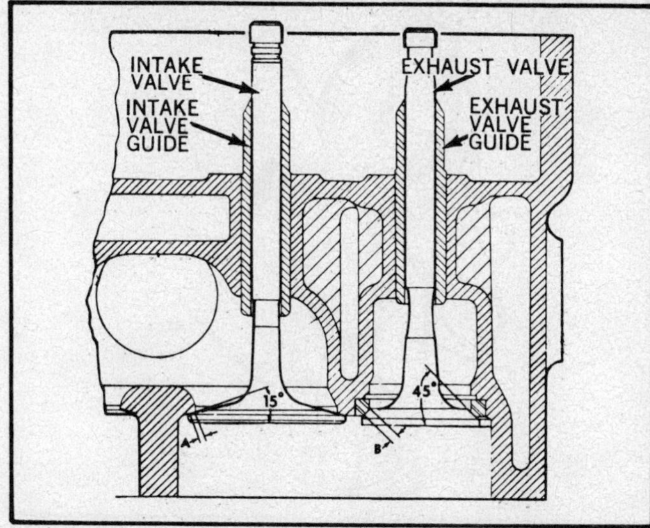

Cross section of valves showing exhaust valve seat insert and intake valve seat without insert. Method of measuring seat angle is illustrated.

have the guide holes bored directly in the cylinder head material. When the clearances become excessive between the valve and guide, the guides can be reamed to an oversize dimension and oversize valves used. The "knurling" process may be used to recondition the inside of the guide surface, if the valve to guide clearance is not excessive.

A machining operation can be used to drill out the non-replaceable guide holes and have a standard type guide installed. This operation should be done by an automotive machine shop, equipped with the special boring machine.

REPLACEABLE GUIDE TYPE

Depending on the type of cylinder head, valve guides may be pressed, hammered, or shrunk in. In cases where the guides are shrunk into the head, replacement should be left to an equipped machine shop. In other cases, the guides are replaced as follows: Press or tap the valve guides out of the head using a stepped drift. Determine the height above the boss that the guide must extend and obtain a stack of washers, their I.D. similar to the guides O.D., of that height. Place the stack of washers on the guide and insert the guide into the boss.

NOTE: Valve guides are often tapered or beveled for installation.

Using the stepped installation tool, press or tap the guides into position. Ream the guides according to the size of the valve stem.

RESURFACING (GRINDING) THE VALVE FACE

Using a valve grinder, resurface the valves according to specifications.

Seat installation tool—typical

CAUTION

Valve face angle is not always identical to valve seat angle.

A minimum margin of $^3/_{64}$ in. should remain after grinding the valve. The valve stem tip should also be squared and resurfaced, by placing the stem in the V-block of the grinder and turning it while pressing lightly against the grinding wheel.

RESURFACING THE VALVE SEATS USING A GRINDER

Select a pilot of the correct size and a coarse stone of the correct seat angle. Lubricate the pilot if necessary and install the tool

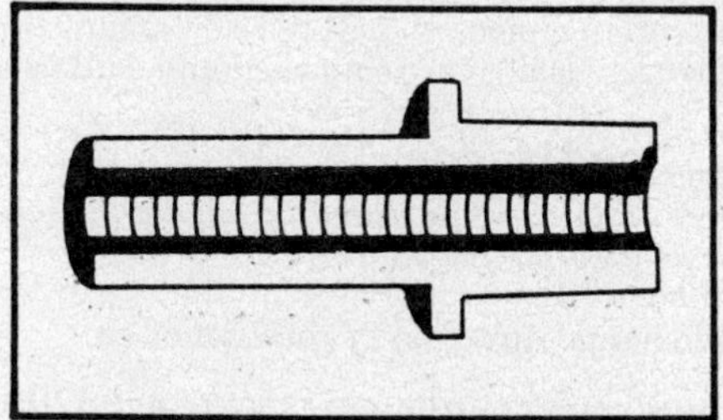

Cross section of knurled valve guide

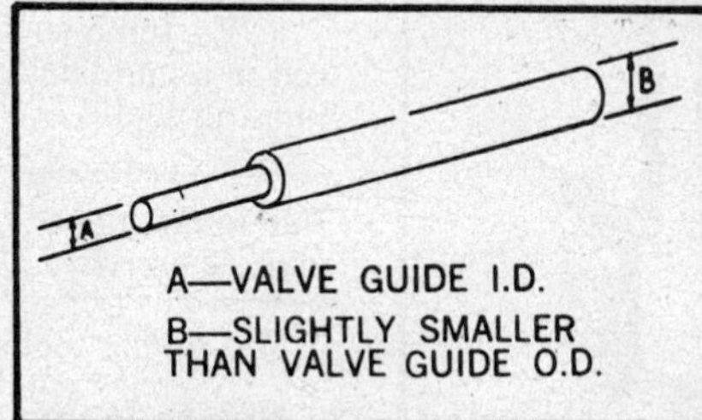

Valve guide removal tool

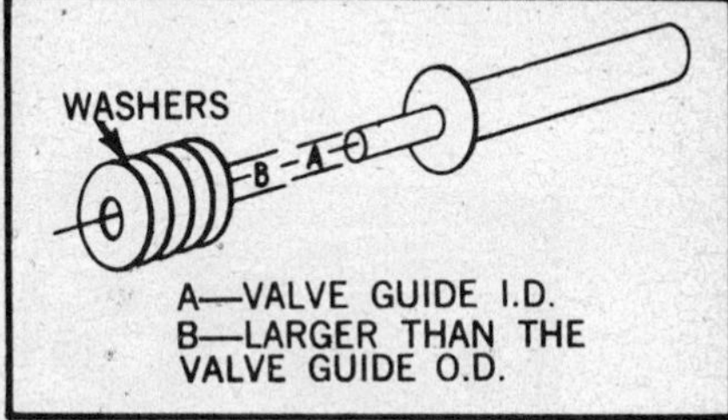

Valve guide installation tool with washer stack

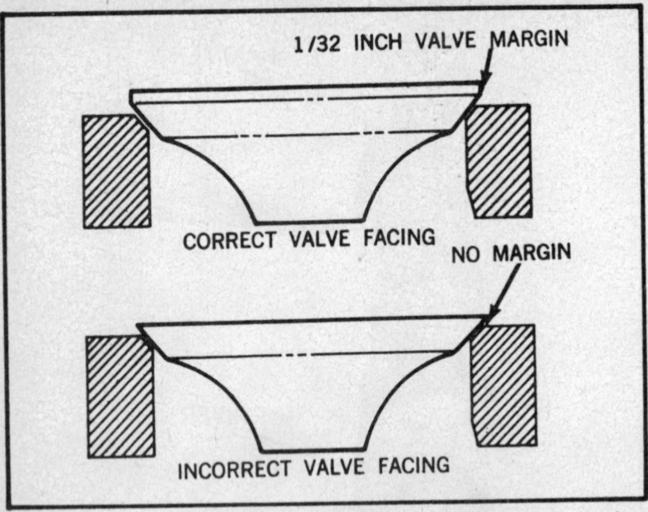

Correct and incorrect grinding of the valve face with proper margin indicated

Checking valve seat run-out with a dial gauge

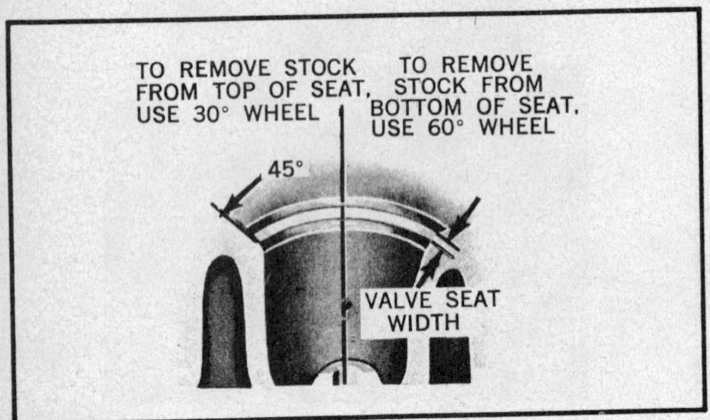

Centering and narrowing valve seat with correction stone

Grinding valve seats

in the valve guide. Move the stone on and off the seat at approximately two cycles per second, until all flaws are removed from the seat. Install a fine stone and finish the seat. Center and narrow the seat using correction stones. Intake seat width – $^{1}/_{16}$–$^{5}/_{64}$ in. Exhaust seat width – $^{3}/_{64}$–$^{1}/_{16}$ in.

CHECKING THE VALVE SEAT CONCENTRICITY

1. Coat the valve face with Prussian blue dye, install the valve and rotate it on the valve sat. If the entire seat becomes coated and the valve is known to be concentric, the set is concentric.
2. Install a dial gauge pilot into the guide and rest the arm on the valve seat. Zero the gauge and rotate the arm around the seat. Runout should not exceed 0.002 in.

LAPPING THE VALVES

NOTE: Valve lapping is done to ensure efficient sealing of resurfaced valves and seats. Valve lapping alone is not recommended for use as a resurface procedure.

1. Invert the cylinder head, lightly lubricate the valve stems and install the valves in the head as numbered. Coat valve seats with fine grinding compound and attach the lapping tool suction cup to a valve head.

NOTE: Moisten the suction cup.

2. Rotate the tool between the palms, changing position and lifting the tool often to prevent grooving. Lap the valve until a smooth polished seat is evident. Remove the valve and tool and rinse away all traces of grinding compound.
3. Fasten a suction cup to a piece of drill rod and mount the rod in a hand drill. Proceed as above, using the hand drill as a lapping tool.

Due to the higher speeds involved when using the hand drill, care must be exercised to avoid grooving the seat.

4. Lift the tool and change direction of rotation often.

NOTE: Many manufacturers do not recommend the lapping of valves to the seats after each has been reground. However, for the rebuilder to be certain a perfect

Hand lapping the valve to the seat

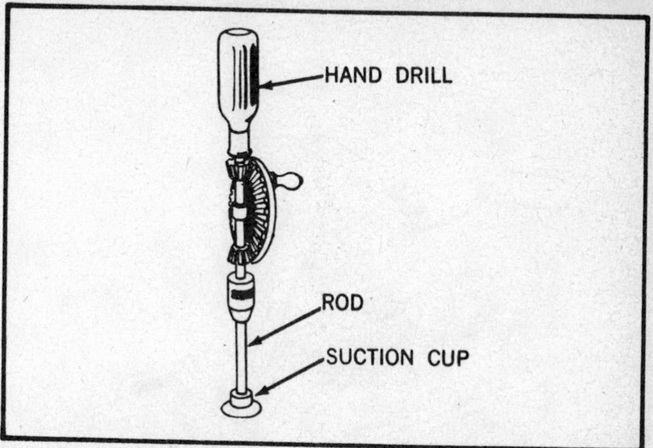

Mechanical valve lapping tool

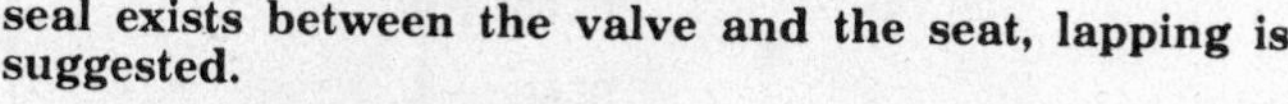

seal exists between the valve and the seat, lapping is suggested.

CHECK THE VALVE SPRINGS

Test the spring pressure at the installed and compressed (installed height minus valve lift) height using a valve spring tester. Springs used on small displacement engines (up to 3 liters) should be ± 1 lb. of all other springs in either position. A tolerance of ± 5 lbs. is permissable on larger engines.

INSTALL VALVE STEM SEALS

Due to the pressure differential that exists at the ends of the intake valve guides (atmospheric pressure above, manifold vacuum below), oil is drawn through the valve guides into the intake port. This has been alleviated somewhat since the addition of positive crankcase ventilation, which lowers the pressure above the guides. Several types of valve stem seals are available to reduce blow-by. Certain seals simply slip over the stem and guide boss, while others require that the boss be machined. Recently, Teflon guide seals have become popular. Consult a parts supplier or machinist concerning availability and suggested usages.

NOTE: When installing seals, ensure that a small amount of oil is able to pass the seal to lubricate the valve guides; otherwise, excessive wear may result.

INSTALL THE VALVES

Lubricate the valve stems and install the valves in the cylinder head as numbered. Lubricate and position the seals (if used, see above) and the valve springs. Install the spring retainers, compress the springs and insert the keys using needlenose pliers or a tool designed for this purpose.

NOTE: Retain the keys with wheel bearing grease during installation.

CHECK VALVE SPRING INSTALLED HEIGHT

Measure the distance between the spring pad and the lower edge of the spring retainer and compare to specifications. If the installed height is incorrect, add shim washers between the spring pad and the spring.

CAUTION

Use only washers designed for this purpose.

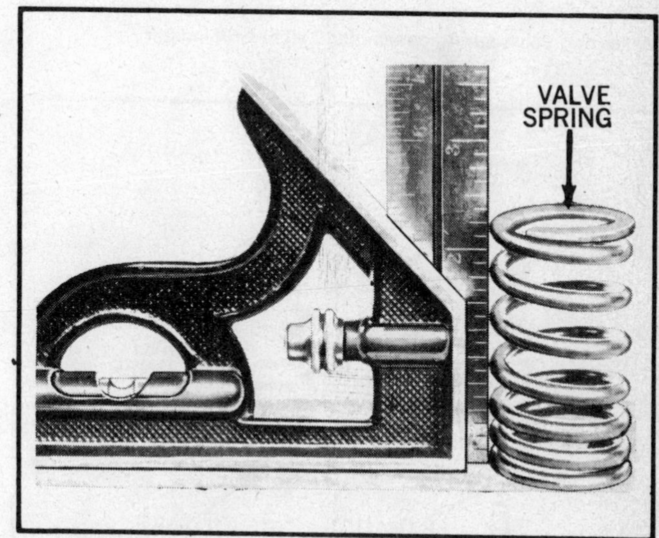

Checking valve spring for free length and squareness

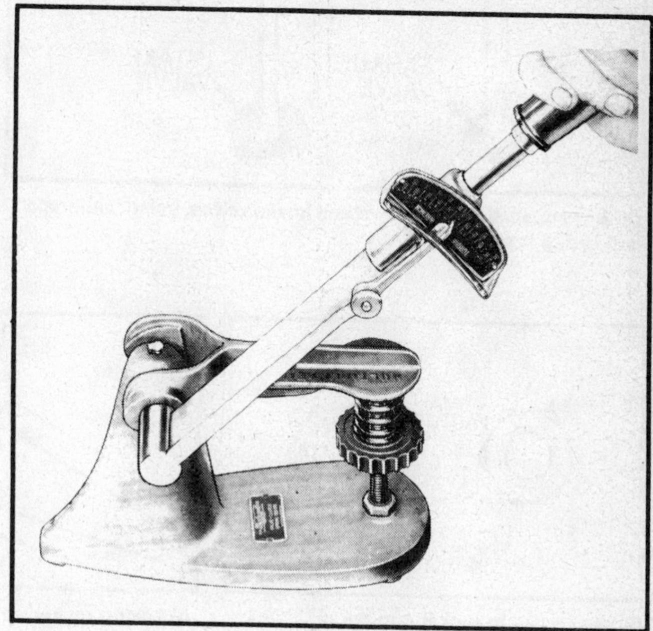

Testing valve spring compressed height

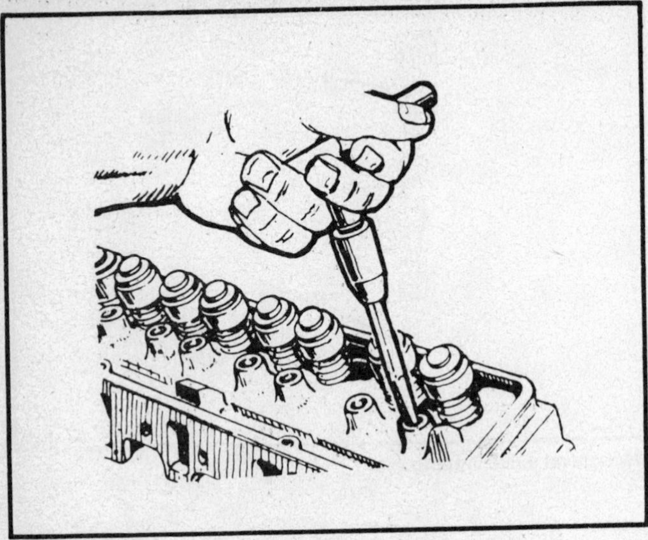

Measuring valve spring assembled height with caliper

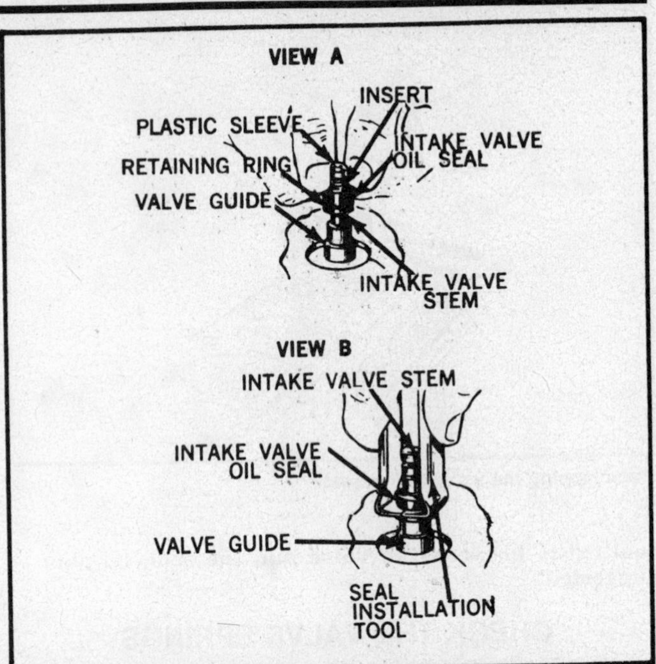

Installing intake valve oil seals, Perfect Circle type, using plastic sleeve and special installation tool

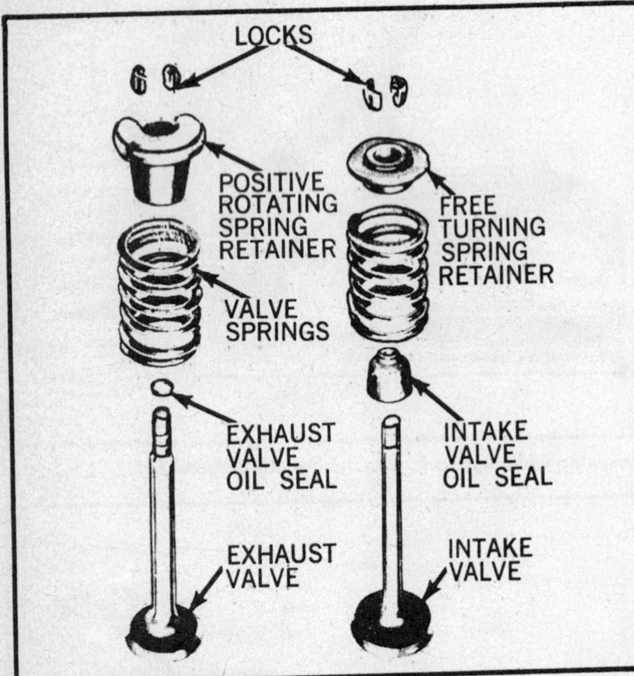

Oil seal installation on exhaust and intake valves, using "umbrella" and O-ring type seals

INSPECT THE ROCKER ARMS, BALLS, STUDS and NUTS

Visually inspect the rocker arms, balls, studs and nuts for cracks, galling, burning, scoring, or wear. If all parts are intact, liberally lubricate the rocker arms and balls and install them on the cylinder head. If wear is noted on the rocker arm at the point of valve contact, grind it smooth and square, removing as little material as possible. Replace the rocker arm if excessively worn. If a rocker stud shows signs of wear, it must be replaced. If a rocker nut shows stress cracks, replace it.

INSPECT THE ROCKER SHAFT(S) AND ROCKER ARMS

Remove rocker arms, springs and washers from rocker shaft.

NOTE: Lay out parts in the order in which they are removed.

Inspect rocker arms for pitting or wear on the valve contact point, or excessive bushing wear. Bushings need only be replaced if wear is excessive, because the rocker arm normally contacts the shaft at one point only. Grind the valve contact

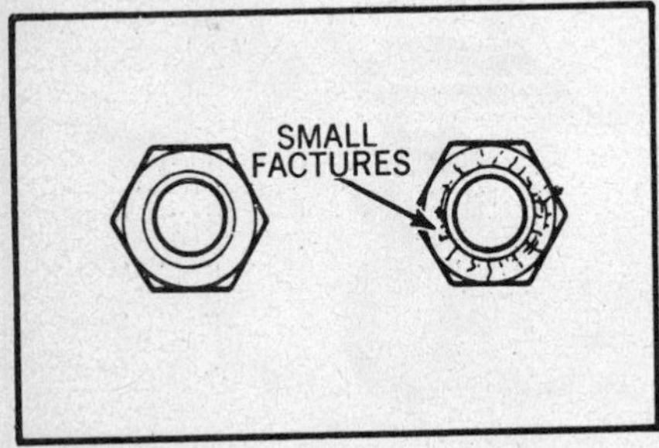

Stress cracks in rocker arm nut

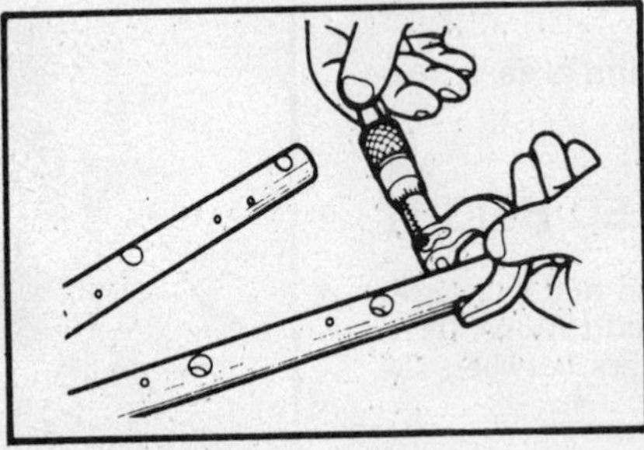

Checking rocker arm shaft O.D. with micrometer

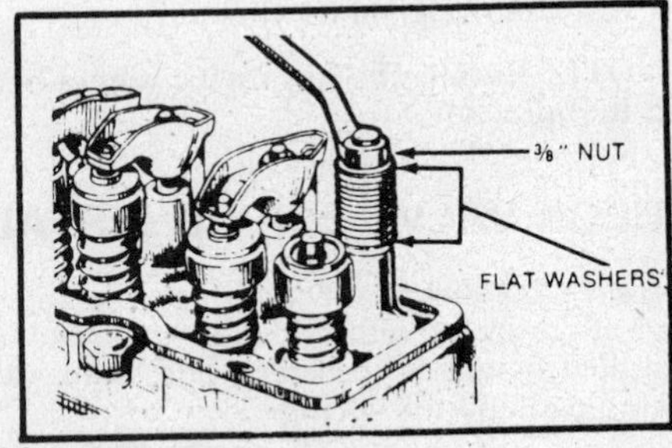

Checking rocker arms

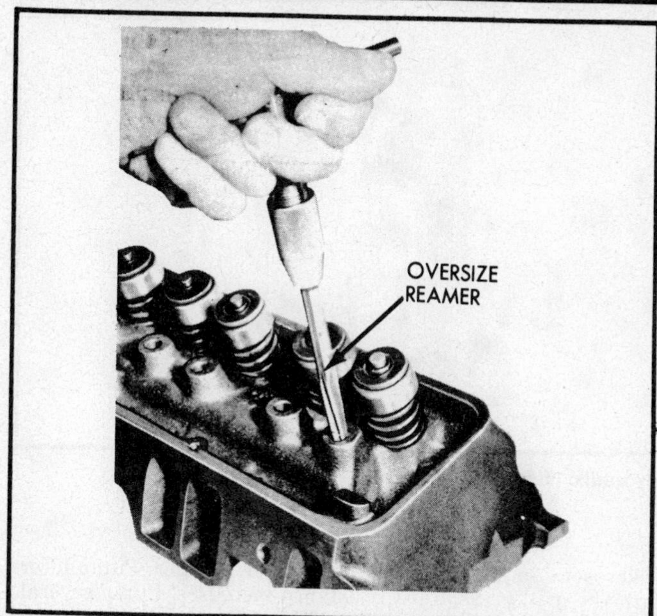

Reaming the stud bore for oversize rocker studs

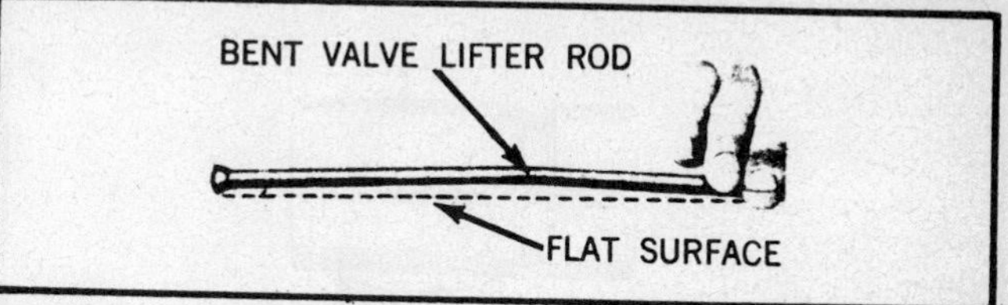

Checking for bent push rod

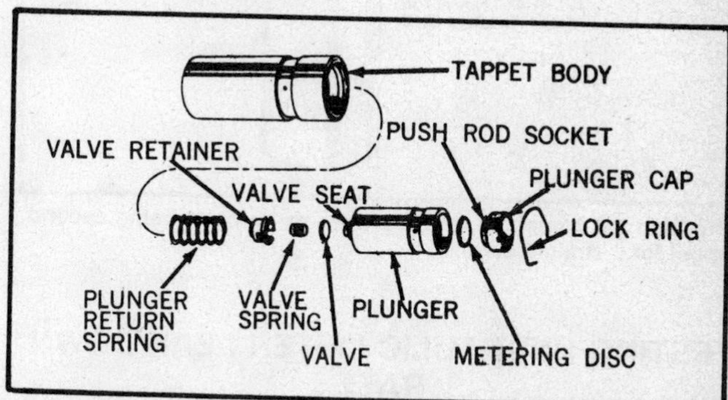

Exploded view of hydraulic lifter—typical

Removing a pressed in rocker stud

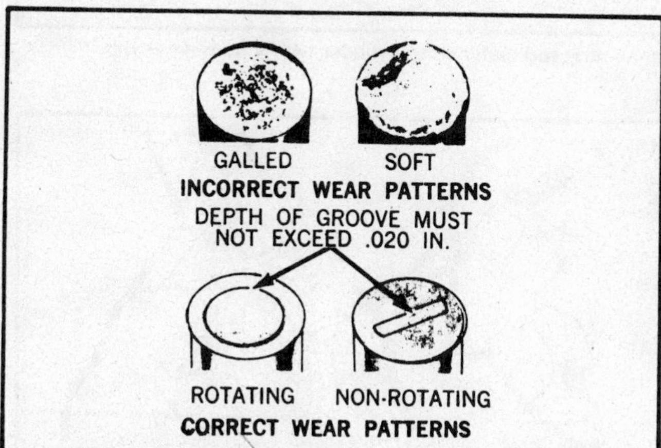

Wear patterns on base of lifter bodies

point of rocker arm smooth if necessary, removing as little material as possible. If excessive material must be removed to smooth and square the arm, it should be replaced. Clean out all oil holes and passages in rocker shaft. If shaft is grooved or worn, replace it. Lubricate and assemble the rocker shaft.

REPLACING ROCKER STUDS

In order to remove a threaded stud, lock two nuts on the stud and unscrew the stud using the lower nut. Coat the lower threads of the new stud with Loctite and install.

Two alternative methods are available for replacing pressed in studs. Remove the damaged stud using a stack of washers and a nut or use a stud puller. In the first, the boss is reamed 0.005–0.006 in. oversize and an oversize stud pressed in. Control the stud extension over the boss using washers, in the same manner as valve guides. Before installing the stud, coat it with white lead and grease. To retain the stud more positively, drill a hole through the stud and boss and install a roll pin. In the second method, the boss is tapped and a threaded stud installed. Retain the stud using a locking compound.

INSPECT THE PUSHRODS

Remove the pushrods and if hollow, clean out the oil passages using fine wire. Roll each pushrod over a piece of clean glass. If a distinct clicking sound is heard as the pushrod rolls, the rod is bent and must be replaced.

The length of all pushrods must be equal. Measure the length of the pushrods, compare to specifications and replace as necessary.

INSPECT THE VALVE LIFTERS

MECHANICAL OR HYDRAULIC

Remove lifters from their bores and remove gum and varnish, using solvent. Clean walls of lifter bores. Check lifters for concave wear as illustrated. If face is worn concave, replace lifter and carefully inspect the camshaft. Lightly lubricate lifter and insert it into its bore. If play is excessive, an oversize lifter must be installed (where possible). Consult a machinist concerning feasibility. If play is satisfactory, remove, lubricate and reinstall the lifter.

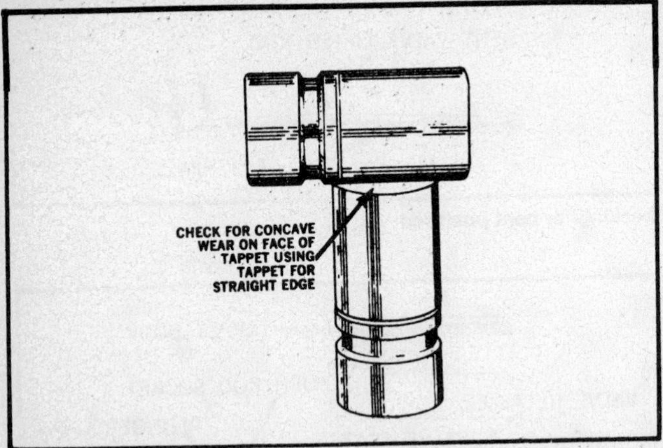

Checking the tappet for concave wear on its base, using second tappet for a straight edge

Hydraulic lifter leakdown tester—typical

TESTING HYDRAULIC LIFTER LEAK DOWN RATE

Special testers are available for the checking of the hydraulic lifter leak down rate. Special instructions accompanying the testers should be followed by the rebuilder. If the tester is not available, the following alternate method can be used.

Submerge lifter in a container of kerosene. Chuck a used pushrod or its equivalent into a drill press. Position container of kerosene so pushrod acts on the lifter plunger. Pump lifter with the drill press, until resistance increases. Pump several more times to bleed any air out of lifter. Apply very firm, constant pressure to the lifter and observe rate at which fluid bleeds out of lifter. If the fluid bleeds very quickly (less than 15 seconds), lifter is defective. If the time exceeds 60 seconds, lifter is sticking. In either case, recondition or replace lifter. If lifter is operating properly (leak down time 15–60 seconds) lubricate and reinstall.

ENGINE BLOCK RECONDITIONING

MARKING MAIN AND CONNECTING ROD CAPS

Using a punch, mark the corresponding main bearing caps and saddles according to position (i.e., one punch on the front main cap and saddle, two on the second, three on the third, etc.). Using number stamps, identify the corresponding connecting rods and caps, according to cylinder (if no numbers are present). Remove the main and connecting rod caps and place sleeves of plastic tubing over the connecting rod bolts, to protect the journals as the crankshaft is removed.

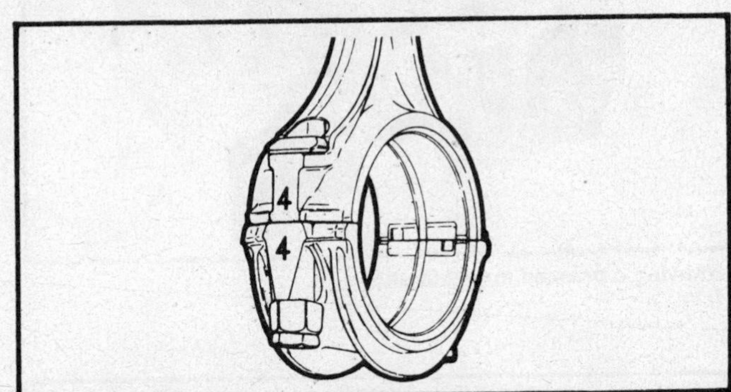

Connecting rod matched to cylinder with a number stamp

REMOVE THE RIDGE

In order to facilitate removal of the piston and connecting rod, the ridge at the top of the cylinder (unworn area; see illustration) must be removed. Place the piston at the bottom of the bore and cover it with a rag. Cut the ridge away using a ridge reamer, exercising extreme care to avoid cutting too deeply. Remove the rag and remove cuttings that remain at the piston.

CAUTION

If the ridge is not removed and new rings are installed, damage to rings will result.

REMOVING THE PISTON AND CONNECTING ROD

Invert the engine and push the pistons and connecting rods out of the cylinders. If necessary, tap the connecting rod boss with a wooden hammer handle, to force the piston out.

Scribe connecting rod matchmarks

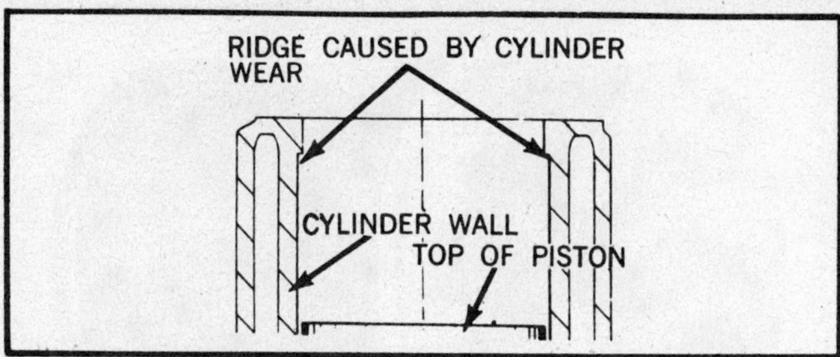

Cylinder bore ridge

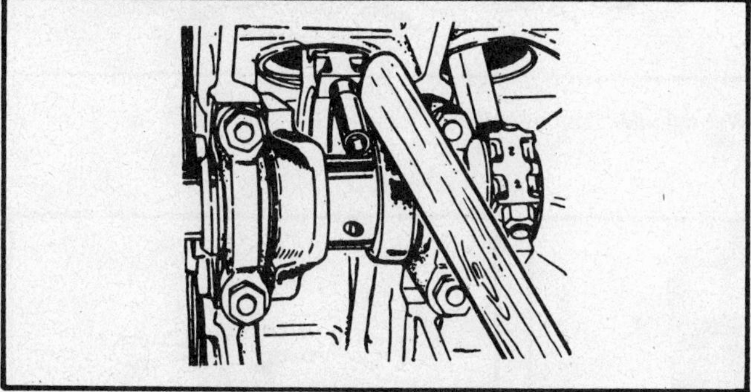

Removing the piston and connecting rod assembly

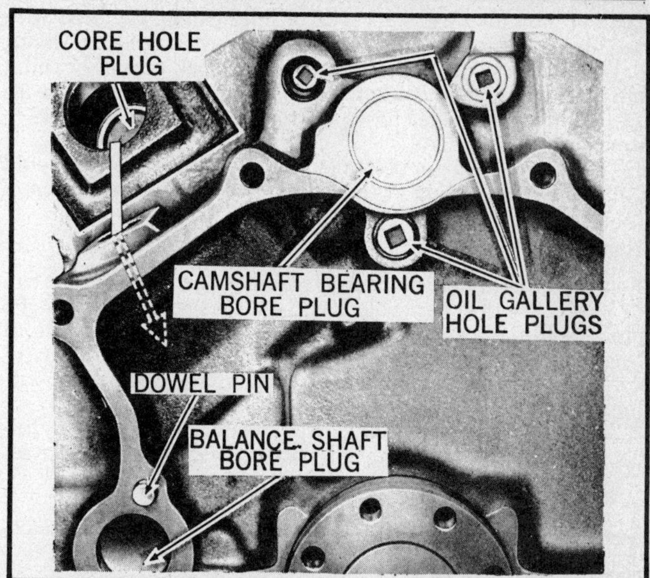

Location of oil gallery plugs, core plugs and camshaft bearing bore plug—V8 engine (some engines may be equipped with a balance shaft)

CAUTION

Do not attempt to force the piston past the uncut cylinder ridge.

REMOVE THE OIL GALLERY PLUGS

Threaded plugs should be removed using an appropriate (usually square) wrench. To remove soft, pressed in plugs, drill a hole in the plug and thread in a sheet metal screw. Pull the plug out by the screw using pliers.

REMOVING FREEZE PLUGS

Drill a hole in the center of the freeze plugs and pry them out using a drift or special puller.

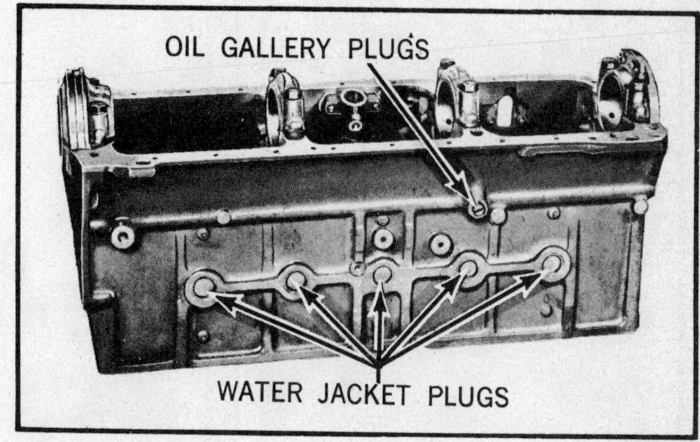

Location of oil galley and water jacket plugs—6 cylinder engine typical

CHECK THE BORE DIAMETER AND SURFACE

Visually inspect the cylinder bores for roughness, scoring, or scuffing. If evident, the cylinder bore must be bored or honed oversize to eliminate imperfections and the smallest possible oversize piston used. The new pistons should be given to the machinist with the block, so that the cylinders can be bored or honed exactly to the piston size (plus clearance). If no flaws are evident, measure the bore diameter using a telescope gauge and micrometer, or dial gauge, parallel and perpendicular to the engine centerline, at the top (below the ridge) and bottom of the bore. Subtract the bottom measurements from the top to determine taper and the parallel to the centerline measurements from the perpendicular measurements to determine eccentricity. If the measurements are not within specifications, the cylinder must be bored or honed and an oversize piston installed. If the measurements are within specifications the cylinder may be used as is, with only finish honing.

CYLINDER SLEEVE LINERS

DRY CYLINDER LINERS

Various engines are fitted with dry type cylinder liners at the

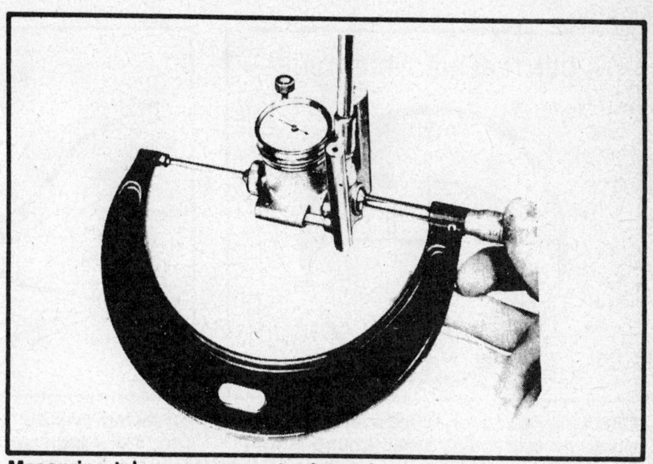

Measuring telescope gauge to determine bore size

time of manufacture. This type of liner can be replaced with the use of special pulling tools at the time of engine overhaul.

When the cylinder bore is part of the block assembly and if only one or two cylinder bores are damaged, sleeves can be installed in the damaged bores to avoid reboring all cylinders to an oversize condition.

The services of a competent automotive machine shop should be used for the boring of the cylinders and the installation of the liners.

WET CYLINDER LINERS

Removable cylinder liners are used in varied engines that can be lifted from the engine block without the use of pullers or of a press. Soft metal rings are used at the base of the liners to seal between machined surfaces on the engine block and the cylinder liner, to prevent coolant from entering the engine lubricating system.

The cylinder head gasket is used to seal the top of the cylinder liner and the cylinder head. Should the cylinder head be re-

Wet cylinder liner—typical

Cylinder reboring machine

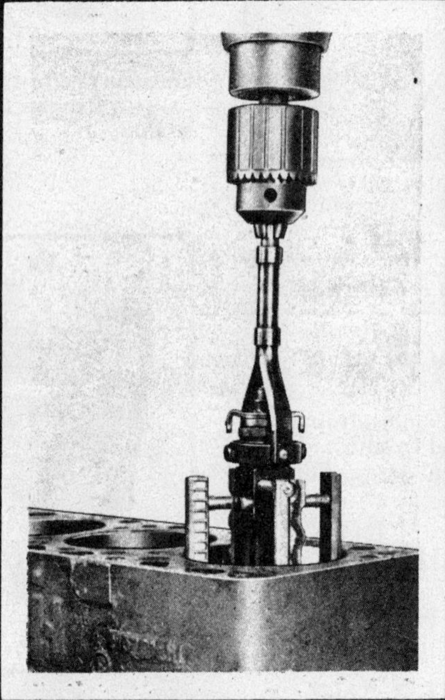

Cylinder honing tool

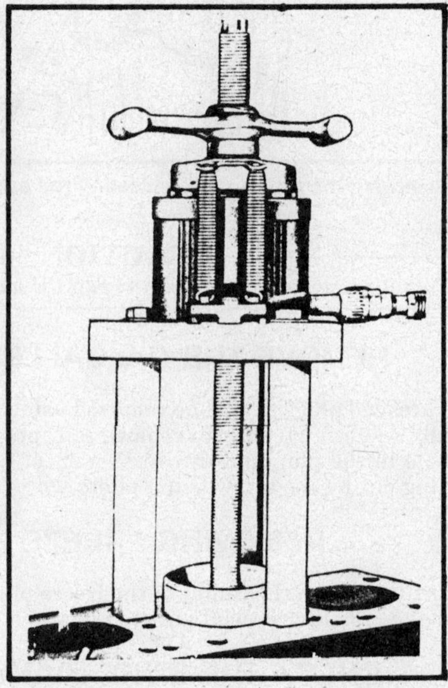

Removing cylinder sleeve with the use of hydraulic tool

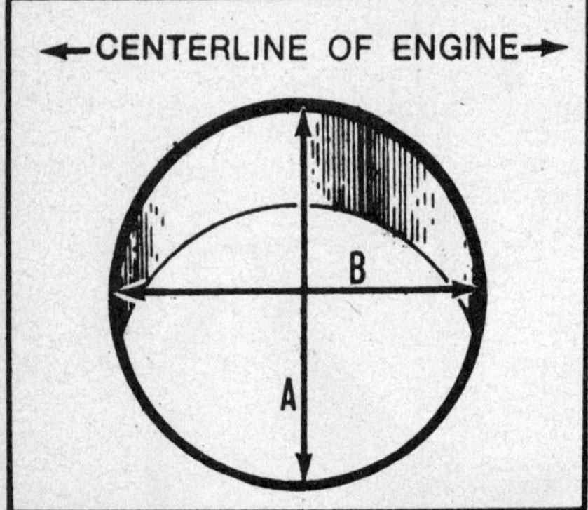

Checking points for cylinder bore out-of-round measurement. Out-of-round is difference between measurement A and B

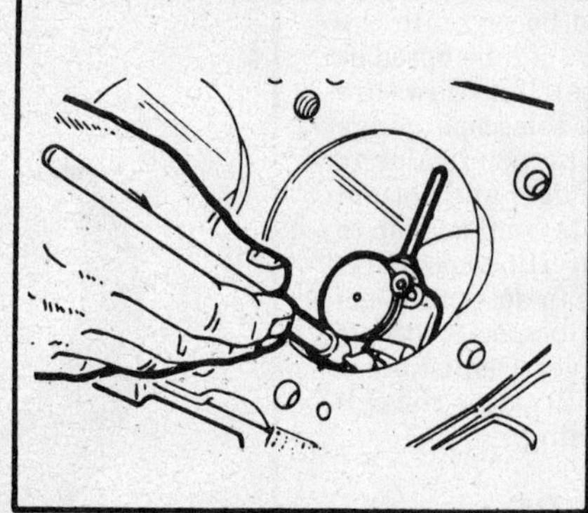

Checking cylinder bore taper and out-of-round dial indicator cylinder bore gauge

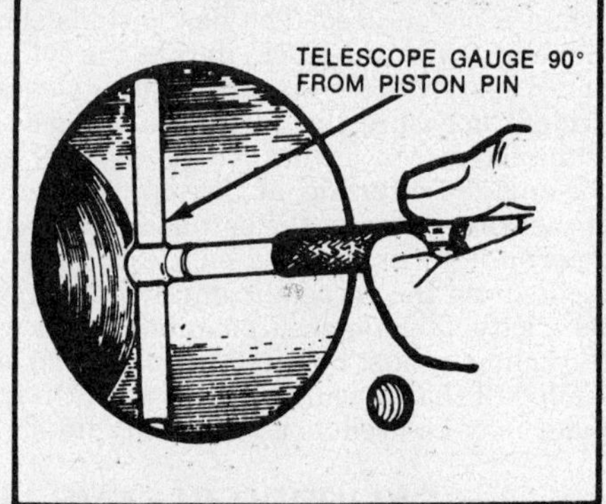

Measuring cylinder bore with telescope gauge

moved or the engine overhauled, a projection of approximately 0.002–0.006 in. (depending upon engine manufacturer's specifications) should exist at the liner top, above the surface of the engine block. If the projection is not present, new sealing rings should be installed at the bottom of the cylinder liners to prevent coolant leakage or compression loss.

Installation of pistons, rings and liners are installed as sets to control the weight and balance of the components.

CHECK THE CYLINDER BLOCK BEARING ALIGNMENT

Remove the upper bearing inserts. Place a straightedge in the bearing saddles along the centerline of the crankshaft. If clearance exists between the straightedge and the center saddle, the block must be linebored.

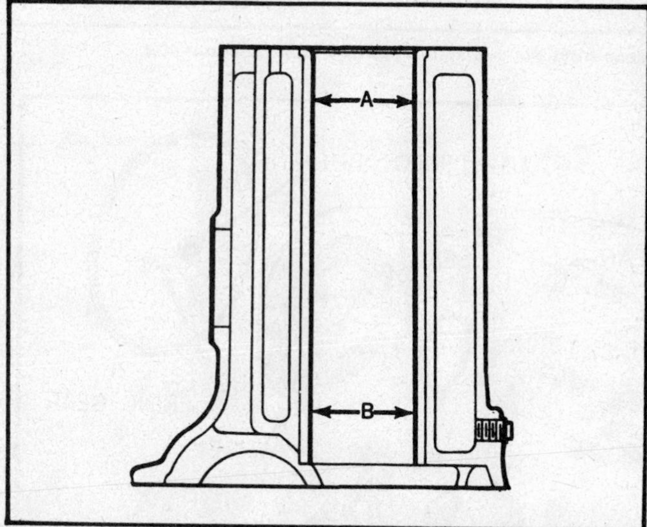

Checking points for cylinder bore taper measurement. Taper is difference between measurement A and B

Checking main bearing saddle alignment

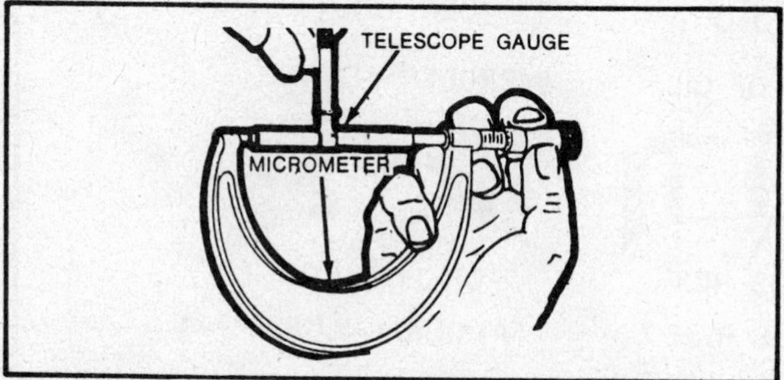

Measuring cylinder gauge to determine bore size

HOT-TANK THE BLOCK

Have the block hot-tanked to remove grease, corrosion and scale from the water jackets.

NOTE: Consult the operator to determine whether the camshaft bearings will be damaged during the hot-tank process.

SERVICE THE CRANKSHAFT

Ensure that all oil holes and passages in the crankshaft are open and free of sludge. If necessary, have the crankshaft ground to the largest possible undersize.

Have the crankshaft magnafluxed, to locate stress cracks. Consult a machinist concerning additional service procedures, such as surface hardening (e.g., Nitriding, Tuftriding) to improve wear characteristics, cross drilling and chamfering the oil holes to improve lubrication and balancing.

Measure the main bearing journals at each end twice (90° apart) using a micrometer, to determine diameter, journal taper and eccentricity. If journals are within tolerances, reinstall bearing caps at their specified torque. Using a telescope gauge and micrometer, measure bearing I.D. parallel to piston axis and at 30° on each side of piston axis. Subtract journal O.D. from bearing I.D. to determine oil clearance. If crankshaft journals appear defective, or do not meet tolerances, there is no need to measure bearings; for the crankshaft will require grinding and/or.undersize bearings will be required. If bearing appears defective, cause for failure should be determined prior to replacement.

Refer to the failure diagnosis section to help you determine the cause of the failure.

CHECK THE BLOCK FOR CRACKS

Visually inspect the block for cracks or chips. The most common locations are as follows:

1. Adjacent to freeze plugs
2. Between the cylinders and water jackets
3. Adjacent to the main bearing saddles
4. At the entrance bottom of the cylinders

Check only suspected cracks using spot check dye (see introduction). If a crack is located, consult a machinist concerning possible repairs.

Magnaflux the block to locate hidden cracks. If cracks are located, consult a machinist about feasibility of repair.

NOTE: Engine blocks that are porous or have sand holes, can be repaired with metallic plastic where coolant or oil pressure does not exist. Do not attempt to repair cracked blocks with the metallic plastic.

CHECK THE BLOCK DECK FOR WARPAGE

Using a straightedge and feeler gauges, check the block deck for warpage in the same manner that the cylinder head is checked (see Cylinder Head Reconditioning). If warpage exceeds specifications, have the deck resurfaced.

NOTE: In certain cases a specification for total material removal (Cylinder head and block deck) is provided. This specification must not be exceeded.

CHECK THE DECK HEIGHT

The deck height is the distance from the crankshaft centerline to the block deck. To measure, invert the engine and install the crankshaft, retaining it with the center main cap. Measure the distance from the crankshaft journal to the block deck, parallel to the cylinder centerline. Measure the diameter of the end (front and rear) main journals, parallel to the centerline of the cylinders, divide the diameter in half and subtract it from the previous measurement. The results of the front and rear measurements should be identical. If the difference exceeds 0.005 in., the deck height should be corrected.

NOTE: Block deck height and warpage should be corrected together.

INSTALL THE OIL GALLERY PLUGS AND FREEZE PLUGS

Coat freeze plugs with sealer and tap into position using a piece of pipe, slightly smaller than the plug, as a driver. To ensure retention, stake the edges of the plugs. Coat threaded oil

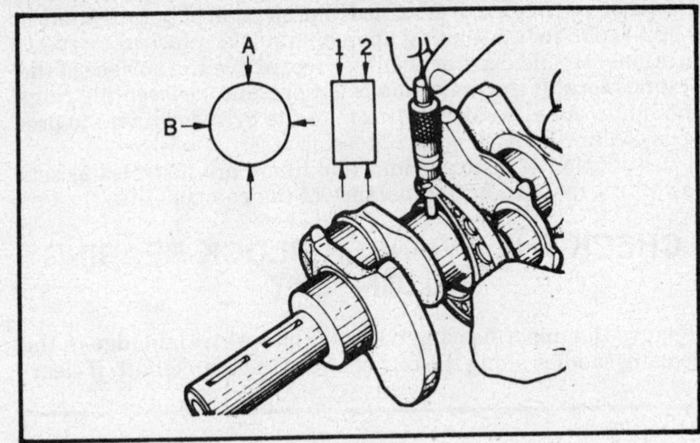

Measuring the crankshaft journals with a micrometer

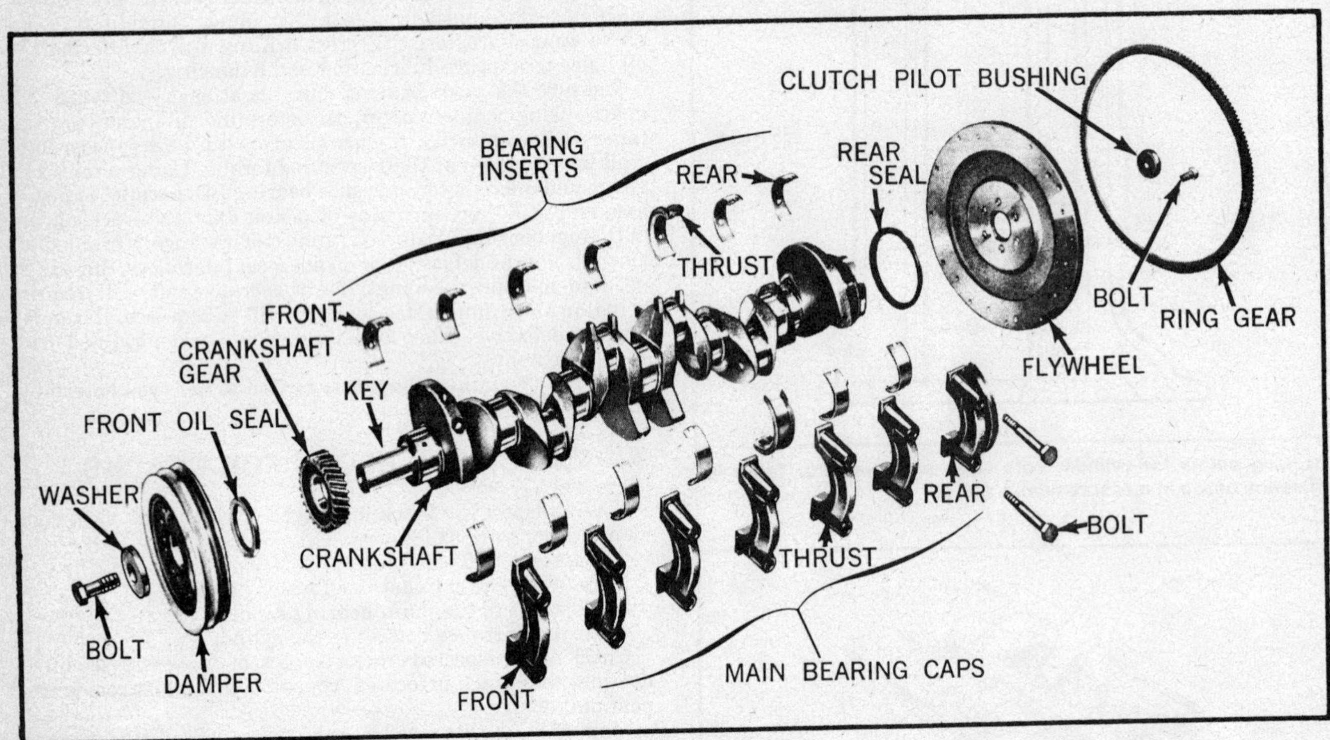

Crankshaft assembly—typical

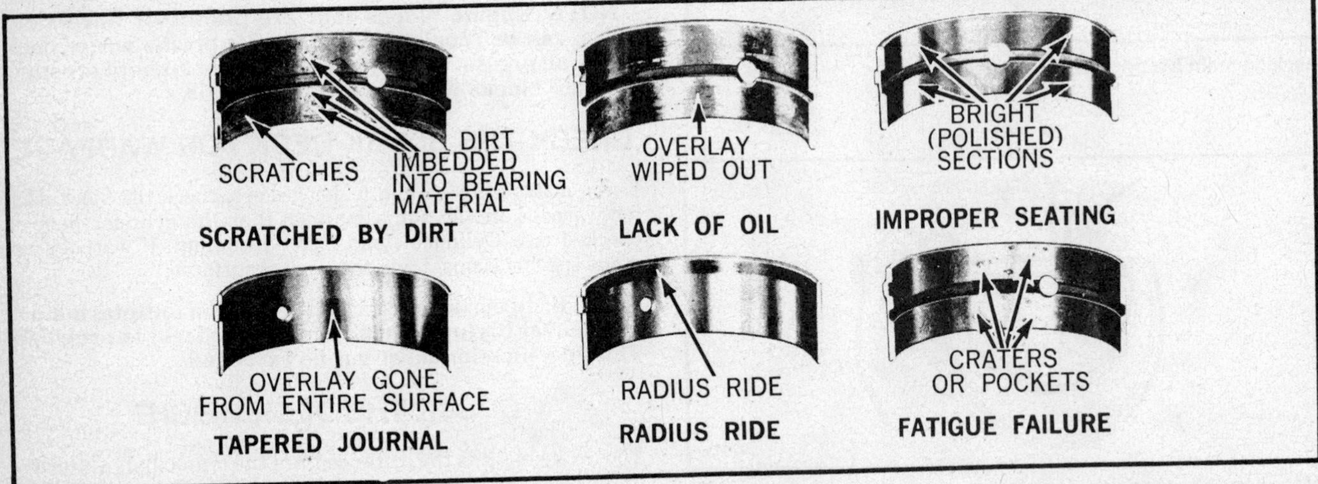

Causes of crankshaft bearing failures

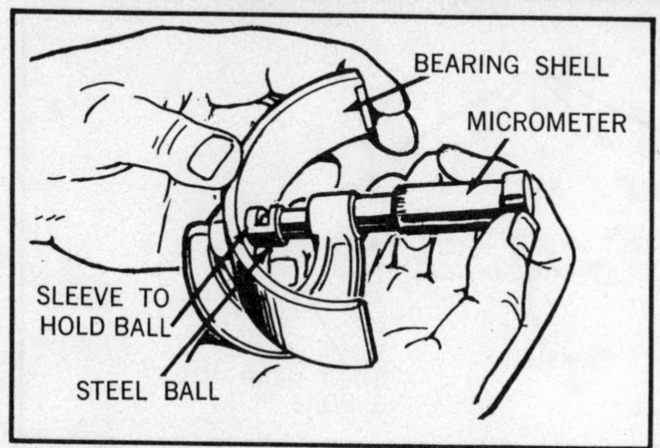

Measuring bearing insert thickness with special ball

Checking the camshaft for straightness

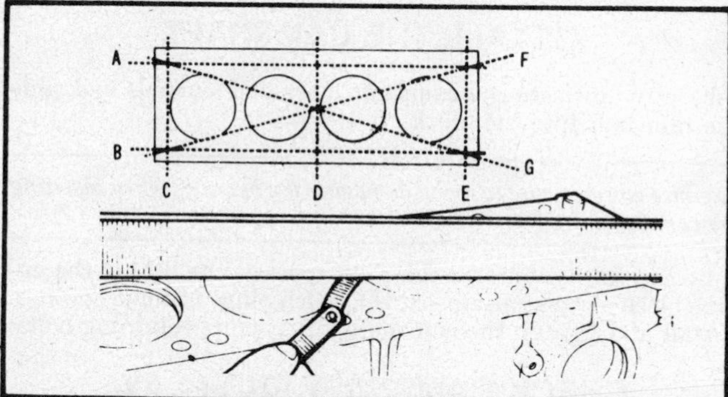

Checking the cylinder block for distortion

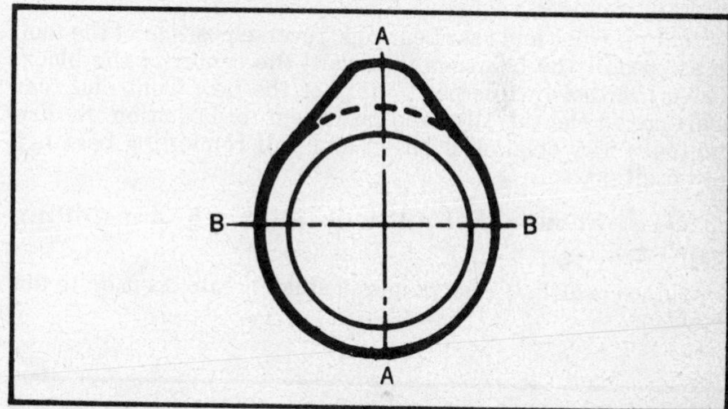

Camshaft lobe measurement—lift is difference between A and B measurements

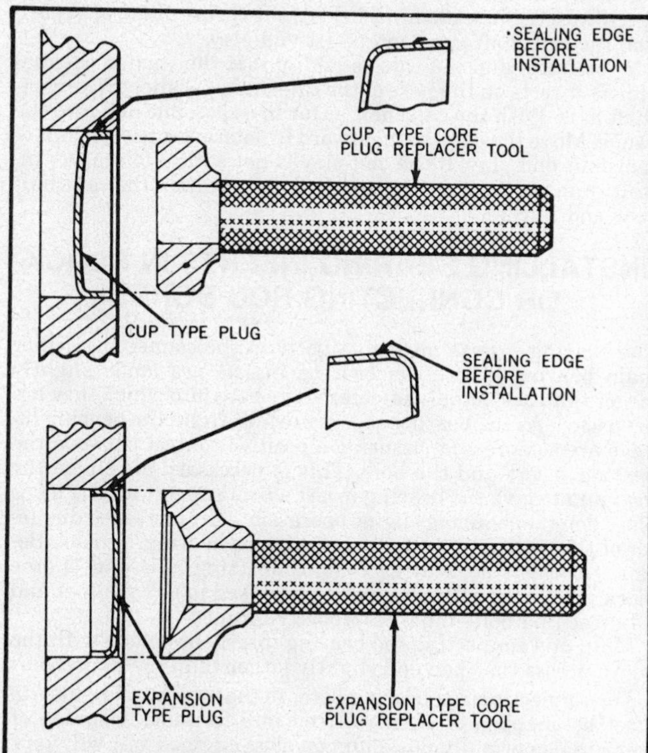

Installation of cup type and expansion type core plugs with special tools

gallery plugs with sealer and install. Drive replacement soft plugs into block using a large drift as a driver.

Rather than reinstalling lead plugs, drill and tap the holes and install threaded plugs, where possible.

CLEAN AND INSPECT THE CAMSHAFT

Degrease the camshaft, using solvent and clean out all oil holes. Visually inspect cam lobes and bearing journals for excessive wear. If a lobe is questionable, check all lobes as indicated below. If a journal or lobe is worn, the camshaft must be reground or replaced.

NOTE: If a journal is worn, there is a good chance that the bushings are worn.

If lobes and journals appear intact, place the front and rear journals in V-blocks and rest a dial indicator on the center journal. Rotate the camshaft to check straightness. If deviation exceeds 0.001 in., replace the camshaft.

Check the camshaft lobes with a micrometer, by measuring the lobes from the nose to base and again at 90°. The lift is determined by subtracting the second measurement from the first. If all exhaust lobes and all intake lobes are not identical with specs, the camshaft must be reground or replaced.

REPLACE THE CAMSHAFT BEARINGS

If excessive wear is indicated or if the engine is being completely rebuilt, camshaft bearings should be replaced as follows: Drive the camshaft rear plug from the block. Assemble the removal puller with its shoulder on the bearing to be removed. Gradually tighten the puller nut until bearing is removed. Remove remaining bearings, leaving the front and rear for last.

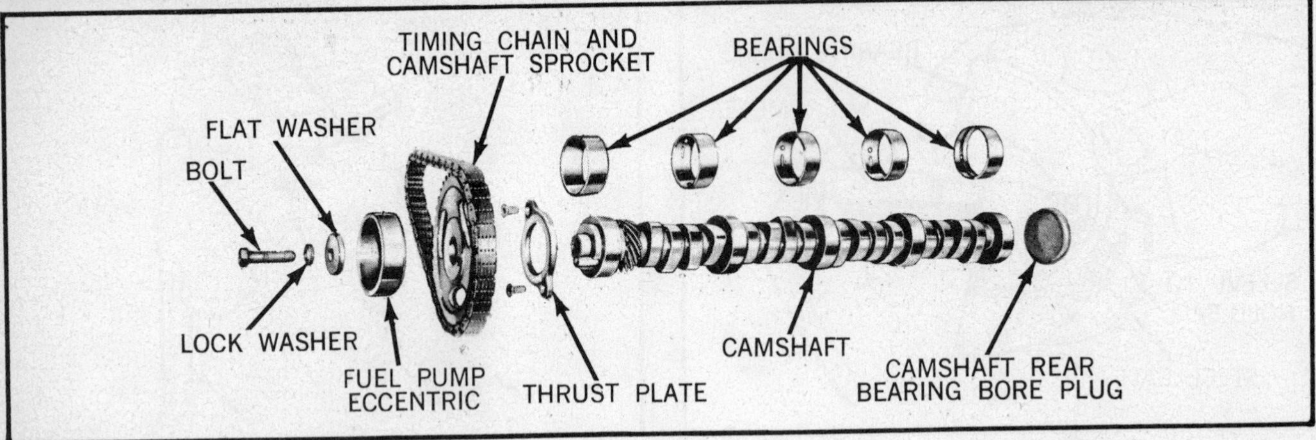

Chain driven camshaft assembly—typical

To remove front and rear bearings, reverse position of the tool, so as to pull the bearings in toward the center of the block. Leave the tool in this position, pilot the new front and rear bearings on the installer and pull them into position. Return the tool to its original position and pull remaining bearings into position.

NOTE: Ensure that oil holes align when installing bearings.

Replace camshaft rear plug and stake it into position to aid retention.

Removing and installing cam bearings with special puller tool—typical

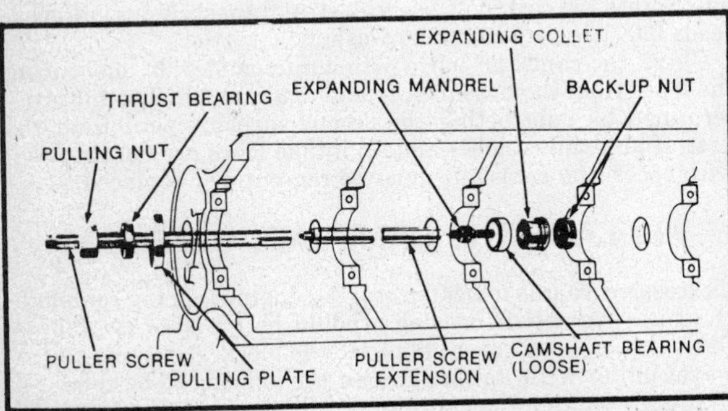

Checking camshaft alignment with Vee blocks and dial indicator

INSTALL THE CAMSHAFT

Liberally lubricate the camshaft lobes and journals and slide the camshaft into the block.

CAUTION

Exercise extreme care to avoid damaging the bearings when inserting the camshaft.

Be careful not to force the shaft towards the rear of the engine block as this can unseat the welch plugs in some engines. Install and tighten the camshaft thrust plate retaining bolts.

CHECK CAMSHAFT END-PLAY

1. Using feeler gauges, determine whether the clearance between the camshaft boss (or gear) and backing plate is within specifications. Install shims behind the thrust plate, or reposition the camshaft gear and retest end-play.
2. Mount a dial indicator stand so that the stem of the dial indicator rests on the nose of the camshaft, parallel to the camshaft axis. Push the camshaft as far in as possible and zero the gauge. Move the camshaft outward to determine the amount of camshaft end-play. If the end-play is not within tolerance, install shims behind the thrust plate or reposition the camshaft gear and retest.

INSTALLING BEARING INSERTS IN BLOCK OR CONNECTING ROD BORES

The bearing inserts must fit tightly in the connecting rod or main bearing bores. The bearing inserts are made slightly larger than the actual diameter of the bore into which they are to be used. As the bearing caps are drawn tight, the bearing inserts are compressed, assuring a positive contact between the bearing insert and the bore. This is necessary to relieve the heat and to give the bearing insert a firm support for the loads place don them during engine operation. This increased diameter of the bearing insert is referred to as bearing "crush". Because of this, the bearing caps, connecting rods and engine block must not be filed, lapped or reworked in any manner and all attaching bolts must be properly torqued.

Main and connecting rod bearing inserts are made with the width across the open end slightly larger than the main bearing or connecting rod bearing bore, so that the bearing inserts must be snapped or lightly forced into its seat. A spread of 0.025 in. is normally minimum on most engines, but will vary from engine to engine. (Some bearing kits will have instructions for the proper installation of the inserts.)

To adjust the bearing spread of the thick wall bearings, such

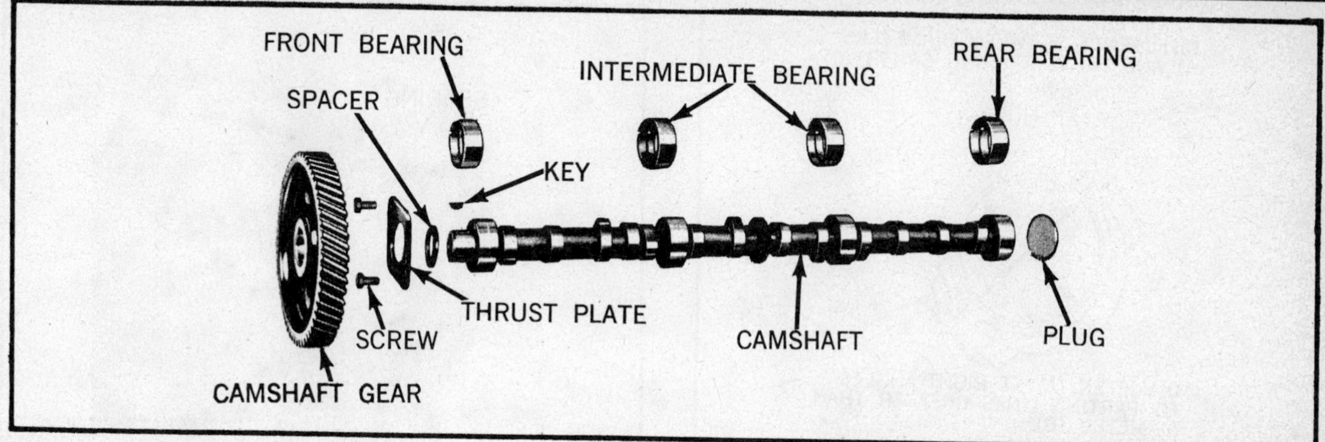

Gear driven camshaft assembly—typical

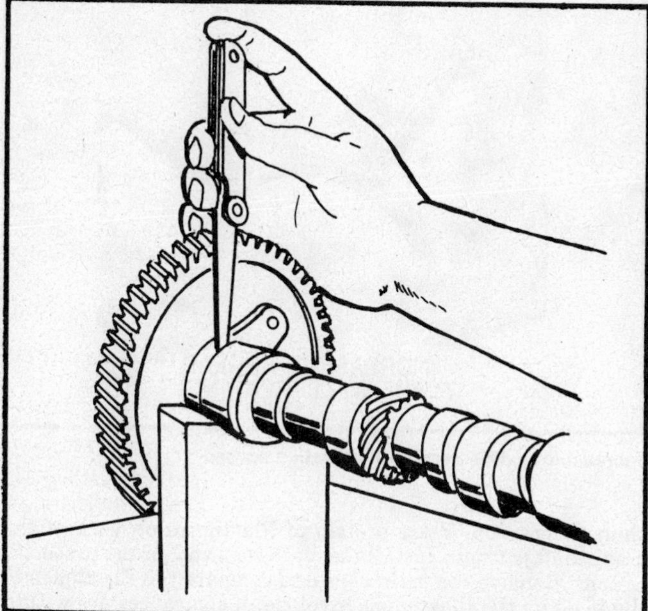

Checking clearance between timing gear and thrust plate with feeler gauge

1. PUSH CAM TO REAR OF ENGINE
2. SET DIAL ON ZERO
3. PULL CAM FORWARD AND RELEASE

Checking camshaft end-play with dial indicator

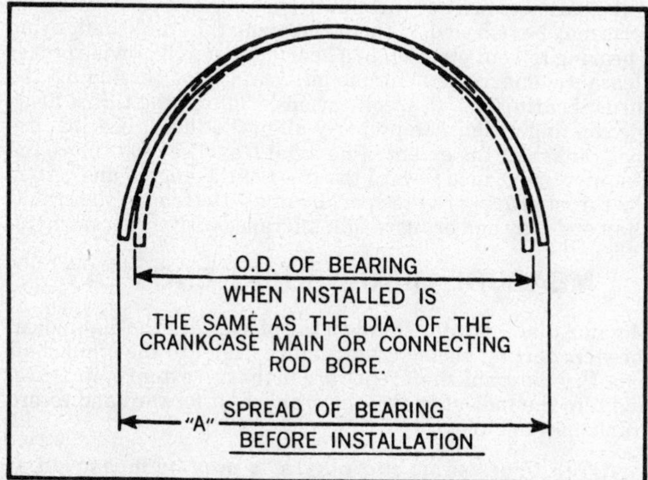

Illustration of bearing insert spread

as main bearing inserts, place one end of the bearing insert on a wood block and strike the other end with a soft mallet to decrease the spread. To increase the spread, place the bearing insert ends on a wood block and strike the back of the insert with a soft mallet, squarely and lightly. The bearing spread on the thin walled bearing inserts, such as connecting rod bearing inserts, can be adjusted by hand, either spreading with the thumbs and forefingers of both hands, or by squeezing the bearing insert by the palm of the hand to decrease the spread. Check the spread distance often during the adjustment procedure.

INSTALL THE REAR MAIN SEAL

Position the block with the bearing saddles facing upward. Lay the rear main seal in its groove and press it lightly into its seat. Place a piece of pipe the same diameter as the crankshaft journal into the saddle and firmly seat the seal. Hold the pipe in position and trim the ends of the seal flush if required.

INSTALL THE CRANKSHAFT

Thoroughly clean the main bearing saddles and caps. Place the upper halves of the bearing inserts on the saddles and press into position.

NOTE: Ensure that the oil holes align.

Press the corresponding bearing inserts into the main bearing caps. Lubricate the upper main bearings and lay the crank-

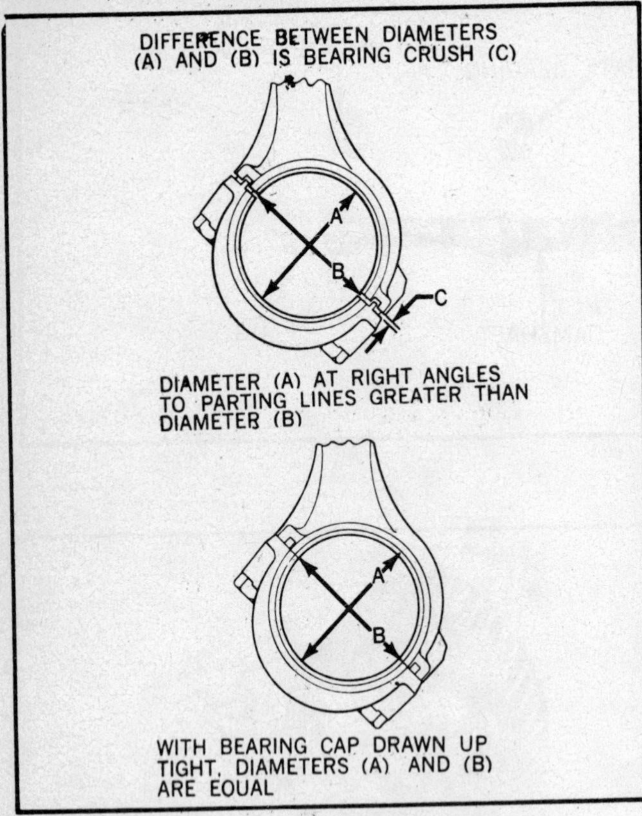

Bearing crush in connecting rod bore

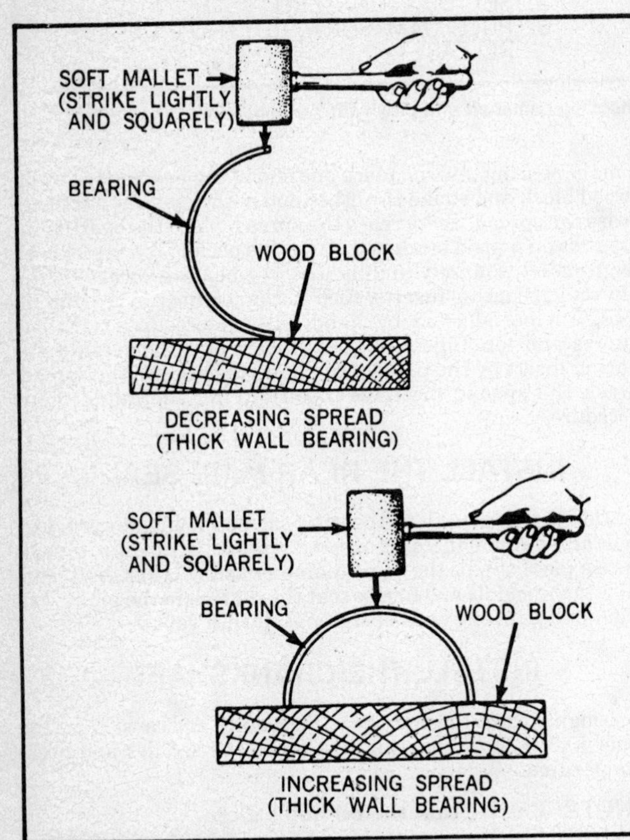

Increasing and decreasing thick-walled bearing spread

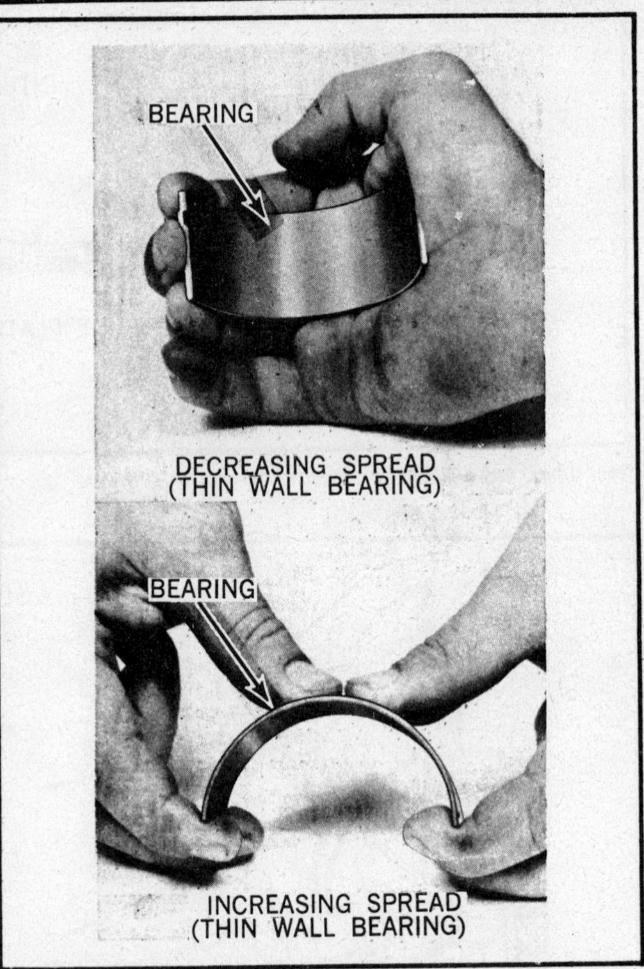

Increasing and decreasing thin-walled spread

shaft in position. Place a strip of Plastigage on each of the crankshaft journals, install the main caps and torque to specifications. Remove the main caps and compare the Plastigage to the scale on the Plastigage envelope. If clearances are within tolerances, remove the Plastigage, turn the crankshaft 90°, wipe off all oil and retest. If all clearances are correct, remove all Plastigage, thoroughly lubricate the main caps and bearing journals and install the main caps.

If clearances are not within tolerance, the upper bearing inserts may be removed, without removing the crankshaft, using a bearing roll out pin. Roll in a bearing that will provide proper clearance and retest. Torque all main caps, excluding the thrust bearing cap, to specifications. Tighten the thrust bearing cap finger tight. To properly align the thrust bearing, pry the crankshaft the extent of its axial travel several times, the last movement held toward the front of the engine and torque the thrust bearing cap to specifications. Determine the crankshaft end-play and bring within tolerance with thrust washers.

MEASURE CRANKSHAFT END-PLAY

Mount a dial indicator stand on the block, with the dial indicator stem resting on the crankshaft parallel to the crankshaft axis. Pry the crankshaft rearward to the full extent of its travel and zero the indicator. Pry the crankshaft forward and record crankshaft end-play.

NOTE: Crankshaft end-play also may be measured at the thrust bearing, using feeler gauges.

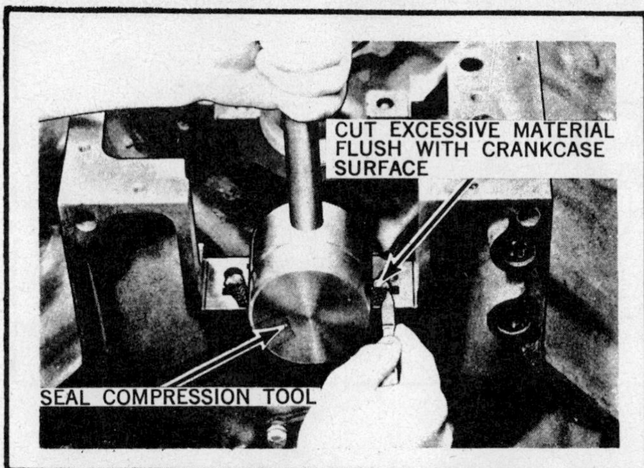

Seating rear main bearing seal

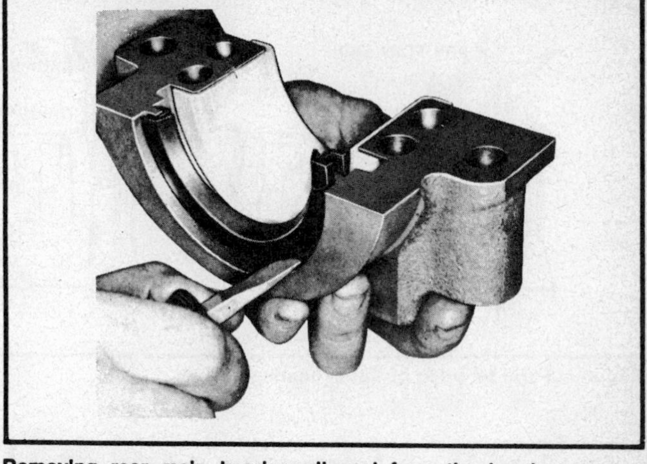

Removing rear main bearing oil seal from the bearing cap—preformed seal type

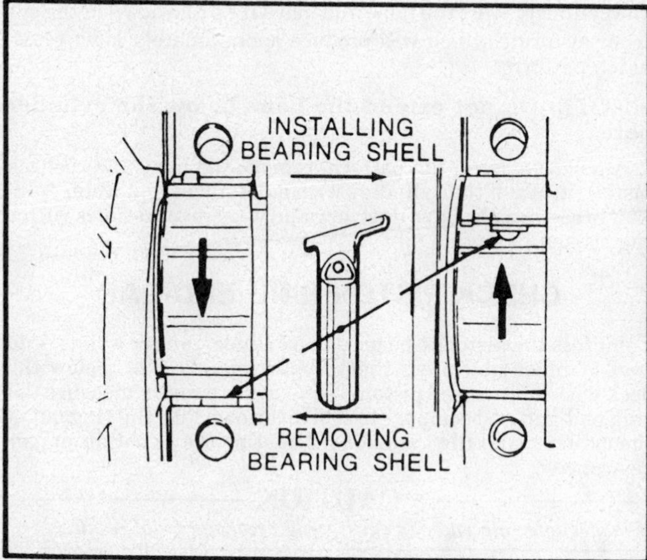

Main bearing insert identification—typical

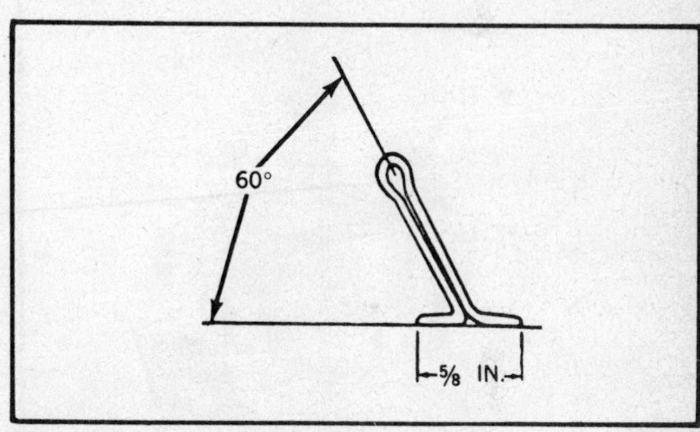

Bearing insert roll-out pin made from cotter pin

Removing and installing main bearing inserts with roll-out pins (cross section of crankshaft journal)

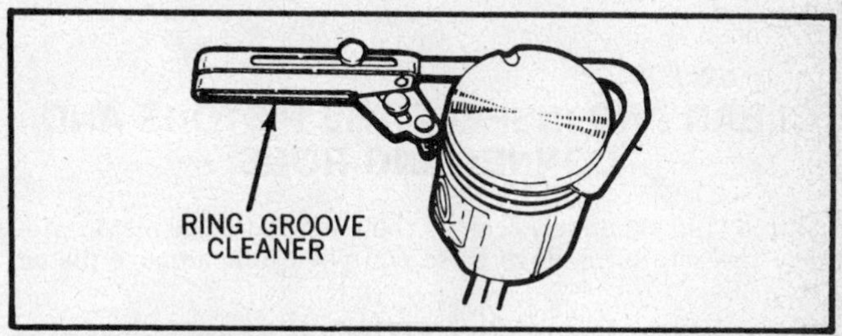

Cleaning piston ring grooves—typical

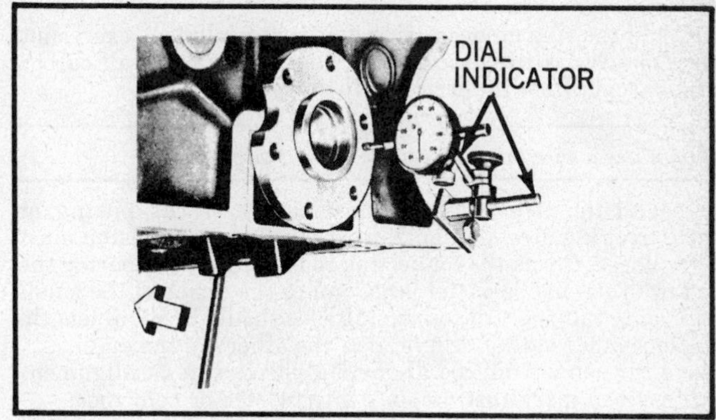

Checking crankshaft end-play—typical

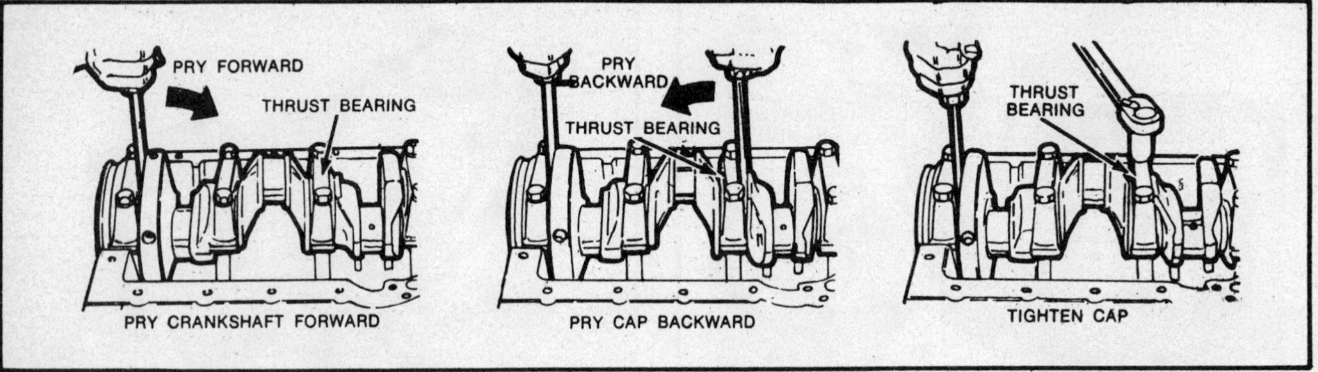

Alignment and torquing of thrust bearing

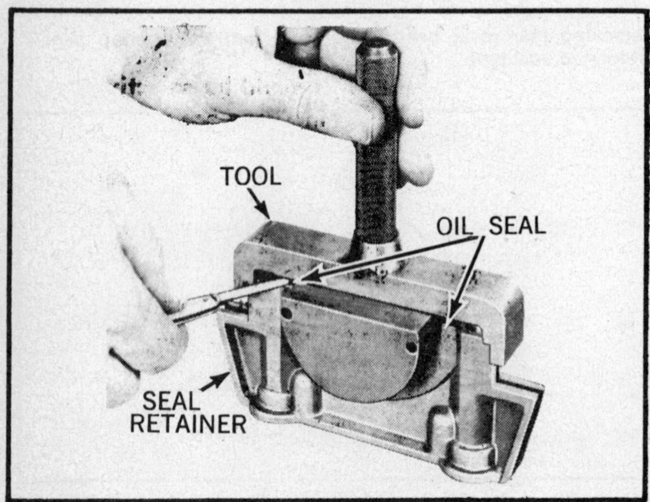

Installing rear main bearing oil seal in bearing cap

CLEAN AND INSPECT THE PISTONS AND CONNECTING RODS

Using a ring expander, remove the rings from the piston. Remove the retaining rings (if so equipped) and remove piston pin.

CAUTION

If the piston pin must be pressed out, determine the proper method and use the proper tools; otherwise the piston will distort.

Clean the ring grooves using an appropriate tool, exercising care to avoid cutting too deeply. Thoroughly clean all carbon and varnish from the piston with solvent.

CAUTION

Do not use a wire brush or caustic solvent on pistons.

Inspect the pistons for scuffing, scoring, cracks, pitting, or excessive ring groove wear. If wear is evident, the piston must be replaced. Check the connecting rod length by measuring the rod from the inside of the large end to the inside of the small end using calipers. All connecting rods should be equal length. Replace any rod that differs from the others in the engine. Have the connecting rod alignment checked in an alignment fixture by a machinist. Replace any twisted or bent rods.

Magnaflux the connecting rods to locate stress cracks. If cracks are found, replace the connecting rod.

FINISH HONE THE CYLINDERS

Chuck a flexible drive hone into a power drill and insert it into the cylinder. Start the hone and move it up and down in the cylinder at a rate which will produce approximately a 60° cross-hatch pattern.

NOTE: Do not extend the hone below the cylinder bore.

After developing the pattern, remove the hone and recheck piston fit. Wash the cylinders with a detergent and water solution to remove abrasive dust, dry and wipe several times with a rag soaked in engine oil.

CHECK PISTON RING END-GAP

Compress the piston to be used in a cylinder, one at a time, into that cylinder and press them approximately 1 in. below the deck with an inverted piston. Using feeler gauges, measure the ring end-gap and compare to specifications. Pull the ring out of the cylinder and file the ends with a fine file to obtain proper clearance.

CAUTION

If inadequate ring end-gap exists, ring breakage could result.

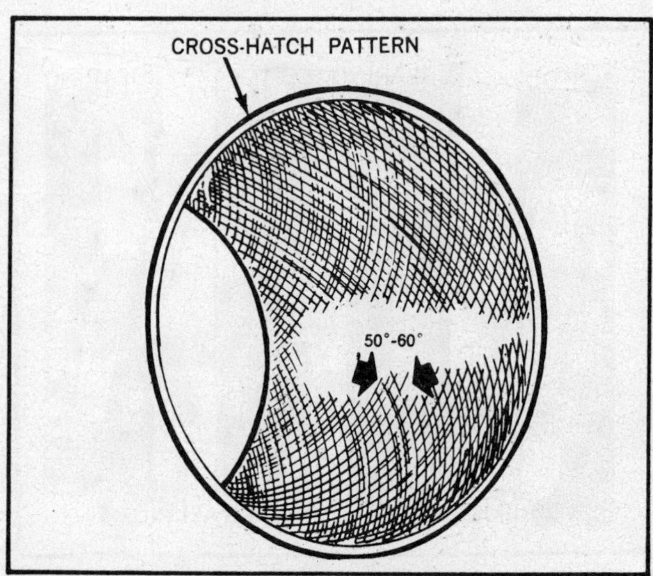

Cross hatching of cylinder bore by finish honing

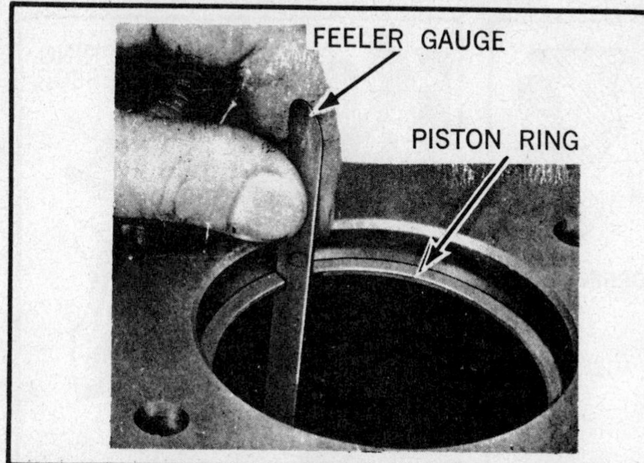

Checking ring gap in cylinder bore

FIT THE PISTONS TO THE CYLINDERS

Using a telescope gauge and micrometer, or a dial gauge, measure the cylinder bore diameter perpendicular to the piston pin, 2 ½ in. below the deck. Measure the piston perpendicular to its pin on the skirt. The difference between the two measurements is the piston clearance. If the clearance is within specifications or slightly below (after boring or honing), finish honing is all that is required. If the clearance is excessive, try to obtain a slightly larger piston to bring clearance within specifications. Where this is not possible, obtain the first oversize piston and hone (or if necessary, bore) the cylinder to size.

ASSEMBLE THE PISTONS AND CONNECTING RODS

Inspect piston pin, connecting rod, small end bushing and piston bore for galling, scoring or excessive wear. If evident, replace defective part(s). Measure the I.D. of the piston boss and connecting rod small end and the O.D. of the piston pin. If within specifications, assemble piston pin and rod.

CAUTION

CAUTION: If piston pin must be pressed in, determine the proper method and use the proper tools; otherwise the piston will distort.

Install the lock rings; ensure that they seat properly. If the parts are not within specifications, determine the service method for the type of engine. In some cases, piston and pin are serviced as an assembly when either is defective. Others specify reaming the piston and connecting rods for an oversize pin. If the connecting rod bushing is worn, it may in many cases be replaced. Reaming the piston and replacing the rod bushing are machine shop operations.

INSTALL THE PISTON RINGS

Inspect the ring grooves in the piston for excessive wear or taper. If necessary, recut the groove(s) for use with an overwidth ring or a standard ring and spacer. If the groove is worn uniformly, overwidth rings or standard rings and spacers may be installed without recutting. Roll the outside of the ring around the groove to check for burrs or deposits. If any are found, remove with a fine file. Hold the ring in the groove and measure side clearance. If necessary, correct as indicated above.

NOTE: Always install any additional spacers above the piston ring.

The ring grooves must be deep enough to allow the ring to seat below the lands. In many cases, a "go-no-go" depth gauge will be provided with the piston rings. Shallow grooves may be corrected by recutting, while deep grooves require some type of filler or expander behind the piston. Consult the piston ring supplier concerning the suggested method. Install the rings on the piston, lowest ring first, using a ring expander.

NOTE: Position the ring markings as specified by the manufacturer.

INSTALL THE PISTONS

Press the upper connecting rod bearing halves into the connecting rods and the lower halves into the connecting rod caps. Position the piston ring gaps according to specifications and lubricate the pistons. Install a ring compressor on the piston and press two long (8 in.) pieces of plastic tubing over the rod bolts. Using the plastic tubes as a guide, press the piston into the bore and onto the crankshaft with a wooden hammer handle. After seating the rod on the crankshaft journal, remove the tubes and install the cap nuts finger tight. Install the remain-

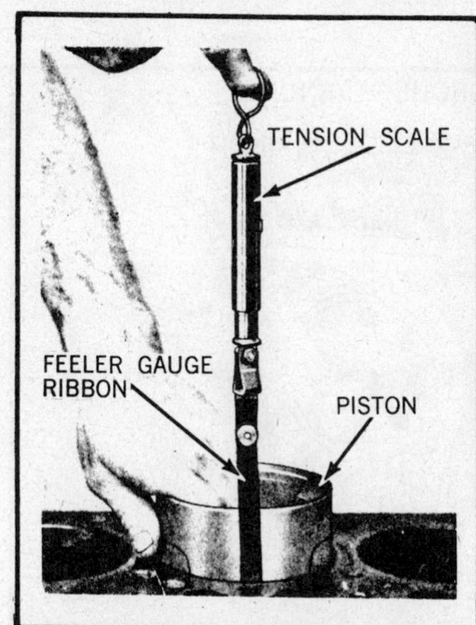

Checking piston to cylinder bore clearance

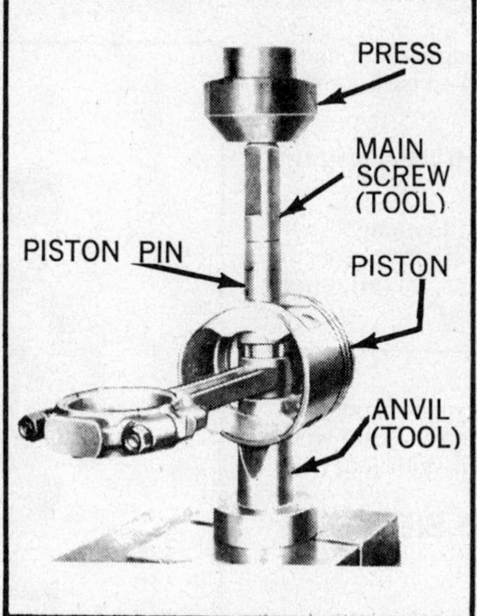

Removing or installing piston pin

Installing rings on piston with the use of an expander tool

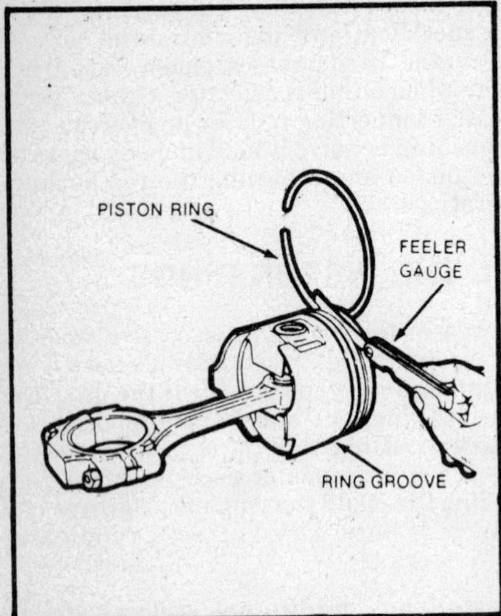

Checking ring to groove side clearance

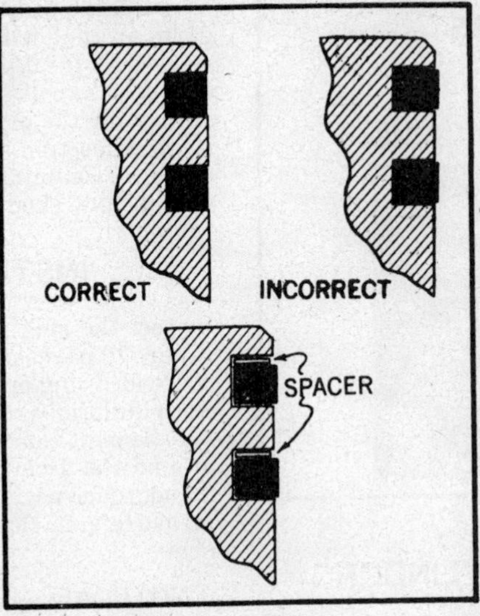

Correct ring spacer installation

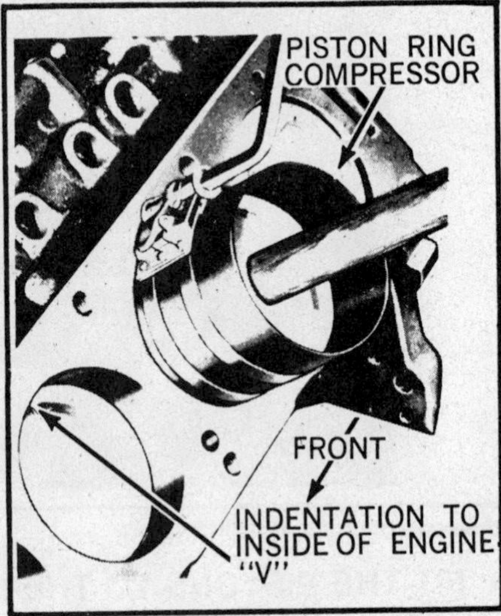

Installing piston assembly with straight sided ring compressor tool

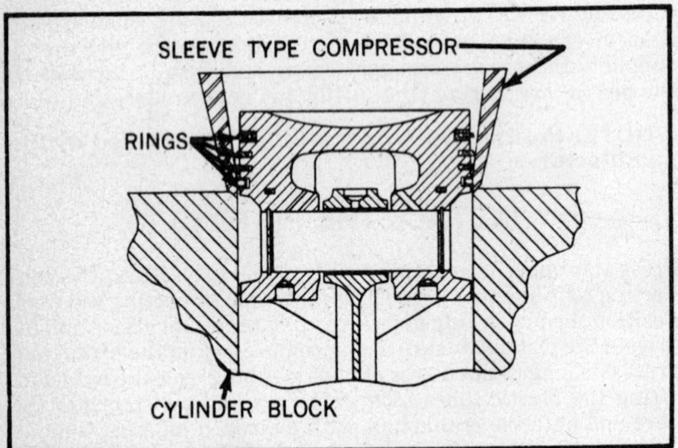

Installing piston assembly with a tapered sleeve type ring compressor tool

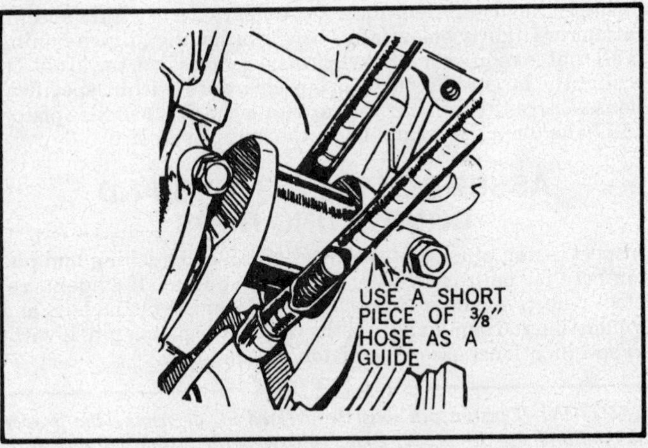

Tubing used as a guide during piston-connecting rod installation

ing pistons in the same manner. Invert the engine and check the bearing clearance at two points (90° apart) on each journal with Plastigage.

NOTE: Do not turn the crankshaft with Plastigage installed.

If clearance is within tolerances, remove all Plastigage, thoroughly lubricate the journals and torque the rod caps to specifications. If clearance is not within specifications, install different thickness bearing inserts and recheck.

CAUTION

Never shim or file the connecting rods or caps.

Always install plastic tube sleeves over the rod bolts when the caps are not installed, to protect the crankshaft journals.

CHECK CONNECTING ROD SIDE CLEARANCE

Determine the clearance between the sides of the connecting rods and the crankshaft, using feeler gauges. If clearance is below the minimum tolerance, the rod may be machined to pro-

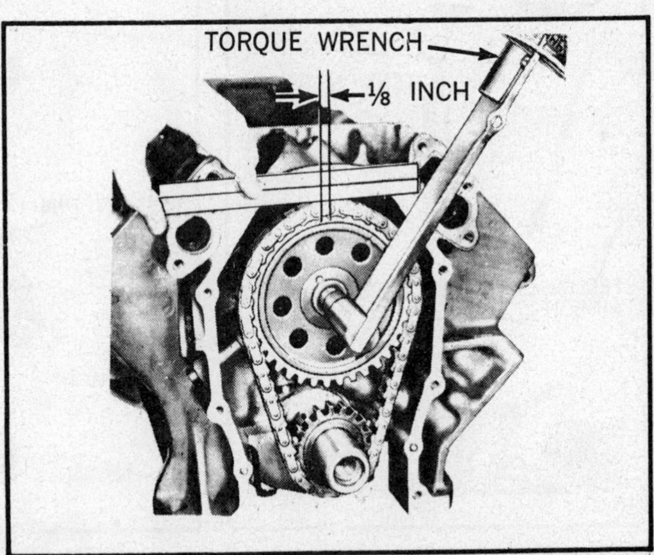

Using torque wrench to measure timing chain deflection

vide adequate clearance. If clearance is excessive, substitute an unworn rod and recheck. If clearance is still outside specifications, the crankshaft must be welded and reground, or replaced.

INSPECT THE TIMING CHAIN

Visually inspect the timing chain for broken or loose links and replace the chain if any are found. If the chain will flex sideways, it must be replaced.

NOTE: If the original timing chain is to be reused, install it in its original position.

INSPECT THE TIMING CHAIN DEFLECTION

Different methods are used by the engine manufacturers to measure the timing chain deflection and to determine the condition of the chain. Three such methods are as follows:

1. Rotate the crankshaft in a counterclockwise direction to remove the slack on the left side of the chain. Make a reference mark on the block and measure from the mark to the outside of the chain, halfway between the camshaft and crankshaft sprockets. Rotate the crankshaft in the opposite direction and remove the slack from the right side of the chain. Force the chain outward on the left side and measure from the original reference mark to the chain. The difference between the first and second measurements is the amount of chain deflection. The allowable deflection can be from 1/4–1/2 in., depending upon the manufacturer.
2. The second method of chain deflection measurement is to block the crankshaft to prevent movement. Using a torque wrench and socket on the camshaft sprocket bolt and placing a scale even with the edge of a chain link, apply 30 ft. lbs. (w/cylinder head on block) or 15 ft. lbs. (w/cylinder head off block) in the direction of engine rotation and obtain a reference point on the scale to link. Apply 30 ft. lbs. (w/cylinder head on block) or 15 ft. lbs. (w/cylinder head off block) in the opposite direction and measure the chain movement on the scale. The measurement should not exceed 1/8 in.
3. A third method of measuring timing chain deflection is to rotate the crankshaft clockwise until the No. 1 piston is on its firing stroke at TDC. The damper timing mark should point to TDC on the timing degree indicator. Remove the valve cover to expose the rocker arms of the companion or opposite cylinder to the No. 1 piston. Install a dial indicator on the push rod or rocker arm of the exhaust valve of this opposite or companion cylinder in a manner to register the push rod or rocker arm upward movement. Zero the dial indicator and slowly turn the crankshaft counterclockwise until the slightest movement is recorded on the dial indicator. Stop and observe the damper timing mark for the number of degrees of travel from TDC. If the reading on the timing degree indicator exceeds 6–8 degrees, replace the timing chain and sprockets.

OVERHEAD CAM TIMING CHAINS

Timing chains for the overhead cam engines are difficult to examine for looseness due to the chain tensioners used to maintain a controlled tension on the chain while in use. The chains are usually checked off the engine by measurement of a predetermined number of links with the chain stretched tight. Should the measurement of the links exceed the manufacturer's specifications, the chain should be replaced.

Another method is to wrap the chain around the sprockets and measure each chain/sprocket diameter. Should the manufacturer's specifications be exceeded, the chain and sprocket should be replaced. Where no specifications exist, the repairperson must make a professional determination to either replace the chain and sprockets or not.

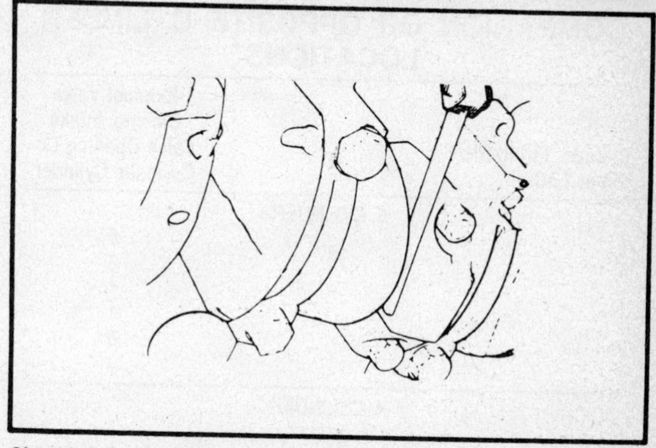

Checking connecting rod end clearance with feeler gauge blade

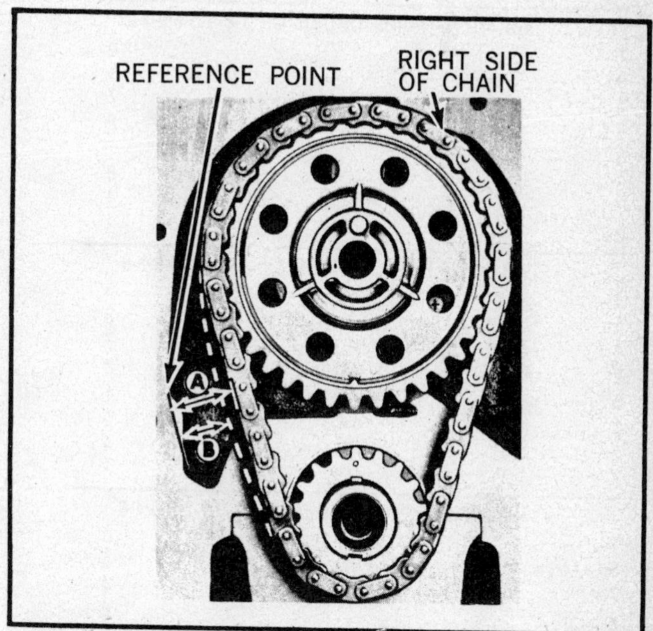

Checking timing chain deflection using point on engine blocks as reference point

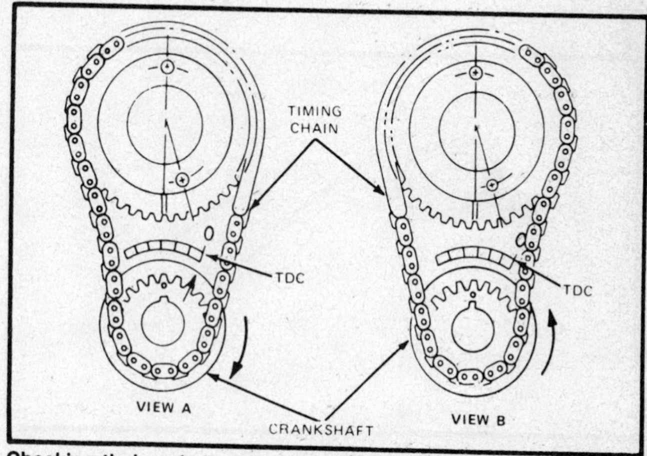

Checking timing chain deflection with timing indicator scale

COMPANION OR OPPOSITE CYLINDER LOCATIONS

Cylinder Firing-Piston at TDC	Exhaust Valve Closing, Intake Valve Opening On Opposite Cylinder
6 CYLINDER	
1	6
5	2
3	4
6	1
2	5
4	3
4 CYLINDER	
1	4
3	2
4	1
2	3
V-8 WITH FIRING ORDER OF 1-8-4-3-6-5-7-2	
1	6
8	5
4	7
3	2
6	1
5	8
7	4
2	3
V-8 WITH FIRING ORDER OF 1-5-4-2-6-3-7-8	
1	6
5	3
4	7
2	8
6	1
3	5
7	4
8	2
V-8 WITH FIRING ORDER OF 1-3-7-2-6-5-4-8	
1	6
3	5
7	4
2	8
6	1
5	3
4	7
8	2

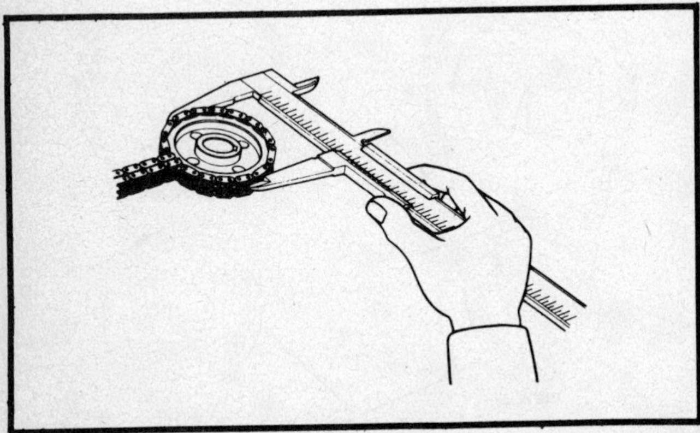

Example of timing chain/sprocket measurement

TIMING BELT INSPECTION

The timing belt should be inspected for hardness, separation of plys, cracks, worn or missing teeth and abnormal side wear. If the timing belt is removed for any reason, a new belt must be installed. Do not re-use the old belt.

CHECK TIMING GEAR BACKLASH AND RUNOUT

Mount a dial indicator with its stem resting on a tooth of the camshaft gear. Rotate the gear until all slack is removed and zero the indicator. Rotate the gear in the opposite direction until slack is removed and record gear backlash. Mount the indicator with its stem resting on the edge of the camshaft gear, parallel to the axis of the camshaft. Zero the indicator and turn

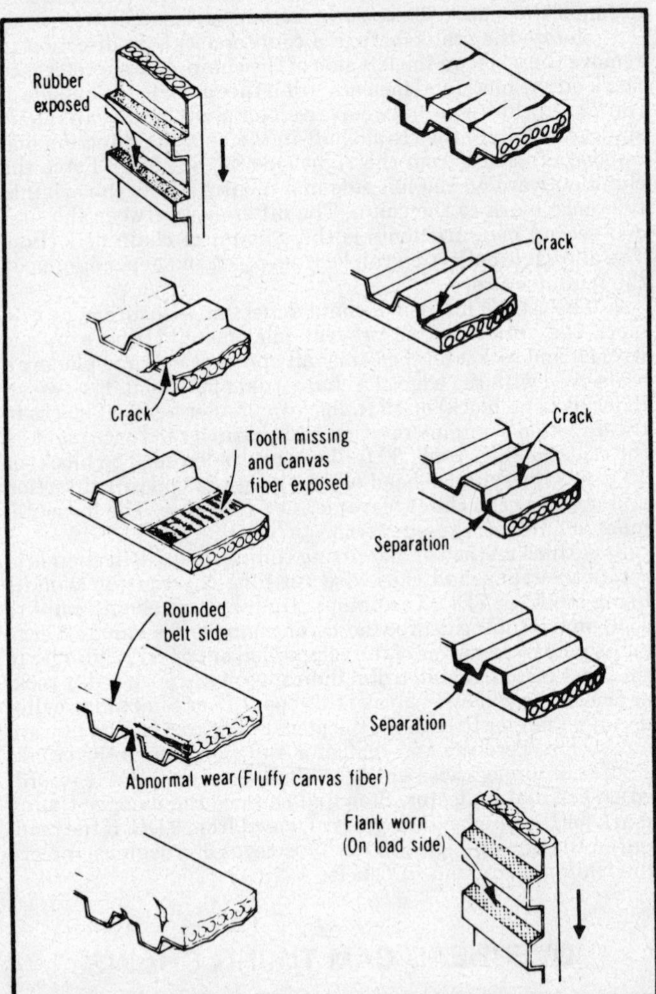

Flaw conditions of timing belt

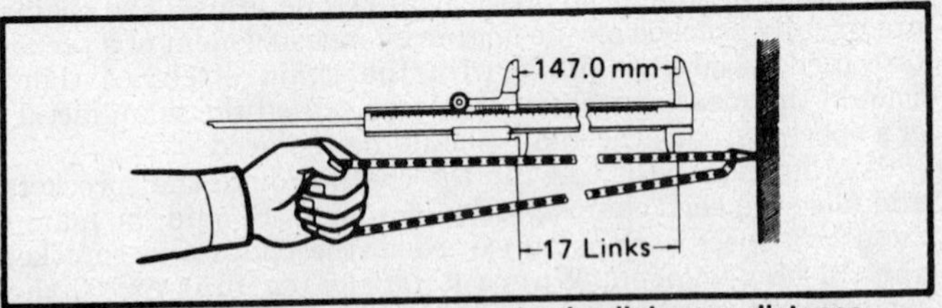

Example of timing chain measurement using links as a distance factor

the camshaft gear one full turn, recording the runout. If either backlash or runout exceed specifications, replace the worn gear(s).

OIL PUMP

Three major types of oil pumps are used, positive gear type (with or without crescent), rotor type and the trochoid type. Regardless of the type pump used, a determination must be made, by measurements and examination, in regards to the re-use, overhaul or replacement of the oil pump assembly.

NOTE: It is recommended to replace the oil pump assembly with a new unit when a major engine overhaul is done.

Inspection

The oil pump and its components must be inspected for any of the following conditions.

1. Worn, pitted or damaged gear teeth surfaces.
2. Abnormal gear side wear, scores or burrs.
3. Oil pump body and gear pockets for abnormal wear, scores, burrs, grooves or nicks.
4. Correct measurement of internal components and body to manufacturer's specifications.
5. Pressure regulator valve for wear, scores, nicks or burrs.
6. Pressure regulator spring for distortion, breakage, correct length and tension.

Priming the Oil Pump

Before the engine start-up, the oil pump must be primed. Manufacturers vary in their recommendations with either engine oil or petroleum jelly used as the priming agent. Whenever possible, follow the manufacturer's recommended priming procedure.

Completing the Rebuilding Process

Following the above procedures, complete the rebuilding process as follows:

Fill the oil pump with oil, or petroleum jelly, to prevent cavitating (sucking air) on initial engine start up. Install the oil pump and the pickup tube on the engine. Coat the oil pan gasket as necessary and install the gasket and the oil pan. Mount the flywheel and the crankshaft vibrational damper or pulley on the crankshaft.

NOTE: Always use new bolts when installing the flywheel.

Inspect the clutch shaft pilot bushing in the crankshaft. If the bushing is excessively worn, remove it with an expanding puller and a slide hammer and tap a new bushing into place.

Position the engine, cylinder head side up. Lubricate the lifters and install them into their bores. Install the cylinder head and torque it as specified in the car section. Insert the pushrods (where applicable) and install the rocker shaft(s) (if so equipped) or position the rocker arms on the pushrods. If solid lifters are utilized, adjust the valves to the "cold" specifications.

Mount the intake and exhaust manifolds, the carburetor(s), the distributor and spark plugs. Adjust the point gap and the static ignition timing. Mount all accessories and install the engine in the car. Fill the radiator with coolant and the crankcase with high quality engine oil.

BREAK-IN PROCEDURE

Before starting the engine, be sure all coolant hoses are attached and tight, the coolant level is correct, a new oil filter is installed and the crankcase filled with the proper level of oil.

The oil pump should be primed and if possible, the engine lubrication system should be charged with a pressure tank. Adjust the tappets (if required), the timing and carburetor as accurately as possible.

Start the engine and adjust the throttle to an approximate engine speed of 1000 to 2000 rpm, until the engine reaches normal operating temperature, normally within 20–30 minutes.

CAUTION

Do not leave the vehicle unattended during the warm-up period. Observe the engine operation and check for any oil or coolant leaks. Stop the engine immediately if a problem exists, to avoid engine damage.

After the engine has "run-in", lower the idle speed and stop the engine. Retorque the cylinder head bolts as required.

NOTE: Engines with aluminum heads or blocks must be allowed to cool to room temperature before any bolts are retorqued.

After rechecking the coolant and oil levels, make any further adjustments as necessary.

Follow the manufacturer's recommended driving break-in procedure or as a general rule, the following procedures may be used.

Drive the vehicle on the highway and accelerate from 30–50 mph, approximately 10–15 times, traffic flow permitting, to properly seat the piston rings to the cylinder walls. If traffic flow does not permit this procedure, accelerate the engine rapidly during shifting through the intermediate gears. The vehicle should be put in light duty service for the first 50 miles and sustained high speed should be avoided during the first 100 miles. Most important: Do not lug the engine. (Lugging exists when the engine does not respond to further opening of the throttle.)

INDEX

INDEX

GENERAL INFORMATION—DIESEL ENGINES

Diesel engines have basically the same internal components as gasoline powered engines. The major differences are the type of fuel used and the manner in which the fuel is directed to the combustion chamber. The diesel engine also lacks the conventional spark type ignition, but depends upon the increase of temperature of the air in the cylinder as it is compressed by the upward piston movement within the cylinder. As the piston nears its top dead center (TDC) position, the fuel is injected into the cylinder in a spray or atomized state and, due to the high temperature of the compressed air, the mixture of fuel and air ignites, forcing the piston downward in a proper developing stroke due to the expanding gases.

Diesel engine are manufactured in two major styles, four and two cycle engines. Both are used in vehicle applications in the transportation field.

It is easier to understand the function of the diesel engine parts when a general understanding of what happens in the combustion chamber during each of the four piston strokes, comprising the four cycles, is explained.

In order for the diesel engine to function properly, valves and injectors must act in direct relation to each other and to the four strokes of the engine. The intake and exhaust valves are camshaft operated, linked by tappets or cam followers, pushrods and rocker arms. the injectors are operated by a pump timed to the crankshaft and/or camshaft rotation to provide a spray of fuel into the combustion chamber at the precise moment for efficient combustion.

STROKES OF THE FOUR CYCLE DIESEL ENGINE

Intake Stroke

During the intake stroke, the piston travels downward with

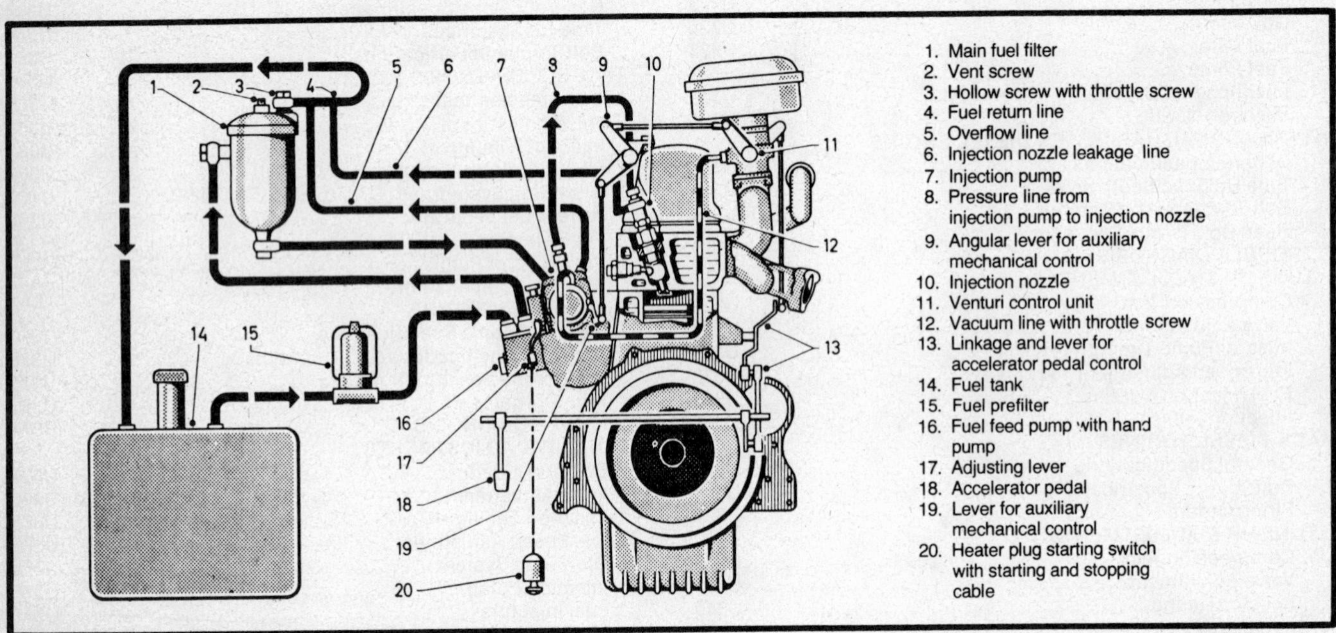

Diesel engine fuel supply system—typical

FUEL FEED OPERATING PRINCIPLE COMPARISON CHART

<table>
<tr><th>Stroke</th><th>Diesel</th><th>Fuel Injection</th><th>Carburetor</th></tr>
<tr><td>INDUCTION OR INTAKE</td><td>Intake of air only</td><td>Intake of air only. Injection of fuel during induction</td><td>Intake of an air-fuel mixture, measured by the carburetor</td></tr>
<tr><td>COMPRESSION</td><td>High compression of the air: Example—Ratio of 22.2/1. Temperature 600°C.</td><td colspan="2">Compression of the mixture Example—Ratio of 8.8/1. Temperature 380°C.</td></tr>
<tr><td>End of stroke</td><td>Injection of fuel which ignites spontaneously</td><td colspan="2">Ignition of the mixture by the spark plug.</td></tr>
<tr><td>IGNITION OR POWER</td><td>Combustion and expansion</td><td colspan="2">Combustion and expansion</td></tr>
<tr><td>EXHAUST</td><td colspan="3">Discharge of the burnt gasses</td></tr>
</table>

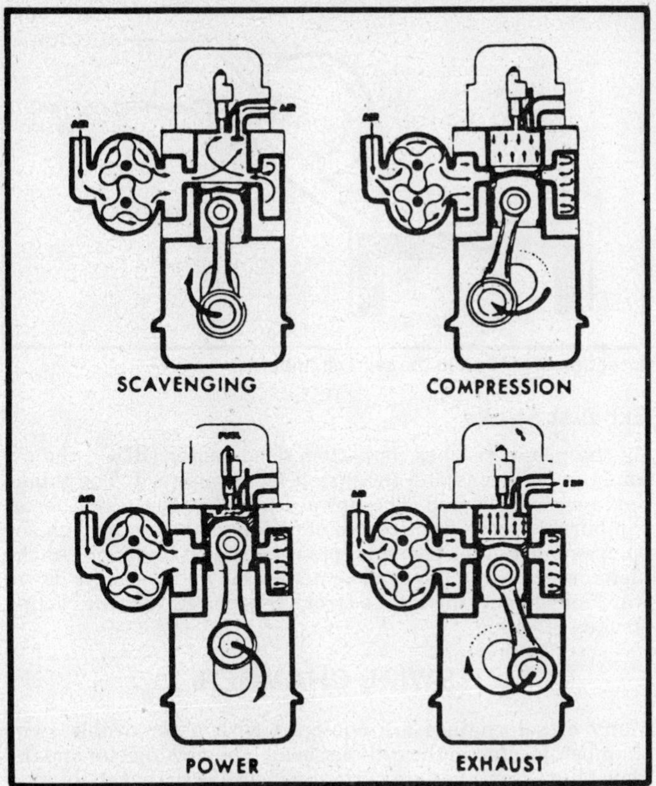

Two stroke diesel engine—In-line

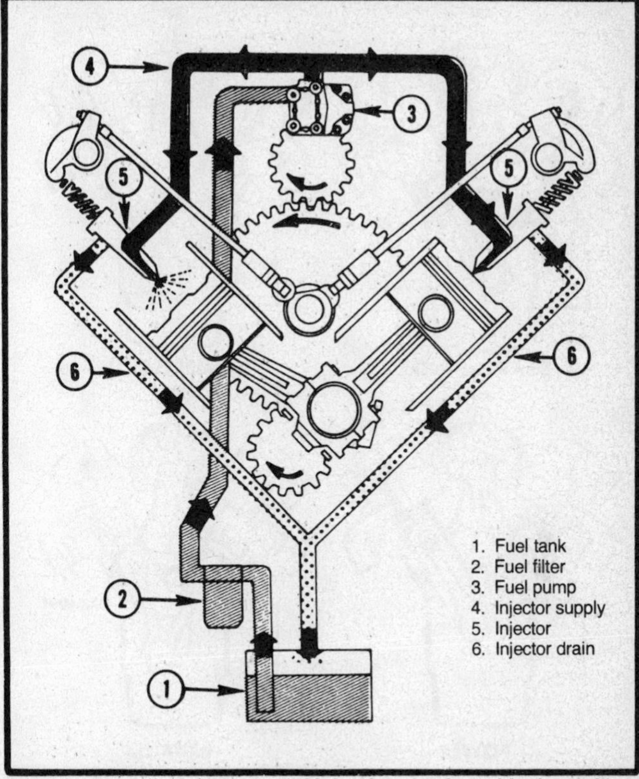

Cross section of a cam operated injection nozzle and fuel supply

the intake valve open and the exhaust valve closed. The downward travel of the piston allows and draws atmospheric air into the cylinder from the induction system. On turbocharged engines, the induction system is pressurized as the turbocharger forces more air into the cylinder. The intake charge consists of air only and contains no fuel mixture.

Compression Stroke

At the end of the intake stroke with the piston at bottom dead center, (BDC), the intake valve closes and the piston starts upward on its compression stroke. The exhaust valve remains closed. At the end of the compression stroke., air in the combustion chamber has been forced by the piston to occupy a smaller space than it occupied at the beginning of the stroke. Thus, compression ratio is the direct proportion of the amount of space the air occupied in the combustion chamber before and after being compressed. Diesel engine compression ratios range from approximately 14:1 to 22:1 in comparison to the gasoline engine compression of from 7.5:1 to 9.5:1. Compressing the air into a small space causes the temperature of the air to a point high enough to ignite the fuel, which has a flash point under the temperature level. During the last part of the compression stroke and the early part of the power stroke, a small metered charge of fuel is injected into the combustion chamber and ignited by the existing hot compressed air.

Power Stroke

During the beginning of the power stroke, the piston is pushed downward by the burning and expanding gases. Both the intake and exhaust valves remain closed. As more fuel is added to the cylinder and burns, the gases become hotter and expand more to force the piston downward and thus add driving force to the crankshaft rotation.

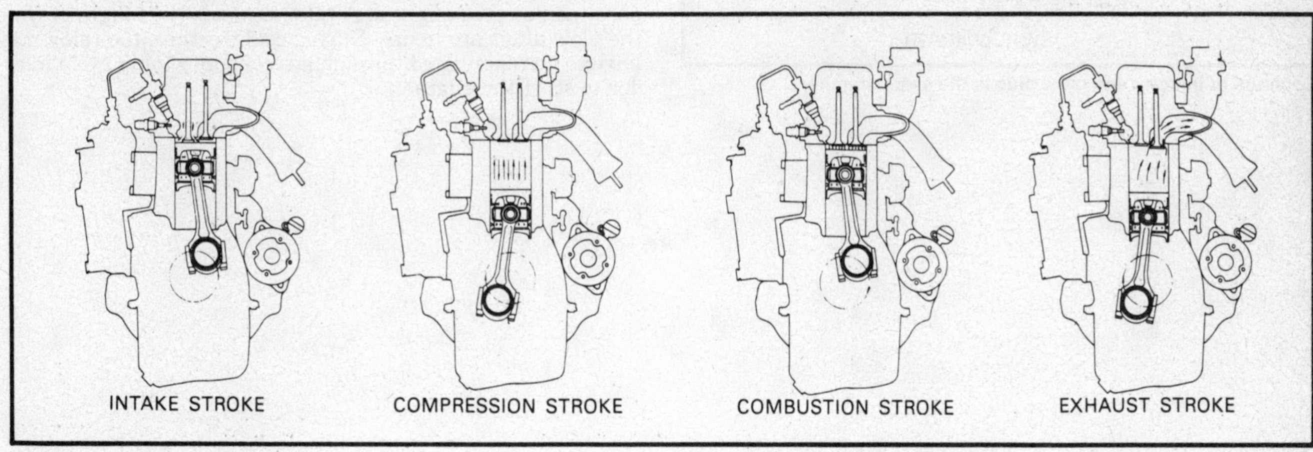

Diesel engine four cycle strokes

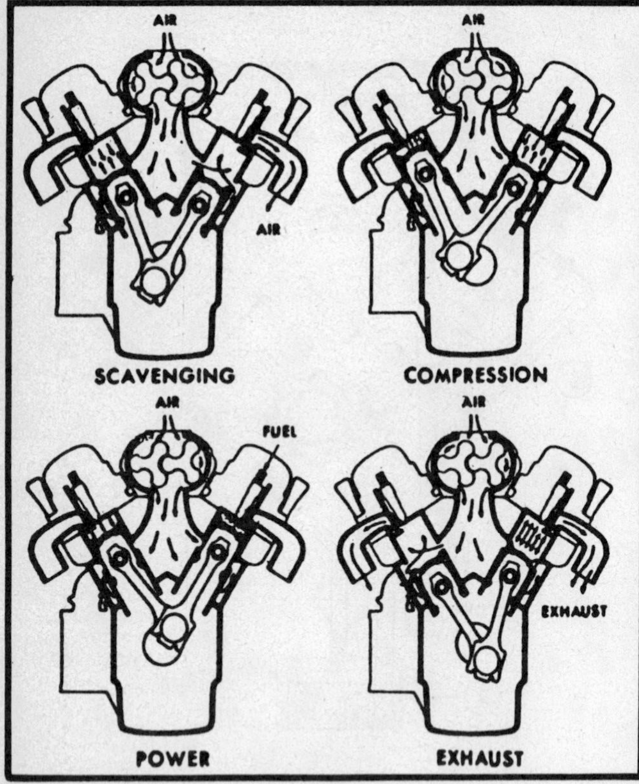

Two stroke diesel engine—V-8 engine

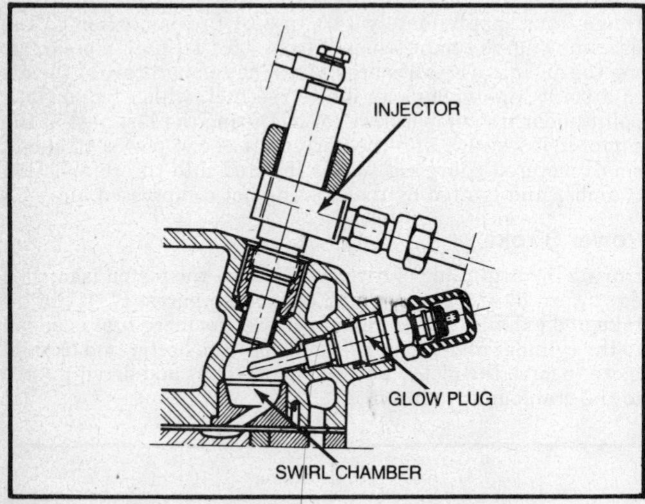

Location of injector and glow plug in the swirl chamber

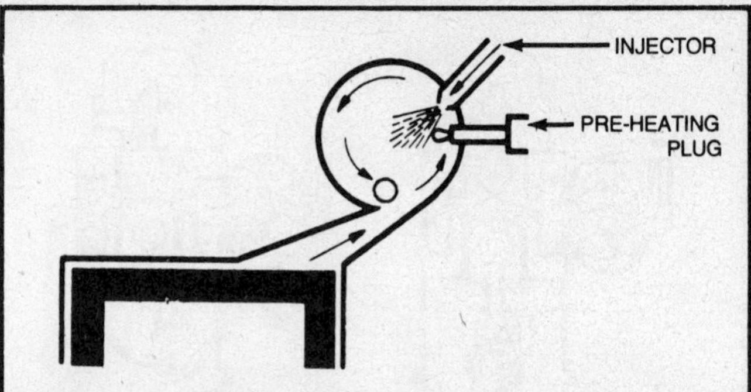

Direction of air flow in the swirl chamber

Exhaust Stroke

As the piston reaches its bottom dead center (BDC), the exhaust valve opens and the piston moves upward. The intake valve remains closed. The upward travel of the piston forces the burned gases from the combustion chamber through the open exhaust valve port and into the exhaust manifold. As the piston reaches the top dead center (TDC) and starts its downward movement, the intake stroke is repeated and the cycling strokes continue.

SWIRL CHAMBER

Many diesel engines are equipped with a removable swirl chamber, located in the cylinder head. The fuel injector and the glow plug assemblies are normally installed so that their operating ends are exposed in the chamber. The chamber capacity is normally equal to $^3/_4$ of the total volume of the air at the end of the compression stroke.

The purpose of the swirl chamber is to produce a strong turbulence of air, which progressively increases as the piston approaches top dead center (TDC) on the compression stroke. The fuel is injected and swirled by the air and, as soon as ignition begins, the pressure in the chamber increases, forcing the air, the burned gases and unburned fuel towards the cylinder. This causes the piston to descend and reverse the direction of the swirl, causing a more intense turbulence and a better combustion of the fuel. This aids in obtaining a low fuel consumption rate.

GLOW PLUGS

Electrically operated glow plugs are used to heat the combustion chamber prior to cold weather and initial engine starts. The glow plugs resemble the spark plugs of the conventional gasoline powered engines. A relay controls the length of time the glow plugs are in use. During cold weather, the relay may have to be reactivated through a second glow plug cycle in order to start the engine.

CATERPILLAR DIESEL ENGINES

3208, 3306, 3406 AND 3408 SERIES

GENERAL ENGINE SPECIFICATIONS

Engine Series	No. of Cylinders	Cu. In. Disp.	Bore × Stroke (in.)	Max. Horsepower	Torque SAE @ rpm	Firing Order Right Hand Rotation	Low Idle rpm	Governor Limit rpm	Compression Ratio
3208	8	636	4.5 × 5.0	160 @ 2800	365 @ 1400	1-2-7-3-4-5-6-8	650	3030	16.4:1
3208②	8	636	4.5 × 5.0	165 @ 2600	398 @ 1300	1-2-7-3-4-5-6-8	650	3030	16.4:1
3208③	8	636	4.5 × 5.0	175 @ 2800	425 @ 1400	1-2-7-3-4-5-6-8	650	3030	16.4:1
3208	8	636	4.5 × 5.0	175 @ 2800	400 @ 1400	1-2-7-3-4-5-6-8	650	3030	16.4:1
3208②	8	636	4.5 × 5.0	185 @ 2600	452 @ 1400	1-2-7-3-4-5-6-8	650	3030	16.4:1
3208③	8	636	4.5 × 5.0	200 @ 2800	490 @ 1400	1-2-7-3-4-5-6-8	650	3070	16.4:1
3208	8	636	4.5 × 5.0	210 @ 2800	485 @ 1400	1-2-7-3-4-5-6-8	650	3040	16.4:1
3208②	8	636	4.5 × 5.0	225 @ 2600	560 @ 1400	1-2-7-3-4-5-6-8	650	2800	16.4:1
3208	8	636	4.5 × 5.0	250 @ 2600	610 @ 1400	1-2-7-3-4-5-6-8	650	2825	16.4:1
3208	8	636	4.5 × 5.0	250 @ 2800	610 @ 1400	1-2-7-3-4-5-6-8	650	3030	16.4:1
3306	6	638	4.75 × 6.0	245 @ 2100	860 @ 1350	1-5-3-6-2-4	600	2100	15.0:1
3306③	6	638	4.75 × 6.0	245 @ 2200	820 @ 1300	1-5-3-6-2-4	650	2200	17.5:1
3306	6	638	4.75 × 6.0	250 @ 1800	860 @ 1350	1-5-3-6-2-4	600	1800	15.0:1
3306	6	638	4.75 × 6.0	260 @ 1900	860 @ 1350	1-5-3-6-2-4	600	1900	15.0:1
3306	6	638	4.75 × 6.0	270 @ 2000	860 @ 1350	1-5-3-6-2-4	600	2000	15.0:1
3306③	6	638	4.75 × 6.0	270 @ 2200	775 @ 1400	1-5-3-6-2-4	650	2200	17.5:1
3406	6	893	5.4 × 6.5	350 @ 1800	1200 @ 1200	1-5-3-6-2-4	750	1800	14.5:1
3406③	6	893	5.4 × 6.5	350 @ 1800	1225 @ 1200	1-5-3-6-2-4	750	1800	14.5:1
3406	6	893	5.4 × 6.5	350 @ 2100	1200 @ 1200	1-5-3-6-2-4	750	2100	14.5:1
3406	6	893	5.4 × 6.5	380 @ 2100	1245 @ 1200	1-5-3-6-2-4	750	2100	14.5:1
3406	6	893	5.4 × 6.5	400 @ 2100	1265 @ 1300	1-5-3-6-2-4	750	2100	14.5:1
3406	6	893	5.4 × 6.5	280 @ 2100	1015 @ 1200	1-5-3-6-2-4	750	2100	14.5:1
3406	6	893	5.4 × 6.5	300 @ 2100	1054 @ 1200	1-5-3-6-2-4	750	2100	14.5:1
3406	6	893	5.4 × 6.5	325 @ 2100	1050 @ 1200	1-5-3-6-2-4	750	2100	14.5:1
3406③	6	893	5.4 × 6.5	380 @ 2100	1285 @ 1200	1-5-3-6-2-4	750	2100	14.5:1
3406	6	893	5.4 × 6.5	290 @ 1800	1000 @ 1200	1-5-3-6-2-4	750	1800	14.5:1
3406③④	6	893	5.4 × 6.5	300 @ 1900	1054 @ 1200	1-5-3-6-2-4	750	1900	14.5:1
3406④	6	893	5.4 × 6.5	305 @ 1900	1050 @ 1200	1-5-3-6-2-4	750	①	14.5:1
3406④	6	893	5.4 × 6.5	350 @ 1900	1165 @ 1200	1-5-3-6-2-4	750	1900	14.5:1
3406	6	893	5.4 × 6.5	375 @ 2100	1145 @ 1400	1-5-3-6-2-4	750	①	14.5:1
3406⑤	6	893	5.4 × 6.5	250 @ 1600	1000 @ 1200	1-5-3-6-2-4	750	1600	14.5:1
3406⑤	6	893	5.4 × 6.5	285 @ 1600	1090 @ 1200	1-5-3-6-2-4	750	1600	14.5:1
3406⑤	6	893	5.4 × 6.5	300 @ 1600	1200 @ 1200	1-5-3-6-2-4	750	1600	14.5:1
3406⑤	6	893	5.4 × 6.5	330 @ 1600	1320 @ 1200	1-5-3-6-2-4	750	1600	14.5:1
3408③	V-8	1099	5.4 × 6.0	450 @ 2100	1350 @ 1500	1-8-4-3-6-5-7-2	600	2100	15.3:1
3408	V-8	1099	5.4 × 6.0	450 @ 2100	1460 @ 1200	1-8-4-3-6-5-7-2	700	2100	14.5:1
3408④	V-8	1099	5.4 × 6.0	420 @ 1900	1460 @ 1200	1-8-4-3-6-5-7-2	650	3030	15.5:1

① 280PC—2260 325PC—2285
280DI—2300 360PC—2300
② On-highway ratings
③ California use only
④ Economy (1900 rpm)
⑤ Economy (1600 rpm)

TUNE-UP SPECIFICATIONS

Engine Series	Valve Clearance Intake (in.)	Valve Clearance Exhaust (in.)	Injection Pump Timing (deg.)	Injection Nozzle Pressure (psi)	Idle Speed (rpm)	Maximum No-Load Speed (rpm)
3208	.015	.025	16B	2750–2900	650	①
3306	.015	.025	17–19B	1200–2350	600–650	①
3406	.015	.030	②	③	750	①
3408	.015	.030	④	③	600–700	①

① See General Engine Specifications Chart
② Precombustion Chamber Type-All—9–11°BTDC
Direct Injection Type
Pump No. 9–49—28–30° BTDC
9–798—27–29° BTDC
9–2626—27–29° BTDC
9–512 thru 9–215—27–29° BTDC
9–3384—27–29° BTDC
9–3702—27–29° BTDC
9–3746—27–29° BTDC
9–3839—27–29° BTDC
9–3939—27–29° BTDC
9–5435—27–29° BTDC
9–3702—25.5–27.5° BTDC
9–3839—21.5–23.5° BTDC
③ Precombustion Chamber Type: 400–750 psi
Direct Injection Type: 2400–3100 psi
④ Precombustion Chamber Type: 10–12° BTDC
Direct Injection Type: 27–29° BTDC

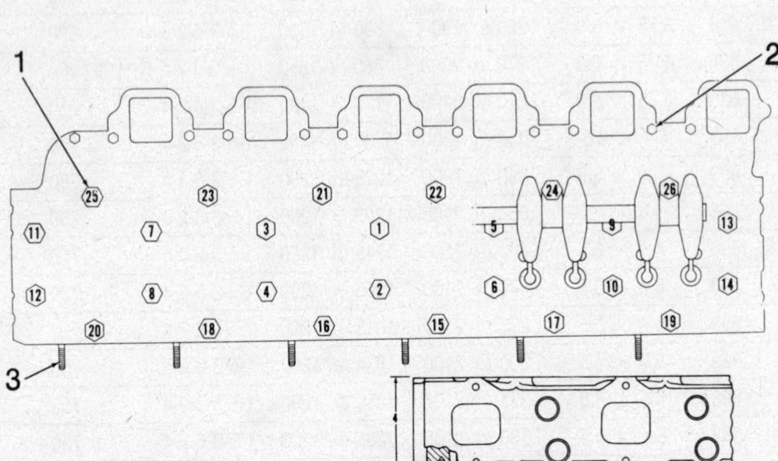

① Large bolts (3/4 inch). Put engine oil on all bolt threads and tighten the bolts in the following sequence:
Step 1: Tighten bolts from 1 to 20 in number sequence to 200 ± 20 ft. lbs. (270 ± 25 N·m)
Step 2: Tighten bolts from 1 to 20 in number sequence to 330 ± 15 ft. lbs. (450 ± 20 N·m)
Step 3: Tighten bolts from 1 to 20 in number sequence again to 330 ± 15 ft. lbs. (450 ± 20 N·m)
Step 4: Install the rocker arm shafts (1) for the engine valves.
Step 5: Tighten bolts from 21 to 26 in number sequence to 200 ± 20 ft. lbs. (270 ± 25 N·m)
Step 6: Tighten bolts from 21 to 26 in number sequence to 330 ± 15 ft. lbs. (450 ± 20 N·m)
Step 7: Tighten bolts from 21 to 26 in number sequence again to 330 ± 15 ft. lbs. (450 ± 20 N·m)
Step 8: Tighten the twelve small bolts (2) to 32 ± 5 ft. lbs. (43 ± 7 N·m)
② Small bolts (3/8 inch). See step 8.
③ Torque for twelve studs in cylinder head 20 ± 3 ft. lbs. (25 ± 4 N·m)
④ Height of cylinder head (new) 4.440 ± .010 in. (112.78 ± 0.25 mm)

Head bolt torque sequence—3406 Series (© Caterpillar Tractor Co.)

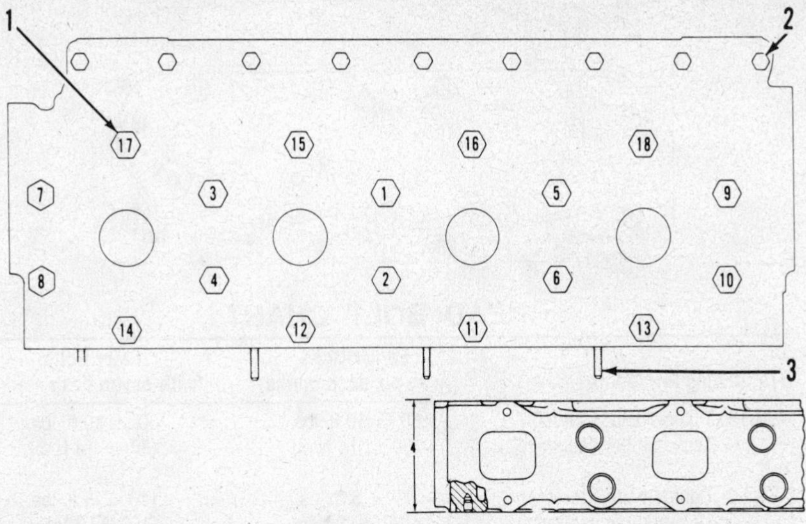

① Large bolts (3/4 inch). Put engine oil on all bolt threads and tighten the bolts in the following step sequence:

Step 1: Tighten bolts from 1 to 14 in number sequence to 200 ± 20 ft. lbs. (270 ± 25 N·m)

Step 2: Tighten bolts from 1 to 14 in number sequence to 330 ± 15 ft. lbs. (450 ± 20 N·m)

Step 3: Tighten bolts from 1 to 14 in number sequence again to 330 ± 15 ft. lbs. (450 ± 20 N·m)

Step 4: Install the rocker arms for the engine valves.

Step 5: Tighten bolts from 15 to 18 in number sequence to 200 ± 20 ft. lbs. (270 ± 25 N·m)

Step 6: Tighten bolts from 15 to 18 in number sequence to 330 ± 15 ft. lbs. (450 ± 20 N·m)

Step 7: Tighten bolts from 15 to 18 in number sequence again to 330 ± 15 ft. lbs. (450 ± 20 N·m)

Step 8: Tighten the nine small bolts (2) to 32 ± 5 ft. lbs. (43 ± 7 N·m)

② Small bolts (3/8 inch). See step 8.

③ Torque for eight studs in each cylinder head 20 ± 3 ft. lbs. (25 ± 4 N·m)

④ Height of cylinder head (new) 4.440 ± .010 in. (112.78 ± 0.25 mm)

Head bolt torque sequence—3408 Series (© Caterpillar Tractor Co.)

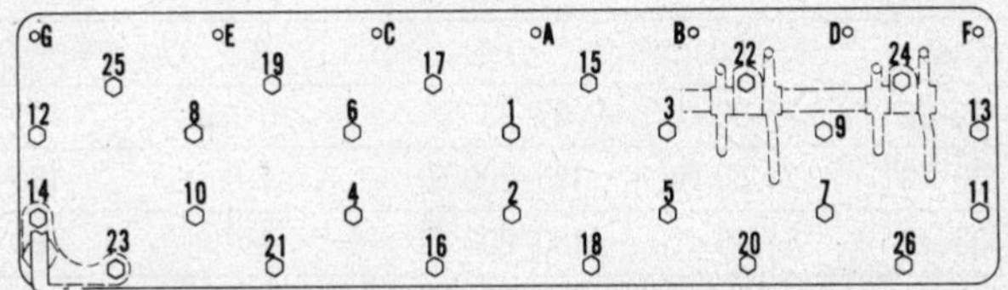

Step 1. Tighten all bolts in number sequence to 115 ft. lbs. (155 Nm)

Step 2. Tighten all bolts in number sequence to 172 ft. lbs. (233 Nm)

Step 3. Tighten all bolts in number sequence to 198 ft. lbs. (267 Nm)

Step 4. Tighten all bolts in letter sequence to 37 ft. lbs. (50 Nm)

Cylinder head bolt torque sequence—3306 Series (© Caterpillar Tractor Co.)

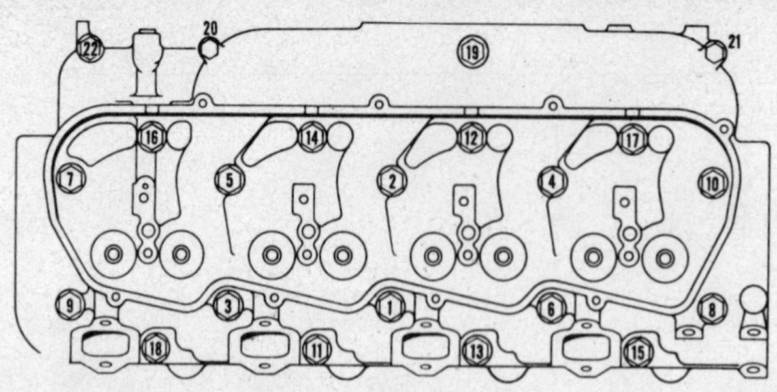

HEAD BOLT CHART

Tightening Procedure	Earlier Bolts (with six dash marks)	Later Bolts (with seven dash marks)
Step 1: Tighten bolts 1 through 18 in number sequence to:	60 ± 10 ft. lbs. (80 ± 14 N·m)	60 ± 10 ft. lbs. (80 ± 14 N·m)
Step 2: Tighten bolts 1 through 18 in number sequence to:	95 ± 5 ft. lbs. (130 ± 7 N·m)	110 ± 5 ft. lbs. (150 ± 7 N·m)
Step 3: Again tighten bolts 1 through 18 in number sequence to:	95 ± 5 ft. lbs. (130 ± 7 N·m)	110 ± 5 ft. lbs. (150 ± 7 N·m)
Torque for head bolts 19 through 22 (tighten in number sequence to)	32 ± 5 ft. lbs. 43 ± 7 N·m)	

Cylinder head bolt torque sequence—3208 Series (© Caterpillar Tractor Co.)

ENGINE TORQUE SPECIFICATIONS

(All measurements in ft. lbs.)

Engine Series	Cylinder Head	Intake Manifold	Exhaust Manifold	Conn. Rod	Main Bearing Caps	Damper to Crankshaft Bolt	Flywheel to Crankshaft	Oil Pump Mounting Bolts	Oil Pan Bolts
3208	①	—	32	30 ②	30 ④	460	55	18	17
3306	⑤	—	32–38	27–33 ③	27–33 ③	210–250	130–170	—	—
3406	315–345	—	33–43	54–66 ④	180–200 ④	—	180–220	—	—
3408	315–345	—	33–43	54–66 ④	180–200 ④	—	180–220	—	—

NOTE: On 3208 engines the early head bolts are identified by six marks; later bolts have seven marks.

① Large bolts (early): 60 then 95 ft. lbs.
Large bolts (late): 60 then 110 ft. lbs.
Small bolts: 32 ft. lbs.

② Plus 60°

③ Plus 90°

④ Plus 120°

⑤ Numbered bolts: 115 then 172–198
Lettered bolts: 27–37

CHILTON'S THREE "C's" DIESEL ENGINE DIAGNOSIS PROCEDURE

Condition	Cause	Correction
Hard Starting—Engine Turns Freely	1. Cold outside temperatures. 2. No fuel getting to engine-clogged filters, empty tank, plugged or kinked lines. 3. Fuel shut-off solenoid is not energized 4. Fuel shut-off solenoid is stuck. 5. Fuel transfer pump delivering less than 10 psi. ② 6. Injection timing incorrect. 7. Fuel injection pump drive slipping 8. Incorrect valve adjustment. 9. Defective fuel nozzle. 10. Restriction in exhaust system. 11. Air or water in fuel system.	1. Install block heater. 2. Replace fuel filter, refill fuel tank or clear fuel lines as necessary. 3. Check solenoid operation and repair or replace as necessary. 4. Replace fuel shut-off solenoid. 5. Check fuel pressure at transfer pump. 6. Reset injection timing. 7. Replace injection pump drive. 8. Check and adjust valve clearance. 9. Replace fuel injector. 10. Repair as necessary. 11. Drain fuel system and flush or bleed.
Hard Starting—Engine Will Not Turn or Turns Slowly	1. Battery voltage too low. 2. Defective cable or connection from battery to starter. 3. Defective starter or solenoid. 4. Interior engine condition preventing engine from turning. 5. Transmission or power take-off (PTO) problem, preventing engine from turning.	1. Recharge or replace battery. 2. Repair connection or replace cable. 3. Replace starter or solenoid. 4. Check for seized engine components or hydrostatic lock. 5. Check and repair as necessary.
Engine Misfires ①	1. Fuel injection lines installed in improper firing order. 2. Defective injection nozzles or pump. 3. Incorrect valve lash. 4. Sticking valves. 5. Incorrect injection timing. 6. Fuel transfer pump delivering less than 10 psi. 7. Faulty high pressure fuel line. 8. Poor compression. 9. Air or water in fuel system. 10. Malfunctioning automatic timing advance. 11. Defective head gasket. 12. Fuel leakage from line nut or line adapter. 13. Clogged fuel filter caused by wax build-up in fuel.	1. Check injection line routing to injection pump. 2. Replace injection nozzles or pump assembly. 3. Adjust valve clearance. 4. Overhaul as necessary. 5. Reset injection timing. 6. Check transfer pump pressure. 7. Replace fuel line. 8. Check compression pressures. 9. Bleed or drain as necessary. 10. Replace automatic timer or refer pump to specialist for calibration. 11. Replace head gasket. 12. Tighten fuel connection or replace. 13. Replace fuel filter and install fuel line heater to prevent fuel waxing.
Excessive Black or Gray Smoke (ENGINE RUNS SMOOTH) ②	1. Insufficient combustion air, clogged air cleaner or manifold, malfunctioning turbocharger. 2. Defective fuel nozzle. 3. Incorrect injection timing. 4. Incorrect fuel ratio control setting or injector rack setting. 5. Restriction in exhaust system. 6. Valve leakage or incorrect adjustment.	1. Replace air filter element. Check turbocharger operation. 2. Clean or replace fuel nozzle. 3. Reset injection timing. 4. Remove injection pump and calibrate on test stand. 5. Repair as necessary. 6. Adjust valve lash or overhaul as required.

CHILTON'S THREE "C's" DIESEL ENGINE DIAGNOSIS PROCEDURE

Condition	Cause	Correction
(ENGINE RUNS ROUGH)	1. Engine misfire. 2. Air in fuel system. 3. Malfunctioning automatic timing advance. 4. Incorrect injection timing.	1. Follow procedure outlined above. 2. Bleed air from fuel system. 3. Replace automatic timer assembly. 4. Reset injection timing.
Excessive White or Blue Smoke	1. Cold outside temperatures. 2. Extended idling period. 3. High crankcase oil level. 4. Worn piston rings or cylinder liners. 5. Engine misfire. 6. Incorrect injection timing. 7. Incorrect valve adjustment. 8. Malfunctioning automatic timing advance 9. Defective fuel nozzle.	1. Reset fuel ratio on injector rack. 2. Increase engine rpm periodically. 3. Correct oil level. 4. Replace piston rings or cylinder liners. 5. Follow procedure outlined above. 6. Reset injection timing. 7. Adjust valve lash. 8. Replace automatic timer. 9. Clean or replace fuel nozzle.
Excessive Oil Consumption	1. Worn valve guides. 2. Scored rings or liners. 3. High crankcase oil level. 4. Engine misfire.	1. Replace valve guides. 2. Replace rings or cylinder liner. 3. Correct crankcase oil level. 4. Follow procedure outlined above.
Lack of Power	1. Improperly adjusted accelerator linkage. 2. Failed fuel nozzle. ① 3. Improper grade of fuel. 4. Turbocharger clogged or dragging. 5. Air induction leaks. ③ 6. Improper injection timing. 7. Excessive valve lash. 8. Fuel supply pressure less than 10 psi. ② 9. Faulty timing advance.	1. Adjust accelerator linkage. 2. Clean or replace fuel nozzle. 3. Drain and refill fuel tank. 4. Check turbocharger operation. 5. Correct as necessary. 6. Reset injection timing. 7. Adjust valves. 8. Check fuel supply pump pressure. 9. Check automatic timer operation.
Low Oil Pressure	1. Lubricating oil diluted with fuel. 2. Excessive clearances in bearings in crankcase or timing gears. 3. Defective oil pump or relief valve. 4. Crankcase oil level excessive. 5. Oil temperature too high—faulty cooler or cooler relief valve.	1. Drain and refill crankcase. 2. Replace bearings, check gear backlash. 3. Replace oil pump or relief valve. 4. Correct oil level. 5. Check oil cooler and lines.
Coolant Temperature Too High	1. Combustion gases leaking into coolant. 2. Low coolant level. 3. Faulty water pump. 4. Faulty thermostat. 5. Injection timing incorrect. 6. Pinched shunt line	1. Replace head gasket and check for cracks in block or head. 2. Top up cooling system. 3. Replace water pump. 4. Replace thermostat. 5. Reset injection timing. 6. Replace shunt line.

① When trouble shooting for misfiring, operate the engine at the speed where misfire is most noticeable. Loosen each injector pump fuel nut, one at a time. The cylinder or cylinders which effect performance the least should be tested for a defective fuel nozzle or pump first.

② Fuel transfer pump output should be 10–20 psi at cranking speed. At full load, the rating is 25 psi, and at high idle, 30 psi.

③ In testing for poor performance or smoke, remember that they can result from either fuel system defects or engine mechanical defects. An air intake restriction across the air cleaner of 30 in. of water, or an exhaust system restriction of more than 15 in. of water can cause smoke and poor performance because of lack of oxygen and compression. If fuel system inspection reveals no problem on cylinders that misfire, a compression test and measurement of intake and exhaust manifold pressures should be the next step.

TUNE-UP AND ADJUSTMENTS

Every engine tune-up should include the following checks and/or adjustments.

1. Compression test (if applicable).
2. Valve clearance adjustment.
3. Fuel injection pump timing.
4. Fuel rack settings (if necessary).
5. Engine idle speed setting.
6. Maximum no-load speed setting (governor adjustment).
7. Glow plug system check (if equipped).

NOTE: Efficiency of emission controls and engine performance depends on adherence to proper operation and maintenance recommendations and use of recommended fuels and lubrication oils.

Locating Top Dead Center/Compression Position for No. 1 Piston

3208 SERIES

1. Remove the plug from timing hole in the front cover. Put timing bolt in timing hole.
2. Turn the crankshaft clockwise (as seen from front of engine) until bolt will go into the hole in the drive gear for the camshaft.
3. Remove the valve cover on the right side of the engine (as seen from rear of engine). The two valves at the right front of the engine are the intake and exhaust valves for No. 1 cylinder.
4. The intake and exhaust valves for No. 1 cylinder must now be closed and the timing pointer will be in alignment with the TDC–1 on the damper assembly. The No. 1 piston is now at top center on the compression stroke.

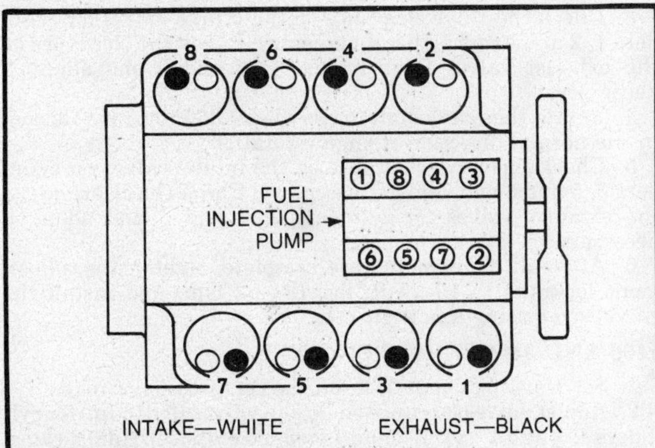

Valve and injector pump location—3208 Series
(© Caterpillar Tractor Co.)

3306 SERIES

NOTE: No. 1 piston at top dead center (TDC) on its compression stroke is the starting point for all timing procedures.

1. Remove the starter motor and install the engine turning tool group or equivalent.
2. Remove the valve cover.
3. Rotate the engine clockwise (as viewed from the flywheel end) 30 degrees to remove the free play from the timing gears.

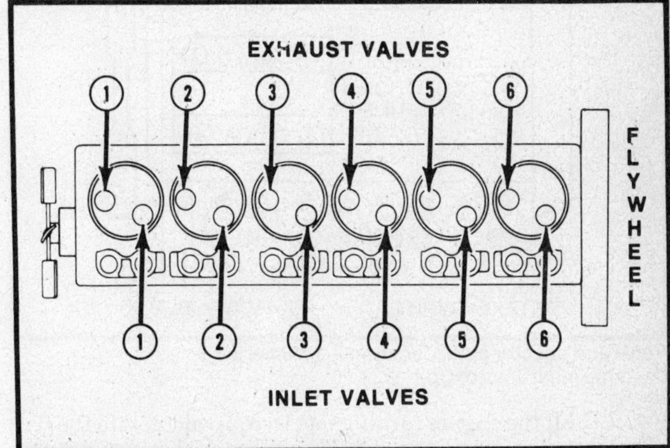

Cylinder and valve location—3306 Series
(© Caterpillar Tractor Co.)

4. Remove the plug from the timing hole in the flywheel housing. Rotate the crankshaft until a $^3/_8$ in.–16NC bolt, 2.0 in. (50.8mm) long can be threaded into the flywheel through the timing hole in the flywheel housing. No. 1 piston is now at TDC. If the crankshaft is turned beyond TDC, repeat Steps 3 and 4 again.
5. The intake and exhaust valves for No. 1 cylinder should be closed. Check by moving the rocker arms by hand slightly up and down.
6. If the No. 1 piston is not on its compression stroke, remove the timing bolt, rotate the crankshaft counterclockwise 360° and install the timing bolt as previously described.

3406 SERIES

No. 1 piston at top dead center on the compression stroke is the starting point of all timing procedures. The timing bolt is kept in storage on the engine and can be installed in either the right or left side of the engine.

NOTE: There are two threaded holes in the flywheel which are in alignment with removal plugged holes in the left and right front of the flywheel housing. The two holes in the flywheel are at different distances from the center of the flywheel so that the timing bolt cannot be put in the wrong hole.

1. Remove the bolts and covers from the flywheel housing.

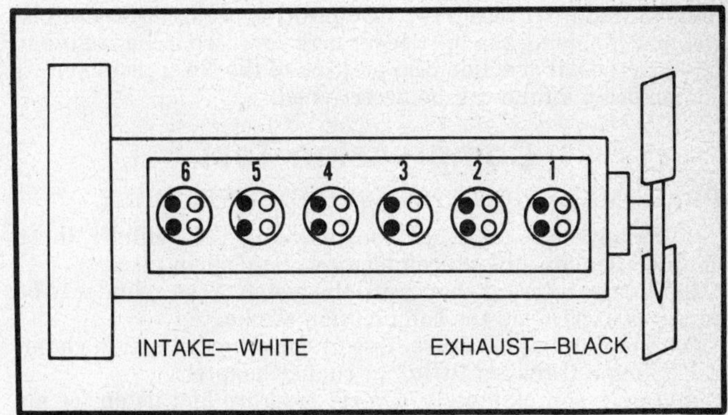

Cylinder and valve location—3406 Series
(© Caterpillar Tractor Co.)

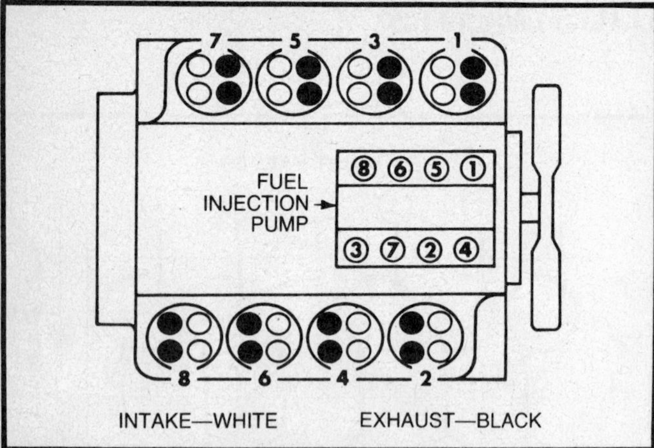

Valve and injector pump location—3408 Series
(© Caterpillar Tractor Co.)

2. Install the engine turning tool or equivalent, into the flywheel housing, until the shoulder of the tool is against the housing. Attach a turning handle to the flywheel rotator and turn the flywheel while holding the timing bolt in either hole in the housing. Stop the rotation when the timing bolt can be installed in the threaded hole of the flywheel.

3. To be assured that the No. 1 piston is at TDC on its compression stroke, remove the valve rocker arm cover. The No. 1 cylinder valves should be closed and the rocker arms should be movable up and down, with hand pressure.

4. If the No. 1 cylinder is not on its compression stroke, rotate the crankshaft 360° and install the timing bolt.

5. If the flywheel was not turned in the direction of normal engine rotation, or was turned past the timing hole, turn the flywheel clockwise (opposite the direction of normal engine rotation) approximately 30 degrees. This operation is to be sure the play is removed from the timing gears when the engine is put on top dead center.

NOTE: The engine is observed from the flywheel end when the direction of rotation is given.

6. Turn the flywheel counterclockwise until the hole in the flywheel is aligned with the timing bolt. When the timing bolt can be turned freely in the threaded hole in the flywheel, the No. 1 piston is on top dead center.

7. If the hole in the flywheel is turned beyond the hole in the flywheel housing, turn the flywheel back (clockwise) a minimum of 30 degrees beyond the hole in the flywheel Then turn the flywheel counterclockwise towards the housing hole again.

3408 SERIES

The No. 1 piston at top dead center on the compression stroke is the starting point for all timing procedures. By referring to the 3406 procedure to locate the TDC position of No. 1 cylinder piston and removing the left rocker arm cover from the engine to observe the valve action, the position of the No. 1 piston on its compression stroke can be ascertained.

Compression Test

PRECOMBUSTION CHAMBER ENGINES ONLY

1. Remove the fuel injection nozzle of the cylinder to be checked, leaving the precombustion chamber in place.

2. Rotate the crankshaft until the piston of the cylinder to be tested is at TDC on the compression stroke.

3. Adapt an air-pressure hose to the pre-combustion chamber, using a threaded fitting or rubber adapter.

4. Apply approximately 100 psi pressure and listen for air leakage at the air cleaner inlet, exhaust outlet and crankcase breather. On turbocharged engines, it may be necessary to remove the air inlet and exhaust outlet connections to detect leakage. Air through the air intake indicates a leaky intake valve, air through the exhaust indicates a leaky exhaust valve and air through the crankcase breather indicates problems with pistons, rings, or liners. If there is valve leakage, check the valve clearance.

Valve Adjustment

3208 SERIES

1. Remove valve covers.

2. Rotate the crankshaft in a clockwise direction until the piston of No. 1 cylinder is at TDC on the compression stroke. The TDC–1 mark on the damper or pulley will align with the timing pointer.

3. Adjust the lash for intake and exhaust valves of cylinders 1 and 2. Adjust the inlet valve for 0.015 in. lash and the exhaust for 0.025 in. lash. Lash adjustment is accomplished by loosening the locknut, adjusting the screw to the dimension of the feeler gauge and then holding the screw while retightening the locknut to 19–25 ft. lbs. Recheck the adjustment to ensure it was not disturbed during the tightening of the locknut.

4. Rotate the crankshaft 180° clockwise, so the VS mark will align with the pointer. Adjust lash for all valves of cylinders 7 and 3.

5. Rotate the crankshaft 180° clockwise again, until the TDC mark on the damper or pulley aligns with the pointer. Adjust the lash of all valves on cylinders 4 and 5.

6. Again rotate the crankshaft 180° clockwise (the VS mark will again align on engines so equipped). Adjust the lash for cylinders 6 and 8.

7. Replace the valve covers.

3306 SERIES

Valve clearance is measured between the rocker arm and the valve stem. When the valve clearance is checked, adjustment is not necessary if the measurement is within the range specified in the tune-up chart.

1. Set the No. 1 cylinder at TDC on its compression stroke.

2. Remove the valve cover.

3. Check the valve clearance on the intake valves for cylinders 1, 2 and 4 and adjust if necessary. Check the clearance on the exhaust valves for cylinders 1, 3 and 5 and adjust if necessary.

4. Rotate the crankshaft (or flywheel) 360° (one revolution) in the normal direction of engine rotation.

5. Check the valve clearance on the intake valves for cylinders 3, 5 and 6 and adjust if necessary. Check the clearance on the exhaust valves for cylinders 2, 4 and 6 and adjust if necessary.

6. After all adjustments are complete, tighten the adjustment locknuts to 19–25 ft. lbs. (24–32 Nm) and install the valve cover using a new gasket.

3406 AND 3408 SERIES ENGINES

1. Set No. 1 piston at TDC on the compression stroke.

2. Adjust valve clearance on intake valves (0.015 in.) for cylinders 1, 2 and 4 (cyl. 1, 2 and 7 on 3408 engines). Adjust clearance on exhaust valves (0.030 in.) for cylinders 1, 3 and 5 (1, 3, 4 and 8 on 3408 engines).

3. Following each adjustment, tighten the valve adjustment screw nut to 22 ft. lbs. Recheck adjustment.

4. Remove the timing bolt and rotate the flywheel 360° in the direction of engine rotation. This will align No. 6 piston at TDC on the compression stroke. Replace the timing bolt in the flywheel.

5. Adjust valve clearance on intake valves (0.015 in.) for cylinders 3, 5 and 6 (3, 4, 6 and 8 on 3408 engines). Adjust valve clearance on exhaust valves (0.030 in.) for cylinders 2, 4 and 6 (2, 5, 6 and 7 on 3408 engines).

6. Repeat Step 3.

7. Remove the timing bolt when adjustments are complete.

Bridge Adjustment

3406 AND 3408 SERIES

NOTE: Valves must be fully closed for this procedure.

1. Loosen the adjustment screw locknut and turn adjustment screw out several turns.
2. Keep the bridge in contact with the valve stem opposite the adjustment screw by hand during adjustment.
3. Turn the adjustment screw clockwise until contact with the valve stem is made. Turn the screw another 30 degrees.
4. Tighten the locknut to 22 ft. lbs. (28 Nm).

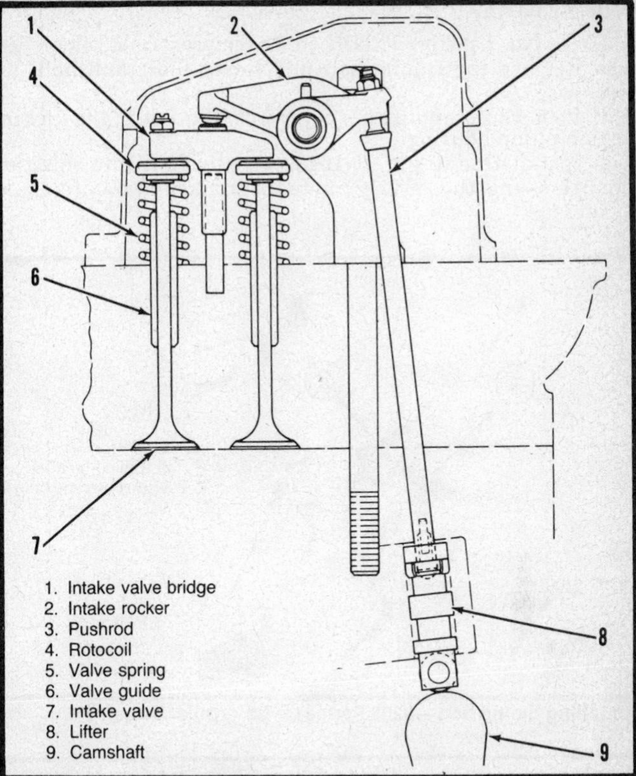

Typical bridged valve mechanism—intake valve illustrated, exhaust valve similar—3406 and 3408 Series
(© Caterpillar Tractor Co.)

Injection Pump Timing

3208 SERIES

The timing of the fuel injection pump can be changed to make compensation for movement in the taper sleeve drive or worn timing gears. The timing can be checked and, if necessary, changed using the following method.

1. Remove bolt from the timing pin hole.
2. Turn the crankshaft clockwise (as seen from front of engine) until timing pin goes into the notch in the camshaft for the fuel injection pumps.

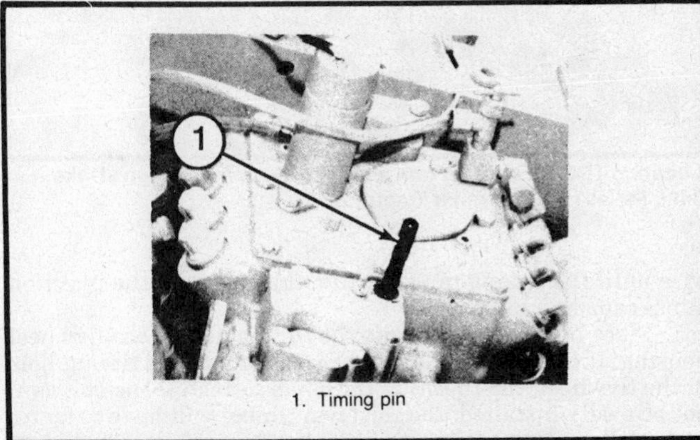

Timing pin installed in injector housing—3208 Series
(© Caterpillar Tractor Co.)

3. Remove the plug from timing hole in the front cover. Put timing bolt through the front cover and into the hole with threads in the timing gear.
4. If the timing pin is in the notch in the camshaft for the fuel injection pumps and bolt goes into the hole in the timing gear through timing hole the timing of the fuel injection pump is correct.
5. If bolt does not go in the hole in the timing gear with timing pin in the notch in the camshaft, use the following procedure.

   a. Remove nuts and the cover for the tachometer drive assembly.

   b. Remove the tachometer drive shaft and washer from the camshaft for the fuel injection pumps. Tachometer drive shaft and washer are removed as an assembly.

   c. Put puller on the camshaft for the fuel injection pumps. Tighten bolts until the drive gear on the camshaft for the fuel injection pumps comes loose.

   d. Remove the puller.

   e. Turn the crankshaft clockwise (as seen from front of engine) until timing bolt goes into the hole in the timing gear. With timing pin in the notch in the camshaft for the fuel injection pumps and bolt in the hole in the timing gear, the timing for the engine is correct.

   f. Install washer and tachometer drive shaft. Tighten tachometer drive shaft to:
   Earlier: 80 ± 5 lb. ft. (110 ± 7 N;pdm)
   Later: 110 ± 10 lb. ft. (150 ± 14 N;pdm)
   Then remove timing pin.

   g. Turn the crankshaft two complete revolutions clockwise (as seen from front of engine) and put timing pin and bolt in again. If timing pin and bolt can not be installed do Steps a through f again.

   h. Remove bolt from the timing gear and install in holding hole. Install the plug in timing hole. Remove timing pin and install bolt. Install cover for the tachometer drive assembly.

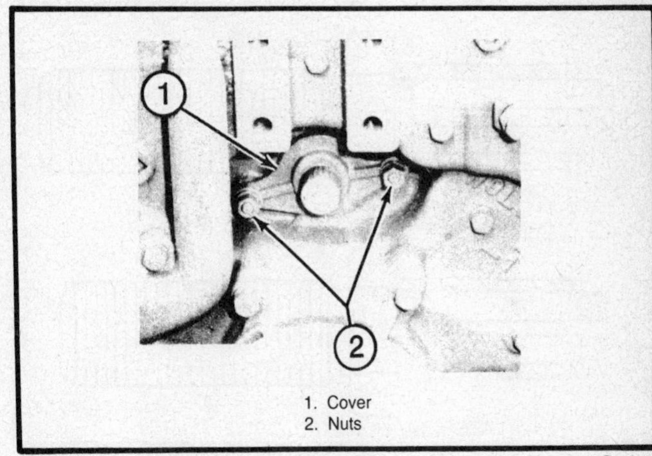

Location of tachometer drive assembly (© Caterpillar Tractor Co.)

3306 SERIES

1. Set No. 1 piston at TDC on its compression stroke.
2. Remove the timing bolt and rotate the crankshaft 30° clockwise.
3. Remove the timing pin cover from the side of the fuel injection pump housing.
4. Install timing pin 7N1048 or equivalent into injection pump housing, then slowly rotate the crankshaft counterclockwise until the timing pin slips into the groove in the injection pump camshaft.
5. Place the timing bolt into the timing hole in the flywheel housing. If the bolt can be hand-threaded into the timing hole in the flywheel, the injection timing is correct. If the bolt cannot be easily installed, the injection timing will have to be reset as follows:
6. Remove the mounting nuts and cover from the timing gear housing.
7. Loosen the bolt holding the automatic advance unit to the fuel pump camshaft.
8. Loosen the automatic timing advance unit from the injection pump camshaft using a suitable puller.
9. Remove the timing bolt from the flywheel housing and rotate the flywheel clockwise 60° BTDC of No. 1 piston.
10. Tighten the automatic timing advance unit bolt finger tight, making sure the timing pin is still in the groove of the injection pump camshaft.
11. Slowly rotate the crankshaft counterclockwise until the timing bolt can be installed in the flywheel.
12. Install adapter FT1560 or equivalent on the timing advance unit. Install a torque wrench on the adapter and apply a torque of 45–50 ft. lbs. (60–70 Nm) in a clockwise direction as viewed from the front of the engine. While holding the torque on the adapter, tighten the retaining bolt on the timing advance unit to 180–220 ft. lbs. (245–295 Nm).
13. Remove the timing bolt from the flywheel and the timing pin from the injection pump.
14. Rotate the crankshaft counterclockwise two revolutions. If the timing pin can be installed in the injection pump and the timing bolt fits into the flywheel, the injection timing is correct. If not, repeat Steps 6 through 13.

3406 SERIES

1. Install the timing pin through the hole in the pump housing and into the notch in the camshaft.

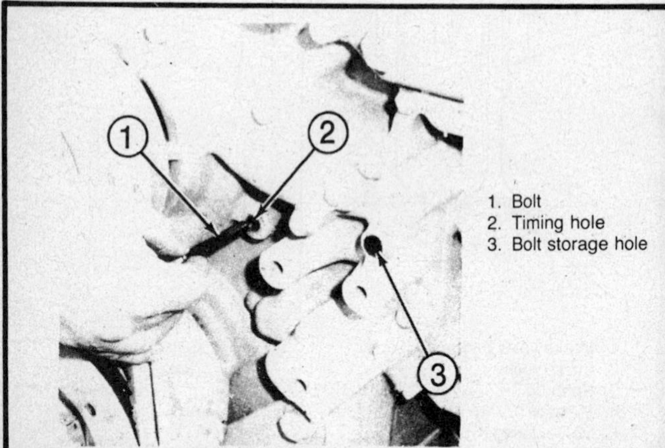

Installing timing bolt—3208 Series (© Caterpillar Tractor Co.)

Injection pump timing pin cover (1)—3306 Series (© Caterpillar Tractor Co.)

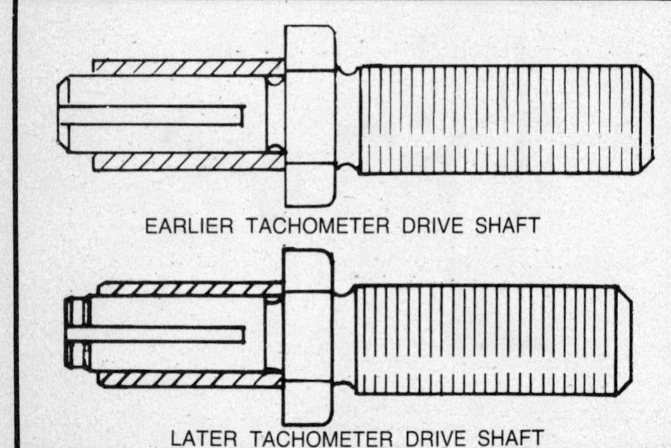

Tachometer drive comparison (© Caterpillar Tractor Co.)

Timing pin (1) installed in injection pump—3306 Series (© Caterpillar Tractor Co.)

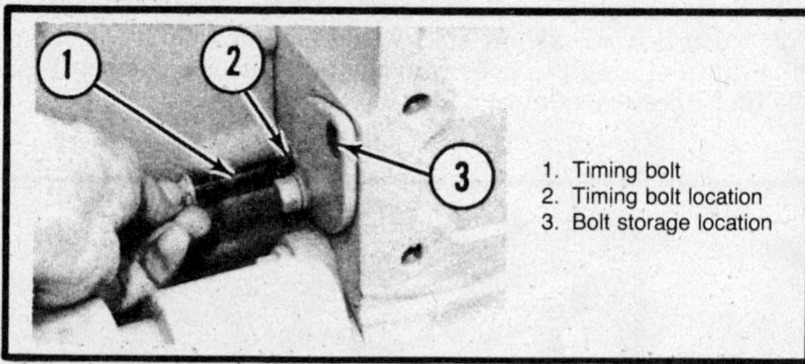

Locating TDC for number one piston on its compression stroke—3406 Series (© Caterpillar Tractor Co.)

2. Loosen four bolts (one bolt on earlier engines) holding the automatic timing advance unit to the drive shaft for the fuel injection pump.
3. Tap the automatic timing advance unit with a soft faced hammer to loosen it from the end of the drive shaft for the fuel injection pump.
4. Place the No. 1 piston at TDC, if not previously done.
5. On earlier engines, tighten the bolt to 15 ft. lbs. torque. Remove the timing pin and tighten the bolt to a final torque of 110 ft. lbs. On later engines, tighten the four bolts to 25 ft. lbs. and remove the timing pin. Tighten to a torque of 50 ft. lbs. and then to a final torque of 100 ft. lbs.
6. Remove the timing bolt from the flywheel.
7. Turn the crankshaft two complete revolutions and recheck the timing for correctness.
8. If the timing is not correct, repeat the timing procedure.

3408 SERIES

1. With the No. 1 piston on its compression stroke and at TDC, remove the cover or the air-fuel ratio control (if equipped).
2. On later engines, remove the plug from the front of the injection pump housing. Install the timing pin (tapered end first) through the hole in the pump housing and into the timing notch in the fuel pump camshaft.
3. If the timing is correct, the timing pin will go into the notch of the camshaft and the timing bolt will turn into the threaded hole in the flywheel. If the timing is not correct, it will have to be changed. If the timing requires adjustment, continue on to the next step.
4. Remove the timing pin, the access cover and loosen the four retaining bolts of the automatic timing advance unit.

NOTE: Be sure the timing pin is removed before the four bolts are loosened.

5. Tighten the four bolts finger-tight to hold the unit against the timing gears when the gears are turned to prevent play or backlash.
6. Remove the timing bolt and turn the flywheel until the timing pin will go into the groove in the injection pump camshaft.
7. Turn the flywheel clockwise (opposite the direction of engine rotation) a minimum of 30° to remove any play in the timing gears at top dead center.
8. Turn the engine in the direction of normal rotation until the No. 1 piston is at the TDC of its compression stroke. Turn the threaded timing bolt into the hole in the flywheel.
9. Tighten the four automatic timing advance unit retaining bolts to 20 ft. lbs. Remove the timing pin from the injection pump housing.
10. Tighten the four advance unit retaining bolts to 100 ft. lbs. and remove the timing bolt from the flywheel.

Location of timing hole plug—3408 Series (later engines) (© Caterpillar Tractor Co.)

11. Rotate the crankshaft two complete revolutions and recheck the timing to be sure the timing pin will go into the injector housing camshaft and the timing bolt will go into the flywheel. If the timing is incorrect, complete the procedure again.
12. If the timing is correct, be sure to remove the timing pin and the timing bolt.

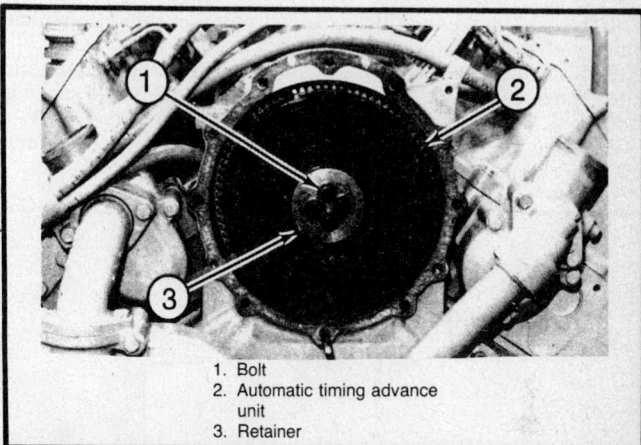

1. Bolt
2. Automatic timing advance unit
3. Retainer

Automatic timing advance unit—3408 Series (© Caterpillar Tractor Co.)

Timing pin installed in the injector housing—3406 Series (© Caterpillar Tractor Co.)

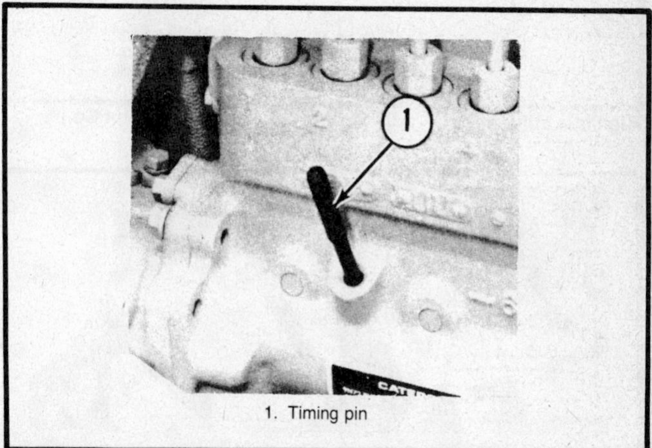

1. Timing pin

Timing pin installed in the injector housing—3408 Series (early engines) (© Caterpillar Tractor Co.)

Idle Speed Adjustment

3208 SERIES

NOTE: This procedure covers the basic idle and maximum speed adjustment only. If the governor requires overhaul, the fuel injection pump should be removed and referred to a properly equipped specialist for calibration.

1. Check the engine idle speed with an accurate mechanical tachometer and connecting cable.
2. If the low idle requires adjustment, loosen the locknut and turn the low idle adjustment bolt until the correct idle speed is obtained. Tighten the locknut and recheck idle speed.
3. Move the governor lever to the full load position and check the high idle rpm. If the high idle requires adjustment, remove the small cover at the top rear of the injection pump to expose adjusting screw.
4. Loosen the locknut and turn the adjustment screw to obtain the correct high idle specification. Return the governor lever to the low idle position and then back to full load and recheck adjustment.
5. After adjustment is complete, tighten the locknut and install the adjustment screw cover on the injection pump. Whenever the high idle speed is adjusted, the balance point should also be checked.

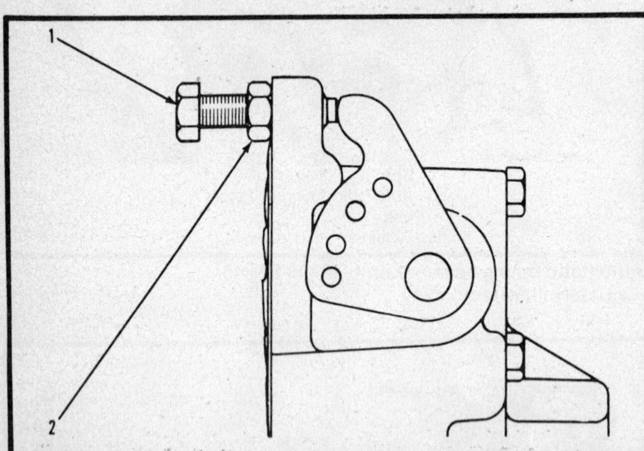

Loosen locknut (2) and turn adjusting bolt (1) to adjust low idle—3208 Series (© Caterpillar Tractor Co.)

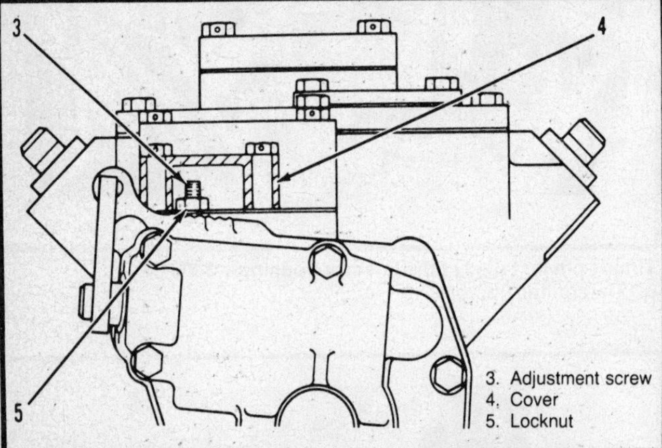

High idle adjustment—3208 Series (© Caterpillar Tractor Co.)

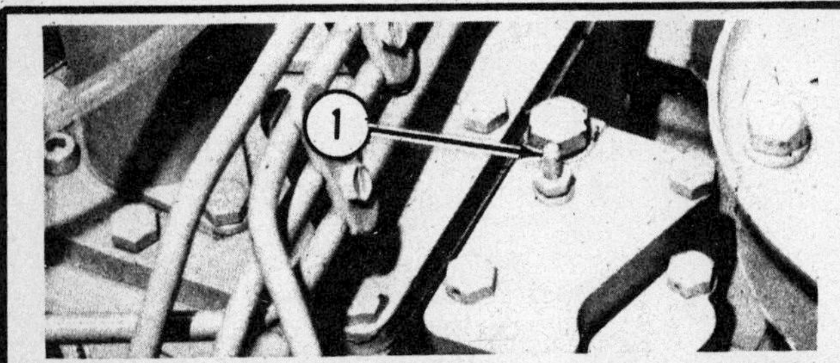

Location of brass terminal (1)—3208 Series (© Caterpillar Tractor Co.)

Checking Balance Point

NOTE: Checking the balance point of the engine is a method of making an engine performance diagnosis. If the balance point and high idle rpm are correct, the fuel system of the engine is operating properly.

1. Connect a mechanical tachometer to the engine by using the tachometer drive takeoff and cable adaptor.
2. Connect a continuity light to the brass terminal screw on the cover for the load stop. Connect the other end to a good ground on the fuel system.
3. Start the engine and allow it to reach operating temperature.
4. Run the engine at high idle and record the engine speed. Add load on the engine slowly until the continuity light just comes on. This is the engine balance point. Record the engine speed at the balance point, repeating the check procedure several times to make sure the readings are accurate.
5. Stop the engine and compare the rpm values taken during testing with the Rack Setting Information chart. If the balance point is correct, the fuel system is working properly. If the balance point is incorrect, adjust the high idle rpm adjusting bolt until the correct value is obtained.

Idle Speed Adjustment

3306 SERIES

NOTE: This procedure covers basic adjustment only. If the idle and high rpm values are not obtainable by adjustment of the set screws, the fuel injection pump governor must be adjusted by a fuel injection specialist.

1. Connect an accurate mechanical tachometer to the engine.
2. Start the engine and allow it to reach operating temperature. Check the low and high idle rpm speed, with no load on the engine, by moving the governor control lever.
3. To adjust the low idle, move the governor control lever to the low idle position. Loosen the locknut on the low idle adjustment screw and turn until the correct idle speed is obtained. Increase the engine speed and return to low idle to check the adjustment.
4. To adjust high idle, cut the lockwire and remove the cover over the high idle adjustment screw.
5. Loosen the locknut and turn the high idle adjustment screw to obtain the correct value. Decrease the engine speed then return to high idle to check the adjustment.
6. Once the adjustment is made, tighten the locknut and replace the cover. Reinstall a new lockwire and seal on the cover after all adjustment procedures are complete.

Checking Balance Point

NOTE: The balance point for the 3306 engine is 20 rpm higher than full load speed.

1. Connect a mechanical tachometer to the engine using the tachometer drive.
2. Connect a continuity light to the brass terminal screw on the injection pump, located at the rear of the governor housing. Connect the other end of the light to a good ground on the fuel system.

3. Start the engine and allow it to reach operating temperature.
4. Run the engine at high idle and record the rpm reading.
5. Add load slowly to the engine until the continuity light just comes on. This is the balance point. Record the engine speed (rpm) at the balance point. Repeat the operation several times to assure an accurate reading.
6. Stop the engine and compare the values recorded with the specifications listed in the Fuel Rack Setting chart.
7. If the full load speed is not correct, adjust the high idle as required to bring the value within specifications.

NOTE: If the high idle speed is out of tolerance and the full load speed is correct, look for a weak governor spring.

Low Speed Governor Control Adjustment

1. Start the engine and allow it to idle.
2. engage the governor control. The engine should speed up to 1600 ± 50 rpm and maintain that value.
3. If the rpm needs adjustment, loosen the locknut and turn the adjusting screw clockwise to lower the rpm and counterclockwise to raise the rpm. Once the adjustment is complete, tighten the locknut to 6–12 ft. lbs. (8–16 Nm).
4. With the engine running at 1600 rpm, apply a maximum load. The engine speed should be 1500 ± 45 rpm.
5. If adjustment is necessary, repeat Step 3. Torque the locknut when adjustment is complete.
6. Remove the load and when engine speed is stable at no-load rpm, disengage the governor control to allow the engine to return to low idle.

Idle Speed Adjustment

3406 SERIES

NOTE: This procedure covers basic adjustment only. If the idle speed specifications cannot be obtained with these adjustments, the injection pump will have to be recalibrated by a qualified specialist.

1. Attach an accurate mechanical tachometer to the engine using the 1P7448 tachometer cable or equivalent.
2. Start the engine and allow it to reach operating temperature. Check the low idle rpm reading and compare it to specifications.
3. Before adjusting the idle speed, make sure the governor linkage is in the low idle position. Remove the adjustment bolt cover and turn the low idle adjustment bolt as necessary to either increase or decrease the idle speed.
4. Increase the engine speed and return the governor linkage to the low idle position, then recheck the idle speed setting. Repeat this procedure whenever any adjustment is made until the rpm setting is correct.
5. Move the governor linkage to the high idle position and measure the rpm value with the tachometer.
6. If adjustment is necessary, turn the high idle adjustment bolt as necessary to adjust the high idle engine speed.
7. After adjustment, return the linkage to the low idle position, then back to high idle and record the rpm reading. Repeat this operation until the high idle is correct.
8. Once all adjustment procedures are complete, replace the cover over the adjusting bolts. When the cover is installed on the governor, the idle adjustment screws fit into holes in the cover. The shape of the holes will not let the idle adjustment screws turn once the cover is installed. Install a new wire and seal to the bolt cover.

Checking Balance Point

NOTE: The balance point check of the engine is a method to diagnose engine performance. If the balance point and high idle speed are correct, the fuel system is functioning properly.

1. Connect a mechanical tachometer to the engine tachometer drive hookup.
2. Connect a continuity tester to the brass terminal screw on the governor housing. Connect the other end of the tester to a good ground on the fuel system.
3. Start the engine and allow it to reach normal operating temperature.
4. Raise the engine speed to the high idle position by moving the governor lever. Record the rpm value as measured by the tachometer.
5. Add load on the engine slowly until the continuity light just comes on. This is the engine balance point. Record the engine speed (rpm) at the balance point.
6. Stop the engine and compare the readings taken with the specifications in the Rack Setting Information chart.
7. If the balance point is correct, the governor setting is adjusted correctly. If the balance point is not correct, adjust the high idle rpm until the specifications are obtained.

CAUTION

Do not adjust the rpm above the range given for high idle specifications as damage to the engine can result.

Idle Speed Adjustment

3408 SERIES

NOTE: This procedure is for minor adjustment only. If the idle speed cannot be brought into specifications by these adjustments, the fuel injection pump will have to be recalibrated by a specialist.

1. Attach an accurate mechanical tachometer to the tachometer drive coupling on the engine using the 1P7448 tachometer cable or equivalent.
2. Start the engine and allow it to reach operating temperature.
3. Measure the idle speed and compare it with the specifications listed in the Tune-Up chart.
4. If the low idle needs adjustment, move the governor lever to the low idle position and turn the adjusting screw on the injection pump until the correct low idle rpm is obtained.
5. Raise the engine rpm, then return the governor lever to the low idle position and check the adjustment. Tighten the locknut when all adjustments are complete.
6. Move the governor lever to the high idle position and check the rpm value on the tachometer. Compare high idle speed to the specifications listed in the Tune-Up chart.
7. If the high idle needs adjustment, remove the cover at the top rear of the governor and turn the high idle adjustment bolt as necessary to either increase or decrease the high idle speed.
8. Return the linkage to the low idle position and then back to high idle and check the rpm value again. Repeat this operation several times to assure an accurate reading.
9. Once the correct high idle setting is obtained, replace the cover over the high idle adjustment bolt. When the cover is installed on the governor, the adjustment screw fits into a hole shaped to prevent the idle adjustment from moving after the cover is installed. Install a new wire and seal when all adjustments are complete.

Checking Balance Point

NOTE: The balance point check of the engine is a method of diagnosing engine performance. If the balance point and high idle speed are correct, the fuel system is operating properly.

1. Connect a mechanical tachometer to the engine.
2. Connect one end of a continuity tester to the brass terminal screw on the governor housing. Connect the other end to a good ground on the fuel system.

NOTE: On earlier engines, the brass terminal is located on top of the governor cover.

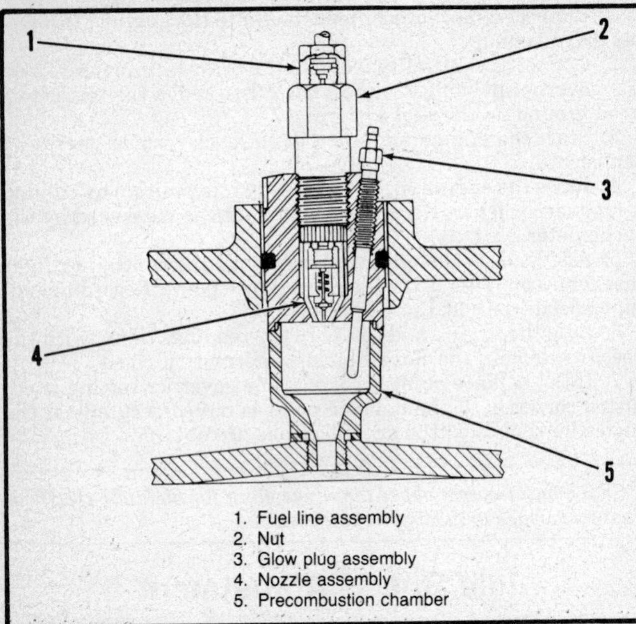

Injection valve and pre-combustion chamber—typical (© Caterpillar Tractor Co.)

3. Start the engine and allow it to reach normal operating temperature.
4. Move the governor lever to the high idle position and record the engine speed (rpm).
5. Add load to the engine slowly until the circuit tester light just comes on. This is the balance point. Record the engine speed (rpm) when the test light comes on, then repeat the procedure several times to make sure the readings are correct.
6. Stop the engine and compare the readings with the information given in the Rack Setting Information chart.
7. If the balance point is not correct, adjust the high idle rpm until the proper specification is obtained.

CAUTION

Do not adjust the high idle above the range given in the specifications chart. Damage to the engine can result.

Glow Plugs

Removal and Installation

ALL MODELS

1. Remove the valve cover.
2. Disconnect the glow plug clip from the fuel injection line, then remove the wire from the glow plug connector.
3. Remove the glow plug from the precombustion chamber with socket 5P127 or equivalent. Inspect the glow plug for damage, carbon buildup or a melted heating element. Perform a continuity test to verify glow plug operation before installing.
4. Installation is the reverse of removal. Coat the threads with anti-seize compound and install using removal socket tool. Torque the glow plugs to 8–12 ft. lbs. (11–17 Nm).
5. Install wire connector and glow plug clip.

NOTE: The glow plug wire should be on the same side of the fuel line as the glow plug.

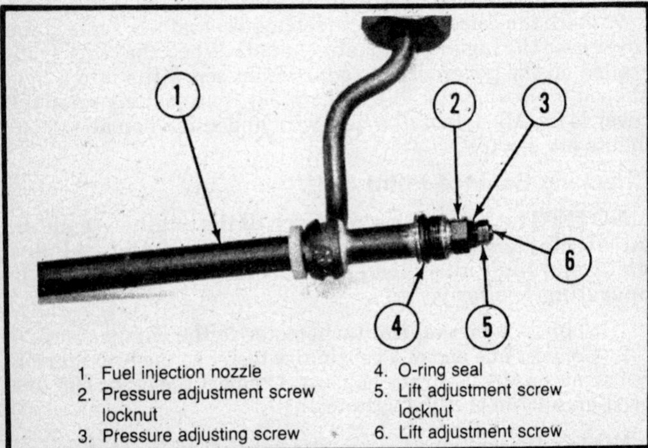

Fuel injection nozzle components (© Caterpillar Tractor Co.)

Fuel Injection Nozzles

Removal and Installation

3208 SERIES

1. Remove the rocker arm shafts.
2. Disconnect the fuel injection line and nozzle from the adapter. Cap all fuel line fittings immediately to prevent contamination of the fuel system with dirt.
3. Remove the clamp and the spacer holding the fuel injection nozzle in place.
4. Using a twisting motion, carefully pull the fuel injector out of the head. Remove the adapter from the head and remove the injection nozzle.
5. Check the injection nozzle for leakage, opening pressure and spray pattern with a suitable test bench. Remove the carbon seal dam and compression seal and discard.
6. Installation is the reverse of removal. Install a new carbon seal dam and compression seal and make sure the bore in the cylinder head and fuel inlet fittings are clean.

3306 SERIES

1. Remove the fuel injection lines. Do not let the tops of the injection nozzles turn when the fuel lines are loosened or the nozzles will be damaged.
2. Remove the hold down clamp and install nozzle puller 6V3129 or equivalent.

NOTE: Cap all open fuel lines and fittings to prevent contamination of the fuel system during service.

3. Move the screw out of the puller enough to engage the inside lip of the puller on the lower stepped diameter of the nozzle.
4. With the nozzle bleed screw aligned with the clearance hole in the puller, turn the screw in until the tip of the button goes into the thread in the hole for the nozzle clamp bolt.

CAUTION

Do not exceed 12 ft. lbs. (17 Nm) of torque on the screw in the removal tool to loosen the nozzle in the bore. Over torquing can cause the stem of the nozzle to bend or break off.

5. If the nozzle cannot be removed with the puller, a slide hammer must be used to loosen the nozzle in the bore.

NOTE: Hold the slide hammer so the center line of the tool is the same as the extended center line of the fuel injection nozzle. This will prevent distortion which can cause the nozzle to bend or break off.

6. If the slide hammer is necessary for removal of the injector it must be replaced as the impact will damage the nozzle. If the puller is used to remove the injector, remove and replace the carbon dam seal on the front of the nozzle.
7. Installation is the reverse of removal. Make sure the bore is clean and free of debris before installing the fuel injector. Use seal installer 8S2252 or equivalent to install the carbon dam seal on the injector nozzle.

8. Install a new seal on the fuel injection nozzle and place the nozzle in position with the bleed screw away from the rocker arm cover. The nozzle should slide into the bore smoothly with a slight twisting motion and moderate pressure. Do not force the injector into the bore. Once the nozzle is installed, install the hold-down clamp and fuel injection lines.

CAUTION

Do not let the tops of the injection nozzles turn when the fuel lines are tightened. The nozzles will be damaged if the top of the nozzle turns in the body.

3406 AND 3408 SERIES WITH PRECOMBUSTION CHAMBERS

1. Remove the valve cover.
2. Disconnect the clips from the fuel lines and remove the lines from the engine. Cap all fuel line openings immediately to prevent contamination of the fuel system.
3. Remove the hold down nut from the injector and carefully remove the injector from the precombustion chamber.
4. Installation is the reverse of removal. Torque the hold down nut to 50–60 ft. lbs. (68–82 Nm).
5. Install the fuel lines and torque the line nuts to 25–35 ft. lbs. (37–47 Nm).

CAUTION

When tightening the fuel line nuts, be careful not to damage the O-ring seals on the inner fuel lines.

3406 AND 3408 SERIES WITH DIRECT INJECTION

1. Remove the valve covers.
2. Disconnect the fuel line assemblies from the cylinder head and injectors and remove them from the engine. Cap all fuel line openings immediately to prevent contamination of the fuel system.
3. Remove the hold down nut on the injector and use extractor 5P6729 or equivalent to remove the injector from the cylinder head.

NOTE: If the extractor tool will not loosen the injector, a special puller tool 1P3075 will be necessary for removal.

4. Once the injector is removed from the engine, the nozzle assembly and seal may be removed from the injector body.
5. Installation is the reverse of removal. Coat the injector seal with clean diesel fuel before installing injector into the head. Torque the injector hold down nut to 50–60 ft. lbs. (68–82 Nm).
6. Install the fuel lines and torque the line nuts to 25–35 ft. lbs. (33–47 Nm).

Injection Pump and Governor

Removal and Installation

3208 SERIES

1. Remove the air cleaner, injection lines and intake manifold.
2. Remove the plug from the cover in the pump housing. Install the injection timing pin and turn the engine clockwise until the timing pin drops into the notch in the pump camshaft.
3. Remove the tachometer drive housing and disconnect the tachometer drive shaft.
4. Pull the drive gear free of the shaft using 5P2371 puller plate or equivalent. Tighten the puller bolts evenly until the drive gear is free of the shaft.
5. Remove the plug from the timing hole in the front cover and install a $^5/_{16}$ in.–18NC bolt, $2^1/_2$ in. long. Turn the crankshaft until the bolt can be installed in the timing gear and is in the center of the timing hole. The camshaft for the injection pump is now in correct time to the engine.
6. Remove the fuel line and mounting bolts from the injection pump and carefully lift the injection pump and governor assembly clear as a unit.
7. Installation is the reverse of removal. Align the fuel injection pump housing and governor assembly in position on the engine. Install the mounting bolts and fuel lines.
8. Install the tachometer drive shaft and torque early designs (recognized by the beveled end) to 75–85 ft. lbs. (101–115 Nm). Torque later tachometer drive to 100–120 ft. lbs. (135–163 Nm).
9. Check the injection timing. To check the timing, remove the timing pin and the bolt, then turn the crankshaft two revolutions clockwise and reinstall the timing pin and bolt back into place as before. If the timing pin or bolt cannot be installed, the fuel injection pump camshaft must be put into time again before proceeding on to the next step. See Injection Timing.
10. If the injection timing is correct, remove the bolt from the timing gear and install the plug into the timing hole.
11. Remove the timing pin from the timing slot in the injection pump camshaft and install the tachometer drive cover.
12. Install the air intake manifold, fuel injection lines and air cleaner. Torque all fuel injection line nuts to 25–35 ft. lbs. (33–47 Nm).

Removal and Installation

3306 SERIES

1. Remove the fuel ratio control, shutoff solenoid and fuel injection lines.

NOTE: Cap all fuel lines and connections to prevent dirt contamination of the fuel system.

2. Remove the cover from the timing gear housing.
3. Loosen the timing gear center bolt, leaving a gap of 0.125 in. (3.2mm) between the washer and weight assembly.
4. Use a suitable puller to remove the timing gear assembly from the fuel injection pump camshaft.
5. Remove the tube assembly located just behind the fuel filter housing.
6. Remove the mounting bolts that hold the fuel injection pump and governor assembly to support.
7. Remove the bolts holding the heat shield in position.
8. Remove the turbocharger oil supply line and oil return line.
9. Remove the mounting nuts holding the fuel injection pump and governor in place.
10. Carefully lift the fuel injection pump and governor off the engine as an assembly.

NOTE: Since the fuel injection pump and governor assembly weigh 62 lbs., a nylon strap and shop hoist is recommended for removal and installation of the injection pump.

11. Remove the fuel filter and base, tube assembly and drain lines from the fuel injection pump assembly.
12. Installation is basically the reverse of removal. Set the engine No. 1 piston at TDC on its compression stroke as previously described.
13. Install the timing tool 6V4186 or equivalent in the fuel injection pump housing. Push on the tool lightly while turning the fuel injection pump camshaft until the tool engages the slot in the camshaft. When the timing tool engages the slot, the fuel injection pump is in the No. 1 piston TDC position.
14. Make sure the O-ring seals are in position on the injection pump housing and governor. Coat the O-rings lightly with clean engine oil.
15. Place the fuel injection pump housing and governor assembly in position on the timing gear plate and the oil manifold. Install the mounting nuts that hold the injection pump housing to the timing gear plate and the governor housing to the oil manifold.

CAUTION

After the fuel injection pump housing and governor are installed on the timing gear plate, make sure the rack is free to move. The O-ring seal on the drive end of the injection pump can hold the rack and prevent free movement. If the rack does not move freely, the engine can overspeed and be damaged.

16. Install the bolt and washer that hold the weight assembly to the injection pump camshaft. Install the washer with the large outside diameter toward the bolt head, then tighten the bolt finger tight only.
17. Install adapter FT1560 or equivalent on the timing gear. Using a torque wrench, apply a counter–force of 50 ft. lbs. (68 Nm) on the adapter while tightening the timing gear center bolt to 180–220 ft. lbs. (245–295 Nm).
18. Check the injection timing by removing the timing pin from the injection pump and the timing bolt from the flywheel. Turn the crankshaft clockwise (as viewed from the front) approximately ½ turn, then reinstall the timing pin. While the crankshaft is turned slowly clockwise, lightly push on the timing pin until it engages the slot in the injection pump camshaft. Install the timing bolt in the flywheel.

NOTE: The timing is correct when the pin is in the groove on the injection pump camshaft and the timing bolt can be installed into the flywheel. Any results other than these will require the injection timing to be reset. See "Injection Timing–3306 Series."

19. If the injection timing is correct, install the cover on the timing gear housing.
20. Install the heat shield.
21. Install the turbocharger oil supply line and oil return line, along with the clip that holds the lines.
22. Remove the timing pin from the injection pump and install the cover and gasket.
23. Install the tube assembly that runs behind the fuel filter.
24. Remove the timing bolt and install the plug in the flywheel housing. Remove the crankshaft turning tool and reinstall the starter assembly.
25. Install the breather assembly on the rocker arm cover, if removed, install the fuel injection lines, shutoff solenoid and fuel ratio control. Tighten the fuel injection line nuts to 25–35 ft. lbs. (33–47 Nm).

CAUTION

Do not let the tops of the fuel nozzles turn when torquing the fuel line nuts to specifications. The nozzles will be damaged if the top of the nozzle turns in the body.

Injection Pump and Governor

Removal

3406 SERIES (EARLY GOVERNOR)

1. Remove the fuel shutoff solenoid and fuel ratio control from the injection pump assembly.
2. Set the engine at TDC, remove the plug from the side of the fuel injection pump housing and install timing pin 8S2291 or equivalent through the hole and into the notch in the injection pump camshaft. If the tool will not fit into the notch, follow the procedures under Injection Pump Timing before proceeding with removal.
3. Disconnect fuel lines from the fuel injection pump housing, then disconnect the fuel injection lines from the pump housing. Cap all open fuel connections to prevent dirt from contaminating the fuel system.
4. Remove the bolts which hold the bracket to the governor housing.
5. Fasten a nylon strap to the injection pump housing and connect to a shop hoist. Remove the bolts holding the injection pump assembly to the cylinder block.
6. Remove the bolts holding the fuel injection pump housing to the fuel injection pump and governor housing, then carefully lift the injection pump and governor clear as an assembly.

NOTE: The use of a shop hoist is recommended since the injection pump and governor assembly weigh 70 lbs.

7. To install, see the procedures under "Installation (Early and Late Governors)."

Removal

3406 SERIES (LATE GOVERNOR)

1. Remove the fuel shutoff solenoid and fuel ratio control from the injection pump assembly.
2. Set the No. 1 piston at TDC on its compression stroke.
3. Install timing bolt 8F8804 or equivalent into the flywheel. Remove the plug from the side of the injection pump housing and install timing pin 8S2291 or equivalent through the hole and into the notch in the injection pump camshaft.

NOTE: If the timing pin cannot be installed into the notch on the injection pump camshaft, follow the instructions under Fuel Injection Timing before proceeding.

4. Disconnect the fuel lines from the injection pump. Disconnect the fuel injection lines from the injection pump housing and cap all open fuel connections to prevent dirt from contaminating the fuel system.
5. Remove the bolts holding the bracket to the governor housing.
6. Fasten a nylon strap and hoist to the injection pump housing and remove the bolts holding the injection pump housing to the cylinder block. Remove the bolts holding the injection pump housing to the injection pump and governor drive housing, then carefully lift the injection pump and governor as an assembly.

NOTE: The use of a shop hoist is necessary since the injection pump assembly weighs 70 lbs.

Installation

3406 SERIES (EARLY AND LATE GOVERNOR)

1. Using a nylon strap and shop hoist, carefully place the fuel injection pump housing and governor in position on the fuel injection pump and governor drive housing.
2. Install the bolts that hold the injection pump housing to the injection pump and governor drive. Install the bolts that hold the injection pump housing to the cylinder block.
3. Install the bracket to the governor housing.
4. Remove the fuel line caps and install the injection lines and fuel lines. Torque all fuel line nuts to 25–35 ft. lbs. (33–47 Nm). Do not let the tops of the fuel nozzles turn when the fuel line nuts are tightened or the nozzles will be damaged.
5. Remove the timing pin from the fuel injection pump and the timing bolt from the flywheel. Turn the crankshaft two complete revolutions clockwise (as seen from the front) and check the fuel injection timing. If the timing is not correct, follow the procedure outlined under Injection Timing.
6. If the injection timing is correct, install the plug into the injection pump housing and flywheel cover.
7. Remove the engine turning tool, if used and install the cover. Install the fuel ratio control and shutoff solenoid.

NOTE: Further disassembly and adjustment of the fuel injection pump and governor assembly should be referred to a qualified specialist.

CAUTION

Whenever starting a diesel engine after any injection pump removal or service, uncover the intake manifold (or turbocharger inlet) and have a flat piece of steel on hand to cover the inlet and shut down the engine should overspeeding occur. Keep fingers away from the portion of the steel plate that covers the air inlet since the suction force is considerable.

Injection Pump and Governor

Removal and Installation

3408 SERIES

1. Remove the fuel injection lines and cap all openings to prevent contamination of the fuel system.
2. Set the No. 1 piston on TDC of its compression stroke and remove the bolts holding the automatic timing advance device cover.
3. Remove the bolts, retainer and automatic timing advance device.
4. Disconnect the fuel lines from the transfer pump.
5. Disconnect the lines from the fuel injection pump housing and air-fuel ratio control. Cap all open lines.
6. Remove the bolt from the governor linkage.
7. Remove the bolts from the bracket holding the fuel injection pump housing to the cylinder block and the bolts holding the housing to the block.
8. Fasten a nylon strap and hoist to the injection pump and governor assembly, then slide the pump and governor assembly to the rear and carefully lift it clear of the engine. Further disassembly of the governor should be referred to a qualified specialist.

NOTE: Since the injection pump and governor assembly weigh 110 lbs., the use of a hoist is necessary during removal and installation procedures.

9. Once the injection pump is clear, remove the three O-ring seals and discard if worn or damaged.
10. Installation is the reverse of removal. Make sure the outer surface of the fuel system and the surfaces that come in contact with it are clean.
11. Install the O-rings on the injection pump housing.
12. Hoist the injection pump and governor assembly as a unit and lower it into position on the engine. Install the bolts that hold the pump housing to the cylinder block.
13. Install the bolts and bracket holding the injection pump housing to the block.
14. Connect the governor linkage and the line to the air-fuel ratio control.
15. Connect the fuel lines to the transfer pump and fuel injection lines to the pump housing. Torque the injection line caps to 25–35 ft. lbs. (33–47 Nm).
16. Place automatic timing advance device in position in the housing. Install the retainer and bolts.
17. Check injection pump timing by inserting timing pin into the groove on the pump camshaft. Remove the timing plug in the pump housing and insert timing pin 5P4185 or equivalent. If the timing pin cannot be inserted into the camshaft groove, the injection timing will have to be reset. See the procedures outlined under "Injection Timing."
18. If the injection timing is correct, tighten the mounting bolts on the timing device to 20 ft. lbs. (25 Nm) and remove the timing pin.
19. Retorque the mounting bolts to 95–105 ft. lbs. (128–142 Nm), then turn the crankshaft two complete revolutions and recheck injection timing by repeating Step 16.
20. If the timing is correct, install the plug into the injection pump housing and reinstall the timing advance device cover.

CAUTION

Whenever starting a diesel engine after any injection pump removal or service, uncover the intake manifold (or turbocharger inlet) and have a flat piece of steel on hand to cover the inlet and shut down the engine, should overspeeding occur. Keep fingers away from the portion of the steel plate that covers the air inlet since the suction force is considerable.

CUMMINS DIESEL ENGINES

GENERAL ENGINE SPECIFICATIONS

Engine Model	Bore & Stroke	Piston Disp. Cu. In.	Maximum Horsepower @ R.P.M.	Torque @ R.P.M.	Firing Order: Right Hand Rotation	Firing Order: Left Hand Rotation	Lube Oil Pressure @ Governed Speed
V-378-155	4⅝ × 3¾	378	155 @ 3300	280 @ 1900	1-4-2-5-3-6	—	—
VT-378-155	4⅝ × 3¾	378	155 @ 3300	280 @ 1900	1-4-2-5-3-6	—	—
V-504-210	4⅝ × 3¾	504	210 @ 3300	375 @ 1900	1-5-4-8-6-3-7-2	1-2-7-3-6-8-4-5	—
VT-504-210	4⅝ × 3¾	504	210 @ 3300	375 @ 1900	1-5-4-8-6-3-7-2	1-2-7-3-6-8-4-5	—
V-555-210	4⅝ × 4⅛	555	210 @ 3300	445 @ 1900	1-5-4-8-6-3-7-2	1-2-7-3-6-8-4-5	40 @ 3300
V-555-225	4⅝ × 4⅛	555	225 @ 3000	425 @ 1800	1-5-4-8-6-3-7-2	1-2-7-3-6-8-4-5	40 @ 3300
V-555-240	4⅝ × 4⅛	555	240 @ 3300	445 @ 1900	1-5-4-8-6-3-7-2	1-2-7-3-6-8-4-5	40 @ 3300
VT-555-225	4⅝ × 4⅛	555	225 @ 3000	425 @ 1800	1-5-4-8-6-3-7-2	1-2-7-3-6-8-4-5	40 @ 3300
VT-555-240	4⅝ × 4⅛	555	240 @ 3300	445 @ 1900	1-5-4-8-6-3-7-2	1-2-7-3-6-8-4-5	40 @ 3300
LTA-10-240	4.9 × 5.4	611	240 @ 2100	750 @ 1300	1-5-3-6-2-4	—	35/45 @ 2460
LTA-10-270	4.9 × 5.4	611	270 @ 2100	840 @ 1300	1-5-3-6-2-4	—	35/45 @ 2460
Super-250	5½ × 6½	927	250 @ 2100	710 @ 1575	1-5-3-6-2-4	1-4-2-6-3-5	50 @ 2100
NHE-225	5½ × 6	855	225 @ 2100	—	1-5-3-6-2-4	1-4-2-6-3-5	—
NTC-230	5½ × 6	855	230 @ 2100	805 @ 1600	1-5-3-6-2-4	1-4-2-6-3-5	50 @ 2100
Formula 230	5½ × 6	855	230 @ 1900	805 @ 1300	1-5-3-6-2-4	1-4-2-6-3-5	40 @ 1900

GENERAL ENGINE SPECIFICATIONS

Engine Model	Bore & Stroke	Piston Disp. Cu. In.	Maximum Horsepower @ R.P.M.	Torque @ R.P.M.	Firing Order Right Hand Rotation	Firing Order Left Hand Rotation	Lube Oil Pressure @ Governed Speed
NH-230	5½ × 6	855	220 @ 2100	—	1-5-3-6-2-4	1-4-2-6-3-5	—
NTC-230-S	5½ × 6	855	—	—	1-5-3-6-2-4	1-4-2-6-3-5	—
NHF-240	5½ × 6	855	240 @ 1800	—	1-5-3-6-2-4	1-4-2-6-3-5	50 @ 2100
Power Torque-240	5½ × 6	855	240 @ 2100	900 @ 1300	1-5-3-6-2-4	1-4-2-6-3-5	50 @ 2100
Formula-240	5½ × 6	855	240 @ 1800	900 @ 1300	1-5-3-6-2-4	1-4-2-6-3-5	—
NTC-250-S	5½ × 6	855	—	—	1-5-3-6-2-4	1-4-2-6-3-5	—
NHH-250	5½ × 6	855	250 @ 2100	—	1-5-3-6-2-4	1-4-2-6-3-5	—
NTC-250	5½ × 6	855	250 @ 2100	855 @ 1575	1-5-3-6-2-4	1-4-2-6-3-5	40 @ 2100
NHC-250	5½ × 6	855	250 @ 2100	850 @ 1300	1-5-3-6-2-4	1-4-2-6-3-5	40 @ 2100
Formula 250	5½ × 6	855	250 @ 1900	850 @ 1300	1-5-3-6-2-4	1-4-2-6-3-5	40 @ 2000
NTE-235	5½ × 6	855	235 @ 2100	650 @ 1575	1-5-3-6-2-4	1-4-2-6-3-5	50 @ 2100
NTF-255	5½ × 6	855	—	—	1-5-3-6-2-4	1-4-2-6-3-5	—
NHF-265	5½ × 6	855	—	—	1-5-3-6-2-4	1-4-2-6-3-5	—
Power Torque-270	5½ × 6	855	270 @ 2100	1000 @ 1300	1-5-3-6-2-4	1-4-2-6-3-5	35 @ 2100 (no load)
Formula-270	5½ × 6	855	270 @ 1800	1000 @ 1300	1-5-3-6-2-4	1-4-2-6-3-5	35 @ 2100 (no load)
NHCT-270	5½ × 6	855	270 @ 2100	740 @ 1575	1-5-3-6-2-4	1-4-2-6-3-5	40 @ 2100
Power Torque-270	5½ × 6	855	270 @ 1950	825 @ 1575	1-5-3-6-2-4	1-4-2-6-3-5	40 @ 2100
NTC-290	5½ × 6	855	290 @ 2100	930 @ 1300	1-5-3-6-2-4	1-4-2-6-3-5	40 @ 2100
NTCC-290	5½ × 6	855	290 @ 2100	835 @ 1575	1-5-3-6-2-4	1-4-2-6-3-5	40 @ 2100
Formula 290	5½ × 6	855	290 @ 1900	930 @ 1300	1-5-3-6-2-4	1-4-2-6-3-5	40 @ 1900
NTCE-290	5½ × 6	855	—	—	1-5-3-6-2-4	1-4-2-6-3-5	—
NTF-295	5½ × 6	855	—	—	1-5-3-6-2-4	1-4-2-6-3-5	—
NTFE-295	5½ × 6	855	—	—	1-5-3-6-2-4	1-4-2-6-3-5	—
Power Torque-300-D	5½ × 6	855	—	—	1-5-3-6-2-4	1-4-2-6-3-5	—
NTC-300	5½ × 6	855	300 @ 2100	1000 @ 1300	1-5-3-6-2-4	1-4-2-6-3-5	35 @ 2100 (no load)
Formula-300	5½ × 6	855	300 @ 1800	1000 @ 1300	1-5-3-6-2-4	1-4-2-6-3-5	35 @ 2100 (no load)
Power Torque-300	5½ × 6	855	300 @ 2300	875 @ 1600	1-5-3-6-2-4	1-4-2-6-3-5	40 @ 2100
Power Torque-330	5½ × 6	855	330 @ 2300	930 @ 1500	1-5-3-6-2-4	1-4-2-6-3-5	40 @ 2100
NTC-335	5½ × 6	855	335 @ 2100	930 @ 1575	1-5-3-6-2-4	1-4-2-6-3-5	50 @ 2100
NTCC-335	5½ × 6	855	335 @ 2100	930 @ 1500	1-5-3-6-2-4	1-4-2-6-3-5	50 @ 2100
NHHTC-335	5½ × 6	855	—	—	1-5-3-6-2-4	1-4-2-6-3-5	—
NTCE-350	5½ × 6	855	350 @ 2100	1120 @ 1300	1-5-3-6-2-4	1-4-2-6-3-5	—
NTC-350	5½ × 6	855	350 @ 2100	1120 @ 1300	1-5-3-6-2-4	1-4-2-6-3-5	40 @ 2100
NTCC-350	5½ × 6	855	350 @ 2100	1065 @ 1400	1-5-3-6-2-4	1-4-2-6-3-5	40 @ 2100
Formula 350	5½ × 6	855	350 @ 1900	1120 @ 1300	1-5-3-6-2-4	1-4-2-6-3-5	40 @ 1900
NTF-365	5½ × 6	855	—	—	1-5-3-6-2-4	1-4-2-6-3-5	—
NTA-370	5½ × 6	855	370 @ 2100	1015 @ 1575	1-5-3-6-2-4	1-4-2-6-3-5	50 @ 2100
NT-380	5½ × 6	855	380 @ 2300	855 @ 1600	1-5-3-6-2-4	1-4-2-6-3-5	40 @ 2300
NTA-380	5½ × 6	855	380 @ 2300	855 @ 1500	1-5-3-6-2-4	1-4-2-6-3-5	40 @ 2300
NTA-400	5½ × 6	855	400 @ 2100	1000 @ 1575	1-5-3-6-2-4	1-4-2-6-3-5	40 @ 2100
NTC-400	5½ × 6	855	400 @ 2100	1150 @ 1500	1-5-3-6-2-4	1-4-2-6-3-5	40 @ 2100

GENERAL ENGINE SPECIFICATIONS

Engine Model	Bore & Stroke	Piston Disp. Cu. In.	Maximum Horsepower @ R.P.M.	Torque @ R.P.M.	Firing Order Right Hand Rotation	Firing Order Left Hand Rotation	Lube Oil Pressure @ Governed Speed
NTA-420	5½ × 6	855	420 @ 2300	1045 @ 1725	1-5-3-6-2-4	1-4-2-6-3-5	40 @ 2300
Twin Turbo-475	5½ × 6	855	475 @ 2100	1430 @ 1400	1-5-3-6-2-4	1-4-2-6-3-5	—
V-903	5½ × 4¾	903	280 @ 2600	700 @ 1575	1-5-4-8-6-3-7-2	—	50 @ 2600
VT-903	5½ × 4¾	903	300 @ 2400	795 @ 1600	1-5-4-8-6-3-7-2	—	50 @ 2400
Formula 903	5½ × 4¾	903	290 @ 2200	795 @ 1600	1-5-4-8-6-3-7-2	—	50 @ 2200
V-903	5½ × 4¾	903	280 @ 2600	—	1-5-4-8-6-3-7-2	1-2-7-3-6-8-4-5	—
V-903	5½ × 4¾	903	295 @ 2600	—	1-5-4-8-6-3-7-2	1-2-7-3-6-8-4-5	—
VT-903	5½ × 4¾	903	320 @ 2600	—	1-5-4-8-6-3-7-2	1-2-7-3-6-8-4-5	—
VT-903	5½ × 4¾	903	400 @ 2600	—	1-5-4-8-6-3-7-2	1-2-7-3-6-8-4-5	—
Formula VT-300	5½ × 4¾	903	300 @ 2200	860 @ 1400	1-5-4-8-6-3-7-2	1-2-7-3-6-8-4-5	—
VT-400	5½ × 4¾	903	400 @ 2600	—	1-5-4-8-6-3-7-2	1-2-7-3-6-8-4-5	—
VTA-903-T	5½ × 4¾	903	450 @ 2600	—	1-5-4-8-6-3-7-2	1-2-7-3-6-8-4-5	—
VTB-903	5½ × 4¾	903	275 @ 2100	—	1-5-4-8-6-3-7-2	1-2-7-3-6-8-4-5	—
KT-450	6¼ × 6¼	1150	450 @ 2100	1350 @ 1500	1-5-3-6-2-4	1-4-2-6-3-5	50 @ 2100
KTA-525	6¼ × 6¼	1150	525 @ 2100	1650 @ 1300	1-5-3-6-2-4	1-4-2-6-3-5	50 @ 2100
KTA-600	6¼ × 6¼	1150	600 @ 2100	1650 @ 1600	1-5-3-6-2-4	1-4-2-6-3-5	50 @ 2100

FIRING ORDERS

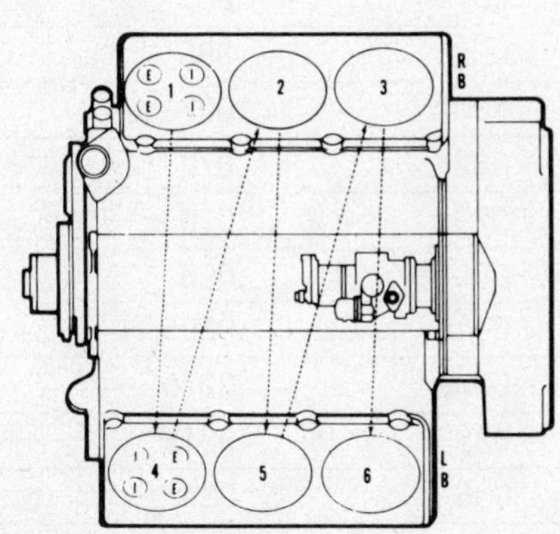

Firing order and cylinder location—378 Series
(© Cummins Engine Co.)

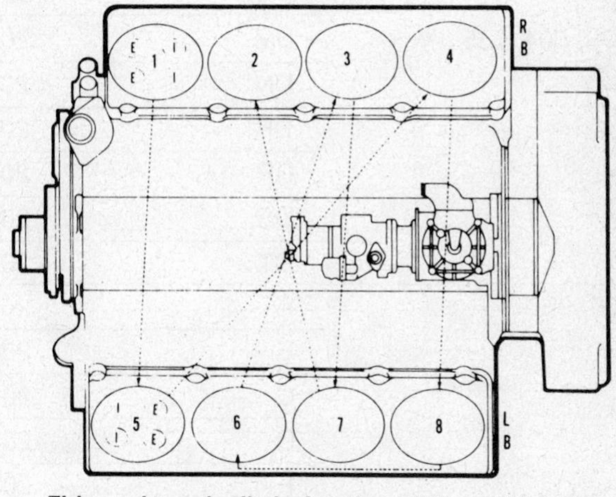

Firing order and cylinder location—504 and 555 Series
(© Cummins Engine Co.)

FIRING ORDERS

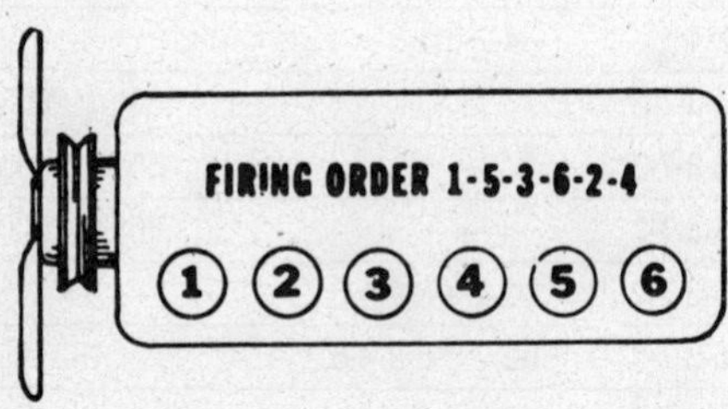

Firing order and cylinder location—611, 855 and KT1150 Series
(© Cummins Engine Co.)

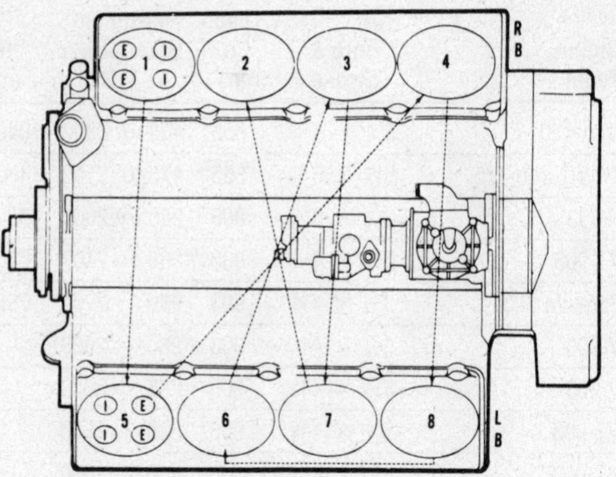

Firing order and cylinder location—903 Series
(© Cummins Engine Co.)

INJECTION TIMING SPECIFICATIONS

Engine Series	Timing Code	Piston Travel (Inches)	Push Rod Travel (Inches)		
			Nominal	Fast	Slow
378, 504, 555	DA	.2032	.050	.048	.052
	DC	.2032	.056	.054	.058
	DD	.2032	.062	.060	.064
	DB	.2032	.061	.059	.063
	DE	.2032	.078	.076	.080
	DG	.2032	.048	.046	.050
	DF	.2032	.065	.063	.067
	DH	.2032	.071	.0695	.0725
	DJ	.2032	.074	.072	.076
	DK	.2032	.102	.100	.104
	DL	.2032	.095	.093	.097
378, 504, 555	DM	.2032	.087	.085	.089
	DN	.2032	.098	.095	.101
	DP	.2032	.100	.097	.103
	DR	.2032	.082	.079	.085
	DS	.2032	.079	.076	.082
	DT	.2032	.069	.066	.072
855, 927	A	.2032	.0415	.0395	.0435
	B	.2032	.0295	.0275	.0315
	C	.2032	.0335	.0315	.0355
	D	.2032	.036	.034	.038
	E	.2032	.029	.028	.030

INJECTION TIMING SPECIFICATIONS

Engine Series	Timing Code	Piston Travel (Inches)	Push Rod Travel (Inches)		
			Nominal	Fast	Slow
855, 927	Y	.2032	.039	.037	.041
	Z	.2032	.026	.024	.028
	AA	.2032	.031	.030	.032
	AC	.2032	.028	.027	.029
	AF	.2032	.045	.044	.046
	AH	.2032	.035	.034	.036
	AI	.2032	.034	.033	.035
	AK	.2032	.041	.040	.042
	AN	.2032	.046	.045	.047
	AQ	.2023	.042	.041	.043
	AS	.2032	.036	.035	.037
	AT	.2032	.030	.029	.031
	AU	.2032	.049	.048	.050
	AV	.2032	.050	.049	.051
	AW	.2032	.060	.059	.061
	AX	.2032	.055	.054	.056
	AY	.2032	.040	.039	.041
	AZ	.2032	.059	.058	.060
	BA	.2032	.028	.027	.029
	BB,CM	.2032	.100	.099	.101
	BC	.2032	.024	.023	.025
	BD	.2032	.095	.094	.096
	BH,CH	.2032	.052	.051	.053
	BI,CB,CN	.2032	.105	.104	.106
	BM	.2032	.053	.052	.054
	BS	.2032	.072	.071	.073
	BT	.2032	.081	.080	.082
	BU	.2032	.065	.064	.066
	BV	.2032	.062	.061	.063
	BW	.2032	.067	.066	.068
	BY	.2032	.070	.069	.071
	CC	.2032	.115	.114	.115
	CD	.2032	.074	.073	.075
	CE	.2032	.026	.025	.027
	CF	.2032	.038	.037	.039
	CO	.2032	.0635	.0625	.0645
	CP	.2032	.120	.119	.121
	CR	.2032	.110	.109	.111

INJECTION TIMING SPECIFICATIONS

Engine Series	Timing Code	Piston Travel (Inches)	Push Rod Travel (Inches)		
			Nominal	Fast	Slow
903	J	.2032	.049	.046	.052
	AG	.2032	.066	.063	.069
	BE	.2032	.059	.056	.062
	BK	.2032	.069	.066	.072
	BF	.2032	.079	.076	.082
	Q	.2032	.054	.051	.057
	AB	.2032	.078	.075	.081
	BG	.2032	.094	.091	.097
	BX	.2032	.083	.080	.086
	BZ	.2032	.089	.086	.092
	CG	.2032	.092	.089	.095
	BN	.2032	.084	.081	.087
	CG	.2032	.094	.091	.097
	CS	.2032	.111	.108	.114
1150	AE	.2032	.108	.106	.110
	AM	.2032	.118	.116	.120
611	CX	.2032	.080	.078	.082
	CY	.2032	.075	.073	.077

VALVE AND INJECTOR ADJUSTMENT SPECIFICATIONS—903 AND 611 SERIES

Adjustment Limits Using Indicator Method of Adjustment

Engine Series	Injector Plunger Travel	Valve Clearance Inch (mm)	
		Intake	Exhaust
903	1.2 TO 1 ROCKER LEVER RATIO—INJECTOR LEVER P/N 196565		
	0.180 ± 0.001 (4.57 ± 0.003)	0.012 (0.30)	0.025 (0.64)
	1 TO 1 ROCKER LEVER RATIO—INJECTOR LEVER P/N 211399		
	0.187 ± 0.001 (4.75 ± 0.03)	0.012 (0.30)	0.025 (0.64)
611	0.1975–0.1985 (5.01–5.04)	0.014 (0.036)	0.027 (0.069)

VALVE AND INJECTOR ADJUSTMENT SPECIFICATIONS—1150 SERIES
Uniform Plunger Travel Adjustment Limits

	Injector Plunger Travel Inch (mm)		Valve Clearance Inch (mm)	
Oil Temp.	Adj. Value	Recheck Limit	Intake	Exhaust
Cold	0.304 (7.72)	0.3035 to 0.3045 (7.709 to 7.734)	0.014 (0.36)	0.027 (0.69)
Hot	0.303 (7.70)	0.3025 to 0.3035 (7.684 to 7.709)	0.014 (0.36)	0.027 (0.69)

VALVE AND INJECTOR ADJUSTMENT SPECIFICATIONS—1150 AND 611 SERIES
Injector and Valve Set Position①

		Set Cylinder	
Bar in Direction	Pulley Position	Injector	Valve
Start	A	3	5
Adv. To	B	6	3
Adv. To	C	2	6
Adv. To	A	4	2
Adv. To	B	1	4
Adv. To	C	5	1

① Firing order: 1-5-3-6-2-4

VALVE AND INJECTOR ADJUSTMENT SPECIFICATIONS—855 SERIES
Uniform Plunger Travel Adjustment

	Injector Plunger Travel Inch (mm)		Valve Clearance Inch (mm)	
Oil Temp.	Adj. Value	Recheck Limit	Intake	Exhaust
		ALUMINUM ROCKER HOUSING		
Cold	0.170 (4.32)	0.169 to 0.171 (4.29 to 4.34)	0.011 (0.28)	0.023 (0.58)
Hot	0.170 (4.32)	0.169 to 0.171 (4.29 to 4.34)	0.008 (0.20)	0.023 (0.58)
		CAST IRON ROCKER HOUSING		
Cold	0.175 (4.45)	0.174 to 0.176 (4.42 to 4.47)	0.011 (0.28)	0.023 (0.58)
Hot	0.175 (4.45)	0.174 to 0.176 (4.42 to 4.47)	0.008 (0.20)	0.023 (0.58)

VALVE AND INJECTOR ADJUSTMENT SPECIFICATIONS—855 SERIES
Injector and Valve Set Position①

Bar in Direction	Pulley Position	Set Cylinder Injector	Set Cylinder Valve
Start	A or 1-6 VS	3	5
Adv. To	B or 2-5 VS	6	3
Adv. To	C or 3-4 VS	2	6
Adv. To	A or 1-6 VS	4	2
Adv. To	B or 2-5 VS	1	4
Adv. To	C or 3-4 VS	5	1

① Engine firing order: right hand: 1-5-3-6-2-4

VALVE AND INJECTOR ADJUSTMENT SPECIFICATIONS—855 SERIES
Injector and Valve Set Position①

Bar in Direction	Pulley Position	Set Cylinder Injector	Set Cylinder Valve
Start	1-6 VS	2	4
Adv. To	3-4 VS	6	2
Adv. To	2-5 VS	3	6
Adv. To	1-6 VS	5	3
Adv. To	3-4 VS	1	5
Adv. To	2-5 VS	4	1

① Engine firing order: left hand 1-4-2-6-3-5

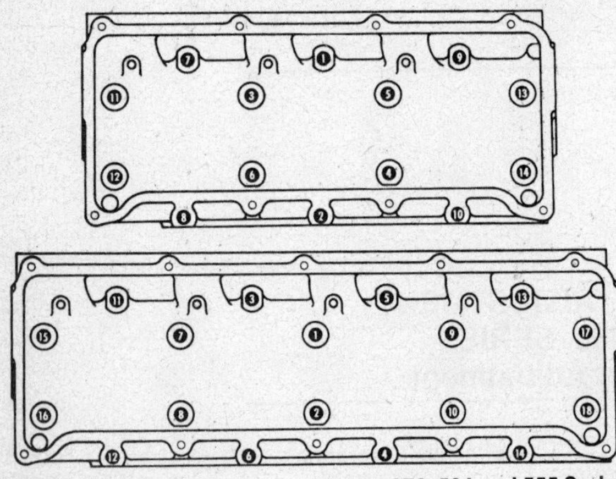

Cylinder head bolt torque sequence—378, 504 and 555 Series
(© Cummins Engine Co.)

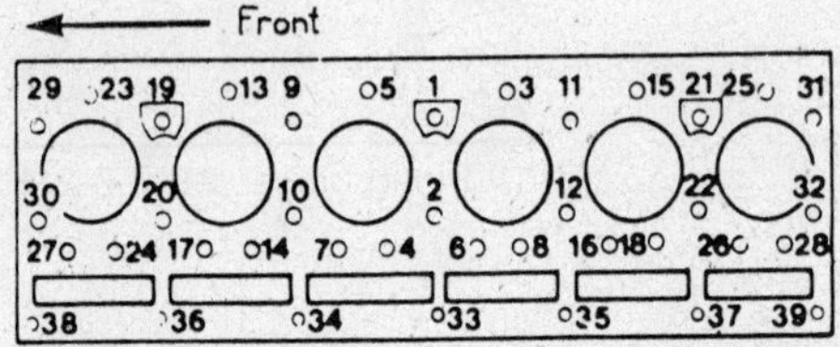

Cylinder head bolt torque sequence—855 Series
(© Cummins Engine Co.)

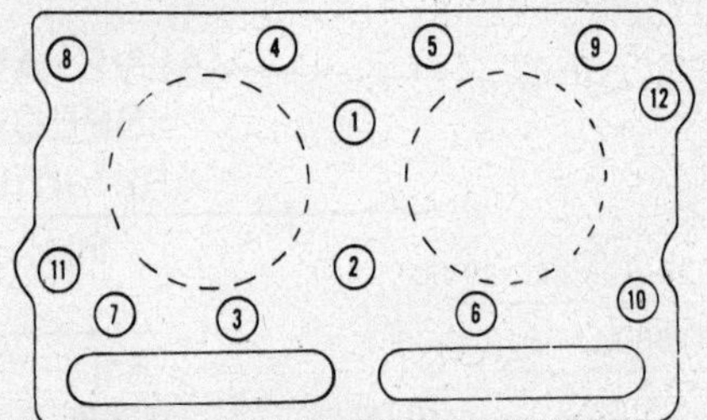

Cylinder head bolt torque sequence—1150 Series
(© Cummins Engine Co.)

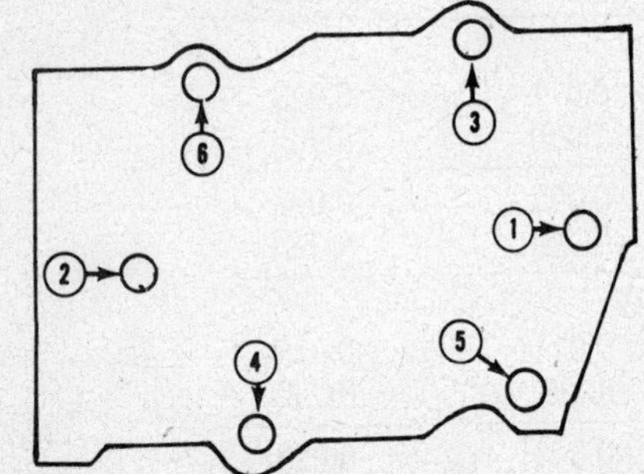

Cylinder head bolt torque sequence—611 Series
(© Cummins Engine Co.)

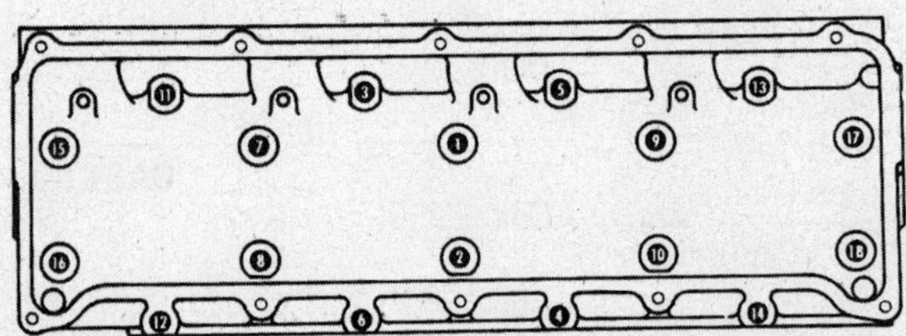

Cylinder head bolt torque sequence—903 Series
(© Cummins Engine Co.)

TORQUE SPECIFICATIONS

(For each step, tighten following the specified torque pattern to the torque figure indicated below. All readings are in foot pounds unless otherwise indicated. Degrees of rotation refers to the rotation of the nut or capscrew.)

Operation	903 Series Engines	855 Series Engines	378, 504, 555 Series Engines	1150 Series Engines	611 Series Engines
Cylinder Head Bolts①					
Step 1	50–80	20–25	80–90	40–60	75
Step 2	115–135	80–100	110–115	110–130	125
Step 3	175–185	265–305		180–190	175
Step 4	200–240			250–260	loosen fully
Step 5	280–300				75
Step 6					125
Step 7					175
Main Bearing Capscrew⑨					
Step 1	50	80–90⑩	55–65	190–200	50
Step 2	140–170	160–170	115–125	440–450	105
Step 3	300–320	250–260	165–175	loosen fully	155
Step 4	loosen fully	loosen fully	loosen fully	190–200	loosen fully
Step 5	50	80–90	55–65	440–450	50
Step 6	140–170	160–170	115–125		105
Step 7	300–320	250–260	165–175		155
Side Capscrews					
Step 1	25		35–40		
Step 2	70–75		65–70		
Step 3	140–150		100–110		
Connecting Rod Bolts②					
Step 1	55–60	70–75	25–30	70–80	50
Step 2	90–100	140–150	50–55	140–150	105
Step 3	loosen fully	loosen fully	loosen fully	210–220	155
Step 4	30–40	25–30	25	loosen fully	loosen fully
Step 5	60–70	70–75	60 degrees	70–80	50
Step 6	95–110	140–150		140–150	105
Step 7				210–220	155
Oil Pan Bolts③					
Step 1	30–35	35–40	15–17 (5/16″ bolts)	30–35 (3/8″ bolts)	35
Step 2				40–45 (7/16″ bolts)	
Step 3				60–70 (9/16″ bolts)	
Flywheel Housing	50–55	150	70–75	140–160	145
Flywheel④					
Step 1	180–200	200–220	55–60	100–120	50
Step 2			135–145	200–220	95
Step 3					145
Crankshaft Adapter Capscrews	330–350		135–140		
Valve Crosshead Adjustment Locknut⑤	25–30	25–30	25–28	25–30	30
Intake Manifold⑥					
Step 1	30–35	20–25	10	30–35	
Step 2			20		
Step 3			34–37		
Exhaust Manifold⑦	40–45		30–32	40–45	50
Crankshaft Vibration Damper					
Step 1	200–205		30–35	65–75	105
Step 2			110–120		
Crankshaft Drive Pulley					
Step 1			20		105
Step 2			90–100		

TORQUE SPECIFICATIONS

(For each step, tighten following the specified torque pattern to the torque figure indicated below. All readings are in foot pounds unless otherwise indicated. Degrees of rotation refers to the rotation of the nut or capscrew.)

Operation	903 Series Engines	855 Series Engines	378, 504, 555 Series Engines	1150 Series Engines	611 Series Engines
Crankshaft Pulley/Vibration Damper⑧					
Step 1		85	30–35	160–180	105
Step 2			110–120	320–340	

① 555 Series engines; a) 25–30, b) 80–90, c) 135–140
1150 Series engines; torque readings are for Cadium Plated head gasket, if a Lubricated head gasket is used torque gasket as follows: a) 40–60, b) 140–160, c) 240–260, d) 350–370

② 555 Series engines; a) 40–45, b) 75–80, c) loosen fully, d) 55, e) 60 degrees

③ 555 Series engines; 28–31 when ⅜″ bolts are used
855 Series engines; torque the capscrews that hold the oil pan to the rear cover plate to 15–20 ft. lbs. Tighten the capscrews that hold the oil pan to the flywheel housing to 70–80 ft. lbs.
903 Series engines; torque the smaller diameter bolts at the rear of the oil pan to 16–19 foot pounds

④ 855 Series engines; 190–200 when capscrews with safety wire are used

⑤ 903 Series engines; 30–35 when using a torque wrench adapter
855, 378, 504, 555, and 1150 Series engines; 22–26 when using a torque wrench adapter
1150 Series engines; when using a torque wrench adapter on a Jacobs Brake Crosshead

⑥ 855 Series engine; 22–27 when using a steel cover

⑦ 855 Series engine; 40 when washers or lockplates are not used

⑧ 855 Series engines; if ½″ grade 8 capscrews are used, torque to 115–125, ⅝″ grade 8 capscrews are used, torque to 180–200, ⅝″ grade 5 capscrews are used torque to 150–170
555 Series engines; tighten to a final torque of 135–140 ft. lbs.

⑨ 855 Series engines; torque the 1 in. capscrews to a) 100–110, b) 200–210, c) 300–310 d) loosen completely and repeat steps a thru c

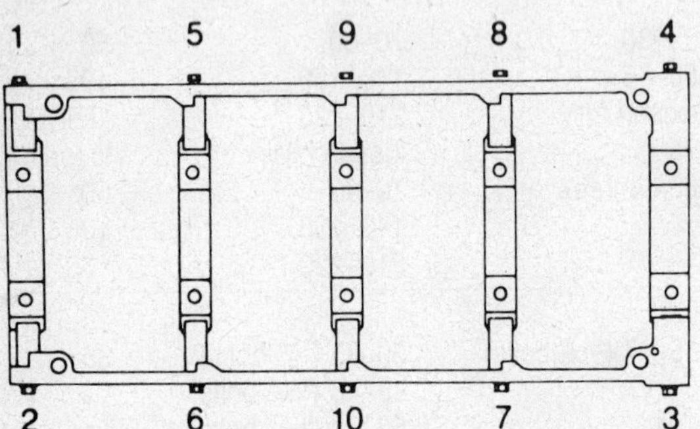

All V8 Series (© Cummins Engine Co.)

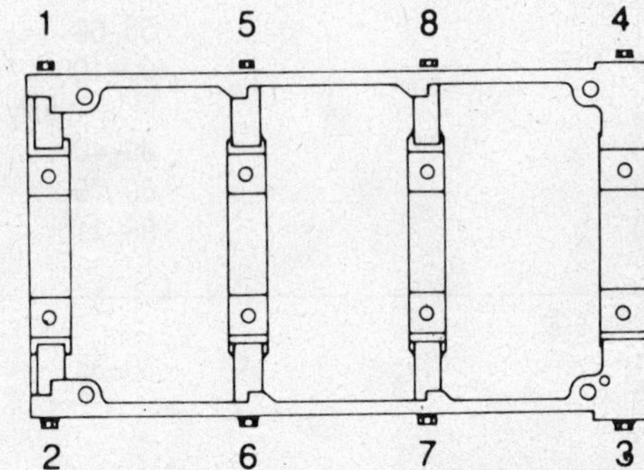

All V6 Series (© Cummins Engine Co.)

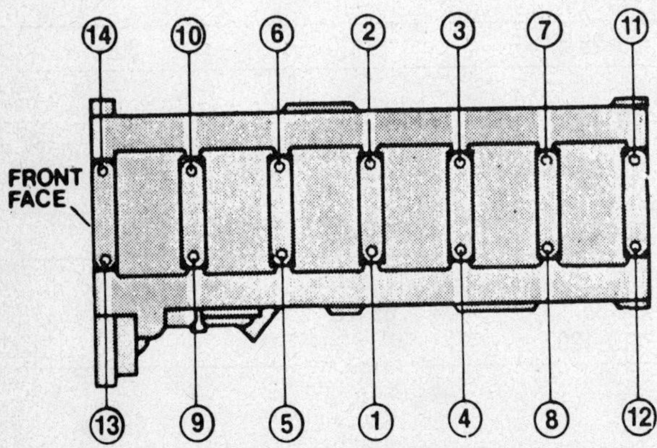

L-10 Series (© Cummins Engine Co.)

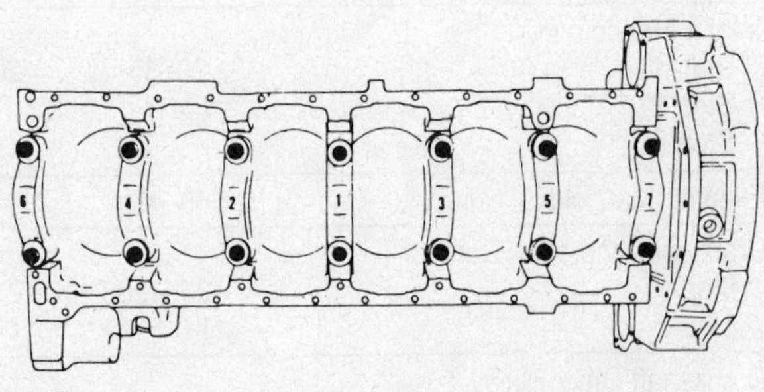

KTA 1150 Series (© Cummins Engine Co.)

CHILTON'S THREE "C's" DIESEL ENGINE DIAGNOSIS PROCEDURE

Condition	Cause	Correction
Hard Starting or Failure to Start	1. Fuel shut off valve closed or fuel tank empty.	1. Check fuel shut-off and fuel level.
	2. Inferior quality fuel.	2. Drain and refill fuel tank.
	3. Restricted fuel lies.	3. Clear fuel lines.
	4. Fuel pump pressure regulation faulty.	4. Check fuel pressure.
	5. Plugged injector spray holes.	5. Clean fuel injectors.
	6. Broken fuel pump drive shaft.	6. Repair fuel pump.
	7. Gear pump gears scored or worn.	7. Replace fuel pump.
	8. Injector inlet or drain connections loose.	8. Check connections.
	9. Water in fuel.	9. Drain and refill fuel tank.
	10. Air leaks in fuel suction line.	10. Correct as necessary.
	11. Incorrect injector timing.	11. Reset injection timing.
	12. Valve leakage.	12. Check valves.
	13. Restricted air intake.	13. Clear air intake.
	14. Engine in need of overhaul.	14. Correct as necessary.
	15. Incorrect valve timing.	15. Reset valve timing.
Engine Runs but Misses	1. Restricted fuel lines.	1. Clear fuel lines.
	2. Water in fuel or poor quality fuel.	2. Drain and refill fuel tank.
	3. Air leaks in fuel suction line.	3. Correct as necessary.
	4. Injectors improperly adjusted or plugged.	4. Clean and check injectors.
	5. Low compression, intake or exhaust valves leaking.	5. Check valves for wear or damage.
	6. Leaking supercharger air connection.	6. Check all intake connections.
	7. Restricted drain line.	7. Clear drain line.
	8. Stuck injector plunger.	8. Check fuel injector plungers.
	9. Improper valve and injector adjustments.	9. Check valve clearance and injector opening pressure.
Excessive Smoke	1. Restricted fuel system drain lines.	1. Clear fuel lines.
	2. Plugged injector spray holes.	2. Clean fuel injectors.
	3. Inferior quality fuel.	3. Drain and refill fuel system.
	4. Engine fuel rate too high.	4. Reset maximum fuel delivery.
	5. Injectors improperly adjusted.	5. Check injector operation.
	6. Intake manifold or cylinder head gasket leak.	6. Correct as necessary.
	7. Restricted air intake.	7. Replace filter element.
	8. High exhaust back pressure.	8. Check for exhaust restriction.
	9. Broken or worn piston rings.	9. Repair as necessary.
	10. Engine in need of overhaul.	10. Repair as necessary.
	11. Incorrect valve timing.	11. Reset valve timing.
	12. Worn or scored cylinder liners or pistons.	12. Repair as necessary.
Low Power or Loss of Power	1. Inferior quality fuel.	1. Drain and refill fuel system.
	2. Water in fuel.	2. Drain water separator and tank.
	3. Fuel suction line leaking.	3. Repair as necessary.
	4. Restricted fuel lines.	4. Clear fuel lines.
	5. Low fuel pressure.	5. Check delivery pressure.
	6. Plugged injector spray holes.	6. Clean fuel injectors.
	7. Dirty fuel filters or screens.	7. Replace filters and clean screens.
	8. Improper valve and injector adjustments.	8. Check valve clearance and injector operation.
	9. Improperly adjusted throttle linkage.	9. Check throttle linkage.
	10. High speed governor set too low.	10. Adjust governor setting.
	11. Air in system.	11. Bleed air from fuel system.
	12. Sticking stop control (fuel shut off).	12. Replace stop control.
	13. Restricted air intake.	13. Replace filter element.
	14. High exhaust back pressure.	14. Check for exhaust restriction.
	15. Intake manifold or cylinder head gasket leakage.	15. Repair as necessary.
	16. Low compression—intake or exhaust valve leakage.	16. Overhaul as necessary.
	17. Broken or worn piston rings.	17. Replace piston rings.
	18. Incorrect bearing clearances.	18. Replace worn bearings.
	19. Worn or scored cylinder liners or pistons.	19. Replace cylinder liners.
	20. Engine in need of overhaul.	20. Repair as necessary.
	21. Incorrect valve timing.	21. Reset valve timing.
	22. Dirty air cleaner.	22. Replace filter element.
	23. Overheating engine.	23. Check cooling system operation.

CHILTON'S THREE "C's" DIESEL ENGINE DIAGNOSIS PROCEDURE

Condition	Cause	Correction
Excessive Fuel Consumption	1. Inferior quality fuel.	1. Drain and refill fuel system.
	2. Restricted fuel system drain lines.	2. Clear fuel lines.
	3. Fuel rate set too high.	3. Reset maximum fuel delivery.
	4. Fuel leaks—external or internal.	4. Correct as necessary.
	5. Plugged injector spray holes.	5. Clean fuel injectors.
	6. Injectors not adjusted properly.	6. Check injector opening pressure.
	7. Cracked injector body or cup.	7. Replace injector.
	8. Restricted air intake.	8. Replace air cleaner element.
	9. High exhaust back pressure.	9. Check exhaust restriction.
	10. Engine overloaded.	10. Correct as necessary.
	11. Incorrect bearing clearances.	11. Replace worn bearings.
	12. Engine in need of overhaul.	12. Correct as necessary.
Excessive Oil Consumption	1. External or internal oil leaks.	1. Correct as necessary.
	2. Cylinder oil control not working.	2. Repair as necessary.
	3. Wrong grade oil for climatic conditions.	3. Drain and refill crankcase.
	4. Broken or worn piston rings.	4. Repair as necessary.
	5. Engine in need of overhaul.	5. Overhaul as required.
	6. Worn or scored cylinder liners or pistons.	6. Replace cylinder liners or pistons.
Low Lubrication Oil Pressure	1. Oil suction line restricted.	1. Clear oil suction line.
	2. Oil pump or pressure regulator valve not working properly.	2. Check oil pump and regulator valve.
	3. Crankcase oil level too low.	3. Top up crankcase oil level.
	4. Wrong grade of oil for conditions.	4. Drain and refill crankcase.
	5. Insufficient coolant.	5. Top up cooling system.
	6. Worn water pump.	6. Replace water pump.
	7. Coolant thermostat not working.	7. Replace thermostat.
	8. Loose fan belts.	8. Tighten fan belts.
	9. Clogged coolant passages.	9. Flush cooling system.
	10. Clogged oil cooler.	10. Replace oil cooler.
	11. Radiator core openings restricted.	11. Repair as necessary.
	12. Air in cooling system.	12. Bleed cooling system.
	13. Insufficient radiator capacity.	13. Repair as necessary.
	14. Leaking coolant hoses, connections or gaskets.	14. Correct as necessary.
	15. Incorrect bearing clearances.	15. Replace worn bearings.
	16. Engine in need of overhaul.	16. Repair as necessary.
	17. Engine overloaded.	17. Correct as necessary.

TUNE-UP AND ADJUSTMENTS

COMPRESSION TEST

The only accepted means of checking engine compression is by a Blow-By Test which requires the use of a special measuring tools, gauges and engine dynamometer. This procedure is usually accomplished with the engine removed and set up in a test cell. No other compression test procedure is recommended by the manufacturer.

VALVE SET MARK ALIGNMENT (VS)

378, 504, 555 SERIES ENGINES

1. Turn the crankshaft in the proper direction of rotation until the no. 1 "VS" mark on the vibration damper or the crankshaft pulley is aligned with the pointer.
2. In this position, both the intake and exhaust valves must be closed for cylinder no. 1. If this is not the case, advance the crankshaft one revolution. Refer to engine firing order, if required.

NOTE: Do not use the fan blades to rotate the engine.

3. Adjust the injector plunger and then the crossheads and valves of the first cylinder. Turn the crankshaft in the direction of rotation to the next "VS" mark.

NOTE: Two complete revolutions of the crankshaft are needed to set the injectors and valves. Injectors and valves can be adjusted for only one cylinder at any on "VS" setting.

4. Continue turning the crankshaft and making the proper adjustments until all injectors and valves have been serviced.

378, 504, 555 and 855 SERIES ENGINES (TORQUE METHOD)

1. If used, pull the compression release lever to allow crankshaft rotation without engine compression.
2. Loosen the injector rocker lever adjusting nut on all cylinders to distinguish between cylinders adjusted and those not adjusted during the procedure.
3. Turn the engine in normal direction of rotation until the appropriate valve set mark for the cylinder being adjusted aligns with the pointer on the gear case cover.
4. Check the rocker levers on the two cylinders indicated on the crankshaft pulley, only one pair the levers should be loose. This is the cylinder to be adjusted after first setting the injector plunger.

CAUTION

If equipped with Top Stop Injectors, the plunger travel can only be adjusted with the injectors removed from the engine, using a special adjusting tool. Bent push rods can result, if not properly adjusted. Refer to Top Stop Injector Adjustment Procedure.

5. The injector plungers are adjusted with a torque wrench and screw driver adapter to specific torque setting. Turn the adjusting screw down until the plunger contacts the cup and advance an additional 15 degrees to squeeze the oil from the cup.
6. Loosen the adjusting screw one turn, then tighten the adjusting screw in two or three passes with a torque wrench and adapter to 60 ft. lbs. (hot or cold engine) on the 378, 504 and 555 series engines and 72 ft. lbs. (hot or cold engine) on the 855 series engine.

NOTE: If the rocker housing is cast iron on the 855 series engines, the cold engine setting is 48 inch lbs. and the hot engine setting is 72 inch lbs.

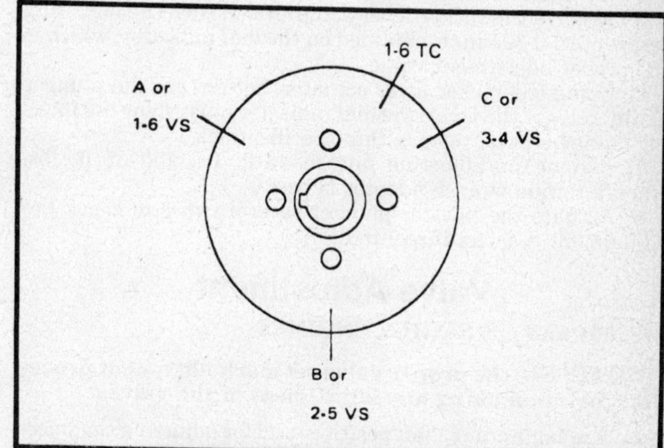

Valve set (VS) marking location on pulley—855 Series
(© Cummins Engine Co.)

7. After adjusting the injector plunger travel, set the crossheads and valve clearances to specifications.

NOTE: On the 378, 504 and 555 series engines, after all the injectors and valves have been adjusted and the engine warmed up to 140 degrees F. (oil temperature), reset the injectors.

1150 SERIES ENGINES

NOTE: See the proper valve set mark alignment procedure before making any injector plunger adjustments.

1. Install tool 3375007 (indicator support) or equivalent with its extension on the injector plunger top at number 4 cylinder.

NOTE: Make sure that the indicator extension is secure in the indicator stem and not against the rocker lever.

2. Using tool 3375010 (rocker lever actuator) or equivalent, depress the injector plunger until the plunger is bottomed in the cup. This is necessary to squeeze the oil from the cup.
3. Allow the injector plunger to rise, bottom again and then set the dial indicator at zero with the injector plunger bot-

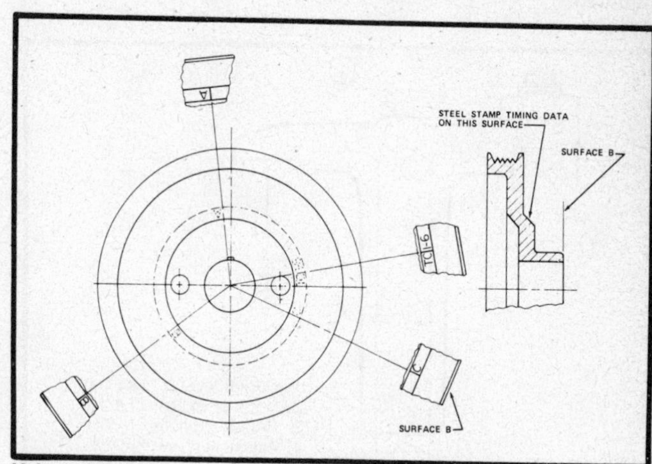

Valve set (VS) marking location on pulley—KT1150 Series
(© Cummins Engine Co.)

tomed. At this point, check the extension contact with the plunger top.

4. Allow the plunger to rise and then bottom again to check the zero dial indicator setting.

5. Remove the rocker lever actuator and turn the adjusting screw until 0.304 in. is obtained on the dial indicator, which is the proper adjustment value.

6. Using the rocker lever actuator, bottom out the plunger again, release the lever, the dial indicator must show the injector plunger travel to be within specifications.

7. Torque the adjusting nut 40–45 ft. lbs. (30–35 ft. lbs. when a torque wrench adapter is used).

8. Actuate the injector plunger several times to check the adjustment. Correct if required.

Valve Adjustment

378, 504 and 555 SERIES ENGINES

NOTE: See the proper valve set mark alignment procedure before making any adjustment of the valves.

1. The same crankshaft position used for adjusting the injectors is used for adjusting the valves.

2. While adjusting the valves, be sure that the compression release, if equipped, is in the released position.

3. Loosen the locknut and back off the adjusting screw. Insert the feeler gauge between the rocker lever and the top of the crosshead.

4. Adjust the valve to the proper specification. Turn the screw down until the lever just touches the gauge. Lock the adjusting screw in this position with the locknut.

5. Torque the locknut 40–45 ft. lbs. (30–35 ft. lbs. if a torque wrench adapter is used).

NOTE: Make a final valve adjustment after the injectors are adjusted and the engine is at proper operating temperature.

1150 SERIES ENGINES

NOTE: See the proper valve set mark alignment procedure before making any adjustment to the valves.

1. Before adjusting the valves on number 2 cylinder, be sure that the crossheads are properly adjusted.

2. Insert the correct thickness feeler gauge between the rocker lever and the crosshead. Adjust the valve to specifications.

3. Turn the adjusting screw down until the rocker lever just touches the feeler gauge. Torque the adjusting locknut 40–45 ft. lbs.(30–35 ft. lbs. if a torque wrench adapter is used).

4. Continue this procedure until all the valves are properly adjusted.

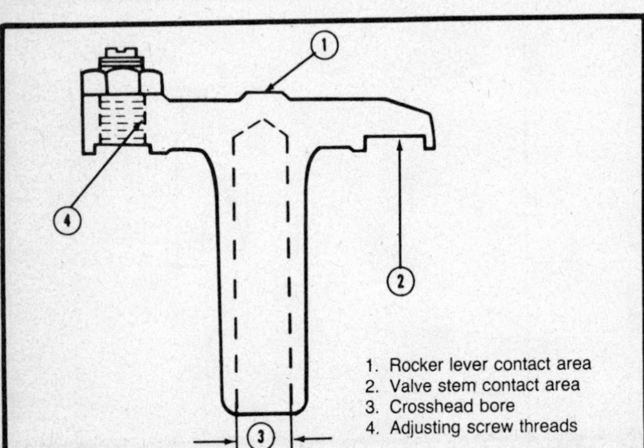

Normal crosshead wear points—typical (© Cummins Engine Co.)

Injector and Valve Adjustment

903 SERIES ENGINES

1. Rotate the crankshaft in the proper direction of rotation until a "VS" mark on the flange aligns with the pointer on the front cover.

2. There are two cylinder numbers at each "VS" mark. The injector and the valves on one of these two cylinders are now ready to be adjusted.

NOTE: Adjust the valves and the injector on the cylinder that has the intake and exhaust valves closed.

3. After making the proper adjustment, rotate the crankshaft to align the next "VS" mark with the pointer. Adjust the valves and injectors in the same sequence as the engine firing order.

4. Install tool ST–1170 (indicator stand assembly) and tool 3375006 (dial indicator assembly) in place. Install the indicator extension on top of the injector plunger.

NOTE: Be sure the indicator extension is tight in the indicator stem and is not touching the rocker lever.

5. Turn the adjusting screw for the injector lever clockwise until the injector plunger touches the cup.

6. Turn the adjusting screw counterclockwise one-half turn. Turn the adjusting screw clockwise again until the injector plunger touches the injector cup. Set the dial on the indicator to zero.

7. Turn the adjusting screw counterclockwise until the dial indicator tool shows a total reading of .187 in. for a 1 to 1 rocker lever ratio-injector lever, p/n–211399 or .180 in. for 1.2 to 1 rocker lever ratio-injector lever p/n–196565.

611 AND 1150 SERIES ENGINES

1. Rotate the crankshaft in the normal direction of engine rotation and align the "A" valve set mark on the accessory drive pulley with the pointer on the gear cover. Make sure the intake and exhaust valves on number 5 cylinder are closed.

2. Install the injector travel adjustment kit or equivalent to the injector to be adjusted. Make sure the stem of the dial indicator is correctly installed and does not touch the rocker lever.

CAUTION

Do not tighten the injector adjusting screw more than the amount outlined in the following procedure. The injector can be damaged if the screw is too tight.

3. Turn the adjusting screw clockwise until the injector plunger is at the bottom of its travel. Turn the adjusting screw an additional ¼ turn clockwise to remove the fuel from the injector cup. Turn the adjusting screw ½ turn clockwise to the bottom of the injector plunger travel.

4. Adjust the dial indicator to zero.

5. Turn the adjusting screw counterclockwise until the dial indicator shows the value given in the adjustment chart.

6. Once the adjustment is complete, tighten the adjusting screw locknut to 40–45 ft. lbs. Recheck the adjustment.

7. Once the injector adjustment is complete, adjust the intake and exhaust valve clearance to specifications. Refer to the chart for adjustment sequence.

Top Stop Injector Adjustment

855 SERIES ENGINES

1. A cold set zero clearance setting is made at the same injector adjustment as with the dial indicator method.

CAUTION

Top Stop injector plunger travel can only be adjusted when the injectors are removed from the engine, using adjusting tool 3375160.

2. When the engine crankshaft has been set in the proper position for the injector to be adjusted, tighten the adjusting screw until all lash is removed from the injector train. Then tighten the adjusting screw one additional turn to properly seat the links and to squeeze oil from the socket surfaces.

3. Back the adjusting screw off until the spring washer contacts stop. Adjust the zero clearance. Using torque wrench, tighten the screw to 5–6 inch lbs. torque.

NOTE: Zero clearance is defined as the condition where the link is slightly loaded. If a torque wrench is not available, zero clearance can be set at the point where the link is slightly loaded, but just free enough to be rotated by hand.

4. Hold the adjusting screw with a screwdriver and tighten the locknut to 40–45 ft. lbs. (30–35 ft. lbs. when using a torque wrench adapter).

Crosshead Adjustment

NOTE: See the proper valve set mark alignment procedure before making any adjustments to the crossheads.

1. On 1150 series engines, position the crossheads over the guides with the adjusting screws toward the water passage in the rocker housing.
2. Loosen valve crosshead adjusting screw locknut and back off screw one turn.
3. Use light finger pressure at the rocker lever contact surface to hold crosshead in contact with valve stem nearest the push rod.
4. Turn adjusting screw down until it contacts its mating valve stem.
5. On some engines it may be necessary to advance the set screw an additional twenty to thirty degrees to straighten the stem on its guide.
6. Hold the adjusting screw in this position and tighten the locknut to the proper specification.
7. Check clearance between crosshead and valve spring retainer with wire gauge. There must be a minimum of 0.025 in. clearance at this point.

Injector Plunger Adjustment

378, 504, 555 AND 855 SERIES ENGINES

NOTE: See the proper valve set mark alignment procedure before making any injector plunger adjustments.

1. On 378, 504 and 555 series engines, tighten the injector holddown capscrew to 30–35 ft. lbs.
2. Turn the adjusting screw until the plunger contacts the cup. Advance the screw an additional 15 degrees to squeeze the oil from the cup.

NOTE: This adjustment will aid in distinguishing between cylinder adjusted and not adjusted.

3. Turn the engine in the direction of rotation until a valve set mark ("VS") aligns with the boss on the gear case cover.
4. Check the valve rocker levers on the two cylinders aligned as indicated on the pulley. On one cylinder of the pair, both rocker levers will be free and both valves will be closed; this is the cylinder to adjust.
5. Adjust the injector plunger first, then the crossheads and valves to the proper specification.

903 SERIES ENGINES

Information on valve set mark ("VS") alignment can be found under the Injector and Valve Adjustment procedure located in this section.

1150 SERIES ENGINES

1. Turn the engine in the direction of rotation until "A" valve set mark on the pulley is aligned with the pointer on the gear housing cover.

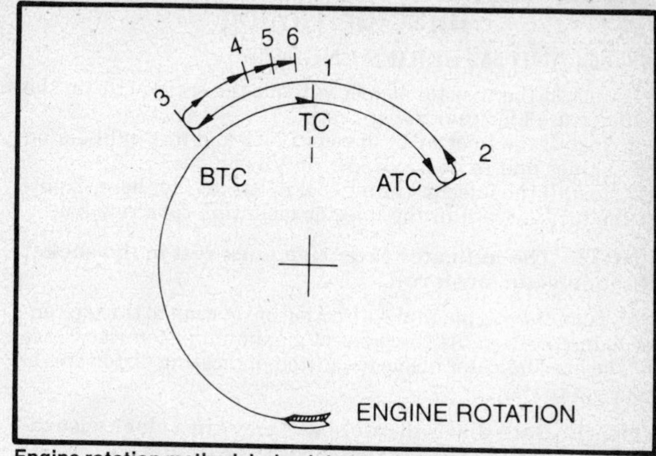

Engine rotation method during injection timing procedure—378, 504 and 555 Series (© Cummins Engine Co.)

2. In this position the injector plunger for no. 3 or no. 4 cylinder will be at the top of its travel and the rocker levers for no. 5 or no. 2 cylinder will be closed.
3. The injector and valves for any one cylinder cannot be set at the same time.

NOTE: CPL (control parts list)—480 engines (California) require injector setting of .184 in..

4. Torque the adjusting screw locknuts 40–45 ft. lbs. (30–35 ft. lbs. when using a torque wrench adapter).
5. Actuate the injector plunger several times to check the adjustment. Valves must be within specification.

NOTE: Use the same engine position used to set the injectors to set the valves for the same cylinder.

6. Adjust the valve clearance by putting the correct feeler gauge between the rocker lever and the crosshead contact pads. Adjust the valves to specification by turning the adjusting screw down until the rocker lever touches the feeler gauge.

NOTE: Make sure that the valve tappet rollers are against the lobe on the camshaft before adjusting the valves.

7. Continue through the firing order until all components requiring adjustments have been adjusted.

NOTE: Be sure to turn the crankshaft to the next "VS" mark each time the valves or injector is adjusted on a particular cylinder.

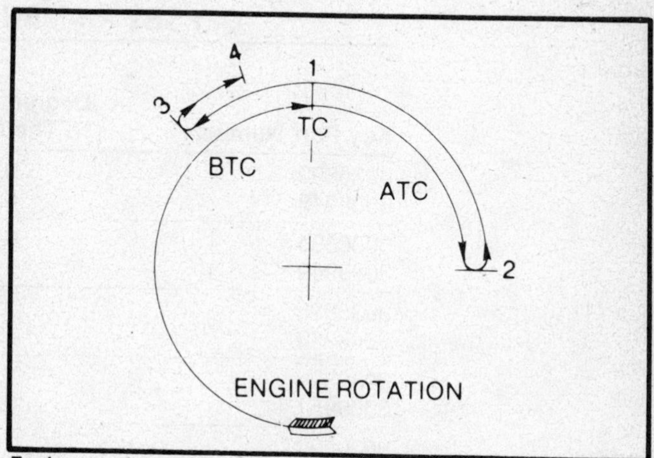

Engine rotation method during injection timing procedure—611, 855, 903 and KT1150 Series (© Cummins Engine Co.)

Injector Timing

378, 504 AND 555 SERIES ENGINES

1. Install the injector tappet without the spring clip on the cylinder used for the timing check.
2. Install the injector push rod in no.2 and no.6 cylinder on V8 engines and in no.5 cylinder on V6 engines.
3. Install the injector timing tool in the injector bore. Tighten the tool in place in the injector mounting capscrew hole.

NOTE: The indicator extension must rest in the socket of the injector push rod.

4. Turn the engine in the direction of rotation to the top center firing position. At the point of maximum piston rise, "zero in" the dial indicator above the piston, indicating piston travel from top center.

NOTE: Both dial indicators will move in a clockwise direction when on the correct stroke for timing.

5. Turn the engine in the direction of rotation to sixty degrees after top center (2). At this point the top of the moving plunger should be in line with the sixty degree groove on the fixed scale of the indicator gauge.
6. Set the indicator above the push rod to 0.020 in. of its fully compressed position and "zero in" the dial indicator.
7. Turn the engine in the opposite direction of rotation to sixty degrees before top center (3), or until the sixty degree mark on the plunger in the injector bore is in line with the groove on the retainer.

NOTE: This alignment mark is the same alignment mark as indicated in Step number 5.

8. Be sure that the piston travel dial indicator has 0.0250 in. travel.
9. Turn the engine in the direction of rotation until the dial indicator above the piston shows that the piston has traveled to the location shown at the first check point.
10. Compare the reading to the piston travel specification reading which is located in the injector timing specification chart.
11. Read the push rod travel on the dial indicator above the push rod and check that reading against the specification in the injector timing specification chart.
12. If the push rod travel is greater than the specification, the timing is slow. If the push rod travel is less than the specification, the timing is fast. A new camshaft key must be installed to bring the reading within specification. Select and install the next advance or retard camshaft timing key to correct the problem.

NOTE: Maximum push rod travel variation between the cylinders should not exceed 0.003 in.. Each 0.006 in. offset of the camshaft key is equal to 0.0025 in. push rod indicator travel at the 0.2032 piston travel check point.

13. Recheck engine injection timing as required.

611 SERIES ENGINE

NOTE: The injection timing of the LTA-10 engine can be adjusted by changing the camshaft key which controls the position of the camshaft lobes during the operating cycles of the engine. If an offset camshaft key is installed so that the arrow marked on the top of the key is toward the engine, the timing will be retarded. If the arrow facing away from the engine, the timing will be advanced.

1. Install the injection timing tool 3375522 or equivalent in the injector bore of the No. 1 cylinder. The open end of the mounting foot must be toward the camshaft.
2. Use the alignment tool to align the push rod plunger rod, then tighten the clamp handle.
3. Install the injector push rod between the injector camshaft follower and the plunger rod.
4. Turn the accessory drive shaft in the direction of engine rotation (clockwise) until both plunger rods of the timing fixture move together in an up direction.

NOTE: The engine is on the compression stroke when both plunger rods move up at the same time.

5. Turn the accessory drive shaft until the piston plunger rod reaches its full upward travel position. The piston is now at TDC.
6. Move the piston travel gauge so the contact tip is in the center of the plunger rod. Lower the gauge so the contact tip is fully compressed and then raise the gauge 0.025 in. (0.063mm) and lock it in this position.
7. Turn the accessory drive shaft in the normal direction of engine rotation (clockwise) to 90° ATDC. Loosen the set screw for the push rod travel dial gauge so the contact tip is in the center of the plunger rod. Lower the gauge so the contact tip is fully compressed, then raise the gauge 0.025 in. (0.063mm) and lock it in this position. Zero the dial gauge.
8. Turn the accessory drive shaft in the opposite direction of engine rotation (counterclockwise) to TDC, then continue turning until the crankshaft is at 45° BTDC. This will take up the gear lash in the engine.
9. Turn the accessory drive shaft slowly clockwise until the piston travel gauge is at 0.2032 in. (5.16mm) BTDC.

OFFSET CAMSHAFT KEY CHART

Key Part Number	Degree of Offset (To The Camshaft)	Change in Push Rod Travel mm	Change in Push Rod Travel inch
3030893	0.25	0.051	0.002
3009948	0.50	0.102	0.004
3030894	0.75	0.152	0.006
3009949	1.00	0.203	0.008
3030895	1.25	0.254	0.010
3009950	1.50	0.305	0.012
3030896	1.75	0.356	0.014
3009951	2.00	0.406	0.016
3030897	2.25	0.457	0.018
3030898	2.50	0.508	0.020

CAUTION

If the crankshaft is turned beyond the 0.2032 in. (5.16 mm) BTDC position, the crankshaft must be turned counterclockwise back to the 45°BTDC position and a new approach started

10. Read the push rod travel gauge. This figure represents the injection timing value. Compare the reading to the specifications listed in the Injection Timing Chart and adjust if necessary by means of an offset camshaft key.

855 SERIES ENGINES

1. Install the injector timing tool in the injector sleeve. engage the rod of the push rod tool into the injector push tube socket. Secure the tool in place by tightening the holddown bolts by hand.

NOTE: The two dial indicator gauges used for this procedure must have a total travel of 0.250 in..

2. Loosen both of the indicator supports. Rotate the crankshaft in the direction of rotation to top dead center. In this position the piston travel plunger will be near the full upward position. Adjust both indicators to their fully compressed position.

NOTE: To prevent damage to the indicator dials, raise them approximately 0.020 in. and lock them in place with the setscrew.

3. To assure that the piston is at top dead center on the compression stroke rotate the crankshaft back and forth. Top dead center is indicated by the maximum clockwise position of the piston travel indicator pointer. Align the piston travel indicator face to "zero" with the pointer and lock the tool in place.

NOTE: Both dial indicators move in the same direction when the cylinder is on the proper stroke. If this is not the case, turn the crankshaft one complete revolution to place the cylinder on the compression stroke and then repeat Step number three.

4. Rotate the crankshaft in the direction of rotation to ninety degrees after top dead center. Turn the push tube travel indicator and align "zero" with the pointer. Lock the tool in place.
5. Turn the crankshaft in the opposite direction of rotation to forty-five degrees before top dead center.
6. Turn the crankshaft in the direction of rotation until a reading of 0.2032 in. before top dead center is reached on the piston travel indicator.
7. The push rod travel indicator should read in line with the specification outlined in the injection timing specification chart.
8. If the push rod travel is greater than the specification given, engine timing is slow. If the push rod travel is less than the specification given, engine timing is fast. Correct as required by adding or removing cam follower gaskets.
9. Remove cam follower gaskets on right hand rotation engines to retard timing and add cam follower gaskets on left hand engines to retard engine timing.

NOTE: Adjustments to the engine timing are made by changing the thickness of the cam follower housing gaskets. Before making any adjustments to the cam follower gasket check to see that the cam follower capscrews are torqued 30–35 ft. lbs. Also make sure that the indicator tool is functioning properly and not bottoming or binding.

903 SERIES ENGINES

1. Install the injector timing fixture in the injector bore of cylinder no. 2 or no. 6. The indicator extension must be in the socket of the injector push rod. Using the capscrew hole for mounting the injector, tighten the tool in position.

NOTE: The spring clip must not be on the tappet when checking injection timing. Be sure to install the clip after the injection timing has been set.

2. Turn the crankshaft in the direction of rotation to the top center of the compression stroke. At the point of maximum piston rise, put the dial indicator above the piston and set it at the "zero" position.

NOTE: Both of the dial indicators will move in a clockwise direction when on the correct stroke for timing.

3. Turn the crankshaft sixty degrees after top center (2). At this point the top of the moving plunger must be in line with the sixty degree groove on the scale.
4. Set the dial indicator above the push rod to the "zero" position.
5. Turn the crankshaft in the direction opposite of rotation (3) until the sixty degree mark on the plunger aligns with the groove on the retainer (same index mark as indicated in Step 3).
6. On VTB engines, turn the crankshaft in the direction opposite rotation (3) until the indicator gauge above the piston reads 0.250–0.300 in. before top center.
7. Turn the crankshaft in the direction of rotation (4) until the dial indicator gauge shows that the piston has moved to 0.2032 in. before top center.
8. The travel on the dial indicator gauge above the push rod should be in line with the specification in the injection timing specification chart.
9. If the push rod travel is greater than the specification the timing is slow. If the push rod travel is less than the specification the timing is fast. A new camshaft key must be installed to bring the reading within specification.
10. Select and install the next advance or retard timing key that will bring the reading within specification.

NOTE: The maximum push rod travel difference between cylinders is not to exceed 0.003 in. Each 0.007 in. offset of the key is equal to 0.0025 in. travel of the push rod indicator.

11. Recheck injection timing as required.

1150 SERIES ENGINES

1. Position timing fixture in injector well. Engage push rod indicator in injector push tube socket. Hand tighten holddowns evenly.
2. If adaptor block is used, attach block to housing then secure rod indicator to block. Mount tools straight in cylinder and over push rod tube. Loosen indicators in their supports to prevent damage when turning the engine.

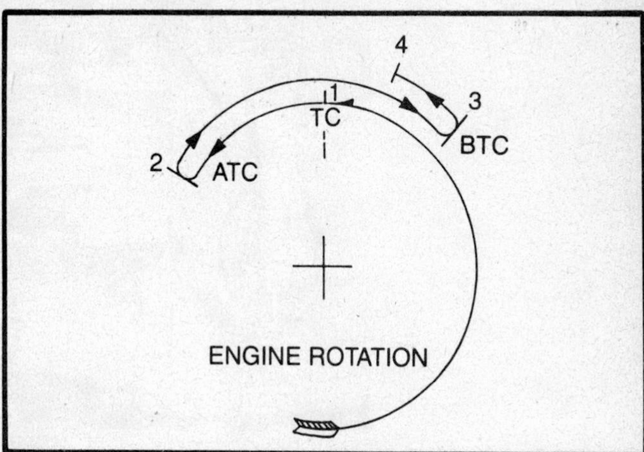

Engine rotation method during injection timing procedure—903VTB Series (© Cummins Engine Co.)

3. Turn crankshaft in direction of rotation to bring piston to be checked to TDC firing position.
4. Position piston indicator to compress stem within 0.010 in. of inner travel stop. Secure indicator.
5. Check for exact "zero" (TDC) with dial indicator.
6. Turn crankshaft in direction of rotation to 90 degrees ATDC. Position pushrod indicator on follower to 0.020 in. from inner travel stop. Secure indicator.
7. Turn crankshaft back to a position 45 degrees BTDC.
8. Slowly turn engine in direction of rotation until piston indicator is positioned at 0.0032 in. before "zero" on the dial indicator. This is equivalent to 0.2032 in. BTC.
9. The travel on the dial indicator gauge above the push rod should be in line with the specification in the injection timing specification chart.
10. If the push rod travel is greater than the specification the timing is slow. If the push rod travel is less than the specification the timing is fast. A new camshaft key must be installed to bring the reading within specification.
11. Select and install the next advance or retard timing key that will bring the reading within specification.
12. Recheck the injection timing as required.

Governor Adjustments

ALL ENGINES

The accuracy of the following adjustments changes with the condition of the engine, engine loads and the reliability of the test gauges used in performing the operations. The following adjustments can not be performed on a cold engine, engine oil temperature must be at least 165 degrees Fahrenheit. Also, the valves and the injectors must be correctly adjusted.

Idle Speed with "Type R" Fuel Pump

NOTE: Before the engine idle speed is adjusted the engine must be warmed up completely (at least 165 degrees Fahrenheit oil temperature). Idle speed adjustments must never be made on a cold engine.

1. Remove the pipe plug from the spring assembly cover.
2. Install the idle adjusting tool in the spring assembly cover.

NOTE: Be sure to operate the engine long enough to expel all of the air from the fuel system after the idle adjusting tool has been installed in the spring assembly cover.

3. The idle adjusting screw is held in place by a spring clip. Turn the idle adjustment screw in to increase the engine speed and out to decrease the engine speed.
4. 580–620 rpm is the factory recommended idle speed which is intended as a reference point. Changes can be made to this speed. Care must be taken so component cyclic vibrations are not created by extreme variations in the idle speed.
5. Remove the idle adjusting tool from the spring cover assembly. Replace the pipe plug.

NOTE: On the mechanical variable speed (MVS) governor fuel pump, the maximum and minimum idle speed adjusting screws are located on the governor cover.

6. To adjust the idle, loosen the rear idle speed adjustment screw locknut. Turn the adjustment screw in or out until the proper idle has been achieved.
7. Tighten the adjustment screw locknut immediately to prevent air from entering the system.

Idle Speed with "Type G" Fuel Pump

NOTE: Before the engine idle speed is adjusted the engine must be warmed up completely (at least 165 degrees Fahrenheit oil temperature). Idle speed adjustments must never be made on a cold engine.

1. Remove the pipe plug from the spring pack cover.
2. The idle adjustment screw is held in position by a spring clip. Using the idle adjusting tool, adjust the idle by turning the screw in to increase the engine speed or out to decrease the engine speed.

NOTE: The idle adjusting tool will not let the spring pack cover leak while the idle is being adjusted.

3. The factory recommended idle speed, which is intended as a reference point is 580–620 rpm for 855 and 1150 series engines, 625–675 rpm for 903 series engines and 600–650 rpm for 378, 504 and 555 series engines. Changes can be made from these engine speeds. Extreme care must be exerted so component cyclic vibrations are not created by extreme variations in the idle speed.

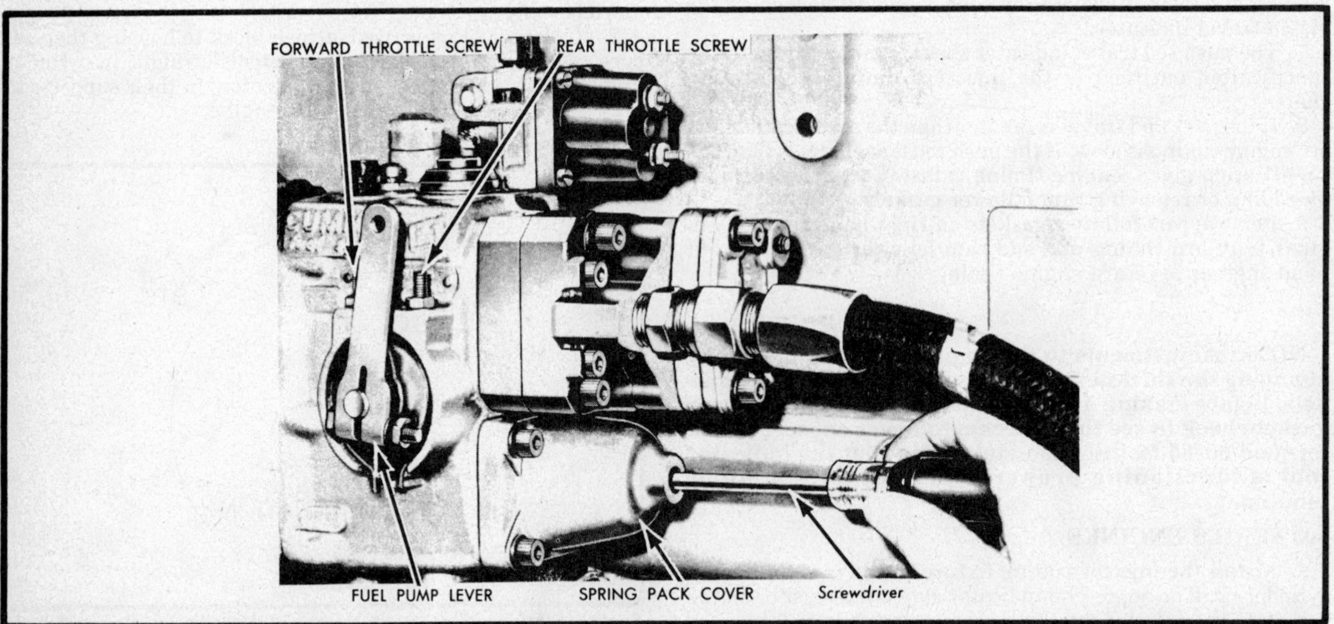

Fuel pump adjustments (© Cummins Engine Co.)

NOTE: The engine idle speed specification is located on the engine dataplate. It is under the emission control information on the dataplate. The engine idle speed on some models will exceed the specification given in Step three.

4. Replace the pipe plug after removing the idle speed adjusting tool.

NOTE: On the variable speed (VS), mechanical variable speed (MVS) and the special variable speed (SVS) governors the maximum and minimum idle speed adjusting screws are located on the governor cover.

5. To adjust the idle speed, loosen the rear idle adjustment screw locknut. Turn the adjustment screw in or out until the correct idle speed is achieved.

NOTE: Do not set the special variable speed (SVS) governor idle in power takeoff applications to less than 1100 rpm.

6. Tighten the idle speed adjusting screw locknut immediately to prevent air from entering the system.

Cut-Off Setting

1. At full throttle increase the engine load until the engine speed is pulled down at least 100 rpm below the rated engine speed.
2. Decrease the engine load slowly, while watching the fuel manifold pressure gauge.

NOTE: The pressure gauge will increase with the decreasing engine load. When the governor begins restricting fuel, the manifold pressure will begin decreasing with the decreasing engine load.

3. Continue decreasing the engine load until the fuel manifold pressure reaches its peak and then decreases one to two psi. This is the governor cut-off point.
4. The governor cut-off speed should be 20–50 rpm higher than the rated engine speed. This is to make sure that the governor is not restricting fuel before the rated engine speed.
5. If the governor cut-off point is higher or lower than the specification given, remove or add adjusting shims behind the governor high speed spring as required.
6. Recheck the governor cut-off point as required.

Maximum No-Load Speed

NOTE: Before performing this test be sure that the engine is at the proper operating temperature and that all of the air is removed from the fuel system.

1. With the transmission in neutral, or the clutch fully disengaged, open the throttle and hold it fully open.
2. Note the maximum engine speed. This speed should be ten to twelve percent greater than the governor cut-off speed, depending upon the engine loads (fans, pumps etc.).

NOTE: This test must not be used to check or make governor speed adjustments. This test is of secondary importance and should not be considered unless the no-load speed reading is significantly greater than the specification.

3. If the no-load speed is significantly greater than the specification given the governor assembly must be examined for a potential problem.

Throttle Leakage

ALL ENGINES

1. Operate engine to purge all air from system.
2. Adjust throttle control linkage so that pump throttle just contacts the front throttle stop screw when throttle is closed.
3. Place transmission in neutral, open throttle fully and let engine run at high idle—no load.
4. Using a stop watch, check the time required for throttle release to 1000 rpm movement. Repeat several times.
5. If engine begins to stall upon deceleration, increase throttle leakage.
6. Note position of leakage adjusting screw. Turn screw in while checking engine operation until deceleration time is increased 1 to 2 seconds.
7. If engine decelerates too slowly, it may be necessary to decrease leakage.
8. Note position of adjusting screw. Back out screw as engine decelerates until engine tends to stall. Turn screw in until deceleration time is increased 1 to 2 seconds.

Glow Plugs

1. Remove the engine preheater adapter and the glow plug from the intake manifold.
2. Remove the nozzle and the clamping washer from the adapter.
3. Clean the adapter and the nozzle with carburetor cleaner (or equivalent).

NOTE: Be sure that the nozzle screen and the spray holes are open and clean. Check the O-ring for damage.

4. Check the glow plug on a six or twelve volt source, as applicable. Replace as required.

NOTE: Six and twelve volt glow plugs are not interchangeable.

5. Assemble the clamp washer and the nozzle to the adapter.
6. Torque the nozzle to 15–20 ft. lbs. and bend the washer over one of the hexagonal sides of the nozzle.
7. Reinstall the assembled adapter into the intake manifold.

Fuel Pump

The PT (pressure-time) fuel pump is driven by the air compressor at engine speed. The engine speed governor is incorporated in the fuel pump. The tachometer is coupled to the fuel pump main shaft. The fuel pump supplies fuel under high pressure to the injectors; one for each cylinder.

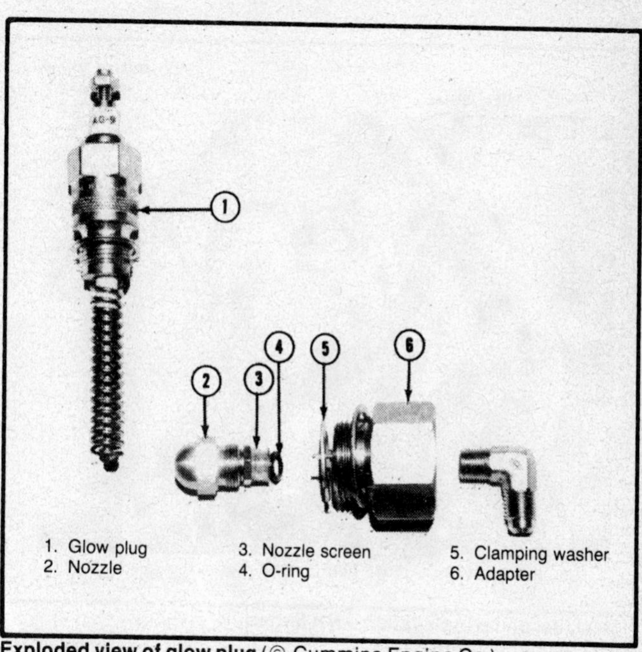

Exploded view of glow plug (© Cummins Engine Co.)

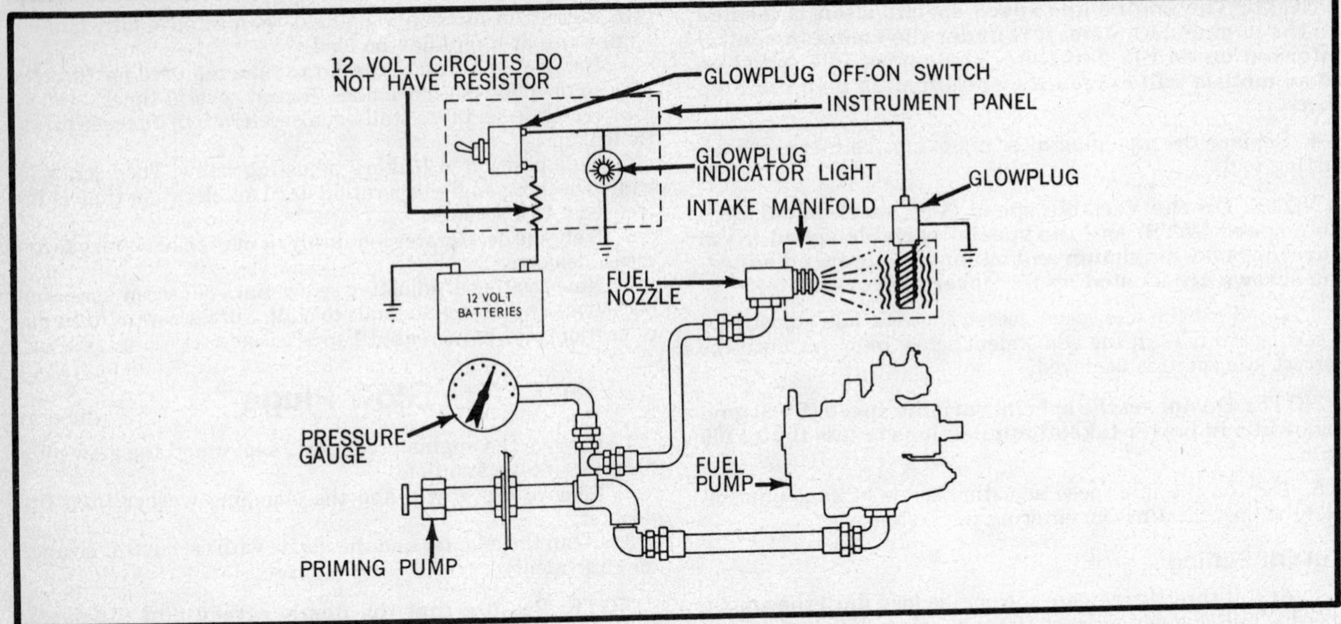

Preheater operation (© Cummins Engine Co.)

The fuel injectors meter and inject fuel into the cylinders. The injectors are operated and timed by push rods actuated by the camshaft and cam followers. Engine timing can be varied by changing the injector lifter adjustments.

The variable-speed, mechanical governor has two purposes: it maintains sufficient fuel delivery to the injectors for idling with the throttle control in idling position and it cuts off fuel to the injectors above maximum rate rpm.

Removal and Installation

855, 611 and 1150 SERIES ENGINES

1. Remove, as required, all of the necessary components and linkages in order to properly remove the unit from the vehicle.
2. Remove the fuel supply line and the drain line from the fuel pump and the cylinder head (fuel manifold—1150 series engines).

NOTE: Some engines may have front mounted fuel supply and drain tubing.

3. If equipped, remove the throw-away fuel filter.
4. Remove the fuel pump from the governor drive or the air compressor assembly. Lift out the drive buffer or the splined coupling.
5. Installation is the reverse of removal. Torque the fuel pump mounting bolts 30–35 ft. lbs. Be sure to use new gaskets when making connections that require the use of gaskets.

378, 504, 555 AND 903 SERIES ENGINES

NOTE: On naturally aspirated 378, 504 and 555 series engines using a variable speed (VS) fuel pump and air compressor, it is not necessary to remove the air intake manifold.

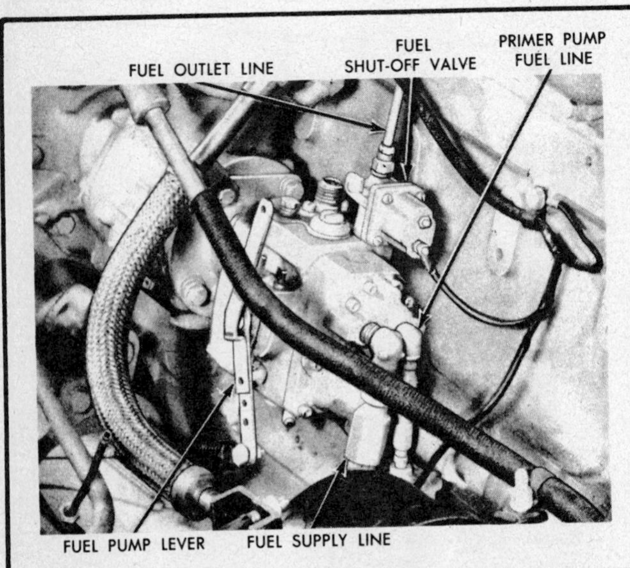

Typical fuel pump installation—NH Series (© Cummins Engine Co.)

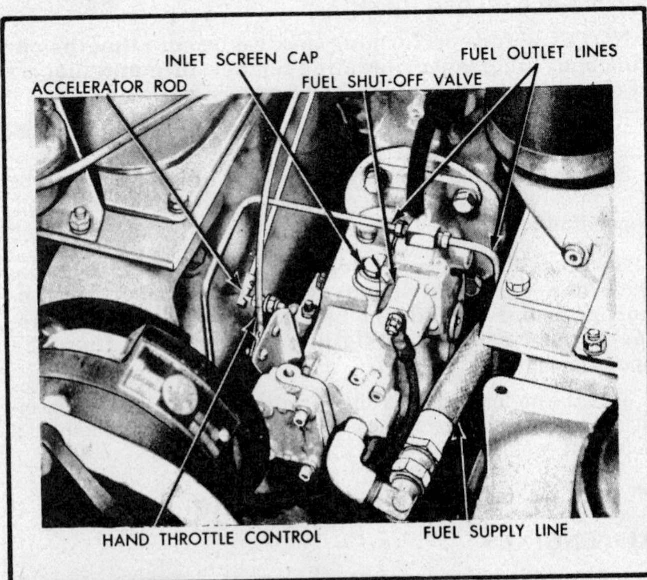

Typical fuel pump installation—V6 Series (© Cummins Engine Co.)

1. Remove, as required, all the necessary components and linkages in order to properly remove the unit from the vehicle.
2. Remove the intake manifold retaining bolts. Remove the intake manifold and the intake crossover from the engine.

NOTE: On naturally aspirated engines it will be necessary to remove the air crossover assembly first.

3. Remove the fuel supply line and the drain line from the fuel pump and the cylinder head.
4. Remove the retaining bolts securing the fuel pump to the air compressor. Remove the unit from the vehicle.
5. Remove the drive buffer or spider from the air compressor shaft.
6. Installation is the reverse of removal. Torque the fuel pump mounting bolts 30–35 ft. lbs. Be sure to use new gaskets when making connections that require the use of gaskets.

Injectors

Removal and Installation

1. Remove, as required, all the necessary linkages and components in order to gain access to the engine valve cover.
2. Remove the valve cover retaining bolts and remove the cover.
3. Remove the injector holddown plate.
4. Using the proper injector removal tool, remove the injector from the cylinder head.

NOTE: Do not use a screwdriver or a pry bar to remove the injectors as damage may occur.

5. Before installing the injector assembly, lubricate the O-rings with the proper grade and type lubricating oil.
6. On 378, 504 and 555 series engines, install the injector into the cylinder head. Align the injector so that the bottom screen is toward the center of the engines.

NOTE: To seat Type "D" injectors in the cylinder head, fabricate a T-handle from $^5/_8$ in. bar stock. Drill a $^5/_{16}$ in. hole, $^1/_2$ in. deep from the bottom and braze in a Type "D" injector link. Place this assembly on top of the injector in place. Install the injector links (if removed) with the part number to the top.

7. On 611 and 855 series engines, start the injector into its bore from the intake side of the engine. The injectors are to be installed with the filter screen at the twelve o'clock position (Type "D" injectors may be turned to any position). Place a valve spring compressor or equivalent on top of the injector plunger coupling and apply force to secure the injector in place.
8. On 903 and 115 series engines, install the injector into the cylinder head. Use the injector removal tool to properly seat the injectors.

NOTE: On 903 series engines, align the injector so that the screen is toward the center of the engine. Install the retaining rings over the injector.

9. On 378, 504 and 555 series engines, install the holddown clamps lockwashers and capscrews. Torque the capscrews 30–35 ft. lbs.
10. On 611, 855 and 1150 series engines, place the holddown plate over the injector body and install the holddown screws. Do not tighten at this time. Carefully insert the injector plunger link. Torque the holddown screws 11–13 ft. lbs.
11. Check the injector plunger for freedom after tightening the retaining clamps on all series engines.
12. On 903 series engines, install the injector links into the center of the injector plunger.
13. Continue the installation procedure in the reverse order of the removal.

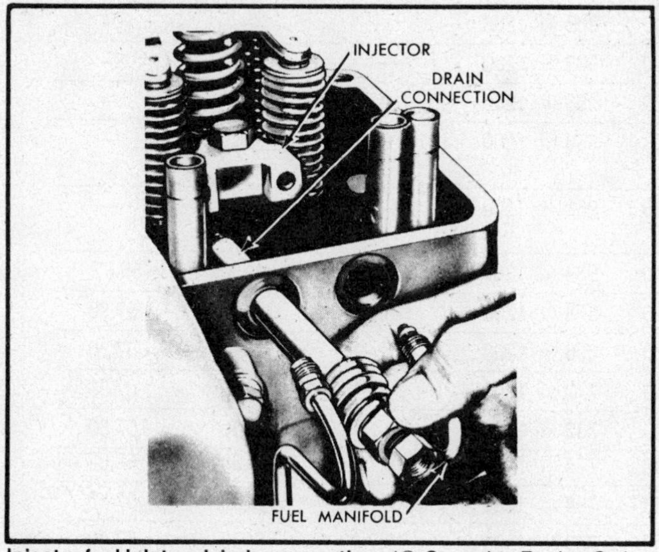

Injector fuel inlet and drain connections (© Cummins Engine Co.)

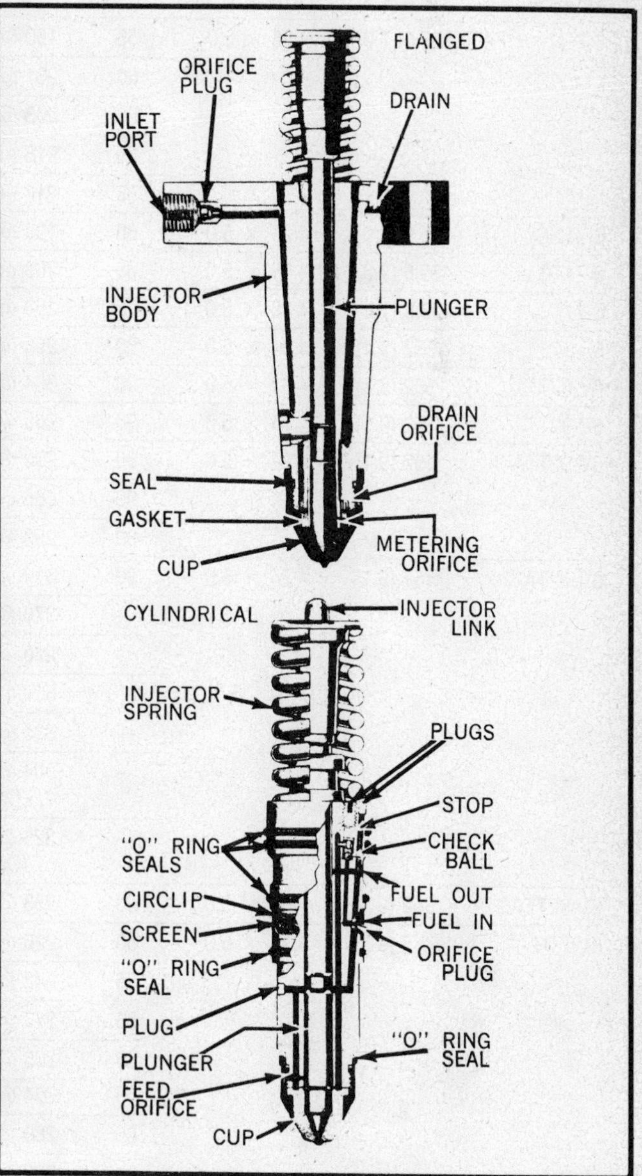

Flanged and cylindrical injectors (© Cummins Engine Co.)

DETROIT DIESEL ENGINES

GENERAL SPECIFICATIONS
Detroit Diesel Engines

Number of Cylinder and Engine Models	Cubic Inch (Liter)	Bore and Stroke (Inches)	Injector Size (Cu-mm)	Horse Power @ rpm (SAE Net)	Torque @ rpm (SAE Net)	Compression Ratio	Governor Full Load rpm②	Taxable Horsepower
4-53N	212 (3.5)	3.875 × 4.50	50	126 @ 2800	265 @ 1800	21.0:1	2800	24.02
			50	120 @ 2800	270 @ 1800	21.0:1	2800	24.02
4-53TGTC	212 (3.5)	3.875 × 4.50	60	161 @ 2500	388 @ 1800	18.7:1	2500	24.02
4-53TC	212 (3.5)	3.875 × 4.50	55	146 @ 2500	361 @ 1800	18.7:1	2500	24.02
6V-53N	318.4 (5.2)	3.875 × 4.50	50	190 @ 2800	414 @ 1800	21.0:1	2800	36.04
6V-53T	318.4 (5.2)	3.875 × 4.50	50	194 @ 2600	510 @ 1800	21.0:1	2600	36.04
6V-53TC	318.4 (5.2)	3.875 × 4.50		—	—	21.0:1	—	36.04
6V-53TAC	318.4 (5.2)	3.875 × 4.50		—	—	21.0:1	—	36.04
6-71N	425.6 (7.0)	4.25 × 5.0	55	180 @ 1950	533 @ 1200	18.7:1	2100	43.45
			60	201 @ 2100	552 @ 1200	18.7:1	2100	43.45
			60	203 @ 2100	586 @ 1200	18.7:1	2100	43.45
			65	218 @ 2100	588 @ 1600	18.7:1	2100	43.45
			65	219 @ 2100	575 @ 1600	18.7:1	2100	43.45
6-71NC	425.6 (7.0)	4.25 × 5.0	60	198 @ 2100	556 @ 1200	18.7:1	2100	43.45
6-71TC	425.6 (7.0)	4.25 × 5.0	65	263 @ 2100	780 @ 1400	18.7:1	2100	43.45
6-71T	425.6 (7.0)	4.25 × 5.0	75	263 @ 2100	780 @ 1400	17.0:1	2100	43.45
6V-92	552 (9.1)	4.84 × 5.0	80	258 @ 2100	719 @ 1400	19.0:1	2100	56.2
6V-92T	552 (9.1)	4.84 × 5.0	90	304 @ 2100	868 @ 1400	17.0:1	2100	56.2
6V-92TT	552 (9.1)	4.84 × 5.0	90	265 @ 1950	948 @ 1200	17.0:1	1950	56.2
6V-92TTA	552 (9.1)	4.84 × 5.0	90	290 @ 1900	926 @ 1300	17.0:1	1900	56.2
			90	265 @ 1950	938 @ 1400	17.0:1	1950	56.2
			90	253 @ 1950	926 @ 1300	17.0:1	1950	56.2
6V-92TA	552 (9.1)	4.84 × 5.0	90	314 @ 2100	926 @ 1300	19.0:1	2100	56.2
			—	270 @ 1800	963 @ 1200	—	—	—
			—	270 @ 2100	963 @ 1200	—	—	—
			—	307 @ 1800	963 @ 1200	—	—	—
			—	330 @ 2100	963 @ 1200	—	—	—
			—	304 @ 1800 (Calif.)	958 @ 1200	—	—	—
			—	325 @ 2100 (Calif.)	958 @ 1200	—	—	—
6V-92TTAC	552 (9.1)	4.84 × 5.0	90	253 @ 1950	934 @ 1300	17.0:1	1950	56.23
8V-71N	567.5 (9.3)	4.25 × 5.0	50	226 @ 1950	673 @ 1200	18.7:1	1950	57.80
			55	242 @ 1950	696 @ 1200		1950	57.80
			55	245 @ 1950	772 @ 1200	18.7:1	1950	57.80
			60	265 @ 2100	732 @ 1200	18.7:1	2100	57.80
			60	264 @ 2100	775 @ 1200	18.7:1	2100	57.80
			65	289 @ 2100	758 @ 1600	18.7:1	2100	57.80
			65	283 @ 2100	789 @ 1600	18.7:1	2100	57.80

GENERAL SPECIFICATIONS
Detroit Diesel Engines

Number of Cylinder and Engine Models	Cubic Inch (Liter)	Bore and Stroke (Inches)	Injector Size (Cu-mm)	Horse Power @ rpm (SAE Net)	Torque @ rpm (SAE Net)	Compression Ratio	Governor Full Load rpm②	Taxable Horsepower
8V-71T	567.5 (9.3)	4.25 × 5.0	65	293 @ 2100	845 @ 1400	17.0:1	2100	57.80
			70	320 @ 2100	900 @ 1400	17.0:1	2100	57.80
			75	335 @ 2100	940 @ 1600	17.0:1	2100	57.80
8V-71TT	567.5 (9.3)	4.25 × 5.0	75	299 @ 1950	974 @ 1300	17.0:1	1950	57.80
			75	300 @ 1950	1027 @ 1300	17.0:1	1950	57.80
8V-71TA	567.5 (9.3)	4.25 × 5.0	65	297 @ 2100	917 @ 1200	17.0:1	2100	57.80
			70	324 @ 2100	978 @ 1200	17.0:1	2100	57.80
			75	349 @ 2100	1038 @ 1200	17.0:1	2100	57.80
8V-71TTA	567.5 (9.3)	4.25 × 5.0	75	288 @ 1950	1038 @ 1200	17.0:1	1950	57.80
8V-71TAC	567.5 (9.3)	4.25 × 5.0	75	329 @ 1200	1032 @ 1200	17.0:1	2100	57.80
8V-92	736 (12.1)	4.84 × 5.0	80	342 @ 2100	962 @ 1400	19.0:1	2100	74.8
8V-92T	736 (12.1)	4.84 × 5.0	90	412 @ 2100	1201 @ 1400	19.0:1	2100	74.8
8V-92TT	736 (12.1)	4.84 × 5.0	90	360 @ 950	1212 @ 1400	19.0:1	1950	74.8
			90	414 @ 2100	1212 @ 400	17.0:1	2100	74.8
			75	355 @ 1800	1150 @ 1200	17:1	—	—
			90	365 @ 1950	1250 @ 1300	17:1	—	—
			90	445 @ 2100	1250 @ 1300	17:1	—	—
			—	355 @ 1800 (Calif.)	1130 @ 1300	17:1	—	—
			—	440 @ 2100 (Calif.)	1250 @ 1300	17:1	—	—
8V-92TTA	736 (12.1)	4.84 × 5.0	90	348 @ 1950	112 @ 1400	17.0:1	1950	74.8
8V-92TTAC	736 (12.1)	4.84 × 5.0	90	348 @ 1950	1200 @ 1400	17.0:1	1950	74.8
12V-71	851 (13.95)	4.25 × 5.0	55	371 @ 2100	1090 @ 1200	18.7:1	2100	86.7
12V-71N	851 (13.95)	4.25 × 5.0	60	390 @ 2100	1078 @ 1200	18.7:1	2100	86.7
V8-8.2NA①	500.4 (8.2)	4.25 × 4.41	—	153 @ 3000	332 @ 1200	18.3:1	3000	57.8
V8-8.2T①	500.4 (8.2)	4.25 × 5.00	—	193 @ 3000	414 @ 1800	17.0:1	3000	57.8

①—4 cycle "fuel pincher"
②—Idle speed listed in Tune-up Specifications
N—4 valves
NA—Natural aspirited
T—Turbocharges
TT—Fuel Squeezer
A—Aftercooler
C—California engines

CRANKSHAFT AND BEARING SPECIFICATIONS

(Measurements in inches)

Engine Series	Main Bearing Journal Diameter	Main Bearing Clearance	Shaft End-Play ①	Rod Bearing Journal Diameter	Rod Bearing Clearance
53 in-line 4 cylinder	2.999–3.000	0.001–0.004	0.004–0.011	2.449–2.2500	0.0015–0.0045
53 6V	3.499–3.500	0.001–0.004	0.004–0.011	2.749–2.750	0.0011–0.0041
71 in-line 6 cylinder	3.499–3.500	0.0014–0.014	0.004–0.014	2.749–2.750	0.0014–0.0044
71 8V, 12V	4.499–4.500	0.0016–0.0050	0.004–0.011	2.999–3.000	0.0010–0.0040
92-6V-8V	4.4985–4.5002	0.0014–0.0055	0.004–0.012	2.9985–3.002	0.0008–0.0045
V8, 8.2 liter	4.0594–4.0605	0.0015–0.0056	—	—	—

① Shaft thrust taken at rear bearing on two cycle engines and at number four on four cycle engines.

LINER, PISTON AND PIN SPECIFICATIONS

(Measurements in inches)

Engine Series	Liner		Piston		Piston Pin		
	Inside Diameter	Depth of Flange Below Block	Diameter At Skirt	Clearance Skirt to Liner	Diameter	Pin to Brushing Clearance	Pin to Rod Brushing Clearance
53 non-turbo	3.8752–3.8767	0.0465–0.0500	3.8699–3.8721	0.0031–0.0068	1.3746–1.3750	0.0025–0.0034	0.0010–0.0019
turbo	3.8752–3.8767	0.0465–0.0500	3.8669–3.8691	0.0061–0.0098	—	—	—
71-All	Long Port 4.2295–4.2511	0.450–0.0500	—	—	Trunk type 1.4996–1.5000	0.0025–0.0034	0.0025–0.0034
	Short Port 4.2495–4.2516	①			Cross head type 1.4996–1.5000	③	③
71-trunk type piston	—	—	4.2433–4.2455	Long Port 0.0040–0.0078 Short Port 0.0040–0.0083	—	—	—
71E	—	—	Two valve cylinder head 4.2433–4.2455	0.0040–0.0078	—	—	—
	—	—	Four valve cylinder head (60 cmm-ing.) 4.2433–4.2455	0.0040–0.0078	—	—	—
	—	—	Four valve cylinder head (70 cmm-ing.) 4.2418–4.2440	0.0055–0.0093	—	—	—
71M	—	—	4.2418–4.2440	0.0055–0.0093	—	—	—
71N	—	—	4.2413–4.2435	0.0060–0.0098	—	—	—
71T	—	—	4.2413–4.2435	0.0060–0.0098	—	—	—
71N and 71T	—	—	Cross head pistons 4.2428–4.2450 ④	0.0045–0.0083	1.4996–1.5000	②	②

LINER, PISTON AND PIN SPECIFICATIONS

(Measurements in inches)

Engine Series	Liner		Piston		Piston Pin		
	Inside Diameter	Depth of Flange Below Block	Diameter At Skirt	Clearance Skirt to Liner	Diameter	Pin to Brushing Clearance	Pin to Rod Brushing Clearance
V-71	Long port 4.2495–4.2511	0.450–0.500	Trunk type pistons		1.4996–1.5000	0.0025–0.0034	0.0025–0.0034
	Short port 4.2495–4.2516		Two valve cyl. head 4.2443–4.2455	0.004–0.0078	—	—	—
	—	—	Four valve cyl. head (60 cmm-ing.) 4.2433–4.2455	0.004–0.0078	—	—	—
	—	—	(70 cmm-ing.) 4.2428–4.2450	0.0045–0.0083	—	—	—
V-71N	—	—	4.2428–4.2450	0.0045–0.0083	—	—	—
V-71T	—	—	4.2393–4.2415	0.0080–0.0118	—	—	—
V-71N, V-71T	—	—	4.2428–4.2450 ③	0.0045–0.0083	1.4996–1.500	②	②
V-92	4.8391–4.8415	0.0418–0.482	Cross Head Type Pistons 4.8318–4.8343 ④	0.0051–0.0097	1.4996–1.5000	②	②
V8-8.2 Liter	Cylinder bore 4.250	—	—	Non-turbo 0.0047–0.0059 Turbo 0.0054–0.0066	—	—	—

① Low block—height of flange above block—0.0020–0.0060

② Slipper bearing bushing—thickness at center—0.0870–0.0880 inch. Clearance (edge of bushing to groove in piston) 0.0005–0.0105 inch.

③ Diameter above and below piston pin may be 4.2414 inch.

④ Diameter above and below piston pin may be 4.8280 inch.

RING SPECIFICATIONS

(Measurement in inches)

Engine Series	Compression Rings		Oil Rings	
	Gap	Clearance	Gap	Clearance
53	Chrome—0.0200–0.0460	No. 1—(top) 0.0030–0.0060 No. 2—0.0070–0.0100	0.0100–0.0250	0.0015–0.0055
	Cast iron—0.0200–0.0360	No. 3 & 4—0.0050–0.0080 No. 3 & 4—21:1 comp. ratio 0.0045–0.0070		
71 w/trunk pistons	0.0180–0.0430	No. 1—(top) 0.0095–0.0130 No. 2—0.0075–0.0110 No. 3 & 4—0.0055–0.0090	0.0080–0.0230	0.0015–0.0055

RING SPECIFICATIONS

(Measurement in inches)

Engine Series	Compression Rings		Oil Rings	
	Gap	Clearance	Gap	Clearance
71E w/trunk pistons	No. 1 (top fire ring) 0.0230–0.0380 No. 2, 3 & 4 0.0180–0.0430	No. 1 (top fire ring) 0.0230–0.0380 2—0.0095–0.0130 3—0.0075–0.0110 4—0.0055–0.0090	0.0080–0.0230	0.0015–0.0055
71M w/trunk pistons	No.1 (top fire ring) 0.0230–0.0380 No. 2, 3 & 4 0.0180–0.0430	No. 1 (top fire ring) 0.0040–0.0070 No. 2—0.0095–0.0130 No. 3—0.0075–0.0110 No. 4—0.0055–0.0090	0.0080–0.0230	0.0015–0.0055
71N	No. 1 (top fire ring) 0.0230–0.0380 No. 2, 3 & 4 0.0180–0.0430	No. 1 (top fire ring) 0.0040–0.0060 No. 2—0.0100–0.0130 No. 3 & 4—0.0040–0.0070	0.0080–0.0230	0.0015–0.0055
71T w/trunk pistons	0.0180–0.0430	No. 1—0.0095–0.0130 No. 2—0.0075–0.0110 No. 3 & 4—0.0055–0.0090	Two rings in lower groove 0.0050–0.0140 One ring in upper groove 0.0050–0.0140	Two rings in lower groove 0.0015–0.0055 One ring in upper groove 0.0010–0.0035
71N and 71T w/cross head pistons	No. 1 (top fire ring) 0.0230–0.0380 No. 2 & 3—0.0180–0.0430 Seal ring—0.0020–0.0210	No. 1 (top fire ring) 0.0010–0.0050 No. 2—0.0100–0.0130 No. 3—0.0040–0.0070 Seal ring—0.0005–0.0030	Two rings in lower groove (71 N & T engines) 0.0080–0.0230 Two rings in upper groove (71N engine) 0.0080–0.0230 One ring in upper groove (71 T engine) 0.0050–0.0140 Two rings in upper groove (71 T engine) 0.0080–0.0230	Lower groove 0.0015–0.0055 Upper groove 0.0010–0.0035
V-92N-A and V-92T	No. 1 (top fire ring) 0.0250–0.0450 No. 2 & 3—0.0250–0.0450 Seal ring—0.0020–0.0170	No. 1 (top fire ring) 0.0010–0.0050 No. 2—0.0100–0.0130 No. 3—0.0040–0.0070 Seal ring—0.0005–0.0030	Two rings in lower groove (turbo & non-turbo) 0.0100–0.0250 Two rings in upper groove (turbo) 0.0070–0.0170 Two rings in upper groove (non-turbo) 0.0100–0.0250	0.0015–0.0055
V8, 8.2 liter	0.010–0.020	Top—0.0027–0.0055 Lower—0.0020–0.0035	0.010–0.020	0.002–0.0033

VALVE SPECIFICATIONS

(Measurements in inches)

Engine Series	Stem Diameter	Valve Guide Inside Diameter (Protrusion, Flush or Recess)	Clearance Stem to Guide	Valve Head to Cylinder Head
53 two valve head	0311–0315	0.0020–0.0040	0.0020–0.0040	0.002 protr. to 0.037
Current four valve head	0.7450–0.2488	0.3125–0.2517	0.0017–0.0035	Flush to 0.024 recess
Former four valve head	0.5475–0.2222	0.2004–0.2515	0.0020–0.0018	0.006 protr. to 0.0018

VALVE SPECIFICATIONS

(Measurements in inches)

Engine Series	Stem Diameter	Valve Guide Inside Diameter (Protrusion, Flush or Recess)	Clearance Stem to Guide	Valve Head to Cylinder Head
71 in-line Two valve	0.3417–0.3425	0.3445–0.3445	0.0022–0.0038 0.005 recess 0.017 protr.	45° two valve
Four valve	0.3100–0.3105	0.3125–0.3135	0.0020–0.0035 0.002 recess 0.028 protr. 30 ° current two and four valve 0.023 recess to 0.006 protr.	30° former two and four
V-71 Two Valve Four valve	0.03417–0.3425 0.34100–0.3105	0.03445–0.3455 0.3125–0.3135	0.0020–0.0038 0.0020–0.0035	30° former two and four valve 0.0020 recess to 0.028 protr. 30° current two and four valve 0.023 recess to 0.006 protr.
V92	0.3100–0.3108	0.3125–0.3135	0.0017–0.0035	0.023 recess to 0.006 protr.
V8, 8.2 liter	—	—	—	—

VALVE CLEARANCE

(Measurements in inches)

Engine Series	Type	Cold		Hot	
		Go	No-Go	Go	No-Go
53	Two valve	0.010	0.012	0.008	0.010
	Four valve	0.025	0.027	0.023	0.025
71	In-line	0.015 -	0.017	0.013	0.015
V-71	Two valve	0.011	0.013	0.008	0.010
	Four valve	0.015	0.017	0.013	0.015
V-92	—	0.015	0.017	0.013	0.015
V8, 8.2 liter	Intake	—	—	0.012	—
	Exhaust	—	—	0.014	—

FIRING ORDERS

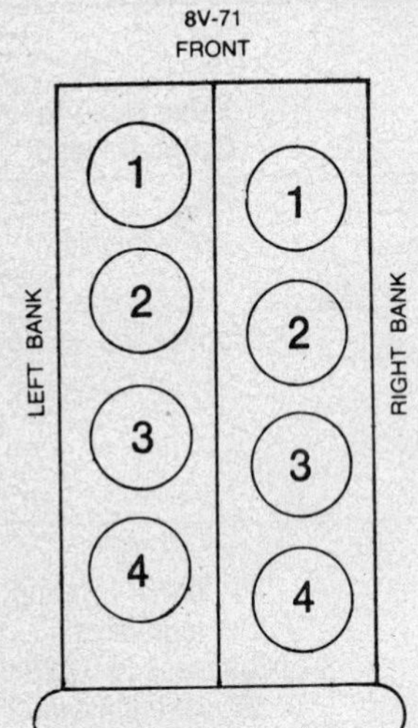

Firing order:
RH 1L-3R-3L-4R-4L-2R-2L-1R
LH 1L-1R-2L-2R-4L-4R-3L-3R

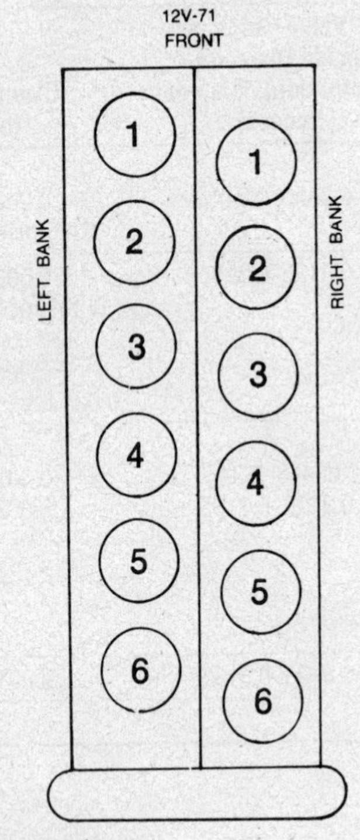

Firing order:
RH 1L-5L-3R-4R-3L-4L-2R-6R-2L-6L-1R-5R
LH 1L-5R-1R-6L-2L-6R-2R-4L-3L-4R-3R-5L

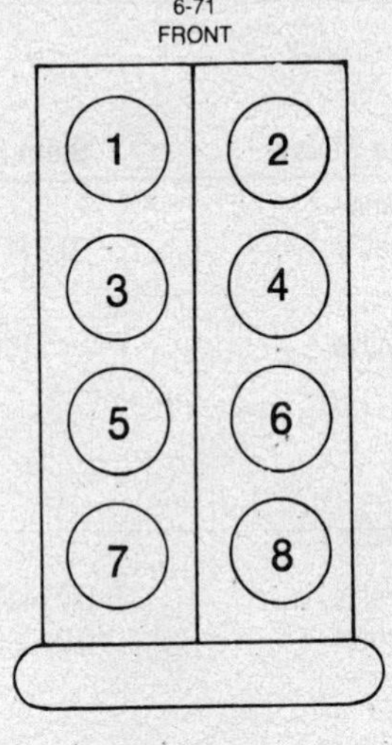

Firing order:
RH 1-8-4-3-6-5-7-2

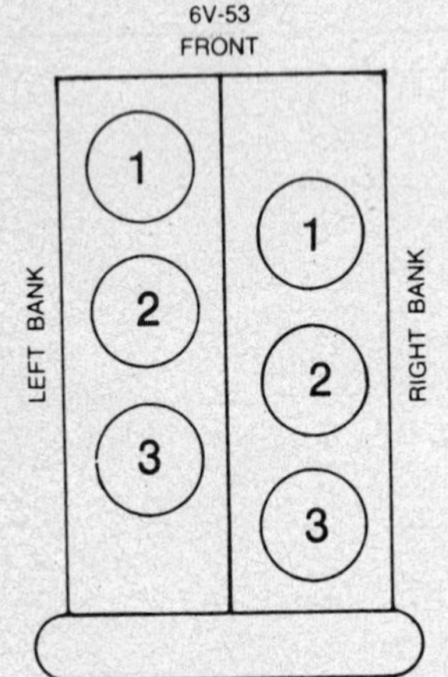

Firing order:
RH 1L-3R-3L-2R-2L-1R
LH 1L-1R-2L-2R-3L-3R

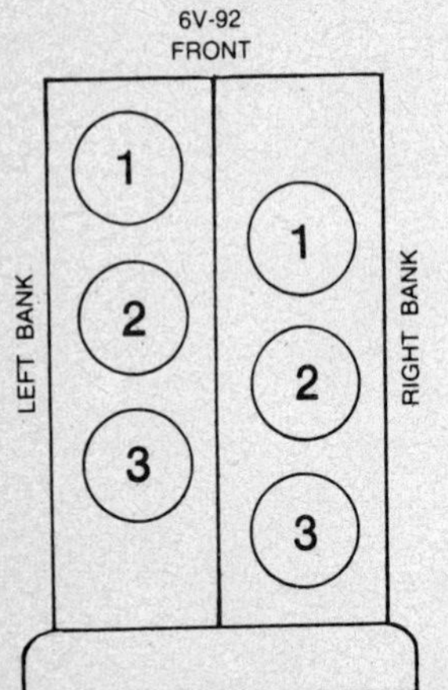

Firing order:
RH 1L-3R-3L-2R-2L-1R
LH 1L-1R-2L-2R-3L-3R

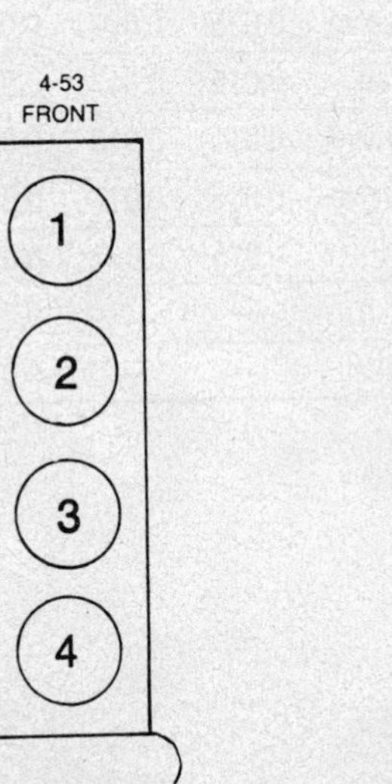

Firing order:
RH 1-3-4-2
LH 1-2-4-3

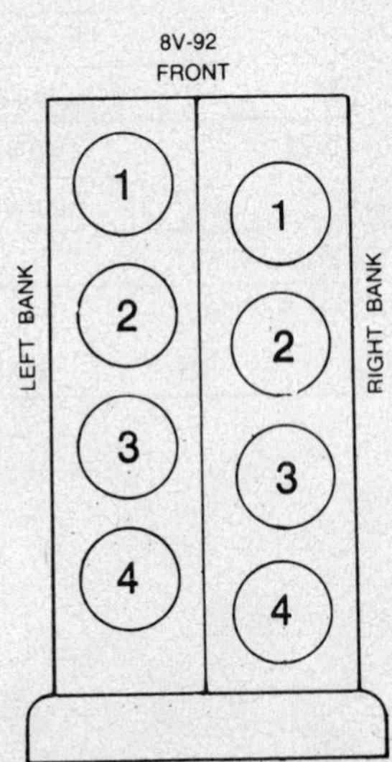

Firing order:
RH 1L-3R-3L-4R-4L-2R-2L-1R
LH 1L-1R-2L-2R-4L-4R-3L-3R

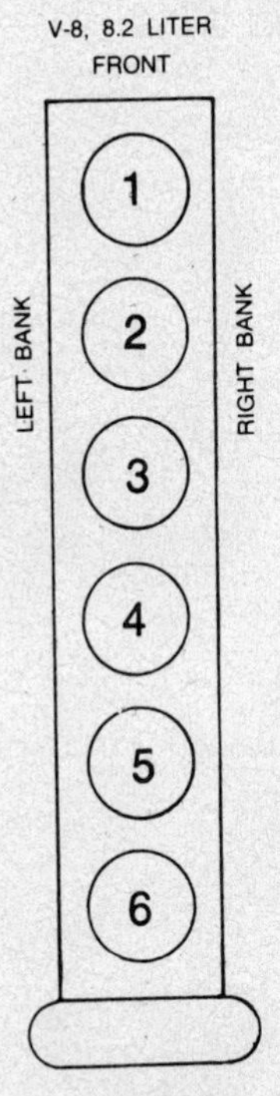

Firing order:
RH 1-5-3-6-2-4
LH 1-4-2-6-3-5

HEAD BOLT TORQUE SEQUENCE

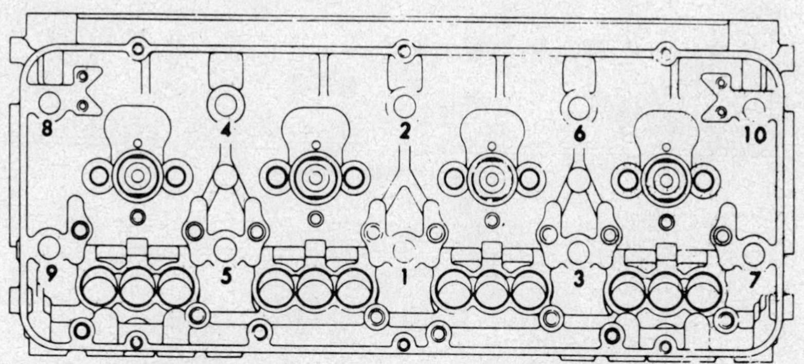

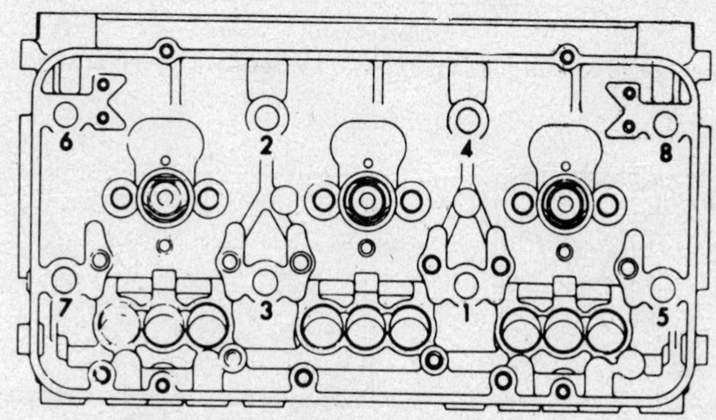

Cylinder head bolt torque sequence—53 Series (© General Motors Corp.)

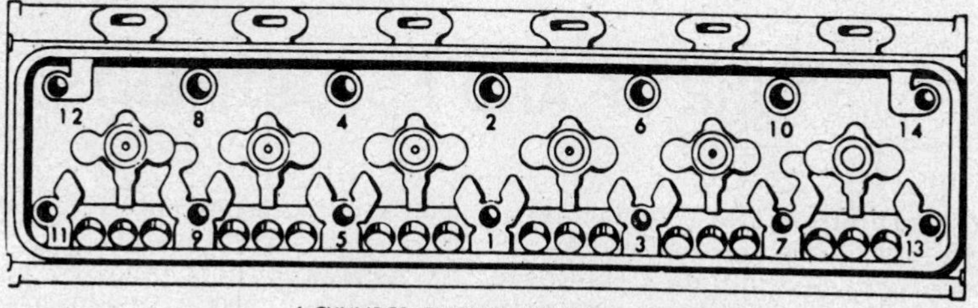

Cylinder head bolt torque sequence—71 in-line Series (© General Motors Corp.)

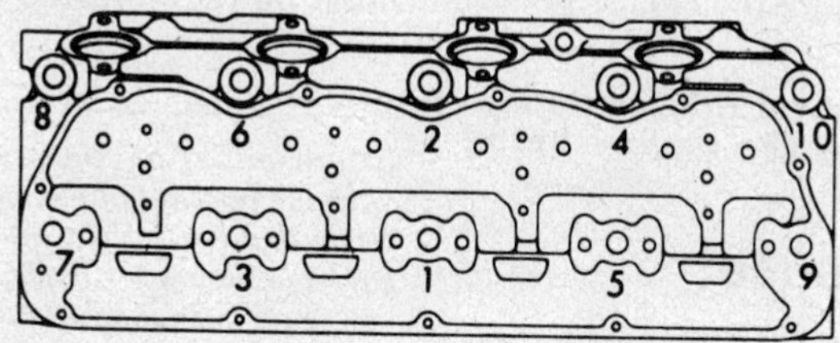

Cylinder head bolt torque sequence—V8, 8.2 Liter Series (© General Motors Corp.)

TORQUE SEQUENCES

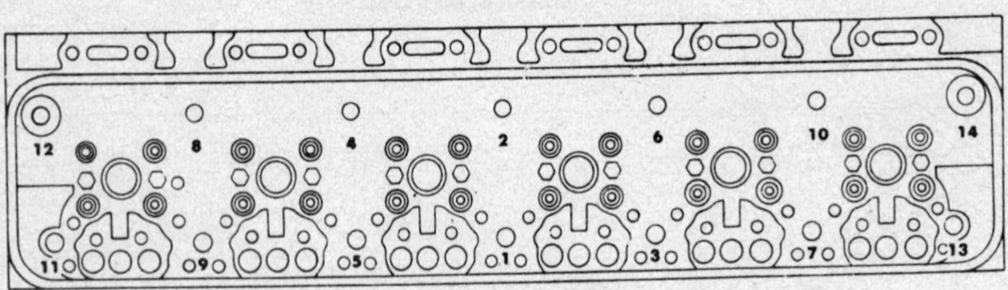

CYLINDER HEAD FOR 12V ENGINE

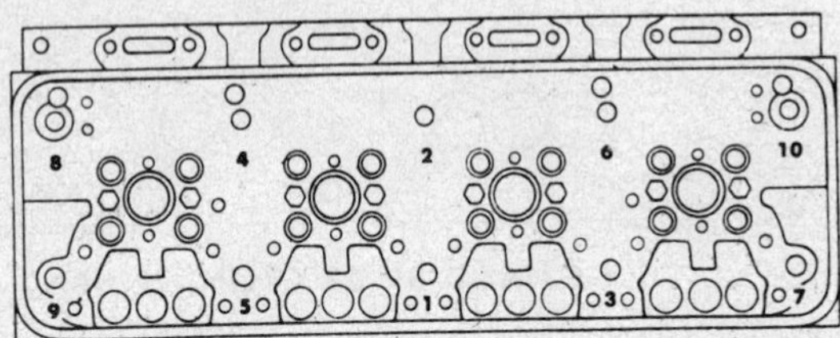

CYLINDER HEAD FOR 8V ENGINE

Cylinder head bolt torque sequence—71 V Series (© General Motors Corp.)

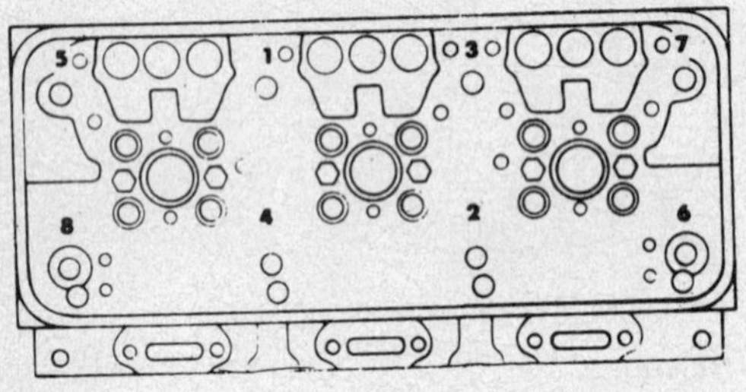

CYLINDER HEAD FOR 6V ENGINE

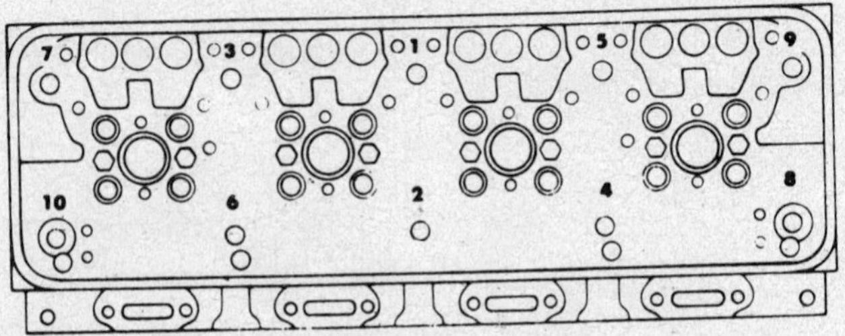

CYLINDER HEAD FOR 8V ENGINE

Cylinder head bolt torque sequence—92 Series (© General Motors Corp.)

TUNE UP AND ADJUSTMENTS

NOTE: Before tune-up procedure is started it is important that air cleaners and fuel filters are serviced as described in applicable maintenance manuals. Crankcase breather tube and air box drains must be clean and unobstructed. Air box drains may be cleaned with compressed air.

Scheduled tune-ups are done at mileage or time intervals at the discretion of the owner/operator or when the engine's performance is unsatisfactory. Many times, minor adjustments of the valves, injector mechanism and governors, along with the renewal of fuel and air filters will restore the engine performance to normal.

NOTE: Refer to the Emission Control Information label for specifications concerning the engine being serviced.

Tune Up Sequence

To completely tune-up an engine, all adjustments except bridge balancing adjustment and exhaust valve cold setting must be performed only after engine has reached its normal operating temperature.

Results obtained from an engine tune-up are usually unsatisfactory, unless a step-by-step, systematic and orderly approach is used. Proceed in the following sequence.

NOTE: If a supplementary governing device is used, such as a load limit device, it must be disconnected prior to the tune-up. After the governor and injector rack adjustments are made, the supplementary governing device must be reconnected and adjusted.

CAUTION

Before starting an engine after an engine speed control adjustment or after the removal of the engine governor cover, the serviceman must verify that the injector racks move to the no-fuel position when the governor stop lever is placed in the stop position. Engine overspeed will result if the injector racks cannot be positioned at the no-fuel position with the governor stop lever.

SERIES 53

WITH MECHANICAL GOVERNOR

1. Adjust the exhaust valve clearance.
2. Time the fuel injectors.
3. Adjust the governor gap.
4. Position the injector rack control levers.
5. Adjust the maximum no-load speed.
6. Adjust the idle speed.
7. Adjust the buffer screw.
8. Adjust the throttle booster spring (variable speed governor only).
9. Adjust the supplementary governing device, if equipped.

WITH HYDRAULIC GOVERNOR

1. Adjust the exhaust valve clearance.
2. Time the fuel injectors.
3. Adjust the fuel rod.
4. Position the injector rack control levers.
5. Adjust the load limit screw.
6. Compensation adjustment (PSG only).
7. Adjust the speed droop.
8. Adjust the maximum no-load speed.

SERIES 71, IN–LINE

WITH MECHANICAL GOVERNOR

1. Adjust the exhaust valve clearance.
2. Time the fuel injectors.
3. Adjust the governor gap.
4. Position the injector rack control levers.
5. Adjust the maximum no-load speed.
6. Adjust the idle speed.
7. Adjust the buffer screw.
8. Adjust the throttle booster spring (variable speed governor only).
9. Adjust the supplementary governing device, if equipped.

WITH HYDRAULIC GOVERNOR

1. Adjust the exhaust valve clearance.
2. Time the fuel injectors.
3. Adjust the fuel rod.
4. Position the injector rack control levers.
5. Adjust the load limit screw.
6. Compensation adjustment (PSG governors only).
7. Adjust the speed droop.
8. Adjust the maximum no-load speed.

SERIES V–71

WITH MECHANICAL GOVERNOR

1. Adjust the exhaust valve clearance.
2. Time the fuel injectors.
3. Adjust the governor gap.
4. Position the injector rack control levers.
5. Adjust the maximum no-load speed.
6. Adjust the idle speed.
7. Adjust the Belleville spring for "TT" horsepower.
8. Adjust the buffer screw.
9. Adjust the throttle booster, spring (variable speed governor only).
10. Adjust the supplementary governing device, if equipped.

WITH HYDRAULIC GOVERNOR

1. Adjust the exhaust valve clearance.
2. Time the fuel injectors.
3. Adjust the governor linkage.
4. Position the injector rack control levers.
5. Adjust the load limit screw.
6. Compensation adjustment (PSG governors only).
7. Adjust the speed droop.
8. Adjust the maximum no-load speed.

SERIES 92

WITH MECHANICAL GOVERNOR

1. Adjust the exhaust valve clearance.
2. Time the fuel injectors.
3. Adjust the governor gap.
4. Position the injector rack control levers.
5. Adjust the maximum no-load speed.
6. Adjust the idle speed.
7. Adjust the Belleville spring for "TT" horsepower.
8. Adjust the buffer screw.
9. Adjust the throttle booster spring (variable speed governor only).
10. Adjust the supplementary governing device, if equipped.

WITH HYDRAULIC GOVERNOR

1. Adjust the exhaust valve clearance.
2. Time the fuel injectors.
3. Position the injector rack control levers.
4. Adjust the governor linkage.
5. Adjust the load limit screw.
6. Compensation adjustment (PSG governors only).
7. Adjust the speed droop.
8. Adjust the maximum no-load speed.

SERIES V8, 8.2 (FUEL PINCHER)

1. Adjust the intake and exhaust valve clearances.
2. Time the fuel injectors.
3. Position the injector rack control levers.

Compression Test

The compression pressures of the cylinders can be checked as follows:

1. Have the engine at normal operating temperature.
2. Remove the fuel pipes from the injector and fuel connection on number one cylinder.
3. Remove the injector and install the pressure gauge with adaptor in its place.
4. Fabricate a jumper connection between the fuel inlet and return manifold connection to permit the fuel from the inlet manifold to flow directly to the return manifold.
5. Start the engine and run at 600 (700 for four cycle engine) rpm. Record the compression pressure.

CAUTION

Do not crank the engine with the starter motor to obtain the compression pressures.

6. Stop the engine and move the pressure gauge with adaptor and the jumper fuel connection to the next cylinder. Re-install the injector and fuel line in the cylinder just tested.
7. Repeat the procedure with each cylinder until all have been tested.
8. The variation in cylinder compression pressures should not exceed 25 psi at 600 (700 for four cycle engine) rpm.
9. The average cylinder compression pressure will range from 390 to 425 psi, at or near sea level, for the two cycle engines, while the compression pressure for the four cycle engine (V8, 8.2 liter) is approximately 630 psi for the naturally aspirated engines and 550 psi for the turbocharged engines, at sea level and at 700 rpm.

Bridge Balancing Adjustment

WITH FOUR VALVE CYLINDER HEAD

The exhaust valve bridge assembly is adjusted and the adjustment screw locked securely at the time the cylinder head is installed on the engine. Until wear occurs with the operation of the engine, no further adjustment is required on the exhaust valve bridge.

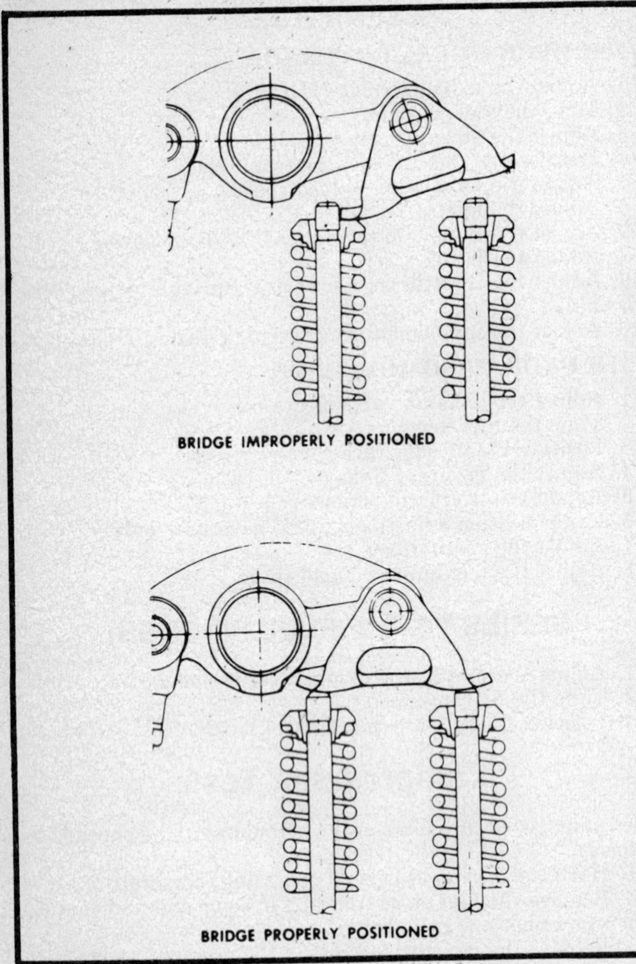

Relationship of properly positioned exhaust valve bridge on four valve cylinder head (© General Motors Corp.)

1. Remove injector fuel jumper lines, then remove rocker arm shaft brackets. Lift rocker arms and swing back to provide access to valve bridge.
2. Remove bridge and spring (when used) from guide. Place in vise.
3. Loosen adjusting screw lock nut.
4. Install bridge on bridge guide without spring.
5. Press straight down on the pallet surface of bridge. Turn adjusting screw until it just touches the valve stem, then turn screw an additional $\frac{1}{8}$ to $\frac{1}{4}$ turn and tighten lock nut finger tight.
6. Remove bridge and place in a vise. With screwdriver, hold screw from turning and tighten lock nut on the adjusting screw. Complete the operation by tightening the lock nut to 25 ft. lbs. torque, being sure that screw does not turn.

CAUTION

Do not tighten while on engine, as binding may damage bridge, guide and valve.

7. Apply engine oil to bridge and bridge guide.
8. Reinstall the bridge in its original position without the bridge spring.
9. Place a 0.0015" feeler under each end of the bridge.

NOTE: Feeler used at inner end of bridge must be narrow enough to fit in bridge locating groove. Pressing down on the pallet surface of the bridge, both feelers must be tight. If both feelers are not tight, readjust the screw as previously instructed.

10. Remove the bridge and reinstall in its original position with the bridge spring (when used) in place.
11. Adjust remaining bridges as instructed in previous steps.
12. Reconnect fuel jumper lines to injectors and connectors.

Valve Clearance Adjustment

Whenever the valve operating mechanism is changed or moved, the cylinder head overhauled or replaced, new or original valves reworked, the valve clearance must be adjusted. An initial adjustment must be made with the engine cold and prior

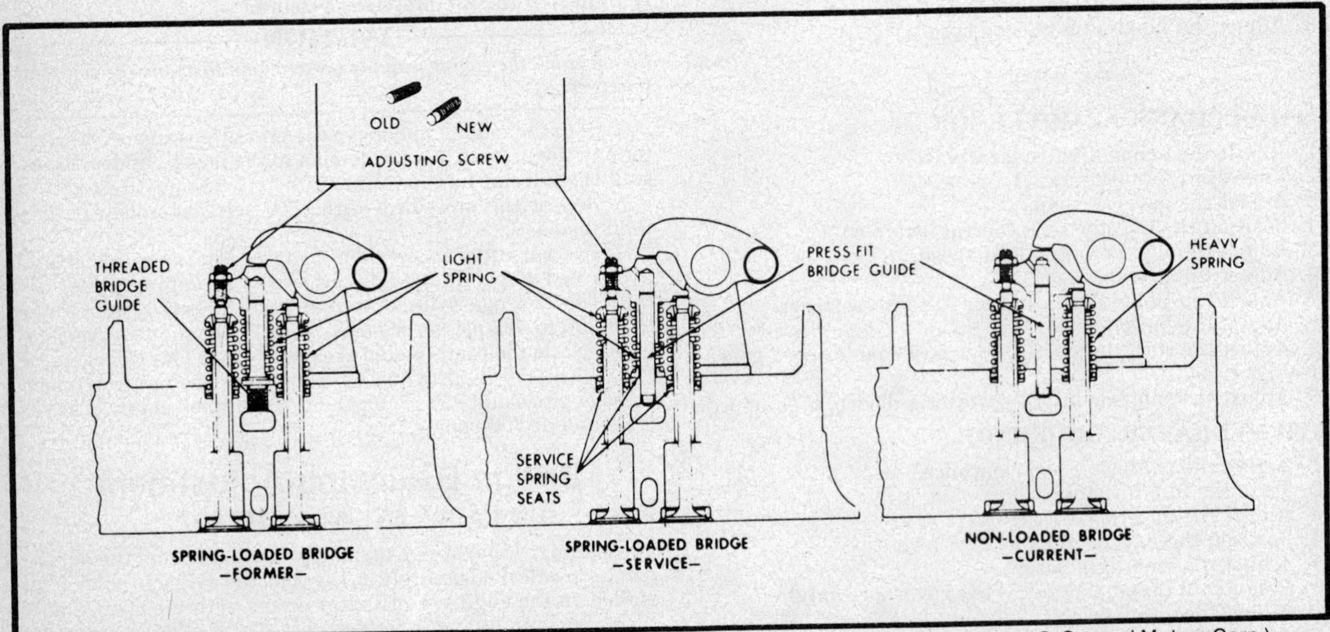

Exhaust valve bridge used with four valve cylinder head with former, service and current bridge guide usage (© General Motors Corp.)

to engine start-up to avoid valve damage. After the engine has reached normal operating temperature, a recheck of the valve clearance must be done. A valve clearance specification chart follows the adjusting procedures for the engine series. All two cycle engine exhaust valves can be adjusted in their firing order sequence during one crankshaft revolution, while the four cycle engine exhaust and intake valves can be adjusted in their firing order sequence during two crankshaft revolutions.

Valve Adjustment Procedure

TWO VALVE CYLINDER HEAD—TWO CYCLE ENGINE

COLD

1. Remove the valve rocker covers from the engine if not previously done.
2. Secure the governor speed control lever in the IDLE speed position or STOP position, if a stop lever is provided.
3. Rotate the crankshaft with a crankshaft rotating tool or with the starting motor until the injector follower is fully depressed on the cylinder that the valves are to be adjusted.

CAUTION

Do not allow the crankshaft bolt to loosen, if used to turn the crankshaft.

4. Loosen the exhaust valve rocker arm pushrod lock nut.
5. Place a feeler gauge blade, 0.001 in. thicker than specifications between the exhaust valve stem and the rocker arm. Adjust the pushrod to obtain a smooth pull on the feeler gauge blade.
6. With the feeler gauge blade removed, hold the pushrod with the proper sized wrench and tighten the locknut securely.
7. Recheck the clearance. A feeler gauge blade, 0.001 in. thinner than specifications, should pass freely between the valve stem and the rocker arm, but a 0.001 in. thicker blade should not pass through. Readjust the pushrod as necessary.
8. Rotate the crankshaft until the next cylinder injector follower in the firing order, is fully depressed. Adjust and check the exhaust valve clearance for that cylinder.
9. Adjust and check the remaining exhaust valve clearance as outlined. Install the valve rocker covers.

HOT

1. With the engine at normal operating temperature, have the injector follower fully depressed on the number one cylinder in the firing order and verify the final exhaust valve clearance as listed in the specification chart for the engine series.
2. The final clearance is correct if a feeler gauge blade 0.001 in. thinner than the hot specification clearance, will pass freely between the end of the valve stem and the rocker arm, but a 0.001 in. thicker blade than the hot specification clearance will not pass through.
3. Continue checking the exhaust valve clearance of the cylinders in the firing order sequence.
4. Install the valve rocker covers.

FOUR VALVE CYLINDER HEAD—TWO CYCLE ENGINE

The exhaust valves bridge balance must be properly adjusted before any valve clearances are checked. Refer to the Exhaust Valve Bridge Balance Adjustment section for the proper adjustment procedure. After having balanced the exhaust valve bridges, do not disturb the bridge adjusting screws. Make all valve adjustments with the pushrods only.

COLD

1. Remove the valve rocker covers from the engine, if not previously done.

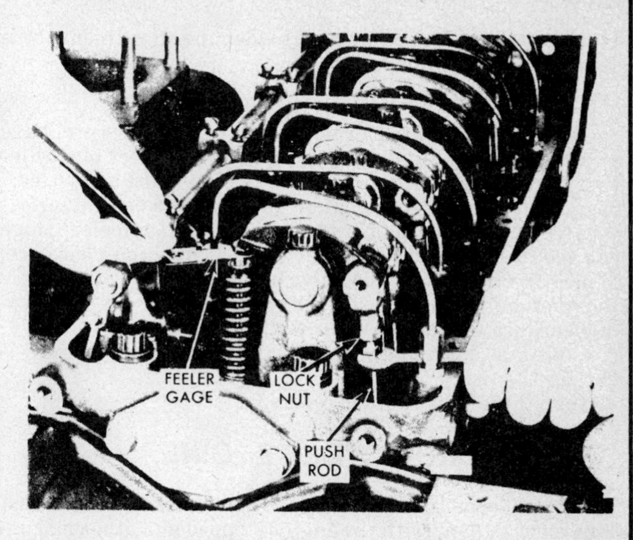

Adjusting valve clearance—two valve cylinder head
(© General Motors Corp.)

2. Secure the governor speed control lever in the IDLE speed position or STOP position, if a stop lever is provided.
3. Rotate the crankshaft with a crankshaft rotating tool or with the starting motor until the injector follower is fully depressed on the cylinder that the valves are to be adjusted.

CAUTION

Do not allow the crankshaft bolt to loosen, if used to turn the crankshaft.

4. Loosen the exhaust valve rocker arm pushrod locknut.
5. Place a feeler gauge blade 0.001 in. thicker than specifications between the valve bridge and the valve rocker arm pallet. Adjust the pushrod to obtain a smooth pull on the feeler gauge blade.
6. With the feeler gauge blade removed, hold the pushrod with the proper sized wrench and tighten the locknut securely.
7. Recheck the clearance. A feeler gauge blade, 0.001 in. thinner than specifications, should pass freely between the valve bridge and the valve rocker arm pallet, but a 0.001 in. thicker blade should not pass through. Readjust as required.
8. Rotate the crankshaft until the next cylinder injector follower in the firing order is fully depressed. Adjust and check

Adjusting valve clearance—spring loaded valve bridge
(© General Motors Corp.)

the exhaust valve clearance for that cylinder as in the previous steps.

9. Install the valve rocker covers when the adjustment of the exhaust valves are complete.

HOT

1. With the engine at normal operating temperature, have the injector follower fully depressed on the number one cylinder in the firing order and verify the final exhaust valve clearance as listed in the specification chart for the engine series.
2. The final or hot adjustment is correct if a feeler gauge blade 0.001 in. thinner than the hot specification clearance, will pass freely between the valve bridge and the valve rocker arm pallet, but a 0.001 in. thicker blade than the hot specification clearance will not pass through.
3. Continue checking the exhaust valve clearance of the cylinders in the firing order sequence.
4. Install the valve rocker covers.

FOUR CYCLE ENGINE

The valve clearance adjustment on the intake and exhaust valves must be done with the engine stopped and at normal operating temperature. The valve clearance is adjustable by means of a set screw and lock nut arrangement, located at the pushrod end of the rocker arms.

CAUTION

Before any adjustments are done, the repairman must determine that the injector racks move to the no-fuel position when the governor stop lever is placed in the STOP position.

NOTE: A shutdown solenoid is mounted to the engine governor and must be energized to the RUN position or removed from the governor prior to connecting the governor linkage to the rack control shaft or engine overspeed may occur. The solenoid is designed to hold the fuel shutdown in the STOP position at all times except when energized and should the injector racks be held in the full fuel position and connected to the governor while the shutdown is in the STOP position, the injectors will be locked at full rack with maximum fuel being injected into the engine.

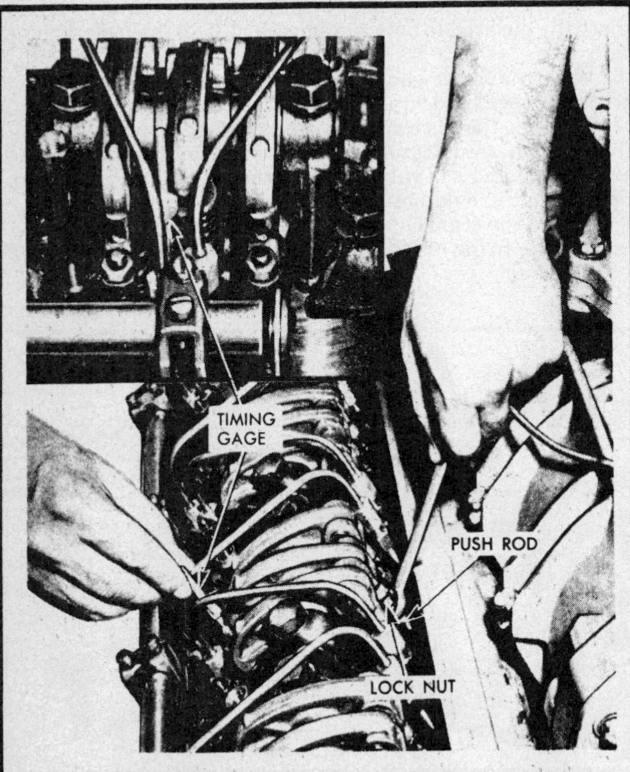

Timing fuel injector—V type engine (© General Motors Corp.)

1. Remove the valve rocker covers, if not previously done.
2. Manually or with the starter motor, bring the piston of the number one cylinder to TDC position. An indication of TDC is the downward movement of the injector rocker arm.
3. Insert the feeler gauge blade of correct thickness, between the end of the appropriate valve stem and the rocker arm. Adjust the clearance until the gauge blade is a snug fit between the valve stem and the rocker arm. Lock the adjusting nut securely and recheck the clearance.
4. After adjusting the intake and exhaust valves of the number one cylinder to specifications, rotate the crankshaft until the next cylinder in the firing order sequence is at TDC. Adjust the intake and exhaust valves in the same manner as was done on the valves of number one cylinder.
5. Continue in the firing order sequence until all valves have been adjusted.
6. Install the valve rocker covers.

Injector Timing

TWO CYCLE ENGINES

To time the injectors properly, the injector follower must be adjusted to a definite height in relation to the injector body.

1. Position the governor speed control lever in the idle speed position and if a stop lever is provided, secure it in the stop position.
2. Rotate the crankshaft either with the starter motor or manually, until the exhaust valves are fully depressed on the particular cylinder to be timed.

CAUTION

If the engine is turned manually by the bolt on the front of the crankshaft, do not turn the crankshaft in a left-hand direction of rotation or the bolt may be loosened.

NOTE: Injector timing gauges are available through the manufacturer or through major tool suppliers.

3. Place the small end of the injector timing gauge in the hole provided in the top of the injector body with the flat of the gauge towards the injector follower.

NOTE: Refer to Tune-up Charts for tool and dimension specifications.

4. Should the injector timing dimension need to be adjusted, loosen the injector rocker arm pushrod locknut. Turn the pushrod and adjust the injector rocker arm until the extended part of the gauge will just pass over the top of the injector follower.
5. Hold the pushrod and tighten the locknut. Recheck the adjustment and readjust the pushrod as necessary.
6. Rotate the engine to the next cylinder in the firing order, until the exhaust valves are fully depressed and adjust the fuel injectors as required. Continue the engine rotation and adjustment until all injectors have been checked and/or adjusted.
7. Install the valve rocker covers on the engine.

FOUR CYCLE ENGINES

An injector timing gauge, Kent-Moore J29014, has been developed and designed for timing the injectors on the V8, 8.2 engines, using Base Circle (BC) or Top Dead Center (TDC) methods. The specially designed gauge dial has two sections with red numbers on the inner perimeter of the dial for Top Dead

Center timing and black numbers on the outer perimeter of the dial for Base Circle timing. A stepped master gauge block is used to calibrate the dial indicator for each timing method. The lower step is for the calibration when used with the Base Circle method and the upper step is used when calibrating for the Top Dead Center method.

CAUTION

When using the Kent-Moore gauge or an equivalent, follow the manufacturer's recommended calibration procedures before attempting to adjust the fuel injection timing, using either method.

Base Circle Method

A Base Circle injector timing height specification label is located on the front of the left bank rocker cover. The information on the label is valid for each cylinder until a major overhaul is done and components such as the crankshaft, camshaft, cylinder block or gear train are changed. New Base Circle injector height measurements for each cylinder must then be recorded and attached to the engine.

To time the injectors utilizing the dimensions on the injector timing label, located on the left rocker cover, calibrate the dial indicator as per the manufacturer's instructions, using the black numbers on the outer perimeter of the dial.

1. Position the number one cylinder injector rocker arm so that approximately two full threads are showing above the locknut.
2. Rotate the crankshaft until the number one cylinder injector rocker arm is at the top of its stroke (on its cam base circle).
3. Place the dial indicator tool on the top of the injector follower with the indicator probe sitting on the injector ledge projection. engage the two spring loaded pins to the injector spring coil to secure the gauge to the injector.
4. Slowly rotate the engine crankshaft until the number one cylinder injector follower descends between 0.5 to 1.0mm. The injector timing can then be set on cylinders three, four, six and eight.
5. Remove the dial indicator tool from the number one cylinder injector and place it on the number three cylinder injector and secure it in place.
6. Adjust the rocker arm adjusting screw until the specific timing dimension is indicated on the dial indicator for that specific cylinder, as listed on the injector timing height label, attached to the engine valve rocker cover. Continue the adjustments with the indicator tool on cylinders four, six and eight injectors, without moving the engine crankshaft. As each separate injector timing height is adjusted per cylinder, tighten the locknuts securely.
7. Remove the dial indicator from the number eight injector and rotate the crankshaft approximately 360° until number six injector follower is on its cam base circle. Install the dial indicator on the number six injector follower and rotate the crankshaft until the injector follower descends approximately 0.5 to 1.0mm. The injector timing height can then be adjusted on cylinders one, two, five and seven as was done in Steps 5 and 6.

NOTE: The dial indicator should be rechecked for proper calibration during the injector timing height adjustment procedures.

Establishing a Precision Top Dead Center (T.D.C.) Position

Whenever an engine component is changed, such as a crankshaft, camshaft, cylinder block or gear train is replaced, any previous determined injector heights are no longer valid. To conform to the Federal E.P.A. and California exhaust emission specifications, the former injector timing heights are incorrect and must be removed from the engine. The new dimensions are determined by the following procedures and must be measured and the measurements recorded on a sticker, which is to be placed on the front of the left rocker cover.

Measurement Procedures

1. With the cylinder head off the engine block, a special tool is placed in the number eight cylinder which limits the piston stroke and locates number one cylinder in the TDC position of the compression stroke. One complete turn of the crankshaft may have to be made to place the number one piston on the compression stroke. If so, remove tool until the complete turn has been made.

CAUTION

With the special tool in place in the number eight cylinder bore, do not attempt to rotate the engine crankshaft, other than by hand.

2. With the number eight piston firmly against the special tool, remove the dust cover from the flywheel housing, if not previously removed. A timing pin guide hole is located in the lower front of the flywheel housing.
3. The flywheel has four equally spaced holes (90°) for the timing pin to engage.

NOTE: A special tool, consisting of a timing pin and guide are available to the repairman.

4. Install the timing pin and guide into the flywheel housing and lock the guide bolts in place. engage the timing pin in the mating hole in the flywheel to retain the TDC position of number one cylinder.
5. Remove the special positioning tool from number eight cylinder and without moving the crankshaft, install the cylinder head assembly.
6. With the cylinder head and components in place, position all injector rocker arm adjusting screws so that approximately two full threads are above a snug locknut.
7. With the timing pin still engaged in the flywheel hole representing number one cylinder piston at TDC on its compression stroke, set the properly calibrated dial indicator tool on the top of the injector follower so that the probe rests on the projecting injector body ledge. Secure the indicator to the injector spring coil.
8. Using the red numbers on the inner perimeter of the dial, adjust the number one cylinder injector rocker arm so that the reading on the dial corresponds with the following specifications. Tighten the locknut and remove the dial indicator from the injector assembly.
   a. 50 State Turbo Engine: 44.75mm
   b. California Naturally Aspirated: 44.45mm
   c. 49 States Naturally Aspirated: 43.80mm
9. Remove the timing pin from the flywheel hole and gently rotate the crankshaft clockwise 90° and reinstall the timing pin in the next timing hole in the flywheel. This position represents the next cylinder in the firing order, which is number eight. Repeat Steps 7 and 8 and adjust the injector rocker arm to specifications.
10. Continue the procedure in Step 9, followed by Steps 7 and 8 until all injector rocker arms have been adjusted. The firing order is 1,8,4,3,6,5,7 and 2.

NOTE: While adjusting the injector rocker arms with the cylinders at TDC on the compression stroke, the intake and exhaust valves can be adjusted cold, allowing 0.001 to 0.002 in. more tolerance than specifications. Recheck as previously outlined with the engine at normal operating temperature for final clearance.

CAUTION

Do not allow the timing pin and guide to remain in the flywheel and flywheel housing after the injectors have been adjusted. Damage to the special tools and engine components can result if an attempt is made to start the engine.

Recording Base Circle Timing Heights

After a major overhaul with component parts replacement, new dimensions must be obtained for the injector timing height measurement and recorded on a new label to be affixed to the engine as previously outlined. The procedure is as follows.

1. Rotate the crankshaft until the number one cylinder piston is almost at TDC on its compression stroke.
2. Install a properly calibrated dial indicator tool on the injector rocker arm and secure. Rotate the crankshaft until the rocker arm begins its downward travel, between 0.5 and 1.0mm. Recheck the calibration of the dial indicator tool on its stepped master gauge block. Place the dial indicator successively on the top of numbers eight, four, three and six injectors and read the timing heights for each injector.
3. Record the measurements per cylinder on a new Base Circle timing label.
4. Remove the dial indicator tool and rotate the crankshaft nearly one complete turn. Install the dial indicator on the number six injector rocker arm and rotate the crankshaft until the rocker arm has depressed between 0.5 and 1.0mm.
5. Remove the dial indicator and recalibrate on the stepped master gauge block. Install the dial indicator on the tops of injectors of cylinders five, seven, two and one, successively and record the readings on the Base Circle Timing label.
6. The new Base Circle Timing heights must be kept with the engine to facilitate timing for future service until major changes are again made.

Maximum No-Load Engine Speed Adjustment

SERIES 4-53, 6V-53 ENGINES

Should a reconditioned or replacement governor be installed on the engine, the no-load maximum engine speed setting should be checked and adjusted to the rpm specifications listed on the engine name plate to insure against engine overspeeding. Two types of governor springs are used and are classified as type A and type B. Type A governors have a spring housing covering an extended spring from the governor housing, while the type B governor has only a spring cover with the spring assembly flush with the housing. Adjust each type governor as follows.

TYPE A

1. Loosen the locknut and back off the high-speed spring retainer several turns. Start the engine and slowly increase the speed. If the engine exceeds the required no-load speed before the speed control lever reaches the end of its travel, back off the spring retainer a few additional turns.
2. With the engine at normal operating temperature and no-load on the engine, place the speed control lever in the maximum speed position. Turn the high-speed spring retainer in until the engine is operating at the recommended no-load speed.
3. The maximum no-load speed varies with the full-load operating speed and is called "droop." The reason for "droop" is to ensure the governor will move the injector racks into the full-fuel position at the desired engine rpm by having the governor set approximately 150 to 200 rpm higher at the no-load rpm, than the full-load speed. An example would be if the full-load speed is to be 2600 rpm, then the no-load speed setting should be 2800 rpm to insure the governor will move the injector racks to the full-fuel position at the desired full-load speed.
4. Hold the spring retainer and tighten the locknut.

TYPE B

1. Start the engine and bring to normal operating temperature. Have the engine at no-load.
2. Place the speed control lever in the maximum speed position and note the engine rpm.
3. If the engine rpm is out of specifications, stop the engine and adjust as follows:
   a. Remove the high speed spring retainer with a special remover tool and withdraw the high-speed spring and plunger assembly from the governor housing.

NOTE: To prevent the low speed spring and cap from dropping into the governor, do not jar the high-speed assembly during its removal.

   b. Remove the high speed spring from the high speed spring plunger and add or remove the shims as required to establish the desired engine no-load speed.

NOTE: The engine speed will increase approximately 10 rpm for each 0.010 in. shim added to the shim pack.

   c. Install the high-speed spring on the plunger and install the spring assembly into the governor housing.
   d. Tighten the spring retainer securely. The maximum no-load speed varies with the full-load operating speed desired. An example would be if the full-load speed setting should be 2800 rpm, then the no-load speed setting should be 2940 rpm to ensure that the governor will move the injector racks to the full-fuel position at the desired full-load speed.
4. Start the engine and recheck the no-load speed. Repeat the addition or deletion of shims as necessary to establish the no-load speed as required.

SPEED DROOP SPECIFICATIONS

Full Load RPM	Maximum Governor Droop—RPM
TYPE A GOVERNOR	
0-1200	200
1201-1400	175
1401-1600	150
1601-1800	160
1801-2000	170
2001-2200	180
2201-2400	190
2401-2600	200
2601-2800	210
TYPE B GOVERNOR	
2401-2600	150
2601-2800	140

Idle Speed Adjustment

NOTE: The maximum no-load speed must be properly adjusted before the idle speed is adjusted.

1. The engine must be at normal operating temperature and the buffer screw backed out to avoid contact with the differential lever. Turn the idle speed adjusting screw until the engine is operating at approximately 15 rpm below the recommended idle speed of 500 to 600 rpm. This may vary with the engine application.

NOTE: If the engine has a tendency to stall during deceleration, install a new buffer screw. The later buffer screw uses a heavier spring and restricts the travel of the differential lever to the off (no-fuel) position.

2. Hold the idle screw and tighten the locknut.

3. Install the high-speed spring retainer cover and tighten the two bolts.

Buffer Screw Adjustment

NOTE: The idle speed must be properly adjusted before the buffer screw is reset.

1. With the engine at normal operating temperature, turn the buffer screw in so it contacts the differential lever as lightly as possible and still eliminates engine roll.

NOTE: Do not increase the engine idle speed more than 15 rpm with the buffer screw.

2. Recheck the maximum no-load speed. If it has increased more than 25 rpm, back off the buffer screw until the increase is less than 25 rpm.
3. Hold the buffer screw and tighten the locknut.
4. If the engine is equipped with a supplementary governing device, adjust it as required.

SERIES 71 INLINE, V–71

STANDARD GOVERNOR

1. Loosen the locknut and back off the high speed spring retainer approximately five turns.
2. With the engine at normal operating temperature and with no-load on the engine, move the speed control lever in the full fuel position. Turn the high speed spring retainer in until the recommended no-load speed is reached.
3. Hold the high speed spring retainer and tighten the locknut.

EARLY DUAL RANGE GOVERNOR

After positioning the injector rack control levers and setting the idle speed, set the maximum engine speeds. With the spring housing assembly mounted on the governor, the piston and sleeve assembly assembled and the low maximum speed adjusting screw extended from the spring housing approximately $^{3}/_{4}$ in. beyond the lock nut, proceed as follows:

CAUTION

Do not apply air pressure to the governor until performing Step 1h.

NOTE: Be sure the buffer screw projects $^{5}/_{8}$ in. from the lock nut to prevent its interference while adjusting the maximum no-load speeds.

NOTE: To prevent air leakage between the piston and sleeve assembly, coat the mating threads with sealant.

1. Set the high maximum no-load speed.
   a. Start the engine and place the speed control lever in the maximum speed position.
   b. Loosen the lock nut and turn the low maximum speed adjusting screw in until the desired no-load high maximum speed is obtained.
   c. Stop the engine and remove the spring housing. Note the distance the sleeve extends beyond the spring housing.

CAUTION

Do not permit the seal ring on the piston to slide past the air inlet port, since the seal ring will be damaged.

   d. Remove the piston and sleeve from the bottom of the spring housing.
   e. Turn the piston until the sleeve extends from the bottom of the piston the same distance the sleeve extends beyond the spring housing, Step c.
   f. Check the adjustment by installing the piston and sleeve in the spring housing. The piston should be flush to $^{1}/_{64}$ in. below the bottom of the spring housing when it is tight against the adjustment screw.

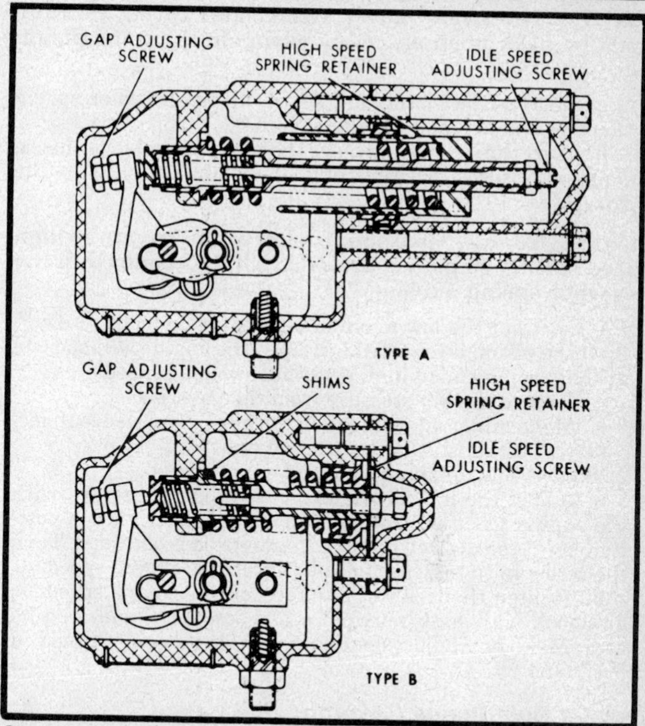

Cross section of type A and type B governors used with the 53 inline Series (© General Motors Corp.)

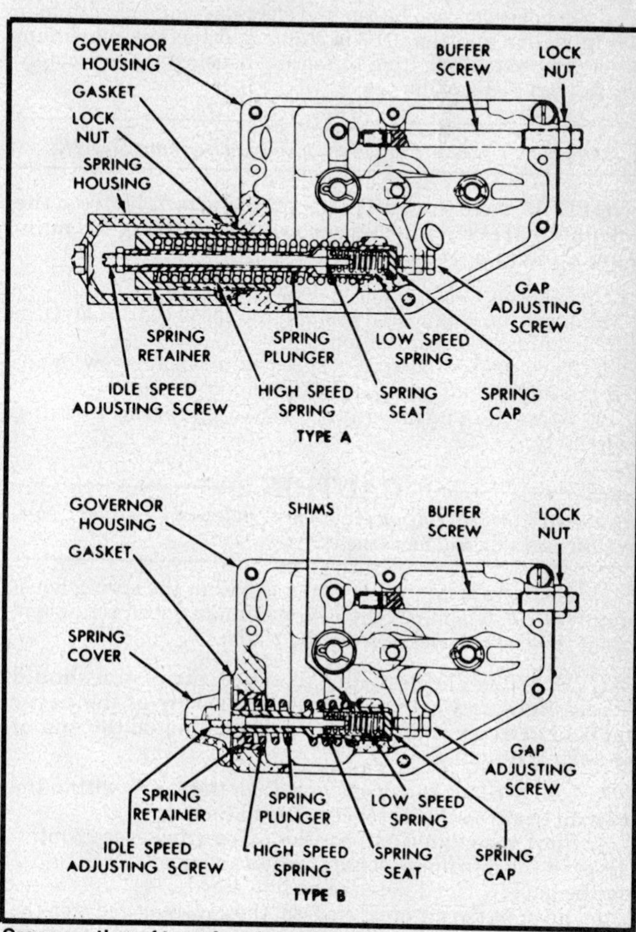

Cross section of type A and type B governors used with 53 V Series engines (© General Motors Corp.)

NOTE: The cover, cover gasket and spring housing must be held as an assembly when checking the piston position.

g. Replace the piston and sleeve in the governor spring housing and assemble to the governor.

h. Start the engine and place the speed control lever in the maximum speed position and apply air pressure to the governor.

NOTE: To overcome the tension of the governor high speed spring, 50 psi air pressure will be required in the governor spring housing.

i. Back out the low maximum speed adjustment screw ¼ in. If the piston is adjusted correctly, the engine will operate at the recommended high maximum no-load speed.

j. Remove the air pressure from the governor.

k. Make minor adjustment on the piston and sleeve if necessary to establish the exact speed desired.

2. Set the low maximum no-load engine speed.

a. Adjust the low maximum speed adjusting screw, with the engine speed control lever in the maximum speed position, until the desired low maximum speed is obtained. Turn the screw in to increase or out to decrease engine speed.

b. Tighten the lock nut and recheck the engine speed.

3. Check both high maximum and low maximum engine speeds. Make any adjustment that is necessary as outlined in Steps 1 and 2.

Current Dual Range Governor

After positioning the injector rack control levers, set the maximum engine speeds. With the spring housing assembly mounted on the governor, the piston and sleeve assembled with four .100 in. shims and ten .010 in.shims and the low maximum speed screw extending from the spring housing approximately 1 ¼ in., proceed as follows:

CAUTION

Do not apply air pressure to governor until performing Step 1f.

NOTE: Be sure the buffer screw projects ⅝ in. from the lock nut to prevent interference while adjusting the maximum no-load speeds.

1. Set the high maximum no-load speed.

a. Start the engine and position the speed control lever in the maximum speed position.

b. Turn the low maximum speed adjustment screw in until the high maximum speed desired is obtained.

c. Stop the engine and remove the spring housing assembly.

CAUTION

Do not permit the seal ring on the piston to slide past the air inlet port, since the seal ring will be damaged.

d. Note the distance the piston is within the spring housing when it is against the low maximum speed screw and then remove the sleeve from the piston.

NOTE: When checking this distance, the piston should be held tight against the adjustment screw of the cover that is held in position, with its gasket, against the end of the spring housing.

e. Remove a quantity of shims from the shims within the piston, equal to the distance noted in Step d.

f. Start the engine and position the engine speed control lever in the maximum speed position and apply air pressure to the governor and note the engine speed.

g. Remove the air pressure from the governor and stop the engine, then install or remove shims as required to obtain the correct high maximum no-load speed. Removing shims will decrease the engine speed and adding shims will increase the engine speed.

NOTE: Each .010 in. shim removed or added will decrease or increase the engine speed approximately 10 rpm.

2. Set the low maximum no-load engine speed.

a. Adjust the low maximum speed adjusting screw, with the speed control lever held in the maximum speed position, until the desired low maximum is obtained. Turn the screw in to increase or out to decrease the engine speed.

b. Recheck the engine speed and readjust if necessary.

3. Check both the high maximum and low maximum engine speeds. Make any adjustment that is necessary as outlined in Steps 1 and 2.

Adjusting Idle Speed

1. With the buffer screw backed out to avoid contact with the differential lever, turn the idle speed adjusting screw until the engine operates approximately 15 rpm below the recommended speed.

NOTE: The spring housing will have to be removed on the series 71 in-line engines to uncover the idle speed adjusting screw.

2. The recommended idle speed is 450 on in-line engines and 500 rpm for trucks and highway coaches and 400 rpm for city coaches on the V–71 engines.

3. Hold the idle screw and tighten the locknut.

4. Install the high speed spring retainer cover on the V–71 engines and the spring housing on the 71 in-line engines.

Adjusting the Buffer Screw

1. Turn the buffer screw in until it contacts the differential lever as lightly as possible and still eliminates engine roll. Do not increase the engine idle speed more than 15 rpm with the buffer screw.

2. Recheck the maximum no-load speed. If it has increased more than 25 rpm, back off the buffer screw until the increase is less than 25 rpm. Tighten the locknut.

Governor and Injector Rack Control Adjustments

MECHANICAL LIMITING SPEED GOVERNORS SERIES 4–53, 6V–53 ENGINES

CAUTION

Before attempting governor and injector rack adjustments, disconnect any supplementary governing devices. After the adjustments are made, reconnect and adjust the supplementary governing devices.

Governor Gap Adjustment

1. Have the engine stopped and at normal operating temperature. Remove the governor high speed spring retainer cover.

2. Back out the buffer screw or de-energize the fast idle cylinder, until the screw extends approximately ⅝ in. from the locknut.

CAUTION

Do not back the buffer screw out beyond the limits given or the control link lever may become disengaged from the differential lever.

3. **4–53 engines:**

a. Remove the valve rocker cover, start the engine and adjust the idle speed screw to obtain an idle speed of between 500 and 600 rpm.

b. Stop the engine and remove the governor cover.

6V–53 engines:

a. Start the engine and adjust the idle speed screw to obtain the desired idle speed of from 500 to 600 rpm or that stamped on the engine specification label. Tighten the lock nut.

NOTE: Turbocharged engine governors include a starting aid screw and lock nut threaded into the governor gap adjusting screw.

b. Stop the engine and remove the valve rocker covers.

4. Start the engine and control the speed by manually operating the injector control tube lever on the 4–53 engines and by the differential lever on the 6V–53 engines. Do not overspeed the engine, but keep the speed between 800 to 1000 rpm.

5. Check the gap between the low-speed spring cap and the high-speed spring plunger with a 0.0015 in. feeler gauge blade. If the gap is incorrect, reset the gap adjusting screw until the gap is correct. Tighten the adjusting screw locknut and recheck the gap. Readjust as required.

6. Stop the engine and install the governor cover, except on turbocharged models. These models have an internal starting aid screw and locknut that must be adjusted before the cover is installed. The starting aid screw is adjusted after the rack control levers are properly positioned.

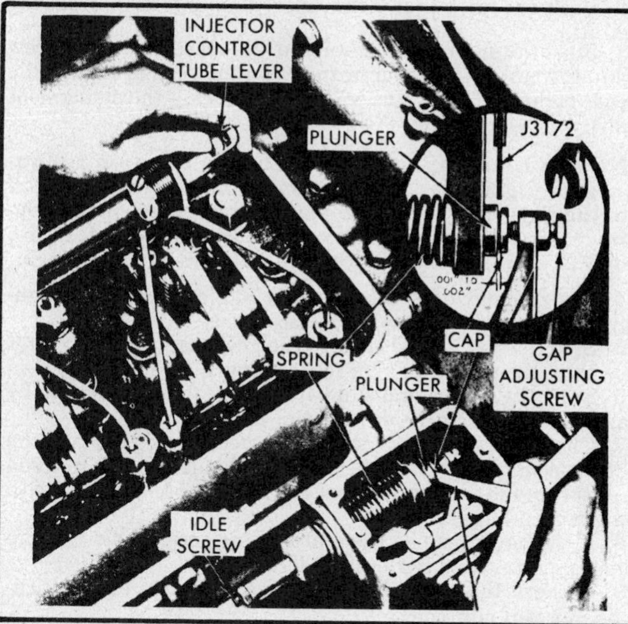

Adjusting gap, double weight governor—71 in-line Series
(© General Motors Corp.)

SERIES 71 – IN-LINE

Governor Gap Adjustment

CAUTION

The engine manufacturer recommends that if the governor gap is to be adjusted with the engine in the vehicle, the fan assembly be removed to prevent personal injury, due to the closeness of the blades to the governor location.

SINGLE WEIGHT GOVERNOR

1. Have the engine stopped, at normal operating temperature and supplementary governing devices disconnected.

2. Remove the governor high-speed spring retainer cover. Backout the buffer screw or fast idle cylinder until it extends approximately ⅝ in. from the lock nut.

3. Start the engine and loosen the idle speed adjusting screw locknut. Adjust the idle screw to obtain the desired idle speed.

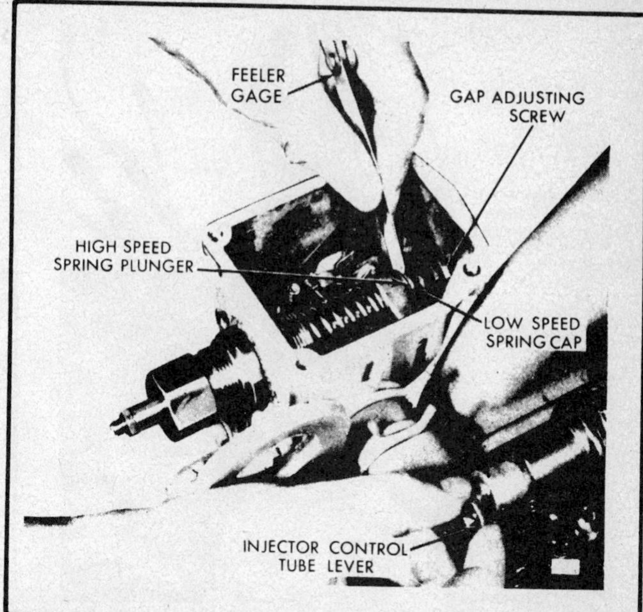

Adjusting governor gap—typical of 53 in-line Series
(© General Motors Corp.)

Minimum idle speeds are 500 rpm for trucks and highway coaches and 400 rpm for city coaches.

NOTE: Current limiting speed governors used in turbocharged engines include a starting aid screw threaded into a boss on the governor housing.

4. After the idle has been adjusted, stop the engine and remove the governor cover and lever assembly, along with the valve rocker cover.

5. Remove the fuel rod from the differential lever and the injector control tube lever.

6. Check the gap between the low-speed spring cap and the high-speed spring plunger with a special gauge measuring 0.170 in.

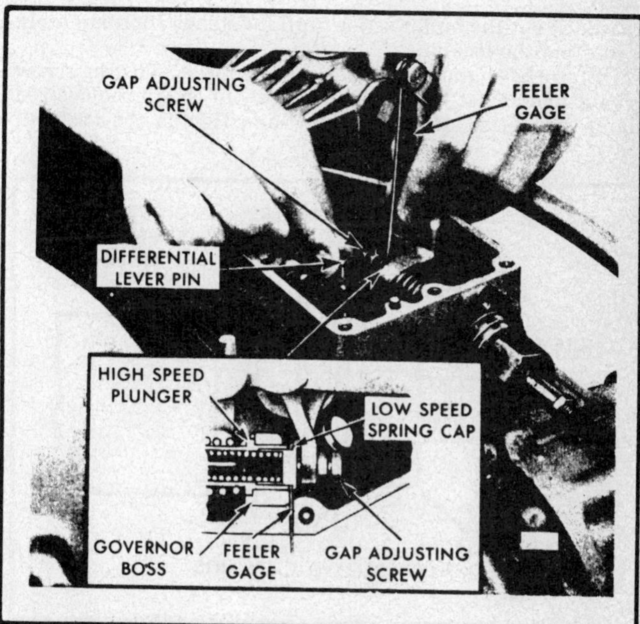

Adjusting governor gap—typical of 53 V Series
(© General Motors Corp.)

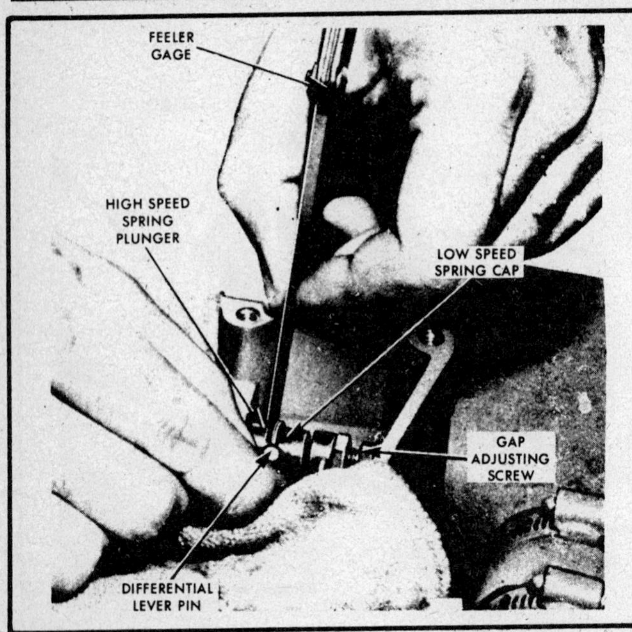

Adjusting gap, double weight governor—71 V and 92 Series
(© General Motors Corp.)

NOTE: Be sure the external starting aid screw is backed out far enough to make it ineffective when making the gap check and adjustment.

7. If required, loosen the locknut and move the gap adjusting screw until a slight drag is felt on the measuring tool. Hold the adjusting screw and tighten the locknut. Recheck the gap and adjust as necessary.

8. Install the fuel rod between the governor and the injector control tube lever. Install the governor cover and lever assembly.

DOUBLE WEIGHT GOVERNOR

1. The engine must be at normal operating temperature and stopped. Remove the governor high-speed spring retainer cover.

2. Back out the buffer screw until it extends approximately ⅝ in. from the locknut.

3. Start the engine and loosen the idle speed adjusting screw locknut and adjust the idle speed screw to obtain the desired engine idle speed. Hold the screw and tighten the locknut.

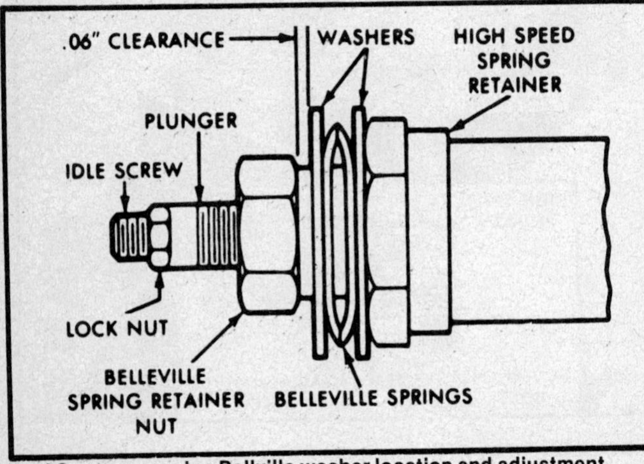

Fuel Squeezer engine Bellville washer location and adjustment
(© General Motors Corp.)

(Minimum engine idle speeds are 500 rpm for trucks and highway coaches and 400 rpm for city coaches.)

4. Stop the engine and remove the governor cover and lever assembly, also the valve rocker cover and the fuel rod from the differential lever and the injector control tube lever.

5. Start the engine and run between 800 and 1000 rpm by manually operating the control tube lever.

6. Check the gap between the low-speed spring cap and the high speed plunger with a 0.0015 in. feeler gauge blade. Reset the gap adjusting screw if the adjustment is incorrect. Hold the gap adjusting tool and tighten the locknut.

7. Recheck the governor gap and readjust as necessary. Stop the engine and install the fuel rod between the differential lever and the control tube lever.

8. Install the governor cover and lever assembly.

SERIES 6V, 8V, 12V–71 ENGINES EXCEPT FUEL SQUEEZER SERIES 6V, 8V–92 ENGINES EXCEPT FUEL SQUEEZER

DOUBLE WEIGHT GOVERNOR

1. Have the engine at normal operating temperature and stopped. Remove the high-speed spring retainer cover.

2. Back out the buffer screw approximately ⅝ in. from the locknut.

3. Start the engine and loosen the idle speed adjusting screw locknut. Adjust the idle screw to obtain the desired engine idle speed. Tighten the locknut without disturbing the adjustment screw.

NOTE: Limiting speed governors used on turbocharged engines include a starting aid screw threaded into the governor housing on current engines, or the governor gap adjusting screw on early engines. A nylon patch is used in place of locknuts on the early engines.

4. The recommended idle speed is 500 for trucks and highway coaches and 400 rpm for city coaches.

5. Stop the engine and remove the governor cover and lever assembly. Remove the valve rocker covers.

6. Start the engine and run between 1100 and 1300 rpm by manually operating the differential lever.

7. Check the gap between the low-speed spring cap and the high-speed plunger with a feeler gauge blade of 0.002 to 0.004 in. If the gap is incorrect, re-set the gap to specifications with the gap adjusting screw.

8. If the governor has the starting aid screw, hold the gap adjusting screw and tighten the locknut.

9. Recheck the gap with the engine operating at specifications. Reset if necessary.

10. Stop the engine and install the governor cover and lever assembly.

NOTE: If the governor has the starting aid screw, do not install the cover at this time.

SINGLE WEIGHT GOVERNOR

The governor gap is checked and adjusted using the same procedure as with the double weight governor. The exceptions are in the measurement of the gap between the low-speed spring cap and the high speed spring plunger. A special gauge is used with a measurement of 0.200 in.

FUEL SQUEEZER ENGINE GOVERNOR SETTINGS

ALL SERIES AS APPLICABLE

The tune-up of the Fuel Squeezer engine is the same as a standard engine. Certain exceptions are noted and are as follows.

a. Prior to the engine tune-up, the Belleville spring (washer) retainer nut must be backed out until there is approximately 0.060 in. clearance between the washer and the retaining nut.

b. Set the running engine governor gap at 0.002 to 0.004 in. at 1100 to 1300 rpm with the engine idle reset to 500 rpm.

c. After completion of the tune-up, consisting of setting injector timing, valve clearance, governor gap, injector rack and engine speeds, adjust the Belleville spring device (TT-tailor torqued).

Belleville Spring Adjustment

The adjustment of the Belleville springs (washers) for the TT horsepower can be accomplished by two methods, depending upon the equipment available to the Service facilities. The methods are:

a. Idle drop method.
b. Power reduction factor.

The operation of the Belleville springs (washers) can be better understood if a brief explanation is presented to the repairman. The spring force of the Belleville springs (washers) works with the governor weights to pull the injector racks out of fuel as the engine speed is increased. Conversely, as the engine speed is reduced by the increased load, the high-speed spring overcomes the force of the Belleville springs (washers) and moves the injector racks to an increased fuel position. The racks move progressively into more fuel to maintain the constant horsepower until the racks are in full fuel at a speed near 1500 rpm.

The Belleville springs (washers) working in conjunction with the limiting speed governor, gives the Fuel Squeezer engines the ability to maintain a reasonably constant horsepower over a wide speed range and its 6% torque rise per one hundred rpm.

The tune-up of the Fuel Squeezer engine is the same as the standard engine except for the following exceptions.

NOTE: Special tachometer or engine, chassis or output shaft dynamometer must be available to reset the Belleville spring (washer) "TT" (tailor torque) device correctly.

1. Prior to tuning the Fuel Squeezer engine, backout the Belleville spring (washer) retainer nut until approximately 0.060 in. clearance exists between the washer and the retainer nut.

2. When adjusting the governor gap, set the running engine governor gap at 0.002 to 0.004 in. at 1100 to 1300 rpm with the idle speed adjusted to 500 rpm.

3. After completing the standard engine tune-up of setting the valve clearance, setting injector timing, governor gap, injector racks and engine speeds, adjust the Belleville springs (washer).

Idle Drop Method

The idle drop method is an effective, accurate means of setting the Belleville springs (washers) to "tailor torque" the horsepower. An electronic tachometer is mandatory, with accuracy within one rpm, since each one rpm error in setting the idle drop results in a two or three horsepower error.

When using the special tachometer, follow the manufacturer's procedures, keeping in mind the following important point. The flywheel has either 102 or 118 teeth and must be known before attempting the adjustment with the electronic tachometer, because impulses are electronically picked up from the flywheel to measure the rpm. When the flywheel part number or type is not known, measure the distance from the camshaft housing cover lower bolt head to the outer circumference of the flywheel bell housing. If the distance is approximately 1¼ in., a 118 tooth flywheel is used and if the distance is 2 ½ in., a 102 tooth flywheel is used.

1. Perform the standard engine tune-up. Set the no-load speed as required by the engine type, injector size and governor. Refer to the accompanying chart.

Adjusting engine idle—V8, 8.2L Series (© General Motors Corp.)

2. Disconnect the accelerator linkage from the governor speed control lever, if not previously done.

3. Operate the engine until normal operating temperature has been reached and stabilized.

4. From the accompanying chart, using the engine type, injector size and governor, select the initial and specified idle drop numbers for the rated "TT" horsepower and rated speed at which the engine is to operate.

5. Set the initial speed with the idle adjusting screw to specifications.

6. With the governor speed control lever in the idle position, turn the Belleville spring (washer) retainer nut clockwise on the plunger until the specified idle drop speed is obtained. Secure the retaining nut with the locking screw. When the specified idle speed is achieved, the engine is power controlled to the "TT" horsepower rating.

NOTE: The idle speeds must be exact and steady. If not, check for binding or rubbing in the fuel control system components.

7. Lower the idle speed to the specific operating idle speed, using the idle speed adjusting screw.

8. Adjust the buffer screw and starting aid screw.

Power Reduction Factor Method

The power reduction factor method is used to set the "TT" engine horsepower to a specific percentage below full throttle horsepower, with the engine/vehicle on an engine, chassis or output shaft dynamometer.

A general outline is presented for the Belleville spring (washer) adjustment, along with a power reduction factor chart, for use with the dynamometer.

1. The standard engine tune-up should be performed. The throttle delay piston must be removed and the Belleville spring (washer) retainer nut backed off until a clearance of 0.060 in. exists between the washers and the retaining nut.

2. Refer to the accompanying chart and set the no-load speed as required by the engine type, injector size and governor.

3. Operate the engine until normal operating temperature is reached and stabilized.

4. Using the engine, chassis or output shaft dynamometer, measure the full throttle horsepower at 100 rpm below the rated engine speed with the Belleville springs (washers) loose. Record the horsepower reading.

CAUTION

Satisfactory power adjustment can be obtained only if the full throttle horsepower and adjusted horsepower, as in Step 4, are obtained with the engine cooling in the same mode, such as operating or not operating.

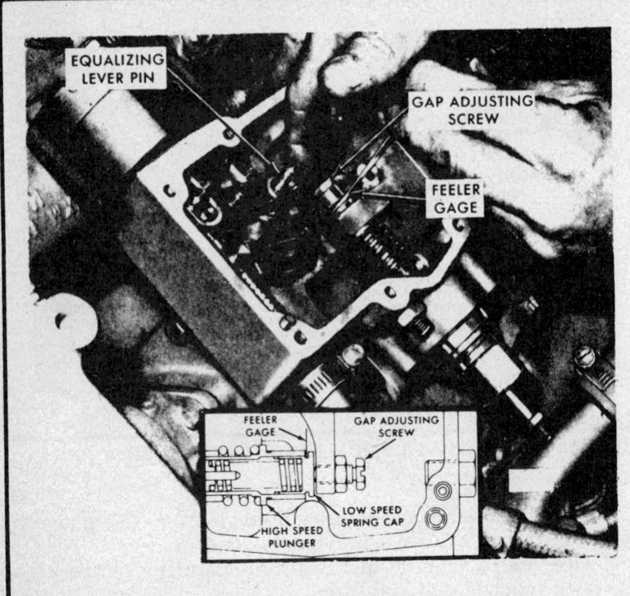

Adjusting governor gap—V8, 8.2L Series
(© General Motors Corp.)

5. Select the power reduction factor in the accompanying chart for the proper engine type, desired rated horsepower and rated engine speed.

6. Multiply the horsepower recorded in Step 4 by the factor selected from the chart. Record this value.

7. Adjust the Belleville spring (washer) retainer nut clockwise so that the observed horsepower is reduced to that recorded in Step 6 at 100 rpm below the rated engine speed, with the governor speed control lever in the maximum speed position and the fan in the same operating mode. Verify that the engine is obtaining the adjusted "TT" horsepower, within 5%, at rated engine speed. If the adjusted "TT" horsepower cannot be obtained at the rated engine speed, governor droop interference may be the cause. If necessary, to eliminate droop interference, readjust the engine no-load speed from 150 to 175 rpm above the rated engine speed and repeat the power reduction factor method.

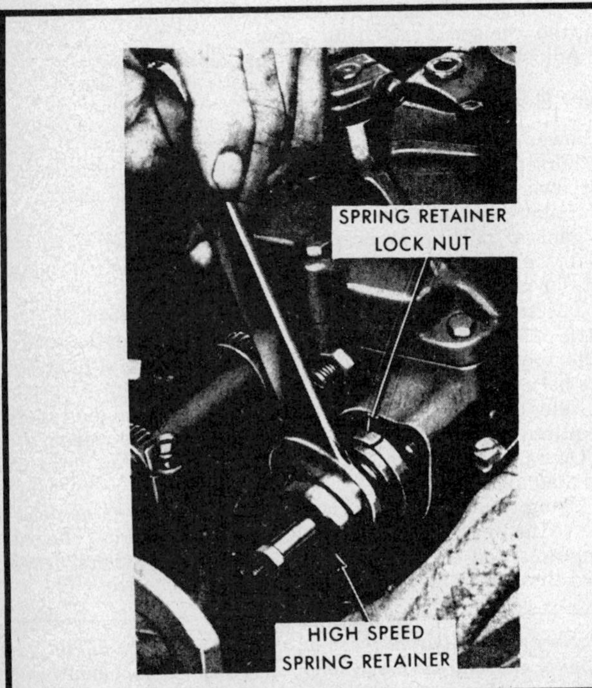

Adjusting maximum no-load engine speed—V8, 8.2L Series
(© General Motors Corp.)

8. Check the idle speed and if necessary, re-set to idle speed specifications.

9. Adjust the buffer screw and starting aid screw.

Flexispec Engine Governor Adjustment

When it is desirable to adjust the Fuel Squeezer "TT" engine to obtain a non-"TT" maximum rated horsepower, proceed as follows:

1. Adjust the engine governor to obtain a no-load speed 175 rpm above the desired rated speed.

CAUTION

Do not exceed a full load speed of 2100 rpm or a no-load speed of 2275 rpm.

2. Position the Belleville spring (washer) retainer to obtain approximately 0.060 in. clearance between the Belleville spring (washer) and the retainer, *with the engine stopped.*

Limiting Speed Mechanical Governor Adjustment

V8, 8.2 LITER ENGINE

Prior to starting the engine for governor adjustment, verification of the valve clearance, timing of the injectors, adjustment of the injector rack control mechanism and fuel shut-off must be accomplished.

Governor Gap and Initial Idle Adjustment

1. Remove the governor cover, adjust the static idle gap to 0.216 in. and reinstall the governor cover.

2. Remove the high speed spring retainer cover and back out the buffer screw until it extends $^5/_8$ in. beyond the governor housing.

3. Loosen the locknut and adjust the idle screw to protrude approximately $^{11}/_{32}$ in. beyond the locknut.

4. Adjust the high speed adjusting nut to 1.63 in. from the governor body.

5. Start the engine and run until normal operating temperature is reached.

6. Adjust the idle speed to 700 rpm and tighten the locknut.

7. Stop the engine and remove the governor cover. Restart the engine and bring the engine to 1500 rpm by the manual operation of the differential lever.

CAUTION

Do not overspeed the engine during this operation.

8. Check the gap between the low speed spring cap and the high speed spring plunger with a feeler gauge blade of 0.002 to 0.004 in. thickness. If the gap setting is incorrect, reset the gap adjusting screw. Tighten the locknut and recheck the gap. Readjust as required.

9. Reinstall the governor cover with the pin of the speed control lever projecting into the slot of the differential lever.

10. If the gap setting has to be changed, the racks will have to be rechecked and adjusted as necessary.

CAUTION

Before starting an engine after a speed control adjustment or after the removal of the governor cover and lever, the repairman must determine that the injector racks move to the no-fuel position when the governor stop lever is in the STOP position. Engine overspeed can result if the racks cannot be positioned at the no-fuel position with the governor stop lever.

11. During the governor cover installation, the roll pin in the fuel shut off control shaft must be located between the side wall of the governor and the long screw in the equalizer lever. After the cover has been installed, check the operation of the speed control and the fuel shut off.

Maximum No-load Engine Speed Adjustment

To ensure the engine speed will not exceed the recommended no-load speed, adjust the maximum no-load speed as follows:

1. Loosen the high-speed spring retainer locknut and back off the retainer several turns. Start the engine and increase the engine speed gradually. If the speed exceeds the required no-load speed before the speed control lever reaches the end of its travel, back off the spring retainer a few additional turns.
2. With the engine at normal operating temperature and no-load on the engine, place the speed control lever in the maximum speed position. Turn the high speed spring retainer until the engine is operating at the recommended no-load speed.
3. Tighten the high speed spring retainer locknut and re-check the no-load speed. Reset as required.

CAUTION

The maximum no-load speed specification is to be obtained from the engine emission plate or the governor identification plate.

4. Adjust the engine idle speed with the buffer screw backed out to avoid contact with the equalizing lever. Turn the idle speed adjusting screw until the engine idles at the recommended speed of 700 rpm.
5. Hold the idle adjusting screw and tighten the locknut.
6. Increase the engine speed to 1500/2000 rpm and close the throttle and re-check the idle speed.
7. Set the throttle to the RUN position and set the no-load rpm to 3150 rpm, without the buffer adjusted.
8. Install the high speed spring retainer cover on the governor housing.

Buffer Screw Adjustment

After the idle speed is correctly adjusted, set the buffer screw as follows:

1. Have the engine at normal operating speed and running at idle. Turn the buffer screw in so that it contacts the equalizing lever as lightly as possible and still eliminates engine roll.

NOTE: Do not increase the engine idle speed more than 15 rpm with the buffer screw adjustment.

2. Re-check the maximum no-load speed as listed on the engine emission plate or the governor identification plate. If the maximum no-load speed has increased by more than 100 rpm, back off the buffer screw until the increase in rpm is less than 100.
3. Hold the buffer screw and tighten the locknut.
4. Inspect the operation of the shutdown lever while running at the no-load rpm with the throttle in the RUN position. If the engine does not shut off, back out the buffer screw until it does. Re-lock the locknut.

Positioning the Rack Control Levers

The position of the injector racks determine the amount of fuel injected into each cylinder and ensures equal distribution of the load. Certain engines use spring loaded injector tube assemblies that have yield springs at each injector rack control lever and only one screw and locknut to hold the injector rack in position. The single screw and locknut arrangement is adjusted in the same manner as the two screw rack control levers.

SERIES 4–53, 6–71 ENGINES

Adjust the rear injector rack first to establish a guide for adjusting the remaining injector rack control levers.

1. Disconnect any linkage attached to the speed control lever and turn the idle speed adjusting screw until $\frac{1}{2}$ in. of threads project from the locknut, with the nut against the high speed plunger.

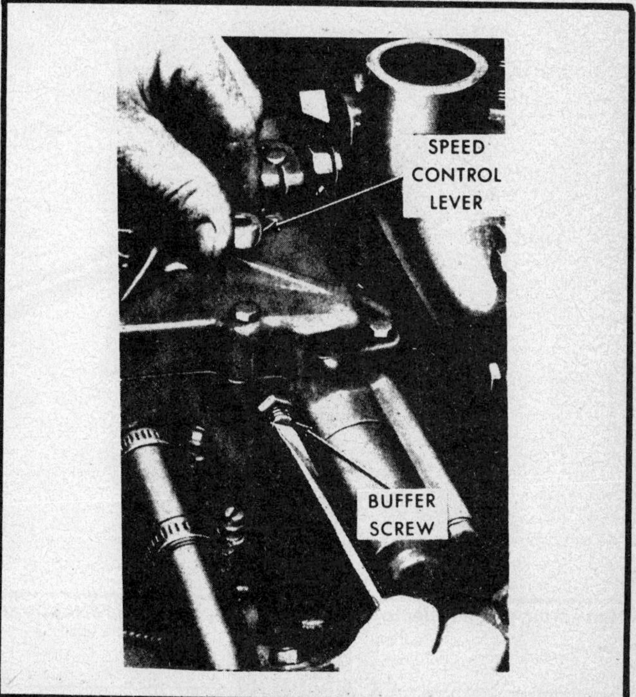

Adjusting the buffer screw—V8, 8.2L Series
(© General Motors Corp.)

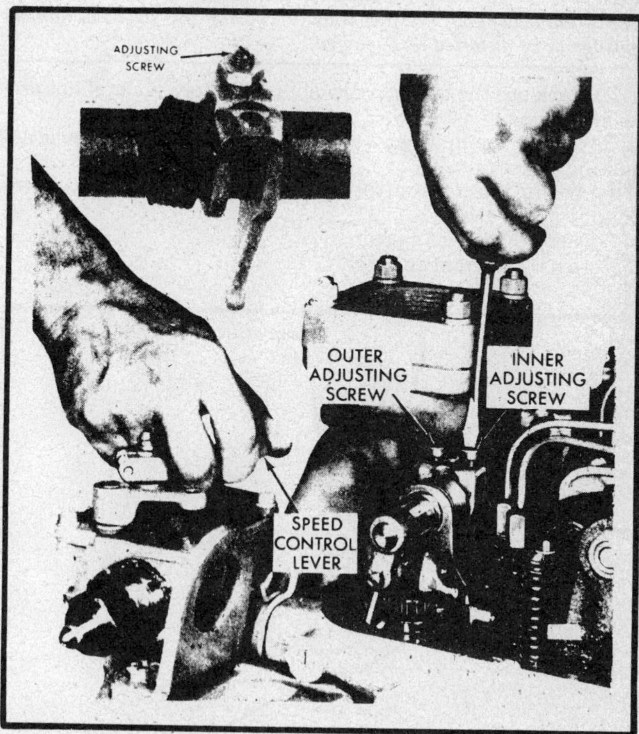

Positioning the injector rack control lever, typical of in-line engines. Single adjusting screw illustrated
(© General Motors Corp.)

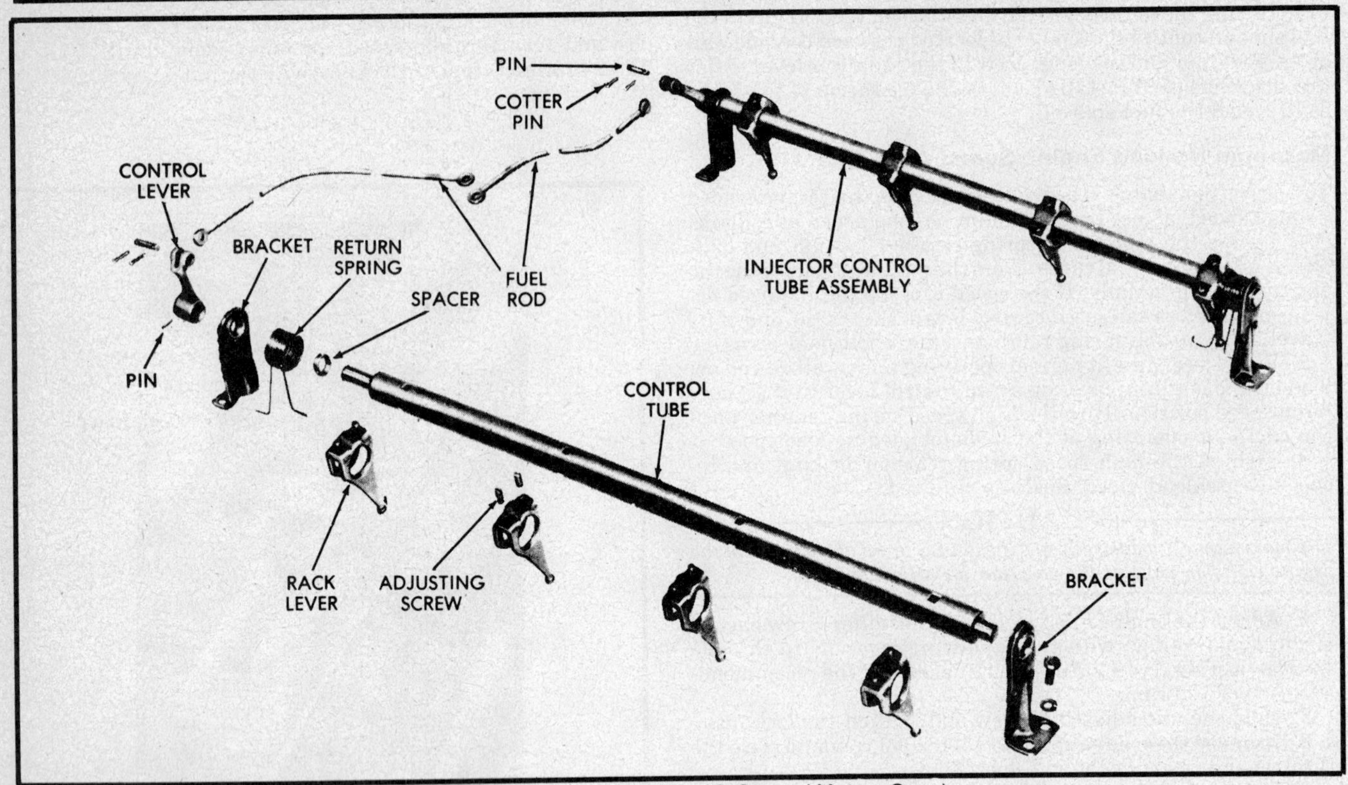

Non-spring loaded injector control tube—typical of all two cycle engines (© General Motors Corp.)

CAUTION

A false fuel rack setting could result if the idle speed adjusting screw is not backed out as noted. This adjustment lowers the low speed spring tension for easier compression, allowing the closing of the low speed gap without bending the fuel rods or causing the yield mechanism springs to be distorted or damaged.

2. Back out the buffer screw approximately $^5/_8$ in., if not previously done.
3. Loosen the inner and outer injector rack control lever adjusting screws.

The specific injector control rack lever adjustment for each engine is as follows:

Series 4–53: rear injector
Series 6–71: front injector

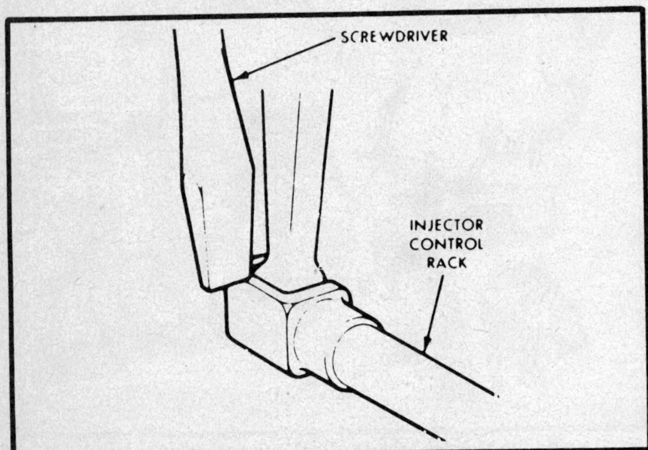

Checking injector rack spring action—typical of all two cycle engines (© General Motors Corp.)

NOTE: Be certain all levers are free on the injector control tube.

4. Move the speed control lever to the full fuel position and hold with a light finger pressure. Turn the inner adjusting screw on the specified injector rack control lever down until a slight movement of the control lever is observed or more resistance is noted when attempting to turn the adjusting screwdriver. This places the rear injector rack in the full fuel position. Turn down the outer adjusting screw until it bottoms lightly on the injector control tube, then alternately tighten both the inner and the outer adjusting screws. A torque of 24 to 36 inch lbs. is recommended.
5. To verify the proper rack adjustment, hold the speed control lever in the full fuel position and press down on the injector rack with a screwdriver or other object and note the "rotating" movement of the injector control rack. The injector control rack should also spring back when the downward pressure is released.
6. If the rack does not return to its original position, it is too loose. To correct this condition, back off on the outer adjusting screw and tighten the inner adjusting screw.
7. If the setting is too tight, more effort is needed to move the speed control lever to the end of its travel. To correct this condition, back off the inner adjusting screw slightly and tighten the outer adjusting screw slightly.

CAUTION

The adjustment of the specified injector rack control lever should result in placing the governor linkage and the control tube assembly in the same position as when the engine is running at full load.

8. To adjust the remaining injector rack control levers, remove the clevis pin from the fuel rod and the injector control tube lever. Hold the injector control racks in the full fuel position by means of the lever on the end of the control tube. Turn down the inner adjusting screw on the injector rack control lever of the adjacent injector until the injector rack has moved

into the full fuel position and the inner adjusting screw is bottomed on the injector control tube. Then alternately tighten both the inner and outer adjusting screw. A torque of 24 to 36 inch lbs. is recommended.

9. Recheck the specified injector rack to be sure it has remained snug on the ball end of the injector rack control lever while the adjacent injector rack was adjusted. If the rack of the specified injector has become loose, back off the inner adjusting screw slightly on the adjacent injector rack control lever. Tighten the outer adjusting screw slightly. When the settings are correct, the racks of both injectors must be snug on the ball ends of their respective rack control levers.

10. Adjust and position the remaining injector rack control levers as outlined in Steps 8 and 9.

11. Connect the fuel rod to the injector control tube lever.

12. Turn the idle speed adjusting screw in until a projection of $^3/_{16}$ in. from the locknut exists, in order to start the engine.

SERIES 6V–53, 8V–71, 12V–71, 6V–92, 8V–92 ENGINES

NOTE: Should the engine be equipped with the single adjusting screw and locknut, make the rack control lever adjustment in the same manner as the two screw units.

The following procedures are outlined for the two screw units.

The letters R and L indicate the injector location in the right and left cylinder head banks, viewed from the rear of the en-

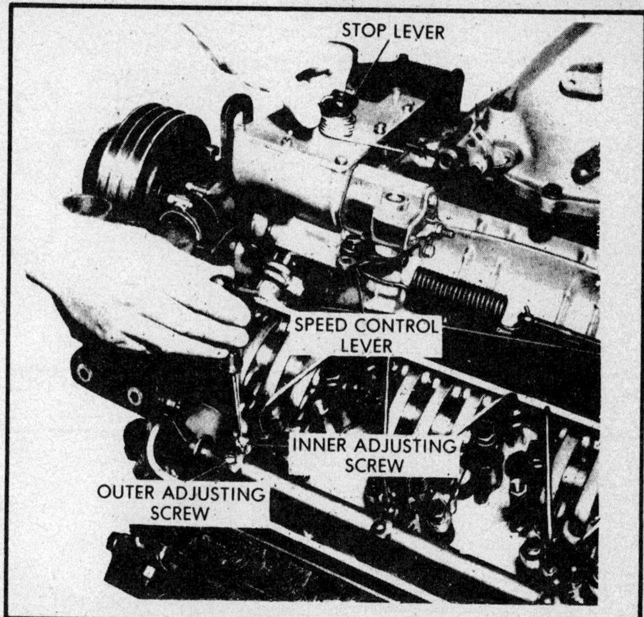

Adjusting of number one injector rack control lever—92 Series and typical of other engine series (© General Motors Corp.)

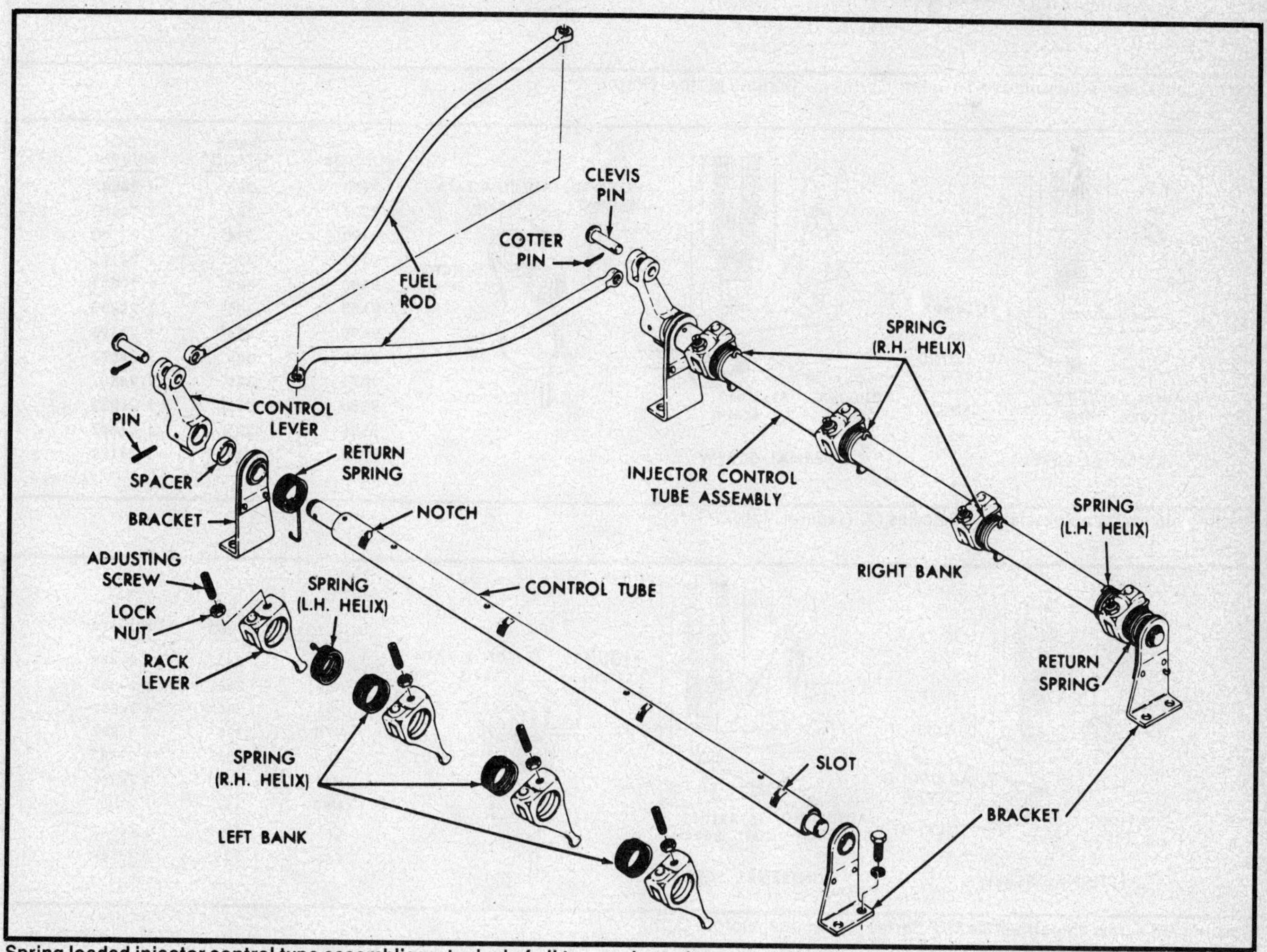

Spring loaded injector control type assemblies—typical of all two cycle engines (© General Motors Corp.)

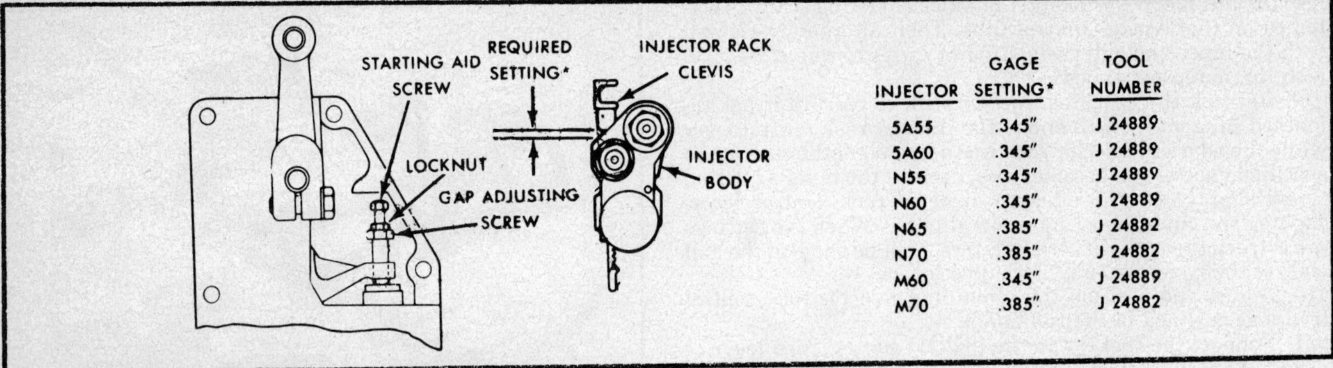

INJECTOR	GAGE SETTING*	TOOL NUMBER
5A55	.345"	J 24889
5A60	.345"	J 24889
N55	.345"	J 24889
N60	.345"	J 24889
N65	.385"	J 24882
N70	.385"	J 24882
M60	.345"	J 24889
M70	.385"	J 24882

Starting aid screw adjustment—53 Series (© General Motors Corp.)

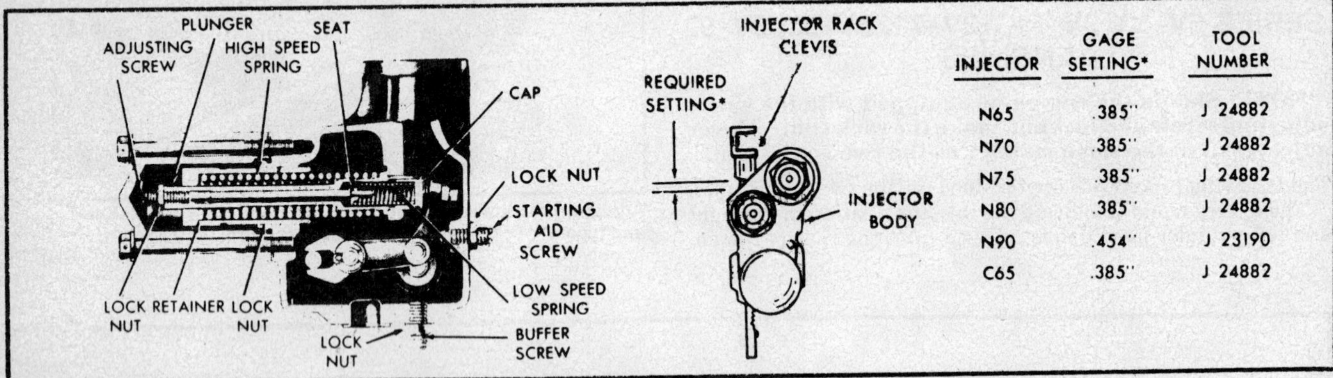

INJECTOR	GAGE SETTING*	TOOL NUMBER
N65	.385"	J 24882
N70	.385"	J 24882
N75	.385"	J 24882
N80	.385"	J 24882
N90	.454"	J 23190
C65	.385"	J 24882

Starting aid screw adjustment—71 in-line Series (© General Motors Corp.)

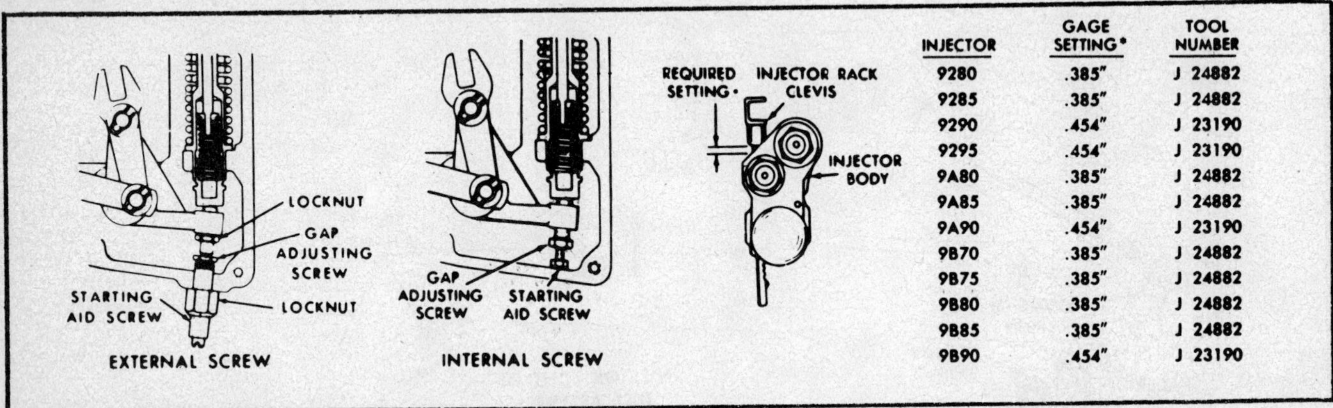

INJECTOR	GAGE SETTING*	TOOL NUMBER
9280	.385"	J 24882
9285	.385"	J 24882
9290	.454"	J 23190
9295	.454"	J 23190
9A80	.385"	J 24882
9A85	.385"	J 24882
9A90	.454"	J 23190
9B70	.385"	J 24882
9B75	.385"	J 24882
9B80	.385"	J 24882
9B85	.385"	J 24882
9B90	.454"	J 23190

Starting aid screw adjustment—92 Series (© General Motors Corp.)

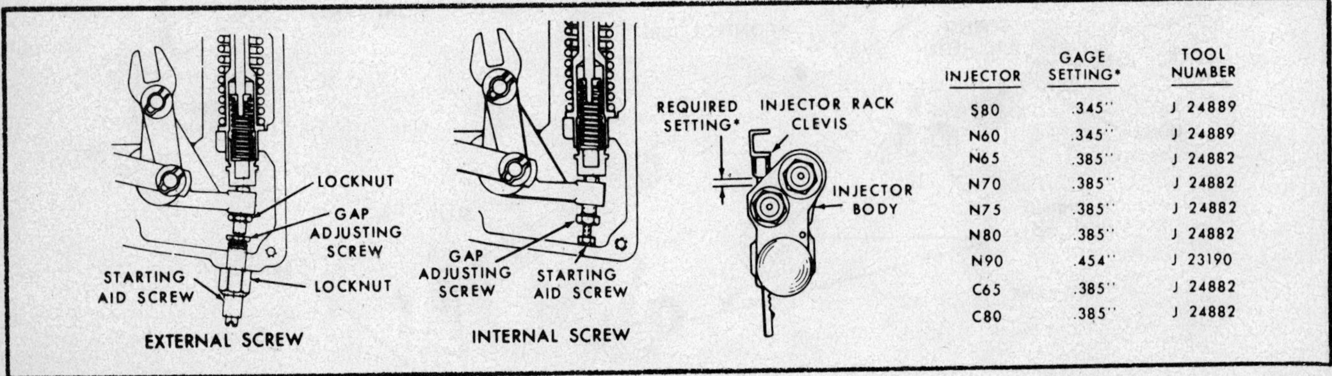

INJECTOR	GAGE SETTING*	TOOL NUMBER
S80	.345"	J 24889
N60	.345"	J 24889
N65	.385"	J 24882
N70	.385"	J 24882
N75	.385"	J 24882
N80	.385"	J 24882
N90	.454"	J 23190
C65	.385"	J 24882
C80	.385"	J 24882

Starting aid screw adjustment—71 V Series (© General Motors Corp.)

gine. The cylinders are numbered, starting at the front of the engine on each cylinder bank. Adjust the specific injector rack control lever first to establish a guide for adjusting the remaining injector rack control levers.

1. The specific injector rack control lever to be adjusted first, per engine, is as follows:
   a. 6V–53: 3 left, then 3 right.
   b. 8V–71, 12V–71, 6V–92, 8V–92: 1 left, then 1 right
2. Disconnect the linkage attached to the speed control lever.
3. Turn the idle speed adjusting screw out until approximately ½ in. of the thread projects from the locknut, with the locknut against the high speed plunger.

CAUTION

A false fuel rack setting could result if the idle speed adjusting screw is not backed out as noted. This adjustment lowers the low speed spring tension for easier compression, allowing the closing of the low speed gap without bending the fuel rods or causing the yield mechanism springs to be distorted or damaged.

4. Back out the buffer screw approximately ⅝ in., if not already done.
5. Remove the clevis pin from the fuel rod and the right cylinder bank injector control tube lever.
6. Loosen all of the inner and outer injector rack control lever adjusting screws on both injector control tubes. Be sure all levers are free on the tubes.
7. Move the speed control lever to the maximum speed position and hold in place with light finger pressure. Turn the inner adjusting screw on the specified injector rack control lever down until a slight movement of the control tube lever is observed or an increase in resistance is noted in the turning effort of the adjusting screwdriver. This will place the specified injector in the full fuel position. Turn down the outer adjusting screw until it bottoms lightly on the injector control tube. Alternately tighten both the inner and outer adjusting screws to a torque of 24 to 36 inch lbs.

CAUTION

The adjustment of the specified injector rack control lever should result in placing the governor linkage and the control tube assembly in the same position as when the engine is running at full load.

8. To verify the proper rack adjustment, hold the speed control lever in the full fuel position and press down on the injector rack with a screwdriver or other object and note the "rotating" movement of the injector control rack. The injector control rack should also spring back when the downward pressure is released.
9. If the rack does not return to its original position, it is too loose. To correct this condition, back off on the outer adjusting screw and tighten the inner adjusting screw by the same amount.
10. If the setting is too tight, the injector rack becomes tight before the speed control lever reaches the end of its travel, resulting in more effort required to move the speed control lever to the end of its travel. To correct this condition, back off the inner adjusting screw slightly and tighten the outer adjusting screw slightly.
11. Remove the clevis pin from the fuel rod and the left bank injector control tube lever.
12. Insert the clevis pin in the fuel rod and the right cylinder bank injector control tube lever and position the specified injector rack control lever as outlined in Step 7.
13. Insert the clevis pin in the fuel rod and the left cylinder bank injector control tube lever. Repeat the check on the one or three left and one or three right injector rack control levers as outlined in Step 7. Check for and eliminate any deflection which may occur at the bend in the fuel rod where it enters the cylinder head.
14. To adjust the remaining injector rack control levers, remove the clevis pin from the fuel rods and the injector control tube levers, hold the injector control racks in the full fuel position by means of the lever on the end of the control tube and proceed as follows:
   a. Turn the inner adjusting screws of the injector rack control lever inward until the screw bottoms.

NOTE: The injector control rack should be in the full fuel position.

   b. Turn in the outer adjusting screw until it bottoms on the injector control tube.
   c. While holding the control tube lever in the full fuel position, adjust the inner and outer adjusting screws to obtain the same condition as outlined in Step 7. Tighten the screws to a torque of 24 to 36 inch lbs.

CAUTION

After the specified injector rack control levers are adjusted, do not try to alter their settings. All other adjustments are made on the remaining control racks.

15. When the adjustment of all injector rack control levers have been done, recheck their settings and correct as required. All of the control racks must have the same "spring" condition with the control tube lever in the full fuel position.
16. Insert the clevis pin in the fuel rod and the injector control levers. Turn the adjusting screw for the engine idle inward until $^3/_{16}$ in. of the screw projects from the locknut to permit starting of the engine.
17. Replace the valve covers on the engine and complete the assembly.

Adjustment of Starting Aid Screw—Turbocharged Engines Series 6V–53

1. With the engine stopped, place the governor stop lever in the RUN position and the speed control lever in the IDLE position.

NOTE: The starting aid screw has a locknut while the gap adjusting screw has a self-lock patch.

2. Hold the gap adjusting screw to prevent it from turning and adjust the starting aid screw to obtain the required clearance, 0.016 in. (.397mm), between the shoulder of the number three right (3R) injector rack clevis and the counterbore in the injector body.
3. When the adjustment is completed, tighten the locking nut on the starting aid screw to prevent oil leakage as well as locking the screw setting.
4. Position the stop lever in the RUN position and move the speed control lever from the IDLE position to the maximum speed position. Return the speed control lever back to the IDLE position and recheck the injector rack clevis-to-body clearance.

NOTE: Movement of the governor speed control lever is to take up clearances in the governor linkages. The clevis to body clearance can be increased or reduced by the movement of the starting aid screw.

5. Start the engine and recheck the running gap 0.0015 in. and if necessary, reset it. Stop the engine and install the governor cover in place on the governor housing.

V8, 8.2 LITER ENGINE

1. Remove the valve rocker covers, if not previously done.
2. Loosen the clamp bolts in the left and right shaft control levers.
3. Check to determine that the number one rack control lever has been correctly located and the set screw tight and bottomed. This lever is not adjustable.

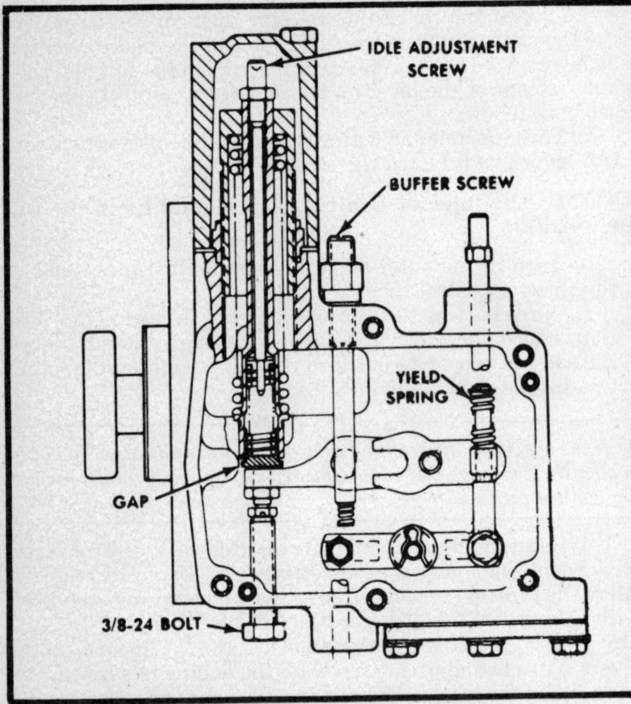

Setting gap at low speed spring cap—V8, 8.2L Series (© General Motors Corp.)

4. Rotate the left control shaft until the number one injector is in the full fuel position.

NOTE: A special injector rack control pin is available to provide a light spring load on the control shaft to hold the number one injector in the full fuel position.

5. Loosen the adjusting screws in the three remaining levers on the left bank as required to be sure that only number one injector is at full fuel position and at zero lash.
6. Tighten the number three set screw until a zero lash has been obtained between the injector rack and the injector rack control lever.
7. Recheck number one injector to make sure that zero lash has not been lost. If no zero lash exists, back off the adjusting screw on the number three injector rack control lever and retighten slowly.
8. Repeat this procedure on injectors numbers five and seven.

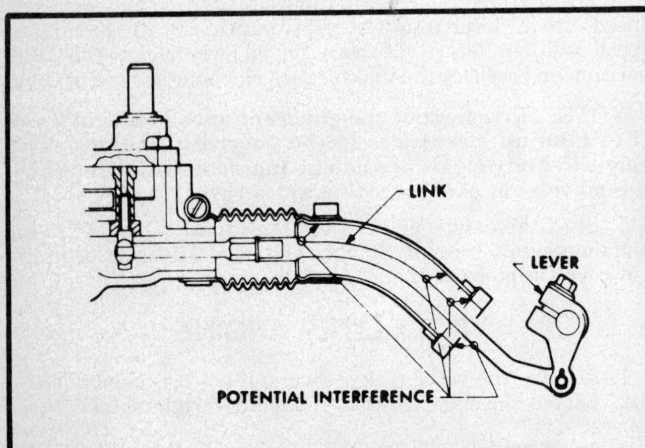

Operational interference check points of the governor fuel rods to cylinder head or tubes—V8, 8.2L Series (© General Motors Corp.)

9. Remove the injector rack control pin tool from the left cylinder head, if used. Check the rack control assembly for freedom of movement. The injector rack assembly must return to the no-fuel position without any hesitation.
10. Refer to Steps three through ten and adjust the numbers two, four, six and eight injector rack control levers on the right bank.

Control Connection Adjustment

1. Remove the governor cover and the screw plug from the side of the governor housing, opposite the spring rack.
2. Install a $^3/_8$ × 24 bolt, with a minimum of 1 $^1/_2$ in. of thread, into the tapped hole. Screw the bolt inward until the gap at the low speed spring cap is reduced to 0.0015 to 0.000 in.. Install the governor cover.
3. Remove or energize the shutdown solenoid.
4. Hold the governor speed control lever in the full fuel position. The special injector rack control pin can be used to hold the racks in position.
5. Rotate the left bank injector control shaft to hold the injector racks firmly in the full fuel position and hold the left shaft control lever lightly in the direction towards the governor.
6. Carefully, tighten the bolt in the left shaft control lever.
7. Move the governor speed control lever to the idle position and back to the full fuel position. Spongy action indicates yield spring action near the full fuel position and should not be felt.
8. Repeat Steps four through seven for the right bank adjustment.

NOTE: The governor fuel rods should be free of any interference with the cylinder heads or tubes. Check the locknut on the governor fuel rod to be sure it is tight.

9. With the speed control lever held in the full fuel position, attempt to push each injector rack towards full fuel with finger pressure against the flat end of the rack. If movement is greater than 0.002 to 0.003 in., loosen the left and right lever bolts and repeat the adjusting procedure.
10. Repeat the governor shut off lever check.
11. Remove the long $^3/_8$ in. bolt from the governor housing and install the threaded plug in the housing.
12. Install the rocker covers and solenoid, if removed.

Fuel System

The fuel system includes the fuel pump, fuel injectors, fuel injector tubes, fuel strainer and filter, fuel manifolds (internal and external) and the fuel lines.

FUEL PUMP

The fuel pumps used on the Detroit Diesel engines are positive displacement gear type pumps and are available in either left or right hand rotation to service the varied engine applications. The different rotation pumps are not interchangeable, nor can a pump made for one rotation, be rebuilt for the opposite rotation because the relief valve can only be installed in one position in the pump body. Regardless of rotation, two differently rated pumps are used, a standard pump with $^1/_4$ in. wide gears and a high capacity pump with $^3/_8$ in. wide gears. These pumps are not completely interchangeable without exchanging exterior fittings and lines. The fuel pumps are located at the following areas on the varied engines.

a. **Series 53 in-line:** Mounted on the governor weight housing and driven by the governor weight shaft.
b. **Series 53V:** Mounted on the governor and driven by the accessory drive gear.
c. **Series 71 in-line:** Mounted on the rear end plate cover of the blower and driven by the blower lower rotor. Special engine applications are driven by the balance shaft and are mounted to a special flywheel housing cover.

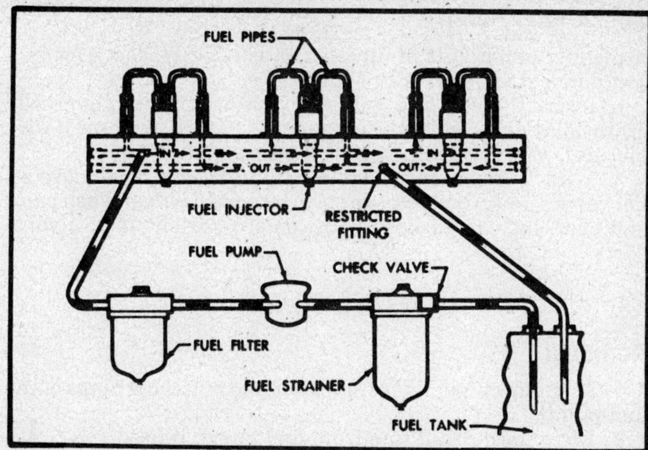

FUEL PIPES
IN
OUT
FUEL INJECTOR
RESTRICTED FITTING
FUEL PUMP
CHECK VALVE
FUEL FILTER
FUEL STRAINER
FUEL TANK
Schematic of typical two cycle in-line engine fuel system
(© General Motors Corp.)

FUEL PIPES
RESTRICTED TEE
FUEL INJECTOR
FUEL PUMP
CHECK VALVE
FUEL FILTER
FUEL STRAINER
FUEL TANK
Schematic of typical two cycle V engine fuel system
(© General Motors Corp.)

d. **Series 71V, 92:** Mounted to the governor housing and driven by the end of the right hand helix (spiral) rotor.

e. **Series V8, 8.2 liter:** Mounted to the governor weight housing and driven by the governor weight shaft.

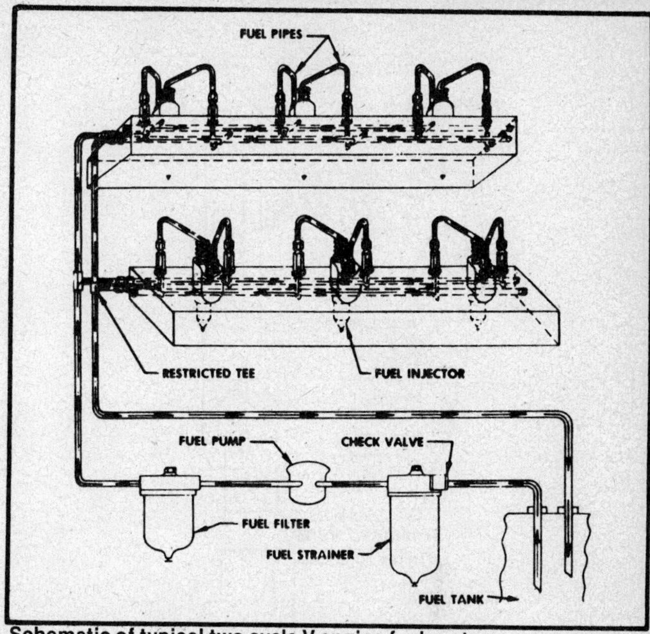

TESTS

If engine operation indicates insufficient supply of fuel to the injectors and the fuel level is not low in the supply tank, check the fuel flow between the restricted fitting in the fuel return passage in the cylinder head and the fuel supply tank.

Fuel Flow Check

1. Disconnect the fuel return line from the fitting at the fuel tank and hold the open end of the pipe in a convenient receptacle.

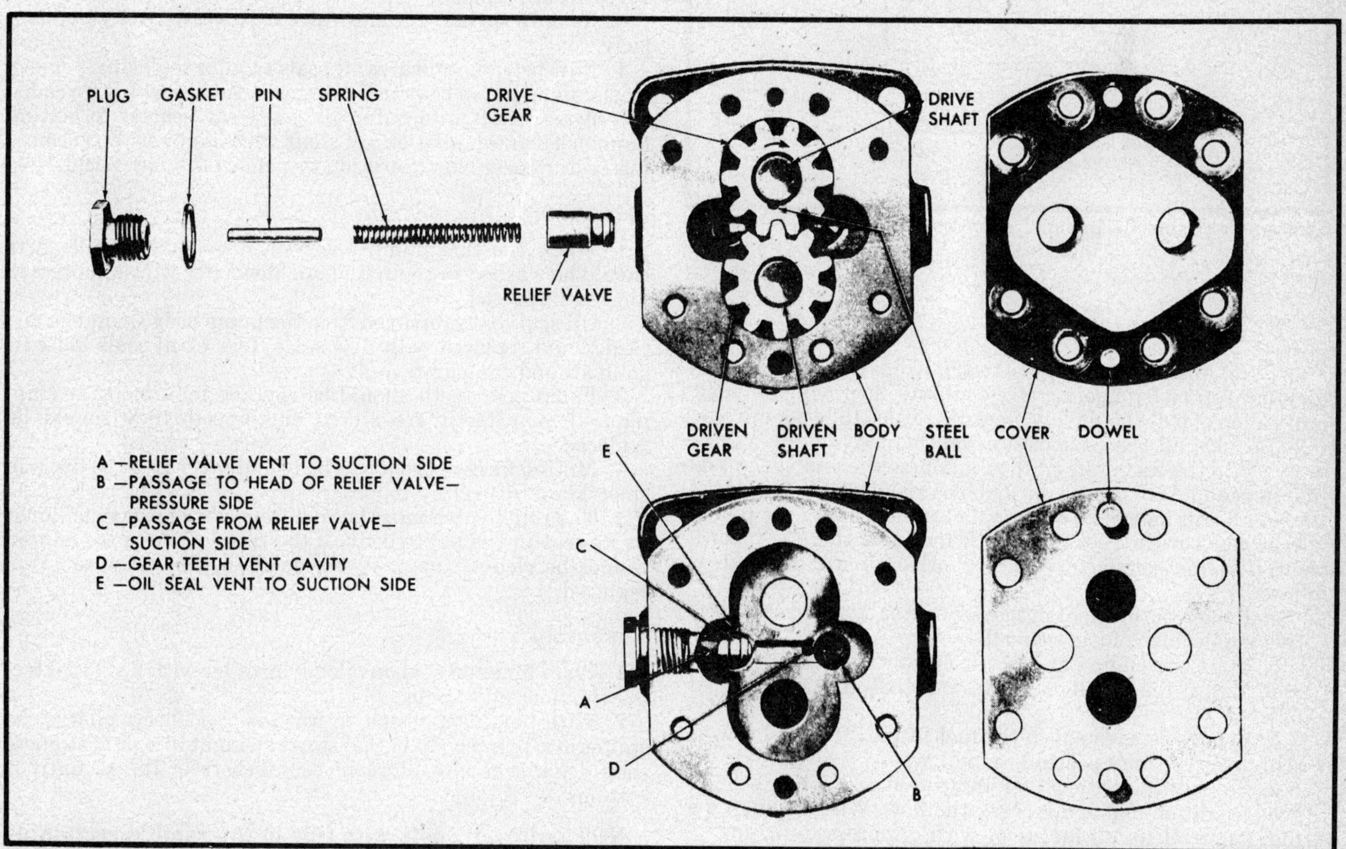

PLUG
GASKET
PIN
SPRING
DRIVE GEAR
DRIVE SHAFT
RELIEF VALVE
DRIVEN GEAR
DRIVEN SHAFT
BODY
STEEL BALL
COVER
DOWEL
A —RELIEF VALVE VENT TO SUCTION SIDE
B —PASSAGE TO HEAD OF RELIEF VALVE—PRESSURE SIDE
C —PASSAGE FROM RELIEF VALVE—SUCTION SIDE
D —GEAR TEETH VENT CAVITY
E —OIL SEAL VENT TO SUCTION SIDE
A
B
C
D
E
Cross section of fuel pump and component parts—typical of all Series (© General Motors Corp.)

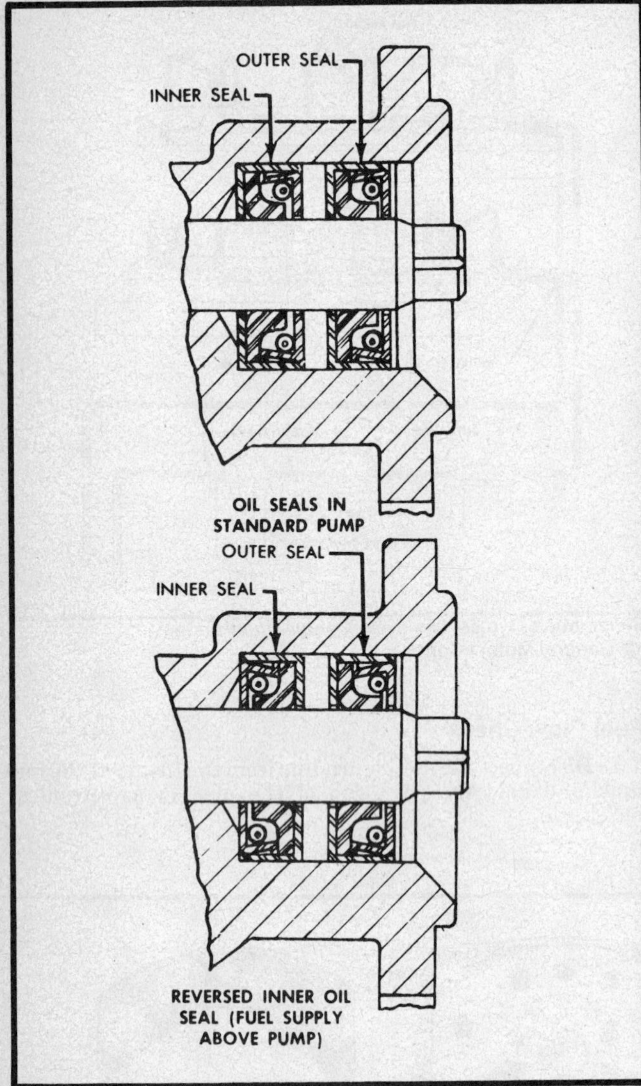

Seal location in the fuel pump (© General Motors Corp.)

2. Start and run the engine at 1200 rpm and measure the fuel flow return for a period of one minute. Approximately one half gallon of fuel should flow from the return tube per minute.

3. Be sure all connections are tight so that no air will be drawn into the fuel system; then immerse the end of the fuel line in the fuel container. Air bubbles rising to the surface of the liquid will indicate a leak on the suction side of the pump.

4. Whenever the fuel flow check indicates there is insufficient flow for satisfactory engine performance, proceed as follows:

a. Renew the element in the strainer as outlined in respective applicable vehicle manual.

b. Start the engine and run it at 1200 rpm to check the fuel flow. If the fuel flow is still unsatisfactory continue as follows.

c. Renew the element in the fuel filter. If the fuel flow is still unsatisfactory continue as follows.

d. Substitute another fuel pump that is known to be in good condition and again check the flow. When changing a fuel pump, clean all fuel lines with compressed air and be sure all fuel line connections are tight.

Check Fuel Pump

If the fuel pump fails to function satisfactorily, check for broken pump shaft, or dirt in relief valve.

1. Insert the end of a wire through one of the pump body drain holes, then crank the engine momentarily and see if wire vibrates. Vibration will be felt if pump shaft rotates.

2. Without removing the pump from the engine, remove relief valve screw, then remove spring, pin and valve. Wash parts and blow out valve cavity with compressed air. Install valve parts.

FUEL PUMP

Removal

1. Disconnect fuel lines from inlet and outlet openings of the fuel pump.

2. Disconnect drain line from fuel pump, if used.

3. Unscrew three pump attaching bolt and washer assemblies and withdraw pump.

4. Check drive coupling and if broken, replace.

Disassembly

With the fuel pump removed from the engine, disassemble the pump as follows:

1. Remove eight cover bolts, then withdraw the pump cover away from the pump body and off the two cover dowels.

2. Withdraw drive shaft, drive gear and gear retaining ball as an assembly from the pump body.

3. Remove drive gear, if necessary, from shaft being careful not to misplace the locking ball.

4. Remove driven gear and shaft as an assembly from pump body.

5. Remove valve screw, holding hand on screw to relieve valve spring tension.

6. Remove spring, pin and valve from valve cavity in pump body.

7. If inspection indicates oil seals require replacing, remove by clamping pump body in a bench vise and screwing threaded end of tool shaft into outer oil seal (seal nearest to bolting flange). Then tap pilot end of shaft with hammer thus removing seal. Repeat this operation to remove the inner seal.

Inspection

1. When the fuel pump has been disassembled, all parts should be washed in clean fuel oil, blown dry with compressed air and inspected.

2. Oil seals once removed from the pump body should be discarded and replaced with new seals. Lips of oil seals must fit snug around the pump shaft.

3. Pump gear teeth should be checked for scoring or chipping. If gear teeth are scored or chipped, they should be replaced.

4. Mating faces of the pump body and cover must be flat and smooth and fit tightly together.

5. The relief valve must be free from score marks and must fit its seat in the pump body. If the relief valve is scored and cannot be cleaned up with crocus cloth, the valve must be replaced.

Assembly

1. Place inner oil seal on pilot of installer with lip of seal facing shoulder on handle.

2. With pump supported on wood blocks, insert pilot of installer into pump body so seal starts straight into pump flange, then drive seal into place in counterbore of flange until it bottoms.

NOTE: Install seals with lips in the same direction as removed.

3. Place adaptor on pilot end of installer with shorter end of adaptor against shoulder on installer. Position outer oil seal on adaptor with lip of seal facing adaptor, then insert pilot of installer into pump so seal starts straight in pump flange and drive seal into pump body until the shoulder of adaptor contacts body.
4. Clamp pump body in soft jaws of bench vise with relief valve cavity up. Lubricate the outside diameter of relief valve and place valve in cavity with hollow end up. Insert spring inside the valve and pin inside of spring. With gasket in place next to head of valve screw place screw over spring and thread into pump body.
5. Install fuel pump drive gear, if removed, over plain end of drive shaft with slot in gear facing plain end of shaft. This operation is very important. Press gear beyond locking ball retaining hole. Then place ball in hole and press gear back until end of slot contacts ball.
6. Lubricate pump shaft and insert square end of shaft into opening at gear side of pump body and through the two oil seals.
7. Place driven gear shaft and gear assembly in pump body with chamfered end of gear teeth facing pump body.
8. Lubricate gears and shafts with clean engine oil.
9. Apply a thin coat of reputable sealer on face of pump cover outside of gear pocket area, then place cover against pump body with two dowel pins in cover entering holes in pump body. The cover can be installed in only one position over the two shafts.
10. Secure cover in place.
11. After assembly, rotate pump shaft by hand to make certain that parts rotate freely. If binding exists, it may be necessary to tap corner of pump cover with a hammer to relieve binding.

Installation

1. Affix a new gasket to pump body and locate pump drive coupling over square end of fuel pump drive shaft.
2. Install fuel pump on engine and secure.
3. Connect inlet and outlet fuel lines to the fuel pump.
4. Connect drain tube, if used, to pump body.
5. Prime fuel system before starting the engine.

FUEL INJECTORS

Two types of fuel injectors, the crown and the needle valve, are used on all the Detroit Diesel two cycle engines, except the series 92, which uses only the needle valve type fuel injector. The fuel injector used on the V8, 8.2 liter four cycle engine is a version of the needle valve fuel injector, utilizing a different type fuel supply arrangement.

To vary the power output of the engine, injectors having different fuel output capacities are used and are governed by the helix (spiral) angle of the plunger and type of spray tip used. Each fuel injector has a circular disc pressed into a recess at the front of the injector body for identification of the relative size of the injector. It is imperative that the correct injectors are used for each engine application. If the injectors are mixed, erratic operation and possible damage to the engine could result.

Each injector control rack is actuated by a lever on the injector control tube, which is connected to the governor by a fuel rod. These controls can be adjusted independently to permit a uniform setting of all injector racks.

The injectors used in engines with a four valve cylinder head, require an offset injector body due to the restricted area around the exhaust valve mechanism. A narrower injector clamp is used with the offset injector body and can be used with the standard injector bodies. Certain other injectors, designated as "S" types, utilize a clamp that is positioned lower on the injector body.

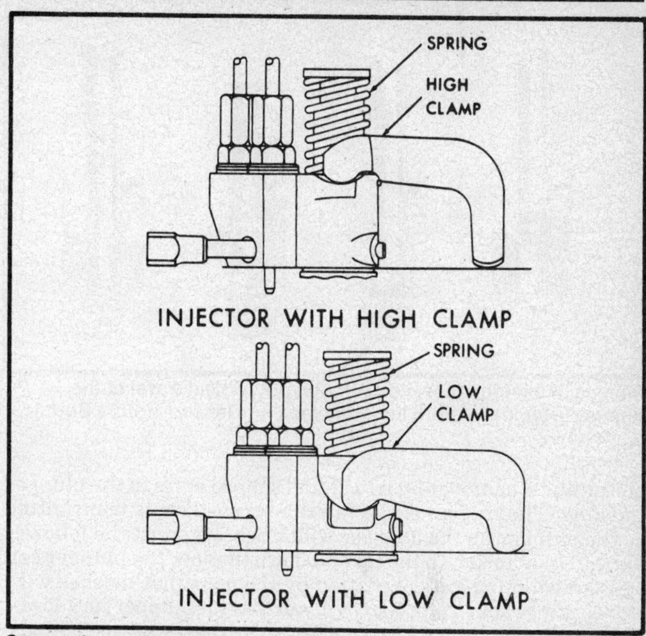

Comparison of high and low injector clamps (© General Motors Corp.)

INJECTOR OPERATION CROWN AND NEEDLE TYPES

After passing through the filter element inlet passage, the fuel oil fills the supply chamber between the bushing and the spill deflector, in addition, the area under the injector plunger within the bushing is also filled. The plunger operates up and down in the bushing, the bore of which is open to the fuel supply in

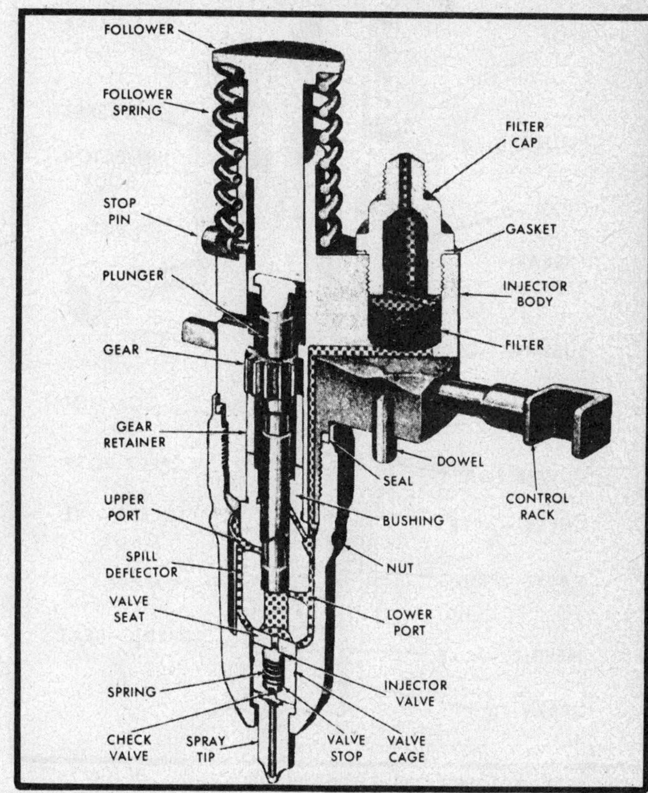

Cross section of crown type fuels injector (© General Motors Corp.)

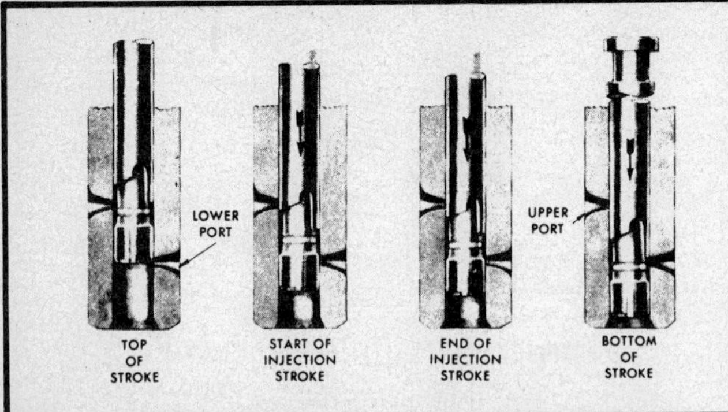

Phases of injector operation through the vertical travel of the plunger—typical of both injector types (© General Motors Corp.)

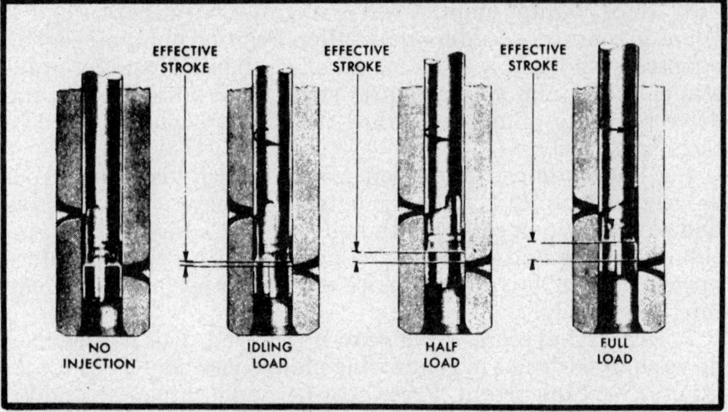

Metering of fuel from NO-LOAD to FULL LOAD—typical of both injector types (© General Motors Corp.)

the annular chamber by two funnel shaped ports in the plunger bushing. The motion of the injector rocker arm is transmitted to the plunger by the follower which bears against the follower spring. In addition to the up and down motion, the plunger can be rotated, during its operation by the gear that meshes with the control rack. To properly meter the fuel, upper and lower helix (spiral) grooves are machined in the lower part of the plunger. The relation of the helixes (spirals) to the two ports, change with the rotation of the plunger.

As the plunger moves downward, under pressure of the injector rocker arm, a portion of the fuel that is trapped below the plunger is then forced up through a central passage in the plunger, into the fuel metering recess and into the supply chamber through the upper port, until the upper port is closed off by the upper helix (spiral) of the plunger. With the upper and lower ports both closed off, the remaining fuel under the plunger is subjected to increased pressure by the continued downward movement of the plunger.

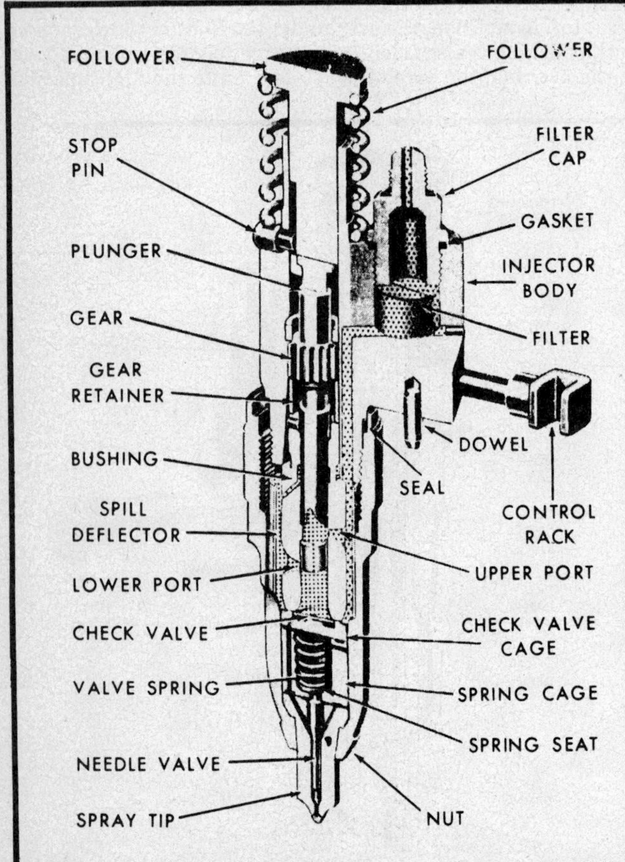

Cross section of needle valve type fuel injector (© General Motors Corp.)

CROWN INJECTOR

When sufficient pressure is built up, the injector valve is lifted off its seat and the fuel is forced through small orifices in the spray tip and atomized into the combustion chamber. A check valve, mounted in the spray tip, prevents air leakage from the combustion chamber to flow into the fuel injector if the valve is accidentally held open by a small particle of dirt or other reasons.

NEEDLE VALVE INJECTOR

When sufficient pressure is built up, a flat, non-return check valve is opened. The fuel in the check valve cage, spring cage, tip passage and tip fuel cavity is compressed until the pressure force acting upward on the needle valve, is sufficient to open the valve against the downward force of the valve spring. As the needle valve lifts off its seat, the fuel is forced through the small orifices in the spray tip and atomized into the combustion chamber.

When the lower land of the plunger uncovers the lower port in the bushing, the fuel pressure below the plunger is relieved and the valve spring closes the needle valve, ending the injection cycle. A relief passage for excess pressure, has been provided in the spring cage to permit bleed-off of fuel leaking past the needle pilot in the tip assembly.

A check valve located directly below the bushing, prevents leakage from the combustion chamber compression pressures to enter the fuel injector, should the valve be accidentally held open by a small particle of dirt or other reasons.

BOTH TYPE INJECTORS

The injector plunger is then returned to its original position by the injector follower spring. On the return upward movement of the plunger, the high pressure cylinder within the bushing, is again filled with fuel oil through the ports. The constant circulation of fresh cool fuel oil through the injector, renews the fuel supply in the chambers and helps cool the injector, while effectively removing all traces of air which could accumulate in the fuel system an interfere with the accurate metering of the fuel.

The fuel injector outlet opening is directly adjacent to the inlet opening, on both types of injectors.

Changing the position of the helixes by the rotation of the plunger, retards or advances the closing of the ports and the beginning and the ending of the injection period. At the same time, it increases or decreases the amount of fuel injected into the cylinders.

Injector Removal

1. Clean and remove the valve rocker cover from the engine.
2. Remove the fuel pipes from the injector and the fuel connectors. Cap the open fittings to prevent foreign material from entering the fuel supply system.
3. Crank the engine or bar the flywheel to bring the outer ends of the pushrods of the injector and valve rocker arms in line horizontally.
4. Remove the two rocker shaft bracket bolts and swing the rocker arms away from the injector and valves.
5. Remove the injector clamp bolt, the special washer and the clamp.
6. Loosen the inner and outer adjusting screws on the injector rack control lever and slide the lever away from the injector.

NOTE: Certain engines have only one adjusting screw and locknut.

7. Lift the injector from its seat in the cylinder head.
8. Cover the injector hole in the cylinder head to prevent objects from dropping into the combustion chamber.
9. Clean the exterior of the injector with clean fuel oil and dry with compressed air.

Injector Tests

Numerous fuel injector test stands are available to test the injection operation out of the engine. The type and manufacturer of the test stand is determined by the repairman's decision, experience and availability. Regardless of the manufacturer or type, the operating instructions must be read, understood and the procedures followed by the repairman, as outlined, during the testing procedures.

CAUTION

The fuel, sprayed from an injector during a test, can penetrate the skin, enter the bloodstream and cause serious infection. Therefore, it is extremely important to use the proper equipment and to follow the manufacturer's operating instructions.

NOTE: Detroit Diesel Allison recommends the use of Kent Moore test stands for the injector testing. References throughout the text will be directed to the Kent Moore test stands or their equivalent.

INJECTOR CONTROL RACK AND PLUNGER MOVEMENT TEST

ALL ENGINE SERIES

1. Place the injector in the injector fixture and rack freeness tester (Kent Moore J22396 or equivalent).
2. Position the handle contact screw on the center of the top of the injector follower. Adjust the handle contact screw as required.
3. Place the injector control rack in the NO-FUEL position and hold in place. Push the tester handle down and depress the follower to the end of its stroke.
4. Very slowly, release the pressure on the handle while moving the control rack up and down, until the follower reaches the end of its travel.
5. The rack should fall freely of its own weight. If the rack does not fall freely, loosen the injector nut, turn the tip and retighten the nut. It may be necessary to loosen and tighten the nut several times.
6. Should the control rack not free-up, change the injector nut. If necessary, dissassemble the injector to locate and repair the misaligned parts.

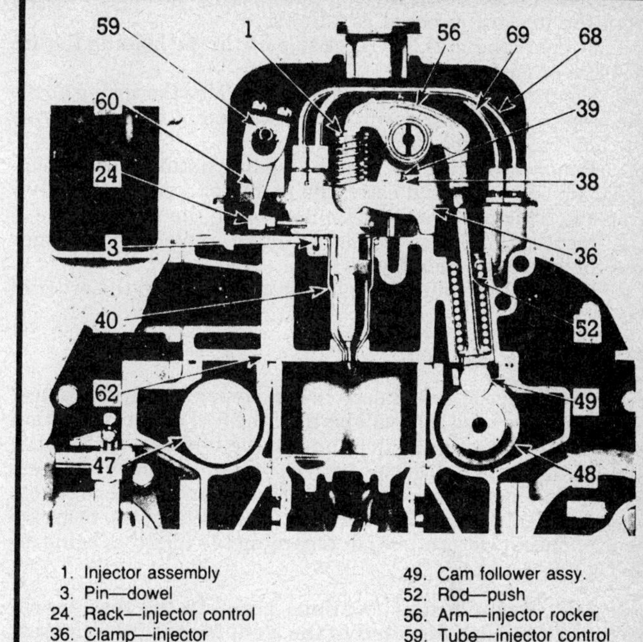

Fuel injector mounting—typical of two cycle engines (© General Motors Corp.)

VISUAL INSPECTION OF THE PLUNGER

ALL ENGINE SERIES

A small area on the bottom helix (spiral) and the lower portion of the upper helix (spiral), if chipped, will not be indicated by any tests. The plunger must be removed from the injector and

Removing the injector from the cylinder head—typical of all series (© General Motors Corp.)

examined under a magnifying glass. To remove the plunger from the injector, proceed as follows:

1. Support the injector, right side up, in the holding fixture (J22396 or equivalent).
2. Compress the follower spring, then raise the spring above the stop pin with a screwdriver or equivalent tool. Withdraw the pin from the injector body.
3. Remove the injector from the holding fixture. Turn the injector upside down and catch the spring and plunger as they drop out. This prevents dirt from entering the injector.
4. Inspect the plunger and, if chipped, replace the plunger and the bushing assembly.
5. Reinstall the plunger, follower and spring in the order of removal.

Fuel Injector Tests

When testing the fuel injectors for proper operation, a test bench must be used that will parallel the fuel system operation of the engine during the holding and the injection cycle of the fuel injector. Regardless of the type or name brand of the test bench equipment used, the manufacturer's recommended test procedures must be followed during the injector tests, to arrive at a conclusive determination regarding the injectors being either good or bad.

NOTE: Various specifications noted in the test procedure outlines are directed to the Kent Moore injector test bench, which utilizes both a pressure gauge (psi) and a high pressure reference gauge, which indicates the relative acceptability of the needle valve injectors and is to be used as a troubleshooting and diagnosis aid only. This test indicator allows comparative testing of the needle valve injector without disassembly. The exact injector valve opening pressure on this type of injector unit can only be determined by the needle valve tip test, using the test stand and special adapters. When using an equivalent injector test bench, its manufacturer's specifications and test procedures must be followed to arrive at the same conclusions as with the Kent Moore test bench.

Injector Valve Opening and Spray Pattern Test

CROWN INJECTORS

SERIES 53, 71 ENGINES

1. Clamp the injector securely in the test bench and make all connections as required. Purge the air from the test fuel system as outlined by the manufacturer.
2. With the fuel rack control in the full-fuel position, operate the pump lever rapidly until the valve opening pressure of 450 to 850 psi is reached and the spray pattern occurs.
3. Check that all the tip spray holes are open and the pattern of the spray is acceptable.

NEEDLE VALVE INJECTORS

SERIES 53, 71 AND 92 ENGINES

1. Clamp the injector securely in the test bench and make the required connections. Purge the air from the test fuel system as outlined by the manufacturer.
2. With the fuel rack control in the full-fuel position, operate the pump lever rapidly, 40 to 80 strokes per minute.
3. The beginning and the ending of the fuel injection should be sharp, with a finely atomized spray and with no drops of test oil forming on the tip of the injector.
4. Observe the indicator on the reference gauge, just before the injection cycle ends. Use the following reference values to determine the relative acceptability of the injectors, when using the Kent Moore test bench or an equivalent.

Series 53 Engines	
All except injector L-40	127 minimum to 146 maximum
Injector L-40	116 minimum to 127 maximum
Series 71 Engines	
All except injectors N-90, 7B5E, B55E and B65	125 minimum to 146 maximum
Injectors N-90, 7B5E, B55E and B65	138 minimum to 162 maximum
Series 92 Engines	
All injectors	138 minimum to 162 maximum

NOTE: This reference value is to be used as a troubleshooting and diagnosis guide which allows comparative testing of the injectors without disassembly.

Injector High Pressure Test

BOTH TYPE INJECTORS

This test is made to determine the sealing of the filter cap gaskets, body plugs and the nut sealing rings.

1. Have the injector clamped in the test bench securely and the test fuel system purged of air.
2. Operate the pump to build up a pressure of 1600 to 2000 psi.
3. Hold the pressure and check for leakage from the sealing units and repair as necessary.

Injector Holding Pressure Test

BOTH TYPE INJECTORS

This test will determine the sealing of the body to bushing mating surfaces in the injector and also indicates proper plunger to bushing fit.

1. Have the injector clamped in the test bench securely and the test fuel system purged of air.
2. Operate the pump to build up a pressure of 500 psi (700 psi for needle valve injector).
3. A pressure drop from 450 to 250 psi in less than 15 seconds indicates leakage and repairs are required.

Spray Tip Test

NEEDLE VALVE INJECTORS

1. Mount the injector in the test bench securely with the appropriate adapters. Purge the test fuel system of air. Mount the spray guard, if equipped.
2. Pump the operating lever approximately 40 strokes per minute to stimulate the action of the tip functioning in the engine.
3. Note the psi pressure at which the needle valve opens. The opening pressure should be between 2200 and 3300 psi. The opening and closing action should be sharp and produce a normal, finely atomized spray pattern.
4. If the valve opening is less than 2200 psi and/or the atomization is poor, a weak valve spring or a poor needle valve seat is indicated.
5. If the valve opening pressure is within 2200–3300 psi, check for tip leakage as follows:
   a. With the pump, build up a pressure of 1500 psi and hold it for 15 seconds.
   b. There should be no fuel droplets formed on the tip, although a slight wetting at the tip is permissible.

Needle Valve Lift Test

1. Using a special dial indicator and base assembly tool, zero the dial indicator plunger by placing the base on a flat surface so that the plunger and the base are on the same plane.
2. Place the spray tip and the needle valve assembly tight against the bottom of the gauge base with the quill of the needle valve in the hole of the dial indicator plunger.
3. The needle valve lift can be read from the dial indicator. The lift should be 0.008 to 0.018 in. If the lift exceeds 0.018 in., the tip assembly must be replaced. If the lift is less than 0.008 in., an indication of foreign matter exists between the needle valve and the tip seat.
4. If the needle valve lift is within specifications, install a new needle valve spring and recheck the valve opening pressure and valve action.
5. Low valve opening or poor fuel atomization with a new spring and seat indicates the spray tip and needle valve assembly must be replaced.

Fuel Output Test

BOTH TYPE INJECTORS

A calibrator type test bench must be used that can automatically actuate the injector, under controlled conditions, to simulate the actual operation of the injector while in the engine. The test bench must be able to count the injection strokes, supply the test fuel at a specific pressure and have means of measuring the delivered fuel from the injector. Using this method, a set of injectors can be selected that will inject the same amount of fuel in each cylinder at a given throttle setting, thus resulting in a smooth running, well balanced engine.

V8, 8.2 LITER ENGINE

1. Install the injector in the test bench and make all required connections. Purge the air from the test fuel system.
2. Operate the pump lever of the test bench to obtain approximately 40 strokes per minute and note the pressure at which the needle valve opens. The opening pressure should be between 2700 and 3400 psi with a sharp opening and closing, producing a finely atomized spray.
3. If the valve opening pressure is below 2700 psi and/or the atomization of the fuel is poor, the cause is usually a worn or fatigued valve spring. Replace the valve spring and retest.
4. If the valve opening is within specifications, check for tip leakage by holding pressure of 1500 psi for approximately 15 seconds. There should be no fuel droplets formed.

NOTE: A slight wetting of the valve tip end is permissible.

5. If the spray tip seat is satisfactory, check the holding time for a pressure drop of 2000 to 1500 psi. The time lapse should not be less than 20 seconds. If the pressure drops in less than 20 seconds, replace the needle valve and tip assembly. Retest the unit.
6. If the needle valve passes the above tests, the lift test can be omitted. If not, proceed as follows:
   a. Using a special dial indicator and base assembly tool, zero the dial indicator plunger by placing the base on a flat surface so that the plunger and the base are on the same plane.
   b. Place the spray tip and the needle valve assembly tight against the bottom of the gauge base with the quill of the needle valve in the hole of the dial indicator plunger.
   c. The needle valve lift can be read from the dial indicator. The lift should be 0.010 to 0.014 in. (0.25 to 0.35mm). If the lift exceeds 0.014 in. (0.35mm), the tip assembly must be replaced. If the lift is less than 0.010 in. (0.25mm), an indication of foreign matter exists between the needle valve and the tip seat.
   d. If the needle valve lift is within specifications, install a new needle valve spring and recheck the valve opening pressure and valve action.
   e. Low valve opening or poor fuel atomization with a new spring and seat indicates the spray tip and needle valve assembly must be replaced.

CROWN TYPE INJECTOR

Disassembly

If required, the injector may be disassembled in the following manner:

1. Support injector upright in injector assembly fixture and remove filter caps, springs, filter elements and gaskets.

NOTE: Whenever injector is disassembled, filter elements and gaskets should be discarded and replaced with new filters and gaskets.

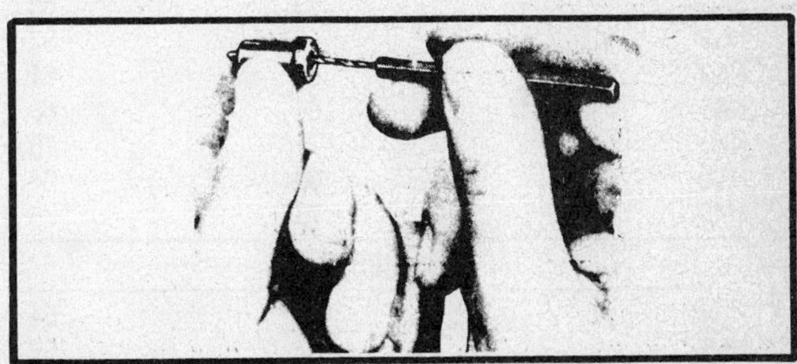

Cleaning the injector spray tip—needle valve and crown types (© General Motors Corp.)

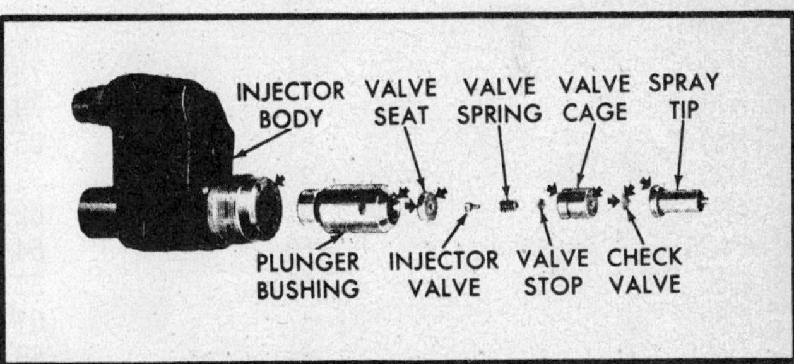

Crown injector sealing surfaces that may require lapping (© General Motors Corp.)

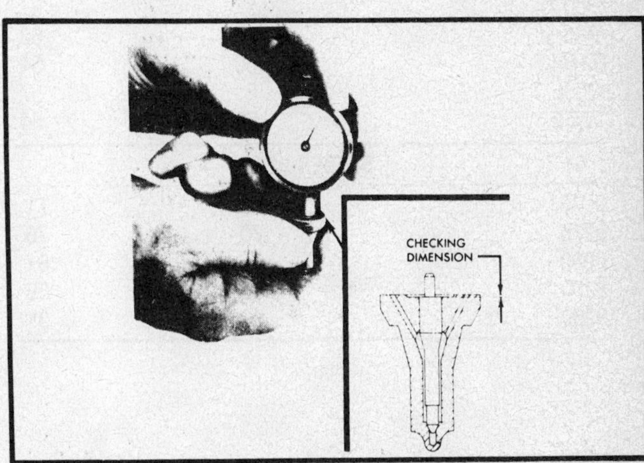

Checking the needle valve fuel injector lift with a dial indicator (© General Motors Corp.)

FUEL OUTPUT SPECIFICATION CHART

Needle Valve Injector

Injector	Calibrator J 22410 Min.	Calibrator J 22410 Max.
SERIES 53		
N35	38	41
L40	41	46
N40	42	47
N45	47	52
N50	50	55
C40	42	47
C45	47	52
C50	50	55
5A55	56	61
5A60	63	68
N55	53	57
N60	57	61
N65	64	68
N70	71	75
M60	60	64
M70	73	76
SERIES 71		
71N5	50	54
N55	53	57
N60	57	61
N65 (white tag)	64	68
N65 (brown tag)	64	68
HN65	70	72
N70	71	75
N75	75	79
N80	81	85
N90	87	92
M95	97	102
71C5	50	54
C55	53	57
C60	57	61
C65	64	68
C70	71	75
B55	53	57
B60	57	61
B65	64	68
71B5	50	54
B55E	53	57
7B5E	50	54
SERIES 92①		
9270	65	71
9275	70	76
9280	75	81
9285	80	86
9290	85	91

Injector	Calibrator J 22410 Min.	Calibrator J 22410 Max.
SERIES 92①		
9295	90	96
9A80	75	81
9C70	65	71
9C75	70	76
9C80	75	81
9C90	85	91
7G65	67	72
7G70	72	77
7G75	77	82
9A85	80	86
9A90	85	91
9200	95	101
9215	110	116
9B70	65	71
9B75	70	76
9B80	75	81
9B85	80	86
9B90	85	91

① First digit identify injector for series "92" engines.

CROWN INJECTORS

Injector	Min.	Max.
HV55	52	56
5S8	50	54
6E8	53	57
6S8	53	57
55E	55	59
S55	55	59
HV6	59	63
S60	59	63
60	60	64
HE6	60	64
60E	60	64
S65	64	68
70	71	75
HV7	71	75
S70	71	75
80	78	82
HV8	80	84
S80	80	84
90	87	92
HV9	87	92
S90	87	92
35	36	40
40	39	43
45	44	48
S40	43	47
S45	48	52
S50	52	56

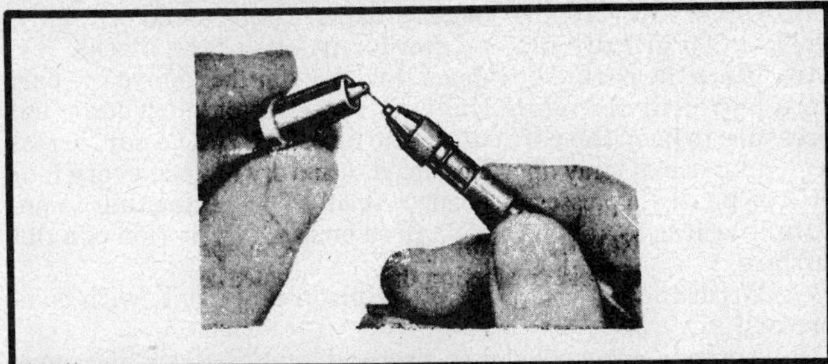

Cleaning the injector spray tip orifices—needle valve and crown types (© General Motors Corp.)

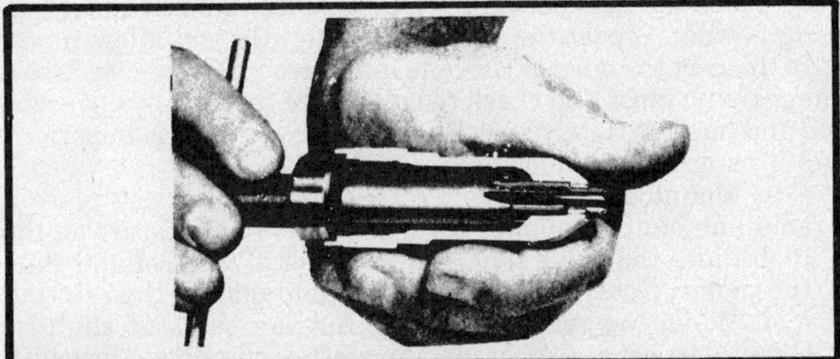

Cleaning the injector nut spray tip seal—typical of needle valve and crown type injectors (© General Motors Corp.)

2. Compress follower spring. Then, using a screwdriver, raise spring above stop pin and withdraw pin. Allow follower spring to rise gradually.
3. Remove plunger follower, spring and plunger as an assembly.
4. Reverse the injector in the fixture and loosen nut from injector body.
5. Remove the spray tip and valve parts off bushing and place in a clean receptacle until ready for assembly.
6. When an injector has been in use for some time, the spray tip, even though clean on the outside, may not be pushed readily from the nut with the fingers. In this event, support the nut on a wood block and drive the tip down through the nut.
7. Remove spill deflector and seal ring from injector nut.
8. Remove plunger bushing, gear retainer and gear from injector body.
9. Withdraw injector control rack from injector body.

Injector Service

1. Wash all injector parts in clean fuel oil or another suitable solvent. Dry them with filtered compressed air. Use extra care when cleaning passages, drilled holes, etc.
2. Clean out the spray tip with a reamer. Turn the reamer clockwise during cleaning. Wash the spray tip, dry it with compressed air and then clean the spray tip orifices with a 0.005 in. diameter wire.

NOTE: The wire end must be honed until it is smooth, free of burrs and the end tapered a distance of $^1/_{16}$ in., by a stone, before using it for cleaning purposes.

After the orifice cleaning, again wash the spray tip in fuel oil or solvent and dry it.

3. Clean fuel and rack holes with appropriate cleaning brushes and then blow all passages dry with compressed air.
4. When handling the injector plunger, never touch the finished surfaces with the fingers. Wash the plunger and its bushing in clean fuel oil and dry it with compressed air. Wrap tissue paper around the bushing cleaner tool and out the bushing bore. Submerge the parts in clean fuel oil to protect them from corrosion during the remaining steps of injector service.

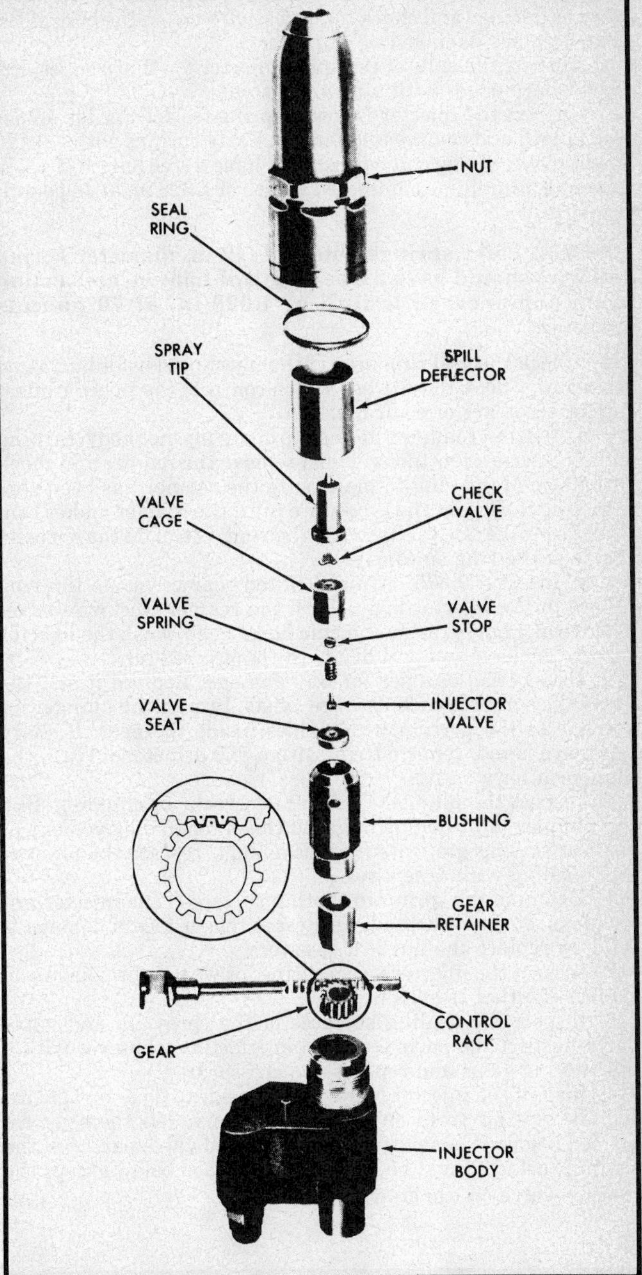

Exploded view of the crown injector and component parts location (© General Motors Corp.)

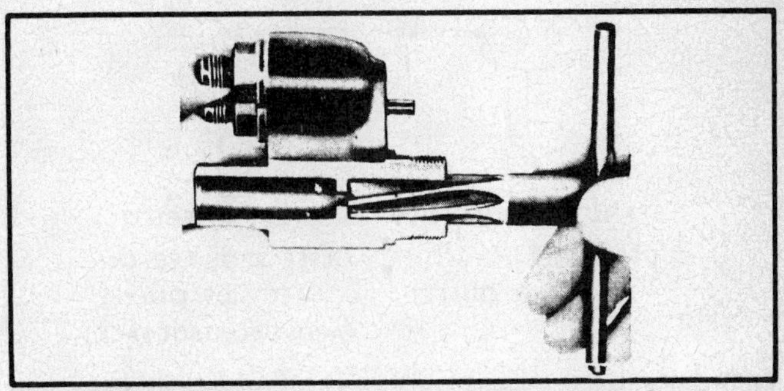

Cleaning the injector body—typical (© General Motors Corp.)

5. Inspect the control rack and rack gear teeth for excessive wear or damage and check for excessive wear in the bore of the gear. Replace damaged or worn parts.

6. Inspect the ends of the spill deflector for sharp edges. Remove sharp edges with a medium stone.

7. Inspect the injector follower spring for defects, for proper free length and compressed length. Early springs with a 0.120 in. diameter spring coil wire should have a free length of 1.659 in. and a minimum compressed length of 1.028 in. at 48 pounds pressure.

NOTE: Later springs with a 0.142 in. diameter spring coil wire should have a free length of 1.504 in. and a minimum compressed length of 1.028 in. at 70 pounds pressure.

8. Check the seal ring area of the injector body for burrs and scratches. Check the surface which contacts the injector bushing for scratches or scuff marks.

a. Insert a reamer into the top of the injector body, turning it clockwise a few turns. Then, remove the reamer and check the face of the ring to make sure the reamer has been contacting it. Repeat the procedure until the reamer makes contact over the entire surface of the ring. Clean up the opposite side of the ring similarly.

b. Insert a 0.375″ straight fluted reamer inside the ring bore in the injector body. Turn the reamer clockwise to remove any burrs inside the ring bore. Then, wash the injector body in clean fuel and dry with compressed air.

9. Inspect the plunger for any damage. Replace it and the bushing as a set if such damage exists. Inspect the plunger for damage at the portion which rides inside the gear. If sharp edges are found, remove them with a 500 grit stone. Wash the plunger after stoning.

10. Inspect the plunger bushing for cracks or chipping. Slip the plunger into the bushing and check for free movement. If wear or scoring prevents free movement, replace the plunger and bushing with a new set.

11. Examine the spray tip seating surface of the injector nut for nicks, burrs, or brinelling. Reseat the surface if damage is mild, or replace the nut if it is severe.

12. Inspect the injector valve spring for wear or breakage and replace if either is evident.

13. Inspect the sealing surfaces of the spray tip and valve parts. Inspect the parts for any imperfection whatever with a magnifying glass and replace as necessary.

14. Inspect the injector body, bushing, spray tip and valve assembly seating surfaces and, if necessary, lap them as described below. Whenever reinstalling used valve parts, all the sealing surfaces must be lapped as described below except the injector valve on the crown valve.

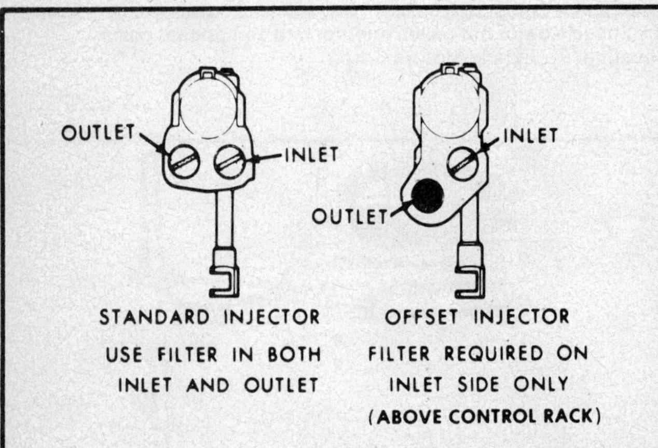

Filter location within the injector body (© General Motors Corp.)

15. Clean the lapping blocks, using compressed air only. Spread 600 grit dry lapping powder on one of the blocks.

16. Place the part to be lapped flat on the block. Move the part back and forth in a figure eight motion, applying just sufficient pressure to keep the part flat on the block. Draw the part across a clean piece of tissue paper placed on a flat surface every four or five passes to clean it. Inspect it after each cleaning to ensure that it is lapped just enough to ensure production of a flat surface.

17. Wash the part in cleaning solution and dry it with compressed air.

18. Apply lapping powder to a second lapping block and move the part lightly across the block just a few times to give it a smooth surface. Wash the part in cleaning solution and dry it with compressed air.

19. Place the part on a third lapping block and, without lapping powder, repeat the process very lightly just a few times.

20. Inspect the edge of the hole in the crown valve seat. Use a magnifying glass and check to make sure the seat is a true circle and has a perfectly smooth surface. If the edge is imperfect, lap it as described below:

a. Mount a deburring tool in a drill motor and place a small amount of lapping powder and oil in a mixture on the tool. Place the valve seat over the pilot of the tool and start the motor. Gently touch the valve seat against the rotating tool. When the seat is uniform, flat lap the seat slightly. Clean the part and examine the width of the edge. The width of the chamfer at the edge of the hole should be 0.002–0.005 in.. A greater width will lower the pop pressure of the injector.

21. Wash all parts that have been lapped in a suitable solvent and dry with compressed air. Clean the inside of the injector bushing by wrapping clean tissue around a bushing cleaner tool and rotating it inside the bushing.

Injector Assembly

Before starting to assemble an injector, it is necessary to have an extremely clean bench on which to work and place the parts. Since the plunger and bushing are matched parts, they must be considered as one piece and, if one is replaced, both must be replaced.

Assemble Injector Filters

New filters and gaskets should always be used when reassembling injectors.

1. Holding the injector body right side up, place a filter in each of the fuel cavities in the top of the injector body. Note that the fuel filters have a dimple in one end. When assembling the filters, always have the dimple at the bottom.

2. Place a spring above each filter, a new gasket up against the shoulder of each filter cap, lubricate the threads and tighten the filter cap in place in the injector body to a torque of 65 to 75 ft. lbs., using a $^9/_{16}$ in. deep socket wrench. It is important that the filter caps be tightened securely so as to compress the gaskets and effect a good seal with the injector body. Also, when the caps are tightened, they compress the filter springs which hold the filters securely in place so all fuel entering the injector is properly filtered.

3. Install covers on injector filter caps to prevent any dirt particles from entering injector. Be sure covers are clean.

Assemble Rack and Gear

When rack and gear are assembled, the marked tooth of the gear must be engaged between the two marked teeth on the rack.

1. Hold the injector body bottom end up and slide the rack through the proper hole in the body. The two marked teeth can then be observed when looking into the bore for the gear from the bottom of the injector body. The injector rack can be placed in the injector body in only one position and have the tooth marks show in the opening for the gear.

2. Holding the rack in position so the tooth marks show, slide the gear into proper engagement with the rack.

3. Slide gear retainer down on top of gear; then place plunger bushing down onto retainer with locating pin in bushing guided into slot of injector body.

Assemble Injector Valve Parts

1. Support the body of the injector in an injector assembly fixture with the bottom end up.

2. Locate the seal ring on the shoulder of the body. Slide the spill deflector over the barrel of the bushing.

3. Place the valve seat on the end of the bushing. Insert the stem of the valve into one end of the valve spring and the valve stop into the opposite end. Lower the valve cage over the assembly so that the stop seats in the cage. Position the valve cage on the valve seat.

4. Locate the check valve on the center of the cage. Place the spray tip over the check valve and against the cage. Then, lubricate the threads and carefully pilot the nut over the spray tip and check valve assembly. The tip will slide through the hole in the small end of the nut.

5. Screw the nut into place, making sure the valve assembly doesn't shift. If they do shift, turn the end of the spray tip with the fingers while screwing the nut onto the body by hand.

6. Tighten the injector nut to 55–65 ft. lbs.

CAUTION

Do not exceed the specified torque. Improper sealing and stretching of the injector nut could result.

Assemble the Plunger and Follower

1. Slide the head of the plunger onto the follower. Insert the assembly through the plunger spring and onto the injector.

2. Invert the injector in the fixture, so the connector is upward and push the rack all the way in. Insert the free end of the plunger into the top of the injector body.

3. Start the stop pin into position in the injector body so the bottom coil of the follower spring rests on the flange on the stop pin. With the follower slot and the injector body hole in alignment and the flat side of the plunger positioned to engage the flat side of the gear, press down on the top of the follower and press the follower stop pin into position. The follower will have to be pressed down until the slot and hole are aligned and allow the pin to go in.

Check Spray Tip Concentricity

This step must be performed to ensure that the spray tip and injector nut are concentric within 0.008 in. for correct alignment of the tip in the spray tip hole of the cylinder head.

1. Mount the injector in a concentricity gauge.

2. Zero the dial indicator. Rotate the injector one full turn and note the highest reading on the dial.

3. If the run out exceeds 0.008 in., remove the injector from the gauge, loosen the injector nut, re-center the spray tip and retorque the nut to 55–65 ft. lbs.

4. If repeated attempts fail to center the tip within the specified runout, the assembly of the injector is unsatisfactory.

NEEDLE VALVE TYPE INJECTOR

Disassembly

1. Support the injector in the assembly fixture and remove the filter caps, gaskets and filter elements. Discard used filters and gaskets.

NOTE: A filter is used in the inlet side only on the offset injector. No filter is required in the outlet side.

2. Compress the follower spring and use a screwdriver to raise the spring above the stop pin and withdraw the pin. Release the follower spring gradually.

a. **V8–8.2 liter:** Compress the follower spring slightly and rotate the follower counterclockwise until the roll pin aligns with the release slot in the body. Remove the follower, plunger and spring as an assembly.

3. Remove the plunger follower and plunger assembly from the body. Remove the follower spring.

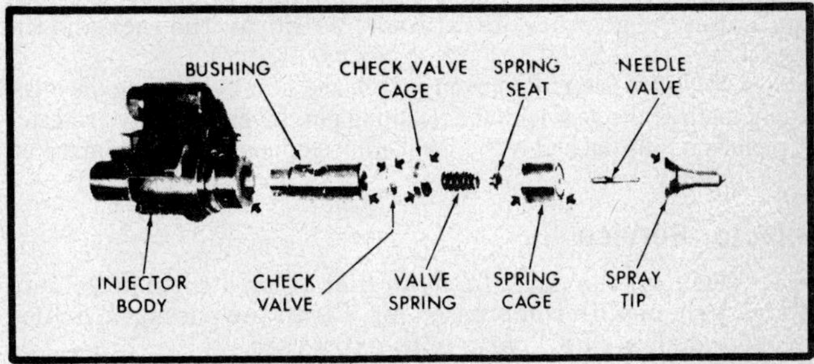

Needle valve injector sealing surfaces that may require lapping
(© General Motors Corp.)

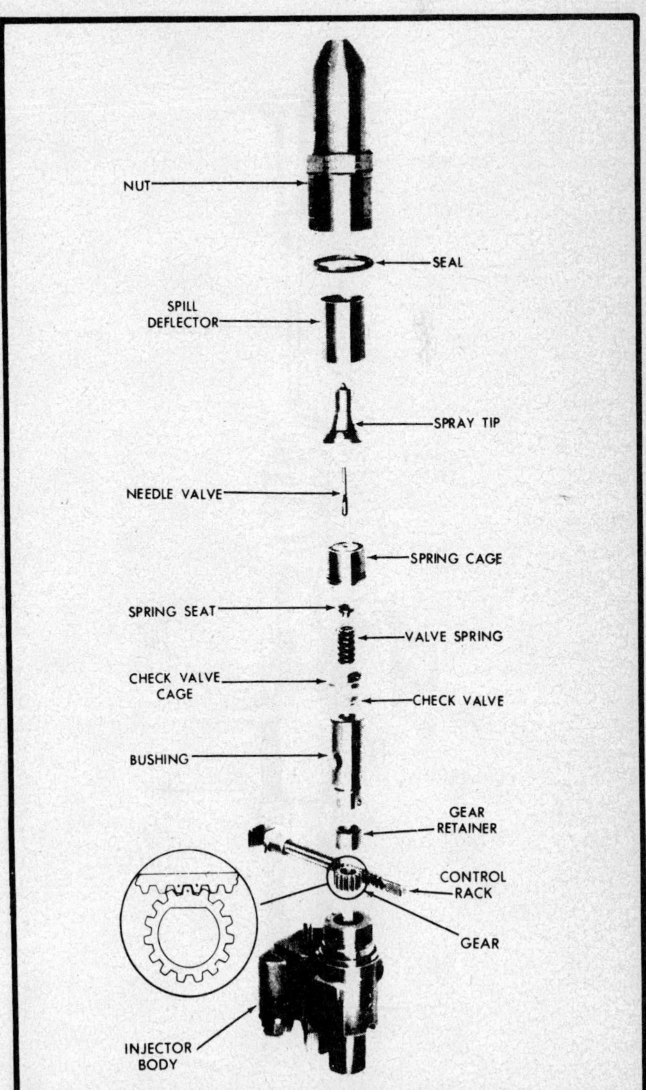

Exploded view of needle valve type injector tip assembly
(© General Motors Corp.)

4. Reverse the position of the injector in the fixture and, with a socket wrench, loosen the body nut. Remove the nut by carefully lifting it straight up to avoid dislodging the spray tip and valve parts. Remove the spray tip and valve parts and place them in a clean receptacle.

5. If you can't easily push the spray tip off the nut, support the nut on a wood block and drive the tip down through the nut using a special tool.

6. Remove the spill deflector, if equipped. Lift the bushing straight out of the body.

7. Remove the body from the holding fixture. Invert the body and catch the gear and its retainer. Withdraw the rack and the seal ring.

a. **V8, 8.2 Liter:** Remove the rack and gear by aligning the missing tooth of the gear with the retaining pin. Invert the body and catch gear as it falls out and withdraw the injector control rack from the injector body.

Injector Service

1. Wash all the parts in clean fuel oil or a suitable solvent and dry them with compressed air. Clean the passages, drilled holes and slots in all parts with extra care.

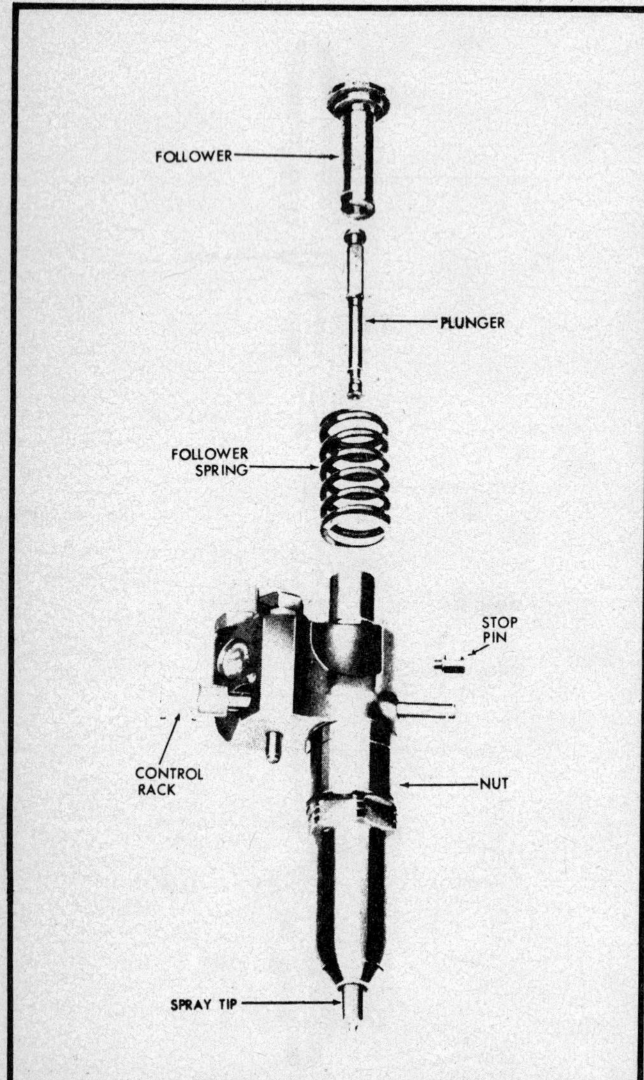

Injector plunger follower and component parts location—typical of both types of injectors (© General Motors Corp.)

2. Clean the spray tip with a special reamer, turning the reamer in a clockwise direction. Wash the spray tip and dry it with compressed air. Clean the orifices with a pin vise using 0.005" diameter wire for tips with 0.005–0.0055 in. diameter holes and a 0.006 in. wire for tips with 0.006 in. diameter holes. Hone the end of the wire to remove burrs and taper the end $^1/_{16}$ in. back from the tip with a stone. Allow the wire to protrude $^1/_8$ in. from the holder. After cleaning, wash the spray tip in clean fuel oil and dry it with compressed air.

NOTE: During reaming of the spray tip, avoid contacting the needle valve seat.

3. Clean and brush all injector body passages with an appropriate brush. Dry all passages with compressed air.

4. Insert a reamer into the top of the injector body, turning it clockwise a few turns. Then, remove the reamer and check the face of the ring to make sure the reamer has been contacting it. Repeat the procedure until the reamer makes contact over the entire surface of the ring. Clean up the opposite side of the ring similarly.

5. Insert a 0.375 in. straight fluted reamer inside the ring bore in the injector body. Turn the reamer clockwise to remove any burrs inside the ring bore. Then, wash the injector body in clean fuel and dry with compressed air.

6. Use the two types of carbon removing tools to remove carbon deposits from the spray tip seat and the lower end of the injector nut. The tool to be used should be inserted carefully and turned clockwise. Be careful not to remove metal or set up burrs.

7. Wash the injector nut in clean fuel oil and dry with compressed air. Wash the plunger and bushing with clean fuel oil and dry with compressed air, avoiding contact with the finished plunger surfaces.

8. Submerge all parts in a receptacle containing clean fuel oil. Keep all parts of each injector assembly together.

9. Inspect the teeth on the control rack and control rack gear for excessive wear or damage. Check for excessive wear in the bore of the gear. Replace any damaged or worn parts.

10. Inspect the ends of the spill deflector for sharp edges or burrs which could create burrs on the injector body or nut. Remove burrs with a medium stone.

11. Perform the following steps:

a. **All series except V8, 8.2 liter:** Inspect the injector follower spring for defects, for proper free length and compressed length. Early springs with a 0.120 in. diameter spring coil wire should have a free length of 1.659 in. and a minimum compressed length of 1.028 in. at 48 pounds pressure.

b. Later springs with a 0.142 in. diameter spring coil wire should have a free length of 1.504 in. and a minimum compressed length of 1.028 in. at 70 pounds pressure.

c. **V8, 8.2 liter:** The injector follower spring should have a diameter of 0.160 in. and a free length of 1.865 in. With a compression pressure of 98 pounds, the length should not be under 1.248 in.

12. Check the seal ring area for burrs or scratches. Check the surface which contacts the injector bushing for scratches, scuff marks, etc. Lap this surface if it is faulty.

13. Inspect the plunger for scoring, chipping, or excessive wear. Check for sharp edges where the plunger rides in the gear. If sharp edges exist, remove them with a 500 grit stone. Wash the plunger after stoning. Inspect the plunger bushing for cracks or chipping. Check the locating pin in the bushing and replace it if it is damaged or sheared off. Check the plunger and bushing for free movement. Replace badly worn, chipped, or scored plungers and bushings with a new assembly.

14. Examine the spray tip seating surface of the injector nut for nicks, burrs, or brinelling. Reseat the seating surface, if necessary, or replace the nut if it is severely damaged.

15. Inspect the injector valve spring and replace it if it is worn or broken.

16. Inspect the sealing surfaces. Examine the surfaces under a magnifying glass for burrs, nicks, erosion, cracks, chipping, or excessive wear and replace as necessary. Check the spray tip for enlarged orifices and replace it if necessary.

17. Examine the needle valve for wear, scoring, or damage to the quill where it contacts the spring seat. If the needle valve is scored or damaged, replace the spray tip assembly. Lap all surfaces indicated by arrows as described below. Lap also the sealing surfaces of new parts to remove burrs or nicks picked up during handling.

18. Clean three lapping blocks with compressed air only. Spread 600 grit dry lapping powder on two of the blocks.

19. Place each part flat on the block. Using a figure eight motion, move the part back and forth across the block, maintaining just sufficient pressure to keep the part completely in contact with the block.

20. After each five passes, clean the part with tissue paper by placing the paper on a flat surface and drawing the part across it. Lap the part just until it is flat; avoid excessive lapping. When the part is flat, wash it in solvent and dry with compressed air.

21. Repeat the lapping process very briefly on the second block. Then, wash and dry the part as before.

22. Lap the part very, very lightly on the third block without the use of powder. Wash again and dry with compressed air.

Injector Assembly

1. Insert the new filters slotted end up, in the fuel cavities, as required. Place new gaskets on the filter caps, coat the threads with oil and install the caps, torquing them to 65–75 ft. lbs. Install clean shipping caps on the filter caps.

2. With the injector body bottom end up, slide the rack through the hole in the body. Look into the bore and slide the rack back and forth until you can see the two drill marks. Hold the rack in this position while placing the gear in the injector body and meshing the teeth of the gear so the drill marks align. Place the gear retainer on top of the gear, align the bushing locating pin with the slot in the injector body and slide the end of the bushing into place.

3. Mount the injector in a holding fixture with the bottom end up. Install a new seal ring on the shoulder of the body and then position the spill deflector over the barrel of the bushing. Place the check valve on top of the center of the bushing and then place the check valve cage over the valve and against the bushing.

4. Insert the spring seat inside the valve spring and insert the assembly into the spring cage with the spring seat going first. Place the spring cage, spring seat and valve spring assembly, with the valve spring down, on top of the check valve cage. Insert the needle valve (tapered end down) into the spray tip.

CAUTION

When installing a new spray tip assembly in a former injector, a new valve spring seat must also be installed. The current needle valve has a shorter quill.

5. Place the spray tip and needle valve on top of the spring cage with the small end of the needle valve in the hole in the spring cage. Lube the threads of the injector nut and then carefully position the nut and screw it in place by hand, watching carefully to make sure the valve assembly does not shift. If the valve parts are not centrally located, assembly may be eased by turning the end of the spray tip while screwing the nut onto the body.

6. **All series, except V8, 8.2 liter:** Invert the injector in the fixture and push the control rack all the way in. Place the follower spring and stop pin on the body so the bottom coil of the spring rests on the narrow flange of the pin. Slide the head of the plunger into the slot in the follower and then position the plunger and follower over the injector body and align the slot in the follower with the stop pin hole in the body. Align the flat side of the plunger with the flat in the gear and lower the plunger and follower straight into the gear and injector body until the follower rests on the spring.

7. **V8, 8.2 liter:** Press down on the follower while rotating clockwise until it contacts the guide slot and then release the follower. Press down on the follower and press the stop pin into the slot in the follower until the spring drops into the stop pin slot. Invert the injector and use a special socket wrench and torque drive to tighten the nut to 75–85 ft. lbs. (70–80 ft. lbs. V8, 8.2 liter).

8. Place the injector in a concentricity gauge. Zero the dial indicator. Rotate the injector 360° and note the total run-out indicated. If the run-out exceeds 0.008 in., attempt to recenter the spray tip by removing the injector from the gauge and loosening the nut. After retorquing the nut (75–85 ft. lbs.) and placing the unit back into the gauge, recheck the concentricity.

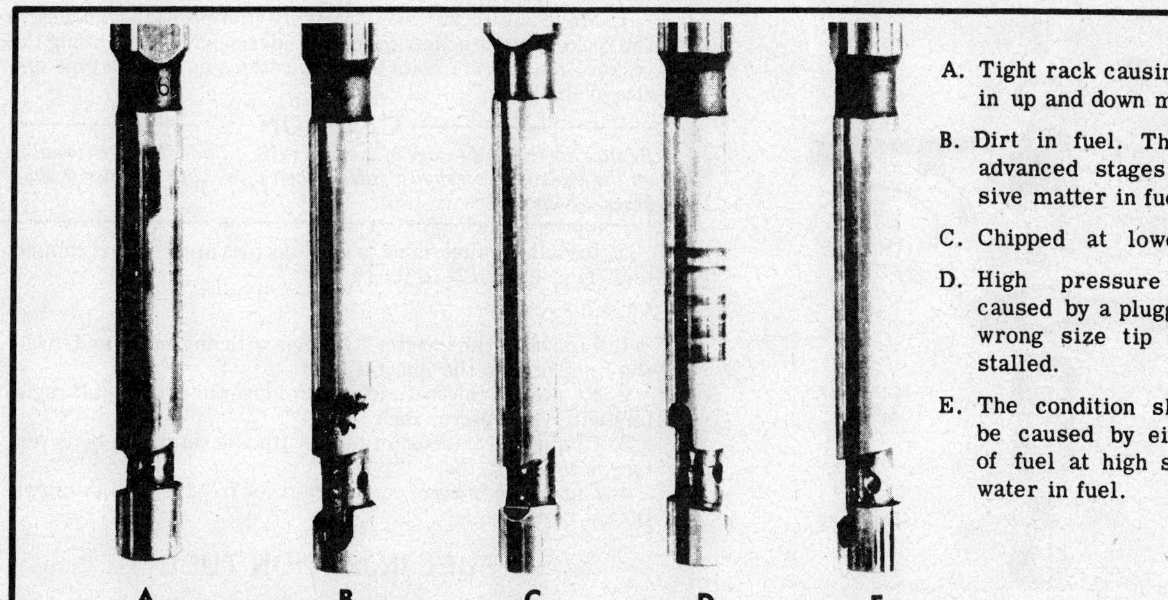

A. Tight rack causing binding in up and down movement.

B. Dirt in fuel. This shows advanced stages of abrasive matter in fuel.

C. Chipped at lower helix.

D. High pressure scoring caused by a plugged tip or wrong size tip being installed.

E. The condition shown can be caused by either lack of fuel at high speeds or water in fuel.

Damaged and usable plungers (© General Motors Corp.)

If several attempts fail to bring the concentricity within specifications, check the entire injector assembly.

Injector Testing

ALL SERIES

Before placing a reconditioned injector in service, all of the tests (except the visual inspection of the plunger) previously outlined in this section under Injector Tests must be performed again.

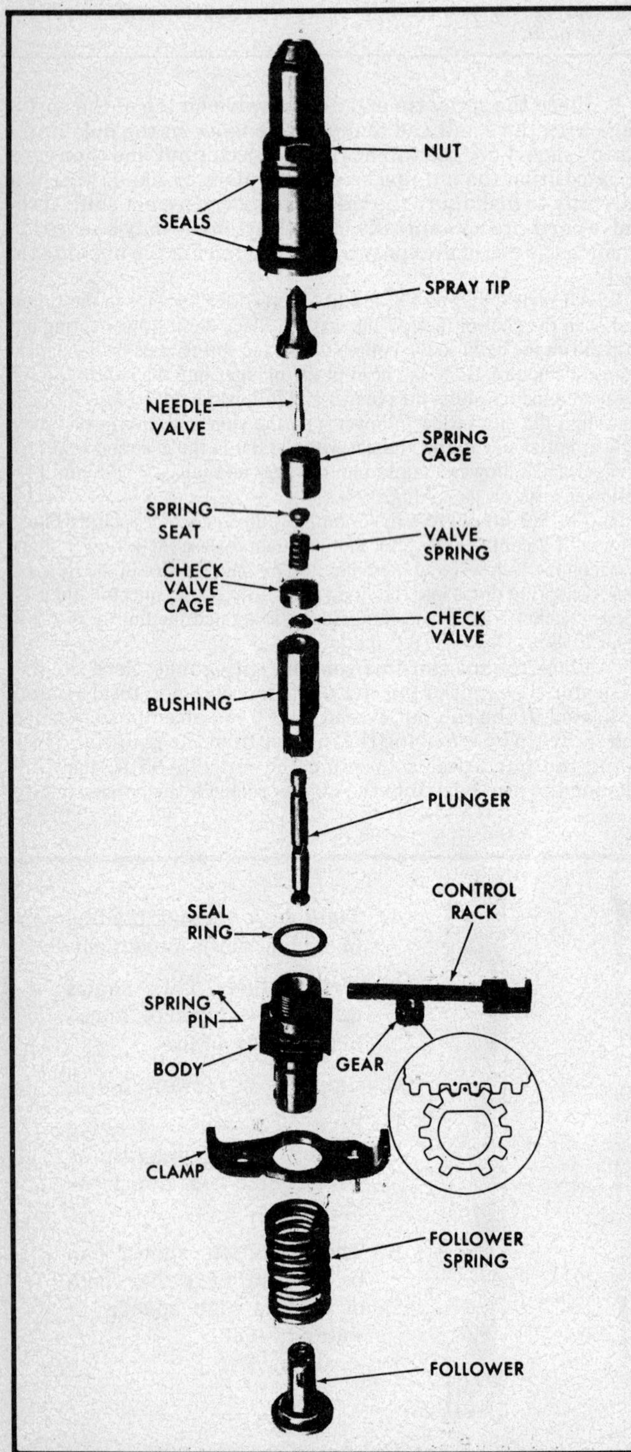

Exploded view of needle valve injector used on the V8, 8.2L Series (© General Motors Corp.)

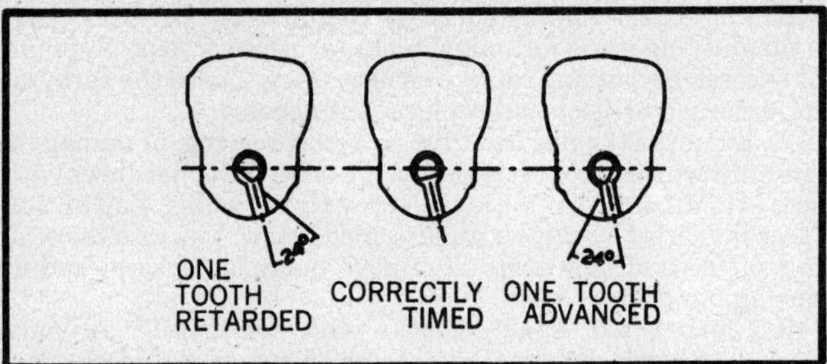

Injector rack to gear timing (© General Motors Corp.)

If an injector is not to be used immediately, caps should be installed on the injector caps. The injector test oil remaining in the injector after the fuel output test will serve as a rust preventive while the injector is in storage.

Injector Installation

Before installation of an injector in the cylinder head(s), the carbon should be removed from the beveled seat of the injector tube. This will assure correct alignment of the injector and prevent stresses from being exerted against the spray tip. Use the special injector tube bevel reamer tool to clean the carbon from the injector tubes.

CAUTION

Care must be taken to remove ONLY carbon so that the proper clearance between the injector body and the cylinder head is maintained.

NOTE: Pack the flutes of the reamer with grease to retain the carbon removed from the tube.

ALL MODELS, EXCEPT V8, 8.2 LITER

1. With the injectors filled with fuel oil, insert the injector into the injector tube with the dowel pin in the injector body, seated in the locating hole in the cylinder head.
2. Slide the injector rack control lever over so that it registers with the injector rack.
3. Install the injector clamp, the special washer with the curved side towards the injector clamp and the bolt. Torque the bolt to 20–25 ft. lbs.

NOTE: Check the injector control rack for freedom of movement. Over-torquing can cause binding or sticking.

4. Move the rocker arm assembly into position and secure the rocker arm brackets to the cylinder head by tightening the rocker arm bracket bolts to specifications as per the type and size of the bolts.

CAUTION

Be sure the exhaust bridge of the four valve cylinder heads are resting on the ends of the exhaust valves when tightening the rocker shaft bracket bolts.

5. Install the fuel pipes to the injectors and the fuel connectors. Tighten to 12–15 ft. lbs.

V8, 8.2 LITER

1. Lubricate the injector "O" rings with engine oil and insert the injector into the injector tube.
2. Rotate the injector rack control lever over so that it registers with the injector rack.
3. Clamp the injector in place with the retaining bolts and torque to 7–9 ft. lbs.
4. Check the injector control rack for freedom of movement. Do not over torque.

FUEL INJECTION TUBE

The cylinder head(s) must be removed before the injection tube can be removed or replaced.

FORD V8 6.9L DIESEL

General Description

The 6.9L diesel engine is a four cycle naturally aspirated V–8 with overhead valves. The right bank of cylinders are numbered 1, 3, 5, 7, with number 1 being at the front. The firing order is 1–2–7–3–4–5–6–8.

The crankcase has been especially designed to withstand the loads of diesel operation and utilizes a four bolt main bearing to assure a rigid, inflexible support for the rotating parts. The crankcase also has internal piston oil cooling jets which direct oil to the underside of the piston.

The crankshaft is a five main bearing unit with fore and aft thrust controlled at the center (NO. 3) bearing. Heavy-duty forged steel connecting rods are attached to the crankshaft, two to each bearing throw. The piston pin is a free floating type permitting the pin to move or float freely in piston and rod. The pin is held in place with pin retaining snap-rings.

The camshaft is supported by five insert-type bearings pressed into the block and is driven by a drive gear keyed to the crankshaft. The end thrust of the camshaft is controlled by a thrust flange located between the front camshaft journal and the camshaft drive gear.

The aluminum-alloy pistons are fitted with two compression rings and one oil ring.

The hydraulic valve tappets minimize engine noise and maintain zero valve lash or tappet clearance. This eliminates the need for periodic adjustment. The hydraulic valve tappets also incorporate camshaft roller followers for improved camshaft wear characteristics.

The cylinder head assemblies feature pre-combustion chambers which provide superior combustion characteristics. The cylinder heads used on the engine are equipped with positive valve-rotating mechanisms located at the bottom of the intake and exhaust valve springs.

The engine is equipped with a fully closed crankcase ventilation system. The crankcase depression regulator (CDR) valve is mounted on the intake manifold and provides a connection between the valley pan and the intake manifold, to regulate crankcase pressure.

The rotary-type injection pump is located between the cylinder heads in a recess in the front of the engine. The engine governor is integral with the fuel injection pump. Operating principles and service instructions for the fuel system components are also provided in this Section.

The 6.9L engine is made for Ford Motor Company by International Harvester Company.

GENERAL ENGINE SPECIFICATIONS

Engine No. Cyl. Displacement (liters)	Fuel Distribution	Horsepower @ rpm	Torque @ rpm (ft. lbs.)	Bore × Stroke (in.)	Compression Ratio	Oil Pressure @ 2000 rpm
V8 (6.9)	Rotary Injection	170 @ 3,300	307 @ 1,800	4.00 × 4.18	20.7:1	40–60

DIESEL TUNE-UP SPECIFICATIONS

Engine No. Cyl. Displacement (liters)	Static Injection Timing	Fuel Injection Order	Valve Clearance	Injection Nozzle Opening Pressure (psi)	Intake Valve Opens (deg)	Idle Speed ① (rpm)	
						Man.	Auto.
V8 (6.9)	①	1-2-7-3-4-5-6-8	②	1850	—	600–700	600–700

Note: The underhood specifications sticker often reflects changes made in production. Sticker figures must be used if they disagree with those in the above chart.

① See underhood sticker for fast idle speed.

② Hydraulic lifters used (not adjustable).

TORQUE SPECIFICATIONS

All readings in ft. lbs.

Engine No. Cyl. Displacement (liters)	Cylinder Head Bolts	Rod Bearing Bolts	Main Bearing Bolts	Crankshaft Pulley Bolt	Flywheel to Crankshaft Bolts	Manifold	
						Intake	Exhaust
V8 (6.9)	①	46–51 ②	95 ③	90	44–50 ④	24	30

① First pull 40 ft. lbs., second pull 65 ft. lbs., final 75 ft. lbs.

② First tighten to 38 ft. lbs., then to 46–51 ft. lbs.

③ First tighten to 75 ft. lbs., then to 95 ft. lbs.

④ Apply thread locking sealant before installation.

DYNAMIC TIMING SPECIFICATIONS

Fuel Cetane Value	Altitude 0-3000 Ft ①	Altitude Above 3000 Ft ①
38–42	6° ATDC	7° ATDC
43–46	5° ATDC	6° ATDC
47–50	4° ATDC	5° ATDC

① Installation or resetting tolerance for dynamic timing is ± 1°. Service limit is ± 2°.

FIRING ORDERS

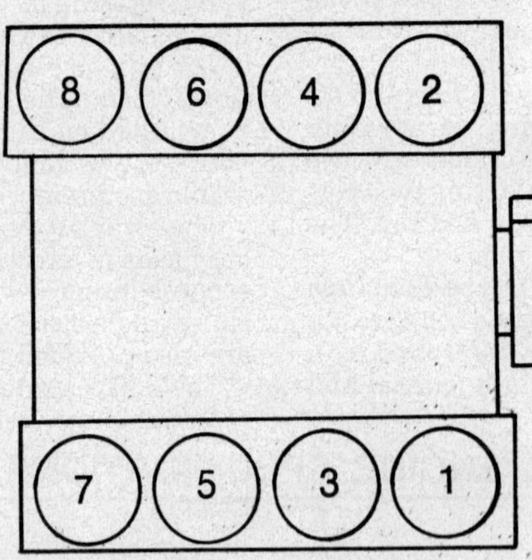

Firing order: 1-2-7-3-4-5-6-8

CHILTON'S THREE "C's" DIESEL ENGINE DIAGNOSIS PROCEDURE

Condition	Cause	Correction
Rough Idle	Improper adjustment	Adjust idle
	Accelerator control cable binding	Repair or lubricate
	Air or water in the fuel system	Clear air or water from fuel system
	Injection nozzle clogged	Check and clean injector nozzles
	Improper valve clearance	Check valve adjustment
	Injection pump malfunction	Check injection pump
Poor Performance	Air cleaner clogged	Check element
	Accelerator control cable binding	Check control cable for free movement
	Restricted fuel flow (water or air)	Check lines and filter
	Incorrect injection timing	Check injection timing
	Injection pump malfunction	Replace injection pump
Excessive Exhaust Smoke	Restricted air cleaner	Check element
	Air or water in fuel filter	Remove air or water from fuel system
	Improper grade fuel	Check fuel in tank
	Incorrect injection timing	Check injection timing
	Injection pump malfunction	Replace injection pump
	Injector nozzle stuck open	Check injector nozzles

CHILTON'S THREE "C's" DIESEL ENGINE DIAGNOSIS PROCEDURE

Condition	Cause	Correction
Excessive Fuel Consumption	Restricted air cleaner	Check element
	Leak in fuel lines	Check for leaks
	Incorrect idle speed	Check idle
	Restricted exhaust system	Check exhaust
	Improper grade fuel	Check fuel in tank
	Injection pump malfunction	Check injection pump operation
Loud Knocking In Engine	Defective fuel injector	Replace fuel injector

Note: If the problem persists after performing these preliminary checks, disassembly and inspection of internal engine components may be necessary for further diagnosis.

TUNE-UP AND ADJUSTMENTS

Compression Test

1. Be sure that the battery is properly charged. Operate the engine until the engine is at normal operating temperature. Turn the ignition switch off. Remove the air cleaner and disconnect injection pump solenoid leads from injection pump to prevent accidental engine starting. Then remove all the glow plugs.
2. Install a compression gauge Rotunda® 19–0001 or equivalent in No. 1 cylinder glow plug hole.
3. Crank the engine (with the ignition switch off) at least five pumping strokes and record the highest reading indicated. Note and record the approximate number of compression strokes required to obtain the highest reading.
4. Repeat the check on each cylinder, cranking the engine approximately the same number of compression strokes. Record all readings.

CAUTION

Do not add oil to cylinder. This could cause hydrostatic lock.

Test Conclusion

The indicated compression pressures are considered normal if the lowest reading cylinder is at least 75 percent of the highest. Variations lower than 75 percent imply an improperly seated valve or worn or broken piston rings.

Hydraulic Roller Cam Follower

The cam followers are the hydraulic type and are not adjustable. If a hydraulic tappet noise is present, any of the following could be the cause:

1. Excessive collapsed tappet gap.
2. Sticking tappet plunger.
3. Tappet check valve not functioning properly.
4. Air in lubrication system.
5. Leakdown rate too rapid.
6. Excessive valve guide wear.

Excessive collapsed tappet gap may be caused by loose rocker arm fulcrum bolts, or wear of tappet roller, pushrod, rocker arm, rocker arm fulcrum or valve tip. With tappet collapsed, using tool T83T–6500–A, bleed-down wrench or equivalent, check gap between valve tip and rocker arm to determine if any other valve train parts are damaged, worn, or out of adjustment.

A sticking tappet plunger may be caused by dirt, chips, or varnish inside the tappet. The sticking can be corrected by disassembling the tappet and removing the dirt, chips or varnish that is causing the condition.

A tappet check valve that is not functional may be caused by an obstruction such as dirt or chips preventing it from closing when the cam lobe is lifting the tappet, or it may be caused by a broken check valve spring.

Air bubbles in the lubrication system will prevent the tappet from supporting the valve spring load and may be caused by too high or too low an oil level in the oil pan, or by air being drawn into the system through a hole, crack, or leaking gasket on the oil pump pickup tube.

If the leakdown time is below the specified time for used tappets, noisy operation may result. If no other cause for noisy tappets can be found, the leakdown rate should be checked and any outside the specification should be replaced.

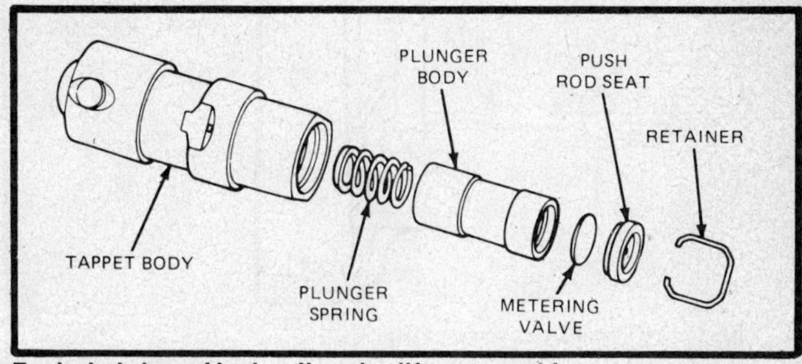

Exploded view of hydraulic valve lifter assembly
(© Ford Motor Co.)

Leakdown Test

CAUTION

Tappets cannot be checked with engine oil in them. Only the testing fluid can be used.

Assembled tappets can be tested with tool 6500–E or equivalent to check the leakdown rate. The leakdown rate specification is the time in seconds for the plunger to move a specified distance of its travel while under a 50 lb. (22.68 kg) load. Test the tappets as follows:

1. Disassemble and clean the tappet to remove all traces of engine oil.

NOTE: Do not mix parts from different tappets. Parts are select-fitted and are not interchangeable.

2. Place the tappet in the tester, with the plunger facing upward. Pour hydraulic tappet tester fluid into the cup to a level that will cover the tappet assembly. The fluid can be purchased from the manufacturer of the tester.

NOTE: Using kerosene or any other fluid will not provide an accurate test.

3. Place the $^5/_{16}$ in. steel ball provided with the tester in the plunger cap.
4. Adjust the length of the ram so that the pointer is $^1/_{16}$ in. (1.59mm) below the starting mark when the ram contacts the tappet plunger, to facilitate timing as the pointer passes the start timing mark. Use the center mark on the pointer scale as the stop timing point instead of the original stop timing mark at the top of the scale.
5. Work the tappet plunger up and down until the tappet fills with fluid and all traces of air bubbles have disappeared.
6. Allow the ram and weight to force the tappet plunger downward. Measure the exact time it takes for the pointer to travel from the start timing to the stop timing marks of the tester.
7. A tappet that is satisfactory must have a leakdown rate (time in seconds) within the minimum and maximum limits specifications.
8. If tappet is not within specifications, replace it with a new tappet. It is not necessary to disassemble and clean new tappets before testing, because the oil contained in new tappets is test fluid.
9. Remove fluid from cup and bleed fluid from tappet by working plunger up and down. This step will aid in depressing the tappet plungers when checking the valve clearance.

INJECTOR TIMING

STATIC TIMING

1. Loosen the injection pump to mounting nuts.
2. Rotate the injection pump to bring the mark on the pump into alignment with the mark on pump mounting adapter.
3. Visually recheck the alignment of the timing marks and tighten injection pump mounting nuts.

DYNAMIC TIMING

1. Bring the engine up to normal operating temperature.
2. Stop the engine and install a dynamic timing meter, Rotunda® 78–0100 or equivalent, by placing the magnetic probe pick-up into the probe hole.

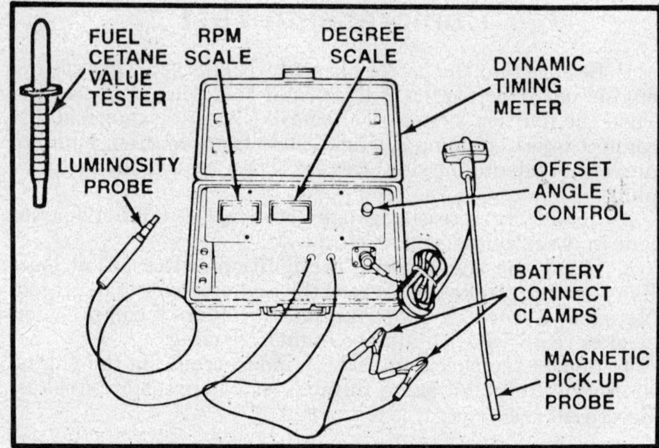

Injection pump timing tools (© Ford Motor Co.)

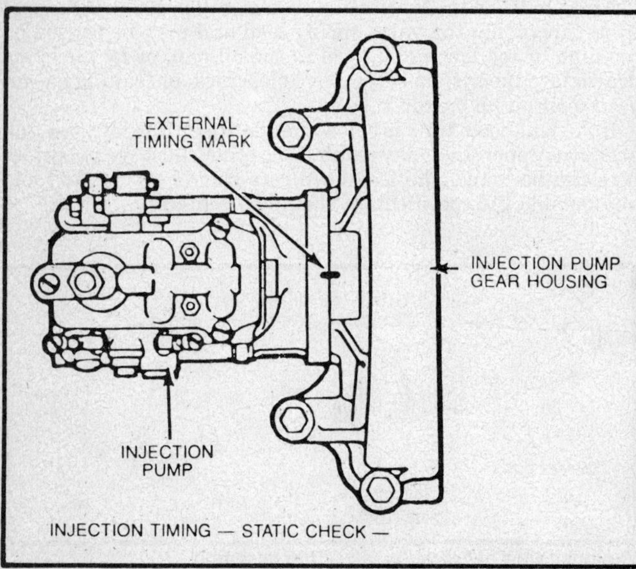

Injection pump timing marks (© Ford Motor Co.)

3. Remove the No. 1 glow plug wire and remove the glow plug, install luminosity probe and tighten to 12 ft. lbs. (16 Nm). Install the photocell over the probe.
4. Connect a dynamic timing meter to the battery and adjust the offset of the meter.
5. Set the transmission in neutral and raise the rear wheels off the ground. Using Rotunda® 14–0302, throttle control, set the engine speed to 1400 rpm with no accessory load. Observe the injection timing on the dynamic timing meter.

NOTE: Obtain a fuel sample from the vehicle and check the cetane value using the tester supplied with the Ford special tools 78–0100 or equivalent. Refer to the dynamic timing chart to find the correct timing in degrees.

6. If dynamic timing is not within ± 2° of specification, then injection pump timing will require adjustment.
7. Turn the engine off. Note the timing mark alignment. Loosen the injection pump-to-adapter nuts.

8. Rotate the injection pump clockwise (when viewed from the front of engine) to retard and counterclockwise to advance timing. Two degrees of dynamic timing is approximately 0.030 in. (.75mm) of timing mark movement.
9. Start the engine and recheck the timing. If the timing is not within ± 1° of specification, repeat Steps 7 through 9.
10. Turn off the engine. Remove the dynamic timing equipment. Lightly coat the glow plug threads with anti-seize compound, install the glow plug and tighten to 12 ft. lbs. (16 Nm). Connect the glow plug wires.

Idle Speed

Curb Idle Adjustment

1. Place the transmission in neutral or park.
2. Bring the engine up to normal operating temperature.
3. Idle speed is measured with manual transmission in neutral and automatic transmission in drive with the wheels blocked.
4. Check the curb idle speed, using Rotunda® 99–0001 or equivalent magnetic pick-up tachometer. Adjust the idle speed to 600–700 rpm.

NOTE: Always check the underhood emissions control information label, for the latest idle and adjustment specifications.

5. Place the transmission in neutral or park and momentarily speed up the engine. Allow the rpm to drop to idle and recheck the idle speed. Readjust if necessary.

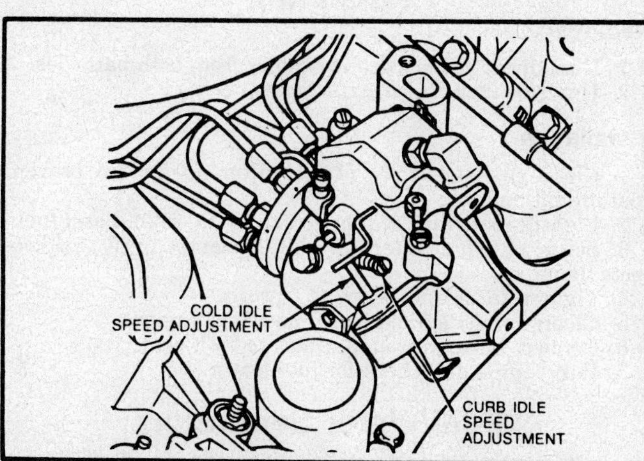

Idle speed adjustment screws on 6.9L engine injection pump (© Ford Motor Co.)

Fast Idle Adjustment

1. Place the transmission in neutral or park.
2. Start the engine and bring up to normal operating temperature.
3. Disconnect the wire from the fast idle solenoid.
4. Apply battery voltage to activate the solenoid plunger.
5. Speed up the engine momentarily to set the plunger.
6. The fast idle should be between 850–900 rpm. Adjust the fast idle by turning the solenoid plunger in or out.
7. Speed up the engine momentarily and recheck the fast idle. Readjust as necessary.
8. Remove the battery voltage from the solenoid and install the wire to the solenoid.

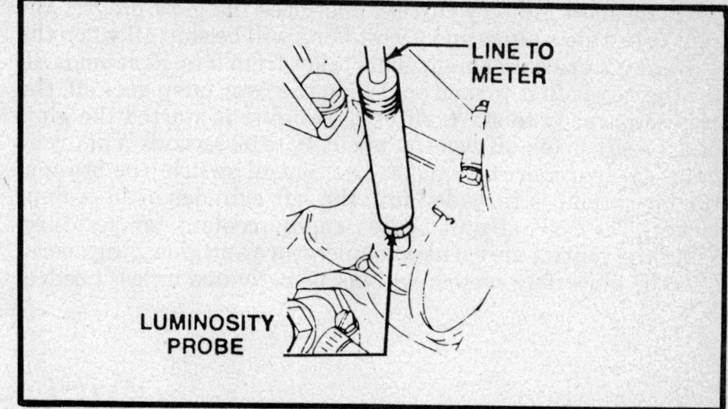

Installing luminosity probe—typical (© Ford Motor Co.)

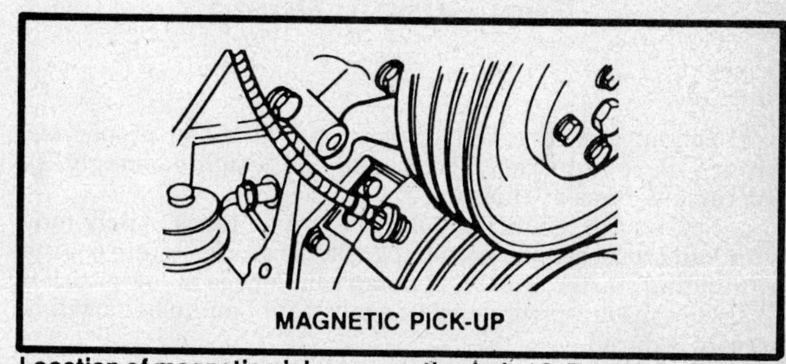

Location of magnetic pick-up mounting hole (© Ford Motor Co.)

Glow Plug System

The 6.9L diesel engine utilizes an electric glow plug system to aid in the start of the engine. The function of this system is to pre-heat the combustion chamber to aid ignition of the fuel.

The system consists of eight glow plugs (one for each cylinder), control switch, power relay, after glow relay, wait lamp latching relay, wait lamp and the eight fusible links located between the harness and the glow plug terminal.

On initial start with a cold engine, the glow plug system operates as follows: The glow plug control switch energizes the power relay (which is a magnetic switch) and the power relay

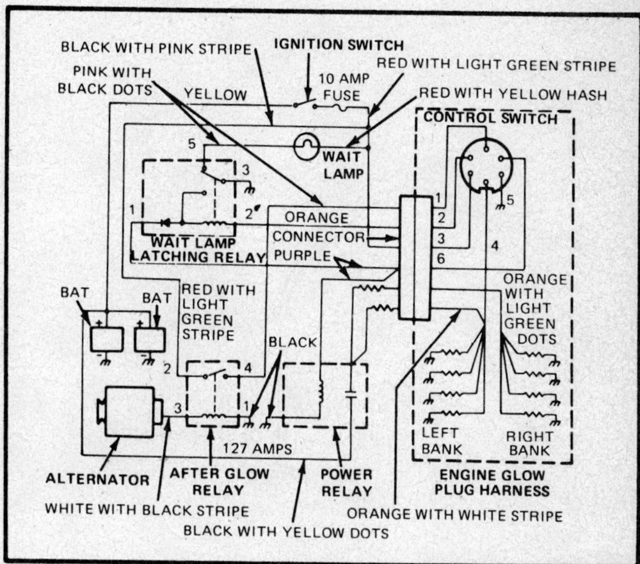

Schematic of glow plug electrical circuit (© Ford Motor Co.)

contacts close. Battery current energizes the glow plugs. Current to the glow plugs and a wait lamp will be shut off when the glow plugs are hot enough. This takes from 2 to 10 seconds after the key is first turned on. When the wait lamp goes off, the engine is ready to start. After the engine is started the glow plugs begin an on-off cycle for about 40 to 90 seconds. This cycle helps to clear start-up smoke. The control switch (the brain of the operation) is threaded into the left cylinder head coolant jacket. The control unit senses engine coolant temperature. Since the control unit senses temperature and glow plug operation the glow plug system will not be activated unless needed. On a restart (warm engine) the glow plug system will not be activated unless the coolant temperature drops below 165°F (91°C).

The fast start system utilizes 6 volt glow plugs in a 12 volt system to achieve rapid heating of the glow plug, a cycling device is required in the circuit.

CAUTION

Never bypass the power relay of the glow plug system. Constant battery current (12 volts) to glow plugs will cause them to overheat and fail, possibly resulting in severe engine damage.

FUEL SYSTEM

Fuel Supply Pump

Removal

1. Loosen the threaded connections with the proper size wrench (flare nut wrench preferred) and retighten snugly. Do not remove lines at this time.
2. Loosen the mounting bolts one to two turns. Apply force with hand to loosen fuel pump if gasket is stuck. Rotate engine, by nudging starter, until fuel pump cam lobe is at low position. At this position, spring tension against fuel pump bolts will be greatly reduced.
3. Disconnect fuel supply pump inlet, outlet and fuel return line.

CAUTION

Use care to prevent combustion of spilled fuel.

4. Remove fuel pump attaching bolts and remove pump and gasket. Discard old gasket.

Installation

1. Remove all fuel pump gasket material from engine and from fuel supply pump if, reinstalling used pump.
2. Install attaching bolts into fuel supply pump and install a new gasket on bolts. Position fuel supply pump to mounting pad. Turn attaching bolts alternately and evenly and tighten to specification.

NOTE: Cam must be at its low position before attempting to install fuel supply pump. If it is difficult to start the mounting bolts, remove the pump and reinstall with lever on bottom side of cam.

3. Install fuel outlet line. Start fitting by hand to avoid crossthreading.
4. Install inlet line and fuel return line.
5. Start engine and observe all connections for fuel leaks for two minutes.
6. Stop engine and check all fuel supply pump fuel line connections. Check for oil leaks at pump mounting pad.

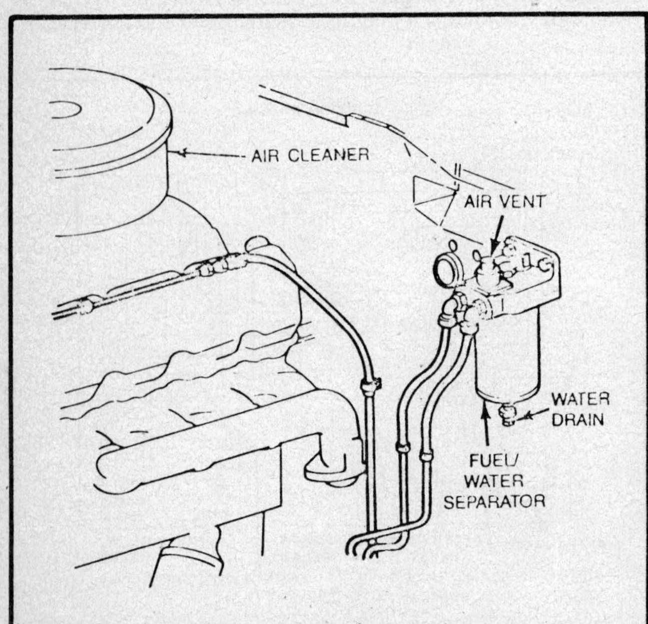

Draining water/fuel separator (© Ford Motor Co.)

Fuel Filter

Removal

1. Disconnect battery ground cables from both batteries.
2. Unscrew fuel filter from adapter.

Installation

1. Clean gasket surface of fuel filter adaptor to prevent contamination.
2. Lightly coat filter sealing gasket with clean diesel fuel.
3. Screw new fuel filter onto filter adapter until seal contacts flange.
4. Tighten filter another $1/2$ to $3/4$ turn.
5. Clean up any spilled fuel from top of engine.
6. Connect battery ground cables to both batteries.
7. Run engine and check for fuel leaks.

Fuel/Water Separator

The 6.9L diesel engine is equipped with fuel/water separator in the fuel supply line. A "Water in Fuel" indicator light is provided on the instrument panel to alert the operator. The light should glow when the ignition switch is in the START position to indicate proper light and water sensor function. If the light glows continuously while the engine is running, the water must be drained from the separator as soon as practical to prevent damage to the fuel injection system.

Injection Nozzles

Removal

NOTE: Before removing nozzle assemblies, clean exterior of each nozzle assembly and the surrounding area with clean fuel oil or solvent to prevent entry of dirt into the engine when nozzle assemblies are removed. Also, clean fuel inlet and fuel leak-off piping connections. Blow dry with compressed air.

1. Remove the fuel line retaining clamp(s) from the nozzle lines that are to be removed.
2. Disconnect the nozzle fuel inlet (high pressure) and fuel leak-off tees from each nozzle assembly and position out of the way. Cover the open ends of the fuel inlet and outlet or nozzles with protective caps, to prevent dirt from entering.
3. Remove the injection nozzles by turning them counterclockwise. Pull the nozzle assembly with the copper washer attached from the engine. Cover the nozzle fuel opening and spray tip, with plastic caps, to prevent the entry of dirt.

NOTE: Remove the copper injector nozzle gasket from the nozzle bore with special tool, T71P–19703–C, or equivalent, whenever the gasket does not come out with the nozzle.

4. Place the nozzle assemblies in a fabricated holder as they are removed from the heads. The holder should be marked with numbers corresponding to the cylinder numbering of the engine. This will allow for re-installation of the nozzle in the same ports they were removed from.

Installation

1. Thoroughly clean nozzle bore in cylinder head before reinserting nozzle assembly with nozzle seat cleaner, special tool T83T–9527–A or equivalent. Make certain that no small particles of metal or carbon remain on the seating surface. Blow out the particles with compressed air.
2. Remove the protective cap and install a new copper gasket on the nozzle assembly, with a small dab of grease.

NOTE: Anti-seize compound or equivalent should be used on nozzle threads to aid in installation and future removal.

3. Install the nozzle assembly into the cylinder head nozzle bore.
4. Tighten the nozzle assembly to 33 ft. lbs. (45 Nm).
5. Remove the protective caps from nozzle assemblies and fuel lines.
6. Install the leak-off tees to the nozzle assemblies.

NOTE: Install two new O-ring seals for each fuel return tee.

7. Connect the high pressure fuel line and tighten, using a flare nut wrench.
8. Install the fuel line retainer clamps.
9. Start the engine and check for leaks.

Nozzle Testing

Where ideal conditions of good combustion, specified engine temperature control and absolutely clean fuel prevail, nozzles will require little attention. Nozzle trouble is usually indicated by one or more of the following symptoms:

1. Smoky exhaust (black)
2. Loss of power
3. Misfiring
4. Increased fuel consumption
5. Combustion knock
6. Engine overheating

When faulty nozzle operation is suspected on an engine that is misfiring or puffing black smoke, a simple test can be made to determine which cylinder(s) is causing the problem.

1. Run the engine at the rpm, which makes the misfire most pronounced.
2. Momentarily loosen the high pressure fuel inlet line connection on one nozzle assembly one half turn. Then re-tighten the connection.
3. Check each cylinder in the same manner. If one nozzle is found where loosening makes no difference in the misfiring, or puffing of black smoke stops, that nozzle should be tested.

NOTE: It is advisable to test all nozzles before cleaning them.

1. Remove the nozzle(s) to be tested.
2. Prepare Rotunda® #14–6300 (test stand) or equivalent for making the tests. Fill the reservoir with clean calibration fluid. Open the tester valve slightly and operate the tester handle to expel air from the tester and outlet pipe. Operate the tester until solid fluid (without air bubbles) flows from the end outlet pipe. Close the tester valve.
3. Connect the injection nozzle to the test stand.
4. Bleed the air from the nozzles. Open the stand valve and operate the tester handle for several quick strokes to expel air from the injection nozzle. Fluid should flow from the spray holes in the nozzle tip.

CAUTION

Always wear approved safety glasses when operating the nozzle tester. Avoid contacting the spray with any open flame or sparks. Do not smoke during testing.

NOTE: Use only approved SAE No. 208629 calibration fluid in the tester or (SAE J968D or ISO 4113).

CAUTION

During testing keep hands and skin away from the spray, since the liquid leaves the nozzle tip with sufficient force to penetrate the skin and cause serious injury. If available, enclose the nozzle tip in a transparent receptacle.

5. Check the nozzle opening pressure. Open the gauge valve and pump the handle slowly until the nozzle sprays. Observe the gauge to determine opening pressure. Normal operating pressure of the nozzle is 2100–2150 psi (14,480–14,824 kPa) and the service minimum is 1850 psi (12,756 kPa).

NOTE: Chatter will vary from nozzle to nozzle as will the sound. While nozzle chatter is acceptable, a lack of chatter is not a reason to condemn a nozzle.

6. Check the tip leakage by operating the test pump to maintain a constant pressure at 200 psi (1379 kPa) below opening pressure. The nozzle tip should remain dry without an accumulation of fuel drops at the tip spray holes. A slight wetting after about 5 seconds is permissible if no droplets are formed.

NOTE: Wiping the nozzle tip with the fingers will draw fuel from the nozzle giving a false test result. Use a clean, dry and lint free cloth to wipe the tip dry before testing.

7. Check return port fuel leak-off, operate the test pump and observe the return port during spray. A leak-off rate of one or two drops per tester stroke is acceptable. If fuel squirts from the return port, the nozzle is faulty and must be replaced.
8. Operate the tester with smooth even strokes and observe the spray pattern. Concentrate on the first three in.es of spray from the end of the nozzle. The spray should be finely atomized in an even straight pattern. The pattern should be concentric (not lopsided). Fuel should not come out in droplets or a solid stream. If a nozzle fails the spray test, clean the nozzle and repeat the spray test.
9. Soak the nozzles in a cold decarbonizing solution for one hour, or use a sonic nozzle cleaner, if available.
10. Install the nozzle(s), run the engine and check for leaks.

Injection Pump

NOTE: Before removing any fuel lines, clean exterior with clean fuel oil or solvent to prevent entry of dirt into engine when fuel lines are removed.

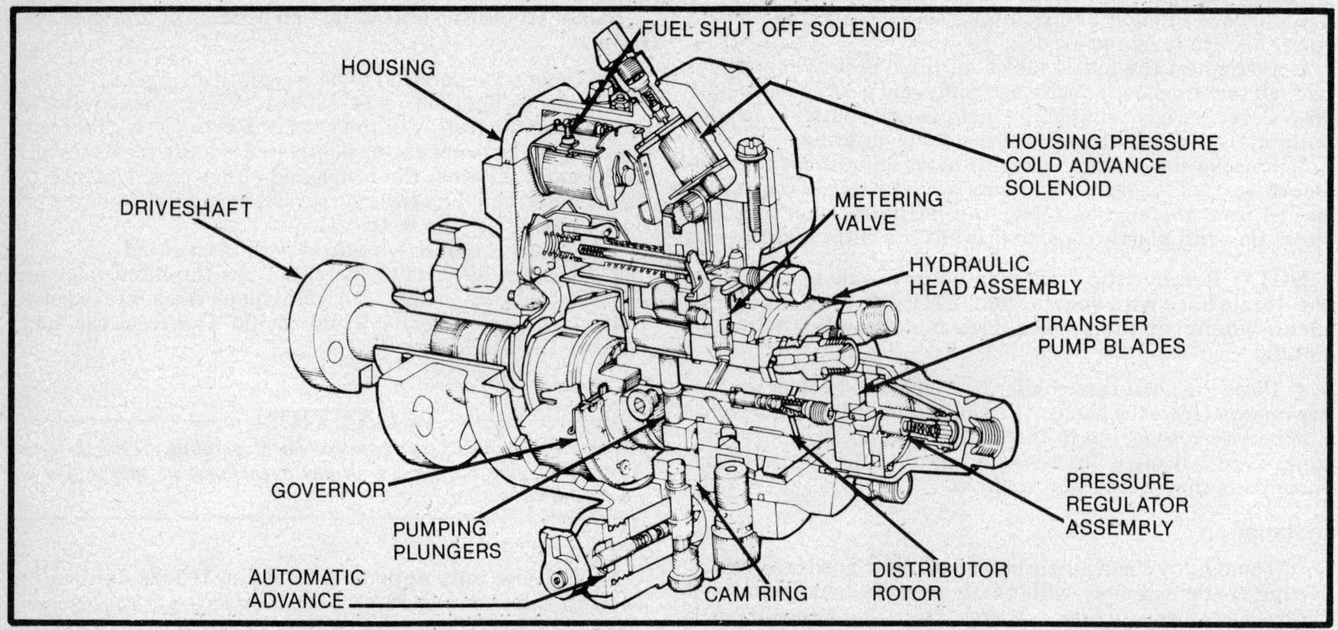

Cross section of injection pump—6.9L Engine (© Ford Motor Co.)

CAUTION

Do not wash or steam clean engine while engine is running. Serious damage to injection pump could occur.

Removal

1. Disconnect battery ground cables from both batteries.
2. Remove engine oil filler neck.
3. Remove bolts attaching injection pump to drive gear.
4. Disconnect electrical connectors to injection pump.
5. Disconnect accelerator cable and speed control cable from throttle lever, if so equipped.
6. Remove air cleaner and install intake opening cover, Tool T83T–9424–A or equivalent.
7. Remove accelerator cable bracket, with cables attached, from intake manifold and position out of the way.

NOTE: All fuel lines and fittings must be capped using Fuel System Protective Cap Set T83T–9395–A, or equivalent, to prevent fuel contamination.

8. Remove fuel filter-to-injection pump fuel line and cap fittings.

Location of injection pump attaching bolts (© Ford Motor Co.)

9. Remove and cap injection pump inlet elbow.
10. Remove and cap injection pump fitting adapter.
11. Remove fuel return line on injection pump, rotate out of the way and cap all fittings.

NOTE: It is not necessary to remove injection lines from injection pump to remove injection pump. If lines are to be removed, loosen injection line fittings at injection pump before removing it from engine.

12. Remove fuel injection lines from nozzles and cap lines and nozzles.
13. Remove three nuts attaching injection pump to injection pump adapter.
14. If injection pump is to be replaced, loosen injection line retaining clips and injection nozzle fuel lines and cap all fittings at this time with protective cap set T83T–9395–A or equivalent. Do not install injection nozzle fuel lines until new pump is installed in engine.
15. Lift injection pump, with nozzle lines attached, up and out of engine compartment.

CAUTION

Do not carry injection pump by injection nozzle fuel lines as this could cause lines to bend or crimp.

Installation

1. Install new O-ring on drive gear end of injection pump.
2. Move injection pump down and into position.
3. Position alignment dowel on injection pump into alignment hole on drive gear.
4. Install bolts attaching injection pump to drive gear and tighten to specification.
5. Install nuts attaching injection pump to adapter. Align scribe lines on injection pump flange and injection pump adapter and tighten to 14 ft. lbs. (19 Nm).
6. If injection nozzle fuel lines were removed from injection pump install at this time.
7. Remove caps from nozzles and fuel lines and install fuel line nuts on nozzles and tighten to 22 ft. lbs. (30 Nm).
8. Connect fuel return line to injection pump.
9. Install injection pump fitting adapter with a new O-ring.

10. Clean old sealant from injection pump elbow threads, using clean solvent and dry thoroughly. Apply a light coating of pipe sealant on elbow threads.
11. Install elbow in injection pump adapter and tighten to a minimum of 6 ft. lbs. (8 Nm). Then tighten further, if necessary, to align elbow with injection pump fuel inlet line, but do not exceed 360° of rotation or 10 ft. lbs. (13 Nm).
12. Remove caps and connect fuel filter-to-injection pump fuel line.
13. Install accelerator cable bracket to intake manifold.
14. Remove intake manifold cover and install air cleaner.
15. Connect accelerator and speed control cable, if so equipped, to throttle lever.
16. Install electrical connectors on injection pump.
17. Clean injection pump adapter and oil filler neck sealing surfaces.
18. Apply a ⅛ in. bead of RTV Sealant on adapter housing.
19. Install oil filler neck and tighten to specifications.
20. Connect battery ground cables to both batteries.
21. Run engine and check for fuel leaks.
22. If necessary, purge high pressure fuel lines of air by loosening connector one half to one turn and cranking engine until solid fuel, free from bubbles, flows from connection.
23. Check and adjust injection pump timing.

CAUTION

Keep eyes and hands away from nozzle spray. Fuel spraying from the nozzle under high pressure can penetrate the skin and cause infection. Medical attention should be provided immediately in the event of skin penetration.

Bleeding Fuel System

If necessary, purge high pressure fuel lines of air by loosening connector one half to one turn and cranking engine until solid fuel, free from bubbles, flows from connection. Tighten the fuel line fitting and start the engine to check for fuel leaks.

Fuel Control

On-off fuel control is provided by an electric solenoid located in the diesel injection pump housing cover. Current is supplied to the solenoid when the ignition switch is turned on. If no fuel is supplied with the ignition switch in the on position, check for current at the solenoid terminal before condemning the solenoid.

Fuel Lines

Removal

NOTE: Before removing any fuel lines, clean exterior with clean fuel oil, or solvent to prevent entry of dirt into fuel system when fuel lines are removed. Blow dry with compressed air.

1. Disconnect battery ground cables from both batteries.
2. Remove air cleaner and cap intake manifold opening with Ford Tool T83T–9424–A or equivalent.
3. Disconnect accelerator cable and speed control cable, if so equipped, from injection pump.
4. Remove accelerator cable bracket from intake manifold and position out of the way with cable(s) attached.

NOTE: To prevent fuel system contamination, cap all fuel lines and fittings with protective cap set.

5. Disconnect fuel line from fuel filter to injection pump and cap all fittings.

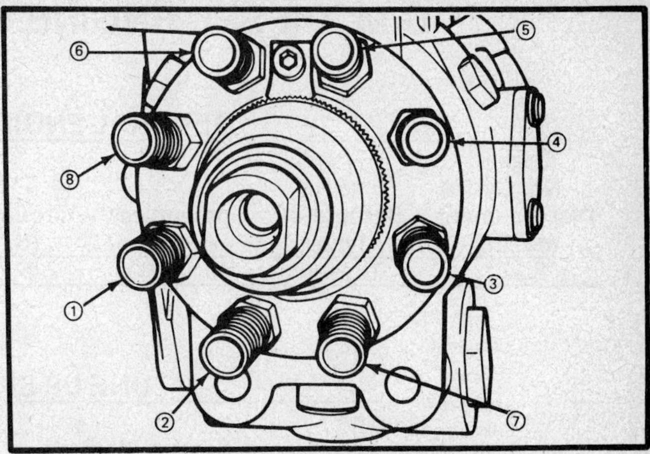

Cylinder location on injection pump delivery lines
(© Ford Motor Co.)

6. Disconnect and cap nozzle fuel lines at nozzles.
7. Remove fuel line clamps from fuel lines to be removed.
8. Remove and cap injection pump inlet elbow.
9. Remove and cap inlet fitting adapter.
10. Remove injection nozzle lines, one at a time, from injection pump.

NOTE: Fuel lines must be removed following this sequence: 5–6–4–8–3–1–7–2. Install caps on each end of each fuel line and pump fitting as it is removed and identify each fuel line accordingly.

Installation

1. Install fuel lines on injection pump, one at a time and tighten to 22 ft. lbs. (30 Nm).

NOTE: Fuel lines must be installed in the sequence: 2–7–3–1–8–4–6–5.

2. Clean old sealant from injection pump elbow, using clean solvent and dry thoroughly.
3. Apply a light coating of pipe sealant on elbow threads.
4. Install elbow in injection pump adapter and tighten to a minimum of 6 ft. lbs. (8 Nm) then tighten further, if necessary, to align elbow with injection pump fuel inlet line, but do not exceed 360° of rotation or 10 ft. lbs. (13 Nm).
5. Remove caps from fuel lines and connect lines to nozzles and tighten to 22 ft. lbs. (30 Nm).
6. Uncap and connect fuel line from fuel filter to injection pump and tighten.
7. Install fuel line retaining clamps and tighten.
8. Install accelerator cable bracket on intake manifold.
9. Connect accelerator and speed control cable, if so equipped, to injection pump throttle lever.
10. Remove intake manifold cover and install air cleaner.
11. Connect battery ground cables to both batteries.
12. Run engine and check for fuel leaks.
13. If necessary, purge high pressure fuel lines of air by loosening connector one half to one turn and cranking engine until solid fuel, free from bubbles, flows from connection.

CAUTION

Keep eyes and hands away from nozzle spray. Fuel spraying from the nozzle under high pressure can penetrate the skin.

G.M. DIESEL ENGINE 5.7 LITER, 350 CU. IN. V8

GENERAL ENGINE SPECIFICATIONS

Engine No. Cyl. Displacement (cu. in.)	Carburetor Type	Horsepower @ rpm	Torque @ rpm (ft. lbs.)	Bore × Stroke (in.)	Compression Ratio	Oil Pressure @ 2000 rpm
8-350	Diesel	125 @ 3600	225 @ 1600	4.057 × 3.385	22.5:1	40

TUNE-UP SPECIFICATIONS

Year	Engine No. Cyl. Displacement (cu. in.)	Timing (deg) Man. Trans.	Timing (deg) Auto. Trans.	Minimum Compression (lbs)	Valves Intake Opens (deg)	Fuel Pump Pressure (psi) ②	Idle Speed (rpm) Man. Trans.	Idle Speed (rpm) Auto. Trans.
1980	8-350	—	①	275	16	5.5–6.5	—	600
1981	8-350	—	①	275	16	5.5–6.5	—	575/600
1982–'84	8-350	—	4 at DC	275	16	5.5–6.5	—	600

NOTE: The underhood specifications sticker often reflects tune-up changes made in production. Sticker figures must be used if they disagree with those in this chart.

① Align the timing marks on the injection pump and drive flange.

② Fuel transfer pressure given—Injection pump = 8-12 PSI @ 1000 rpm (take the reading at the injection pump pressure tap—injector opening can be as high as 1225 psi).

TORQUE SPECIFICATIONS

(All readings in ft. lbs.)

Engine	Cylinder Head Bolts	Rod Bearing Bolts	Main Bearing Bolts	Crankshaft Bolt	Flywheel to Crankshaft Bolts	Manifold Intake	Manifold Exhaust
350	130 ①	42	120	200–310	60	40 ①	25

① Clean and dip entire bolt in engine oil before tightening to obtain a correct torque reading.

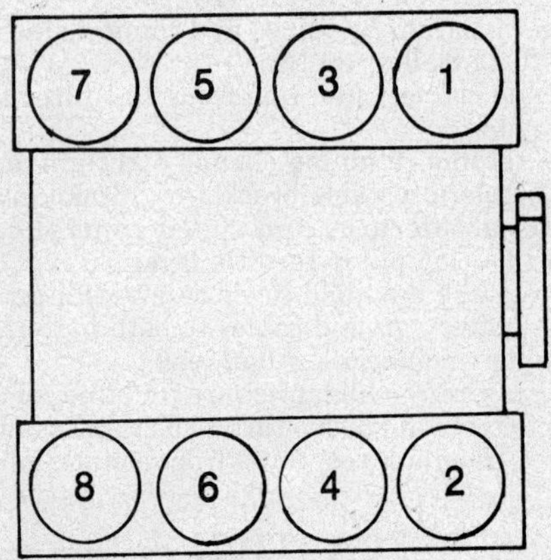

Engine firing order 1-8-4-3-6-5-7-2 (© General Motors Corp.)

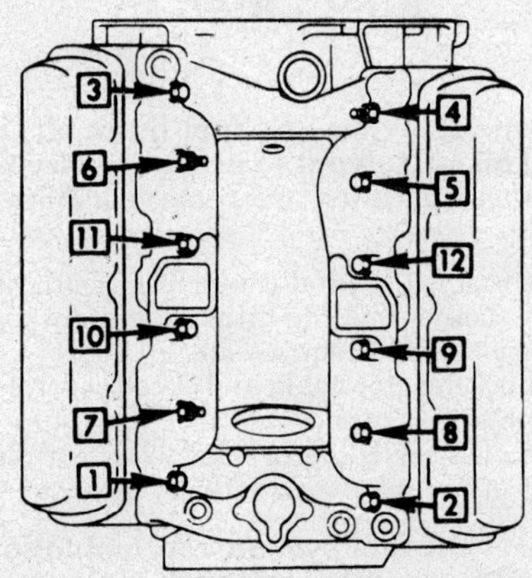

Intake manifold bolt torque sequence (© General Motors Corp.)

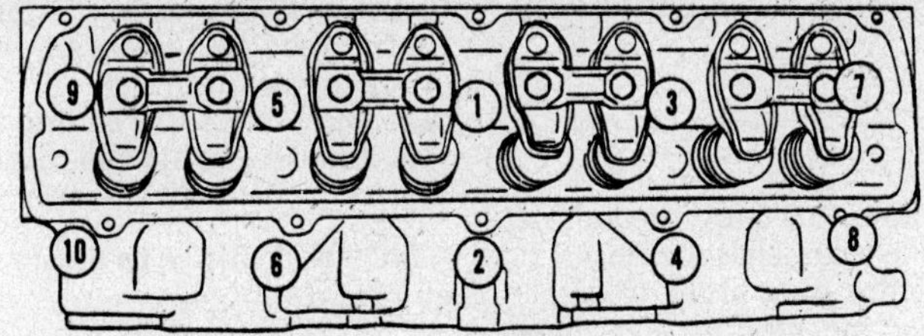

Cylinder head bolt torque sequence (© General Motors Corp.)

TUNE-UP AND ADJUSTMENTS

Compression Test

When checking the compression, always make sure that the batteries are at or near full charge. The total reading for any given cylinder is not as important as the difference between all cylinders. The cylinder with the lowest reading should not be less than 70% of the one with the highest reading and no cylinder should be less than 275 psi.

1. Remove the air cleaner and cover the air crossover.
2. Disconnect the wire from the fuel solenoid terminal on the injection pump.
3. Tag and disconnect all glow plug wiring and then remove the glow plugs.
4. Screw a compression gauge into the hole of the cylinder that is being checked.
5. Crank the engine. Six "puffs" per cylinder should be enough for an accurate reading. Normal compression will build up quickly and evenly if the cylinder is OK.

NOTE: Never add oil to any cylinder during a compression test, as extensive damage may result.

6. Installation is in the reverse order.

Valve Adjustment

This engine uses hydraulic valve lifters; no adjustment is necessary or possible.

Injection Timing

Adjustment

1980–81 MODELS

For the engine to be properly timed, the marks on the top of the injection pump adapter and the flange of the injection pump must be in alignment. This is done with the engine turned off.

1. Loosen the three pump retaining nuts with the proper tool.
2. Use a one in. open end wrench on the boss at the front of the injection pump and rotate the pump until the two timing marks align.
3. Tighten the retaining nuts to 35 ft. lbs. and then adjust the throttle rod.

Establishing A New Timing Mark

When a new injection pump adapter has been installed you will need to make a new timing mark also.

1. File off the original mark on the adapter. DO NOT file off the mark on the pump flange.
2. Position the no. 1 cylinder at TDC of the compression stroke.
3. Align the mark on the vibration balancer with the zero mark on the indicator. The position of the injection pump driven gear should be offset to the right when the No. 1 cylinder is at TDC.
4. Install a special timing tool into the pump adapter. Torque the tool toward the no. 1 cylinder to 50 ft. lbs.

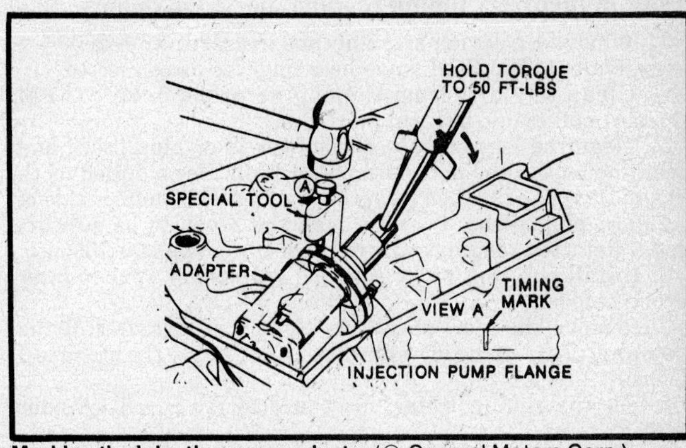

Marking the injection pump adapter (© General Motors Corp.)

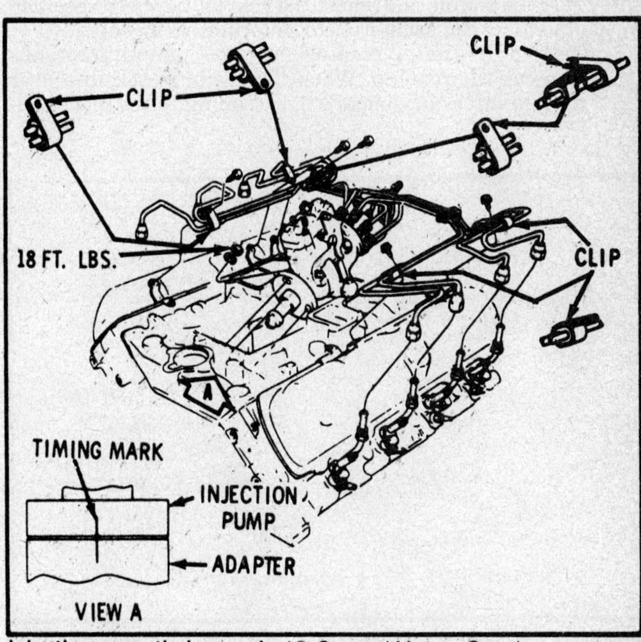

Injection pump timing marks (© General Motors Corp.)

5. Mark the pump adapter, remove the special tool and install the injection pump.

Checking Timing

1982 AND LATER

The timing meter J–33075 or equivalent picks up the engine speed and crankshaft position from the crankshaft balancer. It uses a luminosity signal through a glow plug probe to determine combustion timing. Certain engine malfunctions may cause incorrect timing readings. Engine malfunctions should be corrected before a timing adjustment is made. The marks on the pump and adapter flange will normally be aligned within 0.050 in. (1.27mm).

NOTE: Alignment of timing marks may be used in emergency situations (i.e. timing meter not available). However for optimum engine operation, the timing should be adjusted with the timing meter as soon as possible.

1. Place transmission selector lever in park, apply parking brake and block drive wheels.
2. Start the engine and let it run at idle until fully warmed up. Then shut off the engine.

NOTE: Failure to have the engine fully warmed up will result in incorrect timing reading and adjustments.

3. Remove air cleaner assembly and install cover J–26996–1 or equivalent. The EGR valve hose must be disconnected.
4. Clean any dirt from the engine probe holder (RPM counter) and crankshaft balancer rim.
5. Clean the lens on both ends of the glow plug probe and clean the lens in the photo-electric pick-up. Use a dulled tooth pick to scrape the carbon from the combustion chamber side of the glow plug probe. Look through the probe to be sure its clean. Retarted readings will result if the probe is not clean.
6. Install the rpm probe into the crankshaft rpm counter (probe holder).
7. Remove the glow plug from No. 1 cylinder. Install the glow plug probe in the glow plug opening. Torque the probe to 9 ft. lbs. (12 Nm).
8. Set the timing meter offset selector to the 8 cylinder setting.
9. Connect the battery leads; red to positive, black to negative.
10. Start the engine and adjust the rpm to the speed specified on the "Vehicle Emission Control Information Label".
11. Observe the timing reading then at 2 minute intervals, again observe the reading. When the readings stabilize over the 2 minute interval, compare that reading to the one specified on the "Vehicle Emission Control Information Label". The timing reading, when set to specification will be "Negative" (after top dead center).
12. Disconnect the timing meter.
13. Lubricate only the threads of the removed glow plug with lubricant 9985462 or equivalent.

NOTE: Failure to apply the correct lubricant can cause engine damage.

14. Install the removed glow plug. Torque the glow plug to 15 ft. lbs. (21 Nm).
15. Install the air cleaner being certain to reconnect the EGR valve hose.

Adjusting Timing

1982 AND LATER

1. Shut off the engine.
2. Note the relative position of the marks on the pump flange and pump intermediate adapter.
3. Loosen the bolts holding the pump to the adapter to a point where the pump can be rotated. Use a 1" open end wrench. (Tool J–25304 has the proper offset on the handle to clear the fuel return line).
4. Rotate the pump to the left to advance the timing and to the right to retard the timing. The width of the mark on the intermediate adapter is about 2/3 degree. Move the pump the amount that is needed and tighten the pump retaining bolts to 35 ft. lbs. (47 Nm).
5. Start the engine and recheck the timing reading as outlined previously. Reset and recheck the timing if needed.
6. Reset the fast and curb idle speeds. Both procedures are in this section.
    a. Sooty or dirty probes will result in retarded readings.
    b. The luminosity probe will soot up very fast when used in a cold engine.
    c. Wild needle fluctuations on the timing meter indicate a cylinder not firing properly. Correction of this condition must be made prior to adjusting the timing.

Mechanical Governor

The governor serves the purpose of maintaining the desired engine speed within the operating range under varying load conditions. The limits of throttle travel are set by throttle linkage screws for proper slow idle and maximum high idle. The governor operates automatically and is not adjustable. The maximum high idle is factory set and should not be adjusted at any time. The slow and A/C fast idle settings are adjustable.

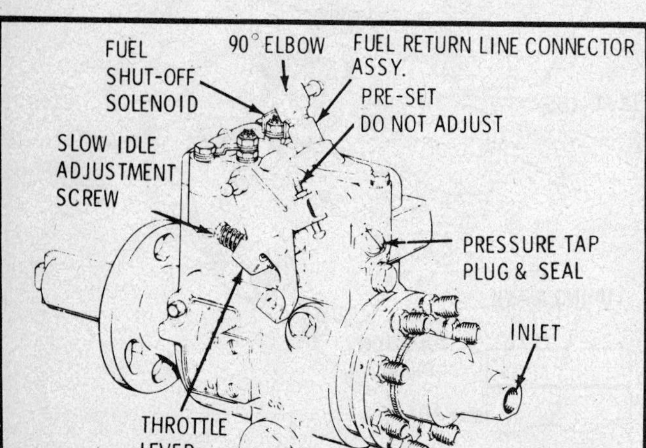

Injection pump slow idle adjustment (© General Motors Corp.)

IDLE SPEED

Slow Idle Adjustment

1. Run the engine until it reaches normal operating temperature.
2. Insert the probe of a magnetic pickup tachometer into the timing indicator hole.
3. Set the parking brake and block the drive wheels.
4. Place the transmission in Drive and turn the A/C off (if so equipped).
5. Turn the slow idle adjustment screw on the injection pump to obtain the idle speed specified on the emission control label.

Fast Idle Solenoid Adjustment

1. Set the parking brake and block the drive wheels.
2. Run the engine until it reaches normal operating temperature.
3. Place the transmission in Drive and disconnect the compressor clutch wire.

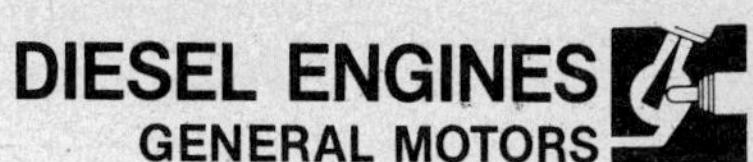

4. Turn the A/C on. On cars without A/C, disconnect the solenoid wire and then connect jumper wires to the solenoid terminals. Ground one wire and connect the other to the battery, this will activate the solenoid.

5. Adjust the fast idle solenoid plunger to obtain the specified rpm.

THROTTLE ROD

Adjustment

1. Check timing.
2. Remove the clip from the cruise control rod (if so equipped) and disconnect the rod from the throttle lever assembly.
3. Disconnect the detent cable from the throttle assembly.
4. Loosen the lock nut on the pump rod and shorten it several turns.
5. Rotate the lever assembly to the full throttle position and hold it there.
6. Lengthen the pump rod until the injection pump lever just contacts the full throttle stop.
7. Release the lever assembly and tighten the pump rod lock nut.
8. Remove the pump rod from the lever assembly and reconnect the detent cable.

DETENT CABLE

Adjustment

NOTE: The throttle rod must be adjusted before adjusting the detent cable.

1. Depress and hold the metal lock tab on the cable upper end.
2. Move the slider through the fitting, away from the lever assembly, until it stops against the metal fitting.
3. Release the metal tab, rotate the lever assembly to the full throttle stop and then release it.
4. Reconnect the pump rod and the cruise control rod (if equipped).

Vacuum Regulator Valve

Adjustment

1. Note the location of the two vacuum hoses and remove the valve. (When installing, the valve must be adjusted.)
2. Remove the air crossover, disconnect the throttle rod from the throttle lever and loosen the vacuum regulator valve injection pump bolts.
3. Place the carburetor angle gauge adapter on the injection pump throttle lever. Place the angle gauge on the adapter.
4. Rotate the throttle lever to wide open throttle and set the angle gauge to zero degrees. Center the bubble in the level and reset the angle gauge to 50 degrees.
5. Rotate the throttle lever to ceter the bubble. Apply an outside vacuum source of 18–22 in. to the inboard port of the vacuum valve. Rotate the valve clockwise to obtain 7–8 in. of vacuum.

Glow Plugs

Eight glow plugs are used to heat the prechamber to aid in starting. They are essentially small heaters that turn on when the ignition switch is turned to the "RUN" position prior to starting the engine. They remain on for a short time after starting and then automatically shut off.

There are two types of glow plugs used on G.M. diesels; the "fast-glow" type and the "slow-glow" type. The fast-glow type use pulsing current applied to 6 volt glow plugs, while the slow-glow type use a continuous current applied to 12 volt glow plugs.

An easy way to tell the plugs apart is that the fast-glow (6V) plugs have a 5/16 in. wide electrical connector plug, while the slow glow (12V) connector is 1/4 in. wide. Do not attempt to interchange any parts of these two glow plug systems.

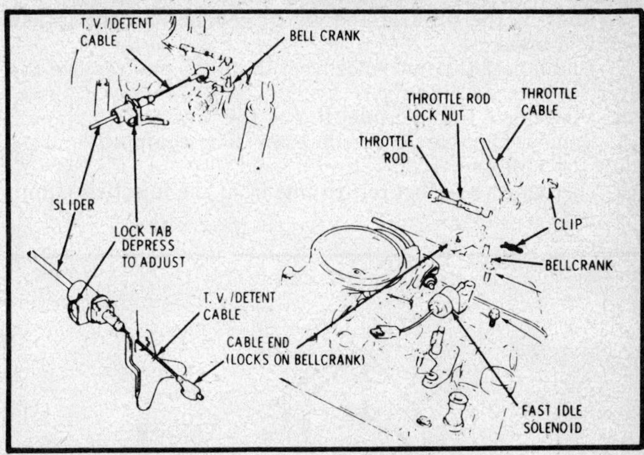

Detent cable adjustment (© General Motors Corp.)

Removal and Installation

NOTE: Use extreme care when removing a glow plug as the tip may break off; requiring cylinder head removal.

1. Tag and disconnect the electrical connectors.
2. Using the large hex nut, loosen the glow plug and carefully lift it out of the cylinder head.
3. Installation is in the reverse order.

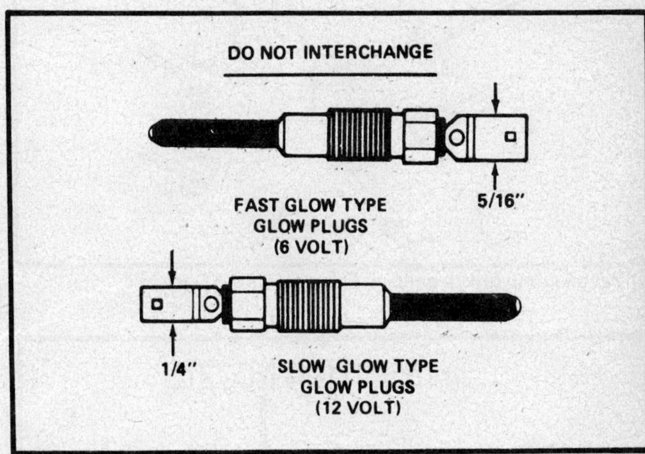

Glow plug identification (© General Motors Corp.)

Injection Pump

Removal

1. Remove the air cleaner.
2. Remove the filters and pipes from the valve covers and air crossover.
3. Remove the air crossover and cap the intake manifold with screened covers or tape.
4. Disconnect the throttle rod and return spring.
5. Remove the bellcrank.

6. Remove the throttle and detent cables from the intake manifold brackets.
7. Disconnect the fuel lines from the filter and remove the filter.
8. Disconnect the fuel inlet line at the pump.
9. Remove the rear A/C compressor (if so equipped) and remove the fuel line.
10. Disconnect the fuel return line from the injection pump.

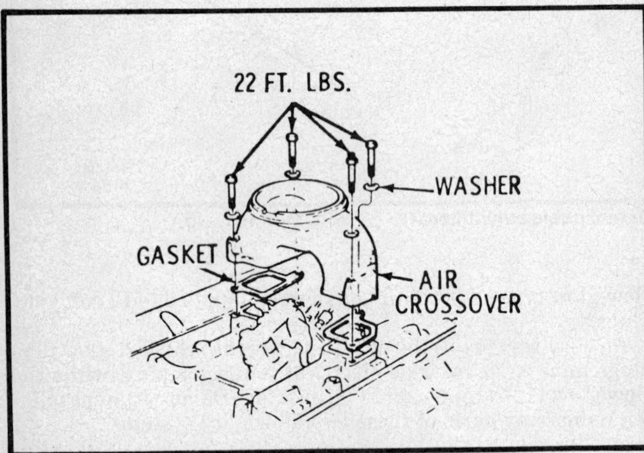

Typical air crossover (© General Motors Corp.)

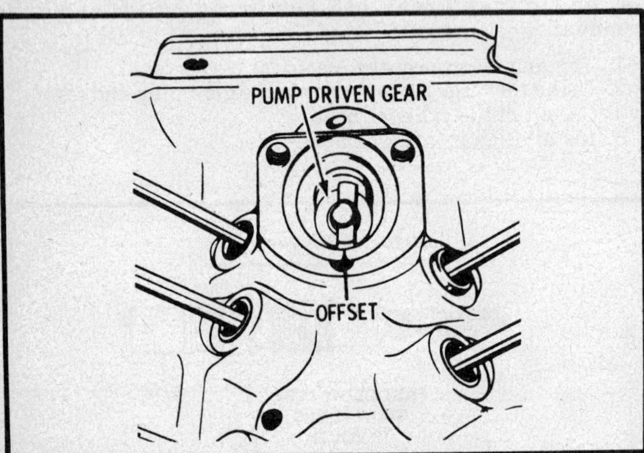

Offset on pump driven gear (© General Motors Corp.)

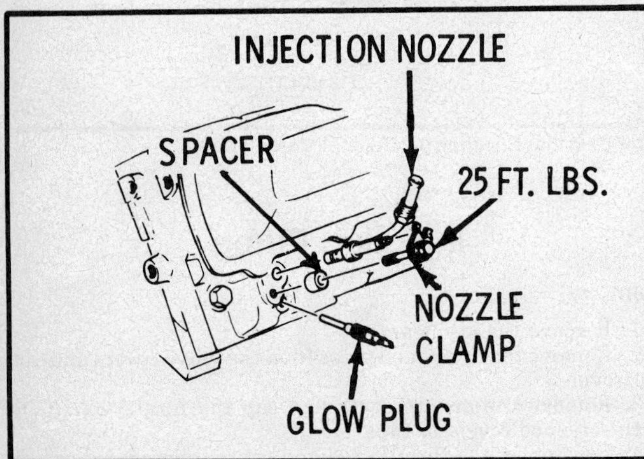

Injector nozzle installation (© General Motors Corp.)

11. Remove the clamps and pull the fuel return lines from each injection nozzle.
12. Using two wrenches, disconnect the high pressure lines at the nozzles.
13. Remove the three injection pump retaining nuts.
14. Remove the pump and cap all lines and nozzles.

Installation

1. Remove the protective caps from all lines and nozzles. Place the engine on TDC for the no. 1 cylinder. The mark on the harmonic balancer on the crankshaft will be aligned with the zero mark on the timing tab and both valves for no. 1 cylinder will be closed. The index mark on the injection pump driven gear should be offset to the right when no. 1 is at TDC. Check that all of these conditions are met before continuing.
2. Line up the offset tang on the pump driveshaft with the pump driven gear and install the pump.
3. Install, but do not tighten the pump retaining nuts.
4. Connect the high pressure lines at the nozzles.
5. Using two wrenches, torque the high pressure line nuts to 25 ft. lbs.
6. Connect the fuel return lines to the nozzles and pump.
7. Align the timing mark on the injection pump with the line on the pump adaptor and torque the mounting nuts to 35 ft. lbs.

NOTE: A one in. open end wrench on the boss at the front of the injection pump will aid in rotating the pump to align the marks.

8. Adjust the throttle rod.
9. Install the fuel inlet line between the transfer pump and the filter.
10. Install the rear A/C compressor brace (if so equipped).
11. Install the bellcrank and clip.
12. Connect the throttle rod and return spring.
13. Adjust the transmission cable.
14. Start the engine and check for fuel leaks.
15. Remove the screened covers or tape and install the air crossover.
16. Install the tubes in the airflow control valve in the air crossover and install the ventilation filters in the valve covers.
17. Install the air cleaner.
18. Start the engine and allow it to run for two minutes. Stop the engine, let it stand for two minutes, then restart. This permits the air to bleed off within the pump.

Injectors

Removal and Installation

1980–84

The injectors on these engines are simply unscrewed from the cylinder head, after the fuel lines have been removed, much like a spark plug. Be careful not to damage the injector tip and make sure that the copper gasket is removed from the cylinder head if it does not come off with the injector.

Clean the carbon build-up from the tip of the injector. Installation is in the reverse.

NOTE: 1981 and later engines use two types of injectors; CAV Lucas and Diesel Equipment. When installing the inlet fittings, tighten to 45 ft. lbs. on the Diesel Equipment injector and to 25 ft. lbs. on the CAV injector.

Injection Pump Fuel Lines

When any fuel lines are to be removed, clean all the fittings before loosening. Immediately cap all lines, nozzles and fittings to maintain system cleanliness.

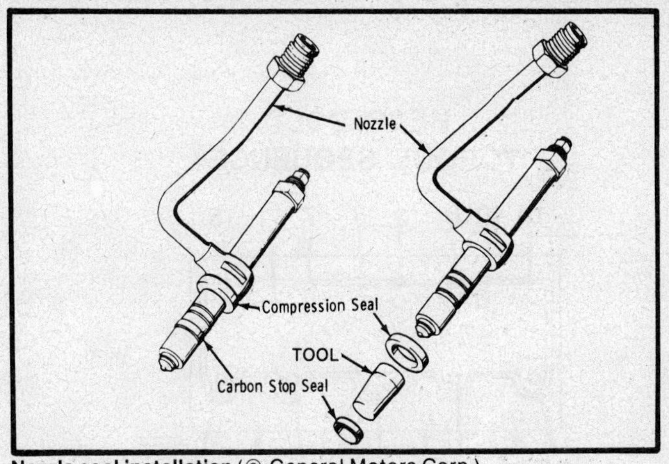

Nozzle seal installation (© General Motors Corp.)

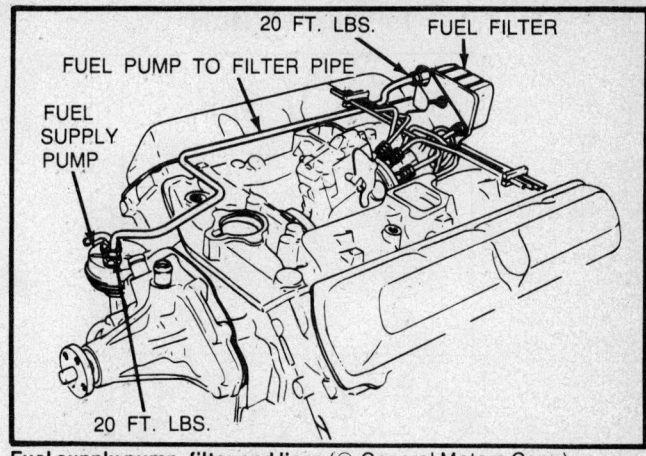

20 FT. LBS.
FUEL FILTER
FUEL PUMP TO FILTER PIPE
FUEL SUPPLY PUMP
20 FT. LBS.

Fuel supply pump, filter and lines (© General Motors Corp.)

G.M. DIESEL ENGINE 6.2 LITER, 379 CU. IN. V8

GENERAL ENGINE SPECIFICATIONS

Engine No. Cyl. Displacement (cu. in.)	Carburetor Type	Horsepower @ rpm	Torque @ rpm (ft lbs)	Bore × Stroke (in.)	Compression Ratio	Oil Pressure @ 2000 rpm
8–379	Diesel	130 @ 3600	240 @ 2000	3.98 × 3.80	21.5:1	NA

NA—Not available

TUNE-UP SPECIFICATIONS

Engine No. Cyl. Displacement (cu. in.)	Ignition Timing (deg)①		Compression (lbs)	Valves Intake Opens (deg)	Fuel Pump Pressure (psi)	Idle Speed (rpm)①	
	Man Trans.	Auto. Trans.				Slow	Fast
8–379			275	NA	5.5–6.5	575/550	700

NOTE: The underhood specifications sticker often reflects tune-up specification changes made in the production run. Sticker figures must be used if they differ with those in this chart.

① Where two figures are separated by a slash, the first is for manual trans, the second is for auto trans.

NA—Not available

TORQUE SPECIFICATIONS

All readings in ft. lbs.

Engine	Cylinder Head Bolts	Rod Bearing Bolts	Main Bearing Bolts	Crankshaft Bolt	Flywheel to Crankshaft Bolts	Manifold	
						Intake	Exhaust
379	88–103	44–52	①	140–162	NA	25–37	18–25

NA—Not available

① Inner: 105–117
Outer: 94–105

Engine firing order: 1-8-7-2-6-5-4-3

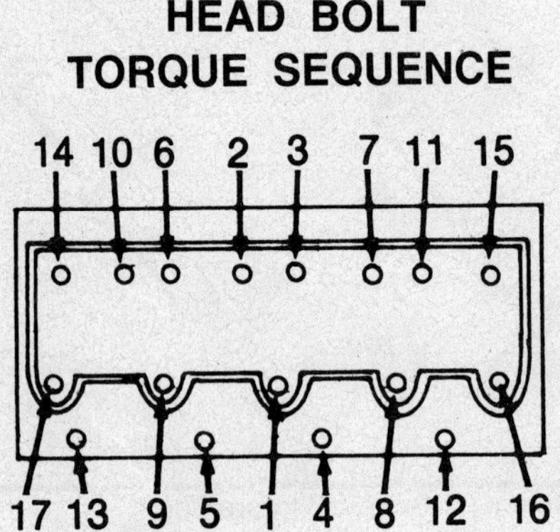

Cylinder head torque sequence

DESCRIPTION

The 6.2 liter, 379 cu. in. V8, 4 cycle diesel is developed and produced by Chevrolet. It is a totally new engine designed specifically for truck application with heavy duty usage in mind.

The base of the engine (short block) is very similar in design to a V8 gasoline engine; the major difference being the cylinder heads, combustion chamber, fuel distribution system, air intake manifold and the method of ignition. The cylinder block, crankshaft, main bearings, connecting rods and pistons look much the same as their gasoline engine counterparts, although they are of much heavier construction due to the higher compression ratio required to ignite diesel fuel. The intake and exhaust manifolds are of special design and construction.

The cylinder head incorporates a 17 bolt head design which locates 5 bolts around each cylinder. This helps gasket durability. It also includes a high swirl pre-combustion chamber which mixes fuel and air to provide an efficient fuel burn and low emissions. A special cavity in the piston top further assists in mixing the combustion products for complete burning.

Main bearing caps all use 4 bolts instead of the normal 2 to provide rigid support for the crankshaft and minimize stress. The rolled fillet nodular iron crankshaft utilizes a torsional damper, tuned to reduce vibrations.

The engine also uses roller hydraulic lifters running on a forged steel camshaft.

TUNE-UP AND ADJUSTMENT

Compression Test

When checking the compression, always make sure that the batteries are at or near full charge. The total reading for any given cylinder is not as important as the difference between all cylinders. The cylinder with lowest reading should not be less than 70% of the one with the highest reading and no cylinder should be less than 275 psi.

1. Remove the air cleaner and cover the air crossover.
2. Disconnect the wire from the fuel solenoid terminal on the injection pump.
3. Tag and disconnect all glow plug wiring and then remove the glow plugs.
4. Screw a compression gauge into the hole of the cylinder that is being checked.
5. Crank the engine. Six "puffs" per cylinder should be enough for an accurate reading. Normal compression will build up quickly and evenly if the cylinder is OK.

NOTE: Never add oil to any cyinder during a compression test, as extensive damage may result.

6. Installation is in the reverse order.

Valve Adjustment

This engine uses roller hydraulic valve lifters; no adjustment is necessary or possible.

Injection Timing

Adjustment

For the engine to be properly timed, the marks on top of the engine front cover and the injection pump flange must be aligned. This is done with the engine turned off.

1. Loosen the three pump retaining nuts.
2. Use the proper tool and rotate the pump until the two timing marks are in alignment.
3. Tighten the retaining nuts to 30 ft. lbs. and then adjust the throttle rod.

Establishing a New Timing Mark

When a new front cover has been installed, a new timing mark will also be required.

1. Remove the injection pump and then position the No. 1 cylinder at TDC of the compression stroke.
2. Install a special timing tool into the injection pump. Do not use a gasket.
3. The slot on the injection pump gear should be in the vertical 6 o'clock position and the timing marks on the gears will be aligned. If not, remove the tool and rotate the engine 360°.
4. Fasten the gear to the fixture and tighten.
5. Install a 10mm nut to the upper housing stud to hold the fixture flange nut finger tight.
6. Torque the large bolt (18mm) counterclockwise (toward left bank) to 50 ft. lbs. Tighten the 10mm nut.
7. Make sure that the crankshaft has not rotated and the fixture did not bind on the 10mm nut.
8. Strike a scriber with a mallet to mark the TDC position on the front cover.
9. Remove the tool, install the injection pump and attach the gear to the pump hub.
10. Adjust injection timing.

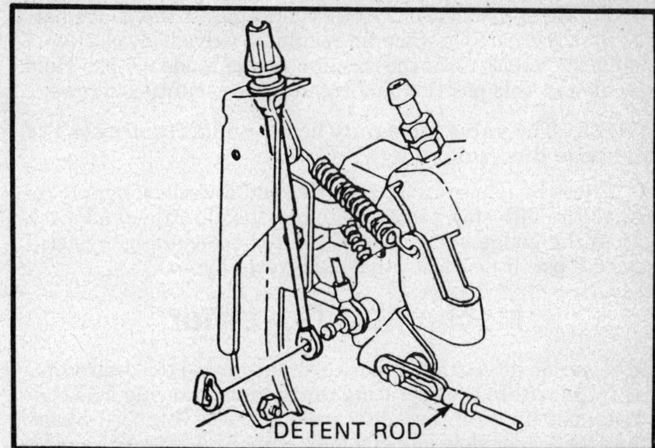

Accelerator linkage (© General Motors Corp.)

Throttle Position Switch Adjustment

1. Loose assemble throttle position switch to the injection pump with the throttle lever in the closed position.
2. Attach an ohmmeter across the IGN (pink) and EGR (yellow) terminals or wires.
3. Insert the proper "switch-closed" gauge block between the gauge boss on the injection pump and the wide open stop screw on the throttle shaft.
4. Rotate and hold the throttle lever against the gauge block.
5. Rotate the throttle switch clockwise (facing throttle switch) until continuity just occurs (high meter reading) across the IGN and EGR terminals or wires. Hold the switch body in this position and tighten the mounting screws.

NOTE: The switch point must only be set while rotating the switch body in the clockwise direction.

6. Release the throttle lever and allow it to return to the idle position. Remove the "switch-closed" gauge bar and insert a "switch-open" gauge bar.
7. Rotate the throttle lever against the "switch-open" gauge bar. There should be no continuity across the IGN and EGR terminals or wires.
8. If no continuity exists, the switch is set properly. If there is continuity, the switch must be reset by repeating the entire procedure again.

Transmission Vacuum Regulator Valve

Adjustment

1. Attach the vacuum regulator valve snugly, but loosely, to the injection pump. The switch body must be free to rotate on the pump.
2. Apply approximately 9–10 psi of vacuum to the inboard nipple. Attach a vacuum gauge to the outboard nipple.
3. Insert a vacuum regulator valve gauge bar between the gauge boss on the injection pump and the wide open stop screw on the throttle lever.

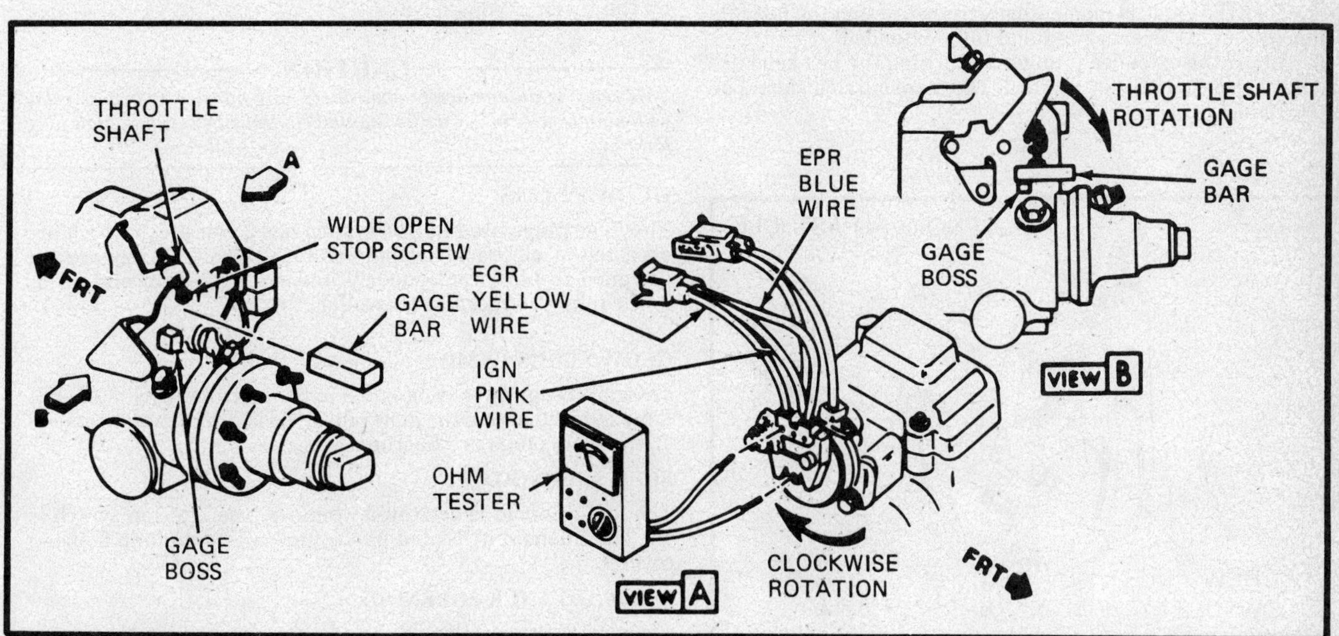

Throttle position switch adjustment (© General Motors Corp.)

4. Rotate and hold the throttle shaft against the gauge bar.
5. Slowly rotate the vacuum regulator valve body clockwise (facing the valve) until the vacuum gauge reads 5.6 psi. Hold the valve at this position and tighten the mounting screws.

NOTE: The valve must only be set while rotating in the clockwise direction.

6. Check by releasing the throttle shaft and allowing it to return to the idle stop position. Rotate the throttle shaft back against the gauge bar and check that the vacuum gauge still reads 5.6 psi. If not, the valve must reset again.

Mechanical Governor

The governor serves the purpose of maintaining the desired engine speed within the operating range under varying load conditions. The limits of throttle travel are set by throttle linkage screws for proper slow idle and maximum high idle. The governor operates automatically and is not adjustable. The maximum high idle is factory set and should not be adjusted at any time. The slow and A/C fast idle settings are adjustable.

Idle Speed

Slow Idle Adjustment

1. Run the engine until it reaches nornal operating temperature.
2. Set the parking brake and block the drive wheels.
3. Remove the air cleaner and turn all accessories off.
4. Install a diesel tachometer
5. Turn the low idle speed screw on the injection pump until the proper idle is obtained. Automatic transmissions should be in Drive and manual transmissions should be in Neutral.
6. Disconnect the tachometer and install the air cleaner.

Fast Idle Speed Adjustment

1. Run the engine until it reaches normal operating temperature.
2. Set the parking brake and block the drive wheels.
3. Disconnect the connector from the fast idle solenoid. Connect an insulated jumper wire between the positive battery terminal and the solenoid terminal. This will energize the terminal.
4. Open the throttle momentarily to ensure that the fast idle solenoid plunger is energized and fully extended.
5. Adjust the extended plunger by turning the hex head until the proper fast idle is obtained. The transmission should be in Neutral.

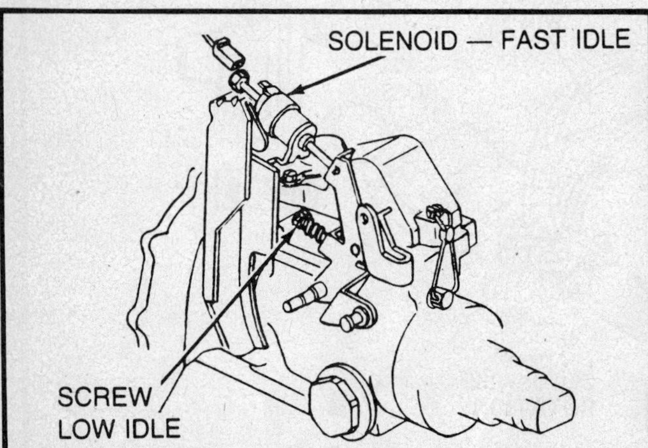

Idle speed adjustment (© General Motors Corp.)

6. Remove the jumper wire, reinstall the solenoid connector and disconnect the tachometer.

Glow Plugs

Eight glow plugs are used to preheat the chamber as an aid to starting. They are essentially small 12 volt heaters that turn on when the ignition switch is turned to the "Run" position prior to starting the engine. They remain on for a short time after starting and them automatically shut off.

Removal and Installation

NOTE: Use extreme care when removing the glow plugs as the tip may break off; requiring cylinder head removal to retrieve it.

1. Tag and disconnect the electrical connectors.
2. Using the large hex nut, loosen the plug and carefully pull it out of the cylinder head.
3. Installation is in the reverse order.

System Operation

The 6.2 liter diesel glow plug control system consists of a thermal controller, glow plug relay, 6 volt glow plugs and a "Glow Plugs" lamp. Other components which have no function in controlling glow plug operation but are part of the electrical system start and run operations are: fuel solenoid, fast idle and cold advance solenoids, cold advance temperature switch and the TCC, ECR and EPR solenoids.

They are 6 volt glow plugs (operated at 12 volts) that turn on when the ignition key is turned to the run position. They remain pulsing a short time after starting, then automatically turn off.

CONTROLLER

The thermal controller is mounted in the water passage at the rear of the engine. Thermostatic elements within the controller are designed to open or close the ground circuit to the glow plug relay as necessary to control the pre-heat and afterglow cycles of glow plug operation.

GLOW PLUG RELAY

The glow plug relay located on the left inner fender panel provides current to the glow plugs. The relay is pulsed on and off by the thermal controller.

CAUTION

This relay is automatically controlled. Any attempt to bypass relay with jumper wire or rewire for manual control may result in glow plug failure.

GLOW PLUGS

The glow plugs used in this system are 6 volt plugs which are operated at electrical system voltage (12 volts). They are not designed to burn continuously and are pulsed on and off as needed, by the thermal controller.

GLOW PLUGS LAMP

The glow plugs lamp is mounted in the instrument cluster. The lamp is wired across the glow plugs and is illuminated whenever the glow plugs are heating.

FUEL SOLENOID

The fuel solenoid is activated whenever the ignition switch is on. The solenoid is located in the fuel injection pump housing cover.

COLD ADVANCE SOLENOID

The cold advance solenoid, also located in the injection pump cover, is controlled by a cold advance temperature switch

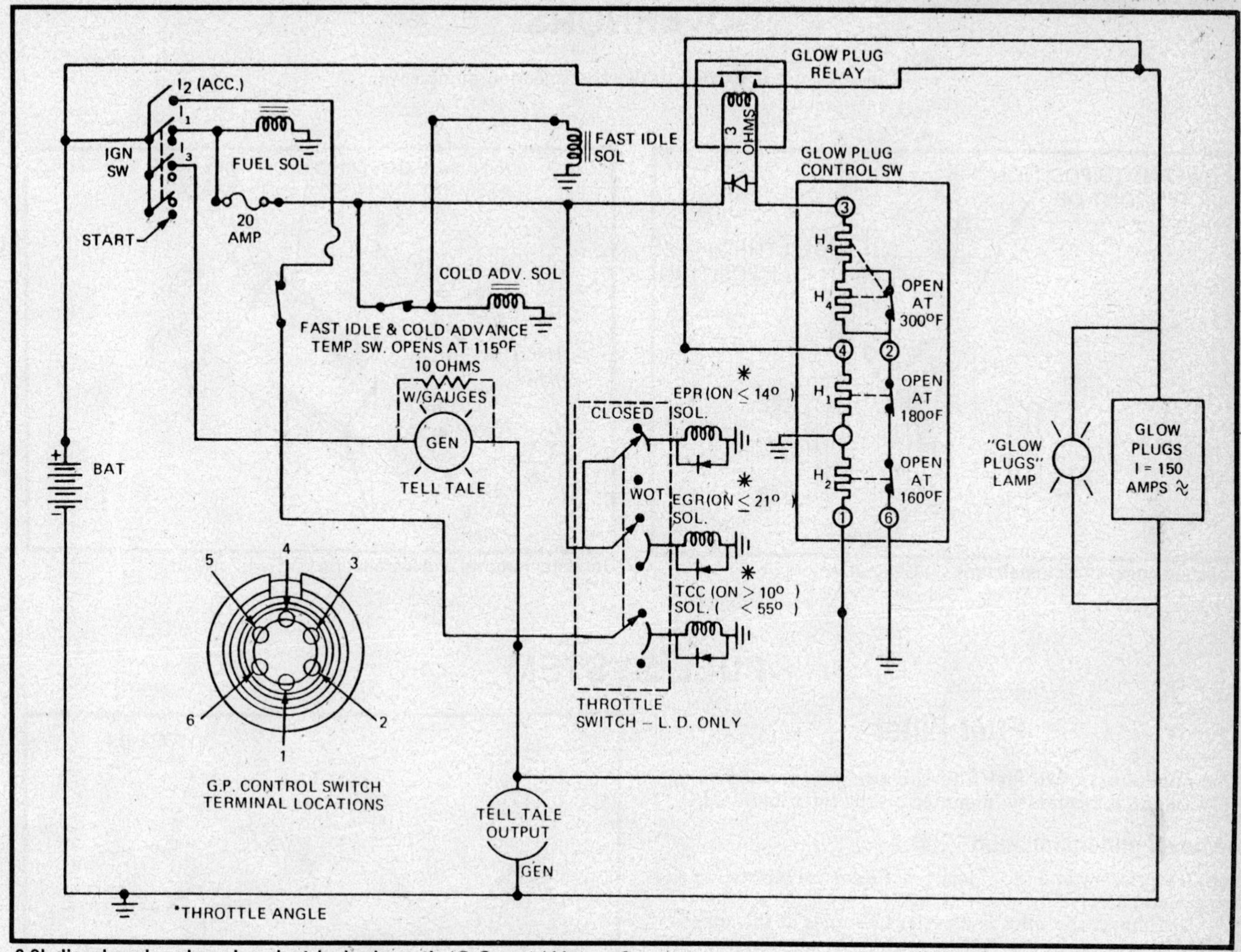

6.2L diesel engine glow plug electrical schematic (© General Motors Corp.)

which activates this solenoid and the fast idle solenoid at a specified minimum temperature. The switch should be closed below 90°F and open above 122°F.

CIRCUIT OPERATION – COLD START

With the ignition switch in "Run" the following events take place simultaneously.

1. The fuel solenoid is energized opening the fuel metering valve. The fuel heater is powered provided the temperature is low enough to require heating of the fuel.
2. Battery voltage is applied to the fast idle solenoid and cold advance solenoid through the fast idle/cold advance temperature switch (when closed).
3. Battery current flows through the thermal controller circuits and through the glow plug relay coil to ground.
4. The glow plugs lamp which is wired across the glow plugs, comes on whenever the glow plugs are powered.
5. The thermal controller starts the glow plugs heating cycle.

Initially, the glow plugs are activated continuously for a period of 7½ to 9 seconds at 0°F. The glow plugs then begin to pulse on and off at a rate determined by the thermal characteristics of the controller. The initial current brings the glow plug preheat chamber up to the temperature required for cold starting. The pulse cycle (on and off) acts to maintain chamber temperature to provide stable engine warm up. As the engine warms up, the thermal controller turns off all current to the relay de-energizing the glow plugs completely. The controller is capable of varying glow plug operation as required (up to one minute) when the engine is started warm and little or no heating is necessary.

Controller failure as in the case of prolonged preheat (more than 9 seconds) would cause a circuit breaker in the controller to open, cutting off glow plug operation completely.

GOVERNORS

The governor is located under the injection pump cover.

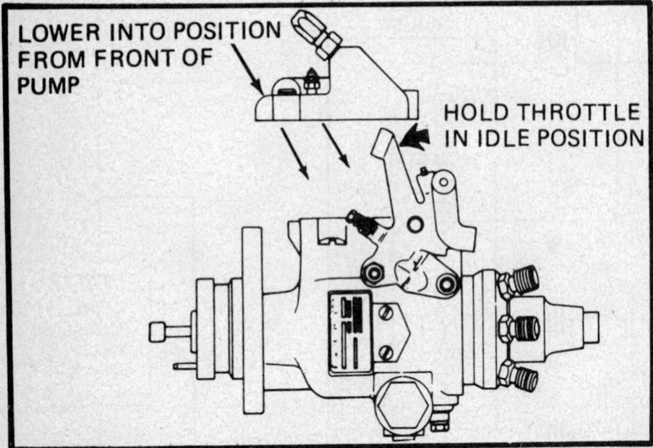

Injection pump cover installation (© General Motors Corp.)

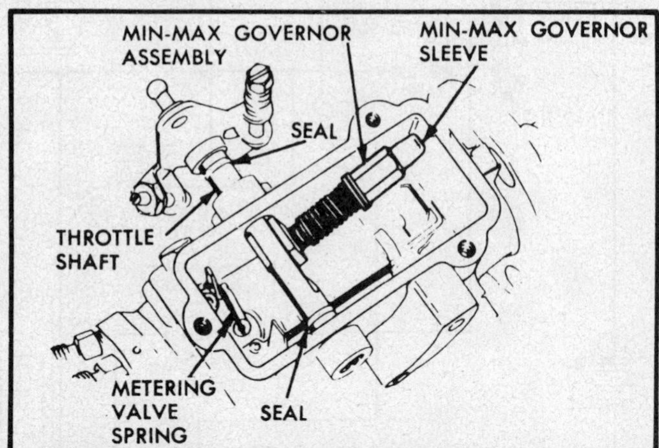

Governor removal and installation (© General Motors Corp.)

FUEL SYSTEM

Fuel Filter

This engine uses two fuel filters; a primary, located on the firewall and a secondary, mounted on the inlet manifold.

Removal and Installation

Both the primary and secondary fuel filters are serviced in the same manner.

1. Disconnect the inlet and outlet fuel lines at the adapter.
2. Unscrew mounting bolts and remove adapter from the inlet/firewall.
3. Unscrew filter from adapter.

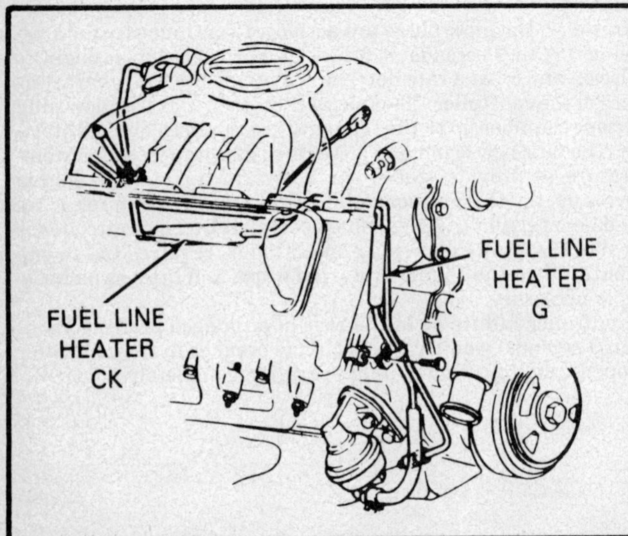

Fuel line heater location on varied models
(© General Motors Corp.)

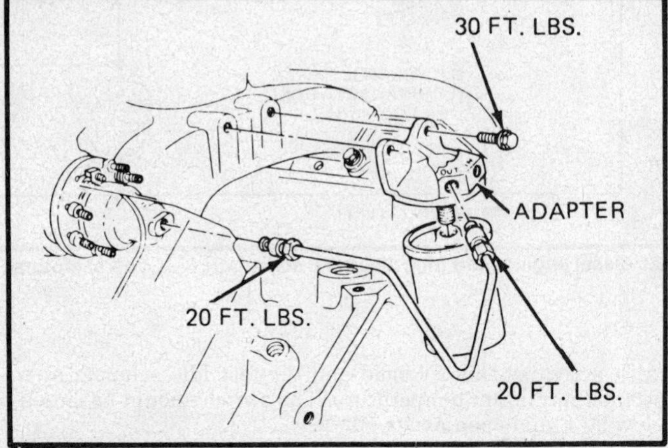

Secondary fuel filter on CK models—Other models similar
(© General Motors Corp.)

4. Anytime either of the filters are removed or replaced, refill with clean diesel fuel to prevent stalling after start up and to avoid long engine cranking time.
5. Screw the filter onto the adapter.
6. Remount the adapter and install the fuel lines.
7. Run engine and check for leaks.

Water Drain

Water can be drained from the primary fuel filter only.

1. Open the petcock on top of the primary filter housing.
2. Place a drain pan below the filter and open the petcock on the bottom of the filter.

NOTE: A length of hose can be attached to the petcock to direct the drained fuel below the frame.

3. When all water is drained, close both petcocks tightly. If all fuel in the filter has been drained, remove the filter and fill it with clean diesel fuel.

4. Start the engine and let it run briefly. It may run rough at first until all air is purged from the system. If roughness continues, check that both petcocks are closed tightly.

Fuel Line Heater

Removal and Installation

1. Disconnect the batteries and remove the air cleaner.
2. Remove the crankcase ventilator bracket from the intake manifold and position it out of the way.
3. Disconnect the fuel lines to the secondary fuel filter and then remove the filter.
4. Loosen the vacuum pump hold-down clamp and rotate the pump to gain access to the manifold bolts.
5. Remove the intake manifold. Install screened covers or tape over the openings.
6. Remove all but #5 and #7 fuel injection lines. Cap all lines, nozzles and fittings.
7. Disconnect the fuel line at the fuel supply pump.
8. Disconnect the fuel line clip and the wire connector.
9. Remove the fuel line heater and the fuel line to the primary filter.
10. Installation is in the reverse order.

Fuel Supply Pump

These engines use a small mechanical fuel pump (much like the ones on gasoline engines) to deliver fuel from the tank and lines to the injection pump.

Removal and Installation

1. Disconnect and plug the two fuel lines.
2. Remove the two mounting bolts.
3. Remove the pump and gasket.
4. Install the pump and gasket. Tighten the mounting bolts to 27 ft. lbs.
5. Install both fuel lines.
6. Start the engine and check for leaks.

Injection Pump

Removal

1. Disconnect the batteries.
2. Remove the fan and the fan shroud.

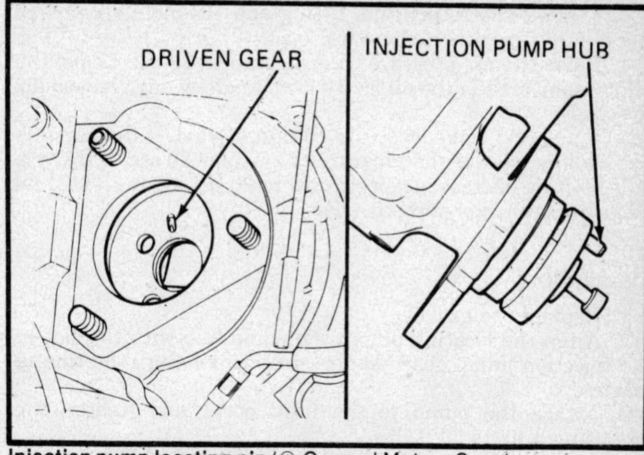

Injection pump locating pin (© General Motors Corp.)

3. Remove the intake manifold.
4. Remove all fuel lines. Cap all lines, nozzles and fittings.
5. Disconnect the accelerator cables at the injection pump. Disconnect the detent cable if applicable.
6. Tag and disconnect all necessary wires and hoses at the injection pump.
7. Disconnect the fuel return line and the line at the pump.
8. If equipped with AC, remove the AC hose retainer bracket.
9. Remove the oil filler tube complete with PCV vent hose assembly.
10. Scribe or paint a mark on the front cover and align, alignment mark on pump and front cover.
11. It will be necessary to rotate the engine in order to gain access to the injection pump retaining bolts through the oil filler neck hole.
12. Remove the pump-to-front cover nuts, remove the pump and cap all lines and fittings.

Testing

1. Drain all fuel from the pump.
2. Connect an air line to the pump inlet connection. Make sure that the air supply is clean and dry.

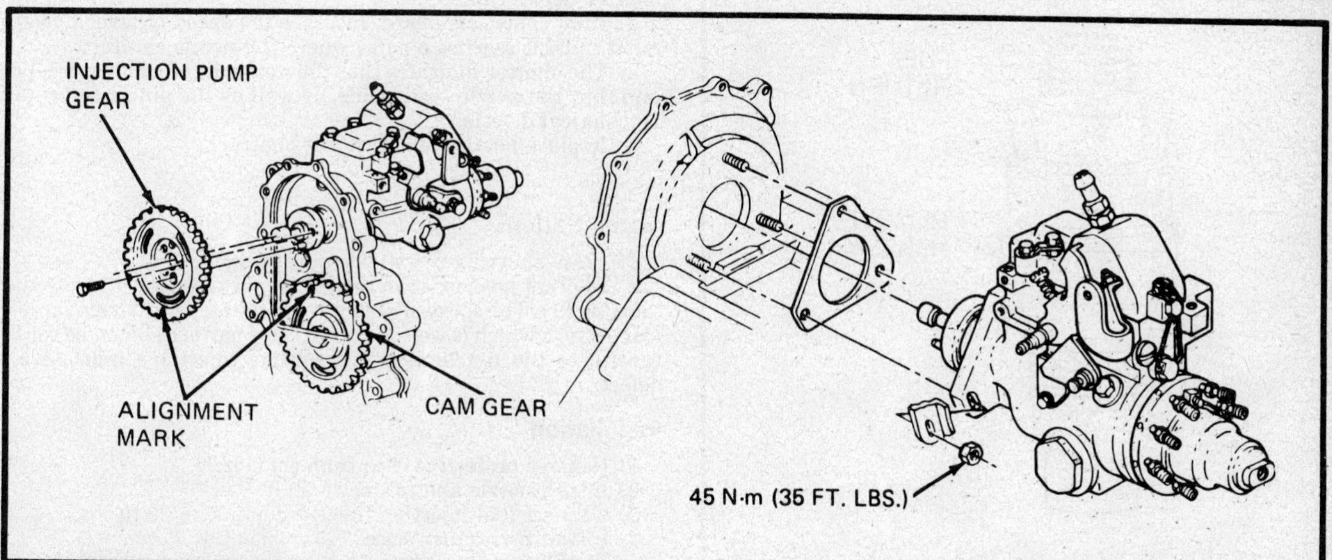

Injection pump installation (© General Motors Corp.)

3. Seal off the return line fitting and completely immerse the pump in a bath of clean test oil.
4. Raise the air pressure in the pump to 20 psi. Leave the pump immersed in the oil for 10 min. to allow any trapped air to escape.
5. Watch for leaks after the 10 min. period. If the pump is not leaking, reduce the pressure to 2 psi for 30 sec. If there is still no leak, increase the pressure to 20 psi again. If still no leaks are seen, the pump is OK.

Installation

1. Replace the gasket.
2. Align the locating pin on the pump hub with the slot in the injection pump gear. At the same time, align the timing marks.
3. Attach the pump to the front cover and tighten the mounting nuts to 30 ft. lbs.
4. Attach pump-to-drive gear and tighten the bolts to 20 ft. lbs.
5. Install the oil filler tube along with the PCV vent hose assembly.
6. Install the AC hose retainer bracket if removed.
7. Install the fuel line at the pump and tighten to 20 ft. lbs. Install the fuel return line.
8. Connect all wires and hoses. Connect the accelerator cable.
9. Connect the injection lines.
10. Install the intake manifold.
11. Install the fan shroud, the fan and connect the batteries.

Injection Nozzle

Removal

1. Disconnect the batteries.
2. Disconnect the fuel line clip and remove the fuel return hose.
3. Remove the fuel injection line.
4. Remove the injection nozzle using the special tool if possible. If not, use a 30mm open end wrench. Be sure to remove the nozzle using the large 30mm hex nut. Failure to do this will result in damage to the injection nozzle. Always cap the nozzle and lines to prevent damage and contamination.

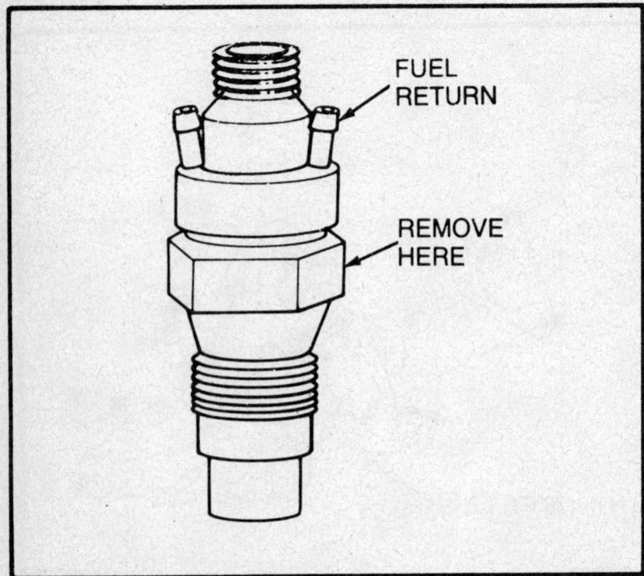

Injection nozzle (© General Motors Corp.)

Testing

If all of the following tests are satisfied, the nozzle holder can be installed in the engine without any changes. If any one of the tests is not satisfied, the complete nozzle holder assembly must be replaced.

Preparation

1. Connect the nozzle holder assembly to the test line.
2. Close the shutoff valve to the pressure gauge.
3. Fill and flush the nozzle holder assembly with test oil by activating the lever repeatedly and briskly. This will apply test oil to all functionally important areas of the nozzle and purge it of air.

Obtaining Pressure Check

1. Open shutoff valve at pressure gauge ¼ turn.
2. Depress lever of tester slowly. Note at what pressure the needle of the pressure gauge stopped, indicating an increase in pressure (nozzle does not chatter) or at which pressure the pressure dropped substantially (nozzle chatters). The maximum observed pressure is the opening pressure.
3. The opening pressure should not fall below the lower limit of 1600 psi.
4. Replace nozzles which fall below the lower limit.

Leakage Test

1. Further open shutoff valve at pressure gauge (½ to 1 ½ turns).
2. Blow-dry nozzle tip.
3. Install two clear plastic lines (approximately 1–1 ½ in.) over leak-off connections.
4. Depress lever of manual test stand slowly until gauge reads a pressure of 1380 psi. Observe tip of nozzle. A drop may form but not drop off within a period of 10 seconds.
5. Replace the nozzle holder assembly if a droplet drops off the nozzle bottom within the 10 seconds.

Chatter Test

1. Close shutoff lever at pressure gauge.
2. Depress lever of manual test stand slowly noting whether chatter noises can be heard.
3. If no chatter is heard, increase the speed of lever movement until it reaches a point where the nozzle chatters.
4. The chatter indicates that the nozzle needle moves freely and that the nozzle seat, guide, as well as the pintle, have no mechanical defects.
5. Replace nozzles which do not chatter.

Spray Pattern

1. Close shutoff valve at pressure gauge.
2. Depress lever of manual test stand downward abruptly and quickly. The spray should have a tight, evenly shaped conical pattern which is well atomized. This pattern should be concentric to the nozzle axis. Streamlike injections indicate a defect.

Installation

1. Remove protective caps from the nozzle.
2. Install nozzle and torque to 50 ft. lbs.
3. Connect fuel injection line, torque nut to 20 ft. lbs.
4. Install fuel return hose.
5. Install fuel line clip.
6. Connect battery.

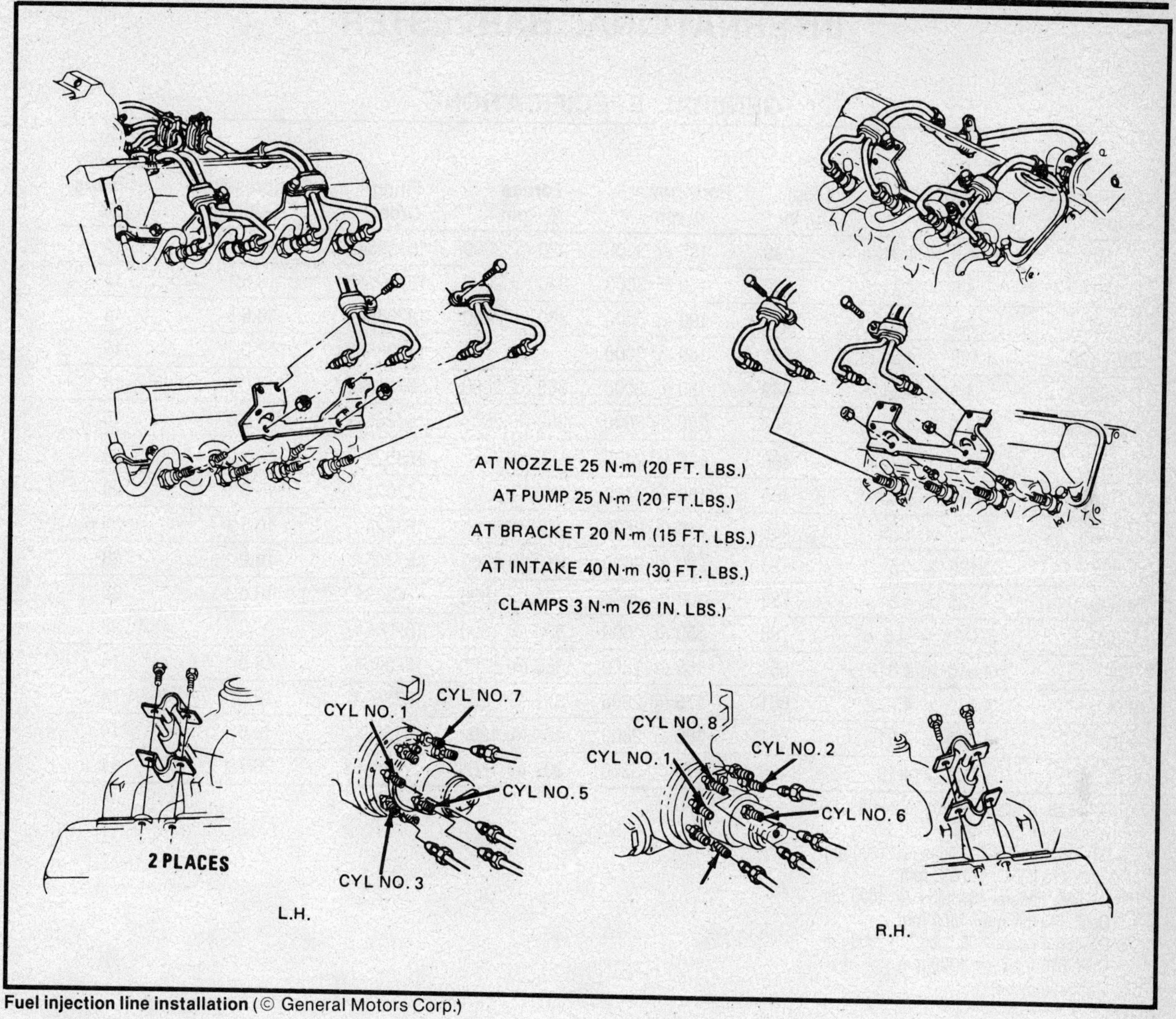

AT NOZZLE 25 N·m (20 FT. LBS.)
AT PUMP 25 N·m (20 FT.LBS.)
AT BRACKET 20 N·m (15 FT. LBS.)
AT INTAKE 40 N·m (30 FT. LBS.)
CLAMPS 3 N·m (26 IN. LBS.)
2 PLACES
CYL NO. 1
CYL NO. 7
CYL NO. 5
CYL NO. 3
L.H.
CYL NO. 8
CYL NO. 1
CYL NO. 2
CYL NO. 6
R.H.

Fuel injection line installation (© General Motors Corp.)

CYL NO. 8
CYL NO. 6
CYL NO. 4
CYL NO. 2
CYL NO. 7
CYL NO. 5
CYL NO. 3
CYL NO. 1
CYL NO. 8
CYL NO. 1
CYL NO. 3
CYL NO. 4
CYL NO. 7
CYL NO. 2
CYL NO. 6
CYL NO. 5

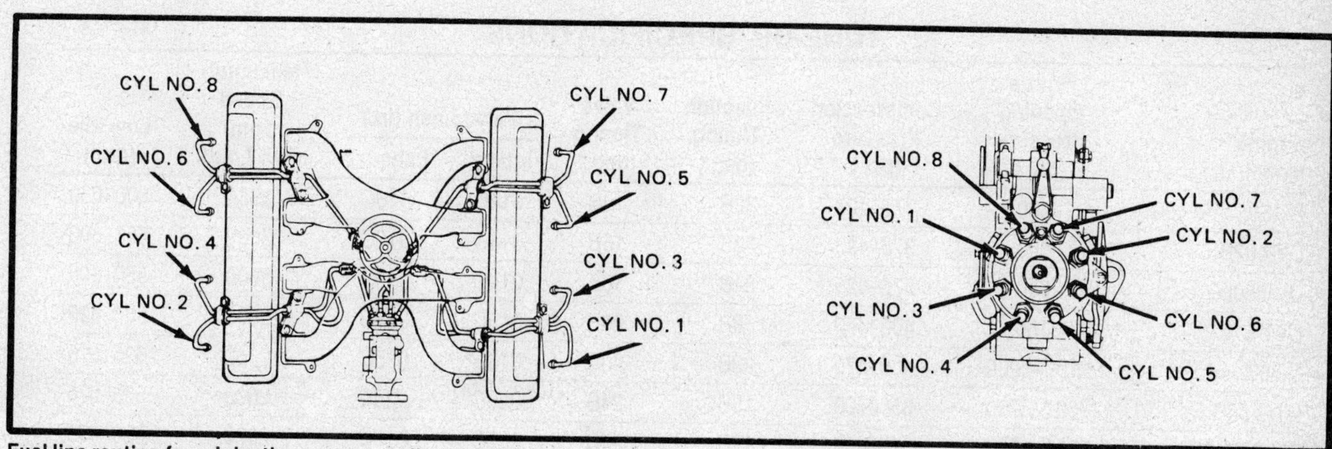

Fuel line routing from injection pump to cylinders (© General Motors Corp.)

INTERNATIONAL HARVESTER

GENERAL SPECIFICATIONS

Engine Model	Bore & Stroke	Displ. Cu. In.	Horsepower @ rpm	Torque @ rpm	Firing Order	Compression Ratio	Oil Capacity w/Filters (qts)
D-150	4.5 × 4.3125	549	150 @ 3000	320 @ 2000	18736542	16.6:1	14
D-170	4.5 × 4.3125	549	170 @ 3000	340 @ 2000	18736542	16.6:1	14
D-190	4.5 × 4.3125	549	190 @ 3000	360 @ 2000	18736542	16.6:1	14
DV-462B	4.125 × 4.3125	461	160 @ 3000	①	18736542	17.0:1	16
DV-550B	4.5 × 4.3125	549	180 @ 3000	365 @ 2000	18736542	17.0:1	16
DV-550B	4.5 × 4.3125	549	200 @ 3000	389 @ 2000	18736542	17.0:1	16
DT-466	4.30 × 5.35	466	165 @ 2400	②	153624	16.3:1	20
DT-466	4.30 × 5.35	466	180 @ 2400	③	153624	16.3:1	20
DT-466	4.30 × 5.35	466	210 @ 2600	④	153624	16.3:1	20
V-800	5.3125 × 4.5	798	280 @ 2600	812 @ 1600	18736542	16.0:1	38
V-800	5.3125 × 4.5	798	300 @ 2600	725 @ 1800	18736542	16.0:1	38
V-800	5.3125 × 4.5	798	350 @ 2600	820 @ 1800	18736542	16.0:1	38
9.0L	4.510 × 4.312	551	165 @ 2800	366 @ 1200	18736542	19.0:1	14
9.0L⑤	4.510 × 4.312	551	175 @ 2800	371 @ 1600	18736542	19.0:1	14
9.0L	4.510 × 4.312	551	180 @ 2800	401 @ 1200	18736542	19.0:1	14
6.9L	4 × 4.18	420	170 @ 3300	307 @ 1800	12734568	20.7:1	11

① DV-462B: available in 307 or 341 ft.lbs. versions @ 2000 rpm
② DT-466: Federal-420 ft.lbs. @ 1600 rpm Calif.-418 ft.lbs. @ 1600 rpm
③ DT-466: Federal-464 ft.lbs. @ 1600 rpm Calif.-469 ft.lbs. @ 1600 rpm
④ DT-466: Federal-508 ft.lbs. @ 1800 rpm Calif.-518 ft.lbs. @ 1800 rpm
⑤ California model

TUNE-UP SPECIFICATIONS

Engine Model	Nozzle Opening Pressure (psi.)	Compression Pressure (psi.)	Injection Timing (deg.)	Valve Timing (deg.)	Valve Lash (in.)		Maximum Speed (rpm) Full Load	Low Idle (rpm)
					Intake	Exhaust		
D-150, 170, 190	2800	375–425	32B	16B	.014C	.016C	3350	600–650
DV-462B	2300	375–425	32B	16B	.014C	.016C	3000	550–600
DV-550B	2300	375–425	34B	16B	.014C	.016C	3000	550–600
DVT-573	3150	400–470	8B	20B	.013C	.025C	2600	575–625
V-800	3100–3200	400–470	22B	30B	.013C	.025C	2600	625–675
DTI-466B	3600–3750	350–400	15B①	24B	.020C	.025C	2600	625–675
DT-466/466B	3600–3750	375–425	17B②	24B	.020C	.025C	2600	625–675

TUNE-UP SPECIFICATIONS

Engine Model	Nozzle Opening Pressure (psi.)	Compression Pressure (psi.)	Injection Timing (deg.)	Valve Timing (deg.)	Valve Lash (in.)		Maximum Speed (rpm) Full Load	Low Idle (rpm)
					Intake	Exhaust		
9.0L	3075–3225	450–525	16B	16B	.012	.016	2800	625–675
6.9L	2100–2150	—	③	—	④	④	3300	600–700

① Figure is for engine off. Timing @ 700 rpm is 17B
② Engine off or 700 rpm for 210 hp models
13B w/engine off for 190 hp models
15B @ 700 rpm for 190 hp models
③ Align timing marks and set dynamic timing (see text)
④ Hydraulic followers used (clearance is not adjustable)

ENGINE TORQUE SPECIFICATIONS

(ft. lbs.)

Engine Model	Cyl. Head	Main Brg.	Conn. Rod	Nozzle Clamps	Camshaft Flange	Flywheel	Crankshaft Pulley/ Damper	Camshaft Gear Nut
D-150, 170, 190	105–110	110–115①	55②	14–16	40–50	110–115	260–290	200–225
DV-462B, 550B	110	130①	55	15	40	110	325	200
466 Series	165	115	130	20	20	110–125	125	85
V-800	220	390③	130	35	30	235	425④	30
9.0L	⑤	125–135⑥	55②	14–16	40–45	110–115	260–290	200–225
6.9L	⑦	95⑧	⑨	—	—	38	90	12–18

① Tie bolts: 50 ft. lbs.
② Plus 1/6 turn more
③ Cross bolts: 160 ft. lbs. to be torqued after cap bolts
④ Gear nut
⑤ Step 1-torque to 50 ft. lbs. Step 2-90 ft. lbs. Step 3-110 ft. lbs.
⑥ Tie Bolts: 40–45 ft. lbs.
⑦ Step 1-40 ft. lbs., Step 2-65 ft. lbs., Step 3-75 ft. lbs.
⑧ Step 1-75 ft. lbs., Step 2-95 ft lbs.
⑨ Step 1-38 ft. lbs., Step 2-46–51 ft. lbs.

HEAD BOLT TORQUE SEQUENCE

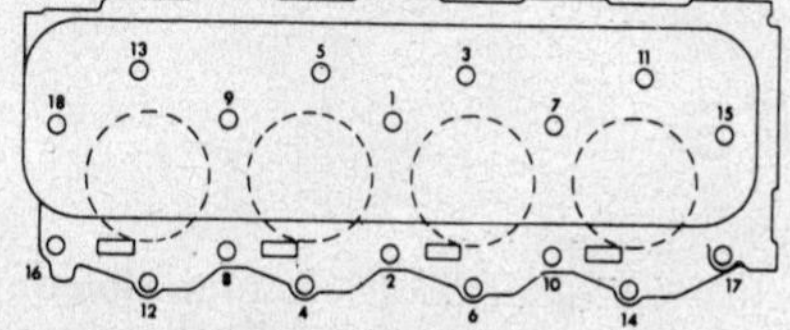

DV-462 and 550 head bolt tightening sequence

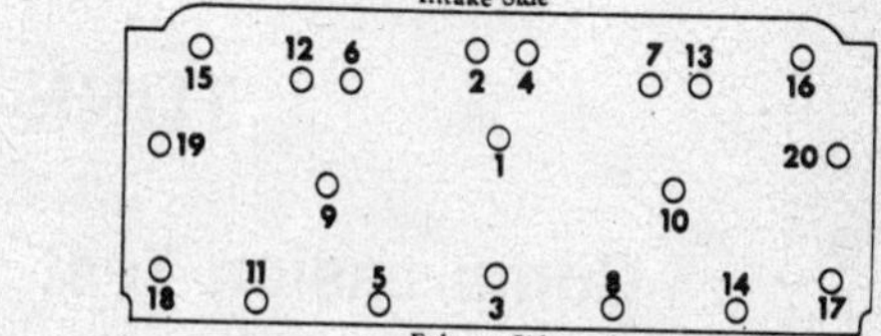

V-800 head bolt tightening sequence

FRONT →
INTAKE SIDE

	22	14	6	3	12	21	
25		15	8	1	10	17	26
24		18	9	2	7	16	23
	20	11	4	5	13	19	

466 series head bolt tightening sequence

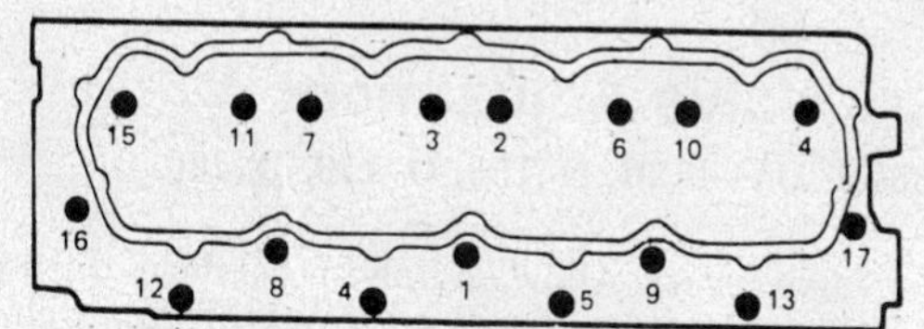

Head bolt torque sequence—6.9L engine

CHILTON'S THREE "C's" DIESEL ENGINE DIAGNOSIS PROCEDURE

Condition	Cause	Correction
Engine fails to start	1. Tank empty, tank valve closed. 2. Plugged filter or fuel lines. 3. Defective damper valve. 4. Defective transfer pump. 5. Plugged injector line. 6. Defective pump plunger.	1. Refill fuel tank; open valve. 2. Clean or replace as necessary 3. Replace damper valve. 4. Replace transfer pump. 5. Clear fuel line. 6. Replace pump plunger.
Engine hard to start	1. Cranking speed too slow (below 250 rpm). 2. Swirl destroyer stuck open 3. Accelerator fails to reach full fuel position. 4. Improper fuel. 5. Water in fuel. 6. Improper injection timing. 7. Poor compression.	1. Check starter. 2. Check operation. 3. Check linkage operation. 4. Drain and refill fuel tank. 5. Drain and refill fuel tank and lines. 6. Reset injection timing. 7. Check compression.
Erratic engine operation	1. Improper fuel. 2. Inadequate transfer pump pressure. 3. Injection lines leaking. 4. Incorrect injector timing. 5. Faulty injector nozzle. 6. Poor compression.	1. Drain and refill fuel tank. 2. Check fuel pressure. 3. Tighten or replace fuel line(s). 4. Reset injection timing. 5. Replace faulty injector. 6. Check compression.
Low power without smoke	1. Accelerator linkage travel restricted. 2. Governor high idle adjustment incorrect. 3. Low transfer pump pressure. 4. Low fuel supply pressure. 5. Improper maximum fuel setting. 6. Injector plungers worn. 7. Exhaust system restricted. 8. Swirl destroyer in "on" position 9. Air cleaner slightly restricted. 10. Faulty injector nozzles. 11. Improper injection timing.	1. Check linkage operation. 2. Adjust governor. 3. Check fuel pressure. 4. Check fuel pressure. 5. Reset maximum fuel. 6. Replace injectors. 7. Check exhaust flow. 8. Check operation. 9. Replace air cleaner element. 10. Replace injection nozzles. 11. Reset injection timing.
Engine smokes, but with no loss in power	1. Faulty Nozzles. 2. Faulty maximum fuel setting.	1. Replace injection nozzles. 2. Reset maximum fuel delivery.
Engine smokes and lacks power	1. Swirl destroyer on 2. Air cleaner restricted. 3. Faulty nozzles. 4. Injector pump out of time. 5. Loss of compression in one cylinder. 6. Maximum fuel setting substantially too high.	1. Check operation. 2. Replace air cleaner element 3. Replace injection nozzles. 4. Reset injection timing. 5. Check compression. 6. Reset maximum fuel delivery.
Lube oil diluted with fuel	1. Faulty nozzles. 2. Incorrect delivery valve torque. 3. Faulty pump plunger. 4. Damaged pump barrel seat. 5. Cracked pump housing.	1. Replace injection nozzles. 2. Retorque delivery valve. 3. Replace pump plunger. 4. Replace seal. 5. Replace injection pump.

TUNE-UP AND ADJUSTMENTS

Compression Test

Refer to the Ford V8 6.9L Diesel Engine section for service information on IH 6.9L Diesel engine.

Valve Adjustment

9.0L, DV–550B, DV–462B, D–150, D–170, D–190 ENGINES

1. Remove valve covers. Allow engine to cool down until all parts are at uniform temperature. See the specifications chart for valve clearance.

2. Rotate the engine in the normal direction of rotation until the no. 1 intake valve just starts to open. Adjust both valves on no. 6 cylinder.

3. Continue rotating the engine until no. 8 intake valve is just opening and adjust valves on no. 5 cylinder.

4. Rotate the engine until no. 7 intake valve is just opening and adjust the valves on no. 4 cylinder.

5. Rotate the engine until no. 3 intake valve is just opening on no. 2 cylinder.

6. Rotate the engine until no. 6 intake is just opening and adjust the valves on no. 1 cylinder.

7. Rotate the engine until no. 5 intake is just opening and adjust the valves on no. 8 cylinder.

8. Rotate the engine until no. 4 intake is just opening and adjust the valves on no. 7 cylinder.

9. Rotate the engine until no. 2 intake is just opening and adjust the valves on no. 3 cylinder.

V–800 ENGINE

1. Bring the number one piston to its compression stroke position with the timing indicator on the TDC mark. Rotate both the intake and exhaust valve push rods to be sure that the cam is on its off-lift position and the valves are closed on the number one cylinder.

2. With the number one cylinder piston in its compression position at TDC, adjust the intake valves for cylinders 1, 2, 4 and 5. Adjust the exhaust valves for cylinders 1, 3, 7 and 8.

3. Turn the crankshaft one complete revolution until the number six cylinder piston is at its compression position at TDC. Adjust the intake valves for cylinders 3, 6, 7 and 8. Adjust exhaust valves for cylinders 2, 4, 5 and 6.

CAUTION

Do not attempt to adjust the valves with the engine running, as severe internal engine damage could result.

4. The procedure to adjust the bridge valve lash on the V–800 engine is as follows:

a. Loosen the bridge adjusting screw nut and back out the screw. Press down on the rocker arm at the point of contact with the bridge.

b. Turn the adjusting screw down until it contacts the valve stem, then turn the screw an additional 30 degrees. Hold the screw and tighten the locknut to 20–25 ft. lbs. (27–34 Nm).

c. To set the lash, loosen the rocker lever screw and nut. Insert a feeler gauge between the rocker arm and the bridge. Turn the screw until the proper specifications are obtained. Intake 0.013 in. (0.33mm) and exhaust 0.025 in. (0.64mm).

d. Tighten the locknut to 30–35 ft. lbs. (41–47 Nm).

DT–466, DT AND DTI–466 ENGINES

1. With the valve cover removed, turn the crankshaft until the number one piston is on the compression stroke and the timing pointer is on line with the TDC mark on the vibration damper.

2. Six valves are adjusted when the number one piston is at TDC and the remaining six valves are adjusted when the crankshaft is rotated one complete revolution, placing the number six piston at TDC position on the compression stroke.

3. With the number one piston at TDC, adjust the intake valves of cylinders 1, 2 and 4. Adjust the exhaust valves of cylinders 1, 3 and 5.

4. After rotating the crankshaft one full revolution and placing the number six piston at TDC, adjust the intake valves of cylinders 3, 5 and 6. Adjust exhaust valves of cylinders 2, 4 and 6.

Injection Pump Timing

D–150,170 AND 190

1. Position the shut-off control valve in the SHUT-OFF position.

2. Rotate the engine in the direction of normal rotating until No. 1 cylinder is on the compression stroke. Continue rotating until the 32B mark reaches the pointer.

NOTE: The engine should be turned manually; if the timing mark is passed, back up at least 1/4 revolution past the mark and approach it again.

3. Release the shut-off control.

4. Remove the delivery valve, spring and fill piece from the No. 1 pumping element and install a drip spout. The drip spout can be made from a length of injection pipe and a connector nut.

Maximum PSI	Minimum PSI
260	195
280	210
300	225
320	240
340	255
360	270
380	285
400	300
420	315
440	330

Engine Model	Comp. PSI	Cranking RPM ②
DV-462B, DV-550B	375–425	①
D-150, D-170, D-190	375–425	①
V-800	400–470	235
9.0 Liter	450–525	200
D-466	375–425	①

① Measured at cranking motor speed
② At sea level

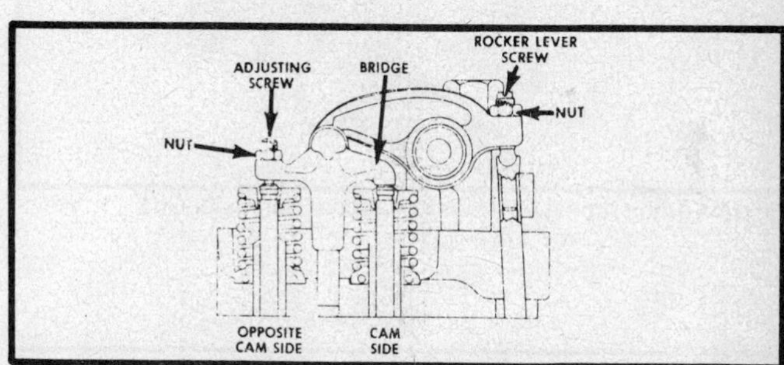

Valve lash adjustment (© International Harvester Co.)

5. Position the control rack at the load position as follows:

a. Hold the accelerator lever in the full forward position.

b. Slowly move the shut-off lever rearward. A distinct click will be heard as the rack moves from the excess fuel to the full load position. On pumps with a torque capsule (D–150, 170), a spring clip is used to prevent spring collapse in the torque capsule.

6. Supply fuel to the pump gallery. Fuel should flow from the drip spout at the rate of one drop every three to five seconds. If this rate is not observed, the pump must be removed from the engine and the injection pump drive flange must be repositioned on the engine.

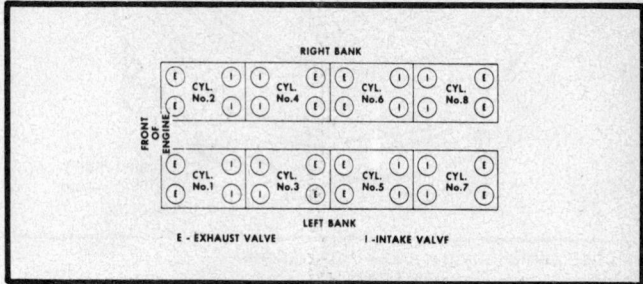

Valve arrangement (© International Harvester Co.)

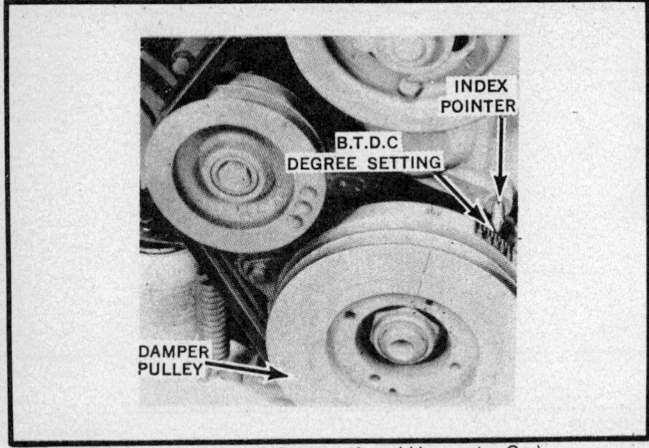

Timing mark and pointer (© International Harvester Co.)

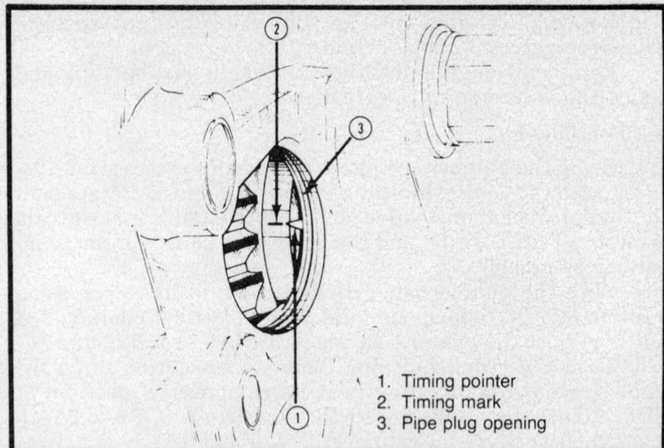

Injection pump timing marks—late models (© International Harvester Co.)

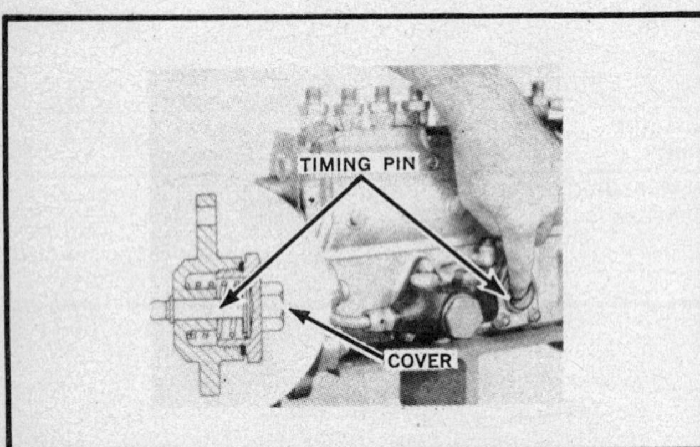

Injection pump timing pin (© International Harvester Co.)

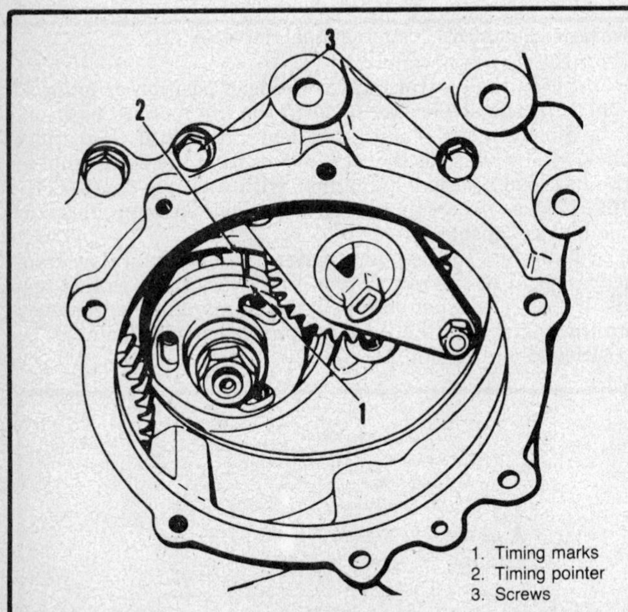

Injection pump timing marks—early models (© International Harvester Co.)

DV–462B AND DV550B ENGINES

1. Put engine shutoff control in "shut-off" position.
2. Remove the cap from the timing pin on the left side of the injector pump.
3. Loosen No. 1 injector nozzle in its bore. Rotate the engine. When the nozzle pops up, start watching the timing mark and pointer on the front of the engine.

NOTE: Nozzle hold-down bolts must be threaded in at least two turns.

4. Stop rotating the engine when the pointer indicates 34 degrees BTDC on 550B engines, or 32 degrees on 462B engines. If damper is turned beyond the proper mark, turn the engine backwards until it has passed at least ¼ of a turn beyond the mark.
5. Attempt to insert the timing pin into the slot in the pump camshaft. If the pin cannot be inserted, repeat Steps 3–5. If the pin can be inserted, adjust timing as described below.
6. Remove upper and lower halves of the air cleaner and, where necessary, the manifold crossover adapter. Cover manifold openings.
7. Disconnect the accelerator rod and control cable at the governor.
8. Clean the pump and connections with diesel fuel. Disconnect the low pressure and the injector lines and the pump lube oil line. Cap all openings.
9. Remove the pump stabilizing brackets. Remove the adapter mounting bolts which hold the adapter and housing to the front cover.
10. Pull the pump rearward, freeing the drive flange tangs from the middle disc and remove it.
11. Install the coupling onto the tangs of the drive shaft, with the blind holes in the center of the coupling facing the pump.
12. Position the drive flange of the pump so that its tangs are horizontal and the timing pin can be engaged with the pump camshaft.
13. Locate the pump on the engine, carefully engaging the drive flange tangs with the coupling. Secure the adapter and pump to the rear of the engine front cover with the mounting bolts.
14. Install the stabilizing brackets.

466 SERIES

1. Remove the pump from the engine.
2. Remove the pump drive gear and install the pump and mounting adapter plate on the timing case cover.
3. Secure the pump and adapter plate with two bolts.
4. Set the engine timing mark at the specified static setting. The line on the pump must be in line with the timing pointer.

5. Install the drive gear and mesh it with the idler gear. Do not tighten the bolt at this time.

6. Hold the pump shaft and rotate the drive gear counterclockwise to remove backlash. Tighten the bolts to 30 ft. lbs.

NOTE: Disregard any timing marks on the idler gear.

7. Connect the fuel lines and oil supply line.

8. Install the injection lines and tighten the fittings to 30 ft. lbs. Secure the line clamps.

9. Connect and adjust the governor control linkage.

10. If the pump is equipped with a port closure lock plug, remove it and install the regular plug.

11. If the engine is not timed correctly, reposition the crankshaft to the specified timing mark. Remove the three bolts from the pump drive gear and rotate the pump driveshaft EXACTLY one revolution. The pump is now timed and the engine will start.

NOTE: It is impossible to align the marks inside the pump and the timing marks on the drive hub at the same time.

12. Install the pump access cover.

V–800

1. Remove pump from engine.
2. Remove the cover from the rear of the mounting adapter.
3. Reach through the opening with a deep socket and loosen the pump drive capscrews. Rotate the pump camshaft to bring each of the six capscrews around into view.
4. Remove the timing pin cover.
5. Rotate the pump camshaft while holding in on the notch in the camshaft. Install the timing pin holding tool to keep the pin depressed.
6. Scribe timing marks on gear and align with scribe mark on advance unit.
7. Install and lubricate a new O-ring on the flange of the pump mounting adapter.
8. Push pump into place on engine, engaging camshaft gear and compressor idle gear.
9. Visually check, through the adapter opening, that the injection pump gear bolt is near the center of the slotted hole in the advance unit. If not, the pump is out of time one tooth in either direction.
10. Push pump into engagement with the camshaft gear and air compressor idler gear. Before O-ring enters bore, align the mounting holes in the pump flange with those in the front plate.

NOTE: When the pump is installed, the gear should have rotated far enough clockwise to allow the gear bolts to be positioned in the middle of the slots in the advance unit. If alignment is not correct, remove the pump, rotate the gear one tooth and reinstall.

11. Install all pump mounting bolts.
12. Using a deep socket, reach in through the access hole and tighten the first gear bolt to 50 ft. lbs.
13. Remove the timing pin holding tool. Make sure that the timing pin is completely released.
14. Torque the five remaining bolts to 50 ft. lbs. each, by rotating the crankshaft through two revolutions, stopping each 120° to tighten the next bolt.
15. Recheck static timing at the vibration damper. It should be 22° BTDC at # 1 compression.
16. Install the access cover and gasket and the timing pin cap.

9.0L ENGINE

1. Block the fuel shut-off control in the OFF position to prevent accidental starting of the engine.
2. Rotate the engine in the normal direction of rotation (clockwise as viewed from the front of the engine) until the No. 1 cylinder is at TDC on the compression stroke. Continue to rotate the engine until the 16 degree mark on the crankshaft pulley is aligned with the engine timing pointer. In this position, the pumping element for the No. 1 cylinder is at the start of injection.

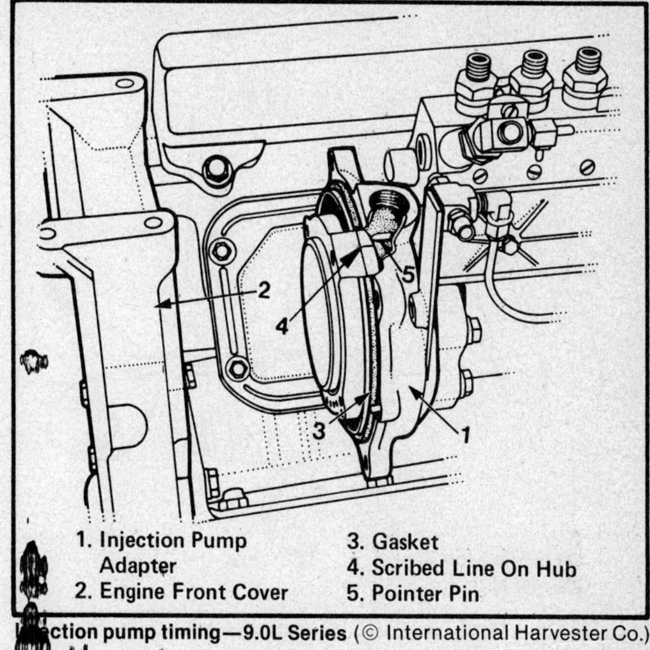

Injection pump timing—9.0L Series (© International Harvester Co.)

NOTE: If the engine is turned beyond the specified timing mark, back up at least ¼ turn from the mark and begin the approach again in the normal direction of rotation. Do not back engine to align timing marks.

3. To be sure the No. 1 cylinder is on its compression stroke, loosen the injection nozzle hold down bolt from the No. 1 nozzle slightly. Watch for the nozzle to pop up while slowly rotating the engine. To prevent the nozzle from coming out of the head, always make sure three threads on the hold down bolt are engaged in the mounting hole.

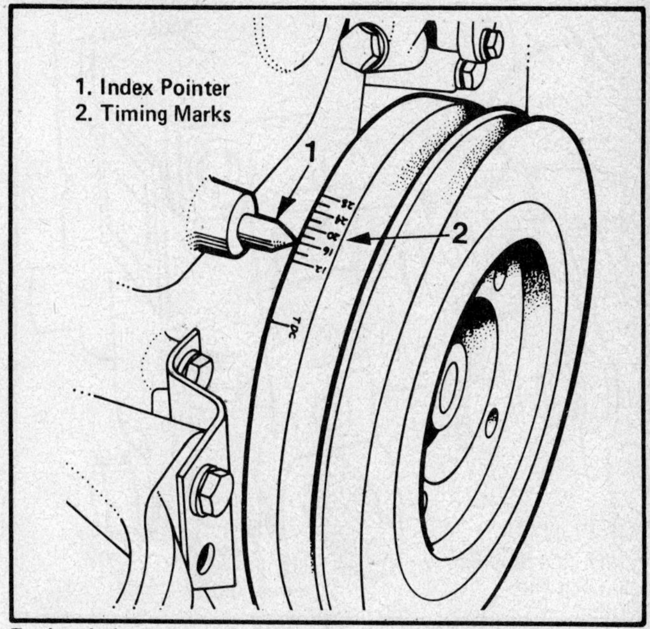

Engine timing marks and pointer location—typical (© International Harvester Co.)

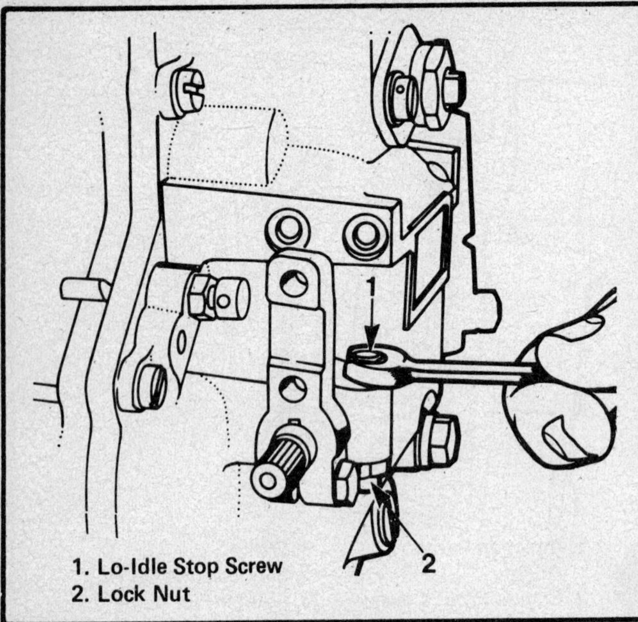

Idle speed adjustment—typical (© International Harvester Co.)

4. Remove the sight plug on top of the injection pump adapter housing. The scribed line on the pump must be aligned with the pointer pin. If the marks do not align, it will be necessary to reset the pump to engine timing.
5. Before the timing adjustment can be made, it will be necessary to drain the coolant, remove the fan drive, fan, hub assembly, water outlet, water return tube and drive gear cover.
6. Loosen the injection pump drive gear mounting bolts and rotate the injection pump hub to align the hub with the pointer pin. Once aligned, tighten the mounting bolts and recheck alignment.
7. Once the timing is set, reinstall all removed components and refill cooling system.

Maximum no-load adjustment—typical
(© International Harvester Co.)

NOTE: To minimize timing inaccuracies during pointer and scribed line alignment viewing, threads must be seen around the circumference of the viewing hold.

Idle Speed Adjustment

ALL ENGINES

1. Bring engine to operating temperature. Note tachometer reading. Lo-idle speed is given in the "Tune-Up Specifications" chart.
2. If necessary to adjust the lo-idle, loosen the locknut and turn clockwise to reduce rpm, or counterclockwise to increase it. Tighten the locknut.
3. Operate the engine up to hi-idle three times and allow it to return to lo-idle. If the adjustment is not correct, repair binding in the linkage.

Maximum No-Load Speed Adjustment

ALL ENGINES

NOTE: Maximum no-load governed speed (hi-idle) is the point of engine speed where governor prevents engine rpm from going higher. Hi-idle adjustment is located at accelerator lever stop screw and is initially made on pump calibrating stand. Minor adjustment can be made on engine as follows:

1. With engine running and at normal operating temperature, push control lever to its full forward position-lever against hi-idle stop.
2. Read tachometer and note highest engine rpm. (Make sure tachometer is accurate.)
3. If governed speed does not reach specified limit, check throttle linkage to make sure,lever is not restricted.
4. If governed speed is not within specified limits, remove seal on locknut of hi-idle stop screw and reset hi-idle adjustment. Turn stop screw out (counterclockwise) to reduce hi-idle or turn in (clockwise) to increase hi-idle. Tighten locknut and recheck hi-idle speed. When adjustment is correct, reseal locknut.

Fuel Injection Nozzles

Removal and Installation

ALL ENGINES

1. Before removing nozzle assemblies, clean exterior of each nozzle assembly and the surrounding area with clean fuel oil or solvent to prevent entry of dirt into engine when nozzle assemblies are removed. Also, clean fuel inlet and fuel leak-off piping connections.
2. Disconnect fuel inlet (high pressure) and fuel leak-off pipes from each nozzle assembly. Cover open ends of pipes to prevent entry of dirt.
3. Remove nozzle mounting bolt and hold down clamp. Pull nozzle assembly with washer and seal from engine. If assembly seems stuck, rotate it slightly to break it loose from carbon deposits in the cylinder head recess. Be careful not to strike the nozzle tip against any hard surface during removal.
4. Installation is the reverse of removal.

NOTE: Cover nozzle assembly fuel inlet and leak-off openings with plastic caps to prevent entry of dirt. Also protect nozzle tip.

Injection Pump

Removal

DV-462B, DV-550B, D-150, 170 AND 190 ENGINES

1. Remove the upper and lower halves of the air cleaner and,

where necessary, the manifold crossover adapter. Cover manifold openings.

2. Disconnect the accelerator rod and control cable at the governor.

3. Clean the pump and connections with diesel fuel. Disconnect low pressure and injector lines and the pump lube oil line. Cap all openings.

4. Remove the pump stabilizing brackets. Remove the adapter mounting bolts which hold the adapter and housing to the front cover.

5. Pull the pump rearward, freeing the drive flange tangs from the middle disc and remove it.

Inspection

1. Inspect pump mounting flange and the bosses of the rear mounting bracket.
2. Inspect the drive flange for damage, wear, or loose mounting.
3. Torque the securing nut to 75 ft. lbs.

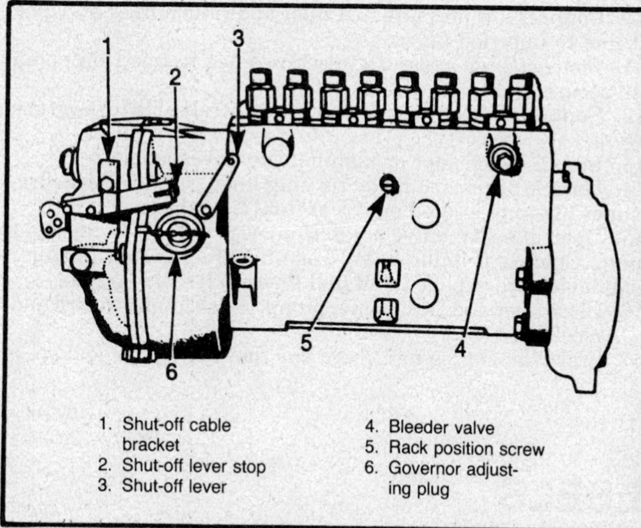

Right side view of injection pump—typical
(© International Harvester Co.)

Installation

1. Install the coupling onto the tangs of the drive shaft, with the blind hole in the center of the coupling facing the pump.
2. Position the drive flange of the pump so that its tangs are horizontal and the timing pin can be engaged with the pump camshaft.
3. Locate the pump on the engine, carefully engaging the drive flange tangs with the coupling. Secure the adapter and pump to the rear of the engine front cover with the mounting bolts.
4. Install the stabilizer brackets.

466 SERIES ENGINES

Removal and Installation

1. Disconnect the governor control linkage at the pump.
2. On units equipped with a Bowden shut-off wire, disconnect the control linkage from the shut-off lever.
3. On units equipped with an electric shut-off, disconnect the wire.
4. Disconnect the following lines from the pump:
   a. Lube oil supply line
   b. Primary filter-to-supply pump tube
   c. Supply pump-to-final filter tube
   d. Final filter-to-injection pump hose

NOTE: Cap all lines as soon as they are disconnected.

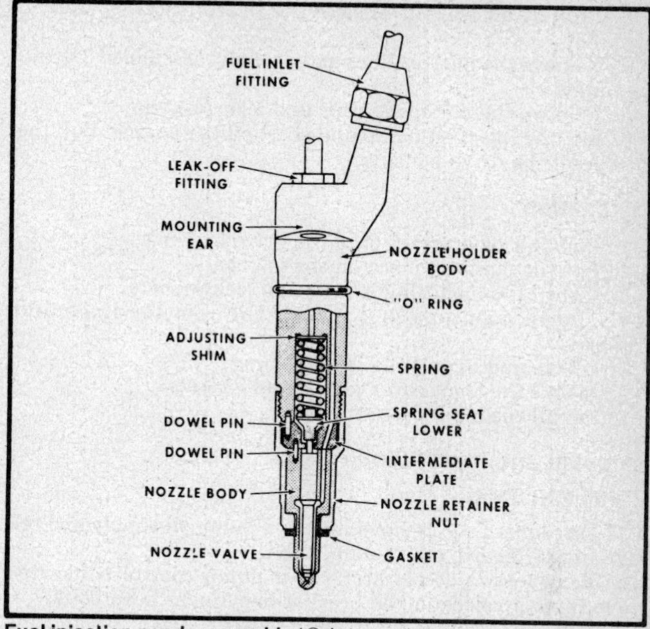

Fuel injection nozzle assembly (© International Harvester Co.)

   e. Pump-to-injector lines
   f. Fuel return line
5. Remove the pump access cover.
6. Remove the two bolts securing the pump mounting plate adapter to the front cover. Remove the pump and adapter plate.
7. To install, see the section under Injection Pump Timing.

Removal

DVT-573 ENGINE

1. Remove air compressor.
2. Remove the front cover plates and gaskets from the heads.

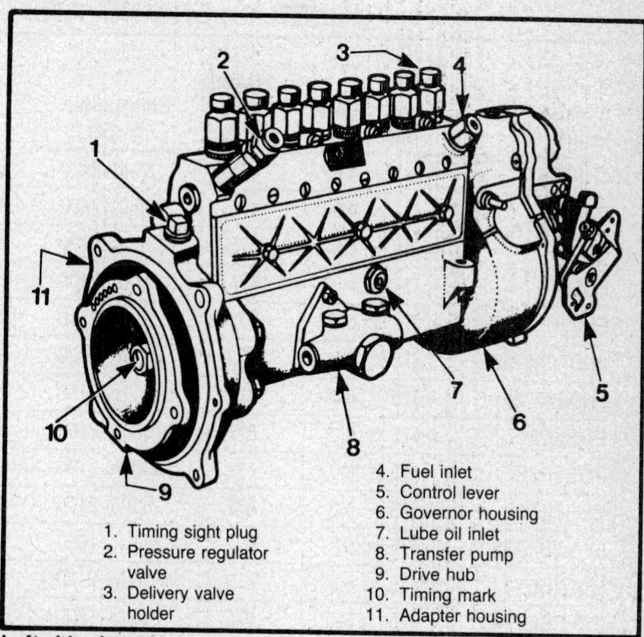

Left side view of injection pump—typical
(© International Harvester Co.)

3. Remove all leak-off lines at the injector nozzles. Cap all openings.
4. Remove the injector lines and dampers assembled. Cap all openings.
5. Remove the mounting caps and lockwashers.
6. Lift the injection pump and shaft off the engine. Pull the gasket off the drive housing.

Installation

1. Install a new gasket onto the drive housing.
2. Put the pump in place on the engine.
3. Install the mounting screws and lockwashers.
4. Uncap openings and install the injector lines and dampers.
5. Uncap and install the leak-off lines.
6. Install the front cover plates and gaskets.
7. Install the air compressor.

Removal and Installation

V-800 ENGINE

1. Disconnect and remove injection pump oil supply and return lines. Remove oil pressure tube.
2. Remove two accelerator rod-to-pump control bolts. Remove three accelerator rod bracket-to-cylinder head bolts.
3. Remove accelerator rod and bracket.
4. Remove pump bracket-to-engine bolt.
5. Support pump and remove the five attaching bolts.
6. Slide the pump rearward clear of the drive gear.
7. To install, follow instructions under Injector Pump Timing.

Removal

9.0L ENGINE

1. Drain engine coolant from radiator and engine block.
2. Disconnect accelerator and shut off control cables from governor.
3. Before disconnecting fuel lines, clean pump and connections with clean diesel fuel.
4. Disconnect injection lines, low pressure lines and lube oil line from pump. Remove fuel line brackets as necessary. Use plastic caps or plugs to protect openings from dirt.
5. Remove fan drive, water outlet and return tube, injection pump drive gear cover and drive gear.
6. Remove four injection pump adapter to engine front cover mounting bolts. Remove two support bracket bolts on right side of pump and two mounting bracket nuts underneath injection pump, remove pump.
7. Installation is the reverse of removal. Inspect pump mounting flange at rear of engine front cover. Also inspect injection pump stabilizer brackets and drive gear for damage or wear.
8. Secure mounting adapter and injection pump to rear of engine front cover with four mounting bolts.
9. Install stabilizing brackets to side at rear of pump housing.
10. Connect low pressure fuel inlet and return lines and lube oil line to injection pump.
11. Connect high pressure injection lines to injection pump and secure fuel line brackets.
12. Connect accelerator rod and stop control cable to governor levers.
13. Install air cleaner or manifold crossover adapter.
14. Unlock primer pump by turning knob counter clockwise. Primer pump is located on top of final filter base.
15. Open bleeder valve located on right front of injection pump. Operate priming pump and allow fuel to flow until all air bubbles are expelled and fuel flows in a solid stream.
16. Close vent and lock primer pump. (Push knob forward and turn clockwise)
17. Start the engine and check the fuel system for leaks.

MACK DIESELS

GENERAL ENGINE AND TUNE-UP SPECIFICATIONS

Engine Model	Bore × Stroke (Inches)	Piston Displ. Cu. In.	Horsepower @ rpm	Torque @ rpm	Firing Order	Governor Speed No Load	Idle Speed rpm	Injection Pump Timing (deg.)
END475	4.53 × 4.92	475	155 @ 2400	385 @ 1500	1-5-3-6-2-4	2600	450	30°B
ENDT475	4.53 × 4.92	475	190 @ 2400	470 @ 1500	1-5-3-5-2-4	2600	500	24°B
ET477	4.53 × 4.92	475	210 @ 2400	510 @ 1500	1-5-3-6-2-4	2600	450–500	18°B
EDT477	4.53 × 4.92	475	157 @ 2400	510 @ 1500	1-5-3-6-2-4	2600	450–500	18°B
ENDT(B)673	4.875 × 6.0	672	225 @ 2100	653 @ 1600	1-5-3-6-2-4	2280	525–575	29°B
ENDT(B)673C	4.875 × 6.0	672	250 @ 2100	700 @ 1500	1-5-3-6-2-4	2280	525–575	28°B
END(B)673E	4.875 × 6.0	672	180 @ 2100	540 @ 1400	1-5-3-6-2-4	2280	500–575	30°B
ET(B)673	4.875 × 6.0	672	260 @ 2100	775 @ 1500	1-5-3-6-2-4	2350	600–650	26°B
ET(B)673E	4.875 × 6.0	672	200 @ 2100	600 @ 1500	1-5-3-6-2-4	2310	600–650	28°B
ETY(B)673E	4.875 × 6.0	672	200 @ 2100	600 @ 1500	1-5-3-6-2-4	2310	600–650	18°B
ETAY(B)673A	4.875 × 6.0	672	315 @ 1900	1050 @ 1450	1-5-3-6-2-4	2225	600–650	21°B
ETAZ(B)673	4.875 × 6.0	672	320 @ 2100	1000 @ 1500	1-5-3-6-2-4	2310	525–575	24°B
ETAZ(B)673A	4.875 × 6.0	672	315 @ 1900	1050 @ 1450	1-5-3-6-2-4	2225	600–650	24°B
ETAZ(B)673C	4.875 × 6.0	672	295 @ 1800	985 @ 1400	1-5-3-6-2-4	2185	600–650	24°B

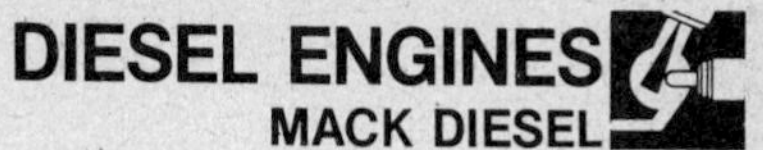

GENERAL ENGINE AND TUNE-UP SPECIFICATIONS

Engine Model	Bore × Stroke (Inches)	Piston Displ. Cu. In.	Horsepower @ rpm	Torque @ rpm	Firing Order	Governor Speed No Load	Idle Speed rpm	Injection Pump Timing (deg.)
ENDT(B)675	4.875 × 6.0	672	235 @ 2100	906 @ 1200	1-5-3-6-2-4	2310	525–575	26–27°B
ETY(B)675	4.875 × 6.0	672	235 @ 2100	906 @ 1200	1-5-3-6-2-4	2350	600–650	16°B
ENDT(B)676	4.875 × 6.0	672	285 @ 1800	1080 @ 1200	1-5-3-6-2-4	2310	525–575	22°B
ETA(B)676B	4.875 × 6.0	672	302 @ 2100	1150 @ 1200	1-5-3-6-2-4	2370	600–650	25°B
ETAY(B)676	4.875 × 6.0	672	283 @ 2100	1080 @ 1200	1-5-3-6-2-4	2310	525–575	18°B
ETAY(B)676D	4.875 × 6.0	672	285 @ 1800	1080 @ 1200	1-5-3-6-2-4	2100	525–575	18°B
END707	5.00 × 6.0	707	200 @ 2100	557 @ 1600	1-5-3-6-2-4	2280	500–575	30°B
END711	5.00 × 6.0	707	211 @ 2100	602 @ 1600	1-5-3-6-2-4	2280	500–575	30°B
E6-200	4.875 × 6.0	672	200 @ 2100	600 @ 1500	1-5-3-6-2-4	2350	600–650	21°B
EC6-235	4.875 × 6.0	672	235 @ 2100	700 @ 1500	1-5-3-6-2-4	2280	525–575	13°B
EM6-237	4.875 × 6.0	672	237 @ 1800	906 @ 1200	1-5-3-6-2-4	2350	①	③
EM6-237R	4.875 × 6.0	672	237 @ 1800	906 @ 1200	1-5-3-6-2-4	2100	525–575	21°B
E6-250	4.875 × 6.0	672	250 @ 2100	750 @ 1500	1-5-3-6-2-4	2350	600–650	19°B
EMC6-250	4.875 × 6.0	672	250 @ 1800	950 @ 1200	1-5-3-6-2-4	2290	525–575	17°B
E6-260	4.875 × 6.0	672	260 @ 2100	775 @ 1500	1-5-3-6-2-4	2350	525–575	20°B
EM6-285	4.875 × 6.0	672	285 @ 1800	1065 @ 1400	1-5-3-6-2-4	2150	525–575	23°B
EM6-285R	4.875 × 6.0	672	285 @ 1700	1065 @ 1400	1-5-3-6-2-4	2050	525–575	22°B
E6-315	4.875 × 6.0	672	315 @ 1900	1050 @ 1450	1-5-3-6-2-4	2225②	①	25°B
EC6-330	4.875 × 6.0	672	330 @ 1950	1065 @ 1400	1-5-3-6-2-4	2150	525–575	16°B
E6-350	4.875 × 6.0	672	350 @ 1950	1132 @ 1400	1-5-3-6-2-4	2150	525–575	22°–23°B
ENDT(B)865	5.25 × 5.0	866	322 @ 2400	1100 @ 1350	1-5-4-8-6-3-7-2	2650	600–650	25°B
ENDT(B)866	5.25 × 5.0	866	375 @ 2200	1040 @ 1600	1-5-4-8-6-3-7-2	2500	600–650	25°B
EM9-400	5.375 × 5.50	998	392 @ 2100	1520 @ 1230	1-5-4-8-6-3-7-2	2420	600–650	17°B
EM9-400R	5.375 × 5.50	998	400 @ 1700	1520 @ 1230	1-5-4-8-6-3-7-2	1970	600–650	17°B
EMC9-400	5.375 × 5.50	998	392 @ 2100	1520 @ 1230	1-5-4-8-6-3-7-2	2420	600–650	13°B
EMC9-400R	5.375 × 5.50	998	400 @ 1700	1520 @ 1230	1-5-4-8-6-3-7-2	1970	600–650	13°B
EM6-225	4.875 × 6.0	672	225 @ 2100	844 @ 1260	1-5-3-6-2-4	2325	525–575	25°B
EM6-250R	4.875 × 6.0	672	250 @ 1700	940 @ 1260	1-5-3-6-2-4	1950	600–650	④
EM6-275	4.875 × 6.0	672	275 @ 2100	1038 @ 1260	1-5-3-6-2-4	2315	525–575	25°B
EM6-275L	4.875 × 6.0	672	275 @ 1700	1275 @ 1020	1-5-3-6-2-4	1900	525–575	22°B
EM6-275R	4.875 × 6.0	672	275 @ 1600	1038 @ 1260	1-5-3-6-2-4	1770	525–575	23°B
EMC6-285	4.875 × 6.0	672	283 @ 2100	1080 @ 1200	1-5-3-6-2-4	2290	525–575	14°B
EMC6-285R	4.875 × 6.0	672	285 @ 2100	1080 @ 1200	1-5-3-6-2-4	2050	525–575	14°B
EM6-300	4.875 × 6.0	672	300 @ 2100	1125 @ 1260	1-5-3-6-2-4	2330	525–575	24°B
EM6-300R	4.875 × 6.0	672	300 @ 1700	1125 @ 1260	1-5-3-6-2-4	2150	525–575	24°B
ER-315R	4.875 × 6.0	672	315 @ 1800	1050 @ 1405	1-5-3-6-2-4	2225	600–650	25°B
ER-325	4.875 × 6.0	672	325 @ 1950	1050 @ 1400	1-5-3-6-2-4	2150	525–575	24°B
ER-325R	4.875 × 6.0	672	325 @ 1950	1050 @ 1400	1-5-3-6-2-4	2030	525–575	24°B
E6-350R	4.875 × 6.0	672	350 @ 1800	1131 @ 1400	1-5-3-6-2-4	2050	525–575	22°–23°B
EC6-350	4.875 × 6.0	672	350 @ 1950	1131 @ 1400	1-5-3-6-2-4	2200	525–575	17°B
EM9-400R	5.375 × 5.50	998	400 @ 1900	1520 @ 1530	1-5-4-8-6-3-7-2	2175	600–650	—

GENERAL ENGINE AND TUNE-UP SPECIFICATIONS

Engine Model	Bore × Stroke (Inches)	Piston Displ. Cu. In.	Horsepower @ rpm	Torque @ rpm	Firing Order	Governor Speed No Load	Idle Speed rpm	Injection Pump Timing (deg.)
EMC9-400R	5.375 × 5.50	998	400 @ 1900	1520 @ 1230	1-5-4-8-6-3-7-2	2175	600–650	—
E9-440	5.375 × 5.50	998	440 @ 1800	1495 @ 1350	1-5-4-8-6-3-7-2	2100	600–650	—

① American Bosch pump-525-575 rpm
Robert Bosch pump-600-650 rpm
② American Bosch pump-2100 rpm
③ United Technologies Diesel systems pump-21°B
Robert Bosch pump-20°B
④ United Technologies Diesel systems pump-22°B
Robert Bosch-25°B

ENGINE TORQUE SPECIFICATIONS

Engine Series	Cylinder Head (Ft. Lbs.)	Main Bearing Bolts (Ft. Lbs.)	Connecting Rod Bolts (Ft. Lbs.)	Rocker Bracket Caps (Ft. Lbs.)	Flywheel Mounting Nuts (Ft. Lbs.)
END475/ ENDT475	140	Nut-150 Stud-155	80	40	149④
ET477	140	155	81	35	140④
Current Production 6 Cylinder	⑤⑥	1 1/16″-200 5/8″-175	150	35	190①
ENDT 865,866	225	350①②	150③	35	190①
998⑦	⑧	350①②	175①	55	180

① Oiled
② Buttress screw 100 ft. lbs.
③ 170–180 ft. lbs. on part #367GCA3178A (connecting rod only).
④ Use lock plates.
⑤ Oil all cylinder head capscrew bosses, capscrew threads and washers with SAE #30 engine oil prior to assembly. Do not oil the threads in the cylinder block. Tighten capscrews individually on any one head in the proper sequence. Also:
1. Tighten all to 50 ft. lbs.
2. Repeat, in sequence, to 125 ft. lbs.
3. Finally tighten to 200 ft. lbs.
After run-in procedure, in sequence, back off each capscrew individually until free, then retorque same capscrew to 220 ft. lbs.

⑥ Oil all cylinder head stud nut bosses, stud nut threads, and washers with SAE #30 engine oil prior to assembly. Do not oil threads in cylinder block. Tighten stud nuts individually on any one head in the proper sequence. Also:
1. Tighten all to 50 ft. lbs.
2. Repeat, in sequence, to 125 ft. lbs.
3. Finally tighten to 175 ft. lbs.
After run-in procedure, in sequence, back off each stud nut individually until free, then retorque same nut to 175 ft. lbs.

⑦ 998 cubic inches
⑧ Oil all cylinder head capscrew threads and washers with SAE #30 engine oil prior to assembly. Tighten capscrews individually on any one head in the proper sequence. Also:
1. Tighten all to 50 ft. lbs.
2. Repeat, in sequence, to 175 ft. lbs.
3. Finally tighten to 220 ft. lbs.
After run-in procedure, in sequence, back off each capscrew individually until free, then retorque same capscrew to 220 ft. lbs.

FIRING ORDERS

FRONT OF ENGINE

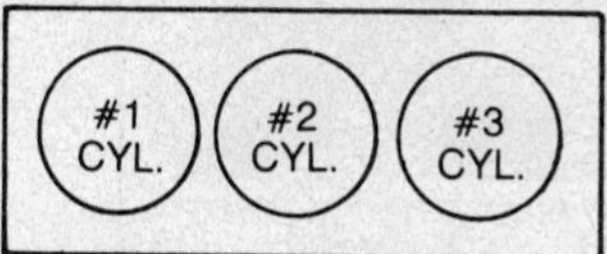

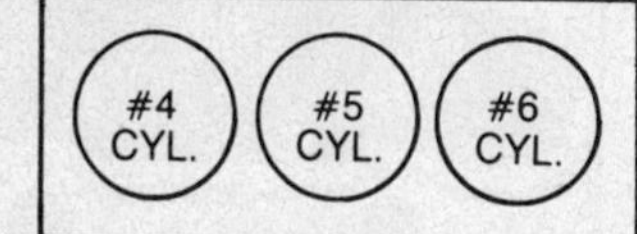

All 6 cylinder engines: 1-5-3-6-2-4

FRONT OF ENGINE

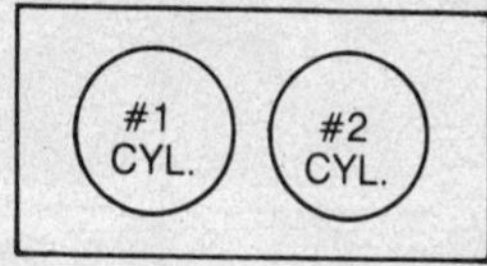

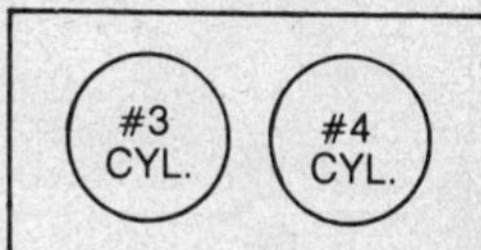

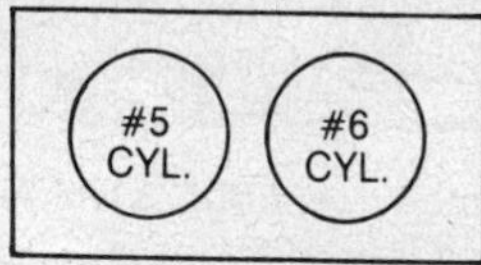

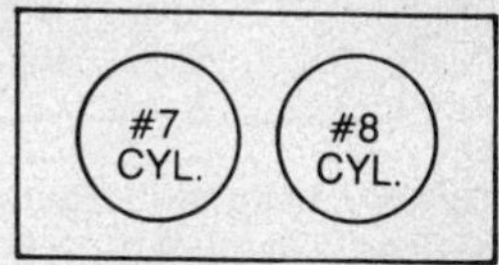

All V8 engines: 1-5-4-8-6-3-7-2

TORQUE SEQUENCES

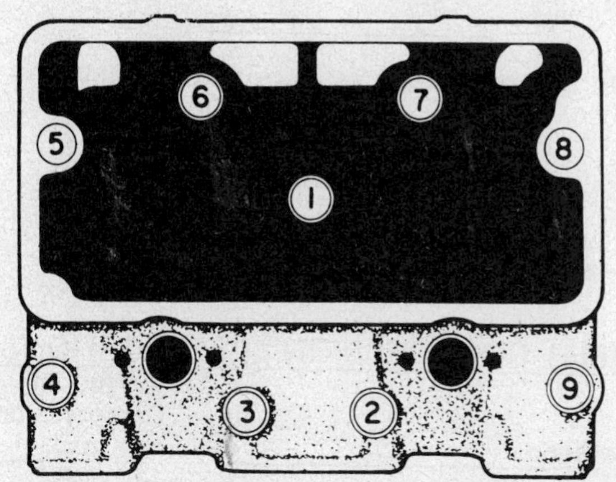

Cylinder head nut torquing sequence, END475 engine series

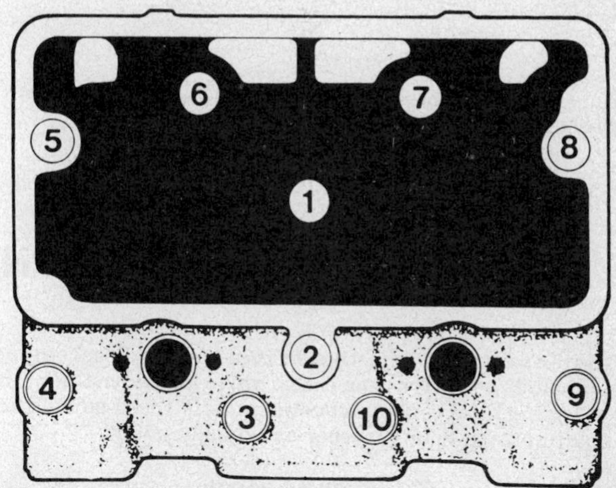

Cylinder head bolt torquing sequence, 475 series 6 cylinder

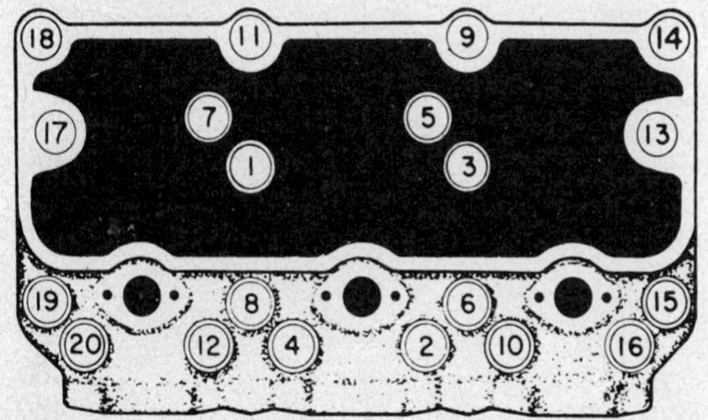

Cylinder head nut torquing sequence, END, T673 and 711 engine series (5/8 in. stud)

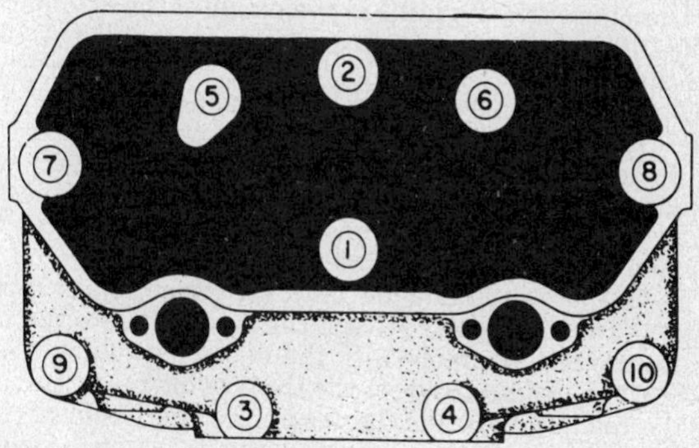

Cylinder head nut torquing sequence, END, T and 864 engine series

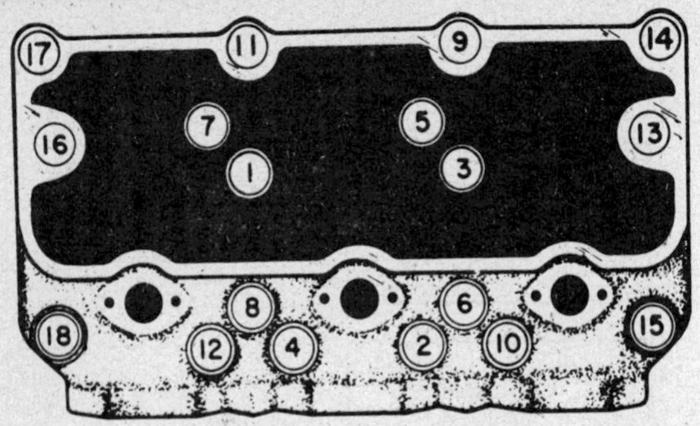

Cylinder head nut torquing sequence, END673 and 711 engine series (¾ in. stud at 15 and 18 locations)

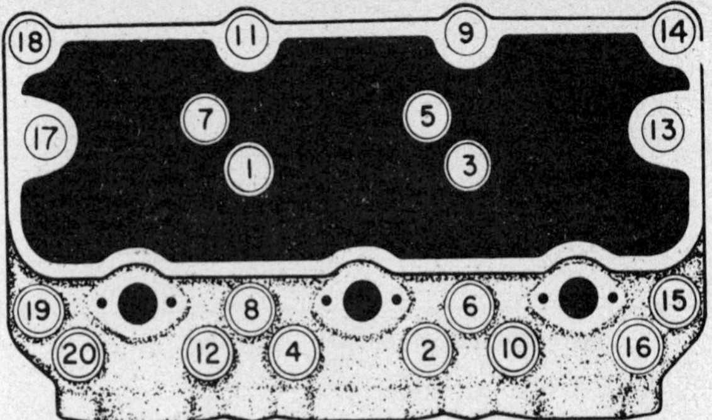

Cylinder head bolt torquing sequence, 6 cylinder current production (⅝ in. studs)

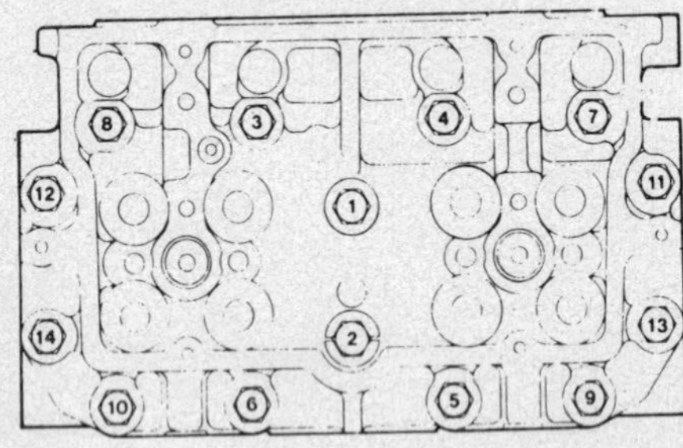

Cylinder head bolt torquing sequence, EMC9-400R, EMC9-400, EM9-400R and EM9-400 engines

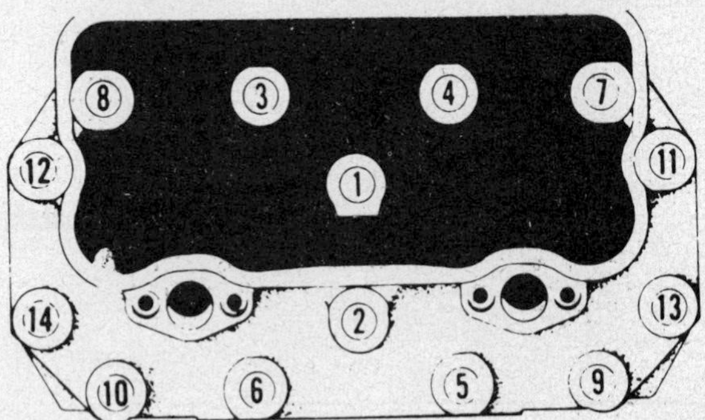

Cylinder head bolt torquing sequence, ENDT and ENDDT V8 series

TUNE-UP AND ADJUSTMENTS

A good tune-up and adjustment procedure for diesel engines should include a compression check, valve lash adjustment, injection timing, fuel control adjustment, idle speed adjustment and maximum no-load governor speed adjustment.

Compression

If referral to the chart indicates low compression could be the cause of the malfunction, test the compression of each cylinder as described:

1. Operate the engine at fast idle until it reaches operating temperature. Stop the engine.
2. Disconnect the fuel line at the nozzle of the cylinder to be checked. Place a container near the open end of the line to catch the fuel.
3. Remove the injection nozzle and holder assembly. Clean carbon from the nozzle tip with a special wire brush.
4. Remove carbon from the cylinder head nozzle hole with a special reamer and wire brush. Use an air gun to remove loose carbon. Crank the engine a few times with the starter to remove any remaining loose material.
5. Install a special adapter onto the gauge, place a copper gasket on the adapter and insert the assembly into the nozzle hole. Secure the assembly with the injector hold-down nuts.
6. Start the engine and set the throttle for 1,000 rpm. Compare the reading with the figures on the chart below.
7. Remove the gauge. Reinstall the injection nozzle and holder with a new gasket washer and holder dust seal. Make sure only one gasket washer is used.

NORMAL COMPRESSION SPECIFICATIONS

Engine Series	Normal Compression (psi)
END475	540
ENDT475	470
ET477	470
END(B)673E	530
ENDT(B)673	575
ENDT(B)673C	460
ET(B)673	460
ET(B)673E	460
ETY(B)673E	635
ETAY(B)673A	460
ETAZ(B)673	460
ETAZ(B)673A	460
ETAZ(B)673C	460
ENDT(B)675	460
ETY(B)675	585
ENDT(B)676	460
ETA(B)676B	460
ETAY(B)676	460
ETAY(B)676D	460
END707	530
END711	530

MINIMUM COMPRESSION PRESSURE PSI

Engine Series	Altitude Feet 0	2,000	4,000	6,000	8,000	10,000	12,000	14,000
Non-turbocharged six cylinder	530	500	460	430	390	360	340	310
Turbocharged/charged air cooling six cylinder	475	445	415	385	355	325	295	275
V8—866 cu. in. 14.95:1 ①	485	455	425	385	355	335	305	285
V8—866 cu. in. 15.7:1 ①	540	410	480	440	410	380	350	330
V8—400 series ②	585	555	525	495	465	435	405	375

① Compression ratio
② 998 cubic inches

8. Repeat the test for the remaining cylinders.
9. Compare readings with each other. They should be within 50 psi.
10. Check all nozzle holder and fuel line fittings for proper torque. Start the engine and make sure there are no fuel leaks.

Valve Adjustment

CAUTION

To avoid damage to pistons, always set valve lash under cold static conditions (coolant temperature below 100°F and engine turned to the off position).

6 CYLINDER

Adjust inlet and exhaust valve clearances at TDC of the compression stroke. Follow the firing order when making adjustments. The firing order for all Mack 6 cylinder diesel engines is 1–5–3–6–2–4.

Mark the vibration damper at three 120° increments. Start with the TDC mark for number one cylinder (already marked on damper) and place a white mark $12^9/_{32}$ in. in both direections from the number one cylinder mark. Use these marks to rotate the engine to TDC for each successive piston in the firing order.

1. Set number one cylinder piston on TDC of the compression stroke, using the mark on the vibration damper.
2. Loosen the adjusting screw locknut on the inlet and exhaust rocker arms.
3. Adjust the inlet and exhaust valve lash to specified clearance.
4. Tighten the adjusting screw locknuts.
5. Recheck the valve lash.
6. Turn the crankshaft, in the direction of normal engine rotation placing number five piston at TDC of the compression stroke. Adjust the valve clearances as previously outlined.
7. Continue rotating the crankshaft through the firing order, stopping at each cylinder TDC compression stroke, to adjust the valve clearance.

NOTE: When adjusting exhaust valve clearances on engines equipped with Mack Dynatard® engine brake, use Mack special tool MVT–36–6 or equivalent.

V8 ENGINES

Set the V8 valve lash in firing order with the piston at TDC of the compression stroke. The firing order of all Mack V8 diesel engines is 1–5–4–8–6–3–7–2. Present production Mack V8 vibration dampers have four timing marks spaced 90° apart, indicating TDC for each cylinder piston. On earlier models only the number one cylinder piston is marked. When not marked, chaulk three more white marks on the damper at 90° intervals.

VALVE CLEARANCE SPECIFICATIONS

(Valve stem to rocker arm)

Engine Series	Cold Static Inlet	Exhaust
END475	.014	.108
ENDT475	.014	.028
ET477	.014	.028
6 Cyl ①	.016	.024
All V8	.016	.026

① Includes all Mack 6 cylinder engines in production as of August 31, 1980.

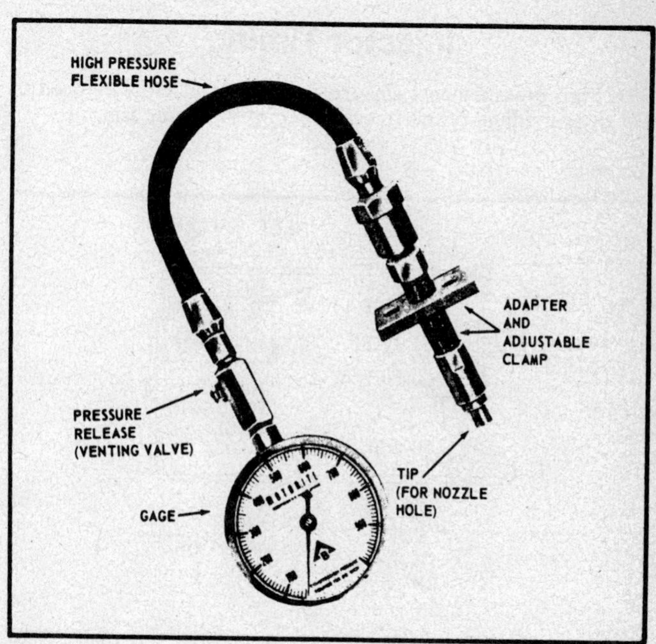

Compression tester (© Mack Trucks, Inc.)

Valve timing mark location on vibration damper
(© Mack Trucks, Inc.)

1. Set the number one cylinder piston on TDC of the compression stroke, using the timing marks on the vibration damper as a guide.
2. Loosen the adjusting screw locknuts on the inlet and exhaust rocker arms.
3. Adjust the inlet valve lash to 0.016 in. and the exhaust valve lash to 0.026 in..

NOTE: When adjusting exhaust valve clearances on engines equipped with Mack Dynatard® engine brake use Mack special tool MVT–36–6 or equivalent.

4. Tighten the adjusting screw locknuts and recheck the valve lash.
5. Adjust all valves in the firing order in same manner as outlined for number one cylinder.

Injector Timing

The high pressure port closure stand method must be used to check and adjust Mack injection pump to engine timing.

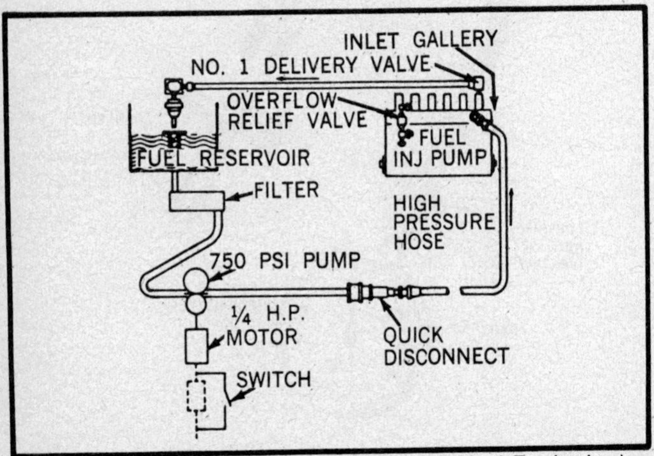

High pressure port closing system diagram (© Mack Trucks, Inc.)

NOTE: Port closing is defined as the point at which the fuel coming from an injection pump delivery valve changes from a steady stream to a few drops.

When the Mack diesel engine is timed correctly the vibration damper/flywheel timing mark will be at the specified degrees, at the same time as the port closure of the number 1 cylinder fuel delivery valve.

NOTE: Injection timing specifications are found on the injection pump name plate or EPA emission plate.

Adjust the timing by following the same procedure for all Mack 6 or 8 cylinder engines equipped with American Bosch (APE) or Robert Bosch (PES) injection pumps.

Special Tools

The following Mach special tools (or equivalent) will be required in order to complete the high pressure port closure timing procedure:

1. Portable high pressure – port closing timer (Bacharach part o. 72–7010) or high pressure hand supply pump (Robert Bosch no. 1–687–222–039).
2. Timing plug gauge for American Bosch injection pump (J24345–1).
3. Timing plug gauge for Robert Bosch injection pump (J24345–2).

END475 timing marks aligned (© Mack Trucks, Inc.)

High Pressure Port Closing Stand Timing Procedure

1. Cap or connect injection lines on all except number 1 delivery valve outlet.
2. Remove all return fuel lines at the overflow relief valve union fittings. Cap the relief valve port connectors.
3. Connect the high pressure line from the portable closure stand to the fuel inlet of the injection pump gallery.
4. Connect the stand return line from the number 1 cylinder delivery valve holder to the portable port closure stand.
5. Check the timing.
   a. Secure the injection pump stop lever in run position.
   b. On pumps equipped with a retard start device, remove the control rack cap plug and insert the correct timing plug gauge. (American Bosch J24345–1 and Robert Bosch J24345–2).

CAUTION

On Mack Scania engines equipped with a Robert Bosch injection pump the damper cylinder must be removed from the pump to prevent damage to the damper cylinder.

c. When equipped with a Mack Puff Limiter, apply 30 PSI minimum air pressure to the puff limiter air cylinder. The air pressure must be applied before the high pressure fuel is delivered to the pump or mistiming will occur.

d. Activate the throttle lever several times and secure it in the full load position.

e. Introduce fuel pressure to the pump gallery.

NOTE: Fuel pressure applied prior to securing the throttle lever may prevent proper port closing.

f. Slowly rotate the engine, bringing up the number one cylinder piston on its compression stroke. Stop rotating the engine immediately when the fuel stream from number cylinder delivery valve changes to fuel drops (port closing).

g. Check the timing mark on the damper/flywheel. The mark should be at the degrees specified on the pump name plate.

6. If the pump to engine timing differs from specification, then adjust it.

a. Shut off the port closure stand.

b. Loosen the injection pump drive coupling capscrews.

c. Move the injection pump drive coupling in the reverse of normal rotation until the coupling is at the end of its adjusting slots. Lightly tighten the capscrews.

d. Rotate the engine until number one cylinder piston comes up on its compression stroke. Stop rotating the engine, when the specified degrees show on the vibration damper or flywheel.

e. Repeat Step 5. Adjust the drive coupling as needed to correct the timing.

7. When the timing is correct turn off the port closure stand, torque the drive coupling capscrews, remove the timing plug gauge and install the control rack cap plug.

8. Remove the caps from the overflow relief valve union port connections and install all fuel return lines.

Control Rack and Governor

Mack injection pump rack control is accomplished by a mechanical governor mounted on the end of the pump. The governor provides a coupling between the accelerator linkage and the injection pump rack, thereby, regulating fuel delivery in response to pedal position, load and engine speed.

NOTE: Mack fuel injection pumps are factory sealed. No adjustments should be made by other than Mack authorized repair stations, or the engine warranty may be voided.

Adjust Idle Speed

The low idle setting is the only adjustment that can be made on Mack injection pumps without breaking a protective lead seal. All other adjustments require the breaking of seals, which if broken by unauthorized personnel voids the pump and engine warranty.

Special Tools

The Mack special tool J28559 Digistrobe or equivalent magnetic pickup type tachometer is needed to check and adjust engine idle speed.

Checking Low Idle Speed

1. Locate and mark the TDC line on the vibration damper.
2. Connect the J28559 Digistrobe to the required power source (Check equipment instructions).
3. Set the Digistrobe at the recommended low idle speed.
4. Start the engine and direct the flash of the Digistrobe at the vibration damper. The mark on the vibration damper should appear to be stopped and the digital read out should equal the specified low idle speed. If the low idle speed is out of specification, adjust it.

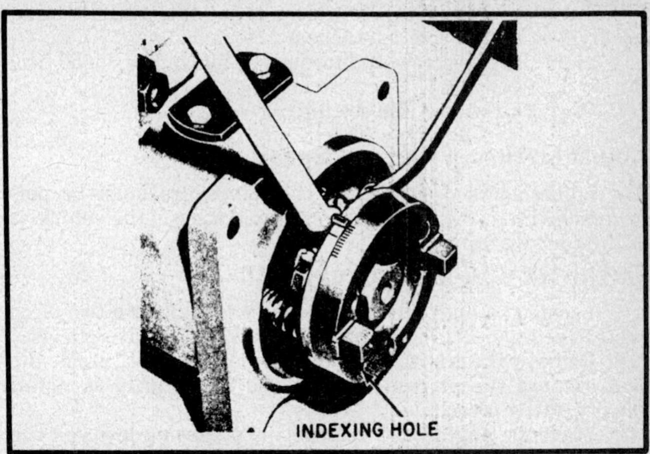

Adjusting injection pump coupling on END864 engine (© Mack Trucks, Inc.)

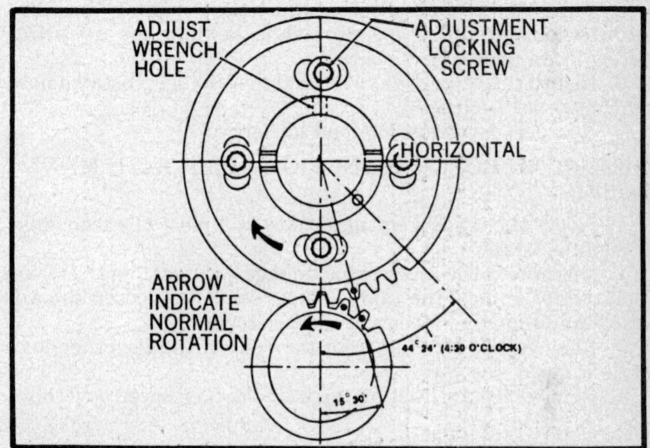

Position of drive coupling tangs and timing marks just prior to pump installation (© Mack Trucks, Inc.)

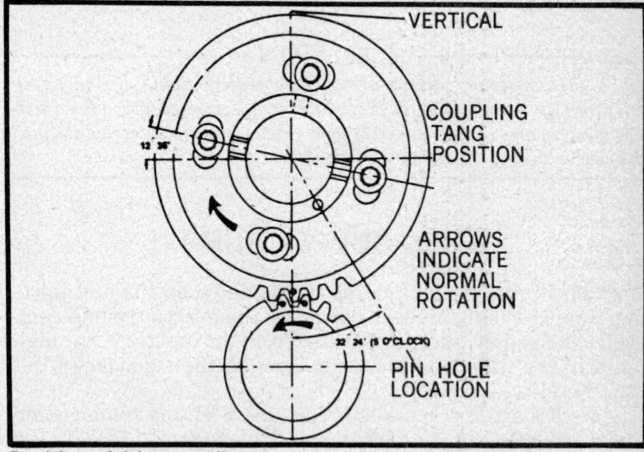

Position of drive coupling tangs and timing marks with No. 1 piston at TDC (© Mack Trucks, Inc.)

Adjusting Low Idle Speed

The low idle adjusting screw is located on the top of the throttle housing cover.

1. Connect the J28559 Digistrobe or equivalent tachometer and set it to the specified low idle rpm.
2. Start the engine and flash the Digistrobe on the vibration damper.

3. Loosen the low idle screw locknut and turn the idle screw until the specified rpm is reached.
4. Hold the idle screw and torque the locknut to 45–50 inch lbs.
5. Recheck the low idle setting.

Adjust Maximum No-Load Speed

The adjustments described in this procedure must be performed by an authorized Mack service station if the vehicle is still under warranty.

AMERICAN BOSCH INJECTION PUMP

1. Locate the high idle adjustment screw under a two-piece protective cover behind the throttle linkage operating lever.
2. Remove the throttle linkage operating lever, break the seal, remove the protective cover and temporarily re-install the operating lever.
3. Start the engine and remove the operating lever on the governor until it contacts the high idle adjusting screw.
4. If the engine rpm is above or below specification, loosen the locknut on the adjusting screw.
5. Turn the adjusting screw until the correct rpm is obtained. Retighten the locknut while holding the adjusting screw in an unchanged position.
6. Install the protective cover and the linkage. Install a new tamper-proof lead seal.
7. Recheck maximum no-load idle speed.

AMERICAN BOSCH INJECTION PUMP WITH MAXI-MISER

1. Apply the truck's spring brakes and place the transmission in neutral.
2. Disconnect the accelerator linkage springs from the injection pump, remove the tamper-proof seals and loosen the air line retaining clip on the valve lifter cover.
3. Remove the air line from the rear of the governor and slide it out of the way.
4. Remove the air inlet fitting from the dual speed governor.
5. Loosen the air inlet cap.
6. Install a master tachometer so that it can be seen as work is performed on the pump. Start the engine, warm it up and secure the accelerator lever in the high idle position.
7. Use an allen wrench to turn the adjusting screw until the correct rpm is obtained.
8. When the rpm is adjusted to specification, tighten the air inlet cap without disturbing the adjusting screw.
9. Install the air inlet fitting and connect the air line to the dual speed governor.
10. Remove the master tachometer, reconnect the accelerator linkage and install new tamper-proof seals.

NOTE: If the vehicle equipped with a Maxi-Miser is to be Dyno tested, the Maxi-Miser must be temporarily deactivated in order to check the power at governed speed. Apply shop air to the governor to deactivate it.

ROBERT BOSCH INJECTION PUMP

1. Locate the high idle adjustment screw on the side of the injection pump.
2. Identify the lead seal and protective cover arrangement which must be removed to gain access to the adjustment screw.
3. Pry out the tamper-proof lead seal.
4. Remove the screw and protective cover. Loosen the high idle locknut.
5. With the throttle lever in the full throttle position, turn the adjusting screw in until there is clearance between the throttle lever and the adjusting screw.
6. Turn the adjusting screw out until it just contacts the throttle lever. Give the screw an additional $\frac{1}{4}$ turn out to prevent the governor's internal linkage from binding.
7. If the engine rpm is still below the governed speed no-load specification, the pump must be removed and recalibrated.
8. If the engine rpm is too high, continue turning the adjusting screw out until the correct rpm is reached. Carefully tighten the locknut, while holding the proper rpm setting.
9. Install the protective cover and a new tamper-proof seal.

FUEL SYSTEM

CAUTION

Mack fuel injection pumps are factory sealed including the pump drive timing gear cover. If the truck is under warranty, all adjustments or repairs should be made by a Mack authorized service station. Otherwise the warranty may be voided.

FUEL SUPPLY PUMP

Most Mack fuel supply pumps are mounted on the fuel injection pump housing and are driven by the injection pump camshaft. The supply pump draws fuel from the fuel tank, through the primary filter and pumps it through the secondary filter into the injection pump.

Some Robert Bosch fuel systems use a Viking combination fuel transfer pump and tachometer drive to provide fuel to the injection pump and drive the tachometer. The unit is driven off from the auxiliary shaft.

FUEL INJECTION PUMP

All current production Mack engines use either the American Bosch (APE) or the Robert Bosch (PES) injection pumps.

Removal – 6 Cylinder

1. Loosen the inner support bracket bolts.
2. Remove the upper and lower support brackets.
3. Remove the lower pump to cylinder block bracket.
4. Remove all fuel line brackets and fuel lines from the pump. Cap all fuel lines to prevent dirt from entering and fuel from spilling.
5. Remove the drive coupling bolts and drive coupling.
6. Remove the pump from the engine.

Installation – 6 Cylinder

1. Rotate the engine in the normal direction until number one piston comes up on the compression stroke. At the same time bring the mark on the vibration damper flywheel to the number of degrees specified on the valve cover. The injection pump driveshaft flange lugs should now be in the horizontal position and the indexing pin hole at the 4 o'clock position.
2. Grease the front (non-counterbored) face of the coupling and mount it on the pump driveshaft flange. Center the coupling ring side to side.
3. Remove the adapter inspection hole cover.
4. Assemble the injection pump upper support bracket (if used) to the injection pump and tighten the bolts.
5. Rotate the pump coupling drive flange until the lugs are in a vertical plane and the indexing hole is at a 7 o'clock position.
6. Mount the pump assembly on the engine. As the pump moves into position the indexing pin can be observed through the adaptor inspection hole.

7. Install the adaptor to cylinder block bolts and tighten them.
8. Assemble the injection pump lower support bracket to the cylinder block and tighten the bolts lightly. Install and tighten the support bracket to cylinder block bolts.
9. Check the coupling ring for approximately $^{3}/_{32}$ in. end float.
10. Set the timing by the high pressure (port closing) stand method.

Removal – V8 Engine

1. Remove the hardware and pump bolts.
2. Remove the drive coupling bolts and drive coupling.
3. Remove all fuel line brackets and fuel lines from the injection pump. Cap all fuel lines to prevent dirt from entering and fuel from spilling.
4. Remove the pump from the engine.

Installation – V8 Engine

1. Rotate the engine in the normal direction until the number one piston is at TDC of the compression stroke. The timing mark on the drive coupling should be centered between the two timing marks on the auxiliary drive shaft gear. The pin hole location should be at the five o'clock position and the coupling tangs at $12^{1}/_{2}$ degrees off from horizontal.
2. Rotate the engine backwards approximately 40 degrees.
3. Rotate the engine in the normal direction again until the vibration damper timing reads at the degrees specified on the pump name plate. In this position, the drive coupling tangs will be approximately horizontal and the pin hole will be between the 4 and 5 o'clock position. The gear timing marks will be approximately $15^{1}/_{2}$ degrees to the right.
4. Install the pin and ring assembly on the injection pump drive coupling.
5. Install the injection pump. Connect all fuel lines and fuel line brackets.
6. Recheck the port closing timing.

Fuel Filters

The primary filter is located between the fuel tank and the fuel supply pump. The primary filter is color coded red. A secondary fuel filter is located between the fuel supply pump and the fuel injection pump. The secondary fuel filter is color coded green. For all current production models the filters are the spin on type.

Removal

1. Clean the area around the filter and the adapter with solvent. Dry the area with compressed air.
2. Break the filters loose with a filter wrench. Both filters have right hand threads.
3. Wipe the sealing surface clean on the adapter before installing a new filter.

Installation

NOTE: Mack service filters contain detailed installation procedures. If package procedures conflict with this procedure, the package instructions should be followed.

1. Apply a thin film of engine oil to the filter sealing gasket.
2. Pre-prime the filters by filling them with filtered fuel. Prime the filter through the small outer holes on the top of the filter. Do not add the fuel through the center core.
3. Apply a thin coat of clean engine oil to the sealing gasket. Tighten the filter one full turn by hand after the gasket contacts the adapter.

Fuel Injector Service

The fuel injectors in Mack diesel engines receive metered fuel at injection pressure from the injector pump. The nozzles are used to provide effective atomization of the fuel through use of a nozzle valve and discharge nozzle, which insure sharp start-up and cutoff of fuel flow and production of four high velocity streams which will effectively penetrate to all parts of all combustion chamber.

The nozzle body at the lower end of the injector consists of the hole type nozzle, the seat for the nozzle valve and the fuel passage. The nozzle valve spindle extends upward to the top of the nozzle holder, where there is an adjustable spring for maintenance of precise injector pop pressure. Controlled clearance between the nozzle body and the nozzle valve lubricates the mechanism. A leak-off fitting at the top of the injector returns excess fuel to the fuel tank.

Injector nozzles should be removed and checked after 50,000 to 75,000 miles, or if troubleshooting reveals poor performance. Extreme care must be taken to ensure absolute cleanliness during nozzle service. It must also be remembered that oil leaving an injector nozzle is moving at extreme speed. Contact with the skin will usually result in penetration. Therefore, testing must be carried out in a manner that will protect the skin from nozzle discharge.

NOTE: If an injector is suspected of malfunction, it can be located as follows: run the engine at idle, loosen the high pressure fitting to the suspected injector at the injection pump ($^{1}/_{2}$ turn). This will cut off the fuel to the nozzle. Retighten the fitting. If the cylinder is not restored to firing, then the nozzle should be removed and checked completely.

Removal

1. Clean the cylinder head around the nozzles and the tubing connections with solvent. Blow dry with compressed air.
2. Remove the leak-off lines, carefully recovering the copper gaskets.
3. Remove the high pressure fuel lines and install protector plugs in their open ends.
4. Remove the nuts from the hold down studs. Use a small pry bar to remove nozzles, gripping them under the hold-down flanges at a point near to the nozzle body. Use penetrating oil to aid removal if the nozzle is especially tight.
5. Place nozzles in a rack in order of removal so they may be installed in the engine in original order. Plug the nozzle ports in the cylinder head(s).

Testing

1. Clean carbon from the nozzle with a special wire brush.
2. Mount the nozzle holder assembly in a tester. Make sure the tester is filled with clean fuel.
3. Close the pressure gauge valve (to protect the gauge). Operate the actuating lever at about 25 strokes per minute to expel air and settle the spring and nozzle loading column.
4. Open the pressure gauge valve one half turn and slowly operate the actuating lever to raise the pressure to the point where the nozzle opens. Carefully watch the gauge and note the exact pressure at which the nozzle opens. Also check the characteristics of the flow to ensure that no leakage or dripping course occurs after the end of injection.
5. Compare the opening pressure with the figure specified in the nozzle opening pressure chart and adjust the nozzle to specifications if necessary.
6. Wipe the nozzle tip dry. Operate the actuating lever slowly to bring pressure to within 100 psi of opening pressure (20 psi with END 475 nozzles) and maintain the pressure for five seconds. If drops of fuel form or if the nozzle sprays slightly, reject it.

7. Close the gauge valve (to protect the gauge) and operate the lever at about 15 strokes per minute. The spray pattern formed should be sharp, solid and with uniform quantities and angles between orifices. Use short, rapid strokes on END 475 nozzles to produce a good spray pattern. Reject a nozzle with a poor spray pattern.

8. On all but 475 series nozzles, test the nozzle to make sure it makes a chattering sound. Operate the actuating handle so the stroke takes about two seconds. Close the pressure gauge valve. A distinct and regular chattering sound must be produced, although an occasional variation is acceptable. Reject a nozzle which does not pass the chatter test.

Disassembly

NOTE: The American Bosch ($^{21}/_{17}$mm) injectors do not have an opening pressure adjusting screw; therefore, the opening spring pressure cannot be released for disassembly. In order to disassemble this type of injector, soak the assembly in carbon solvent, then place it in the Mack tool disassembly fixture TSE–77108 (or equivalent). The disassembly fixture must be used in order to avoid damage to the index dowel pins, holder and nozzle. With the fixture in a soft jawed vise, loosen the upper cap and then remove the cap by hand turning. Remove the nozzle assembly from the fixture to complete the disassembly.

1. Loosen the opening pressure adjusting screw all the way to relieve all downward pressure.
2. Position the nozzle assembly on a suitable block in a vise. Remove the upper cap nut.
3. Loosen the locknut, if the nozzle is equipped with one and loosen the opening pressure adjusting screw all the way to relieve all downward pressure.
4. Use a special wrench to remove the spring retaining capnut. Remove the pressure adjusting spring and spindle assembly.
5. Invert the holder assembly in a softjawed vise and remove the nozzle capnut. Remove the nozzle body and valve assembly. Keep these two parts together as they are a mated assembly. Reinstall nozzle cap nut loosely.

Inspection

1. Wash all parts in a safe solvent and inspect for wear as described below:
   a. Check the spring for corrosion and pitting and replace if they are evident.
   b. Check spindle for straightness within 0.010 in. T.I.R.
   c. Check the lapped surfaces of the nozzle body and holder for cracks and scratches. Replace parts that are cracked and lap parts which are slightly scratched. If the holder lapped surface is spalled more than .003" deep in the needle valve area, it must be replaced rather than resurfaced.
   d. Remove the locating dowels from the holder very carefully to prevent damaging the lapped surface. Check the spring retaining cap nut to make sure the bleed hole is open.
   e. Clean the pressure chamber of the nozzle body with a special scraper, as shown in the illustration.
   f. Using a special needle and vise, clean the nozzle body holes. Be careful to avoid breaking the needle inside the discharge holes, as fragments may prove to be impossible to remove.
   g. Lift the valve about ⅓ of its length out of the nozzle body, hold the body at 45 degrees from the vertical and release the valve. It should slide back freely. If the valve is not free, work the valve in the nozzle body using a special polishing tallow. Clean the nozzle valve and body in solvent and blow dry.
   h. Check the nozzle valve lift using a straightedge and dial indicator. See the injection Nozzle Opening Pressure Chart for specifications. Place the nozzle in a fixture and run a straightedge across the top of the nozzle body. Mount a dial indicator right above the needle valve and zero it. While holding the straightedge, raise the needle valve with a pair of tweezers just until the lower portion of the valve contacts the straightedge. Hold the valve in position while reading the dial indicator. If the valve lift is not to specification, the assembly must be replaced.
   i. If the injector uses a filter in the fuel inlet connection, clean it by reverse flushing it with compressed air.
   j. Check the ends of the high pressure fuel tubes to make sure they are open. Ream ENDT 864 lines to .085" and all others to .078". Flush out the chips.

Assembly

1. Place the injection nozzle holder in a soft jawed vise.
2. Position the nozzle body and valve onto the holder, aligning dowel pins and holes carefully.
3. Install the nozzle cap nut, using a special centering sleeve during the initial tightening. Remove the centering sleeve and torque the cap nut to specification, using a special adapter.
4. Invert the holder and install the spindle and pressure adjusting spring. Tighten the pressure adjusting screw and lock it in position with the locknut.
5. Install the injector in a test stand and adjust opening pressure as described in the section on service.
6. Install the nozzle holder with a new gasket and install and tighten upper capnuts.

Installation

1. Remove copper nozzle tip gasket from the hole in the cylinder head. Clean the nozzle cavity with a special reamer and wire brush. Check the gasket seat for trueness and cleanliness. Crank the engine over by hand to blow loose carbon from the cavity.
2. Apply an anti-seize compound to the outside diameter of nozzle and holder and position the assembly in the head with a new nozzle tip gasket and dust seal O-ring. The nozzle tip gasket may be held in place with a small amount of grease.
3. Seat the nozzle squarely and then install and tighten hold down nuts evenly.
4. Install the high pressure fuel lines and torque nuts carefully so that tubing will not be distorted.
5. Install the leak-off lines with their copper gaskets.
6. Operate the engine and check for leaks. Retighten fittings as necessary.

Bleeding Fuel System

Whenever the injection pump, supply pump, fuel lines or fuel filter(s) have been removed, bleed out all air before attempting to start the engine. Air bubbles in the system will enter the injection pump and cause hard starting and erratic engine performance.

Past production models equipped with a hand priming pump on the injection pump, can be bled (primed) by the following procedure.

1. Disconnect the transfer pump (supply pump) outlet connection.
2. Prime the system with the hand primer, until a solid stream of fuel runs out of the outlet connection.
3. Retighten the transfer pump outlet.
4. Disconnect or loosen the fuel inlet connection at the pump gallery.
5. Prime the system with the hand primer until a solid stream of fuel is obtained.

NOTE: If fuel cannot be obtained by hand priming, check the fuel lines for leaks. Check the lines from the fuel supply tank to the fuel transfer (supply) pump.

6. Connect and tighten the gallery inlet fitting.

21 MM INJECTION NOZZLE SPECIFICATIONS

Engine Series	Nozzle Opening Pressure—PSI	Valve Lift-In	Injection Pump	Holes	Hole Diameter Inch (mm)
END475	1985 to 2035	0.015	PES	4	0.011 (0.280)
ENDT475	2840 to 2890	0.015	PES	5	0.010 (0.252)
ENDT673	3000 to 3050	0.014	APE/PES	4	0.0126 (0.320)
ENDT673C	3000 to 3050	0.014	APE/PES	5	0.0126 (0.320)
ET673②	3000 to 3050	0.014	APE/PES	5	0.0126 (0.320)
END673E	3000 to 3050	0.019	PES	5	0.0126 (0.320)
END673E	3000 to 3050	0.014	APE	5	0.0126 (0.320)
ENDT675①	3000 to 3050	0.014	APE	5	0.0126 (0.320)
ENDT675	3000 to 3050	0.019	PES	5	0.0126 (0.320)
END707	3000 to 3050	0.019	PES	5	0.0126 (0.320)
END711	3000 to 3050	0.019	PES	5	0.0126 (0.320)

① To November, 1977 on APE injection pumps only
② To January, 1979

21/17MM INJECTION NOZZLE SPECIFICATIONS

Engine Series	Nozzle Opening Pressure—PSI	Valve Lift-In	Injection Pump	Holes	Hole Diameter Inch (mm)
AMERICAN BOSCH INJECTION NOZZLE AND HOLDER					
ENDT676	4200 to 4350	0.014	APE	5	0.0126 (0.320)
ENDT675C	3300 to 3450	0.014	APE	6	0.0126 (0.320)
ETAZ673	4200 to 4350	0.014	APE	5	0.0126 (0.320)
ENDT675①	3800 to 3950	0.014	APE	5	0.0126 (0.320)
ETAY673	4200 to 4350	0.014	APE	5	0.0126 (0.320)
ETAY676	4200 to 4350	0.014	APE	5	0.0126 (0.320)
ETZ675	3800 to 3950	0.014	APE	5	0.0126 (0.320)
ETY675	3800 to 3950	0.014	APE	5	0.0126 (0.320)
ROBERT BOSCH INJECTION NOZZLE AND HOLDER					
ENDT676	4200 to 4400	0.019	PES	5	0.0126 (0.320)
ENDT675C	3800 to 3950	0.014	PES	5	0.0126 (0.320)
ETAZ673	4200 to 4400	0.019	PES	5	0.0126 (0.320)
ET673②	3800 to 3950	0.014	PES	5	0.0126 (0.320)
ETAY676	4200 to 4400	0.019	PES	5	0.0126 (0.320)
ETY675	3800 to 3950	0.014	PES	5	0.0126 (0.320)
ETZ675	3800 to 3950	0.014	PES	5	0.0126 (0.320)
ETAY673	4200 to 4400	0.019	PES	5	0.0126 (0.320)
ETY673E	3800 to 3950	0.014	PES	5	0.0126 (0.320)
MACK SCANIA ONLY					
ET477	2990 to 3060	0.011	PES	5	0.010 (0.252)

① Begining November 1, 1977
② Beginning January, 1979 production

6 CYL.① INJECTION NOZZLE SPECIFICATIONS

Engine Model	Nozzle Opening Pressure—PSI	Valve Lift-In	Injection Pump	Holes	Hole Diameter Inch (mm)
E6-200	3000–3150	—	PES	5	.0126(0.320)
EM6-225	4250–4400	—	PES	5	.0126(0.320)
EC6-235	3800–3950	—	APE	5	.0126(0.320)
EM6-237	②	—	③	5	④
EM6-237R	3800–3950	—	APE	5	.0126(0.320)

6 CYL.① INJECTION NOZZLE SPECIFICATIONS

Engine Model	Nozzle Opening Pressure—PSI	Valve Lift-In	Injection Pump	Holes	Hole Diameter Inch (mm)
E6-250	4250–4400	—	PES	5	.0126(0.320)
EM6-250	4200–4400	—	③	5	④
EM6-250R	4200–4400	—	③	5	⑤
EMC6-250	4200–4350	—	APE	5	.0126(0.320)
E6-260	3800–3950	—	APE	5	.0126(0.320)
EM6-275	4200–4350	—	APE	5	.0126(0.320)
EM6-275L	4200–4350	—	PLM	5	.0126(0.320)
EM6-275R	4200–4350	—	APE	5	.0126(0.320)
EM6-285	4200–4400	—	③	5	.0126(0.320)
EM6-285R	4200–4350	—	APE	5	.0126(0.320)
EMC6-285	4200–4350	—	APE	5	.0126(0.320)
EMC6-285R	4200–4350	—	APE	5	.0126(0.320)
EM6-300	4200–4350	—	APE	5	.0126(0.320)
EM6-300R	4200–4350	—	APE	5	.0126(0.320)
E6-315	4250–4400	—	PES	5	.0126(0.320)
E6-325	4200–4350	—	PLM	5	.0126(0.320)
EC6-330	4200–4350	—	PLM	5	.0126(0.320)
E6-350	4300–4450	—	PLM	5	.0126(0.320)
E6-350R	4200–4350	—	PLM	5	.0126(0.320)
EC6-350	4200–4350	—	PLM	5	.0126(0.320)

①Includes all mack 6 cylinder engines in production as of August 31, 1980.

②United Technologies Diesel systems pump: 3800–3950
Robert Bosch Pump: 4250–4400

③United Technologies Diesel systems pump: APE
Robert Bosch pump: PES

④United Technologies Diesel systems pump: .0126(0.320)
Robert Bosch pump: .0120(0.305)

⑤United Technologies Diesel systems pump: .0118(0.300)
Robert Bosch pump: .0126(0.320)

V-8 INJECTION NOZZLE SPECIFICATIONS

Engine Series	Nozzle Opening Pressure—PSI	Valve Lift-In	Injection Pump	Holes	Hole Diameter Inch (mm)
ENDT(B) 865,866	3800–3950	—	APE	6	0.011(0.28)
400 Series①	4200–4350	—	APE	6	0.011(0.28)

①998 cubic inches

7. Disconnect the overflow line on the injection pump and continue priming, until a solid stream of fuel runs out.
8. Connect and tighten the overflow line.
9. Secure the hand priming handle and start the engine.

NOTE: Check the Robert Bosch system for an open bleed line on the secondary filter. If equipped, use the bleed line to prime the system. Start the engine before opening the bleed line. Close the bleed line as soon as a solid stream of fuel is obtained.

10. When the engine is operating normally, check the filters and lines for leaks.

When current production models, not equipped with a hand priming pump, need to be bled, use one of two alternate procedures:

First Alternate Bleeding Procedure

1. Attach a manual or electric low pressure pump (15–20 psi) to the inlet side of the primary fuel filter.
2. Disconnect or loosen the overflow valve fitting.
3. Using clean fuel, pump the system out until all of the air is expelled from the overflow valve.
4. Reconnect and tighten the overflow valve.

Second Alternate Bleeding Method

1. Completely remove the overflow valve from the injection pump gallery, to provide resistance free fuel flow.
2. Press a shop air nozzle wrapped with a shop towel onto the fuel tank filler spout. Pressurize the fuel tank. Any air escaping past the shop towel will prevent excessive pressure in fuel tank.
3. Continue the pressure until a solid stream of fuel is obtained at the overflow port.
4. Install the overflow valve.

Fuel Cut Off Controls

INJECTION PUMP SWITCH

V8 ENGINES WITH AMERICAN BOSCH V-TYPE PUMPS

The switch is located on the rack cap end of the injection pump. It is a micro-type switch. The switch is engaged by the rack extension and activates the system at zero fuel only. The switch is pre-adjusted and under normal operation needs no further adjustment. If adjustment proves necessary:

1. Measure the height of each of the three electrical terminals on the top cover of the Dynatard switch. Each must extend at least $\frac{1}{2}$ in. above the cover. If not, remove the cover and adjust the terminal by loosening the locknuts.
2. Cut and remove the seal wire from the switch side cover, remove the side cover, rectifier and gasket. Position the engine brake toggle switch on the dash to the ON position activate the electrical circuit to the engine brake switch.
3. Depress the microswitch contact button with a screwdriver and check for continuity with a circuit tester.
4. If continuity is good, check the adjustment of the engine brake adjusting screw. Connect the circuit tester from the engine terminals to ground. Push the control rack extension in to the stop position and the light should go on. If not, turn the adjusting screw until it does.
5. Loosen the cap screw on the end of the rack extension just enough to remove the adjusting screw and bracket. Place a straight edge along the forked end of the adjusting screw bracket and measure the clearance between the straight edge and the screw. Loosen the locknut and adjust the screw to obtain a clearance of 0.138–0.142 in. and tighten the locknut.
6. Slide the adjusting screw bracket between the control rack extension and capscrew and tighten the capscrew. Replace the switch side cover and rectifier. Install a new gasket and secure with a pump seal.

SIX AND V8 ENGINE WITH AMERICAN BOSCH INJECTION PUMP, EXCEPT V-TYPE PUMP

This switch is a small contact type and is an integral part of the governor housing cover. The switch assembly is activated by the cam nose and fulcrum lever assembly and activates the system at zero fuel only. If adjustment is necessary follow either of the two following procedures:

WITH INTERNAL PUFF LIMITER

A 0.070 in. feeler gauge and a gauge plug, part #J24659 are necessary for this adjustment.

1. Measure the adjusting screw extension from the first locknut. The screw should extend $\frac{1}{8}$ in. If not, loosen both locknuts and adjust the screw. Tighten the locknuts.
2. Place the pump stop lever in the RUN position.
3. Remove the rack cap plug.

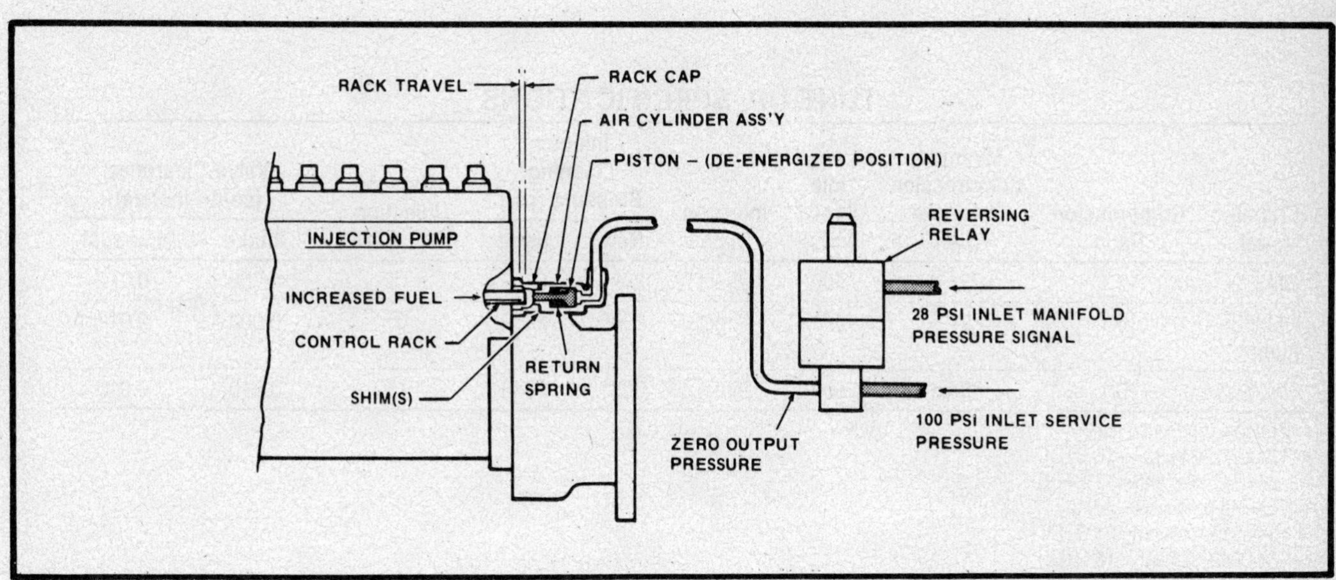

Normal operating position of Puff Limiter—typical (© Mack Trucks, Inc.)

NOTE: On 6–cylinder models, the rack cap may have to be held to prevent its turning when removing the plug or installing the gauge plug.

4. Position the lockring flush against the head of the gauge to allow maximum exposure of the plug gauge screw threads.
5. Screw the special gauge plug into the rack cap until it contacts the rack. Continue to screw it in until it bottoms internally in the injection pump, placing the rack in the full OFF position.
6. Position and lock the lockring by turning it clockwise flush against the rack cap.

CAUTION

To keep the lockring fixed in this position, screw it in on the set screws placed 180° apart.

7. Turn the special gauge plug counterclockwise until the 0.070 in. feeler gauge can be inserted between the lockring and the cap.
8. Attach the electrical continuity tester to the contact terminal and ground.
9. Loosen the two adjusting screw locknuts on the engine brake switch adjusting screw.
10. Turn the adjusting screw slowly, counterclockwise until continuity is broken.
11. Turn the screw slowly clockwise until continuity is just achieved. Tighten the inner locknut without disturbing the setting.
12. Place the contact terminal in the upright position and tighten the outer locknut.

WITH ANEROID PUFF LIMITER – ROBERT BOSCH PUMP

Special gauge plug #J24660 is necessary for this adjustment.

1. Place the injection pump stop lever in the RUN position.
2. Remove the rack cap plug.
3. Screw the plug gauge into the rack cap until it contacts the rack. Continue to screw it in until it bottoms internally in the full OFF position.
4. Move the throttle from idle to wide open several times. Return and securely retain it against the idle stop by using the throttle return spring or its equivalent.
5. Connect the continuity tester between the contact terminal and ground.
6. Loosen the two adjusting screw locknuts on the engine brake switch adjusting screw.
7. Turn the adjusting screw counterclockwise until continuity occurs at the tester.
8. Turn the adjusting screw slowly clockwise until the point at which continuity breaks. Then turn it one full turn more, clockwise.
9. Tighten the inner locknut without disturbing the setting.
10. Return the terminal to the upright position and tighten the outer locknut.
11. Remove the plug gauge and install the rack cap securely.

PUMPS WITH MACK PUFF LIMITER

1. Run the engine to normal operating temperature and establish a smooth idle of 550 rpm.
2. Loosen both nuts on the pump brake switch.
3. On American Bosch Pumps, turn the adjusting screw clockwise; on Robert Bosch Pumps, turn the adjusting screw counterclockwise until the Dynatard brake comes on.
4. Turn the screw in the opposite direction one full turn.
5. Tighten the jam nut and wire nut. Check the setting by noting that the brake drops out between 1000 and 700 rpm.

MERCEDES DIESEL ENGINES
OM352, OM352A, OM355/5 ENGINES

TUNE-UP SPECIFICATIONS

Engine Model	Compression Ratio	Minimum Compression Pressure (psi)	Idle Speed (rpm)	Injection Type	Injector Opening Pressure (psi) New	Injector Opening Pressure (psi) Used	Start of Injection (deg. BTDC)	Valve Clearance (cold—inches) Intake	Valve Clearance (cold—inches) Exhaust
OM352	17:1	284.5	600	Direct	2986	2559	①	0.008	0.012
OM352A (turbo)	16:1	284.5	600	Direct	2986	2559	②	0.008③	0.012③
OM355/5	16:1	284.5	500	Direct	2631	2346	15	0.010	0.016

① Engine production codes:
344.912–344.937—18°BTDC
344.942–344.945—17°BTDC

② Engine production codes:
344.912–344.937—21°BTDC
344.942–344.945—18°BTDC

③ 1979 and later: intake–0.010 exhaust 0.016

GENERAL ENGINE SPECIFICATIONS

Engine Model	No. Cyl. Displacement (cu. in.)	Horsepower @ rpm (SAE net)	Torque @ rpm (SAE net)	Firing Order	Bore × Stroke	Governed Speed	Oil Pressure @ rpm (psi)
OM352	6-346	130 @ 2800	260 @ 1800	1-5-3-6-2-4	3.82 × 5.04	2800	36.3 @ 2800
OM352A (turbo)	6-346	156 @ 2800	310 @ 2100	1-5-3-6-2-4	3.82 × 5.04	2800	36.3 @ 2800
OM355/5	5-589	181 @ 2200	455 @ 1600	1-2-4-5-3	5.04 × 5.90	2200	36.3 @ 2200

FIRING ORDERS

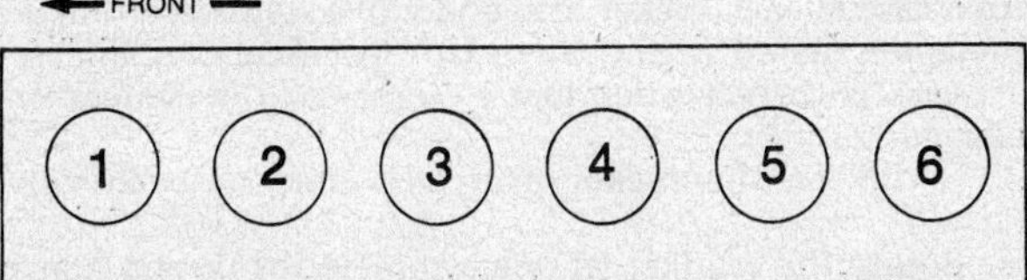

Firing order OM352 and OM352A engines: 1-5-3-6-2-4

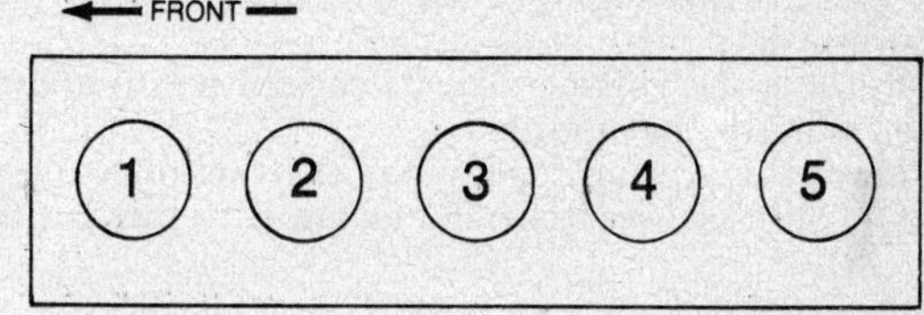

Firing order OM355/5 engines: 1-2-4-5-3

TORQUE SPECIFICATIONS

(All readings in foot-pounds)

Engine Model	Cylinder Head	Rocker Support	Exhaust Manifold	Connecting Rod	Main Bearing Cap	Damper-to-Crankshaft (center bolt)	Flywheel	Nozzle Holder	Oil Pan	Valve Cover
OM352 & OM352A	①	80	36	79.5 + 90°	42 + 90°	398	29 + 90°	50	③	18
OM355/5	②	72	44	58	167	543	51 + 90°	51	21	18

① Three steps: 1st—43.5, 2nd—65, 3rd—80
② Three steps: 1st—29.0, 2nd—56, 3rd—87
③ M6 Grade bolt: 36
M8 Grade bolt: 54

TORQUE SEQUENCES

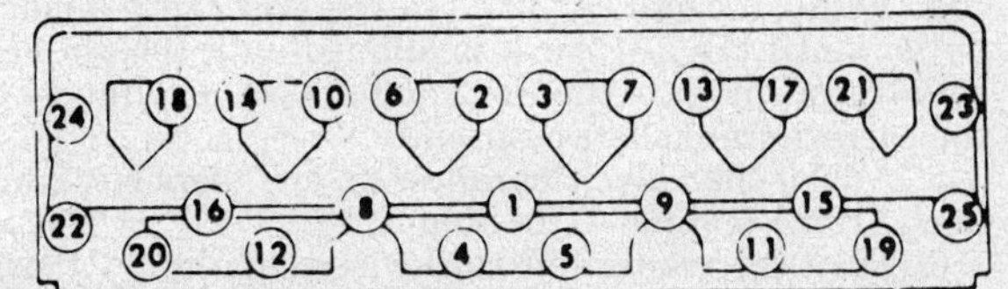

Cylinder head nut torque sequence—OM352 and OM352A engines

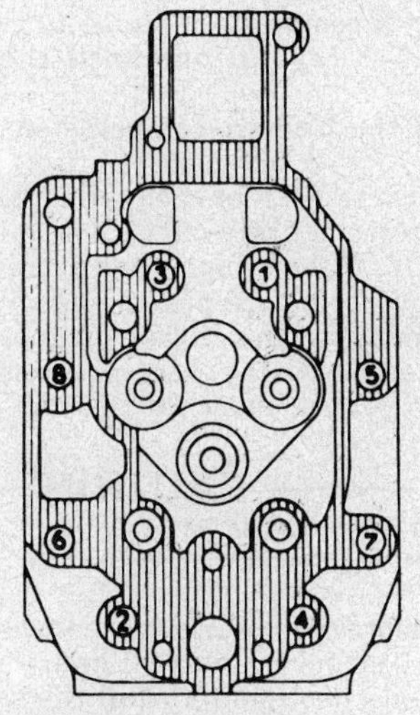

Cylinder head bolt torque sequence—OM355/5 engines

TUNE-UP AND ADJUSTMENTS

Every engine tune-up should include the following:
1. Compression test.
2. Valve adjustment.
3. Fuel injection pump timing.
4. Fuel rack settings (if necessary).
5. Engine idle speed setting.
6. Maximum no-load speed setting.

Cylinder Compression

Testing

1. Adjust the valve clearances as outlined later in the tune-up section.
2. Operate the engine until it reaches normal operating temperature.
3. Remove the valve cover. Be careful not to allow foreign matter to enter the engine.
4. Move the accelerator lever of the fuel injection pump to the "fuel shut-off" position and fasten it in this position with wire.

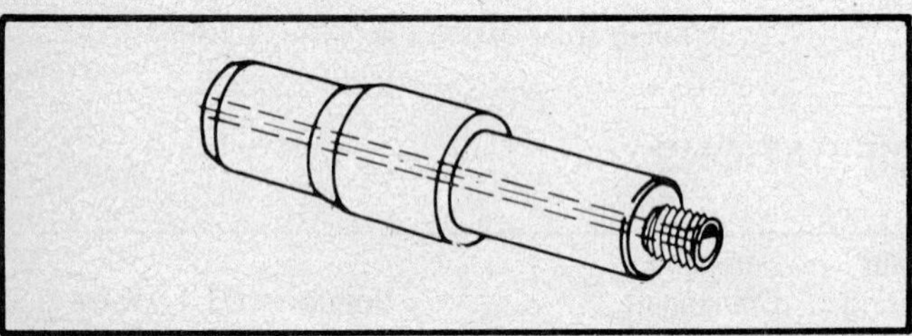

Compression tester adapter (© Mercedes Benz of North America)

5. Disconnect the fuel injection lines at the injection nozzles.
6. Remove the fuel leak-off line from the cylinder head sidewall.
7. Remove the No. 1 injection nozzle hold-down nut. Using a special nozzle holder puller, remove the No.1 nozzle holder.
8. Clean the nozzle holder seat in the cylinder head and crank the engine to remove any surrounding dirt or carbon flakes.
9. Install a compression test adaptor and secure it to the head with the nozzle holder nut. Tighten the nut to 50 ft. lbs.
10. Connect a compression gauge to the adaptor and crank the engine 5–8 revolutions until the highest reading is obtained.
11. Record the highest compression pressure which was attained.
12. Repeat Steps 7–11 for each cylinder. If any cylinder seems low on compression, first squirt 1 fl.oz. oil into the cylinder and repeat Step 10. If the compression increases, the compression pressure is bypassing the piston rings, which will require engine disassembly for an accurate diagnosis. If the compression does not increase with the extra oil present in the cylinder, the valves, valve guides and/or the cylinder head gasket could be at fault.

CAUTION

Do not exceed 1 fl.oz. of oil or engine damage may occur.

13. If all compression pressure are within limits, reinstall the injection nozzles and the leak-off line. Reconnect the injection lines at the injectors and reinstall the valve cover.
14. Unfasten the accelerator lever of the injection pump and return it to the normal position.

Valve Adjustment

OM352 AND OM352A ENGINES

1. Remove the valve cover. Be careful not to allow foreign matter to enter the engine.
2. Rotate the crankshaft until the OT marks on the vibration damper pulley and the timing case cover are aligned. This position should be top dead center/compression for the No. 1 cylinder. To verify this, hand-spin the No. 1, 2, 3, 5, 7 and 9 push rods. If the pushrods will not spin by hand, turn the crankshaft one more revolution and again line-up the OT marks.
3. Loosen the rocker arm lock nuts on valves 1, 2, 3, 5, 7 and 9. Identify the intake and exhaust valves and adjust the clearance between each rocker arm and valve stem according to the dimensions listed in the Tune-Up Specifications Chart. The clearance is correct when just a slight drag is evident on the feeler gauge.
4. Retighten the rocker arm lock nuts as each valve is adjusted.
5. Rotate the crankshaft one complete revolution and align the OT marks on the vibration damper pulley and the timing case cover. The No. 4, 6, 8, 10, 11 and 12 push rods should be free to rotate.
6. Loosen the rocker arm lock nuts for the No. 4, 6, 8, 10, 11 and 12 valves. Adjust the valve clearances in the same manner as in Step 3.
7. After the adjustments have been completed, turn the engine several revolutions and recheck all of the valve clearances.
8. Reinstall the valve cover using a new valve cover gasket.

NOTE: The valve cover gasket MUST be replaced any time the cover is removed. This gasket is also used as an air intake gasket. Failure to replace the gasket could result in excessive oil consumption.

OM355/5 ENGINES

1. Remove the valve covers. Mark the covers so that they may be reinstalled in their original locations. Be careful not to allow foreign matter to enter the engine.
2. Rotate the engine to position the No. 1 piston at top dead center compression; the OT marks on the crankshaft pulley and the timing case cover must be aligned. To verify this, hand spin the pushrods of the No. 1 cylinder. If the pushrods will not spin by hand, turn the crankshaft one more revolution and again line-up the OT marks.
3. Loosen the rocker arm lock nuts of the No. 1 cylinder. Identify the intake and exhaust valves and adjust the clearance between each rocker arm and valve stem according to the dimensions listed in the Tune-Up Specifications Chart. The clearance is correct when just a slight drag is evident on the feeler gauge. Retighten the lock nuts.
4. Rotate the crankshaft clockwise past the 3–5 mark on the pulley until the 2–4 mark is aligned with the pointer. Hand spin the pushrods of the No. 2 and the No. 4 cylinders to verify the correct crankshaft position.
5. Adjust the valve clearances on cylinders No. 2 and No. 4 in the same manner as in Step 3.
6. Turn the crankshaft clockwise past the OT marks until the 3–5 mark is aligned with the pointer. Adjust the valve clearances on cylinders No. 3 and No. 5 in the same manner as in Step 3.
7. After the adjustments have been completed, turn the engine several revolutions and recheck all of the valve clearances.
8. Install the valve covers in their original locations using new valve cover gaskets.

Injection Pump Timing

OM352 AND OM352A ENGINES

1. Thoroughly clean the injection pump and the surrounding area.
2. Remove the clutch housing dust shield.
3. Bring the No. 1 piston to top dead center compression, aligning the FB (fuel beginning) marks of the vibration damper pulley and the timing case pointer using either of the following two methods:
    a. Remove the valve cover. Turn the crankshaft clockwise while observing the rocker arm movement of the No.6 cylinder. As the No.6 exhaust valve is closing and the No.6 intake valve is opening, the No.1 cylinder should be on its compression stroke and the OT marks on the vibration damper and timing case pointer should be aligned. Turn the crankshaft ¼ turn counterclockwise since the OT point is beyond the FB point. Turn the crankshaft clockwise (to remove the gear backlash) and align the FB indicators.
    b. Remove the valve cover. Turn the crankshaft clockwise while observing the closing of the exhaust valve of the No.6 cylinder. Continue to turn the crankshaft until the FB indicators are aligned.
4. Remove the breather tube from the timing gear housing.

NOTE: Use Steps 5 and 6 only if the pump was removed previously.

5. Install the pump and align the marked tooth of the pump drive gear with the housing pointer.
6. Install the five pump support bolts through the support plate and torque the bolts to 36 ft. lbs. Loosen the four screws holding the pump to the support plate.
7. If the pump had not been removed previously, disconnect the No. 1 injection line from the injection pump.
8. Remove the half moon clamps from the No.1 and 2 delivery valve holders.
9. Remove the No.1 delivery valve holder, filler piece, compression spring and check valve needle.
10. Reinstall only the No. 1 delivery valve holder.
11. Attach a drip tube to the delivery valve holder.

NOTE: Do not use an old high pressure fuel line as a drip tube as this will cause inaccurate results.

12. If the pump had been removed previously, connect the fuel supply lines to the fuel transfer pump and the fuel filter(s).
13. Connect the fuel supply line from the fuel filter to the injection pump.

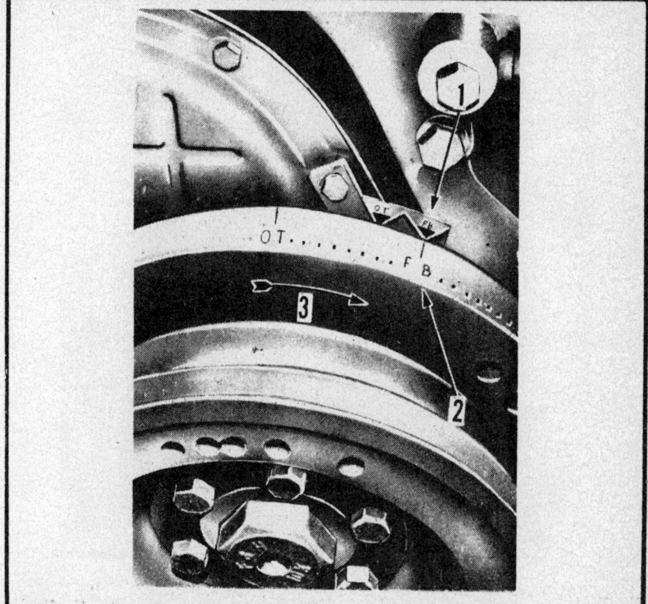

Aligning the FB (fuel beginning) mark prior to injection pump timing—OM355/5 engine (© Mercedes Benz of North America)

NOTE: The existing fuel supply of the vehicle or a fuel reservoir attached to the fuel inlet port of the injection pump can be used to supply fuel to the injection pump.

14. Open the bleeder at the front of the injection pump low pressure fuel gallery. Operate the fuel feed hand pump until fuel from the bleeder valve is completely free of air bubbles. Close the bleeder valve.

NOTE: If the vehicle's own fuel supply is used to supply fuel to the pump (as opposed to an external reservoir), actuate the hand pump to maintain a positive pressure.

15. Attach a spring to the injection pump throttle lever to keep the lever in the full forward (full load) position.
16. Push the top of the injection pump towards the engine (retard). A steady stream of fuel should flow from the drip tube attached to the No.1 delivery valve holder.
17. Slowly pull the top of the pump away from the engine (advance) until the fuel flow is reduced to one drop per 15–20 seconds.

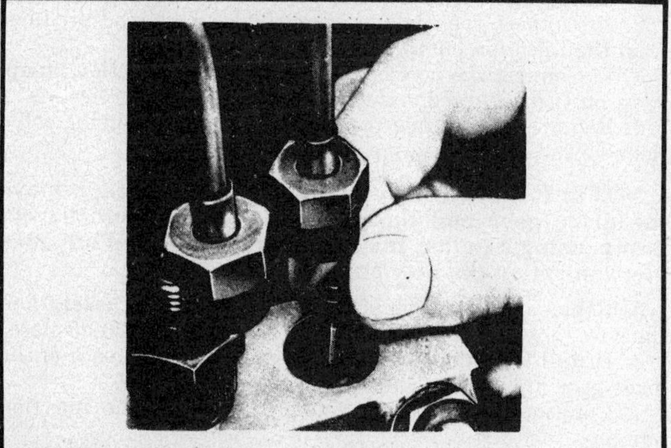

Removing the check valve needle of the delivery valve—OM352 and OM352A engines (© Mercedes Benz of North America)

Fuel reservoir installed for injection timing procedure—OM352 and OM352A engines (© Mercedes Benz of North America)

Aligning the FB (fuel beginning) marks prior to injection pump timing—OM355/56 engine (© Mercedes Benz of North America)

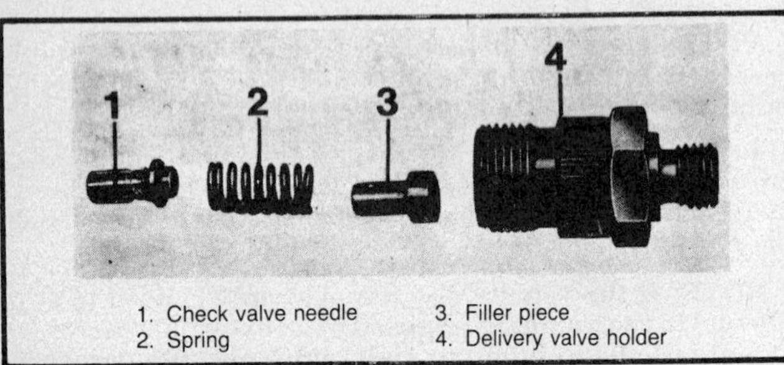

1. Check valve needle
2. Spring
3. Filler piece
4. Delivery valve holder

Delivery valve components (© Mercedes Benz of North America)

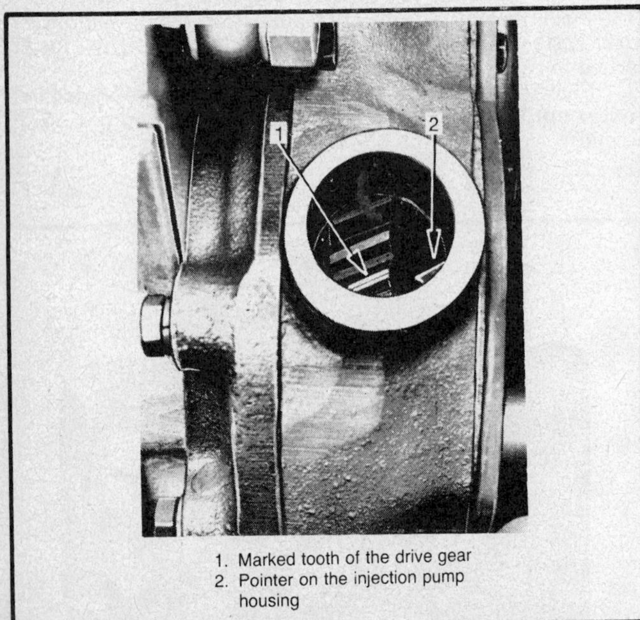

1. Marked tooth of the drive gear
2. Pointer on the injection pump housing

Aligning the injection pump drive gear with the pump housing pointer—OM352 and OM352A engines (© Mercedes Benz of North America)

18. Tighten one of the injection pump bolts to lock the injection pump.
19. Recheck the timing as follows:
   a. Turn the engine ¼ turn counterclockwise. A steady stream of fuel should again flow from the drip tube.
   b. Turn the engine clockwise until the fuel flow slows to one drop per 15–20 seconds. The FB indicators should now be aligned.
20. Tighten the remaining injection pump mounting bolts. Torque all of the mounting bolts to 36 ft. lbs.
21. Remove the auxiliary fuel reservoir, if used.
22. Detach the drip tube from the delivery valve holder and remove the delivery valve holder.
23. Reassemble the delivery valve according to the accompanying illustration.
24. Install the delivery valve holder and torque to 33 ft. lbs.
25. Replace the half moon clamping segments and torque the segment screw to 5 ft. lbs.
26. Install the injection line(s) and the fuel supply line (if a fuel reservoir was used).
27. Install the oil line and bleed the fuel system as described later in this section.
28. Install the valve cover (using a new gasket), breather tube and clutch housing cover.

OM355/5 ENGINE

1. Rotate the engine crankshaft clockwise and align the FB mark on the vibration damper with the timing case pointer.

NOTE: If the FB mark was moved past the pointer, turn the crankshaft counterclockwise a minimum of ⅙ of a turn to account for gear backlash.

2. Check that the advance fly weights are in the "rest" position by looking through the inspection hole of the advance mechanism.
3. Check that the FB marks on the injection pump flywheel and the pump pointer are aligned.
4. If the FB marks are not aligned, loosen both nuts on the slotted flange segment and turn the pump flywheel to align the FB marks. Tighten the segment in this position.
5. Install the inspection hole plug into the advance mechanism.

Injection Pump

Removal and Installation

OM352 AND OM352A ENGINES

1. Rotate the engine crankshaft until the FB (fuel beginning) mark on the vibration damper is aligned with the FB mark of the pointer on the timing case. Also, check that the marked tooth of the injectionpump drive gear is aligned with the pointer on the pump housing.
2. Disconnect the fuel injection, fuel return and oil lines from the injection pump.
3. Disconnect the accelerator rod from the injection pump. Also, on turbocharged engines, disconnect the aneroid line
4. Remove the five injection pump-to-support housing bolts. Remove the injection pump.

NOTE: If the injection pump is to be replaced, remove the drive gear and timing advance unit from the old pump, using a puller. Install the drive gear and advance mechanism on the new pump.

5. Replace the injection pump-to-drive housing gasket. Hold the new gasket in place by applying grease to the flange plate.
6. Install the injection pump with the marked tooth of the drive gear aligned with the pump housing pointer.
7. Connect the lines and accelerator rod to the injection pump.
8. Install the hollow screw with the single small hole on the lube oil filter end of the oil supply line.

9. If a new or remanufactured pump is installed, remove the pump side cover and fill the pump with ½ quart of engine oil.
10. Refer to the injection pump timing procedure to properly time the injection pump.

OM355/5 ENGINE

1. Remove the air filter and the air filter bracket.
2. Drain the coolant from the engine.
3. Remove the power steering pump flange screws. Remove the pump and wire it out of the way.
4. Disconnect the air, water and oil lines from the auxiliary air compressor.
5. Remove the snapring, nut and lock washer from the air compressor pivot bolt.
6. Remove the clamp screw from the compressor mounting bracket and loosen the adjustment screw.
7. Remove the V-belts and remove the air compressor.
8. Rotate the engine crankshaft clockwise until the FB (fuel beginning) mark on the vibration damper is aligned with the pointer on the timing case cover.

Removing the injection pump drive gear with a puller (© Mercedes Benz of North America)

9. Remove the inspection hold plug from the advance mechanism and check the position of the advance flyweights through the inspection hole. The slash mark on each flyweight should be aligned with the mark on the corresponding flyweight.
10. Align the following marks:
    a. injection pump-to-flywheel marks
    b. fine adjustment marks
    c. flange to advance housing marks

NOTE: If the marks from Steps 9 and 10 are not visible, rotate the crankshaft 360° clockwise and again align the FB mark with the timing case pointer. Repeat Steps 9 and 10 if necessary.

11. Disconnect the fuel return and oil lines from the injection pump.
12. Disconnect the accelerator linkage from the injection pump.
13. Disconnect the injection lines from the injection pump as previously outlined.
14. Remove the screws from the injection pump flywheel flange.
15. Remove the injection pump mounting screws and remove the injection pump.

NOTE: If a new or remanufactured pump is to be installed, fill the injection pump with ½ quart of engine oil through the oil return port.

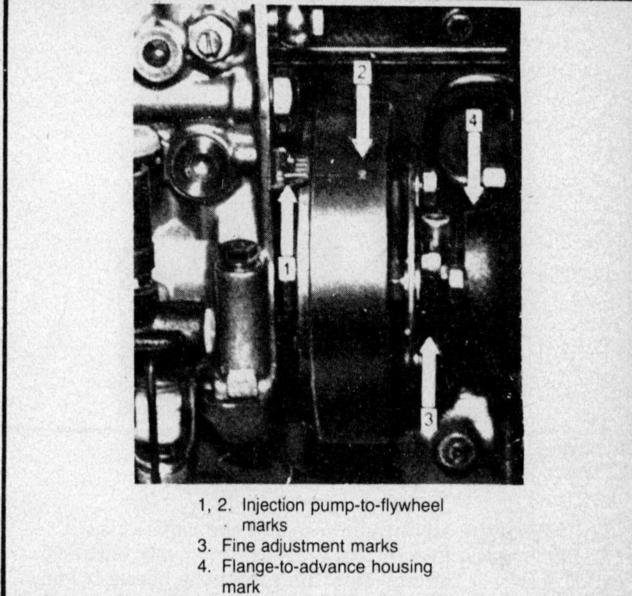

1, 2. Injection pump-to-flywheel marks
3. Fine adjustment marks
4. Flange-to-advance housing mark

Marks which must be aligned prior to injection pump removal—OM355/5 engine (© Mercedes Benz of North America)

16. Installation is the reverse of the previous steps. Refer to the injection pump timing procedure to properly time the injection pump.

NOTE: With the engine running, a minimum flexing of the pump flex plates should be evident. If the flexing seems excessive, slide the segment flange on the shaft as necessary to minimize the flexing.

Fuel Injection Nozzles

Removal and Installation

OM352 AND OM352A ENGINES

1. Drain the coolant from the engine.

Advance mechanism flyweights as viewed through the inspection hole—OM355/5 engine (© Mercedes Benz of North America)

Removing the injection nozzle holder with a puller (© Mercedes Benz of North America)

2. Remove the air intake hose and the valve cover.
3. Remove the fuel return lines as previously outlined.
4. Disconnect the injection lines from the nozzle holders.
5. Remove the nozzle holder nut(s) from the cylinder head.
6. Using a special nozzle holder puller remove the nozzle holder(s) from the cylinder head along with the copper sealing washers.

NOTE: If the copper washers must be replaced, use new washers of the same thickness as the original washers.

7. Remove the nozzle holder protective sleeve from the cylinder head using the appropriate special tool.
8. Remove the O-ring from the cylinder head groove. Apply silicone grease to the I.D. of this O-ring during installation.
9. Installation is the reverse of the previous steps. Note the following during installation:
   a. Apply Permatex type sealant to the nozzle holder protective sleeve threads before installing the sleeve.
   b. Torque the protective sleeve to 43 ft. lbs.
   c. Make sure the alignment lug of the nozzle holder is positioned in the cylinder head recess.
   d. Torque the nozzle holder nut to 43–51 ft. lbs.

OM355/5 ENGINES

1. Remove the air filter and the air filter bracket.
2. Drain the coolant from the engine.
3. Remove the valve covers. Mark the covers so that they may be reinstalled in their original locations. Be careful not to allow foreign matter to enter the engine.
4. Remove the rocker arm assemblies. Mark each assembly so that it may be reinstalled in its original location.
5. Disconnect the injection lines from the nozzle holder.
6. Remove the fuel filter bowls and the breather from the push rod cover.
7. Loosen the injection line flare and lock nuts at the cylinder head junctions. Turn the lines away from the nozzle holders.
8. Remove the nozzle holder ring nut from each nozzle holder.
9. Remove the nozzle holders using a nozzle holder pulling tool.
10. Remove the copper nozzle holder washers.

NOTE: If the copper washer must be replaced, use new washers of the same thickness as the original washers.

11. Remove the protective sleeves with an appropriate special tool.
12. Remove the O-rings from the cylinder head.
13. Installation is the reverse of the previous steps. Refer to Step 9 of the OM352 and OM352A procedure. It is recommended to bleed the fuel system prior to starting the engine.

Fuel bleeder valves on the fuel filter housing (© Mercedes Benz of North America)

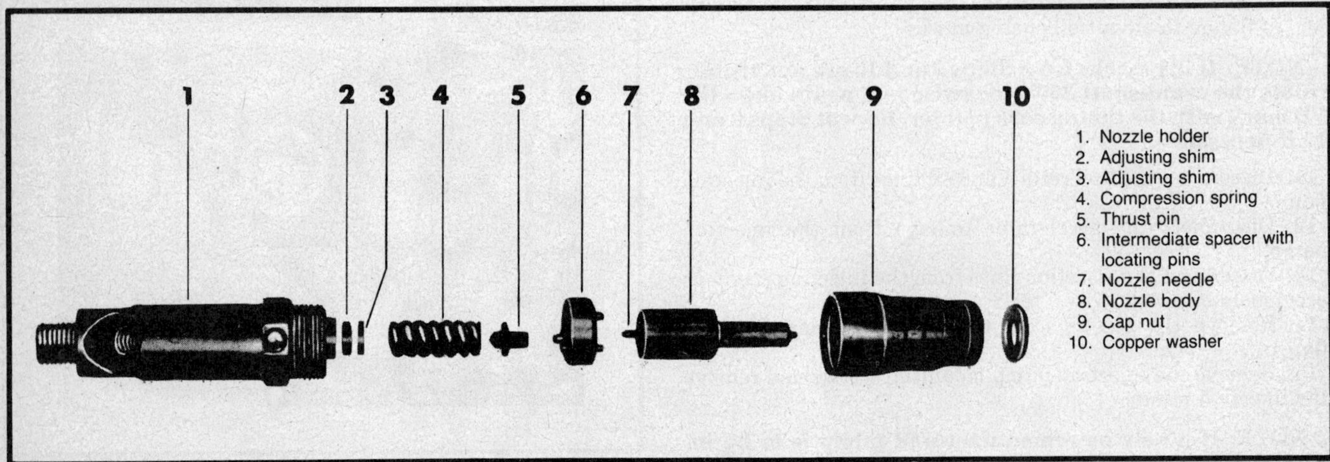

Exploded view of injection nozzle (© Mercedes Benz of North America)

Fuel System Bleeding

To insure proper engine operation, the fuel system must be completely free of air. Normally, the system is bled continuously through the return line to the fuel filter housing when the engine is running. It is recommended to manually bleed the fuel system after the fuel tank has been run dry or after major fuel system servicing.

1. Open the bleeder valve on the fuel filter housing.
2. Operate the fuel feed hand pump until fuel from the bleeder valve is completely free of air bubbles.
3. Close the fuel filter housing bleeder valve.
4. Open the bleeder valve at the front of the injection pump low pressure fuel gallery.
5. Operate the fuel feed hand pump until fuel from the bleeder valve is completely free of air.
6. Close the low pressure gallery bleeder valve.
7. Tighten the hand pump.

NOTE: Any air remaining in the system will be forced out after a few minutes of engine operation.

Fuel bleeder valve at low pressure fuel gallery of the injection pump (© Mercedes Benz of North America)

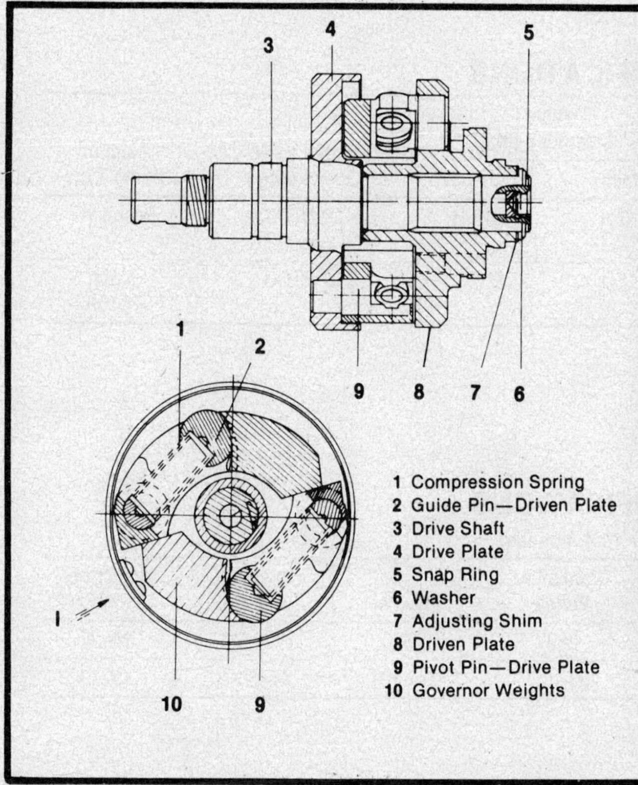

Cross section of injection timing advance mechanism—OM355/5 engine (© Mercedes Benz of North America)

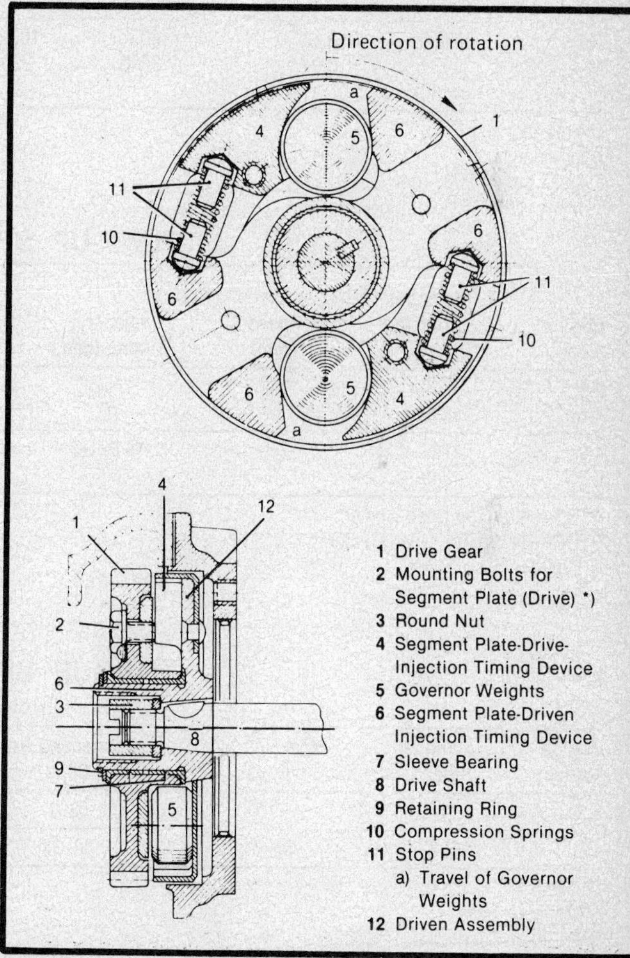

Cross section of injection timing mechanism—OM352 and OM352A engines (© Mercedes Benz of North America)

MITSUBISHI 4 CYL 143.2 CU.IN.(2.3L), 6 CYL 243.5 CU.IN. (4.0L)

GENERAL ENGINE SPECIFICATIONS

Engine Model	Engine Displacement	Bore × Stroke (in.)	Horsepower @ rpm	Torque ft. lbs. @ rpm	Compression Ratio	Compression Pressure (psi)	Oil Pressure @ idle (psi)	Firing Order
2.3L① (turbo)	2346 cc (143.2 cu. in.)	3.59 × 3.54	80 @ 4200	125 @ 2100	21:1	384 @ 250 rpm	28	1-3-4-2
4.0L ②	3998 cc (243.5 cu. in.)	3.62 × 3.94	100 @ 3700	163 @ 2200	20:1	425	③	1-5-3-6-2-4

①4 cylinder
②6 cylinder
③42-71 psi @ 2000 rpm

TUNE-UP SPECIFICATIONS

Engine Model	Injection Pressure (psi)	Idle Speed (rpm)	Injection Timing (deg.)	Valve Clearance (in.) Intake	Valve Clearance (in.) Exhaust	Intake Valve Opens (deg.)	Injection Pump Type
2.3L 4 cyl	1707–1849	750	2 ATDC ①	.010 H	.010 H	20 BTDC	Bosch VE
4.0L 6 cyl	1707–1849	750	18 BTDC	.012C	.012C	32 BTDC	Bosch PE56A

ATDC—After Top Dead Center
BTDC—Before Top Dead Center
①TDC for high altitude

TORQUE SPECIFICATIONS

(All measurements in foot pounds)

Engine Model	Cylinder Head	Main Bearing Caps	Connecting Rod Caps	Crankshaft Pulley	Flywheel	Injection Nozzle	Injection Pump②
2.3L	90①	79①	58①	289	65①	44–58	18–25
4.0L	76–83③	55–61	33–34	123–137	94–101	44–50④	15–19

①Oiled
②Mounting bolts
③84-90 on hot engine
④17-26 on fuel lin cap 33-39 on nozzle body pieces

TORQUE SEQUENCES

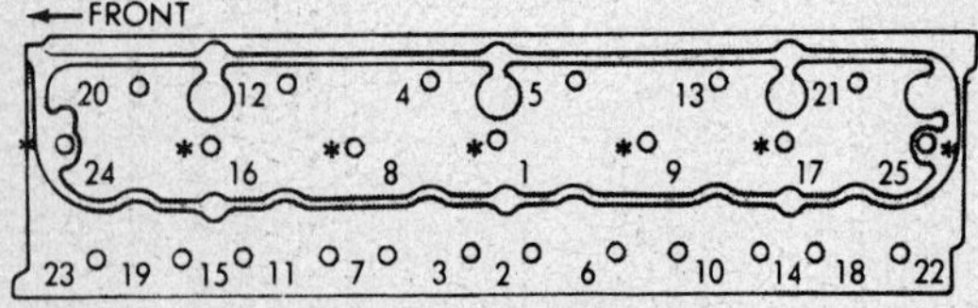

Head bolt torque sequence—4.0L engine

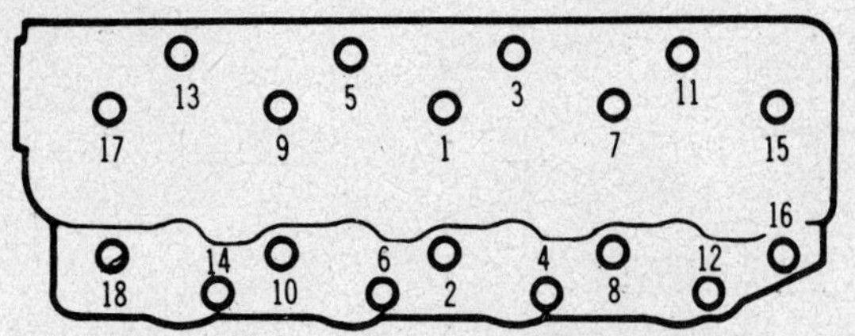

Head bolt torque sequence—2.3L engine

CHILTON'S THREE "C's" DIESEL ENGINE DIAGNOSIS PROCEDURE

Condition	Cause	Correction
Rough Idle	Improper adjustment	Adjust idle
	Accelerator control cable binding	Repair or lubricate
	Air or water in the fuel system	Clear air or water from fuel system
	Injection nozzle clogged	Check and clean injector nozzles
	Improper valve clearance	Check valve adjustment
	Injection pump malfunction	Check injection pump
Poor Performance	Air cleaner clogged	Check element
	Accelerator control cable binding	Check control cable for free movement
	Restricted fuel flow (water or air)	Check lines and filter
	Incorrect injection timing	Check injection timing
	Injection pump malfunction	Replace injection pump
Excessive Exhaust Smoke	Restricted air cleaner	Check element
	Air or water in fuel filter	Remove air or water from fuel system
	Improper grade fuel	Check fuel in tank
	Incorrect injection timing	Check injection timing
	Injection pump malfunction	Replace injection pump
	Injector nozzle stuck open	Check injector nozzles
Excessive Fuel Consumption	Restricted air cleaner	Check element
	Leak in fuel lines	Check fo leaks
	Incorrect idle speed	Check idle
	Restricted exhaust system	Check exhaust
	Improper grade of fuel	Check fuel in tank
	Injection pump malfunction	Check injection pump operation
Loud Knocking In Engine	Defective fuel injector	Replace fuel injector

NOTE: If the problem persists after performing these preliminary checks, disassembly and inspection of internal engine components may be necessary for further diagnosis.

TUNE-UP AND ADJUSTMENTS

The Mitsubishi diesel engine tune-up should include the following checks and/or adjustments:

1. Compression test.
2. Valve adjustment.
3. Injection timing.
4. Injector pressure test and inspection.
5. Idle speed adjustment.
6. Glow plug operation check.

Compression Test

2.3L 4 CYLINDER

NOTE: Valve clearances set too close will result in poor compression readings. If a valve rotator fails, compression will also be low.

Compression on the diesel engine can be checked with a screw in compression gauge adaptor installed in the fuel injector or glow plug hole. The compression gauge should have a capacity of at least 500 psi. Individual cylinder pressures should not vary more than 10%.

4.0L 6 CYLINDER

1. Remove the glow plugs.
2. Install cylinder compression pressure adaptor into glow plug mounting hole and attach compression gauge to adaptor.
3. Disconnect the fuel control motor to cut off the fuel input.
4. Crank the engine and read the compression value for the cylinder being tested.
5. At a cranking speed of 170 rpm, the compression pressure should read between 285–426 psi. If the compression pressure is below 285 psi, the need for engine repair is indicated.
6. Test all cylinders and verify that the compression values are within 10% of each other.

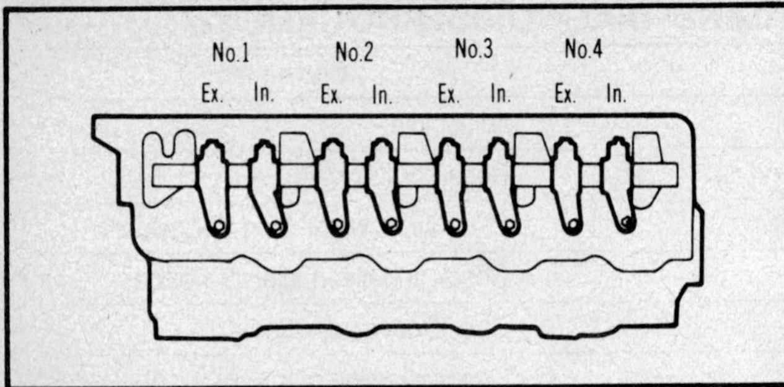

Adjusting valve clearance on 2.3L engine
(© Mitsubishi Motors Corp.)

ADJUST VALVES AT TOP OF COMPRESSION STROKE

I = INTAKE VALVE
E = EXHAUST VALVE

CYLINDER NO.	1		2		3		4		5		6	
VALVE ARRANGEMENT	E	I	E	I	E	I	E	I	E	I	E	I

Intake and exhaust valve arrangement—4.0L engine
(© Mitsubishi Motors Corp.)

Valve Adjustment

2.3L 4 CYLINDER

NOTE: The valves should be adjusted with the engine at normal operating temperature.

1. Set the No. 1 piston at TDC on its compression stroke. Remove the valve cover.
2. Loosen the locknut and adjust the No. 1 and No. 2 intake and the No. 1 and No. 3 exhaust valves to specifications. Tighten the locknut and recheck clearance.
3. Rotate the crankshaft one revolution (No.4 cylinder at TDC), then loosen the locknut and adjust the No.3 and No.4 intake and the No.2 and No.4 exhaust valves to specifications. Tighten the locknut and recheck clearance. Reinstall the valve cover.
4. Check and adjust the idle speed if necessary.

4.0L 6 CYLINDER

1. Stop the engine and remove the valve cover.
2. Set the No. 1 cylinder at TDC on its compression stroke.
3. Insert a feeler gauge of specified thickness into the clearance between the valve stem end and the rocker arm. Adjust as required by loosening the locknut and turning the adjusting screw.
4. Repeat the procedure for each cylinder to adjust the remaining valves. Always use a new gasket when installing the valve cover.

Injection Pump Timing

2.3L 4 CYLINDER

NOTE: This procedure requires the use of a special prestroke measuring adaptor and dial gauge.

1. Set the No. 1 piston at TDC on its compression stroke. Make sure the timing marks on the camshaft sprocket and injection pump sprocket are aligned with the timing marks.
2. Loosen the nuts securing the injection lines to the fuel injection pump at the pump delivery valves. Do not allow the delivery valves on the fuel injection pump to loosen when loosening fuel line connections.
3. Loosen the injection pump mounting bolts slightly to allow pump movement for adjustment.
4. Check that the measuring adaptor push rod protrudes 10mm (0.4 in.). Protrusion may be adjusted by the inner nut on the measuring adaptor.
5. Remove the timing plug from the injection pump and install the measuring adaptor with dial indicator.
6. Turn the crankshaft counterclockwise until the notch on the pulley is 30° BTDC on the compression stroke of No. 1 piston. Zero the dial indicator, then turn the crankshaft slightly from side to side to make sure the dial indicator does not move from the zero position.
7. Turn the crankshaft in the normal direction of rotation (clockwise) to 2° ATDC and check that the dial indicator reads 1 ± 0.03mm (.0394 ± .0011 in.).
8. If the dial indicator does not read the specified value, tilt the injection pump body right or left until the correct reading is obtained. Tighten the mounting bolts.
9. Repeat Steps 7 and 8 to check the adjustment.
10. Remove the timing gauge and measuring adaptor.
11. Install the copper gasket and timing plug in injection pump. Torque fuel line connections to specifications.

4.0L 6 CYLINDER

1. Disconnect the battery ground cable.
2. Disconnect the fuel shutoff rod at the injection pump lever by snapping the rod over the ball stud.
3. Clean all grease and dirt away from the No.1 delivery valve, pipe and pump area.

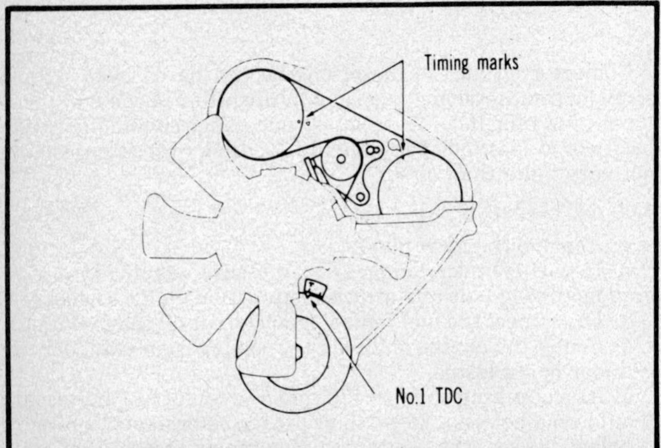

Correct alignment of timing marks at TDC on 2.3L engine
(© Mitsubishi Motors Corp.)

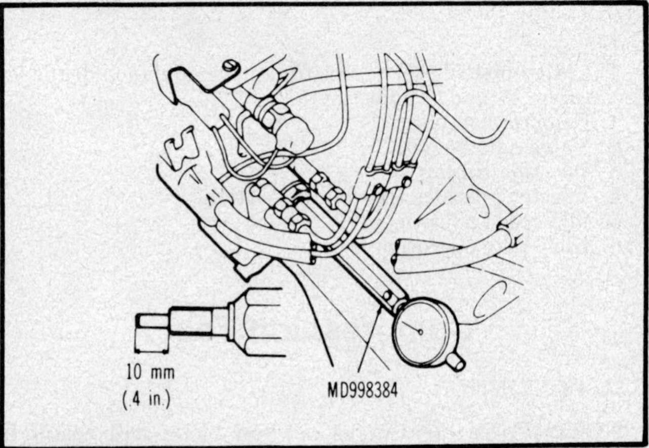

Prestroke measuring adapter installed in the injection pump—2.3L engine (© Mitsubishi Motors Corp.)

Injection pump timing scale—4.0L engine
(© Mitsubishi Motors Corp.)

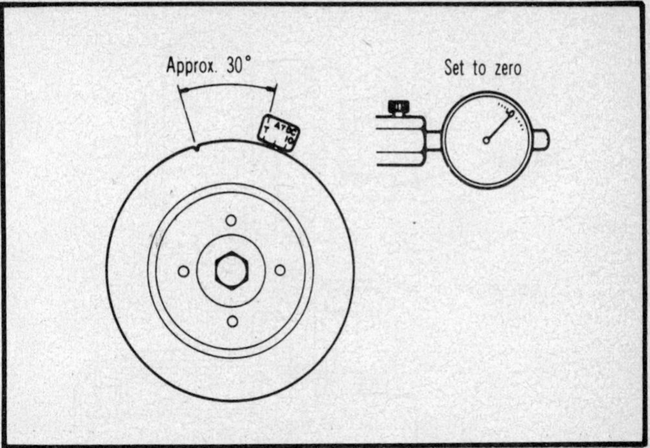

Turn the crankshaft clockwise to zero the dial indicator—2.3L engine (© Mitsubishi Motors Corp.)

4. Turn the engine in the normal direction of rotation (clockwise) until the No.1 piston is at TDC on its compression stroke.
5. Continue turning the engine $1^3/_4$ turns more.
6. Disconnect the No. 1 injection pipe from the delivery valve.

CAUTION

When disconnecting the injection pipe(s) at the delivery valve(s), hold the delivery valve holder(s) stationary and loosen the injection pipe fitting. Do not turn the delivery valve holder as this will disturb the delivery valve calibration.

7. Turn the engine in the normal direction of rotation very slowly and stop when fuel begins to emerge from the delivery valve holder. This is the point when injection begins.
8. Check the injection timing point on the scale on the back of the crankshaft damper. If the timing is correct, the mark should be at the standard valve shown on the Vehicle Emission Control Information Label on the valve cover, minus 2 degrees.
9. If the timing is not at the standard mark, minus 2 degrees, loosen the four pump-to-flange plate nuts and rotate the pump to advance or retard the timing. The crankshaft angle varies by 6 degrees per division on the pump flange scale.
10. Tighten the pump flange nuts.

Idle Speed Adjustment

2.3L 4 CYLINDER

NOTE: Before adjusting idle, turn all lights and accessories off and place the transmission in neutral.

1. Start and warm up the engine to normal operating temperature.
2. Run the engine for more than 5 seconds at 2000–3000 rpm, then let the engine idle for 2 minutes.
3. Connect diesel tachometer and check the idle speed. If the idle speed is beyond specifications, adjust by turning the idle speed adjusting screw. Be careful not to disturb any other screws.

4.0L 6 CYLINDER

1. Remove cover and gasket from tachometer takeoff on right side of engine in front of oil filter assembly. Install mechanical tachometer adapter and attach mechanical tachometer and drive cable.
2. Turn hand throttle counterclockwise and pull all the way out. Depress accelerator to floor and crank engine. Hold accelerator to floor after engine starts. Allow engine to warm up until some speed is attained (1250–1500 rpm). Release accelerator slowly until engine runs smoothly. When engine begins to warm, turn hand throttle clockwise to reduce engine speed to idle.

Timing marks on crankshaft damper—4.0L engine
(© Mitsubishi Motors Corp.)

CAUTION

If a new injection pump has been installed, do not allow engine speed to rise above 1300 rpm. If engine overspeeds, it may run away and damage or destroy itself.

3. Be sure that governor control lever is at idling position before attempting to adjust idle speed.

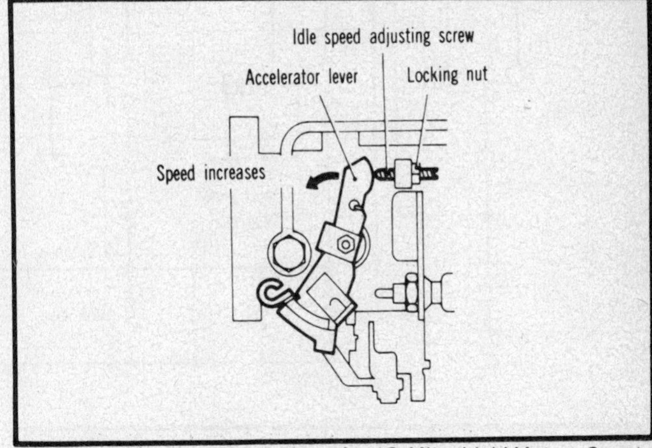

Idle speed adjustment on 2.3L engine (© Mitsubishi Motors Corp.)

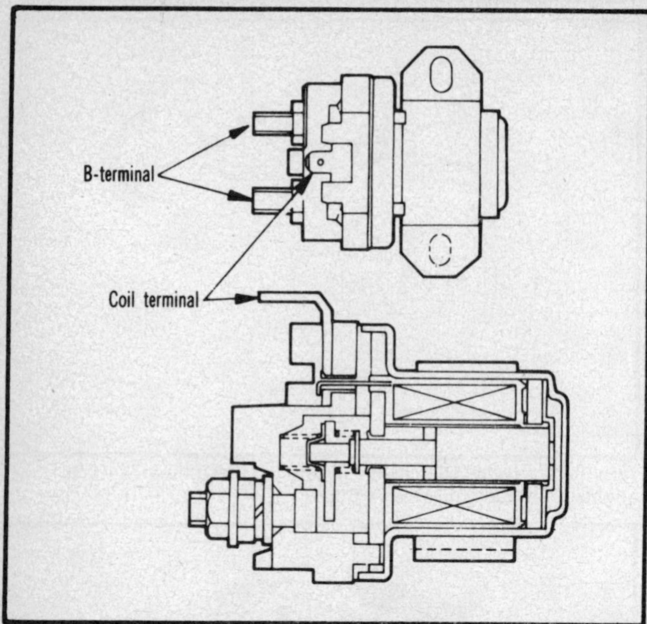

Glow plug relay (© Mitsubishi Motors Corp.)

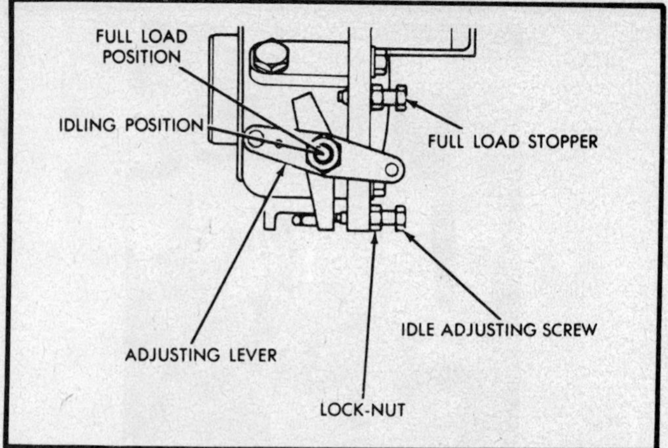

Idle speed adjustment—4.0L engine (© Mitsubishi Motors Corp.)

4. Check tachometer. If idle speed is not between 600 and 70 rpm, adjust idle speed.

5. Loosen idle adjusting screw locknut. Adjust screw as necessary to set idle to specifications. Turn adjusting screw IN to increase idle speed: OUT to decrease idle speed.

6. When idle speed is as specified, tighten idle adjusting screw locknut. Recheck idle speed to be sure it has not shifted.

Glow Plug Systems

2.3L 4 CYLINDER

The Quick Glow System has two main circuits to maintain the glow plug at constant temperature and to shorten the preheating time substantially. One circuit applies battery voltage (12 volts) to the glow plug. The other is the heat stabilization circuit which decreases voltage applied to the glow plug by changing the power source circuit to the dropping resistor when the glow plug reaches the design temperature.

The Quick Glow System operates when the coolant temperature is below 86°F. When the ignition key is turned to the ON position, the indicator light on the dash is lit and No.1 and No.2 glow plug relays are on. Actual current flow to the glow plugs is made by the No.1 glow plug relay only. When the START

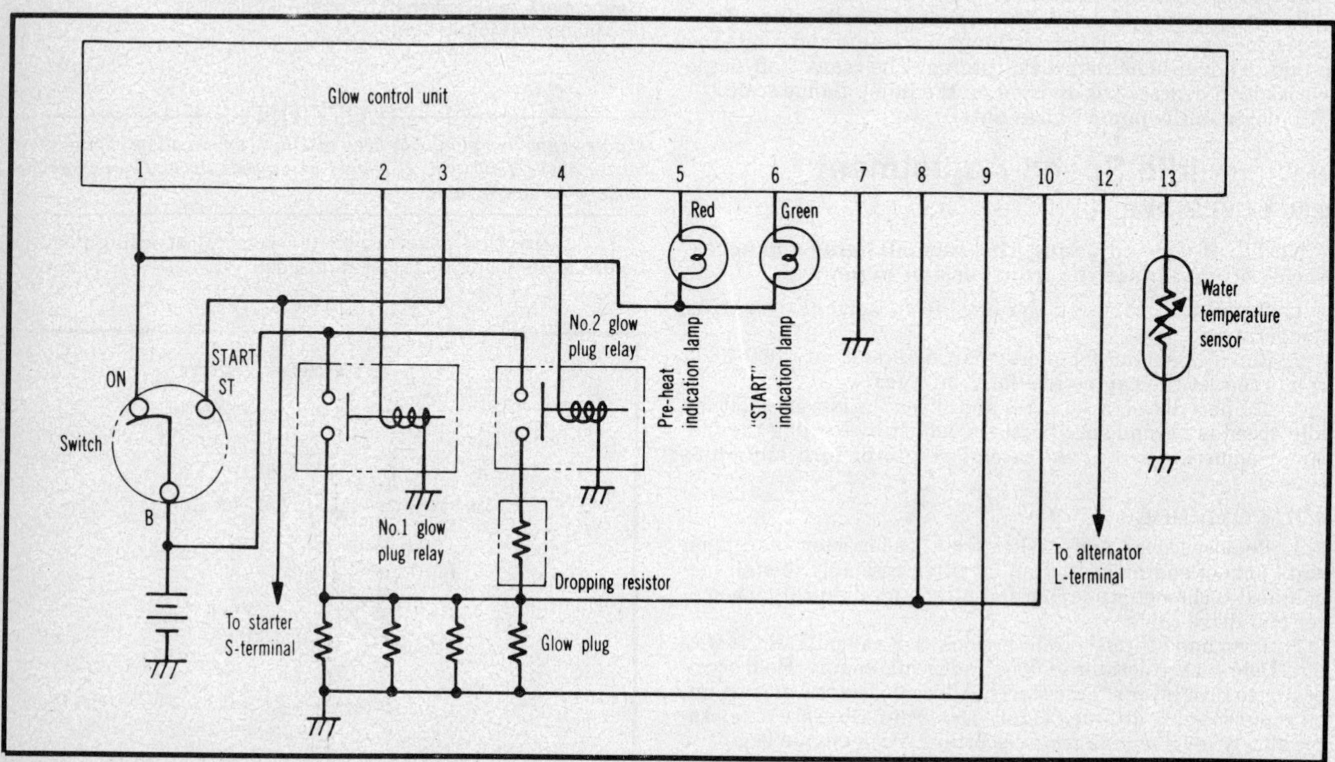

Electrical schematic of quick glow plug system (© Mitsubishi Motors Corp.)

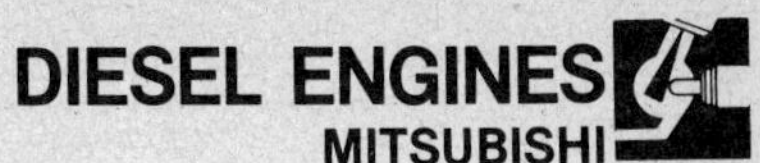

light is on and the key is turned to the START position, current flow to the glow plugs is continued by the No.2 relay. After the engine is started, after-glow is continued by the No.2 glow plug relay.

Testing Glow Plug

1. Remove the glow plug and check for damage or deformation of the pin.
2. Check the resistance between the terminal and body, then check for open or short circuit in the plug itself.

NOTE: Standard resistance is 0.1 ohm at 68°F.

Testing Glow Plug Relay

The glow plug relay is functioning if there is continuity between the B terminals when 6 volts is applied between the glow plug relay and coil terminal.

Testing Dropping Resistor

Check the terminals' resistance, then check for a short circuit. Normal resistance value is 130 milliohms. If no shorts are found and the resistance is as specified, the dropping resistor is good.

4.0L 6 CYLINDER

Electrically operated glow plugs are used to heat the combustion chambers prior to cold weather and initial engine starts. The glow plugs resemble the spark plugs of the conventional gasoline powered engines. A relay controls the length of time the glow plugs are in use. During cold weather, the relay may have to be reactivated through a second glow plug cycle in order to start the engine.

Testing

1. Tag and disconnect the electrical connectors.
2. Using the large hex nut, loosen the glow plug and carefully lift it out of the cylinder head.
3. Check continuity between glow plug end and glow tip with an ohm meter.
4. Installation is in the reverse order.

NOTE: Use extreme care when removing a glow plug as the tip may break off; requiring cylinder head removal. Carefully clean carbon from glow plug tip before reinstalling.

Fuel Filter

2.3L 4 CYLINDER

A fuel filter is provided to protect the injection pump from dirt and water in and out of the fuel tank. The fuel filter has a fuel heater built in to prevent the interruption of fuel flow due to parrafin flakes at low ambient temperatures. A hand pump is incorporated by the inlet valve on the fuel filter mount. The bottom of the fuel filter forms a sediment trap and the accumulation of water will trigger a warning light on the dash.

NOTE: The fuel heater is activated when the fuel temperature is below 38°F as determined by the fuel temperature sensor. The fuel heater light on the dash will illuminate when the fuel heater is functioning.

Removal and Installation

1. Disconnect the water level sensor connector, fuel heater connector and fuel temperature sensor connector.
2. Loosen filter cartridge by hand or by using a band wrench. If the pump body is to be removed, disconnect the fuel lines and loosen the mounting bolts.
3. Remove the water level sensor from the cartridge by lightly clamping the sensor in a vise and turning the cartridge.

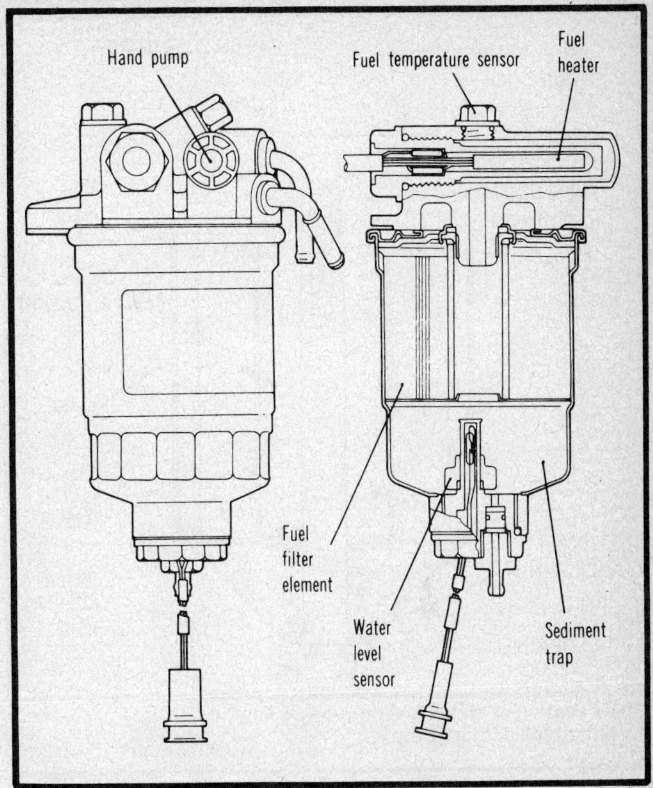

Diesel fuel filter on 2.3L engine (© Mitsubishi Motors Corp.)

4. Transfer the sensor to the new cartridge and lubricate the sealing gasket with diesel fuel.
5. Install in reverse order of removal. Bleed the fuel system.

Bleeding the Fuel System

NOTE: The fuel system should be bled whenever the filter is changed or any lines have been disconnected.

1. Loosen the air plug on the fuel filter assembly.
2. Pull out the hand pump knob by turning it to the left.
3. Pump the hand pump until the fuel coming out of the air plug hole has no air bubbles in it.
4. Tighten the air plug, then continue to pump until the operation of the hand pump feels heavy. Lock the pump knob by turning it to the right while holding it in.

Draining Water From The Fuel Filter

NOTE: If water accumulates in the fuel filter during operation, a warning light on the dash will illuminate.

1. Loosen the drain plug on the fuel filter.
2. Pull out the hand pump by turning the knob to the left.
3. Drain water by pumping the hand pump until pure diesel fuel flows, then tighten the drain plug.
4. Check that the warning indicator has gone out.

4.0L 6 CYLINDER

The six cylinder diesel fuel system has three fuel filters. One is part of the gauge sending unit assembly immersed in the fuel tank at the end of the fuel line. This filter does not normally need servicing, but can be replaced if necessary.

The second filter (strainer), a gauze-type filter between the fuel supply tank and the feed pump, is located at the inlet port of the feed pump. It operates under suction and removes large-size particles of dirt and foreign matter. This filter should be removed and cleaned every 12,000 miles. Clean the wire gauze

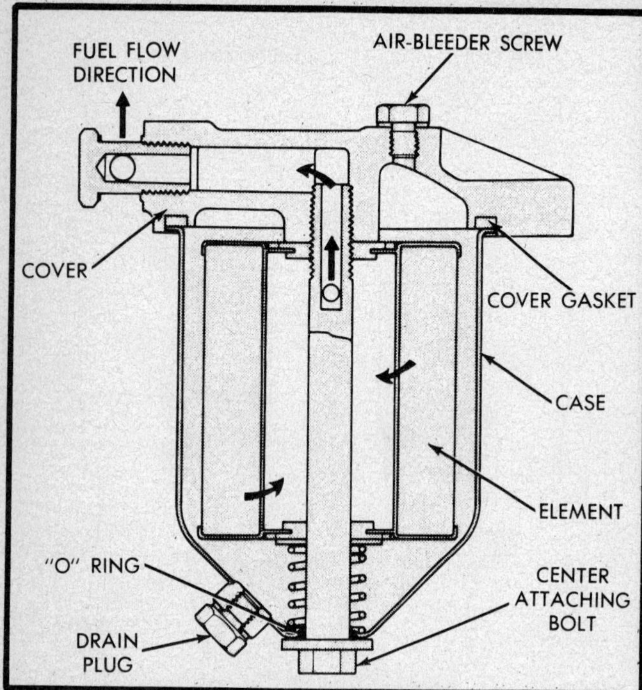

Cross section of diesel fuel filter—4.0L engine
(© Mitsubishi Motors Corp.)

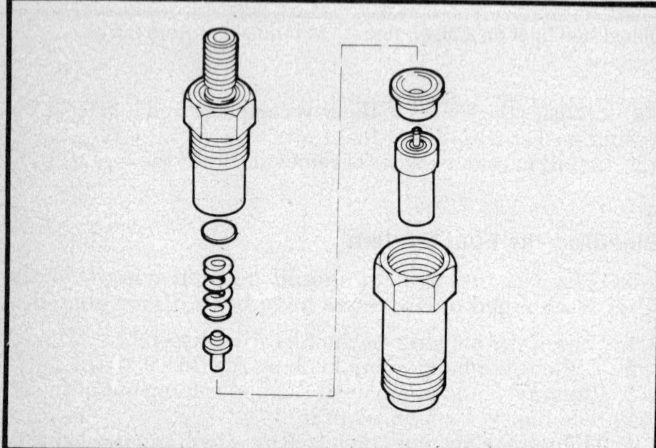

Exploded view of diesel fuel injector for 2.3L engine
(© Mitsubishi Motors Corp.)

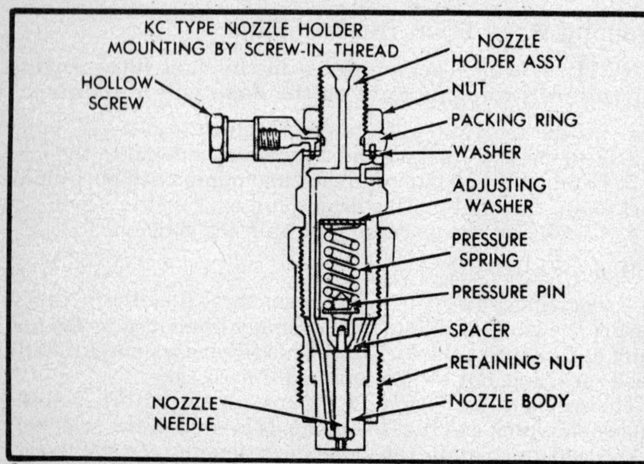

Cross section of fuel injector for 4.0L engine
(© Mitsubishi Motors Corp.)

in a suitable solvent to remove entrapped foreign matter. After cleaning, reinstall filter and fuel line connector and bleed air from the fuel system.

The third filter is a paper element throw away type installed at the back of the intake manifold and installed between the feed pump and the injection pump. A clogged filter will fail to supply a sufficient quantity of fuel to the engine, causing poor performance or erratic operation. Inspect the fuel filter element every 12,000 miles.

Removal and Installation

1. Loosen the air plug at top of fuel filter. Remove the drain plug or open the petcock at the bottom and allow fuel to drain.
2. Remove the center bolt and separate the case from the cover.
3. Inspect the paper filter element for excessive sediment buildup. If the element appears clogged, replace at this time.
4. Clean inside of case thoroughly before installing element.
5. Install new cover gasket and O-ring and reassemble case to cover. Reinstall drain plug or close petcock.
6. Bleed air from fuel system before placing vehicle in operation. Replace the fuel filter element every 24,000 miles.

Bleeding the Fuel System

Air trapped in the fuel system can cause inadequate fuel injection, poor operation and hard starting. Whenever the fuel system is serviced, it should be bled of trapped air in the proper sequence.

1. Loosen the fuel filter petcock or valve and operate the priming pump on the feed pump. If the filter is filled with fuel, fuel containing air bubbles will be discharged from the petcock or valve. Continue pumping until the discharged fuel contains no more air bubbles. Then tighten the fuel valve or petcock securely.
2. Loosen the air bleeder screw at the top of the injection pump and operate the priming pump. Continue pumping until all air is bled from the fuel in the pump reservoir. Then close the air bleeder screw securely.

Injection Nozzles

Removal and Installation

2.3L 4 CYLINDER

1. Remove the fuel delivery lines from the injectors and injection pump. Remove the lines as an assembly and cap all open fuel fittings on the injection pump immediately to prevent contamination with dirt or grease.
2. Remove the fuel return pipe nuts, then remove the fuel return line.
3. Remove the injection nozzle assembly from the cylinder head with special tool MD998387 or equivalent.
4. Installation is the reverse of removal. Torque fuel injector to 44–50 ft. lbs. Replace the heat shields.

NOTE: Exercise care when handling the fuel injector. It is a high precision part that is easily damaged by dirt or dropping.

4.0L 6 CYLINDER

1. Clean the injection nozzle connection before disassembly.
2. Remove the injection line from the nozzle assembly at the cylinder. Cap the fuel line opening to prevent contamination of the fuel system.
3. Remove the fuel injector from the head using a suitable socket tool.
4. Installation is the reverse of removal. Torque the fuel injector to 44–50 ft. lbs. Torque the fuel line nut to 17–26 ft. lbs.

NOTE: Exercise care when handling the fuel injector. It is a high-precision assembly that is easily damaged by dirt or dropping.

Injection Pump

Removal and Installation

2.3L 4 CYLINDER

1. Remove the timing belt upper cover.
2. Remove the nut and washer securing the injection pump sprocket.

NOTE: Be careful not to drop the nut and washer into lower cover.

3. Turn the crankshaft to bring No. 1 piston to TDC on its compression stroke.
4. Use a suitable gear puller to loosen the sprocket from the taper section of the drive shaft. Do not remove the sprocket; carefully set it in the timing belt lower cover with the belt engaged.
5. Remove the two water hoses from the wax element. Keep the end of the removed water hose higher than the cylinder head to prevent coolant drainage.
6. Disconnect the boost compensator hose at the injection pump.
7. Remove the fuel injection lines from the injection pump. Make sure the delivery valves do not turn when loosening the pipe connections at the pump.
8. Remove the injection pump support bracket bolts.
9. Remove the injection pump mounting nuts and remove the injection pump from the engine.

CAUTION

Do not turn the crankshaft with the injection pump removed

10. Installation is the reverse of removal. Make sure the timing marks on the camshaft sprocket and crankshaft pulley are aligned with their respective timing marks.
11. After mounting injection pump, carefully install injection pump sprocket and belt. Make sure that the injection pump drive shaft key is not misplaced or dropped.
12. Adjust injection timing and bleed the fuel system.

NOTE: If found to be defective, the injection pump must be replaced with a new or rebuilt unit. Any injection pump overhaul should be referred to an authorized Bosch diesel injection specialist.

Injection Pump

Removal

4.0L 6 CYLINDER

1. Disconnect battery negative cable at battery.
2. Disconnect fuel shutoff rod at stop lever. Rod end snaps over stop lever ball stud.
3. Remove steering pump and mounting bracket assembly from engine and set aside.
4. Clean dirt, paint and any other foreign material from fuel line, hose fittings and injection pipes at injection pump.
5. Drain engine oil. Remove dipstick and dipstick tube.
6. Disconnect throttle cable and linkage from injection pump control lever.
7. Remove throttle control bracket assembly from block, injection pump and control motor bracket. Set to one side.
8. Disconnect fuel supply line to fuel feed pump, loosening anchor clamps as necessary.
9. Disconnect fuel filter hoses from fuel feed pump and injection pump. Replace hollow bolts with seals into pumps to prevent dirt entry.
10. Turn engine crankshaft until No. 1 piston is positioned between 7 degrees BTDC and TDC on the compression stroke. Check pointer. It should be about midway between TDC and the 14 degree line on the crankshaft damper.

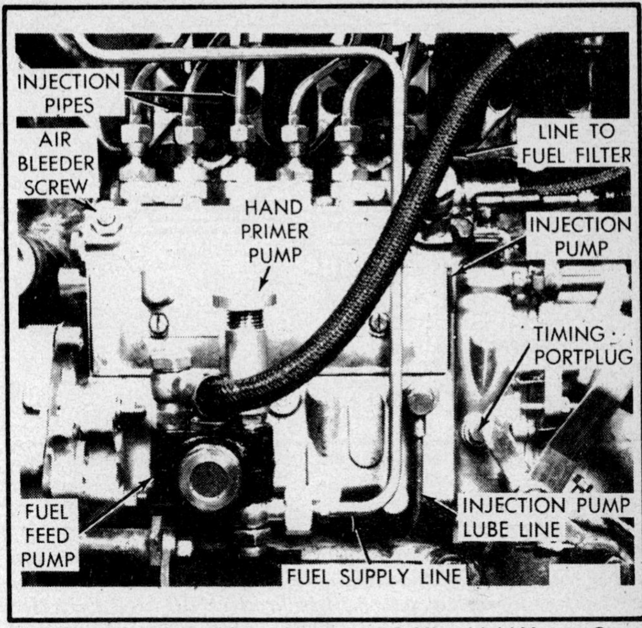

Injection pump assembly—4.0L engine (© Mitsubishi Motors Corp.)

11. Disconnect injection pipes from delivery valves and move away from block.

CAUTION

When disconnecting the injection pipe(s) at the delivery valve(s), hold the delivery valve holder(s) stationary and loosen the injection pipe fitting. Do not turn the delivery valve holder as this will disturb the delivery valve calibration.

12. Cap open delivery valves to prevent dirt from entering. Disconnect injection pump lube line at block fitting near starter motor forward end.
13. Injection pump assembly is attached to engine by five screws and one bolt. Front screws extend through timing case and engine front plate into pump flange plate. Rear bolt fastens flange plate to engine front plate. Remove these six fasteners.
14. Pull injection pump rearward to disengage from engine front plate and timing gear case. Twist pump toward block and continue pulling rearward until automatic timer is free of case.

Installation

1. Loosen four nuts attaching injection pump to mounting flange plate. Align center timing mark on pump flange with pointer on plate.
2. Be sure O-ring seal is in place on forward face of pump mounting flange.
3. Remove threaded timing port plug on governor housing behind control lever to expose pump camshaft bushing timing mark. Turn pump drive gear to align timing mark on camshaft bushing with pointer on governor. Guide plate notch on drive gear will be at approximately 8 o'clock point as viewed from front.
4. Be sure that crankshaft is still positioned between TDC and 7 degrees BTDC. See Removal, Step 10, with No. 1 piston on compression stroke.
5. Insert automatic timer into timing gear case. Turn injection pump in until against block. Then turn pump drive gear clockwise or counterclockwise to mesh drive and idler gears. Push pump forward into timing gear case and turn away from block to align attachment holes.

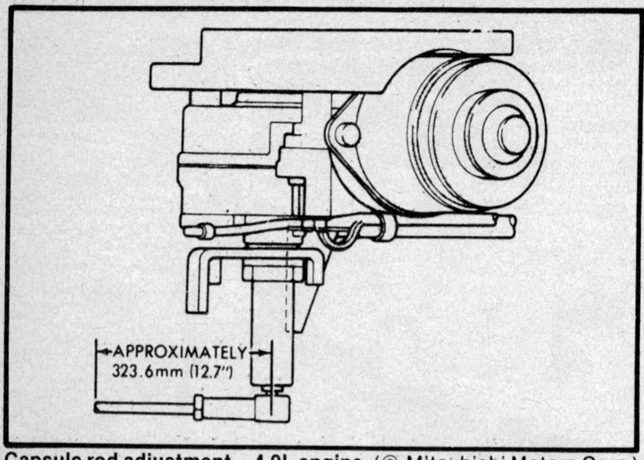

Capsule rod adjustment—4.0L engine (© Mitsubishi Motors Corp.)

CAUTION

Correct gear mesh is assured by drive gear guide plate. If pump cannot be pushed forward manually until flange plate seal diameter contacts engine front plate, gear mesh is incorrect. DO NOT ATTEMPT TO FORCE PUMP INTO POSITION. Retract pump and turn drive gear as needed to achieve correct gear mesh.

6. Attach the pump to the timing gear case. Turn the crankshaft opposite rotation direction until it reaches the specified timing mark. The governor pointer and pump camshaft bushing timing marks should now be aligned. If not, the pump must be removed and installed again.
7. When the timing marks are aligned, install the governor housing timing port plug and continue with the pump installation by reversing the removal procedure. However, do not yet connect No. 1 injection pipe or battery cable.
8. Refill crankcase with specified engine oil.
9. Bleed air from fuel filter and injection pump.
10. Check injection timing point. Adjust as required, following procedures under Injection Timing in this section.

CAPSULE ROD

Adjustment

1. Check capsule rod installation at motor drive lever. With the injection pump lever in the DRIVE position, the drive lever at the motor should be between the two marks.
2. Turn the drive lever with a prybar until it is nearly straight up and down, pointing upward.
3. Disconnect the capsule rod. Be sure that the injection pump stop lever is in the DRIVE position.
4. Loosen the capsule rod lock nut and adjust rod length until the drive lever is properly positioned between the match marks.
5. Tighten the lock nut and install the capsule rod to the drive lever. The nominal length of the capsule rod is 322.6mm (12.7 in.).

DATSUN/NISSAN 4 CYLINDER 2.2L (SD22) DIESEL ENGINE

GENERAL ENGINE SPECIFICATIONS

Engine Type	Engine Displace-ment-cc (cu. in.)	Fuel Delivery	Advertised Horsepower @ rpm	Advertised Torque @ rpm (ft. lbs.)	Bore and Stroke (in.)	Advertised Compres-sion Ratio	Oil Pressure (psi/idle)
SD22 2.2L 4 cyl	2164 (132)	Diesel Injection	61 @ 4000	102 @ 1800	3.27 × 3.94	21.6:1	60

DIESEL ENGINE TUNE-UP SPECIFICATIONS

Engine Type	Injector Opening Pressure (psi)	Low Idle (rpm)	Dashpot Speed (rpm)	Valve Clearance (in.)		Intake Valve Opens (deg.)	Injection Timing rpm	Firing Order
				Intake	Exhaust			
SD22	1422-1493	550-700	1280-1350	.014	.014	28B	20 BTDC	1-3-4-2

TORQUE SPECIFICATIONS

(All readings in ft. lbs. unless noted)

Engine Type	Engine Displace-ment cc (cu. in.)	Cylinder Head Bolts	Rod Bearing Bolts	Main Bearing Bolts	Crank-shaft Pulley Bolts	Fly-wheel to Crank-shaft Bolts	Manifolds	
							Intake	Exhaust
SD22 2.2L 4cyl	2164 (132)	94 large 40 small	36–40	123–127	217–239	33–36	11–13	11–13

TORQUE SEQUENCES

Cylinder head bolt torque sequence

CHILTON'S THREE "C's" DIESEL ENGINE DIAGNOSIS PROCEDURE

Condition	CAUSE	CORRECTION
Rough Idle	Improper adjustment	Adjust idle
	Accelerator control cable binding	Repair or lubricate
	Air or water in the fuel system	Clear air or water from fuel system
	Injection nozzle clogged	Check and clean injector nozzles
	Improper valve clearance	Check valve adjustment
	Injection pump malfunction	Check injection pump
Poor Performance	Air cleaner clogged	Check element
	Accelerator control cable binding	Check control cable for free movement
	Restricted fuel flow (water or air)	Check lines and filter
	Incorrect injection timing	Check injection timing
	Injection pump malfunction	Replace injection pump
Excessive Exhaust Smoke	Restricted air cleaner	Check element
	Air or water in fuel filter	Remove air or water from fuel system
	Improper grade fuel	Check fuel in tank
	Incorrect injection timing	Check injection timing
	Injection pump malfunction	Replace injection pump
	Injector nozzle stuck open	Check injector nozzles
Excessive Fuel Consumption	Restricted air cleaner	Check element
	Leak in fuel lines	Check for leaks
	Incorrect idle speed	Check idle
	Restricted exhaust system	Check exhaust
	Improper grade of fuel	Check fuel in tank
	Injection pump malfunction	Check injection pump operation
Loud Knocking In Engine	Defective fuel injector	Replace fuel injector

Note: If the problem persists after performing these preliminary checks, disassembly and inspection of internal engine components may be necessary for further diagnosis.

TUNE-UP AND ADJUSTMENTS

Compression Test

1. Warm up the engine.
2. Remove the injection nozzle.
3. Install compression test adapter into nozzle mounting hole and attach compression gauge.
4. Measure the compression pressure by cranking the engine. Use the same number of compression strokes to measure each cylinder. The standard compression is 427 psi and the limit is 356 psi. There should be no more than 43 psi difference between each cylinder.

NOTE: The engine compression measurement should be made as quickly as possible.

Valve Adjustment

1. Warm up the engine to normal operating temperature.
2. Remove the air cleaner and valve rocker cover.
3. Turn the crankshaft so that the No. 1 cylinder is set at TDC on the compression stroke.
4. Adjust the clearances of the No. 1,2,3 and 5 valves, if necessary, by loosening the rocker arm lock nut and turning the adjusting screw.
5. Rotate the crankshaft so that the No. 4 cylinder is at TDC/compression and adjust the No. 4,6,7 and 8 valves, if necessary.

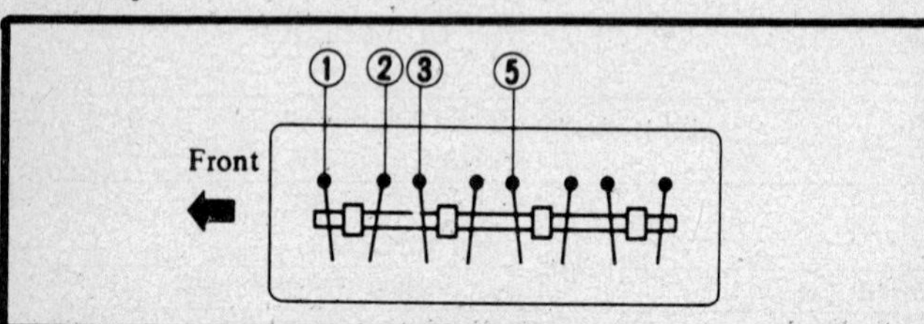

2.2L engine valve adjustment—step one
(© Nissan Motor Corp. of USA)

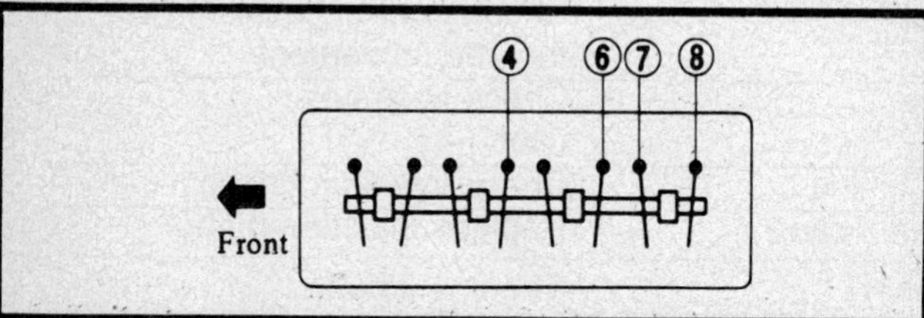

2.2L engine valve adjustment—step two
(© Nissan Motor Corp. of USA)

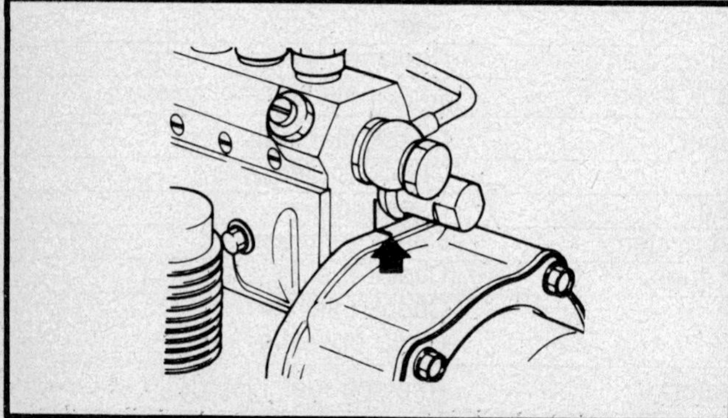
Timing marks on pump and engine front plate
(© Nissan Motor Corp. of USA)

NOTE: When checking the clearances, the feeler gauge should move with a very slight drag.

6. Install the cylinder head cover.

Injection Timing

1. Check the timing marks on the pump and engine front plate and align if necessary.
2. Turn the crankshaft pulley in the direction of rotation and align the timing marks.
3. Remove all injection tubes and governor hoses.
4. Remove the No. 1 lock plate and delivery valve holder and pull out the delivery valve stopper and spring.

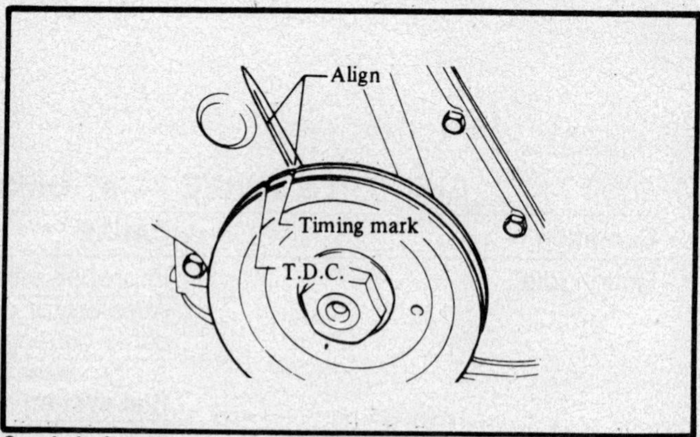

Crankshaft pulley alignment marks
(© Nissan Motor Corp. of USA)

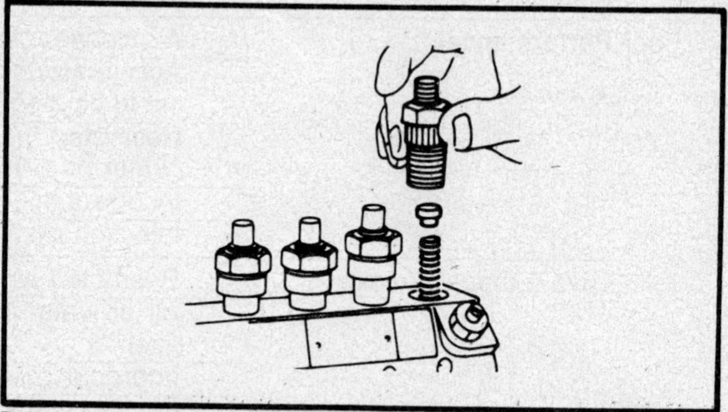
Delivery valve stopper and spring (© Nissan Motor Corp. of USA)

5. Install the delivery valve holder without the stopper and spring.
6. Connect the fuel hose so that fuel can be supplied by the priming pump.
7. Connect test tube to the No. 1 delivery valve holder.
8. Push the injection pump assembly fully down toward the engine side.
9. While feeding fuel by operating the priming pump, slowly move the injection pump until the fuel flow from the No. 1 injection tube stops.
10. Tighten the pump in this position and check that the timing marks on the pump and front plate are aligned. If not, stamp a new mark on the front plate.

11. Remove the No.1 injection tube and delivery valve holder and reinstall spring and stopper, then reinstall delivery valve and torque to 22–25 ft. lbs. (29–34 Nm).

12. Connect governor and fuel hoses and bleed the fuel system.

Idle Speed Adjustment

1. Start the engine and allow it to reach operating temperature. Stop the engine.
2. Attach diesel tachometer to No. 1 injection line. Remove the clamp on No. 1 line to obtain a more accurate reading.
3. Start the engine and check the idle speed with the tachometer. Make sure the accelerator linkage is not binding.
4. If the idle speed is not as specified in the Tune-Up chart, make sure the throttle control knob is pushed all the way in before adjusting.
5. If adjustment is necessary, loosen the idle adjusting screw locknut and turn the idle adjusting screw until the proper idle speed is obtained. Race the engine and allow it to return to idle, then recheck the adjustment.
6. After idle adjustment is complete, tighten the locknut.

NOTE: After every idle speed adjustment, adjust the dashpot (if equipped) by maintaining an engine speed of 1280–1350 rpm, loosening the dash pot locknut, then operating the dash pot and adjusting the tip until it contacts the control lever.

Glow Plug System

The auto-glow system used on the 2.2 liter engine consists of the following components:

1. Glow plug mounted in the engine block.

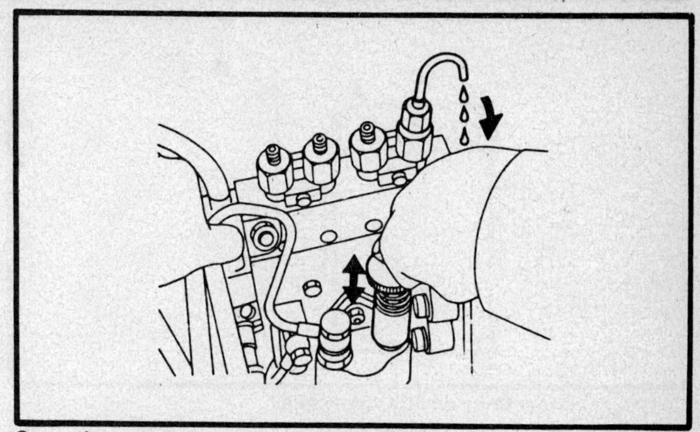

Operating priming pump to check fuel flow (© Nissan Motor Corp. of USA)

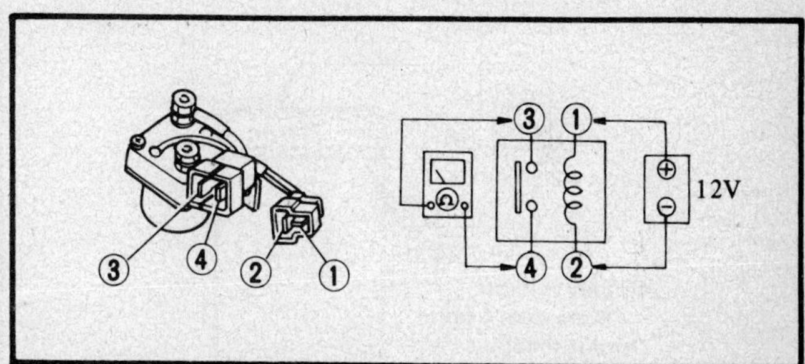

Terminal location on glow plug relay (© Nissan Motor Corp. of USA)

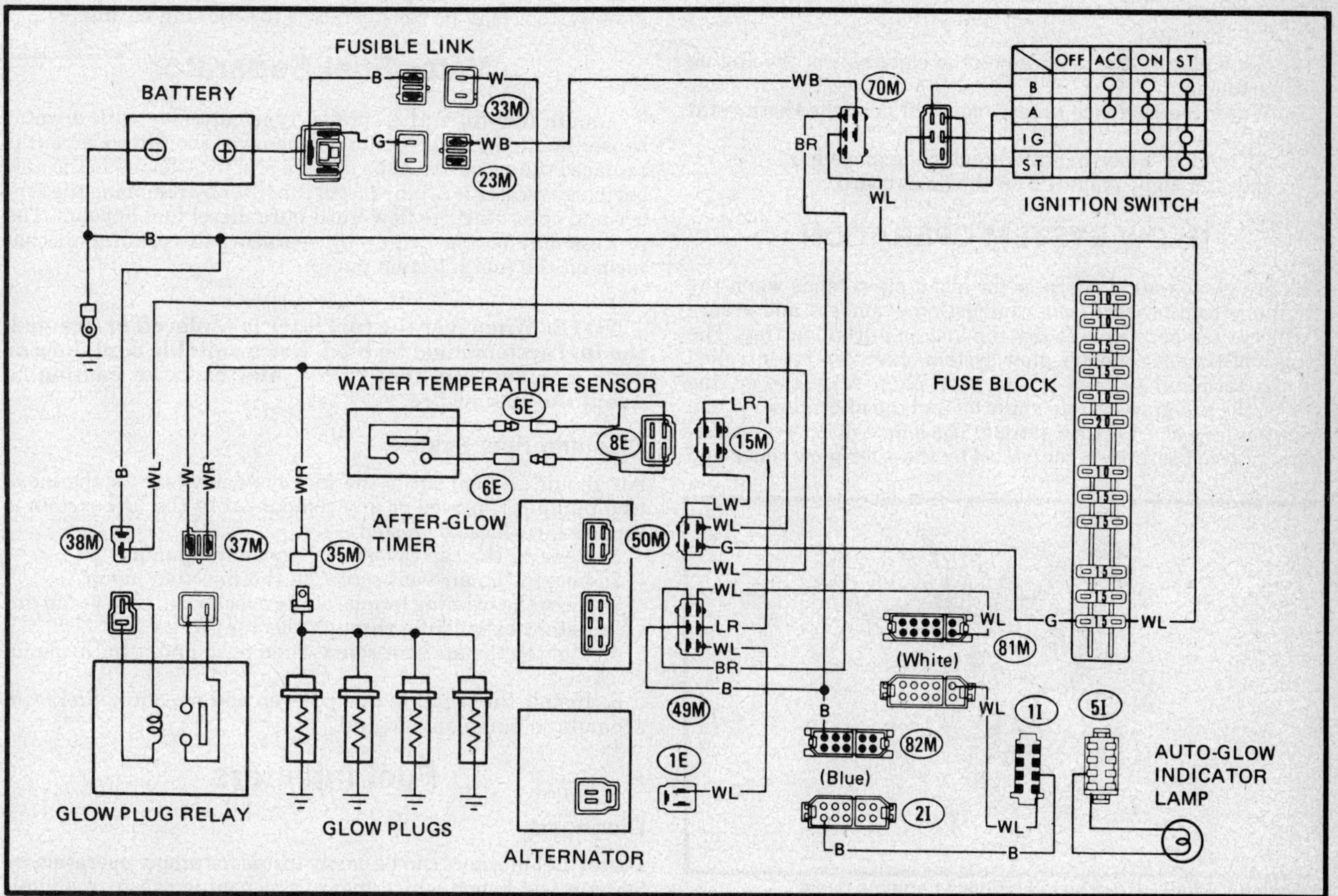

Electrical schematic of auto-glow plug system—early type (© Nissan Motor Corp. of USA)

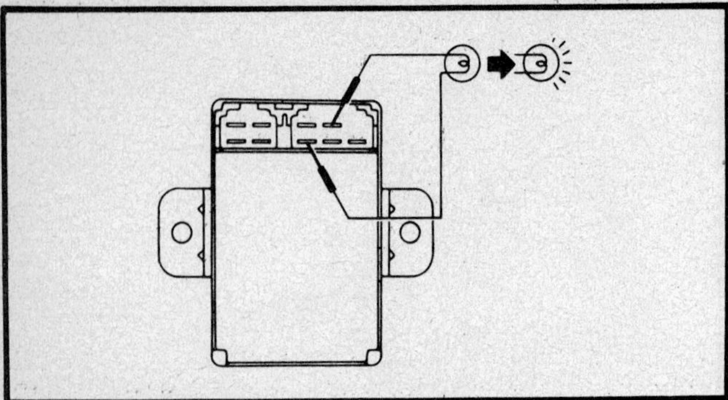

Test light connections on after-glow relay
(© Nissan Motor Corp. of USA)

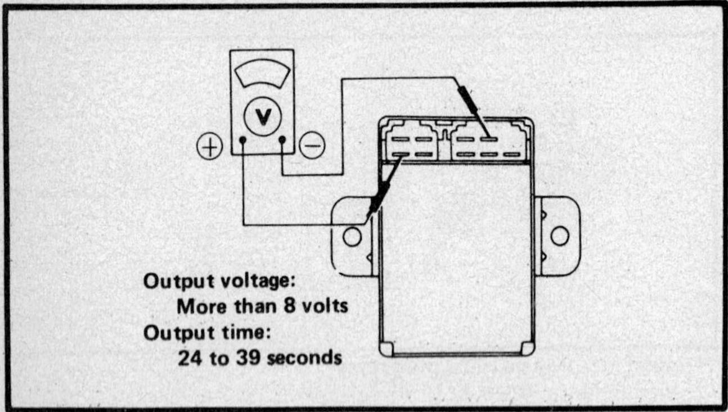

Voltmeter test on after-glow relay (© Nissan Motor Corp. of USA)

2. Glow plug relay mounted on the right side of the engine compartment.
3. Water temperature sensor mounted near the thermostat housing.
4. After-glow timer mounted under the glove box.
5. Indcator light mounted on the dash board.

GLOW SYSTEM OPERATION

The pre-glow system operates for about six seconds when the engine is cold to warm the combustion chambers and assure sufficient temperatures to fire the fuel on initial starting. The length of time for the pre-glow system operation is controlled by the terminal voltage of the glow plug. After the engine starts, the pre-glow system shuts off and the after-glow system operates for a short length of time. The length of time the after-glow system operates is controlled by the after-glow timer and could be anywhere from 1 to 48 seconds. The after-glow timer shuts off the glow system when the terminal voltage at the glow plugs exceeds 7 volts.

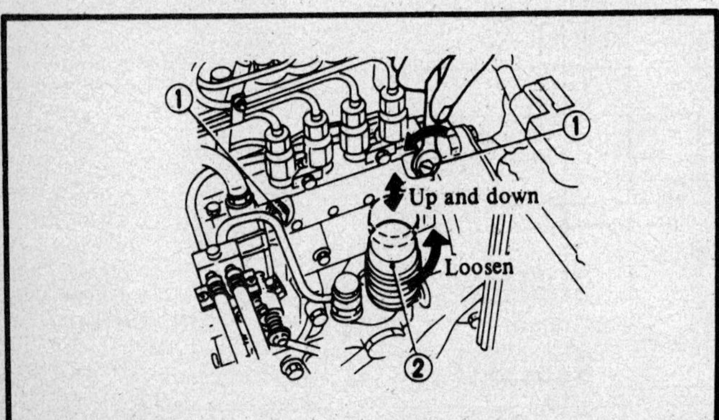

Bleeding the fuel system by operating the priming pump
(© Nissan Motor Corp. of USA)

Glow System Testing

A simple continuity test can determine if a glow plug is functioning normally. Remove the glow plug and apply 12 volts to the connector while grounding the body. The heating element should glow within 15 seconds.

CAUTION

Exercise care to avoid a possibly serious burn during testing. Remember that the glow plug tip will be hot for a time after testing. Do not apply current any longer than 15 seconds.

The water temperature sensor is checked by measuring the resistance (ohms) across the sensor connector terminals while heating the sensor body in water. The resistance should be about 12 ohms at 14°F and drop to about 1 ohm at 122°F.

The glow plug relay is tested by removing it and making sure continuity exists between terminals 1 and 2. Apply 12 volts between terminals 1 and 2 and check for continuity between 3 and 4. Continuity between terminals 3 and 4 should not exist when battery voltage is removed.

The after-glow timer unit may be checked by connecting a test lamp or voltmeter as illustrated. Turn the ignition ON and measure the length of time the test light stays on. At an engine temperature of around 68°F the test light should glow for approximately 8–12 seconds. Output voltage should be at least 8 volts.

NOTE: Disconnect the lead wire from the S terminal of the starter before testing.

If the glow time and output voltage are as described, the glow system may be considered as functioning normally.

Water/Fuel Separator

The main fuel filter is a spin-on type cartridge with a water sensor mounted in the bottom. Whenever the filter element is replaced the sensor must be remove and transferred to the new cartridge. Water is drained from the filter by removing the sensor and observing the flow until pure diesel fuel appears. The process may be speeded up by operating the priming mechanism on the fuel injection pump.

NOTE: Whenever the fuel filter is replaced or drained, the fuel system must be bled. Use a suitable container or rags to catch any fuel runoff and exercise caution to avoid the risk of fire.

Bleeding Fuel System

Air should be bled out of the fuel system whenever the injection pump is removed or any component in the fuel system is repaired, replaced or tested.

1. Remove the cap covering the priming pump.
2. Loosen the air vent screw on the injection pump.
3. Turn the priming pump counterclockwise, then pump until air stops exhausting through the vent screw.
4. Tighten the air vent screw, then push and turn the pump clockwise.
5. Install the priming pump cover and wipe any fuel from around the pump and engine.

Fuel Injectors

Diagnosis

Diesel fuel injectors can be easily tested for proper operation by using a test bench which measures opening pressure and allows visual inspection of the spray pattern. A defective injector can cause a variety of problems such as hard starting, rough idle, lack of power, excessive smoke or fuel consumption and audible knocks in the engine. An abnormal engine knock is one of the most obvious symptoms of a defective injector. Injector nozzle opening pressure can be adjusted by changing the shim inside the injector body. A shim thickness change of 0.04mm (0.0016 in.) will change opening pressure by 68 psi.

NOTE: All fuel injection systems are sensitive to dirt. When working on the injection system, everything must be kept clean. Make it a practice to wipe every pipe connector before removing it.

Removal and Installation

1. Remove the injection tube assembly.
2. Remove the spill tube assembly. To prevent the spill tube from breaking, remove it by gripping the nozzle holder.
3. Remove the injection nozzle assembly with suitable tool.
4. Installation is the reverse of removal. Torque injection nozzle assembly to 43–51 ft. lbs. (59–69 Nm).
5. Bleed the fuel system.

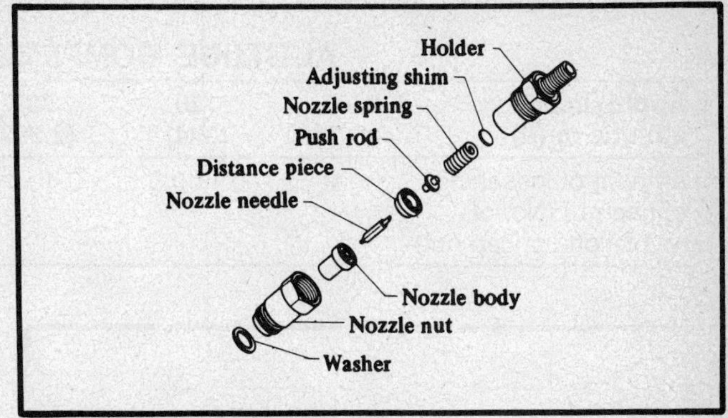

Exploded view of 2.2L engine fuel injector
(© Nissan Motor Corp. of USA)

Injection Pump

GENERAL INFORMATION

The SD22 engine uses a Kiki-Bosch PE type inline injection pump. The pump is driven by a gear with a timing device that automatically advances the start of fuel delivery (timing) in response to increases in engine rpm. A fuel supply pump with a hand primer is mounted on the side and driven by an eccentric located between two cams of the injection pump.

A control mechanism consisting of mechanical linkage and an electronic control unit (D.P.C. module) controls the START, STOP and DRIVE operation of the injection pump. On some models, a high altitude compensator is mounted on a bracket at the rear of the injection pump housing. The oil sump is connected to the engine lubrication system, providing the injection pump with filtered oil, but the pump diaphragm must be oiled at regular intervals as part of normal injection pump maintenance.

NOTE: Datsun/Nissan recommends that all internal injection pump overhaul procedures be performed at an authorized Kiki-Bosch service facility because of the specialized equipment needed for proper calibration.

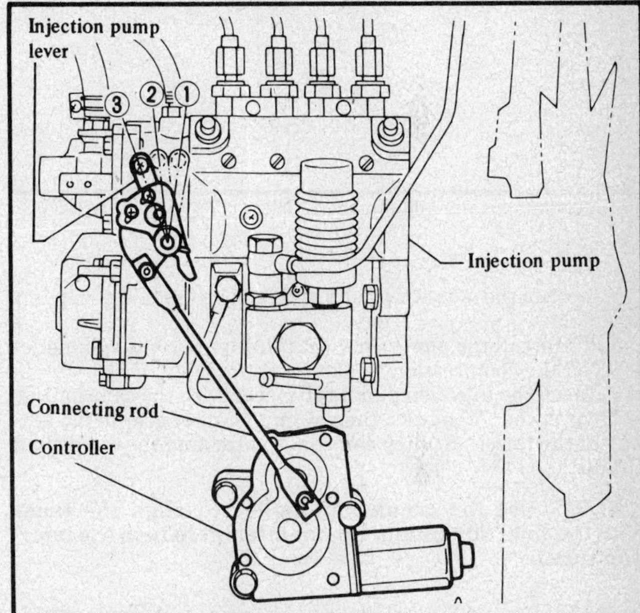

Injection pump control mechanism
(© Nissan Motor Corp. of USA)

INJECTION PUMP CONTROL MECHANISM

The injection pump control system is wired through the ignition switch in order to start, operate or stop the diesel injection pump. The control mechanism is controlled by the injection pump control unit (D.P.C. module) to regulate the amount of fuel injection by operating the injection pump lever. When the ignition is in the START position, the injection pump lever is set to increase the amount of fuel delivered. After the engine starts (key in the ON position), the lever moves to the normal driving position. When the key is turned OFF, the pump lever moves to the STOP position and cuts off all fuel to the engine.

NOTE: The engine can be stopped manually by turning the key OFF and moving the control lever away from the injection pump to the STOP position by hand.

Removal and Installation

1. Remove Tem-coupling with fan and radiator.
2. Remove the fuel lines as a unit from the pump and injectors. Cap the open ends of the injectors and delivery nozzles to prevent dirt from entering the fuel system.
3. Disconnect the governor hoses, fuel hoses and oil feed pipe bolt.
4. Disconnect pump controller connecting rod.
5. Remove the timing gear cover on injection pump.
6. Remove the timer round nut.
7. Remove the timer assembly using special tool ST19530000 or equivalent.

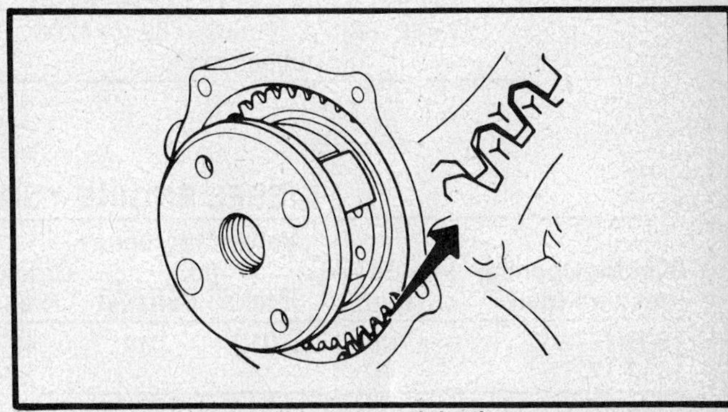

Correct alignment of timing marks on injection pump gears
(© Nissan Motor Corp. of USA)

ALTITUDE COMPENSATOR ADJUSTMENT

Approximate altitude m (ft)	0 (0)	120 (394)	700 (2,297)	1,300 (4,265)	2,000 (6,562)	2,700 (8,859)	3,400 (11,155)
Amount of loosening of cap nut (No. of revolutions of cap nut)	0	0.1~0.3	0.4~0.8	0.9~1.3	1.4~1.8	1.9~2.3	2.4~2.6

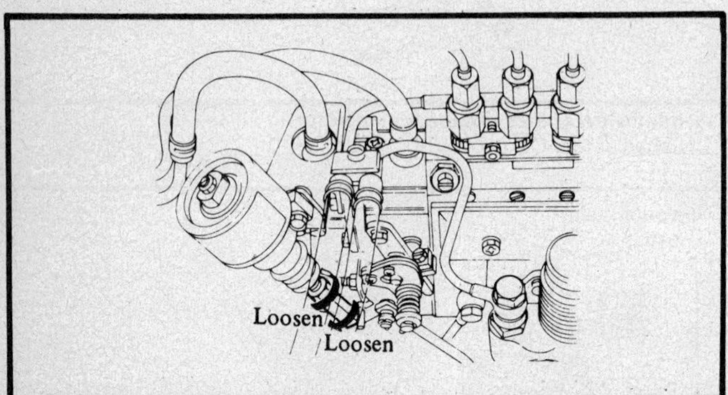

Altitude compensator adjustment (© Nissan Motor Corp. of USA)

8. Loosen the mounting bolts and remove the injection pump assembly.
9. To install the pump, first set the engine No. 1 cylinder at TDC on the compression stroke.
10. Mesh the injection pump drive gear with the camshaft idler gear at the "Y" marks, then align the timer gear to the keyway of the injection pump camshaft by turning the crankshaft pulley.

NOTE: Use the crankshaft pulley to align the timer with the injection pump. Do not attempt to turn the injection pump.

11. Secure the timer assembly with a lockwasher and round nut. Torque to 14–18 ft. lbs. (20–25 Nm).
12. Align pump mark to front cover mark.
13. Set injection timing as previously described.
14. Install all disconnected hoses and linkage in the reverse order of removal.
15. Install radiator and fan with Tem-coupling. Refill the cooling system.
16. Install the fuel lines and bleed the fuel system.

ALTITUDE COMPENSATOR

Adjustment

1. Check for loose connections before attempting adjustment. Connect hand vacuum pump and make sure compensator control rod is free and moves when vacuum is applied.
2. Disconnect the diesel pump controller rod.
3. Loosen lock nut and cap nut of the compensator and turn the cap nut until it just touches the control rod. Temporarily tighten the lock nut.
4. Determine the altitude (feet above sea level) in the area where the vehicle is to be operated.

NOTE: Any area that is above 4000 ft. in elevation is considered a High Altitude Area.

5. Refer to the chart to determine the number of cap nut revolutions necessary to adjust the compensator push rod. Tighten the lock nut after adjustment.
6. Reconnect the pump control rod.

TOYOTA DIESEL ENGINE

GENERAL ENGINE SPECIFICATIONS

Engine Type	Engine Displacement Cu. In. (cc)	Fuel Delivery	SAE Net Horsepower (@ rpm)	SAE Net Torque @ rpm (ft lbs)	Bore x Stroke (in.)	Compression Ratio	Oil Pressure @ rpm (psi)
L	133.5 (2188)	Fuel Injection	62 @ 4200	93 @ 2400	3.54 x 3.38	21.5:1	11.4 @ 700

DIESEL ENGINE TUNE-UP SPECIFICATIONS

Injector Opening Pressure (psi)	Idle Speed (rpm)	Valve Clearance (in.) Intake	Valve Clearance (in.) Exhaust	Cranking Compression Pressure @ 250 rpm	Maximum Compression Variance③	Firing Order
1636-1778① 1492-1777②	700	.010	.014	427 psi maximum 284 psi minimum	71 psi	1-3-4-2

① New ② Used ③ Between highest and lowest cylinder readings

FIRING ORDER

Firing order: 1-3-4-2

TORQUE SPECIFICATIONS

(All readings in ft. lbs.)

Engine Type	Engine Displacement Cu. In. (cc)	Cylinder Head Bolts	Rod Bearing Bolts	Main Bearing Bolts	Crankshaft Pulley Bolt	Flywheel-to-Crankshaft Bolts	Manifolds Intake	Manifolds Exhaust
L	133.5 (2188)	84-90	37-43	71-81	69-75	84-90	8-11	11-15

TORQUE SEQUENCES

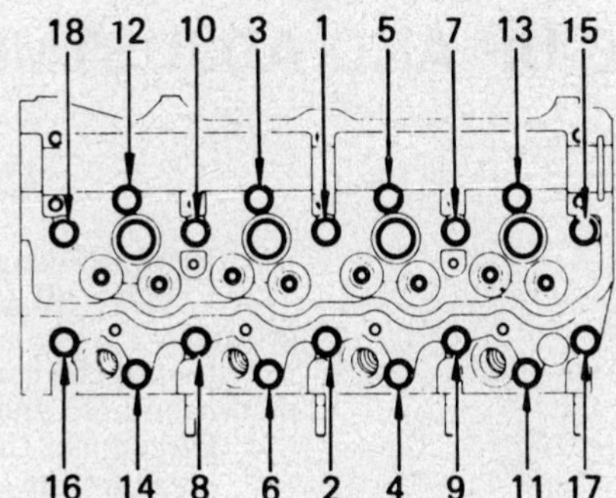

Cylinder head bolt tightening sequence

CHILTON'S THREE "C's" DIESEL ENGINE DIAGNOSIS PROCEDURE

Condition	CAUSE	CORRECTION
Rough Idle	Improper adjustment	Adjust idle
	Accelerator control cable binding	Repair or lubricate
	Air or water in the fuel system	Clear air or water from fuel system
	Injection nozzle clogged	Check and clean injector nozzles
	Improper valve clearance	Check valve adjustment
	Injection pump malfunction	Check injection pump
Poor Performance	Air cleaner clogged	Check element
	Accelerator control cable binding	Check control cable for free movement
	Restricted fuel flow (water or air)	Check lines and filter
	Incorrect injection timing	Check injection timing
	Injection pump malfunction	Replace injection pump
Excessive Exhaust Smoke	Restricted air cleaner	Check element
	Air or water in fuel filter	Remove air or water from fuel system
	Improper grade fuel	Check fuel in tank
	Incorrect injection timing	Check injection timing
	Injection pump malfunction	Replace injection pump
	Injector nozzle stuck open	Check injector nozzles

CHILTON'S THREE "C's" DIESEL ENGINE DIAGNOSIS PROCEDURE

Condition	CAUSE	CORRECTION
Excessive Fuel Consumption	Restricted air cleaner	Check element
	Leak in fuel lines	Check for leaks
	Incorrect idle speed	Check idle
	Restricted exhaust system	Check exhaust
	Improper grade of fuel	Check fuel in tank
	Injection pump malfunction	Check injection pump operation
Loud Knocking In Engine	Defective fuel injector	Replace fuel injector

Note: If the problem persists after performing these preliminary checks, disassembly and inspection of internal engine components may be necessary for further diagnosis.

TUNE-UP AND ADJUSTMENTS

The Toyota type L diesel engine tune-up should include the following inspections and/or repairs;

1. Compression test.
2. Valve adjustment.
3. Injection timing check and/or adjustment.
4. Injector pressure test and inspection.
5. Idle speed adjustment.
6. Glow system operation check.

Valve clearance adjustment sequence
(© Toyota Motor Sales, USA)

Compression Test

1. Bring the engine to normal operation temperature.
2. Remove all glow plugs. Make sure the load wire is not grounded.
3. Install the compression gauge adapter into the glow plug mounting hole and connect the compression gauge.
4. Disconnect the fuel cut solenoid wire connector.
5. Measure the compression pressure while cranking the engine with the starter. Refer to the specifications.

NOTE: The number of compression strokes used in determining the maximum compression should be the same for all cylinders tested.

Valve Adjustment

NOTE: The engine should be at normal operating temperature when adjusting the valves.

1. Stop the engine and remove the valve cover.
2. Set the No.1 cylinder to TDC on the compression stroke.
3. Adjust the valves indicated by the arrows on the illustration. Valve clearance is measured between the valve stem and the rocker arm adjusting screw.

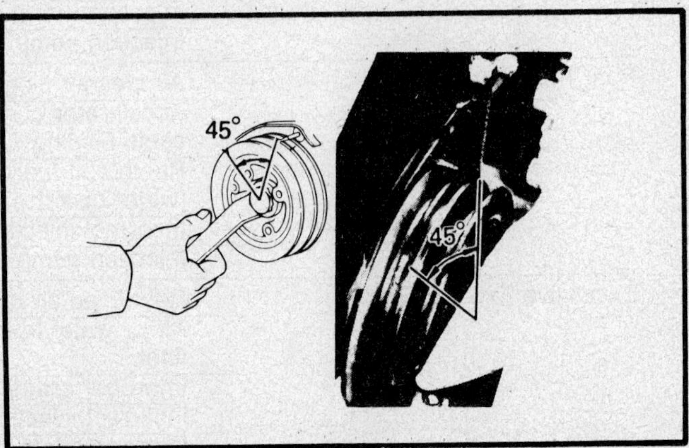

Correct placement of crankshaft to measure injection pump stroke (© Toyota Motor Sales, USA)

4. Rotate the crankshaft 360 degrees and adjust the remaining valves.

NOTE: Do not start the engine with the valve cover removed.

Injection Timing

1. Remove the injection pump head bolt.
2. Install the plunger stroke measuring tool and dial indicator to the injection pump head plug.
3. Rotate the crankshaft clockwise and set either the No.1 or No.4 cylinder 45 degrees BTDC on the compression stroke.
4. Zero the dial indicator.
5. Slowly rotate the crankshaft pulley until the No. 1 or No. 4 cylinder is at TDC/compression.
6. Measure the piston plunger stroke on the dial indicator. It should be 1.0mm (0.0394 in.).
7. If the stroke is not correct, loosen the injection pump retaining bolts, the union nuts of the injection pipes on the pump side and the union bolt of the fuel inlet pipe on the pump side.
8. Adjust the piston plunger stroke by slightly tilting the injection pump body. If the stroke is less than specifications, adjust the pump towards the engine, If the stroke exceeds specifications, adjust the pump away from the engine.
9. Tighten the injection pump bolts to 11–15 ft. lbs., making sure the stroke does not change during tightening.
10. Tighten the union nuts to 17–22 ft. lbs. and tighten the fuel inlet fitting to 15–18 ft. lbs.
11. Remove the measuring tool and dial gauge, then torque the distributor head bolt to 8–9 ft. lbs. Replace the washer when installing the head bolt.

NOTE: Bleed air from the fuel pipes by loosening the pipes at the injectors and cranking the engine.

Idle and Maximum Speed Adjustment

1. Warm the engine to normal operating temperature and allow it to idle.
2. Turn the idle adjustor knob counterclockwise; the knob should return to its locked position.
3. Turn the engine off and remove the accelerator connection rod.
4. Connect a tachometer to the engine according to the manufacturers recommendations.
5. Start the engine and check the engine rpm at idle. The idle engine speed should be 700 rpm.

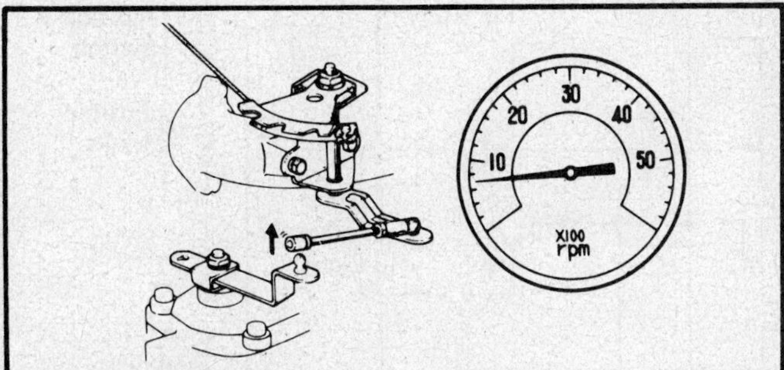

Remove accelerator connecting rod to check idle
(© Toyota Motor Sales, USA)

6. If adjustment is necessary, turn the idle adjusting screw on the fuel injection pump as required to obtain the 700 rpm idle speed.
7. Fully depress the injection pump lever, note the maximum engine speed and release the accelerator pedal immediately. The maximum engine speed should be 4900 rpm.
8. If adjustment is necessary, remove the wire seal of the maximum speed adjusting screw, if so equipped.
9. Using Toyota special service tool #092785–54020 or its equivalent, loosen the locknut of the maximum speed adjusting screw.
10. Turn the maximum speed adjusting screw until the proper maximum engine speed is obtained.
11. Install the accelerator connecting rod and adjust its length so that there is no slack in the accelerator cable.
12. Check that the idle speed increases as the idle adjuster knob is pulled outward. Turn the knob counterclockwise so that the rpm returns to the idle specification.
13. Turn the engine off and disconnect the tachometer from the engine.
14. Road test the vehicle and verify adjustments are correct.

High Altitude Modification

In order to improve the emission control in designated high or low altitude areas (above or below 4000 feet), a modification procedure has been developed for the L-series diesel engine. These modification procedures will result in better engine performance and improved fuel economy when the engine is operated in either high or slow altitude areas. A sticker must be affixed to the engine compartment whenever a modification to a high altitude specification is performed and removed when the diesel engine has been re-adjusted for low altitude operation. The emission control labels are available from the manufacturer.

Modification Procedure

HIGH ALTITUDE OPERATION (ABOVE 4,000 FEET)

1. Remove the injection pump head bolt.
2. Install the plunger stroke measuring tool and dial indicator to the injection pump head plug.
3. Rotate the crankshaft clockwise and set No.1 cylinder 45 degrees before TDC on the compression stroke.
4. Zero the dial indicator.
5. Slowly rotate the crankshaft pulley until the No.1 cylinder is at TDC.
6. Measure the piston plunger stroke on the dial indicator.
7. Loosen the injection pump bolts, all union nuts of the injection pipe on the injection pump side and the union bolt of the fuel inlet pipe on the pump side.
8. Adjust the pump plunger stroke to 1.12mm (0.0441 in.), by slightly tilting the injection pump body towards the engine, if the stroke is less and away from the engine if the stroke is more than specifications.

NOTE: Be sure the engine is at TDC when making this adjustment.

9. After adjusting the pump stroke, tighten the injection pump bolts to 11–15 ft. lbs., making sure the stroke does not change during the tightening.
10. Tighten the union nuts the 17–22 ft. lbs. and the fuel inlet bolt to 15–18 ft. lbs.
11. Remove the measuring tool and the dial indicator. Install the pump head bolt with a new washer and torque to 8–9 ft. lbs.

NOTE: Bleed the air from the fuel lines by loosening the pipes at the injectors and cranking the engine.

12. Follow the instructions under "Idle Speed Adjustment"and set the engine idle speed to 700 rpm. Affix a new High Altitude Adjustment label too the underside of the hood, next to the existing Vehicle Emission Control Information label.

Low Altitude Operation (Below 4000 Feet)

To adjust a high altitude vehicle to low altitude specifications, follow the procedure outlined under "Injection Timing." Be sure to remove the high altitude emission label after the adjustment.

Glow Plug System

GENERAL INFORMATION

When the coolant temperature is below 104 degrees F. (40 degrees C.), the glow plug system is designed to preheat the combustion chambers in order to provide sufficient temperature to fire the fuel on initial starting of the engine. When functioning properly, the glow plug indicator should light for 4.5 seconds when the temperature is below the preset standard and 0.5 seconds when the temperature is above the preset standard. Components of the glow plug system are not serviceable and is found to be defective, must be replaced as a unit.

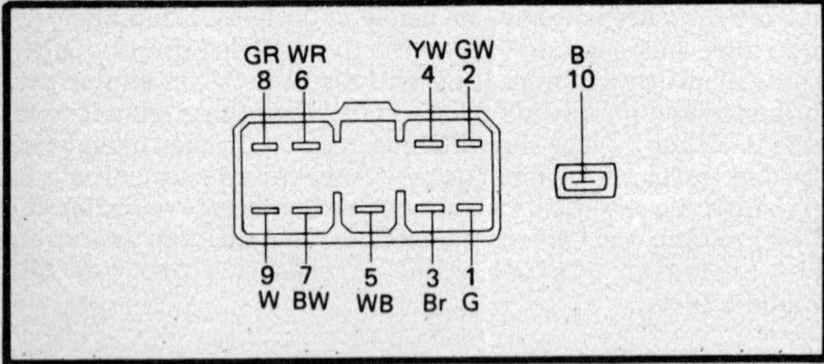

Pre-heating timer connector locations
(© Toyota Motor Sales, USA)

NOTE: If a glow plug is found to be defective, it is a good policy to replace the complete set.

The glow plug system consists of the following components:

1. Preheating timer located behind the left kick panel.
2. Glow plug relay No.1 located on the left front fender, in the engine compartment.
3. Glow plug relay No.2 located under the right fender, in the engine compartment.
4. Glow plugs mounted on the left side of the engine.
5. Glow plug current sensor located above the No.3 glow plug.
6. Resistor located on the back surface of the intake manifold.
7. Water temperature sensor located on the right side of the engine block.

Glow Plug Diagnosis

Glow System Testing

NOTE: Before beginning any test procedures, make sure the battery voltage is 12 volts with the engine switch off and that the fusible link in the glow system is intact.

1. Test glow plug relay No.1 by checking for continuity between terminal g and E. There should be no continuity between terminals +B and G. Apply 12 volts between terminals g and E and again test for continuity between +B and G. Continuity should now be present. Any result other than these, replace glow plug relay No.1.
2. Check glow plug relay No.2 by repeating the same procedure used for testing relay No.1. Again, if the test results differ from those described, replace glow plug relay No.2.

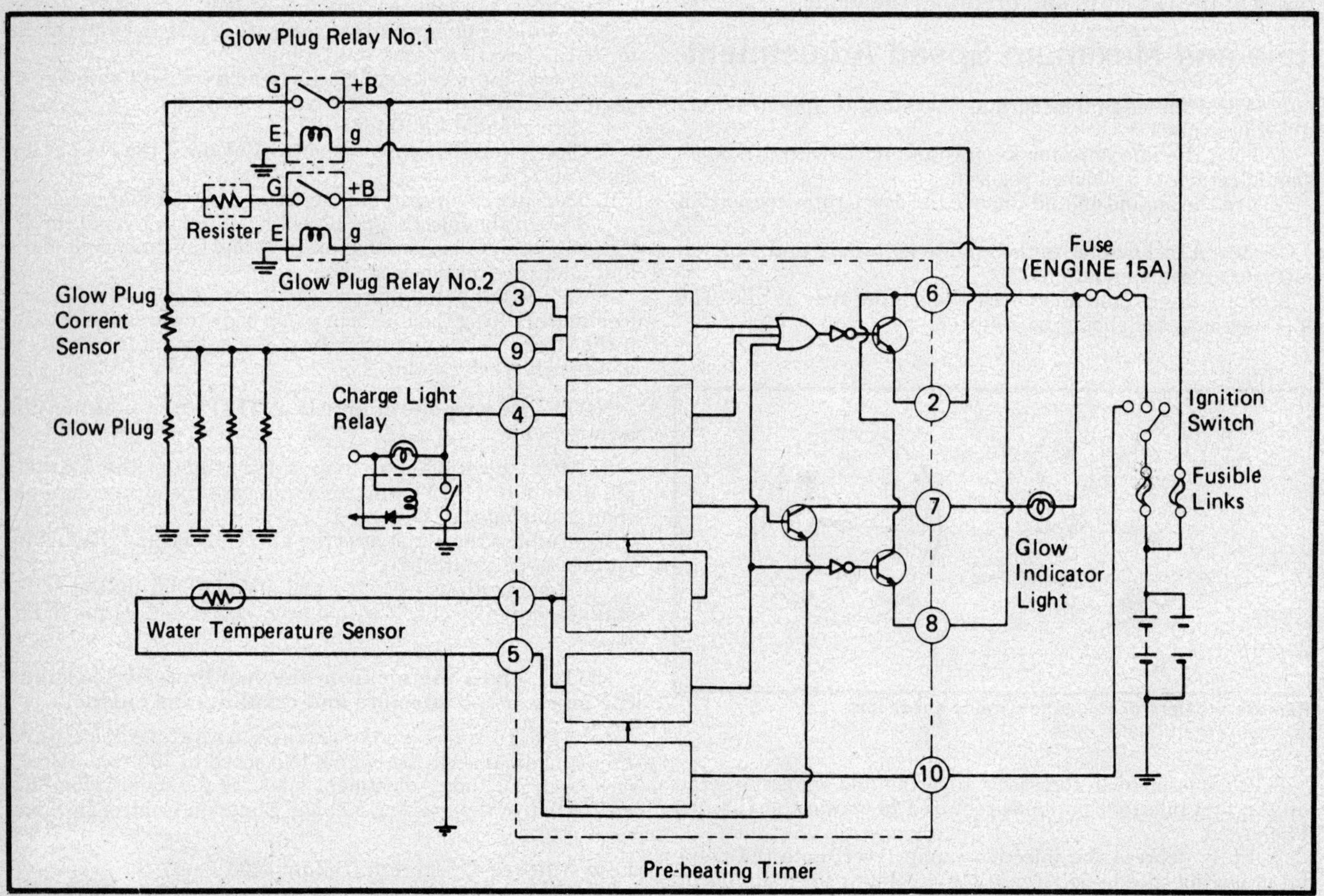

Electrical schematic of glow plug system (© Toyota Motor Sales, USA)

3. Measure the glow plug resistance with the glow plug installed in the cylinder head. Attach an ohmmeter leads to the input connector pin of the glow plug and the engine block. The ohmmeter should read 0.14 ohms @ 68 degrees F. If the resistance is not correct, replace the glow plug or set.

4. Check the glow plug current sensor by confirming that there is continuity between the current sensor terminals If no continuity exists, replace the glow plug current sensor.

5. Check the resistor located on the back surface of the intake manifold by measuring the resistance with an ohmmeter between the input pin connection and the resistor body. It should read approximately zero ohms. If the resistance is incorrect, replace the resistor.

6. Check the coolant temperature sensor by removing the connector and measuring the resistance between the water temperature sensor terminals. Refer to the chart for resistance values at various temperatures. Replace the water temperature sensor if the resistance values are incorrect.

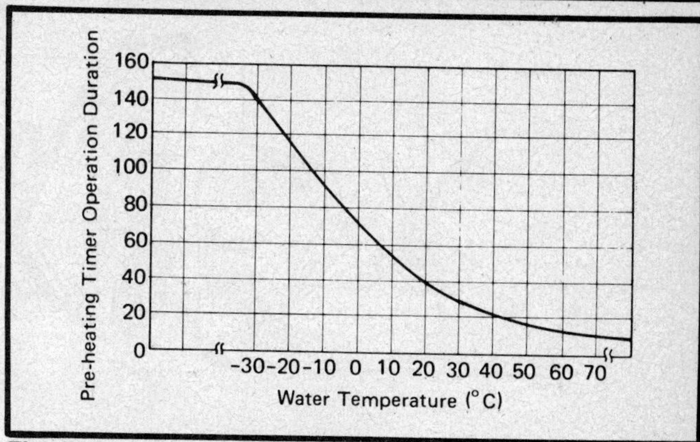

Time/temperature chart for timer test
(© Toyota Motor Sales, USA)

FUEL SYSTEM

Fuel Filter/Sedimentor (Water Separator)

The Toyota 2.2L, type L diesel engine uses an inline, cartridge type spin-on fuel filter element that is replaced just like an oil filter. The sedimentor function is to separate water and particulates from the fuel before it reaches the injection pump. When the water in the sedimentor reaches a dangerous level, a warning light will illuminate on the dash to indicate that the sedimentor must be drained. To drain the sedimentor, open the drain cock and turn the priming handle counterclockwise to free it. Pump the priming handle until pure diesel fuel appears, then close the drain cock and tighten the priming handle.

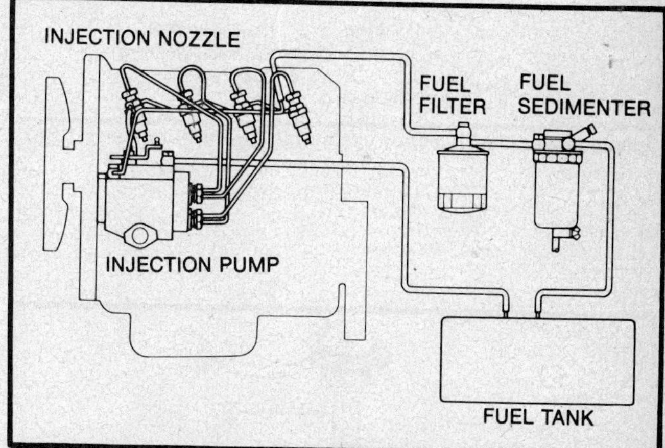

Fuel system components for the 2.2L diesel engine
(© Toyota Motor Sales, USA)

Injection Pump

Removal and Installation

1. Disconnect the cables which are positioned above the valve cover and move the cables aside. Remove the valve cover.
2. Disconnect the cables from both batteries.
3. Rotate the engine (clockwise only), until the TDC mark on the pulley is aligned with the pointer. Check that the valves of the No.1 cylinder are closed (rocker arms loose). If the valves are not closed, rotate the crankshaft one complete revolution and again align the TDC mark with the pointer.
4. Disconnect the fuel injection lines at the injection pump and at the injectors. Remove the injection fuel lines.
5. Disconnect the fuel feed lines at the injection pump and plug the line.
6. Remove the engine cooling fan, belts and water pump pulley.
7. Remove the crankshaft pulley, using an appropriate puller.
8. Remove the timing belt cover.
9. Using a piece of chalk or paint, mark the relationship between the timing gears and the timing belt.
10. Remove the timing belt idler pulley and the timing belt.
11. Remove the injection pump drive gear, using an appropriate puller.
12. Note the factory made timing marks next to the outer pump fastener. This mark signifies the required relationship between the pump and the timing case assembly. Align this mark during the installation.
13. Unbolt and remove the injection pump.
14. Installation of the pump is the reverse of the removal procedure. Install the belt in accordance with the marks that were made or aligned during the removal.
15. Reset the injector timing.

Fuel Injectors

Diagnosis

Diesel fuel injectors can be easily tested for proper operation by using a test bench which measures opening pressure and al-

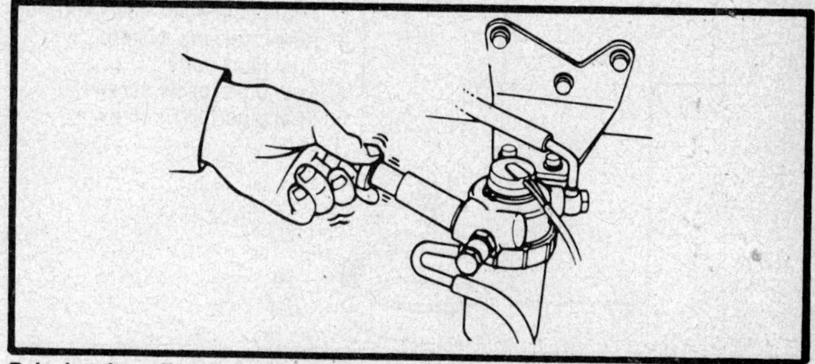

Priming handle on fuel sedimenter (© Toyota Motor Sales, USA)

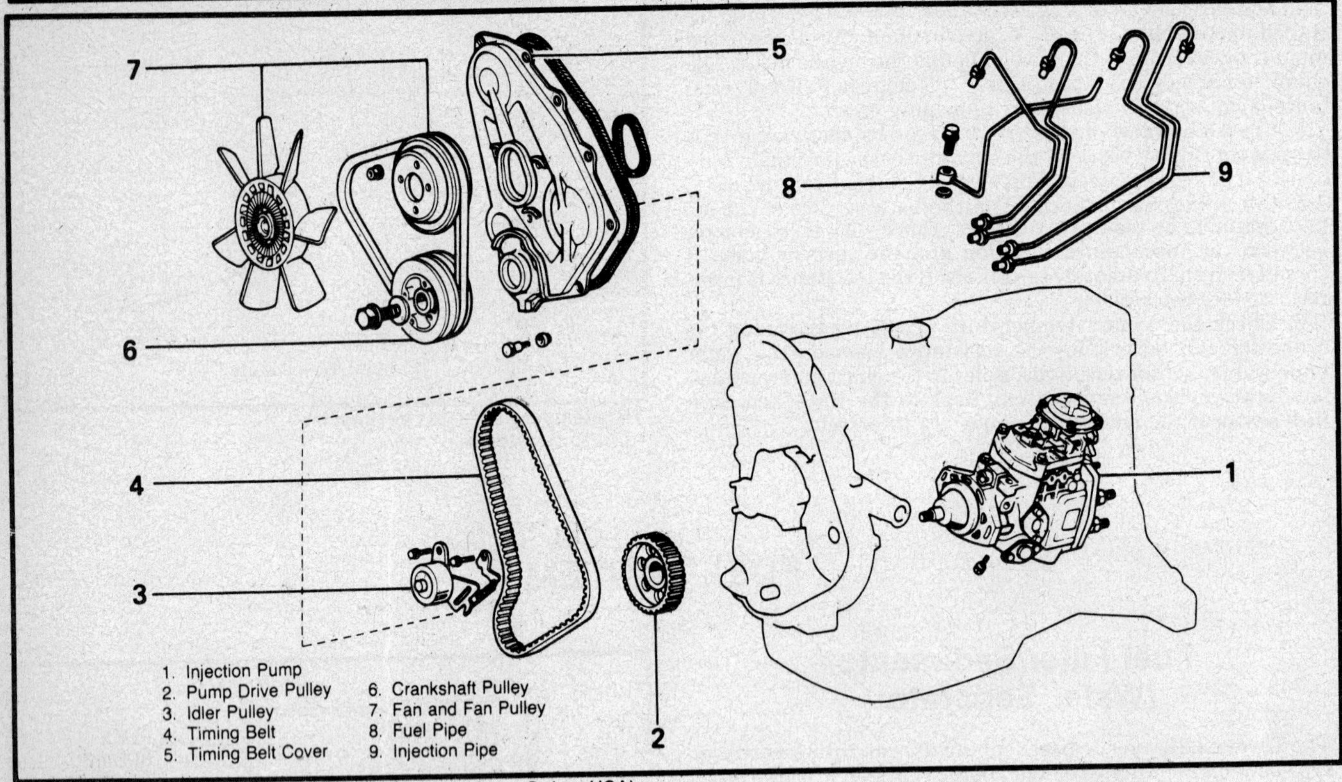

Components of fuel injection system (© Toyota Motor Sales, USA)

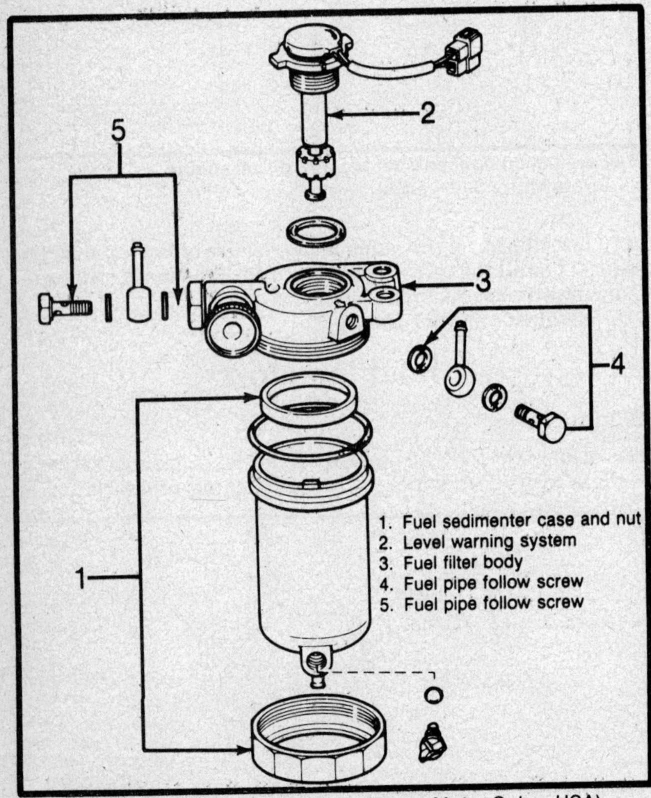

Exploded view of fuel sedimenter (© Toyota Motor Sales, USA)

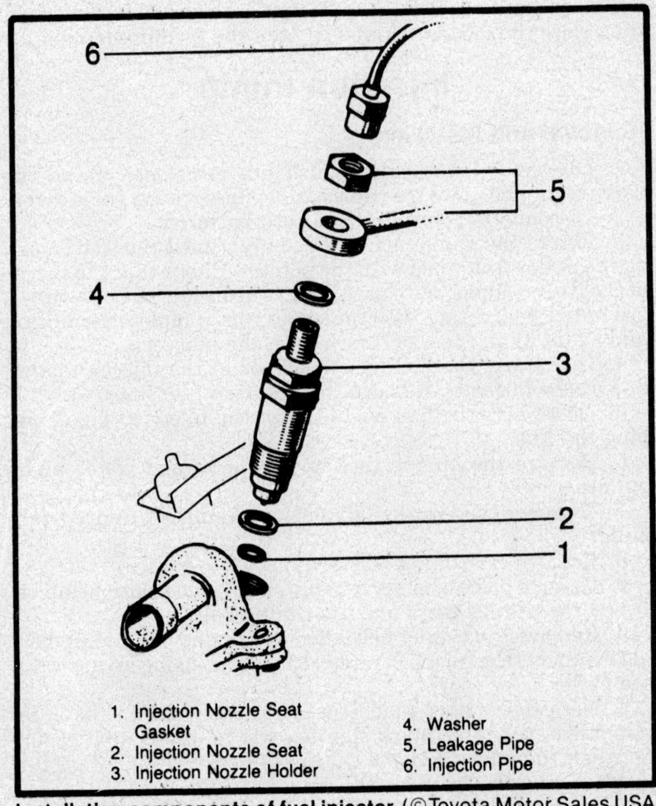

Installation components of fuel injector (©Toyota Motor Sales,USA)

lows visual inspection of the spray pattern. An incorrect spray pattern can cause a variety of problems, such as hard starting, rough idle, lack of power, excessive smoke or fuel consumption and audible knocks in the engine. An abnormal engine knock is one of the most obvious symptoms of a defective injector. Injector nozzle opening pressure can be adjusted by adding or removing shims, located within the injector body. A shim thickness change of 0.05mm (0.0020 in.) will change the opening pressure by 71 psi.

Removal and Installation

1. Remove the injection fuel lines.
2. Remove the leakage pipe from the injectors and note the location of each sealing washer.
3. Remove the nozzle(s) from the cylinder head, noting the position of the nozzle seats and seat gaskets.

CAUTION

Do not allow dirt to enter the engine through the nozzle holes.

NOTE: Remove accumulations of carbon from the nozzle holes.

4. Keep the injectors in order so that they may be installed in their original positions.
5. Install the injector assembly, noting that;
   a. The nozzle seat is installed between the injector and the seat gasket.
   b. The nozzle seat must be positioned with the concave side of the seat towards the injector.
6. Position a wrench on the hex of the nozzle body (NOT the nozzle retaining nut) and torque to 44–57 ft. lbs.

NOTE: After any service is performed on the diesel fuel system, pump the priming handle on the fuel sedimentor assembly 30–40 times to purge air from the fuel system.

VOLVO DIESEL ENGINES

D60A, TD60A, TD70D, TD70E, TD70F

GENERAL ENGINE SPECIFICATIONS

Engine Series①	Displacement (cu. in.)	Horsepower @ rpm (net)	Torque @ rpm (ft. lb.)	Bore & Stroke (in.)	Compression Ratio	Oil Pressure (psi)②	Firing Order
D 60 A	334	120 @ 2800	260 @ 1500	3.875 × 4.724	17.0:1	43–71	1-5-3-6-2-4
TD 60 A	334	180 @ 2800	376 @ 1900	3.875 × 4.724	16.0:1	43–71	1-5-3-6-2-4
TD 70 D	409	165 @ 2400	413 @ 1400	4.125 × 5.118	16.0:1	42–71	1-5-3-6-2-4
TD 70 E	409	205 @ 2400	492 @ 1400	4.125 × 5.118	14.5:1	40–70	1-5-3-6-2-4
TD 70 F	409	230 @ 2400	605 @ 1400	4.125 × 5.118	14.5:1	40–65	1-5-3-6-2-4

①All engines are in-line 6 cylinder
②7 psi @ idle

TUNE-UP SPECIFICATIONS

Engine Series	Injection Timing (deg.)	Injector Opening Pressure (psi)	Low Idle (rpm)	High Idle (rpm)	Maximum Full Load Speed (rpm)	Compression Pressure (psi @ rpm)	Valve Lash (in.)	
							Intake	Exhaust
D 60 A	22–23B	2844①	600–650	3000–3100	2800	355 @ 200	0.016C	0.018C
TD 60 A	21–22B	2844①	600–650	3000–3100	2800	327 @ 200	0.016C	0.018C
TD 70 D	18–19B	2488②	475–525	2550–2650	2400	340 @ 180	0.016C	0.018C
TD 70 E	20–21B	2844③	475–525	2550–2650	2400	327 @ 180	0.016C	0.022C
TD 70 F	18–19B	3840④	475–550	2650–2750	2400	325 @ 180	0.016C	0.022C

B—Before top dead center
①New nozzle—2958 psi
②New nozzle—2560–2673 psi
③New nozzle—2915–3029 psi
④New nozzle—3900–4020 psi

FIRING ORDER

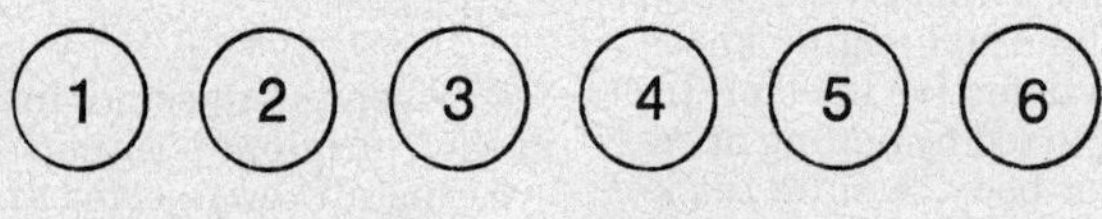

Firing order—all engines

TORQUE SPECIFICATIONS

(All measurements in foot pounds)

Engine Series	Cylinder Head Bolts	Conn. Rod Brg. Bolts	Main Brg. Bolts	Crankshaft Damper Bolt	Flywheel-Crankshaft	Injection Pump Flange	Injectors
60 (All)	123	116	101	188	116–130	14–18①	14
70 (All)	137 long 100 short③	115	100	45②	115–130	50	15

① Element fastener
② Center bolt: 188 ft. lbs.
③ TD70F engine:
First pass—36 ft. lbs.
Second pass—118 ft. lbs.
Final torque—60° turn in sequence

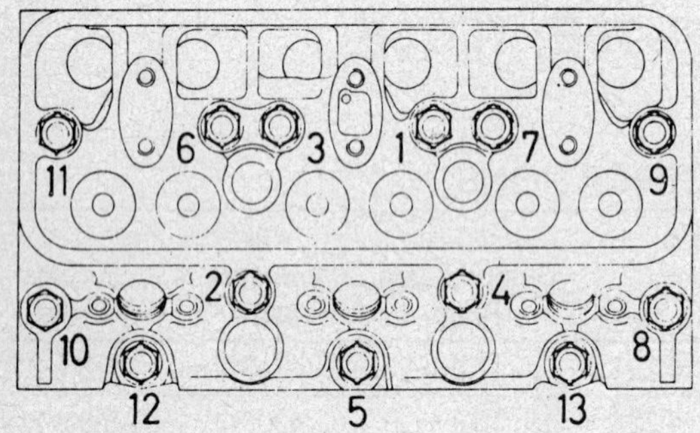

Head bolt torque sequence—60 Series
(© Volvo North America Corp.)

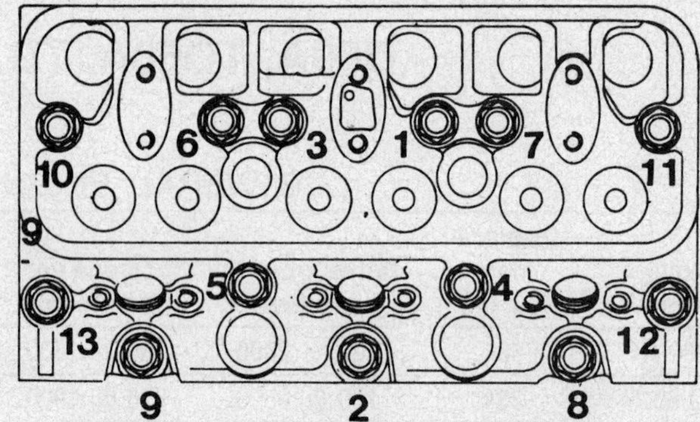

Head bolt torque sequence—70 Series
(© Volvo North America Corp.)

CHILTON'S THREE "C's" DIESEL ENGINE DIAGNOSIS PROCEDURE

Condition	Cause	Correction
Rough Idle	Improper adjustment	Adjust idle
	Accelerator control cable binding	Repair or lubricate
	Air or water in the fuel system	Clear air or water from fuel system
	Injection nozzle clogged	Check and clean injector nozzles
	Improper valve clearance	Check valve adjustment
	Injection pump malfunction	Check injection pump
Poor Performance	Air cleaner clogged	Check element
	Accelerator control cable binding	Check control cable for free movement
	Restricted fuel flow (water or air)	Check lines and filter
	Incorrect injection timing	Check injection timing
	Injection pump malfunction	Replace injection pump

CHILTON'S THREE "C's" DIESEL ENGINE DIAGNOSIS PROCEDURE

Condition	Cause	Correction
Excessive Exhaust Smoke	Restricted air cleaner	Check element
	Air or water in fuel filter	Remove air or water from fuel system
	Improper grade fuel	Check fuel in tank
	Incorrect injection timing	Check injection timing
	Injection pump malfunction	Replace injection pump
	Injector nozzle stuck open	Check injector nozzles
Excessive Fuel Consumption	Restricted air cleaner	Check element
	Leak in fuel lines	Check for leaks
	Incorrect idle speed	Check idle
	Restricted exhaust system	Check exhaust
	Improper grade of fuel	Check fuel in tank
	Injection pump malfunction	Check injection pump operation
Loud Knocking In Engine	Defective fuel injector	Replace fuel injector

Note: If the problem persists after performing these preliminary checks, disassembly and inspection of internal engine components may be necessary for further diagnosis.

TUNE-UP AND ADJUSTMENTS

Valve Adjustment

ALL ENGINES

NOTE: The engine must be cold to adjust the valve clearance. Do not attempt to adjust the valves with the engine running

1. Make sure the stop control is pulled out.
2. Remove the inspection cover beneath the flywheel casing. Remove the rocker covers.
3. Rotate the engine in the normal direction of rotation until the No.1 piston is at top dead center on the compression stroke. (0° on the flywheel).
4. Adjust valves 1,2,4,5,7 and 9 to specifications.
5. Rotate the engine one turn so that the No.6 piston is at top dead center on the compression stroke (0° on the flywheel).
6. Adjust valves 3, 6, 8, 10, 11 and 12 to specifications.
7. Once all adjustments are complete, push in the stop control and install the valve covers.

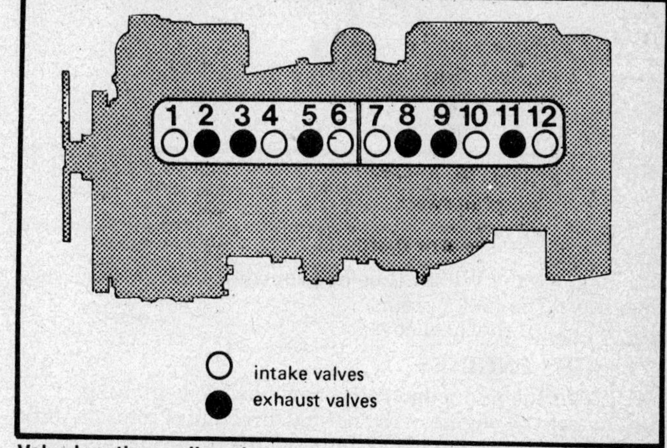

Valve location—all engines (© Volvo North America Corp.)

Injection Pump Timing

60 SERIES ENGINES

1. Set the No.1 piston at top dead center on the compression stroke.
2. Remove the inspection plate from the flywheel housing and check alignment of timing marks. Turn the engine in the normal direction of rotation until the timing gradations show 22–23° (D60) or 21–22° (TD60) opposite the pointer.
3. Install a Wilbar tube or equivalent to the delivery pipe for No.1 cylinder.
4. Bleed the fuel system. Remove the delivery pipe for No. 1 cylinder and bleed the discharge valve and Wilbar tube by turning the injection pump shaft back and forth a few times.
5. Move the throttle control lever to the full throttle position and fasten it there with a spring or similar device.
6. Pull the stop arm back as far as possible and then return it to the operating position. This will set the control rod to the full load position.

NOTE: If the stop arm is not pulled all the way back, then returned to the operating position, the control rod will stop at the cold start position, giving an inaccurate adjustment.

7. Turn the pump shaft in the opposite direction of normal rotation and check that the fuel level in the Wilbar tube moves. Open the valve on the Wilbar tube and allow the level to drop to the middle of the sight glass.
8. Turn the pump shaft in the normal direction of rotation in small increments until the fuel level in the tube starts to rise. The point at which the fuel level just starts to rise is the start of injection for the No. 1 cylinder.
9. Check that the flywheel marks coincide with the pump adjustments in Steps 7 and 8. If the pump requires adjustment, loosen the pump drive bolts and turn the pump shaft as necessary after setting the timing marks on the flywheel as outlined in Step 2.

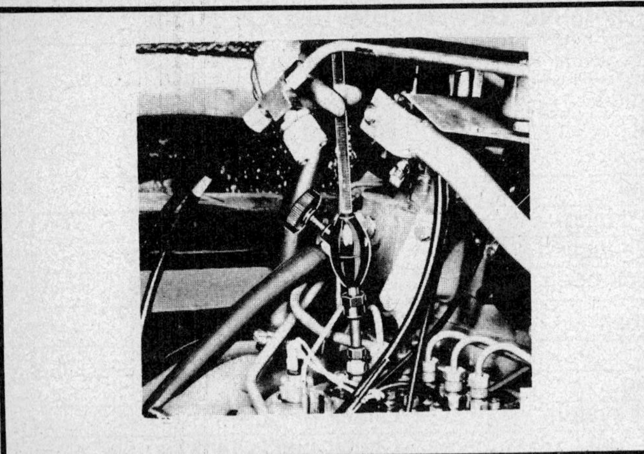

Injection pump adjustment with Wilbar tube (© Volvo North America Corp.)

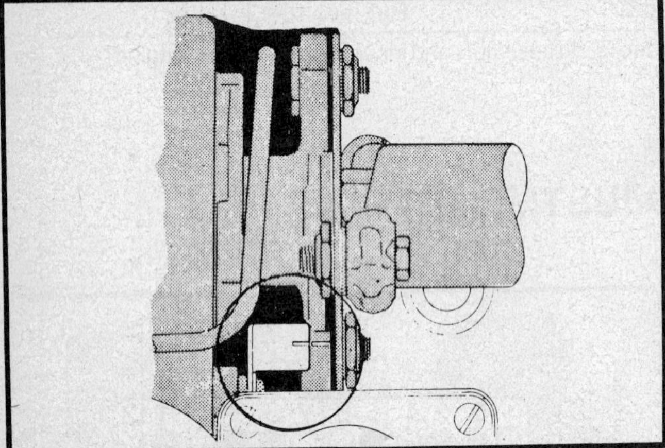

Setting the pump coupling–70 Series (© Volvo North America Corp.)

10. Once all adjustments are complete, tighten the drive bolts.
11. Remove the Wilbar tube and reinstall the No. 1 delivery pipe. Bleed the fuel systems.
12. Reinstall flywheel cover.

70 SERIES ENGINES

1. Clean the pump and components before beginning.
2. Rotate the engine in the normal direction of rotation until the No.1 piston is at top dead center on the compression stroke.

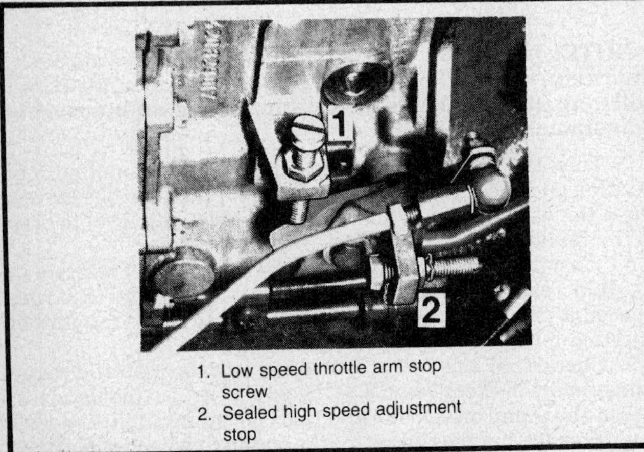

1. Low speed throttle arm stop screw
2. Sealed high speed adjustment stop

Speed setting—60 Series (© Volvo North America Corp.)

3. Continue to turn the engine slowly until the timing marks on the flywheel align with the proper marks as given in the Tune-Up Specifications chart for injection timing. Make sure the sighting line from the mark on the flywheel over the pointer to the eye is at right angles from the flywheel. If viewed from the side, it is possible to err by a few degrees.
4. Make sure the pump coupling rear flange alignment mark is opposite the mark on the pump end adjusting plate. If the marks do not line up, loosen the coupling bolts and align the marks.
5. Check the adjustment by turning the engine back ½ turn, then foreward in the normal direction of rotation until the firing position for No. 1 cylinder is indicated by the alignment marks on the flywheel.
6. Once all adjustments are complete, tighten the flange bolts.

Idle Speed Adjustment

ALL MODELS

1. Check that the accelerator linkage is operating properly and that there is no play.
2. Run the engine to normal operating temperature.
3. Turn the throttle stop screw to obtain 475–525 rpm for the 70 series and 600–650 rpm for the 60 series.

Maximum No-Load Speed Adjustment

ALL MODELS

1. Run the engine to normal operating temperature.
2. Break the lead seal on the speed stop.
3. Run the engine at maximum speed and check that the speed arm on the injection pump touches the maximum speed stop.
4. Adjust the stop to obtain 3000–3100 rpm for the 70 series and 2550–2650 rpm for the 60 series. Replace the lead seal.

Starting Heater

ALL MODELS

The starting heater is electrically operated and consists of three band elements connected in series and placed in-line before the intake manifold. Its function is to facilitate cold starting at low ambient temperatures, thereby reducing exhaust smoke. When energized by the ignition switch, the element heats up to approximately 1292°F to warm the intake air. The heater can be used for several minutes after starting the engine to prevent stalling due to the cold intake air.

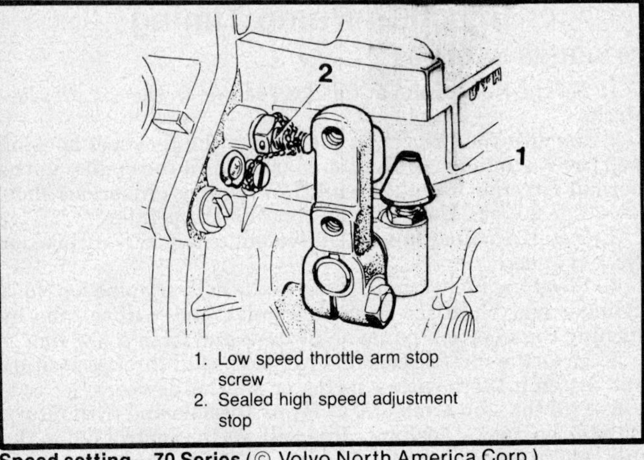

1. Low speed throttle arm stop screw
2. Sealed high speed adjustment stop

Speed setting—70 Series (© Volvo North America Corp.)

Testing

Check the starting heater with a voltmeter by turning the ignition switch to the GLOW position and checking the voltage drop across each outer band element. It should be approximately 8 volts. If no voltage is indicated, check the battery, all cable connections, the ignition switch and the wiring past the relay. If after these check the starting heater is still not the correct voltage, replace the heater.

CAUTION

Because of the nature of operation, any type of starting spray can be ignited by the starting heater and cause an explosion in the intake manifold. For this reason, do not attempt to use any type of starting fluid on any Volvo diesel engine.

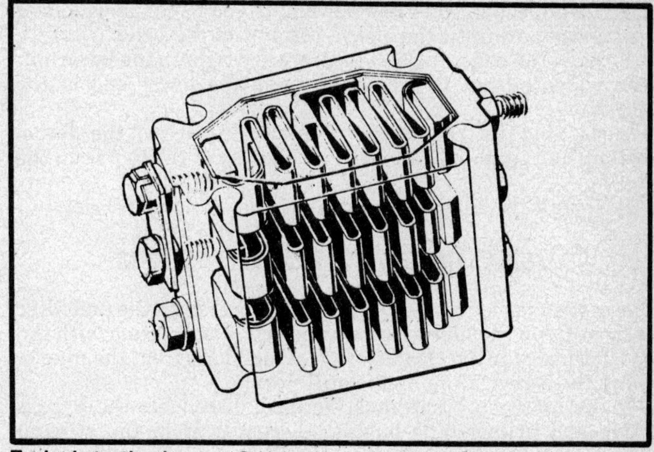

Typical starting heater (© Volvo North America Corp.)

Fuel Injector

Removal and Installation

ALL MODELS

1. Remove the rocker arm covers.
2. Remove the fuel delivery lines and cap them.
3. Remove the injector holddown bolts and pull out the injectors. If injectors are difficult to remove, use tool Volvo #2683 and 2991 or equivalent. Clean the copper sleeve contact surface.
4. Installation is the reverse of removal. Torque bolts to 14 ft. lbs.

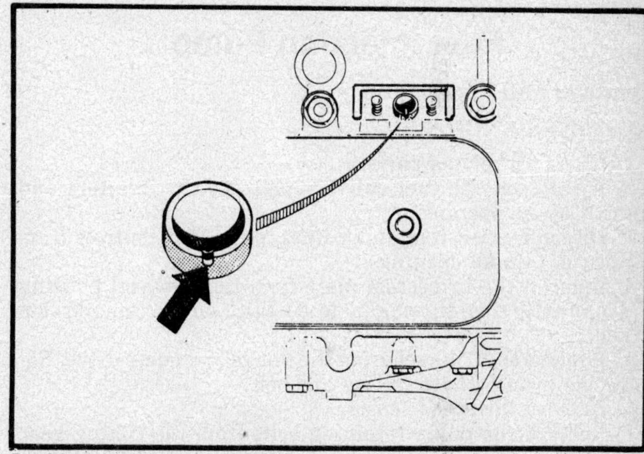

Position the injector sleeve recess during installation (© Volvo North America Corp.)

Fuel Injector Sleeve

Removal and Installation

ALL MODELS

NOTE: The cab member or gear lever carrier may have to be removed, depending on which sleeve is to be pulled.

1. Remove the injector as described above.
2. Using extractor, Volvo #2128 or its equivalent, pull the sleeve from the head.
3. Remove the O-ring from the head.
4. Clean the O-ring groove and the sealing surface between the head and sleeve. Install a new O-ring.
5. Manually turn the engine until the piston corresponding to the sleeve being worked on, is at bottom dead center. This can be determined by removing the inspection cover on the flywheel.
6. Install the sleeve with Volvo tool #6008, or its equivalent, as follows:
   a. Unscrew the tool widening pin and place the sleeve on the tool.
   b. Back off the tool spindle nut.
   c. Screw in the widening pin.
   d. Coat the outside of the sleeve with clean engine oil and push the tool and sleeve into the head. Check that the index mark (recess) for the sleeve points straight upwards.

Injector removal with special tool (© Volvo North America Corp.)

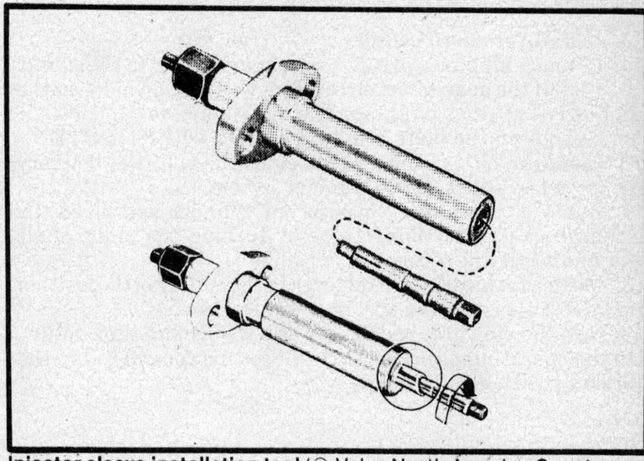

Injector sleeve installation tool (© Volvo North America Corp.)

7. Install the injector holddown nuts and force the widening tool downward until the sleeve bottoms in the head.

8. Hold the widening tool securely and tighten the large nut. The widening pin is pressed through the lower end of the sleeve.

9. Tighten the nut until the tool spindle is free of the sleeve. Pull up on the spindle and remove the rest of the tool from the sleeve.

10. Install the injector and cab member or lever carrier.

BLEEDING THE FUEL SYSTEM

The system is bled at the bleeder screw located on the fuel filter carrier. Open the bleeder screw and prime the system with the hand primer until a clean stream of fuel flows from the nipple. Close the screw while fuel is still flowing.

If the injection pump must be bled, disconnect the bypass valve and prime until bubbles disappear from the stream. Close the connection while fuel is still flowing. Do not bleed at the pressure equalizer.

Fuel Injection Pump

Removal and Installation

6O SERIES ENGINES

1. Clean all related parts.
2. Disconnect the fuel delivery pipes at the injectors and pump. Cap all openings.
3. Disconnect all remaining lines, pipes and controls from the pump. Cap all openings.
4. Remove the inspection plate from the flywheel housing and manually turn the engine to #1 TDC, on the compression stroke.
5. Remove the bolts securing the flange and pump drive. Remove the intermediate section and bolt.
6. Remove the speed sensor.
7. Remove the pump retaining bolts from the timing gear case and lift off the pump.
8. Before installing the pump, make sure that there is 1 pt. of oil in the unit.
9. Turn the engine manually until the timing gradations show 22–23° (D60) or 21–22° (TD60) opposite the pointer.
10. Adjust the pump camshaft until the mark on the end of the shaft inclines about 20° obliquely towards the cylinder block.
11. Apply chassis grease to the sealing ring at the front of the pump.
12. Install the pump on the timing gear case and tighten the bolts.

NOTE: The pump must be positioned so that the stud bolts are opposite the oval holes in the pump.

13. Install the speed sensor.
14. Connect all pipes, except the delivery pipes, to the pump.
15. Install the gear wheel clamp, lock washer and bolts on the pump drive at front of pump. The bolts must be $^{5}/_{16}$ UNC × 45mm. Tighten the bolts snugly. DO NOT OVERTIGHTEN.
16. Install a Wilbar tube, or its equivalent, to the delivery pipe for #1 cylinder. Bleed the fuel system.
17. Remove the delivery pipe for #1 cylinder and bleed the discharge valve and Wilbar tube by turning the pump shaft back and forth a few times.
18. Move the throttle control lever to the full throttle position and hold it there with a spring or similar device.
19. Pull the stop arm back as far as possible and then return it to the operating position. This will set the control rod to the full load position.

NOTE: If the stop arm is not pulled all the way back, then returned to the operating position, the control rod will stop at the cold-start position, giving a faulty adjustment.

20. Turn the pump shaft in the opposite direction of normal rotation and check that the fuel level in the Wilb;auar tube moves. Open the valve on the Wilbar tube and allow the level to drop to the middle of the sight glass.
21. Turn the pump shaft in the normal direction in small increments until the fuel in the level tube starts to rise. The point at which the fuel just starts to rise is the injection point for #1 cylinder.
22. Tighten the bolts at the front of the pump between the flange and the pump gear.
23. Manually turn the engine to check that the flywheel markings coincide with the pump adjustments in Steps 20 and 21.
24. When all adjustments are correct, tighten the pump drive bolts and install the flywheel housing inspection plate.
25. Remove the Wilbar tube, connect the delivery pipes and install the controls. Install the cover on the timing gear case.
26. Start the engine and check for leaks.

Removal and Installation

70 SERIES ENGINES

1. Clean all related parts.
2. Disconnect all pipes, lines and controls from the pump. Cap all openings.
3. Manually turn the engine to #1 cylinder TDC compression. Check the rocker arms and timing marks.
4. Mark the position of the pump coupling nuts for exact reassembly.
5. Remove the bolts from the pump coupling. Separate the rear flange from the intermediate section of the pump coupling.

NOTE: The position of the nuts must not be changed during removal and installation.

6. Unbolt and remove the pump. Be careful to avoid damage to the steel discs.
7. Before installing the pump, make sure that the unit is correctly filled with oil.
8. While observing the timing marks, manually rotate the engine until the pointer is opposite the 20° mark. Check the mark from a straight-on angle. Viewing from the side can cause an error of several degrees.
9. Loosen the pump coupling clamp bolt and position the pump on the bracket. Push the coupling forward on the shaft.
10. Install the pump coupling rear flange on the shaft. Turn it until the index line on the flange is opposite the index line on the setting plate.
11. Install the intermediate section of the pump coupling on the flange by sliding the coupling on the shaft from the auxiliary drive gear end. Make certain the domed washers are located between the rear flange of the coupling and the steel discs. Tighten the bolts. Make certain that the nuts are in the previously marked positions.
12. Tighten the pump coupling clamp bolt and check that the steel disc are not distorted.
13. Check that the timing marks on the pump and coupling coincide with the flywheel indexed at the 20° mark. This can be accomplished by rotating the engine ½ turn opposite normal rotation, then back to the #1 firing position.
14. Install all pipes, lines and controls, then bleed the fuel system. Start the engine and check for leaks.

INDEX

Carburetor Identification

All carburetors are identified by code numbers, either stamped on the attaching flange side, the main body or on a metal tag, retained by a bowl cover screw. This identifying number is most important to the repairman in order to obtain the correct carburetor replacement or parts and to properly adjust the carburetor when matched to a specific engine.

Angle Degree Tool

An angle degree tool is recommended by Rochester Products Division, for use to confirm adjustments to the choke valve and related linkages on their late model two and four barrel carburetors, in place of the plug type gauges.

Decimal and degree conversion charts are provided for use by technicians who have access to an angle gauge and not plug gauges. It must be remembered that the relationship between the decimal and the angle readings are not exact, due to manufacturers tolerances.

To use the angle gauge, rotate the degree scale until zero (0) is opposite the pointer. With the choke valve completely closed, place the gauge magnet squarely on top of the choke valve and rotate the bubble until it is centered. Make the necessary adjustments to have the choke valve at the specified degree angle opening as read from the degree angle tool.

NOTE: The carburetor may be off the engine for adjustments. Be sure the carburetor is held firmly during the use of the angle gauge.

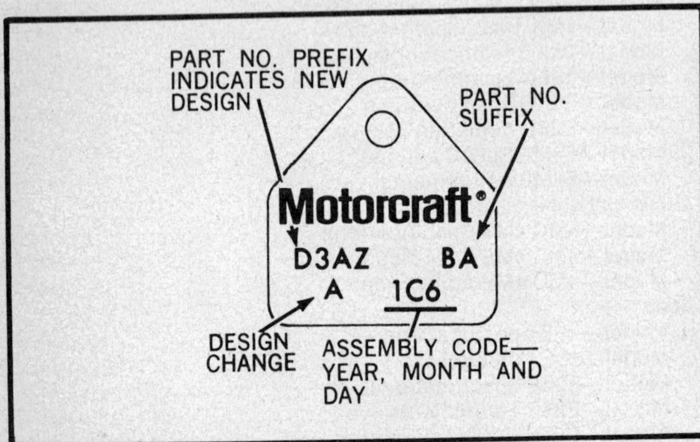

Motorcraft carburetors for Ford usage—typical (© Ford Motor Co.)

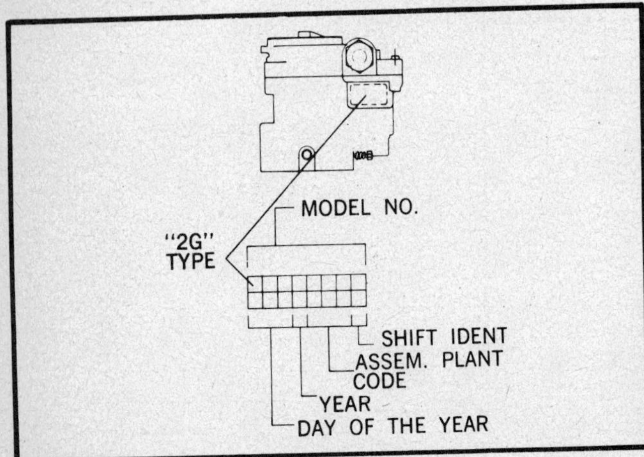

Rochester two barrel models—typical (© General Motors Corp.)

Emission Calibration Numbers

Emission calibration numbers are used by Ford Motor Company to provide the technician with the necessary specifications to adjust a specific engine to the proper emission control levels.

The calibration numbers are listed on the lower right of the Vehicle Emission Control Information label, which is attached to the engine valve cover.

The information on the decal must be used when differences exist between the decal and other specification tables, unless otherwise noted by Ford Motor Company.

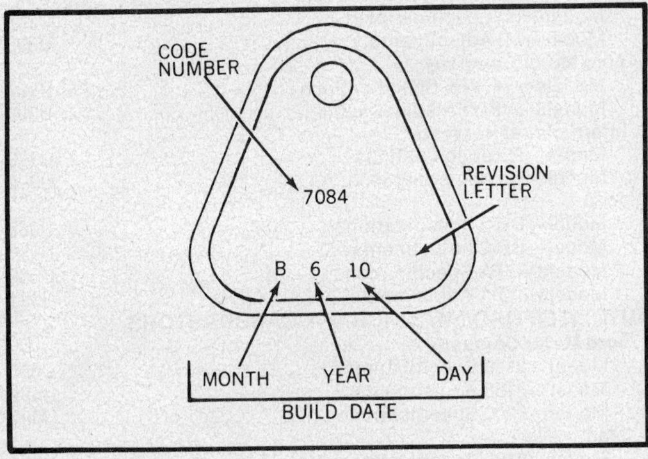

Carter carburetors for Jeep usage—typical (© Jeep Corp.)

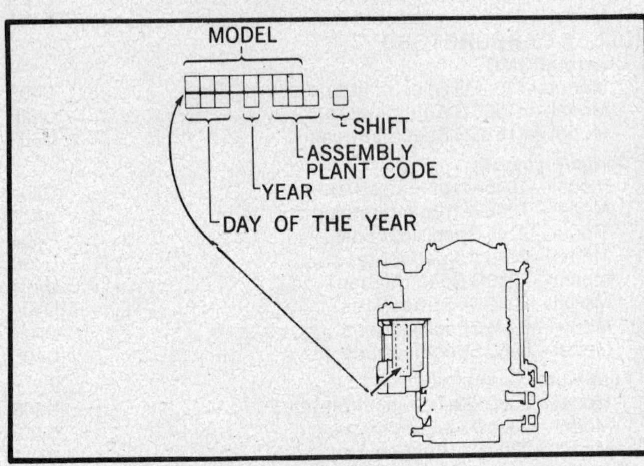

Rochester one barrel models—typical (© General Motors Corp.)

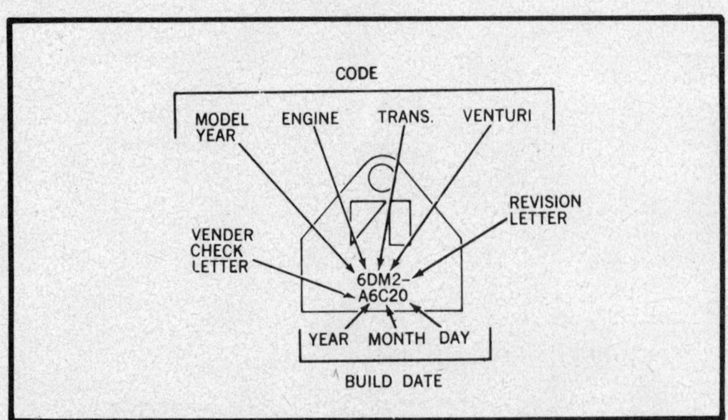

Motorcraft carburetors for Jeep usage—typical (© Jeep Corp.)

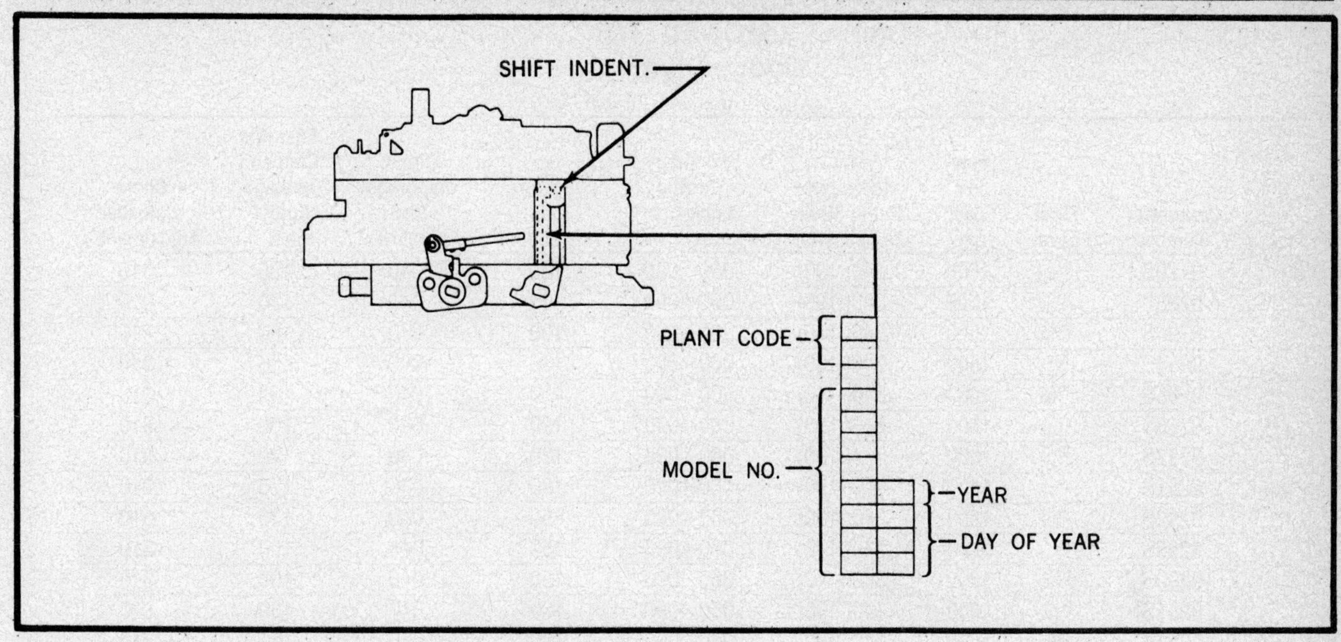

Rochester four barrel models—typical (© General Motors Corp.)

Carter

MODEL BBD
Dodge/Plymouth

(All measurements in inches)

Year	Carburetor Number	Float Level	Choke Unloader	Fast Idle Cam Setting	Choke Valve Initial Opening w/Vacuum Kick	Fast Idle Speed (rpm)	Accelerator Pump Setting	Step-up Piston Gap
'80–'82	8146S	.250	.310	.070	.070	1500	.500	.035
	8147S	.250	.310	.110	.150	1500	.500	.035
'82	8348S	.250	.310	.070	.130	1600	.500	.035
	8352S	.250	.310	.070	.130	1600	.500	.035
'83	8146S	.250	.310	.070	.070	1500	.470	.035
	8147S	.250	.310	.110	.150	1500	.470	.035
	8371S	.250	.280	.070	.130	1600	.470	.035
	8374S	.250	.280	.070	.130	1400	.470	.035
	8359S	.250	.280	.070	.130	1400	.470	.035
	8358S	.250	.280	.070	.130	1400	.470	.035
'84	8387S	.250	.310	.110	.150	1700	.470	.035
	8386S	.250	.310	.070	.070	1500	.470	.035
	8374S	.250	.280	.070	.130	1400	.470	.035
	8359S	.250	.280	.070	.130	1400	.470	.035
	8358S	.250	.280	.070	.130	1400	.470	.035

Note: Choke is fixed on all models

MODEL TQ
Dodge/Plymouth

(All measurements in inches)

Year	Carburetor Number	Float Level	Fast Idle Speed (rpm)	Accelerator Pump Stroke Adjustment①	Secondary Throttle Lock-Out Adjustment	Vacuum Kick Adjustment	Choke Diaphragm Rod Adjustment	Fast Idle Cam and Linkage Adjust-ment③	Choke Unloader Adjustment②
'80	9279S	29/32	1600	.340(.190)	.060–.090	.130	.040	.130	.310
	9288S	29/32	1600	.340(.190)	.060–.090	.120	.040	.120	.310
	9296S	29/32	1500	.340(.140)	.060–.090	.100	.040	.100	.310
	9254S	29/32	1500	.340(.190)	.060–.090	.130	.040	.100	.310
	9265S	29/32	1600	.340(.140)	.060–.090	.150	.040	.100	.310
	9255S	29/32	1600	.340(.190)	.060–.090	.120	.040	.100	.310
	9252S	29/32	1600	.340(.190)	.060–.090	.120	.040	.120	.310
	9251S	29/32	1600	.340(.190)	.060–.090	.120	.040	.120	.310
	9292S	29/32	1600	.340(.190)	.060–.090	.150	.040	.130	.310
	9298S	29/32	1600	.340(.140)	.060–.090	.150	.040	.100	.310
	9299S	29/32	1600	.340(.140)	.060–.090	.150	.040	.100	.310
	9281S	29/32	1600	.340(.190)	.060–.090	.180	.040	.130	.310
	9261S	29/32	1600	.340(.190)	.060–.090	.130	.040	.130	.310
'81	9311S	29/32	1500	.340	.060–.090	.150	.040	.100	.310
	9314S	29/32	1500	.340	.060–.090	.150	.040	.100	.310
	9325S	29/32	1500	.340	.060–.090	.120	.040	.100	.310
	9329S	29/32	1600	.340	.060–.090	.130	.040	.100	.310
	9330S	29/32	1500	.340	.060–.090	.130	.040	.100	.310
	9331S	29/32	1700	.340	.060–.090	.110	.040	.100	.310
	9332S	29/32	1700	.340	.060–.090	.110	.040	.100	.310
	9357S	29/32	1800	.340	.060–.090	.130	.040	.100	.310
	9358S	29/32	1700	.340	.060–.090	.180	.040	.100	.310
	9359S	29/32	1500	.340	.060–.090	.130	.040	.100	.310
'82	9342S	29/32	1600	.340	.060–.090	.130	.040	.100②	.310
	9375S	29/32	1800	.340	.060–.090	.130	.040	.130②	.310
	9376S	29/32	1700	.340	.060–.090	.130	.040	.130②	.310
	9379S	29/32	1500	.340	.060–.090	.130	.040	.130②	.310
'83	9342S	29/32	1600	.340(.390)	.060	.130	.040	.100②	.310
	9375S	29/32	1800	.340(.390)	.060	.130	.040	.130②	.310
	9379S	29/32	1500	.340(.390)	.060	.130	.040	.130②	.310
	9376S	29/32	1700	.340(.390)	.060	.180	.040	.100②	.310
'84	9386S	29/32	1600	.340(.190)	.060–.090	.170	.040	.100	.310
	9387S	29/32	1500	.340(.190)	.060–.090	.150	.040	.100	.310
	9379S	29/32	1500	.340(.190)	.060–.090	.130	.040	.130	.310
	9376S	29/32	1700	.340(.190)	.060–.090	.180	.040	.100	.310

Note: Choke is fixed on all models
① Stage I (Stage II). No Stage II adjustment on 1981–82 models
② Measure at the lowest edge of the choke valve on the throttle lever side
③ Set the linkage with idle on the second highest step of the cam

MODELS YF/YFA
Ford

(All measurements in inches)

Year	Carburetor Number	Float Level	Float Drop	Choke Unloader Setting	Choke Setting	Dash Pot Plunger	Initial Choke Opening
'80	E0TE–9510 ABA,FA, LA,KA	.69	1.53	.28	①	—	.290
	ACA,ARA	.69	1.53	.28	①	—	.320
	AEA,AFA, ALA,AKA, ATA,CA, GA	.69	1.53	.28	①	—	.230
'81	E0TE–9510 AMA,FA	.69	—	.28	Index	—	.290
	D5TE–9510 CA,VA	.69	—	.28	Index	—	.290
	AGB	3/8	—	.28	1 Rich	—	.230
	E1TE–9510 UA,ARA, ARB	.78	—	.28	Index	—	.230
	AUA,VA	.78	—	.28	2 Rich	—	.300
	AZA,GA	.78	—	.330	2 Rich	—	.320
'82	E2TE–AMA E2UE–EA	.78	—	.28	Index	—	.230
	E2TE BZA,BVA	.78	—	.28	Index	—	.270
	CEA,JA	.78	—	.320	2 Rich	—	.330
	YA,AAA	.78	—	.280	Index	—	.300
	MA,ANA	.78	—	.280	2 Rich	—	.300
	KA	.78	—	.330	2 Rich	—	.320
	AAA	.78	—	.280	Index	—	.300
	EZUE–DA	.78	—	.330	2 Rich	—	.320
'83–'84	E37E–9510 LB,NB, RB,TB	.65	—	.270	Gray②	—	.320
	E37E–9510 BB	.65	—	.270	Yellow②	—	.320
'85	E5TE-9510 DA	.65	—	.270	Gray②	—	.320
	VA,UA,TA, BA,RA,SA, JA	.78	—	.330	Red②	—	.360
	FA	.78	—	.330	Red②	—	.340
	HA	.78	—	.330	Red②	—	.320
	DA,MA,CA③	.78	—	.330	Red②	—	.360
	D5TE-9510 AGB	3/8	—	.280	—	—	.230
	EOTE-9510 AMB,FB	.69	—	.280	Index	—	.290

①See Ford calibration specifications
②Choke cap index plate color
③Feedback carburetor

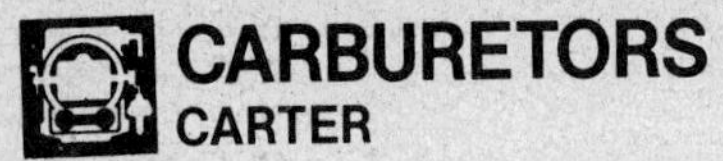

MODEL TQ
International

(All measurements in inches)

Year	Carburetor Number	Float Level	Fast Idle Speed (rpm)	Auto Choke Setting	Fuel Bowl Vent Clearance	Accelerator Pump Stroke Adjustment	Secondary Throttle Lock-Out Adjustment	Metering Rod Adjustment	Vacuum Kick Adjustment	Vacuum Pull-off Choke Adjustment	Fast Idle Cam and Linkage Adjustment	Choke Unloader Adjustment
'80–'81	TQ91285	.91 ± .030 (Old Needles) .88 ± .030 (New Needles)	1600	1/4 Rich	.800–.830	Primary① .328–.358 Secondary① .120–.260	.060–.090	.468 ± .031	Vac. High .440–.460 Vac. Low .235–.255	.840–.880	.089–.109	.280–.320
	TQ6591S, 6550S	1.06	1550–1600	1 Rich	.800–.830	Primary .328–.358 Secondary .120–.260	.060–.090	15/32	Vac. High .335–.355 Vac. Low .250–.270	.840–.880 (6550S only)	.089–.109	.280–.320
	TQ6590S, 6552S, 6551S	1.06	1550–1600	1 Rich	.800–.830	Primary .328–.358	.060–.090	15/32	Vac. High .335–.355 Vac. Low .250–.270	.840–.880 (6551S only)	.089–.109	.280–.320

① Rod in inner hole

MODEL BBD–2
Jeep

(All measurements in inches)

Year	Carburetor Number	Float Level	Step-up Piston Gap	Initial Choke Clearance	Fast Idle Cam Setting	Choke Cover Setting	Choke Unloader (Min.)	Fast Idle Speed (rpm)①
'80	8256	.250	.035	.128	.093	2 Rich	.280	1850
	8257	.250	.035	.128	.095	2 Rich	.280	1700
	8253	.250	.035	.128	.095	2 Rich	.280	1850
	8254	.250	.035	.120	.086	2 Rich	.280	1700
	8255	.250	.035	.140	.093	2 Rich	.280	②
	8277	.250	.035	.116	.081	1 Rich	.280	1700
'81	8302	.250	.035	.140	.095	1 Rich	.280	1850
	8303	.250	.035	.140	.095	1 Rich	.280	1700
	8311	.250	.035	.120	.085	1 Rich	.280	1700
	8306	.250	.035	.140	.095	1 Rich	.280	1700
	8312	.250	.035	.140	.095	1 Rich	.280	②
	8307	.250	.035	.140	.095	1 Rich	.280	1700
'82–'83	8338	.250	.035	.140	.095	1 Rich	.280	1850
	8339	.250	.035	.140	.095	1 Rich	.280	1700
	8340	.250	.035	.150	.110	1 Rich	.280	1700
	8341	.250	.035	.150	.150	1 Rich	.280	1700
	8349	.250	.035	.128	.095	2 Rich	.280	②
	8351	.250	.035	.130	.095	Index	.280	1700
'84–'85	8383	.250	.035	.140	.095	1 Rich	.280	1850
	8384	.250	.035	.140	.095	1 Rich	.280	1700

① On second step of fast idle cam with TCS solenoid and EGR disconnected.

② Manual transmission 1700 rpm and automatic transmission 1850 rpm

MODEL YFA
Jeep

(All measurements in inches)

Year	Carburetor Number	Float Level	Fast Idle Cam Setting Index	Initial Choke Clearance	Choke Cover Setting	Choke Unloader (Min.)	Fast Idle Speed (rpm)①	Bowl Vent Opens
'83	7452	.600	.175	.280	Fixed	.280	2300	2 Step
	7453	.600	.175	.280	Fixed	.280	2000	2 Step
	7454	.600	.175	.280	Fixed	.280	2300	2 Step
	7455	.600	.175	.280	Fixed	.280	2000	2 Step
'84	7700	.600	.175	.240	Fixed	.280	2000	—
	7701	.600	.175	.240	Fixed	.280	2300	—
	7702	.600	.175	.240	Fixed	.280	2000	—
	7703	.600	.175	.240	Fixed	.280	2300	—
'85	7704	.600	.175	.280	Fixed	.280	2000	—
	7705	.600	.175	.280	Fixed	.280	2300	—
	7706	.600	.175	.280	Fixed	.280	2000	—
	7707	.600	.175	.280	Fixed	.280	2300	—

① Engine hot, EGR valve disconnected

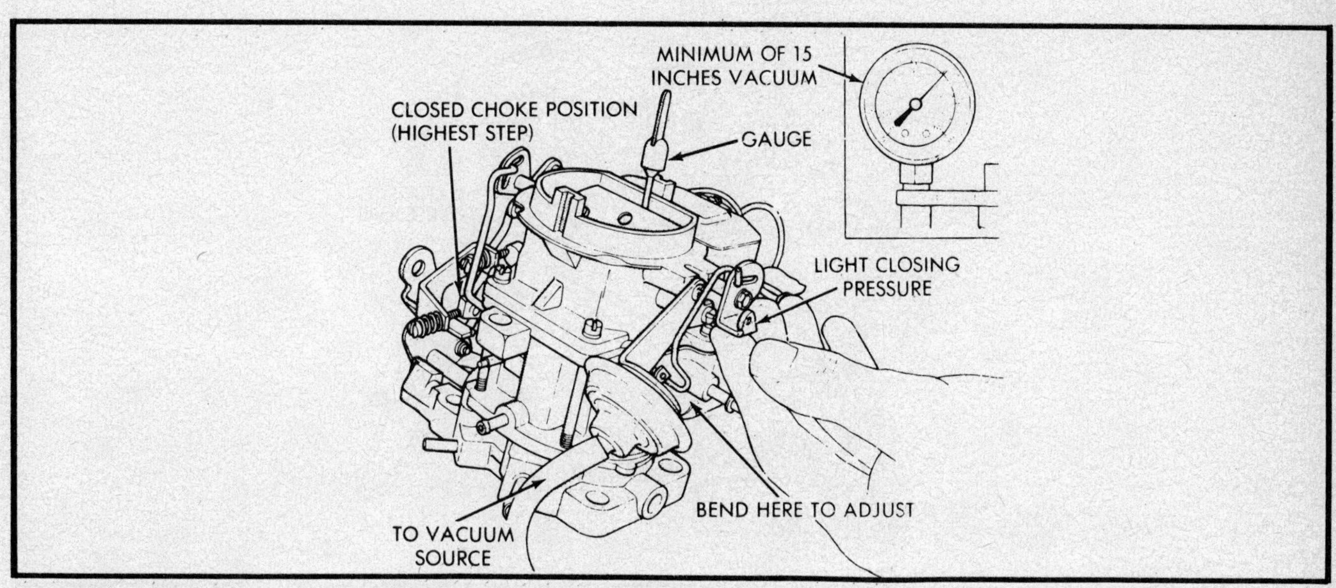

Adjustment of initial opening (vacuum kick)—BBD carburetor (© Chrysler Corp.)

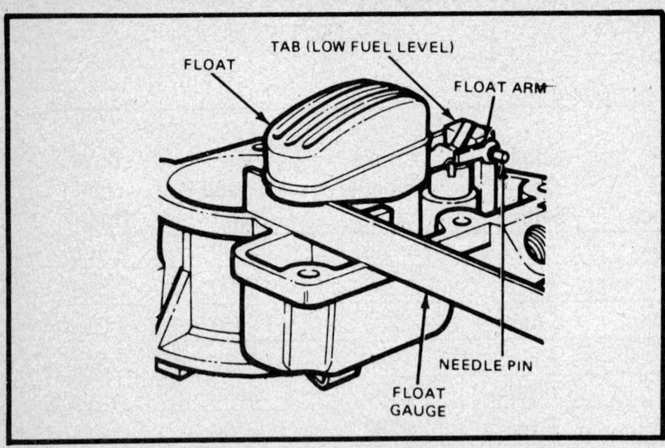

Measurement of float drop—YF/YFA carburetor
(© Ford Motor Co.)

Adjusting choke unloader—BBD carburetor

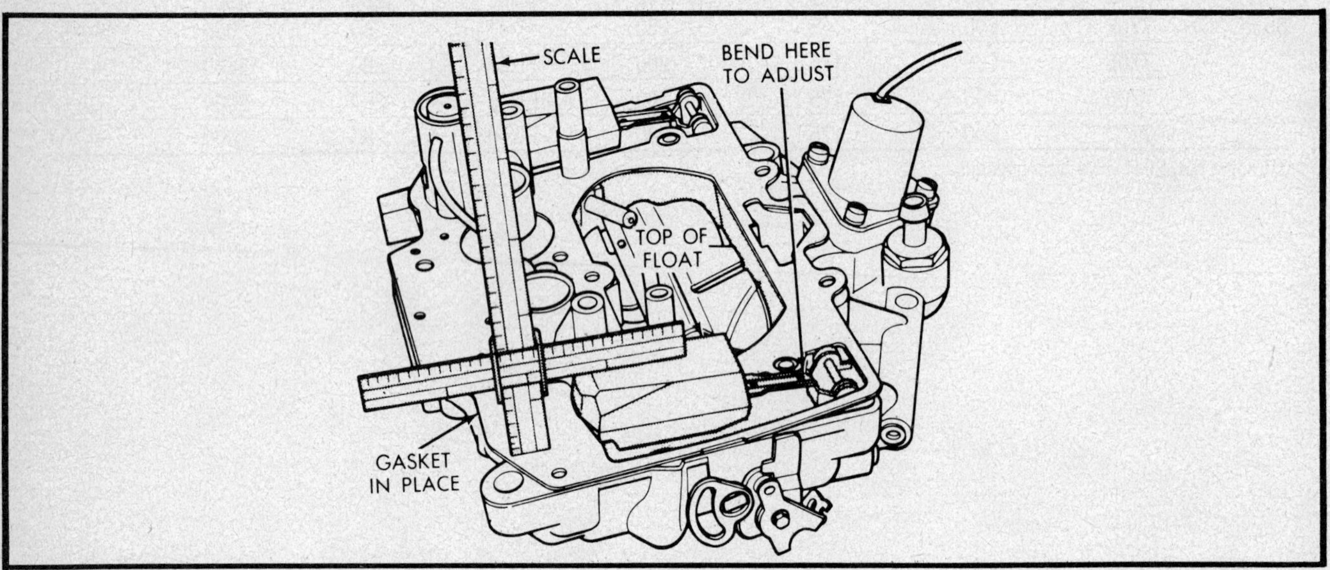

Carter TQ float height measurement (© Chrysler Corp.)

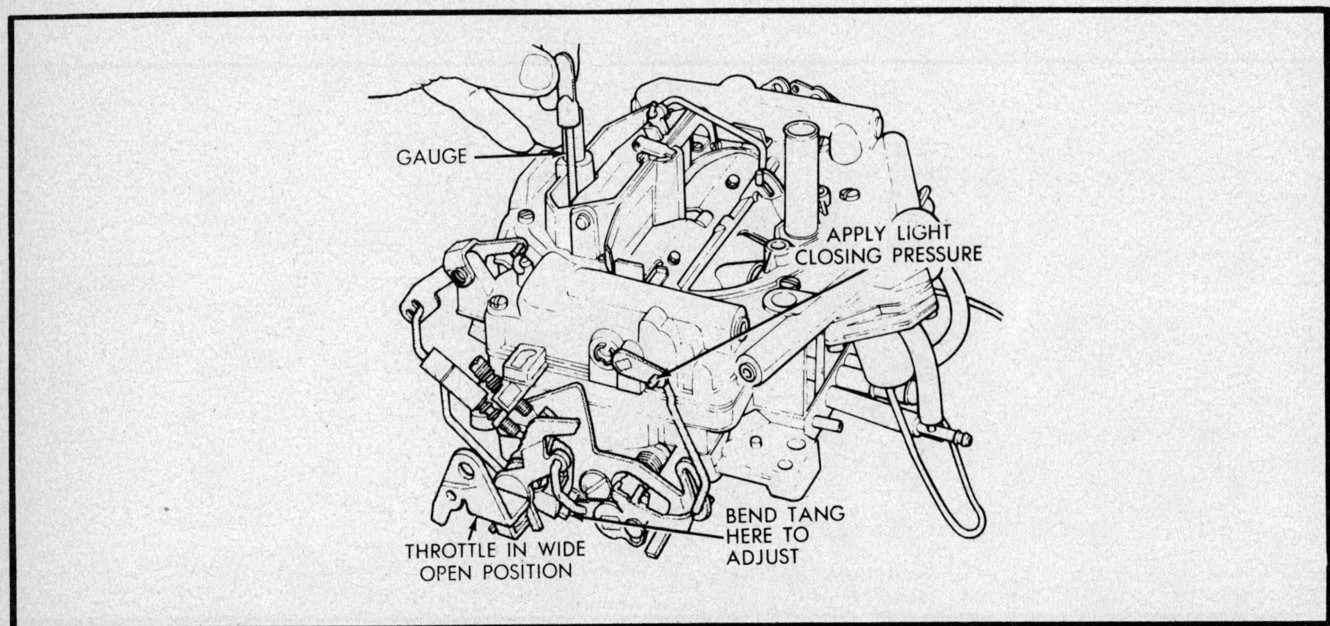

Carter TQ choke unloader adjustment (© Chrysler Corp.)

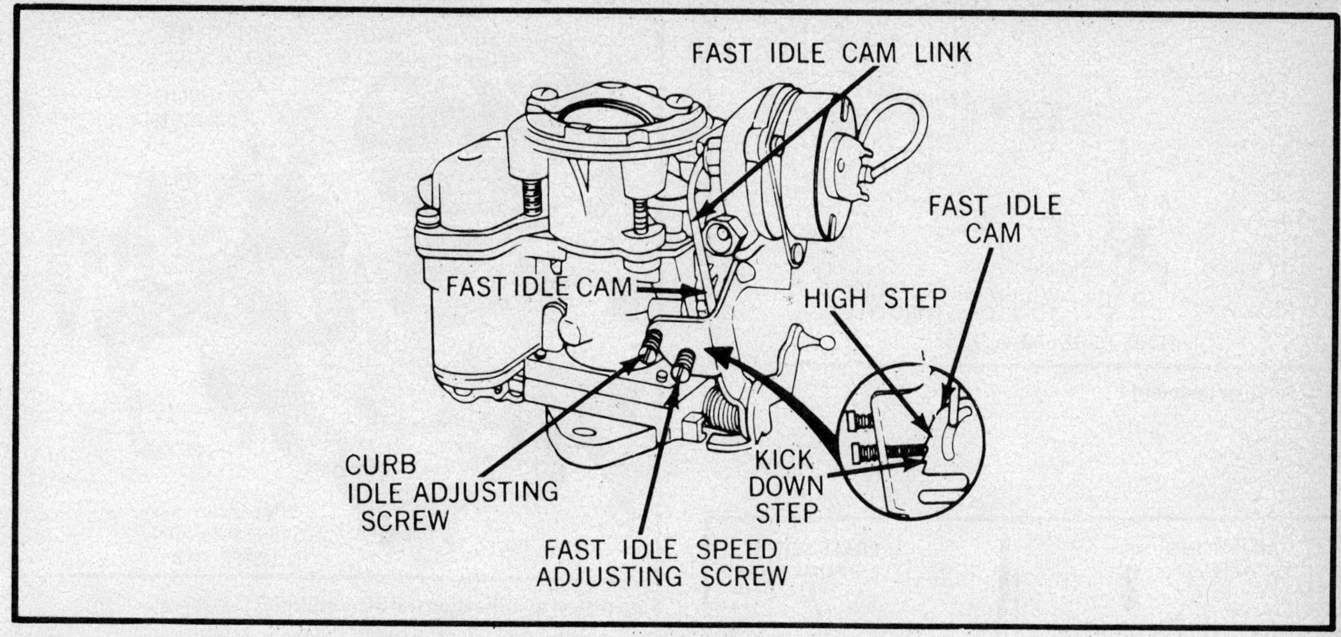

Typical adjustment points—YF carburetor with electric choke (© Ford Motor Co.)

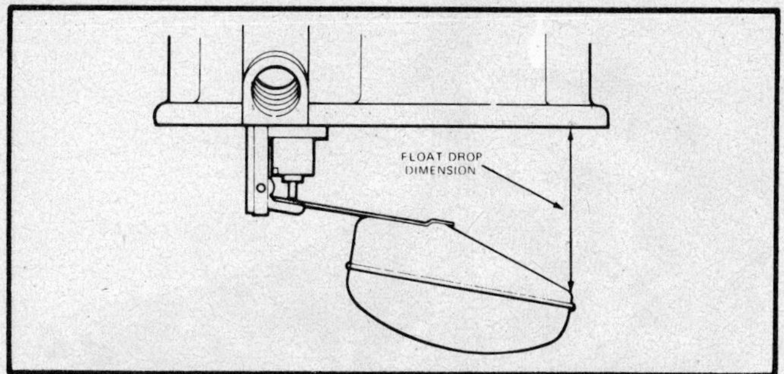

Measurement of float drop—YF carburetor (© Jeep Corp.)

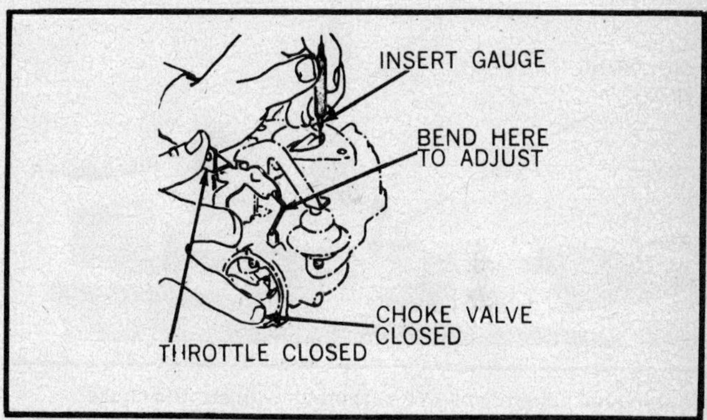

BBS fast idle adjustment

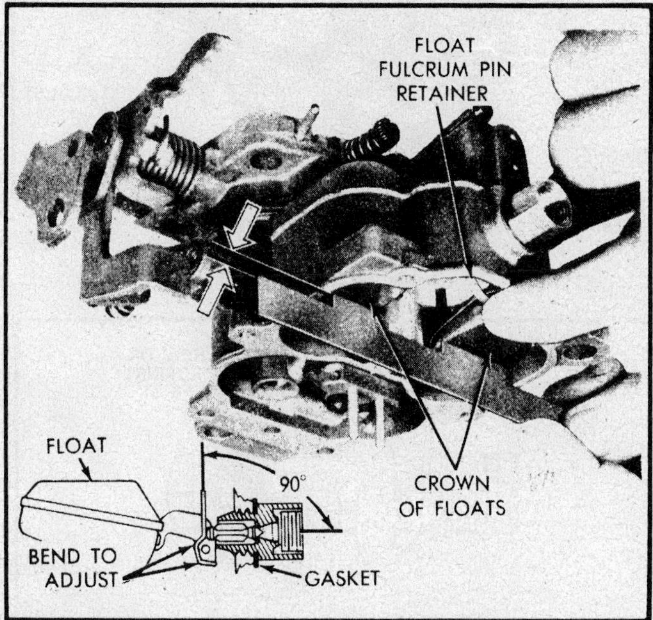

Adjusting float level with bowl inverted—BBD carburetor (© Chrysler Corp.)

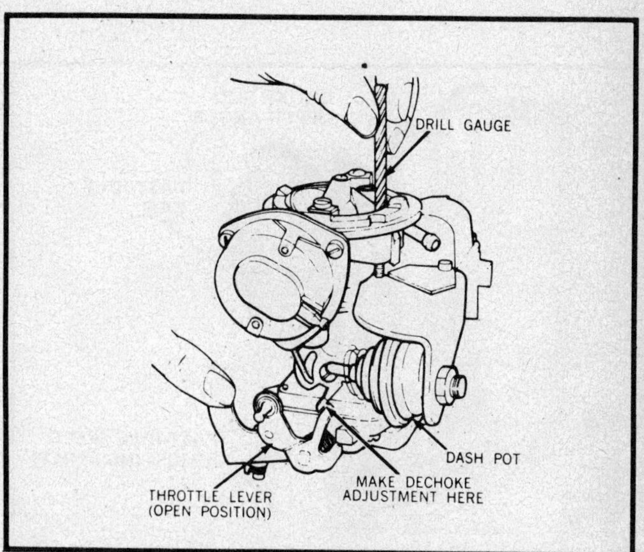

Choke plate unloader (dechoke) adjustment—typical YFA carburetor (© Ford Motor Co.)

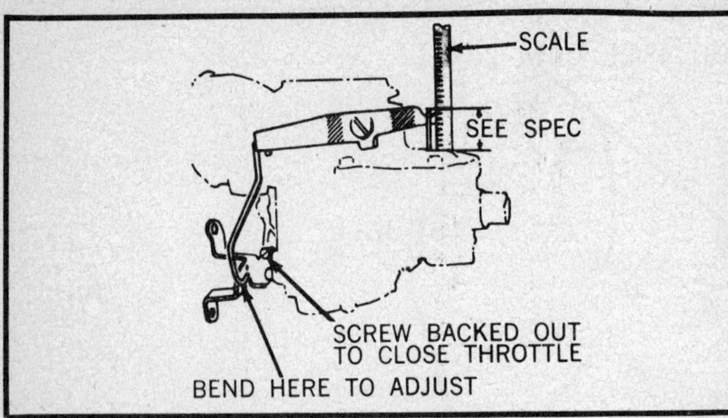

BBS pump adjustment

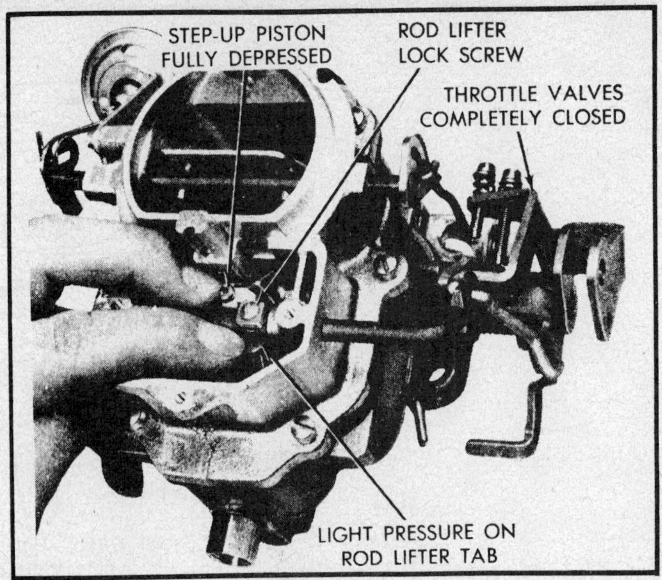

Step piston qualification—BBD carburetor (© Chrysler Corp.)

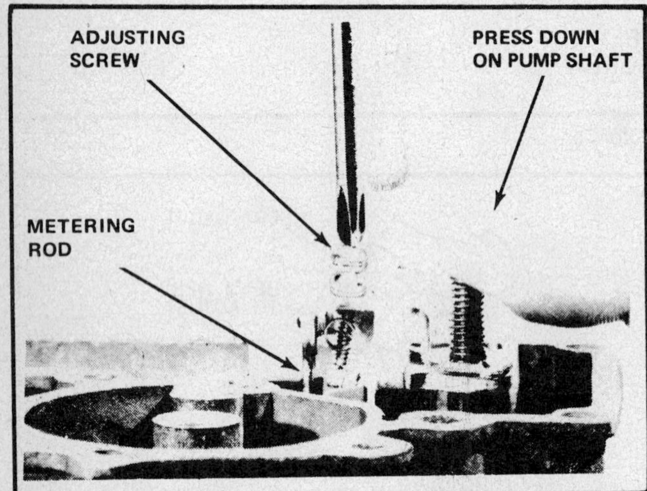

Metering rod adjustment—YF carburetor with electric choke (© Jeep Corp.)

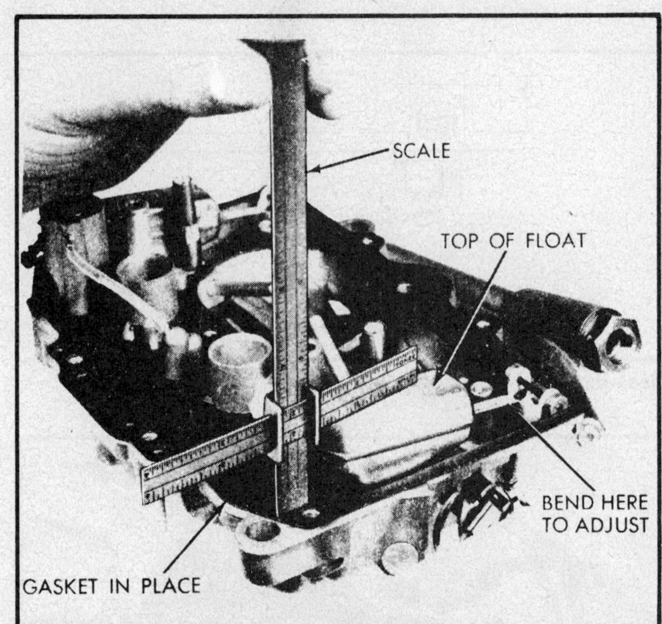

Carter Thermo-Quad® float height measurement (© Chrysler Corp.)

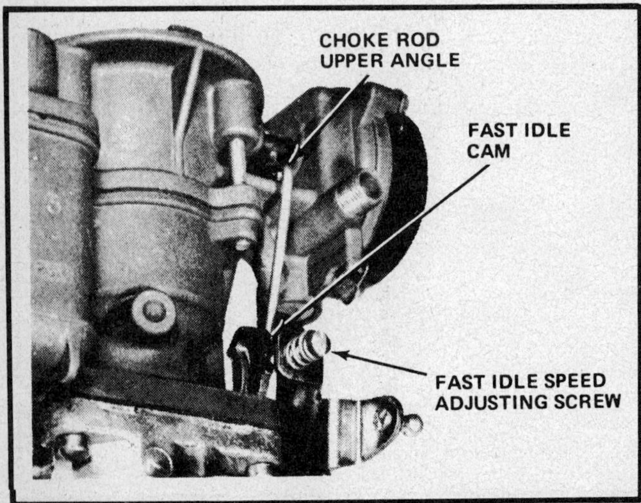

Fast idle cam and linkage adjustment—YF carburetor (© Jeep Corp.)

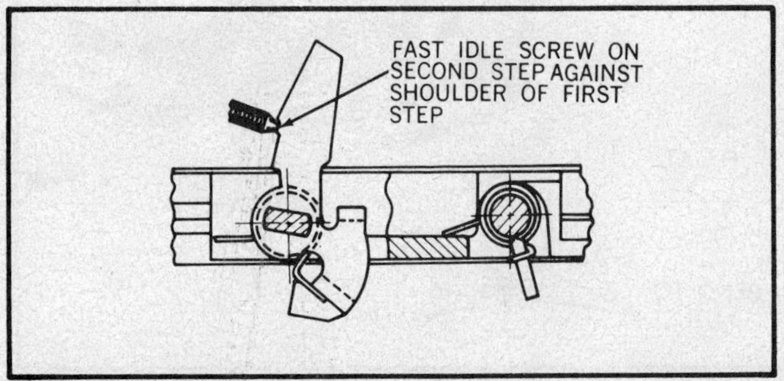

Carter Thermo-Quad® fast idle speed adjustment cam position (© Chrysler Corp.)

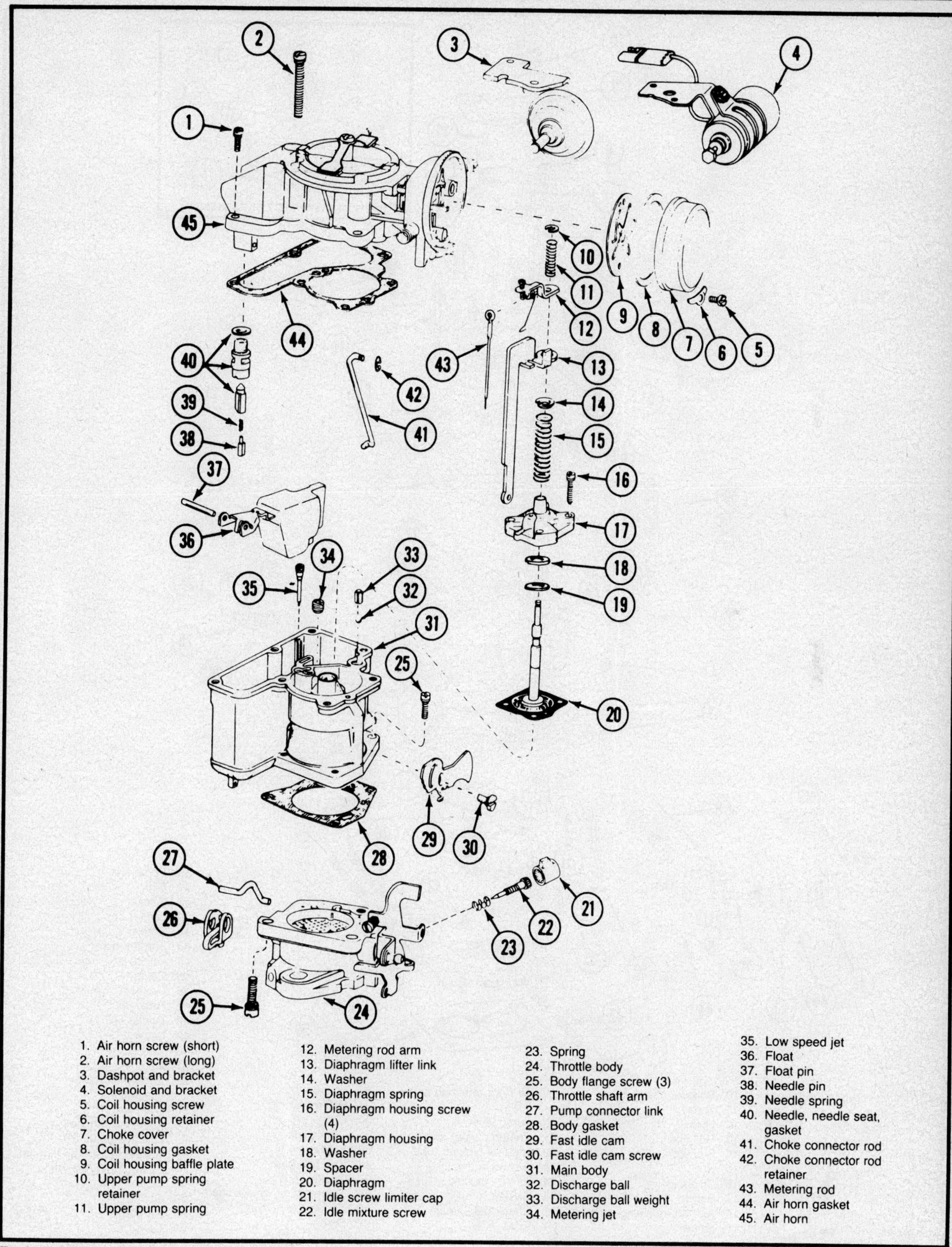
1. Air horn screw (short)
2. Air horn screw (long)
3. Dashpot and bracket
4. Solenoid and bracket
5. Coil housing screw
6. Coil housing retainer
7. Choke cover
8. Coil housing gasket
9. Coil housing baffle plate
10. Upper pump spring retainer
11. Upper pump spring
12. Metering rod arm
13. Diaphragm lifter link
14. Washer
15. Diaphragm spring
16. Diaphragm housing screw (4)
17. Diaphragm housing
18. Washer
19. Spacer
20. Diaphragm
21. Idle screw limiter cap
22. Idle mixture screw
23. Spring
24. Throttle body
25. Body flange screw (3)
26. Throttle shaft arm
27. Pump connector link
28. Body gasket
29. Fast idle cam
30. Fast idle cam screw
31. Main body
32. Discharge ball
33. Discharge ball weight
34. Metering jet
35. Low speed jet
36. Float
37. Float pin
38. Needle pin
39. Needle spring
40. Needle, needle seat, gasket
41. Choke connector rod
42. Choke connector rod retainer
43. Metering rod
44. Air horn gasket
45. Air horn

Exploded view of YF carburetor—typical (© Jeep Corp.)

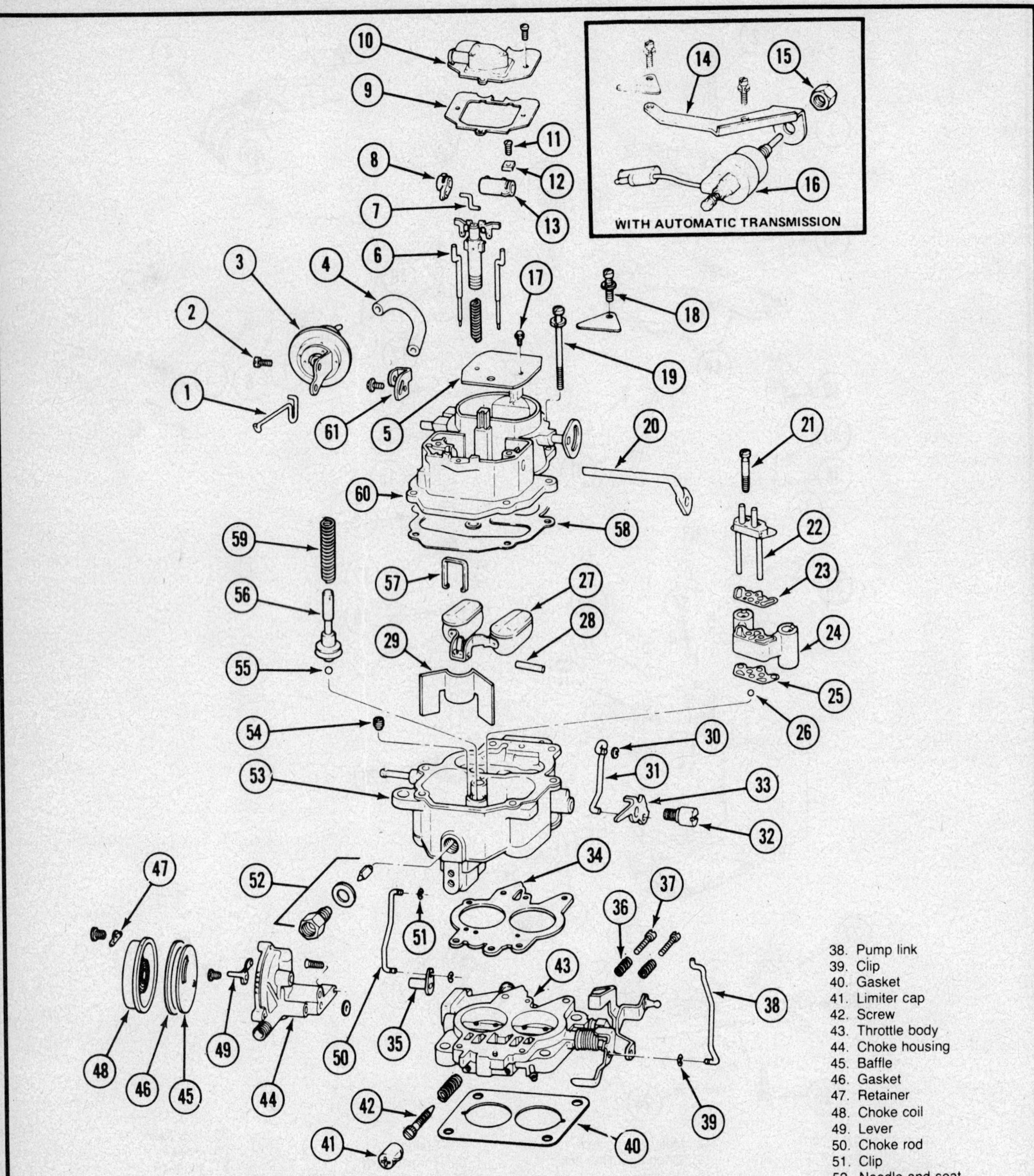

WITH AUTOMATIC TRANSMISSION

1. Diaphragm connector link
2. Screw
3. Choke vacuum diaphragm
4. Hose
5. Valve
6. Metering rod
7. S-Link
8. Pump arm
9. Gasket
10. Rollover check valve
11. Screw
12. Lock
13. Rod lifter
14. Bracket
15. Nut
16. Solenoid
17. Screw
18. Air horn retaining screw (short)
19. Air horn retaining screw (long)
20. Pump lever
21. Venturi cluster screw
22. Idle fuel pick-up tube
23. Gasket
24. Venturi cluster
25. Gasket
26. Check ball (small)
27. Float
28. Fulcrum pin
29. Baffle
30. Clip
31. Choke link
32. Screw
33. Fast idle cam
34. Gasket
35. Thermostatic choke shaft
36. Spring
37. Screw
38. Pump link
39. Clip
40. Gasket
41. Limiter cap
42. Screw
43. Throttle body
44. Choke housing
45. Baffle
46. Gasket
47. Retainer
48. Choke coil
49. Lever
50. Choke rod
51. Clip
52. Needle and seat assembly
53. Main body
54. Main metering jet
55. Check ball (large)
56. Accelerator pump plunger
57. Fulcrum pin retainer
58. Gasket
59. Spring
60. Air horn
61. Lever

Carter BBD two barrel carburetor—typical (© Chrysler Corp.)

1. Fuel inlet nut and gasket
2. Idle compensator screw
3. Idle compensator
4. Idle compensator gasket
5. "E" retainer
6. Primary diaphragm choke pull-off rod washer
7. Primary diaphragm choke pull-off rod
8. Auxiliary diaphragm choke pull-off rod (if equipped)
9. Choke lever screw
10. Choke lever
11. Choke connector rod
12. Countershaft lever screw
13. Countershaft, lever, outer
14. Countershaft lever spring
15. Countershaft lever, inner
16. Fast idle cam rod
17. Throttle connector rod
18. Cover plate screw
19. Metering rod cover plate (opposite pump)
20. Metering rod cover plate (pump side)
21. Step-up piston cover plate
22. Step-up piston and hanger assembly
23. Metering rod
24. Step-up piston spring
25. Bowl cover screw
26. IH part number location
27. Bowl cover assembly
28. Float pin
29. Float assembly
30. Needle, seat, and gasket
31. Pump passage tube
32. Bowl cover gasket
33. Secondary metering jet
34. Primary metering jet
35. Quad rings
36. Pin spring retainer
37. Bowl vent valve lever, upper
38. Bowl vent valve lever spring
39. Bowl vent valve arm
40. Bowl vent valve grommet
41. Rivet plug
42. Pump housing screw
43. Pump housing
44. Pump housing gasket
45. Discharge check needle
46. Pump arm screw
47. Pump arm
48. Pump "S" link
49. Air valve lock plug
50. Air valve adjustment plug
51. Air valve spring
52. Pump intake check assembly
53. Plunger assembly
54. Plunger spring
55. Main body
56. Main body gasket
57. Step-up piston lifter
58. Step-up piston lifter lever pin
59. Solenoid and diaphragm choke pull-off bracket screw
60. Solenoid
61. Solenoid operating lever screw
62. Curb idle speed screw and lever
63. Bowl vent lever, lower
64. Throttle shaft washer
65. Hose
66. Primary diaphragm choke pull-off bracket
67. Auxiliary choke pull-off and dashpot
68. Auxiliary choke pull-off and bracket (if equipped)
69. Dashpot and bracket
70. Limiter cap
71. Idle mixture screw
72. Idle mixture screw spring
73. Throttle body assembly
74. Carter part number location
75. Low idle speed screw

Exploded view of a typical late model Thermo-Quad® (© Chrysler Corp.)

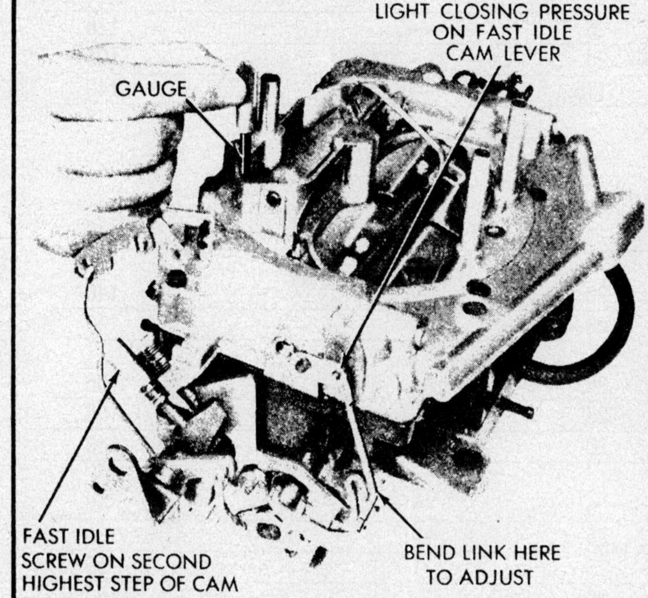

Adjustment of fast idle cam setting—Thermo-Quad® carburetor (© Chrysler Corp.)

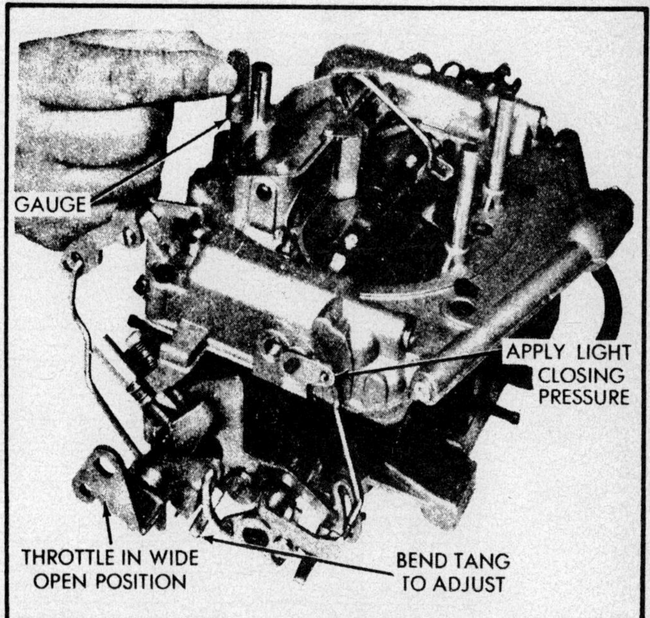

Choke unloader adjustment—Thermo-Quad® carburetor (© Chrysler Corp.)

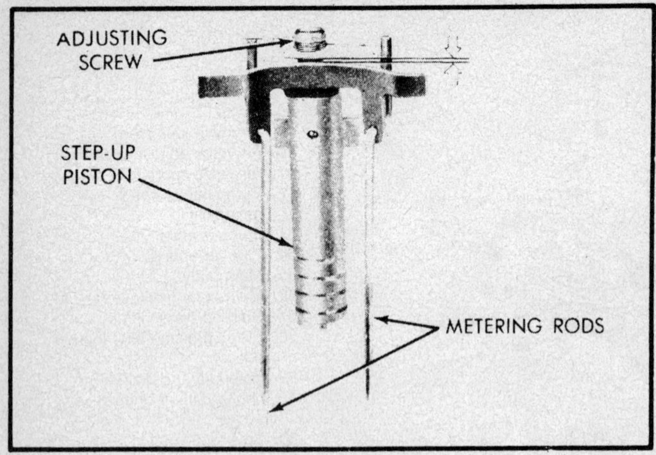

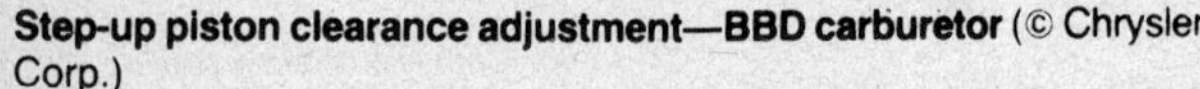
Step-up piston clearance adjustment—BBD carburetor (© Chrysler Corp.)

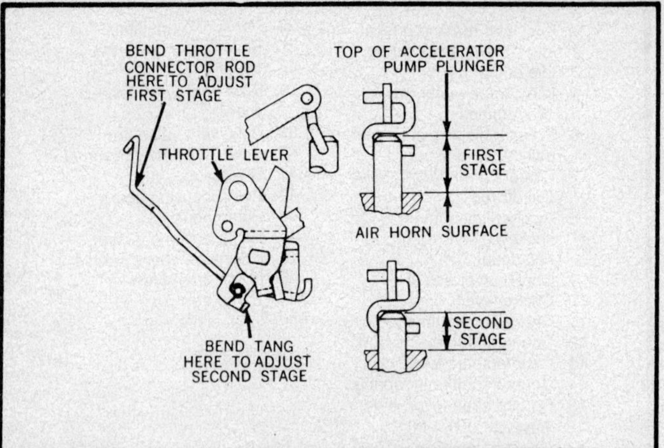

Adjustment of the primary and secondary accelerator pump—Thermo-Quad® carburetor (© Chrylser Corp.)

Autolite/Ford/Motorcraft

MODEL 2150
Ford

(All measurements in inches)

Year	Carburetor Number	Float Level (Dry)	Choke Unloader Setting	Choke Setting	Accelerator Pump Rod Location	Fuel Level (Wet)	Choke Pulldown Setting (Min)
'80	E0TE-9510 BGA, CYA, GZA, ABA, BEA	.810	—	.20	—	—	.140
	BHA	.810	—	.20	—	—	.135
	BRA, DDA	.810	—	.20	—	—	.128
	CFA, EAA	.810	—	.25	—	—	.128
	CVA, NA	.875	—	.20	—	—	.105
	BYA	.875	—	.115	—	—	.140
	BSA Calibration Number: 0-59J-R0 0-59G-R10	.875	—	.115	—	—	.140
	0-59J-R10 0-59H-R10	.875	—	.20	—	—	.140
	DCA	.875	—	.25	—	—	.140
	AAA, PA, SA, TA, VA	.810	—	.25	—	—	.185
	AA	.810	—	.25	—	—	.105
	CLA	.875	—	.20	—	—	.140
	BLA, BFA, BZA	.875	—	.25	—	—	.148
	CCA, CBA	.875	—	.25	—	—	.159
	EDA, DGA	.875	—	.25	—	—	.155
	EEA, EFA	.875	—	.20	—	—	.160
	DEA, ECA	.875	—	.25	—	—	.175
	DFA	.875	—	.25	—	—	.185

MODEL 2150
Ford

(All measurements in inches)

Year	Carburetor Number	Float Level (Dry)	Choke Unloader Setting	Choke Setting	Accelerator Pump Rod Location	Fuel Level (Wet)	Choke Pulldown Setting (Min)
'81	E1TE-9510 BJA, CHA, BCA	31/64	—	.250	V notch	—	.148
	BTA	31/64	—	.250	V notch	—	.130
	BVA	7/16	—	.200	V notch	—	.130
	CEA, CFA	31/64	—	.200	V notch	—	.160
	CAA, BYA	31/64	—	.250	V notch	—	.175
	BSA	31/64	—	.250	V notch	—	.130
	CCA	31/64	—	.250	V notch	—	.155
	BZA, CBA	31/64	—	.250	V notch	—	.180
	CNA, CMA, CPA, CRA, CSA, CKA, CLA	7/16	—	.200	V notch	—	.125
	E1UE-9510 KA	31/64	—	.250	V notch	—	.180
	GA	7/16	—	.200	V notch	—	.130
	HA	31/64	—	.200	V notch	—	.125
'82	E2TE- BNA, CGA	7/16	.200	V notch	2	.810	.125
	BMA, CFA	7/16	.250	V notch	2	.810	.125
	DAA, CYA	7/16	.250	V notch	2	.810	.115–.135
	BEA	7/16	.200	V notch	2	.810	.130
	BLA	7/16	.200	V notch	2	.810	.125
	AYA, BEA, CJA, BFA	7/16	.200	V notch	2	.810	.130
	E2UE-JA	31/64	.200	V notch	2	.875	.130
	E2TE-BAA, BBA	7/16	.200	V notch	2	.810	.130
	CKA	7/16	.200	V notch	2	.810	.120
	E2UE-FA E1UE-JA	31/64	.200	V notch	3	.875	.120
	E2UE-KA	31/64	.200	V notch	2	.875	.120
	E2TE-BPA,BRA	31/64	.200	V notch	2	.875	.120
	E2UE-ANA AAA AKA E2UE-RA	31/64	.250	V notch	3	.875	.170–.190
	E2UE-SA	31/64	.250	V notch	3	.875	.182
	E2UE-HA ABA E1UE-KA	31/64	.250	V notch	3	.875	.170–.190
	E2TE-BHA BGA	31/64	.250	V notch	4	.875	.180
	E2TE-DCA E2TE-DBA	31/64	.250	V notch	3	.875	.170–.190
	E2TE-BKA BJA	31/64	.250	V notch	4	.875	.175
	E2TE-DDA DEA	31/64	.250	V notch	3	.875	.170–.190

MODEL 2150
Ford

(All measurements in inches)

Year	Carburetor Number	Float Level (Dry)	Choke Unloader Setting	Choke Setting	Accelerator Pump Rod Location	Fuel Level (Wet)	Choke Pulldown Setting (Min)
'83	E3TE-9510						
	BCA						
	BFA						
	BBA						
	BGA	—	.25	V notch	3	.810	.115–135
	AUA	7/16	.20	V notch	3	.810	.142
	BHA	7/16	.20	V notch	3	.810	.152
	AYA	7/16	.25	V notch	4	.810	.137
	AVA	7/16	.25	V notch	3	.810	.149
	BJA	7/16	.20	V notch	4	.810	.157
	BLA	7/16	.20	V notch	3	.810	.157
	BEA	7/16	.20	V notch	3	.810	.149
	BMA	7/16	.20	V notch	4	.810	.150
	E3UE-9510						
	CA,FA	31/64	.20	V notch	3	.875	.120
	BA,KA	31/64	.20	V notch	2	.875	.120
	E3TE-9510						
	BAA,BPA	31/64	.25	V notch	3	.875	.130
	E2UE-9510						
	DA						
	EA						
	ANA						
	AKA	31/64	.25	V notch	3	.875	.180
	E37E-9510						
	LB	.650	.27	—	—	—	.320
	E37E-9510						
	ABA						
	AAA						
	ADA	7/16	.250	V notch	4	.810	.126–.146
'84	E37E-9510						
	AEA	7/16	.200	V-notch	4	.810	.136
	E4TE-9510						
	AUA	31/64	.200	V-notch	4	.875	.150
	AFA	31/64	.200	V-notch	3	.875	.144
	ADA	7/16	.200	V-notch	4	.810	.152
	ACA	7/16	.200	V-notch	4	.810	.155
	ATA	31/64	.200	V-notch	3	.875	.130
'85	E57E-9510				4	.810④	.136
	BA,CA	1/16	.250	3-Rich			
	E5TE-9510			V-notch	4	.875	.150
	YA	9/32	.220				
	ACA	9/32	.200	3 Rich	4	.875	.150
	AAA	1/4	.200	V-notch	4	.810	.155
	PA	1/4	.200	3 Rich	4	.810	.152
	E3UE-9510	31/64	.250	V-notch	3	.875	.180
	EA,DA						

① Wet float setting 1980 only

② For choke settings see the Ford Calibration Specifications 1980 only

③ For 1979 carburetor specifications see Ford Calibration Specifications

MODEL 7200
1981 Ford

(All measurements in inches)

Year	Carburetor Number	Float Level (Dry)	Float Drop	Choke Unloader Setting	Choke Setting	Dash Pot Plunger	Initial Choke Setting
'81	E1TE-9510 YA,AHA	1.455①	—	—	Index	—	—
	ZA	1.040①	—	—	Index	—	—

① ± .025 inches

MODEL 7200
1982–'83 Ford

(All measurements in inches)

Year	Carburetor Number	Float Setting	Float Drop	Control Vacuum Regulator	Pulldown Timing	Pump lever Lash
'82	E1TE-2A, AHA E2TE-CDA, CCA	1.070–1.010	1.490–1.430	.245–.255	2–5 sec.	.010①
'83	E3TE-9510– BVA, BYA	1.070–1.010	1.490–1.430	.245–.255	2–5 sec.	.010①

① Plus one turn counter-clockwise.

MODEL 2100
Jeep

(All measurements in inches)

Year	Carburetor Number	Float Level (Dry)	Fuel Level (Wet)	Initial Choke Valve Clearance	Fast Idle Cam Setting ②	Choke Cover Setting	Choke Unloader Valve Clearance	Fast Idle Speed ①	Bowl Vent Clearance	Rod Pump Location Hole
'80	ODMJ12	.375	.093	.125	.113	2 Rich	.300	1500	.120	3
	ODM2JC	.375	.093	.120	.106	2 Rich	.300	1500	.120	3
	ODA2J2	.375	.093	.120	.106	2 Rich	.300	1600	.120	3
	ODA2J	.375	.093	.128	.113	2 Rich	.300	1600	.120	3
	ODM2A	.375	.093	.128	.113	2 Rich	.360	1500	.120	3

① TCS solenoid and EGR disconnected, fast idle screw on 2nd cam step.
② Measured between choke valve and air horn, fast idle screw on 2nd cam step.

MODEL 2150
Jeep

(All measurements in inches)

Year	Carburetor Number	Float Level (Dry)	Fuel Level (Wet)	Initial Choke Valve Clearance	Fast Idle Cam Setting ②	Choke Cover Setting	Choke Unloader Valve Clearance	Fast Idle Speed ①	Bowl Vent Clearance	Rod Pump Location Hole
'80	ORHM2	.575	.930	.104	.081	2 Rich	.348	1500	.120	3
	ORHA2	.575	.930	.104	.081	2 Rich	.350	1600	.120	3
'81	DMJ2	.375	.930	.125	.113	2 Rich	.300	1500	.120	3
	DA2J	.375	.930	.128	.113	1 Rich	.300	1600	.120	3
	DM2A	.375	.930	.128	.113	1 Rich	.360	1500	.120	3
	RHM2	.575	.930	.104	.081	2 Rich	.348	1500	.120	3
	RHA2	.575	.930	.113	.086	2 Rich	.350	1600	.120	3

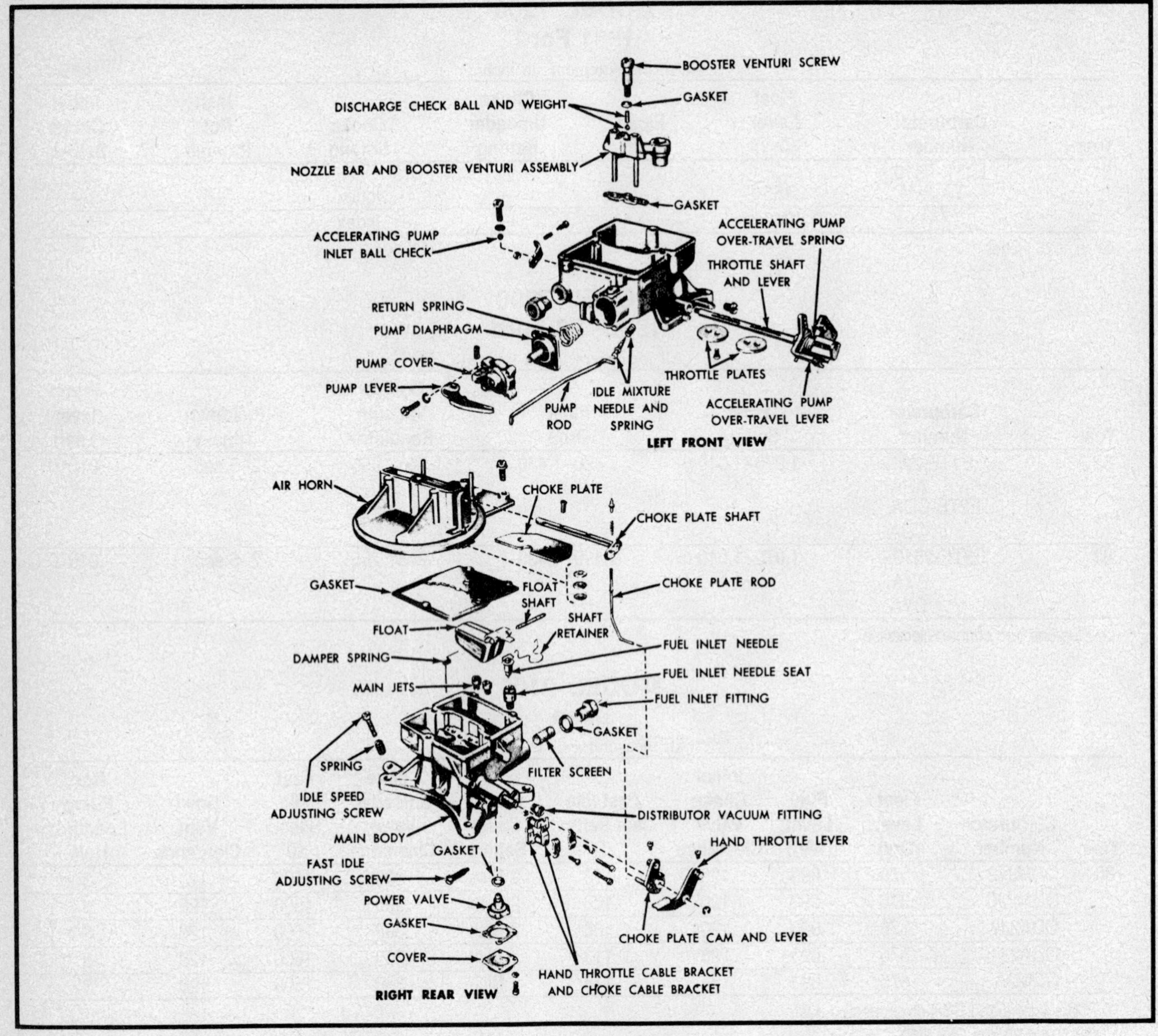

Exploded view of model 2100 carburetor (with manual choke, manual throttle, and automatic choke mechanisms shown)
(© Ford Motor Co.)

MODEL 2150
Jeep

(All measurements in inches)

Year	Carburetor Number	Float Level (Dry)	Fuel Level (Wet)	Initial Choke Valve Clearance	Fast Idle Cam Setting ②	Choke Cover Setting	Choke Unloader Valve Clearance	Fast Idle Speed ①	Bowl Vent Clearance	Rod Pump Location Hole
'82	2RHM2	19/64–23/64 ③	.930	.116	.076	1 Rich	.350	1500	.120	—
	2RHA2	19/64–23/64 ③	.930	.116	.076	1 Rich	.350	1600	.120	—
'84–'85	4RHA2	.575	.930	.136	.086	2 Rich	.350	1600	.120	—
	5RHA2	.328	.930	.118	.076	Y	.420	1600	—	—

① TCS solenoid and EGR disconnected, fast idle screw on 2nd cam step

② Measured between choke valve and air horn fast idle screw on 2nd cam step

③ Measured from machined bowl surface to a point 1/8 inch from float tip with the needle seated

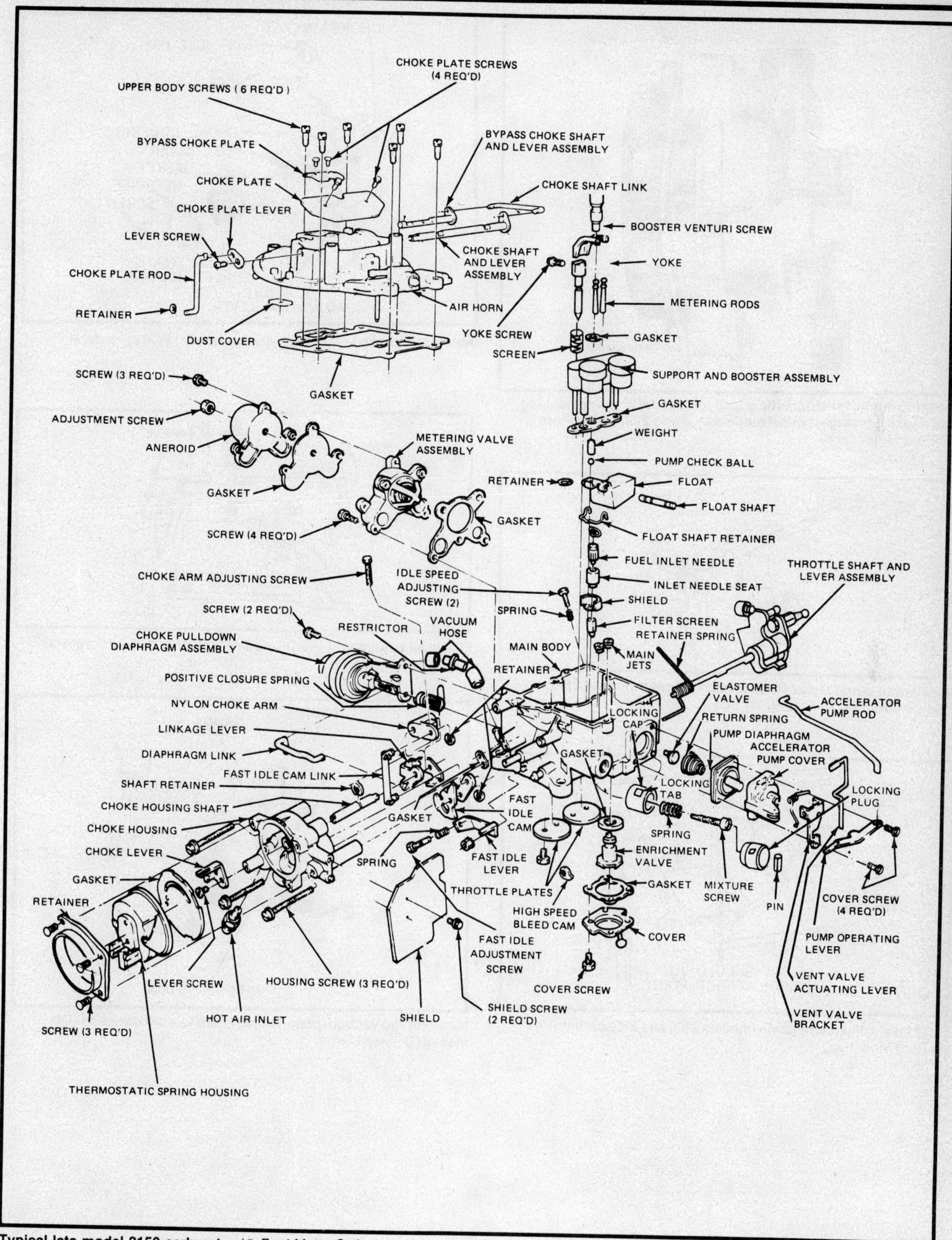
CHOKE PLATE SCREWS (4 REQ'D)
UPPER BODY SCREWS (6 REQ'D)
BYPASS CHOKE PLATE
BYPASS CHOKE SHAFT AND LEVER ASSEMBLY
CHOKE PLATE
CHOKE SHAFT LINK
CHOKE PLATE LEVER
BOOSTER VENTURI SCREW
LEVER SCREW
CHOKE SHAFT AND LEVER ASSEMBLY
YOKE
CHOKE PLATE ROD
METERING RODS
AIR HORN
RETAINER
DUST COVER
YOKE SCREW
GASKET
SCREEN
SUPPORT AND BOOSTER ASSEMBLY
SCREW (3 REQ'D)
GASKET
GASKET
ADJUSTMENT SCREW
WEIGHT
ANEROID
METERING VALVE ASSEMBLY
PUMP CHECK BALL
RETAINER
FLOAT
GASKET
FLOAT SHAFT
GASKET
SCREW (4 REQ'D)
FLOAT SHAFT RETAINER
FUEL INLET NEEDLE
THROTTLE SHAFT AND LEVER ASSEMBLY
CHOKE ARM ADJUSTING SCREW
IDLE SPEED ADJUSTING SCREW (2)
INLET NEEDLE SEAT
SHIELD
SCREW (2 REQ'D)
SPRING
FILTER SCREEN
RESTRICTOR
VACUUM HOSE
RETAINER SPRING
CHOKE PULLDOWN DIAPHRAGM ASSEMBLY
MAIN BODY
MAIN JETS
RETAINER
POSITIVE CLOSURE SPRING
ELASTOMER VALVE
NYLON CHOKE ARM
ACCELERATOR PUMP ROD
LOCKING CAP
RETURN SPRING
LINKAGE LEVER
PUMP DIAPHRAGM
ACCELERATOR PUMP COVER
DIAPHRAGM LINK
GASKET
FAST IDLE CAM LINK
LOCKING TAB
SHAFT RETAINER
LOCKING PLUG
FAST IDLE CAM
CHOKE HOUSING SHAFT
GASKET
CHOKE HOUSING
SPRING
CHOKE LEVER
ENRICHMENT VALVE
SPRING
FAST IDLE LEVER
GASKET
MIXTURE SCREW
GASKET
RETAINER
THROTTLE PLATES
COVER SCREW (4 REQ'D)
PIN
HIGH SPEED BLEED CAM
FAST IDLE ADJUSTMENT SCREW
COVER
PUMP OPERATING LEVER
LEVER SCREW
HOUSING SCREW (3 REQ'D)
VENT VALVE ACTUATING LEVER
COVER SCREW
SHIELD SCREW (2 REQ'D)
VENT VALVE BRACKET
HOT AIR INLET
SHIELD
SCREW (3 REQ'D)
THERMOSTATIC SPRING HOUSING

Typical late model 2150 carburetor (© Ford Motor Co.)

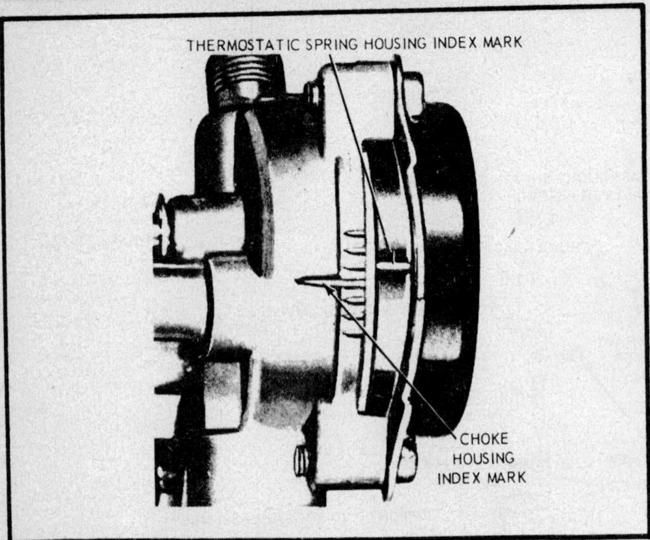

Indexing marks for automatic choke thermostatic spring housing and choke housing—typical models 2100 and 2150 carburetors (© Ford Motor Co.)

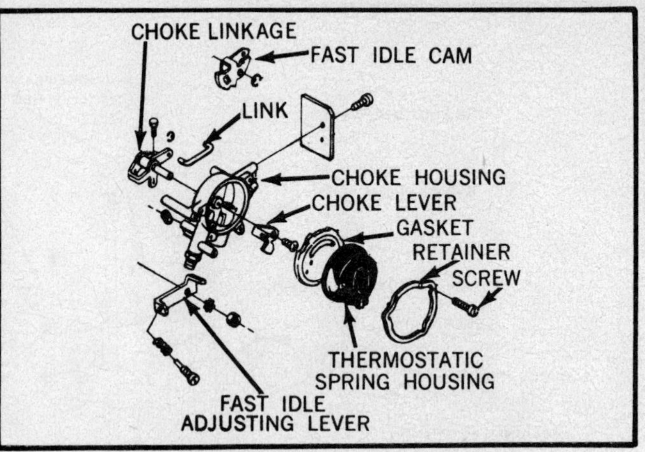

Automatic choke assembly (typical)—model 2100 carburetor

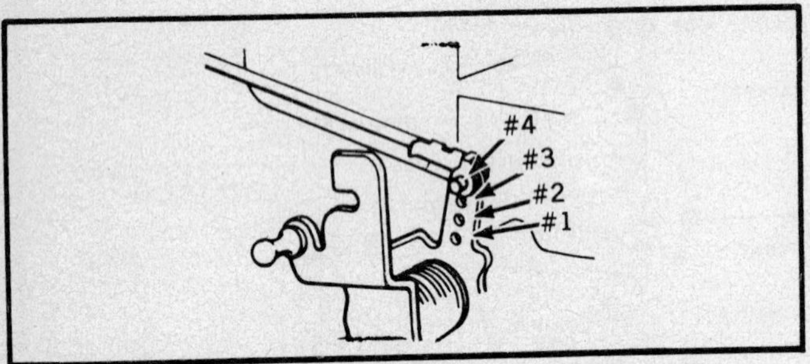

Accelerator pump stroke hole location—typical models 2100 and 2150 carburetors (© Ford Motor Co.)

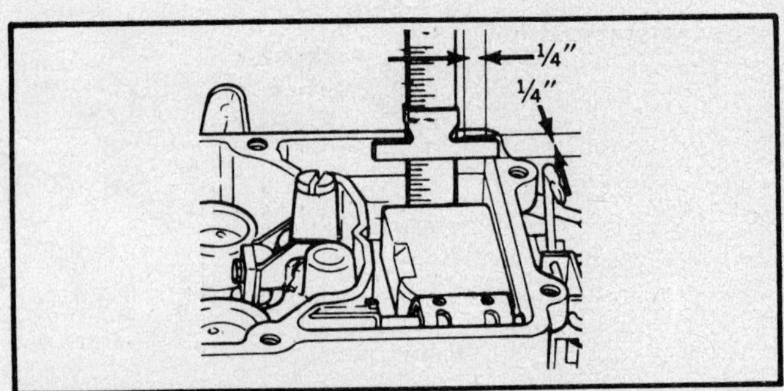

Fuel level adjustment (wet)—models 2100 and 2150 carburetors (© Ford Motor Co.)

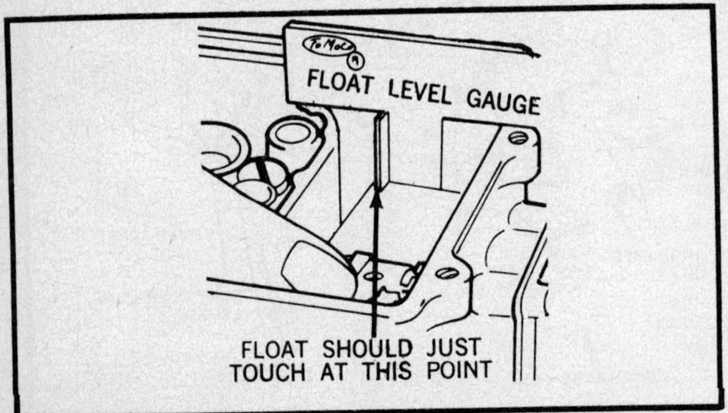

Float level adjustment (dry)—models 2100 and 2150 carburetors (© Ford Motor Co.)

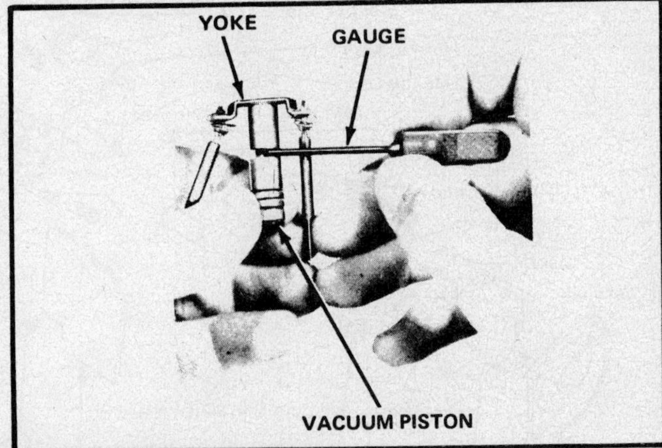

Metering rod vacuum piston adjustment to a clearance of .120 inches (© Jeep Corp.)

Holley

MODEL 4150EG
Chevrolet/GMC

(All measurements in inches)

Year	Carburetor Number	Float Level (Dry)	Accelerator Pump (Min.)	Fast Idle (rpm)	Air Vent Clearance	Fast Idle Mechanical Clearance
'80–'84	R8848A	②	.015	2200	.045–.075	.031
	R8849A	②	.015	2200	.045–.075	.031
	R8852A	②	.015	2200	.045–.075	.031
	R8853A	②	.015	2200	.045–.075	.031
	R8856A	②	.015	2200	.045–.075	.031
	R8850A	②	.015	2200	—	.031
	R8851A	②	.015	2200	—	.031
	R8854A	②	.015	2200	—	.031
	R8855A	②	.015	2200	—	.031
	R8857A	②	.015	2200	—	.031
'85	All Numbers (Federal and Canadian)	②	#1	③	.045–.075	.031
	All Numbers (California	②	#1	③	—	.031

① Primary bowl—.197
Secondary bowl—.166
② Primary bowl—.194
Secondary bowl—.213

Note: Secondary set screw should be ½ turn open
③ See underhood specifications sticker

MODEL 4152EG
Chevrolet/GMC

(All measurements in inches)

Year	Carburetor Number	Dry Float Level		Secondary Set Screw	Fast Idle	Pump Cam Position
		Primary	Secondary			
'85	All	.194	.213	½ turn open	.031①	#1 hole

① Mechanical setting

MODEL 1945
Dodge/Plymouth

(All measurements in inches)

Year	Carburetor Number	Dry Float Level	Choke Unloader	Pump Stroke	Pump Rod Hole	Fast Idle Cam Position	Fast Idle Speed	Initial Choke Opening
'80	R8978A	①	.250	1.70	1	.080	1600	.130
	R8720A	①	.250	1.61	2	.090	1600	.130
	R9107A	①	.250	1.70	1	.080	1600	.100
	R9106A	①	.250	1.61	2	.080	1600	.100
	R8979A	①	.250	1.70	1	.080	1600	.130
	R8721A	①	.250	1.61	2	.080	1600	.130
'81	R9131A	①	.250	1.61	2	.090	1600	.130
	R9132A	①	.250	1.61	2	.090	1600	.130
	R9134A	①	.250	1.61	2	.090	1600	.130
	R9152A	①	.250	1.61	2	.080	1800	.130
	R9153A	①	.250	1.61	2	.080	1800	.130
	R9399A	①	.250	1.61	2	.080	1800	.130

MODEL 1945
Dodge/Plymouth

(All measurements in inches)

Year	Carburetor Number	Dry Float Level	Choke Unloader	Pump Stroke	Pump Rod Hole	Fast Idle Cam Position	Fast Idle Speed	Initial Choke Opening
'82	R9132A	①	.250		2	.090	1600	.130
	R9134A	①	.250		2	.090	1600	.130
	R9153A	①	.250		2	.080	1800	.130
	R9399A	①	.250		2	.080	1800	.130
	R9762A	①	.250		2	.090	1600	.130
	R9765A	①	.250		2	.080	1800	.130
'83	R40055A	①	.250		2	.080	1600	.130
	R40056A	①	.250		2	.080	1600	.130
	R9399-1A	①	.250		2	.080	1800	.130
	R9134-1A	①	.250		2	.090	1800	.130
'84	R40088A	①	.250	1.61	2	.080	1600	.130
	R40089A	①	.250	1.61	2	.080	1600	.130
	R40102A	①	.250	1.70	1	.080	1800	.130
	R40103A	①	.250	1.61	2	.090	1600	.130
'85	R40102A	①	.250	1.70	1	.080	1800	.130
	R40244A	①	.250	1.61	2	.090	1600	.130
	R40159	①	.250	1.61	2	.080	1600	.130
	R40160	①	.250	1.61	2	.090	1600	.130

Note: Choke setting is fixed and non-adjustable.

① Flush with top of bowl cover gasket, carb inverted

MODEL 2245
Dodge/Plymouth

(All measurements in inches)

Year	Carburetor Number	Float Level (Dry)	Choke Unloader	Choke Setting	Pump Rod Location (Hole)	Fast Idle Cam Position	Fast Idle Speed (rpm)	Initial Choke Opening
'80–'81	R7871A	3/16	.170	Fixed	1	.110	1700	.150
'82	R9816A	3/16	.170	Fixed	3	.110	1700	.150
'83	R9816A	5/32–7/32	.170	Fixed	2	.110	1700	.150

① Fixed setting

② Float drop—bottom of float to be parallel with air horn bottom

MODEL 2280, 2280G
Dodge/Plymouth

(All measurements in inches)

Year	Carburetor Number	Float Level ①	Choke Vacuum Kick	Fast Idle Cam	Fast Idle (rpm)	Choke Unloader	Bowl Vent Valve
'80	R8999A	5/16	.130	.070	1600	.310	.030
	R9000A	5/16	.130	.070	1600	.310	.030
	R9001A	5/16	.150	.070	1600	.310	.030
	R9209A	5/16	.150	.070	1600	.310	.030
	R9224A	5/16	.150	.070	1600	.310	.030
'81	R9135A	9/32	.110	.070	1500	.310	—
	R9136A	9/32	.130	.070	1500	.310	—
	R9151A	9/32	.110	.070	1500	.310	—
	R9437A	9/32	.130	.070	1500	.310	—
'82	R9491A	7/32–10/32	.140	.052	1500	.200	—
	R9493A	7/32–10/32	.140	.052	1500	.200	—
	R9572A	7/32–10/32	.140	.052	1500	.200	—

MODEL 2280, 2280G
Dodge/Plymouth

(All measurements in inches)

Year	Carburetor Number	Float Level①	Choke Vacuum Kick	Fast Idle Cam	Fast Idle (rpm)	Choke Unloader	Bowl Vent Valve
'83	R9499A	9/32	.140	.052	1500	.200	—
	R9951A	9/32	.140	.052	1500	.200	—
'84	R9951A	9/32	.140	.070	1500	.250	—
	R40093A	9/32	.140	.052	1500	.200	—
'85	R40164	9/32	.140	.070	1600	.150	.035
	R40167	9/32	.140	.070	1600	.150	.035
	R40172A	9/32	.140	.070	1450	.200	.035

① Measured from surface of fuel bowl to the toe of each float

MODEL 6145
Dodge/Plymouth

(All measurements in inches)

Year	Carburetor Number	Float Setting	Choke Vacuum Kick	Choke Unloader Adjustment	Fast Idle Cam Position	Fast Idle (rpm)	Pump Piston Stroke
'83	R40029A	①	.150	.250	.090	1600	1.70
	R40030A	①	.150	.250	.090	1600	1.61
'84	R40098A	①	.150	.250	.070	1600	1.61
	R40099A	①	.150	.250	.070	1600	1.61
'85	R40161	①	.150	.250	.060	1600	1.75
	R40162	①	.150	.250	.070	1600	1.75

① With bowl inverted, float lungs just touch a straightedge run along gasket surface.

② 1450 rpm with manual transmission

MODEL 6280
Dodge/Plymouth

(All measurements in inches)

Year	Carburetor Number	Float Level	Choke Vacuum Kick	Fast Idle Cam	Choke Unloader	Accelerator Pump Stroke	Fast Idle Speed	Propane Idle Speed
'85	R40132	①	.150	.070	.250	②	1400	710
	R40133	①	.130	.070	.150	②	1625③	775④

① Measured from surface of fuel bowl to top of each float

② Flush with top of bowl vent

③ 1450 rpm with manual transmission

④ 740 rpm with manual transmission

MODEL 2300C
Ford

(All measurements in inches)

Year	Carburetor Number	Fuel Level (Wet)	Pump Cam Location	Pulldown Setting	Choke Setting	Choke Unloader
'83	E2TE-9510-DPA	①	1	.210–.230	3 Rich	.300

MODEL 2300 EG
Ford

(All measurements in inches)

Year	Carburetor Number	Float Level	Float Drop	Choke Unloader Setting	Choke Setting	Dash Pot Plunger	Initial Choke Setting
'80	E0TE–9510 PA, PB, BCA, BCB, EVA, EYA	①	—	—	—	—	.375
'81	D9TE–9510 ABC, APA	①	—	—	Manual	—	.350–.400

① Check float level to the bottom of the sight plug in the carburetor

MODEL 2300EG
Ford

(All measurements in inches)

Year	Carburetor Number	Fuel Level (Wet)	Pump Lever Location	Power Valve Timing	Pulldown Setting
'82	D9TE APA AGA	①	# 2	9.5-7.0/3.0-.5	.350–.400
	E0TE-PA E2TE-NA	①	# 1	9.5-7.0/3.0-.5	.350–.400

MODEL 2300EG
Ford

(All measurements in inches)

Year	Carburetor Number	Fuel Level (Wet)	Pump Lever Location	Enrichment Valve Ident.	Main Jet Ident.
'83	D9TE-APA E2TE-AGA E0TE-PA E2TE-NA	①	—	12	58
'84–'85	D9TE-9510 APA, PA	①	#2	12	58
	E2TE-9510 AGA, NA	①	#2	12	58

① At bottom of sight plug

MODEL 4150EG
Ford

(All measurements in inches)

Year	Carburetor Number	Float Level (Dry)	Float Drop	Choke Unloader Setting	Choke Setting	Dash Pot Plunger	Initial Choke Setting
'80	D9HE–9510 CA, DA, EA, FA	①	—	—	—	—	—
	E0HE–9510 CA,EA	①	—	—	—	—	—
'81	D9HE–9510 CA,EA	①	—	—	Manual	—	—

① Check float level to the bottom of the sight plug in the carburetor

MODEL 4180EG
Ford

(All measurements in inches)

Year	Carburetor Number	Float Level (Dry)	Float Drop	Choke Unloader Setting	Choke Setting	Dash Pot Plunger	Initial Choke Setting
'80	E0TE-9510 ETA, JB, EUA, RB, JA, RA, ERA, MB, SB, SA, ESA, MA	①	—	—	—	—	.210
	D9TE-9510 AHE, EBA, ETA, EUA	①	—	—	—	—	.210
'81	D9TE-9510 EBA, AHE, ETA, EUA	①	—	—	Manual	—	.185–.235
	E0TE-9510 RA, JA, MA, SA	①	—	—	Manual	—	.185–.235

① Check float level to the bottom of the sight plug in the carburetor

MODEL 4180EG
Ford

(All measurements in inches)

Year	Carburetor Number	Fuel Level (Wet)	Choke Pulldown Setting	Pump Lever Location	Power Valve Timing
'82	E2TE-CSA, AJA CUA, CTA, AKA, CVA E0TE-SA495 D9TE-EVA495	①	.180–.440	#1	9.5-7.0/3.0-.5

① At bottom of sight plug

MODEL 4180C
Ford

(All measurements in inches)

Year	Carburetor Number	Fuel Level (Wet)	Choke Pulldown Setting	Choke Unloader Setting	Choke Setting	Pump Lever Location	Enrichment Valve Indent.
'80	D9TE-9510 DKA	①	—	.300–.330	—	—	②
'81	D9TE-9510 BKA	①	—	—	5 Rich	—	③
'82	E1UE-RA	①	.200–.220	.295–.335	2 Rich	#1	④
'83	E3TE-9510-PC 9510-PC	①	.210–.230	.300–.330	3 Rich	#1	11
	E3TE-9510-SB 9510-TB	①	.210–.230	.300–.330	3 Rich	#1	8

MODEL 4180C
Ford

(All measurements in inches)

Year	Carburetor Number	Fuel Level (Wet)	Choke Pulldown Setting	Choke Unloader Setting	Choke Setting	Pump Lever Location	Enrichment Valve Indent.
'84	E4TE-9510-ARA	①	.185	.300	Index	#1	13
	E3TE-9510 PD	①	.220	.295–.335	3 Rich	#1	8
	TC	①	.210–.230	.300–.330	3 Rich	#1	8
	RD	①	.200	.315	3 Rich	#1	8A
	SC	①	.210–.230	.315	3 Rich	#1	8A

① At bottom of sight plug
② Initial choke setting .210 in.
③ Initial choke setting .195–.225
④ Power valve timing 9.5–7.0/3.0–.5

MODEL 4190EG

Year	Carburetor Number	Fuel Level (Wet)	Enrichment Valve Ident.	Pump Cam Location	Primary Main Jet	Secondary Main Jet
'83	E2TE- CMA CNA	①	12	#1	62	68
'84–'85	E2TE-9510 AGA, NA	①	12	#2	58	—
	CMA, CNA	①	12	#1	62	683
	CPA, CRA	①	12	#1	62	683
	E3HE-9510 AA, BA, CA, DA	①	12	#1	62	683

① At bottom of sight plug

MODEL 1920
International

(All measurements in inches)

Year	Carburetor Number	Float Level	Fuel Level	Fast Idle Speed (rpm)	Auto Choke Setting	Dash-Post Setting	Fuel Bowl Vent Clearance	Pump Piston Stroke Adjustment	Fast Idle Cam Pos. Adjustment (Top Step—Hot)	Choke Vac. Pulldown (Kick) Adjustment	Choke Unloader Adjustment	Choke qualification Adjustment
'79–'81	7771	①	11/16 ± 1/32	2200	1 Lean	—	—	25/32	—	—	.235–.295	.150–.180

① Flush with top edge of bowl and with fuel inlet valve held closed

MODEL 1940C
International

(All measurements in inches)

Year	Carburetor Number	Float Level	Fuel Level	Automatic Choke	Dash Pot Setting	Choke Unloader	Fast Idle (rpm)	Curb Idle (rpm)	Pump Stroke	Idle %CO
'79–'81	7771	①	11/16 ± 1/32	1 Rich	.100–.130	.235–.295	2200	675–725	25/32	0.3–1.5

① Flush with top edge of bowl, with fuel inlet valve held closed

MODEL 2210C
International

(All measurements in inches)

Year	Carburetor Number	Float Level	Fuel Level	Fast Idle Speed	Choke Setting	Choke Unloader	Choke Qualification Adjustment
'79–'81	6620-1 7309	.180	½①	2000	②	.198–.258	.040–.070
	7214, 7214-1	.180	½①	1800	Preset	.228 ± .030	.135 ± .015
	7309, 6620-2, 7133, 7940 8241	.180	½①	2200	②	.198–.258	.040–.070
	7657, 7217, 8244	.180	½①	1800	Preset	.198–.258	.120–.150

①@ 5.5 psi

②Choke with index marks—1 notch lean (restrained)
Choke without index marks—preset (unrestrained)

MODEL 2300, 2300C, 2300G, 2300EG
International

(All measurements in inches)

Year	Carburetor Number	Fuel Level	Fast Idle (rpm)	Governor No load (rpm)	Governor Full load (rpm)	Fast Idle (rpm)	Curb Idle (rpm)	Idle % CO
'79–'81	8736	⅜	2200	4000	3800	1450 ± 50	625–675	1.0–3.0
	7922	⅜	2400	3800	3600	1350 ± 50	525–575	0.5–2.5
	8741	⅜	2000	3400	3200	1350 ± 50	500–550	1.0–2.0
	9072	⅜	2000	3800	3600	1350 ± 50	625–675	1.0–3.0
	8242	⅜	2000	4000	3800	1450 ± 50	625–675	1.0–3.0
	9076	⅜	2400	3800	3600	1350 ± 50	525–575	0.5–2.0
	8245	⅜	2400	3800	3600	1350 ± 50	525–575	0.5–2.0
	8248	⅜	2000	3400	3200	1350 ± 50	500–550	1.0–2.0
	8232	⅜	2200	4000	3800	1350 ± 50	650–700	2.0
	8180	⅜	2200	4000	3800	1300 ± 50	650–700	1.5
	8236	⅜	2400	3800	3600	1350 ± 50	525–575	0.5–2.5
	8235	⅜	2400	3800	3600	1350 ± 50	525–575	0.5–2.5
	8238	⅜	2000	3400	3200	1350 ± 50	500–550	1.5–3.0

MODELS 4150G, 4150EG
International

(All measurements in inches)

Year	Carburetor Number	Fuel Level	Fast Idle Setting (rpm)	Governor Speed No-Load (rpm)	Governor Speed Full-Load (rpm)	Curb Idle Speed (rpm)	Idle Mixture Setting % CO
'80 (Federal)	6803-3	①	2000	3800	3600	650–700	2.0 Max
	7215	①	2400	3800	3600	525–575	0.5–2.5
	7251	①	2400	3800	3600	525–575	0.5–2.5
	6911	①	2000	3400	3200	500–550	1.5–3.0
'80 (Calif.)	7028, 7529	①	②	3800	3600	625–675	0.5–1.5
	7218, 7218-1	①	2400	3800	3600	525–575	0.5–2.5
	7581	①	2400	3800	3600	525–575	0.5–2.5
	7921	①	2400	3800 ± 50	—	525–575	0.5–2.5
'80 (50 States)	7029, 7029-1	①	2400	3800	3600	525–575	0.5–2.5
	6974	①	2000	3400	3200	500–550	1.0–2.0

①Primary ⅜ in., Secondary ⅝ in.

②Mechanical setting-.015–.020 in.

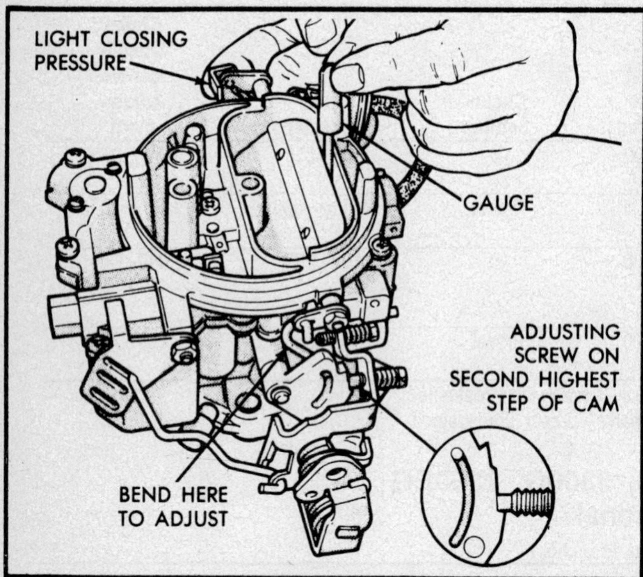

Fast idle cam position adjustment—models 2210, 2210C and 2245 carburetors (© Chrysler Corp.)

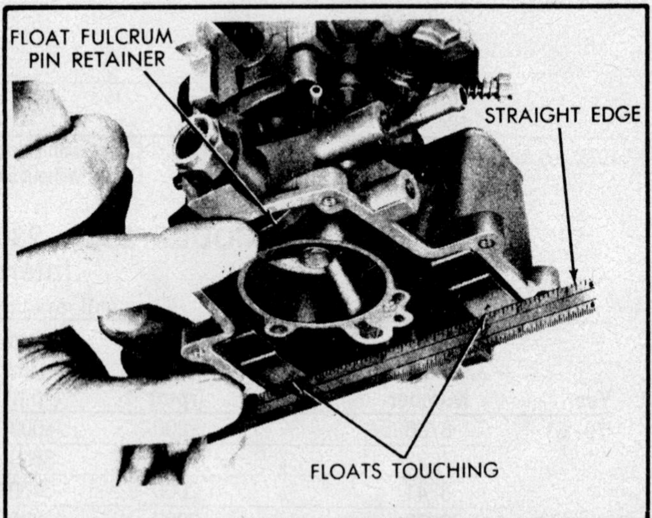

Adjusting the fuel level with the bowl inverted—model 1945 carburetor (© Chrysler Corp.)

Checking float setting—model 1920 one barrel (© Chrysler Corp.)

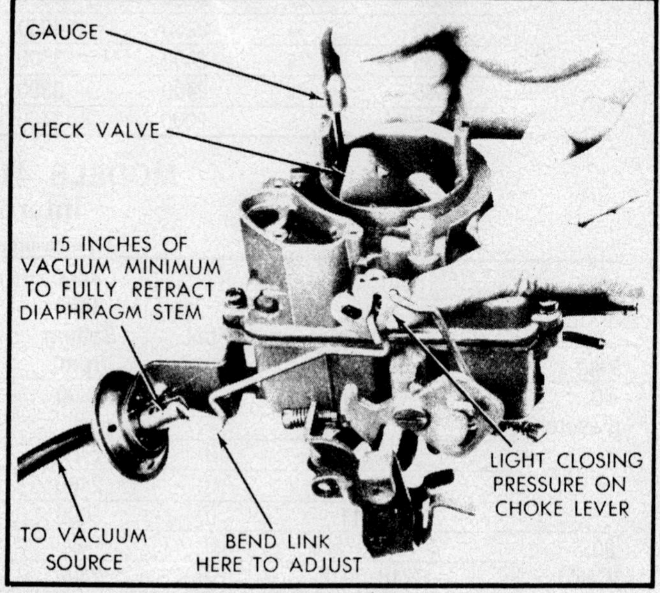

Choke valve initial setting (vacuum kick)—model 1945 carburetor (© Chrysler Corp.)

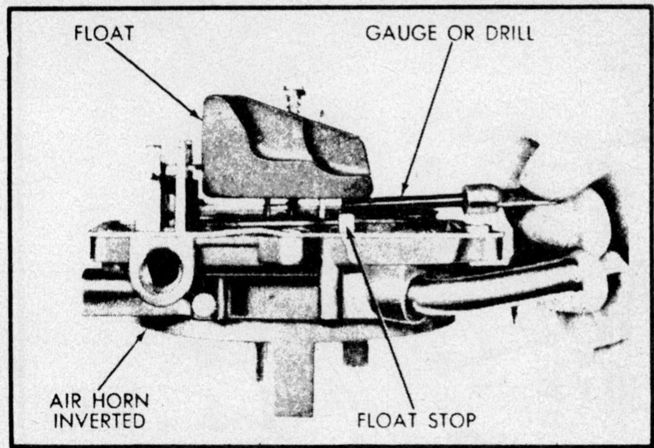

Adjusting the float level—models 2210, 2210C and 2245 carburetors (© Chrysler Corp.)

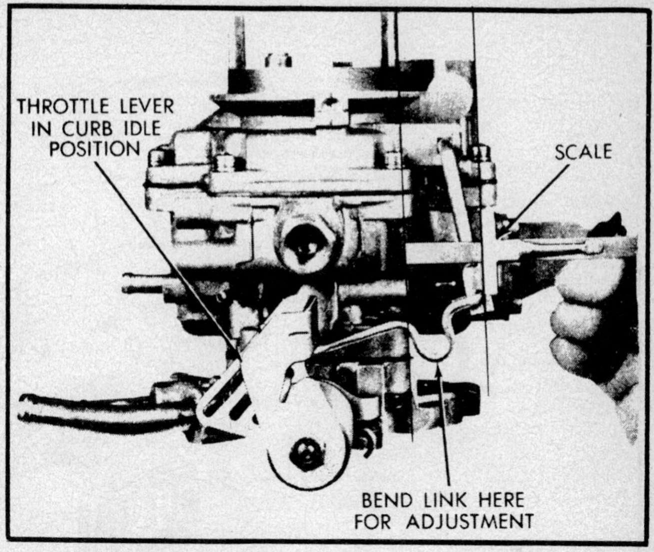

Accelerator pump piston stroke adjustment—model 1945 carburetor (© Chrysler Corp.)

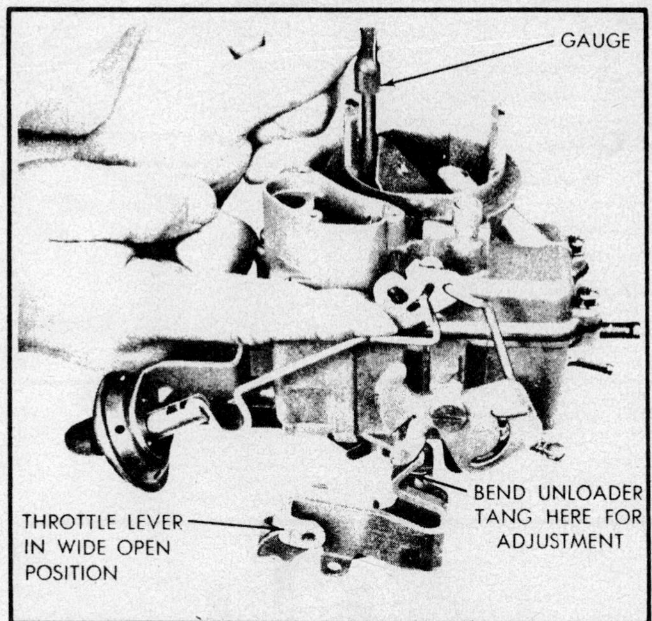

Choke valve unloader adjustment—model 1945 carburetor (© Chrysler Corp.)

Checking the accelerator pump lever clearance—Holley 4150 typical (© Ford Motor Co.)

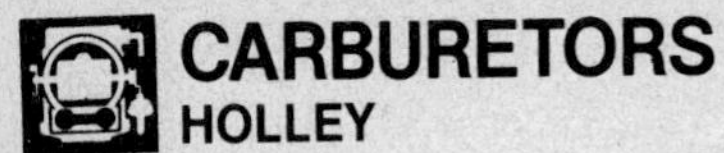

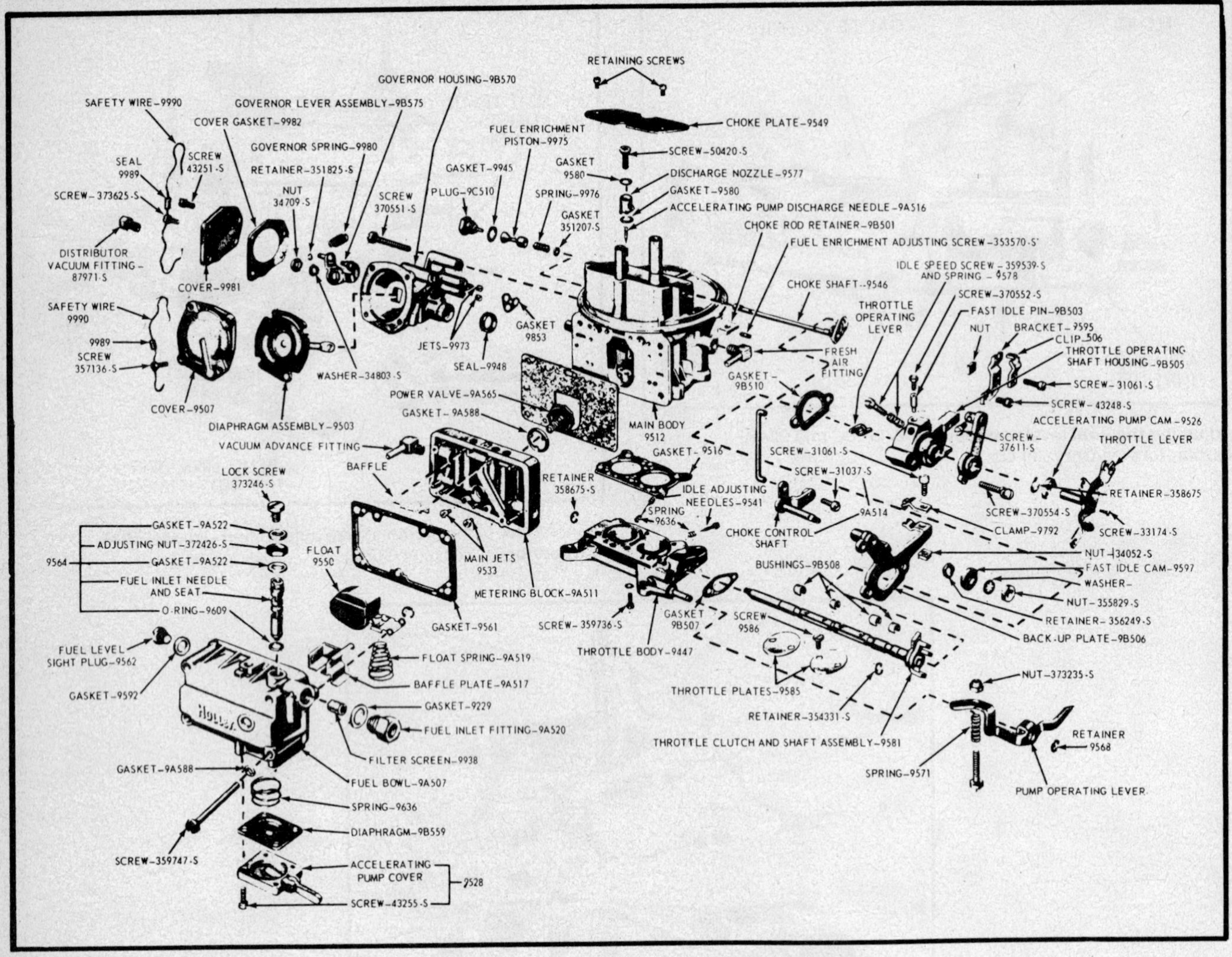

RETAINING SCREWS
GOVERNOR HOUSING–9B570
SAFETY WIRE–9990
GOVERNOR LEVER ASSEMBLY–9B575
COVER GASKET–9982
CHOKE PLATE–9549
FUEL ENRICHMENT PISTON–9975
GOVERNOR SPRING–9980
SCREW–50420-S
SEAL 9989
SCREW 43251-S
RETAINER–351825-S
GASKET–9945
GASKET 9580
DISCHARGE NOZZLE–9577
NUT 34709-S
SCREW 370551-S
PLUG–9C510
SPRING–9976
GASKET–9580
SCREW–373625-S
ACCELERATING PUMP DISCHARGE NEEDLE–9A516
GASKET 351207-S
CHOKE ROD RETAINER–9B501
FUEL ENRICHMENT ADJUSTING SCREW–353570-S
DISTRIBUTOR VACUUM FITTING–87971-S
IDLE SPEED SCREW–359539-S AND SPRING–9578
CHOKE SHAFT–9546
COVER–9981
SCREW–370552-S
THROTTLE OPERATING LEVER
FAST IDLE PIN–9B503
SAFETY WIRE 9990
NUT
BRACKET–9595
CLIP–506
GASKET 9853
THROTTLE OPERATING SHAFT HOUSING–9B505
9989
JETS–9973
FRESH AIR FITTING
SCREW 357136-S
SEAL–9948
SCREW–31061-S
WASHER–34803-S
GASKET–9B510
SCREW–43248-S
POWER VALVE–9A565
COVER–9507
GASKET–9A588
MAIN BODY 9512
ACCELERATING PUMP CAM–9526
DIAPHRAGM ASSEMBLY–9503
SCREW–37611-S
THROTTLE LEVER
VACUUM ADVANCE FITTING
GASKET–9516
SCREW–31061-S
BAFFLE
SCREW–31037-S
LOCK SCREW 373246-S
RETAINER 358675-S
IDLE ADJUSTING NEEDLES–9541
RETAINER–358675
SPRING 9636
9A514
SCREW–370554-S
GASKET–9A522
CLAMP–9792
SCREW–33174-S
ADJUSTING NUT–372426-S
CHOKE CONTROL SHAFT
FLOAT 9550
MAIN JETS 9533
NUT–34052-S
9564
GASKET–9A522
BUSHINGS–9B508
FAST IDLE CAM–9597
FUEL INLET NEEDLE AND SEAT
WASHER
METERING BLOCK–9A511
NUT–355829-S
O-RING–9609
SCREW 9586
RETAINER–356249-S
GASKET–9561
SCREW–359736-S
GASKET 9B507
BACK-UP PLATE–9B506
FUEL LEVEL SIGHT PLUG–9562
THROTTLE BODY–9447
FLOAT SPRING–9A519
NUT–373235-S
GASKET–9592
BAFFLE PLATE–9A517
THROTTLE PLATES–9585
GASKET–9229
RETAINER–354331-S
RETAINER 9568
FUEL INLET FITTING–9A520
THROTTLE CLUTCH AND SHAFT ASSEMBLY–9581
FILTER SCREEN–9938
GASKET–9A588
SPRING–9571
FUEL BOWL–9A507
PUMP OPERATING LEVER
SPRING–9636
DIAPHRAGM–9B559
SCREW–359747-S
ACCELERATING PUMP COVER
9528
SCREW–43255-S

Holley two barrel—typical

UNDERSIDE SURFACE OF AIR HORN
BOTTOM EDGE OF FLOAT SHOULD BE PARALLEL

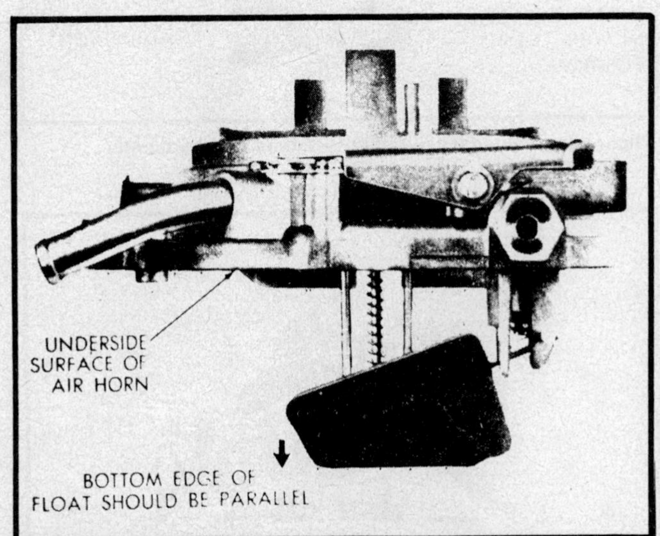

Adjusting the float drop—models 2210, 2210C and 2245 carburetors (© Chrysler Corp.)

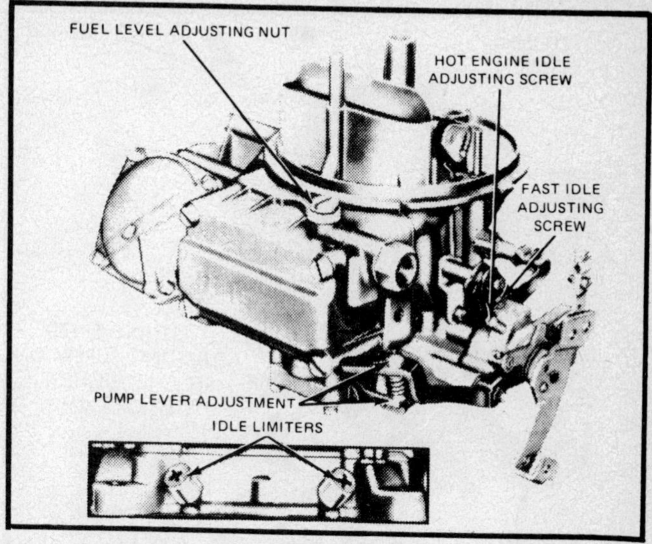

Adjustment location—model 2300 carburetor (© Chrysler Corp.)

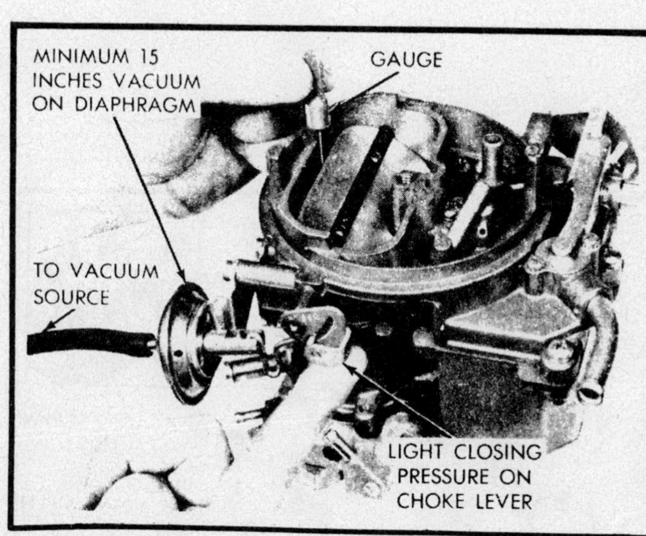

Adjusting the initial choke valve setting—models 2210, 2210C and 2245 carburetors (© Chrysler Corp.)

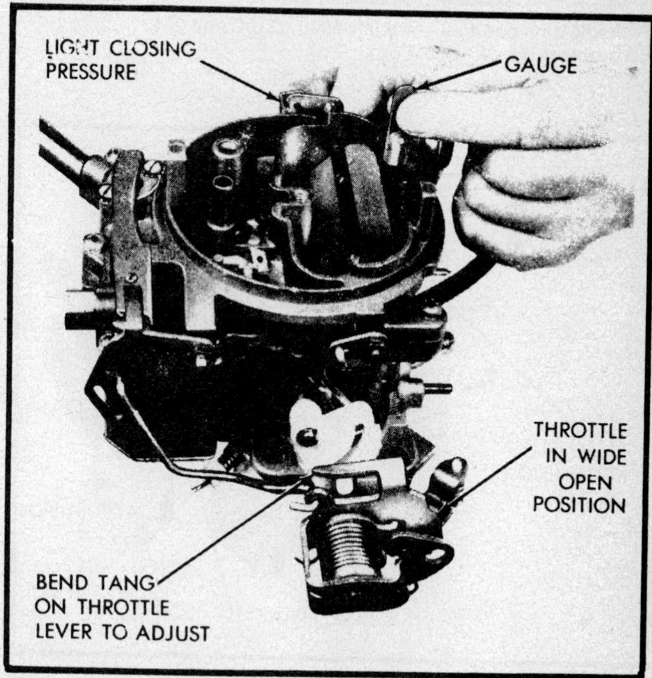

Choke unloader adjustment—models 2210, 2210C and 2245 carburetors (© Chrysler Corp.)

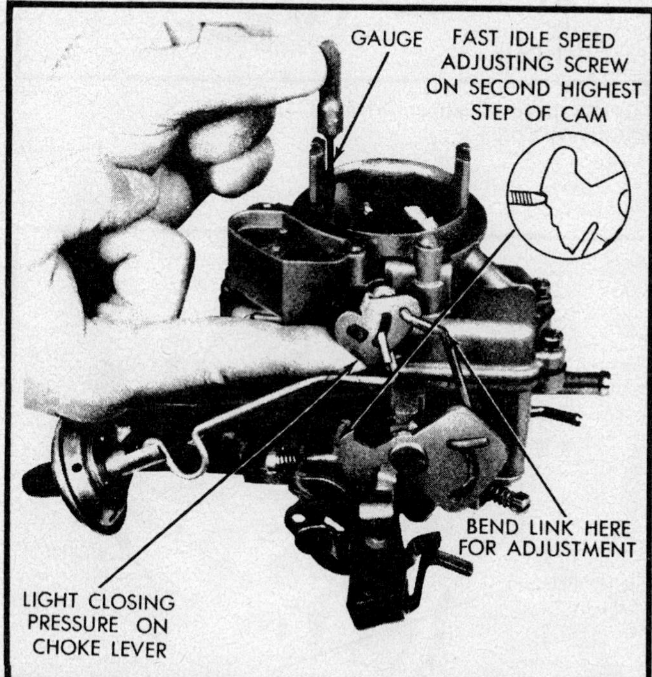

Fast idle cam-to-choke valve adjustment—model 1945 carburetor (© Chrysler Corp.)

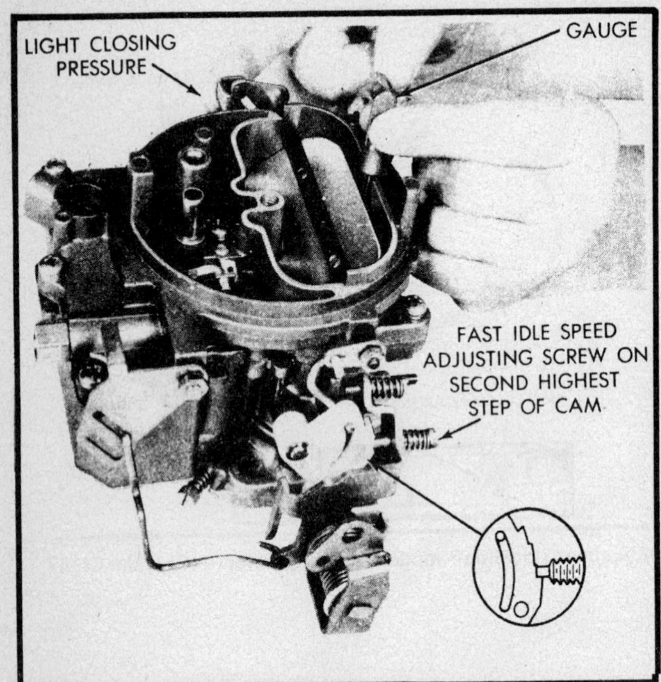

Fast idle cam position—models 2210, 2210C and 2245 carburetors (© Chrysler Corp.)

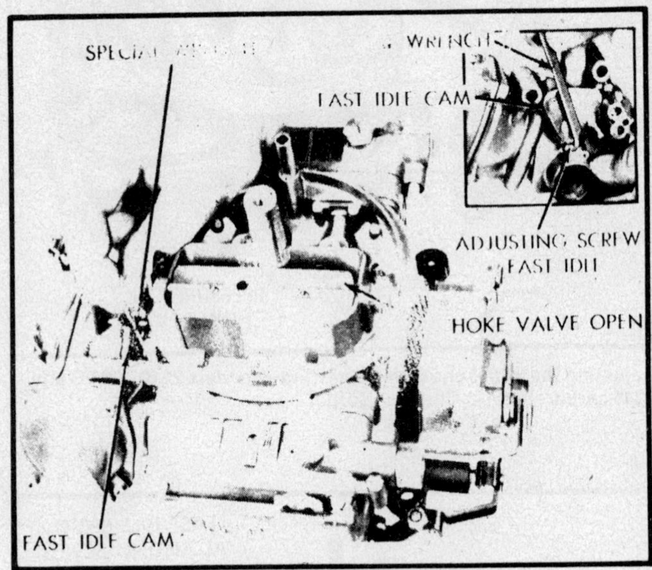

Fast idle speed adjustment—Holley 4150 typical (© Chrysler Corp.)

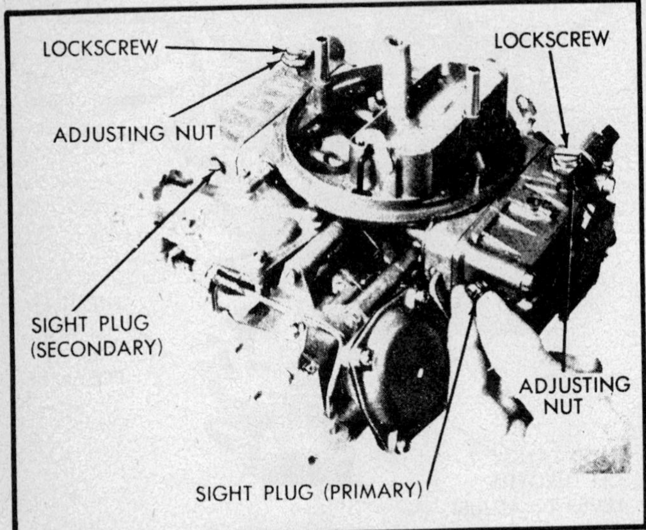

Fuel level sight plug location—Holley 4150 typical (© Chrysler Corp.)

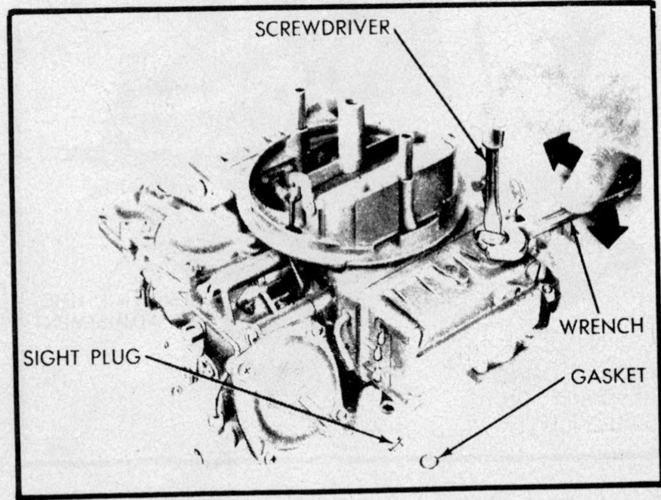

Adjusting the fuel level—Holley 4150 typical (© Chrysler Corp.)

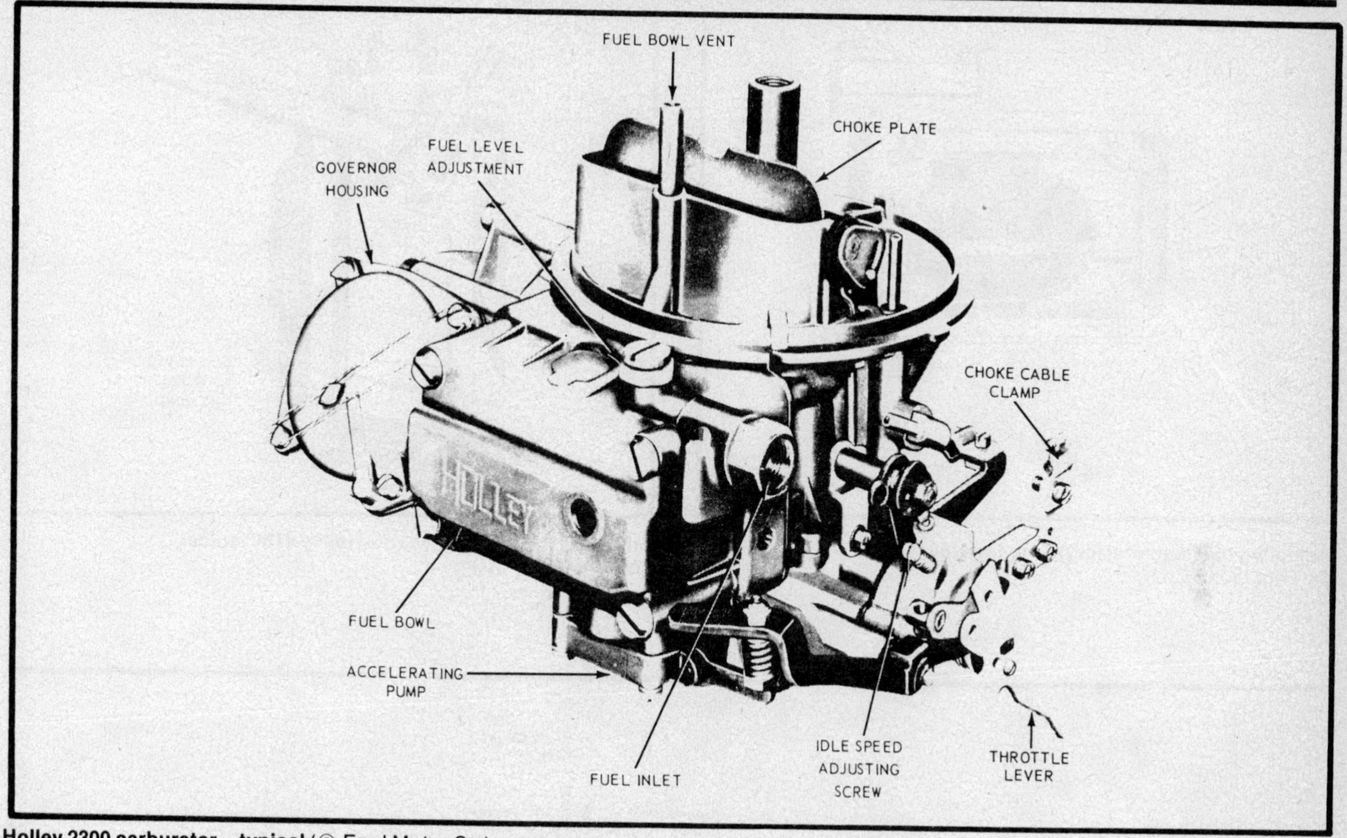

FUEL BOWL VENT
CHOKE PLATE
FUEL LEVEL ADJUSTMENT
GOVERNOR HOUSING
CHOKE CABLE CLAMP
FUEL BOWL
ACCELERATING PUMP
IDLE SPEED ADJUSTING SCREW
THROTTLE LEVER
FUEL INLET

Holley 2300 carburetor—typical (© Ford Motor Co.)

SECONDARY FUEL BOWL
MAIN BODY
SECONDARY THROTTLE OPERATING DIAPHRAGM
PRIMARY FUEL BOWL
ACCELERATING PUMP ASSEMBLY
THROTTLE BODY
GOVERNOR ASSEMBLY

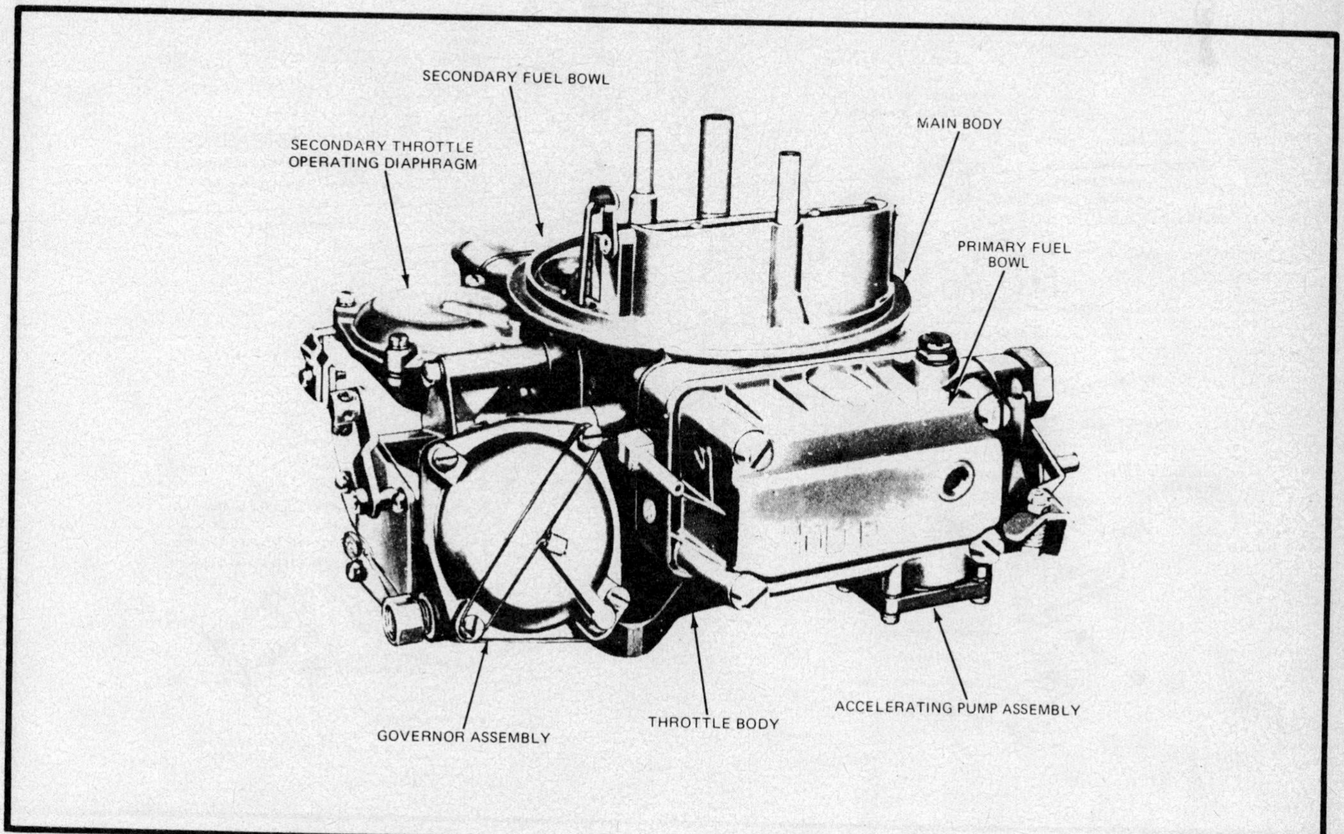

Holley 4150 carburetor—typical (© Ford Motor Co.)

TURN ADJUSTING NUT
UNTIL FLOAT IS PARALLEL
WITH TOP OF BOWL
(HOLDING BOWL UPSIDE DOWN)

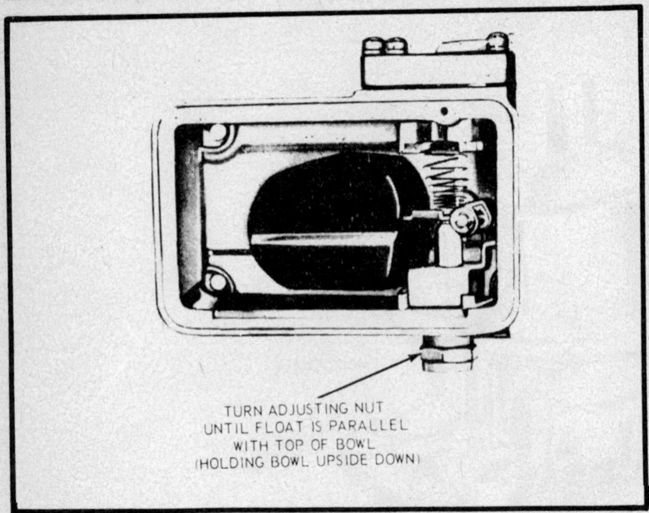

Adjusting the float level (dry)—Holley 4150 typical
(© Ford Motor Co.)

LOCK SCREW
ADJUSTING NUT
FUEL LEVEL
SIGHT PLUG
OPENING

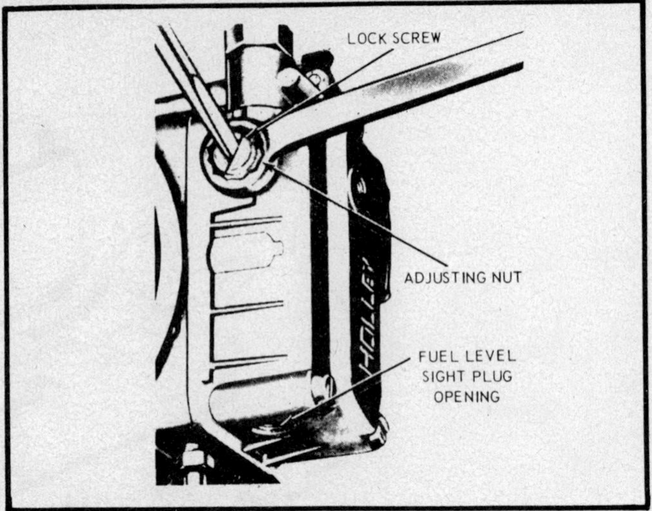

Adjusting the fuel level (wet)—Holley 4150 typical
(© Ford Motor Co.)

DIAPHRAGM
ASSEMBLY
COVER
AIR CLEANER ANCHOR SCREW
SECONDARY
HOUSING
ACCELERATING PUMP DISCHARGE NOZZLE
ACCELERATING PUMP DISCHARGE NEEDLE
DIAPHRAGM SPRING
CHOKE SHAFT
SECONDARY
VACUUM
CHECK BALL
CHOKE ROD PICK-UP LEVER AND BUSHING
FAST IDLE CAM PLUNGER
FUEL LEVEL SIGHT
PLUG AND GASKET
FAST IDLE PIN
GOVERNOR BY-PASS JETS
GOVERNOR SPRING PIN
CHOKE
ROD
GOVERNOR
HOUSING
CHOKE
ROD
SEAL
SECONDARY FUEL BOWL
CHOKE CONTROL LEVER
SECONDARY FUEL BOWL GASKET
GOVERNOR HOUSING COVER
SECONDARY METERING BLOCK
GOVERNOR SPRING
CHOKE PLATE
SPRING
GOVERNOR LEVER
GOVERNOR VACUUM FITTING
FUEL TRANSFER TUBE
BALANCE TUBE
GOVERNOR DIAPHRAGM COVER
O-RING SEAL
WASHER
METERING BLOCK GASKET
PLUNGER
SPRING
GOVERNOR DIAPHRAGM
CLEAN AIR FITTING
FAST IDLE CAM AND SHAFT ASSEMBLY
PRIMARY
METERING BLOCK
MAIN BODY
GOVERNOR HOUSING SEAL
DISTRIBUTOR VACUUM FITTING
POWER VALVE
LOCK SCREW
IDLE LIMITER
THROTTLE BODY-TO-MAIN BODY GASKET
BAFFLE
GASKET
POWER
VALVE
GASKET
THROTTLE OPERATING
HOUSING PLATE
FUEL LEVEL ADJUSTING NUT
FUEL INLET
NEEDLE
AND SEAT
GASKET
SECONDARY
THROTTLE PLATES
SHAFT
BUSHINGS
IDLE
ADJUSTING
NEEDLE
FUEL LEVEL SIGHT PLUG
AND GASKET
FLOAT
WASHER
O-RING
BAFFLE
PLATE
MAIN JETS
IDLE LIMITER
SECONDARY THROTTLE SHAFT
SPACER
FLOAT SPRING
THROTTLE CONNECTING ROD
THROTTLE BODY
THROTTLE SHAFT DRIVER
FILTER SCREEN
FUEL INLET FITTING
THROTTLE
OPERATING LEVER
ACCELERATING PUMP
OPERATING LEVER
PRIMARY FUEL BOWL
PRIMARY THROTTLE
PLATES
HOT ENGINE
IDLE SCREW
DIAPHRAGM SPRING
PRIMARY THROTTLE
SHAFT
DIAPHRAGM ASSEMBLY
ACCELERATING PUMP COVER
THROTTLE
OPERATING HOUSING
THROTTLE
PICK-UP LEVER
ACCELERATING
PUMP CAM

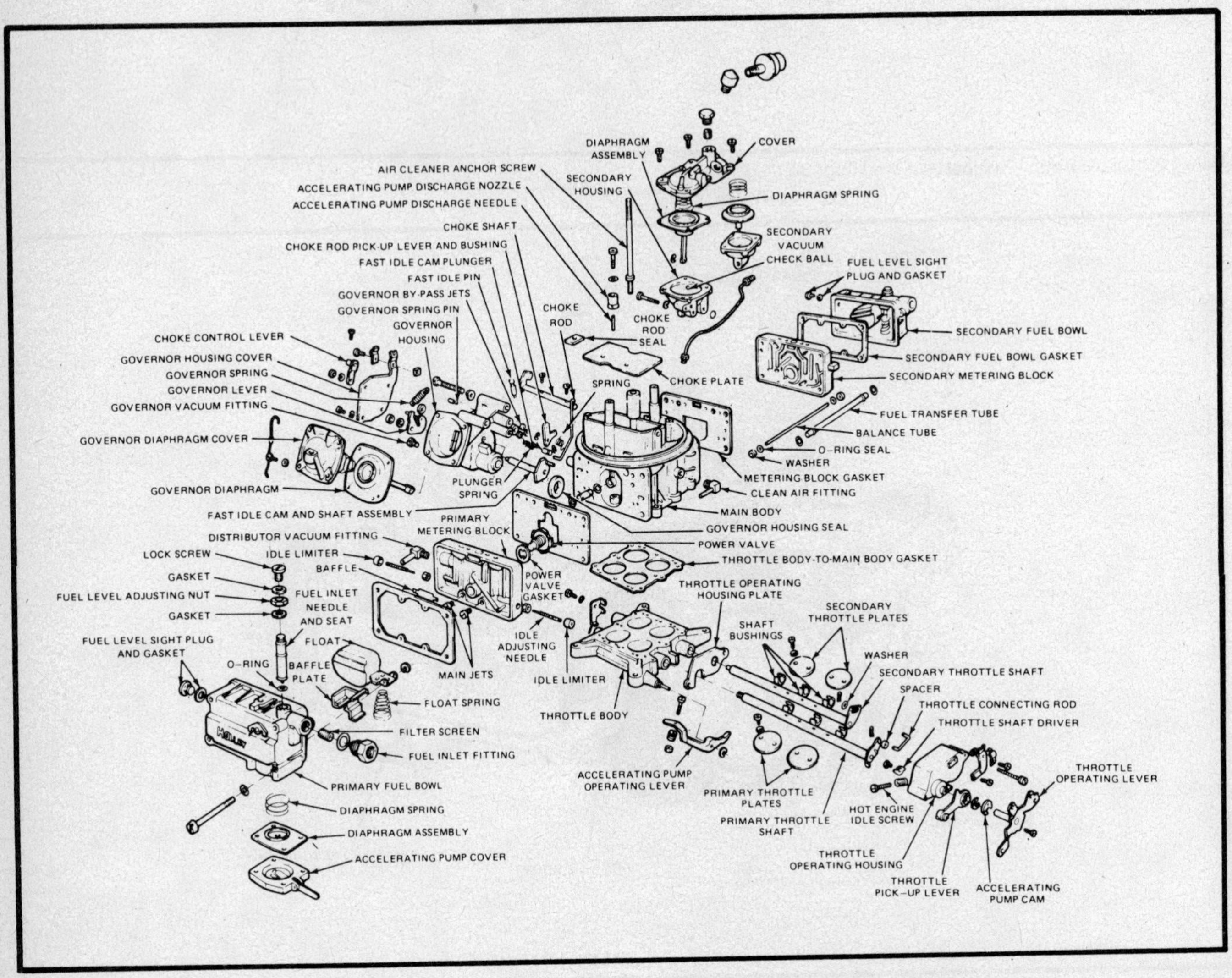

Holley four barrel—typical

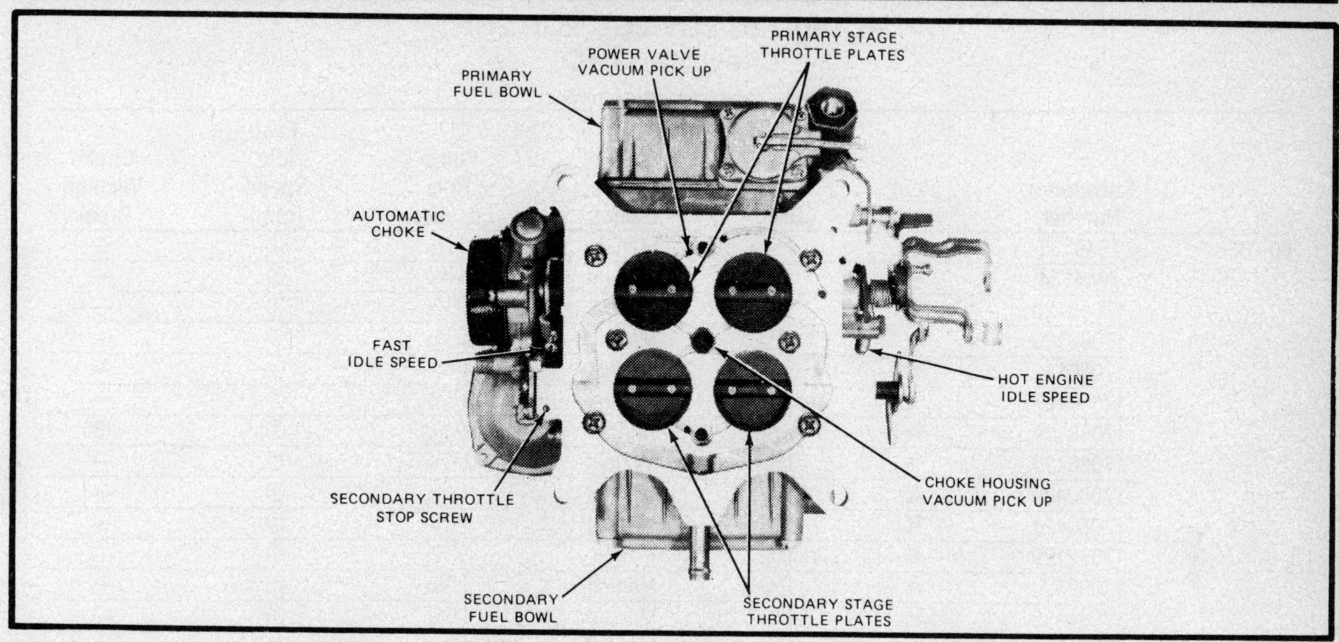

Bottom view—Holley 4160C carburetor (© Ford Motor Co.)

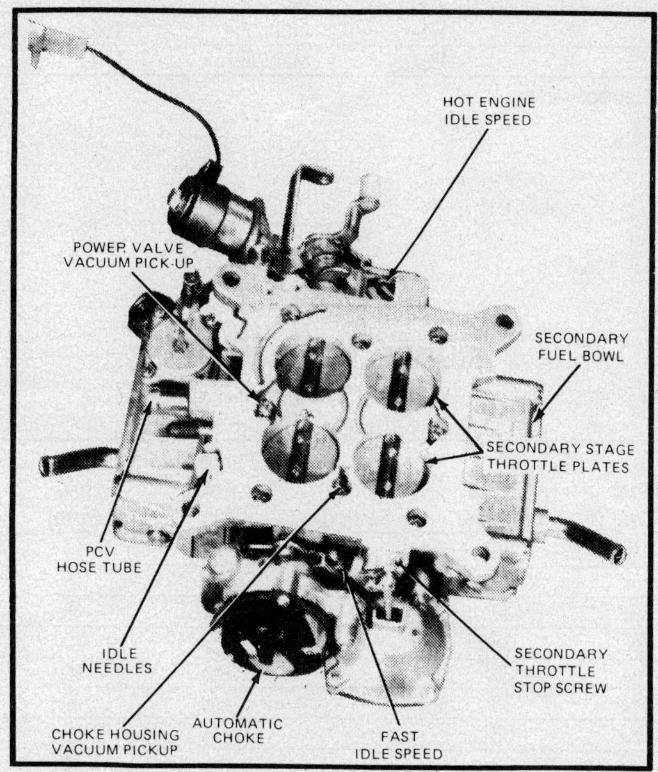

Bottom view—Holley 4180C carburetor (© Ford Motor Co.)

MODEL 2G/2GV/2GC/2GE/2GF
Chevrolet/GMC

(All measurements in inches)

Year	Carburetor Number	Float Level	Float Drop	Choke Setting	Pump Rod Location	Fast Idle Speed (rpm)	Choke Vacuum Break
'80–'86	7044133	11/16	19/32	Manual	19/16	①	—
	7044134	11/16	19/32	Manual	17/16	①	—
	17058120	11/16	19/32	Manual	121/32	①	—
	17080120	5/8	19/32	Manual	121/32	①	—
	17080126	5/8	19/32	Manual	121/32	①	—
	17080127	5/8	19/32	Manual	121/32	①	—
	17080129	5/8	19/32	Index	121/32	①	.130
	17080420	5/8	19/32	Manual	121/32	①	—
	17080423	5/8	19/32	Manual	121/32	①	—
	17080424	5/8	19/32	Manual	121/32	①	—
	17082129	5/8	19/32	Manual	121/32	①	—
	17082420	5/8	19/32	Manual	115/32	①	—
	17084432	5/8	19/32	Manual	115/32	①	—
	17084433	5/8	19/32	Manual	121/32	①	—
	17085120	5/8	19/32	Manual	115/32	①	—
	17085126	5/8	19/32	Manual	115/32	①	—
	17085464	5/8	19/32	Manual	115/32	①	—
	17085465	5/8	19/32	Manual	121/32	①	—

① See Tune-Up Specifications or underhood sticker

MODEL M2MC/M2ME
Chevrolet/GMC

(All measurements in inches ro degrees)

Year	Carburetor Number	Float Level	Choke Unloader	Choke Setting	Pump① Rod Adj.	Fast② Idle (rpm)	Fast Idle Cam Setting	Choke Vacuum Break
'80	17080100	7/16	38°	—	9/32	③	38°	29°
	17080102	7/16	38°	—	9/32	③	38°	29°
	17080142	7/16	38°	—	9/32	③	38°	29°
	17080143	7/16	38°	—	9/32	③	38°	29°
	17080145	7/16	38°	—	9/32	③	38°	29°
'81	17081101	13/32	38°	—	5/16	③	38°	29°
	17081103	13/32	38°	—	5/16	③	38°	29°
	17081142	13/32	38°	—	5/16	③	38°	29°
	17081143	13/32	38°	—	5/16	③	38°	29°
	17081144	13/32	38°	—	5/16	③	38°	29°
	17081145	13/32	38°	—	5/16	③	38°	29°

Note: Specified angle for use with angle degree tool

① Rod installed in the inner hole of the pump lever (nearest the carburetor)

② Manual transmission—1300 rpm in neutral

③ See underhood emissions label for idle speed specifications

MODEL 1ME/1M/1MEF
Chevrolet/GMC

(All measurements in inches)

Year	Carburetor Number	Float Level	Choke Unloader Setting	Choke Setting	Fast Idle Speed (rpm)	Metering Rod Setting	Fast Idle Cam 2nd Step	Choke Vacuum Break
'80	17080009	11/32	.520	②	2400	.090	.275	.400
	17080309	11/32	.520	②	2400	.090	.275	.400
	17080359	11/32	.520	②	2400	.090	.275	.400
'81–'83	17081009	11/32	.520	②	③	.090	.275	.400
	17081309	11/32	.520	②	③	.090	.275	.400
	17081329	11/32	.520	②	③	.090	.275	.400
'84–'86	17081009	11/32	.520	②	③	.090	.275	.400
	17084329	11/32	.520	②	③	.090	.275	.400
	17085009	11/32	.520	②	③	.090	.275	.400
	17085036	11/32	.520	②	③	.090	.275	.400
	17085044	11/32	.520	②	③	.090	.275	.400
	17085045	11/32	.520	②	③	.090	.275	.400
	17086096	11/32	.520	②	③	.090	.275	.400
	17086101	11/32	.520	②	③	.090	.275	.400
	17086102	11/32	.520	②	③	.090	.275	.400

① .090 inches on medium duty truck applications
② Not adjustable
③ See emission label under hood
④ Lower edge of choke valve

MODEL 2SE
Chevrolet/GMC

(All measurements in inches)

Year	Carburetor Number	Float Level	Choke Unloader①	Choke Setting	Pump Rod Adj.③	Fast Idle (rpm)	Fast Idle Cam 2nd step①	Choke Vacuum Break①
'80	17080621	1/8	41°	⑤	9/16	④	17°	22°
	17080622	1/8	41°	⑤	9/16	④	17°	22°
	17080623	1/8	41°	⑤	9/16	④	17°	22°
	17080626	1/8	41°	⑤	9/16	④	17°	22°
	17080720	1/8	41°	⑤	9/16	④	17°	22°
	17080721	1/8	41°	⑤	9/16	④	17°	23.5°
	17080722	1/8	41°	⑤	9/16	④	17°	20°
	17080723	1/8	41°	⑤	9/16	④	17°	23.5°
'81	17081621	3/16	38°	⑤	5/8	④	15°	38°
	17081622	3/16	38°	⑤	5/8	④	15°	38°
	17081623	3/16	38°	⑤	5/8	④	15°	38°
	17081624	3/16	38°	⑤	5/8	④	15°	38°
	17081625	3/16	38°	⑤	5/8	④	15°	38°
	17081626	3/16	38°	⑤	5/8	④	15°	38°
	17081627	3/16	38°	⑤	5/8	④	15°	38°
	17081629	3/16	41°	⑤	5/8	④	15°	38°
	17081630	3/16	38°	⑤	5/8	④	15°	38°
	17081633	3/16	38°	⑤	5/8	④	15°	38°
	17081720	3/16	41°	⑤	5/8	④	15°	38°

MODEL 2SE
Chevrolet/GMC

(All measurements in inches)

Year	Carburetor Number	Float Level	Choke Unloader①	Choke Setting	Pump Rod Adj.③	Fast Idle (rpm)	Fast Idle Cam 2nd step①	Choke Vacuum Break①
'81	17081721	3/16	41°	⑤	5/8	④	15°	38°
	17081725	3/16	41°	⑤	5/8	④	15°	38°
	17081726	3/16	41°	⑤	5/8	④	15°	38°
	17081727	3/16	41°	⑤	5/8	④	15°	38°

①Use angle degree tool or change over to decimal equivalent on the conversion chart at the end of this section

②1 notch counterclockwise

③Measure distance from air horn casting

④See emissions label underhood for exact rpm specification

⑤Riveted choke cap is not adjustable under normal circumstances

MODEL 2SE
Chevrolet/GMC

(All measurements in inches or degrees)

Year	Carburetor Number	Float Level	Choke Coil Lever	Choke Rod①	Primary Vacuum Break	Secondary Vacuum Break	Air Valve Rod	Choke Unloader
'82	17082334	3/16	.085	15°	26°	38°	1°	42°
	17082335	3/16	.085	15°	26°	38°	1°	42°
	17082336	3/16	.085	15°	26°	38°	1°	42°
	17082337	3/16	.085	15°	26°	38°	1°	42°
	17082338	3/16	.085	15°	26°	38°	1°	42°
	17082339	3/16	.085	15°	26°	38°	1°	42°
	17082341	3/16	.085	15°	30°	37°	1°	42°
	17082342	3/16	.085	15°	30°	37°	1°	42°
	17082344	3/16	.085	15°	30°	37°	1°	42°
	17082345	3/16	.085	15°	30°	37°	1°	42°
	17082431	3/16	.085	15°	24°	38°	1°	42°
	17082433	3/16	.085	15°	24°	38°	1°	42°
	17082480	3/16	.085	15°	26°	38°	1°	42°
	17082481	3/16	.085	15°	26°	38°	1°	42°
	17082482	3/16	.085	15°	23°	38°	1°	42°
	17082483	3/16	.085	15°	26°	38°	1°	42°
	17082484	3/16	.085	15°	26°	38°	1°	42°
	17082485	3/16	.085	15°	26°	38°	1°	42°
	17082486	3/16	.085	15°	28°	38°	1°	42°
	17082487	3/16	.085	15°	28°	38°	1°	42°
	17082488	3/16	.085	15°	28°	38°	1°	42°
	17082489	3/16	.085	15°	28°	38°	1°	42°
	17082348	7/16	.085	22°	26°	32°	1°	40°
	17082349	7/16	.085	22°	28°	32°	1°	40°
	17082350	7/16	.085	22°	26°	32°	1°	40°
	17082351	7/16	.085	22°	28°	32°	1°	40°
	17082353	7/16	.085	22°	28°	35°	1°	30°
	17082355	7/16	.085	22°	28°	35°	1°	30°

MODEL 2SE
Chevrolet/GMC

(All measurements in inches or degrees)

Year	Carburetor Number	Float Level	Choke Coil Lever	Choke Rod①	Primary Vacuum Break	Secondary Vacuum Break	Air Valve Rod	Choke Unloader
'83	17083410	3/16	.085	15°	23°	38°	1°	42°
	17083411	3/16	.085	15°	26°	38°	1°	42°
	17083412	3/16	.085	15°	23°	38°	1°	42°
	17083413	3/16	.085	15°	26°	38°	1°	42°
	17083414	3/16	.085	15°	23°	38°	1°	42°
	17083415	3/16	.085	15°	26°	38°	1°	42°
	17083416	3/16	.085	15°	23°	38°	1°	42°
	17083417	3/16	.085	15°	26°	38°	1°	42°
	17083419	3/16	.085	15°	28°	38°	1°	42°
	17083421	3/16	.085	15°	26°	38°	1°	42°
	17083423	3/16	.085	15°	28°	38°	1°	42°
	17083425	3/16	.085	15°	26°	38°	1°	42°
	17083427	3/16	.085	15°	26°	38°	1°	42°
	17083429	3/16	.085	15°	28°	38°	1°	42°
	17083560	3/16	.085	15°	28°	38°	1°	42°
	17083562	3/16	.085	15°	28°	38°	1°	42°
	17083565	3/16	.085	15°	28°	38°	1°	42°
	17083569	3/16	.085	15°	28°	38°	1°	42°
	17083348	7/16	.085	22°	30°	32°	1°	40°
	17083349	7/16	.085	22°	30°	32°	1°	40°
	17083350	7/16	.085	22°	30°	32°	1°	40°
	17083351	7/16	.085	22°	30°	32°	1°	40°
	17083352	7/16	.085	22°	30°	35°	1°	40°
	17083353	7/16	.085	22°	30°	35°	1°	40°
	17083354	7/16	.085	22°	30°	35°	1°	40°
	17083355	7/16	.085	22°	30°	35°	1°	40°
	17083360	7/16	.085	22°	30°	32°	1°	40°
	17083361	7/16	.085	22°	28°	32°	1°	40°
	17083362	7/16	.085	22°	30°	32°	1°	40°
	17083363	7/16	.085	22°	28°	32°	1°	40°
	17083364	7/16	.085	22°	30°	35°	1°	40°
	17083365	7/16	.085	22°	30°	35°	1°	40°
	17083366	7/16	.085	22°	30°	35°	1°	40°
	17083367	7/16	.085	22°	30°	35°	1°	40°
	17083390	13/32	.085	28°	30°	35°	1°	38°
	17083391	13/32	.085	28°	30°	35°	1°	38°
	17083392	13/32	.085	28°	30°	35°	1°	38°
	17083393	13/32	.085	28°	30°	35°	1°	38°
	17083394	13/32	.085	28°	30°	35°	1°	38°
	17083395	13/32	.085	28°	30°	35°	1°	38°
	17083396	13/32	.085	28°	30°	35°	1°	38°
	17083397	13/32	.085	28°	30°	35°	1°	38°
'84	17084348	11/32	.085	22°	30°	32°	1°	40°
	17084349	11/32	.085	22°	30°	32°	1°	40°
	17084350	11/32	.085	22°	30°	32°	1°	40°
	17084351	11/32	.085	22°	30°	32°	1°	40°
	17084352	11/32	.085	22°	30°	35°	1°	40°
	17084353	11/32	.085	22°	30°	35°	1°	40°
	17084354	11/32	.085	22°	30°	35°	1°	40°
	17084355	11/32	.085	22°	30°	35°	1°	40°

MODEL 2SE
Chevrolet/GMC

(All measurements in inches or degrees)

Year	Carburetor Number	Float Level	Choke Coil Lever	Choke Rod ①	Primary Vacuum Break	Secondary Vacuum Break	Air Valve Rod	Choke Unloader
'84	17084360	5/32	.085	22°	30°	32°	1°	40°
	17084362	5/32	.085	22°	30°	32°	1°	40°
	17084364	5/32	.085	22°	30°	35°	1°	40°
	17084366	5/32	.085	22°	30°	35°	1°	40°
	17084390	7/16	.085	28°	30°	38°	1°	38°
	17084391	7/16	.085	28°	30°	38°	1°	38°
	17084392	7/16	.085	28°	30°	38°	1°	38°
	17084393	7/16	.085	28°	30°	38°	1°	38°
	17084394	7/16	.085	28°	30°	40°	1°	38°
	17084395	7/16	.085	28°	30°	40°	1°	38°
	17084396	7/16	.085	28°	30°	40°	1°	38°
	17084397	7/16	.085	28°	30°	40°	1°	38°
	17084410	11/32	.085	15°	23°	38°	1°	42°
	17084412	11/32	.085	15°	23°	38°	1°	42°
	17084425	11/32	.085	15°	26°	36°	1°	40°
	17084427	11/32	.085	15°	26°	36°	1°	40°
	17084560	11/32	.085	15°	24°	34°	1°	38°
	17084562	11/32	.085	15°	24°	34°	1°	38°
	17084569	11/32	.085	15°	24°	34°	1°	38°
'85	17085348	5/32	.085	22°	32°	36°	1°	40°
	17085350	5/32	.085	22°	32°	36°	1°	40°
	17085351	11/32	.085	22°	32°	36°	1°	40°
	17085352	5/32	.085	22°	30°	34°	1°	40°
	17085354	5/32	.085	22°	30°	34°	1°	40°
	17085355	11/32	.085	22°	30°	34°	1°	40°
	17085360	5/32	.085	22°	32°	36°	1°	40°
	17085362	5/32	.085	22°	32°	36°	1°	40°
	17085363	11/32	.085	22°	32°	36°	1°	40°
	17085364	5/32	.085	22°	30°	34°	1°	40°
	17085366	5/32	.085	22°	30°	34°	1°	40°
	17085367	11/32	.085	22°	30°	34°	1°	40°
	17085372	5/32	.085	22°	32°	36°	1°	40°
	17085374	5/32	.085	22°	32°	36°	1°	40°

Note: Specified angle for use with angle degree tool.
① Adjust with fast idle cam on 2nd step.

MODEL E2SE
Chevrolet/GMC

(All measurements in inches or degrees)

Year	Carburetor Number	Float Level	Choke Coil Lever	Choke Rod①	Primary Vacuum Break	Secondary Vacuum Break	Air Valve Rod	Choke Unloader
'83	17083356	13/32	.085	22°	25°	35°	1°	30°
	17083357	13/32	.085	22°	25°	35°	1°	30°
	17083358	13/32	.085	22°	25°	35°	1°	30°
	17083359	13/32	.085	22°	25°	35°	1°	30°
	17083368	1/8	.085	22°	25°	35°	1°	30°
	17083370	1/8	.085	22°	25°	35°	1°	30°
	17083450	1/8	.085	28°	27°	35°	1°	45°
	17083451	1/4	.085	28°	27°	35°	1°	45°
	17083452	1/8	.085	28°	27°	35°	1°	45°
	17083453	1/4	.085	28°	27°	35°	1°	45°
	17083454	1/8	.085	28°	27°	35°	1°	45°
	17083455	1/4	.085	28°	27°	35°	1°	45°
	17083456	1/8	.085	28°	27°	35°	1°	45°
	17083630	1/4	.085	28°	27°	35°	1°	45°
	17083631	1/4	.085	28°	27°	35°	1°	45°
	17083632	1/4	.085	28°	27°	35°	1°	45°
	17083633	1/4	.085	28°	27°	35°	1°	45°
	17083634	1/4	.085	28°	27°	35°	1°	45°
	17083635	1/4	.085	28°	27°	35°	1°	45°
	17083636	1/4	.085	28°	27°	35°	1°	45°
	17083650	1/8	.085	28°	27°	35°	1°	45°
	17083430	11/32	.085	15°	26°	38°	1°	42°
	17083431	11/32	.085	15°	26°	38°	1°	42°
	17083434	11/32	.085	15°	26°	38°	1°	42°
	17083435	11/32	.085	15°	26°	38°	1°	42°
'84	17072683	9/32	.085	28°	25°	35°	1°	45°
	17074812	9/32	.085	28°	25°	35°	1°	45°
	17084356	9/32	.085	22°	25°	30°	1°	30°
	17084357	9/32	.085	22°	25°	30°	1°	30°
	17084358	9/32	.085	22°	25°	30°	1°	30°
	17084359	9/32	.085	22°	25°	30°	1°	30°
	17084368	1/8	.085	22°	25°	30°	1°	30°
	17084370	1/8	.085	22°	25°	30°	1°	30°
	17084430	11/32	.085	15°	26°	38°	1°	42°
	17084431	11/32	.085	15°	26°	38°	1°	42°
	17084434	11/32	.085	15°	26°	38°	1°	42°
	17084435	11/32	.085	15°	26°	38°	1°	42°
	17084452	5/32	.085	28°	25°	35°	1°	45°
	17084453	5/32	.085	28°	25°	35°	1°	45°
	17084455	5/32	.085	28°	25°	35°	1°	45°
	17084456	5/32	.085	28°	25°	35°	1°	45°
	17084458	5/32	.085	28°	25°	35°	1°	45°
	17084532	5/32	.085	28°	25°	35°	1°	45°
	17084534	5/32	.085	28°	25°	35°	1°	45°
	17084535	5/32	.085	28°	25°	35°	1°	45°
	17084537	5/32	.085	28°	25°	35°	1°	45°
	17084538	5/32	.085	28°	25°	35°	1°	45°
	17084540	5/32	.085	28°	25°	35°	1°	45°
	17084542	1/8	.085	28°	25°	35°	1°	45°
	17084632	9/32	.085	28°	25°	35°	1°	45°

MODEL E2SE
Chevrolet/GMC

(All measurements in inches or degrees)

Year	Carburetor Number	Float Level	Choke Coil Lever	Choke Rod①	Primary Vacuum Break	Secondary Vacuum Break	Air Valve Rod	Choke Unloader
'84	17084633	9/32	.085	28°	25°	35°	1°	45°
	17084635	9/32	.085	28°	25°	35°	1°	45°
	17084636	9/32	.085	28°	25°	35°	1°	45°
'85	17085356	4/32	.085	22°	25°	30°	1°	30°
	17085357	9/32	.085	22°	25°	30°	1°	30°
	17085358	4/32	.085	22°	25°	30°	1°	30°
	17085359	9/32	.085	22°	25°	30°	1°	30°
	17085368	4/32	.085	22°	25°	30°	1°	30°
	17085369	9/32	.085	22°	25°	30°	1°	30°
	17085370	4/32	.085	22°	25°	30°	1°	30°
	17085371	9/32	.085	22°	25°	30°	1°	30°
	17085452	5/32	.085	28°	25°	35°	1°	45°
	17085453	5/32	.085	28°	25°	35°	1°	45°
	17085458	5/32	.085	28°	25°	35°	1°	45°

Note: Specified angle for use with angle degree tool

① All models: Lean mixture screw–2½ turns
Idle mixture screw–4 turns

MODEL E4ME
Chevrolet/GMC

(All measurements in inches or degrees)

Year	Carburetor Number	Float Level	Rich Mixture Screw	Idle Mixture Needle Turns	Air Valve Spring Turns	Choke Rod	Front Vacuum Break	Rear Vacuum Break	Air Valve Rod	Choke Unloader	Idle Air Bleed Valve
'83	17083202	11/32	—	3 3/8	7/8	20°	—	27°	—	38°	①
	17083203	11/32	—	3 3/8	7/8	38°	—	27°	—	38°	①
	17083204	11/32	—	3 3/8	7/8	20°	—	27°	—	38°	①
	17083207	11/32	—	3 3/8	7/8	38°	—	27°	—	38°	①
	17083216	11/32	—	3 3/8	7/8	20°	—	27°	—	38°	①
	17083218	11/32	—	3 3/8	7/8	20°	—	27°	—	38°	①
	17083236	11/32	—	②	7/8	20°	—	27°	—	38°	1.756
	17083506	7/16	—	②	7/8	20°	27	36°	—	36°	1.756
	17083508	7/16	—	②	7/8	20°	27	36°	—	36°	1.756
	17083524	7/16	—	②	7/8	20°	25	36°	—	36°	1.756
	17083526	7/16	—	②	7/8	20°	25	36°	—	36°	1.756
'84	17084201	11/32	4/32	3 3/8	7/8	20°	27°	—	.025	38°	①
	17084205	11/32	4/32	3 3/8	7/8	38°	27°	—	.025	38°	①
	17084208	11/32	4/32	3 3/8	7/8	20°	27°	—	.025	38°	①
	17084209	11/32	4/32	3 3/8	7/8	38°	27°	—	.025	38°	①
	17084210	11/32	4/32	3 3/8	7/8	20°	27°	—	.025	38°	①
	17084507	7/16	4/32	②	1	20°	27°	36°	.025	36°	①
	17084509	7/16	4/32	②	1	20°	27°	36°	.025	36°	①
	17084525	7/16	4/32	②	1	20°	25°	36°	.025	36°	①
	17084527	7/16	4/32	②	1	20°	25°	36°	.025	36°	①

MODEL E4ME
Chevrolet/GMC

(All measurements in inches or degrees)

Year	Carburetor Number	Float Level	Rich Mixture Screw	Idle Mixture Needle Turns	Air Valve Spring Turns	Choke Rod	Front Vacuum Break	Rear Vacuum Break	Air Valve Rod	Choke Unloader	Idle Air Bleed Valve
'85	17085202	11/32	4/32	3 3/8	7/8	20°	27°	—	.025	38°	①
	17085203	11/32	4/32	3 3/8	7/8	20°	27°	—	.025	38°	①
	17085204	11/32	4/32	3 3/8	7/8	20°	27°	—	.025	38°	①
	17085207	11/32	4/32	3 3/8	7/8	38°	27°	—	.025	38°	①
	17085218	11/32	4/32	3 3/8	7/8	20°	27°	—	.025	38°	①
	17085502	7/16	—	②	7/8	20°	26°	36°	.025	39°	①
	17085503	7/16	—	②	7/8	20°	26°	36°	.025	39°	①
	17085506	7/16	—	②	1	20°	27°	36°	.025	36°	①
	17085508	7/16	—	②	1	20°	27°	36°	.025	36°	①
	17085524	7/16	—	②	1	20°	25°	36°	.025	36°	①
	17085526	7/16	—	②	1	20°	25°	36°	.025	36°	①

Note: Specified angle for use with angle degree tool
Lean mixture screw-1.304 gauge
Choke stat lever-.120 gauge
① Preset with 1.756 gauge, final adjustment on vehicle
② Preset 3 turns, final adjustment on vehicle

MODEL M4MC/4MV QUADRAJET
Chevrolet/GMC

(All measurements in inches)

Year	Carburetor Number	Float Level	Choke Unloader	Choke Setting	Pump① Rod Adj.	Fast Idle Cam 2nd Step	Choke Vacuum Break
'80	17080201	15/32	42°	②	9/32	46°	23°
	17080205	15/32	42°	②	9/32	46°	23°
	17080206	15/32	42°	②	9/32	46°	23°
	17080224	15/32	42°	②	9/32	46°	23°
	17080290	15/32	42°	②	9/32	46°	26°
	17080291	15/32	42°	②	9/32	46°	26°
	17080292	15/32	42°	②	9/32	46°	26°
	17080295	15/32	42°	②	9/32	46°	23°
	17080297	15/32	42°	②	9/32	46°	23°
	17080503	15/32	42°	②	9/32	46°	26°
	17080506	15/32	42°	②	9/32	46°	26°
	17080508	15/32	42°	②	9/32	46°	26°
	17080523	15/32	42°	②	9/32	26°	23°
	17080524	15/32	42°	②	9/32	46°	23°
	17080525	15/32	42°	②	9/32	46°	23°
	17080526	15/32	42°	②	9/32	46°	23°
	17080226	15/32	42°	②	9/32	46°	23°
	17080227	15/32	42°	②	9/32	46°	23°

MODEL M4MC/4MV QUADRAJET
Chevrolet/GMC

(All measurements in inches)

Year	Carburetor Number	Float Level	Choke Unloader	Choke Setting	Pump① Rod Adj.	Fast Idle Cam 2nd Step	Choke Vacuum Break
	17080527	15/32	42°	②	9/32	46°	23°
	17080528	15/32	42°	②	9/32	46°	23°
	17080213	3/8	40°	②	9/32	37°	30°
	17080215	3/8	40°	②	9/32	37°	30°
	17080513	3/8	40°	②	9/32	37°	30°
	17080515	3/8	40°	②	9/32	37°	30°
	17080229	3/8	40°	②	9/32	37°	30°
	17080529	3/8	40°	②	9/32	37°	30°
	17080225	15/32	42°	②	9/32	46°	23°
	17080212	3/8	40°	②	9/32	30°	24°
	17080512	3/8	40°	②	9/32	30°	24°
'81	17080212	3/8	40°	②	9/32	30°	24°
	17080213	3/8	40°	②	9/32	30°	23°
	17080215	3/8	40°	②	9/32	30°	23°
	17080298	3/8	40°	②	9/32	30°	23°
	17080507	3/8	40°	②	9/32	30°	23°
	17080512	3/8	40°	②	9/32	30°	24°
	17080513	3/8	40°	②	9/32	30°	23°
	17081200	15/32	42°	②	9/32	23°	24°
	17081201	15/32	42°	②	9/32	23°	23°
	17081205	15/32	42°	②	9/32	23°	23°
	17081206	15/32	42°	②	9/32	23°	23°
	17081220	15/32	42°	②	9/32	23°	23°
	17081226	15/32	42°	②	9/32	23°	24°
	17081227	15/32	42°	②	9/32	—	24°
	17081290	13/32	42°	②	9/32	24°	23°
	17081291	13/32	42°	②	9/32	24°	23°
	17081292	13/32	42°	②	9/32	24°	23°
	17081506	13/32	36°	②	9/32	36°	23°
	17081508	13/32	36°	②	9/32	36°	23°
	17081524	13/32	36°	②	5/16③	36°	25°
	17081526	13/32	36°	②	5/16③	36°	25°

Note: Specified angle for use with angle degree tool

① Place the pump arm linkage in the inner hole of the arm, except on carburetors with a 5/16 pump rod height (see ③)

② 1980 and 1981 choke cover are riveted in position and are not adjustable under normal conditions

③ On carburetors with 5/16 pump rod height, place the pump arm linkage in the outer hole of the arm

MODEL M4MC/M4ME QUADRAJET
Chevrolet GMC

(All measurements in inches or degrees)

Year	Carburetor Number	Float Level	Pump Rod Hole	Pump Rod Setting	Choke Rod ① Setting	Air Valve Rod	Vacuum Break Front	Vacuum Break Rear	Air Valve Turns	Choke Unloader	Propane Enrichment (rpm)
'82	17080212	3/8	inner	9/32	46°	.025	24°	30°	3/4	40°	②
	17080213	3/8	inner	9/32	37°	.025	23°	30°	1	40°	②
	17080215	3/8	inner	9/32	37°	.025	23°	30°	1	40°	②
	17080298	3/8	inner	9/32	37°	.025	23°	30°	1	40°	②
	17080507	3/8	inner	9/32	37°	.025	23°	30°	1	40°	②
	17080512	3/8	inner	9/32	46°	.025	24°	30°	3/4	40°	②
	17080513	3/8	inner	9/32	37°	.025	23°	30°	3/4	40°	②
	17082213	3/8	inner	9/32	37°	.025	23°	30°	1	40°	②
	17082220	13/32	inner	9/32	46°	.025	24°	34°	7/8	39°	②
	17082221	13/32	inner	9/32	46°	.025	24°	34°	7/8	39°	150
	17082222	13/32	inner	9/32	46°	.025	24°	34°	7/8	39°	50
	17082223	13/32	inner	9/32	46°	.025	24°	34°	7/8	39°	100
	17082224	13/32	inner	9/32	46°	.025	24°	34°	7/8	39°	50
	17082225	13/32	inner	9/32	46°	.025	24°	34°	7/8	39°	150
	17082226	13/32	inner	9/32	46°	.025	24°	34°	7/8	39°	50
	17082227	13/32	inner	9/32	46°	.025	24°	34°	7/8	39°	50
	17082230	13/32	inner	9/32	46°	.025	26°	36°	7/8	39°	②
	17082231	13/32	inner	9/32	46°	.025	26°	36°	7/8	39°	②
	17082234	13/32	inner	9/32	46°	.025	26°	36°	7/8	39°	②
	17082235	13/32	inner	9/32	46°	.025	26°	36°	7/8	39°	②
	17082290	13/32	inner	9/32	46°	.025	24°	34°	7/8	39°	②
	17082291	13/32	inner	9/32	46°	.025	24°	34°	7/8	39°	②
	17082292	13/32	inner	9/32	46°	.025	24°	34°	7/8	39°	②
	17082293	13/32	inner	9/32	46°	.025	24°	34°	7/8	39°	100
	17082506	13/32	inner	9/32	46°	.025	23°	36°	7/8	39°	50
	17082508	3/8	inner	9/32	46°	.025	23°	36°	7/8	39°	50
	17082513	13/32	inner	9/32	46°	.025	23°	30°	3/4	40°	②
	17082524	13/32	outer	5/16	46°	.025	25°	36°	7/8	39°	20
	17082526	13/32	outer	5/16	46°	.025	25°	36°	7/8	39°	20
'83	17080201	15/32	inner	9/32	46°	.025	—	23°	7/8	42°	②
	17080205	15/32	inner	9/32	46°	.025	—	23°	7/8	42°	②
	17080206	15/32	inner	9/32	46°	.025	—	23°	7/8	42°	②
	17080213	3/8	inner	9/32	37°	.025	23°	30°	1	40°	②
	17080290	15/32	inner	9/32	46°	.025	—	26°	7/8	42°	②
	17080291	15/32	inner	9/32	46°	.025	—	26°	7/8	42°	②
	17080292	15/32	inner	9/32	46°	.025	—	26°	7/8	42°	②
	17080298	3/8	inner	9/32	37°	.025	23°	30°	1	40°	②
	17080507	3/8	inner	9/32	37°	.025	23°	30°	1	40°	②
	17080513	3/8	inner	9/32	37°	.025	23°	30°	1	40°	②
	17082213	9/32	inner	9/32	37°	.025	23°	30°	1	40°	②
	17083234	13/32	inner	9/32	46°	.025	—	26°	7/8	39°	20
	17083235	13/32	inner	9/32	46°	.025		26°	7/8	39°	100
	17083290	13/32	inner	9/32	46°	.025	—	24°	7/8	39°	40
	17083291	13/32	inner	9/32	46°	.025	—	24°	7/8	39°	100
	17083292	13/32	inner	9/32	46°	.025	—	24°	7/8	39°	40
	17083293	13/32	inner	9/32	46°	.025	—	24°	7/8	39°	100
	17083298	3/8	inner	9/32	37°	.025	23°	30°	1	40°	②
	17083507	3/8	inner	9/32	37°	.025	23°	30°	1	40°	②
	17080212	3/8	inner	9/32	46°	.025	24°	30°	3/4	40°	②
	17080512	3/8	inner	9/32	46°	.025	24°	30°	3/4	40°	②

MODEL M4MC/M4ME QUADRAJET
Chevrolet GMC

(All measurements in inches or degrees)

Year	Carburetor Number	Float Level	Pump Rod Hole	Pump Rod Setting	Choke Rod① Setting	Air Valve Rod	Vacuum Break Front	Vacuum Break Rear	Air Valve Turns	Choke Unloader	Propane Enrichment (rpm)
'83	17083220	13/32	inner	9/32	46°	.025	—	24°	7/8	39°	150
	17083221	13/32	inner	9/32	46°	.025	—	24°	7/8	39°	150
	17083222	13/32	inner	9/32	46°	.025	—	24°	7/8	39°	50
	17083223	13/32	inner	9/32	46°	.025	—	24°	7/8	39°	150
	17083224	13/32	inner	9/32	46°	.025	—	24°	7/8	39°	50
	17083225	13/32	inner	9/32	46°	.025	—	24°	7/8	39°	150
	17083226	13/32	inner	9/32	46°	.025	—	24°	7/8	39°	50
	17083227	13/32	inner	9/32	46°	.025	—	24°	7/8	39°	50
	17083230	13/32	inner	9/32	46°	.025	—	26°	7/8	39°	20
	17083231	13/32	inner	9/32	46°	.025	—	26°	7/8	39°	100
'84	17084200	13/32	inner	9/32	46°	.025	—	26°	7/8	39°	②
	17084206	13/32	inner	9/32	46°	.025	—	26°	7/8	39°	20
	17084211	13/32	inner	9/32	46°	.025	—	26°	7/8	39°	②
	17084220	13/32	inner	9/32	46°	.025	—	26°	7/8	39°	80
	17084221	13/32	inner	9/32	46°	.025	—	26°	7/8	39°	80
	17084226	13/32	inner	9/32	46°	.025	—	24°	7/8	39°	30
	17084227	13/32	inner	9/32	46°	.025	—	24°	7/8	39°	30
	17084228	13/32	inner	9/32	46°	.025	—	26°	7/8	39°	80
	17084229	13/32	inner	9/32	46°	.025	—	26°	7/8	39°	80
	17084230	13/32	inner	9/32	46°	.025	—	26°	7/8	39°	20
	17084231	13/32	inner	9/32	46°	.025	—	26°	7/8	39°	40
	17084234	13/32	inner	9/32	46°	.025	—	26°	7/8	39°	20
	17084235	13/32	inner	9/32	46°	.025	—	26°	7/8	39°	80
	17084290	13/32	inner	9/32	46°	.025	—	24°	7/8	39°	30
	17084291	13/32	inner	9/32	46°	.025	—	26°	7/8	39°	100
	17084292	13/32	inner	9/32	46°	.025	—	24°	7/8	39°	30
	17084293	13/32	inner	9/32	46°	.025	—	26°	7/8	39°	100
	17084294	13/32	inner	9/32	46°	.025	—	26°	7/8	39°	30
	17084298	13/32	inner	9/32	46°	.025	—	26°	7/8	39°	30
'85	17084500	12/32	inner	9/32	37°	.025	23°	30°	1	40°	②
	17084501	12/32	inner	9/32	37°	.025	23°	30°	1	40°	②
	17084502	12/32	inner	9/32	46°	.025	24°	30°	7/8	40°	②
	17085000	12/32	inner	9/32	46°	.025	24°	30°	7/8	40°	②
	17085001	12/32	inner	9/32	46°	.025	23°	30°	1	40°	②
	17085003	12/32	inner	9/32	46°	.025	23°	—	7/8	35°	②
	17085004	13/32	inner	9/32	46°	.025	23°	—	7/8	35°	②
	17085205	13/32	inner	9/32	20°	.025	26°	38°	7/8	39°	②
	17085206	13/32	inner	9/32	46°	.025	—	26°	7/8	39°	20
	17085208	13/32	inner	9/32	20°	.025	26°	38°	7/8	39°	10
	17085209	13/32	outer	3/8	20°	.025	26°	36°	7/8	39°	50
	17085210	13/32	inner	9/32	20°	.025	26°	38°	7/8	39°	10
	17085211	13/32	outer	3/8	20°	0.25	26°	36°	7/8	39°	50
	17085212	13/32	inner	9/32	46°	.025	23°	—	7/8	35°	②
	17085213	13/32	inner	9/32	46°	.025	23°	—	7/8	35°	②
	17085215	13/32	inner	9/32	46°	.025	—	26°	7/8	32°	②
	17085216	13/32	inner	9/32	20°	.025	26°	38°	7/8	39°	②
	17085217	13/32	inner	9/32	20°	.025	26°	36°	1/2	39°	②
	17085219	13/32	inner	9/32	20°	.025	26°	36°	1/2	39°	②
	17085220	13/32	outer	3/8	20°	.025	—	26°	7/8	32°	75
	17085221	13/32	outer	3/8	20°	.025	—	26°	7/8	32°	75

MODEL M4MC/M4ME QUADRAJET
Chevrolet GMC

(All measurements in inches or degrees)

Year	Carburetor Number	Float Level	Pump Rod Hole	Pump Rod Setting	Choke Rod① Setting	Air Valve Rod	Vacuum Break Front	Vacuum Break Rear	Air Valve Turns	Choke Unloader	Propane Enrichment (rpm)
'85	17085222	13/32	inner	9/32	20°	.025	26°	36°	1/2	39°	20
	17085223	13/32	outer	3/8	20°	.025	26°	36°	1/2	39°	50
	17085224	13/32	inner	9/32	20°	.025	26°	36°	1/2	39°	20
	17085225	13/32	outer	3/8	20°	.025	26°	36°	1/2	39°	50
	17085226	13/32	inner	9/32	20°	.025	—	24°	7/8	32°	20
	17085227	13/32	inner	9/32	20°	.025	—	24°	7/8	32°	20
	17085228	13/32	inner	9/32	46°	.025	—	24°	7/8	39°	30
	17085229	13/32	inner	9/32	46°	.025	—	24°	7/8	39°	30
	17085230	13/32	inner	9/32	20°	.025	—	26°	7/8	32°	20
	17085231	13/32	inner	9/32	20°	.025	—	26°	7/8	32°	40
	17085235	13/32	inner	9/32	46°	.025	—	26°	7/8	39°	80
	17085238	13/32	outer	3/8	20°	.025	—	26°	7/8	32°	75
	17085239	13/32	outer	3/8	20°	.025	—	26°	7/8	32°	75
	17085290	13/32	inner	9/32	46°	.025	—	24°	7/8	39°	30
	17085291	13/32	outer	3/8	46°	.025	—	26°	7/8	39°	100
	17085292	13/32	inner	9/32	46°	.025	—	24°	7/8	39°	30
	17085293	13/32	outer	3/8	46°	.025	—	26°	7/8	39°	100
	17085294	13/32	inner	9/32	46°	.025	—	26°	7/8	39°	②
	17085298	13/32	inner	9/32	46°	.025	—	26°	7/8	39°	②

Note: Specified angle for use with angle degree tool. Choke coil lever setting is .120 in. for all carburetors.

① Second step of fast idle cam
② See Underhood Specifications sticker

QUADRAJET MODELS
Dodge/Plymouth

Year	Carburetor Number	Float Level	Air Valve Spring Turns	Fast Idle cam	Choke Rod	Vacuum Kick	Air Valve Rod	Choke Unloader	Propane rpm
'85	1785408	13/32	1/2	20°	.143	27°①	.025	38°②	800
	1785409	13/32	5/8	20°	.143	27°①	.025	38°②	750
	1785415	13/32	1/2	20°	.143	27°①	.025	38°②	800
	1785416	13/32	3/4	20°	.143	27°①	.025	38°②	800

Note: Specified angle for use with angle gauge tool

① Plug gauge-.214 in.
② Plug gauge-.345 in.

MODEL 2SE/E2SE
Jeep

(All measurements in inches or degrees)

Year	Carburetor Number	Float Level	Pump Stem Height	Fast② Idle Cam	Fast Idle (rpm)	Air① Valve Link	Primary Vacuum Break	Choke Unloader	Choke Setting
'81	17081790	.208	.128	25°	2400	2°	19°	32°	③
	17081791	.256	.128	25°	2600	2°	19°	32°	③
	17081796	.208	.128	25°	2400	2°	—	19°	③
	17081797	.208	.128	25°	2600	2°	—	19°	③
'82	17082380	.169	1.28	18°	2400	2°	21°	34°	③
	17082381	.169	1.28	18°	2400	2°	21°	34°	③
	17082389	.169	.128	18°	2400	2°	19°	34°	③

Note: Specified angle for use with angle degree tool

①Maximum degree setting
②2nd step on cam
③Tamper resistant—riveted cover

MODEL 2SE/E2SE
Jeep

(All measurements in inches or degrees)

Year	Carburetor Number	Float Level	Air Valve Windup	Choke Coil Lever	Fast Idle Cam 2nd Step	Primary Vacuum Break	Secondary Vacuum Break	Air Valve Rod	Choke Unloader
'83–'84	17084581	5/32	1	.085	22°	26°	32°	1°	40°
	17084580	5/32	1	.085	22°	26°	32°	1°	40°
	17084582	5/32	1	.085	22°	26°	32°	1°	40°
	17084583	5/32	1	.085	22°	26°	32°	1°	40°
	17084384	1/8	1	.085	22°	25°	30°	1°	40°
'85–'86	17085380	5/32	1	.085	22°	26°	32°	1°	40°
	17085381	5/32	1	.085	22°	26°	32°	1°	40°
	17085382	5/32	1	.085	22°	26°	32°	1°	40°
	17085383	5/32	1	.085	22°	26°	32°	1°	40°
	17085384	1/8	1	.085	22°	25°	30°	1°	40°

Note: Specified angle for use with angle degree tool

MODEL E2SE
Jeep

(All measurements in inches)

Year	Carburetor Number	Float Level	Pump Stem Height	Fast Idle Cam 2nd step	Fast Idle (rpm)	Air ① Valve Link	Choke Unloader	Choke Setting
'81	170811796	.208	.128	25°	2400	2°	19°	②
	170811797	.208	.128	25°	2600	2°	19°	②
'82	17082389 ③	.169	.128	18°	2400	2°	34°	②

① Maximum degree setting
② Tamper resistant—Riveted choke cover
③ Primary vacuum break setting is 19°.

MODEL E2SE

(All measurements in inches)

Year	Carburetor Number	Float Level	Air Valve Windup	Choke Coil Lever	Fast Idle Cam 2nd Step	Primary Vacuum Break	Secondary Vacuum Break	Air Valve Rod	Choke Unloader
'83	17084384	1/8	1	.085	22°	25°	30°	1°	40°

DCH3HO

(All measurements in inches)

Float Needle Valve Stroke	Primary Throttle Valve Adjustment	Secondary Throttle Opening Point	Kick Lever Adjustment
.059	.050–.059①	.24–30	②

① Applies to manual trans. automatic trans- .059–.069

② Zero clearance between kick lever screw and return plate—throttle fully closed.

MODEL DCH340
Chevrolet S-10

(All measurements in inches)

Float Needle Valve Stroke	Primary Throttle Valve Adjustment	Secondary Throttle Opening Point	Kick Lever Adjustment
.059	.050–.059①	.24–.30	②

① Applies to manual trans. automatic trans- .059–.069

② Zero clearance between kick lever screw and return plate—throttle fully closed.

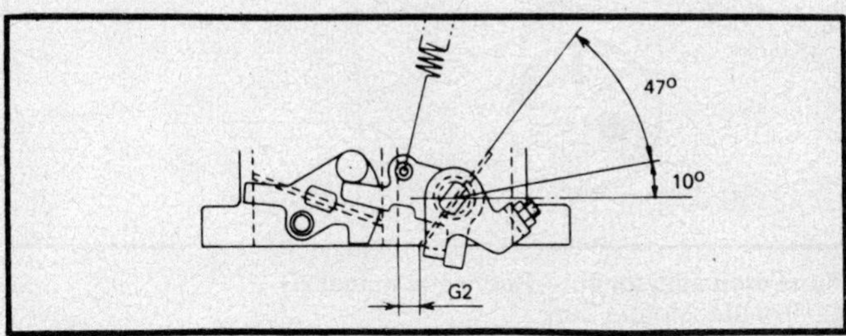

Secondary throttle opening point clearance—DCH340

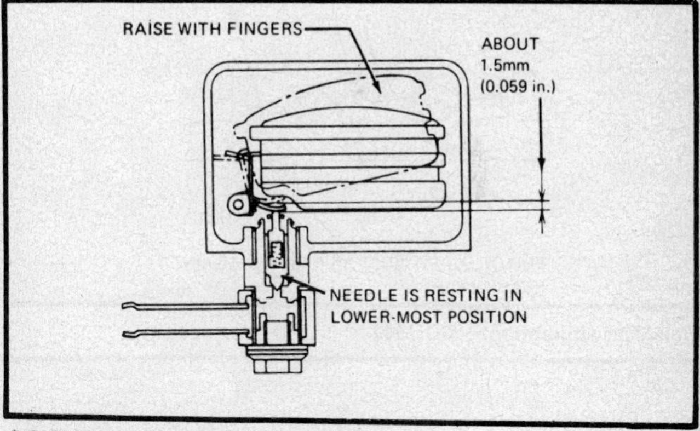

DCH340 needle valve stroke adjustment

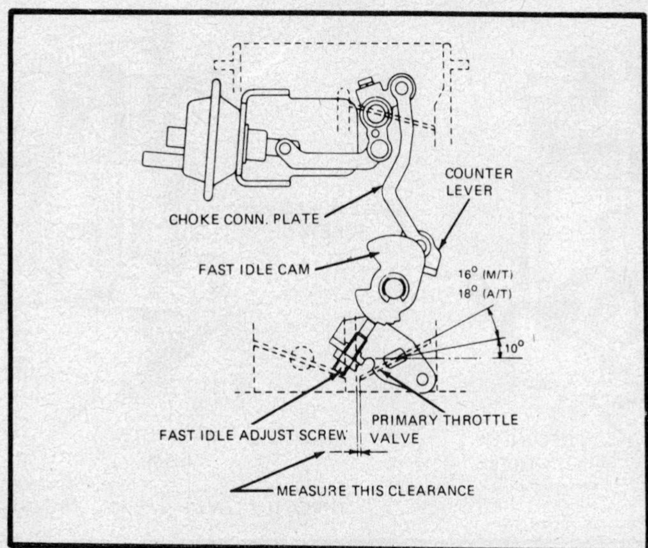

Primary throttle valve adjustment—DCH340

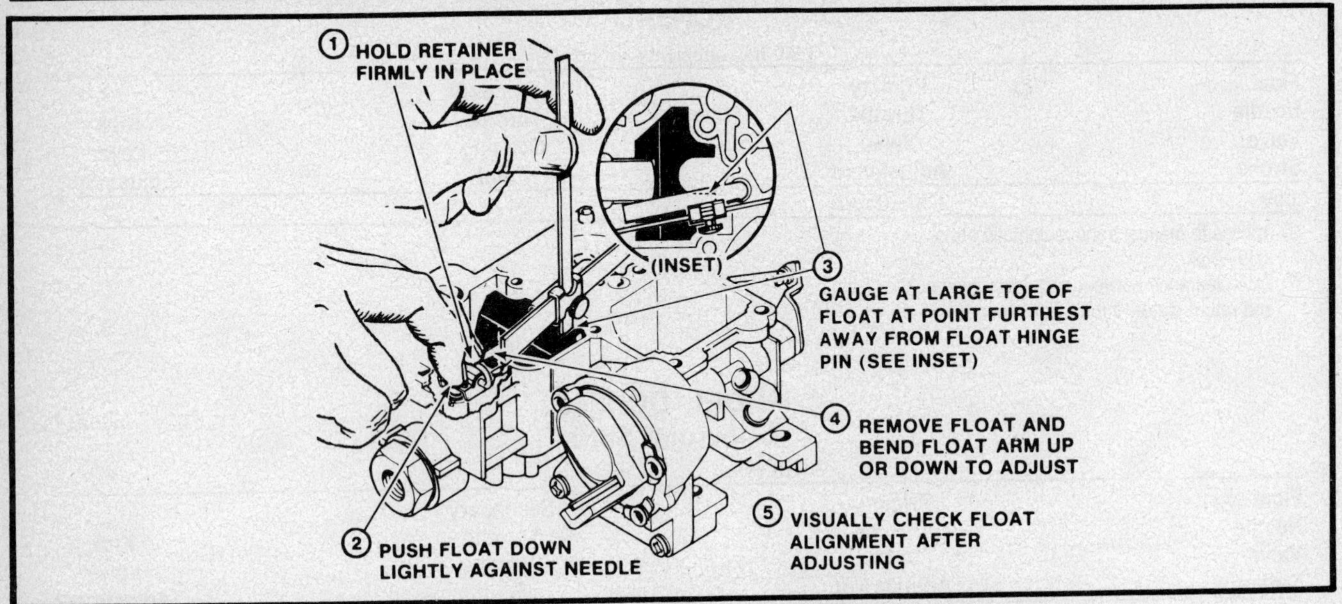

Setting float level—model 2SE carburetor (© General Motors Corp.)

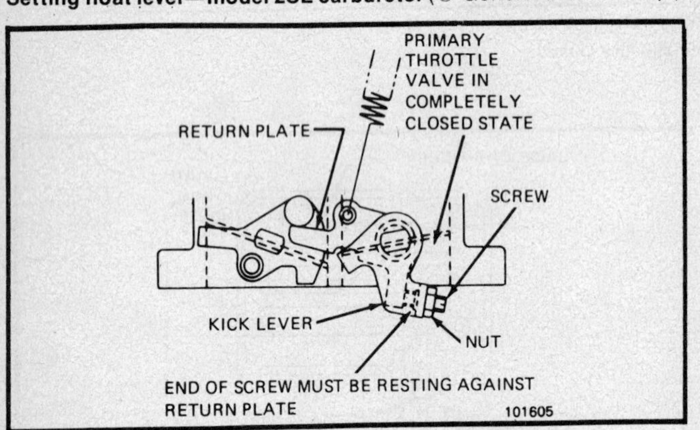

Kick lever adjustment—DCH340

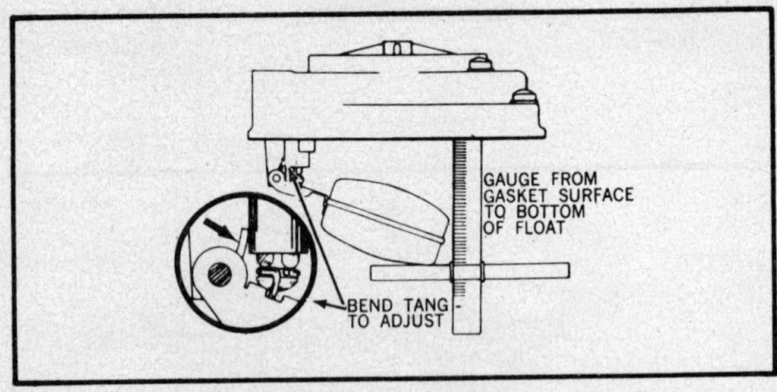

Float drop adjustment—Rochester model 2G (© General Motors Corp.)

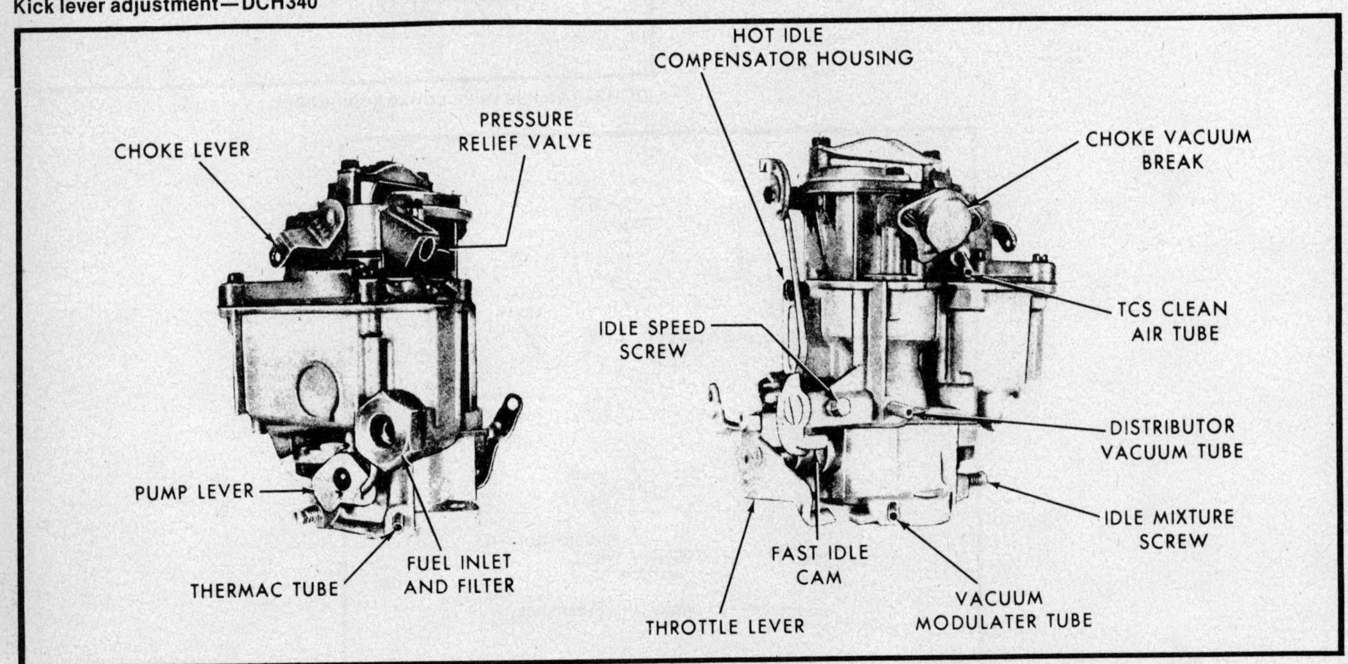

Rochester Monojet® carburetor—typical (© General Motors Corp.)

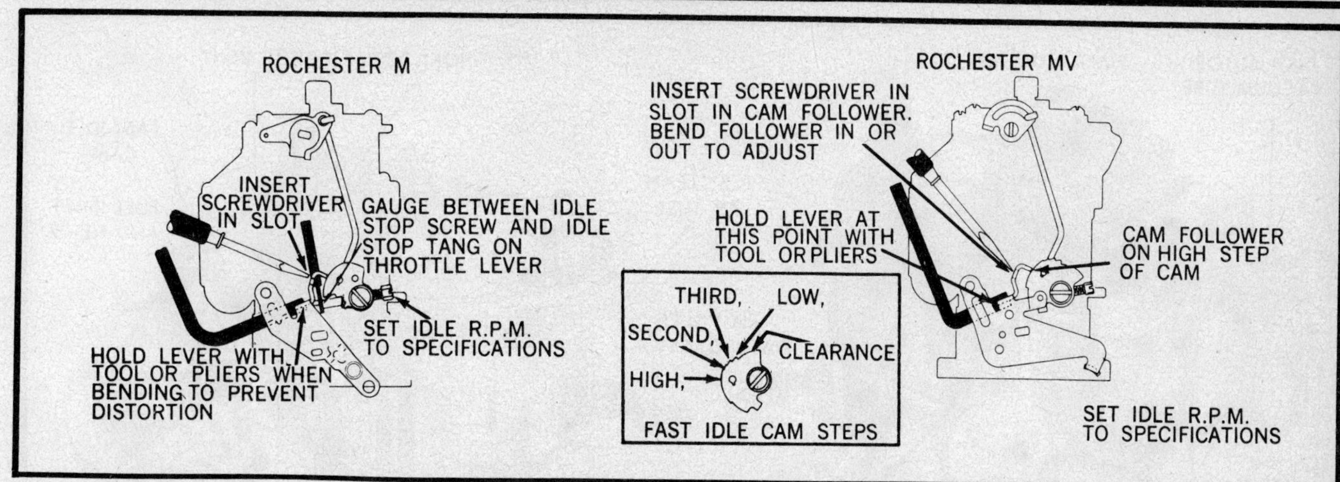

Fast idle adjustment—Monojet® carburetor (© General Motors Corp.)

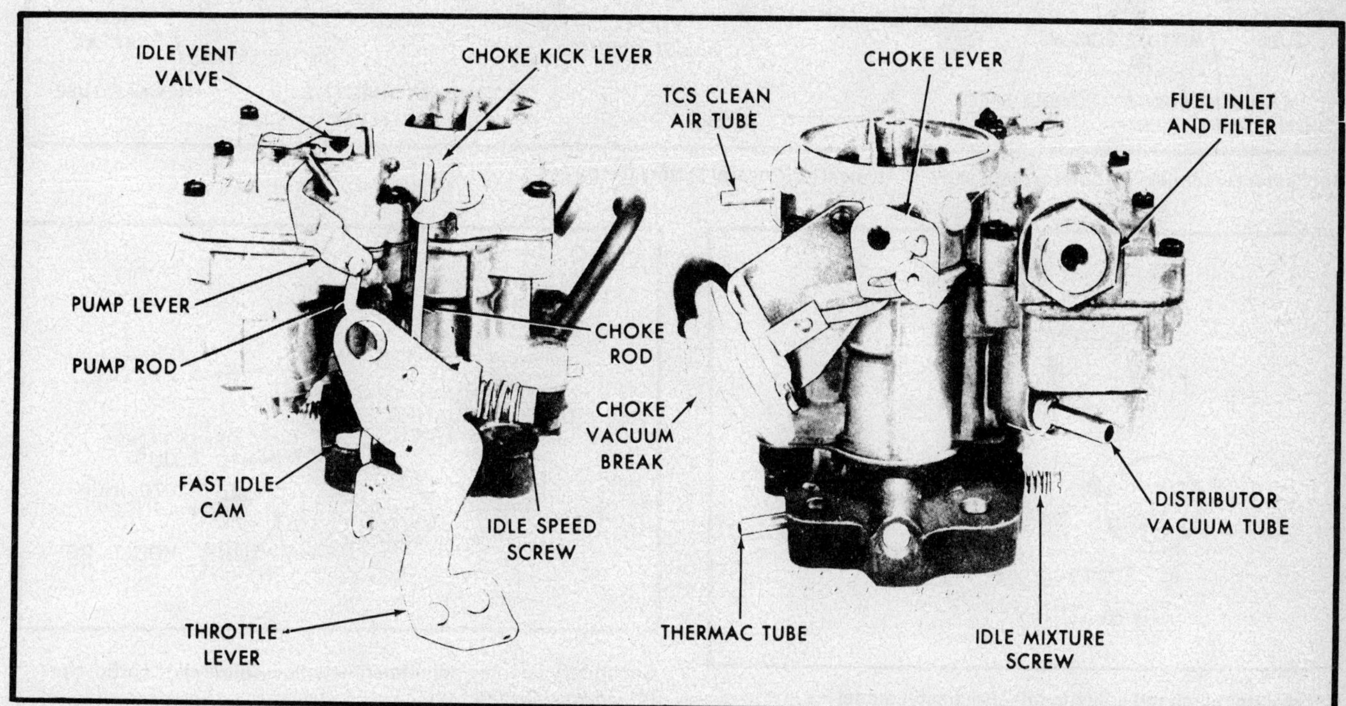

Rochester model 2GV—typical (© General Motors Corp.)

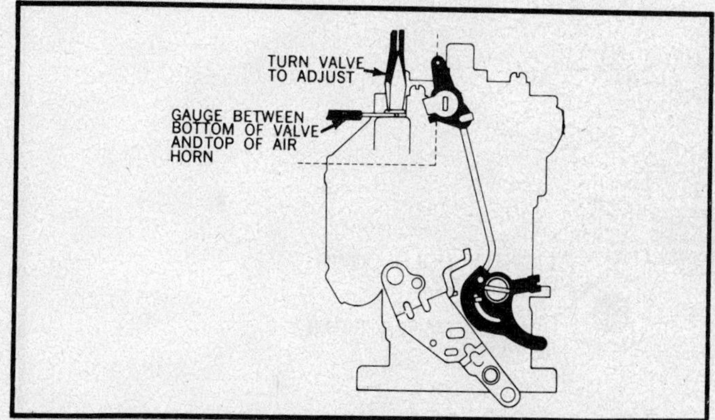

Idle vent adjustment—Monojet® carburetor
(© General Motors Corp.)

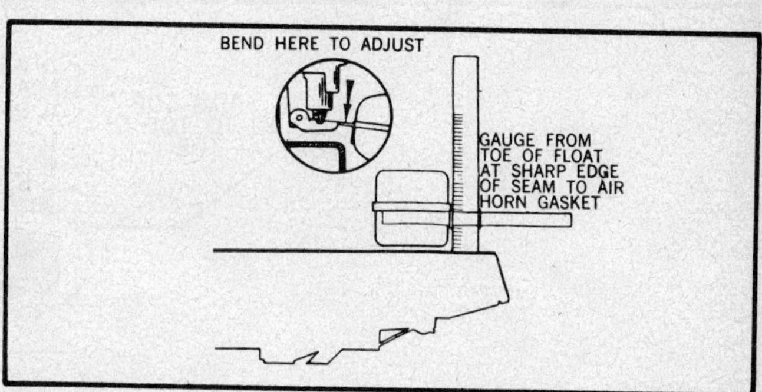

Float level adjustment—Rochester model 2G
(© General Motors Corp.)

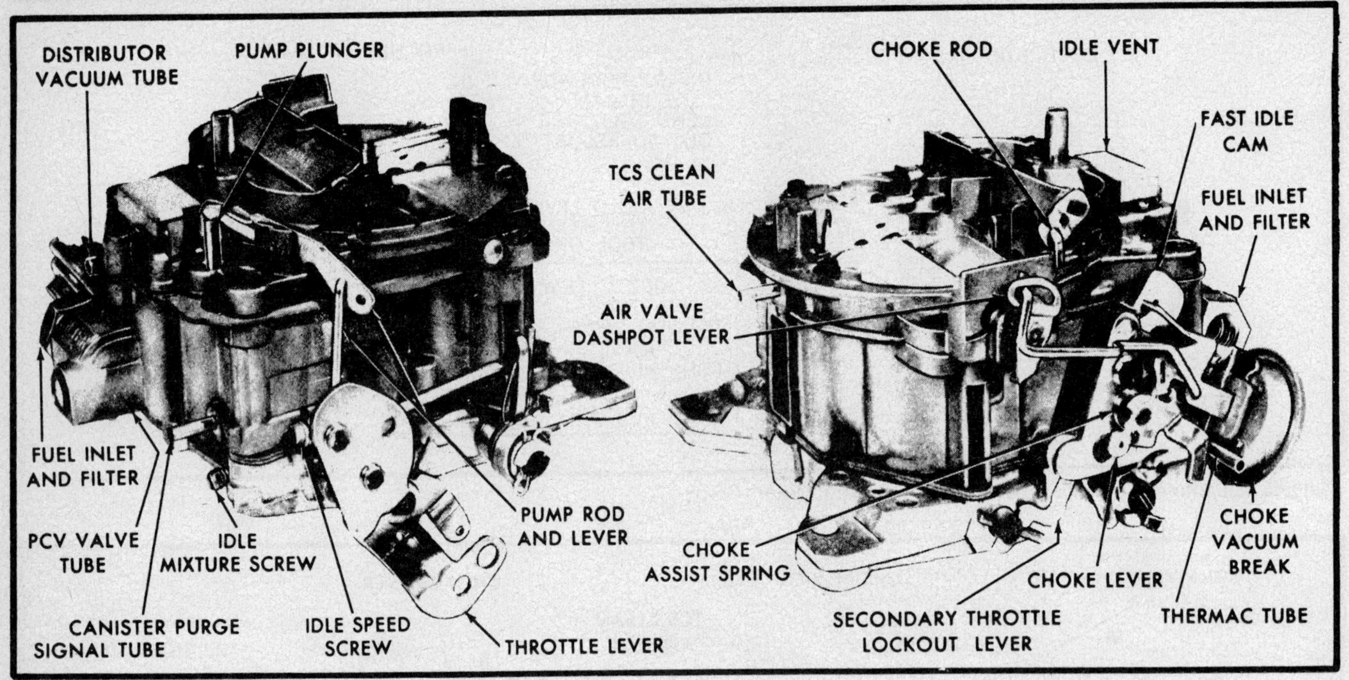

Rochester Quadrajet® carburetor (4MV shown)—typical (© General Motors Corp.)

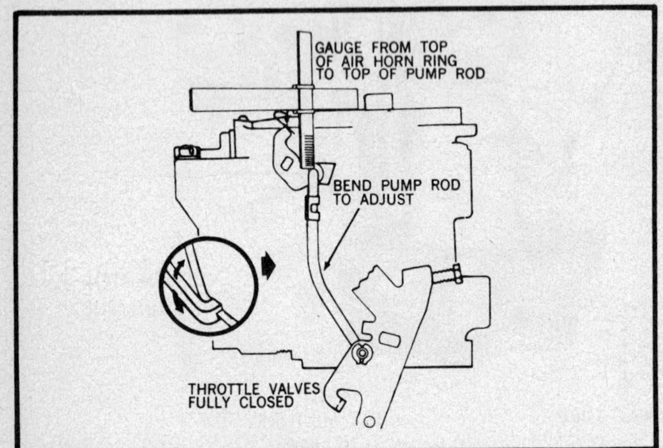

Accelerator pump rod adjustment—Rochester model 2G

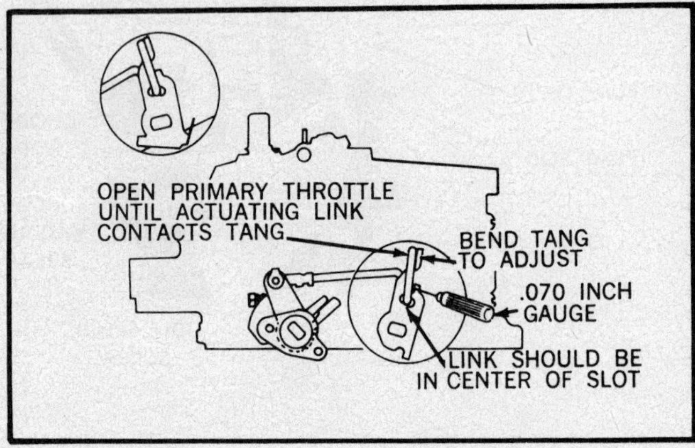

Secondary opening adjustment—typical Quadrajet® carburetor (© General Motors Corp.)

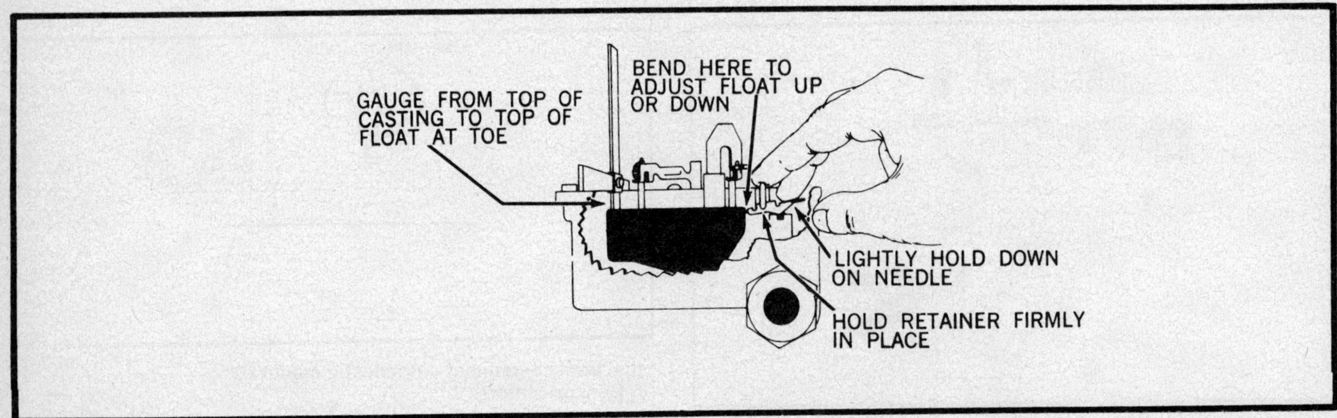

Float level adjustment—Monojet® carburetor (© General Motors Corp.)

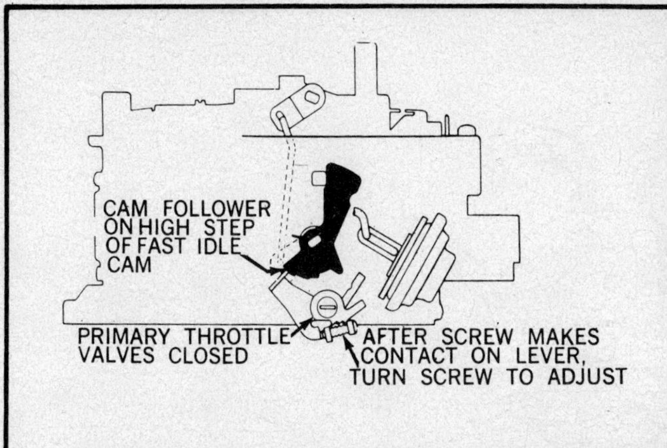

Fast idle adjustment—typical Quadrajet® carburetor
(© General Motors Corp.)

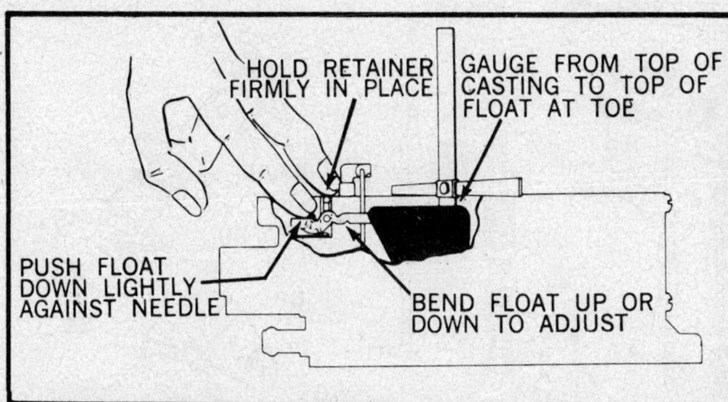

Float level adjustment—typical Quadrajet® carburetor
(© General Motors Corp.)

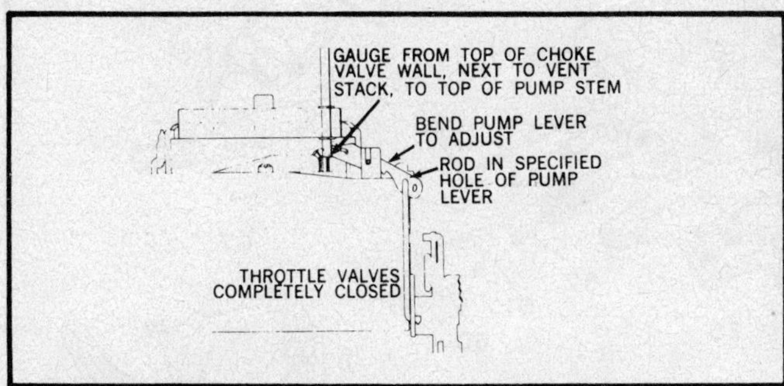

Pump rod adjustment—typical Quadrajet® carburetor
(© General Motors Corp.)

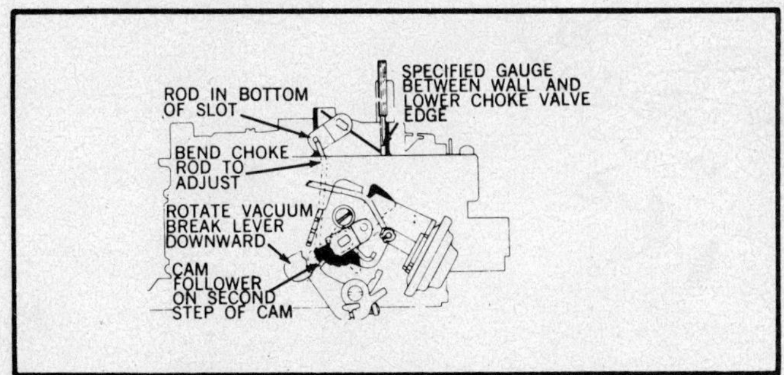

Choke rod adjustment—typical Quadrajet® carburetor
(© General Motors Corp.)

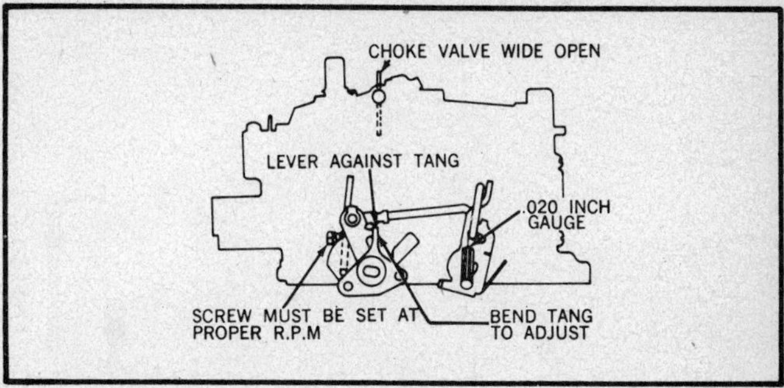

Secondary closing adjustment—typical Quadrajet® carburetor
(© General Motors Corp.)

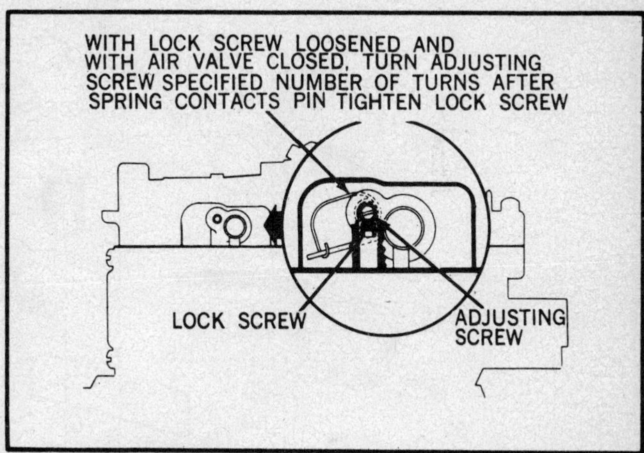

Air valve spring adjustment—typical Quadrajet® carburetor
(© General Motors Corp.)

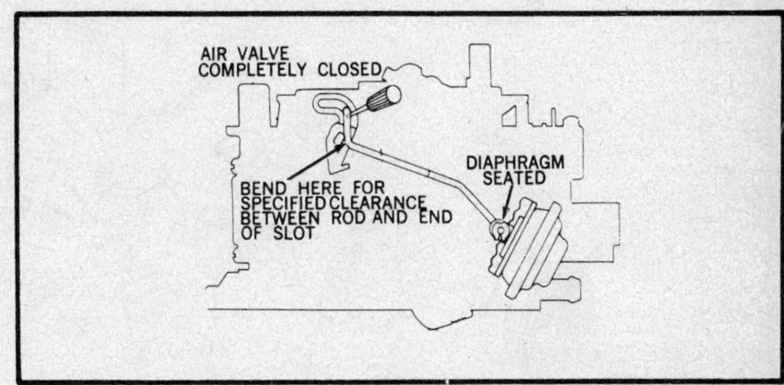

Air valve dashpot adjustment—typical Quadrajet® carburetor
(© General Motors Corp.)

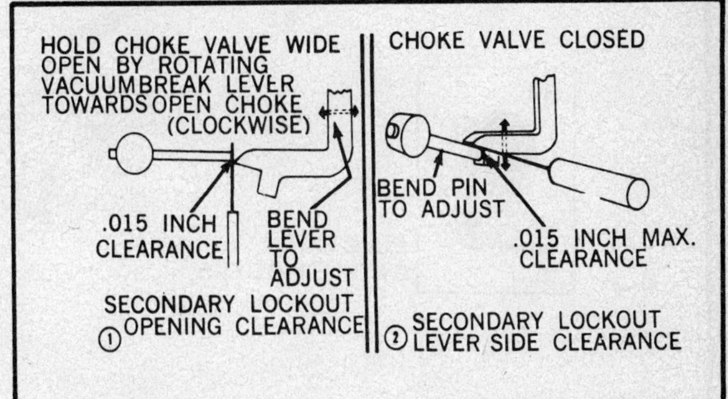

Secondary lockout adjustment—typical Quadrajet® carburetor
(© General Motors Corp.)

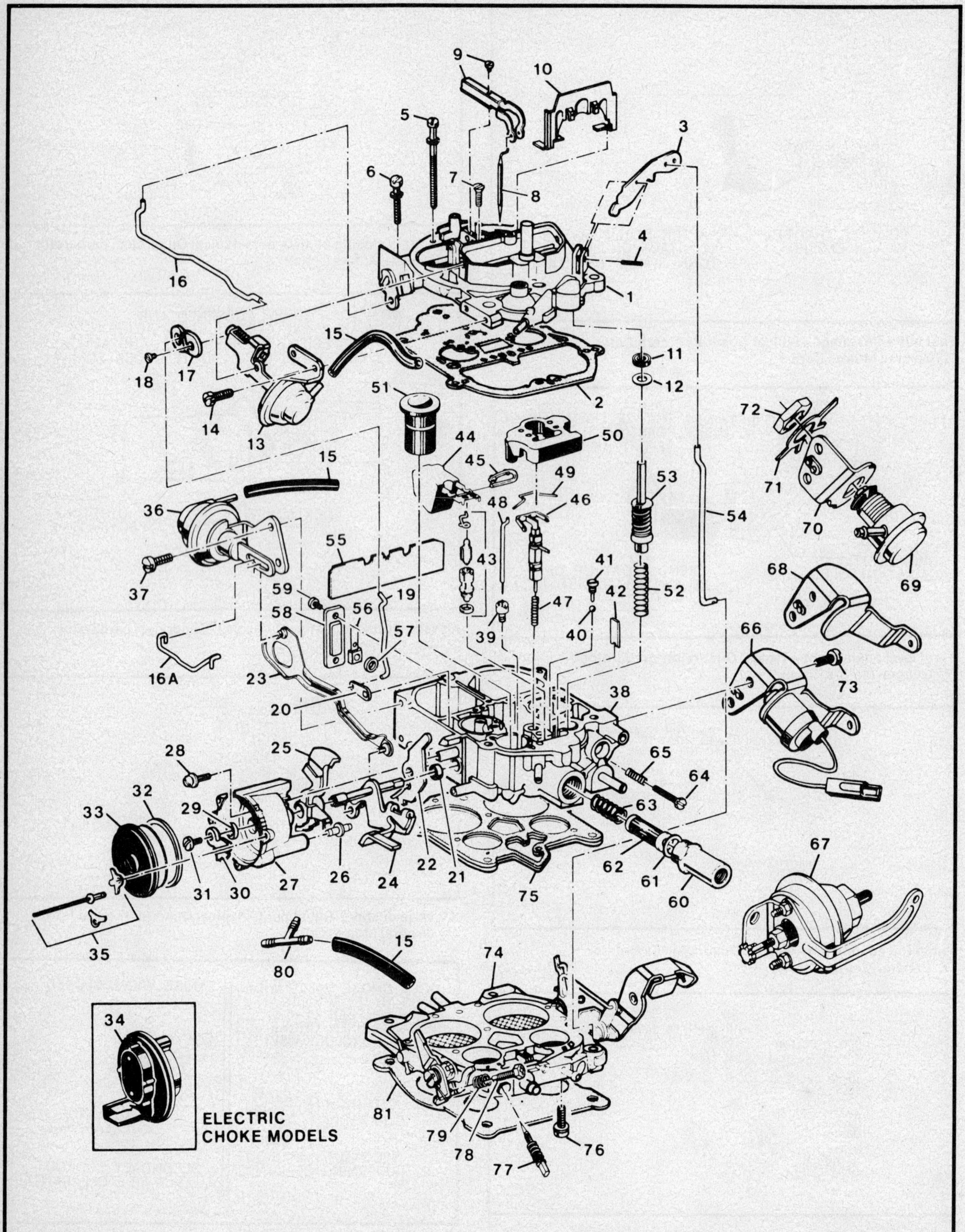

ELECTRIC CHOKE MODELS

M4MC/M4ME carburetor exploded view (© General Motors Corp.)

1. Air Horn Assy.
2. Gasket—Air Horn
3. Lever—Pump Actuating
4. Roll Pin—Pump Lever Hinge
5. Screw—Air Horn Long (2)
6. Screw—Air Horn Short ( )
7. Screw — Air Horn Countersunk (2)
8. Metering Rod—Secondary (2)
9. Holder and Screw—Secondary Metering Rod
10. Baffle—Secondary Air
11. Seal—Pump Plunger
12. Retainer—Pump Seal
13. Vac. Break Control & Bracket—Front
14. Screw—Control Attaching (2)
15. Hose—Vacuum
16. Rod—Air Valve
16A. Rod—Air Valve (Truck)
17. Lever—Choke Rod (Upper)
18. Screw—Choke Lever
19. Rod—Choke
20. Lever—Choke Rod (Lower)
21. Seal—Intermediate Choke Shaft
22. Lever—Secondary Lockout
23. Link—Rear Vacuum Break
24. Int. Choke Shaft & Lever
25. Cam—Fast Idle
26. Seal—Choke Housing to Bowl (Hot Air Choke)
27. Kit—Choke Housing
28. Screw—Choke Housing to Bowl
29. Seal—Intermediate Choke Shaft (Hot Air Choke)
30. Lever—Choke Coil
31. Screw—Choke Coil Lever
32. Gasket—Stat Cover (Hot Air Choke)
33. Stat Cover & Coil Assy. (Hot Air Choke)
34. Stat Cover & Coil Assy. (Electric Choke)
35. Kit — Stat Cover Attaching
36. Rear Vacuum Break Assembly
37. Screw—Vacuum Break Attaching (2)
40. Ball—Pump Discharge
41. Retainer—Pump Discharge Ball
42. Baffle—Pump Well
43. Needle & Seat Assembly
44. Float Assembly
45. Hinge Pin — Float Assembly
46. Power Piston Assembly
47. Spring—Power Piston
48. Rod—Primary Metering (2)
49. Spring—Metering Rod Retainer
50. Insert—Float Bowl
51. Insert—Bowl Cavity
52. Spring—Pump Return
53. Pump Assembly
54. Rod—Pump
55. Baffle—Secondary Bores
56. Idle Compensator Assembly
57. Seal—Idle Compensator
58. Cover—Idle Compensator
59. Screw—Idle Compensator Cover (2)
60. Filter Nut—Fuel Inlet
61. Gasket—Filter Nut
62. Filter—Fuel Inlet
63. Spring—Fuel Filter
64. Screw—Idle Stop
65. Spring — Idle Stop Screw
66. Idle Speed Solenoid & Bracket Assembly
67. Idle Load Compensator & Bracket Assembly
68. Bracket—Throttle Return Spring
69. Actuator—Throttle Lever (Truck Only)
70. Bracket—Throttle Lever Actuator (Truck Only)
71. Washer—Actuator Nut (Truck Only)
72. Nut—Actuator Attaching (Truck Only)
73. Screw—Bracket Attaching (2)
74. Throttle Body Assembly
75. Gasket—Throttle Body
76. Screw—Throttle Body (3)
77. Idle Mixture Needle & Spring Assy. (2)
78. Screw — Fast Idle Adjusting
79. Spring — Fast Idle Screw
80. Tee—Vacuum Hose
81. Gasket—Flange

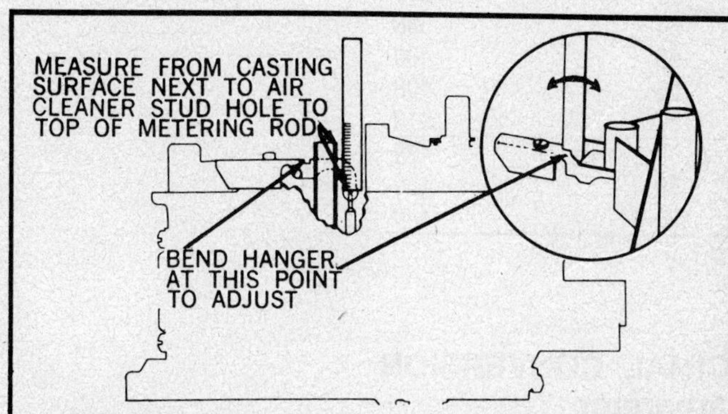

Secondary metering adjustment—typical Quadrajet® carburetor (© General Motors Corp.)

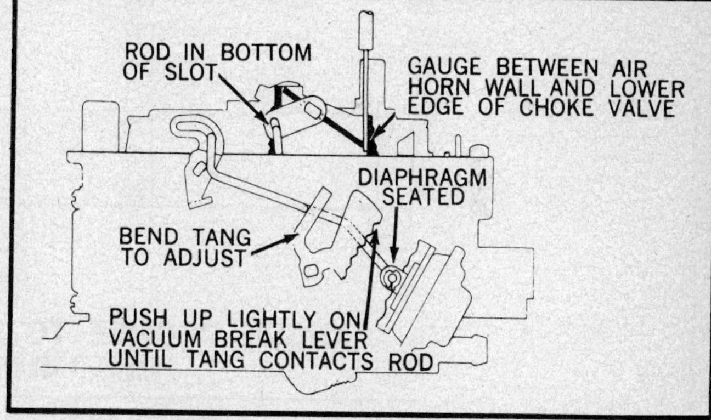

Vacuum break adjustment—typical Quadrajet® carburetor (© General Motors Corp.)

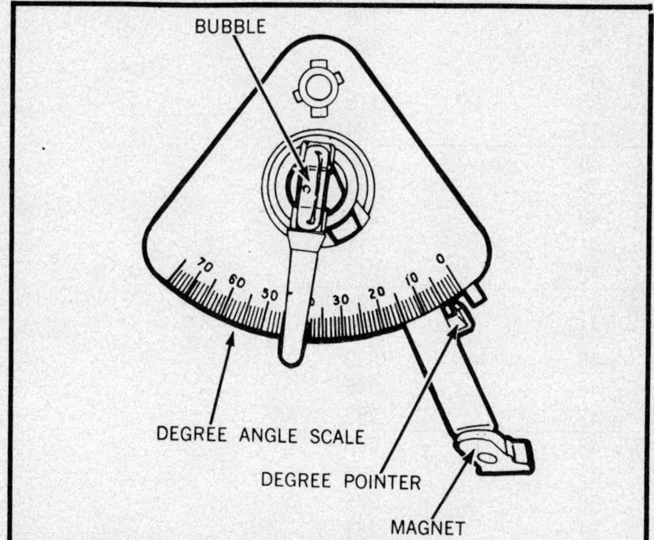

Degree angle tool—typical (© Kent-Moore Tools)

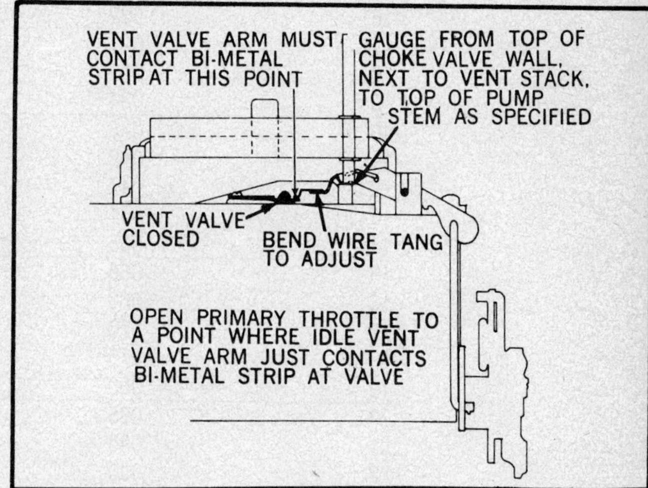

Idle vent adjustment—typical Quadrajet® carburetor (© General Motors Corp.)

ANGLE DEGREE TO DECIMAL CONVERSION
Model M2MC, M2ME and M4MC Carburetor

Angle Degrees	Decimal Equiv. Top of Valve	Angle Degrees	Decimal Equiv. Top of Valve
5	.023	33	.203
6	.028	34	.211
7	.033	35	.220
8	.038	36	.227
9	.043	37	.234
10	.049	38	.243
11	.054	39	.251
12	.060	40	.260
13	.066	41	.269
14	.071	42	.277
15	.077	43	.287
16	.083	44	.295
17	.090	45	.304
18	.096	46	.314
19	.103	47	.322
20	.110	48	.332
21	.117	49	.341
22	.123	50	.350
23	.129	51	.360
24	.136	52	.370
25	.142	53	.379
26	.149	54	.388
27	.157	55	.400
28	.164	56	.408
29	.171	57	.418
30	.179	58	.428
31	.187	59	.439
32	.195	60	.449

ANGLE DEGREE TO DECIMAL CONVERSION
Model 4MV Carburetor

Angle Degrees	Decimal Equiv. Top of Valve	Angle Degrees	Decimal Equiv. Top of Valve
5	.019	33	.158
6	.022	34	.164
7	.026	35	.171
8	.030	36	.178
9	.034	37	.184
10	.038	38	.190
11	.042	39	.197
12	.047	40	.204
13	.051	41	.211
14	.056	42	.217
15	.060	43	.225
16	.065	44	.231
17	.070	45	.239
18	.075	46	.246
19	.080	47	.253
20	.085	48	.260
21	.090	49	.268
22	.095	50	.275
23	.101	51	.283
24	.106	52	.291

ANGLE DEGREE TO DECIMAL CONVERSION
Model 4MV Carburetor

Angle Degrees	Decimal Equiv. Top of Valve	Angle Degrees	Decimal Equiv. Top of Valve
25	.112	53	.299
26	.117	54	.306
27	.123	55	.314
28	.128	56	.322
29	.134	57	.329
30	.140	58	.337
31	.146	59	.345
32	.152	60	.353

TPS ADJUSTMENT SPECIFICATIONS
Chevrolet/GMC Models

Year	Engine Code	TPS Voltage
'83	H	.51
	G	.51
	F	.40
	L	.40
'84	B	.255
	X	.31
	Z	.255
	G	.48
	H	.48
	G	.48
	F	.41
	L	.41
'85	G	.48
	H	.48
	G	.48
	F	.41
	L	.41
	N	.25

Note: Measure voltage with throttle at curb idle position, ignition ON, engine and A/C OFF. All values ± 0.1 volt.

FORD CALIBRATION NUMBERS
LIGHT TRUCK ONLY

Year	Emission Calibration Number	Choke Pulldown Setting	Choke Unloader Setting	Choke Cap Setting	Float Setting (Dry)	Float Level (Wet)	Pump Lever Location
'82	2-55D-R0	.125	.200	V-Notch	7/16	.810	#2
	2-56D-R0	.125	.250	V-Notch	7/16	.810	#2
	2-56D-R10	.115–.135	.250	V-Notch	7/16	.810	#2
	2-57G-R0	.130	.200	V-Notch	7/16	.810	#2
	2-58H-R0	.125	.200	V-Notch	7/16	.810	#2
	2-51D-R0	.270	.28	Index	.78	—	—
	2-51E-R0	.270	.28	Index	.78	—	—
	2-51F-R0	.270	.28	Index	.78	—	—
	2-51G-R0	.270	.28	Index	.78	—	—
	2-51K-R0	.230	.28	Index	.78	—	—
	2-51L-R0	.230	.28	Index	.78	—	—
	2-51P-R0	.320	.330	2 Rich	.78	—	—
	2-51P-R10	.320	.330	2 Rich	.78	—	—
	2-51S-R0	.320	.330	2 Rich	.78	—	—
	2-51T-R0	.320	.330	2 Rich	.78	—	—
	2-51X-R0	.300	.28	Index	.78	—	—

Year	Emission Calibration Number	Choke Pulldown Setting	Choke Bi-Metal I.D.	Cam Index Setting		Choke Unloader	Float Level (Dry)
	2-51Y-R0	.300	.28	Index	.78	—	—
	2-52G-R0	.300	.28	2 Rich	.78	—	—
	2-52H-R0	.300	.28	2 Rich	.78	—	—
	2-52K-R0	.300	.28	2 Rich	.78	—	—
	2-52L-R0	.300	.28	2 Rich	.78	—	—
	2-52S-R0	.320	.330	2 Rich	.78	—	—
	2-52T-R0	.320	.330	2 Rich	.78	—	—
	2-52Y-R0	.300	.28	Index	.78	—	—
	2-53D-R0	.130	.200	V-Notch	7/16	.810	#2
	2-53F-R0	.130	.200	V-Notch	7/16	.810	#2
	2-53G-R0	.130	.200	V-Notch	7/16	.810	#2
	2-53H-R0	.130	.200	V-Notch	7/16	.810	#2
	2-53K-R0	.130	.200	V-Notch	7/16	.810	#2
	2-53X-R1	.130	.200	V-Notch	7/16	.810	#2
	2-54D-R0	.125	.200	V-Notch	7/16	.810	#2
	2-54F-R0	.130	.200	V-Notch	31/64	.875	#2

FORD CALIBRATION NUMBERS
LIGHT TRUCK ONLY

Year	Emission Calibration Number	Choke Pulldown Setting	Choke Bi-Metal I.D.	Cam Index Setting	Choke Unloader		Float Level (Dry)
	2-54G-R0	.125	.200	V-Notch	7/16	.810	#2
	2-54H-R0	.130	.200	V-Notch	31/64	.875	#2
	2-54K-R0	.125	.200	V-Notch	7/16	.810	#2
	2-54L-R0	.125	.200	V-Notch	7/16	.810	#2
	2-54P-R0	—	—	Index	1.070–1.010	—	—
	2-54R-R0	—	—	Index	1.070–1.010	—	—
	2-54X-R1	.120	.200	V-Notch	7/16	.810	#2
	1-63T-R0	—	—	Index	1.070–1.010	—	—
	1-63T-R10B	—	—	Index	1.070–1.010	—	—
	1-64H-R2	.120	.200	V-Notch	31/64	.875	#3
	1-64R-R1	—	—	—	1.070–1.010	—	—
	1-64S-R0	—	—	—	1.070–1.010	—	—
	1-64T-R0	—	—	—	1.070–1.010	—	—
	1-64T-R10	—	—	—	1.070–1.010	—	—
	2-63Y-R10B	—	—	Index	1.070–1.010	—	—
	2-64X-R0	.120	.200	V-Notch	31/64	.875	#2
	2-64Y-R10B	—	—	Index	1.070–1.010	—	—
'83	3-41D-R01	.320	REL	.140	.22		.650
	3-41D-R10	.320	REL	.140	.22		.650
	3-41P-R02	.320	REL	.140	.22		.650
	3-41P-R11	.320	REL	.140	.22		.650
	3-41P-R12	.320	REL	.140	.22		.650
	3-49S-R01	.320	REL	.140	.22		.650
	3-49S-R10	.320	REL	.140	.22		.650
	3-49S-R11	.320	REL	.140	.22		.650
	3-49X-R01	.320	REL	.140	.22		.650
	3-49X-R11	.320	REL	.140	.22		.650
	3-50S-R01	.320	REL	.140	.22		.650
	3-50S-R11	.320	REL	.140	.22		.650
	3-50X-R10	.320	REL	.140	.22		.650
	3-50X-R11	.320	REL	.140	.22		.650
	3-55D-R00	.115–.135	2080ME350	V-Notch	.25		.810①
	3-56D-R00	.115–.135	2080ME350	V-Notch	.25		.810①
	3-51D-R00	.270	EC	.140	.28		.780
	3-51E-R01	.270	EB	.140	.28		.780
	3-51F-R00	.270	EC	.140	.28		.780
	3-51G-R00	.270	EC	.140	.28		.780
	3-51H-R00	.270	EB	.140	.28		.780
	3-51K-R00	.270	EB	.140	.28		.780
	3-51L-R00	.270	EB	.140	.28		.780
	3-51P-R00	.320	EC	.140	.330		.780
	3-51R-R00	.320	EC	.140	.330		.780
	3-51R-R10	.320	EC	.140	.330		.780
	3-51S-R00	.320	EC	.140	.330		.780
	3-51S-R10	.320	EC	.140	.330		.780
	3-51T-R00	.320	EC	.140	.330		.780
	3-51T-R10	.320	EC	.140	.330		.780
	3-51V-R00	.300	EB	.140	.28		.780
	3-51X-R00	.300	EB	.140	.28		.780
	3-51Z-R00	.300	EB	.140	.28		.780
	3-52E-R00	.270	EC	.140	.28		.780
	3-52F-R00	.300	EC	.140	.28		.780
	3-52G-R00	.300	EC	.140	.28		.780
	3-52K-R00	.300	EC	.140	.28		.780
	3-52R-R00	.320	EC	.140	.330		.780
	3-52R-R10	.320	EC	.140	.330		.780
	3-52S-R00	.320	EC	.140	.330		.780
	3-52S-R10	.320	EC	.140	.330		.780
	3-52T-R00	.320	EC	.140	.330		.780
	3-52T-R10	.320	EC	.140	.330		.780
	3-52V-R00	.300	EB	.140	.28		.780
	3-52Y-R00	.300	EB	.140	.28		.780
	3-52Z-R00	.300	EB	.140	.28		.780
	3-53F-R00	.142	2100MF	V-Notch	.20		7/16
	3-53G-R00	.142	2100MF	V-Notch	.20		7/16
	3-53K-R00	.142	2100MF	V-Notch	.20		7/16
	3-53L-R00	.142	2100MF	V-Notch	.20		7/16
	3-53W-R00	.152	2100MF400	V-Notch	.20		7/16
	3-53Y-R00	.152	2100MF400	V-Notch	.20		7/16
	3-53Z-R00	.152	2100MF400	V-Notch	.20		7/16
	3-54E-R00	.137	2100MF	V-Notch	.25		7/16
	3-54F-R00	.149	2100KH	V-Notch	.25		7/16
	3-54J-R00	.137	2100MF	V-Notch	.25		7/16
	3-54L-R00	.149	2100KH	V-Notch	.25		7/16
	3-54P-R00	.157	2080ME400	V-Notch	.20		7/16
	3-54R-R00	.157	2080ME400	V-Notch	.20		7/16
	3-54T-R00	.157	2100ME400	V-Notch	.20		7/16
	3-54W-R00	.149	2120KH400	V-Notch	.20		7/16
	3-54Y-R00	.150	2100MF400	V-Notch	.20		7/16
	3-54Z-R00	.150	2100MF400	V-Notch	.20		7/16
	1-63T-R12	②	③	.355–.365④	.245–.255⑤		1.010–1.070
	1-63T-R13	②	③	.355–.365④	.245–.255⑤		1.010–1.070
	1-64H-R02	.120	2150ME	V-Notch	.20		31/64
	1-64T-R12	②	③	.355–.365	.245–.255⑤		1.010–1.070
	1-64T-R13	②	③	.355–.365	.245–.255⑤		—
	2-63Y-R11	②	③	.355–.365④	.245–.255⑤		1.010–1.070
	2-63Y-R12	②	③	.355–.365④	.245–.255⑤		1.010–1.070
	3-64X-R00	.120	2100ME	V-Notch	.20		31/64
	2-64Y-R11	②	③	.355–.365	.245–.255⑤		1.010–1.070
	2-64Y-R12	②	③	.355–.365	.245–.255⑤		1.010–1.070

FORD CALIBRATION NUMBERS
LIGHT AND HEAVY TRUCKS

Year	Emission Calibration Number	Choke Setting	Fast Idle (RPM) High Cam	Fast Idle (RPM) Kick Down①	Choke Valve Pull Down
'80	0-51F-RO	Index	—	1600	—
	0-51G-RO	2 Rich	—	1400	—
	0-51H-RO	2 Rich	—	1400	—
	0-51L-RO	Index	—	1400	—
	0-51M-RO	Index	—	1400	—
	0-51S-RO	Index	—	1600	—
	0-51T-RO	Index	—	1600	—
	0-52H-RO	2 Rich	—	1400	—
	0-52J-RO	2 Rich	—	1400	—
	0-52L-RO	2 Rich	—	1400	—
	0-52M-RO	2 Rich	—	1400	—
	0-52S-RO	Index	—	1600	—
	0-53D-RO	3 Rich	2000	—	—
	0-53G-RO	3 Rich	2000	—	—
	0-53H-RO	3 Rich	2000	—	—
	0-53K-RO	3 Rich	2000	—	—
	0-53L-RO	3 Rich	2000	—	—
	0-53N-RO	3 Rich	2500	—	—
	0-53Q-RO	3 Rich	2500	—	—
	0-53S-RO	3 Rich	2500	—	—
	0-54D-RO	3 Rich	2000	—	—
	0-54F-RO	3 Rich	2000	—	—
	0-54G-RO	Index	2000	—	—
	0-54H-RO	3 Rich	2000	—	—
	0-54K-RO	Index	2000	—	—
	0-54L-RO	3 Rich	2000	—	—
	0-54M-RO	3 Rich	2100	—	—
	0-54N-RO	1 Rich	2400	—	—
	0-54P-RO	3 Rich	2000	—	—
	0-54Q-RO	1 Rich	2400	—	—
	0-54R-RO	3 Rich	2100	—	—
	0-54T-RO	3 Rich	2000	—	—
	0-54V-RO	3 Rich	2100	—	—
	0-60A-RO	3 Rich	2000	—	—
	0-59C-RO	3 Rich	2000	—	—
	0-59G-RO	3 Rich	2000	—	—
	0-59G-R10	3 Rich	2000	—	—
	0-59H-RO	3 Rich	2000	—	—
	0-59H-R10	3 Rich	2000	—	—
	0-59J-RO	3 Rich	2000	—	—
	0-59J-R10	3 Rich	2000	—	—
	0-59S-RO	3 Rich	2000	—	—
	0-60B-RO	3 Rich	2000	—	—
'81	1-57G-R1	—	2200	—	—
	1-58G-RO	—	2000	—	—
	1-51D-RO	—	—	1400	—
	1-51D-R10	—	—	1400	—
	1-51E-RO	—	—	1400	—
	1-51F-RO	—	—	1400	—
	1-51G-RO	—	—	1400	—
	1-51H-RO	—	—	1400	—
	1-51K-RO	—	—	1400	—
	1-51L-RO	—	—	1400	—
	1-51E-R10	—	—	1400	—
	1-51F-R10	—	—	1400	—
	1-51G-R10	—	—	1400	—
	1-51H-R10	—	—	1400	—
	1-51K-R10	—	—	1400	—
	1-51L-R10	—	—	1400	—
	1-51S-RO	—	—	1400	—
	1-51S-R10	—	—	1400	—
	1-51T-RO	—	—	1400	—
	1-52G-RO	—	—	1400	—
	1-52H-RO	—	—	1400	—
	1-52K-RO	—	—	1400	—
	1-52L-RO	—	—	1400	—
	1-52G-R10	—	—	1400	—
	1-52H-R10	—	—	1400	—
	1-52K-R10	—	—	1400	—
	1-52L-R10	—	—	1400	—
	1-52S-RO	—	—	1400	—
	1-52T-RO	—	—	1400	—
	1-53D-RO	—	2200	—	—
	1-53F-RO	—	2200	—	—
	1-53G-RO	—	2200	—	—
	1-53H-RO	—	2200	—	—
	1-53K-RO	—	2200	—	—
	1-53D-R10	—	2200	—	—
	1-53G-R10	—	2200	—	—
	1-53K-R10	—	2200	—	—
	1-59A-RO	—	2000	—	—
	1-59B-RO	—	2000	—	—
	1-59H-RO	—	2000	—	—
	1-59K-RO	—	2000	—	—
	1-60A-RO	—	2200	—	—
	1-60B-RO	—	2200	—	—
	1-60H-R1	—	2000	—	—
	1-60J-RO	—	2000	—	—
	1-60K-RO	—	2000	—	—
	1-63T-RO	—	1700	—	—
	1-64A-RO	—	2000	—	—
	1-64G-R1	—	2000	—	—
	1-64H-R2	—	2000	—	—
	1-64R-R1	—	1650	—	—
	1-64S-RO	—	1650	—	—
	1-64T-RO	—	1650	—	—

①Kickdown—2nd step of fast idle cam

FORD CALIBRATION NUMBERS MEDIUM AND HEAVY TRUCK

Year	Emission Calibration Number	Choke Pulldown Setting	Choke Unloader Setting	Choke Cap Setting	Float Setting (Dry)	Float Level (Wet)	Pump Lever Location
'82	5-77-R1	.230	.28	1 Rich	3/8	—	—
	5-78-R1	.230	.28	1 Rich	3/8	—	—
	5-77G-R12	.290	.28	Index	.69	—	—
	9-77S-R10	.290	.28	Index	.69	—	—
	9-78J-R0	.290	.28	Index	.69	—	—
	9-78J-R11	.290	.28	Index	.69	—	—
	7-79-R1	.130	.250	V-Notch	31/64	.875	#3
	7-80-R0	.130	.250	V-Notch	31/64	.875	#3
	2-75J-R17	.170–.190	.250	V-Notch	31/64	.875	#3
	2-76J-R17	.170–.190	.250	V-Notch	31/64	.875	#3
	7-75A-R11	.173	.250	V-Notch	31/64	.875	#3
	7-75A-R12	.173	.250	V-Notch	31/64	.875	#3
	7-75J-R14	.170–.190	.250	V-Notch	31/64	.875	#3
	7-76A-R11	.182	.250	V-Notch	31/64	.875	#3
	7-76A-R12	.182	.250	V-Notch	31/64	.875	#3
	7-76J-R11	.170–.190	.250	V-Notch	31/64	.875	#3
	7-76J-R13	.170–.190	.250	V-Notch	31/64	.875	#3
	7-76J-R14	.170–.190	.250	V-Notch	31/64	.875	#3
	7-76J-R15	.170–.190	.250	V-Notch	31/64	.875	#3
	9-83G-R12	.350–.400	—	—	—	①	②
	9-83H-R11	.180–.440	—	—	—	①	#1
	9-83H-R14	.180–.440	—	—	—	①	#1
	9-73J-R11	.180	.250	V-Notch	31/64	—	#4
	9-73J-R12	.180	.250	V-Notch	31/64	—	#4
	9-73J-R13	.170–.190	.250	V-Notch	31/64	—	#3
	9-73J-R14	.170–.190	.250	V-Notch	31/64	—	#3
	9-74J-R11	.175	.250	V-Notch	31/64	—	#4
	9-74J-R12	.175	.250	V-Notch	31/64	.875	#4
	9-74J-R13	.165–.185	.250	V-Notch	31/64	.875	#3
	9-74J-R14	.165–.185	.250	V-Notch	31/64	.875	#3
	9-87G-R11	.180–.440	—	—	—	①	#1
	9-97J-R12	.200–.220	.295–.335	2 Rich	—	①	#1

① At bottom of sight plug
② #1-E0TE-PA, E2TE-NA; #2-E2TE-AGA, D9TE-APA

FORD CALIBRATION NUMBERS MEDIUM AND HEAVY TRUCK

Year	Emission Calibration Number	Choke Pulldown Setting	Choke Bi-Metal I.D.	Cam Index Setting	Choke Unloader	Float Level (Dry)
'83	5-77-R01	.230	A2	.110	.28	3/8
	5-78-R01	.230	A2	.110	.28	3/8
	9-77J-R12	.290	A2	.140	.28	.69
	9-77S-R10	.290	A2	.140	.28	.69
	9-78J-R00	.290	A2	.140	.28	.69
	9-78J-R11	.290	A2	.140	.28	.69
	7-79-R01	.130	TR3	V-Notch	.25	31/64
	7-80-R00	.130	TB4	V-Notch	.25	31/64
	2-75A-R10	.180	TB3	V-Notch	.25	31/64
	2-75J-R20	.180	TB3	V-Notch	.25	31/64
	2-76A-R10	.180	TB3	V-Notch	.25	31/64
	2-76J-R20	.180	TB3	V-Notch	.25	31/64
	9-83G-R12	.350–.400	—	—	—	⑥
	9-83G-R14	.210–.230	47R-292A	—	.300	⑥
	9-83H-R11	—	—	—	—	⑥
	9-83H-R14	—	—	—	—	⑥
	9-87G-R11	—	—	—	—	⑥
	9-97J-R13	.210–.230	47R-692A	—	.300–.330	⑥
	3-98S-R00	.210–.230	47R-692A	—	.300–.330	⑥

① Wet float level
② Adjust for timing of 4–7 seconds
③ E2TE-9848-CA
④ On 2nd step of cam
⑤ Refers to vacuum regulator setting
⑥ Bottom of sight plug-wet level

INDEX

GASOLINE ENGINE EMISSION CONTROL

Introduction

The emission control devices required by law on trucks are determined by weight classification and were considered either "light duty" or "heavy duty" applications, with the Gross Vehicle Weight (GVW) of 6000 lbs. as the dividing line. State and Federal Government regulations have now mandated a new weight standard from the 6000 lbs. GVW to a new GVW of 8500 lbs. or less as "light duty" and a GVW of 8500 lbs. or more as "heavy duty" applications.

The light duty emission devices are normally the same as used on the passenger cars.

During certain model years, passenger carrying vehicles, such as window vans with greater GVW of 6000 lbs. were also considered to be light duty models and must comply with the light duty emission control requirements.

Heavy duty truck models use fewer emission control devices than the light duty models, although more emission controls are being required in each succeeding year to comply with the changing emission control regulations and requirements.

The State of California remains stringent in their emission control standards and throughout this section, reference will be made to either the California, High Altitude or to the Federal engines. (Federal referring to the remaining 49 states, High Altitude referring to areas above 4000 ft. (1,219 meters).

Engine Modifications

Internal engine modifications have been made from year to year by redesigning the following:

1. Lowering the compression ratios to allow the use of low or nonleaded fuels.
2. Combustion chambers and piston modifications for a more efficient air/fuel flow rate and burning time.
3. Camshaft modification to improve valve timing and to increase valve overlap periods.
4. Higher engine operating temperatures and increased cooling areas.
5. Balanced fuel induction manifolds to properly balance the air/fuel flow to the cylinders.
6. Other modifications include changes in metals used in the construction of the engines and components to allow the opera-

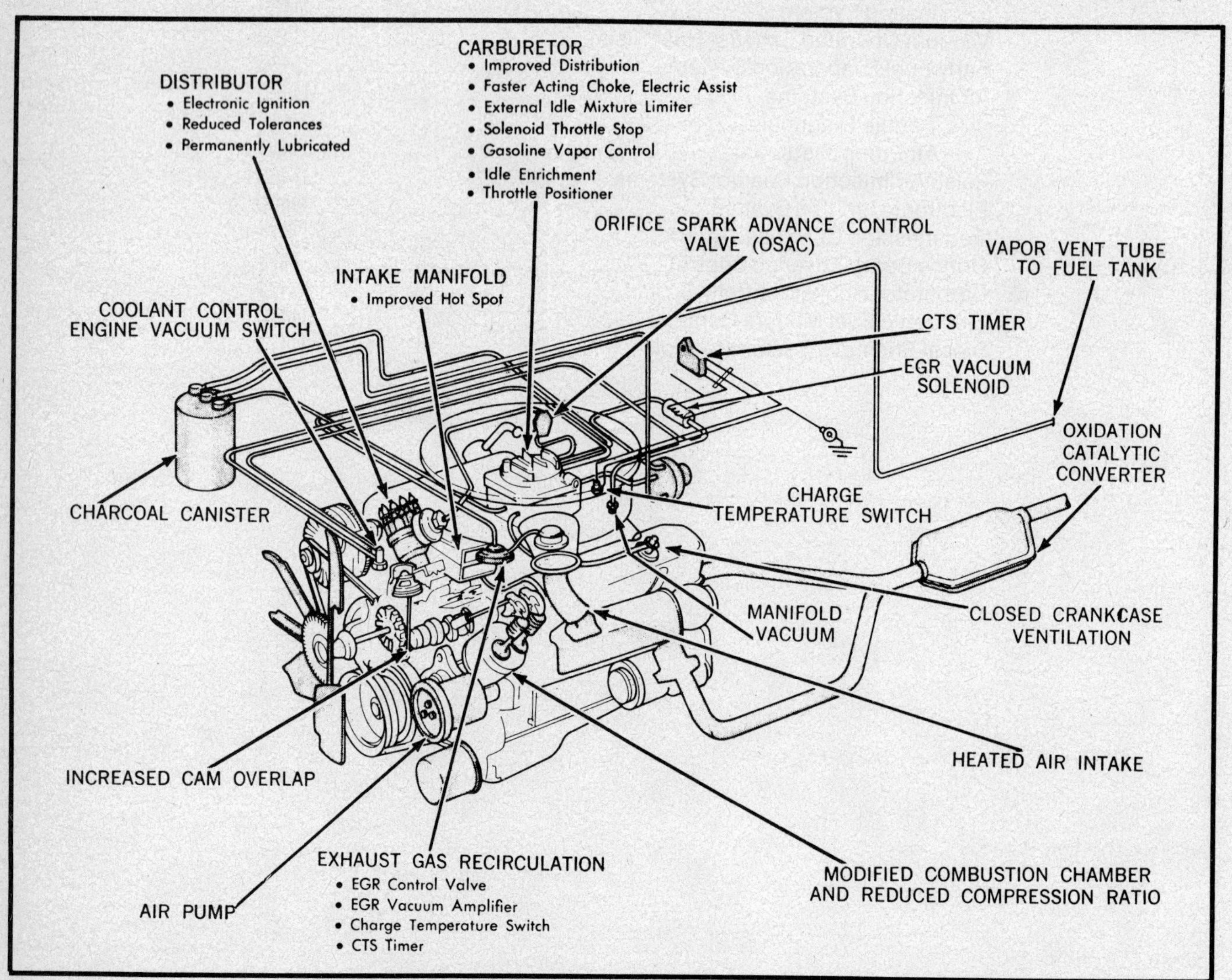

Emission Control System—Typical of light duty emission operation (© Chrysler Corp.)

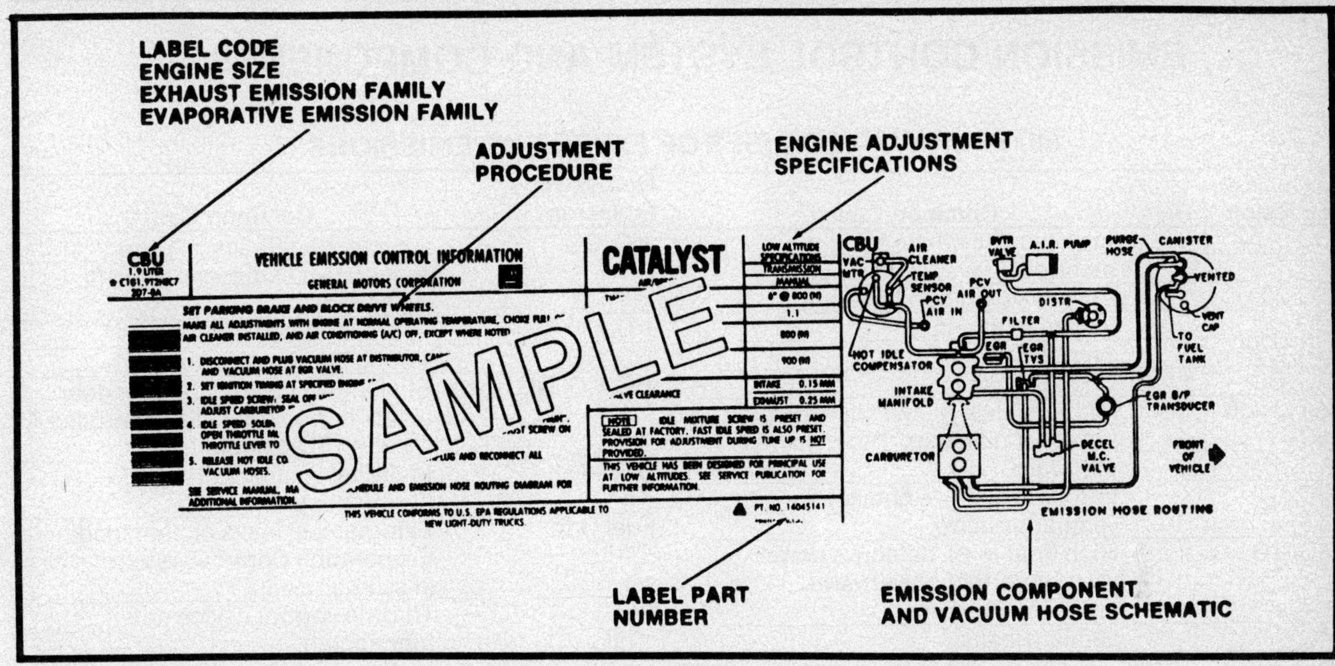

Emission Certification label, including vacuum hose schematic. Typical of all manufacturers (© General Motors Corp.)

tion of the engine with non-leaded, non-lubricating fuels.

External engine modifications have been made to the carburetors and distributors to provide the proper air/fuel mixture and to provide the proper timing of the ignition spark to insure the engine emission levels remain within the legislated limits, while providing the best engine performance and fuel economy at varying speeds and loads.

Emission Control Systems

In order to control the engine crankcase, fuel and exhaust emissions, three major systems have been designated.

1. Crankcase controls are used to provide a more complete scavenging of the crankcase vapors and to route the vapors to the engine fuel induction system for burning with the air/fuel mixture.
2. Evaporation controls are used to prevent the emission of gasoline vapors from the fuel tank and carburetor, into the atmosphere. Charcoal canisters are used to store the gasoline vapors during periods of engine shutdown and during periods of engine operation, the gasoline vapors are drawn into the fuel induction system and burned with the air/fuel mixture.
3. Exhaust controls are used to limit the emission of Carbon Monoxide (CO), Hydrocarbons (HC) and Oxides of Nitrogen (NOx) from the engine exhaust. Numerous controls are used on the engines and the exhaust systems to perform this removal of pollutants.

Emission Certification Label

An Emission Certification label is attached to either the engine or engine compartment sheet metal and should be consulted before any adjustments are made to the engine.

NOTE: It is a good practice to copy the information from the Emission Certification label and keep with the owners manual, in case the label becomes mutilated or lost.

MAINTENANCE

In order for the emission controls to function properly, maintenance must be performed at regular intervals, either by time or mileage increments. Owner manuals will normally contain a maintenance schedule for services to be done and should be followed for longer emission systems and vehicle life.

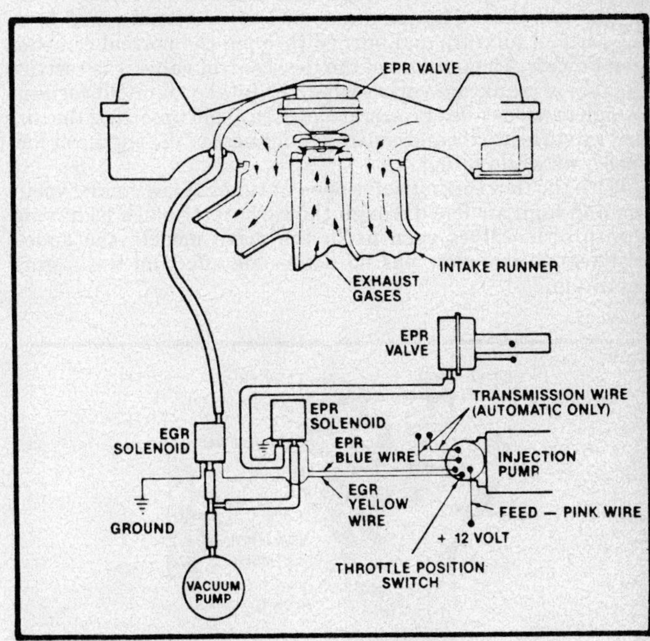

Vacuum switched EGR EPR control schematic 6.2 L engine (© General Motors Corp.)

EMISSION CONTROL SYSTEM AND COMPONENTS

MOST COMMON CAUSES OF EXCESSIVE EMISSIONS

Excessive Emission	Common Cause
CO	Inproper idle mixture.
CO	Incorrect idle speed.
HC, NO_x	Advanced ignition timing.
HC	Retarded timing.
HC, CO	Dirty air cleaner.
HC, CO	Choke sticking.
Very High HC	Ignition miss, fouled spark plugs, improper plug gap, disconnected plug wire.
HC, CO	Improper positive crankcase ventilation valve.
HC, CO	High float level, defective power valve, incorrect power valve, incorrect metering.
HC	Vacuum leaks.

Excessive Emission	Common Cause
HC, CO	Air Injection Reactor Pump inoperative or disconnected (if equipped).
HC, CO, NO_x	Improper grade of fuel.
HC, NO_x	Wrong spark plugs (too hot).
HC, CO, NO_x	Sticking air cleaner damper door (with Thermostatically Controlled Air Cleaner) (if so equipped).
HC, NO_x	Improper vacuum advance, (if so equipped).
Fuel Odor	External fuel leaks or damaged Evaporation Control System (if so equipped).
HC	Throttle control device not functioning.

CRANKCASE EMISSION CONTROL SYSTEM

Positive Crankcase Ventilation (PCV) System

With the engine operating, crankcase ventilation air is drawn through an air cleaner mounted filter assembly, through a hose to the crankcase air inlet, down into the crankcase and up to the rocker arm chamber, out through a flow control valve and into a hose connected to the base of the carburetor or to the intake manifold. The crankcase vapors are then mixed with the air/fuel mixture and burned through the normal combustion process. The purpose of the flow control valve is to restrict the flow of crankcase vapors when the intake manifold vacuum is high (such as idle or coast models), to avoid upsetting the air/fuel mixture at idle and causing roughness of the engine at low speeds or while idling.

With the flow control valve open at times of low engine vacuum and high air flow through the carburetor (such as having the throttle valves open as in the drive model), the added crankcase vapor flow has no noticeable effect on the engine operation.

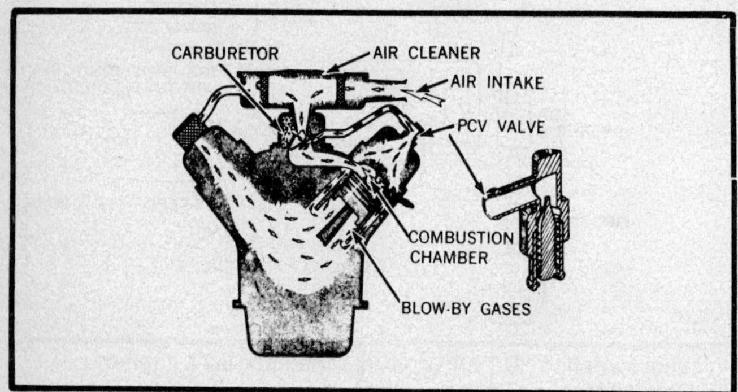

Closed crankcase ventilation system (© Chrysler Corp.)

CRANKCASE CONTROL TESTING

Checking crankcase vacuum is the most effective way to test any PCV system. If there is vacuum in the crankcase, then the major part of the system has to be working.

On many models, you can effectively test the system with a vacuum gauge designed for testing the PCV system. It is best to test the system at the fresh air intake, that is, where a large, open tube enters the air cleaner, often at a filter. Leave the PCV valve and its hose, and the oil filler cap, in place. Disconnect the fresh air hose at the air cleaner and test at the end of the hose.

One can also test the system at the oil filler hole. In this case, disconnect the fresh air hose at the air cleaner and use some positive means to plug it such as a cork or clean rag. Start the engine and leave it idling in Park or Neutral.

It may take a few seconds for the vacuum to build up enough to operate the gauge. Make sure you allow time for the full force of the vacuum to take effect. If you don't get any vacuum, pull the PCV valve from the valve cover and hold your finger over the open end. You should soon feel full manifold vacuum. If you feel vacuum here, but did not get an indication of vacuum at the oil filler hole or fresh air intake, check for a clogged fresh air intake hose, or leaks at the grommets, valve covers, or oil pan gasket. Often, simply tightening pan or cover bolts will cure the problem.

If there's no vacuum at the PCV valve, check for a clogged valve or hose, or a poor connection. In some cases, the hose is attached to a fitting that's screwed into the intake manifold and the fitting could be loose.

If still uncertain about the condition of the PCV valve or system, you can make some additional checks. You can remove the valve and shake it. If it rattles, this is an indication that it's probably working although in rare cases the valve may still malfunction sometimes. If the valve does not rattle, the inner plunger is stuck and it must be replaced.

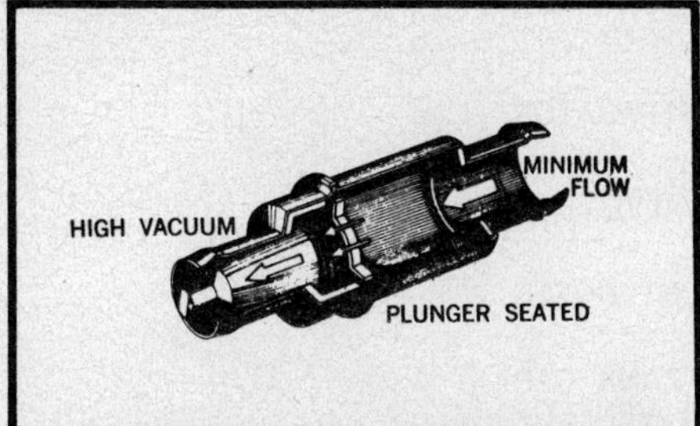

PCV valve at low engine speed or during idle (© International Harvester Co.)

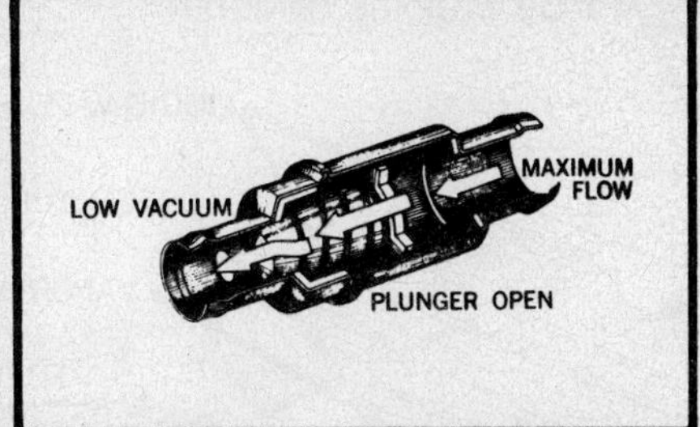

PCV valve operation at high engine speed (© International Harvester Co.)

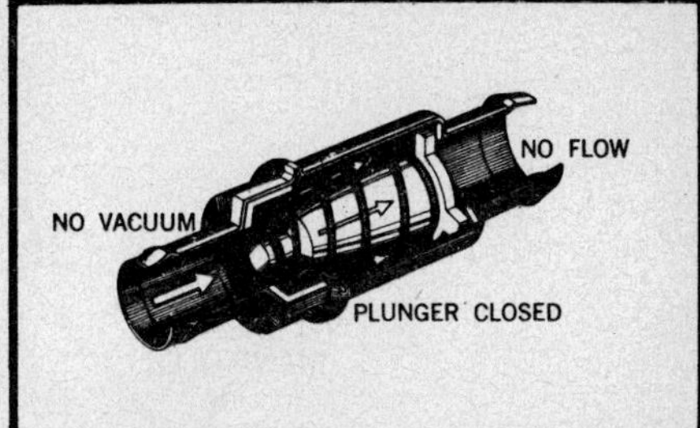

PCV valve operation with engine off or during backfire (© International Harvester Co.)

Jeep specifies that closing off the open end of the PCV valve should result in a 50 rpm drop at idle. If the engine drops less than this or does not change speed, the valve is clogged.

With any vehicle, if the engine idles roughly and you can restore a smooth idle by closing off the open end of the PCV valve, this is a sure sign that the valve must be replaced.

EVAPORATION EMISSION CONTROL SYSTEM

To prevent the emission of gasoline vapors into the atmosphere from the gasoline tank and carburetor vents, vapors are routed by hoses to one or more charcoal filled canisters for storage while the engine is stopped and are routed from and/or through the canister(s) to the engine fuel induction system, when the engine is operating.

On single canister arrangements, the throttle valve is normally used as purge valve, with the vapor hoses routed to the intake manifold or to the carburetor base. On some vehicle models, the purging of the canister is accomplished by air movement through the air cleaner snorkel and into the engine, by having the purge hose connected from the canister to the snorkel.

On dual canister arrangements, the purging action of the

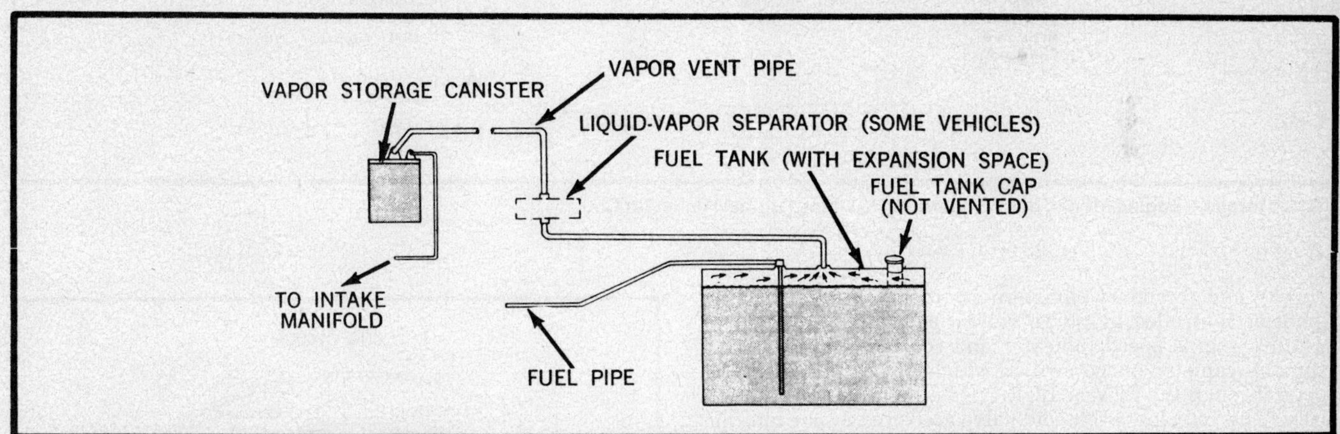

Schematic view of gasoline evaporation system (© International Harvester Co.)

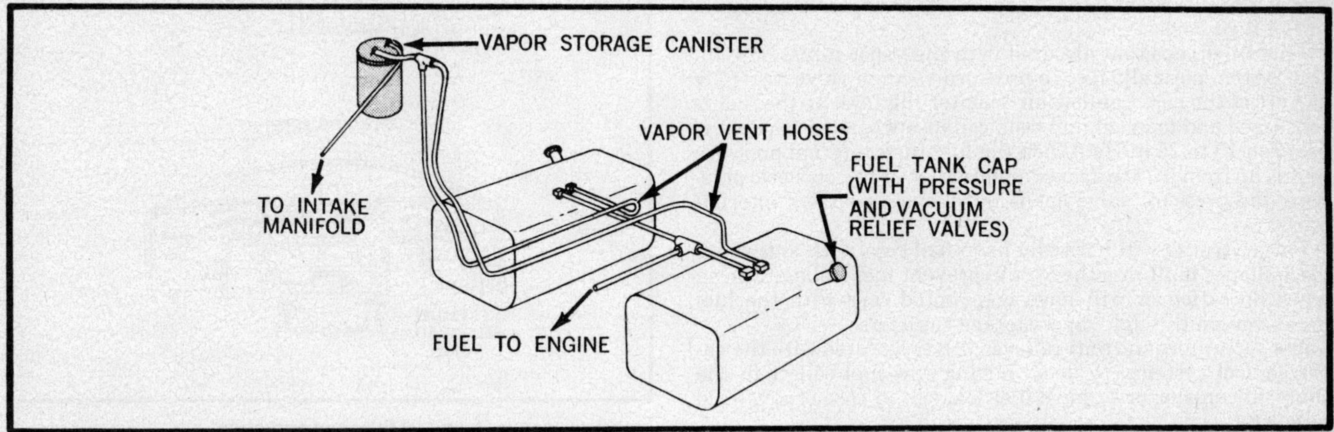

Typical single vapor storage canister arrangement with twin fuel tanks (© International Harvester Co.)

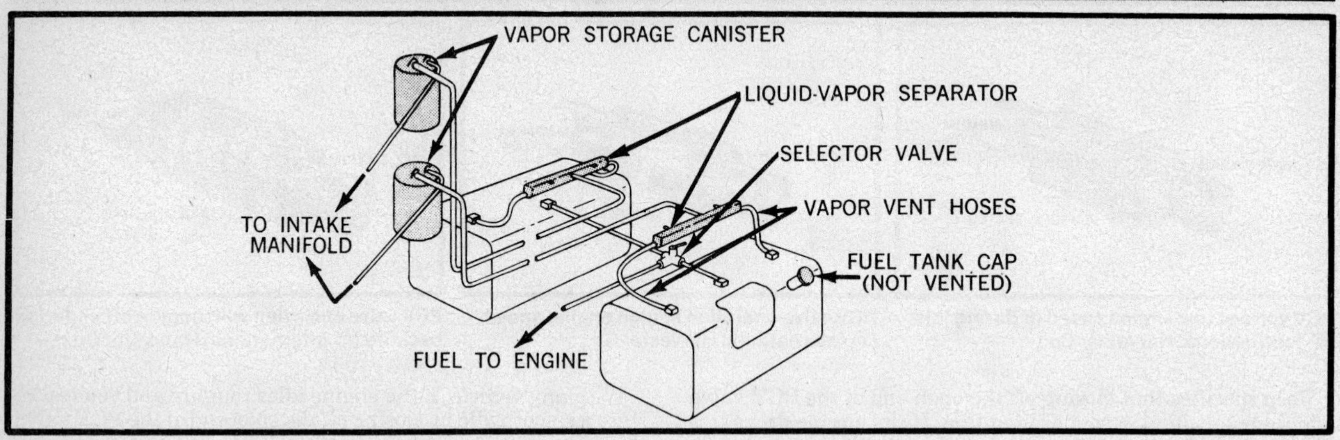

Typical double vapor storage canister arrangement with twin fuel tanks (© International Harvester Co.)

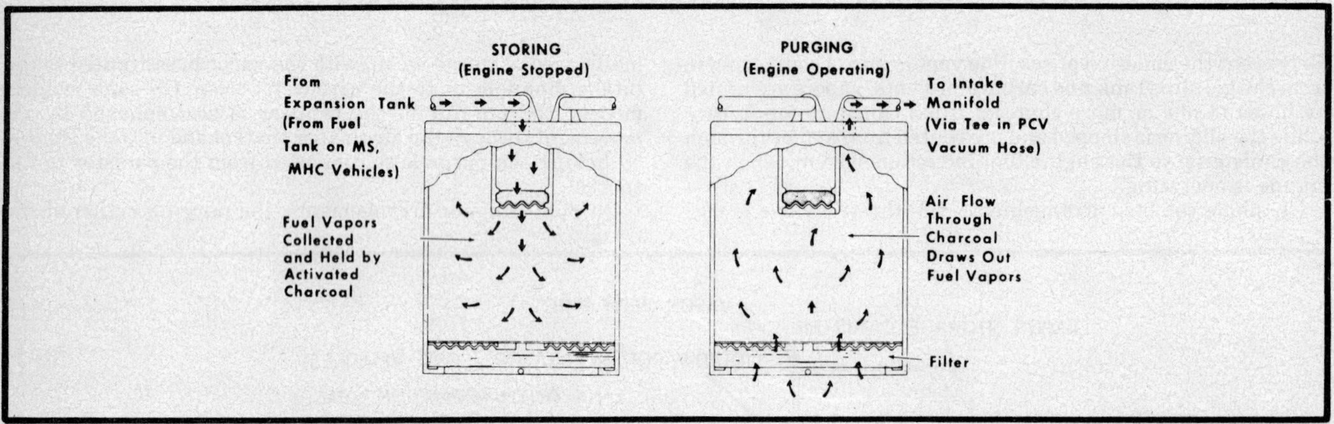

Vapor storage—Engine off and during operation (© International Harvester Co.)

primary and secondary canisters are triggered by a vacuum signal or controlled by purge valves, controlled by manifold vacuum, engine speed indicator and coolant temperature to open the canister purge switch, which allows the vapors to purge through the PCV or EGR system and into the engine.

On some vehicles, a solenoid valve activated by the ignition switch allows intake vacuum to purge the canister. When the ignition is turned off, the solenoid valve closes to retain the vapors in the system. Valve failure occurs in the closed position and can result in lean running due to the existence of a vacuum in the float bowl.

Fuel filler caps that are used with the vapor Emission Control System normally have a pressure-vacuum valve assembly as part of the cap, to allow air to enter the tank as the fuel is consumed and to avoid fuel tank collapse when the vacuum is between 15 to 25 in.Hg. When the fuel tank internal pressure builds up from 0.75 to 2.0 psi (nominal) over atmospheric pressure, the pressure valve opens to relieve the excess internal pressures.

Larger trucks will normally have fuel caps with anti-surge mechanisms built into the caps to prevent fuel spillage during truck operation or will have non-vented caps with the fuel tanks vented through vapor storage canisters.

Vapor separators and anti-rollover valves are used with the vapor control systems, to avoid having raw fuel collect in the charcoal canister or to have fuel leakage in case of a vehicle rollover.

Note: Should fuel tanks or fuel tank filler caps be re-

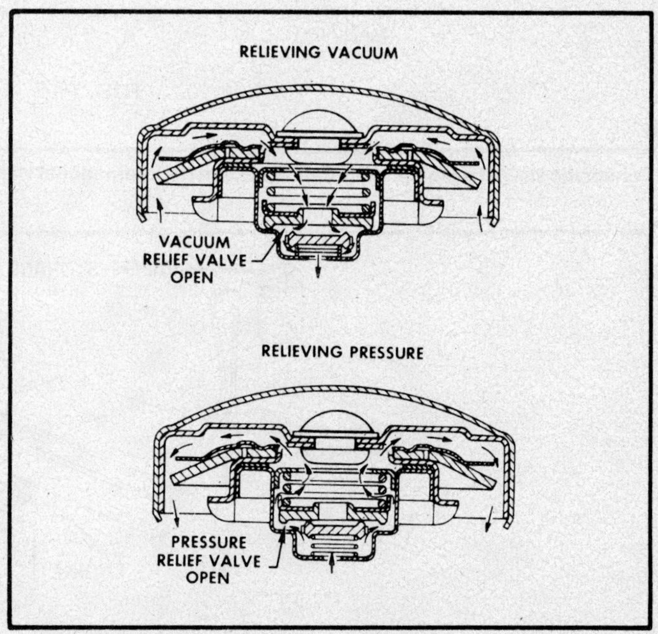

Pressure vacuum type fuel filler cap operation (© International Harvester Co.)

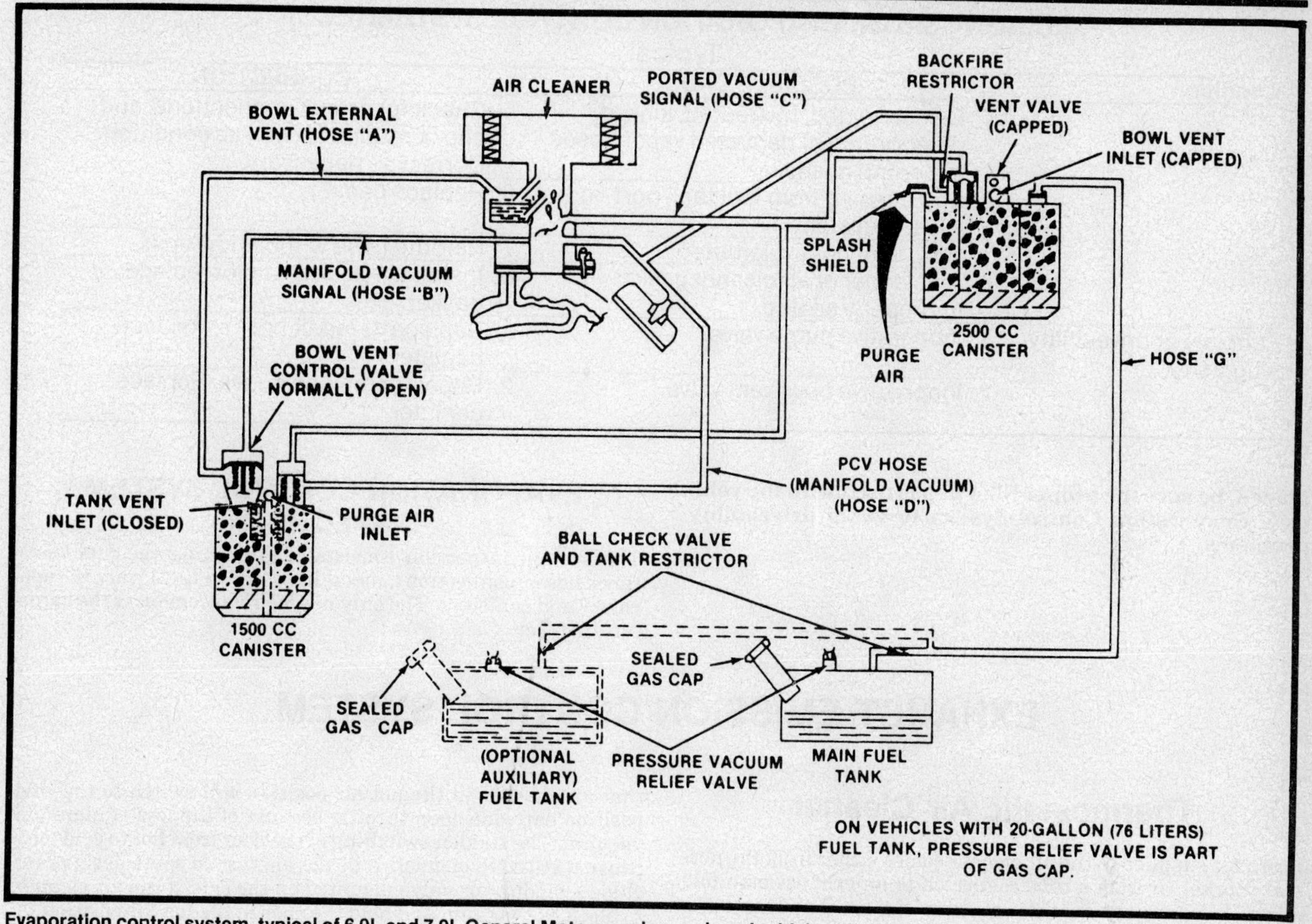

Evaporation control system, typical of 6.0L and 7.0L General Motors engine equipped vehicles (© General Motors Corp.)

DIAGNOSIS OF EVAPORATION CONTROL SYSTEM (ECS)
Typical

Condition	POSSIBLE CAUSE	CORRECTION
Evidence of fuel loss or fuel vapor odor	Hoses not connected correctly	Check connections
A. From area of fuel tank or fuel cap. Perform pressure check to determine possible causes	1. Leaking or plugged fuel evaporator hoses.	1. Repair or replace hoses as necessary.
	2. Leaking fuel cap.	2. Repair or replace as necessary.
	3. Leaking fuel filler.	3. Repair or replace as necessary.
	4. Fuel filler neck gasket surface nicked, burred, or dented.	4. Repair or replace as necessary.
	5. Leaking sending unit or gasket.	5. Repair or replace as necessary.
	6. Leaking tank switch unit (Dual tank system).	6. Replace unit.
	7. Inoperative tank switch unit (Dual tank system).	7. Replace unit.
B. From under hood. Perform pressure check to determine possible causes	1. Fuel leaking from fuel lines, fuel pump or carburetor.	1. Tighten fuel line. Repair or replace fuel pump or carburetor as necessary.
	2. Cracked or damaged canisters.	2. Repair or replace canisters as necessary.
	3. Inoperative bowl vent valve	3. Repair or replace hoses. Replace canister.
	4. Inoperative purge valve.	4. Repair or replace hoses. Replace canister.

DIAGNOSIS OF EVAPORATION CONTROL SYSTEM (ECS)
Typical

Condition	POSSIBLE CAUSE	CORRECTION
	5. Disconnected, misrouted, kinked, deteriorated or damaged vapor hoses or control hoses.	5. Check for proper connections, and check routing as well as condition. Correct as necessary.
	6. Cap missing from fuel tank port on lower canister.	6. Replace cap.
	7. Bowl vent hose misrouted.	7. Reroute hose without low spot.
	8. Air cleaner or air cleaner gasket improperly seated.	8. Install air cleaner and/or replace gasket.
Poor idle or driveability sluggish·	1. Inoperative purge valve.	1. Replace or repair hoses. Replace canister.
	2. Inoperative bowl vent valve.	2. Repair or replace hoses. Replace canister.

placed, be sure the proper filler cap is used with the vehicle's Evaporation Control System to avoid driveability problems.

EVAPORATION CONTROL SYSTEM INSPECTION

The system inspection consists of examining the fuel resistance hoses, connections, metal lines, nylon lines, valves, separators and canisters. The only needed replacement is the canister air filter.

EXHAUST EMISSION CONTROL SYSTEM

Thermostatic Air Cleaner

Fresh air supplied to the air cleaner comes either from the normal snorkel, or from a tube connected to an exhaust manifold stove. A door in the snorkel regulates the source of incoming air so that a warm engine always takes in warm air, approximately 100°F. The door may be controlled by a thermostatic spring or expansion bulb, or it may be vacuum operated. The vacuum operated designs use a thermostatic bimetal switch inside the air cleaner that bleeds off vacuum as the engine warms up, and regulates the position of the air door. On all late models, the snorkel is connected to a long tube so it takes in cooler air from outside the engine compartment. In hot climates the cool air tube is necessary because underhood air can easily reach 200°F.

Vacuum operated air doors are all designed so that the air cleaner takes in cold air when there is no vacuum. This means that an air door in the hot air position will switch to the cold position oat wide open throttle because of the loss of manifold vacuum. The sudden switching of the door from hot to cold may cause a stumble or misfire in the engine, so some designs include a modulator valve mounted on the side of the air cleaner to block the vacuum and hold the door in the hot air position. A small thermostat inside the modulator opens it when the underhood temperatures reach normal. Other designs use a delay valve that allows the air door to move to the cold position slowly, to prevent stumble.

NON–VACUUM TYPE AIR CLEANERS

Testing

To test the non-vacuum type of heated air cleaner, start with an engine that is cold enough to have the air door in the hot air

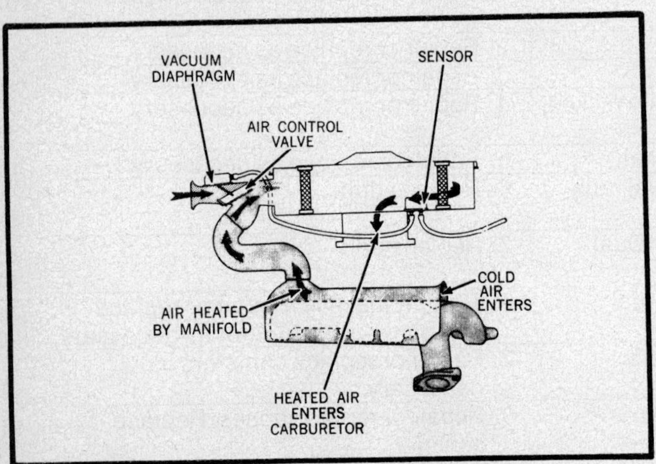

Vacuum operated air cleaner operation (© Chrysler Corp.)

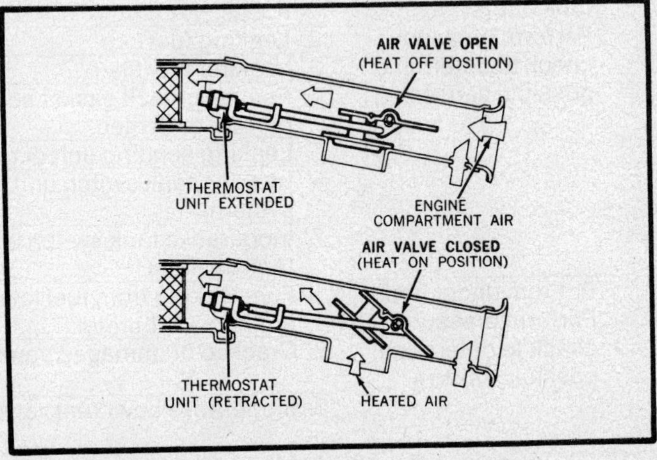

Thermostatic controlled air cleaner operation—typical (© Jeep Corp.)

position. Remove the top of the air cleaner and put a thermometer inside the cleaner, then replace the cover without the nuts. Start the engine and watch the air door through the end of the air cleaner. You may have to remove some air ducting to be able to see the air door. As soon as the air door starts to move from the hot air position, lift the top off the air cleaner and read the temperature. If the temperature is between 130 and 150°F, the thermostat is working correctly. If not, replace the thermostat.

CAUTION

Do not replace the thermostat if the temperature is off by only a few degrees. It must be considerably out of specification, or perhaps not opening at all, to affect the running of the vehicle.

VACUUM TYPE AIR CLEANERS

Testing

To test the vacuum type of heated air cleaner, inspect the air door with the engine off. It should be in the cold air position. Start he engine. If the engine is cold, the air door should move to the hot air position. As the engine warms up, the air door should move to a mid position, depending on the outside air temperature.

If the outside air is extremely cold, the air door may stay in the hot air position indefinitely. On a warm day, after the engine warms up the air door should move to the cold air position. If it doesn't, the temperature sensor inside the air cleaner might be faulty, or the air door itself might be hanging up. Check the air door by running a hose from manifold vacuum to the vacuum motor. Connect and disconnect the hose to see if the air door moves freely. If the air door is free, check out the hoses for leaks or blockage. If the hoses are okay, the trouble must be in the temperature sensor, and it should be replaced.

Modulators are used in the air cleaner vacuum line on some engines. The modulator mounts on the side of the air cleaner and has two hose connections, one to the air cleaner temperature sensor, and the other to the vacuum motor. Below 50–80°F, the modulator is a one-way check valve, which allows vacuum to move the air door to the hot air position, but traps the vacuum so the door will not jump back to the cold air position during acceleration. This prevents a stumble.

After the modulator warms up, the check valve unseats so that the vacuum can pass freely in either direction, and the air door then operates normally. The connections for the modulator are important. The connection in the center goes to the vacuum motor, and the connection on the edge goes to the vacuum source, which is the temperature sensor.

To test the modulator on a cold engine, apply enough vacuum to the edge port to move the air door to the hot position. Then remove the hose from the port, and the air door should stay in the hot position. Make the same test when the engine is warmed up, and the air door should move to the cold position when you pull off the hose.

Deceleration Control Devices

Deceleration (especially sudden release of the throttle) produces more hydrocarbon and CO emissions than any other gas engine operating mode. Because of high manifold vacuum, both compression and turbulence in the cylinder are at a minimum. At the same time, fuel laying in the manifold under cruise or acceleration conditions may suddenly be evaporated and pass through the engine practically unburned.

As a result of these combustion/emissions problems, many vehicles, especially those using high rpm engines and manual transmissions, are equipped with devices which slow or limit closing of the throttle when the vehicle is at a slow down speed. In some cases, ignition timing may be advanced.

When improperly adjusted or malfunctioning, these systems may cause: engine racing and difficult shifting; inconsistent behavior of the engine when the throttle is released, also causing difficult shifting, or backfiring.

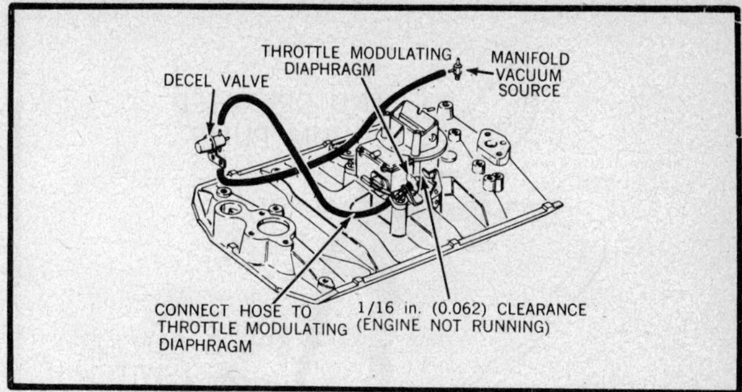

Typical vacuum throttle modulating system (© Jeep Corp.)

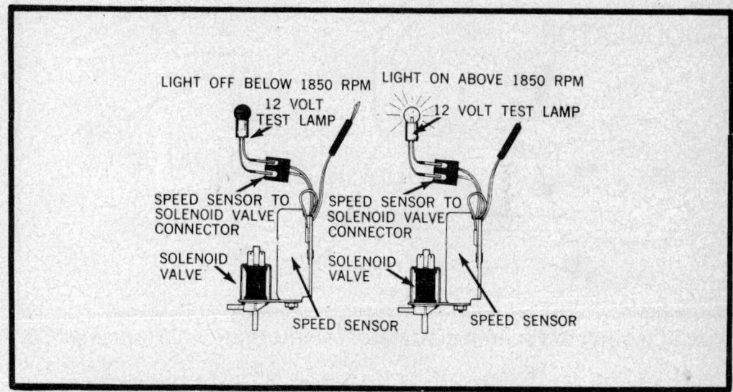

Testing of electric speed sensor switch
(© International Harvester Co.)

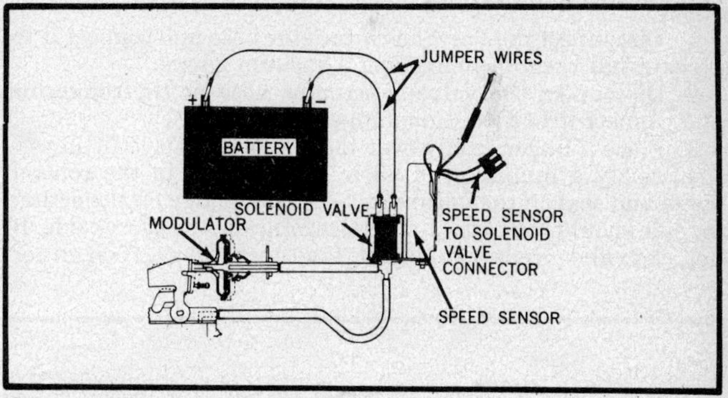

Testing of electric solenoid valve with engine running
(© International Harvester Co.)

Since such a system can radically raise engine idle speed, you should make sure adjustments are to specification and that all elements of the system are snugly connected and working smoothly.

CHEVROLET/GMC Throttle Return Control System

HEAVY DUTY EMISSIONS, THROUGH 1982

A throttle return control system (TRC) is used on some California truck engines. When the truck is coasting against the engine, the control valve is open to allow vacuum to operate the throttle lever actuator. The throttle lever actuator then pushes the throttle lever slightly open reducing the HC (hydrocarbon) emission level during coasting. When manifold vacuum drops below a predetermined level, the control valve closes, the throttle lever retracts, and the throttle lever closes to the idle position.

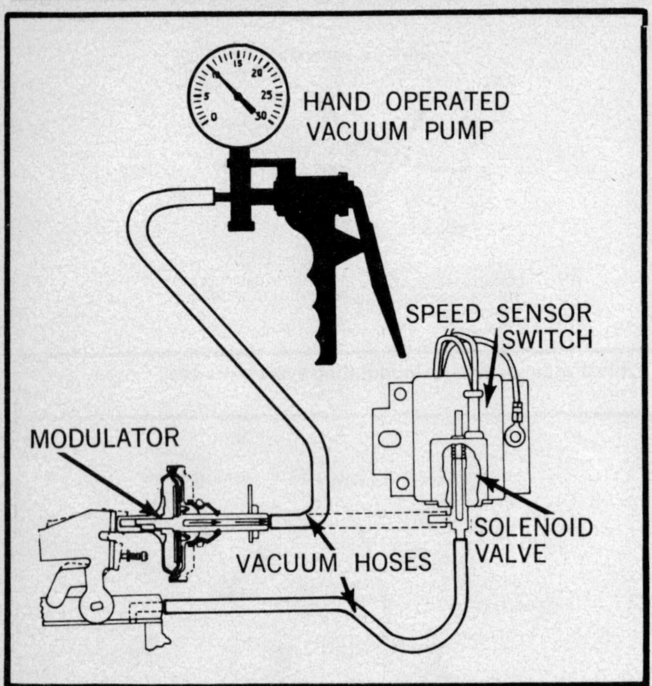

Typical testing of vacuum modulator (© International Harvester Co.)

CONTROL VALVE

Check and Adjustment

1. Disconnect the valve-to-carburetor hose and connect it to an external vacuum source and a vacuum gauge.
2. Disconnect the valve-to-actuator hose at the connector and connect it to a vacuum gauge.
3. Place a finger firmly over the end of the bleed fitting.
4. Apply a minimum of 23 in.Hg. vacuum to the control valve and seal off the vacuum source. The gauge on the actuator side should read the same as the gauge on the source side. If not, the valve needs adjustment. If vacuum drops off on either side (with the finger still on the bleed fitting), the valve is defective and should be replaced.
5. With a minimum of 23 in.Hg. vacuum in the valve, remove the finger from the bleed fitting. The vacuum level in the actuator side will drop to zero and the reading on the source side will drop to a value that will be the valve set point of 21.5 in.Hg. If the valve is not within ½ in.Hg vacuum of the specified valve set point, adjust the valve.
6. Gently pry off the conical plastic cover.
7. Turn the adjusting screw in (clockwise) to raise the set point or out (counterclockwise) to lower the set point.
8. Recheck the valve set point.
9. If necessary, repeat the adjustment.

THROTTLE VALVE

Check and Adjustment

1. Disconnect the valve-to-actuator hose at the valve and connect it to an external vacuum source.
2. Apply 20 in.Hg. vacuum to the actuator and seal the vacuum source. If the vacuum gauge reading drops, the valve is leaking and should be replaced.
3. Check the throttle lever, shaft, and linkage for freedom of operation.
4. Start the engine and warm it to operating temperature.
5. Note the idle rpm.
6. Apply 20 in.Hg. vacuum to the actuator and manually operate the throttle. Allow it to close against the extended actuator plunger. Note the engine rpm.
7. Release and reapply 20 in.Hg. vacuum to the actuator and note the rpm at which the engine speed increases (do not assist the actuator).
8. If the engine speed obtained in Step 7 is not within 150 rpm of that obtained in Step 6, then the actuator may be binding. If the binding cannot be corrected, replace the actuator.
9. Release the vacuum from the actuator and the engine speed should return to within 50 rpm of the speed noted in Steps 4 and 5.

To adjust the actuator:

10. Turn the screw on the actuator plunger until the specified TRC speed range (1475–1525 rpm) is obtained.

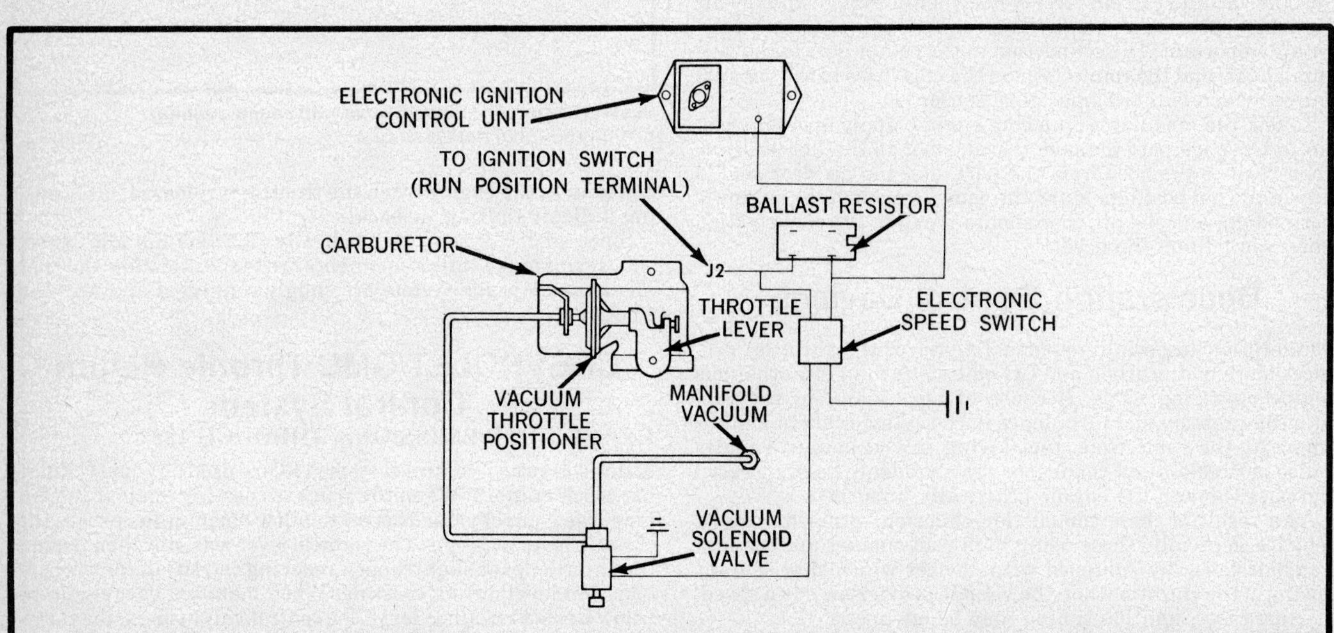

Typical throttle positioner system used on Chrysler Corp. vehicles having California Emission requirements (© Chrysler Corp.)

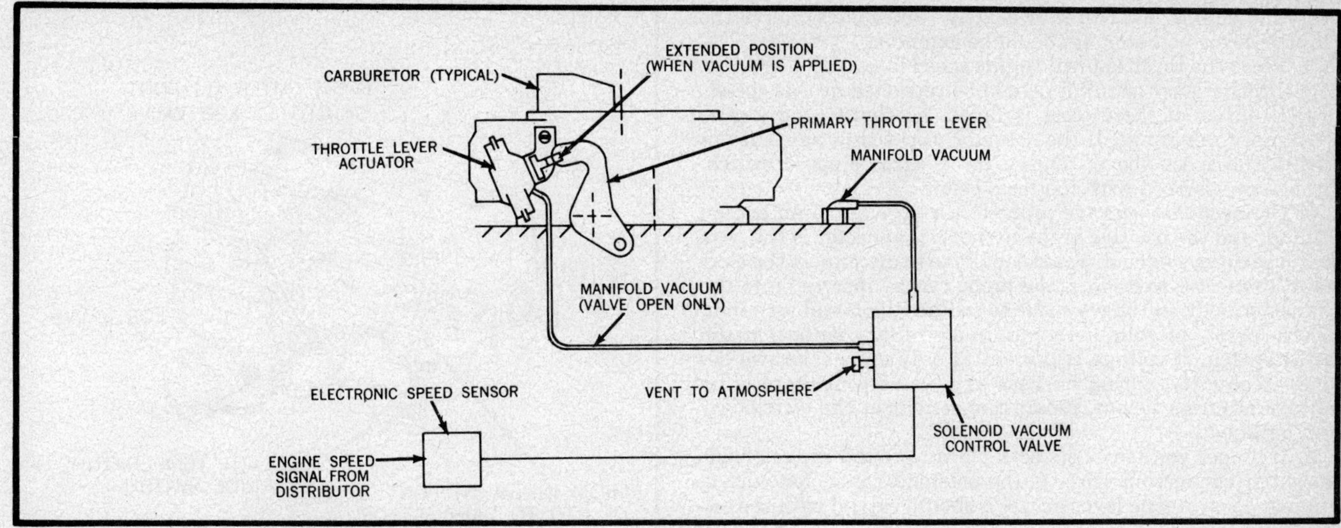

Typical throttle return control system used on GM vehicles (© General Motors Corp.)

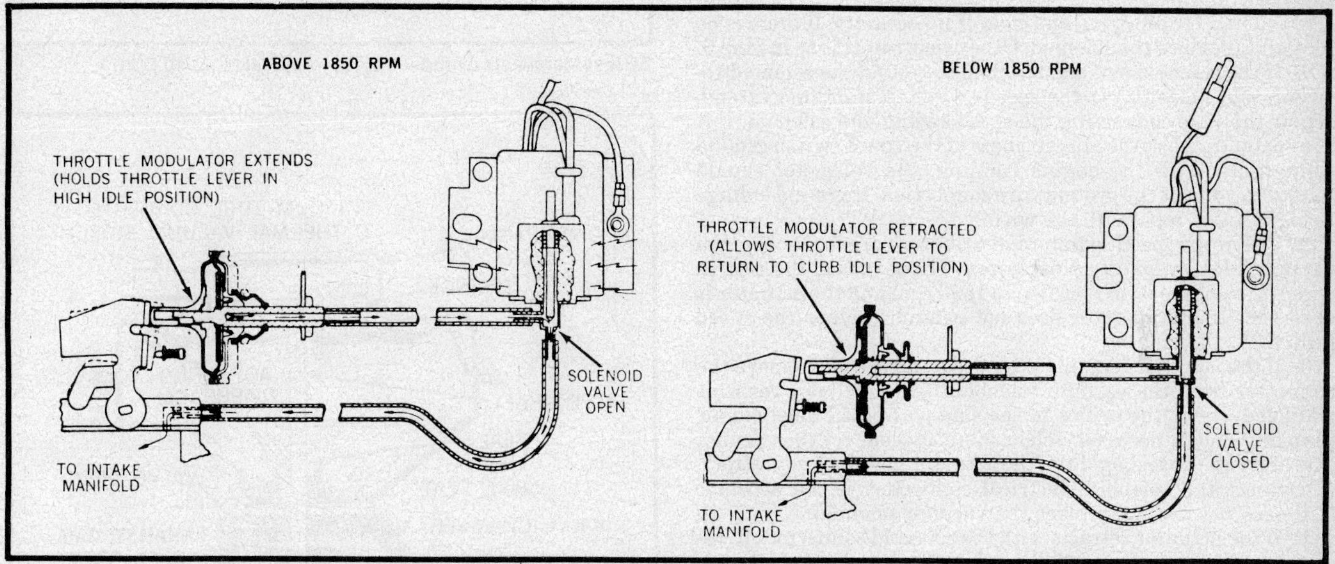

Typical throttle modulator operation used on I.H. vehicles (© International Harvester Co.)

Chevrolet/GMC Throttle Return Control System

HEAVY DUTY EMISSIONS, 1983 AND LATER

The Throttle Rerturn Control system used on 1983 and later trucks with heavy duty emission controls, consists of a vacuum operated throttle lever actuator, an electronic speed sensor, and a solenoid vacuum control valve, which converts the sensor's electronic signal to vacuum to actuate the system. The system opens the throttle slightly beyond its curb idle position to reduce hydrocarbons when the engine is overrunning.

Problems with the system would be indicated by inconsistent idle speed or unaccustomed engine braking or backfiring. Troubleshoot the system as described below.

1. Inspect all vacuum hoses for cracks or bad connections and replace as necessary. Make sure wiring connectors are firmly attached at the distributor, speed switch, and vacuum solenoid.

2. Connect a tachometer sensitive enough to measure a change of 10 rpm to the distributor TACH terminal. Then,

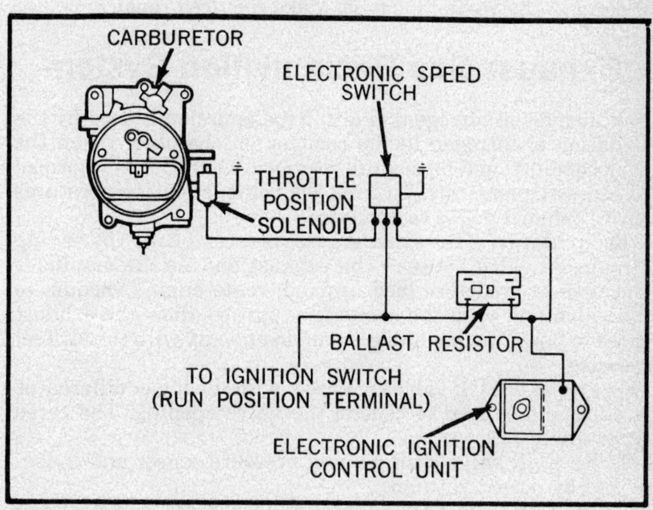

Typical throttle positioner electrical circuitry used on Chrysler Corp. vehicles (© Chrysler Corp.)

start the engine and run it at exactly 1890 rpm. Observe the throttle lever actuator. It should be extended.

3. Close the throttle until engine speed is exactly 1700 rpm. The throttle lever actuator should be retracted at this speed.

4. If either of these tests is failed, accelerate the engine within a wider range. If the actuator works this way, but not within the specs above, replace the electronic speed switch. Otherwise, proceed with the tests below.

5. Connect the negative probe of a voltmeter to an engine ground, and the positive probe to the hot connector of the wire to the vacuum solenoid. You do not have to disconnect the electrical connector to do this, the probe can be inserted into the connector body on the wire side to contact the metal terminal. Check for 12–14 volts here and, in a similar manner, at the speed switch. If voltage is present at only one of the two devices, repair the wiring harness as necessary. If there is no voltage at either device, repair connections at the distributor and bulkhead.

6. If proper voltage exists both places, ground the solenoid-to-switch connecting wire at the solenoid connector with a jumper. The throttle lever actuator should extend with the engine running.

7. If it does not extend, disconnect the hose at the side port of the solenoid that connects to the actuator. Check the orifice inside the port for plugging and clear it if necessary. If there is no plugging, replace the solenoid. Otherwise, retest it as in Step 6.

8. If the solenoid extended in Step 6, ground the solenoid-to-switch wire terminal at the speed switch. If it did not extend, repair the wire connecting the speed switch and solenoid. If it does extend, check the effectiveness of the speed switch ground connection. With the engine running, the voltmeter should read zero volts at the ground wire connection. If ground voltage is high, make repairs to the wiring.

9. Check the speed switch-to-distributor wire for proper connection. Make repairs as necessary. Then, repeat the test in which the engine is accelerated to 1890 rpm and the actuator is observed. If the actuator does not extend, replace the speed switch.

10. If the actuator remains extended at all speeds, remove the connector from the vacuum solenoid. If the actuator remains extended, check the orifice in the side port of the solenoid for plugging and, if necessary, clear it out. Reconnect the vacuum line and run the test again. If the actuator now does not retract, disconnect the solenoid electrical connector. If the actuator still does not retract, replace the vacuum solenoid.

11. If the actuator retracts with the solenoid connector off, reconnect and then remove the speed switch connector. If the actuator now retracts, replace the speed switch. If the actuator does not retract, the solenoid-to-switch wire is shorted to ground in the wiring harness. Make required repairs.

Exhaust Gas Recirculation System

NOx (oxides of nitrogen) is a tailpipe emission caused by the oxidation of nitrogen in the combustion chamber. When the peak combustion temperature goes over 2500°F, NOx is formed in excessive amounts. To keep the combustion temperatures down, exhaust gas is recirculated.

Recirculation of the exhaust gases is accomplished by having a movable valve between the exhaust and intake manifolds and upon a predetermined demand, route engine vacuum to the valve and open the connecting port to allow the exhaust gases to flow into the intake manifold and mix with the air/fuel mixture.

Three types of EGR valves are used, with the major differences in the method used to control the valve opening. The three types are as follows:

1. An EGR valve with no back pressure sensor and is controlled by ported vacuum.

2. An EGR valve with an integral back pressure sensor and is controlled by ported vacuum and exhaust gas back pressure.

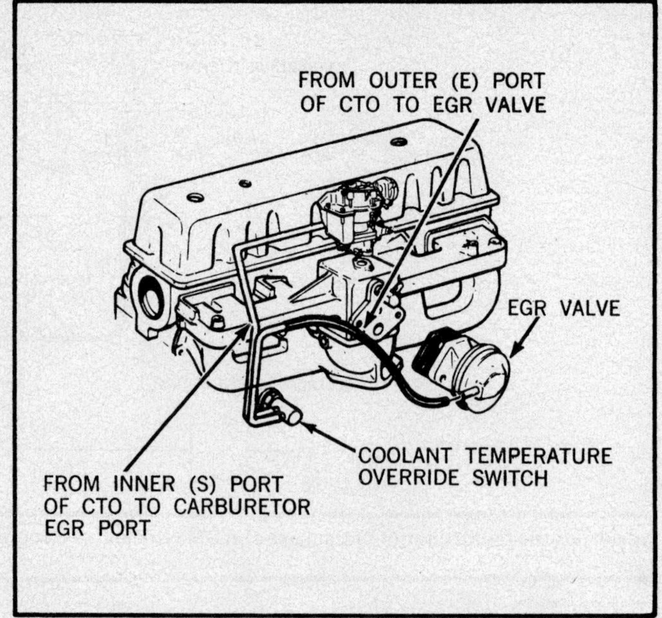

EGR system—six cylinder engine—typical (© Jeep Corp.)

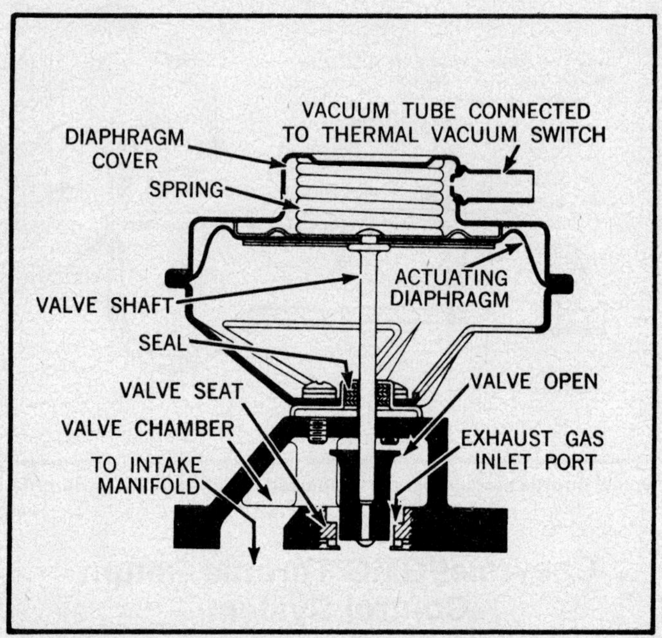

Cross section of ported vacuum signal EGR valve (© General Motors Corp.)

Both positive and negative type transducers are used to react to either high or low exhaust gas back pressures.

3. An EGR valve with an external, non-integral back pressure sensor and is controlled by ported vacuum and exhaust gas back pressure.

NOTE: Venturi vacuum is used as a triggering agent when a vacuum amplifier is used in the EGR system.

Several different types of controls are used to turn the vacuum to the EGR valve on and off. Most of them have to do with engine temperature, as described later.

When the EGR valve hose is connected to the base of the carburetor, without a separate amplifier, the system is operated by ported vacuum. The hose may not run directly from the

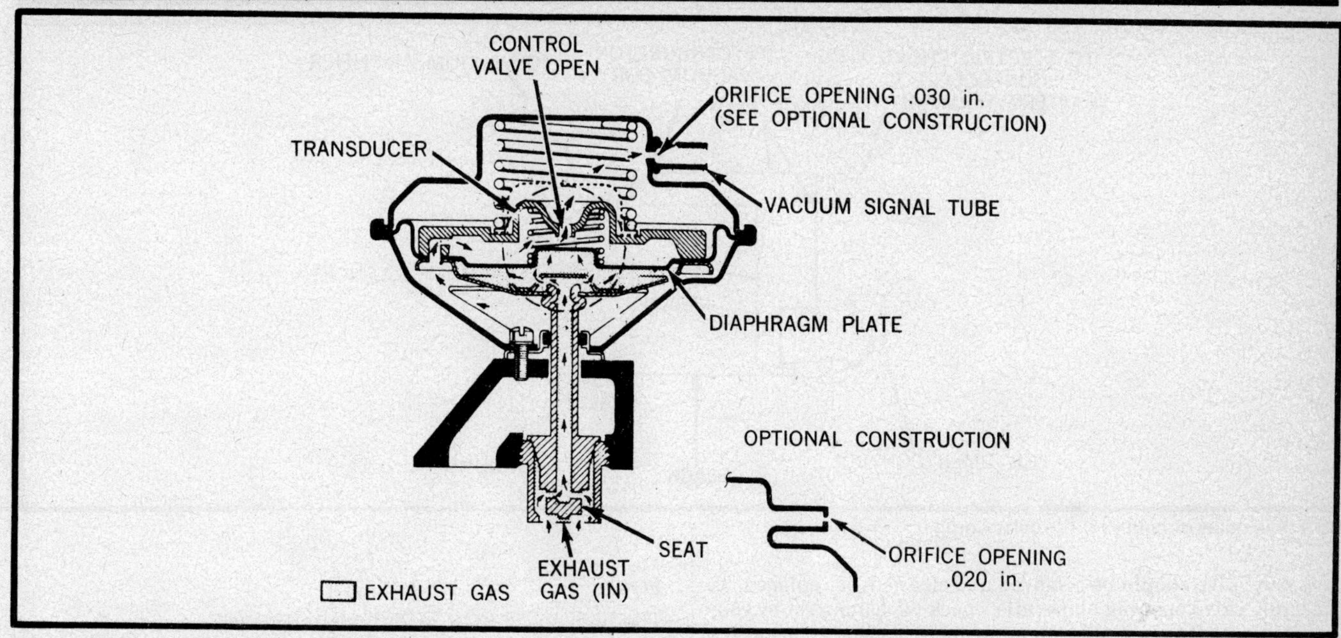

Cross section of positive back pressure EGR valve (© General Motors Corp.)

EGR valve to the carburetor, but may go through a temperature control valve of some sort. In a ported vacuum system, the vacuum to operate the EGR valve is taken from a port that is above the throttle plate at idle, and thus not subject to vacuum. Because there is no vacuum, the spring in the EGR valve closes it, and the exhaust gas does not recirculate. As the throttle is opened, the port is exposed to vacuum, and the EGR valve opens.

Vacuum systems, with an amplifier, are the most complicated, because of the number of hoses. Manifold vacuum is connected to the amplifier by a hose, and then connects to the EGR valve. The amplifier also connects to venturi vacuum. At idle there is no venturi vacuum, but above idle the air moves through the carburetor venturi fast enough to create a vacuum. This slight amount of vacuum opens the amplifier, which then allows manifold vacuum to open the EGR valve.

Temperature controls for EGR systems come in many different designs. They are all made so that the EGR valve stays closed when the engine or the outside air is cold. After the engine or the outside air warms up, the temperature control allows the EGR valve to operate normally.

TESTING EGR SYSTEMS

Testing of the EGR systems should verify that the EGR valve is closed at idle, open above idle, and that the exhaust gas is actually recirculating. If the EGR valve sticks open at idle, the engine will run very rough, or may not even start. If this hap-

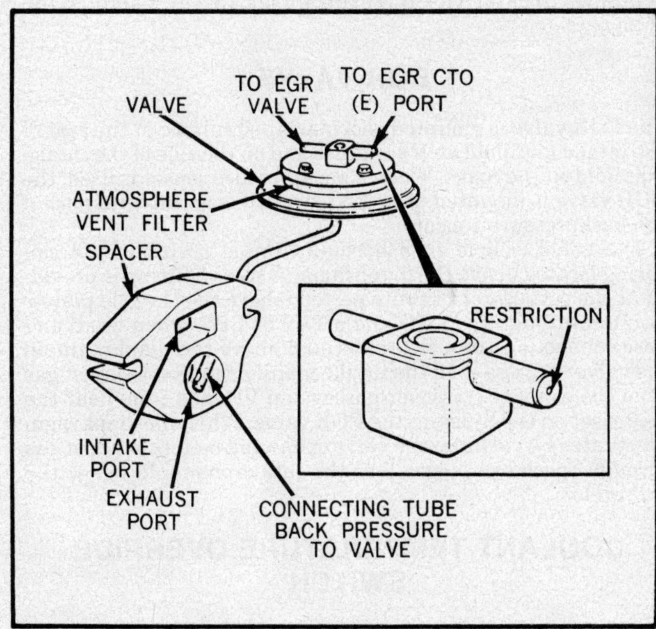

EGR valve with external, non-integral back pressure sensor (© Jeep Corp.)

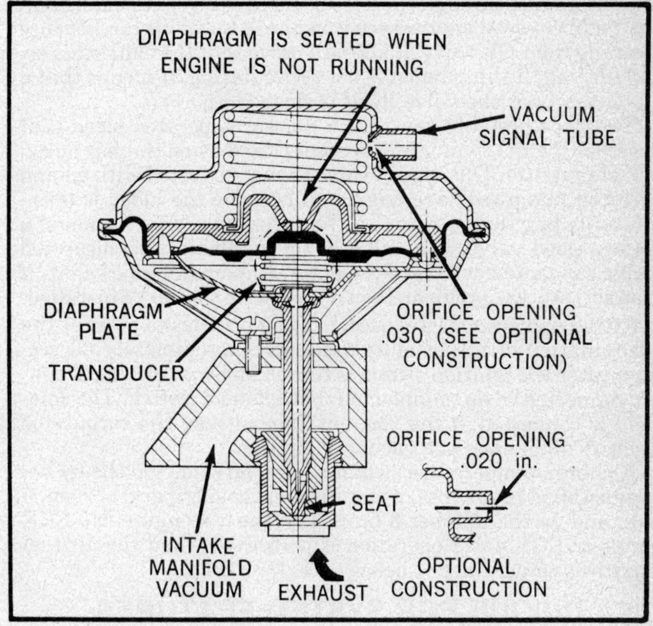

Cross section of negative back pressure EGR valve (© General Motors Corp.)

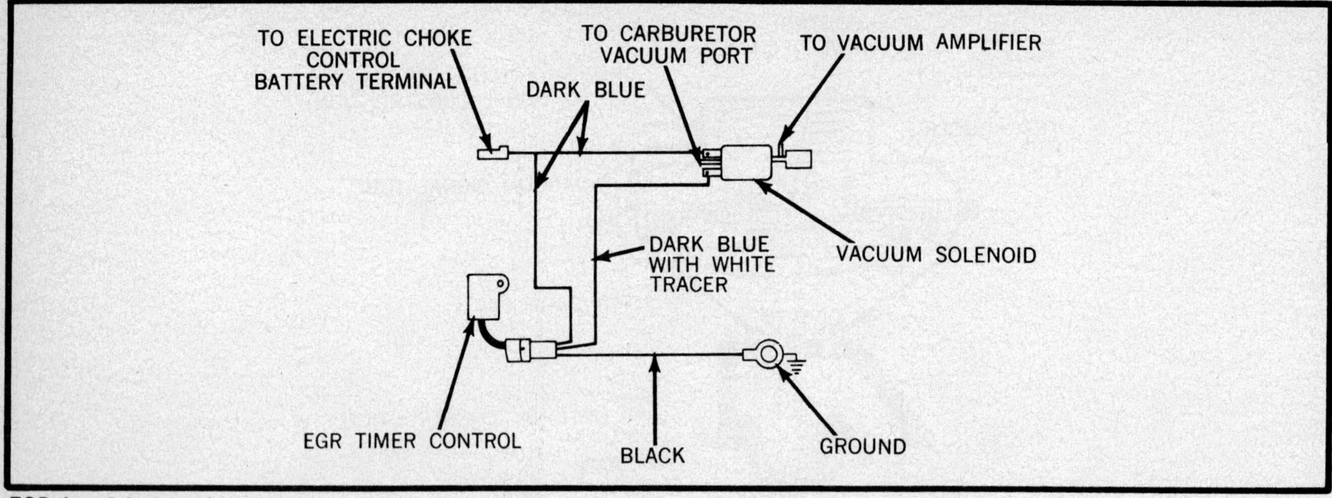

EGR time delay circuitry (© Chrysler Corp.)

pens the valve should be removed and cleaned, or replaced. To check for valve opening above idle, check with a mirror or your fingers to see if the diaphragm or stem moves when the engine is at a fast idle in Park or Neutral. If the diaphragm does not move when the throttle is opened, there is either a problem with vacuum, or the valve is stuck closed. With a vacuum gauge connected to the EGR port, you should see vacuum on the gauge when the throttle is opened. EGR valves should not leak when tested with a hand vacuum pump. If they do they must be replaced.

To find out if the exhaust gas is actually recirculating, use a hand vacuum pump or mouth suction through a hose to open the EGR valve with the engine idling. If the engine runs rough or dies, you know the exhaust gas is recirculating. If the engine does not run rough, make a second test at 2500 rpm. Opening the EGR valve at that rpm should cause a change in engine speed. If it does, you know the exhaust gas is recirculating. To make the 2500 rpm test, remove and plug the hose from the EGR port. Attach your suction hose to the EGR valve before running the engine at 2500 rpm. Simply pulling off the EGR hose at 2500 rpm is not a valid test, because the extra air entering the engine through the hose could cause a speed change all by itself. On most engines you won't have to go this far, because opening the EGR valve at idle will prove that the exhaust is recirculating. If the exhaust is not recirculating, it means that a passageway or the valve itself is clogged up.

The back-pressure sensor is a pressure-operated bleed that disables the EGR valve and keeps it closed when there is no exhaust pressure. This type of valve cannot be tested with a hand vacuum pump with the engine off because the bleed is open. The only practical way to test the valve is by substitution of a known good valve. If a valve is not available, the suspected valve can be removed, and the holes temporarily taped shut. If this corrects the problem, then a new valve should be installed.

EGR delay systems are used on some vehicles to prevent the recirculation of the exhaust gases for approximately 60 seconds after the ignition switch is turned on by an electrical timer, connected to an engine mounted solenoid switch. The solenoid is connected in the vacuum line between the carburetor venturi nipple and the vacuum amplifier.

A charge temperature switch is used on some models by being installed in the intake manifold on the number 6 branch, 6 cyl., and on the number 8 branch on the V8 engine. No EGR timer or EGR valve operation is permitted when the air/fuel mixture temperature is below 60°F. (16°C).

UNIQUE EGR SYSTEM FEATURES

Certain vehicles use EGR system features other than the standard ones previously described. These are covered below.

FORD

The high speed EGR modulator subsystem consists of a speed sensor, an electronic module and a solenoid vacuum valve. The speed sensor, driven by the speedometer cable, provides an AC signal in relation to engine speed, to the electronic module. The electronic module processes the information from the speed sensor and sends a signal to the high speed modulator (vacuum solenoid) valve. When the vehicle speed exceeds the module trigger speed, the solenoid vacuum valve closes which, in turn, causes the EGR valve to close.

JEEP

The EGR system consists of a diaphragm actuated flow control valve (EGR valve), coolant temperature override switch (EGR CTO) and connecting hoses. From 1980, a Thermal Vacuum Switch, located in the air cleaner, was added to control the vacuum signal between the EGR and CTO.

The purpose of the EGR system is to limit the formation of oxides of nitrogen by diluting the fresh air intake charge with a metered amount of exhaust gas, thereby reducing the peak temperatures of the burning gases in the combustion chambers.

EGR VALVE

The EGR valve is mounted on a machined surface at the rear of the intake manifold on V8 engines and on the side of the intake manifold on the Sixes. When a backpressure sensor is used, the EGR valve is mounted on a spacer which is an integral part of the backpressure sensor.

The valve is held in a normally closed position by a coil spring located above the diaphragm. A special fitting is provided at the carburetor to route ported (above the throttle plates) vacuum through the CTO and a TVS or BPS (when used) and hose connections to a fitting located above the diaphragm on the valve. A passage in the intake manifold directs exhaust gas from the exhaust crossover passage on V8s and from near the heat riser on the Sixes, to the EGR valve. When the diaphragm is actuated by vacuum, the valve opens and meters exhaust gas through special passages into the intake manifold below the carburetor.

COOLANT TEMPERATURE OVERRIDE SWITCH

This switch is located in the intake manifold at the coolant passage adjacent to the oil filler tube on V8s and on the left side of the cylinder block on the Sixes. The outer port of the switch is connected to either the EGR valve or BPS (when used). The inner port is connected by a hose to the EGR fitting at the carburetor. When the coolant temperature reaches 115°F., the inner port of the switch opens and a vacuum signal is applied to the EGR valve. This vacuum signal is subject to regulation by the BPS when used.

THERMAL VACUUM SWITCH (TVS)

The TVS is located in the air cleaner and functions as an on/off switch controlled by air cleaner air temperature. The TVS controls the vacuum passage between the EGR CTO valve and the EGR valve. Air temperature in the 40–50°F. range cause the TVS to limit the vacuum applied to the EGR valve, thus improving cold engine driveability.

EXHAUST BACKPRESSURE SENSOR (BPS)

This device is used on some models in conjunction with the EGR system.

The BPS monitors exhaust backpressure and permits EGR operation only when engine operating conditions are favorable. The BPS units are variously calibrated, are not serviceable and must be replaced with the identical part as a unit when necessary.

The BPS consists of a diaphragm valve and a spacer connected by a metal tube projecting into an exhaust port in the spacer body. The EGR valve mounts directly on the spacer. On some six cylinder engines, the sensor is integral with the EGR valve.

In operation, the metal tube connecting the diaphragm valve to the spacer routes exhaust backpressure from the particular exhaust port to the sensor. When the backpressure reaches a certain level the diaphragm valve spring pressure is overcome, permitting a vacuum signal to the EGR valve, providing that the CTO switch is open.

Thus, EGR operation is only permitted when the engine is warmed up sufficiently and exhaust backpressure relatively high, such as during acceleration and at some cruising speeds. When temperature or backpressure conditions are not met, the vacuum signal is vented to the atmosphere from a vent at the diaphragm valve.

Catalytic Converter

A catalytic converter is a chamber in the exhaust system that contains a catalyst. When hydrocarbons or carbon monoxide pass over the catalyst, they react with the oxygen in the exhaust and are converted into harmless water and carbon dioxide. The catalyst inside the converter is made in two forms. General Motors, and Jeep use the pellet form, in which loose pellets are packaged into the converter and can be emptied out and changed, if necessary. Ford, International, and Chrysler use the monolithic (honeycomb) catalyst, which is built into the converter shell and is not replaceable. On Ford, International and Chrysler products the entire converter must be replaced if it goes bad.

NOTE: Both the pellet and the monolithic types may be used in conjunction with each other on later vehicle applications.

There is no way to test a converter in the field to see if it is actually working. Tailpipe readings may be used to set carburetor idle mixtures, when the car maker requires it, but taking a tailpipe reading to determine if the converter is working is not possible.

The one field check that is recommended in all cases is to inspect for mechanical damage. If a converter gets overheated, the catalyst can melt and block the exhaust. Pellets or pieces of the catalyst may even come out the tailpipe while the engine is running. If this happens, the pellets or the entire converter must be changed.

Checking for a melted converter that restricts the exhaust can be done with a vacuum gauge connected to the engine. Run the engine at about 2500 rpm in Park or Neutral. If the vacuum reading is steady, the exhaust is okay. If the vacuum reading slowly drops, it indicates a buildup of pressure in the exhaust.

The use of leaded fuel will slowly destroy the efficiency of the catalyst until finally, after several tanks full, it won't do its job any more. If used long enough, leaded fuel can even cause catalyst plugging to the point that the engine will not run.

Do not change the catalyst if the vehicle has been run on only one tank or less of leaded fuel. Switching back to lead free fuel will allow the catalyst to recover and be almost as efficient as it was.

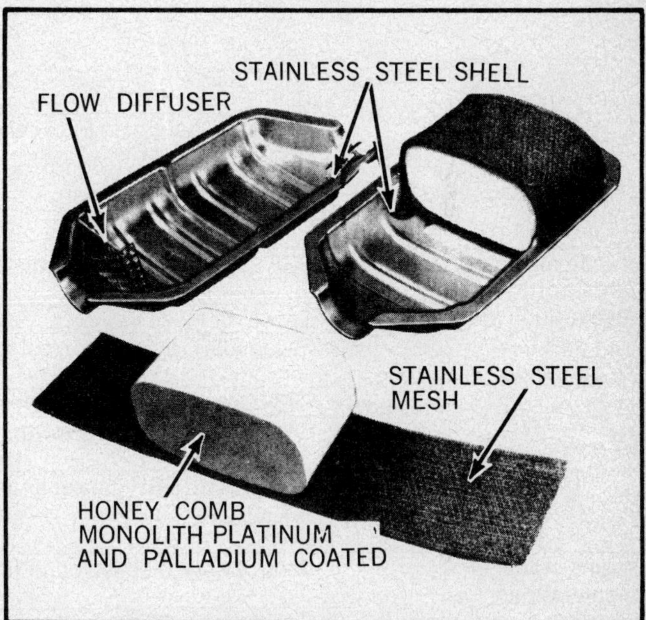

Cut-away view of catalytic converter using honey comb monolith catalyst (© Chrysler Corp.)

Cut-away view of pellet type catalytic converter with exhaust flow shown (© General Motors Corp.)

DIAGNOSIS OF EXHAUST GAS RECIRCULATION SYSTEM
Typical

Condition	POSSIBLE CAUSE	CORRECTION
Engine idles abnormally rough and/or stalls	1. EGR valve vacuum hoses misrouted.	1. Check EGR valve vacuum hose routing. Correct as required.
	2. Leaking EGR valve.	2. Check EGR valve for correct operation.
	3. EGR valve gasket failed or loose EGR attaching bolts.	3. Check EGR attaching bolts for tightness. Tighten as required. If not loose, remove EGR valve and inspect gasket. Replace as required.
	4. EGR thermal control valve and/or EGR-TVS.	4. Check vacuum into valve from carburetor EGR port with engine at normal operating temperature and at curb idle speed. Then check the vacuum out of the EGR valve. If the two vacuum readings are not equal within ± (1.7 kPa) ½ in. Hg., then proceed to EGR vacuum control diagnosis.
	5. Improper vacuum to EGR valve at idle.	5. Check vacuum from carburetor EGR port with engine at stabilized operating temperature and at curb idle speed. If vacuum is more than (-3.3 kPa) 1.0 in. Hg., refer to carburetor idle diagnosis.
Engine runs rough on light throttle acceleration and has poor part load performance	1. EGR valve vacuum hose misrouted.	1. Check EGR valve vacuum hose routing. Correct as required.
	2. Check for loose valve.	2. Torque valve.
	3. Failed EGR vacuum control valve.	3. Same as listing in "Engine Idles Rough" condition.
	4. TVS open below 54°C (130°F.)	4. Clean EGR passage of all deposits.
	5. Sticky or binding EGR valve.	5. Remove EGR valve and inspect. Replace as required.
	6. Wrong or no EGR gasket and/or spacer.	6. Check and correct as required. Install new gasket, install spacer (if equipped), torque attaching parts.
Engine stalls on decelerations	1. Control valve blocked or air flow restricted.	1. Check internal control valve function per service procedure.
	2. Restriction in EGR vacuum line or valve vacuum signal tube.	2. Check EGR vacuum lines for kinks, bends, etc. Remove or replace hoses as required. Check EGR vacuum control valve function. Check EGR valve for excessive deposits causing sticky or binding operation. Replace valve.
	3. Sticking or binding EGR valve.	3. Remove EGR valve and replace valve.
Part throttle engine detonation	1. Control valve blocked or air flow restriction.	1. Check internal control valve function.
	2. Insufficient exhaust gas recirculation flow during part throttle acceleration.	2. Check EGR valve hose routing. Check EGR valve operation. Repair or replace as required. Check EGR thermal control valve and/or EGR-TVS. Replace valve as required. Check EGR passages and valve for excessive deposit. Clean as required.
	Note: ***Non-Functioning EGR valve could contribute to part throttle detonation.***	
	3. Control valve blocked or flow restricted.	3. Check EGR.
	Note: ***Detonation can be caused by several other engine variables. Perform ignition and carburetor related diagnosis.***	
Engine starts but immediately stalls when cold	1. EGR valve hoses misrouted.	1. Check EGR valve hose routings.
	2. EGR TVS system malfunctioning when engine is cold.	2. Perform check to determine if the EGR thermal control valve and/or EGR-TVS are operational. Replace as required.
	Notice: ***Stalls after start can also be caused by carburetor problems.***	

CONVERTER OVERHEAT PROTECTION

Engine controls are used to prevent the converter from being damaged by overheating due to overly rich fuel mixtures during periods of deceleration.
The controls are named differently by the manufacturers, but are all designed to accomplish the same purpose and to operate basically in the same manner. To prevent the engine from operating at a rich mode when the throttle plates are closed during deceleration, electrical and/or mechanical means are provided to hold the throttle plates open at predetermined engine speeds, in order to lean the air/fuel mixture as necessary to control the exhaust emissions. The engine control should be inoperative under engine speeds of 1800 to 2000 rpms to avoid engine overrun or vehicle overspeed in slow traffic.

The various parts are as follows:

1. The throttle lever actuator is mounted as part of the carburetor assembly and operates when vacuum is applied to it from a separate solenoid vacuum control valve.
2. The solenoid vacuum control valve is controlled by a signal from the electronic speed sensor or a throttle modulator deceleration valve vacuum signal to allow vacuum to be routed to the throttle lever actuator.
3. Electronic speed sensor is mounted near or included with the distributor and senses the engine speed and sends a signal to the solenoid vacuum control valve as long as the preset speed is exceeded.

Testing The System

To test the electrical speed sensor system, place the transmission in neutral or park and set the hand brake. With a tachometer attached to the engine, increase the engine speed to approximately 2000 rpm. The solenoid or modulator stem should extend to hold the carburetor throttle lever off curb idle setting. As the engine speed is reduced to below 1800 rpm, the solenoid or modulator stem should retract to the off position. A hand held vacuum pump and test lamp can be used to test the individual components of the system.

To test the vacuum operated system, without an electrical sensor, 21 to 22 in.Hg. must be directed to the decel valve to open the port to direct vacuum to the throttle modulating diaphragm, located on the carburetor base. With the vacuum present, the stem of the modulating diaphragm will be extended. Release of the vacuum should allow the stem of the modulating diaphragm to retract.

Vacuum Operated Exhaust Heat Riser Valves

Exhaust heat riser valves have been used for many years to force part of the engine exhaust through a passageway under the intake manifold for the purpose of preheating the fuel mixture. The heat valve was spring loaded into the closed position, but heat would make the spring relax so that during high speed operation or after warmup the exhaust would push it open.

Many engines now use vacuum operated heat valves, controlled by a vacuum switch that is sensitive to engine temperature. On these systems, manifold vacuum is used to close the valve and force the exhaust gases through the crossover passage in the intake manifold. All the systems have a temperature valve that shuts the vacuum off when the engine warms up.

A coolant temperature-sensitive vacuum switch is mounted on the intake manifold coolant passage and has two hose connections. It actually does triple duty because it also controls the vacuum supply to the idle enrichment system and the air switching valve.

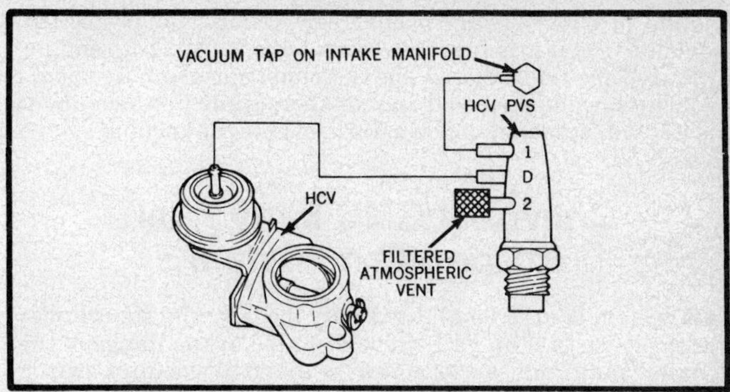

Exhaust heat control valve vacuum circuit using a ported vacuum coolant switch—typical (© Ford Motor Co.)

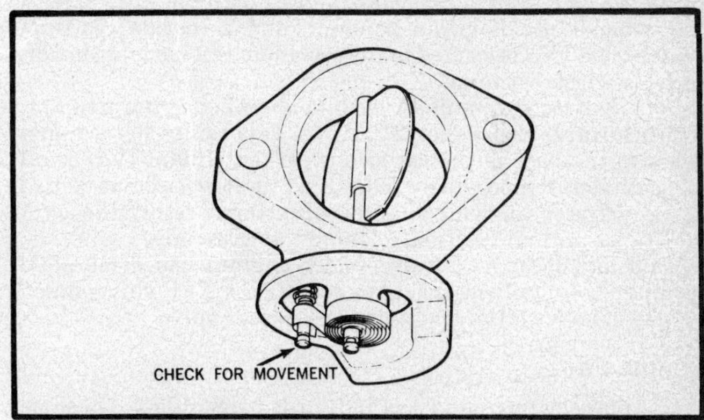

Spring controlled exhaust heat control valve—typical (© Ford Motor Co.)

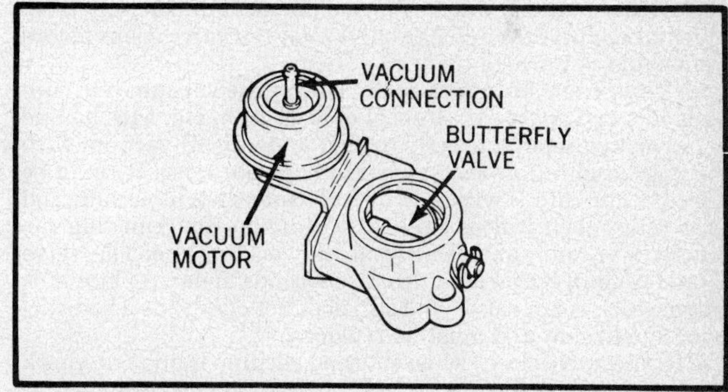

Vacuum operated exhaust heat control valve—typical (© Ford Motor Co.)

A second type vacuum switch has three hose connections, but one of them is a vent with a filter to keep the dirt out.

A third control uses wither a coolant vacuum switch, or a vacuum solenoid connected to an oil temperature switch. The coolant vacuum switch has two hose connections and a vent when it controls the heat valve only. When it is tied into other emission control systems, it can have as many as five hose connections and a vent. Some models also have a check valve in the hose so that vacuum will be trapped in the heat valve actuator when the engine is accelerated. This keeps the heat valve in the closed position and prevents a rattle.

VACUUM OPERATED EXHAUST HEAT RISER VALVES

Testing

Testing the vacuum operated heat riser valve is a matter of

making sure it closes and opens freely. Using hand protection, move it to see if it is free on a warm engine. On a cold engine, the valve should be closed and disconnecting the hose should allow it to open. On a cold engine, there should be vacuum at the vacuum actuator and on a warm engine the vacuum should be shut off.

Chevrolet/GMC Early Fuel Evaporation System

This system is used on all light duty models. The six cylinder system consists of an EFE valve mounted at the flange of the exhaust manifold, an actuator, a thermal vacuum switch (TVS) and a vacuum solenoid. The TVS is on the right side of the engine, forward of the oil pressure switch. The TVS is normally closed and sensitive to oil temperature.

The V8 EFE system consists of an EFE valve at the flange of the exhaust manifold, an actuator, and a thermal vacuum switch. The TVS is located in the coolant outlet housing and directly controls vacuum.

In both systems, manifold vacuum is applied to the actuator, which in turn, closes the EFE valve. This routes hot exhaust gases to the base of the carburetor. When coolant (V8) or oil (six cylinder) temperatures reach a set limit, vacuum is denied to the actuator, allowing an internal spring to return the actuator to its normal position, opening the EFE valve.

1983 and later 4.8L six cylinder engines use a manifold mounted thermostatic spring to actuate the EFE valve, much as was done with the traditional heat riser valve.

Diagnosis

1. Allow the engine to cool until it is below 105°F. On some V8 engines, the EFE valve actuator arm is protected by a two-piece metal cover. Remove the cover if so equipped.
2. Start the engine while watching the EFE valve. The actuator link should be pulled into the diaphragm housing. If so, continue to run the engine to check that the valve opens before the engine is warmed up.
3. If the valve fails to close disconnect the vacuum line running to it and apply a vacuum of at least 10 in.Hg. with a hand pump or by tapping directly to engine manifold vacuum with the engine idling. If the valve still does not close, it could be seized. Lubricate it with a manifold heat valve lubricant, and then retest it. If it does close, test it further by removing the source of vacuum and sealing off the vacuum line. The valve should remain closed for at least 20 seconds, if not, replace it. A valve which is not seized and still does not close, has a bad vacuum diaphragm and must be replaced.
4. If the valve closes when external vacuum is applied, check the rest of the system for loose, kinked, pinched, plugged or cracked hoses and repair or replace parts as required. Also make sure vacuum is getting through the TVS or EFE vacuum solenoid (with engine still below 105°F). Replace the thermostatic control device, if necessary.
5. Warm up the engine to operating temperature. If the valve does not open, check the engine thermostat to ensure the engine reaches operating temperature. Check the TVS or EFE solenoid to ensure vacuum is cut off before the engine reaches operating temperature; and check the valve to ensure it is not mechanically bound in the cold position. If these checks do not reveal the reason the valve won't open, there is no air bleed effect in the diaphragm and the valve must be replaced.

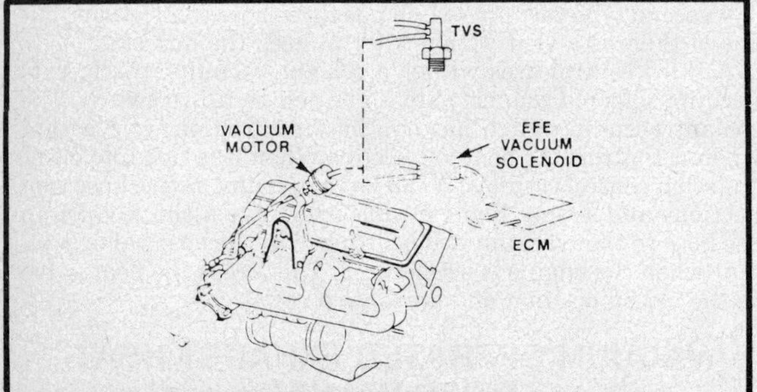

Chevrolet/GMC EFE systems use either a TVS or EFE vacuum solenoid to shut off the EFE valve when the engine warms up (© General Motors Corp.)

Air Injection Systems

A belt-driven air pump supplies air to small tubes positioned in the exhaust port near each exhaust valve. The air mixes with unburned hydrocarbons in the exhaust and the hydrocarbons actually burn up in the exhaust system. Air injection systems are used on engines with catalytic converters, so that the converter gets enough air to keep the reaction going.

All Chevrolet/GMC meduim duty trucks with gasoline engines, having Federal Emissions standards for 1985 and later, can be identified by their usage of two charcoal canister, twin air pumps on V8 engines and a "Check Engine " indicator light on the dash.

Plumbing on air injection systems varies considerably. A check valve is used between the pump and the exhaust port nozzle to keep hot exhaust gases from traveling up the plumbing and destroying the pump. V8s use two check valves. An anti-backing valve, also called bypass valve or diverter valve, is used between the pump and the check valve. Usually, the diverter valve is mounted on the pump or near it. A small sensing hose connects the diverter valve to intake manifold vacuum. When the vacuum rises during deceleration, the diverter valve opens and sends the pump air into the atmosphere. This prevents the overrich deceleration mixture in the exhaust system from exploding or backfiring out the tailpipe.

Some models started using a diverter valve that has the small hose connection on the end instead of the side. The older diverter valve was normally in the running position, but the new one is normally in the dump position. The old valve allowed the air to pass through the engine exhaust ports regardless of whether the small sensing line was hooked up. The new valve, being normally in the dump position, must have the small sensing line hooked up to manifold vacuum, which pulls the valve mechanism from the dump position into the normal running position.

The new style valve will not go into the dump position automatically during deceleration. To get the valve to dump, a vacuum differential valve (VDV) is connected in the sensing line. Manifold vacuum goes through the VDV and then to the diverter valve. When the manifold vacuum increases during deceleration, the VDV closes the sensing line. This shuts off the vacuum to the diverter valve, and the valve goes into the dump position.

A further refinement of this is to connect the sensing line to ported (above the throttle plates) vacuum instead of manifold vacuum and eliminate the VDV. In this situation, the diverter valve only receives vacuum above idle, because the vacuum port in the carburetor throat is above the throttle plate at idle. So whenever the engine idles, the diverter valve goes to the dump position. It also dumps during deceleration, because the throttle at that time is in the idle position.

Some systems have a delay valve, similar to a spark delay valve, in the sensing hose. This delays for a few seconds, the drop in vacuum when the throttle closes, so that the air is not dumped every time the driver takes his foot off the throttle in traffic.

Temperature controls are also used in the sensing hose hookup. Usually, the temperature valve shuts the vacuum off when

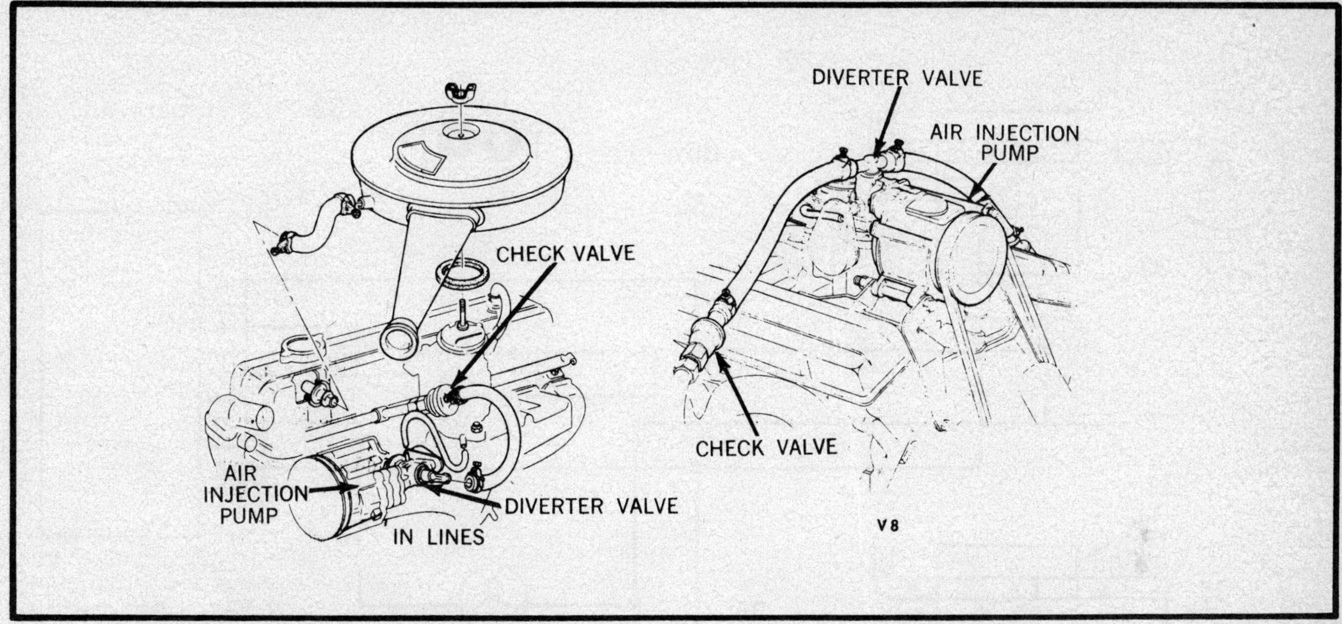

Air Injection system—typical (© General Motors Corp.)

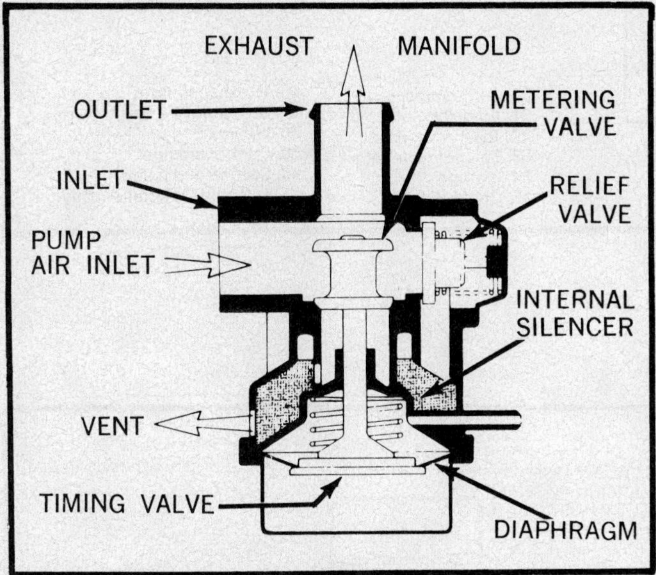

Diverter valve with internal muffler (© General Motors Corp.)

the engine is cold, so that the pump air doesn't go to the engine exhaust ports until the engine warms up.

An idle vacuum valve is used to operate in conjunction with the vacuum delay valve, to provide backfire control, full time idle dumping of secondary air during cold engine operation, deceleration or extended idle periods of ½ to 2 minutes or more. The valve also provides cold temperature protection for the catalyst and a cold EGR valve lockout.

AIR PUMP

Tests

CAUTION

Do not hammer on, pry or bend the pump housing while tightening the drive belt or testing the pump.

Before proceeding with the tests, check the pump drive belt tension. If the belt squeals when the engine is running, the pump may be dragging or seized. Remove the belt and turn the pump by hand to check for seizure. Disregard any chirping, squealing, or rolling sounds from inside the pump when turning it by hand, as these are normal.

Check the hoses and connections for leaks. Hissing or a blast of air is indicative of a leak. Soapy water, applied lightly around the area in question, is a good method for detecting leaks.

To test air output, disconnect the air hose from the pump wherever it is convenient. If you disconnect it from one check valve on a V8, the other hose should also be disconnected and plugged for the test. Run the engine at idle and feel the blast of air from the hose with your hand. Increase the engine speed to 1500 rpm and feel the blast of air again. If the blast increases, and is steady, the pump is okay.

PUMP NOISE

Diagnosis

The air pump is normally noisy. As engine speed increases, the noise of the pump will rise in pitch. The rolling sound of the pump bearings is normal. However, if this sound becomes objectionable at certain speeds, the pump may be defective and will have to be replaced.

A continual hissing sound from the air pump pressure relief valve at idle indicates a defective valve. Replace the relief valve. If the pump rear bearing fails, a continual knocking sound will be heard. Since the rear bearing is not separately replaceable, the pump will have to be replaced as an assembly.

ANTI-BACKFIRE VALVE

Tests

1. Detach the hose which runs from the bypass valve to the check valve.
2. Connect a tachometer to the engine. With the engine running at normal idle speed, check to see that air is flowing from the bypass valve hose connection.
3. Speed the engine up, so that it is running at 1,500–2,000 rpm. Allow the throttle to snap shut.

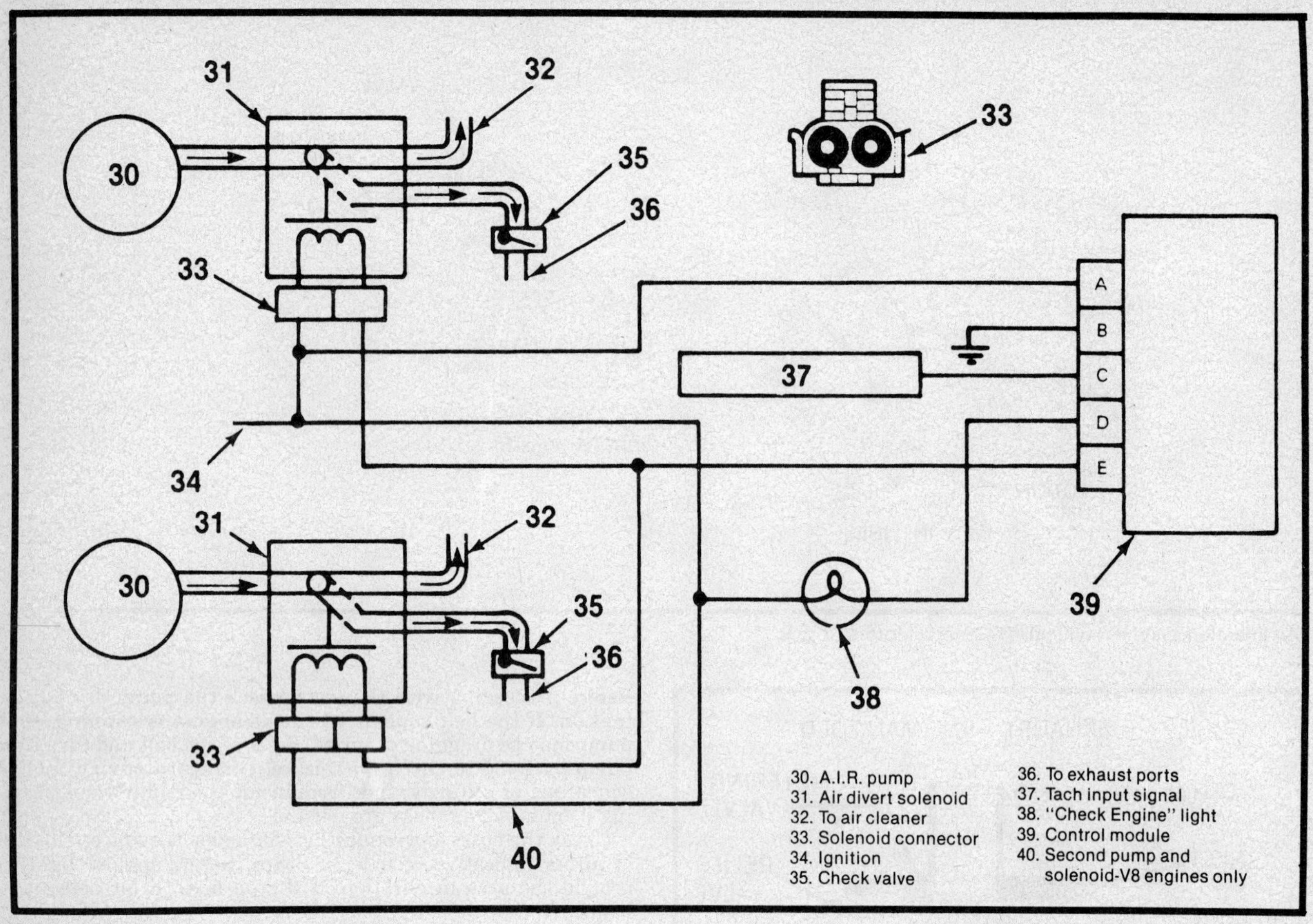

30
31
32
33
34
35
36
37
38
39
40
A
B
C
D
E
30. A.I.R. pump
31. Air divert solenoid
32. To air cleaner
33. Solenoid connector
34. Ignition
35. Check valve
36. To exhaust ports
37. Tach input signal
38. "Check Engine" light
39. Control module
40. Second pump and solenoid-V8 engines only

Schematic of A.I.R. system (© General Motors Corp.)

AIR FLOW BYPASSED THROUGH SILENCING MATERIAL AND EXHAUST PORTS
BYPASS VALVE CLOSED
FROM AIR PUMP
MANIFOLD VACUUM
FROM AIR PUMP
RELIEF VALVE (RELIEVES EXCESSIVE PUMP PRESSURE)
BYPASS VALVE OPEN
TO AIR MANIFOLD
CRUISING
(STEADY MANIFOLD VACUUM)
DECELERATING
(INCREASED MANIFOLD VACUUM)

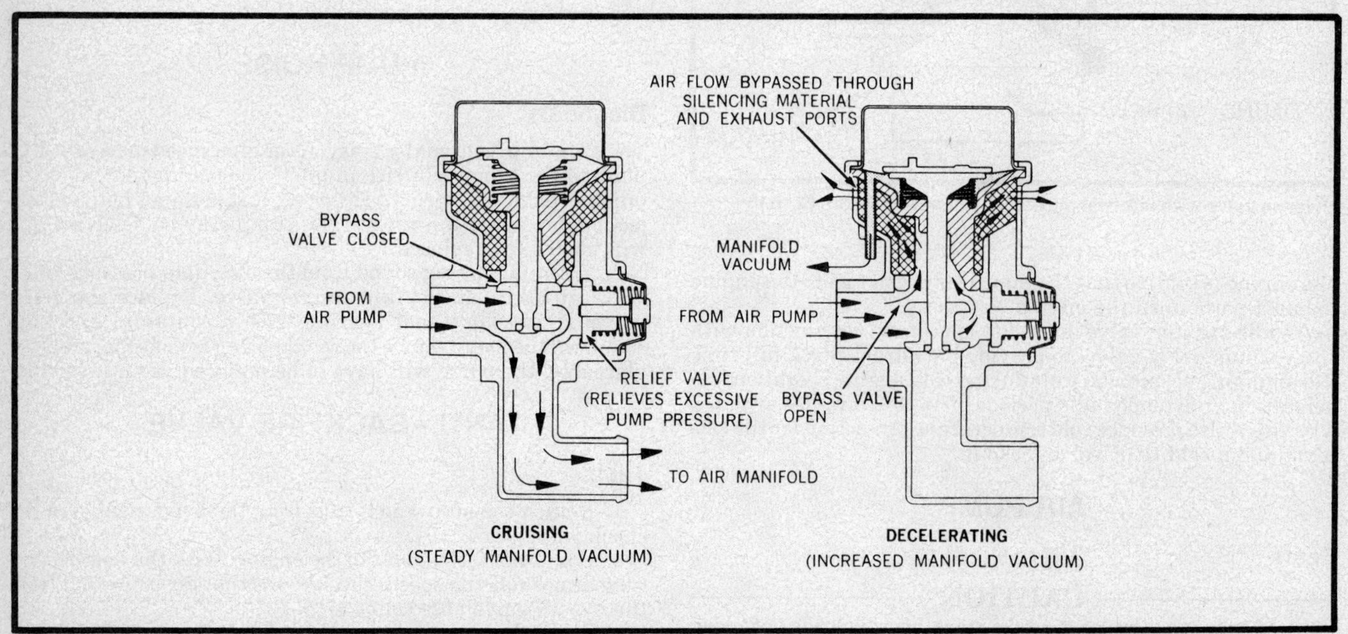

Diverter valve operation (© International Harvester Co.)

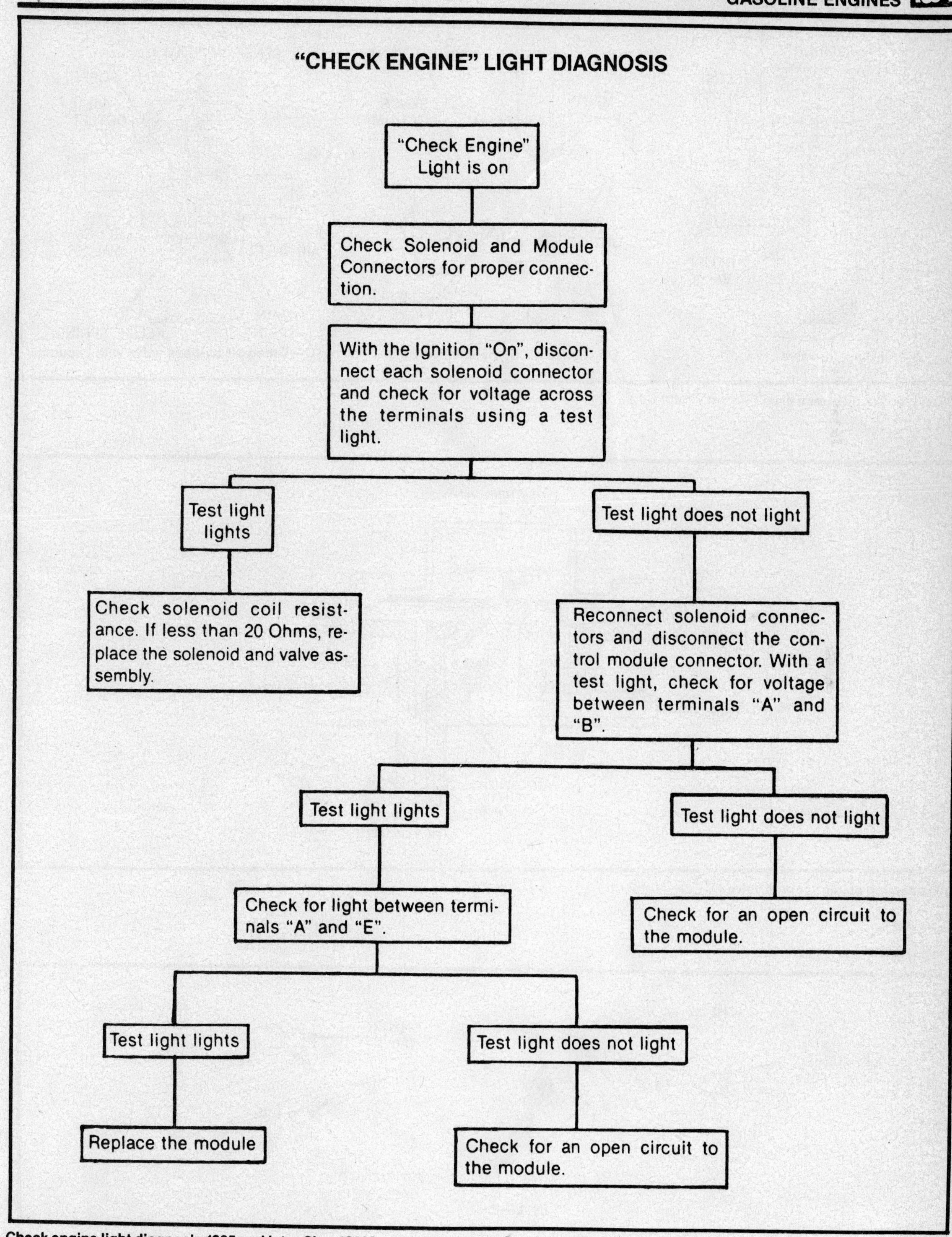
"CHECK ENGINE" LIGHT DIAGNOSIS
"Check Engine" Light is on
Check Solenoid and Module Connectors for proper connection.
With the Ignition "On", disconnect each solenoid connector and check for voltage across the terminals using a test light.
Test light lights
Test light does not light
Check solenoid coil resistance. If less than 20 Ohms, replace the solenoid and valve assembly.
Reconnect solenoid connectors and disconnect the control module connector. With a test light, check for voltage between terminals "A" and "B".
Test light lights
Test light does not light
Check for light between terminals "A" and "E".
Check for an open circuit to the module.
Test light lights
Test light does not light
Replace the module
Check for an open circuit to the module.

Check engine light diagnosis 1985 and later Chev./GMC medium duty trucks with gasoline engine. (© General Motors Corp.)

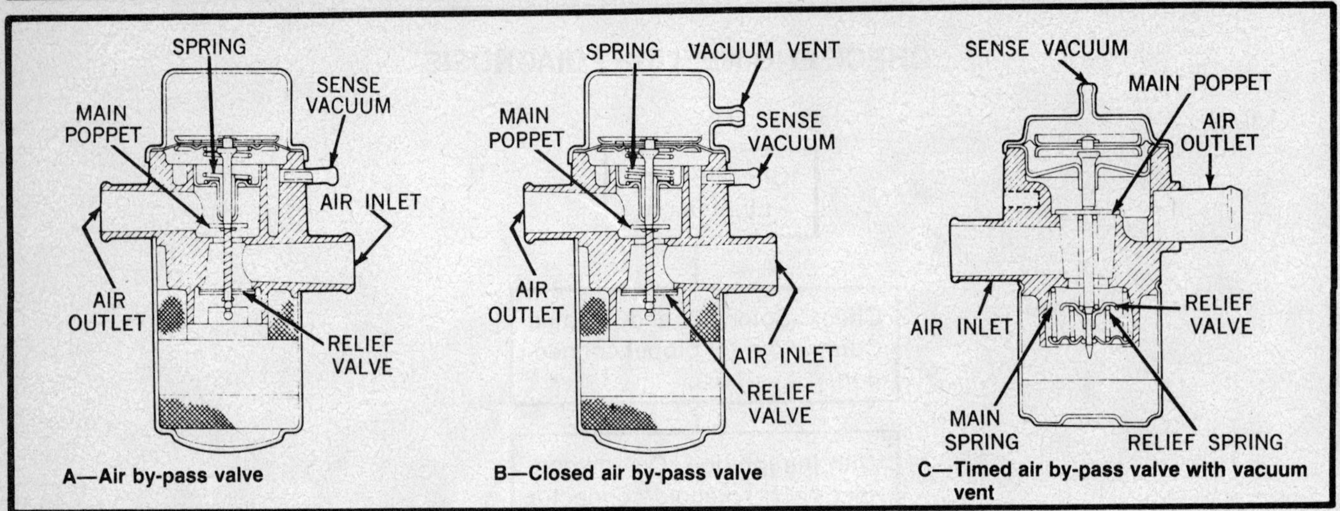

Three types of diverter valves (© Ford Motor Co.)

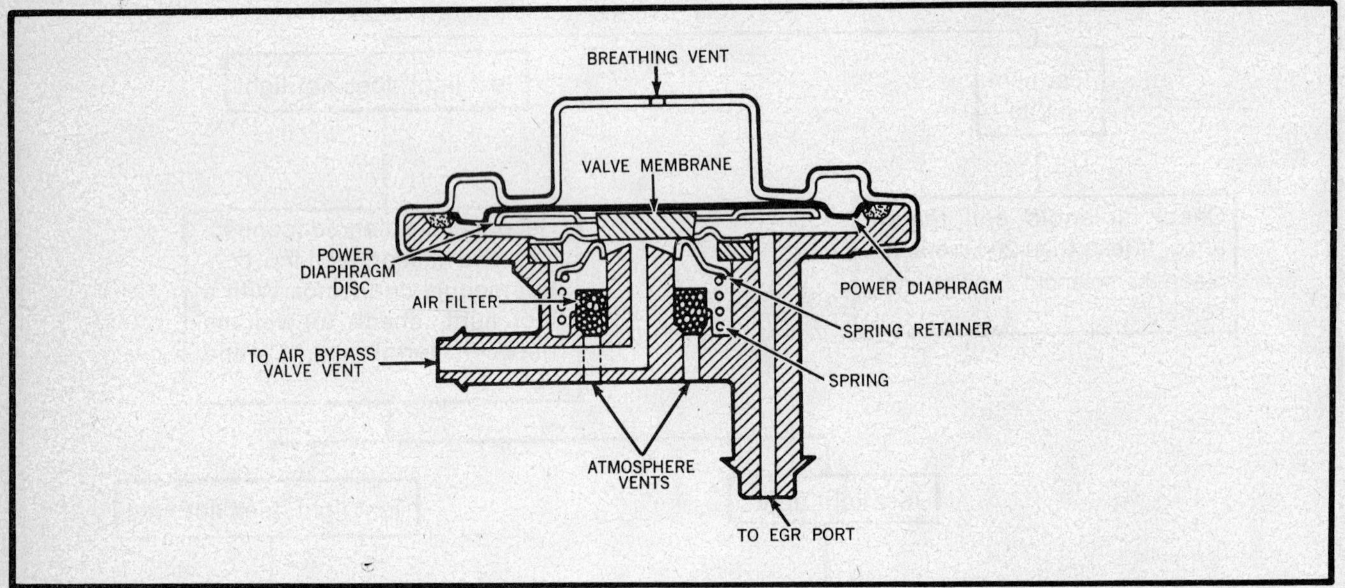

Cross section of idle vacuum valve (© Ford Motor Co.)

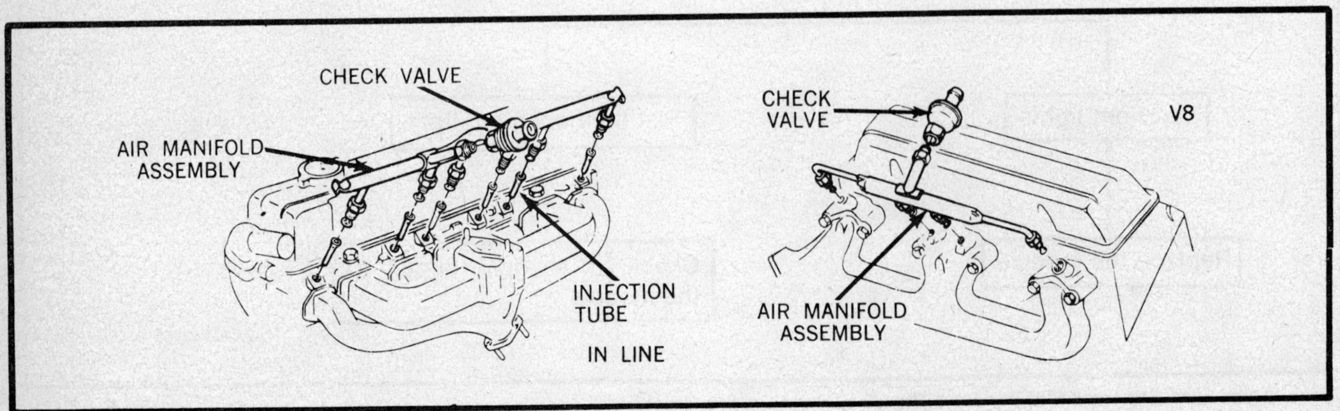

Air Injection tubes (© General Motors Corp.)

AIR INJECTION REACTOR SYSTEM DIAGNOSIS CHART

Condition	Possible Cause	Correction
No air supply—accelerate engine to 1500 rpm and observe air flow from hoses. If the flow increases as the rpm's increase, the pump is functioning normally. If not, check possible cause.	Loose drive belt.	Tighten to specifications.
	Leaks in supply hose.	Locate leak and repair.
	Leak at fittings.	Tighten or replace clamps.
	Air expelled through by-pass valve:	
	a. Connect a vacuum line directly from engine manifold vacuum to by-pass valve.	If this corrects the problem, go to step b. If not, replace air by-pass valve.
	b. Connect vacuum line from engine manifold vacuum source to by-pass valve through vacuum diffential valve directly, by passing the differential vacuum delay and separator valve.	If this corrects the problem, check differential vacuum, delay and separator valve and vacuum source line for plugging. Replace as required. If it doesn't, replace vacuum differential valve.
	Check valve inoperative.	Disconnect hose and blow through hose toward check valve. If air passes, function is normal. If air can be sucked from check valve, replace check valve.
	Pump failure.	Replace pump.
Excessive pump noise, chirping, rumbling, knocking, loss of engine performance.	Leak in hose.	Locate source of leak using soap solution and correct.
	Loose hose	Reassemble and replace or tighten hose clamp.
	Hose touching other engine parts.	Adjust hose position.
	Vacuum differential valve inoperative.	Replace vacuum differential valve.
	By-pass valve inoperative.	Replace by-pass valve.
	Pump mounting fasteners loose.	Tighten mounting screws as specified.
	Pump failure.	Replace pump.
	Check valve inoperative.	Replace check valve.
Excessive belt noise.	Loose belt.	Tighten to spec.
	Seized pump.	Replace pump.
Excessive pump noise. Chirping.	Insufficient break-in.	Run vehicle 10–15 miles at interstate speeds. Recheck.
Centrifugal filter fan damaged or broken.	Mechanical damage.	Replace centrifugal filter fan.
Exhaust tube bent or damaged.	Mechanical damage.	Replace exhaust tube.
Poor idle or driveability.	A defective A.I.R. system cannot cause poor idle or driveability.	Do not replace A.I.R. system.

4. The flow of air from the bypass valve at the check valve hose connection should stop momentarily and air should then flow from the exhaust port on the valve body or the silencer assembly.

5. Let the throttle snap shut several times. If the flow of air is not diverted into the atmosphere from the valve exhaust port or if it fails to stop flowing from the hose connection, check the vacuum lines and connections. If these are tight, either the bypass valve or one of the accessory valves in the small sensing hose is defective and must be replaced.

6. A leaking diaphragm will cause the air to flow out both the hose connection and the exhaust port at the same valve.

7. Late model systems should stop flowing at idle, as described earlier. If not,the bypass valve or accessory valve is defective.

CHECK VALVE

TEST

Remove the hose from the check valve. With the engine running at 1,500 rpm in Park or Neutral, hold the back of your hand near the check valve to test for exhaust gas leakage. If the valve leaks, it must be replaced.

NOTE: Vibration and flutter of the valve at idle is a

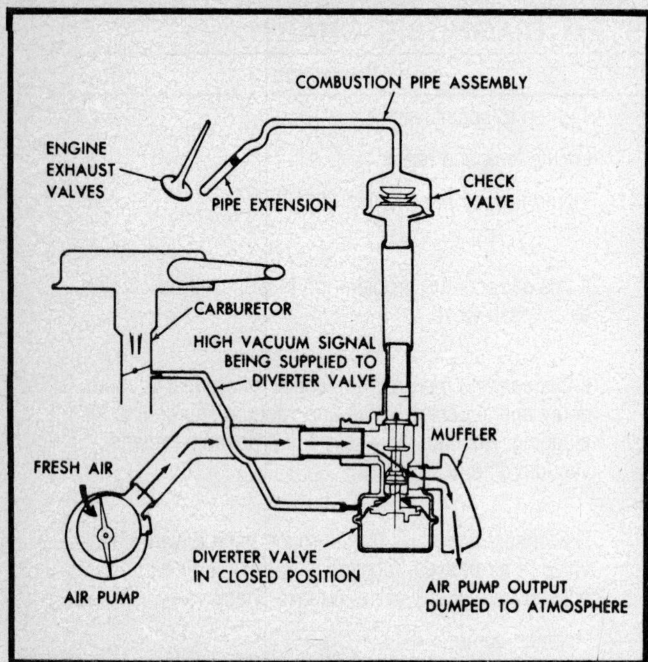

Diverter valve operation—air exhausted—typical (© General Motors Corp.)

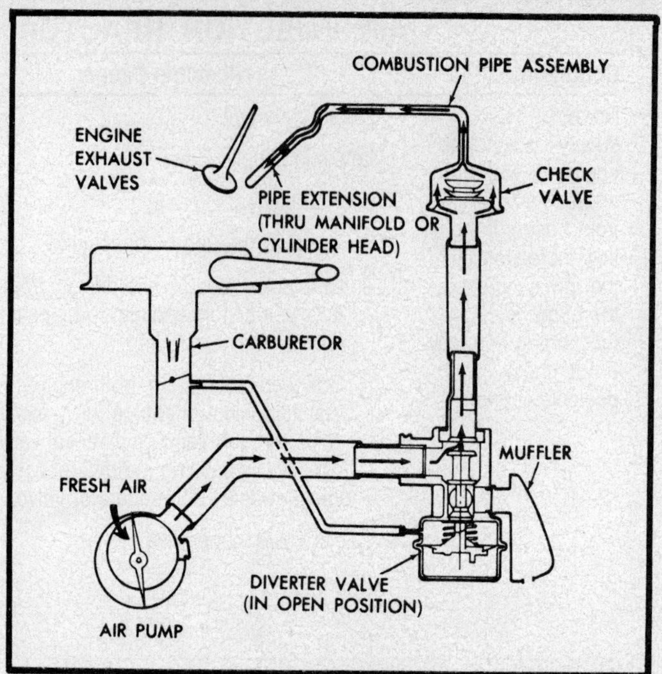

Air injection system operation—typical (© General Motors Corp.)

normal condition caused by exhaust pulsations. It does not mean that the valve is defective.

VACUUM DIFFERENTIAL VALVE

TEST

1. Disconnect the small sensing hose at the bypass valve and connect a vacuum gauge to the hose. With the engine idling in Park or Neutral, the gauge should read full manifold vacuum.

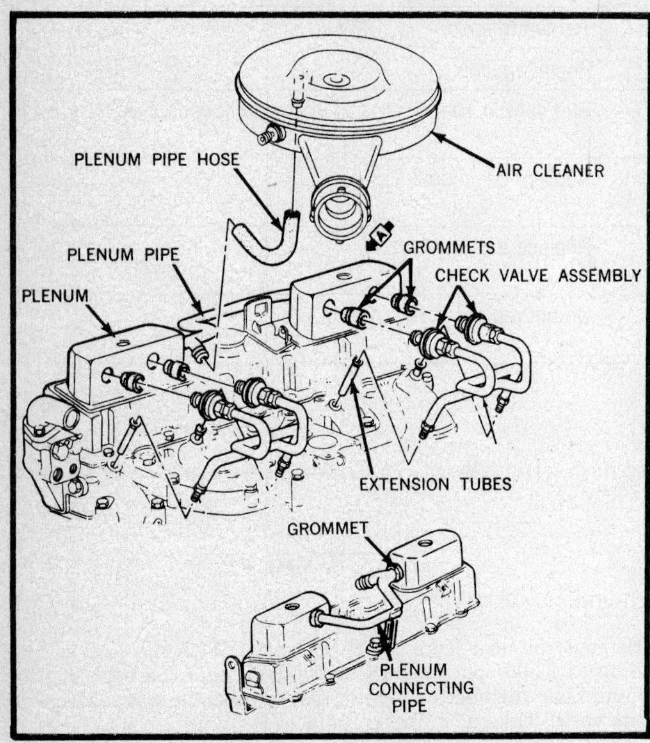

Pulse Air Injection Reactor (PAIR) system (© General Motors Corp.)

2. Run the engine at a steady 2500 rpm in Park or Neutral, and release the throttle. As the engine decelerates, the vacuum gauge should drop close to zero, then return to full manifold vacuum as the engine speed drops to idle. If not, the VDV is defective and must be replaced.

NOTE: The small hose nozzle should be connected to manifold vacuum.

AIR PUMP FILTER

REPLACEMENT

Several American truck brands employ a standard type of air pump filter that requires periodic replacement. Proceed as follows:

1. Disconnect the air and vacuum hoses from the diverter valve.
2. Loosen the pump pivot and adjusting bolts and remove the drive belt.
3. Remove the pivot and adjusting bolts from the pump. Remove the pump and the diverter valve as an assembly.

CAUTION

Do not clamp the pump in a vise or use a hammer or pry bar on the pump housing.

4. To change the filter, break the plastic fan from the hub. It is seldom possible to remove the fan without breaking it.
5. Remove the remaining portion of the fan filter from the pump hub. Be careful that filter fragments do not enter the air intake hole.
6. Position the new centrifugal fan filter on the pump hub. Place the pump pulley against the fan filter and install the securing screws. Torque the screws alternately to 95 inch lbs. and the fan filter will be pressed onto the pump hub.
7. Install the pump on the engine and adjust its drive belt.

Pulse Air Injection Reactor Systems

GM PAIR

The Pulse Air Injection Reactor (PAIR) system is installed on

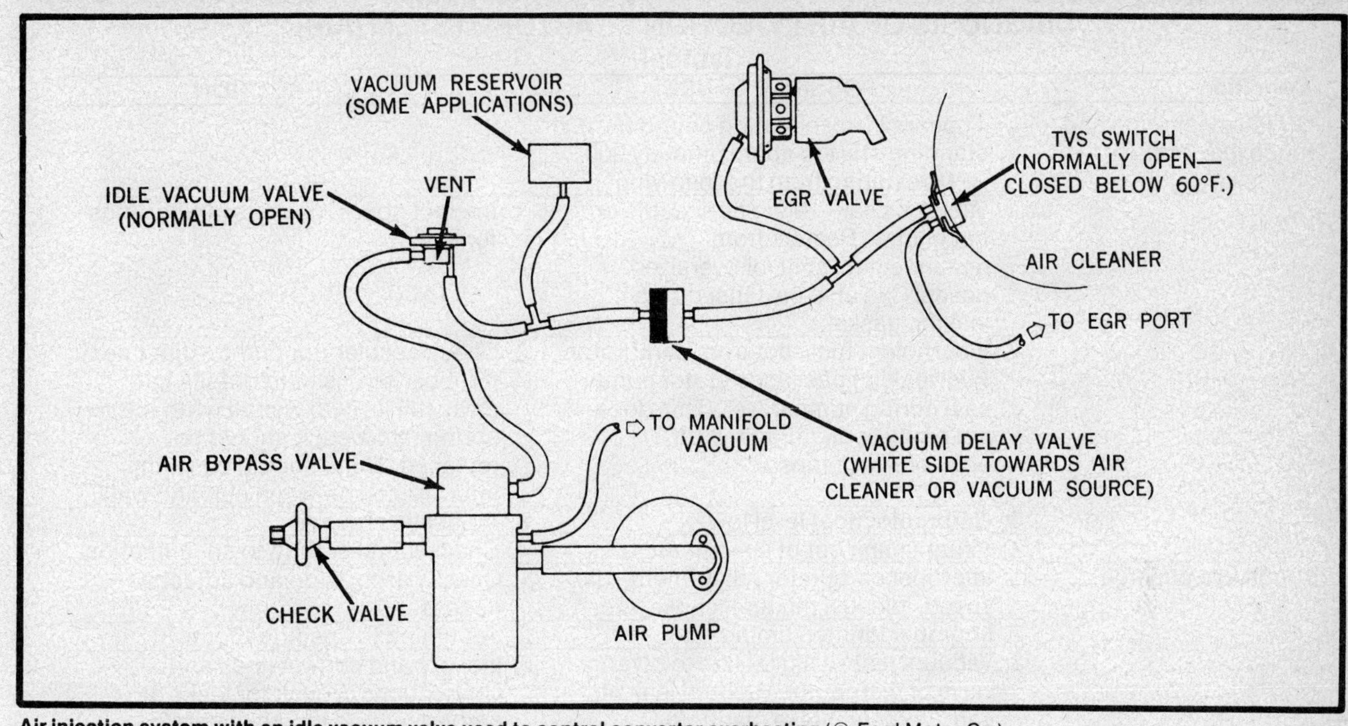

Air injection system with an idle vacuum valve used to control converter overheating (© Ford Motor Co.)

DIAGNOSIS OF AIR INJECTION REACTOR SYSTEM (AIR)
Typical

Condition	POSSIBLE CAUSE	CORRECTION
Pump noisy	1. Hose disconnected or leaking.	1. Connect or replace.
	2. Belt loose.	2. Tighten.
	3. Faulty relief valve (if mounted in pump).	3. Replace valve.
	4. A "chirping" noise may be prevalent on new pump.	4. Allow break-in time.
	5. A continuous "knocking" noise is indicative of rear bearing failure.	5. Replace pump.
	6. Improper belt tension.	6. Adjust.
	7. Seized or binding pump.	7. Replace.
	8. Bent or misaligned pulleys.	8. Inspect belt alignment. Replace pulleys.
Backfire in exhaust system	Rich Fuel Mixture Caused by:	
	1. Inoperative choke—misadjusted or sticking closed.	1. Inspect choke operation—correct as necessary.
	2. Inoperative vacuum break.	2. Replace vacuum break.
	3. Use of manual choke; generally overchoking.	3. Closer control of choking period.
	4. Air cleaner element restricted.	4. Replace element.
	5. Improper crankcase vent maintenance.	5. Inspect system. Replace PCV valve. Check fitting at carburetor—may be plugged with crankcase deposits.
	6. High fuel level.	6. Adjust float level.
	7. Diverter valve stuck in open position.	7. Check valve—replace if defective.
	8. Diverter valve hose disconnected.	8. Correct hose routing.
Backfire or popping in inlet manifold	1. Leaking inlet manifold.	1. Check manifold bolts for tightness.
	2. Incorrect ignition timing.	2. Check timing and set to specifications.

DIAGNOSIS OF AIR INJECTION REACTOR SYSTEM (AIR)
Typical

Condition	POSSIBLE CAUSE	CORRECTION
Off idle hesitation and rough idle (hot)	Appears in acceleration period from a standing start to approximately 900 RPM resulting from the following:	
	1. Vacuum Leak—More noticeable on hot engine. Results from unconnected, split, or oversized hoses. Can also be caused by a leaking gasket.	1. Inspect hoses, gaskets, and fittings for leaks.
	2. Insufficient fuel shot from carburetor. Fuel leaking past accelerator pump seal during pump travel. (This does not apply to diaphragm type accelerator pumps.)	2. Check accelerator pump adjustment. If rubber seal is hard or falls into cavity by its own weight (with return spring removed) it should be replaced. There should be slight interference between cup and wall.
	3. Carburetor float level low.	3. Adjust as required.
	4. Initial timing out of specification.	4. Check initial setting to specification.
Rough idle or surge	1. Improper carburetor adjustment, idle speed, idle fuel mixture, choke, etc.	1. Check carburetion and adjust as necessary.
	2. Improper ignition timing.	2. Set timing to specifications.
	3. Vacuum leak at signal line to diverter valve or distributor. Vacuum leak at carburetor or intake manifold.	3. Inspect and correct lines and connections. Check for leaks at carburetor and intake manifold gasket.
Engine idle speed high	1. Throttle linkage sticking or obstructed by hoses.	1. Inspect linkage and eliminate points of interference.
	2. Idle speed set incorrectly.	2. Reset idle speed to specifications.
Engine "Diesels"—after ignition is turned off	1. Idle speed too high.	1. Reset idle to specifications.
	2. Solenoid set improperly. Low octane fuel.	2. Reset idle to specifications.
	3. Vacuum leak.	3. Inspect hoses, gaskets and fittings. Correct as necessary.
Overheated exhaust system	1. Ignition timing retarded—excessive burning in exhaust system.	1. Reset timing to specifications.
	2. Incorrect or missing pressure relief valve plug in air pump.	2. Check for correct plug. Install if missing.
Charred, deteriorated supply hose	1. Defective check valve.	1. Replace check valve.
Constant air noise	1. Broken hose.	1. Replace hose.
	2. Diverter valve stuck closed.	2. Replace diverter valve.

the small inline 6 cylinder engine, used in General Motors light duty trucks, through 1983. The PAIR system uses no air pump, but relies on the negative and positive exhaust gas impulses to draw fresh air into the exhaust manifold to assist in the further burning of the hydrocarbons (HC) before leaving the tailpipe.

Four individual check valves are used to prevent the exhaust gases from entering the fresh air intake chamber plenums. Two sets of pipes are used, one set in the front section of the exhaust manifold and the second set in the rear section of the exhaust manifold.

Two sets of plenum chambers are used and connected to the carburetor air cleaner by a common hose, for the fresh air intake. During periods of high engine rpm, the check valves will remain closed to prevent the flow of exhaust gases to the engine air cleaner.

Failure Diagnosis

1. Inspect the pulse air valve and pipes for leakage or defective operation. Check for a hissing noise, indicating exhaust or intake air leakage.

2. If one or more of the check valves are defective, exhaust gases will enter the carburetor area and cause poor driveability such as stalling, surge, or poor performance.

PULSE AIR INJECTION REACTOR SYSTEM

Inspection

1. Burned off paint on the rocker arm plenum chambers indicates a defective pulse air valve. Rubber grommets and hoses will deteriorate and can cause a hissing noise.

2. Inspect the carburetor for pieces of rubber hoses or grommets, indicating an overheating of the components.

3. Inspect the operation of the pulse air valve by applying at least 17 in.Hg. at the grommet end of the valve. A drop of 6 in.Hg. in two seconds is allowed.

Electronic Ignition System

A change has been made through the model years from the conventional distributors to the electronic ignition systems for more precise ignition control.

Different types are available from the manufacturers, but the operation of the systems are basically the same. Greater dependability, higher secondary voltages and less need for adjustments are the important factors considered in using this system for emission control.

Refer to the individual truck sections and to the Electrical section for expanded information.

DISTRIBUTOR CONTROLS

All distributor controls act in some way to change or eliminate vacuum advance during certain operation conditions. Usually, the control cuts down on the amount of vacuum advance, in effect retarding the spark, so that the exhaust will get hotter and burn up hydrocarbon and carbon monoxide emissions before they go out the tailpipe.

The distributor vacuum advance unit might be connected, according to factory design, to either manifold vacuum or ported (above the throttle plates) carburetor vacuum. Either way, the vacuum spark advance curve is approximately the same for all running conditions above idle. At idle, however, the manifold vacuum hookup results in full advance, while the ported hookup gives zero advance. If the hoses are hooked up the wrong way, the addition or lack of advance will affect idle speed, requiring a readjustment of the throttle position to bring the idle speed back to specifications. When this is done, emissions will usually be high, so it is important to keep the hoses hooked up correctly.

DUAL DIAPHRAGM DISTRIBUTORS

These distributors have two hose connections, one in the normal position, and the other closer to the distributor body. The hose fitting next to the body is for the retard diaphragm, and is connected to manifold vacuum. The retard diaphragm affects the spark only at idle, when there is no vacuum on the advance diaphragm. In effect, the retard diaphragm provides a movable resting place for the advance diaphragm. When ported vacuum is not acting on the advance diaphragm, it returns to the neutral or no-advance position against the retard diaphragm. At idle, manifold vacuum pulls the retard diaphragm to the retard position and the advance diaphragm follows along to retard the spark.

Testing Dual Diaphragm Distributors

To test a dual diaphragm distributor, connect a timing light to the engine. Remove the retard hose from the distributor and plug the hose. With the engine running, increase the speed to a fast idle and watch the timing marks. The timing should advance. If not, either the vacuum unit is faulty, the vacuum port is plugged, or there is a temperature control device that is shutting off the vacuum. Apply hand pump or mouth suction vacuum to the advance diaphragm and the timing should advance. If not, the distributor or advance unit must be repaired or replaced. Failure to advance could be caused by a faulty diaphragm or a sticky advance plate.

Remove the advance hose from the vacuum unit and read the timing at normal idle speed. Remove the plug that was inserted in the retard hose, and check for full manifold vacuum at the end of it. If there is no vacuum, temperature controls may be shutting it off.

Connect the hose to the retard diaphragm, or apply vacuum from another source. The timing should immediately retard

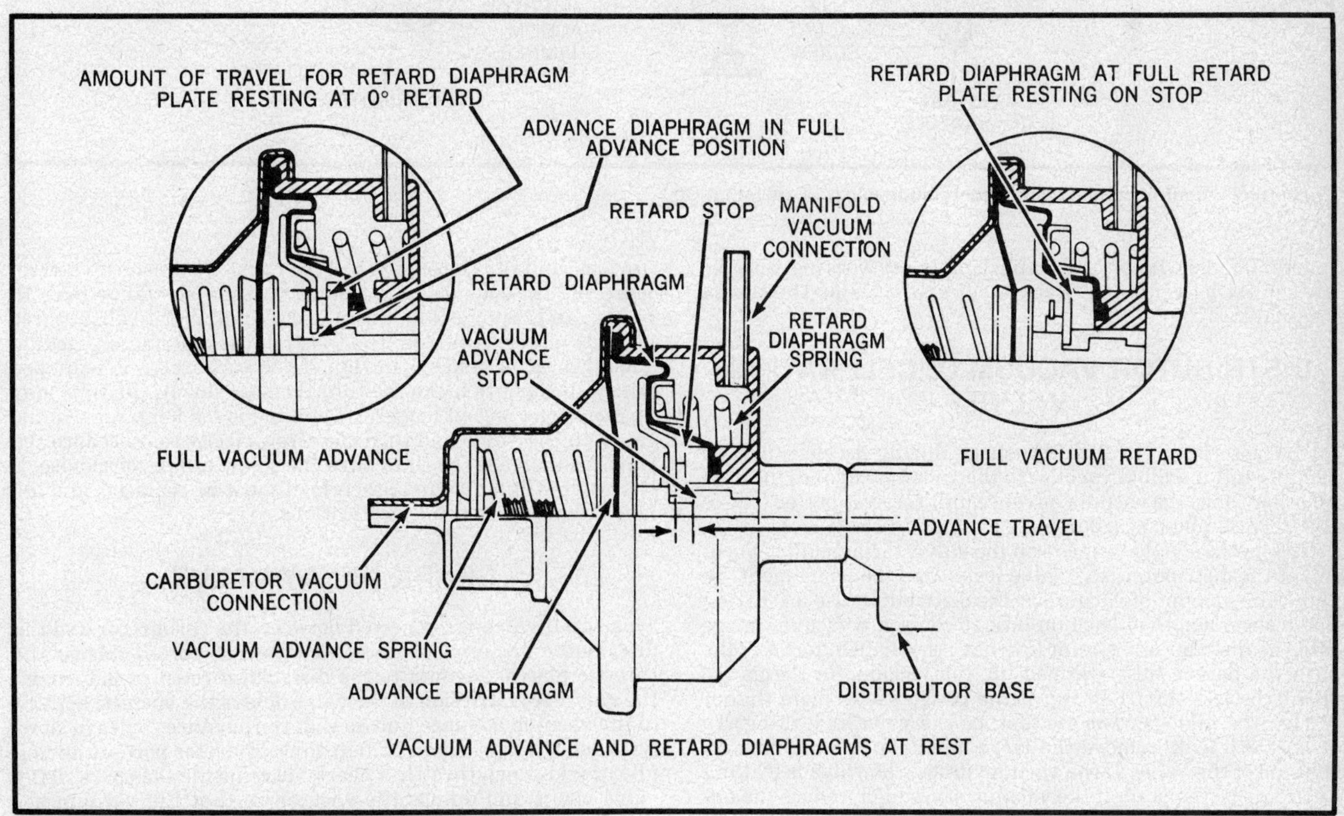

Dual diaphragm vacuum advance mechanism (© Ford Motor Co.)

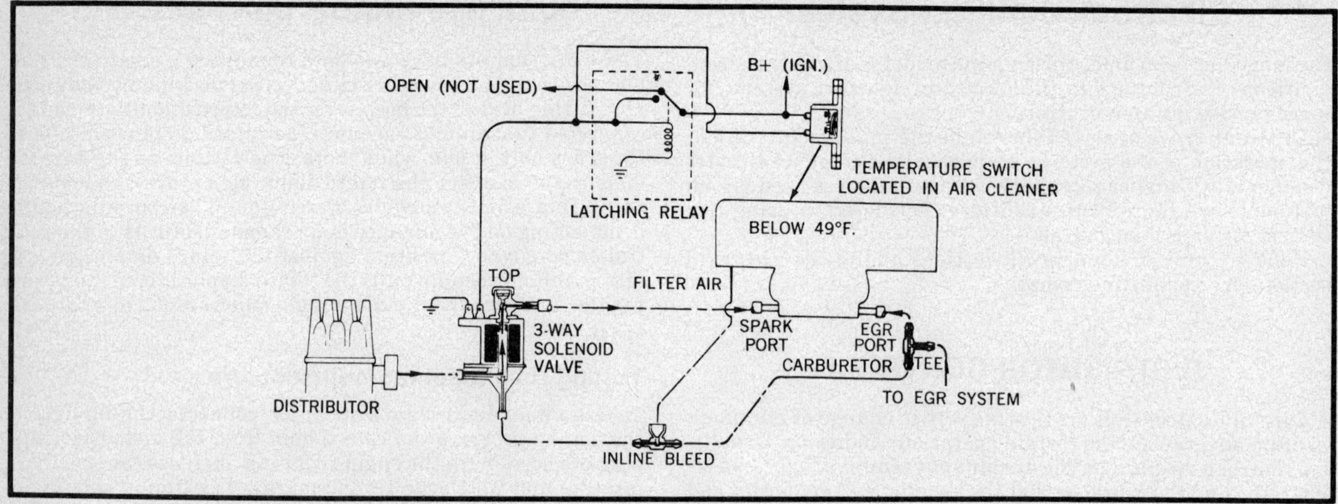

Schematic of Cold Temperature Activated Vacuum (CTAV) system below 49 degrees F. This system is used on some California vehicles (© Ford Motor Co.)

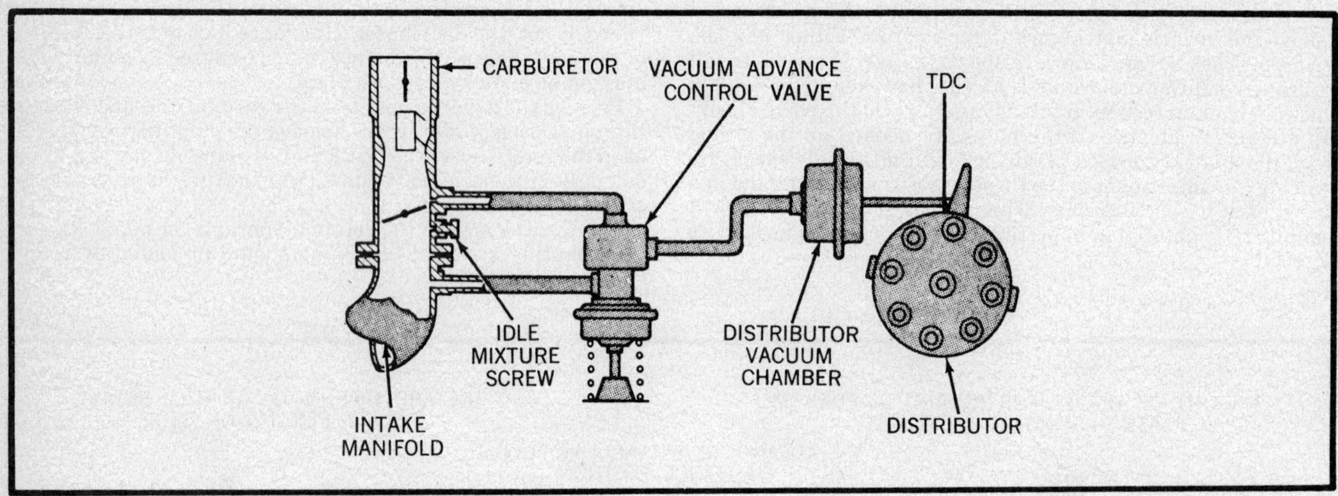

Carburetor—control valve—distributor relationship (© Ford Motor Co.)

several degrees. If not, the diaphragm is not working, and the unit must be replaced. Reconnect all hoses as they were originally.

DISTRIBUTOR VACUUM DECELERATION VALVE

Its purpose is to advance the spark during deceleration, by sending full manifold vacuum to the vacuum advance unit. At all other times the vacuum advance unit receives ported (above the throttle plates) carburetor vacuum.

Three checks should be made on the valve: the amount of vacuum at the distributor, any valve leaks, and the adjustment. To check the amount of vacuum at the distributor, use a T-fitting and a short length of vacuum hose to connect a vacuum gauge into the distributor vacuum line near the distributor. At idle, with the engine fully warmed up, the vacuum on the gauge should be less than 1 in.Hg. If the gauge shows more than 1 in.Hg., the idle speed is too fast, or the valve is leaking. To check for a leak, remove the large manifold vacuum hose on the side of the valve. If the vacuum drops, the valve is leaking and must be replaced. If the vacuum stays high, reduce the engine idle speed so that the port in the carburetor is covered.

To check the valve adjustment, connect the manifold vacuum hose and run the engine at 2000 rpm for 5 seconds. Then release the throttle. The distributor vacuum should go over 16 in.Hg.. and stay there for about one second. Within about three seconds after you release the throttle, the distributor vacuum should drop to below 6 in.Hg.. If the carburetor is equipped with a dashpot to make the throttle close slowly, the time may be about one second longer. If the time is too long, remove the cover on the valve and turn the screw clockwise to reduce the time. To increase the time, turn the screw counterclockwise. If the valve will not adjust properly, it must be replaced, and the new valve adjusted to specifications.

SPARK DELAY VALVE

This small valve is connected between the carburetor and the distributor vacuum advance, so that the ported (above the throttle plates) vacuum to the distributor must pass through the valve. A restriction in the valve delays the vacuum applied to the vacuum advance unit so that the advance comes in slowly. When there is no vacuum at the carburetor port, as during idle or wide open throttle a check valve inside the spark delay valve opens and dumps the vacuum so that the vacuum advance unit returns to the no-advance position without any delay.

Spark delay valves can be tested for correct operation and leaks with a source of vacuum such as a hand vacuum pump or a running engine, and a vacuum gauge. Connect the vacuum gauge to the distributor side of the valve, and the vacuum source to the other side. The gauge should rise slowly until it reads the amount of vacuum available. The time to rise to the maximum reading should be from one to 28 seconds. If the vacuum gauge does not read anything, the valve is plugged. If the vacuum reads instantly, without any delay, the valve is open. In either case, the spark delay valve must be replaced. To test the check valve part of the spark delay valve, remove the vacuum source and the vacuum gauge should drop instantly to zero without any delay. If there is any delay, the spark delay valve is defective and must be replaced.

TEMPERATURE ACTIVATED VACUUM (TAV) AND COLD TEMPERATURE ACTIVATED VACUUM (CTAV) SYSTEMS

This system switches the vacuum source back and forth between the carburetor spark port and EGR port, according to the air temperature. A three-nozzle vacuum solenoid is used. Below approximately 55°F, outside air temperature, the temperature switch is open and the solenoid is not energized. In this position, the solenoid connects the spark port to the vacuum advance unit. Above 55°F, the temperature switch closes and energizes the solenoid. In this position, the solenoid connects the EGR port to the vacuum advance unit.

The temperature switch is located in the air cleaner and a latching relay is on the firewall. Once the temperature switch has closed, the relay latches so that any sudden rush of cold air through the air cleaner will not cycle the solenoid on and off. The latching relay keeps the solenoid energized as long as the ignition switch is on. When the ignition switch is turned off, the relay unlatches and the system is ready for the next start, whether the air temperature is hot or cold. If the air at the temperature switch is over 55°F, the latching relay will come on when the ignition switch is turned on.

Testing

Test the system with a vacuum gauge connected to the vacuum advance hose at the distributor. With the temperature above 65°F. (to be sure the temperature switch has closed) a vacuum should be present from the EGR port. If the EGR port hose is disconnected and the vacuum drops, the system is working. When making a cold test, the vacuum should come from the spark port hose, so disconnecting that hose should make the vacuum drop. Because both ports are above the throttle plate, the throttle must be opened slightly to get vacuum at the hose.

Identifying the spark port and EGR ports on the carburetor is easy if they are marked. If there is no marking on the carburetor, connect two vacuum gauges, one to each port. At idle, there should not be any vacuum. If vacuum is present, it usually means the engine is idling too fast. Close the throttle slightly to slow down the idle and the vacuum should drop to almost zero.

When the throttle is opened, vacuum should be present on one gauge before the other. The gauge that gets vacuum first is connected to the spark port.

ORIFICE SPARK ADVANCE CONTROL (OSAC)

It is a mechanism that delays the application of vacuum to the distributor vacuum advance unit. When the throttle is opened, the carburetor port is exposed to vacuum. This vacuum goes through a hose to the OSAC valve and then to the distributor vacuum advance. The OSAC valve is sometimes mounted on the firewall and sometimes on the air cleaner. Inside the OSAC valve is a calibrated orifice that delays the vacuum as much as 27 seconds, depending on the calibration of the valve.

Some OSAC valves have temperature control that senses the temperature inside the air cleaner or inside the plenum chamber behind the firewall, depending on where the valve is mounted. If the valve contains temperature control, it will be wide open below 60°F, bypassing the orifice and allowing vacuum advance without any delay. Above 60°F, the bypass closes and the delay takes over.

Testing

To test the valve, connect a vacuum gauge to the DIST connection on the valve. With the engine idling, you should have no reading on the gauge. If there is a reading, the engine is idling too fast. With the engine idling, open the throttle to a fast idle and hold it steady. The vacuum on the gauge will rise slowly until it reaches a maximum reading. If not, there is something wrong with the system and you should check out the hoses and the carburetor port, or replace the valve is necessary.

VACUUM REDUCER VALVE

Inserted between the manifold vacuum source and the distributor, this valve reduces the vacuum acting on the advance diaphragm by about 3 in.Hg.. This valve is always used on a system that includes a distributor thermal vacuum switch. The vacuum advance unit operates on ported (above the throttle plates) vacuum, except when the engine overheats above 225°F. This opens the thermal vacuum switch and sends full manifold vacuum through the vacuum reducer valve to the advance unit. Thus, the vacuum reducer valve is only operating when the engine is overheated.

Testing

To test the valve, connect a vacuum gauge to the TVS nozzle and a hand vacuum pump to the MAN nozzle. When you pump up 15 in.Hg.. vacuum on the hand pump, the vacuum on the separate gauge should be 3 to 4 in.Hg. lower. Both gauges should hold the vacuum without leakdown. If not, the valve is defective and must be replaced.

RETARD DELAY VALVE

When the throttle is suddenly opened, engine vacuum drops immediately and this causes the vacuum advance to move quickly from the advance position to the neutral or no-advance position. A retard delay valve is a restriction with a one-way check valve. It allows the vacuum to act on the vacuum advance unit normally, but when the vacuum drops, the delay valve traps the vacuum in the advance unit and lets it out slowly. It takes several seconds for the advance unit to return to the neutral position.

Some models have the retard delay valve hooked up so that it only operates when the engine is cold. At normal operating temperature the delay is bypassed.

Testing

Testing of the delay valve can be done with a hand vacuum pump. Connect the pump to the MAN side of the valve, or the side that connects to the vacuum source on the engine. Connect a separate vacuum gauge to the other side of the valve. When the hand pump is operated, the vacuum will rise on both the pump gauge and the separate gauge equally. When the release is pulled, the pump gauge will drop to zero immediately, but the separate gauge will take several seconds to drop to zero. If it doesn't work that way, the delay valve is defective and must be replaced.

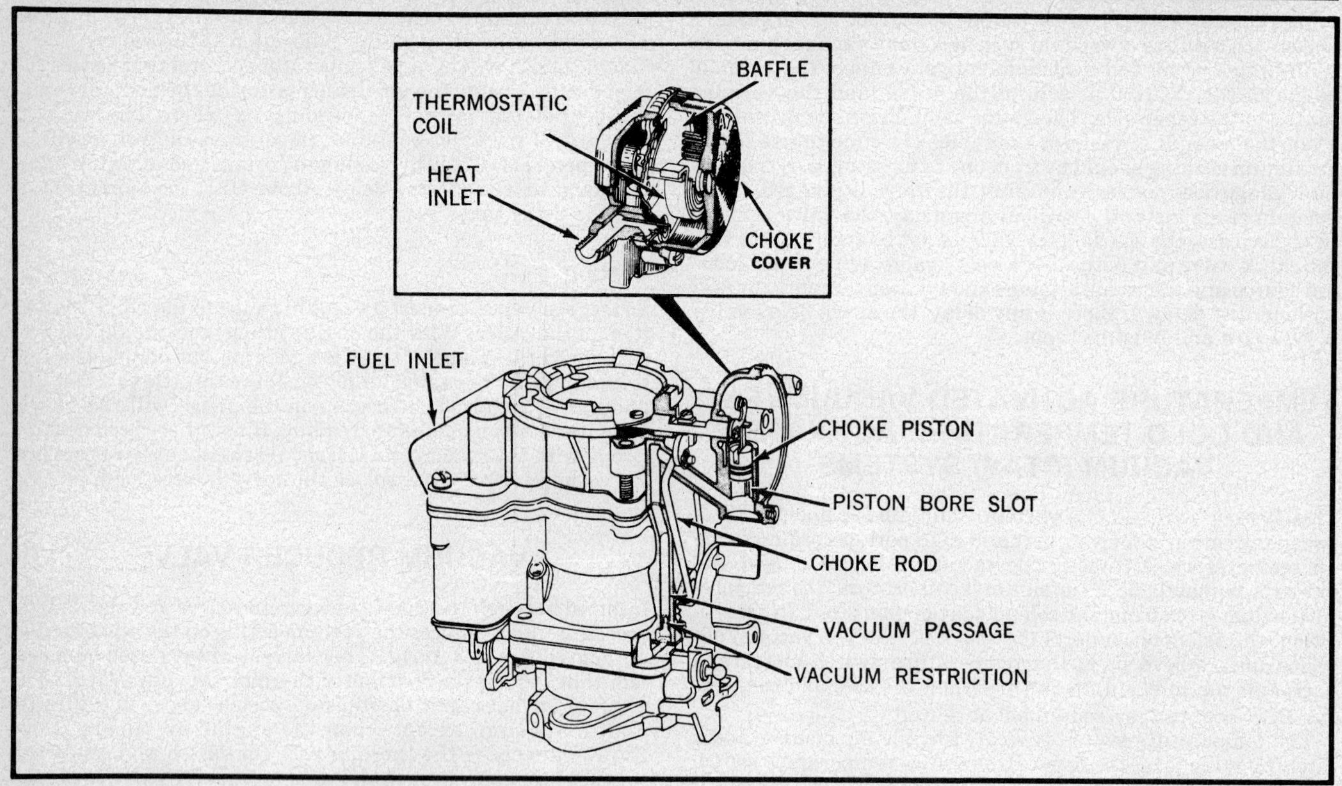

Non-electric choke assembly used with choke stove in the exhaust manifold—typical (© Jeep Corp.)

COLD START SPARK ADVANCE

A coolant sensitive vacuum switch (PVS) is combined with a delay valve (distributor retard control valve) to provide retard delay when the engine coolant is below 128°F. The hose routing is set up so that the vacuum advance unit operates on manifold vacuum through the retard delay valve when the engine is cold and on ported vacuum through a spark delay valve when the engine is warm. The system also has an overheat PVS that switches the vacuum advance over to manifold vacuum (through the spark delay valve) when the engine coolant gets over 235°F.

Testing

Testing the spark delay valve is covered in this section under Spark Delay Valve. Testing for the distributor retard control valve is the same as for the retard delay valve in this section.

When the 128° PVS is cold, connection No. 2 is blocked and D and 1 are connected. When it is over 128°F No. 1 is blocked and D and 2 are connected.

Carburetor Choke Controls

NON–ELECTRIC CHOKE

A non-electric choke uses a "stove" on the exhaust manifold or a well on the intake manifold to provide heat. When the well is used, the choke coil is surrounded by the warm intake manifold, heated by the exhaust crossover passage. When the stove is used, the choke housing is connected to engine vacuum and a long tube pulls the heated air from the stove into the choke housing to heat up the choke coil and cause the choke to open as the engine warms up. When an electric choke is used, it can be in addition to all the above, or it can be the only source of choke heat, depending on the design.

ELECTRIC CHOKE

The electric choke has a small heater next to the choke coil. This heater receives its current from different sources, depending on the car maker.

Ford Motor Company and Jeep chokes are powered from the alternator "center tap," which produces about 7 volts. As the alternator is only putting out voltage when the engine is running, the electric choke is automatically shut off when the engine is off. It is important that the choke is connected only to the special "center tap" provided on the alternator. The description "center tap" refers to the construction of the alternator wiring and not to the location of the connection.

Inside is a thermostatic switch that turns on the heating element at approximately 80°F. Above that, the element stays on as long as the engine is running. The 80°F figure was selected because the engine is warm enough at that temperature to keep running without the choke. When the heater comes on,

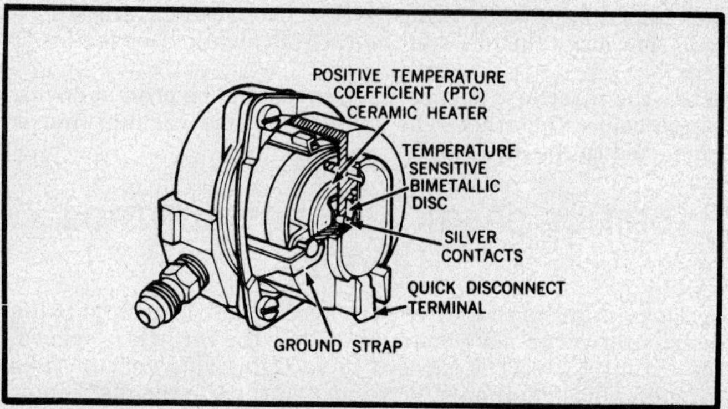

Electric choke assembly—used with choke stove (© Ford Motor Co.)

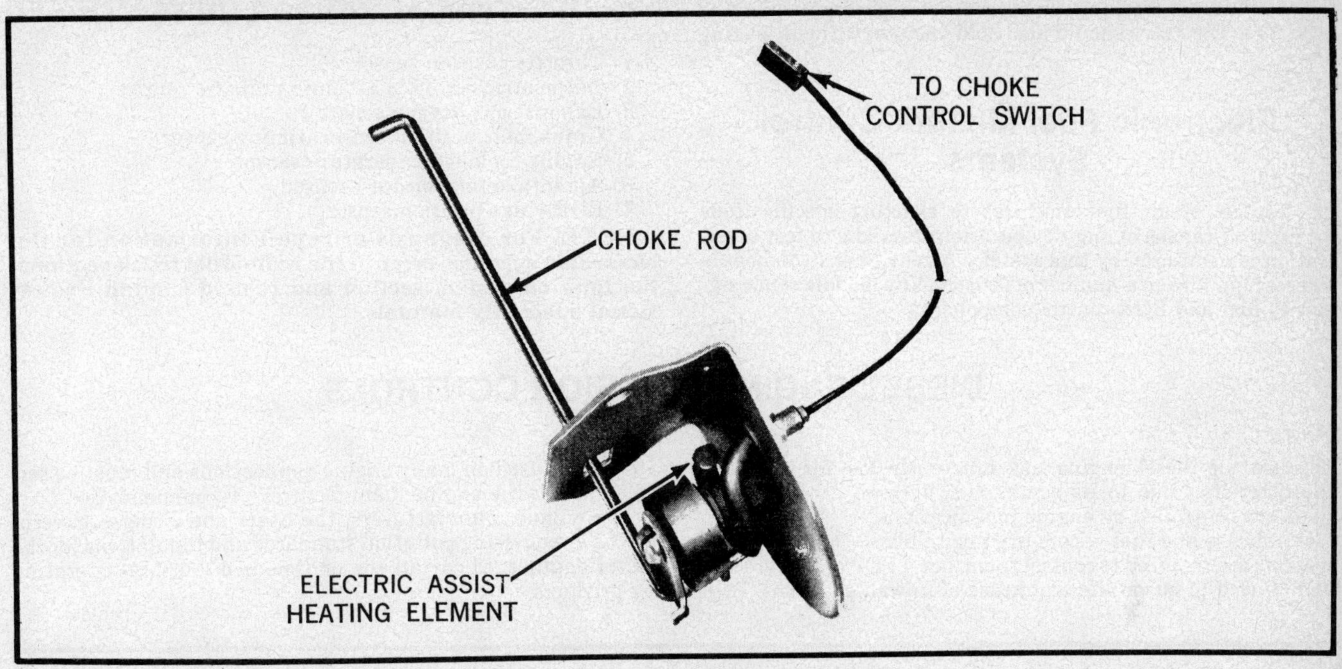

Manifold well type choke assembly—electric assembly illustrated. Both electric and non-electric types used (© Chrysler Corp.)

the choke opens very quickly. When the engine is shut off and cools down, the choke switch may stay on to as low as 65°F at the choke housing. On a warm restart, where the choke switch was still on, the heating element would heat up the choke and open it shortly after the engine started.

Chrysler Corporation vehicles with an electric choke use a well type choke, which receives the both from the intake manifold and the electric choke heater. A separate choke control unit is mounted on top of the intake manifold and connected to the heater with a wire. This wire disconnects at the choke control unit only, not at the heater.

Choke control units may be single and double stage. The double stage is recognized by the external resistor alongside the unit. The single stage unit turns on the choke heater at approximately 60°F. and off at 110°F. The double stage unit keeps the heater on below 60°F., but the current runs through the resistor. At approximately 60°F., the resistor is taken out of the circuit and the heater gets full current. At 110°F., the control unit turns the heater off.

Testing can be done with a non-powered test light on the choke terminal to find out if the heater is on or off. The ignition switch must be on. If the light glows, you know the control unit is on. On two-stage units, the light will glow dimly when the resistor is in the circuit and brightly when the resistor is out. The current to the control unit comes from the ignition switch and there is no fuse.

Chevrolet and GMC use an electric choke that is mounted on the carburetor. The choke has a dual element behind the coil spring. Whenever the engine is running, the choke heater is in operation. Below 50–70°F., a bimetal snap disc in the choke cover turns off the large section of the heating element so that only the small section gives off heat. Above 50–70°F., the disc switches on the large heating element for faster choke opening.

Current to the choke is controlled by a three-terminal oil pressure switch. One of the terminals is a ground for the red oil pressure light on the instrument panel. The other two terminals are a switch in series between the ignition switch and the choke heater. Oil pressure operates the switch so that the choke gets current only when the engine is running. The circuit is fused through the backup light or transmission fuse in the fuse block.

NOTE: Failure of the choke heater circuit will cause the oil pressure light to go on.

IDLE ENRICHMENT SYSTEM

In order to reduce the cold engine stalling, a metering system is used to relate to the carburetor, rather than to the choke. The system enriches the carburetor mixtures in the curb idle and fast idle modes. The carburetor will have the complete idle system enriched during periods of cold to semi-cold operating conditions. The idle enrichment valve is manifold vacuum controlled and opens or closes a passageway that admits extra air to the idle circuit.

Some models have a coolant temperature control valve, mounted on a coolant passage and connected by hose between the manifold vacuum source and the idle enrichment valve. When the engine is cold, the valve is open and allows vacuum to operate the idle enrichment valve to richen the idle fuel mixture. When the engine warms up, the valve closes and cuts off the vacuum to the coolant temperature valve.

A vacuum solenoid may be included in the vacuum hose arrangement to provide EGR valve delay while the engine is cold.

Testing

Testing the system can be done on a cold engine by disconnecting the hose at the carburetor and connecting a vacuum gauge to the hose. Start the engine and note the length of time that vacuum appears on the gauge. At the end of the timed period, the gauge should drop to zero. Allow the engine to warm up to operating temperature and make the test again. This time you should not see any vacuum on the gauge, because the CCIE (coolant control idle enrichment), valve should be closed. If there is no timer, you will see vacuum for several minutes after a cold start, until the engine warms up.

To check the effect of the idle enrichment use a hand vacuum pump on the idle enrichment valve on the carburetor. With vacuum applied, the valve will be closed, richening the idle, and changing the idle speed. Release the vacuum and the speed should go back where it was. If there is no speed change, either the valve is not working, or a carburetor passage is blocked with dirt. The valve should also hold vacuum without leaking down.

Electronic Fuel Mixture Control Systems

The control of air fuel mixtures to exacting specifications through all ranges of engine operation from idle to fast acceleration is monitored by this system. A central control module receives input from a number of sensors. The module sends signals to fuel and EGR control components.

TYPICAL SENSOR UNITS

1. Throttle position sensor
2. Barometric/manifold absolute pressure sensor
3. Exhaust gas oxygen sensor
4. Crankshaft position sensor (timing sensor)
5. Engine coolant temperature sensor
6. Air intake temperature sensor
7. EGR valve position sensor

NOTE: For diagnosis or repair information for the electronic systems, refer to the individual truck sections, the ignition system section and related Chilton Professional speciality manuals.

DIESEL ENGINE EMISSION CONTROLS

Because the diesel engine has inherently low air pollution characteristics due to its combustion system, exhaust emissions are controlled by engine modifications.

Crankcase and fuel vapors are negligible so that no special systems are required to control them, but a PCV crankcase system is used to purge the crankcase of unwanted fumes. EGR valves are used on many engine applications and must be serviced as per the engine manufacturer's recommendations.

The engine manufacturers, the State and Federal governments are devising pollution standards and regulations for the diesel engines, to curtail the emissions of harmful operating by-products.

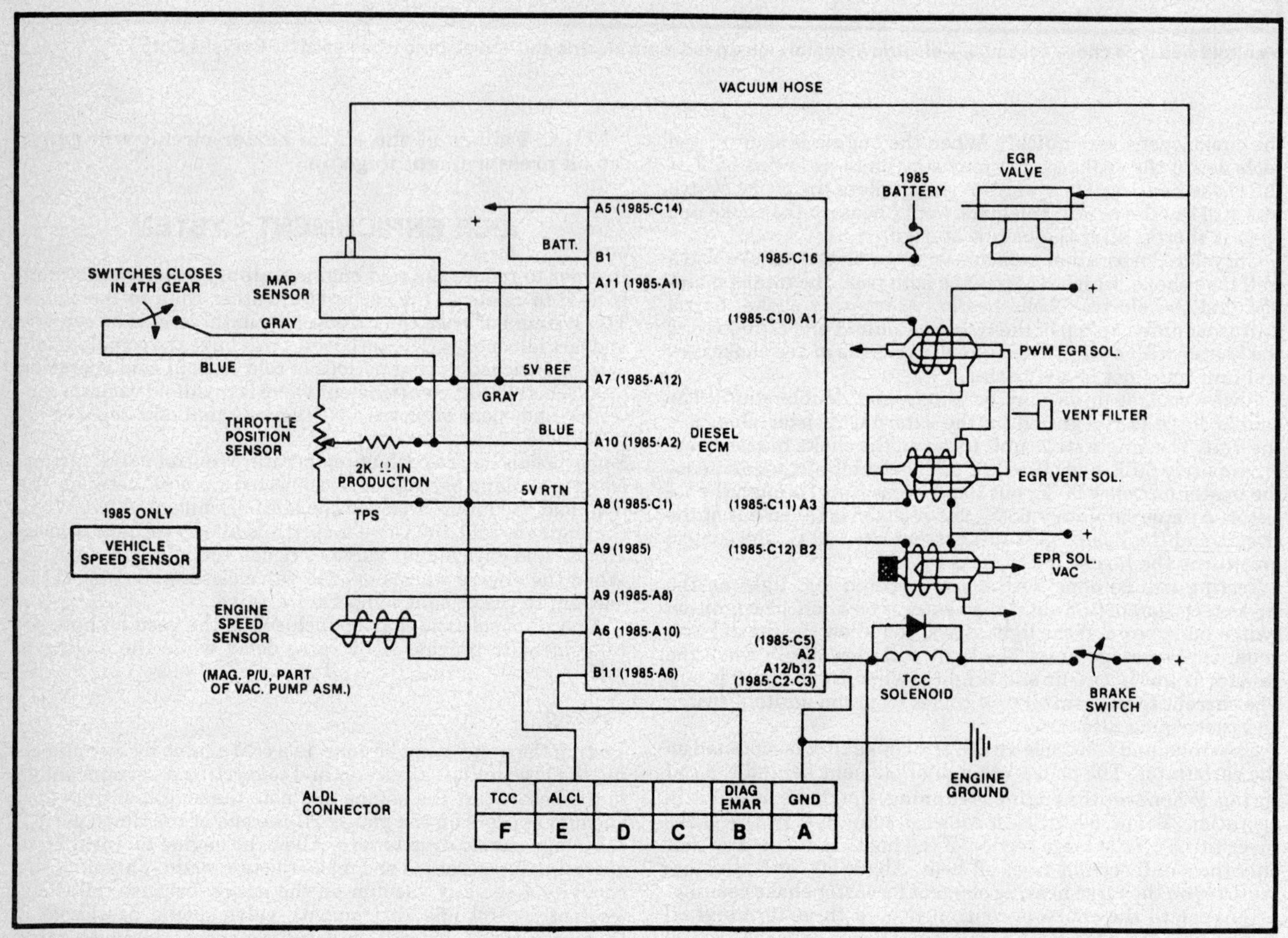

6.2 Diesel Electronic Control System (© General Motors Corp.)

INDEX

MANUAL STEERING

POWER STEERING

STEERING TROUBLE DIAGNOSIS
Manual Steering

Condition	Possible Cause	Correction
Excessive Play or Looseness in the Steering	1. Steering gear shaft adjusted too loose or shaft and/or bushing badly worn.	1. Replace worn parts and adjust according to instructions.
	2. Excessive steering gear worm end play due to bearing adjustment.	2. Adjust according to instructions.
	3. Steering linkage loose or worn.	3. Replace worn parts.
	4. Front wheel bearings improperly adjusted.	4. Adjust wheel bearings.
	5. Steering arm loose on steering gear shaft.	5. Inspect for damage to the gear shaft and steering arm, replace parts as necessary.
	6. Steering gear housing attaching bolts loose.	6. Tighten the attaching bolts to specifications.
	7. Steering arms loose at steering knuckles.	7. Tighten according to specifications.
	8. Working pins or bushings.	8. Replace king pins and bushings.
	9. Loose spring shackles.	9. Adjust or replace parts as necessary.
Hard Steering	1. Low or uneven tire pressure.	1. Inflate the tires to recommended pressures.
	2. Insufficient lubricant in the steering gear housing or in steering linkage.	2. Lubricate as necessary.
	3. Steering gear shaft adjusted too tight.	3. Adjust according to instructions.
	4. Improper caster or toe-in.	4. Align the wheels.
	5. Steering column misaligned.	5. See "Steering Gear Alignment."
Wheel Tramp (Excessive Vertical Motion of Wheels)	1. Incorrect tire pressure.	1. Inflate the tires to recommended pressures.
	2. Improper balance of wheels, tires and brake drums.	2. Balance as necessary.
	3. Loose tie rod ends or steering connections.	3. Inspect and repair as necessary.
	4. Worn or inoperative shock absorbers.	4. Replace the shock absorbers.
	5. Excessive run-out of brake drums, wheels or tires.	5. Repair or replace as required.
Shimmy	1. Badly worn and/or unevenly worn tires.	1. Rotate tires or replace if necessary.
	2. Wheels and tires out of balance.	2. Balance wheel and tire assemblies.
	3. Worn or loose steering linkage parts.	3. Replace parts are required.
	4. Worn king pins and bushings.	4. Replace king pins and bushings.
	5. Loose steering gear adjustments.	5. Adjust steering gear as necessary.
	6. Loose wheel bearings.	6. Adjust wheel bearings.
	7. Improper caster setting.	7. Adjust caster to specifications.
	8. Weak or broken springs.	8. Replace as required.
	9. Incorrect tire pressure or tire sizes not uniform.	9. Check tire sizes and inflate tires to recommended pressure
	10. Faulty shock absorbers.	10. Replace as necessary.
Pull to One Side (Tendency of the Vehicle to Veer in one Direction Only)	1. Incorrect tire pressure or tires not uniform.	1. Check tire sizes and inflate the tires to recommended pressures.
	2. Wheel bearings improperly adjusted.	2. Adjust wheel bearings.
	3. Dragging brakes.	3. Inspect for weak, or broken brake shoe spring, binding pedal.
	4. Improper caster, camber or toe-in.	4. Adjust to specifications.
	5. Grease, dirt, oil or brake fluid on brake linings.	5. Inspect, replace and adjust as necessary.
	6. Broken or sagging rear springs.	6. Replace the rear springs.
	7. Bent front axle, linkage or steering knuckle.	7. Replace the parts as necessary.
	8. Worn or tight king pin bushings.	8. Lubricate or replace as necessary.
Wander or Weave	1. Improper caster, camber or toe-in.	1. Adjust to specifications.
	2. Worn king pin and bushings.	2. Replace parts as required.
	3. Worn or improperly adjusted front wheel bearings.	3. Adjust or replace parts as necessary.
	4. Loose spring shackles.	4. Adjust or replace parts as necessary.
	5. Incorrect tire pressure or tire sizes not uniform.	5. Check tire sizes and inflate tires to recommended pressure.
	6. Loose steering gear mounting bolts.	6. Tight to specifications.

STEERING TROUBLE DIAGNOSIS
Manual Steering

Condition	Possible Cause	Correction
Wander or Weave	7. Tight king pin bushings. 8. Tight king pin thrust bearings.	7. Lubricate or ream to proper fit. 8. Adjust to .001 to .005 inch cleareance.

MANUAL STEERING GEAR

STEERING GEAR ALIGNMENT

Before any steering gear adjustments are made, it is recommended that the front end of the truck be raised and a thorough inspection be made for stiffness or lost motion in the steering gear, steering linkage and front suspension. Worn or damaged parts should be replaced, since a satisfactory adjustment of the steering gear cannot be obtained if bent or badly worn parts exist.

It is also very important that the steering gear be properly aligned in the truck. Misalignment of the gear places a stress on the steering worm shaft, therefore a proper adjustment is impossible. To align the steering gear, loosen the steering gear-to-frame mounting bolts to permit the gear to align itself. Check the steering gear to frame mounting seat. If there is a gap at any of the mounting bolts, proper alignment may be obtained by placing shims where excessive gap appears. Tighten the steering gear-to-frame bolts. Alignment of the gear in the truck is very important and should be done carefully so that a satisfactory, trouble-free gear adjustment may be obtained.

Gemmer Worm and Double Roller Tooth Type

WITH SCREW ADJUSTED MESH

The steering gear is of the worm and roller type with a 24 to 1 gear ratio. The cross shaft is straddle mounted with a bearing surface at the top and bottom points of the shaft mounting areas. The three tooth cross shaft roller is mounted in ball bearings. The proper lubricant used in the gear box is S.A.E. 90 Extreme Pressure Lubricant.

The external adjustments given below will properly adjust the steering gear.

WORM BEARING

ADJUSTMENT

1. Turn the steering wheel about one full turn from straight ahead and secure it so it doesn't move.

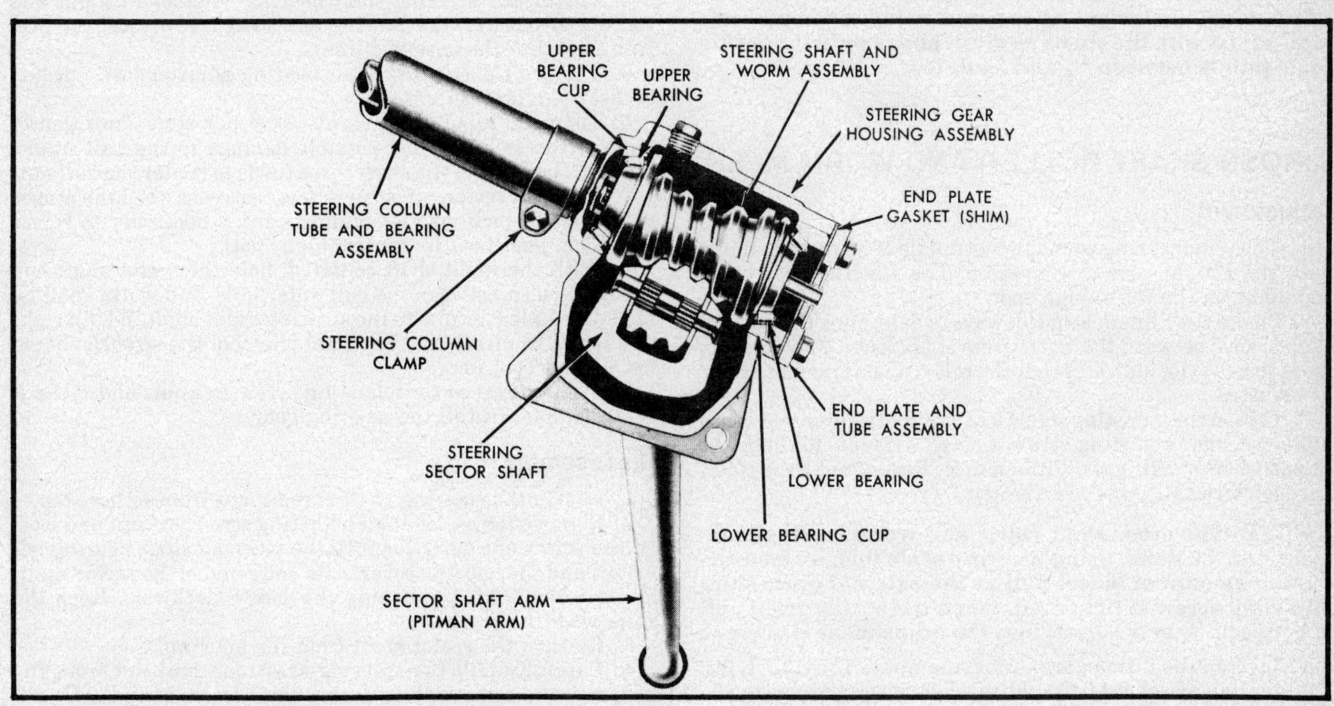

Worm and roller type steering gear (© Ford Motor Co.)

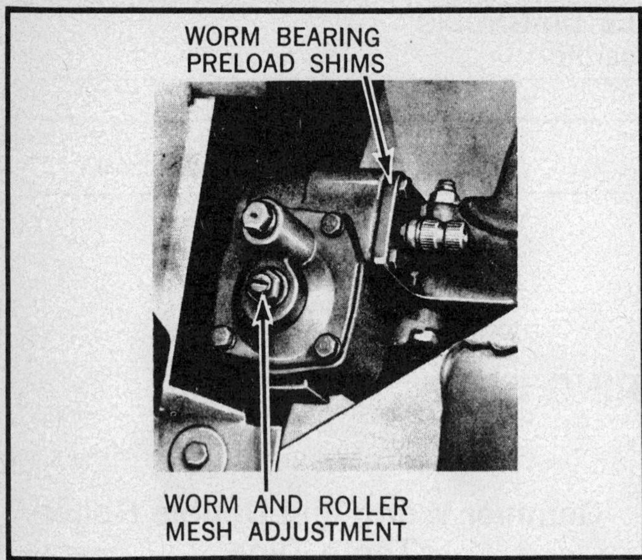

Steering gear adjustments (© Ford Motor Co.)

2. Determine if there is any worm gear end-play by shaking the front wheel sideways and noting if there is any end movement that may be felt between the steering wheel hub and the steering jacket tube. (Be sure any movement noted is not looseness in the steering jacket tube.)

3. If end play is present, adjust the worm bearings by loosening the four cover cap screws about $^{1}/_{2}$ in. Separate the top shim, using a knife blade, and remove it. Do not damage the remaining shims or gaskets.

4. Replace the cover and recheck the end-play again. If necessary, repeat Steps 2 and 3 until the end-play movement is as small as possible without tightening the steering gear too much.

NOTE: Adjustment may be done with the Pitman arm disconnected. With the steering wheel turned about one full turn from straight ahead and using a spring scale tool, adjust with the shims as given above until the spring scale pull is between $^{1}/_{4}$ and $^{5}/_{8}$ ft. lbs.

CROSS SHAFT ROLLER AND WORM MESH

Adjustment

1. Turn the steering wheel to the middle of its turning limits with the Pitman arm disconnected. The steering gear roller should be on the worm high spot.

2. Shake the Pitman arm sideways to determine the amount of clearance between the worm cross shaft roller. Movement of more than $^{1}/_{32}$ in. indicates that the roller and worm mesh must be adjusted.

3. Loosen the adjusting screw lock nut and tighten the external cross shaft adjusting screw a small amount. Recheck the clearance by shaking the Pitman arm. Repeat until the clearance is correct. (Do not overtighten.)

NOTE: The cross shaft roller and worm mesh adjustment may be done, using a spring scale tool, by measuring the amount of wheel pull as the external cross shaft adjusting screw is tightened. When the spring scale pull is between $^{7}/_{8}$ and 1 $^{1}/_{8}$ ft. lbs., the adjustment is correct.

4. Tighten the Pitman arm attaching nut to 100–125 ft. lbs. The steering wheel nut (if loosened) should be tightened to 15–20 ft. lbs. torque.

Disassembly

1. Remove steering gear oil seal, using a suitable puller.
2. Remove cross shaft, using an arbor to prevent bearings from dropping out.
3. Remove cover, shims and cover gasket.
4. Remove worm gear, thrust bearings and bearing cups.

Assembly

1. Clean and inspect all parts, replace as necessary.

NOTE: If either thrust bearing is excessively worn, replace them both.

2. Reassemble steering gear, using new oil seal.
3. Perform worm bearing and cross shaft roller and worm mesh adjustments.
4. Lubricate to specifications.

Ford Steering Gear-Recirculating Ball Type

STEERING WORM AND SECTOR GEAR

Adjustment

The ball nut assembly and the sector gear must be adjusted properly to maintain a minimum amount of steering shaft end play and a minimum amount of backlash between the sector gear and the ball nut. There are only two adjustments that may be done on this steering gear and they should be done as given below:

1. Remove the steering gear from the vehicle.
2. Loosen the locknut on the sector shaft adjustment screw and turn the adjusting screw counterclockwise about three turns.
3. Measure the worm bearing preload by attaching an inch lbs. torque wrench to the input shaft. Note the reading required to rotate input shaft about 1 $^{1}/_{2}$ turns either side of center. If the torque reading is not about 4–5 inch lbs., adjust the gear as given in the next step.
4. Loosen the steering shaft bearing adjuster lock nut and tighten or back off the bearing adjusting screw until the preload is within the specified limits.
5. Tighten the steering shaft bearing adjuster lock nut and recheck the preload torque.
6. Turn the input shaft slowly to either stop. Turn gently against the stop to avoid possible damage to the ball return guides. Then rotate the shaft three turns to center the ball nut.
7. Turn the sector adjusting screw clockwise until the proper torque (9–10 inch lbs.) is obtained that is necessary to rotate the worm gear past its center (high spot).
8. With the input shaft centered, hold the sector shaft and check the lash between the ball nuts, balls, and worm shaft by applying 15 lbs. torque to the steering input shaft in both right and left turn directions. The total travel of the wrench should not exceed 1 $^{1}/_{4}$ in..
9. Tighten the sector adjusting screw locknut, and recheck the backlash. Install the steering gear.

Disassembly

1. Rotate the steering shaft three turns from either stop.
2. Remove the sector shaft adjusting screw locknut and loosen the screw one turn. Remove the steering shaft bearing adjuster, and the housing cover bolts and remove the sector shaft. Remove the shaft by turning the screw clockwise. Keep the shim with the screw.
3. Remove the sector shaft from the housing.
4. Carefully pull the steering shaft and ball nut from the housing, and remove the steering shaft lower bearing. Do not run the ball nut to either end of the worm gear to prevent dam-

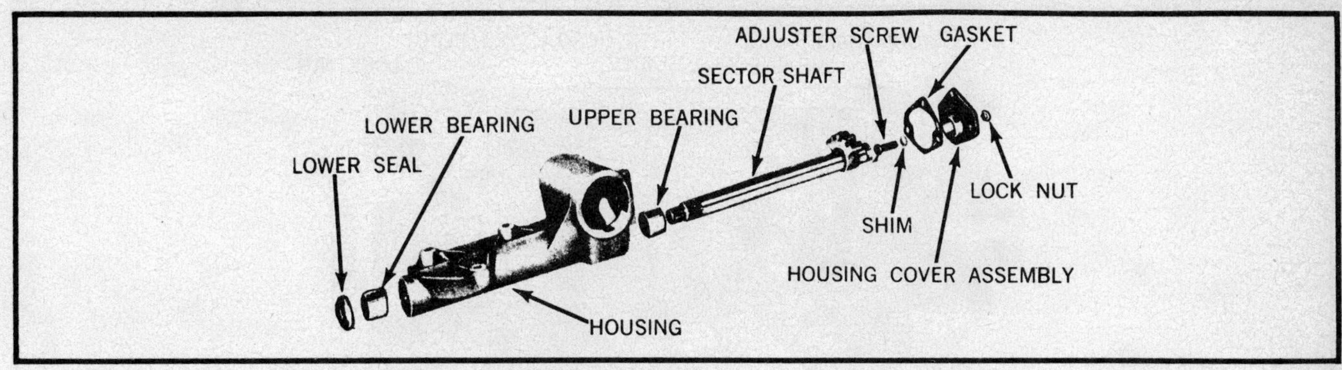

Sector shaft and housing—Ford recirculating ball model (© Ford Motor Co.)

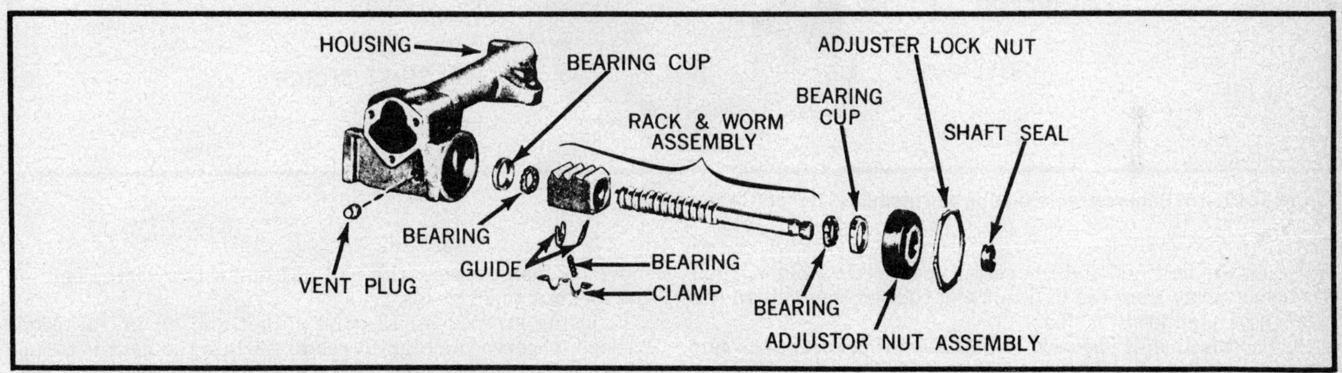

Steering shaft and related parts—Ford recirculating ball model (© Ford Motor Co.)

aging the ball return guides. Disassemble the ball nut only if there are signs of binding or tightness.

5. To disassemble the ball nut, remove the ball return guide clamp and the ball return guides from the ball nut. Keep ball nut clamp side up until ready to remove the ball bearings.

6. Turn the ball nut over and rotate the worm shaft from side to side until all 50 balls have dropped out into a clean pan. With all balls removed, the nut will slide off the wormshaft.

7. Remove the upper bearing cup from the bearing adjuster and the lower cup from the housing. It may be necessary to tap the housing or the adjuster on a wooden block to jar the bearing cups loose.

Inspection

1. Carefully clean and inspect all parts. If the inspection shows bearing damage, the sector shaft bearing and the oil seal should be pressed out.

2. If the sector shaft bearing and oil seals were removed, press new bearings and oil seals into the housing. Do not clean, wash, or soak seals in cleaning solvent.

3. Apply the recommended steering gear lubricant to the housing and seals, filling the pocket between the sector shaft bearings.

Assembly

1. Install the bearing cup in the lower end of the housing and a bearing cup in the adjuster nut. Install a new seal in the bearing adjuster if the old seal was removed.

2. Apply gear lube to the outside of the worm shaft and the inside of the ball nut. Lay the steering shaft down, and position the ball nut on the shaft with the guide holes upward and the shallow end of the teeth to the left of the steering wheel position. Align the grooves in worm and ball nut by sighting through the guide holes.

3. Insert the ball guides into the holes in the ball nut, lightly tapping them, if necessary, to seat them.

4. Insert 25 balls into the hole in the top of each ball guide. If necessary, rotate the shaft slightly to distribute the balls evenly in the circuit.

5. Install the ball guide clamp, tightening the screws to the proper torque. Check that the worm shaft rotates freely.

6. Coat the threads of the steering shaft bearing adjuster, the housing cover bolts, and the sector adjusting screw with a suitable oil-resistant sealing compound. Do not apply sealer to female threads and do not get sealer on the steering shaft bearings.

7. Coat the worm bearings, sector shaft bearings, and gear teeth with steering gear lubricant.

8. Clamp the housing in a vise, with the sector shaft axis horizontal, and place the steering shaft lower bearing in its cup. Place the steering shaft and ball nut assemblies in the housing.

9. Position the steering shaft upper bearing on top of the worm gear and install the steering shaft bearing adjuster, adjuster nut, and the bearing cup. Leave the nut loose.

10. Adjust the worm bearing preload according to the instructions given earlier.

11. Position the sector adjusting screw and adjuster shim, and check for a clearance of not more than 0.002 in. between the screw head and the end of the sector shaft. If the clearance exceeds 0.002 in., add enough shims to reduce the clearance to under 0.002 in. clearance.

12. Start the sector shaft adjusting screw into the housing cover. Install a new gasket on the cover.

13. Rotate the steering shaft until the ball nut teeth mesh with the sector gear teeth, tilting the housing so the ball will tip toward the housing cover opening.

14. Lubricate the sector shaft journal and install the sector shaft and cover. With the cover moved to one side, fill the gear with lubricant (about 0.97 lb.). Push the cover and the sector shaft into place, and install the two top housing bolts. Do not tighten the bolts until checking to see that there is some lash

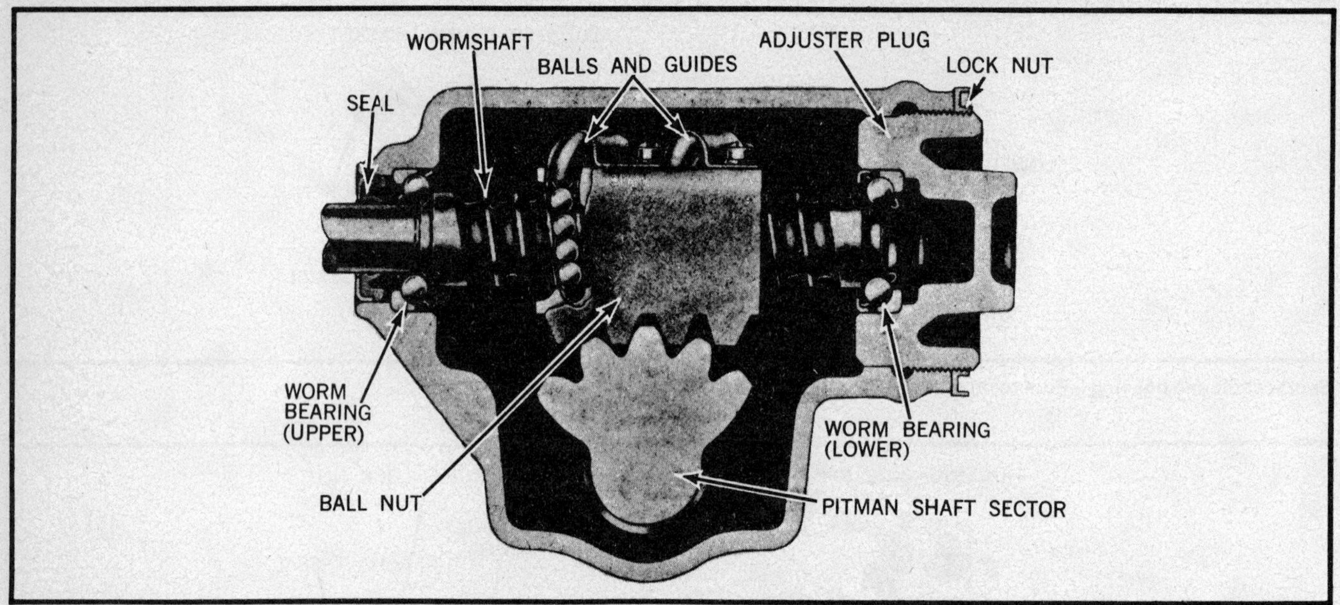

Cross section of Saginaw recirculating ball model (© General Motors Corp.)

between the ball nut and the sector gear teeth. Hold or push the cover away from the ball nut and tighten the bolts to the proper torque (30–40 ft. lbs.).

15. Loosely install the sector shaft adjusting screw lock nut and adjust the sector shaft mesh load as given earlier. Tighten the adjusting screw lock nut.

Saginaw Recirculating Ball Type

The steering gear is of the recirculating ball nut type. the ball nut, mounted on the worm gear, is driven by means of steel balls which circulate in helical grooves in both the worm and nut. Ball return guides attached to the nut serve to recirculate the two sets of balls in the grooves. As the steering wheel is turned to the right, the ball nut moves upward. When the wheel is turned to the left, the ball nut moves downward.

The sector teeth on the pinion shaft and the ball nut are designed so that they fit the tightest when the steering wheel is straight ahead. This mesh action is adjusted by an adjusting screw which moves the pinion shaft endwise until the teeth mesh properly. The worm bearing adjuster provides proper preloading of the upper and lower bearings.

Before doing the adjustment procedures given below, ensure that the steering problem is not caused by faulty suspension components, bad front end alignment, etc. Then, proceed with the following adjustments.

STEERING WORM AND SECTOR

Adjustment

1. Tighten the worm bearing adjuster plug until all end play has been removed, then loosen $^1/_4$ turn.
2. Use an $^{11}/_{16}$ in. 12 point socket to carefully turn the wormshaft all the way into the right corner then turn back about $^1/_2$ turn.
3. Tighten the adjuster plug until the proper thrust bearing preload is obtained (5–8 inch lbs.). Tighten the adjuster plug locknut to 85 ft. lbs.
4. Turn the wormshaft from one stop to the other counting the number of turns. Then turn the shaft back exactly half the number of turns to the center position.
5. Turn the lash (sector shaft) adjuster screw clockwise to remove all lash between the ball nut and sector teeth. Tighten the locknut to 25 ft. lbs.
6. Using an $^{11}/_{16}$ in. 12 point socket and an in. lb. torque wrench, observe the highest reading while the gear is turned through the center position. It should be 16 inch lbs. or less.
7. If necessary repeat Steps 5 and 6.

Disassembly

1. Place the steering gear in a vise, clamping onto one of the mounting tabs. The wormshaft should be in a horizontal position.
2. Rotate the wormshaft from stop to stop and count the total number of turns. Turn back exactly halfway, placing the gear on center.
3. Remove the three self locking bolts which attach the sector cover to the housing.
4. Using a plastic hammer, tap lightly on the end of the sector shaft and lift the sector cover and sector shaft assembly from the gear housing.

NOTE: It may be necessary to turn the wormshaft by hand until the sector will pass through the opening in the housing.

5. Remove the locknut from the adjuster plug and remove the adjuster plug assembly.
6. Pull the wormshaft and ball nut assembly from the housing.

NOTE: Damage may be done to the ends of the ball guides if the ball nut is allowed to rotate to the end of the worm.

7. Remove the worm shaft upper bearing from inside the gear housing.
8. Pry the wormshaft lower bearing retainer from the adjuster plug housing and remove the bearing.
9. Remove the locknut from the lash adjuster screw in the sector cover. Turn the lash adjuster screw clockwise and remove it from the sector cover. Slide the adjuster screw and shim out of the slot in the end of the sector shaft.
10. Pry out and discard both the sector shaft and wormshaft seals.

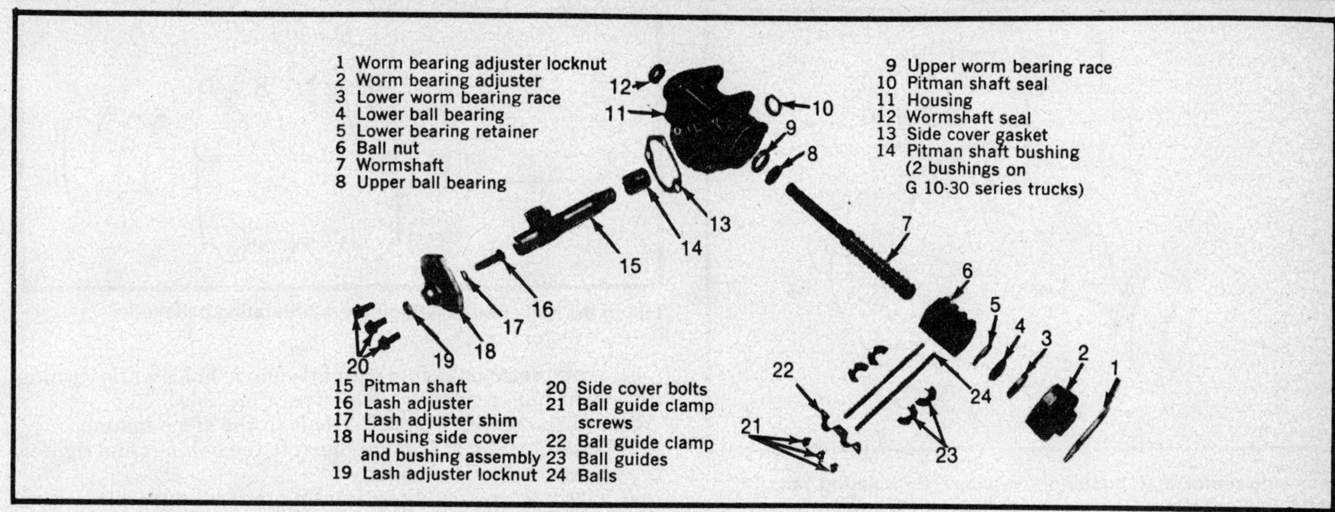

Exploded view of Saginaw recirculating ball model (© General Motors Corp.)

Inspection

1. Wash all parts in cleaning solvent and blow dry with an air hose.
2. Use a magnifying glass and inspect the bearings and bearing caps for signs of indentation, or chipping. Replace any parts that show signs of damage.
3. Check the fit of the sector shaft in the bushings in the sector cover and housing. If these bushings are worn, a new sector cover and bushing assembly or housing bushing should be installed.
4. Check steering gear wormshaft assembly for being bent or damaged.

SHAFT SEAL

Replacement

1. Remove the old seal from the pump body.
2. Install the new seal by pressing the outer diameter of the seal with a suitable size socket.

NOTE: Make sure the socket is large enough to avoid damaging the external lip of the seal.

SECTOR SHAFT BUSHING

Replacement

1. Place the steering gear housing in an arbor press.
2. Press the sector shaft bushing from the housing.

CAUTION

Service bushings are bored to size and require no further reaming.

SECTOR COVER BUSHING

Replacement

1. The sector cover bushing is not serviced separately. The entire sector cover assembly including the bushing must be replaced as a unit.

BALL NUT SERVICE

If there is any indication of binding or tightness when the ball nut is rotated on the worm the unit should be disassembled, cleaned and inspected as follows:

Removing the bearing retainer from the worm bearing adjuster—Saginaw recirculating ball model (© General Motors Corp.)

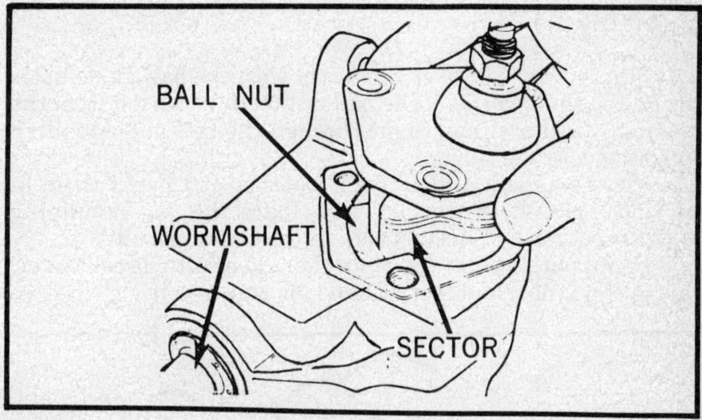

Removing sector shaft assembly—Saginaw recirculating ball model (© Ford Motor Co.)

BALL NUT

Disassembly

1. Remove the screws and clamp retaining the ball guides in the ball nut. Pull the guides out of the ball nut.
2. Turn the ball nut upside down and rotate the wormshaft back and forth until all the balls have dropped out of the ball nut. The ball nut can now be pulled endwise off the worm.

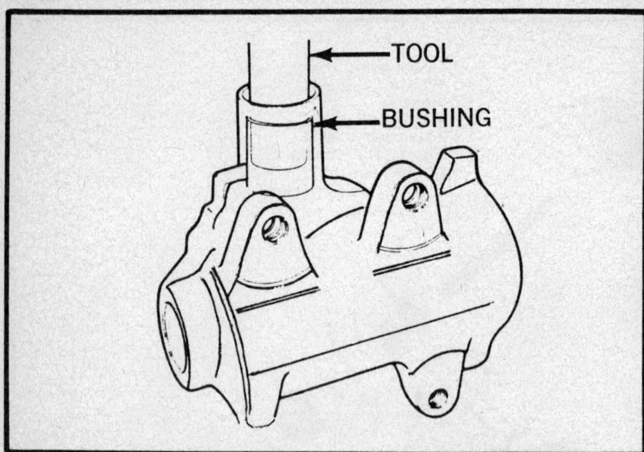

Removing sector shaft bushing—Saginaw recirculating ball model (© Ford Motor Co.)

Removing worm shaft lower bearing cup from the adjuster plug—Saginaw recirculating ball model (© Ford Motor Co.)

3. Wash all parts in solvent and dry them with air. Use a magnifying glass and inspect the worm and nut grooves and the surface of all balls for signs of indentation. Check all ball guides for damage at the ends. Replace any damaged parts.

Assembly

1. Slip the ball nut over the worm with the ball guide holes up and the shallow end of the ball nut teeth to the left from the steering wheel position. Sight through the ball guide to align the grooves in the worm.
2. Place two ball guide halves together and insert them in the upper circuit in the ball nut. Place the two remaining guides together and insert them in the lower circuit.
3. Count out 25 balls and place them in a suitable container. This is the proper number of balls for one circuit.

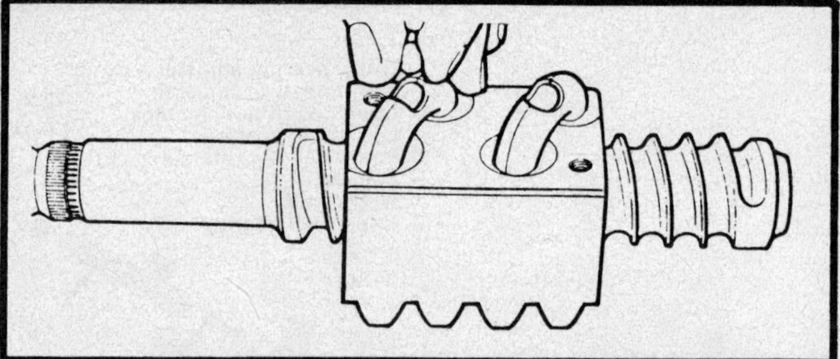

Filling the ball circuits—Saginaw recirculating ball model (© Ford Motor Co.)

4. Load the 25 balls into one of the guide holes while turning the wormshaft gradually away from that hole.
5. Fill the remaining ball circuit in the same manner.
6. Assemble the ball guide clamp to the ball nut and tighten the screws to 18–24 inch lbs.
7. Check the assembly by rotating the ball nut on the worm to see that it moves freely. Do not rotate the ball nut to the end of the worm threads as this may damage the ball guides.

Assembly

1. Coat the threads of the adjuster plug, sector cover bolts and lash adjuster with a non-drying oil resistant sealing compound.

NOTE: Do not apply compound to the female threads. Use extreme care when applying compound to the bearing adjuster so that it does not come in contact with the wormshaft bearing.

2. Place the steering gear housing in a vise with the wormshaft bore horizontal and the sector cover opening up.
3. Make sure that all seals, bushings and bearing cups are installed in the gear housing and that the ball nut is installed on the wormshaft.
4. Slip the wormshaft upper bearing assembly over the wormshaft and insert the wormshaft and ball nut assembly into the housing, feeding the end of the shaft through the upper ball bearing cup and seal.
5. Place the wormshaft lower bearing assembly in the adjuster plug bearing cup and press the stamped retainer into place with a suitable size socket.
6. Install the adjuster plug and locknut into the lower end of the housing while carefully guiding the end of the wormshaft into the bearing until nearly all end play has been removed from the wormshaft.
7. Position the lash adjuster including the shim in the slotted end of the sector shaft.

NOTE: End clearance should not be greater than 0.002. If the end clearance is greater than 0.002 a shim package is available with thicknesses of 0.063, 0.065, 0.067, 0.069.

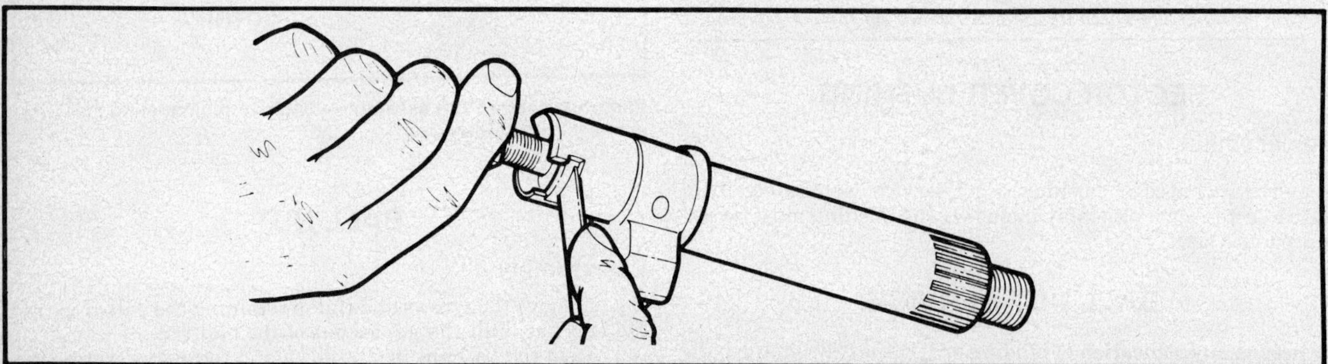

Checking lash adjuster end clearance—Saginaw recirculating ball model (© Ford Motor Co.)

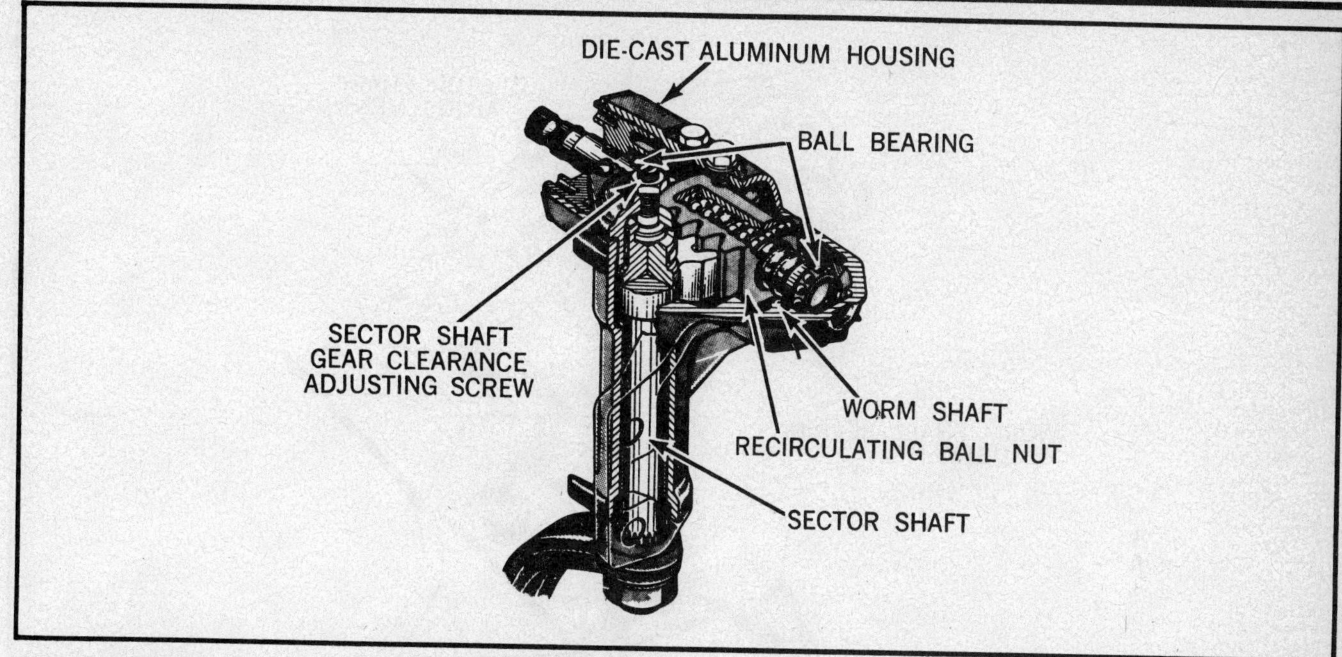

Chrysler recirculating ball type steering gear (© Chrysler Corp.)

8. Lubricate the steering gear with 11 oz. of steering gear grease. Rotate the wormshaft until the ball nut is at the other end of its travel and then pack as much new lubricant into the housing as possible without losing out the sector shaft opening. Rotate the wormshaft until the ball nut is at the other end of its travel and pack as much lubricant into the opposite end as possible.
9. Rotate the wormshaft until the ball nut is in the center of travel. This is to make sure that the sector shaft and ball nut will engage properly with the center tooth of the sector entering the center tooth space in the ball nut.
10. Insert the sector shaft assembly including lash adjuster screw and shim into the housing so that the center tooth of the sector enters the center tooth space in the ball nut.
11. Pack the remaining portion of the lubricant into the housing and also place some in the sector cover bushing hole.
12. Place the sector cover gasket on the housing.
13. Install the sector cover onto the sector shaft by reaching through the sector cover with a screwdriver and turning the lash adjuster screw counterclockwise until the screw bottoms, then back the screw off one-half turn. Loosely install a new lock nut onto the adjuster screw.
14. Install and tighten the sector cover bolt to 30 ft. lbs.

Chrysler Recirculating Ball Type

The steering gear is of the recirculating ball nut type. The ball nut, mounted on the worm gear, is driven by means of steel balls which circulate in helical grooves in both the worm and nut. Ball return guides attached to the nut serve to recirculate the two sets of balls in the grooves. As the steering wheel is turned to the right, the ball nut moves upward. When the wheel is turned to the left, the ball nut moves downward.

The sector teeth on the pinion shaft and the ball nut are designed so that they fit the tightest when the steering wheel is straight ahead. This mesh action is adjusted by an adjusting screw which moves the pinion shaft endwise until the teeth mesh properly. The worm bearing adjuster provides proper preloading of the upper and lower bearings.

WORM BEARING PRE-LOAD

Adjustment

1. Remove the steering gear arm and lockwasher from the sector shaft, using a suitable gear puller.
2. Remove the horn button or horn ring.
3. Loosen the sector-shaft adjusting screw locknut, and back out the adjusting screw about two turns.
4. Turn the steering wheel two complete turns from the straight ahead position, and place an in. lb. torque wrench on the steering shaft nut.
5. Rotate the steering shaft at least one turn toward the straight ahead position while measuring the torque on the torque wrench. The torque should be between 1 $^1/_8$ and 4 $^1/_2$ inch lbs. to move the steering wheel. If torque is not within these limits, loosen the worm shaft bearing adjuster locknut and turn the adjuster clockwise to increase the preload or counterclockwise to decrease the preload. When the preload is correct, hold the adjuster screw steady and tighten the locknut. Recheck preload.

BALL NUT RACK AND SECTOR MESH

Adjustment

NOTE: This adjustment can be accurately made only after proper preloading of worm bearing.

1. Turn steering wheel gently from one stop to the other, counting the number of turns. Turn the steering wheel back exactly half way, to the center position.
2. Turn the sector–shaft adjusting screw clockwise to remove all lash between ball nut rack and the sector gear teeth, then tighten adjusting screw locknut to 35 ft. lbs.
3. Turn the steering wheel about $^1/_4$ turn away from the center or high spot position. With the torque wrench on the steering wheel nut measure the torque required to turn the steering wheel through the high spot at the center position. The reading should be between 8 and 11 inch lbs. This is the total of the worm shaft bearing preload and the ball nut rack and sector

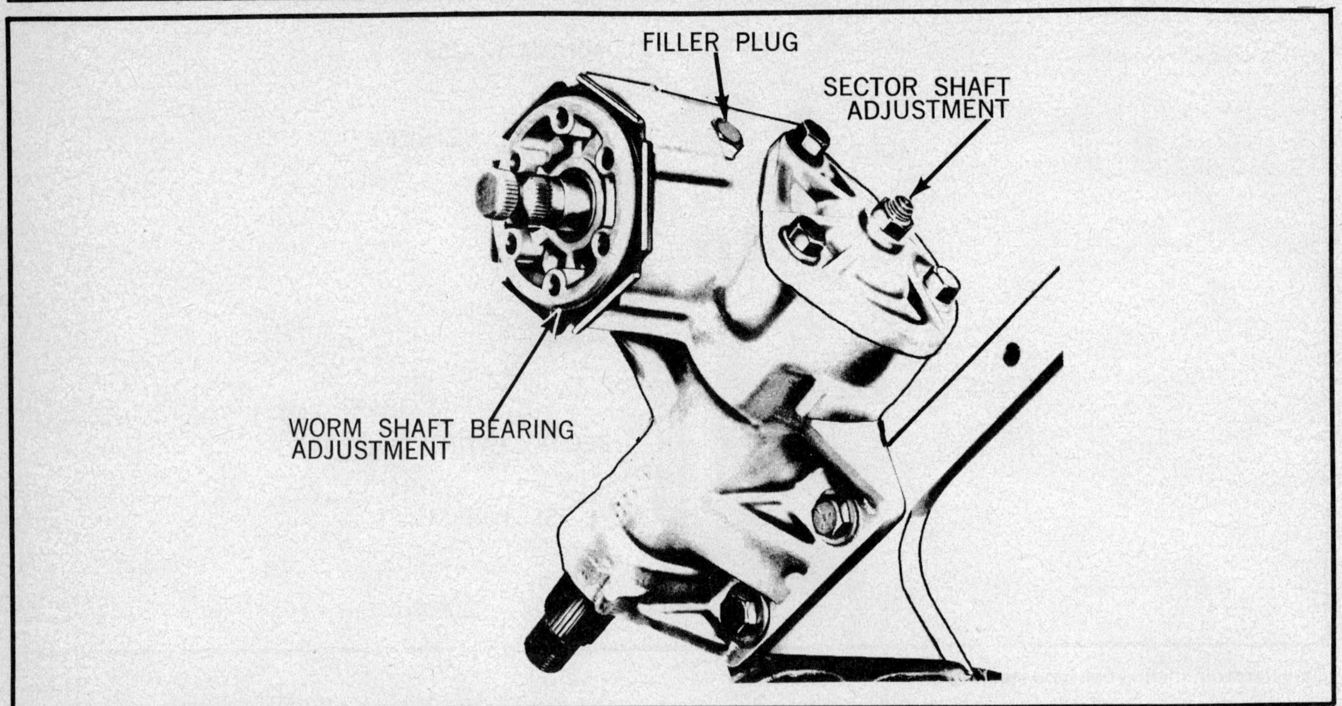

Steering gear adjustment locations (© Chrysler Corp.)

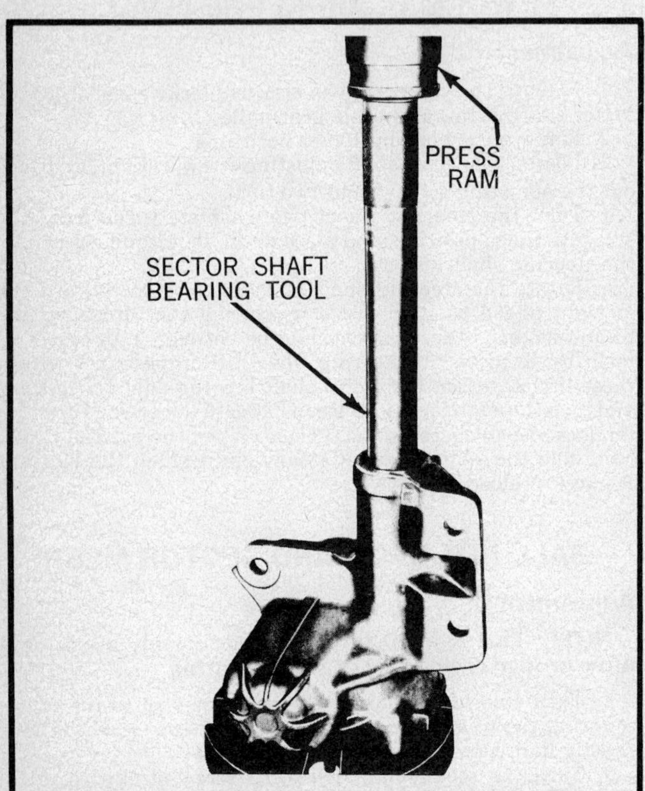

Removing the sector shaft inner and outer bearings (© Chrysler Corp.)

gear mesh load. Readjust the sector-shaft adjustment screw if necessary to obtain a correct torque reading.

4. After completing the adjustments, place the front wheels in a straight ahead position, and with the steering wheel and steering gear centered, install the steering arm on sector-shaft. Tighten the steering arm retaining nut to 180 ft. lbs.

STEERING GEAR

Disassembly and Assembly

1. Attach the steering gear assembly to a holding fixture and put the holding fixture in a bench vise. Thoroughly clean the outside surface before disassembly.
2. Loosen the sector-shaft adjusting screw locknut, and back out the adjusting screw about two turns to relieve the mesh load between the ball nut rack and the sector gear teeth.
3. Position the steering gear worm shaft in a straight ahead position.
4. Remove the attaching bolts from the sector-shaft cover and slowly remove the sector-shaft while sliding an arbor tool into the housing. Remove the locknut from the adjusting screw and remove the screw from the cover by turning it clockwise. Slide the adjustment screw and its shim out of the slot in the end of the sector-shaft.
5. Loosen the worm shaft bearing adjuster locknut with a brass drift (punch) and remove the locknut. Hold the worm shaft steady while unscrewing the adjuster. Slide the worm adjuster off the shaft.

CAUTION

Handle the adjuster carefully to avoid damaging the aluminum threads. Also, do not run the ball nut down to either end of the worm shaft to avoid damaging the ball guides.

6. Carefully remove the worm and ball nut assembly. This assembly is serviced as a complete assembly only and is not to be disassembled or the ball return guides removed or disturbed.
7. Remove the sector-shaft needle bearing by placing the gear housing in an arbor press; insert a tool in the lower end of the housing and press both bearings through the housing. The sector-shaft cover assembly, including a needle bearing or bushing, is serviced as an assembly.

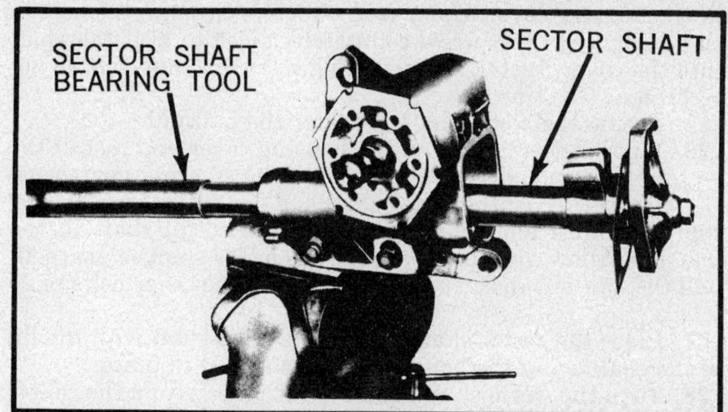

Removing the sector shaft (© Chrysler Corp.)

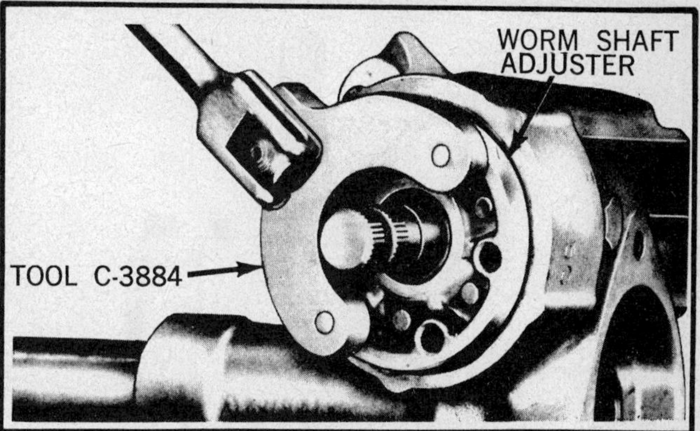

Removing the wormshaft adjuster (© Chrysler Corp.)

8. Remove the worm shaft oil seal from the worm shaft bearing adjuster by inserting a blunt punch behind the seal and tapping alternately on each side of the seal until it is driven out of the adjuster.
9. Remove the worm shaft in the same manner as that given in Step 8. *Be careful not to cock the bearing cup and distort the adjuster counter bore.*
10. Remove the lower cup if necessary. Pull the bearing cup out.
11. Wash all parts in clean solvent and dry thoroughly. Inspect all parts for wear, scoring, pitting, etc. Test operation of the worm shaft and ball nut assembly. If ball nut does not travel smoothly and freely on the worm shaft or if there is binding, replace the assembly.

NOTE: Extreme care must be taken when handling the aluminum worm bearing adjuster to avoid thread damage. Also, be careful not to damage the threads in the gear housing. Always lubricate the worm bearing adjuster before screwing it into the housing.

12. Inspect the sector-shaft for wear and check the fit of the shaft in the housing bearings. Inspect the fit of the shaft pilot bearing in the housing. Be sure the worm shaft is not bent or damaged.
13. Install the sector-shaft lower needle bearing. Press the bearing into the housing about $\frac{7}{16}$ in. below the end of the bore to leave space for the new oil seal.
14. Install the upper needle bearing in the same manner and press it into the inside end of the housing bore flush with the inside end of the bore surface.
15. Install the worm shaft bearing cups (upper and lower) by placing them and their spacers in the adjuster nut and press them into place.
16. Install the worm shaft oil seal by placing the seal in the worm shaft adjuster with the metal seal retainer up. Drive the seal into place with a suitable sleeve until it is just below the end of the bore in the adjuster.

NOTE: Apply a coating of steering gear lubricant to all moving parts during assembly. Also, put lubricant on and around oil seal lips.

17. Clamp the holding fixture and housing in a bench vise with the bearing adjuster opening upward. Place a thrust bearing in the lower cup in the housing.
18. Hold the ball nut from turning and insert the worm shaft and ball nut assembly into the housing with the end of the worm shaft resting in the thrust bearing. Place the upper thrust bearing on the worm shaft. Thoroughly lubricate the threads on the adjuster and the threads in the housing.
19. Place a protective sleeve of tape over the splines on the worm shaft to avoid damaging the seal. Slide the adjuster assembly over the shaft.

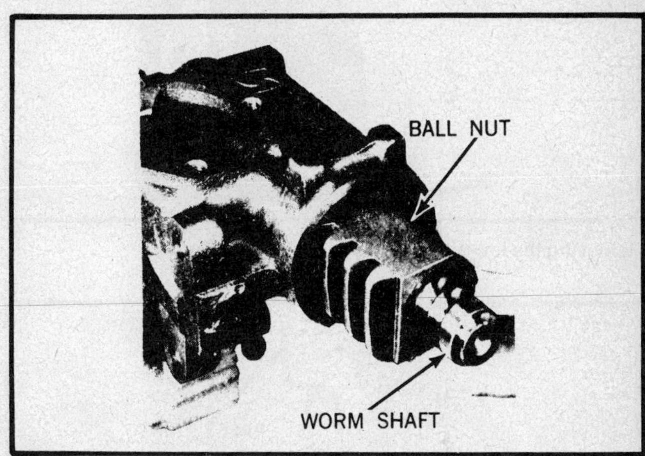

Removing the wormshaft and ball nut assembly
(© Chrysler Corp.)

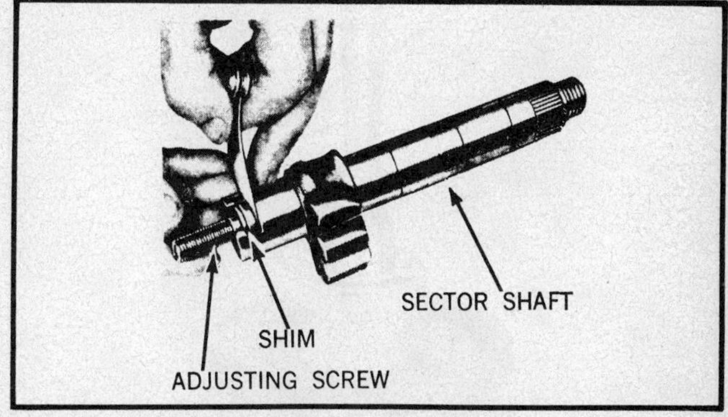

Measuring the sector shaft adjusting screw and clearance
(© Chrysler Corp.)

20. Thread the adjuster into the housing and tighten the adjuster to 50 ft. lbs. while rotating the worm shaft to seat the bearings.
21. Loosen the adjuster so no bearing preload exists. Tighten the adjuster for a worm shaft bearing preload of 1 $\frac{1}{8}$ to 4 $\frac{1}{2}$ inch lbs. Tighten the bearing adjuster locknut and recheck the preload.
22. Before installing the sector-shaft, pack the worm shaft cavities in the housing above and below the ball nut with steering gear lubricant. A good grade of multi-purpose lubricant

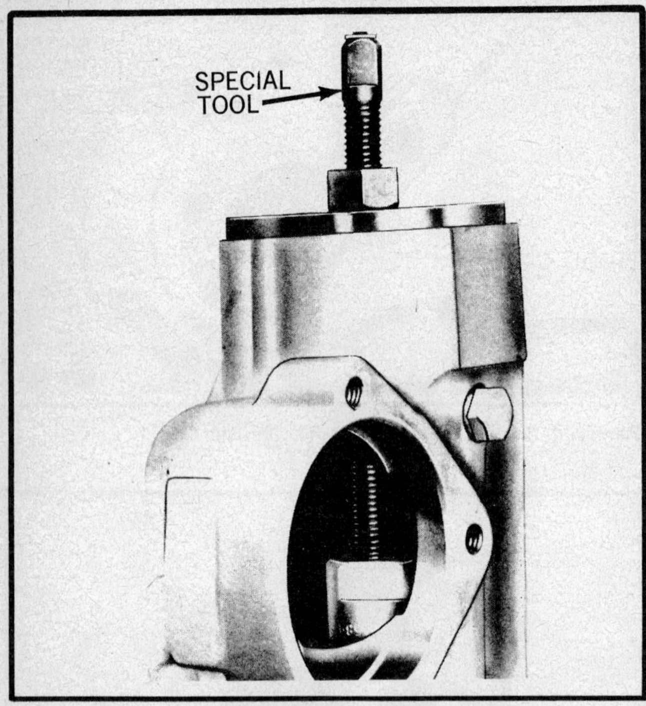

Removing the lower bearing cup (© Chrysler Corp.)

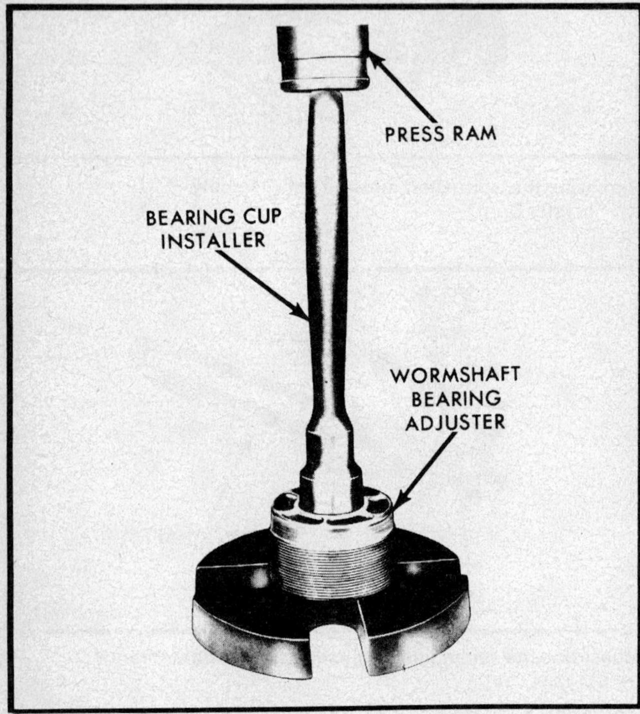

Installing the wormshaft upper bearing cup (© Chrysler Corp.)

may be used if steering gear lubricant is not available. *Do not use gear oil.* Pack enough lubricant into the worm cavities to cover the worm.

23. Slide the sector-shaft adjusting screw and shim into the slot in the end of the shaft. Check the end clearance for no more than 0.004 in. clearance. If the clearance is not within the limit, remove old shim and install a new shim, available in three different thicknesses, to get the proper clearance.

24. Start the sector-shaft and adjuster screw into the bearing in the housing cover. Using a screwdriver through the hole in the cover, turn the screw counterclockwise to pull the shaft into the cover. Install the adjusting screw locknut, but do not tighten at this time.

25. Rotate the worm shaft to center the ball nut.

26. Place a new gasket on the housing cover and install the sector-shaft and cover aasembly into the steering gear housing. Be sure to coat the sector-shaft and sector teeth with steering gear lubricant before installing the sector-shaft in the housing. Allow some lash between the sector-shaft sector teeth and the ball nut rack. Install and tighten the cover bolts to 25 ft. lbs.

27. Place the sector-shaft seal on the cross-shaft with the lip of the seal facing the housing. Press the seal in place.

28. Turn the worm shaft about $^1/_4$ turn away from the center of the high spot position. Using a torque wrench and a $^3/_4$ in. socket on the worm shaft spline, check the torque needed to rotate the shaft through the high spot. The reading should be between 8 and 11 inch lbs. Readjust the sector-shaft adjusting screw until the proper reading is obtained. Tighten the locknut to 35 ft. lbs. and recheck sector-shaft torque.

SECTOR-SHAFT OIL SEAL

Replacement

1. Remove the steering gear arm retaining nut and lockwasher.
2. Remove seal with a seal puller or other appropriate tool.
3. Place a new oil seal onto the splines of the sector-shaft with the lip of the seal facing the housing.
4. Remove the tool, and install the steering gear arm, lockwasher, and retaining nut. Tighten the nut to 180 ft. lbs. torque.

Ross Worm and Roller Steering Gear

The steering gear is of the worm and roller type, with shim adjustments provided for the worm gear bearings and an adjusting screw for the sector shaft adjustment.

This steering gear assembly is manufactured in different housing configurations, but the disassembly, assembly and adjustments are basically the same. The different models are identified by the size of the sector shaft.

BEARING PRELOAD

Adjustment

1. Loosen the four cap screws which fasten the end cover to the steering gear housing.

Models	Sector Shaft Diameter
254, 301	1¼ inch
376, 378	1⅜ inch
408	1½ inch
504	1¾ inch

2. Alternately tighten the cap screws evenly and rotate the worm gear shaft. Tighten the screws to 18 to 22 ft. lbs.
3. If necessary, remove the end cover and either add or subtract from the number of shims, and repeat Steps 1 and 2 to obtain the correct bearing preload.

WORM GEAR AND ROLLER GEAR BACKLASH

Adjustment

1. Loosen the locknut and turn the adjustment at the side

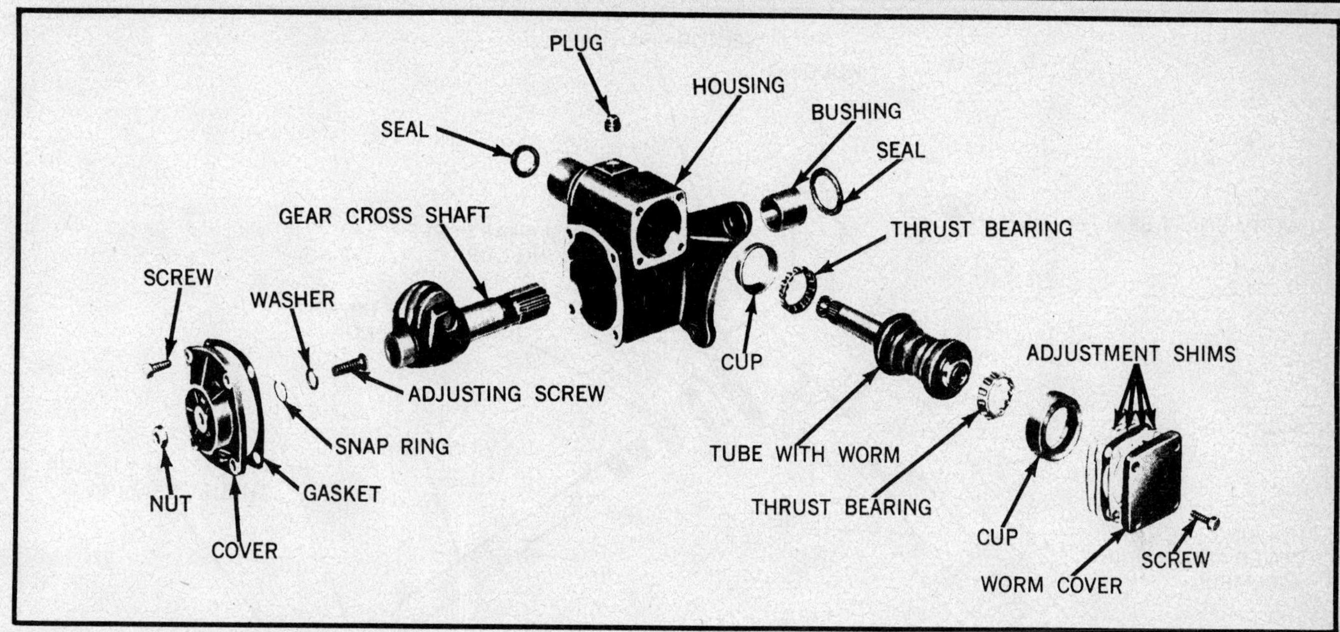

Ross worm and roller steering gear (© Chrysler Corp.)

cover counterclockwise until the worm gear shaft turns freely through its entire range of travel.

2. Count the number of turns necessary to rotate the worm gear shaft through its entire range of travel.

3. Turn the shaft back exactly half the number of turns to the center position.

4. Turn the shaft back and forth through its center of travel and tighten the adjustment screw to obtain a rolling torque requirement of 7 to 12 inch lbs.

5. Hold the adjustment screw in position and torque the locknut to 16–20 ft. lbs.

6. Recheck the rolling torque and repeat the above procedure if necessary.

Disassembly

1. Drain the lubricant from the gear.
2. Make index marks on the roller gear and shaft assembly and on the steering arm to assure correct alignment during reassembly.
3. Remove the nut and lockwasher from the shaft.
4. Using a puller remove the arm from the shaft.

NOTE: Do not use a hammer or wedge to remove the steering arm or damage to the gear and shaft assembly may result.

5. Remove the four side cover attaching screws and remove the cover and roller gear and shaft assembly as a unit.
6. Remove the locknut from the adjustment screw and turn the screw clockwise until it is completely unthreaded from the side cover, then remove the roller gear and shaft assembly from the cover.
7. Remove the four end cover attaching screws and remove the cover from the housing.
8. Withdraw the worm gear and shaft assembly from the housing.
9. Remove the lower and upper bearing cups and ball bearings from the shaft.
10. Remove and discard both the worm gear shaft and roller gear shaft housing oil seals.

Inspection

1. Clean all parts with a suitable cleaning solvent and blow dry with an air hose.
2. Check the steering gear housing for cracks, leaks or breaks and replace if damaged.
3. Examine the roller gear to assure that it has proper freedom of movement and does not have excessive lash or roughness. Replace if necessary.
4. Check the adjustment screw of the roller gear and shaft assembly for excessive end play. If end play exceeds 0.015 inch, remove the retaining ring, thrust washer and screw from the gear and shaft assembly and replace with new parts.
5. Inspect the roller gear and shaft needle bearings for wear or damage. Insert a shaft through each bearing and check for clearance. If clearance exceeds 0.010 inch, replace the bearings. Either needle bearing may be removed by pressing out with a piloted mandrel. When pressing in a new bearing make sure that the face of the bearing is flush with the bearing boss of the cover or housing.
6. Inspect the worm gear and shaft assembly for wear, scoring or pitting. Polish the assembly with a fine abrasive cloth or replace if necessary.
7. Check the upper and lower ball bearings and cups of the worm gear and shaft assembly for wear and damage. Replace the ball bearings as a full set if worn or damaged.

Assembly

1. Press new oil seals into the worm gear shaft and roller gear shaft oil seal bores of the housing with the longer lip of each seal facing into the housing.
2. Lubricate the worm gear and shaft assembly and upper ball bearing and cup with SAE 80 gear lubricant.
3. Install the bearing and cup on the shaft.
4. Carefully install the shaft assembly into the steering gear housing.
5. Lubricate the lower end of the worm gear and shaft assembly and lower ball bearing and cup with SAE 80 gear lubricant.
6. Install the bearing, cups and spacer on the shaft.
7. Position the shims and end cover on the steering gear housing and install the four cap screws loosely.
8. Adjust the bearing preload.
9. Position the tapped hole of the side cover to the adjustment screw of the roller gear and shaft assembly and thread the adjustment screw counterclockwise into the cover until the end of the shaft just touches the inner face of the cover.

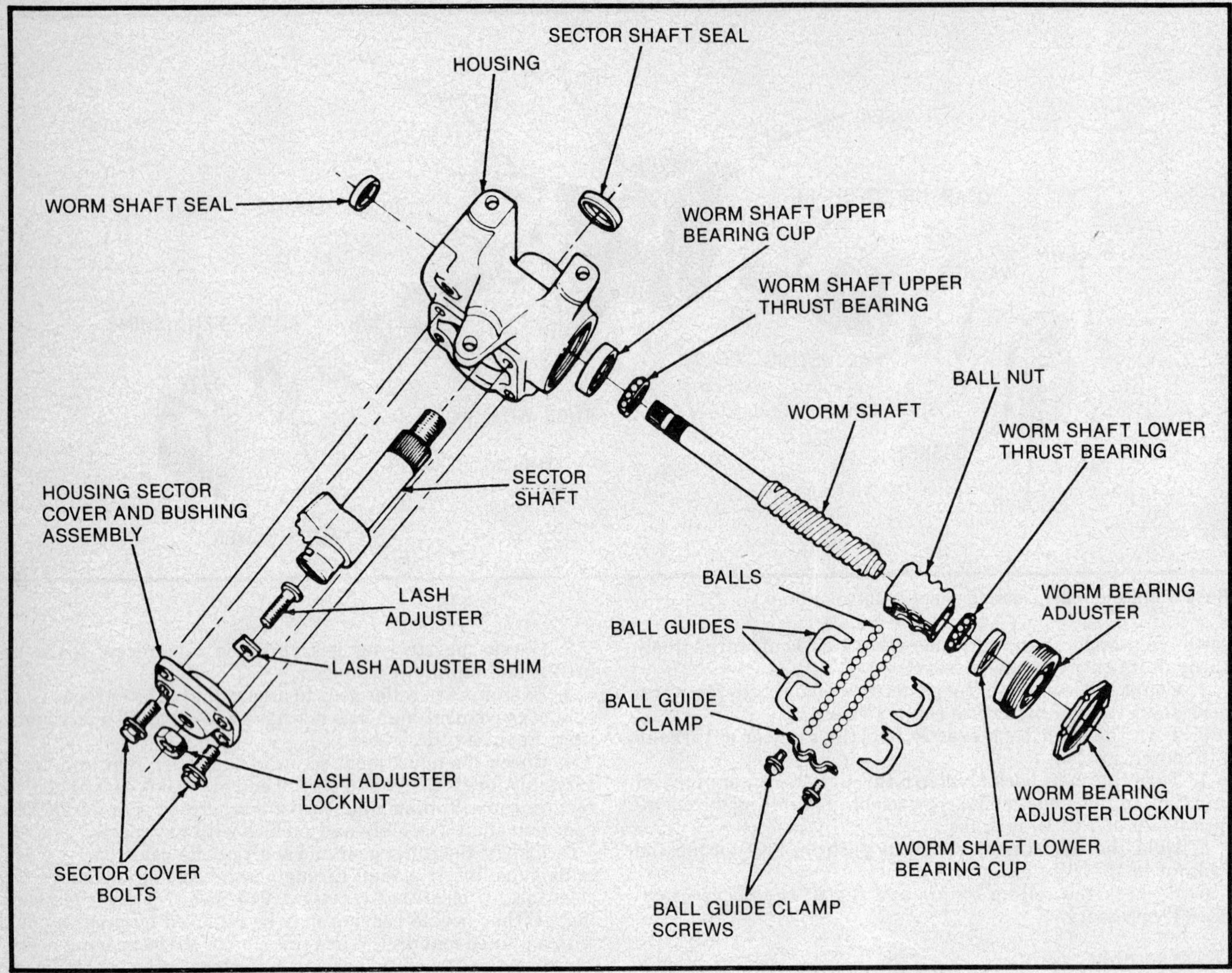

Koyo steering gear-exploded view (© Ford Motor Co.)

10. Install a locknut loosely on the adjustment screw.
11. Install a new side cover gasket.
12. Lubricate the roller gear with SAE 80 gear lubricant.
13. Carefully insert the gear and shaft assembly into the steering gear housing. The roller gear and worm gear must mesh to seat the side cover to the housing.
14. Tighten the side cover capscrews to 18–22 ft. lbs.
15. Make a worm gear and roller gear backlash adjustment.
16. Clamp the exposed section of the roller gear and shaft assembly firmly into a soft jaw vise.
17. Align the index marks made during disassembly and position the steering arm to the splined end of the shaft.
18. Install the lockwasher and nut on the shaft threads and tighten the nut to draw the arm into position on the splines.
19. Fill the steering gear housing to the required level with SAE 80 gear lubricant.

Koyo

PRELOAD AND MESHLOAD

Adjustment (Gear Removed From Vehicle)

1. Tighten the sector cover bolts to 40 ft. lbs.
2. Loosen the preload adjuster locknut and tighten the worm bearing adjuster nut until all end play has been removed. Lubricate the wormshaft seal with a drop of Type F automatic transmission fluid.
3. Using a $^{11}/_{16}$ in., 12 point socket and an inch lbs. torque wrench, turn the wormshaft all the way to the right. Measure the left turn torque required to rotate the wormshaft at a constant speed for approximately 1 $^{1}/_{2}$ turns. This torque reading is preload.
4. Tighten or loosen the adjuster nut as required until the correct preload of 7–9 inch lbs. is obtained. Tighten the adjuster locknut to 187 ft. lbs.
5. Rotate the wormshaft from stop to stop, counting the total number of turns, then turn back halfway, placing the gear at the center. (Approximately 7 turns stop to stop.)
6. Again, using the tools in Step 3, observe the highest reading while the wormshaft is turned approximately 90° either way across center. If the highest reading (meshload) is within 12–14 in lbs. and at least 4 inch lbs. over the preload, turn the sector shaft adjusting screw as required.
7. Hold the sector shaft adjusting screw and tighten the locknut to 25 ft. lbs.

Disassembly

1. Rotate the steering shaft from stop to stop, counting the

total number of turns. Then turn exactly half-way back, placing the gear on center.

2. Remove the sector adjusting cover bolts, then remove the sector shaft with the cover. Remove the cover from the shaft by turning the screw clockwise. Keep the shim with the screw.

3. Using a special locknut wrench, loosen the worm bearing adjuster locknut and remove the adjuster plug and wormshaft thrust bearing.

4. Carefully pull the wormshaft and ball nut assembly from the housing and remove the upper thrust bearing.

NOTE: To avoid damage to the return guides, keep the ball nut from running down to either end of the worm.

5. Pry out the sector shaft and wormshaft seals and discard them.

NOTE: Individual parts for this manual steering gear are not availabe for service. Do not disassemble. If the worm cannot rotate freely in the ball nut, replace the entire assembly.

6. The adjuster/plug bearing cup can be removed using a puller tool and slide hammer.

7. The housing bearing cup can be removed from the housing using a hammer and a suitable size bearing driver or socket.

8. The sector cover bushing is not serviceable. If found to be defective the entire sector cover including the bushing must be replaced.

9. The sector shaft needle bearing is serviced only as part of the housing unit and is not serviced separately. If one or more needles fall out, they may be cleaned and put back using steering gear lube to hold them in place.

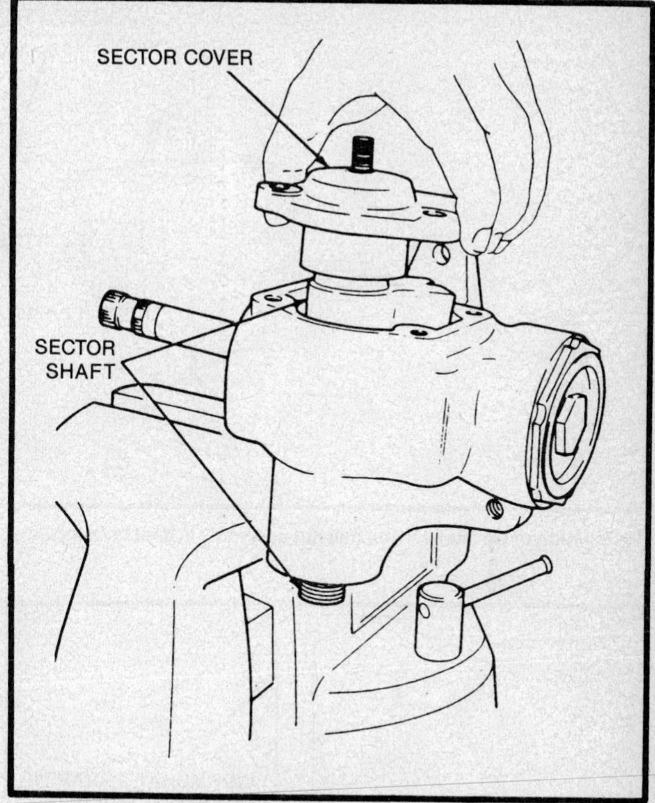

Sector shaft removal (© Ford Motor Co.)

Inspection

1. Wash all parts in a cleaning solvent and dry thoroughly with air.
2. Inspect all bearings and bushings for wear.
3. Inspect the ball nut gear for chipping.
4. Inspect the ball nut and wormshaft for tightness and binding.
5. Inspect the housing for cracks.
6. Inspect the sector gear teeth for chipping.
7. Check the clearance between the sector adjusting screw head and the bottom of the sector shaft T-slot. If the clearance is more than 0.004 in. install a new shim as required to reduce the clearance to 0.004 in. or less. A steering gear lash adjuster kit is available containing five different size shims. While holding the sector adjusting screw, turn the sector shaft back and forth. The sector shaft must turn freely. If the sector shaft does not turn freely, increase the T-slot clearance using an appropriate shim from the lash adjuster kit. Make sure the resulting clearance is not more than 0.004 in.

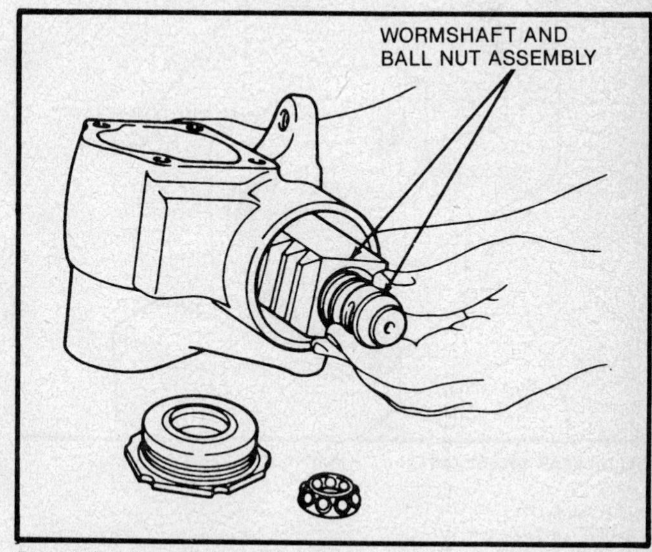

Removal of wormshaft and ball nut assembly (© Ford Motor Co.)

Assembly

1. If the wormshaft bearing cup was removed from the housing, install a new cup Using Tool T82T–3504–AH, or equivalent.

2. If the adjuster plug bearing cup was removed, install a new cup using Tool T82T–3504–AH or equivalent.

3. Install the sector shaft seal in the housing using Tool T82T–3504–AH, or equivalent. Press the seal until it bottoms out.

4. Tap the womshaft seal in the housing, using a suitable size socket and a hammer. Assemble the seal flush with the housing surface.

5. Clamp the steering gear housing in a vise with the wormshaft bore horizontal and the sector cover opening up.

6. Apply steering gear grease to the wormshaft bearings, sector shaft needle bearing in the housing and the sector cover bushing.

7. Slip one of the wormshaft bearings over the wormshaft splined end. Insert the wormshaft and ball nut assembly into the housing. Feed the splined end of the wormshaft through the bearing cup and seal. Place the remaining wormshaft thrust bearing in the adjuster plug bearing cup.

8. Install the adjuster plug and locknut into the housing opening being careful to guide the wormshaft end into the bearing until nearly all end play has been removed from the wormshaft.

9. Position the sector adjusting screw and shim into the sector shaft slot. Check the clearance between the screw head and

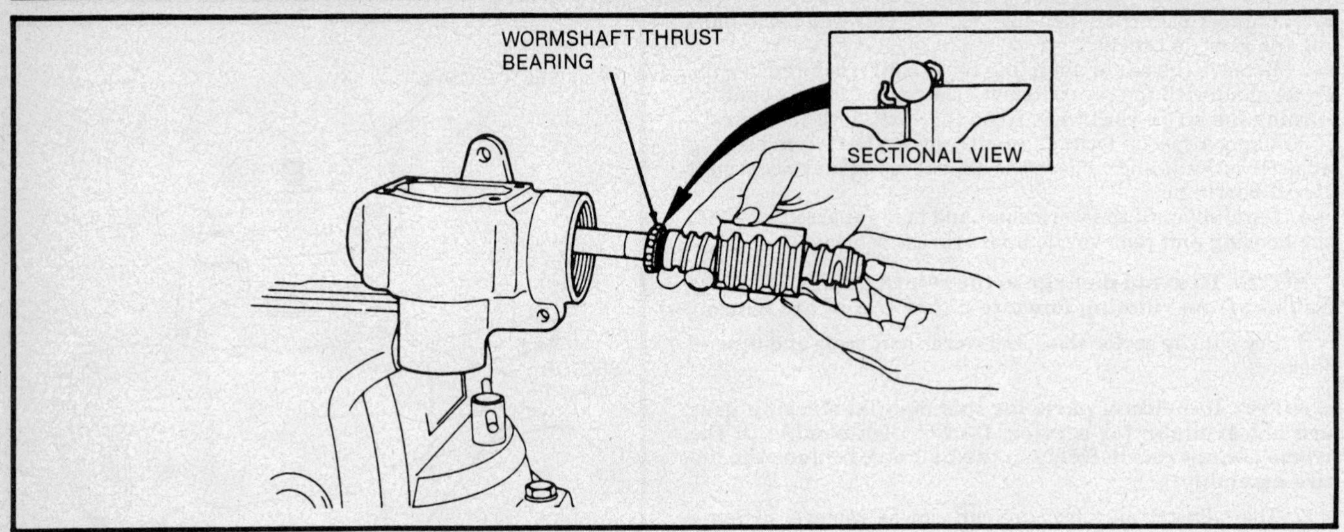

Installation of wormshaft and ball nut assembly in gear housing (© Ford Motor Co.)

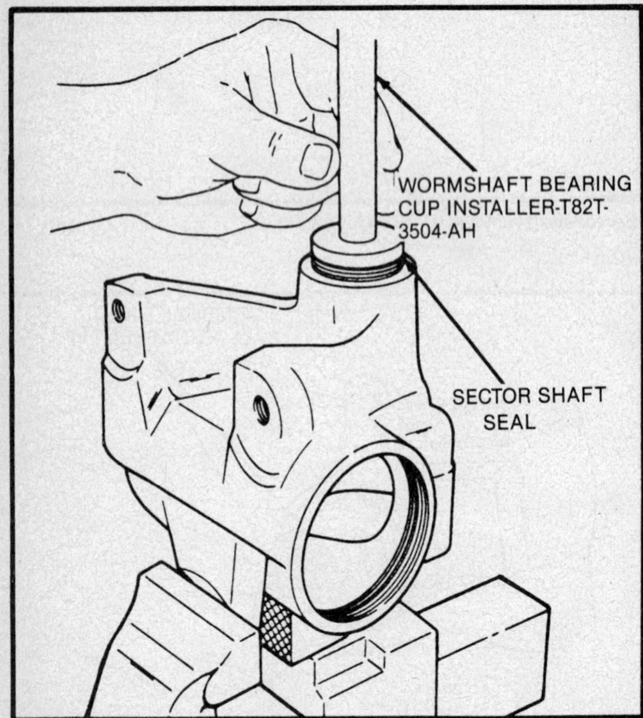

Sector shaft seal installation (© Ford Motor Co.)

the sector shaft T-slot. Refer to Step 7 under Inspection above.

10. Lubricate the steering gear with 14.8 ounces by weight of steering gear grease. Rotate the wormshaft until the ball nut is near the end of its travel. Pack as much grease into the housing as possible without loosing it out at the sector shaft opening. Rotate the wormshaft to move the ball nut near the other end of its travel and pack more grease into the housing.

11. Rotate the wormshaft until the ball nut is in the center of its travel.

12. Insert the sector shaft assembly containing the adjuster screw and shim into the housing so that the center tooth of the sector gear enters the center rack tooth space in the ball rut. Rotate the ball nut teeth slightly up to aid in alignment of the gear teeth and installation of the sector shaft.

13. Pack the remaining grease into the housing.

14. Apply a $^{1}/_{8}$ in. wide by $^{1}/_{8}$ in. high bead of silicone rubber sealant to the mating surfaces of the sector cover and the housing. After waiting about 5 minutes, engage the sector adjuster screw with the tapped hole in the center of the center cover by turning the screw counterclockwise until the sector cover is flush with the housing.

15. Install the sector cover to housing attaching washer and bolts. Do not torque the bolts unless there is a lash between the sector shaft and wormshaft. The lash can be obtained by turning the screw counterclockwise.

16. Tighten the sector cover attaching bolts to 40 ft. lbs.

17. Adjust the steering gear preload and meshload. Refer to adjustments above.

POWER STEERING

GENERAL INFORMATION

The procedures for maintaining, adjusting, and repairing the power steering systems and components discussed in this chapter are to be done only after determining that the steering linkages and front suspension systems are correctly aligned and in good condition. All worn or damaged parts should be replaced before attempting to service the power steering system. After correcting any condition that could affect the power steering, do the preliminary tests of the steering system components.

STEERING TROUBLE DIAGNOSIS
Power Steering

Condition	Possible Cause	Correction
Hard Steering	1. Low or uneven tire pressure.	1. Inflate the tires to recommended pressures.
	2. Insufficient lubricant in the steering gear housing or in steering linkage.	2. Lubricate as necessary.
	3. Steering gear shaft adjusted too tight.	3. Adjust according to instructions.
	4. Improper caster or toe-in.	4. Align the wheels.
	5. Steering column misaligned.	5. See "Steering Gear Alignment."
	6. Loose, worn or broken pump belt.	6. Adjust or replace belt.
	7. Air in system.	7. Bleed air from system.
	8. Low fluid level in the pump reservoir.	8. Fill to correct level.
	9. Pump output pressure low.	9. See "Pressure Test."
	10. Leakage at power cylinder piston rings. (Linkage type).	10. Replace piston rings and repair as required.
	11. Binding or bent cylinder linkage. (Linkage type).	11. Replace or repair as required.
	12. Valve spool and/or sleeve sticking. (Linkage type).	12. Free-up or replace as required.
Intermittent or No Power Assist	1. Belt slipping and/or low fluid level.	1. Adjust or replace belt. Add fluid as necessary.
	2. Piston or rod binding in power cylinder. (Linkage type).	2. Repair or replace piston and rod.
	3. Sliding sleeve stuck in control valve. (Linkage type).	3. Free-up or replace sleeve.
	4. Improper pump operation.	4. Refer to "Power Steering Pump."
Poor or No Recovery from Turns	1. Improper caster setting.	1. Adjust to specifications.
	2. Steering gear adjustments too tight.	2. Adjust according to instructions.
	3. Improper spool nut adjustment. (Linkage type).	3. Adjust according to instructions.
	4. Valve spool installed backwards. (Linkage type).	4. Install valve spool correctly.
	5. Low tire pressure.	5. Inflate tires to recommended pressure.
	6. Tight steering linkage.	6. Lubricate as necessary.
	7. King pins frozen.	7. Lubricate as necessary.
Lack of Effort (Both Turns)	1. Improper sector shaft adjustment.	1. Adjust Sector Shaft.
	2. Pressure plates on wrong side of reactions rings.	2. Gear Recondition.
Lack of Effort (Left Turn Only)	1. Left turn reaction seal "O" ring worn, damaged or missing.	1. Gear Recondition.
	2. Left turn reaction oil passageway not drilled in housing or cylinder head.	2. Replace parts as required.
	3. Left turn reaction ring sticking in cylinder head.	3. Replace parts as required.
Lack of Effort (Right Turn Only)	1. Right turn U-shaped reaction seal worn, damaged, or missing.	1. Gear Recondition.
	2. Right turn reaction oil passageway not drilled in housing head, or ferrule pin.	2. Replace parts as required.
	3. Right turn reaction ring sticking in housing head.	3. Replace parts as required.
Lack of Assist (Left Turn Only)	1. Left turn reaction seal "O" ring worn, damaged, or missing.	1. Gear Recondition.
Lack of Assist (Right Turn Only)	1. Right turn U-shaped reaction seal worn, damaged, or missing.	1. Gear Recondition.
	2. Worm sealing ring (teflon) worm sleeve seal, ferrule pin "O" ring damaged or worn.	2. Gear Recondition.
	3. Excessive internal leakage thru piston end plug and/or side plugs.	3. Replace worm-piston assembly.

STEERING TROUBLE DIAGNOSIS
Power Steering

Condition	Possible Cause	Correction
Lack of Assist (Both Turns)	1. Low oil level in pump reservoir (usually accompanied by pump noise).	1. Fill to proper level.
	2. Loose pump belt.	2. Adjust belts.
	3. Pump output low.	3. Pressure test pump.
	4. Engine idle too low.	4. Adjust engine idle.
	5. Excessive internal leakage thru piston end plug and/or side plugs.	5. Replace worm-piston assembly.

PRELIMINARY TESTS

Lubrication

Proper lubrication of the steering linkage and the front suspension components is very important for the proper operation of the steering systems of trucks equipped with power steering. Most all power steering systems use the same lubricant in the steering gear box as in the power steering pump reservoir, and the fluid level is maintained at the pump reservoir.

With power cylinder-assist power steering, the steering gear is of the standard mechanical type and the lubricating oil is self contained within the gear box and the level is maintained by the removal of a filler plug on the gear box housing. The control valve assembly is mounted on the gear box and is lubricated by power steering oil from the power steering pump reservoir, where the level is maintained.

AIR BLEEDING

Air bubbles in the power steering system must be removed from the fluid. Be sure the reservoir is filled to the proper level and the fluid is warmed up to operating temperature. Then, turn the steering wheel through its full travel three or four times until all the air bubbles are removed. Do not hold the steering wheel against its stops. Recheck the fluid level.

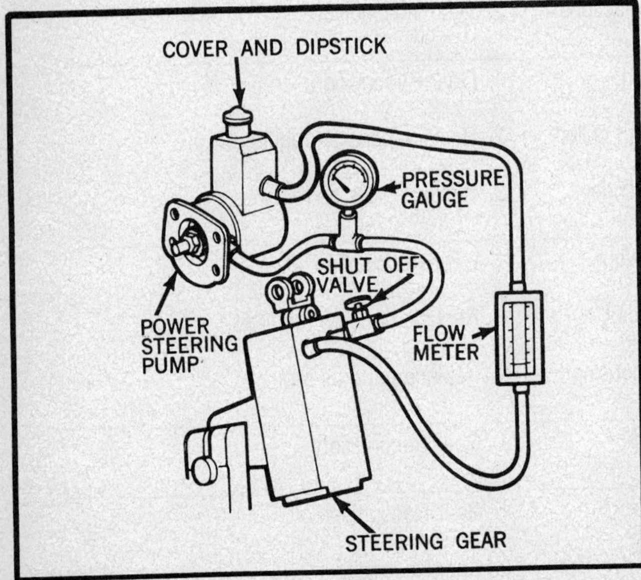

Testing power steering hydraulic system for internal leakage using a pressure gauge, shut off valve and flow meter—typical
(© Ford Motor Co.)

FLUID LEVEL

Inspection

1. Run the engine until the fluid is at the normal operating temperature. Then, turn the steering wheel through its full travel three or four times, and shut off the engine.
2. Check the fluid level in the steering reservoir. If the fluid level is low, add enough fluid to raise the level to the Full mark on the dipstick or filler tube.

PUMP BELT

Inspection

1. Inspect the pump belt for cracks, glazing, or worn places. Using a belt tension gauge, check the belt tension for the proper range of adjustment. The amount of tension varies with the make of truck and the condition of the belt. New belts (those belts used less than 15 minutes) require a higher figure. The belt deflection method of adjustment may be used only if a belt tension gauge is not available. The belt should be adjusted for a deflection of $^1/_4$ to $^3/_8$.

Fluid Leaks

Check all possible leakage points (hoses, power steering pump, or steering gear) for loss of fluid. Turn engine on and rotate the steering wheel from stop to stop several times. Tighten all loose fittings and replace any defective lines or valve seats.

Turning Effort

Check the turning effort required to turn the steering wheel after aligning the front wheels and inflating the tires to the proper pressure.

1. With the vehicle on dry pavement and the front wheel straight ahead, set the parking brake and turn the engine on.
2. After a short warm-up period for the engine, turn the steering wheel back and forth several times to warm the steering fluid.
3. Attach a spring scale to the steering wheel rim and measure the pull required to turn the steering wheel one complete revolution in each direction. The effort needed to turn the steering wheel should not exceed the limits specified.

NOTE: This test may be done with the steering wheel removed and a torque wrench applied on the steering wheel nut.

Power Steering Pump Flow

Since the power steering pump provides all the power assist in a power steering system, the pump must operate properly at all times for the system to work. After performing all the checks given above, the power steering pump may be tested for proper flow by the following procedures:

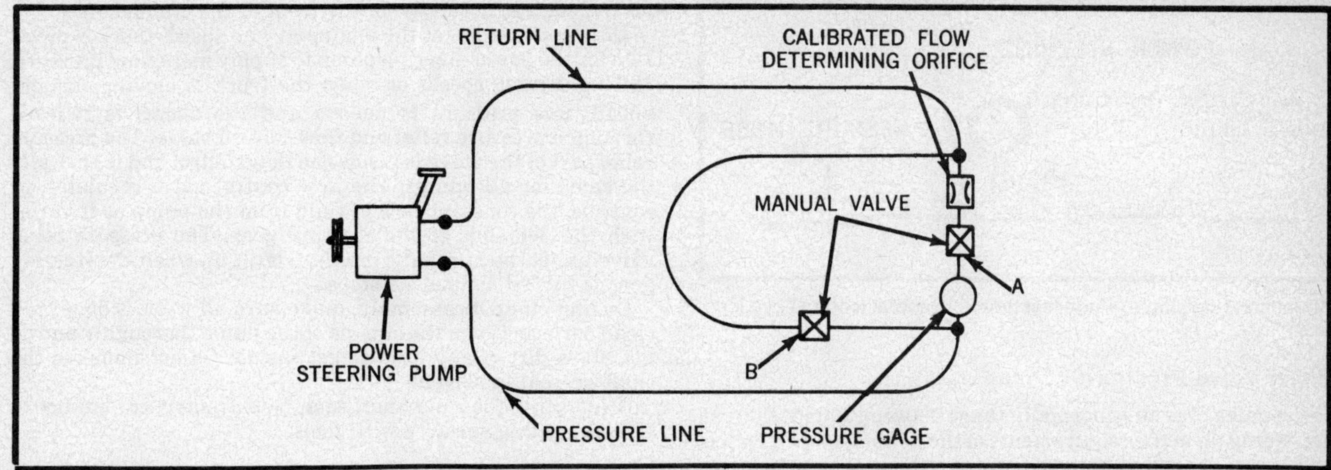

Power steering pump test circuit diagram (© Ford Motor Co.)

TWO GAUGES AND FLOW METER

Testing

1. Disconnect the pressure and return lines at the power steering pump and connect the test pressure and return lines. The test lines are connected to a pressure gauge and two manual valves.
2. Open the two manual valves, connect a tachometer to the engine, and start the engine. Run the engine at idle speed until the reservoir fluid temperature reaches about 165–175 degrees Fahrenheit. This temperature must be maintained during the test. Manual valve B may be partially opened to create a back pressure of no more than 350 psi to aid the temperature rise. Reservoir fluid must be at the proper level.
3. After the engine and the reservoir fluid are sufficiently warmed up, close the manual valve B. Note the pressure gauge reading. It must be a minimum of 620 psi.
4. If the pressure reading is below the minimum acceptable pressure, the pump is defective and must be repaired. If the pressure reading is at or above the minimum value, the pump is normal. Open manual valve B and proceed to the pump fluid pressure test.

POWER STEERING PUMP FLUID PRESSURE

Testing

1. Keep the lines and pressure gauge connected as in the Pump Flow Test.
2. With manual valve A and B opened fully, run the engine at the proper idle speed. Then, close manual valve A and manual valve B, in that order.

CAUTION

Do not keep both valves closed for more than 5 seconds since the fluid temperature will increase abnormally and cause unnecessary wear to the pump.

3. With both manual valves closed, the pressure reading should be as given in the specifications. If the pressure is below the minimum reading, the pump is defective and must be repaired. If the pressure reading is at or above the minimum reading, the pump is normal and the power steering gear or power assist control valve must be checked.

Checking the Oil Flow and Pressure Relief Valve in the Pump Assembly

When the wheels are turned hard right, or hard left, against the stops, the oil flow and pressure relief valves come into action. If these valves are working and are not stuck there should be a slight buzzing noise.

CAUTION

Do not hold the wheels in the extreme position for over three or four seconds because, if the pressure relief valve is not working, the pressure could get high enough to damage the system.

Single Gauge

1. Install the test presure gauge (O–2000 psi) between the power steering pump and the control valve.
2. With the fluid at a temperature of 170 to 190°F, the engine running above idle and the shut-off valve open, observe the pressure reading while moving the wheels to the end of their right and left travel.
3. If the gauge registers the correct relief valve pressure, the hydraulic system should be satisfactory. If pressure cannot be built up on either side of the gear, internal pump or gear problems exist.

NOTE: A shuttle valve equipped power cylinder may register a sharp drop-off in pressure at the end of the wheel travel and is considered normal.

4. To check the pump, close the shut-off valve and observe the pressure gauge. The pressure reading should be at relief valve pressure.

NOTE: Do not keep the shut-off valve closed longer than 15 seconds as damage to the pump could occur.

5. Repeat the closing of the shut-off valve twice more and record the highest pressure reading each time.
6. If the pressure readings are within 50 lbs. of each other and with-in the pump relief valve specifications, the pump operation is normal.
   Example: Pump specifications 900 to 1500 psi.
   Readings: 1st–1310 psi, 2nd–1290 psi, 3rd–1320
7. If the readings are high but do not repeat within 50 lbs. of each other, the flow control valve can be sticking. If 100 lbs. difference is noted below the low listed specification, replace the flow valve and recheck the system.

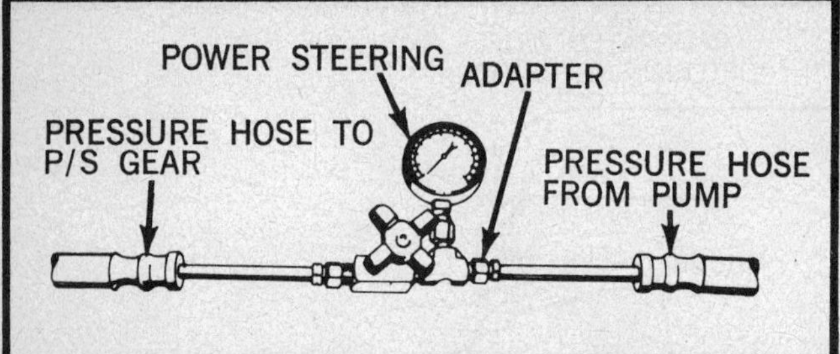

Power steering single gauge test unit (© General Motors Corp.)

Relief Valve Pressure

Relief valve pressures normally range between 800 to 2000 psi, depending upon the requirements of the power steering system and the axle application used on the vehicle. The lighter the truck, the less pressure is needed to operate the steering system, while the opposite is true of the heavier vehicles.

The minimum pressures with the wheels straight ahead and at engine idle should be in the 80 to 120 psi range.

POWER STEERING HOSE

Inspection

Inspect both the input and output hoses of the power steering pump for worn spots, cracks, or signs of leakage. Replace hose if defective, being sure to reconnect the replacement hose properly. Many power steering hoses are identified as to where they are to be connected by special means, such as fittings that will only fit on the correct pump fitting, or hoses of special lengths.

Test Driving Truck to Check the Power Steering

When test driving to check power steering, drive at a speed between 15 and 20 mph. Make several turns in each direction. When a turn is completed, the front wheels should return to the straight ahead position with very little help from the driver.

If the front wheels fail to return as they should and yet the steering linkage is free, well oiled and properly adjusted, the trouble is probably due to misalignment of the power cylinder or improper adjustment of the spool valve.

The power steering pump supplies all the power assist used in power steering systems of all designs. There are various designs of pumps used by the truck manufacturers but all pumps supply power to operate the steering systems with the least effort. All power steering pumps have a reservoir tank built onto the oil pump. These pumps are driven by belt turned by pulleys on the engine, normally on the front of the crankshaft.

During operation of the engine at idle speed, there is provision for the power steering pump to supply more fluid pressure. During driving speeds or when the truck is moving straight ahead, less pressure is needed and the excess is relieved through a pressure relief and flow control valve. The pressure relief part of the valve is inside the flow control and is basically the same for all pumps. The flow control valve regulates, or controls, the constant flow of fluid from the pump as it varies with the demands of the steering gear. The pressure relief valve limits the hydraulic pressure built up when the steering gear is turned against its stops.

During pump disassembly, make sure all work is done on a clean surface. Clean the outside of the pump thoroughly and do not allow dirt of any kind to get inside. Do not immerse the shaft oil seal in solvent.

If replacing the rotor shaft seal, be extremely careful not to scratch sealing surfaces with tools.

T/C Series Power Steering Pump

The TC Series Power Steering Pump is a vane type, constant displacement pump. This pump will use a remote fluid reservoir. A pressure relief valve inside the flow control valve limits pump pressure. The TC series pump will be used on the Isuzu Diesel Engine.

RETURN TUBE

Removal

1. Plug return tube to prevent chips from entering pump.
2. Use a tap, washers, and nut to remove damaged return tube.

INSTALLATION

1. Using Loctite® Solvent 75559 and Loctite® 290 adhesive, coat the end of new return tube.
2. Using a press, press tube into housing until bottomed.

ROTATING GROUP

Removal

1. Using a small punch in the access hole, remove the retaining ring.
2. Using a $^5/_8$ in. piece of bar stock or suitable brass drift, press on pressure plate hub from drive shaft side of housing until thrust plate can be removed.
3. The O-ring seal in housing must be removed next. It is now possible to remove the remaining parts of the rotating

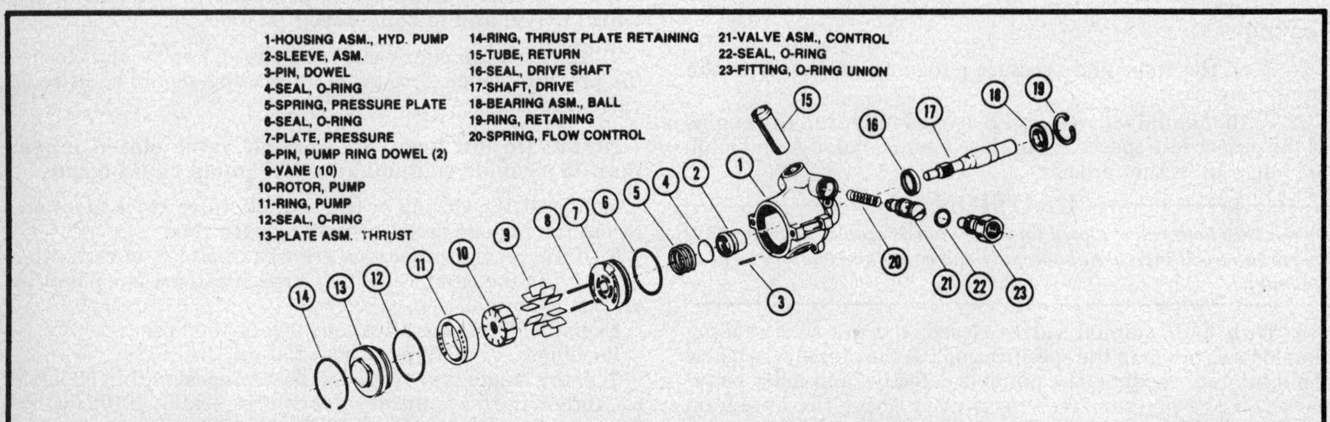

TC series—power steering pump

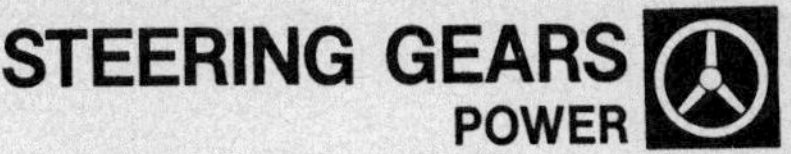

STEERING TROUBLE DIAGNOSIS
Power Steering Pump

Condition	Possible Cause	Correction
Intermittent Assist	1. Flow control valve sticking.	1. Pressure test pump and service as necessary.
	2. Slipping belt.	2. Adjust belt.
	3. Low fluid level.	3. Inspect and correct fluid level.
	4. Low pump efficiency.	4. Pressure test pump and service as necessary.
No Assist	1. Pump seizure.	1. Replace pump.
	2. Broken slipper spring(s).	2. Recondition pump or replace as necessary.
	3. Flow control bore plug ring not in place.	3. Replace snap ring. Inspect groove for depth.
	4. Flow control valve sticking.	4. Pressure test pump and service as necessary.
No Assist When Parking Only	1. Wrong pressure relief valve.	1. Install proper relief valve.
	2. Broken "O" ring on flow control bore plug.	2. Replace "O" ring.
	3. Loose pressure relief valve.	3. Tighten valve. DO NOT ADJUST.
	4. Low pump efficiency	4. Pressure test pump and service as necessary.
Noisy Pump	1. Low fluid level.	1. Inspect and correct fluid level.
	2. Belt noise.	2. Inspect for pulley alignment, paint or grease on pulley and correct. Adjust belt.
	3. Foreign material blocking pump housing oil inlet hole.	3. Remove reservoir, visually check inlet oil hole and service as necessary.
Pump Vibration	1. Pump hose interference with sheet metal or brake lines.	1. Reroute hoses.
	2. Belt loose.	2. Adjust belt.
	3. Pulley loose or out of round.	3. Replace pulley.
	4. Crankshaft pulley loose or damaged.	4. Replace crankshaft pulley.
	5. Bracket pivot bolts loose.	5. If unable to tighten, replace bracket.
Pump Leaks	1. Cap or filler neck leaks.	1. Correct fluid level.
	2. Reservoir solder joints leak.	2. Resolder or replace reservoir as necessary.
	3. Reservoir "O" ring leaking.	3. Inspect sealing area of reservoir. Replace "O" ring or reservoir as necessary.
	4. Shaft seal leaking.	4. Replace seal.
	5. Loose rear bracket bolts.	5. Tighten bolts.
	6. Loose or faulty high pressure ferrule.	6. Tighten fitting to 24 foot-pounds or replace as necessary.
	7. Rear bolt holes stripped or casting cracked.	7. Repair, if possible, or replace pump.
Objectionable "Hiss"	1. Noisy valve	1. Do not replace valve unless "hiss" is extremely objectionable. A replacement valve will also exhibit sight noise and is not always a cure for the objection.
Rattle or Chuckle Noise in Steering Gear	1. Gear loose on frame.	1. Check gear mounting bolts. Torque bolts to specifications.
	2. Steering linkages looseness.	2. Check linkage pivot points for wear. Replace if necessary.
	3. Pressure hose touching other parts of truck.	3. Adjust hose position. Do not bend tubing by hand.
	4. Loose Pitman shaft over center adjustment. **NOTE:** A slight rattle may occur on turns because of increased clearance off the "high point". This is normal and clearance must not be reduced below specified limits to eliminate this slight rattle.	4. Adjust
	5. Loose Pitman arm.	5. Torque Pitman arm pinch bolt.

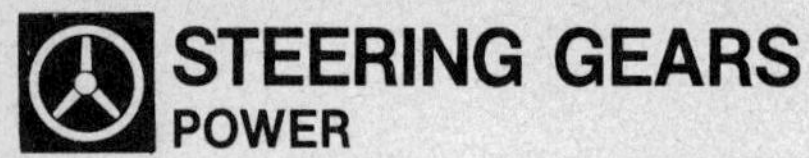

STEERING TROUBLE DIAGNOSIS

Power Steering Noise

Condition	Possible Cause	Correction
Squawk Noise in Steering Gear When Turning or Recovering From a Turn	1. Dampener O-ring on valve spool cut. 2. Loose or worn valve.	1. Replace dampener O-Ring. 2. Replace valve.
Chirp Noise in Steering Gear	1. Gear relief valve.	1. Replace relief valve.
Chirp Noise in Steering Pump	1. Loose belt.	1. Adjust belt tension.
Belt Squeal (Particularly Noticeable at Full Wheel Travel and Standstill Parking)	1. Loose belt.	1. Adjust belt tension.
Growl Noise in Steering Pump	1. Excessive back pressure in hoses or steering gear caused by restriction.	1. Locate restriction and correct. Replace part if necessary.
Growl Noise in Steering Pump (Particularly Noticeable at Standstill Parking)	1. Scored pressure plates, thrust plate or rotor. 2. Extreme wear of cam ring.	1. Replace parts and flush system. 2. Replace parts.
Groan Noise in Steering Pump	1. Low oil level. 2. Air in the oil. Poor pressure hose connection.	1. Fill reservoir to proper level. 2. Torque connector. Bleed system.
Rattle or Knock Noise in Steering Pump	1. Loose pump pulley nut.	1. Torque nut.
Rattle Noise in Steering Pump	1. Vanes not installed properly. 2. Vanes sticking in rotor slots.	1. Install properly. 2. Repair or replace.
Swish Noise in Steering Pump	1. Defective flow control valve.	1. Replace part.
Whine Noise in Steering Pump	1. Pump Shaft bearing scored.	1. Replace housing and shaft. Flush and bleed system.

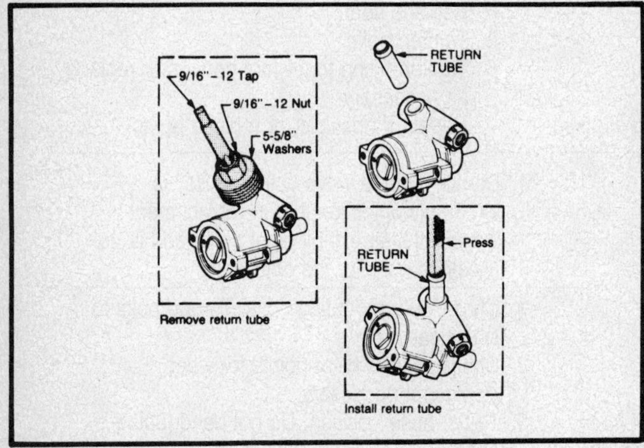

Return tube removal and installation

group from housing. It may still be necessary to use a press to remove the pressure plate.

4. Remove O-ring seal from the sleeve assembly and dispose.

Installation

1. Lubricate new O-ring seal and install into sleeve assembly.

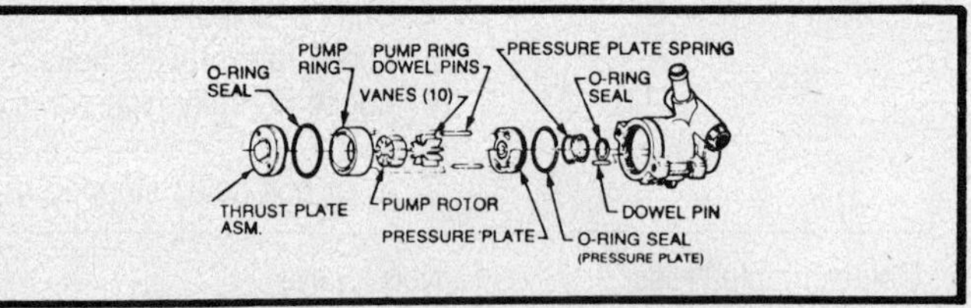

Rotating group removal

2. Insert dowel pin in housing.
3. Install spring over sleeve assembly in housing.
4. Lubricate O-ring seal and install on pressure plate.
5. Mark top of pressure plate directly over dowel pin hole in plate. This will help line up hole with dowel pin.
6. Install pressure plate in housing. Be sure dowel pin and hole in pressure plate engage properly.
7. Install two (2) pump ring dowel pins in holes in pressure plate. Slide pump ring over these two pins. Be sure identification marks on pump ring are facing upward.
8. Install rotor with counter bore side toward drive shaft end of housing. Add ten vanes.
9. Lubricate O-ring seal and install in housing.
10. Install thrust plate in housing, making sure that dimples in thrust plate line up with bolt holes in housing and that thrust plate engages pump ring dowel pins.

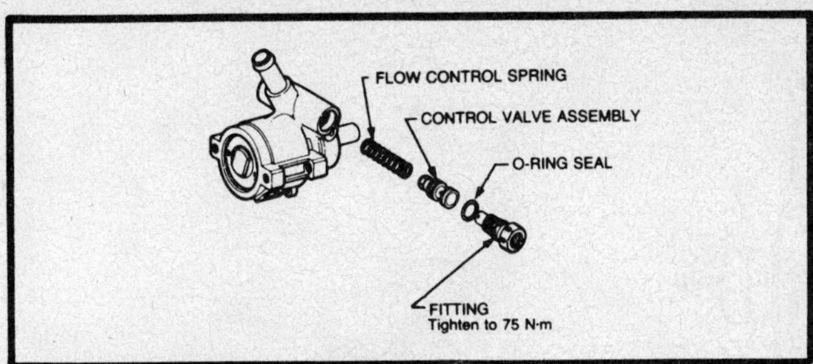

Control valve removal and installation

11. Using a press, press on thrust plate far enough to install retaining ring.
12. Install retaining ring with opening of ring centered with bolt hole in housing nearest to access hole.

DRIVE SHAFT & BEARING

Removal

1. Remove retaining ring with snap ring pliers.
2. Remove drive shaft and bearing assembly.
3. Remove the bearing using a press.

INSTALLATION

1. Using a press, install the bearing on the driveshaft.
2. Slide bearing assembly into housing while rotating drive shaft so shaft serrations engage with rotor.
3. Bottom bearing in housing.
4. Install retaining ring with beveled side outward.

CONTROL VALVE

REMOVAL & INSTALLATION

1. Remove the fitting and O-ring.
2. Remove the control valve assembly.
3. Remove the flow control spring.
4. Replace damaged or defective parts.
5. Installation is the reverse of removal.

DRIVE SHAFT SEAL

Removal & Installation

1. Using a seal puller carefully remove the seal from the housing.
2. Check housing for damage.
3. Install the new seal using a suitable socket. Drive the seal into the housing until it bottoms.

SLEEVE ASSEMBLY

Removal & Installation

1. Remove the driveshaft and bearing assembly as previously outlined.
2. From the driveshaft side of the housing remove sleeve assembly using a punch.
3. Using a suitable socket, press sleeve assembly into housing from pressure plate side.
4. Be sure sleeve assembly is fully seated in housing.

Pump Overhaul

VANE TYPE POWER STEERING PUMP

The vane type power steering pump is used in Saginaw steering systems. The operation is basically the same as that of the roller type pumps. Centrifugal force moves a number of vanes outward against the pump ring, causing a pumping action of the fluid to the control valve.

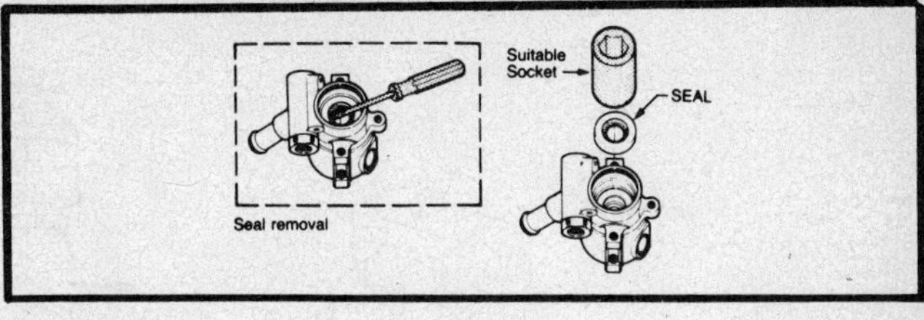

Seal removal

Removal

1. Disconnect hoses at the pump, securing them in a raised position to prevent oil drainage. Cap or cover the ends of the hoses to keep dirt out.
2. Install two caps on the pump fittings to prevent oil drainage.
3. Loosen the bracket-to-pump mounting nuts, move pump toward engine slightly, and remove the pump drive belt.
4. Remove the bracket-to-pump bolts and remove the pump from the truck.
5. While holding the drive pulley steady, loosen and remove the pulley attaching nut. Slide the pulley off the shaft.

NOTE: Do not hammer the pulley off the shaft.

Installation

1. To install the pump on the truck, reverse the removal procedure. Always use a new pulley nut, tightening it to 35–45 ft. lbs. torque.
2. After reconnecting the hoses to the pump, fill the reservoir with fluid and bleed the pump of air by turning the drive pulley counterclockwise (as viewed from the front) until air bubbles do not appear.
3. Install the pump drive belt over the pulley, move the pump against the belt until tight enough, then tighten the mounting bolts and nuts.
4. Bleed the air from the system.

Disassembly

1. Clean the outside of the pump in a non-toxic solvent before disassembling.
2. Mount the pump in a vise, being careful not to squeeze the front hub too tight.
3. Remove the union and seal.
4. Remove the reservoir retaining studs and separate the reservoir from the housing.
5. Remove the mounting bolt and union O-rings.
6. Remove the filter and filter cage; discard the element.
7. Remove the end plate retaining ring by compressing the retaining ring and then prying it out with a removal tool. The retaining ring may be compressed by inserting a small punch in the $^{1}/_{8}$ in. diameter hole in the housing and pushing in until the ring clears the groove.
8. Remove the end plate. The end plate is spring-loaded and should rise above the housing level. If it is stuck inside the housing, a slight rocking or gentle tapping should free the plate.
9. Remove the shaft woodruff key and tap the end of the shaft gently to free the pressure plate, pump ring, rotor assembly, and thrust plate. Remove these parts as one unit.
10. Remove the end plate O-ring. Separate the pressure plate, pump ring, rotor assembly, and thrust plate.

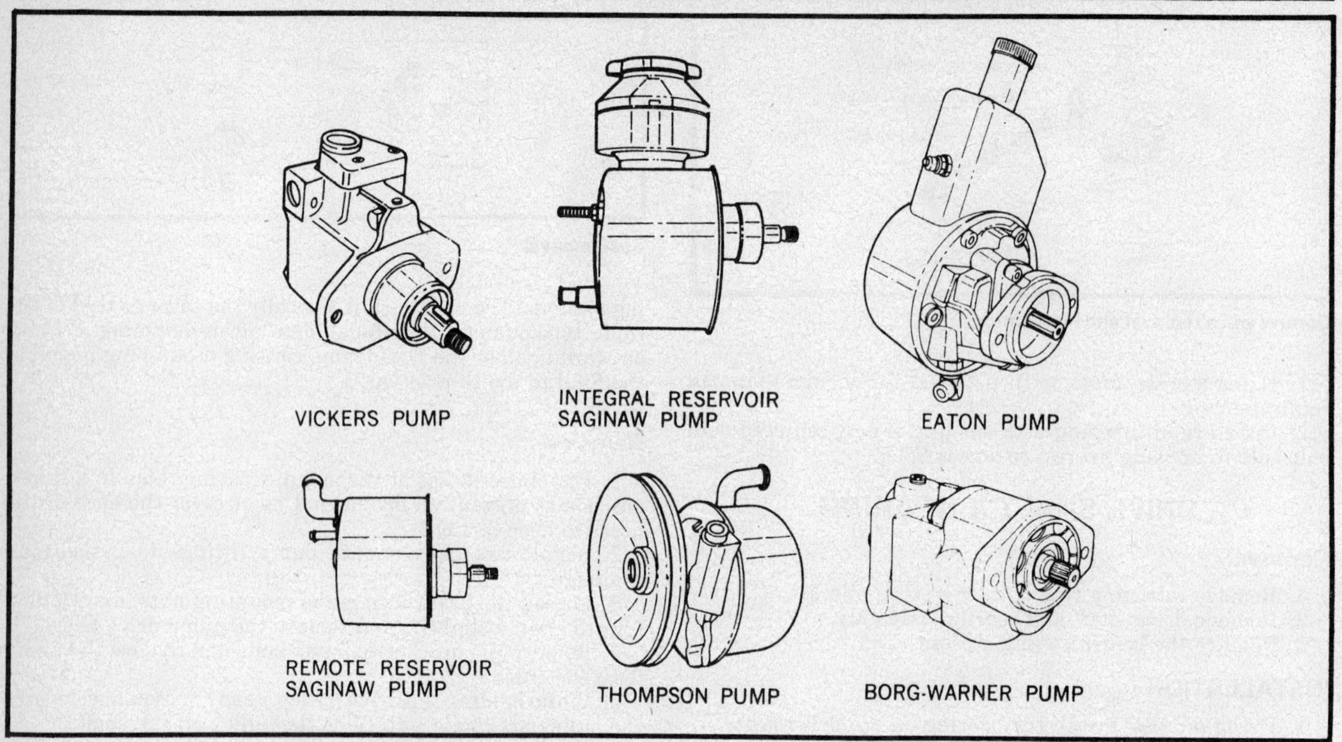

Identification of power steering pumps used on General Motors trucks—typical (© General Motors Corp.)

Inspection

Clean all metal parts in a non-toxic solvent and inspect them as given below:

1. Check the flow control valve for free movement in the housing bore. If the valve is sticking, see if there is dirt or a rough spot in the bore.
2. Check the cap screw in the end of the flow control valve for looseness. Tighten if necessary being careful not to damage the machined surfaces.
3. Inspect the pressure plate and the pump plate surfaces for flatness and check that there are no cracks or scores in the parts. Do not mistake the normal wear marks for scoring.
4. Check the vanes in the rotor assembly for free movement and that they were installed with the radiused edge toward the pump ring.
5. If the flow control valve plunger is defective, install a new part. The valve is factory calibrated and supplied as a unit.
6. Check the drive shaft for wornsplines, breaks, bushing material pick-up, etc.

Removing end plate ring (© General Motors Corp.)

7. Replace all rubber seals and O-rings removed from the pump.
8. Check the reservoir, studs, casting, etc. for burrs and other defects that would impair operation.

Assembly

1. Install a new shaft seal in the housing and insert the shaft at the hub end of housing, splined end entering mounting face side.
2. Install the thrust plate on the dowel pins with the ported side facing the rear of the pump housing.
3. Install the rotor on the pump shaft over the splined end. Be sure the rotor moves freely on the splines. Countersunk side must be toward the shaft.
4. Install the shaft retaining ring. Install the pump ring on the dowel pins with the rotation arrow toward the rear of the pump housing. Rotation is clockwise as seen from the pulley.
5. Install the vanes in the rotor slots with the radius edge towards the outside.
6. Lubricate the outside diameter and chamfer of the pressure plate with petroleum jelly so as not to damage the O-ring and install the plate on the dowel pins with the ported face toward the pump ring. Seat the pressure plate by placing a large socket on top of the plate and pushing down with the hand.
7. Install the pressure plate spring in the center groove of the plate.
8. Install the end plate O-ring. Lubricate the outside diameter and chamfer of the end plate with petroleum jelly so as not to damage the O-ring and install the end plate in the housing, using an arbor press. Install the end plate retaining ring while pump is in the arbor press. Be sure the ring is in the groove and the ring gap is positioned properly.
9. Install the flow control spring and plunger, hex head screw end in bore first. Install the filter cage, new filter stud seals and union seal.
10. Place the reservoir in the normal position and press down until the reservoir seats on the housing. Check the position of the stud seals and the union seal.

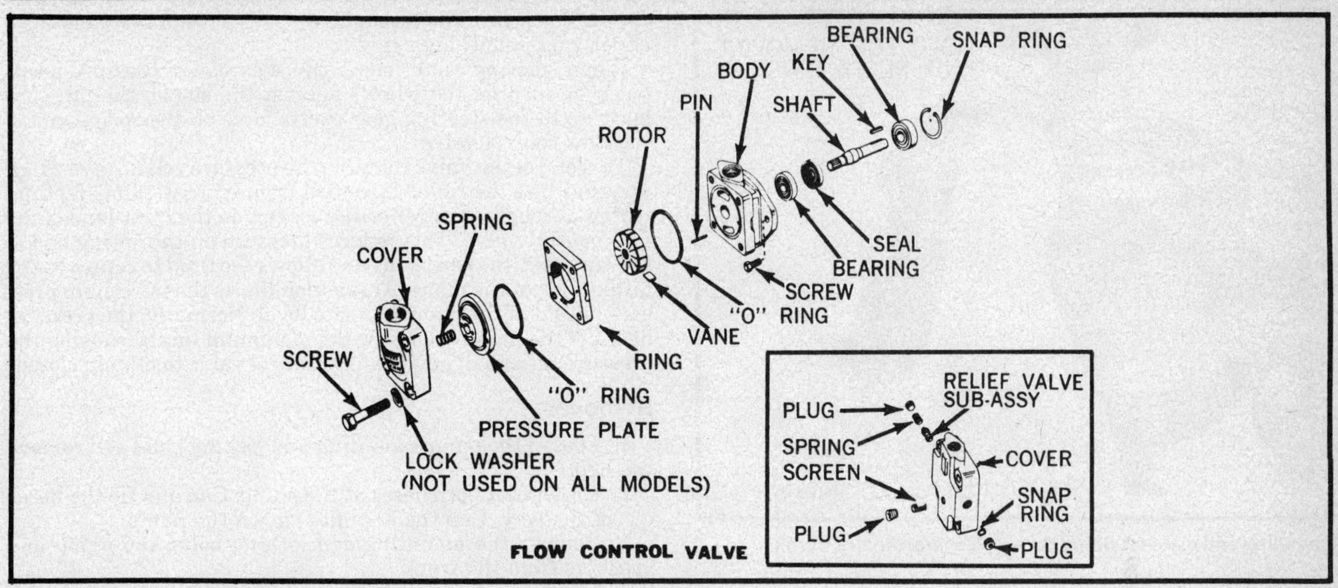

Exploded view of vane type pump—Vickers (© International Harvester Co.)

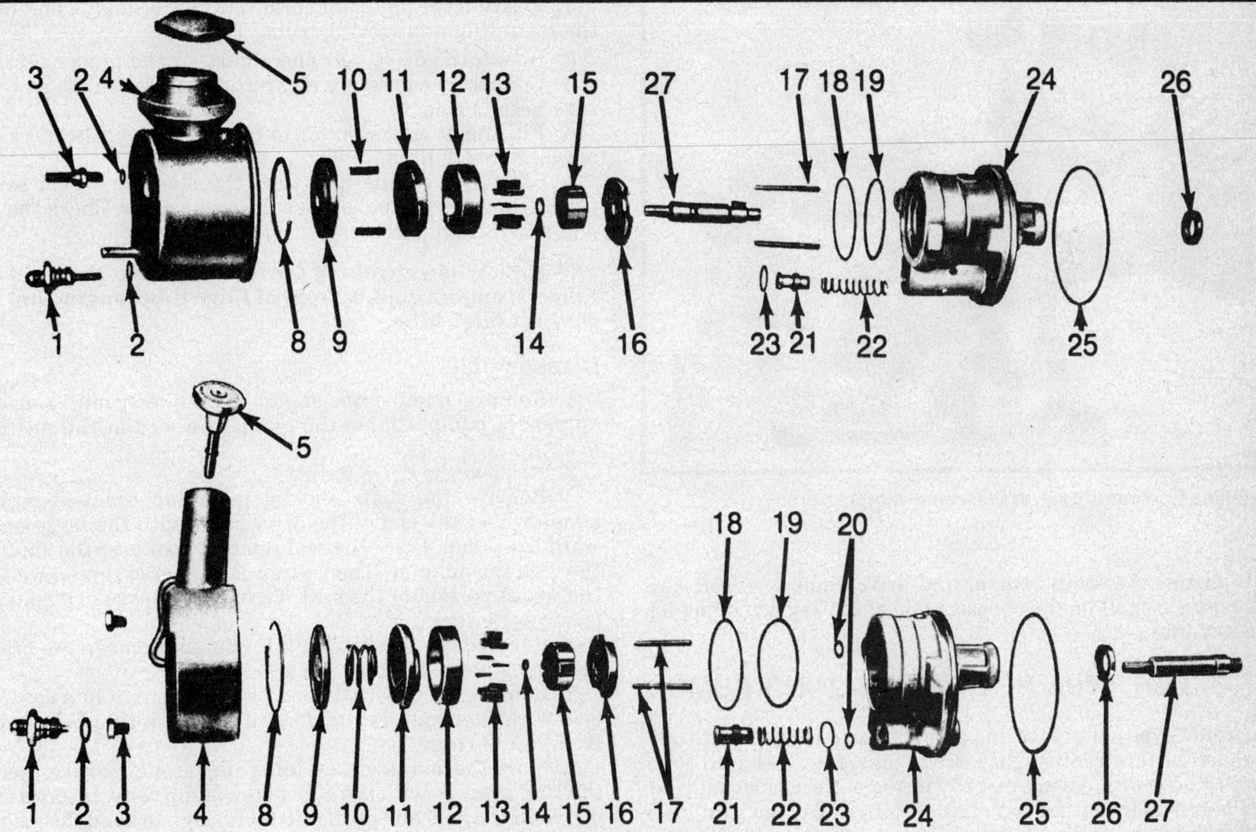

1 Union
2 Union "O" ring seal
3 Mounting studs
4 Reservoir
5 Dip stick and cover
8 End plate retaining ring
9 End plate
10 Spring
11 Pressure plate
12 Pump ring
13 Vanes
14 Drive shaft retaining ring
15 Rotor
16 Thrust plate
17 Dowel pins
18 End plate "O" ring
19 Pressure plate "O" ring
20 Mounting stud square ring
21 Flow control valve
22 Flow control valve spring
23 Flow control valve square ring seal
24 Pump housing
25 Reservoir "O" ring seal
26 Shaft seal
27 Shaft

Vane type power steering pumps (© General Motors Corp.)

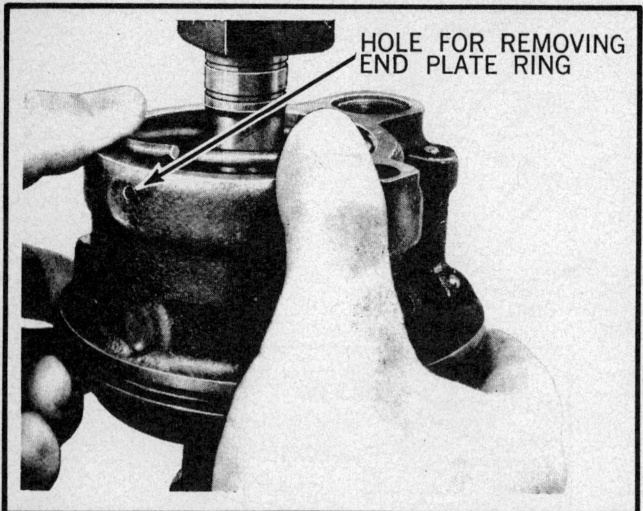

Installing end plate retaining ring (© General Motors Corp.)

Installing flow control valve (© General Motors Corp.)

11. Install the studs, union, and drive shaft woodruff key. Support the shaft on the opposite side of the key when tapping the key into place.

ROLLER TYPE POWER STEERING PUMP

The roller type power steering pump is designed similar to other constant flow centrifugal force pumps. A star-shaped rotor forces 12 steel rollers against the inside surface of a cam ring. As the rollers follow the eccentric pattern of the cam ring, oil is drawn into the inlet ports and exhausted through the discharge ports while the rollers are moved into v shaped cavities of the rotor, forcing oil into the high pressure circuit. A flow control valve permits a regulated amount of fluid to return to the intake side of the pump when excess output is produced during high speed operation. This reduces the power needs to drive the pump and minimizes temperature build-up.

The flow control valve used in one make of pump is a two-stage valve. Fluid under high pressure passes through two holes into a metering circuit located in a sealed passage. At low speed, about 2.7 gpm. passes to the gear. As speed increases and the valve moves, excess fluid is bypassed to the inlet and the valve blocks flow through one hole. This drops the flow to about 1.6 gpm. at high speeds.

When steering conditions produce excessive pressure needs (such as turning the wheels against the stops), the pressure built up in the steering gear exerts force on the spring end of the flow control valve.

This end of the valve contains the pressure relief valve. High pressure lifts the relief valve ball from its seat, allowing fluid to flow through a trigger orifice located in the front land of the flow control valve. This reduces pressure on the spring end of the valve which then opens and allows the fluid to return to the intake side of the pump. This action limits the maximum pressure output of the pump to a safe level. Normally, the pressure needs of the pump are below the maximum limits, causing the pressure relief ball and the flow control valve to remain closed.

Removal

1. Loosen the pump mounting and locking bolts and remove the belt.
2. Disconnect both hoses at the pump. Cap and tie the hoses out of the way. Cap the hose fittings on the pump.
3. Remove the mounting and locking bolts, the pump and brackets from the truck.

Installation

1. Position the pump and brackets on the engine and install the mounting and locking bolts.
2. Install the drive belt and adjust for the proper tension.
3. Connect the pressure and return hoses, using a new pressure hose O-ring.
4. Fill the pump reservoir to the top of the filler neck with power steering fluid.
5. Start the engine and turn the steering wheel several times from stop to stop to bleed the pump of air. Check the level and add fluid if necessary.

NOTE: When checking the level, see that the level is as follows: engine cold-bottom of filler tube; engine hot-half way up filler tube.

Disassembly

1. Remove pump from engine, drain reservoir, and clean outside of pump. Clamp the pump in a vise at the mounting bracket.
2. Remove the drive pulley.
3. Remove the shaft seal by installing the seal remover adapter over the end of the drive shaft with the large end toward the pump. Place the seal remover tool over the shaft and through the adapter. Then, screw the tapered thread well into the metal portion of the seal. Tighten the large drive nut and remove the seal.
4. Remove the pump from the vise and remove the bracket mounting bolts. Remove the bracket.
5. Remove the reservoir and place the pump in a soft-faced vise with the shaft down. Discard the mounting bolt and the reservoir O-rings.
6. Move the end cover retaining ring around until one end of the ring lines up with the hole in the pump body. Insert a small punch in the hole and push it in far enough to bend the ring so a screwdriver can be inserted between the ring and the housing. Remove the ring.
7. Remove the end cover and spring from the housing. It may be necessary to tap the cover gently to loosen it in the housing.
8. Remove the pump from the vise and turn the pump over so the rotating pump may come out of the housing. Tap the end of the drive shaft to loosen these parts. Lift the pump body off the rotating group. Check that the seal plate is removed from the bottom of the housing bore.
9. Discard the O-rings from the pressure plate and end cover.

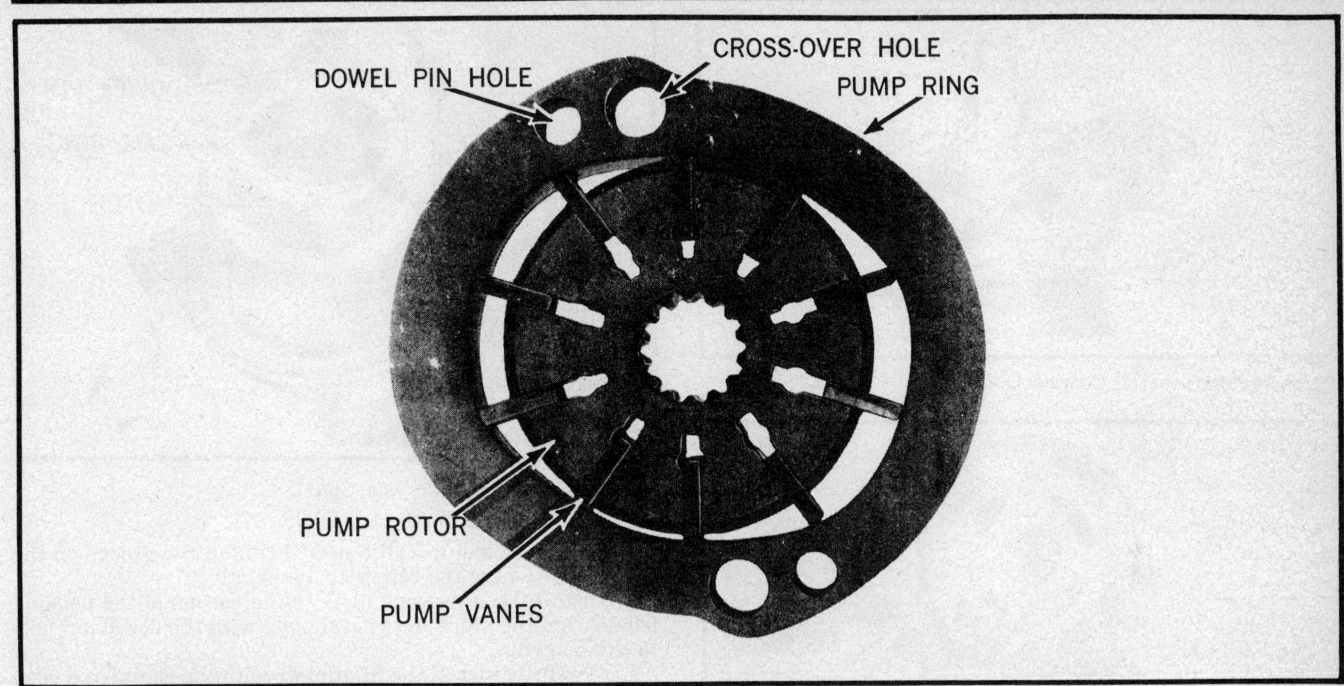

Correct vane assembly (© General Motors Corp.)

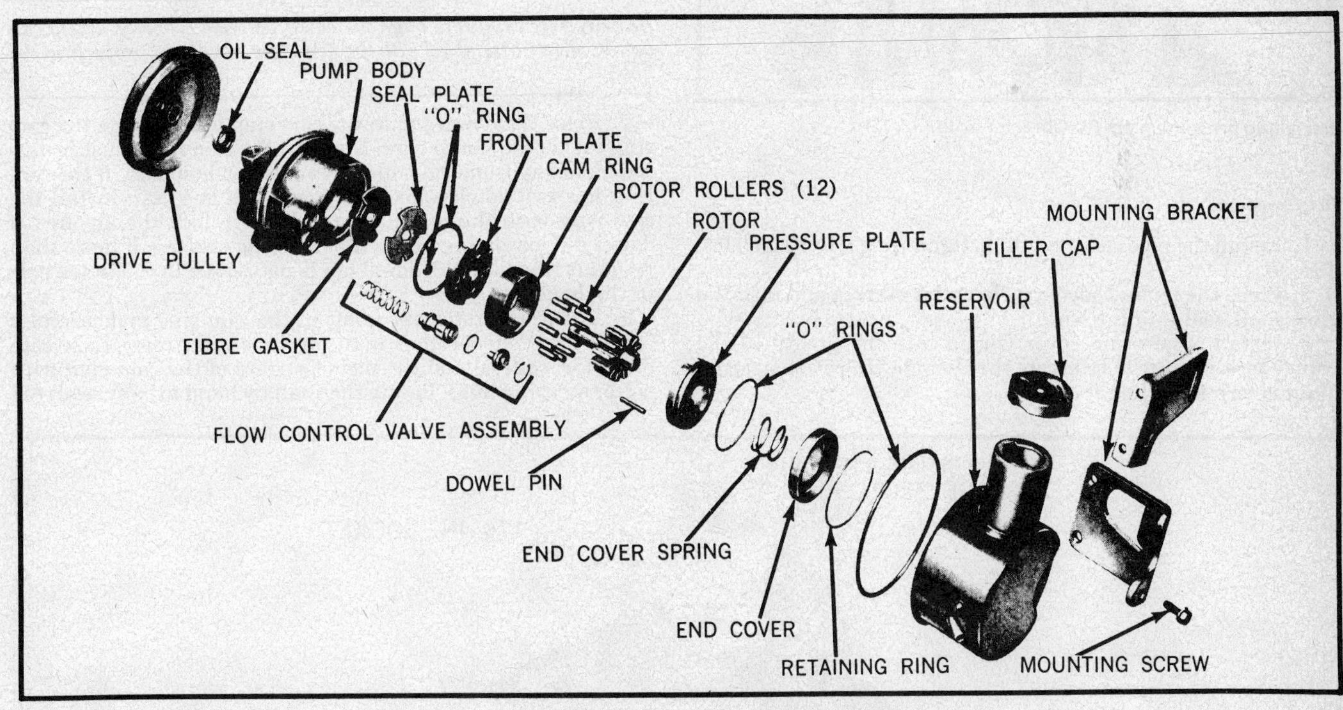

Roller type power steering pump (© General Motors Corp.)

10. Remove the snap-ring, bore plug, flow control valve and spring from the housing. Discard the O-ring. If necessary to dismantle the flow control valve for cleaning, see the procedure for disassembly.

Inspection

1. Remove the clean out plug with an Allen wrench.
2. Wash all metal parts in clean, non-toxic solvent. Blow out all passages with compressed air and air dry all cleaned parts.
3. Inspect the drive shaft for excessive wear and the seal area for nicks or scoring. Replace if necessary.
4. Inspect the end plates, rollers, rotor and cam ring for nicks, burrs, or scratches. If any of the components are damaged enough to cause poor operation of the pump, all the interior parts may have to be replaced to prevent later failures.
5. Inspect the pump body drive shaft bushing for excessive wear. Replace the pump body and bushing as one assembly.

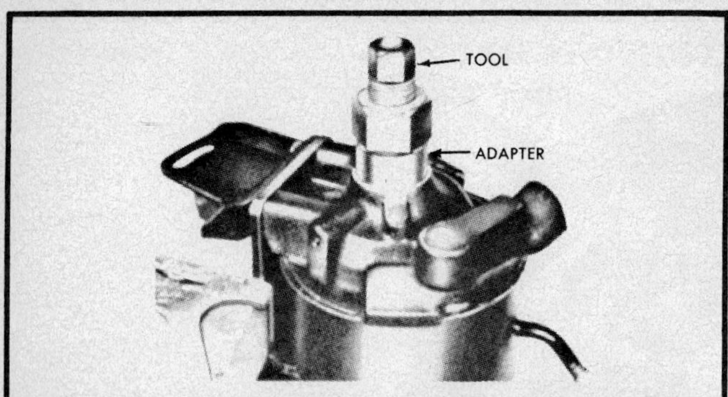

Removing shaft seal (© Chrysler Corp.)

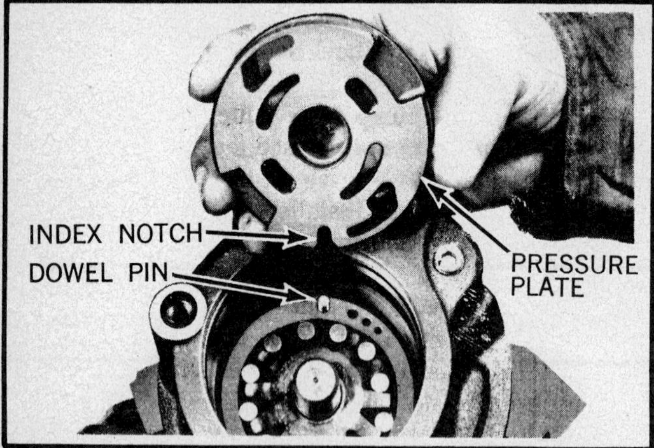

Installing pressure plate (© Chrysler Corp.)

Assembly

1. Install the pipe clean out plug, tightening it to 80 inch lbs. torque.
2. Place the pump body on a clean flat surface and install a new shaft seal into the bore.
3. Install a new end cover O-ring into the groove in the pump bore. Be sure to lubricate the O-ring with power steering fluid before installing it.

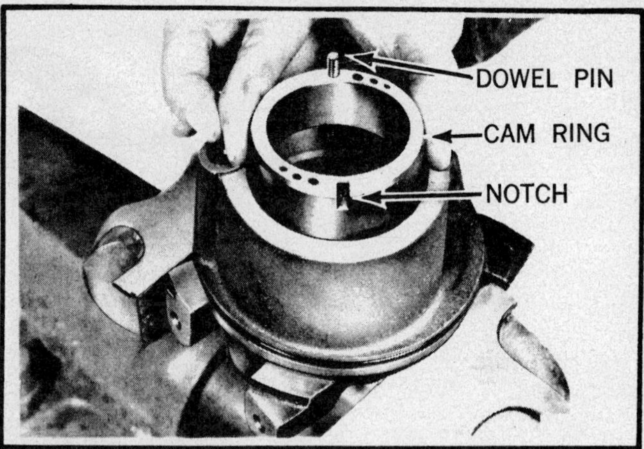

Installing cam ring (© Chrysler Corp.)

4. Lubricate and install a new O-ring in the groove on the pump body where the reservoir fits snugly.
5. Install the brass seal plate to the bottom of the housing bore. Align the notch in the seal plate with the dowel pin hole in the housing.
6. Carefully install the front plate with the chamfered edge down in the pump bore. Align the index notch in the plate with the dowel pin hole in the housing.

CAUTION

Be extremely careful to align the dowel pin hole properly. Pump can be completely assembled with the dowel pin not seated properly in the hole.

7. Place the dowel pin in the cam ring and position the cam ring inside the pump bore. Notch in the cam ring must be facing up (away from the pulley end of pump housing). If the cam ring has two notches, one machined and one cast, install the cam ring with the machined notch up. Check the amount of dowel pin extending above the cam ring surface. If more than $^{3}/_{16}$ in. is showing, the dowel pin is not seated in the index hole in the housing.
8. Install the rotor and shaft in the cam ring and carefully install the 12 steel rollers in the cavities of the rotor. Lubricate the rotor, rollers, and the inside surface of the cam ring with power steering fluid. Rotate the shaft by hand to be sure all the

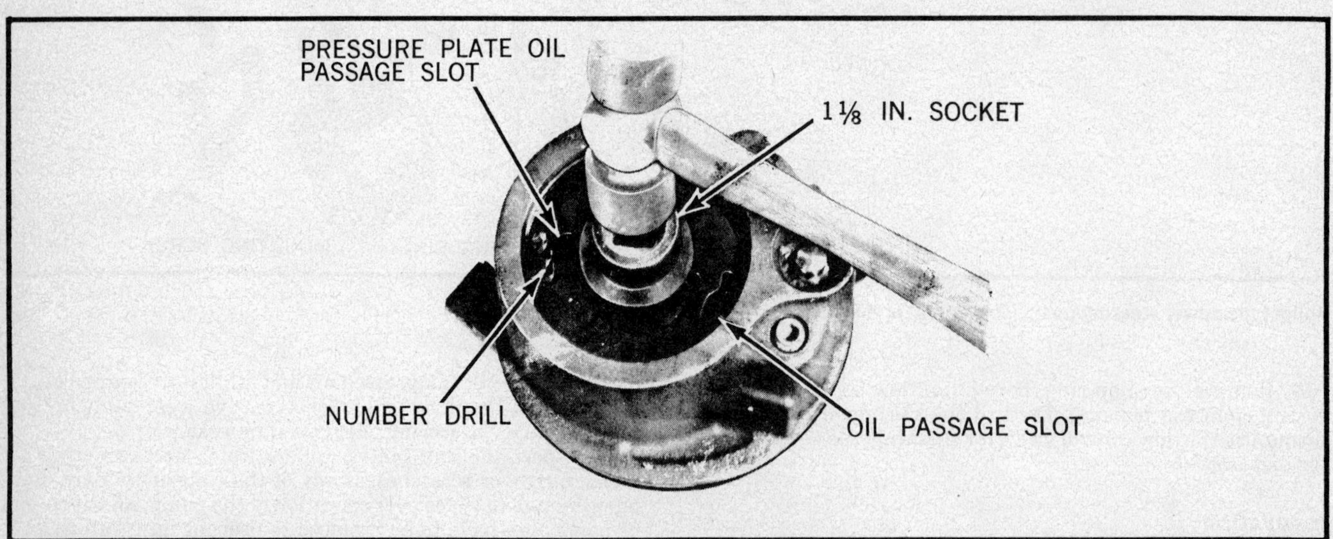

Seating pressure plate (© Chrysler Corp.)

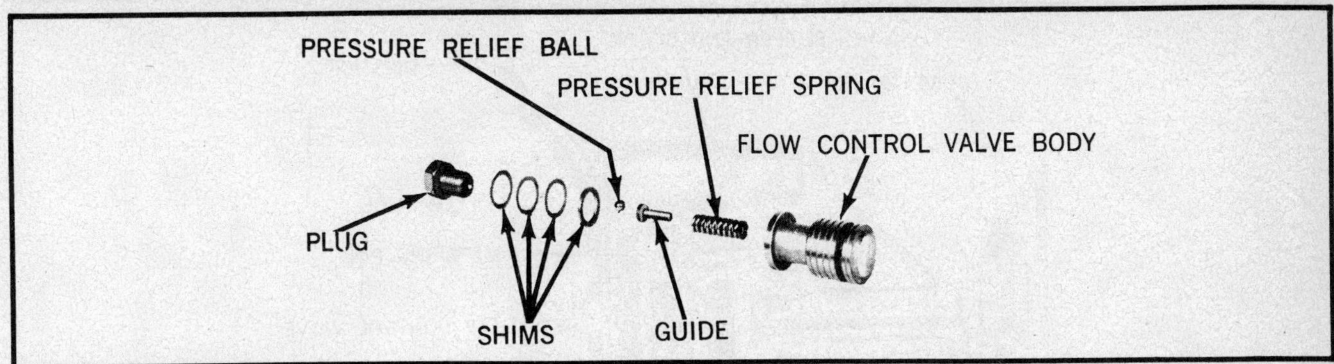

Flow control valve (© Chrysler Corp.)

rollers are seated parallel with the shaft and are not sticking or binding.

9. Position the pressure plate by carefully aligning the index notch on the plate with the dowel pin and inserting a clean drill (number 13 to 16) in the cam ring oil hole next to the dowel pin notch until it bottoms on the housing floor.

10. Lubricate and install a new O-ring on the pressure plate. Position the pressure plate in the pump bore so that the dowel pin is in the index notch on the plate and the drill extends through the oil passage in the pressure plate. Seat the pressure plate on the cam ring using a clean 1 $^1/_8$ in. socket and a soft-faced hammer to tap it gently. Remove the drill and inspect the plate at both oil passage slots to be sure that the plate is squarely seated on the cam ring.

11. Place the large coil spring over the raised portion of the installed pressure plate.

12. Place the end cover, lip edge facing up, over the spring. Press the end cover down below the retaining ring groove. Install the retaining ring in the groove. Be sure the end cover chamfer is squarely seated against the snap-ring.

13. Replace the reservoir mounting bolt seal.

14. Lubricate the flow control valve assembly with power steering fluid and insert the valve spring and valve in the bore. Install a new O-ring on the bore plug, lubricate with fluid, and carefully install in the bore. Install the snap-ring with the sharp edge up. Do not depress the bore plug more than $^1/_{16}$ in. below the snap-ring groove.

15. Place the reservoir on the pump body and visually align the mounting bolt hole. Tap the reservoir down on the pump with a plastic-faced hammer.

16. Remove the pump from the vise and install the mounting brackets with the mounting bolts on the pump. Tighten the bolts to 18 ft. lbs. torque.

17. Install the drive pulley by using the installer tool as follows: place the pulley on the end of the shaft and thread the installer tool into the $^3/_8$ in. threaded hole in the end of the shaft. Put the installer shaft in a vise and tighten the drive nut against the thrust bearing, pressing the pulley on the shaft until it is flush. Do not try to press the pulley on the shaft without the special installer tool since the pump interior will be damaged by any other installation procedure. A small amount of drive shaft end play will be seen when the pulley is installed. This end play is necessary and will be minimized by a thin coat of oil between the rotor and the end plates when the pump is operating.

18. Install the pump assembly on the engine, install the drive belt and hoses (use new O-ring on pressure hose), and check for leaks.

FLOW CONTROL VALVE

Disassembly

1. After removing the pump from the engine and the reservoir from the pump, remove the snap-ring and plug from the flow bore. Discard the O-ring.

2. Depress the control valve against the spring pressure and allow the valve to spring out of the bore. If the valve is stuck in the bore or it did not come out of the bore far enough, it may be necessary to tap the housing lightly to remove it.

3. If the valve has dirt or foreign particles on it or in its bore, the rest of the pump needs cleaning. The hoses should be flushed and the steering gear valve body reconditioned. If the valve bore is badly scored, replace the pump body and the flow control valve.

4. Remove any nicks or burrs by gently rubbing the valve with crocus cloth. Clamp the valve land in a vise with soft-jaws and remove the hex head ball seat and shims. Note the number and gauge (thickness) of the shims on the ball seat. They must be re-installed for the same shim thickness to keep the same value of relief pressure.

5. Remove the valve from the vise and remove the pressure relief ball, guide, and spring.

Assembly

1. Insert the spring, guide and pressure relief ball in the end of the flow control valve.

2. Install the hex head plug using the exact number and thickness shims that were removed. Tighten the plug to 80 inch lbs. torque.

3. Lubricate the valve with power steering fluid and insert the flow control valve spring and valve in the housing bore. Install a new O-ring on the bore plug, lubricate with fluid and carefully install into the bore. Install the snap-ring. Do not depress the bore plug more than $^1/_{16}$ in. beyond the snap-ring groove.

SLIPPER TYPE POWER STEERING PUMP

The slipper type power steering pump is a belt-driven constant displacement assembly that uses a number of spring-loaded slippers in the pump rotor to force fluid from the inlet side to the flow control valve. Openings in the metering pin allow a flow of about two gpm. of fluid to the steering gear before the flow control valve directs the excess fluid to the inlet side of the pump again. Maximum pressure in the pump is limited by the pressure relief valve which opens when the pressure exceeds the maximum limits.

The slipper type power steering pump discussed in this section is used on Ford trucks and is called the Ford-Thompson power steering pump.

Removal

1. Drain the fluid from the pump reservoir by disconnecting the fluid return hose at the pump. Then, disconnect the pressure hose from the pump.

2. Remove the mounting bolts from the front of the pump.

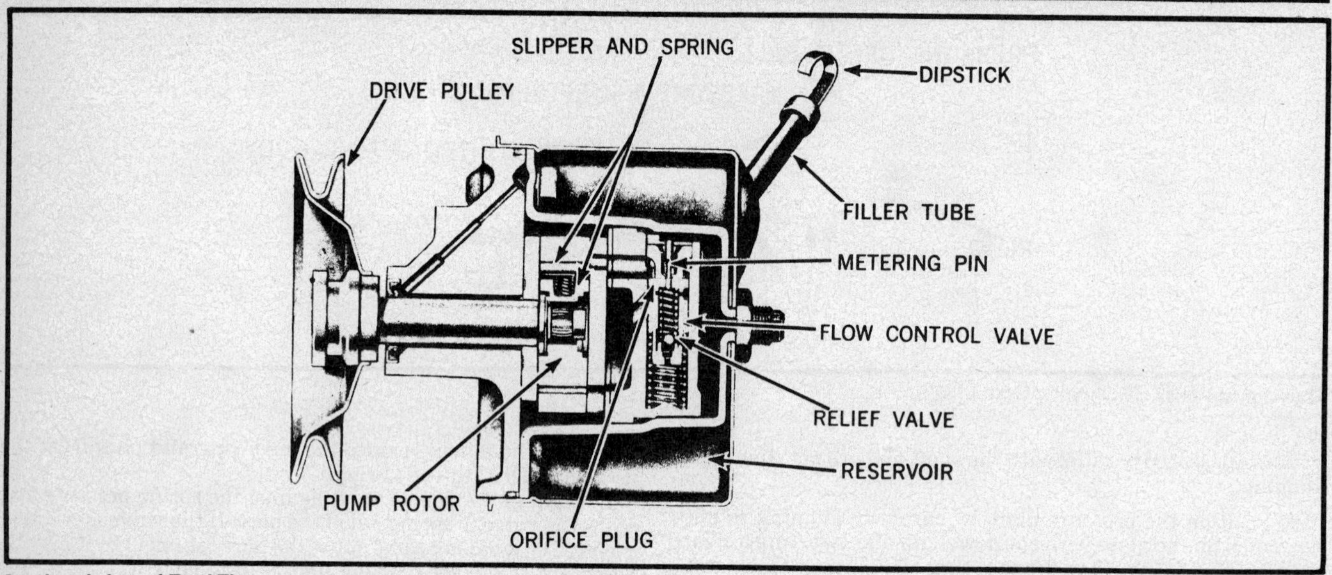

Sectional view of Ford Thompson power steering pump (© Ford Motor Co.)

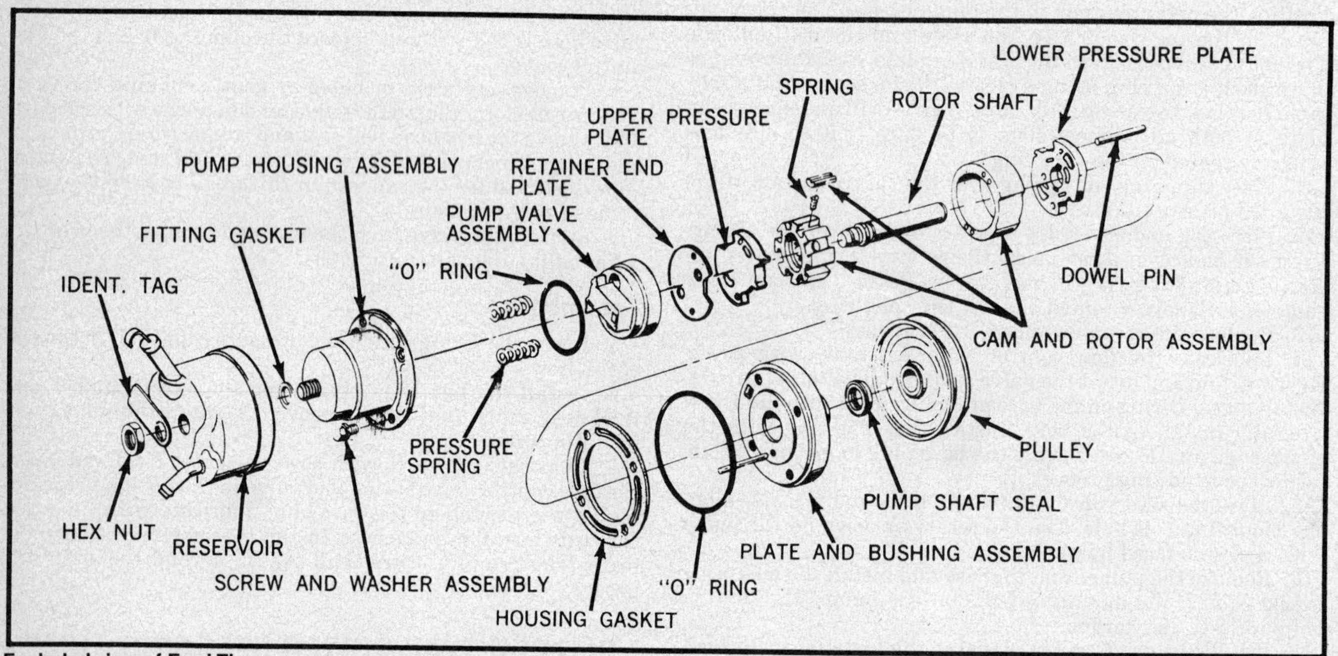

Exploded view of Ford Thompson power steering pump (© Ford Motor Co.)

On eight cylinder engines, there is a nut on the rear of the pump that must be removed. After removing all the mounting bolts and nuts from the pump, move the unit inward to loosen the belt tension and remove the belt from the pulley. Then remove the pump from the engine.

Installation

1. Position the pump on the mounting bracket and loosely install the mounting bolts and nuts. Put the drive belt over the pulley and move the pump outward against the belt until the proper belt tension is obtained. Measure the belt tension with a gauge for the proper adjustment. Only in cases where a belt tension gauge is not available should the belt deflection method be used. If the belt deflection method is used, be sure to check the belt with a tension gauge at the earliest time since the deflection method is not accurate.
2. Tighten the mounting bolts and nuts to the specified torque limits.
3. Tighten the pressure hose fitting hex nut to the proper torque. Then connect the pressure hose to the pump and tighten the hose nut to the proper torque.
4. Connect the fluid return hose to the pump and tighten the clamp.
5. Fill the pump reservoir with power steering fluid and bleed the air bubbles from the system.
6. Check for leaks and recheck the fluid level. If necessary, add fluid to raise the level properly.

Disassembly

1. Drain as much fluid from the pump as possible after removing the pump from the truck.
2. Install a $^3/_8$ X 16 in. capscrew in the end of the pump shaft

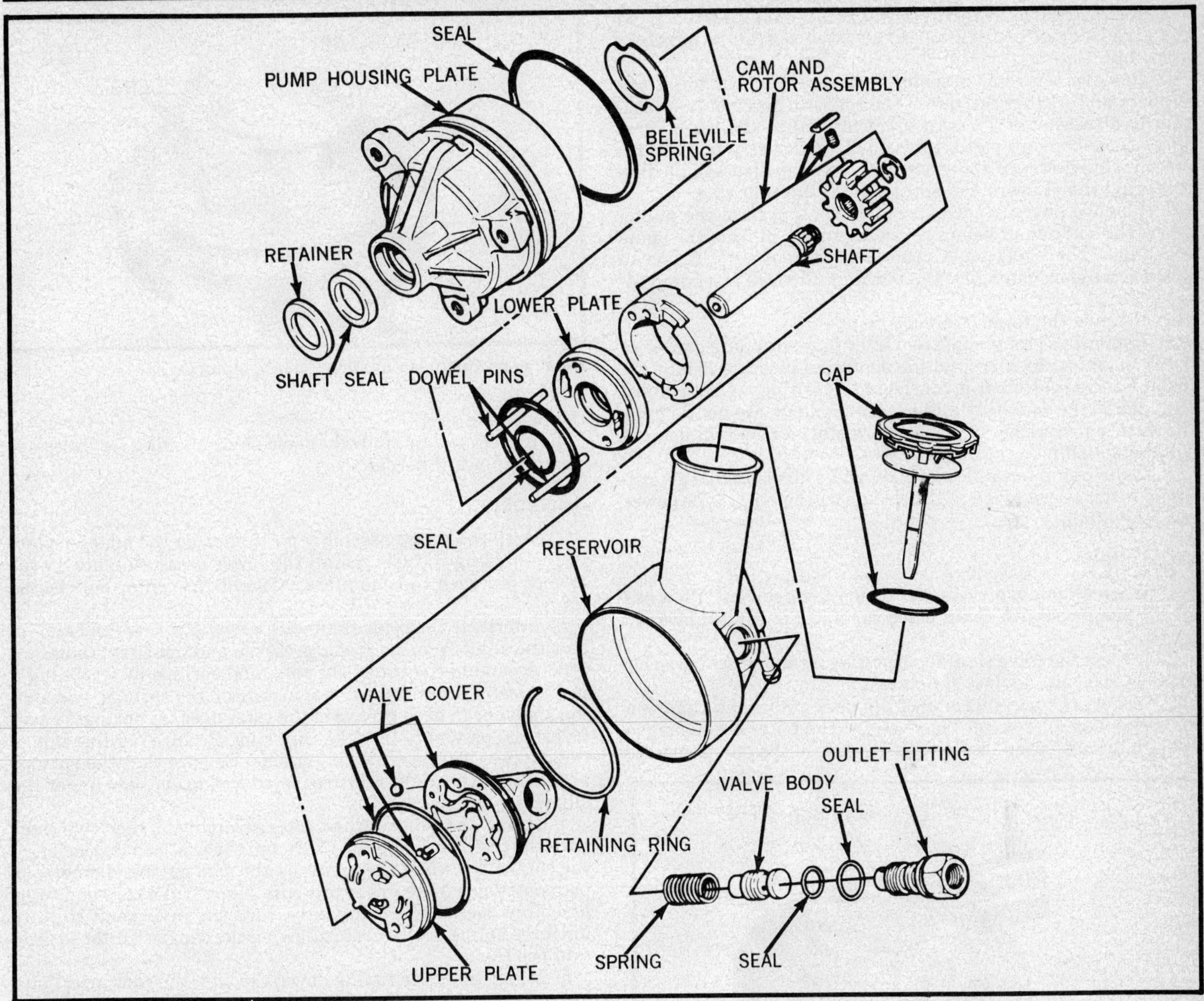

Exploded view of model C-11 slipper type pump (© Ford Motor Co.)

to avoid damaging the shaft end with the pulley remover tool. Install the pulley remover tool on the pulley hub and place the pump and remover tool in a vise. Hold the pump steady and turn the tool nut counterclockwise to draw the pulley off the shaft. The pulley must be removed without in and out pressure on the pump shaft to avoid damaging the internal thrust washers.

3. Remove the pump reservoir by installing the pump in a holding fixture with an adapter plate in a vise with the reservoir facing up.
4. Remove the outlet fitting hex nut and any other attaching parts from the reservoir case.
5. Invert the pump so the reservoir is now facing down. Using a wooden block, remove the reservoir by tapping around the flange until the reservoir is loose. Remove the reservoir O-ring seal and the outlet fitting gasket from the pump.
6. Again invert the pump assembly in the vise, remove the pump housing holding bolts and the pump housing.
7. Remove the housing cover, the O-ring seal and the pressure springs from inside the pump housing. Remove the pump cover gasket and discard it.
8. Remove the retainer end plate and upper pressure plate. In some pumps, the end plate and the upper pressure plate are made as one unit.

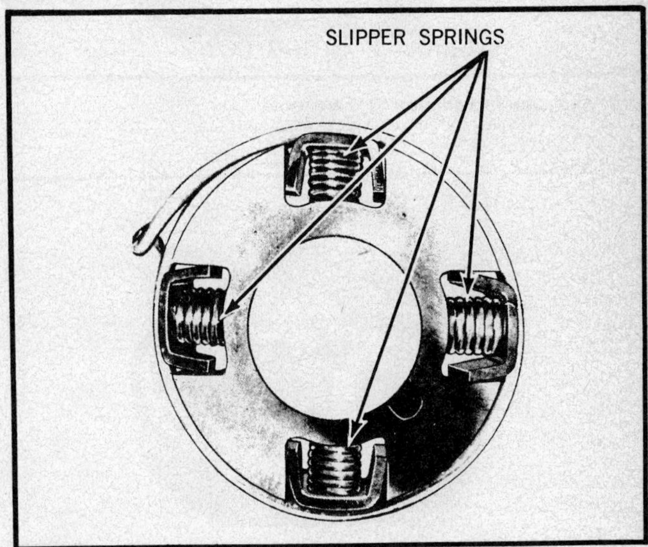

Correct slipper installation—Chrysler models (© Chrysler Corp.)

9. Remove the loose fitting dowel pin. Be careful not to bend the fixed dowel pin which remains in the housing plate assembly.

10. Remove the rotor assembly being careful not to let the slippers and springs fall out of the rotor. It may not be necessary to disassemble the rotor assembly unless the lower pressure plate, housing plate, rotor shaft and/or seal is to be replaced. However, the rotor assembly may be disassembled by removing the slippers and springs from the cam ring.

11. Remove any rust, dirt, burrs, or scoring from the pulley end of the rotor shaft before removing the shaft from the housing plate. The shaft must come out without restrictions to avoid scoring or damaging the bushing. Remove the pump rotor shaft.

12. Remove the lower pressure plate.

13. Remove the rotor shaft seal after first wrapping a piece of 0.005 in. shim stock around the shaft and pushing it into the inside of the seal until it touches the bushing. With a sharp tool, pierce the seal body and pry the seal out. Do not damage the bushing, housing, or the shaft. Install a new seal using a soft-faced hammer.

14. If the pump has a flow control valve, disassemble according to instructions given in the section on the roller type power steering pump.

Inspection

1. Wash all metal parts in clean, non-toxic solvent. Blow out all oil passages with compressed air and air dry all cleaned parts.

2. Inspect the drive shaft for excessive wear and seal area for nicks or scoring. Replace if necessary.

3. Inspect the pressure plates, slippers, rotor, and cam ring for nicks, burrs, or scratches. If any of the parts are damaged enough to cause poor operation or binding of the pump, replace

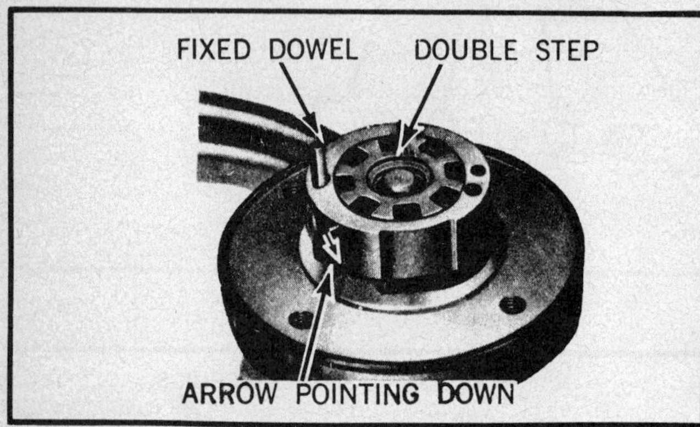

Cam and rotor installation (© Ford Motor Co.)

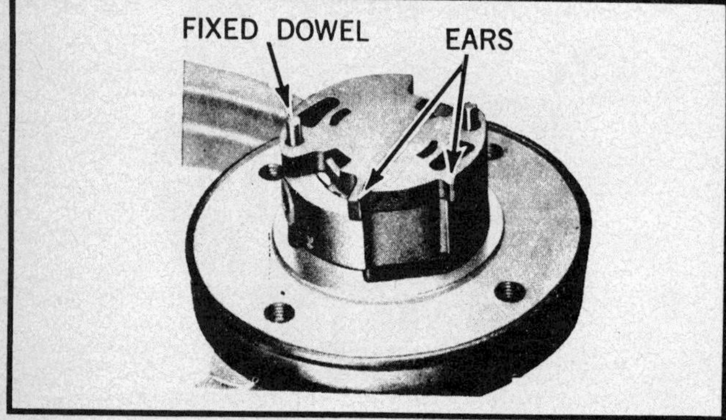

Upper pressure plate installation (© Ford Motor Co.)

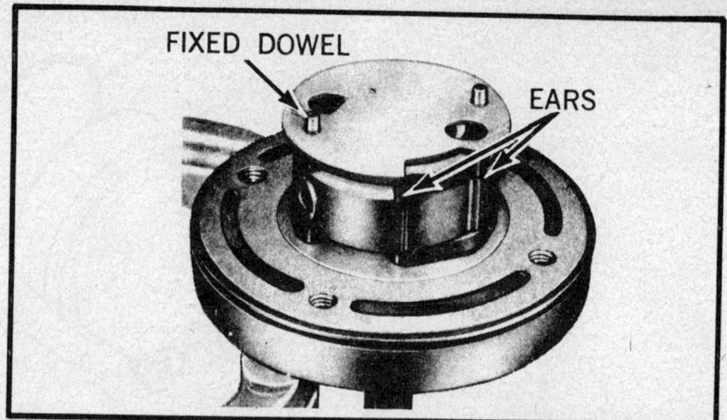

Retainer end plate installation (© Ford Motor Co.)

the defective part.

4. Inspect the pump body drive shaft bushing for excessive wear. Replace if necessary.

Assembly

1. With the pump assembly positioned on the adapter plate in the holding fixture, install the lower pressure plate on the anchor pin with the chamfered slots at the center hole facing up.

2. Lubricate the rotor shaft with power steering fluid and insert the shaft into the lower pressure and housing plates.

3. Assemble the rotor, slippers, and springs by wrapping a piece of wire around the rotor, installing the springs, and sliding a slipper in each groove of the rotor over the springs. Then, insert the assembly into the cam ring. Be sure the flat side of the slippers are toward the left side. Be sure that the springs are installed straight and are not cocked to one side under the slippers.

4. Install the cam ring and rotor assembly on the drive shaft with the fixed dowel passing through the first hole to the left of the cam notch when the arrow on the cam outside diameter is pointing toward the lower pressure plate. If the cam and rotor assembly does not seat properly, turn the rotor shaft slightly until the spline teeth mesh, allowing the cam and rotor to drop into position.

5. Insert the loose fitting dowel through the cam insert and lower pressure plate into the hole in the housing plate assembly. When both dowels are installed properly, they will be the same height.

6. Install the upper pressure plate so the tapered notch is facing down against the cam insert. The fixed dowel should pass through the round dowel hole and the loose dowel through the long hole. The slot between the ears on the outside of the pressure plate should match the notch on the cam insert.

7. Install the retainer end plate so the slot on the end plate matches the notches on the upper pressure plate and the cam insert.

8. Install the pump valve assembly O-ring seal on the pump valve assembly. Do not twist the seal.

9. Place the pump valve assembly on top of the retainer end plate with the large exhaust slot on the pump valve in line with the outside notches of the cam, upper pressure plate, and retainer end plate. All parts must be fully seated. If correctly installed, the relief valve stem will be in line with the lube return hole in the pump housing plate.

10. Put small amounts of vaseline on the pump housing plate to hold the cover gasket in place. Install the cover gasket in place.

11. Insert the pressure plate springs into the pockets in the pump valve assembly.

12. Plug the intake hole in the housing.

13. Lubricate the inside of the housing and the housing cover seal with power steering fluid. Install two studs for use as posi-

Correct slipper installation—Ford models (© Ford Motor Co.)

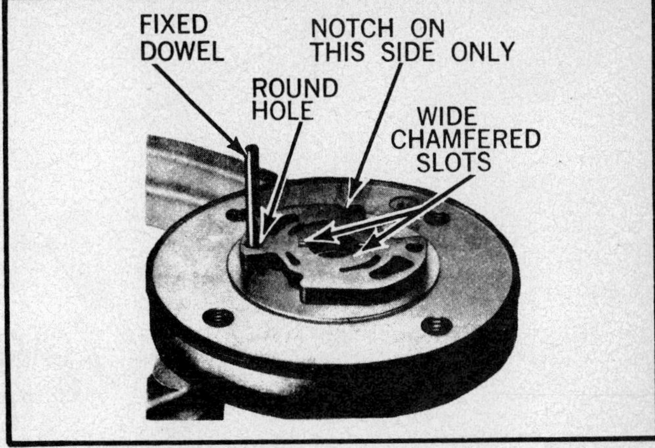

Lower pressure plate installed (© Ford Motor Co.)

tioning guides, one in the bolt hole nearest the drain hole and the other in the bolt hole on the opposite side of the housing plate.

14. Align the small lube hole in the housing rim and the lube hole in the housing plate. Install the housing, using a steady, even, downward pressure. Do not jar the pressure spring out of position. Remove the guide studs and loosely install the housing retaining bolts finger tight.

15. Tighten the retaining bolts evenly to 28–32 ft. lbs. until the housing flange contacts the gasket.

16. Install a $^3/_8$–16 hex head screw into the end of the rotor shaft and put a torque wrench on it. Check the amount of torque needed to rotate the rotor shaft. If the torque is more than 15 inch lbs., loosen the retaining bolts slightly and rotate the rotor shaft. Then, retighten the retaining bolts evenly. Do not use the pump if the shaft torque exceeds 15 inch lbs.

17. Release the pin in the bench holding fixture and shake the pump assembly back and forth. If there is a rattle, the pressure springs have fallen out of their seats and must be reinstalled.

18. Install the reservoir O-ring seal on the housing plate without twisting it. Lubricate the seal and install the reservoir, aligning the notch in the reservoir flange with the notch in the outside edge of the pump housing plate and bushing assembly. Using only a soft-faced hammer, tap at the rear outer corners of the reservoir. Inspect the assembly to be sure the reservoir is fully seated on the housing plate.

19. Install the identification tag (if one was removed) on the outlet valve fitting. Install the outlet valve fitting nut and tighten to 48–45 ft. lbs. torque.

20. Turn the pump assembly over and install the pulley using the tool used to remove the pulley. Turn the tool nut clockwise to draw the pulley on the shaft until it is flush with the shaft end. Do not exert inward and outward pressures on the shaft to avoid damaging the internal thrust areas. Remove the tool.

BORG WARNER POWER STEERING PUMP

The Borg Warner pump is a gear-type power steering pump and is used on on series of diesel engines. The pump is mounted directly to the engine and is gear driven. A bolt-on oil flow control valve is attached to the pump assembly.

VICKERS POWER STEERING PUMP

Disassembly

1. Clamp pump in vise with cover end up and remove cover screws. Lift off cover and remove O-ring.

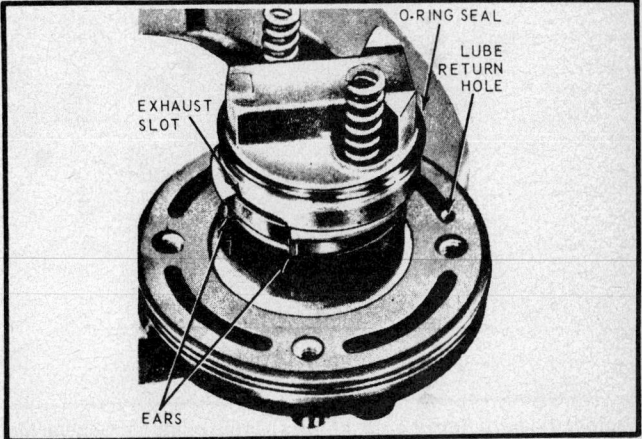

Valve and pressure spring installation (© Ford Motor Co.)

2. If pump is equipped with flow control valve, remove plug spring and valve subassembly.
3. Remove pressure plate and spring.
4. Mark position of ring and remove it along with locating pin.
5. Separate vanes from rotor and slide rotor from shaft.
6. Turn pump body over and remove shaft key and outer bearing snap ring. Tap on splined end of shaft with a soft hammer to force it out of housing.
7. If bearing is to be removed, support the inner race and press shaft out of bearing.
8. Pull shaft seal out of body.
9. Press inner bearing out of body.

Assembly

1. Coat all parts with hydraulic fluid before assembly.
2. If flow control valve is used, assemble components into cover. If cover has a blind bore, install spring first, then valve. Install snap ring and plug. Install screen and retaining plug.
3. Press shaft into outer bearing while supporting inner race. Press inner bearing into body using a driver on the outer race.
4. Install seal. Seals should be assembled with holes facing the shaft end of the pump. Lube lip with petroleum jelly.
5. Slide driveshaft in place until outer bearing is sealed. Install bearing retaining snap ring in body.
6. Install new O-ring in body. Insert ring locating pins in body and assemble ring so that arrow points in direction of rotation.

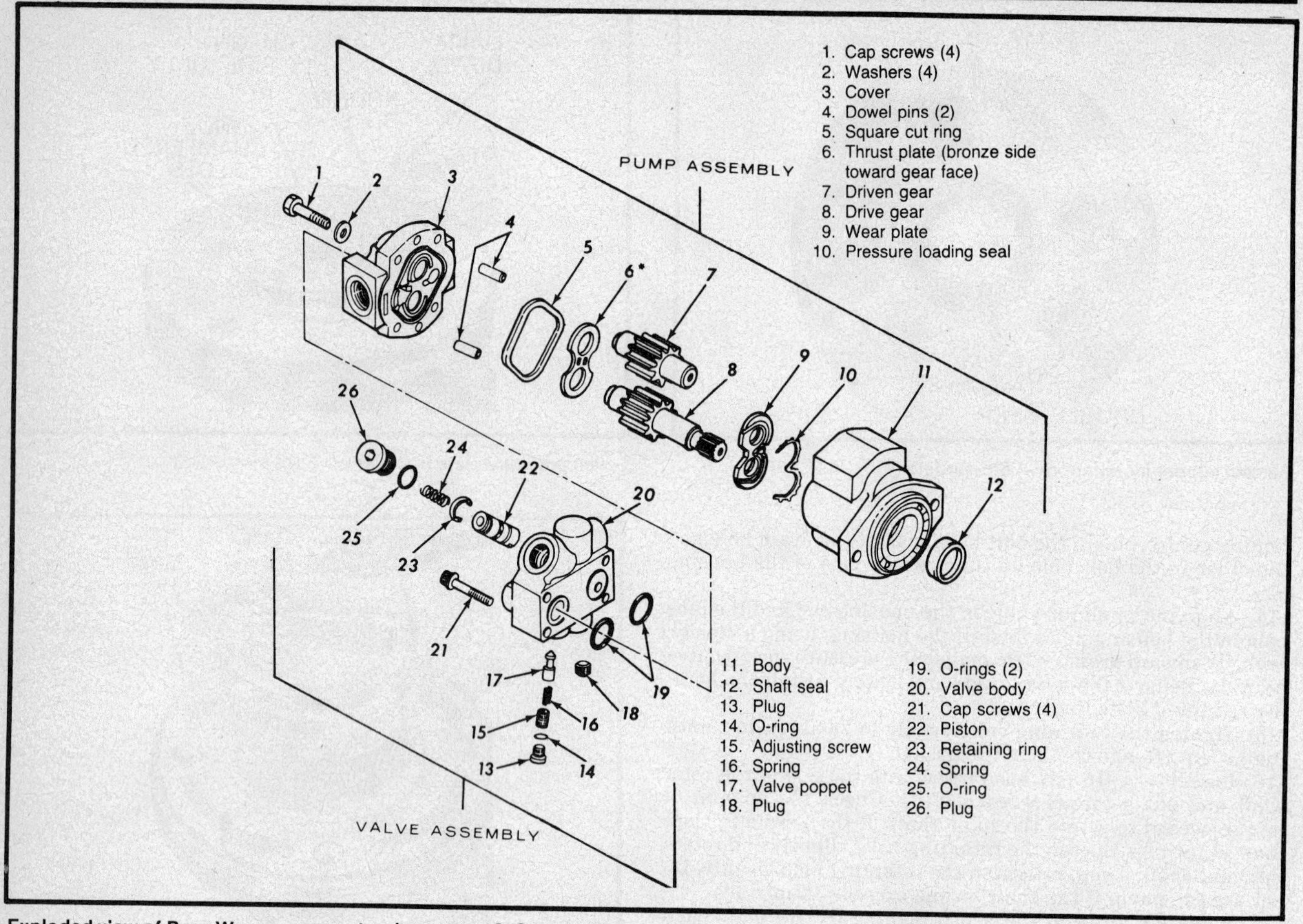

PUMP ASSEMBLY
VALVE ASSEMBLY
1. Cap screws (4)
2. Washers (4)
3. Cover
4. Dowel pins (2)
5. Square cut ring
6. Thrust plate (bronze side toward gear face)
7. Driven gear
8. Drive gear
9. Wear plate
10. Pressure loading seal
11. Body
12. Shaft seal
13. Plug
14. O-ring
15. Adjusting screw
16. Spring
17. Valve poppet
18. Plug
19. O-rings (2)
20. Valve body
21. Cap screws (4)
22. Piston
23. Retaining ring
24. Spring
25. O-ring
26. Plug

Exploded view of Borg Warner power steering pump (© General Motors Corp.)

1 Control valve assembly
2 Control valve spring
3 Valve cover plug
4 Cover
5 Pressure plate spring
6 Pressure plate
7 O-ring seal
8 Ring
9 Rotor
10 Vane
11 Pump body
12 Inner shaft bearing
13 Seal
14 Pump shaft
15 Shaft key
16 Outer shaft bearing
17 Snap ring
18 Shaft nut
19 Foot bracket screw
20 Foot bracket (optional)
21 Valve Body pin
22 Orifice plug
23 Valve cover plug
24 Snap ring
25 Cover screw
26 Screen plug
27 Screen

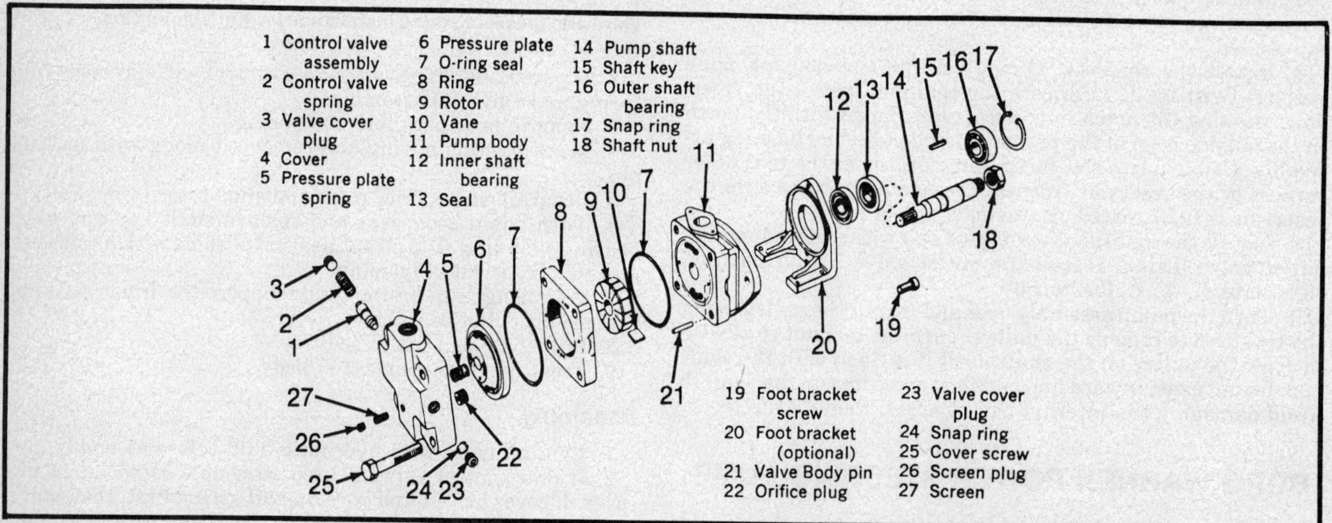

Vickers V2000 series pump (© Mack Trucks Inc.)

7. Install rotor on shaft and insert vanes in rotor slots. Be sure radiused edge of vanes is toward the ring.

8. Place pressure plate over locating pins and flat against ring.

9. Insert pressure plate spring in pressure plate recess, then install cover using new O-ring. Be sure outlet port in cover is in correct position with respect to inlet port in body. Tighten attaching bolts to specified torque. Check binding.

VTM 27 AND VTM 42 SERIES

Disassembly

NOTE: Two versions of the VTM 27 are in use. The non-current production pump uses needle bearings on the shaft; the current models use ball bearings and dispense with the thrust spacers.

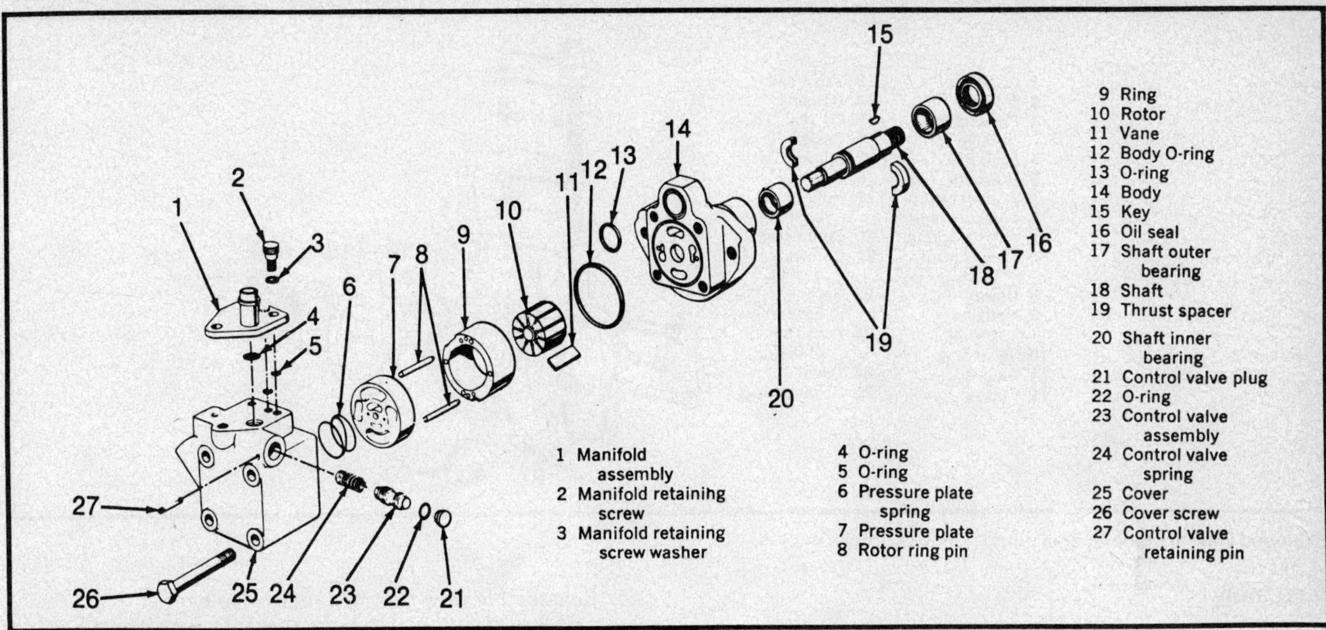

Vickers VTM27 series pump-non current models (© Mack Trucks Inc.)

1. If the pump has an attached reservoir, remove it before working by removing wing nut, washer, cover and gasket. Lift washer, filter retainer, spring and filter element from stud. Remove reservoir stud and nut, two reservoir retaining screws, baffle and reinforcing plate. Separate reservoir from pump. Discard O-rings.
2. If pump has manifold instead of reservoir, remove it along with attaching cap screws, copper washer and O-rings.
3. Clamp pump mounting flange in a vise with soft jaws. Remove cover attaching bolts and separate cover from body.
4. Remove pressure plate spring and pressure plate.
5. Remove ring, locating pins and rotor and vane assembly. Remove and discard O-rings found between body and cover.
6. Mount cover in a vise and drive relief valve retaining pin out. Do not allow relief valve plug and subassembly to fall from bore. Remove plug, valve and spring from bore.
7. Non-current VTM 27: support shaft outer end of pump body on a two inch pipe coupling and using an arbor press, remove the shaft assembly, shaft thrust spacers, outer needle bearing and shaft seal.
8. Current VTM 27 and all VTM 42: remove large snap ring retaining ball bearing in body. Press shaft and bearing assembly from body. Remove snap ring that retains bearing on shaft and remove bearing if not serviceable.
9. Inner bearing, if used, and seal in current production pumps, can be driven from body using a pin punch.

Assembly

NOTE: Lubricate all parts in hydraulic fluid before assembly. For non-current production VTM 27 pump, use Steps 1 thru 4 and Steps 9 thru 15. For current production VTM 27 and 42 pumps use Steps 5–15.

1. Install inner bearing by pressing into body with an arbor press.
2. Assemble thrust spacers on shaft and install shaft in pump body.
3. Press outer needle bearing over shaft and into pump body to $^1/_{64}$ in. past seal shoulder. This gives 0.010–0.015 in. end play.
4. Position seal on body and press into place until it contacts locating shoulder.
5. Press inner bearing into body.
6. Press seal into body.
7. Press ball bearing on shaft and secure with snap ring.
8. Install shaft and bearing assembly into body. Install snap ring.
9. Install locating pins in pump body. Install ring over pins according to direction of rotation.
10. Install rotor with chamfered edge towards inner ring contour.
11. Install vanes with radiused edge towards inner ring contour.
12. Install pressure plate.
13. Insert O-ring in body, then install pressure plate spring and cover. Tighten cover screws to torque.
14. Place spring and valve assembly in relief bore. Position valve with hex towards spring. Insert plug, with O-ring, in bore and hold in place while driving in new retaining pin.
15. Install reservoir or manifold as required. Place new O-rings over reservoir outlet tube and use copper washer on screw which enters oil passage if manifold is used. Assemble reservoir.

MACK-SCANIA PUMP

Disassembly

1. Remove cover retaining cap screws.
2. Tap cover with soft mallet to separate from housing.
3. Remove housing O-ring from groove in pump housing.
4. Remove lock ring from shaft and lift rotor assembly out of housing.
5. Remove key from shaft and tap shaft out of housing.
6. Remove oil seal.
7. Remove connector from valve body.

CAUTION

Take care when removing connector as it compresses the flow control spring and could cause injury if not restrained when unscrewed.

8. Remove flow control spring.
9. Turn cover assembly over and tap lightly to remove valve assembly.
10. Use suitable pliers and remove snap ring.
11. Remove piston and spring from valve body.

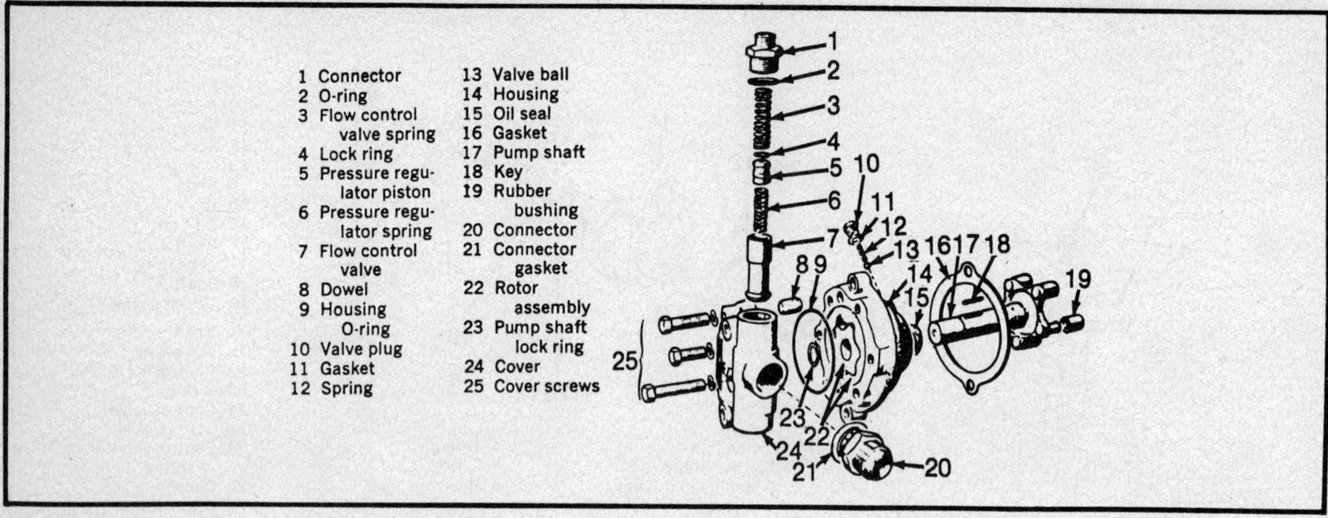

Exploded view of Mack-Scania pump (© Mack Trucks Inc.)

Assembly

1. Install spring and piston in flow control valve body and secure with snap ring.
2. Position valve body into pump cover and install spring.
3. Position new O-ring on connector and install in cover.
4. Install new oil seal in housing.
5. Position rotor assembly in housing and install shaft, aligning keyway in shaft with key slot in rotor.
6. Install key in shaft and rotor.
7. Install lockring on shaft and position new O-ring on housing.
8. Install cover-to-housing aligning dowelpins.
9. Install cover.
10. Turn shaft to be sure pump rotates freely with no binding.

EATON PUMP

Disassembly

1. Remove coupling assembly from pump shaft.
2. Place pumps in soft jawed vise and remove cover attaching screws. Separate cover from body.
3. Remove cover and O-ring seal. Do not lose O-ring retainer.
4. Mark rotors for reference. Remove pump shaft, key, snap ring and inner rotor from pump body.
5. Remove outer rotor by turning body over and tapping on a soft surface.
6. Slide rotor and key off pump shaft.
7. Remove oil seal from body.
8. Disassemble flow control relief valve by:
   a. Remove connector, O-ring and flow control valve spring.
   b. Tap cover on soft surface to dislodge valve assembly.
   c. Remove relief valve by pushing valve into flow control valve and removing snap ring. Remove valve and spring.

Assembly

NOTE: Lubricate all parts before assembly.

1. Install new oil seal in pump body. Press seal in place using a driver on outer edge of seal.
2. Install inner rotor and key on shaft and insert shaft and rotor assembly into body, coupling end front.
3. Place outer rotor in body. Be sure rotors are aligned according to marks made during disassembly.
4. Locate O-rings in body and insert thrust washer in cover. Place cover in position on body and tighten to torque.
5. Reassemble flow control relief valve by:
   a. Insert spring and relief valve into flow control valve, small end first.
   b. Push relief valve into flow control valve far enough to allow installation of snap ring.
   c. Install valve assembly into pump body, narrow land first, insert spring and install connector using new O-ring.

Bendix Linkage-Type Power Steering System

The Bendix linkage-type power steering is a hydraulically controlled system composed of an integral pump and fluid reservoir, a control valve, a power cylinder, connecting fluid lines, and the steering linkage. The hydraulic pump, which is driven by a belt turned by the engine, draws fluid from the reservoir and provides pressure through hoses to the control valve and the power cylinder. There is a pressure relief valve to limit the pressures within the steering system to a safe level. After the fluid has passed from the pump to the control valve and the power cylinder, it returns to the reservoir.

CONTROL VALVE CENTERING SPRING

Adjustment

1. Raise the truck and remove the spring cap attaching screws and remove the spring cap.

CAUTION

Be very careful not to position the hoist adapters of two post hoists under the suspension and/or steering components. Place the hoist adapters under the front suspension lower arms.

2. Tighten the adjusting nut snug (about 90–100 inch lbs.); then, loosen the nut $^1/_4$ turn (90 degrees). Do not turn the adjusting nut too tight.
3. Place the spring cap on the valve housing. Lubricate and install the attaching screws and washers. Tighten the screws to 72–100 inch lbs. torque.
4. Lower the truck and start the engine. Check the steering effort using a spring scale attached to the steering wheel rim for a pull of no more than 12 lbs.

POWER STEERING CONTROL VALVE

Removal

1. Raise the truck and support safely. If a two post hoist is

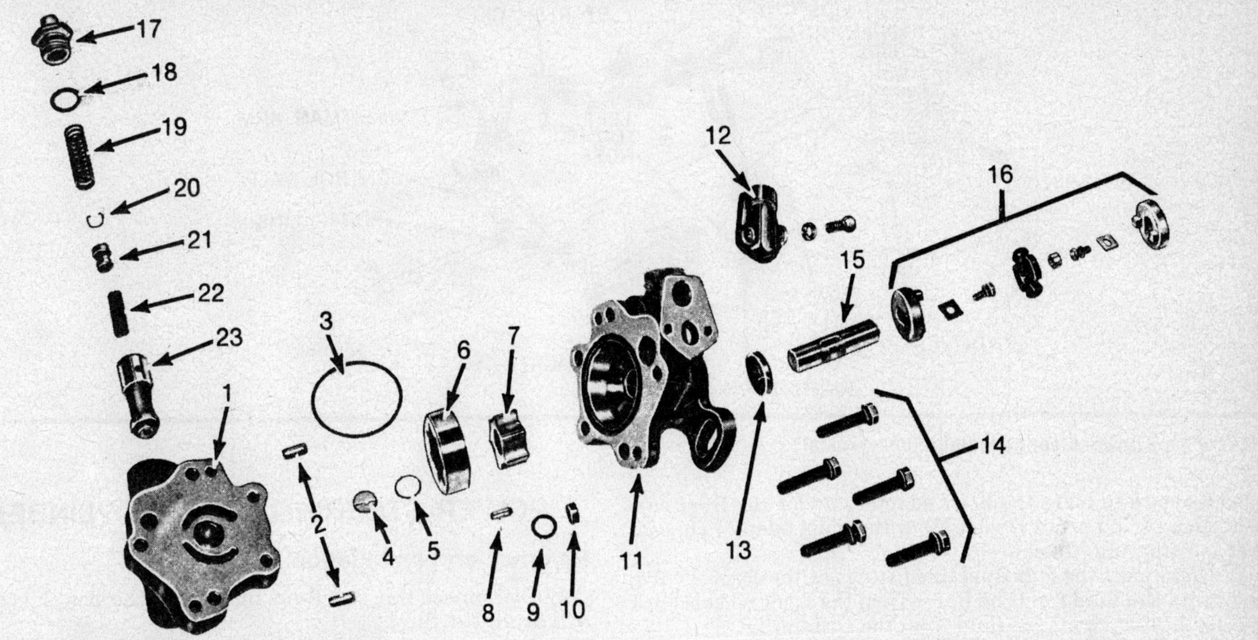

1 Cover
2 Cover dowel
3 Body O-ring
4 Thrust washer
5 Snap ring
6 Outer rotor
7 Inner rotor
8 Drive pin
9 Bypass O-ring
10 Bypass O-ring retainer
11 Body
12 Outlet adapter
13 Oil seal
14 Cover screws
15 Pump shaft
16 Coupling assembly
17 Hose connector
18 Connector O-ring
19 Flow control valve spring
20 Valve retainer snap ring
21 Relief valve
22 Relief valve spring
23 Flow control valve

Exploded view of Eaton pump (© Mack Trucks Inc.)

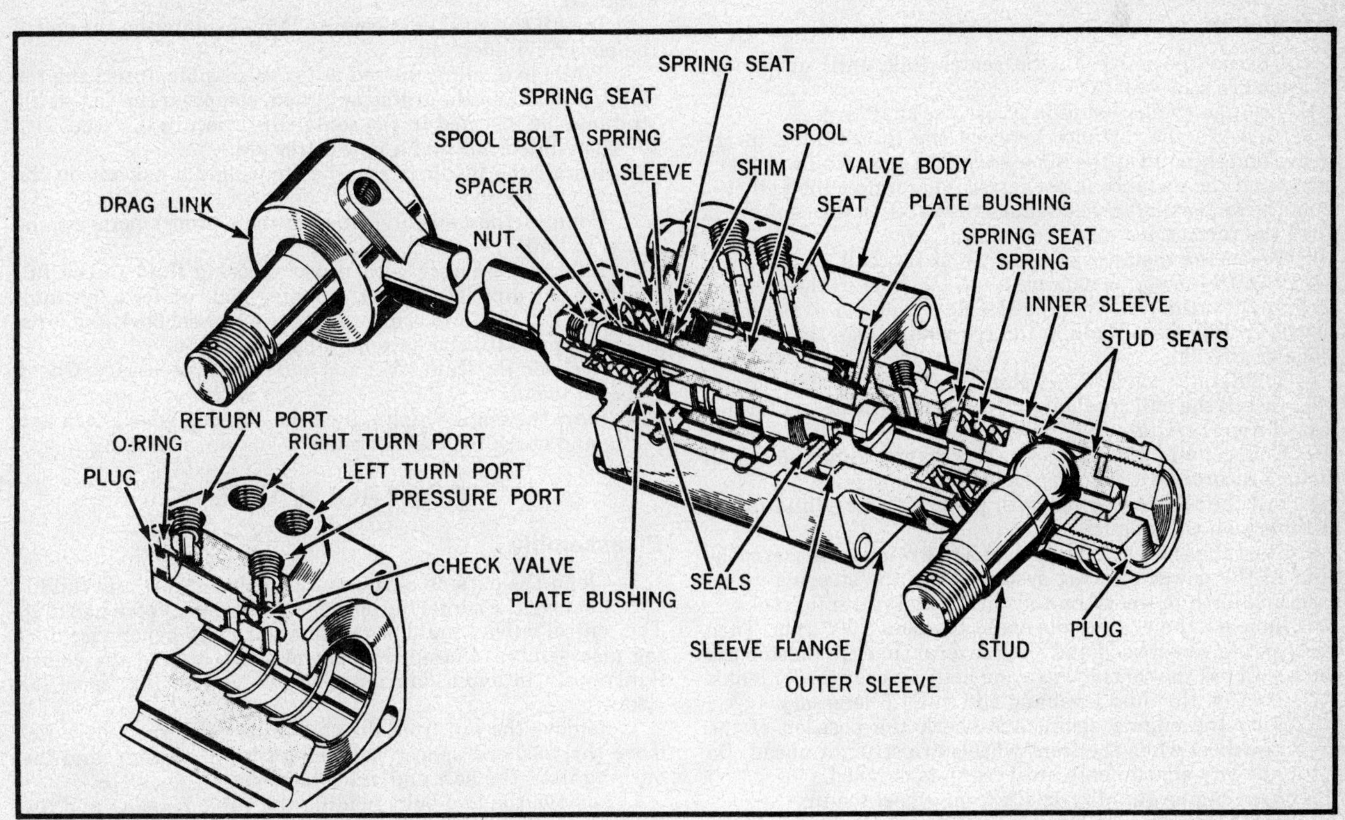

Control valve cross section—typical (© Ford Motor Co.)

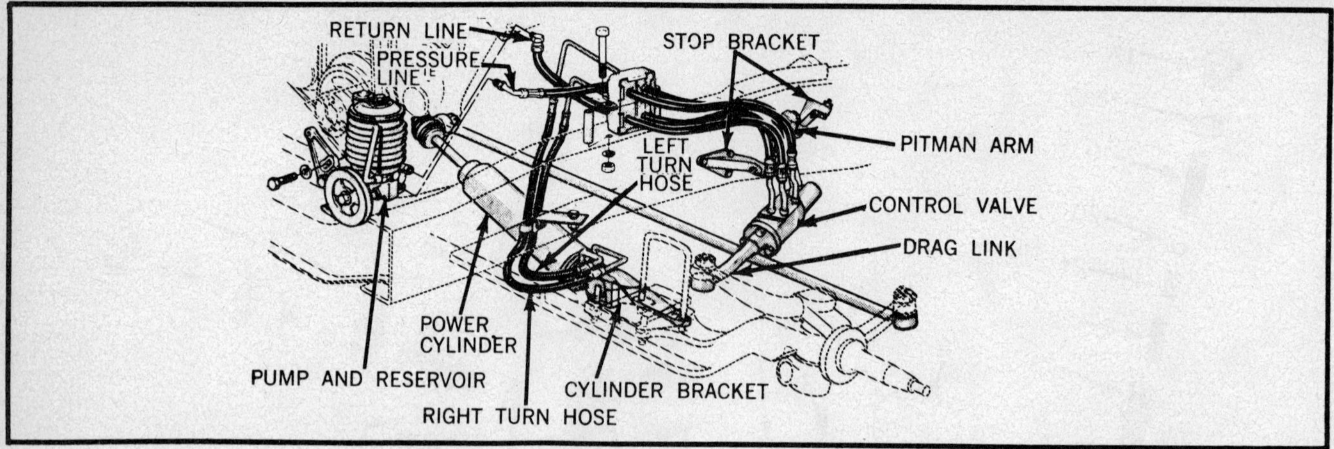

Linkage type power steering installation—typical (© Ford Motor Co.)

used, be sure to place the hoist adapters under the front suspension steering arms. Do not allow the hoist adapters to contact the steering linkage.

2. Disconnect the four fluid line fittings at the control valve and drain the fluid from the lines. Turn the front wheels back and forth to force all the fluid from the system.
3. Loosen the clamping nut and bolt at the right end of the sleeve.
4. Remove the roll pin from the steering arm-to-idler arm rod through the slot in the sleeve.
5. Remove the control valve ball stud nut.
6. Remove the ball stud from the sector shaft arm.
7. After turning the front wheels fully to the left, unthread the control valve from the center link steering arm-to-idler arm rod.

Installation

1. Thread the valve on the center link until about four threads are still visible.
2. Position the ball stud in the sector shaft arm.
3. Measure the distance between the grease plug in the sleeve and the stud at the inner end of the left spindle connecting rod. If the distance is not correct, disconnect the ball stud from the sector shaft arm and turn the valve on the center link until the correct distance is obtained.
4. When the distance is correct and the ball stud is positioned in the sector shaft arm, align the hole in the steering arm-to-idler arm rod with the slot near the end of the valve sleeve. Install the roll pin in the rod hole to lock the valve in place on the rod.
5. Tighten the valve sleeve clamp bolt to the proper torque.
6. Install the ball stud nut and tighten to the proper torque. Install a new cotter pin.
7. Connect all fluid lines to the control valve and tighten all fittings securely. Do not over-tighten.
8. Fill the fluid reservoir with power steering fluid to the full mark on the dipstick.
9. Start the engine and run it for a few minutes to warm the fluid in the power steering system. Turn the steering wheel back and forth to the stops and check the system for leaks.
10. Increase the engine idle speed to about 1000 rpm. Turn the steering wheel back and forth several times, then stop the engine. Check the control valve and hose connections for leaks.
11. Recheck the fluid level and add fluid if necessary.
12. Start the engine again, and check the position of the steering wheel when the front wheels are straight ahead. Do not make any adjustments until toe-in is checked.
13. With engine running, check front wheel toe-in.
14. Check steering wheel turning effort which should be equal in both directions.

POWER STEERING POWER CYLINDER

Removal and Installation

1. Disconnect the two fluid lines from the power cylinder and drain the fluid.
2. Remove the pal nut, attaching nut, washer and the insulator from the end of the power cylinder rod. Remove the cotter pin and castellated nut holding the power cylinder stud to the center link.
3. Disconnect the power cylinder stud from the center link.
4. Remove the insulator sleeve and washer from the end of the power cylinder.
5. Inspect the tube fittings and seats in the power cylinder for nicks, burrs, or other damage. Replace the seats or tubes if damaged.
6. Install the washer, sleeve and the insulator on the end of the power cylinder rod.
7. While extending the rod as far as possible, insert the rod in the bracket on the frame and then, compress the rod so the stud may be inserted in the center link. Secure the stud with the castellated nut and a new cotter pin.
8. Install the insulator, washer, nut, and a pal nut on the power cylinder rod.
9. Connect the two fluid lines to their proper ports on the power cylinder.
10. Fill the reservoir with power steering fluid to the full mark on the dipstick. Start the engine and run for a few minutes to warm the fluid. Turn the steering wheel back and forth to the stops to fill the system. Stop the engine.
11. Recheck the fluid level and add fluid if necessary. Check for fluid leaks.
12. Start the engine again, turn the steering wheel back and forth, and check for leaks while the engine is running.

CONTROL VALVE

Disassembly

1. Clean the outside of the control valve of dirt and fluid.
2. Remove the centering spring cap from the valve housing. The control valve should be put in a soft-faced bench vise during disassembly. Clamp the control valve around the sleeve flange only to avoid damaging the valve housing, spool, or sleeve.
3. Remove the nut from the end of the valve spool bolt. Remove the washers, spacer, centering spring, adapter, and the bushing from the bolt and valve housing.
4. Remove the two bolts holding the valve housing and the sleeve together. Separate the valve housing and the sleeve.
5. Remove the plug from the sleeve. Push the valve spool out

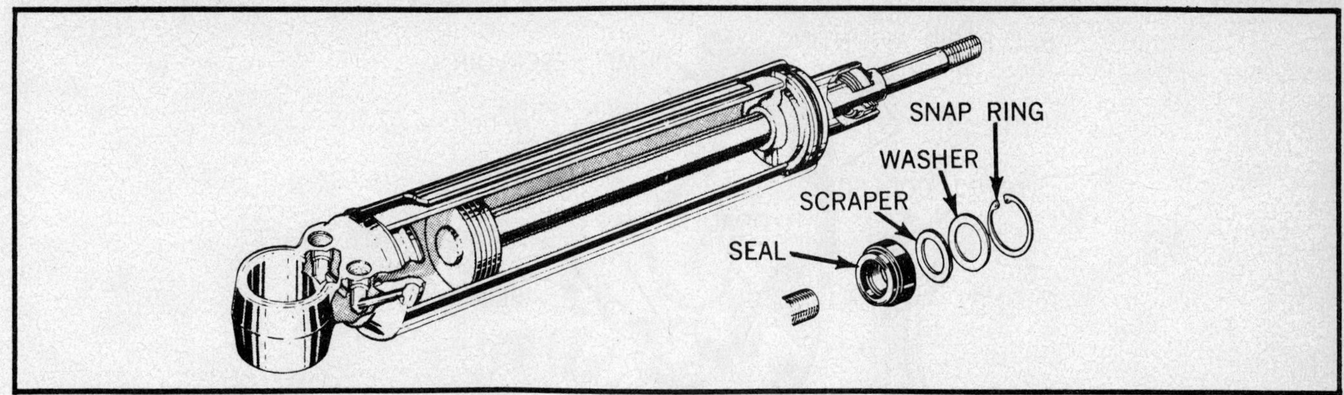

Phantom view of power cylinder—typical (© Ford Motor Co.)

of the centering spring end of the valve housing, and remove the seal from the spool.

6. Remove the spacer, bushing and valve housing.

7. Drive the pin out of the travel regulator stop with a punch and hammer. Pull the head of the valve spool bolt tightly against the travel regulator stop before driving the pin out of the stop.

8. Turn the travel regulator stop counterclockwise in the valve sleeve to remove the stop from the sleeve.

9. Remove the valve spool bolt, spacer, and rubber washer from the travel regulator stop.

10. Remove the rubber boot and clamp from the valve sleeve. Slide the bumper, spring, and ball stud seat out of the valve sleeve and remove the ball stud socket from the sleeve.

11. Remove the return port hose seat and the return port relief valve.

12. Remove the spring plug and O-ring. Then remove the reaction limiting valve.

13. Replace all worn or damaged hose seats by using an Easy-Out screw extractor or a bolt of proper size as a puller. Tap the existing hole in the hose seat, using a starting tap of the correct size. Remove all metal chips from the hose seat after tapping. Place a nut and washer on a bolt of the same size as the tapped hole. The washer must be large enough to cover the hose seat port. Insert the bolt in the tapped hole and remove the hose seat by turning the nut clockwise and drawing the bolt out. Install a new hose seal in the port, and thread a bolt of the correct size in the port. Tighten the bolt enough to bottom the seal in the port.

Assembly

1. Coat all parts of the control valve assembly with power steering fluid. Seals should be coated with lubricant before installation.

2. Install the reaction limiting valve, spring and plug. Install the return port relief valve and the hose seat.

3. Insert one of the ball stud seats (flat end first) into the ball stud socket, and insert the threaded end of the ball stud into the socket.

4. Place the socket in the control valve sleeve so that the threaded end of the ball stud can be pulled out through the slot.

5. Place the other ball stud seat, spring, and bumper in the socket. Install and securely tighten the travel regulator stop.

6. Loosen the stop just enough to align the nearest hole in the stop with the slot in the ball stud socket and install the stop pin in the ball stud socket, travel regulator stop, and valve spool bolt.

7. Install the rubber boot, clamp, and the plug on the control valve sleeve. Be sure the lubrication fitting is turned on tightly and does not bind on the ball stud socket.

8. Insert the valve spool in the valve housing, rotating it while installing it.

9. Move the spool toward the centering spring end of the housing, and place the small seal bushing and spacer in the sleeve end of the housing.

10. Press the valve spool against the inner lip of the seal and, at the same time, guide the lip of the seal over the spool with a small screwdriver. Do not nick or scratch the seal or the spool during installation.

11. Place the sleeve end of the housing on a flat surface so that the seal, bushing and spacer are at the bottom end; then push down the valve spool until it stops.

12. Carefully install the spool seal and bushing in the centering spring end of the housing. Press the seal against the end of the spool, guiding the seal over the spool with a small flat tool. Do not nick or scratch the seal or the spool during installation.

13. Pick up the housing, and slide the spool back and forth in the housing to check for free movement.

14. Place the valve sleeve on the housing so that the ball stud is on the same side of the housing as the ports for the two power cylinder lines. Install the two bolts in the sleeve, and torque them to the proper torque.

15. Place the adapter on the centering spring end of the housing, and install the bushing, washers, spacers and centering spring on the valve spool bolt.

16. Compress the centering spring and install the nut on the bolt. Tighten the nut snug (about 90–100 inch lbs.); then, loosen it not more than $^1/_4$ turn. Do not over-tighten to avoid breaking the stop pin at the travel regulator stop.

17. Move the ball stud back and forth to check for free movement.

18. Lubricate the two cap attaching bolts. Install the centering spring cap on the valve housing, and tighten the two cap bolts to the proper torque.

19. Install the nut on the ball stud so that the valve can be put in a vise. Then, push forward on the cap end of the valve to check the valve spool for free movement.

20. Turn the valve around in the vise, and push forward on the sleeve end to check for free movement.

POWER CYLINDER SEAL

Removal

1. Clamp the power cylinder in a vise and remove the snapring from the end of the cylinder. Do not distort or crack the cylinder in the vise.

2. Pull the piston rod out all the way to remove the scraper, bushing, and seals. If the seals cannot be removed in this manner, remove them by carefully prying them out of the cylinder with a sharp pick. Do not damage the shaft or seal seat.

Installation

1. Coat the new seals with power steering fluid and place the

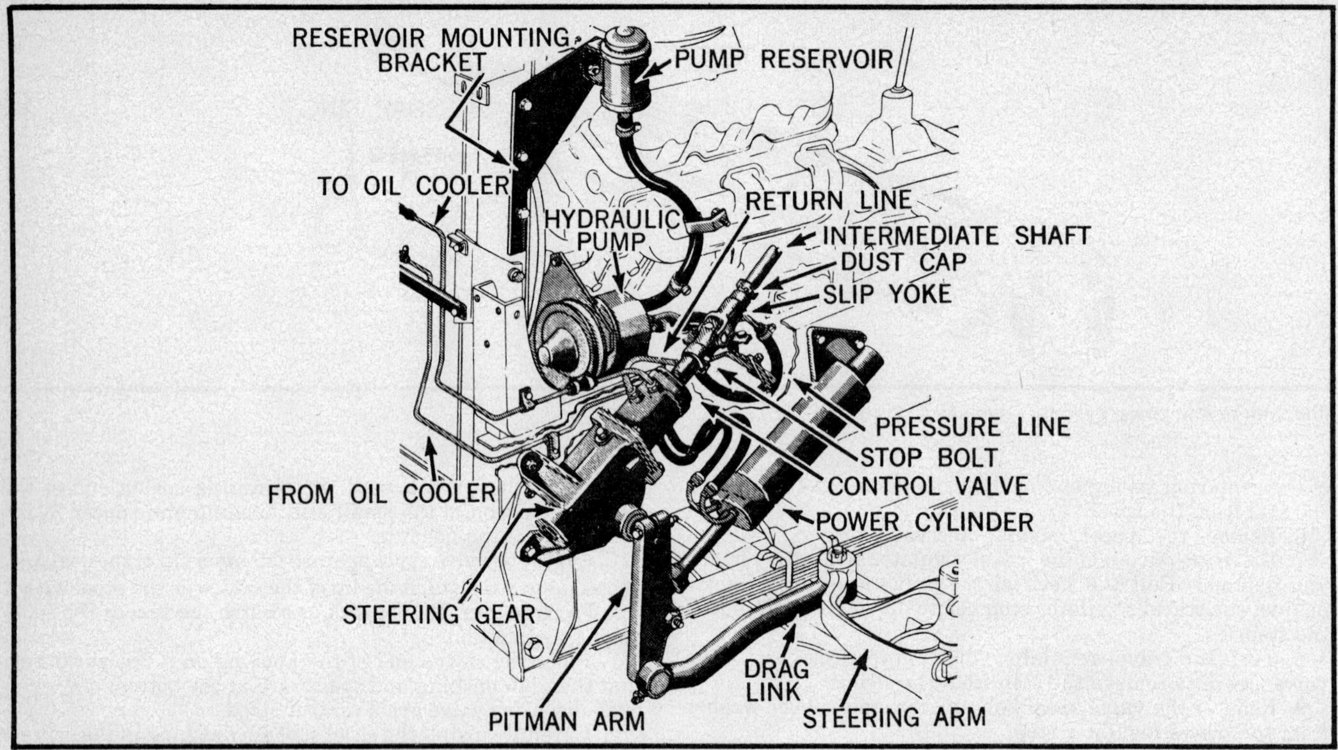

General Motors power steering system—tilt cab—typical (© General Motors Corp.)

parts on the piston rod. Coat with grease or lubricant.

2. Push the rod in all the way, and install the parts in the cylinder with a deep socket slightly smaller than the cylinder opening.

POWER STEERING PUMP

Removal and Replacement

To remove or install the power steering pump, see the section on the slipper type pump.

Saginaw Linkage-Type Power Cylinder

Removal

1. Remove the two hoses which are connected to the cylinder and drain fluid into a container.
2. Remove power cylinder from frame bracket.
3. Remove cotter pin and nut and pull stud out of relay rod.
4. Remove cylinder from vehicle.

Inspection

1. Check seals for leaks around cylinder rod. If leaks are found, replace seals.
2. Check hose connection seats for damage and replace if necessary.
3. For service other than seat or seal replacement, it is necessary to replace the power cylinder.
4. The ball stud may be replaced by removing snap-ring.

Disassembly and Assembly

1. To remove piston rod seal, remove snap-ring and pull out on rod. Remove back-up washer, piston rod scraper and piston rod seal from rod.
2. To remove the ball stud, depress the end plug and remove the snap-ring. Push on the end of the ball stud and the end plug, spring, spring seat, ball stud and seal may be removed. If the ball seat is to be replaced, it must be pressed out.
3. Reverse disassembly procedure. Be sure snap-ring is properly seated.

Installation

1. Install power cylinder on vehicle in reverse of removal procedure.
2. Reconnect the hydraulic lines, fill system and bleed out air as described in the installation and balancing section of control valve servicing.

POWER STEERING HOSES

Carefully inspect the hoses. When installing, be sure to place in such a position as to avoid all chafing or other abuse when making sharp turns.

Saginaw Rotary-Type Power Steering

The rotary-type power steering gear is designed with all components in one housing.

The power cylinder is an integral part of the gear housing. A double-acting type piston allows oil pressure to be applied to either side of the piston. The one-piece piston and power rack is meshed to the sector shaft.

The hydraulic control valve is composed of a sleeve and valve spool. The spool is held in the neutral position by the torsion bar and spool actuator. Twisting of the torsion bar moves the valve spool, allowing oil pressure to be directed to either side of the power piston, depending upon the directional rotation of the steering wheel, to give power assist.

On many trucks of the General Motors Corporation, a modified version of the rotary valve power steering system provides

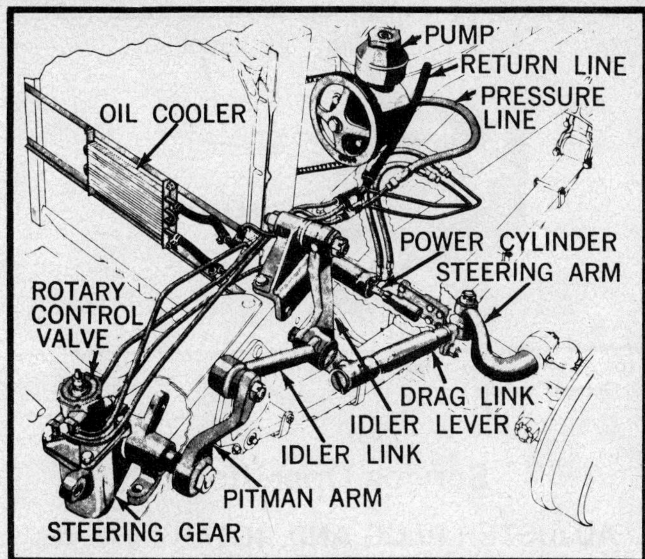

General Motors power steering system—conventional cab—typical (© General Motors Corp.)

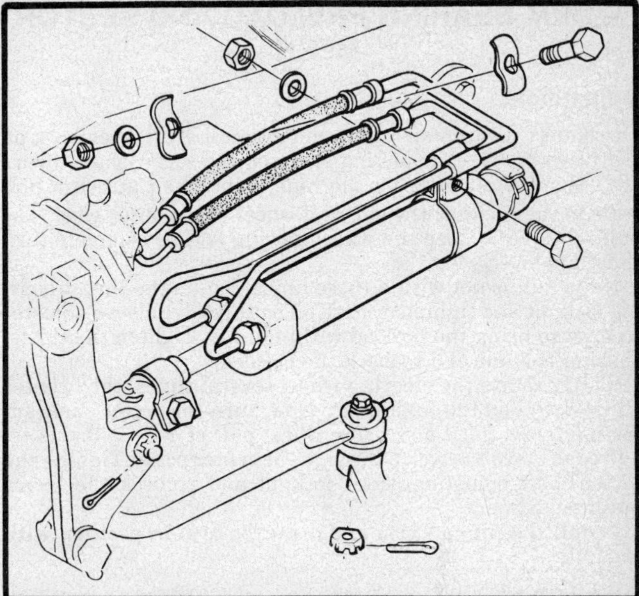

General Motors side mounted power cylinder (© General Motors Corp.)

variable ratio steering to assist the driver to steer the truck easier and safer. The steering gear ratio will vary from a high ratio of about 16:1 while steering straight ahead to a lower gear ratio of about 12.1:1 while making a full turn to either side.

ROLLER PUMP

Removal

Remove the reservoir cover and use a suction gun to empty the reservoir. Disconnect the hoses from the pump and tie them in a raised position to prevent oil drainage. Loosen the pump adjusting screw and remove the pump belt, then take out the retaining bolts and remove the pump and reservoir.

Installation

Position the pump assembly and install the retaining bolts. Be sure there is clearance between the pump bracket and the engine front support bracket. Install the hoses and place the pump belt on the pulley. Adjust the belt to $^1/_2$ in. deflection, then tighten the adjusting screw.

Connect the hoses to the pump assembly. Fill the reservoir to within $^1/_2$ in. of the top with Dexron® 11 automatic transmission fluid.

Start the engine and rotate the steering wheel several times to the right and left to expel air from the system, then recheck the oil level and install the reservoir cover.

POWER STEERING UNIT

This unit uses Dexron®II automatic transmission fluid. The fluid capacity is 4 $^1/_2$ pints.

Bleeding the System

Fill the pump reservoir to within $^1/_2$ in. of the top. Start and run the engine to attain normal operating temperatures. Now, turn the steering wheel through its entire travel three or four times to expel air from the system, then recheck the fluid level.

Checking Steering Effort

Run the engine to attain normal operating temperatures. With the wheels on a dry floor, hook a pull scale to the spoke of the steering wheel at the outer edge. The effort required to turn the steering wheel should be $3^1/_2$–5 lbs. If the pull is not within these limits, check the hydraulic pressure.

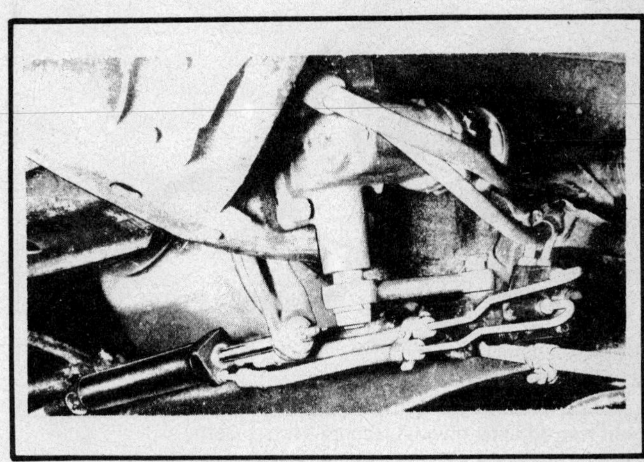

Typical light duty power cylinder (© General Motors Corp.)

Pressure Test

To check the hydraulic pressure, disconnect the pressure hose from the gear. Now connect the pressure gauge between the pressure hose from the pump and the steering gear housing. Run the engine to attain normal operating temperatures, then turn the wheel to a full right and a full left turn to the wheel stops.

Hold the wheel in this position only long enough to obtain an accurate reading.

The pressure gauge reading should be within the limits specified. If the pressure reading is less than the minimum needed for proper operation, close the valve at the gauge and see if the reading increases. If the pressure is still low, the pump is defective and needs repair. If the pressure reading is at or near the minimum reading, the pump is normal and needs only an adjustment of the power steering gear or power assist control valve.

WORM BEARING PRELOAD AND SECTOR MESH

Adjustment

Disconnect the pitman arm from the sector shaft, then back off on the sector shaft adjusting screw on the sector shaft cover.

Center the steering on the high point, then attach a pull scale to the spoke of the steering wheel at the outer edge. The pull required to keep the wheel moving for one complete turn should be $^1/_2$–$^2/_3$ lbs.

If the pull is not within these limits, loosen the thrust bearing locknut and tighten or back off on the valve sleeve adjuster locknut to bring the preload within limits. Tighten the thrust bearing locknut and recheck the preload.

Slowly rotate the steering wheel several times, then center the steering on the high point. Now, turn the sector shaft adjusting screw until a steering wheel pull of 1–1 $^1/_2$ lbs. is required to move the worm through the center point. Tighten the sector shaft adjusting screw locknut and recheck the sector mesh adjustment.

Install the pitman arm and draw the arm in position with the nut.

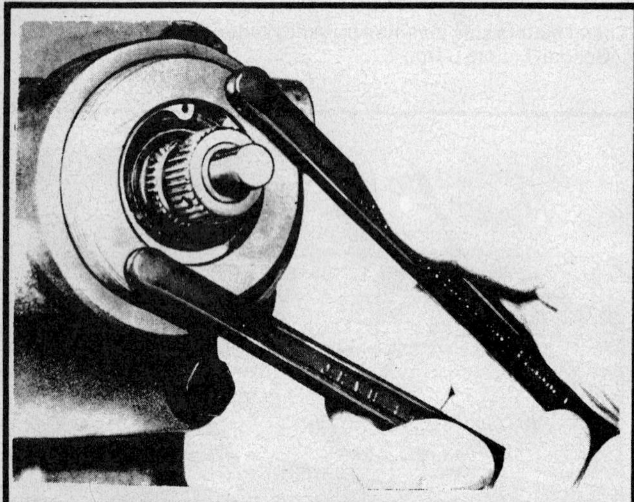

Removing adjuster plug (© General Motors Corp.)

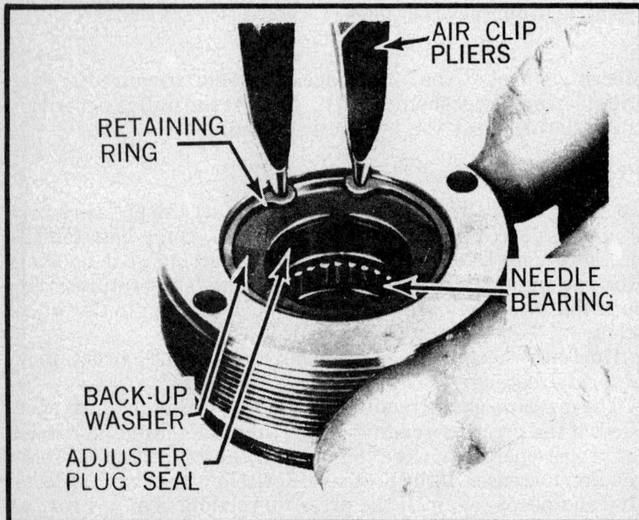

Removing adjuster plug seal retainer ring
(© General Motors Corp.)

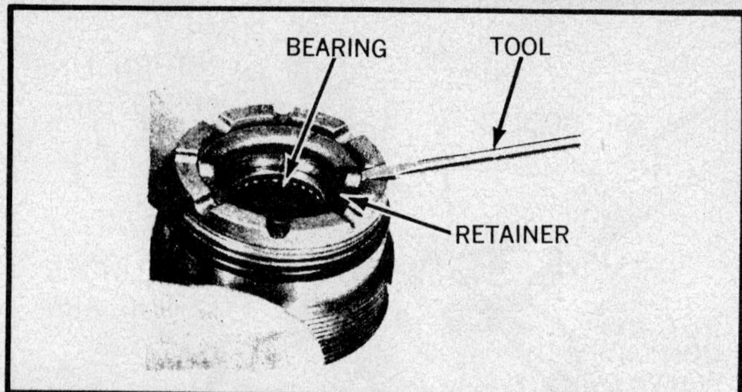

Exploded view of adjuster plug assembly
(© General Motors Corp.)

Service Operations

ADJUSTER PLUG AND ROTARY VALVE

Removal

1. Thoroughly clean exterior of gear assembly. Drain by holding valve ports down and rotating worm back and forth through entire travel.
2. Place gear in vise.
3. Loosen adjuster plug locknut with punch. Remove adjuster plug with spanner.
4. Remove rotary valve assembly by grasping stub shaft and pulling it out.

ADJUSTER PLUG

Disassembly & Assembly

1. Remove upper thrust bearing retainer with screwdriver. Be careful not to damage bearing bore. Discard retainer. Remove spacer, upper bearing and races.
2. Remove and discard adjuster plug O-ring.
3. Remove stub shaft seal retaining ring (Truarc pliers will help) and remove and discard dust seal.
4. Remove stub shaft seal by prying out and discard.
5. Examine needle bearing and, if required, remove same by pressing from thrust bearing end.
6. Inspect thrust bearing spacer, bearing rollers and races.
7. Reassemble in reverse of above.

ROTARY VALVE

Disassembly

Repairs are seldom needed. Do not disassemble unless absolutely necessary. If the O-ring seal on valve spool dampener needs replacement, perform this portion of operation only.

1. Remove cap-to-worm O-ring seal and discard.
2. Remove valve spool spring by prying on small coil with a small tool to work spring onto bearing surface of stub shaft. Slide spring off shaft. Be careful not to damage shaft surface.
3. Remove valve spool by holding the valve assembly in one hand with the stub shaft pointing down. Insert the end of pencil or wood rod through opening in valve body cap and push spool until it is out far enough to be removed. In this procedure, rotate to prevent jamming. If spool becomes jammed it may be necessary to remove stub shaft, torsion bar and cap assembly.

Assembly

NOTE: All parts must be free and clear of dirt, chips, etc., before assembly and must be protected after.

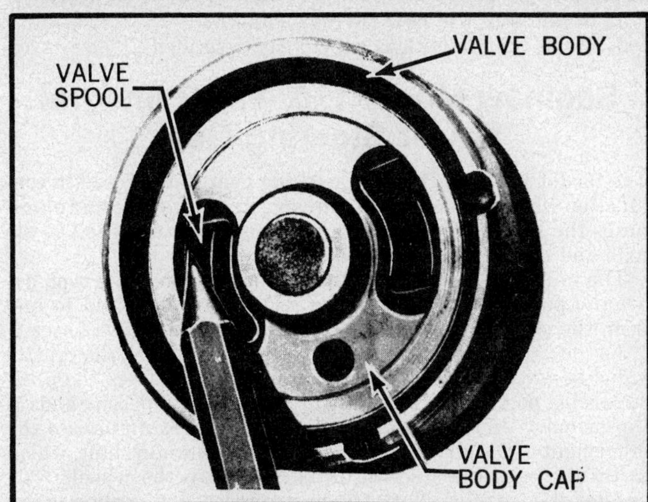

Separating valve spool from valve body (© General Motors Corp.)

1. Lubricate three new back-up O-ring seals with automatic transmission oil and reassemble in the ring grooves of valve body. Assemble three new valve body rings in the grooves over the O-ring seals by carefully slipping over the valve body.

NOTE: If the valve body rings seem loose or twisted in the grooves, the heat of the oil during operation will cause them to straighten.

2. Lubricate a new dampener O-ring with automatic transmission fluid and install in valve spool groove.
3. Assemble stub shaft torsion bar and cap assembly in the valve body, aligning the groove in the valve cap with the pin in the valve body. Tap lightly with soft remainder of assembly. Valve body pin must be in the cap groove. Hold parts together during the remainder of assembly.
4. Lubricate spool. With notch in spool toward valve body, slide the spool over the stub shaft. Align the notch on the spool with the spool drive pin on stub shaft and carefully engage spool in valve body bore. Push spool evenly and with slight rotating motion until it reaches the drive pin. Rotate slowly, with some pressure, until notch engages pin. Be sure dampener O-ring seal is evenly distributed in the spool groove.

CAUTION

Use extreme care because spool to valve body clearance is very small. Damage is easily caused.

5. With seal protector over stub shaft, slide valve spool spring over shaft, with small diameter of spring going over shaft last. Work spring onto shaft until small coil is located in stub shaft groove.
6. Lubricate a new cap to O-ring seal and install in valve body.

ADJUSTER PLUG AND ROTARY VALVE

Installation

1. Align narrow pin slot on valve body with valve body drive pin on the worm. Insert the valve assembly into gear housing by pressing against valve body with finger tips. Do not press on stub shaft or torsion bar. The return hole in the gear housing should be fully visible when properly assembled.

CAUTION

Do not press on stub shaft as this may cause shaft and cap to pull out of valve body, allowing the spool dampener O-ring seal to slip into valve body oil grooves.

2. With seal protector over end of stub shaft, install adjuster plug assembly into gear housing snugly with spanner, then back plug off approximately one-eighth turn. Install plug locknut but do not tighten. Adjust preload as described in the adjustment section.
3. After adjustment, tighten locknut.

PITMAN SHAFT

Removal and Installation

1. Completely drain the gear assembly and thoroughly clean the outside.
2. Place gear in vise.
3. Rotate stub shaft until pitman shaft gear is in center position. Remove side cover retaining bolts.
4. Tap end of pitman shaft with soft hammer and slide shaft out of housing.
5. Remove and discard side cover O-ring seal.
6. The seals, washers, retainers and bearings may now be removed and examined.
7. Examine all parts for wear or damage and replace as required.
8. Install in reverse of above. Make proper adjustment as described in adjustment section.

RACK-PISTON NUT AND WORM ASSEMBLY

Removal

1. Completely drain the gear assembly and thoroughly clean the outside.

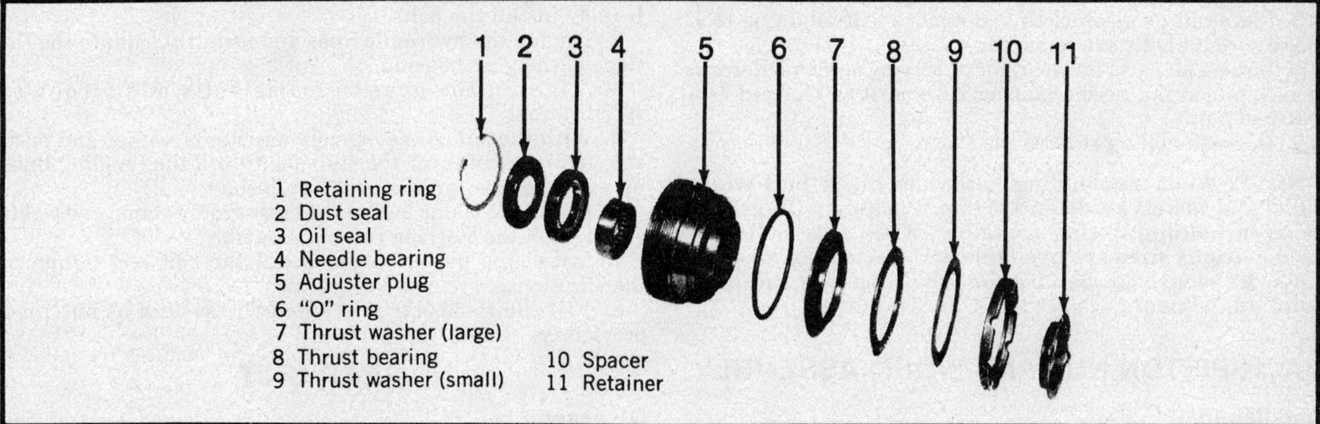

Removing thrust bearing retainer (© General Motors Corp.)

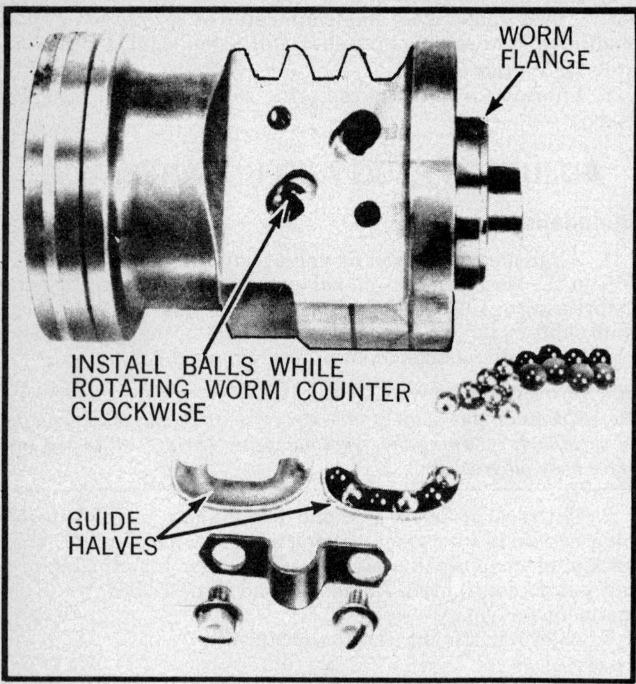

Installing balls in rack piston (© General Motors Corp.)

2. Remove pitman shaft assembly as previously described.
3. Rotate housing end plug retaining ring so that one end of ring is over hole in gear housing. Spring one end of ring so pin punch can be inserted to lift it out.
4. Rotate stub shaft to full left turn position to force end plug out of housing.
5. Remove and discard housing end plug O-ring seal.
6. Remove rack-piston nut end plug with $^{1}/_{2}$ square drive.
7. Insert special tool in end of worm. Turn stub shaft so that rack-piston nut will go into tool and then remove rack-piston nut from gear housing.
8. Remove adjuster plug and rotary valve assemblies as previously described.
9. Remove worm and lower thrust bearing and races.
10. Remove cap O-ring seal and discard.

RACK-PISTON NUT AND WORM

Disassembly and Assembly

1. Remove and discard piston ring and back-up O-ring on rack piston nut.
2. Remove ball guide clamp and return guide.
3. Place nut on clean cloth and remove ball retaining tool. Make sure all balls are removed.
4. Inspect all parts for wear, nicks, scoring or burrs. If worm or rack-pinion nut need replacing, both must be replaced as a matched pair.
5. In reassembling reverse the above.

NOTE: When assembling, alternate black and white balls, and install guide and clamp. Packing with grease helps in holding during assembly. When new balls are used, various sizes are available and a selection must be made to secure proper torque when making the high point adjustment.

RACK-PISTON NUT AND WORM ASSEMBLY

Installation

1. Install in reverse of removal procedure.
2. In all cases use new O-ring seals.
3. Make adjustments as previously described.

Saginaw Model 170, 170-D Integral Power Steering Gear

The model 170, 170-D power steering gear unit is used in conjunction with the heavier pitman and steering arms, and eliminates the need for power cylinder assist units attached to the axle and to the steering linkage.

The unit uses a remote mounted, belt driven, vane type hydraulic pump for fluid pressure and directs the fluid to and from the gear unit by the use of pressure and return hoses.

As the vehicle operator turns the steering wheel, the control valve is moved within the gear housing, and closes the pressure relief port and directs fluid pressure to the opposite ends of the primary and secondary pistons. The pressure assists the movement of the pistons as they rotate the pitman shaft, which in turn, moves the steering linkage to turn the wheels. The greater the turning effort, the more pressure is applied to the piston ends, therefore assuring the operator a smooth hydraulic assist in turning at all times.

As the steering effort to the steering wheel is stopped, the control valve is returned to its neutral position, the fluid pressure to the piston ends are equalized on both sides, the pressure is directed to the relief port and returned to the pump reservoir, and the steering gear is returned to the neutral or straight ahead position.

Adjustments

There are no on-the-vehicle adjustments of the integral type steering gear.

Removal

1. Center the steering gear and remove the pitman arm bolt.
2. Spread the pitman arm clamp boss slightly to remove the arm. Do not spread the arm clamp boss over 0.004 inch.
3. Remove the pot joint to stub shaft clamp bolt, loosen the steering column assembly and pull upward until the shaft coupling clears the stub shaft.
4. Disconnect the hydraulic lines and plug them. Remove the steering gear attaching bolts and with the aid of an assistant, turn the gear in a vertical position and lower the gear between the frame and the inner fender panel.

Installation

1. Install adapter plate to the gear assembly, if removed. (Install the lower forward bolt through the adapter plate before attaching it to the gear housing.)
2. With the gear in a vertical position, (stub shaft up), move the gear upward between the fender panel and the frame. Loosely install the bolts.
3. Unplug the hydraulic lines and install them into the fittings of the gear housing.
4. Tighten the gear to frame bolts and torque to specifications.
5. With the aid of one or more assistants, center and push the steering shaft over the stub shaft until the coupling lines up with the cross groove in the stub shaft.
6. Install the clamp bolt in the cross groove clamp and tighten. Tighten the steering column assembly.
7. Install the pitman arm, install the bolt and torque to specifications.
8. Fill the reservoir and bleed the system as outlined previously.

GEAR UNIT

Disassembly

1. Place the steering gear box in a holding fixture or a vise.

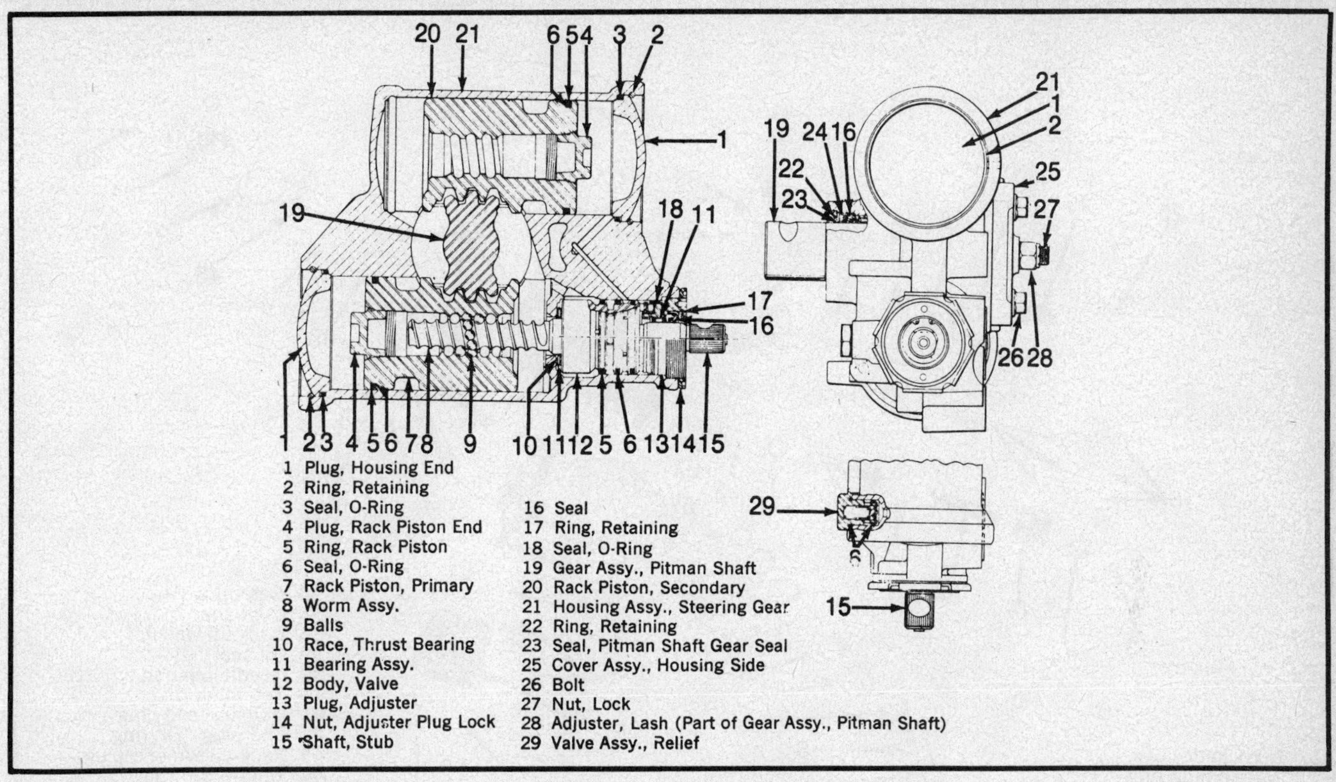

Integral power steering gear and control unit—models 170-170D (© General Motors Corp.)

With a small pin punch, dislodge the end cover retaining rings from their grooves in the primary and secondary piston housings and pry them out.

2. Turn the stub shaft counterclockwise to force the cover from the primary cylinder. Remove the cover and O- ring seal.

3. Remove the rack piston end plug, the sector preload adjuster nut, and the four side cover bolts.

4. Using a $^1/_4$ in. Allen wrench, turn the preload adjusting nut clockwise until the side cover separates from the sector shaft and remove the cover.

5. Turn the stub shaft counterclockwise until the sector shaft teeth are out of engagement with the teeth of the rack piston.

NOTE: The secondary piston end cover is stuck, turn the stub shaft counterclockwise until the rack piston bottoms in the housing, then engage the sector end tooth in the center tooth spacing on the primary rack piston. Turn the stub shaft counterclockwise until the secondary rack piston forces the end cover from the housing.

6. Remove the secondary rack piston from the bore in the gear housing. Do not remove the end plug unless it is to be replaced.

7. Rotate the stub shaft clockwise until the teeth of the sector and the rack piston clear each other and the rack piston can move freely.

8. Insert a ball retainer tool or its equivalent into the bore of the rack piston. Turn the stub shaft counterclockwise while holding the tool firmly against the worm, forcing the rack piston over the tool and retaining the recirculating balls in place. Remove the rack piston from the housing.

9. Rotate the sector shaft teeth to clear the housing and remove the shaft from the gear housing.

10. Remove the adjuster plug lock nut and with the aid of a spanner wrench, remove the adjuster plug from the stub shaft end of the gear housing.

11. Remove the valve and worm as an assembly with the thrust bearings and races and separate the worm from the valve assembly.

ADJUSTER PLUG

Disassembly and Assembly

1. Reinstall the adjuster plug into the gear housing and snug it finger tight. Remove the snap retaining ring and the back-up washer.

2. Remove the seal from the plug by prying the seal outward, being careful not to damage the bore.

3. Pry the thrust bearing retainer from the bore. Remove the spacer, washer, bearing and second washer.

4. The needle bearing assembly can be removed from the plug by driving it out.

5. The assembly of the plug can be accomplished by the reversal of the disassembly procedure. Install new O-rings, seals, and bearings as needed and lubricate the parts with power steering fluid.

VALVE AND STUB SHAFT

Disassembly and Assembly

1. Hold the valve assembly by hand with the stub shaft down. Lightly tap the stub shaft against a wood block until the cap is raised from the valve body approximately $^1/_4$ inch.

2. Remove the shaft assembly from the spool by disengaging the shaft pin, and remove the spool from the valve body by rotating it.

3. Remove and discard the O-rings and replace the teflon rings if needed.

4. The assembly is in the reverse of disassembly. All parts should be lubricated with power steering fluid.

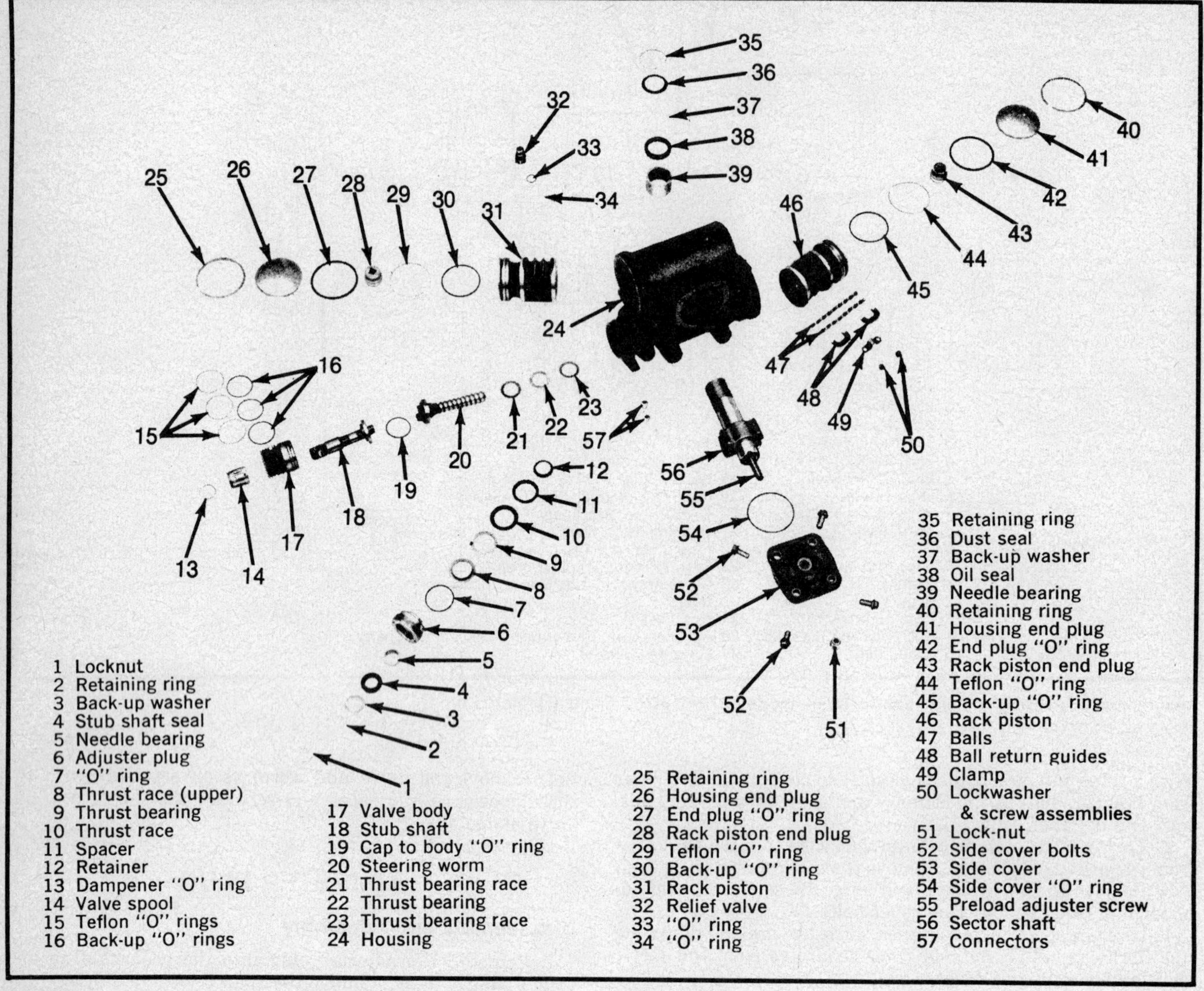

Exploded view of models 170–170D steering gear (© Chrysler Corp.)

NOTE: The valve body pin must mate with the cap notch before the valve body is assembled into the gear assembly and a new O-ring placed in the shaft end of the valve body assembly.

PRIMARY RACK PISTON

Disassembly

1. Remove the two screws from the ball return clamp. Remove the guide, retaining tool and the recirculating balls.
2. Remove the teflon ring and O-ring from the rack piston.

Assembly

1. Install the teflon and O-rings.
2. Slide the worm into the rack piston and rotate the worm to align the grooves with the ball return guide hole nearest the piston ring.
3. While turning the worm shaft, feed 28 balls into the rack piston.

NOTE: The silver and black balls must be alternately installed as the black balls are 0.005 inch smaller than the silver balls.

4. Place the remaining 6 balls alternately into the ball return guide, holding the balls in place with grease. Install the guide into the holes of the rack piston, retaining with the guide clamps and screws.
5. Install the ball retaining tool in place of the worm shaft, being careful not to allow any balls to drop.

NOTE: When installing the teflon rings, looseness will be noticed. The teflon rings will heat-shrink when the gear is operated. Therefore, care must be exercised when assembling the internal parts into the housing, to insure that all parts are lubricated with power steering fluid and not forced during the reassembly. The seals and O-rings may be damaged if this is allowed to happen.

SECONDARY RACK PISTON

No disassembly is necessary on this unit unless the teflon and O-rings are to be replaced.

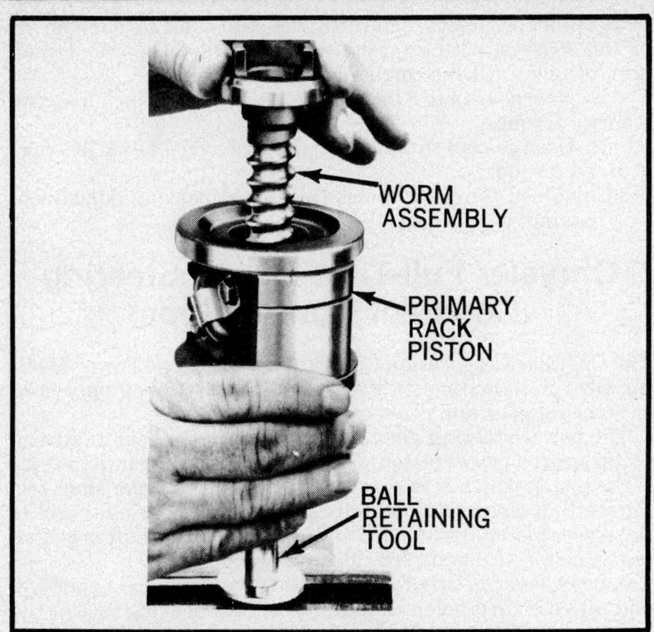

Removing worm shaft while installing a ball retainer tool
(© Chrysler Corp.)

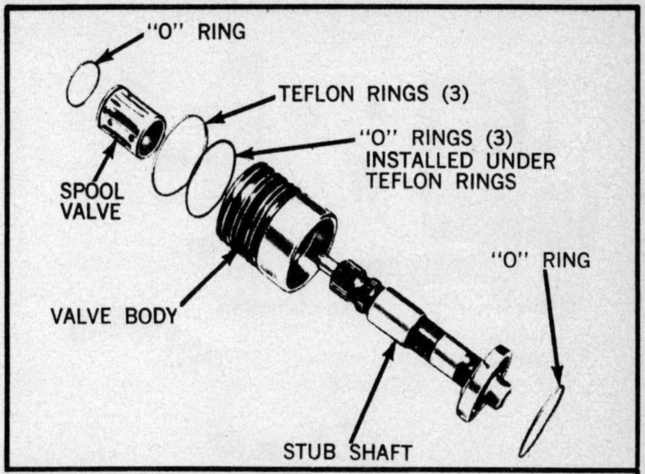

Exploded view of valve body and stub shaft (© Chrysler Corp.)

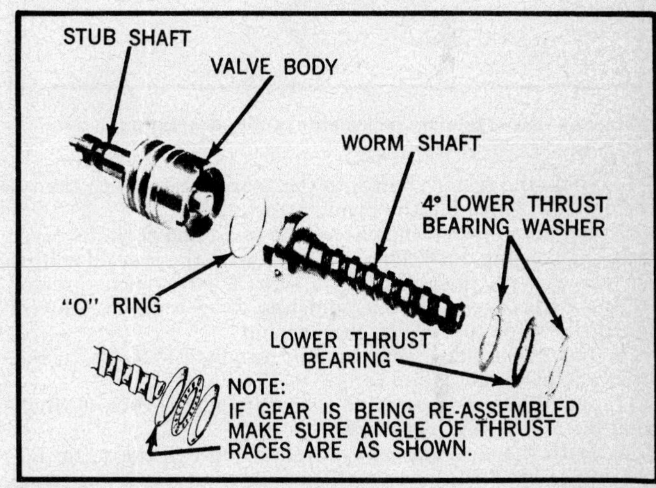

Exploded view of worm shaft and valve body (© Chrysler Corp.)

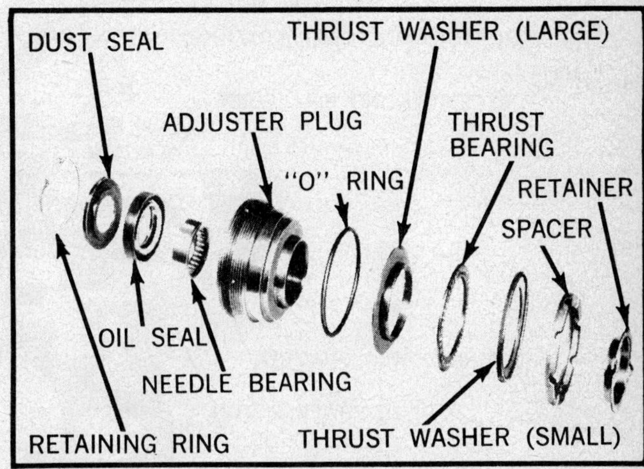

Exploded view of adjuster plug (© Chrysler Corp.)

GEAR UNIT

Assembly and Adjustment

1. Install the thrust washer, bearing and second thrust washer over the end of the worm and lubricate with power steering fluid.

NOTE: The tapered surfaces of the washers should be parallel to each other and the cupped side towards the stub shaft.

2. Install the O-ring in the valve body so that it is seated against the lower shaft cap and lubricate the valve body, rings and seals with power steering fluid.
3. Align the narrow notch in the valve body with the pin in the worm and install the unit into the gear housing, by exerting pressure on the valve body and not the stub shaft.
4. The return hole in the gear housing should be fully uncovered when the valve body is fully seated. Screw in the adjuster plug assembly and seat it against the valve body.
5. Adjust the thrust bearing preload by torquing the adjuster plug to 20 ft. lbs. to seat the thrust bearings.
6. Mark the steering housing in line with one of the tool hole locations on the adjuster plug. Measure counterclockwise $^3/_{16}$ to $^1/_4$ inch and remark the housing.
7. Loosen the adjuster until the tool hole is in line with the second mark on the steering housing and install the lock nut and tighten while maintaining the alignment of the adjuster tool hole with the mark on the housing.
8. With the aid of a torque wrench, turn the stub shaft evenly and observe the torque reading. The reading should be from 4 to 10 inch pounds.
9. Continue the adjustment as necessary to obtain the specified torque reading.
10. With the ball retaining tool in position, lubricate and install the primary rack piston into the gear housing until the retaining tool bottoms against the center of the worm.
11. Turn the stub shaft clockwise to thread the rack piston onto the worm. Keep the retaining tool tight against the worm while turning the stub shaft.
12. Remove the ball retainer tool when the rack piston is completely threaded onto the worm. Center the rack teeth in the sector shaft opening.
13. Install the secondary rack piston in the gear housing and line up the center tooth space with the teeth of the primary rack piston.

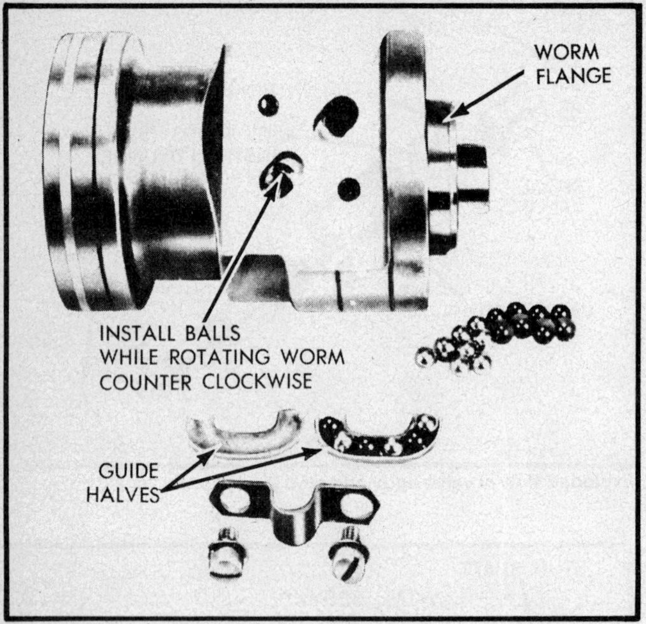

Exploded view of primary rack piston (© Chrysler Corp.)

14. Slide the sector shaft into the gear housing with the tapered teeth engaging the primary rack piston.
15. Install a new O-ring on the side cover and push the cover into the housing until contact is made with the preload adjuster screw. With the aid of a $^{1}/_{4}$ inch Allen wrench inserted through the cover, turn the adjusting screw counterclockwise until the cover bottoms on the housing.
16. Install the side cover bolts and torque to 45 ft. lbs. Install the rack piston plug and torque to 75 ft. lbs.
17. Install the primary and secondary end covers, O-rings, and install the retainer rings.
18. With the steering gear on center, tighten the sector adjusting screw. Install and tighten the lock nut and check the overcenter torque while rotating the stub shaft through an arc of 180 degrees, with a torque wrench. Adjust the sector shaft accordingly until the correct torque is obtained.

a. New gears 4 to 8 inch lbs., but not over 18 inch lbs. combined torque.

b. Used gears 4 to 5 inch lbs., but not over 14 inch lbs. combined torque.

c. Combined torque includes the thrust bearing adjustment reading, over-center and internal friction.

Chrysler Full-Time Power Steering (Constant Control Type)

The Chrysler Corporation Constant Control Type Power Steering Gear System consists of a hydraulic pressure pump, a power steering gear and connecting hoses.

The power steering gear housing contains a gear shaft and sector gear, a power piston with gear teeth milled into the side of the piston which is in constant mesh with the gear shaft sector teeth, a worm shaft which connects the steering wheel to the power piston through a coupling. The worm shaft is geared to the piston through recirculating ball contact.

A pivot lever is fitted into the spool valve at the upper end and into a drilled hole in the center thrust bearing race at the lower end. The center thrust bearing race is held firmly against the shoulder of the worm shaft by two thrust bearings, bearing races and an adjusting nut. The pivot lever pivots in the spacer which is held in place by the pressure plate.

When the steering wheel is turned to the left the worm shaft moves out of the power piston a few thousandths of an inch, the center thrust bearing race moves the same distance since it is clamped to the worm shaft. The race thus tips the pivot lever and moves the spool valve down, allowing oil under pressure to flow into the left-turn power chamber and force the power piston down. As the power piston moves, it rotates the cross-shaft sector gear and, through the steering linkage, turns the front wheels.

On a right turn the worm shaft moves into the power piston, the center thrust bearing race thus tips the pivot lever and moves the spool valve up, allowing oil under pressure to flow into the right power chamber and force the power piston up.

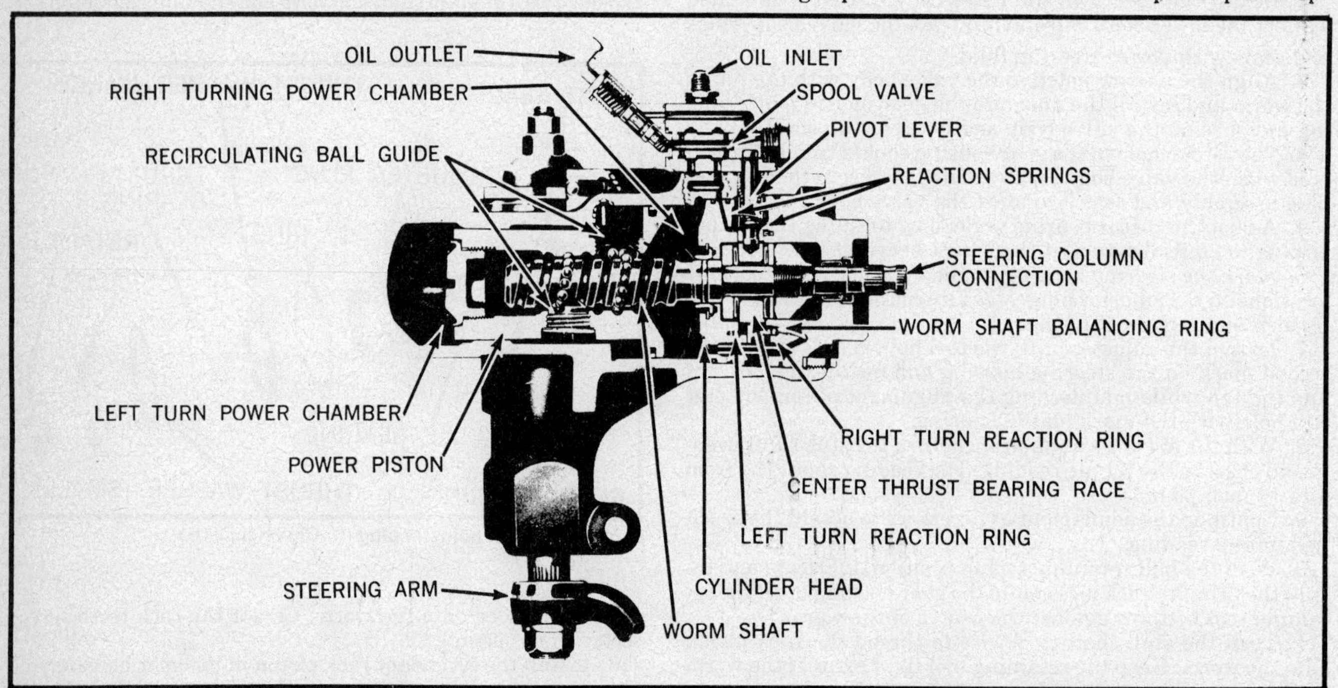

Cross section of Chrysler power steering gear (© Chrysler Corp.)

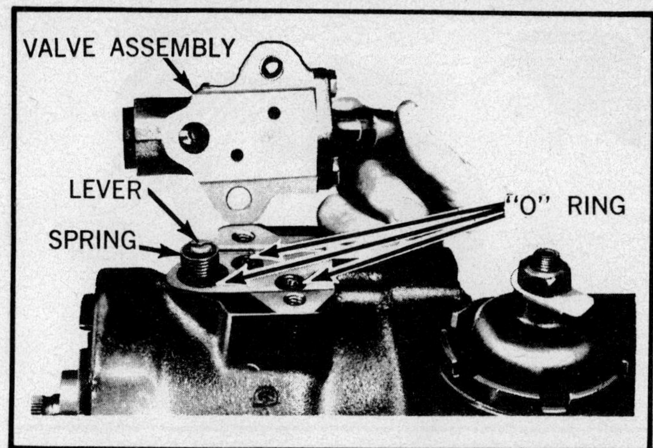

Removing valve body assembly (© Chrysler Corp.)

Removing pilot lever (© Chrysler Corp.)

Pressure Test

Connect the pressure test hoses with the pressure gauge installed between the pump and steering gear.

Now, fill the reservoir to the level mark, then start the engine and bleed the system. Allow the engine to idle until the fluid in the reservoir is between 150° F. and 170° F. Now turn the steering wheel to the extreme right and check the pressure reading, then turn to the extreme left and check the reading again. The gauge reading should be equal in each direction. If not, it indicates excessive internal leakage in the unit.

The pressure should agree with the specifications in Pump section for satisfactory power steering operation.

Reconditioning

1. Drain gear by turning worm shaft from limit to limit with oil connections held downward. Thoroughly clean outside.
2. Remove valve body attaching screws, body and three O-rings.
3. Remove pivot lever and spring. Pry under spherical head with a small bar.

NOTE: Take care not to collapse slotted end of valve lever as this will destroy bearing tolerances of the spherical head.

4. Remove steering gear arm from sector shaft.
5. Remove snap-ring and seal back-up washer.
6. Remove seal, using proper tool to prevent damage to relative parts.
7. Loosen gear shaft adjusting screw locknut and remove gear shaft cover nut.
8. Rotate wormshaft to position sector teeth at center of piston travel. Loosen power train retaining nut.

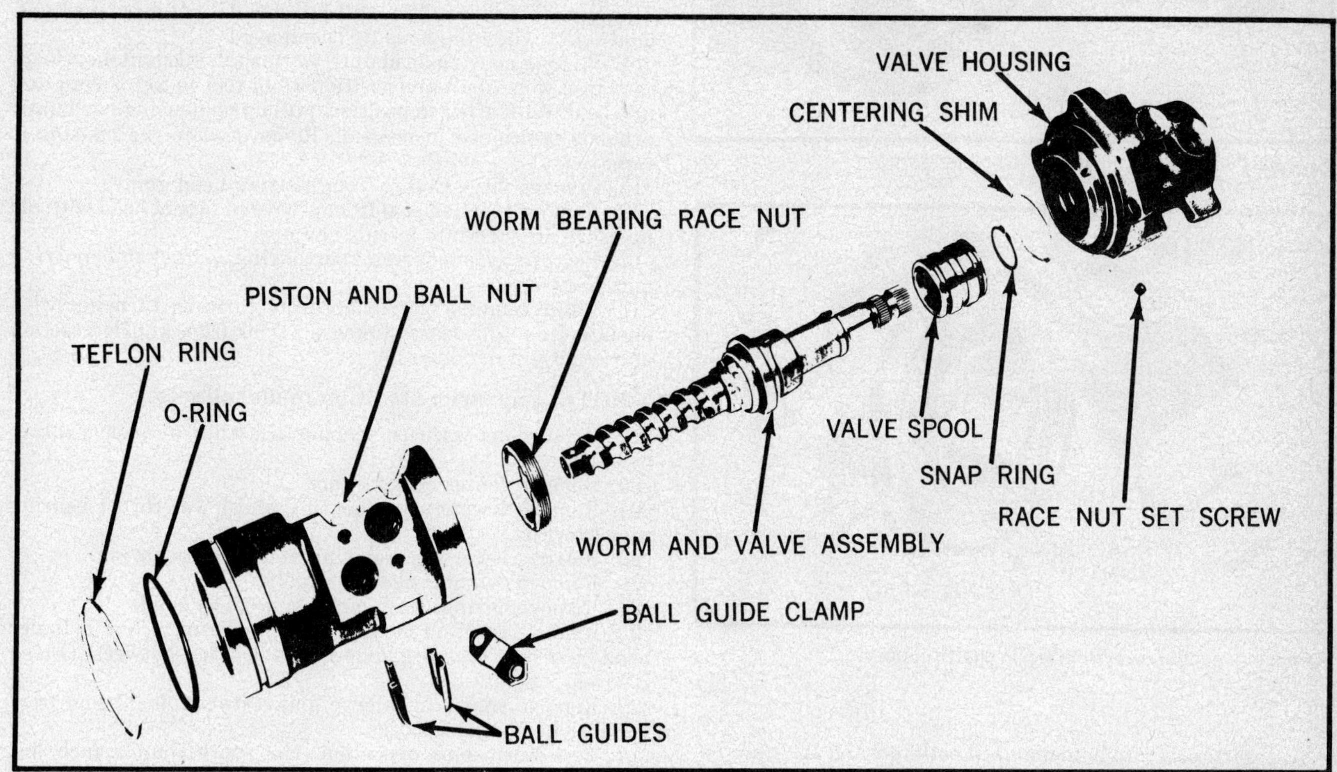

Ball nut and valve housing (© Ford Motor Co.)

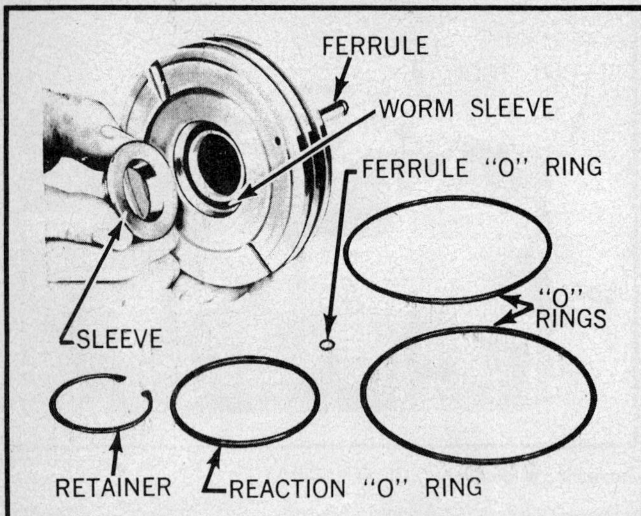

Removing cylinder head oil seal (© Chrysler Corp.)

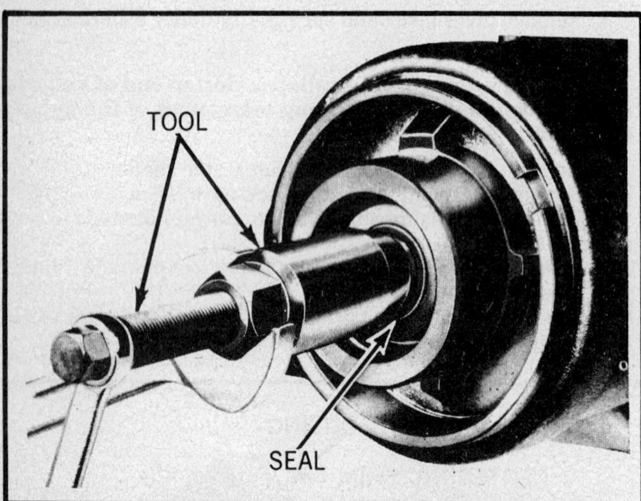

Removing worm shaft oil seal (© Chrysler Corp.)

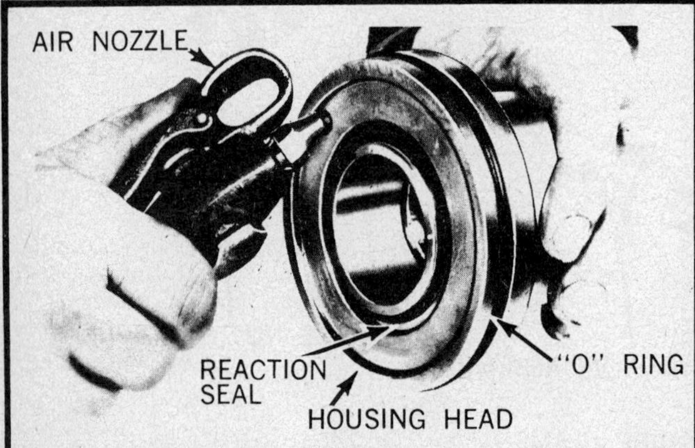

Removing reaction seal from worm shaft support (© Chrysler Corp.)

9. Insert tools into housing until both tool and shaft are engaged with bearings.
10. Turn worm shaft either to full left or full right (depending

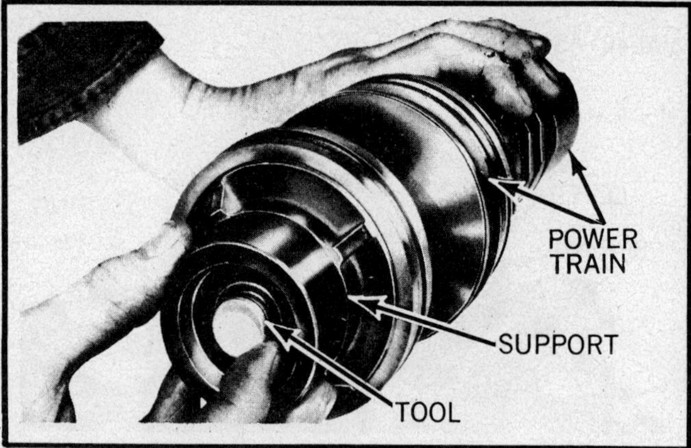

Retaining bearing rollers with arbor tool (© Chrysler Corp.)

on car application) to compress power train parts. Then remove power train retaining nut as mentioned above.
11. Remove housing head tang washer.
12. While holding power train completely compressed, pry on piston teeth with a small bar, using shaft as a fulcrum, and remove complete power train.

NOTE: Maintain close contact between cylinder head, center race and spacer assembly and the housing head. This will eliminate the possibility of reactor rings becoming disengaged from their grooves in cylinder and housing head. It will prohibit center spacer from separating from center race and cocking in the housing. This could make it impossible to remove the power train without damaging involved parts.

13. Place power train in soft-jawed vise in vertical position. The worm bearing rollers will fall out. Use of arbor tool will hold roller when the housing is removed.
14. Raising housing head until wormshaft oil shaft just clears the top of wormshaft and position arbor tool on top of shaft and into seal. With arbor in position, pull up on housing head until arbor is positioned in bearing. Remove when the housing is removed.
15. Remove large O-ring from housing head groove.
16. Remove reaction seal from groove in face of head with air pressure directed into ferrule chamber.
17. Remove reactor spring, reactor ring, worm balancing ring and spacer.
18. While holding wormshaft from turning, turn nut with enough force to release staked portions from knurled section and remove nut.

NOTE: Pay strict attention to cleanliness.

19. Remove upper thrust bearing race (thin) and upper thrust bearing.
20. Remove center bearing race.
21. Remove lower thrust bearing and lower thrust bearing race (thick).
22. Remove lower reaction ring and reaction spring.
23. Remove cylinder head assembly.
24. Remove O-rings from outer grooves in head.
25. Remove reaction O-ring from groove in face of cylinder head. Use air pressure in oil hole located between O-ring grooves.
26. Remove snap-ring, sleeve and rectangular oil seal from cylinder head counterbore.
27. Test wormshaft operation. Not more than 2 inch lbs. should be required to turn it through its entire travel, and with a 15 ft. lb. side load.

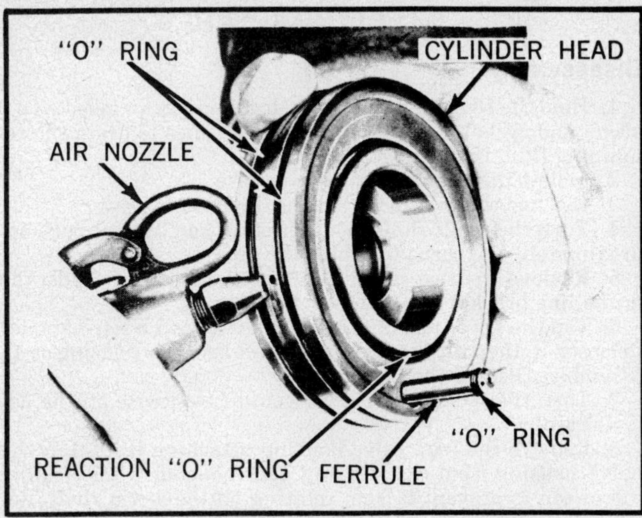

Removing reaction seal from cylinder head (© Chrysler Corp.)

NOTE: The worm and piston is serviced as a complete assembly and should not be disassembled.

28. Shaft side play should not exceed 0.008 in. under light pull applied 2 $^{5}/_{16}$ in. from piston flange.
29. Assemble in reverse of above, noting proper adjustments and preload requirements following.
30. When cover nut is installed, tighten to 20 ft. lbs. torque.
31. Valve mounting screws should be tightened to 200 inch lbs. torque.
32. With hoses connected, system bled, and engine idling roughly, center valve unit until not self-steering. Tap on head of valve body attaching screws to move valve body up, and tap on end plug to move valve body down.
33. With steering gear on center, tighten gear shaft adjusting screw until lash just disappears.
34. Continue to tighten $^{3}/_{8}$ to $^{1}/_{2}$ turn and tighten locknut to 50 ft. lbs.

Ford Integral Power Steering Gear

The Ford integral power steering unit is a torsion-bar type.

The torsion bar power steering unit includes a worm and one-piece rack piston, which is meshed to the gear teeth on the steering sector shaft. The unit also includes a hydraulic valve, valve actuator, input shaft and torsion bar assembly which are mounted on the end of the worm shaft and operated by the twisting action of the torsion bar.

The torsion-bar type of power steering gear is designed with the one piece rack-piston, worm and sector shaft in one housing and the valve spool in an attaching housing. This makes possible internal fluid passages between the valve and cylinder, thus eliminating all external lines and hoses, except the pressure and return hoses between the pump and gear assembly.

The power cylinder is an integral part of the gear housing. The piston is double acting, in that fluid pressure may be applied to either side of the piston.

A selective metal shim, located in the valve housing of the gear is for the purpose of tailoring steering gear efforts. If efforts are not within specifications they can be changed by increasing or decreasing shim thickness as follows:

1. Efforts heavy to the left-increase shim thickness.
2. Efforts light to the left-decrease shim thickness.

Adjustments

The only adjustment which can be performed is the total over center position load, to eliminate excessive lash between the sector and rack teeth.

1. Disconnect the Pitman arm from the sector shaft.
2. Disconnect the fluid return line at the reservoir, at the same time cap the reservoir return line pipe.
3. Place the end of the return line in a clean container and cycle the steering wheel in both directions as required, to discharge the fluid from the gear.
4. Turn the steering wheel to 45 degrees from the left stop.
5. Using an in. lb. torque wrench on the steering wheel nut, determine the torque required to rotate the shaft slowly through an approximately $^{1}/_{8}$ turn from the 45 degree position.
6. Turn the steering gear back to center, then determine the torque required to rotate the shaft back and forth across the center position. Loosen the adjuster nut, and turn the adjuster screw until the reading is 11–12 inch lbs. greater than the torque 45 degrees from the stop. Tighten the lock nut while holding the screw in place.
7. Recheck the readings and replace the Pitman arm and the steering wheel hub cover.
8. Correct the fluid return line to the reservoir and fill the reservoir with specified lubricant to the proper level.

VALVE CENTERING SHIM

Removal and Installation

1. Hold the steering gear over a drain pan in an inverted position and cycle the input shaft several times to drain the remaining fluid from the gear.
2. Mount the gear in a soft-jawed vise.
3. Turn the input shaft to either stop then, turn it back approximately $1^{3}/_{4}$ turns to center the gear.
4. Remove the two sector shaft cover attaching screws, the brake line bracket and the identification tag.
5. Tap the lower end of the sector shaft with a soft-faced hammer to loosen it, then lift the cover and shaft from the housing as an assembly. Discard the O-ring.
6. Remove the four valve housing attaching bolts. Lift the valve housing from the steering gear housing while holding the piston to prevent it from rotating off the worm shaft.
7. Remove the valve housing and the lube passage O-rings and discard them.
8. Place the valve housing, worm and piston assembly in the bench mounted holding fixture with the piston on the top.
9. Rotate the piston upward (back off) 3 $^{1}/_{2}$ turns.
10. Insert tool T66P–3553–C or equivalent (with the arm facing away from the piston) into a bolt hole in the valve housing. Rotate the arm into position under the piston.
11. Loosen the Allen head race nut set screw from the valve housing.
12. Using tool T66P–3553–B or equivalent, loosen the worm bearing race nut.
13. Lift the piston-worm assembly from the valve housing. During removal hold the piston to prevent it from spinning off at the shaft.
14. Change the power steering valve cèntering shim.
15. Install the piston-worm assembly into the valve housing. Hold the piston worm to prevent it from spinning off of the shaft.
16. Install the worm bearing race nut and torque to 2–8 inch lbs. using tool T66P–3553–B or equivalent.
17. Install the race nut set screw (Allen head) through the valve housing.
18. Rotate the piston upward (back off) $^{1}/_{2}$ turn and remove tool T66P–3553–C or equivalent.
19. Remove the valve housing, worm, and piston assembly from the holding fixture.
20. Position a new lube passage O-ring in the counterbore of the gear housing.
21. Apply vaseline to the teflon seal on the piston.
22. Place a new O-ring on the valve housing.

23. Slide the piston and valve into the gear housing being careful not to damage the teflon seal.

24. Align the lube passage in the valve housing with the one in the gear housing, and install but do not tighten the attaching bolts.

25. Rotate the ball nut so that the teeth are in the same place as the sector teeth. Tighten the four valve housing attaching bolts to 35–45 ft. lbs.

26. Position the sector shaft cover O-ring in the steering gear housing. Turn the input shaft as required to center the piston.

27. Apply vaseline to the sector shaft journal; then, position the sector shaft and cover assembly in the gear housing. Install the brake line bracket, steering gear identification tag and the two sector shaft cover attaching studs.

28. Position an in. lb. torque wrench on the gear input shaft and adjust the meshload to approximately 4 inch lbs. Then, torque the sector shaft cover attaching studs to 55–70 ft. lbs.

29. After the cover attaching bolts have been tightened to specification, adjust the mesh load to 17 inch lbs. with an in. lb. torque wrench.

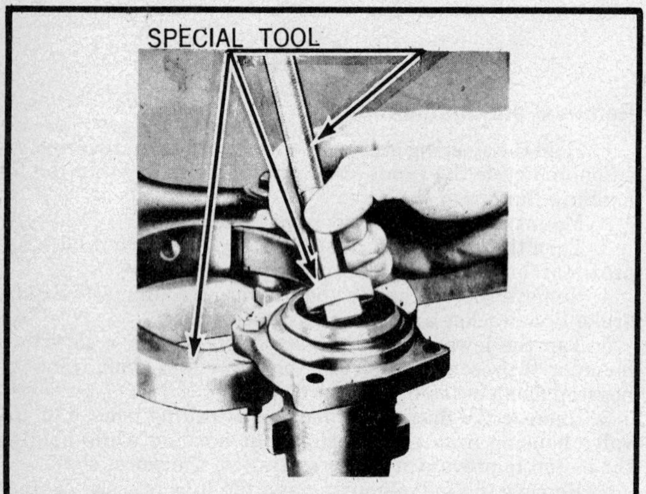

Removing bearing and oil seal (© Ford Motor Co.)

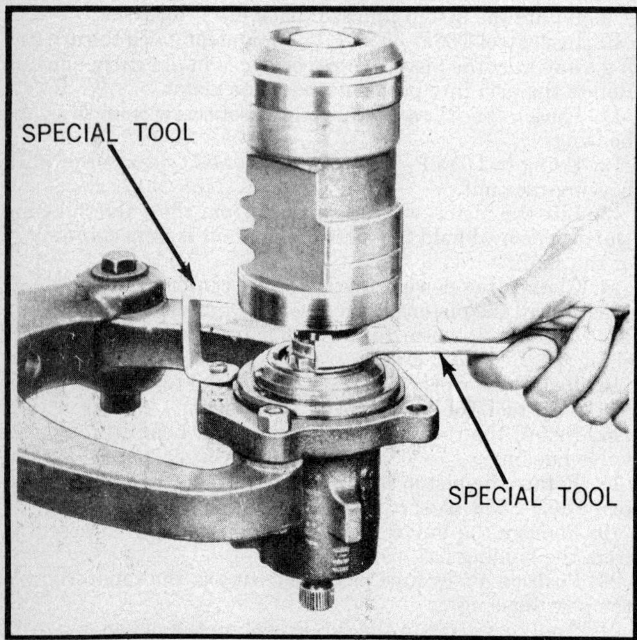

Removing worm bearing race nut (© Ford Motor Co.)

STEERING GEAR

Disassembly

1. Hold the steering gear over a drain pan in an inverted position and cycle the input shaft several times to drain the remaining fluid from the gear.
2. Mount the gear in a soft-jawed vise.
3. Remove the lock nut from the adjusting screw.
4. Turn the input shaft to either stop then, turn it back approximately $1^3/_4$ turns to center the gear.
5. Remove the two sector shaft cover attaching studs, the brake line bracket and the identification tag.
6. Tap the lower end of the sector shaft with a soft-hammer to loosen it, then lift the cover and shaft from the housing as an assembly. Discard the O-ring.
7. Turn the sector shaft cover counterclockwise off the adjuster screw.
8. Remove the four valve housing attaching bolts. Lift the valve housing from the steering gear housing while holding the piston to prevent it from rotating off the worm shaft. Remove the valve housing and the lube passage O-rings and discard them.
9. Stand the valve body and piston on end with the piston end down. Rotate the input shaft counterclockwise out of the piston allowing the ball bearings to drop into the piston.
10. Place a cloth over the open end of the piston and turn it upside down to remove the balls.
11. Remove the two screws that attach the ball guide clamp to the ball nut and remove the clamp and the guides.
12. Install the valve body assembly in the holding fixture (do not clamp in a vise) and loosen the race nut screw (Allen head) from the valve housing and remove the worm bearing race nut.
13. Carefully slide the input shaft, worm and valve assembly out of the valve housing. Due to the close diametrical clearance between the spool and housing, the slightest cocking of the spool may cause it to jam in the housing.
14. Remove the shim from the valve housing bore.

VALVE HOUSING

Removal & Installation

1. Remove the dust seal from the rear of the valve housing and discard the seal.
2. Remove the snap-ring from the valve housing.
3. Turn the fixture to place the valve housing in an inverted position.
4. Insert special tool in the valve body assembly opposite the seal end and gently tap the bearing and seal out of the housing. Discard the seal. Caution must be exercised when inserting and removing the tool to prevent damage to the valve bore in the housing.
5. Remove the fluid inlet and outlet tube seats with an EZ-out if they are damaged.
6. Coat the fluid inlet and outlet tube seats with vaseline and position them in the housing. Install and tighten the tube nuts to press the seats to the proper location.
7. Coat the bearing and seal surface of the housing with a film of vaseline.
8. Seat the bearing in the valve housing. Make sure that the bearing is free to rotate.
9. Dip the new oil seal in gear lubricant; then, place it in the housing with the metal side of the seal facing outward. Drive the seal into the housing until the outer edge of seal does not quite clear the snap-ring groove.
10. Place the snap-ring in the housing; then, drive on the ring until the snap-ring seats in its groove to properly locate the seal.
11. Place the dust seal in the housing with the dished side (rubber side) facing out. Drive the dust seal into place. The seal

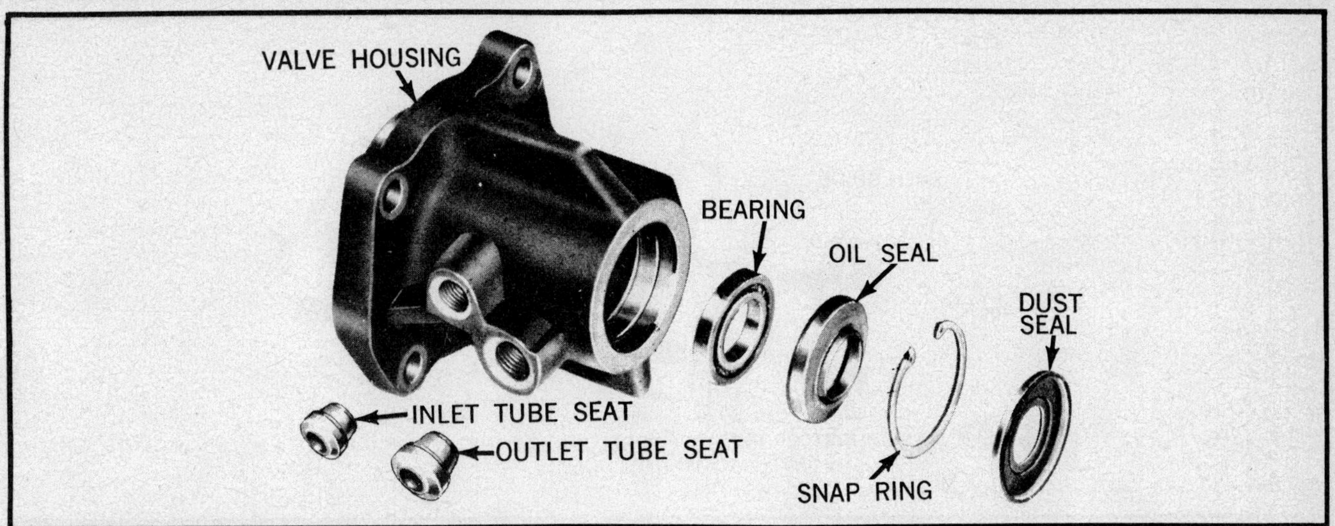

Valve housing disassembled (© Ford Motor Co.)

must be located behind the undercut in the input shaft when it is installed.

WORM AND VALVE

Removal & Installation

1. Remove the snap-ring from the end of the actuator.
2. Slide the control valve spool off the actuator.
3. Install the valve spool evenly and slowly with a slight oscillating motion into the flanged end of valve housing with the valve identification groove between the valve spool lands outward, checking for freedom of valve movement within the housing working area. The valve spool should enter the housing bore freely and fall by its own weight.
4. If the valve spool is not free, check for burrs at the outward edges of the working lands in the housing and remove with a hard stone.
5. Check the valve for burrs and if burrs are found, stone the valve in a radial direction only. Check for freedom of the valve again.
6. Remove the valve spool from the housing.
7. Slide the spool onto the actuator making sure that the groove in the spool annulus is toward the worm.
8. Install the snap-ring to retain the spool. The beveled ID of the snap-ring must be assembled toward the spool.
9. Check the clearance between the spool and the snap-ring. The clearance should be between 0.0005–0.035 inch. If the clearance is not within these limits, select a snap-ring that will allow a clearance of 0.002 inch.

PISTON AND BALL NUT

Removal and Installation

1. Remove the teflon ring and the O-ring from the piston and ball nut.
2. Dip a new O-ring in gear lubricant and install it on the piston and ball nut.
3. Install a new teflon ring on the piston and ball nut being careful not to stretch it any more than necessary.

STEERING GEAR HOUSING

Removal and Installation

1. Remove the snap-ring and the spacer washer from the lower end of the steering gear housing.
2. Remove the lower seal from the housing. Lift the spacer washer from the housing.
3. Remove the upper seal in the same manner as the lower seal. Some housings require only one seal and one spacer.
4. Dip both sector shaft seals in gear lubricant.
5. Apply lubricant to the sector shaft seal bore of the hous-

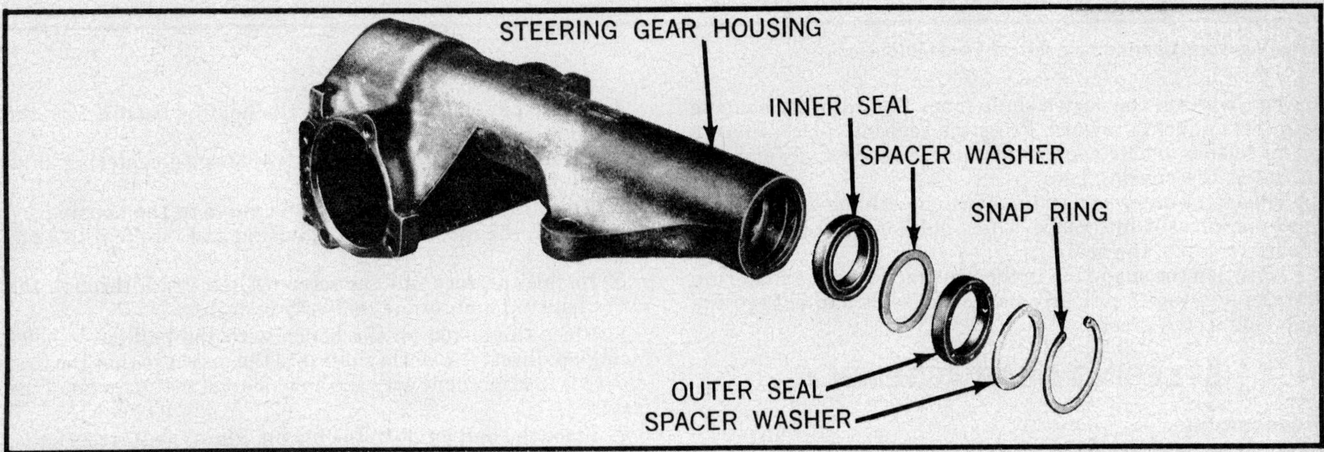

Steering gear housing and sector shaft seal assembly (© Ford Motor Co.)

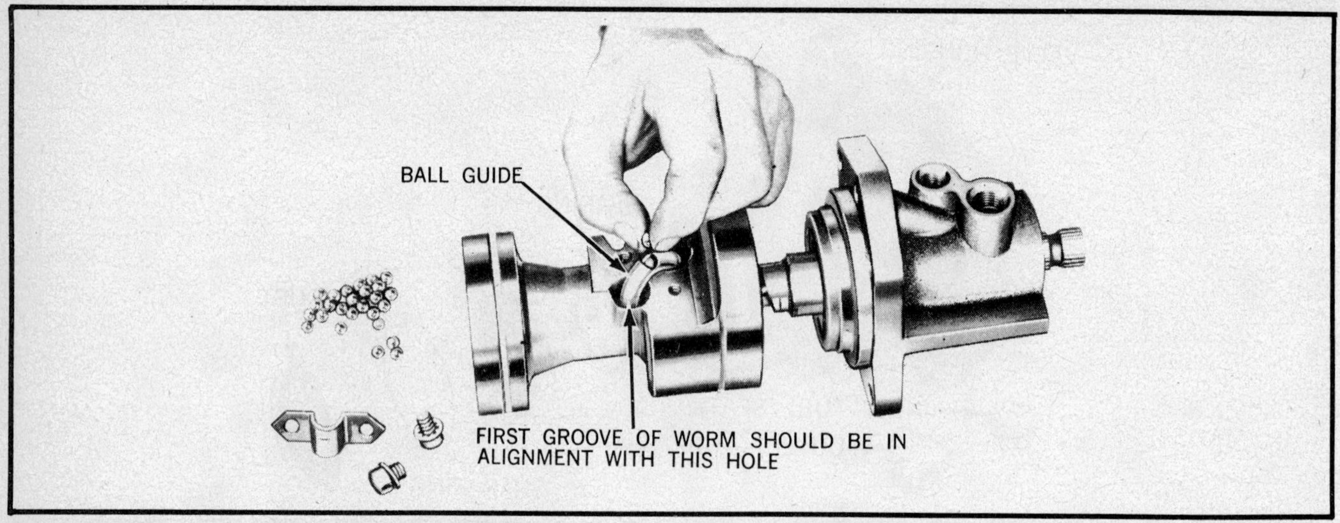

Loading balls into the ball guides (© Ford Motor Co.)

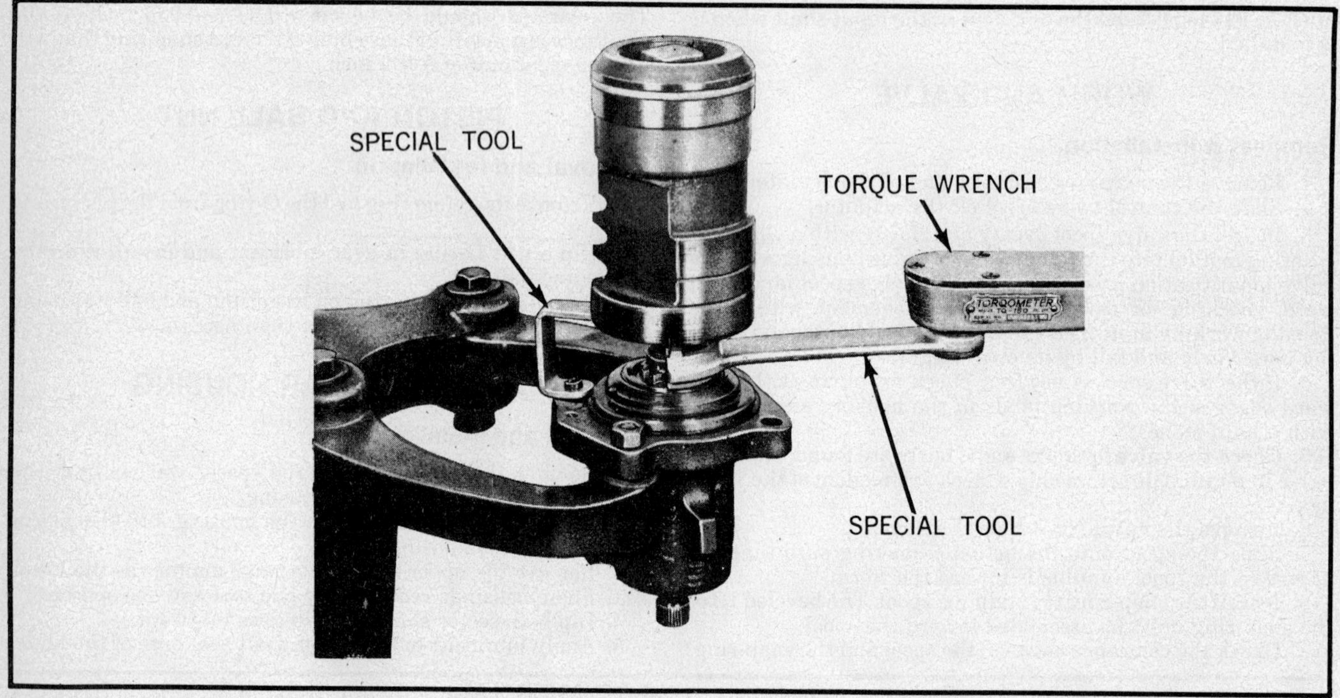

Installing worm bearing race nut (© Ford Motor Co.)

ing and position the sector shaft inner seal into the housing with the lip facing inward. Press the seal into place. Place a spacer washer (0.090 inch) on top of the seal and apply more lubricant to the housing bore.

6. Place the outer seal in the housing with the lip facing inward and press it into place. Then, place a 0.090 inch spacer washer on top of the seal.

7. Position the snap-ring in the housing. Press the snap-ring into the housing to properly locate the seals and engage the snap-ring in the groove.

STEERING GEAR ASSEMBLY

Disassembly

NOTE: Do not clean, wash, or soak seals in cleaning solvent.

1. Mount the valve housing in the holding fixture with the flanged end up.
2. Place the required thickness valve spool centering shim in the housing.
3. Carefully install the worm and valve in the housing.
4. Install the race nut in the housing and torque it to 42 ft. lbs.
5. Install the race nut set screw (Allen head) through the valve housing and torque to 20–25 inch lbs.
6. Place the piston on the bench with the ball guide holes facing up. Insert the worm shaft into the piston so that the first groove is in alignment with the hole nearest to the center of the piston.
7. Place the ball guide in the piston. Place the 27 to 29 balls, depending on the piston design, in the ball guide turning the worm in a clockwise direction as viewed from the input end of

the shaft. If all of the balls have not been fed into the guide upon reaching the right stop, rotate the input shaft in one direction and then in the other while installing the balls. After the balls have been installed, do not rotate the input shaft or the piston more than $3^1/_2$ turns off the right stop to prevent the balls from falling out of the circuit.

8. Secure the guides in the ball nut with the clamp.
9. Position a new lub passage O-ring in the counterbore of the gear housing.
10. Apply petroleum jelly to the teflon seal on the piston.
11. Place a new O-ring on the valve housing.
12. Slide the piston and valve into the gear housing being careful not to damage the teflon seal.
13. Align the lube passage in the valve housing with the one in the gear housing and install but do not tighten the attaching bolts.
14. Rotate the ball nut so that the teeth are in the same plane as the sector teeth. Tighten the four valve housing attaching bolts to 35–45 ft. lbs.
15. Position the sector shaft cover O-ring in the steering gear housing. Turn the input shaft as required to center the piston.
16. Apply vaseline to the sector shaft journal then position the sector shaft and cover assembly in the gear housing. Install the brake line bracket, the steering identification tag and two sector shaft cover attaching bolts. Torque the bolts to 55–70 ft. lbs.
17. Attach an in. lb. torque wrench to the input shaft. Adjust the mesh load to 17 inch lbs.

Ross HF–54 and HF–64 Integral Power Steering Gear

The Ross model HF–54, HF–64 integral power steering gears have a hydraulically operated control valve, a power cylinder (piston rack and housing) and a mechanical means of steering control, all incorporated in a main housing with oil pressure supplied by an engine driven pump.

UNLOADER VALVE

Adjustment

This unloader valve adjustment is for right turn only on HF–54 model gears and for both turns on HF–64 Model gears. Prior to performing the following procedure, obtain the vehicle's straight ahead position by driving the vehicle with hands off the steering wheel thus allowing the unit to find its own center. Now mark the steering column to steering wheel with chalk or masking tape.

1. Check the front wheel turning angles and adjust as required with the wheels off the ground.
2. Position the wheels straight ahead and lower the vehicle.
3. **Right turn-HF–54 or HF–64 gears:** With the engine at idle, the vehicle standing still and the fluid at normal operating temperature, rotate the steering wheel to the right the prescribed number of turns.
4. Hold in this position. Loosen the locknut and turn the unloader valve pressure adjusting screw until an audible hiss is heard. Tighten the locknut.
5. Return the wheel to a straight ahead position while the vehicle is moving. With the vehicle standing still, again rotate the steering wheel the prescribed turns; then, check for the audible hiss. Readjust if necessary as in Step 4 and check once more as in this step. It is important to remember that the HF–64 gear has a pitman arm stop for the right turn cast on the gear housing. The pitman arm must not contact this stop prior to contacting the unloader valve. When the hiss is heard during the adjustment, the clearance between the pitman arm and the cast stop should be $^{11}/_{16}$ to $^1/_8$ inch minimum.
6. **Left turn-HF–64 gear only:** Repeat Steps 3, 4, and 5 while rotating the steering wheel to the left 1 $^3/_4$ turns.

Model	Turns
H-54	1¾
H-64—2 port	1¼
H-64—4 port	1½

SECTOR SHAFT

Adjustment

1. Disconnect the drag link from the Pitman arm.
2. Center the steering wheel. Grasp the Pitman arm and check it for free movement (lash) between the sector shaft and the rack piston.
3. If free movement is noted (lash), remove the steering gear from the vehicle.
4. Loosen the sector shaft adjustment screw locknut on the side cover.
5. After rotating the input shaft through its full travel for a minimum of five cycles, adjust the sector shaft adjusting screw to provide 15–20 in. lb. torque as the input shaft is rotated 90 degrees each side of center.
6. Back out the adjusting screw one turn and note the torque required to move the input shaft 90 degrees each side of the center position. Move the adjusting screw in to provide an increase in torque of 2–4 inch lbs. at a point within 45 degrees each side of center after the adjusting screw jam nut is first tightened snug. Now torque to a final 20–25 ft. lbs. The input torque of the completely assembled gear, minus hydraulic oil, should not exceed 15 inch lbs. for the full travel of the output shaft.
7. Install the steering gear in the vehicle.
8. Connect the drag link to the Pitman arm.
9. Connect the pump lines and refill the system with the specified fluid.

Disassembly

1. Rotate the input shaft so the index mark on the end of the sector shaft is perpendicular to the centerline of the gear (straight-ahead position).
2. Remove the side cover attaching screws and washers.
3. Tap lightly on the end of the sector shaft with a soft hammer to disengage the side cover seal and allow the housing to drain.
4. Remove all nicks, burrs, rust and paint before removing the shaft. Lift the side cover and sector shaft from the housing as an assembly.
5. Remove the sector shaft seal adapter attaching screws and remove the adapter from the housing.
6. Remove the four screws that attach the control valve adapter to the housing.
7. Remove the control valve and rack piston from the housing as an assembly.
8. Remove the sector shaft adjustment screw lock nut. Turn the adjustment clockwise until free of the side cover.
9. Remove the unloader valve retainer, unloader valves, rod and the spring from the rack piston.
10. If all parts appear undamaged, do not disassemble the rack piston assembly. If there is evidence of damage, place the rack piston on a clean surface with the ball return guides facing upward. Remove the two ball return guide retainer attaching screws, lock washers, guide retainer, guide and balls. It may be necessary to tilt the rack piston over a clean pan and oscillate the worm shaft to empty the rack of all the balls. Lift the worm shaft from the rack after all the balls have been removed.
11. Carefully hold the input shaft in a vise equipped with soft jaws. Remove the snap-ring, washer, bronze washer, cup, seal

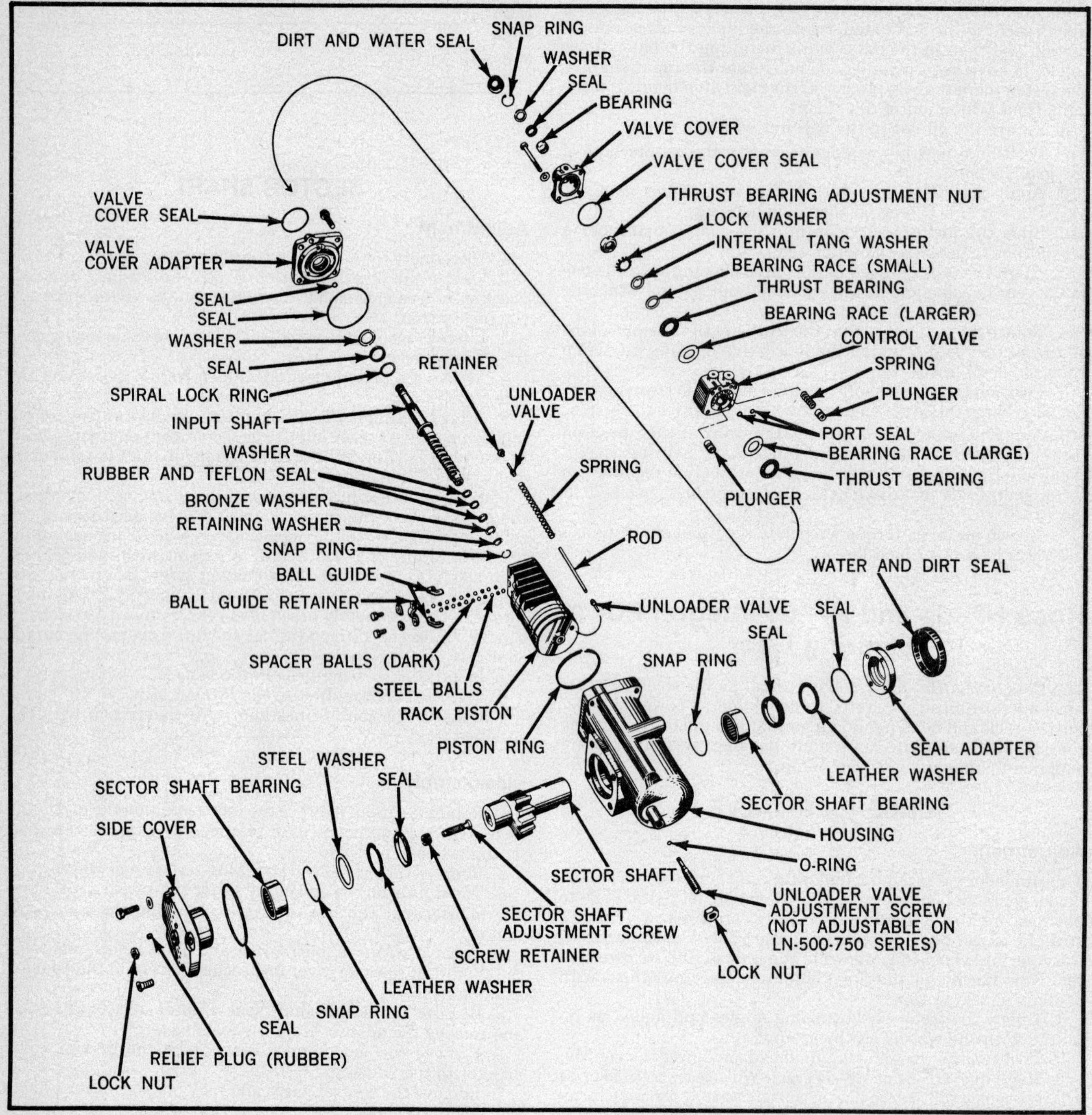

Exploded view of Ross model H-54 steering gear (© Ford Motor Co.)

and washer. It may be necessary to cut the teflon cup off the shaft.

12. Remove the valve cover dirt and water seal.
13. Remove the four valve cover attaching screws. Lift the cover from the control valve.
14. Unstake the thrust bearing adjustment nut lock washer and remove the adjustment nut.
15. Remove the lock washer, internal tang washer, bearing race (small), thrust bearing and the large bearing race.
16. Lift the control valve and the control valve adapter from the input shaft.
17. Remove spiral lock ring, seal and washer from the counterbore of the valve cover adapter. Discard the washer and seal.
18. Do not disassemble the valve unless absolutely necessary. The valve is the control center of the hydraulic system. The major parts, which are the body and spool, are machined to very close tolerances and with precision machined edges. The spool and valve body are selectively fitted at the factory, and therefore these two parts are not separately replaceable. If either is damaged or excessively worn, the complete valve assembly should be replaced. Good performance of power steering is not assured if a mismatched valve spool and body are used. Care should be exercised in the handling of these parts to

prevent damage. Sealing edges of the valve bore and the spool should not be broken. This will result in excessive leakage and reduced hydraulic power. If valve parts should drop out during gear disassembly, reassemble the valve as follows:

a. Clean all parts with a clean petroleum base solvent and blow dry with clean, dry air.

b. Insert the valve spool in the control valve making certain that the machined identification groove in the ID of one end of the spool is toward the gear housing.

c. There are 7 sets of plungers, each set having one reaction spring. Insert the 6 solid centering plunger sets first along with one spring per set. The remaining plunger set should be inserted in the valve body with the small hole on each plunger facing outboard.

Cleaning and Inspection

1. All parts should be cleaned in a clean petroleum base solvent and blown dry with clean dry air. Avoid wiping parts with a cloth, since lint may cause binding and sticking of closely fitted components.
2. Inspect the worm grooves in the rack piston and on the input shaft for wear scores. Inspect the OD of the rack piston and the ring or teeth for wear or scores. On the HF–64 gear, the ball nut and input shaft are serviced as a matched assembly. Therefore, both must be replaced if either are worn or damaged. The rack piston is not matched.
3. Inspect the inside ends of the ball return guides for wear or damage.
4. Inspect the housing bore for wear or scores of being cracked and replace as required.
5. Inspect the sector shaft teeth for wear or the bearing surfaces for wear or scores.
6. Replace the sector shaft bearings if worn or damaged.

NOTE: The sector shaft bearing in the side cover is replaced as part of the side cover assembly.

7. Replace all seals at time of disassembly.

Assembly

1. Lubricate all rubber parts prior to assembly.
2. If the sector shaft bearing was removed from the steering gear housing, install the snap-ring in the outboard side of the housing (HF–54 gear only).
3. Place the steering gear housing in a press with the side cover area on a wood block to prevent damage to the machined area.
4. Position the bearing on the housing with the numbered end facing up. Carefully press the bearing into the housing until the outer surface is flush. Use a tool that pilots in the ID of the bearing and contacts the bearing end surface.
5. Coat the unloader valve pressure adjusting screw O-ring liberally with clean grease or oil. Carefully slide it into the groove on the non-threaded end of the adjusting screw.
6. Thread the adjusting screw into the lower end of the housing leaving $^7/_8$ inch of the screw exposed. Install the lock nut on the adjusting screw and tighten it securely.
7. Carefully secure the input shaft in a vise equipped with soft jaws to permit access to both ends of the shaft.
8. On HF–54 gears, slide the bearing race (large) thrust bearing, control valve (with cylinder ports toward the shoulder), bearing race (small), internal tang washer, lock washer and thrust bearing adjustment nut. On HF–64 gears, slide the thrust bearing race washer, spacer, control valve (with cylinder ports toward the shoulder), needle thrust bearing, thrust bearing race washer, tang washer, lock washer and thrust bearing adjustment nut.
9. Tighten the adjustment nut to 20 ft. lbs., then back it off $^1/_2$–1 lock washer tangs. Bend one tang of the lock washer into the slot provided on the adjustment nut. When adjusted in this manner, the control valve should rotate freely on the shaft with a torque of 2–3 $^1/_2$ inch lbs. and have no perceptible end play.
10. Assemble a new washer seal and the spiral lock ring in the counterbore of tbe valve cover adapter. Make sure that the lip of seal is facing toward the spiral lock ring.
11. Coat a new valve cover seal and two new cylinder port seals with grease to retain them in place. Position the seals in the recesses provided in the control valve cover adapter on the surface adjacent to the control valve.
12. Reposition the input shaft in the vise securing the serrated end.
13. Slip the adapter over the worn groove end of the input shaft. Align the cylinder port seals with the ports in the control valve. Install one of the attaching bolts finger tight to facilitate assembly.
14. Assemble the washer (steel), a new rubber seal, new teflon cup with the lip toward the seal, bronze washer and retaining washer. Compress the washer and seal, then install the snap-ring on the end of the input shaft. Make sure that the snap-ring is fully seated in the groove and the recessed area of the retaining washer.
15. Secure the rack piston in a soft-jawed vise with the ball guide holes facing upward.
16. Carefully expand the piston ring and install it in the piston groove.
17. Place the two unloader valves, spring, and rod in the rack piston. Apply a drop of sealer to the threads of the retainer. Install and torque the retainer to 25 ft. lbs.
18. Coat the input shaft seal at the end of worm with grease and place it in the rack piston bore.
19. Assemble sixteen balls while rotating the input shaft counterclockwise. The black spacer balls and the polished steel balls must be installed alternately. Coat the ball return guides with grease to retain the balls, then install the six remaining balls in the guides making sure that the balls in the guide alternate with the last balls installed in the rack piston. If a ball is lost, no more than three black spacer balls may be used for replacement. Secure the guide retaining clip to the rack piston with two screws and washers. Torque the screws to 30–35 ft. lbs. and bend the tab of the locking washer against the flat.
20. Grip the serrated end of the sector shaft in a soft-jawed vise.
21. Coat the head of the sector shaft adjusting screw with grease. Position the head of adjusting screw into the slot in the end of sector shaft.
22. Install a new sector shaft adjustment screw retainer in the end of shaft. Tighten the retainer to permit free rotation of screw without perceptible end play. Stake the retainer in the two slots provided and recheck the rotation effort.
23. If the pressure relief plug has been removed or ruptured, press a new one into the side cover until it is flush with the surface.
24. Assemble the snap-ring, steel washer (with taper toward the snap-ring), leather washer and the two piece seal into the side cover. The seal has "Oil Side" molded into one side and must be visible after installation.
25. Coat the end of sector shaft with lubricant. Rotate the sector shaft adjusting screw counterclockwise to thread it into the side cover. Rotate the screw until a firm stop is reached. Make sure that the shaft seal has not fallen out of position.
26. Place the outer seal in the seal adapter. Then install the leather washer and inner seal making sure that the side having the mold "Oil Side" is visible after installation.
27. If the input shaft needle bearing has been removed from the control valve cover it must be installed with a tool that will pilot in the bearing and have clearance in the cover bore. The bearing must be pressed from the part number end and to a depth of 1 $^1/_8$ inches from the face of the valve cover. After installation of the bearing, make sure that all rollers rotate freely.
28. Install the seal on the control valve cover with the lip facing toward the needle bearing. Coat the washer with grease

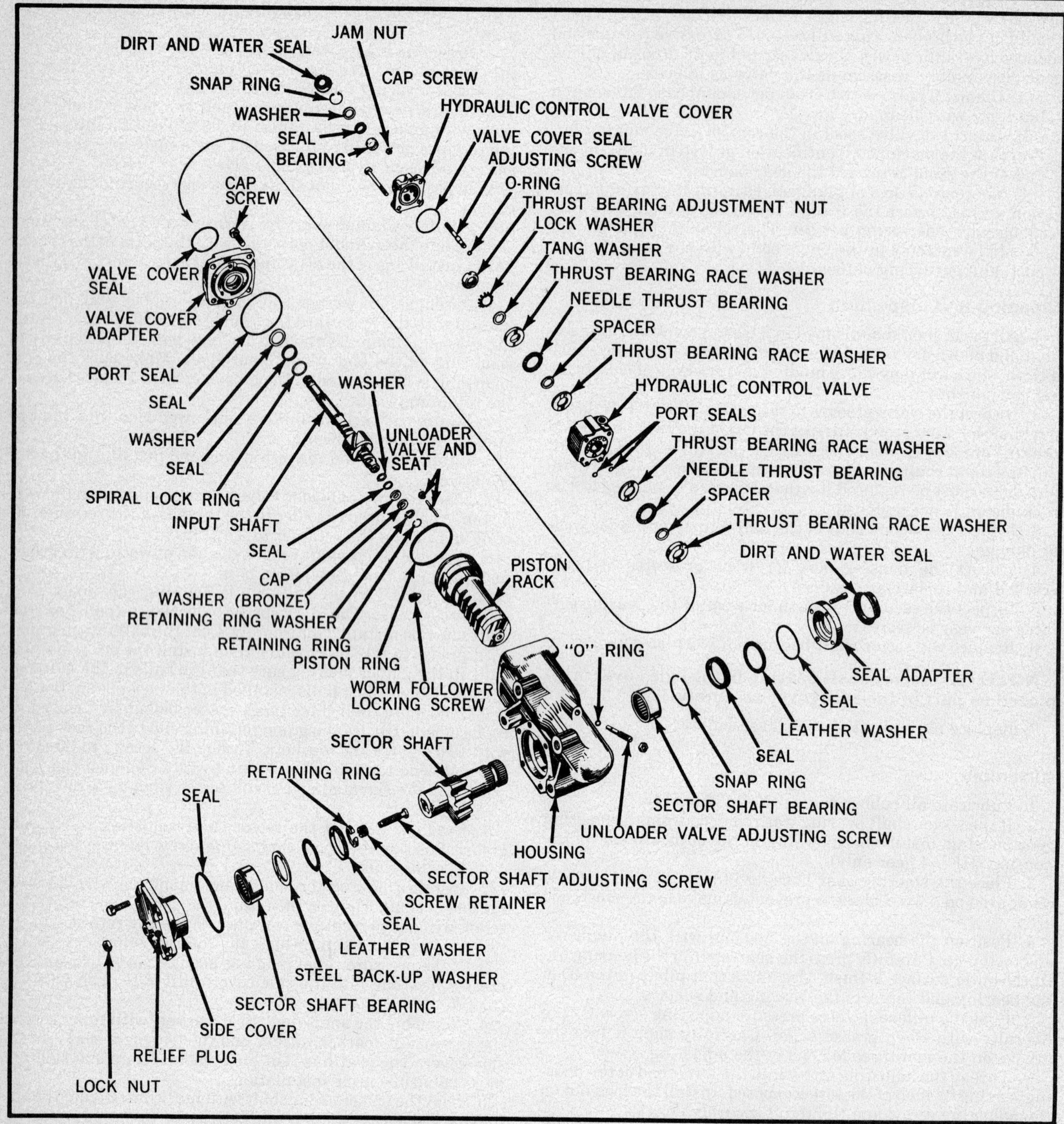

Exploded view of Ross model H-64 steering gear (© Ford Motor Co.)

and install it on the cover. Install the snap-ring to secure the seal and washer.

29. Pack the new dirt and water seal with grease and install it on the control valve cover.

30. Secure the steering gear housing in a vise equipped with soft jaws.

31. Lubricate the steering gear housing bore. Start the rack piston into the bore, then compress the ring and move the piston into position so that the teeth are visible through the side cover opening. Install the four adapter-to-housing attaching bolts. Remove the one bolt that was previously installed.

32. Lubricate a new valve cover seal with grease and position it in the recess of the valve cover.

33. Slide the valve cover onto the input shaft and install the four cover-to-control valve attaching bolts.

34. Rotate the input shaft as required to align the center tooth of the rack piston (marked tooth) with the side cover opening.

35. Lubricate a new side cover O-ring and position it on the side cover.

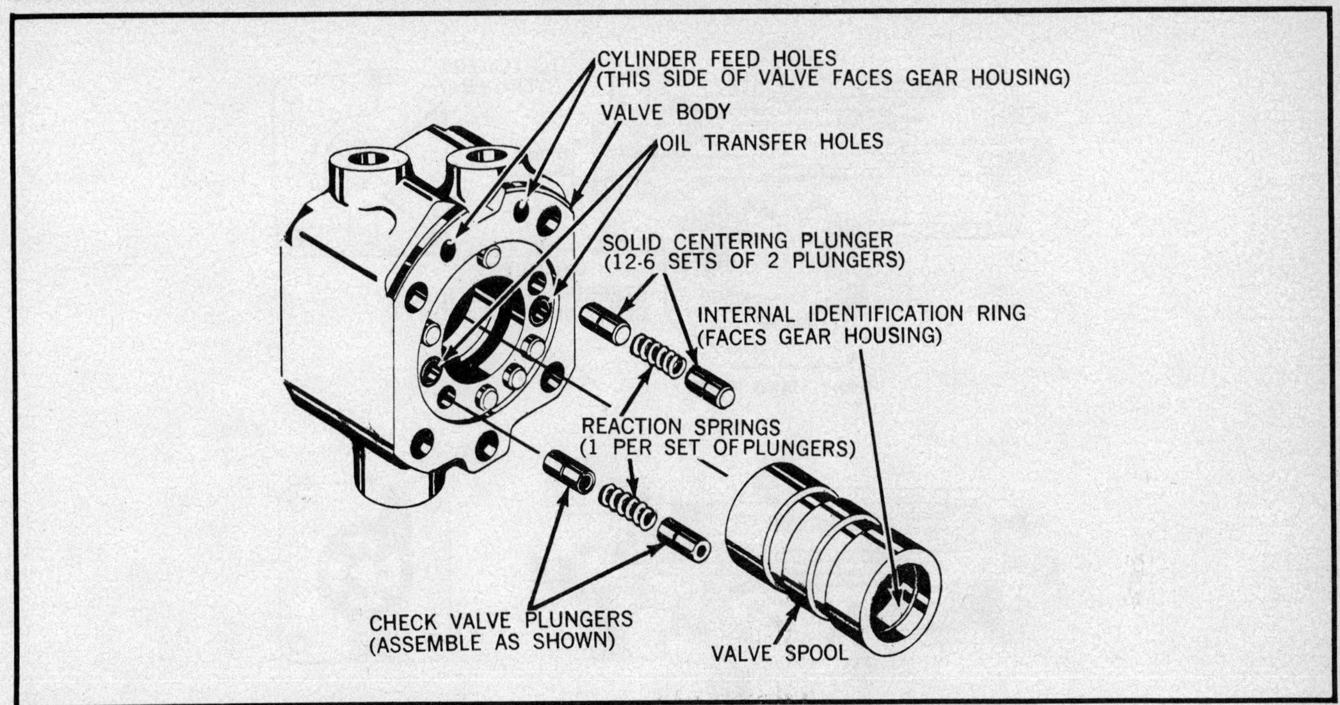

Hydraulic control valve assembly (© Ford Motor Co.)

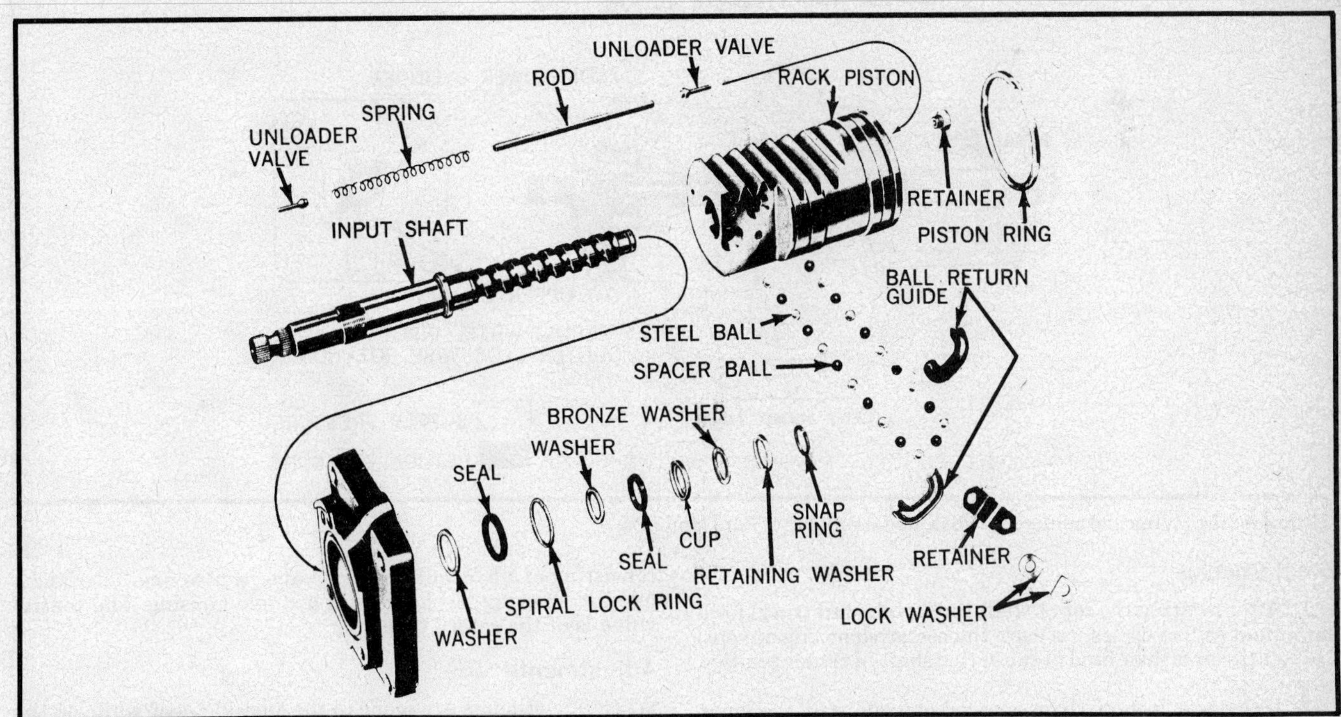

Input shaft seals and retainers—models HF-54 (models HF-64 similar) (© Ford Motor Co.)

36. Position the sector shaft and side cover to the steering gear housing making sure that the center tooth (marked tooth) engages the center space (marked space).
37. Install the four side cover attaching bolts and lock washers. Torque the bolts to 45–55 ft. lbs.
38. Adjust sector shaft adjustment screw as outlined in the Sector Shaft Adjustment.
39. Cover the sector shaft serrations with a layer of scotch tape to prevent damage to the seal in the adapter.
40. Position the adapter over the sector shaft and on the housing. Install and tighten the attaching bolts.
41. Pack the seal adapter outer seal with grease, then install it on the adapter to prevent water entry.

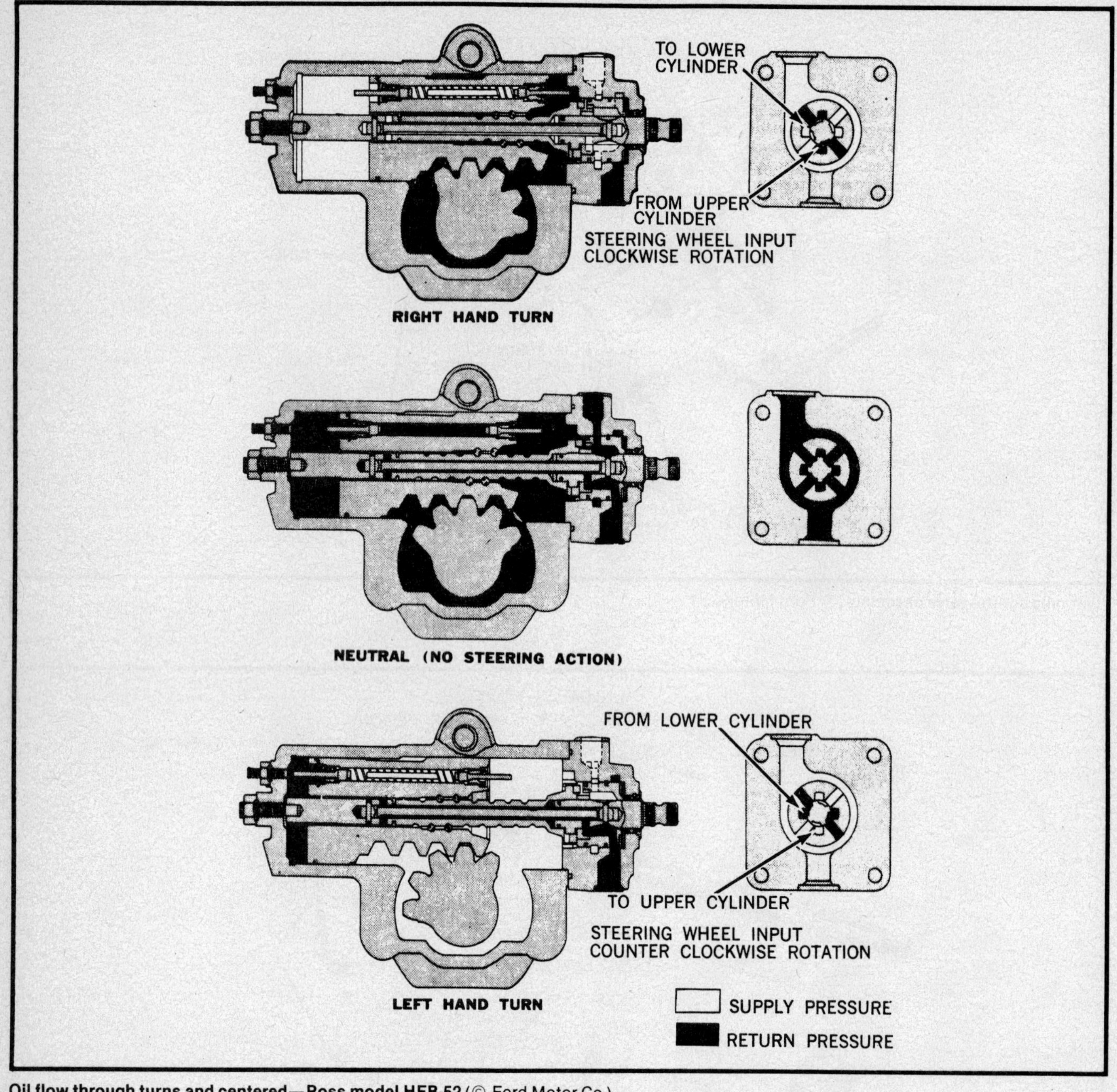

Oil flow through turns and centered—Ross model HFB-52 (© Ford Motor Co.)

Final Checks

1. After rotating the input shaft through its full travel for a minimum of five cycles, recheck the sector shaft adjustment. No rotational lash or bind of the sector shaft in center position is permissible.
2. If the gear is properly assembled and adjusted, the input torque of the empty gear should not exceed 15 inch lbs. over full travel of 95 degrees at the output shaft.
3. Reverse-torque applied to output shaft for full gear travel should not exceed 50 ft. lbs.

Ross Model HFB–52 Integral Power Steering Gear

The model HFB–52 power steering gear is a fully integral unit, consisting of a hydraulic control valve, a power cylinder and a manual steering mechanism in a single housing. The control valve is of the rotory type.

Adjustments

When adjustments are made to the steering gear while on the vehicle, disconnect the Pitman arm or drag link and the input coupling. Leave the plumbing attached and allow the engine to idle while performing the adjustments.

SECTOR SHAFT

Adjustment

1. Loosen the locknut and adjust the screw to provide a torque at the worm gear of 23–28 inch lbs. as the steering gear is moved 90 degrees from each side of center.

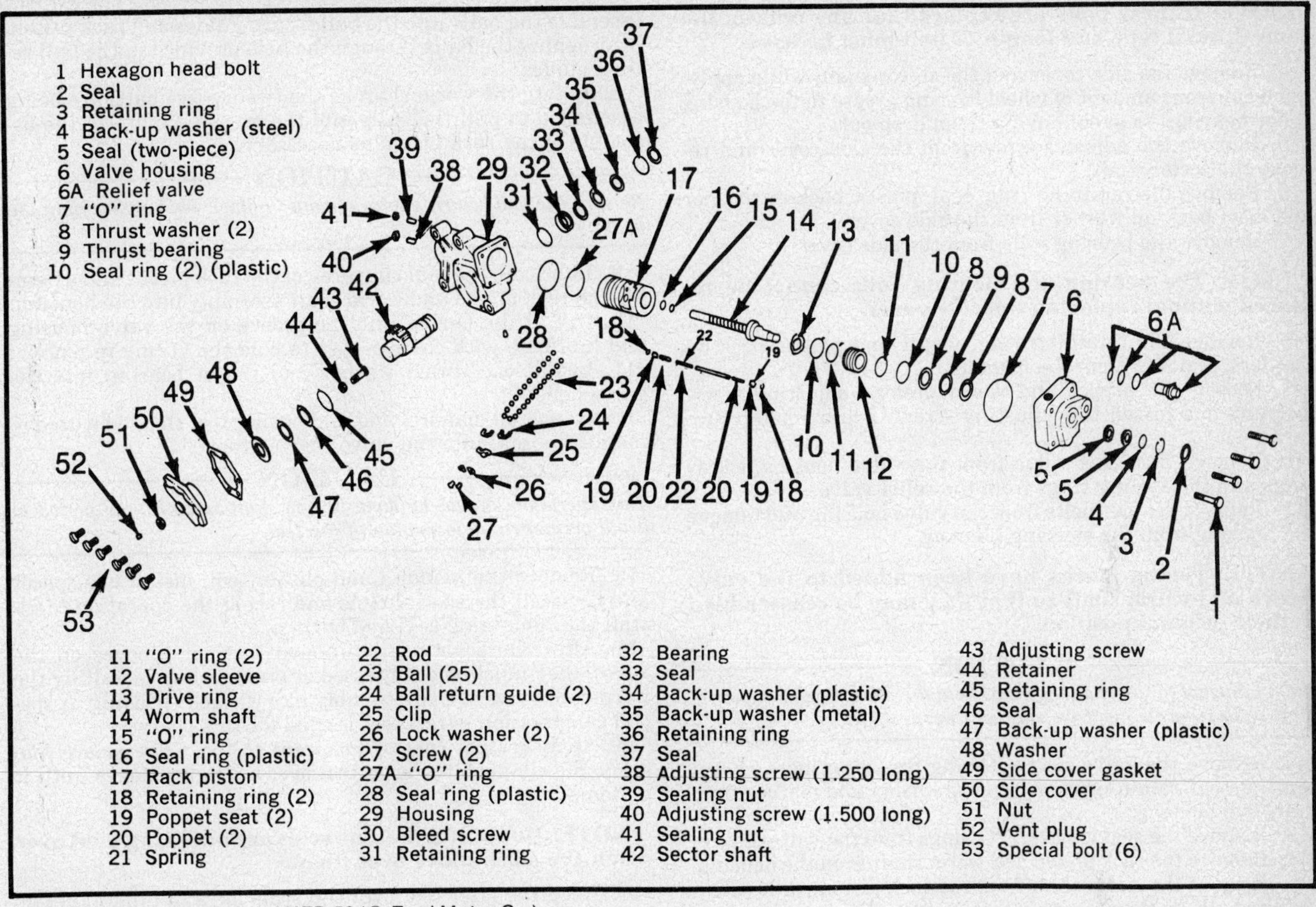

Exploded view Ross model HFB-52 (© Ford Motor Co.)

2. Back out the adjusting screw one turn and note the torque necessary to move the worm shaft 90 degrees from each side of center.

3. Rotate the adjusting screw to provide a rise in torque of 2 to 4 inch lbs. at a point within 45 degrees from each side of center. Tighten the locknut to 40–45 ft. lbs.

4. The torque to rotate the worm shaft must not exceed 26 inch lbs. at any point of steering gear travel.

WORM PRELOAD

Adjustment

1. Loosen the adjustment screw jam nut and tighten the adjusting screw to 25–30 inch lbs.

2. Tighten the jam nut to 40–50 ft. lbs. while holding the adjusting screw so that it does not rotate.

3. The purpose of the adjustment is to put a light preload on the worm thrust bearing assembly. The input shaft must rotate smoothly and without binding through the full steering gear travel with a maximum torque of 26 inch lbs.

Poppet Adjusting Screws

The steering gear must be in the vehicle for this adjustment. The purpose of the adjustment is to set the poppet adjusting screw so the poppet contacts the adjusting screw just before full wheel cut is reached. When at full wheel cut (steering against axle stops), the poppet should be fully tripped and the pressure shown on a pressure gauge in the supply line should be between 200 and 500 psi.

1. Install a pressure gauge in the oil supply line to the steering gear.

2. Note the oil pressure when turning the wheels against the axle stops.

3. If the pressure reading is less than the pressure relief setting, back the poppet adjusting screw out until the system is operating at relief pressure when the wheels are against the axle stops.

4. Turn the poppet adjusting screw in until the pressure reading is less than 500 psi when the wheels are against the axle stops.

5. Lock the adjusting screw jam nut and tighten the sealing nut to 12 to 18 ft. lbs. Remove the pressure gauge from the system.

CAUTION

Do not operate the steering system at relief pressure for more than a few seconds at a time or damage to the system may result due to excessive heat generation.

STEERING GEAR

Disassembly

1. Place the steering gear in a vise in a horizontal position. Note the timing mark on the end of the sector shaft. Position this mark in a vertical position with the steering gear in the center of its travel.

2. Remove the sector shaft seal from the housing and loosen the sector shaft adjusting screw jamnut.

3. Place a drain pan under the steering unit and remove the six special ring head bolts from the side cover.

NOTE: If these bolts are replaced for any reason, the same special type and length of bolt must be used.

4. Remove the side cover and the sector shaft, while applying a generous amount of wheel bearing grease to the housing roller bearings to avoid having them drop out.
5. Remove the adjuster screw from the side cover and remove the sector shaft.
6. Remove the retaining ring, seal, plastic back-up washer and steel back-up washer from the side cover.
7. Remove the bearing rolls from the side cover.

NOTE: The bearing and bearing rolls cannot be replaced without replacing the side cover.

8. Remove the retaining ring, metal and plastic back-up washers, and seal from the housing.
9. Loosen the poppet and worm preload adjusting screw locknuts and loosen the adjusting screws approximately two turns.
10. Remove the relief valve from the valve housing, the O rings and the sealing rings from the relief valve.
11. Remove the four bolts from the valve housing and remove the housing from the steering housing.

NOTE: Timing marks have been added to the valve sleeve and worm shaft so that they may be reassembled in their original position.

CAUTION

Do not attempt to unbend tangs that hold the drive ring to the worm shaft or to separate the drive ring and worm shaft.

12. Remove the valve sleeve, O-ring thrust washers, thrust bearing, seal, retaining ring, back-up washer and seal cup from the valve housing.
13. Remove the seal rings and O-rings from the valve sleeve.
14. Remove the rack piston and worm shaft from the housing.
15. Remove the worm shaft from the rack piston while catching the balls as they come out, after removing the ball return guides.

NOTE: A complete new set of twenty-five matched balls will be required if any of the balls are lost.

16. No further need of disassembly is needed unless there is evidence of damage to the remaining parts.

Inspection

1. Inspect the rack piston teeth and worm groove for excessive wear.
2. Inspect the worm shaft helical groove for brinelling. (Surface indentations.)
3. Inspect the housing bore for abnormal wear or marks that would affect sealing and cause the steering gear to leak internally.
4. Inspect all bearings and contact surfaces.
5. Wash all parts in clean solvent and blow dry with air.

Assembly

1. Install all hard parts as necessary and use new seals, gaskets and sealing rings.
2. Assemble all sealing rings onto rack piston.
3. Apply clean wheel bearing grease to the housing bearing rolls to retain them.
4. Assemble poppet seat, retaining ring into the rack piston and tighten the poppet seat to 20–25 ft. lbs.
5. Assemble the O-ring and sealing ring onto the worm shaft, using special installation and compression tools to avoid damage.
6. Lubricate the seal ring area and assemble the worm shaft into the rack piston.
7. Assemble the ball return guides into the rack piston and assemble the balls into the ball return guides and rack piston, by dropping the balls through the hole provided in the ball return guides.
8. Rotate the worm shaft as the twenty-five balls are being assembled to pull the balls into the groove. Complete the assembly of the rack piston as necessary.

CAUTION

Be sure the ball return guides remain in place while assembling the balls.

9. Lubricate the seal ring area of the rack piston and assemble the rack piston and worm shaft assembly into the housing.
10. Install the O-ring into the groove on the valve housing and lubricate with clean grease to hold the O-ring in place.
11. Install the thrust washer and thrust bearing into the valve housing.
12. A tapered mandrel and seal pusher tool should be used to install the seal into the valve sleeve groove.

CAUTION

This operation should be done in one short smooth time period to avoid permanent deformation of the seal.

13. Remove the mandrel and pusher tool, install one spacer and reinstall the special tools and repeat the operation to install the remaining seal and O-ring.
14. After the seals are positioned in their grooves on the valve, they must be compressed or sized, before installing the worm and valve sleeve assembly into the gear housing. A special compression (sizer) tool is used for this operation.
15. Apply a light coat of lubricant to the valve sleeve and seals. Slowly push the sizer tool over the valve sleeve until it bottoms.

NOTE: Be careful that the seals are not being bent over when the sizer slides over them.

16. Keep the sizer tool over the seals for a minimum of one minute and then remove the sizer tool.
17. Apply lubricant to the seal ring areas of the valve sleeve.
18. Assemble the thrust washer to the end of the valve sleeve and hold the washer with grease. Install the valve sleeve into the valve housing. The distance from the face of the valve housing to the face of the valve sleeve should be approximately 0.400 inch.
19. Align the timing marks on the valve sleeve and the worm shaft. Assemble the valve housing onto the worm shaft.

Valve housing installation—Ross model HFB-52
(© Ford Motor Co.)

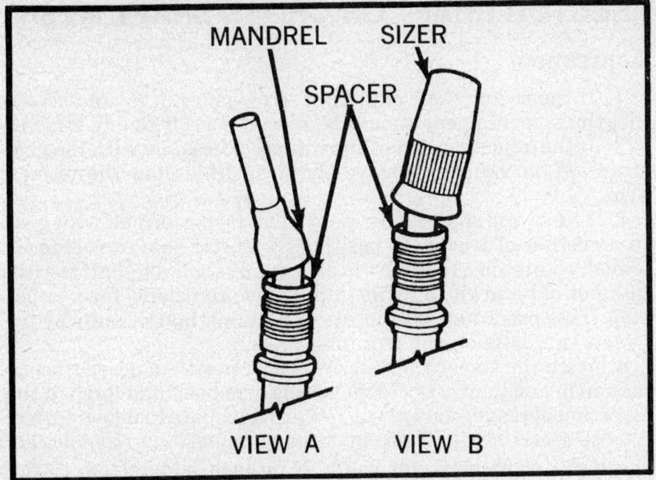

Mandrel for installation of seals (view A), and sizer tool for seals (view B)—Ross model HFB-52 (© Ford Motor Co.)

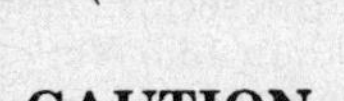

CAUTION

The drive ring teeth must engage the notches in the valve sleeve.

20. Use a $^{13}/_{16}$ X 12 point box end wrench to rotate the worm shaft, in order to pull the valve housing against the steering housing. Install the four bolts into the housing and torque to 45–50 ft. lbs.

21. Locate the rack piston near the center of the steering gear travel and turn the adjusting screw in no more than 10 ft. lbs., and back the adjusting screw out one turn.

22. Measure the torque required to rotate the worm shaft through 90 degrees from each side of center. The torque should not exceed 15 inch lbs. Tighten the lock nut to 40–50 ft. lbs.

23. *Important:* After tightening the lock nut, the rotating torque for the worm shaft must rise 4 to 7 inch lbs. above the previously checked torque.

24. Assemble the forty bearing rolls to the bearing race inside the side cover, using grease to hold the rolls in place.

25. Assemble the steel and plastic back-up washers, seal and retaining ring into the side cover and install the seal in the side cover with the flat side towards the bearing.

26. Lubricate the short bearing area of the sector shaft and install in the side cover. Screw the adjusting screw in to the side cover until it bottoms. The side cover should rotate freely on the sector shaft with no appreciable axle movement.

27. Press the vent plug into the side cover until flush. Put locknut on the adjusting screw.

28. Position rack piston in the center of the steering gear travel. Align the center tooth on the sector shaft with the third notch from the sealing ring end on the rack piston and using a new side cover gasket, install the sector shaft and side cover assembly, into the steering housing.

CAUTION

Do not dislodge the bearing rolls while installing the sector shaft into the steering housing.

29. Install the six special bolts and torque them to 150 to 170 ft. lbs.

30. Adjust the side cover adjusting screw to provide a 23 to 28 inch lbs. torque at the worm shaft as the steering gear is moved 90 degrees from each side of center. Back out the adjusting screw one turn and note the torque required to move the worm shaft through 90 degrees of center. Move the adjusting screw in to provide a rise in torque of 2 to 4 inch lbs. at a point 45 degrees of center. Tighten the locknut to 40–45 ft. lbs. and recheck the rotating torque. It should not exceed 26 inch lbs. at any point of steering gear travel.

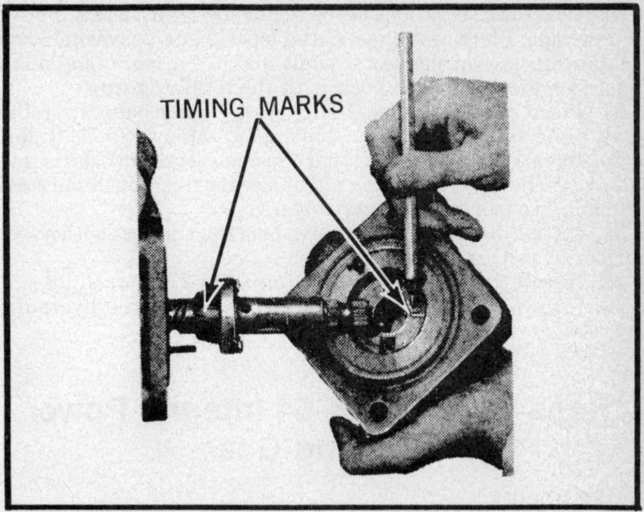

Timing marks on valve seal and worm shaft—Ross model HFB-52 (© Ford Motor Co.)

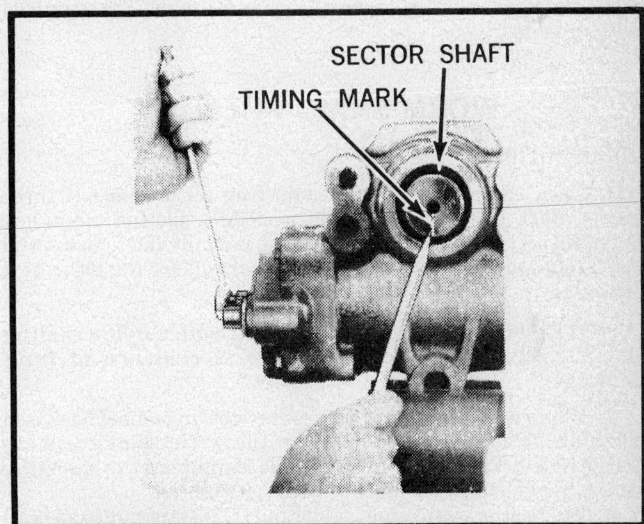

Sector shaft timing mark—Ross model HFB-52 (© Ford Motor Co.)

Sector shaft seal assembly positioning—Ross model HB-52 (© Ford Motor Co.)

31. Cover the serrations of the sector shaft with a seal protector or tape. Place seal, plastic and metal back-up washers and retaining ring on the sector shaft and use a seal installation tool to press into place. Lock with the retaining ring.
32. Place the O-ring, seal ring, and O-ring onto the relief valve and assemble into the housing. Tighten to 25–35 ft. lbs.
33. Install O-ring onto the seal cup and install both parts into the valve housing. With the aid of a seal driver, push the steel back-up washer into the valve housing.
34. Install the seal into the valve housing and seat with a seal driver or soft punch and hammer.
35. Install the bleed screw and torque to 27–33 inch lbs.
36. Install the unit on the vehicle and bleed the hydraulic system.

Ross Model HFB–64 Integral Power Steering Gear

Adjustments

If access to the steering gear is possible, the following adjustments can be made with the gear installed on the vehicle. If access is not possible, remove the gear to make the required adjustments.

WORM SHAFT PRELOAD

Adjustment

1. Back off the worm shaft adjusting screw jam nut three turns. Back off the worm shaft preload adjusting screw one turn. Inspect the threads between the jam nut and housing end for foreign matter. Clean the threads or replace the jam nut if necessary.

NOTE: The jam nut is a special nut with a nylon sealing surface. Replace the nut if there is evidence of fluid leakage.

2. While a helper lightly moves the steering wheel back and forth about one inch total, tighten the worm shaft adjusting screw to 7–8 Nm (60–70 in-lb). While tightening the adjusting screw, make sure the jam nut does not tighten.
3. Torque the worm shaft adjusting screw jam nut to 95–110 Nm (70–80 ft-lb) making sure that the worm shaft preload adjusting screw does not move. The purpose of this adjustment is to put a light preload on the worm thrust bearings. After adjustments has been made there should be no perceptible in and out movement of the input shaft as it is rotated from right turn to left turn and back. The input shaft should rotate smoothly and without binding through full travel of the gear with a maximum torque of 6.2 Nm (55 in-lb).

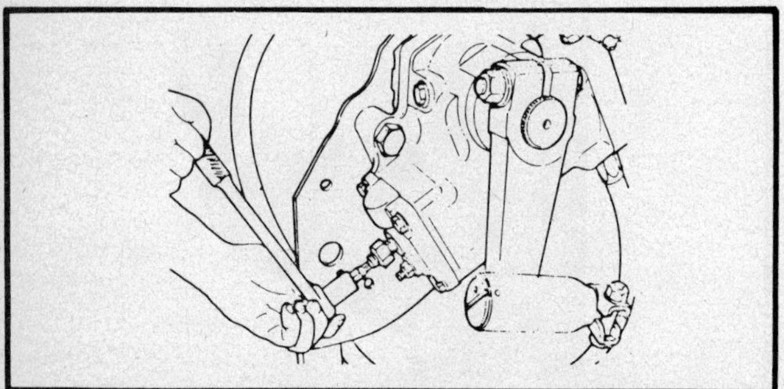

Worm shaft preload adjustment—loosening or tightening adjusting screw (© Ford Motor Co.)

SECTOR SHAFT OR CROSS SHAFT MESH

Adjustment

1. If the sector shaft adjusting screw jam nut is not accessible, the steering gear should be removed prior to adjustment.
2. If the adjusting screw and nut are accessible with the gear installed on vehicle, remove the drag link from the pitman arm.
3. The sector shaft adjustment must be performed with gear in its center of travel. To position the sector shaft on center of travel, rotate the steering wheel or input shaft one-half the full number of handwheel turns (input shaft rotations) from either stop. This procedure will locate the timing marks midway between two bolts on the trunnion cover.
4. With the sector shaft in the center position, grasp the pitman arm and gently try to move this arm back and forth in the direction of travel. Finger-tip force is adequate to detect lash of a loose sector shaft. There must be no movement (freeplay) of the input shaft or sector shaft. If no lash is detected, do not adjust.
5. If lash is detected, loosen jam nut and move the adjusting screw clockwise until the sector shaft and rack piston are in contact. Use no more than 13.5 Nm (10 ft-lb) of torque. Then, turn the adjusting screw counterclockwise one turn. At this point there should be lash at the pitman arm.
6. To adjust, slowly turn the adjusting screw clockwise until no lash is felt at the pitman arm. Hold the adjusting screw in place and tighten the jam nut to 54–61 Nm (40–45 ft-lb).
7. Recheck the pitman arm for lash. Turn the steering wheel or input shaft $^{1}/_{4}$ turn each side of center. No lash should be felt. If lash exists, repeat Steps 3–7.
8. Reconnect drag link to pitman arm and install gear if necessary.

STEERING GEAR

Disassembly

If it is necessary to disassemble any of the component parts, make sure a clean work bench is used. All parts should be cleaned in clear, clean solvent and blown dry with air. Keep each part separate to avoid nicks and burrs.

CAUTION

Avoid wiping parts with cloth as lint may actually cause binding and sticking of the closely fitted parts.

NOTE: Never steam clean or high-pressure wash hydraulic steering gear assemblies. Do not force or abuse close fitted parts as damage may result.

1. Position steering gear in a vise with worm shaft in a horizontal position. Check timing mark located on end of sector shaft, position this mark in vertical direction with steering gear in center of steering gear travel.
2. Remove seal by prying out with a screwdriver.
3. Remove the four trunnion cover bolts. Remove the trunnion cover. Remove and discard the "O"-ring, the plastic backup washer and the two-piece seal.
4. Remove any paint or corrosion from serrated end of sector shaft and loosen jam nut on sector shaft adjusting screw. Tape the serrated end of the sector shaft to protect the bearing rolls during removal.
5. Place suitable pan under steering gear for fluid to drain and remove six "special ring head" bolts from side cover.

NOTE: These bolts have a special ring located on bolt head for sealing purposes. If these bolts are replaced, they must be replaced with the same "special" type and length of bolt.

6. Remove side cover and sector shaft assembly; a soft ham-

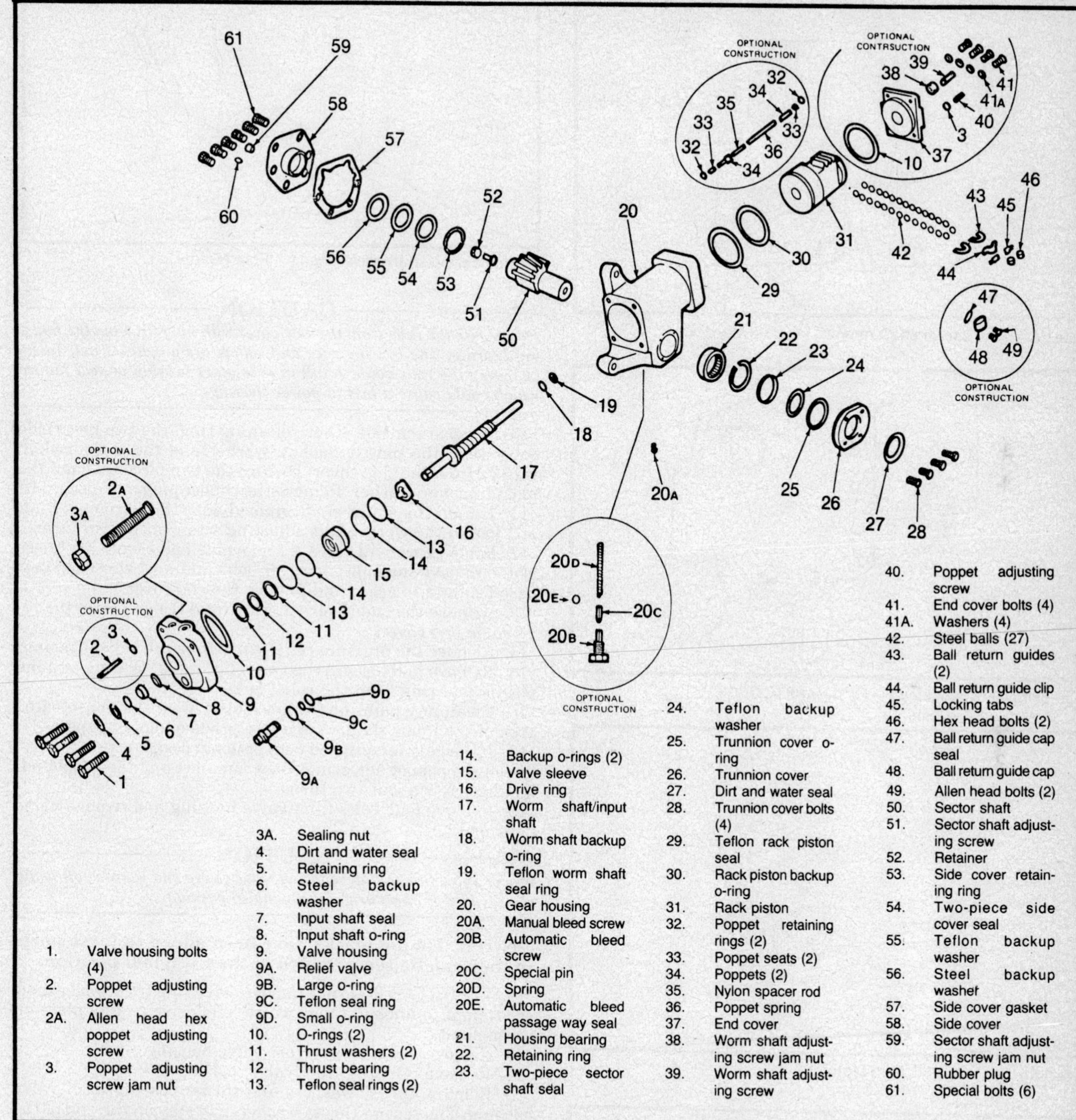

HFB-64 power steering gear—exploded view (© Ford Motor Co.)

mer or wooden handle may be used to remove sector shaft by tapping on the end of the sector shaft.

NOTE: When sector shaft is being removed, stop when the bearing rolls are half exposed and apply a generous amount of clean wheel bearing grease to retain needle bearings in housing bearing. The needle bearings can fall out if they are not held in place with grease. If any of the rolls are lost, the bearing rolls must be replaced as a matched set. Bearing tool J26738 or its equivalent may also be used to retain the rolls.

7. Check to make sure all needle bearing rolls are in place after sector shaft is removed.
8. Remove sector shaft adjusting screw nut.
9. Remove the sector shaft adjusting screw through side cover and remove sector shaft.

NOTE: By placing the side cover exterior side down and lifting the sector shaft out vertically, the side cover bearing rolls will fall into the side cover where they may be easily collected. Take care not to lose any rollers during disassembly of assembly or the complete side cover assembly will have to be replaced.

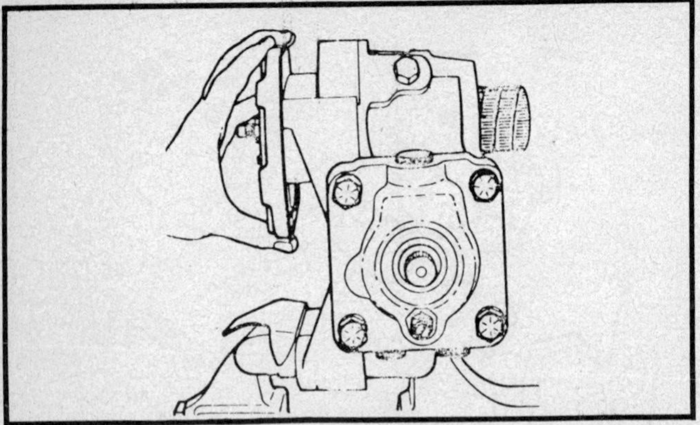

Side cover and sector shaft removal (© Ford Motor Co.)

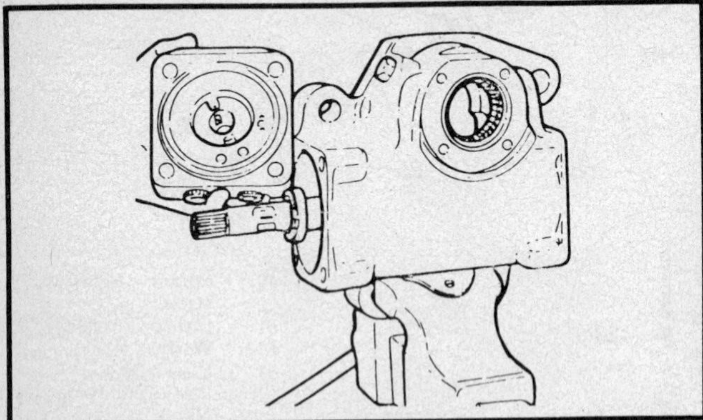

Removing valve housing (© Ford Motor Co.)

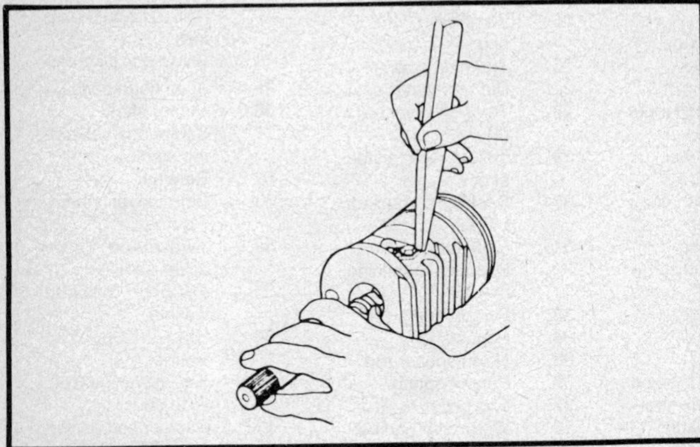

Bending lock tangs (© Ford Motor Co.)

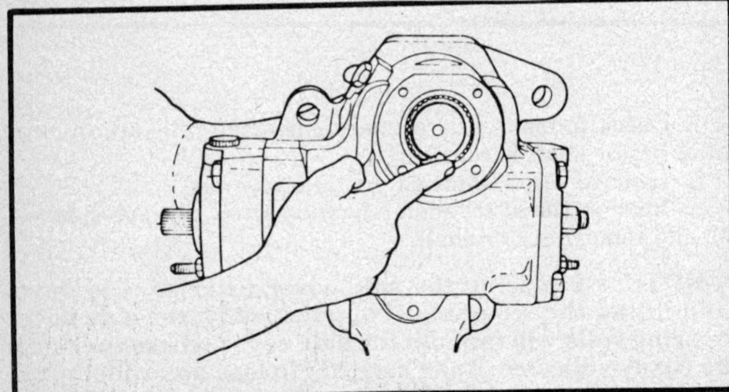

Retaining bearing bolts (© Ford Motor Co.)

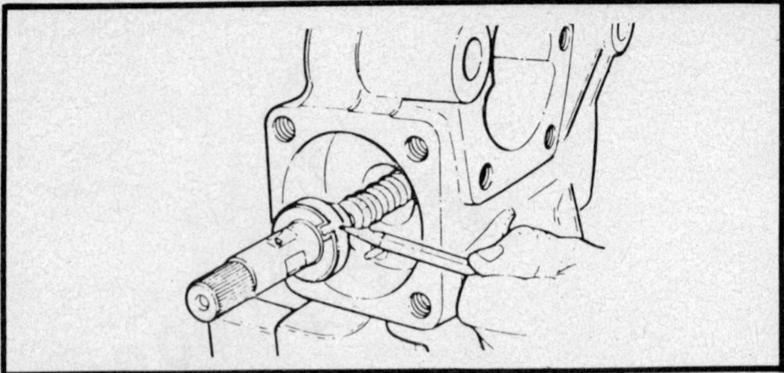

Worm bearing shaft drive rings (© Ford Motor Co.)

CAUTION

Do not mix the rolls from the side cover with the rolls from the housing bearing. The bearing race and rollers are a matched set. Interchanging the rolls could result in premature bearing or seal failure which could cause a loss of power steering.

10. Remove the side cover retaining ring, the two-piece side cover seal, the plastic backup washer and the steel backup washer from the side cover. Discard the two-piece seal and the plastic backup washer. Remove the rubber plug and discard it.
11. Loosen the worm shaft preload adjusting screw jam nut and loosen the worm shaft adjusting screw about two turns.
12. Some gears will have a removable end cover. For these gears, remove the four end cover bolts and washers. Then prepare for fluid to drain and remove the end cover.
13. Remove the end cover "O"-ring from the groove in the removable end cover.
14. Remove the pressure relief valve from the valve housing.
15. Remove and discard the two relief valve "O"-ring and the plastic seal ring from the relief valve.
16. Clean any paint or foreign matter from the nonserrated area of the input shaft with a fine grade of emery paper.
17. If the gear is equipped with optional design poppet valves, loosen the poppet adjusting screw jam nuts and the poppet adjusting screw about two turns.
18. Remove four bolts from valve housing and remove valve housing.

CAUTION

Proper valve function depends on valve sleeve and worm shaft being reassembled in their original assembled position.

NOTE: Timing marks have been added to these parts so they can be reassembled in their original position.

19. IMPORTANT: Do not remove drive ring from worm shaft or attempt to unbend tangs which hold drive ring in place on worm shaft.
20. Remove valve sleeve from valve housing.
21. Remove "O" ring from valve housing.
22. Remove thrust washers and thrust bearing from valve housing. The second thrust washer may stay on the end of the valve sleeve. If so, remove it from the sleeve.
23. Remove seal from valve housing with a screwdriver.
24. Remove retaining ring, (steel) back-up washer, seal cup and "O" ring from valve housing.
25. Inspect thrust bearing and thrust washers for wear marks or brinelling, replace if damaged.
26. Remove seal rings and O-rings from valve sleeve. Do not damage the valve sleeve.
27. Remove rack piston and worm shaft assembly from housing.

NOTE: For gears with a removable end cover, remove the rack piston assembly from the long end of the housing (bottom of gear) to prevent the plastic piston seal from getting caught in the sector shaft cavity.

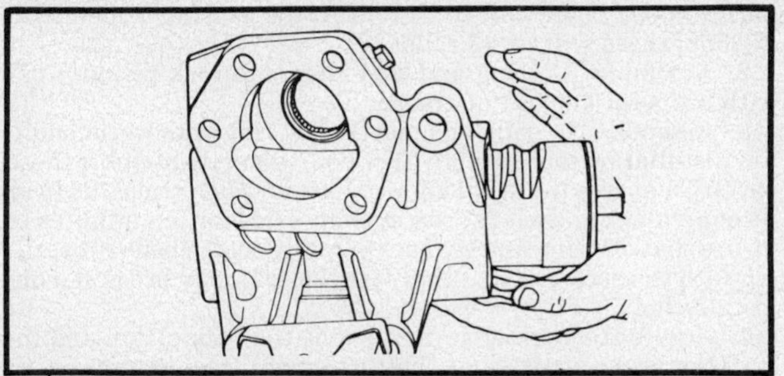
Rack piston and worm shaft removal (© Ford Motor Co.)

28. Lay rack piston and worm shaft assembly on a clean rag to keep from rolling and to catch balls as they come out.
29. For rack pistons with a ball return guide cap remove the two allen head bolts. Remove the ball return guide cap and ball return guide cap seal.
30. Some rack pistons may have a ball return guide clip instead of the cap. In this case, bend the tangs down on the two locking tabs. Remove the two hex head bolts. Remove the clip.
31. Remove ball return guides and balls from rack piston. Ball return guides are closely fitted into rack piston and may have to be removed by carefully inserting a pry tool between rack piston and ball return guides. To remove balls, turn rack piston over so balls can roll out as worm shaft is rotated in each direction by small amounts.

NOTE: Assembly contains a set of twenty-seven matched balls; special care must be exercised to not lose them. A complete new matched set of balls will be required if any balls are lost.

33. Inspect rack piston teeth and worm groove for excessive wear marks.
34. Remove seal ring and "O"-ring from rack piston.
35. Remove and discard the plastic worm shaft seal ring and "O"-ring.
36. If gear has the automatic air bleed assembly, remove the screw and passageway seal from the housing. Then, tilt the housing upside down so that the special pin and spring fall out.
37. If the gear is equipped with poppet valves in the rack piston, they will usually not require servicing. If it is necessary, however, position the rack piston in a soft-jawed vise. Then, remove two poppet retaining rings, two poppet seats, two poppets, the nylon spacer rod and the poppet spring.

Inspection

Check to make sure that all sealing surfaces and seal cavities are free from nicks and corrosion. If any part is nicked or corroded where sealing occurs, the part must be replaced to insure proper sealing and gear function.

Wash all parts in clean petroleum-based solvent. Blow dry with air only.

1. Inspect the rack piston teeth for cracks and wear. If a step can be detected by running a fingernail horizontally across the teeth surface, both the rack piston and sector shaft must be replaced.
2. Inspect the rack piston internal ball-track-grooves and the worm shaft grooves for brinelling (dents) or spalling (flaking). If either condition exists, all of the following parts must be replaced: the rack piston, the worm shaft/input shaft assembly, the balls, the drive ring and the valve sleeve.
3. Visually inspect the upper shaft seal area near the input shaft serrations for nicks, and run a fingernail edge across the sealing surface to detect steps.

NOTE: The input shaft is pinned to the worm shaft by the torsion bar pin, and the assembly is flexible and may appear slightly bent at this joint. This slight bend is normal.

Ball removal (© Ford Motor Co.)

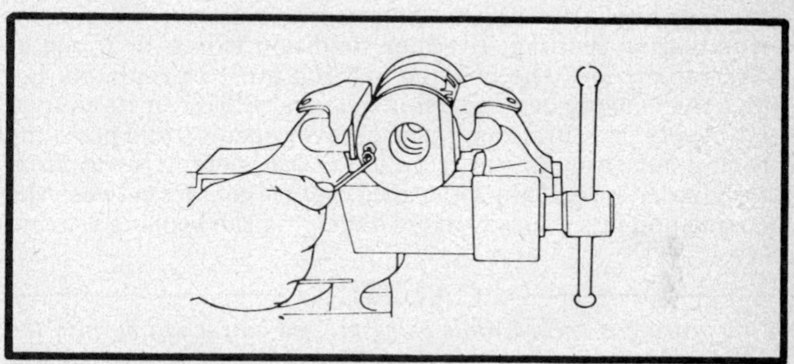
Poppet valve service (© Ford Motor Co.)

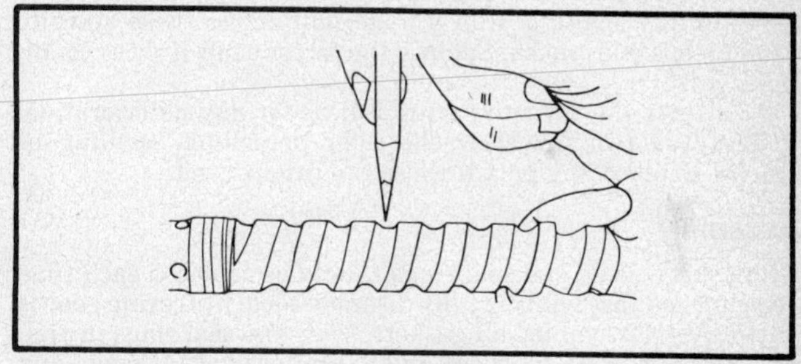
Worm shaft inspection (© Ford Motor Co.)

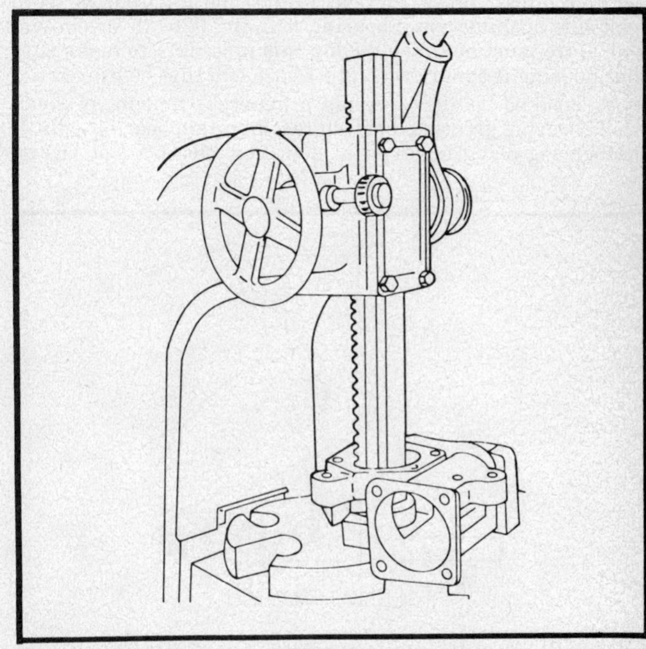
Housing bearing removal (© Ford Motor Co.)

4. Inspect the housing cylinder bore where normal scoring marks running lengthwise through the bore maybe noticed. Replace the housing only if it has been tested for internal leakage and it has been determined that the scoring, and not damaged seals, is responsible for the excessive internal leakage.

NOTE: In running this test, make sure that excessive internal leakage can only be attributed to the housing and not to the new seals in the worm shaft rack piston and valve sleeve.

5. Inspect the housing faces for nicks that would prevent proper sealing. Replace the gear housing if these nicks are present and cannot be easily removed with a fine-toothed flat file without changing the dimensional characteristics.

6. Inspect the housing bearing and the side cover bearing for brinelling or spalling. If either condition exists, or if one or more rolls is lost, the housing bearing must be replaced. Remove the housing bearing using mandrel J26738 or its equivalent. Apply pressure from the side cover opening and press the bearing out through the trunnion cover opening, away from the cylinder bore. Maintain a good, square contact between the housing and press base to avoid damaging the housing bearing bore.

CAUTION

If the bearing is cocked while being pressed out, it will burnish the bore, causing it to become oversized. If this happens, the housing will have to be replaced.

7. Inspect the sector shaft bearing and sealing surface for brinelling or spalling. Run a fingernail across these areas to detect steps and cracks. Replace the sector shaft if these conditions exist.

8. Inspect the thrust bearing rollers for any deterioration. Inspect the two thrust washers for brinelling, spalling or cracks. Replace any part if these conditions exist.

Assembly

All gaskets, seals and seal rings should be replaced each time steering gear assembly is fully disassembled; if steering gear is partially disassembled all gaskets, seals and seal rings in area affected should be replaced. Individual seals, seal rings and gaskets or complete seal kits are available.

1. If required, press new bearing into housing from the trunnion side opening using bearing mandrel J26738, or equivalent. Care must be taken during this procedure to make sure that housing is square with press base and that bearing is not in a "crooked" position. Apply a generous amount of clean wheel bearing grease to bearing race to retain bearing rolls. If the bearing being installed is identified BR–866–1 or has no part number, there will be 44 rolls. If the bearing is identified F83508, there will be 43 rolls.

2. Assemble "O" ring and seal ring onto rack piston. Coat with a liberal amount of grease.

3. Assemble "O" ring and plastic seal ring onto worm shaft, use installation tool J26650–01 or equivalent, to asemble these parts. Compress the seal ring with compression tool J26649 or its equivalent and set the worm shaft aside for ten minutes to insure that the ring and seal are properly seated before installing into the rack piston, otherwise the seal may break during installation.

4. Grease the sealing surface inside the rack piston and install the worm shaft/input shaft assembly into the rack.

5. Assemble ball return guides into rack piston. Make sure they are properly seated.

CAUTION

Do not seat guides with a hammer. Damage to guides can result in subsequent lockup or loss of steering.

6. Assemble ball into ball return guides and rack piston; drop balls thru hole provided in ball return guides. Rotate worm shaft as balls are being assembled to pull balls down into groove, assemble twenty-seven balls.

CAUTION

Make sure ball return guides stay down in place in rack piston while assembling balls.

7. For gears equipped with the ball return guide cap, grease the cap seal and place it in the seal groove of the cap. Assemble the cap so that the seal makes full contact with the rack piston surface. Install the two allen head bolts and tighten them to 18–23 Nm (13–17 ft-lbs).

8. For gears equipped with the ball return guide clip, install it so that both bolt hole faces are in full contact with the rack piston surface. Install the two lock tabs and the two hex head bolts. Tighten the bolts to 18–23 Nm (13–17 ft lbs). Finish by bending the locking tabs up against the bolt head flats.

CAUTION

Rotate the worm shaft from one end of travel to the other to make certain the balls have been installed properly. If you cannot rotate the worm shaft, you will have to remove the balls and reassemble them. If a gear is installed on a truck with the worm shaft unable to rotate, the gear will not function correctly and damage may result.

9. Apply a generous amount of clean grease to seal ring area of rack piston and very carefully assemble rack piston and worm shaft assembly into housing so as not to damage the seals. For gears with a removable end cover, install the rack piston and worm shaft assembly into the long end of the gear

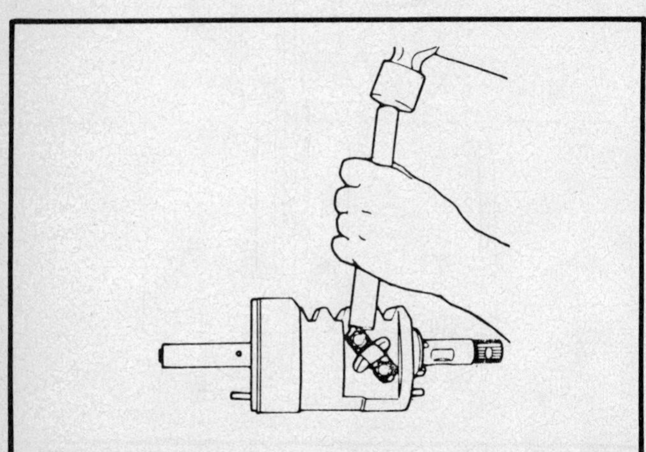

Bending clip locking tabs (© Ford Motor Co.)

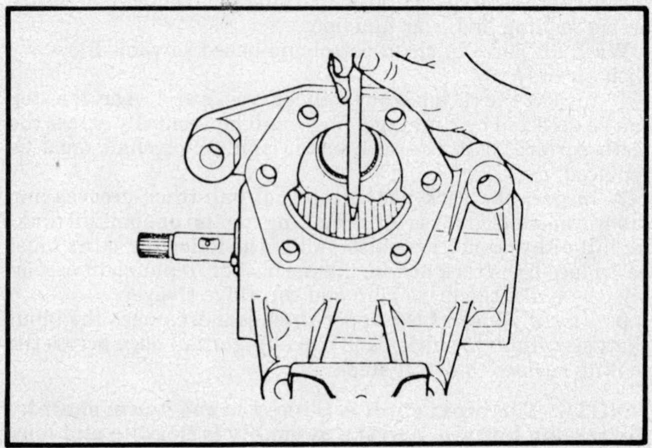

Positioning rack teeth (© Ford Motor Co.)

housing so that the plastic rack piston seal goes in last.

10. Rotate the rack piston and worm shaft assembly in the housing so that the rack teeth are exposed in the sector shaft cavity of the housing.

11. Assemble the worm shaft adjusting screw jam nut onto the nonslotted end of the worm shaft preload adjusting screw so that the seal on the jam nut faces the end cover or closed end of the housing.

12. If the gear is equipped with poppet valves, assemble the poppet valve adjusting screw and jam nut and the other poppet valve adjusting screw and jam nut in the same manner as described for the worm shaft adjusting screw and jam nut.

NOTE: The poppet valve adjusting screws, may not be the same length. If they are not, assemble the shorter adjusting screw into the end cover or closed end of the housing, a few turns. If this procedure is not followed exactly, the poppet assembly may break and lockup the steering gear.

13. Install the worm shaft preload adjusting screw into the end cover or closed end of the gear housing a few turns. Final adjustment will be made later.

14. If the gear is equipped with the removable end cover, apply clean grease to the "O"-ring groove in the end cover. Install the new end cover "O"-ring into the groove. When installed, the "O"-ring will extend slightly above the machined surface of the end cover.

15. If the gear is equipped with the removable end cover, install the four end cover bolts and washers. Torque to 143–156 Nm (105–115 ft. lbs).

16. Grease the two new backup "O"-rings and the two new plastic seal rings and install onto the valve sleeve using seal installation tool J26647 or its equivalent.

17. Use the compression tool J26648 or its equivalent to compress the plastic seal rings. Leave this compression tool on for 10 minutes, to ensure that the seals are properly seated. Otherwise, the valve sleeve will be difficult to assemble into the valve housing and the seal may be cut during installation.

18. Apply clean grease to the "O"-ring groove in the valve housing. Install the new valve housing "O"-ring into the groove. When installed, the valve housing "O"-ring should extend slightly above the machined surface of the valve housing.

19. Apply a generous amount of clean grease to one thrust washer. Place the valve housing exterior side down on a flat surface and place the thrust washer into the valve housing, making sure to center the washer.

20. Apply a generous amount of clean grease to the thrust bearing. Install the bearing into the valve housing and onto the first thrust washer, making sure to center the bearing on the washer.

CAUTION

The thrust washer and the thrust bearing must be flat and centered in the counterbore surface of the valve housing. Otherwise, the thrust washer could break when the valve housing is placed onto the gear housing, causing the steering gear to malfunction.

21. Remove the compression tool from the valve sleeve. Apply more grease to the valve sleeve seals, and grease the thrust washer face on the end of the valve sleeve without the drive slots.

Place the second thrust washer onto this face. This thrust washer must be securely on the valve sleeve, otherwise it can crack and cause the steering gear to malfunction.

22. Locate the timing mark on the valve sleeve, a faint, punched mark on the chamfered edge of the sleeve. Make a corresponding mark on the front face with a felt marker.

23. Assemble the valve sleeve, with the second thrust washer attached, into the valve housing thrust-washer end first. When the valve sleeve is properly in place, the valve sleeve face should measure approximately 0.400 in. (10–16mm) below the face of the valve housing.

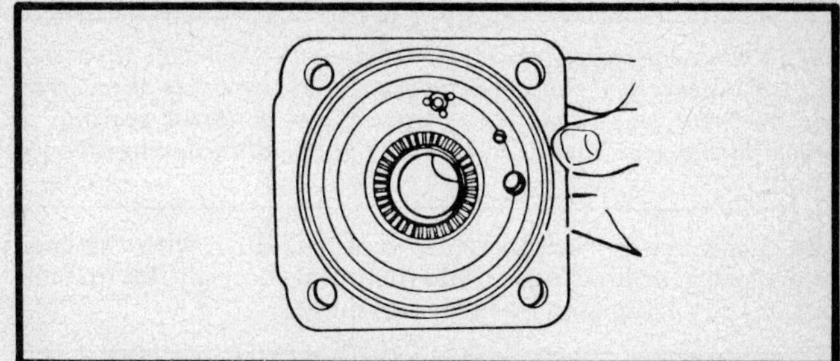

Thrust bearing installation (© Ford Motor Co.)

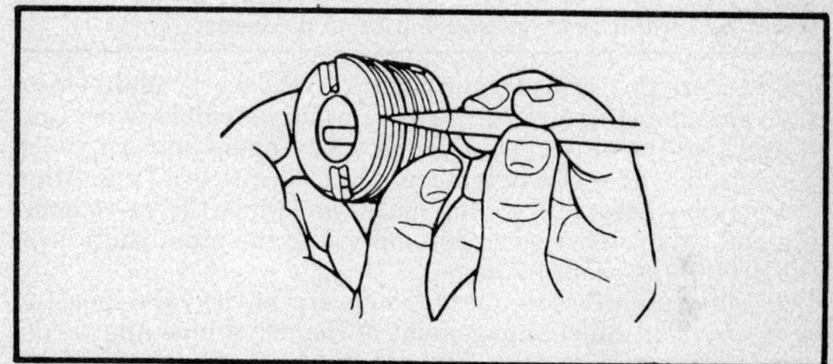

Valve timing mark (© Ford Motor Co.)

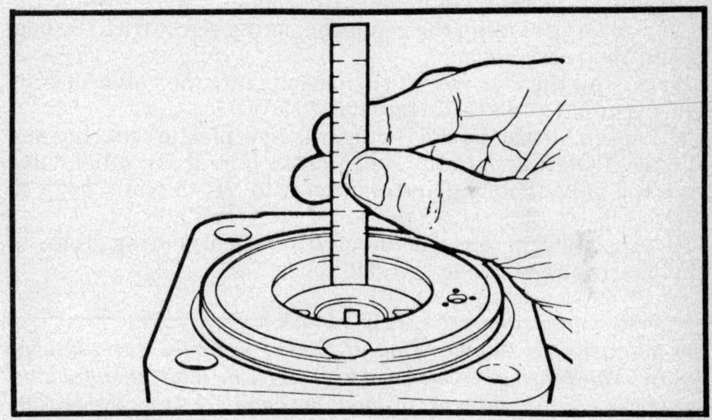

Valve sleeve correctly installed (© Ford Motor Co.)

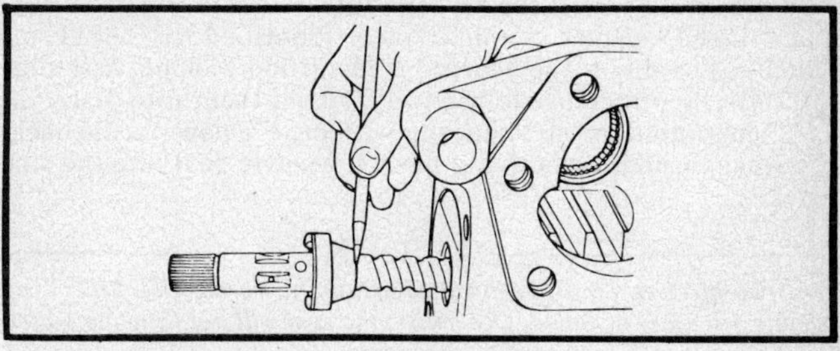

Worm shaft timing mark (© Ford Motor Co.)

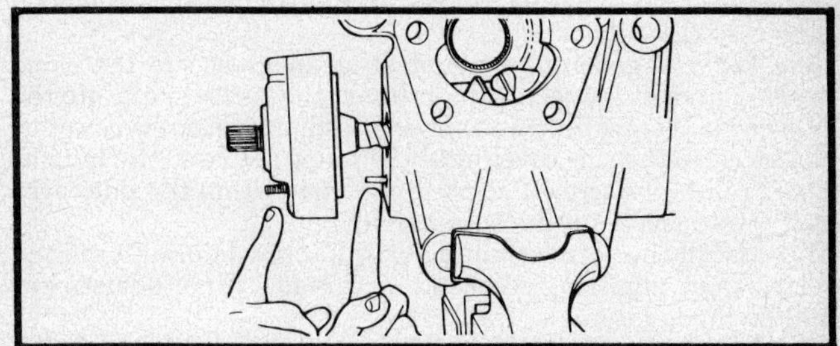

Poppet adjusting screw alignment (© Ford Motor Co.)

CAUTION

Do not force the valve sleeve down into the valve housing. Make sure the valve sleeve seal rings are compressed. Misassembly or incorrect measurement may cause the thrust washers or thrust bearings to break during gear operation, resulting in a malfunctioning steering gear.

24. Position the rack piston so that it is flush with the open end of the gear housing. Rotate the worm shaft until it extends out of the rack piston as far as it will go.

CAUTION

Worm shaft and valve sleeve are assembled and sold as matched sets. Use only pre-matched sets for replacement. Never mate an old sleeve with a new worm or a new sleeve with an old worm.

25. Locate the scribed timing mark on the worm shaft. Grasp the valve housing and valve sleeve as an assembly, with your thumbs on the valve housing and your fingers applying pressure on the valve sleeve to keep it in the valve housing. Align the previously located timing marks and place the valve housing and valve sleeve as an assembly onto the input shaft until the drive lugs are fully engaged.
26. Maintain pressure on the valve end of the valve housing to insure continued engagement of the drive lugs and thrust bearing package. Continuing pressure, rotate the input shaft to bring the valve housing into contact with the gear housing face. If the gear is equipped with poppet valves, rotate the valve housing to align the poppet adjusting screw with the poppet in the rack piston.
27. Install the four valve housing bolts into the valve housing and tighten to 143–156 Nm (105–115 ft-lbs).
28. Assemble the new "O"-ring, the new plastic seal ring and the new "O"-ring onto the relief valve. Install the relief valve into the valve housing and tighten it to 34–48 Nm (25–35 ft-lbs).
29. Apply a generous amount of clean wheel bearing grease to the bearing race inside the side cover.

CAUTION

Do not substitute another kind of grease, use only wheel bearing grease. This bearing is sealed and will receive no lubrication from the hydraulic fluid in the gear. Without the correct grease, the bearing could wear prematurely.

30. Assembly the bearing rolls into the side cover bearing race. If the bearing is unmarked or identified BR-866-1, assemble 44 rolls. If the bearing is identified F83508, assemble 43 rolls. Apply grease to the rolls to hold them into place.
31. Assemble the steel backup washer, the new plastic backup washer, and the new two-piece side cover seal into the side cover.

CAUTION

The two-piece seal must be installed so that the words "OIL SIDE" are visible after it is installed. Otherwise, the seal will not function which could result in a loss or power steering.

32. Assemble the side cover retaining ring into the ring groove of the side cover.
33. Apply a generous amount of clean grease to the short bearing area of the sector shaft. Insert the sector shaft into the side cover. Screw in the sector shaft adjusting screw counterclockwise in the side cover until the screw reaches solid height. Then, rotate the screw clockwise one turn so that the side cover will rotate freely on the sector shaft.
34. Install the sector shaft adjusting screw jam nut onto the sector shaft adjusting screw a few threads. Final adjustment will be made later.
35. Press the rubber plug into the hole provided in the side cover until the plug is flush.

CAUTION

Do not weld or otherwise plug this hole in any permanent manner. This is a safety vent which functions only if the side cover seal fails. If this seals fails and the plug cannot vent, the steering gear may lockup or otherwise malfunction.

36. Apply clean grease to the new side cover gasket and assemble it onto the side cover. Apply enough grease to hold the gasket in place.
37. There are four teeth on the rack piston. Position the rack piston so that the tooth space identified by the pencil, between the second and third teeth, is in the center of the sector shaft opening. This will center the rack piston in the opening.

CAUTION

If the rack piston is not centered, gear travel will be severely limited in one direction.

38. Clean off any old tape on the sector shaft. Retape the serrations and bolt groove with one layer of clean masking tape. Install the sector shaft and side cover into the gear housing as an assembly. Make sure that the center tooth of the sector shaft engages the center space (between the second and third teeth) of the rack piston.

CAUTION

As the sector shaft is placed through the housing bearing, do not knock any of the bearing rolls out of the bearing race. Do not pinch the side cover gasket. If either occurs, the bearing or seal may fail prematurely resulting a loss of power steering assist.

39. Install the six special side cover bolts into the side cover and torque them to 300–325 Nm (220–240 ft-lbs).
40. Place the trunnion cover exterior face down and install the new plastic backup washer.
41. Install the new two-piece sector shaft seal so that the words "OIL SIDE" are visible after the seal is in place.

CAUTION

The words "OIL SIDE" must be visible on the seal after it is in place. If not, the seal will not function and a loss of power steering assist may occur.

42. Grease the new trunnion cover "O"-ring and install it into the trunnion cover "O"-ring groove.
43. Visually inspect the housing bearing to make sure that all the bearing rolls are in place. Then, install the trunnion cover. Install the four trunnion cover bolts and tighten them to 20–30 Nm (15–22 ft-lbs). Install a new dirt and washer seal.
44. Apply clean grease to the input shaft seal assembly, and to the input shaft. Install the new two-piece input shaft seal, flat side out, and the steel backup washer, using seal driving tool. Install the retaining ring.
45. Pack the area around the input shaft with clean water-resistant grease, and install the dirt and water seal by tapping into place with a hammer and soft punch.

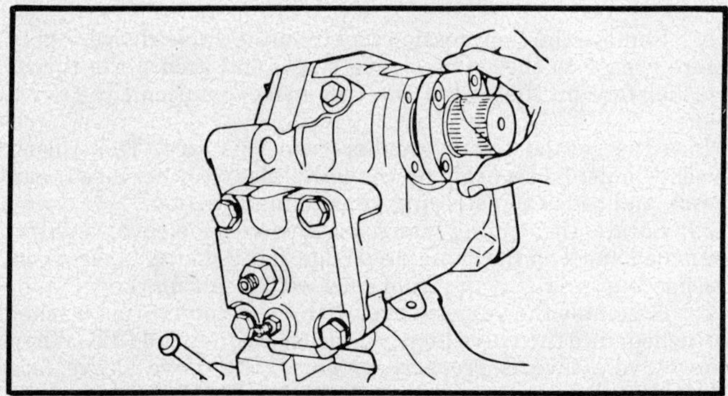

Trunnion cover installation (© Ford Motor Co.)

46. If the gear is equipped with the automatic bleed screw, position the steering gear so that the cylinder bore axis is vertical and the input shaft is pointing down. Then install the spring, the special pin and the automatic bleed screw into the housing. Torque the screw to 22–27 Nm (16–20 ft-lbs).

CAUTION

If the automatic bleed assembly is improperly assembled, there may be a loss of power steering in one direction.

47. If the gear is equipped with the manual bleed screw, install it in the gear housing and tighten to 3–4 Nm (27–33 in-lbs).

Before installing the gear on the vehicle, proceed to make the final adjustments.

Final Adjustments

1. Screw the wormshaft preload adjusting screw finger tight until it contacts the worm shaft. Apply 7–14 Nm (5–10 ft-lbs) of torque. Back screw out one turn.
2. To center the steering gear, align the sector shaft timing mark halfway between two trunnion cover bolts. The timing mark should be perpendicular to the center line of the cylinder bore.
3. Adjust the sector shaft adjusting screw while you rotate the input shaft 90 degrees each side of center, until the input shaft reaches a torque of 2.8–3.4 Nm (25–30 in-lbs).
4. Back out the adjusting screw one turn. Note the torque now required to rotate the input shaft through 90 degrees each side of center. Then move the adjusting screw in to increase the noted torque by 0.23 to 0.68 Nm (2 to 6 in-lbs). The increase should be noted at a point within 45 degrees each side of center.
5. Tighten the sector shaft adjusting screw jam nut to 54–68 Nm (40–50 ft-lbs). The torque now required to rotate the input shaft should not exceed 2.3 Nm (20 in-lbs), at any point in the steering gear travel. If it does exceed 2.3 Nm (20 in-lbs), repeat Step 4.
6. Adjust the worm shaft preload adjusting screw to increase the maximum noted input torque by 1.1 to 1.7 Nm (10 to 15 in-lbs), while rotating the input shaft 45 degrees each side of center. Make sure the worm shaft adjusting screw jam nut does not contact the closed end of the housing or end cover while making this adjustment. Torque the jam nut to 95–108 Nm (70–80 lb-ft), making sure that the adjusting screw does not move.

ROSS HFB 64 INTEGRAL POWER STEERING GEAR TORQUE LIMITS

Part	Torque Limits (ft-lbs)	N•m
Hexagon Head Bolt (Valve Housing)	105–115	142–156
Relief Valve	25–35	34–47
Screw (Ball Return Guide Cap)	15–19	20–26
Sealing Nut (Worm Shaft Adjusting Screw)	70–80	95–109
Nut (Sector Shaft Adjusting Screw)	40–45	54–61
Special Bolt (Side Cover)	220–240	299–326
Bolt Assembly, Pitman Arm Clamp, 3/4-16 (Grade 8)	220–300	299–406
Trunnion Cover Bolt	15–22	20–30
Bleed Screw	16–20	22–27

7. The torque now required to rotate the input shaft through complete travel of the steering gear should not exceed 4 Nm (35 in-lbs). If it does not exceed 4 Nm (35 in-lbs), repeat Step 6.

Sheppard Integral Type System

The Sheppard Integral Power Steering Gear is manufactured in two series. A low pressure gear designed to operate in a range of 0–1300 psi and a high pressure series designed to operate up to 2000 psi. Some models of the Sheppard gear are available in a low or high ratio. To determine low or high ratio, disconnect the master gear drag link, turn the steering wheel from full left to full right and count the number of turns. If the total turns is 5 or less, the ratio is low. Over 5 turns is high ratio. The Sheppard Gear requires the use of 10w–40 (API SD–SE) motor oil. When filling the reservoir, start the engine and turn the steering wheel from left to right and continue filling until the proper level is reached and maintained. A replaceable filter element is located in the pump reservoir. To lubricate the dirt and salt seals in the bearing cap and flush out any contaminants that may have passed these seals, chassis grease should be added with low pressure when the vehicle is serviced. If equipped with a miter gear box (angle drive) use Fisk Magic ball bearing grease or equivalent.

OPERATION

The actuating shaft (connected to the steering column) is threaded to accommodate the actuating valve which is centered within the piston by reversing springs. The valve moves in a linear (straight) motion within the piston permitting the edges of the valve to overlap mating edges on the inside of the piston. This causes high pressure oil to build up at one end of the piston. The higher pressure on one end of the piston causes the piston to move in the bore of the gear housing. The output shaft and pinion gear are engaged to a rack gear machined into one side of the piston. As the piston moves, the output shaft and Pitman arm are rotated by the rack and pinion gear. When rotation or input from the actuating shaft ceases, pressure on, or movement of the actuating valve stops and the reversing springs at the ends of the valve center the valve in the piston relieving the high pressure then power to the steering ceases.

Movement of the actuating valve, to control oil pressure is controlled by the deflection of the reversing spring at either end of the valve. Total movement of the valve is approximately 0.040 inch. Relief valve plungers or adjustable stops are provided at the bearing cap and cylinder head. When the plungers are adjusted properly, they will automatically unload the hydraulic system if the wheels are turned to either extreme direction.

Identification

Each Sheppard gear has markings for identification. A number is cast into the steering gear housing and identifies the basic family to which the steering gear belongs. Stamped letters and numbers are on an exposed machined surface of the housing which identifies that particular unit. A serial number is also stamped on the gear to identify the month and year when the gear was built.

STEERING GEAR

Disassembly

WITHOUT MITER GEARBOX

1. Loosen the plunger locknut and remove the relief valve plungers.

NOTE: Later production steering gears may have slotted and recessed relief plunger. The later style plungers are removed and adjusted with a straight bladed screw driver.

SHEPPARD POWER STEERING
Operating Pressure and Oil Flow Specifications

Models	Ratio	Oil Flow (GPM) U.S. Minimum	Oil Flow (GPM) U.S. Maximum
LOW PRESSURE			
188	—	1.9	2.4
191	—	2.2	2.7
39	—	3.6	4.4
491	—	4.3	5.3
51	—	4.8	6.0
59	—	5.7	7.0
HIGH PRESSURE SERIES			
192	—	2.2	2.7
252, 292	—	3.2	4.0
372, 382, 352	—	3.6	4.4
392, 392S	—	3.6	4.4
492, 492S	—	4.3	5.3
592	—	5.7	7.0
DUAL SYSTEMS			
292W/292 Slave	Low	4.5	5.5
	High	4.0	5.0
372-382W/292 Slave	Low	5.0	6.0
	High	4.0	4.5
392W/392 Slave	Low	5.0	6.0
	High	4.0	5.0
392W/292 Slave	Low	5.0	6.0
	High	4.0	5.0
492W/492 Slave	Low	6.0	7.0
	High	5.0	6.0
592W/592 Slave	Low	8.0	9.0
	High	7.0	8.0

—Not applicable

2. Remove the housing cover bolts and tap on the end of the output shaft to loosen the cover.
3. Remove the output shaft and gear assembly from the housing.
   a. Before moving, check the scribe marks on the rack and gear for alignment purposes during reassembly.
   b. If the marks can not be seen make your own so that the parts can be easily timed during reassembly.
4. Leave the gear on the output shaft unless replacement is necessary.
   a. To disassemble the output shaft and gear, remove the screws which secure the gear retaining nut.
   b. Turn the retaining nut counterclockwise and remove the nut.
   c. Press the output shaft out of the gear.
5. Mark the cylinder head and housing for reassembly and remove the cylinder head and gasket.

NOTE: Some units do not use a gasket here. In their place will be square cut ring seals on the cylinder and bearing caps.

6. Mark the bearing cap and housing for reassembly and remove the bearing cap attaching bolts.
7. Turn the bearing cap and actuating shaft out of the actuating valve.
8. Disassemble the bearing and actuating shaft only if a defect is suspected.

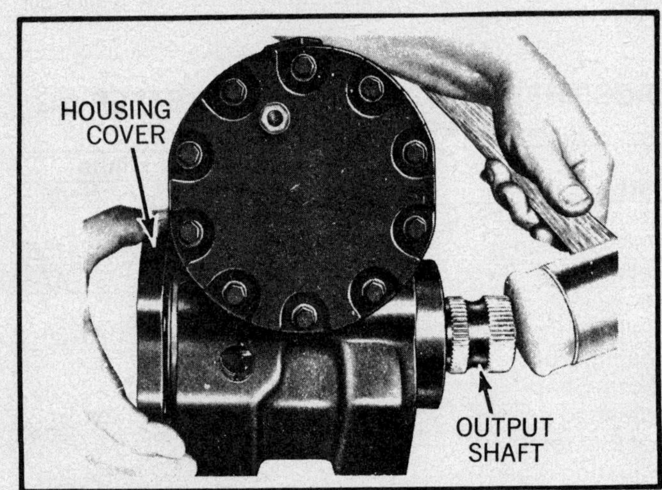

Removing output shaft (© Mack Trucks Inc.)

   a. To disassemble, remove the lock-pin from the retaining nut.
   b. Use a spanner wrench and remove the retaining nut.
   c. Tap or press the actuating shaft out of the bearing cap.

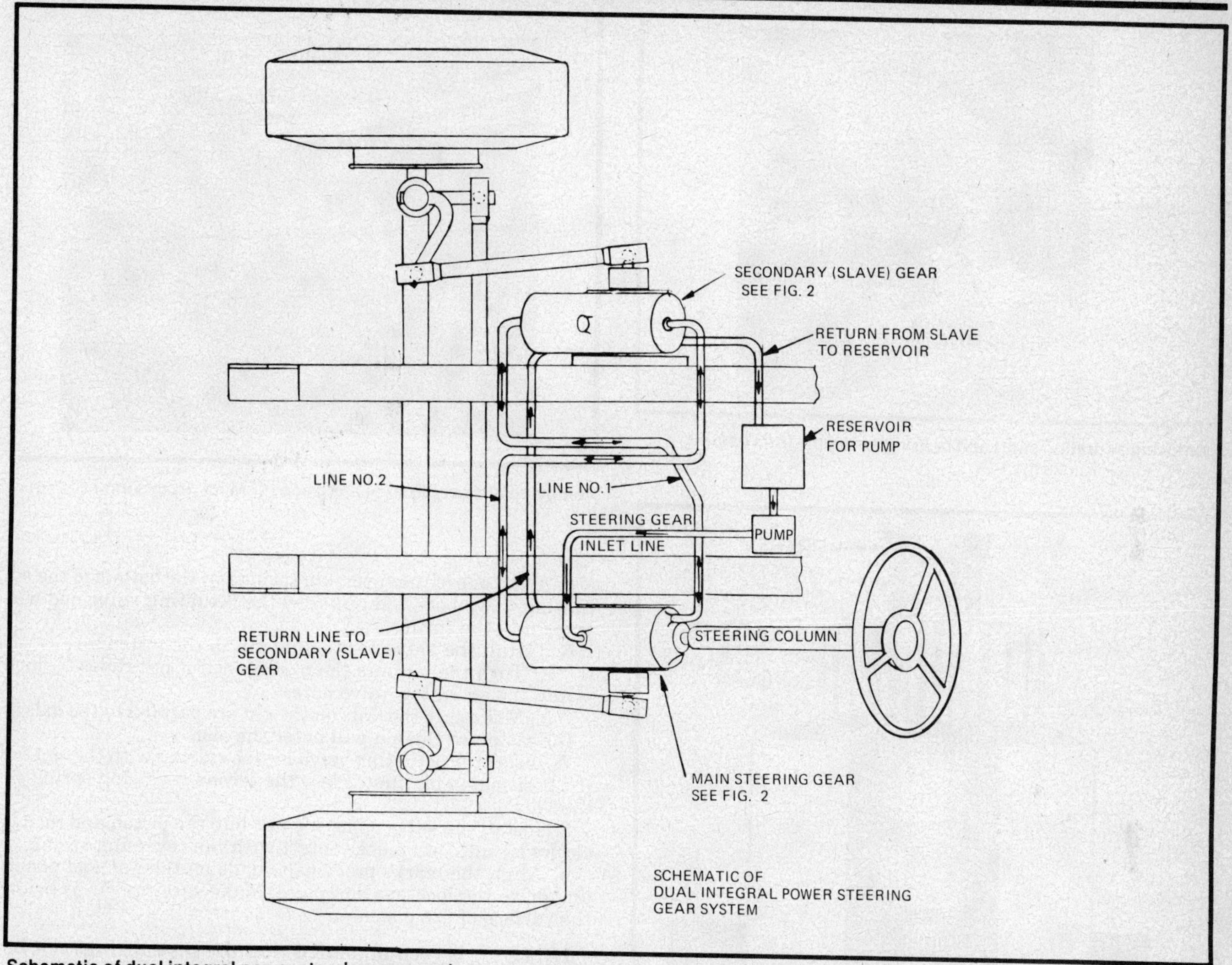

SECONDARY (SLAVE) GEAR SEE FIG. 2
RETURN FROM SLAVE TO RESERVOIR
RESERVOIR FOR PUMP
LINE NO.2
LINE NO.1
STEERING GEAR INLET LINE
PUMP
RETURN LINE TO SECONDARY (SLAVE) GEAR
STEERING COLUMN
MAIN STEERING GEAR SEE FIG. 2
SCHEMATIC OF DUAL INTEGRAL POWER STEERING GEAR SYSTEM

Schematic of dual integral power steering gear system (© Mack Trucks Inc.)

NOTE: The bearing and actuating shaft is serviced as a unit and should not be disassembled after removing from the bearing cap.

d. Pry the dirt seal from the bearing cap.
e. Drive the oil seal from the bearing cap.

9. Pull the piston assembly out of the housing.
10. Mark the piston and valve adjusting nut for reassembly. Remove the lock pin from the nut, then remove the nut.
11. Remove the reversing spring and without forcing, remove the actuator valve from the piston.
12. Remove the valve positioning pin.
13. Remove the second reversing spring from the piston.
14. Remove the piston rings.
15. Remove the valve seats, balls and spring from the piston.

CAUTION

Be careful when removing the valve seats as the balls are spring loaded.

16. Remove the output shaft seal.
17. If it is necessary to replace the output shaft bushings in either the housing or cover, use a puller.

Assembly

1. Clean all parts individually in a solvent and replace any parts that are worn or broken.

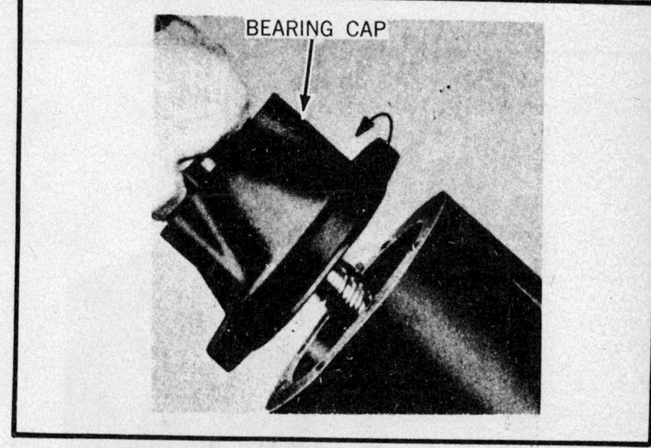

Removing bearing cap and actuating shaft (© Mack Trucks Inc.)

2. If removed, press new cover or housing bushings flush with the inside face.
3. Install a new output shaft seal.
4. Insert a valve spring, ball and seat into each bore.

NOTE: Be sure the valve seats are flush with or below the surface of the piston.

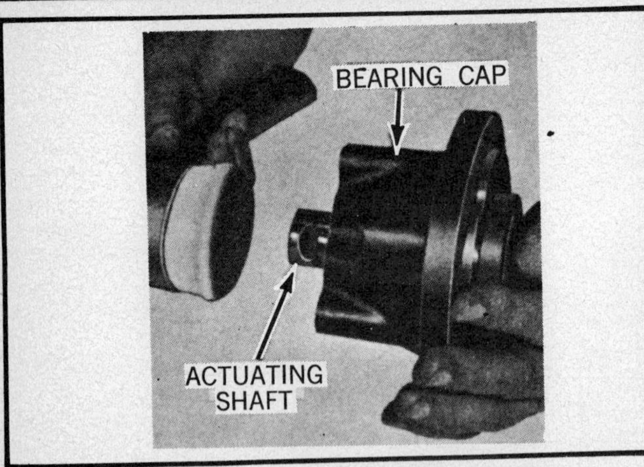

Removing actuating shaft and bearing assembly from bearing cap (© Mack Trucks Inc.)

Removing dirt seal from bearing cap (© Mack Trucks Inc.)

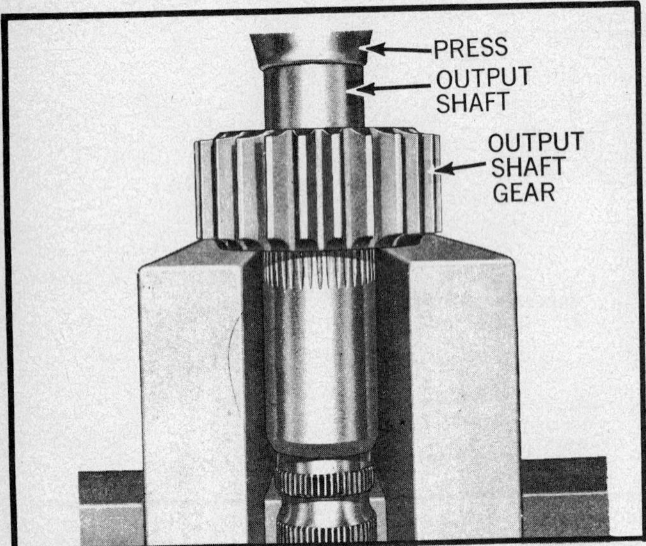

Removing output gear from shaft (© Mack Trucks Inc.)

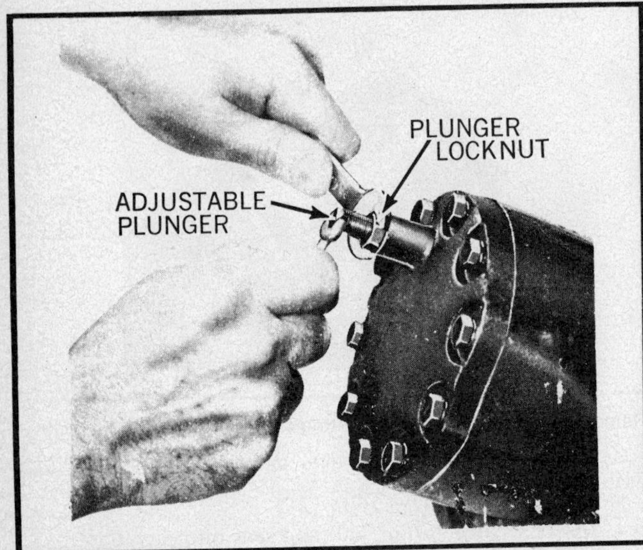

Removing relief valve plunger (© Mack Trucks Inc.)

5. Place one of the reversing springs on the bottom of the actuating valve bore and center so the actuating valve end will enter into the spring.
6. Install the valve positioning pin in the piston.
   a. Turn the pin into the piston until it protrudes $^1/_4$ inch into the actuating valve bore.
   b. Make sure the flats on the pin are parallel to the axis of the piston so the pin will enter the slot.
7. Insert the actuating valve into the piston with the slot for the positioning pin first. Place the second reversing spring on the valve.
8. Install the valve adjusting nut into the piston and turn it clockwise until it makes contact with the reversing spring.
9. Align the marks previously made on the nut and piston and drive the lock-pin into place. Make sure the pin is below the surface of the piston.

NOTE: It is recommended that the piston rings not be reinstalled on the piston assembly of the Sheppard Power Steering Gear during an overhaul. The unit will operate properly without the rings. Production steering gears will have the rings omitted, and may be encountered upon disassembly of the steering gear.

10. Coat the piston and housing bore with oil.
11. Install the piston into the housing with the actuating valve end towards the bearing cap end of the housing.
12. Install the cylinder head and use a new gasket.
   a. Align the marks so the head will be in the correct position and the relief valve plunger will line up with the relief valve in the piston.
   b. Torque the attaching bolt. $^5/_{16}$ bolts to 20 ft. lbs.; $^3/_8$ bolts to 33 ft. lbs.
13. Press a new oil and dirt seal into the bearing cap.
14. If removed previously, press the actuating shaft and bearing assembly into the bearing cap.
15. Install the actuating shaft bearing retaining nut and insert the locking pin.

NOTE: When using a new retaining nut the hole for the lockpin must be drilled after the nut is seated. Use a $^3/_{32}$ inch drill and drill the nut $^3/_{16}$ inch deep through the hole in the bearing cap.

16. Thread the actuating shaft into the actuating valve and install the bearing cap with a new gasket.
   a. Align the marks on the cap and housing to insure the plunger lining up with the relief valve.

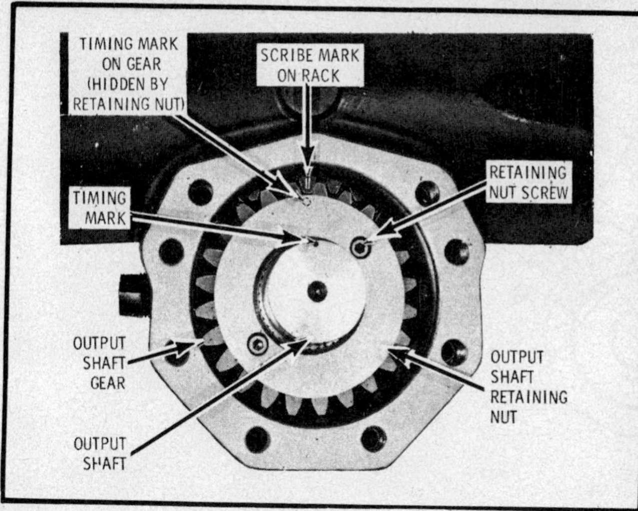

Output shaft and gear alignment marks (© Mack Trucks Inc.)

Removing oil seal from bearing cap

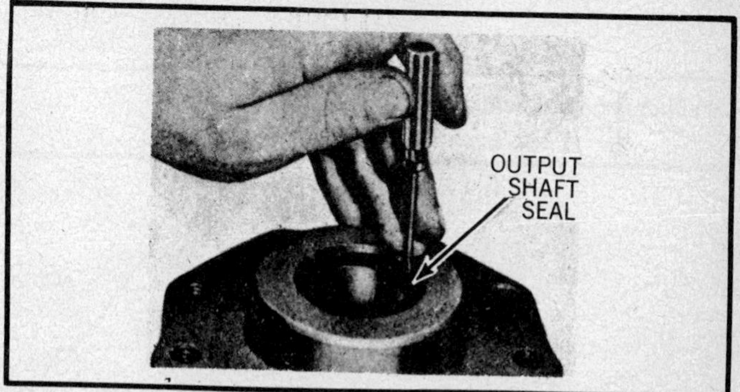

Removing output shaft seal (© Mack Trucks Inc.)

b. Hold the bearing cap in the proper position and turn the actuating shaft until the bearing cap is seated.

c. Torque the attaching bolts: $^5/_{16}$ bolts to 20 ft. lbs.; $^3/_8$ bolts to 33 ft. lbs.

17. Install the output shaft on the gear if it was previously disassembled.

Align the marks on the output shaft and the gear and press the gear on the shaft.

18. Insert the output shaft and gear assembly into the gear housing and make sure the timing mark on the gear is aligned with the mark on the rack.

NOTE: It may be necessary to make another scribe mark on the rack if the original mark is difficult to see when the output shaft gear is in place. It is important that the rack and gear are correctly timed.

19. Install the output shaft gear retaining nut and tighten against the gear while aligning the holes in the nut and the gear. Install and tighten the two retaining nut screws.

20. Place a new O-ring in the groove and install the housing cover.

a. Tap the cover with a soft hammer to seat it properly.

b. Install the attaching bolts and tighten: $^7/_{16}$ bolts to 20–36 ft. lbs.; $^5/_8$ bolts to 100 ft. lbs.

21. Use new O-rings and install the relief valve plungers. Turn into the bearing cap or cylinder head approximately six turns.

22. Install the gear in the vehicle and make the final relief valve plunger adjustments. See the Relief Valve Plunger Adjustment for procedures.

Removing piston assembly from housing (© Mack Trucks Inc.)

STEERING GEAR

Disassembly

WITH MITER GEARBOX

1. Loosen the locknut and remove the relief valve plunger in the cylinder head.
2. Remove the housing cover bolts and tap on the end of the output shaft to loosen the cover.
3. Remove the output shaft and gear assembly from the housing.

a. Before removing, check the scribe marks on the rack and gear for alignment purposes during reassembly.

b. If the marks cannot be seen, make your own so that the parts can be easily timed during reassembly.

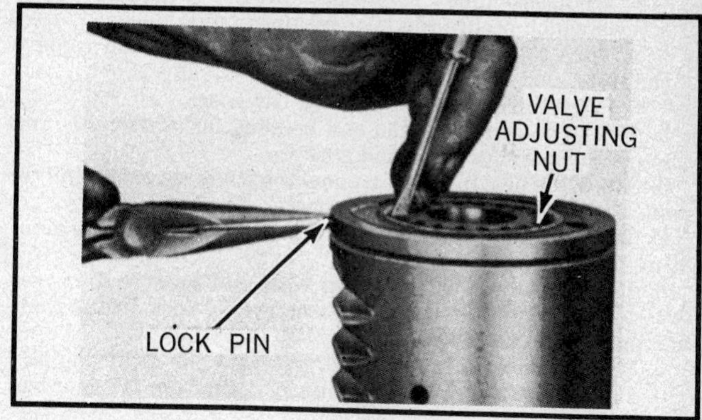

Removing valve positioning pin (© Mack Trucks Inc.)

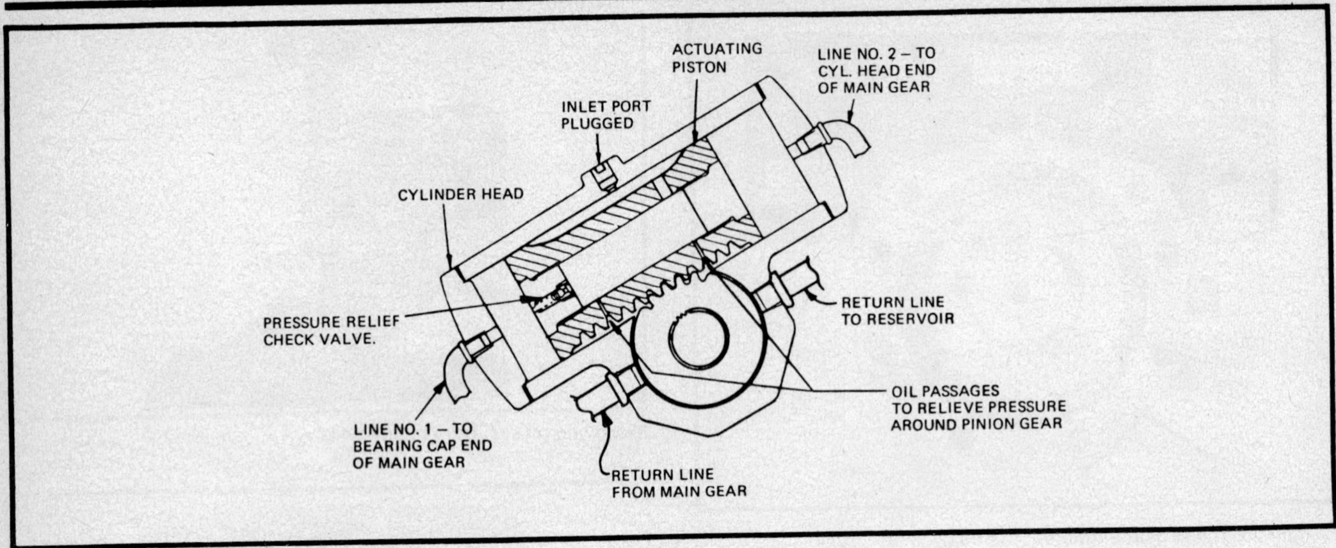

Secondary gear assembly (© Mack Trucks Inc.)

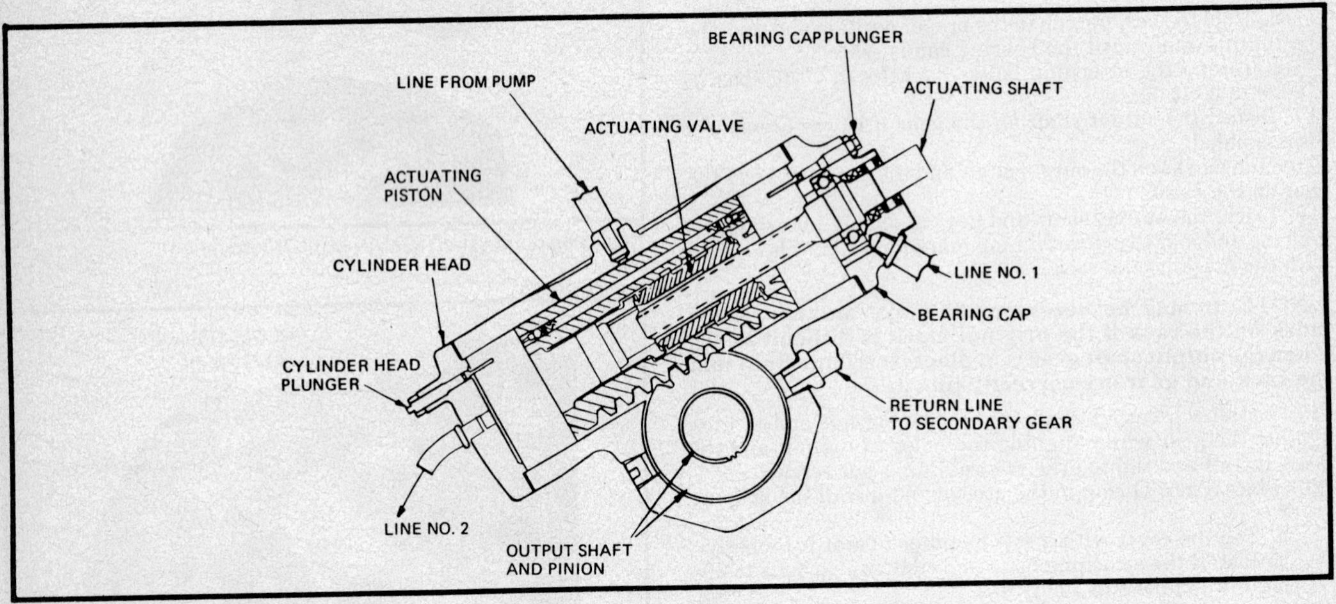

Main gear assembly (© Mack Trucks Inc.)

4. Leave the gear on the output shaft unless replacement is necessary.
   a. To disassemble the output shaft and gear, remove the screws which secure the gear retaining nut.
   b. Turn the retaining nut counterclockwise and remove the nut.
   c. Press the output shaft out of the gear.
5. Mark the cylinder head and housing for reassembly and remove the cylinder head and gasket.
6. Mark the bearing cap and housing for reassembly and remove the bearing cap attaching bolts.
7. Turn the bearing cap and actuating shaft out of the actuating valve.
8. Remove the cover attaching bolts and remove the cover with the input shaft and bearing assembly. Check for the shaft and gear timing marks.
9. Remove the input gear by driving out the retaining pin.
10. Pull the bearing retaining nut lock-pin from the gear box cover.
11. Use a spanner wrench and turn the bearing retainer nut counterclockwise and remove it from the gearbox cover.
12. Remove the bearing and input shaft assembly from the cover using a soft hammer.
13. If necessary, the shaft can be driven or pressed out of the bearing.
14. Remove the seal from the cover.
15. Remove the bolts, including the one hidden inside the housing, that attaches the gearbox housing to the bearing cap. Tap the gearbox with a soft hammer to loosen it, then lift it from the bearing cap.
16. Remove the bearing cap O-ring.
17. Remove the gear retaining nut and washer from the shaft and pull the gear off the shaft.
18. Mark the bearing retaining nut at the pin hole location for reassembly.
19. Remove the lock pin from the bearing cap and remove the bearing retaining nut.
20. Remove the shims located next to the bearing and save for reassembly.
21. Remove the bearing cap to housing screws.

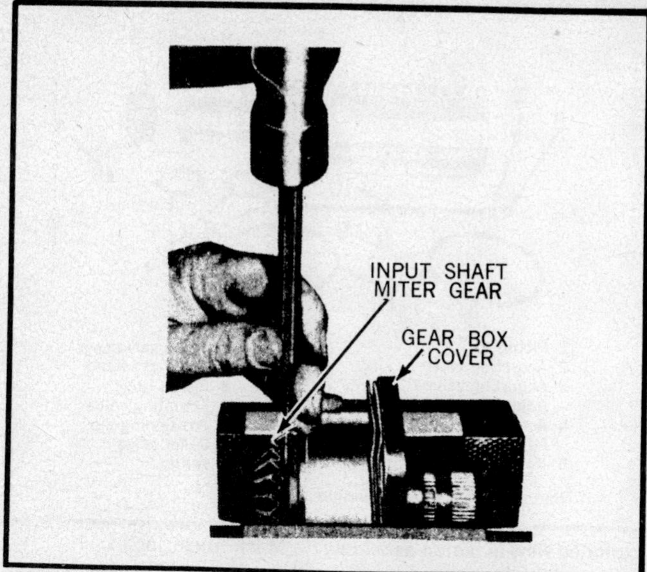

Removing miter gear retaining pin (© Mack Trucks Inc.)

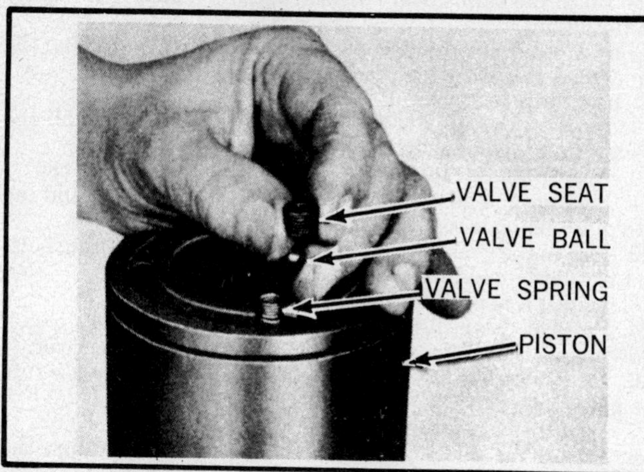

Removing relief valve from piston (© Mack Trucks Inc.)

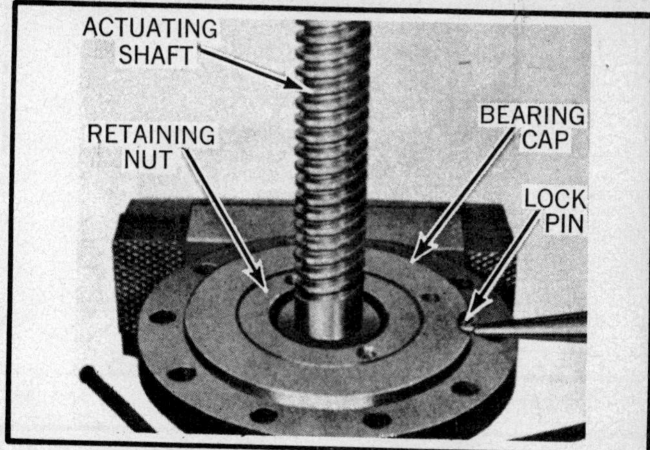

Disassembling bearing cap and actuating shaft (© Mack Trucks Inc.)

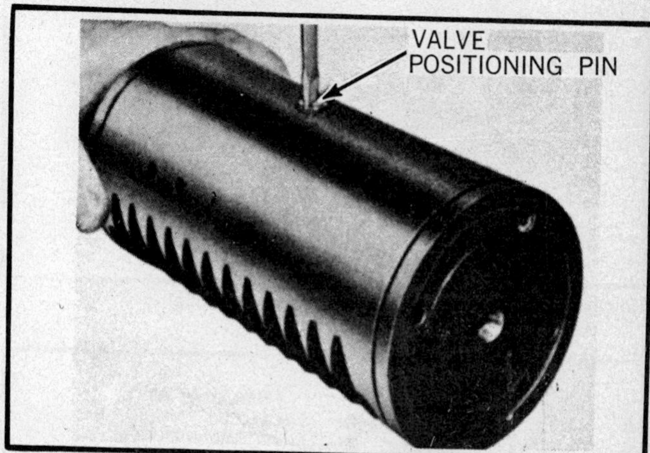

Removing valve adjusting nut lockpin (© Mack Trucks Inc.)

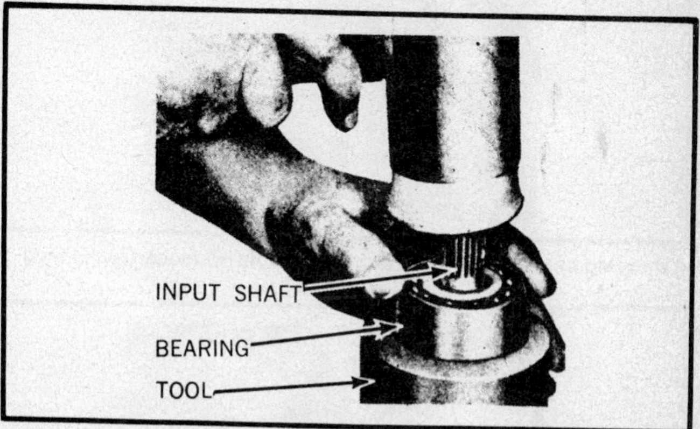

Removing bearing from input shaft (© Mack Trucks Inc.)

22. Note the timing marks on the actuating shaft and valve for reassembly then turn and unscrew the bearing cap and shaft assembly out of the valve.
23. Remove the actuating shaft and bearing from the bearing cap by tapping easily with a soft hammer.
24. If necessary, remove the fixed plunger from the bearing cap. Pry the plunger lock-pin out far enough from the cap to be gripped with pliers then withdraw the pin completely.

NOTE: Do not remove the fixed plunger unless damaged.

25. Remove the oil seal from the bearing cap.
    a. On non-current models, pry the seal from the bearing cap.
    b. On current models, holes in the cap are provided so that the seal may be driven out with a punch.

Assembly

1. Clean all parts individually in a solvent and replace any parts that are worn or broken.
2. Position a new seal in the bearing cap so that the lip faces the piston side and press into place.
3. If the fixed plunger was removed insert it in the bearing cap and install the retaining pin. Make sure the pin is below the surface of the bearing cap.
4. Press the bearing on the actuating shaft.
5. Press the shaft and bearing assembly into the bearing cap without damaging the seal.
6. Screw the actuating shaft into the actuating valve and align the timing marks.
7. Install the bearing cap attaching bolts and tighten. $^5/_{16}$ bolts to 20 ft. lbs.; $^3/_8$ bolts to 33 ft. lbs.

Removing bearing retaining nut lockpin (© Mack Trucks Inc.)

Removing hidden capscrew holding gearbox housing (© Mack Trucks Inc.)

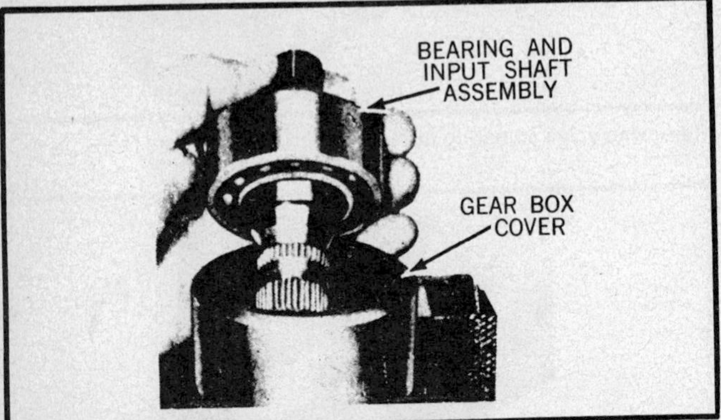

Removing bearing and input shaft assembly (© Mack Trucks Inc.)

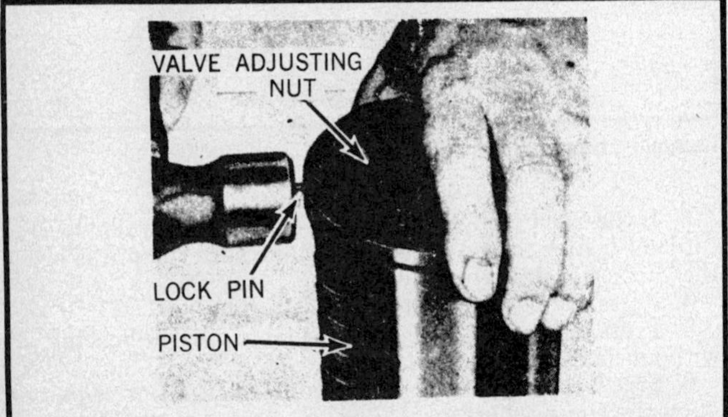

Installing valve adjusting nut and lock pin (© Mack Trucks Inc.)

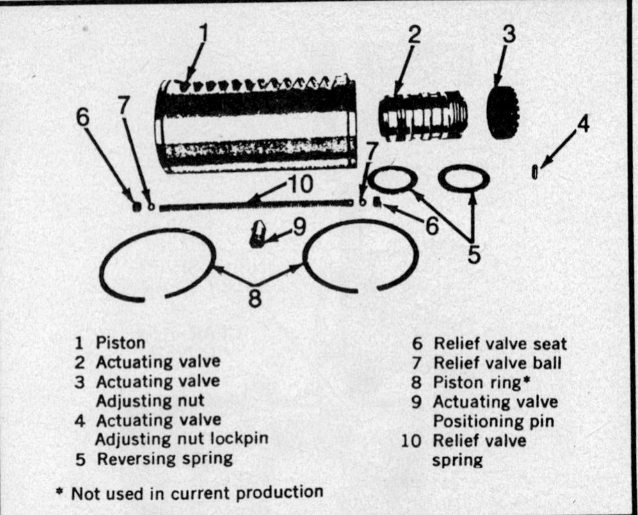

Exploded view of piston assembly (© Mack Trucks Inc.)

8. Place the shims over the bearing and install the bearing retaining nut.
   a. Tighten the nut against the bearing while aligning the mark on the nut with the lock-pin hole.
   b. Install the lock-pin.
9. Position the gear on the actuating shaft and install the washer and nut.
10. Install a new O-ring in the groove in the bearing cap.
11. Position the gearbox housing on the bearing cap and tap into place using a soft hammer.
12. Install the gearbox housing to bearing cap retaining bolts and washers including the bolt inside the housing.
13. Install a new cover seal.
14. Press or drive the input shaft into the bearing.
15. Install the bearing and shaft assembly into the cover.
16. Install the bearing retaining nut and turn clockwise into the cover.
17. Install the bearing retaining nut lock-pin.
18. Install the miter gear on the input shaft and align the timing marks.
19. Install the retaining pin.
20. Install the cover assembly and shim on the gearbox housing.
21. Fill the gearbox housing with the correct grade of grease through the grease fitting.

FINAL ADJUSTMENTS

Bleeding Air from System

SINGLE STEERING

1. After installing the gear but before installing the Pitman arm, the air must be bled from the system. Fill the pump reservoir with the recommended oil (10w–40 motor oil). It will be necessary to continue filling after starting the engine and during the bleeding process to keep the oil at the proper level.
2. Set the parking brake, chock the wheels, start engine and allow to idle. Turn the steering wheel from left to right making three complete cycles to remove all the air from the steering system.
3. Stop engine. Check oil level and add as necessary. Install Pitman arm.

DUAL STEERING

1. With the steering gears installed, the Pitman arms may be installed if there is no clearance problem with the Pitman arm striking any object when full travel is used. Install the

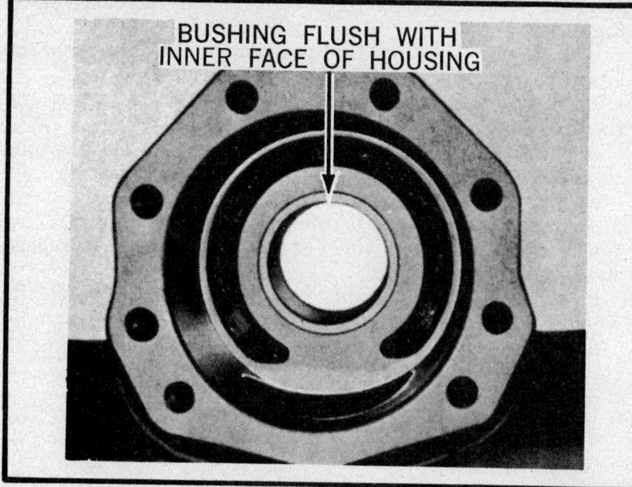

Installing housing bushing (© Mack Trucks Inc.)

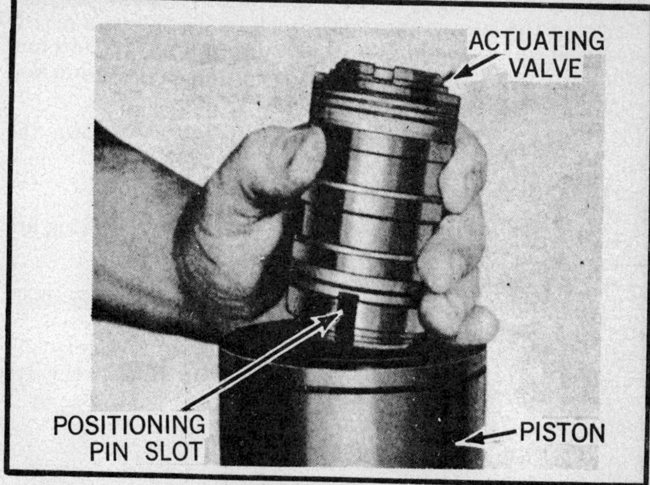

Installing actuating valve (© Mack Trucks Inc.)

arms checking carefully to see that the timing mark on the output shaft and the timing mark on the Pitman arm are aligned. Torque to specifications, depending on the attachment method used (lockwasher and hex nut, set screw and press fit, or nut with locking cap screw).

2. Fill the pump reservoir, set the parking brake, start engine and allow to run at a fast idle speed.

3. With the engine running and the drag links disconnected, turn the steering wheel to the left and hold until the secondary or slave gear Pitman arm moves to its full travel. Turn the steering wheel to the right and hold until the secondary gear Pitman arm again moves to its full travel. Repeat this process three or more times. Keep checking the reservoir for oil level and add as required.

4. Connect the drag link to the master gear, but do not connect the drag link to secondary gear at this time. Turn the steering wheel to left and hold until the secondary gear Pitman arm moves the full travel. Turn to the right and hold until the secondary gear again moves to its full travel. Repeat three times. Turn the steering wheel until the secondary gear Pitman arm lines up with the drag link. Install the Pitman arm.

NOTE: Do not move the Pitman arm by hand or air will be drawn into the system.

5. Check oil level, add as necessary.

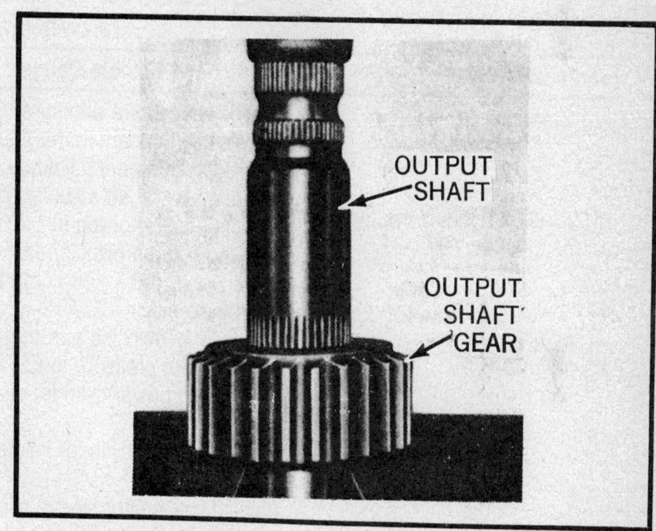

Pressing gears on output shaft (© Mack Trucks Inc.)

RELIEF VALVE PLUNGER

Adjustment

This adjustment should be made periodically and any time the gears, springs, axle, etc. are disturbed. The adjustment is important because it protects the pump, steering gear, and steering linkage from overloading when the wheels are at full turn. Steering gears using the miter gearbox do not have an adjustable plunger at the gearbox end.

WITH MITER GEARBOX

1. With the power off check the right and left steering angles (See the steering angle procedures in the General Repair Section.)

2. Turn the adjustable plunger in the cylinder head inward until it bottoms.

3. Return the wheels to the straight forward position and start the engine to operate the power steering.

4. For the right turn adjustment, proceed as follows:

a. Slowly turn the steering wheel to the right until the hydraulic assist is stopped (resistance in the wheel is felt). The wheel should not be forced beyond this point.

b. Hold the wheel at this position and measure the clearance between the axle turn circle stop screw and boss or stopnut on the back of the knuckle.

c. Set clearance by adjusting the drag link.

d. Loosen the drag link clamp and lengthen the link to decrease clearance and shorten the length to increase the clearance.

e. After the adjustment has been made, measure the clearance again.

5. For left turn adjustment, proceed as follows:

a. Slowly turn the steering wheel to the left until the hydraulic assist is stopped (resistance in the wheel is felt). The wheel should not be forced beyond this point.

b. Hold the wheel at this position and measure the clearance between the axle turn circle stop-screw and boss or stopnut.

c. The clearance should be $^1/_8$ inch. If the clearance is incorrect, adjust the relief valve plunger at the lower end of the cylinder.

d. Turn the valve in to increase clearance and out to decrease clearance.

NOTE: If it is impossible to obtain accurate adjustments in the previous steps, check to see that the arrow stamped on the output shaft is indexed with the notched mark on the steering lever. The spline groove marked with a zero is not the index point.

6. Tighten all clamps and lock-nuts and shut down the engine.

WITHOUT MITER GEARBOX

1. With the power off, check the right and left steering angles (see the steering angle procedures).
2. Turn the adjustable plungers all the way in.
3. Start the engine and run at a fast idle so the power steering operates.
4. For the left turn adjustment, proceed as follows:
   a. Turn the steering wheel to the left until the relief valve contacts the plunger. This can be felt by an increased steering effort.
   b. Hold the wheel at this position and do not force the wheel beyond this point.
   c. Check the clearance between the axle stop-screw and the boss.
   d. Turn the bearing cap upper plunger outward until the clearance is $^1/_8$ inch between the stop-screw and boss.
   e. Tighten the lock-nut.
5. For the right turn adjustment, proceed as follows:
   a. Turn the steering wheel to the right until an increased steering effort is felt.
   b. Hold the wheel at this position and do not force the wheel beyond this point.
   c. Turn the cylinder head plunger outward until there is a clearance of $^1/_8$ inch between the stop-screw and boss.
   d. Tighten the locknut.

STEERING TROUBLE DIAGNOSIS
Power Steering

Condition	Possible Cause	Correction
Hard Steering	1. Low or uneven tire pressure.	1. Inflate the tires to recommended pressures.
	2. Insufficient lubricant in the steering gear housing or in steering linkage.	2. Lubricate as necessary.
	3. Steering gear shaft adjusted too tight.	3. Adjust according to instructions.
	4. Improper caster or toe-in.	4. Align the wheels.
	5. Steering column misaligned.	5. See "Steering Gear Alignment."
	6. Loose, worn or broken pump belt.	6. Adjust or replace belt.
	7. Air in system.	7. Bleed air from system.
	8. Low fluid level in the pump reservoir.	8. Fill to correct level.
	9. Pump output pressure low.	9. See "Pressure Test."
	10. Leakage at power cylinder piston rings. (Linkage type).	10. Replace piston rings and repair as required.
	11. Binding or bent cylinder linkage. (Linkage type).	11. Replace or repair as required.
	12. Valve spool and/or sleeve sticking. (Linkage type).	12. Free-up or replace as required.
Intermittent or No Power Assist	1. Belt slipping and/or low fluid level.	1. Adjust or replace belt. Add fluid as necessary.
	2. Piston or rod binding in power cylinder. (Linkage type).	2. Repair or replace piston and rod.
	3. Sliding sleeve stuck in control valve. (Linkage type).	3. Free-up or replace sleeve.
	4. Improper pump operation.	4. Refer to "Power Steering Pump."
Poor or No Recovery from Turns	1. Improper caster setting.	1. Adjust to specifications.
	2. Steering gear adjustments too tight.	2. Adjust according to instructions.
	3. Improper spool nut adjustment. (Linkage type).	3. Adjust according to instructions.
	4. Valve spool installed backwards. (Linkage type).	4. Install valve spool correctly.
	5. Low tire pressure.	5. Inflate tires to recommended pressure.
	6. Tight steering linkage.	6. Lubricate as necessary.
	7. King pins frozen.	7. Lubricate as necessary.
Lack of Effort (Both Turns)	1. Improper sector shaft adjustment.	1. Adjust Sector Shaft.
	2. Pressure plates on wrong side of reactions rings.	2. Gear Recondition.

STEERING TROUBLE DIAGNOSIS
Power Steering

Condition	Possible Cause	Correction
Lack of Effort (Left Turn Only)	1. Left turn reaction seal "O" ring worn, damaged or missing. 2. Left turn reaction oil passageway not drilled in housing or cylinder head. 3. Left turn reaction ring sticking in cylinder head.	1. Gear Recondition. 2. Replace parts as required. 3. Replace parts as required.
Lack of Effort (Right Turn Only)	1. Right turn U-shaped reaction seal worn, damaged, or missing. 2. Right turn reaction oil passageway not drilled in housing head, or ferrule pin. 3. Right turn reaction ring sticking in housing head.	1. Gear Recondition. 2. Replace parts as required. 3. Replace parts as required.
Lack of Assist (Left Turn Only)	1. Left turn reaction seal "O" ring worn, damaged, or missing.	1. Gear Recondition.
Lack of Assist (Right Turn Only)	1. Right turn U-shaped reaction seal worn, damaged, or missing. 2. Worm sealing ring (teflon) worm sleeve seal, ferrule pin "O" ring damaged or worn. 3. Excessive internal leakage thru piston end plug and/or side plugs.	1. Gear Recondition. 2. Gear Recondition. 3. Replace worm-piston assembly.
Lack of Assist (Both Turns)	1. Low oil level in pump reservoir (usually accompanied by pump noise). 2. Loose pump belt. 3. Pump output low. 4. Engine idle too low. 5. Excessive internal leakage thru piston end plug and/or side plugs.	1. Fill to proper level. 2. Adjust belts. 3. Pressure test pump. 4. Adjust engine idle. 5. Replace worm-piston assembly.

FRONT SUSPENSION TROUBLE DIAGNOSIS

UNEVEN TIRE WEAR

1. Tire pressure's low
2. Excessive camber
3. Tires out of balance
4. Tires overloaded
5. Out of round tires and rims
6. Caster incorrect
7. Toe-in incorrect
8. High speed driving into turns
9. Unequal tire size
10. Improper tracking
11. Bent or worn steering and suspension components

STEERING WHEEL SPOKE POSITION NOT PROPERLY CENTERED

1. Steering gear set off "high-spot"
2. Improper toe-in
3. Relationship between lengths of tie-rods not equal
4. Bent steering components
5. Steering wheel improperly placed on steering shaft

HARD STEERING

1. Tire pressure low
2. Wheel spindle bent
3. Steering assembly binding or maladjusted
4. Tie rod ends tight
5. Caster excessive
6. Kingpins or ball joints too tight
7. Lack of lubrication to steering and suspension units.

SHIMMY

1. Tire pressure incorrect
2. Tires of unequal size
3. Loose wheel bearings
4. Loose steering arms or steering gear adjustment
5. Steering gear loose on frame
6. Loose or broken steering linkage rods or internal adjustment parts
7. Spring shackles loose
8. Ball joints or kingpins and bushings worn
9. Front end alignment out of specifications
10. Wheels and tires out of balance
11. Wheels and tires out of round or loose on hub
12. Shock absorbers worn out.
13. U-bolts loose on axle to spring.
14. Worn or out-of-round brake drum or rotor (shimmy felt upon brake application)

WANDER OR WEAVE

1. Tire pressure incorrect
2. Tires of unequal size
3. Bent spindle
4. Wheel bearings loose or worn
5. Kingpins worn or bent
6. Kingpins tight in steering knuckle or bushings
7. Steering gear assembly too tight or too loose
8. Too little caster
9. Too much or too little chamber
10. Too much or too little toe-in
11. Front axle bent or shifted
12. Springs broken
13. Frame diamond shaped
14. Rear axle housing shifted or bent
15. Steering linkage tight or binding
16. Lack of lubrication to front suspension or steering linkage
17. Defective power steering assembly

FRONT END RIDES HARD

1. Improper tire pressure
2. Springs broken or too stiff
3. Shock absorbers too stiff or malfunctioning
4. Front end alignment incorrect
5. Loose suspension components

VEHICLE STEERS TO ONE SIDE AT ALL TIMES

1. Incorrect caster setting
2. Incorrect camber setting
3. Incorrect kingpin inclination or wheel support angle
4. Unequal tire pressure or tire size
5. One side brake drag

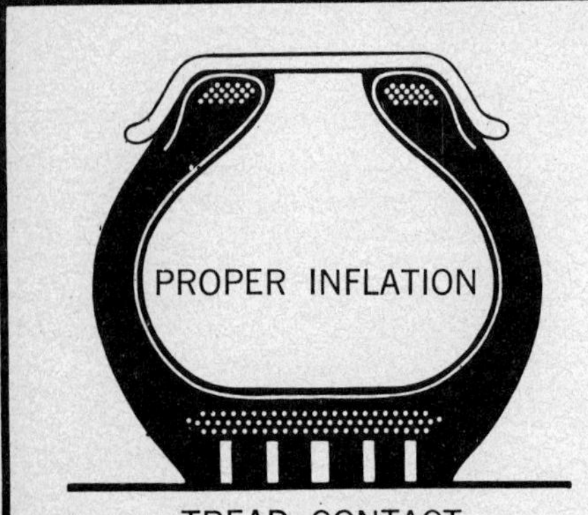

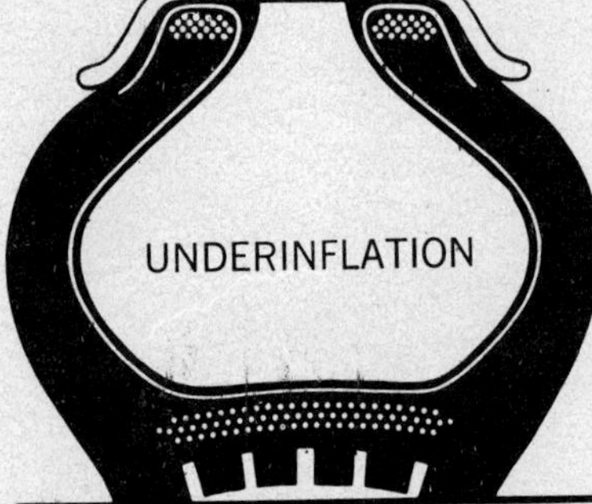

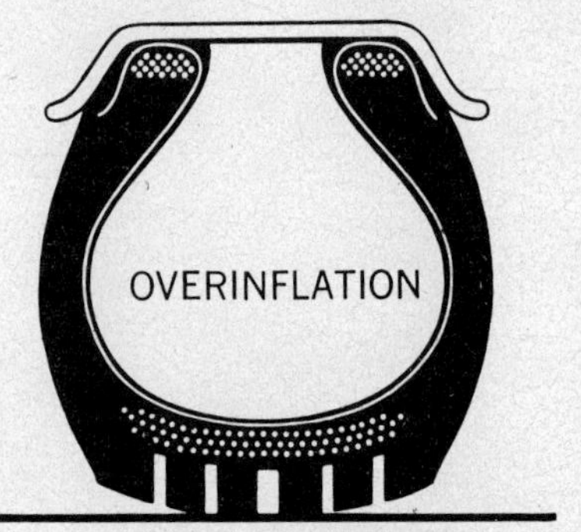

Comparison of normal, under and over tire inflation and effect on the tire thread (© Rubber Manufacturers Association)

6. Unequal shock absorber control
7. Bent or damaged steering and suspension components
8. Uneven or weak spring condition, front or rear
9. Broken center or shackle bolts
10. Frame bent causing improper tracking

NOISY FRONT END

1. Lack of, or improper lubrication
2. Loose steering linkage
3. Loose suspension parts
4. Loose brake parts
5. Worn universal (FWD)
6. Worn differential (FWD)
7. Loose sheet metal

LUBRICATION LEAKING INTO DRUM OR ON ROTOR

1. Excessive differential lubricant (FWD)
2. Clogged axle housing vent (FWD)
3. Damage or worn universal driveshaft oil seal (FWD)
4. Loose steering knuckle flange bearings (FWD)
5. Defective outer seal
6. Rough spindle to oil seal surface
7. Wheel bearings overpacked or use of wrong lubricant
8. Clogged oil slinger drain
9. Cracked steering knuckle outer flange

EXCESSIVE TIRE WEAR

1. Incorrect wheel alignment
2. Failure to rotate tires
3. Improper tire inflation
4. Overload or improperly loaded vehicle
5. High tire temperature operation
6. Excessive speed, quick starts and quick stops
7. Bent suspension, frame or wheel parts
8. Tires out of balance
9. Uneven brake application
10. Excessive hard turning of tandem and spread axle wheels

Wheel Alignment

For a truck to have safe steering control with a minimum of tire wear, certain established rules must be followed. These rules fix the values of planes, angles and radii relative to each other and to truck and tire dimensions. Some factors are built in, with no provision for adjustment; others are adjustable within limits. The entire system depends upon all value factors, separately and combined. It is therefore difficult to change some of the established settings without influencing others.

This system is called steering geometry or wheel alignment and requires a complete check of all the factors involved. Definitions of these factors and the effect each one has on the truck are given in the following paragraphs. For adjustment data relative to each separate truck and year, refer to the individual truck sections.

STEERING WHEEL POSITION

Always check steering wheel alignment in conjunction with and at the same time as toe-in. In fact, the steering wheel spoke position, with the truck on a straight section of highway, may be the first indication of front end misalignment.

If the truck has been wrecked, or indicates any evidence of steering gear or linkage disturbance, the Pitman arm should be disconnected from the sector shaft. The steering wheel (or gear) should be turned from extreme right to extreme left to determine the halfway point in its turning scope. This will be the spot on the gear that is in action during straight ahead driving and in which position the steering gear should be adjusted. With the steering wheel in the straight-ahead position and the steering gear adjusted to zero lash status, reconnect the Pitman arm.

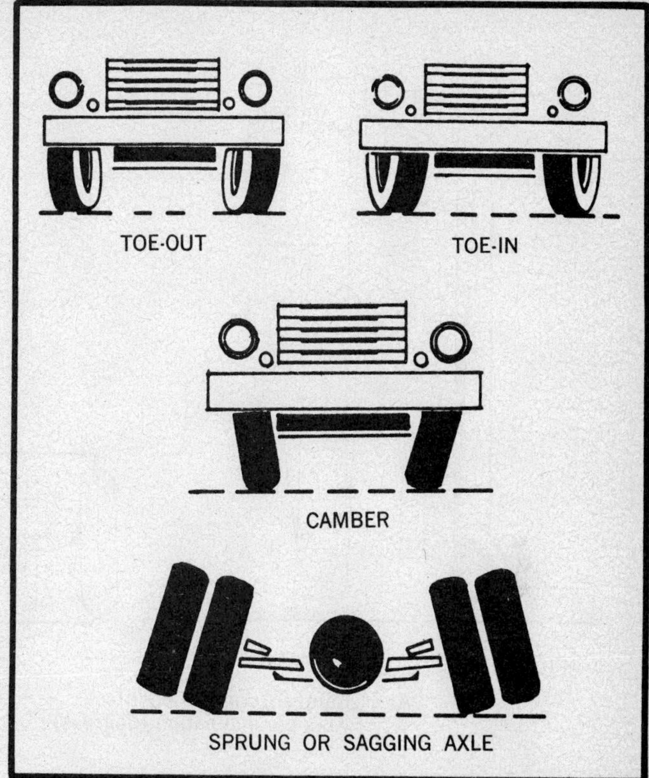

Exaggerated views of alignment problems
(© General Motors Corp.)

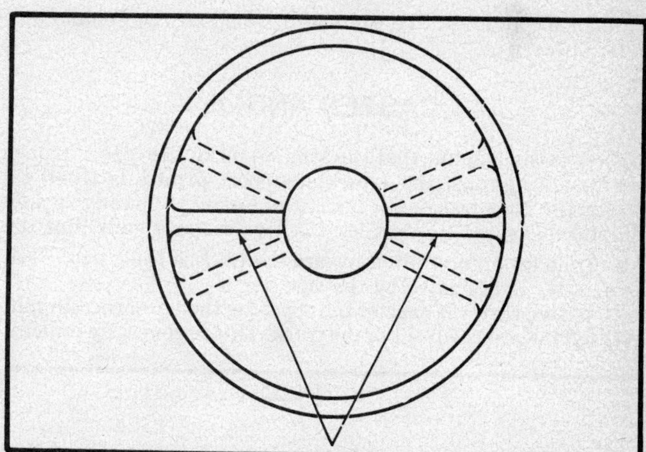

Steering wheel position

Steering Geometry

CAMBER ANGLE

Camber is the amount that the front wheels are inclined outward or inward at the top. Chamber is spoken of, and measured, in degrees from the perpendicular. The purpose of the

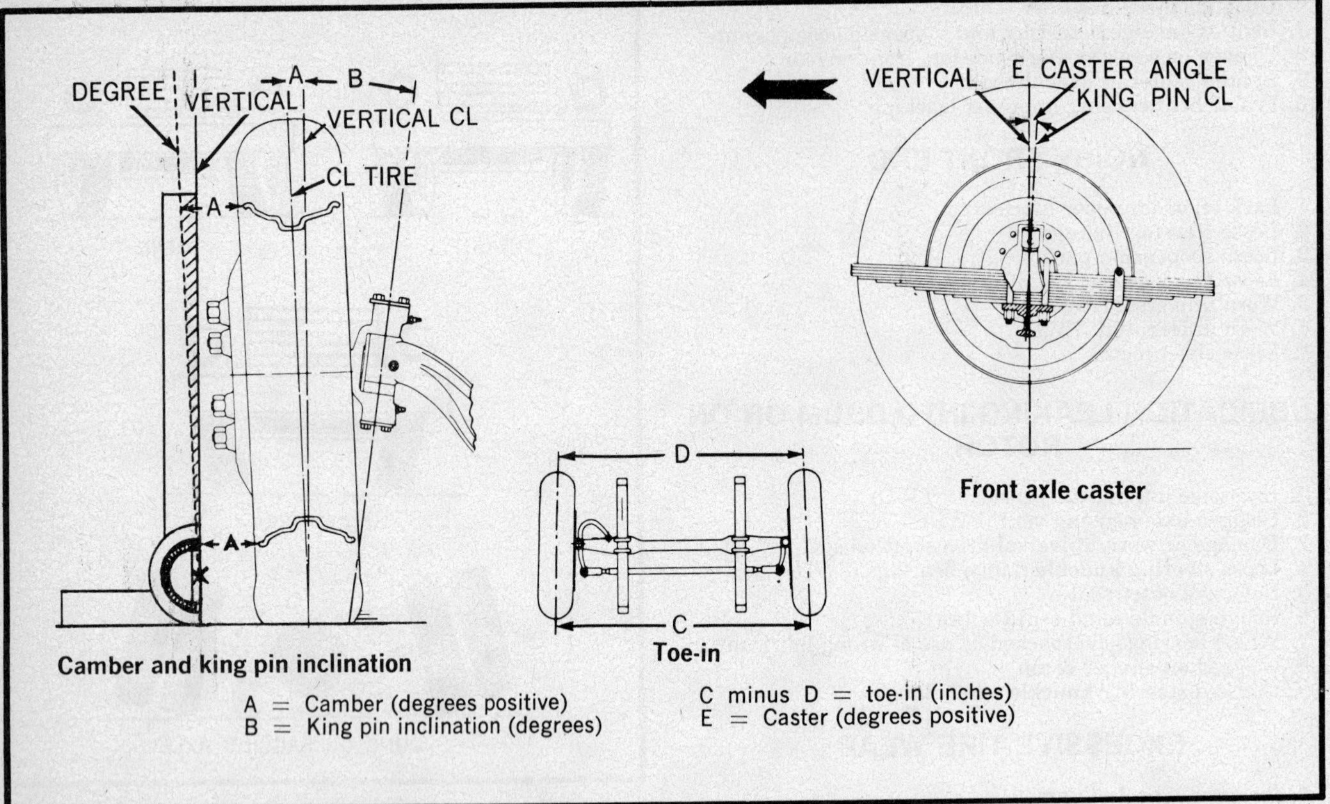

Steering geometry (© General Motors Corp.)

camber angle is to take some of the load off the spindle outboard bearing.

CASTER ANGLE

Caster is the amount that the kingpin (or in the case of trucks without king-pins, the knuckle support pivots) is tilted towards the back or front of the truck. Caster is usually spoken of, and measured, in degrees. Positive caster means that the top of the kingpin is tilted toward the back of the truck. Positive caster is indicated by the sign "+".

Negative caster is exactly the opposite; the top of the kingpin is tilted toward the front of the truck. This is generally indicated by the sign "-". Negative caster is sometimes referred to as reverse caster.

The effect of positive caster is to cause the truck to steer in the direction in which it tends to go. Positive caster in the front wheels may cause the truck to steer down off a crowned road or steer in the direction of a cross wind. For this reason, a number of our modern trucks are arranged with negative caster so that the opposite is true; the truck tends to steer up a crowned road and into a cross wind.

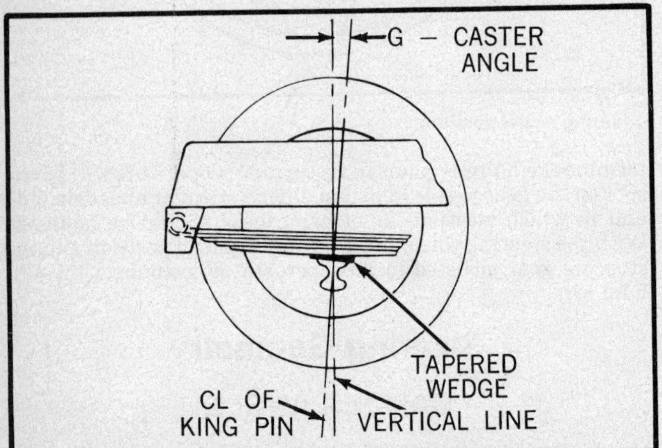

Use of tapered wedge between the axle and spring to adjust caster angle (© International Harvester Co.)

Correction

Caster angle specifications are based on the vehicle load limits, which will usually result in a level frame.

Since load requirements may vary, the frame does not always remain level and must be considered when determining the correct caster angle.

To measure the from angle, the vehicle should be on a smooth and level surface. Place a bubble protractor on the frame rail and measure the degree of frame tilt and in what direction, either front or rear.

Two methods of determining caster angles are used. The first method is to determine the caster angle from the wheel with alignment equipment, and the second method is to obtain the desired caster angle from the specification charts. The frame angle is then added to or subtracted fro the caster angles as necessary. The two methods are outlined. Examples and diagrams are provided for use by the repairman to assist in determining the proper caste angle to use.

FIRST METHOD

1. Determine the frame angle.
   a. Frame high at rear–frame angle is negative.
   b. Frame low at rear–frame angle is positive.

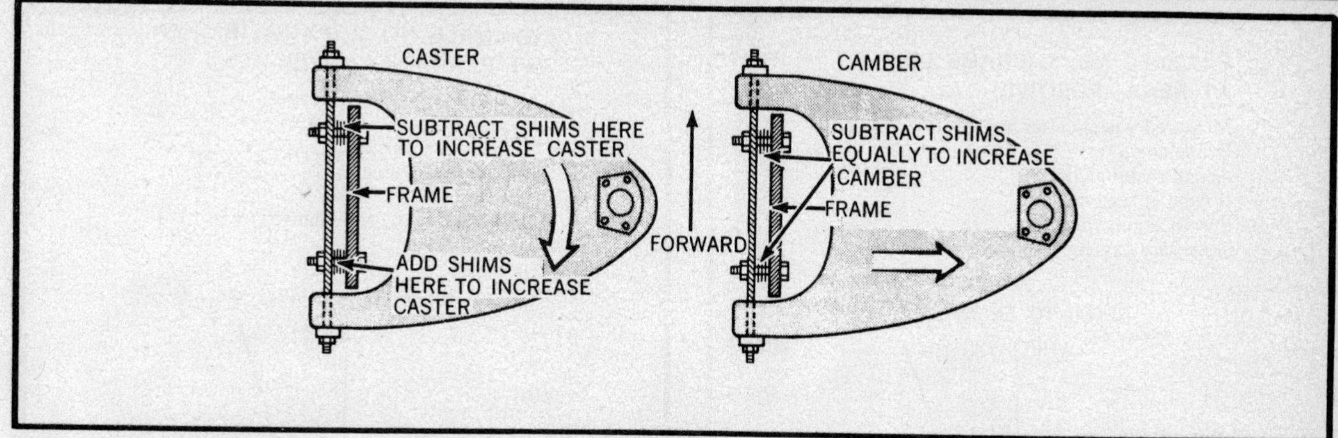

Caster-camber adjustment on upper arm front suspension (© General Motors Corp.)

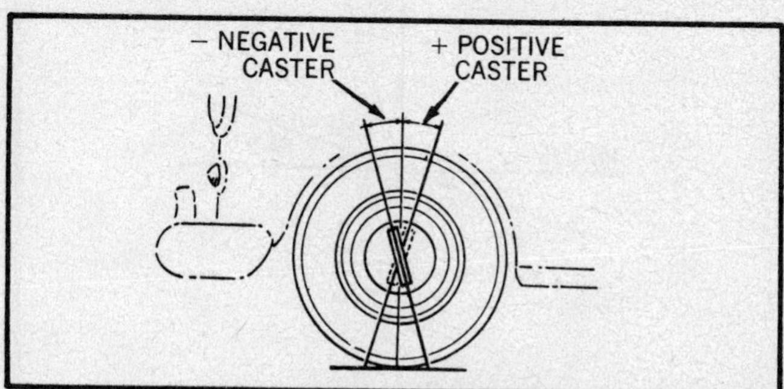

Caster angle showing positive and negative caster

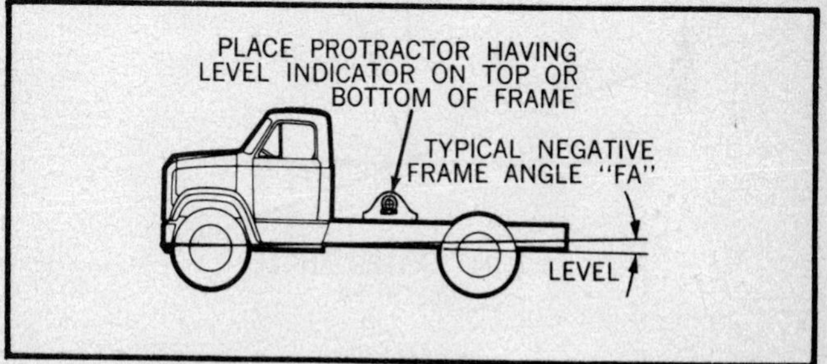

Frame angle determination-first method
(© General Motors Corp.)

2. Determine the caster angle at the wheel with the alignment checking equipment.
3. Add or subtract frame angle from or to the determined caster angle.
   a. Negative frame angle is added to positive caster angle.
   b. Positive frame angle is subtracted from positive caster angle.
   c. Negative frame angle is subtracted from negative caster angle.
   d. Positive frame angle is added to negative caster angle.
4. Determine the correct caster angle and the specified caster angle and correct on the vehicle. Use the following examples as guides.

SECOND METHOD

1. Measure the frame angle.
   a. Front of frame down–frame angle positive.
   b. Front of frame up–frame angle negative
2. From the specifications, determine the specified or desired caster setting.
3. Add or subtract the frame angle from the specified caster setting.
   a. Positive frame angle is subtracted from the specified setting.
   b. Negative frame angle is added to the specified caster setting.
4. Using wheel alignment equipment, obtain the measured caster angle from the wheel and determine the corrected specified setting, using the following examples as guides.

ANGLE OF KINGPIN INCLINATION

In addition to the caster angle, the kingpins (or knuckle support pivots) are also inclined toward each other at the top. This angle is known as kingpin inclination and is usually spoken of, and measured, in degrees.

The effect of kingpin inclination is to cause the wheels to steer in a straight line, regardless of outside forces such as crowned roads, cross winds, etc., which may tend to make it steer at a tangent. As the spindle is moved from extreme right to extreme left it apparently rises and falls. Notice that it reaches its highest position when the wheels are in the straight-ahead position. In actual operation, the spindle cannot rise and fall because because the wheel is in constant contact with the ground.

Therefore, the truck itself will rise at the extreme right turn and come to its lowest point at the straight-ahead position, and again rise for an extreme left turn. The weight of the truck will tend to cause the wheels to come to the straight-ahead position, which is the lowest position of the truck itself.

INCLUDED ANGLE

Included angle is the name given to that angle which includes kingpin inclination and camber. It is the relationship between the centerline of the wheel and the centerline of the kingpin (or the knuckle support pivots). This angle is build into the knuckle (spindle) forging and will remain constant throughout the life of the truck, unless the spindle itself is damaged.

When checking a truck on the front end stand, always measure kingpin inclination as well as camber unless some provision is made on the stand for checking condition of the spindle. Where no such provision is made, add the kingpin inclination inclination to the camber for each side of the truck. These totals should be exactly the same, regardless of how far from the norm the readings may be.

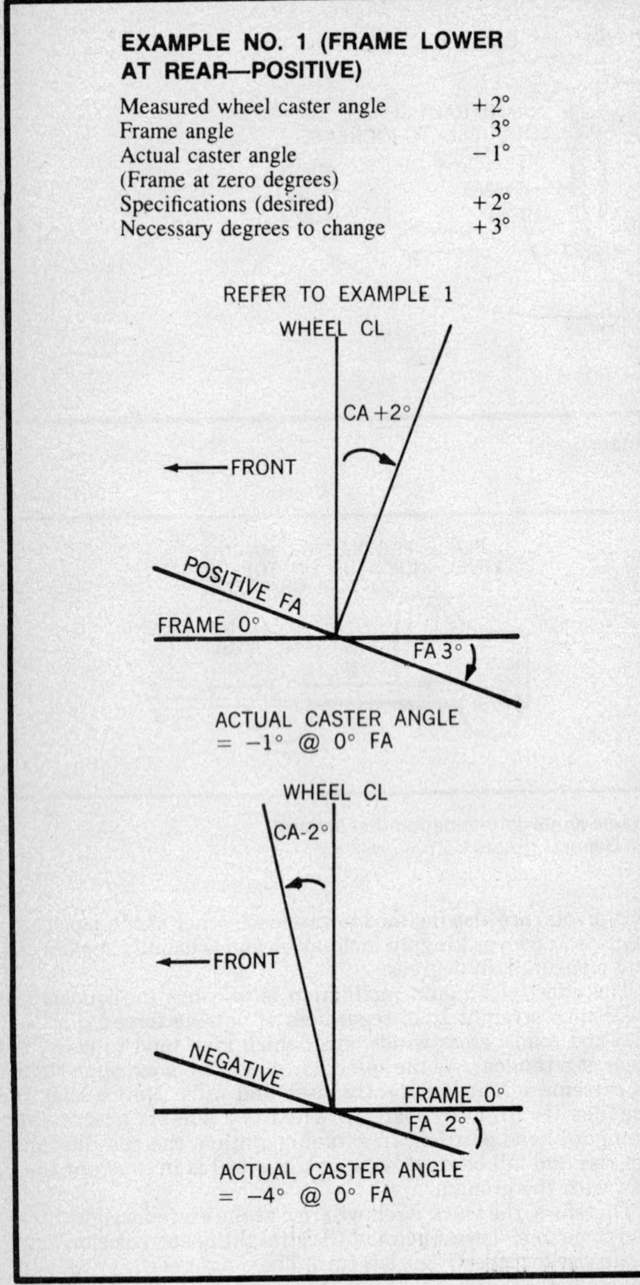

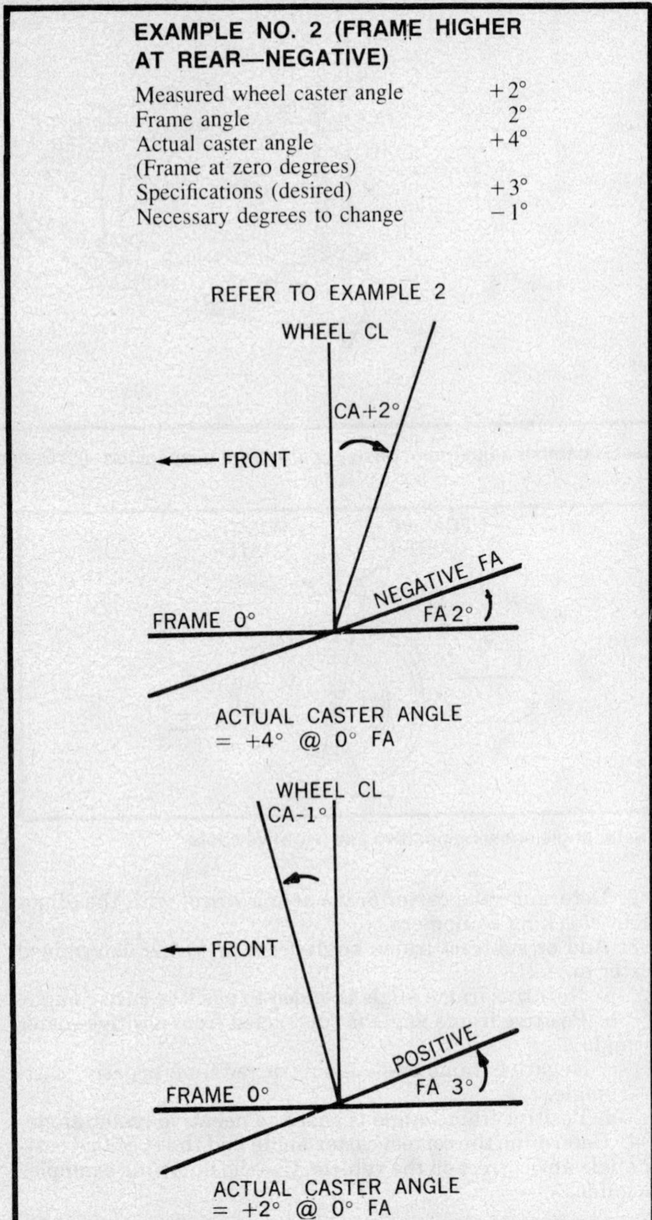

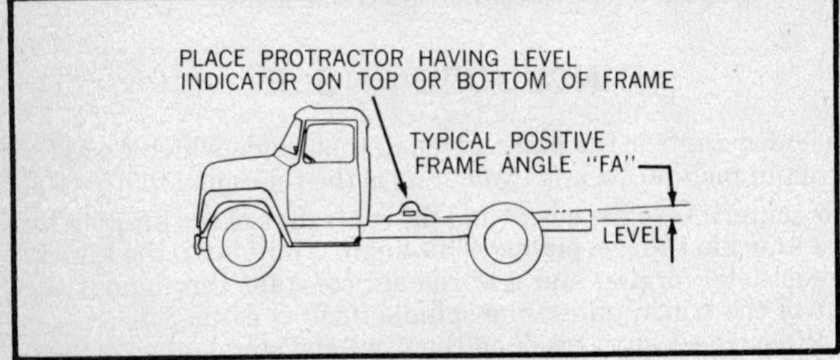

Frame angle determination-second method
(© International Harvester Co.)

For example, the left side of the truck checks 5 $^1/_2$° kingpin inclination and 1° positive camber–total 6 $^1/_2$°. Since both sides check exactly the same for the included angle, it is unlikely that both spindles, in this instance, are bent. Adjusting to correct for camber will automatically set correct kingpin inclination.

A bent spindle would show up like this: left side of the truck has $^3/_4$° positive camber, 5 $^1/_4$° kingpin inclination–6° included angle. Right side of truck has 1 $^1/_4$° positive camber, 6° kingpin inclination–total 7 $^1/_4$° included angle. One of these spindles is bent and if adjustments are made to correct camber, the kingpin inclination will be incorrect due to the bent spindle.

Since the most common cause of a bent spindle is striking the curb when parking, which causes the spindle to bend upward, the side having the greater included angle usually has the bent spindle. It will be found impossible to achieve good alignment and minimum tire wear unless the bent spindle is replaced.

TOE–IN

Toe-in is the amount that the front wheels are closer together at the front than they are at the back. This dimension is usually spoken of, and measured, in inches or fractions of inches.

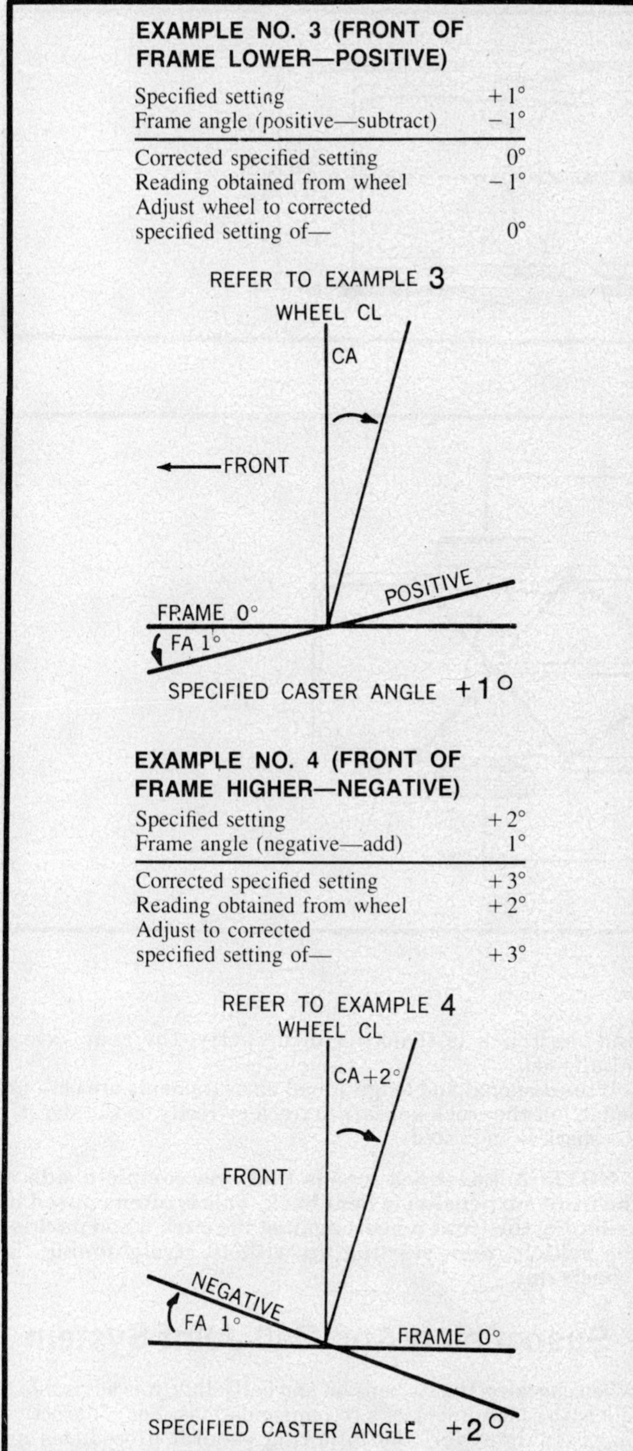

EXAMPLE NO. 3 (FRONT OF FRAME LOWER—POSITIVE)

Specified setting	+1°
Frame angle (positive—subtract)	−1°
Corrected specified setting	0°
Reading obtained from wheel	−1°
Adjust wheel to corrected specified setting of—	0°

EXAMPLE NO. 4 (FRONT OF FRAME HIGHER—NEGATIVE)

Specified setting	+2°
Frame angle (negative—add)	1°
Corrected specified setting	+3°
Reading obtained from wheel	+2°
Adjust to corrected specified setting of—	+3°

Generally speaking, the wheels are toed-in because they are cambered. When a truck operates with 0° camber it will be found to operate with zero toe-in. As the required camber increases, so does the toe-in. The reason for this is that the cambered wheel tends to steer in the direction in which it is cambered. Therefore it is necessary to overcome this tendency of the wheel by compensating very slightly in the direction opposite to that in which it tends to roll. Caster and camber both have an effect on toe-in. Therefore toe-in is the last thing on the front end which should be corrected.

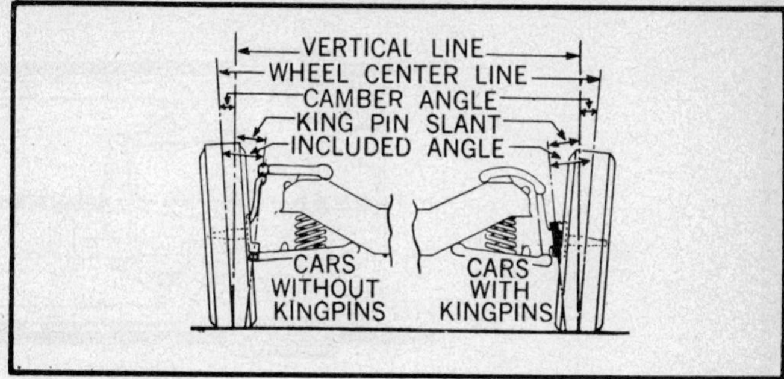

Camber, king pin slant and included angle

TOE—OUT STEERING RADIUS

When a truck is steered into a turn, the outside wheel of the vehicle scribes a much larger circle than the inside wheel. Therefore, the outside wheel must be steered to a somewhat less angle than the inside wheel. This difference in the angle is often called toe-out.

The change in angle from toe-in in the straight-ahead position to toe-out in the turn is caused by the relative position of the steering arms to the kingpin and to each other.

If a line were drawn from the center of the kingpin through the center of the steering arm-tie rod attaching hole at each wheel, these lines would be found to cross almost exactly in the center of the rear axle.

If the front end angles, including toe-in, are set correctly, and the toe-out is found to be incorrect, one or both of the steering arms are bent.

TRACKING

While tracking is more a function of the rear axle and frame, it is difficult to align the front suspension when the truck does not track straight. Tracking means that the centerline of the rear axle follows exactly the path of the centerline of the front axle when the truck is moving in a straight line.

On trucks that have equal tread, front and rear, the rear tires will follow in exactly the thread of the front tires, when moving in a straight line. However, there are many trucks whose rear tread is wider than the front tread. On such trucks, the rear axle tread will straddle the front axle tread an equal amount on both sides, when moving in a straight line.

Perhaps the easiest way to check a truck for tracking is to stand directly in back of it and watch it more in a straight line down the street. If the observer will stand as near to the center of the truck as possible, he can readily observe, even with the difference in perspective between the front and rear wheels, whether or not they are tracking properly. If the truck is found to track incorrectly, the difficulty will be found in either the frame or in the rear axle alignment.

Another more accurate method to check tracking is to park the truck on a level floor and drop a plumb-line from the extreme outer edge of the front suspension lower A-frame. Use the same drop point on each side of the truck. Make a chalk lie where the plumb-line strikes the floor. Do the same with the rear axle, selecting a point on the rear axle housing for the plumb-line.

Measure diagonally from the left rear mark to the right front mark and from the right rear mark to the left front mark. These two diagonal measurements should be exactly the same. A $^{1}/_{4}$ in. variation is acceptable.

If the diagonal measurements taken are different, measure from the right rear mark to the right front mark and from the left rear to the left front. These two measurements should also be the same within $^{1}/_{4}$ in..

If the diagonal measurements are different, but the longitu-

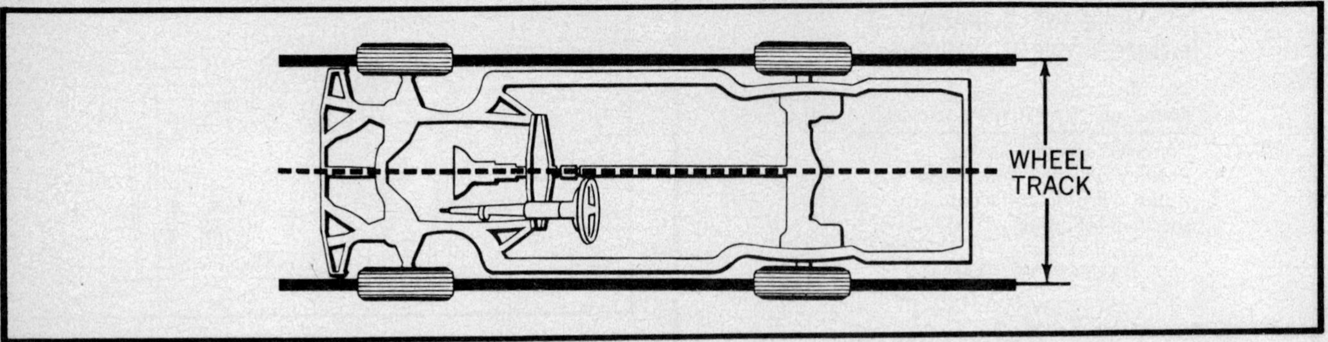

Typical parallel wheel track (© Hunter Engineering Co.)

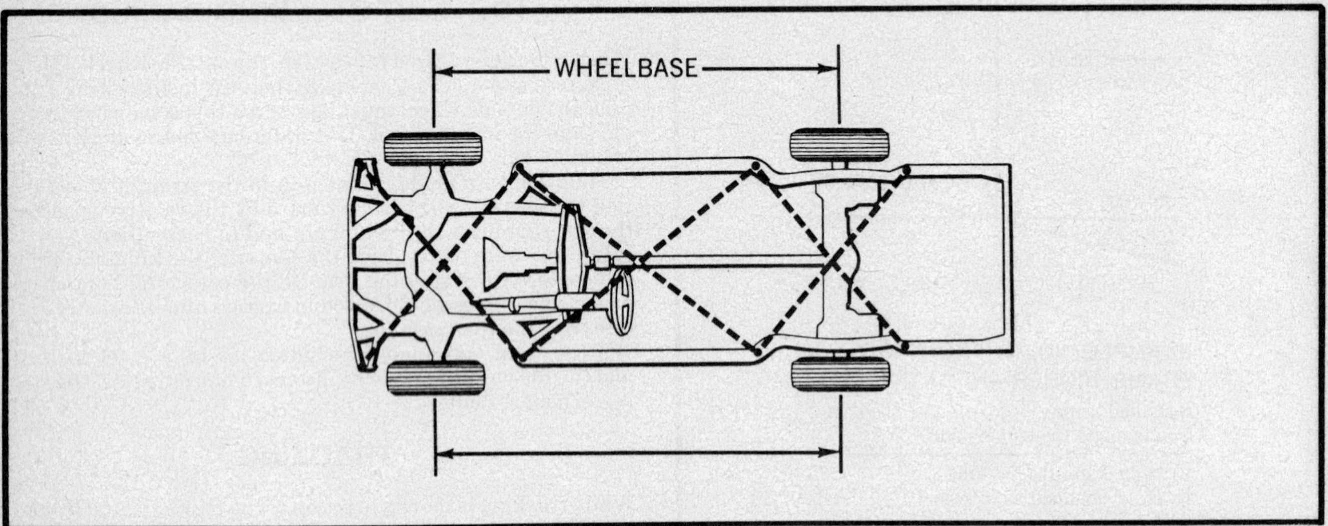

Measuring corresponding points of frame (© Hunter Engineering Co.)

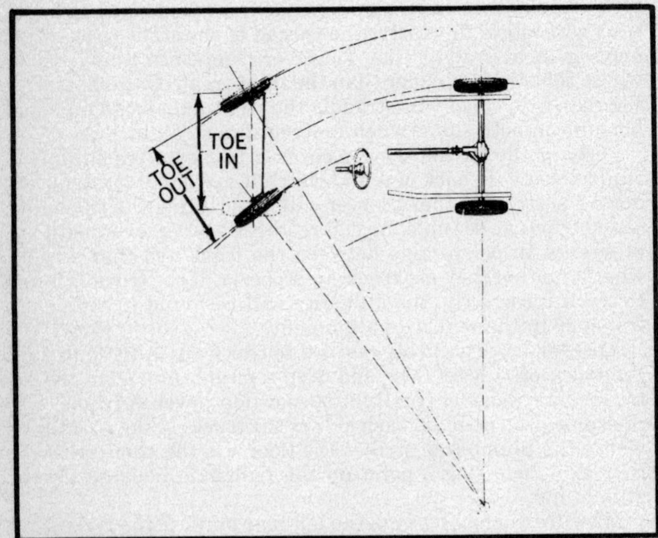

Steering geometry on turns (© Chrysler Corp.)

dinal measurements are the same, the frame is swayed (diamond shaped).

However, in the event that the diagonal measurements are unequal and the longitudinal measurements are also unequal, and the truck is tracking incorrectly, the rear axle is misaligned.

If the diagonal and longitudinal measurements are both unequal, but the truck appears to track correctly on the street, a kneeback is indicated.

NOTE: A kneeback means that one complete side of the front suspension is bent back. This is often caused by crimping the front wheels against the curb when parking the vehicle, then starting up without straightening the wheels out.

Suspension And Ball Joint System

When checking the suspension and ball joints, it is advisable to follow the manufacturer's recommendations. For all practical purposes, however, the following general procedures are applicable.

SUSPENSION SYSTEM

Inspection

This check is made with the ball joints fully loaded, so that suspension elements other than the ball joints may be checked.
When the front spring or torsion bar is supported by lower control arm, the jackstand should be located under the front crossmember or frame.
When the front spring i supported by the upper control arm, the jackstand should be located under the lower control arm.

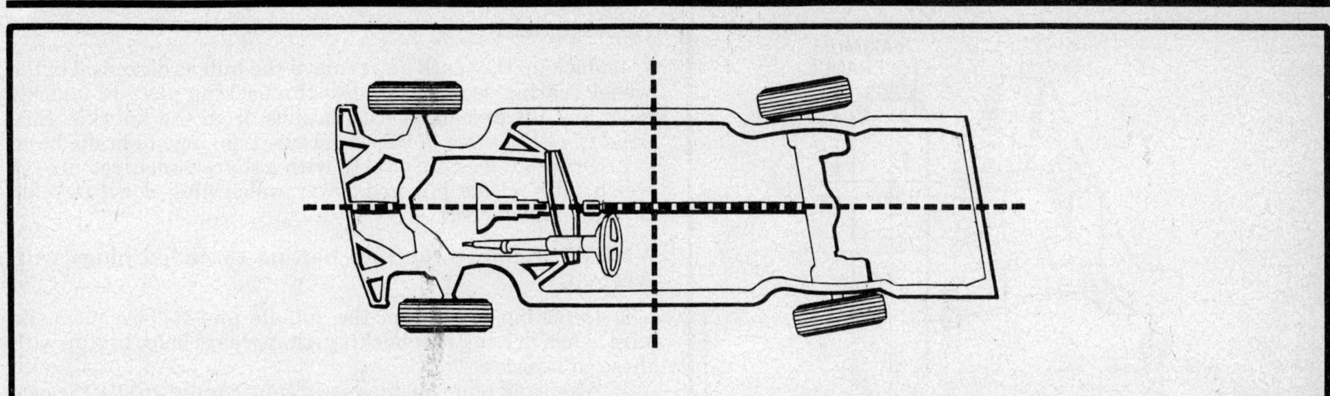

Bent frame, diamond shaped (© Hunter Engineering Co.)

Vertical or horizontal movement at the road wheel should not exceed the following:

1. Up to and including 16 in. – ¼ in.
2. 16 to 18 in. – ⅓ in.
3. More than 18 in. – ½ in.

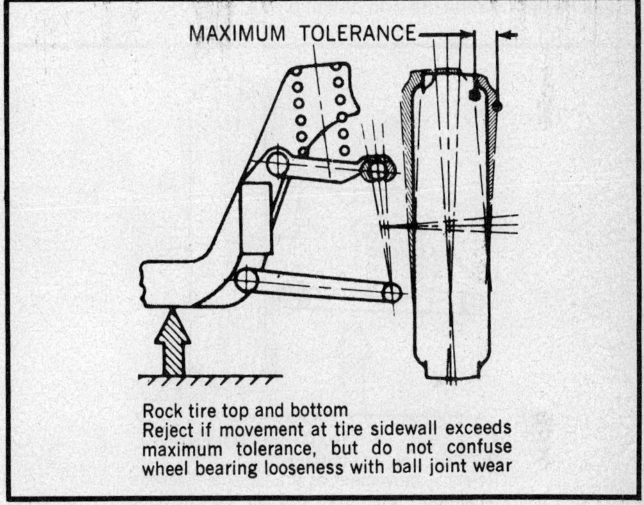

MAXIMUM TOLERANCE
Rock tire top and bottom
Reject if movement at tire sidewall exceeds maximum tolerance, but do not confuse wheel bearing looseness with ball joint wear

Check ball joint radial (side play)

Ball Joint

Inspection

When checking the ball joints for any wear, they must be free of any load.

When the front spring or torsion bar is supported by the lower control arm, the jackstand should be positioned under the lower control arm.

When the front spring is supported by the upper control arm, the jackstand should be located under the front crossmember or frame.

Replace the upper ball joint if any noticeable play is present in the joint when the spring is supported by the upper control arm; If the sideplay (horizontal motion) of the wheel, when rocked, exceed specifications; or if the up and down (vertical motion) exceed specifications.

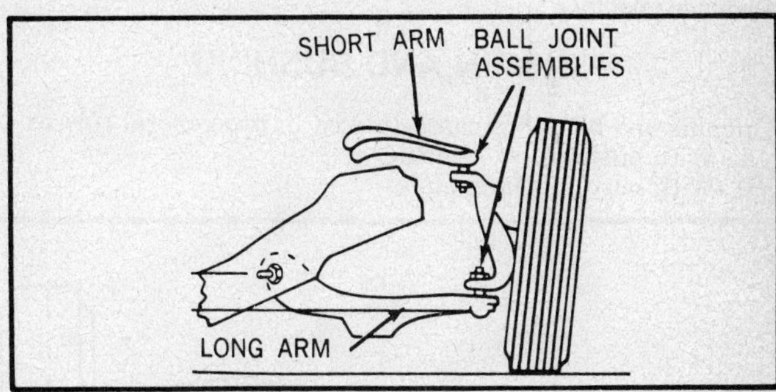

Use of control arms and ball joints for independent suspension

WHEEL BEARING AND SEAL

Replacement

NOTE: Refer to individual truck section for oil filled hub service.

1. Place jack under lower suspension arm. Remove hub cover and grease cap. Remove spindle nut, keyed washer and outer bearing. Slide off hub and drum.

NOTE: In some cases, drum removal may require loosening of brake adjustment.

2. At this point, brakes and drums should be inspected for their condition.
3. With hub and drum on bench, remove seal and inner bearing. Thoroughly clean all parts. Drive out inner and outer races of roller type. Use care not to mar the bearing surfaces.
4. Pack bearings with approved lubricant. When replacing cups, use a bearing race driver if possible. If a punch is used, make sure it is blunt and then drive parts in every carefully to avoid cocking the bearings.
5. Install new grease seal in hub. Assemble hub and drum on spindle and replace the outer bearing, key washer and nut.
6. A common method of adjustment is to tighten to zero clearance and then back off to first cotter pin castellation. Some manufacturers recommend tightening to approximately 10 to 12 ft. lbs., then backing off nut ⅙ turn. If cotter pin hole does not line up, loosen slightly.
7. Readjust brake if necessary and install grease cap and hub cover. Remove jack.

NOTE: When disc brakes are used on the front wheels, the calipers must be removed before the rotors can be taken from the spindle. Hang the calipers by wire from the frame rail so the weight of the caliper is not on the brake hose. The bearing and seal replacement procedure is the same as for the drum brakes.

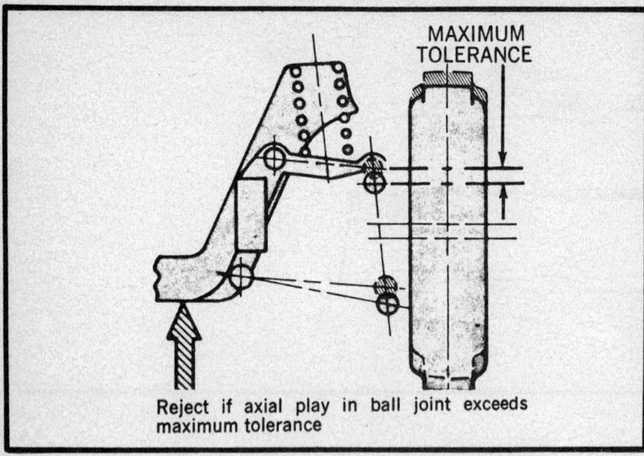

MAXIMUM
TOLERANCE
Reject if axial play in ball joint exceeds maximum tolerance

Check ball joint axial (up and down) play

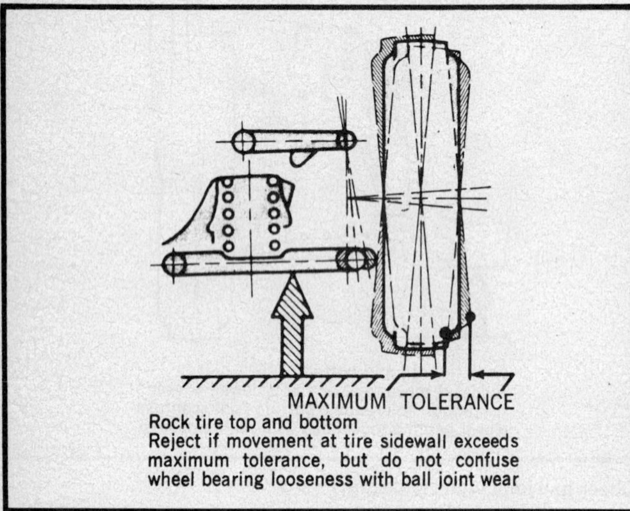

Maximum tolerance

KINGPIN AND BUSHING

Kingpins and bushings can be placed in two general classes:

A. With bushings in knuckle.
B. With bushings in spindle.

Replacement

1. Jack up the truck and remove the hub as described in the wheel bearing section. Remove the backing plate to knuckle bolts and lift assembly, with brakes, from the knuckle. Suspend it with a piece of wire to prevent damage to brake hose.
2. Drive out lock pin or bolt. with a sharp punch, remove top welch plug. Drive pin and lower welch plug down through knuckle and support.

NOTE: Remove top and bottom threaded plugs with wrench.

3. Drive bushings from the spindle and replace them. Be sure, when driving new bushing, that grease holes line up with those in knuckle.
4. Align and ream bushings to a snug running fit for the new kingpin.
5. Insert the kingpin through the top of the spindle, support, thrust bearing (with shims to control vertical play) and into the spindle bottom. Keep the kingpin in proper rotation so that the lockpin can be inserted. Install lockpin or bolt. Install upper and lower welch plugs.
6. Install backing plate with steering arms and lubricate properly.
7. Install hubs, drums and wheels, then remove jack.

BALL JOINT

Replacement

UPPER BALL JOINT – RIVETED TYPE

On some trucks, the upper ball joint is riveted to the control arm. Place jack under lower arm and raise wheel clear off the floor. Remove wheel. Remove nut from ball joint. If joint is being replaced, it may be driven out with a heavy hammer. If threads are to be saved, a spreader tool should be used.

After removing joint from knuckle support, cut off rivets at upper arm. Drilling rivets eases this job.

To replace the ball joint: install in upper arm, using special bolts supplied with new joint. Do not use ordinary bolts.

Next, set the taper into the upper end of the knuckle support and install nut and cotter pin. Check alignment.

THREADED TYPE

On some trucks, the upper ball joint is threaded into the control arm.

Place jack under lower control arm and relieve load on torsion bar. Raise wheel clear of floor. Remove wheel. Remove nut from ball joint. If ball joint is being replaced, it may be driven

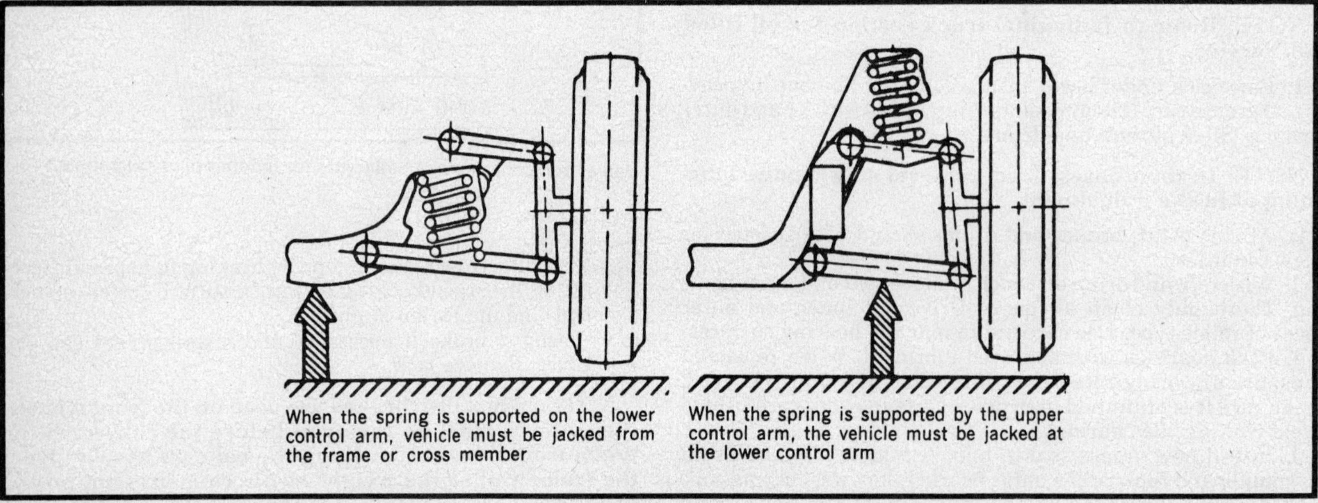

When the spring is supported on the lower control arm, vehicle must be jacked from the frame or cross member
When the spring is supported by the upper control arm, the vehicle must be jacked at the lower control arm

Steering and suspension jacking procedure

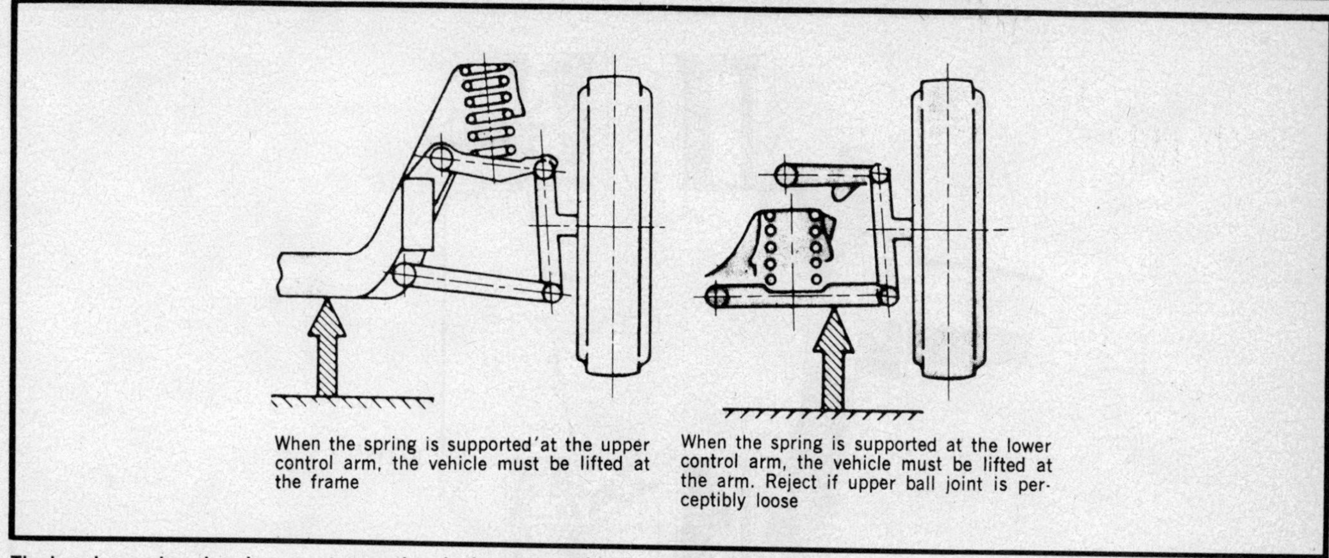

When the spring is supported at the upper control arm, the vehicle must be lifted at the frame
When the spring is supported at the lower control arm, the vehicle must be lifted at the arm. Reject if upper ball joint is perceptibly loose

The bearing and seal replacement procedure is the same as for the drum brakes

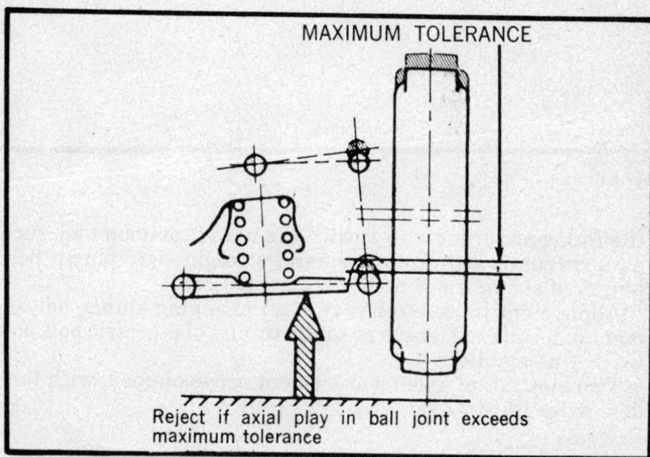

Check ball joint axial (up and down) play

out with a heavy hammer. If threads are to be saved, use a spreader tool.

After removing from knuckle support, the ball joint can be unscrewed from the support arm. Special tools are recommended for this operation.

When replacing the ball joint, be sure to engage the threads into the control arm squarely. Torque to 125 ft. lbs. If this torque cannot be obtained, check for bad threads in arm or on joint. Install new balloon seal.

Place joint in knuckle and install nut. Reload torsion bar (if so equipped) and reset height.

LOWER BALL JOINT

Removal and Installation

PRESSED TYPE

These ball joints are pressed into support arms. To replace pressed-in units, it is necessary to remove the front spring and support arm.

After removing wheel and drum, loosen nut slightly at ball joint taper and hammer lightly around area to loosen. If new ball joints are being installed, it is not necessary to protect the threads.

Place support arm in an arbor press with a suitable tool and press ball joint from the arm.

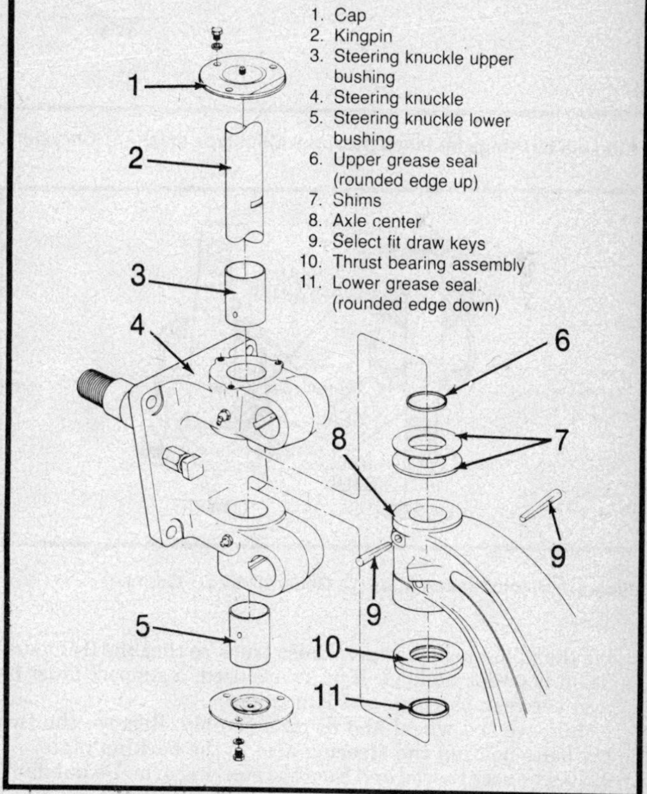

Exploded view of spindle bolt and bushing attachment of a steering knuckle—typical (© General Motors Corp.)

Install ball joint by reversing the pressing procedure.

NOTE: Special tools of the C-clamp type are available and an be used n some trucks to avoid removal of front spring and support arm.

INTEGRAL TYPE

On some trucks, the lower ball joint is integral with the steering arm and is not serviced separately. To service this unit, re-

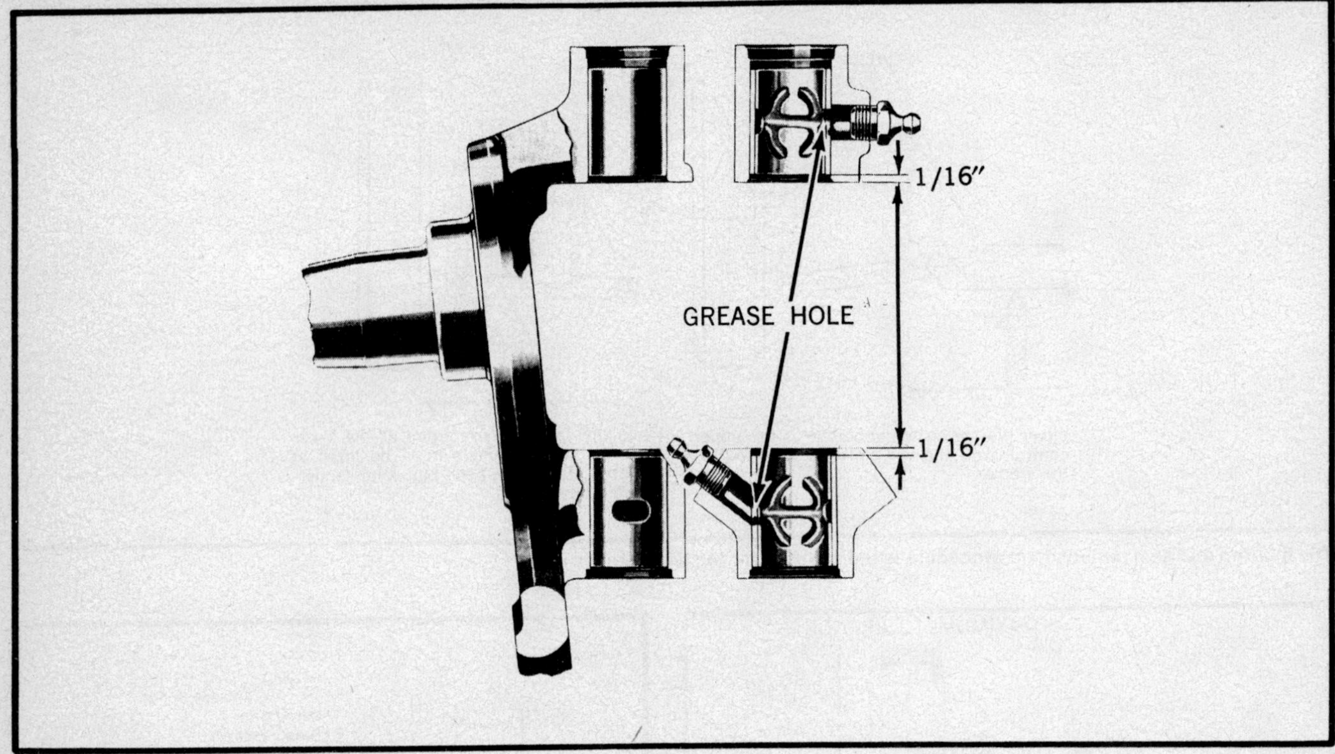

King pin bushings installed (Reverse Elliot type axle) (© Chrysler Corp.)

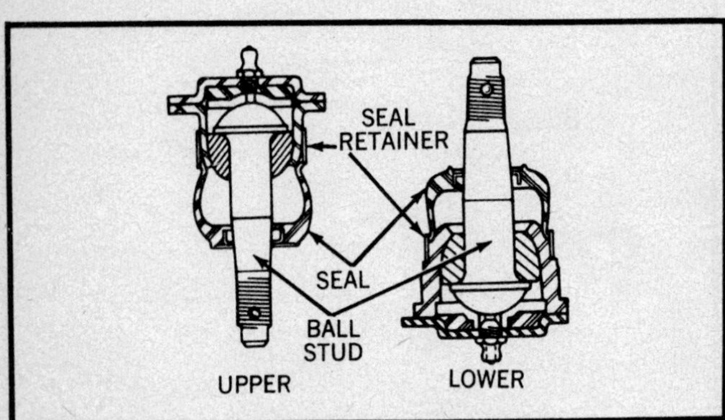

Typical ball joint assemblies (© General Motors Corp.)

move the upper arm bumper. Raise truck so that the front suspension is under no load. If jacks are used, a support must be placed between the jack and K-member.

1. Remove the wheel and drum assembly. Remove the two lower bolts holding the steering arm to the backing plate.
2. Disconnect tie-rod end from the steering arm. Do not damage seal.
3. Remove the ball joint stud from the lower control arm. A spreading tool will aid in this operation.
4. Install new seal on ball joint. Bolt the steering arm to the backing plate. Insert the ball joint into control arm and torque nut.
5. Connect the tie-rod end. Install drum and wheel.

REAR SUSPENSION

Axle Alignment

Rear suspensions can be checked for alignment in relation to the frame and front wheels with the use of common tool, such as a carpenter's (framing) square, straightedge, plumb bob, length of string (cord) and/or a trammel bar.

Adjustment procedures vary from changing shims, adjustment of torque rod length or to the timing of eccentric bolt and washer assemblies.

Two methods of axle measurement are explained, with tandem axles illustrated.

METHOD A

1. Locate a point on both frame rails for a measuring device, such as a straight edge, to run perpendicular from the frame to the ground. This distance is optional, but must be the same measurement on both sides.
2. Attach a long string (cord) to an object behind the rear axle. Be sure the string reaches to the measuring device or beyond.
3. Position two 1 x 2 x 2 in. wood blocks on the rear wheel rim bead, one forward of the rim and the second on the rear of the rim at axle height.
4. Draw the steering around the rear of the wheels at axle height and pull the string tight so as to just contact the rear and front wood blocks. Extend the string to the area of the measuring device, used in Step one.
5. Measure the distance between the string and the measuring device and record.
6. Repeat the measuring operation on the opposite side of the axle.
7. The two distances (left and right sides) should be equal. If not, the rear axle housing must be adjusted.

NOTE: By moving the wheel 180° and remeasuring, a bent wheel can be found by the difference in the measurements.

METHOD B

1. Clamp a straight edge to the top of the frame rail ahead of

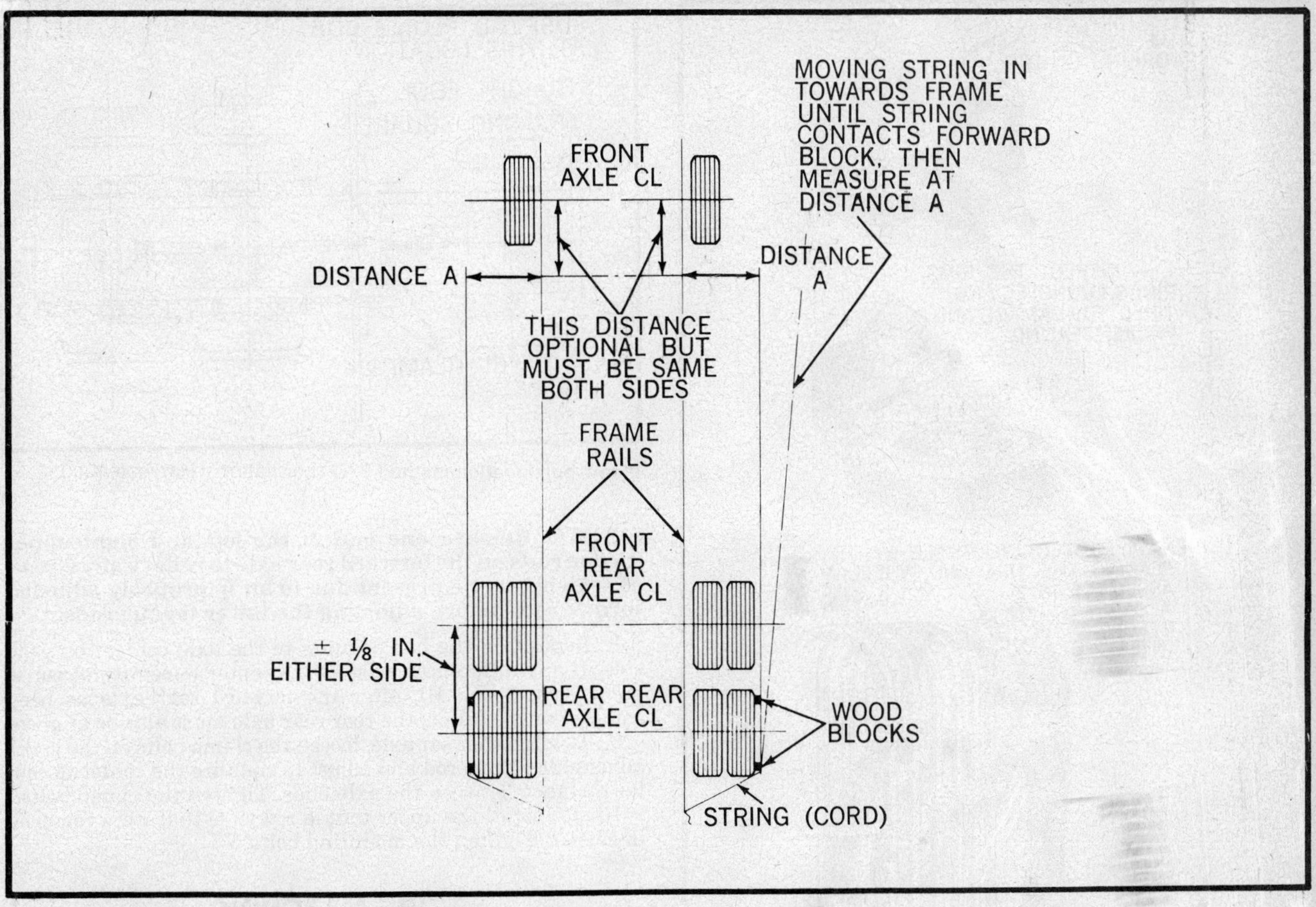

Rear axle and suspension alignment-using method A (© Ford Motor Co.)

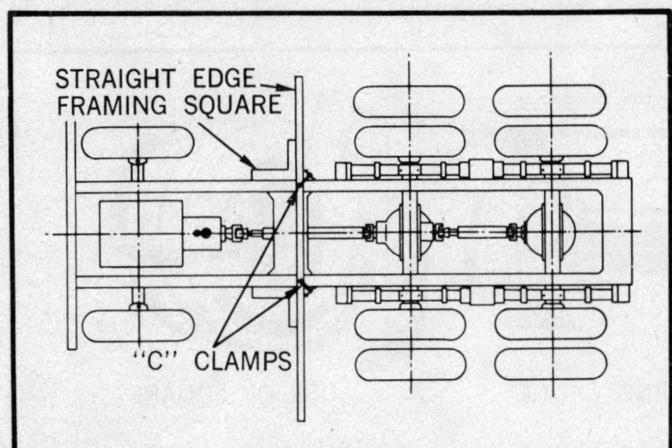

Straightedge location-method B (© International Harvester Co.)

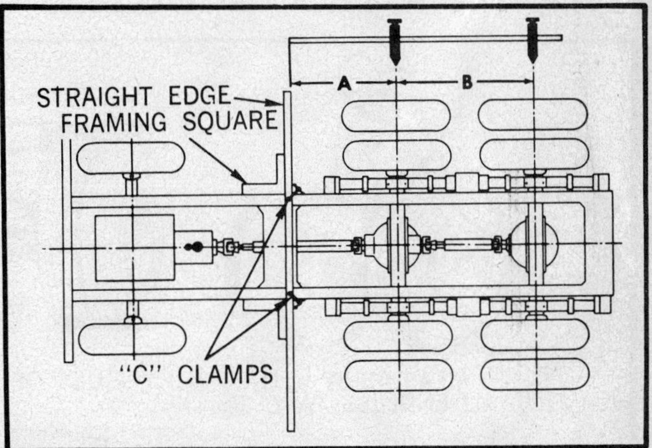

Measurements of axles and suspension to the plumb bob and straightedge-method (© International Harvester Co.)

the forward rear axle. Use a framing square against the straight-edge and the outside surface of the frame siderail to insure the straightedge is perpendicular to the frame.

2. Suspend a plumb bob from the straightedge in front of the tire and on the outboard side of the forward rear axle.

3. Position a bar with pointers that can be engaged in the center holes of the rear axles.

4. Measure the distance between cord of the plumb bob and the pointer on the forward axle and record (dimension A).

5. Position the plumb bob and bar on the opposite side of the vehicle and measure as outlined in paragraph 4. Record the result.

6. Any difference in dimensions from side to side must be equalized if the difference exceeds 0.0625 in.

7. Equalize the dimensions by loosening the clamp bolts on the lower adjustable torque rod on the forward rear axle and adjusting the length of the torque rod. Tighten the clamp bolts.

Tire safety-remember the word D.I.P. (© General Motors Corp.)

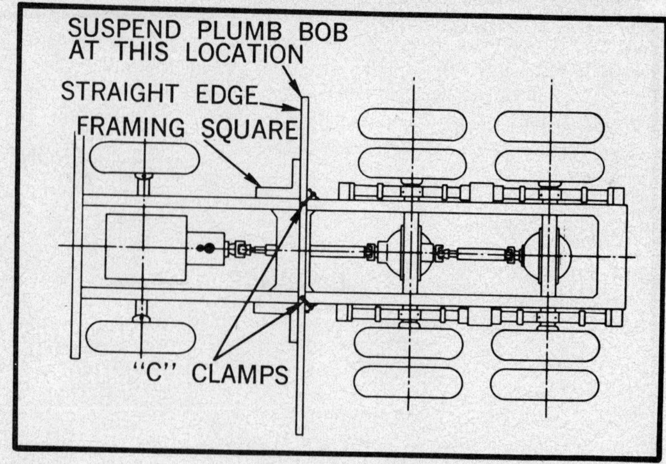

Plumb bob location-method B (© International Harvester Co.)

NOTE: Remove one end of the left and right upper torque rods on the forward rear axle to relieve any stresses which may be present due to an improperly adjusted torque rod, before adjusting the lower torque rods.

8. Reposition the bar pointers to the axle centers on each side. If any differences exist in the center to center measurement, (dimension B), after the forward rear axle as been squared to the frame, the rear rear axle must also be aligned.
9. To align the rear axle, loosen the clamp bolts on the lower adjustable torque rod and adjust to equalize the center to center distance between the axle ends. Tighten the clamp bolts.
10. Reinstall the upper torque rod ends that were removed in Step 7. Tighten the mounting bolts.

TIRE MATCHING

Proper tire matching is essential on tandem drive units to avoid excessive tire wear, scuffing and possible damage to the

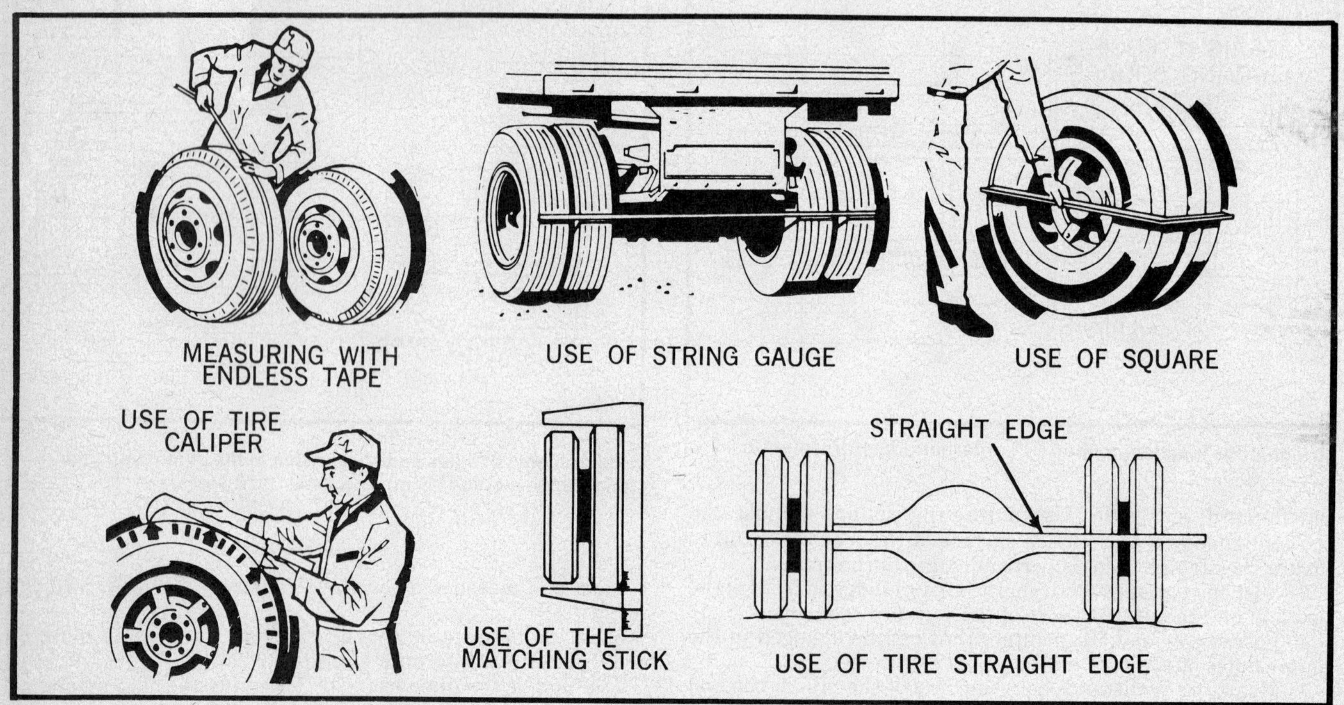

Tools used for tire matching (© General Motors Corp.)

drive unit. Most manufacturers recommend the tires to be matched to within $^1/_8$ in. of the same rolling circumference. Both driving axle tire circumferences should be matched as closely as possible to avoid excessive tandem axle lubricant temperatures.

Numerous means are available for measurement purposes, a few of which follow:

1. Endless tape or Pi tape
2. String gauge
3. Square
4. Tire caliper
5. Matching stick
6. Tire straight edge

TIRE REPLACEMENT

Specialized tools and equipment have been designed for use in the replacement of a tire on multipiece rims. The manufacturers instructions should be followed in the use of the machines in the amounting and dismounting of tires to avoid personal injury.

For the safety of the repairman, the word "D.I.P." should be remembered when working with tires and wheels.

1. D–DEFLATE–The tire before working on it.
2. I–INSPECT–The rim, rings, lug holes and tires for damage and proper sealing.
3. P–PROTECT–Yourself by placing the tire and wheel assembly in a cage before inflating.

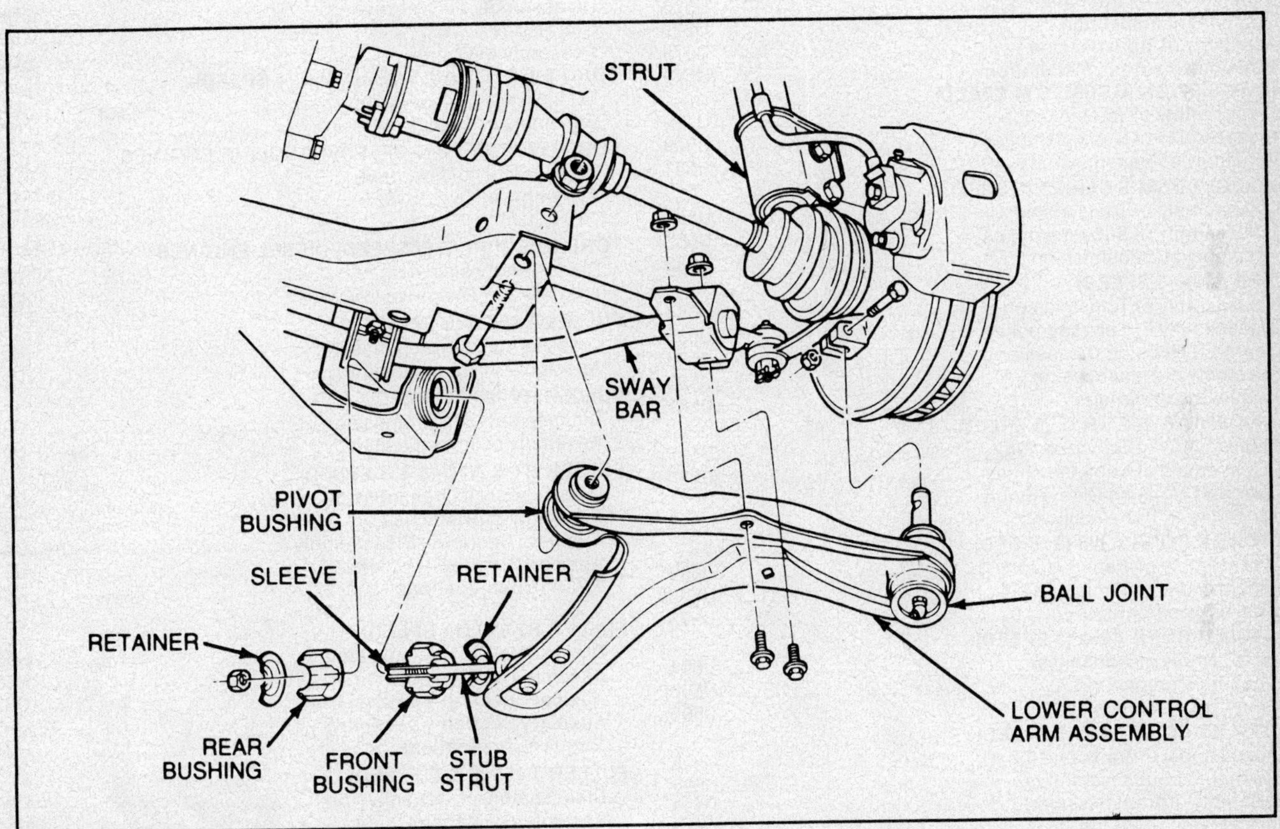

Typical front suspension inspection points

INDEX

INDEX

Sequence of Diagnosis

In order to determine the problems that may exist in a transmission, a systematic diagnosis procedure should be followed to locate and repair the malfunction.

1. Consult with the owner or operator to identify the problem.
2. Road test, whenever possible with the owner or operator, to verify the problem is within the transmission and not caused by a related component.
3. Verify that all controls are operating properly and in good condition.
4. With the unit removed from the vehicle, inspect it prior to the disassembly.
5. During the disassembly, inspect the varied parts to locate the source of the problem.
6. Replace companion gears to defective or worn gears. Do not reinstall a part that does not have a long service life remaining.
7. Make any modifications or changes as recommended by the manufacturer.

Transmission Diagnosis and Troubleshooting

Noises with Transmission in Neutral (Always Leave Main Box in Neutral, Auxiliary in Gear When Idling)

1. Misalignment of transmission.
2. Worn flywheel pilot bearing.
3. Worn or scored countershaft bearings.
4. Worn or rough reverse idler gear.
5. Sprung or worn countershaft.
6. Excessive backlash in gears.
7. Worn mainshaft pilot bearing.
8. Scuffed gear tooth contact surface.
9. Insufficient lubrication.
10. Use of incorrect grade of lubricant.

Noises with Transmission in Gear

1. Worn or rough mainshaft rear bearing.
2. Rough, chipped or tapered sliding gear teeth.
3. Noisy speedometer gears.
4. Excessive end play of mainshaft gears.
5. Refer to conditions listed above under noises with transmission in neutral.

Growling, Humming and Grinding

1. Pitted, chipped or cracked gears.
2. Damaged gears or chips in lubricant from failed power-take-off.
3. Excessive gear wear from high mileage or overloading.

Hissing, Thumping and Bumping

1. Bad bearings on way to failure.
2. Broken bearings and retainers.

Metallic Rattles

1. Engine torsional vibration.
2. Clutch disc assembly worn or without torsional vibration dampers.
3. Engine idle speed too low.
4. Rough engine idle.
5. Excessive backlash in power take off mounting.

Squealing, Gear Whine and Gear Seizure

1. One of the free running gears seizing on thrust face or fluted diameter momentarily, then letting go.
2. Whine of excessive backlash in mating gears or improper shimming of power take off unit.

Walking or Jumping out of Gear

CAUSES OUTSIDE TRANSMISSION

1. Improperly positioned forward remote control which limits full travel forward and backward from the remote neutral position.
2. Improper adjustment or length shift rods or linkage that limits travel of forward remote from neutral position.
3. Loose bell cranks, sloppy ball and socket joints.
4. Shift rods, cables, etc., too spongy, flexible, or not secured properly at both ends.
5. Worn or loose engine mounts if forward unit is mounted to frame.
6. Forward remote mount too flimsy, loose on frame, etc.
7. Set screws loose at remote control joints.
8. Air shift system partially inoperative.
9. Transmission and engine out of alignment either vertically or horizontally.

CAUSES INSIDE TRANSMISSION

1. Shift tower or cover loose or interlock balls or pins worn or springs broken.
2. Shift fork pads not square with shift rod bore.
3. Shift rod poppet springs broken.
4. Shift rod poppet notches worn.
5. Shift rod bent or sprung out of line.
6. Shift fork pads or groove in sliding gear or collar worn excessively.
7. Shift fork pads not square with rod bore.
8. Worn taper on gear teeth, spacers or bearings.
9. Backing rings or retaining rings not installed properly on rear unit.

Hard Shifting

PRELIMINARY INVESTIGATION

1. Not enough clutch pedal free play.
2. Worn or inoperative clutch hydraulic cylinder.
3. Worn or loose clutch shaft, levers.
4. Worn or loose throwout bearing or carrier.
5. Low air pressure to main auxiliary unit shift cylinder.
6. Air leaks in cylinders, control lines or cab control valve.
7. Improper remote control function.
8. No lubricant in remote control units.
9. No lubricant in (or grease fittings on) U-joints or swivels of remote controls.

UNSYNCHRONIZED (CONSTANT MESH) TRANSMISSIONS

1. Lack of lubricant or wrong lubricant used causing build-up of sticky varnish and sludge deposits on splines of shaft and gears.
2. Sliding clutch gears tight on splines of shaft.
3. Clutch teeth burred over, chipped or badly mutilated due to improper shifting.
4. Driver not familiar with proper shifting procedure for this transmission. Also includes proper shifting if used with two speed axle, auxiliary, etc.
5. Clutch or drive gear pilot bearing seized, rough, or dragging.
6. Clutch brake engaging too soon when clutch pedal is depressed.

SYNCHRONIZED TRANSMISSION

1. Badly worn or bent shift rods.
2. Loose or flimsy remote controls, spongy or flexible rods and/or cables preventing full application of force to hold and synchronize gears.
3. Further, driver may not be able to feel the synchronizer action which usually results in a snap type shift.
4. Synchronizer bronze or aluminum rings worn or steel chips imbedded in rings prevent proper synchronization.
5. Damaged synchronizer such as broken poppet springs, poppets jammed, loose or broken blocker pins.
6. Free running gears, seized or galled on either the thrust face or diameters.

Sticking in Gear

1. Clutch not releasing.
2. Inoperative slave power units.
3. Sliding clutch gears tight on splines.
4. Chips wedged between or under splines of shaft and gear.
5. Improper adjustment, excessive wear or lost motion in shifter linkage.
6. Clutch brake set too high on clutch pedal locking gears behind hopping guard.

Crash Shifting or Raking Gears

SYNCHRONIZED TRANSMISSIONS

1. Raking of gears during manual shift may be caused by a defective synchronizer or improper shifting technique for synchronized transmission.
2. Occurs with cold, heavy oil, but synchronizer begins to work properly when transmission oil reaches normal operating temperature.
3. Heavy oil prevents the synchronizer cone from breaking through oil film and doing job properly.
4. Glazing of synchronizer cones due to use of E.P. addition in multi-purpose axle lubricant.
5. Synchronizer cones worn smooth causing loss of clutching action, which causes failure to control engine speed drop off during upshift, failure to bring engine speed nearly up to governor speed when driver shifting, and attempted shifting without using clutch.
6. Blocker pin detents worn resulting in loss of blocker action.
7. Blocker pins loose, broken or turned over.

Oil Leaks

1. Oil level too high.
2. Wrong lubricant in unit.
3. Non-shielded bearing used at front or rear bearing cap (where applicable.)
4. Seals (if used) defective or omitted from bearing cap, wrong type seal used, etc.
5. Screwback threads in bearing caps off location, worn out, or filled with varnish, sludge, dirt, etc.
6. Transmission breather omitted, plugged internally, etc.
7. Capscrews loose, omitted or missing from remote control, shifter housing, bearing caps, P.T.O. or covers, etc.
8. Welch "seal" plugs loose or missing entirely from machine openings in case.
9. Oil drain back openings in bearing caps or case plugged with varnish, dirt, covered with gasket material, etc.
10. Broken gaskets, gaskets shifted or squeezed out of position, pieces still under bearing caps, clutch housing, P.T.O. and covers, etc.
11. Cracks or holes in castings.
12. Drain plug loose.
13. Also possibility that oil leakage could be from engine.
14. Internal O-ring worn in air cylinders, leaking air into transmission, pressurizing transmission.

Vibration

ORIGINATING IN TRANSMISSION

1. Sprung mainshafts and countershaft.
2. Gears that have seized to shaft and broken loose.
3. Bearings that are extremely worn allowing rotating shafts to oscillate from intended centers.

ORIGINATING ELSEWHERE BUT APPARENTLY IN TRANSMISSION

1. Drive lines out of static or dynamic balance.
2. Out of phase, wrong drive line working angles.
3. Worn crosses and bearings in U-joints.
4. Loose mounting or worn center bearings.
5. Worn and pitted teeth on ring gear and pinion of driving axle(s).
6. Wheels out of balance.
7. Warped parking brake drum or disc.

Bearing Failure

1. Dirt, always abrasive enters through seals, breathers, dirty containers.
2. Lapping action of fine steel particles from balls and raceways.
3. Entry of chips from hammers, chisels, punches during disassembly and assembly.
4. Bearing jammed with chip(s) may turn on shaft or in housing.
5. Brinnelling, ball depressions, spalling.
6. Excessive looseness under load scrubs shaft and bearing bore.
7. Failure due to heat. Failure of lubricant circulation. Lubricant deterioration or low level.
8. Radically tight bearing caused by expansion of inner race when mounted on shaft or compression of outer race when pressed into housing. Off-square mounting producing heat at retainers.

Air Shift System Diagnosis and Troubleshooting

Failure to Shift

LOW AIR PRESSURE IN SHIFT SYSTEM

1. Low air pressure in brake system air tank.
2. Air pressure regulator out of adjustment.
3. Air pressure regulator defective.
4. Leaks in controls, valves or air lines.
5. Frozen lines or valves during cold weather.

INTERNAL SHIFT CYLINDER(S) WEAK OR INOPERATIVE

1. Worn O-ring on piston shift bar, or piston rod, bad gaskets.
2. Cover insert valve inoperative.
3. Main air valve inoperative.

EXTERNAL SHIFT CYLINDERS WEAK OR INOPERATIVE

1. Worn O-rings on piston rod, or defective gaskets.
2. Cylinder link clevis, or cylinder anchor pivot excessively worn or poor link adjustment.

COVER INSERT VALVE INOPERATIVE

1. Leaking at retainer nut or external O-ring.
2. Piston jammed or by-passing air.

MAIN AIR VALVE INOPERATIVE

1. No air from drivers shift valve.
2. Excessive O-ring or piston wear with air by-passing or leaking in one or both range positions.
3. Actuating piston held by jammed actuating pin in shift bar housing remaining in protruded position.
4. Plunger rusted causing excess moisture.

DRIVER SHIFT VALVE(S) INOPERATIVE

1. No air to drivers shift valve(s).
2. Valve(s) worn or defective.

MECHANICAL RESISTANCE OR BLOCK TO INTERNAL RANGE OR AUXILIARY GEAR SECTION

1. Worn shift bar(s) jammed or broken poppets or interlock pins, or springs.
2. Internal shift fork, clutch gear, or synchro wear or failure.

Slow Shifting

LOW AIR PRESSURE IN SHIFT SYSTEM

1. Low air pressure in brake system air tank.
2. Air pressure regulator out of adjustment.
3. Air pressure regulator defective.
4. Leaks in controls, valves or air lines.
5. Frozen lines or valves during cold weather.

INTERNAL SHIFT CYLINDERS WEAK SLOW RESPONSE

1. Worn O-ring on piston, shift bar, or piston rod/bad gasket.
2. Cover insert valve slow.
3. Main air valve slow.

COVER INSERT VALVE SLOW RESPONSE

1. Leaking at retainer nut or external O-ring.
2. Piston dragging or by-passing air.

MAIN AIR VALVE SLOW RESPONSE

1. Low air from drivers shift valve.
2. Excessive O-ring or piston wear with air by-passing or leaking in one or both range positions.
3. Rust, moisture from air tank.

EXTERNAL SHIFT CYLINDER(S) SLOW RESPONSE

1. Cylinder shaft locknut under clevis worked loose allowing shaft to back out of adjustment. Cylinder shaft will not return to neutral position.
2. Air leaks around cylinder shaft or piston.
3. Air cylinder cap anchor pin hole worn excessively, allowing cylinder to be loose during shifts to gear positions.
4. Air cylinder shaft slightly bent causing piston to bind in cylinder.
5. Fittings on cylinders, regulator leaking, or fittings from main air supply ahead of rear unit shifting system, leaking before it reaches rear unit air system.
6. Pinched air line at regulator or cylinders.
7. Lockwire on regulator fatigued or broken apart, allowing regulator setting screw to back off, producing low air pressure to shifting system.
8. Regulator (non-adjustable) defective.
9. Filter contamination blow off butterfly nut not tight or seated properly.
10. Cab control valve dry of O-ring lubrication or excessive dirt in unit that will adhere to rotor.
11. Worn O-rings in cab control valve under rotor.
12. Cab control valve loose on shift lever.

Crash Shifting or Raking of Gears

HIGH AIR PRESSURE

1. Improperly set pressure regulator (adjustable type).
2. Defective regulator.
3. Regulator or valve freeze-up in cold weather.
4. Poor driver technique.
5. Failure to control engine speed drop off during upshift.
6. Failure to bring engine up to near governed speed when downshifting.

Transfer Case Diagnosis and Troubleshooting

Slips Out of Gear (High-Low)

1. Shifting poppet spring weak.
2. Bearing broken or worn.
3. Shifting fork bent.
4. Improper control rod adjustment.

Slips Out of Front Wheel Drive

1. Shifting poppet spring weak or broken.
2. Bearing worn or broken.
3. Excessive shaft end-play.
4. Shifting fork bent.

Hard Shifting

1. Lack of lubricant.
2. Shift lever binding on shaft.
3. Shifting poppet ball scored.
4. Shifting fork bent.
5. Low tire pressure.

Backlash

1. Companion yoke loose.
2. Transfer case loose on mounts.
3. Internal parts excessively worn.

Noisy

1. Low lubricant level.
2. Bearings improperly adjusted or excessively worn.
3. Gears worn or damaged.
4. Improper alignment of driveshafts or U-joints.

Oil Leakage

1. Excessive amount of lubricant in case.
2. Vent clogged.
3. Gaskets or seals leaking.
4. Bearings loose or damaged.
5. Driveshaft yoke mating surfaces scored.

Overheating

1. Excessive or insufficient amount of lubricant.
2. Bearing adjustment too tight.

CLEANING OF TRANSMISSION COMPONENTS

Cleanliness of parts, tools, and work area is of the utmost importance. All transmission components (except bearing assemblies) should be cleaned in cleaning solvent and dried with compressed air before any inspection or work is begun. Great care should be taken when cleaning bearings. Bearings should always be cleaned separately from other parts in clean cleaning solvent and not gasoline. They must never be cleaned in a hot solution tank. It is advisable that they be soaked in cleaning fluid and then tapped against a block of wood in order to free any solidified lubricant that may be trapped inside. Rinse bearings thoroughly in clean solvent and then dry them with moisture-free compressed air being careful not to spin the bearings with the air stream. Rotate each bearing slowly and inspect rollers or balls for any signs of excessive wear, roughness, or damage. Those bearings not in excellent condition must be replaced. If they pass this inspection, they should be dipped in clean oil and wrapped in clean lintless cloth to protect them until installation.

INSPECTION OF TRANSMISSION COMPONENTS

All parts must be completely and carefully inspected and replaced for any signs of wear, stress, discoloration or warpage due to excessive heat. Whenever available, the magna flux process should be used on all parts except roller and ball bearings, to detect small cracks unseen by the eye. Inspect the breather assembly to see that it is not clogged or damaged and check all threaded parts for stripped or cross threads. Oil passages must be cleared of obstructions by the use of air pressure or brass rods and all gaskets, oil seals, lock wires, cotter pins, and snap rings are to be replaced. Small nicks or burrs in gears or splines can be removed with a fine abrasive stone. It is important that any housings or covers having cracks or other damage should be replaced and not welded. Synchronizers, not in excellent condition, must be replaced. The bronze synchronizer cone should be checked for wear or for any steel chips that may have become imbedded in it. Springs must be inspected for free length, compressed length, distortion, or collapsed coils.

NOTE: The splines on many clutch gears, mainshafts, etc., are equipped with a machined relief called a "hopping guard". With the clutch gear engaged, the mating gear is free to slip into this notch, preventing the two gears from separating or "walking out of gear" under various load conditions. This is not a worn or chipped gear. Do not grind or discard the gear.

Check all shafts for spline wear or damage. If the mainshaft 1st and reverse sliding gear or clutch hub have worn into the sides of the splines, the shaft should be replaced. Shift forks, shift rods, interlock balls and pins must be replaced if scored, worn, distorted or damaged.

MANUAL TRANSMISSION SERVICE

AMC (Jeep)

Model AX4 is a 4-speed manual transmission while AX5 is a 5-speed manual transmission. Both transmissions have synchromesh engagement in all forward gears controlled by a floor shift mechanism integrated into the transmission top cover.

NOTE: The following components and materials must be replaced whenever the transmission is overhauled. Lip-type oil seals, lock nuts, all roll pins and all snaprings.

Disassembly

1. Remove the clutch housing.
2. Remove the straight screw plug, spring and ball using a Torx bit to remove the screw plug, and a magnet to remove spring and ball.
3. Remove five adapter housing bolts and one nut.
4. Remove the shift lever housing set bolt and lock plate.
5. Remove the plug at the rear of the shift fork shaft.
6. Remove the large magnet to pull the shaft out.
7. Remove the select lever from the top while rotating.
8. Remove the five adapter housing bolts two studs and one nut.
9. Using a plastic hammer, tap and remove the extension housing. Leave the gasket attached to the intermediate plate.
10. Remove the front bearing retainer and outer snaprings from the two front bearings.
11. Separate the intermediate plate from the transmission case using a small plastic hammer and remove the case.
12. Mount the intermediate plate in a vise. Be careful not to damage the plate.

NOTE: Before placing the intermediate plate in a vise, insert bolts, washers, and nuts in the open holes at the bottom of plate. Tighten vise against these bolts to prevent damage to the plate.

13. Remove the straight screw plug, locking balls and springs using a Torx bit and magnet.
14. Remove the five slotted spring pins using a hammer and punch and then remove the two E-rings from the shift rails The locking ball from the reverse shift head and locking ball and pin from the intermediate housing will fall from the holes so be sure to catch them with a magnet.
15. Pull out the shift fork shaft No. 4 from the intermediate plate and catch the locking ball.
16. Remove shift fork shaft No.4 and the 5th gear fork.
17. Pull out shift fork shaft No.5 from the intermediate plate, and remove it with the reverse shift head. The interlock pins will fall from their hole. If they do not come out, remove them with a magnet.
18. Remove the shift fork shaft No. 3 from the intermediate plate and catch the interlock pins. The interlock pin will fall from the hole so be sure to catch it. If it does not come out, remove it with a magnet.
19. Remove shift fork shaft No. 1 from the intermediate plate being careful not to drop the interlock pin.

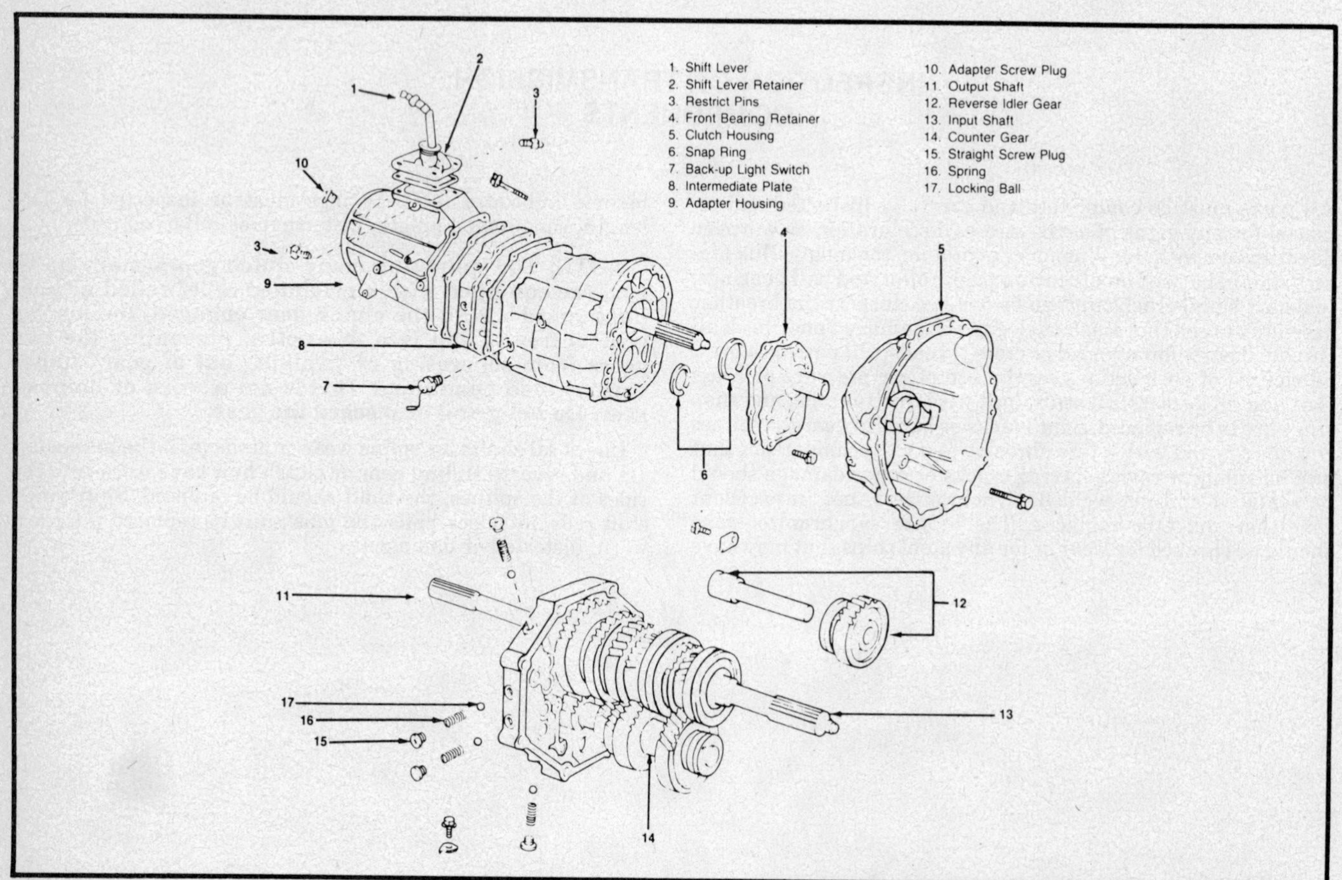

Jeep 4-5 speed

20. Remove shift fork shaft No. 2, shift fork No. 2 and shift fork No.1.
21. Remove the reverse idle gear shaft stopper, reverse idler gear and shaft.
22. Remove the reverse shift arm from the reverse shift arm bracket.
23. Using a feeler gauge, measure the counter fifth gear thrust clearance. Standard Clearance: 0.004–0.012 in.
24. Engage two gears to lock the output shaft. Using a hammer and chisel, loosen the staked part of the nut on the counter shaft.
25. Remove the lock not disengage the gears.
26. Remove the gear spline piece No. 5, synchronizer ring, needle roller bearing and counter fifth gear using tool J-22888 or equivalent.
27. Remove the spacer and use a magnet to remove the ball.
28. Remove the reverse shift arm bracket.
29. remove the rear bearing retainer bolts with a Torx bit and the snapring using snapring pliers.
30. Remove the output shaft, counter gear and input shaft as a unit from the intermediate plate by pulling on the counter gear and tapping on the intermediate plate with a plastic hammer.
31. Remove the input shaft with fourteen needle roller bearing from the output shaft.
32. Remove the counter rear bearing from the intermediate plate.
33. Measure the thrust clearance of each gear. Standard Clearance: 0.004–0.010 in.
34. Using two awls and a hammer, tap out the snapring.
35. Using a press, remove the fifth gear, rear bearing, first gear and the inner race.
36. Remove the needle roller bearing.
37. Remove the synchronizer ring, second gear.
39. Remove the needle roller bearing.
40. Remove the snapring from hub sleeve No. 2.
41. Using a press, remove the hub sleeve, synchronizer ring, and third gear.
42. Remove the needle roller bearing.

Component Inspection

Output Shaft and Inner Race

1. Check the output shaft and inner race for wear or damage.
2. Using calipers, measure the output shaft flange thickness. Minimum Thickness. Minimum Thickness: 0.189 in.
3. Using calipers, measure the inner face flange thickness. Minimum Thickness: 0.157 in.
4. Using a micrometer, measure the outer diameter of the output shaft journal surface. 2nd Gear Minimum: 1.495 in., 3rd Gear Minimum: 1.377 in.
5. Using a micrometer, measure the outer diameter of the inner race. Minimum Diameter: 1.535 in.
6. Using a dial indicator, measure the shaft runout. Maximum Runout: 0.002 in.

First Gear Oil Clearance

1. Using a dial indicator, measure the oil clearance between the gear and inner race with the needle roller bearing installed. Standard Clearance: 0.0004 in. to 0.0013 in.
2. Using a dial indicator, measure the oil clearance between the gear and shaft with the needle roller bearing installed. Standard Clearance: 2nd and 3rd Gears: 0.0004 in. to 0.0013 in., Counter 5th Gear: 0.0004 in. to 0.0013 in.

Synchronizer Ring Inspection

1. Check for wear or damage. Turn the ring and push it in to check the braking action.
2. Measure the clearance between the synchronizer ring

Thickness mm (in.)	
2.05–2.10	(0.0807–0.0827)
2.10–2.15	(0.0827–0.0846)
2.15–2.20	(0.0846–0.0866)
2.20–2.25	(0.0866–0.0886)
2.25–2.35	(0.0886–0.0906)
2.30–2.35	(0.0906–0.0925)

back and the gear spline end. Standard Clearance: 0.040 in. to 0.078 in., Minimum Clearance 0.031 in.

Shift Fork and Hub Sleeve Clearance

1. Using a feeler gauge, measure the clearance between the hub sleeve and shift fork. Maximum Clearance: 0.039 in.

Input Shaft and Bearing Inspection and Removal

1. Check for wear or damage. If necessary, remove the bearing snapring using snapring pliers and remove the bearing.
2. Using a press, remove the bearing.
3. Using a press a tool J-34603 or equivalent, install the new bearing.
4. Select a snapring that will allow minimum axial play and install it on the shaft.

Counter Gear and Bearing Inspection

1. Check the gear teeth for werar or damage.
2. Check the bearing for wear or damage.

Counter Gear Front Bearing Replacement

1. Using snapring pliers, remove the snapring.
2. Check the bearing for wear or damage.

Counter Gear Front Bearing Replacement

1. Using snapring pliers, remove the snapring.
2. Press out the bearing using tool J-22912-01 or equivalent, press in the bearing and inner race.
5. Select a snapring that will allow minimum axial play and install it on the shaft.

Thickness mm (in.)	
2.05–2.10	(0.0807–0.0827)
2.10–2.15	(0.0827–0.0846)
2.15–2.20	(0.0846–0.0866)
2.20–2.25	(0.0866–0.0886)
2.25–2.30	(0.0886–0.0906)
2.30–2.35	(0.0906–0.0925)

Front Bearing Retainer Inspection

1. Check retainer for damage.
2. Check the oil seal lip for wear or damage.

Oil Seal Replacement

1. Using a awl, pry the old seal out of the housing.
2. Press in the new oil seal using tool J-34602 or equivalent.
3. The oil seal depth is 0.441 in. to 0.480 in. from the housing to transmission surface to the top edge of the seal.

Reverse Restrict Pin replacement

1. Check for wear or damage.
2. Using a Torx bit, remove the screw plug.
3. Using a hammer and pin punch, drive out the slotted spring pin.
4. Pull off the lever housing and slide out the shaft.
5. Install the lever housing.
6. Using a hammer and pin punch, drive out the slotted spring pin.

7. Using a Torx bit, install and torque the screw plug to 27 ft. lbs. torque.

Adapter Housing and Oil Seal Inspection and Replacement

1. Check the adapter housing for wear or damage.
2. Replace the oil seal with tool J-29184 or equivalent.

OUTPUT SHAFT

Assemble

1. Install the clutch hub No. 1 and No. 2 into hub sleeves along with the shifting keys. Install the key springs so their gaps are not in line.
2. Install the shifting springs under the shifting keys.
3. Apply gear oil on the output shaft and 3rd gear needle roller bearing.
4. Place the 3rd gear synchronizer ring on the gear and align the ring slots with the shifting keys.
5. Install the needle roller bearing in the 3rd gear and hub sleeve No. 2.
6. Select a new snapring (2) that will allow minimum axial play and install it on the shaft.
7. Using a feeler gauge, measure the 3rd gear thrust clearance. Standard Clearance: 0.004 in to 0.010 in.
8. Apply gear oil on the output shaft and 2nd gear needle bearing.
9. Place the 2nd gear synchronizer ring on the 2nd gear and align the ring slots with the shifting keys.
10. Install the needle roller bearing in the 2nd gear.
11. Using a press install the 2nd gear and hub sleeve No.1.
12. Install the first gear locking ball in the output shaft.
13. Apply gear oil to the needle roller bearing.
14. Assemble the first gear, synchronizer ring, needle roller bearing and bearing inner race.

Thickness mm (in.)	
1.75–1.80	(0.0689–0.0709)
1.80–1.85	(0.0709–0.0728)
1.85–1.90	(0.0728–0.0748)
1.90–1.95	(0.0748–0.0768)
1.95–2.00	(0.0768–0.0787)
2.00–2.05	(0.0788–0.0807)
2.05–2.10	(0.0807–0.0827)

15. Install the assembly on the output shaft, with the synchronizer ring slots aligned with the shifting keys.
16. Turn the inner race to align it with the locking ball.
17. Install the output shaft rear bearing using tool J-34603 or equivalent and a press.
18. Install the bearing on the output shaft with the outer race snapring groove toward the rear. Hold the 1st gear inner race to prevent it from falling.
19. Measure the 1st and 2nd gear thrust clearance with a feeler gauge. Standard Clearance: 0.004 in to 0.010 in.
20. Install 5th gear on the output shaft using tool J-35603 or equivalent and a press.
21. Select a snapring that will allow minimum axial play.
22. Using the proper tools tap the snap into position.
23. Apply multi-purpose grease to the fourteen needle bearings and install them in the input shaft.
24. Install the output shaft into the intermediate plate by pulling on the output shaft and tapping on the intermediate plate.
25. Install the input shaft to the output shaft with the synchronizer ring slots aligned with the shifting keys.
26. Install the counter gear into the intermediate plate while holding the counter gear, and install the counter rear bearing with a suitable driver.

Thickness mm (in.)	
2.67–2.72	(0.1051–0.1071)
2.73–2.78	(0.1075–0.1094)
2.79–2.84	(0.1098–0.1118)
2.85–2.90	(0.1122–0.1142)
2.91–2.96	(0.1146–0.1165)
2.97–3.02	(0.1169–0.1189)
3.03–3.08	(0.1193–0.1213)
3.09–3.14	(0.1217–0.1236)
3.15–3.20	(0.1240–0.1260)
3.21–3.26	(0.1264–0.1283)
3.27–3.32	(0.1287–0.1307)

27. Install the bearing snapring using snapring pliers. Be sure the snapring is flush with the intermediate plate surface.
28. Using a Torx bit, install and tighten the screws to 13 ft. lbs. torque.
29. Install the reverse shift arm bracket and tighten the bolts to 13 ft. lbs. torque.
30. Install the ball and spacer.
31. Install the shifting keys and hub sleeve No.3 onto the counter 5th gear. Install the key springs positioned so the end gaps are not in line.
32. Install shifting key springs under the shifting keys.
33. Apply gear oil to the needle roller bearing and install the counter 5th gear with hub sleeve No.3 and needle roller bearings.
34. Install the synchronizer ring on gear spline piece.
35. Using tool J-28406 or equivalent drive in gear spline piece No.5 with the synchronizer ring slots aligned with the shifting keys. When installing gear spline piece No. 5, support the counter gear in front with a 3 to 5 lb. hammer or equivalent.
36. Engage two gears to lock the output shaft.
37. Install and tighten the lock nut to 90 ft. lbs. torque on the counter shaft.
38. Stake the lock nut.
39. Disengage the gears.
40. Measure the counter fifth gear thrust clearance using a feeler gauge. Standard Clearance: 0.004 in to 0.012 in.
41. Install the reverse shift arm to the pivot of the reverse shift arm bracket.
42. Install the reverse idler gear on the shaft.
43. Align the reverse shift arm shoe to the reverse idler gear groove and insert the reverse idler gear shift to the intermediate plate.
44. Install the reverse idler gear shaft stopper and tighten the bolt to 13 ft. lbs. torque.
45. Place shift forks No. 1 and No. 2 into groove of hub sleeves No. 1 and No. 2 and install fork shaft No.2 to the shift fork No.1 and No. 2 through the intermediate plate.
46. Apply multi-purpose grease to the interlock pins.
47. Using a magnet and a suitable tool, install the interlock pin onto the intermediate plate.
48. Install the interlock pin into the shaft hole.
49. Install fork shaft No. 1 to shift fork No. 1 through the intermediate plate.
50. Using a magnet and a suitable tool, install the interlock pin into the intermediate plate.
51. Install the interlock pin into the shaft hole.
52. Install fork shaft No.3 to the reverse shift arm through the intermediate plate.
53. Install the reverse shift head into fork shaft No. 5.
54. Insert fork shaft No. 5 to the intermediate plate and put in the reverse shift head to the shift fork No. 3.
55. Using a magnet and a suitable tool, install the locking ball into the reverse shift head hole.
56. Shift hub sleeve No. 3 to the 5th speed position.
57. Place shift fork No. 3 into the groove of hub sleeve No. 3

and install fork shaft No.4 to shift fork No. 3 and reverse shift arm.

58. Using a magnet and a suitable tool, install the locking ball into the intermediate plate and insert fork shaft No. 4 to the intermediate plate.

59. Check the interlock by positioning the shift fork shaft No.1 to the 1st speed position.

60. Fork shafts No. 2, No. 3, No. 4 and No. 5 should not move.

61. Using a pin punch and a hammer, drive in new slotted springs pins in each shift fork, reverse shift arm and reverse shift head.

62. Install two fork shaft E-rings.

63. Apply liquid sealer to the screw plugs.

64. Install the locking balls, springs and screw plugs with a Torx bit and tighten to 14 ft. lbs. torque. Install the short spring into the tower of the intermediate plate.

65. Remove the intermediate plate from the vise.

66. Remove the bolts, nuts, washers and gasket.

Transmission Case Installation

1. Align each bearing outer race, each fork shaft end and reverse idler gear with the holes in the case and install the case on the intermediate plate. If necessary, tap on the case with a plastic hammer.
2. Instll two new bearing snaprings.
3. Install front bearing retainer with a new gasket.
4. Apply liquid sealer to the bolts.
5. Install and tighten the bolts to 12 ft. lbs. torque.
6. Instll the new gasket to the intermediate plate.
7. Install the adapter housing.
8. Install and tighten the adapter bolts to 27 ft. lbs. torque.
9. Install the shift lever housing.
10. Insert the shift lever into the adapter and shift lever housing.
11. Install and tighten shift lever housing bolt with a lock plate to 28 ft. lbs. torque. Lock the lock plate.
12. Install and tighten the adapter screw plug to 13 ft. lbs. torque.
13. Apply liquid sealer to the plug.
14. Install the locking ball, spring and screw plug and tighten the plug to 14 ft. lbs. torque.
15. Check to see that the input shaft and output shafts rotate smoothly.
16. Check to see that shifting can be done smoothly to all positions.
17. Install the black restrict pin on the reverse gear/5th gear side.
18. Install the remaining pin and tighten the pins 20 ft. lbs. torque.
19. Install the shift lever retainer with a new gasket and tighten the bolts to 13 ft. lbs. torque.
20. Install the back-up light switch and tighten to 27 ft. lbs. torque.
21. Install the clutch housing and tighten the bolts to 27 ft. lbs. torque.

Chevrolet/GM S Series

77mm 4-SPEED TRANSMISSION

Disassembly

1. Remove drain plug and drain lubricant from transmission.
2. Thoroughly clean the exterior of the transmission assembly.
3. Using a hammer and punch, remove the roll pin that attaches the offset lever to shift rail.
4. Remove extension housing attaching bolts. Separate the extension housing from the transmission case and remove housing and offset lever as an assembly.
5. Remove detent ball and spring from offset lever and remove roll pin from extension housing or offset lever.
6. Remove transmission shift cover attaching bolts. Pry the shift cover loose using the proper tool and remove cover from transmission case.
7. Remove clip that retains reverse lever to reverse lever pivot bolt.
8. Remove reverse lever pivot bolt and remove reverse lever and fork as an assembly.
9. Using a hammer and punch, mark position of front bearing cap to transmission case. Remove front bearing cap bolts and remove bearing cap.
10. Remove small retaining and large locating snaprings from front drive gear bearing.
11. Install bearing puller J-22912-01 on front bearing and puller J-8433-1 with two bolts on end of drive gear and remove and discard bearing. A new bearing must be used when assembling the transmission.
12. Remove retaining and locating smaprings from rear bearing and mainshaft. Install puller J-22912-01 on bearing and puller J-8433-1 with two bolts (J-33171) on end of mainshaft and remove and discard used bearing. A new bearing must be used when assembling transmission.
13. Remove drive gear from mainshaft and transmission case as shown.
14. remove mainshaft from transmission case by tipping mainshaft down at the rear and lifting shaft out through shift cover opening.
15. Using a hammer and punch, remove rollpin retaining reverse idler gear shift in transmission case. Remove idler gear and shaft from case.
16. Remove countershaft from rear of case using loading tool J-26624. Remove countershaft gear and loading tool as an assembly from case along with thrust washers.

Mainshaft Disassembly

1. Scribe alignment mark on third/fourth synchronizer hub and sleeve for reassembly. remove retaining snapring and remove third/fourth synchronizer assembly from mainshaft.
2. Slide third gear off mainshaft.
3. Remove second gear retaining snapring. Remove tabbed thrust washer, second gear and blocker ring from mainshaft.
4. Remove first gear thrust washer and roll pin from mainshaft. Use pliers to remove roll pin.
5. Remove first gear and blocker ring from mainshaft.
6. Scribe alignment mark on first/second synchronizer hub and sleeve for reassembly.
7. Remove synchronizer springs and keys from first/second sleeve and remove sleeve from shaft.

NOTE: Do not attempt to remove the first/second hub from the mainshaft. The hub and mainshaft are assembled and machined as a unit.

8. Remove loading Tool J-26624, roller bearings, spacers and thrust washers from the countershaft gear.

Drive Gear Disassembly

1. Remove roller bearings from cavity of drive gear.

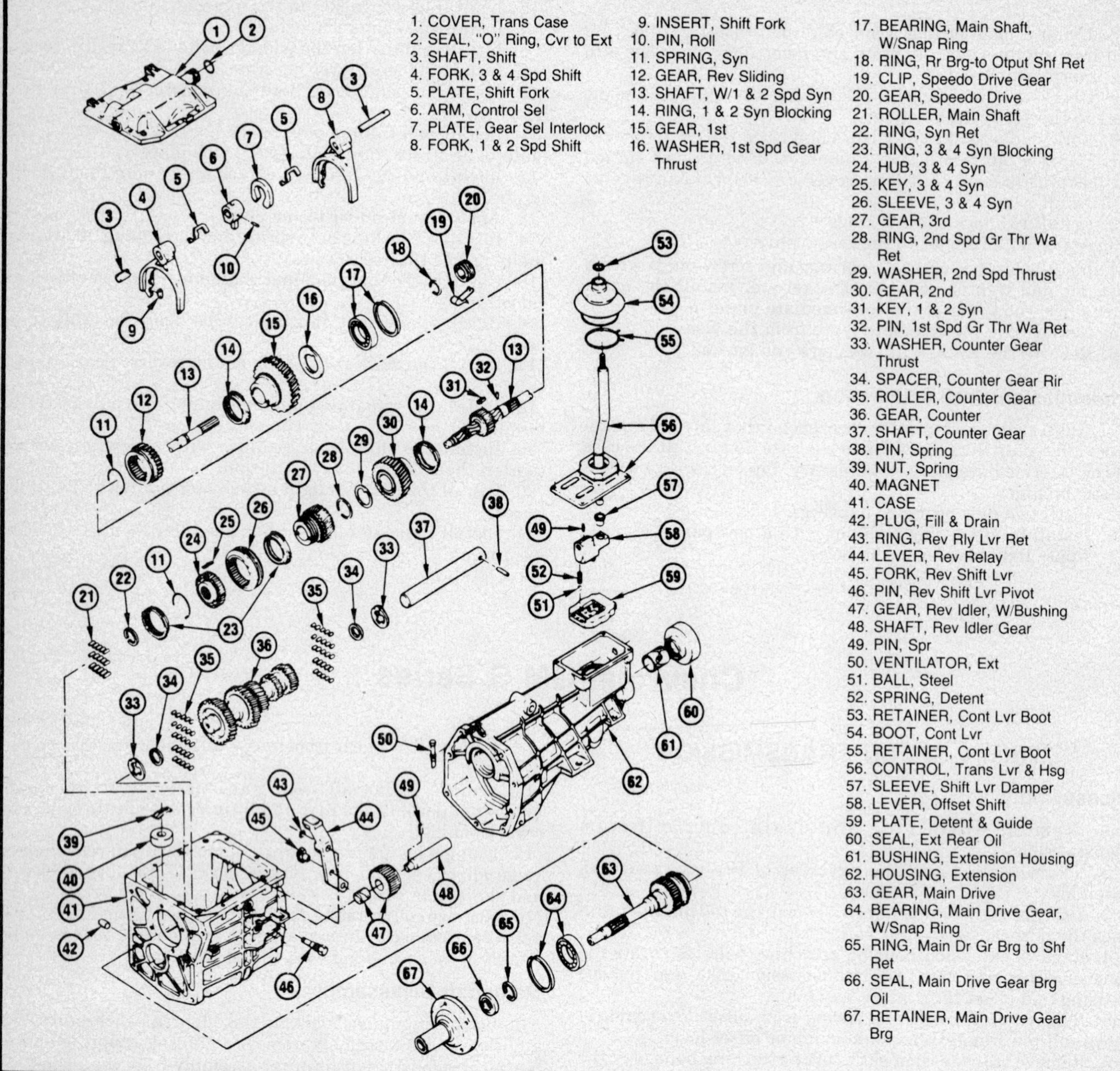

77mm four speed transmission

2. Wash parts in a cleaning solvent.
3. Inspect gear teeth for wear.
4. Inspect drive shaft pilot for wear.

Cover Disassembly

1. Place selector arm plates and shift rail in neutral position (centered).
2. Rotate shift rail until selector arm disengages from selector arm plates and roll pin is accessible.
3. Remove selector arm roll pin using a pin punch and hammer.
4. Remove shift rail, shift forks, selector arm plates, selector arm, interlock plate and roll pin.
5. Remove shift cover to extension housing "O" ring seal using a suitable tool.
6. Remove nylon inserts and selector arm plates from shift forks. Note position of inserts and plates for assembly reference.

Assembly

1. Install nylon inserts and selector arm plates in shift forks.
2. If removed, install shift rail plug. Coat edges of plug with sealer before installing.
3. Coat shift rail and rail bores with light weight grease and insert shift rail in cover. install rail until flush with inside edge of cover.
4. Place first/second shift fork in cover with fork offset facing rear of cover and push shift rail through fork. The first/second shift fork is the larger of the two forks.
5. Position selector arm and C-shaped interlock plate in cover and insert shift rail through arm. Widest part of interlock

plate must face away from cover, and selector arm roll pin hole must face downward and toward rear of cover.

6. Position third/fourth shift fork in cover with fork offset facing rear of cover. Third/fourth shift fork selector arm plate must be under first/second shift for selector arm plate.

7. Push shift rail through third/fourth shift fork and into front bore in cover.

8. Rotate shift rail until selector arm plate at forward end of rail faces away from, but is parallel to cover.

9. Align roll pin holes in selector arm and shift rail and install roll pin. Roll pin must be flush with surface of selector arm to prevent pin from contacting selector arm plates during shifts.

10. Install a new shift cover to extension housing "O" ring seal. Coat "O" ring seal with transmission lubricant.

Drive Gear Assembly

1. Coat roller bearings and drive gear bearing bore with light weight grease. Install roller bearings into bore of drive gear.

Mainshaft Assembly

1. Coat mainshaft and gear bores with transmission lubricant.

2. Install first/second synchronizer sleeve on mainshaft, aligning marks previously made.

3. Install synchronizer keys and springs into the first/second synchronizer sleeve. Engage tang end of springs into the same synchronizer key but position open ends of springs so they face away from one another.

4. Place blocking ring on first gear and install gear and ring on mainshaft. Be sure synchronizer keys engage notches in first gear blocking ring.

5. Install first gear roll pin in mainshaft.

6. Place blocking ring on second gear and install gear and ring on mainshaft. Be sure synchronizer keys engage notches in second gear blocking ring. Install second gear thrust washer and snap ring on mainshaft. Be sure thrust washer tab is engaged in mainshaft notch.

7. Measure second gear end play using feeler gauge. Insert gauge between gear and thrust washer. End play should be 0.004 in to 0.014 in. If end play is over 0.014 in., replace thrust washer and snap ring and inspect synchronizer hub for excessive wear.

8. Place blocking ring on third gear and install gear and ring on mainshft.

9. Install thrid/fourth synchronizer sleeve on hub, aligning marks previously made.

10. Install synchronizer keys and springs in third/fourth synchronizer sleeve. Engage tang end of each spring in same key but position open ends of springs so they face away from one another.

11. Install third/fourth synchronizer assembly on the mainshaft with machined groove in hub facing forward. Install snapring on mainshaft. Be sure synchronizer keys are engaged in notches in third gear blocker ring.

12. Install Tool J-26624 into countershaft gear. Using a light weight grease, lubricate roller bearings and install into bores at front and rear of countershaft gear. Install roller bearing retainers on Tool J-26624.

Transmission Assembly

1. Coat countershaft gear thrust washers with grease and position washer in case.

2. Position countershaft gear in case and install countershaft from rear of case. Be sure that thrust washers stay in place during installation of countershaft and gear.

3. Position reverse idler gear in case with shift lever groove facing rear of case and install reverse idler shaft from rear of case. Install roll pin in shaft and center pin in shaft.

4. Install mainshaft assembly into the case. Do not disturb position of synchronizer assemblies during installation.

5. Install fourth gear blocking ring in third/fourth synchronizer sleeve. Be sure synchronizer keys ingaged in notches in blocker ring.

6. Install drive gear into case and engage with mainshaft.

7. Position mainshaft first gear against the rear of the case. Using a new baring, start front bearing onto drive gear. Align bearing with bearing bore in case and drive bearing onto drive gear and into case using Tool J-25234.

8. Install front bearing retaining and locating snaprings.

9. Apply a $\frac{1}{8}$ in. diameter bead of RTV sealant, #732 or equivalent, on case mating surface of front bearing cap. Install bearing cap aligning marks previously made. Apply non-hardening sealer on attaching bolts and install bolts. Torque bolts to specification.

10. Install first gear thrust washer with oil grove facing first gear on mainshaft, aligning slot in washer with first gear roll pin.

11. Using a new bearing, position rear bearing on mainshaft. Align bearing with bearing bore in case and drive bearing into case using Tool J-25234.

12. Install locating and retaining snaprings on rear bearing.

13. Install speedometer gear and retaining clip on mainshaft.

14. Apply non-hardening sealer to threads of reverse lever pivot bolt and start bolt into case. Engage reverse lever fork in the reverse idler gear and reverse lever on pivot bolt. Tighten bolt to specifications and install retaining clip.

15. Rotate drivegear and mainshaft gear. If blocker rings tend to stick on gears, release the rings by gently prying them off the cones.

16. Apply a $\frac{1}{8}$ in. diameter bead or RTV Sealant, #732 or equivalent, on the cover mating surface of transmission. Place reverse lever in neutral, and position cover on case.

17. Install 2 dowel type bolts first to align cover on case. Install remaining cover bolts and torque to specifications. The offset lever to shift rail roll pin hole must be in the vertical position after cover installation.

18. Apply a $\frac{1}{8}$ in. diameter bead of RTV Sealant, #732 or equivalent, on the extension housing to transmission case mating surface.

19. Place extension housing over mainshaft to a position where shift rail is in shift cover opening.

20. Install detent spring in offset lever. Place ball in neutral guide plate detent position. Apply pressure on the offset lever, slide offset lever onto shift rail and seat extension housing to transmission case.

21. Install extension housing retaining bolts. Torque bolts to specifications.

22. Align hole in offset lever and shift rail and install roll pin.

23. Fill transmission to its proper level with recommended lubricant.

Five Speed Transmission

Disassembly

1. Remove drain bolt on transmission case and drain lubricant.

2. Thoroughly clean the exterior of the transmission assembly.

3. Using pin punch and hammer, remove roll pin attaching offset lever to shift rail.

4. Remove extension housing to transmission case bolts and remove housing and offset lever as an assembly. Do not attempt to remove the offset lever while the extension housing is still bolted in place. The lever has a positioning lug engaged in the housing detent plate which prevents moving the lever far enough for removal.

5. Remove detent ball and spring from offset lever and remove roll pin from extension housing or offset lever.

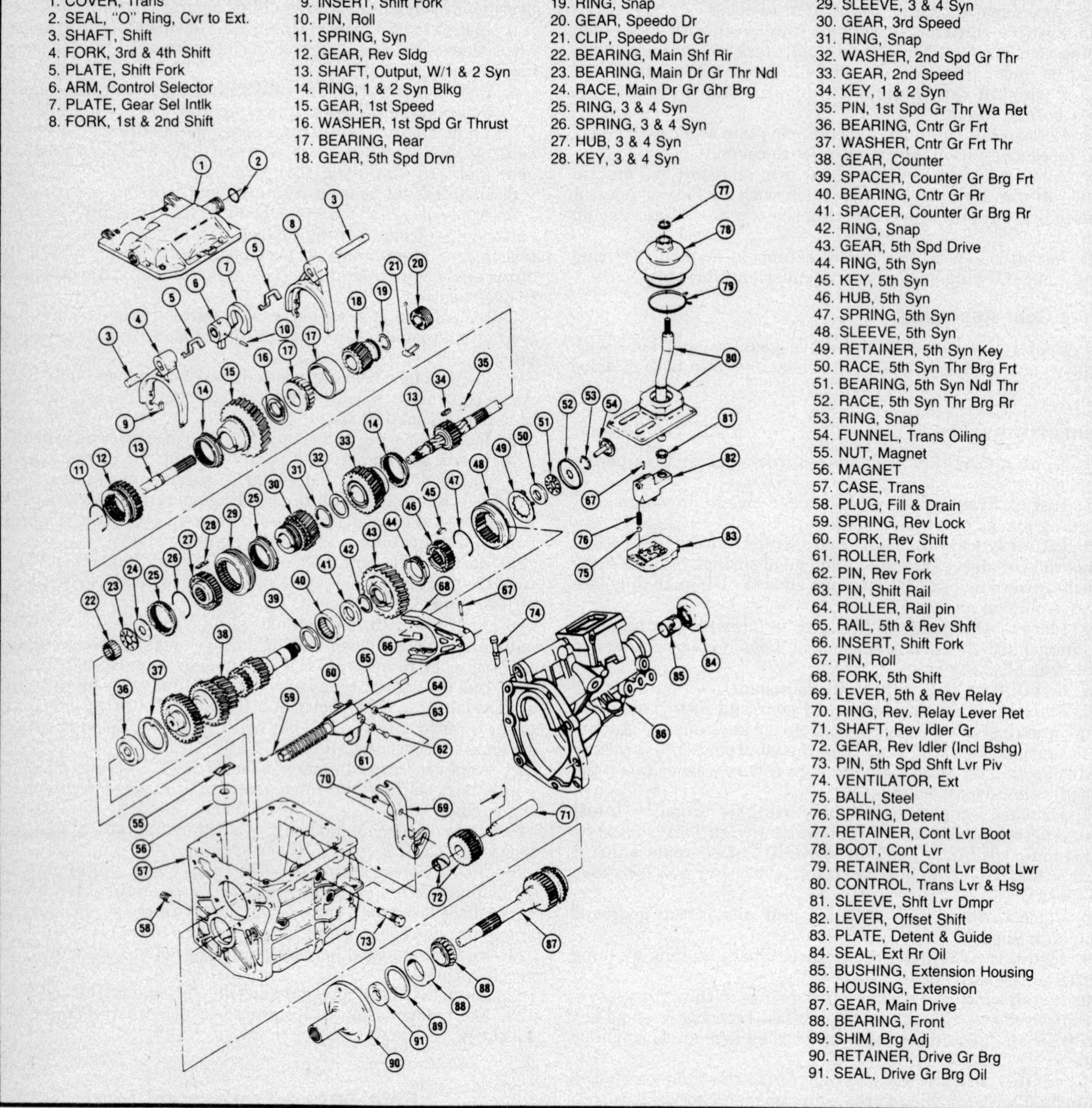

77mm five speed transmission

6. Remove plastic funnel, thrust bearing race and thrust bearing from rear of counter shaft. The countershaft rear thrust bearing, bearing washer and plastic funnel may be found inside the extension housing.

7. Remove bolts attaching transmission cover and shift fork assembly and remove cover. Two of the transmission cover attaching bolts are alignment-type dowel bolts. Note the location of these bolts for assembly reference.

8. Using a punch and hammer, drive the roll pin from the fifth gearshift fork while supporting the end of the shaft with a block of wood.

9. Remove fifth synchronizer gear snapring, shift fork, fifth gear synchronizer sleeve, blocking ring and fifth speed drive gear from rear of counter shaft.

10. Remove snapring from fifth speed driven gear.

11. Using a hammer and punch, mark both bearing cap and case for assembly reference.

12. Remove front bearing cap bolts and remove front bearing cap. Remove front bearing race and end play shims from front bearing cap.

13. Rotate drive gear until flat surface faces counter shaft and remove drive gear from transmission case.

14. Remove reverse lever C-clip and pivot bolt.

15. Remove mainshaft rear bearing race and then tilt mainshaft assembly upward and remove assembly from transmission case.

16. Unhook overcenter link spring from front of transmission case.

17. Rotate fifth gear/reverse shift rail to disengage rail from reverse lever assembly. Remove shift rail from rear of transmission case.
18. Remove reverse lever and fork assembly from transmission case.
19. Using hammer and punch, drive roll pin from forward end of reverse idler shaft and remove reverse idler shaft, rubber "O" ring and gear from the transmission case.
20. Remove rear countershaft snapring and spacer.
21. Insert a brass drift through drive gear opening in front of transmission case and, using an arbor plress, carefully press countershaft rearward to remove rear counter shaft bearing.
22. Move countershaft assembly rearward, tilt countershaft upward and remove from case. Remove countershaft front thrust washer and rear bearing spacer.
23. Remove countershaft front bearing from transmission case using an arbor press.

Mainshaft Disassembly

1. Remove thrust bearing washer from front end of mainshaft.
2. Scribe reference mark on third/fourth synchronizer hub and sleeve for reassembly.
3. Remove third/fourth synchronizer blocking ring, sleeve, hub and third gear as an assembly from mainshaft.
4. Remove snapring, tabbed thrust washer, and second gear from mainshaft.
5. Remove fifth gear with Tool-J-22912-01 or its equal and arbor press. Slide rear bearing of mainshaft.
6. Remove first gear thrust washer, roll pin, first gear and synchronizer ring form mainshaft.
7. Scribe reference mark on first/second synchronizer hub and sleeve for reassembly.
8. Remove synchronizer spring and keys form first/reverse sliding gear and remove gear from mainshaft hub. do not attempt to remove the first second reverse hub from mainshaft. The hub and shaft are assembled and machined as a matched set.

Drive Gear Disassembly

1. Remove bearing race, thrust bearing, and roller bearings from cavity of drive gear.
2. Using Tool- J-22912-01 or its equal and arbor press, remove bearing from drive gear.
3. Wash parts in a cleaning solvent.
4. Inspect gear teeth and drive shaft pilot for wear.

Drive Gear Assembly

1. Using Tool J-22912-01 or its equal with an arbor press, install bearing on drive gear.
2. Coat roller bearings and drive gear bearing bore with grease. Install roller bearings into bore of drive gear.
3. Install thrust bearing and race in drive gear.

Mainshaft Assembly

1. Coat mainshaft and gear bores with transmission lubricant.
2. Install first/second synchronizer sleeve on mainshaft hub aligning marks made at disasssembly.
3. Install first/second synchronizer keys and springs. Engage tang end of each spring in same synchronizer key but position open end of springs opposite of each other.
4. Install blocker ring and second gear on mainshaft. Install tabbed thrust washer and second gear retaining snapring on mainshaft. Be sure washer tab is properly seated in mainshaft notch.
5. Install blocker ring and first gear on mainshaft. Install first gear roll pin and then first gear thrust washer.
6. Slide rear bearing on mainshaft.
7. Install fifth speed gear on mainshaft using Tool J-22912-01 and arbor press. Install snapring on mainshaft.
8. Install third gear, third/fourth synchronizer assembly and thrust bearing on mainshaft. Synchronizer hub offset must face forward.

Assembly

1. Coat countershaft front bearing bore with Loctite 601, or equivalent, and install front countershaft bearing flush with facing of case using an arbor press.
2. Coat countershaft tabbed thrust washer with grease and install washer so tab engages depression in case.
3. Tip transmission case on end and install countershaft in front bearing bore.
4. Install countershaft rear bearing spacer. Coat countershaft rear bearing with grease and install bearing using Tool J-29895 and sleeve J-33032, or its equivalent. The bearing when correctly installed will extend beyond the case surface 0.125 inch.
5. Position reverse idler gear in case with shift lever groove facing rear of case and install reverse idler shaft from rear of case. Install roll pin in idler shaft.
6. Install assembled mainshaft in transmission case. Install rear mainshaft bearing race in case.
7. Install drive gear in case, and engage in third/fourth synchronizer sleeve and blocker ring.
8. Install front bearing race in front bearing cap. Do not install shims in front bearing cap at this time.
9. Temporarily install front bearing cap.
10. Install fifth speed/reverse lever, pivot bolt and retaining clip. Coat pivot bolt threads with non-hardening sealer. Be sure to engage reverse lever fork in reverse idler gear.
11. Install countershaft rear bearing spacer and retaining snap ring.
12. Install fifth speed gear on countershaft.
13. Insert fifth speed/reverse rail in rear of case and install into reverse fifth speed lever. Rotate rail during installation to simplify engagement with lever. Connect spring to front of case.
14. Position fifth gear shift fork on fifth gear synchronizer assembly and install synchronizer on countershaft and shift fork on shift rail. Make sure roll pin hole in shift fork and shift rail are aligned.
15. Support fifth gear shift rail and fork on a block of wood and install roll pin.
16. Install thrust race against fifth speed synchronizer hub and install snap ring. Install thrust bearing against race on countershaft. Coat both bearing and race with petroleum jelly.
17. Install lipped thrust race over needle-type thrust bearing and install plastic funnel into hole in end of counter shaft gear.
18. Temporarily install extension housing and attaching bolts. Turn transmission case on end, and mount a dial indicator on extension housing with indicator on the end of mainshaft.
19. Rotate mainshaft and zero dial indicator. Pull upward on mainshaft until end play is removed and record reading. Mainshaft bearings require a preload of 0.001–0.005 in. to set preload, select a shim pack measuring 0.001–0.005 in. greater than the dial indicator reading recorded.
20. Remove front bearing cap and front bearing race Install necessary shims to obtain prelaod and reinstall bearing race.
21. Apply a $\frac{1}{8}$ in. bead of RTV sealant, #732 or equivalent, on case mating surface of front bearing cap. Install bearing cap aligning marks made during disassembly and torque bolts to specification.
22. Remove extension housing.
23. Move shift forks on transmission cover and synchronizer sleeves inside transmission to the neutral position.
24. Apply a $\frac{1}{8}$ in. bead of RTV sealant, #732 or equivalent, or cover mating surface of transmission.
25. Lower cover onto case while aligning shift forks and syn-

chronizer sleeves. Center cover and install the two dowel bolts. Install remaining bolts and torque to specification. The offset lever to shift rail roll pin hole must be in the vertical position after cover installation.

26. Apply a 1/8 in. bead of RTV Sealant, #732 or equivalent, on extension housing to transmission case mating surface.

27. Install extension housing over mainshaft and shift rail to a position where shift rail just enters shift cover opening.

28. Install detent spring into offset lever and place steel ball in neutral guide plate detent. Position offset lever on steel ball and apply pressure on offset lever and at the time seat extension housing against transmission case.

29. Install extension housing bolts and torque to specification.

30. Align and install roll pin in offset lever and shift rail.

31. Fill transmission to its proper level with lubricant.

Clark 280V Series Transmissions

FIVE SPEED TRANSMISSIONS

The Clark 280V series transmissions are available in two direct drive and an overdrive ratio. The 285V has normal steps between the gears while the 282V has a "short fourth", meaning a small step between direct and fourth, which can be used to split the step with a two speed axle. The OD model is designated 280VO and has the OD gear as an integral part of the gear train. The direct drive and overdrive types of gear trains differ in gear ratios and in the power flow. However, the basic construction of the transmissions are the same.

Disassembly

1. Remove the remote control or shift tower from the control

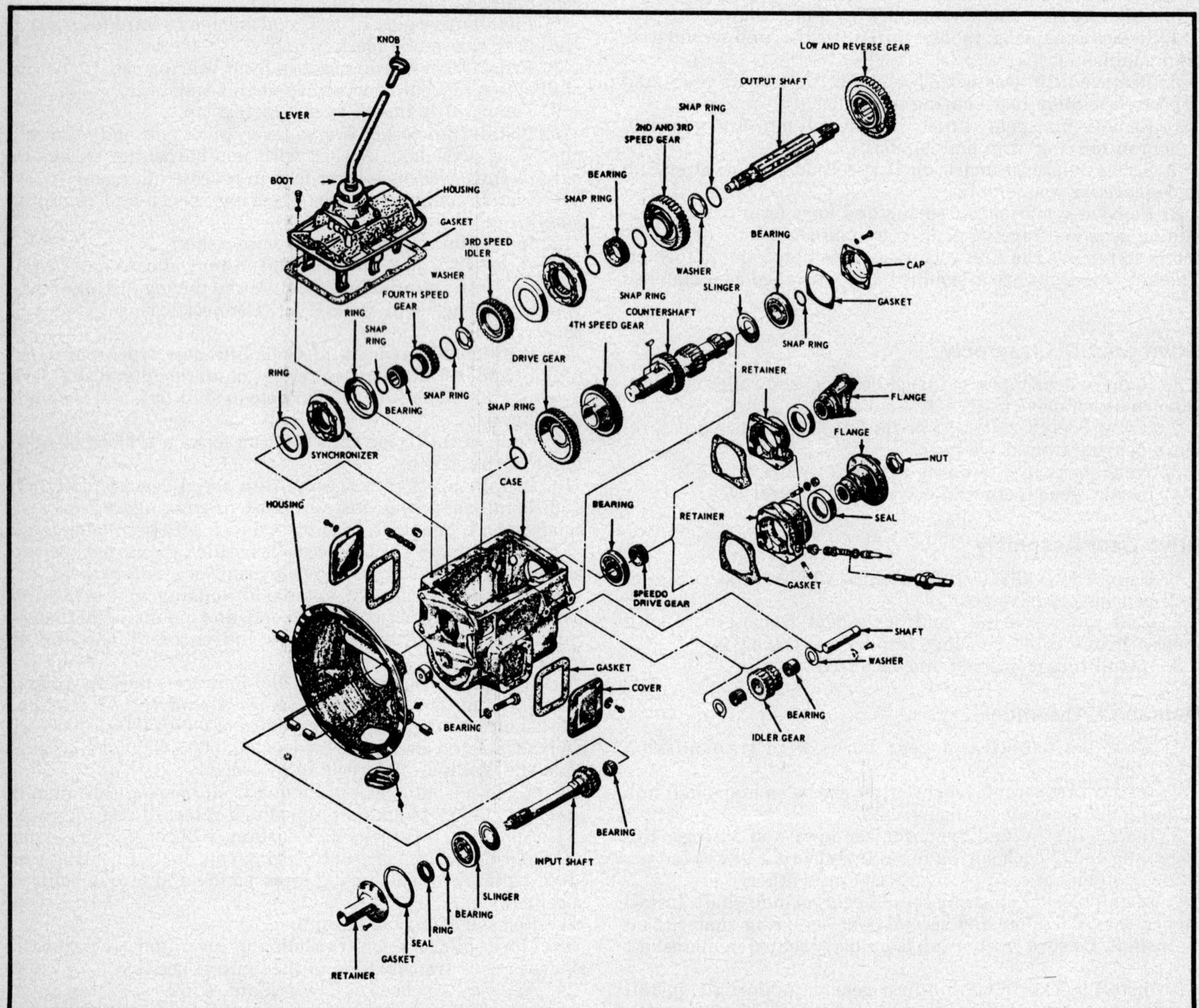

Exploded view Clark 280V transmission (© Ford Motor Co.)

cover. Remove the control cover capscrews and lock washers. Remove the control cover assembly from the transmission. Remove the back-up light switch.

2. Remove the universal joint assembly and the drive shaft from the parking brake drum.

3. Remove the parking brake drum. Disconnect the parking brake actuating lever from the linkage.

4. Remove the transmission spline flange. Remove the bolts holding the carrier plate to the transmission housing. Slide the plate with the brake shoes and retaining springs off the transmission.

5. Lock the transmission in two gears and remove the brake drum retaining nut. Remove the brake drum.

6. Remove the output shaft rear bearing retainer and the speedometer drive gear.

7. Remove the countershaft rear bearing retainer. Remove the bearing snapring.

8. Remove the input shaft bearing retainer and pull the input shaft out of the case. Be careful not to drop the output shaft pilot bearing rollers into the transmission case.

9. Move the output shaft rearward until the rear bearing is exposed. Remove the rear bearing with a suitable bearing puller.

10. Lift the output shaft out of the transmission case.

11. Remove the reverse idler shaft using the special tool. Lift the reverse idler gear, bearing and thrust washer out of the case.

12. Move the countershaft rearward until the rear bearing is exposed. Remove the bearing and the oil slinger with a suitable puller.

13. Lift the countershaft out of the case.

14. If the countershaft front bearing or the pilot bearing is to be replaced, remove the clutch housing from the transmission.

15. Press the pilot bearing out of the transmission case. Do not hammer or drive the bearing out of the bearing bore.

OUTPUT SHAFT

Disassembly

1. Remove the first reverse gear from the output shaft.

2. Clamp the output shaft, front end facing up, in a soft jawed vise. Remove the fourth/fifth speed synchronizer assembly from the shaft. Remove the snap ring retaining the fourth gear and remove the shift hub sleeve and the fourth gear.

3. Remove the third gear snapring and lift the locating washer and the gear off the shaft.

4. Lift the second/third speed synchronizer off the shaft.

5. Remove the snapring retaining the second/third speed gear shift hub sleeve and lift the sleeve off the shaft.

6. Remove the second gear snapring and remove the locating washer and the gear.

Assembly

1. Install the output shaft, forward end up, in a soft jawed vise.

2. Install the second gear lower snapring and the locating washer on the output shaft. Install the second gear on the output shaft with the clutching teeth facing upward. Install the upper snapring.

3. Install the second/third shift hub sleeve and snapring. While pressing downward on the second gear to compress the lower helical snapring, check the gap between the second gear and the upper snapring. This gap must be minimum of 0.006 in.

4. Install the second/third speed synchronizer assembly on the shaft.

5. Install the third gear on the shaft with clutching teeth facing downward. Install the third gear locating washer and snapring.

6. Install the fourth gear with the clutching teeth facing upward.

7. Install the bottom cone of the fourth/fifth synchronizer over the clutching teeth of the fourth gear.

8. Install the fourth/fifth shift sleeve hub. Be sure the chamfered side is facing down. Install the snapring.

9. Install the fourth/fifth synchronizer on the shift hub sleeve.

10. Reverse the output shaft and install the first/reverse gear with the shift fork facing downward. A minimum of 0.006 in. end play must be maintained on all mainshaft gears. Synchronizer end play on both synchronizers must be maintained at 0.060 in. minimum and 0.160 in. maximum.

INPUT SHAFT

Disassembly

1. Remove the bearing retaining snapring from the input shaft. Remove the bearing, using the special tool.

Assembly

1. Install the oil slinger and press the bearing on the input shaft. Be sure the snapring groove is facing the forward end of the shaft.

NOTE: To prevent damage to the bearing, apply pressure on the inner race of the bearing only.

2. Install the bearing snapring.

COUNTERSHAFT

Disassembly

1. Remove the snapring at the forward end of the countershaft.

2. Place the countershaft assembly in a hydraulic press, and press the drive gear off the shaft.

3. Remove the key from the shaft and press the fourth gear off the shaft. Remove the remaining key.

Assembly

1. Install the fourth speed gear key in the slot on the shaft. Position the fourth gear on the shaft with the long hub facing toward the front.

2. Install the countershaft main drive gear key in the keyway in the shaft. Install the countershaft drive gear on the shaft with the long hub facing toward the rear. Install the snapring on the countershaft.

GEAR SHIFT HOUSING

Disassembly

NOTE: It is not necessary to disassemble the gear shift housing assembly to determine if the parts are worn. Note the condition of the shifter fork shafts and forks by visual inspection. If the forks are excessively worn or if they bind when shifted, disassemble the gear shift housing assembly to make repairs. Check the interlocking system.

1. With the control cover in neutral, pry the fourth/fifth shift fork to the fourth speed position (toward the rear of the cover). Remove the front rail support capscrews and remove the front rail support.

2. Remove the interlock tapered pin supports. Note the position of the interlock tapered pins for reassembly.

3. Remove the rear rail support capscrews and remove the rear rail support.

4. Remove the first/reverse shift fork and rail assembly. Remove the fourth, fifth, second, and third shift fork and rail assembly. Use caution so as not to lose the interlock cross pin, interlock tapered pins, or the mesh lock poppet balls.

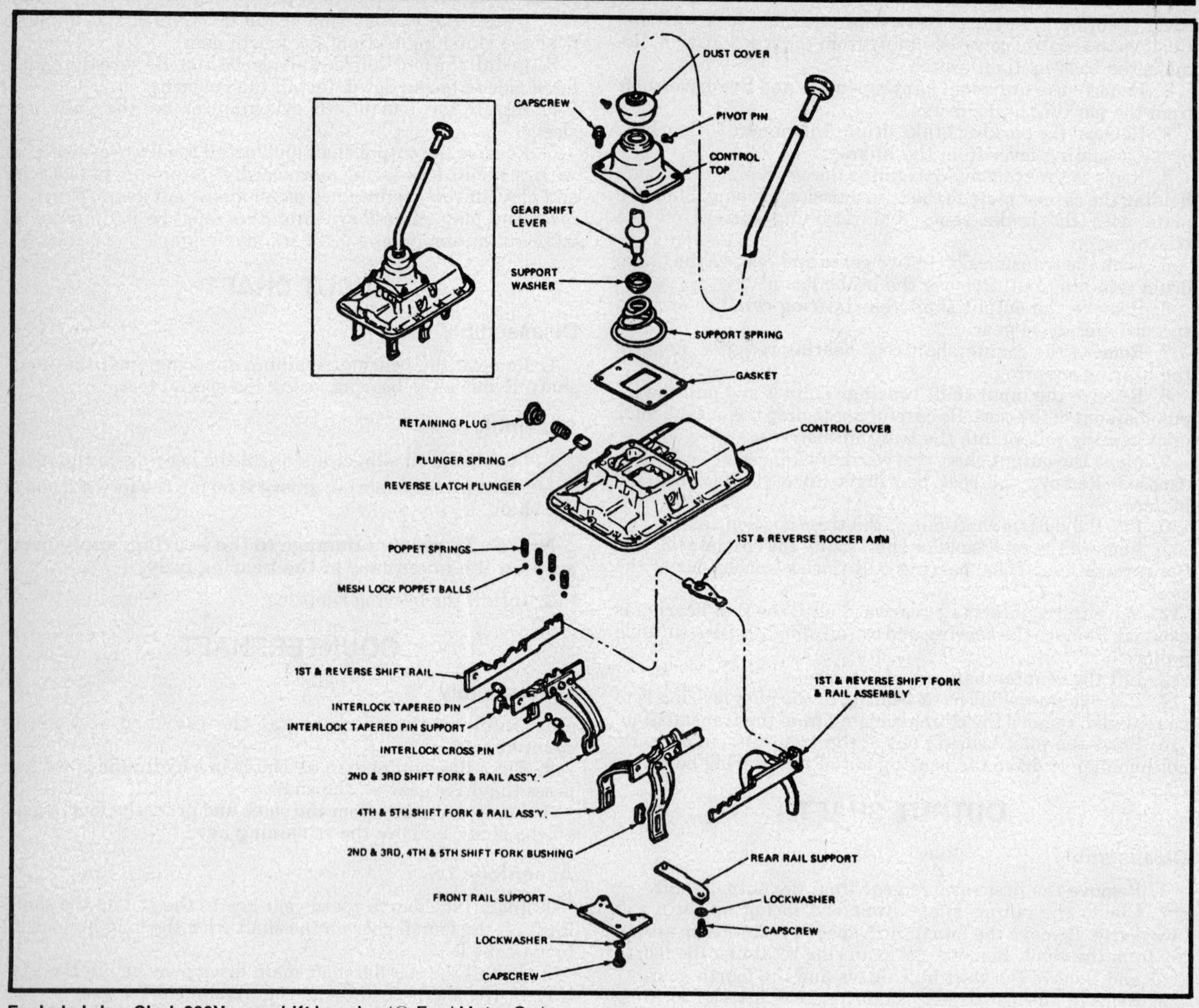

Exploded view Clark 280V gear shift housing (© Ford Motor Co.)

5. Remove the first/reverse shift rail. Remove the four mesh lock poppet balls. Remove the four poppet springs.
6. Remove the first/reverse rocker arm. Remove the reverse latch plunger spring retaining plug and the reverse latch plunger spring and plunger.
7. If the fork bushings are worn, secure the fork in a soft jawed vise and remove the worn bushings with a drift. Install new bushings in the fork. Turn the fork over on the anvil of the vise and secure the bushings in the fork, using a prick punch and upsetting the bushing metal on the outside of the fork.

Assembly

1. Position the first/reverse rocker arm on the pivot pin. Install the reverse latch plunger, spring and retaining plug. Tighten the plug securely.
2. Install the four poppet springs and the four mesh lock poppet balls. Note the first/reverse shift fork rail poppet ball in the pocket.
3. Align one tapered interlock cross pin with the hole in the first/reverse shift rail. Position the rail on the poppet ball, in neutral position with the interlock pin aligned with the first interlock tapered pin. Install the second interlock tapered pin.
4. Align the pin with the interlock cross pin hole.
5. Position the fourth/fifth shift fork and rail assembly on the poppet ball in neutral position. Slightly raise the rear of the rail and align the second interlock tapered pin with the cross hole in the rail. Note the positions of the tapered interlock pins and the shift rails.
6. Install the first/reverse shift fork and rail assembly on the poppet ball in a neutral position. Align the first/reverse rocker arm in the notch at the rear of the rail. Position the rear rail support.
7. Install the rail support capscrews and washers. Tighten the capscrews slightly. Install the interlock tapered pin supports. Tap the fourth/fifth shift fork to the rear (fourth speed position).
8. Position the front rail support and install the capscrews and washers. Tighten the front and rear support capscrews 20–25 ft. lbs.
9. Tap the fourth/fifth shift fork and rail assemble forward to a neutral position.

TRANSMISSION

Assembly

1. Coat the countershaft needle bearings with grease and install them in the front countershaft bore.

2. Tip the rear of the countershaft down and lower it into the case. Push the countershaft forward and insert the shaft through the bearing.

3. Position the countershaft rear bearing oil slinger and bearing on the shaft. Drive the bearing in to the bearing bore in the case. The countershaft drive gear should be supported while driving the shaft to prevent damage to the front bearing. Install the rear bearing retainer.

4. Coat the reverse idler thrust washers with grease and position them in the case.

5. Insert the two roller bearings in the reverse idler bear bore. Place the gear assembly in position in the transmission case, with the small gear toward the rear of the case.

6. Insert the reverse idler shaft through the hole in the case through the reverse idler gear and into the forward support boss. Drive the reverse idler shaft into the case until the slot in the shaft is lined up with the lock bolt hole. Install the retainer in the slot and secure the retainer with the lock bolt. Tighten the bolt to specifications.

7. Tilt the rear of the output shaft assembly downward and insert the end of the shaft through the output shaft bore in the case. Lower the front end of the output shaft until it is in line with the pilot bearing opening. Move the assembly forward into position.

8. Insert the pilot bearing in the input shaft bore.

9. Position the input shaft and bearing assembly in the forward end of the transmission case. Tap the front end of the shaft with a soft faced hammer until the snapring is seated against the case. Be sure the clutching teeth of the input shaft gear mesh with the fifth speed synchronizer without binding.

10. Position a new gasket on the input shaft bearing retainer. Be sure that the oil return holes in the retainer and gasket are aligned with the holes in the transmission case.

11. Install the lock washers and bolts on the input shaft bearing retainer and tighten the bolts to specifications.

12. Position the output shaft rear bearing on the shaft and drive the bearing into the bore until the snapring is seated against the case.

TORQUE SPECIFICATIONS

	ft. lbs.
Companion flange nut	350–420
Countershaft rear bearing cap	20–25
Input shaft bearing retainer	20–25
Output shaft bearing retainer	20–25
Reverse idler shaft lock bolt	20–25
Shift control to case	20–25
Shift cover to case	20–25
Shift tower to shift cover	20–25
Transmission to clutch housing	60–80

LUBRICANT CAPACITY

	Pints
Clark 280V series	8

13. Position the countershaft rear bearing cap and gasket on the case and install the lock washers and bolts. Tighten the bolts to specification.

14. Install the speedometer drive gear on the output shaft and position a new oil seal in the output shaft bearing retainer. Be sure the seal is correctly installed. Position a new gasket and the bearing retainer on the case and install the cock washers and bolts. Tighten the bolts to specification.

15. Install the parking brake drum and companion flange assembly. Tighten the yoke retaining nut to specification.

16. With the transmission in neutral, position the control cover over the gears, aligning the shift forks in the shift cover with the gear shift hubs. If the control cover is in neutral and the transmission is in neutral, the transmission drive gear should turn without the brake drum or output shaft turning. Install the capscrews and washers. Tighten 20 to 25 ft. lbs. Install the remote control or shift tower in the control cover. Tighten the capscrews 20 to 25 ft. lbs.

Clark 390V and 280 VHD Series

FIVE SPEED TRANSMISSIONS

The Clark 390V and 280VHD series transmissions are five speed units and have split pin synchronizers in all gears except low and reverse. The shift forks have replaceable bronze inserts and numerous needle bearings. Two tapered roller bearings and one large straight roller bearing is used to support the power shafts. Certain differences exist between the transmissions, but are both basically the same.

Disassembly

1. Remove the remote control or shift tower from the control cover. Remove the control cover capscrews and lockwashers. Remove the control cover assembly from the transmission. Remove the back-up light switch.

2. Remove the universal joint assembly and the drive shaft from the parking brake drum.

3. Remove the parking brake drum. Disconnect the parking brake actuating lever from the linkage.

4. Remove the transmission spline flange. Remove the bolts holding the carrier plate to the transmission housing. Slide the plate with the brake shoes and retaining springs off the transmission.

5. Lock the transmission in two gears and remove the brake drum retaining nut. Remove the brake drum from the output shaft.

6. Remove the output shaft rear bearing retainer and the speedometer drive gear.

7. Remove the countershaft rear bearing retainer, then remove the bearing snapring.

8. Remove the input shaft bearing retainer and pull the input shaft out of the case. Be careful not to drop the output shaft pilot bearing rollers into the transmission case.

9. Force the output shaft rearward until the rear bearing is exposed. Working with a bearing puller, remove the rear bearing from the bore.

10. Lift the output shaft out of the case.

11. Remove the reverse idler shaft using special tool. Lift the reverse idler gear, bearing and thrust washer out of the transmission case.

12. Move the countershaft rearward until the rear bearing is exposed. Remove the bearing and oil slinger with a suitable gear puller.

13. Lift the countershaft from the case.

14. If the countershaft front bearing or pilot bearing is to be replaced, remove the clutch housing from the transmission.

15. Press the pilot bearing out of the case. Do not hammer or

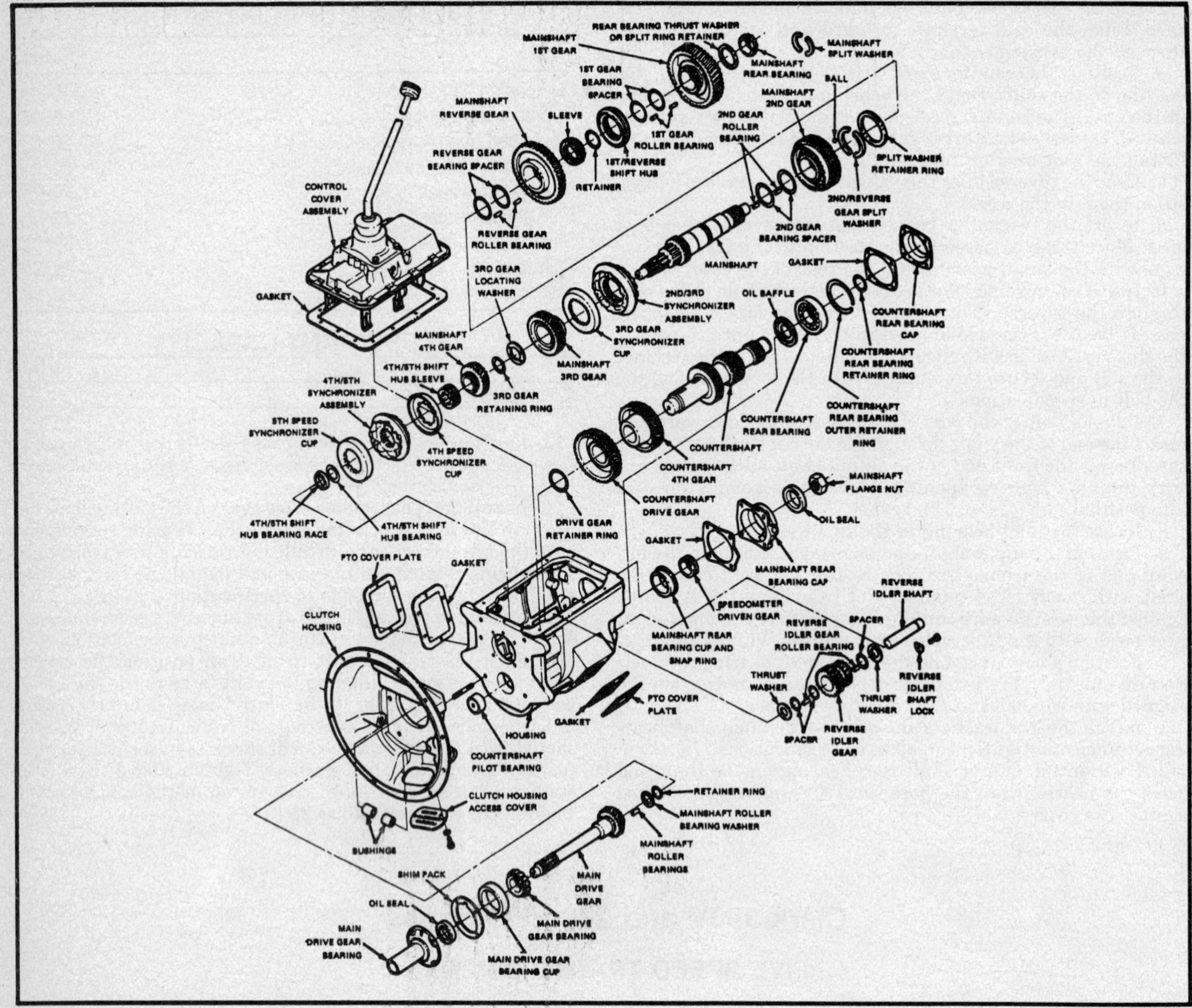

Exploded view Clark 390V transmission (© Ford Motor Co.)

drive the bearing out as damage or distortion to the bearing bore will result.

OUTPUT SHAFT

Disassembly

1. Clamp the output shaft, front end facing upward, in a soft jawed vise. Remove the fifth gear synchroninizer and the fourth and fifth gear synchronizer assembly.
2. Remove the shift hub thrust bearing and race.
3. Remove the fourth and fifth shift hub sleeve and the fourth speed synchronizer ring. Remove the fourth gear.
4. Remove the third gear snapring, locating washer. Lift the third gear off the shaft.
5. Remove the third gear synchronizer ring and the synchronizer assembly.

NOTE: There is a variation in the mainshaft first gear retention. One version has a split washer and a split washer retainer ring. Working with a three legged puller, pull against the split washer retainer ring to remove the rear bearing. The other version of the mainshaft first gear retention is a thrust washer between the first gear and the rear bearing. In this version there is not enough room to get a puller behind the thrust washer and it will be necessary to pull on the first gear.

6. Remove the rear bearing and the first gear. Be sure not to lose the needle bearings under the first gear.
7. Remove the first and reverse shift hub sleeve retainer and remove the shift hub and sleeve.
8. Remove the reverse gear. Be sure not to lose the needle bearings under the reverse gear.
9. Remove the second gear retainer and the second gear.

Assembly

1. Install the output shaft, forward end up, in a soft jawed vise.
2. Position the third gear on the output shaft with the clutching teeth down. Install the locating washer and snapring.
3. Turn the output shaft over and install the third gear synchronizer ring and the second and third synchronizer assembly.

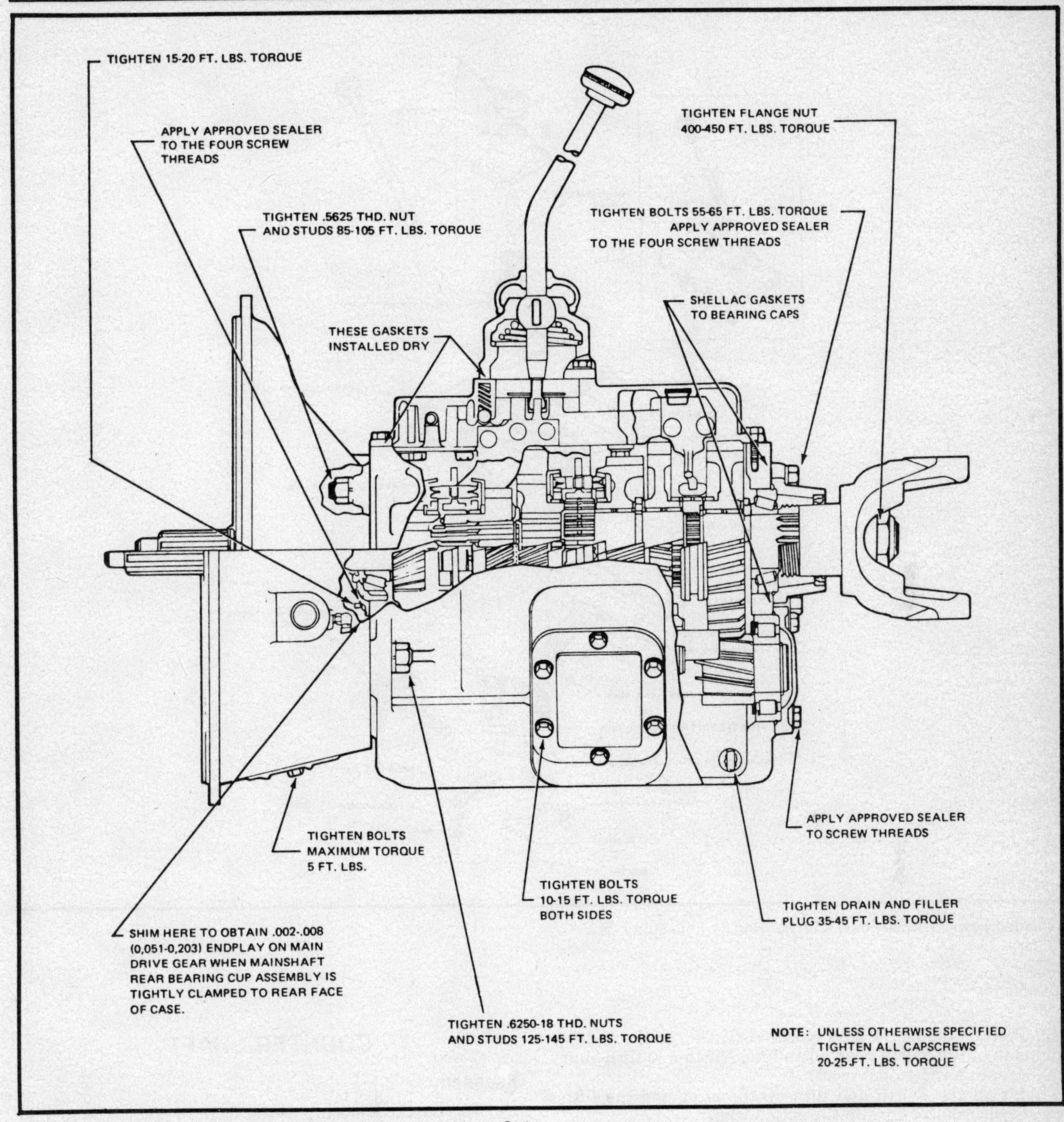
TIGHTEN 15-20 FT. LBS. TORQUE
APPLY APPROVED SEALER TO THE FOUR SCREW THREADS
TIGHTEN FLANGE NUT 400-450 FT. LBS. TORQUE
TIGHTEN .5625 THD. NUT AND STUDS 85-105 FT. LBS. TORQUE
TIGHTEN BOLTS 55-65 FT. LBS. TORQUE APPLY APPROVED SEALER TO THE FOUR SCREW THREADS
SHELLAC GASKETS TO BEARING CAPS
THESE GASKETS INSTALLED DRY
APPLY APPROVED SEALER TO SCREW THREADS
TIGHTEN BOLTS MAXIMUM TORQUE 5 FT. LBS.
TIGHTEN BOLTS 10-15 FT. LBS. TORQUE BOTH SIDES
TIGHTEN DRAIN AND FILLER PLUG 35-45 FT. LBS. TORQUE
SHIM HERE TO OBTAIN .002-.008 (0,051-0,203) ENDPLAY ON MAIN DRIVE GEAR WHEN MAINSHAFT REAR BEARING CUP ASSEMBLY IS TIGHTLY CLAMPED TO REAR FACE OF CASE.
TIGHTEN .6250-18 THD. NUTS AND STUDS 125-145 FT. LBS. TORQUE
NOTE: UNLESS OTHERWISE SPECIFIED TIGHTEN ALL CAPSCREWS 20-25 FT. LBS. TORQUE

Torque specifications—Clark 390V transmission (© Ford Motor Co.)

4. With the clutching teeth of the second gear down, coat the inside diameter of the gear with a high quality heavy grease. This will hold the needle rollers in place during assembly. Install the first row of needle rollers.
5. Position the bearing spacer and install the second row of bearings. Position the outer bearing spacer.
6. Install the second gear on the output shaft, using caution so as not to catch the needle rollers on the edge of a spline or snap-ring groove.
7. Install the second gear split washer locating ball and split washer on the output shaft. Install the retaining ring over the split washer.
8. Coat the inside of the reverse gear with grease and install the bearing spacers and the bearings.
9. Install the reverse gear on the output shaft, position the shift hub sleeve and the shift hub, and install the shift hub sleeve snapring.
10. Install the spacers and bearings in the first gear and install the gear on the output shaft.
11. Install the first gear retaining washer. Install the output shaft bearing. Be sure that the bearing is tight against the washer.
12. Turn the output shaft over and install the fourth gear with the clutching teeth facing upward.

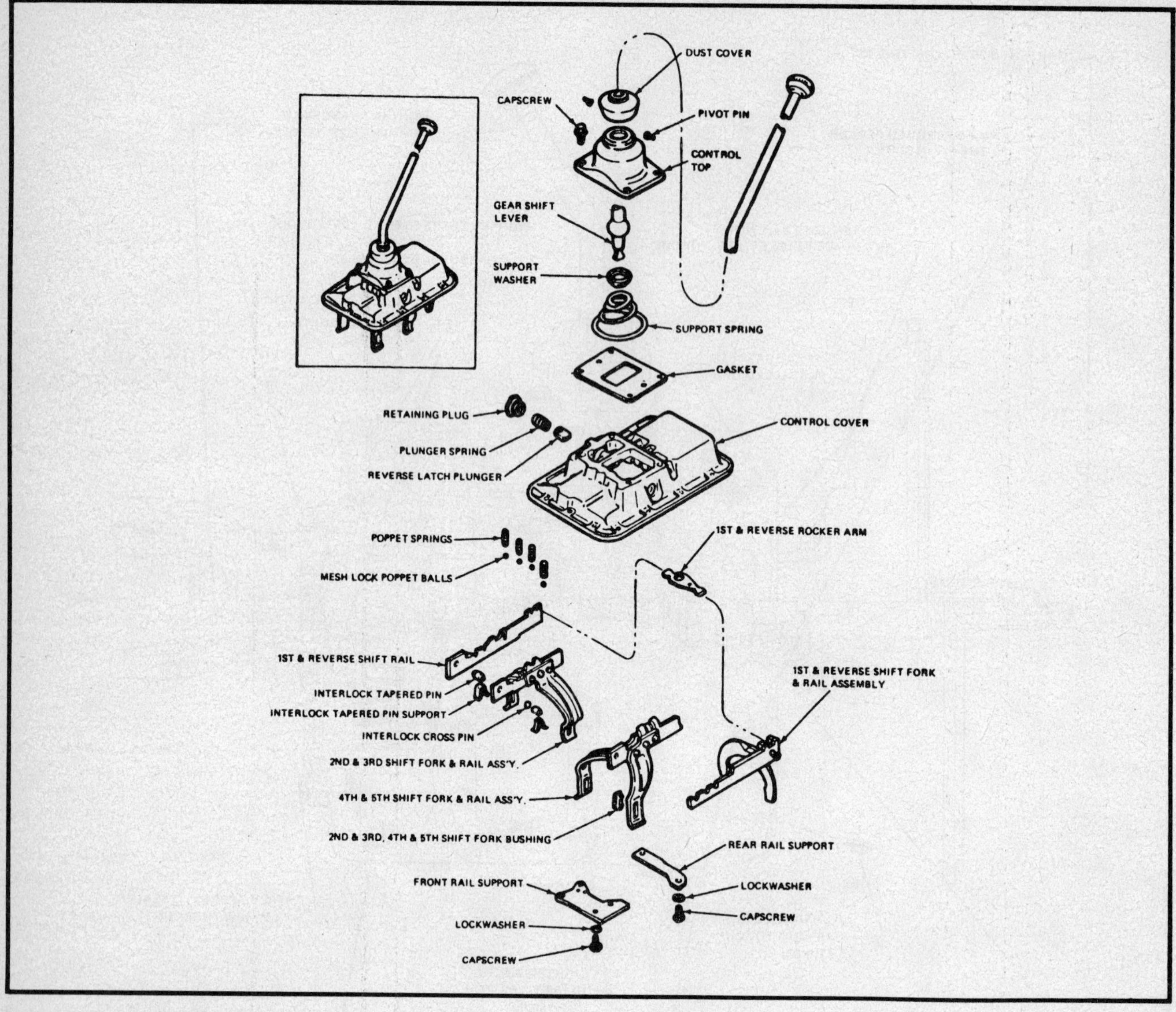

Exploded view Clark 390V gear shift housing (© Ford Motor Co.)

13. Position the fourth gear synchronizer ring on the clutching teeth of the fourth gear. Install the fourth and fifth shift hub sleeve on the output shaft.
14. Install the fourth and fifth synchronizer and the fifth speed synchronizer ring on the output shaft.
15. Install the thrust bearing and race.

INPUT SHAFT

Disassembly

1. Remove the bearing snapring from the input shaft. Remove the bearing with the special tool.
2. Remove the needle bearing retainer and the washer. Remove the needle bearings.

Assembly

1. Press the bearing on the input shaft.
2. Install the needle bearings, the washer and snapring.

COUNTER SHAFT

Disassembly

1. Remove the snapring at the forward end of the counter shaft.
2. Place the countershaft assembly in a hydraulic press, and press the drive gear off the shaft.
3. Remove the key from the shaft and press the fourth/speed gear off the shaft. Remove the remaining key.

Assembly

1. Install the fourth/speed gear key in the slot on the shaft. Position the fourth/speed gear on the shaft with the long hub facing toward the front.
2. Install the countershaft main drive gear key in the keyway on the shaft. Install the countershaft drive gear on the shaft with the long hub facing toward the rear. Install the snapring on the countershaft.

GEAR SHIFT HOUSING

Disassembly

NOTE: It is not necessary to disassemble the gear shift housing assembly to determine if the parts are worn. Note the condition of the shifter fork shafts and the forks by visual inspection. If the forks are excessively worn, or if they bind when shifted into the various positions, disassemble the gear shift housing. Check the interlocking system.

1. With the control cover in neutral, pry the fourth/fifth speed shift fork to the fourth speed position (toward the rear of the cover). Remove the front rail support capscrews and remove the front rail support.
2. Remove the interlock tapered pin supports. Note the position on the interlock tapered pins for reassembly.
3. Remove the rear rail support capscrews and remove the rear rail support.
4. Remove the first/reverse shift fork and rail assembly, remove the fourth, fifth, second and third shift fork and rail assembly. Use caution so that the interlock cross pin, interlock tapered pins, or the mesh lock poppet balls are not lost.
5. Remove the first/reverse shift rail. Remove the four mesh lock poppet balls, and then remove the four poppet springs.
6. Remove the first/reverse rocker arm. Remove the reverse latch plunger spring retaining plug and the reverse latch plunger spring and plunger.
7. If the fork bushings are worn, secure the fork in a soft jawed vise and remove the worn bushings with a suitable drift. Install the new bushings in the fork. Turn the fork over on the anvil of the vise and secure the bushing in the fork, using a pick punch and upsetting the bushing metal on the outside of the fork.

Assembly

1. Position the first/reverse rocker arm on the pivot pin. Install the reverse latch plunger, spring and the retaining plug. Tighten the plug securely.
2. Install the four poppet springs and the four mesh lock poppet balls.
3. Align one tapered interlock cross pin with the hole in the first/reverse shift rail. Position the rail on the poppet ball, with the rail in the neutral position. Note the position of the tapered interlock pin in relation to the rail.
4. Install the interlock cross pin in the second/third shift rail. Position the rail on the poppet ball, in neutral position with the interlock pin aligned with the first interlock pin aligned with the first tapered pin. Install the second interlock tapered pin. Align the pin with the interlock cross pin hole.
5. Position the fourth/fifth shift fork rail assembly on the poppet ball in the neutral position. Slightly raise the rear of the rail and align the second interlock tapered pin with the cross hole in the rail. Note the positions of the tapered interlock pins in the shift rails.
6. Install the first/reverse shift fork and rail assembly on the poppet ball in a neutral position. Align the first/reverse rocker arm in the rear of the rail.
7. Install the rail support capscrews and washers. Tighten the capscrews slightly. Install the interlock tapered pin supports. Tap the fourth/fifth shift fork to the rear (fourth speed position).
8. Position the front rail support and install the capscrews and washers. Tighten the front and rear support capscrews 20–25 ft. lbs.
9. Tap the fourth/fifth shift fork and rail assembly forward to a neutral position.

TRANSMISSION

Assembly

1. Coat the front counter shaft needle bearings with grease and install them in the front countershaft bore.
2. Tap the rear of the countershaft down and lower into the case. Push the countershaft forward and insert the shaft into the front bearing.
3. Position the countershaft rear bearing oil slinger and bearing on the shaft. Drive the bearing into the bore. The countershaft drive gear should be supported while driving the shaft to prevent damage to the front bearing. Install the rear bearing retainer.
4. Coat the reverse idler thrust washer with grease and position them in the transmission case.
5. Insert the bearings in the reverse idler bore. Place the gear assembly in position in the case, with the small gear toward the rear of the case.
6. Insert the reverse idler shaft through the hole in the case through the reverse idler gear and into the forward support boss. Drive the reverse idler shaft into the case until the slot in the shaft is lined up with the lock bolt hole. Install the retainer in the slot and secure the retainer with the lock bolt. Tighten the bolt to specification.
7. Tilt the rear of the output shaft assembly downward and insert the end of the shaft through the output shaft in the bore in the case. Lower the front end of the output shaft until it is in line with the pilot bearing opening. Move the assembly forward into position.
8. Insert the pilot bearing in the input shaft bore.
9. Position the input shaft and bearings in the forward end of the transmission case. Tap the front end of the shaft with a soft faced hammer until the snapring is seated against the case. Be sure the clutching teeth of the input shaft gear mesh with the fifth speed synchronizer without binding.
10. Position a new gasket on the input shaft bearing retainer. Be sure that the oil return holes in the retainer and gasket are aligned with the holes in the transmission case.
11. Install the lock washers and bolts on the input shaft bearing retainer and tighten the bolts to specification.
12. Position the output shaft rear bearing on the shaft and drive the bearing into the bore until the snapring is seated against the case.
13. Position the countershaft rear bearing cap and gasket on the case and install the lock washers and bolts. Tighten to specification.
14. Install the speedometer drive gear on the output shaft, and position a new oil seal in the output shaft bearing retainer. Be sure the seal is correctly installed. Position a new gasket and the bearing retainer on the case and install the lock washers and bolts. Tighten to specification.
15. Install the parking brake drum and companion flange assembly. Tighten the yoke retaining nut to specification.
16. With the transmission in neutral, position the control cover over the gears, aligning the shift forks in the shift cover with the gear shift hubs. If the control cover is in Neutral and the transmission is in Neutral, the transmission drive gear should turn without the brake drum or output shaft turning. Install the capscrews and washers, and tighten 20 to 25 ft. lbs. Install the remote control or shift tower in the control cover. Tighten the capscrews 20 to 25 ft. lbs.

Chrysler Corporation

A-230 THREE SPEED TRANSMISSION

The A-230 is a three speed transmission equipped with two synchronizer units to assist in the engagement of all forward gears. Lubricant capacity is 5 pints.

Disassembly

SHIFT HOUSING AND MECHANISM

1. Shift to second gear.
2. Remove side cover. If shaft O-ring seals need replacement. Pull shift forks out of shafts. Remove nuts and operating levers from shafts. Deburr and remove the shafts.

DRIVE PINION RETAINER AND EXTENSION HOUSING

1. Remove pinion bearing retainer from front of transmission case. Pry off retainer oil seal for clearance. With a brass drift, tap drive pinion as far forward as possible. Rotate cut away part of second gear next to countershaft gear. Shift second–third synchronizer sleeve forward. Remove speedometer pinion adapter retainer. Work adapter and pinion out of extension housing.
2. Unbolt extension housing. Break housing loose with plastic hammer and carefully remove.

IDLER GEAR AND MAINSHAFT

1. Insert dummy shaft in case to push reverse idler shaft and key out of case.
2. Remove dummy shaft and idler rollers.
3. Remove both tanged idler gear thrust washers.
4. Remove mainshaft assembly through rear of case.

COUNTERSHAFT GEAR AND DRIVE PINION

1. Using a mallet and dummy shaft, tap the countershaft rearward enough to remove key. Drive countershaft out of case, being careful not to drop the washers.
2. Lower countershaft gear to bottom of case.
3. Remove snapring from pinion bearing outer race (outside front of case).

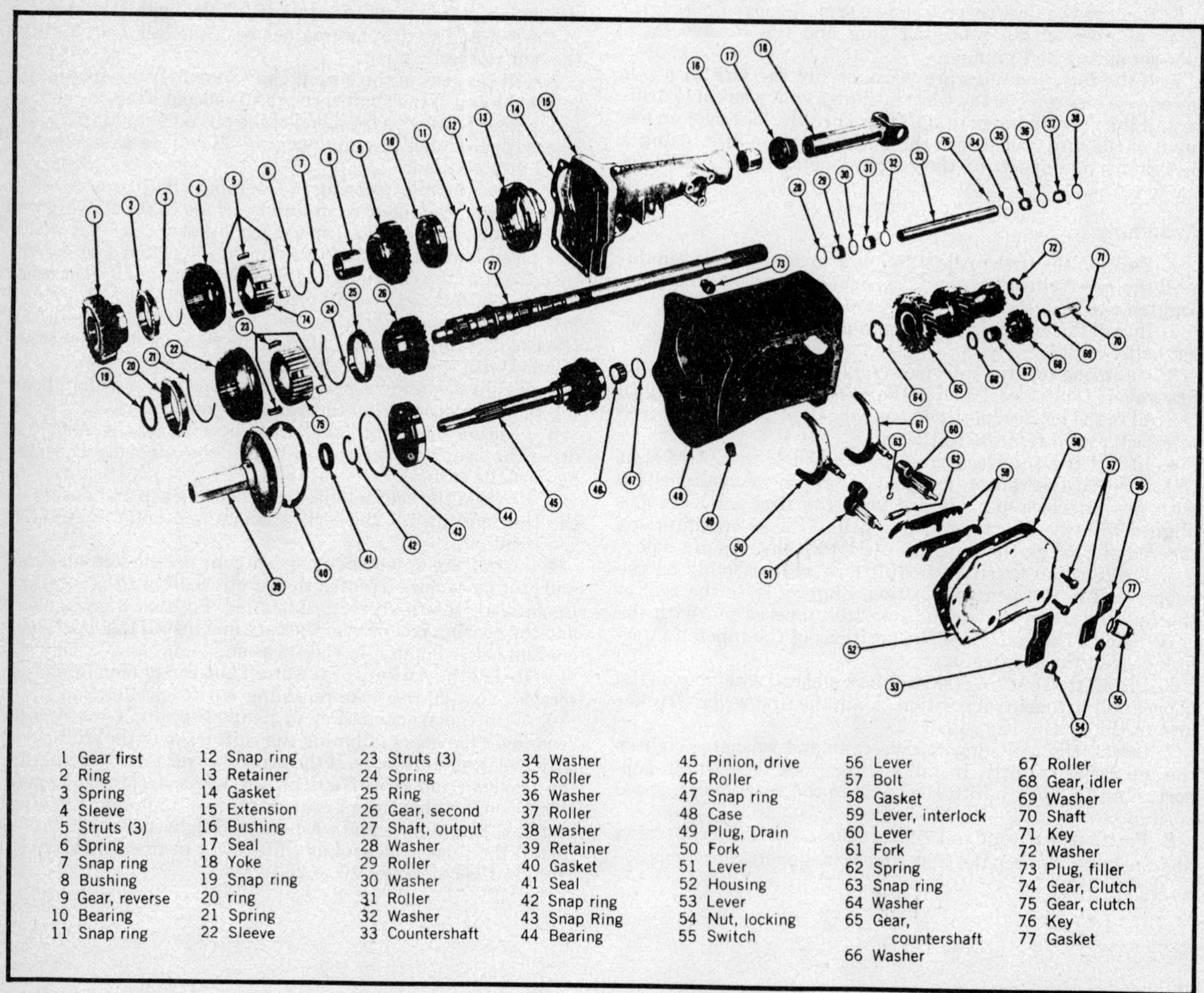

A-230 three speed transmission (© Chrysler Corp.)

4. Drive pinion shaft into case with plastic hammer. Remove assembly through rear of case.

5. If bearing is to be replaced, remove snapring and press off bearing.

6. Lift counter shaft gear and dummy shaft out through rear of case.

MAINSHAFT

1. Remove snapring from front end of mainshaft along with second gear stop ring and second gear.

2. Spread snapring in mainshaft bearing retainer. Slide retainer back off the bearing race.

3. Remove snapring at rear of mainshaft. Support front side of reverse gear. Press bearing off mainshaft.

4. Remove from press. Remove mainshaft bearing and reverse gear from shaft.

5. Remove snapring and first/reverse synchronizer assembly from shaft. Remove stop ring and first gear rearward.

Cleaning and Inspection

See Cleaning and Inspection instructions at the beginning of the Transmission section.

Assembly

COUNTERSHAFT GEAR

1. Slide dummy shaft into countershaft gear.

2. Slide one roller thrust washer over dummy shaft and into gear, followed by 22 greased rollers.

3. Repeat Step 2, adding one roller thrust washer on end.

4. Repeat steps 2 and 3 at other end of countershaft gear. There is a total of 88 rollers and 6 thrust washers.

5. Place greased front thrust washer on dummy shaft against gear with tangs forward.

6. Grease rear thrust washer and stick it in place in the case, with tangs rearward. Place countershaft gear assembly in bottom of transmission case until drive pinion is installed.

PINION GEAR

1. Press new bearing on pinion shaft with snapring groove forward. Install new snapring.

2. Install 15 rollers and retaining ring in drive pinion gear.

3. Install drive pinion and bearing assembly into case.

4. Position countershaft gear assembly by positioning it and thrust washers so countershaft can be tapped into position. Be careful to keep the countershaft against the dummy shaft to keep parts from falling between them. Install key in countershaft.

5. Tap drive pinion forward for clearance.

MAINSHAFT

1. Place a stop ring flat on the bench. Place a clutch gear and a sleeve on top. Drop the struts in their slots and insert a strut spring with the tang inside on strut. Turn the assembly over and install second strut spring, tang in a different strut.

2. Slide first gear and stop ring over rear of mainshaft and against thrust flange between assembly over rear of mainshaft, first and second gears on shaft.

3. Slide first/reverse synchronizer indexing hub slots to first gear stop ring lugs.

4. Install first/reverse synchronizer clutch gear snapring on mainshaft.

5. Slide reverse gear and mainshaft bearing on shaft, supporting inner race of bearing. Be sure snapring groove on outer race is forward.

6. Install bearing retaining snapring on mainshaft. Slide snapring over the bearing and seat it in groove.

7. Place second gear over front of mainshaft with thrust surface against flange.

8. Install stop ring and second/third synchronizer assembly against second gear. Install second/third synchronizer clutch gear snapring on shaft.

9. Move second/third synchronizer sleeve forward as far as possible. Install front stop ring inside sleeve with lugs indexed to struts.

10. Rotate cut out on second gear toward countershaft gear for clearance.

11. Insert mainshaft assembly into case. Tilt assembly to clear cluster gears and insert pilot rollers in drive pinion gear. If assembly is correct, the bearing retainer will bottom to the case without force. If not, check for a misplaced strut, pinion roller, or stop ring.

REVERSE IDLER GEAR

1. Place dummy shaft into idler gear. Insert 22 greased rollers.

2. Position reverse idler thrust washers in case with grease.

3. Position idler gear and dummy shaft in case. Install idler shaft and key.

EXTENSION HOUSING

1. Remove extension housing yoke seal. Drive bushing out from inside housing.

2. Align oil hole in bushing with oil slot in housing. Drive bushing into place. Drive new seal into housing.

3. Install extension housing and gasket to hold mainshaft and bearing retainer in place.

DRIVE PINION BEARING RETAINER

1. Install outer snapring on drive pinion bearing. Tap assembly back until snap-ring contacts case.

2. Using seal installer tool or equivalent, install a new seal in retainer bore.

3. Position main drive pinion bearing retainer and gasket on front of case. Coat threads with sealing compound, install bolts, torque to 30 ft. lbs.

GEARSHAFT MECHANISM AND HOUSING

1. If removed, place two interlock levers in pivot pin with spring hangers offset toward each other, so that spring installs in a straight line. Place E-clip on pivot pin.

2. Grease and install new O-ring seals on both shift shafts. Grease housing bores and insert shafts.

3. Install spring on interlock lever hangers.

4. Rotate each shift shaft fork bore to straight up position. Install shift forks through bores and under both interlock levers.

5. Position second/third synchronizer sleeve to rear, in second gear position. Position first–reverse synchronizer sleeve to middle of travel, in neutral position. Place shift forks in the same positions.

6. Install gasket and gearshift mechanism. The bolt with the extra long shoulder must be installed at the center rear of the case. Torque bolts to 15 ft. lbs.

7. Install speedometer drive pinion gear and adapter. Range number on adapter, which represents the number of teeth on the gear, should be in 6 o'clock position.

TORQUE SPECIFICATIONS

Manual A-203 3-Speed	ft. lbs.
Back up light switch	15
Extension housing bolts	50
Drive pinion bearing retainer bolts	30
Gearshift operating lever nuts	18
Transmission to clutch housing bolts	50
Transmission cover retaining bolts	12
Transmission drain plug	25

Chrysler Corporation

A-250 THREE SPEED TRANSMISSION

The A-250 is a three speed transmission equipped with a synchronizer between second and third gears. Lubricant capacity is 4 ½ pints.

Disassembly

1. Remove case cover and gasket.
2. Measure the synchronizer "float" with a pair of feeler gauges. Measurement is made between the synchronizer outer ring pin and the opposite synchronizer outer ring. This measurement must be made on two pins 180 degrees apart with equal gap on both ends for "float" determination. The measurement should be between 0.060 in. to 0.117 in. A snug fit should be maintained between feeler gauge and pins.
3. Remove the bolt and retainer holding the speedometer pinion adapter in the extension housing. Carefully work the adapter and pinion out of the extension housing.

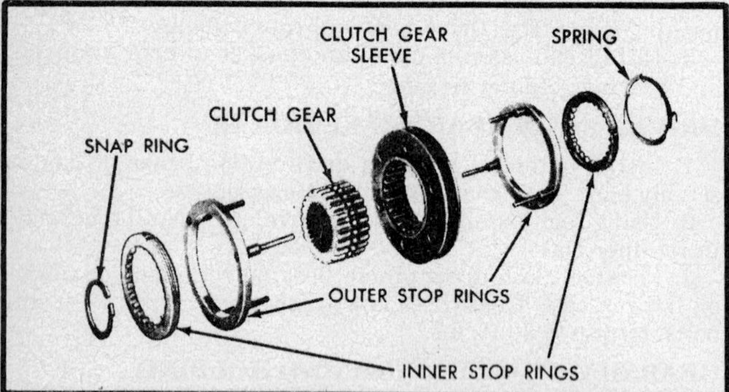

Exploded view A-250 synchronizer (© Chrysler Corp.)

4. Remove extension housing bolts and extension housing.
5. Remove the bolts that attach the drive pinion bearing retainer to case, then slide the retainer off the pinion. Pry the seal out of retainer using a suitable tool. Be cautious not to nick or scratch the bore.
6. Rotate the drive pinion so that the blank clutch tooth area is opposite the countershaft for removal clearance.
7. Slide drive pinion assembly slightly out of case. Move the synchronizer front inner stop ring from the short splines on the pinion shaft. Slowly remove drive pinion assembly.
8. Remove snapring that holds bearing on pinion shaft. Remove pinion bearing washer. Using an arbor press, press pinion shaft out of bearing. Remove oil slinger.
9. Remove snapring and bearing rollers from the end of the drive pinion.
10. Remove clutch gear retaining snapring from the mainshaft.
11. Remove the mainshaft bearing securing snapring from case.
12. Slide mainshaft and bearing rearward out of case while holding the gears as they drop free.
13. Remove the snapring from mainshaft and press the bearing off of mainshaft.
14. Remove the synchronizer components, second gear, first/reverse gear and shift forks from case.

NOTE: Steps 15 thru 18 need only be performed if gear shift lever seals are leaking.

15. Remove the shift levers from the shift shafts.
16. Drive out the tapered retaining pin from the first/reverse shift shaft. Remove the shift shaft from inside the case.

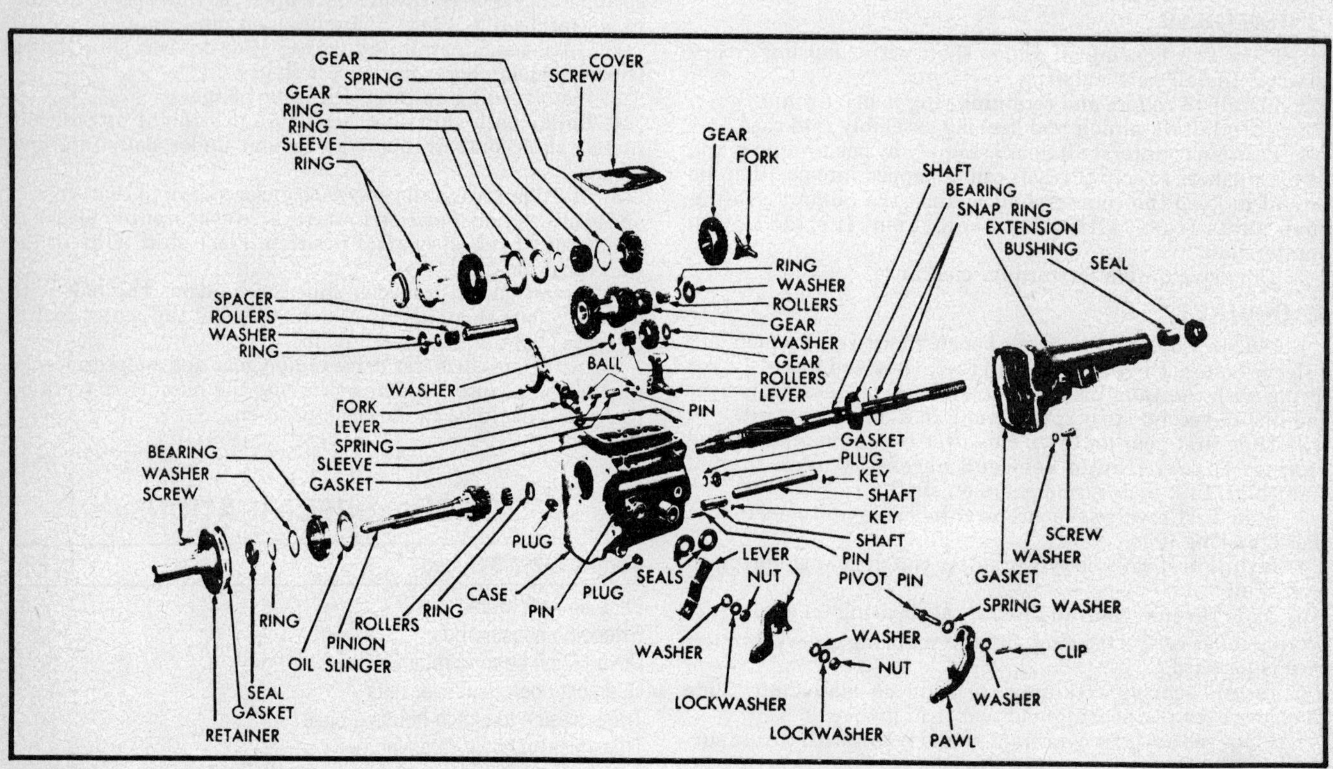

Exploded view A-250 transmission (© Chrysler Corp.)

NOTE: As the detent balls are spring loaded, when the shafts are removed the balls will drop to the bottom of the transmission case.

17. Remove the interlock sleeve, spring and both detent balls from case. Drive tapered retaining pin out of second–third shaft and remove shaft from case.
18. Drive shift shaft seals out of case with a suitable drift.
19. Check end play of countershaft gear with a feeler gauge. The end play should be between 0.005 in. to 0.022 in. This measurement is used to determine if a new thrust washer is necessary during reassembly.
20. Using a countershaft bearing arbor, drive the countershaft towards the rear of the case until the small key can be removed from the countershaft.
21. Drive the countershaft the rest of the way out of the case, keeping the arbor tight against the end of the countershaft. This will prevent loss of roller bearings.
22. Remove the countershaft gear, front thrust washer and rear thrust washer from the case.
23. Remove the bearing rollers, spacer ring and center spacer from the countershaft gear.
24. Drive the reverse idler gear shaft out of the transmission case using a suitable drift. Remove the Woodruff key from the end of the reverse idler shaft.
25. Remove the reverse idler gear and thrust washers out of the case. Remove the bearing rollers from the gear.

Cleaning and Inspection

See Cleaning and Inspection instructions at the beginning of the Transmission section.

Assembly

1. Slide the countershaft gear bearing roller spacer over arbor tool. Coat the bore of gear with lubricant and slide tool and spacer into gear bore.
2. Lubricate the bearing rollers with heavy grease and install two rows of 22 rollers each in both ends of gear in area around arbor. Cover with heavy grease and install bearing spacer rings in each end of gear and between roller rows.
3. If countershaft gear end play was found to be excessive during disassembly, install new thrust washers. Cover with heavy grease and install thrust washer and thrust needle bearing and cap at each end of countershaft gear and over arbor. Install gear and arbor in the case, and make sure that tabs on rear thrust washer slide into grooves in the case.
4. Drive the arbor forward out of the countershaft gear and through the bore in the front of the case using the countershaft and a soft faced hammer. When the countershaft is almost in place, make certain the keyway in the countershaft is aligned with the key slot in the rear of the case. Insert the shaft key and continue to drive the countershaft into the case until the key is bottomed in the slot.
5. Position special arbor tool in the reverse idler gear and install the 22 roller bearings using a heavy grease.
6. Place the front and rear thrust washers at each end of the reverse idler gear. Position the assembly in the transmission case with the chamfered end of the gear teeth towards the front. Make sure that the thrust washer tabs engage the slots in case.
7. Insert reverse idler shaft into the bore at rear of case with keyway to the rear, pushing the arbor towards the front of the case.
8. When the keyway is aligned with the slot in the case, insert the key in the keyway. Drive the shaft forward until the key is seated in the recess.

NOTE: Steps 9 through 14 need only be performed if the shift levers have been disassembled.

9. Place new shift shaft seals in the case and drive it into position with suitable drift.
10. Carefully slide the first/reverse shift shaft into the case and lock into place with a tapered retaining pin. Position the lever so that the center detent is aligned with the interlock bore.
11. Install the interlock sleeve into the bore followed by a detent ball, spring and pin.
12. Install remaining detent ball and hold in place with detent ball holding tool.
13. Depress the detent ball and carefully install the second/third shift shaft. Align center detent with detent ball and secure lever with tapered retaining pin.
14. Install shift levers and tighten retaining nuts to 18 ft. lbs.
15. Press the bearing on the mainshaft and select and install snapring that gives minimum end play.
16. Move shift lever to reverse position, and then place the first/reverse gear and shift fork in the case. Both shift forks are offset toward the rear of the transmission case.
17. Assemble the synchronizer parts with shift fork and second gear.
18. Place the second gear assembly in the transmission case and insert the shift fork into its lever.
19. Install the mainshaft carefully through the gear assembly until it bottoms in rear of case.
20. Install synchronizer clutch gear snapring on mainshaft.
21. Select and install mainshaft bearing snapring in case.
22. If "float" measurement was found to be outside specifications, install or remove shims to place "float" within range.
23. Install oil slinger on drive pinion shaft and slide against the gear.
24. Slide the bearing over the pinion shaft with snapring groove away from gear, then seat bearing on shaft using an arbor press.
25. Install keyed washer between bearing and retaining snapring groove.
26. Secure bearing and washer with selected thickness snapring. If large snapring around bearing was removed, install it at this time.
27. Place drive pinion shaft in a vise with soft faced jaws and install the 14 roller bearings in the shaft cavity. Coat the roller bearings with a heavy grease and install retaining ring in groove.
28. Rotate the drive pinion so that the blank clutch tooth area is next to the countershaft. Guide the drive pinion through the front of case and engage the inner stop ring with the clutch teeth. Then seat pinion bearing. The pinion shaft is fully seated when the snapring is in full contact with the case.
29. Install a new seal in the pinion bearing retainer.
30. Position retainer assembly and new gasket on the case. Use sealing compound on bolts and tighten to 30 ft. lbs.
31. Slide the extension housing and a new gasket over mainshaft. Guide shaft through bushing and oil seal. Use sealing compound on the bolt used in the hole tapped through the transmission case. Install remaining bolts and tighten all to 50 ft. lbs.
32. Install the transmission cover and gasket and tighten cover bolts to 12 ft. lbs.
33. Rotate the speedometer pinion gear and adapter assembly so that the number on the adapter corresponding to the number of teeth on the gear is in the 6 o'clock position as the assembly is installed.
34. Fill the transmission with the proper lubricant and install the drain plug and tighten to 25 ft. lbs. Install the back-up light switch and tighten to 15 ft. lbs.
35. Rotate the drive pinion shaft and check operation of transmission by running the transmission through all gear ranges.

Chrysler Corporation

A-390 THREE SPEED TRANSMISSION

The A-390 is a three speed synchromesh transmission. Lubricant capacity is 4 ½ pints.

Disassembly

1. Remove the bolts that attach the cover to the case. Remove the cover and gasket.
2. Remove the long spring that retains the detent plug in the case. Remove the detent plug with a small magnet.
3. Remove the bolt and retainer securing the speedometer pinion adapter to the transmission case. Carefully work the adapter and pinion out of the extension housing.
4. Remove the bolts that attach the extension housing to the transmission case. Slide the extension housing off the output shaft.
5. Remove the bolts that attach the input shaft bearing retainer to the case. Slide the retainer off the shaft. Using a suitable tool, pry the seal out of the retainer. Be careful not to nick or scratch the bore in which the seal is pressed or the surface on which the seal is bottomed.
6. Remove the lubricant fill plug from the right side of the case. Working through the fill plug opening, drive the roll pin out of the countershaft with a ¼ in. punch.
7. Working with the countershaft bearing arbor and a soft faced hammer, tap the countershaft toward the front of the case with the arbor tool to remove the expansion plug from the countershaft bore at the front of the case. The countershaft is a loose fit in the case and will slide easily.
8. Insert the arbor tool through the front of the case and

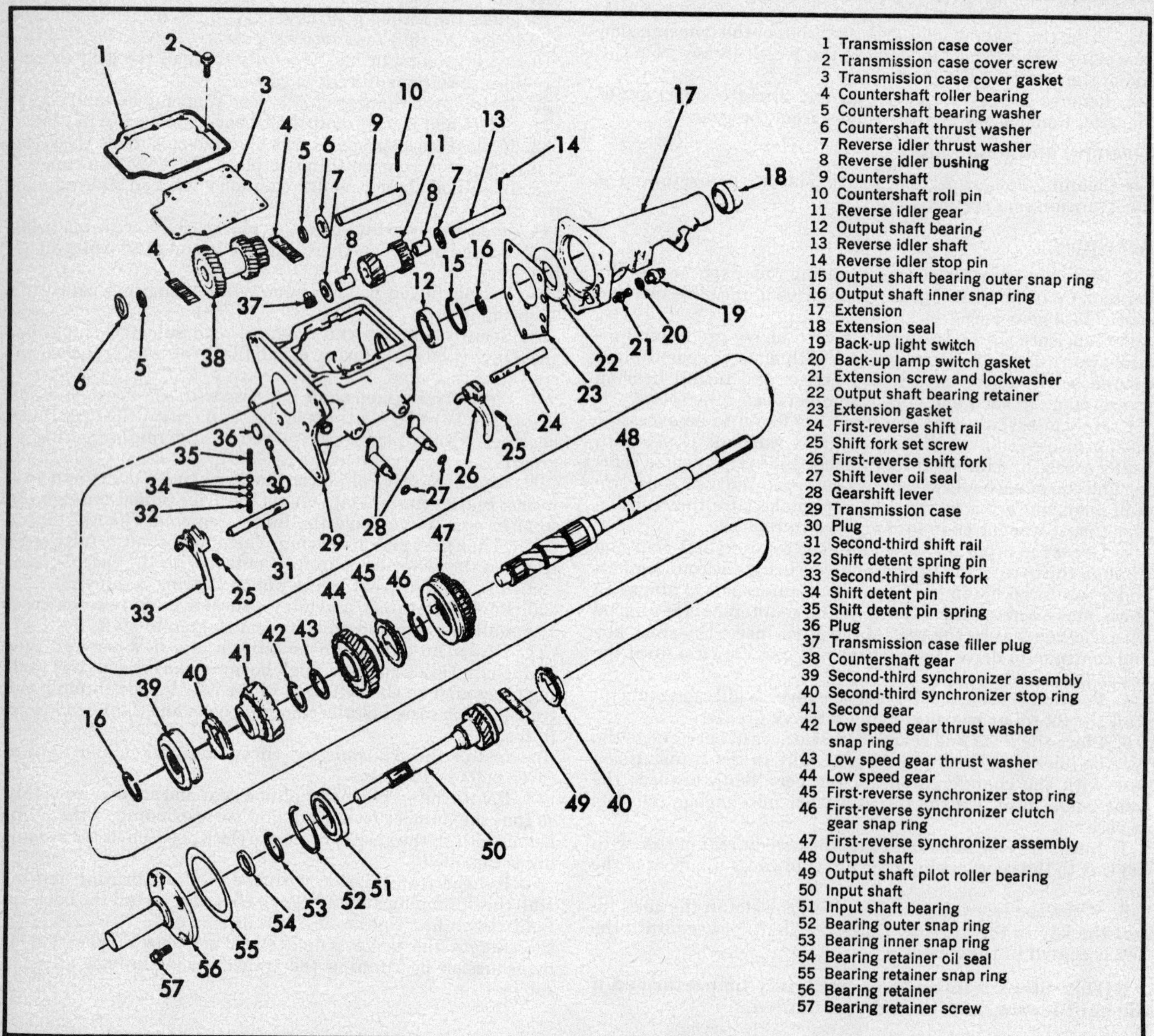

Exploded view A-390 transmission (© Chrysler Corp.)

push the countershaft out of the rear of the case so the roll pin hole in the countershaft does not travel through the roller bearings. The countershaft gear will drop to the bottom of the case. Remove the countershaft from the rear of the case.

9. Place both shift levers in neutral (center) position.
10. Remove the input shaft assembly and stop ring from the front of the case.
11. Remove the set screw that secures the first/reverse shift fork to the shift rail. Slide the first/reverse shift rail out through the rear of the case.
12. Move the second/third shift fork rearward for access to the set screw. Remove the set screw from the fork. Using a suitable tool, rotate the shift rail one quarter turn.
13. Lift the interlock plug from the case with a magnet.
14. Tap on the inner end of the second/third shift rail to remove the expansion plug from the front of the case. Remove the shift rail through the front of the case.
15. Remove the second/third shift rail detent plug and spring from the detent bore with a magnet.
16. Tap the output shaft assembly rearward until the output shaft bearing clears the case. Remove both shift forks. Remove the snapring that retains the output shaft bearing to the output shaft.
17. Assemble the output shaft bearing removal tool over the output shaft and bearing. Remove the output shaft bearing.
18. Remove the output shaft assembly through top of the case.
19. Using a suitable drift, drive the reverse idler gear shaft toward the rear, and out of the transmission case.
20. Lift the reverse idler gear and thrust washer out of the case.
21. Remove the countershaft gear, arbor assembly, and thrust washers from the bottom of the case.
22. Remove the countershaft roll pin from the bottom of the case.
23. Remove the snapring that retains the second/third synchronizer clutch gear and sleeve assembly on the output shaft. Slide the second/third synchronizer assembly off the end of the output shaft.

NOTE: Do not separate the second/third synchronizer clutch gear, sleeve, struts, or spring unless inspection reveals that a replacement is necessary.

24. Slide the second gear and stop ring off the output shaft.
25. Remove the snapring and thrust washer retaining the first gear. Slide the first gear and stop ring off the output shaft.
26. Remove the snapring that retains the first/reverse synchronizer hub on the output shaft. The first/reverse synchronizer hub is a press fit on the output shaft. To avoid damage to the synchronizer, remove the synchronizer hub using an arbor press. Do not attempt to remove or install the hub by hammering or prying.

Overhaul

SHIFT LEVERS AND SEALS

1. Remove the operating levers from their respective shafts. Remove any burrs from the shafts to avoid damage to the case.
2. Push the shift levers out of the transmission case. Remove and discard the O-ring seal from each shaft.
3. Lubricate the new seals with transmission oil and install them on the shafts.
4. Install the shift levers in the case.
5. Install the operating levers and tighten the retaining nuts to 18 ft. lbs.

INPUT SHAFT BEARING AND ROLLERS

1. Remove the snapring securing the bearing on the input shaft. Carefully press the input shaft out of the bearing with an arbor press.
2. Remove the fifteen bearing rollers from the cavity in the end of the input shaft.

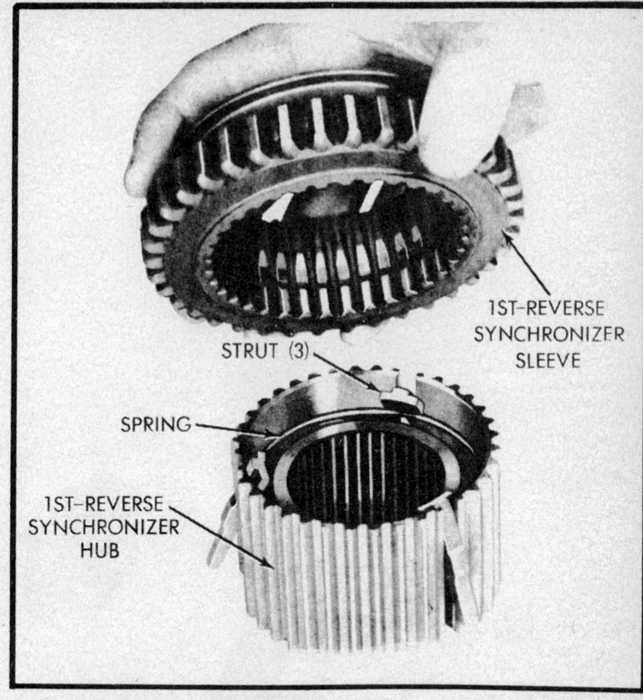

Assembling the first/reverse synchronizer—A-390 transmission (© Chrysler Corp.)

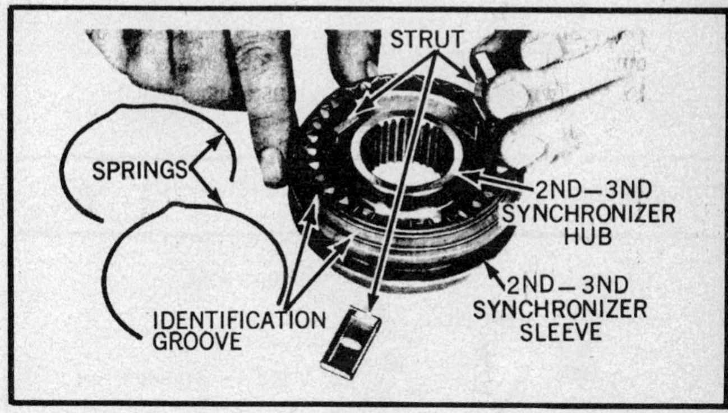

Assembling the second/third synchronizer—A-390 transmission (© Chrysler Corp.)

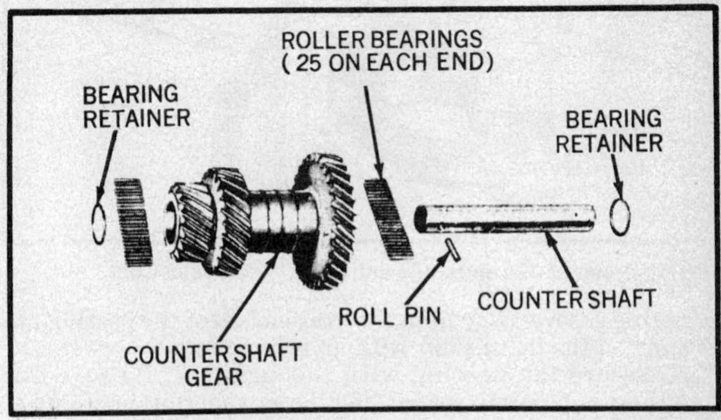

Exploded view A-390 countershaft and gear (© Chrysler Corp.)

3. Install the 15 bearing rollers in the cavity of the input shaft. Coat the rollers with a thin film of grease to retain them during installation.
4. Slide the input shaft bearing over the input shaft,

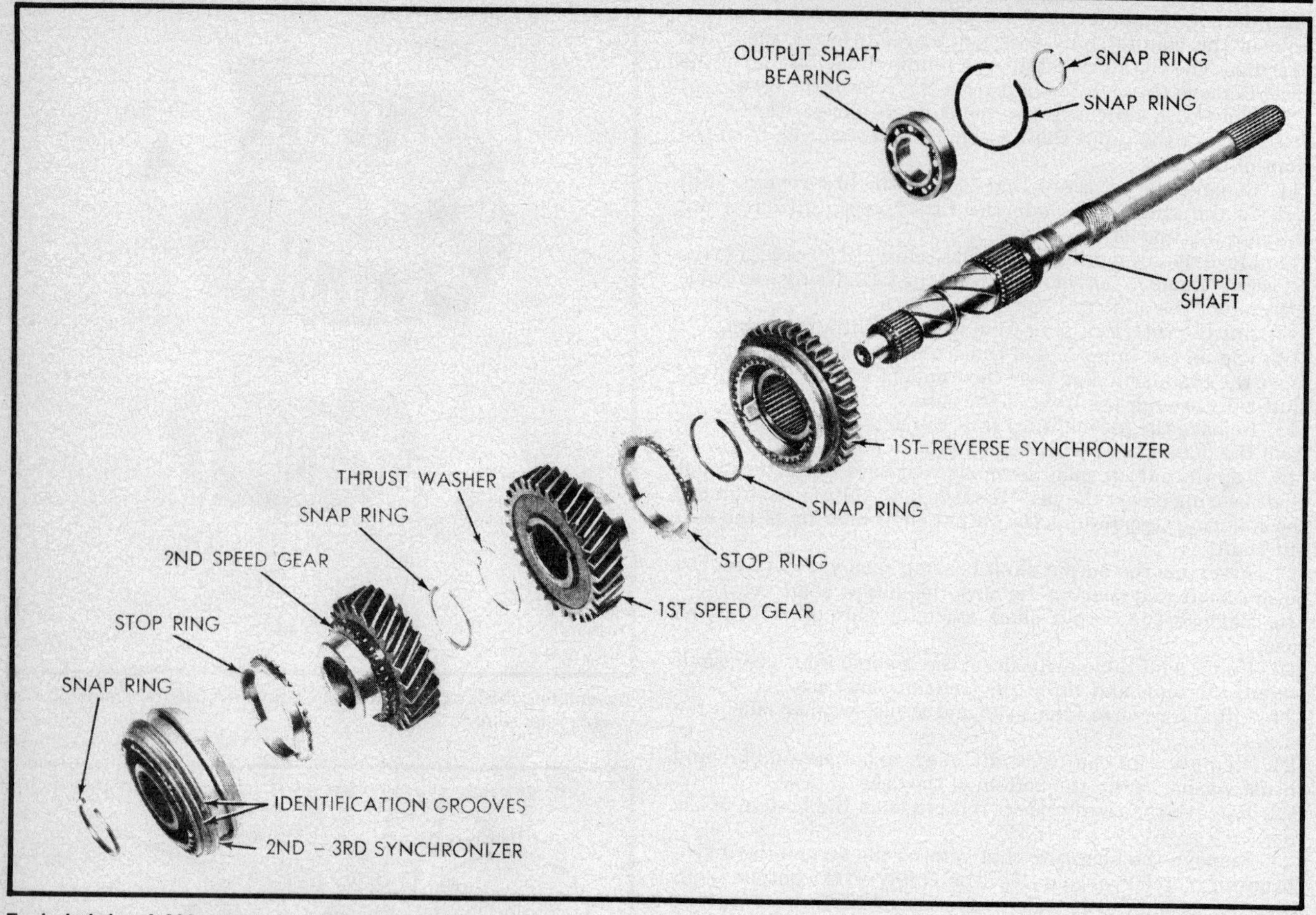

Exploded view A-390 output shaft assembly (© Chrysler Corp.)

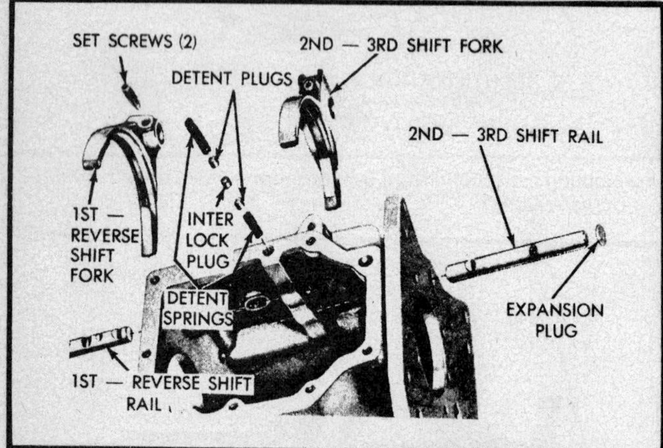

Exploded view A-390 shift rails and forks (© Chrysler Corp.)

snapring groove away from the gear end. Seat the bearing assembly on the input shaft with an arbor press.

5. Secure the bearing with the snapring. Be sure the snapring is properly seated. If a large snapring around the bearing was removed, be sure to install it at this time.

SYNCHRONIZERS

NOTE: If either synchronizer is to be disassembled, mark all parts so that they will be reassembled in the same position. Do not mix parts from the two synchronizers.

1. Push the synchronizer hub off each synchronizer sleeve.
2. Separate the struts and springs from the hubs.
3. Install the spring on the front side of the first/reverse synchronizer hub, making sure that all three strut slots are fully covered. Hang the three struts on the spring and in the slots with the wide end of the strut inside the hub.
4. With the alignment marks on the hub and sleeve aligned, push the sleeve down on the hub until the struts are in the neutral detent. Place the stop ring on top of the synchronizer assembly.
5. With the alignment marks on the second/third synchronizer sleeve and hub aligned, slide the sleeve on the hub. Drop in the three struts in the strut slots. Install the spring with the hump in the center, into the hollow of the strut. Turn the assembly over and install the other spring so that the hump in the center of the spring is inserted in the same strut. Place the stop ring on each end of the synchronizer assembly.

COUNTERSHAFT GEAR AND BEARING

1. Remove the countershaft bearing arbor, the roller bearings and the two bearing retainers from the countershaft gear.
2. Coat the bore in each end of the countershaft gear with grease.
3. Insert the countershaft arbor and install twenty five roller bearings and the retainer washer in each end of the countershaft gear.
4. Position the countershaft gear and arbor assembly in the transmission case. Align the gear bore and the thrust washers with the bores in the case and install the countershaft.
5. Using a feeler gauge, check the countershaft gear end play. The end play should be within 0.004 in. to 0.018 in. If the clearance is not within limits, replace the thrust washers.

6. After establishing the correct end play, install the arbor tool in the countershaft gear and lower the gear and tool out of the bottom of the transmission case.

Assembly

1. Coat the countershaft gear thrust surfaces in the case with a thin film of grease and position the two thrust washers in place. Place the countershaft gear and arbor assembly in the proper position in the bottom of the transmission case. The countershaft gear will remain in the bottom of the case until the output and input shafts are installed.
2. Coat the reverse idler gear thrust surfaces in the case with a thin film of grease and position the two thrust washers in place. Install the reverse idler gear in the case and align the gear bore with the thrust washers in the case bore. Install the reverse idler shaft.
3. Measure the reverse idler gear end play with a feeler gauge. End play should be 0.004 in. to 0.018 in. If the clearance is not within limits, replace the thrust washers. If the end play is correct, leave the reverse idler gear in place.
4. Lubricate the output shaft splines and the machined surfaces with transmission oil.
5. Slide the first/reverse synchronizer onto the output shaft with the fork groove toward the front. The first/reverse synchronizer hub is a press fit on the output shaft. To eliminate the possibility of damage to the hub, install the hub using an arbor press. Do not attempt to install the hub by hammering or driving. Secure the hub on the output shaft with the snapring.
6. Slide the first gear and stop ring onto the output shaft, aligning the slots in the stop ring with the struts. Install the thrust washer and snapring.
7. Slide the second gear and stop ring on the output shaft.
8. Install the second/third synchronizer assembly on the output shaft. Rotate the second gear to index the struts with the slots in the stop ring. Secure the synchronizer with a snapring.
9. Position the output shaft assembly in the transmission case. Place the transmission in a vertical position with the front of the case flat on the work bench. Place a 1 $\frac{1}{4}$ inch block of wood under the end of the output shaft. The block of wood will hold the output shaft assembly up during installation of the output shaft bearing.
10. Install the large snapring on the output shaft bearing. Place the bearing on the output shaft with the large snapring up. Drive the bearing on the shaft until it is seated on the shaft. Secure the bearing on the output shaft with the snapring. Return the transmission to a horizontal position.
11. Insert both shift forks in the case and in their proper sleeves. Push the output shaft assembly into position and tap it forward until the output shaft bearing is seated in the transmission case.
12. Install the shortest detent spring followed by a detent plug into the case. Place the second/third synchronizer assembly in the second gear position.
13. Align the second/third shift fork and install the second/third shift rail. The second/third shift rail is the shortest of the two shift rails. It will be necessary to depress the detent plug to enter the shift rail in the bore. Move the rail inward until the detent plug engages the forward notch (second gear position).
14. Secure the fork to the rail with the set screw. Move the synchronizer to the neutral position.
15. Install a new expansion plug in the transmission case.
16. Install the interlock plug in the transmission case with a magnet. If the second/third shift rail is in the neutral position, the top of the interlock plug will be slightly lower than the surface of the first/reverse shift rail bore.
17. Align the first/reverse fork and install the first/reverse shift rail. Move the rail inward until the center notch (neutral) is aligned with the detent bore. Secure the fork to the rail with the set screw.
18. Using a suitable tool, install a new oil seal in the input shaft bearing retainer bore.
19. Coat the bore of the input shaft gear with a thin film of grease. A thick, heavy grease will plug the lubricant holes and prevent lubrication of the roller bearings. Install the fifteen roller bearings in the bore.
20. Place the stop ring, slots aligned with the struts, into the second/third synchronizer. Tap the input shaft assembly into place in the case while holding the output shaft to prevent the roller bearings from dropping.
21. Roll the transmission over so that it rests on both the top edge and the shift levers. The countershaft gear will drop into place. Using a suitable tool, align the countershaft gear and thrust washers with the bore in the transmission case.
22. Working from the rear of the case, slide the countershaft into position being careful to keep the countershaft in contact with the arbor to avoid dropping parts out of position. Be sure that the roll pin hole in the countershaft aligns with the roll pin hole in the case.
23. Install the roll pin. Install a new expansion plug in the countershaft bore at the front of the case. Install the plug flush or below the face of the case to prevent interference with the clutch housing.
24. Slide the extension housing, with a new gasket, over the output shaft and against the case. Coat the attaching bolt threads with a sealing compound. Install and tighten the attaching bolts to 50 ft. lbs.
25. Install the input shaft bearing retainer and a new gasket. Make sure that the oil return slot is at the bottom. Coat the threads with a sealing compound, install the attaching bolts and tighten to 30 ft. lbs.
26. Install the remaining detent plug into the case followed by the detent spring.
27. Install the filler plug and the back-up light switch. Pour lubricant over the entire gear train while rotating the input shaft and the output shaft.
28. Place the cover and a new gasket on the transmission. Coat the attaching screw threads with a sealing compound. Install and tighten the attaching screws to 22 ft. lbs.

TORQUE SPECIFICATIONS

	ft. lbs.
Cover to case screws	22
Back-up light switch	15
Extension housing to case bolts	
50	
Extension housing to cross member bolts	50
Gearshift lever nuts	18
Input shaft bearing retainer bolts	30
Shift fork to shift rail set screw	10
Transmission to clutch housing bolts	50
Transmission drain plug	25
Transmission filler plug	15

Chrysler Corporation

FOUR SPEED OVERDRIVE TRANSMISSION

The four speed overdrive transmission is a four speed unit with all forward gears synchronized. Third gear is direct, while the fourth gear is the overdrive ratio. Lubricant capacity is 7 pints.

Disassembly

GEARSHIFT HOUSING AND MECHANISM

1. If available, mount transmission in a repair stand.
2. Disconnect gearshift control rods from the shift control levers and the transmission operating levers.
3. Remove the two gearshift control housing mounting bolts.
4. Remove gearshift control housing from the transmission extension housing or mounting bracket (if so equipped).
5. Remove the gearshift control housing mounting bracket bolts, then remove the bracket (if so equipped).
6. Remove back-up light switch (if so equipped).
7. Remove output companion flange nut and washer, if used, then pull the flange from the mainshaft (output shaft).
8. Remove gearshift housing to transmission case attaching bolts.
9. With all levers in the neutral detent position, pull housing out and away from the case. If first and second, or third and fourth shift forks remain in engagement with the synchronizer sleeves, move the sleeves and remove forks from the case.
10. Remove nuts, lock washers and flat washers that hold first/second, and third/fourth speed shift operating levers to the shafts.
11. Disengage shift levers from the flats on the shafts and remove levers. Remove the E-ring on the overdrive four speed.

EXTENSION HOUSING, MAINSHAFT AND MAIN DRIVE PINION

1. Remove the bolt and retainer holding the speedometer pinion adapter in the extension housing, then remove the pinion adapter.
2. Remove the bolts attaching the extension housing to the transmission case.
3. Rotate the extension housing on the output shaft to expose the rear of the countershaft. Install one bolt to hold the extension in place.
4. Drill a hole in the countershaft extension plug at the front of the case.
5. Reaching through this hole, push the countershaft to the rear to expose the Woodruff key, when exposed, remove it. Push the countershaft forward against the expansion plug, and using a brass drift, tap the countershaft forward until the expansion plug is removed.
6. Using a countershaft arbor, push the countershaft out the rear of the case, but don't let the countershaft washers fall out of position. Lower the cluster gear to the bottom of the transmission case.
7. Remove the bolt and rotate the extension back to the normal position.
8. Remove the drive pinion attaching bolts and slide the retainer and gasket from the pinion shaft, then pry the pinion or seal from the retainer. When installing the new seal, don't nick or scratch the seal bore in the retainer or the surface on which the seal bottoms.
9. Using a brass drift, tap the pinion and bearing assembly forward and remove through the front of the case.
10. Slide the third and overdrive synchronizer sleeve slightly forward, slide the reverse idler gear to the center of its shaft, and tap the extension housing rearward. Slide the housing and mainshaft assembly out and away from the case.
11. Remove the snapring holding the third and overdrive synchronizer clutch gear and sleeve assembly to the mainshaft, then remove the synchronizer assembly.
12. Slide the overdrive gear and stop ring off the mainshaft. Using pair of long nose pliers, compress the snap ring holding the mainshaft bearing in the extension housing. With it compressed, pull the mainshaft assembly and bearing out of the extension housing.
13. Remove the snapring holding the mainshaft on the shaft. The bearing is removed by inserting steel plates on the front side of the first speed gear, then pressing the mainshaft through the bearing being careful not to damage the gear teeth.
14. Remove the bearing, retainer ring, first speed gear and stop ring from the shaft.
15. Remove the snapring. Remove the first and second clutch gear and sleeve assembly from the mainshaft.
16. Remove the drive pinion bearing inner snapring, then using an arbor press, remove the bearing. Remove the snapring and bearing rollers from the cavity in the drive pinion.
17. Remove the countershaft gear from the bottom of the case, then remove the arbor, needle bearings, thrust washers and spacers from the center of the countershaft gear.
18. Remove the reverse gearshift lever detent spring retainer, gasket, plug, and detent ball spring from the rear of the case.
19. The reverse idler gear shaft is a tight fit in the case and will have to be pressed out.
20. If there is oil leakage visible around the reverse gearshift lever shaft, push the lever shaft in and remove it from the case. Remove the detent ball from the bottom of the transmission case and remove the shift fork from the shaft and detent plate.

Assembly

REVERSE SHAFT

Follow the first four steps only if you removed the reverse shaft in the disassembly procedure.

1. Install a new oil seal O-ring on the lever shaft and coat the shaft with grease; insert it into its bore and install the reverse fork in the lever.
2. Install the reverse detent spring and gasket; insert the ball and spring and install the plug and gasket.
3. Place the reverse idler gear shaft in position in the end of the case and drive it in far enough to position the reverse idler gear on the protruding end of the shaft with the fork slot toward the rear. While doing this, engage the slot with the reverse shift fork.
4. With the reverse idler gear correctly positioned, drive the reverse gear shaft into the case far enough to install the Woodruff key. Drive the shaft in flush with the end of the transmission case. Install the back-up light switch and gasket.

COUNTERSHAFT GEAR AND DRIVE PINION

1. Coat the inside bore of the countershaft gear with a thin film of grease and install the roller bearing spacer with an arbor into the gear, center the spacer and arbor.
2. Install the roller bearings and a spacer ring on each end.
3. Replace worn thrust washers, coat the new ones with grease and install them over the arbor with the tang side toward the case boss.
4. Install the countershaft assembly into the case and allow the gear assembly to sit on the bottom of the case so that the thrust washers won't come out of position.
5. Press the drive pinion bearing on the pinion shaft. Make sure the outer snap ring groove is toward the front end and the bearing is seated against the shoulder on the gear.

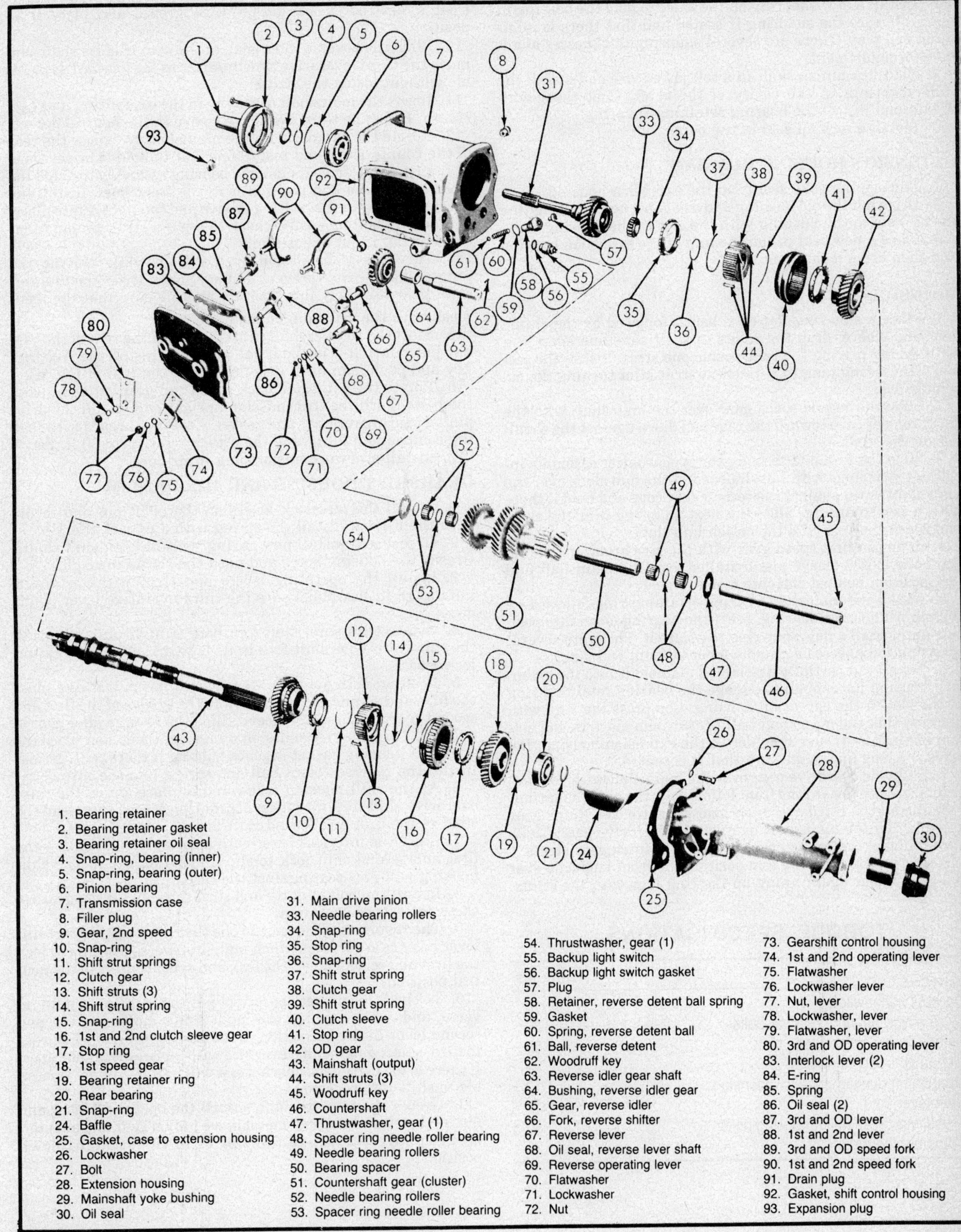
1. Bearing retainer
2. Bearing retainer gasket
3. Bearing retainer oil seal
4. Snap-ring, bearing (inner)
5. Snap-ring, bearing (outer)
6. Pinion bearing
7. Transmission case
8. Filler plug
9. Gear, 2nd speed
10. Snap-ring
11. Shift strut springs
12. Clutch gear
13. Shift struts (3)
14. Shift strut spring
15. Snap-ring
16. 1st and 2nd clutch sleeve gear
17. Stop ring
18. 1st speed gear
19. Bearing retainer ring
20. Rear bearing
21. Snap-ring
24. Baffle
25. Gasket, case to extension housing
26. Lockwasher
27. Bolt
28. Extension housing
29. Mainshaft yoke bushing
30. Oil seal
31. Main drive pinion
33. Needle bearing rollers
34. Snap-ring
35. Stop ring
36. Snap-ring
37. Shift strut spring
38. Clutch gear
39. Shift strut spring
40. Clutch sleeve
41. Stop ring
42. OD gear
43. Mainshaft (output)
44. Shift struts (3)
45. Woodruff key
46. Countershaft
47. Thrustwasher, gear (1)
48. Spacer ring needle roller bearing
49. Needle bearing rollers
50. Bearing spacer
51. Countershaft gear (cluster)
52. Needle bearing rollers
53. Spacer ring needle roller bearing
54. Thrustwasher, gear (1)
55. Backup light switch
56. Backup light switch gasket
57. Plug
58. Retainer, reverse detent ball spring
59. Gasket
60. Spring, reverse detent ball
61. Ball, reverse detent
62. Woodruff key
63. Reverse idler gear shaft
64. Bushing, reverse idler gear
65. Gear, reverse idler
66. Fork, reverse shifter
67. Reverse lever
68. Oil seal, reverse lever shaft
69. Reverse operating lever
70. Flatwasher
71. Lockwasher
72. Nut
73. Gearshift control housing
74. 1st and 2nd operating lever
75. Flatwasher
76. Lockwasher lever
77. Nut, lever
78. Lockwasher, lever
79. Flatwasher, lever
80. 3rd and OD operating lever
83. Interlock lever (2)
84. E-ring
85. Spring
86. Oil seal (2)
87. 3rd and OD lever
88. 1st and 2nd lever
89. 3rd and OD speed fork
90. 1st and 2nd speed fork
91. Drain plug
92. Gasket, shift control housing
93. Expansion plug

Exploded view Chrysler overdrive transmission (© Chrysler Corp.)

6. Install a new snapring on the shaft to hold the bearing in place. Be sure the snapring is seated and that there is minimum end play. There are several snapring thicknesses available for adjustment.

7. Place the pinion shaft in a soft jawed vise and install the roller bearings in the cavity of the shaft. Coat them with grease and install the bearing retaining snapring.

8. Install a new oil seal in the bore.

EXTENSION HOUSING BUSHING

1. Remove the yoke seal from the extension housing.

2. Drive out the old bushing and drive in a new one, aligning the oil hole in the bushing with the slot in the housing.

3. Place a new seal in the opening of the extension housing and then drive it into place.

MAINSHAFT

1. Place a stop ring flat on a bench followed by the clutch gear and sleeve, drop the struts in their slots and snap in a strut spring placing the tang inside one strut. Install the second strut spring tang in a different strut after turning the assembly over.

2. Slide the second speed gear over the mainshaft with the synchronizer cone toward the rear and down against the shoulder on the shaft.

3. Slide the first and second gear synchronizer assembly including stop rings with lugs indexed in the hub slots, over the mainshaft down against the second gear cone and hold it there with a new snapring. Slide the next snapring over the shaft and index the lugs into the clutch hub slots.

4. Slide the first speed gear with the synchronizer cone toward the clutch sleeve just installed over the mainshaft and into position against the clutch sleeve gear.

5. Install the mainshaft bearing retaining ring followed by the mainshaft rear bearing, press the bearing down into position and install a new snap ring to secure it. There are several snapring thicknesses available for minimum end play.

6. Install the partially assembled mainshaft into the extension housing far enough to engage the bearing retaining ring in the slot in the extension housing. Compress the ring with pliers so that the mainshaft ball bearing can move in and bottom against its thrust shoulder in the extension housing. Release the ring and make sure that it is seated.

7. Slide the overdrive gear over the mainshaft with the synchronizer cone toward the front followed by the gears snapring.

8. Install the third overdrive gear synchronizer clutch gear assembly on the mainshaft against the overdrive gear. Make sure to index the rear stop ring with the clutch gear struts.

9. Install the snapring and position the front stop ring over the clutch gear again lining up the ring lugs with the struts. Coat a new extension gasket with grease and place it in position.

10. Slide the reverse idler gear to the center of its shaft and move the third–overdrive synchronizer as far forward as possible without losing the struts.

11. Insert the mainshaft assembly in the case tilting it as necessary. Place the third overdrive sleeve in the neutral detent.

12. Rotate the extension on the mainshaft to expose the rear of the countershaft and install one bolt to hold it in position.

13. Install the drive pinion and bearing assembly through the front of the case and position it in the front bore. Install the outer snapring in the bearing groove and tap lightly into place. If it doesn't bottom easily, check to see if a strut, pinion roller or stop ring is out of position.

14. Turn the transmission upside down while holding the countershaft gear to prevent damage. Then lower the countershaft gear assembly into position making sure that the teeth mesh with the drive pinion gear.

15. Start the countershaft into the bore at the rear of the case and push until it is in about halfway, then install the Woodruff key and push it in until it is flush with the rear of the case.

16. Rotate the extension back to normal position and install the bolts. Turn the transmission upright and install the drive pinion bearing retainer and gasket. Coat the threads with sealing compound and tighten the attaching bolts to 30 ft. lbs.

17. Install a new expansion plug in its bore.

GEARSHIFT HOUSING AND MECHANISM

1. Install the interlock levers on the pivot pin and secure with the E-ring. Install the spring with a pair of pliers.

2. Grease and install new O-ring seals on both shift shafts. Grease the housing bores and push the shafts through.

3. Install the operating levers and tighten the retaining nuts to 18 ft. lbs. Make sure the third overdrive lever points down.

4. Rotate each shift shaft fork bore straight up and install the third overdrive shift fork in its bore and under both interlock levers.

5. Position both synchronizer sleeves in neutral and place the first and second gear shift fork in the groove of the first and second gear synchronizer sleeve. Slide the reverse idler gear to neutral. Turn the transmission on its right side and place the gearshift housing gasket in place holding it there with grease. Install the reverse detent ball and spring into the case bore.

6. As the shift housing is lowered in place, guide the third overdrive shift fork into its synchronizer groove then lead the shaft of the first and second shift lever.

7. Raise the interlock lever with a suitable tool to allow the first and second shift fork to slip under the levers. The shift housing will now seat against the case.

8. Install the bolts lightly and shift through all the gears to check for proper operation.

9. The reverse shift lever and the first and second gear shift lever have cam surfaces which mate in reverse position to lock the first and second lever, the fork and synchronizer in the neutral position.

10. To check for proper operation, put the transmission in reverse, and, while turning the input shaft, move the first and second lever in each direction. If it locks up or becomes harder to turn, select a new shift lever size with more or less clearance. If there is too little cam clearance, it will be difficult or impossible to shift into reverse.

11. Grease the reverse shaft, install the operating lever and nut, and install the speedometer drive pinion gear and adapter, making sure the range number is in the straight down position.

TORQUE SPECIFICATIONS

	ft. lbs.
Back up light switch	15
Drive pinion bearing, retainer bolts	30
Extension housing to case bolts	50
Gearshift to mounting plate	24
Gearshift mounting plate to extension	12
Shift lever nuts	18
Transmission to clutch housing bolts	50
Transmission drain plug	25

Chrysler A-412 Manual Transaxle

Gear reduction, ratio selection and differential functions are combined in a single unit. The transaxle assembly is housed in a two piece magnesium case. One piece is the transmission housing and the other piece is the clutch and differential assembly housing.

Disassembly

1. Remove the clutch push rod.
2. Remove the dirve flange dust plug. snapring, cone washer drive flange and drive flange oil seal.
3. Remove the selector shaft cover, push out the selector shaft and remove the selector shaft oil seal.
4. Remove the mainshaft bearing retaining nut rubber plugs, and remove the clutch release bearing end cover. While removing, hold the clutch release lever in upward position to avoid loading end cover and damaging case threads.
5. Remove the release bearing and the sleeve.
6. Remove the circlips from the torque shaft, and remove the clutch torque shaft, return spring and release lever.
7. Remove the mainshaft bearing retainer nuts. The three studs and clips will drop into the case.
8. Remove the case attaching bolts, the reverse idler shaft set screw and the backup light switch. Remove the transmission case, and mark the shims for installation reference.
9. Remove the reverse shift fork supports and remove the reverse shift fork.
10. Remove the mainshaft assembly and pinion shaft fourth speed gear.
11. Disassemble the mainshaft by removing the bearing and fourth speed gear, the third/fourth synchronizer and third speed gear and needle hearing.

NOTE: Synchronizers are serviced as an assembly.

12. Remove the shift rail "E" clips, and remove the shift forks assembly.
13. Remove the clutch push rod seal and bushing assembly.
14. On the pinion shaft, remove the snapring, third speed gear, and needle bearing.
15. Remove the reverse gear idler shaft.
16 Complete pinion shaft disassembly by removing the first/second gears synchronizer, the second speed gear sleeve, the first gear stop ring and the first speed gear. The inner sleeve for second speed gear and the first speed gear are removed together.

NOTE: Before installing the puller to remove the synchronizer, remove the plastic thrust bottom, and install Tool L-4443-4 or equivalent in the pinion shaft. The pinion shaft bearing retainer is notched in two places for puller jaws.

17. Remove the pinion shaft retainer and first gear thrust washer, and remove the pinion shaft.

Differential Repair

1. Remove the axle shaft circlips.
2. Remove differential bearing cone and cup. Bearing cones and cups are matched sets and must be replaced as assemblies.
3. Remove the side gears.
4. Remove the pinion shaft snapring, and drive out the pinion shaft. Pinion shaft gears and plastic thrust washer can now be removed from differential case. When installing pinion shaft be sure to align plastic thrust washer with case to avoid damaged to thrust washer holes.
5. Drill out the ring gear rivets. The new ring gear is installed with bolts and nuts.

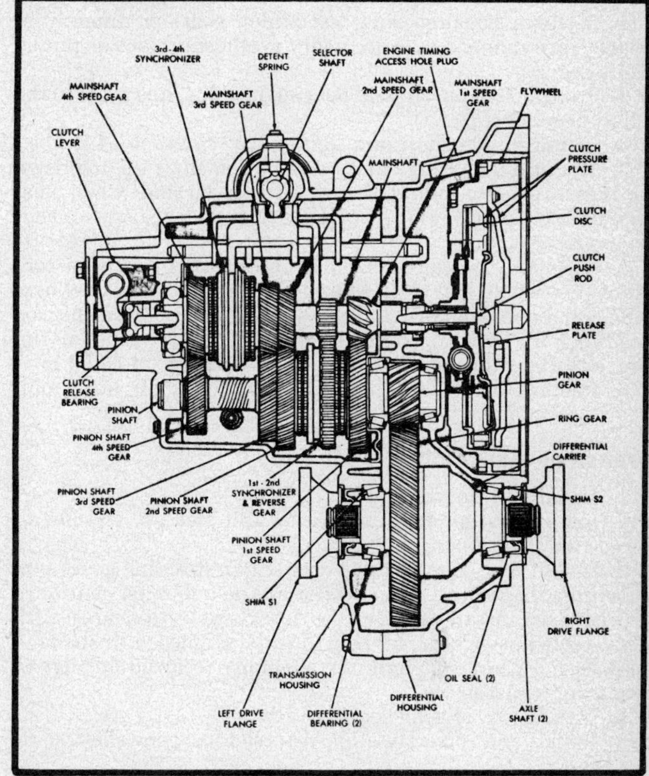

Chrysler A-412 transaxle

Differential Bearing Preload Adjusting

NOTE: Differential Bearing Preload adjustment is necessary after replacement of the transmission case, clutch housing, differential case or differential bearings.

1. Install cup of bearing (opposite ring gear) with shim S2 in clutch/differential housing. Shim S2 is always 0.039 in. thick.
2. Install outer race on ring gear side without shim S1 in transmission housing.
3. Install differential in its housing.
4. Place transmission housing in position with gasket and tighten five bolts to 14 ft. lbs.
5. Install a dial indicator, and move the differential up and down for measurement reading.

NOTE: Do not turn differential when measuring because bearings will settle and give incorrect reading.

6. Correct bearing preload is obtained by adding a constant figure 0.015 in. to measured reading. For example, measured reading plus preload is 0.035 in. the constant figure is 0.015 in. add them together and you get 0.050 which is the shim thickness.
7. Remove the transmission case, and drive out the outer bearing cup.
8. insert selected shim S1; the thickest shim first. Shims are available in sizes ranging from 0.006 in. to 0.031 in.
9. Drive in bearing cup and install transmission housing with gasket and tighten. Before installing transmission housing, remove one axle shaft to check turning torques

Checking Turning Torque

1. Lubricate bearings with transmission oil, and check for

the following turning torque, new bearings 10.4 to 21.7 inch lbs. used bearings minimum 2.7 inch lbs.

Pinion Shaft Bearing Preload Adjustment

1. If clutch housing, ring and pinion gears or differential bearing are changed, it is necessary to adjust prelaod on pinion shaft bearing.
2. Place a 0.65 mm shim in bearing housing, and press in the small bearing cup.
3. Install pinion shaft and tighten cover nuts to 14 ft. lbs.
4. Mount a dial gauge and move pinion shaft up and down for measurement reading. Do not turn pinion shaft when measuring because bearings will settle and give incorrect measurement.
5. Specified bearing prelaod is obtained by adding a constant figure 0.20 mm to measured reading and shim thickness 0.65 mm. For example, installed shim is 0.025 in. the measured reading is 0.012 in. the preload is 0.008, which is a constant figure, and the shims are available from 0.025 in. to 0.055 in.
6. Remove ball bearing retainer, pinion shaft and small bearing cup and 0.65 mm shim. Install correct shim.

Transaxle Assembly

1. Install the pinion shaft.
2. Install first gear thrust washer flat side up, and install pinion shaft retainer.
3. Install first gear and stop ring and first/second gears synchronizer. The lowest thrust collar on the hub must go toward second gear. Install the sleeve with reverse teeth nearest fifth gear. Slots in synchronizer ring must be aligned with struts in first/second gears synchronizer assembly to avoid damage to stop ring on assembly.
4. Install second gear bearing race.
5. Install and correctly align reverse idler gear shaft.
6. Install needle bearing and second speed gear.
7. Install third speed gear. Select and install a retaining snapring which wil provide 0.000 to less than 0.004 in. end play.
8. Install the mainshaft and third/fourth gears synchronizer assembly.
9. Install fourth speed gear mainshaft needle bearing and mainshaft fourth speed gear.
10. Install fourth speed gear and snapring on pinion shaft.
11. Use Tool L-4442 to correctly adjust mainshaft position to specifications.
12. Adjust mainshaft end play only if transmission case, clutch housing or mainshaft has been changed.
13. Install shift forks and "E" clips.
14. Install reverse shift fork and support brackets.
15. Use guide pins to install transmission case on clutch housing. Be sure pinion shaft is aligned with pinion shaft needle bearing in transmission case.
16. Install mainshaft bearing snapring.
17. Install reverse idler shaft bolt and install selector shaft assembly.
18. Install mainshaft bearing retainer and washer.
19. Install clutch torque shaft, return spring, release lever and circlips.
20. Install release bearing and sleeve.
21. Install the clutch release bearing end cover and mainshaft bearing retainer nut rubber plug.
22. Install selector shaft cover.
23. Install back-up light switch.
24. Install the detent plunger. Adjust the plunger as follows. Loosen lock nut. Tighten adjusting sleeve until gap can be seen between lock ring and adjusting sleeve. Loosen adjusting sleeve $1/4$ turn. Hold adjusting sleeve in this position and tighten lock nut.
25. install the clutch push rod and the selector shaft boot seal.

A-412 MANUAL TRANSAXLE TORQUE SPECIFICATIONS

Clutch Housing Case Bolt	250 in/lbs
Clutch Housing Case Stud	250 in/lbs
Release Bearing End Cover Screw	105 in/lbs
Back-up Light Switch	144 in/lbs
Electronic Timing Probe Retainer	80 in/lbs
Gearshift Selector Shaft Cover	35 ft/lbs
Gearshift Detent Body Lock Nut	175 in/lbs
Drain Plug	175 in/lbs
Fill Plug	175 in/lbs
Pinion Shaft Bearing Retainer Bolt	29 ft/lbs
Mainshaft Ball Bearing Retaining Nut	155 in/lbs
Reverse Idler Shaft Set Screw	175 in/lbs
Reverse Idler Fork Bracket—Clutch Housing Screw	105 in/lbs

Chrysler A-460 Manual Transaxle

Intermediate Shaft Assembly

The 1–2 and 3–4 shift forks and synchronizer stop rings are interchangeable. However, if parts are to be reused, reassemble then in their original position. When assembling the intermediate shaft, make sure all gears turn freely and have a minimum of 0.003 in. end play.

INPUT SHAFT

Shim thickness calculation need only be done if any of the following parts are replaced. Refer to Bearing Adjustment Procedure to determine the proper shim thickness for correct bearing preload and proper bearing turning torque.

1. Transaxle case.
2. Input shaft seal retainer.
3. Bearing retainer plate.
4. Rear end cover.
5. Input Shaft.
6. Input shaft bearings.

DIFFERENTIAL

Shim thickness calculation need only be done if any of the following parts are replaced. Refer to Bearing Adjustment Procedure to determine the proper shim thickness for correct bearing preload and proper bearing turning torque.

1. Transaxle case.
2. Differential bearing retainer.
3. Extension housing.
4. Differential case.
5. Differential bearings.

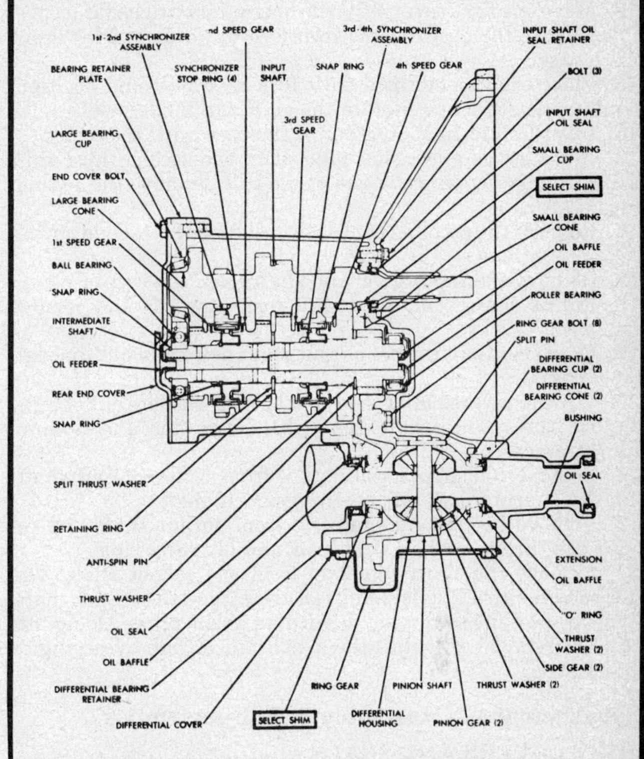

A-460 manual transaxle

BEARING ADJUSTMENT PROCEDURE

1. Take extreme care when removing and installing bearing cups and cones. Use only an arbor press for instllation, as a hammer may not properly align the bearing cup or cone. Burrs or nicks on the bearing seat will give a false end play reading while gauging for proper shims. Improperly seated bearings cups and cones are subject to low mileage failure.
2. Bearing cups and cones should be replaced if they show signs of pitting or heat distress. If distress is seen on either the cup or bearing rollers, both cup and cone must be replaced.
3. Bearing end play and drag torque specifications must be maintained to avoid premature bearing failures. Used (original) bearing may lose up to 50% of the original drag torque after break in.

NOTE: All bearing adjustments must be made with no other component interference or gear mesh.

4. Replace bearings as a pair. for example, if one differential bearing is defective, replace both differential bearings. If one input shaft bearing is defective, replace both input shaft bearings.
5. Bearing cones must be reused if removed.
6. Turning torque readings should be obtained while smoothly rotating in either direction (breakaway reading is not indicative of the true turning torque).

Ford 3.03 Three Speed Transmission

The Ford 3.03 is a fully synchronized three speed transmission. All gears except reverse are in constant mesh. Forward speed gear changes are accomplished with synchronizer sleeves.

Disassembly

1. Drain the lubricant by removing the lower extension housing bolt.
2. Remove the case cover and gasket.
3. Remove the long spring that holds the detent plug in the case and remove the detent plug with a small magnet.
4. Remove the extension housing and gasket.
5. Remove the front bearing retainer and gasket.
6. Remove the filler plug on the right side of the transmission case. Working through the plug opening, drive the roll pin out of the case and countershaft with a $\frac{1}{4}$ inch punch.
7. Hold the countershaft gear with a hook. Install dummy shaft and push the countershaft out of the rear of the case. As the countershaft comes out, lower the gear cluster to the bottom of the case. Remove the countershaft.
8. Remove the snapring that holds the speedometer drive gear on the output shaft. Slip the gear off the shaft and remove the gear lock ball.
9. Remove the snapring that holds the output shaft bearing. Using a special bearing puller, remove the output shaft bearing.

10. Place both shift levers in the neutral (center) position.
11. Remove the set screw that holds the first/reverse shift fork to the shift rail. Slip the first/reverse shift rail out through the rear of the case.
12. Move the first/reverse synchronizer forward as far as possible. Rotate the first/reverse shift fork upwards and lift it out of the case.
13. Place the second/third shift fork in the second position. Remove the set screw. Rotate the shift rail 90 degrees.
14. Lift the interlock plug out of the case with a magnet.
15. Remove the expansion plug from the second/third shift rail by lightly tapping the end of the rail. Remove the second/third shift rail.
16. Remove the second/third shift rail detent plug and spring from detent bore.
17. Remove the input gear and shaft from the case.
18. Rotate the second/third shift fork upwards and remove from case.
19. Using caution, lift the output shaft assembly out through top of case.
20. Lift the reverse idler gear and thrust washers out of case. Remove the countershaft gear, thrust washer and dummy shaft from case.
21. Remove the snapring from the front of the output shaft. Slip the synchronizer and second gear off shaft.
22. Remove the second snapring from output shaft and remove the thrust washer, first gear and blocking ring.
23. Remove the third snapring from the output shaft. The first/re-verse synchronizer hub is a press fit on the output shaft. Remove the synchronizer hub with an arbor press. Do not attempt to remove or install the synchronizer hub by prying or hammering.

Disassembly and Assembly of Sub-Assemblies

SHIFT LEVERS AND SEALS

1. Remove shift levers from the shafts. Slip the levers out of case. Discard shaft sealing O-rings.
2. Lubricate and install new O-rings on shift shafts.
3. Install the shift shafts in the case and secure shift levers.

INPUT SHAFT BEARINGS

1. Remove the snapring securing the input shaft bearing. Using an arbor press, remove the bearing..
2. Press the input shaft bearing onto shaft using correct tool.

SYNCHRONIZERS

1. Scribe alignment marks on synchronizer hubs before disassembly. Remove each synchronizer hub from the synchronizer sleeves.
2. Separate the inserts and insert springs from the hubs. Do not mix parts from the separate synchronizer assemblies.
3. Install the insert spring in the hub of the first/reverse synchronizer. Be sure that the spring covers all the insert grooves. Start the hub on the sleeve making certain that the scribed marks are properly aligned. Place the three inserts in the hub, small ends on the inside. Slide the sleeve and reverse gear onto hub.
4. Install one insert spring into a groove on the second/third synchronizer hub. Be sure that all three insert slots are covered. Align the scribed marks on the hub and sleeve and start the hub into the sleeve. Position the three inserts on the top of the retaining spring and push the assembly together. Install the remaining retainer spring so that the spring ends cover the same slots as the first spring. Do not stagger the springs. Place a synchronizer blocking ring on the ends of the synchronizer sleeve.

COUNTERSHAFT GEAR BEARINGS

1. Remove the dummy shaft, needle bearings and bearing retainers from the countershaft gear.
2. Coat the bore in each end of the countershaft gear with grease.
3. Hold the dummy shaft in the gear and install the needle bearings in the case.
4. Place the countershaft gear, dummy shaft, and needle bearings in the case.
5. Place the case in a vertical position. Align the gear bore and the thrust washers with the bores in the case and install the countershaft.
6. Place the case in a horizontal position. Check the countershaft gear end play with a feeler gauge. Clearance should be between 0.004 in. to 0.018 in. If clearance does not come within specifications, replace the thrust washers.
7. Install the dummy shaft in the countershaft gear and leave the gear at the bottom of the transmission case.

Assembly

1. Cover the reverse idler gear thrust surfaces in the case with a thin film of lubricant, and install the two thrust washers in the case.
2. Install the reverse idler gear and shaft in the case. Align the case bore and thrust washers with gear bore and install the reverse idler shaft.
3. Measure the reverse idler gear end play with a feeler

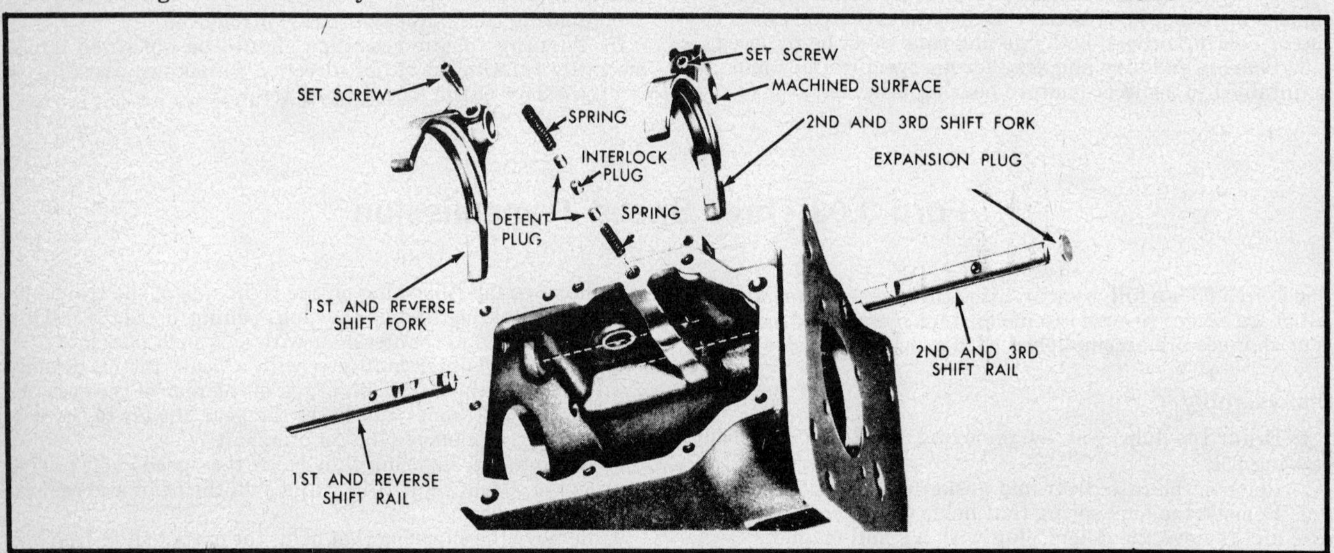

Exploded view Ford 3.03 shift rails and forks (© Ford Motor Co.)

Rotating second/third shift rail—Ford 3.03 transmission (© Ford Motor Co.)

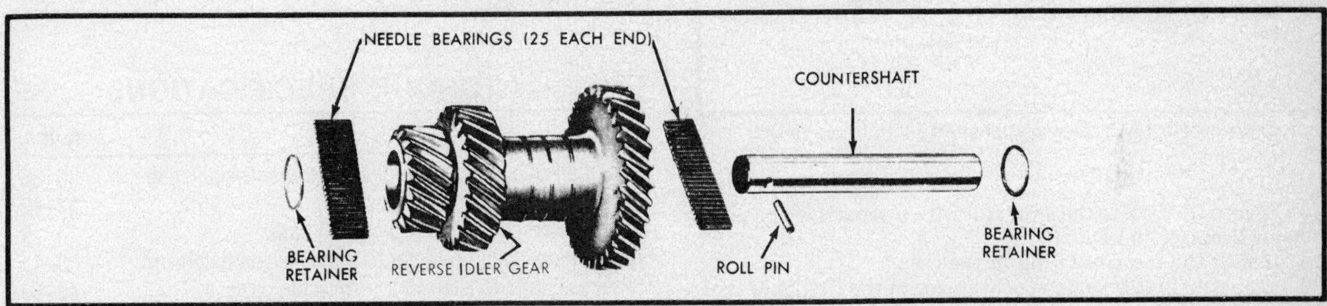

Exploded view Ford 3.03 countergear (© Ford Motor Co.)

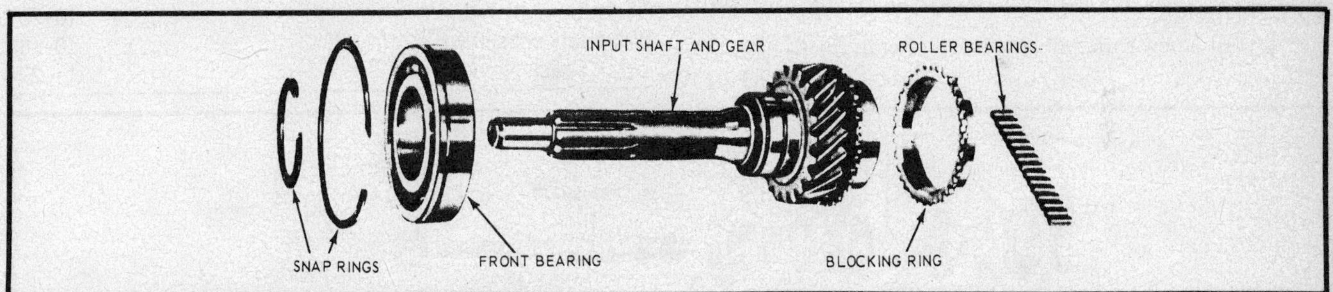

Exploded view Ford 3.03 input shaft gear (© Ford Motor Co.)

gauge, clearance should be between 0.004 in. to 0.018 in. If end play is not within specifications, replace the thrust washers. If clearance is correct, leave the reverse idler gear in case.

4. Lubricate the output shaft splines and machined surfaces with transmission oil.

5. The first/reverse synchronizer hub is a press fit on the output shaft. Hub must be installed in an arbor press. Install the synchronizer hub with the teeth-end of the gear facing towards the rear of the shaft. Do not attempt to install the first/reverse synchronizer with a hammer.

6. Place the blocking ring on the tapered surface of the first gear.

7. Slide the first gear on the output shaft with the blocking ring toward the rear of the shaft. Rotate the gear as necessary to engage the three notches in the blocking ring with the synchronizer inserts. Install the thrust washer and snapring.

8. Slide the blocking ring onto the tapered surface of the second gear. Slide the second gear with blocking ring and the second/third synchronizer on the mainshaft. Be sure that the tapered surface of second gear is facing the front of the shaft and that the notches in the blocking ring engage the synchronizer inserts. Install the snapring and secure assembly.

9. Cover the core of the input shaft with a thin coat of grease. A thick film of grease will plug lubricant holes and cause damage to bearings.

10. Install the input shaft through the front of the case and insert snapring in the bearing groove.

11. Install the output shaft assembly in the case. Position the second/third shift fork on the second/third synchronizer.

12. Place a detent plug spring and a plug in the case. Place the second–third synchronizer in the second gear position (toward the rear of the case). Align the fork and install the second/third shift rail. It will be necessary to depress the detent plug to install the shift rail in the bore. Move the rail forward until the detent plug enters the forward notch (second gear).

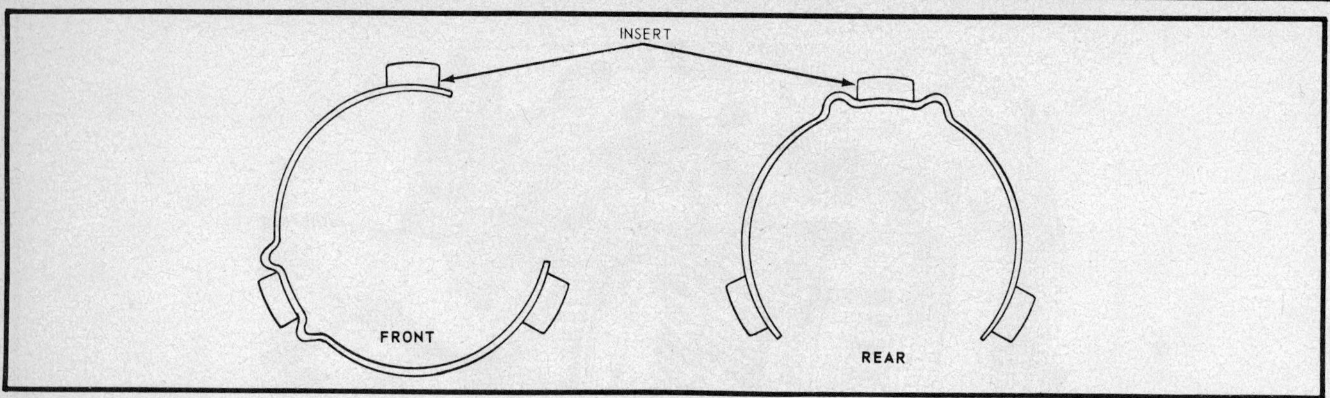

First/reverse synchronizer insert spring installation Ford 3.03 (© Ford Motor Co.)

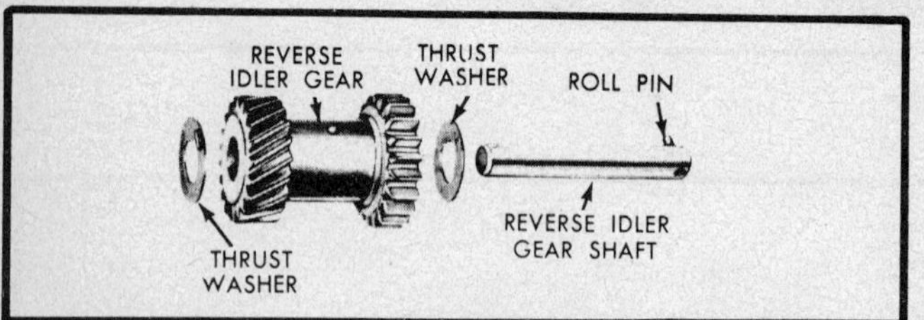

Exploded view Ford 3.03 reverse idler shaft (© Ford Motor Co.)

13. Secure the fork to the shift rail with a set screw and place the synchronizer in neutral.

14. Install the interlock plug in the case.

15. Place the first/reverse synchronizer in the first gear position (towards the front of the case). Place the shift fork in the groove of the synchronizer. Rotate the fork into position and install the shift rail. Move the shift rail inward until the center notch (neutral) is aligned with the detent bore. Secure shift fork with set screw.

16. Install a new shift rail expansion plug in the front of the case.

Lubricant Refill Capacity

	U.S. Pints	Imp. Pints
Ford Type 3.03	3.5	3.0

TORQUE SPECIFICATIONS

	ft. lbs.
Input shaft gear bearing retainer to transmission case	30–36
Transmission to flywheel housing	37–42
Transmission cover to transmission case	14–19
Speedometer cable retainer to transmission extension	3–4.5
Transmission extension to transmission case	42–50
Flywheel housing to engine	40–50
Gear shift lever to cam and shaft assembly lock nuts	18–23
U-Joint flange to output shaft	60–80
Filler plug	10–20
Shifter fork set screws	10–18
T.R.S. switch to case	15–20

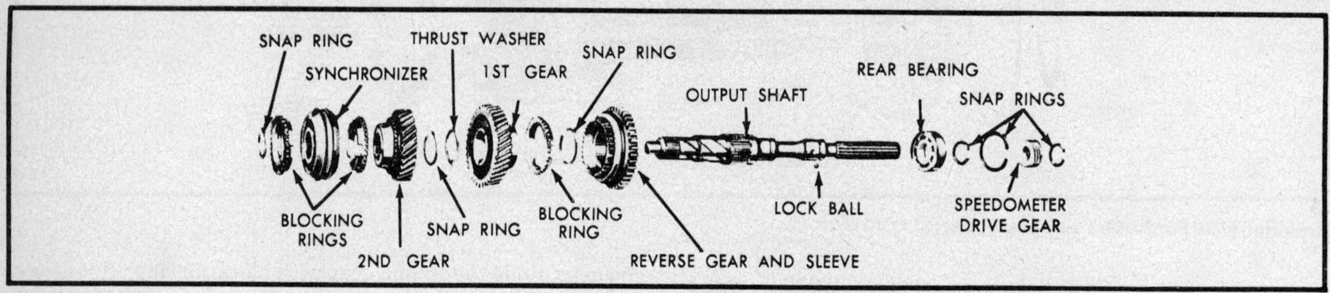

Exploded view Ford 3.03 output shaft (© Ford Motor Co.)

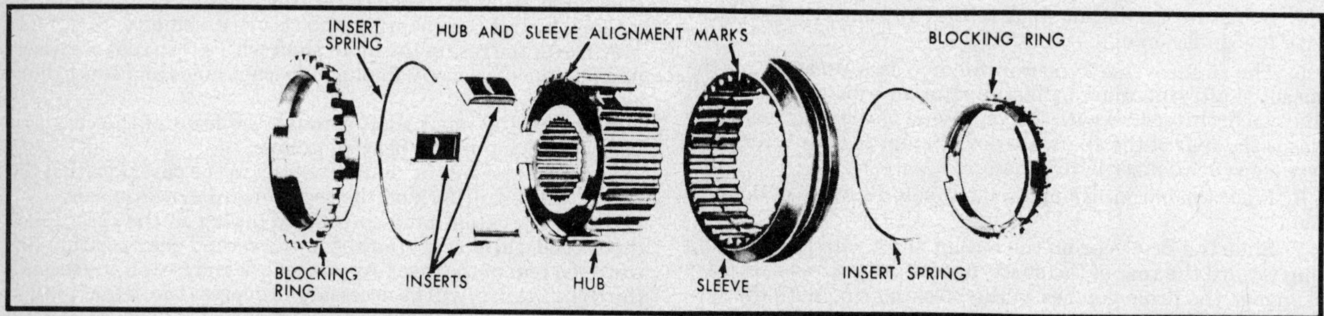

Exploded view Ford 3.03 second/third synchronizer (© Ford Motor Co.)

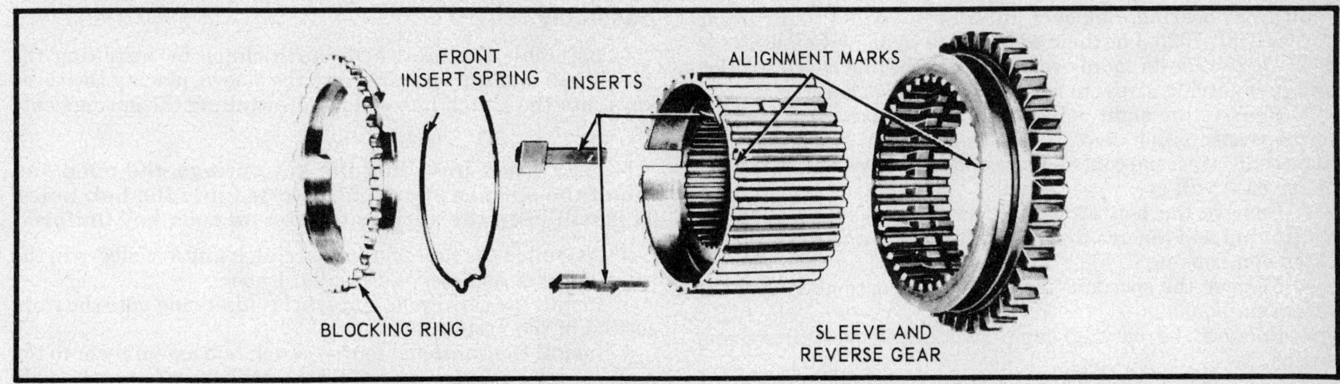

Exploded view Ford 3.03 first/reverse synchronizer (© Ford Motor Co.)

17. Hold the input shaft and blocking ring in position and move the output shaft forward to seat the pilot in the roller bearings on the input gear.
18. Tap the input gear bearing into place while holding the output shaft. Install the front bearing retainer and gasket. Torque attaching bolts to specifications.
19. Install the large snapring on the rear bearing. Place the bearing on the output shaft with the snapring end toward the rear of the shaft. Press the bearing into place using a special tool. Secure the bearing to the shaft with the snapring.
20. Hold the speedometer drive gear lock ball in the detent and slide the speedometer drive gear into position. Secure with snapring.
21. Place the transmission in the vertical position. Using a suitable tool insert it through the drain hole in the bottom of the case, align the bore of the countershaft gear and the thrust washer with the bore in the case.
22. Working from the rear of the case, push the dummy shaft out of the countershaft gear with the countershaft. Align the roll pin hole in the countershaft with the matching hole in the case. Drive the shaft into place and install the roll pin.
23. Position the new extension housing gasket on the case with sealer. Install the extension housing and torque to specification.
24. Place the transmission in gear and pour gear oil over entire gear train while rotating the input shaft.
25. Install the remaining detent plug and long spring in case.
26. Position cover gasket on case with sealer and install cover. Torque cover bolts to specifications.
27. Check operation of transmission in all gear positions.

Ford Four Speed Transmission (Diesel Engines)

Disassembly

1. If not already drained, remove the drain plug and drain the transmission fluid into a suitable container. Remove the fork and release bearing from the clutch housing.
2. Install transmission in Holding Fixture T57L-500-B. Remove six bolts attaching the front cover to the transmission case and remove the front cover shim and gasket.
3. Remove front cover oil seal.
4. Remove the input shaft snapring.
5. Remove outer snapring on input shaft bearing. Install Bearing Collet tool T75L-7025-E or its equal on main input

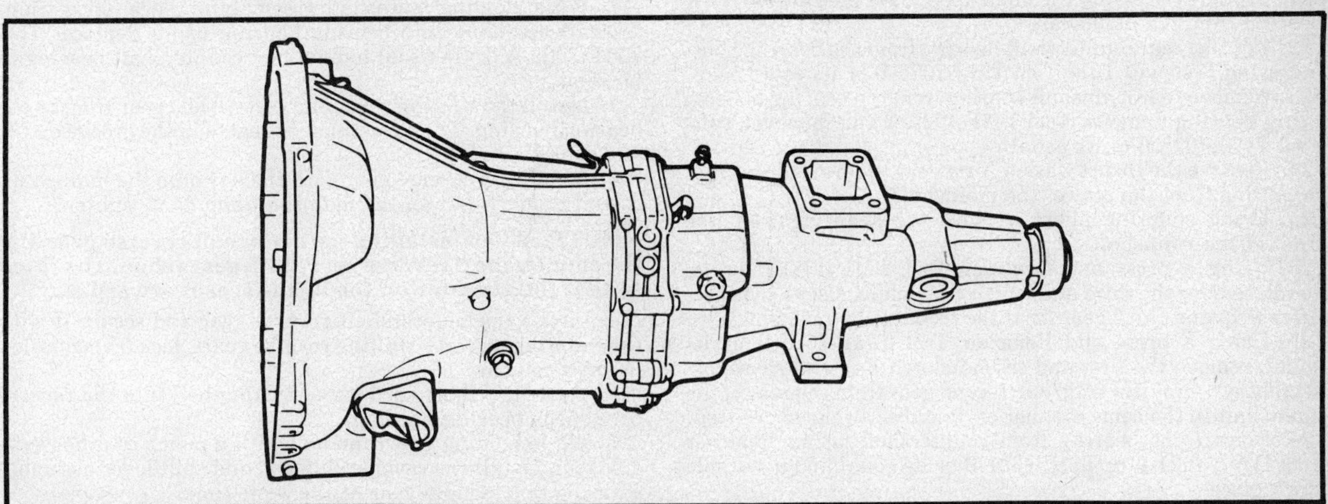

Four speed manual (diesel engine)

shaft front bearing, Remover Tube T75L-7025-B and Forcing Screw T75L-7025-J or their equal. slide Bearing Collet Sleeve T75L-7025-G or its equal over remover tube and bearing collet, and turn forcing screw to remove input shaft bearing.

6. Remove the eight bolts attaching the extension housing to the transmission case., Slide the extension housing off the mainshaft, with the control lever end laid down and to the left as far as it will go.

7. Remove the bolt attaching the control lever end to the control rod and remove the control lever end and rod from the extension housing.

8. Remove the speedometer driven gear assembly from the extension housing.

9. Remove the back-up lamp switch and neutral sensing switch.

10. Remove the snapring that secures the speedometer drive gear on the mainshaft. Slide the speedometer drive gear off the mainshaft and remove the lock ball.

11. Install Bearing Pusher Tool T83T-7111-A or its equal over countershaft front bearing. Turn forcing screw to force countershaft, together with the countershaft front bearing, from the transmission housing.

12. Slide Bearing Holder and Gear Shaft Assembly from the transmission housing.

13. Remove three spring cap bolts, three springs and shift locking balls. The reverse spring is shortest. The lower ball is spring loaded, and will pop out.

14. Remove the reverse shift rod and shift fork assembly and reverse gear from the bearing housing.

15. Remove roll pins fixing shift forks to the rods. Push each of the shift rods rearward through the fork and bearing housing and remove the shift rods and forks.

NOTE: Mark 3rd–4th and 1st–2nd shift forks before removal to simplify installation.

16. Remove the lower reverse shift rod locking ball and spring, and the interlock pins from the bearing housing.

17. Straighten the tab of the lockwasher. Lock transmission synchronizers into any two gears and remove the mainshaft lock nut using Adapter Tool T83T-7025-A and Tool Shaft T77J-7025-C or its equal.

18. Remove the snapring from the rear end of the countershaft and slide off the counter reverse gear.

19. Remove the five bearing cover bolts and cover, and the reverse idler gear shaft from the bearing housing.

20. With a soft hammer, tap the rear end of the mainshaft and countershaft in turn, being careful not to damage the shafts, and remove these shafts from the bearing housing.

21. Carefully separate the input shaft and caged needle roller bearing from the mainshaft.

22. Remove rear countershaft bearing from the bearing housing using Remover Tube Tool T77J-7025-B or its equal.

23. Remove rear mainshaft bearing from the bearing housing using Bearing Remover Tool T77F-4222-A and Remover Tube Tool T77J-7025-B or its equal.

24. Remove the thrust washer, first gear, sleeve and synchronizer ring from the rear of the mainshaft.

25. Using snapring pliers, remove the snapring from the front of the mainshaft.

26. Using a press and Remover Tool T71P-4621-B or its equal, remove the third and fourth clutch hub, sleeve, synchronizer ring and third gear from the front of the mainshaft.

27. Using a press and Remover Tool T71P-4621-B or its equal, remove the first and second clutch hub and sleeve assembly synchronizer ring, and second gear from the rear of the mainshaft in the same manner as described in the above step.

28. Press front bearing from countershaft using Remover Tool D79L-4621-A or T71P-4621-B or its equal and a suitable stock piece.

29. Perform cleaning and inspection procedures described in a separate section of this manual.

Assembly

1. Assemble the third and fourth clutch by installing the clutch hub and synchronizer into the sleeve, placing the three keys into the clutch hub slots and installing the springs onto the hub.

NOTE: When installing the key springs, the open end tab of the springs should be inserted into the hub holes. This will keep the springs tension on each key uniform

2. Assemble the first and second clutch hub and sleeve in the same manner as described in Step 1 above.

3. Install the third gear and synchronizer ring onto the front section of the mainshaft.

4. Install the third and fourth clutch hub assembly onto the mainshaft by using a press. Hold assembly together and slowly press into place.

5. Fit the snapring on the mainshaft.

6. Install the second gear, synchronizer ring onto the rear section of the mainshaft.

7. Install the first and second clutch hub assembly onto the mainhshaft by using a press.

8. Install the synchronizer ring, first gear with sleeve, and thrust washer onto the mainshaft.

9. Install the input shaft and the needle roller bearing to the mainshaft.

10. Check the countershaft rear bearing clearance. Measure the depth of the countershaft bearing bore in the bearing housing using a depth micrometer (D80P-4201-A or Equivalent). Then, measure the countershaft bearing height. The difference between the two measurements, indicates the required thickness of the adjusting shim. The clearance should be less than 0.0039 in. The adjusting shims are available in the following thickness, 0.0039 in. and 0.0118 in.

11. Check the mainshaft bearing clearance in the same manner as for the countershaft rear bearing clearance. The clearance should be less than 0.0039 in. The adjusting shims are available in the following thickness, 0.0039 in and 0.0118 in.

12. Position proper shim on countershaft rear bearing and press into bearing housing using Installer Tool T77J-7025-B.

13. Position proper shim on mainshaft bearing and press into bearing housing using Insttaller Tool T77J-7025-K or its equal.

14. Position front bearing on countershaft and press into place using Bearing Repalcer Tool T71P-7025-A or its equal.

15. Mesh counter shaft and mainshaft assembly and positon the two on the bearnig housing. Make certain that thrust washer is installed on mainshaft assembly at the rear of the first gear.

16. While holding mainshaft assembly in place, press countershaft assembly into bearing housing using Replacer Tool T71P-7025-A or its equal to hold rear countershaft bearing in housing.

17. Install the bearing cover and reverse idle gear shaft to the bearing housing. The cover must be seated in the groove on the idle gear shaft.

18. Install the reverse gear with the key onto the mainshaft. Install the lock nut on the mainshaft and hand tighten.

NOTE: When installing the mainshaft reverse gear and the countershaft reverse gear, both gears should be fitted so that the chamfer on the teeth faces rearward.

19. Install the countershaft reverse gear and secure it with the snapring. After installing reverse gears, lock transmission in any two gears.

20. Insert the short spring and locking ball into the reverse bore of the bearing housing.

21. While holding down the ball with a punch or other suitable tool, install the reverse shift rod and shift lever assembly with the reverse idle gear at the same time.

22. Using the dummy shift rails (Tool Number T72J-7280 or its equal), install each shift fork rod and interlock pins.

23. Install the first and second shift fork and third and fourth shift fork to their respective clutch sleeves.
24. Align the roll pin holes of each shift fork and rod. Install the new roll pins.

NOTE: When assembling the shift fork and control end, a new roll pin should be installed with a pin slit positioned in the direction of the shift rod axis.

25. Install the shift locking balls and springs into their respective positions and install the spring cap bolt. The short spring and ball are installed in the reverse bore.
26. Apply a thin coat of Silicone Sealer D6AZ-19562-B, or equivalent, on both contacting surfaces of the bearing housing.
27. Install the bearing housing assembly to the transmission case.
28. Temporarily attach the bearing housing to the transmission with two top and two bottom bolts and tighten the extension housing mounting bolts to position the countershaft front bearing in the bore.

NOTE: If necessary, remove plugs from bell housing shift rod bores to align shift rods. After installation of bearing housing assembly is complete, reinstall plugs using a silicone sealer (D6AZ-19562-B or equivalent).

29. Tighten the mainshaft locknut 116 to 174 ft. lbs. using Adapter T83T-7025-A and Tool Shaft T77J-7025-C or equivalent.
30. Bend a tab on the lockwasher using Staking Tool T77J-7025-F or equivalent.
31. Install the speedometer drive gear with the lock ball onto the mainshaft and secure it with a snapring.
32. With the outer snapring in place on the main driveshaft front bearing, place bearing, shim 38917-2S, and Adapter Tool T75L-7025-N or equivalent over the input shaft.
33. Thread the Replacer Shaft T75L-7025-K or equal onto the Adapter Tool. Install the Replacer Tube T75L-7025-B or equal over the Replacer shaft and install the nut and washer on the forcing screw.
34. Slowly tighten the nut until the adapter is secure on the input shaft. Make certain that all tools are aligned.
35. Tighten the nut on the forcing screw until the bearing outer snapring is seating against the housing. Remove the installation tools.
36. Install the input shaft snapring.
37. Install the speedometer driven gear assembly to the extension housing and attach with the bolt and lock plate.
38. Insert the shift control lever through the holes from the front side of the extension housing.
39. Install the control lever end to the control lever and tighten the attaching bolt 20–25 ft. lbs.
40. Install the back-up lamp switch and neutral sensing switch to the extension housing and tighten the switches 20–25 ft. lbs.
41. Remove the bolts installed previously to temporarily hold the bearing housing.
42. Apply a thin coat of Silicone Sealer D6AZ-19562-B or equivalent on the contacting surface of the bearing housing and extension housing.
43. Install the extension housing to the bearing housing with the control lever and laid down to the left as far as it will go. Tighten the eight attaching bolts. Check to ensure that the control rod operates properly.

Ford Four Speed Transmission (Gasoline Engines)

Disassembly

1. Remove the nuts attaching the bell housing to the transmission case. Remove the bell housing and gasket.
2. Remove the drain plug and drain lubricant from the transmission. Clean the metal filings from the magnet of the drain plug (if necessary). Install the drain plug.
3. Place transmission in neutral.
4. Remove the four bolts attaching the gearshift lever retainer to the extension housing. Remove the gearshift lever retainer and gasket.
5. Remove the six bolts attaching the extension housing to the transmission case.
6. Raise the control lever to the left and slide toward the rear of the transmission. Slide the extension housing off the mainshaft, being careful not to damaged the oil seal.
7. If required, remove the bolt attaching the gearshift control lower end to the gearshift control lever, and remove the control lever end and control lever.
8. If required, remove the back-up lamp switch from the extension housing.
9. Remove the anti spill seal from the output shaft and discard (a seal is not necessary for assembly).
10. Remove the snapring that secures the speedometer drive gear to the mainshaft. Slide the drive gear off the mainshaft, and remove the lock ball.
11. Evenly loosen the fourteen bolts securing the transmission case cover to the transmission case and remove the cover and gasket.
12. Remove the three spring cap bolts the detent springs and the detent balls with a magnet from the transmission case.

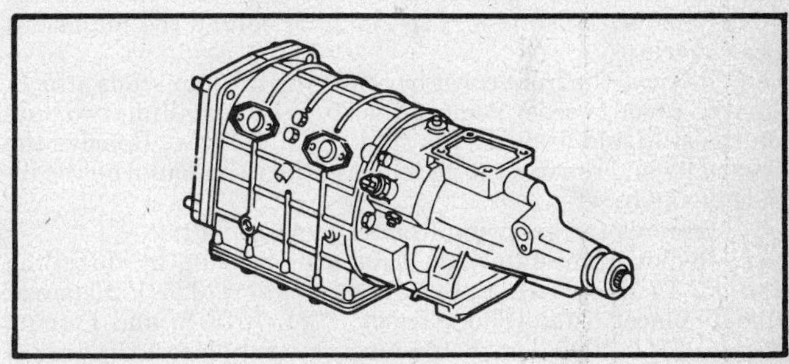

Four speed manual (Gasoline engine)

13. Remove the four bolts attaching the blind covers to the transmission case and remove the blind covers and gaskets.
14. Slide the reverse shift fork shaft assembly and reverse idler gear out of the transmission case.
15. Shift the transmission into fourth gear. This will provide adequate space to drive out the roll pin. With a small drift, drive the roll pin from third and fourth fork assembly. Slide the third and fourth shift fork shaft out of the rear of the transmission case.
16. Remove the roll pin from the first and second shift fork. Slide the first and second shift fork shaft assembly out the rear of the transmission case. Remove both interlock pins.
17. Reinstall the reverse idler gear to lock the gears. Install the Synchronizer Ring Holder and countershaft Spacer (T77J-7025-E) or its equal between the fourth speed synchronizer ring and synchromesh gear on the mainshaft. Shift the trans-

mission gear into second gear to lock the mainshaft and prevent the assembly from rotating.

18. Straighten the bent portion of the lockwasher with a chisel.

19. Remove the locknut and washer using Locknut Wrench Adapter T82T-7003-CH and Locknut Wrench, T77J-7025-C or their equal. Slide the reverse/idler gear off the mainshaft.

20. Remove the key from the mainshaft.

21. Remove the reverse idler gear.

22. Remove the snapring from the rear end of the countershaft. Slide the countershaft reverse gear off the countershaft.

23. Remove the four bearing retainer attaching bolts.

24. Remove the baring retainer together with the reverse idler gear shaft.

25. To remove the countershaft rear bearing, install Puller, T77J-7025-H; Puller Rings, T77J-7025-J; Remover Tube, T77J-7025-B; and Forcing Screw, T75L-7025-J or their equal. Squarely insert the jaws of the puller behind the front bearing retainer ring in the two recessed areas of the case.

NOTE: The retainer ring may need to be turned to position the split in the retainer ring midway between the recessed area, before the puller is installed. This will reduce the possibility of the retainer ring becoming distorted as the bearing is removed.

26. Turn the forcing screw clockwise to remove the bearing.

27. To remove the mainshaft rear bearing, install Puller T77J-7025-H; Puller Rings, T77J-7025-J; Remover and Replacer Tube (Long Tube), T75L-7025-C and Forcing Screw, T75L-7025-J or their equal. Squarely insert the jaws of the puller behind the rear mainshaft bearing retainer ring in the two recessed areas of the case.

NOTE: The retainer ring may need to be turned to position the split in the ring midway between the recessed areas before the puller is installed. This will reduce the possibility of the retainer ring becoming distorted as the bearing is removed.

28. Turn the forcing screw clockwise to remove the bearing.

29. Remove the shim and spacer from behind the mainshaft rear bearing.

30. Remove the front cover by removing the four studs attaching the cover to case. Remove the studs by installing two nuts on the stud and drawing the stud out of the case. Remove the four bolts and remove the cover. Save the shim found on the inside of the cover.

31. Remove the snapring from the input shaft.

32. Remove the mainshaft drive gear bearing by installing Puller, T77J-7025-H; Puller Rings, T77J=7025-J; Remover and Replacer Tube (Short Tube), T75L-7025-B; and Forcing Screw, T75L-7025-J or their equal. Squarely insert the jaws of the puller behind the mainshaft drive gear bearing retainer ring in the two recessed areas of the case.

NOTE: The retainer ring may need to be turned to position the split in the ring midway between the recessed areas before the puller is installed. This will reduce the possibility of the retainer ring becoming distorted as the bearing is removed.

33. Turn the forcing screw clockwise to remove the bearing.

34. Rotate both shift forks so that the main gear train will fall to the bottom of the case. Remove the shift forks. Rotate the input shaft so that one of the two flats on the input shaft face upward.

35. Insert Synchronizer Ring Holder and Countershaft Spacer, T77J-7025-E or its equal between the first gear on the countershaft and the rear of the case.

36. Remove the snapring from the front of the countershaft.

37. Install Forcing Screw, T75L-7025-J; Press Frame, T77J-7025-N; and Press Frame Adapter, T82T-7003-BH or their equal against the countershaft assembly.

38. Turn the forcing screw clockwise to press the countershaft rearward. Press the countershaft (3/16 inch movement) until it contacts the Synchronizer Ring Holder and Countershaft Spacer.

39. To remove the countershaft front bearing, install Puller, T77J-7025-H; Puller Rings, T77J-7025-J; Remover Tube, T77J-7025-B; and Forcing Screw, T75L-7025-J or their equal. Squarely insert the jaws of the puller behind the front bearing retainer ring in the two recessed areas of the case.

NOTE: The retainer ring may need to be turned to position the split in the ring midway between the recessed areas, before the puller is installed. This will reduce the possibility of the retainer ring becoming distorted as the bearing is removed.

40. Turn the forcing screw clockwise to remove the bearing.

41. Remove the shim from behind the countershaft front bearing.

42. Remove the input shaft from the transmission case. Remove the synchronizer ring and caged bearing from the main driveshaft.

43. Remove the countershaft from the transmission case.

44. Remove the inner race of the countershaft center bearing from the countershaft in a press frame using Axle Bearing Seal Plate, T75L-1165-B and Pinion Bearing Cone Remover, D79L-4621-A or their equal.

45. Remove the mainshaft and gear assembly from the transmission case.

46. Remove the snapring from the front of the mainshaft.

47. Slide the third/fourth clutch hub and sleeve assembly, the third synchronizer ring, and third gear off of the front of the mainshaft. Do not mix the synchronizer rings.

48. Slide the thrust washer, first gear, and gear sleeve off the rear mainshaft. Press the bushing from the first gear using a press and suitable presssing stock.

49. Remove the first and second clutch hub and sleeve assembly from the mainshaft.

50. Clean and inspect transmission case, gears, bearings, and shafts

Assembly

Before beginning the assembly procedure, three measurements must be performed: Mainshaft Thrust Play, Countershaft Thurst Play and Mainshaft Bearing clearance.

Mainshaft Thrust Play

Check the mainshaft thrust play by measuring the depth of the mainshaft bearing bore in the transmission rear cage by using a depth micrometer (D80P-4201-A) or its equal. Then measure the mainshaft rear bearing height. The difference between the two measurements indicates the required thickness of the adjusting shim. The standard thrust play is 0–0.0039 in. Adjusting shims are available in 0.0039 in. and 0.0118 in.

Countershaft Thrust Play

Check the countershaft thrust play by measuring the depthmicrometer (D80P-4201-A) or its equal. Then measure the countershaft front bearing height. The difference between the two measurements indicates the required thickness of the adjusting shims. The standard thrust play is 0–0.0039 in. Adjusting shims are available in 0.0039 in. and 0.0118 in. sizes.

Mainshaft Bearing Clearance

Check the main driveshaft bearing clearance by measuring the depth of the bearing bore in the clutch adapter plate with a depth micrometer, D80P-4201-A or its equal. Make sure the micrometer is on the second step of the plate. Measure the bearing height. The difference between the two measurements indicates the required adjusting shim thickness. The standard clearance is 0 to 0.0039 in. If an adjusting shim is required, select one to bring the clearance to within specifications.

1. Assemble the first and second synchromesh mechanism by installing the clutch hub to the sleeve, placing the three synchronizer keys into the clutch hub key slots and installing the key springs to the clutch hub.

NOTE: When installing the Key springs, the open end tab of the springs should be inserted into the hub holes with the springs turned in the same direction. This will keep the spring tension on each key uniform.

2. Assemble the third and fourth synchromesh mechanisms in the same manner as first and second synchromesh mechanism.
3. Place the synchronizer ring on the third gear to the front of the mainshaft with the synchronizer ring toward the front.
4. Slide the third and fourth clutch hub and sleeve assembly to the front of the mainshaft, making sure that the three synchronizer keys in the synchromesh mechanism engage the notches in the synchronizer ring. Note the proper direction of the third and fourth clutch hub and sleeve assembly.
5. Install the snapring to the front of the mainshaft.
6. Place the synchronizer ring on the second gear and slide the second gear to the mainshaft with the synchronizer ring toward the rear of the shaft.
7. Slide the first and second clutch hub and sleeve assembly to the mainshaft with the oil grooves of the clutch hub toward the front of the mainshaft. Make sure that the three synchronizer keys in the synchromesh mechanism engage the notches in the second synchronizer ring.
8. Insert the first gear sleeve in the mainshaft.
9. Press the bushing in the first gear using a press and suitable press stock.
10. Place the synchronizer ring on the first gear and slide the first gear onto the mainshaft with the synchronizer ring facing the front of the shaft. Rotate the first gear as necessary to engage the three notches in the synchronizer ring with the synchronizer keys.
11. Install the original thrust washer on the mainshaft.
12. Position the mainshaft and gears assembly in the case.
13. Position the caged bearing in the front end of the mainshaft.
14. Place the synchronizer ring on the input shaft (fourth gear), and install the input shaft to the front end of the mainshaft, making sure that the three synchronizer keys in the third and fourth synchromesh mechanism engage the notches in the synchronizer ring.
15. Position the first and second shift fork and third-and fourth shift fork in the groove of the clutch hub and sleeve assembly.
16. Press the inner race of the countershaft rear bearing onto the countershaft using Center Bearing Replacer, T77J-7025-K or its equal.
17. Position the countershaft gear in the case, making sure that the countershaft gear engages each gear of the mainshaft assembly.
18. Install the correct shim in the mainshaft rear bearing bore as determined in the Mainshaft Thrust Play Measurement.
19. Position the main drive gear bearing and the mainshaft rear bearing into the proper bearing bores. Be sure the synchronizer and shifter forks have not been moved out of position.
20. Install the Dummy Bearing Replacer, T75L-7025-Q; Mainshaft Front Bearing Replacer, T82T-7003-DH; Replacer Tube, T77J-7025-M; Press Frame Adapter, T82T-7003-BH; and Press Frame, T77J-7025-N or their equal on the case. Position the Synchronizer Ring Holder and Countershaft Spacer, T77J-7025-E or their equal between the mainshaft drive gear and synchronizer ring. Turn the forcing screw on the press frame until both bearings are properly seated.
21. Install the main drive gear bearing snapring.

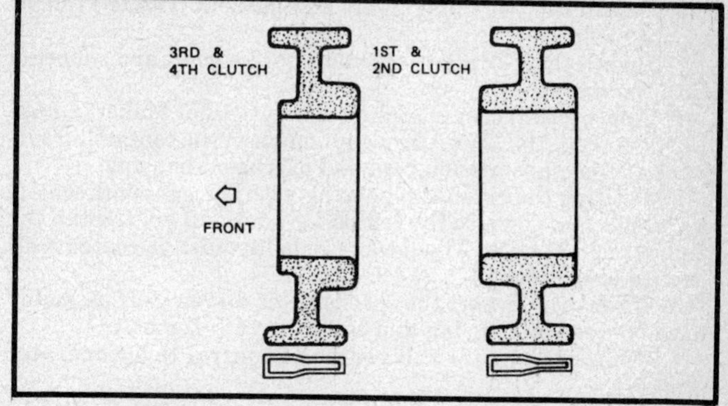

Clutch hub assembly direction)

22. Place the correct shim in the countershaft front bearing bore as determined by the Countershaft Thrust Play Mesurement.
23. Position the countershaft front and rear bearings in the bores and install the tools. Turn the forcing screw until the bearing is properly seated. Use the rear bearing as a pilot.
24. Install the snapring to secure the countershaft front bearing.
25. Install the bearing retainer together with the reverse idler gear shaft to the transmission case and tighten the four attaching bolts.
26. Slide the counter reverse gear onto the countershaft with the chamfer to the rear. Install the snapring to secure the counter reverse gear.
27. Install the key on the mainshaft.
28. Slide the reverse gear and lockwasher(tab facing outward) onto the mainshaft (chamfer on teeth should be to rear). Install a new locknut and hand tighten.
29. Shift into second gear and reverse gear to lock rotation of the mainshaft. Tighten the locknut 145 to 203 ft. lbs. using the Locknut Wrench (T77J-7025-C) and Locknut Adapter, T82T-7003-CH or their equal.
30. Place the fourth and third clutch sleeve in third gear using Synchronizer Ring Holder and Countershaft Spacer, T77J-7025-E or its equal.
31. Check the clearance between the synchronizer key and the exposed edge of the synchronizer ring with a feeler gauge. If the measurement is greater than 0.079 in., the synchronizer key can pop out of position. To correct this, change the thrust washer (selective fit) between the mainshaft rear bearing and the first gear. Available thrust washer sizes are 0.098, 0.118, and 0.138.
32. Check the clearance again with a feeler gauge. If the clearance is within specifications, bend the tab of the lockwasher.
33. Slide the first and second shift fork shaft assembly into the case (from rear of case). Install the roll pin. Secure the first and second shift fork to the fork shaft by staking the roll pin. Be sure to use a new roll pin.
34. Insert the interlock pin into the transmission using the lockout pin replacer tool.
35. Slide the third and fourth shift fork shaft assembly into the case (from rear of case). Secure the third and fourth shift fork to the fork shaft by staking the roll pin. Place transmission in neutral. Be sure to use a new roll pin.
36. Insert the interlock pin into the transmission.
37. Slide the reverse fork shaft assembly and reverse idler gear into the transmission case from the rear of the case with the gear chamfer forward. Secure the reverse shift fork to the fork shaft by staking the roll pin. Be sure to use a new roll pin.
38. Position the three detent balls and three springs into the case place copper washer on the top two bolts and install the three spring cap bolts.

39. Install the two blind covers and gaskets. Tighten the attaching bolts.
40. Install the lock all, speedometer drive gear, and snapring onto the mainshaft.
41. Apply a thin coat of sealing agent, Gasket Maker, E2AZ-19562-A (ESEM4G234-A2) or equivalent to the contacting surfaces of the transmission case and extension housing.
42. Position the extension housing with the gearshift control lever end laid down to the left as far as it will go. tighten the four attaching bolts. The lower two bolts must be coated with Loctite or equivalent.
43. If removed, insert the speedometer driven gear assembly to the extension housing and secure it with the bolt.
44. Check to ensure the gearshift control lever operates properly.
45. Install the transmission case cover gasket and cover with drain plug to rear. Install and tighten the fourteen attaching bolts.
46. Position the gasket and gearshift lever retainer to the extension housing, and tighten the four attaching bolts.
47. Install the correct size shim on the second step of the clutch adapter plate as determined by the Mainshaft Bearing Clearance Measurement.
48. Coat the clutch adapter plate with sealer, Gasket Maker, E2AZ-19562-A (ESEM4G234-A2) or equivalent. Install the clutch adapter plate to the transmission case and tighten the four bolts and four studs.
49. Remove the filler plug and install 3.0 pints of Ford Manual Transmission Lube, D8DZ-19C547-A (ESPM2C83-C) or equivalent. Reinstall filler plug and tighten 18 to 29 ft. lbs.

Ford Four Speed Overdrive Transmission

The Ford four speed overdrive transmission is fully synchronized in all forward gears. The four speed shift control is serviced as a unit and should not be disassembled. The lubricant capacity is 4.5 pints.

Disassembly

1. Remove retaining clips and flat washers from the shift rods at the levers.
2. Remove shift linkage control bracket attaching screws and remove shift linkage and control brackets.
3. Remove cover attaching screws. Then lift cover and gasket from the case. Remove the long spring that holds the detent plug in the case. Remove the plug with a magnet.
4. Remove extension housing attaching screws. Then, remove extension housing and gasket.
5. Remove input shaft bearing retainer attaching screws. Then, slide retainer from the input shaft.
6. Working a dummy shaft in from the front of the case, drive the countershaft out the rear of the case. Let the countergear assembly lie in the bottom of the case. Remove the set screw from the first/second shift fork. Slide the first/second shift rail out of the rear of the case. Use a magnet to remove the interlock detent from between the first/second and third/fourth shift rails.

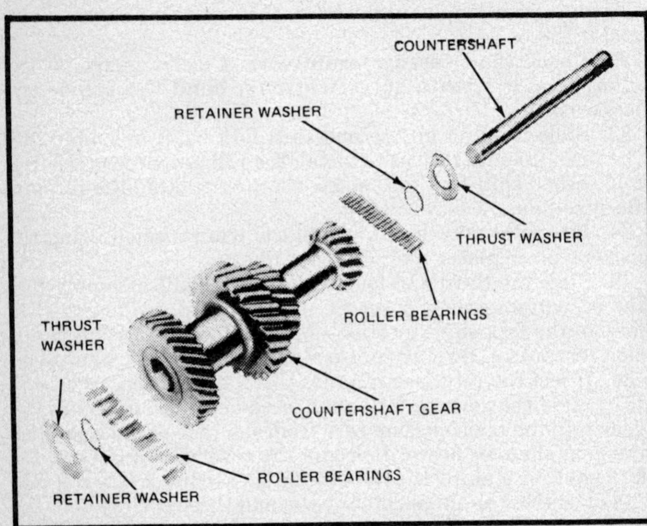

Exploded view of countershaft gear (© Ford Motor Co.)

7. Locate first/second speed gear shift lever in neutral. Locate third/fourth speed gear shift lever in third speed position. On overdrive transmissions, locate third/fourth speed gear shift lever in the fourth speed position.
8. Remove the lockbolt that holds the third–fourth speed shift rail detent spring and plug in the left side of the case. Remove spring and plug with a magnet.
9. Remove the detent mechanism set screw from top of case. Then, remove the detent spring and plug with a small magnet.
10. Remove attaching screw from the third/fourth speed shift fork. Tap lightly on the inner end of the shift rail to remove the expansion plug from front of case. Then, withdraw the third/fourth speed shift rail from the front. Do not lose the interlock pin from rail.
11. Remove attaching screw from the first and second speed shift fork. Slide the first/second shift rail from the rear of case.
12. Remove the interlock and detent plugs from the top of the case with a magnet.
13. Remove the snapring or disengage retainer that holds the speedometer drive gear to the output shaft, then remove speedometer gear drive ball.
14. Remove the snapring used to hold the output shaft bearing to the shaft. Pull out the output shaft bearing.
15. Remove the input shaft bearing snaprings. Use a press to remove the input shaft bearing. Remove the input shaft and blocking ring from the front of the case.
16. Move output shaft to the right side of the case. Then, maneuver the forks to permit lifting them from the case.
17. Support the thrust washer and first speed gear to prevent sliding from the shaft, then lift output shaft from the case.
18. Remove reverse gear shift fork attaching screw. Rotate the reverse shift rail 90°, then, slide the shift rail out the rear of the case. Lift out the reverse shift fork.
19. Remove the reverse detent plug and spring from the case with a magnet.
20. Using a dummy shaft, remove the reverse idler shaft from the case.
21. Lift reverse idler gear and thrust washers from the case. Be careful not to drop the bearing rollers or the dummy shaft from the gear.
22. Lift the countergear, thrust washers, rollers and dummy shaft assembly from the case.
23. Remove the next snapring from the front of the output shaft. Then, slide the third/fourth synchronizer blocking ring and the third speed gear from the shaft.
24. Remove the next snapring and the second speed gear thrust washer from the shaft. Slide the second speed gear and the blocking ring from the shaft.

25. Remove the snapring, then slide the first/second synchronizer, blocking ring and the first speed gear from the shaft.

26. Remove the thrust washer from rear of the shaft.

Unit Repairs

CAM AND SHAFT SEALS

1. Remove attaching nut and washers from each shift lever, then remove the three levers.
2. Remove the three cams and shafts from inside the case.
3. Replace the old O-rings with new ones that have been well lubricated.
4. Slide each cam and shaft into its respective bore in the transmission.
5. Install the levers and secure them with their respective washers and nuts.

SYNCHRONIZERS

1. Push the synchronizer hub from each synchronizer sleeve.
2. Separate the inserts and springs from the hubs. Do not mix parts of the first–second with parts of third–fourth synchronizers.
3. To assemble, position the hub in the sleeve. Be sure the alignment marks are properly indexed.
4. Place the three inserts into place on the hub. Install the insert springs so that the irregular surface (hump) is seated in one of the inserts. Do not stagger the springs.

COUNTERSHAFT GEAR

1. Dismantle the countershaft gear assembly.
2. Assemble the gear by coating each end of the countershaft gear bore with grease.
3. Install dummy shaft in the gear. Then install 21 bearing rollers and a retainer washer in each end of the gear.

REVERSE IDLER GEAR

1. Dismantle reverse idler gear.
2. Assemble reverse idler gear by coating the bore in each end of reverse idler gear with grease.
3. Hold the dummy shaft in the gear and install the 22 bearing rollers and the retainer washer into each end of the gear.
4. Install the reverse idler sliding gear on the splines of the reverse idler gear. Be sure the shift fork groove is toward the front.

INPUT SHAFT SEAL

1. Remove the seal from the input shaft bearing retainer.
2. Coat the sealing surface of a new seal with lubricant, then press the new seal into the input shaft bearing retainer.

Assembly

1. Grease the countershaft gear thrust surfaces in the case. Then, position a thrust washer at each end of the case.
2. Position the countershaft gear, dummy shaft, and roller bearings in the case.
3. Align the gear bore and thrust washers with the bores in the case. Install the countershaft.
4. With the case in a horizontal position, countershaft gear endplay should be from 0.004 in. to 0.018 in. Use thrust washers to obtain play within these limits.
5. After establishing correct endplay, place the dummy shaft in the countershaft gear and allow the gear assembly to remain on the bottom of the case.
6. Grease the reverse idler gear thrust surfaces in the case, and position the two thrust washers.
7. Position the reverse idler gear, sliding gear, dummy, etc., in place. Make sure that the shift fork groove in the sliding gear is toward the front.
8. Align the gear bore and thrust washers with the case bores and install the reverse idler shaft.
9. Reverse idler gear endplay should be 0.004 in. to 0.018 in. Use selective thrust washers to obtain play within these limits.

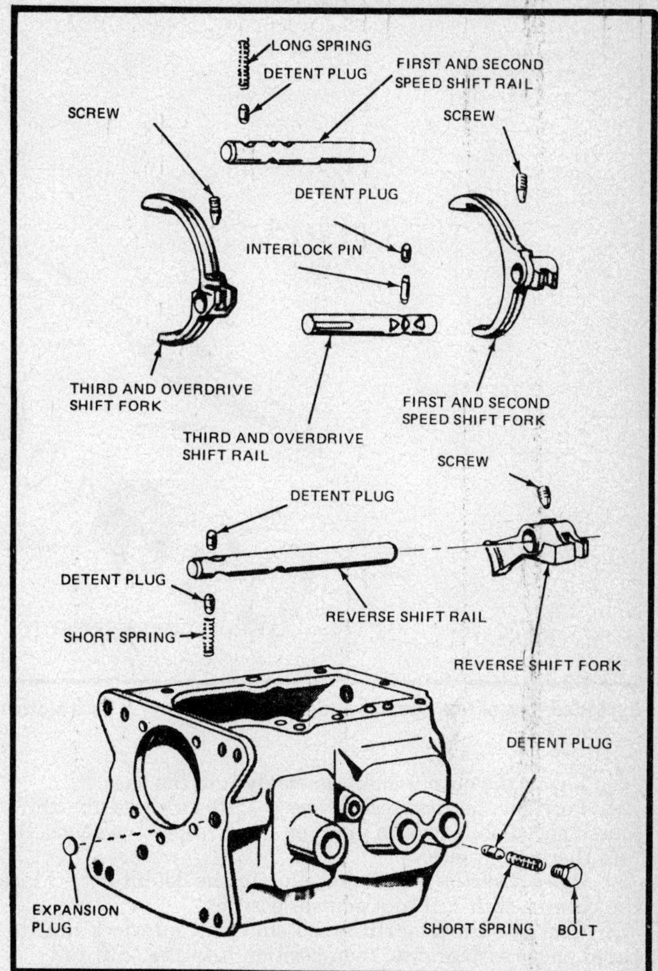

Exploded view of shift mechanism Ford four speed overdrive (© Ford Motor Co.)

10. Position reverse gear shift rail detent spring and detent plug in the case. Hold the reverse shift fork in place on the reverse idler sliding gear and install the shift rail from the rear of the case. Lock the fork to the rail with the Allen head set screws.
11. Install the first/second synchronizer onto the output shaft. The first and reverse synchronizer hub are a press fit and should be installed with gear teeth facing the rear of the shaft.

On overdrive transmissions, first and reverse synchronizer hub is a slip fit.

12. Place the blocking ring on second gear. Slide second speed gear onto the front of the shaft with the synchronizer coned surface toward the rear.
13. Install the second speed gear thrust washer and snapring.
14. Slide the fourth gear onto the shaft with the synchronizer coned surface front.
15. Place a blocking ring on the fourth gear.
16. Slide the third/fourth speed gear synchronizer onto the shaft. Be sure that the inserts in the synchronizer engage the notches in the blocking ring. Install the snapring onto the front of the output shaft.
17. Put the blocking ring on the first gear.
18. Slide the first gear onto the rear of the output shaft. Be sure that the inserts engage the notches in the blocking ring and that the shift fork groove is toward the rear.
19. Install heavy thrust washer onto the rear of the output shaft.

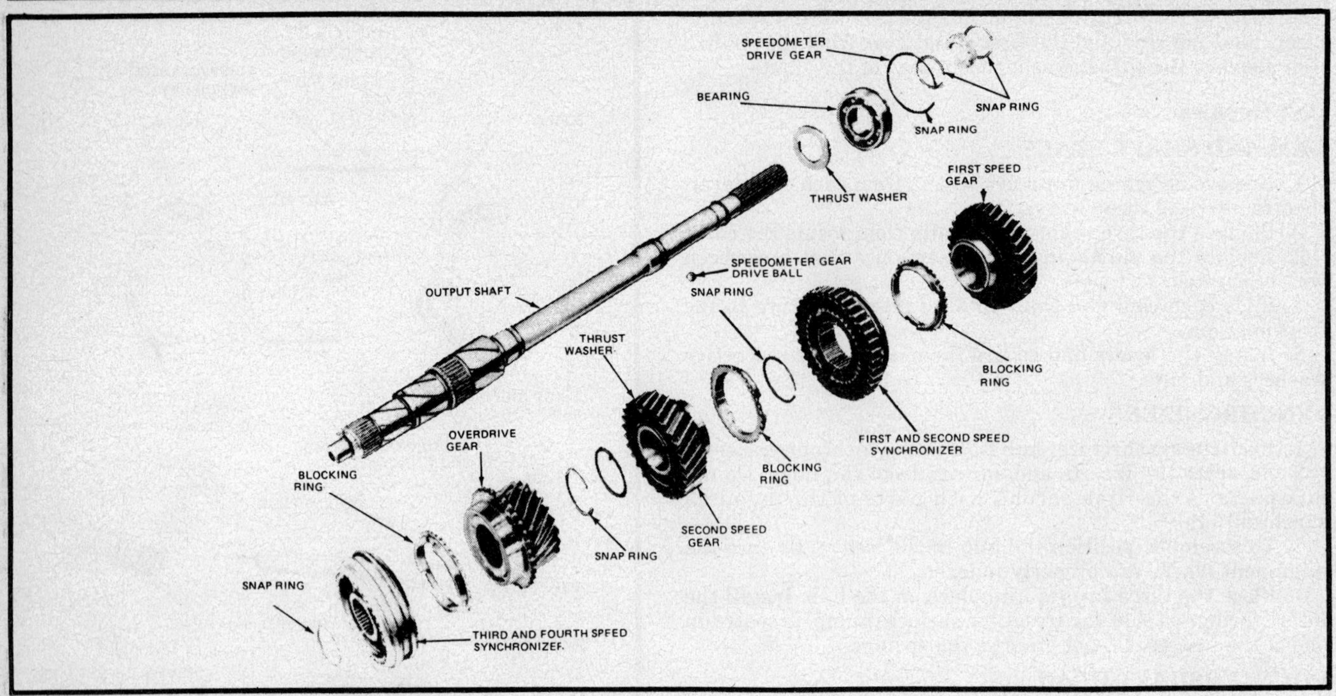

Exploded view of four speed overdrive transmission (© Ford Motor Co.)

20. Lower the output shaft assembly into the case.

21. Position the first/second speed shift fork and the third/fourth speed shift fork in place on their respective gears. Rotate them into place.

22. Place a spring and detent plug in the detent bore. Place the reverse shift rail into neutral position.

23. Coat the third/fourth speed shift rail interlock pin (tapered ends) with grease, then position it in the shift rail.

24. Align the third/fourth speed shift fork with the shift rail bores and slide the shift rail into place. Be sure that the three detents are facing the outside of the case. Place the front synchronizer into fourth speed position and install the set screw into the third/fourth speed shift fork. Move the synchronizer to neutral position. Install the third/fourth speed shift rail detent plug, spring and bolt into the left side of the transmission case. Place the detent plug (tapered ends) in the detent bore.

25. Align first/second speed shift fork with the case bores and slide the shift rail into place. Lock the fork with the set screw.

26. Coat the input gear bore with a small amount of grease. Then install the 15 bearing rollers.

27. Put the blocking ring in the third/fourth synchronizer. Place the input shaft gear in the case. Be sure that the output shaft pilot enters the roller bearing of the input shaft gear.

28. With a new gasket on the input bearing retainer, dip attaching bolts in sealer, install bolts and torque 30 to 36 ft. lbs.

29. Press on the output shaft bearing, then install the snapring to hold the bearing.

30. Position the speedometer gear drive ball in the output shaft and slide the speedometer drive gear into place. Secure gear with snapring.

31. Align the countershaft gear bore and thrust washers with the bore in the case. Install the countershaft.

32. With a new gasket in place, install and secure the extension housing. Dip the extension housing screws in sealer, then torque screws 42 to 50 ft. lbs.

33. Install the filler plug and the drain plug.

34. Pour E.P. gear oil over the entire gear train while rotating the input shaft.

35. Place each shift fork in all positions to make sure they function properly. Install the remaining detent plug in the case, followed by the spring.

36. With a new cover gasket in place, install the cover. Dip attaching screws in sealer, then torque screws 14 to 19 ft. lbs.

37. Coat the third/fourth speed shift rail plug bore with sealer. Install a new plug.

38. Secure each shift rod to its respective lever with a spring washer, flat washer and retaining pin.

39. Position the shift linkage control bracket to the extension housing. Install and torque the attaching screws 12 to 15 ft. lbs.

Ford Single Rail Four Speed, Overdrive Transmission

The Single Rail Overdrive (SROD) transmission is a four speed unit that has all forward speeds synchronized. A single control rod (rail) connects the shift lever to the transmission shift lever rails. The lubricant capacity is 4.5 pints.

Disassembly

1. Remove the lower extension housing bolt to drain the transmission.

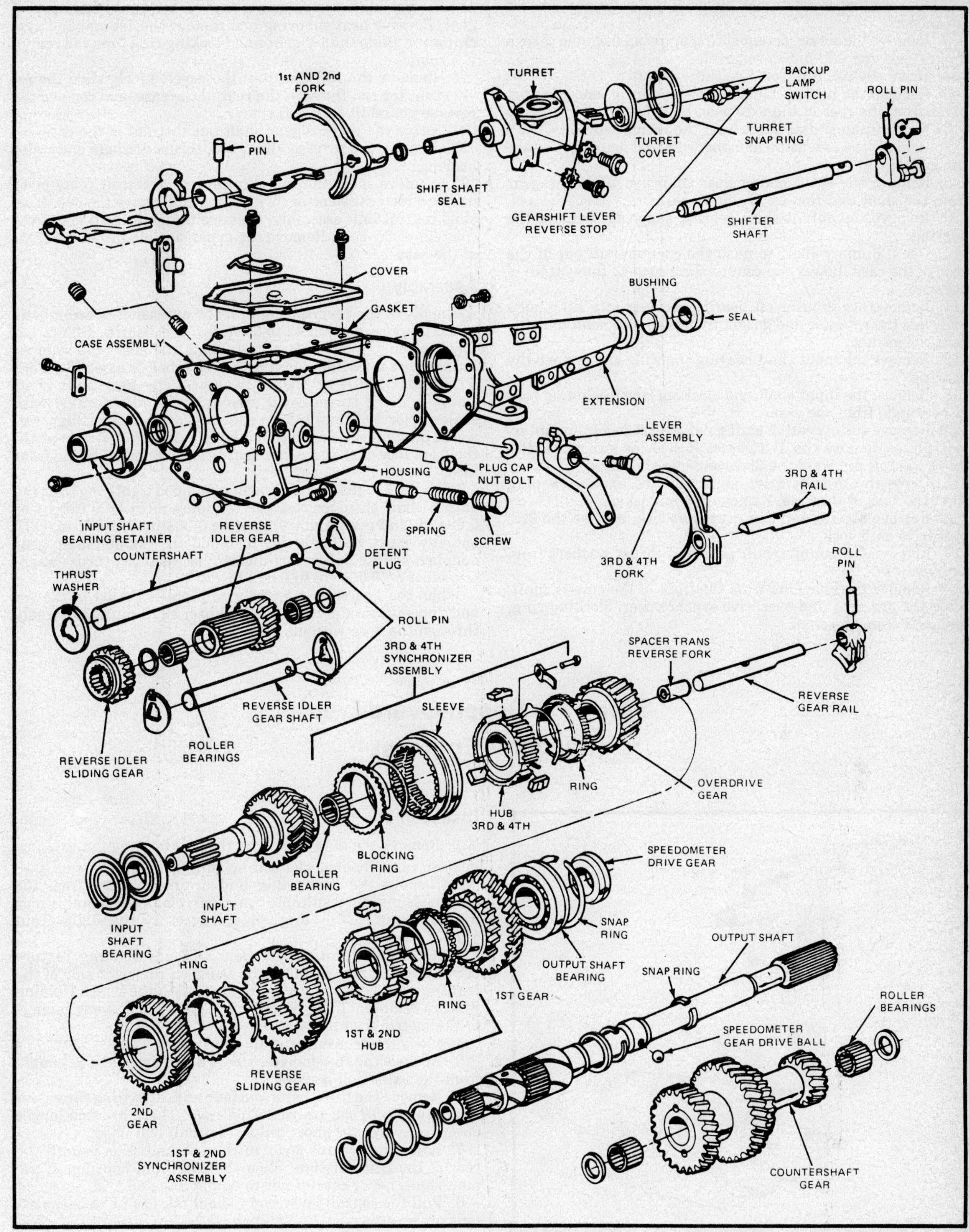

Disassembly of single rail four speed overdrive transmission (© Ford Motor Co.)

2. Remove the cover screws. Remove the cover and discard the gasket.

3. Remove the screw, detent spring and plug from the case; a magnetized rod will aid in removal.

4. Drive the roll pin from the shifter shaft.

5. Remove the backup lamp switch, snapring, and the dust cover from the rear of the extension housing.

6. Remove the shifter shaft from the turret assembly.

7. Remove the extension housing bolts and housing; discard the gasket.

8. Remove the speedometer gear snapring. Slide the gear from the shaft and remove the drive ball.

9. Remove the output shaft bearing snapring. Remove the bearing.

10. Use a dummy shaft to push the countershaft out of the rear of the case. Lower the countershaft gear to the bottom of the case.

11. Remove the input shaft bearing retainer attaching bolts and slide the retainer and gasket from the input shaft and discard the gasket.

12. Remove the input shaft bearing snapring and remove the bearing.

13. Remove the input shaft and blocking ring (including roller bearings) from the case.

14. Remove the overdrive shift pawl, gear selector and interlock plate. Remove the 1–2 gearshift selector arm plate. Remove the roll pin from the 3rd/overdrive shift fork.

15. Drive the 3rd/overdrive shift rail and expansion plug from the rear of the case. Remove the mainshaft.

16. Remove the 1st and 2nd gear shift fork; remove the 3rd/overdrive shift fork.

17. Remove the countershaft gear and thrust washers from the case.

18. Remove the snapring from the front of the output shaft. Slide the 3rd gear and overdrive synchronizer, blocking ring, and gear from the shaft.

19. Remove the next snapring and washer and remove second gear. Remove next snapring and remove the 1st and 2nd synchronizer. Slide the 1st gear and blocking ring from the rear of the shaft.

20. Remove the roll pin from the reverse fork, slide the reverse shifter rail through the rear of the case, and remove the reverse gearshift fork and spacer.

21. Drive the reverse gear shaft out the rear of the case.

22. Remove the reverse idler gear, thrust washers and roller bearings.

23. Remove the retaining clip, reverse gearshift relay lever and reverse gear selector fork pivot pin. Remove the overdrive shift control link assembly. Remove the shift shaft seal from the rear of the case. Remove the expansion plug from the front of the case.

Assembly

Assembly is the reverse. Tighten the extension housing bolts in a criss cross pattern 42 to 50 ft. lbs. The bearing rollers, extension housing bushing, shifter shaft and gear shift damper bushing are to be lubricated with grease before assembly (Ford #ESW-M1C109-A or the equivalent). The gear shift shaft sleeve and the turret cover assembly should be coated with sealer prior to installation. The intermediate and high rail welch plug must be seated firmly; it must not protrude above the front face of the case, nor seat below 0.6 in. below the front face.

With the 1st gear thrust washer clamped tightly against the output shaft shoulder, 1st gear endplay must be 0.005 in. to 0.024 in. 2nd gear endplay must be 0.003 in. to 0.021 in. O.D. endplay must be 0.009 in. to 0.023 in. Countershaft gear endplay, checked after installation between the thrust washers, must be 0.004 in. to 0.018 in.

When the gearshift selector arm plate is seated in the 1st and 2nd shift fork plate slot, the shifter shaft must pass freely through the bore without binding.

Ford Five Speed Overdrive (Gasoline Engines)

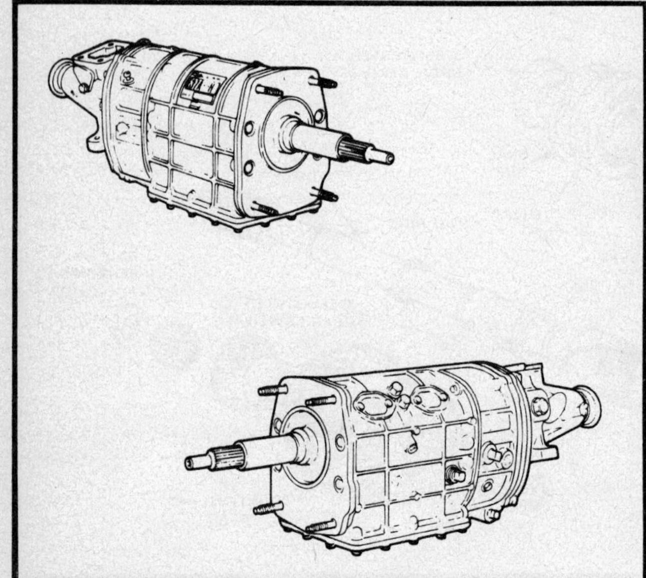

Ranger five speed overdrive

Disassembly

1. Remove the nuts attaching the bell housing to the transmission case. Remove the bell housing gasket.

2. Remove the drain plug and drain lubricant from the transmission into a suitable container. clean the metal filings from the magnet of the drain plug, if necesary. Install the drain plug.

3. (Optional) Position the Bench Mount Holding Fixture (T57L-500-B) or its equal to the studs on the right side of the transmission housing. Secure in place with the Bench Holding Fixture Adapter (T77J-7025-D) or its equal to prevent damage to the metric stud threads.

4. Place the transmission in neutral.

5. Remove the speedometer sleeve and driven gear assembly from the extension housing.

6. Remove the three bolts and four nuts attaching the extension housing to the transmission case. There are two longer outer bolts and one short center (bottom) bolt used.

7. Raise the control lever to the left and slide toward the rear of the transmission. Slide the extension housing off the mainshaft, being careful not to damage the oil seal.

8. Pull the control lever and rod out the front end of the extension housing.

9. If required, remove the back-up lamp switch from the extension housing.

10. Remove the anti-spill seal from the mainshaft and discard (A seal is not necessary for assembly.).
11. Remove the snapring that secures the speedometer drive gear to the mainshaft. Slide the drive gear off the mainshaft, and remove the lock ball.
12. Evenly loosen the fourteen bolts securing the transmission case cover to the transmission case. Remove the cover and gasket.
13. Mark the shift rails and forks to aid during transmission assembly. Remove the roll pins attaching the shift rod ends to the shift rod and remove the shift rod ends.
14. Gently pry the bearing housing away from the transmission case using the proper tool and being careful not to damage the housing or case. Slide the bearing housing off the mainshaft.
15. Remove the snapring and washer retaining the mainshaft rear bearing to the mainshaft.
16. Assembly the Bearing Puller Ring Tool (T77J-7025-J), Bearing Puller Tool (T77J-7025-H), and Forcing Screw (T75L-7025-J) on the Remover and Replacer Tube Tool (T75L-7025-B) or their equal. Slide the tool assembly over the mainshaft and engage the puller jaws behind the rear bearing. Tighten the jaws evenly onto the bearing with a wrench, then turn the forcing screw to remove the mainshaft rear bearing.
17. Remove the snapring from the rear end of the countershaft. Assemble the Bearing Puller Tool (T77J-7025-H), Bearing Puller Ring (T77J-7025-J) and Forcing Screw (T75L-7025-J) onto the Remover Tube (T77J-7025-B) or their equal. Slide the tool assembly over the countershaft and engage the puller jaws behind the countershaft rear bearing. Tighten the jaws evenly onto the bearing with a wrench, then turn the forcing screw to remove the bearing.
18. Remove the counter fifth gear and spacer from the rear of the countershaft.
19. Tap the housing with a plastic hammer, if necessary, and remove center housing. Remove the reverse idler gear and two spacers with housing.
20. Remove the cap screw from center housing and remove idler gear shaft.
21. Remove the three spring cap bolts. The two bolts on the case upper portion are 17mm and the bolt on the case side is 14mm. Remove the detent springs and the detent balls with a magnet from the transmission case.
22. Remove the four bolts attaching the blind covers to the transmission case and remove the blind covers and gaskets.
23. Remove the roll pin from the fifth and reverse shift fork. Slide the fifth and reverse shift fork shaft out of the transmission case.
24. Shift the transmission into fourth gear. This will provide adequate space the drive out the roll pin. With a small drift, drive the roll pin. With a small drift, drive the rollpin from third and fourth shift fork. Slide the third and fourth shift fork shaft out of the rear of the transmission case.
25. Remove the roll pin from the first and second shift fork. Slide the first and second shift fork shaft assembly out the rear of the transmission case. Remove both interlock pins.
26. Remove the snapring that secures the fifth gear to the mainshaft.
27. Remove the thrust washer and lock ball, fifth gear and synchronizer ring from the rear of the mainshaft.
28. Install the Synchronizer Ring Holder and Countershaft Spacer (T77J-7025-E) or its equal between the fourth-speed synchronizer ring and synchromesh gear on the mainshaft. Shift the transmission into second gear to lock the mainshaft and prevent the assembly from rotating.
29. Straighten the staked portion of the mainshaft bearing locknut with the Staking Tool (T77J-7025-C) or its equal. Using the Locknut Wrench ((T77J-7025-C) or its equal. remove the mainshaft bearing locknut.
30. Slide the reverse gear and clutch hub assembly off the mainshaft.
31. Remove the counter reverse gear from the countershaft.
32. If installed, remove the transmission from the holding fixture and set on a workbench.
33. Remove the bolts attaching the mainshaft center bearing cover to the transmission and remove the bearing cover.
34. To remove the countershaft center bearing, install Puller T77J-7025-H, Puller Rings T77J-7025-J, Remover Tube T77J-7025-B, and Forcing Screw T75L-7025-J or their equal. Squarely insert the jaws of the puller behind the center bearing retainer ring in the recessed areas of the case.

NOTE: The retainer ring may need to be turned to position the split in the retainer ring midway between the recessed areas before the puller is installed. this will reduce the possibility of the retainer ring becoming distorted as the bearing is removed.

35. Turn the forcing screw to remove the bearing.
36. To remove the mainshaft center bearing, install Puller T77J-7025-H, Puller Rings T77J-7025-J, Long Remover Tube T75L-7025-C and Forcing Screw T75L-7025-J or their equal. Squarely insert the jaws of the puller behind the jaws of the puller behind the rear mainshaft bearing retainer ring in the tow recessed areas of the case.
37. Turn the forcing screw clockwise to remove the bearing.
38. Remove the shim an spacer from behind the mainshaft rear bearing along with the bearng.
39. Remove the front cover by first removing the four studs attaching the cover to case. Remove the studs by installing two nuts (10mm x 1.5) on the stud and drawing the stud out of the case. Remove the four 14mm bolts and remove the cover. Save the shim found on the inside of the cover.
40. Remove the snapring from the input shaft.
41. Remove the input shaft bearing by installing Puller T77J-7025-H, Puller Rings T77J-7025-J, Remover Tube T75L-7025-B, and Forcing Screw T75L-7025-J or their equal. Squarely insert the jaws of the puller behind the input shaft bearing retainer ring in the two recessed areas of the case.

NOTE: The retainer ring may need to turned to position the slit in the ring midway between the recessed areas before the puller is installed.

42. Turn the forcing screw clockwise to remove the bearing.
43. Rotate both shift forks so that the main gear train will fall to the bottom of the case. Remove the shift forks. Rotate the input shaft so that one of the two flats on the input shaft faces upward.
44. Remove the snapring from the front of the countershaft.
45. Remove Synchronizer Ring Holder T77J-7025-E or its equal from the front of the case and insert between the first gear on the counter shaft and the rear of the case.
46. Install Forcing Screw T75L-7025-J, Press Frame T77j-7025-N, and Press Frame Adapter T82T-7003-BH or their equal against the countershaft assembly.
47. Turn the forcing screw clockwise to press the countershaft rearward. Press the countershaft ($^3/_{16}$ inch movement) until it contacts the Synchronizer Ring Holder and Countershaft Spacer.
48. To remove the countershaft front bearing, first remove the press frame. The, install Puller T77J-7025-H, Puller Rings T77J-7025-J, Remover Tube T777J-7025-B, and Forcing Screw T75L-7025-J or their equal. Squarely insert the jaws of the puller behind the front bearing retainer ring in the two recessed areas of the case.

NOTE: The retainer ring may need to be turned to position the split in the ring midway between the recessed areas before the puller is installed.

49. Turn the forcing screw clockwise to remove the bearing.
50. Remove the shim form behind the countershaft front bearing.
51. Remove the countershaft from the transmission case.
52. Remove the input shaft from the transmission case. Re-

move the synchronizer ring and caged bearing from the mainshaft.

53. Remove the mainshaft and gear assembly from the transmission case.

54. Remove the inner race of the countershaft center bearing from the countershaft in a press frame using Axle Bearing Seal Plate T75L-1165-B and Pinion Bearing Cone Remover D79L-4621-A or their equal.

55. Remove first gear and first and second synchronizer ring. Remove snapring retainer from mainshaft. Do not mix synchronizer rings.

56. Install Bearing Remover Tool T71P-4621-B or its equal between second and third gear.

57. Press the mainshaft out of third gear and third and fourth clutch hub sleeve.

58. Press the first and second clutch hub and sleeve assembly, and first gear sleeve from the mainshaft.

59. Clean and inspect the case, gears, bearings and shafts.

Assembly

NOTE: As each part is assembled, Coat the part with manual transmission oil D8DZ-19C547-A (ESP-M2C83-C) or equivalent. Before beginning the assembly procedure, three measurements must be performed: Mainshaft Thrust Play, Countershaft Thrust Play and Mainshaft Bearing Clearance.

Mainshaft Thrust Play

Check the mainshaft thrust play by measuring the depth of the mainshaft bearing bore in the transmission rear case by using a depth micrometer (D80P-4201-A). Then the measure the mainshaft rear bearing height. The difference between the two mesurements indicates the required thickness of the adjusting shim. The standard thrust play is 0 to 0.0039 in. Adjusting shims are available in 0.0039 in. and 0.0118 in. sizes.

Countershaft Thrust Play

Check the countershaft thrust play by measuring the depth of the countershaft front bearing bore in the transmission case by using a depth micrometer (D80P-4201-A). Then measure the countershaft front bearing height. The difference between the two measurements indicates the required thickness of the adjusting shims. The standard thrust play is 0 to 0.0039 in. Adjusting shims are available in 0.0039 in. and 0.0118 in.sizes.

Mainshaft Bearing Clearance

Check the mainshaft bearing clearance by measuring the depth of the bearing bore in the clutch adapter plate with a depth micrometer, D80P-4201-A. Make sure the micrometer is on the second step of the plate. Measure the bearing height. The difference between the two measurements indicates the required adjusting shim thickness. The standard clearance is 0 to 0.0039 in. If an adjusting shim is required, select one to bring the clearance to within specifications.

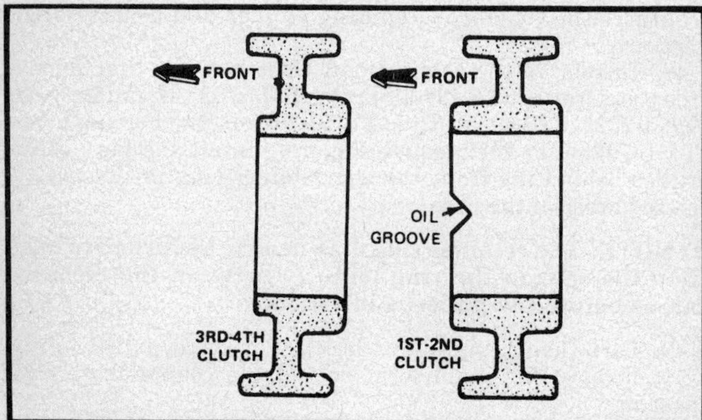

Clutch hub assembly direction

1. Assemble the first and second synchromesh mechanism and the third and fourth synchromesh mechanism by installing the clutch hub to the sleeve. Place the three synchronizer keys into the clutch hub key slots and install the key springs to the clutch hub.

NOTE: When installing the key springs, the open end tab of the springs should be inserted into hub holes with springs turned in the same direction. This will keep the spring tension on each key uniform.

2. Place the synchronizer ring on the second gear and position the second gear to the mainshaft with the synchronizer ring toward the rear of the shift.

3. Slide the first and second clutch hub and sleeve assembly to the mainshaft with the oil grooves of the clutch hub toward the front of the mainshaft. Make sure that the three synchronizer keys in the synchromesh mechanism engage the notches in the second synchronizer ring.

4. Press into position using press and suitable replacer tool.

5. Insert the first gear sleeve on the mainshft.

6. Place the synchronizer ring on the third gear along with the caged roller bearing and slide the third gear to the front of the mainshaft with the synchronizer ring toward the front.

7. Press the third and fourth clutch hub and sleeve assembly to the front of the mainshaft. Make sure that the three synchronizer keys in the synchromesh mechanism engage the notches in the synchronizer ring. Note the proper direction of the third and fourth clutch hub and sleeve assembly.

8. Install the snapring to the front of the mainshaft.

9. Slide the needle bearing for the first gear to the mainshaft.

10. Place the synchronizer ring on the first gear. Slide the first gear on to the mainshaft with the synchronizer ring facing the front of the shaft. Rotate the first gear, as necessary, to engage the three notches in the synchronizer ring with the synchronizer keys.

11. Install the original thrust washer to the mainshaft.

12. Position the mainshaft and gear assembly in the case.

13. Position the first and second shift fork and third and fourth shift fork in the groove of the clutch hub and sleeve assembly.

14. Position the caged bearing in the front end of the mainshaft.

15. Place the synchronizer ring on the input shaft (fourth gear) and install the input shaft to the front end of the mainshaft. Make sure that the three synchronizer keys in the third and fourth synchromesh mechanism engage the notches in the synchronizer ring.

16. Press the inner race of the countershaft rear bearing onto the countershaft using Center Bearing Replacer T77J-7025-K or its equal.

17. Position the countershaft gear in the case, Making sure that the countershaft gear engages each gear of the mainshaft assembly.

18. Install the correct shim on the mainshaft center bearing as determined in the Mainshaft Thrust Play Mesurement.

19. Position the input shaft bearing and the mainshaft center bearing to the proper bearing bores. Be sure the synchronizer and shifter forks have not been moved out of position.

20. Install the Synchronizer Ring Holder ToolT77J-7025-E or its equal between the fourth synchronizer ring and the synchromesh gear on the mainshaft.

21. Install the Dummy Bearing Replacer T82T-7003-DH, Replacer Tube T77J-7025-M, and Press Frame T77J-7025-N or their equal on the case. Turn the forcing screw on the press frame until both bearings are properly seated.

22. Install the input shaft bearing snapring. Be sure that the

synchronizer and shift forks are properly positioned during seating of bearings. After bearings are seated, make certain that both synchronizers operate freely.

23. Place the correct shim in the countershaft front bearing bore.

24. Position the countershaft front and center bearings in the bores and install the tools. Turn the forcing screw until the bearing is properly seated. Use the center bearing as a pilot.

25. Install the snapring to secure the countershaft front bearing.

26. Remove the synchronizer ring holder.

27. Install the bearing cover to the transmission case and tighten the four attaching bolts. Tighten 41 to 59 ft. lbs.

28. Install the reverse idler gear and shaft with a spacer on each side of shaft.

29. Slide the counter reverse gear (chamfer side forward) and spacer onto the countershaft.

30. Slide the thrust washer, reverse gear, caged roller bearings and clutch hub assembly onto the mainshaft. Install a new locknut (hand tight).

31. Shift into second gear and reverse gear to lock the rotation of the mainshaft. Tighten the locknut 115 to 175 ft. lbs. using the Locknut Wrench T77J-7025-C or its equal.

32. Stake the locknut into the mainshaft keyway using the staking tool.

33. Place the fourth and third clutch sleeve in third gear using Synchronizer Ring Holder and Countershaft Spacer T77J-7025-E.

34. If new synchronizers have been installed, Check the clearance between the synchronizer key and the exposed edge of the synchronizer ring with a feeler gauge. If the measurement is greater than 0.079 in., the synchronizer key can pop out of position. To correct this, change the thrust washer (selective fit) between the mainshaft center bearing and the first gear Available thrust washer sizes are 0.089,0.118 and 0.138.

35. If new synchronizers were installed, check the clearance again with a feeler gauge, If the clearance is within specifications, bend the tab of the lockwasher.

36. Position the fifth synchronizer ring on the fifth gear. Slide the fifth gear onto the mainshaft with the synchronizer ring toward the front of the shft. Rotate the fifth gear, as necessary, to engage the three notches in the synchronizer ring with the synchronizer keys in the reverse and clutch hub assembly.

37. Install the lock ball and thrust washer on the rear of the fifth gear.

38. Install the snapring on the rear of the thrust washer. Check the clearance between the thrust washer and the snapring. If the clearance is not within 0.0039 in. to 0.0118 in., select the proper size thrust washer to bring the clearance within specifications.

39. Slide the first and second shift fork shaft assembly into the case (front rear of case). Secure the first and second shift fork shaft assembly into the case). Secure the first and second shift fork to the fork shaft with the roll pin. Be sure to use a new roll pin.

40. Insert the interlock pin into the transmission using the lockout pin replacer tool.

41. Shift transmission into fourth gear. Slide the third and fourth shift fork shaft into the case, from rear of case. Secure the third and fourth shift fork to the fork shaft with the roll pin. Insert interlock pin. Be sure to use a new roll pin.

42. Shift synchronizer hub into fifth gear. Position reverse and fifth fork on the clutch hub and slide the reverse and fifth fork shaft into the case (from rear of case). Secure the reverse and fifth shift fork to the fork shaft with the roll pin. Be sure to use a new roll pin.

43. Install the two blind covers and gasket. Tighten the attaching bolts 23 to 34 ft. lbs.

44. Position the three detent balls and three springs into the case and install the spring cap bolts.

45. Apply a thin coat of Gasket Maker E2AZ-19562-A (ESE-M4G234-A2) or equivalent to the contacting surfaces of the center housing and transmission case.

46. Position the center housing on the case. Align the reverse idler gear shaft boss with the center housing attaching bolt boss. Install and tighten the idler shaft capscrew and tighten 41 to 59 ft. lbs.

47. Slide the counter fifth gear to the countershft.

48. Position the countershaft rear bearing on the countershaft. Press into positon using the Adjustable Press Frame T77J-7025-N and Forcing Screw T75L-7025-J or their equal.

49. Install the thrust washer and snapring to the rear of the countershaft rear bearing. Check the clearance between the thrust washer and the snapring using a feeler gauge.

50. If the clearance is not within 0.0000 in. to 0.0059 in., select the proper size thrust washer to bring the clearance within specifications, 0.0748, 0.0787, 0.0827, or 0.0866.

51. If installed, remove filler plugs. Position the mainshaft rear bearing on the mainshaft. Press into place using the adjustable Press Frame T77J-7025-N, Dummy Bearing T75L-7025-QI and Forcing Screw T75L-7025 or their equal.

52. Install the thrust washer and snapring to the rear of the mainshaft rear bearing. Check the clearance between the thrust washer and the snapring. The Clearance should be 0.0000 in. to 0.0039 in. If the clearance is not within specifications, replace the thrust washer to bring the clearance within specifications, 0.0787, 0.0846, or 0.0906.

53. Apply a thin coat of Gasket Maker E2AZ-19562-A (ESE-M4G234-A2) or equivalent to the contacting surfaces of the bearing housing and center housing.

54. Position the bearing housing on the center housing.

55. Install each shift fork shaft end onto the proper shift fork shaft. (Note the scribe marks made during disassembly) and secure with roll pins.

56. Install the lock ball. Speedometer drive gear, and snapring onto the mainshaft.

57. If removed, install control lever and rod in extension housing.

58. Apply a thin coat of Gasket Maker E2AZ-19562-A (ESE-M4G234-A2) or equivalent to the contacting surfaces of the bearing housing and extension housing.

59. Position the extension housing in the bearing housing with the gearshift control lever end laid down to the left as far as it will go. Tighten the attaching bolts and nuts 60 to 80 ft. lbs. There are two longer outer bolts and one shorter center (bottom) bolt used.

60. If removed, insert the speedometer driven gear assembly to the extension housing and secure it with the bolt.

61. Check the ensure the gearshift control lever operates properly.

62. Install the transmission case cover gasket and cover with drain plug to the rear. Install and tighten the fourteen attaching bolts 23 to 34 ft. lbs..

63. Install the correct size shim on the second step of the front cover as determined by the mainshaft bearing clearance measurement.

64. Coat the front cover with Gasket Maker E2AZ-19562-A (ESE-M4G234-A2) or equivalent. Install the front cover to the transmission case and tighten the four bolts and four studs.

65. Install 3.0 pints of Ford Manual Transmission Lube D8DZ-19C547-A (ESP-M2C83-C) or equivalent. Reinstall the filler plugs and tighten 18 to 29 ft. lbs.

Ford Five Speed Overdrive (Diesel Engines)

Disassembly

1. If not already drained, remove the drain plug and drain the transmission fluid into a suitable container. Remove the fork and release bearing from the transmission case.
2. Install the transmission in Bench Mounted Holding Fixture, T57L-500-B or its equal. Remove the six bolts attaching the front cover to the transmission case and remove the front cover, shim (located in cover) and gasket.
3. Remove the front cover oil seal using Inner Seal Removal Tool, T75P-3504-G and Impact Slide Hammer, T50T-100-A or their equal.
4. Remove the input shaft snapring.
5. If installed, remove the gearshift lever. Remove the four bolts and remove the retainer and gasket from the extension housing.
6. Remove the outer retaining ring on the input shaft bearing. Install Bearing Collet Tool, T75L-7025-E on the input shaft bearing, and Remover Tube, T75L-7025-B and Forcing Screw T75L-7025-J or their equal. Slide Bearing Collet Sleeve, T75L-7025-G or its equal over the Remover Tube and Bearing Collet, and turn the forcing screw to remove the input shaft bearing.
7. Remove the bolt that attaches the control lever end to the control rod an remove the control lever end and rod from the extension housing.
8. Remove the eight bolts attaching the extension housing to the intermediate housing and transmission housing. Slide the extension housing off the output shaft with the control lever end laid down and to the left as far as to will go.
9. Remove the speedometer driven gear assembly from the extension housing.
10. Remove the back-up lamp switch and the neutral safety switch.
11. Remove the grommet from the end of the output shaft. Remove the snapring that secures the speedometer drive gear on the output shaft. Slide the speedometer drive gear off the output shaft and remove the lock ball.
12. Install Bearing Pusher Tool, T83T-7111-A or its equal over the countershaft front bearing. Turn the forcing screw to force the countershaft (together with the countershaft front bearing) from the transmission case. Remove the pusher tool assembly. The countershaft front bearing may remain in the transmission case. Remove the Bearing with a suitable driver.
13. Remove and discard the roll pin from the 1–2 shift fork. Remove the circlip from the rail. Remove the upper cap bolt and with a magnet, remove the spring and detent ball from the bore. Remove the 1–2 shift fork.

NOTE: Note the position of the 1–2 shift fork in relation to the 3–4 shift fork for positioning during reassembly. The shift forks and rails are not interchangeable. Check the position of the shift rail and the relationship of the detent slots to the bore for positioning during reassembly. The three detent slots in the shift rails face towards the cap bolts.

14. Remove the roll pin from the 3–4 shift fork. Remove the circlip from the rail. Remove the middle cap bolt and with a magnet, remove the spring and detent ball from the bore. Remove the 3–4 shift fork and rail. An inerlock pin will drop out of the bore when the 3–4 shift rail is removed. Note the position of the shift rail and the relationship of the detent slots to the bore for positioning during reassembly.
15. Remove the circlip and washer form the 5R (Reverse) shift rail. Remove the bottom cap bolt and with a magnet, remove the shorter length spring and detent ball.
16. Drive the roll pin from the 5R shift lever and remove the lever from the rail. With a magnet remove the other detent ball and shorter length spring from the bottom (5R) bore.
17. Gently pry the intermediate housing away from the bearing housing. Remove the gear and bearing assembly out of the intermediate housing.
18. Install the gear train and bearing housing assembly in a fabricated holding tool positioned in a vise. A soft jawed vise may be used in place of the holding tool.
19. Remove the bottom cap bolt and with a magnet, remove the shorter length spring and detent ball from the bore. Drive the roll pin out of the 5R shift fork and discard. Remove the 5R shift rail. An interlock pin will drop out of the bore when the 5R shift rail is removed.

NOTE: Note the position of the 5R shift fork in relation to the bearing housing for positioning during reassembly. Check the position of the shift rail and the relationship of the detent slots to the bore for positioning during reassembly. The three detent slots in the shift rail face toward the cap bolt.

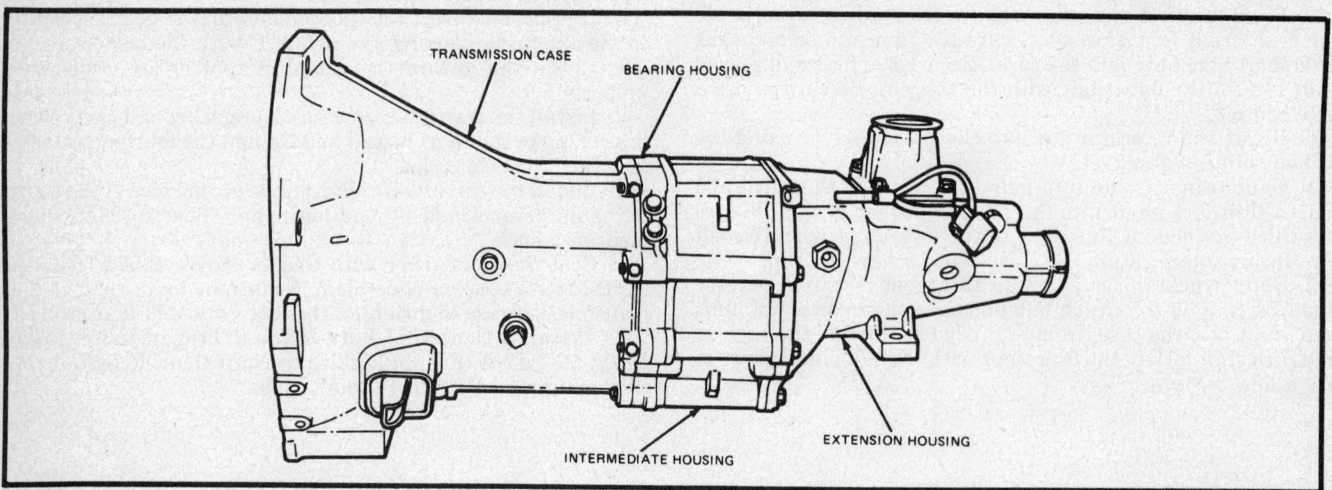

Five speed manual overdrive (diesel engine)

20. Remove the retaining ring from the output shaft ball bearing. Remove the thrust washer.

21. To remove the output shaft rear bearing, place Shaft Protectors, D80L-625-2 and D80L-625-3 or their equal on the end of the output shaft. It may be necessary to hold the shaft protectors in place with putty. Install Puller, T77J-7025-H, Collet (2), T77J-7025-J or their equal against the bearing so the jaws of the puller are against the rear of the bearing. Place Tube (Long), T75L-7025-C or its equal over the output shaft. Install Forcing Screw, T75L-7025-J or its equal into the tube and turn the forcing screw clockwise to remove the bearing. Discard the bearing and install a new one during reassembly.

22. Remove the snapring from the countershaft rear bearing. Install Puller. T77J-7025-H, Collet (2), T77J-7025-J, Tube (Short, T77J-7025-B) and Forcing Screw, T75L-7025-J or their equal. Turn the forcing screw clockwise and remove the bearing. Discard the bearing and install a new one during reassembly.

23. Remove the retaining ring, thrust washer and lock ball from the output shaft.

24. Remove the fifth gear and sleeve from the countershaft. The collar of the fifth gear faces towards the bearing housing.

25. Remove the reverse gear from the countershaft. The collar of the counter/reverse gear faces towards the bearing housing.

26. Remove the fifth gear form the output shaft and remove the 5R sychronizer ring.

27. Straighten the peen on the locknut with Staking Tool, T77J-7025-F or its equal. Lock the transmission gears in reverse and any forward gear. Install Lock Nut Wrench T77J-7025-C or its equal on the locknut and remove the locknut and discard.

28. Remove the 5R synchronizer assembly from the output shaft.

29. Pry the reverse gear caged needle bearing. Sleeve and thurst washer from the output shaft.

30. Remove the snapring and remove the reverse idler gear from the idler shaft. Remove the keyed thrust washer from the shaft.

31. Remove the five bolts that attach the bearing cover to the bearing housing and remove the cover.

32. If required, remove the bolt retaining the idler shaft to the bearing housing and drive the plate and shaft assembly out of the housing.

33. With a soft hammer. tap the rear end of the output shaft and countershaft in turn, being careful not to damage the shafts. Remove the shafts form the bearing housing.

34. Carefully separate the input shaft, caged needle bearing and synchronizer ring from the output shaft.

35. Press the rear countershaft bearing from the bearing housing using Remover Tube Tool, T77J7025-B or its equal.

36. Press the rear output shaft bearing from the bearing housing using Bearing Remover Tool, T77F-4222-A and Remover Tube Tool, T77J-7025-B or their equal.

37. Remove the thrust washer, first gear, sleeve and synchronizer ring from the rear of the output shaft.

38. Using snapring pliers, remove the snapring from the front of the output shaft.

39. Using a press and Remover Tool, T71P-4621-B or its equal, remover the third and fourth hub, sleeve, synchronizer ring and third gear from the front of the output shaft.

40. Using a press and Remover Tool,T71P-4621-B or its equal, remove the first and second hub and sleeve assembly synchronizer ring, and second gear from the rear of the output shaft in the same manner as described in the previous step.

41. Press the front bearing from the countershaft using Remover Tool D79L-4621-A or T71P-4621-B and suitable press stock.

42. Inspect all parts.

Assembly

1. Assemble the 3–4 synchronizer assembly by installing the keys in the hub and sliding the sleeve over the hub and keys. Install the springs onto the hub.

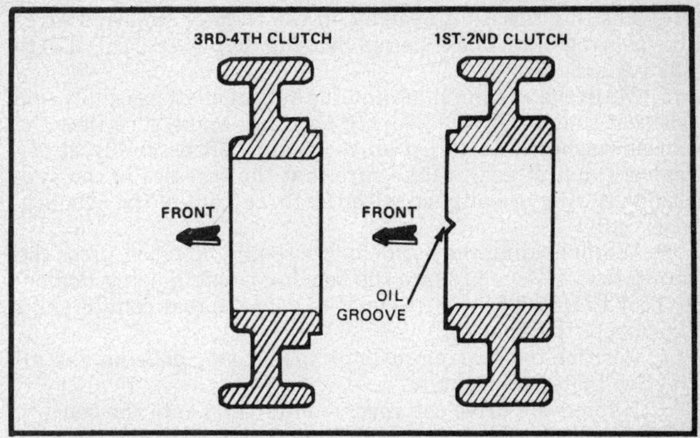

Synchronizer hub installation

NOTE: When installing the springs, the open end tab of the springs should be inserted into the hub holes. This will keep the spring tension on each key uniform.

2. Assemble the 1–2 synchronizer assembly in the same manner as described in Step 1. Assemble the 5R synchronizer assembly as also described in Step 1 and install the retaining ring in the 5R assembly.

3. Install the third gear and synchronizer ring onto the front section of the output shaft.

4. Install the 3–4 synchronizer assembly onto the output shaft by using a press. Hold the assembly together and slowly press in place. Make sure the three recesses in the synchronizer ring are aligned with the three keys in the synchronizer hub. Note the proper direction of the hub. The recesses in each synchronizer sleeve must face each other.

5. Fit the snapring on the output shaft.

6. Instll the second gear, synchronizer ring onto the rear section of the output shaft.

7. Install the 1–2 synchronizer assembly onto the output shaft by using a press. Hold the assembly together and slowly press in place. Make sure the three keys recesses in the synchronizer ring are aligned with the three keys in the synchronizer hub. Note the proper direction of the hub. The recesses in the synchronizer sleeve must face each other.

8. Install the synchronizer ring, first gear with sleeve, and thrust washer onto the output shaft.

9. Install the input shaft and the needle roller bearing to the output shaft.

10. Check the countershaft rear bearing clearance. Measure the depth of the countershaft bearing bore in the bearing housing with a depth micrometer (D80P-4201-A or equivalent). Install the retaining ring on the bearing and with a depth micrometer measure the distance betwen the inside edge of the ring and the end of the bearing. The difference between the two measurements indicates the required thickness of the adjusting shim. The clearance should be less than 0.0039 in. The adjusting shims are available in 0.0039 in. and 0.0118 in. sizes.

11. Check the output shaft bearing clearance. Measure the depth of the bearing bore with a depth micrometer. Measure the width of the bearing with a micrometer. The difference between the two measurements indicates the required thickness of the adjusting shim. The clearance should be less than 0.0039 in. Adjusting shims are available in 0.0039 in. and 0.0118 in. sizes.

12. Position the proper shim on the countershaft rear bearing and press into the bearing housing using Installer Tool, T77J-7025-B or its equal.

13. Position the proper shim on the output shaft bearing and press the bearing into the bearing housing using Installer Tool, T77J-7025-K or its equal.

14. Position the front bearing on the countershaft and press the bearing into place using Bearing Replacer Tool, T71P-7025-A or its equal.

15. Mesh the countershaft and the output shaft assembly and position the two in the bearing housing. Make sure that the thrust washer is installed on the mainshaft assembly at the rear of the first gear. Make sure that the recesses in the synchronizer ring are aligned with the three keys in the synchronizer hub.

16. While holding the mainshaft assembly in place, press the countershaft assembly into the bearing housing using Replacer Tool T71P-7025-A or its equal to hold the rear countershaft bearing in the housing.

17. Position the bearing cover on the bearing housing. Install the five bolts and tighten.

18. If removed, drive the reverse idler shaft into the bearing housing. Install the bolt and tighten.

19. Install the thrust washer, sleeve, caged needle bearing and reverse gear on the output shaft.

20. Install the reverse gear on the countershaft. The offset on the gear must face the bearing housing.

21. Place the keyed thrust washer so the tab is in the groove in the bearing housing. Install the reverse idler gear so the squared portion of the gear faces the bearing housing. Make sure the reverse idler gear and reverse gear are in mesh. Install the spacer and snapring on the idler shaft.

22. Install the 5R synchronizer assembly on the output shaft.

23. Lock the transmission in Reverse and any forward gear. Install a new locknuton the output shaft and tighten 94 to 152 ft. lbs. using Locknut Wrench, T77J-7025-C or its equal.

24. Bend the tab on the locknut with Staking Tool, T77J-7025-F or its equal.

25. Install the 5R synchronizer ring and gear on the output shaft. Make sure the three recesses in the synchronizer ring are aligned with the three keys in the synchronizer hub.

26. Install the sleeve and the counter fifth gear on the countershaft.

27. Install the lock ball in the output shaft and position the thrust washer so the slot in the washer is over the lock ball. Install the retaining ring.

28. Position the output shaft assembly in a press and press the output shaft bearing on the shaft using Dummy Bearing Replacer, T75L-7025-Q or its equal and an appropriate length of press stock. Install the thrust washer and retaining ring.

29. Position the countershaft in a press and press the countershaft rear bearing on the shaft using Dummy Bearing Replacer, T75L-7025-Q or its equal and an appropriate length of press stock. Install the thrust washer and retaining ring.

30. Position all synchronizers in the neutral position. Install the shorter length spring and detent ball in the bottom (5R) bore. Compress the ball and spring with Dummy Shift Rail Tools, T72J-7280 or its equal and install the dummy shift rail in the bore. Install the 5R shift rail in the bottom bore and make sure the three detent slots in the rail face the cap bolt and the interlock slot in the 5R rail baces towards the 1–2 bore. Install the interlock pin through the top bore so it is positioned in the channel between the 5R rail bore and 3–4 rail bore. Install the 3–4 rail in the housing and make sure the three detent slots in the rail face the middle bore. Insert the interlock pin in the channel the 3–4 rail and the 1–2 rail bore. Install the 1–2 shift rail in the housing so the three detent slots in the rail face the top bore.

NOTE: The interlock pins are identical and all four detent balls are identical. The springs for the 5R or bottom bore are of a shorter length than the other two springs.

31. Install the first and second shift fork and the third and fourth shift forks to their respective sleeves.

32. Align the roll pin holes of each shift fork and rod. Install new roll pins.

NOTE: When installing the shift fork and control end, a new roll pin should be installed with a pin slit positioned in the direction of the shift rod axis. If not removed, remove the shift levers from the shift rails. Remember from which rail each lever was removed for correct installation upon assembly.

33. Install the detent balls and springs into their respective bores and install the three cap bolts. The shorter length spring is installed in the bottom (reverse) bore.

34. Install the circlips on the 1–2 and 3–4 shift rails. Install the circlip and washer on the 5R shift rail.

35. Apply a thin coating of Silicone Sealer D6AZ-19562-B or equivalent to the mating surfaces of the transmission case and the bearing housing. Install the transmission case on the bearing housing.

36. Apply a thin coating of Silicone Sealer, D6AZ-19562-B or equivalent to the mating surfaces of the bearing housing and intermediate housing. Install the intermediate housing to the bearing housing.

37. Position the shift lever gates on the appropriate shift rails. Install new roll pins.

38. Place the lock ball in the output shaft and position the speedometer drive gear over the ball. Install the snapring. Install the grommet on the end of the output shaft.

39. Apply a thin coating of Silicone Sealer, D6AZ-19562-B or equivalent to the extension housing and the intermediate housing. Slide the extension housing over the output shaft (the control lever must be moved to the far left) and onto the extension housing. Install the bolts and tighten.

NOTE: If necessary, remove the plugs from the transmission case shift rod bores to align the shift rods. After the installation of the bearing housing assembly, reinstall the plugs using Silicone Sealer, D6AZ-19562-B or equivalent.

40. With the outer snapring in place on the input shaft front bearing, place the bearing, shim and Adapter Tool, T75L-7025-N or its equal over the input shaft.

41. Thread the Replacer Shaft, T75L-7025-K or its equal onto the Adapter Tool. Install the Replacer Tube, T75L-7025-B or its equal over the Replacer Shaft and install the nut and washer on the forcing screw.

42. Slowly tighten the nut until the adapter is securely on the input shaft. Make sure the tools are aligned.

43. Tighten the nut on the forcing screw until the bearing outer snapring is seated. Remove the installation tools.

NOTE: The input shaft bearing retaining ring must be flush with the transmission case. If not flush, it will be necessary to tap on the end of the input shaft with a soft hammer until the bearing is seated.

44. Install the input shaft snapring.

45. Measure the distance between the end of the installed input bearing in the transmission case with a depth micrometer. Measure the distance between the bearing cover gasket and the bottom of the bearing bore in the cover. The difference between the two measurements is the clearance between the outer bearing race and the front cover. The clearance should be less than 0.0039 inch. Clearance can be adjusted by installing an adjusting shim. Shims are available in sizes of 0.006 inch and 0.012 inch.

46. Install a new oil seal in the front cover using Installer Tool, T71P-7025-A. Install the shim in the recess in the front cover.

47. Apply gear lubricant to the lip of the oil seal inside the front cover and install the front cover to the transmission case. Install the six bolts and tighten.

48. Install the control lever end to the control lever and tighten the attaching bolt 20–25 ft. lbs.

49. Install the back-up lamp switch and the neutral safety

switch to the extension housing and tighten the switches 20–25 ft. lbs.

50. Install the gearshift lever retainer and gasket to the extension housing. Install the four bolts and tighten 20–27 ft. lbs. If required, install the gearshift lever.

51. Install the release bearing and fork.

The Fuller Transmissions

When working with the Fuller transmissions, many similarities will be found among the different transmission models. Top gear ratios can be changed in the service field from direct to overdrive, or vice-versa. A deep reduction gear can be added to provide for greater initial torque. For these reasons, the model numbers of the transmissions are most important and should be referred to during minor or major repairs.

A unique feature of this transmission family is that the input shaft and the front drive gear are not integral and can be changed separately on many of the models.

Air pressure is used to provide the shifting of the transmission to and from high and low ranges. Air pressure is also used to shift in and out of the deep reduction gearing, when used.

Fuller T-905-A Five Speed

NOTE: The disassembly and assembly of the basic T-905-A transmission is the same as the RT-910 transmission, after all exterior components have been removed from them. The exceptions are that the right countershaft bearing on the T 905-A must be removed before the mainshaft is lifted from the case, also the T-905 has two keys in the mainshaft. To disassemble, follow the steps 1 thru 9 then refer to Fuller RT-910 ten speed main transmission disassembly procedures.

Disassembly

1. Remove the bolts that attach the shifting bar housing to the transmission case. Tap the housing free from the transmission case.
2. Lock the mainshaft by engaging two gears at one time with the sliding clutches.
3. Remove the companion flange attaching nut, then the flange.
4. Remove the rear bearing cover attaching screws and pry off the cover.
5. Remove the speedometer drive gear, spacer, and bearing washer from the output shaft.
6. Remove the rear bearing from the output shaft.
7. Remove the lock wire and the two flat key attaching screws. Lift the two keys from the output shaft and remove the shaft.
8. Remove the clutch release mechanism from the flywheel housing.
9. Remove the bolts and nuts that attach the flywheel housing to the transmission case.

Assembly

NOTE: Refer to the Fuller RT-910 ten speed transmission assembly procedures for assembly of the basic transmission, then proceed as follows.

1. Place a new flywheel housing gasket on the front of the transmission case.
2. Position the flywheel housing on the six studs and install the nuts, bolts and lockwashers.
3. Position the output shaft on the coupling gear and install the two flat keys and attaching bolts. Tighten the bolts and secure with lock wire.
4. Install the rear bearing on the output shaft.
5. Position the bearing washer and the drive gear or spacer on the output shaft.
6. Use a new bearing cover gasket and install the bearing cover on the case.

Fuller RT-906 Six Speed

The RT-906 transmission has six forward speeds and two reverse speeds. The transmission includes a three speed front section and a two speed auxiliary or range section, both contained in one case. First through third speeds are obtained by using the three gear ratios in the front section through the low speed gear of the range section. Fourth through sixth speeds are obtained by using the three gear ratios in the front sections through the high speed (direct drive) range gear.

SEPARATION OF THE MAIN AND AUXILIARY SECTIONS

1. After the transmission assembly is removed, disconnect the air hoses at the air valve.
2. Remove the air filter and air regulator valve assemblies.
3. Remove the four bolts attaching the air valve to the adapter plate and remove the valve.
4. Remove the alignment sleeve, spring, and actuating pin from the air valve adapter plate. Then remove the plate from the transmission.
5. With the transmission in neutral, remove the gear shift housing cover. Drain the transmission lubricant.
6. Lock the transmission in two gears and remove the U-Joint flange.
7. Remove the bolts that attach the auxiliary section to the transmission case. Install three puller screws in the tapped holes of the rear plate and tighten them alternately and evenly, to move the auxiliary section to the rear just far enough to break the gasket seal.

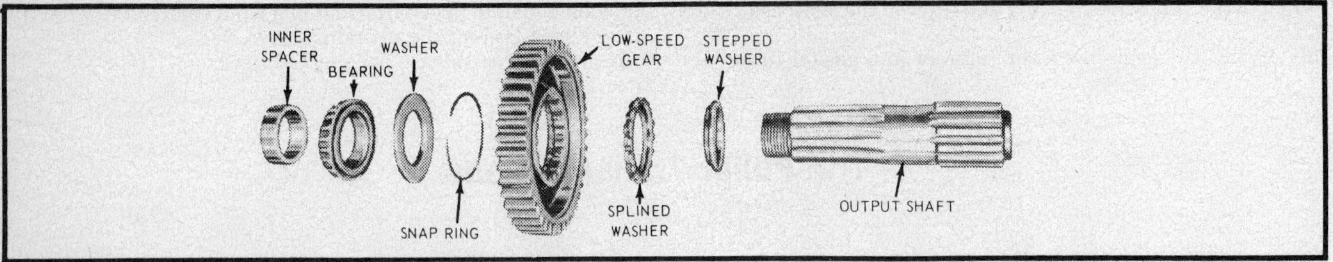

Output shaft auxiliary section (© Ford Motor Co.)

8. Attach a chain hoist to the auxiliary section and separate it from the transmission.
9. Remove the bolts and nuts that attach the clutch housing to the transmission and remove the housing.

MAIN TRANSMISSION

NOTE: Refer to Fuller T-905-A five speed transmission section for disassembly and assembly of the main transmission.

AUXILIARY SECTION

Disassembly

1. Remove the shift cylinder cover bolts and remove the cover.
2. Remove the nut from the end of the shifter shaft. Using puller screws, remove the piston from the shift cylinder.
3. Remove the bolts that attach the shift cylinder housing to the rear plate.
4. Cut the lock wires and remove the set screws from the shifting fork. It may be necessary to rotate the shift cylinder housing to expose the set screws.
5. Push the shifter shaft to the inside, through the fork hub, and out of the cylinder housing. Remove the shifting fork and the shift cylinder housing from the plate.
6. Remove the countershaft gear by removing the snapring and pressing the gear from each shaft.
7. Disassemble the synchronizer by removing the direct (high range) cone synchronizer ring from the pins of the low speed synchronizer ring. Be careful not to lose the three springs located in the bores of the direct cone synchronizer.
8. Remove the sliding clutch gear from the pins of the low speed synchronizer.
9. Remove the inner bearing spacer from the output shaft.
10. Using the front face of the low speed gear as a base, press the shaft through the gear, washers and bearing.

Assembly

1. Install the stepped and splined washers on the output shaft. Make sure the small diameters are toward the threaded end of the shaft.
2. Install the low speed gear on the output shaft with the flat side up. Then, install the cone-shaped washer with the flat side against the gear.
3. Install the bearing on the shaft with the taper toward the threaded end.
4. Install the inner bearing spacer on the shaft and against the bearing.
5. With the low speed synchronizer ring on a bench with the pins up, install the clutch sliding gear on the pins.
6. Install the three springs in the direct synchronizer and press the direct synchronizer over the pins of the low speed synchronizer ring.
7. Install the key on each countershaft and press the countershaft onto each drive gear.
8. Install the snapring on the front of each countershaft.
9. With the rear plate on a bench, place the front cup of the rear bearing into the rear bore of the plate. (Taper to the inside).
10. Place the bearing outer spacer on the front cup.
11. Place the rear cup on the spacer and tap the two cups and spacer into the rear plate bore.
12. Place the rear plate over the output shaft. Make sure that the bearing on the shaft is seated on the rear plate front bearing cup.
13. Install the rear bearing on the output shaft.
14. If the rear bearing cover was removed install a new oil seal and replace the cover. Use a star washer at the hole which intersects with the speedometer bore.
15. Install the synchronizer assembly on the output shaft, with the low-speed synchronizer ring toward the low speed gear.
16. To install and time the auxiliary countershafts, mark the gear tooth which is stamped O on the small diameter low range gear of each countershaft. This tooth will be aligned with the keyway in the countershaft drive gear. These two teeth, one on each countershaft, must mesh at the same time with the output shaft low speed gear, and be in directly opposite positions.
17. Mark any two adjacent teeth on the output shaft low speed gear. Then, mark the two adjacent teeth, which are directly opposite the 1st set marked. There should be the same number of teeth between the markings on each side of the gear.
18. Place the rear plate assembly on wood blocking, with the threaded end of the output shaft up. Make sure the blocking is also placed under the synchronizer assembly to prevent it from dropping from the output shaft.
19. Place each countershaft into position and place wood blocking under each shaft. For correct timing be sure to place the marked teeth of the countershafts into mesh with the marked teeth of the low speed gear.
20. Install the rear bearing on each countershaft. Recheck the gears to be sure that they are correctly timed.
21. Position a rear bearing retainer plate on each countershaft and install the attaching bolts and lock wire. Install the rear bearing covers.
22. Install a new O-ring in the shift cylinder bore if necessary.
23. Position the shifting fork on the sliding clutch gear and install the shift cylinder into the bore of the rear plate.
24. Insert the threaded end of the shifter shaft through the front of the shift cylinder, through the shifting fork hub and into the cylinder bore. Install the set screws and lock wire.
25. Install new O-rings on the shift cylinder position if they were removed.
26. Install the piston in the shift cylinder bore.
27. Install the cover on the shift cylinder.

JOINING THE MAIN AND AUXILIARY SECTIONS

1. Attach the clutch housing to the transmission case.

2. Using a chain hoist, attach the auxiliary section to the transmission. It may be necessary to rotate the drive gear to properly mesh the gears.

3. With the transmission locked in two gears, install the speedometer drive gear and U-joint flange on the mainshaft. If the speedometer drive gear is not used, be sure to install a replacement spacer of the same width.

4. Install the gearshift housing cover.

5. Install the air valve plate and housing.

6. Install the air filter and air regulator valve assemblies and connect the hoses at the valve.

7. Fill transmission with the specified fluid.

Fuller RT-9509, RT-12509, RTO-958LL, RTO-1258LL, RT-11509
Eight And Nine Speed Transmissions

This transmission is the twin countershaft design. The mainshaft gears, when not engaged, float between the countershaft gears, eliminating the need for gear sleeves and bushings. All gears are constant mesh with spur type teeth. There are nine progressive forward ratios and two reverse, consisting of a five speed front section and a synchronized two speed range auxiliary section.

SEPARATION OF THE MAIN AND AUXILIARY SECTIONS

1. After the transmission assembly is removed, remove the shifter bar housing assembly.

2. Lock the transmission in gear and remove the output yoke nut from the tailshaft.

3. Remove the output yoke and the speedometer drive gear.

4. Separate the auxiliary section from the case by removing the capscrews and using three puller screws to break the gasket seal.

5. Use a chain hoist to support the weight and pull the auxiliary section rearward from the transmission case.

MAIN TRANSMISSION

Disassembly

1. Remove the clutch housing.

2. Remove the rear coupling snapring from the mainshaft.

3. Cut the lockwire and remove the three capscrews that attach the bearing retainer to the case.

4. Insert three puller screws in the tapped holes in the retainer ring and tighten evenly to pull the assembly from the case bore.

5. Remove the snapring and press or drive the retainer ring and bearing from the auxiliary drive gear. To remove the left idler gear, the reverse gear on the mainshaft must first be moved forward to provide the necessary clearance.

6. Remove the snapring from the inside diameter of the mainshaft reverse gear.

7. Move the mainshaft gear as far forward as possible into engagement with the sliding clutch.

8. Use an inside jaw puller and remove the auxiliary countershaft front bearing outer race from the left reverse idler gear bore.

9. Inside the case, turn the elastic stop nut from the threads of the reverse idler shaft and remove the washer.

10. Unscrew the plug from the end of the idler shaft and attach an impact puller. Pull the idler shaft from the gear and idler boss while holding the gear and thrust washer inside the case. Remove the gear and thrust washer from the case.

12. If necessary remove bearing inner race, cup and washer.

13. If necessary press the bearing from the reverse idler gear. It may be necessary to remove the bearings from the right

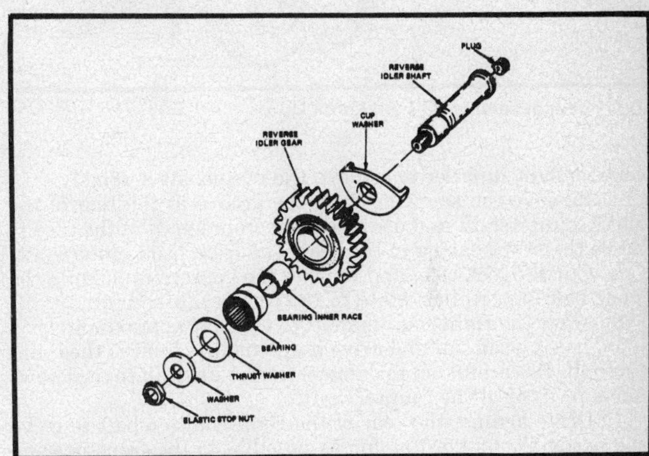

Reverse idler gear assembly (© Ford Motor Co.)

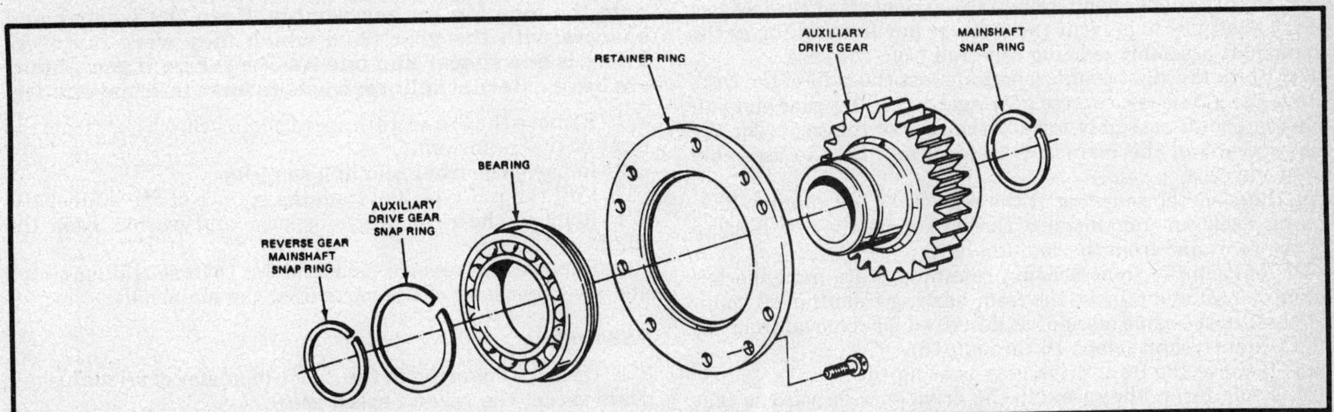

Auxiliary drive gear assembly (© Ford Motor Co.)

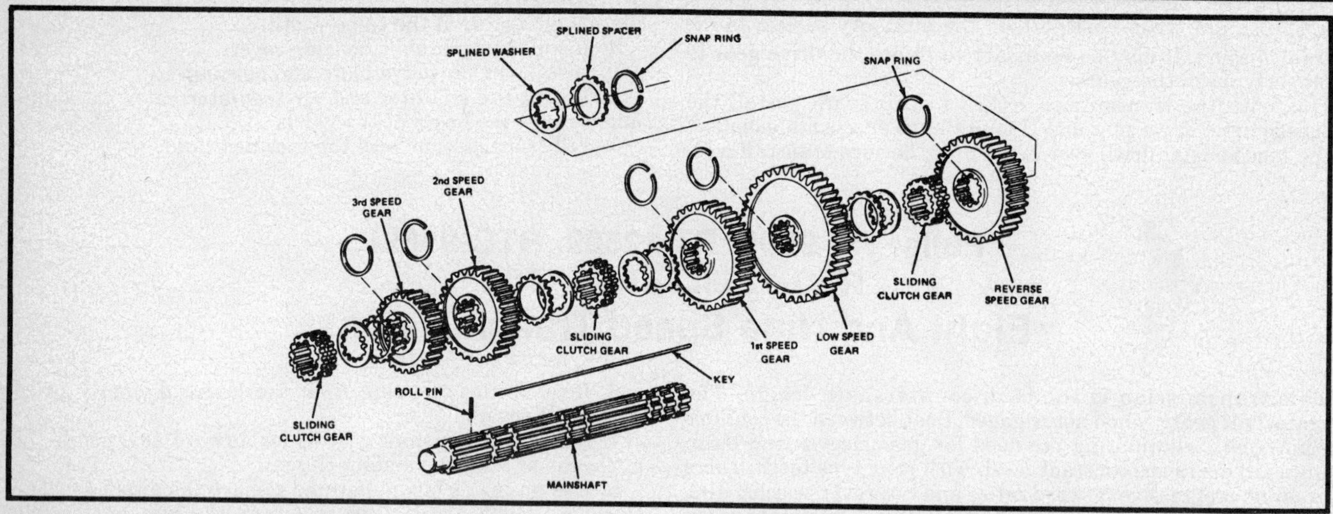

Mainshaft assembly (© Ford Motor Co.)

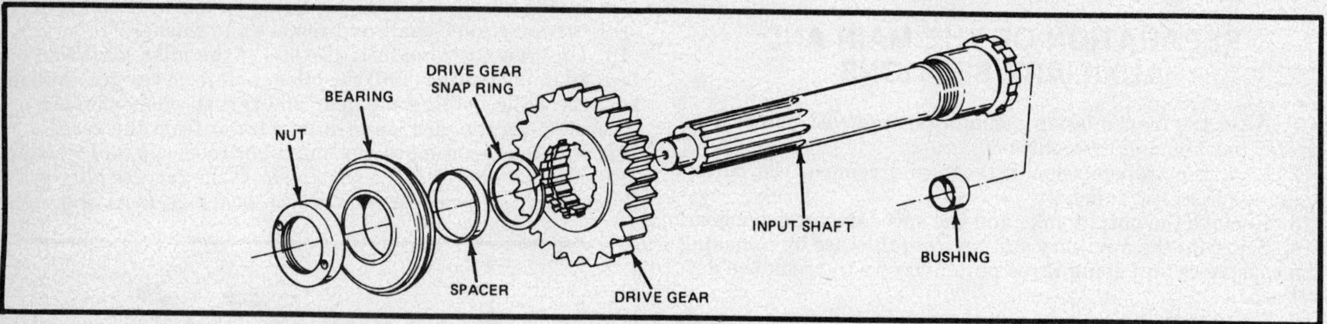

Drive gear assembly (© Ford Motor Co.)

countershaft in order to remove the mainshaft assembly.

14. Remove the snapring from the groove at the rear of the right countershaft and use a soft bar from inside of the case to move the rear bearing to the rear, and from the countershaft.

15. Cut the lockwire, and remove the capscrews holding the front bearing retainer plate to the right countershaft.

16. Move the right countershaft to the rear approximately $1/2$ inch, using a soft bar and drive it against the front of the countershaft. Be careful not to damage the retainer plate capscrews holes in front of the countershaft.

17. Drive against the rear of the right countershaft to move the assembly forward as far as possible so the front bearing snapring is exposed.

18. Using a puller or pry bars remove the front bearing.

19. Place a rubber band around the mainshaft at the location of the shaft key to prevent the rod type key from falling as the mainshaft assembly is being removed from the case.

20. Block the right countershaft against the wall of the case. Move the mainshaft reverse gear against the 1st gear and pull the mainshaft assembly toward the rear of the case. Tilt the forward end of the mainshaft upward and lift the assembly from the case.

21. Remove the snapring at the rear of the left countershaft. Using a soft bar from inside of the case, move the rear bearing to the rear, and from the countershaft.

22. Remove the front bearing retaining plate from the left countershaft and remove the front bearing from the left countershaft in the same manner as described for removal from the right countershaft (steps 16 through 18).

23. Remove the front drive gear bearing cover.

24. From inside the case, tap the drive gear forward so that the snapring can be removed from the bearing. Use a soft bar and move the drive gear forward if necessary.

25. Move the drive gear assembly to the inside of the case and remove from the case.

26. Remove the countershaft assemblies from the case.

27. Pull the outer race of the auxiliary countershaft bearing from the right reverse idler gear bore.

28. Remove the right reverse idler gear and shaft and disassemble as previously described for the left reverse idler gear (steps 9 through 13).

MAINSHAFT

Disassembly

NOTE: When removing washers, spacers and gears, note the location for reassembly. Keep the washer and spacers with the gear from which they were removed. There is one spacer and one washer for each gear. Spacers have external splines; washers have internal splines.

1. Remove the 3rd and 4th speed sliding clutch gear from the front of the mainshaft.
2. Remove the front coupling snapring.
3. Pull the rod type key from the splines of the mainshaft.
4. Remove the reverse gear spacer and washer from the shaft.
5. Remove the reverse gear and 1st reverse sliding clutch and the remainder of the parts from the mainshaft.

Assembly

1. Install a snapring in the inside diameter of all mainshaft gears except the reverse speed gear.
2. Make sure the roll pin is in place in the bore between splines near the pilot end of the mainshaft.

NOTE When replacing parts on the mainshaft assembly the resetting or axial clearances for mainshaft gears may be necessary. Washers are available in six thicknesses to obtain the correct limits. Always use the low limit washer in the reverse, 1st and 3rd speed gear positions. In most cases, when setting up the reverse gear clearance, the low limit washer will give the correct clearance. However, if desired, this clearance can be measured before the mainshaft assembly is installed in the case. This is done by securing the reverse gear in position on the mainshaft with the reverse gear snapring and the front coupling snapring, then securing the auxiliary drive gear assembly in position on the rear of the mainshaft with the rear coupling snapring.

3. With the forward end of the mainshaft in a vise, place a 3rd speed gear washer over the rear of the shaft and move downward to the lowest radial groove in the shaft, flat side up. Rotate the washer to align the internal splines with the splines of the mainshaft. Temporarily install the key in the spline to keep the washer aligned, pushing down against the roll pin.
4. Install the 3rd speed gear spacer with the flat side down.
5. Install the 3rd speed gear on a spacer with the clutching teeth down.
6. Install the 2nd speed gear with the clutching teeth up.
7. Install a spacer in the hub of the 2nd speed gear with the flat side up.
8. Remove the key and install a 2nd speed gear washer with the flat side down, aligning splines with the mainshaft. Use a feeler gauge between the hub of the gears to obtain a reading. Change the washer as required for the correct end play specifications.
9. Relocate the key to the lockwashers in position.
10. Install the 1st and 2nd speed sliding clutch gear and align the keyway in the sliding clutch gear with a key.
11. Remove the key and install the 1st speed gear washer with the flat side up.
12. Install the 1st speed gear spacer, with the flat side down.
13. Install the 1st speed gear with the clutching teeth down.
14. Install the low speed gear with the clutching teeth up.
15. Install the low speed gear spacer in the hub of the gear with the flat side up.
16. Remove the key and install the low speed gear washer with the flat side down and the splines aligned. Use a feeler gauge between the hub of the gears and change the washer if required to obtain the correct end play specifications.
17. Relocate the key to the lockwashers in position.
18. Install the low/reverse sliding clutch gear and align the keyway with the key.
19. Install the reverse gear on the sliding clutch gear and engage it with both the low and reverse gear.
20. Remove the key and install the reverse gear washer in the radial groove on the mainshaft. Align the splines and relocate the key.
21. Install the reverse spacer with the flat side down.
22. Install the snapring in the second radial groove from the top. Install it so that the gap between the ends of the snapring is placed at the location of the key in the spline.

NOTE: The key is not held in place by the snapring, it is held in position by the hub of the auxiliary drive gear when installed.

23. Temporarily place a rubber band on the mainshaft to hold the key in position during installation of the mainshaft assembly.
24. Remove the assembly from the vise and install the 3rd and 4th speed sliding clutch gear.

DRIVE GEAR

Disassembly

1. Free the bearing nut where it is peened to the shaft.
2. Using an appropriate tool remove the bearing nut from the drive shaft, left hand thread.
3. Press the shaft through the bearing and gear using the rear face of the drive gear as a base.
4. Check the bushing in the pocket end of the drive shaft and

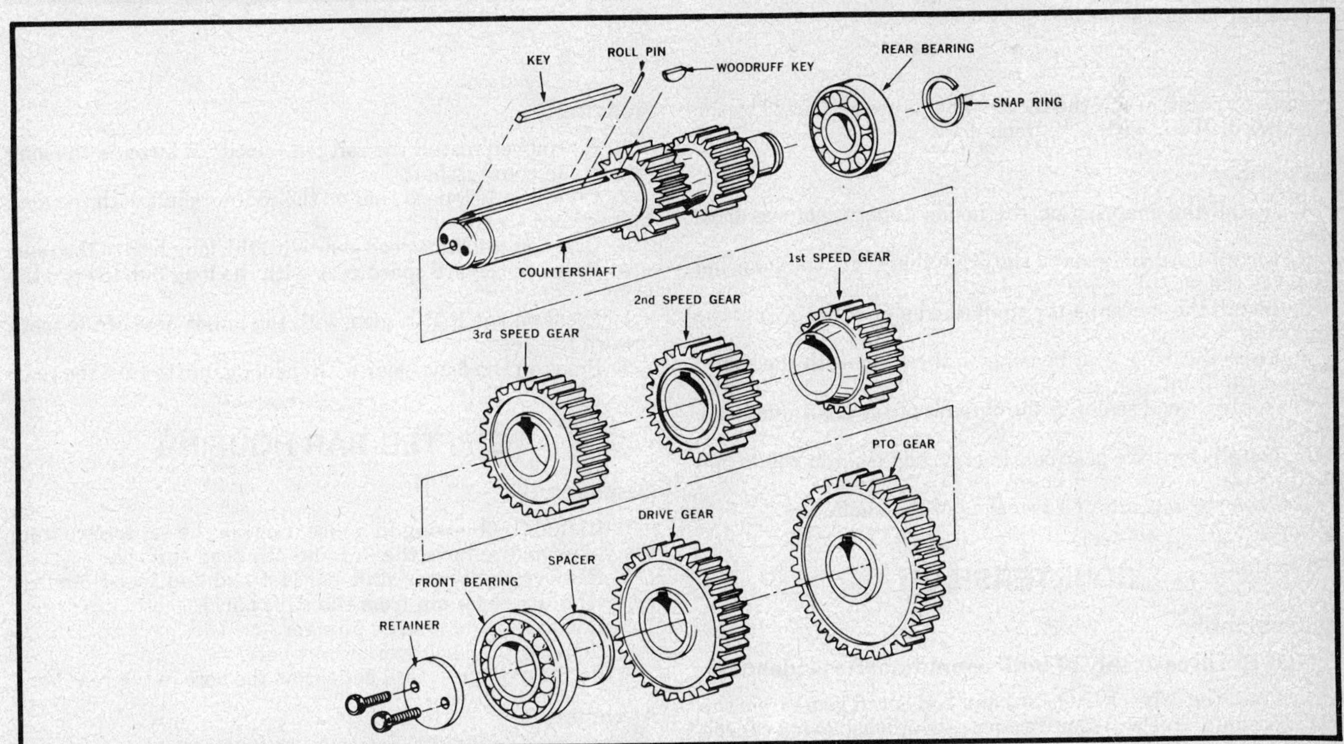

Exploded view of the countershaft assemblies (© Ford Motor Co.)

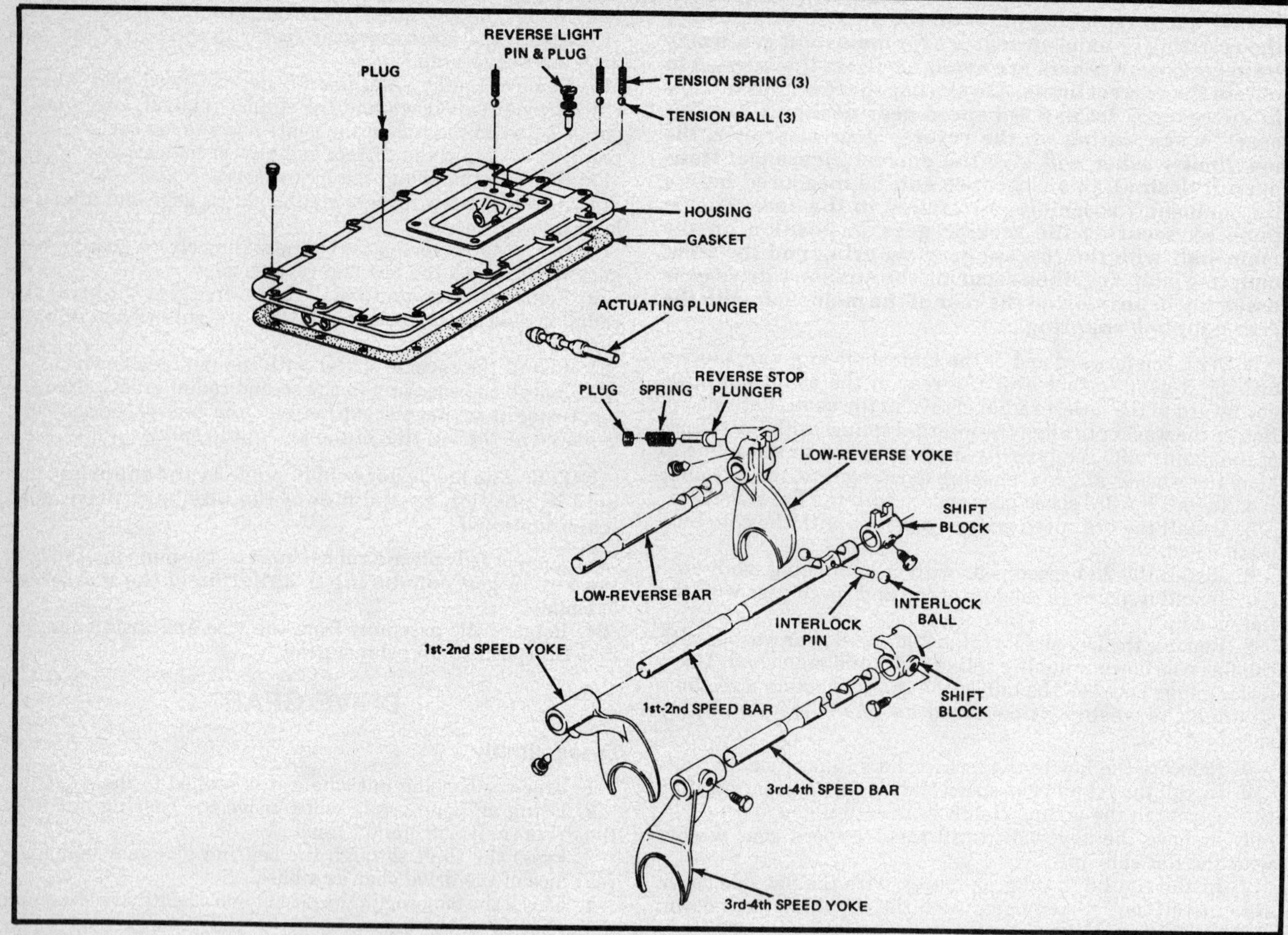

Shifter bar housing assembly (© Ford Motor Co.)

replace as necessary. If the three oil holes are restricted by the bushing drill out with a $^5/_{32}$ inch drill.

Assembly

1. Install the snapring on the inside diameter of the drive gear.
2. Install the drive gear on the drive shaft with the snapring towards the front.
3. Install the spacer on the shaft and against the gear of the snapring.
4. Press the drive gear bearing on the shaft with the shield toward the front.
5. Apply thread sealer to the threads of the shaft and bearing nut.
6. Install the drive gear bearing nut and tighten 250 to 300 ft. lbs.
7. Peen the nut into the two slots of the shaft.

COUNTERSHAFT

Disassembly

NOTE: Disassembly of both countershafts is identical.

1. Press the drive, P.T.O., 3rd and 2nd speed gears from the countershaft. This will require a press of at least 25 ton capacity. Never use the P.T.O. gear as a base for pressing.
2. Press the 1st speed gear from the countershaft.

Assembly

1. If removed install the roll pin, Woodruff key and the long key in the countershaft.
2. Press the 1st speed gear on the countershaft with the long hub toward the front.
3. Press on the 2nd speed gear with the long hub to the rear.
4. Press on the 3rd speed gear with the long hub toward the front.
5. Press on the P.T.O. gear with the bullet nose of the teeth toward the rear.
6. Press on the drive gear with the long hub toward the rear.

SHIFTER BAR HOUSING

Disassembly

1. Clamp the housing in a vise, remove the set screws from the yokes and remove the 3rd and 4th peed shift bar.
2. Remove the center shift bar (1st and 2nd speed) and remove the interlock pin from the shift bar.
3. Remove the actuating plunger.
4. Remove the low/reverse shift bar.
5. Remove the interlock balls from the bore in the rear boss.

Assembly

1. Install the housing in a vise with the short shift bar at the bottom and the rear of the housing to the right.

2. Install the shift bars through the rear bores of the housing with the neutral and shift notches to the rear. Keep the bars in the neutral position when installed.

3. Install the low/reverse shift bar and yoke. If previously disassembled, install the reverse stop plunger, spring and plug in the bore in the low/reverse yoke until 1 $^1/_4$ to 2 threads protrude. Make sure the plunger can fully depress into the bore at the yoke slot. Stake the plug through the small hole in the yoke.

4. Install the yoke set screw and tighten 45 to 55 ft. lbs. Wire securely.

5. Install the actuating plunger.

6. Install the $^3/_4$ inch interlock ball in the rear boss.

7. Install the 1st and 2nd speed shift bar in the center rear boss in the housing through the shift block, center boss and 1st and 2nd speed yoke. Insert the interlock pin in the bore in the neutral notch of the shift bar as the neutral notch of the bar enters the rear bar of the housing. The shift block is installed with the wire support to the rear and the yoke is installed with the fork to the rear. Keep the shift bar so that the interlock pin remains in the vertical position during the remainder of assembly. Rotation of the bar will allow the interlock pin to jam into the tension spring bores.

8. Install the yoke and shift block setscrews and tighten 45 to 55 ft. lbs. Wire securely.

9. Install the second $^3/_4$ inch interlock ball in the rear boss.

10. Install the 3rd and 4th speed shift bar in the top rear bore of the housing through the shift block, center boss and the 3rd and 4th speed yoke, with the fork to the front. Install the block and yoke setscrews and tighten 45 to 55 ft. lbs. Wire securely.

11. Install the three tension balls in the bores at the shift bar locations.

12. Install the tension springs over the tension balls. The green coded spring is installed in the 3rd and 4th speed shift bar location. (Left side).

MAIN TRANSMISSION

Assembly

NOTE: Before starting assembly make certain that all magnetic discs are in place in the bottom of the case.

1. Install the plug in the right reverse idler gear shaft.
2. Install the cup washer on the shaft.
3. Install the bearing inner race on the shaft against the cup washer.
4. If previously removed, press the needle bearing into the bore of the reverse idler gear.
5. Insert the threaded end of the idler shaft through the lower right hole at the rear of the transmission case. As the shaft is inserted through the bore install the thrust washer and reverse idler gear. Make certain the needle bearings in the gear seat on the inner race evenly before completing installation of the shaft.
6. Install the elastic stop nut and washer on the shaft and tighten 50 to 60 ft. lbs.
7. Using an appropriate driver install the auxiliary countershaft front bearing outer race in the right reverse idler gear shaft bore.
8. On the drive gear of each countershaft mark the gear tooth which aligns with the keyway in the shaft. This tooth will be stamped with an "O".
9. Place the left countershaft assembly (47 tooth P.T.O. gear) into position in the case. Do not install the bearings.
10. Mark any two adjacent gear teeth on the drive gear. Then mark the two adjacent teeth which are directly opposite the first set marked. There should be the same number of teeth between the marking on each side of the gear.
11. Insert the drive gear through the bore from inside the case. Work the drive gear past the countershafts and seat the bearing in the front bore.
12. Install the snapring in the groove in the bearing.
13. Use a block to center the rear of the left countershaft in the case bore.
14. Mesh the mark tooth on the left countershaft with the marked teeth on the drive gear.
15. Install the spacer on the countershaft and using a suitable driver, install the front bearing in the bore and on the left countershaft.
16. Remove the block at the rear of the left countershaft and install the rear bearing in the case bore using a suitable driver.
17. Install the bearing retainer plate on the front of the left countershaft and tighten the cap screws 50 to 65 ft. lbs. Wire securely.
18. Install the snapring in the groove at the rear of the countershaft.
19. From inside the case, insert the rear of the mainshaft assembly through the rear bearing bore and lower the assembly into position.
20. Move the mainshaft assembly forward to seat the pilot end of the shaft into the bushing in the pocket of the drive gear

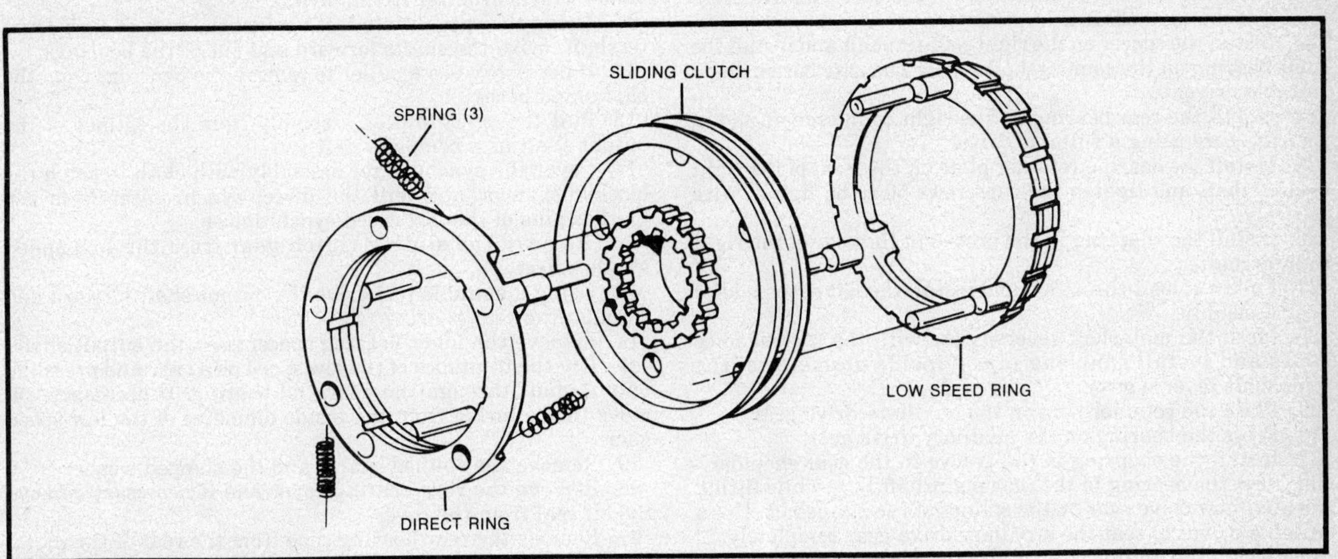

Exploded view of synchronizer assembly—RT0-1258LL transmission (© Eaton Corp.)

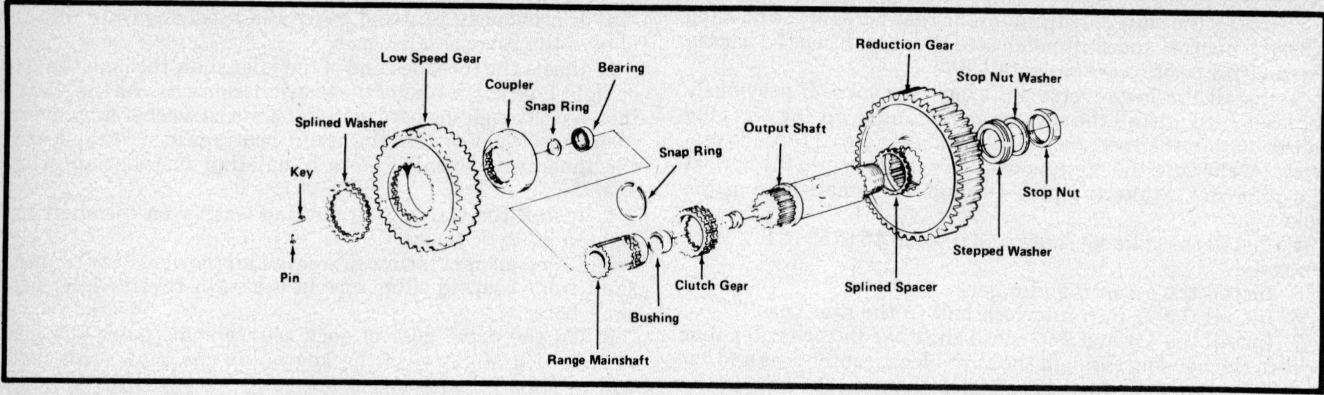

Exploded view of the deep reduction gear and output shaft—RT0-1258LL auxiliary section (© Eaton Corp.)

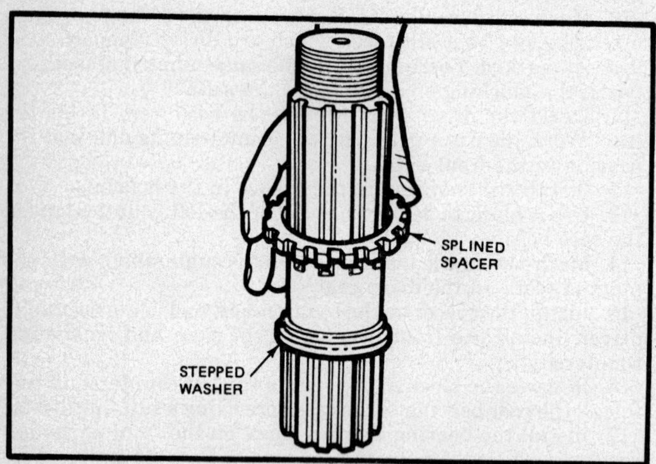

Output shaft splined spacer and stepped washer
(© Ford Motor Co.)

shaft. Remove the rubber band that was temporarily installed at the rear of the mainshaft.

21. Mesh the timing tooth on the right countershaft with the timing teeth marked on the drive gear. Mesh the countershaft gears with the mainshaft gears.

22. Center the rear of the right countershaft in the case bore and center the rear of the mainshaft in the bore. Accurate centering of the mainshaft is important.

23. Install the spacer on the right countershaft and install the front bearing on the countershaft and in the case bore using a suitable driver.

24. Install the rear bearing on the right countershaft and in the case bore using a suitable driver.

25. Install the bearing retainer plate on the front of the right countershaft and tighten the capscrews 50 to 65 ft. lbs. Wire securely.

26. Install the snapring in the groove in the rear of the right countershaft.

27. Follow steps 1 through 7 and install the left reverse idler gear assembly.

28. Mesh the mainshaft reverse gear with the reverse idler gears and install snapring in the inside diameter of the mainshaft reverse gear.

29. Place the retainer ring on the auxiliary drive gear.

30. Press the bearing on the auxiliary drive gear.

31. Install the snapring in the groove in the gear shoulder.

32. Seat the bearing in the rear mainshaft bore while fitting the auxiliary drive gear on the splines of the mainshaft. Use a suitable driver to seat the auxiliary drive gear completely.

33. Secure the retainer ring with capscrews and tighten 35 to 45 ft. lbs. Wire in groups of three.

34. Install the rear coupling snapring in the groove at the rear of the mainshaft.

35. Install the gasket and the front drive gear bearing cover. Tighten the capscrews 35 to 45 ft. lbs.

AUXILIARY SECTION

Disassembly

1. Remove the capscrews holding the shift cylinder cover to the housing.
2. Remove the elastic stop nut from the rear of the shift bar.
3. Cut the lockwire and remove the two yoke set screws.
4. Push the shift bar to the rear and remove the bar and piston from the shift cylinder housing.
5. If necessary, remove the O-rings from the inside diameter and outside diameter of the piston.
6. Remove the yoke.
7. Remove the shift cylinder housing from the auxiliary section plate.
8. Remove the two countershaft rear bearing covers from the plate.
9. Remove the snapring from the rear of each countershaft.
10. To remove the countershafts, place the auxiliary section plate on wooden blocks so that the front of the countershafts are approximately two inches from the work bench surface. Also place blocking under the synchronizer assembly to prevent the synchronizer from moving.
11. Using the appropriate tool against the rear of each countershaft, drive the shafts forward and out of the bearings.
12. If necessary use a puller to remove the bearings from the shafts and bores.
13. Pull the synchronizer assembly from the splines of the output shaft as a complete unit.
14. Cover the synchronizer assembly with cloth to catch the blocker springs, and pull the direct synchronizer from the blocker pins of the low speed synchronizer.
15. Remove the sliding clutch gear from the low speed synchronizer.
16. Using a suitable tool drive the output shaft forward and through the rear bearing.
17. Remove the inner bearing spacer from the output shaft.
18. Use the front face of the low speed as a base and press the output shaft through the gear and bearing. If necessary, remove the snapring from the inside diameter of the low speed gear.
19. Remove the splined spacer and the stepped washer.
20. Remove the rear bearing cover and if necessary remove the oil seal from the cover.
21. Remove the rear bearing cone from the rear of the plate.
22. Remove the two bearing cups and outer spacer from the rear of the output shaft bore in the auxiliary section plate.

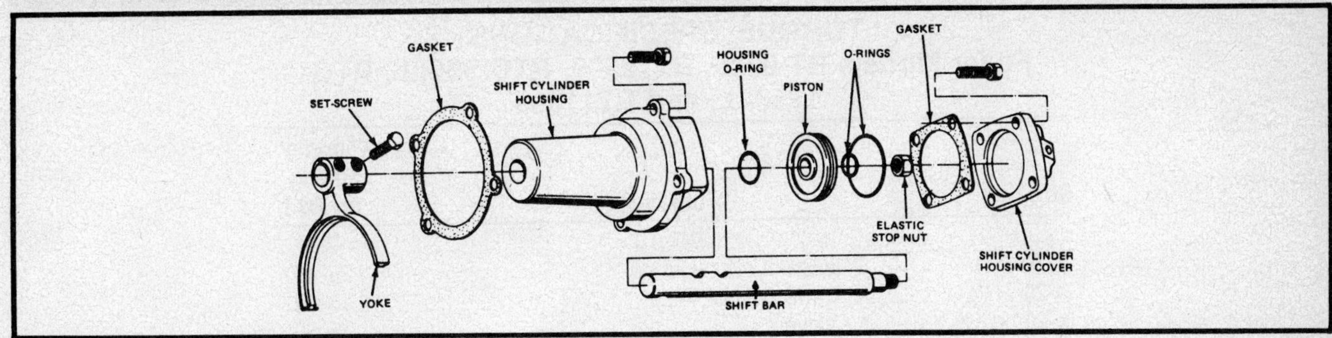

Range shift cylinder assembly (© Ford Motor Co.)

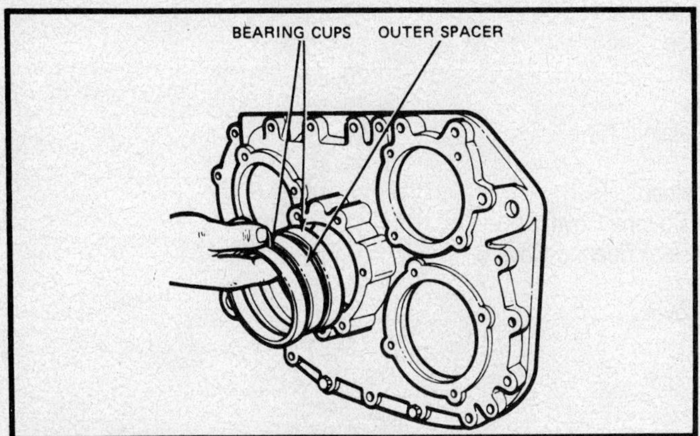

Output shaft bearing cups and spacer (© Ford Motor Co.)

Assembly

1. Install the stepped washer and the splined spacer on the output shaft.
2. If removed, install the snapring in the inside diameter of the low speed gear.
3. Install the low speed gear on the output shaft and on the splined spacer with the flat side of the gear toward the threaded end of the output shaft.
4. Install the washer on the shaft against the flat side of the low speed gear.
5. Install the front bearing cone on the shaft against the washer with the taper toward the threaded end of the output shaft. The front and rear bearing cones are a matched set. Make sure the correct cone for the cup is used as indicated by markings. Heating of the bearing cones for installation is recommended, provided the bearing is not heated over 275 degrees F. Heat lamps are recommended as a heating source.
6. Install the inner bearing spacer on the output shaft against the bearing cone.
7. Install the front bearing cup in the rear bore of the plate with the tapered end toward the front of the output shaft.
8. Install the outer spacer on the front bearing cup and use a soft bar to tap it evenly into the bore.
9. Install the rear bearing cup on the outer spacer and use a soft bar to tap it evenly into the bore until the lip seats against the housing.
10. Place the sliding clutch gear on the pins of the low speed synchronizer.
11. Install the three springs in the direct synchronizer.
12. Place the direct synchronizer over the blocker pins of the low speed synchronizer and compress the springs to fully seat it.
13. On the small diameter (low range) gear of each countershaft, mark the gear tooth which is stamped with an "O".
14. Mark any two adjacent teeth on the output shaft low speed gear, then mark the two adjacent teeth which are directly opposite the 1st set marked.
15. Place the synchronizer assembly with the flat side down on blocking about two inches high.
16. Place the output shaft into position on the synchronizer assembly, meshing the splines of the shaft with the synchronizer sliding clutch gear.
17. With the bearing inner race installed on the front of each auxiliary countershaft, place both countershafts against the output shaft while meshing the marked tooth on each countershaft low range gear between two of the marked teeth on the output shaft low speed gear.
18. Place the auxiliary section plate down onto the shafts and center the shafts in the bearing bores.
19. Heat and install the rear bearing cone on the output shaft.
20. If previously removed, install the oil seal in the rear bearing cover.
21. Install the cover and gasket on the plate and tighten the capscrews 35 to 45 ft. lbs. The capscrew with the brass washer is installed in the hole which passes through the speedometer drive bore.
22. Use a soft bar and install the auxiliary countershaft rear bearings onto the shafts and into the bore. Use a bearing driver to complete the installation. Be careful not to damage the bearings. It may be necessary to block up the outer edges of the plate to install the rear bearings.
23. Install the snapring in the groove on each countershaft.
24. Install the rear bearing covers and gaskets and tighten the capscrews 35 to 45 ft. lbs.
25. Insert the shift cylinder housing in the bore on the auxiliary section plate and tighten the capscrews 35 to 45 ft. lbs.
26. If previously removed, install the O-ring in the range shift cylinder.
27. Install the yoke into the sliding clutch gear of the synchronizer and insert the shift bar, the non threaded end first through the rear of the range shift cylinder and yoke hub. Secure the yoke to the bar with set screws and tighten 45 to 55 ft. lbs. Lockwire securely.
28. If previously removed, install the range shift piston O-rings.
29. Secure the piston to the shift bar with the elastic stop nut and tighten 80 to 90 ft. lbs.
30. Install the range shift cylinder cover and gasket and tighten the capscrews 35 to 45 ft. lbs.

JOINING OF MAIN AND AUXILIARY SECTIONS

1. Position the auxiliary section suspended from a chain hoist at the rear of the transmission case. Move the auxiliary section evenly onto the rear of the transmission with the gasket in place between the sections. The two countershaft drive gears will mesh with the auxiliary drive gear, and the front of the countershafts with the inner race of the bearings installed

TORQUE SPECIFICATIONS
Fuller Models RT-9509, RT12509, RTO-958LL, RTO-1258LL, and RT11509

Size	Location	Torque Rating (ft. lbs.)
	BOLTS	
3/8-16 × 1 1/4	Gear Shift Lever Housing	35–45
1/4-20 × 7/8	Air Valve Adaptor Plate	15–20
1/4-20 × 1 3/4	Air Valve	15–20
3/8-16 × 3/4	Air Regulator—Filter Bracket	20–25
3/8-16 × 1 1/4	Shifter Bar Housing	35–45
3/8-16 × 1 3/4	Auxiliary Section to Case	35–45
3/8-16 × 2	Auxiliary Section to Case	35–45
1/2-13 × 1 1/2	Clutch Housing to Case	70–80
1/2-13 × 3 1/2	Clutch Housing to Case	70–80
3/8-16 × 1	Auxiliary Drive Gear Retainer Ring	35–45
3/8-16 × 1 1/4	Front Bearing Cover	35–45
1/2-20 × 1	C/S Front Bearing Retainer	50–65
3/8-16 × 2 3/4	Auxiliary Section Rear Bearing Cover	35–45
3/8-16 × 1 1/4	Auxiliary Countershaft Rear Bearing Covers	35–45
3/8-16 × 1	Range Shift Cylinder	35–45
3/8-16 × 1	Range Shift Cylinder Cover	35–45
3/8-16 × 3/4	PTO Cover, Small①	18–23 (12–15 with oil filter)
7/16-14 × 1 1/4	PTO Cover, Large	50–65
	NUTS	
2.00-16	Output Yoke	425–525
1/2-13	Gear Shift Knob Jam Nut	31–42
5/8-18	Clutch Housing to Case	140–150
5/8-18	Reverse Idler Shafts	50–60
2 1/8-16	Drive Gear Bearing Nut	250–300
5/8-18	Range Shift Piston	80–90

END PLAY LIMITS

Reverse Speed Gear	0.005–0.038 in.②
Forward Speed Gears	0.005–0.012 in.

① Installing capscrews with more than 23 ft. lbs. of torque will force corners of PTO cover away from case with resultant oil leakage.

② Washers are used to obtain the correct limits; six thicknesses are available as follows:

Limits	Color Code
0.248–0.250	White
0.253–0.255	Green
0.258–0.260	Orange
0.263–0.265	Purple
0.268–0.270	Yellow
0.273–0.275	Black

will seat in the two bearing outer races installed in the reverse idler gearshaft bore of the front section.

NOTE: The auxiliary section can also be installed by setting the front section vertically on wood blocks and by lowering the auxiliary section evenly on the transmission.

2. Install the capscrews that secure the auxiliary section to the transmission case and tighten 35 to 45 ft. lbs.
3. Install the speedometer drive gear.
4. Lock the transmission in gear and install the output yoke. Tighten the yoke 425 to 525 ft. lbs.
5. Install the shifter bar housing assembly.

Fuller RT–610 Ten Speed Transmission

This transmission is the twin countershaft design. Engine torque is split between the two countershafts. Floating mainshaft gears are held in radial position by rotation of the countershaft gears. Axial position is maintained by washers. Gears are clutched to the mainshaft by short sliding clutch gears on the mainshaft, which engage internal splines in the gear hubs.

Ten speeds are obtained by a five speed main section and a two speed range section. The five gear ratios in the main section are used once through reduction in low range and again in high (direct) range.

All ten speeds are controlled by one gearshift lever and a range control button. Range shifts are automatic after being pre selected.

SEPARATION OF THE MAIN AND AUXILIARY SECTIONS

1. Disconnect the two nylon air lines at the air valve on the transmission.
2. Remove the gearshift lever housing, lever and control valve as a unit.
3. Disconnect the air line between the valve and regulator.
4. If necessary remove the street ell and reducer from the regulator.
5. Remove the air regulator and filter assembly.
6. Remove the two air lines between the air valve and cylinder in the auxiliary.
7. Remove the air valve and fittings.
8. Remove the actuating spring and pin from the bore in the transmission.
9. Remove the control housing from the shift bar housing.
10. Lift the shift bar housing from the transmission.
11. Lock the transmission by engaging two speeds with the mainshaft sliding clutch gears. Remove the elastic stop nut from the output shaft. Pull the flange or yoke straight to the rear and off of the shaft.
12. Remove the capscrews that attach the main and auxiliary sections. Insert puller screws in the housing and evenly move the auxiliary section to the rear.
13. Remove the clutch release mechanism if so equipped.
14. Remove the front gear cover.

MAIN TRANSMISSION

Disassembly

1. Remove the right countershaft snapring from the rear bearing bore of the case. Using a soft bar and hammer against the rear of the countershaft, move the assembly forward to expose the snapring groove in front of the bearing.

NOTE: It may be necessary to use a punch between the hub of the countershaft drive gear and inner race of the bearing to move the gear forward on the shaft.

2. Use the snapring which was removed from the rear bore and install it in the exposed snapring groove. Loosen the capscrews at the bearing retaining rings on the auxiliary drive gear.
3. Using a soft bar and hammer against the front of the countershaft, move the shaft to the rear as far as possible. This will move the front bearing forward on the shaft. Again using a soft bar and a hammer move the countershaft as far forward as possible to unseat the front bearing from the case bore. Use a puller and remove the bearing.
4. Use a curved soft bar and hammer and from inside the case move the rear countershaft bearing to the rear far enough to expose the snapring in the groove of the bearing. Install the

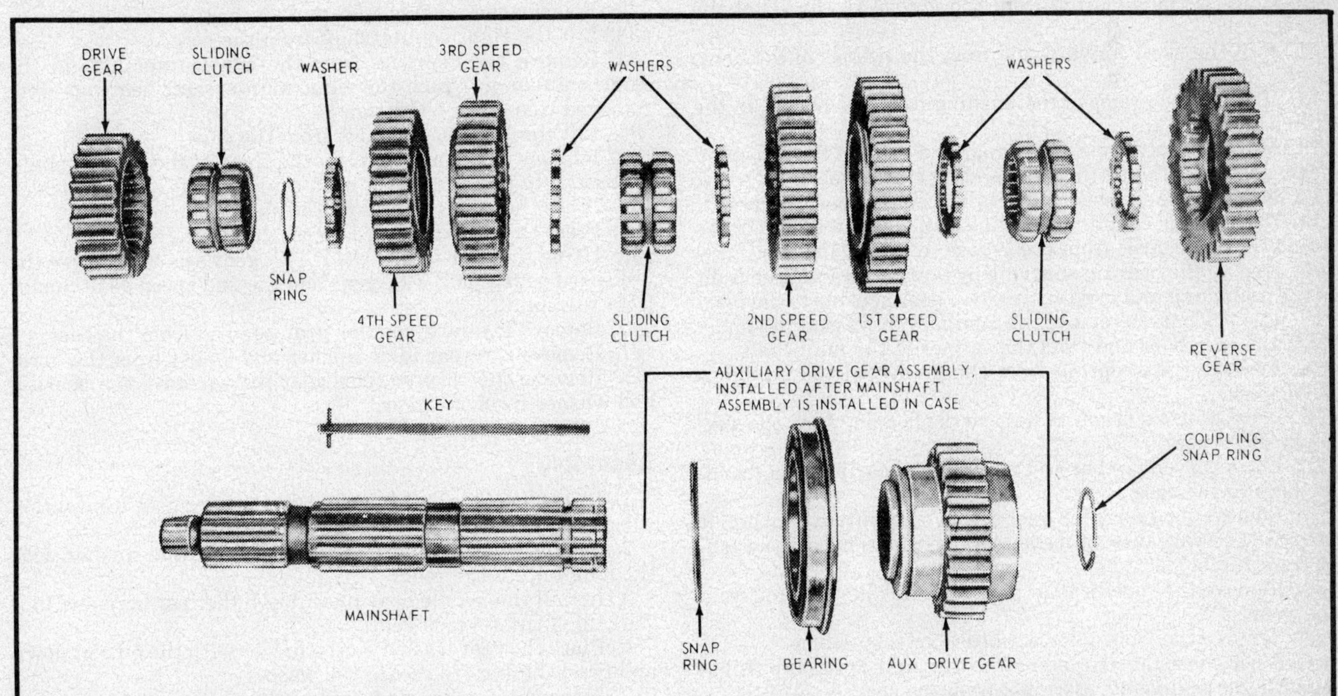

Main and auxiliary drive gear—exploded view (© Ford Motor Co.)

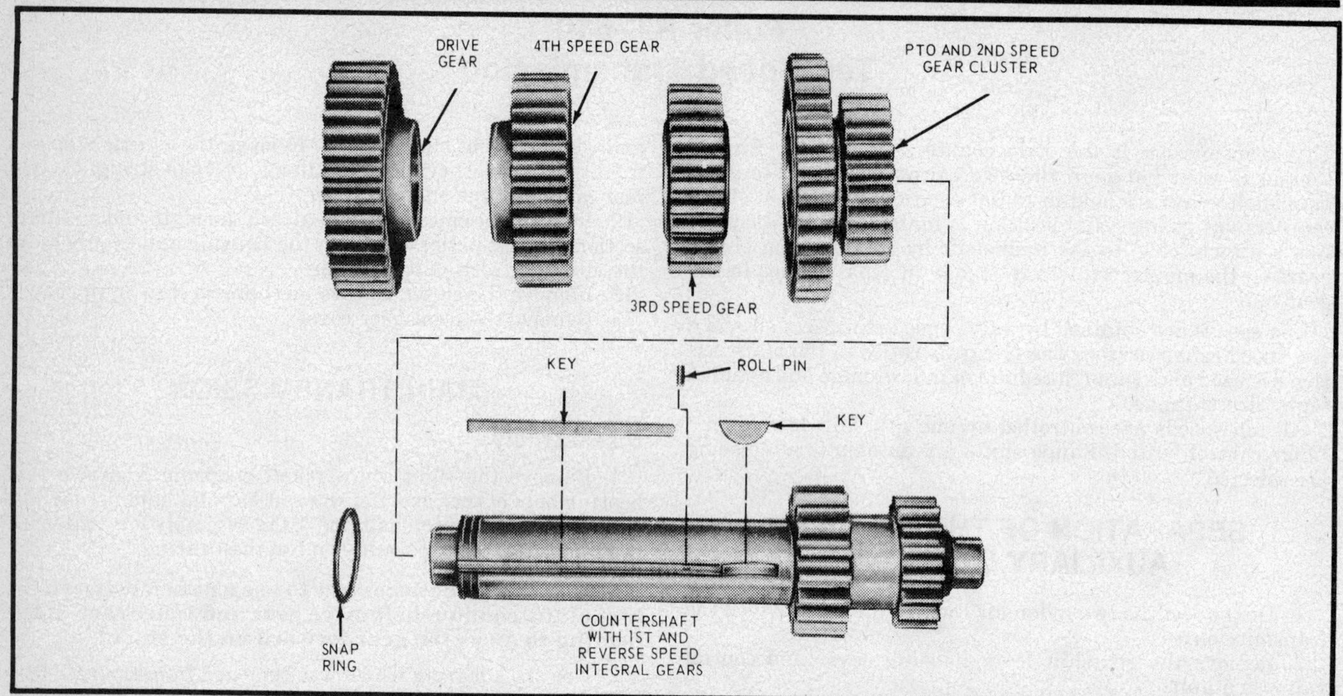

Front section countershaft—exploded view (© Ford Motor Co.)

snapring used on the front bearing and use pullers to remove the bearing.

5. Move the drive gear and shaft forward as far as possible.
6. Remove the bearing retaining snapring from the groove in the shaft.
7. Hold the shaft in position and tap the drive gear forward to unseat the bearing from the case.
8. Use a puller and remove the bearing.
9. Remove the drive gear washer.
10. Remove the snapring from the groove in the ID of the drive gear.
11. Pull the shaft forward and from the splines of the drive gear.
12. If necessary, remove the bushing from the pocket in the clutch shaft.
13. Move the drive gear to the rear and against the 4th speed gear, engaging the teeth of the sliding clutch gear.
14. Remove the two bearing retainer rings from the case.
15. Remove the coupling snapring, located in the bore of the auxiliary drive gear, from the groove in the mainshaft.
16. Expose the bearing snapring by tapping against the front of the mainshaft and moving the drive gear bearing to the rear.
17. Use pry bars to remove the auxiliary drive gear assembly from the case bore and from the splines of the mainshaft.
18. Remove the snapring from the groove in the auxiliary drive gear.
19. Press or use a driver to remove the bearing from the auxiliary drive gear.
20. Use a curved pry bar and remove the bearing from the idler bore in the case.
21. Remove the rear idler washer and holder from the bore. It may be necessary to bend the holder lugs and remove the washer from the holder.
22. Remove the reverse idler gear and the idler bearing from the gear.
23. Remove the front idler washer from the case.
24. Block the right countershaft to the right as far as possible and lift the mainshaft assembly from the case.
25. Remove the drive gear and the 4th/5th sliding clutch from the mainshaft.
26. Inside the hub of the 4th speed gear, remove the snapring from the groove in the mainshaft.
27. Remove the 4th speed gear and washer.
28. Remove the 3rd speed gear and washer.
29. Remove the 2nd/3rd speed sliding clutch.
30. Remove the long key from the slot in the mainshaft and remove the 2nd speed gear and washer and the 1st speed gear and washer.
31. Remove the 1st/reverse sliding clutch.
32. Remove the reverse gear and washer.
33. Lift the right countershaft from the case.
34. Remove the bearings from the left countershaft in the same manner in which the right countershaft bearings were removed (see steps 1 through 8).
35. Lift the left countershaft from the case.
36. Remove the snapring from the front of the countershaft. Disassembly procedures for each countershaft are identical.
37. Press the drive gear from the shaft.
38. Press the 4th speed gear from the shaft.
39. Using the rear face of the P.T.O. gear as a base, press the 3rd speed gear, the P.T.O. gear and the 2nd speed gear cluster from the shaft.
40. Remove the reverse idler gear bearing from the case.
41. Remove the rear idler washer and holder from the bore.
42. Remove the reverse idler gear then remove the bearing and washer from the gear.

Assembly

1. Install the small, flat, right reverse idler gear front washer on the pin in the lower right of the case.
2. Set the reverse gear in position next to the washer with the long hub to the rear.
3. Install the needle bearing through the rear bore and into the hub of the reverse gear.
4. Place the rear washer in the holder with the oil slot down and bend the lugs to secure the washer.
5. Place the washer and holder into the reverse gear case bore with the oil slots toward the gear and the holder flange to the rear.

6. Install the auxiliary countershaft front bearing into the reverse gear case bore to hold the gear into position.

7. Install the roll pin, long key, and Woodruff key in the slots of the countershaft.

8. Press the P.T.O. and 2nd speed gear cluster on the countershaft, P.T.O. gear to the front.

9. Press the 3rd speed gear on the shaft with the long hub to the rear.

10. Press the 4th speed gear on the shaft with the long hub to the front.

11. Press the drive gear on the shaft with the shaft with the long hub to the rear.

12. Install the snapring on the groove at the front of the shaft.

13. On the drive gear of each countershaft mark the gear tooth which is aligned with the keyway in the shaft. The tooth will be stamped with an O.

14. Place the left then the right countershaft into position in the case but do not install the bearings.

15. Place the mainshaft in a vise with the pilot end down. Keep the keyway free for insertion of the long key.

NOTE: Each mainshaft gear is held in place by locking the gear splined washer to the mainshaft with a key. There is one splined washer for each gear. Splined washers for the reverse, 1st, 2nd, and 3rd speed gears are identical; the 4th speed splined washer is of a smaller diameter.

16. Install the 2nd speed gear washer and insert the key from the bottom.

17. Install the 2nd speed gear on the splined washer with the clutching teeth down.

18. Install the 1st speed gear on the shaft and against the 2nd speed gear with the clutching teeth up.

19. Insert the splined washer in the hub of the 1st speed gear and install the key.

20. Install the 1st reverse sliding clutch and align the slot in the clutch with the key.

22. Install the reverse gear splined washer and lock with the key.

23. Reposition the assembly in the vise with the pilot end up.

24. Install the 2nd/3rd speed sliding clutch.

25. Install the 3rd speed gear splined washer; lift the key to install the washer under the pin in the key to lock in position.

26. Install the 3rd speed gear on the mainshaft, fitting the gear splines on those of the washer.

27. Install the 4th speed gear on the mainshaft with the clutching teeth up and against the 3rd speed gear.

28. Install the 4th speed gear splined washer on the mainshaft and in the hub of the 4th speed gear.

29. Install the snapring in the groove in the mainshaft which will hold the 4th speed gear in position on the shaft.

30. Install the 4th–5th speed sliding clutch on the mainshaft and place in engagement with the 4th speed gear.

31. Mark the timing teeth on the drive gear (5th speed gear). Mark the two adjacent teeth on the drive gear. Mark the two adjacent teeth on the drive gear which are directly opposite the first set marked. There should be the same number of teeth between the markings on each side of the gear.

32. Install the drive gear on the mainshaft and against the 4th speed gear with the snapring groove in the drive gear to the front.

33. Remove the assembly from the vise and install the reverse gear on the rear of the mainshaft. Engage the splines of the gear with those of the splined washer on the mainshaft.

34. Move both countershafts toward the case wall as far as possible.

35. Place the mainshaft in position in the case and block under the front of it to center it in the front bore of the case.

36. Press the bearing on the auxiliary drive gear with the snapring towards the gear.

37. Install the bearing retaining snapring.

38. Center the mainshaft in the rear bore of the case and install the auxiliary drive gear.

39. Seat the auxiliary drive gear bearing in the rear bore of the case.

40. In the hub of the auxiliary drive gear, install the coupling snapring in the groove of the mainshaft.

41. Install the two bearing retainer plates on the case.

42. Attach both upper and lower plates, using a double locking lug for each plate.

43. Install the bushing in the pocket of the clutch shaft. Make sure it is flush with the shaft and that the oil hole is not plugged.

44. Install the clutch shaft in the splines of the drive gear, moving the gear forward against the inside wall of the case.

45. Install the ring in the groove of the ID of the drive gear.

46. Install the drive gear spacer on the shaft.

47. Install the drive gear bearing on the shaft and into the case bore.

48. Install the bearing retaining snapring in the groove of the clutch shaft with the taper to the outside.

49. Mesh the left countershaft with the mainshaft gears, placing the marked timing tooth on the countershaft drive gear into proper mesh with the two marked timing teeth on the main drive gear.

50. Hold the left countershaft in position and install the front and rear bearings. Center the rear of the left countershaft in the rear bore of the case with a wood block. Partially install the front bearing on the countershaft and the case bore. Partially install the rear bearing on the countershaft and in the case bore. Use a flanged bearing driver to complete sealing of both bearings.

51. Install the snapring in the rear bore of the case.

52. Place the right countershaft into mesh with the mainshaft gears, placing the marked timing tooth on the countershaft drive gear into proper mesh with the two marked timing teeth on the main drive gear.

53. Hold the right countershaft in position and install the front and rear bearings in the same manner as installed on the left countershaft.

54. Install the snapring in the groove in the rear bore of the case.

55. Install the left reverse/idler gear on the pin in the upper left of the case.

56. Install the needle bearing in the hub of the reverse/idler gear.

57. Set the reverse/idler gear into position with the long hub to the rear.

58. Place the rear washer in the holder, with the oil slot down, and bend the lugs to secure the washer.

59. Place the washer and the holder in the reverse gear case bore with the oil slots toward the gear and the holder flange to the rear.

60. Install the auxiliary front bearing into the reverse gear case bore to hold the reverse idler gear assembly into position.

SHIFTING BAR HOUSING

Disassembly

1. Remove the shifting bar housing from the transmission.

2. Remove the tension spring cover from the housing.

3. Tilt the housing and remove the tension springs and balls from the bores in the top of the housing.

4. Set the housing in a vise with the plunger side up.

5. Cut the lock wires and remove the screws, then move the top and center shifter shafts to the rear and out of the housing. Remove the shifter fork from each shaft. As the neutral detent in the center shaft clears the housing boss remove the interlock pin.

6. Remove the actuating plunger from the bore in the housing.

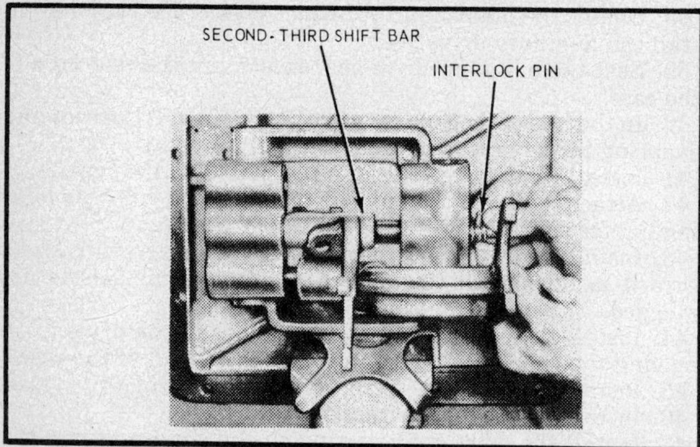

Removing the shift rod interlock pin (© Ford Motor Co.)

7. Move the lower shifter shaft to the rear and out of the housing. Remove the shifter fork from the shaft. Do not lose the interlock balls as the lower shaft is removed.

Assembly

1. Install the shifter shaft through the rear bores of the housing with the neutral detent notches to the rear. Keep the shaft in the neutral position when installed.
2. Place the housing in a vise with the plunger side up.
3. Install the first and reverse speed shifter shaft in the bottom bore and through the shifting fork. Install the set screw and the lock wire.
4. Install the actuating plunger in the front opening of the housing and a three-quarter inch interlock ball in the rear opening.
5. Position the 2nd/3rd speed shifter shaft in the center bore and through the shift block and fork. Install the interlock pin in the bore at the neutral notch. Install the set screws and secure with lock wire.

NOTE: Keep the shifter shaft so that the interlock pin remains in a vertical position during the completion of the assembly. Rotating the shaft will cause the interlock pin to jam into the tension spring bores.

6. Install a $^3/_4$ inch ball in the rear opening of the housing.
7. Position the 4th/5th speed shifter shaft in the upper bore and through the shifting block and fork. Install the set screws and secure with lock wire.
8. Remove the gearshift housing from the vise and install the three detent balls and springs into the top of the housing.

AUXILIARY SECTION

Disassembly

1. Use pullers and remove the bearing from the front of the tailshaft.
2. Remove the rear bearing cover and if necessary the cover seal.
3. Remove the speedometer gear and washer.
4. Remove the inside housing. Use a long punch and move the outer races of the countershaft rear bearings to the rear around $^1/_2$ inch.
5. Pull the countershafts forward and out of the housing.
6. Pull the bearing inner race from the rear of the countershafts.
7. Remove the snapring from the groove in the front of the shaft.
8. Press the drive gear forward and from the shaft.
9. Remove the air cylinder cover.
10. Remove the nut and lockwasher from the air cylinder piston shaft then use air to remove the piston.
11. If necessary, remove the O-ring from the piston then remove the copper seal from the shaft.
12. Move the synchronizer assembly, shift yoke and piston shaft forward and out of the housing as a complete assembly.
13. Remove the shaft and yoke from the synchronizer assembly.
14. Cut the lock wire, turn out the two lock screws and remove the yoke from the shaft.
15. Place the larger low speed sliding clutch ring on the bench.
16. Turn and pull upward to remove the high range synchronizer from the pins.
17. Remove the sliding clutch from the low range synchronizer pins.
18. Remove the dust seal, and air port extension from the top of the housing.
19. Remove the air cylinder from the housing and remove the O-ring from the cylinder if necessary.
20. Drive or press against the rear of the tailshaft to remove the low speed gear and tailshaft assembly forward and from the rear bearing.
21. Remove the rear washer and the low speed gear from the rear of the shaft.
22. Remove the splined washer from the hub of the low speed gear.
23. Move the mainshaft rear bearing to the rear and out of the housing.
24. Use a driver to remove the countershaft rear bearings from the housing.

Assembly

1. Make sure the magnetic cleaner is installed in the recess in the auxiliary case.

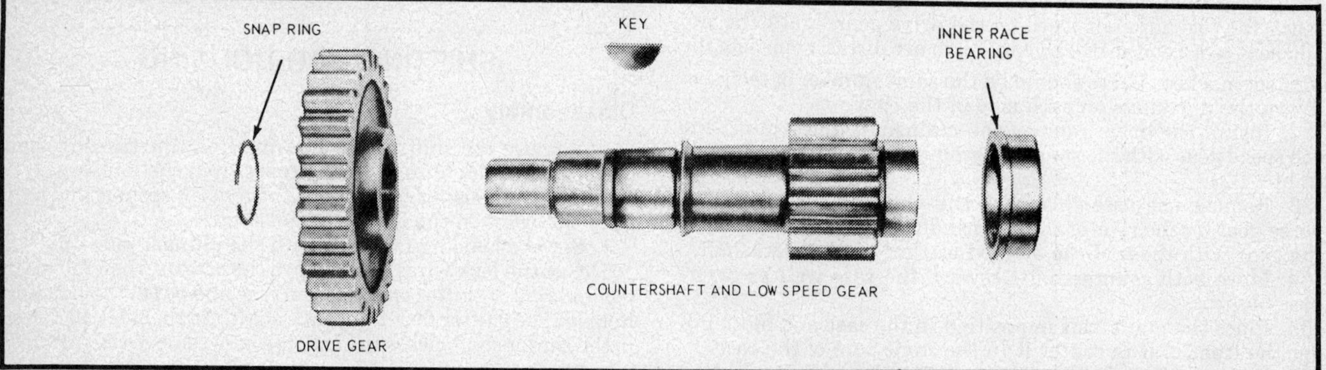

Auxiliary section countershaft—exploded view (© Ford Motor Co.)

2. Mark any two adjacent low gear teeth. Then mark the two adjacent teeth which are directly opposite the first set marked. There should be the same number of teeth between the markings on each side of the gear.

3. Place the splined spacer in the hub of the low speed gear with the shoulder to the rear.

4. Install the low speed gear and spacer over the rear of the shaft and against the shoulder with the clutching teeth to the front.

5. Install the low speed gear rear washer on the shaft and against the gear with the camfer to the rear.

6. Set the tailshaft with the forward end down and place the auxiliary housing over the rear of the shaft so that the shaft extends through the rear bore.

7. Seat the mainshaft rear bearing on the shaft and in the bore.

8. Install the O-ring in the slot in the small bore in the range shift air cylinder.

9. Install the cylinder in the housing with the small bore in the cylinder aligned with the air port in the top of the auxiliary.

10. Install the dust cover and air port extension through the housing and into the bore of the air cylinder.

11. Place the shifting yoke on the piston shaft with the fork towards the threaded end.

12. Align the slots in the shaft with the bores in the yoke hub and install the two lock screws. Secure with safety wire.

13. Place the yoke in the slot of the sliding clutch. The threaded end of the piston shaft is toward the larger low range synchronizer.

14. Place the entire assembly into the housing, thread the splined sliding clutch on the tailshaft and insert the piston shaft through the cylinder bore.

15. Install the copper seal on the threaded end of the piston shaft.

16. Install the O-ring on the OD of the piston.

17. Install the piston on the shaft and against the copper washer, with the flat side of the piston out. Then install the lockwasher and nut on the shaft.

18. Install the gasket and cylinder cover.

19. Place the larger low speed ring face down on a bench with the pins up.

20. Place the sliding clutch, recessed side up, on the pins of the low speed ring.

21. Install the three springs in the bores in the high speed synchronizer ring.

22. Place the high speed synchronizer ring over the pins of the low speed synchronizer ring, seating the springs against the pins.

23. Apply pressure to the high speed synchronizer ring to compress the springs and seat the pins of the low speed synchronizer fully into the bores of the ring.

24. If necessary, install the keys in the keyways of the countershafts.

25. Press the drive gear on each countershaft with the long hub to the rear.

26. Install a snapring on the front of each countershaft.

27. Install a bearing inner race on the rear of each countershaft.

28. Mark the tooth on the countershaft low speed gear that is aligned with the keyway in the drive gear. This gear tooth will be stamped with an O.

29. Seat the outer races of the countershaft rear bearings only partially in the bores, just enough to stay in place.

30. Place the countershafts into position in the housing, inserting the inner races into the partially installed outer races.

31. As the countershafts are installed, mesh the marked low speed gear tooth on each countershaft between each set of marked gear teeth on the low speed gear.

32. With the countershafts in position, complete the installation of the countershaft rear bearings on the shaft and into the case bore.

33. Install the speedometer rear gear and washer on the tailshaft and if removed install the oil seal in the rear bearing cover.

34. Install the rear bearing cover and install the bearing on the front of the tailshaft.

JOINING OF THE MAIN AND AUXILIARY SECTIONS

1. Install the drive gear bearing cover.
2. Install the clutch housing.
3. If so equipped, install the clutch release mechanism. The two reverse gears, including the washers, must be in perfect alignment with the center of the case bores as the front of the auxiliary countershafts must be inserted in these parts during auxiliary installation. Use a heavy grease to hold the washers in place. Check the rear of the front section to make sure all the snaprings have been installed.
4. Install the auxiliary section on the front section, aligning the auxiliary section on the dowel pins and the extended portion of the auxiliary countershafts with the reverse idler gears. It may make assembly easier if someone slowly rotates the clutch shaft during installation.
5. Secure the auxiliary section with the capscrews.
6. Lock the transmission by engaging the two gears with the mainshaft sliding clutches.
7. Install the companion flange on the splines of the tailshaft.
8. Make sure the shift bars are in the neutral position. Place the sliding clutches on the mainshaft in the neutral position.
9. Install the shifting bar housing on the transmission, fitting the yokes into the yoke slots of the corresponding clutch gears.
10. Make sure the shifting notches on the bars in the shifting bar housing are aligned in the neutral position.
11. Install the gearshift lever housing on the shifting bar

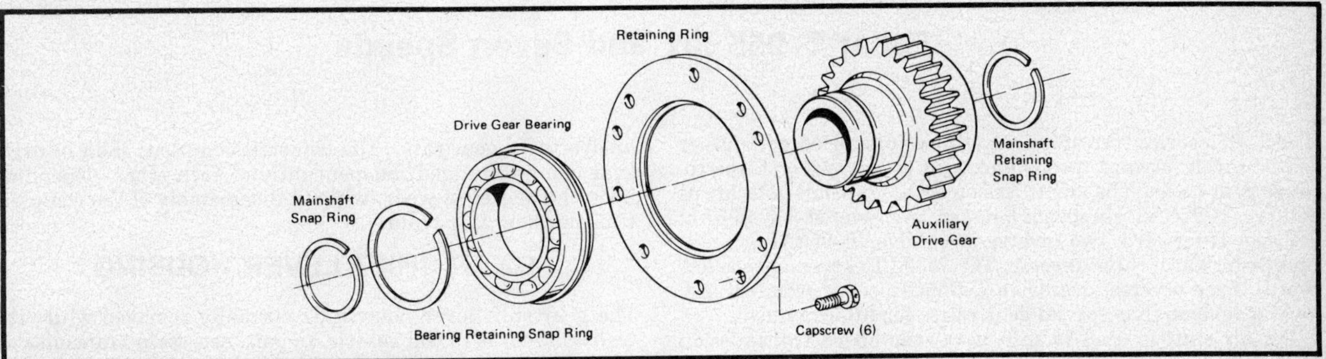

Auxiliary drive gear mechanism (© Eaton Corp.)

TORQUE SPECIFICATIONS
Fuller Model RT-610 Tenspeed

Location	Thread Size & Length	Torque (ft. lbs.)
	BOLTS	
Air Filter	¼-20 × ½	15–20
Air Valve	¼-20 × 1¾	15–20
Air Filter to Case	⅜-16 × ¾	20–25
PTO Cover, Right (used with oil filter)	⅜-16 × ¾	12–15
Bearing Retainer	⅜-16 × 1	35–45
Rear Bearing Cover	⅜-16 × 1	35–45
Front Bearing Cover, Top	⅜-16 × 1¼	35–45
Front Bearing Cover, Bottom	⅜-16 × 1¼	35–45
Air Cylinder Cover	⅜-16 × 1½	35–45
Shift Lever Housing	⅜-16 × 1¼	35–45
Tension Spring Cover	⅜-16 × 1¼	35–45
Auxiliary to Transmission	⅜-16 × 1¼	35–45
Shift Bar Housing	⅜-16 × 1¼	35–45
Rear Bearing Cover	⅜-16 × 2¾	35–45
PTO Cover or TCB-6 Brake Cover, Bottom	7/16-14 × 1¼	50–65
Clutch Housing to Case	½-13 × 1¼	70–75
	NUTS	
Clutch Housing Studs	⅝-18	170–180
Rear Support Studs	⅝-18	170–180
Air Piston	½-20	60–70
Output Shaft	1½-18	380–470

housing, fitting the lower end of the lever into the notches in the shifting block and yokes.

12. Install the attaching capscrews, except the capscrew at the left rear corner as this is used to secure the air line.
13. Install the fittings on the air valve.
14. Install the actuating pin and spring in the bore in the transmission.
15. Check the bore in the air valve and make sure the piston is either in a forward or rear position, then install the alignment sleeve in the air valve. The piston can be moved with air or a pencil.
16. Install the air valve on the transmission and tighten the capscrews evenly. The actuating plunger in the case fits into the alignment sleeve in the air valve.
17. Install the fittings in the shift cylinder.
18. Install the high range air line between the air port in the rear cover of the air cylinder and the side rear port of the air valve.
19. Install the low range air line from the air port in the top of the cylinder to the side air port in the air valve.
20. Secure the regulator to the bracket with the exhaust port away from the transmission, then tighten the two capscrews which attach the bracket to the filter.
21. If previously removed, install the bushing and the 90 degree fitting in the output port of the air regulator. The fitting faces toward the gearshift lever housing.
22. Install the air regulator and filter on the left side of the transmission.
23. Install the air line between the output port of the air regulator and the tee of the supply port of the air valve.
24. Install the black nylon air line from the output of the control valve to the air port in the hexagonal end cap of the air valve.
25. Install the white nylon air line from the in port of the control valve to tee in the supply port of the air valve.

Fuller T–955 Six and Seven Speeds

The T–955 series transmissions are manufactured with either six or seven forward speeds and with either two or three reverse gear ratios. The identification of the transmissions are as follows. T–955AL: six speeds forward, two reverse, TO–955AL: six speeds forward, two reverse, overdrive, T–955ALL: seven speeds forward, three reverse, TO–955ALL: seven speeds forward, three reverse, overdrive T–955GL: six speeds forward, two in reverse (has special gear ratios for highway use).

An air shift is used to shift the seven speed transmission both in and out of the Lo-Lo forward gears and the Lo-Lo reverse gears. The transmission gears can be converted to obtain an overdrive gear ratio. The transmission input shaft or drive gear can be changed independently of each other, depending upon the degree of wear, without disassembly of the complete transmission gear train.

GEAR SHIFT LEVER HOUSING

The gear shift lever housing is normally removed while the transmission is in the vehicle, to gain necessary transmission removal clearance. The retaining bolts are removed and the housing lifted from the shift bar housing. The installation is done in the reverse of the removal procedure with the transmission back in the vehicle.

SHIFT BAR HOUSING

Removal

1. Remove the two retaining bolts holding the tension spring cover. Remove the cover, the four tension springs and the four steel balls.
2. Remove the reverse light pin and plug, if necessary. Remove the air breather.
3. Remove the sixteen retaining bolts from the shift bar housing. Lift the housing from the transmission case.

Disassembly

1. Mount the shift housing in a soft jawed vise with the shortest shift rail to the top. Cut and remove all lock wires.

NOTE: As the shift rails are removed from the shift bar housing, the shift yokes and blocks will be free to drop. As the parts are removed, they should be marked and kept in their proper order for ease of assembly.

2. Remove the lockscrew from the short shift rail (5th–6th speed) and remove from the housing. It may be necessary to remove the plug, spring and plunger from the shift yoke.
3. Remove the lockscrew from the 3rd/4th shift rail and remove the rail from the housing. The interlock pin will drop from the rail as it clears the housing web. Do not lose it.
4. Remove the two lockscrews from the 2nd/reverse shift rail and remove the rail.
5. Remove the two lockscrews from the 1st/low reverse shift rail and remove the rail from the housing.
6. As the 1st/low reverse shift rail is removed from the housing, three interlock balls will fall from the housing.

Assembly

1. The assembly of the shift bar housing is in the reverse of the removal procedure. Be sure to install the interlock pin in the 3rd/4th shift rail during the assembly.
2. Install the lockscrews and tighten securely. Install the lockwire and position wire to avoid interference during the shifting operation.

Installation

1. Position the shift levers, yokes and blocks in the neutral position. Position all internal gears of the transmission in the neutral position and install the housing onto the transmission case. Secure the housing with the retaining bolts.
2. Install the four tension balls, springs and the tension spring cover in place and secure with the two retaining bolts.
3. If removed, install the reverse light pin and plug. Install the air breather if previously removed.
4. Install the air shift tubing and fitting to the rear of the transmission.

CLUTCH HOUSING

Removal

1. If equipped, remove the upshift brake assembly from the front bearing cover.
2. Remove the four retaining bolts and the six retaining nuts from the front of the clutch housing and remove the housing from the transmission case.

COMPANION FLANGE OR YOKE

Removal

1. Lock the transmission in two gears and remove the retaining nut from the output shaft.
2. Pull the companion flange or yoke from the output shaft and remove the speedometer drive gear or spacer from the flange or yoke.

AUXILIARY REAR SECTION

Removal

1. Remove the nineteen retaining bolts and insert three bolts into the threaded holes in the flange of the auxiliary section.

NOTE: On the T–955AL and GL series, it may be necessary to remove the plate at the top right corner of the auxiliary section to allow access to the top right retaining bolts.

2. Tighten the three puller bolts and break the gasket seal between the case and the auxiliary section. Use a chain hoist to remove the rear housing auxiliary section from the transmission case. Reinstall the output shaft nut to avoid damage to the threads of the output shaft during the housing removal.

AUXILIARY DRIVE GEAR ASSEMBLY

Removal

1. Cut the lockwires and remove the six retaining bolts from the retaining plate that holds the auxiliary drive gear assembly to the transmission case.
2. Remove the snapring from the rear of the mainshaft.
3. Install three puller screws in the tapped holes on the retainer plate and move the gear assembly from the transmission case.
4. Remove the snapring from the groove on the front of the auxiliary drive gear.
5. Support the assembly by the retaining ring and drive the gear down and from the bearing, freeing the retaining ring.

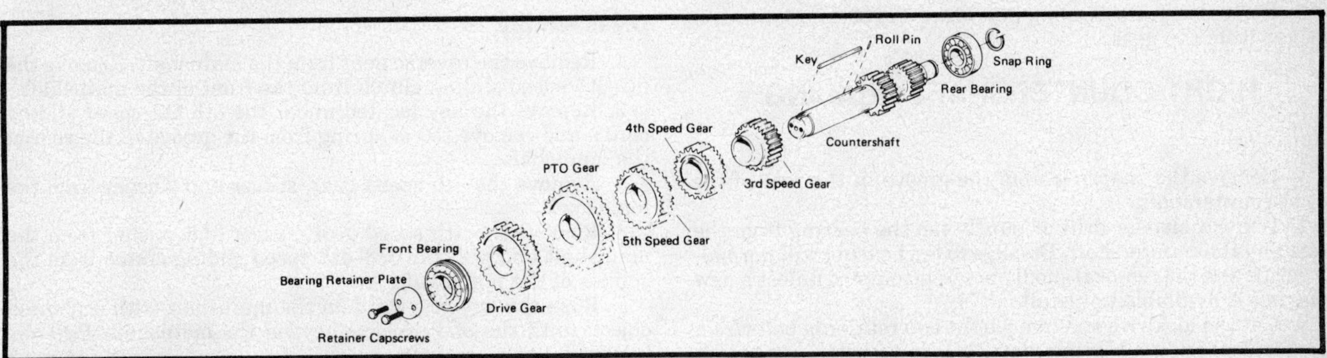

Countershaft—exploded view (© Eaton Corp.)

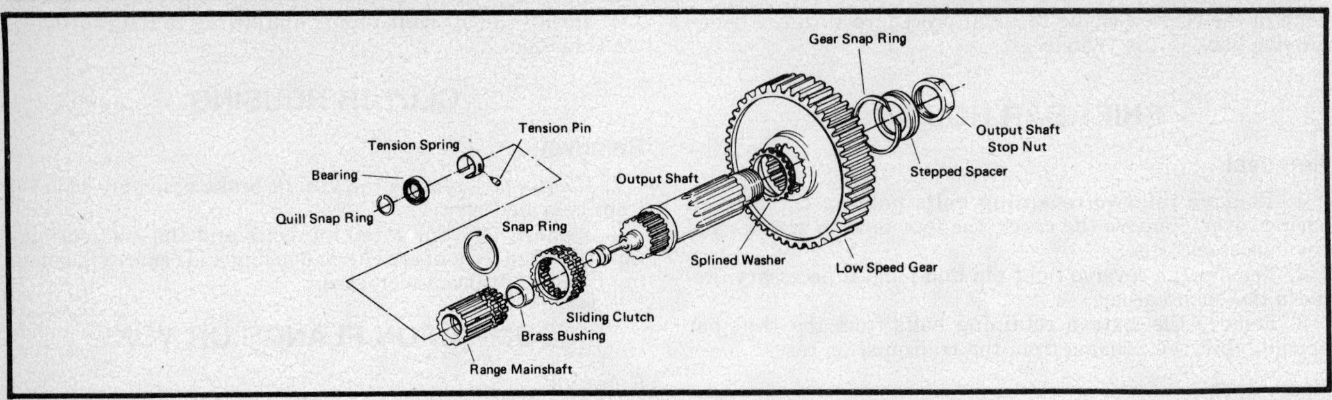

Exploded view of range mainshaft (© Eaton Corp.)

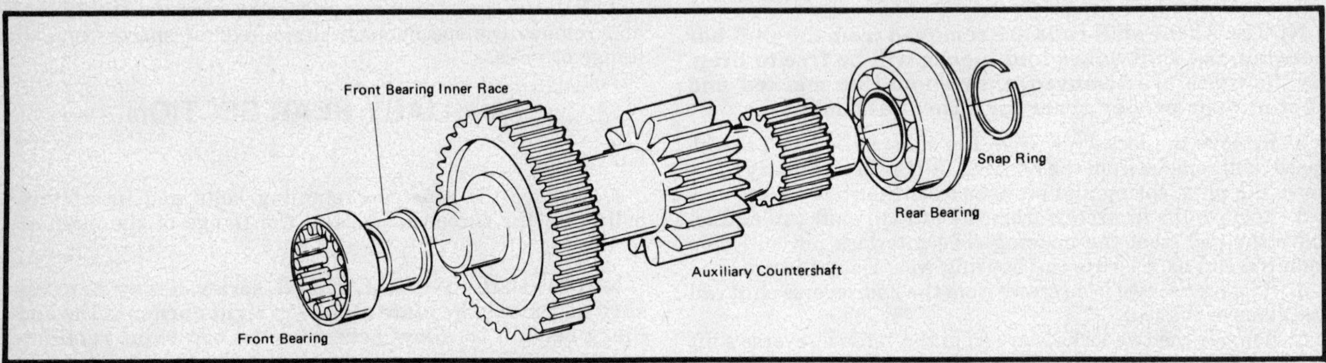

Auxiliary countershafts—exploded view (© Eaton Corp.)

LEFT REVERSE IDLER GEAR ASSEMBLY

Removal

1. Remove the snapring from the inside diameter of the hub of the mainshaft reverse gear. Move the reverse gear forward on the mainshaft and against the first speed gear, engaging the splines of both the first and reverse speed gears with the splines of the sliding clutch gear.
2. Remove the elastic stop nut and washer from the end of the idler shaft.
3. Using an inside jaw type puller, remove the left and right auxiliary countershaft case bearings.
4. Remove the plug from the end of the idler shaft and insert a threaded puller into the tapped hole. Hold the gear and the thrust washer in place and pull the idler shaft from the transmission case.
5. Remove the reverse idler gear from the case. Remove the thrust and rear washers from the case.
6. If necessary, the bearing inner race and bearing can be removed from the gear.

RIGHT COUNTERSHAFT BEARING

Removal

1. Remove the snapring from the groove in the rear of the right countershaft.
2. Using a slender drift or punch, tap the bearing from the case and the countershaft. Damage to the bearing will normally result and the removal should not be attempted unless a new bearing is available to install.
3. Cut the lockwire and remove the two retaining bolts from the front bearing retaining plate. It may be necessary to lock the transmission in two speeds to remove the retaining bolts.
4. Drive the countershaft to the rear as far as possible with a soft bar and hammer. Reverse the procedure and using the soft bar and hammer, drive the countershaft as far forward as possible to unseat the bearing from the transmission case.
5. Using a bearing puller, remove the bearing from the countershaft front end. Block the countershaft against the side of the case.

MAINSHAFT ASSEMBLY

Removal

1. With the right countershaft blocked to the side of the case, pull the mainshaft to the rear as far as possible.
2. Tilt the front of the mainshaft up and move the assembly forward while lifting the assembly from the case.
3. Use caution as the reverse gear is free to slide from the end of the mainshaft.

Disassembly

1. Remove the reverse gear from the mainshaft. Remove the 5th/6th speed sliding clutch from the front of the mainshaft.
2. Remove the key located under the 5th/6th speed sliding clutch and remove the snapring from the groove in the rear of the mainshaft.
3. Remove the 5th speed gear, spacer and washer from the mainshaft.
4. Remove the 4th speed gear, spacer and washer from the mainshaft and pull the 3rd–4th speed sliding clutch from the splines of the mainshaft.
5. Push the key rearward on the mainshaft with a pointed object, until the end projects beyond the mainshaft. Pull the key from the mainshaft.
6. Remove the reverse gear washer and spacer from the

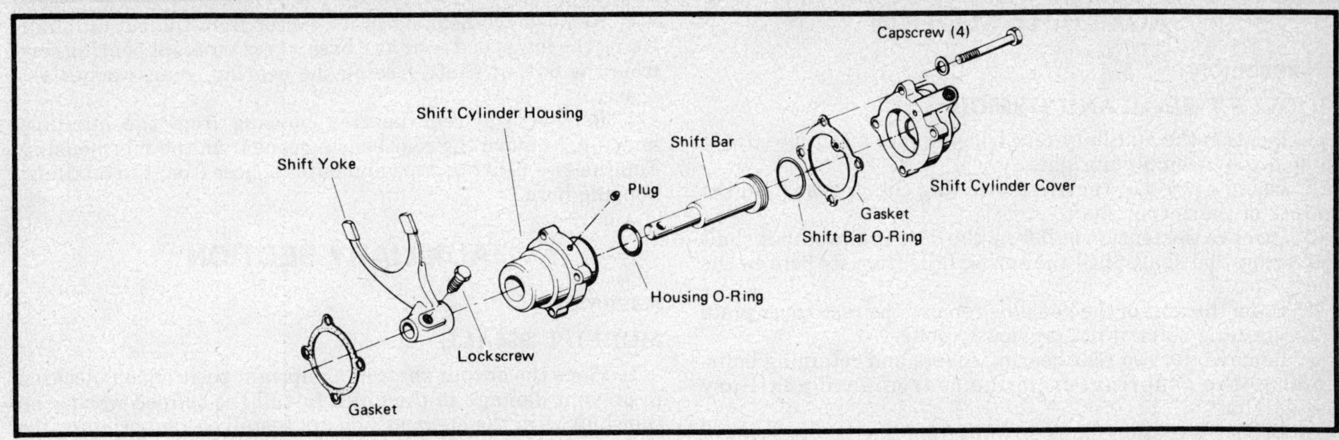

Low gear shift cylinder—exploded view (© Eaton Corp.)

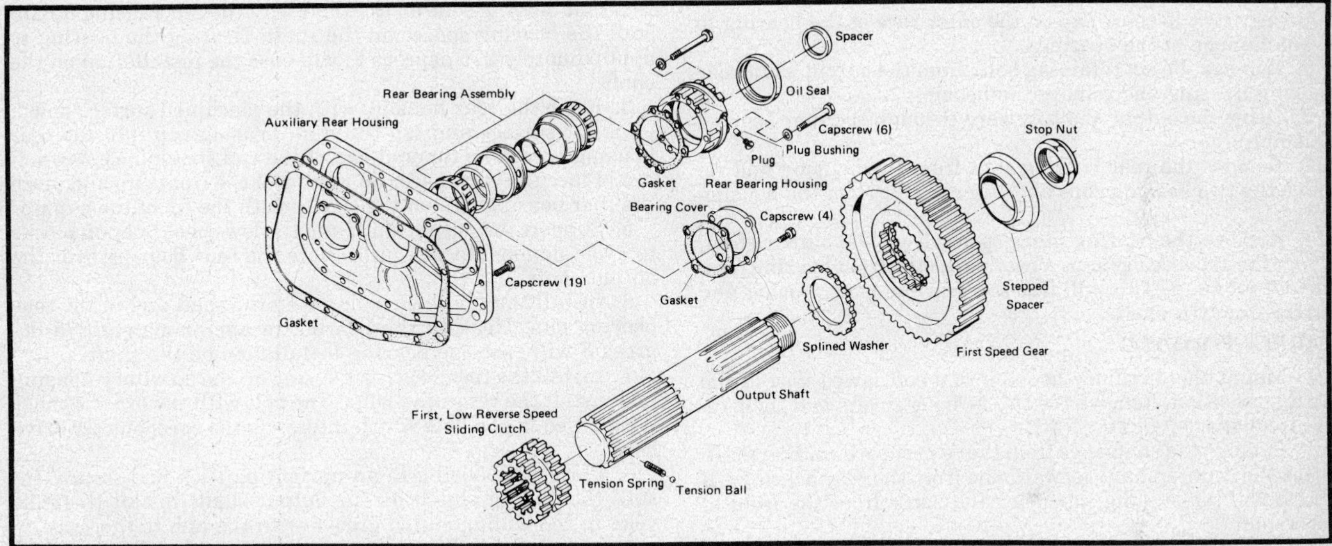

First speed gear, output shaft and rear bearing assembly (© Eaton Corp.)

mainshaft. Pull the reverse/2nd speed sliding clutch from the splines of the mainshaft.

7. Remove the second and third speed gears, washers and spacers from the mainshaft.

INPUT SHAFT AND DRIVE GEAR ASSEMBLY

Removal

1. Remove the retaining bolts from the front bearing cover and remove the cover.
2. Tap the drive gear forward from the inside of the case and remove the snapring from the front bearing.
3. Move the drive gear assembly towards the inside of the case and move past the countershaft assemblies. Remove the drive gear assembly from the case.
4. Relieve the bearing nut where it is peened to the shaft and remove the nut from the shaft. The nut has a left hand thread.
5. Press the shaft through the bearing and gear. If necessary, remove the snapring from the inside of the gear.
6. Check the bushing in the pocket of the input gear and replace if necessary.

COUNTERSHAFT ASSEMBLIES

Removal

1. Grasp the countershaft assembly, either right or left and remove both from the case.

Disassembly

NOTE: Except for the number of teeth on the P.T.O. gears, the countershaft assemblies are identical. The disassembly and assembly of the countershafts are the same procedures.

1. Press the 6th, P.T.O., 5th and 4th speed gears from the countershaft, followed by the removal of the 3rd speed gear. Remove the key and roll pin.

RIGHT REVERSE IDLER GEAR ASSEMBLY

The removal and disassembly of the right reverse idler gear assembly is the same procedure as the removal and disassembly of the left reverse idler gear assembly. Refer to the appropriate section.

AUXILIARY SECTION

Disassembly

MODELS T–955AL AND T–955GL

1. Position the auxiliary rear housing into a soft jawed vise to hold the assembly upright.
2. Using a pry bar, remove the sliding clutch gear from the splines of the output shaft.
3. Remove the tension ball from the bore in the output shaft and rotate the shaft until the spring falls from its bore in the shaft.
4. From the rear of the housing, remove the rear cover plate and retaining bolts, if not previously done.
5. Remove the two rear bearing covers and retaining bolts. Remove the snaprings from the rear of each auxiliary countershaft.
6. Drive the countershafts forward from the bearings with a soft bar and hammer. Do not allow the shaft assemblies to drop.
7. With the countershafts out, remove the bearings from the housing, front to rear. Tap on the outer race of the bearing to avoid damage to the bearings.
8. Remove the six retaining bolts from the output shaft rear bearing housing and remove the housing.
9. Drive the output shaft forward through the rear bearing assembly.
10. Remove the rear bearing cone from the housing and remove the two bearing cups and outer spacer from the housing bore.
11. Remove the bearing inner spacer from the output shaft. Using the 1st speed gear as a base, press the front bearing from the output shaft. This will free the bearing, gear, washer and spacer from the shaft.

MODEL T–955ALL

1. Mount the auxiliary housing in a soft jawed vise in the upright position. Remove the two bearing covers and their retaining bolts.
2. Remove the snaprings from the rear of each countershaft. Drive the countershafts forward and from the rear bearings. If necessary, remove the inner bearing races from the front of each shaft.
3. Tap the bearings to the rear and from the case bores.
4. Pry the sliding clutch forward and off the splines of the range mainshaft. Rotate the mainshaft until the sliding clutch retaining plunger falls from its bore in the mainshaft. Remove the key from its groove in the mainshaft.
5. Rotate the splined washer inside the 1st speed gear until its teeth align with the grooves in the mainshaft, freeing the gear.
6. Remove the 1st speed gear from the mainshaft, along with the coupler.
7. Cut the lockwires and remove the lockscrew on the low speed shift yoke.
8. From the rear side of the case, remove the air cylinder cover and retaining bolts.
9. Pull the shift bar to the rear and from the cylinder housing. Remove the O-ring from the large diameter of the bar, if necessary.
10. Remove the cylinder housing from the auxiliary housing case. If necessary, remove the O-ring from the bore in the housing.
11. Remove the shift yoke from the sliding clutch assembly. Remove the snapring from the front of the output shaft quill.
12. Use two pry bars and move the mainshaft forward and off the quill. Remove the bearing from the bore of the mainshaft and, if necessary, remove the brass bushing, snapring and tension spring.
13. Remove the sliding clutch from the splines of the output shaft. Drive the output shaft forward and from the rear bearing assembly.
14. Remove the bearing inner spacer from the output shaft. Using the low speed gear as a base, press the front bearing cone from the output shaft, freeing the bearing, gear, washer and spacer.
15. Remove the rear bearing housing from the auxiliary housing. Remove the rear bearing cone from the rear housing. Tap the two bearing cups and outer spacer from the auxiliary housing bore.

AUXILIARY SECTION

Assembly

MODEL T–955ALL

1. Place the output shaft in an upright position, on blocking to prevent damage to the quill. Install the splined washer on the shaft with the stepped side up. Install the snapring in the groove of the low speed gear and install the gear on the shaft, with the clutching teeth down.
2. Install the rear washer on the shaft, flat side up. Install the front bearing cone on the shaft with the taper facing up. Install the bearing spacer on the shaft. Heating the bearing to approximately 275 degrees F. will ease the installation on the shaft.
3. Place the rear housing with the machined surface down, on a flat surface and tap the front bearing cup into the rear housing bore. The tapered end of the cup should face down.
4. Place the cup spacer on the top of the front cup and place the rear bearing cup on the spacer with the lip of the cup up.
5. Support the output shaft and the low speed gear on blocks to avoid damage to the quill. Place the rear housing over the output shaft.
6. Install the rear bearing cone on the shaft and in the rear bearing cup. Heating the bearing to approximately 275 degrees F will ease the bearing installation on the shaft.
7. Install the rear bearing housing on the auxiliary housing and install the retaining bolts. The bolt with the brass washer is installed in the hole which intersects the speedometer drive bore.
8. Place the housing in an upright position and secure. Install the sliding clutch on the output shaft. Install the shift yoke in the sliding clutch groove with the hub to the front.
9. Install the shift cylinder housing in the bore of the auxiliary housing with the small air channel to the right. Install the O-ring in the bore of the cylinder housing, if previously removed.
10. Install the O-ring, if previously removed, into the large diameter of the shift bar and insert the bar into the cylinder housing, making sure that the front of the bar passes through the shift yoke hub.
11. Align the hole in the shift bar and install the yoke lockscrew. Secure with a lockwire.
12. Install the shift cylinder cover on the housing and align the air channel with the channel in the cylinder housing. Secure the cover with the retaining bolts.
13. Install the bearing in the front of the mainshaft and the snapring on the outside diameter of the mainshaft (rear groove).
14. Install the tension spring inside the mainshaft, aligning the hole in the spring with the bore in the shaft. Install the brass bushing in the shaft bore.
15. Tap the mainshaft evenly onto the output shaft quill with the bearing facing to the front. Install the coupler on the mainshaft, clutching teeth to the rear.
16. Install the first speed gear on the shaft with the machined face of the gear to the rear. Install the splined washer on the shaft and in the hub of the gear.
17. Rotate the splined washer to lock the gear onto the shaft. Install the key in the mainshaft keyway with the tab locked under the tooth on the gear.
18. Hold the key in position while rotating the shaft and in-

sert the clutch retainer in the bore of the shaft. Install the sliding clutch on the shaft.

19. Mark any two teeth on the first speed gear and then mark the two teeth directly opposite. Mark the tooth on the first speed gear of each countershaft that is marked with an "O". If previously removed, heat and install the bearing inner races on each of the countershaft front ends with the shoulders towards the gear.

20. Install the countershaft rear bearings into the case bores with an appropriate driver tool.

21. Align the marked tooth on each countershaft to the marked teeth on the first speed gear and seat the countershafts into the rear bearings with a soft bar and hammer.

22. Drive the countershafts into the bearings until the snapring groove is visible. Install the snapring on each countershaft end. Install the two bearing covers and retaining bolts.

MODELS T-955AL AND T-955GL

1. Place the output shaft in an upright position with the threaded end up and install the splined washer on the shaft.

2. Place the first speed gear on the shaft and engage the splines of the gear with the splines of the washer. Place the stepped washer on the shaft with the flat side up.

3. Heat the bearing to approximately 275 degrees F. and install on the shaft with the taper up. Install the bearing spacer on the output shaft.

4. Lay the rear housing on a flat surface with the machined side down. Install the front bearing cup in the bearing bore of the housing, with the wide diameter to the front. Install the spacer on the top of the front bearing cup and install the rear bearing cup on the spacer with the wide diameter to the rear.

5. Tap the cups and spacer into place in the bearing bore of the rear housing.

6. With the output shaft still in the upright position, install the rear housing over the shaft and allow the bearing on the shaft to seat in the cup.

7. Heat the rear bearing to approximately 275 degrees F and install on the output shaft with the taper facing down.

8. Install the rear bearing housing and the retaining bolts. The retaining bolt with the brass washer should be placed in the hole that intersects the speedometer drive bore.

9. Support the rear housing in an upright position. Mark any two adjacent teeth on the first speed gear and then mark the two teeth directly opposite.

10. Locate the tooth on each countershaft with the marking "O" and mark with an indicating paint. If previously removed, heat and install the countershaft inner bearing race on the front of each shaft with the shoulder towards the gear.

11. Install the countershaft rear bearings into the rear housing bearing bores with a bearing driver.

12. Mesh the marked tooth on one of the countershafts between two of the marked teeth on the first speed gear. Start the shaft into the rear bearing and drive the shaft inward until the snapring groove is exposed on the rear of the countershaft. Repeat the installation procedure for the second countershaft. Install the snaprings in the groove of each countershaft. Install the two bearing covers and the retaining bolts.

13. Install the tension spring and ball in the output shaft. Using a blunt instrument, hold the tension ball down in its bore and install the sliding clutch on the shaft and over the ball.

MAINSHAFT

Assembly

1. Position the mainshaft in a vise with the front end down. Position the roll pin in the keyway.

2. Install the third speed gear splined washer on the shaft with the flat side up. Unless specified, the large notch on the washers should be installed on the opposite side of the shaft from the keyway.

3. Rotate the washer on the shaft until a notch aligns with the keyway and install the key in the keyway. Install the splined spacer on the shaft with the flat side against the washer.

4. Install the third speed gear on the shaft, clutching teeth down and engaging the splines of the spacer.

5. Position the second speed gear on the third speed gear with the clutching teeth up. Install the second speed splined spacer on the shaft and in the hub of the second speed gear with the flat side up.

6. Remove the key from the keyway and install the washer, flat side down, in the hub of the gear and turn the washer until a notch aligns with the keyway. Reinstall the key back in the keyway.

7. Install the second/reverse speed sliding clutch on the shaft with the large notch over the keyway.

8. Remove the key and install the reverse gear splined washer on the shaft with the flat side up.

9. Turn the washer on the shaft until a notch aligns with the keyway and reinstall the key.

10. Install the spacer on the shaft and against the washer with the flat side down.

11. Install the snapring in the groove in the mainshaft, behind the end of the key.

12. Remove the mainshaft assembly from the vise and turn the assembly with the front end upward. Lock in the vise. Install the third/fourth speed sliding clutch on the shaft with the large notch over the keyway.

13. Install the fourth speed gear washer on the shaft with one notch fitting over the key and resting on the shoulder of the shaft with the flat side up.

14. Install the spacer on the shaft with the flat side down. Place the fourth speed gear on the shaft with the clutching teeth down and engaging the splines of the spacer.

15. Place the fifth speed gear on the fourth speed gear with the clutching teeth up. Install the spacer with the flat side up, on the shaft and in the hub of the fifth speed gear.

16. Install the washer on the shaft and in the hub of the fifth speed gear with the flat side down.

17. Align the large notch of the washer with the keyway and install the key, fitting the tapered end in the washer notch and the pin in the hole in the keyway.

18. Install the fifth/sixth speed sliding clutch on the shaft with the large notch over the key.

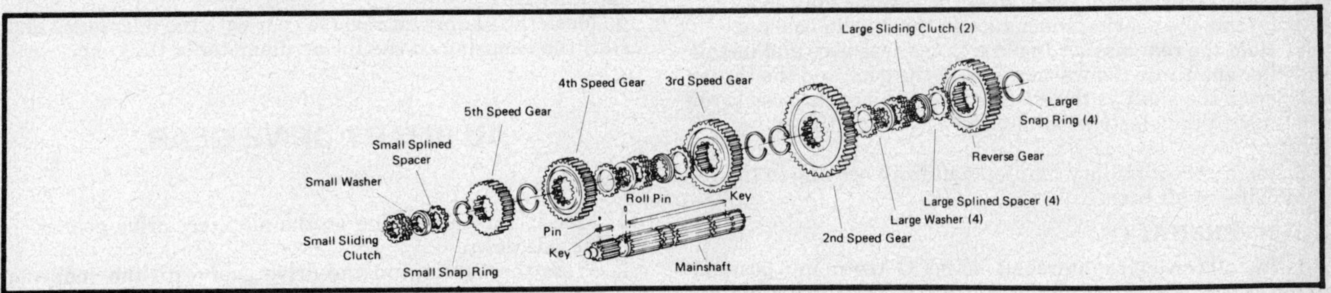

Mainshaft assembly—exploded view (© Eaton Corp.)

19. Remove the assembly from the vise and install the reverse gear on the shaft with the clutching teeth forward and engaging the splines of the sliding clutch. Engage the second speed clutch so that the reverse and second speed gears are as close together as possible.

20. Set the mainshaft assembly aside until the remaining transmission components are assembled.

COUNTERSHAFTS

Assembly

NOTE: Except for the number of teeth on the P.T.O. gears, the two countershafts are identical and the assembly procedure is the same.

1. Install the roll pin and key in each countershaft.
2. Press the third speed gear on the shaft with the long hub down. Press the fourth speed gear on the shaft with the long hub up.
3. Press the fifth speed gear on the shaft with the long hub down.
4. Press the P.T.O. gear on the shaft with the bullet nose of the teeth facing upward. Press the sixth speed gear on the shaft with the long hub upward.
5. Mark the timing teeth on each countershaft drive gear with a marking paint. The timing teeth are aligned with the keyway and are stamped with an "O". The P.T.O. gear positions are with the 47 tooth P.T.O. gear on the left side and the 45 tooth P.T.O. gear on the right side.

DRIVE GEAR

Assembly

1. Install the snapring in the hub of the drive gear.
2. Install the drive gear on the splines of the input shaft with the snapring to the front.
3. Install the spacer on the shaft and against the snapring.
4. Install the drive gear bearing on the shaft and coat the locknut threads with a Loctite® compound.
5. Install the locking nut (left hand thread) and torque 250 to 300 ft. lbs. Peen the nut into the two slots of the shaft.
6. Mark any two adjacent teeth on the drive gear and mark two teeth directly opposite. Install the pocket bushing if needed.

NOTE: If a new bushing is installed flush with the shaft pocket and the three oil holes are restricted, drill out with a $^5/_{32}$ inch drill. The radial clearance between the bushing and the pilot on the mainshaft should be 0.040 to 0.045 inch.

TRANSMISSION CASE

Reassembly

1. Install the three magnetic discs on the bottom of the case. An oil resistant adhesive can be used to hold them in place.
2. Install the plug in the end of the reverse idler shaft. Press the needle bearing into the bore of the reverse idler gear.
3. Install the bearing inner race in the needle bearing.
4. Hold the rear washer in place in the case bore and install the idler shaft into the washer. Install the gear and the thrust washer on the shaft as the shaft is inserted into the case bore.
5. Install the elastic stop nut and washer on the end of the shaft.
6. Install the auxiliary countershaft front bearing in the reverse idler shaft bore.

COUNTERSHAFTS

1. Install the left countershaft (47 P.T.O. teeth) into position in the case and then install the right (45 P.T.O. teeth) countershaft into position, but do not install the bearings.

DRIVE GEAR ASSEMBLY

1. Insert the drive gear assembly into the case and move the input shaft out through the bearing bore.
2. After working the drive gear through the countershaft teeth, seat the bearing in the bore and install the snapring in the outer groove of the bearing.

TIMING THE LEFT COUNTERSHAFT AND THE DRIVE GEAR

1. Center the rear of the left countershaft in the case bore. If a centering tool is not available, use wooden blocks or equivalent.
2. Mesh the marked tooth on the countershaft gear between two of the marked teeth on the drive gear.
3. Using a bearing driver or equivalent, install the front bearing on the countershaft and into the case bearing bore.
4. Remove the centering block from the rear of the case and install the rear countershaft bearing on the shaft and into the case bearing bore.
5. Install the bearing retainer plate on the front of the shaft. Tighten the retaining bolts and wire securely.
6. Install the snapring in the groove at the rear of the countershaft.

MAINSHAFT

1. From inside the case, insert the rear of the mainshaft assembly through the rear bearing bore and lower the assembly into position. Use caution as the reverse gear is free and could fall or be misaligned.
2. Move the mainshaft forward and seat the pilot end of the shaft into the bushing of the drive/input shaft assembly. Center the rear of the mainshaft in the bearing bore.

RIGHT COUNTERSHAFT INSTALLATION AND TIMING

1. Mesh the marked timing tooth on the right countershaft between the two marked timing teeth on the drive gear. Be sure the left countershaft timing tooth is still meshed between the two marked teeth on the drive gear.
2. Center the rear of the right countershaft and recheck the centering of the mainshaft.
3. Install the front bearing on the right countershaft and in the case bore.
4. Install the rear bearing on the shaft and in the case bore.
5. Install the bearing retainer plate on the front of the right countershaft and secure it with the retaining bolts and wire.
6. Install the snapring on the rear of the countershaft in the groove provided.

LEFT REVERSE IDLER GEAR ASSEMBLY

1. Install the plug in the idler shaft. Press the needle bearing into the reverse idler gear, if not previously done.
2. Install the inner race in the bearing of the gear.
3. Hold the rear washer in place in the case bore and insert the shaft into the washer. Install the gear and thrust washer on the shaft as the shaft is pushed on through the case bore.
4. Install the elastic stop nut and washer on the end of the shaft. Install the auxiliary countershaft front bearing in the reverse idler bore.
5. Mesh the mainshaft reverse gear with the idler gears and install the snapring in the inside diameter of the gear.

AUXILIARY DRIVE GEAR

Assembly

1. Place the retainer ring on the auxiliary drive gear with the flat side down.
2. Press the bearing on the drive gear with the snapring against the retainer ring.
3. Install the snapring in the groove at the rear of the gear

hub. Seat the bearing in the rear case bore, fitting the drive gear on the splines of the mainshaft.

4. Secure the retaining ring to the housing with the retaining bolts. Tighten and secure with wire.

5. Install the rear coupling snapring in the groove on the rear of the mainshaft.

CLUTCH HOUSING, AUXILIARY HOUSING

Installation

The installation of the clutch housing and the auxiliary housing is accomplished in the reverse of the removal procedure.

Fuller T–1056 Series Six Speed

The T–1056 transmission is of the twin countershaft design and has six forward speeds. The transmission has a progressive shift from 1st to 6th speeds without the use of an auxiliary gear set.

GEAR SHIFT LEVER HOUSING

The gear shift lever housing is normally removed while the transmission is in the vehicle, to gain necessary transmission removal clearance.

Removal and Installation

1. Place the transmission in neutral and remove the four retaining bolts.

2. Lightly jar the housing to break the gasket seal and lift the housing assembly from the shift bar housing.

3. Place a cover over the open hole to prevent foreign material from entering the transmission.

4. The installation is normally done when the transmission is reinstalled into the vehicle, and is in the reverse order of the removal procedure.

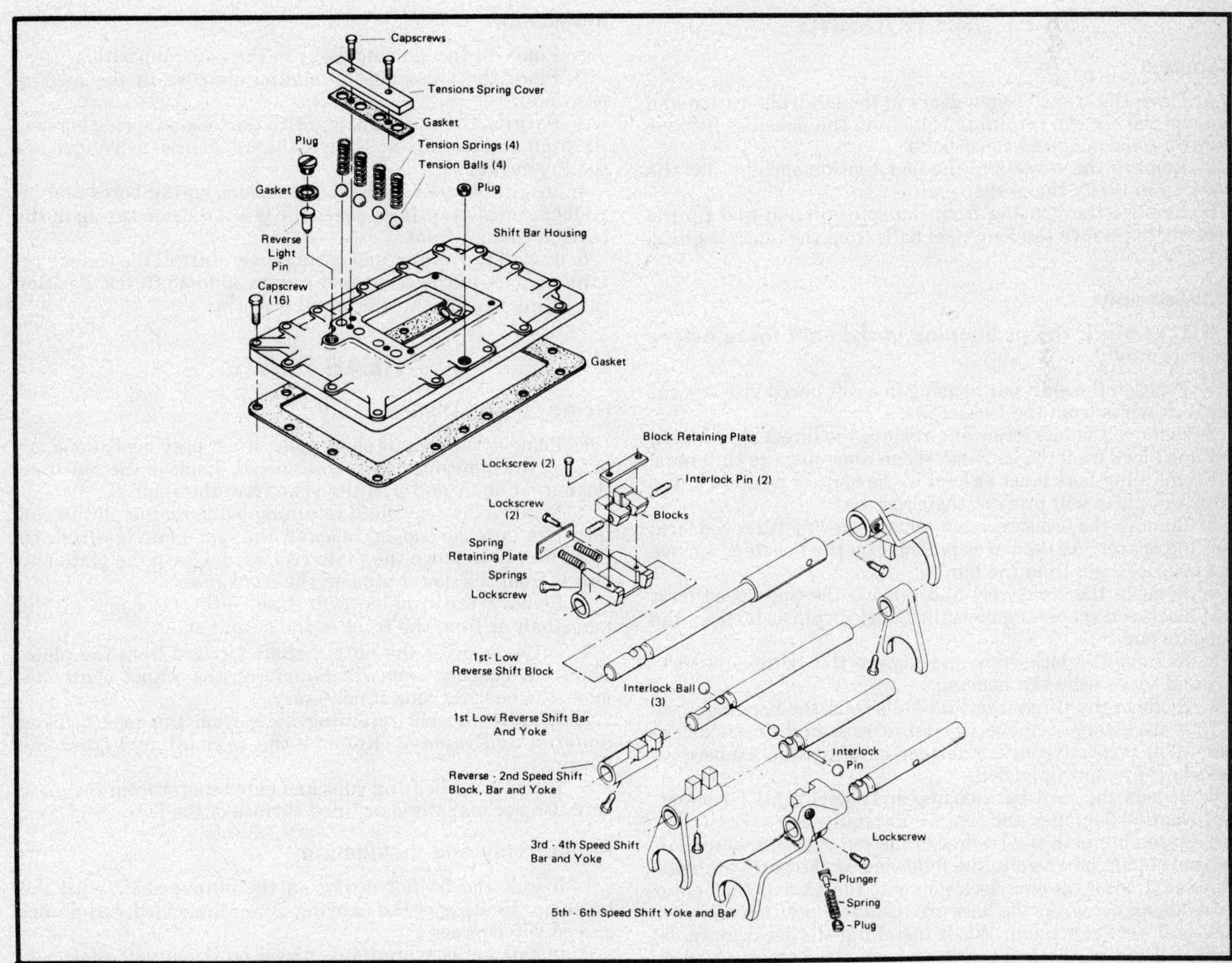

Exploded view of the shift bar housing assembly (© Eaton Corp.)

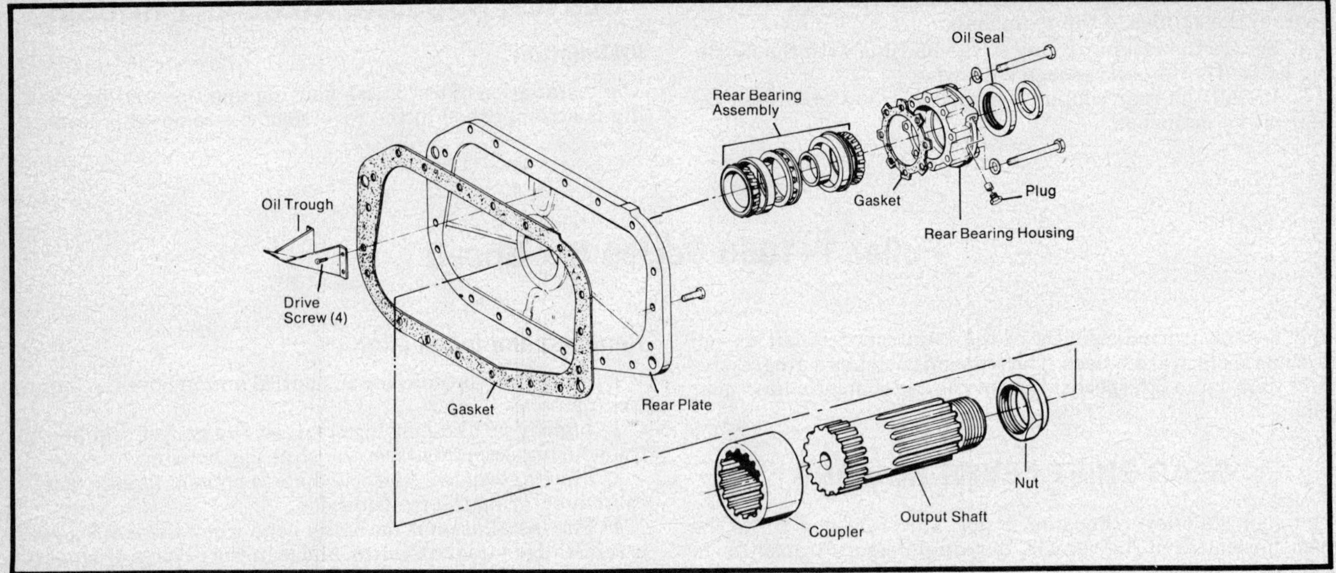

Rear plate assembly—exploded view (© Eaton Corp.)

SHIFT BAR HOUSING

Removal

1. Have the transmission gears in the neutral position and remove the sixteen retaining bolts from the housing. Remove the two tension spring cover bolts.
2. Remove the cover and the four tension springs. Jar the housing to break the gasket seal.
3. Remove the housing from the transmission and tip the housing to remove the four steel balls from the tension spring bores.

Disassembly

NOTE: Mark the positioning of the shift forks before their removal.

1. Position the shift bar housing in a soft jawed vise and cut the lock wires from the lockscrews.
2. Remove the lockscrew and remove the direct speed yoke, bar and block from the housing. When removing the shift bars, the remaining bars must be kept in the neutral position or the interlock parts will prevent their removal.
3. Remove the lockscrew and remove the 3rd/4th speed fork, bar and spacer. As the bar is pulled from the housing, remove the interlock pin from the bar.
4. Remove the lockscrew and remove the 2nd speed fork, bar, block and spacer. Remove the interlock pin as it clears the housing end.
5. Remove the lockscrew and remove the 1st/reverse fork, bar and block from the housing.
6. Remove the three interlock balls from the housing.
7. If necessary, remove the 1st/reverse and direct blocks from their respective forks. Caution must be exercised because the plugs are spring loaded.
8. Inspect the shift bar housing and components for abnormal wear or damages and replace as required.
9. Assembly is in the reverse of the removal procedure. Attention should be given to the following as the parts are reassembled. Install the interlock pins into the bars as they enter the housing bores. As the bars are installed, position an interlock ball between them. When installing the lockscrews, be sure the end of the lockscrew seats in the bore of the bar. Torque the lockscrews 35 to 45 ft. lbs. Use lockwire on each of the lockscrews.

Installation

1. Place all the shifting forks in the neutral position.
2. Place the transmission sliding clutches in the neutral position.
3. Position the shift housing with the tension spring bores to the front and seat the housing to the transmission, using a new sealing gasket.
4. Install the four balls in the tension spring bores and install the tension springs. Place the green tension spring in the bore on the left front.
5. Install the gasket and spring cover. Install the sixteen retaining bolts in the cover and torque 35 to 45 ft. lbs. Position the lifting eyes in their original positions.

REAR PLATE

Removal and Disassembly

1. Remove the output shaft yoke, if not previously done, by locking the transmission in two speeds. Remove the nut from the output shaft and pull the yoke from the shaft.
2. Remove the rear plate retaining bolts. Re-install three of the bolts into the tapped holes in the rear plate and tighten them evenly to move the plate rearward. Grasp the plate and pull it from the dowel pins on the front case.
3. Remove the coupler gear from either the end of the mainshaft or from the front of the output shaft.
4. Drive or press the output shaft forward from the plate. The front bearing cone will remain on the output shaft. Remove the bearing cone if necessary.
5. Remove the six retaining bolts from the rear bearing housing and remove. Remove the rear oil seal from the housing.
6. Tap the two bearing cups and outer spacer from the plate bore. Do not mar the machined surface of the bore.

Reassembly and Installation

1. Install the front bearing on the output shaft with the taper up. Heating of the bearing is recommended, but do not exceed 275 degrees F.
2. Install the bearing inner spacer on the output shaft.
3. Place the front bearing cup over the plate bore with the thick side up. Place the bearing on the cup and position the

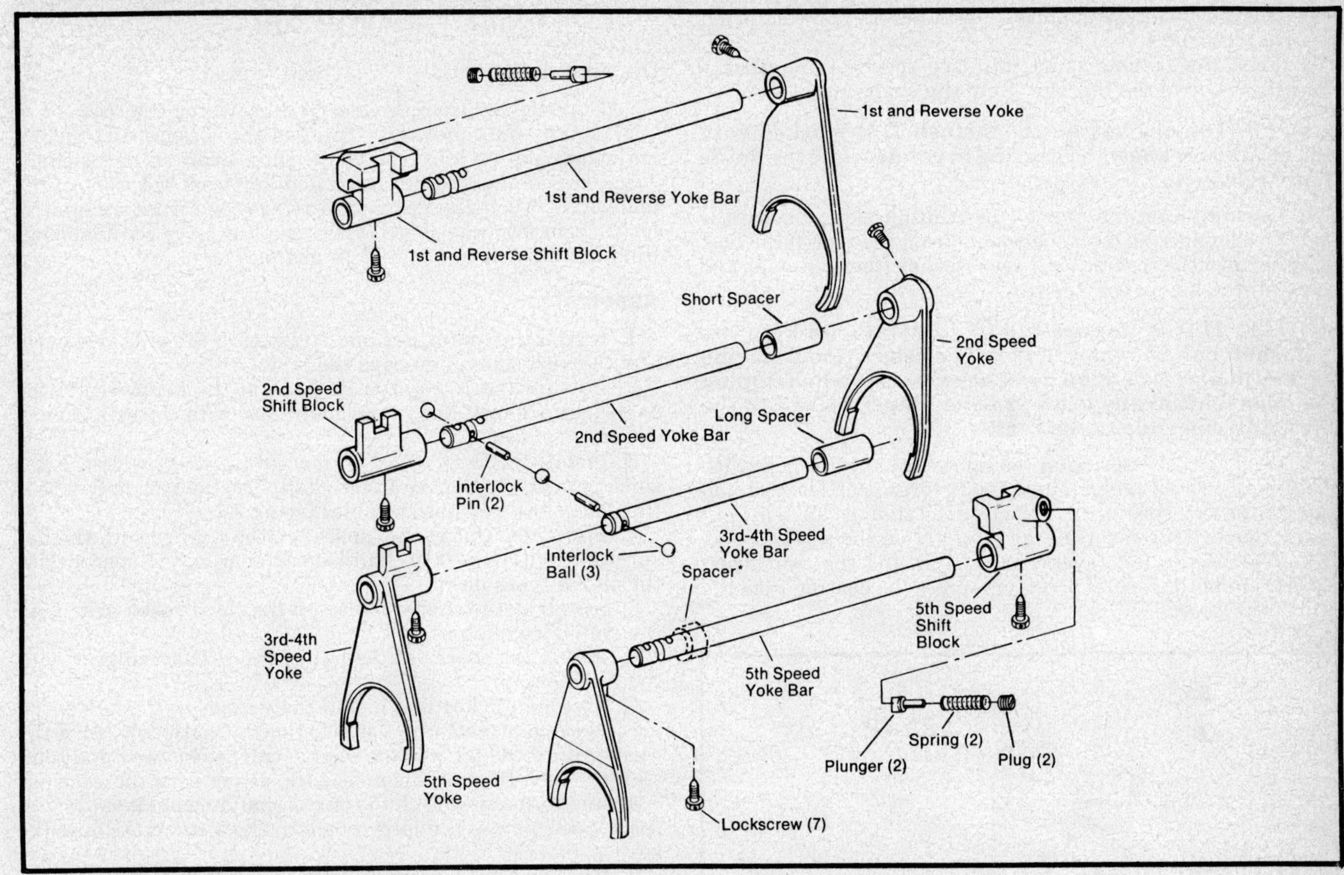

Shift bar, yokes and blocks (© Eaton Corp.)

rear bearing cup on the spacer with the lop up. Drive the three components into the bore at the same time. The bearings and cups are matched sets and should be paired with each other during the installation.

4. Position the rear plate over the output shaft. Heat the rear bearing to not over 275 degrees F and install onto the output shaft. Be sure the lip of the rear cup does not move away from the plate during the bearing installation.

5. Install the new rear oil seal into the bearing housing. Install the bearing housing onto the rear plate using a new gasket.

6. Be sure that one of the notches in the face of the housing aligns with the oil port on the mating surface of the plate. Install the six retaining bolts. It is recommended by the manufacturer that an oil trough be installed on the rear plate of transmissions not equipped. The retaining bolt with the brass washer is to be installed in the hole intersecting the speedometer drive gear bore.

7. Install the coupler onto the mainshaft or the output shaft. Install the rear plate assembly and gasket onto the front case dowel pins, while engaging the coupler with the shaft splines. Rotate the output shaft as necessary to engage the splines.

8. Install the retaining bolts and torque 35 to 45 ft. lbs.

CLUTCH COVER HOUSING

Removal and Installation

1. To remove the clutch housing, remove the retaining nuts and bolts, tap the housing to break the gasket seal and pull the housing forward off the studs.

2. To install, reverse the removal procedure, using a new gasket. Torque the nuts and bolts to the following specifications.

Aluminum Clutch Housing:

Nuts	140–150 ft. lbs.
Bolts	70–80 ft. lbs.

Iron Clutch Housing:

Nuts	180–200 ft. lbs.
Bolts	80–100 ft. lbs.

FRONT CASE

Disassembly

1. With the rear plate off the front case, remove the mainshaft rear snapring and pull the second speed mainshaft gear from the mainshaft.

2. Remove the positioning snapring and the second speed washer from the mainshaft.

3. Lock the transmission in two speeds and remove the two rear countershaft nuts.

4. Cut the locking wires and turn the lockscrews out that secure the twoidler shaft retaining plates and the mainshaft plate.

5. From the front of the gear box, cut the lockwires and remove the lockscrews. Remove the two front countershaft bearing retaining plates.

6. Drive both countershafts rearward as far as possible with a soft bar and driving mall.

7. With the use of a special pulling tool, remove the second speed gears from the countershafts.

8. Remove the keys from the countershafts.

9. Using a slide type hammer impact puller, remove the left reverse idler shaft.

10. Lock the transmission into two speeds and pull the mainshaft key to the rear and from the shaft.

NOTE: The keyway on the mainshaft is marked with an "O". Do not allow the gearing to rotate while the key is being removed.

11. Working from the rear of the transmission, remove the two washers and the mainshaft plate from the rear of the box.

12. Remove the reverse gear rear washer from the shaft and reinstall the key in the keyway.

NOTE: If it is impossible to reinstall the key, the mainshaft can be removed from the case without having the key in place. Caution must be exercised when tipping the mainshaft as the gearing is no longer locked to the shaft and can slide to the rear.

13. Remove the snapring in the hub of the reverse gear with the use of a small probe. Move the reverse gear forward and against the first speed gear, engaging the sliding clutch in both gears. Remove the reverse gear spacer from the shaft.

14. Remove the left reverse idler gear and the two thrust washers from the case. If necessary, press the bearing from the hub of the gear.

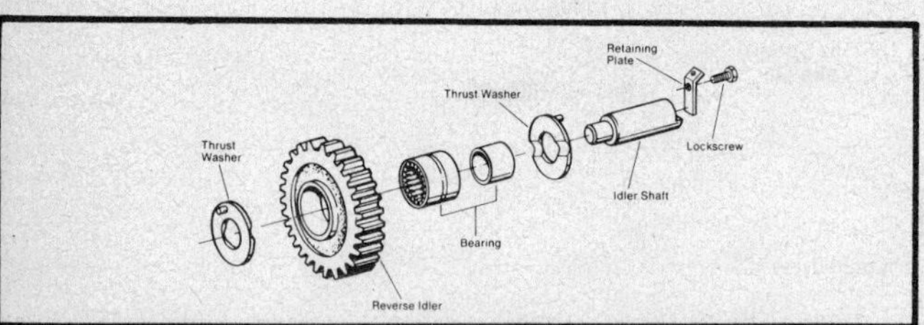

Reverse idler gear (© Eaton Corp.)

15. Using a long drift and driving mall, remove the right countershaft rear bearing to the rear and out of the case. The removal procedure will ruin the bearing and its removal should not be done unless replacement of the bearing is planned.

16. Drive the front of the right countershaft to the rear until the front of the shaft is free of the front bearing. Drive against the rear of the shaft to move the bearing forward and out of the case.

17. Remove the front bearing retaining bolts, tap the cover to break the gasket seal and remove the cover over the input shaft.

18. From inside the transmission case, drive the input shaft and bearing forward until the bearing clears the case. Do not completely remove the input shaft assembly.

19. With the front of the countershaft still engaged with the drive gear, swing the rear of the countershaft as far to the right as possible.

20. Slide the mainshaft to the rear, tip the front upward and remove the mainshaft assembly from the case. The reverse idler is loose and can fall from the shaft during the removal. The right reverse idler shaft can be removed with an impact puller tool to aid in the removal of the mainshaft.

21. Move the right countershaft as far to the rear as possible and swing the front of the shaft intowards the middle of the case. Tip the front of the countershaft upward and remove from the case.

22. Remove the left countershaft in the same manner as the right countershaft.

23. If not previously removed, pull the right reverse idler shaft from the transmission case. Remove the gear and the two thrust washers. Replace the reverse idler bearing with a press, if required.

MAINSHAFT

Disassembly

1. Pull the key from the mainshaft towards the rear.

2. Turn the gearing to release the washers from the mainshaft splines and remove the three gears from the shaft.

3. Remove the sliding clutch and key from the front of the mainshaft. Turn the gearing to release the washers and remove them from the shaft. If necessary, remove the snaprings from the hubs of the mainshaft gears.

Assembly

1. Install the mainshaft into a vise with the pilot end down and the vise clamping above the pilot.

2. Be sure the roll pin is in place in the keyway and the snaprings are installed in the gear hubs, with the exception of the reverse gear.

3. Install the third speed washer on the shaft with the flat side up. Lock the washer on the shaft with the key, noting that the end of the key has the holes facing up.

4. Install the third speed spacer on the washer with the flat surface down. Install the third speed gear on the spacer with the clutch teeth down.

5. Install the first speed gear on the third speed gear with the clutching teeth up.

6. Install the spacer in the hub of the first speed gear with the flat side up.

7. Remove the key and install the washer in the hub of the first speed gear with the flat side down. Cautiously, turn the washer until the large notch aligns with the keyway and reinstall the key. During this procedure, do not turn the gearing.

8. Install the sliding clutch on the shaft and against the first speed gear, noting the large notch in the clutch goes over the key.

9. Remove the key and install the reverse gear washer on the shaft with the flat surface up. Reinstall the key.

10. Remove the shaft assembly from the vise and reinstall it with the pilot end up. Do not allow the key to slide down out of position. Retain with a rubber band, if necessary.

11. Install the sliding clutch on the shaft with the large notch over the keyway.

12. Install the fourth speed spacer on the shaft with the flat surface up.

13. Install the fourth speed gear on the spacer with the clutching teeth down.

14. Install the fifth speed gear on the fourth speed gear and install the spacer in the hub of the fifth speed gear, with the flat side up.

15. Install the washer in the spacer with the flat side down. Turn the washer to align the large notch with the keyway.

16. Install the key in the keyway with the tapered end in the large notch of the washer and the pin in the key way hole.

17. Install the sliding clutch on the shaft with the large notch over the key way. Lay the assembly aside to be installed into the case later.

COUNTERSHAFTS

Disassembly

1. The two countershafts are identical and are disassembled in the same manner.

2. The countershaft is pressed from the gears using a press with at least 25 ton capacity.

3. Use the fifth speed gear as a base during the pressing operation. Remove the key and roll pin as required.

Assembly

1. The assembly of the countershafts are in the reverse of the disassembly procedure. Exercise caution while doing the press work to avoid cocking the gears on the shafts.

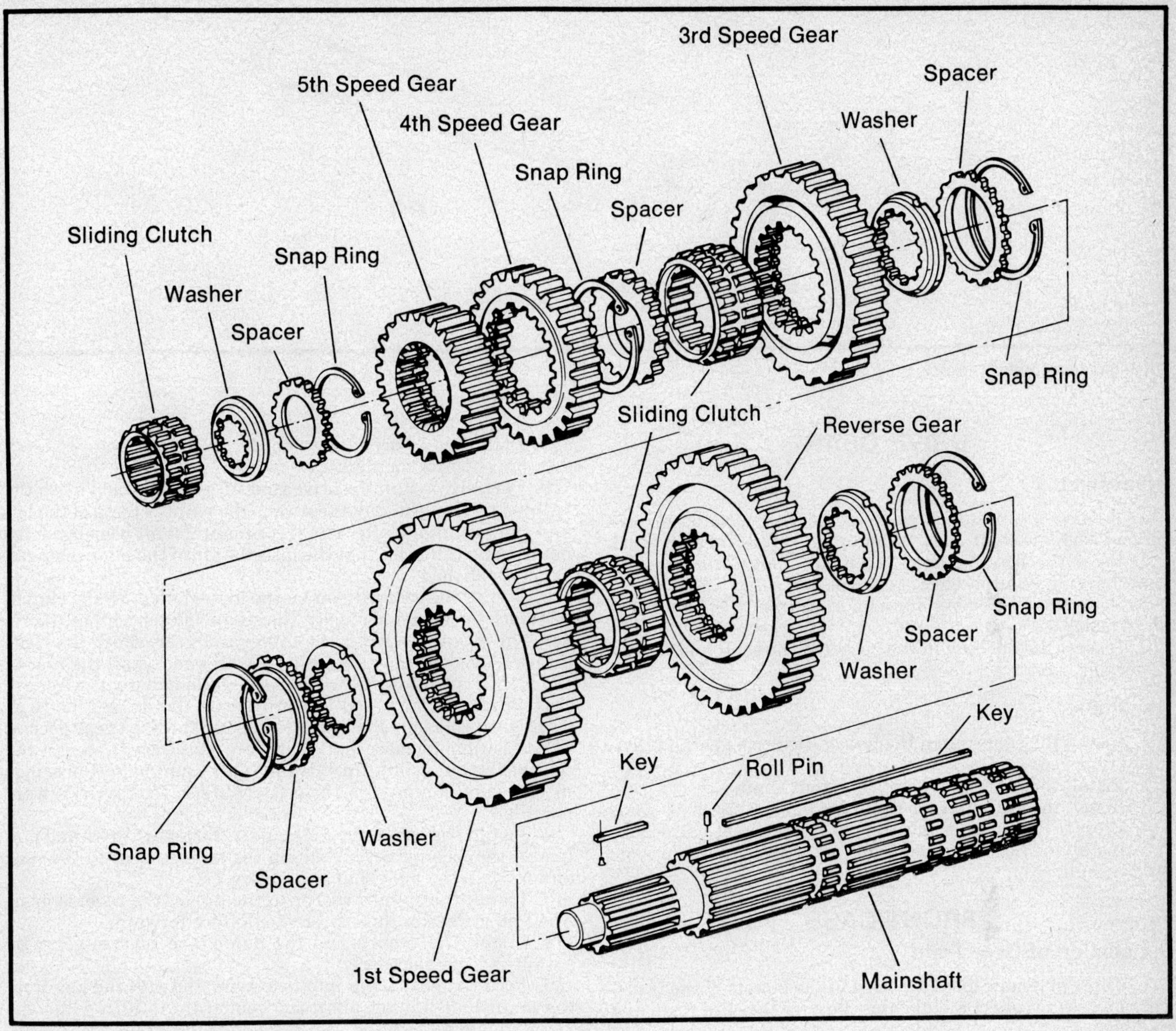

3rd Speed Gear
Spacer
5th Speed Gear
4th Speed Gear
Washer
Snap Ring
Spacer
Sliding Clutch
Snap Ring
Washer
Spacer
Snap Ring
Sliding Clutch
Reverse Gear
Snap Ring
Spacer
Washer
Key
Key
Roll Pin
Snap Ring
Washer
Spacer
1st Speed Gear
Mainshaft

Mainshaft assembly—exploded view (© Eaton Corp.)

4th Speed Gear
5th Speed Gear
Drive Gear
Front Bearing
Retainer Plate
Lockscrews
Roll Pin
Key
Rear Bearing
Countershaft
3rd Speed Gear

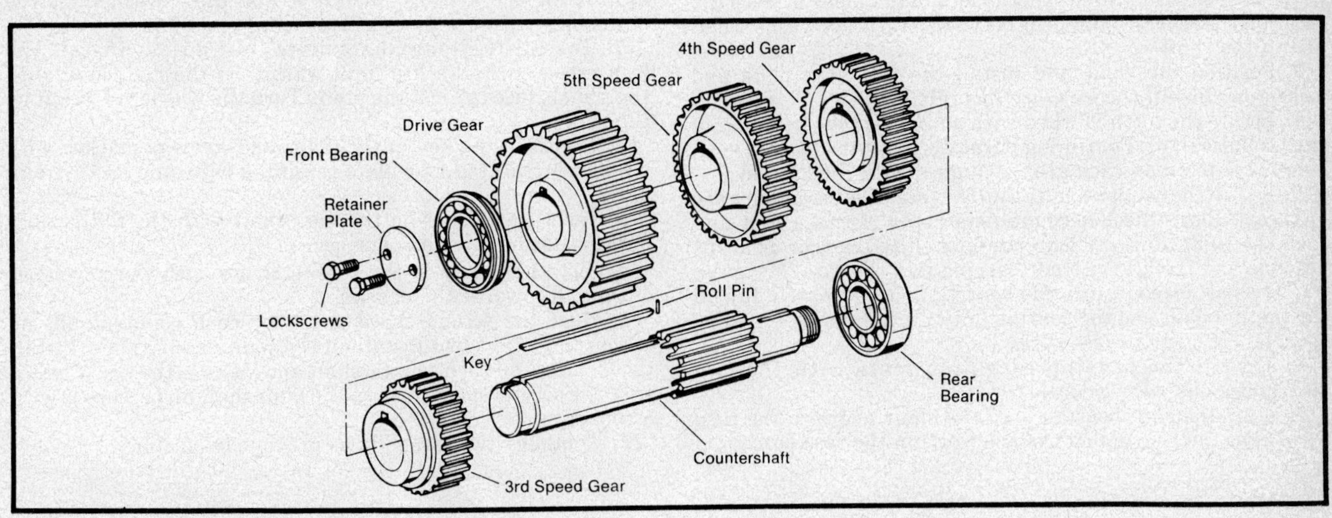

Countershaft assembly—exploded view (© Eaton Corp.)

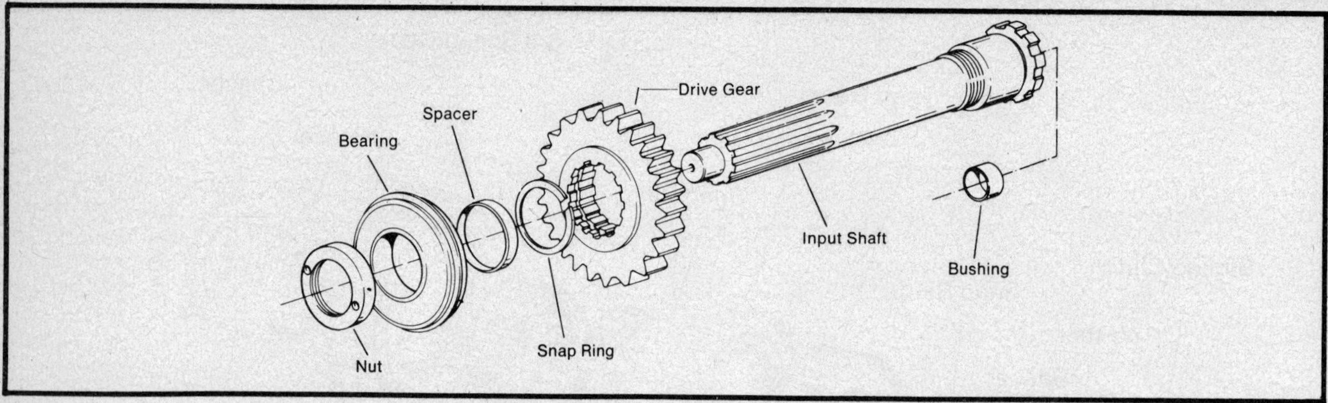

Drive gear assembly (© Eaton Corp.)

DRIVE GEAR

Disassembly

1. Remove the peened area of the bearing nut and remove the nut from the shaft. The nut and shaft threads are left hand.
2. Press the bearing from the input shaft. This frees the gear, bearing and spacer for removal.
3. If necessary, remove the snapring from the hub of the drive gear.
4. Inspect the bushing in the pocket of the shaft and replace if worn or defective.

Assembly

1. Install the snapring in the hub of the drive gear, if previously removed.
2. Install the drive gear onto the input shaft.
3. Install the spacer on the shaft and against the drive gear.
4. Press the bearing in place on the shaft (shield side down).
5. Install the nut on the shaft and peen the nut into the slots on the shaft.

FRONT CASE

Installation of Gear Train

1. Three magnetic discs are used in the bottom of the transmission case to collect metal chips. Be sure they are clean and in place.
2. Install the thrust washers for the right reverse idler gear in the case, mating the washer pins into the holes in the case. Position the reverse idler gear between the thrust washers and install the shaft.
3. Position the shaft and install the retaining plate and lockscrew. Install the lockwire securely.
4. Locate the tooth marked with an "O" on the large gear of each countershaft. For timing purposes, paint the tooth of each gear. This tooth on each gear is aligned with the keyway.
5. Install the countershafts into the case. The assemblies are identical. Place the left countershaft into the case first and then the right. Pull the left countershaft to the rear as far as possible and install the front bearing into the case. Move the countershaft forward into the bearing and alternately tap on the countershaft and the bearing until the bearing is seated on the shaft and in the case bore.
6. Install the bearing retaining plate with the two lockscrews and wire securely.
7. Start the rear bearing onto the shaft and into the case bore. Seat the bearing on the shaft and in the case bore.
8. Paint two adjacent teeth on the drive gear and two teeth directly opposite for timing purposes.
9. Partially install the drive gear into the case and mesh the painted teeth of the drive gear with the painted teeth of the left and right countershafts. The right countershaft bearings have not been installed wo that the installation of the mainshaft can be accomplished.
10. Install the reverse gear on the mainshaft with the clutching teeth forward and engage the sliding clutch so that the reverse gear is flat against the first speed gear. Block the right counter<chshaft towards the case wall and install the rear of the mainshaft through the case web while moving the front of the mainshaft down and forward. Move the drive gear rearward until the mainshaft pilot seats into the drivegear pocket.
11. Position the mainshaft rear plate on the case to center the rear of the mainshaft. Install the right countershaft bearings in the same manner as the left countershaft bearings were installed.
12. Install the left reverse idler gear, thrust washers and pin. Install the locking wire. Position the reverse gear to the rear and remove the mainshaft rear plate.
13. Install the splined spacer in the hub of the reverse gear. The flat surface of the spacer should face forward.
14. Install the snapring in the hub of the reverse gear. Be sure it is locked properly.
15. Lock the gear train into two gears and pull the key from the mainshaft. Do not allow the gear train to turn while the key is removed.
16. Install the large washer on the mainshaft and turn it to lock it on the splines. Install a low limit washer on the mainshaft with the flat surface facing rearward.
17. Install the mainshaft plate, but do not install the lockscrews. Install a low limit washer on the mainshaft with the flat surface against the plate. Turn the washer to lock it on the shaft.
18. Reinstall the key in the mainshaft keyway marked with an "O". Install the four plate retaining bolts and lock wire in pairs.
19. Install a washer on the mainshaft with the flat surface out and secure with a snapring.
20. Install the key in the countershafts with the key taper down and towards the bearing.
21. Heat the second speed gears for each countershaft, no more than 275F° and install on the countershaft ends. Install the locknuts on each countershaft and stake to the key way. Install the second speed gear on the mainshaft and secure it with a snapring.
22. Complete the assembly as previously outlined.

Fuller RT-, RTF-, RTOF-9513 and RT-12513 Thirteen Speed Transmission

This transmission is the twin countershaft design. Engine torque is split between the two countershafts. The mainshaft gears, when not engaged, float between the countershaft gears, eliminating the need for gear sleeves and bushings. These transmissions have 13 progressive forward ratios and two reverse, consisting of a five speed front section, a synchronized two speed range section and an overdrive splitter gear.

SEPARATION OF THE MAIN AND AUXILIARY SECTIONS

1. With the transmission assembly removed from the vehicle and the air lines disconnected, remove the capscrews which attach the auxiliary housing to the transmission case.
2. Install puller screws in the tapped holes in the housing and tighten evenly to move the auxiliary section to the rear to break the gasket seal.
3. Attach a chain hoist to the housing and separate the auxiliary section from the transmission.

MAIN TRANSMISSION

Disassembly

1. Remove the mainshaft rear coupling snapring from the groove in the mainshaft, located inside the bore of the drive gear.
2. Cut the lock wire and remove the capscrews that attach the bearing retainer ring to the case.
3. Insert three puller screws in the taped holes in the retainer ring and tighten evenly to pull the assembly from the case bore.
4. Secure the gear in a vise and remove the snapring from the auxiliary drive gear.
5. Press or drive the bearing retainer ring and bearing from the auxiliary drive gear. To remove the left reverse idler gear, move the reverse gear forward on the mainshaft to provide the necessary clearance.
6. Move the mainshaft reverse gear to the rear as far as possible and remove the snapring from the ID of the gear.
7. Move the mainshaft reverse gear forward and against the low speed gear and into engagement with the sliding clutch gear.
8. Remove the auxiliary countershaft front bearing from the reverse idler bore.
9. Remove the elastic stop nut and washer from the reverse idler shaft.
10. Remove the plug from the bore of the reverse shaft.
11. Insert an impact puller and remove the reverse idler shaft. This will unseat the countershaft front bearing of the auxiliary section from the case bore.
12. As the reverse idler shaft is moved to the rear, remove the thrust washer and gear from the shaft and case.
13. If necessary, remove the bearing inner race which is a slip fit from the reverse idler shaft.
14. If necessary, press the bearing from the bore of the reverse idler gear. Remove the cup from the bore.
15. Remove the bearing retainer snapring from the groove at the rear of the right countershaft.
16. Using a blunt punch, from within the case, move the countershaft rear bearing to the rear and from the shaft.
17. Remove the bearing retainer plate from the front of the right countershaft.
18. Using a soft bar move the right countershaft to the rear approximately $\frac{1}{2}$ inch.
19. Move the countershaft assembly forward to fully expose the front bearing snapring. Remove the front bearing by using a puller or pry bar.
20. Block the right countershaft toward the case wall, as far forward as possible.
21. With the main shaft reverse gear against the 1st speed gear, pull the mainshaft to the rear and from the case.
22. Remove the snapring from the groove at the rear of the left countershaft.
23. Using a blunt punch, from within the case, move the countershaft rear bearing to the rear and from the shaft.
24. Remove the bearing retainer plate from the front of the left countershaft.
25. Using a soft bar against the front of the countershaft, move the countershaft to the rear approximately $\frac{1}{2}$ inch.
26. Move the left countershaft forward until the front bearing snapring is exposed.
27. Pull or pry the front bearing from the shaft.
28. Remove the front bearing cover cap screws.
29. From inside the case, use a soft bar and hammer to move the drive-gear forward, while removing the cover as the drive gear bearing is moved.
30. Remove the snapring from the drive gear bearing.
31. Move the drive gear assembly to the rear, past the countershaft gears and out of the case.
32. Remove the right and left countershafts from the case.
33. Repeat steps 6 thru 12 to remove the right reverse idler assembly.

DISASSEMBLY OF THE MAIN TRANSMISSION SUBASSEMBLIES

Disassembly

MAINSHAFT

1. Remove the 3rd and 4th speed sliding clutch gear from the mainshaft.
2. Remove the mainshaft front coupling snapring from the rear of the mainshaft.
3. Remove the long key from the mainshaft and the reverse gear spacer and washer.
4. Remove the reverse gear and first/reverse sliding clutch. Keep the washers and spacers with the gear from which they were removed. The spacers have external splines and the washers have internal splines.
5. Work the washers, spacers and gears from the mainshaft. It will be necessary to turn the washers, located under each gear, to align with the splines of the mainshaft.
6. If necessary, remove the snap rings from the groove in the ID of each gear.

Assembly

1. Mount the mainshaft in a vise with the front end up and keeping the keyway clear.
2. Install the snapring in the groove of the ID of all the mainshaft gears except the reverse gear.
3. Install the reverse gear washer on the mainshaft in the fifth radial groove from the top. Turn the square slot in the ID of the washer to align with the keyway in the shaft. Install with the flat side down.
4. From the bottom, install the long key in the keyway in the mainshaft so that the forward end is moved through the slot in the reverse gear washer. Keep the snap ring groove to the rear and to the outside.
5. Install the low speed sliding clutch gear on the mainshaft,

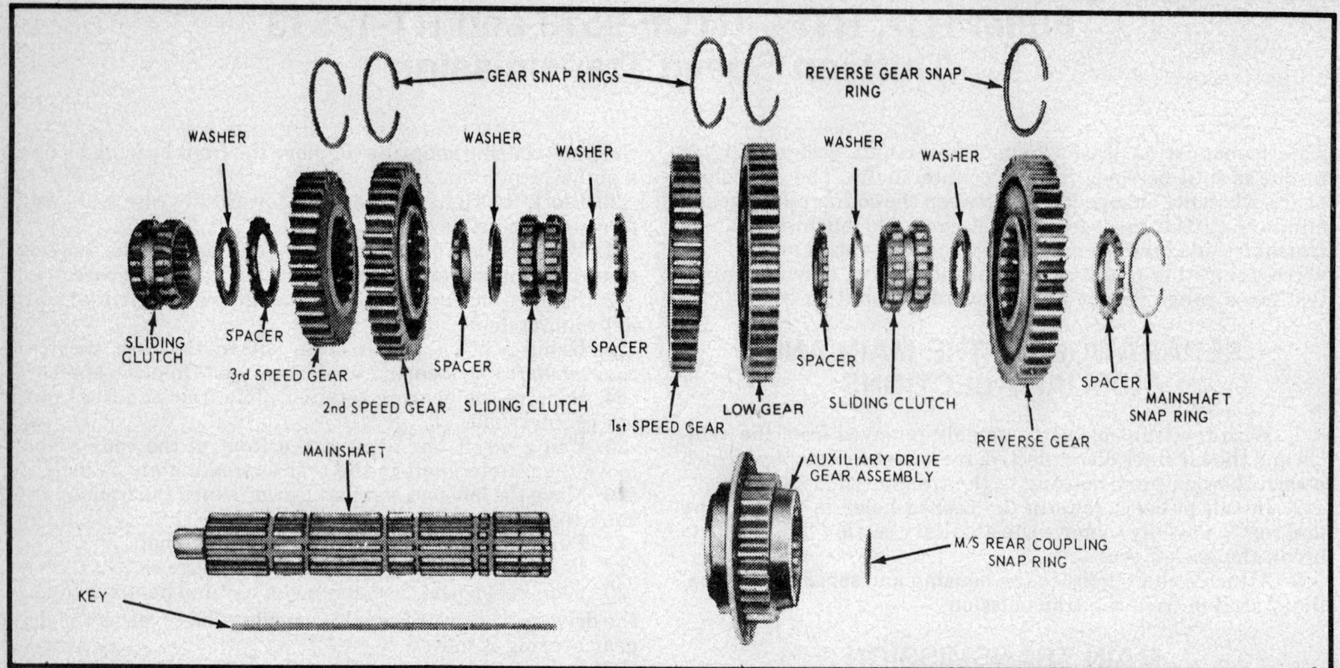

Mainshaft assembly (© Ford Motor Co.)

aligning the large slot in the ID of the gear with the key in the shaft.

6. Install the low low speed gear washer, flat side up, on the mainshaft in the fourth radial groove from the top. Turn the square slot in the ID of the washer to align with the keyway in the shaft.

7. Move the key upwards through the slot in the low low speed gear washer until the front of the key is level with the third radial groove from the top.

8. Install the low low speed gear spacer, flat side down, on the mainshaft and against the washer.

9. Install the low low speed gear, snap ring up, on the mainshaft, engaging the splines of the gear with the splines of the spacer.

10. Install the 1st speed gear, snapring down, on the mainshaft and against the low low speed gear.

11. Install the 1st speed gear spacer, flat side up, on the mainshaft, engaging the splines of the gear with the splines of the spacer.

12. Install the 1st speed gear washer, flat side down, on the mainshaft and against the 1st speed spacer.

13. Turn the 1st speed gear washer until the square slot in the ID aligns with the keyway of the mainshaft.

14. Move the key upwards to engage the 1st speed gear washer and continue to move the key until it reaches the 2nd radial groove in the top of the mainshaft.

15. Install the 1st/2nd speed sliding clutch on the mainshaft, aligning the large slot in the ID of the clutch gear with the key in the shaft.

16. Install the 2nd speed gear washer on the mainshaft and in the 2nd radial groove from the top in the mainshaft.

17. Turn the washer until the square slot in the ID aligns with the keyway in the mainshaft, and move the key upward to engage the washer. Install the washer with the flat side up.

18. Install the 2nd gear spacer on the mainshaft with the flat side against the washer.

19. Install the 2nd speed gear, flat side up, on the mainshaft, engaging the splines of the gear with the splines of the washer.

20. Install the 3rd speed gear, snapring down, on the mainshaft and against the 2nd speed gear.

21. Install the 3rd gear speed gear spacer, on the mainshaft, flat side up, engaging the splines of the gear with the splines of the spacer.

22. Install the 3rd speed gear washer on the mainshaft with the flat side towards the spacer.

23. Align the slot in the ID of the washer with the keyway in the shaft and move the key upwards to engage the 3rd speed gear washer.

24. Install the 3rd/4th speed sliding clutch gear, aligning the large slot in the clutch gear with the keyway in the shaft.

25. Remove the assembly from the vise and move the long key until the snapring groove in the key aligns with the second snap ring groove from the end of the mainshaft.

26. Install the reverse gear, with the snapring groove to the rear, on the rear of the mainshaft, and move as far forward as possible into engagement with the sliding clutch gear.

27. Install the reverse gear spacer on the end of the mainshaft with the flat side against the washer.

28. Install the front mainshaft coupling snapring on the mainshaft and key while securing the key to the mainshaft at the second snapring groove from the end of the mainshaft.

DRIVE GEAR

Disassembly

1. Remove the drive gear bearing nut from the shaft (left hand thread).

2. Using the rear face of the drive gear as a base, mount the assembly in a press, and press the shaft through the gear to unseat the bearing, spacer and drive gear from the shaft.

3. If necessary, remove the snapring from the ID of the drive gear.

Assembly

1. Install the snapring in the ID of the drive gear.

2. Install the drive gear on the shaft with the snapring of the gear towards the front.

3. Install the drive gear spacer on the shaft and against the snapring.

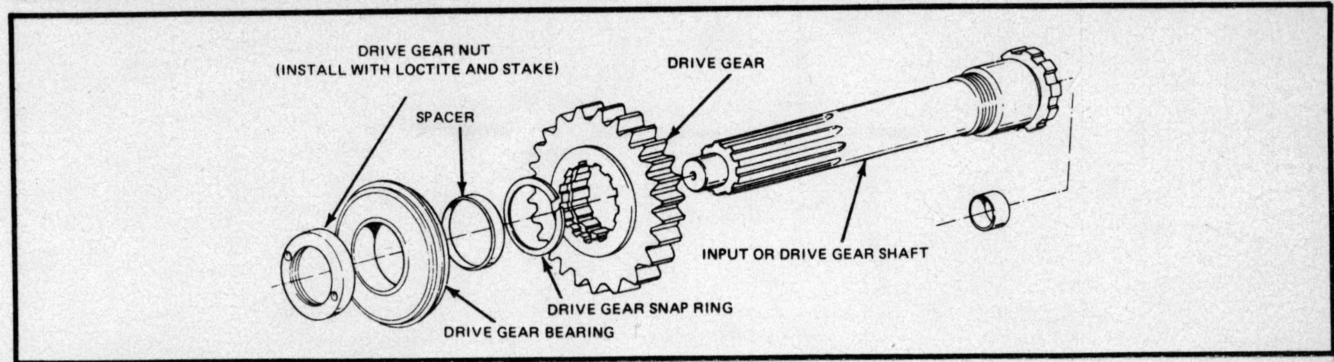

Drive gear assembly (© Ford Motor Co.)

4. Press the drive gear bearing on the shaft with the shield towards the front.
5. Install the bearing nut on the shaft (left hand thread) and torque 250 to 300 ft. lbs. Peen the nut.

COUNTERSHAFT

Disassembly

NOTE: Both countershafts are disassembled in the same manner.

1. Press the 2nd/3rd P.T.O. and 4th speed gears from the countershaft.
2. Press the 1st speed gear from the countershaft.
3. Remove the long key, Woodruff key, and pin from the countershaft if necessary.

Assembly

1. Install the Woodruff key, long key, and pin if previously removed.
2. Press the 1st speed gear on the countershaft with the long hub to the front.
3. Align the keyway in the gear with the keys in the shaft and press the 2nd speed gear on the countershaft with the long hub towards the rear.
4. Press the 3rd speed gear on the countershaft with the long hub toward the front.
5. Press the P.T.O. gear on the countershaft with the bullet end of the teeth toward the rear.
6. Press the 4th speed gear (drive gear) on the countershaft with the long hub of the gear toward the rear.
7. The left countershaft takes a 47 tooth P.T.O. gear; the right, a 45 tooth P.T.O. gear. After completing assembly of the countershafts, mark both left and right assemblies to correspond with the P.T.O. gears.

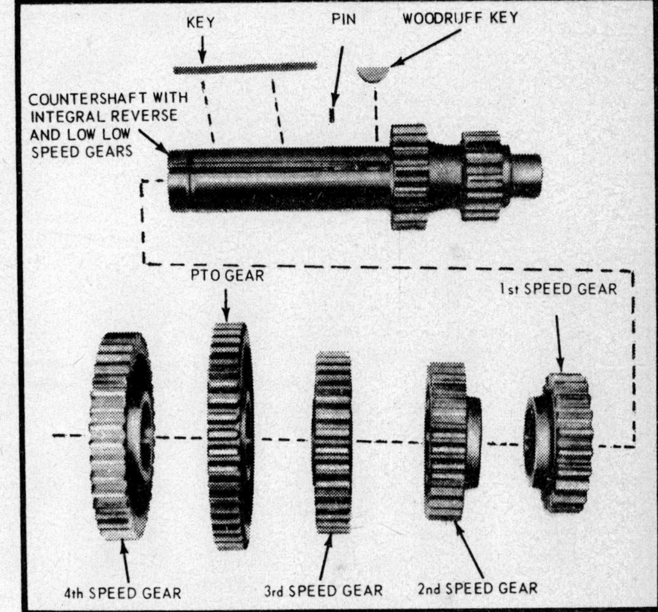

Countershaft assembly (© Ford Motor Co.)

SHIFTER BAR HOUSING

Disassembly

NOTE: Bars not being removed from the housing must be kept in a neutral position or the interlock parts will lock the bars.

1. Tilt the housing and remove the tension springs and balls from the bores in the top of the housing.
2. Place the housing in a vise with the plunger side up.
3. Cut the lock wire and remove the lock screws from each bar just prior to its removal.
4. Move the upper shifter bar to the rear and from the housing, removing the shift block and shift yoke from the bar.
5. Move the center bar to the rear and from the housing, removing the shift block and shift yoke from the bar. As the neutral notch in the shift bar clears the housing boss, remove the interlock pin from the bore in the neutral notch.
6. Remove the actuating plunger from the bore in the housing.
7. Remove the lower bar to the rear and out of the housing, removing the shift yoke from the bar.
8. Two interlock balls will fall from the interlock ball opening in the rear boss of the housing as the last ball is removed.

Assembly

1. Install the housing in a vise with the short bar location at the bottom and the rear of the housing to the right.

NOTE: Shifting bars are to be installed through the rear bores of the housing with the neutral and shift notches to the rear. Keep the bars in the neutral position when installed.

2. Install the low reverse shifter bar into the housing in the lowest bore, installing the shifting yoke on the bar.
3. If previously disassembled, install the reverse stop plunger, spring and plug in the bore until 1 ½ to 2 threads protrude. Stake the plug through a small hole in the yoke.
4. Install the yoke lock screw, tighten and wire securely.
5. Install the actuating plunger in the bore in the left side of the housing with the flat end outward.

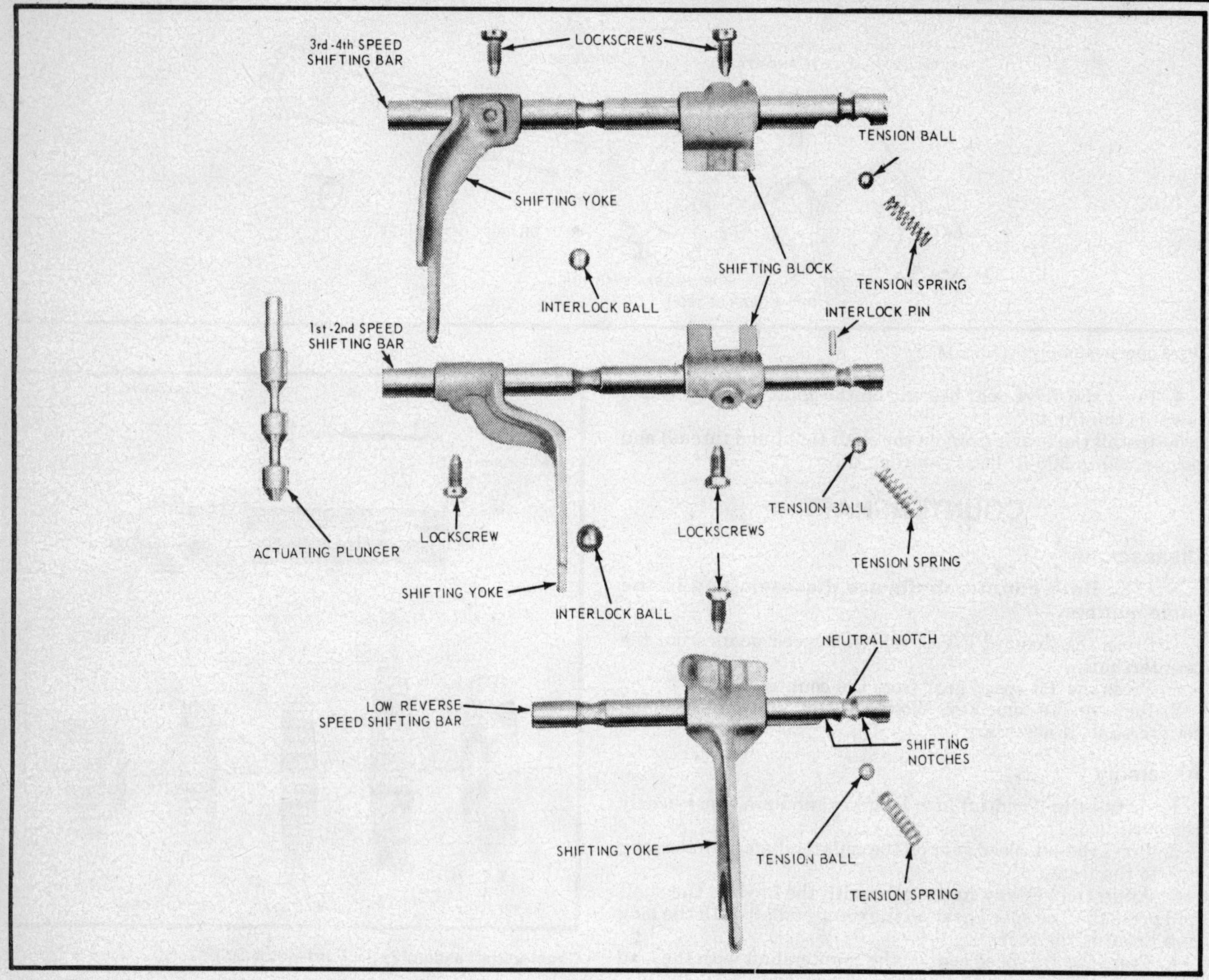

Shifter bar housing assembly (© Ford Motor Co.)

6. Install the $^3/_4$ inch interlock ball in the bore in the rear boss.

7. Install the 1st and 2nd speed shifting bar through the center bore in the housing, through the shifting block, the center boss and the shift yoke. The block is installed with the wire support to the rear. Install the interlock pin in the bore of the neutral notch of the bar as the notch enters the rear bar in the housing.

NOTE: For the remainder of reassembly keep the interlock pin in the vertical position.

8. Install the block and yoke lock screws and tighten and wire securely.

9. Install the $^3/_4$ inch interlock ball in the bore of the rear boss.

10. Install the 3rd/4th speed shifting bar in the top bore of the housing, through the shifting block, the center boss and the 3rd and 4th speed shifting yoke with the fork to the front.

11. Install the block and yoke lock screws and tighten and wire securely.

12. Place the shifting bar assembly on a work bench and install the three tension balls and springs in the top of the housing. The black spring is installed in the left bore (3rd/4th shift bar). Red springs are installed in the other two bores.

AUXILIARY SECTION

Disassembly

1. Remove the shift cylinder cover.
2. Remove the nut from the end of the shifter shaft.
3. Using air on the low range port, remove the piston from the shift cylinder. Do not stand in back of the piston.
4. Remove the bolts that attach the shift cylinder housing to the rear plate.
5. Cut the lock wires and remove the set screws from the shifting fork.
6. Push the shifter shaft to the inside, through the fork hub and out of the cylinder housing. Remove the shifting fork and shift cylinder housing from the plate.
7. If necessary remove the O-rings from the piston and shift cylinder housing.
8. To remove the countershaft assemblies, place the rear plate on wood blocks so that the front of the countershafts are approximately two inches from the work bench. Also place a block under the synchronizer assembly to keep it from moving.
9. Remove the countershaft rear bearing covers.
10. Remove the snaprings from the rear of each countershaft.
11. Tap the rear of the shafts to unseat them from the bearings then using a puller remove the bearings.

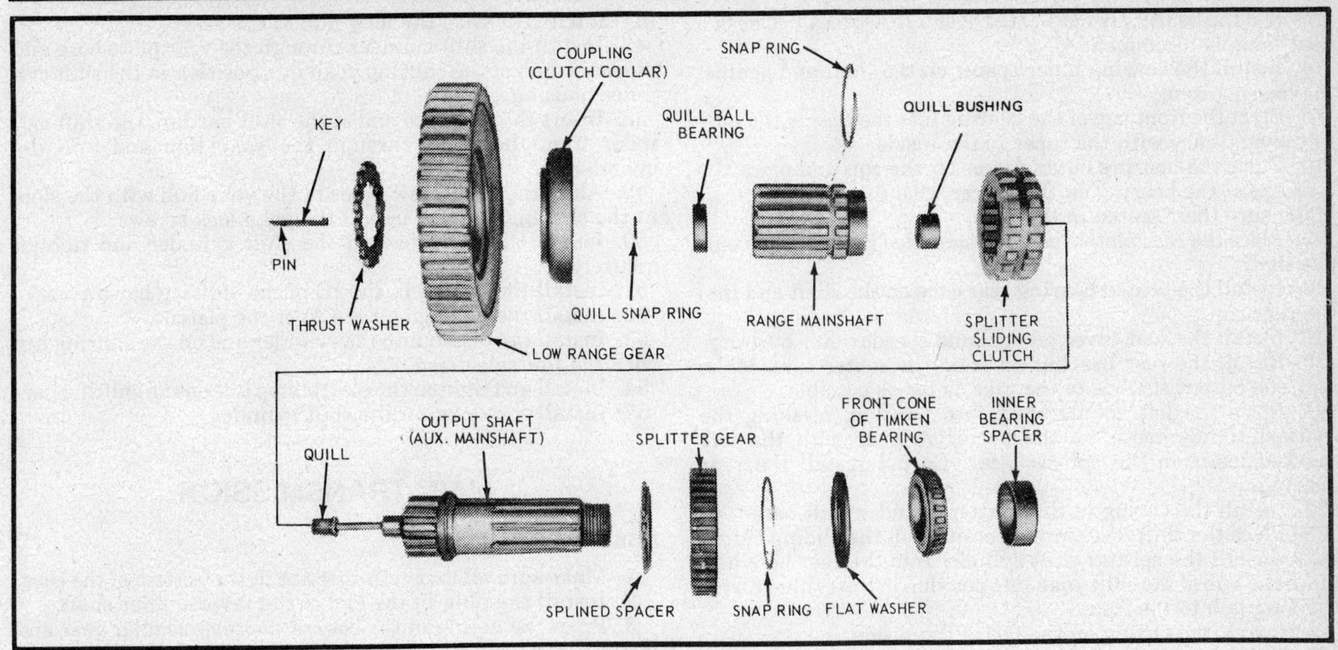

Auxiliary range mainshaft and output shaft—exploded view (© Ford Motor Co.)

12. Pull the synchronizer assembly from the output shaft as a complete unit.
13. Pull the direct (high range) cone synchronizer ring from the pins of the low speed synchronizer ring, covering with a cloth to catch the blocker spring installed in the bores of the direct cone synchronizer. Lay the large low speed ring on a flat surface and pull the direct cone slowly upward.
14. Removing the sliding clutch gear from the pins of the low speed synchronizer.
15. Remove the key from the keyway between the splines of the range mainshaft.
16. Turn the splines of the low speed gear washer, located in the hub of the gear, to align with the splines of the shaft.
17. Remove the low speed gear and splined washer from the shaft.
18. Removing the clutching collar from the shaft.
19. Remove the right countershaft from the auxiliay housing.
20. Remove the splitter gear shift cylinder cover.
21. Cut the lock wire and turn out the lock screw from the shifting yoke.
22. Pull the shifting bar out from the rear of the shift cylinder.
23. If necessary, remove the O-ring from the OD of the piston.
24. Remove the shifting yoke from the sliding clutch gear and withdraw the shift cylinder from the housing.
25. Remove the left countershaft assembly.
26. With a soft bar and hammer or press, move the splitter gear and output shaft assembly forward and out of the rear bearing.
27. Remove the bearing inner spacer from the shaft.
28. Using the front face of the splitter gear as a base, press the tailshaft through the gear and front cone of the bearing, freeing the gear, washer and bearing cone.
29. Remove the splined washer from the gear and if necessary, remove the snapring.
30. Remove the snapring from the front of the quill, then pull the range mainshaft from the quill using the sliding clutch as a base for the puller jaws.
31. If necessary, remove the ball bearing, snapring and bushing from the range mainshaft.
32. Remove the rear bearing cover and remove the oil seal from the cover.
33. Remove the bearing rear cone from the housing.
34. Push the parts to the rear to remove the two cups and outer spacer of the bearing from the housing bore.

NOTE: The auxiliary countershafts, drive gear and overdrive gear are one piece and cannot be disassembled. The two gears are welded to the shaft at the time of manufacturer.

35. If necessary, remove the bearing inner race from the front of the countershaft.

Assembly

1. For timing purposes, mark the tooth on each overdrive gear that is stamped with an O.
2. Install the inner race of the bearing on the front of the countershafts.
3. Install the splitter gear sliding clutch on the splines of the output shaft, internal splines to the rear.
3. If previously removed, install the bushing in the range mainshaft $^1/_{16}$ inch below the face.
4. Install the snapring in the groove at the end of the splines in the range mainshaft.
5. Install the range mainshaft on the quill of the output shaft.
6. Install the front ball bearing in the range mainshaft and on the quill.
7. Install the snapring in the groove on the front of the quill.
8. Install the snapring in the groove of the splitter (overdrive) gear.
9. Mark any two adjacent gear teeth on the splitter gear. Then mark the two adjacent teeth that are directly opposite the first set marked.
10. Install the splined washer on the shaft and against the shaft shoulder.
11. Install the splitter gear on the splined washer with the clutching teeth to the front.
12. Install the rear washer on the output shaft with the flat side to the rear.
13. Install the front cone of the bearing on the shaft and against the washer, taper towards the thread end. Heating the bearing cones to install on the output shaft is recommended,

provided the bearing is not heated over 275 degrees F. Use of a heat lamp is recommended.

14. Install the bearing inner spacer on the shaft and against the bearing cone.

15. Start the front cup of the bearing into the rear of the bore in the auxiliary with the taper to the inside.

16. Place the bearing outer spacer on the cup and place the rear cup of the bearing on the spacer with the lip to the rear. Make sure their seated in the bore.

17. Place the rear plate with the assembled cups over the output shaft.

18. Install the heated bearing rear cone on the shaft and into the rear cup.

19. Install the rear cover oil seal and speedometer bushing.

20. Install the rear bearing cover on the center bore. Make sure the output shaft is to the rear as far as possible.

21. Place the left countershaft into position, meshing the marked timing tooth on the overdrive gear with the two marked teeth on the splitter gear. Do not install the rear bearing.

22. Install the O-ring in the splitter cylinder shift bore.

23. Place the shift yoke fork in position in the sliding clutch gear. Install the splitter shift cylinder into the rear bore and place the hub of the shift yoke into position in the cylinder with the long hub to the front.

24. Install the O-ring on the OD of the piston.

25. From the rear, install the shift bar into the shift cylinder and through the yoke hub.

26. Install the lock screw in the yoke hub and secure with wire.

27. Install the splitter insert valve in the cover, then secure the valve with the exhaust screw.

28. Install the splitter shift cylinder cover with the exhaust screw down and the supply port to the right.

29. Place the right countershaft into position, meshing the marked tooth on the overdrive gear with the two marked teeth of the splitter gear. Do not install the rear bearing.

30. Install the splitter gear clutching collar on the splines of the range mainshaft, against the snapring with the clutching teeth to the rear.

32. Install the low range gear on the range mainshaft and against the clutching collar.

33. Install the splined washer on the range mainshaft and into the hub of the low range gear. Align the splines of the washer with the raised splines of the shaft.

34. Lock the low-range gear into position by inserting the range mainshaft key between the splines of the shaft and washer.

35. Place the larger low speed synchronizer ring on a work bench with the pins upward.

36. Install the sliding clutch gear on the pins with the protruding clutching teeth down.

37. Install the three springs in the bores in the direct synchronizer ring.

38. Place the direct synchronizer ring over the pins of the low speed ring sliding clutch, seating the springs against the pin.

39. Compress the springs and seat the pins of the low speed synchronizer fully into the bores of the plate.

40. Spread the countershaft assemblies and place the assembled synchronizer assembly on the range of the mainshaft, fitting the low range cone into the cone on the low range gear.

41. Set the housing with the front end of the countershafts on a bench. Center the rear of the countershafts in the housing bores. Make sure that the marked teeth on the countershaft overdrive gear are meshed with the marked timing teeth of the splitter gear.

42. Install the rear bearings on the shafts and into the bores.

43. Install the snapring on the rear of each countershaft.

44. Install the rear bearing covers.

45. Install the O-ring in the bore of the shift cylinder.

46. Place the range shifting yoke into the yoke slot of the sliding clutch gear with the long hub to the rear.

47. Install the shift cylinder through the rear plate bore and place the hub of the shifting yoke into position in the shift cylinder housing.

48. Insert the threaded end of the shift bar into the shift cylinder from the front, through the yoke hub and into the cylinder.

49. Align the lock screw holes in the yoke hub with the slots in the shifting bar and install the yoke lock screws.

50. Install the capscrews in the shift cylinder and tighten securely.

51. Install the O-ring in the ID of the shifting bar piston.

52. Install the O-ring on the OD of the piston.

53. Install the piston into the cylinder and on the shifting bar with the flat side down.

54. Install and tighten the elastic stop nut on the shifting bar.

55. Install the cover on the shift cylinder.

MAIN TRANSMISSION

Assembly

1. Make sure all magnetic disc are in the bottom of the case.

2. Install the plug in the end of the reverse idler shaft.

3. Press the needle in the bore of the reverse idler gear and install the cup on the shaft.

4. Insert the threaded end through the lower right wall of the case.

5. As the shaft is moved forward, install the thrust washer and reverse idler gear on the shaft, seating the gear on the inner race of the bearing.

6. Install the washer and the nut on the end of the shaft.

7. Install the auxiliary countershaft front bearing in the reverse idler bore.

8. On the drive gear of each countershaft, mark the gear tooth which aligns with the keyway in the shaft. This tooth will be stamped with an O.

9. Place the left countershaft, with the larger 47 tooth P.T.O. gear, into position in the case. Do not install the bearings.

10. Install the right countershaft, with the 45 tooth P.T.O. gear, into position in the case. Do not install the bearings.

11. Mark any two adjacent gear teeth on the drive gear. Then mark the two adjacent teeth which are directly opposite the first set marked.

12. Make sure the snapring is removed from the drive gear bearing.

13. Insert the drive gear shaft from inside the case and move as far forward as possible.

14. Install the snapring in the groove in the drive gear bearing.

15. Use a block to center the rear of the left countershaft in the case bore.

16. Mesh the marked tooth on the left countershaft drive gear with two marked teeth on the main drive gear.

17. Start the front bearing in the case bore. Center the countershaft assembly and install the front bearing on the shaft and into the case bore.

18. Remove the block at the rear of the shaft and install the rear bearing on the shaft and into the case bore.

19. Install the bearing retainer plate on the front of the countershaft. Tighten and wire the capscrews.

20. Install the snapring in the groove at the rear of the countershaft.

21. Block the right countershaft assembly towards the wall of the case as far as possible to provide clearance for the installation of the mainshaft.

22. With the reverse gear as far forward as possible on the mainshaft, lower the rear of the mainshaft into the case and through the rear bearing bore.

23. Lower the front of the mainshaft into position meshing

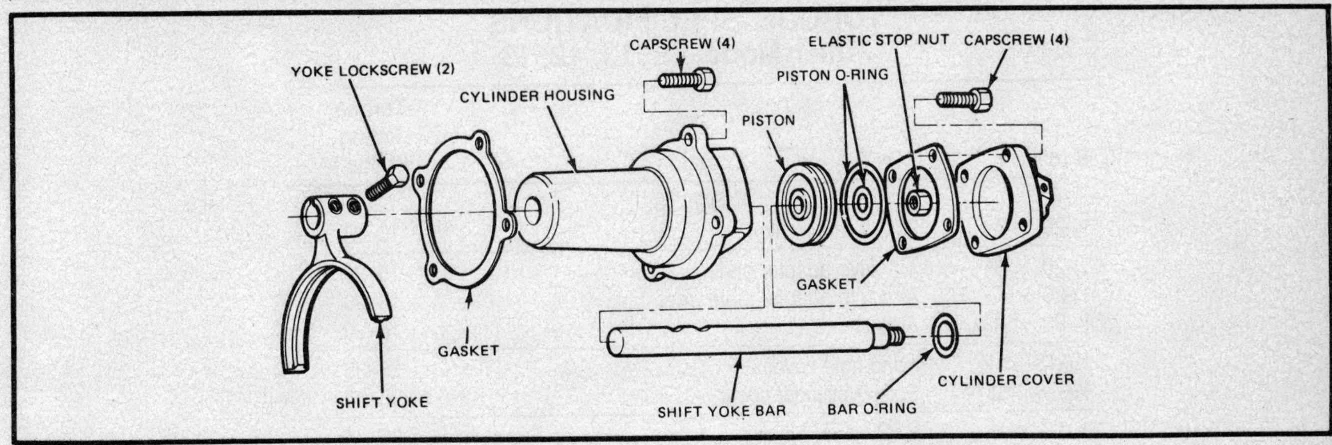

Range shift cylinder—exploded view (© Ford Motor Co.)

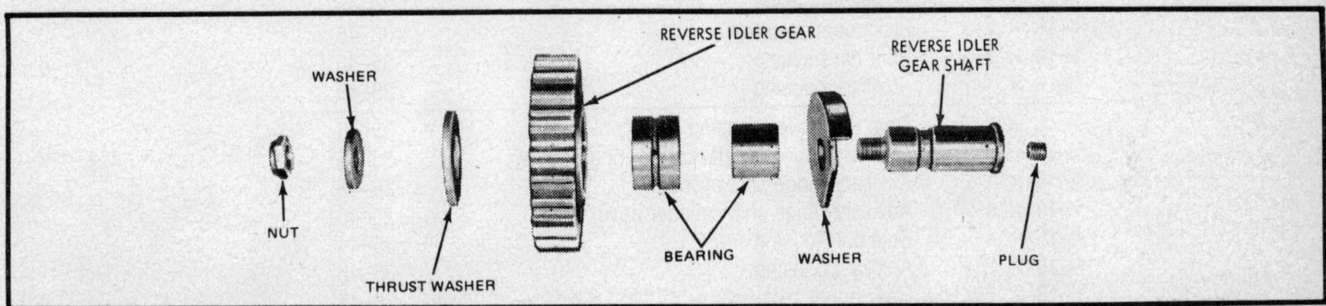

Reverse idler gear assembly—exploded view (© Ford Motor Co.)

the mainshaft gears with the corresponding gears on the left countershaft.

24. Move the right countershaft to mesh gears with the corresponding gears on the mainshaft, and mesh and marked tooth on the countershaft drive gear with the two marked teeth on the main drive gear.

25. Use blocking to center the rear of the right countershaft in the case bore and to center the rear of the mainshaft in the rear bearing bore.

26. Start the front bearing in the case bore. Center the countershaft assembly and install the front bearing on the shaft and into the case bore.

27. Remove the block at the rear of the countershaft and install the rear bearing on the shaft and into the case bore.

28. Install the bearing retainer plate on the front of the countershaft and tighten and wire the capscrews.

29. Install the snapring in the groove at the rear of the countershaft.

30. Repeat steps 1 through 7 to install the left reverse idler gear assembly.

31. Move the reverse gear as far as possible to the rear, against the rear wall of the case, and mesh the teeth with those of the reverse idler gear.

32. Install the snapring in the ID of the reverse gear.

33. Move the reverse gear rearward on the shaft and into the correct position. Install the snapring in the hub of the gear.

32. Place the bearing retainer ring on the auxiliary drive gear.

33. Press the bearing on the drive gear with the snapring towards the retainer.

34. Install the snapring in the groove in the shoulder of the auxiliary drive gear.

35. Install the auxiliary drive gear assembly into the rear case bore.

36. Install all capscrews which attach the retainer ring to the case. Tighten and wire securely.

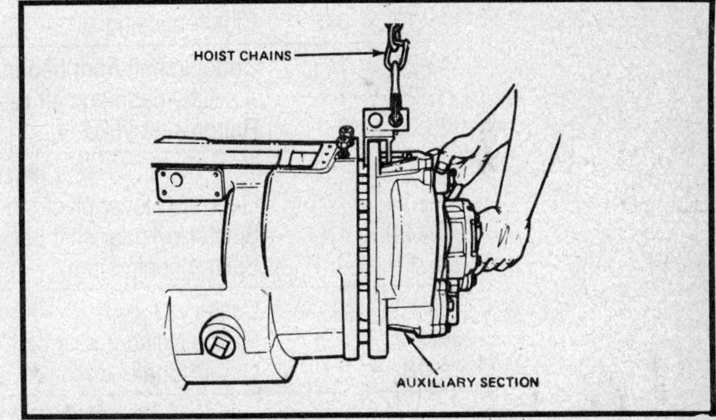

Joining of the auxiliary section (© Ford Motor Co.)

37. Pull the mainshaft as far to the rear as possible and install the rear mainshaft coupling snapring in the groove in the mainshaft located inside the bore of the drive gear.

JOINING OF THE MAIN AND AUXILIARY SECTIONS

1. Make sure the two dowel pins are in place in the rear face of the transmission.

2. Place a chain hoist on the auxiliary assembly and move it evenly onto the rear of the transmission.

3. The two countershaft drive gears will mesh with the auxiliary drive gear and the front of the countershafts will seat in the two bearings installed in the front section. Move the assembly evenly, rotating the drive gear if necessary, to properly mesh the gears.

4. Install the attaching capscrews and connect the air lines.

TORQUE SPECIFICATIONS
Fuller Models 9513, 12513

Size	Location	Torque Rating (ft. lbs.)
	BOLTS	
¼-20 × ½	Air filter to bracket	10–15
¼-20 × ⅝	Air valve adapter plate	15–20
¼-20 × ⅞	Air valve adapter plate, rear	15–20
¼-20 × 1¾	Air valve	15–20
5/16-18 × ½	Hand hole cover	25–35
5/16-18 × 1½	Splitter cylinder cover	25–35
⅜-16 × ¾	PTO cover, small	35–45
⅜-16 × ¾	Air filter bracket to case	35–45
⅜-16 × 1	Auxiliary drive gear bearing retainer	35–45
⅜-16 × 1½	Auxiliary housing	35–45
⅜-16 × 1¼	Front bearing cover	35–45
⅜-16 × 1¼	Shift bar housing	35–45
⅜-16 × 1¼	Auxiliary housing	35–45
⅜-16 × 1¼	Gear shift lever housing	35–45
⅜-16 × 1¼	Auxiliary countershaft rear bearing covers	35–45
⅜-16 × 1¼	Auxiliary range shift cylinder	35–45
⅜-16 × 1¼	Auxiliary range shift cylinder cover	35–45
⅜-16 × 1¾	Shift bar housing	35–45
⅜-16 × 2	Auxiliary housing	35–45
⅜-16 × 2¾	Rear bearing cover	35–45
7/16-14 × 1¼	PTO cover, large	50–65
½-13 × 1½	Clutch housing	70–75
½-13 × 3½	Clutch housing	70–75
½-20 × 1	Countershaft front bearing retainers	50–65
½-20 × 1	Auxiliary countershaft rear bearing retainer	50–65
½-20 × 2	Range shift yoke	50–65
	NUTS	
5/16-24	Gear shift lever pivot pin	15–20
7/16-20	Splitter cylinder shift bar	20–25
⅝-11	Splitter control jam	60–65
⅝-18	Case	170–185
⅝-18	Range cylinder shift bar	70–80
2-16	Output Shaft	425–525
	END PLAY LIMITS	
	Reverse speed gear	0.005–0.038 in.
	Forward speed gears	0.005–0.012 in.

Fuller RT, RTO, RTOF-910, RTF, RT-12510, RT-1110 Ten Speed and RT, RTO-915 Fifteen Speed Transmission

The RT-910, 12510, 1110 series transmissions have ten forward speeds and two reverse, consisting of a five speed front section and two speed auxiliary or range section, both contained in one case. The RT-915 series transmissions have fifteen forward speeds and two reverse, consisting of a five speed front section, which is identical to the RT-910, 12510, 1110 series front section, and a three speed auxiliary or range section. Both sections are contained in one case with the rear plate being extended to accommodate the extra set of gears.

SEPARATION OF MAIN AND AUXILIARY SECTIONS

1. Disconnect the air hoses at the valve.

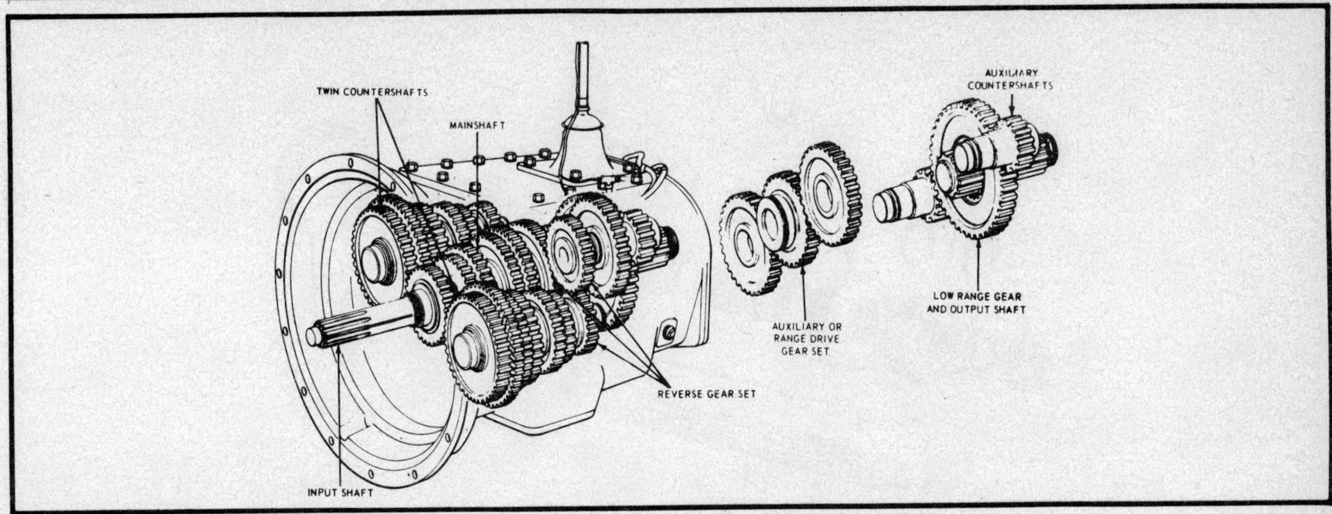

Fuller ten speed transmission (© Ford Motor Co.)

2. Remove the air filter and air regulator valve assemblies.
3. Remove the air valve from the adapter plate.
4. Remove the air valve adapter plate by removing the alignment sleeve, spring, and actuating pin.
5. With the transmission in neutral, remove the gear shift housing cover. Drain the lubricant.
6. Lock the transmission in two gears and remove the U-joint flange.
7. Remove the bolts that attach the auxiliary section to the transmission case. Install three puller screws in the tapped holes of the rear plate and tighten them to move the auxiliary section to the rear just far enough to break the gasket seal.
8. Attach a chain hoist to the auxiliary section and separate from the transmission.
9. Remove the clutch housing from the transmission.

MAIN TRANSMISSION

Disassembly (All Models)

1. Remove the snapring from the inside of the auxiliary drive gear.
2. Remove the mainshaft rear quill support plate from the bore of the auxiliary drive gear and remove the coupling.
3. Remove the coupling snap ring from the rear mainshaft.
4. Remove the bearing retainer ring bolts. Insert three puller screws in the tapped holes of the retainer ring and tighten the bolts evenly to pull the assembly from the case.
5. Place the auxiliary drive gear in a vise and remove the bearing nut. This nut has a left thread. Then, press or drive the bearing retainer ring and the bearing from the gear.
6. Move the mainshaft reverse gear to the rear as far as possible and remove the reverse gear snap ring. Then, move the reverse gear forward and against the low speed gear to mesh with the sliding clutch gear. Remove the snapring and the reverse gear splined spacer from the mainshaft.
7. Working from inside the case, remove the left reverse idler shaft nut and washer.
8. Remove the plug from the reverse idler shaft bore. Using an impact puller, remove the reverse idler gear shaft. Remove the thrust washer and gear.
9. If necessary, remove the bearing inner race from the reverse idler shaft, and the bearing from the bore of the reverse idler gear.
10. Move the mainshaft assembly to the rear as far as possible to separate the mainshaft gears from the countershaft gears. Tilt the front of the mainshaft and lift it from the case.
11. Remove the bearing retainer bolts from the front of the countershaft. Remove the snapring from the rear of the countershaft.
12. Drive the countershaft to the rear as far as it will go. This will partially unseat the front bearing from the shaft and the rear bearing from the case bore.
13. Using a puller, remove the countershaft rear bearing from the shaft and case bore.
14. Move the countershaft forward until the front bearing is clear of the case. Then, extract the front bearing from the shaft.
15. Follow the same procedure for removing the left countershaft bearings.
16. Remove the bolts from the input shaft bearing retainer.
17. Working from inside the case tap the input shaft forward and remove the bearing retainer. Remove the snapring from the input shaft bearing.
18. Move the input shaft assembly from the case.
19. Move the front of the right countershaft toward the center of the case and, at the same time, lift it from the case.
20. Remove the left countershaft in the same way.
21. Working from inside the case, remove the right reverse idler shaft nut and washer.
22. Remove the plug from the reverse idler shaft bore. Using an impact puller, remove the reverse idler gear shaft. Remove the thrust washer and gear.
23. If necessary, remove the inner bearing race from the reverse idler shaft, and the bearing from the base of the reverse idler gear.

MAIN TRANSMISSION SUBASSEMBLIES

Disassembly (All Models)

GEAR SHIFT HOUSING

1. Remove the tension springs and balls from the bores in the top of the housing.
2. Set the housing in a vise with the plunger side up.
3. Remove the shifter shaft lock screws before removing shaft.
4. Move the top and center shifter shafts out of the housing. Remove the shifting fork and block from each shaft. As the neutral detent in the center shaft clears the housing boss, remove the interlock pin.
5. Remove the actuating plunger from housing bore.
6. Move the lower shifter shaft to the rear and out of the housing. Remove the shifting fork from the shaft. Do not lose the interlock balls as the lower shaft is removed.

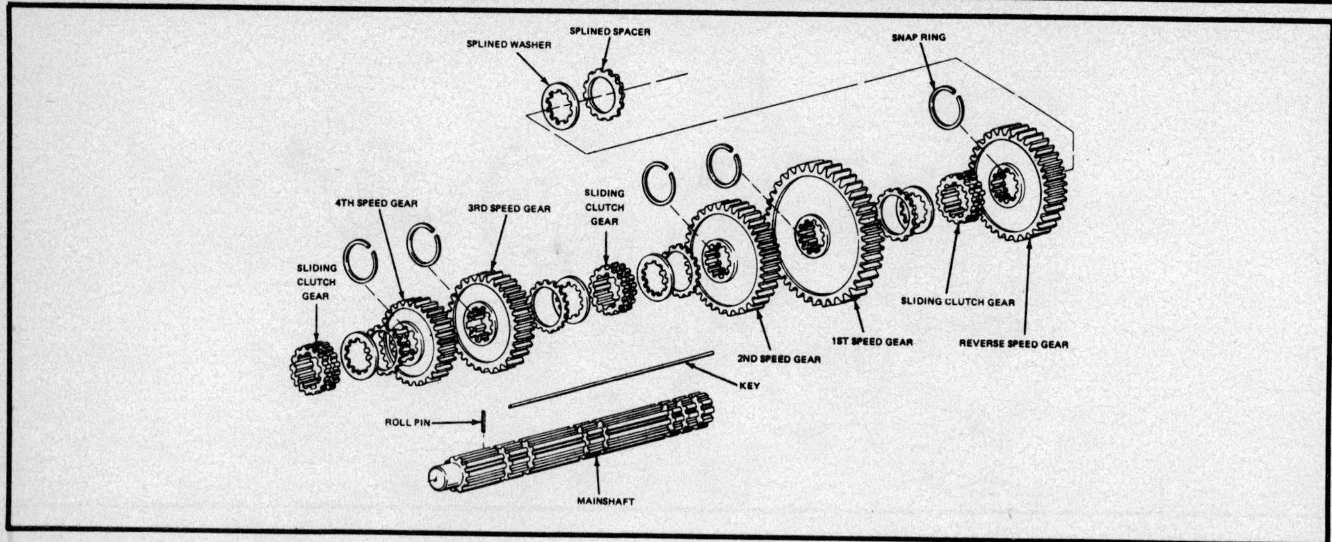

Mainshaft assembly—exploded view (© Ford Motor Co.)

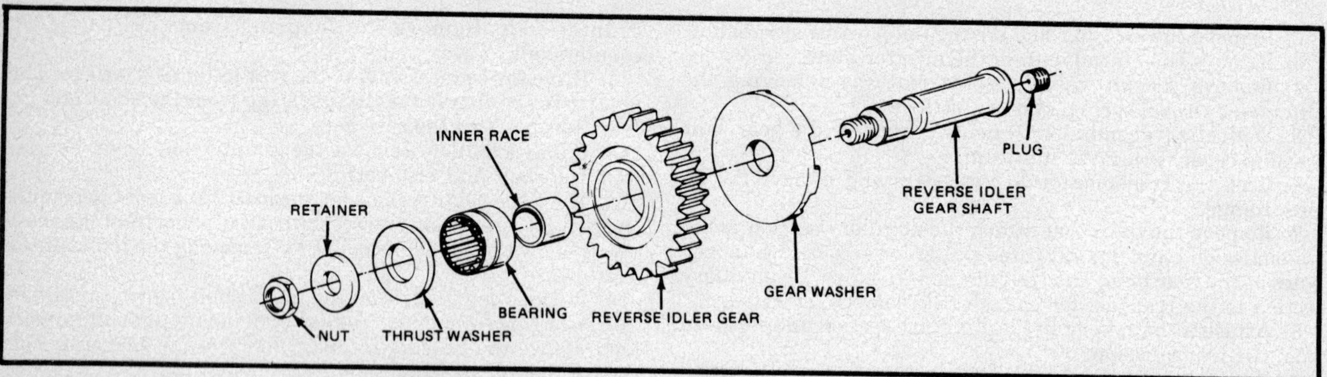

Reverse idler gear assembly—exploded view (© Ford Motor Co.)

MAINSHAFT

1. Remove the fourth/fifth speed sliding clutch gear from the mainshaft.
2. Remove the mainshaft reverse speed gear.
3. Remove the long key located between the splines of the mainshaft.
4. Remove the reverse gear washer and remove the first/reverse sliding clutch gear. Remove the remaining washers, spacers, and gears from the shaft. When removing washers, spacers, and gears, note their location to facilitate the reassembly of the mainshaft. Keep washers and spacers with the gear from which they were removed; there is one spacer and one washer from each gear.
5. If the quill bearing is to be removed, remove the snapring and extract the bearing.
6. If necessary, remove the snaprings from each mainshaft gear.

INPUT SHAFT

1. Mount the shaft in a soft jawed vise. Relieve the peening on the bearing nut, and remove the nut. It has a left thread.
2. Using the rear face of the input shaft gear as a base, mount the assembly in a press, and press the shaft through the gear. This will free the bearings, spacer, and gear from the shaft.

COUNTERSHAFT

NOTE: Both countershafts are identical, except for the number of teeth on the P.T.O. gears, thus, they are disassembled in the same manner.

1. Remove the snapring from the rear of the countershaft.
2. Using the rear face of the reverse gear as a base, press the gear from the countershaft.
3. Using the second speed gear as a base, press the first and second speed gears from the countershaft.
4. Using the fifth speed gear as a base, press the countershaft out of the third, fourth, P.T.O., and fifth speed gears.
5. Remove the three keys and spacer from the countershaft.

AUXILIARY SECTION

Disassembly All Models

1. Remove the shift cylinder cover.
2. Remove the nut from the end of the shifter shaft. Using puller screws, remove the piston from the shift cylinder.
3. Remove the shift cylinder housing bolts.
4. Remove the set screws from the shifting fork. If necessary, rotate the shift cylinder housing to expose the set screws.
5. Push the shifter shaft to the inside, through the fork hub, and out of the cylinder housing. Remove the shifting fork and shift cylinder housing from the plate.

AUXILIARY SECTION SUB-ASSEMBLIES

Disassembly

COUNTERSHAFT ALL MODELS

1. Press the countershaft gear from each shaft.
2. Remove the key from each countershaft.

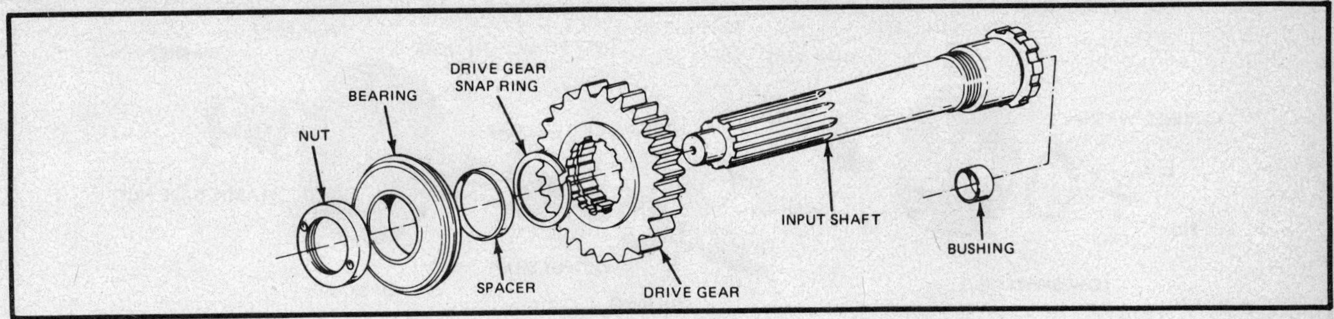

Main transmission input shaft—exploded view (© Ford Motor Co.)

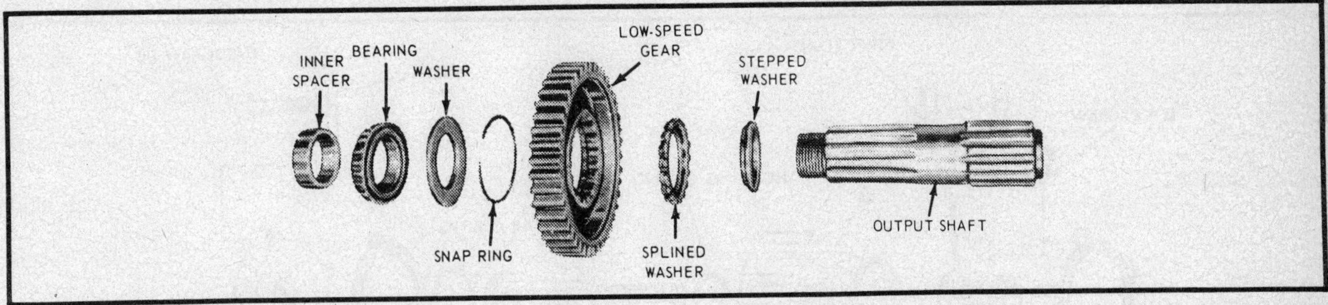

Auxiliary section output shaft (© Ford Motor Co.)

SYNCHRONIZER ALL MODELS

1. Remove the direct (high range) cone synchronizer ring from the pins of the low-speed synchronizer ring. Place a cloth over the ring during removal to catch the three springs installed in the bores of the direct cone synchronizer.
2. Remove the sliding clutch gear from the pins of the low speed synchronizer.

OUTPUT SHAFT EXCEPT RT-915 SERIES

1. Remove the inner bearing spacer from the output shaft.
2. Using the front face of the low speed gear as a base, press out the shaft.
3. Remove the splined and stepped washers from the shaft.

LOW RANGE GEAR RT-915 SERIES

1. Remove the key from the keyway between the splines of the range mainshaft.
2. Turn the splines of the low speed gear washer, located in the hub of the gear, to align with the splines of the shaft.
3. Remove the gear, washer and coupler from the shaft.

DEEP REDUCTION SHIFT CYLINDER RT-915 SERIES

1. Remove the cover from the shift cylinder.
2. Cut the lock wire and turn out the lockscrew from the shift yoke.
3. Push the yoke bar to the rear and remove it from the housing. If necessary, remove the O-ring from the large OD of the bar.
4. Remove the shift yoke and cylinder housing from the rear housing. If necessary, remove the O-ring from the bore in the cylinder housing.

RANGE MAINSHAFT RT-915 SERIES

1. Remove the snapring from the front of the quill.
2. Move the sliding clutch forward and against the snapring of the range mainshaft.
3. Remove the front bearing from the shaft.
4. Remove the snapring from the OD of the mainshaft and if necessary, press the bushing from the mainshaft.

DEEP REDUCTION GEAR AND OUTPUT SHAFT RT-915 SERIES

1. Use a soft bar and hammer to drive the output shaft forward and from the rear bearing.
2. Remove the bearing inner spacer from the shaft.
3. Using the front face of the deep reduction gear as a base, press the shaft through the gear and bearing, freeing the bearing, washer and gear.
4. If necessary, remove the snapring from the ID of the gear.
5. Remove the rear bearing cover and if necessary, the seal from the cover.
6. Remove the bearing rear cone from the rear housing.
7. Remove the two bearing cups and outer spacer from the housing.

AUXILIARY SECTION SUB-ASSEMBLIES

Assembly

OUTPUT SHAFT EXCEPT RT-915 SERIES

1. Set the output shaft on a workbench with the threaded end up. Install the stepped and splined washers on the shaft. Be sure the small diameters are toward the threaded end of the shaft.
2. Install the low speed gear (flat side up) on the shaft. Then, install the cone-shaped washer, with the flat side against the gear.
3. Install the bearing on the shaft, with the taper toward the threaded end.
4. Install the inner bearing spacer on the shaft and against the bearing.

SYNCHRONIZER ALL MODELS

1. Place the low speed synchronizer ring on a work bench with the pins up. Then, install the clutch sliding gear on the pins.
2. Install the three springs into the direct synchronizer ring and place the direct synchronizer over the pins of the low speed synchronizer ring.

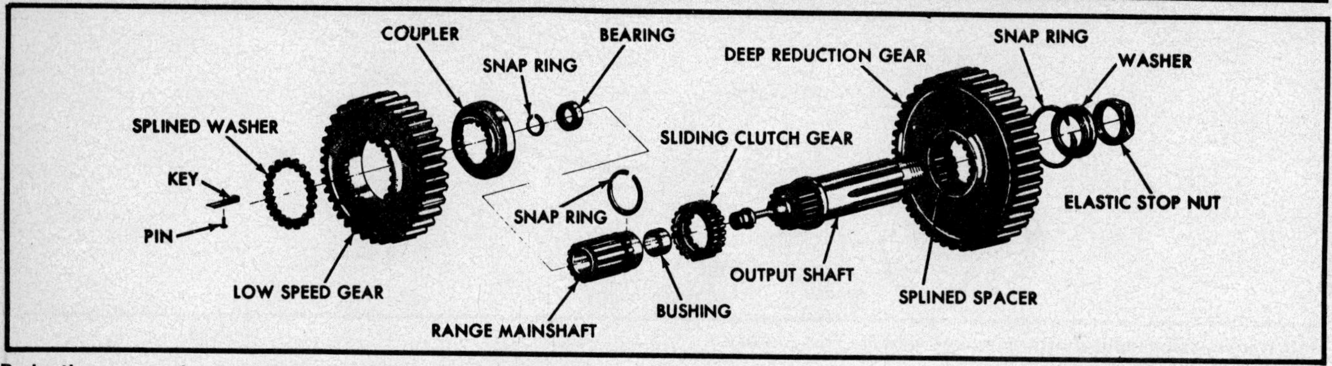

Reduction gear and output shaft assemblies—RT-915 series (© Chrysler Corp.)

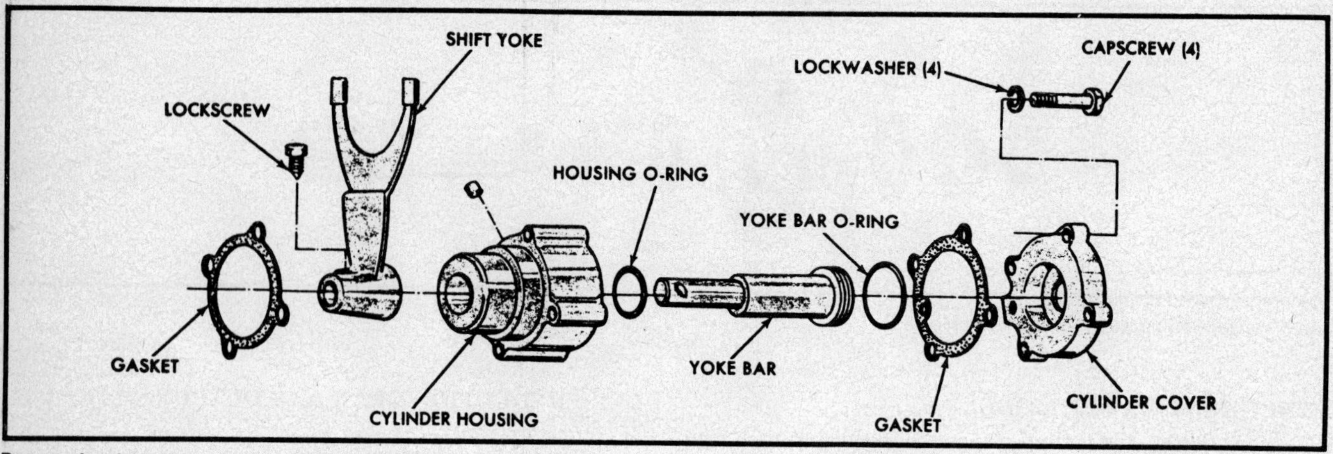

Deep reduction shift cylinder—RT-915 series (© Chrysler Corp.)

3. Compress the springs and fully seat the direct synchronizer on the pins of the low speed synchronizer by pushing the direct synchronizer ring.

COUNTERSHAFT ALL MODELS

1. Install a Woodruff key on each countershaft and press the countershaft onto each drive gear.
2. Install the snapring on the front of each countershaft.

LOW RANGE GEAR RT-915

1. Install the coupler on the shaft, large diameter to the rear.
2. If previously removed, install the snapring in the ID of the low speed gear and install the gear on the shaft and against the coupler, dished side to the front.
3. Install the low speed gear splined washer on the shaft and against the snapring in the hub of the gear. Turn the washer to lock the gear on the shaft.
4. Install the key in the keyway, inserting the thick end between the splines of the washer.

DEEP REDUCTION SHIFT CYLINDER RT-915

1. Install the O-ring in the bore of the shift cylinder and install the shift cylinder housing into the auxiliary housing with the small air channel to the right.
2. Install the shift yoke on the sliding clutch with the lock screw hole to the front and insert the yoke bar from the tear through the shift cylinder and yoke, aligning the indentation in the bar with the lockscrew hole in the yoke.
3. Install the yoke lockscrew and tighten and wire securely.
4. Install the cylinder cover.

RANGE MAINSHAFT ASSEMBLY RT-915

1. Install the snapring in the groove in the OD of the mainshaft.
2. Install the bushing in the shaft, positioning halfway on the rear bearing surface. The distance between the top of the bushing and the lug on the rear mainshaft should be $^7/_{16}$ inch.
3. Install the mainshaft on the quill of the output shaft, seating the bushing on the bearing surface of the quill.
4. Install the front bearing in the mainshaft and on the quill. Seat the bearing with a sleeve driver.
5. Install the snapring in the groove in the front of the quill.

DEEP REDUCTION GEAR AND OUTPUT SHAFT RT-915

1. Place the output shaft, threaded end up, on blocks to protect the quill and install the splined spacer on the shaft with the large diameter down.
2. If previously removed, install the snapring in the groove in the deep reduction gear and install the gear on the shaft with the snapring towards the threaded end.
3. Install the rear on the shaft with the step side towards the gear.
4. Install the front bearing cone on the shaft and against the rear washer. This is a matched bearing; make sure the correct cone and cup are matched. Heating the bearing cones for installation is recommended, provided the bearing is not heated over 275 degrees F.
5. Install the bearing inner spacer on the shaft and against the bearing cone.
6. Mark any two adjacent teeth on the deep reduction gear and then mark the teeth directly opposite.
7. Start the front bearing cup into the bore in the rear housing, taper to the inside, and place the outer spacer and rear cup on the front cup and tap the three evenly into the bore until the lip of the rear cup seats against the housing.
8. Place the rear housing over the output shaft.

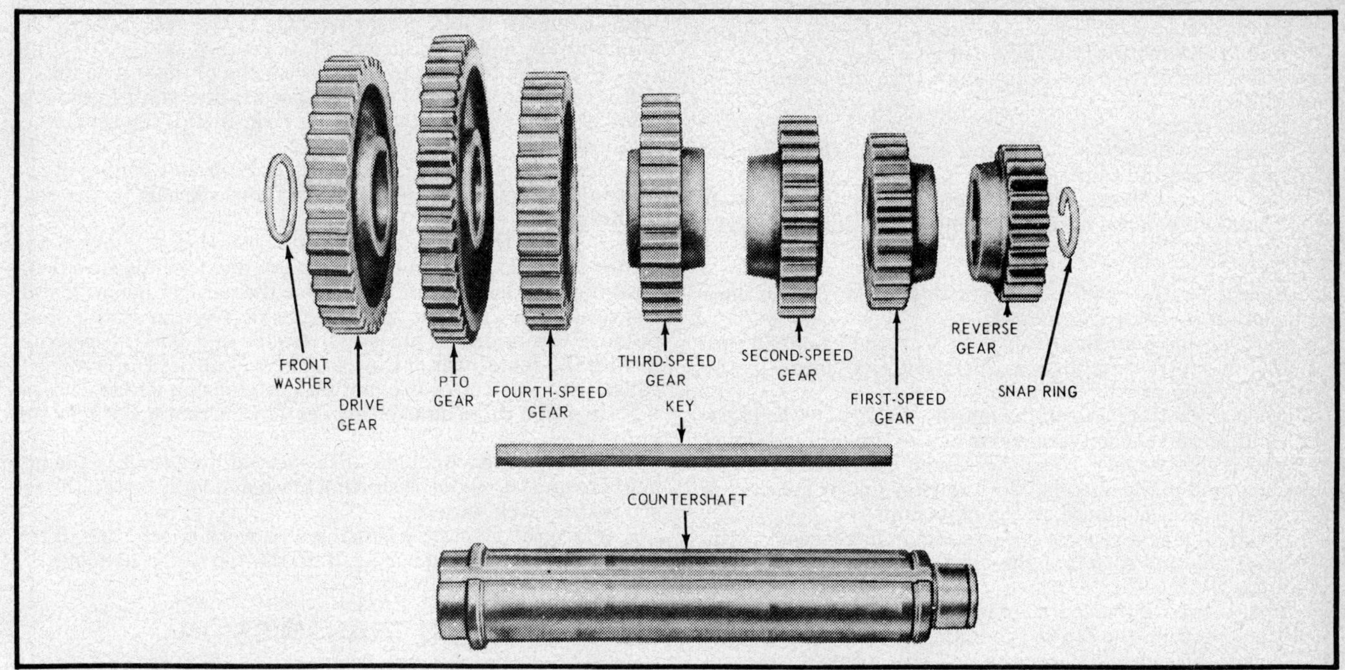

Main transmission countershaft—exploded view (© Ford Motor Co.)

9. Heat the rear bearing cone and install the cone on the shaft and into the rear cup.
10. If previously removed, install the oil seal in the rear bearing cover and install the cover on the housing.
11. Install the sliding clutch gear on the front of the shaft with the yoke slots toward the front.

AUXILIARY SECTION

Assembly All Models

1. With the rear plate on a work bench, place the front cup (taper to the inside) of the rear bearing into the rear bore of the plate.
2. Place the bearing outer spacer on the front cup.
3. Place the rear cup on the spacer and tap the two cups and spacer into the rear plate bore.
4. Place the rear plate over the output shaft. Be sure that the bearing on the shaft is seated on the rear plate front bearing cup.
5. Install the rear bearing on the output shaft.
6. Install a new oil seal in the rear bearing cover if it was removed. Install the cover to the rear plate, using a star washer at the hole which intersects with the speedometer bore.
7. Install the synchronizer assembly on the output shaft, with the low-speed synchronizer ring toward the low speed gear.
8. To install and time the auxiliary countershafts, mark the gear tooth which is stamped O on the small diamater low range gear of each countershaft. This tooth will be aligned with the keyway in the countershaft drive gear. These two teeth, one on each countershaft, must both mesh at the same time with the output shaft low speed gear and be in directly opposite positions.
9. Mark any two adjacent teeth on the output shaft low speed gear. Then, mark the two adjacent teeth, which are directly opposite the first set marked. There should be the same number of teeth between the markings on each side of the gear.
10. Block the rear plate assembly with the threaded end of the output shaft up. Make sure the synchronizer assembly is blocked to prevent it from dropping from the output shaft.
11. Position and block each countershaft. For correct timing, be sure to place the marked teeth of the countershafts into mesh with the marked teeth of the low-speed gear.
12. Install the rear bearing on each countershaft. Recheck the gears for correct timing.
13. Install a rear bearing retainer plate on each countershaft and secure with lockwire. Install the rear bearing covers.
14. Install a new O-ring in the shift cylinder bore if it was removed.
15. Position the shifting fork on the sliding clutch gear, and install the shift cylinder into the bore of the rear plate.
16. Insert the threaded end of the shifter shaft through the front of the shift cylinder, through the shifting fork hub, and into the cylinder bore. Install the set screws and lock wire.
17. Install shift cylinder piston O-rings if they were removed.
18. Position the piston in the shift cylinder bore and secure with the elastic stop nut. Install the shift cylinder piston and torque the elastic stop nut to specifications.
19. Install the cover on the shift cylinder (air port to the upper left).

MAIN TRANSMISSION SUBASSEMBLIES

Assembly All Models

COUNTERSHAFT

NOTE: Except for the number of teeth on the P.T.O. gears, the countershafts are identical and assembled in the same manner.

1. Install the front washer over the rear of the countershaft and insert the keys.
2. Press the countershaft gears on the shaft one at a time; the drive, P.T.O., third, and first speed gears are installed with the long hubs to the rear. The fourth, second, and reverse speed gears are installed with the long hubs to the front. The left countershaft is equipped with a 47 tooth P.T.O. gear; the right side is equipped with a 45 tooth gear. After installing the P.T.O. gear on the countershaft, mark the assembly either left or right to correspond with the installed P.T.O. gear.
3. Install the snapring on the countershaft.

INPUT SHAFT

1. Install the snapring in the drive gear.
2. Install the drive gear on the shaft with the snapring toward the front.
3. Install spacer.
4. Press the drive gear bearing on the shaft, with the snapring toward the front.
5. Torque the bearing attaching nut to specifications (left hand thread). Peen the nut at the slots milled into the shaft.

MAINSHAFT

1. Except for the reverse gear, install a snapring in each mainshaft gear if it was removed.
2. Position the mainshaft in a vise, with the front end up.
3. Install the reverse gear washer (flat side down) in the fifth groove from the top of the mainshaft.
4. From the bottom, install the long key in the keyway of the mainshaft so that the forward end is moved through the slot of the reverse gear washer. Keep the snapring groove in the key to the rear and to the outside. Move the key upward to engage each washer as it is placed on the mainshaft.
5. Install the first/reverse speed sliding clutch gear on the mainshaft, making sure that the keyway is lined up with the key in the shaft.
6. Install the first speed gear washer (flat side up) in the fourth groove from the top of the mainshaft. Then, move the key upward through the slot in the first speed gear washer until the front of the key is level with the third groove from the top.
7. With the flat side down, install the first speed gear spacer on the mainshaft and against the washer.
8. Install the first speed gear on the mainshaft with the snapring up. Make certain the splines of the gear mesh with the splines of the spacer.
9. With the snapring down, install the second speed gear against the first speed gear.
10. Install the second speed gear spacer and washer, with the flat sides down. Move the key upward through the slot in the second speed gear washer until it reaches the second groove from the top of the mainshaft.
11. Align the keyway in the second/third speed sliding clutch with the key, and position the clutch on the mainshaft.
12. Install the third speed gear washer (flat side up) in the second groove from the top of the mainshaft. Then, move the key upward to engage the washer.
13. Install the third speed spacer with the flat side against the washer.
14. Install the third speed gear (snapring up) on the shaft and onto the splines of the spacer.
15. With the snapring down, install the fourth speed gear on the mainshaft and against the third speed gear.
16. With the flat side up, install the fourth speed gear spacer into the fourth speed gear hub.
17. Install the fourth speed gear washer (flat side down) on the mainshaft, and move the key upward to engage the washer.
18. Install the fourth/fifth speed sliding clutch gear, aligning the large slot in the clutch gear with the keyway in the shaft.
19. Install the front quill bearing and snapring if it was removed. When installing the bearing, be sure to use a suitable tool so that the quill is not pushed into the mainshaft.
20. Remove the mainshaft assembly from the vise and align the key groove with the snapring groove in the mainshaft.
21. Install the reverse gear on the mainshaft and engage it with the sliding clutch gear. Do not install the reverse gear spacer and snapring until the mainshaft assembly is installed in the transmisison.
22. Install the front mainshaft coupling snapring on the mainshaft and key, securing the key to the mainshaft.

GEAR SHIFT HOUSING

Install the shifter shaft through the rear bores of the housing with the neutral and detent notches to the rear. Install the shafts in the neutral position.

1. Place the housing in a vise with the plunger side up.
2. Install the first and reverse speed shifter shaft in the bottom bore and through the shifting fork. Install the set screws and lock wire.
3. Install the actuating plunger in the front opening of the housing, and a three-quarter inch interlock ball in the rear opening.
4. Position the second and third speed shifter shaft in the center bore and through the shift block and fork. Be sure to install the interlock pin in the bore at the neutral notch. Install the set screws and lock wire. Do not remove the shifter shaft because the interlock pin must remain in a vertical position during the remainder of the assembly. Rotating the shaft will cause the interlock pin to jam into the tension spring bores.
5. Install a three quarter inch ball in the rear opening of the housing.
6. Position the fourth and fifth speed shifter shaft in the upper bore and through the shifting block and fork. Install the set screws and lock wire.
7. Place the gear shift housing on a work bench. Install the three detent balls and springs into the top of the housing.

MAIN TRANSMISSION

Assembly

1. Install the right reverse idler shaft plug.
2. If removed, install the needle bearings in the bore of the reverse idler gear.
3. If previously removed, install the bearing inner race on the reverse idler shaft.
4. Insert the threaded end of the idler shaft through the right wall of the case. As the shaft is moved forward, install the reverse idler gear, and thrust washer. Be sure the needle bearings in the gear are seated evenly on the shaft inner race before moving the shaft forward. The thrust washer should be placed between the gear and the boss, with the slot toward the gear.
5. Position the washer over the threaded end of the shaft, and secure it with the elastic stop nut.
6. To install and time the countershaft assemblies, mark the drive gear tooth that aligns with the keyway of each countershaft. This tooth will be stamped with an O.
7. Position the left and right countershaft assemblies into the case. Make sure the left countershaft assembly has the larger 47 tooth P.T.O. gear.
8. Mark any two adjacent gear teeth on the input shaft drive gear. Then, mark two adjacent teeth which are directly opposite the first set marked.
9. Install the input shaft through the front bore from inside the case. Move the shaft as far forward as possible and install the snapring on the input shaft bearing.
10. Using a wood block, center the front of the left countershaft in the case bore. Then, mesh the marked tooth on the left countershaft drive gear with the two teeth marked on the input shaft main drive gear.
11. With the countershaft as far to the rear as possible, install the rear bearing on the shaft and into the case bore.
12. Install the front bearing on the countershaft into the case bore.
13. Install the snapring on the rear of the countershaft.
14. Position the bearing retainer plate on the front of the countershaft and secure with the attaching bolts and lock wire.
15. Install the left and right countershaft in the same manner.
16. Bolt the input shaft bearing retainer to the case.
17. Lower the mainshaft assembly into the case. Place a bar across the top of the case and install a support wire under the forward sliding clutch gear.
18. Align the mainshaft assembly, making sure that the

Meshing the countershaft and input drive gears at pre-marked gear teeth (© Ford Motor Co.)

mainshaft gears and the corresponding gears on the countershafts are properly engaged, and that the quill bearing is seated in the pocket of the main drive gear. Remove the support wire and bar. Keep the mainshaft assembly in the forward position during the installation of the left reverse idler gear so that the gears will not slip out of mesh.

19. Install the plug in the left reverse idler shaft.

20. Install the needle bearings in the bore of the reverse idler gear if they were removed.

21. Install the bearing inner race on the reverse idler shaft if it was previously removed.

22. Insert the threaded end of the idler shaft through the left wall of the case. Follow the same procedure as in step numbers 4 and 5.

23. Move the mainshaft reverse gear to the rear so that it engages the reverse idler gears. Then, install the reverse gear spacer (flat side inward) into the hub of the reverse gear. Install the reverse gear snapring.

24. If the auxiliary drive gear was disassembled, place the bearing retainer on the gear and press the bearing into place. Apply antiseize compound to the threads of the drive gear and nut (left hand thread) and install the nut.

25. Bolt the auxiliary drive gear assembly into the rear case bore. Wire the bolts in groups of three.

26. Pull the mainshaft as far to the rear as possible and install the coupling snapring.

27. Place the coupling gear and rear quill support plate in the bore of the auxiliary drive gear, and install the snap ring.

28. Install the auxiliary countershaft front bearings into the reverse idler shaft bores.

JOINING OF MAIN AND AUXILIARY SECTIONS

1. Bolt the clutch housing to the transmission case and torque to specifications.

2. Using a chain hoist, position the auxiliary section to the transmission. It may be necessary to rotate the drive gear to properly mesh the gears. Install and tighten bolts.

3. With the transmission locked in two gears, install the speedometer drive gear and U-joint flange on the mainshaft. Torque the nut to specifications. If the speedometer drive gear is not used, be sure to install a replacement spacer of the same width.

4. Bolt the gear shift housing cover to the transmission.

5. Install the air valve plate and housing.

6. Install the air filter and air regulator valve assemblies, and connect the air hoses at the air valve. Fill the transmission with the proper lubricant.

AIR VALVE

Removal

1. Remove the floor mat and the floor plate.

2. Place the gearshift lever in the neutral position. Drain the air from the system.

3. Disconnect the air line leading from the regulator to the tee fitting on the air valve.

4. Disconnect the two air cylinder lines from the air valve.

5. Disconnect the two nylon air lines from the air valve.

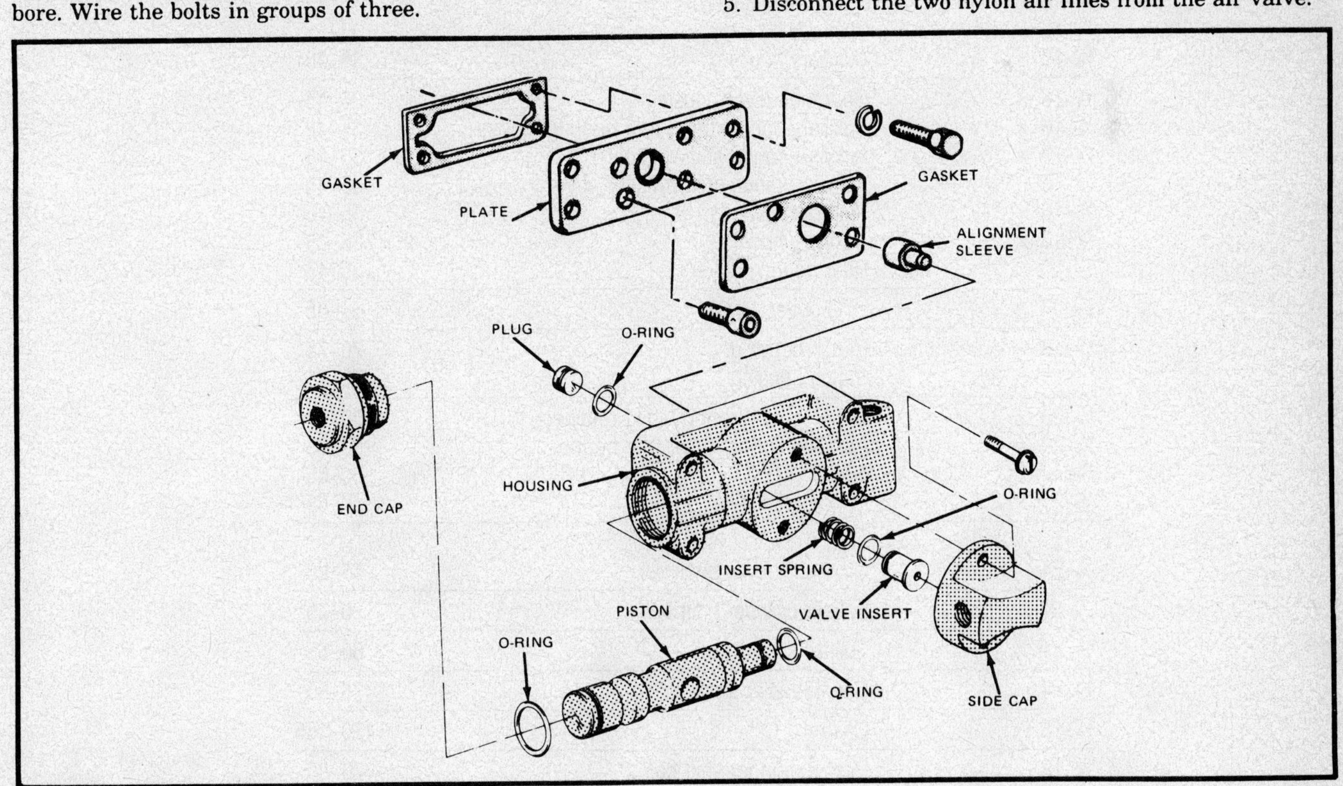

Air valve—exploded view (© Ford Motor Co.)

6. Remove the bolts, the air valve gasket, and the alignment sleeve.
7. Thoroughly clean the valve in cleaning solvent and air dry it.

Disassembly

1. Remove all air line fittings and the vent from the valve.
2. Remove the side cap from the valve body.
3. Remove the valve insert and spring from the piston. Remove the O-ring from the valve insert.
4. Remove the end cap and piston from the valve body. Remove the two O-rings from the piston.
5. Remove the nylon plug from the piston and remove the O-ring from the plug.

Assembly

1. Use all new O-rings and lubricate them with a thin film of vaseline before installing them.
2. Install O-rings on the piston and nylon plug. Install the plug in the piston.
3. Insert the piston in the valve body and install and tighten the end cap.
4. Install the spring into the piston.
5. Install an O-ring on the valve insert and install it in the piston.
6. Tighten the side cap to the valve body with the attaching screws and lock washers.
7. Coat the fittings with sealer and install them in their respective ports. Install the vent in the body.

TORQUE SPECIFICATIONS
Fuller Models 910, 12510, Rt11110 & 915

Size	Location	Torque Rating (ft. lbs.)
	BOLTS	
¼-20 × ½	Air filter to bracket	10–15
¼-20 × ⅝	Air valve adapter plate	15–20
¼-20 × ⅞	Air valve adapter plate rear	15–20
¼-20 × 1¾	Air valve	15–20
5/16-18 × ½	Hand hole cover	23–35
5/16-18 × 1½	Splitter cylinder cover	23–35
⅜-16 × ¾	PTO cover, small	35–45
⅜-16 × ¾	Air filter bracket to case	35–45
⅜-16 × 1	Auxiliary drive gear bearing retainer	35–45
⅜-16 × 1½	Auxiliary housing	35–45
⅜-16 × 1¼	Front bearing cover	35–45
⅜-16 × 1¼	Shift bar housing	35–45
⅜-16 × 1¼	Auxiliary housing	35–45
⅜-16 × 1¼	Gear shift lever housing	35–45
⅜-16 × 1¼	Auxiliary countershaft rear bearing covers	35–45
⅜-16 × 1¼	Auxiliary range shift cylinder	35–45
⅜-16 × 1¼	Auxiliary range shift cylinder cover	35–45
⅜-16 × 1¾	Shift bar housing	35–45
⅜-16 × 2	Auxiliary housing	35–45
⅜-16 × 2¾	Rear bearing cover	35–45
7/16-14 × 1¼	PTO cover, large	50–65
½-13 × 1½	Clutch housing	70–75
½-13 × 3½	Clutch housing	70–75
½-20 × 1	Countershaft front bearing retainers	50–65
½-20 × 1	Auxiliary countershaft rear bearing	50–65
Retainers	50–65	50–65
½-20 × 2	Range shift yoke	50–65
	NUTS	
⅝-24	Gear shift lever pivot pin	15–20
7/16-20	Splitter cylinder shift bar	20–25
⅝-11	Splitter control jam	60–65
⅝-18	Reverse idler shaft	75–80
⅝-18	Case	170–185
⅝-18	Range cylinder shift bar	70–80
2-16	Output shaft	425–525

Installation

1. Place the gear shift lever in the neutral position. The lever must remain in this position until air pressure has entered the system.
2. Apply air pressure to the front port of the air valve to move the pistons to the rear. Failure to comply with these two steps may result in valve damage.
3. Position the alignment sleeve in the valve body.
4. Place a new gasket on the body.
5. Secure the body to the transmission with the attaching screws and lock washers. Tighten the screws to specification.
6. Connect all air lines to the valve as shown.

MASTER CONTROL VALVE

Removal

1. Drain the air from the system.
2. Disconnect the two nylon lines from the fittings.
3. Remove the master control valve from the gearshift lever.

Disassembly

1. Place the control valve with the rear housing (outlet side) on a bench, and remove the front and rear housing attaching bolts.
2. Remove the control button and plunger assembly.
3. Remove the detent balls, springs, and felt seals from the valve housings.
4. Remove the valve plate and O-ring from the rear housing.
5. Lift the valve insert from the front housing, and remove the O-ring.
6. Remove the wave washer installed under the valve insert.
7. If necessary, drive the roll pin from the button. Then remove the control button from the plunger.

Assembly

1. Insert the wave washer in the front housing bore.
2. Insert a new O-ring on the valve insert and install the insert into the front housing.
3. Position a new O-ring into the rear housing bore and install the valve plate.

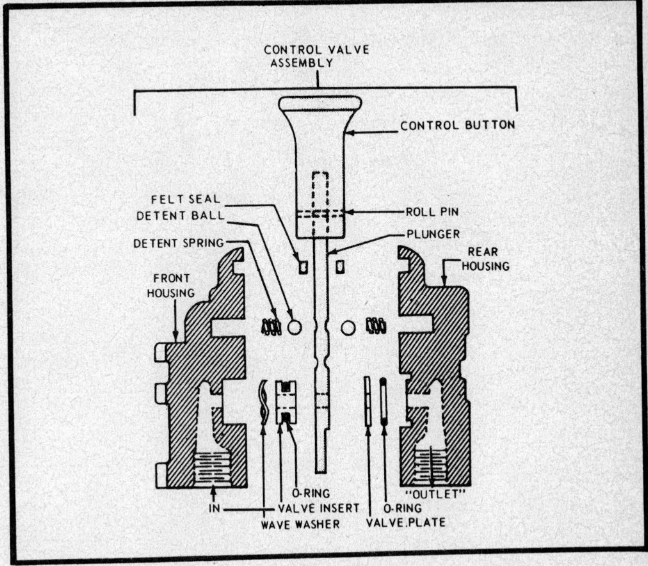

Master control valve—exploded view (© Ford Motor Co.)

4. Install a felt seal into the top of each housing.
5. If the control button was removed, secure it to the plunger with the roll pin.
6. Position the detent balls and springs into the housings and install the control button and plunger assembly. Install the housing attaching screws.

Installation

1. Secure the control valve to the gearshift lever with the attaching clamp. Make sure that the control valve button is six inches below the top surface of the gearshift knob when the button is pulled out. Tighten the clamp.
2. Connect the white nylon air line to the inlet port (right side) of the master control valve.
3. Connect the black nylon air line to the outlet port (left side).

Fuller RT-613, RT-6613 Thirteen Speed

This transmission is the twin countershaft design with 13 forward speeds and 3 reverse. These units consist of a five speed front section and a three speed range or auxiliary section. The twin countershaft design splits the torque evenly between the two countershafts. The mainshaft gears float between the mating gears on the countershafts eliminating gear bushings and sleeves. The transmission uses a countershaft brake which slows down the transmission gearing by forcing a piston against the transmission's P.T.O. gear.

COMPANION FLANGE AND CLUTCH HOUSING

Disassembly

1. Lock the transmission in two speeds, remove the nut from the tailshaft then pull the companion flange or yoke from the splines of the tailshaft.
2. Remove the speedometer drive gear or replacement spacer from the companion flange or yoke.
3. Remove the clutch release mechanism or upshift clutch brake assembly.
4. Remove the six nuts and two bolts and remove the clutch housing.

Assembly

1. Install the clutch housing on the studs in the front case and tighten the nuts 170 to 185 ft. lbs. and the bolts 70 to 75 ft. lbs.
2. Install the speedometer drive gear or spacer on the hub of the yoke or flange.
3. Lock the transmission in two speeds and install the yoke or flange on the splines of the tailshaft.
4. Install the tailshaft nut and tighten 450 to 500 ft. lbs.

GEAR SHIFT LEVER HOUSING

Disassembly

1. Remove the four bolts and lift the assembly from the shift bar housing.

BOOT
PIVOT PIN
CAPSCREW (4)
HOUSING
O-RING
GASKET
LEVER
WASHER
SPRING

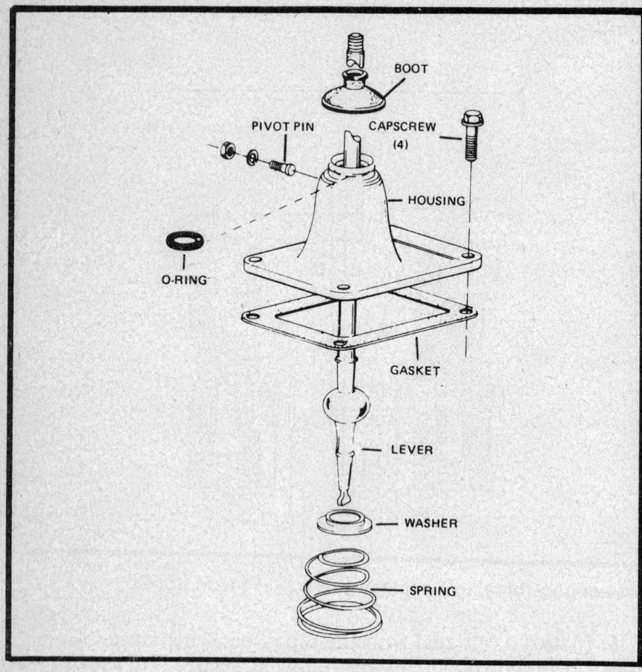

Gear shift lever housing—exploded view (© Ford Motor Co.)

2. Place the assembly upside down in a vise and remove the tension spring by prying it up and over the spring retainers, one coil at a time.
3. Remove the washer and lever from the housing.
4. Remove the housing from the vise and, if necessary, remove the nut, washer, pivot pin, and O-ring.

Assembly

1. If so equipped, install the O-ring in the groove in the housing.
2. Install the lockwasher and nut to secure the pivot pin.
3. Install the gearshift lever in the housing, fitting the pivot pin in the slot in the lever.
4. Install the tension spring washer in the housing.
5. Make sure the shift bar housing is in the neutral position, then install the gear shift lever housing, fitting the lever in the shifting slots in the forks.

SHIFT BAR HOUSING

Disassembly

1. Remove the retaining capscrews and remove the shift bar housing from the transmission.
2. Remove the tension spring cover.
3. Remove the three tension springs and balls.
4. Place the shift bar housing in a vise, cut the lockwire, remove the lockscrew and pull the 1st/reverse shift bar from the housing and remove the yoke.
5. Cut the lock wire, remove the lockscrew and pull the 2nd

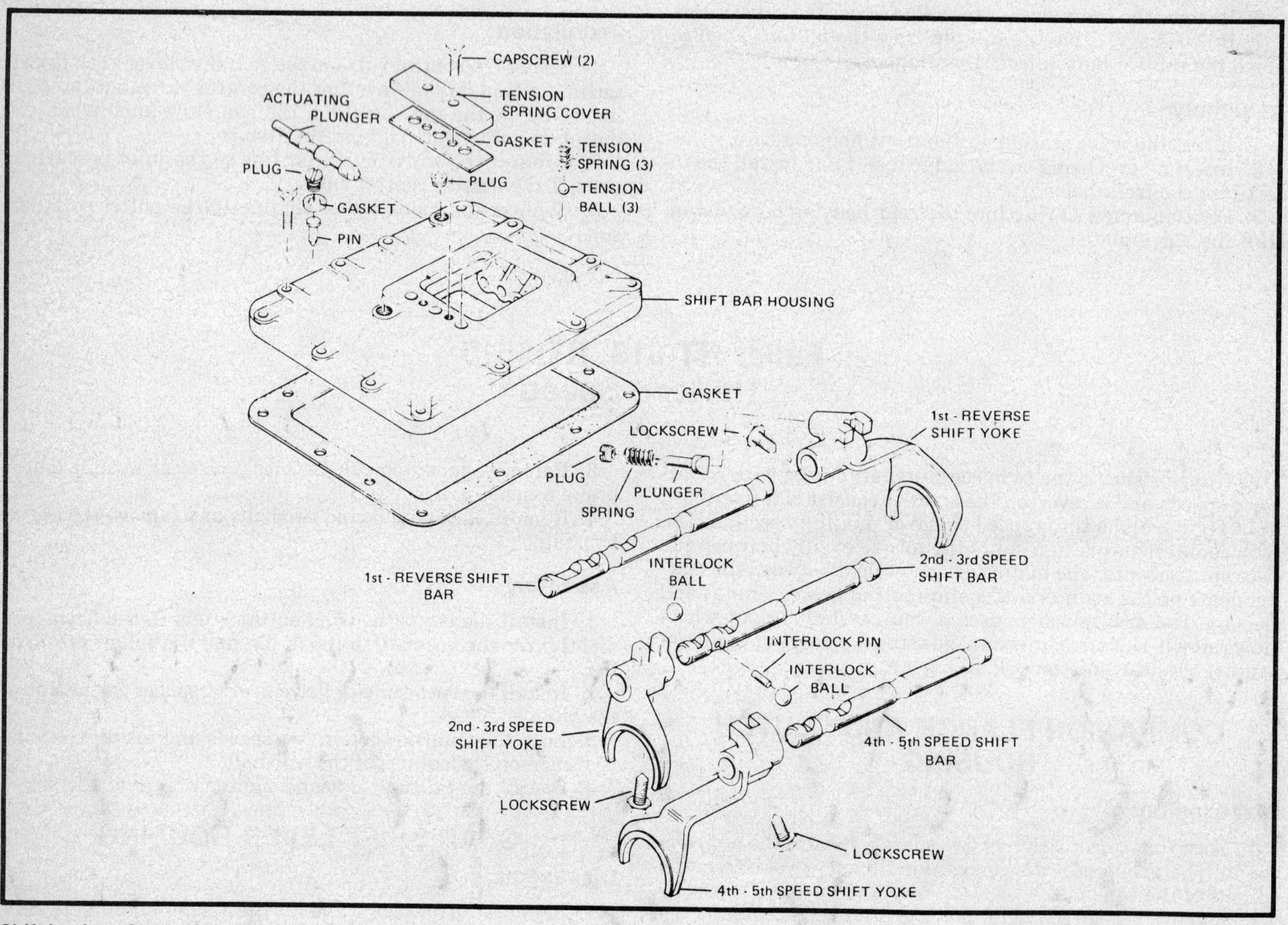

CAPSCREW (2)
ACTUATING PLUNGER
TENSION SPRING COVER
GASKET
TENSION SPRING (3)
PLUG
PLUG
TENSION BALL (3)
GASKET
PIN
SHIFT BAR HOUSING
GASKET
LOCKSCREW
1st - REVERSE SHIFT YOKE
PLUG
PLUNGER
SPRING
1st - REVERSE SHIFT BAR
INTERLOCK BALL
2nd - 3rd SPEED SHIFT BAR
INTERLOCK PIN
INTERLOCK BALL
2nd - 3rd SPEED SHIFT YOKE
4th - 5th SPEED SHIFT BAR
LOCKSCREW
LOCKSCREW
4th - 5th SPEED SHIFT YOKE

Shift bar housing—exploded view (© Ford Motor Co.)

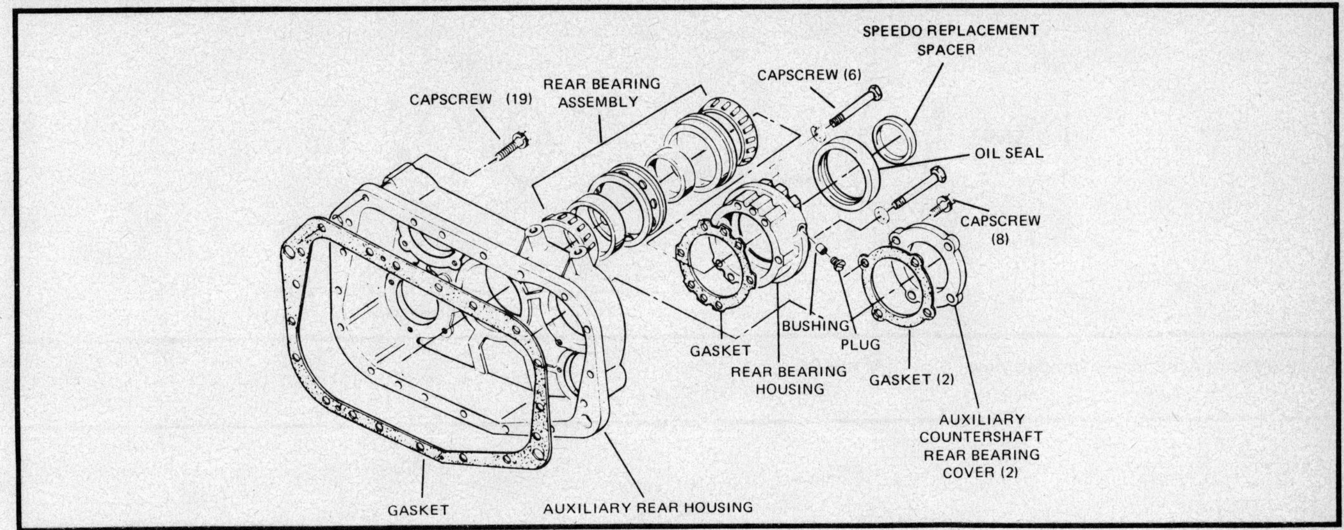

Auxiliary rear housing—exploded view (© Ford Motor Co.)

and 3rd speed shift bar from the housing, removing the interlock pin from the neutral notch then remove the yoke.
6. Remove the actuating plunger from the housing.
7. Cut the lockwire, remove the lockscrew and pull the 4th and 5th speed shift bar from the housing, removing the yoke.
8. Remove the two interlock balls from the web of the housing.

Assembly

1. Install the 4th and 5th speed shift bar and yoke. Tighten the lockscrew and wire securely.
2. Install an interlock ball in the front web.
3. Install the actuating plunger in the rear web.
4. Install the 2nd and 3rd speed shift bar and yoke, inserting the interlock pin in the bore of the neutral notch. Install the yoke lockscrew and tighten and wire securely.
5. Install the interlock ball in the front web.
6. Install the 1st and reverse shift bar and yoke. Install the yoke lockscrew and tighten and wire securely.
7. Remove the assembly from the vise and install the three tension balls and springs.
8. Install the tension spring cover.
9. Make sure the shift yokes and the sliding clutches are in the neutral position, then install the shift bar housing on the transmission.

AUXILIARY REAR HOUSING

Disassembly

1. Remove the cover from the intermediate shift cylinder.
2. Remove the locknut from the shaft in the cylinder.
3. Remove the cylinder housing from the bore in the auxiliary housing by pulling evenly to the rear.
4. Remove the piston from the cylinder housing and, if necessary, remove the O-ring from the OD of the piston.
5. If necessary, remove the O-rings from the cylinder housing and the shaft.
6. Remove the two countershaft bearing covers.
7. Remove the snapring from the rear of both countershafts.
8. Remove the 19 capscrews which attach the rear housing to the intermediate case. Reinsert one capscrew near both dowel pin locations and turn in two or three threads.
9. Insert three puller screws and move the rear housing approximately $1/4$ inch to the rear.
10. Insert flat suitable tool between the auxiliary and intermediate housings.
11. Use a soft bar and a hammer and drive against the rear of both countershafts to move them as far forward as possible. This will move the bearings to the rear on the shaft.
12. Remove the flat suitable tool and the puller screws and move the rear housing to its original position against the intermediate housing by evenly turning in the two remaining capscrews. This will expose the two rear bearing snaprings.
13. Attach a bearing puller to each snapring and remove both rear bearings from the countershafts.
14. Remove the two remaining capscrews. Attach a chain hoist to the rear housing and separate from the intermediate housing. Place the assembly in a vise in the upright position.

Assembly

1. Make sure that the synchronizer assembly is as far forward as possible on the tailshaft, and that the marked teeth on the auxiliary countershafts are facing each other.
2. Using a hoist, move the rear housing into position with the top tipped back slightly to allow the synchronizer assembly to pass through the auxiliary countershafts. Make sure the direct synchronizer is not sliding off the low speed blocker pins. Look through the rear bearing bores and mesh the marked tooth on each countershaft between the two marked teeth on each side of the auxiliary low speed gear. Move the rear housing evenly onto the two dowel pins.
3. Secure the rear housing with the retaining bolts.
4. Use a soft bar and a hammer against the rear of both auxiliary countershafts to seat the front bearings, and use a bearing driver to install the rear bearings on the shafts and in the bore.
5. Install the rear bearing snaprings in the countershaft grooves.
6. Install the rear bearing covers.
7. Install the O-ring on the intermediate shift shaft.
8. Install the intermediate shift cylinder in the rear housing, fitting the shift shaft through the cylinder bore. The cylinder is installed with the small air channel in the housing to the right.
9. Install the O-ring in the OD of the piston, and install the piston on the shaft in the cylinder.
10. Install the elastic stop nut on the shift shaft.
11. Install the shift cylinder cover, aligning the small channel on the cover with the channel in the housing. The insert valve opening on the cover will be facing down.
12. If previously, install the insert valve in the cover with the flat end facing up.
13. Install the insert valve retaining nut.

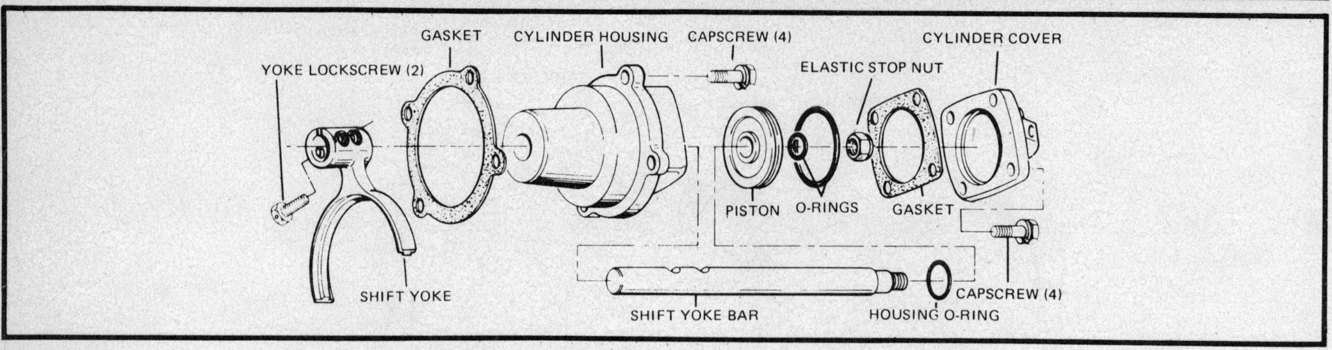

Auxiliary shift cylinder—exploded view (© Ford Motor Co.)

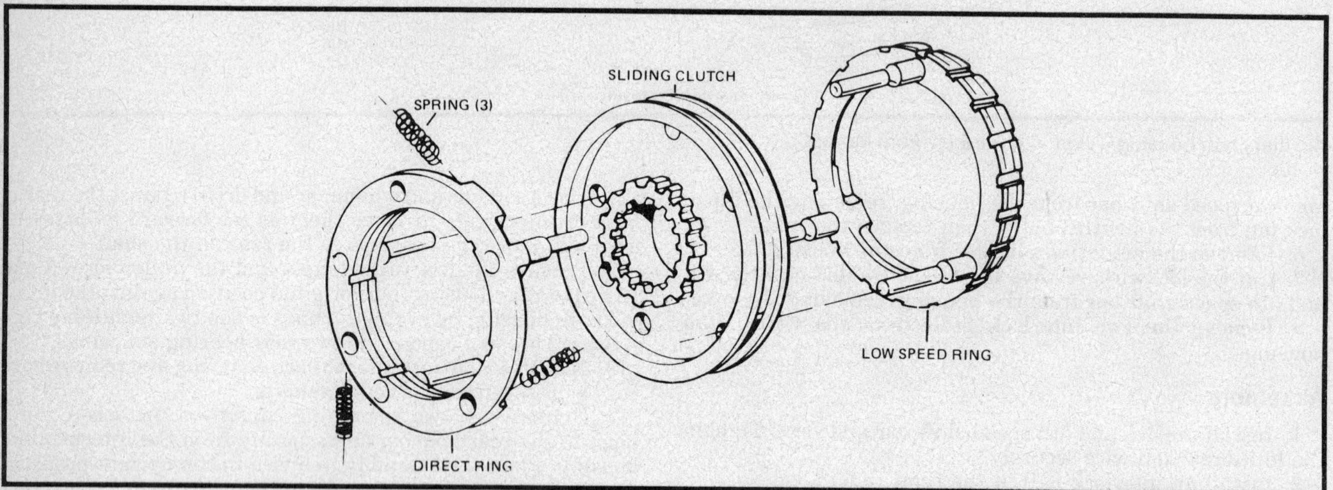

Synchronizer assembly—exploded view (© Ford Motor Co.)

Auxiliary Rear Housing Subassemblies

AUXILIARY SHIFT CYLINDER

Disassembly

1. Remove the cover from the shift cylinder.
2. Remove the locknut from the shifting shaft in the cylinder.
3. Cut the lockwire and remove the two yoke lockscrews.
4. Push the shifting shaft and piston to the rear, and then remove the cylinder housing. Remove the shifting yoke and sliding clutch gear.
5. Remove the piston from the shaft and remove the O-rings on the inner and outer diameters of the piston.
6. Remove the four bolts, and the cylinder housing from the bore in the auxiliary rear housing. Remove the O-ring from the bore in the cylinder housing. Remove the synchronizer assembly from the splines of the tailshaft.

Assembly

1. Install the O-ring in the bore of the shaft cylinder.
2. Install the cylinder housing into the rear housing bore and secure with the bolts.
3. Install the shifting shaft from the front, through the yoke hub and cylinder, aligning the notches with the lockscrew bores in the yoke hub.
4. Install the two yoke lockscrews and tighten and wire securely.
5. Install the O-rings in the ID and OD of the piston.
6. Install the piston on the shifting shaft with the flat side down.
7. Install the locknut on the shifting shaft.
8. Install the shift cylinder cover with the air fitting on the top left side.

SYNCHRONIZER

Disassembly

1. Pull the direct synchronizer from the blocker pins of the low speed synchronizer.
2. Remove the sliding clutch from the low speed synchronizer.

Assembly

1. Install the sliding clutch on the pins of the low speed synchronizer, recessed side up.
2. Install the three springs in the direct synchronizer.
3. Place the direct synchronizer over the low speed blocker pins, seating the springs against the pins.
4. Compress the springs to fully seat the direct synchronizer on the pins of the low speed synchronizer.
5. Place the direct low speed fork into the yoke slot of the sliding clutch, hub to the rear, and install the synchronizer assembly on the splines of the output shaft.

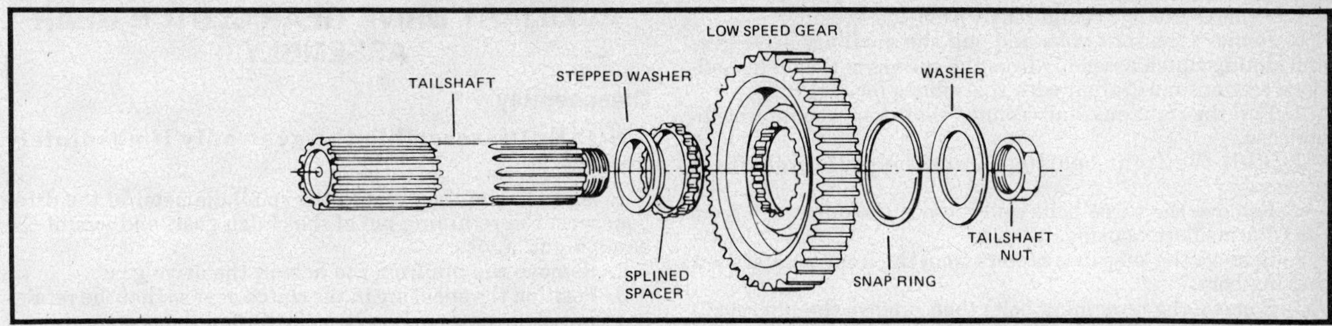

Tailshaft and low speed gear—exploded view (© Ford Motor Co.)

TAILSHAFT AND LOW SPEED GEAR

Disassembly

1. Use a soft bar and hammer against the rear of the tailshaft, to drive the assembly forward and from the rear bearing.
2. Remove the bearing inner sleeve from the shaft.
3. Use the low speed gear as a base to press the bearing from the shaft and to free the gear and rear washer.
4. Remove the splined washer from the shaft.
5. Remove the stepped washer from the shaft.
6. Remove the snapring from the ID of the low speed gear.
7. Remove the rear cover and if necessary, remove the oil seal from the cover.
8. Remove the bearing rear cone.
9. Remove the two bearing cups and outer spacer from the housing bore.

Assembly

1. Install the snapring in the low speed gear.
2. Mark two adjacent teeth on the low speed gear, and mark the two teeth directly opposite.
3. Set the tailshaft on a bench with the threaded end up, and install the low speed gear step washer with the large diameter down.
4. Install ther splined washer onto the shaft and washer.
5. Install the low speed gear on the splined spacer with the teeth down.
6. Install the low speed gear rear washer on the shaft with the camfered ID up.
7. Install the front cone of the rear bearing on the shaft and gainst the washer. Heating the bearing is suggested but not more than 275 degrees F. Use a heating lamp.
8. Install the bearing inner spacer on the shaft.
9. Place the front bearing cup partially into the bore of the housing with the taper to the inside.
10. Place the bearing outer spacer on the front cup, and place the rear bearing cup on the spacer.
11. Tap all three units into the rear bore until the lip of the rear cup seats against the housing.
12. Place the auxiliary rear housing over the end of the shaft, and seat the front bearing cone in the front cup.
13. Install the bearing rear cone on the shaft and into the rear cup. Heating the bearing is suggested but not more than 275 degrees F.
14. Install the oil seal in the rear bearing cover then install the cover. Use a brass washer at the speedometer gear location.

AUXILIARY INTERMEDIATE HOUSING

Disassembly

1. Remove the plate from the rear of the mainshaft.
2. Remove the intermediate drive gear from the shaft and if necessary, remove the two snaprings and plate from ther ID of the intermediate drive gear.
3. Remove the intermediate shifter shaft from the housing.

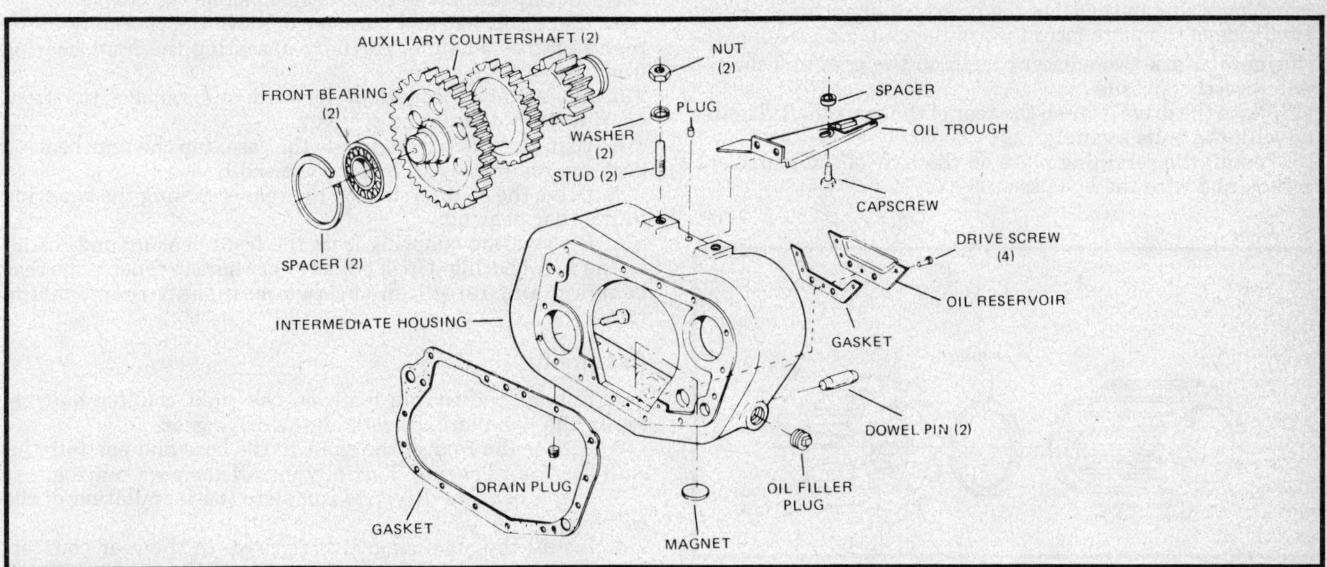

Auxiliary intermediate housing—exploded view (© Ford Motor Co.)

4. Remove the left countershaft from the housing.
5. Remove the shift yoke and pull the auxiliary drive gear and sliding clutch assembly from the splines of the mainshaft. Both sections must align with the splines for removal.
6. Pull the right auxiliary countershaft from the intermediate case.
7. Pull the front bearings from the countershafts if necessary.
8. Remove the three bolts and remove the oil trough from the intermediate housing.
9. Remove the snapring spacers from the front countershaft bearing bores.
10. Remove the remaining bolts then remove the intermediate housing from the transmission.

Assembly

1. Place the intermediate housing on the dowel pins and against the front case. Secure with the retaining bolts. Do not install the bolts in the two top center holes.
2. Place a snapring spacer in both front countershaft bores.
3. Install the oil trough in the intermediate housing with two bolts in the front wall and one bolt in the top of the housing. The spacer is placed between the oil trough and the top of the case.
4. Mark the low speed gear tooth identified with an "O" on each auxiliary countershaft for timing purposes. Then mark the tooth on the intermediate and drive gears which align with that tooth.
5. Install the bearing on the front of each countershaft, seating it against the shaft shoulder.
6. Place the left countershaft into position, but do not completely seat the front bearing in the bore.
7. On the auxiliary drive gear and the sliding clutch assembly, mark the two adjacent teeth on the drive gear, and mark the teeth directly opposite.
8. Install the auxiliary drive gear and sliding clutch assembly on the splines of the mainshaft. Mesh the marked tooth on each countershaft between the marked teeth of the auxiliary drive gear.
9. Place the intermediate shift yoke in the yoke slot of the auxiliary drive gear sliding clutch assembly, hub to the rear.
10. Install the intermediate shift shaft through the bore in the housing and the yoke hub. Secure with the lockscrew and wire.
11. If previously removed, install the snapring, plate, and second snap ring in the ID of the intermediate drive gear. The raised side of the plate faces toward the clutching teeth of the drive gear. Mark two adjacent teeth on the gear and the two teeth directly opposite.
12. Place the drive gear on the rear of the mainshaft. Tighten and wire the bolts securely.
13. Install the retaining plate on the rear of the mainshaft. Tighten and wire the bolts securely.

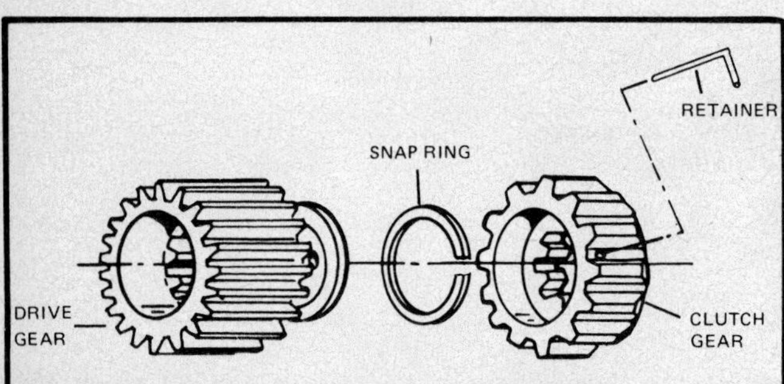

Auxiliary drive gear/clutch assembly—exploded view
(© Ford Motor Co.)

AUXILIARY DRIVE GEAR/CLUTCH GEAR ASSEMBLY

Disassembly

NOTE: Disassemble the gear only if absolutely necessary.

1. Align one of the holes in the small diameter of the drive gear with the retaining pin of the clutch gear, and mount the assembly in a vise.
2. Remove the pin from the hole in the drive gear.
3. Position the snapring in the clutch gear so that the retaining pin hole is approximately $\frac{1}{2}$ inch from the open section of the snap ring. Install a small Allen wrench or equivalent into the retaining pin hole and force down until the snapring is forced out of the groove. Pry the snapring from the groove.
4. Remove the drive gear from the clutch gear, and if necessary, remove the snapring from the clutch gear.

Assembly

1. If previously removed, install the snapring on the drive gear with the large diameter facing out.
2. Place the small diameter of the drive gear inside the clutch gear, and mount the assembly in a vise so that the two gears are forced together. For ease of retaining pin installation, place the snapring so that open section is underneath the retaining pin hole.
3. Pry the snapring into position inside the clutch gear.
4. Align the drive gear hole with the retaining pin hole, then from inside the drive gear, insert the pin with the elbow bend facing away from the clutch gear. Turn the drive gear so that the pin cannot fall out, then bend the end of the retaining pin down in between the teeth of the clutch gear.

FRONT SECTION RIGHT COUNTERSHAFT BEARINGS

Disassembly

1. Loosen, but do not remove the two mainshaft rear bearing retainers.
2. Use a soft bar and hammer against the rear of the right countershaft and drive as far forward as possible to expose the snapring groove in the front bearing.
3. Remove the snapring from the rear countershaft bearing bore, and install in the front bearing snapring groove.
4. Use a soft bar and hammer to move the assembly to the rear as far as possible, partially unseating the front bearing from the shaft.
5. Move the countershaft forward and remove the front bearing with a puller or pry bars.
6. Using a punch from inside the case, tap the rear bearing back approximately $\frac{1}{4}$ inch on the shaft.
7. Drive the countershaft to the rear, exposing the snapring in the rear bearing.
8. Remove the snapring from the front bearing and install on the rear bearing. Use a puller or pry bars to remove the rear bearing, and retighten the two mainshaft rear bearing retainers.

Assembly

1. Engage the timing tooth on the right countershaft between the two marked teeth on the drive gear.
2. Center the rear of the shaft in the bore and partially install the front bearing. Partially install the rear bearing.
3. Use a bearing driver to complete the installation of the bearings.
4. Install the snap ring in the groove in the rear countershaft bearing bore. Drive both countershafts back until the rear bearings seat against the snap rings.

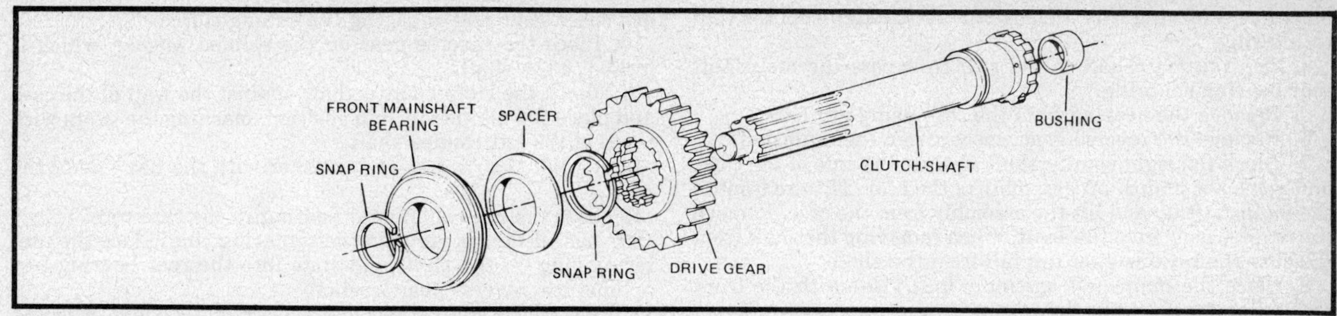

Clutch shaft—exploded view (© Ford Motor Co.)

CLUTCH SHAFT

Disassembly

1. Remove the front bearing cover or upshift clutch brake plate.
2. Move the drive gear and shaft as far forward as possible, and remove the snapring from the groove in the clutch shaft.
3. While holding the shaft in position, tap the drive gear forward to unseat the front mainshaft bearing.
4. Use a puller or pry bar to remove the bearing from the shaft.
5. Remove the spacer from the shaft.
6. Remove the snapring from the ID of the drive gear.
7. Pull the shaft forward and from the splines of the drive gear.
8. Move the drive gear to the rear and against the 4th speed gear, engaging the splines of the sliding clutch.

Assembly

1. If previously removed, install the bushing in the pocket of the clutch shaft. Make sure the oil hole is not plugged.
2. Insert the clutch shaft in the drive gear.
3. Install the snapring in the ID of the drive gear.
4. Install the spacer on the shaft with the flat side against the gear.
5. Install the drive gear bearing on the shaft and in the case bore.
6. Install the snapring in the groove in the shaft with the flat side toward the bearing.
7. Install the front bearing cover.

REVERSE IDLER GEARS

Disassembly

NOTE: The left and right reverse idler gears are disassembled in the same manner.

1. Remove the elastic stop nut and washer from the reverse idler shaft.
2. Push the shaft to the rear and remove from outside the case.
3. Remove the thrust washer and gear from inside the case.
4. Remove the needle bearing from the gear.
5. Assembly is the reverse of the disassembly procedure.

MAINSHAFT

Disassembly

1. Remove the two mainshaft rear bearing retainers, and remove the snapring from the groove in the rear of the mainshaft. Use caution as this will free the spring loaded centering ring.
2. Remove the splined retainer from the mainshaft.
3. Center the front of he mainshaft in the case bore and re-

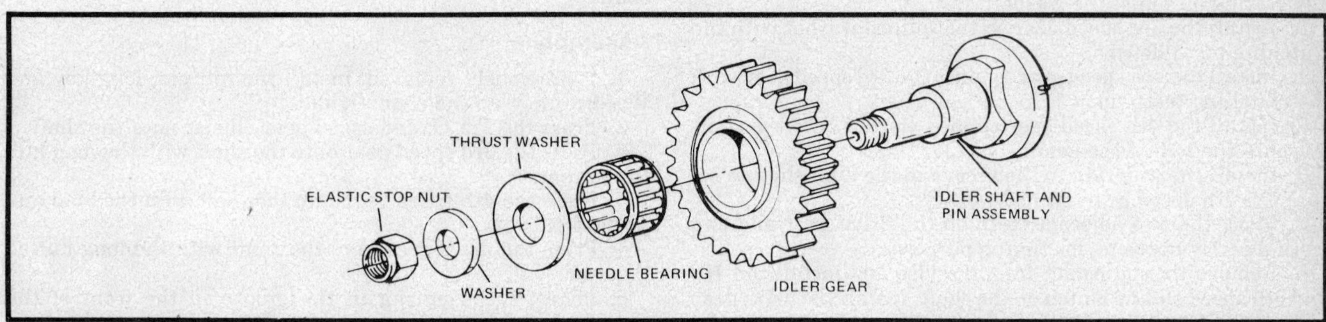

Low reverse idler gear—exploded view (© Ford Motor Co.)

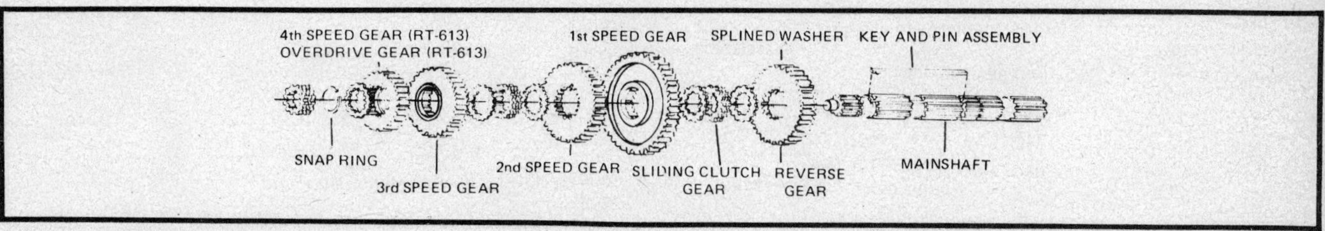

Mainshaft—exploded view (© Ford Motor Co.)

move the centering ring. Remove the six springs from the centering ring.

4. Tap the mainshaft to the rear to expose the mainshaft rear bearing snapring.
5. Remove the bearing from the case using pry bars.
6. Remove the reverse gear washer from the mainshaft.
7. Block the right countershaft against the side of the case, and move the mainshaft assembly to the rear. Tilt the front of the mainshaft up and lift the assembly from the case. Remove the reverse gear from the shaft. When removing the shaft from the case the reverse gear can fall from the shaft.
8. Place the mainshaft assembly in a viser with the front end up, and remove the drive gear.
9. Remove the snapring and splined washer from the 4th speed gear.
10. Remove the 3rd speed gear, key and splined washer.
11. Remove the 2nd and 3rd speed sliding clutch.
12. Remove the assembly from the vise and pull the key from the mainshaft.
13. Remove the reverse gear splined spacer and the 1st and reverse sliding clutch.
14. Remove the 1st and 2d speed gears and splined spacers.

Assembly

1. Place the mainshaft in a vise with the front end down, keeping the keyway free.
2. Install the 2nd speed gear washer and insert the key from the bottom to lock the washer in position.
3. Install the 2nd speed gear on the splined washer with the clutching teeth down.
4. Install the 1st speed gear against the 2nd speed gear with the clutching teeth up.
5. Insert the splined washer in the hub of the 1st speed gear. Align the washer with the mainshaft splines and move the key up to lock the washer in position.
6. Install the 1st and reverse sliding clutch, aligning the slot in the clutch with the key.
7. Install the reverse gear spolined washer, align the keyway and lock in position with the key.
8. Reposition the assembly in a vise with the pilot end up, and pull the key up approximately ½ inch. Install the 2nd and 3rd speed sliding clutch, aligning the slot in the clutch with the key.
9. Install the 3rd speed gear splined washer down over the key and push the key down into position, with the pin in the key resting on top of the washer.
10. Install the 3rd speed gear on the splined washer with the clutching teeth down.
11. Install the 4th speed gear against the 3rd speed gear with the clutching teeth up.
12. Install the 4th speed gear splined washer onto the shaft and into the hub of the gear.
13. Install the snapring in the groove in the mainshaft to secure the 4th speed gear splined washer.
14. Mark the two adjacent teeth on the drive gear and two teeth directly opposite, for timing purposes.
15. Remove the mainshaft from the vise and install the 4th and 5th speed sliding clutch on the shaft. Install the drive gear against the 4th speed gear with the clutching teeth towards the 4th speed gear and engaging the sliding clutch.
16. Place the reverse gear on the splined washer, which is locked to the shaft.
17. Block the right countershaft against the wall of the case and place the mainshaft into position, mashing the gears with those of the left countershaft.
18. Install the reverse gear washer with the flat side to the rear.
19. Seat the mainshaft rear bearing in the case core.
20. Install the six rings in the centering ring. Place the centering ring on the shaft and slide into the rear bearing and against the reverse gear washer.
21. Install the splined retainer washer on the shaft, with the coned surface towards the centering ring.
22. Place the snapring on the shaft against the splined retainer washer.
23. Block against the front of the mainshaft and use a sleeve driver to move the centering ring, retainer washer and snapring forward until the snapring seats in the groove in the mainshaft.
24. Install the rear bearing retainers and secure the bolts with the locking lugs.
25. Slide the drive gear forward off the splines of the sliding clutch and align the timing marks with the marked tooth on the left countershaft.
26. Slide the 4th–5th speed sliding clutch forward to engage the splines of the drive gear.

COUNTERSHAFT

Disassembly

NOTE: The right and left countershafts are disassembled in the same manner.

1. Remove the blocking and lift the right countershaft from the case.
2. Remove the left countershaft bearings in the same manner as those removed from the right and lift the left countershaft from the case.
3. Remove the snapring from the front of each shaft.
4. Press the drive gear and 4th speed gear from eachshaft.
5. Using the rear face of the P.T.O. gear as a base press the 3rd speed gear and the P.T.O./2nd speed gear cluster from each shaft.

Assembly

1. If previously removed, install the roll pin, long key and Woodruff key on the countershaft.
2. Press the P.T.O./2nd speed gear cluster onto the shaft.
3. Press the 3rd speed gear onto the shaft with the long hub to the rear.
4. Press the 4th speed gear into the shaft with the long hub to the front.
5. Press the drive gear onto the shaft with the long hub to the rear.
6. Install the snapring in the groove in the front of the countershaft.

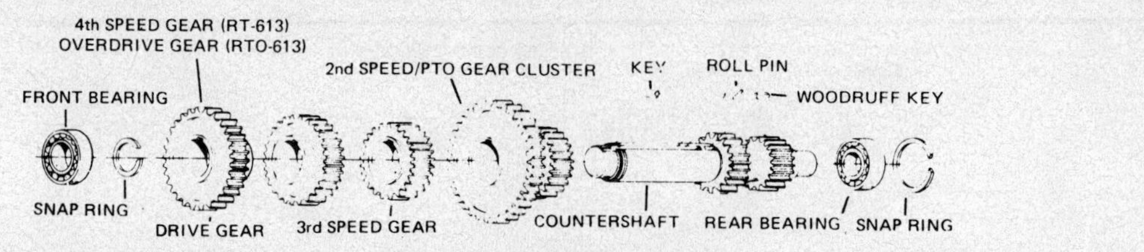

Countershaft—exploded view (© Ford Motor Co.)

TORQUE SPECIFICATIONS
Fuller Models Rt-613

Size	Location	Torque-Rating (ft. lbs.)
	BOLTS	
¼-20 × ½	Air filter to bracket	10–15
¼-20 × ⅝	Air valve adapter plate	15–20
¼-20 × ⅞	Air valve adapter plate rear	15–20
¼-20 × 1¾	Air valve	15–20
5/16-18 × ½	Hand hole cover	23–35
5/16-18 × 1½	Splitter cylinder cover	23–35
⅜-16 × ¾	PTO cover, small	35–45
⅜-16 × ¾	Air filter bracket to case	35–45
⅜-16 × 1	Auxiliary drive gear bearing retainer	35–45
⅜-16 × 1½	Auxiliary housing	35–45
⅜-16 × 1¼	Front bearing cover	35–45
⅜-16 × 1¼	Shift bar housing	35–45
⅜-16 × 1¼	Auxiliary housing	35–45
⅜-16 × 1¼	Gearshift lever housing	35–45
⅜-16 × 1¼	Auxiliary countershaft rear bearing covers	35–45
⅜-16 × 1¼	Auxiliary range shift cylinder	35–45
⅜-16 × 1¼	Auxiliary range shift cylinder cover	35–45
⅜-16 × 1¾	Shift bar housing	35–45
⅜-16 × 2	Auxiliary housing	35–45
⅜-16 × 2¾	Rear bearing cover	35–45
7/16-14 × 1¼	PTO cover, large	50–65
½-13 × 1½	Clutch housing	70–75
½-13 × 3½	Clutch housing	70–75
½-20 × 1	Countershaft front bearing retainers	50–65
½-20 × 1	Auxiliary countershaft rear bearing retainers	50–65
½-20 × 2	Range shift yoke	50–65
	NUTS	
⅝-18	Clutch housing	170–85
⅝-18	Range cylinder shift bar	70–80
2-16	Output shaft	450–500
⅝-24	Gearshift lever pivot pin	15–20
7/16-20	Splitter cylinder shift bar	20–25
⅝-11	Splitter control jam	60–65
⅝-18	Reverse idler shaft	75–80

7. On the drive gear of each shaft mark the gear tooth which is aligned with the keyway. The tooth is also stamped with an "O".

8. Place the left countershaft into position in the case.

9. Center the rear of the countershaft in the case bore and partially install the front bearing on the shaft and in the case bore. Partially install the rear bearing; then use a driver to complete the installation of the front and rear bearing.

10. Install the snapring in the groove in the rear bearing bore.

11. Place the right countershaft into position and install the bearings.

International Harvester T-495 and T- 496 5–Speed Transmissions

The T-495 and T-496 transmissions have five forward speeds with one reverse and are synchronized units. The first and reverse gears are in constant mesh and are engaged by a sliding clutch gear.

CONTROL LEVER AND SHIFT BAR HOUSING

Removal

1. Place the transmission in the reverse position and remove the retaining bolts from the shift bar housing.
2. Lift the shift bar housing assembly from the transmission case.
3. Separate the control lever housing from the shift bar housing by the removal of the four retaining bolts. Do not lose the three poppet springs and steel balls from the top of the shift bar housing.

CONTROL LEVER ASSEMBLY

Disassembly

1. Place the shift lever housing in a soft jawed vise and remove the lever handle (knob).
2. Remove the control lever spring retainer pin, the control lever spring retainer, spring, dust cover and felt washer.
3. Remove the pivot pin snapring. Remove the pivot pin and control lever from the housing.

Assembly

Complete the assembly in the reverse order of the disassembly procedure.

SHIFT BAR HOUSING

Disassembly

1. If not previously removed, lift the poppet springs and balls from the top of the shift bar housing.
2. Remove the lock pins from the first and reverse speed shift block and shift forks.
3. Drive the fourth and fifth speed shift rail out towards the front of the shift bar housing, driving out the shift rail dust cup. Remove the shift fork.
4. Remove the interlock ball and cross pin retainer plug, located on the left outside of the housing just below the poppet ball and spring housing, releasing the interlock ball and pin.
5. Remove the first and reverse speed and the second and third speed shift forks and shift rails from the housing.

Reassembly

1. The reassembly of the shift bar housing is in the reverse of the disassembly procedure. Be sure, during the assembly that the forks and rails are reinstalled in their original positions.

MAIN DRIVE GEAR AND MAINSHAFT

Removal

1. Lock the transmission shafts by engaging two gears at the same time.
2. Remove the flange nut, washer and flange. Remove the parking brake drum and brake band.
3. Remove the rear bearing retainer bolts and retainer from the rear of the transmission. Slide the speedometer gear from the mainshaft.
4. With the transmission still locked in two gears, remove the countershaft rear bearing lock nut.
5. Drive the mainshaft towards the rear of the case to expose the mainshaft rear bearing and snapring. Install a bearing puller to the bearing and pull it from the mainshaft.
6. Remove the front bearing retainer. Remove the drive gear and bearing from the front of the transmission case.
7. Retain the first/reverse gear to the mainshaft with a hose clamp fastened to the mainshaft. Remove the front synchronizer from the shaft, if necessary to gain working space. Position the countershaft slinger impeller in a horizontal plane before removal of the mainshaft to prevent damage to the impeller.
8. Tilt the front on the mainshaft assembly upward and remove the assembly from the transmission case.

MAINSHAFT

Disassembly

1. Remove the fourth and fifth speed synchronizer, if not previously done.
2. Remove the mainshaft front snapring and the clutch gear. Slide the fourth speed gear from the shaft.
3. Remove the third speed gear snapring and thrust washer. Slide the third speed gear from the mainshaft.
4. Remove the second and third speed synchronizer assembly from the mainshaft, along with the hose clamp that was placed on the shaft to assist in the removal of the assembly.
5. Remove the first speed gear thrust washer and the first speed gear from the mainshaft.
6. Remove the select fit snapring, the clutch hub, reverse gear and thrust washer.
7. Remove the second speed gear retaining snapring and the second speed gear.

Reassembly

1. Install the rear synchronizer assembly (second and third speed) on the mainshaft with the wider stop ring fitted in the second gear cavity.
2. Slide the mainshaft third speed gear on to the mainshaft. Install the correct select fit thrust washer which will give 0.002 to 0.006 inch between the snapring and the thrust washer of the third speed gear. The washers are of the following thicknesses. 0.119 to 0.122 inch, 0.123 to 0.126 inch, 0.127 to 0.130 inch, 0.131 to 0.134 inch,
3. Install the third speed snapring and the fourth speed mainshaft gear with the oil slots towards the third speed gear.
4. Install the mainshaft clutch gear with the oil grooves next to the fourth speed gear.
5. Install the mainshaft snapring.

NOTE: This snapring is selective. Select a ring to provide a tight fit, but also be sure the fourth speed gear rotates freely on the mainshaft, after the snapring is installed.

6. Install the second speed gear and the second speed gear select fit thrust washer. Install the snapring.
7. Check the end play of the second speed gear by placing the mainshaft in an upright position in a soft jawed vise. Insert feeler gauges between the second speed gear and the forward part of the mainshaft. Holding the feeler gauges in place, slowly rotate the second speed gear and locate the gear high spot. Insert the proper select fit thrust washer to obtain 0.002 to

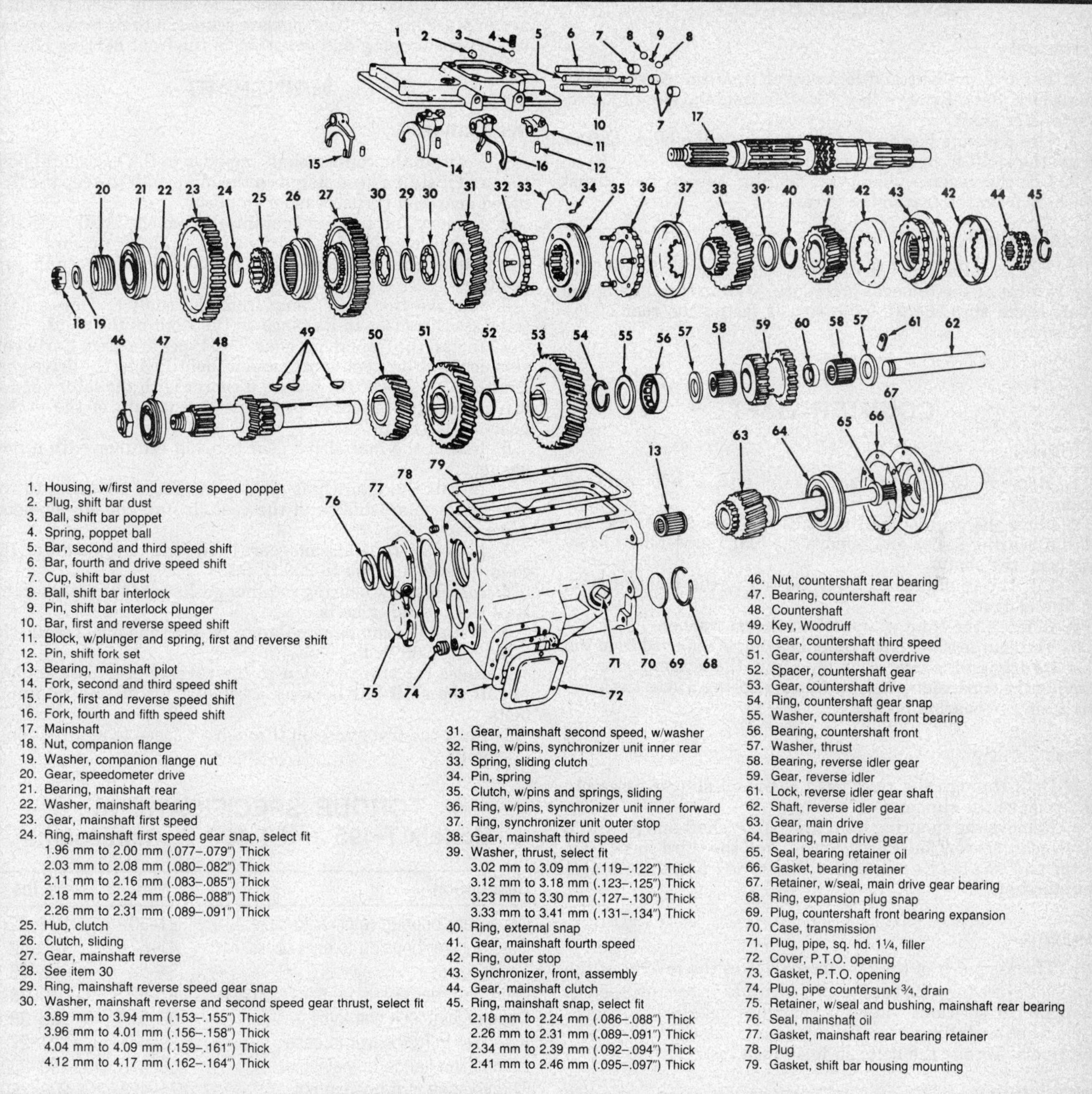

Exploded view of IH T-495 and T-496 transmissions (© IH Co.)

0.006 inch clearance or end play. Select the proper thrust washer as required. 0.153 to 0.155 inch, 0.156 to 0.158 inch, 0.159 to 0. 161 inch, 0.162 to 0.164 inch.

8. To provide a tight fit between the first/reverse clutch hub and the select fit snapring, position the mainshaft in a vise, if removed from step 7. Place the first/reverse clutch hub on the mainshaft and insert a select fit snapring in the mainshaft groove. Check the snapring fit in four locations on the mainshaft and select one for a tight fit. Select one from the following sizes. 0.077 to 0.079 inch, 0.080 to 0.082 inch, 0.083 to 0.085 inch, 0.086 to 0.088 inch, 0.089 to 0.091 inch.

9. Install the select fit thrust washer, the reverse gear and the first/reverse clutch hub to the mainshaft. Install the previously selected snapring (step 8) on the mainshaft.

10. Insert feeler gauges on both sides of the mainshaft, between the first/reverse clutch hub and the reverse gear clutch teeth. Rotate the reverse gear slowly with the feeler gauges in position. A running clearance (end play) should be between 0.002 and 0.007 inch. To obtain the proper clearance, select a thrust washer from the list of selected thrust washers as given in step 7.

11. Install the first speed gear and the first speed gear thrust washer. Force the thrust washer against the shoulder on the mainshaft and insert a feeler gauge between the first speed thrust washer and the first speed gear hub. A running clearance of 0.002 to 0.006 inch should exist. If a minimum of 0. 002 inch running clearance cannot be obtained, a new first speed gear must be installed.

REVERSE IDLER GEAR

Removal

1. Remove the bolt and lockwasher from the reverse idler shaft lock plate. Remove the lock plate from the slot in the reverse idler shaft.
2. Use a prying bar and wedge to remove the idler shaft or drive the shaft from the case with a brass drift.
3. Lift the reverse idler gear, bearing, spacer, and thrust washers from the transmission case.

Installation

1. The installation of the reverse idler gear assembly is in the reverse of the removal procedure. When assemblying the gear, make sure the 21 tooth side is facing the rear of the transmission.

COUNTERSHAFT

Removal

1. Remove the countershaft rear nut, if not removed previously.
2. Move the countershaft towards the rear of the case. Install a bearing puller and remove the rear countershaft bearing from the shaft.
3. Lift the countershaft from the top of the transmission, front end first.
4. Remove the front countershaft thrust washer.
5. The countershaft front roller bearing is removed from the case by driving the expansion plug from the bearing bore, removing the expansion plug retaining snapring. Drive the bearing from the bearing bore.

Disassembly

1. Drill through the rivet head of the oil slinger assembly and remove the slinger.
2. Remove the snapring from the countershaft and press the drive gear, spacer, fourth speed gear, and the third speed gear from the shaft. Remove the Woodruff keys from the countershaft.

Assembly

1. The assembly of the countershaft is in the reverse of the removal procedure. Be sure the Woodruff keys are installed in their proper positions when the gears are installed.
2. When installing the oil slinger, bolts are used in place of the rivets. Torque the bolts 35 to 40 inch lbs.

Installation

1. Install the countershaft into the transmission case in the reverse of the removal procedure. Be sure the thrust washers are in place and the bearings are seated in their bores. Install the expansion plug and snapring in the front bearing bore.

MAINSHAFT

Installation

1. Position the countershaft impeller in the horizontal position and install a hose clamp on the mainshaft to keep the first speed gear and thrust washer in place.
2. Remove the front synchronizer from the shaft assembly and while lifting the front of the shaft assembly upward, place the rear of the shaft into the case and level the shaft into position.
3. Remove the hose clamp from the shaft and install the front synchronizer in its place on the front of the shaft.
4. Install the front drive gear. Two types are used. Early version uses a drive gear spacer and is identified by the drive gear length of 1 $^1/_8$ inch. Do not use a spacer with the later version drive gear, as assembly problems and failure of the pocket bearing will occur.
5. Install the maindrive gear bearing retainer with a new gasket.
6. Install the mainshaft rear bearing and snapring to the rear of the mainshaft and the case. Install the speedometer drive gear.
7. Lock the transmission gears in two speeds and tighten the countershaft nut 200 to 250 ft. lbs.
8. Install a new bearing retainer gasket and the retainer. Install the retaining bolts.
9. Install the companion flange, washer and nut. Torque the nut 190 to 230 ft. lbs.
10. Place the transmission in the reverse gear position and install the shift bar housing assembly. Install the retaining bolts.
11. Shift the transmission through all speed to assure proper assembly.

TORQUE SPECIFICATIONS
Models T-495 and T-496 Transmissions

Description	N·m	ft. lbs.
Drive gear bearing retainer to case	21–30	16–22
Control lever housing to shift cover	41–57	30–42
Cover to case	34–52	25–38
Mainshaft rear bearing retainer to case	41–52	30–38
Countershaft lock bolt to case	33–51	25–38
P.T.O. or P.T.O. cover to case	29–37	21–27
Companion flange to mainshaft	258–312	190–230
Countershaft rear bearing nut	271–423	200–250
Parking brake bracket	142–169	105–125

Muncie Model SM330
Three Speed (83MM)

The G.M. Corporation Model SM 330 (83MM) (Muncie) is a three speed transmission using helical constant mesh gears. The engagement of all gears except reverse is assisted by synchronizers.

TRANSMISSION UNIT

Disassembly

1. Remove side cover and shift forks.
2. Unbolt extension and rotate to line up groove in extension flange with reverse idler shaft. Drive reverse idler shaft and key out of case with a brass drift.
3. Move second/third synchronizer sleeve forward. Remove extension housing and mainshaft assembly.
4. Remove reverse idler gear from case.
5. Remove third speed blocker ring from clutch gear.
6. Expand snapring which holds mainshaft rear bearing. Tap gently on end of mainshaft to remove extension.

GENERAL DATA

Type	3-Speed
Synchromesh gears	1st, 2nd, and 3rd
Model	SM330 (83MM)
Gear ratios	
1st speed	3.03:1
2nd speed	1.75:1
3rd speed	1.00:1
Reverse	3.02:1

7. Remove clutch gear bearing retainer and gasket.
8. Remove snapring. Remove clutch gear from inside case by gently tapping on end of clutch gear.
9. Remove oil slinger and 16 mainshaft pilot bearings from clutch gear cavity.
10. Slip clutch gear bearing out front of case. Aid removal with a screwdriver between case and bearing outer snapring.
11. Drive countershaft and key out to rear.
12. Remove countergear and two tanged thrust washers.

MAINSHAFT

Disassembly

1. Remove speedometer drive gear. Some speedometer drive gears, made of metal, must be pulled off.
2. Remove rear bearing snapring.
3. Support reverse gear. Press on rear of mainshaft to remove reverse gear, thrust washer, and rear bearing. Be careful not to cock the bearing on the shaft.
4. Remove first and reverse sliding clutch hub snapring.
5. Support first gear. Press on rear of mainshaft to remove clutch assembly, blocker ring, and first gear.
6. Remove second and third speed sliding clutch hub snapring.
7. Support second gear. Press on front of mainshaft to remove clutch assembly, second speed blocker ring, and second gear from shaft.

CLEANING AND INSPECTION

For more detailed information, see the "Cleaning and Inspection" instructions at front of transmission section.
1. Wash all parts in solvent.
2. Air dry.

CLUTCH KEYS AND SPRINGS

Replacement

Keys and springs may be replaced if worn or broken, but the hubs and sleeves must be kept together as originally assembled.
1. Mark hub and sleeve for reassembly.
2. Push hub from sleeve. Remove keys and springs.
3. Place three keys and two springs, one on each side of hub, so all three keys are engaged by both springs. The tanged end of the springs should not be installed into the same key.
4. Slide the sleeve onto the hub, aligning the marks.

EXTENSION OIL SEAL AND BUSHING

Replacement

1. Remove seal.
2. Using bushing remover and installer, or other suitable tool, drive bushing into extension housing.
3. Drive new bushing in from rear. Lubricate inside of bushing and seal. Install new oil seal with extension seal installer or suitable tool.

CLUTCH BEARING RETAINER OIL SEAL

Replacement

1. Pry old seal out.
2. Install new seal using seal installer or suitable tool. Seat seal in bore.

MAINSHAFT

Assembly

1. Lift front of mainshaft.
2. Install second gear with clutching teeth up; the rear face of the gear butts against the mainshaft flange.
3. Install a blocking ring with clutching teeth downward. All three blocking rings are the same.
4. Install second and third synchronizer assembly with fork slot down. Press it onto mainshaft splines. Both synchronizer assemblies are identical but are assembled differently. The second/third speed hub and sleeve is assembled with the sleeve fork slot toward the thrust face of the hub; the first-reverse hub and sleeve, with the fork slot opposite the thrust face. Be sure that the blocker ring notches align with the synchronizer assembly keys.

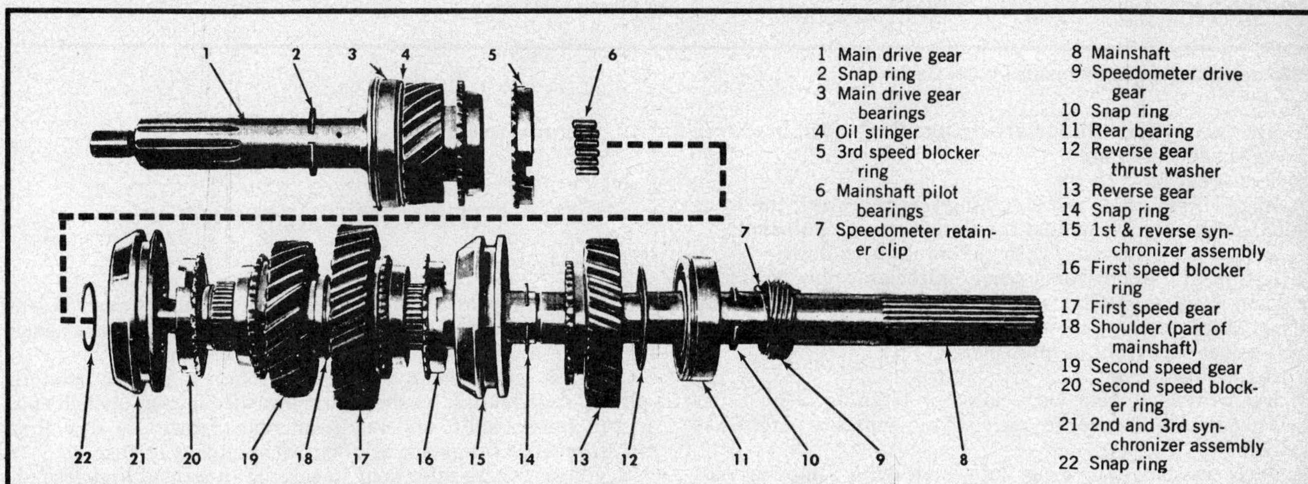

Main drive gear and mainshaft assembly (© GM Corp.)

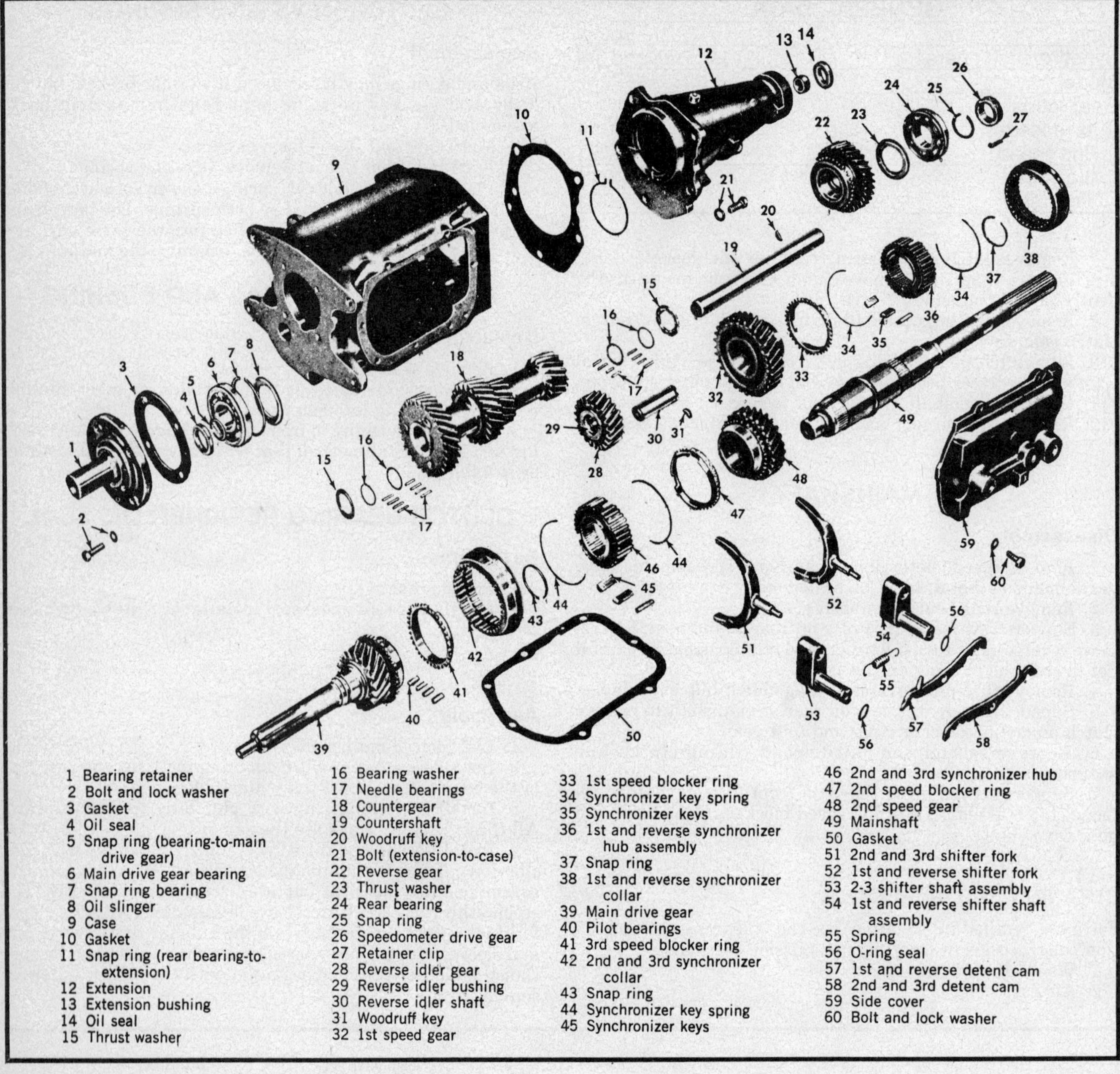

SM330 transmission components (© GM Corp.)

5. Install synchronizer snapring. Both synchronizer snaprings are the same.
6. Turn rear of shaft up.
7. Install first gear with clutching teeth upward; the front face of the gear butts against the flange on the mainshaft.
8. Install a blocker ring with clutching teeth down.
9. Install first and reverse synchronizer assembly with fork slot down. Press it onto mainshaft splines. Be sure blocker ring notches align with synchronizer assembly keys and synchronizer sleeves face front of mainshaft.
10. Install snapring.
11. Install reverse gear with clutching teeth down.
12. Install steel reverse gear thrust washer with flats aligned.
13. Press rear ball bearing onto shaft with snapring slot down.
14. Install snapring.
15. Install speedometer drive gear and retaining clip.

TRANSMISSION UNIT

Assembly

1. Place a row of 29 roller bearings, a bearing washer, a second row of 29 bearings, and a second bearing washer at each end of the countergear. Hold in place with grease.
2. Place countergear assembly through rear case opening with a tanged thrust washer, tang away from gear, at each end. Install countershaft and key from rear of case. Be sure that thrust washer tangs are aligned with notches in case.
3. Place reverse idler gear in case. Do not install reverse idler shaft yet. The reverse idler gear bushing may not be replaced separately, it must be replaced as a unit.

4. Expand snapring in extension. Assemble extension over mainshaft and onto rear bearing. Seat snapring.
5. Load 16 mainshaft pilot bearings into clutch gear cavity. Assemble third speed blocker ring onto clutch gear clutching surface with teeth toward gear.
6. Place clutch gear assembly, without front bearing, over front of mainshaft. Make sure that blocker ring notches align with keys in second/third synchronizer assembly.
7. Stick gasket onto extension housing with grease. Assemble clutch gear, mainshaft, and extension to case together. Make sure that clutch gear teeth engage teeth of countergear anti-lash plate.
8. Rotate extension housing. Install reverse idler shaft and key.
9. Torque extension bolts to 45 ft. lbs.
10. Install oil slinger with inner lip facing forward. Install front bearing outer snapring and slide bearing into case bore.
11. Install snapring to clutch gear stem. Install bearing retainer and gasket and torque to 20 ft. lbs. Retainer oil return hole must be at 6 o'clock.

TORQUE SPECIFICATIONS Muncie-83MM

	ft. lbs.
Extension to case attaching	45
Drain plug	30
Filler plug	15
Side cover attaching bolts	22
Main drive gear retainer bolts	22
Transmission case to clutch housing bolts	45

12. Shift both synchronizer sleeves to neutral positions. Install side cover, inserting shifter forks in synchronizer sleeve grooves.
13. Torque side cover bolts to 20 ft. lbs.

Muncie Model SM465 Four Speed (117mm)

Muncie model CH-465-SM-465 transmission is a four speed transmission using helical gears. The action of all gears except reverse is aided by synchronizers.

TRANSMISSION UNIT

Disassembly

1. Remove transmission cover assembly. Move reverse shifter fork so that reverse idler gear is partially engaged before attempting to remove cover. Forks must be positioned so rear edge of the slot in the reverse fork is in line with the front edge of the slot in the forward forks as viewed through tower opening.
2. Lock transmission into two gears. Remove the universal joint flange nut, universal joint front flange and brake drum assembly.

NOTE: On 4-wheel drive models, use a special tool to remove mainshaft rear lock nut.

3. Remove parking brake and brake flange plate assembly on those vehicles having a driveshaft parking brake.
4. Remove rear bearing retainer and gasket.
5. Slide speedometer drive gear off mainshaft.
6. Remove clutch gear bearing retainers and gasket.
7. Remove countergear front bearing cap and gasket.
8. Using a prybar, pry off countershaft front bearing.
9. Remove countergear rear bearing snaprings from shaft and bearing. Using special tool, remove countergear rear bearings.
10. Remove clutch gear bearing outer race to case retaining ring.
11. Remove clutch gear and bearing by tapping gently on bottom side of clutch gear shaft and prying directly opposite against the case and bearing snapring groove at the same time. Remove fourth gear synchronizer ring. Index cut out section of clutch gear in down position with countergear to obtain clearance for removing clutch gear.
12. Remove rear mainshaft bearing snapring and, using special tools, remove bearing from case. Slide 1st speed gear thrust washer off mainshaft.
13. Lift mainshaft assembly from case. Remove synchronizer cone from shaft.
14. Slide reverse idler gear rearward and move countergear rearward, then lift to remove from case.
15. To remove reverse idler gear, drive reverse idler gear shaft out of case from front to rear using a drift. Remove reverse idler gear from case.

SUBASSEMBLIES TRANSMISSION COVER

Disassembly

1. Remove shifter fork retaining pins and drive out expansion plugs. The third and fourth shifter fork must be removed before the reverse shifter head pin can be removed.
2. With shifter shafts in neutral position, remove shafts. Care should be taken when removing the detent balls and springs since removal of the shifter shafts will cause these parts to be forcibly ejected.
3. Remove retaining pin and drive out reverse shifter shaft.

Assembly

1. In reassembling the cover, care should be taken to install the shifter shafts in order, reverse, 3rd/4th, and 1st/2nd.
2. Place fork detent ball springs and balls in cover.
3. Start shifter shafts into cover and, while depressing the detent balls, push the shafts over the balls. Push reverse shaft through the yoke.
4. With the 3rd–4th shaft in neutral, line up the retaining holes in the fork and shaft. Detent balls should line up with detents in shaft.
5. After 1st and 2nd fork is installed, place two innerlock balls between the low speed shifter shaft and the high speed shifter shaft in the crossbore of the front support boss. Grease the interlock pin and insert it in the 3rd/4th shifter shaft hole. Continue pushing this shaft through cover bore and fork until retainer hole in fork lines up with hole in shaft.
6. Place two interlock balls in crossbore in front support boss between reverse, and 3rd and 4th shifter shaft. Then push remaining shaft through fork and cover bore, keeping both balls in position between shafts until retaining holes line up in fork and shaft. Install retaining pin.
7. Install 1st/2nd fork and reverse fork retaining pins. Install new shifter shaft hole expansion plugs.

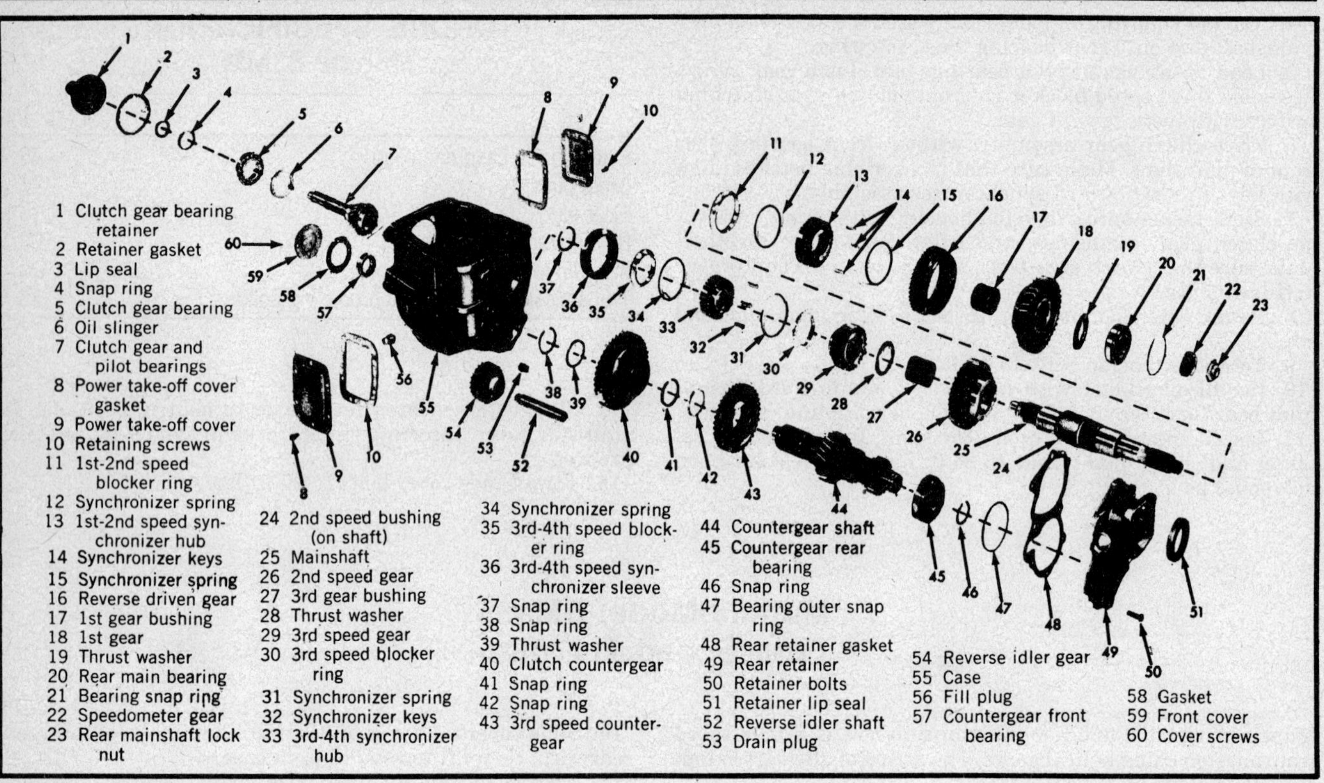

Transmission components (© GM Corp.)

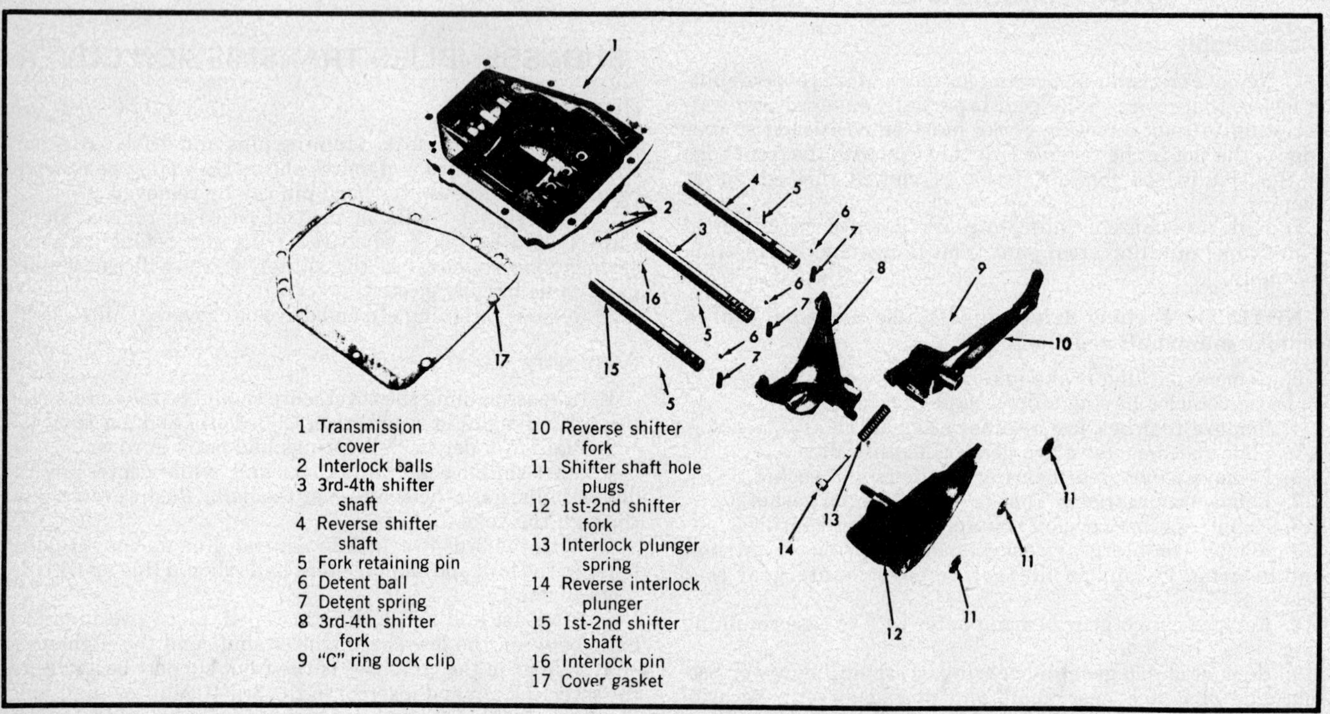

Shift cover assembly components (© GM Corp.)

CLUTCH GEAR AND SHAFT

Disassembly

1. Remove mainshaft pilot bearing rollers from clutch gear if not already removed, and remove roller retainer. Do not remove snapring on inside of clutch gear.

2. Remove snapring securing bearing on steam of clutch gear.

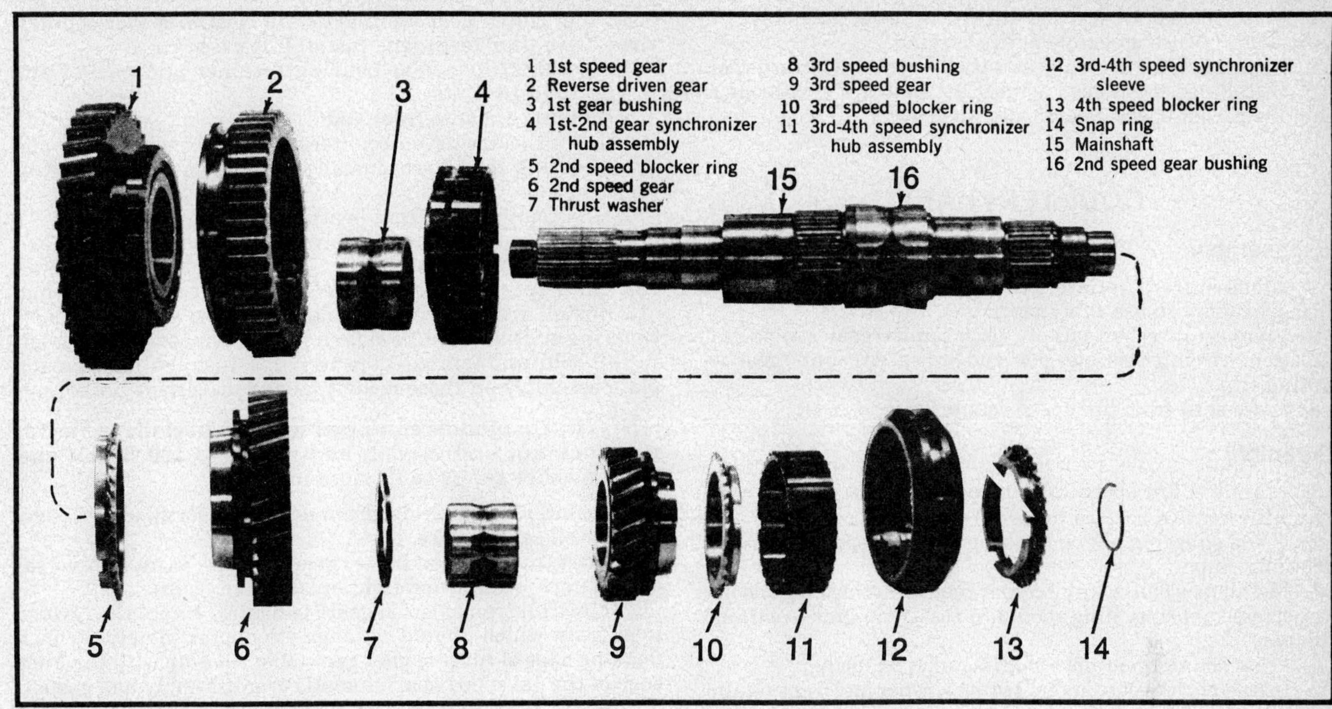

Mainshaft assembly (© GM Corp.)

3. To remove bearing, position a special tool to the bearing and, with an arbor press, press gear and shaft out of bearing.

Assembly

1. Press bearing and new oil slinger onto clutch gear shaft using a special tool. Slinger should be located flush with bearing shoulder on clutch gear. Be careful not to distort oil slinger.
2. Install bearing snapring on clutch gear shaft.
3. Install bearing retainer ring in groove on O.D. of bearing. The bearing must turn freely on the shaft.
4. Install snapring on I.D. of mainshaft pilot bearing bore in clutch gear.
5. Lightly grease bearing surface in shaft recess, install transmission mainshaft pilot roller bearings and install roller bearing retainer. This roller bearing retainer holds bearings in position, and, in final transmission assembly, is pushed forward into recess by mainshaft pilot.

BEARING RETAINER OIL SEAL

Replacement

1. Remove retainer and oil seal assembly and gasket.
2. Pry out oil seal.
3. Install new seal with lip of seal toward flange of tool.
4. Support front surface of retainer in press and drive seal into retainer.
5. Install retainer and gasket on case.

MAINSHAFT

Disassembly

1. Remove first speed gear.
2. Remove reverse driven gear.
3. Press behind second speed gear to remove 3rd/4th synchronizer assembly, 3rd speed gear and 2nd speed gear along with 3rd speed gear bushing and thrust washer.
4. Remove 2nd speed synchronizer ring and keys.
5. Using a press, remove 1st speed gear bushing and 2nd speed synchronizer hub.
6. Without damaging the mainshaft, chisel out the 2nd speed gear bushing.

Inspection

Wash all parts in cleaning solvent and inspect them for excessive wear or scoring.

NOTE: Third and fourth speed clutch sleeve should slide freely on clutch hub but clutch hub should fit snugly on shaft splines. Third speed gear must be running fit on mainshaft bushing and mainshaft bushing should be press fit on shaft. First and reverse sliding gear must be sliding fit on synchronizer hub and must not have excessive radial or circumferential play. If sliding gear is not free on hub, inspect for burrs which may have rolled up on front end of half tooth internal splines and remove by honing as necessary.

Assembly

1. Lubricate with E.P. oil and press onto mainshaft. 1st, 2nd and 3rd speed gear bushings are sintered iron, exercise care when installing.
2. Press 1st and 2nd speed synchronizer hub onto mainshaft with annulus toward rear of shaft.
3. Install 1st and 2nd synchronizer keys and springs.
4. Press 1st speed gear bushing onto mainshaft until it bottoms against hub. Lubricate all bushings with E.P. oil before installation of gears.
5. Install synchronizer blocker ring and 2nd speed gear onto mainshaft and against synchronize hub. Align synchronizer key slots with keys in synchronizer hub.
6. Install 3rd speed gear thrust washer onto mainshaft inserting washer tang in slotted shaft. Then press 3rd speed gear bushing onto mainshaft against thrust washer.
7. Install 3rd speed gear and synchronizer blocker ring against 3rd speed gear thrust washer.
8. Align synchronizer key ring slots with synchronizer as-

sembly keys and drive 3rd and 4th synchronizer assembly onto mainshaft. Secure assembly with snapring.

9. Install reverse driven gear with fork groove toward rear.
10. Install 1st speed gear against 1st and 2nd synchronizer hub. Install 1st speed gear thrust washer.

COUNTERSHAFT

Disassembly

1. Remove front countergear retaining ring and thrust washer. Do not re-use this snapring or any others.
2. Press countershaft out of clutch countergear assembly.
3. Remove clutch countergear and 3rd speed countergear retaining rings.
4. Press shift from 3rd speed countergear.

Assembly

1. Press the 3rd speed countergear onto the shaft. Install gear with marked surface toward front of shaft.
2. Using snapring pliers, install new 3rd speed countergear retaining ring.
3. Install new clutch countergear rear retaining ring. Do not over stress snapring. Ring should fit tightly in groove with no side play.
4. Press countergear onto shaft against snapring.
5. Install clutch countergear thrust washer and front retaining ring.

TRANSMISSION UNIT

Assembly

1. Lower the countergear into the case.
2. Place reverse idler gear in transmission case with gear teeth toward the front. Install idler gear shaft from rear to front, being careful to have slot in end of shaft facing down and flush with case.
3. Install mainshaft assembly into case with rear of shaft protruding out rear bearing hole in case. Rotate case onto front end. Install 1st speed gear thrust washer on shaft, if not previously installed.
4. Install snapring on bearing O.D. and place rear mainshaft bearing on shaft. Drive bearing onto shaft and into case.
5. Install synchronizer cone on mainshaft and slide rearward to clutch hub. Make sure three cut out sections of 4th speed synchronizer cone align with three clutch keys in clutch assembly.
6. Install snapring on clutch gear bearing O.D. Index cut out portion of clutch gear teeth to obtain clearance over countershaft drive gear teeth, and install into case.
7. Install clutch gear bearing retainer and gasket and torque 15 to 18 ft. lbs.
8. Rotate case onto front end.
9. Install snapring on countergear rear bearing O.D., and drive bearing into place. Install snapring on countershaft at rear bearing.
10. Tap countergear front bearing assembly into case.
11. Install countergear front bearing cap and new gasket and torque 20 to 30 inch lbs.
12. Slide speedometer drive gear over mainshaft to bearing.
13. Install rear bearing retainer with new gasket. Be sure snapring ends are in lube slot and cut out in bearing retainer. Install bolts and tighten 15 to 18 ft. lbs. Install brake backing plate assembly on those models having driveshaft brake.

NOTE: On models equipped with 4-wheel drive, install rear lock nut and washer and torque to 120 ft. lbs. and bend washer tangs to fit slots in nut.

14. Install parking brake drum and/or universal joint flange. Lightly oil seal surface.
15. Lock transmission in two gears at once. Install universal joint flange locknut and tighten 90 to 120 ft. lbs.
16. Move all transmission gears to neutral except the reverse idler gear which should be engaged approximately 3/8 inch (leading edge of reverse idler gear taper lines up with the front edge of the 1st speed gear). Install cover assembly and gasket. Shifting forks must slide into their proper positions on clutch sleeves and reverse idler gear. Forks must be positioned as in removal.
17. Install cover attaching bolts and gearshift lever and check operation of transmission.

TORQUE SPECIFICATIONS
Muncie-117MM

	ft. lbs.
Rear bearing retainer	18
Cover bolts	25
Filler plug	35
Drain plug	35
Clutch gear bearing retainer bolts	18
Universal joint front flange nut	95
Power take off cover bolts	18
Parking brake	22
Countergear front cover screws	25
Rear mainshaft lock nut (4 wheel drive models)	95

New Process 435
Four Speed Transmission

TRANSMISSION UNIT

Disassembly

1. Mount the transmission in a holding fixture. Remove the parking brake assembly, if one is installed.
2. Shift the gears into neutral by replacing the gear shift lever temporarily, or by using a bar or a suitable tool.
3. Remove the cover screws, the second screw from the front on each side is shouldered with a split washer for installation alignment.
4. While lifting the cover, rotate slightly counterclockwise to provide clearance for the shift levers. Remove the cover.
5. Lock the transmission in two gears and remove the output flange nut, the yoke, and the parking brake drum as a unit assembly. The drum and yoke are balanced and unless replacement of parts are required, it is recommended that the drum and yoke be removed as a assembly.
6. Remove the speedometer drive gear pinion and the mainshaft rear bearing retainer.
7. Before removal and disassembly of the drive pinion and mainshaft, measure the end play between the synchronizer

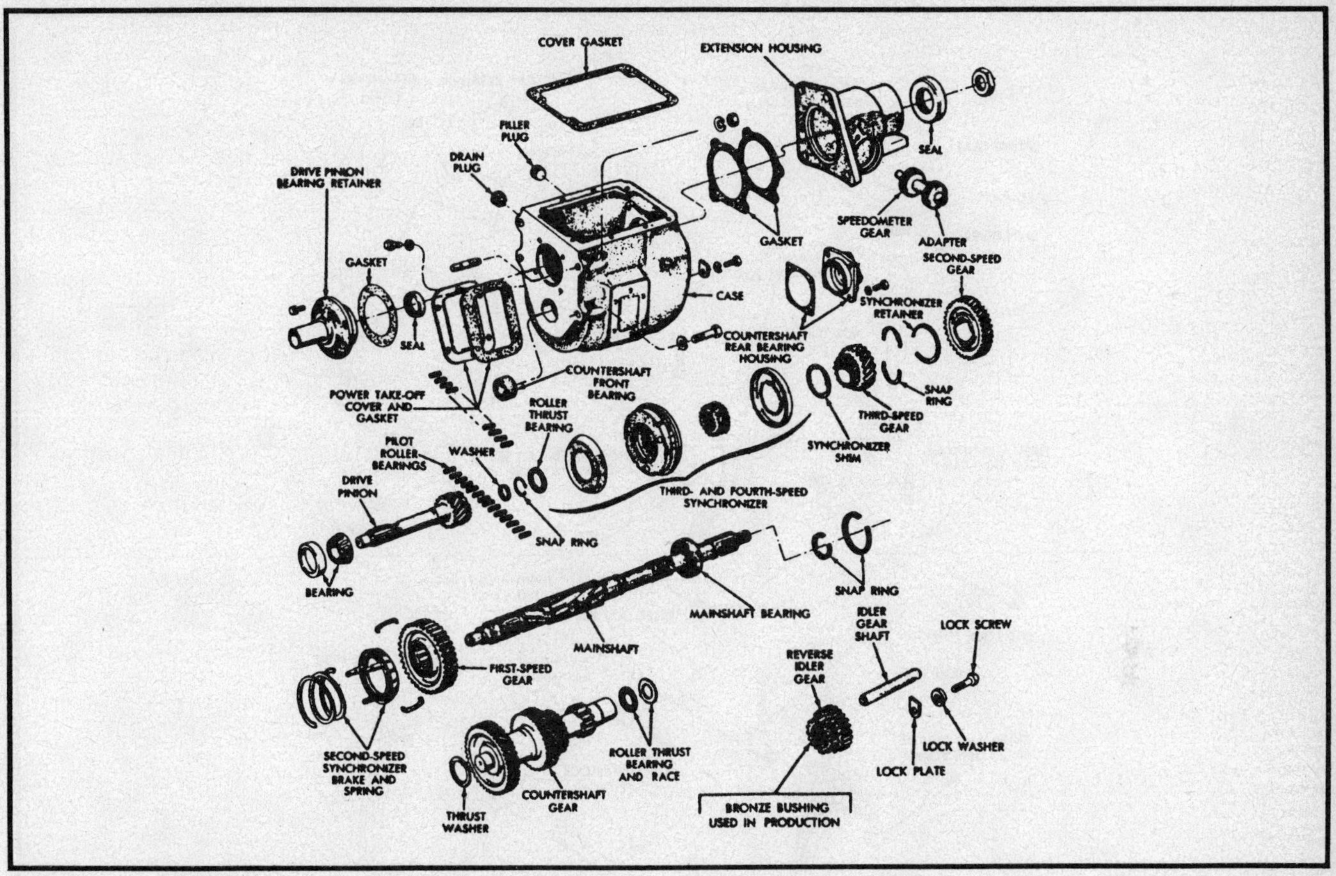

Exploded view of NP435 transmission (© Chrysler Corp.)

stop ring and the third gear. Record this reading for reference during assembly. Clearance should be within 0.050 to 0.070 inch. If necessary, add corrective shims during assembly.

8. Remove the drive pinion bearing retainer.
9. Rotate the drive pinion gear to align the space in the pinion gear clutch teeth with the countershaft drive gear teeth. Remove the drive pinion gear and the tapered roller bearing from the transmission by pulling on the pinion shaft, and rapping the face of the case lightly with a brass hammer.
10. Remove the snapring, washer, and the pilot roller bearings from the recess in the drive pinion gear.
11. Place a brass drift in the front center of the mainshaft and drive the shaft rearward.
12. When the mainshaft rear bearing has cleared the case, remove the rear bearing and the speedometer drive gear with a suitable gear puller.
13. Move the mainshaft assembly to the rear of the case and tilt the front of the mainshaft upward.
14. Remove the roller type thrust washer.
15. Remove the synchronizer and stop rings separately.
16. Remove the mainshaft assembly.
17. Remove the reverse idler lock screw and lock plate.
18. Using a brass drift held at an angle, drive the idler shaft to the rear while pulling.
19. Lift the reverse idler gear out of the case. If the countershaft gear does not show signs of excessive side play or end play and the teeth are not badly worn or chipped, it may not be necessary to replace the countershaft gear.
20. Remove the bearing retainer at the rear end of the countershaft. The bearing assembly will remain with the retainer.
21. Tilt the cluster gear assembly and work it out of the transmission case.
22. Remove the front bearings from the case with a suitable driver.

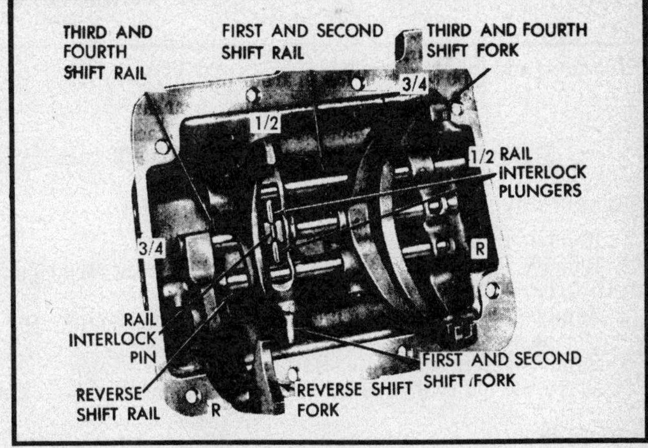

NP435 cover and shift fork assembly (© Chrysler Corp.)

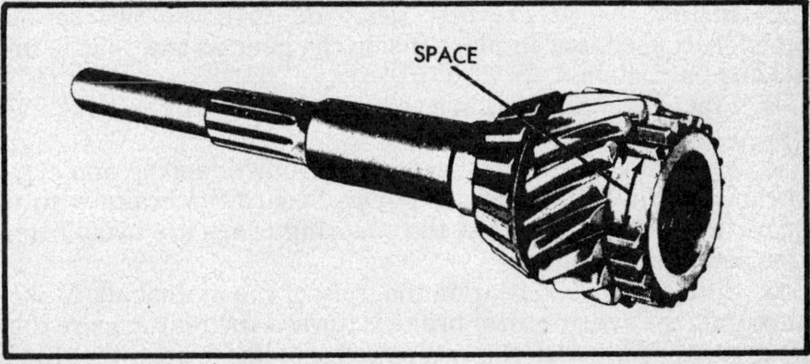

NP435 drive pinion gear showing teeth removal (© Chrysler Corp.)

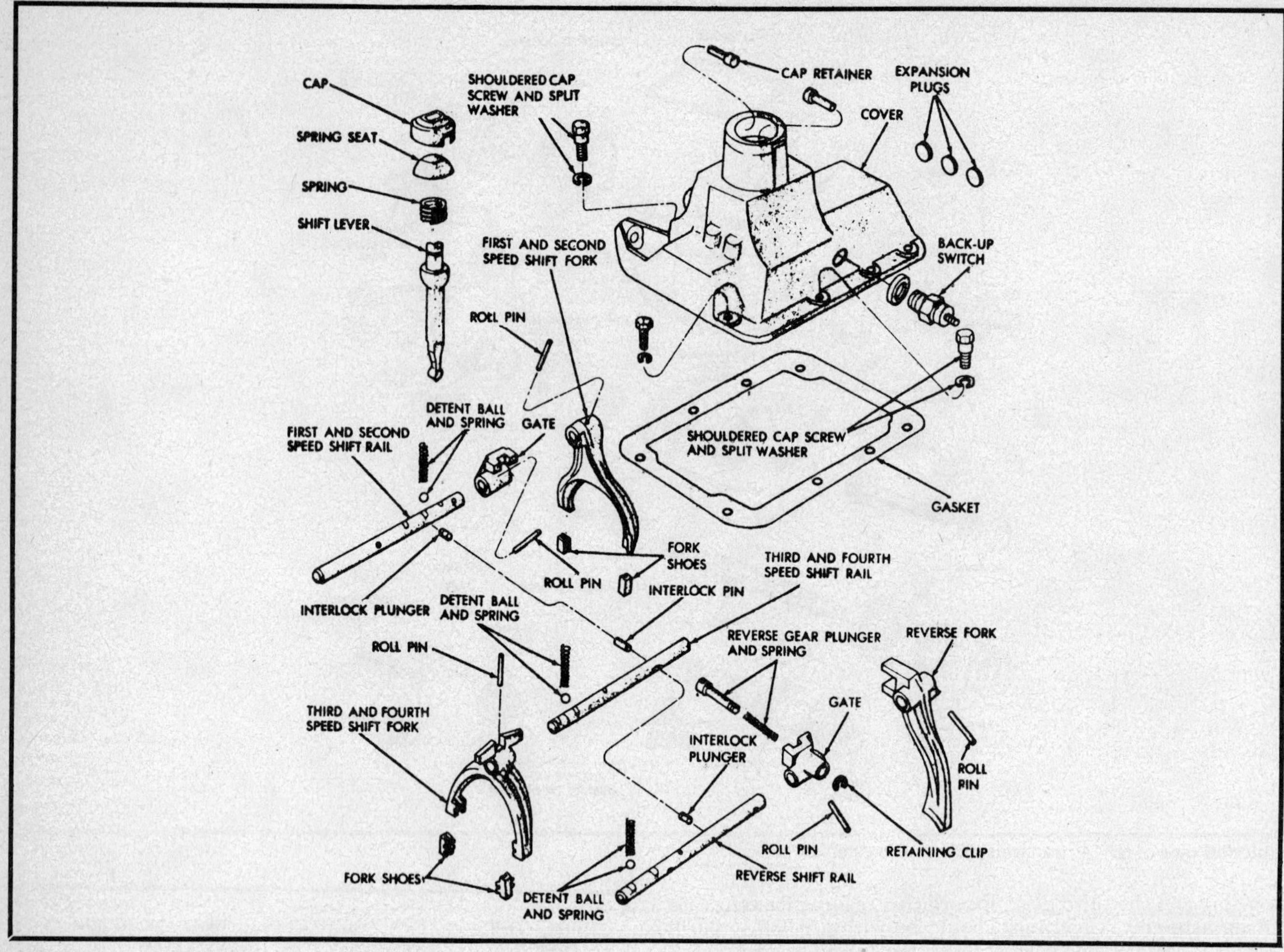

NP435 cover and shift fork assembly (© Chrysler Corp.)

SUBASSEMBLIES MAINSHAFT

Disassembly

1. Remove the clutch gear snapring.
2. Remove the clutch gear, the synchronizer outer stop ring to third gear shim, and the third gear.
3. Remove the special split lock ring with two screw drivers. Remove the second gear and synchronizer.
4. Remove the first/reverse sliding gear.
5. Drive the old seal out of the bearing retainer.

Assembly

1. Place the mainshaft in a soft jawed vise with the rear end up.
2. Install the first/reverse gear. Be sure the two spline springs, if used, are in place inside the gear as the gear is installed on the shaft.
3. Place the mainshaft in a soft jawed vise with the front end up.
4. Assemble the second speed synchronizer spring and synchronizer brake on the second gear. Secure the brake with a snapring making sure that the snapring tangs are away from the gear.
5. Slide the second gear on the front of the mainshaft. Make sure that the synchronizer brake is toward the rear. Secure the gear to the shaft with the two piece lock ring. Install the third gear.
6. Install the shim between the third gear and the third/fourth synchronizer stop ring. Refer to the measurements of end play made during disassembly to determine if additional shims are needed.

NOTE: The exact determination of end-play must be made after the complete assembly of the mainshaft and the main drive pinion is installed in the transmission case.

REVERSE IDLER GEAR

Do not disassemble the reverse idler gear. If it is no longer serviceable, replace the assembly complete with the integral bearings.

COVER AND SHIFT FORK UNIT

NOTE: The cover and shift fork assembly should be disassembled only if inspection shows worn or damaged parts, or if the assembly is not working properly.

Disassembly

1. Remove the roll pin from the first/second shift fork and the shift gate with an "easy out". A square type or a closely wound spiral "easy out" mounted in a tap is preferable for this operation.

2. Move the first/second shift rail forward and force the expansion plug out of the cover. Cover the detent ball access hole in the cover with a cloth to prevent it from flying out. Remove the rail, fork, and gate from the cover.
3. Remove the third/fourth shift rail, then the reverse rail in the manner outlined in steps 1 and 2 above.
4. Compress the reverse gear plunger and remove the retaining clip. Remove the plunger and spring from the gate.

Assembly

1. Install the spring on the reverse gear plunger and hold it in the reverse shift gate. Compress the spring in the shift gate and install the retaining clip.
2. Insert the reverse shift rail in the cover and place the detent ball and spring in position. Depress the ball and slide the shift rail over it.
3. Install the shift gate and fork on the reverse shift rail. Install a new roll pin in the gate and the fork.
4. Place the reverse fork in the neutral position.
5. Install the two interlock plungers in their bores.
6. Insert the interlock pin in the third/fourth shift rail. Install the shift rail in the same manner as the reverse shift rail.
7. Install the first/second shift rail in the same manner as outlined above. Make sure the interlock plunger is in place.
8. Check the interlocks by shifting the reverse shift rail into the Reverse position. It should be impossible to shift the other rails with the reverse rail in this position.
9. If the shift lever is to be installed at this point, lubricate the spherical ball seat and place the cap in place.
10. Install the back-up light switch.
11. Install new expansion plugs in the bores of the shift rail holes in the cover. Install the rail interlock hole plug.

DRIVE PINION AND BEARING RETAINER

Disassembly

1. Remove the tapered roller bearing from the pinion shaft with a suitable tool.
2. Remove the snapring, washer, and the pilot rollers from the gear bore, if they have not been previously removed.
3. Pull the bearing race from the front bearing retainer with a suitable puller.
4. Remove the pinion shaft seal with a suitable tool.

Assembly

1. Position the drive pinion in an arbor press.
2. Place a wood block on the pinion gear and press it into the bearing until it contacts the bearing inner race.
3. Coat the roller bearings with a light film of grease to hold the bearings in place, and insert them in the pocket of the drive pinion gear.
4. Install the washer and snapring.
5. Press a new seal into the bearing retainer. Make sure that the lip of the seal is toward the mounting surface.
6. Press the bearing race into the retainer.

TRANSMISSION UNIT

Assembly

1. Press the front countershaft roller bearings into the case until the cage is flush with the front of the transmission case. Coat the bearings with a light film of grease.
2. Place the transmission with the front of the case facing down. If uncaged bearings are used, hold the loose rollers in place in the cap with a light film of grease.
3. Lower the countershaft assembly into the case placing the thrust washer tangs in the slots in the case, and inserting the front end of the shaft into the bearing.
4. Place the roller thrust bearing and race on the rear end of the countershaft. Hold the bearing in place with a light film of grease.
5. While holding the gear assembly in alignment, install the rear bearing retainer gasket, retainer, and bearing assembly. Install and tighten the cap screws.
6. Position the reverse idler gear and bearing assembly in the case.
7. Align the idler shaft so that the lock plate groove in the shaft is in position to install the lock plate.
8. Install the lock plate, washer, and cap screw.
9. Make sure the reverse idler gear turns freely.
10. Lower the rear end of the mainshaft assembly into the case, holding the first gear on the shaft. Maneuver the shaft through the rear bearing opening. With the mainshaft assembly moved to the rear of the case, be sure the third-fourth synchronizer and shims remain in position.
11. Install the roller type thrust bearing.
12. Place a wood block between the front of the case and the front of the mainshaft.
13. Install the rear bearing on the mainshaft by carefully driving the bearing onto the shaft and into the case, snapring flush against the case.
14. Install the drive pinion shaft and bearing assembly. Make sure that the pilot rollers remain in place.
15. Install the spacer and speedometer drive gear.
16. Install the rear bearing retainer and gasket.
17. Place the drive pinion bearing retainer over the pinion shaft, without the gasket.
18. Hold the retainer tight aginst the bearing and measure the clearance between the retainer and the case with a feeler gauge. End play in steps 19 and 20 below allows for normal expansion of parts during operation, preventing seizure and damage to bearings, gears, synchronizers, and shafts.
19. Install a gasket shim pack 0.010 to 0.015 inch thicker than measured clearance between the retainer and case to obtain the required 0.007 to 0.017 inch pinion shaft end play. Tighten the front retainer bolts and recheck the end play.
20. Check the synchronizer end play clearance 0.050 to 0.070 inch after all mainshaft components are in position and properly tightened. Two sets of feeler gauges are used to measure the clearance. Care should be used to keep both gauges as close as possible to both sides of the mainshaft for best results.

NOTE: In some cases, it may be necessary to disassemble the mainshaft and change the thickness of the shims to keep the end play clearance within the specified limits, 0.050 to 0.070 inch. Shims are available in two thicknesses.

21. Install the speedometer drive pinion.
22. Install the yoke flange, drum, and drum assembly.
23. Place the transmission in two gears at once, and tighten the yoke flange nut.

TORQUE SPECIFICATIONS
New Process 435

	ft. lbs.
Cover screws	20–40
Drive gear retaining screw	15–25
Front countershaft retainer screw	15–25
Front countershaft bearing washer screw	12–22
Flange nut	125
Mainshaft rear retainer screw	15–25
Rear countershaft retainer screw	15–25
PTO cover screws	8–12
Filler and drain plugs	25–45
Reverse idler shaft lock screw	20–40
Brake link shoulder screw	20–40

LUBRICANT CAPACITY

New Process 435	7 pt.

24. Shift the gears and/or synchronizers into all gear positions and check for free rotation.
25. Cover all transmissions components with a film of transmission oil to prevent damage during start up after initial lubricant fill up.
26. Move the gears to the neutral position.
27. Place a new cover gasket on the transmission case, and lower the cover over the transmission.
28. Carefully engage the shift forks into their proper gears. Align the cover.
29. Install a shouldered alignment screw with split washer in the screw hole second from the front of the cover. Try out gear operation by shifting through all ranges. Make sure everything moves freely.
30. Install the remaining cover screws.

New Process 445 Four Speed Transmission

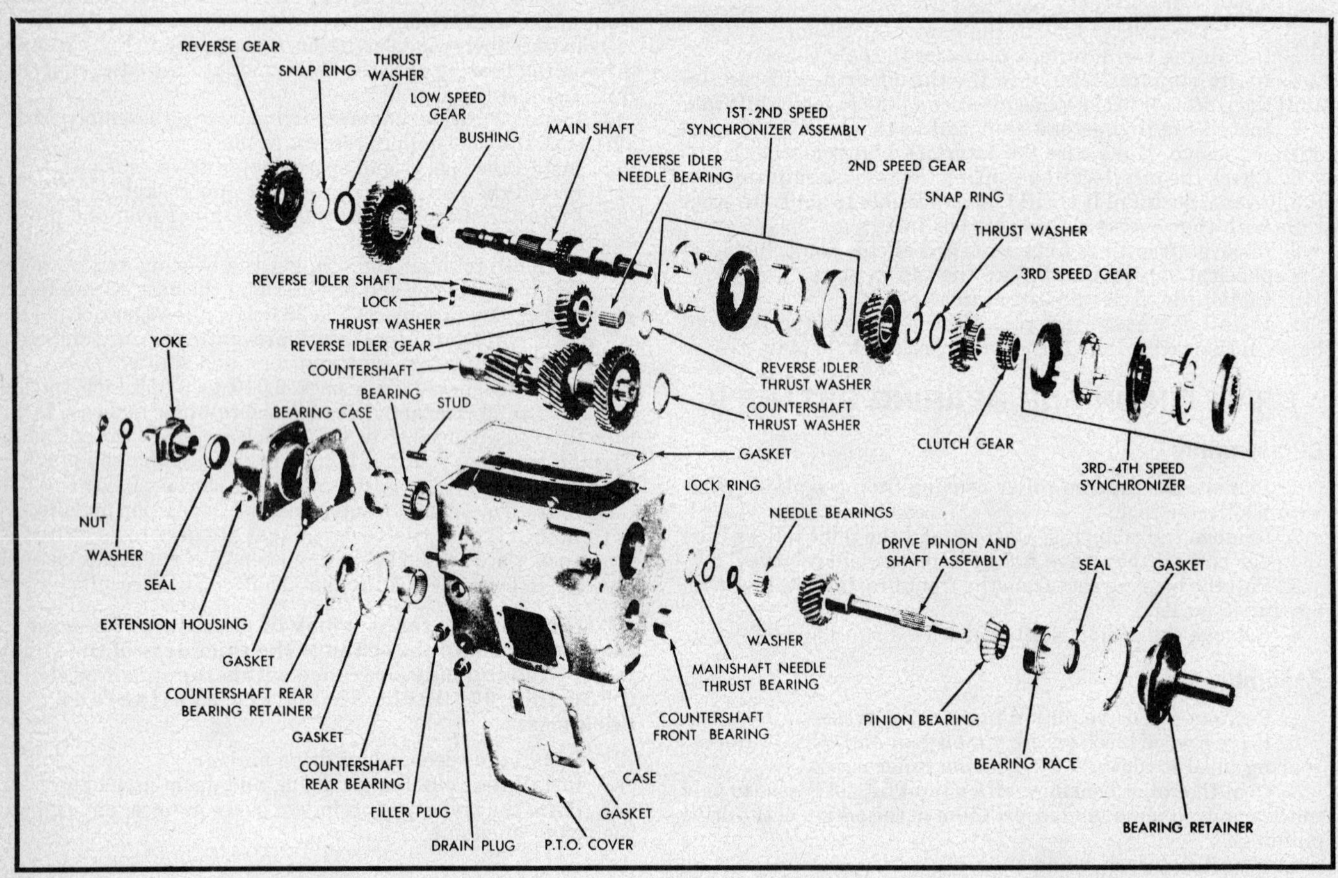

NP445 transmission—exploded view (© Chrysler Corp.)

TRANSMISSION UNIT

Disassembly

1. Place the transmission in a holding fixture and drain the lubricant.
2. Shift the transmission gears into neutral. Remove the gearshift cover attaching bolts. Note that the two bolts opposite the tower are shouldered to properly position the cover. Lift the cover straight up and remove.
3. Lock the transmission in two gears at once and remove the mainshaft nut and yoke.
4. Loosen and remove the extension housing bolts. Remove the mainshaft extension housing and the speedometer drive pinion.
5. Remove the bolts from the drive pinion front bearing retainer and pull the bearing retainer and gasket off.
6. Rotate the drive pinion gear to align the pinion gear flat with the countershaft drive gear teeth. Remove the drive pinion gear and the tapered roller bearing from the transmission.
7. Remove the mainshaft thrust bearing.
8. Push the mainshaft assembly to the rear of the transmission and tilt the front of the mainshaft up.
9. Remove the mainshaft assembly from the transmission case.
10. Remove the reverse idler lock screw and lock plate.
11. Using a suitable size brass drift, carefully drive the reverse idler shaft out the REAR of the case. Do not attempt to drive the reverse idler shaft forward. This will damage the transmission case and the reverse idler shaft.

12. Remove the countershaft rear bearing retainer.
13. Slide the countershaft to the rear, then up and out of the case.
14. Drive the countershaft forward, out of the bearing and the case.

SUBASSEMBLIES MAINSHAFT

Disassembly

1. Place the mainshaft in a soft jawed vise with the front end up.
2. Lift the third/fourth synchronizer and high speed clutch off the mainshaft.
3. Remove the third gear.
4. Remove the second gear snapring. Lift off the thrust washer.
5. Remove the second gear.
6. Remove the first/reverse synchronizer and clutch gear.
7. Install the mainshaft in the vise rear end up.
8. Remove the tapered bearing from the shaft with a suitable gear puller.
9. Remove the first gear snapring and thrust washer.
10. Remove the first gear.

Assembly

1. Lubricate all parts with transmission lubricant prior to assembly.
2. Place the mainshaft in a soft jawed vise with the rear end up.
3. Slide the first gear over the mainshaft, with the clutch gear facing down. Install the thrust washer and snapring.
4. Install the revese gear over the end of the mainshaft with the fork groove facing down.
5. Install the mainshaft rear bearing on the mainshaft with a sleeve of suitable size. Press the bearing on its inner race.
6. Install the mainshaft in the vise with the front end facing up.
7. Install the first/reverse synchronizer.
8. Install the second gear on the mainshaft.
9. Install the keyed thrust washer, ground side toward the second gear and secure with the snapring.
10. Install the third gear and one shim on the mainshaft.
11. Install the third fourth synchronizer over the mainshaft. Make sure that the slotted end of the clutch gear is positioned toward the third gear.

COVER AND SHIFT FORK UNIT

Disassembly

NOTE: The cover and shift fork assembly should be disassembled only if inspection shows worn or damaged parts, or if the assembly is not working properly.

1. Remove the roll pin from the first/second shift fork and the shift gate. Use a square-type or spirial wound "easy-out" mounted in a tap handle for these operations.
2. Move the first/second shift rail rearward and force the expansion plug out of the cover. Cover the detent ball access hole in the cover with a cloth to prevent it from flying out. Remove the rail fork, and gate from the cover.
3. Remove the third/fourth shift rail, then the reverse rail in the manner outlined in steps 1 and 2 above.
4. Compress the reverse gear plunger and remove the retaining clip. Remove the plunger and spring from the gate.

Assembly

1. Apply a thin film of grease on the interlock slugs and slide them into the openings in the shift rail supports.
2. Install the reverse shift rail through the reverse shift fork plate and the reverse shift fork.
3. Secure the reverse shift plate and the shift fork with the roll pins. Install the interlock pin in the third-fourth shift rail. Hold in place with a thin film of grease.
4. Slide the third/fourth shift rail into the rail support from the rear of the cover. Slide the rail through the third-fourth shift fork and poppet ball and spring. Secure the third/fourth shift fork with the roll pin.
5. Install the interlock pin in the first/second shift rail and secure with a light coat of grease. Slide the first/second shift rail into the case, through the shift fork and shift gate. Hold the poppet ball and spring down until the shaft rail passes.
6. Secure the first-second shift rail and gate with the roll pins.

TRANSMISSION UNIT

Assembly

1. Install the countershaft front bearing in the case using a 1 ³⁄₈ inch socket as a driver. Grease the needle bearings prior to installation. Hold the bearings in place with a socket of suitable size while seating the bearing retainer. Drive the retainer in until it is flush with the case.
2. Install the tanged thrust washer on the countershaft with the tangs facing out. Install the countershaft in the transmission case.
3. Install the countershaft rear bearing retainer over the rear bearing. Use a new washer and position the retainer with the curved segment toward the bottom of the case.
4. Install the reverse idler gear into the case with the chamfered section facing the rear. Hold the thrust washer and needle bearings in position.
5. Slide the reverse idler shaft into the case, from the rear, and through the reverse idler gear. Make sure that the lock notch is down and at the rear of the case.
6. Install the reverse idler shaft lock and bolt.
7. Place the mainshaft in a soft jawed vise with the front end facing up.
8. Install the drive gear on top of the mainshaft.
9. Measure the clearance between the high speed synchronizer and the drive gear with two feeler gauges. If the clearance is greater than 0.043 to 0.053 inch, install synchronizer shims between the third gear and the synchronizer brake drum. After the required shims have been installed, remove the drive gear from the mainshaft.
10. Install the mainshaft into the transmission case. Place the thrust washer over the pilot end of the mainshaft.
11. Position the drive gear so that the cutaway portion of the gear is facing down. Slide the drive gear into the front of the case and engage the mainshaft pilot in the pocket of the drive gear.
12. Slip the drive gear front bearing retainer over the shaft on gasket, and do not secure with bolts.
13. Install the mainshaft rear bearing retainer. Tighten the screws to specifications.
14. Hold the retainer against the front of the transmission case and measure the clearance between the front bearing retainer and the front of the case with a feeler gauge. Record the measurement and remove the bearing retainer.
15. Install a gasket pack on the front bearing retainer which is 0.010–0.015 inch thicker than the clearance measured in Step 14.Install the front bearing retainer and torque attaching screws to specification.
16. The end play float of the front synchronizer must be checked before installation of the transmission cover assembly. Measure the end play "float" by inserting two feeler gauges opposite one another between the third gear and the synchronizer

stop ring. Accurate measurement can be made only after all mainshaft parts are in place and torqued to specification.

17. If the front synchronizer end play "float" does not fall between 0.050–0.070 inch, shims should be added or removed as required, from between the third gear and the synchronizer stop ring.

18. Install the yoke retaining nut on the rear of the mainshaft. Shift the transmission into two gears at the same time and torque the yoke nut to 125 ft. lbs.

19. Shift the transmission into neutral.

20. Install the cover gasket.

21. Shift the transmission into second gear. Shift the cover into second.

22. Carefully lower the cover into position. It may be necessary to position the reverse gear to permit the fork to engage its groove.

23. Install the cover aligning screws (shouldered) and tighten with fingers only.

24. Install the remaining cover screws and tighten to specifications.

LUBRICANT CAPACITY

New Process 445	7½ pts.

TORQUE SPECIFICATIONS New Process 445

	ft. lbs.
Cover screws	20–40
Drive gear retaining screw	15–25
Front countershaft retaining screw	15–25
Front countershaft bearing washer screw	12–22
Flange nut	125
Mainshaft rear retainer screw	15–25
Rear countershaft retainer screw	15–25
PTO cover screws	8–12
Filler and drain plugs	25–45
Reverse idler shaft lock screw	20–40
Brake link shoulder screw	20–40

New Process 7550 and 7590 Five Speed Transmissions

TRANSMISSION UNIT

Disassembly

1. Mount the transmission in a housing fixture and remove the parking brake assembly.
2. Shift the gears into neutral.
3. Remove the shift cover screws, the second screw from the front on each side is shouldered with split washers for installation alignment.
4. Lift the cover and turn slightly either way to clear the shift forks, remove the cover.
5. Lock the transmission in two gears at once and remove the output flange nut.
6. Remove the brake drum and yoke assembly by tapping with a brass hammer.

NOTE: The drum and yoke assembly are balanced and unless replacement of parts is required, it is recommended that the drum and yoke be removed as a single unit.

7. Remove the brake band assembly bracket and support bolts and lock washers. Remove the brake band assembly as a complete unit.
8. Before removal and disassembly of the drive pinion and mainshaft, measure the end-play between the synchronizer stop ring and the fourth gear. Record this measurement for reference during assembly. The correct end-play is 0.050 to 0.070 inch. Note any difference from the limits so that corrective shims can be added or removed as required.
9. Remove the drive pinion bearing retainer.
10. Remove the drive pinion gear and ball bearing from the transmission by pulling on the shaft and rapping the face of the case with a brass hammer.
11. Remove the speedometer drive pinion and the mainshaft rear bearing retainer.
12. Place a brass drift in the front center of the mainshaft and drive the mainshaft to the rear.
13. Pull the rear bearing from the mainshaft with a suitable gear puller.
14. Once the mainshaft rear bearing has cleared the case, remove the rear bearing and the speedometer gear with a suitable puller.
15. Move the mainshaft assembly to the rear and tilt the front of the mainshaft up.
16. Hold the first/reverse gear and the fourth/fifth synchronizer to keep them from sliding off the shaft, remove the mainshaft from the transmission case.
17. Remove the reverse idler lock screw and lock plate.
18. Using a brass drift, held at an angle, drive the idler shaft to the rear while pulling.
19. Lift the reverse idler gear and thrust washers out of the case. Loose needle bearings are usually replaced. Never mix old and new bearings.
20. Remove the countershaft rear bearing retainer, gasket and bearing.
21. Tip the countershaft upward and remove it from the case. Remove the thrust washer from the front end of the countershaft.
22. Remove the countershaft front needle bearing from the case bore by tapping on the bearing cage from inside the case, with a suitable driver.

SUBASSEMBLIES DRIVE PINION

Disassembly

1. Remove the snapring and washer holding the pilot needle bearings in place and remove the bearings.
2. Relieve the staked area, remove the drive pinion ball bearing retainer nut and remove the ball bearing. The ball bearing retainer nut has left hand threads.
3. Remove the snapring from the drive pinion ball bearing.
4. Remove the seal from the drive pinion bearing retainer.

Assembly

1. Grease the loose pilot bearings to hold them in place and insert them into the pocket of the drive gear. Install the washer and snapring.
2. Press the large bearing on the pinion shaft. Make sure the bearing is properly seated.

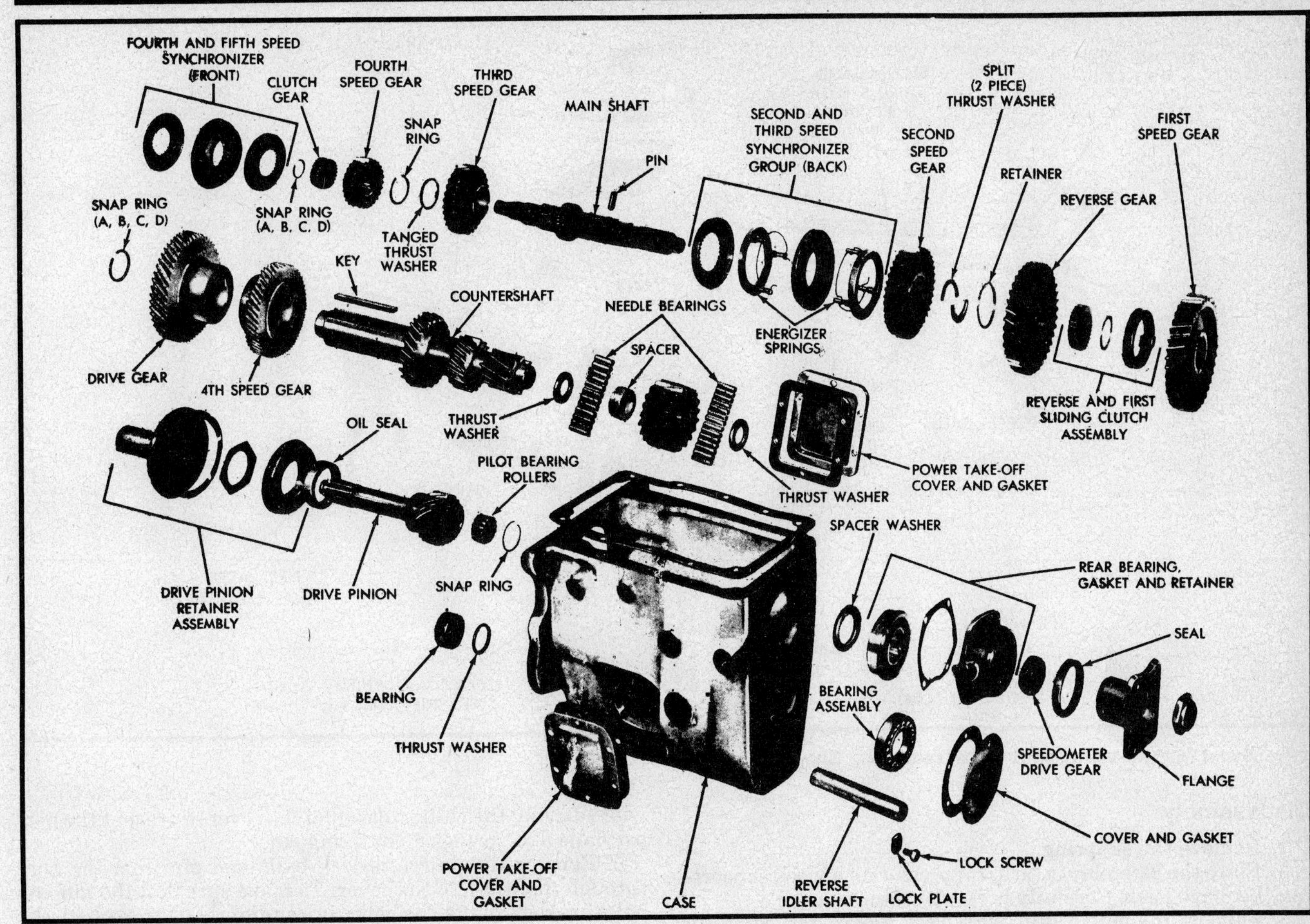

NP7550 and 7590 transmission—exploded view (© Chrysler Corp.)

3. Install the bearing retainer nut and tighten securely. Stake in place.
4. Install the snapring on the large bearing. Make sure the snapring is properly seated. The bearing retainer nut has left hand threads.

MAINSHAFT

Disassembly

1. Remove the spacer washer and the first gear from the mainshaft.
2. Remove the retaining ring and the first/reverse clutch and clutch gear assembly.
3. Remove the reverse gear.
4. Remove the second gear retaining thrust washer. This two piece split washer consists of two halves held in position on the mainshaft by a pin in a hole on the mainshaft together with a retaining ring.
5. Remove the second gear.
6. Remove the second/third synchronizer assembly. The second/third clutch gear is integral with the mainshaft.
7. Remove the snapring and the fourth/fifth synchronizer assembly and clutch gear.
8. Remove the fourth gear, retain the shims for assembly.
9. Remove the retaining snapring, tanged thrust washer and the third gear.

Assembly

1. Place the mainshaft, front end up, in a soft jawed vise.
2. Place the third gear on the shaft with the clutching teeth facing down. Install the tanged thrust washer and the one piece snap ring.
3. Place the fourth gear on the shaft with the clutching teeth up.
4. Check the end-play measurements recorded during disassembly and select shims to provide 0.050 to 0.070 inch end-play between the fourth gear and the fourth/fifth synchronizer.
5. Place the fourth/fifth synchronizer clutch gear, with the oil slots down, on the mainshaft. Select a snapring of the greatest possible thickness to eliminate all end-play of the clutch gear.
6. Remove the mainshaft from the vise and install the second-third synchronizer group. The synchronizer sleeve is marked "Front" for proper installation.
7. Place the second speed gear on the mainshaft.
8. Place the thrust washer retaining pin in the hole in the mainshaft and position the two thrust washer halves. Install the thrust washer retaining ring with the large diameter contacting the second gear.
9. Install the reverse gear.
10. Position the reverse/first clutch gear on the shaft. Install the retaining snapring. Select a snapring with the greatest possible thickness to eliminate all end-play of the clutch gear.
11. Position the sliding clutch on the clutch gear. Install the first gear on the mainshaft.
12. Place the spacer washer on the mainshaft.

COUNTERSHAFT

It is only necessary to disassemble the countershaft if inspection shows signs of damage or malfunction.

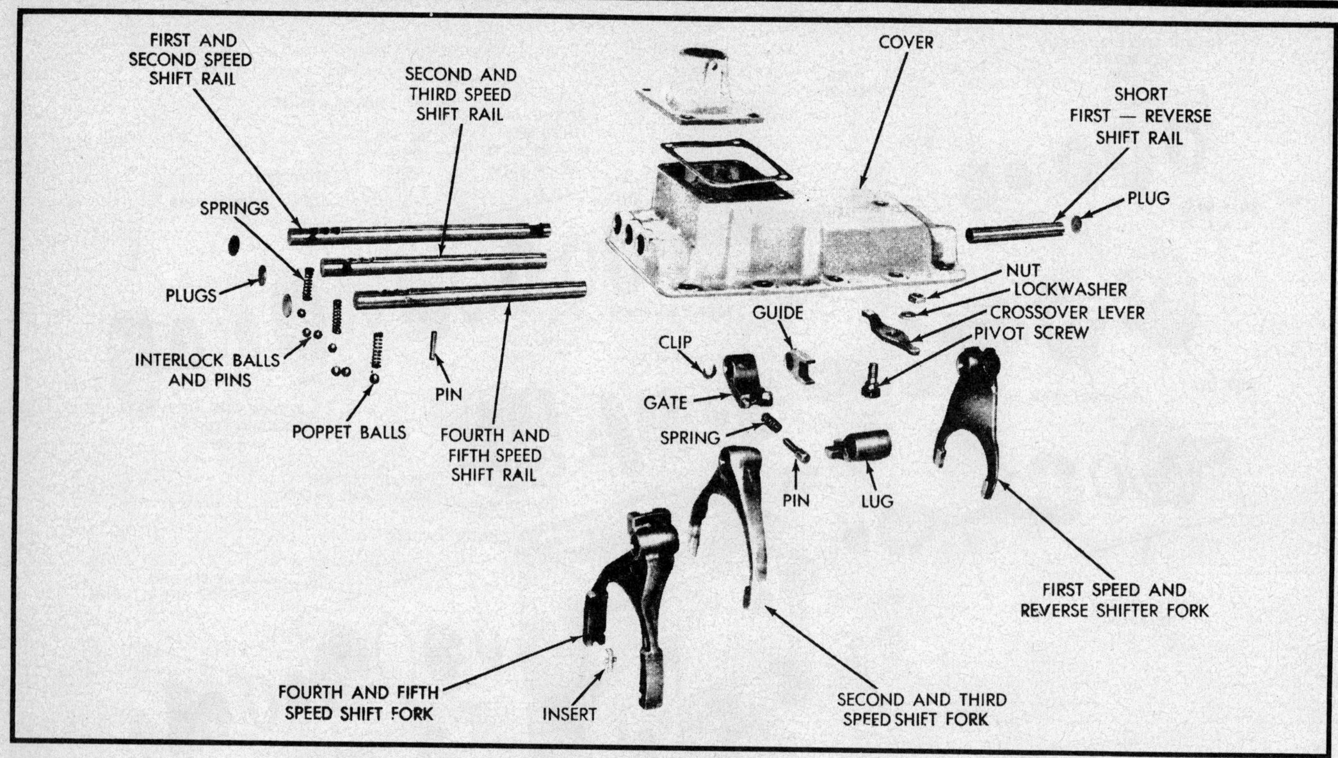

NP7550 and 7590 cover and shift fork assembly (© Chrysler Corp.)

Disassembly

1. Remove the snapring.
2. Place the assembly in an arbor press with a block supporting the drive gear. Carefully press the shaft out.
3. Support the fourth gear with wood blocks and carefully drive the shaft out.
4. Remove the key.

Assembly

1. Place the key in position on the countershaft.
2. Press the gears on the countershaft until properly seated. Make sure that the key does not move out of position as the gears are being pressed on the shaft.
3. Install the snapring on the countershaft. Select a snapring with the greatest possible thickness to eliminate all possible end-play.
4. Install the washer on the countershaft drive gear.

COVER AND SHIFT FORK UNIT

The cover and shift fork assembly should be disassembled only if inspection shows worn or damaged parts, or if the assembly is not working properly.

Disassembly

1. Mount the cover assembly in a soft jawed vise. Mark each fork and rail for location during assembly.
2. Place the shift forks in neutral. Remove the spiral roll pins from the shift forks and lugs. The roll pins may be removed by working with a "easy-out" mounted in a tap handle.
3. Drive the short first/reverse shift rail toward the rear and out of the shift cover. Remove the fork.
4. Remove the first/reverse shift rail pivot bolt and nut. Remove the crossover level.
5. Drive the fourth/fifth and the second/third shift rail forward and out of the shift cover. Remove the long first/reverse shift rail in the same manner. Place a cloth over the shift rails while driving the shift rails out of the cover to prevent the poppet balls and springs from flying out.
6. Remove the four interlock balls and pin from the bore through the width of the cover. To make sure that the pin and balls are out, shake the cover or tap lightly on a wood block.

Assembly

1. Push the long first/reverse shift rail into the cover bore far enough to permit the installation of the gates, poppet ball and springs and the roll pins. Move the shift rail into neutral position.
2. Place a small quantity of grease on the four interlock balls and pin.
3. Place two balls in the interlock bore. Move both of the balls toward the shift rail to seat the ball in the neutral notch.
4. Grease the interlock pin and place it in the hole located in the second-third shift rail. Install the second/third shift rail, gate, and fork as outlined in step 1. Move the rail into neutral.
5. Install the remaining balls into the interlock bore.
6. Push the fourth/fifth shift rail into the cover bore and install the shift fork as outlined in step 1. Move the shift rail into neutral.
7. Place the crossover lever in position in the cover in such a way that the short first/reverse shift rail, fork, and roll pin can be installed. Install the short first/reverse shift rail and parts.
8. Reposition the crossover level to mate in the notches in both the long and short first/reverse shift rails.
9. Install the pivot bolt through the crossover level and the cover. Install the retaining nut and washer.
10. Install new expansion plugs in the shift cover.

TRANSMISSION UNIT

Assembly

1. Coat all parts and assemblies with transmission fluid prior to assembly. This will insure that there is no damage during initial start up.

2. Install the front bearing assembly into the countershaft bearing bore in the case.

3. Grease the thrust washer and place in position in the transmission case.

4. Install the countershaft front bearing journal into the front bearing and seat it against the thrust washer. Be sure to keep the centerline of the countershaft aligned with the rear bearing bore during installation to prevent damage to the countershaft front bearing. Install the countershaft rear bearing assembly, gasket, and cover. Tighten the screws to specification.

5. Check the counter shaft end clearance, it should be 0.008 to 0.020 inch. Clearance can be adjusted by changing the countershaft rear bearing cover gasket.

6. With the reverse idler needle bearings held in place on each side of the spacer with grease, place the reverse idler gear and thrust washer in position in the case.

7. Drive the shaft through the case and gear using a hammer and a brass drift. Be sure that the needles stay in place and that the lock strap slot in the shaft will line up so that the lock strap, cap, and cap screw can be installed.

8. Install the lock strap on the shaft and tighten the cap screw securely.

9. Carefully lower the rear end of the mainshaft into the case while holding the first gear and washer on the shaft.

10. Place a hardwood block at the front of the mainshaft and drive the mainshaft bearing onto the shaft and into the case.

11. Install the drive pinion by carefully driving on the bearing outer race, forcing it into the case while guiding the front end of the mainshaft into the pilot bearing pocket. Make sure the bearing is fully seated.

12. Replace the retainer oil seal, pressing the seal into the retainer until the seal makes contact with its seat. Do not press beyond this point.

13. Install the bearing retainer and gasket and torque the screws to specification.

14. Install the speedometer drive gear on the output shaft.

15. Install the oil seal on the mainshaft flange, pressing the seal on until it makes contact with its seat. Do not press beyond this point.

16. Place the gasket on the output shaft bearing retainer, and install the retainer on the case. Tighten the screws to specifications.

17. Position the universal joint flange and brake drum on the output shaft.

18. Shift the transmission into two gears at the same time, and install the flange nut. Tighten to specifications.

19. Check the fourth/fifth synchronizer end-play "float" as follows. With all transmission parts in place, with the exception of the cover, place two feeler gauges between the fourth-fifth synchronizer and the stop ring. End-play should be 0.050 to 0.070 inch. If end-play is not within limits, shims should be added or removed, as required, from between the fourth-fifth synchronizer and the stop ring. Reassemble and recheck the end-play.

20. Check the second/third synchronizer end-play "float" as follows. With all transmission parts in place, with the exception of the cover, place two feeler gauges between the second/third synchronizer and the outer stop ring. End-play should be 0.070 to 0.090 inch. If the end-play is not within limits, install new parts as required. Shims cannot be used at this point. Reassemble and recheck the end-play.

21. Place the transmission gears and the shift cover in neutral.

22. Position the cover gasket on the transmission.

23. Carefully lower the cover into position on the transmission. Make sure that all shift forks engage their grooves correctly.

24. Install the shouldered aligning screws and split washers, in the second hole from the front, and tighten finger tight.

25. Install the remaining screws and tighten all screws to specification.

26. Shift the transmission through all gear ranges to be sure that the transmission is working properly.

LUBRICANT CAPACITY

New Process 7550 & 7590	18¼ pts.

TORQUE SPECIFICATIONS
New Process 7550 & 7590

	ft. lbs.
Cover screws	20–40
Drive gear retaining screw	15–25
Front countershaft retaining screw	15–25
Front countershaft bearing washer screw	12–22
Flange nut	125–175
Mainshaft rear retainer screw	20–40
Rear countershaft retainer screw	20–40
PTO cover screws	8–12
Filler and drain plugs	25–45
Reverse idler shaft lock screw	20–40
Bar brake screw	70–110
Bell housing screw	70–110
Brake link shoulder screw	25–45

New Process 540 and 542 Five Speed Transmissions

TRANSMISSION UNIT

Disassembly

1. Place the transmission on a stand or a bench.

2. Shift the transmission into the 2nd speed for the 540 and 3rd speed for the 542.

3. Remove the screws and remove the transmission cover by lifting upward and carefully rotating the housing counterclockwise. Note the location of the alignment screws. The alignment screws use split type lockwashers.

On the 542 transmission, it may be necessary to move the 1st speed gear back slightly allowing the offset curve in the shift fork to clear the rim of the gear.

4. Lock the transmission in two gears and remove the output flange nut, with the yoke and parking brake drum as an assembly. The drum and yoke are balanced and unless replaced it is recommended that the drum and yoke be removed as a unit assembly.

5. Before removal and disassembly of the drive pinion and mainshaft measure the end play between the synchronizer out-

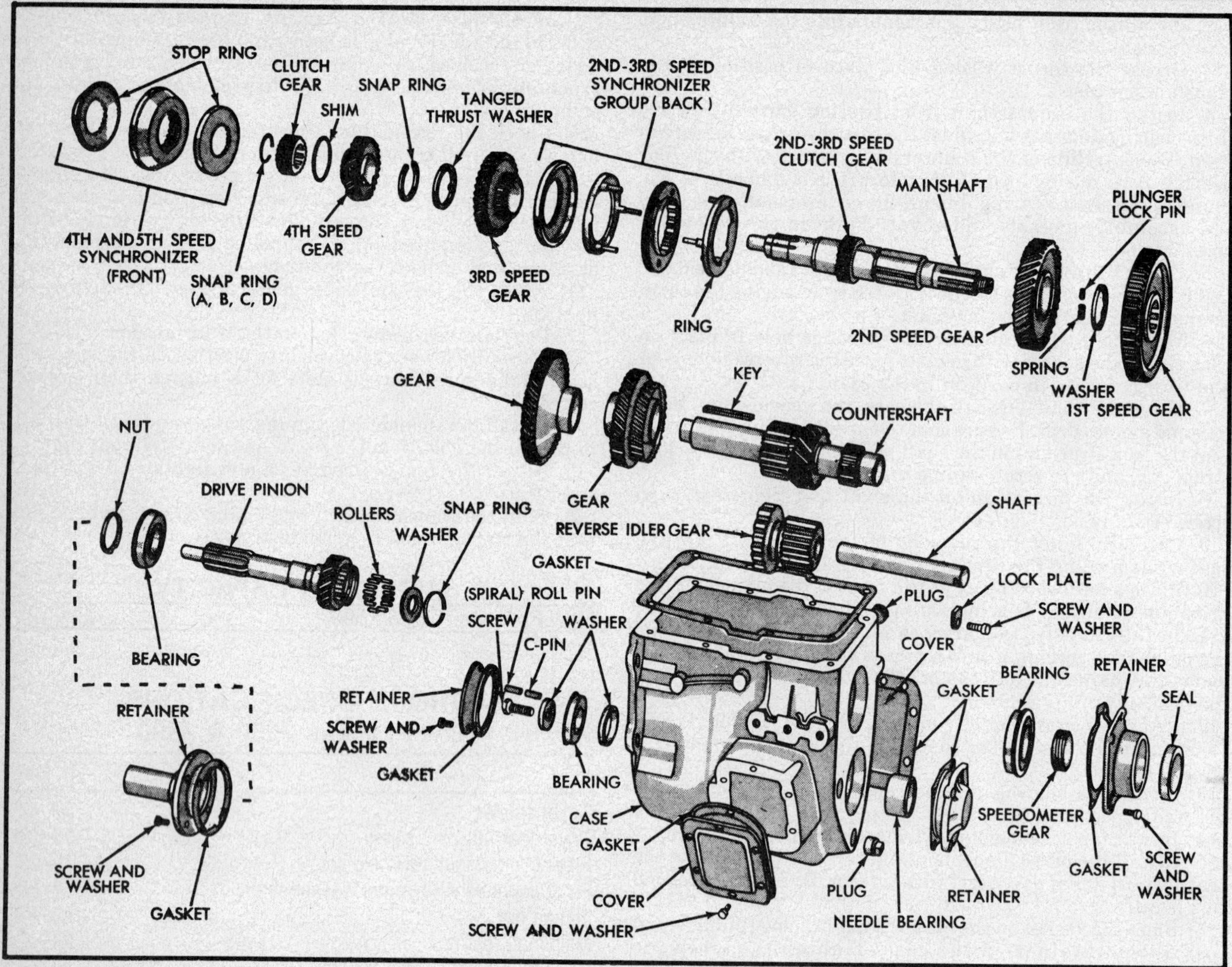

NP540 transmission—exploded view (© Chrysler Corp.)

er stop ring and the 4th speed gear. Record the reading for reference during reassembly and shim as necessary to obtain the ideal end play of 0.050 to 0.070 inch.

6. Remove the drive pinion bearing retainer.
7. Remove the drive pinion assembly from the case while pulling on the shaft and tapping with a small hammer.
8. Remove the mainshaft rear bearing retainer and speedometer drive gear.
9. Using a brass hammer, tap the front of the mainshaft rearward to drive the rear bearing from its bore then using a puller remove the bearing from the mainshaft.
10. Remove the mainshaft assembly from the case by lifting the front end upward and forward until the 1st speed can pass through the notch areas in the case.
11. Remove the reverse idler lock screw and lock plate.
12. With a brass drift held at an angle drive the idler shaft to the rear and pull the shaft.
13. Lift the reverse idler gear from the shaft.
14. On the 542 transmission, push the bearing retainer including the needle bearings and radial thrust bearing out the back of the case. On the 542 transmission, the countershaft must be laid in the bottom of the case to make easier the reverse idler gear removal.
15. Remove the reverse gear shaft with the integral gear, sliding gear and thrust washer.
16. Push the caged front needle bearing out of the case.
17. Remove the countershaft front bearing cover and gasket.
18. To prevent the countershaft from turning, insert a hammer handle between the gear set and the case.
19. Remove the spiral roll pin, screw, retaining washer and C-pin.
20. After removing the gear bearing retainer cap screws, drive against the front end of the countershaft with a brass drift, driving through the front bearing toward the rear, until the countershaft rear bearing and retainer cap comes out of the case. On the 542 transmission, the idler gear must be removed before the countershaft can be removed from the case.
21. Remove the bearing and cap from the countershaft and lift the countershaft from the case.
22. Remove the countershaft front bearing from the bore in the case by tapping the outer bearing race from inside the case.

SUBASSEMBLIES MAINSHAFT

Disassembly

1. Remove the 1st speed gear from the mainshaft.
2. Remove the 2nd speed gear by depressing the plunger lock, and rotating the splined thrust washer. On the 542 remove the snapring and thrust washer.
3. Remove the 2nd/3rd speed synchronizer unit.
4. Clamp the mainshaft in a soft jawed vise and remove the

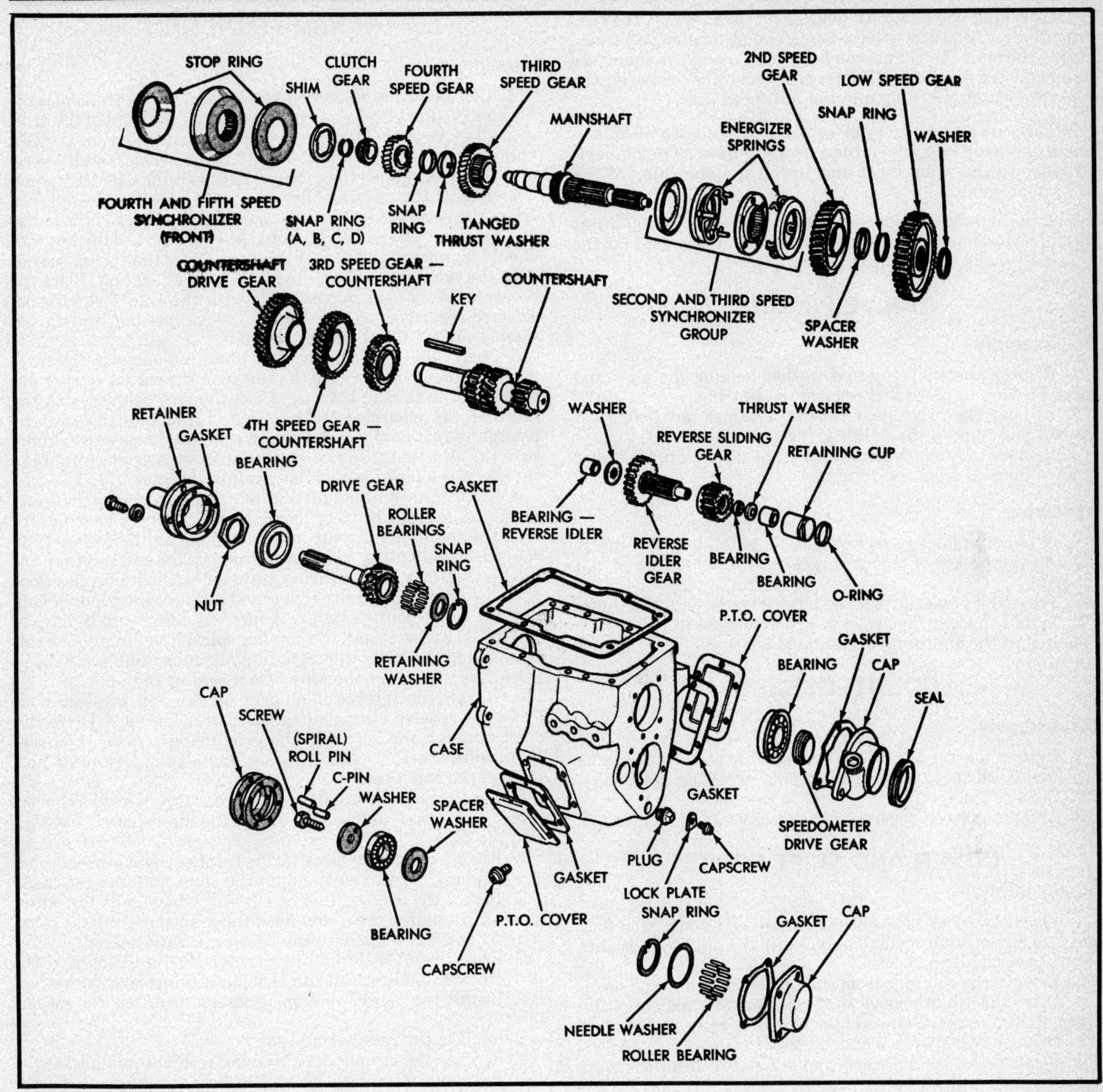

NP542 transmission—exploded view (© Chrysler Corp.)

4th and 5th speed synchronizer assembly, clutch gear snapring and clutch gear.

5. Remove the 4th speed gear and shim.

6. Remove the 3rd speed gear snapring and tanged washer. Remove the 3rd speed gear.

Assembly

1. Place the mainshaft with the forward end up in a soft jawed vise.

2. Place the 3rd speed gear on the shaft with the clutching teeth facing down. Install the one piece snapring and thrust washer.

3. Place the 4th speed gear on the shaft with the clutching teeth up. Refer to the end-play dimension recorded earlier and select shims to provide 0.050 0.070 inch end play between the gear and the front synchronizer.

4. Place the 4th/5th speed synchronizer clutch gear with the oil slots down on the mainshaft. Select a snapring of the greatest possible thickness to eliminate all end play of the clutch gear.

5. Remove the mainshaft from the vise and install the 2nd/3rd speed synchronizer group. The synchronizer sleeve is marked "FRONT" for proper installation.

6. Place the 2nd speed gear on the shaft. On the 540 lock in place by installing the plunger spring, plunger and splined washer. Push in the washer and lock by rotating until the splines are aligned. On the 542 install the thrust washer and snapring. Place the 1st speed gear on the shaft with fork groove facing the front end of the shaft.

7. Checking the end play float (0.050 to 0.090) at the rear synchronizer (2nd/3rd speeds) is mandatory and be performed during the mainshaft. This can be done by using two equal size feeler gauges diametrically opposite each other between the 3rd speed outer stop ring and the 3rd speed gear.

NOTE: To get the proper reading make sure all of the parts are properly assembled and the gauges are inserted close to the mainshaft and up on the shoulder of the 3rd speed gear.

8. If the end-play is less that 0.070 or more than 0.090 shims cannot be used and new component parts must be used for the assembly of the synchronizer group.

DRIVE PINION

Disassembly

1. Remove the snapring and washer holding the pilot and roller bearing in place and remove the bearing.
2. Remove the drive gear bearing retainer nut (left hand thread) and remove the ball bearing.
3. Remove the snapring from the drive gear ball bearing and remove the seal from the retainer.

Assembly

1. Grease the pilot rollers to hold them in place and insert them in the pocket of the drive gear. Install the washer and snapring.
2. Press and properly seat the large bearing onto the shaft.
3. Install the bearing retainer nut and stake in place.
4. Install the snapring on the large bearing.

COUNTERSHAFT

Disassembly

1. Place the assembly in a suitable arbor press with blocks supporting 3rd speed gear and carefully press the shaft out.
2. Remove the key.
3. Assembly is the reverse of the disassembly procedure.

COVER AND SHIFT FORKS

Disassembly

1. Place the cover in a soft jawed vise and mark each fork and rail for location at assembly. Shift the shifter rails into neutral position.
2. Remove the roll pins from the shifter forks and rail ends.
3. Drive the 4th/5th speed shift rails forward and out of the cover, then, the remaining center (2nd/3rd) rail.
4. Drive out the reverse and 1st speed rails.
5. Remove the six interlock balls and two interlock pins from the shift rail support.

Assembly

1. Drive the reverse rail into the housing only far enough to install the reverse gate, poppet ball and spring. Continue to drive the rail through the support until the reverse fork can be installed, then finish driving in the rail and install the welch plug.
2. Install the 1st speed rail in a similar manner.
3. Place a small quantity of grease on the six interlock balls.
4. Shift the reverse and 1st speed rails into neutral and install the interlock balls in the shift rail support.
5. Install the 4th/5th speed shift rail and fork and the 2nd/3rd speed shift rail, fork and rail end in the same manner described in step 1, then install the interlock pins.

TRANSMISSION UNIT

Assembly

1. Lay the countershaft in the bottom of the transmission. Make sure the spacer washer is in place in the front of the drive gear. The reverse idler gear should be installed on the 542 transmission, however on the 540 transmission, install the reverse idler gear after the countershaft installation is complete.
2. Install the reverse idler gear on the 542 transmission. Drive the reverse idler front bearing into the bore of the transmission case. The end of the front bearing with the thicker wall should be toward the rear of the case. Place the thrust washer with the tangs forward on the front of the idler shaft. Place the reverse sliding gear on the shaft with the shift fork channel forward, followed by the radial thrust bearing and thrust washer on the small end of the shaft.
3. Insert the reverse idler gear shaft assembly in the front needle bearing. Make sure the tangs on the thrust washer are seated in the slots in the case. Push the rear bearing with the retainer cup encircled by the oiled O-ring into the case far enough to install the lock plate, washer and cap screw. Make sure the oil hole is fully in view as seen looking down into the case, and the lock plate is flat against the case.
4. With the countershaft front bearing journal protruding through the front bearing bore, install the front bearing. Install the countershaft rear needle bearing on the 540 and the roller bearing on the 542. Install the gasket and retainer.
5. Install the front bearing retainer washer into position, with the large roll pin through it and in the corresponding hole in the countershaft. Install a $^5/_8$ inch cap screw and tighten to 100 to 135 ft. lbs. Install the smaller spiral lock pin into the roll pin leaving the lock pin protruding about one half screw head thickness to prevent the screw from coming out.
6. Install the reverse idler gear on the 540 transmission. Place the reverse idler gear in position in the case. Drive the shaft through the case and the gear using a brass hammer. Make sure the lock plate lines up. Install the lock plate and tighten the cap screw.
7. Carefully guide the first speed gear through the relieved areas in the case, as the rear end of the mainshaft is lowered into the case.
8. Place a hardwood block at the front of the mainshaft and drive the mainshaft bearing onto the shaft and into the case.
9. Install the drive pinion by carefully driving on the outer race while guiding the front end of the mainshaft into the pilot bearing pocket. Make sure the bearing is fully seated.
10. Press the oil seal into the retainer until it makes contact with its seat, then install the bearing retainer and gasket.
11. Install the spacer and speedometer gear on the output shaft.
12. Replace the retainer oil seal.
13. Replace the output shaft bearing retainer and gasket.
14. Position the universal joint flange and brake drum if used on the output shaft.
15. After shifting into two gears at one time, install the output shaft nut.
16. Replace the transmission cover. Place the transmission in third gear and rotate the 2nd/3rd speed synchronizer unit until the pins are aligned.
17. Move the reverse idler gear forward, then, position the housing above the case. Lower the cover into position while guiding the reverse fork through the case and pass the synchronizer pins. Move the first speed gear slightly forward as necessary to engage the fork in the groove in the gear.
18. Install the shouldered aligning screws and split lockwashers in the second hole from the front and tighten thumb tight. Install the remaining cover screws.

Saginaw Three Speed (GM–SM326–76mm)

GENERAL DATA

Type	3-Speed
Synchromesh gears	1st, 2nd, and 3rd
Models SM 326 and SM326 w/Overdrive	
Gar ratios	
1st speed	2.85:1
2nd speed	1.68:1
3rd speed	1.00:1
Reverse	2.95:1

The G.M. Corporation Model SM326 (Saginaw) is a synchromesh three speed transmission using helical constant mesh gears. The engagement of all gears except reverse is assisted by synchronizers.

TRANSMISSION UNIT

Disassembly

1. Remove side cover assembly and shift forks.
2. Remove clutch gear bearing retainer.

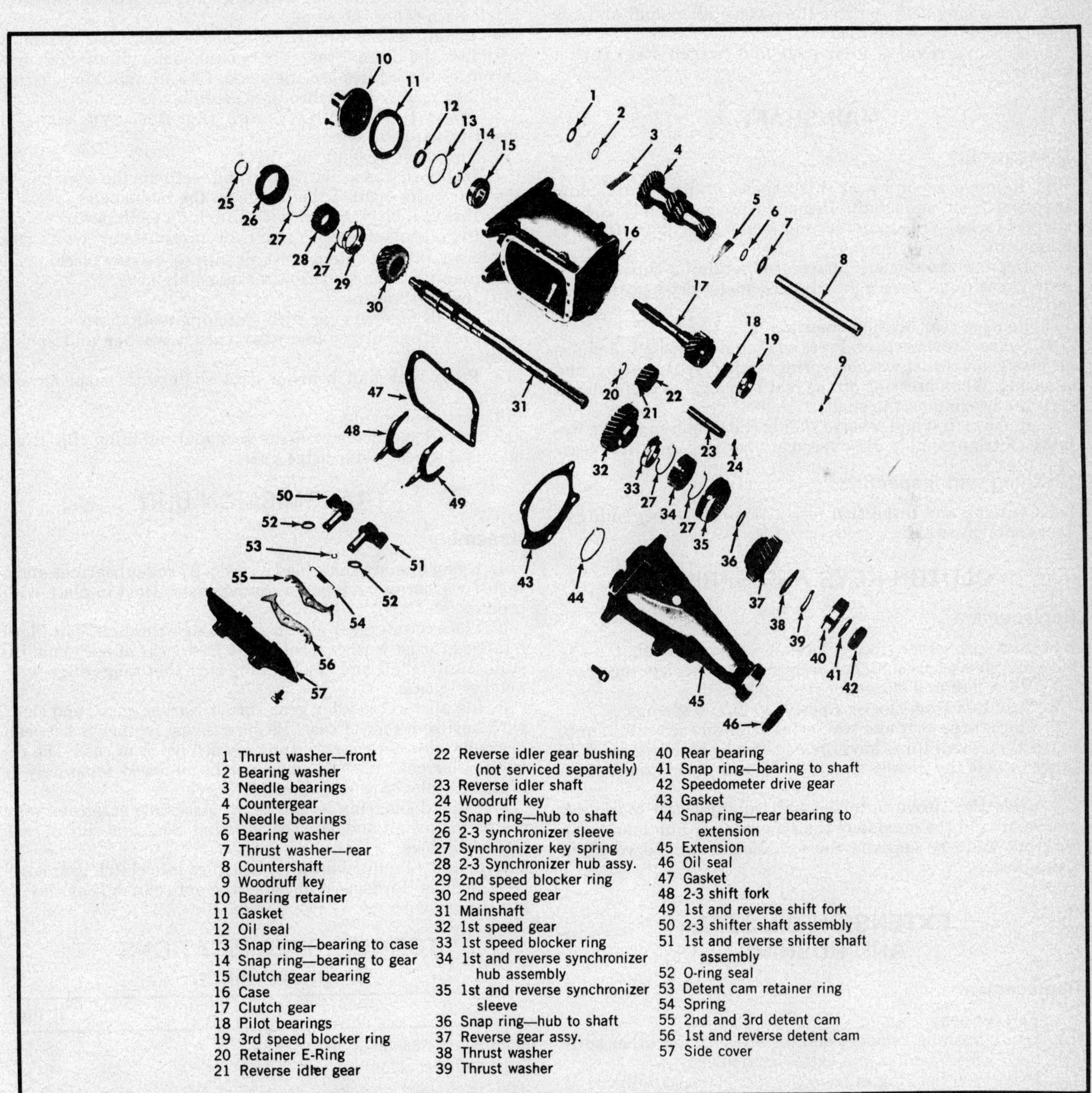

SM326 transmission components (© GM Corp.)

3. Remove clutch gear bearing to gear stem snapring. Pull clutch gear outward until a screwdriver can be inserted between bearing and case. Remove clutch gear bearing.
4. Remove speedometer driven gear and extension bolts.
5. Remove reverse idler shaft snapring. Slide reverse idler gear forward on shaft.
6. Remove mainshaft and extension assembly.
7. Remove clutch gear and third speed blocker ring from inside case. Remove 14 roller bearings from clutch gear.
8. Expand the snapring which retains the mainshaft rear bearing. Remove the extension.
9. Using a dummy shaft, drive the countershaft and key out the rear of the case. Remove the gear, two tanged thrust washers, and dummy shaft. Remove bearing washer and 27 roller bearings from each end of countergear.
10. Use a long drift to drive the reverse idler shaft and key through the rear of the case.
11. Remove reverse idler gear and tanged steel thrust washer.

MAINSHAFT

Disassembly

1. Remove second and third speed sliding clutch hug snapring from mainshaft. Remove clutch assembly, second speed blocker ring, and second speed gear from front of mainshaft.
2. Depress speedometer drive gear retaining clip. Remove gear. Some units have a metal speedometer drive gear which must be pulled off.
3. Remove rear bearing snapring.
4. Support reverse gear. Press on rear of mainshaft. Remove reverse gear, thrust washer, spring washer, rear bearing, and snapring. When pressing off the rear bearing, be careful not to cock the bearing on the shaft.
5. Remove first and reverse sliding clutch hub snapring. Remove clutch assembly, first speed blocker ring, and first gear.

Cleaning and Inspection

See Cleaning and Inspection instructions at the beginning of Transmission section.

CLUTCH KEYS AND SPRINGS

Replacement

Keys and springs may be replaced if worn or broken, but the hubs and sleeves are matched pairs and must be kept together.
1. Mark hub and sleeve for reassembly.
2. Push hub from sleeve. Remove keys and springs.
3. Place three keys and two springs, one on each side of hub, in position, so all three keys are engaged by both springs. The tanged end of the springs should not be installed into the same key.
4. Slide the sleeve onto the hub, aligning the marks. A groove around the outside of the synchronizer hub marks the end that must be opposite the fork slot in the sleeve when assembled.

EXTENSION OIL SEAL AND BUSHING

Replacement

1. Remove seal.
2. Using bushing remover and installer tool, or other suitable tool, drive bushing into extension housing.
3. Drive new bushing in from the rear. Lubricate inside of bushing and seal. Install new oil seal with extension seal installer tool or other suitable tool.

CLUTCH BEARING RETAINER OIL SEAL

Replacement

1. Pry old seal out.
2. Install new seal using seal installer or suitable tool. Seat seal in bore.

MAINSHAFT

Assembly

1. Turn front of mainshaft up.
2. Install second gear with clutching teeth up; the rear face of the gear butts against the flange on the mainshaft.
3. Install a blocker ring with clutching teeth down. All three blocker rings are the same.
4. Install second and third speed synchronizer assembly with fork slot down. Press it onto mainshaft splines. Both synchronizer assemblies are the same. Be sure that blocker ring notches align with synchronizer assembly keys.
5. Install synchronizer snapring. Both synchronizer snaprings are the same.
6. Turn rear of shaft up.
7. Install first gear with clutching teeth up; the front face of the gear butts against the flange on the mainshaft.
8. Install a blocker ring with clutching teeth down.
9. Install first and reverse synchronizer assembly with fork slot down. Press it onto mainshaft splines. Be sure blocker ring notches align with synchronizer assembly keys.
10. Install snapring.
11. Install reverse gear with clutching teeth down.
12. Install steel reverse gear thrust washer and spring washer.
13. Press rear ball bearing onto shaft with snapring slot down.
14. Install snapring.
15. Install speedometer drive gear and retaining clip. Press on metal speedometer drive gear.

TRANSMISSION UNIT

Assembly

1. Using dummy shaft load a row of 27 roller bearings and a thrust washer at each end of countergear. Hold in place with grease.
2. Place countergear assembly into case through rear. Place a tanged thrust washer, tang away from gear at each end. Install countershaft and key, making sure that tangs align with notches in case.
3. Install reverse idler gear thrust washer, gear, and shaft with key from rear of case. Be sure thrust washer is between gear and rear of case with tang toward notch in case. The reverse idler gear bushing may not be replaced separately it must be replaced as a unit with the gear.
4. Expand snapring in extension. Assemble extension over rear of mainshaft and onto rear bearing. Seat snapring in rear bearing groove.
5. Install 14 mainshaft pilot bearings into clutch gear cavity. Assemble third speed blocker ring onto clutch gear clutching surface with teeth toward gear.

TORQUE SPECIFICATIONS Saginaw-76mm

	ft. lbs.
Extension to case attaching bolts	35–55
Drain and filler plugs	10–15
Side cover attaching bolts	18–24
Clutch gear retainer bolts	18–24

6. Place clutch gear, pilot bearings, and third speed blocker ring assembly over front of mainshaft assembly. Be sure blocker rings align with keys in second-third synchronizer assembly.

7. Stick extension gasket to case with grease. Install clutch gear, mainshaft, and extension together. Be sure clutch gear engages teeth of countergear anti-lash plate. Torque extension bolts to 45 ft. lbs.

8. Place bearing over stem of clutch gear and into front case bore. Install front bearing to clutch gear snapring.

9. Install clutch gear bearing retainer and gasket. The retainer oil return hole must be at the bottom. Torque to 10 ft. lbs.

10. Install reverse idler gear shaft E-ring.

11. Shift synchronizer sleeves to neutral positions. Install cover, gasket, and forks, aligning forks with synchronizer sleeve grooves. Torque side cover bolts to 10 ft. lbs.

12. Install speedometer driven gear.

Spicer 5000 Series Five Speed Transmission

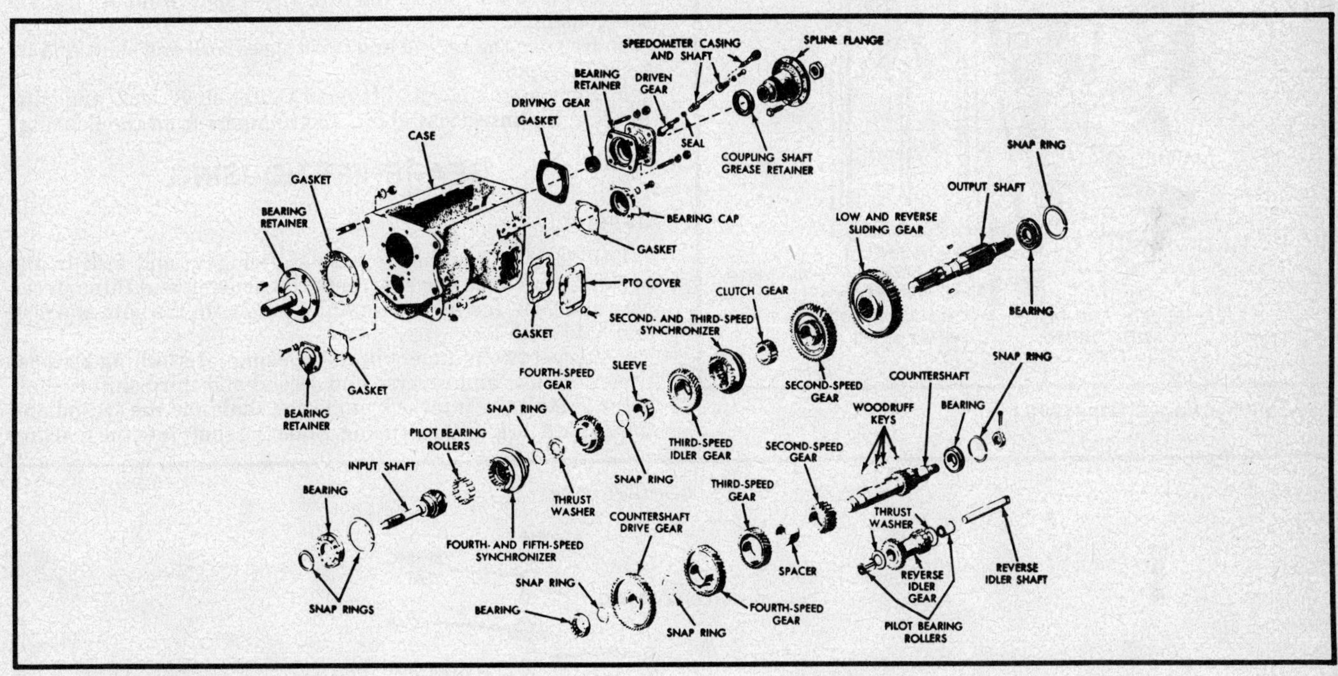

Spicer five speed transmission (© Dana Corp.)

The extra heavy duty five speed transmission (Spicer), is a manually shifted, synchromesh, helical gear type. Fifth forward speed is direct drive. A power take off base is located on the right and left side of the transmission case.

TRANSMISSION UNIT

Disassembly

1. Remove the gear shift housing from the transmission case. Remove the detent balls from the housing and shift the transmission into two gears.

2. Remove the brake drum and spline flange.

3. Remove the brake shoe assembly, the output shaft bearing retainer, speedometer driving gear, and spacer.

4. Remove the countershaft rear bearing retainer, gasket, and countershaft nut.

5. Remove the left side power take off cover.

6. Remove the input shaft bearing retainer and gasket from the case. Using a soft drift, drive the input shaft and front bearing from the case. Remove the pilot rollers from the drive gear.

7. With a hardwood or fiber block placed against the front side of the second-speed gear, drive the input shaft assembly rearward until the output shaft bearing clears the case. Be careful not to hit the second speed gear against the countershaft reverse gear. Remove the bearing from the output shaft.

8. When removing the output shaft from the case, slide off the first speed gear.

9. Using a puller, remove the countershaft rear bearing.

10. Lift the countershaft assembly out of the case.

11. Remove the countershaft front bearing retainer, gasket and bearing from the front of the case.

12. Remove the reverse idler gear, and bearings from the gear bores.

13. Remove any of the 14 output shaft pilot rollers which may have dropped into the case.

OUTPUT SHAFT

Disassembly

1. Remove the fourth and fifth speed synchronizer assembly snapring and thrust washer at the front of the fourth speed gear. Remove the gear.

2. Remove the snapring at the front of the third speed gear sleeve. The second and third speed synchronizer can then be removed by bouncing the front of the output shaft on a block of wood.

3. Press the output shaft out of the second and third speed synchronizer clutch gear and second speed gear.

COUNTERSHAFT

Disassembly

When replacing the countershaft or countershaft gear, press off one gear at a time. To remove the second speed gear use special tool.

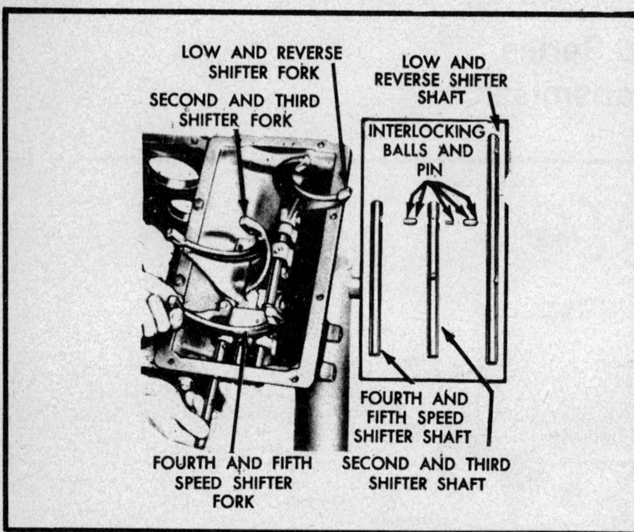

Gearshift housing (© Dana Corp.)

INPUT SHAFT

Disassembly

Remove the input shaft bearing only for replacement. Remove the retaining snapring, and press the bearing off the shaft.

GEARSHIFT HOUSING

Disassembly

1. Attach the gear shift housing to the transmission case. Cut the lock wire from the retaining screws in the shifter forks and gates.
2. Mark the shifter forks, shafts, and gates for correct assembly. Shift the shafts into neutral. Drive out the housing plugs at the front of the shafts.
3. Remove the fourth and fifth speed shaft from the front of the housing.
4. Remove the second and third speed fork and shaft and interlocking pin.
5. Remove the low and reverse shifter shaft, fork, and gate. Remove the interlocking pin and plungers from the housing.

GEARSHIFT HOUSING

Assembly

1. Place the low and reverse shifter gate and fork in the housing, and slide the shaft into the housing and through the gate and fork. Install the retaining screws in the gate and fork and hold with lock wire.
2. Install two plungers in the housing interlocking bore between the low and reverse and second and third shifter shaft bores. Install the interlock pin in the shaft and the second and third speed fork in the housing. Slide the shaft into the housing

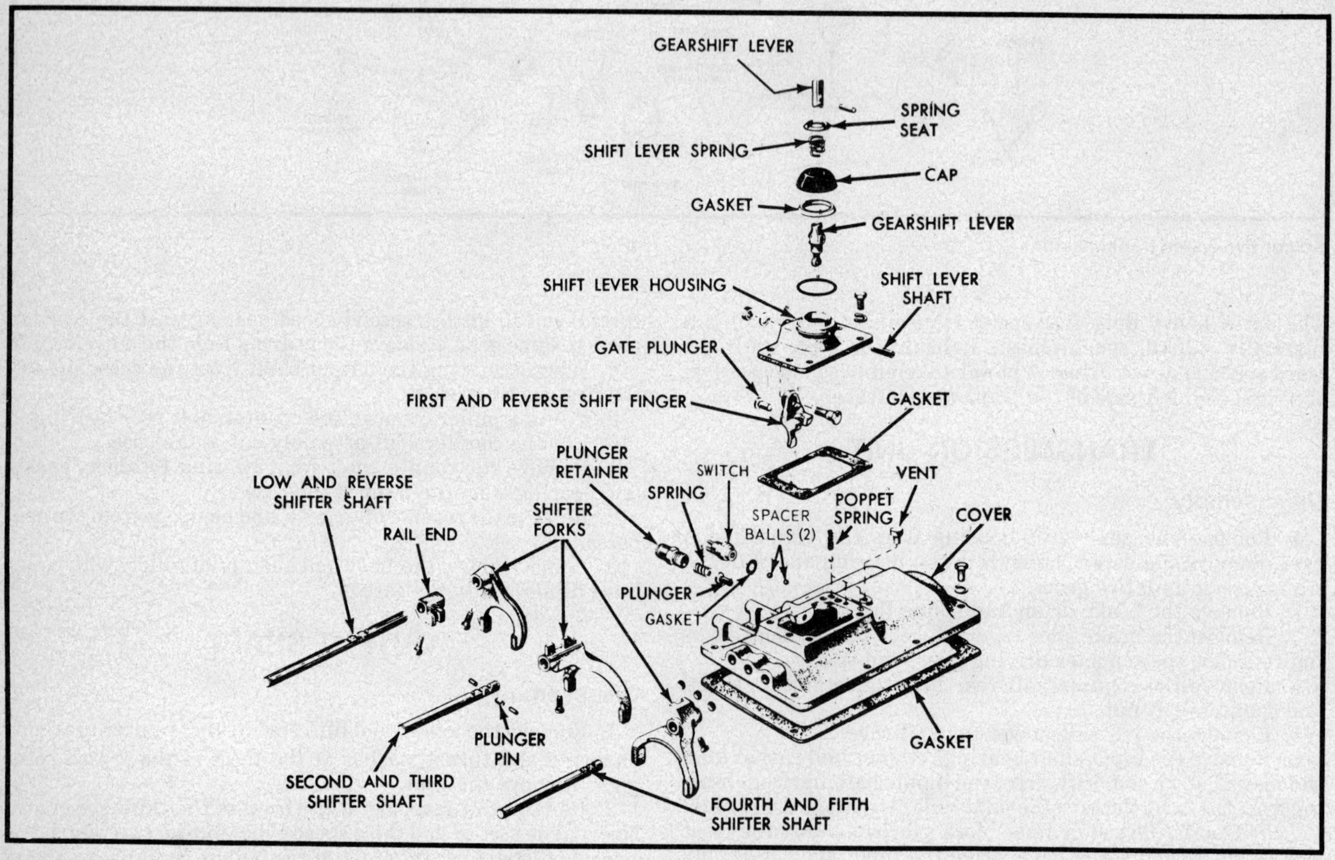

Gearshift housing components (© Dana Corp.)

and through the fork. Install the retaining screw, and lock wire.

3. Install the interlocking pin and plunger in the housing interlocking bore between the second and third speed and fourth and fifth speed shifter shaft guides. Install the fourth and fifth speed shaft and fork. Install the retaining screw and lock wire.

4. Check the interlocking system for correct operation and, using sealer, install the housing plugs. Remove the housing from the transmission case.

TORQUE SPECIFICATIONS
Spicer 5000 Series

Nomenclature		Nuts and/or Bolts and Torque Limits	
Bolt-gear shift lever tower to		3/8–16	7/16–14
gearshift housing		20–25	30–35
Bolt-clutch housing to		7/16–14	9/16–12
trans. case		30–38	70–90
		5/8–11	
		96–120	
Nut-U-joint flange to trans.		1.00–20	1½–18
output shaft		90–125	275–350
	1¼–18		
	225–275		
Nut—drum parking brake to		3/8–24	7/16–20
companion flange		35–45	50–70
Nut—bellcrank to trans.		9/16–18	
		70–90	
Bolt—lever assy. to trans.		3/8–16	
		20–25	
Nut—handbrake anchor bar			
to trans. case (5-speed			
extra-heavy duty only)			
Bolt—bellcrank to trans.			
Bolt—reverse lockout		11/16–16	
plunger retainer		80–100	
Bolt—countershaft rear bearing		5/16–18	7/16–14
retainer		25–30	45–55
		3/8–16	1/2–13
		35–40	67–70
Bolt—countershaft & reverse		5/16–18	7/16–14
idler shaft retainer		25–30	40–45
		3/8–16	1/2–13
		25–37	80–85
		3/8–16	
		18–25	
Bolt—gear shift		5/16–18	3/8–16
housing to trans. case		20–25	30–35
		3/8–16	7/16–14
		35–40	45–50
Bolt—power take off cover		3/8–16	
to trans. case		20–30	
Nut—countershaft bearing lock		1¼–18	
(5-speed extra h.d. &		350–450	
5-speed exclusive)			
Nut—countershaft bearing lock			
(5-speed exclusive h.d.)			
Bolt—input shaft bearing retainer to trans.		5/16–18	7/16–14
case		25–30	40–45
		3/8–16	
		25–30	
Bolt—countershaft		5/16–18	7/16–14
front bearing retainer		25–30	50–55
		3/8–16	
		25–35	

OUTPUT SHAFT

Assembly

1. Place the second speed gear onto the output shaft, with the clutch teeth facing forward.
2. Insert the two Woodruff keys in the output shaft and install the second and third speed synchronizer clutch gear.
3. Place the second and third speed synchronizer, and third speed gear and sleeve on the output shaft. Press the sleeve onto the shaft until it bottoms on the synchronizer clutch gear. The third speed gear sleeve slots must line up with the Woodruff keys in the output shaft.
4. Remove the assembly from the press and install the snapring at the front of the third speed gear sleeve.
5. Install the fourth speed gear, thrust washer, and snapring on the output shaft. Install the fourth and fifth speed synchronizer on the output shaft.

COUNTERSHAFT

Assembly

Install gears and spacer onto shaft and hold with the snaprings. Each gear takes a specific Woodruff key, so install them one at a time.

INPUT SHAFT

Assembly

Press the input shaft bearing onto the shaft using special tool.

TRANSMISSION UNIT

Assembly

NOTE: As a protection against scoring, coat all parts with transmission lubricant.

1. Tap the countershaft front bearing into the case and install retainer and new gasket. Line up the oil return holes in the retainer, gasket and case and torque the retaining bolts 50 to 55 ft. lbs. (30 ft. lbs. for smaller bolts).
2. Place the assembled countershaft in the transmission case into the front bearing.
3. Drive the countershaft rear bearing onto the countershaft and into the case.
4. Install the idler gear bearings, and gear in the case. Drive the idler gear shaft into position, and install the power takeoff cover.
5. Tap the input shaft and bearing into the case. Place the pilot bearing rollers in the input shaft.
6. Install the input shaft bearing retainer without a gasket and tighten the bolts. With a feeler gauge, check the clearance between the bearing retainer and the case to determine gasket size.
7. Install the bearing retainer and gasket, making certain that the oil drain-hole is in line with the gasket and case holes. Torque retainer bolts to 30 ft. lbs., 40 ft. lbs. for the larger bolt.
8. Install the low and reverse gear on the output shaft and place the assembly in the case. Drive the output shaft bearing into position.
9. Shift the transmission into two gears. Install the countershaft nut and torque at 350–450 ft. lbs. Install the countershaft rear bearing retainer and torque the $^{7}/_{16}$ in. bolts to 45 ft. lbs.
10. Install a new oil seal in the output shaft bearing retainer. Place the spacer and speedometer driving gear on the output shaft, and install the bearing retainer. Torque the bolts to specification.
11. Install the parking brake shoe assembly.
12. Install the brake drum and the spline flange. Torque the output shaft nut to specification.
13. Shift the transmission and gear shift housing into neutral, and install the gear shift housing and, using $^{7}/_{16}$ in. bolts, torque to 45 ft. lbs.

Spicer 6000 Series Five Speed Transmissions

GENERAL DATA

Make		Spicer
Type		5-Speed Synchromesh
Models		6852S, 6852K, 6852G, and 6853C
Clutch housing		S.A.E. #2
Gear ratios—all ratios are (to 1)		
Transmission Model	6852G	6852K
1st	6.70	6.70
2nd	3.52	4.02
3rd	1.97	2.49
4th	1.17	1.57
5th	1.00	1.00
Reverse	6.72	6.72
Transmission Model	6852S	6852C
1st	5.71	5.71
2nd	3.20	3.00
3rd	1.89	1.78
4th	1.15	1.00
5th	1.00	0.85
Reverse	5.73	5.73

This transmission is a 5 speed synchromesh helical gear design with direct drive in 5th speed on all models, except the 6853C, which has overdrive in 5th speed.

Engagement of all gears, except first and reverse, is aided by sleeve type synchronizers. All gears are of helical design, with the exception of first and reverse gears. Lubricant capacity is 17 pints.

TRANSMISSION MAINSHAFT

Removal

1. Remove clutch housing and clutch release mechanism as a unit.
2. Engage 2nd and 3rd synchronizer with mainshaft 2nd speed gear, and engage 4th and 5th synchronizer with mainshaft 4th speed or overdrive gear to lock transmission in two gears.
3. Remove companion flange or yoke retaining nut. Use puller to remove flange or yoke.
4. Remove speedometer driven gear and adapter (if used) from mainshaft rear bearing cap.
5. Remove mainshaft and countershaft rear bearing caps and gaskets.
6. Remove cotter pin and countershaft rear bearing nut.
7. Remove speedometer drive gear or spacer from rear end of mainshaft.

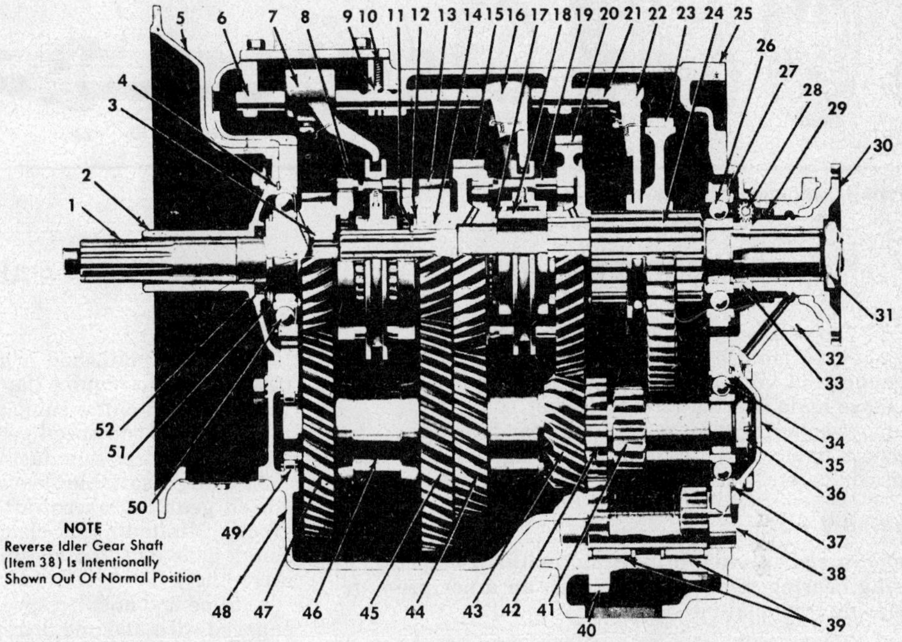

1 Main drive gear
2 Main drive gear bearing cap
3 Mainshaft pilot bearing rollers
4 Snap ring
5 Clutch housing
6 4th and 5th shift rod
7 4th and 5th shift fork
8 4th and 5th synchronizer
9 Poppet ball
10 Poppet spring
11 Snap ring
12 Thrust washer
13 Mainshaft 4th speed or overdrive gear
14 Mainshaft 4th speed or overdrive gear sleeve
15 Mainshaft 3rd speed gear
15 Mainshaft 3rd speed gear
16 2nd and 3rd shift fork
17 Snap ring
18 Mainshaft 2nd and 3rd speed clutch gear
19 2nd and 3rd synchronizer
20 Mainshaft 2nd speed gear
21 1st and reverse shift rod
22 1st and reverse shift fork
23 Mainshaft 1st and reverse sliding gear
24 Mainshaft
25 Shifter housing
26 Mainshaft rear bearing
27 Snap ring
28 Speedometer driven gear
29 Mainshaft rear bearing cap oil seal
30 Companion flange
31 Companion flange nut
32 Mainshaft rear bearing cap
33 Speedometer drive gear
34 Countershaft rear bearing
35 Countershaft rear bearing cap
36 Countershaft rear bearing nut
37 Snap ring
38 Reverse idler gear shaft
39 Reverse idler gear bearings
40 Reverse idler gear
41 Countershaft 1st gear teeth
42 Countershaft reverse gear teeth
43 Countershaft 2nd speed gear
44 Countershaft 3rd speed gear
45 Countershaft 4th speed or overdrive gear
46 Countershaft
47 Countershaft drive gear
48 Transmission case
49 Countershaft front bearing
50 Main drive gear bearing
51 Snap ring
52 Main drive gear bearing cap oil seal

NOTE
Reverse Idler Gear Shaft (Item 38) Is Intentionally Shown Out Of Normal Position

Spicer 6000 series five speed transmission (© Dana Corp.)

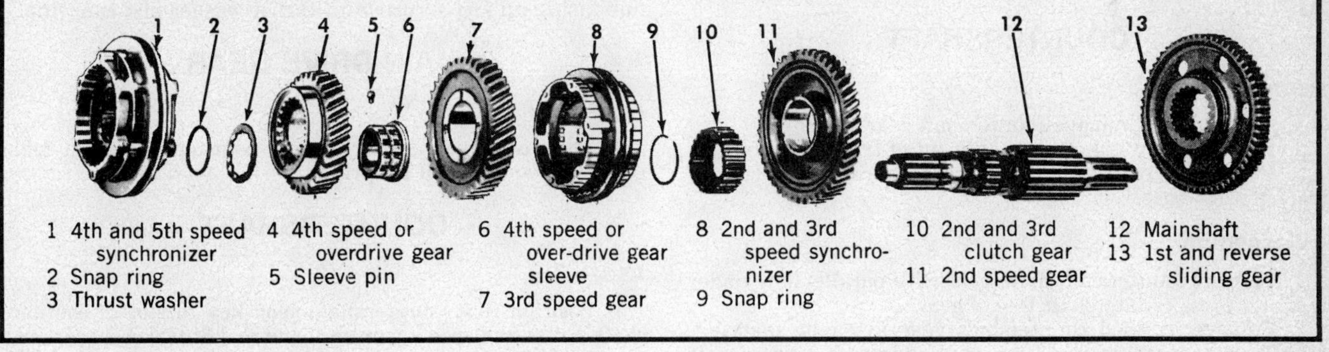

1 4th and 5th speed synchronizer
2 Snap ring
3 Thrust washer
4 4th speed or overdrive gear
5 Sleeve pin
6 4th speed or over-drive gear sleeve
7 3rd speed gear
8 2nd and 3rd speed synchronizer
9 Snap ring
10 2nd and 3rd clutch gear
11 2nd speed gear
12 Mainshaft
13 1st and reverse sliding gear

Mainshaft components (© Dana Corp.)

8. Remove mainshaft rear bearing snapring.
9. Using bearing puller, remove mainshaft rear bearing.
10. Remove mainshaft and gear assembly from the transmission case by clearing it from main drive gear and sliding assembly up and forward out of rear bearing bore.

MAINSHAFT

Disassembly

1. Remove the 1st and reverse sliding gear from mainshaft.
2. Remove 4th and 5th synchronizer.
3. Remove snapring and thrust washer.
4. Slide mainshaft 4th speed or overdrive gear from end of mainshaft.
5. Remove mainshaft 3rd speed gear and mainshaft 4th speed or overdrive gear sleeve.

NOTE: If necessary to press off gear and sleeve, shift 2nd and 3rd synchronizer into engagement with mainshaft 2nd speed gear and support under 3rd speed gear. Be sure to remove sleeve pin from the inside of 4th speed or overdrive gear sleeve.

6. Slide 2nd and 3rd synchronizer from mainshaft.
7. Remove snapring from 2nd and 3rd speed clutch gear.
8. Support mainshaft 2nd speed gear under arbor press and press mainshaft out of 2nd and 3rd speed clutch gear and 2nd speed gear.

Countershaft components (© Dana Corp.)

MAINDRIVE GEAR

Removal

1. Remove 14 mainshaft pilot bearing rollers which may have remained in cavity of main drive gear.
2. Remove main bearing cap and gasket.
3. Remove snapring from main drive gear bearing.
4. Remove main drive gear and bearing assembly from transmission case.

Disassembly

1. Remove main drive gear bearing retaining snapring.
2. Using bearing remover plates with an arbor press, remove bearing from main drive gear.

REVERSE IDLER GEAR

Removal

NOTE: When removing the reverse idler gear shaft, support the gear to prevent it from being damaged.

1. Using remover tool, remove reverse idler gear shaft, gear and bearings.

COUNTERSHAFT

Removal

1. Using puller, remove countershaft rear bearing.
2. Lift the countershaft assembly out of transmission case.
3. Press or drive countershaft front bearing from bore of transmission case.

Disassembly

1. Support countershaft drive gear with parallel bars under hub and press countershaft free of gear.
2. Remove exposed countershaft gear key and snapring. Support 4th speed or overdrive gear and press countershaft free of gear.
3. Follow the same procedure and remove 2nd and 3rd speed gear.
4. Remove the remaining countershaft gear key.

SUBASSEMBLIES

Assembly

Cleanliness is of the utmost importance. The transmission should be rebuilt in a clean working area. All parts, except those actually being worked on should be covered with clean lint-free paper. Avoid nicking, marring, or burring all surfaces.

NOTE: Coat all thrust washers, splines of shafts, and bores of all gears with lubricant to provide initial lubrication thus preventing scoring or galling.

MAINSHAFT

Assembly

1. Position mainshaft in a soft jawed vise, front end up. Fit of new parts may require the use of an arbor press. If so, set up vertically and follow same procedure.
2. Position 2nd speed gear on mainshaft with clutch teeth and synchronizer cone facing up.
3. Using a suitable sleeve, press or drive 2nd and 3rd speed clutch gear on mainshaft. Install snapring in mainshaft groove. Minimum end clearance between 2nd and 3rd speed clutch gear and 2nd speed gear should be 0.004 in. Correct accordingly.
4. Slide 2nd and 3rd speed synchronizer on mainshaft until engaged with 2nd and 3rd speed clutch gear. The 2nd and 3rd speed synchronizer is often assembled backward on the mainshaft. Make sure that the long hub on synchronizer clutch gear faces the 2nd speed gear.
5. Place 3rd speed gear on mainshaft with clutch teeth and synchronizer cone facing downward.
6. Assemble sleeve pin to 4th speed or overdrive gear sleeve with head of pin inside sleeve, with flanged end of sleeve facing the 3rd speed gear, align sleeve pin with splines and press on the mainshaft.
7. Place 4th speed or overdrive gear on sleeve with clutch hub facing up and secure with thrust washer and snapring.

MAIN DRIVE GEAR

Assembly

1. Press or drive main drive gear bearing onto main drive gear shaft and install snapring.

COUNTERSHAFT

Assembly

1. Position first countershaft gear key in slot of countershaft. Press 2nd speed gear and, 2nd and 3rd gear spacer onto countershaft.
2. Install the remaining countershaft gear keys. It may be necessary to dress the keys with a file.
3. Press 3rd speed gear on the countershaft, followed by 4th speed gear, a snapring and drive gear secured by a snapring.

MAINSHAFT

Installation

1. Place mainshaft 1st and reverse sliding gear at an angle in the rear of the transmission case with shift fork collar facing toward front of case.
2. Place 4th and 5th synchronizer on mainshaft. Shift synchronizer clutch collar into engagement with mainshaft 4th speed or overdrive gear to help lock synchronizer in place during installation in case.

3. Lower rear of mainshaft into case, through 1st and reverse sliding gear and out mainshaft rear bearing bore. There must be fourteen pilot bearing rollers in the main drive gear pocket.

4. Lower front of mainshaft to mesh with countershaft gears. Slide rear of mainshaft into pocket of main drive gear.

5. Slide rear bearing onto mainshaft with snapring facing the rear.

6. Tap bearing into case bore with its snapring flush with rear of case.

7. Press speedometer drive gear or spacer onto the mainshaft against bearing. Install new oil seal in mainshaft rear bearing cap.

8. Install gasket with sealing cement and mainshaft rear bearing cap and torque cap screws 35 to 40 ft. lbs. Install speedometer driven gear (when used) through opening in mainshaft rear bearing cap.

9. Engage 2nd and 3rd synchronizer with mainshaft 2nd speed gear, and 4th and 5th synchronizer with mainshaft 4th speed or overdrive gear to lock transmission in two gears.

10. Install companion flange or yoke on mainshaft and secure with a washer and nut at a torque of 320 to 350 ft. lbs.

11. Remove rear bearing cap from countershaft and torque bearing nut to 320 to 350 ft. lbs. and secure with cotter pin.

12. Install gasket and countershaft rear bearing (with sealing cement) and torqe cap screws to 35 to 40 ft. lbs. The projection on the countershaft rear bearing cap locks the reverse idler gear shaft into proper position.

13. Rotate main drive gear to check for free rotation of all gears and shafts.

14. Use pressure type oil can, filled with transmission lubricant (S.A.E. 50 engine oil of good quality) to force oil through holes and end slots of all mainshaft gears to open oil passageways. Using the pressure type oil can, spray gear teeth with transmission lubricant to provide initial lubrication and to prevent corrosion.

MAIN DRIVE GEAR

Installation

1. Install main drive gear and bearing from inside the transmission case, by tapping bearing through case bore.

2. Install snapring on outer race of bearing. Tap bearing rearward, so snapring is flush with case. Install new oil seal in main drive gear bearing cap.

3. Install gasket (with sealing cement) and main drive gear bearing cap to transmission case and torque 60 to 80 ft. lbs. Be sure the oil passages in the bearing cap, gasket and transmission case are all aligned.

4. Coat the pocket of main drive gear with light weight ball and roller bearing grease.

5. Place the fourteen pilot bearing rollers in main drive gear pocket.

REVERSE IDLER GEAR

Installation

1. Install reverse idler gear bearings into gear and install in transmission case, with large gear on idler gear toward front of case. Mesh idler gear with countershaft and align bore of bearings with hole in transmission case.

2. Insert reverse idler gear shaft in rear of case, noting that "flat" on shaft is squared toward countershaft so that it can be locked by rear bearing cap.

3. Set countershaft rear bearing cap in place to check lock of reverse idler shaft. Finger tighten bearing cap screws to prevent countershaft from moving during installation of mainshaft.

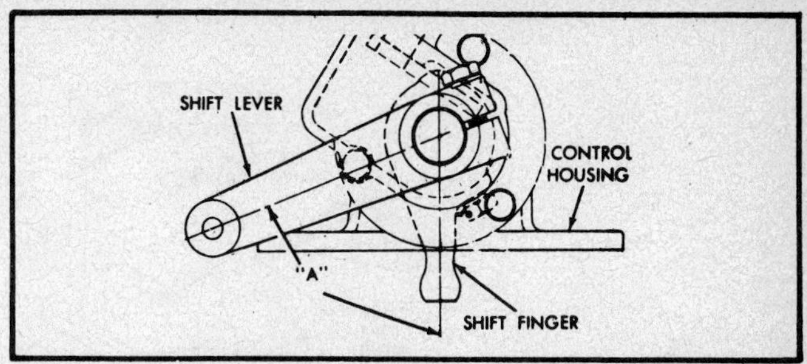

Rod type remote control adjustment (© Dana Corp.)

COUNTERSHAFT

Installation

1. Press countershaft front bearing on front of countershaft.

2. Lower countershaft assembly into case, guiding rear end of shaft out through rear of case.

3. Guide countershaft front bearing into countershaft front bearing bore.

4. Place two strips of flat steel stock, approximately 3/8 inch thick, between countershaft drive gear and wall of case.

5. Seat bearing on shaft (should be tight fit) then remove the two steel strips and tap bearing into bore seating snapring against case.

6. Hand tighten countershaft rear bearing nut.

REMOTE CONTROL ASSEMBLY

Removal

NOTE: The Spicer 6000 transmission uses two different remote control assemblies: prop shaft type and rod type.

1. Remove retainer, plunger pin spring, and plunger.

2. Remove remote control assembly from transmission as described below. Tilt the remote control assembly slightly to the left during removal to prevent the plunger from falling into the transmission.

3. Remove the plunger from the 1st and reverse shift finger.

Installation

1. Coat remote control assembly position on shifter housing.

2. Position plunger in 1st and reverse shift finger; then carefully install remote control assembly as shown, keeping the assembly slightly tilted to the left to prevent the plunger from falling into transmission.

3. Install plunger pin, plunger pin spring, and retainer.

4. Install remote control assembly-to-shifter housing attaching parts. Tighten cap screws firmly.

CONTROL TOWER

Installation

Install control tower as described below only when the transmission is going into storage.

1. Coat gasket with sealing cement and position on shifter housing.

2. Position plunger in 1st and reverse shift finger, then place the assembly and new gasket (with cement) on the shifter housing.

3. Install plunger, plunger spring, and plunger retainer and tighten down the tower with washers and capscrews.

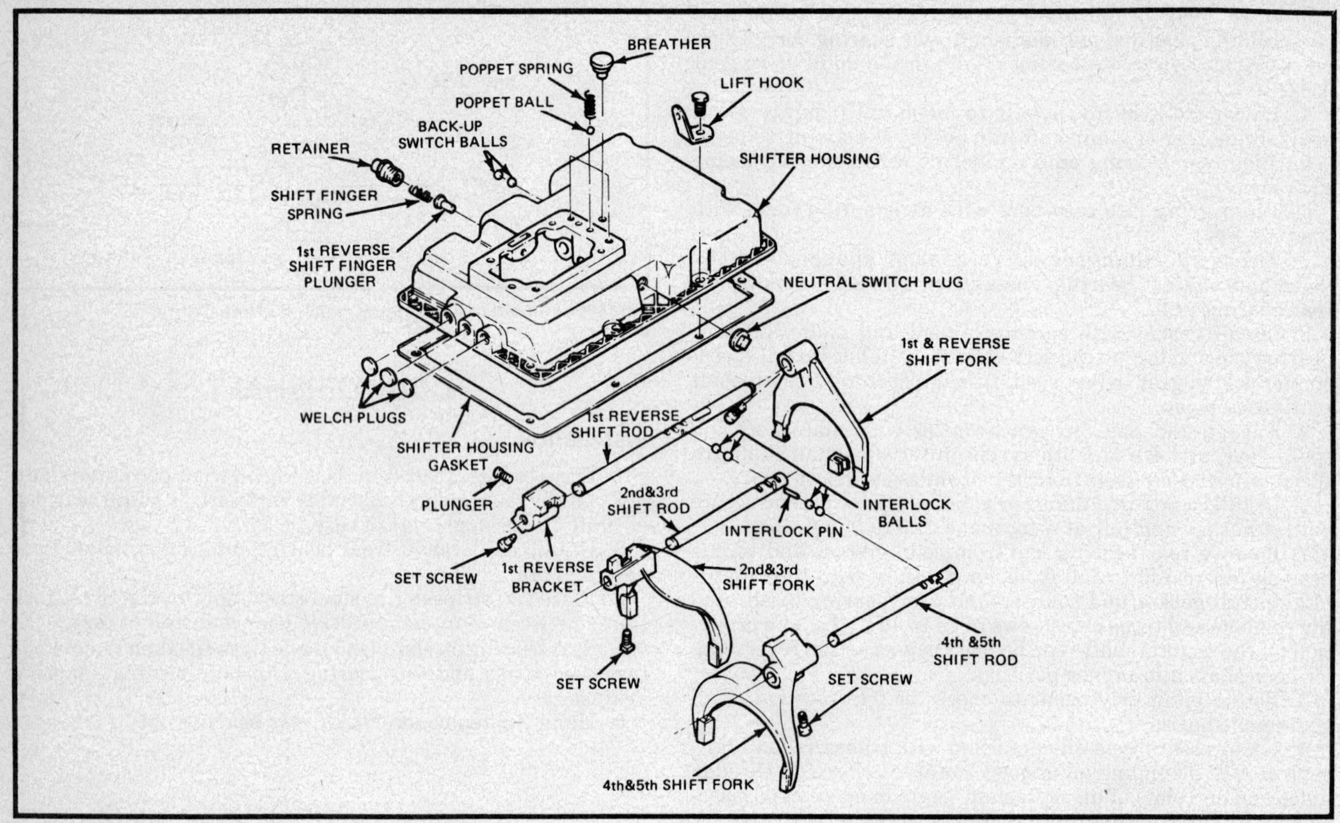

Shifter housing—exploded view (© Dana Corp.)

SHIFTER HOUSING

Removal

NOTE: The Spicer 6000 transmission uses a forward control shifter housing and a center control shifter housing.

1. Remove shifter housing to transmission case attaching parts. Carefully remove forward control shifter housing to prevent loss of the three poppet balls and springs.
2. Carefully remove shifter housing from the case.

Installation

NOTE: Make certain that shift forks and transmission clutch collars are in neutral position.

1. Carefully position shifter housing and gasket (use cement) on transmission case and make sure all three shift forks are in their corresponding shift collar and tighten down.

TORQUE SPECIFICATIONS
Spicer 6000 Series

Location	ft. lbs.
Shift fork set screws	45–50
Main drive gear bearing cap retaining cap screws	60–80
Mainshaft rear bearing cap retaining cap screws	35–40
Mainshaft flange or yoke retaining nut	320–350
Countershaft rear bearing retaining nut	320–350
Countershaft rear bearing cap retaining cap screws	35–40
Clutch housing retaining cap screws	90–95

2. Use small pry bar and check movement of each shift rod for proper shift action. Return shift rods to neutral position. On transmissions using the forward control shifter housing, place the three poppet balls and springs in the shifter housing.

Spicer 50 and 60 Series Five Speed

MAIN TRANSMISSION

Disassembly

1. Remove the shifter housing from the transmission. Lift the housing straight up and use caution not to lose the poppet balls and springs.
2. Use a pry bar and engage the 2nd/3rd speed synchronizer with the 2nd/3rd speed gear, and the 4th/5th speed synchronizer with the 4th/5th speed gear. Lock the transmission in two gears.
3. Using a suitable puller, remove the flange retaining nut from the mainshaft and remove the output flange.
4. Remove the mainshaft rear bearing capscrews and pry the bearing cap from the case. If either bearing or seal needs replacing tap out using a drift or a punch.
5. Remove the speedometer gear from the mainshaft.
6. Remove the capscrews retaining the drive gear front

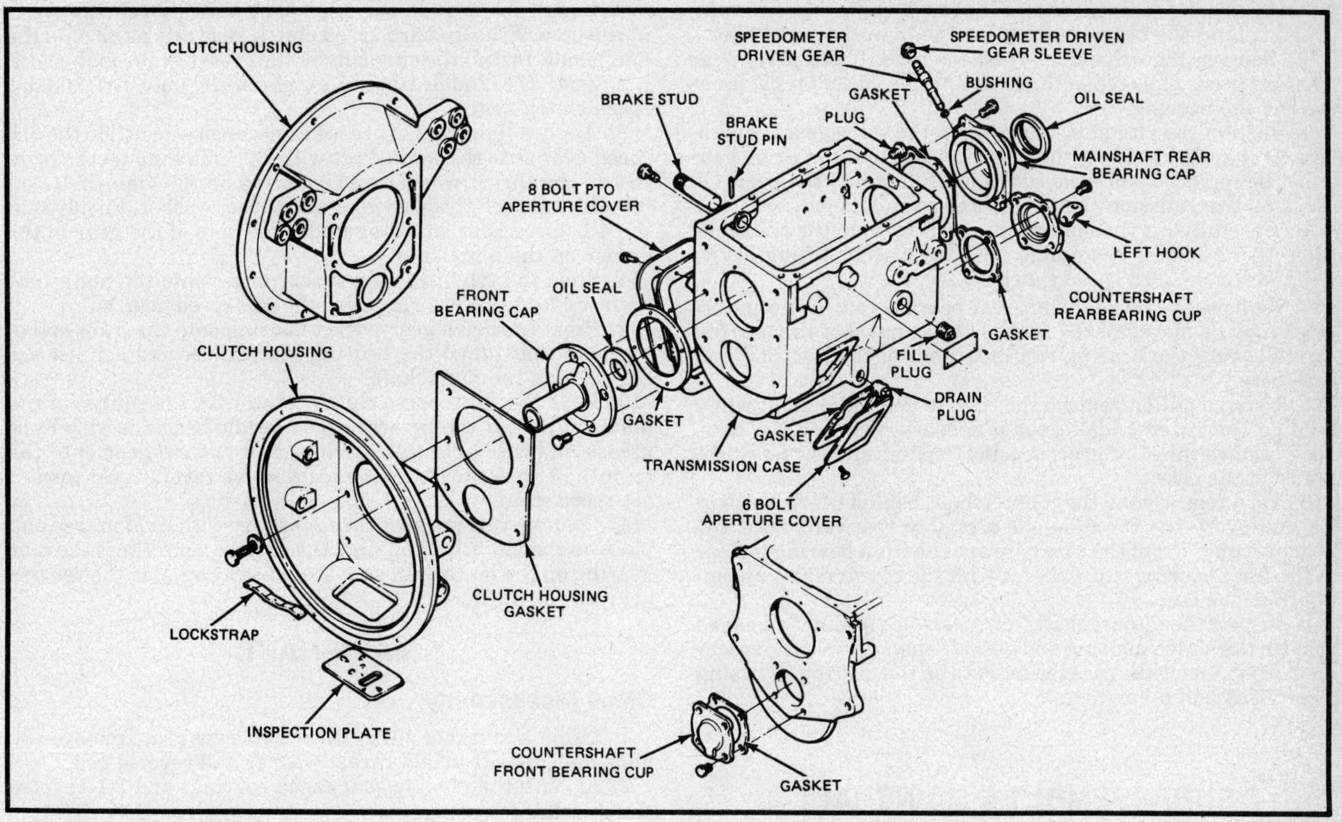

CLUTCH HOUSING
SPEEDOMETER DRIVEN GEAR
SPEEDOMETER DRIVEN GEAR SLEEVE
BRAKE STUD
GASKET
BUSHING
OIL SEAL
BRAKE STUD PIN
PLUG
MAINSHAFT REAR BEARING CAP
8 BOLT PTO APERTURE COVER
LEFT HOOK
FRONT BEARING CAP
OIL SEAL
COUNTERSHAFT REARBEARING CUP
GASKET
CLUTCH HOUSING
FILL PLUG
DRAIN PLUG
GASKET
GASKET
TRANSMISSION CASE
6 BOLT APERTURE COVER
CLUTCH HOUSING GASKET
LOCKSTRAP
INSPECTION PLATE
COUNTERSHAFT FRONT BEARING CUP
GASKET

Typical transmission case (© Dana Corp.)

REVERSE IDLER GEAR
WASHER
CAGED BEARING
SPACER
WASHER
REVERSE IDLER SHAFT

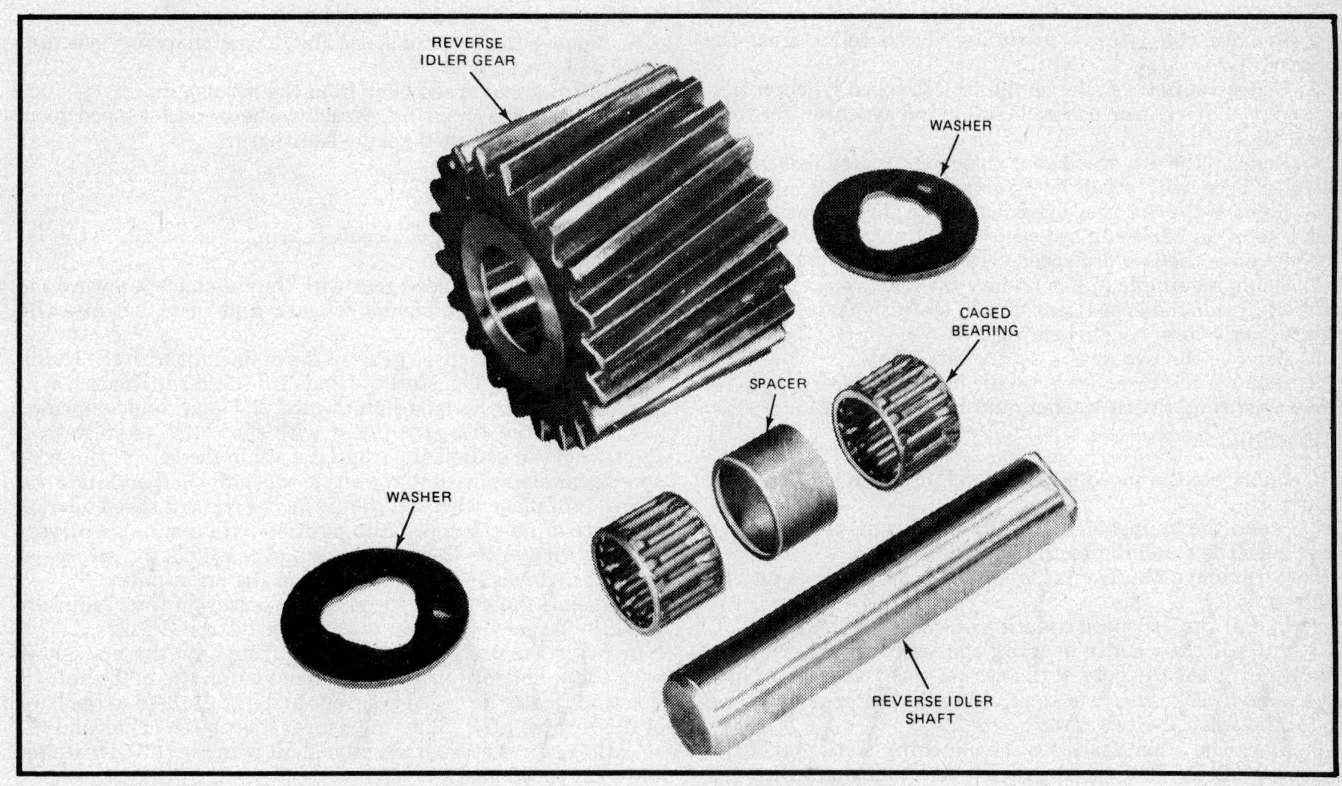

Reverse gear idler shaft assembly (© Ford Motor Co.)

bearing cap and remove the bearing cap. A split ring shim is located behind the bearing cup to set the mainshaft end play.

7. Remove the drive gear from the case. If the drive gear bearing needs to be replaced, use a suitable puller on the inner race of the bearing.

8. Inspect the pocket bearing cup in the drive gear for damage. If it is damaged on the C50 transmission the drive gear must be replaced since the cup is machined into the gear. On the C60 transmission the cup is pressed in and out.

9. Carefully lift the mainshaft assembly from the transmission case by using a suitable hook or another lifting device around the 2nd/3rd speed synchronizer.

10. Remove the countershaft rear bearing cap. The countershaft may be moved to the rear by the removal of the bearing cap, allowing the bearing cup to fall out of the transmission case bore.

11. Using a puller, remove the reverse gear idler shaft while holding the reverse idler gear and bearings inside the case, then remove the idler gear, bearings, spacer and thrust washers from the case.

12. Tie a rope around the countershaft, behind the drive gear. Carefully pry the countershaft assembly rearward until the bearing cup is out of the case bore and the front bearing is clear of the front bearing cup. Carefully lift the countershaft assembly from the case.

13. Inspect the countershaft front bearing cup and if damaged remove the clutch housing and gasket. Then remove the spacer ring. From inside the case tap forward on the bearing cup using a soft drift and a hammer.

SUBASSEMBLIES MAINSHAFT

CM50 Disassembly

1. Using a suitable puller, remove the rear bearing, thrust washer and reverse gear. The caged needle bearings can be removed from the end of the shaft once the reverse gear is removed.

2. Remove the 1st/reverse sliding clutch collar from the mainshaft.

3. Using a suitable puller on the 4th/5th speed synchronizer, remove the drive gear pocket bearing and synchronizer from the mainshaft.

4. Remove the 4th speed gear snapring, located deep inside the gear bore, with a pair of snapring pliers.

5. Remove the 3rd speed gear snapring, thrust washer, 3rd speed gear, and 2nd and 3rd speed synchronizer.

6. Remove the 2nd/3rd speed clutch gear snapring.

7. Using a suitable puller remove the 2nd/3rd speed clutch gear. Pull the 2nd speed gear off the main shaft by hand. Be careful not to lose needle bearings.

8. Remove the two keys from the mainshaft.

9. Remove the three loose needle bearing spacer rings, 1st speed snapring, thrust washer, and 1st speed gear.

Assembly

1. Lubricate the caged bearings and install in the 1st speed gear bore.

2. Stand the mainshaft vertically and install the 1st speed gear with the clutching teeth facing downward.

3. Lubricate the thrust washer and install it on the mainshaft.

4. Install the 1st speed snapring on the mainshaft.

5. Install the needle bearing spacer to the rear of the mainshaft. Coat the bore of the second speed gear with light grease and pack with two rows of needle bearings with one spacer between the two rows.

6. Place the other spacer in the clutching teeth end of the bore. Install the 2nd speed gear on the mainshaft with the clutching teeth facing up.

7. Install the keys in the mainshaft and align the keyways in the bore of the 2nd/3rd speed clutch gear and press onto the mainshaft. Install the snapring in the groove of the mainshaft.

8. Slide the 2nd/3rd speed synchronizer onto the 2nd/3rd speed clutch gear.

9. Apply a light coat of grease as necessary and slide the 3rd speed gear onto the mainshaft with the clutching teeth down. Install the thrust washer and snapring on the mainshaft.

10. Install the 4th speed gear and thrust washer. Firmly seat the 4th speed gear snapring under the bore of the gear in the groove on the mainshaft.

11. Slide the 4th/5th speed synchronizer onto the mainshaft with the larger brass ring over the 4th speed gear hub.

12. Press the drive gear pocket bearing onto the front end of the mainshaft until the bearing is firmly seated against the shoulder on the mainshaft.

13. Slide the 1st/reverse clutch collar over the splines of the mainshaft. Coat the reverse caged needle bearings with light grease and assemble the bearings and reverse gear onto the mainshaft with the clutching teeth of the reverse gear toward 1st speed gear.

14. Coat the reverse gear thrust washer with light grease and place on the mainshaft against the reverse gear. Press the rear bearing on the mainshaft so it seats firmly against the reverse gear thrust washer.

MAINSHAFT

CM60 Disassembly

1. Using a suitable puller on the reverse gear, remove the mainshaft rear bearing, thrust washer and reverse gear.

2. Remove the reverse gear caged bearings and 1st–reverse clutch collar.

3. Remove the 4th/5th speed synchronizer and front drive gear pocket bearing.

4. Remove the 4th/speed gear snapring, thrust washer and 4th speed gear.

5. Using a puller on the 3rd speed gear, remove the 4th speed gear sleeve and 3rd speed gear.

6. Remove the 2nd/3rd speed clutch gear snapring, synchronizer and clutch gear.

7. Lift the 2nd speed gear from the mainshaft.

8. Remove the snapring, thrust washers and 1st speed gear.

9. Remove the caged needle bearings.

Assembly

1. Lubricate the caged needle bearings and install in the 1st speed gear.

2. Install the 1st speed gear with the clutch teeth toward the front, lubricate the thrust washer and install it and the snapring.

3. Slide the 2nd speed gear on the mainshaft with the clutch teeth toward front. Install the 2nd–3rd speed clutch gear, synchronizer (with the long hub toward 2nd gear) and snapring.

4. Install the 3rd–speed gear with the clutch teeth toward the rear of the mainshaft. Align the pin in the bore or the 4th–speed gear sleeve with the spline of the mainshaft and slide the sleeve into place with the flange facing the 3rd speed gear.

5. Drive the 4th speed into position with a suitable driver.

6. Lubricate the thrust washer and assemble the 4th speed gear, thrust washer and snapring on the mainshaft.

7. Install the 4th/5th speed synchronizer on the mainshaft with the larger brass ring toward the 4th speed gear.

8. Press the drive gear pocket bearing onto the mainshaft with the inner race against the shoulder on the mainshaft.

9. Lubricate the caged bearings and install them in the bore of the reverse gear. Slide the 1st/reverse clutch collar and install the reverse gear on the mainshaft with the clutch teeth toward 1st speed gear.

10. Lubricate the thrust washer and install it on the

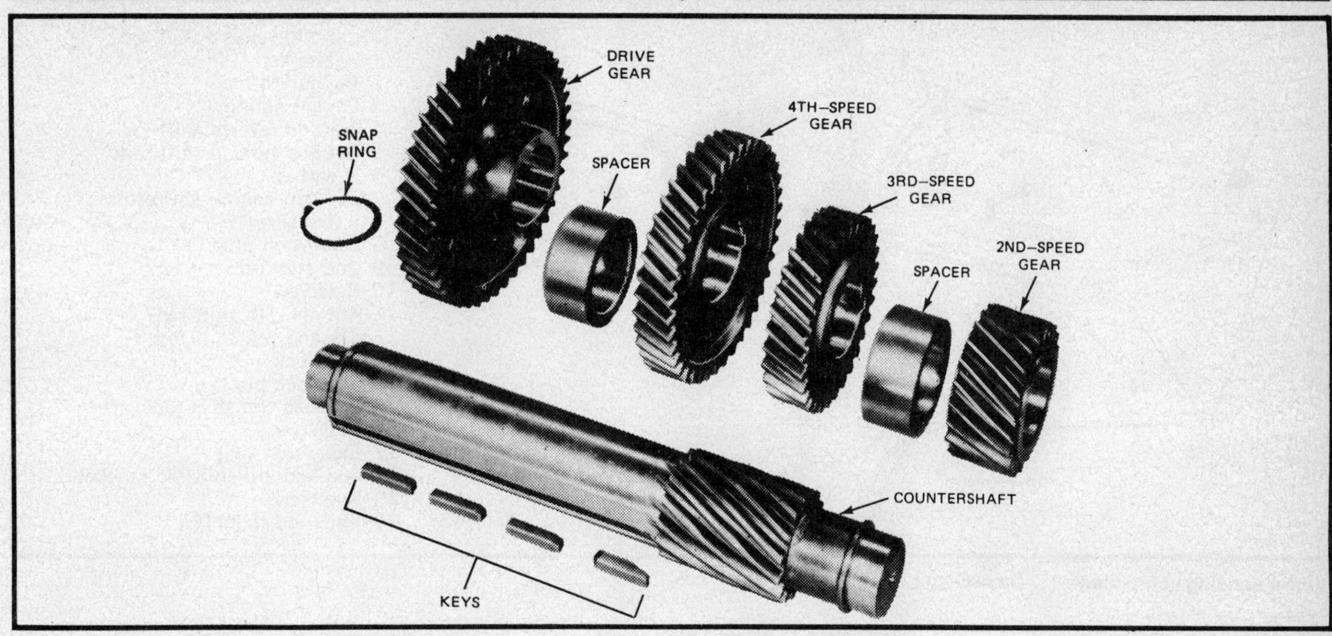

CM60 countershaft assembly (© Ford Motor Co.)

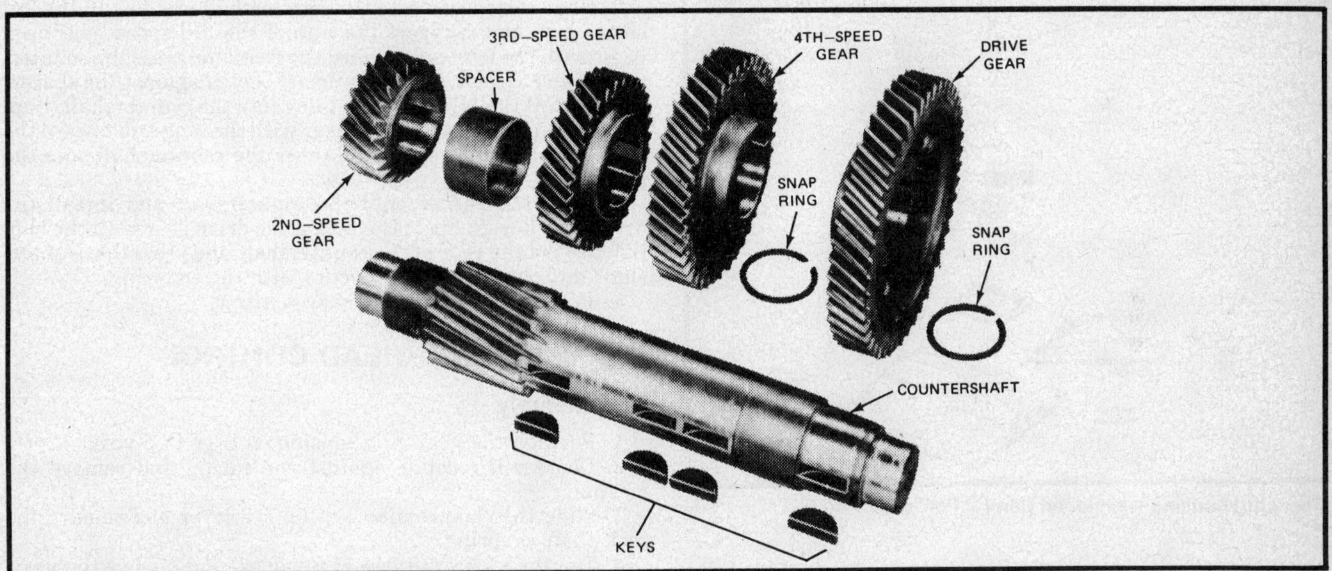

CM50 countershaft assembly (© Ford Motor Co.)

mainshaft against the reverse gear. Press the rear bearing on the main shaft.

COUNTERSHAFT

CM50 Disassembly

1. Using a puller on the inner race remove the front and rear bearings from the countershaft. Remove the drive gear snapring.
2. Support the drive gear as close as possible to the hub and press out the countershaft.
3. Remove the 4th speed gear snapring. Support the 3rd speed gear and press the countershaft until it is free of both the 3rd and 4th speed gears. Remove the gear keys from the countershaft.
4. Slide the spacer off the counrershaft. Support the 2nd speed gear, press out the countershaft and remove the key.

Assembly

1. Seat the 2nd speed gear in the countershaft. Support the hub of the 2nd speed gear on a press (long hub down) and press the countershaft into the gear.
2. Slide the spacer onto the countershaft and position the 3rd speed gear on a press (long hub down) and press the countershaft until the gear is firmly seated against the spacer.
3. Install the 4th speed gear onto the countershaft. Press the countershaft into the 4th speed gear with the long hub toward the front of the countershaft. Secure the gear with the snapring.
4. Position the drive gear key onto the crankshaft. Press the

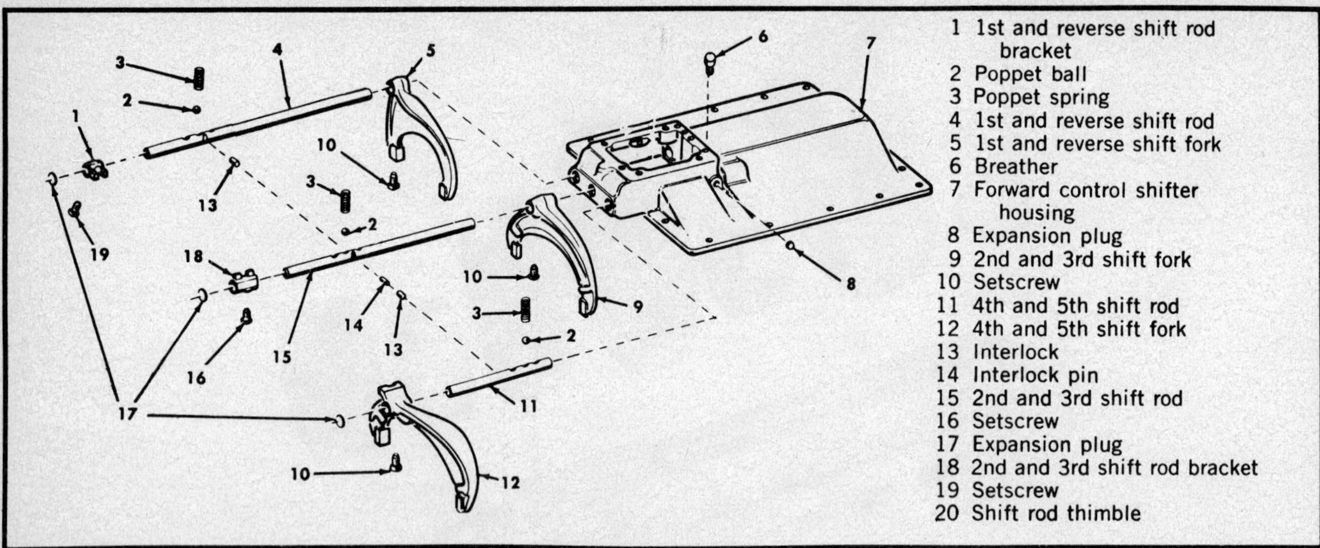

Shifter housing components (© Dana Corp.)

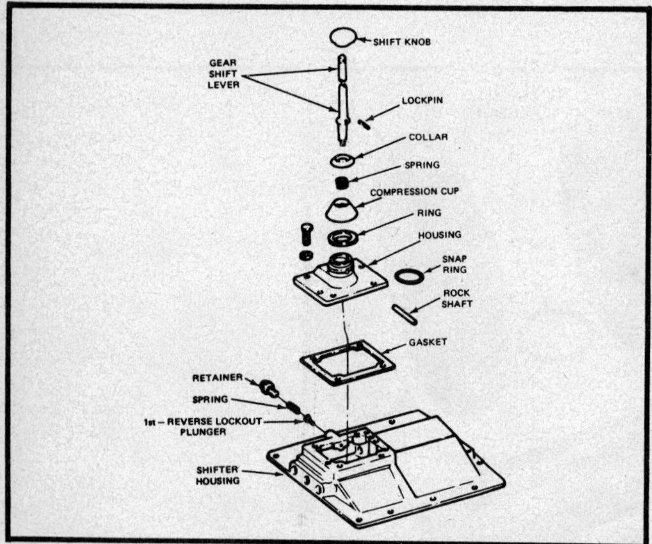

Gear shift housing—exploded view (© Ford Motor Co.)

countershaft into the drive gear with the long hub toward the rear of the coutershaft. Secure the gear with the snapring.

5. Press on the front and rear bearings.

COUNTERSHAFT

CM60 Disassembly

1. Using a puller on the inner race, remove the front and rear bearings. Remove the drive gear snapring.
2. Support the drive gear as close as possible to the hub and press free the drive gear. Remove the key and spacer from the countershaft.
3. Support the 3rd speed gear and press the countershaft free of both the 4th and 3rd speed gears. Remove the two keys and spacer from the countershaft.
4. Support the 2nd speed gear and press the countershaft from the gear.

Assembly

1. Install the 2nd speed gear key. Support the hub of the 2nd speed gear and press the countershaft into the gear while aligning the keyway.
2. Slide the spacer onto the countershaft and install the 3rd speed gear key. Support the hub of the 3rd speed gear on a press with the long hub toward the front and press the countershaft into the gear until it is firmly seated against the spacer.
3. Install the 4th speed gear key into the countershaft. Support the hub of the 4th speed gear with the long hub toward the front of the countershaft and press the countershaft into the gear.
4. Slide the spacer onto the countershaft and install the drive gear key. Support the hub of the drive gear with the long hub toward the rear of the countershaft and press the countershaft into the drive gear. Secure with the snapring.
5. Press on the front and rear bearings.

OVERHEAD CONTROL

Disassembly

1. Position the gearshift housing on edge in a vise.
2. Depress the collar against the spring and remove the lockpin.
3. Slide the compression cup up the lever and remove the rock shaft snapring.
4. Tap the rock shaft free of the dome and remove the gearshift lever and ring.
5. Remove the knob and slide the collar, spring and cup off of the lever.
6. Assembly is the reverse of the disassembly procedure.

SHIFTER HOUSING

Disassembly

1. Remove the three poppet springs and balls from the top of the shifter housing.
2. Turn the shifter upside down and position the 1st/reverse and 2nd/3rd shift forks into the neutral position.
3. Remove the set screw from the 4th/5th shift fork. Tap the 4th/5th shift rod forward with a drift pin until the end of the rod pops the welch plug from the housing. Remove the rod and shift fork.
4. Repeat step 3 for the 2nd/3rd and 1st/reverse shift rods. When the 1st/reverse shift rod is removed, lift both the 1st/reverse shift fork and bracket out of the housing.

5. Remove the interlock balls and back-up switch if necessary.

Assembly

1. Install the lockout plunger in the first/reverse bracket. Lubricate the 1st–reverse shift rod and slide part way into the shifter housing. Align the bracket with the shift rod and slide the rod through the bracket, bosses and 1st–reverse shift fork. Tighten the set screws 40 to 50 ft. lbs.
2. Install the two interlock balls. Lubricate the 2nd/3rd shift rod and slide part way into the housing. Install the interlock pin and hold in place with heavy grease. Align the shift fork with the rod and slide the rod into the boss until in the detent position. Install the set screw and tighten 40 to 50 ft. lbs.
3. Position the 2nd/3rd shift rod in neutral position and install the remaining two interlock balls in the cross hole of the 4th/5th shift rod boss. Slide the 4th/5th shift rod into position and install the shift fork. Tighten the setscrew to 40/50 ft. lbs.
4. Install the welch plug, poppet balls and springs.

MAIN TRANSMISSION

Assembly

1. Using a rope or sling lower the countershaft into the case.
2. If removed, install the countershaft front bearing cup and spacer ring.
3. Position the countershaft front bearing in the front cup and start installation of the rear bearing cup into the case. With the rear bearing properly aligned, drive the rear bearing cup into place in the case bore.
4. Lubricate the caged pocket bearings with 30W oil and install the bearings (with the spacer between the bearings) in the reverse idler gear. Coat the thrust washers with grease to hold the washers against each end of the idler gear. Position the tangs of the washers up and facing outward to align with the slots in the boss inside the case.
5. Hold the idler gear and thrust washers inside the case with the tangs of the washer up. Insert the idler shaft part way into the bore of the case with the shoulder and threaded hole facing out. Carefully align the washer tangs with the slots in the case, and lower the idler gear until it is aligned with the shaft. Insert the shaft into the case through the idler gear with the flat on the shoulder in alignment with position of the flat on the countershaft rear bearing cap. Drive the idler shaft in with a soft mallet until the bottom of the flat is flush with the case.

NOTE: While driving the idler shaft into the case it may be necessary to hold the countershaft rear bearing cup in place using one of the retainer capscrews and a large flat washer.

6. Clean the countershaft rear bearing cap gasket surface and also the gasket surface on the transmission case. Position the countershaft rear bearing cap and gasket to the case with the flat on the side of the cap aligned with the flat on the reverse idler shaft. Tighten the capscrews 60 to 80 ft. lbs. and remove the rope or sling from the countershaft.
7. Attach a suitable hook to the mainshaft assembly and carefully lower the assembly into the case. Mesh the mainshaft gears with the mating countershaft gears.
8. If previously removed press the bearing on the drive gear.
9. Lubricate the pocket bearing on the front of the mainshaft with light grease.
10. Install the drive gear through the front of the transmission case and onto the mainshaft.
11. Assemble the drive gear front bearing cap and gasket on the case. Be sure the oil return hole is properly aligned in the cap, gasket and case. Tighten the cap screws 25 to 32 ft. lbs. The clutch housing removal installation is only required if the countershaft front bearing cup was replaced or the clutch housing was defective.
12. Position the clutch housing gasket on the front of the case and hold in place with a light coat of grease. Be sure the gasket clears the countershaft front bearing spacer. Assemble the clutch housing on the case using the drive gear front bearing cap as a pilot. Tighten the housing capscrews 120 to 150 ft. lbs. Overtightening of the capscrews on the front of the case will distort the end-play of the mainshaft and countershaft.
13. If removed, install the oil seal and bearing cup in the mainshaft rear bearing cap.
14. Lubricate the mainshaft rear bearing with light grease. Assemble the rear bearing cap and gasket on the mainshaft. Apply even pressure on all sides and tighten the capscrews 68 to 80 ft. lbs. Make certain the oil holes in the case, gasket and cap are aligned.
15. Slide the speedometer drive gear onto the mainshaft until it is seated against the shoulder on the mainshaft.
16. Install the output flange, washer and locknut on the mainshaft. Rotate the mainshaft to seat the bearings. Lock the transmission in two gears and tighten the locknut to 500 ft. lbs. Pry on the mainshaft or output flange and check the end play. End-play should measure 0.006 to 0.010 inch. If end-play is not within the prescribed limits, remove the drive gear front bearing cap. Remove the bearing cup from the cap and remove the shim. Measure the thickness of the shim and replace if needed.

NOTE: The countershaft end play specifications are 0.006 to 0.013 inch with "set right" bearings used. End-play should not require checking.

17. Lock the transmission in gear and tighten the output flange locknut 500 to 550 ft. lbs. Shift the transmission into neutral.
18. Install the shifter housing gasket on top of the transmission case. With the shifter forks in neutral, align the forks with the respective synchronizers and 1st reverse clutch collar. Assemble the shifter housing on the case and tighten the cover screws 25 to 32 ft. lbs. Using a small pry bar check the movement of the shift rods for proper operation.

TORQUE SPECIFICATIONS
Spicer 50 and 60 Series

Location	ft. lbs.
Engine to Transmission Bolts	60–80
Countershaft Rear Bearing Cap Capscrews	60–80
Drive Gear Front Bearing Cap Capscrews	25–32
Clutch Housing Capscrews	120–150
Mainshaft Rear Bearing Cap Capscrews	60–80
Output Flange Locknut	500–550
Shifter Housing Cover Screws	25–32
Shifter Fork Setscrews	40–50

Spicer 8000 Series Five Speed

SHIFT HOUSING AND OVERHEAD CONTROL

Removal

1. Remove the overdrive and reverse lockout pins with springs and retainers from both sides of the shift housing.
2. Place a pry bar in the notch of the reverse shift finger and shift the transmission into the reverse gear.
3. Remove the bolts and remove the shift housing.

Disassembly

1. Place the shift lever dome in a vise. Pull up on the grommet, depress the collar against the spring and remove the lock pin.
2. Slide the compression cup up the shaft and remove the rock shaft snapring.
3. Remove the rock shaft and lever, then remove the ball grommet, collar, spring and cup off the lever.
4. Place the shifter housing in a vise with the forks facing out and the front of the housing to the left.
5. Remove the interlock crosshole plug.
6. Hold the reverse shift finger stud and remove the locknut and washer. Tap the stud free of the housing and remove the reverse shift finger. Remove the locknut plunger pin from the counterbore of the shift finger.
7. Cut the lockwire and remove the set screw from the reverse shift rod bracket.
8. Tap the reverse shift fork forward to move the shift rod against the welsh plug. Drive the plug free of the case and tap the fork forward until stopped by the housing. Cut the lockwire and remove the set screw from the reverse fork. Tap the shift rod free of the fork and bracket and out of the housing.
9. Remove the interlock from the cross hole between the rods.
10. Cut the lockwire and remove the set screw from the 3rd and 4th shift fork. Use a soft rod and drive the shift rod forward to remove the welch plug. Remove the rod and shift fork from the housing.
11. Cut the lockwire and remove the set screw from the 1st and 2nd shift rod bracket. Tap the 1st and 2nd shift fork forward to remove the welch plug from the front of the housing. Remove the set screw from the 1st and 2nd fork. Pull the rod free of the fork, bracket and housing.
12. Remove the short interlock from the cross hole between the shift rods.
13. Cut the lock wire and remove the set screws from the 5th speed or overdrive shift rod bracket and shift fork. Drive the shift rod out the front of the cover removing the welch plug. Pull the rod free of the fork, bracket and housing.
14. Remove the four poppet springs from the holes in the shifter housing center boss.

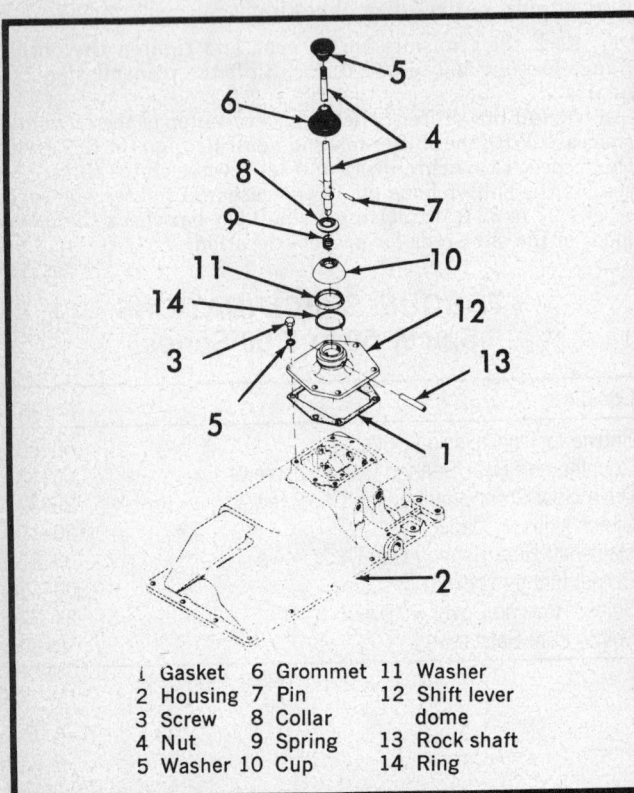

1 Gasket	6 Grommet	11 Washer
2 Housing	7 Pin	12 Shift lever dome
3 Screw	8 Collar	13 Rock shaft
4 Nut	9 Spring	14 Ring
5 Washer	10 Cup	

Shifter housing assembly (© Chrysler Corp.)

Assembly

1. Place the reverse relay shift finger stud in the shift finger.
2. Place the reverse lockout plunger in the reverse relay shift finger.
3. Position the reverse shift finger, and tap the stud through the shift cover housing. Install the nut and washer.
4. Set the four shift rod poppet ball springs in the holes.
5. Place the overdrive lockout plunger in the overdrive shift rod bracket, and slide the overdrive shift rod into the hole in the cover.
6. Place the overdrive rod bracket on the shift rod.
7. Place the poppet ball on the spring, hold it down and slide the rod past it.
8. Position the upper overdrive shift fork on the rod with the long hub of the fork toward the front of the cover. Install the set screws and lock wire.
9. Place a short interlock into the hole in the cover and push it through to the overdrive shift rod.
10. Slide the 1st and 2nd speed shift rod into the second hole from the right side of the front cover. Place the 1st and 2nd shift rod bracket on the rod.
11. Install the small interlock pin on the rod. Place a poppet ball on the poppet spring. Hold the ball and spring compressed and slide the rod past the center boss. Place the 1st and 2nd speed shift fork on the rod, with the long hub toward the front. Install the set screws and lockwire.
12. Install a short interlock into the cover and push it through to the 1st and 2nd speed rod.
13. Slide the 3rd and 4th shift rod into the front of the cover. Place a small interlock pin in the rod. Place the 3rd and 4th speed shift fork on the rod, with the long hub toward the front. Set the poppet ball on the spring and depress it. Slide the rod through the case boss. Line up the holes and install the set screw and lock wire.
14. Place the long interlock in the cover hole and push it over to the 3rd and 4th speed rod.
15. Install the reverse shift rod and position the reverse bracket. Set a poppet ball on the poppet spring, hold it down and push the shift rod past it. Install the reverse shift fork. Install the set screws and wire securely.
16. Install the four expansion plugs in the shift rod holes in the front of the cover, and expand them by striking with a flat ended bar and a hammer.
17. Install the interlock cross-hole plug in the side of the cover.

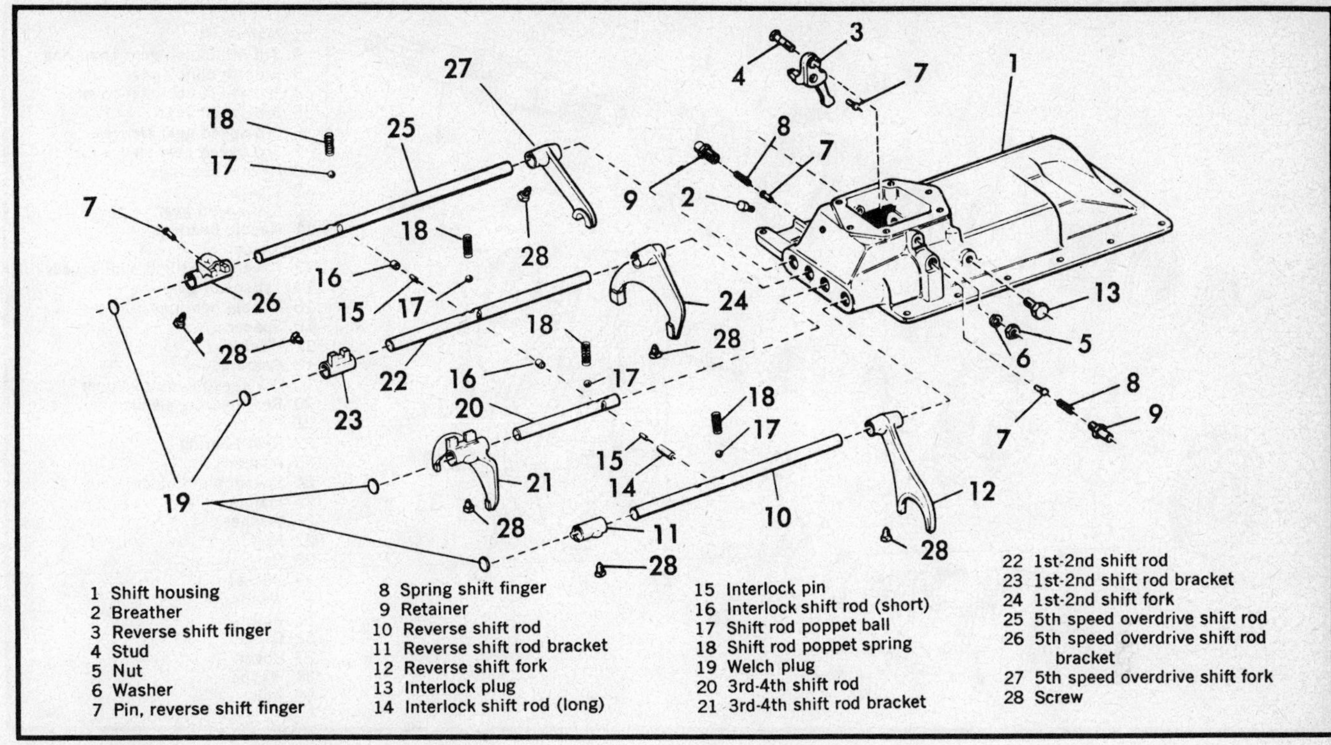

Overhead shift control assembly (© Chrysler Corp.)

TRANSMISSION UNIT

Disassembly

1. Using a bar shift the transmission into the reverse gear and remove the cover from the case.
2. Remove the clutch release cross shaft, yoke, and clutch brake discs.
3. Pull the bearing retainer and the input gear assembly out of the case.
4. Remove the parking brake drum and the speedometer driven gear and bushing.
5. Lock the transmission in two gears, remove the companion flange nut and remove the companion flange with a puller.
6. Remove the mainshaft rear bearing cap.
7. Remove the speedometer gear and the bearing spacer.
8. Tap on the mainshaft 1st speed gear and move the mainshaft as far back to the rear as possible.
9. Using a puller remove the mainshaft rear bearing.
10. Remove the transmission rear cover using a puller.
11. Remove the overdrive shift fork guide rod with a bolt and a puller. Remove the fork from the case.
12. Shift the transmission into two gears. Remove the countershaft rear cotter key and nut.
13. Remove the countershaft overdrive clutch gear by pulling on the collar or by attaching a puller to the three threaded holes in the clutch gear.
14. Remove the 5th or overdrive countershaft gear and thrust washer then pry the gear off the shaft.
15. Tap the mainshaft assembly toward the rear of the case and install a splitter type puller on the mainshaft center bearing outer race. Tap the mainshaft as far forward as possible and then to the rear again until the bearing is loose on the shaft.
16. Remove the mainshaft and gears from the case with the use of a sling. The center bearing and the low speed gear needle bearings will come off during the above operations.
17. Remove the rear bearing retainer.
18. Remove the reverse idler gear. Two identical caged roller bearings support the gear and sleeve.
19. Pry the countershaft assembly toward the rear of the case until a bearing puller can be installed on the rear bearing. Remove the countershaft assembly.

SUBASSEMBLIES MAINSHAFT

Disassembly

1. Place the mainshaft, front end up, in an arbor press.
2. Remove the snapring from the groove behind the front bearing and press the bearing, 3rd and 4th speed clutch gear, mainshaft 3rd speed gear, sleeve and mainshaft 2nd speed gear from the mainshaft.
3. Remove the snapring from between the bearing cap and the drive gear. Pull the cap off toward the front of the drive gear.
4. Remove the left hand threaded nut with a spanner wrench and press the bearing off the shaft.

NOTE: Some early production units used the old style loose needle bearings in the bores of the mainshaft gears. Be careful not to lose them as the gears are removed.

Assembly

1. Press the ball bearing on the input gear with the shielded side of the bearing toward the gear.
2. Install the bearing lock nut on the gear and tighten and stake the nuts.
3. Place the bearing cap over the bearing and press into position.
4. Insert the snapring into the slot in the bearing cap.
5. Use grease and assemble the caged needle bearings onto the shaft diameter just to the front of the center splined area. Install the mainshaft 2nd speed gear over the caged needle bearing, with the clutch teeth toward the rear.

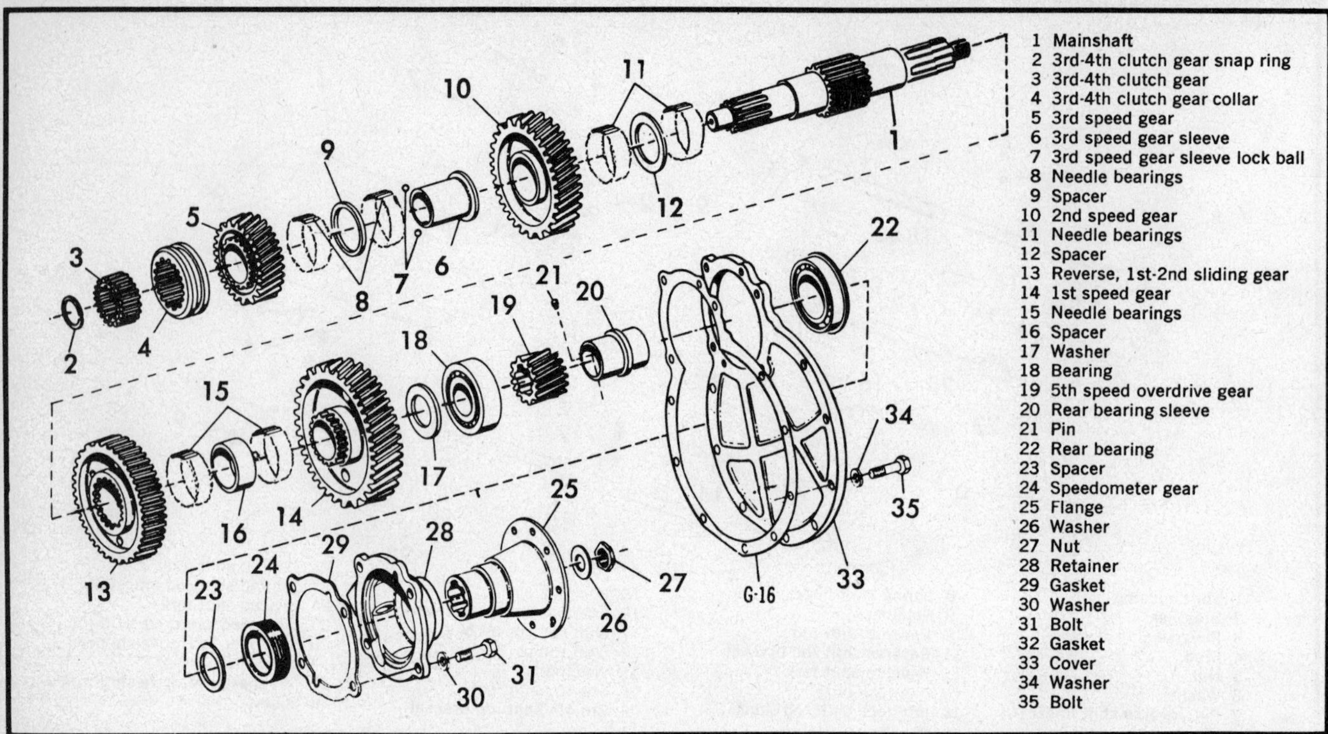

Mainshaft assembly—exploded view (© Chrysler Corp.)

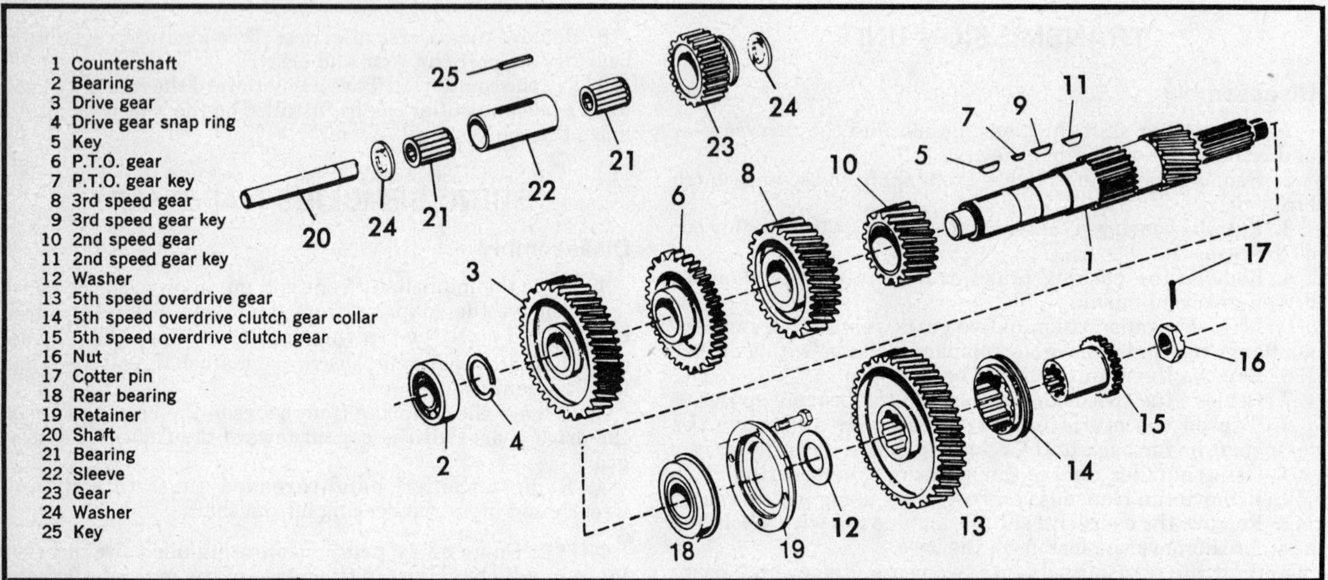

Countershaft and reverse idler gear (© Chrysler Corp.)

6. Install the mainshaft 3rd speed gear sleeve onto the front of the shaft with the flange facing to the rear and the notches aligned with the splines and the balls.

7. Install the caged needle bearings on the mainshaft. Use grease as a retainer.

8. Slide the mainshaft 3rd speed gear over the needle bearings with the clutch teeth toward the front.

9. Press the mainshaft 3rd and 4th speed clutch gear onto the front of the mainshaft with the flat side toward the rear and the clutch hub toward the front.

10. Install the snapring in the groove on the front of the mainshaft.

11. Press the front ball bearing on with the beveled edge of the inner race toward the rear.

12. Press the 3rd and 4th speed clutch collar on the 3rd and 4th speed clutch gear, with the long portion of the hub toward the rear.

13. Slide the 1st and 2nd speed clutch gear onto the splines, with the shift fork collar toward the rear.

14. Using grease, install two rows of 71 needle bearings per row, with the wide spacer between them, on the shaft diameter to the rear of the center splined area.

15. Place the mainshaft 1st speed gear over the needle bearings with the clutch teeth toward the front.

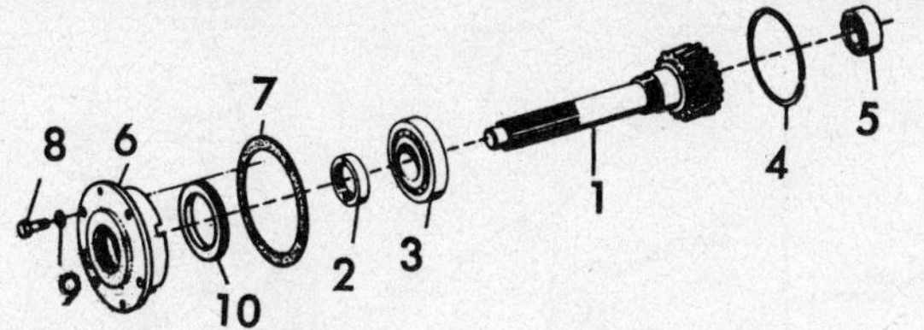

Drive pinion assembly (© Chrysler Corp.)

16. Grease one side of the 1st speed gear thrust washer and place it on the mainshaft with the greased side toward the 1st speed gear.

COUNTERSHAFT

Disassembly

1. Remove the countershaft front bearing with a puller.
2. Remove the snapring from the front of the countershaft.
3. Press the drive gear off the countershaft and the remainder of the gears with a suitable press.

Assembly

1. Position the 2nd gear key and press the 2nd speed gear on the shaft with the chamfered bore toward the front.
2. Insert the 3rd speed gear key and press the 3rd speed gear on the shaft with the long hub of the gear toward the front.
3. Place the P.T.O. gear key in position then press the P.T.O. gear on the shaft with the long hub toward the front.
4. Insert the drive gear key on the shaft then press the drive gear on the shaft with the long hub facing the P.T.O. gear.
5. Install the snapring in its groove in the front of the countershaft. Press the countershaft front bearing on.

TRANSMISSION UNIT

Assembly

1. Lower the countershaft assembly into the case, rear end first and down, so the rear of the countershaft enters the rear bearing bore. Lower the front of the countershaft assembly until the front bearing will enter its bore in the case. Tap the rear bearing until the front bearing enters the bore.
2. Install the countershaft rear bearing, with the snapring toward the rear, in the bore and on the countershaft. Tap in place with a tool that contacts the inner bearing race.
3. Assemble the reverse idler gear, sleeve, key and bearings. Place them in the case with the shift fork collar toward the rear of the transmission case. Make sure the sleeve small diameter is facing toward the front.
4. Install the reverse idler shaft. The tang on the edge of the countershaft rear bearing retainer must align with the flat on the rear end of the shaft.
5. Install the countershaft rear bearing retainer, with the tang locking the idler shaft. Install the bolts and torque to specifications. Install the lockwire.
6. Using a sling lower the mainshaft assembly into the case rear end first. Start the center support bearing over the rear of the shaft and into the case center web with the bearing snapring toward the rear.
7. Install the input gear, bearing and cap, with a new gasket into the front of the case. Pilot the mainshaft front bearing into place in the bore of the input gear. Start but do not tighten the nuts.
8. Drive the mainshaft center support bearing into place.
9. Install the 5th or overdrive gear onto the rear of the mainshaft.
10. Install the 5th or overdrive gear thrust washer and gear onto the rear of the countershaft with the clutch teeth toward the rear. Install the countershaft 5th or overdrive clutch collar and gear with the large diameters of the collar and gear toward the rear. Install the clutch gear nut and torque to specification.
11. Place the pin on the inside of the mainshaft rear bearing sleeve, and press the sleeve onto the rear of the mainshaft 5th or overdrive gear. The ground surface of the hub is to the rear.
12. Install the 5th or overdrive shift fork and shaft guide. The long hub of the shift fork must face toward the front. Place the shift fork guide rod into the hole in the rear of the case, through the shift fork and into the hole in the center web of the case.
13. Install the transmission rear cover, using a new gasket. Do not tighten the bolts.
14. Install the mainshaft rear bearing.
15. Install the mainshaft rear bearing thrust washer and speedometer drive gear.
16. Using a new gasket, install the rear bearing cap onto the transmission cover. Torque the cap bolts to specifications.
17. Place the speedometer driven gear and bushing in the mainshaft rear bearing cap and secure with the two bolts and nuts.
18. Torque the transmission rear cover bolts to specifications.
19. Torque the input gear bearing cap bolts to specifications.
20. Install the clutch release yoke and cross shafts in the clutch housing. Install the clutch brake discs.
21. Shift the transmission and the cover assembly into the reverse position and install the shift cover using a new gasket. Be sure the forks line up with the shift collars. Install the cover bolts and torque to specifications.

Spicer SST-6, SST-6 + 1, SST-1007, Six and Seven Speeds

TRANSMISSION REAR CASE

Disassembly

1. Remove the nut from the end of the output shaft. Remove the yoke or flange.
2. Remove the output shaft bearing cap and gasket.
3. Pull back on the output shaft to expose the snapring and remove the snapring, bearing and thrust spacer from the shaft.
4. Remove the bolts from the piston body and rear cover and remove the piston body and gasket from the case face and off piston.

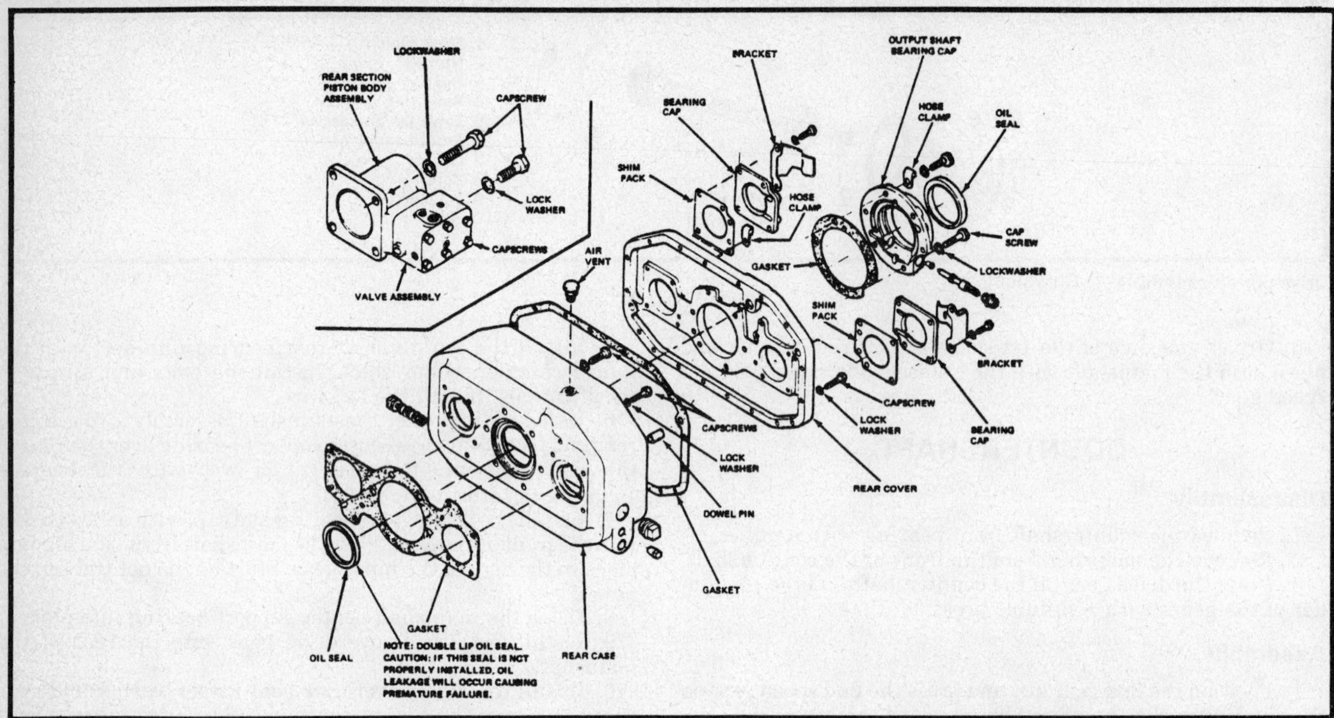

Rear case assembly (© Ford Motor Co.)

5. Remove the shift piston locknut and remove the piston from the shaft.
6. Remove the rear cover and gasket by lifting straight up off the dowel pins.
7. Remove the rear bearing caps with shims from the rear cover.
8. Remove the cups from the countershaft bores of the rear cover.
9. Remove the output shaft and gear from the rear case.
10. Remove the piston shift rod with the fork and stop spacer as an assembly. The curvic clutch collar will pull away with the fork.
11. Remove the curvic clutch collar from the fork and the positive stop spacer of the piston shift rod.
12. Before removing both countershafts, turn the head end gear until the timing marks or paint marks align to each other. Remove both countershafts from the rear case.
13. If the countershaft bearing cones need replacement, use a split puller tool for removal.
14. Remove the selflocking lock nut if so equipped, or unstake the lockwasher tang from the groove of the locknut and remove the locknut. Remove the lockwasher from the end of the shaft.
15. Use a puller tool to remove the pocket bearing from the shaft.
16. Slide the gear and thrust washer from the splines of the shaft.
17. Cut the lockwire from the bolts. Remove the bolts and remove the rear case from the front transmission unit.
18. Inspect the oil seal and replace if necessary.
19. Remove the air vent and replace if necessary.
20. Press the head and timing gears from the countershaft using parallel bars under the gear hub. Press the shaft from the key bore and remove the key from the shaft.

Assembly

1. Install the rear case gasket on the back face of the front unit and install the O-rings into the countershaft bore of the front case.
2. Assemble the rear case on the gasket and secure the rear case to the front case with the bolts and lockwashers. Tighten the $^3/_8$ inch screws 25 to 32 ft. lbs. and the $^1/_2$ inch screws 60 to 80 ft. lbs. Lockwire the bolts.
3. Install the taper bearing cups into the countershaft bores and the output shaft bore seral into the center bore.
4. Install the mainshaft head end gear on the shaft splines. Assemble the thrust washer on the shaft. Install the pocket bearing on the shaft. Tap the bearing on with a tubing pressed against the inner race of the bearing.
5. Install the bearing self locking locknut if so equipped or with lockwasher and locknut. Tighten the locknut 500 to 600 ft. lbs. Bend the tang on the lockwasher if so equipped.
6. Press the key into the keyway of the countershaft. Support the head end timing gear with the long hub end up. Press the shaft into the bore of the gear. Seat the gear face firmly against the shoulder of the shaft.
7. With the cones installed on the countershaft ends, install the countershafts, large OD gear toward the inner face of the rear case. Align the timing marks of the countershaft in mesh with the head end gear timing marks.
8. Install the gasket on the rear case face.
9. If the piston rod, stop spacer and shift fork were previously disassembled, reassemble these parts for installation into the rear case.
10. Assemble the long hub end of the shift fork toward the oil groove end of the piston shaft. Install the set screw and tighten 40 to 50 ft. lbs. and lockwire securely. Assemble the top spacer on the piston end of the rod. Assemble the shift collar on the shift fork pads.
11. Install the complete shift fork and rod sub-assembly into the rear case. Mesh the curvic ring clutch collar into the curvic ring of the gear. Mesh the short end of the piston rod into the rod bore of the rear case.
12. Assemble the gear on the output shaft with the curvic end of the gear toward the shaft shoulder. Install the thrust spacer on the shaft.
13. Install the shaft and gear sub-assembly into the rear case, over the pocket bearing and into the splines of the clutch collar.
14. Install the rear cover and tighten the bolts 25 to 32 ft. lbs.

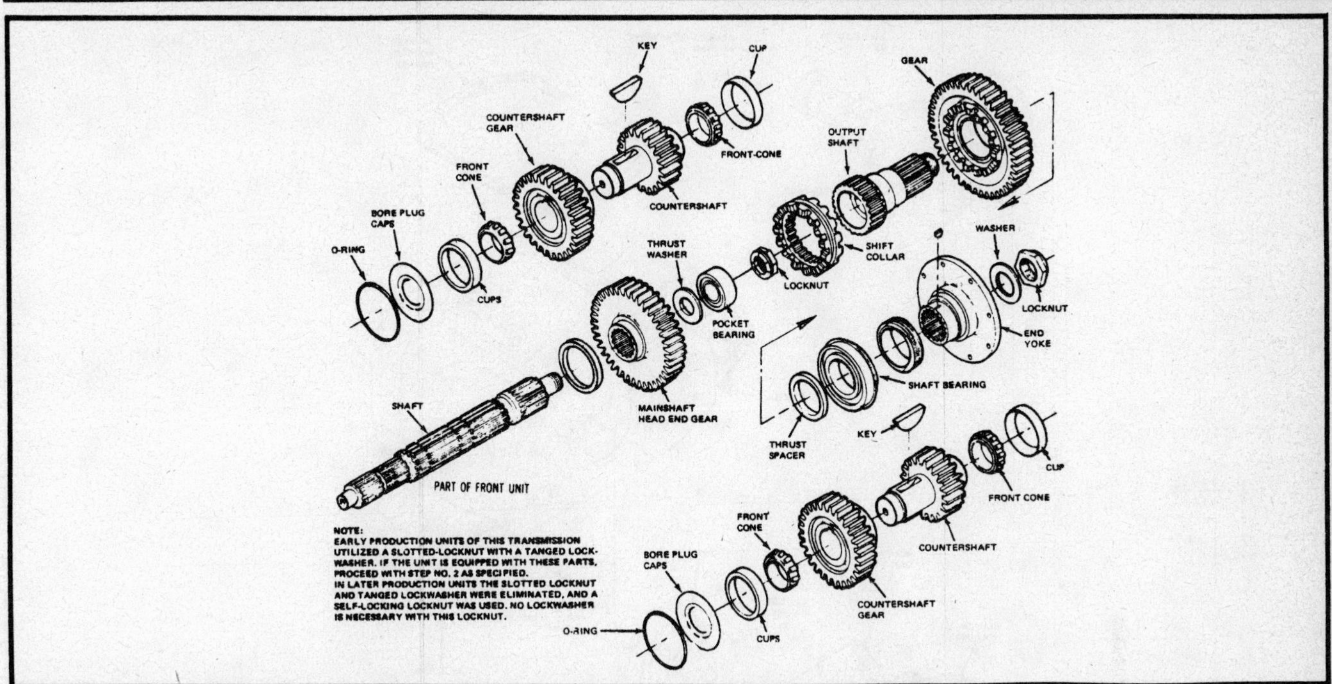

Rear case gears (© Ford Motor Co.)

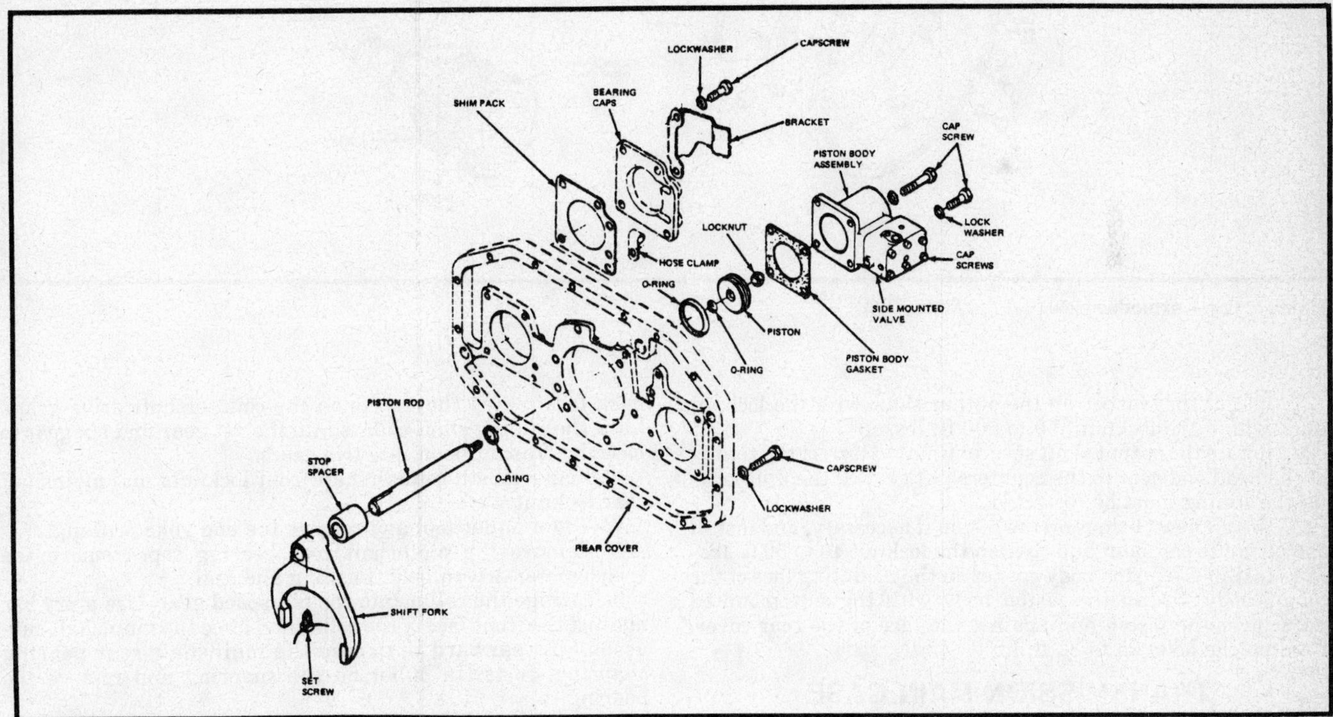

Rear cover (© Ford Motor Co.)

If a new gasket is used it will be necessary to check the end-play of 0.004 to 0.007 inch on the taper bearings of both countershafts.

15. Install the taper bearing cups into the countershaft bores. Allow the back face of the cup to extend out of the cover face approximately $^3/_{32}$ inch.

16. Install the 0.080 inch (average) shim pack with rubberized shims between the over cup OD and against the rear cover face to obtain 0.004 to 0.007 inch countershaft end-play.

17. Insert the 5 inch long $^1/_2$ inch bolt in the tapped hole of the countershaft. Set up a dial indicator at the end face of the countershaft and check end-play.

18. Remove the retaining cap tool and install the bearing caps. Tighten the bolts 25 to 32 ft. lbs.

19. Install the output shaft bearing on the shaft then the cap and gasket. Align the oil return holes and make sure the seal is in place in the bearing cap. Tighten the bolts 60 to 80 ft. lbs.

20. Assemble the end yoke or flange on the output shaft.

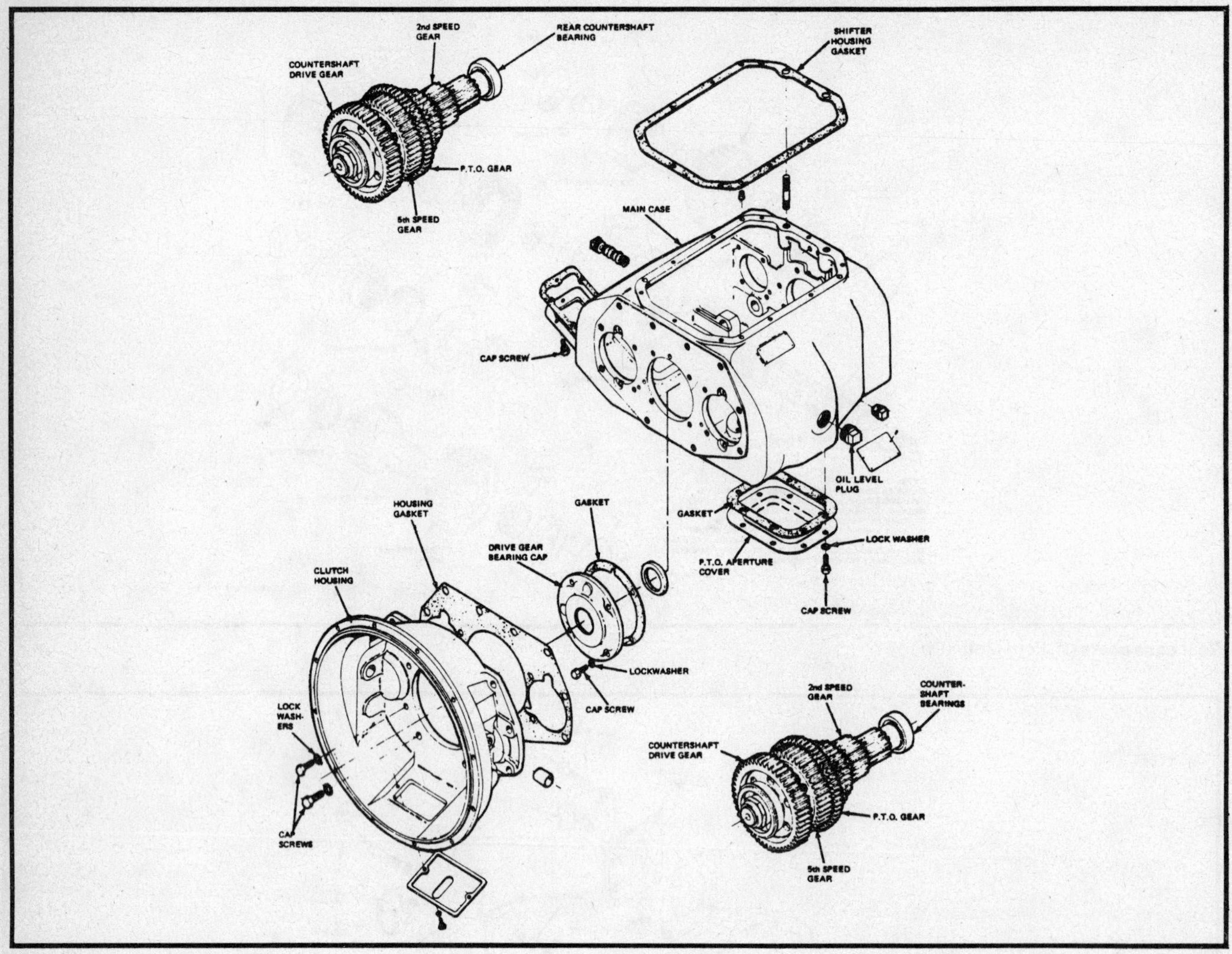

Main section—exploded view (© Ford Motor Co.)

21. Install the washer on the output shaft with the locknut and tighten the locknut 550 to 600 ft. lbs.

22. Rotate the output shaft several times to correct the timing of the head end gear to the countershaft gear. If the unit locks up the timing must be corrected.

23. Install new O-rings on the piston if necessary, and install the piston to the shaft and tighten the locknut 40 to 50 ft. lbs.

24. Install the piston body gasket on the mounting face of the piston body. Install the piston body with the side mounted valve over the piston and against the face of the rear cover. Tighten the bolts 25 to 32 ft. lbs.

TRANSMISSION MAIN CASE

Disassembly

1. Shift the transmission into neutral.

2. Separate the shifter housing from the main case and gasket and lift the housing straight up.

3. Remove the bolt and washer from the long clutch release shaft in the clutch housing. Remove the key and tap free of the yoke. Remove the shaft through the side of the housing.

4. Remove the clutch release bearing, two washers and clutch disc. Remove the six bolts from the clutch housing and tap the housing from the case.

5. Rotate the main drive gear until the timing marks on the back face match the marks on the countershaft drive gears. Lock the sliding shaft collars into the 1st gear and six gear to lock the transmission into two gears.

6. Remove both countershaft front locknuts and mainshaft rear locknut.

7. Use a puller tool and remove the end yoke or flange.

8. Remove the mainshaft rear bearing cap. Remove the speedometer driven gear, bushing and seal.

9. Engage the collar into the 5th speed gear. Use a pry bar against the front face of the collar and force the mainshaft subassembly rearward to expose the mainshaft rear bearing snapring. Install a puller on the snapring and remove the bearing.

10. Remove the thrust washer from the shaft. Remove the split rings from the shaft. Remove the snapring located in the reverse gear bore.

11. Engage the 1st–reverse shift collar under the reverse gear. Slide the reverse gear and collar forward butting the gear against the 1st speed gear. Wire or tie both gears together.

12. Remove the bolts and washers and remove the drive gear bearing cap.

13. Remove the drive gear subassembly by pulling forward on the drive gear splined stem.

14. Using a soft bar on the front end of both countershafts, force the shaft backwards to allow the bearings to creep for-

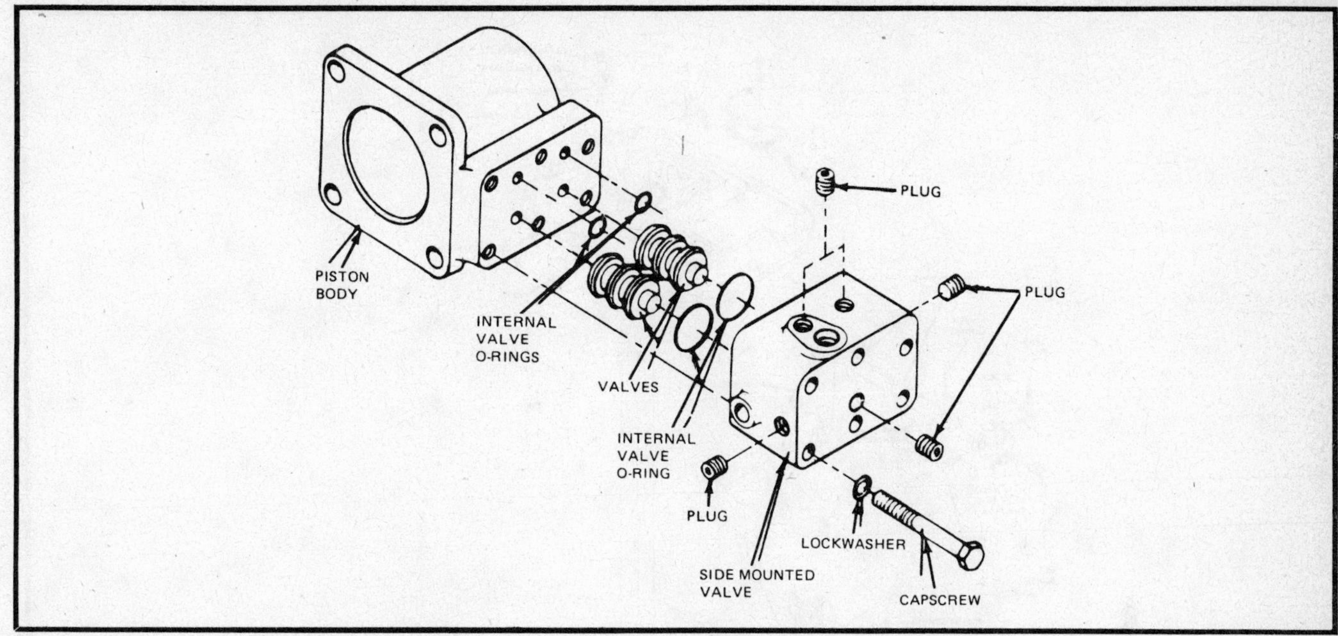

Piston body and valve assemblies (© Ford Motor Co.)

ward to expose the bearing snapring. There are recesses in the case face to allow clearance to install puller tool arms onto the bearing snapring. Remove the bearings from the shaft.

15. Using a pilot tube, long bolt and nut pull out the upper idler gear shaft from the case. Recover the idler gear lockball. Leave the idler gear in place for later removal after the mainshaft subassembly is removed from the case.

16. Place a sling or wire around the 2nd–3rd shift collar to support the mainshaft subassembly. Lift the mainshaft subassembly out with a chain hoist.

17. Remove the upper idler gear subassembly.

18. Looking from the rear of the case, remove the right side countershaft subassembly. Then remove the left side.

19. Using a pilot tube, bolt and nut remove the lower idler gear shaft from the case.

20. Remove the idler gear sub-assembly.

COUNTERSHAFTS AND REVERSE IDLER GEARS

Assembly

1. Place either of the countershaft sub-assemblies on the left side (looking from the rear of the case) with the timing mark "A" of the head gear toward the center of the case. This timing mark must be mated to the drive gear timing mark "V" later in assembly.

2. Install the two idler shaft bearings with the spacer between them into the bore of the reverse idler gears.

3. Take either of the reverse idler gear sub-assemblies and place in the upper boss location. Lay it mesh with the rear countershaft gear teeth. Do not install the reverse idler shaft at this time. Remove the magnetic plug from the case to prevent it from being damaged during installation of the lower right side reverse idler gear.

4. Install the remaining countershaft sub-assembly, placing it inside the main case on the right side. Turn the head end gear around until the timing mark "A" is toward the center of the case. Install the reverse idler gear into position. Roll the idler gear on the mating tooth of the countershaft to find the idler gear bearing bore alignment to the case hole. Install the reverse idler gear shaft and ball into the case. Tap the shaft flush to the case face.

5. Do not install the front or rear countershaft bearings at this time. Let the countershaft lie free at the bottom of the case until the mainshaft sub-assembly is placed into the case.

6. Lower the mainshaft into position and partially mesh with the countershaft gears. Position a pilot tool to spread the position noted in the illustration to allow easier installation of the mainshaft and gears into the case. Leave the hoist and sling in place on the mainshaft for support until all bearings and reverse idler shafts have been installed in the case.

7. Install the thrust washer on the output end of the mainshaft. Push the washer forward and against the thrust washer previously installed, then force both washers against the snapring that is on the rear of the mainshaft.

8. Cut the wire used to tie both gears together then slide the reverse idler gear backwards into approximate location on the reverse gear bore thrust washer.

9. Install the snapring into location in the groove of the bore of the gear.

10. Coat two split rings with heavy grease and install the rings into the recess on the rear of the mainshaft, with the flanges toward the gears.

11. Coat the thrust washer with heavy grease and install it on the mainshaft against the flange face of the split rings.

12. Install the bearing pilot tool for the rear mainshaft bore.

13. Use the front bore bearing pilot tools to support the front end of both countershafts. As the pilot tools are inserted into the front case bores and on the ends of the shaft, keep the timing teeth in correct mesh to each respective gear.

14. With all the timing gears painted, bring the timing teeth of the countershaft head end gears parallel to the bottom of the case or pointing to the center of the case. Position the drive gear timing teeth (two) where they will match and mate to the timing teeth of the countershaft gears.

15. Install the drive gear into the bore of the case until the bearing snapring seats against the face of the main case.

16. Install the front drive gear bearing cap with the gasket. Align the oil return holes of the bearing cap with the oil port holes of the case.

17. Dip the bolts in sealer and use washers to attach the bearing cap to the case. Tighten the bolts 25 to 32 ft. lbs.

18. Remove the bearing pilot tool from the rear case bore and the end of the mainshaft. Slide the three shift collars into the neutral position on the mainshaft.

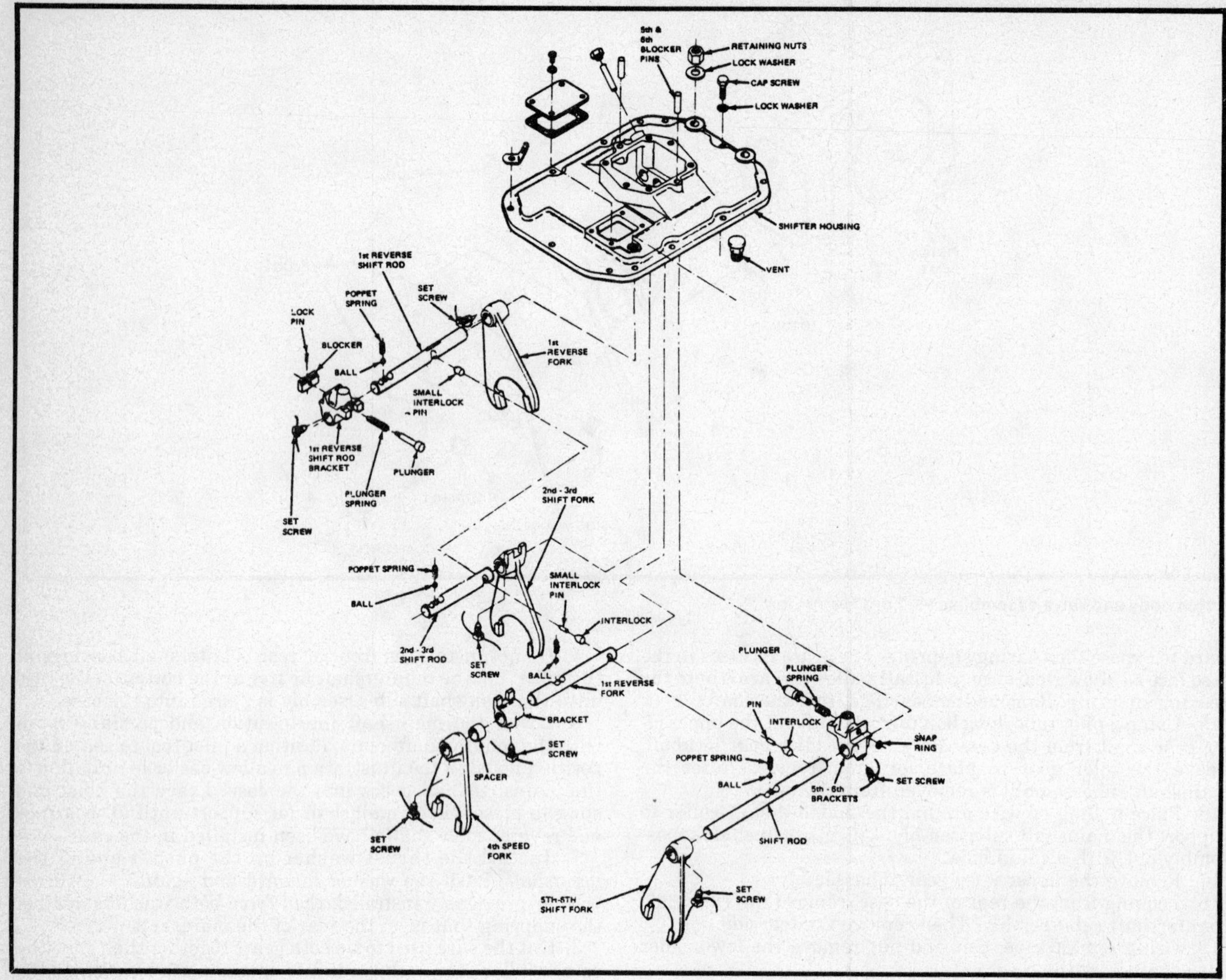

Shifter housing—exploded view (© Ford Motor Co.)

19. Using a pilot tool and a driver install the mainshaft rear bearing on the shaft and into the bore of the case. Seat the bearing snapring against the main case face.
20. Remove the hoist and sling used for installation.
21. Install the reverse idler shaft into the upper reverse idler gear bore. Place the idler shaft lock ball into the shaft ball hole just before entering the recess. With the lock ball locked into the recess, tap the idler shaft end flush to the case face.
22. Use the rear bore countershaft bearing piloting tools to support the rear ends of both countershafts. As the pilot tools are inserted into the bores, keep the timing teeth in correct mesh with each other.
23. Using a countershaft support hook tool, place the rod hooks in the web hole of each gear. Support the tool with a chain hoist hook. Remove the left front bore pilot tool. Install the countershaft bearing using the front face of the pilot tool to drive the bearing on the shaft. Seat the snapring of the bearing to the face of the case.
24. Install the countershaft front lockout on the shaft. Bring the lockout against the bearing face hand tight.
25. Remove the right front pilot tool and install the bearing using the same procedure as in step 23. and 26. Remove the countershaft support hook and install the countershaft front locknut on the shaft, hand tight.
27. Lock the unit in two gears, moving the clutch collar into the reverse gear and the collar into the drive gear. Tighten both countershaft locknuts 550 to 600 ft. lbs.
28. Remove the left rear pilot tool from the countershaft. Install the countershaft rear bearing with the snapring to the outside.
29. Use a pilot tool on the face of the bearing and drive the bearing on the shaft and into the bore of the case. Install the snapring on the shaft.
30. Install the right rear countershaft bearing and snapring in the same manner as the left.
31. Install both countershaft rear bearing caps with gaskets to the case face and tighten the bolts 25 to 32 ft. lbs.
32. Install the end yoke or flange with the washer on the mainshaft output splines. Install the locknut on the mainshaft and tighten 550 to 600 ft. lbs.
33. Move the clutch collar out of the reverse gear and into its neutral position. Leave the collar engaged in the drive gear.
34. Turn the drive gear stem to roll the gear train. If the teeth on the timing marks are in the correct positions, the entire gear train will roll freely, if not the gear train will lock up after a few turns.
35. If the unit locks up, disengage the shift collar from the drive gear. Turn the drive gear in the reverse rotation until the timing marks come into match or close mis-match. If a mismatch appears the shafts must be retimed.

36. Place all the clutch collars in their neutral positions for later installation of the shift housing assembly on the main case.

37. Place a new clutch housing gasket in position.

38. Install the clutch housing using the drive gear bearing cap as a guide. Use sealer on the bolts and tighten the $^5/_8$ inch screws 120 to 150 ft. lbs. and the $^1/_2$ inch 60 to 80 ft. lbs.

39. Install the washer, clutch disc, second washer, and clutch release bearing on the end of the drive gear on the housing. Install the short shaft with the clutch release yoke in the housing. Slide the long shaft from the outside housing into the yoke. Install the key, bolt and washer.

40. Replace the P.T.O. aperture covers and gaskets. Tighten the bolts 25 to 32 ft. lbs.

41. Install the magnetic plug on the right side of the unit and the oil level plug on the left side.

42. Check the shifter cover assembly and make sure all the shift forks are in the neutral position, then install the shifter housing to the main case using a new gasket.

SHIFTER HOUSING

Disassembly

1. Place the shifter housing in a vise with the forks facing out.

2. Cut the lock wires and remove the set screws from the 1st and reverse shift rod bracket and fork.

3. Tap the 1st and reverse shift rod forward to free the fork and bracket from the shift rod.

4. Remove the interlock from the cross hole between the rods.

5. Cut the lockwire and remove the set screw from the 2nd and 3rd shift fork. Tap the rod forward to free the fork and recover the poppet ball.

6. Remove the 4th speed bracket and shift fork and the 5th and 6th speed bracket and shift fork in the same manner as the 1st and reverse and the 2nd and 3rd.

7. Remove the four poppet springs from their holes in the shifter housing front boss.

Assembly

1. Place the shifter housing in a vise with the inside of the housing facing out and with the front of the housing facing left.

2. Apply a light coat of grease to all the bores in the housing and to the shift rods as they are assembled to the housing.

3. Using a poppet assembly tool or equivalent, preload the poppet spring and ball in the poppet detent bore of the top boss or the 5th/6th speed rod location.

4. Select the longest shift rod and enter the longest end from the interlock detent into the rear boss, on the right side of the housing.

5. Assemble the shift rod bracket to the rod with the shift gate downward. Tap the shift rod sharply to remove the poppet ball loading tool in the front boss and continue the assembly until the poppet ball registers in the neutral detent of the shift rod.

6. Install the 5th and 6th shift fork to the rod with the extended hub toward the right. Install the bracket and fork in the proper positions and secure with the set screws and torque 40 to 50 ft. lbs.

7. With the poppet assembly tool or equivalent, preload the poppet spring and ball in the poppet detent bore of the 2nd top opening (4th speed) in the front boss.

8. Coat the small interlock pin of the 4th speed shift rod with heavy grease and insert the pin into the hole of the shift rod. Enter the rod with the interlocking pin to the right, through the rear boss.

9. Install the bracket to the rod with the shift gate down, then install the spacer on the rod. As the shift rod enters the front boss tap the rod sharply to remove the poppet loading tool. Assemble the 4th speed fork to the rod with the extended hub of the fork to the left. Place the shift fork and bracket in its proper position and install the set scew and torque 40 to 50 ft. lbs. Tie with lock wire.

10. Coat the interlock with heavy grease and install the interlock into the access hole of the rear boss through the 2nd and 3rd shift rod bore.

11. With the poppet assembly tool or equivalent, preload the poppet spring and ball in the poppet detent bore.

12. Coat the small interlock with heavy grease and insert the pin into the hole of the 2nd and 3rd shift rod. Enter the rod through the rear boss with the interlock pin to the right.

13. Assemble the 2nd and 3rd shift fork to the rod with the extended hub of the fork to the left. As the shift rod enters the front boss, tap it sharply to remove the poppet loading tool. Install the shift fork in its proper position. Torque the set screw 40 to 50 ft. lbs. and secure with lock wire.

14. Coat the interlock with heavy grease and install the interlock into the access hole of the rear boss with the interlock pin to the right.

15. With a poppet assembly tool or equivalent, preload the poppet spring and ball in the poppet detent bore.

16. Select the 1st and reverse shift rod. Start the end closest to the set screw counter sink hole through the front boss of the housing, then through the middle boss containing the preloading tool. Install the 1st and reverse bracket on the rod after tapping the shift rod sharply to remove the poppet loading tool. Make sure the bracket top boss is down and the shift gate is toward the tower opening. Slide the rod through the rear boss and install the 1st and reverse fork on the rod with the extended hub of the fork to the right. Install the shift fork and rod in the proper position and torque the set screws to 40–50 ft. lbs. Secure with lock wire.

17. Shift the 1st/reverse speed fork into gear and try to shift the other three rods. If functioning correctly the other rods should be locked in neutral.

MAINSHAFT

Disassembly

1. Remove the 5th speed clutch collar. Remove the snapring from the mainshaft groove. Remove the 5th gear sub-assembly then remove the 2nd snapring from the shaft groove.

2. Remove the 4th speed clutch collar, the snapring, then the 4th speed gear sub-assembly.

3. Remove the 3rd speed gear sub-assembly then the snapring from the shaft groove.

4. Remove the 2nd–3rd speed gear shift collar. Remove the snapring under the 2nd speed gear bore. Remove the 2nd speed gear sub-assembly.

5. Cut the holding wire on the 1st and reverse gears. Remove the 1st speed gear sub-assembly, snapring and shift collar from the shaft.

6. Remove the reverse gear sub-assembly from the output end of the shaft.

Assembly

1. Position the mainshaft vertically in a vise.

2. Install the thrust washer on the mainshaft. Let the washer rest on the shoulder near the output splines.

3. Install the snapring in the bottom groove of the mainshaft.

4. Install the 1st/reverse clutch collar on the shaft, with either end of the collar down. Rest the clutch collar on the snapring.

5. Install the 2nd snapring and thrust washer on the shaft. Seat the snapring securely in the groove closest to the 1st and reverse clutch collar.

6. Install the thrust washer and snapring into the 1st speed gear and install the sub-assembly on the shaft, with the 35 degree chamfer in the bore of the gear down toward the clutch collar.

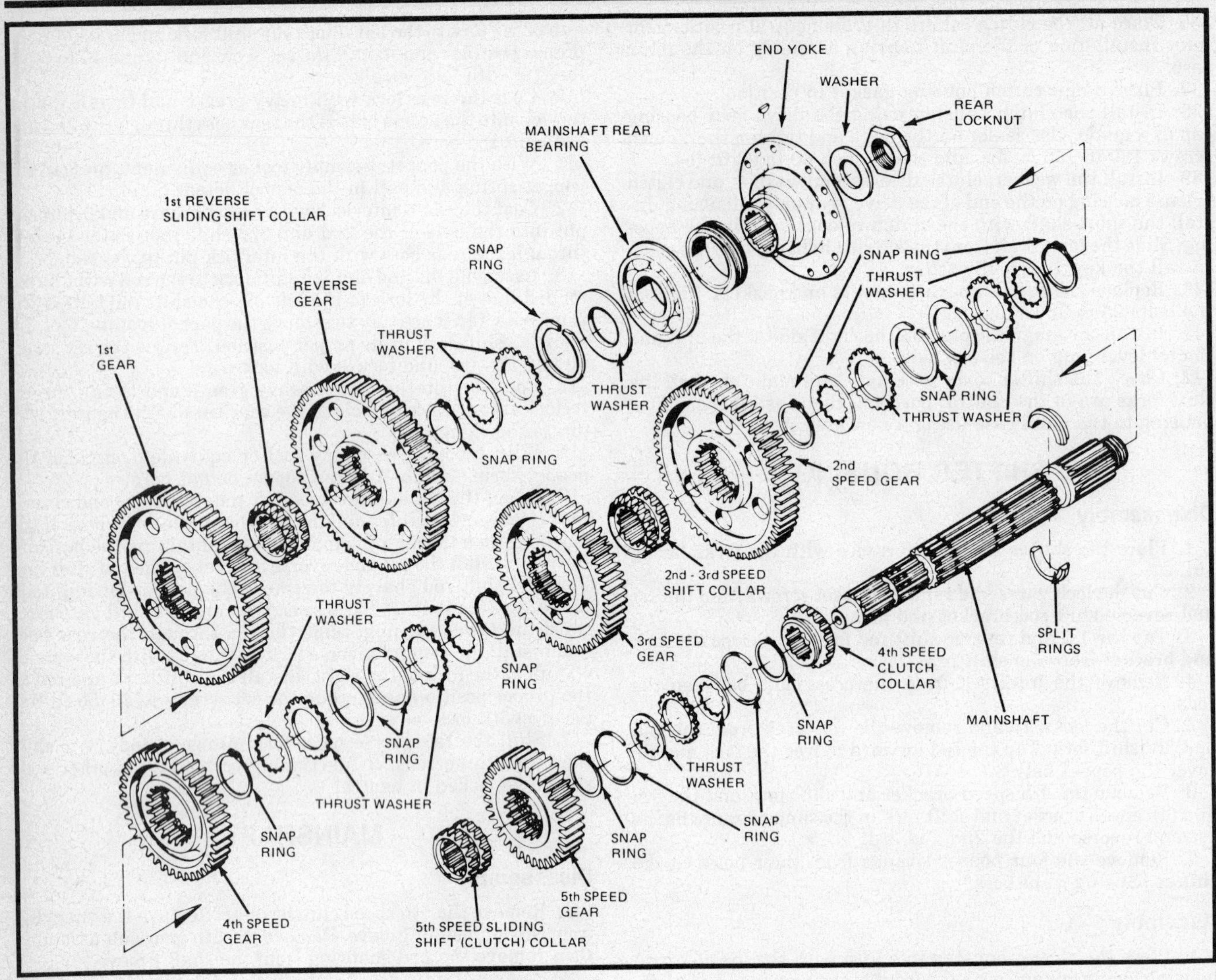

Mainshaft—exploded view (© Ford Motor Co.)

7. Install the 2nd set of washers and snapring into the 2nd speed gear and install the sub-assembly on the shaft, with the 35 degree bore chamfer up. Rest the gear against the face of the 1st speed. Install the 3rd snapring on the shaft under the bore of the 2nd speed gear.

8. Install the 2nd/3rd speed gear clutch collar, either end of the collar down, resting in the bore of the 2nd speed gear.

9. Install the 4th snapring in the groove closest to the 2nd/3rd clutch collar and install the thrust washers on the ring.

10. Install the 3rd snapring into the 3rd speed gear, and install the sub-assembly with the 35 degree chamfer in the bore of the gear down toward the clutch collar. Rest the gear on the washer of the shaft.

11. Install the fourth set of washers and snapring into the 4th speed gear, and install the sub-assembly on the shaft with the 35 degree chamfer bore up. Rest the gear against the face of the 3rd speed gear. Install the fifth snapring in the groove of the shaft under the bore of the 4th speed gear.

12. Install the 4th speed clutch collar on the shaft, with the shift fork collar up. Rest the clutch collar in the bore of the 4th speed gear.

13. Install the first snapring in the shaft groove closest to the 4th speed clutch collar.

14. Install the snapring into the groove of the 5th speed gear. Install the washer, snapring, thrust washer, and second snapring in the gear bore.

15. Install the sub-assembly on the shaft, with the 35 degree bore chamfer up. Rest the gear internal thrust washer on the shaft snapring. Install the 2nd snapring in the shaft groove under the bore of the 5th speed gear.

16. Install the 5th–6th speed clutch collar on the shaft and rest it in the bore of the 5th speed gear.

17. Remove the assembly from the vise and place on a work bench.

18. Slide the 1st/reverse shift collar into the bore of the 1st gear, also slide the thrust washer on the end of the shaft against the snapring.

19. Install the reverse gear on the rear of the shaft and slide it forward onto the clutch collar. Match the OD teeth to the 1st speed gear teeth. Wire or tie the two gears together.

20. Install the remaining parts, relating to the reverse gear and to the rear of the mainshaft, after the mainshaft sub-assembly has been placed into the main case.

COUNTERSHAFT

Disassembly

1. Support the 6th speed gear with parallel bars as close to the hub as possible. Using an arbor press, press the countershaft out of the gear.

2. Remove the 5th speed gear, using a standard puller.

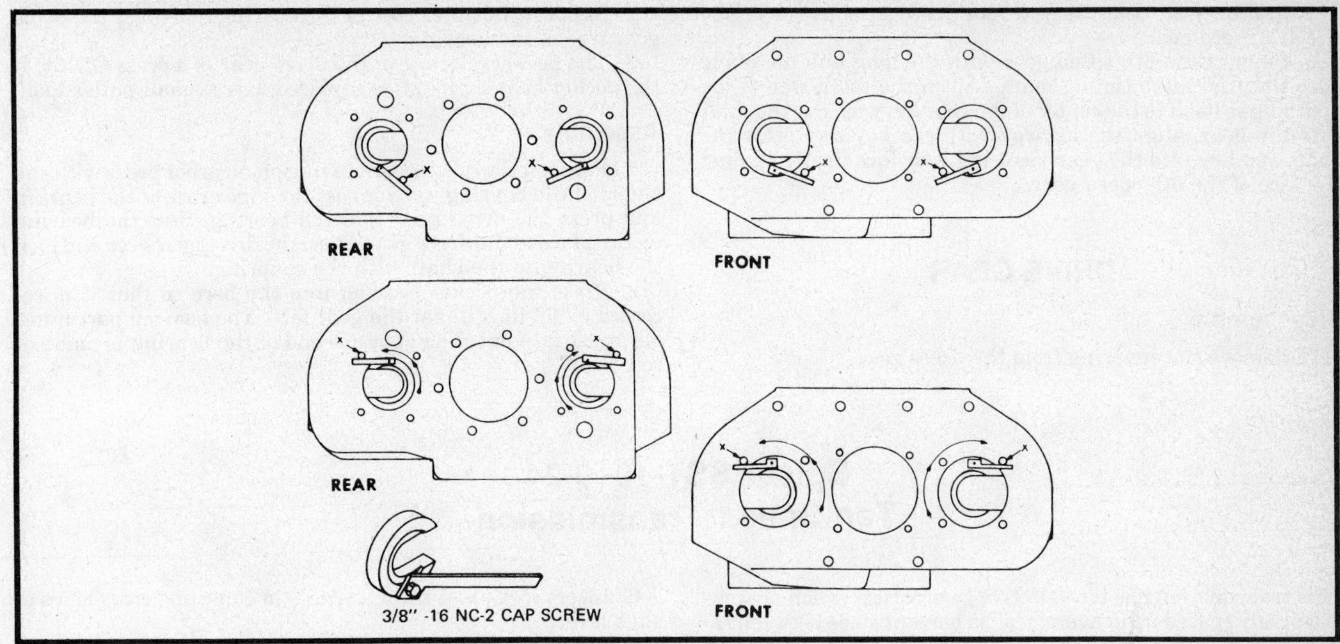

Tool for positioning mainshaft gears in case (© Ford Motor Co.)

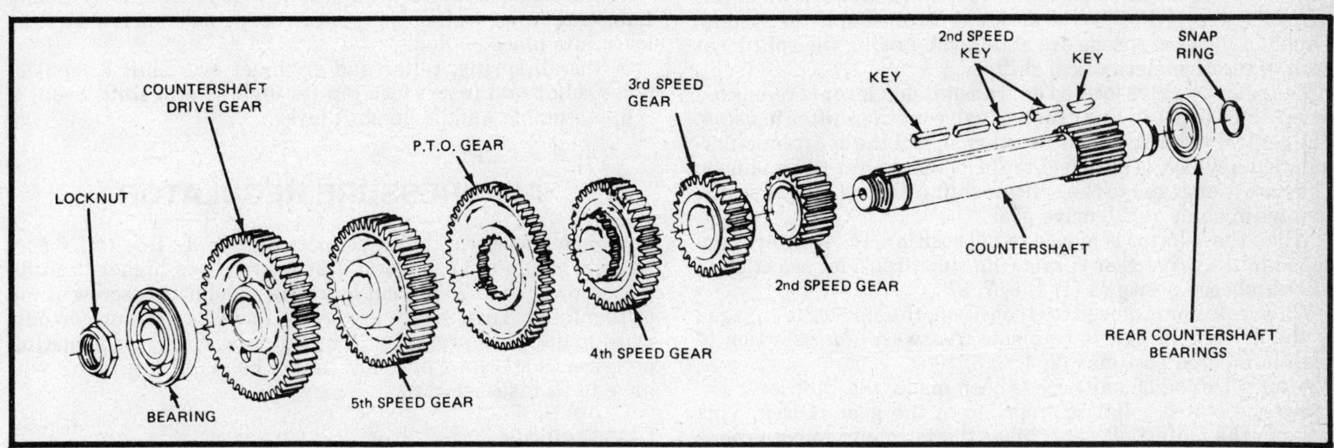

Countershaft—exploded view (© Ford Motor Co.)

3. Lift the P.T.O. gear off the splined teeth of the 4th speed gear.
4. Remove the 4th, 3rd, and 2nd speed gears from the shaft in the same manner as the 6th speed gear.

Assembly

1. Coat the bores of all the gears with oil before pressing on each gear on the countershaft. Install the key for each gear, one at a time, as the countershaft is pressed into the gear bore.
2. Support the 2nd speed gear with either face down. Align the key with the keyway in the gear and press the shaft and key into the gear. Seat the gear face of the shaft firmly against the face of the 2nd speed gear. Make sure the key does not extend beyond the gear face.
3. Install the 3rd and 4th speed gears on the countershaft in the same manner as the 2nd speed gear.
4. Install the P.T.O. gear on the splined teeth of the 4th speed gear with the long hub end against the gear.
5. Support the 5th speed gear with the short end up. Set the shaft into the gear, holding the P.T.O. in place to its mating gear. Align the keyway with the key and press the shaft and

TORQUE SPECIFICATIONS
Spicer SST-6, SST6+1 & SST1007 Series

Part Name	ft. lbs.
Mainshaft flange/yoke locknut	550–600
Left countershaft—front locknut	550–600
Right countershaft—front locknut	550–600
Clutch housing locknuts	
½″ Dia.	60–80
⅝″ Dia.	120–150
Mainshaft front bearing capscrews	25–32
Mainshaft rear bearing capscrews	60–80
Countershafts rear bearing capscrews	25–32
Shifter housing capscrews	25–32
All set screws shift forks, brackets and fingers	40–50

key into the gear. Seat the gear face firmly against the face of the 4th speed gear.

6. Support the 6th speed gear with the long hub up. Make sure that the tooth timing mark "A" on the tooth web of the gear aligns itself to the center of the gear keyway. Set the shaft into the gear, align the keyway with the key and press the shaft and key into the gear. Seat the gear face firmly against the face of the 5th speed gear.

DRIVE GEAR

Disassembly

1. Remove the snapring from the drive gear.
2. Support the outer race of the bearing and press the drive gear free of the bearing.
3. The pocket bearing in the drive gear is a press OD fit. If the pocket bearing must be replaced, use a small puller tool.

Assembly

1. Position the drive gear bearing on an arbor press with the shield of the bearing up. Support the inner race of the bearing and press the drive gear into the bearing. Seat the bearing against face of the drive gear. Turn the drive gear over and lock the bearing to the shaft with the snapring.
2. Press the pocket bearing into the bore so that it is recessed 0.062 inch under the gear face. The bearing part number must face out. The opposite end of the bearing is made of soft metal.

Spicer SST-1010-24 Ten Speed Transmission

This transmission has ten selective gear ratios, which are progressively spaced in an average of 25 percent steps between ratios. It cannot be shifted as a conventional transmission in combination with an auxiliary transmission or a two speed axle. Five basic gears operate in combination with two different selections (Hi or Lo) of an air controlled splitter system. Thus ten forward speeds are obtained by using the splitter at each of the five mechanical shifts.

The selector valve located on transmission lever is connected by air lines to the splitter control valve on the shifter housing. The control valve sends air to either side of the splitter actuating piston which is attached to the splitter shift rod and fork. The fork is engaged to the splitter shift collar on the transmission main shaft at the drive gear.

When the selector is moved to LO position, the splitter is engaged to the drive gear curvic ring side (front) for selection of odd numbered positions (1, 3, 5, 7, 9).

When selector is moved to HI position, the splitter is engaged to the drive gear curvic ring side (rearward) for selection of even numbered positions (2, 4, 6, 8, 10).

After selection of splitter has been made, the shift lever engages the clutch collar appropriate to the gear chosen. This locks in the mainshaft gear, takes the torque from both countershaft gears and delivers torque through the mainshaft to the output yoke.

GEAR SHIFT LEVER

Disassembly

1. Place shift lever dome on edge in vise.
2. Pull up grommet. Depress collar against spring and remove lock pin.
3. Slide compression cup upward on shift lever. Remove rock shaft snapring.
4. Tap rock shaft free of dome, remove shift lever. Remove seal.
5. Remove shift lever handle slide grommet, collar, spring and compression cap off shift lever.
6. Wash all parts and inspect for excessive wear at cross hole in shift lever and rock shaft.
7. Inspect finger end of shift lever for excessive wear. Check spring tension by comparing it with a new spring.

Assembly

1. Hold shift lever so that cross hole aligns with rock shaft cross holes in dome.
2. Insert rock shaft through holes in dome and cross holes of shift lever.
3. Assemble rock shaft snapring to groove of dome and lock rock shaft in place.
4. Lubricate and assemble a new seal to shift lever dome. Lubricate inner wall of compression cup and slide it over shift lever into place on dome.
5. Install spring, collar and grommet over shift lever. Depress collar and insert lock pin through hole in shift lever.
6. Assemble handle on shift lever.

AIR PRESSURE REGULATOR

To bench check regulator, connect air supply line to IN port and air gauge to OUT port. If pressure reads higher than 80 psi, or lower than 75 psi, cut lock wire on adjusting screw at top of regulator. Turn screw inward to increase pressure or outward to decrease pressure. Reinstall lock wire after adjusting pressure. If specified pressure cannot be maintained, unit will have to be disassembled.

Disassembly

1. Remove capscrews and lockwashers from springloaded top cover.
2. Remove spring, inspect for set or breakage. Remove diaphragm, inspect for damage or wear.
3. Remove diaphragm back-up plate and O-ring. Remove plunger pin, spring and O-rings beneath plunger pin. Inspect O-rings beneath and on plunger and plunger spring for wear or damage.

Assembly

1. Place small pin onto plunger pin and install into diaphragm base.
2. Install washer and O-ring, then back-up plate with large O-ring into diaphragm base.
3. Assemble diaphragm to spring retaining cup. Position assembly so diaphragm holes match up with capscrew holes in base.
4. Install pressure spring on retaining plate and place spring seat on top of spring.
5. Assemble top cover over spring with cover holes matching holes in diaphragm base, pre-load spring and secure top cover to base with capscrews and lockwashers.
6. Connect air supply to IN port and a pressure gauge to OUT port, check regulated pressure.

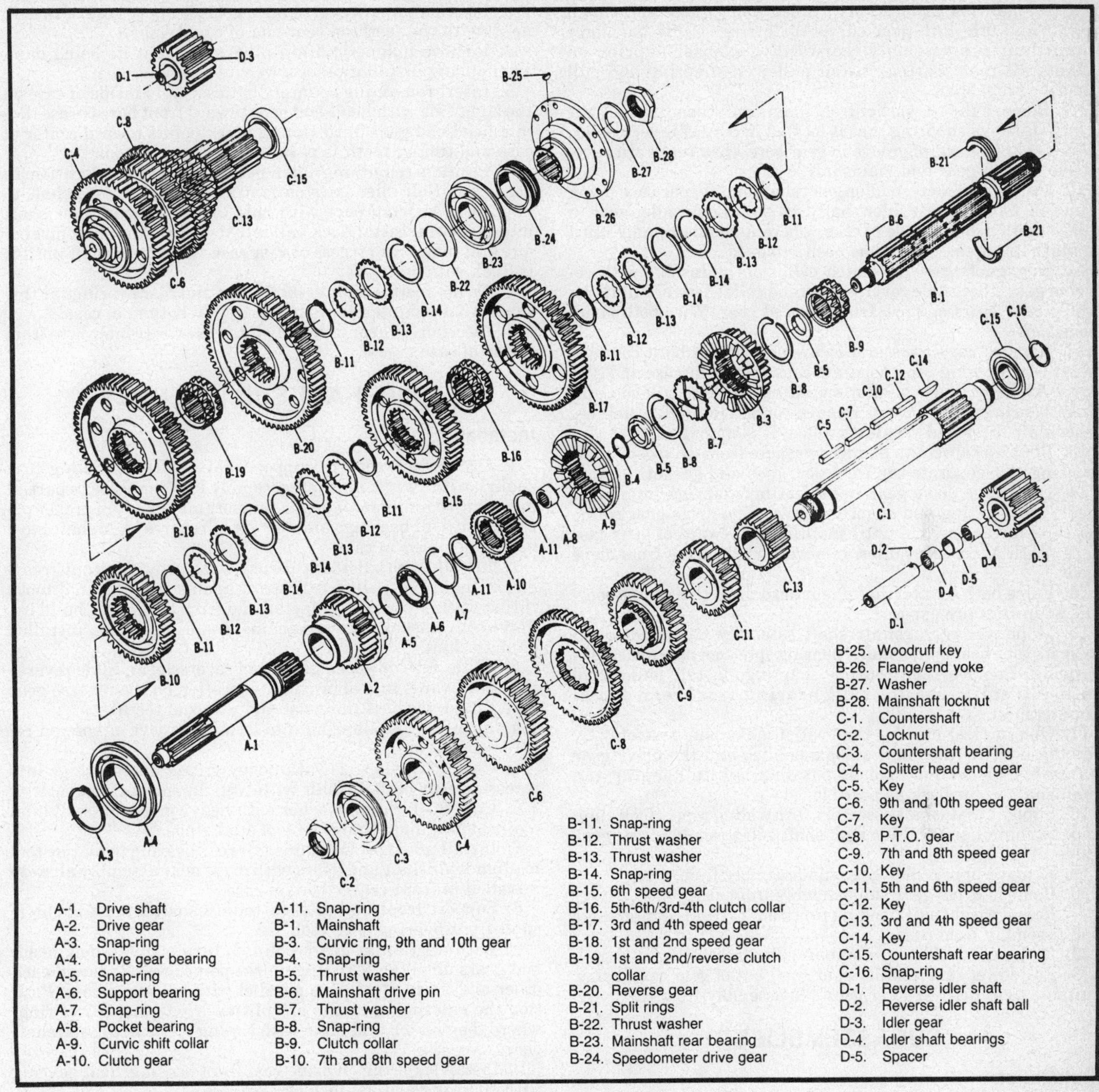

Spicer SST 1010-24 ten speed mainshaft—exploded view (© Ford Motor Co.)

7. Turn adjusting screw inward to increase or outward to decrease pressure until specified pressure of 75 to 80 psi, is obtained. Check by-pass hole for possible air leaks.
8. Install lock wire on adjusting screw.

SUBASSEMBLIES

Removal

1. Remove six clutch housing to gear case external cap screws and lock washers. Remove four internal cap screws and lock washers from inside clutch housing.
2. With a soft hammer, tap clutch housing off gear case and off OD pilot of drive gear front bearing cap. Remove clutch housing gasket.
3. Rotate main drive gear until timing marks on OD of curvic ring of splitter drive gear match and mate with timing marks on back face of the two countershaft head-end drive gears. Lock splitter shift clutch collar into curvic ring of splitter drive gear.
4. Shift clutch collar on mainshaft into 1st–2nd gear to lock transmission in two gears.
5. Remove both countershaft front lock nuts, and yoke lock nut on mainshaft.
6. Remove yoke from mainshaft with suitable tool. Washer will come off with yoke.
7. Remove capscrews and lock washers from mainshaft rear bearing cap. Separate bearing cap from gear case and gasket. Remove speedometer drive gear and bushing, if used. Remove seal if damaged.

8. At mainshaft, place a pry bar between splitter shift clutch collar and 9th–10th gear curvic tooth ring. Using bar, force mainshaft sub-assembly rearward to expose snapring on mainshaft rear bearing. Install puller on snapring and pull bearing from shaft.

9. Remove thrust washer from mainshaft, then remove split rings. Remove snapring that is located in bore of reverse gear. Work snapring out of groove in gear bore, then rearward to remove it from gear and mainshaft.

10. Pull upper reverse idler gear shaft out of gear case using suitable tool. Recover idler shaft lock ball. Leave idler gear in place and force it to side of case, where it should remain until mainshaft sub-assembly has been removed.

11. Engage 1st/reverse clutch collar on mainshaft with reverse gear, then slide reverse gear and collar forward until reverse gear butts against 1st/2nd speed gear. Wire both gears together.

12. Remove capscrews and lockwashers from both countershaft rear bearing caps, separate caps from gear case and gaskets. Air filter and regulator mounting brackets will come off with bearing caps. Do not remove connecting nylon line between air filter and regulator unless it is damaged.

13. Remove capscrews and lockwashers from drivegear front bearing cap, separate cap from gear case and gasket.

14. Disengage drive gear front bearing snapring from drive gear, pull bearing and snapring forward on drive gear spline stem as far as possible until snapring is forward of gear case face. With a suitable puller, remove front bearing from drive gear.

15. Force both countershafts rearward until their front bearing snaprings are exposed.

16. Maneuver each countershaft assembly rearward to expose its rear bearing. Install a bearing split tool on front side of bearing. Remove rear bearing snapring, install puller tool arms on split tool and pull bearing from rear end of countershaft.

17. Obtain clearance for removal of mainshaft assembly by forcing both countershaft sub-assemblies and the drive gear assembly as far forward as possible, while keeping the mainshaft as far back as possible.

18. Support mainshaft assembly with a sling rope. Hook sling rope to chain hoist and lift mainshaft sub-assembly from gear case.

19. Remove upper idler gear sub-assembly from case.

20. Remove drive gear sub-assembly from case.

21. Remove right side (looking from rear of case) countershaft sub-assembly from case.

22. Remove left side countershaft sub-assembly from case.

23. Pull lower reverse idler gear shaft out of gear case, using suitable tool. Recover idler gear sub-assembly from case.

SUBASSEMBLIES

Installation

Timing teeth are designated by a timing mark (letter V) on the head end of both countershafts and the splitter drive gear. Paint the back face of these three gear teeth with a bright color before installing any sub-assemblies.

COUNTERSHAFTS, REVERSE IDLER GEARS AND DRIVE GEAR ASSEMBLY

Installation

1. Insert either countershaft assembly inside gear case on the left side with head-gear towards front bore of case. Turn head-end gear around until timing mark points inward toward center of case and the tooth itself is parallel with bottom of case.

2. Assemble two idler shaft bearings with a spacer between the bore of each reverse idler gear.

3. Position either reverse idler gear in upper bore of case in mesh with the teeth on rear end of countershaft.

4. Remove magnetic drain plug to prevent its being damaged during installation of lower reverse idler gear.

5. Insert remaining countershaft assembly inside of case on the right side with head-end gear toward front bore of case. Rotate head-end gear until timing mark points toward center of case and timing tooth is parallel with case bottom.

6. Position remaining idler gear to lower boss location in gear case. Roll idler gear on mating teeth of countershaft to align gear bearing bore with hole in case. Install idler shaft into gear bore. Install lock ball into its hole in the shaft just before ball comes into recess of gear case. Tap end of shaft until it is flush with case.

7. Do not install countershaft front and rear bearings at this time. Allow countershafts to lay free in bottom of case.

8. Insert drive gear assembly into gear case center bore from inside of case.

MAINSHAFT SUBASSEMBLY

Installation

1. Use a sling rope to support mainshaft, hook sling to a chain hoist, lower mainshaft assembly into gear case in partial mesh with countershaft gears. Support mainshaft in proper position until all bearings and the upper reverse idler shaft have been assembled in case.

2. Install external tooth thrust washer over output (rear) end of mainshaft, slide it forward against the internal tooth thrust washer previously installed during mainshaft build up. Force both washers forward against snapring already installed on mainshaft.

3. Untie 1st/2nd speed gear from reverse gear. Slide reverse gear backwards into approximate location on the reverse gear bore thrust washers (internal and external teeth).

4. Install large snapring into location groove of bore on reverse gear.

5. Coat split rings (2) with heavy grease, install rings into recess on rear of mainshaft with ring flanges facing gears.

6. Coat thick thrust washer with heavy grease, install it on mainshaft against flange face of split rings.

7. Install pilot tool for mainshaft rear bearing bore. Use tool to align mainshaft and gears with drive gear assembly already installed in front center bore of case.

8. Support front end of each countershaft with a countershaft front bearing bore tool.

9. With all timing gears pointed, turn countershaft head-end gears until the V timing marks point inward toward each other and timing teeth are parallel with bottom of case. Position the two timing marks on splitter drive gear (curvic ring) where they match and mate with timing teeth on countershaft gears.

10. Install snapring on drive gear front bearing. Seat bearing with snapring against face of gear case.

11. Install drive gear front bearing cap with gasket. Align oil port holes of case to oil return holes on bearing cap.

12. Dip capscrews in sealer, attach bearing cap to case with cap screws and washers. Torque to specifications.

13. Remove bearing bore pilot tool from case center rear bore and mainshaft. Slide the three clutch collars into their neutral positions on mainshaft.

14. Start inner race of mainshaft rear bearing on mainshaft with mainshaft rear bearing pilot tool against bearing face. Use drive tubing to drive against pilot tool and force bearing onto shaft and into bore of case. Seat bearing snapring against face of case.

15. Loosen hoist tension on sling and remove rope from mainshaft.

16. Install shaft into upper reverse idler gear bore. Insert shaft lock ball in its hole in the shaft just before ball enters recess in case. Tap end of idler shaft flush with case face.

COUNTERSHAFT

Final Assembly and Tie Up

1. Support rear end of each countershaft with a countershaft rear bearing bore pilot tool. As pilot tools are inserted into bores keep timing teeth in correct mesh with each other.
2. As each front piloting tool is removed and a front bearing installed, both countershafts must be held in proper position relative to the timing teeth mesh and the timing marks must be held in place. Using a countershaft support hook tool, place hooks in web hole of head end gear on each countershaft, support tool with a chain hoist.
3. Remove pilot tool from left countershaft front bore. Install left countershaft front bearing, use face of pilot tool on front end of bearing to drive bearing on shaft and into case bore. Seat bearing snapring to face of case.
4. Install left countershaft front lock nut on shaft and hand tighten it against bearing.
5. Remove pilot tool from right countershaft front bore, install right countershaft front bearing in same manner as described for left countershaft.
6. Remove hook tool and chain hoist from countershafts.
7. Install right countershaft front nut on shaft and hand tighten it against bearing.
8. Lock transmission in two gears by engaging splitter shift clutch collar to curvic ring of splitter drive gear and by shifting 1st/2nd reverse clutch collar into 1st/2nd speed gear. Tighten both countershaft front bearing lock nuts to specifications.
9. Remove pilot tool from left countershaft rear bore. Install countershaft rear bearing. Bearing must be assembled with snapring toward outside of transmission case.
10. Use pilot tool tubing to give bearing on shaft and into bore of case. Install snapring on shaft.
11. Remove pilot tool from right countershaft rear bore. Install right countershaft rear bearing in same manner as described for left countershaft.
12. Insert speedometer gear into mainshaft rear bearing cap with oil return holes of bearing cap aligned with port holes in case.
13. Dip bearing cap retaining screws in sealer, install screws with washers. Torque to specifications.
14. Install both countershaft rear bearing caps with gaskets to face of gear case. Install retaining screws and washers and torque to specifications.
15. Install end yoke with washer on mainshaft output splines. Use yoke and flange installer tool.
16. Install mainshaft locknut, torque to specification.
17. Move 1st–2nd reverse clutch collar into its neutral position. Leave splitter shift clutch collar engaged in splitter drive gear.
18. Roll gear train by turning drive gear stem. If tooth timing marks are in correct positions, entire gear train will roll freely. If timing teeth have been aligned wrong or escaped their proper position, gear train will lock up after several turns of drive gear.
19. If unit locks up, disengage shift collar from splitter drive gear. Turn drive gear in reverse rotation until timing marks come into match or close mis-match. If mismatch appears, timing was set incorrectly at time of assembly or timing teeth escaped positioning during final tie up. If this is the case, shafts must be retimed.
20. If timing is correct, shift all clutch collars, except splitter shift collar, into their neutral positions for later installation of shifter housing assembly. Move splitter shift clutch collar into mesh with 9th/10th speed gear so that it will be in proper position for assembly with splitter shift fork.

CLUTCH HOUSING

Installation

1. Using drive gear front bearing cap as a pilot, place clutch housing gasket on front face of gear case.
2. Install clutch housing, using drive gear bearing cap as a guide.
3. Dip capscrews in sealer, install capscrews and washers (six external and eight internal) and torque to specifications.
4. Install clutch release yoke and short shaft to clutch housing. Assemble long shaft to yoke. Align keyway with slots in yoke, assemble key, capscrews and lockwashers.
5. Replace P.T.O. opening covers and gaskets. Tighten retaining screws to specifications.
6. Install magnetic drain plug in right side of case and drain plug in left side.
7. Install shifter housing gasket to gear case.
8. With all shift forks in their neutral position, install shifter housing to gear case so that all shift forks engage their respective clutch collars.

AIR CONTROL AND RELATED PARTS

Installation

1. Assemble mounting brackets to air pressure regulator and air filter assemblies. Mount pressure regulator and bracket to right countershaft rear bearing cap. Mount air filter and bracket to left countershaft rear bearing cap.
2. Connect hose between filter and regulator. Secure with clamp on mainshaft rear bearing capscrew.
3. Install shift lever assembly with retaining screws and lockwashers, torque to specifications.
4. Attach air hose from regulator elbow to control valve tee on top of control valve body. Secure hose with clamp using existing capscrew and lock washer.
5. Connect nylon hose from control valve elbow to selector valve in-port hole fitting.
6. Connect nylon hose from splitter control front elbow to selector valve out-port hole fitting.

SHIFTER HOUSING

Disassembly

1. Remove retaining screws and lock washers and splitter piston housing from shifter housing.
2. Place splitter control in soft jaws of a vise with splitter piston rod shift bracket in the up position. Cut lock wire and remove set screw from bracket.
3. Remove splitter piston housing cover.
4. Remove actuating piston and rod from shift bracket and out of piston by pulling on rod lock nut. If piston O-rings have cuts or flat spots on air sealing surfaces, replace.
5. Remove splitter air valve control body from piston housing.
6. Remove valve plungers (2) from valve body. Inspect O-rings on each plunger for flat spots or cuts on sealing surfaces, replace as needed.
7. Install new O-rings on plungers. Lubricate with Dow silicon grease.
8. Reassemble plungers into valve body, install valve body on piston housing with six retaining screws and lock washers. Torque to specifications.
9. Place piston on actuation piston rod, secure it to rod with lock nut, hand tighten.
10. Install piston and rod into cylindrical housing. As rod end comes through front boss, install shift bracket on rod with extended hub of bracket toward welch plug.
11. Locate shift bracket in its proper position on piston rod. Install set screw, torque to specification, secure with a lock wire.
12. Tighten piston rod lock nut to specifications.
13. Install splitter piston housing cover and gasket, lock washers and retaining screws. Tighten to specifications.
14. Remove shoes from splitter shift fork.
15. Place shifter housing in vise with rods and forks exposed.

16. Remove lock wires and set screws from shift forks.

17. Turn splitter shift rod 90 degrees in either direction to preload poppet detent pin into recess hole of center boss of shifter housing.

18. Tap splitter shift rod to left with a soft drift. As rod clears housing center boss, recover detent pin, remove poppet spring from recess hole in boss. As rod clears splitter fork, remove fork from rod and remove rod from housing front boss.

19. Tap 7th and 8th/9th and 10th shift rod to left. Remove bracket as it clears rod. Recover poppet ball and spring as rod clears front boss. Remove shift fork as it clears rod, then remove rod from front boss.

20. Tap 3rd and 4th/5th and 6th shift rod to left, recover poppet ball and spring from housing boss. Recover shift rod interlock pin if it dislodges during rod movement. Remove shift fork as it clears rod. Remove rod from front boss.

21. Remove housing boss interlock pin located internally in rear boss between 3rd and 4th/5th and 6th, and 7thand 8th/9th and 10th shift rod bores.

22. Tap 1st and 2nd/reverse shift rod to left, remove shift fork as it clears rod. Recover poppet ball and spring from housing boss. Remove bracket sub-assembly as it clears rod, remove rod from front boss.

23. Remove second housing boss interlock pin located internally in boss between 3rd and 4th/5th and 6th and 1st and 2nd/reverse shift rod bores.

24. To disassemble 1st and 2nd/reverse shift bracket, grip trunnion ends in a vise. Shear block retainer pin using a flat head punch against small diameter end of plunger. Strike plunger end with a sharp blow to shear pin. Check block and plunger for excessive wear, check spring for broken coils or loss of tension.

25. Remove vent from top surface of shifter housing.

26. Examine shift fork shoes for excessive wear. Sharp corners should be chamfered to allow entry of oil between shoes and shift collar.

27. Check 1st–reverse blocker pins located on internal side of shifter housing. If pins show excessive wear or galling, drive out with a flat head punch. Press new pin into its hole in shifter housing, flush with top surface of housing. This will allow proper length extension to internal location of shifter housing.

Assembly

1. Grip trunnion ends of 1st and 2nd/reverse shift bracket in a vise. Insert plunger and spring into plunger hole of bracket. Preload plunger with a "C" clamp.

2. Assemble block to bracket so end of plunger enters hole in block. The step on the block must face inward against the block. Assembling the block outward will cause 1st/2nd reverse gear blockout. Align plunger pin hole with block pin hole, install lock pin with a 0.084 inch flat head punch. Tap pin until it is fully seated. Release C-clamp from plunger, move plunger in and out to be sure it moves freely.

3. Place shifter housing on a bench with inside of housing facing up and front of housing to the left.

4. Check all four shift rods to make sure they slide freely in boss bores without excessive radial movement. Coat rods and bores of shifter housing lightly with grease, install rods in bores.

5. Coat interlock pin with heavy grease, insert it into 1st and 2nd/reverse shift rod bore through hole in rear boss.

6. Insert and preload poppet spring and ball in poppet detent bore of 1st and 2nd/reverse rod location.

7. Start end of 1st and 2nd/reverse shift rod and bracket (farthest from setscrew countersunk holes) through rear boss of housing. Assemble bracket on rod with top boss of bracket down, and shift gate towards lower opening. Tap rod sharply to remove poppet loading tool and slide rod into front boss. Assemble shift fork on rod with extended hub of fork to the right. Position fork and bracket on rod, install set screws, tighten to specifications, install lock wires. Move shift rod until poppet ball registers in neutral detent of rod.

8. Install and preload poppet spring and ball in poppet detent bore of 3rd and 4th/5th and 6th shift rod location of boss. Use suitable poppet tool.

9. Select 3rd and 4th/5th and 6th shift rod and fork. Coat small interlock pin (shift rod) with heavy grease, insert into hole of shift rod. Enter rod with interlock pin to the right through rear boss. Assemble fork to rod with fork hub to the left. As rod enters the front boss, tap it sharply to remove poppet loading tool. Position shift fork on rod, install set screw, tighten to specifications, install lock wire. Move shift rod until poppet registers in neutral detent of rod.

10. Coat interlock pin with heavy grease, insert it into 7th and 8th/9th and 10th shift rod bore through hole in rear boss. Install poppet spring and ball in poppet detent bore of 7th and 8th/9th and 10th shift rod location of boss. Use suitable poppet tool.

11. Select 7th and 8th/9th and 10th shift rod, bracket and fork. Enter rod end (farthest from interlock detent) into rear of boss. Assemble bracket on rod with shift gate downward. Tap rod sharply to remove poppet loading tool in front boss. Assemble fork to rod with fork hub to left. Position bracket and fork on rod, install setscrews, torque to specification, secure with lock wire. Move rod until poppet registers in neutral detent of rod.

12. Insert and preload poppet spring and ball in poppet detent bore of splitter shift rod location of boss. Use a suitable poppet tool.

13. Select splitter shift rod and fork. Insert detent end of rod into front boss with detent facing up. Assemble fork to shaft with extended hub of fork to right and hub shift gate down. Tap rod sharply to remove poppet loading tool. Turn rod 180 degrees so poppet pin locates in rod detent. Position fork on rod, install set screw, tighten to specifications, install lock wire. Move rod until poppet registers in left detent of rod. This locates the splitter fork in the LO position of splitter to transmission gear.

14. Shift 1st and 2nd/reverse speed shift fork into gear position. Try to shift the other two shift rods (3rd and 4th/5th and 6th and 7th and 8th/9th and 10th). Rods will be locked in neutral position if interlocks are functioning.

15. Return 1st and 2nd/reverse shift fork to neutral. Check movement of each of the other shift rods to make sure they move readily and completely into each gear position.

16. Turn shifter housing assembly over (top up). Install vent in tapped hole in top of housing, use sealer on threads.

17. Assemble splitter piston housing and splitter control valve body to shifter housing with gasket. As assembly is mounted to housing, be sure to engage pad on splitter piston rod shift bracket into splitter shift fork. Secure assembly to housing with four capscrews with lock washers.

18. Coat trunnions of splitter fork shoes with heavy grease, insert shoes in splitter fork.

MAINSHAFT

Disassembly

1. Remove snapring from front end of mainshaft, slide 9th/10th gear assembly off shaft drive pins.

2. Remove 7th and 8th/9th and 10th clutch collar from shaft.

3. Remove snapring from shaft groove, then remove 7th/8th speed gear sub-assembly.

4. Remove 5th/6th gear sub-assembly, remove snapring from shaft groove.

5. Remove 5th and 6th/3rd and 4th clutch collar from shaft.

6. Remove snapring under 3rd/4th speed gear bore, then remove 3rd/4th speed gear sub-assembly.

7. Remove wire that was used to fasten 1st/2nd speed gear to the reverse gear when mainshaft was removed from gear case.

8. Remove 1st/2nd gear sub-assembly from shaft, remove snapring from shaft groove.
9. Remove 1st/2nd/reverse shift collar from shaft.
10. Remove reverse gear sub-assembly from (rear) output end of shaft.

Assembly

Before assembly, inspect all thrust washers. If they show heavy face galling or tooth wear, they should be replaced. Lubricate old or new thrust washers with 30 weight engine oil on thrust faces as they are assembled to the shaft.

1. Position mainshaft vertically in a vise with output and splines of shaft resting on the bed and soft jaws clamping on the spline area.
2. Install internal tooth thrust washer on mainshaft, let it rest on the shoulder near output splines. The external tooth thrust washer is installed after mainshaft sub-assembly has been installed in gear case.
3. Install snapring in lower groove (output end) of shaft. Make sure ring is seated firmly in groove.
4. Assemble 1st and 2nd/reverse clutch collar on shaft either end of collar down. Rest collar against snapring.

NOTE: Clutch collars are identical parts. They can be installed in any of the gear positions. Either end can be installed on the shaft at the time of assembly.

5. Install 1st/2nd sub-assembly snapring in shaft groove closest to the 1st and 2nd/reverse clutch collar.
6. Install internal tooth thrust washer on shaft so it rests on the snapring.
7. With both thrust washers and large snapring assembled into 1st/2nd speed gear, install 1st/nd sub-assembly on shaft so chamfer in bore of gear extends down toward clutch collar.
8. Assemble second set of thrust washers and large snapring into 3rd/4th speed gear. Install 3rd/4th sub-assembly on shaft with chamfer up. Rest 3rd/4th speed gear against face of 1st/2nd speed gears. Install third (shaft) snapring in shaft groove under bore of 3rd/4th speed gear.
9. Assemble 3rd and 4th/5th and 6th clutch collar so it rests in the bore of 3rd/4th speed gear.
10. Install fourth (shaft) snapring in shaft groove closest to 3rd and 4th/5th and 6th clutch collar.
11. Install two thrust washers (one internal, one external) on shaft, resting them on snapring.
12. Assemble large snapring into 5th/6th speed gear, assemble in bore with gear chamfer down toward clutch collar.
13. Assemble fourth set of washers with large snapring into 7th/8th speed gear. Assemble 7th/8th gear sub-assembly with chamfer up, resting against face of 5th/6th gear. Install fifth snapring in shaft groove under bore of 7th/8th speed gear.
14. Assemble 7th and 8th/9th and 10th speed clutch collar on shaft.
15. If 9th–10th speed gear was disassembled for inspection of thrust washer and large snaprings, reassemble one large snapring in gear bore groove. Install thrust washer and lock parts together with second large snapring.
16. If drive pins on front of mainshaft do not have to be replaced, install 9th/10th sub-assembly on mainshaft.
17. Lock up all 9th–10th gear parts on shaft by installing small snapring in shaft groove. Install curvic shift collar on 9th/10th gear curvic ring.
18. Remove complete assembly from vise and place it on work bench.
19. Slide 1st and 2nd/reverse clutch collar into bore of 1st and 2nd speed gear. Also slide internal tooth thrust washer on rear end of shaft against the snapring.
20. Do not install external tooth thrust washer or large snapring into bore of reverse gear at this time. Assemble reverse gear on rear (output) end of mainshaft. Assemble reverse gear with chamfer of clutch teeth toward clutch collar. Match O.D. teeth of clutch collar to 1st/2nd speed gear internal teeth. Butt both gears together and tie with wire.

COUNTERSHAFT

Disassembly

Use arbor press with parallel bars to remove all gears except 9th and 10th speed gear.

1. Support head-end drive gear with parallel bars as close to hub as possible, press countershaft out of gear.
2. Remove 9th/10th speed gear from countershaft with a puller engaged in the lightener holes in web of gear.
3. Lift P.T.O. gear off splined teeth of 7th/8th speed gear.
4. Support 7th–8th speed gear with parallel bars under gear teeth, press shaft out of gear.
5. Support 3rd/4th speed gear with parallel bars as close to hub as possible, press countershaft out of 5th and 6th/3rd and 4th speed gears.

Assembly

Coat bores of all gears with oil before pressing gears on countershaft. Install key in keyway for one gear at a time. Use mill file to align sides or remove burrs.

1. Press 3rd/4th speed key into place on countershaft. Support 3rd/4th speed gear (either face down). Align key with gear keyway and press shaft and key into gear. Seat gear firmly against face of 1st/2nd speed gear. If necessary tap key flush with gear face.
2. Press the 1 $^{9}/_{19}$ inch 5th/6th speed gear key into place on countershaft. Support 5th–6th speed gear on bars with long hub up. Align key with gear keyway and press shaft and key into gear. Set gear firmly against face of 3rd/4th speed gear. If necessary, tap key back flush with face of gear.
3. Press the 2 $^{3}/_{8}$ inch, 7th/8th speed gear key into place on countershaft. Support 7th/8th speed gear on bars with splined teeth on hub down. Align gear keyway with key and press shaft and key into gear. Seat gear face firmly against face of 5th–6th speed gear. Be sure key is flush with face of gear.
4. Slide P.T.O. gear onto splined teeth of 7th/8th speed gear with long hub of P.T.O. gear against face of 7th/8th speed gear.
5. Press the 2 $^{7}/_{16}$ inch, 9th/10th speed gear key into keyway on the countershaft. Support 9th/10th speed gear on bars with long hub end down. Set shaft into gear holding the P.T.O. gear in mesh with its mating gear. Align gear keyway with key and press shaft and key into gear. Seat gear firmly against face of 7th/8th speed gear. Be sure key is flush with face of gear.
6. Press head-end drive gear key into keyway on countershaft. Support head-end (splitter) drive gear on bars with long hub up. Be sure timing mark on tooth web of gear is in alignment with center of gear keyway. Set shaft into gear, align gear keyway with key, press shaft and key into gear. Seat gear face firmly against face of 9th/10th speed gear. Be sure key is flush with face of gear.

DRIVE GEAR

Disassembly

1. If pocket bearing must be replaced, use a small puller to remove it from pocket of drive gear.
2. Remove clutch gear to shaft outer snapring, remove splitter clutch gear from drive gear splines. Remove clutch gear to shaft outer snapring.
3. Remove large snapring from bore of splitter drive gear, force splitter drive gear off and away from rear bearing.
4. Remove shaft groove to bearing face snapring from drive gear and shaft assembly. Support rear bearing on a press bed and press drive gear and shaft assembly out of bearing.

TORQUE SPECIFICATIONS
Spicer SST-1010 Series

	ft. lbs.
Mainshaft flange/yoke locknut	550–600
Left countershaft—front locknut	550–600
Right countershaft—front locknut	550–600
Clutch housing locknuts	
½″ Dia.	60–80
⅝″ Dia.	120–150
Mainshaft front bearing capscrews	25–32
Mainshaft rear bearing capscrews	60–80
Countershafts rear bearing capscrews	25–32
Shifter housing capscrews	25–32
All set screws (shift forks, bracket and fingers)	40–50
Splitter air control valve body-to-piston housing	7–10
Splitter air piston-to-rod locknut	40–50
Splitter piston housing cover capscrews	13–17
Air regulator pressure	75–80 psi

Assembly

1. Support rear bearing in an arbor press (inner race of bearing). Press drive shaft gear shaft assembly into bearing. Seat snapring in its seat on the shaft.
2. Position the shaft and bearing assembly into bearing bore of splitter drive gear. Seat bearing to the facer of the splitter drive gear and install gear bore groove to bearing snapring.
3. Install clutch gear to shaft inner snapring in groove near bore of splitter drive gear. Assemble splitter clutch gear on shaft and install second (outer) snapring on shaft to secure the clutch gear.
4. Support drive gear sub-assembly in press. Rest the front face of splitter drive gear on press bed. Press pocket bearing into pocket or small inner bore of drive gear and shaft assembly. The bearing with part number JH1812 must be visible when pressed into bore. Press bearing so that it is recessed slightly under gear face.
5. The drive gear assembly must be installed in drive gear case bore from internal side after countershaft assembles have been positioned on bottom of case.
6. Install front bearing and snapring on drive gear assembly and into the case bore from the outside. The drive gear assembly is installed into the gear case later.

Tremec T-150
Three Speed Transmission (77 mm)

The Tremec T-150 (77 mm) transmission is used in varied vehicle applications, with or without transfer cases. The gear selection is controlled by either a top shift housing or by a remote control shift lever assembly. Although some of the gears and case applications are not interchangeable, the gear arrangement is basically the same.

Disassembly

1. Remove the bolts securing the transfer case to the transmission. Remove the transfer case.
2. Remove the transfer case drive gear locknut, flat washer, and drive gear. Remove the large fiber washer from the rear bearing adapter. Move the second-third clutch sleeve forward and the first/reverse sleeve to the rear before removing the locknut.
3. Remove the transmission oil plug and drive the countershaft out of the case with a suitable size drift. Do not lose the countershaft access plug when removing the countershaft. With the countershaft removed the countershaft gear will lie at the bottom of the case, leave it there until the mainshaft is removed.
4. Punch alignment marks in the front bearing cap and the transmission case for assembly reference.
5. Remove the front bearing cap and gasket.
6. Remove the large lock ring from the front bearing.
7. Remove the clutch shaft, front bearing, and the second/third synchronizer assembly. A special tool is required for this operation.
8. Remove the rear bearing and adapter assembly with a brass drift and hammer. Drive the adapter out the rear of the case with light blows from the hammer.
9. Remove the mainshaft assembly. Tilt the spline end of the shaft downward and lift the front end up and out of the case.
10. Remove the countershaft tool and arbor as an assembly. Remove the countershaft thrust washers, countershaft roll pin, and any pilot roller bearings that may have fallen into the case.
11. Remove the reverse idler shaft. Insert a brass drift through the clutch shaft bore in the front of the case and tap the shaft until the end with the roll pin clears the counter bore in the rear of the case. Remove the shaft.
12. Remove the reverse idler gear and thrust washers from the case.
13. Remove the retaining snapring from the front of the mainshaft. Remove the second/third synchronizer assembly and second gear. Mark the hub and sleeve for reference during assembly. Observe the position of the insert springs and the inserts during removal for correct assembly.
14. Remove the insert springs from the second/third synchronizer, remove the three inserts, and separate the sleeve from the synchronizer hub retaining snapring.
15. Remove the snapring and the tabbed thrust washer from the mainshaft and remove the first gear blocking ring.
16. Remove the first/reverse synchronizer hub snapring. Observe the position of the insert springs and the inserts during removal for correct assembly.
17. Remove the first/reverse sleeve, insert spring and the three insert from the hub. Remove the spacer from the rear of the mainshaft. Do not attempt to remove the press fit hub by hammering. Hammer blows will damage the hub and mainshaft.
18. Remove the front bearing retaining snapring and any remaining roller bearings from the clutch shaft.
19. Press the front bearing off the clutch shaft with an arbor press. Do not attempt to remove the bearing by hammering. Hammer blows will damage the bearing and the clutch shaft.
20. Clamp the rear bearing adapter in a soft jawed vise. Do not over tighten.
21. Remove the rear bearing retaining snapring. Remove the bearing adapter from the vise.
22. Press the rear bearing out of the adapter with an arbor press.

Cleaning and Inspection

1. Thoroughly wash all parts in clean solvent and dry with

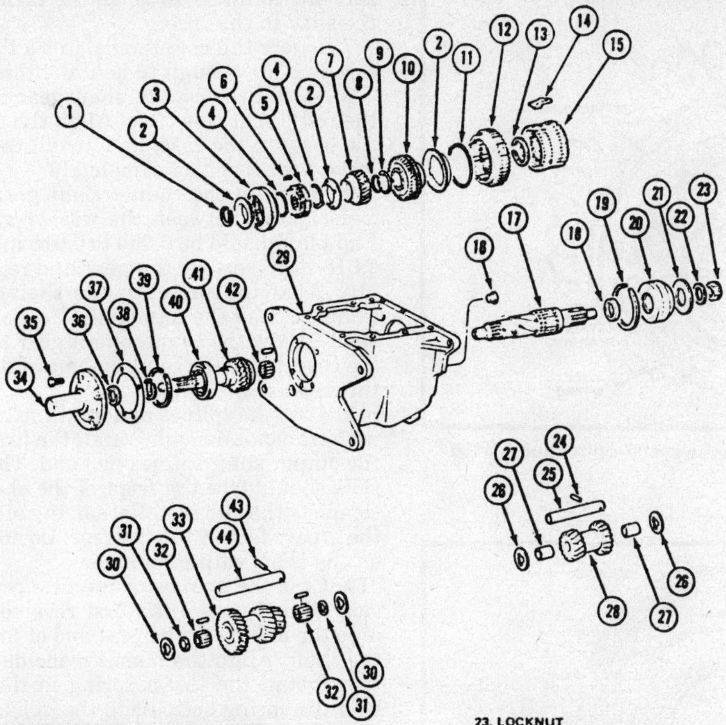

1. MAINSHAFT RETAINING SNAP RING
2. SYNCHRONIZER BLOCKING RINGS (3)
3. SECOND-THIRD SYNCHRONIZER SLEEVE
4. SECOND-THIRD SYNCHRONIZER INSERT SPRING (2)
5. SECOND-THIRD HUB
6. SECOND-THIRD SYNCHRONIZER INSERT (3)
7. SECOND GEAR
8. FIRST GEAR RETAINING SNAP RING
9. FIRST GEAR TABBED THRUST WASHER
10. FIRST GEAR
11. FIRST-REVERSE SYNCHRONIZER INSERT SPRING
12. FIRST-REVERSE SLEEVE AND GEAR
13. FIRST-REVERSE HUB RETAINING SNAP RING
14. FIRST-REVERSE SYNCHRONIZER INSERT (3)
15. FIRST-REVERSE HUB
16. COUNTERSHAFT ACCESS PLUG
17. MAINSHAFT
18. MAINSHAFT SPACER
19. REAR BEARING ADAPTER LOCK RING
20. REAR BEARING AND ADAPTER ASSEMBLY
21. FIBER WASHER
22. FLAT WASHER
23. LOCKNUT
24. ROLL PIN
25. REVERSE IDLER GEAR SHAFT
26. THRUST WASHER
27. BUSHING (PART OF IDLER GEAR)
28. REVERSE IDLER GEAR
29. TRANSMISSIONCASE
30. THRUST WASHER (2)
31. BEARING RETAINER (2)
32. COUNTERSHAFT NEEDLE BEARINGS (50)
33. COUNTERSHAFT GEAR
34. FRONT BEARING CAP
35. BOLT (4)
36. FRONT BEARING CAP OIL SEAL
37. GASKET
38. FRONT BEARING RETAINER SNAP RING
39. FRONT BEARING LOCKRING
40. FRONT BEARING
41. CLUTCH SHAFT
42. MAINSHAFT PILOT ROLLER BEARINGS
43. ROLL PIN
44. COUNTERSHAFT

T-150 transmission—exploded view (© AMC Corp.)

compressed air. Do not dry the bearings with compressed air, use a clean shop cloth.

2. Clean the needle and clutch shaft bearings by placing them in a shallow parts cleaning tray and covering them with solvent. Allow the bearings to air dry on a clean shop cloth.

3. Check the case for the following. Cracks in the bores, bosses, or bolt holes. Stripped threads in bolt holes. Nicks, burrs, rough surfaces in the shaft bores or on the gasket surfaces.

4. Check the gear and synchronizer assemblies for the following. Broken, chipped, or worn gear teeth. Damaged splines on the synchronizer hubs or sleeves. Bent or damaged inserts. Damaged needle bearings or bearing bores in the countershaft gear. Broken or worn teeth or excessive wear of the blocking rings. Wear of galling of the countershaft, clutch shaft, or reverse idler shaft. Worn thrust washers. Nicked, broken, or worn mainshaft or clutch shaft splines. Bent, distorted, or weak snaprings. Worn bushings in the reverse idler gear. Replace the gear if the bushings are worn. Rough, galled, or broken front or rear bearings.

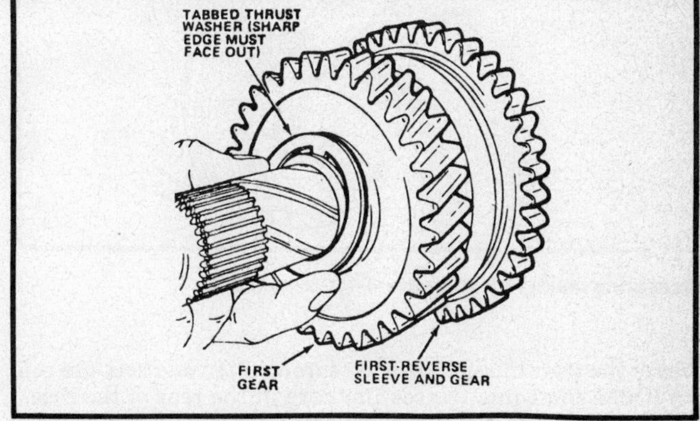

Installing first gear thrust washer on mainshaft—T-150 (© AMC Corp.)

Assembly

1. Lubricate the reverse idler shaft bore and bushings with transmission oil.

2. Coat the transmission case reverse idler gear thrust washer surfaces with petroleum jelly and install the thrust washers in the case. Make sure the locating tangs on the thrust washers are aligned in the slots in the case.

3. Install the reverse idler gear. Align the gear bore, thrust washers, and case bore. Install the reverse idler shaft from the

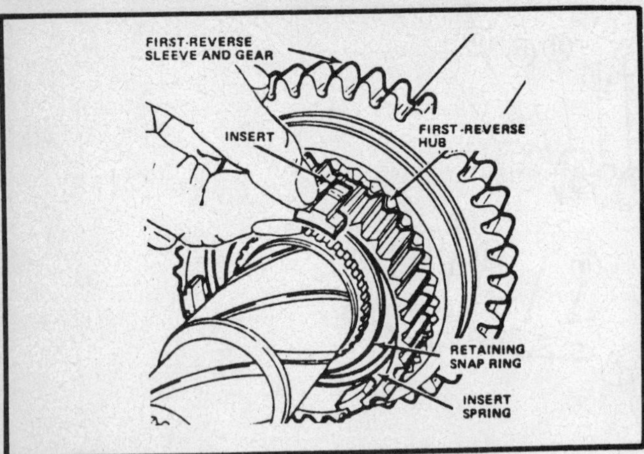

Installing the inserts in the first/reverse synchronizer hub—T-150 (© AMC Corp.)

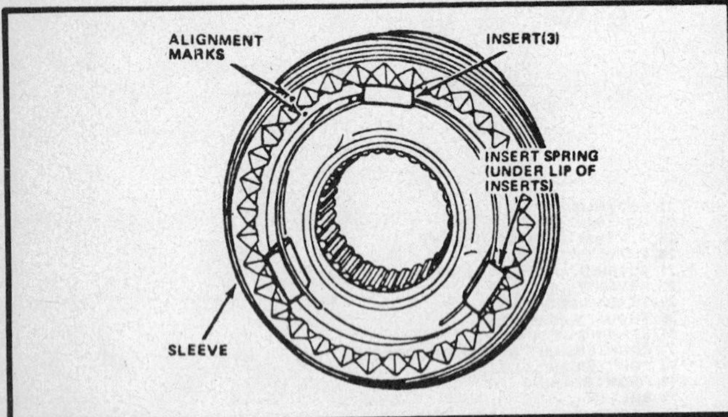

Installing second gear on mainshaft—T-150 (© AMC Corp.)

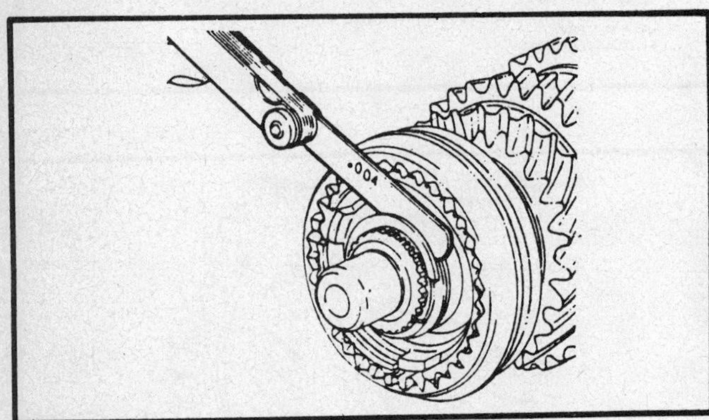

Measuring mainshaft endplay—T-150 (© AMC Corp.)

rear of the transmission case. Be sure to align and seat the roll pin in the shaft into the counter bore in the rear of the case.

4. Measure the reverse idler gear end-play by inserting a feeler gauge between the thrust washer and the gear. End-play should be 0.004 to 0.018 inch. If end play exceeds 0.018 inch, remove the reverse idler gear and replace the thrust washers.

5. Coat the needle bearing bores in the countershaft gear with petroleum jelly. Insert the arbor tool in the bore of the gear and install the (25) needle bearings and the retainer washers at each end of the countershaft gear.

6. Coat the countershaft gear thrust washer surface with petroleum jelly and position the thrust washers in the case. Make sure the locating tangs on the thrust washers are aligned in the slots in the case.

7. Insert the countershaft into the bore at the rear of the case just far enough to hold the thrust washer in place.

8. Install the countershaft gear in the case. Do not install the roll pin at this time. Align the gear bore, thrust washers, the bores in the case, and install the countershaft. Do not remove the arbor tool completely.

9. Measure the countershaft gear end-play by inserting a feeler gauge between the washer and the countershaft gear. End-play should be 0.004 to 0.018 inch. If the end-play exceeds 0.018 inch, remove the gear and replace the thrust washer.

10. When the correct countershaft gear end-play has been obtained, install the countershaft arbor and remove the countershaft. Allow the countershaft gear to remain at the bottom of the case, leave the countershaft in the case enough to hold the thrust washer in place.

11. Coat the splines and machined surfaces on the mainshaft with transmission oil. Install the first/reverse synchronizer on the output shaft splines by hand. The end of the hub with the slots should face the front of the shaft. Use an arbor press to complete the hub installation. Install the retaining snapring in the groove farthest to the rear. Do not attempt to drive the hub on the shaft with a hammer.

12. Coat the splines of the first/reverse hub with transmission oil and install the first reverse sleeve and gear halfway onto the hub, with the gear end of the sleeve facing the rear of the shaft. Align the marks made during disassembly.

13. Install the insert spring in the first/reverse hub. Make sure the spring bottoms in the hub and covers all three insert slots. Position the three "T" shaped inserts in the hub with the small ends in the hub slots and the large ends inside the hub. Push the inserts fully into the hub so they seat on the insert spring, slide the first/reverse sleeve and gear over the inserts until the inserts engage in the sleeve.

14. Coat the bore and the blocking ring surface of first gear with transmission oil and place blocking ring on the tapered surface of the gear.

15. Install the first gear on the output shaft. Rotate the gear until the notches in the blocking ring engage the inserts in the first/reverse synchronizer assembly. Install the tanged thrust washer, sharp end facing out, and retaining snapring on the mainshaft.

16. Coat the bore and blocking ring surface of the second gear with transmission oil. Place the second gear blocking ring on the tapered surface of second gear.

17. Install the second gear on the output shaft with the tapered surface of the gear facing the front of the mainshaft.

18. Install one insert spring into the second/third synchronizer hub. Be sure that the spring covers all three insert slots in the hub. Align the second-third sleeve with the hub using the marks made during disassembly. Start the sleeve onto the hub.

19. Place the three inserts into the hub slots and on top of the insert spring. Push the sleeve fully onto the hub to engage the inserts in the sleeve. Install the remaining insert spring in the exact position as the first spring. The ends of both springs must cover the same slot in the hub and not be staggered. The inserts have a small lip on each end. When they are correctly installed, this lip will fit over the insert spring.

20. Install the second/third synchronizer assembly on the mainshaft. Rotate the second gear until the notches in the blocking ring engage the inserts in the second/third synchronizer assembly.

21. Install the retaining snapring on the mainshaft and measure the end-play between the snapring and the second/third synchronizer hub. The end-play should be 0.040 to 0.014 inch. If the end-play exceeds the limit, replace the thrust washer and all the snaprings on the mainshaft assembly. Install the spacer on the rear of the mainshaft.

22. Install the mainshaft assembly in the case. Be sure that the first/reverse sleeve and gear is in the neutral (centered) position.

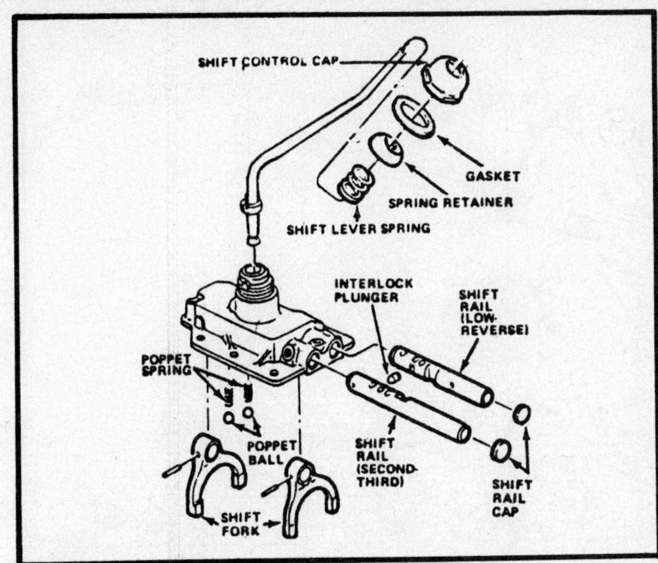

Shift control housing—T-150 (© AMC Corp.)

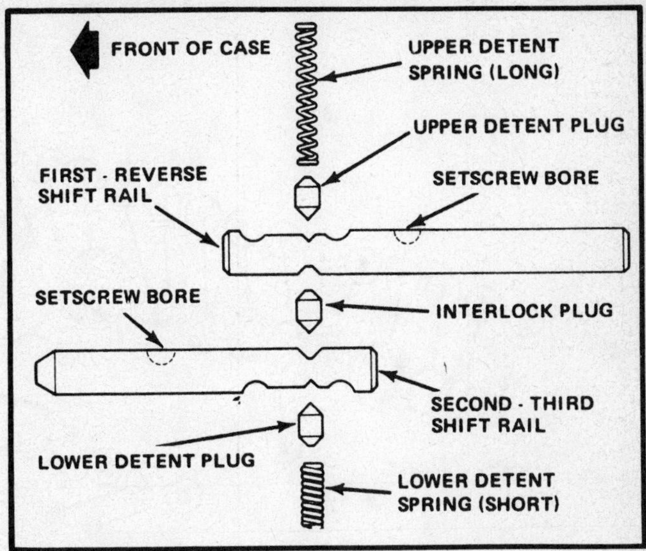

Proper positioning of detent plugs and springs in the remote shifting control shift rails (© AMC Corp.)

23. Press the rear bearing into the rear bearing adapter with an arbor press. Install the rear bearing retaining ring and the bearing adapter lockring.
24. Support the mainshaft assembly and install the rear bearing and adapter assembly in the case. Use a soft faced hammer to seat the adapter in the case.
25. Install the large fiber washer in the rear bearing adapter. Install the transfer drive gear, flat washer, and locknut. Tighten the locknut to 150 ft. lbs. torque.
26. Press the front bearing onto the clutch shaft. Install the bearing retaining snapring on the clutch shaft and the lockring into its groove.
27. Coat the bore of the clutch shaft assembly with petroleum jelly and install the (15) roller bearings in the clutch shaft bore. Do not use chassis grease or a similar heavy grease in the clutch shaft bore. Heavy grease will plug the lubricant holes in the shaft and prevent proper lubrication of the roller bearings.
28. Coat the blocking ring surface of the clutch shaft with transmission oil. Position the blocking ring on the clutch shaft.
29. Support the mainshaft assembly and insert the clutch shaft through the front bearing bore in the case. Seat the mainshaft pilot in the clutch shaft roller bearings. Tap the bearings into place with a soft faced hammer.
30. Apply a thin film of sealer to the front bearing cap gasket and position the gasket on the case. Be sure the cutout in the gasket is aligned with the oil return hole in the case.
31. Remove the front bearing cap oil seal with a suitable tool. Install a new seal with a suitable driver.
32. Install the front bearing cap and tighten the bolts to 33 ft. lbs. Be sure that the marks on the cap and the transmission case are aligned and the oil return slot in the cap lines up with the oil return hole in the case.
33. Make a wire loop about 18 to 20 inches long and pass the wire under the countershaft gear assembly. The wire loop should raise and support the countershaft gear assembly when it is pulled upward.
34. Raise the countershaft gear with the wire. Align the bore in the countershaft gear with the front thrust washer and the countershaft. Start the countershaft into the gear with a soft faced hammer.
35. Align the roll pin hole in the countershaft with the roll pin holes in the case and complete the installation of the countershaft. Install the countershaft access plug in the rear of the case and seat with a soft faced hammer.
36. Install the countershaft roll pin in the case. Use a magnet or needle nose pliers to insert and start the pin in the case. Use a ½ inch punch to seat the pin. Install the transmission filler plug.
37. Shift the synchronizer sleeves through all gear ranges and check their operation. If the clutch shaft and mainshaft appear to bind in the neutral position, check for blocking rings sticking on the first or second gear tapers.
38. Install the transfer case on the transmission. Tighten the attaching bolts to 30 ft. lbs.

SHIFT CONTROL HOUSING

Disassembly

1. Remove the back-up light switch and the transmission controlled spark switch (TCS) if so equipped.
2. Remove the shift control housing cap, gasket, spring retainer, and the shift lever spring as an assembly.
3. Invert the housing and mount in a soft jawed vise.
4. Move the second/third shift rail to the rear of the housing, rotate the shift fork toward the first/reverse rail until the roll pin is accessible. Drive the roll pin out of the fork and rail with a pin punch. Remove the shift fork and the roll pin. The roll pin hole in the shift fork is offset. Mark the position of the shift fork for assembly reference.
5. Remove the second/third shift rail using a brass drift or hammer. Catch the shift rail plug as the rail drives it out of the housing. Cover the shift and poppet ball holes in the cover to prevent the poppet ball from flying out. Mark the location of the shift rail for assembly reference.
6. Rotate the first/reverse shift fork away from the notch in the housing until the roll pin is accessible. Drive the roll pin out of the fork and rail using a pin punch. Remove the shift fork and roll pin. The roll pin hole in the shift fork is offset. Mark the position of the shift fork for assembly reference.
7. Remove the first/reverse shift rail using a brass drift or hammer. Catch the shift rail plug as the rail drives it out of the housing. Cover the shift and poppet ball holes in the cover to prevent the poppet ball from flying out. Mark the location of the shift rail for assembly reference.
8. Remove the poppet balls, springs, and the interlock plunger from the housing.

Assembly

1. Install the poppet springs and the detent plug in the housing.

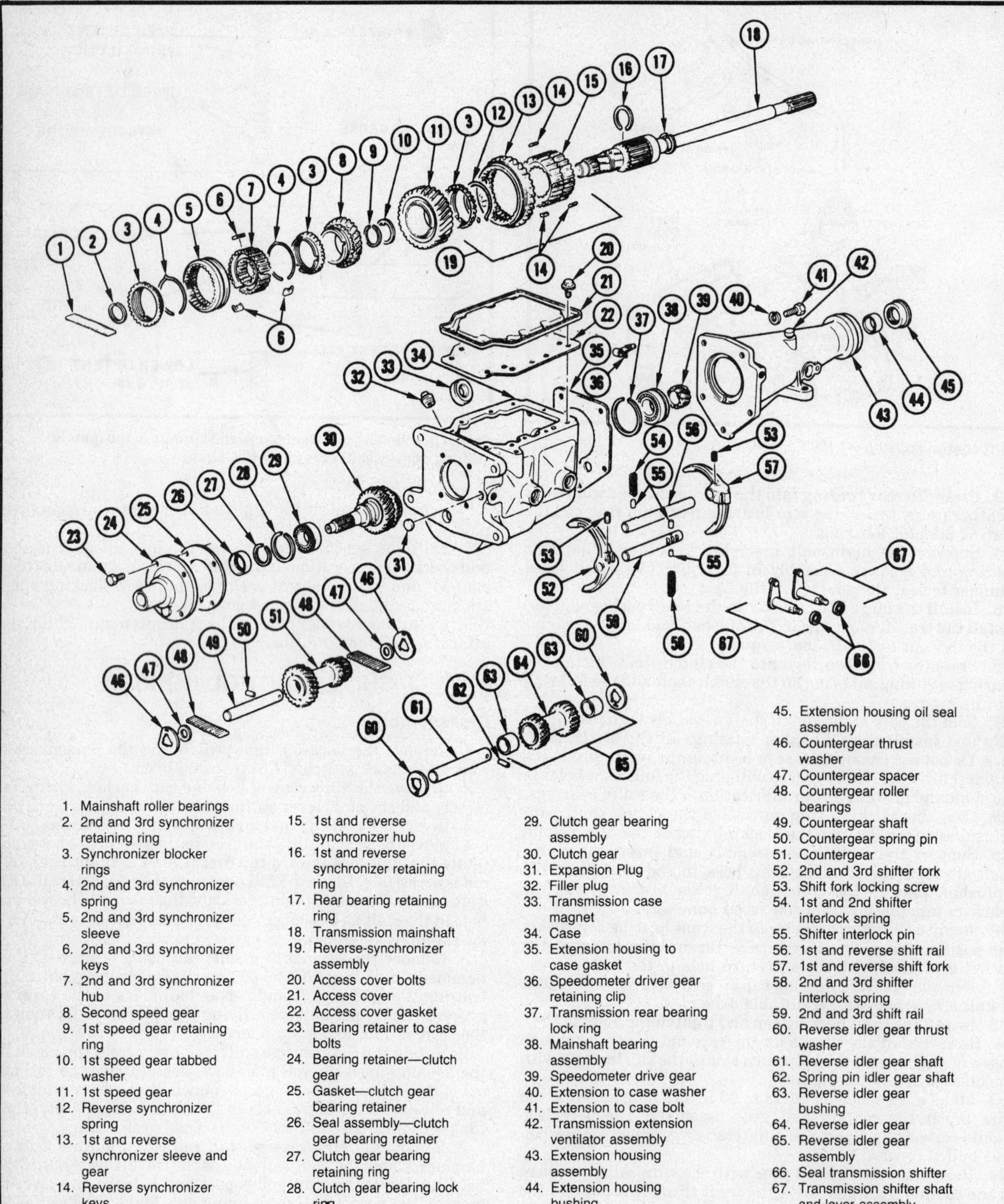
1. Mainshaft roller bearings
2. 2nd and 3rd synchronizer retaining ring
3. Synchronizer blocker rings
4. 2nd and 3rd synchronizer spring
5. 2nd and 3rd synchronizer sleeve
6. 2nd and 3rd synchronizer keys
7. 2nd and 3rd synchronizer hub
8. Second speed gear
9. 1st speed gear retaining ring
10. 1st speed gear tabbed washer
11. 1st speed gear
12. Reverse synchronizer spring
13. 1st anu reverse synchronizer sleeve and gear
14. Reverse synchronizer keys
15. 1st and reverse synchronizer hub
16. 1st and reverse synchronizer retaining ring
17. Rear bearing retaining ring
18. Transmission mainshaft
19. Reverse-synchronizer assembly
20. Access cover bolts
21. Access cover
22. Access cover gasket
23. Bearing retainer to case bolts
24. Bearing retainer—clutch gear
25. Gasket—clutch gear bearing retainer
26. Seal assembly—clutch gear bearing retainer
27. Clutch gear bearing retaining ring
28. Clutch gear bearing lock ring
29. Clutch gear bearing assembly
30. Clutch gear
31. Expansion Plug
32. Filler plug
33. Transmission case magnet
34. Case
35. Extension housing to case gasket
36. Speedometer driver gear retaining clip
37. Transmission rear bearing lock ring
38. Mainshaft bearing assembly
39. Speedometer drive gear
40. Extension to case washer
41. Extension to case bolt
42. Transmission extension ventilator assembly
43. Extension housing assembly
44. Extension housing bushing
45. Extension housing oil seal assembly
46. Countergear thrust washer
47. Countergear spacer
48. Countergear roller bearings
49. Countergear shaft
50. Countergear spring pin
51. Countergear
52. 2nd and 3rd shifter fork
53. Shift fork locking screw
54. 1st and 2nd shifter interlock spring
55. Shifter interlock pin
56. 1st and reverse shift rail
57. 1st and reverse shift fork
58. 2nd and 3rd shifter interlock spring
59. 2nd and 3rd shift rail
60. Reverse idler gear thrust washer
61. Reverse idler gear shaft
62. Spring pin idler gear shaft
63. Reverse idler gear bushing
64. Reverse idler gear
65. Reverse idler gear assembly
66. Seal transmission shifter
67. Transmission shifter shaft and lever assembly

T-150 transmission—exploded view (© AMC Corp.)

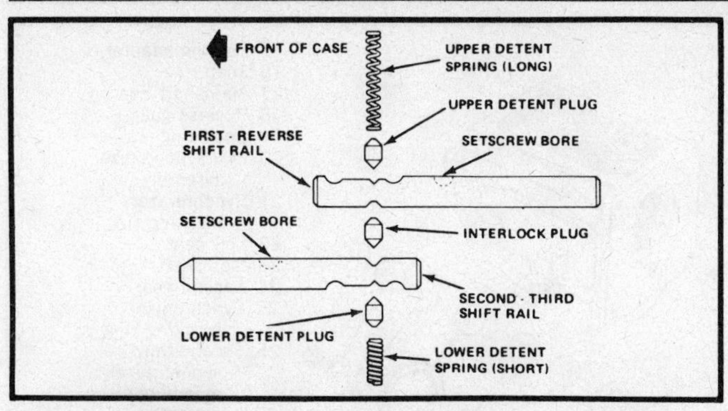

Installation sequence—interlock and detent plugs and springs

2. Insert the first/reverse shift rail into the housing, and install the shift fork on the shift rail.
3. Install the poppet ball on the top of the spring in the first/reverse rail.
4. Using a punch or wooden dowel, push the poppet ball and spring downward into the housing bore and install the first/reverse shift rail.
5. Align the roll pin holes in the first/reverse shift fork and install the roll pin. Move the shift rail to the neutral (center) detent.
6. Insert the second/third shift rail into the housing and install the poppet ball on top of the spring in the shift rail bore.
7. Using a punch or wooden dowel, push the poppet ball and spring downward into the housing bore and install the second/third shift rail.
8. Align the roll pin holes in the second/third shift rail and the shift fork and install the roll pin. Move the shift rail to the neutral (center) position.
9. Install the shift rail plugs in the housing, and remove the shift control cover from the vise.
10. Install the shift lever, shift lever spring, spring retainer, gasket, and the shift control housing cap as an assembly. Tighten the cap securely.
11. Install the back-up light switch and the TCS switch if so equipped.

LUBRICANT CAPACITY

SAE 80-90 gear lube	3 pts.

TORQUE SPECIFICATIONS
Tremec T-150

	ft. lbs.
Back-up light switch	15-20
Fill and drain plugs	10-20
Front bearing cap bolt	30-36
Shift control housing bolts	20-25
Transfer case drive gear locknut	150
Transfer case to transmission bolts	30
TCS switch	18

Warner T–4 and T–5
Four and Five Speed Transmissions

For T–5 procedures, refer to the GM S–Series (5 Speed)

Disassembly

1. Drain the transmission lubricant. 2WD models are not equipped with a drain plug; the fluid must be siphoned from the transmission.
2. Use a pin punch and hammer to remove the offset lever-to-shift rail roll pin.
3. Remove the extension housing (2WD) or the adapter (4WD). Remove the housing and the offset lever as an assembly.
4. Remove the detent ball and spring from the offset lever. Remove the roll pin from the extension housing or adapter.
5. Remove the countershaft rear thrust bearing and race.
6. Remove the transmission cover and shift fork assembly. Two of the transmission cover bolts are alignment type dowel pins. Mark their location so that they may be reinstalled in their original locations.
7. Remove the reverse lever to reverse lever pivot bolt C-clip.
8. Remove the reverse lever pivot bolt. Remove the reverse lever and fork as an assembly.
9. Mark the position of the front bearing cap to case, then remove the bearing cap bolts and cap.
10. Remove the front bearing race and the shims from the bearing cap. Use a small pry bar and remove the front seal from the bearing cap.
11. Rotate the main drive gear shaft until the flat portion of the gear faces the countershaft, then remove the main drive gear shaft assembly.
12. Remove the thrust bearing and 15 roller bearings from the clutch shaft. Remove the output shaft bearing race. Tap the output shaft with a plastic hammer to loosen it if necessary.
13. Tilt the output shaft assembly upward and remove the assembly from the case.
14. Carefully pull off the countershaft rear bearing with the proper puller after marking the position for reinstallation.
15. Move the countershaft rearward and tilt it upward to remove it from the transmission case. Remove the countershaft bearing spacer.
16. Remove the reverse idler shaft roll pin, then remove the reverse idler shaft and gear.
17. Press off the countershaft front bearing. Use the appropriate pullers and remove the bearing from the main drive gear shaft.
18. Remove the extension housing or adapter oil seal and remove the back-up light switch from the case.

OUTPUT SHAFT DISASSEMBLY

1. Remove the thrust bearing washer from the front of the output shaft.
2. Scribe matchmarks on the hub and sleeve of the 3rd–4th synchronizer so that these parts may be reassembled properly.
3. Remove the 3rd–4th synchronizer blocking ring, sleeve and hub as an assembly.
4. Remove the insert springs and the inserts from the 3rd–4th synchronizer and separate the sleeve from the hub.
5. Remove the 3rd speed gear from the shaft.
6. Remove the 2nd speed gear to output shaft snapring, the tabbed thrust washer and the 2nd speed gear from the shaft.

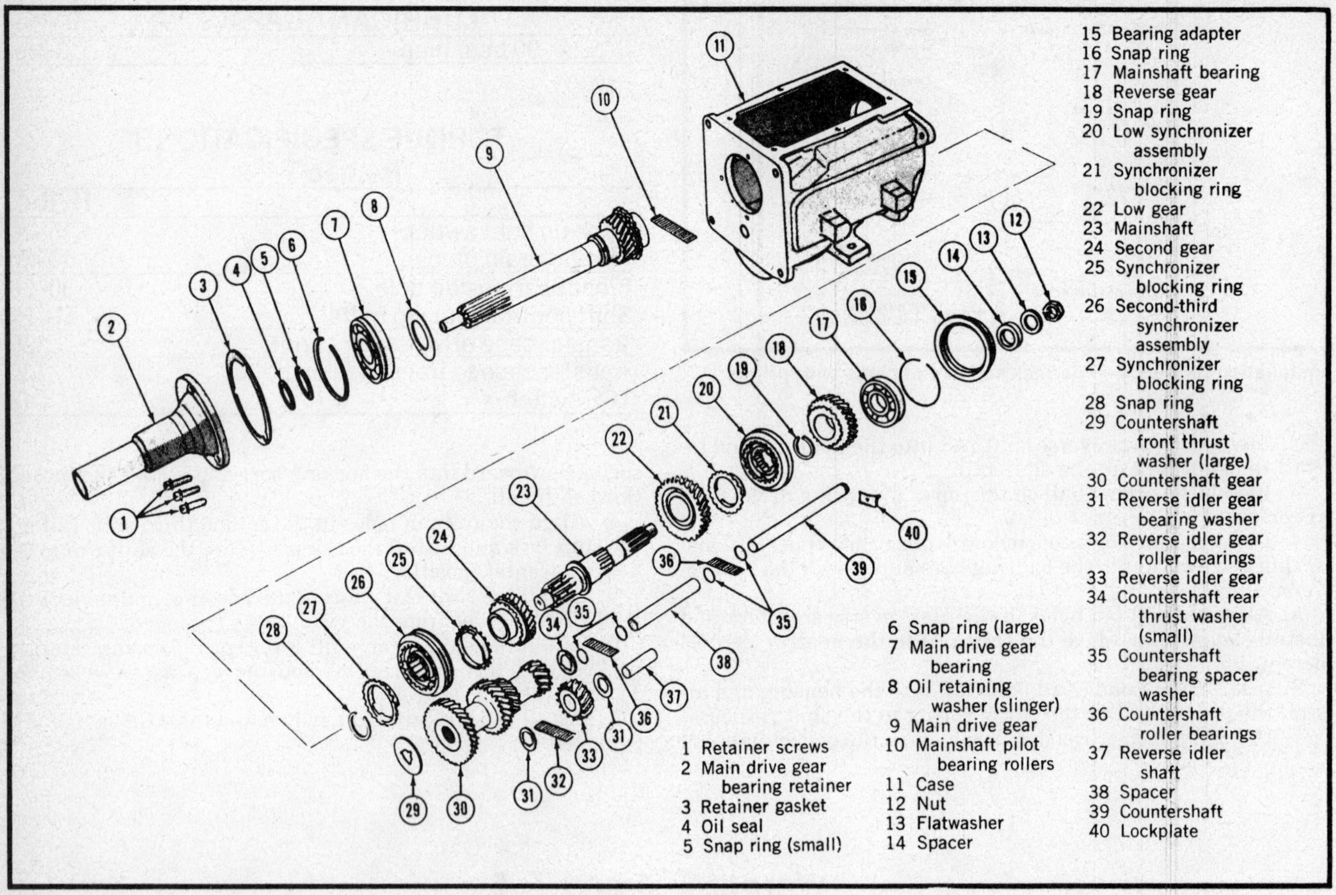

1 Retainer screws
2 Main drive gear bearing retainer
3 Retainer gasket
4 Oil seal
5 Snap ring (small)
6 Snap ring (large)
7 Main drive gear bearing
8 Oil retaining washer (slinger)
9 Main drive gear
10 Mainshaft pilot bearing rollers
11 Case
12 Nut
13 Flatwasher
14 Spacer
15 Bearing adapter
16 Snap ring
17 Mainshaft bearing
18 Reverse gear
19 Snap ring
20 Low synchronizer assembly
21 Synchronizer blocking ring
22 Low gear
23 Mainshaft
24 Second gear
25 Synchronizer blocking ring
26 Second-third synchronizer assembly
27 Synchronizer blocking ring
28 Snap ring
29 Countershaft front thrust washer (large)
30 Countershaft gear
31 Reverse idler gear bearing washer
32 Reverse idler gear roller bearings
33 Reverse idler gear
34 Countershaft rear thrust washer (small)
35 Countershaft bearing spacer washer
36 Countershaft roller bearings
37 Reverse idler shaft
38 Spacer
39 Countershaft
40 Lockplate

T-14A and T-15A three speed transmissions (© Borg Warner Corp.)

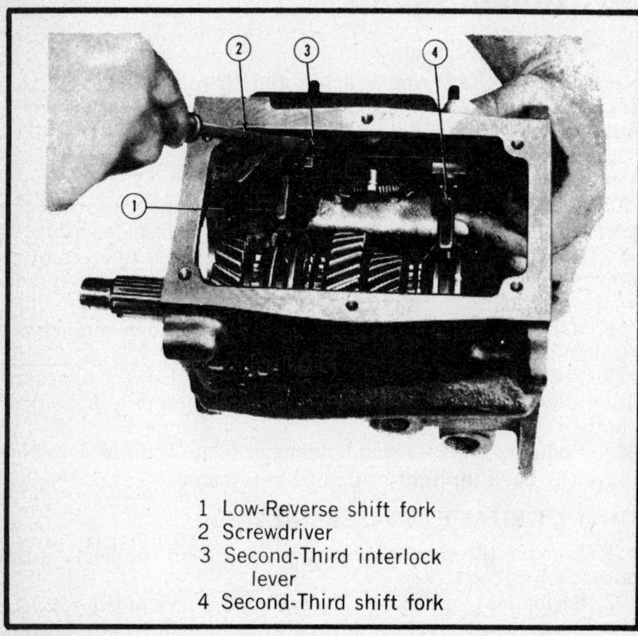

Installing shifter forks (© Borg Warner Corp.)

7. Use an appropriate puller and remove the the output shaft bearing.
8. Remove the 1st gear thrust washer, the roll pin, the 1st speed gear and the blocking ring.
9. Scribe matchmarks on the 1st–2nd synchronizer sleeve and the output shaft.
10. Remove the insert spring and the inserts from the 1st–reverse sliding gear, then remove the gear from the output hub.

OUTPUT SHAFT ASSEMBLY

1. Coat the output shaft and the gear bores with transmission lubricant.
2. Align the matchmarks and install the 1st–2nd synchronizer sleeve on the output shaft hub.
3. Install the three inserts and two springs into the 1st–reverse synchronizer sleeve.

NOTE: The tanged end of each spring should be positioned on the same insert but the open face of each spring should be opposite each other.

4. Install the blocking ring and the 2nd speed gear onto the output shaft.
5. Install the tabbed thrust washer and 2nd gear snapring in the output shaft; be sure that the washer is properly seated in the notch.
6. Install the blocking ring and the 1st speed gear onto the output shaft, then install the 1st gear roll pin.
7. Press the rear bearing onto the shaft.
8. Install the remaining components onto the output shaft: The 1st gear thrust washer. The 3rd speed gear. The 3rd–4th synchronizer hub inserts and the sleeve (the hub offset must face forward). The thrust bearing washer on the rear of the countershaft.

COVER AND FORKS DISASSEMBLY

1. Place the selector arm plates and the shift rail centered in the Neutral position.

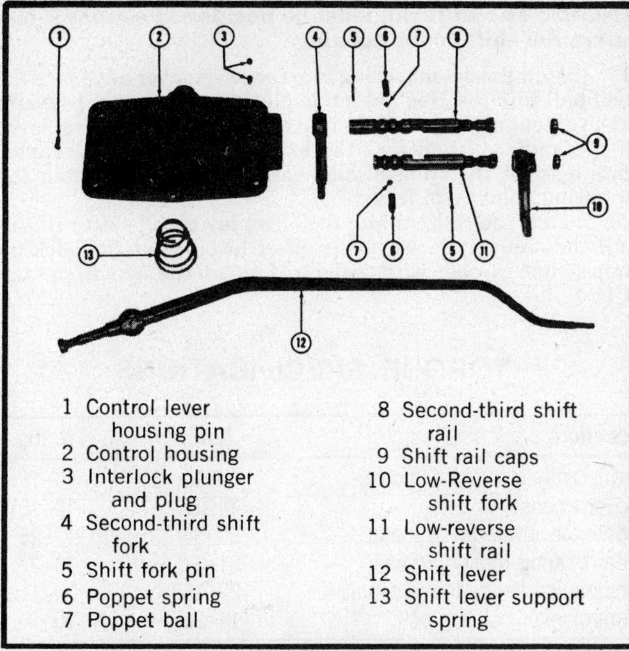

Shift control components (© Borg Warner Corp.)

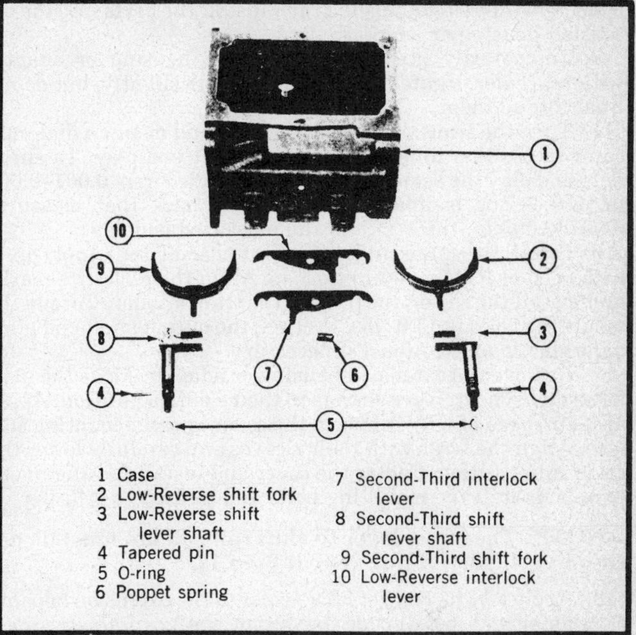

Remote control shift bar housing components (© Borg Warner Corp.)

2. Rotate the shift rail counterclockwise until the selector arm disengages from the selector arm plates; the selector arm roll pin should now be accessible.
3. Pull the shift rail rearward until the selector contacts the 1st–2nd shift fork.
4. Use a $^{3}/_{16}$ in. pin punch and remove the selector arm roll pin and the shift rail.
5. Remove the shift forks, the selector arm, the roll pin and the interlock plate.
6. Remove the shift rail oil seal and O-ring.
7. Remove the nylon inserts and the selector arm plates from the shift forks.

NOTE: Mark the position of the parts so that they may be properly installed.

COVER AND FORK ASSEMBLY

1. Attach the nylon inserts to the selector arm plates and through the shift forks.
2. If removed, coat the edges of the shift rail plug with sealer and install the plug.
3. Coat the shift rail and the rail bores with petroleum jelly, then slide the shift rail into the cover until the end of the rail is flush with the inside edge of the cover.
4. Position the 1st–2nd shift fork into the cover; with the offset of the shift fork facing the rear of the cover. Push the shift rail through the fork. The 1st–2nd fork is the larger of the two forks.
5. Position the selector arm and the C-shaped interlock plate into the cover, then push the shift rail through the arm. The widest part of the interlock plate must face away from the cover and the selector arm roll pin must face downward, toward the rear of the cover.
6. Position the 3rd–4th shift fork into the cover with the fork offset facing the rear of the cover. The 3rd–4th shift selector arm plate must be positioned under the 1st–2nd shift fork selector arm plate.
7. Push the shift rail through the 3rd–4th shift fork and into the front cover rail bore.
8. Rotate the shift rail until the forward selector arm plate faces away from parallel to the cover.
9. Align the roll pin holes of the selector arm and the shift rail and install the roll pin. The roll pin must be installed flush with the surface of the selector arm to prevent selector arm plate to pin interference.
10. Install the O-ring into the groove of the shift rail oil seal, then install the oil seal carefully after lubricating it.

Case Assembly

1. Apply a coat of Loctite® 601, or equivalent, to the outer cage of the front countershaft bearing, then press the bearing into the bore until it is flush with the case.
2. Apply petroleum jelly to the tabbed countershaft thrust washer and install the washer with the tab engaged in the corresponding case depression.
3. Tip the transmission case on end and install the countershaft into the front bearing bore.
4. Install the rear countershaft bearing spacer and coat the rear bearing with petroleum jelly. Install the rear countershaft bearing using the appropriate tools. The rear bearing is properly installed when 0.125 in. is extended beyond the case surface.
5. Position the reverse idler into the case (the shift lever groove must face rearward) and install the reverse idler shaft into the case. Install the shaft retaining pin.
6. Install the output shaft assembly into the transmission case.
7. Install the main drive gear bearing onto the main drive shaft using the appropriate tools. Coat the roller bearings with petroleum jelly and install them in the main drive gear recess. Install the thrust bearing and race.
8. Install the 4th gear blocking ring onto the output shaft. Install the rear output shaft bearing race.
9. Install the main drive gear assembly into the case, engaging the 3rd–4th synchronizer blocking ring.
10. Install a new seal in the front bearing cap and in the rear extension or adapter.
11. Install the front bearing into the front bearing cap but do not (at this time) install the shims. Temporarily install the cap to the transmission without applying sealer.
12. Install the reverse lever, the pivot pin (coat the threads with non-hardening sealer) and the retaining C-clip. Be sure the reverse lever fork is engaged with the reverse idler gear.
13. Coat the countershaft rear bearing race and the thrust

bearing with petroleum jelly, then install the parts into the extension housing or adapter.

14. Temporarily install the extension housing or adapter without sealer, tighten the retaining bolts slightly, but do not final torque them.

15. Turn the transmission case on end and mount a dial indicator in position to measure output shaft end play. To eliminate end play the bearings must be preloaded from 0.001–0.005 in. Check the endplay. Select a shim pack that measures 0.001–0.005 in. thicker than the measured endplay.

16. Install the shims under the front bearing cap. Apply an 1/8 inch bead of RTV sealer to the cap. Align the reference marks and install the cap on the front of the transmission. Torque the mounting bolts to 15 ft. lbs. Recheck the output shaft end play, none should exist. Adjust if necessary.

17. Remove the extension housing or adapter. Move the shift forks and synchronizer sleeves to their neutral position. Apply an 1/8 in. bead of RTV sealer to the cover to case mounting surface. Align the forks with their sleeves and carefully lower the cover into position. Center the cover and install the alignment dowels. Install the mounting bolts and tighten to 9 ft. lbs.

NOTE: The offset lever to shift rail roll pin must be position vertically; if not, repeat Step 17.

18. Apply a 1/8 in. bead of RTV sealer to the extension housing or adapter and install over the output shaft.

NOTE: The shift rail must be positioned so that it just enters the shift cover opening.

19. Install the detent spring into the offset lever and place the steel ball into the Neutral guide plate detent. Apply pressure to the detent spring and offset lever, then slide the offset lever on the shift rail and seat the extension housing or adapter plate against the transmission case. Install and tighten the mounting bolts to 25 ft. lbs.

20. Install the roll pin into the offset lever and shift rail. Install the damper sleeve in the offset lever. Coat the back up lamp switch threads with sealer and install the switch, tighten to 15 ft. lbs.

TORQUE SPECIFICATIONS

Location	N.m.	ft. lbs.
Front bearing retainer to case	14–20	10–15
Cover to case	14–24	10–18
Control levers to lever shafts	20–34	15–25
Rear bearing retainer to case	31–37	23–27
Companion flange to mainshaft	122–163	90–120
Control lever housing bolt	14–20	10–15

Warner T-14A, T-15A Three Speed Transmission

The Warner T-14A, T-15A are fully synchronized three-speed transmissions having helical drive gears throughout. Lubricant capacity is 2 1/2 pints.

TRANSMISSION UNIT

Disassembly

1. Separate transfer case from transmission by removing five capscrews.
2. Remove gearshift housing and disassembly by removing shift rails, poppet balls, springs, and shift forks.
3. Remove nut, flat washer, transfer case drive gear, adapter, and spacer.
4. Remove main drive gear bearing retainer gasket.
5. Remove main drive gear and mainshaft bearing snaprings and bearings.
6. Remove main drive gear and mainshaft assembly.

NOTE: The T-15A transmission must be shifted into second gear to allow removal of the mainshaft and gear assembly.

7. On remote shift models, remove roll pins from lever shafts and housing. From inside case, slide levers and interlock assembly out. Remove forks and lever assemblies.
8. Remove lock plate from reverse idler shaft and countershaft.
9. Drive countershaft out to rear with dummy shaft. Remove countergear and two thrust washers. Remove spacer washers, rollers, and spacer from gear.
10. Drive reverse idler shaft out to rear. Remove gear, washers, and roller bearings.
11. Remove clutch hub snapring and second/third synchronizer assembly.
12. Remove second and reverse gears.
13. Remove clutch hub snapring and low synchronizer assembly.
14. Remove low gear.

SYNCHRONIZER

Disassembly and Assembly

1. Remove springs. low synchronizer has only one spring, second/third, two.
2. Mark sleeve and hub before separating.
3. Remove hub.
4. Remove three shifter plates from hub.
5. Inspect all parts for wear.
6. Assembly in reverse order of disassembly. On second/third unit, make sure that spring openings are 120 degrees from each other, with spring tension opposed.

NOTE: If a synchronized assembly is replaced on a floor shift unit, the shift fork operating the synchronizer being replaced must have the letter A just under the shaft hole on the side opposite the pin.

Inspection

1. Wash all parts in solvent.
2. Air dry but do not spin bearings with air pressure.
3. Check case bearing and shaft bores for cracks or burrs.
4. Check all gears and bronze blocking rings for cracks, and chipped, worn, or cracked teeth. If any gears are replaced, also replace the meshing gears.
5. Check all bearings and bushings for wear or damage.
6. Check that synchronizer sleeves slide freely on clutch hubs.

TRANSMISSION UNIT

Assembly

1. Place reverse idler gear with dummy shaft, roller bearing, and thrust washers in case. Install reverse idler shaft.
2. Assemble countershaft center spacer, four bearing spacers, and bearing rollers in countershaft gear.
3. Install large countergear thrust washer in tront of case.

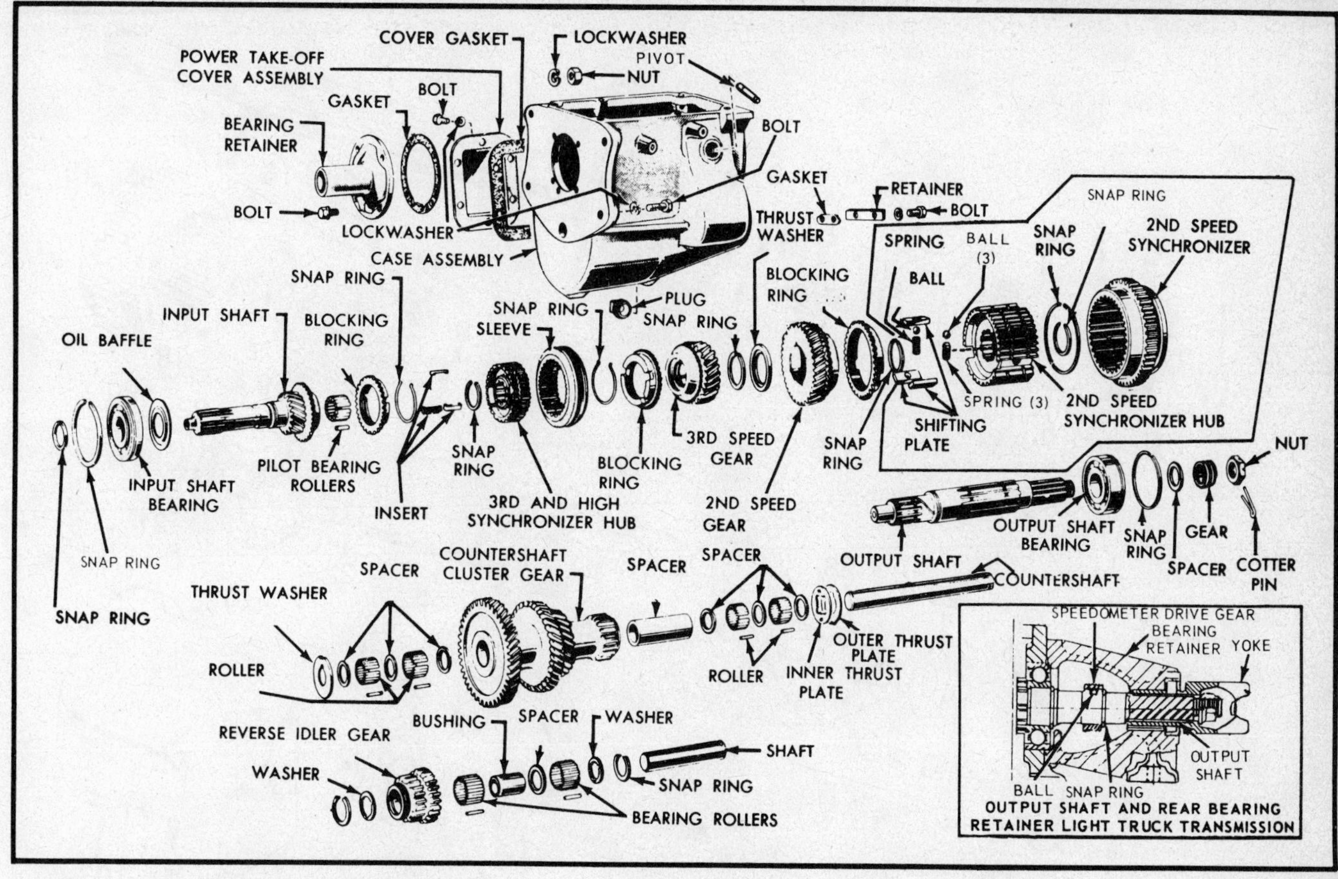

T-18 four speed transmission (© Borg Warner Corp.)

Position small thrust washer on countergear hub with lip facing groove in case. Holding countergear in position, push in countershaft from rear.

4. Install lock plate in slots of reverse idler shaft and countershaft.

5. Install the following components to the mainshaft. Low gear, bronze blocking ring, low synchronizer assembly, the largest snapring that fits in groove, second gear, the bronze blocking ring, second/third synchronizer assembly, the largest snapring that fits in groove and the reverse gea.r

6. Install mainshaft assembly through top of case.

7. Install bronze blocking ring to second/third synchronizer assembly.

8. On remote shift units, install shifter shafts, with new O-rings, into case.

NOTE: T-15 interlock levers are marked as to location. T-14 levers have no marks and are interchangeable.

9. Depress interlock lever while installing shift fork into shift lever and synchronizer clutch sleeve. Install poppet spring. Install tapered pins securing shafts in case.

10. Install main drive gear roller bearings.

11. Install main drive gear and oil slinger into case with cutaway portion of gear toward countergear. Install main drive gear to mainshaft.

12. Using bearing installer and thrust yoke tool, install main drive gear and mainshaft bearings and drive into position. The thrust yoke is needed to prevent damage to the synchronizer clutch.

13. Install main drive gear and mainshaft bearing snaprings. The mainshaft bearing snapring is 0.010 inch thicker than main drive gear bearing snapring.

14. Install mainshaft rear bearing adapter, spacer, transfer case drive gear, flat washer, and nut. Torque nut 130 to 170 ft. lbs.

15. Install main drive gear bearing retainer (with new oil seal) and gasket. Align oil drain holes in retainer and gasket.

16. Install case cover gasket. On remote shift units, install cover gasket with vent holes to left side.

17. Position gear train and floor shift assembly in neutral. Insert shifter forks into clutch sleeves and torque 8 to 15 ft. lbs.

Warner T-18, T-18A and T-19 Series Four Speed

The Warner T-18, T-18A and T-19 transmissions have four forward speeds and one reverse. A P.T.O. opening is provided on certain transmissions, depending upon the models and applications and can be located on either the right or left sides of the case. The T-18 and T-18A transmissions are synchronized in second, third and fourth speeds only, while the T-19 transmis-

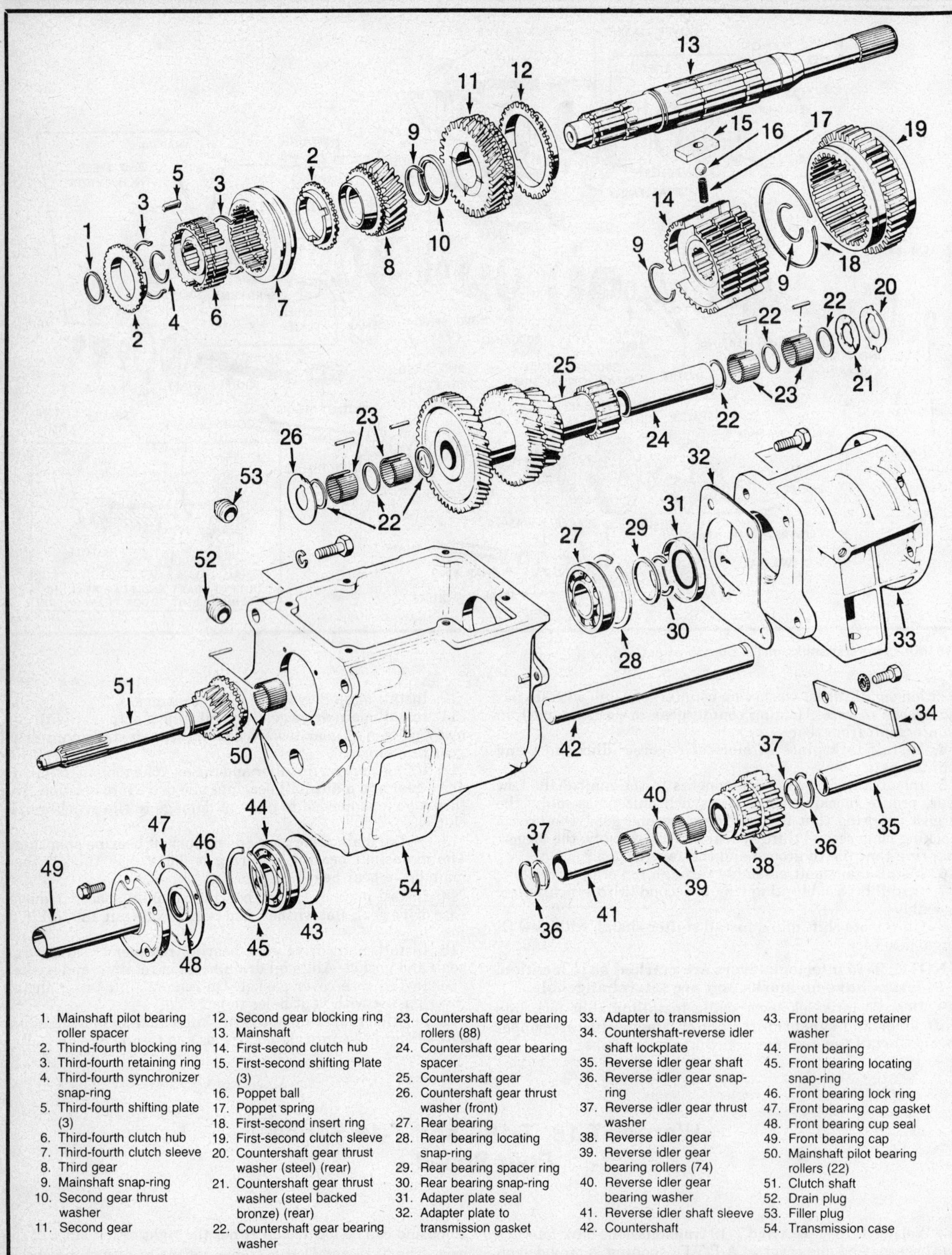

1. Mainshaft pilot bearing roller spacer
2. Thind-fourth blocking ring
3. Third-fourth retaining ring
4. Third-fourth synchronizer snap-ring
5. Third-fourth shifting plate (3)
6. Third-fourth clutch hub
7. Third-fourth clutch sleeve
8. Third gear
9. Mainshaft snap-ring
10. Second gear thrust washer
11. Second gear
12. Second gear blocking ring
13. Mainshaft
14. First-second clutch hub
15. First-second shifting Plate (3)
16. Poppet ball
17. Poppet spring
18. First-second insert ring
19. First-second clutch sleeve
20. Countershaft gear thrust washer (steel) (rear)
21. Countershaft gear thrust washer (steel backed bronze) (rear)
22. Countershaft gear bearing washer
23. Countershaft gear bearing rollers (88)
24. Countershaft gear bearing spacer
25. Countershaft gear
26. Countershaft gear thrust washer (front)
27. Rear bearing
28. Rear bearing locating snap-ring
29. Rear bearing spacer ring
30. Rear bearing snap-ring
31. Adapter plate seal
32. Adapter plate to transmission gasket
33. Adapter to transmission
34. Countershaft-reverse idler shaft lockplate
35. Reverse idler gear shaft
36. Reverse idler gear snap-ring
37. Reverse idler gear thrust washer
38. Reverse idler gear
39. Reverse idler gear bearing rollers (74)
40. Reverse idler gear bearing washer
41. Reverse idler shaft sleeve
42. Countershaft
43. Front bearing retainer washer
44. Front bearing
45. Front bearing locating snap-ring
46. Front bearing lock ring
47. Front bearing cap gasket
48. Front bearing cup seal
49. Front bearing cap
50. Mainshaft pilot bearing rollers (22)
51. Clutch shaft
52. Drain plug
53. Filler plug
54. Transmission case

T-18A transmission—exploded view (© Borg Warner Corp.)

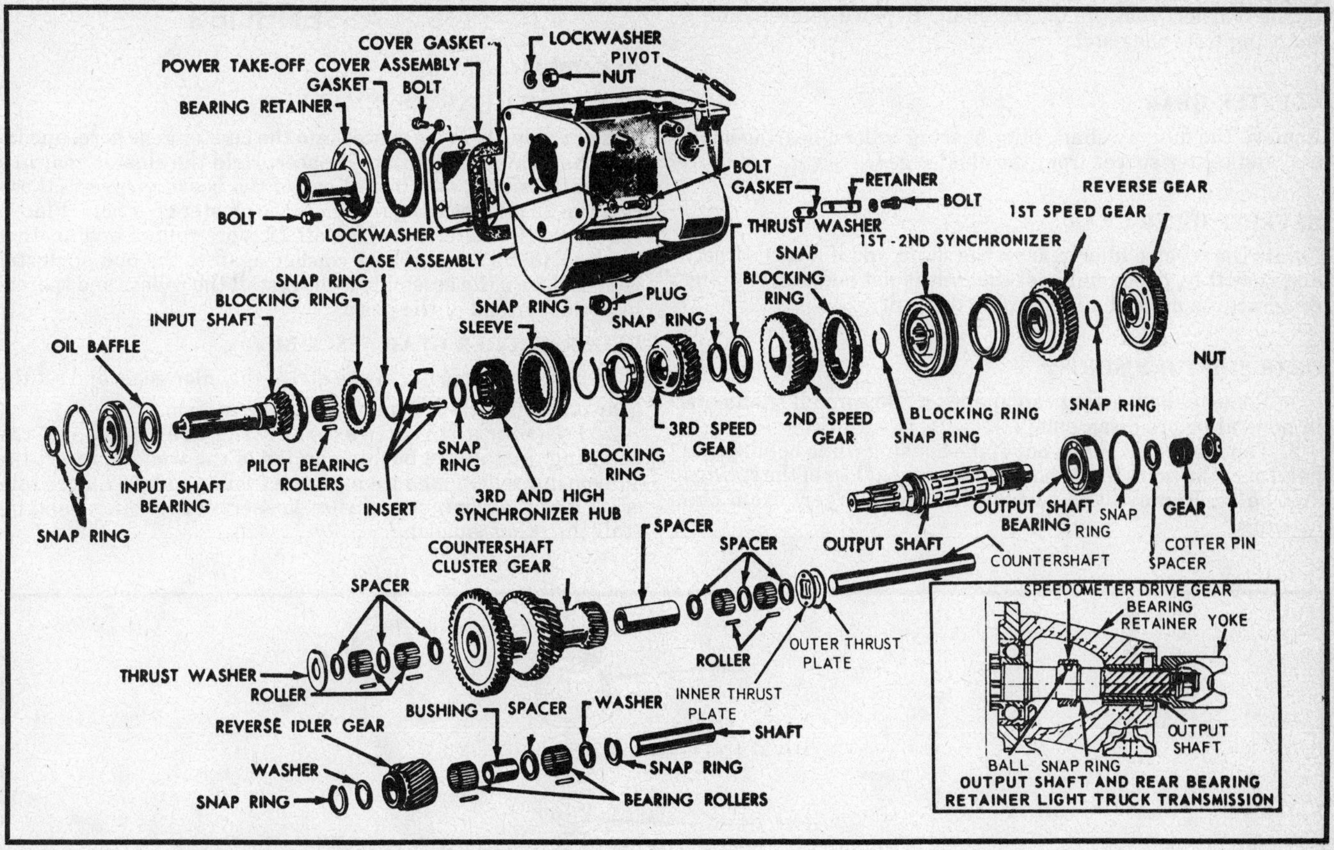

T-19 four speed transmission—exploded view (© Borg Warner Corp.)

sion is synchronized in all forward gears. The disassembly and assembly remains basically the same for the transmission models.

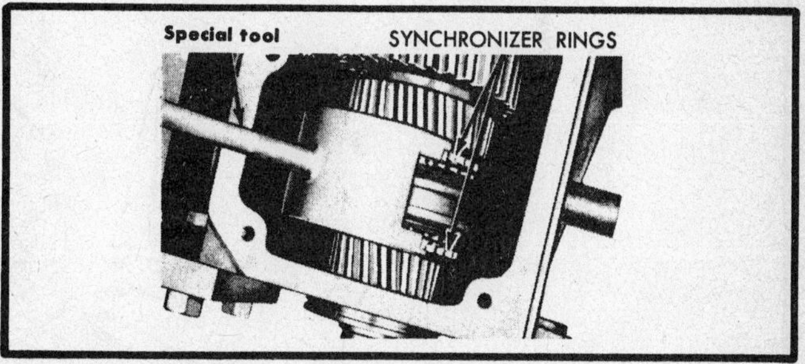

Stop yoke tool (© Borg Warner Corp.)

TRANSMISSION UNIT

Disassembly

1. After draining the transmission and removing the parking brake drum (or shoe assembly), lock the transmission in two gears and remove the U-joint flange, oil seal, speedometer driven gear and bearing assembly. Lubricant capacity is 6 ½ pints.
2. Remove the output shaft bearing retainer and the speedometer drive gear and spacer.
3. Remove the output shaft bearing snapring, and remove the bearing.
4. Remove the countershaft and idler shaft retainer and the P.T.O. cover.
5. After removing the input shaft bearing retainer, remove the snaprings from the bearing and the shaft.
6. Remove the input shaft bearing and oil baffle.
7. Drive out the countershaft (from the front). Keep the dummy shaft in contact with the countershaft to avoid dropping any rollers.
8. After removing the input shaft and the synchronizer blocking ring, pull the idler shaft.
9. Remove the reverse gear shifter arm, the output shaft assembly, the idler gear, and the cluster gear. When removing the cluster, do not lose any of the rollers.

SUBASSEMBLIES

Disassemby

OUTPUT SHAFT

1. Remove the third and high speed synchronizer hub snapring from the output shaft, and slide the third and high speed synchronizer assembly and the third speed gear off the shaft. Remove the synchronizer sleeve and the inserts from the hub. Before removing the two snaprings from the ends of the hub, check the end play of the second speed gear (0.005 to 0.024 inch).
2. Remove the second speed synchronizer snapring. Slide the second speed synchronizer hub gear off the hub. Do not lose any of the balls, springs, or plates. Pull the hub off the shaft, and remove the second speed synchronizer from the second speed gear. Remove the snapring from the rear of the second speed gear, and remove the gear, spacer, roller bearings, and

thrust washer from the output shaft. Remove the remaining snapring from the shaft.

CLUSTER GEAR

Remove the dummy shaft, pilot bearing rollers, bearing spacers, and center spacer from the cluster gear.

REVERSE IDLER GEAR

Rotate the reverse idler gear on the shaft, and if it turns freely and smoothly, disassembly of the unit is not necessary. If any roughness is noticed, disassemble the unit.

GEAR SHIFT HOUSING

1. Remove the housing cap and lever. Be sure all shafts are in neutral before disassembly.
2. Tap the shifter shafts out of the housing while holding one hand over the holes in the housing to prevent loss of the springs and balls. Remove the two shaft lock plungers from the housing.

SUBASSEMBLIES

Assembly

CLUSTER GEAR ASSEMBLY

Slide the long bearing spacer into the cluster gear bore, and insert the dummy shaft in the spacer. Hold the cluster gear in a vertical position, and install one of the bearing spacers. Position the 22 pilot bearing rollers in the cluster gear bore. Place a spacer on the rollers, and install 22 more rollers and another spacer. Hold a large thrust washer against the end of cluster gear and turn the assembly over. Install the rollers and spacers in the other end of the gear.

REVERSE IDLER GEAR ASSEMBLY

1. Install a snapring in one end of the idler gear, and set the gear on end, with the snapring at the bottom.
2. Position a thrust washer in the gear on top of the snapring. Install the bushing on top of the washer, insert the 37 bearing rollers, and then a spacer followed by 37 more rollers. Place the remaining thrust washer on the rollers, and install the other snapring.

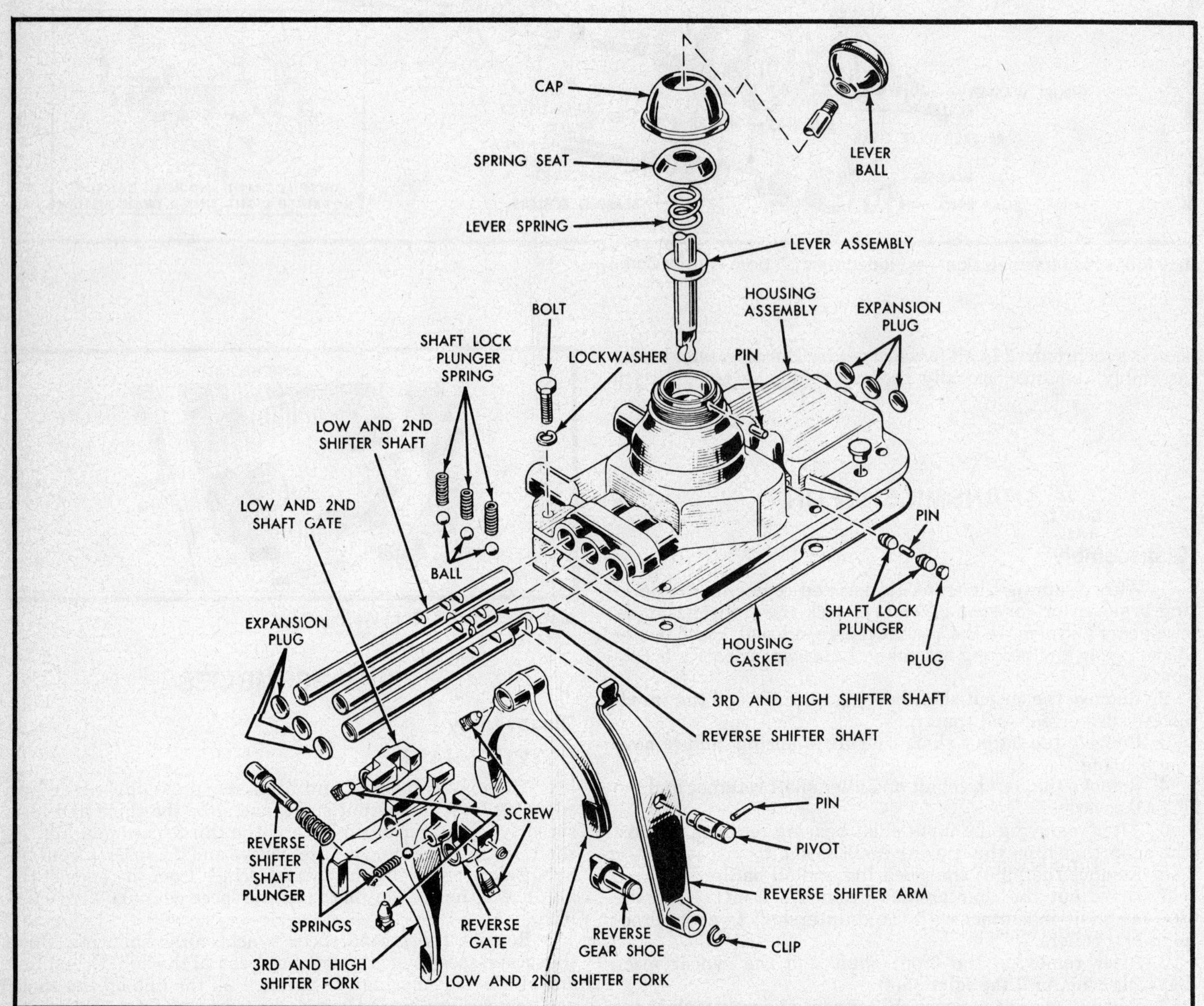

Conventional cab tilt linkage (© Borg Warner Corp.)

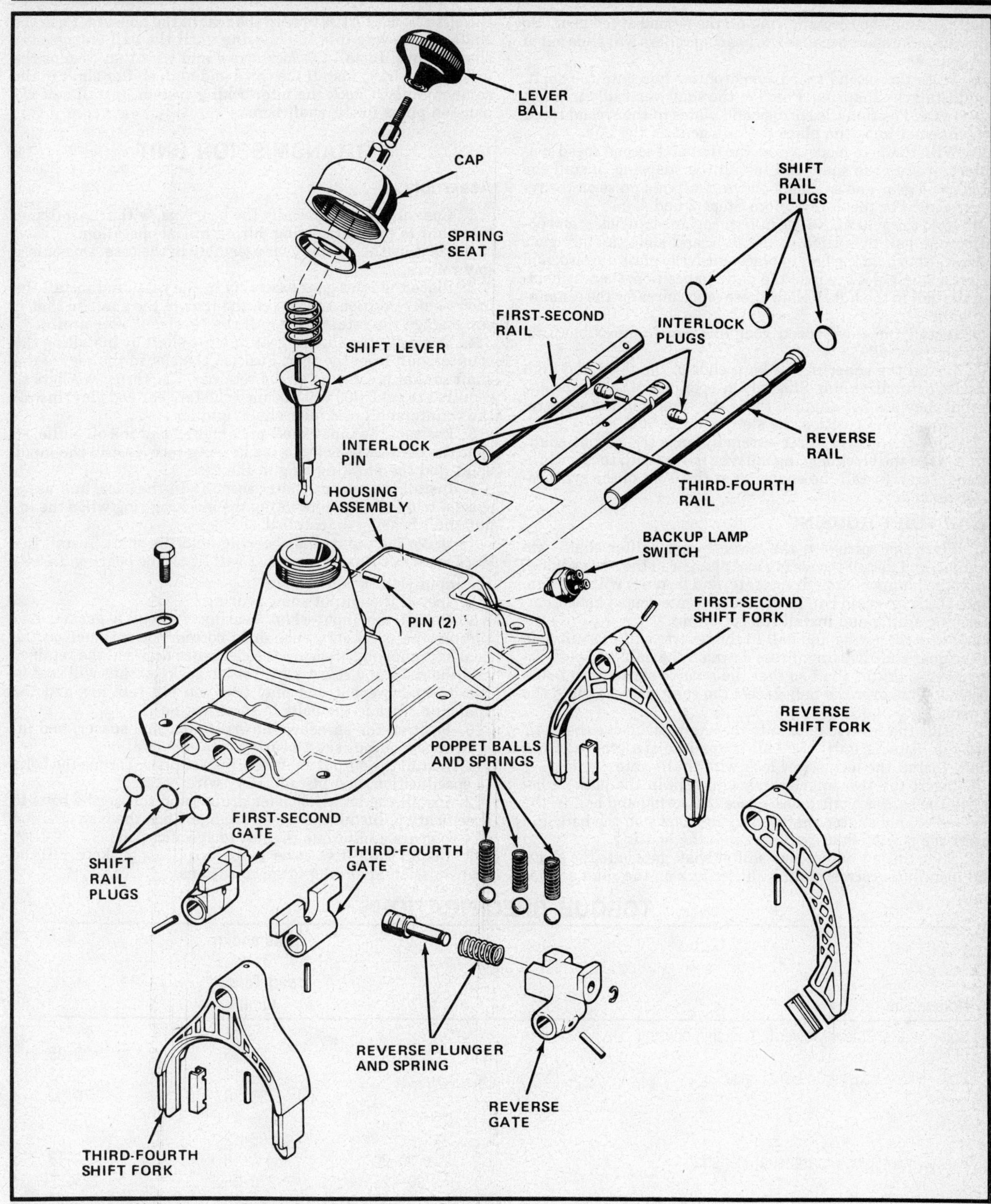

T-18a shift control housing—exploded view (© Borg Warner Corp.)

OUTPUT SHAFT ASSEMBLY

1. Install the second speed gear thrust washer and snapring on the output shaft. Hold the shaft vertically, and slide on the second speed gear. Insert the bearing rollers in the second speed gear, and slide the spacer into the gear. (The T-18 model does not contain second speed gear rollers or spacer). Install the snapring on the output shaft at the rear of the second speed

gear. Position the blocking ring on the second speed gear. Do not invert the shaft because the bearing rollers will slide out of the gear.

2. Press the second speed synchronizer hub onto the shaft, and install the snapring. Position the shaft vertically in a soft jawed vise. Position the springs and plates in the second speed synchronizer hub, and place the hub gear on the hub.

3. With the T-19 model, press the first and second speed synchronizer onto the shaft and install the snapring. Install the first speed gear and snapring on the shaft and press on the reverse gear. For the T-19, ignore Steps 2 and 4.

4. Hold the gear above the hub spring and ball holes, and position one ball at a time in the hub, and slide the hub gear downward to hold the ball in place. Push the plate upward, and insert a small block to hold the plate in position, thereby holding the ball in the hub. Follow these procedures for the remaining balls.

5. Install the third speed gear and synchronizer blocking ring on the shaft.

6. Install the snaprings at both ends of the third and high speed synchronizer hub. Stagger the openings of the snaprings so that they are not aligned. Place the inserts in the synchronizer sleeve, and position the sleeve on the hub.

7. Slide the synchronizer assembly onto the output shaft. The slots in the blocking ring must be in line with the synchronizer inserts. Install the snapring at the front of the synchronizer assembly.

GEAR SHIFT HOUSING

1. Place the spring on the reverse gear shifter shaft gate plunger, and install the spring and plunger in the reverse gate. Press the plunger through the gate, and fasten it with the clip. Place the spring and ball in the reverse gate poppet hole. Compress the spring and install the cotter pin.

2. Place the spring and ball in the reverse shifter shaft hole in the gear shift housing. Press down on the ball, and position the reverse shifter shaft so that the reverse shifter arm notch does not slide over the ball. Insert the shaft part way into the housing.

3. Slide the reverse gate onto the shaft, and drive the shaft into the housing until the ball snaps into the groove of the shaft. Install the lock screw lock wire to the gate.

4. Insert the two interlocking plungers in the pockets between the shifter shaft holes. Place the spring and ball in the low and second shifter shaft hole. Press down on the ball, and insert the shifter shaft part way into the housing.

5. Slide the low and second shifter shaft gate onto the shaft, and install the corresponding shifter fork on the shaft so that the offset of the fork is toward the rear of the housing. Push the shaft all the way into the housing until the ball engages the shaft groove. Install the lock screw and wire that fastens the fork to the shaft. Install the third and high shifter shaft in the same manner. Check the interlocking system. Install new expansion plugs in the shaft bores.

TRANSMISSION UNIT

Assembly

1. Coat all parts, especially the bearings, with transmission lubricant to prevent scoring during initial operation.

2. Position the cluster gear assembly in the case. Do not lose any rollers.

3. Place the idler gear assembly in the case, and install the idler shaft. Position the slot in the rear of the shaft so that it can engage the retainer. Install the reverse shifter arm.

4. Drive out the cluster gear dummy shaft by installing the countershaft from the rear. Position the slot in the rear of the shaft so that it can engage the retainer. Use thrust washers as required to get 0.006 to 0.020 inch cluster gear end play. Install the countershaft and idler shaft retainer.

5. Position the input shaft pilot rollers and the oil baffle, so that the baffle will not rub the bearing race. Install the input shaft and the blocking ring in the case.

6. Install the output shaft assembly in the case, and use a special tool to prevent jamming the blocking ring when the input shaft bearing is installed.

7. Drive the input shaft bearing onto the shaft. Install the thickest select-fit snapring that will fit on the bearing. Install the input shaft snapring.

8. Install the output shaft bearing.

9. Install the input shaft bearing without a gasket, and tighten the bolts only enough to bottom the retainer on the bearing snapring. Measure the clearance between the retainer and the case, and select a gasket (or gaskets) that will seal in the oil and prevent end play between the retainer and the snapring. Torque the bolts to specification.

10. Position the speedometer drive gear and spacer, and install a new output shaft bearing retainer seal.

11. Install the output shaft bearing retainer. Torque the bolts to specification, and install safety wire.

12. Install the brake shoe (or drum), and torque the bolts to specification. Install the U-joint flange. Lock the transmission in two gears and torque the nut to specification.

13. Install the P.T.O. cover plates with new gaskets. Fill the transmission according to specifications.

TORQUE SPECIFICATIONS

Nomenclature		Nuts and/or Bolts and Torque Limits	
Bolt—gear shift lever tower to gearshift housing		3/8–16	7/16–14
		20–25	30–35
Bolt—clutch housing to trans. case		7/16–14	9/16–12
		30–38	70–90
		5/8–11	
		96–120	
Nut—U-joint flange to trans. output shaft	1.00–20	1½–18	1¼–18
	90–125	275–350	225–275
Nut—drum parking brake to companion flange		3/8–24	7/16–20
		35–45	50–70
Nut—bellcrank to trans.		9/16–18	
		70–90	
Bolt—lever assy. to trans.		3/8–16	
		20–25	

TORQUE SPECIFICATIONS

Nomenclature	Nuts and/or Bolts and Torque Limits	
Nut—handbrake anchor bar to trans. case (5-speed extra-heavy duty only)	9/16–18	
	120–130	
Bolt—bellcrank to trans.	3/8–16	
	20–25	
Bolt—reverse lockout plunger retainer	11/16–16	
	80–100	
Bolt—countershaft rear bearing retainer	5/16–18	7/16–14
	25–30	45–55
	3/8–16	1/2–13
	35–40	60–70
Bolt—countershaft & reverse idler shaft retainer	5/16–18	7/16–14
	25–30	40–45
	3/8–16	1/2–13
	25–37	80–85
	3/8–16	
	18–25	
Bolt—gear shift housing to trans. case	5/16–18	3/8–16
	20–25	30–35
	3/8–16	7/16–14
	35–40	45–50
Bolt—power take off cover to trans. case.	3/8–16	
	20–30	
Nut—countershaft bearing lock (5-speed extra h.d. & 5-speed exclusive)	1 1/4–18	
	350–450	
Nut—countershaft bearing lock (5-speed exclusive h.d.)	1 1/2–18	
	350–450	
Bolt—input shaft bearing retainer to trans. case	5/16–18	7/16–14
	25–30	40–45
	3/8–16	
	25–30	
Bolt—countershaft front bearing retainer	5/16–18	7/16–14
	25–30	50–55
	3/8–16	
	25–35	

Warner T-15-D Three Speed Transmission

The Warner T-15-D transmission has three synchronized forward speeds and one reverse. The transmission has either a remote controlled shift lever on the steering column or a top cover shift lever assembly. This transmission can be used with or without a transfer case in the drive line with the use of different extension housing or bearing retainer designs.

MAINSHAFT

Removal

1. Drain the transmission of its lubricant and remove either the top cover or the shift lever assembly from the top of the transmission. Remove the front bearing retainer.
2. Remove the front main drive gear bearing snaprings and remove the bearing from the shaft and transmission case with the aid of a bearing puller or its equivalent.
3. Remove the main drive gear from the transmission case by having the cutaway portion of the gear teeth positioned downward towards the cluster gear. As the gear is removed from the mainshaft, do not lose the needle roller bearing from the bearing pocket.
4. Remove the rear extension housing or the bearing retainer from the rear of the transmission case.
5. Remove the mainshaft rear bearing snaprings and remove the bearing from the mainshaft and transmission case with a bearing puller or its equivalent.
6. Column shift: Position the gears in second speed, move the mainshaft to the left and remove the shift forks.
7. Remove the mainshaft by tilting the front of the assembly upward and lifting it through the top of the case.

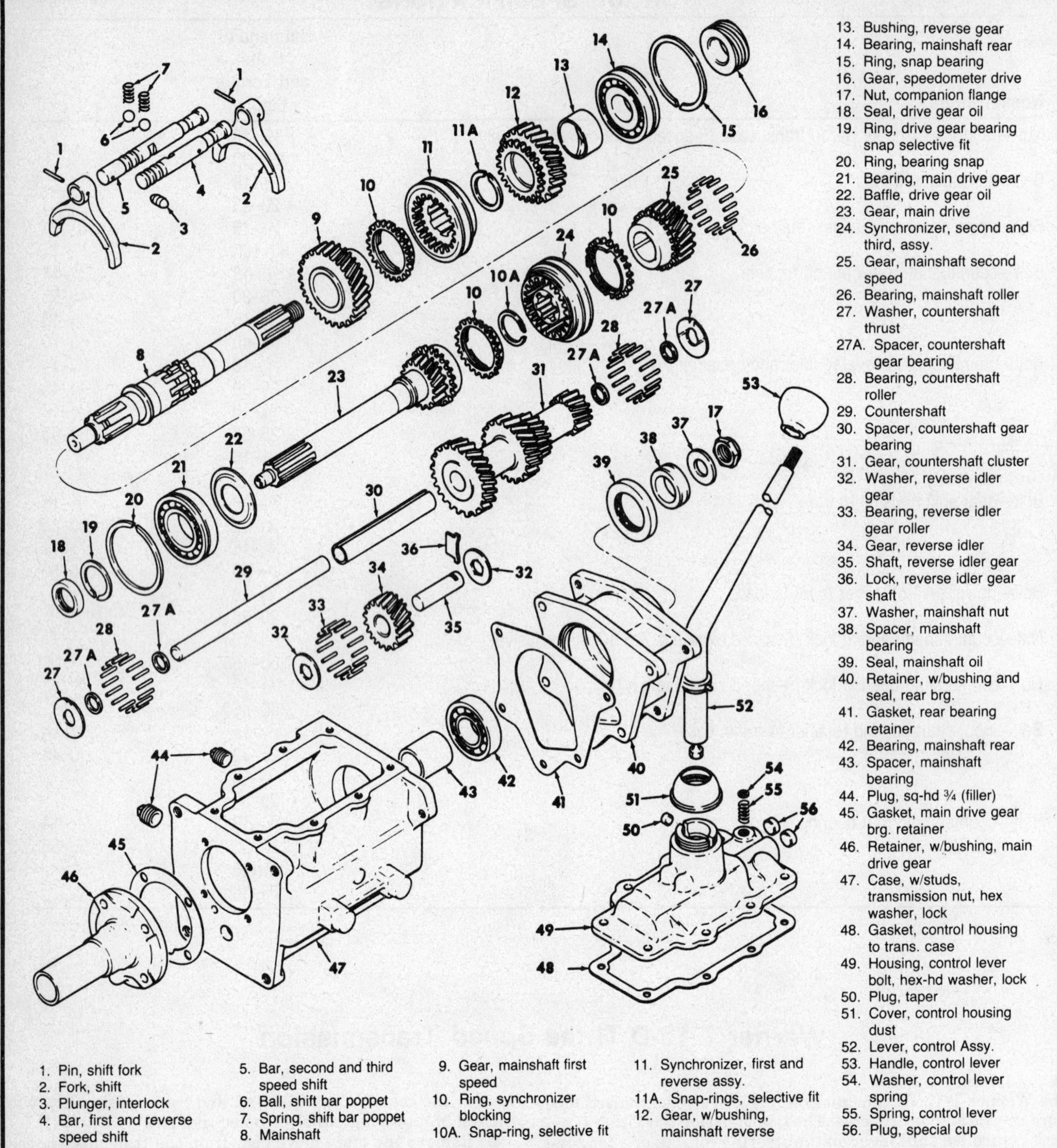

T-15A transmission with top mounted shifter lever—exploded view (© Borg Warner Corp.)

IDLER GEAR, CLUSTER GEAR AND SHAFTS

Removal

1. Tap the reverse idler gear shaft and the countershaft rearward to allow the removal of the lockplate from the slots in both shafts.

2. Using a brass drift, drive the reverse idler gear shaft towards the rear and out of the transmission case. Avoid losing the needle roller bearings from the gear bore.

3. Using a dummy countershaft or its equivalent, drive the countershaft from the rear of the transmission case. Lift the cluster gear assembly from the transmission case. Mark the thrust washer locations.

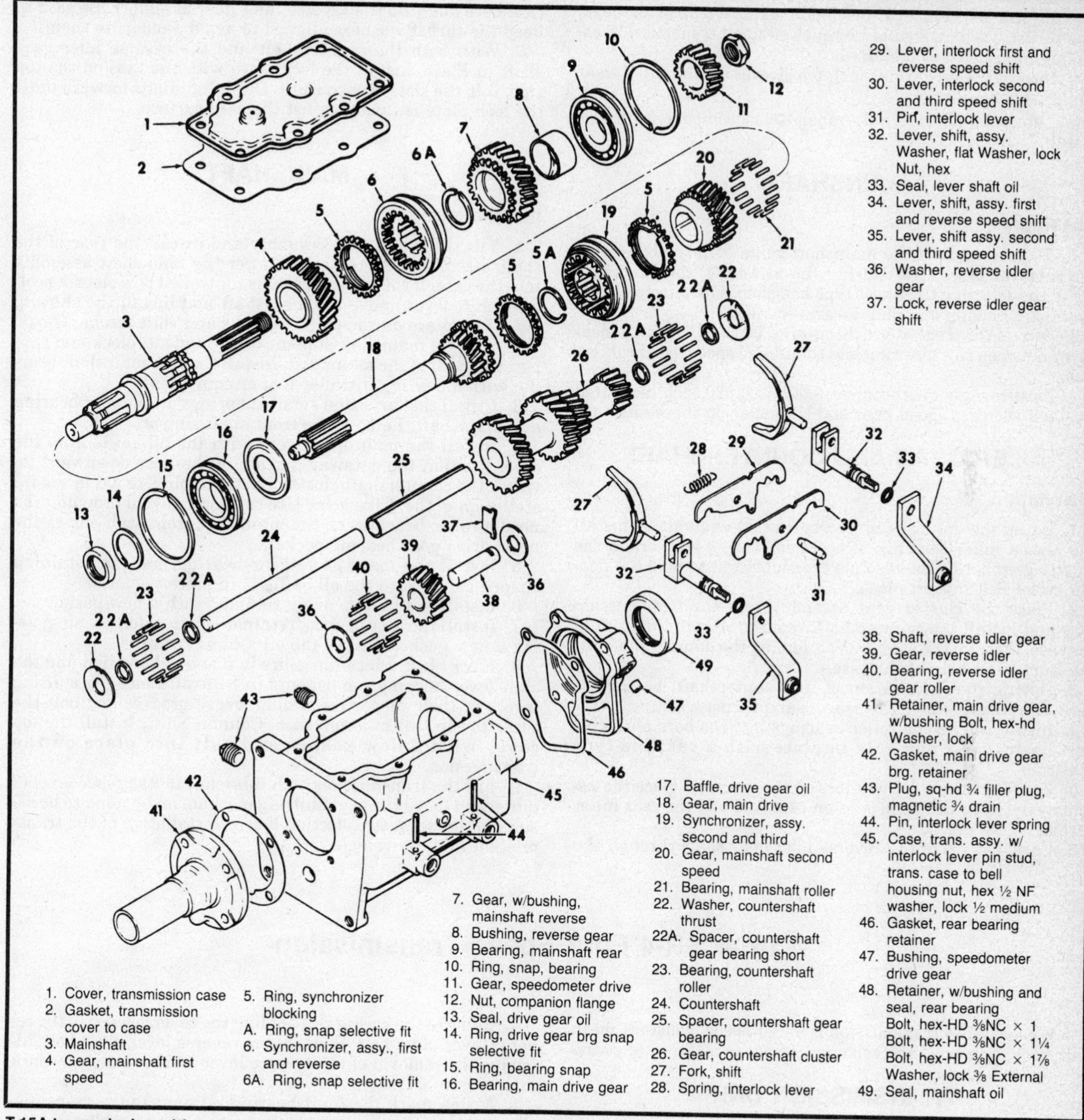

T-15A transmission with remoter shifter lever—exploded view (© Borg Warner Corp.)

MAINSHAFT

Disassembly

1. Remove the second/third speed synchronizer snapring from the front of the mainshaft. Remove the synchronizer from the mainshaft, after matchmarking the sleeve and hub.
2. Remove the second speed gear from the mainshaft.
3. Remove the reverse gear from the rear of the mainshaft. Remove the rear synchronizer (first/reverse) hub snapring.
4. Remove the first/reverse synchronizer unit from the rear of the mainshaft. Only one blocker ring is used with the first/reverse synchronizer assembly as the reverse speed gear is not a synchromesh unit.
5. Remove the first speed gear from the mainshaft.

Cleaning and Inspection

1. Clean the transmission case with solvent and inspect for cracks, worn bearing bores or other damages.
2. Clean and inspect all gears and bronze blocking rings for cracks, chipped or cracked teeth or excessive wear on the teeth. Should a gear require replacement, the meshing gear should be replaced also.

3. Inspect all bearings and bushings for wear or damage. The thrust washers should be renewed upon transmission assembly, if grooved or distorted.
4. Inspect the synchronizer clutch sleeves for abnormal wear and ease of operation.
5. Lubricate all internal transmission components before installation.

MAINSHAFT

Assembly

1. The assembly of the mainshaft gears is in the reverse of the removal procedure. During the assembly, the snaprings are of the selective thickness type and should be selected to obtain the following end-play measurements.
2. Second/third speed synchronizer 0.004 to 0.020 inch measured between the snapring and the second speed synchronizer hub.
3. First/reverse synchronizer 0.005 to 0.020 inch measured between the first speed gear and the collar on the mainshaft.

IDLER GEAR AND COUNTERSHAFT

Installation

1. Using the dummy countershaft or its equivalent, install the needle roller bearings, spacers and thrust washers in the cluster gear bore. Use vaseline type lubricant to hold the needle, roller bearings in place.
2. Place the cluster gear assembly into the transmission case and install the countershaft from the rear to the front of the case, through the cluster gear, forcing the dummy shaft out the front shaft bore of the case.
3. During the installation of the countershaft, be sure to maintain alignment of the spacers and thrust washers.
4. Install the needle roller bearings into the bore of the reverse idler gear and hold in place with a vaseline type lubricant.
5. Position the thrust washers on the gear and place the assembly between the transmission case web and the rear inner surface of the case.
6. Carefully drive the reverse idler gear shaft through the case bore and into the reverse idler gear assembly. Be sure to keep the thrust washers aligned to avoid damage to them.
7. With both the countershaft and the reverse idler gear shaft in Place, install the lock plate with the tabs on the top side, into the slots of each shaft. Drive the shafts forward until the lock plate is flush against the case surface.

MAINSHAFT

Installation

1. Tilt the mainshaft assembly and install the rear of the shaft assembly into the case. Lower the mainshaft assembly into the case. If the transmission is controlled by a steering column shift lever, move the mainshaft and install the shifting forks into place on the clutch sleeves and shift mechanism.
2. Using a mainshaft support or equivalent, block and support the front of the mainshaft. Install the rear mainshaft bearing with a bearing installer tool or equivalent.
3. Install the large and small snaprings on the rear bearing and mainshaft. Remove the front shaft support.
4. Install the main drive gear with the oil baffle, into the case. Position the cutaway portion of the gear downward towards the countershaft/cluster gear assembly, to aid in the installation of the drive gear. Use caution to avoid dropping the needle roller bearings as the mainshaft front stub enters the main drive gear bearing pocket.
5. Install the main drive gear bearing and the retaining snaprings. Be sure the oil baffle is in place.
6. Install the front bearing retainer with a new gasket.
7. Install the rear bearing retainer or extension housing, using a new gasket. Install the oil seal as required.
8. Floor Shift: Place the gears in a neutral position and the shift lever housing components in neutral. Place the shifting levers in their respective sliding sleeve grooves and bolt the cover to the transmission case. Column Shift: Install the top cover with a new gasket and bolt into place on the transmission.
9. Fill the transmission with lubricant to its proper level (3 pints) and move the gear shifting mechanism by hand to be assured of proper gear selection before installation of the transmission into the vehicle.

Warner SR-4 Four Speed Transmission

The Warner SR-4 transmission is a four speed, constant mesh unit, providing synchromesh engagement in all forward gears.

TRANSMISSION UNIT

Disassembly

1. Separate the transmission from the transfer case, if attached.
2. Drain the lubricant from the transmission by removing the lower adapter housing bolt.
3. If the shift lever housing has not been removed, place the shift lever in the neutral position, remove the retaining bolts and lift the shift lever housing from the transmission.
4. Remove the flanged nut holding the offset lever to the shift rail. Remove the offset lever.
5. Remove the adapter housing retaining bolts and the housing from the transmission case.
6. Remove the shift control housing retaining bolts and remove the cover and gasket. Mark the location of the two dowel bolts to reinstall in their original position.
7. Remove the spring clip holding the reverse lever to the reverse lever pivot bolt. Remove the reverse lever pivot bolt, allowing the removal of the reverse lever and reverse lever fork as an assembly.
8. Match mark the front bearing retainer to the transmission case and remove the bearing retainer and gasket.
9. Remove the large and small snaprings from the front and rear ball bearings on the input and output shafts.
10. With the aid of a bearing puller tool or equivalent, remove the input shaft ball bearing and remove the input shaft from the case.
11. Remove the rear (output shaft) bearing from the shaft with the aid of a bearing puller tool or equivalent.
12. Remove the output shaft assembly as a unit from the transmission case. Do not allow the synchronizer sleeves to separate from the hubs during the removal.
13. Push the reverse idler gear shaft rearward and remove the shaft and gear from the case.
14. Using a dummy countershaft, push the countershaft to the rear of the case. Remove the cluster gear assembly and dummy countershaft as a unit, from the transmission case.

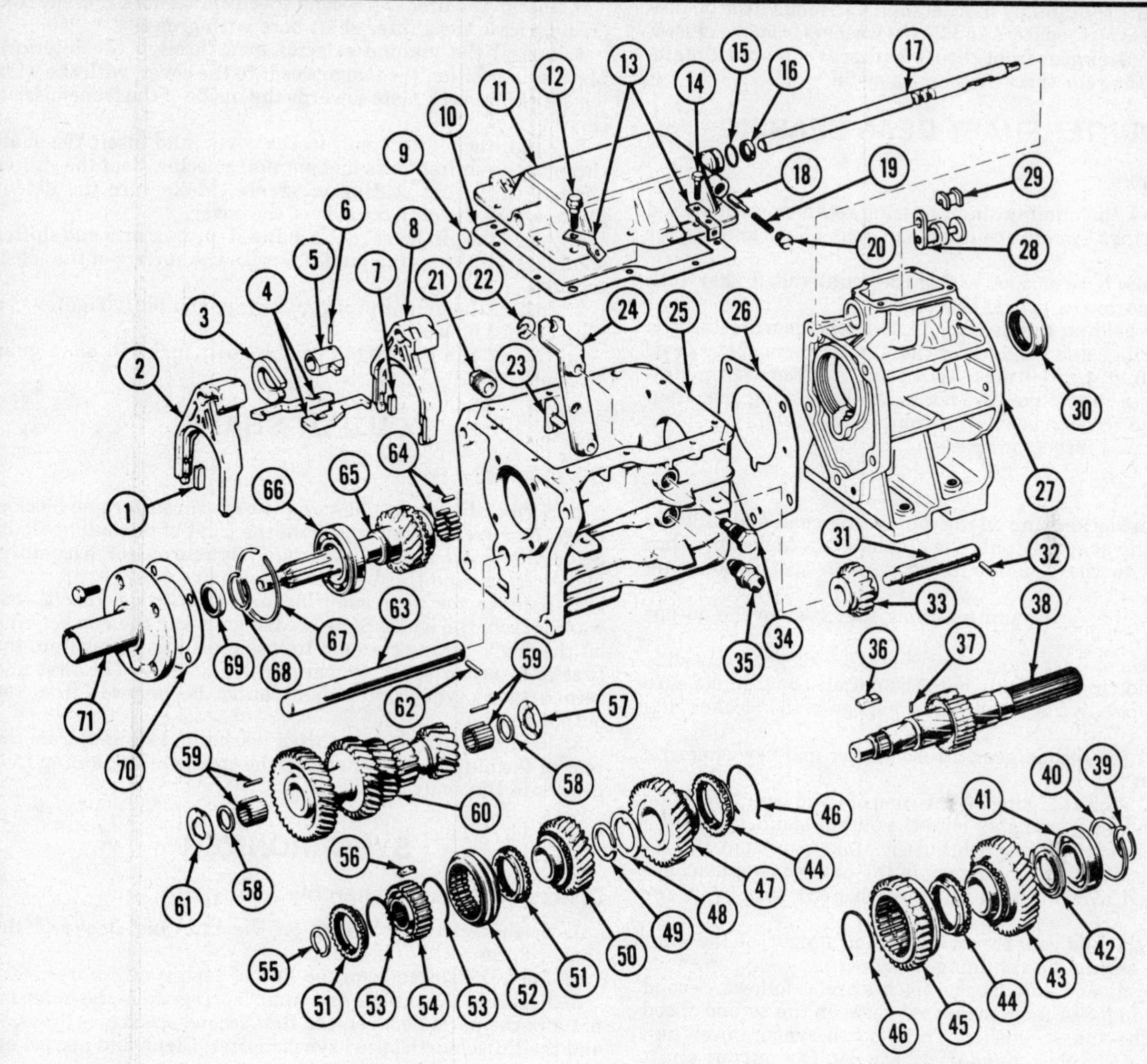

1. Third-fourth shift insert
2. Third-fourth shift fork
3. Selector interlock plate
4. Selector arm plate (2)
5. Selector arm
6. Selector arm roll pin
7. First-second shift fork insert
8. First-second shift fork
9. Shift rail plug
10. Transmission cover gasket
11. Transmission cover
12. Transmission cover dowel bolt (2)
13. Clip
14. Transmission cover bolt (8)
15. Shift rail O-ring seal
16. Shift rail oil seal
17. Shift rail
18. Detent plunger
19. Detent spring
20. Detent plug
21. Fill plug
22. Reverse lever pivot bolt C-clip
23. Reverse lever fork
24. Reverse lever
25. Transmission case
26. Gasket
27. Adapter housing
28. Offset lever
29. Offset lever insert
30. Extension housing oil seal
31. Reverse idler shaft
32. Reverse idler shaft roll pin
33. Reverse idler gear
34. Reverse lever pivot bolt
35. Backup lamp switch
36. First-second synchronizer insert (3)
37. First gear roll pin
38. Output shaft and hub assembly
39. Rear bearing retaining snap-ring
40. Rear bearing locating snap-ring
41. Rear bearing
42. First gear thrust washer
43. First gear
44. First-second synchronizer blocking ring (2)
45. First-reverse sleeve and gear
46. First-second synchronizer insert spring (2)
47. Second gear
48. Second gear thrust washer (tabbed)
49. Second gear snap-ring
50. Third gear
51. Third-fourth synchronizer blocking ring (2)
52. Third-fourth synchronizer sleeve
53. Third-fourth synchronizer insert spring (2)
54. Third-fourth synchronizer hub
55. Output shaft snap-ring
56. Third-fourth synchronizer insert (3)
57. Countershaft gear rear thrust washer (metal)
58. Countershaft needle bearing retainer (2)
59. Countershaft needle bearing (50)
60. Countershaft gear
61. Countershaft gear front thrust washer (plastic)
62. Countershaft roll pin
63. Countershaft
64. Clutch shaft roller bearings (15)
65. Clutch shaft
66. Front bearing
67. Front bearing locating snap-ring
68. Front bearing retaining snap-ring
69. Front bearing cap oil seal
70. Front bearing cap gasket
71. Front bearing cap

SR-4 four speed transmission—exploded view (© Borg Warner Corp.)

15. Separate the dummy countershaft and remove the 50 needle roller bearings, spacers and thrust washers from the cluster gear. The cluster gear front thrust washer is of a plastic material, while the rear thrust washer is metal.

COUNTERSHAFT GEAR BEARING

Replacement

1. Remove the dummy shaft, bearing retainer washers and needle bearings from the countershaft gear. Clean and inspect the parts.
2. Coat the bore at each end of the countershaft gear with grease to retain the needle bearings.
3. While holding the dummy shaft in the gear, install the needle bearings and retainer washers in each end of the gear.
4. Slide first gear off the output shaft, and remove the first speed blocker ring. Take care not to lose the sliding gear from the first and second speed synchronizer assembly.
5. Clean and inspect all parts.

Assembly

1. Place a blocker ring on the cone of first gear, and slide the gear and ring assembly onto the output shaft. Make sure that the inserts in the synchronizer engage in the blocker ring notches.
2. Install the spring pin retaining first gear to the output shaft.
3. Install a blocker ring on the cone of second gear, and slide the gear and ring assembly onto the output shaft. Make sure that the inserts in the synchronizer engage in the blocker ring notches.
4. Install the second gear thrust washer and new snapring on the shaft.
5. Install a blocker ring on the cone of third gear, and slide the gear and ring assembly onto the output shaft. Install the third and fourth speed synchronizer. Make sure that the inserts in the synchronizer engage in the blocker ring notches.
6. Install a new third and fourth gear synchronizer snapring.
7. Place the first gear thrust washer (oil slinger) on the shaft and on the spring pin retaining first gear.
8. Assembly end play measurements are as follows. Second gear 0.004 to 0.014 inch, measured between the second speed gear and the thrust washer. Third/fourth synchronizer hub 0.004 to 0.014 inch, measured between the output shaft snapring and the third speed synchronizer hub.

COVER ASSEMBLY

Disassembly

1. Remove the detent screw, spring and plunger.
2. Pull the shifter shaft rod rearward, rotating it counterclockwise.
3. Remove the spring pin retaining the manual selector and interlock to the shifter shaft.
4. Remove the shifter shaft from the cover taking care not to damage the seal.
5. Remove the manual selector and interlock plate.
6. Remove the first and second speed shifter fork. Remove the third and fourth speed shifter fork.
7. Clean and inspect all parts. Replace the shifter shaft seal and welch plug, if damaged.

Assembly

1. Assemble the two plastic inserts to each shift fork; the two projections on the inside of the inserts fit into the blind holes in the ends of the shift forks. Insert the selector arm plates into the shift forks.
2. Install the third and fourth speed shifter fork into the cover.
3. Install the first and second speed shifter fork into the cover. Lubricate the shifter shaft bore with grease.
4. Install the manual selector arm through the interlock plate, and position the two pieces into the cover, with the wide leg of the interlock plate towards the inside of the transmission case.
5. Align the shifter shaft in the cover, and insert the shaft through the shifter forks and manual selector. Coat the shifter shaft with a light coating of grease. Make sure the detent grooves face the plunger side of the cover.
6. Align the pin holes in the manual selector arm and shifter shaft. Install the spring pin flush with the surface of the selector arm.
7. Install the detent plunger, spring, and plug. Tighten the plug 8 to 12 ft. lbs.
8. Check the operation of the shift forks in each gear position.

OUTPUT SHAFT

Disassembly

1. Scribe alignment marks on the synchronizer and blocker rings. Remove the snapring from the front of the output shaft. Slide the third and fourth speed synchronizer assembly, blocker rings and third gear off the shaft.
2. Remove the next snapring and the second gear thrust washer from the shaft. Slide second gear and the blocker ring off the shaft, taking care not to lose the sliding gear from the first and second speed synchronizer assembly. The first and second speed synchronizer hub cannot be removed from the output shaft.
3. Remove the first gear thrust washer (oil slinger) from the rear of the output shaft. Remove the spring pin retaining first gear onto the shaft.

SYNCHRONIZER

Disassembly and Assembly

1. Scribe reference marks on the hub and sleeve of the synchronizer.
2. Push the sleeve from the hub of each synchronizer.
3. Separate the inserts and insert springs from the hubs. Do not mix the parts between the first/second speed synchronizer and the third/fourth speed synchronizer. Clean and inspect all parts.

NOTE: The first/second speed synchronizer hub is not to be removed from the shaft. They have been assembled and machined as a matched unit during manufacturing to assure concentricity.

4. To assemble, position the sleeve on the hub, aligning the previously marked reference points.
5. Position the three inserts per hub and install the insert springs, being sure that the bent end of the springs are seated in one of the inserts. The springs on each side of the hubs must face in opposite directions and the openings be 180 degrees apart.

TRANSMISSION UNIT

Assembly

1. Coat the countershaft thrust washers with a vaseline type lubricant and position the plastic type washer at the front of the case and the metal washer at the rear of the case.
2. With the 50 needle roller bearings in place in the cluster gear and the dummy countershaft in place, install the countershaft/cluster gear assembly into the case. Be sure the thrust washers are not displaced during the gear installation.
3. Align the cluster gear bore with the case bores and install

the countershaft from the rear to the front of the case, pushing the dummy countershaft from the gear and case.

4. Position the reverse idler gear with the shift lever groove facing to the front and install the shaft from the rear of the case.

5. Being careful not to disturb the synchronizers, install the output shaft assembly into the transmission case. Install the fourth gear blocking ring in the third speed synchronizer sleeve, engaging the inserts on the hub with the grooves of the blocking ring.

6. Install the 15 roller bearings in the input shaft pocket and retain with a vaseline type lubricant. Install the input shaft into the case and engage the shaft in the third/fourth synchronizer, while the stub of the output shaft is installed in the pocket of the input shaft. Do not jam or drop the 15 roller bearings during the input shaft installation.

7. Install the input shaft front bearing. Block the first speed gear against the rear of the case, align the bearing with the bearing bore in the case and drive the bearing completely onto the input shaft and into the transmission case. To identify the front and rear bearings, look for a notch in the front bearing race. The rear bearing has no notch.

8. Install the front bearing retaining and locating snaprings.

9. Install the front bearing cap oil seal and install the cap (bearing retainer) with a new gasket to the transmission case. Install the retaining bolts.

10. Install the first speed thrust washer on the output shaft with the oil grooves facing the first speed gear. Install the rear bearing onto the output shaft and into the case bearing bore. Be sure the first gear thrust washer is engaged on the first gear roll pin before installing the rear bearing.

11. Install the retaining and locating snaprings on the rear bearing and output shaft.

12. Position the reverse lever in the case, on the pivot bolt and install the retaining clip. Tighten the pivot bolt. Be sure the reverse lever fork is engaged in the reverse idler gear.

13. Rotate the input shaft and output shaft gears and blocking rings to insure freeness of movement. Blocking ring to gear clutch tooth face should have a clearance of 0.030 inch.

14. Place the reverse lever in the neutral position and install the cover assembly on the transmission case. Place the two dowel bolts in their original positions and install the remaining retaining bolts.

15. Install a new oil seal in the adapter housing and, using a new gasket, install the adapter housing to the transmission case.

16. Install 3 pints of lubricant into the transmission.

17. Install the offset lever and retain with the flanged nut.

18. Depending upon the installation of the transmission into a vehicle, the shift lever housing can be installed and the transmission attached to the transfer case.

TORQUE SPECIFICATIONS①

	ft. lbs.	N.m.
Backup lamp switch	10	14
Adapter housing bolt	23	31
Detent plug (in housing)	10	14
Fill plug	20	27
Front bearing cap bolt	13	18
Offset lever nut	10	14
Reverse lever pivot bolt	20	27
Shift control housing bolt	10	14
Transmission-to-clutch housing bolt	55	75
Universal joint clamp strap bolt	14	19

① All torque values given in foot-pounds and newton-meters with dry fits unless otherwise specified.

Warner T-176 Four Speed Transmission

The Warner T-176 transmission is a constant mesh unit, synchronized in all forward gears and with one reverse gear.

TRANSMISSION UNIT

Disassembly

1. Remove the transfer case from the rear of the transmission.

2. Remove the shift control housing. Mark the location of the two dowel bolts in the housing.

3. Drain the lubricant from the transmission, if not previously done. Remove the rear adapter housing.

4. With a dummy countershaft tool, remove the countershaft from the transmission, front to rear. Allow the cluster gear to lay on the bottom of the case.

5. Remove the rear bearing locating and retaining snaprings. Remove the rear bearing with a bearing remover tool or equivalent.

6. Match mark the front bearing retainer to the case for easier installation, remove the retaining bolts and the retainer.

7. Remove the locating and retaining snaprings from the front bearing. Remove the front bearing and the input shaft using a puller tool or equivalent.

8. Remove the mainshaft pilot bearing rollers from the input shaft pocket. Engage the third speed synchronizer.

9. Remove the mainshaft assembly by lifting the front of the shaft upward and out.

10. Remove the cluster gear assembly from the case. Locate and remove any thrust washers and needle roller bearings from the case.

11. Tap the reverse idler gear shaft from the case and remove the reverse idler gear and thrust washers.

12. Separate the reverse idler gear from the sliding gear. Do not lose the needle roller bearings.

MAINSHAFT

Disassembly

1. Remove the third/fourth speed synchronizer snapring from the front of the mainshaft.

2. Remove the third/fourth synchronizer from the mainshaft and slide the hub from the sleeve. Remove the inserts and springs. Inspect the blocking rings for wear and damage.

3. Remove the third speed gear and the second speed gear snapring. Remove the second speed gear and the blocking ring. Remove the tabbed thrust washer.

4. Remove the snapring from the first/second synchronizer hub. Remove the hub and the reverse gear with sleeve as an assembly. Match mark the hub and sleeve for assembly references. Remove the inserts and springs as the sleeve is removed.

5. Remove the first speed gear thrust washer from the rear of the shaft and remove the first speed gear and the blocking ring.

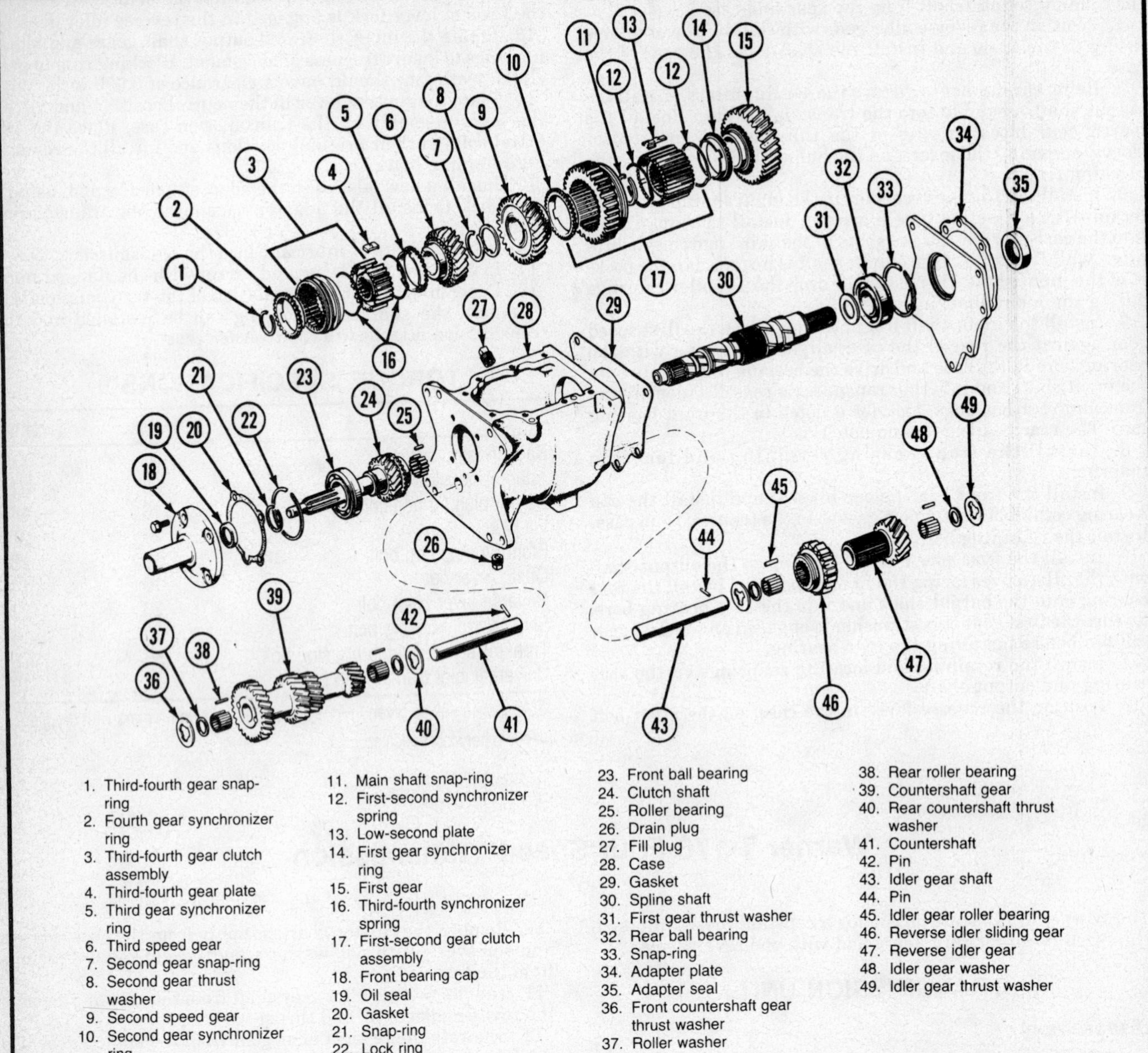

T-176 four speed transmission (© Borg Warner Corp.)

Inspection of Transmission Components

CASE

1. Cracks in the bores, sides, bosses or at bolt holes.
2. Stripped bolt hole threads.
3. Nicks, burrs, roughness on gasket or shaft bore surfaces.

GEARS, SHAFTS AND SYNCHRONIZER UNITS

1. Chipped, broken or worn gear teeth.
2. Damaged splines.
3. Worn or broken teeth or blocking rings.
4. Bent or broken synchronizer inserts or springs.
5. Damaged needle bearings or operating surfaces.
6. Wear or galling of the mainshaft, countershaft, clutch shaft or idler gear shaft.
7. Worn or broken thrust washers.
8. Bent, distorted, broken or weak snaprings.
9. Rough, galled, worn or broken front or rear bearing.

MAINSHAFT

Assembly

1. Assemble the first/second synchronizer hub, inserts and springs. Install the clutch sleeve. Be sure to position the spring ends 180 degrees apart.
2. Install the assembled first/second speed synchronizer hub and the reverse gear with sleeve, on the mainshaft. Secure with a new snapring.
3. Install the first speed gear and blocking ring on the rear of the mainshaft and install the first gear thrust washer.
4. Install a new tabbed thrust washer on the mainshaft with the tab seated in the mainshaft tab bore.
5. Install the second speed gear and the blocking ring on the mainshaft and secure with a new snapring.
6. Install the third speed gear and blocking ring on the mainshaft.

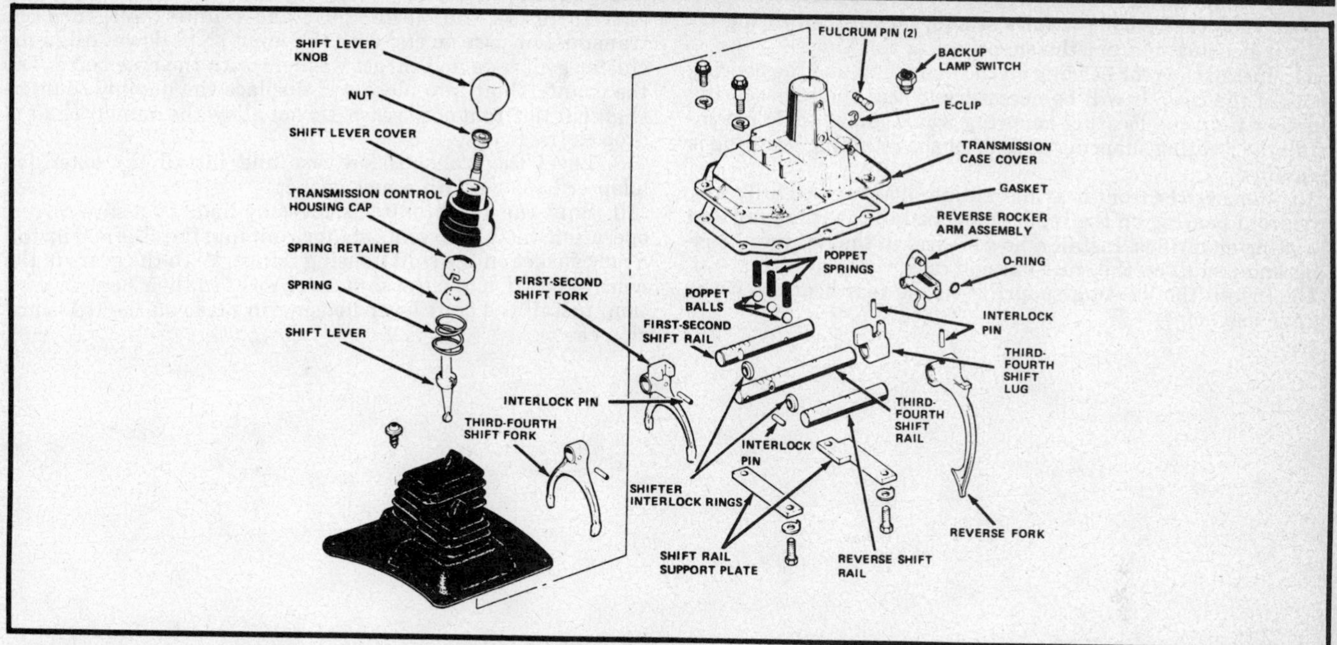

T-176 four speed transmission shift control housing (© Borg Warner Corp.)

7. Assemble the third/fourth speed synchronizer hub, inserts, and springs. Be sure the spring ends are 180 degrees apart.
8. Install the assembled third/fourth speed synchronizer on the mainshaft and secure with a new snapring.
9. The measured end play between the snapring and the third/fourth speed synchronizer should be 0.004 to 0.014 inch.

TRANSMISSION UNIT

Assembly

1. Load the reverse idler gear with the 44 needle roller bearings and a bearing retainer on each end of the gear. Install the sliding gear on the reverse idler gear. Install lubricated thrust washers into the case.
2. Install the reverse idler assembly into the case and install the reverse idler gear shaft.
3. Be sure to engage the thrust washer locating tabs in the case locating slots.
4. Seat the reverse idler gear shaft roll pin into the counterbore in the case. The reverse idler gear end play should be 0.004 to 0.018 inch.
5. Install the 42 needle roller bearings in the cluster gear, using the dummy countershaft as a bearing holder. Use of a vaseline type lubricant is suggested to hold the bearings in place.
6. Position the lubricated thrust washers in place on the inside of the transmission case. Position the thrust washer tabs in the tab slots of the case.
7. Insert the countershaft into the rear case bore, just far enough to hold the rear thrust washer. Lower the cluster gear assembly into the case and align the gear bore with the case bore. Push the countershaft into the cluster gear, displacing the dummy countershaft out the front case bore hole. Do not completely remove the dummy countershaft.
8. Measure the cluster gear end play which should be 0.004 to 0.018 inch. Correct as required and reinstall the dummy countershaft into the cluster gear, pushing the countershaft from the gear.
9. Allow the cluster gear to remain at the bottom of the case until the input and mainshaft has been installed to provide the necessary assembly clearance.
10. With the synchronizers in the neutral position, install the mainshaft assembly into the case.
11. Install the front bearing part way on the input shaft and install the 15 roller bearing in the shaft pocket. Do not use a heavy grease to hold the bearings in the pocket as the grease can plug the lubrication holes. Use only a vaseline type lubricant.
12. Position the blocking ring on the third/fourth synchronizer. Support the mainshaft assembly and insert the input shaft through the front bearing bore of the case. Seat the mainshaft pilot hub into the bearing pocket of the input shaft and tap the front bearing and input shaft into the case, using a soft faced hammer.

T-176 SPECIFICATIONS
Lubricant Capacity and End-Play Tolerances

End-Play Tolerances:
- Countershaft Gear to Case 0.004 to 0.018 inch (0.10 to 0.45 mm)
- Reverse Idler Gear to Case 0.004 to 0.018 inch (0.10 to 0.45 mm)
- Mainshaft Gear Train ..... 0.004 to 0.018 inch (0.10 to 0.45 mm)

Lubricant Capacity .... 3.5 pints (1.7 liters)
Lubricant Type .... SAE 85W-90, APJ GL5

TORQUE SPECIFICATIONS①

	ft. lbs.	N.m.
Backup lamp switch	15	20
Drain and fill plugs	15	20
Front bearing cap bolts	13	18
Shift housing-to-transmission case bolts	13	18
Support plate bolts	18	24

① All torque values given in foot-pounds and newton-meters with dry fits unless otherwise specified.

13. When the bearing is fully seated, install the bearing retainer housing, but not the snaprings at this time.

14. Install the rear bearing on the mainshaft and the bearing bore of the case. It will be necessary to seat the rear bearing further than the locating snapring would allow, so do not install the locating snapring until after the retaining snapring is installed.

15. Remove the front bearing retainer housing and fully seat the front bearing on the input shaft. Install the retaining and locating snaprings. Install a new oil seal in the retainer housing and install on the transmission case.

16. Install the locating snapring on the rear bearing, if not previously done.

17. To install the cluster gear and countershaft, turn the transmission case on end with the input shaft down. Align the cluster gear bore and thrust washers with the case bores. Tap the countershaft into place and displace the dummy countershaft out the front of the case. Do not allow the dummy shaft to drop to the floor.

18. Level the transmission case and install the extension adapter housing with a new gasket.

19. Shift the synchronizer sleeves by hand to insure correct operation. Install 3.5 pints of lubricant into the case and install a new gasket on the shift housing flange. With the gears in the neutral position and the shift lever forks in their neutral position, install the shift lever housing in place on the transmission case.

INDEX

TRANSFER CASE APPLICATION CHART

Model	Chev./GMC	Dodge/Plymouth	Ford	International	Jeep
Borg Warner 13-45			X		
Borg Warner 13-50			X		
Dana 20			X	X	X
Dana 21			X		
Dana 24			X		
Dana 300				X	X
International TC-143				X	
Jeep Selec-Trac 229					X
New Process 203	X		X		
New Process 205	X	X	X	X	
New Process 207	X				
New Process 208	X	X	X		X
New Process 219					X
New Process 228					X
Rockwell T-223		X	X	X	
Spicer 20				X	X
Warner Quadra-Trac					X

TRANSFER CASE

Trouble Analysis

SLIPS OUT OF GEAR (HIGH-LOW)

1. Shifting poppet spring weak.
2. Bearing broken or worn.
3. Shifting fork bent.
4. Improper control rod adjustment.

SLIPS OUT OF FRONT WHEEL DRIVE

1. Shifting poppet spring weak or broken.
2. Bearing worn or broken.
3. Excessive shaft end-play.
4. Shifting fork bent.

HARD SHIFTING

1. Lack of lubricant.
2. Shift lever binding on shaft.
3. Shifting poppet ball scored.
4. Shifting fork bent.
5. Low tire pressure.

BACKLASH

1. Companion yoke loose.
2. Transfer case loose on mounts.
3. Internal parts excessively worn.

NOISY

1. Low lubricant level.
2. Bearings improperly adjusted or excessively worn.
3. Gears worn or damaged.
4. Improper alignment of driveshafts or U-joints.

OIL LEAKAGE

1. Excessive amount of lubricant in case.
2. Vent clogged.
3. Gaskets or seals leaking.
4. Bearings loose or damaged.
5. Driveshaft yoke mating surfaces scored.

OVERHEATING

1. Excessive or insufficient amount of lubricant.
2. Bearing adjustment too tight.

CLEANING & INSPECTION

CLEANING

During overhaul, all components of the transfer case (except bearing assemblies) should be thoroughly cleaned with solvent and dried with air pressure prior to inspection and reassembly.

1. Clean the bearing assemblies as follows.

NOTE: Proper cleaning of bearings is of utmost importance. Bearings should always be cleaned separately from other parts.

a. Soak all bearing assemblies in clean solvent or fuel oil. Bearings should never be cleaned in a hot solution tank.

b. Slush bearings in solvent until all old lubricant is loosened. Hold races so that bearings will not rotate; then clean bearings with a soft bristled brush until all dirt has been removed. Remove loose particles of dirt by tapping bearing flat against a block of wood.

c. Rinse bearings in clean solvent; then blow bearings dry with air pressure.

CAUTION

Do not spin bearings while drying.

d. After drying, rotate each bearing slowly while examining balls or rollers for roughness, damage, or excessive wear. Replace all bearings that are not in first class condition.

NOTE: After cleaning and inspecting bearings, lubricate generously with recommended lubricant, then wrap each bearing in clean paper until ready for reassembly.

2. Remove all portions of old gaskets from parts, using a stiff brush or scraper.

INSPECTION

1. Inspect all parts for discoloration or warpage.
2. Examine all gears and splines for chipped, worn, broken or nicked teeth. Small nicks or burrs may be removed with a fine abrasive stone.
3. Inspect the breather assembly to make sure that it is open and not damaged.

4. Check all threaded parts for damaged, stripped, or crossed threads.
5. Replace all gaskets, oil seals and snap-rings.
6. Inspect housings, retainers and covers for cracks or other damage. Replace the damaged parts.
7. Inspect keys and keyways for condition and fit.
8. Inspect shift forks for wear, distortion or any other damage.
9. Check detent ball springs for free length, compressed length, distortion or collapsed coils.
10. Check bearing fit on their respective shafts and in their bores or cups. Inspect bearings, shafts and cups for wear.

NOTE: If either bearings or cups are worn or damaged, it is advisable to replace both parts.

11. Inspect all bearing rollers or balls for pitting or galling.
12. Examine detent balls for corrosion or brinneling. If shift bar detents show wear, replace them.
13. Replace all worn or damaged parts. When assembling the transfer case, coat all moving parts with recommended lubricant.

Borg Warner 13–45 Transfer Case

This transfer case is a two piece all aluminum part time transfer case. The unit lubrication is done by a positive displacement oil pump. This oil pump, channels the oil flow through drilled holes in the rear output shaft. The oil pump turns with the rear output shaft and allows towing of the vehicle for extended distances without having to disconnect the drive shaft.

Removal

NOTE: Do not proceed with this procedure when the exhaust system is hot.

1. Raise and support the vehicle safely. Drain the gear fluid from the transfer case into a suitable drain pan.
2. Disconnect the four wheel drive indicator switch connector at the transfer case and if so equipped, remove the skid plate from the frame.
3. Disconnect the front driveshaft from the front output yoke. Disconnect the rear drive shaft from the rear output yoke.
4. Disconnect the speedometer driven gear from the transfer case bearing retainer. Remove the retaining clips and shift rod from the transfer case control lever and transfer shift lever.
5. Disconnect the vent hose from the transfer case and remove the heat shield from the engine mount bracket and transfer case.
6. Using a suitable transmission jack or equivalent, support the transfer case. Remove the bolts that hold the transfer case to the transmission.
7. Slide the transfer case rear ward off the transmission output shaft and lower the transfer case from the vehicle. Remove the old gasket between the transfer case and the adapter.

SHIFT LEVER

NOTE: Remove the shift ball only if the shift ball, boot or lever have to be replaced. If any of these parts are not being replaced, remove the shift ball, boot and lever as an assembly.

Removal

1. Remove the plastic insert from the shift ball. Warm the ball with a heat gun or equivalent until it reaches approximately 140°to 180°F. Using a block of wood and a hammer, knock the shift ball off the lever. Be careful not to damage the finish on the shift lever.
2. Remove the rubber boot with the floor pan cover. Disconnect the vent hose from the shift lever.
3. Disconnect the transfer case shift rod from the shift lever. Remove the bolt holding the shift lever to transfer case. Remove the shift lever and bushings.

Installation

1. Position the shift lever and bushings on the transfer case. Install the bolt and tighten to 70 to 90 ft. lbs. Coat the pivots on the shift lever and transfer case lever with a multi-purpose lubricant C1AZ–19590–B or equivalent.
2. Install the shift rod on the pivots and connect the vent hose to the shift lever. Install the rubber boot and floor pan cover.
3. Warm the ball with a heat gun or equivalent until it reaches approximately 140°to 180°F. Using a $^{7}/_{16}$ in. socket and a mallet, tap the ball on to the lever and install the plastic shift pattern insert.
4. Check the transfer case for proper shifting and operation.

TRANSFER CASE

Disassembly

1. Remove the transfer case from the vehicle as previously outlined in this section. Drain the fluid from the case by removing the filler plug from the case half. Remove the speedometer cover.
2. Remove both output shaft yoke nuts and washers. Remove the front and rear output yokes. Remove the four-wheel drive indicator switch.
3. Separate the cover from the case by removing the attaching bolts. Pry the case and cover apart by inserting a suitable tool. Remove the magnetic chip collector from the boss in the bottom of the case half.
4. Slide the shift collar hub off the rear output shaft and compress the shift fork spring . Remove the upper and lower spring retainers from the shaft.
5. As an assembly lift out from the case the four wheel lock-up shift collar. Be careful not to lose the nylon wear pads on the lock-up fork. Note the location of the holes on the nylon wear pad and lock-up fork. Lift the output shaft from the case.
6. Remove the snap ring from the front output shaft and remove the thrust washer. Grip the chain and both sprockets and lift straight up to to remove the drive sprockets, driven sprocket and chain from the output shafts. Remove the thrust washer from the rear output shaft.
7. Lift the front output shaft out from the case. Remove the four oil pump attaching bolts and remove the oil pump rear cover, pick-up tube filter and pump body, two pump pins, pump spring and oil pump front cover from the rear output shaft. Disconnect the oil pump pick-up tube from the pump body.
8. Remove the snap ring that holds the bearing retainer inside the gas. Lift the rear output shaft while tapping on the bearing retainer with a plastic or soft mallet. Lift the rear output shaft and bearing retainer from the case.

NOTE: Two dowel pins will fall into the case when the retainer is removed, be sure note to lose them.

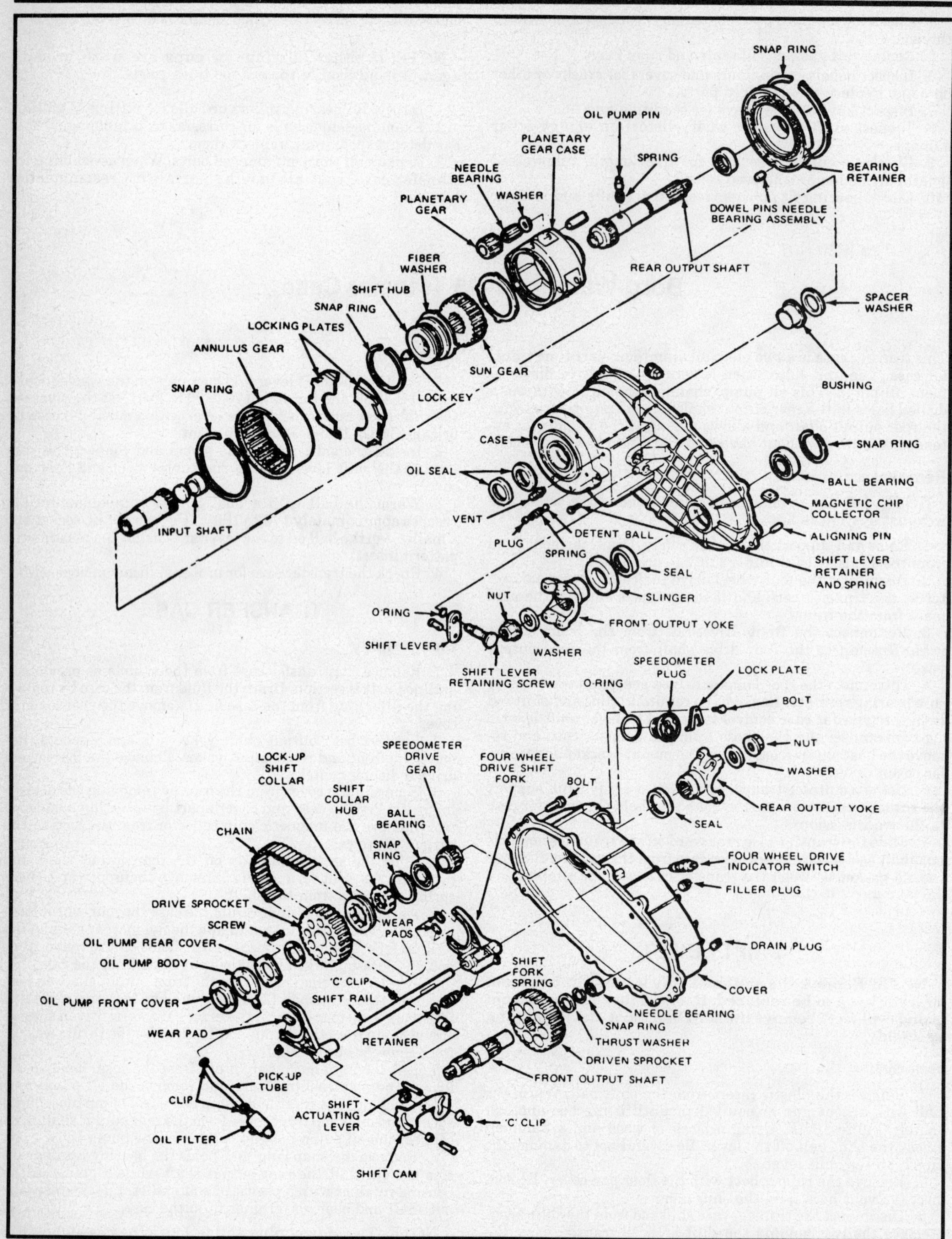

Exploded view of the 1345 transfer case

9. Remove the rear output shaft from the bearing retainer and if necessary, press the needle bearing assembly out from the bearing retainer. Remove the C-clip that holds the shift cam to the shift actuating lever inside the case.

10. Remove the shift lever retaining screw and remove the shift lever from the case. When removing the lever, the shift cam will disengage from the shift lever and may release the detent ball and spring from the case.

11. As an assembly, remove the planetary gear set, shift rail, shift cam, output shaft and shift forks from the case. Be careful not to lose the two nylon wear pads on the shift fork.

12. Remove the spacer washer from the bottom of the case and remove the bushing. Using a drift pin or equivalent, drive out the plug from the detent spring bore.

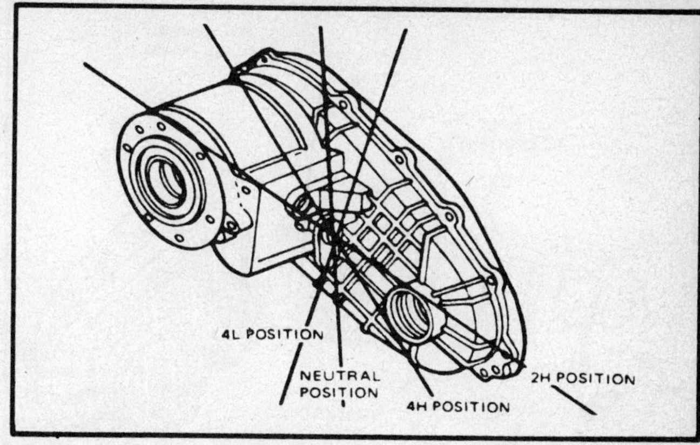

Proper shift lever installation

Assembly

NOTE: Before starting the assembly procedure, lubricate all the internal parts, with DEXRON®II transmission fluid or equivalent.

1. Assemble the planetary gear set, shift rail, shift cam, input shaft and shift fork together as a unit. Be sure that the boss on the shift cam is installed toward the case. Install the spacer washer on the input shaft.

2. Place the rear output shaft in the planetary gear set, being sure that the shift cam engages the shift fork actuating pin. Lay the case on its side and insert the rear output shaft with planetary gear set into the case. Be sure that the spacer washer remains on the input shaft.

3. Install the shift rail into the hole in the case. Install the outer roller bushing into the guide in the case. Remove the rear output shaft and position the shift fork in neutral.

4. Place the shift control lever shaft through the cam and install the clip ring. Be sure that the shift control lever is pointed downward and is parallel to the front face of the case in the neutral position.

5. Check the shift fork and planetary gear engagement. The unit should move freely with out any binding. Press a new needle bearing into the needle bearing retainer using output bearing replacer tool # T80T–7127–C or equivalent.

6. Insert the output shaft through the bearing retainer from the bottom side outward. Insert the rear output shaft pilot into the input shaft rear bushing. Align the dowel holes and lower the bearing into position.

7. Install the dowel pins. Install the snap ring that retains the bearing retainer in the case. Insert the detent ball and spring in the detent bore in the case half.

8. Coat the seal plug with RTV sealant or equivalent. Drive the plug into the case until the lip of the plug is $^{1}/_{32}$ in. below the surface of the case. Peen the case over the plug in two places.

9. Install the oil pump front cover over the output shaft with the flanged side down. The word "TOP" must be facing the top of the transfer case as the position the case id installed in the vehicle.

10. Install the oil pump spring and two pump pins with the flat side outward in the hole in the output shaft. Push both pins in to install the oil pump body, pick-up tube and filter. The rear markings on the pump must be facing upward. Be sure to prime the pump with DEXRON®II transmission fluid or equivalent.

11. Place the oil pump rear cover on the output shaft with the flanged side outward. The word "TOP REAR" is positioned toward the the top of the transfer case in the position the transfer case is installed in the vehicle. Apply Loctite® or equivalent to the oil pump bolts and install the pump cover. Torque the bolts to 3 to 4 ft. lbs. and be sure to rotate the pump while tightening.

NOTE: When the oil pump is correctly installed, it will rotate freely on the output shaft.

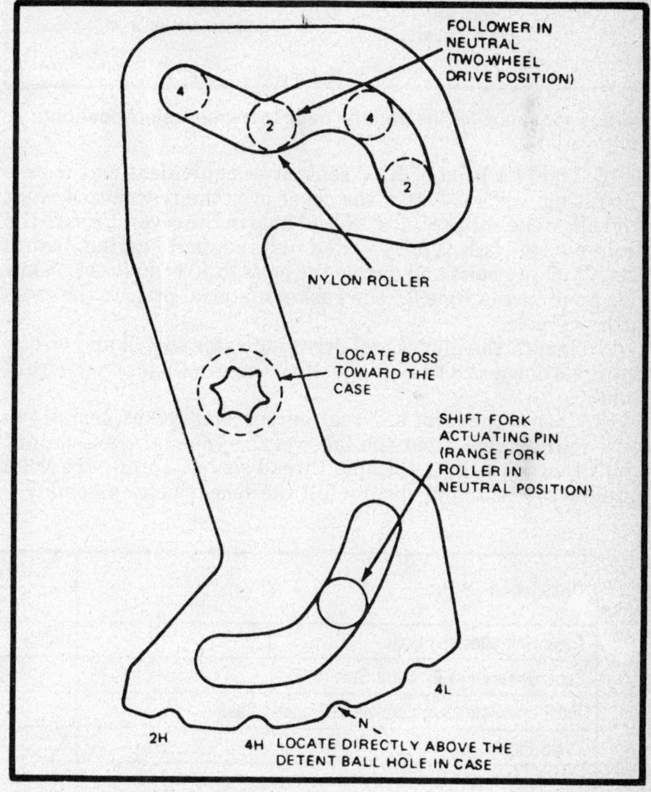

Proper shift cam engagement

12. Install the thrust washer on the rear output shaft next to the oil pump. Install the chain on the drive sprocket and driven sprocket. Lower the chain and sprockets into position in the case. The driven sprocket is installed over the front output shaft and the drive the sprocket is placed on the rear output shaft.

13. Assemble the washer and snap ring behind the driven sprocket. Engage the four wheel drive fork on the shift collar.

14. Slide the shift fork over the shift shaft and the shift collar over the rear output shaft. Be sure that the nylon pads are installed on the shift fork tips and the necked down part of the shift collar lock-up fork are assembled correctly. Note that the location of the holes in the nylon wear pad and the lock-up fork are assembled correctly.

15. Push the four wheel drive shift spring downward and install the upper spring retainer. Push the spring upward and install the lower retainer. Install the shift collar hub on the rear output shaft.

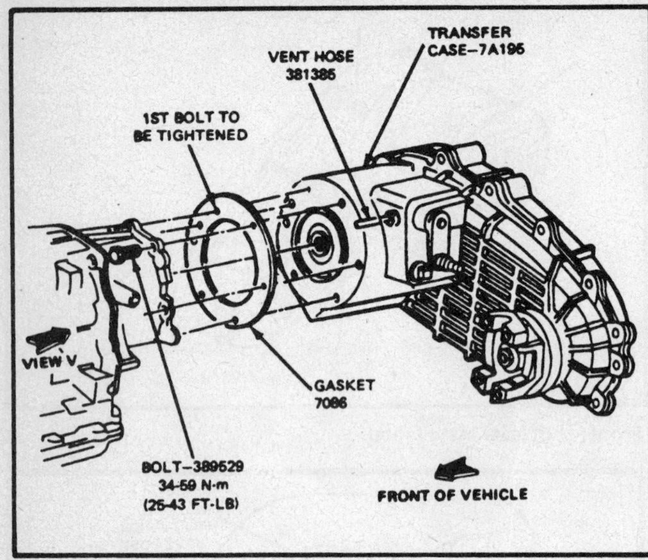

Torque sequence for the transfer case to transmission mounting bolts

16. Apply a bead of RTV sealant or equivalent on the case mounting surface. Lower the cover over the rear output shaft and align the shift rail to its blind hole in the cover. Be sure the front output shaft is fully seated in its support bearing. Install the attaching bolts and torque the bolts to 40 to 45 ft. lbs. Allow one hour curing time for the gasket material prior to the operating vehicle.

17. Install the four wheel drive indicator switch and torque the bolts down at 8 to 12 ft. lbs. Press an oil slinger on the front yoke.

18. Install the front and rear output shaft yokes. Install the anti-spill oil seal. Coat the faces of the yoke nuts and output shaft threads with a suitable thread sealer. Torque the yoke nuts to 100 to 130 ft. lbs. Install the speedometer assembly.

19. Refill the transfer case with 6.5 pints of DEXRON @® II transmission fluid or equivalent. Torque the level plug and the drain plugs to 6 to 14 ft. lbs. Torque the fill plug to 15 to 22 ft. lbs.

20. Install the transfer case as outlined in this section.

21. Start the engine and check the transfer case for correct operation. Stop the engine and check the fluid level, add as necessary.

22. Fluid should drip from the level hole. If the fluid flows out level hole in a stream, the pump may not be operating properly.

Installation

1. Install the heat shield onto the transfer case and place a new gasket between the transfer case and adapter.

2. Raise the transfer case with a suitable transmission jack or equivalent, raise it high enough so that the transmission output shaft aligns with the splined transfer case input shaft.

3. Slide the transfer case forward on to the transmission output shaft and onto the dowel pin. Install transfer case retaining bolts and torque them to 26 to 43 ft. lbs.

4. Connect the rear driveshaft to the rear output shaft yoke and torque the retaining bolts to 20 to 28 ft. lbs. Attach the shift rod to the transfer case shift lever and transfer case control rod and attach with retaining rings.

5. Connect the speedometer driven gear to the transfer case. Connect the four wheel drive indicator switch wire connector at the transfer case.

6. Connect the front driveshaft to the front output yoke and torque the yoke nut to 8 to 15 ft. lbs. Attach the heat shield to the engine mounting bracket and mounting lug on the transfer case.

7. Install the skid plate to the frame. Install the transfer case drain plug and torque the plug to 6 to 14 ft. lbs.

8. Fill the transfer case with 6.5 pints of DEXRON®II transmission fluid or equivalent. Torque the fill plug to 15 to 22 ft. lbs. Start the engine and check the transfer case for correct operation. Stop the engine and check the fluid level, add as necessary.

Description	Torque Limits	
	N-m	Ft-Lbs
Case Half Attaching Bolts	48-54	35-40
Four Wheel Drive Indicator Switch	11-16	8-12
Front and Rear Output Yokes to Transfer Case	163-203	120-150
Drain Plug	13-24	14-22
Fill Plug	21-33	15-25
Transfer Case to Transmission Adapter	34-58	25-43
Heat Shield to Transfer Case	54-61	40-45
Skid Plate to Frame	20-27	15-20
Front Driveshaft to Front Output Yoke	163-203	120-150
Rear Driveshaft to Rear Output Yoke	163-203	120-150

13-45 transfer case torque specifications

Borg Warner 13–50

The Borg Warner 13–50 is a three-piece aluminum part time transfer case. It transfers power from the transmission to the rear axle and when actuated, also to the front drive axle. The unit is lubricated by a positive displacement oil pump that channels oil flow through drilled holes in the rear output shaft. The pump turns with the rear output shaft and allows towing of the vehicle at maximum legal road speeds for extended distances without disconnecting the front and/or rear driveshaft.

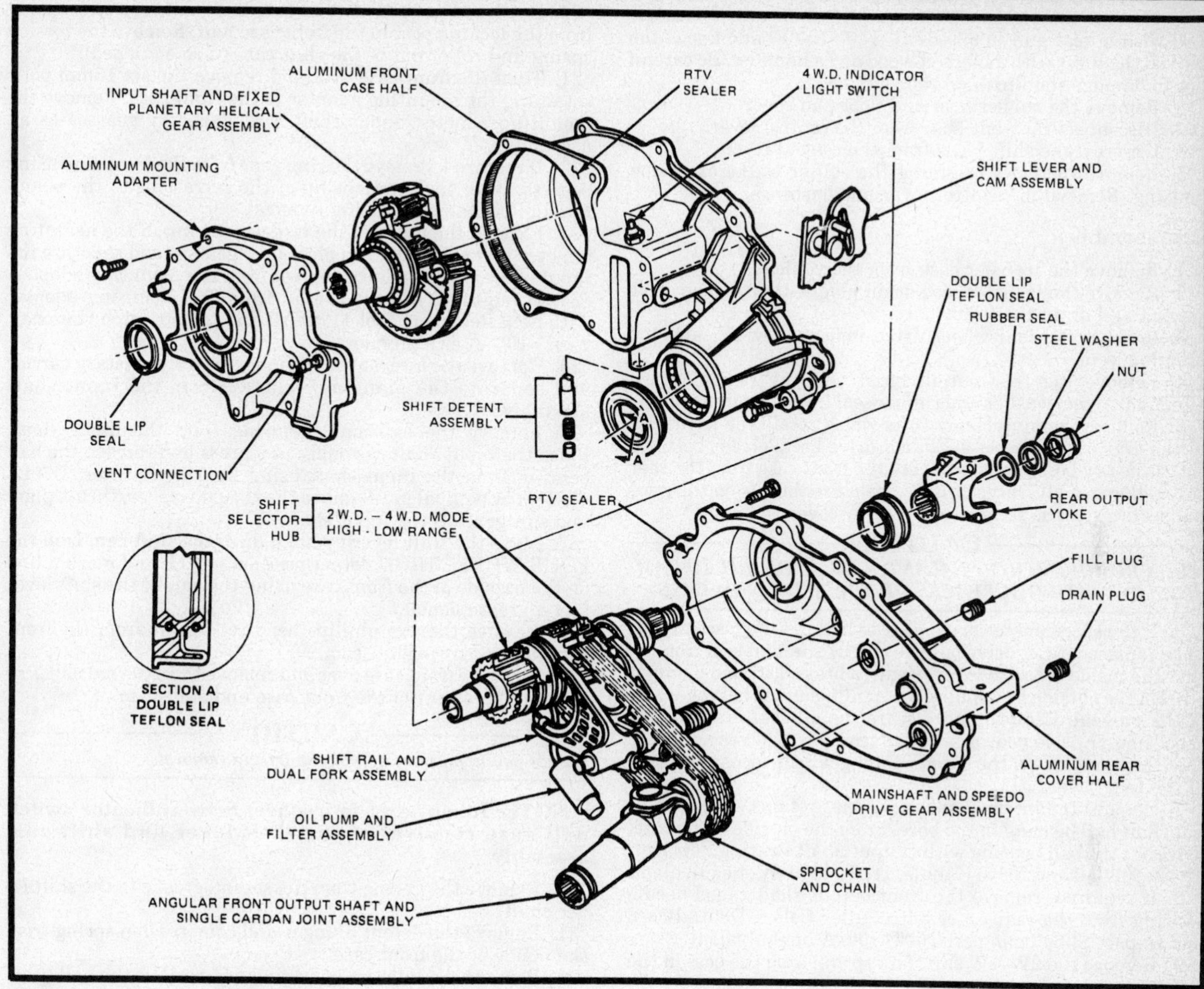

Borg-Warner 13-50 transfer case

Removal

1. Raise the vehicle on a hoist.
2. If so equipped, remove the skid plate from frame.
3. Place a drain pan under transfer case, remove the drain plug and drain fluid from the transfer case.
4. Disconnect the four-wheel drive indicator switch wire connector at the transfer case.
5. Disconnect the front driveshaft from the axle input yoke.
6. Loosen the clamp retaining the front driveshaft boot to the transfer case, and pull the driveshaft and front boot assembly out of the transfer case front output shaft.
7. Disconnect the rear driveshaft from the transfer case output shaft yoke.
8. Disconnect the speedometer driven gear from the transfer case rear cover.
9. Disconnect the vent hose from the control lever.
10. Loosen or remove the large bolt and the small bolt retaining the shifter to the extension housing. Pull on the control lever until the bushing slides off the transfer case shift lever pin. If necessary, unscrew the shift lever from the control lever.
11. Remove the heat shield from the transfer case.

CAUTION

The catalytic converter is located beside the heat shield. Be careful when working around the converter because of the extremely high temperatures generated by the converter.

12. Support the transfer case with a transmission jack.
13. Remove the five bolts retaining the transfer case to the transmission and the extension housing.
14. Slide the transfer case rearward off the transmission output shaft and lower the transfer case from the vehicle. Remove the gasket from between the transfer case and extension housing.

SHIFT LEVER

Removal

NOTE: Remove the shift ball only if the shift ball, boot or lever is to be replaced. If the ball, boot or lever is not being replaced, remove the ball, boot and lever as an assembly.

1. Remove the plastic insert from the shift ball. Warm the ball with a heat gun to 60°–87°C (140°–180°F) and knock the ball off the lever with a block of wood and a hammer. Be careful not to damage the finish on the shift lever.
2. Remove the rubber boot and floor pan cover.
3. Disconnect the vent hose from the control lever.
4. Unscrew the shift lever from the control lever.
5. Remove the bolts retaining the shifter to the extension housing. Remove the control lever and bushings.

Disassembly

1. Remove the transfer case from the vehicle.
2. Remove the transfer case drain plug with a $^3/_8$ inch drive ratchet and drain the fluid.
3. Remove the four-wheel drive indicator switch and the breather vent.
4. Remove the rear output shaft yoke by removing the 30mm nut, steel washer and rubber seal from the output shaft.
5. Remove the nine 15mm bolts which retain the front case to the rear cover. Insert a $^1/_2$ inch drive breaker bar between the three pry bosses and separate the front case from the rear cover. Remove all traces of RTV gasket sealant from the mating surfaces of the front case and rear cover.

CAUTION

WHEN REMOVING RTV SEALANT, TAKE CARE NOT TO DAMAGE THE MATING SURFACES OF THE ALUMINUM CASE.

6. If the speedometer drive gear or ball bearing assembly is to be replaced, first, drive out the output shaft oil seal from either the inside of the rear cover with a brass drift and hammer or from the outside by bending and pulling on the curved-up lip of the oil seal. Remove and discard the oil seal. Remove the speedometer drive gear assembly (gear, clip and spacer). Note that the round end of the speedometer gear clip faces the inside of the rear cover.
7. Remove the internal snap-ring that retains the rear output shaft ball bearing in the bore. From the outside of the case, drive out the ball bearing with Output Shaft Bearing Replacer, T83T–7025–B and Drive Handle, T80T–4000–W or equivalent.
8. If required, remove the front output shaft caged needle bearing from the rear cover with Puller Collet, D80L–100–S and Impact Slide Hammer, T50T–100–A or equivalent.
9. Remove the 2W–4W shift fork spring from the boss in the rear cover.
10. Remove the shift collar hub from the output shaft. Remove the 2W–4W lock-up assembly and the 2W–4W shift fork together as an assembly. Remove the 2W–4W fork from the 2W–4W lock-up assembly. If required, remove the external clip and remove the roller bushing assembly (bushing, shaft and external clip) from the 2W–4W shift fork.
11. If required to disassemble the 2W–4W lock-up assembly, remove the internal snap-ring and pull the lock-up hub and spring from the lock-up collar.
12. Remove the external snap-ring and thrust washer that retains the drive sprocket to the front output shaft.
13. Remove the chain, driven sprocket and drive sprocket as an assembly.
14. Remove the collector magnet from the notch in the front case bottom.
15. Remove the output shaft and oil pump as an assembly.
16. If required to disassemble the oil pump, remove the four 8mm bolts from the body. Note the position and markings of the front cover, body, pins, spring, rear cover, and pump retainer as removed.
17. Pull out the shift rail.
18. Slip the high-low range shift fork out of the inside track of the shift cam. If required, remove the external clip and remove the roller bushing assembly (bushing, shaft and external clip) from the high-low range shift fork.
19. Remove the high-low shift hub from out of the planetary gearset in the front case.
20. Push and pull out the anchor end of the torsion spring from the locking post in the front case half. Remove the torsion spring and roller out of the shift cam (if so equipped).
21. Turn the front case over and remove the six 15mm bolts retaining the mounting adapter to the front case. Remove the mounting adapter, input shaft and planetary gearset as an assembly.
22. If required, remove the ring gear from the front case using a press. Note the relationship of the serrations to the chamfered pilot diameter during removal.
23. Expand the tangs of the large snap-ring in the mounting adapter and pry under the planetary gearset and separate the input shaft and planetary gearset from the mounting adapter.
24. If required, remove the oil from the mounting adapter with Seal Remover, Tool 1175–AC and Impact Slide Hammer, T50T–100–A or equivalent.
25. Remove the internal snap-ring from the planetary carrier and separate the planetary gearset from the input shaft assembly.
26. Remove the external snap-ring from the input shaft. Place the input shaft assembly in a press and remove the ball bearing from the input shaft using Bearing Splitter, D79L–4621–A or equivalent. Remove the thrust washer, thrust plate and sun gear off the input shaft.
27. Move the shift lever by hand until the shift cam is in the FOUR WHEEL HIGH detent position (4WH) and mark a line on the outside of the front case using the side of the shift lever and a grease pencil.
28. Remove the two phillips head set screws from the front case and from the shift cam.
29. Turn the front case over and remove the external clip. Pry the shift lever out of the front case and shift cam.

CAUTION

Do not pound on the external clip during removal.

NOTE: Removal of four-wheel drive indicator switch will ease removal of the shift lever and shift cam assembly.

30. Remove the O-ring from the second groove in the shift lever shaft.
31. Remove the detent plunger and compression spring from the inside of the front case.
32. Remove the internal snap-ring and remove the ball bearing retainer from the front case by tapping on the face of the front output shaft and U-joint assembly with a plastic hammer. Remove the internal snap-ring and drive the ball bearing out of the bearing retainer using Output Shaft Bearing Replacer, T83T–7025–B and Driver Handle, T80T–4000–W or equivalent.

NOTE: The clip is required to prevent the bearing retainer from rotating. Do not discard the clip.

33. Remove the front output shaft and U-joint assembly from the front case. If required, remove the oil seal with Seal Remover, Tool–1175–AC and Impact Slide Hammer, T50T–100–A or equivalent. If required, remove the internal snap-ring and drive the ball bearing out of the front case bore using Output Shaft Replacer, T83T–7025–B and Driver Handle, T80T–4000–W or equivalent.
34. If required, place the front output shaft and U-joint assembly in a vise, being careful not to damage the assembly. Use copper or wood vise jaws.
35. Remove the internal snap-rings that retain the bearings in the shaft.
36. Position the U-Joint Tool, T74P–4635–C or equivalent, over the shaft ears and press the bearing out. If the bearing cannot be pressed all the way out, remove it with vise grip or channel lock pliers.
37. Re-position the U-joint tool on the spider in order to remove the opposite bearing.

38. Repeat the above procedure until all bearings are removed.

Assembly

Before assembly, lubricate all parts with DEXRON @ II, Automatic Transmission Fluid.

1. If removed, start a new bearing into an end of the shaft ear. Support the output shaft in a vise equipped with copper or wood jaws, in order not to damage the shaft.
2. Position the spider into the bearing and press the bearing below the snap-ring groove using U-joint Tool, T74P–4635–C or equivalent.
3. Remove the tool and install a new internal snap-ring on the groove.
4. Start a new bearing into the opposite side of the shaft ear and using the tool, press the bearing until the opposite bearing contacts the snap-ring.
5. Remove the tool and install a new internal snap-ring in the groove.
6. Re-position the front output shaft assembly and install the other two bearings in the same manner.
7. Check the U-joint for freedom of movement. If a binding condition occurs due to misalignment during the installation procedure, tap the ears of both shafts sharply to relieve the bind. Do not install the front output shaft assembly if the U-joint shows any sign of binding.
8. If removed, drive the ball bearing into the front output case bore using Output Shaft Bearing Replacer, T83T–7025–B and Drive Handle, T80T–4000–W or equivalent. Drive the ball bearing in straight, making sure that it is not cocked in the bore. Install the internal snap-ring that retains the ball bearing to the front case.
9. If removed, install the front output oil seal in the front case bore using Output Shaft Seal Installer, T83T–7065–B and Driver Handle, T80T–4000–W or equivalent.
10. If removed, install the ring gear in the front case. Align the serrations on the outside diameter of the ring gear to the serations previously cut in the front case bore. Using a press, start the piloted chamfered end of the ring gear first and press in until it is fully seated. Make sure the ring gear is not cocked in the bore.
11. If removed, install the ball bearing in the bearing retainer bore. Drive the bearing into the retainer using Output Shaft Bearing Replacer, T83T–7025–B and Driver Handle, T80T–4000–W or equivalent. Make sure the ball bearing is not cocked in the bore. Install the internal snap-ring that retains the ball bearing to the retainer.
12. Install the front output shaft and U-joint assembly through the front case seal. Position the ball bearing and retainer assembly over the front output shaft and install in the front case bore. Make sure the clip on the bearing retainer aligns with the slot in the front case. Tap the bearing retainer into place with a plastic hammer. Install the internal snap-ring that retains the ball bearing and retainer assembly to the front case.
13. Install the compression spring and the detent plunger into the bore from the inside of the front case.
14. Install a new O-ring in the second groove of the shift lever shaft. Coat the shaft and O-ring with Multi-Purpose Long-Life Lubricant.

NOTE: Use a rubber band to fill the first groove so as not to cut the O-ring. Discard the rubber band.

15. Position the shift cam inside the front case with the 4WH detent position over the detent plunger. Holding the shift cam by hand, push the shift lever shaft into the front case to engage the shift cam aligning the side of the shift lever with the mark previously scribed on the front case. Install the external clip on the end of the shift lever shaft.
16. Install the two phillips head set screws in the front case and in the shift cam. Tighten the screws to 6.8–9.5 Nm (5–7 ft. lbs.). Make sure the set screw in the front case is in the first groove of the shift lever shaft and not bottomed against the shaft itself. The shift lever should be able to move freely to all detent positions.
17. Slide the sun gear, thrust plate, thrust washer, and press the ball bearing over the input shaft. Install the external snap-ring to the input shaft.

NOTE: The sun gear recessed face and ball bearing snap-ring groove should be toward the rear of the transfer case. The stepped face of the thrust washer should face towards the ball bearing.

18. Install the planetary gear set to the sun gear and input shaft assembly. Install the internal snap-ring to the planetary carrier.
19. Drive the oil seal into the bore of the mounting adapter with Input Shaft Seal Installer, T83–T–7065–A and Driver Handle, T80T–4000–W or equivalent.
20. Place the tanged snap-ring in the mounting adapter groove. Position the input shaft and planetary gearset in the mounting adapter and push inward until the planetary assembly and input shaft assembly are seated in the adapter. When properly seated, the tanged snap-rig will snap into place. Check installation by holding the mounting adapter by hand and tapping the face of the input shaft against a wooden block to ensure that the snap-ring is engaged.
21. Remove all traces of RTV gasket sealant from the mating surfaces of the front case and mounting adapter. Install a bead of RTV gasket sealant on the surface of the front case.
22. Position the mounting adapter on the front case. Install six bolts and tighten to 31–41 Nm (25–30 ft. lbs.).
23. Position the roller on the 90° bent tang of the torsion spring. The larger diameter end of the spring must be installed first.
24. Install the roller into the torsion spring roller track of the shift cam while locating the center spring in the pivot groove in the front case. Push the anchor end of the torsion spring behind the locking post adjacent to the ring gear face.
25. Position the high-low shift hub into the planetary gearset. Slip the high-low shift fork bushing into the high-low roller track of the shift cam and the groove of the high-low shift hub.

NOTE: Make sure the nylon wear pads are installed on the shift fork. Make sure the dot on the pad is installed in the fork hole.

26. Install the shift rail through the high-low fork and make sure the shift rail is seated in the bore in the front case.
27. Install the oil pump front cover over the output shaft with the flanged side down. The word "TOP" must be facing the top of the transfer case as the position the case id installed in the vehicle.
28. Install the oil pump spring and two pump pins with the flat side outward in the hole in the output shaft. Push both pins in to install the oil pump body, pick-up tube and filter. The rear markings on the pump must be facing upward. Be sure to prime the pump with DEXRON® II transmission fluid or equivalent.
29. Place the oil pump rear cover on the output shaft with the flanged side outward. The word "TOP REAR" is positioned toward the the top of the transfer case in the position the transfer case is installed in the vehicle. Apply Loctite® or equivalent to the oil pump bolts and install the pump cover. Torque the bolts to 3 to 4 ft. lbs. and be sure to rotate the pump while tightening.

NOTE: When the oil pump is correctly installed, it will rotate freely on the output shaft.

30. Install the thrust washer on the rear output shaft next to the oil pump. Install the chain on the drive sprocket and driven sprocket. Lower the chain and sprockets into position in the case. The driven sprocket is installed over the front output

shaft and the drive the sprocket is placed on the rear output shaft.

31. If disassembled, assemble the 2W–4W shift fork to the 2W–4W lock up assembly. Install the spring in the lock up collar. Place the lock up hub over the spring and engage the lock up hub in the notches in the lock up collar. Retain the lock up hub to the lock up collar with an internal snap ring.

32. Install the 2W–4W shift fork to the 2W–4W lock up assembly. If removed, make sure the nylon wear pads are installed on the fork. The dot on the pad must be installed in the hole in the fork. Install the 2W–4W lock up collar and hub assembly over the the output shaft and onto the shift rail. If removed, install the shaft, bushing and external clip to the 2W-4W lock up fork.

33. Install the shift collar hub to the output shaft.

34. If removed, drive the gaged needle bearing into the rear cover bore with the needle bearing replacer tool T83T–7127–A and driver handled T80T–4000–W or equivalent.

35. If removed, install the ball bearing in the rear cover bore. Drive the bearing into the rear cover bore with output shaft bearing replacer tool # T83T–7025–B and driver handled T80–4000–W or equivalent. Make sure the ball bearing is not cocked in the bore. Install the internal snap ring that retains the ball bearing to the rear cover.

36. Install the speedometer drive gear assembly into the rear cover bore with round end of the speedometer gear clip facing towards the inside of the rear cover. Drive the oil seal into the rear cover bore with output shaft seal installer tool # T83T–7065–B and driver handle # T80T–4000–W or equivalent.

37. Install the 2W–4W shift fork spring on the inside boss of the rear cover.

38. Prior to final assembly of the rear cover to front case half, the transfer case shift lever assembly should be shifted into "4H" detent position to assure positioning of the shift rail to the rear cover.

39. Coat the mating surface of the front case with a bead of Loctite® sealant or equivalent.

40. Position the rear cover on the front case, making sure that the 2W–4W shift fork spring engages the shift rail and does not fall off the rear cover boss. Install the nine bolts, starting with the bolts on the rear cover and torque the bolts to 23 to 30 ft. lbs.

NOTE: If the rear cover assembly does not seat properly, move the rear cover up and down slightly to permit the end of the shift rail to enter the shift rail hole in the rear cover boss.

41. Install the front and rear output shaft yokes. Install the anti-spill oil seal. Coat the faces of the yoke nuts and output shaft threads with a suitable thread sealer. Torque the yoke nuts to 120 to 150 ft. lbs.

42. Install the four wheel drive indicator switch and torque the bolts down at 23 to 35 ft. lbs.

43. Refill the transfer case with 3.0 pints of DEXRON®II transmission fluid or equivalent. Torque the level plug and the drain plugs to 14 to 22 ft. lbs. Torque the fill plug to 14 to 22 ft. lbs.

44. Install the transfer case as outlined in this section.

45. Start the engine and check the transfer case for correct operation. Stop the engine and check the fluid level, add as necessary.

46. Fluid should drip from the level hole. If the fluid flows out level hole in a stream, the pump may not be operating properly.

Installation

1. Install the heat shield onto the transfer case and place a new gasket between the transfer case and adapter.
2. Raise the transfer case with a suitable transmission jack or equivalent, raise it high enough so that the transmission output shaft aligns with the splined transfer case input shaft.
3. Slide the transfer case forward on to the transmission output shaft and onto the dowel pin. Install transfer case retaining bolts and torque them to 26 to 43 ft. lbs.
4. Connect the rear driveshaft to the rear output shaft yoke and torque the retaining bolts to 20 to 28 ft. lbs. Attach the shift rod to the transfer case shift lever and transfer case control rod and attach with retaining rings.
5. Connect the speedometer driven gear to the transfer case. Connect the four wheel drive indicator switch wire connector at the transfer case.
6. Connect the front driveshaft to the front output yoke and torque the yoke nut to 8 to 15 ft. lbs. Attach the heat shield to the engine mounting bracket and mounting lug on the transfer case.
7. Install the skid plate to the frame. Install the transfer case drain plug and torque the plug to 6 to 14 ft. lbs.
8. Fill the transfer case with 6.5 pints of DEXRON®II transmission fluid or equivalent. Torque the fill plug to 15 to 22 ft. lbs. Start the engine and check the transfer case for correct operation. Stop the engine and check the fluid level, add as necessary.

TORQUE SPECIFICATIONS
Borg-Warner 13-50 Transfer Case

Description	Torque N•m	Torque Ft. Lb.
Breather Vent	8–19	6–14
Case to Cover Bolts	31–41	23–30
Drain and Fill Plug	19–30	14–22
Four-Wheel Drive Indicator Switch	34–47	25–35
Front and Rear Driveshaft Bolts	16–20	12–15
Shift Control Bolts—Large	95–122	70–90
Shift Control Bolts—Small	42–57	31–42
Shift Shaft and Shift Cam Set Screw	6.8–9.5	5–7
Skid Plate to Frame Bolt	30–41	22–30
Transfer Case to Transmission Adapter	34–47	25–35
Upper Shift Control Lever and Heat Shield Bolts	37–50	27–37
Yoke Nut	163–203	120–150
	N•m	In. Lb.
Oil Pump Bolts	4.0–4.5	36–40
Speedometer Screw	2.3–2.8	20–25

NOTE: The output shaft must turn freely within the oil pump. If binding occurs, loosen the four bolts and re-tighten again.

Dana Model 20

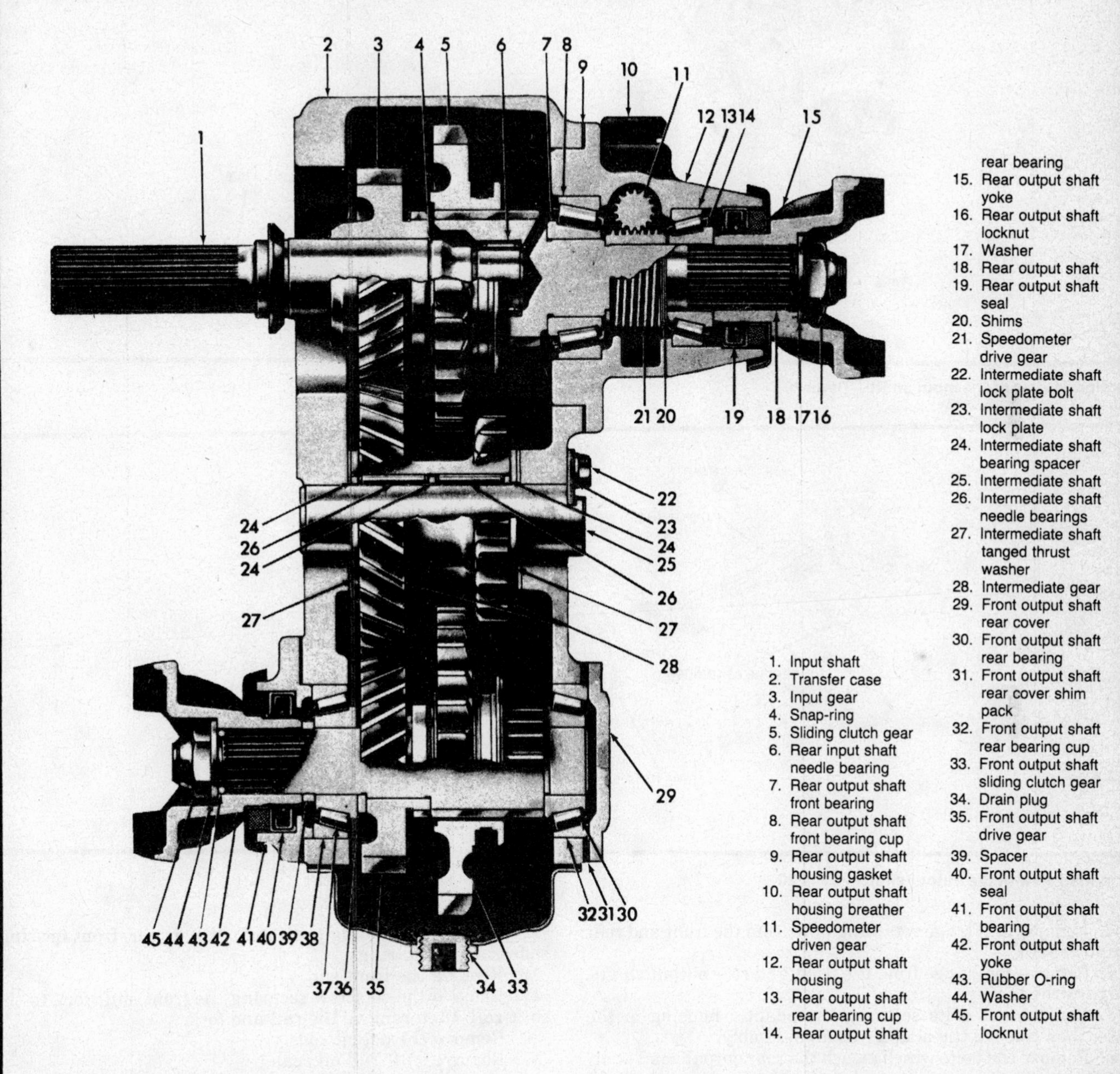

Cross section of Dana model 20 transfer case

The Dana Model 20 is a two-speed gearbox that controls the power from the transmission to the front and rear driving axles. Positions of the transfer case are: four-wheel-drive low (4L), neutral (N), two-wheel-drive high (2H) and four-wheel-drive high (4H).

Disassembly

TRANSFER CASE

1. Clean any dirt from the transfer case and remove the bottom cover plate.
2. Remove the retaining plug, flat washer, detent spring and ball which engages the front drive shift rail detent rod. Then, remove plug from front drive detent rod access hole.
3. Remove the retaining plug, detent spring and ball which engages the rear drive shift rail detent rod.
4. Remove the idler shaft lockplate.
5. Using a hammer and soft drift, drive the idler shaft rearward and out of the case; then lift out the thrust washers and idler gear.

NOTE: When removing the idler gear, do not lose any of the rollers.

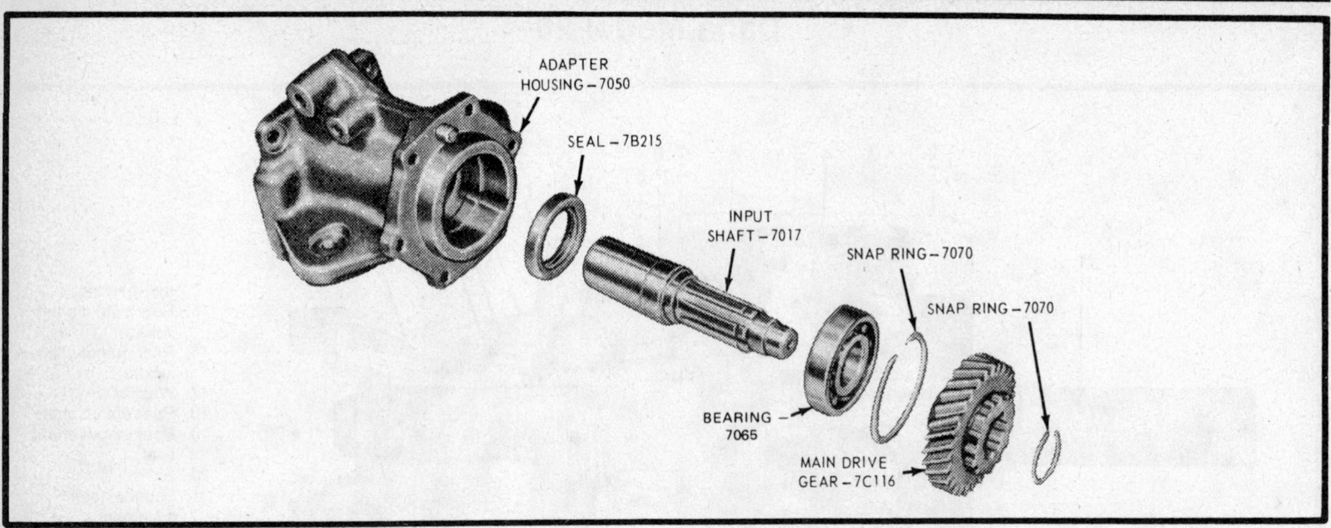

Exploded view of the input shaft—Dana 20

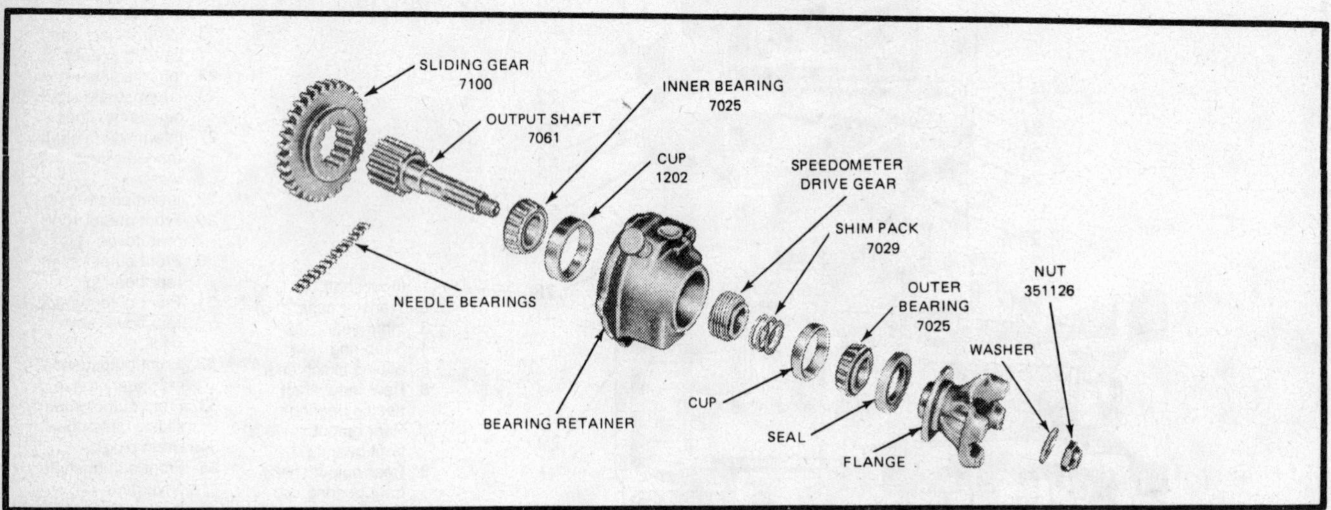

Exploded view of the output shaft—Dana 20

6. Remove the flange retaining nuts from the front and rear output shafts.
7. Remove the flange from the front and rear output shafts. Discard the O-ring.
8. Remove the bolts securing the adapter housing to the case; then remove the adapter as an assembly.
9. Remove the bolts which attach the rear output shaft bearing retainer to the case; then remove the retainer and output shaft as an assembly.

NOTE: Be sure not to lose any of the rollers.

10. Disconnect the shift rail link from the two shift rails.
11. Lift out the rear output shaft sliding gear.
12. Remove the setscrew securing the rear fork to the shift rail; then remove the rear drive shift rail and fork.
13. Remove the front output shaft rear cover and shims. Fasten the shims together.
14. Remove the front output shaft bearing retainer and gasket.
15. Tap the threaded end of the front output shaft; then remove the rear cup.
16. Angle the front output shaft front bearing away from the main drive gear to allow removal of the snap-ring; then tap the shaft and rear bearing out of the case.
17. Lift out the sliding gear, main drive gear, front bearing, spacer and snap-ring.
18. Remove the front cup.
19. Remove the setscrew securing the front shift fork to the shift rail; then remove the rail and fork.
20. Remove the detent rods.
21. Remove shift rail oil seal.

INPUT SHAFT

1. Remove the snap-ring from the front of the shaft.
2. Place the adapter housing and input shaft on a press and force the shaft out of the main drive gear and housing.
3. Remove the bearing retaining snap-ring; then remove bearing.
4. Remove the seal in the adapter housing.

REAR OUTPUT SHAFT

1. Remove needle bearings from bore of shaft.
2. Remove speedometer driven gear.
3. Place bearing retainer and shaft assembly in a press; then force shaft out of retainer.
4. Lift off speedometer drive gear and shims. Tag shims for reassembly.
5. Press out the outer cup, bearing and seal.

6. Remove the inner cup.
7. Remove the inner bearing.

FRONT OUTPUT SHAFT

Using the sliding gear as a base, press rear bearing off shaft.

Assembly

INPUT SHAFT

1. Install a new seal in the adapter housing.
2. Install bearing in the housing and secure with snap-ring.
3. Using the main drive gear as a base, force the input shaft through the housing, seal, bearings and main drive gear. Secure with snap-ring on front of shaft.

REAR OUTPUT SHAFT

1. Press the shaft into the inner bearing.
2. Install outer cup in the bearing retainer.
3. Install the inner cup.
4. Position the outer bearing in the retainer; then place the shims and speedometer drive gear on the shaft. Install shaft in the bearing retainer housing.
5. Place the bearing retainer and shaft in a vise. Install the output shaft flange and torque the retaining nut to specifications.
6. With a dial indicator on the flange end of the shaft, measure end-play. Adjust shim pack between the speedometer drive gear and outer bearing to achieve correct clearance.
7. After setting correct end-play, remove flange and press bearing retainer seal into housing.
8. Install the flange, washer and nut. Tighten the nut to specifications.

FRONT OUTPUT SHAFT

Using a press, force front output rear bearing on shaft.

SHIFT RAIL OIL SEALS

Install the two shift rail oil seals with appropriate tools.

TRANSFER CASE

1. Install the front detent rod in the case.
2. Slide the front drive shift rail all the way into the case and place the shift fork on the rail as it enters the case. Secure the fork to the rail with the setscrew.
3. Position the front output shaft sliding gear in the shift fork.
4. Install the rear detent rod.
5. Slide the rear drive shift rail into the case and position the shift fork on the rail as the rail enters the case. Secure the fork to the rail with the setscrew.

NOTE: The shift rails should be inserted so that the detents are positioned as shown in illustration.

6. While holding the sliding gear and main drive gear in position, install the front output shaft and rear bearing assembly through the two gears.
7. Install the main drive gear spacer and secure with the snap-ring.
8. Install the front output shaft rear bearing cup.
9. Place the front output shaft rear cover and shims on the case and install the attaching bolts.
10. Install the front output shaft front bearing on the shaft. Install the front bearing cup.
11. If the front bearing retainer oil seal was removed, install a new seal. Position the bearing retainer and gasket to the case and install the attaching bolts.
12. Place the rear output shaft rear bearing retainer on a work bench and install 13 needle bearings in the splined hub of the output shaft, using vaseline or grease.
13. Position the rear output shaft rear bearing retainer assembly to the case and install the attaching bolts.
14. Install the rear output shaft sliding gear in the shifting fork and on the splines of the output shaft.
15. Position the adapter housing assembly on the rear output shaft and case. Install the attaching bolts.
16. Install the roller bearings in the bore of the idler shaft gear with vaseline or grease.
17. Position the idler gear and thrust washers in the case; then drive the idler shaft into the rear of the case through the idler gear and thrust washers.

NOTE: After installing the idler shaft, tap the sides of the case to relieve any possible binding.

18. Install the idler shaft lock plate.
19. Secure the shift rail link to the two shift rails.
20. Install the front and rear drive shift rail detent balls, springs and retaining plugs.

NOTE: Be sure that the heavier loaded spring and flat washer are installed in the front drive shift rail.

21. Install the rod access hole plug.
22. Install the flange, washer and retaining nut on each of the output shafts. Be sure to install a new O-ring in the front output shaft flange. Torque the attaching nuts to specifications.
23. With a dial indicator on the front drive output shaft, check the end-play. If not within specifications, adjust the shim pack at the front output shaft rear cover.
24. Place the cover plate on the case and install the attaching bolts.

Dana Model 21

The Dana Model 21 is a single-speed gearbox that transmits power to the front driving axle. There are two positions of the transfer case; front drive axle engaged and front drive axle disengaged.

Disassembly

TRANSFER CASE

1. Clean all dirt from transfer case and drain lubricant.
2. Remove bolts that attach the cover to the top of the case; then remove the cover.
3. Remove the setscrew securing the shift fork to the rail. Tap the shift rail rearward; then remove the rail cap from the rear of the case.

SPECIFICATIONS

END PLAY (IN.)	
Front output shaft	0.001–0.005
Rear output shaft	0.001–0.005
TORQUE LIMITS (FT. LBS.)	
Transfer case to transmission extension bolts	20–30
Transfer case to transmission output shaft nut	60–80
Front output shaft rear cover bolts	25–32
Front output shaft bearing retainer bolts	25–32
Idler shaft cover bolts	25–32
Front and rear output flanges	80–85

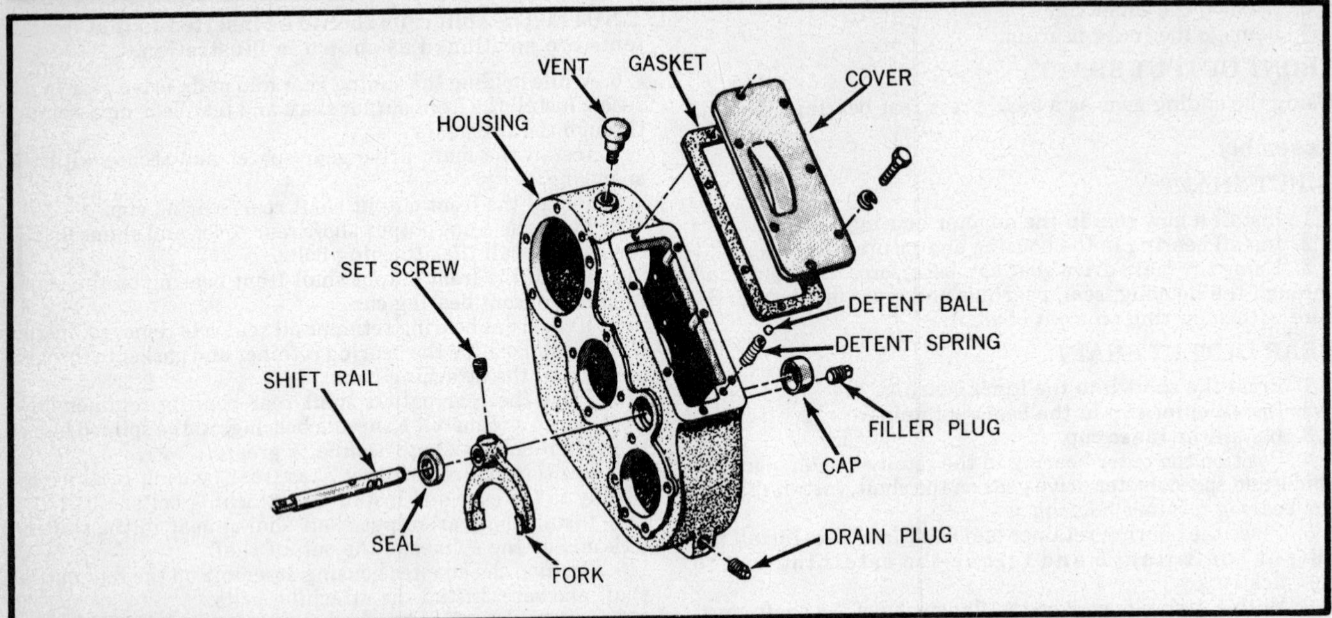

Exploded view of the case housing and shift mechanism—Dana 21

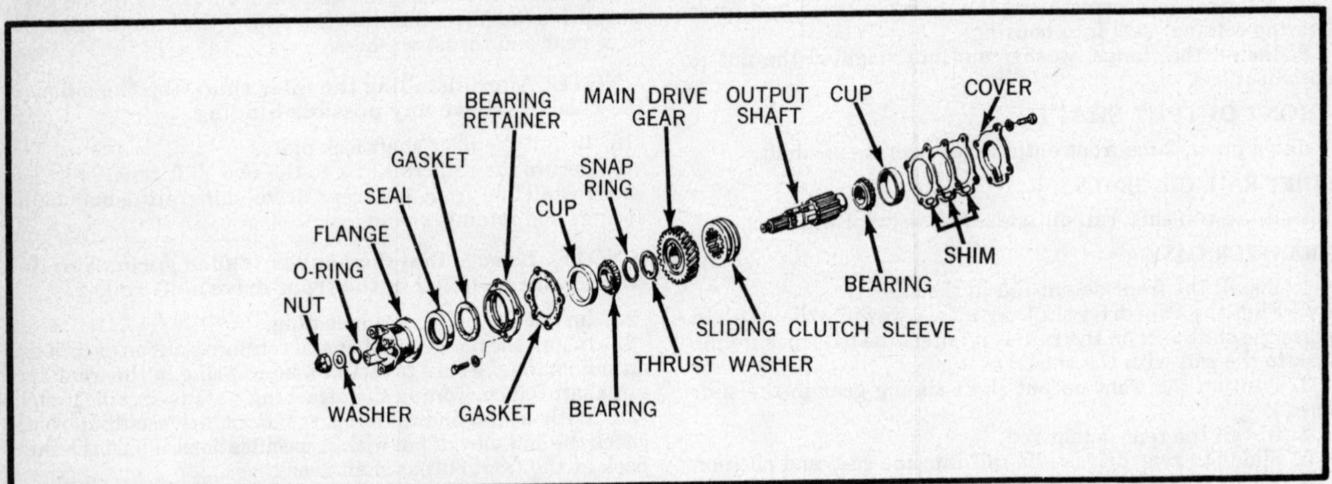

Exploded view of the front output shaft—Dana 21

4. Remove the shift rail and fork.
5. Remove the detent spring and ball which engages the front drive shift rail.
6. Remove the flange attaching nuts, flat washer and O-ring from the front and rear output shafts. Discard the O-rings.
7. Remove the flange from the front and rear output shafts.
8. Remove the bolts that attach the rear output shaft bearing retainer to the case; then remove the retainer and output shaft as an assembly.
9. Remove the front and rear idler shaft covers.
10. Using a hammer and soft drift, drive the idler shaft and rear idler bearing rearward out of the case; then lift out the front bearing and idler gear.
11. Remove the front output shaft bearing retainer and gasket. Remove the retainer seal if it is worn or damaged.
12. Remove the front output shaft rear cover and shims. Tie the shims together for reassembly.
13. Tap the end of the front output shaft toward the front of the case; then remove the front bearing cup. Remove the rear bearing cup by tapping the shaft rearward.
14. Angle the front output shaft front bearing away from the main drive gear to remove the snap-ring from its groove in the shaft. Drive the output shaft and rear bearing out of the case.
15. Remove the sliding gear, main drive gear, front bearing, thrust washer and snap-ring from the case.
16. Remove the shift rail seal.

FRONT OUTPUT SHAFT BEARING

To remove the front output shaft rear bearing, use the sliding gear as a base and press off the bearing.

IDLER SHAFT

1. Remove the snap-ring from the idler shaft.
2. Using the idler gear as a base, press the idler shaft out of the rear bearing.

REAR OUTPUT SHAFT

1. To remove the output shaft from the bearing retainer tap shaft rearward. Remove the shims and spacer.
2. Remove the inner bearing from the output shaft.
3. Place the bearing retainer on a press and force out the outer cup, outer bearing and oil seal.
4. Using a soft drift, drive out the inner bearing cup.

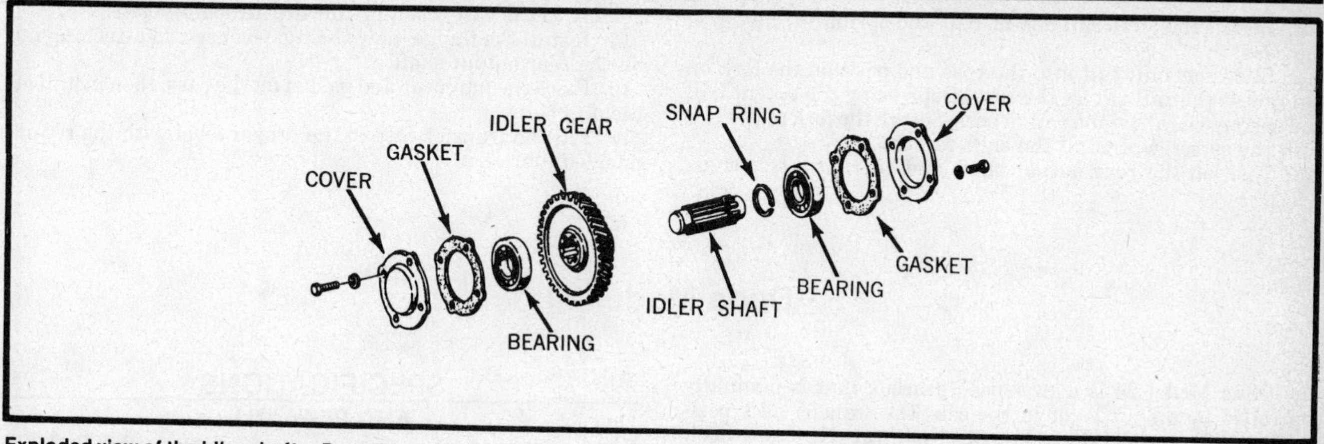

Exploded view of the idler shaft—Dana 21

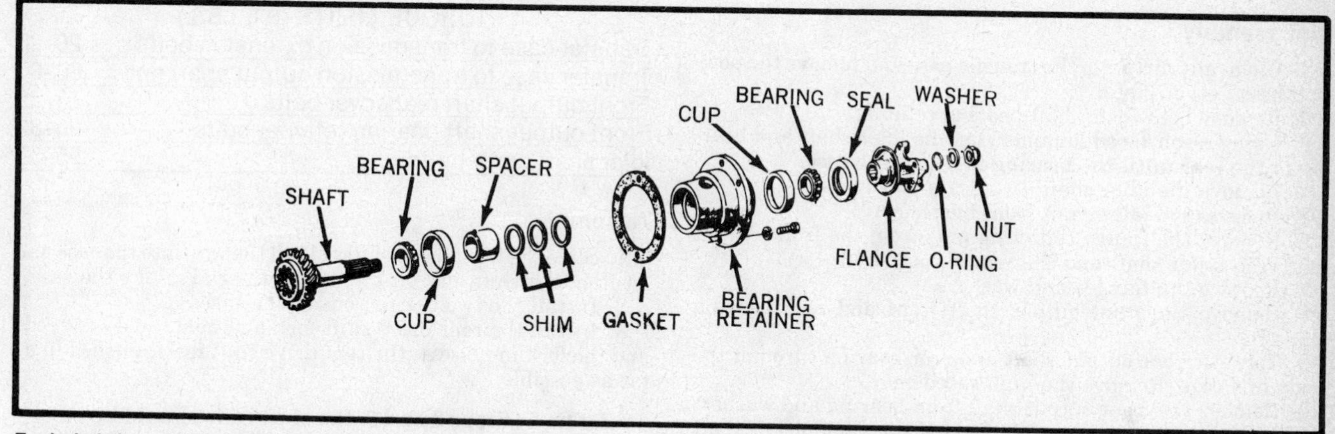

Exploded view of the rear output shaft—Dana 21

Assembly

FRONT OUTPUT SHAFT

Using an arbor press, force rear bearing on front output shaft.

IDLER SHAFT

1. Using a press, install rear idler bearing on the shaft.
2. Install snap-ring.

REAR OUTPUT SHAFT

1. Press the inner bearing on the output shaft.
2. Using a soft-faced hammer, tap the inner bearing cup into the retainer.
3. Install the outer cup.
4. Place spacer and shims on the output shaft; then install the shaft in the bearing retainer housing.
5. Install the outer bearing on the shaft.
6. Place the bearing retainer and output shaft in a vise. Measure end-play with a dial indicator on end of the shaft. If not within specifications, adjust shim pack between the spacer and the front and rear bearing cones.
7. After setting correct end-play, install the bearing retainer seal.

TRANSFER CASE

1. While holding the drive gear, sliding gear and thrust washer in the case, install the front output shaft, from the rear, through the gears and washer. Install the snap-ring.
2. Install the front output shaft rear bearing cup.
3. Place the front output shaft rear cover and shims on the case. After removing old sealant from all mating surfaces with thinner, apply gasket sealer to the attaching bolts and torque to specifications. With the cover installed, apply sealer to the outside edge of the adjusting shims, case and cover joints.
4. Install the front output shaft rear bearing on the shaft. Install the front bearing.
5. If the front bearing retainer oil seal was removed, install a new seal. Position the bearing retainer and gasket to the case and install attaching bolts.
6. Install the flange, new O-ring, washer and attaching nut on the front output shaft.
7. With a dial indicator on the front drive output shaft, check the end-play. If not within specified limits, increase or decrease the shim pack thickness at the front output shaft rear cover.
8. Place the idler gear in the case; then install the idler shaft through the gear. Install the front bearing.
9. Place the front and rear idler covers and gaskets on the case; then install attaching bolts.
10. Install a new shift rail seal.

SPECIFICATIONS

END PLAY (IN.)	
Front output shaft	0.001–0.005
Rear output shaft	0.001–0.005

TORQUE LIMITS (FT. LBS.)	
Transfer case to transmission extension bolts	20–30
Transfer case to transmission output shaft nut	125–150
Front output shaft rear cover bolts	25–32
Front output shaft bearing retainer bolts	25–32
Idler shaft cover bolts	25–32

11. Install the shift rail detent ball and spring in the top of the case.
12. Slide the shift rail into the case and position the fork on the rail as the rail enters the case. Depressing the detent ball and spring will allow the rail to pass. Secure the fork to the rail with the setscrew. Install the shift rail cap.
13. Position the rear output shaft and bearing retainer assembly to the case, then install the attaching bolts.
14. Install the flange, new O-ring, washer and attaching nut on the rear output shaft.
15. Place the top cover and gasket on the case, then install attaching bolts.
16. Fill the transfer case to the proper level with the recommended lubricant.

Dana Model 24

The Dana Model 24 is a two-speed gearbox that is manually controlled by a shift lever in the cab. The transfer case positions are: four-wheel-drive low (4L), neutral (N), two-wheel-drive high (2H) and four-wheel-drive high (4H).

Disassembly

1. Clean any dirt from the transfer case and remove the power take-off cover plate.
2. Remove both idler shaft bearing retainers.
3. Using a soft-faced hammer, tap the idler shaft and bearing to the rear until the bearing is free of the case.
4. Remove the idler shaft, two gears and spacer.
5. Remove the idler shaft front bearing.
6. Remove the flange retaining nuts from the front output shaft, the input shaft and the rear output shaft.
7. Remove the flanges and washers.
8. Remove the front output shaft front and rear bearing retainers.
9. Tap the front output shaft and rear bearing through the gears and case. Remove the high speed gear.
10. Remove the front output shaft front bearing and washer.
11. Remove the setscrew that retains the front drive shaft fork to the shift rail.
12. Remove the front output shaft sliding gear.
13. If the input shaft oil seal is to be replaced, remove it with a four-jaw puller and slide hammer.
14. Remove the input shaft bearing retainer.
15. If the output shaft bearing retainer oil seal is to be replaced, remove it with a puller and slide hammer.
16. Remove the rear output shaft bearing retainer; then remove the speedometer drive assembly.
17. Loosen the rear output shaft assembly from the case by driving on the front end of the input shaft with a soft-faced hammer.
18. Remove the rear output shaft and bearing retainer as an assembly.
19. Tap the input shaft through the front bearing, through the main drive gear, through the sliding gear and out of the case.
20. Lift the main drive gear out of the case and then drive out the input shaft front bearing.
21. Remove the setscrew that retains the rear drive shift fork to the shift rail.
22. Remove the rear output shaft sliding gear.
23. Remove the shift rail link from the two shift rails.
24. Remove the retaining plug, detent spring and ball which engage the front drive shift rail detent rod.
25. Remove the retaining plug detent spring and ball which engages the rear drive shift rail detent rod. Remove the front drive detent rod access hole plug.
26. Pull the front drive shift rail to the furthest outward position.
27. Pull the rear drive shift rail far enough to allow the two detent rods to slide out.
28. Remove the rear drive shift rail and fork.
29. Remove the shift rail seals.

SPECIFICATIONS

END PLAY (IN.)	
Front output shaft	0.003–0.007
Rear output shaft	0.003–0.007
TORQUE LIMITS (FT. LBS.)	
Transfer case to transmission extension bolts	20–30
Transfer case to transmission output shaft nut	60–80
Front output shaft rear cover bolts	25–32
Front output shaft bearing retainer bolts	25–32
Idler shaft cover bolts	25–32

Assembly

1. Slide the front drive shift rail all the way into the case and position the shift fork on the rail as the rail enters the case.
2. Install the two detent rods in the case.
3. Install the rear drive shift fork and hold the detent rods and the fork in place as the rear drive shift rail is pushed in as far as possible.

NOTE: In Steps 2 and 3, the shift rails should be inserted so that the detents are positioned as shown in illustration.

4. Pull the front drive shift rail out to its next detent. This will permit the rear drive shift rail to be pushed in to the full extent of its travel. After pushing the rear drive shift rail all the way in, push the front drive shift rail back to its extreme inward position.
5. Install the rear drive shift detent ball, spring and retaining plug; then install the access hole plug.
6. Install the front drive shift rail detent ball, spring and re-

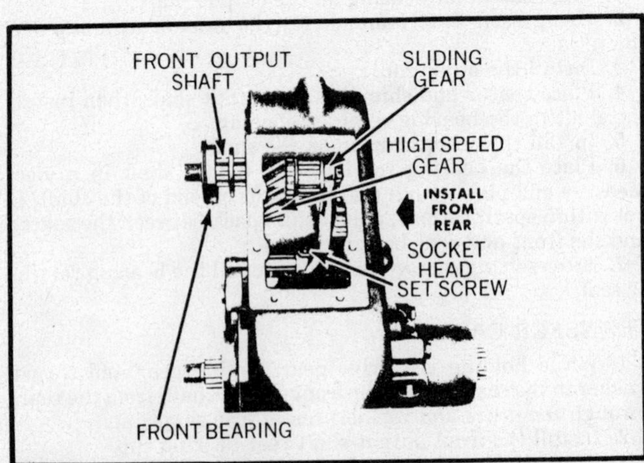

Removing or installing the front output shaft of a Dana 24 transfer case (© Ford Motor Co.)

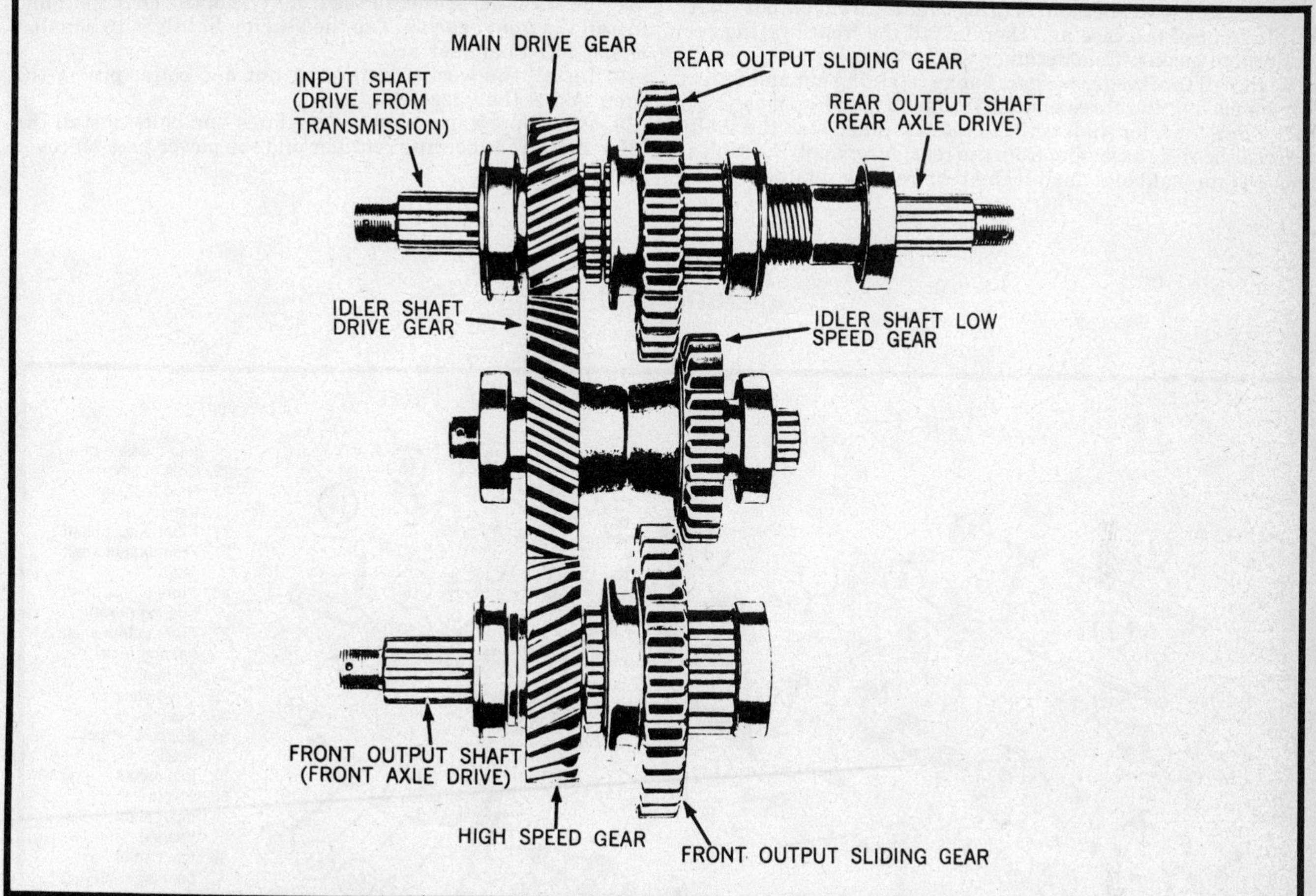

Dana Model 24 gear train—neutral position illustrated (© Ford Motor Co.)

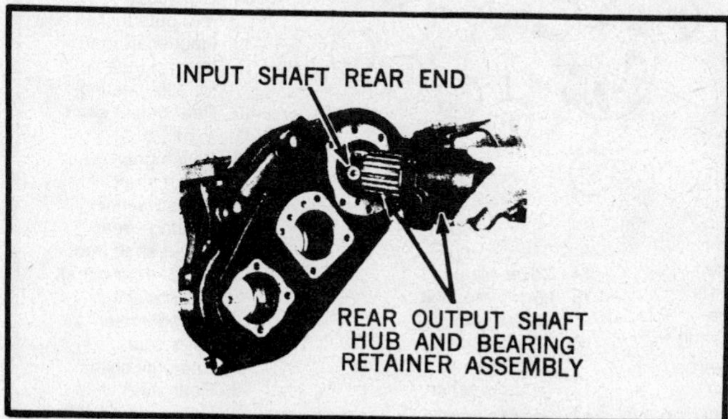

Removing or installing the rear output shaft of the Dana 24 transfer case (© Ford Motor Co.)

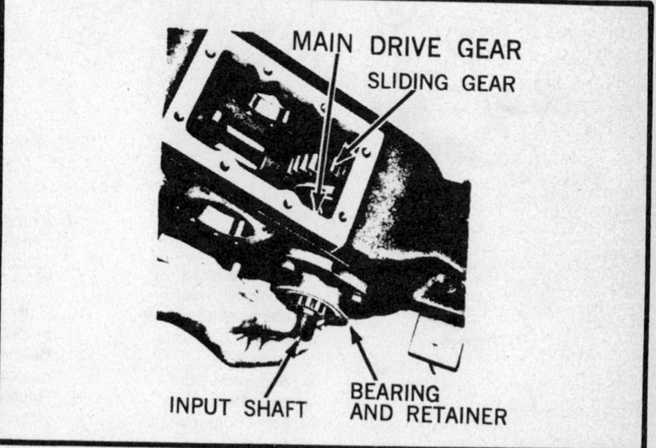

Removing or installing the input shaft of a Dana 24 transfer case (© Ford Motor Co.)

taining plug.

7. Secure the shift rail link in the two shift rails.

8. Place the rear output sliding gear in the shift fork and secure the fork to the rear drive shift rail with the setscrew.

9. Install the input shaft front bearing and retainer assembly. Coat retainer and bolts with sealer.

10. Place the main drive gear in the case; then slide the input shaft into the rear of the case through the main drive gear and through the front bearing and retainer.

11. Install the roller bearings in the splined hub of the rear output shaft assembly with petrolatum jelly or grease. Then install the shaft and bearing retainer assembly, making sure that the output shaft is aligned correctly with the input shaft. Coat the case, bearing retainer and bolts with sealer.

12. Position the front output sliding gear in the shift fork and secure the folk to the front drive shift rail with the setscrew.

13. While holding the sliding gear and high speed gear in position, install the front output shaft and rear bearing assembly through the two gears from the rear of the case.

14. After coating with sealer, install the front output shaft rear bearing retainer and gasket.

15. Install the washer and bearing over the front output shaft at the front of the case and then install the front bearing retainer and gasket. Coat retainer with sealer.

16. Install the flange, washer, flange retaining nut and cotter key on each of the three shafts. Torque to specifications.

17. Place the idler shaft gears in the case and install the shaft and rear bearing assembly from the rear. After applying sealer to the plate and bolts, install the rear bearing retainer.

18. Position the spacer on the front end of the idler shaft and install the front bearing. Tap the bearing lightly with a mallet or soft-faced hammer.

19. Install the washer, retaining nut and cotter pin on the front end of the idler shaft.

20. After applying sealer to the plates and bolts, install the idler shaft front bearing retainer and the power take-off cover plate.

Dana 300

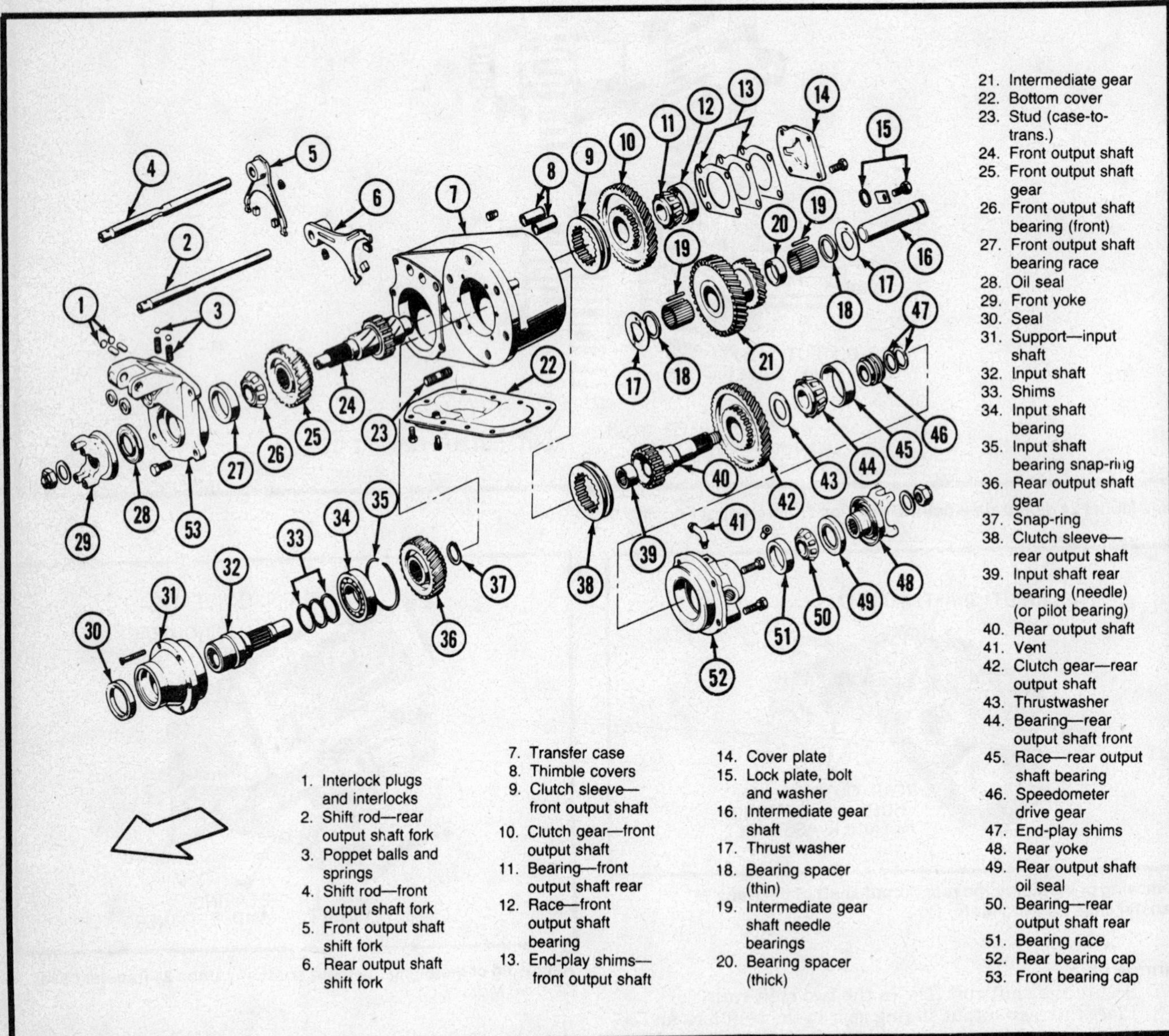

Exploded view of the Dana 300

The 300 is used in Jeep® CJ models only. It has a cast iron case, four gear positions and employs an external floor mounted gearshift linkage for range control. It is a part time, 2 speed unit with undifferentiated high and low ranges. It is used with both manual and automatic transmission. Low range reduction is 2.6:1.

Disassembly

1. Drain the unit and remove the shift lever assembly.

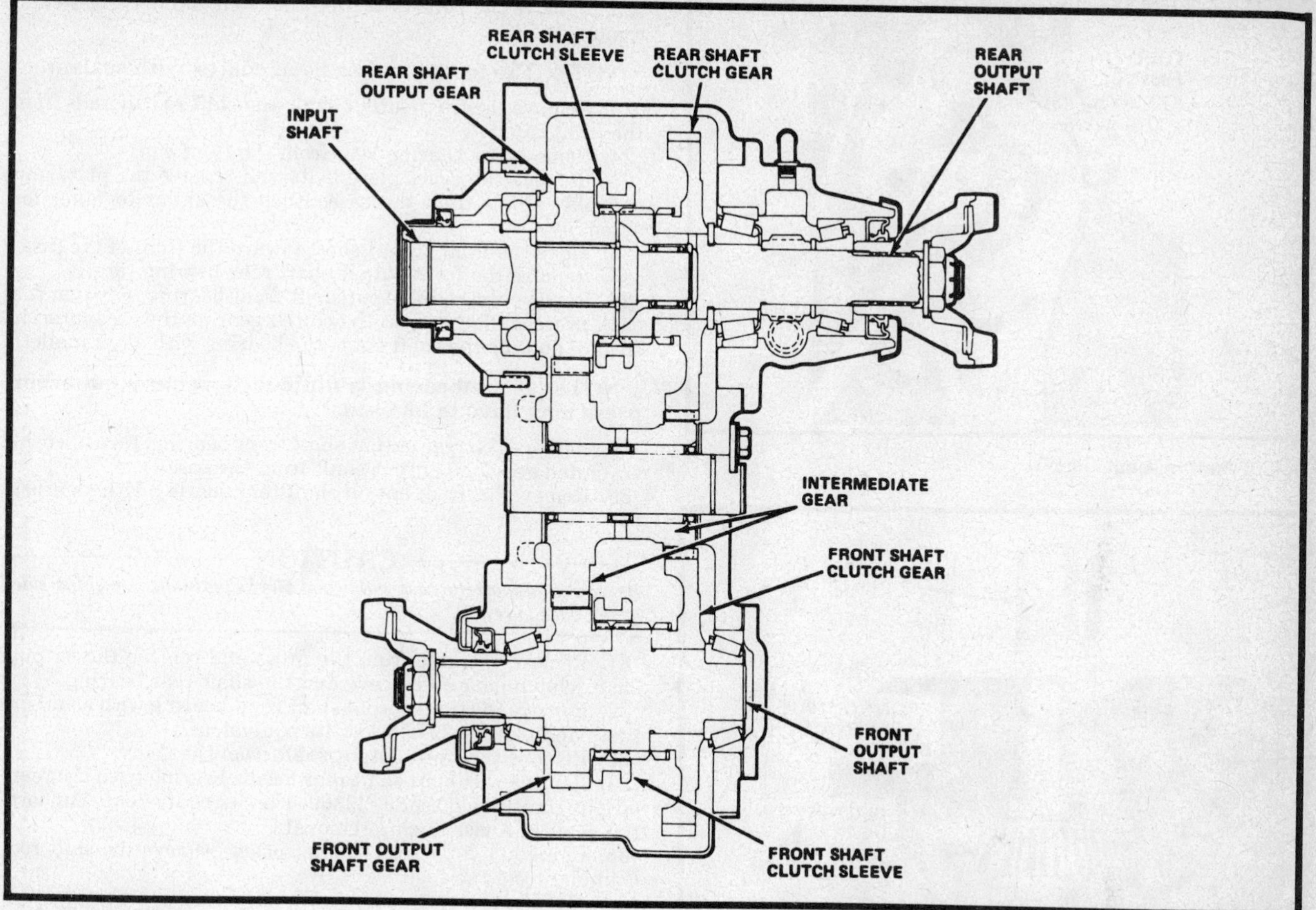

REAR SHAFT CLUTCH SLEEVE
REAR SHAFT CLUTCH GEAR
REAR OUTPUT SHAFT
REAR SHAFT OUTPUT GEAR
INPUT SHAFT
INTERMEDIATE GEAR
FRONT SHAFT CLUTCH GEAR
FRONT OUTPUT SHAFT
FRONT OUTPUT SHAFT GEAR
FRONT SHAFT CLUTCH SLEEVE

Dana 300 power flow

2. Remove the bottom cover.

NOTE: The bottom cover has been coated with a sealant. Use a putty knife to break the seal and work the knife around the bottom of the cover to break it loose. Don't try to wedge the cover off.

3. With a puller, remove the front and rear yokes.
4. Unbolt and remove the input shaft support from the case. The rear output shaft gear and input shaft will come with it as an assembly.

NOTE:The support has been coated with sealant, remove it as you did the bottom cover.

5. Remove the rear output shaft clutch sleeve from the case.
6. Remove and discard the snap ring retaining the rear output shaft gear on the input shaft and remove the gear.
7. Remove and discard the input bearing snapring.
8. Remove the input shaft bearing from the support. Tap the end of the shaft with a soft mallet to aid removal.
9. Remove the input shaft bearing and end-play shims from the shaft with an arbor press.
10. Remove the input shaft oil seal from the support.
11. Unbolt and remove the intermediate shaft lockplate.
12. Remove the intermediate shaft. Tap the shaft out of the case using a brass punch and plastic mallet.
13. Remove and discard the intermediate shaft O-ring seal.
14. Remove the intermediate gear assembly and thrust washers.

NOTE: The thrust washers have locating tabs which must fit into notches in the case at assembly.

Yoke oil seal removal

15. Remove the needle bearings and spacers from the intermediate gear. There are 48 needle bearings and three spacers.
16. Remove the rear bearing cap attaching bolts and remove the cap. A plastic mallet will aid in removal.

NOTE: The rear bearing cap has been coated with sealant.

17. Remove the end play shims and speedometer drive gear from the rear output shaft.

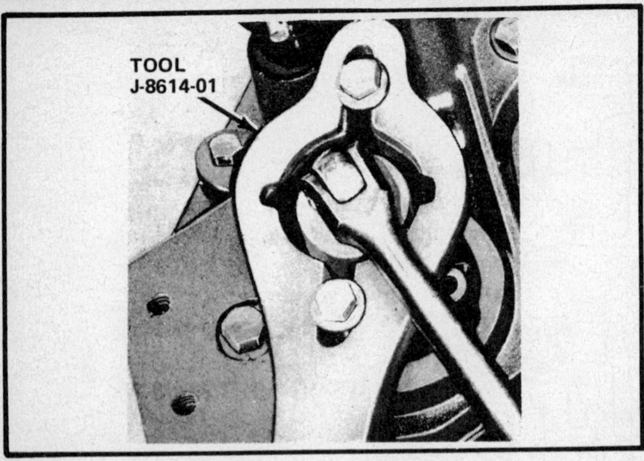

Output shaft yoke nut removal

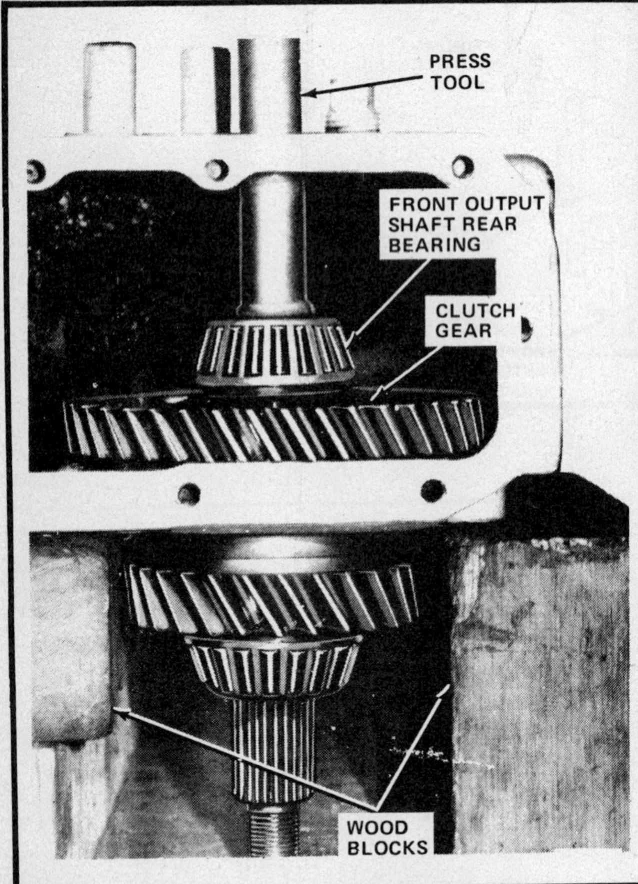

Front output shaft rear bearing removal

18. Remove and discard the rear output shaft oil seal. Remove the bearings and races from the rear cap.
19. Unbolt and remove the front and rear output shaft shift forks from the shift rods.
20. Remove the shift rods. Insert a punch through the clevis pin holes in the rods and rotate the rods while pulling them out of the case.

NOTE: The shift rods are free of the case, take care to avoid losing the shift rod poppet balls and springs.

21. Remove the shift forks from the case.
22. Remove the bolts attaching the front cap to the case and remove the cap.

NOTE: The front cap has been coated with sealant.

23. Remove the front output shaft and shift rod oil seals from the front cap.
24. Remove the bearing race from the front cap.
25. Remove the cover plate bolts and remove the plate and end play shims from the case. Keep the shims together for assembly.
26. Move the front output shaft toward the front of the case.
27. Remove the front output shaft rear bearing race.
28. Remove the rear output shaft front bearing. Position the case on wood blocks. Seat the clutch gear on the case interior surface and tap the shaft out of the bearing with a soft mallet.

NOTE: If the bearing is difficult to remove, an arbor press may have to be used.

29. Remove the rear output shaft front bearing, thrust washer, clutch gear and output shaft from the case.
30. Remove the front output shaft rear bearing with an arbor press.

CAUTION

Be sure to support the case with wood blocks positioned on either side of the case bore.

31. Remove the case from the press and remove the output shaft, clutch gear and sleeve and the shaft rear bearing.
32. Remove the front output shaft front bearing with an arbor press and tool J–22912–01 or its equivalent.
33. Remove the front output shaft from the gear.
34. Remove the input shaft rear needle bearing from the rear output shaft using tool J–29369–1 or its equivalent. Support the shaft in a vise during removal.
35. Using a $^3/_8$ in. drive, $^7/_{16}$ in. socket, remove the shift rod thimbles from the case.

Assembly

Coat all parts with SAE 85W–90 oil before assembly.

1. Apply Loctite® 220 or its equivalent to the thimbles and install them in the case.
2. Install the front output shaft gear on the front output shaft. Be sure that the clutch teeth on the gear face the shaft gear teeth.
3. Install the front bearing on the front output shaft using an arbor press. Be sure that the bearing is seated against the gear.
4. Install the front output shaft in the case and install the clutch sleeve and gear on the shaft.
5. Install the front output shaft rear bearing using an arbor press.

NOTE: Install an old yoke nut on the shaft to avoid damage to the threads.

6. Install the input shaft needle bearings in the rear output shaft with tool J–29179 or its equivalent.
7. Position the rear output shaft clutch gear in the case and insert the rear output shaft into the gear.
8. Install the thrust washer and front bearing on the rear output shaft using an arbor press.
9. Install the shims and bearing on the input shaft using an arbor press.
10. Install a new input shaft seal.
11. Using a new snap-ring, install the input shaft and bearing in the support.
12. Install the rear output shaft gear on the input gear and install a new gear retaining ring.
13. Measure the clearance between the input gear and the gear retaining snap-ring using a feeler gauge. Clearance

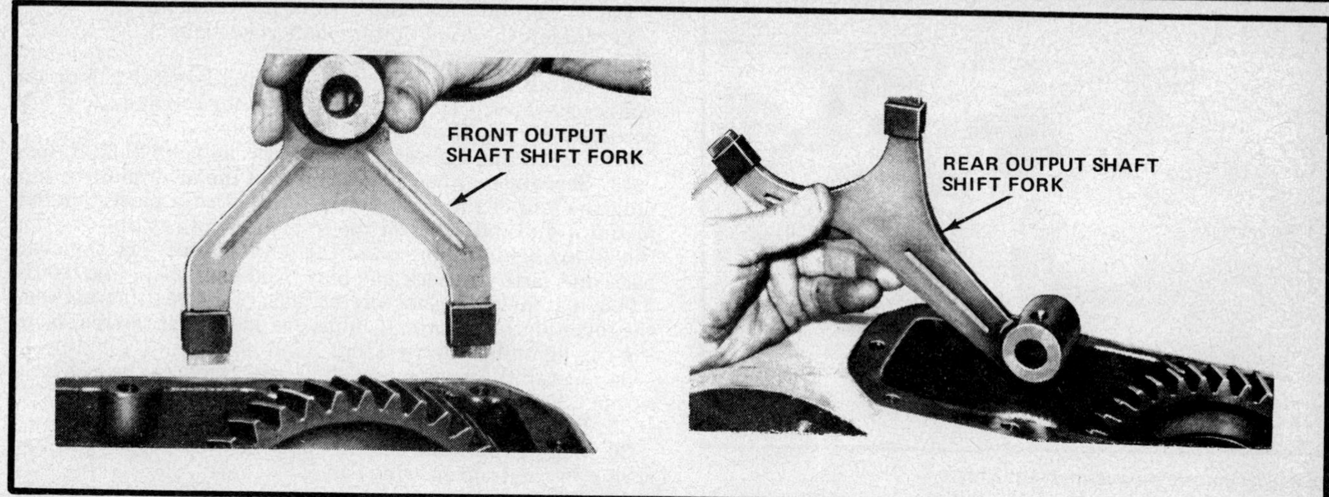

Shift fork installation

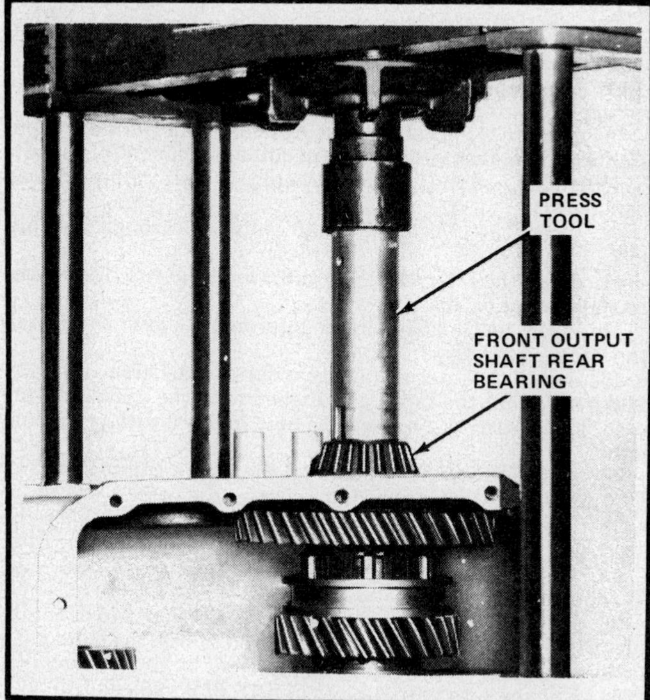

Front output shaft rear bearing installation

should not exceed 0.003 in. If clearance is beyond tolerance, add shims between the input shaft and bearing.

14. Install the clutch sleeve on the rear output shaft.
15. Apply Loctite® 515 or equivalent to the mating surfaces of the input shaft support and install the support assembly, shaft and gear in the case. Use two support bolts to align the support on the case and tap the support into position with a soft mallet. Torque the support bolts to 10 ft. lbs.
16. Install the rear bearing cap front bearing race.
17. Install the rear bearing cap rear bearing race.
18. Position the rear output shaft rear bearing in the rear bearing cap.
19. Install the rear output shaft yoke oil seal.
20. Install the speedometer gear and end-play shims on the rear output shaft.
21. Apply Loctite® 515 or equivalent to the mating surfaces of the cap and install the rear bearing cap. Use two cap bolts to align the cap and tap it into place with a soft mallet.
22. Tighten the cap bolts to 35 ft. lbs.
23. Install the rear output shaft yoke. Torque a new locknut to 120 ft. lbs.
24. Clamp a dial indicator on the rear output shaft bearing

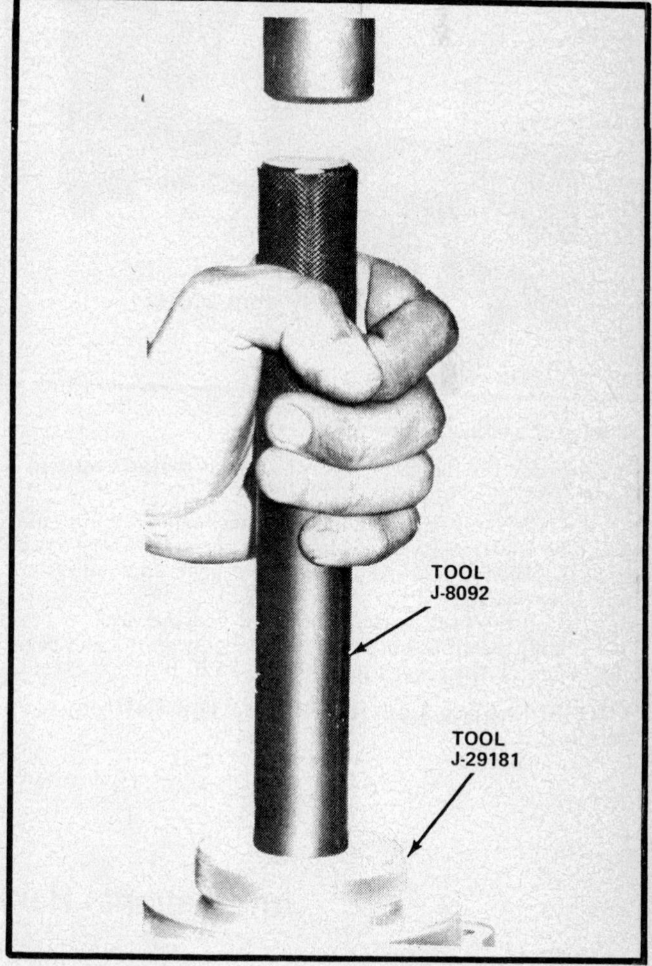

Front output shaft front bearing race installation

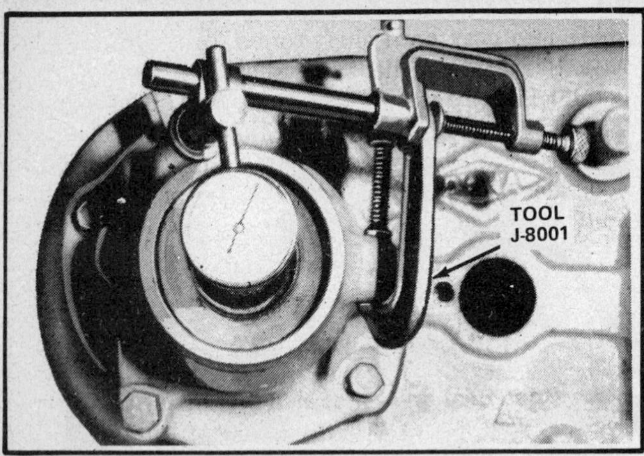

Checking the rear output shaft end-play

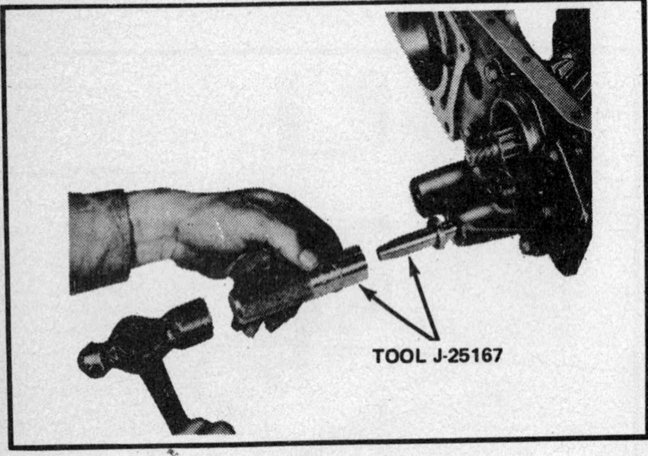

Shift rod oil seal installation

cap. Position the indicator stylus so that it contacts the end of the shaft.

25. Pry the shaft back and forth to check end-play. End-play should be 0.001–0.005 in. If play is not correct, remove or add shims between the speedometer drive gear and the output shaft rear bearing.

26. Install the front output shaft rear bearing race.

27. Install the front output shaft end play shims and cover plate. Tighten the cover plate bolts to 35 ft. lbs.

NOTE: Apply Loctite® 220 to the bolts before installation.

28. Install the front output shaft front bearing race.

29. Install the front output shaft yoke oil seal.

30. Install the shift rod oil seals.

31. Install the front bearing cap, using Loctite® 515 on the mating surfaces. Use two bolts to align the cap and tap it into position with a soft mallet.

32. Install and tighten the bearings cap bolts to 35 ft. lbs.

33. Seat the rear bearing cup against the cover plate by tapping the end of the front output shaft with a plastic mallet. Mount a dial indicator on the front bearing cap and position the stylus against the end of the output shaft. Pry the shaft back and forth to check end-play. End-play should be 0.001–0.005 in. If the play is not correct, add or remove shims between the cover plate and case. If shims are added seat the rear bearing cup again before checking.

34. Install the front output shaft yoke. Tighten the new locknut to 120 ft. lbs.

35. Install the front and rear output shaft shift forks.

36. Install the front output shaft shift rod poppet ball and spring in the front bearing cap.

37. Compress the poppet ball and spring and install the front output shaft shift rod part way in the case.

38. Insert the front output shaft shift rod through the shift fork.

39. Align the setscrew hole in the shift fork and rod. Install and tighten the setscrew to 14 ft. lbs.

40. Install the rear output shaft shift rod poppet ball and spring in the front bearing cap.

41. Compress the ball and spring and install the rear output shaft shift rail part way. The front output shaft shift rod should be in neutral and the interlocks seated in the front bearing cap bore.

42. Insert the rear output shaft shift rod through the shift fork.

43. Align the setscrew holes in the fork and rod. Torque the setscrew to 14 ft. lbs.

44. Insert tool J–25142 in the intermediate gear and install the needle bearings and spacer.

45. Install the intermediate gear thrust washers in the case. Make sure that the tangs are aligned with the grooves in the case. The thrust washers may be held in place with petroleum jelly.

46. Install a new O-ring seal on the intermediate shaft.

47. Position the intermediate gear in the case.

48. Install the intermediate shaft in the case bore. Tap the shaft into the gear until the shaft forces the tool out of the case.

49. Install the intermediate shaft lock plate and bolt. Torque the bolt to 23 ft. lbs.

50. Install the bottom cover, applying Loctite® 515 or equivalent to the mating surfaces. Install and torque the bolts to 15 ft. lbs.

51. Fill the case with 4 pints of SAE 85W–90 gear oil.

International Harvester Model TC–143

The IH Model TC–143 "Silent Drive" transfer case is a chain driven single speed unit. Unlike conventional gear driven transfer cases, this unit has a high-strength link-belt type loop of chain driving two broad-faced sprockets. There is no neutral position. There are two variations of this transfer case; one is frame mounted with a short intermediate drive shaft between the input shaft of the transfer case and the transmission output shaft and the other type is mounted directly to the rear of the transmission.

Disassembly

1. After removing the transfer case from the vehicle and draining all of the lubricant out, clean the outside of the case.

2. Remove the shift cover.

3. Unscrew and remove the indicator light switch from the case.

4. With the rear output shaft flange clamped in a soft jawed vise, remove the flange retaining nut. Remove the flange from

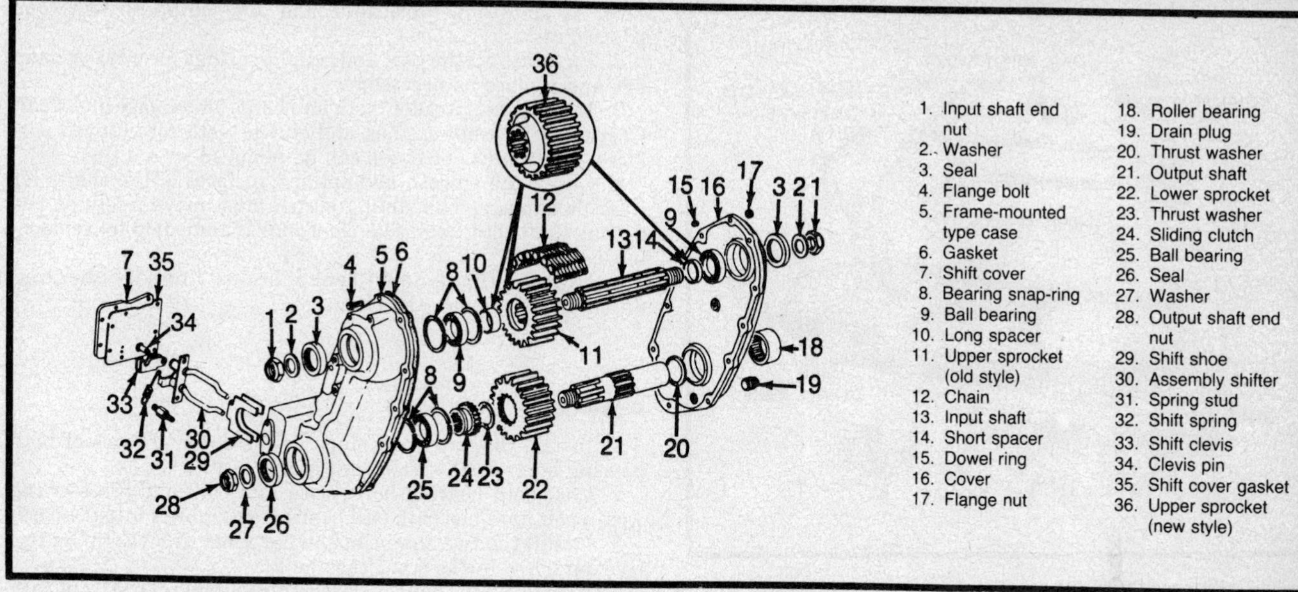

Exploded view of a frame mounted TC143 transfer case

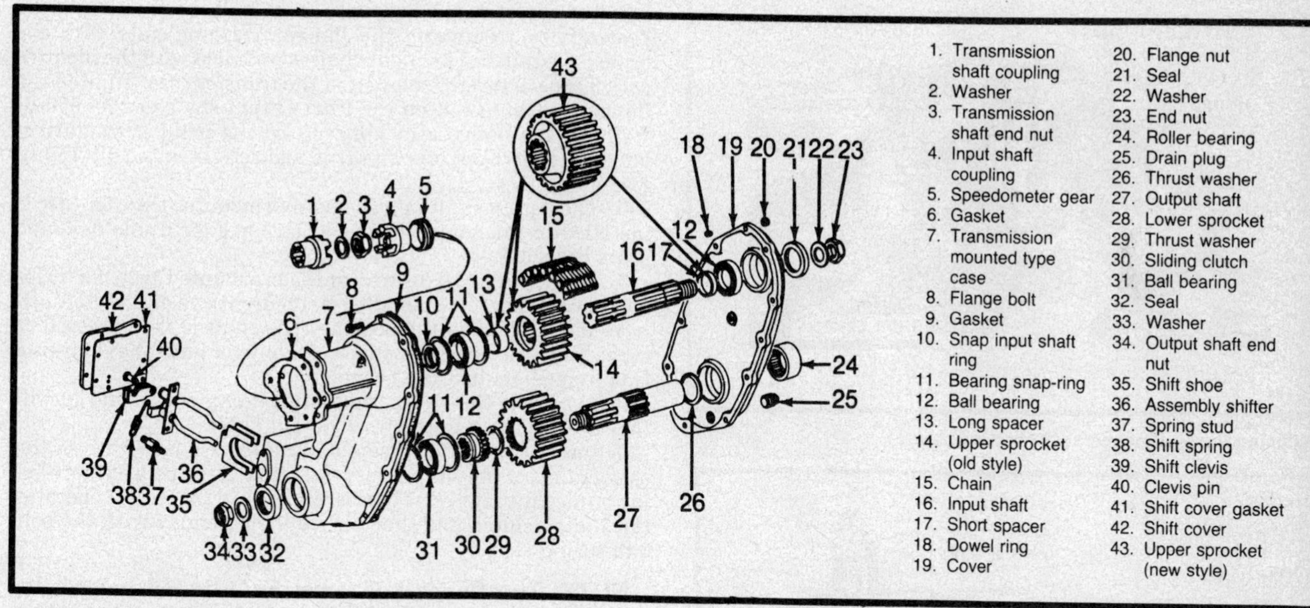

Exploded view of a transmission mounted TC143 transfer case

the vise and remove the flange from the rear output shaft. Use a puller, if necessary.

5. Turn the case so it rests on the flanges and remove the bolts securing the two halves of the case. Lift the top (rear) half of the case from the assembly and discard the gasket.

6. If present, remove the short spacer from the rear side of the input shaft. Also, if the thrust washer did not stay with the cover when removed, remove it now from the front output shaft.

7. With the case again secured in a soft jawed vise, place your thumbs on the ends of the shafts with your fingers under the sprockets. Pull the sprockets together with the chain off the shafts and out of the case as an assembly.

8. Unhook and remove the shift spring.

9. Remove the shift assembly mounting bolt and spring stud from the case.

10. Pull the shift cranks from the bosses inside the case.

11. If present, remove the long spacer from the input shaft and the washer from the front output shaft.

12. Lift the sliding clutch and its shift shoe from the front output shaft.

13. The two shafts are removed from the case with a press or by tapping them out with a soft hammer.

NOTE: If the transfer case is a transmission mounted unit, a snap ring on the input shaft must be removed before the shaft can be removed from the case.

14. After the shafts are removed, remove the oil seals and the bearing snap rings, and press or tap out the two ball bearings.

15. Pry and remove the thrust washer from the boss for the front output shaft roller bearing in the other half of the case.

16. Press the roller bearing cage from the inside and out of the cover.

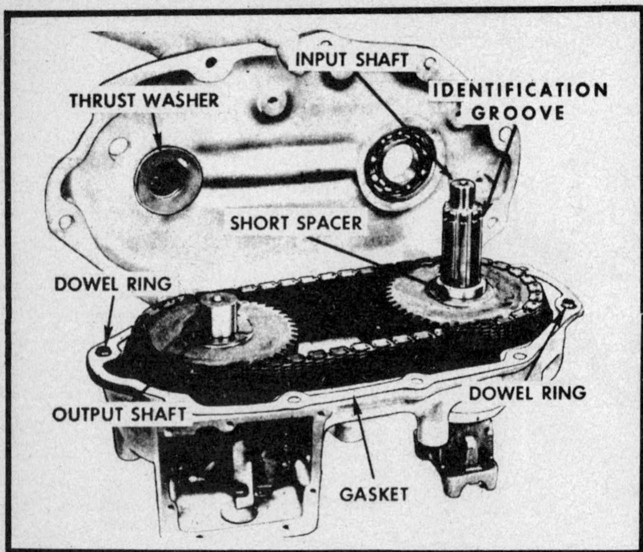

Removing the cover from the case

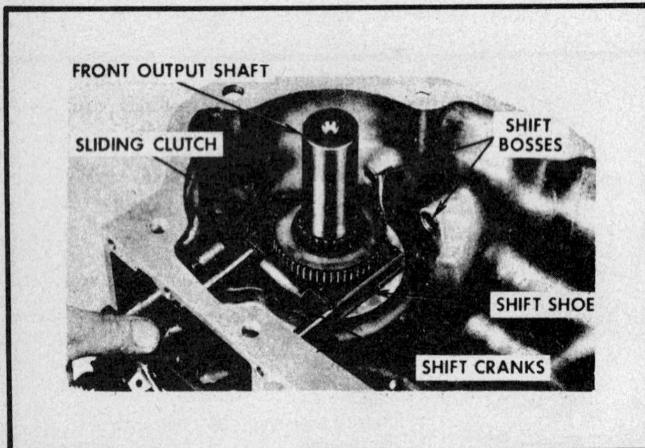

Removing the shift assembly from the case

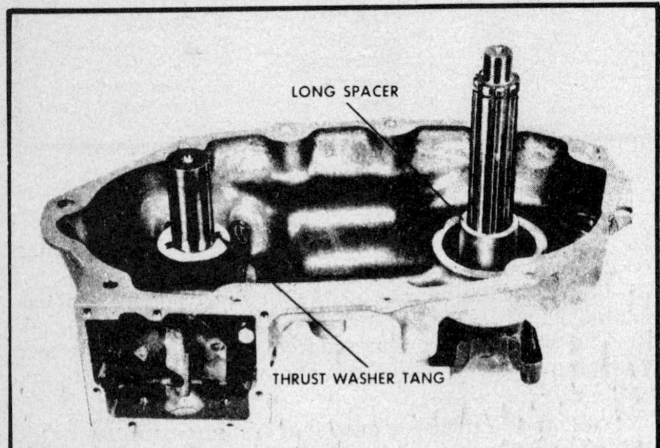

Installing the thrust washer and long spacer

17. Press the ball bearing on the outer race from the outside and out of the cover.

Cleaning and Inspection

1. Clean all parts in solvent, removing all traces of old gaskets, sealants and lubricants, and dry the parts with compressed air.
2. Examine all the ball and roller bearings for wear or damage and replace as necessary.
3. Inspect the sprocket teeth and bores for damage and wear. Check the internal splines and clutch teeth for chipped surfaces. Small nicks or burrs can be removed with a file.
4. Check the smooth and splined surfaces of the shafts for wear or damage. The sliding clutch must move freely on the output shaft, but excessive clearance is remedied by replacement of parts.
5. Examine the chain for bent or broken lines. If either condition exists, replace the chain.

Assembly

1. Install the two snap rings in the outer grooves of both bearing bores in the front half of the case.
2. Coat both bearing bores with lubricant and press or tap with a soft hammer both ball bearing assemblies into the case.
3. Install the two snap rings in the inner grooves of the two bearing bores in the front case half.
4. Install the shaft oil seals from the outside of the front case half. They are best installed with a press.
5. On a frame mounted transfer case, position the lightly lubricated shafts in the bearings, then, pull the shafts into the bearings by tightening the flange attaching nuts with the flanges installed. The input shaft is installed with the identification groove toward the rear of the transfer case. Tighten the flange attaching nut on the front output shaft to 200–250 ft. lbs., and the flange attaching nut on the input shaft until it bottoms, then back off two turns and retighten to 140–150 ft. lbs.
6. The output shaft in transmission mounted transfer case is installed in the same manner as outlined for frame mounted units in step 5.
7. The input shaft in transmission mounted transfer cases has a snap-ring to be installed on the front end of the shaft prior to installation in the bearing. The shaft is then pressed or tapped into the bearing with a soft hammer until the snap-ring is bottomed against the bearing.
8. Assemble the shift shoe to the sliding clutch and install the sliding clutch to the front output shaft.
9. Insert the shifter assembly into the transfer case so the shift cranks of the shifter pass through the shift shoe before being guided into the shift bosses. Make sure the shifter operates the sliding clutch and then secure the assembly with the bolt and spring stud.

NOTE: The flange bolt must be installed before the spring stud because the position of the spring stud when installed prevents the installation of the flange bolts.

10. Install the thrust washer to the front output shaft and the long spacer to the input shaft, if so equipped with a long spacer.

NOTE: Be sure the thrust washer tangs fit down into the splines on the shaft.

11. Lightly lubricate the bores of both sprockets and secure the case in a soft jawed vise by the end of the input shaft.
12. Install the upper sprocket to the outer end of the input shaft. Do not slide the sprocket completely into the case.
13. Position the chain over the sprocket and place the lower sprocket inside the chain.
14. Pull down on the lower sprocket enough to slide the lower sprocket onto the output shaft.
15. Slide both sprockets and chain onto the sprockets as far as they will go.
16. Install the short spacer on the input shaft (not required on later models).

17. Install the shift spring between the spring post and the shifter assembly.

18. Press the ball bearing into the input shaft bore of the rear cover from the inside surface.

19. Press the roller bearing into the output shaft bore of the rear cover from the outside surface until it is flush with the bearing bore.

20. Press the seal for the rear of the input shaft (rear output) into the cover until it is flush.

21. Place the cover on a bench, inside facing up. Coat the back side of the thrust washer with a thin coat of sealant and position it on the roller bearing boss with the tang on the washer mated with the oil passage in the boss.

NOTE :Use the sealant sparingly and make sure none of it enters the bearing or blocks the two oil passages.

22. Position a new gasket and two dowel rings on the mating surface of the case.

23. Position the cover onto the case, guiding the two shafts into their respective bearings. Secure the cover to the case with the attaching nuts and bolts, tightening them to 29–38 ft. lbs.

24. Install the indicator light switch to the case and check its operation with a test light.

25. Install the shift cover gasket and cover on the case and secure it with bolts and lockwashers tightened to 4–6 ft. lbs. *Do not overtighten.*

26. Install the rear output flange on the rear of the input shaft so both the input flange and the output flange are on the same plane. The flanges must be assembled in this manner to prevent vibration.

27. Install the washer and a nylon insert locknut on the shaft tightened to 140–150 ft. lbs. to secure the flange.

Jeep Selec–Trac Model 229

Removal

1. Raise and support the vehicle.
2. Drain the lubricant from the transfer case.
3. Disconnect the speedometer cable and vent hose. Disconnect the transfer case shift lever link at the operating lever.
4. Place a support stand under the transmission and remove the rear crossmember.
5. Mark the transfer case front and rear output shafts at the transfer case yokes and propeller shafts for installation alignment reference.
6. Disconnect the front and rear propeller shafts at the transfer case yokes. Secure the shafts.
7. Disconnect the shift motor vacuum hoses.
8. Disconnect the transfer case shift linkage.
9. Remove the transfer case-to-transmission bolts.
10. Move the transfer case assembly rearward until clear of the transmission output shaft and remove the assembly.
11. Remove all gasket material from the rear of the transmission adapter housing.

RANGE CONTROL LINKAGE

Adjustment

1. Place the range control lever in high range.
2. Insert a $\frac{1}{8}$ inch spacer between gate and lever.
3. Hold the lever in this position.
4. Place range control lever in high range position.
5. Adjust as needed.

Disassembly

1. Remove the drain plug and drain the lubricant from the transfer case.
2. Remove the front and rear yoke nuts and seal washers. Discard the washers.
3. Mark the front and rear yokes for installation alignment reference.
4. Remove the front and rear yokes. Use Tool J–8614–01 or equivalent to remove the yokes if necessary.
5. Place the transfer case on wooden blocks. Cut V-notches in the blocks for clearance for the front case mounting studs.
6. Mark the rear retainer and rear case for assembly reference.
7. Remove the rear retainer bolts and remove the retainer. Use two prybars to pry the retainer off the transfer case. Position the prybars in slots in the retainer and case to pry the retainer loose.
8. Remove the differential shim(s) and speedometer drive gear from the rear output shaft.
9. Remove the bolts attaching the rear transfer case half to the front case half. Note that the bolts used at each end of the transfer case require flat washers.

CAUTION

Insert two prybars in the slots at each end of the rear transfer case half to loosen it. Do not attempt to wedge the transfer case halves apart or the case mating surfaces will be damaged.

10. Remove the rear transfer case half from the front case half using two prybars.
11. Remove the thrust bearing and races from the front output shaft. Note the position of the bearing and races for assembly reference.
12. Remove the oil pump from the rear output shaft. Note the position of the pump for assembly reference. The recessed side of the pump faces the case interior.
13. Remove the rear output shaft from the viscous coupling.
14. Remove the 15 main shaft pilot bearing rollers from the shaft or coupling (if the rollers dropped off during removal of the rear output shaft).
15. Remove the main shaft O-ring from the end of the shaft.
16. Remove the viscous coupling from the main shaft and side gear.
17. Remove the front output shaft, driven sprocket and drive chain assembly. Lift the front shaft, sprocket and chain upward. Tilt the front shaft toward the main shaft. Slide the chain off the drive sprocket and remove the assembly.
18. Remove the main shaft, side gear, clutch gear, drive sprocket and spline gear as an assembly. Place the assembly on a clean shop towel and set aside until the front case disassembly is completed.
19. Remove the front output shaft front thrust bearing assembly from the front case, or from the shaft (if the bearing and races remained on the shaft during removal).
20. Remove the drive chain from the front output shaft and sprocket.
21. Remove the snap-ring that retains the driven sprocket on the front output shaft. Mark the sprocket and shaft for assembly reference and remove the sprocket from the shaft.
22. Remove the mode fork, shift rail, and mode sliding clutch sleeve as an assembly. Mark the sleeve and fork for assembly reference and remove the sleeve from the fork.

NOTE: The mode fork and rail are pinned together so that they will operate as a unit. Remove the pin to separate the two components if necessary.

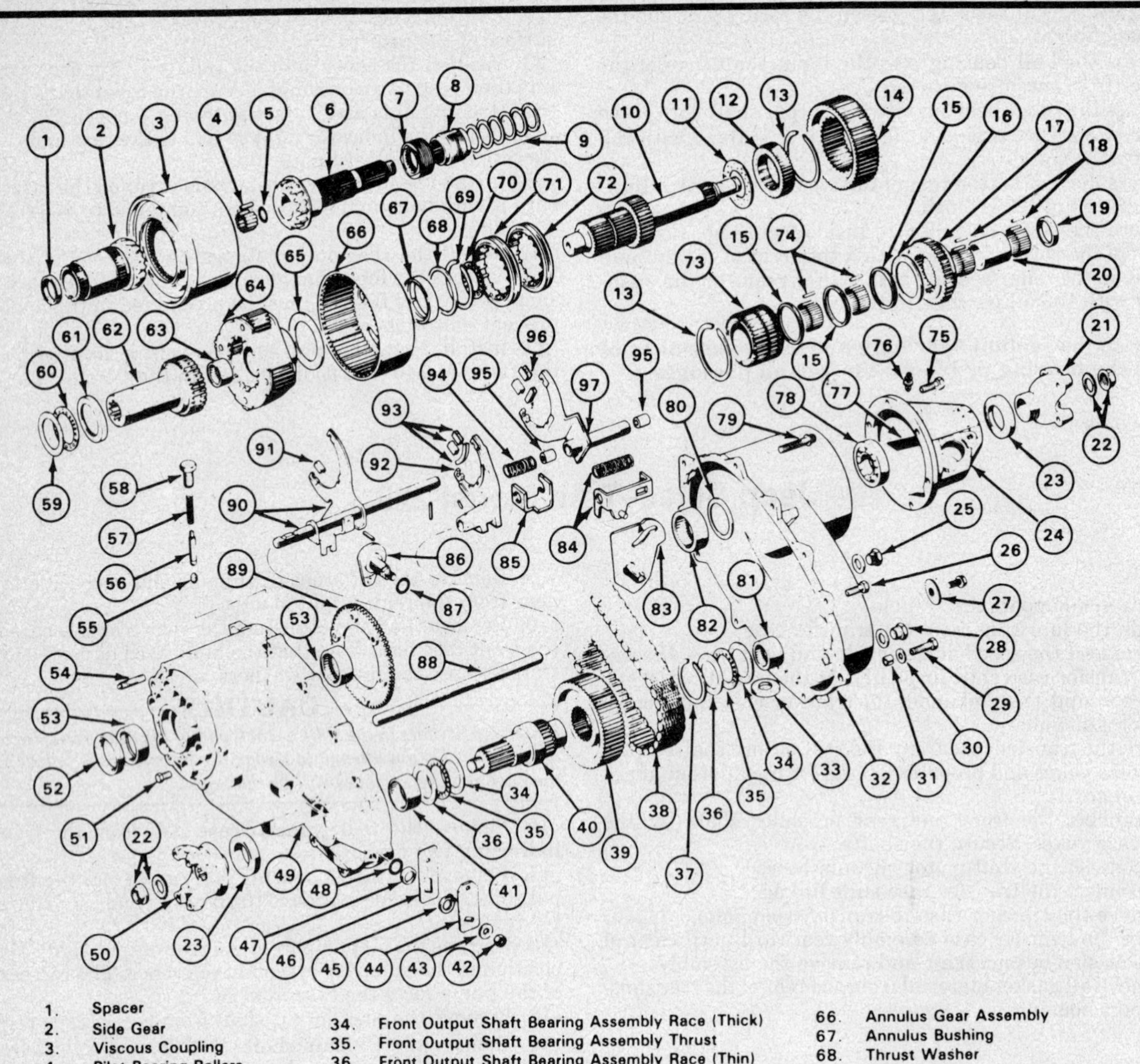

1. Spacer
2. Side Gear
3. Viscous Coupling
4. Pilot Bearing Rollers
5. O-Ring Seal
6. Rear Output Shaft
7. Oil Pump
8. Speedometer Drive Gear
9. Shim Kit
10. Mainshaft
11. Mainshaft Thrust Washer
12. Spline Gear
13. Retaining Ring
14. Sprocket
15. Spacer
16. Sprocket Thrust Washer
17. Viscous Clutch Gear
18. Side Gear Roller (82)
19. Spacer (Short)
20. Spacer (Long)
21. Rear Yoke
22. Nut and Seal Washer
23. Seal
24. Rear Retainer
25. Plug Assembly
26. Bolt
27. Identification Tag
28. Plug Assembly
29. Dowel Bolt
30. Dowel Bolt Washer
31. Case Half Dowel
32. Rear Half Case
33. Magnet
34. Front Output Shaft Bearing Assembly Race (Thick)
35. Front Output Shaft Bearing Assembly Thrust
36. Front Output Shaft Bearing Assembly Race (Thin)
37. Retaining Ring
38. Chain
39. Driven Sprocket
40. Front Output Shaft
41. Front Output Front Bearing
42. Nut
43. Washer
44. Mode Lever
45. Snap Ring
46. Range Lever
47. O-Ring Retainer
48. O-Ring Seal
49. Front Half Case
50. Front Output Yoke
51. Low Range Plate Bolt
52. Input Shaft Oil Seal
53. Input Shaft Bearing
54. Stud
55. Ball
56. Plunger
57. Plunger Spring
58. Screw
59. Input Race
60. Input Thrust Bearing
61. Input Race (Thick)
62. Input Shaft
63. Input Bearing
64. Planetary Gear Assembly
65. Input Gear Thrust Washer
66. Annulus Gear Assembly
67. Annulus Bushing
68. Thrust Washer
69. Retaining Ring
70. Thrust Bearing
71. High Range Sliding Clutch Sleeve
72. Mode Sliding Clutch Sleeve
73. Carrier
74. Carrier Rollers (120)
75. Rear Retainer Bolt
76. Vent
77. Vent Seal
78. Output Bearing
79. Bolt
80. Seal
81. Front Output Rear Bearing
82. Output Shaft Inner Bearing
83. Range Sector
84. Range Bracket (Outer) and Spring
85. Range Bracket (Inner)
86. Mode Sector
87. O-Ring Seal
88. Range Rail
89. Low Range Lockout Plate
90. Mode Fork, Rail and Pin
91. Mode Fork Pad
92. Range Fork
93. Range Fork Pads
94. Range Bracket Spring (Inner)
95. Locking Fork Bushing
96. Locking Fork Pads
97. Locking Fork

Jeep Select Trac 229

TORQUE SPECIFICATIONS
Model 229

Component	Service Set-To Torque
Detent Retainer Bolt	31 N•m (23 ft-lbs)
Drain and Fill Plugs	24 N•m (18 ft-lbs)
Front/Rear Yoke Nuts	163 N•m (120 ft-lbs)
Operating Lever Locknut	24 N•m (18 ft-lbs)
Rear Case-to-Front Case Bolts (All)	31 N•m (23 ft-lbs)
Rear Retainer Bolts	31 N•m (23 ft-lbs)
Transfer Case-to-Transmission Adapter Nuts	35 N•m (26 ft-lbs)
Universal Joint Strap Bolt-to-Transfer Case	19 N•m (170 in-lbs)

23. Remove the locking fork, high range sliding clutch sleeve, fork brackets and fork springs as an assembly. Note the position of the components for assembly reference and disassemble the components for cleaning and inspection.
24. Remove the range sector detent screw and remove the detent spring, plunger and ball.
25. Move the range operating lever downward to the last detent position.
26. Disengage the low range fork lug from the range sector slot.
27. Remove the retaining snap-ring from the annulus gear and remove the thrust washer.
28. Remove the annulus gear, range fork and rail as an assembly. Separate the components for cleaning and inspection.
29. Remove the planetary thrust washer from the planetary assembly hub.
30. Remove the planetary assembly. Grasp the planetary hub and lift the assembly upward to remove it.
31. Remove the main shaft thrust bearing from the input shaft.
32. Remove the input shaft and remove the input shaft thrust bearing and race.
33. Remove the range sector and operating lever attaching nut and lockwasher. Remove the lever.
34. Remove the range sector and shaft from the front case.
35. Remove the range sector O-ring and retainer.

MAIN SHAFT

Disassembly

1. Grasp the drive sprocket and lift the sprocket clutch gear and side gear upward and off the main shaft.
2. Remove the main shaft needle bearings and two bearing spacers from the main shaft; a total of 82 bearings are used; note the spacer position for assembly reference.
3. Remove the spline gear and thrust washer from the main shaft.
4. Remove the side gear, clutch gear, and clutch gear thrust washer from the sprocket carrier and sprocket.
5. Remove the clutch gear and thrust washer from the side gear.
6. Remove one sprocket carrier snap-ring and remove the drive sprocket from the carrier; mark for assembly reference.

CAUTION

The sprocket carrier and main shaft needle bearings are different in size. Take care to avoid intermixing them.

7. Remove the three bearing spacers and all sprocket carrier needle bearings from the carrier; a total of 120 needle bearings are used.
8. Remove the rear output bearing and rear yoke seal from the rear retainer; the bearing is shielded on one side; note the bearing position for assembly reference.
9. Remove the input gear and front yoke seals from the front case; use a screwdriver to pry the seals out of the case.

Cleaning & Inspection

1. Wash all components thoroughly in clean solvent. Ensure that all lubricant, metallic particles, dirt, and foreign material are removed from the surfaces of every component.
2. Apply compressed air to each oil supply port and channel in each transfer case half to remove any obstructions or cleaning solvent residue.
3. Inspect all gear teeth for excessive wear or damage. Inspect all gear splines for burrs, nicks, wear or damage.
4. Remove minor nicks or scratches using an oilstone. Replace any component exhibiting excessive wear or damage.
5. Inspect all snap-rings and thrust washers for excessive wear, distortion and damage. Replace any component exhibiting these conditions.
6. Inspect the transfer case halves and rear retainer for cracks, porosity, damaged mating surfaces, stripped bolt threads and distortion. Replace any component exhibiting these conditions.
7. Inspect the viscous coupling and differential pinions. If the pinions or carrier are damaged or worn excessively, replace the coupling as an assembly only. If the coupling is cracked, leaking, or damaged, replace the coupling as an assembly only.
8. Inspect the condition of all needle, roller, ball and thrust bearings in the front and rear transfer case halves. Also inspect to determine the condition of the bearing bores in both transfer case halves and in the input gear, rear output shaft, side gear, and rear retainer.
9. Replace any component that is excessively worn or damaged. If any shaft, case half or input gear bearing requires replacement, refer to Bushing/Bearing Replacement.

NOTE: The front output shaft thrust bearing race surfaces are heat treated during manufacture. Heat treatment causes a brown or blue discoloration of these surfaces. Do not replace a front output shaft because of this type of discoloration.

BEARING & BUSHING

CAUTION

All of the bearings used in the transfer case must be correctly positioned to avoid blocking the bearing oil supply holes. After replacing any bearing, check the bearing position and ensure that the supply hole is not obstructed by the bearing.

REAR OUTPUT SHAFT BEARING

Removal and Installation

1. Remove the bearing using Remover Tool J-26941 and Slide Hammer J-2619-01 or equivalent. Remove the rear output lip seal using a small awl.
2. Install a replacement lip seal.
3. Install a replacement bearing using Driver Handle J-8092 and Installer Tool J-29166 or equivalent.
4. Remove the tools and inspect the oil supply hole. The bearing must not obstruct the supply hole.

FRONT OUTPUT SHAFT FRONT BEARING

Removal and Installation

1. Remove the bearing using Tools J-8092 and J-29168 or equivalent.
2. Remove the tools and inspect the oil supply hole. The bearing must not obstruct the supply hole.

FRONT OUTPUT SHAFT REAR BEARING

Removal and Installation

1. Remove the bearing using Remover Tool J–26941 and Slide Hammer J–2619–01 or equivalent.

2. Install a replacement bearing using Driver Handle J-8092 and Installer Tool J–29163 or equivalent.

3. Remove the installer tools and inspect the bearing position to ensure the oil supply hole is not obstructed. Also ensure that the bearing is seated flush with the edge of the bore in the case to allow clearance for the thrust bearing assembly.

INPUT GEAR FRONT & REAR BEARINGS

Removal and Installation

1. Remove both bearings simultaneously using Driver Handle J–8092 and Remover Tool J–29170 or equivalent.

2. Install the new bearings one at a time. Install the rear bearing first; then install the front bearing. Use Driver Handle J–8092 and Installer Tool J–29169 or equivalent.

3. Remove the installer tools and inspect the bearing position to ensure the oil supply holes are not obstructed. Also ensure that the bearings are flush with the transfer case bore surfaces.

4. Install a replacement oil seal using seal Installer Tool J-29162 or equivalent.

MAIN SHAFT PILOT BUSHING

Removal and Installation

1. Remove the bushing using Slide Hammer J–2619–01 and Remover Tool J–29369–1 or equivalent.

2. Install a replacement bearing using Driver Handle J-8092 and Installer Tool J–29174 or equivalent.

3. Inspect bushing position to ensure that the oil supply hole is not obstructed.

ANNULUS GEAR BUSHING

Removal and Installation

1. Remove the bushing using Driver Handle J–8092 and Remover/Installer Tool J–29185 or equivalent.

2. Install a replacement bushing using Tools J–8092 and J-29185–2 or equivalent.

3. Remove any chips generated by the bushing removal and/or installation.

REAR OUTPUT BEARING AND REAR YOKE SEAL

Removal and Installation

1. Remove the bearing using a brass drift and hammer.

2. Remove the seal from the retainer using a brass drift and hammer.

CAUTION

The rear output bearing is shielded on one side. Ensure that the shielded side faces the transfer case interior after installation.

3. Install a replacement bearing using Driver Handle J-8092 and Installer Tool J–7818 or equivalent.

4. Install a replacement seal in the retainer using Tool J-29162 or equivalent.

New Process Model 203 (Full Time Four Wheel Drive)

The New Process Model 203 transfer case is a full-time 4WD unit that operates in 4WD at all times. The unit incorporates a differential similar to axle differentials; compensating for different speeds of the front and rear axles resulting from varying speeds while turning and operating over different surfaces.

There are five shift positions with this transfer case; Neutral, High and High Lock, and Low and Low Lock. The Lock positions are used under low traction conditions. In the Lock position, the differential action of the transfer case is eliminated, by locking the front and rear output shafts together. In this mode, neither the front or rear axle can rotate independently of the other.

Disassembly

1. Loosen rear output shaft flange retaining nut and remove front output shaft flange and washer.

2. Tap the front output shaft dust seal away from case assembly. Remove front output shaft bearing retainer and gasket.

3. Position transfer case assembly on blocks with input shaft facing downward.

4. Remove rear output shaft assembly from transfer case. Slide the differential carrier off the shaft.

5. Place a 1 $\frac{1}{2}$ to 2 in. band type hose clamp on input shaft to retain bearings.

6. Lift shift rail and driveout pin retaining shift fork.

7. Remove shift rail poppet ball plug, gasket and ball from case. Use a magnet to remove poppet ball.

8. Push shift rail down, lift up on lockout clutch and remove shift fork from clutch assembly.

9. Remove front output shaft rear bearing retainer. It may be necessary to gently tap front of shaft or cautiously pry retainer from case. Make certain that no roller bearings are lost from rear cover.

10. When necessary, remove rear bearing by pressing.

11. Pry front output shaft front bearing from lower side of case.

12. Remove front output shaft assembly from case.

13. Lift intermediate housing from range box, after removing bolts.

14. Remove chain from intermediate housing.

15. Remove lockout clutch, drive gear and input shaft from range box.

16. Install a 1 $\frac{1}{2}$ to 2 in. band type hose clamp on end of input shaft to retain roller bearings.

17. Pull up on shift rail and remove rail from link.

18. Lift input shaft assembly from range box.

Assembly

1. Position range box with input gear side down, on wood blocks.

2. Place gasket on input housing.

3. Install lockout clutch and drive sprocket on input shaft assembly. Install a 2″ band type hose clamp on end of input shaft to prevent loss of bearings during installation.

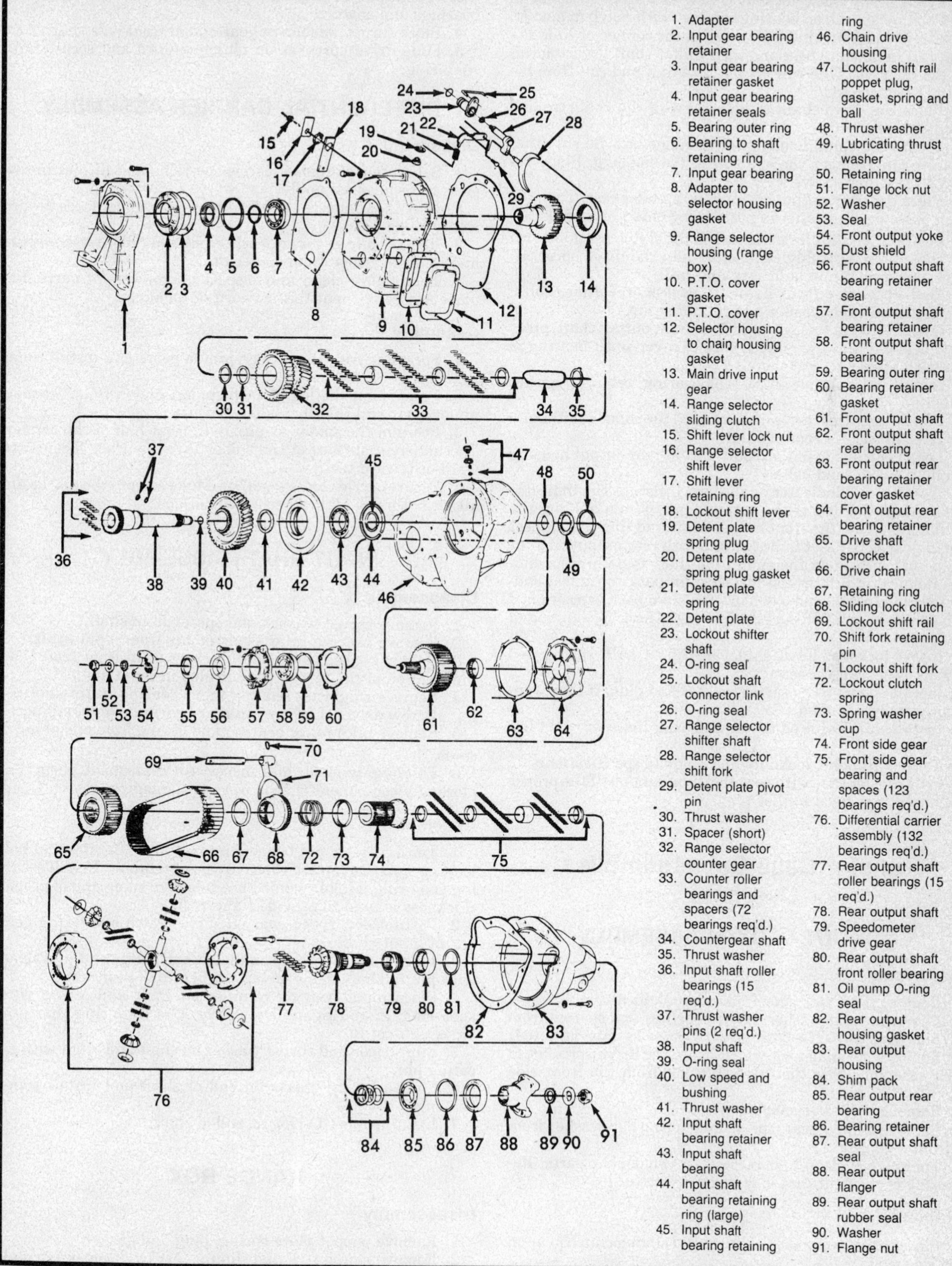
1. Adapter
2. Input gear bearing retainer
3. Input gear bearing retainer gasket
4. Input gear bearing retainer seals
5. Bearing outer ring
6. Bearing to shaft retaining ring
7. Input gear bearing
8. Adapter to selector housing gasket
9. Range selector housing (range box)
10. P.T.O. cover gasket
11. P.T.O. cover
12. Selector housing to chain housing gasket
13. Main drive input gear
14. Range selector sliding clutch
15. Shift lever lock nut
16. Range selector shift lever
17. Shift lever retaining ring
18. Lockout shift lever
19. Detent plate spring plug
20. Detent plate spring plug gasket
21. Detent plate spring
22. Detent plate
23. Lockout shifter shaft
24. O-ring seal
25. Lockout shaft connector link
26. O-ring seal
27. Range selector shifter shaft
28. Range selector shift fork
29. Detent plate pivot pin
30. Thrust washer
31. Spacer (short)
32. Range selector counter gear
33. Counter roller bearings and spacers (72 bearings req'd.)
34. Countergear shaft
35. Thrust washer
36. Input shaft roller bearings (15 req'd.)
37. Thrust washer pins (2 req'd.)
38. Input shaft
39. O-ring seal
40. Low speed and bushing
41. Thrust washer
42. Input shaft bearing retainer
43. Input shaft bearing
44. Input shaft bearing retaining ring (large)
45. Input shaft bearing retaining ring
46. Chain drive housing
47. Lockout shift rail poppet plug, gasket, spring and ball
48. Thrust washer
49. Lubricating thrust washer
50. Retaining ring
51. Flange lock nut
52. Washer
53. Seal
54. Front output yoke
55. Dust shield
56. Front output shaft bearing retainer seal
57. Front output shaft bearing retainer
58. Front output shaft bearing
59. Bearing outer ring
60. Bearing retainer gasket
61. Front output shaft
62. Front output shaft rear bearing
63. Front output rear bearing retainer cover gasket
64. Front output rear bearing retainer
65. Drive shaft sprocket
66. Drive chain
67. Retaining ring
68. Sliding lock clutch
69. Lockout shift rail
70. Shift fork retaining pin
71. Lockout shift fork
72. Lockout clutch spring
73. Spring washer cup
74. Front side gear
75. Front side gear bearing and spaces (123 bearings req'd.)
76. Differential carrier assembly (132 bearings req'd.)
77. Rear output shaft roller bearings (15 req'd.)
78. Rear output shaft
79. Speedometer drive gear
80. Rear output shaft front roller bearing
81. Oil pump O-ring seal
82. Rear output housing gasket
83. Rear output housing
84. Shim pack
85. Rear output rear bearing
86. Bearing retainer
87. Rear output shaft seal
88. Rear output flanger
89. Rear output shaft rubber seal
90. Washer
91. Flange nut

Exploded view of the new process 203 full time transfer case

4. Place input shaft, lockout clutch and drive sprocket in range box. Align tab on bearing retainer with notch in gasket.
5. Engage lockout clutch shift rail to the connector link. Position rail in housing bore and turn shifter shaft lowering rail into the housing. This will prevent the link and rail from becoming disconnected.
6. Place the drive chain in housing with the chain around the outer wall.
7. Secure the chain housing to the range box. Be sure that the shift rail engages the channel of the housing. Place the chain on the input drive sprocket.
8. Place the front output sprocket in transfer case. Turn the clutch drive gear to assist in positioning chain on sprocket.
9. Position the shift fork and rail on the clutch assembly. Install the clutch assembly completely into the drive sprocket. Insert retaining pin in shift fork and rail.
10. Install front output bearing, gasket, retainer, bolts, flange, gasket, seal, washer and retaining nut.
11. If rear bearing was removed from front output shaft, press a new bearing into the outside face of cover until bearing is flush with opening.
12. Install front output shaft, rear bearing, retainer, gasket and bolts.
13. Slip differential carrier assembly on the input shaft. Bolts on carrier must face rear of shaft.
14. Load bearings in pinion shaft, install rear output housing assembly, gasket and bolts.
15. Install a dial indicator on the rear housing. The indicator must contact the end of the output shaft. While holding the rear flange, rotate the front output shaft and find the highest point of gear hop. Reset indicator and with rear output shaft at high point, pull up on the end of the shaft to determine endplay. Remove indicator and install shim pack to control endplay to between 0.00 and 0.005 in.. The shim pack is positioned on the shaft in front of the rear bearing. Check for binding of rear output shaft.
16. Insert lockout clutch shift rail poppet ball, spring and screw plug in transfer case.
17. Install poppet plate spring, gasket and plug, if they were not previously installed.
18. Install shift levers on the range box, if these were not left on vehicle.
19. Torque all bolts, locknuts and plugs to specifications.
20. Fill transfer case with specified lubricant until the proper level is reached. Secure filler plug.

Transfer Case Subassemblies Overhaul

LOCKOUT CLUTCH ASSEMBLY

Disassembly

1. Remove front side gear from input shaft assembly.
2. Remove thrust washer, roller bearings and spacers from front side gear bore. The position of the spacers must be noted.
3. Remove the snap-ring which holds the drive sprocket to clutch assembly. Slip the drive sprocket from the front side gear.
4. Remove the lower snap-ring.
5. Remove sliding gear, spring and spring cup washer from the front side gear.
6. Thoroughly clean and inspect all component parts. Replace any component that is worn or defective.

Assembly

1. Place spring cup washer, spring and sliding clutch gear on front side gear.
2. Secure sliding clutch to front side gear with a snap-ring.
3. Spread petroleum jelly on front side gear and install roller bearings and spacers.
4. Place thrust washer in gear end of front side gear.
5. Slide drive sprocket on clutch splines and secure with snap-ring.

DIFFERENTIAL CARRIER ASSEMBLY

Disassembly

1. Separate differential carrier sections and lift out pinion gear and spider assembly.
2. Note that undercut side of pinion gear spider faces toward front of side gear.
3. Remove pinion thrust washers, pinion roller washer gears and roller bearings from spider unit.
4. Thoroughly clean and inspect all component parts. Replace any component that is worn or damaged.

Assembly

1. Spread petroleum jelly on pinion gears and install roller bearings.
2. Position on the leg of each spider, pinion roller washer, pinion gear and thrust washer.
3. Position the spider assembly in front half of the carrier. The undercut surface of the spider thrust surface face downward or toward teeth.
4. Secure carrier halfs together. Make certain the marks are aligned. Torque all bolts to specifications.

INPUT SHAFT ASSEMBLY

Disassembly

1. Remove thrust washer and spacer from shaft.
2. Remove bearing retainer assembly from input shaft.
3. Hold low speed gear and lightly tap shaft from gear. Note the position of the thrust washer pins in input shaft.
4. Remove snap-ring holding input bearing in retainer using a screw driver. Lightly tap rear bearing out of retainer.
5. Remove pilot roller bearing and O-ring from end of input shaft.
6. Thoroughly clean and inspect all component parts. Replace any component that is worn or damaged.

Assembly

1. Tap or press input bearing into retainer. Be sure that ball loading slots are toward concave side of retainer. Install securing snap ring. Make certain that selective snap-ring of proper thickness is used to provide tightest fit.
2. Position low speed gear on shaft, clutch end facing gear end of input shaft.
3. Place thrust washers on input shaft, align slot in washer with pin in shaft. Slide or tap washers into position.
4. Place input bearing retainer on shaft and secure with snap-ring. Snap-rings are selective. Use snap-ring that provides tightest fit.
5. Slip spacer and thrust washer on shaft and align with locating pin.
6. Spread heavy grease on end of shaft and install roller bearings.
7. Install rubber O-ring at end of shaft.

RANGE BOX

Disassembly

1. Remove poppet plate spring, plug and gasket.
2. Remove clutch fork and sliding gear by disengaging sliding clutch gear from input gear.

3. Remove upper shift lever from shifter shaft.
4. Remove snap-ring and lower shift lever.
5. Push shifter shaft assembly down and remove lockout clutch connector link. The long end of connector link engages poppet plate.
6. Remove shifter shaft assembly and separate shafts. Remove O-rings.
7. When necessary to remove poppet plate, drive pivot shaft out and remove plate and spring from bottom of case.
8. Remove input gear bearing retainer and seal assembly. Release snap-ring from retainer and tap bearing out of assembly.
9. Release snap-ring holding input shaft bearing to shaft and remove bearing.
10. Remove countershaft from cluster gear and case assembly from intermediate case side. Remove cluster gear assembly from range box.
11. Remove cluster gear thrust washers from case.
12. Thoroughly clean and inspect all component parts. Replace any component that is worn or damaged.

Assembly

1. Spread heavy grease in cluster bore and using proper tool install roller bearings and spacers.
2. Spread heavy grease on case and install thrust washers. Engage tab on thrust washers with slot in case.
3. Place cluster gear assembly in case and install countershaft through front of range box and into gear assembly. Flat face of countershaft must be aligned with case gasket.
4. Place bearing on input gear shaft with snap-ring groove facing out, install a new retaining ring. Insert input gear and bearing in housing. The retaining ring used in this operation is a select fit. Use ring that provides the tightest fit.
5. Secure input gear and bearing with a snap-ring.
6. Match up oil slot in retainer with drain hole in case and insert input gear bearing retainer and gaskets. Install bolts and torque to specifications.
7. Spread sealant on pin and install poppet pin and pivot pin in housing.
8. Lubricate and install new O-rings on inner and outer shifter shafts.
9. Insert shifter shafts in housing and engage long end of lockout clutch connector link with outer shifter shaft. Complete this operation before assembly bottoms out.
10. Install lower shift lever and retaining ring.
11. Install upper shift lever and shaft retaining nut.
12. Install shift fork and sliding clutch gear. Push fork up into shifter shaft and engage poppet plate. Move sliding clutch gear onto input shaft gear.
13. Insert poppet plate spring, gasket and plug in housing top. Make certain that spring engages poppet plate.

INPUT GEAR BEARING

Replacement

1. Remove bearing retainer and gasket from housing.
2. Remove and discard snap-ring holding bearing in retainer.
3. Pry bearing from case and remove from shaft.
4. Inspect input gear and bearing retainer for damage or wear. Replace if necessary.
5. Place new bearing and snap-ring on input gear. Using a soft hammer, tap bearing into position. Secure snap-ring.
6. Insert bearing retainer into housing and secure with attaching bolts. Tighten bolts to specifications.

INPUT GEAR RETAINER SEAL

Replacement

1. Remove bearing retainer from housing.
2. Remove seal from retainer by prying.
3. Place new seal on retainer and install with proper seal driver.
4. Install bearing retainer in housing and secure with attaching bolts. Tighten bolts to specifications.

REAR OUTPUT SHAFT HOUSING ASSEMBLY

Disassembly

1. Remove speedometer driven gear from housing.
2. Remove rear output flange and washer, if they have not been removed previously.
3. Using a soft hammer tap on flange end of pinion and remove the pinion. If speedometer drive gear does not come off with pinion reach into case and remove.
4. Remove old seal from bore with suitable prying tool.
5. Remove snap ring retaining rear output rear bearing.
6. Tap bearing out of housing.
7. Install a long drift into rear opening of housing and drive out front output bearing. Remove seal and discard.

Assembly

1. Spread grease on front bearing seal and place in bore. Place bearing in bore and press until it bottoms in housing.
2. Using a soft hammer tap rear bearing into place. Secure with proper snap-ring. Snap-rings are selective, use the one that provides the tightest fit.
3. Place rear seal in bore and drive into position with suitable tool. When seal is in position it should be approximately $\frac{1}{8}$ to $\frac{3}{16}$ in. below housing face.
4. Place speedometer drive gear on output shaft with shims of approximately 0.050 in. thickness. Insert output shaft into carrier through housing front opening.
5. Install flange and washer on output shaft. Leave retaining nut loose until shim requirements are known.
6. Install speedometer driven gear.

FRONT OUTPUT SHAFT BEARING RETAINER SEAL

Replacement

1. Remove old seal from retainer bore.
2. Inspect and clean retainer.
3. Spread sealer on outer edge of new seal.
4. Place new seal in retainer bore and drive into position with proper tool.

FRONT OUTPUT BEARING

Replacement

1. Remove rear cover from case assembly and discard gasket.
2. Press old bearing from cover.
3. Place new bearing on outside face of cover. Cover bearing with a wood block and press into cover until bearing is flush with opening.
4. Place gasket on transfer case and tap cover into position using a soft hammer. Secure cover with attaching bolts and tighten to specifications.

New Process Model 205

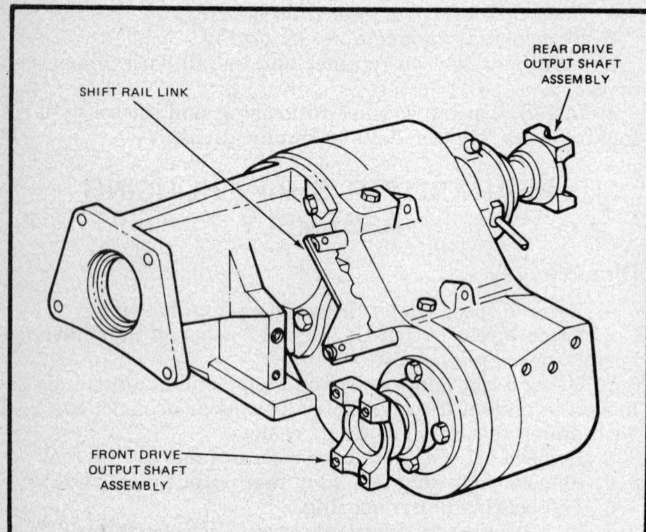

Front view of a model 205 transfer case

The New Process Model 205 transfer case is a two-speed gearbox mounted between the main transmission and the rear axle. The gearbox transmits power from the transmission and engine to the front and rear driving axles.

SPECIFICATIONS

END PLAY (IN.)	
Idler Gear	0.000–0.002 in.
Rear Output Shaft	0.002–0.027 in.
TORQUE LIMITS (FT. LBS.)	
Idler Shaft Locknut	150
Idler Shaft Cover	20
Front Output Shaft Front Bearing Retainer	30–35
Front Output Shaft Yoke Locknut	130–150
Rear Output Shaft Bearing Retainer and Housing	30–35
Rear Output Shaft Yoke Locknut	130–150
P.T.O. Cover	15
Front Output Shaft Rear Bearing Retainer	30-35
Filler and Drain Plugs	30
Case to Frame	130
Case to Adapter	25
Adapter Mount	75
Case Bracket to Frame	
Upper	30
Lower	65
Adapter to Transmission	
Manual Transmission	30–35
Automatic Transmission	30–35

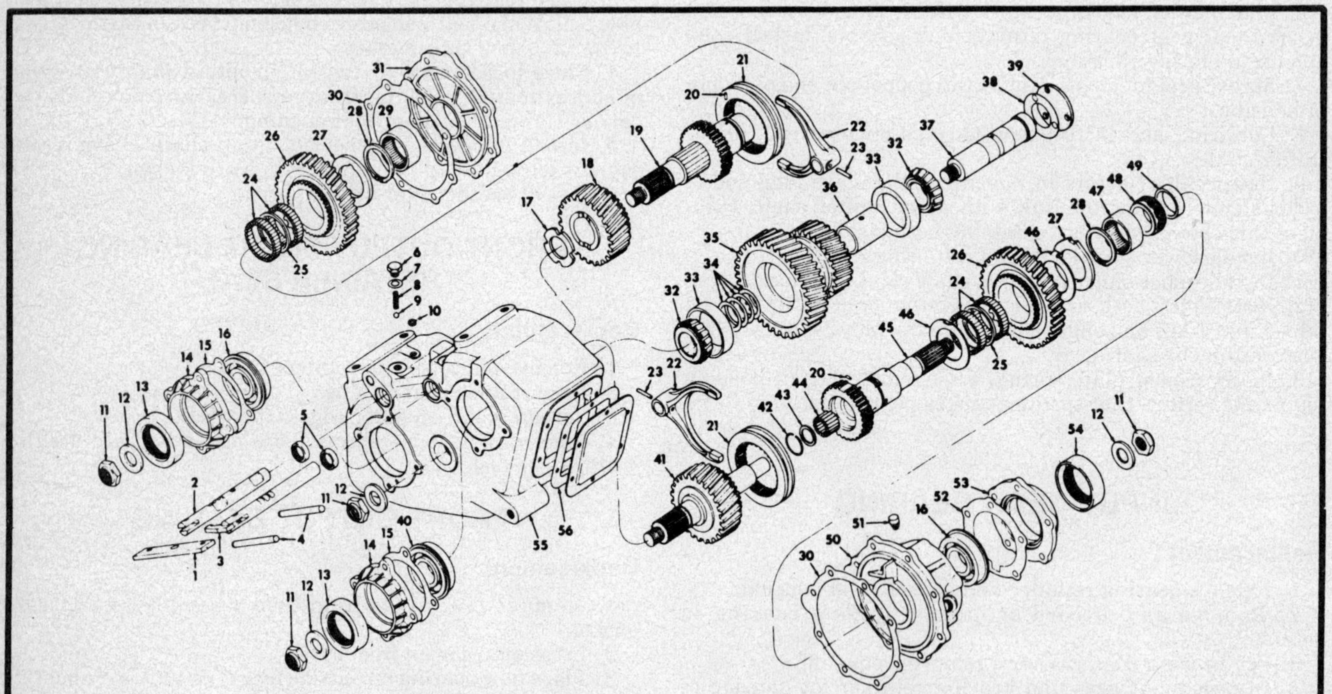

1. Shift lever link
2. Bar
3. Bar
4. Plunger
5. Seal
6. Screw
7. Gasket
8. Spring
9. Ball
10. Plug
11. Nut
12. Washer
13. Seal
14. Retainer
15. Gasket
16. Bearing
17. Washer
18. Gear
19. Shaft
20. Pin
21. Clutch
22. Fork
23. Pin
24. Bearing
25. Spacer
26. Gear
27. Washer
28. Ring
29. Bearing
30. Gasket
31. Retainer
32. Cone
33. Cup
34. Shim set
35. Gear
36. Spacer
37. Shaft
38. Gasket
39. Cover
40. Bearing
41. Shaft
42. Ring
43. Washer
44. Bearing
45. Gear
46. Washer
47. Bearing
48. Gear
49. Spacer
50. Retainer
51. Breather
52. Gasket
53. Retainer
54. Seal
55. Case
56. Gasket

Exploded view of a new process 205 transfer case

Disassembly

TRANSFER CASE

1. Clean the exterior of the case.
2. Remove the nuts from the universal joint flanges.
3. Remove the front output shaft rear bearing retainer, front bearing retainer and drive flange.
4. Tap the front output shaft assembly from the case with a soft hammer. Remove the sliding clutch, front output high gear, washer and bearing from the case.
5. Remove the rear output shaft housing attaching bolts and remove the housing, output shaft, bearing retainer and speedometer gear.
6. Slide the rear output shaft from the housing.

NOTE: Be careful not to lose the 15 needle bearings that will be loose when the rear output shaft is removed.

7. Drive the two 1/4 in. shift rail pin access hole plugs into the transfer case with a punch and hammer.
8. Remove the two shift rail detent nuts and springs from the case. Use a magnet to remove the two detent balls.
9. Position both shift rails in neutral and remove the shift fork retaining roll pins with a long punch.
10. Remove the clevis pin from one shift rail and rail link.
11. Remove the range shift rail first, then the 4WD shift rail.
12. Remove the shift forks and and sliding clutch from the case. Remove the input shaft bearing retainer, bearing and shaft.
13. Remove the cup plugs and rail pins, if they were driven out, from the case.
14. Remove the locknut from the idler gear shaft.
15. Remove the idler gear shaft rear cover.
16. Remove the idler gear shaft, using a soft hammer and a drift.
17. Roll the idler gear assembly to the front output shaft hole and remove the assembly from the case.

Assembly

NOTE: During assembly, lubricate all transfer case internal components with DEXRON®II or petroleum jelly as indicated in the procedure. Do not use chassis lubricant or similar thick lubricants.

1. Install a replacement input shaft and rear output shaft bearing oil seals. Seat the seals flush with the edge of the seal bore or in the seal groove in the transfer case. Coat the seal lips with petroleum jelly after installation.
2. Install the input shaft thrust bearing race in the transfer case counterbore.
3. Install the input gear thrust bearing on the input shaft and install the shaft and bearing in the transfer case.
4. Install the main shaft thrust bearing in the bearing recess in the input shaft.
5. Install the planetary assembly on the input shaft. Ensure that the planetary pinion teeth mesh fully with the input shaft.
6. Install the planetary thrust washer on the planetary hub.
7. Install a replacement sector shaft O-ring and install the retainer in the shaft bore in the transfer case.
8. Install the O-ring on the mode sector shaft and insert the mode sector through the range sector.
9. Install the range sector in the front transfer case half. Install the operating lever and the snap-ring on the range sector shaft.
10. Install the lever, attaching washer, and locknut on the mode sector shaft. Tighten the locknut with 23 Nm (17 ft. lbs.) torque.
11. Assemble the annulus gear, range fork and rail.
12. Install the assembled fork on and over the planetary assembly.
13. Ensure that the annulus gear is fully meshed with the planetary pinions.
14. Engage the range sector lug into the range sector.
15. Install the annulus thrust washer and the annulus retaining ring on the annulus gear hub.
16. Install the detent ball, plunger, spring and retaining screw in the front transfer case half detent bore.
17. Tighten the bolt with 30 Nm (22 ft. lbs.) torque.

CAUTION

The locking mode clutch sleeve and the high range clutch sleeve are not interchangeable. The sleeve splines are different. Ensure that the correct sleeve is installed in the corresponding shift fork.

18. Assemble and install the locking fork, fork bracket, fork springs, and high range clutch sleeves.
19. Ensure that the lug on the fork is seated in the range sector detent slot.
20. Install the range fork lug in the range sector detent notch.
21. Move the range sector to the high range position.
22. Assemble and install the range fork, shift rail and mode clutch sleeve.
23. Install the thrust washer and a replacement O-ring on the main shaft.
24. Install the needle bearings and bearing spacers on the main shaft.
25. Coat the shaft bearing surface and all needle bearings with petroleum jelly.
26. Install the first 41 needle bearings.
27. Install the long bearing spacer, the remaining 41 needle bearings and the remaining short spacer.
28. Be careful to avoid displacing the bearings when the spacers are installed.
29. Use additional petroleum jelly to hold the bearings in place if necessary.
30. Install the spline gear on the main shaft.
31. Take care to avoid displacing the bearings while installing the gear.
32. Install the sprocket carrier in the drive sprocket and install the sprocket carrier snap-rings.
33. Ensure that the carrier and sprocket are aligned according to the reference marks made during disassembly.

NOTE: The sprocket carrier teeth are tapered on one side and the drive sprocket has a deep recess on one side. Ensure that these components are assembled so that the carrier tapered teeth and sprocket recess are on the same side.

34. Install the sprocket carrier bearings and spacers.
35. Coat the carrier bore and all 120 carrier needle bearings with petroleum jelly.
36. Install the center spacer.
37. Install 60 bearings in each end of the carrier and install the remaining two spacers, one at each side of the carrier.
38. Use additional petroleum jelly to hold the bearings in place if necessary.
39. Install the assembled sprocket carrier and drive sprocket on the main shaft. Do not displace the main shaft bearings during installation.
40. Ensure that the recessed side of the drive sprocket is facing downward.
41. Install the clutch gear thrust washer in the main shaft.
42. Position the washer on the sprocket carrier.
43. Install the clutch gear on the side gear.
44. Ensure that the tapered edge of the clutch gear faces the side gear teeth.
45. Install the assembled side gear and clutch gear on the main shaft. Ensure that the side gear is fully seated in the sprocket carrier.
46. Take care to avoid displacing any of the carrier or main shaft needle bearings.
47. Install the main shaft and gear assembly in the case.
48. Ensure that the main shaft is fully seated in the input gear.

49. Install the driven sprocket on the front output shaft and install the sprocket retaining snap-ring. Ensure that the sprocket is installed according to reference marks made during disassembly.
50. Install the front output shaft front thrust bearing assembly in the transfer case front half.
51. Install the thick race in the transfer case and then install the bearing and the thin race.
52. Install the drive chain, front output shaft and driven sprocket.
53. Install the chain on the driven sprocket.
54. Raise and tilt the driven sprocket and chain and install the opposite end of the chain on the drive sprocket.
55. Align the front output shaft with the shaft bore in the transfer case front half and install the shaft in the transfer case.
56. Ensure that the front shaft thrust bearing assembly is seated in the transfer case.
57. Install the front output shaft rear thrust bearing assembly on the front output shaft.
58. Install the thin race first, then install the bearing and thick race.
59. Install the viscous coupling on the side gear and clutch gear.
60. Ensure that the coupling is fully seated on the clutch gear. The clutch gear should be flush with the coupling and the gear teeth should be visible.
61. Coat the main shaft pilot bearing surface and all 15 pilot roller bearings with petroleum jelly and install the bearings on the shaft.
62. Use additional petroleum jelly to hold the bearings in place if necessary.
63. Install the rear output shaft on the main shaft and into the viscous coupling. Ensure that the shaft is completely seated in the coupling.
64. Tap the shaft with a plastic mallet or brass punch to seat it if necessary.
65. Do not displace the pilot bearings during installation of the shaft.
66. Install a replacement rear output shaft bearing seal in the rear transfer case half.
67. Apply a bead of Loctite® 515, or equivalent sealer, to the mating surface of the rear transfer case half.
68. Install the magnet in the case, if removed.
69. Attach the rear transfer case half to the front transfer case half. Ensure that the alignment dowels at the front case half ends are aligned with the bolt holes in the rear case half and mate the rear case half with the front case half.

NOTE: If the rear transfer case half will not mate completely with the front case, inspect for the following: oil in the range fork rail bore, the front output shaft rear thrust bearing assembly is not aligned with the rear case half, the main shaft is not completely seated, the rear case half is not aligned with the oil pump.

70. Install the rear case half to the front case half bolts. Tighten the bolts with 31 Nm (23 ft. lbs.) torque. Ensure that the flat washers are used on the bolts at the case end where the alignment dowels are located.
71. Install the speedometer drive gear on the rear output shaft.
72. Measure the thickness of the shim pack and record.
73. Install a 0.762mm (0.030 in.) shim (approximately) on the rear output shaft.
74. Align the rear retainer on the rear transfer case half and install the retainer. Install the retainer bolts. Tighten the bolts securely but not with the specified torque.
75. Install the front rear output shaft yokes and the original yoke nuts. Tighten the nuts finger-tight only. Check the differential end play.
76. Set the shift lever in the 4-High range position.
77. Position Dial Indicator J–8001 on the rear retainer and position the indicator stylus so it contacts the rear yoke nut.
78. Support the transfer case to prevent the front output yoke from turning.
79. Slowly turn the rear output shaft while maintaining moderate inward pressure on the rear yoke. Turn the rear output shaft at least two full turns to determine the maximum run-out of the shaft.

NOTE: A wrench should be used to turn the yoke to provide the leverage needed to turn the viscous coupling in the transfer case.

80. Set the shaft at its maximum run-out point and zero the dial indicator.
81. Pull upward on the rear output yoke, note the dial indicator pointer position and record it.
82. Remove the retainer. Add or subtract differential shims as necessary to correct the end play. The end play should be between 0.05 and 0.25mm (0.002 to 0.010 in.). The recommended end play is 0.15mm (0.006 in.).
83. After adjusting the end play, remove the front and rear yokes. Discard the original yoke nuts.
84. Apply a bead of Loctite®515, or equivalent sealer, to the retainer mating surface and install the retainer.
85. Apply sealer to the retainer bolts and install the bolts. Tighten the bolts with 31 Nm (23 ft. lbs.) torque.
86. Position the front and rear yokes. Install replacement yoke seal washers and nuts.
87. Tighten the yoke nuts with 163 Nm (120 ft. lbs.) torque. Use Tool J–8614–01 or equivalent to hold the yokes in place while tightening the nuts.
88. Install the detent ball, spring and bolt if these were not installed previously. Apply sealer to the bolt before installing it. Tighten the bolt with 31 Nm (23 ft. lbs.) torque.
89. Install the drain plug and washer.
90. Fill the transfer case with 2.82 liters (6 pints) of DEXRON®II Automatic Transmission Fluid (ATF) and install the fill plug and washer.
91. Tighten the drain and fill plugs with 24 Nm (18 ft. lbs.) torque.
92. Install the plug and washer in the front transfer case half, if removed. Tighten the plug with 24 Nm (18 ft. lbs.) torque.
93. Reinstall transfer case in vehicle.

REAR OUTPUT SHAFT AND YOKE

1. Loosen rear output shaft yoke nut.
2. Remove shaft housing bolts, then remove the housing and retainer assembly.
3. Remove retaining nut and yoke from the shaft, then remove the shaft assembly.
4. Remove and discard snap-ring.
5. Remove thrust washer and pin.
6. Remove tanged bronze washer. Remove gear needle bearings, spacer and second row of needle bearings.
7. Remove tanged bronze thrust washer.
8. Remove pilot rollers, retainer ring and washer.
9. Remove oil seal retainer, ball bearing, speedometer gear and spacer. Discard gaskets.
10. Press out bearing.
11. Remove oil seal from the retainer.

FRONT OUTPUT SHAFT

1. Remove lock nut, washer and yoke.
2. Remove attaching bolts and front bearing retainer.
3. Remove rear bearing retainer attaching bolts.
4. Tap output shaft with a soft-faced hammer and remove shaft, gear assembly and rear bearing retainer.
5. Remove sliding clutch, gear, washer and bearing from output high gear.
6. Remove sliding clutch from the high output gear; then remove gear, washer and bearing.

7. Remove gear retaining snap-ring from the shaft, using large snap-ring picks. Discard ring.
8. Remove thrust washer and pin.
9. Remove gear, needle bearings and spacer.
10. Replace rear bearing, if necessary.

CAUTION

Always replace the bearing and retainer as an assembly. Do not try to press a new bearing into an old retainer.

SHIFT RAILS AND FORKS

1. Remove the two poppet nuts, springs, and using a magnet, the poppet balls.
2. Remove cup plugs on top of case, using a ¼ in. punch.
3. Position both shift rails in neutral, then remove fork pins with a long handled screw extractor.
4. Remove clevis pins and shift rail link.
5. Lower shift rails; upper rail first and then lower.
6. Remove shift forks and sliding clutch.
7. Remove the front output high gear, washer and bearing. Remove the shift rail cup plugs.

INPUT SHAFT

1. Remove snap-ring in front of bearing. Tap shaft out rear of case and bearing out front of case, using a soft-faced hammer or mallet.
2. Tilt case up on power take-off and remove the two interlock pins from inside.

IDLER GEAR

1. Remove idler gear shaft nut.
2. Remove rear cover.
3. Tap out idler gear shaft, using a soft-faced hammer and a drift approximately the same diameter as the shaft.
4. Remove idler gear through the front output shaft hole.
5. Remove two bearing cups from the idler gear.

Assembly

TRANSFER CASE

1. Assemble the idler shaft gears, bearings, spacer and shims, and bearings on a dummy shaft tool and install the assembly into the case through the front output shaft bore, large end first.
2. Install the idler shaft from the large bore side, using a soft hammer to drive it through the bearings, spacer, gears, and shims.
3. Install a washer and new locknut on the end of the idler shaft. Check to make sure the idler gear rotates freely. Tighten the locknut to specification.
4. Install the idler shaft cover with a new gasket so the flat side faces the rear bearing retainer of the front output shaft. Install and tighten the two retaining screws to the proper torque.
5. Install the interlock pins into the interlock bore through the front of the output shaft opening.
6. Start the 4WD shift rail into the front of the case, solid end of the rail first, with the detent notches facing up.
7. Position the shift fork onto the shift rail with the long end facing inward. Push the rail through the fork and into the Neutral position.
8. Position the input shaft and bearing in the case.
9. Start the range shift rail into the case from the front, with the detent notches facing up.
10. Position the sliding clutch to the shift fork. Place the sliding clutch on the input shaft and align the fork with the shift rail. Push the rail through the fork into the Neutral position.
11. Install the roll pins that lock the shift forks to the shift rails with a long punch.
12. Position the front wheel drive high gear and its thrust washer in the case. Position the sliding clutch in the shift fork. Shift the rail and fork into the front wheel drive (4WD-Hi) position, while at the same time, meshing the clutch with the mating teeth on the front wheel drive high gear.
13. Align the thrust washer, high gear and sliding clutch with the bearing bore in the case and insert the front output shaft and low gear into the high gear assembly.
14. Install a new seal in the front bearing retainer of the front output shaft, and install the bearing and retainer and new gasket in the case. Tighten the bearing retainer cap screws to the proper torque.
15. Lubricate the roller bearing in the front output shaft rear bearing retainer, which is the aluminum cover, and install it over the front output shaft and to the case. Install and tighten the retaining screws to the proper torque.
16. Move the range shift rail to the High position and install the rear output shaft and retainer assembly to the housing and input shaft. Use one or two new gaskets, as required, to adjust the clearance on the input shaft pilot. Install the rear output shaft housing retaining bolts and tighten them to specification.
17. Using a punch and sealing compound, install the shift rail pin access plugs.
18. Install the fill and drain plugs and the cross-link clevis pin.

IDLER GEAR

1. Press the two bearing cups in the idler gear.
2. Assemble the two bearing cones, spacer, shims and idler gear on a dummy shaft, with bore facing up. Check end-play.
3. Install idler gear assembly (with dummy shaft) into the case, large end first, through the front output shaft bore.
4. Install idler shaft from large bore side, driving it through with a soft-faced hammer or mallet.
5. Install washer and new locknut. Check for free rotation and measure end-play. Torque locknut to specifications.
6. Install idler shaft cover and new gasket. Torque cover bolts to specifications.

NOTE: Flat side of cover must be positioned towards front output shaft rear cover.

SHIFT RAILS AND FORKS

1. Press the two rail seals into the case.

NOTE: Install seals with metal lip outward.

2. Install interlock pins from inside case.
3. Insert slotted end of front output drive shift rail (with poppet notches up) into back of case.
4. While pushing rail through to neutral position, install shift fork (long end inward).
5. Install input shaft and bearing into case.
6. Install end of range rail (with poppet notches up) into front of case.
7. Install sliding clutch on fork, then place over input shaft in case.
8. Push range rail, while engaging sliding clutch and fork, through to neutral position.
9. Drive new lockpins into forks through holes at top of case.

NOTE: Tilt case on power take-off opening to install range rail lockpin.

FRONT OUTPUT SHAFT AND GEAR

1. Install two rows of needle bearings in the front low output gear and retain with grease.

NOTE: Each row consists of 32 needle bearings and the two rows are separated by a spacer.

2. Position front output shaft in a soft-jaw vise, with spline end down. Place front low gear over shaft with clutch gear facing down; then install thrust washer pin, thrust washer and new snap-ring.

NOTE: Position snap-ring gap opposite the thrust washer pin.

3. Place front drive high gear and washer in case. Install sliding clutch in the shift fork, then put fork and rail into 4-High position, meshing front drive high gear and clutch teeth.

4. Align washer, high gear and sliding clutch and bearing bore. Insert front output shaft and low gear assembly through the high gear assembly.

5. Install front output bearing and retainer with a new seal in the case.

6. Clean and grease rollers in front output rear bearing retainer. Install on case with one gasket and bolts coated with sealant. Torque bolts to specifications.

7. Install front output yoke, washer and locknut. Torque locknut to specifications.

REAR OUTPUT SHAFT

1. Install two rows of needle bearings into the output low gear, retaining them with grease.

NOTE: Each row consists of 32 needle bearings and the two rows are separated by a spacer.

2. Install thrust washer (with tang down in clutch gear groove) onto the rear output shaft.

3. Install output low gear onto shaft with clutch teeth facing downward.

4. Install thrust washer over gear with tab pointing up and away. Install washer pin.

5. Install large thrust washer over shaft and pin. Turn washer until tab fits into slot located approximately 90° away from pin.

6. Install snap-ring and measure shaft end-play.

7. Grease pilot bore and install needle bearings.

NOTE: There are 15 pilot needle bearings.

8. Install thrust washer and new snap-ring in pilot bore.

9. Press new bearing into retainer housing.

10. Install housing on output shaft assembly.

11. Install spacer and speedometer gear. Install rear bearing.

12. Install rear bearing retainer seal.

13. Install bearing retainer assembly on housing, using one or two gaskets to achieve specified clearance. Torque attaching bolts to specifications.

14. Install yoke, washer and locknut on output shaft.

15. Position range rail in high, then install output shaft and retainer assembly on case. Torque housing bolts to specifications.

CASE

1. Install power take-off cover and gasket. Torque attaching bolts to specifications.

2. Install cup plugs at rail pin holes.

NOTE: After installing, seal the cup plugs.

3. Install drain and filler plugs. Torque to specifications.

4. Install shift rail cross link, clevis pins and lock pins.

New Process Model 207

The 207 transfer case is an aluminum case, chain drive, four position unit providing four-wheel drive high and low ranges, a two-wheel high range, and a neutral position. It is a part-time four-wheel drive unit. Torque input in four-wheel high and low ranges is undifferentiated. The range positions on the 207 transfer case are selected by a floor mounted gearshift lever.

The 207 case is a two-piece aluminum case containing front and rear output shafts, two drive sprockets, a shift mechanism and a planetary gear assembly. The drive sprockets are connected and operated by the drive chain. The planetary assembly which consists of a three pinion carrier and an annulus gear provide the four-wheel drive low range when engaged.

TRANSFER CASE

Removal

1. Shift transfer case into 4 Hi.

2. Disconnect negative cable at battery.

3. Raise vehicle and remove skid plate.

4. Drain lubricant from transfer case.

5. Mark transfer case front output shaft yoke and propeller shaft for assembly reference. Disconnect front propeller shaft from transfer case.

6. Mark rear axle yoke and propeller shaft for assembly reference. Remove rear propeller shaft.

7. Disconnect speedometer cable and vacuum harness at transfer case. Remove shift lever from transfer case.

8. Remove catalytic converter hanger bolts at converter.

9. Raise transmission and transfer case and remove transmission mount attaching bolts. Remove mount and catalytic converter hanger and lower transmission and transfer case.

10. Support transfer case and remove transfer case attaching bolts. On vehicles equipped with an automatic transmission, it will be necessary to remove the shift lever bracket mounting bolts from the transfer case adapter in order to remove the upper left transfer case attaching bolt.

11. Separate transfer case from adapter (auto) or extension housing (man.) and remove from vehicle.

Disassembly

1. Remove fill and drain plugs.

2. Remove front yoke. Discard yoke seal washer and yoke nut.

3. Turn transfer case on end and position front case on wood blocks.

4. Shift transfer case to 4 Lo.

5. Remove extension housing attaching bolts. Using a hammer, tap the shoulder on the extension housing to break sealer loose.

6. Remove the snap-ring for the rear bearing from the main shaft and discard.

7. Remove the rear retainer attaching bolts. Using a hammer, tap the shoulder on the retainer to break sealer loose.

8. Remove the rear retainer and pump housing from the transfer case.

9. Remove the pump seal from the pump housing and discard.

10. Remove the speedometer drive gear from the main shaft.

11. Remove the pump gear from the main shaft.

12. Remove the bolts attaching the rear case to the front case and remove rear case. To separate the case, insert a prybar into the slots casted in the case ends and pry upward. DO NOT attempt to wedge the case halves apart at any point on the mating surfaces.

13. Remove the front output shaft and drive chain as an assembly. It may be necessary to raise the main shaft slightly for the output shaft to clear the case.

14. Pull up on the mode fork rail until rail clears range fork and rotate mode fork and rail and remove from transfer case.

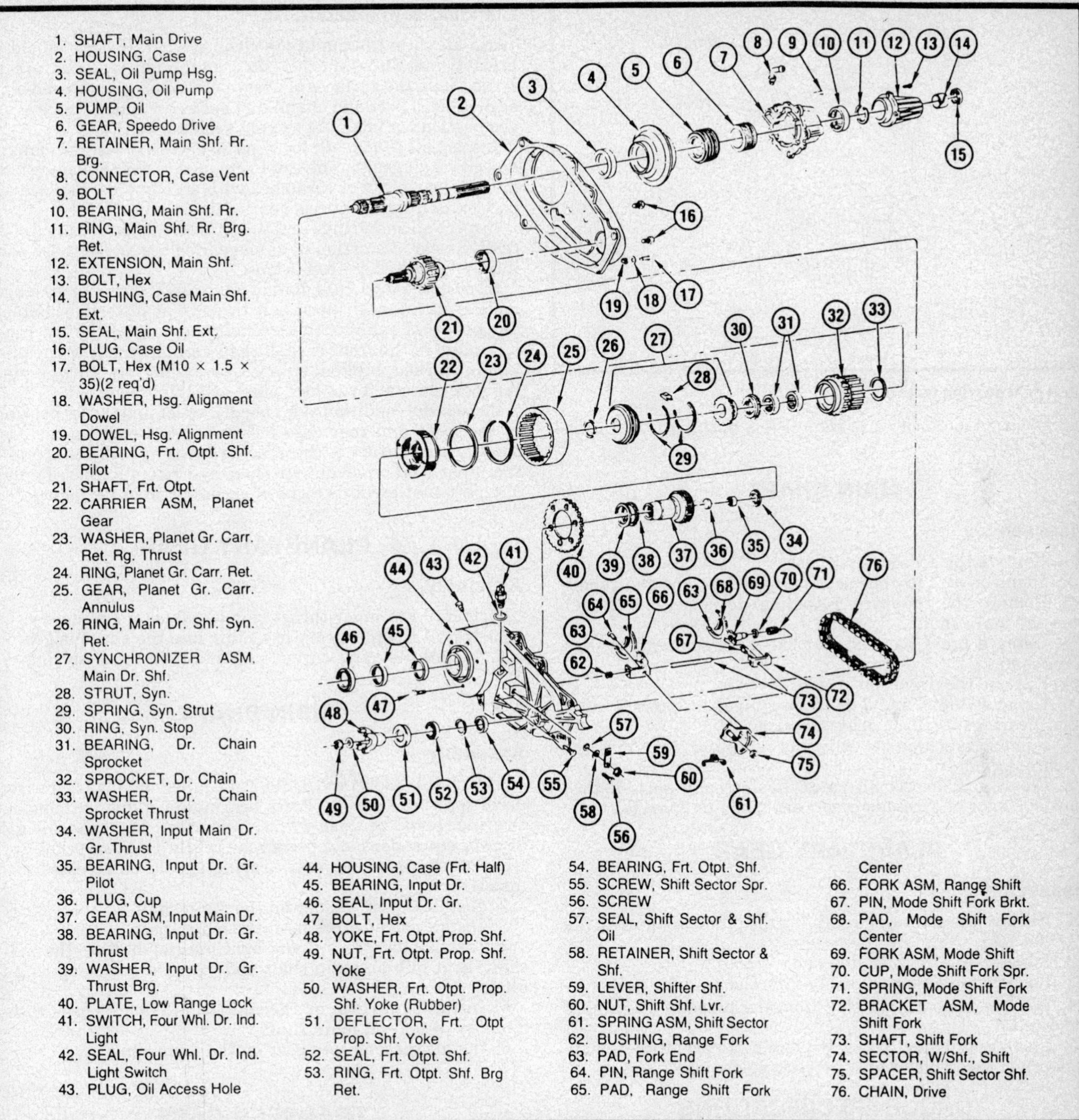

Exploded view of a new process 207 transfer case

15. Pull up on the main shaft until it separates from the planetary assembly. Remove the main shaft from the transfer case.

16. Remove the planetary assembly with the range fork from the transfer case.

17. Remove the planetary thrust washer, input gear thrust bearing and front thrust washer from the transfer case.

18. Remove the shift sector detent spring and retaining bolt.

19. Remove the shift sector, shaft and spacer from the transfer case.

20. Remove the locking plate retaining bolts and lock plate from the transfer case.

21. Remove the input gear pilot bearing using J–29369–1 or equivalent with a slide hammer.

22. Remove the front output shaft seal, input shaft seal and the rear extension seal using a brass drift.

23. Using J–33841 with J–8092 or equivalent, press the 2 caged roller bearings for the front input shaft gear from the transfer case.

24. Using J–29369–2 with J–33367 or a slide hammer, remove the rear bearing for the front output shaft.

25. Using a hammer and drift, remove the rear main shaft bearing from the rear retainer.

26. Using an awl, remove the snap-ring retaining the front output shaft bearing. Using a hammer and drift, remove the bearing from the case.

27. Remove the bushing from the extension housing using J–

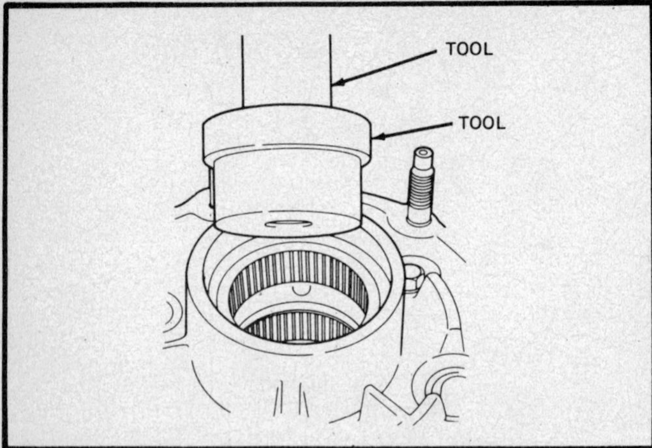

Input gear bearing removal

33839 with J–8092 or equivalent. Press bushing from the extension housing.

MAIN SHAFT

Disassembly

1. Remove the speedometer gear.
2. Using an awl, pry off the pump gear from the main shaft.
3. Remove the snap-ring retaining the synchronizer hub from the main shaft.
4. Using a brass hammer, tap the synchronizer hub from main shaft.
5. Remove the drive sprocket.
6. Using J–33826 and J–8092 or equivalent, press 2 caged roller bearings from the drive sprocket.
7. Remove synchronizer keys and retaining rings from the synchronizer hub.
8. Clean and inspect all parts. Replace any parts if they show evidence of excessive wear, distortion or damage.

PLANETARY GEAR

Disassembly

1. Remove the snap-ring retaining the planetary gear in the annulus gear.
2. Remove outer thrust ring and discard.
3. Remove planetary assembly from the annulus gear.
4. Remove inner thrust ring from the planetary assembly and discard.
5. Clean and inspect parts. Replace any parts if they show evidence of excessive wear, distortion or damage.

TORQUE SPECIFICATIONS
Model 207

Description	N•m	Ft. Lb.
Bolt Locking Plate to Transfer Case	27–40	20–30
Nut-Front Output Yoke	122–176	90–130
Switch Vacuum	20–34	15–25
Nut-Shift Lever	20–27	15–20
Bolt-Transfer Case	27–34	20–25
Bolt-Rear Retainer	20–27	15–20
Bolt-Extension Housing	27–34	20–25
Bolt-Drain-Fill	40–54	30–40
Bolt-Adapter to Transfer Case	26–40	19–29
Bolt-Shift Bracket	65–85	47–62
Bolt-Shift Lever Pivot	120–140	88–103
Bolt-Shift Lever Adjusting	34–48	25–35

Cleaning & Inspection

Wash all parts thoroughly in clean solvent. Be sure all old lubricant, metallic particles, dirt, or foreign material are removed from the surfaces of every part. Apply compressed air to each oil feed port and channel in each case half to remove any obstructions or cleaning solvent residue.

Inspect all gear teeth for signs of excessive wear or damage and check all gear splines for burrs, nicks, wear or damage. Remove minor nicks or scratches with an oil stone. Replace any part exhibiting excessive wear or damage.

Inspect all snap-rings and thrust washers for evidence of excessive wear, distortion or damage. Replace any of these parts if they exhibit these conditions.

Inspect the two case halves for cracks, porosity damaged mating surfaces, stripped bolt threads, or distortion. Replace any part that exhibits these conditions. Inspect the low range lock plate in the front case. If the lock plate teeth or the plate hub is cracked, broken, chipped, or excessively worn, replace the lock plate and the lock plate attaching bolts.

Inspect the condition of all needle, roller and thrust bearings in the front and rear case halves and the input gear. Also, check the condition of the bearing bores in both cases and in the input gear, rear output shaft and rear retainer. Replace any part that exhibits signs of excessive wear or damage.

PLANETARY GEAR

Assembly

1. Install the inner thrust ring on planetary assembly.
2. Install the planetary assembly into the annulus gear.
3. Install the outer thrust ring and then the snap-ring.

MAIN SHAFT

Assembly

1. Using J–33828 and J–8092 or equivalent, install the front drive sprocket bearing. Press bearing until tool bottoms out. Bearing should be flush with front surface. Reverse tool on J–8092 or equivalent and press rear bearing into sprocket until tool bottoms out. The rear bearing should be recessed after installation.
2. Install thrust washer on the main shaft.
3. Install drive sprocket on the main shaft.
4. Install blocker ring and synchronizer hub on the main shaft. Seat hub on main shaft and install a new snap-ring to retain.
5. Install pump gear on the main shaft. Tap the gear with a hammer to seat on main shaft.
6. Install speedometer gear on the main shaft.

TRANSFER CASE

Assembly

All of the bearings used in the transfer case must be correctly positioned to avoid covering the bearing oil feed holes. After installation of bearings, check the bearing position to be sure the feed hole is not obstructed or blocked by a bearing.

1. Install the lock plate in the transfer case. Coat case and lock plate surfaces around bolt holes with Loctite®515 or equivalent.
2. Position the lock plate to the case and align bolt holes in lock plat with case. Install attaching bolts and torque to specification.
3. Install the roller bearings for the input shaft into the transfer case using J–33830 and J–8092 or equivalent. Press bearings until tool bottoms in bore.
4. Install the front output shaft rear bearing, using J–33832

and J–8092 or equivalent. Press bearing until tool bottoms in case.

5. Install the front output shaft front bearing using J–33833 and J–8092 or equivalent. Press bearing until tool bottoms in bore.

6. Install the snap-ring that retains the front output shaft bearing in case.

7. Install the front output shaft seal using J–33834 or equivalent.

8. Install the input shaft seal using J–33831 or equivalent.

9. Install spacer on shift sector shaft and install sector in transfer case. Install shift lever and retaining nut. Torque to specification.

10. Install shift sector detent spring and retaining bolt.

11. Install the pilot bearing into the input gear using J–33829 and J–8092 or equivalent. Press bearing until tool bottoms out.

12. Install the input gear front thrust bearing and input gear in transfer case.

13. Install the planetary gear thrust washer on the input gear. Position range fork on planetary assembly and install planetary assembly into the transfer case.

14. Install the main shaft into the transfer case. Make sure the thrust washer is aligned with the input gear and planetary assembly before installing main shaft.

15. Install mode fork on synchronizer sleeve and rotate until mode fork is aligned with range fork. Slide mode fork rail down through range fork until rail is seated in bore of transfer case.

16. Position drive chain on front output shaft and install chain on drive sprocket. Install front output shaft in the transfer case. It may be necessary to slightly raise the main shaft to seat the output shaft in the case.

17. Install the magnet into pocket of transfer case.

18. Apply ⅛ in. bead of Loctite®515 or equivalent to the mating surface of the front case. Install rear case on the front case aligning dowel pins. Install bolts and torque to 20–25 ft. lbs. Install the two bolts with washers into the dowel pin holes.

19. Install the output bearing into the rear retainer using J–33833 and J–8092 or equivalent. Press bearing until seated in bore.

20. Install pump seal in pump housing using J–33835 or equivalent. Apply petroleum jelly to pump housing tabs and install housing in rear retainer.

21. Apply ⅛ in. bead of Loctite®515 or equivalent to mating surface of rear retainer. Align retainer to case and install retaining bolts. Torque bolts to specification 15–20 ft. lbs.

22. Using a new snap-ring, install snap-ring on main shaft. Pull up on main shaft and seat snap-ring in its groove.

23. Install bushing in extension housing using J–33826 and J–8092 or equivalent. Press bushing until tool bottoms in bore.

24. Install a new seal in the extension housing using J–33843 or equivalent.

25. Apply ⅛ in. bead of Loctite®515 or equivalent to mating surface of extension housing. Align extension housing to the rear retainer and install attaching bolts. Torque bolts to specification 20–25 ft. lbs.

26. Install front yoke on output shaft. Install a new yoke seal washer with a new nut and torque to specification.

27. Install drain plug and torque to specification. Install fill plug.

New Process 208

The 208 is a part-time unit with a two piece aluminum housing. On the front case half, the front output shaft, front input shaft, four wheel drive indicator switch and shift lever assembly are located. On the rear case half, the rear output shaft, bearing retainer and drain and fill plugs are located.

Disassembly

1. Drain the fluid from the case.
2. Remove the attaching nuts from the front and rear output yokes. Remove the yokes and sealing washers.
3. Remove the four bolts and separate the rear bearing retainer from the rear case half.
4. Remove the retaining ring, speedometer drive gear nylon oil pump housing, and oil pump gear from the rear output shaft.
5. Remove the eleven bolts and separate the case halves by inserting a screw driver in the pry slots on the case.
6. Remove the magnetic chip collector from the bottom of the rear case half.
7. Remove the thick thrust washer, thrust bearing and thin thrust washer from the front output shaft assembly.
8. Remove the drive chain by pushing the front input shaft inward and by angling the gear slightly to obtain adequate clearance to remove the chain.
9. Remove the output shaft from the front case half and slide the thick thrust washer, thrust bearing and thin thrust washer off the output side of the front output shaft.
10. Remove the screw, poppet spring and check ball from the front case half.
11. Remove the four wheel drive indicator switch and washer from the front case half.
12. Position the front case half on its face and lift out the rear output shaft, sliding clutch and clutch shift fork and spring.
13. Place a shop towel on the shift rail. Clamp the rail with a vise grip pliers so that they lay between the rail and the case edge. Position a pry bar under the pliers and pry out the shift rail.

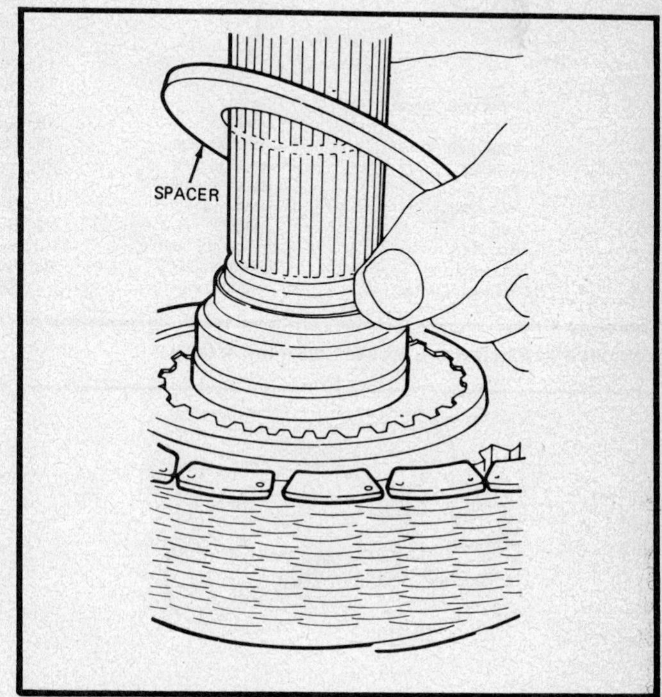

Drive sprocket thrust washer

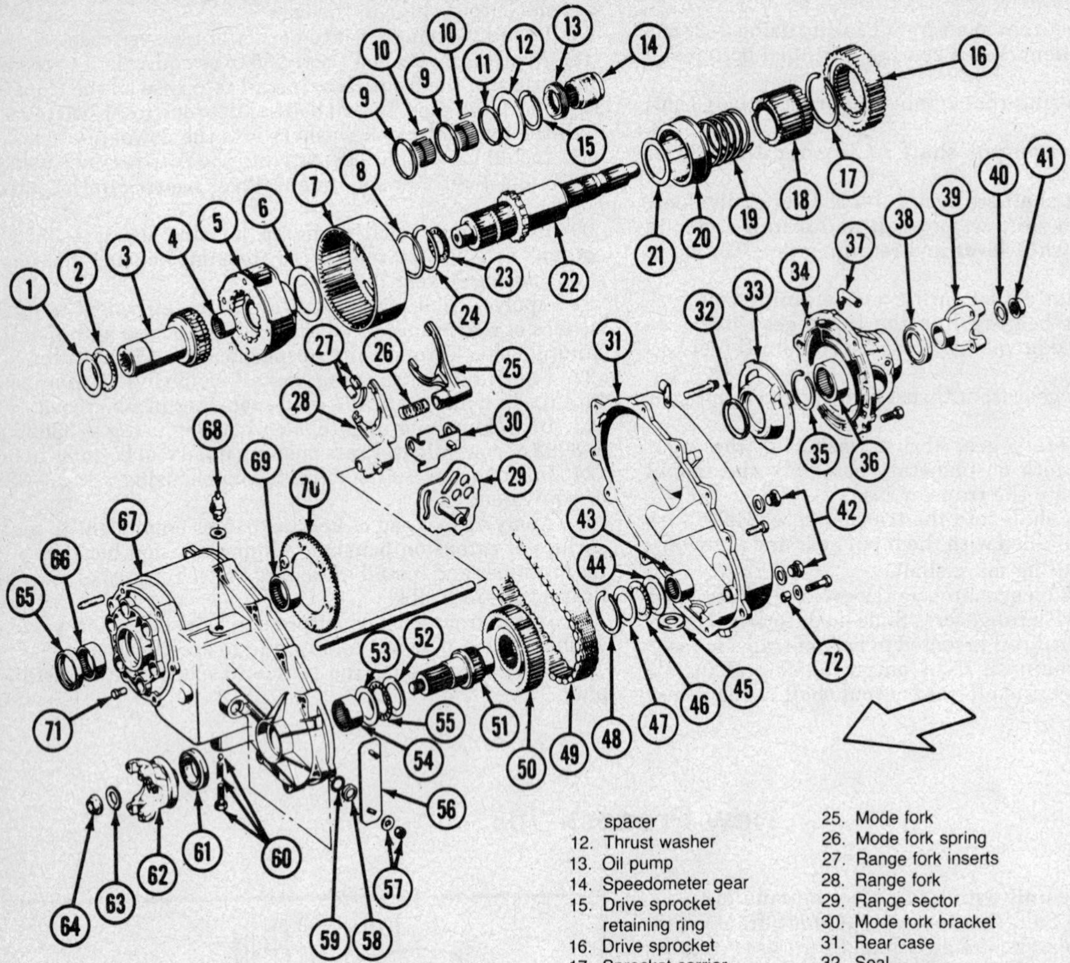

1. Input gear thrust washer
2. Input gear thrust bearing
3. Input gear
4. Mainshaft pilot bearing
5. Planetary assembly
6. Planetary thrust washer
7. Annulus gear
8. Annulus gear thrust washer
9. Needle bearing spacers
10. Mainshaft needle bearings (120)
11. Needle bearing spacer
12. Thrust washer
13. Oil pump
14. Speedometer gear
15. Drive sprocket retaining ring
16. Drive sprocket
17. Sprocket carrier stop ring
18. Sprocket carrier
19. Clutch spring
20. Sliding clutch
21. Thrust washer
22. Mainshaft
23. Mainshaft thrust bearing
24. Annulus gear retaining ring
25. Mode fork
26. Mode fork spring
27. Range fork inserts
28. Range fork
29. Range sector
30. Mode fork bracket
31. Rear case
32. Seal
33. Pump housing
34. Rear retainer
35. Rear output bearing
36. Bearing snap-ring
37. Vent tube
38. Rear seal
39. Rear yoke
40. Yoke seal washer
41. Yoke nut
42. Drain and fill plugs
43. Front output shaft rear bearing
44. Front output shaft rear thrust bearing race (thick)
45. Case magnet
46. Front output shaft rear thrust bearing
47. Front output shaft rear thrust bearing race (thin)
48. Driven sprocket retaining ring
49. Drive chain
50. Driven sprocket
51. Front output shaft
52. Front output shaft front thrust bearing race (thin)
53. Front output shaft front thrust bearing race (thick)
54. Front output shaft front bearing
55. Front output shaft front thrust bearing
56. Operating lever
57. Washer and locknut
58. Range sector shaft seal retainer
59. Range sector shaft seal
60. Detent ball, spring and retainer bolt
61. Front seal
62. Front yoke
63. Yoke seal washer
64. Yoke nut
65. Input gear oil seal
66. Input gear front bearing
67. Front case
68. Lock mode indicator switch and washer
69. Input gear rear bearing
70. Lockplate
71. Lockplate bolts
72. Case alignment dowels

Exploded view of the new process 208 transfer case

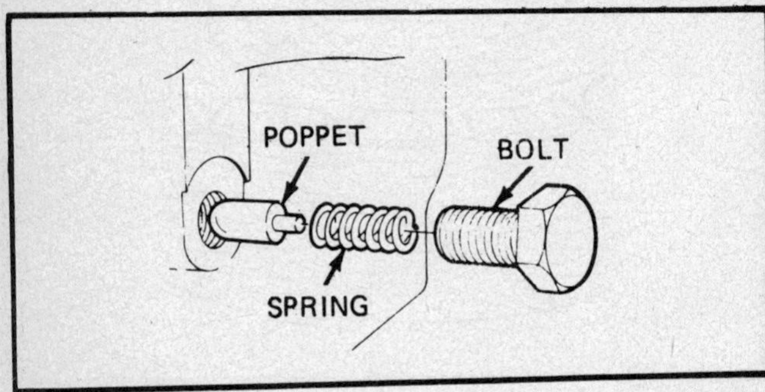

Poppet, spring and bolt

14. Remove the snap ring and thrust washer from the planetary gear set assembly in the front case half.

15. Remove the annulus gear assembly and thrust washer from the front case half.

16. Lift the planetary gear assembly from the front case half.

17. Lift out the thrust bearing, sun gear, thrust bearing and thrust washer.

18. Remove the six bolts and lift the gear locking plate from the front case half.

19. Remove the nut retaining the external shift lever and washer. Press the shift control shaft inward and remove the shift selector plate and washer from the case.

20. From the rear output shaft, remove the snap-ring and thrust washer retaining the chain drive sprocket and slide the sprocket from the drive gear.

21. Remove the retaining ring from the sprocket carrier gear.

22. Carefully slide the sprocket carrier gear from the rear output shaft. Remove the two rows of 60 loose needle bearings. Remove the three separator rings from the output shaft.

Assembly

1. Slide the thrust washer against the gear on the rear output shaft.

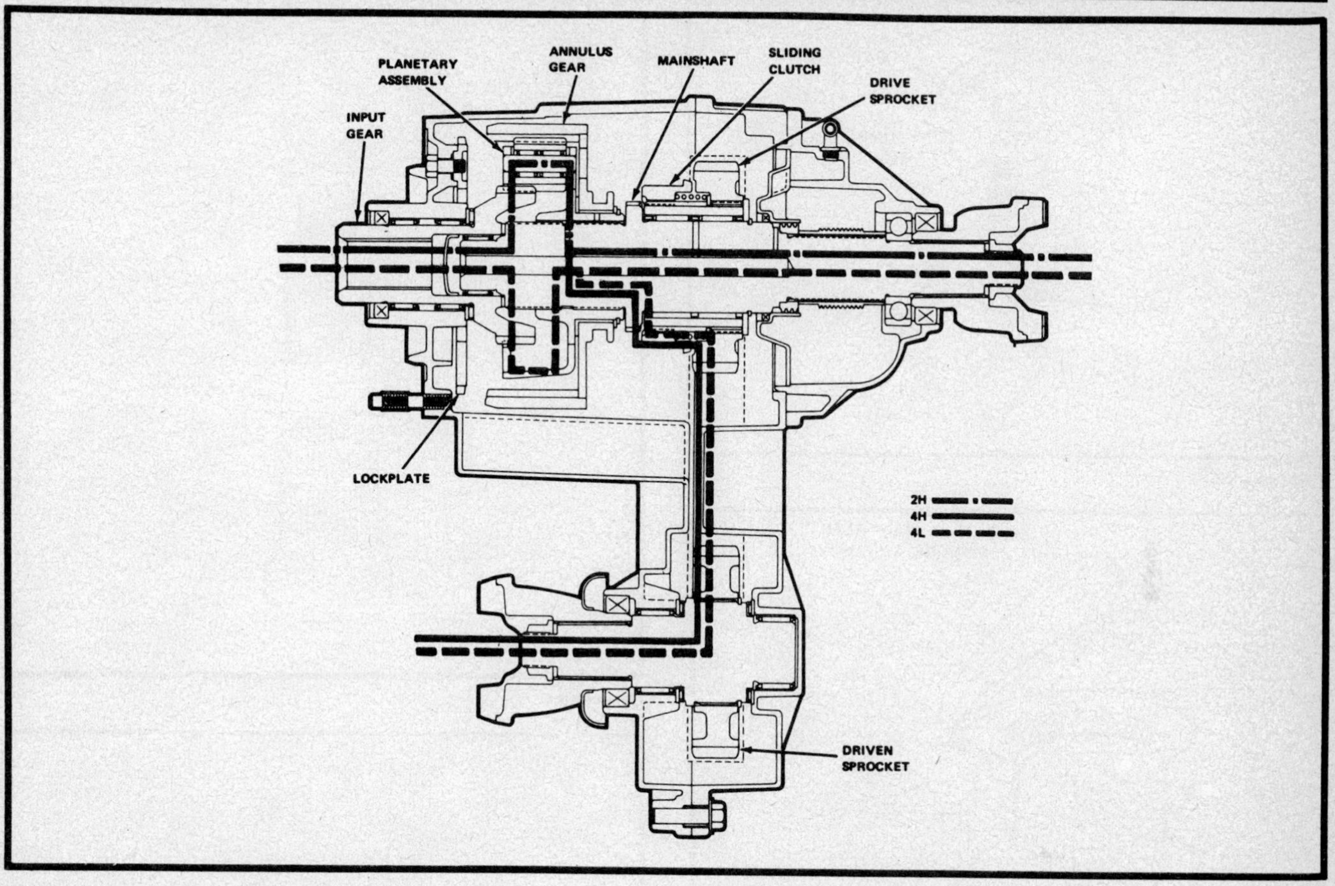

Power flow new process 208 transfer case

Driven sprocket retaining snap-ring

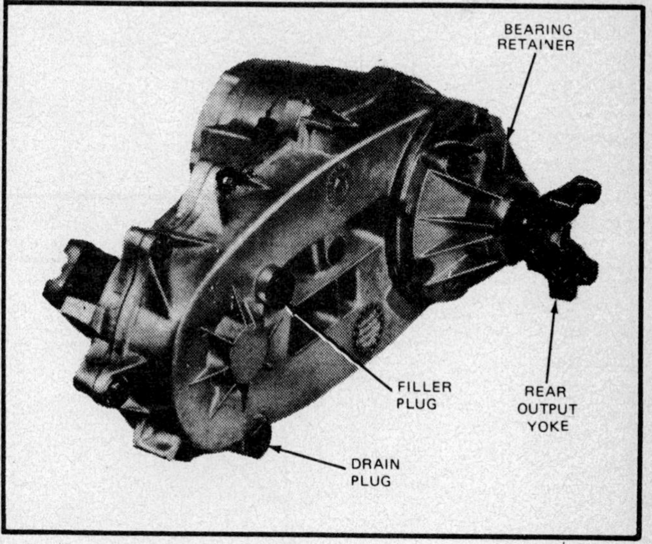

New process 208 rear case view

2. Place the three space rings in position on the rear output shaft. Liberally coat the shaft with petroleum jelly and install the two rows (60 each) of needle bearings in position on the rear output shaft.

3. Carefully slide the sprocket gear carrier over the needle bearings. Be careful not to dislodge any of the needles.

4. Install the retaining ring on the sprocket gear.

5. Slide the chain drive sprocket onto the sprocket carrier gear.

6. Install the thrust washer and snap ring on the rear output shaft.

7. Install the shift selector plate and washer through the front of the case.

8. Place the shift lever assembly on the shift control shaft and torque the nut to 14–20 ft. lbs.

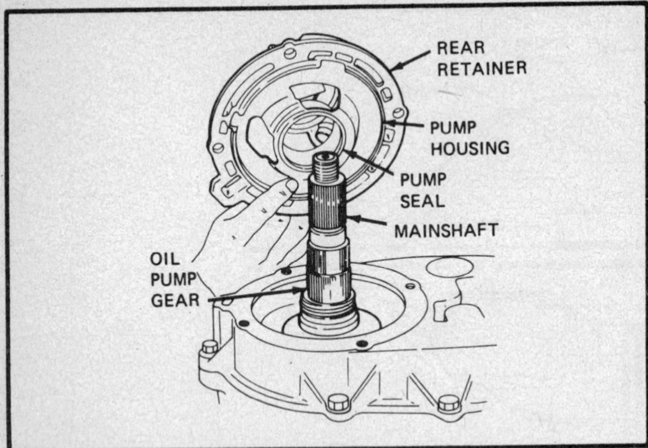

Rear retainer

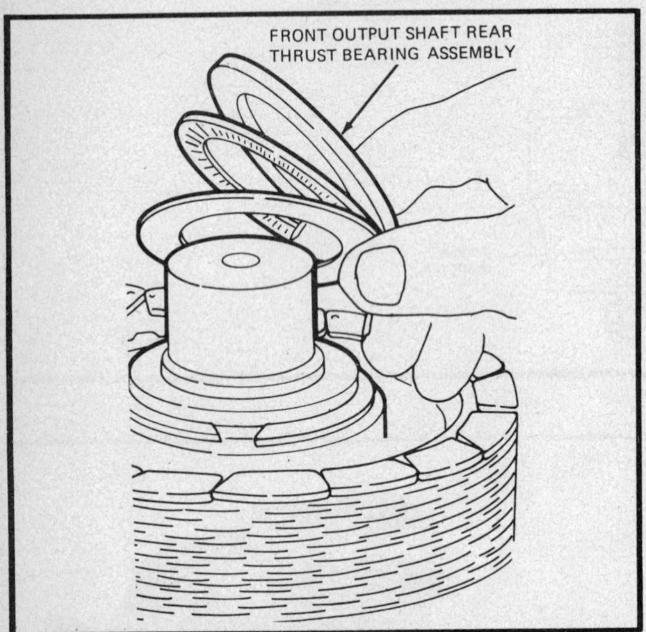

Front output shaft rear thrust washer

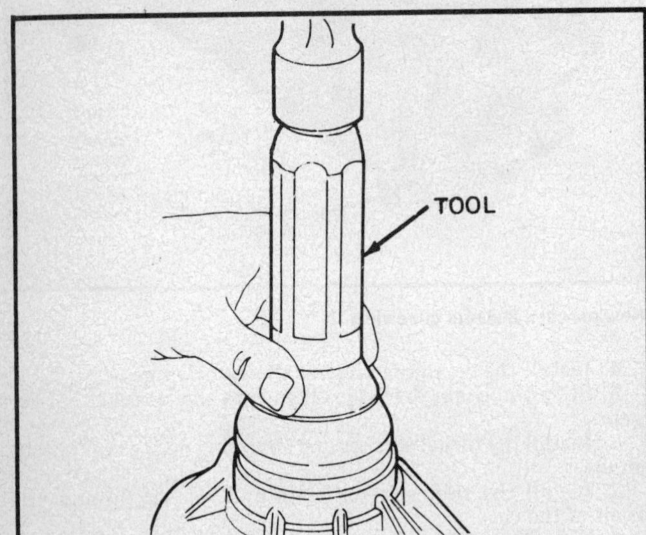

Rear seal installation

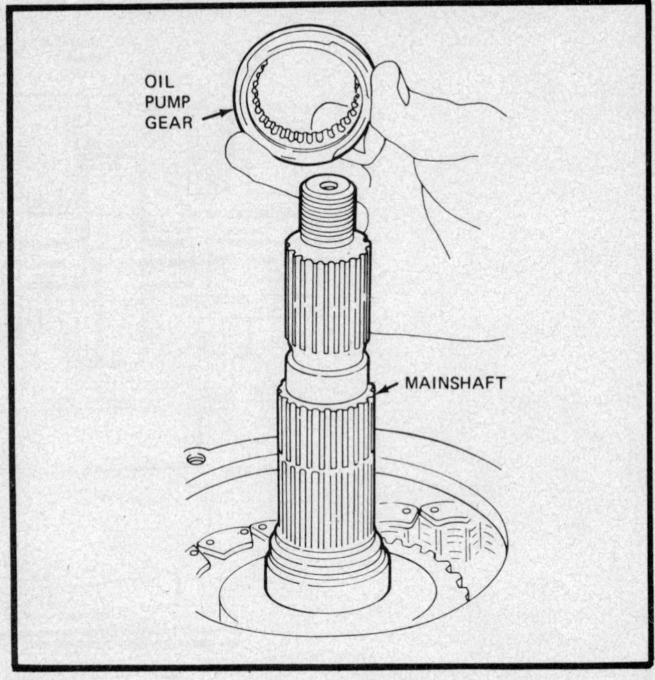

Oil pump

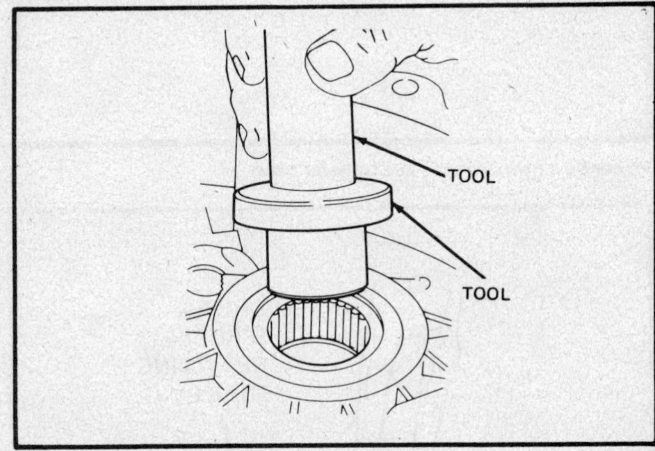

Front output shaft rear bearing installation

9. Place the locking plate in the front case half and torque the bolts to 25–35 ft. lbs.

10. Place the thrust bearing and washer over the input shaft of the sun gear. Insert the input shaft through the front case half from the inside and insert the thrust bearing.

11. Install the planetary gear assembly so the fixed plate and planetary gears engage the sun gear.

12. Slide the annulus gear and clutch assembly with the shift fork assembly engaged, over the hub of the planetary gear assembly. The shift fork pin must engage the slot in the shift selector plate. Install the thrust washer and snap ring.

13. Position the shift rail through the shift fork hub in the front case. Tap lightly with a soft hammer to seat the rail in the hole.

14. Position the sliding clutch shift fork on the shift rail and place the sliding clutch and clutch shift spring into the front case half. Slide the rear output shaft into the case.

15. On the output side of the front output shaft, assemble the thin thrust washer, thrust bearing, and thick thrust washer and partially insert the front output shaft into the case.

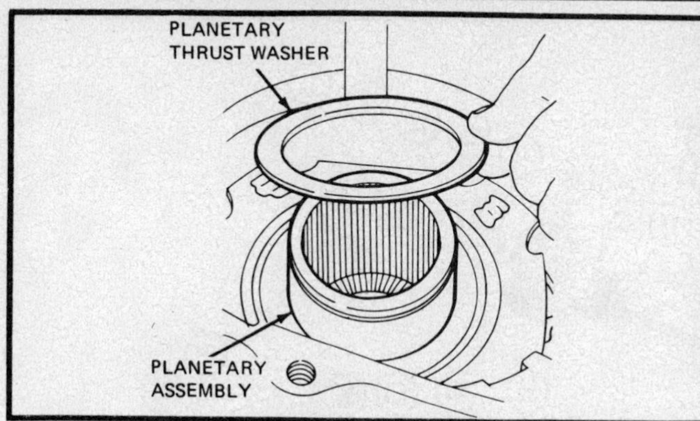

Planetary thrust washer and planetary assembly

16. Place the drive chain on the rear output shaft drive gear. Insert the rear output shaft into the front case half and engage the drive chain on the front output shaft drive gear. Push the front output shaft into position in the case.

17. Assemble the thin thrust washer, thrust bearing and thick thrust washer on the inside of the front output shaft drive gear.

18. Position the magnetic chip collector into position in the front case half.

19. Place a bead of RTV sealant completely around the face of the front case half and assemble the case halves being careful that the shift rail and forward output shafts are properly retained.

20. Alternately tighten the bolts to 20–25 ft. lbs.

21. Slide the oil pump gear over the input shaft and slide the spacer collar into position.

22. Engage the speedometer drive gear onto the rear output shaft and slide the retaining ring into position.

23. Use petroleum jelly to hold the nylon oil pump housing in position at the rear bearing retainer. Apply a bead of RTV sealant around the mounting surface of the retainer and carefully position the retainer assembly over the output shaft and onto the rear case half. The retainer must be installed so that the vent hole is vertical when the case is installed.

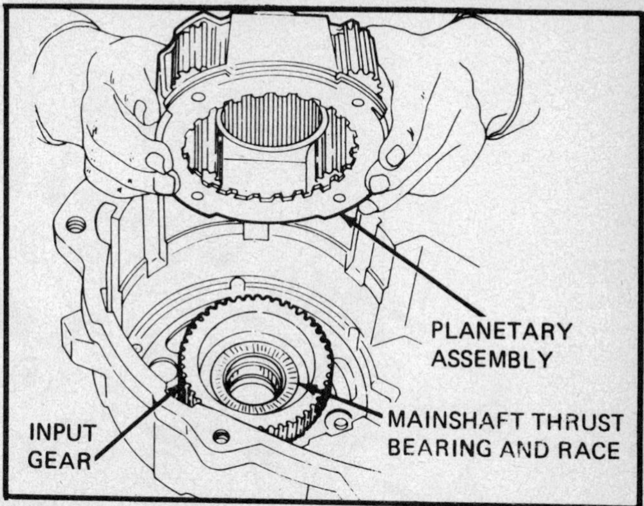

Input gear, mainshaft thrust bearing and planetary installation

24. Torque the retainer bolts alternately to 20–25 ft. lbs.

25. Place a new thrust washer under each yoke and install the yokes on their respective shafts. Place the oil slinger under the front yoke. Torque the nuts to 90–130 ft. lbs.

26. Install the poppet ball, spring and screw in the front case half. Torque the screw to 20–25 ft. lbs.

27. Install the 4WD indicator switch and washer and tighten to 15–20 ft. lbs.

28. Fill the unit with 6 pints of Ford CJ fluid or DEXRON®II.

New Process 219

Introduced in the 1980 model year of Jeep® vehicles as the Quadra-Trac®, this is a full-time unit. The 4WD mode is fully differentiated in 4H only. The 4L and Lock ranges are undifferentiated. The 4H differentiation is accomplished by a torque biasing viscous coupling and an open differential connected to the coupling. Two drive sprockets and an interconnecting drive chain are used to distribute input torque.

Disassembly

1. Drain the lubricant from the case.
2. Remove the front and rear output shaft yokes and discard the yoke seal washers and yoke nuts.
3. Mark the rear retainer and rear case for an alignment reference.
4. Unbolt and remove the rear retainer. If necessary, use a soft mallet to loosen the retainer. Under no circumstances should the retainer be pried off.
5. Remove the differential shims and speedometer drive gear from the rear output shaft. Mark the shims for reference.
6. Remove the rear output bearing snap-ring and remove the bearing from the retainer using a soft mallet.

NOTE: The rear output bearing has one side shielded. Note this for reassembly.

7. Remove the rear output shaft seal from the retainer using a screwdriver or punch.
8. Position the front case assembly on wood blocks. The blocks should have V cuts made in them for more positive support of the case.
9. Remove the case halve bolts. The case halves may be pried apart using a screwdriver in the notches provided at the case ends.

NOTE: The two case end bolts have flat washers and alignment dowels. Note their location for assembly.

10. Remove the rear output shaft and viscous coupling as an assembly. Tap the shaft with a plastic mallet if necessary.
11. Remove the O-ring seal and pilot roller bearings from the main shaft.
12. Remove the rear output shaft from the viscous coupling.
13. Remove the shift rail spring from the rail.
14. Remove the plastic oil pump from the shaft bore in the rear case. Note the pump position for assembly reference. The end with the recess must face the shaft bore when installed.
15. Remove the rear output shaft bearing seal from the case. A screwdriver may be used to pry it out.
16. Remove the front output shaft thrust bearing assembly. Remove the thick washer, bearing and thin washer.
17. Remove the driven sprocket retaining snap-ring.
18. Remove the drive sprocket, drive chain, driven sprocket, side gear clutch and clutch gear as an assembly. Place the assembly on a workbench and mark the components for assembly.

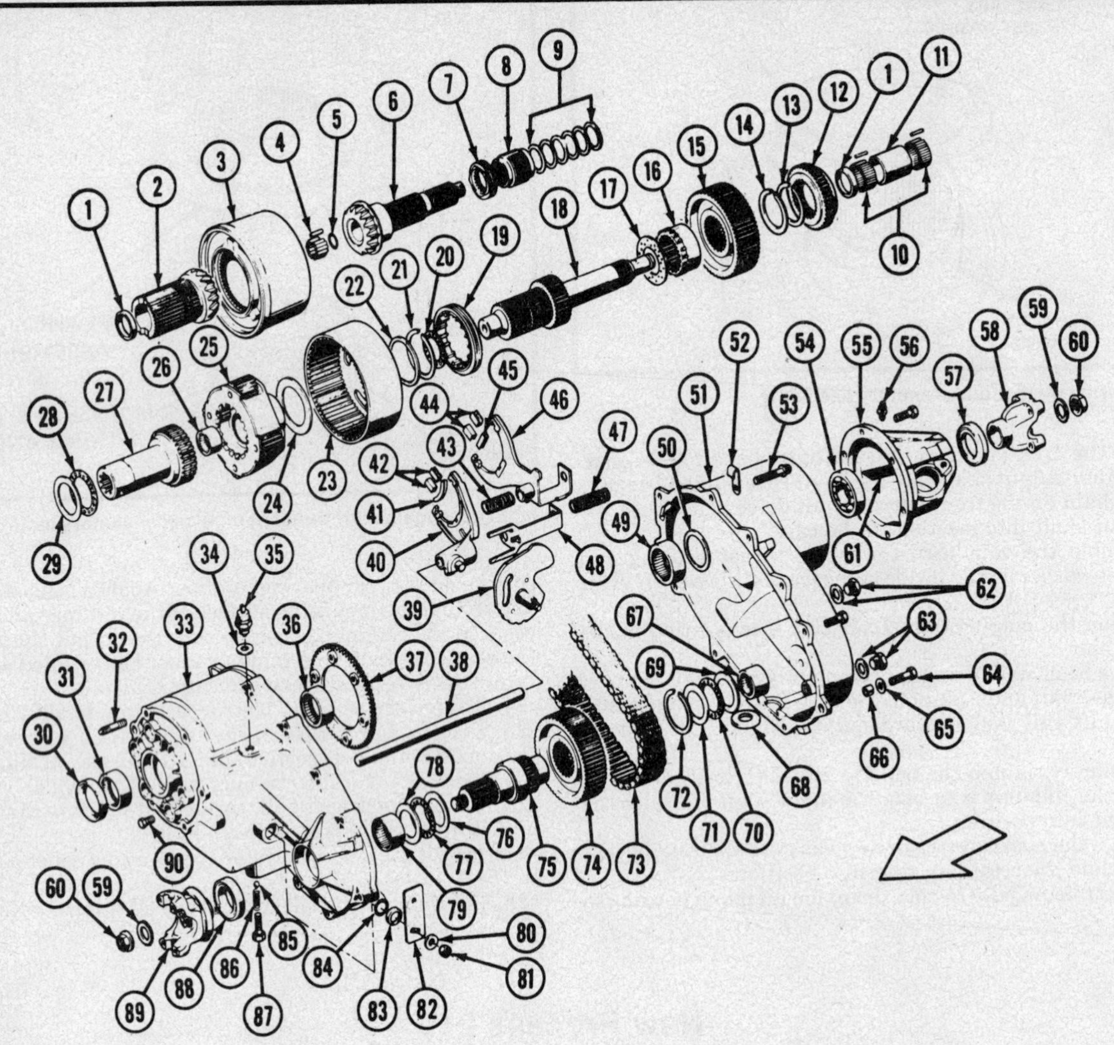

1. Mainshaft rear bearing spacer—short (2)
2. Side gear
3. Viscous coupling and differential assembly
4. Mainshaft rear pilot roller bearings (15)
5. Mainshaft O-ring
6. Rear output shaft
7. Oil pump
8. Speedometer gear
9. Differential end play shims (selective)
10. Mainshaft needle bearings (82)
11. Mainshaft rear bearing spacer
12. Clutch gear
13. Clutch gear locating ring
14. Drive sprocket locating ring
15. Drive sprocket
16. Side gear clutch
17. Mainshaft thrust washer
18. Mainshaft
19. Clutch sleeve
20. Mainshaft thrust bearing
21. Annulus gear retaining ring
22. Annulus gear thrust washer
23. Annulus gear
24. Planetary thrust washer
25. Planetary assembly
26. Mainshaft front pilot bearing
27. Input gear
28. Input gear thrust bearing
29. Input gear thrust bearing race
30. Input gear oil seal
31. Input gear front bearing
32. Front case mounting stud (6)
33. Front case
34. Lock mode indicator switch gasket
35. Lock mode indicator switch
36. Input gear rear bearing
37. Low range lockplate
38. Shift rail
39. Range sector
40. Range fork
41. Range fork insert
42. Range fork pads
43. Mode fork spring
44. Mode fork pads
45. Mode fork insert
46. Mode fork
47. Shift rail spring
48. Mode fork bracket
49. Rear output shaft bearing
50. Rear output shaft bearing seal
51. Rear case
52. Wiring clip
53. Spline bolt
54. Rear output bearing
55. Rear retainer
56. Vent
57. Output shaft oil seal
58. Rear yoke
59. Yoke seal washer
60. Yoke locknut
61. Vent chamber seal
62. Fill plug and gasket
63. Drain plug and gasket
64. Rear case bolt
65. Washer (2)
66. Case alignment dowel
67. Front output shaft rear bearing
68. Magnet
69. Front output shaft rear thrust bearing race (thick)
70. Front output shaft rear thrust bearing
71. Front output shaft rear thrust bearing race (thin)
72. Driven sprocket retaining snap-ring
73. Drive chain
74. Driven sprocket
75. Front output shaft
76. Front output shaft front thrust bearing race (thin)
77. Front output shaft front thrust bearing
78. Front output shaft front thrust bearing race (thick)
79. Front output shaft front bearing
80. Washer
81. Locknut
82. Operating lever
83. Range sector shaft seal retainer
84. Range sector shaft seal
85. Detent ball
86. Detent spring
87. Detent retaining bolt
88. Front output shaft seal
89. Front yoke
90. Lockplate bolts

Exploded view of the new process 219 transfer case

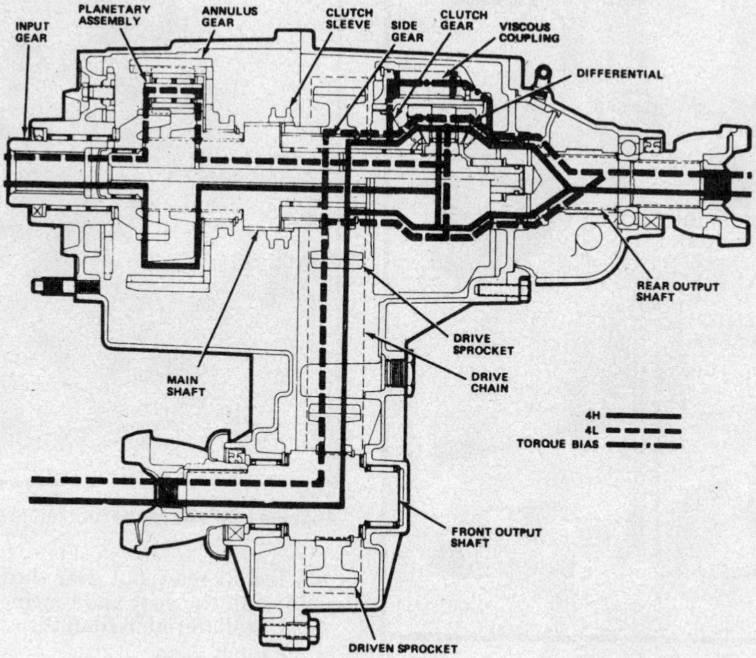

Power flow new process 219 transfer case

19. Remove the needle bearings and spacers from the main shaft and side gear bore. A total of 82 bearings and three spacers is used.
20. Remove the side gear/clutch gear assembly from the drive sprocket. Remove two snap-rings and remove the clutch gear from the side gear.
21. Remove the side gear clutch, main shaft thrust washer and remaining main shaft needle bearing spacer.
22. Remove the front output shaft and shaft thrust bearing assembly. Note the installation sequence of the bearing assembly.
23. Remove the front output shaft seal from the front case using a screwdriver or punch.
24. Remove the shift rail spring from the shift rail.
25. Remove the clutch sleeve, mode fork and spring as an assembly.
26. Remove the main shaft thrust washer and main shaft. Grasp the shaft and pull it straight up and out.
27. Move the range operating lever downward to the last detent position.
28. Disengage the range fork lug from the range sector slot.
29. Remove the annulus gear retaining snap-ring and thrust washer.
30. Remove the annulus gear and range fork.
31. Remove the planetary thrust washer from the hub.
32. Remove the planetary assembly.
33. Remove the main shaft thrust bearing from the input gear.
34. Remove the input gear and remove the input gear thrust bearing and race.
35. Remove the range selector detent ball and spring retaining bolt and remove the detent ball and spring.
36. Remove the range selector and operating lever attaching nut and lockwasher, and remove the lever.

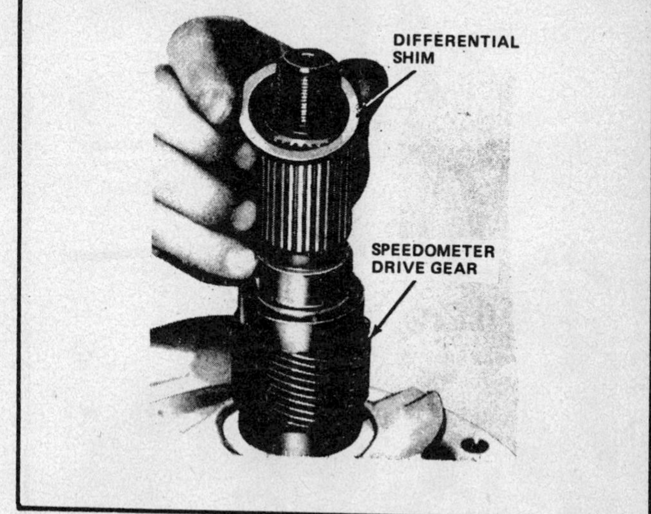

Differential shim, speedometer gear and oil pump

37. Remove the range selector.
38. Remove the range selector O-ring and retainer.
39. Remove the input gear oil seal from the front case with a screwdriver.

Assembly

Lubricate all parts before assembly with 10W–30 motor oil. Petroleum jelly will be indicated for some assemblies. Do not use chassis lube or other heavy lubricants.

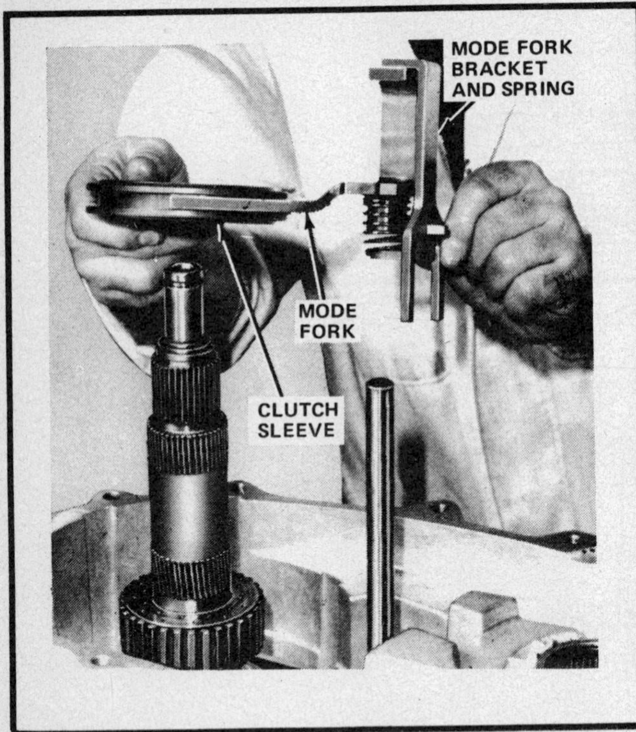

Clutch sleeve and mode fork removal and installation

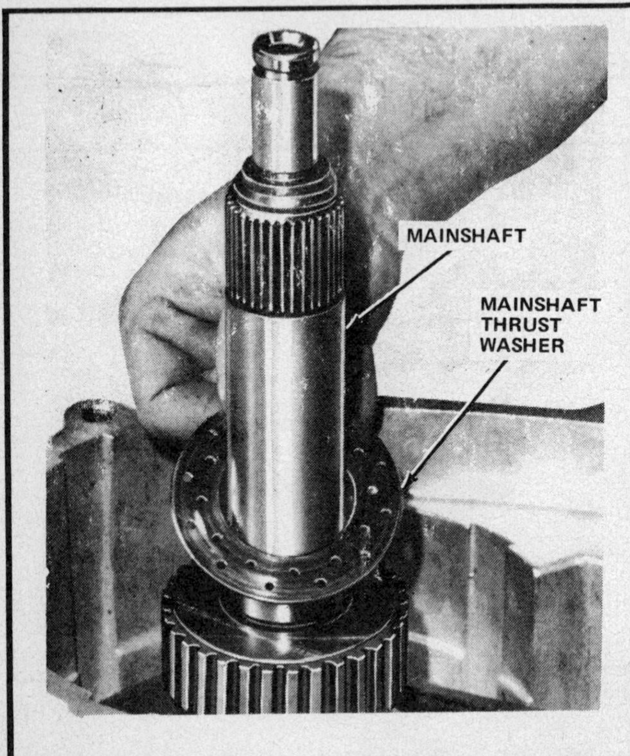

Mainshaft and thrust washer

1. Install new input gear and rear output shaft bearing oil seals. Seat the seals flush with the edge of the seal bore or with the seal groove in the case. Coat the seal lips with petroleum jelly after installation.
2. Install the input gear thrust bearing race in the case counterbore.

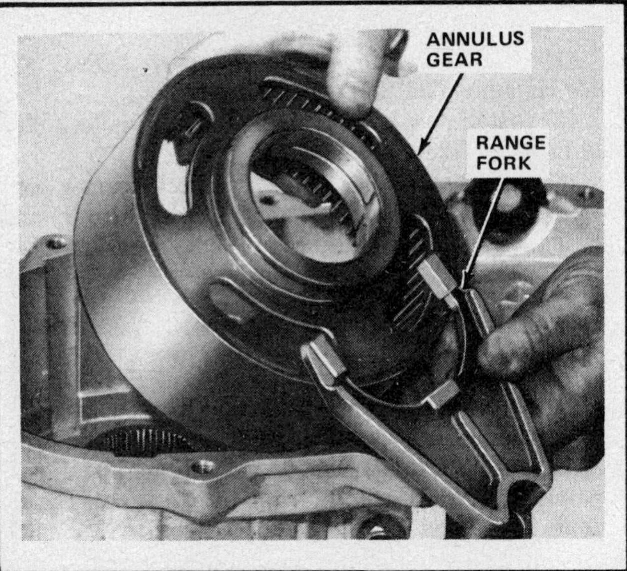

Annulus gear and range fork removal and installation

3. Install the input gear thrust bearing on the input gear and install the gear and bearing in the case.
4. Install the main shaft thrust bearing in the bearing recess in the input gear.
5. Install the planetary assembly on the input gear. Make sure that the planetary pinion teeth mesh fully with the input gear.
6. Install the planetary thrust washer on the planetary hub.
7. Install a new sector shaft O-ring and retainer in the shaft bore in the case.
8. Install the range selector in the front case. Install the operating lever on the sector shaft and install the lever attaching washer and locknut on the shaft. Tighten the locknut to 17 ft. lbs.
9. Install the detent spring, ball and retaining bolt in the front case detent bore. Tighten the bolt to 22 ft. lbs.
10. Move the range selector to the last detent position.
11. Assemble the annulus gear and range fork. Install the assembled fork and gear over the planetary assembly. Be sure that the annulus gear is fully meshed with the planetary pinions.
12. Insert the range fork lug in the range detent slot.
13. Install the annulus thrust washer and retaining ring on the annulus gear hub.
14. Align the main shaft thrust washer in theinput gear, if necessary.
15. Install the main shaft. Be sure the shaft is fully seated in the input gear.
16. Install the main shaft thrust washer on the main shaft.
17. Install the short main shaft needle bearing spacer on the shaft.
18. Apply a liberal coating of petroleum jelly to the main shaft needle bearing surface and install 41 of the 82 needle bearings on the shaft. Be sure the bearings seat on the short spacer.
19. Install the long needle bearing spacer on the shaft. Lower the spacer onto the previously installed needle bearings carefully to avoid displacing them.
20. Align the shift rail bore in the case with the bore in the range fork and install the shift rail.

NOTE: Remove all traces of oil from the case shift rail bore before installing the rail. Oil in the case bore may prevent the rail from seating completely and prevent rear case installation.

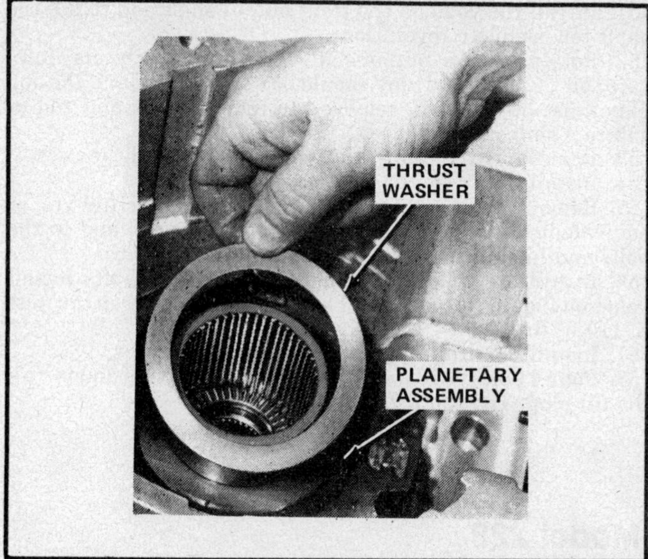

Planetary thrust washer removal and installation

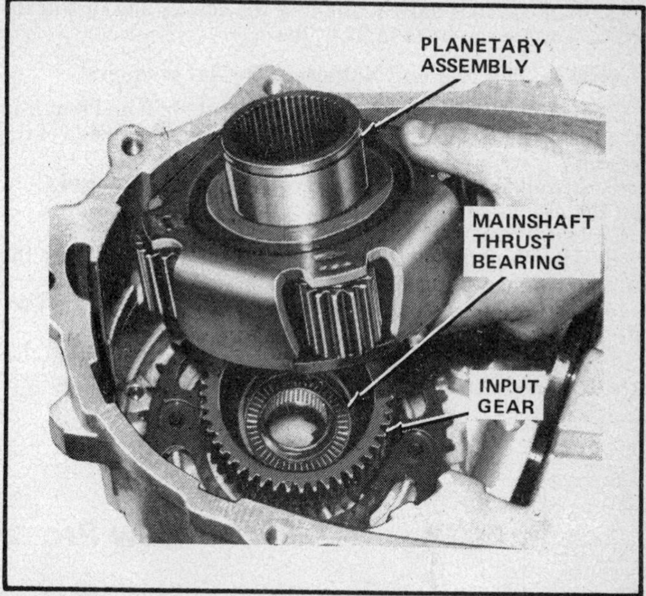

Planetary assembly removal and installation

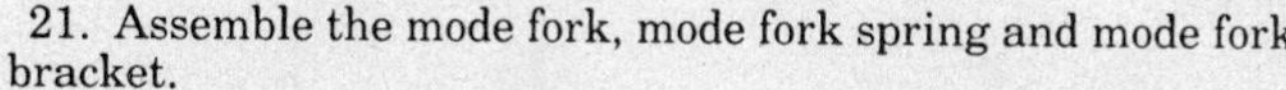

21. Assemble the mode fork, mode fork spring and mode fork bracket.
22. Install the clutch sleeve in the mode fork. Be sure the sleeve is positioned so that the ID numbers on the sleeve face upward when the sleeve is installed.
23. Align the clutch sleeve and mode fork assembly with the shift rail and install the assembly on the shift rail and main shaft. Be sure that the clutch sleeve is meshed with the main shaft gear.
24. Lubricate the remaining 41 needle bearings and place them on the main shaft.
25. Install the side gear clutch on the main shaft with the teeth facing downward. Be sure the gear teeth mesh with the clutch sleeve.
26. Install the remaining short main shaft needle bearing spacer. Install the spacer carefully to avoid displacing previously installed bearings.
27. Install the front output shaft front thrust bearing in the front case. Correct sequence is thick race, bearing, thin race.
28. Install the front output shaft in the front case.
29. Install the clutch gear on the side gear. The tapered side of the clutch gear teeth must face the side gear teeth.
30. Install the clutch gear and drive sprocket locating snap-rings on the side gear. Install the snap-rings so that they face each other.
31. Position the drive and driven sprockets in the drive chain and install the assembled side and clutch gears in the drive sprocket.
32. Install the assembled drive chain, sprockets and side gear on the main shaft and front output shaft. Align the sprockets with the shaft, keeping the assembly level and carefully lower the assembly onto both shafts simultaneously. Do not displace any of the needle bearings.
33. Install the driven sprocket retaining snap-ring.
34. Install the front output shaft rear thrust bearing assembly on the front output shaft. Correct installation sequence is thin race, thrust bearing, thick race.
35. Install the shift rail spring on the shift rail.
36. Install a new O-ring on the main shaft pilot bearing hub.
37. Coat the main shaft pilot roller bearing hub and bearings with a liberal amount of petroleum jelly and install the rollers on the shaft.
38. Install the rear output shaft in the viscous coupling. Be sure it is fully seated.
39. Install the assembled viscous coupling and rear output shaft on the main shaft. Align the main shaft pilot hub with the pilot bearing bore in the rear output shaft and carefully lower the assembly onto the main shaft. Take care to avoid displacing the roller bearings.

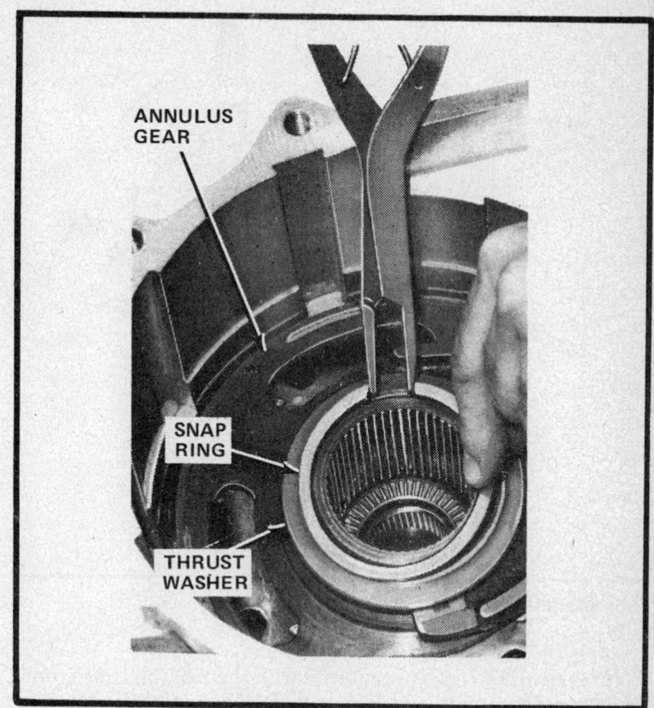

Annulus gear snap-ring and thrust washer

40. Align the clutch gear teeth with the viscous coupling teeth and seat the coupling fully onto the clutch gear.

NOTE: When correctly installed, the clutch gear teeth will not be visible or extend out of the coupling.

41. Install the magnet in the front case, if removed.
42. Clean the mating surfaces of the case halves thoroughly.
43. Apply Loctite®515 or equivalent to the mating surfaces and all attaching bolts.

44. Join the case halves, aligning the dowels and install the bolts. Torque the bolts to 22 ft. lbs.

NOTE: The two end bolts require flat washers.

45. Install the oil pump on the rear output shaft and seat it in the case. The side with the recess should face the inside of the case.
46. Install the speedometer drive gear and differential shift, on the output shaft.
47. Install the vent chamber seal in the rear retainer.
48. Align and install the rear retainer on the case. Make the retainer finger tight only.
49. Install the yoke on the rear output shaft. Make the yoke finger tight only.
50. Mount a dial indicator on the rear retainer. Position the indicator stylus so that it contacts the top of the yoke nut.
51. Install the yoke on the front output shaft and rotate the shaft ten complete revolutions.
52. Rotate the front output shaft again and note the play indicated on the dial. End play should be 0.002–0.010 in. If the end play must be adjusted, remove the rear retainer and add or subtract shims as required.
53. Remove both output shaft yokes and discard the nuts.
54. Install the front and rear yoke seals.
55. Remove the rear retainer bolts, apply Loctite®515 or equivalent to the mating surface of the retainer and to the bolts and install the bolts. Torque them to 22 ft. lbs.
56. Install new yoke seal washers on the output shafts, install yokes on the shafts and install new yoke nuts. Tighten the nuts to 110 ft. lbs.
57. Install the drain plug and tighten to 18 ft. lbs.
58. Pour 4 pints of 10W–30 motor oil into the case and install the fill plug. Tighten it to 18 ft. lbs.

New Process Model 228

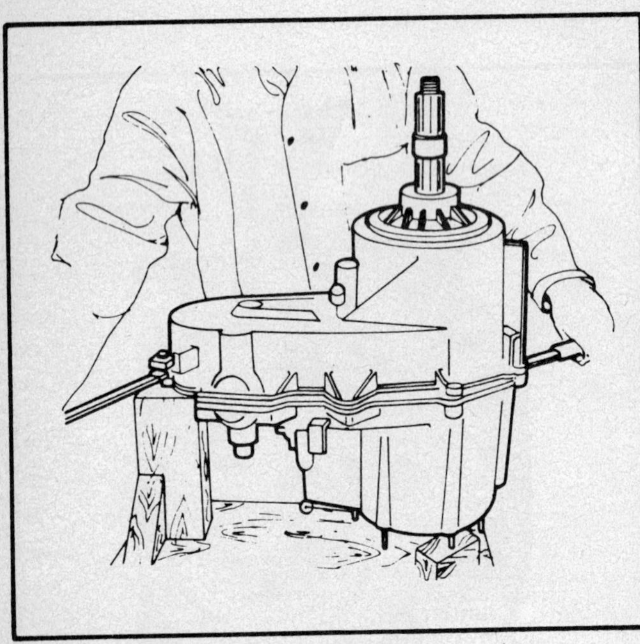

Separating the transfer case halves

The 228 transfer case is very similar to the 229 full time transfer case used on previous Jeep models. The main difference in these two transfer cases, is that the 228 uses a differential unit in place of the viscous coupling. It also uses modified shift collars to preclude engine run away during a delayed shift.

SHIFT MOTOR

Removal and Installation

1. Disconnect the shift motor link from the range lever and discard the lever grommet.
2. Remove the nut and bolt that hold the shift motor bracket to the transfer case and remove the bracket and motor as an assembly. Slide the shift boot inside and remove the E-ring that holds the motor in the bracket.
3. Remove the motor from the transfer case.
4. Replace old gaskets with new gaskets where ever necessary and installation is the reverse order of the removal procedure.

228 TRANSFER CASE

Removal

1. Raise and support the vehicle safely. Drain the lubricant out of the transfer case into a suitable drain pan.
2. Disconnect the speedometer cable and vent hose. Disconnect the transfer case shift lever link at the opening lever.
3. Place a suitable jack stand or equivalent, under the transmission and removew the rear crossmember. Mark the transfer case front and rear output shafts at the transfer case yokes and propeller shafts for installation alignment reference.
4. Disconnect the front and rear propeller shafts at the transfer case yokes and secure the shafts along the frame. Disconnect the shift motor vacuum hoses and the transfer case shift linkage.
5. Place a suitable transmission jack under the transfer case. Remove the transfer case to transmission mounting bolts and move the transfer case assembly rearward until it clears the transmission output shaft.
6. Lower the jack with the transfer case on it and remove the transfer case from the vehicle. Remove all gasket material from the rear of the transmission adapter housing.

Disassembly

1. Drain all the lubricant from the transfer case and remove the front and rear yoke nuts along with their seal washers. Discard the seal washers.
2. Mark the front and rear yokes for easy installation alignment reference and remove the front and rear yokes. It may be necessary to use tool # J–8614–01 or equivalent to remove the yokes.
3. Place the transfer case on wooden blocks. Cut V-notches in the blocks of wood so there is clearance for the front case mounting studs. Mark the retainer and the rear case for easy assembly reference.
4. Remove the rear retainer bolts and pry off the retainer with a suitable pry bar. Remove the differential shim(s) and speedometer drive gear from the rear output shaft.
5. Remove the bolts that attach the rear transfer case half to the front case half. Be sure to get the washer that are used with the bolts on each end of the transfer case.

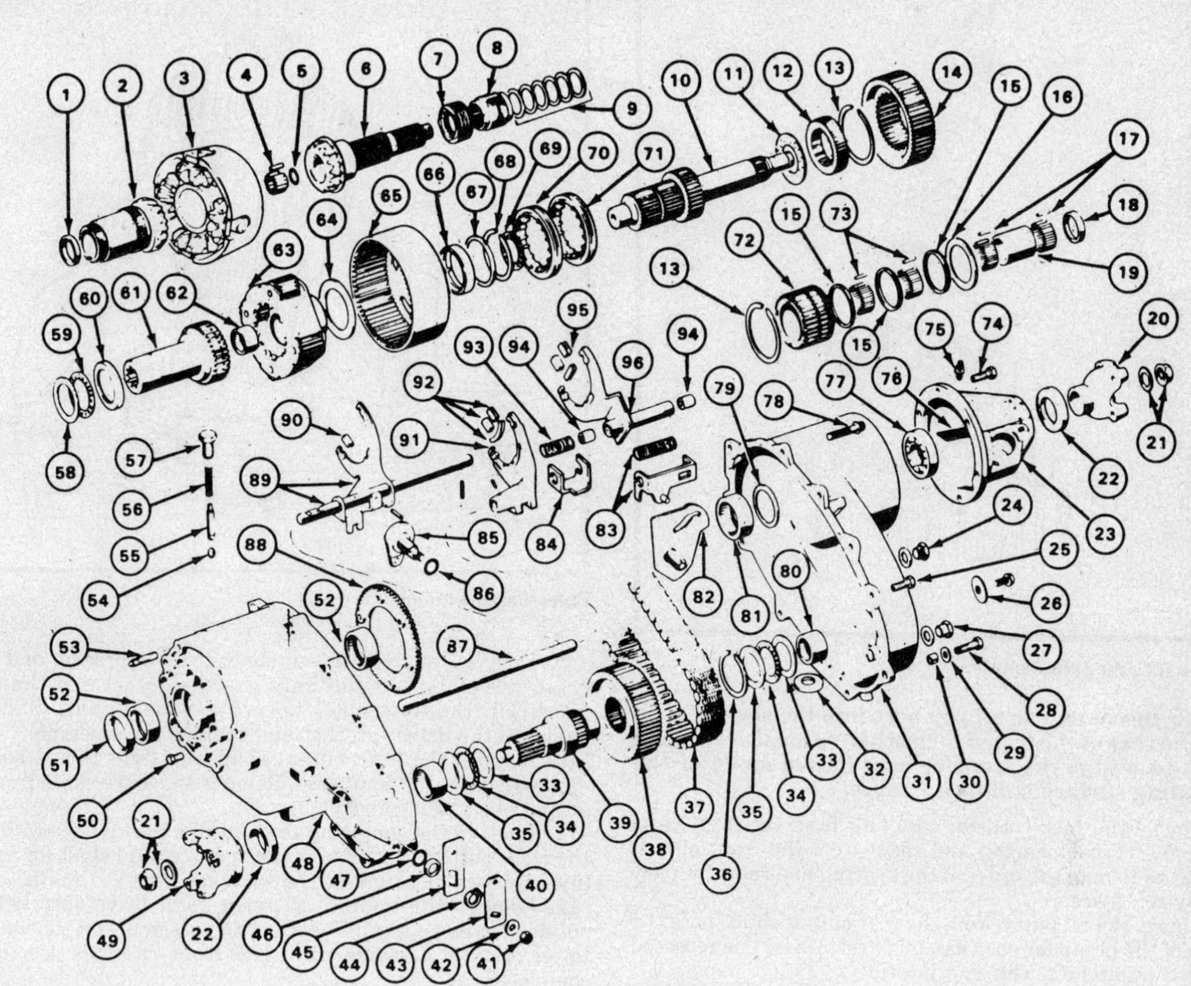

1. Spacer
2. Side gear
3. Differential
4. Pilot bearing rollers (15)
5. O-ring seal
6. Rear output shaft
7. Oil pump
8. Speedometer drive gear
9. Shim kit
10. Mainshaft
11. Mainshaft thrust washer
12. Spline gear
13. Retaining ring
14. Sprocket
15. Spacer
16. Sprocket thrust washer
17. Side gear roller (82)
18. Spacer (short)
19. Spacer (long)
20. Rear yoke
21. Nut and seal washer
22. Seal
23. Rear retainer
24. Plug assembly
25. Bolt
26. Identification tag
27. Plug assembly
28. Dowel bolt
29. Dowl bolt washer
30. Case half dowell
31. Rear half case
32. Magnet
33. Front output shaft bearing assembly race (thick)
34. Front output shaft bearing assembly thrust
35. Front output shaft bearing assembly race (thin)
36. Retaining ring
37. Chain
38. Driven sprocket
39. Front output shaft
40. Front output front bearing
41. Nut
42. Washer
43. Mode lever
44. Snap ring
45. Range lever
46. O-ring retainer
47. O-ring seal
48. Front half case
49. Front output yoke
50. Low range plate bolt
51. Input shaft oil seal
52. Input shaft bearing
53. Stud
54. Ball
55. Plunger
56. Plunger spring
57. Screw
58. Input race
59. Input thrust bearing
60. Input race (thick)
61. Input shaft
62. Input bearing
63. Planetary gear assembly
64. Input gear thrust washer
65. Annulus gear assembly
66. Annulus bushing
67. Thrust washer
68. Retaining ring
69. Thrust bearing
70. High range sliding clutch sleeve
71. Mode sliding clutch sleeve
72. Carrier
73. Carrier rollers (120)
74. Rear retainer bolt
75. Vent
76. Vent seal
77. Output bearing
78. Bolt
79. Seal
80. Front output rear bearing
81. Output shaft inner bearing
82. Range sector
83. Range bracket (outer) and spring
84. Range bracket (inner)
85. Mode sector
86. O-ring seal
87. Range rail
88. Low range lockout plate
89. Mode fork, rail and pin
90. Mode fork pad
91. Range fork
92. Range fork pads
93. Range bracket spring (inner)
94. Locking fork bushing
95. Locking fork pads
96. Locking fork

Exploded view of the 228 transfer case

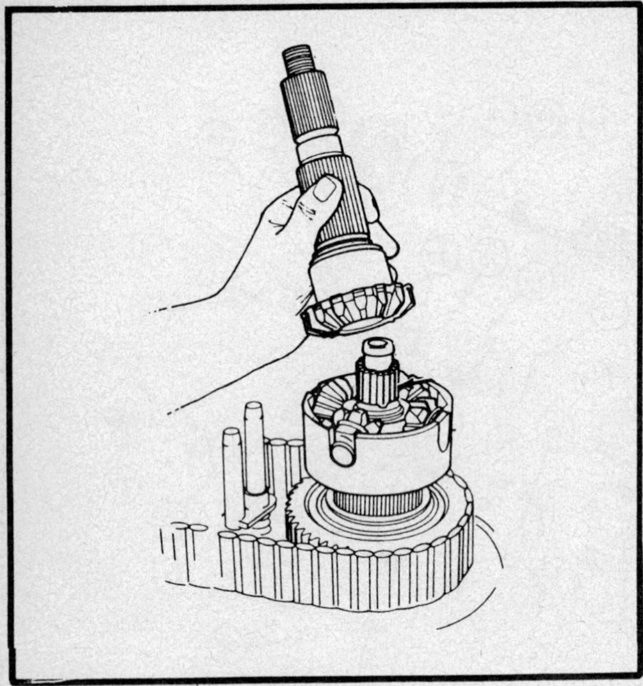

Removing the rear output shaft

NOTE: Insert two small pry bars into the slots at each end of the rear of the transfer case half to loosen it. Do not attempt to wedge the transfer case halves apart or the case mating surface will be damages.

6. Remove the rear transfer case half from the front case. Remove the thrust bearing and races from the front output shaft and be to note the order of the bearing and races for easy assembly reference.

7. Remove the oil pump from the rear output shaft, note the position of the pump for easy assembly reference. The recessed side of the pump faces the case interior.

8. Remove the rear output shaft from the main shaft and remove the 15 main needle bearing rollers from the shaft or coupling. Remove the main shaft O-ring from the end of the shaft. Remove the differential from the main shaft and side gear.

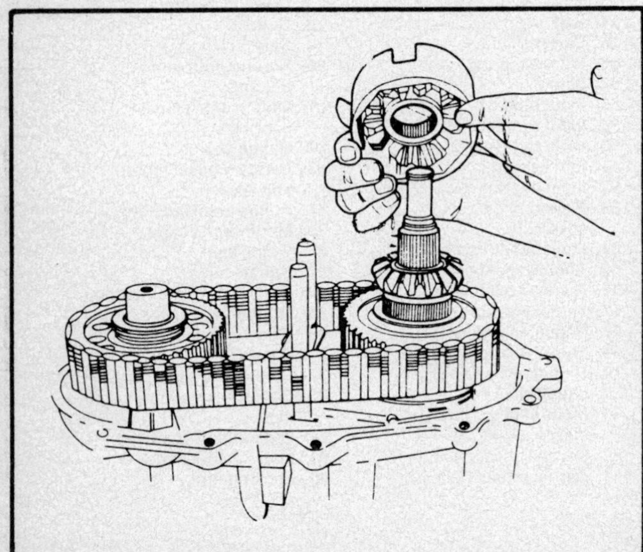

Removing the differential

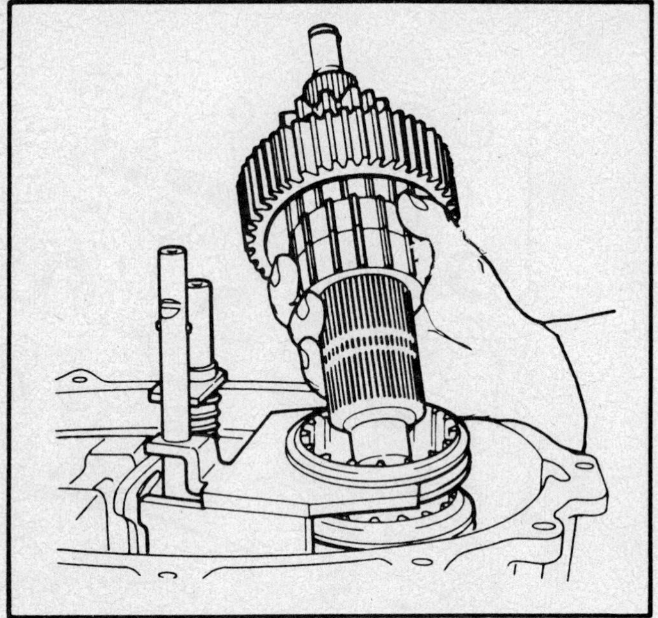

Removing the mainshaft

9. Remove the front output shaft, driven sprocket and drive chain assembly. Lift the front shaft, sprocket and chain upward. Tilt the front shaft toward the main shaft. Slide the chain off the drive sprocket and remove the assembly.

10. Remove the front output shaft and front thrust bearing assembly from the front case. Remove the drive chain from the output shaft and sprocket.

11. Remove the snap ring that retains the riven sprocket on the front output shaft. Mark the sprocket and shaft for assembly reference and remove the sprocket from the shaft.

12. Remove the main shaft, side gear, drive sprocket and spline gear as an assembly. Place the assembly on a clean shop towel and set it aside until the front case disassembly is completed.

13. Remove the mode fork, shift rail and mode sliding clutch sleeve as an assembly. Mark the sleeve and fork for easy assembly reference and remove the sleeve from the fork.

NOTE: The mode fork and rail are pinned together so that they will operate as a unit. Remove the pin to separate the two components if necessary.

14. Remove the locking fork, high range sliding clutch sleeve, fork brackets and fork spring as an assembly. Be sure to take note of the position of these components for an easy assembly reference.

15. Remove the range sector detent screw and remove the detent spring, plunger and ball. Move the range operating lever downward to the last detent position and disengage the low range fork lug from the range sector slot.

16. Remove the retaining snap ring from the annulus gear and remove the thrust washer. Remove the annulus gear, range fork and rail as an assembly and separate the components for cleaning and inspection.

17. Remove the planetary thrust washer from the planetary assembly hub. Remove the planetary assembly, by grasping the planetary hub and lifting the assembly upward.

18. Remove the main shaft thrust bearing from the input shaft. Remove the input shaft, input shaft thrust bearing and race.

19. Remove the range sector and operating lever attaching nut and lockwasher. Remove the lever.

20. Remove the range sector and shaft from the front case and remove the range sector O-ring and retainer.

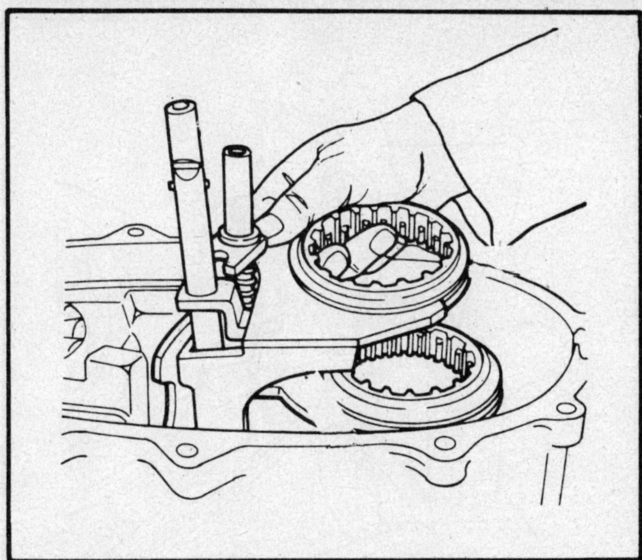

Removing the mode fork and shift rail assembly

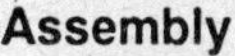

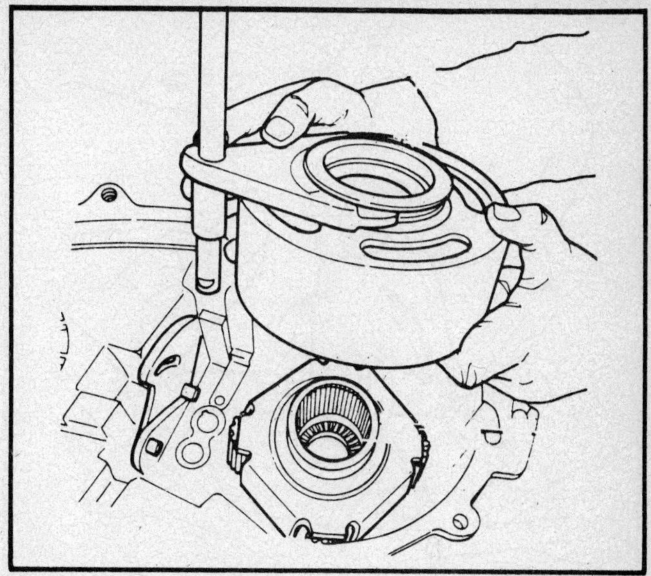

Removing the annulus gear

Assembly

NOTE: During the assembly, lubricate all of the transfer case internal components with DEXRON®II transmission fluid or petroleum jelly as indicated in the procedure. Do not use chassis lubricant or similar thick lubricants.

1. Install a replacement input shaft and rear output shaft bearing oil seals. Set the seals flush with the edge of the seal bore or in the seal groove in the transfer case. Coat the seal lips with petroleum jelly after installation.
2. Install the input shaft thrust bearing race in the transfer case counterbore. Install the input gear thrust bearing on the input shaft and install the shaft and bearing in the transfer case.
3. Install the main shaft thrust bearing in the bearing recess in the input shaft. Install the planetary assembly on the input shaft. Ensure that the planetary pinion teeth mesh fully with the input shaft.
4. Install the planetary thrust washer on the planetary hub. Install a replacement sector shaft O-ring and install the retainer in the shaft bore in the transfer case.
5. Install the O-ring on the mode sector shaft and insert the mode sector through the range sector. Install the range sector in the front of transfer case half. Install the operating lever and the snap ring on the range sector shaft.
6. Install the lever, attaching washer and lock nut on the mode sector shaft. Torque the lock nut to 17 ft. lbs. Assemble the annulus gear, range fork and rail. Install the assembled fork on and over the planetary assembly.
7. Be sure that the annulus gear is fully meshed with the planetary pinions. Engage the range sector lug into the range sector.
8. Install the annulus thrust washer and the annulus retaining ring onto the annulus gear hub. Install the detent ball, plunger, spring and retaining screw in the front transfer case half detent bore. Torque the retaining screw to 22 ft. lbs.

NOTE: The locking mode clutch sleeve and the high range clutch sleeve are not interchangeable. The sleeve splines are different. So be sure that the correct sleeve is installed in the proper shift fork. Also, the sleeves must be replaced as a set.

9. Assemble and install the locking fork, fork bracket, fork springs and high range clutch sleeves. Be sure that the lug on the fork is seated in the range sector detent slot.

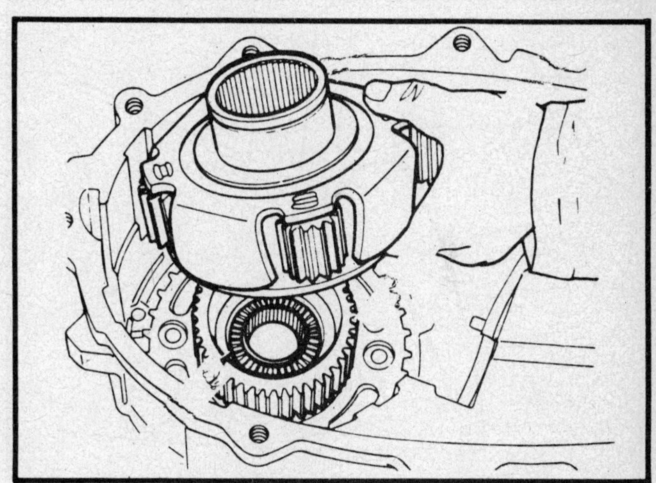

Removing the planetary assembly

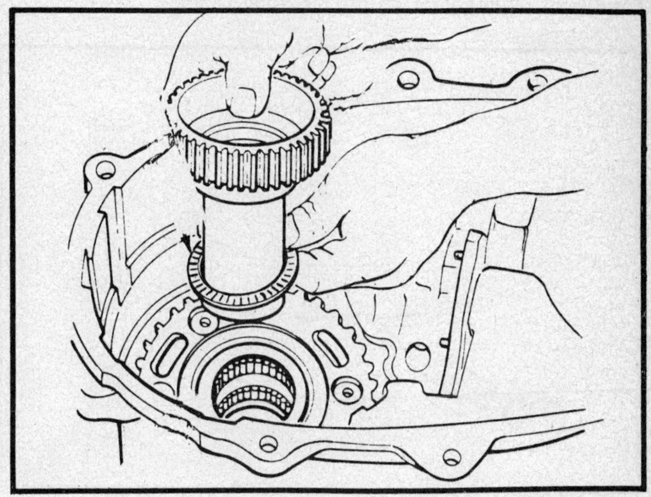

Removing the input shaft assembly

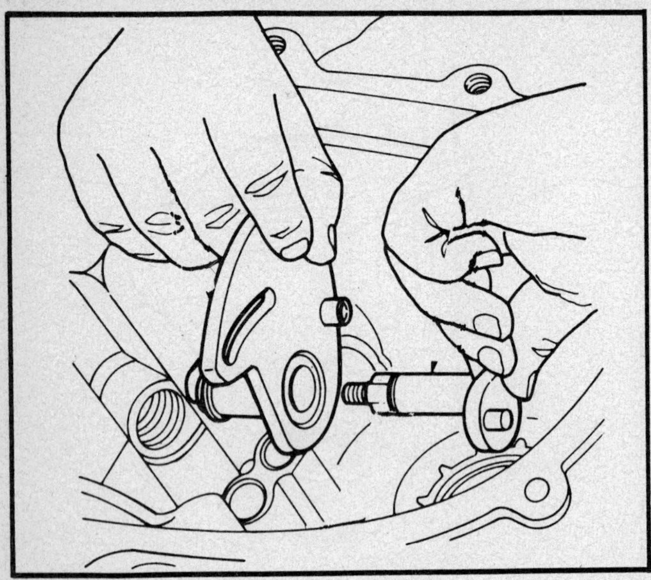

Installing the mode sector shaft into the range sector

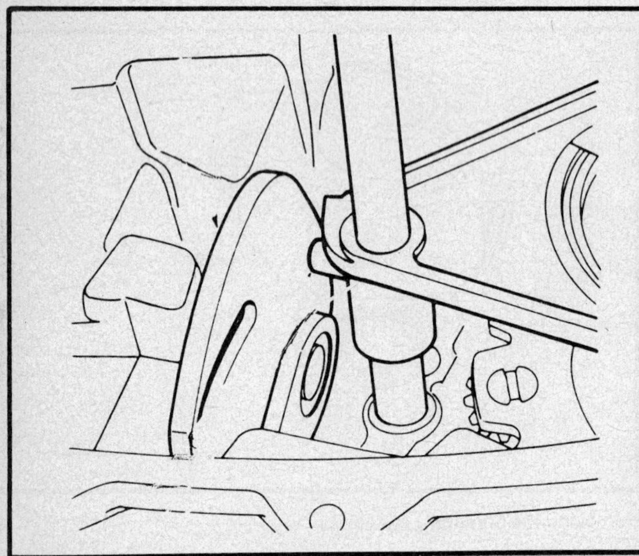

Engage the range sector lug into the range sector

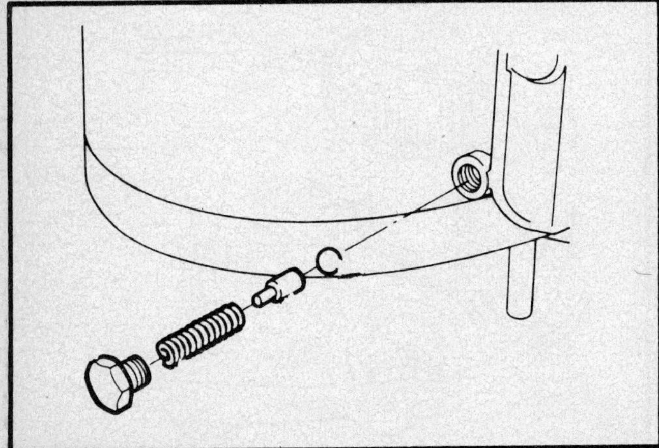

Installing the detent ball assembly

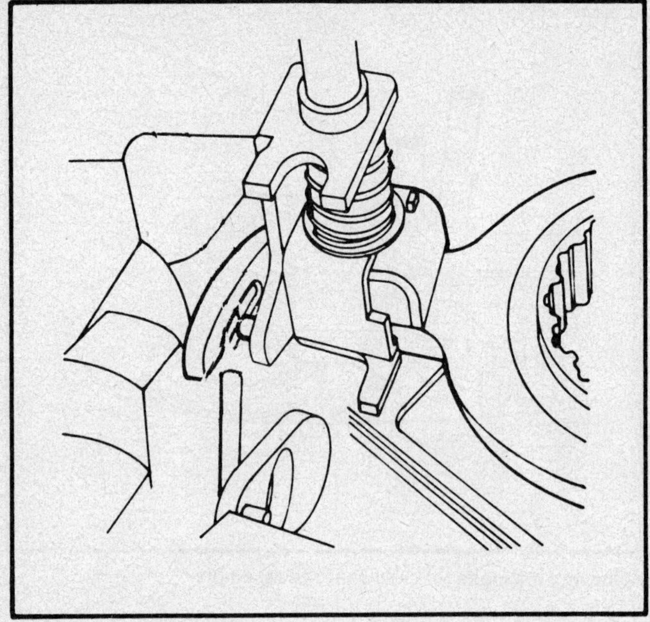

Installing the locking fork

10. Install the range fork lug in the range sector detent notch. Move the range sector to the high range position. Assemble and install the range fork, shift rail and mode clutch sleeve.

NOTE: Steps 11 to 16 are to be used if the main shaft was disassembled, when the transfer case was disassembled.

11. Install the thrust washer and a replacement O-ring on the main shaft. Install the needle bearings and bearing spacers on the main shaft. Coat the shaft bearing surface and all needle bearings with petroleum jelly.
12. Install the first 41 needle bearings and install the long bearing spacer, the remaining 41 needle bearings and the remaining short spacer. Be careful to avoid displacing the bearing when the spacers are installed. Apply additional petroleum jelly to hold the bearing in place if necessary.
13. Install the spline gear on the main shaft, be careful not to displace the bearing while installing the gear. Install the sprocket carrier in the drive sprocket and install the sprocket carrier snap rings. Make sure that the carrier and sprockets are aligned according to the reference marks made during disassembly.

NOTE: The sprocket carrier teeth are tapered on one side and the drive sprocket has a deep recess on one side. Be sure that these components are assembles so that the carrier tapered teeth and sprocket recess are on the same side.

14. Install the sprocket carrier bearings and spacers. Coat the carrier bore and all the 120 carrier needle bearings with petroleum jelly. Install the center spacer.
15. Install the 60 needle bearings in each end of the carrier and install the remaining two spacers, one at each side of the carrier. Apply additional petroleum jelly to hold the bearings in place if necessary.
16. Install the assembled sprocket carrier and drive sprocket on the main shaft. Do not displace the main shaft bearing during installation. Be sure that the recessed side of the drive sprocket is facing downward.
17. Install the trust washer in the main shaft, position the washer on the sprocket carrier. Install the side gear on the main shaft and be sure that the side gear is fully seated in the

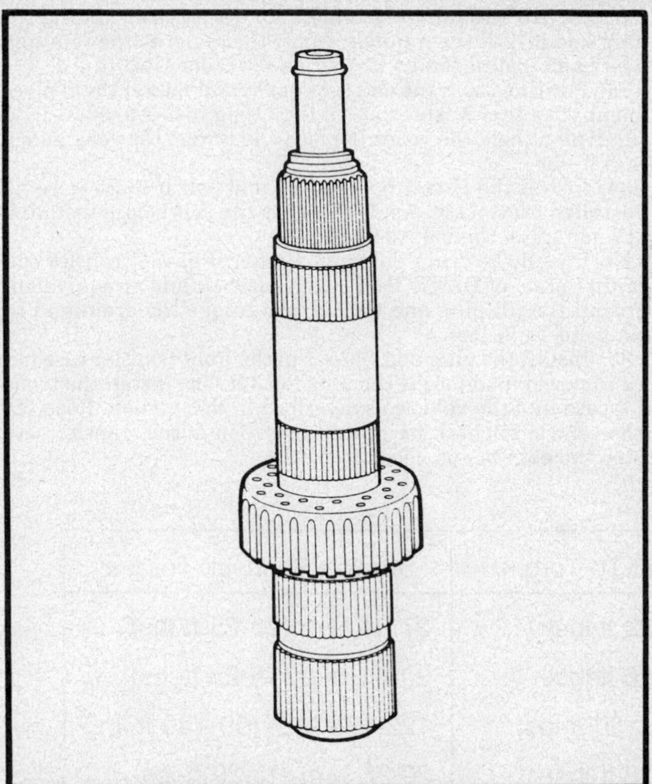

Installing the needle bearing and bearing spacers on the mainshaft

sprocket carrier. Be careful not to displace any of the carrier or main shaft needle bearings.

18. Install the main shaft and gear assembly in the case, making sure that the main shaft is fully seated in the input gear. Install the driven sprocket on the front output shaft and install the sprocket retaining snap ring. Be sure that the sprocket is installed according to the reference marks made during disassembly.

19. Install the front output shaft front thrust bearing assembly in the transfer case front half. Install the thick race in the transfer case and then install the bearing and the thin race.

20. Install the drive chain, front output shaft and driven sprocket. Install the chain on the driven sprocket. Raise and tilt the driven sprocket and chain and install the opposite end of the chain on the drive sprocket.

21. Align the front output shaft with the shaft bore in the transfer case front half and install the shaft in the transfer case. Be sure that the front shaft thrust bearing assembly is seated in the transfer case.

22. Install the front output shaft rear thrust bearing assembly on the front output shaft. Install the tin race first, then install the bearing and the thick race. Install the differential on the side gear, making sure that the differential is fully seated.

23. Coat the main shaft pilot bearing surface and all 15 needle bearings with petroleum jelly and install thew bearing on the shaft. Apply additional petroleum jelly to hold the bearings in place if necessary.

24. Install the rear output shaft on the main shaft and into the differential, making sure that the shaft is completely seated. If necessary tap the shaft with a plastic mallet or equivalent to seat the shaft. Do not displace the pilot bearing during shaft installation.

25. Install the oil pump and the rear output shaft. Install the oil pump with the recessed side facing down. Install a replacement rear output shaft bearing seal in the rear transfer case half.

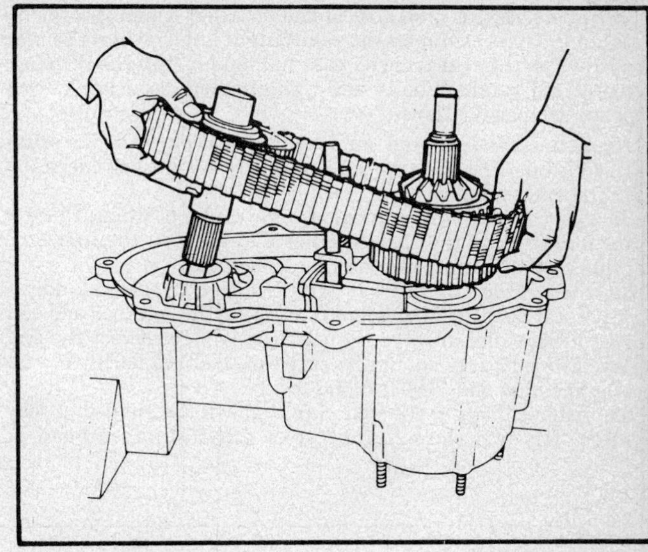

Installing the drive chain, front output shaft and driven socket

26. Apply a bead of Loctite®515 sealant or equivalent, to the mating surface of the rear transfer case half. Install the magnet in the case and attach the rear transfer case half to the front transfer case half. Be sure that the alignment dowels at the front case half ends are aligned with the bolt holes in the rear case half and mate the rear case half with the front case half.

NOTE: If the rear transfer case half will not mate completely with the front case. Inspect the following; oil in the range fork rail bore, the front output shaft rear thrust bearing assembly is not aligned with the rear case half, the main shaft is not completely seated or the rear case half is not aligned with the oil pump.

27. Install the rear case half to the front case half bolts. Torque the bolts to 23 ft. lbs. Be sure that the flat washers are used on the bolts at the case end where the alignment dowels are located. Install the speedometer drive gear on the rear output shaft.

Checking the end play on the rear output shaft

28. Measure the thickness of the shim pack and record. Install a 0.030 in. shim on the rear output shaft. Align the rear retainer on the rear transfer case half and install the retainer. Install the retainer bolts and tighten them securley, do not torque to specifications.

29. Install the front and rear output shaft yokes and the original yoke nuts. Tighten the yoke nuts finger tight and check the differential end play.

30. Set the shift lever in the 4-high range position. Place a dial indicator on the rear retainer and position the indicator stylus so that it contacts the rear yoke nut.

31. Pull upward on the rear output yoke, note the dial indicator pointer position and record it. Remove the retainer and add or subtract differential shims as necessary to correct the end play. The end play should be between 0.002 to 0.010 in. The recommended end play is 0.006 in.

32. After adjusting the end play, remove the front and rear yokes. Discard the original yoke nuts. Apply a bead of Loctite®515 sealant or equivalent, to the retainer mating surface and install the retainer. Apply the sealer to the retaining bolts and install the bolts. Torque the bolts to 23 ft. lbs.

33. Position the front and rear yokes and install the replacement yoke seal washers and nuts. Using tool # J–8614–01 or equivalent hold the yokes in place and torque the yoke nuts to 120 ft. lbs.

34. Install the detent ball, spring and bolt if these were not installed previously. Apply sealer to the bolt before installing it and torque the bolt to 23 ft. lbs.

35. Install the drain plug and washer. Fill the transfer case with 7 pints of DEXRON®II transmission fluid or equivalent. Install the fill plug and washer and torque the drain and fill plugs to 18 ft. lbs.

36. Install the plug and washer in the front transfer case half (if removed) and torque the plug to 18 ft. lbs. Install the transfer case into the vehicle as described in this section. Road test the vehicle to check for proper operation of the transfer case, stop the engine and check for leaks.

Component	Service Set-To Torque	Service Recheck Torque
Detent Retainer Bolt	31 N·m (23 ft-lbs)	27-34 N·m (20-25 ft-lbs)
Drain and Fill Plugs	24 N·m (18 ft-lbs)	20-34 N·m (15-25 ft-lbs)
Front/Rear Yoke Nuts	163 N·m (120 ft-lbs)	122-176 N·m (90-130 ft-lbs)
Operating Lever Locknut	24 N·m (18 ft-lbs)	20-27 N·m (15-20 ft-lbs)
Rear Case-to-Front Case Bolts (All)	31 N·m (23 ft-lbs)	27-34 N·m (20-25 ft-lbs)
Rear Retainer Bolts	31 N·m (23 ft-lbs)	27-34 N·m (20-25 ft-lbs)
Transfer Case-to-Transmission Adapter Nuts	35 N·m (26 ft-lbs)	27-41 N·m (20-30 ft-lbs)
Universal Joint Strap Bolt-to-Transfer Case Yoke	19 N·m (170 in-lbs)	16-23 N·m (140-200 in-lbs)

228 transfer case torque specifications

Rockwell T–223

The Rockwell T–223 transfer case is a two speed unit used to transmit power to both the front and rear driving axles. The transfer case is mounted behind the transmission and is driven by a short drive shaft. A parking brake drum is mounted to the case on the opposite side of the front output shaft.

It is intended and recommended by the manufacture that only through severe operating conditions or poor traction, should the four wheel drive unit be engaged.

Disassembly

TRANSFER CASE

1. Clean the exterior of the case and remove the three driving yokes from the input and output shafts, using a slide hammer.
2. Remove the retaining screws and lift the top cover and gasket. Discard the gasket and clean the mating surfaces.

SHIFT COMPONENTS

1. Remove the detent springs and remove the detent balls with a magnet.
2. Pull both of the shift shafts out through the front of the case. If the shafts cannot be removed this way, drive the shafts and expansion plugs out through the rear of the case.
3. Remove the shift shaft oil seals from the front of the case.
4. Lift the range and declutch shift forks from the case.

FRONT OUTPUT SHAFT

1. Remove the front output shaft bearing cap and gasket and pull the shaft and declutch collar from the case.
2. Slide a long bar through the front output shaft gear and tap out the small and large expansion plugs in the brake hub.

PARKING BRAKE

1. Cut the wire lock and remove the retaining screws from the brake drum, and remove the brake drum from the hub.

2. Remove the brake hub retaining snap ring and remove the brake hub from the front output shaft, using a large gear puller.

3. Disconnect the brake shoe return springs and remove the brake shoes and lever.

4. Remove the brake backing plate mounting bolts and remove the backing plate, washer, deflector plate and washer.

NOTE: Do not try to remove the front output shaft at this time. The idler shaft must be removed first, due to the interference of the gears.

IDLER SHAFT

1. Remove the idler shaft front and rear bearing caps. Wire the forward bearing cap shims together for reassembly.
2. Remove the screws and retainer plate from the front end of the idler shaft and press the idler shaft out through the rear of the case.
3. Lift the Low gear, spacer and front bearing from the case.
4. Remove the High gear and tap the idler shaft front bearing cup from the case.
5. Remove the retaining snap-ring and press the bearing from the idler shaft.

FRONT OUTPUT GEAR

1. After removing the idler shaft assembly, remove the front output shaft rear bearing cap and gasket.
2. Remove the bearing retaining snap-ring and tap the front output gear and bearing into the case. Reach through the cover opening and lift the gear and bearing out of the case.
3. The bearing has to be pressed off the front output shaft.

REAR OUTPUT SHAFT

1. Remove the retaining screws and lift the rear output shaft front and rear bearing caps off the case. Wire the shims together for reassembly.
2. Remove the speedometer drive gear and spacer.
3. Block the rear output gear with a piece of wood and press the rear output shaft and front bearing out of the case. The rear output gear and rear bearing can be lifted out through the cover opening.

INPUT SHAFT

1. Remove the input shaft front and rear bearing covers and wire the shims together for reassembly.
2. Place a block of wood between the sliding gear and the case and press out the input shaft and front bearing.

NOTE: If the gear should cock and become bound on the shaft, try to block it evenly with an additional piece of wood. Do not pound on the shaft.

3. Lift the sliding gear, drive gear, and spacer from the case.
4. Remove the front bearing from the input shaft.

Assembly

INPUT SHAFT

1. Slide the input shaft front bearing onto the input shaft with the shielded side against the shaft shoulder.
2. Start the input shaft into the case. Mount the sliding gear, spacer and drive gear with its bushing onto the input shaft, working through the cover opening.
3. Tap the input shaft into position using a suitable sleeve placed against the inner race of the front bearing and a soft hammer.
4. Position the input shaft front cover and the original shim pack plus an additional 0.010 in. shim on the case. Tighten the retaining screws to the proper torque.
5. Install the rear thrust washer on the shaft and install the rear bearing with the shielded side toward the inside of the case.
6. Position a new gasket on the rear bearing cover and install the cover. Tighten the retaining screws to the proper torque.
7. Mount a dial indicator to the transfer case with the stem against the front end of the input shaft and check the amount of end play present. Remove enough shims from under the front bearing cover to provide 0.003 to 0.005 in. end play. Tighten the front bearing cover retaining screws to specification.

REAR OUTPUT SHAFT

1. Press the front bearing onto the rear output shaft.
2. Hold the rear output gear in position inside the case and slide the shaft through it.
3. Install the front bearing cup and the original shim pack plus an additional 0.010 in. shim, together with the front bearing cover. Install the retaining screws and tighten them to specifications.
4. Press the rear bearing onto the rear output shaft and tap the bearing cup into place.
5. Install the speedometer drive gear and spacer on the shaft.
6. Position a new gasket and the bearing cap and oil seal over the shaft. Install the retaining screws and tighten them to the proper torque.
7. Rotate the shaft to seat the bearings, then install a dial indicator against the rear end of the shaft to check the end play. Remove enough shims from under the front bearing cap to provide zero end-play and zero preload.

FRONT OUTPUT GEAR

NOTE: The front output gear must be installed in the case before the idler shaft assembly is installed.

1. Install the ball bearing on the front output gear hub.
2. Position the gear and bearing in the case and install the retaining snap ring on the bearing.
3. Install the rear bearing cap over a new gasket and tighten the retaining screws to the proper torque.

IDLER SHAFT

1. Press the rear bearing onto the idler shaft and install the retaining snap-ring.
2. Hold the high gear in position inside the case and tap the idler shaft through it with a soft hammer. The short hub side of the gear faces toward the rear of the case.
3. Install the gear spacer on the idler shaft, then install the low gear with the long hub toward the front of the case.
4. Install the rear bearing cup in the case and install the rear bearing cap with a new gasket, tightening the retaining screws to the proper torque.
5. Drive the front bearing onto the idler shaft while holding the shaft rigid to avoid damaging the rear bearing and cup. Install the bearing retainer plate, torque the retaining screws and lock wire them.
6. Tap the front bearing cup into place in the case.
7. Install the front bearing cap with the original shim pack and some extras in order to set up the shaft end play. Torque the front bearing cap retaining screw to specification.
8. Mount a dial indicator on the case with the stem set against the inside face of the lower gear. Check the amount of end play by working the assembly back and forth with a pry bar. Remove enough shims to arrive at 0.003 to 0.005 in. end-play.

FRONT OUTPUT SHAFT

1. Install the ball bearing onto the front output shaft with the retaining snap-ring toward the front.
2. Install the sliding declutch collar onto the shaft and install the shaft into the case.

3. With the shaft in position, install the bearing cap with a new gasket and torque the retaining screws to specification.

PARKING BRAKE

1. Mount the brake backing plate to the case, together with the deflector and stamped washer, with a new gasket between the backing plate and the case. Tighten the retaining screws with star washers to the proper torque.
2. Position the brake lever on the backing plate.
3. Position the brake shoes on the backing plate with the actuating pawl in the web slot.
4. Install the brake shoe return springs.
5. Slide the brake hub onto the splines of the front output shaft and install the retaining snap ring.
6. Install the brake drum with the attaching lockwashers and screws. Tighten the screws to specification and insert lock wires.
7. Install the expansion plugs. The smaller plug goes in the bore of the front output gear.

SHAFT COMPONENTS

1. Install the new shift shaft oil seals in the case.
2. Position the declutch fork in the shift collar.
3. Lubricate the declutch shift shaft and slide it into the case and through the shift fork bore.
4. With the shift shaft in position insert the set screw. Tighten the screw and lock wire it to the fork.
5. Position the range shift fork in the sliding gear.
6. Slide the range shift shaft through the bore of the fork and install the set screw. Tighten the set screw and lock wire it to the shift fork.
7. Install the expansion plugs at the rear of the case and flatten them to expand them.
8. Place the detent balls and springs in position in the case bores and install the case cover with a new gasket, tightening them to the specified torque.
9. Install the driving yokes on the shafts with their lockwashers and retaining nuts and tighten them to the proper torque.

Spicer Model 20

The Spicer Model 20 transfer case is essentially a two-speed gear box located at the rear of the standard transmission, which provides low and direct gear ranges. It also provides a mean of connecting the power to the front axle.

Disassembly

1. Remove cover and gasket from bottom of transfer case.
2. Remove the front drive shift bar poppet spring access hole plugs from front output shaft bearing retainer. If necessary to remove shift bar lock plungers, remove the two expansion plugs from the housing.
3. Remove the idler gear shaft lock plate bolt and lock plate from rear of transfer case.
4. Using a hammer and brass drift, remove idler gear shaft, driving from the front end of the transfer case (opposite slotted end of shaft). As shaft passes thrust washers, remove washers. Remove idler gear with bearings and spacers as a sub-assembly. Remove bearings and spacer from bore of idler gear.
5. Remove end yoke retaining lock nuts from the front and rear output shafts. Using a suitable puller, remove the end yokes from both shafts.
6. Remove steady springs from shift lev<chers. Remove setscrew securing shift lever pivot pin. Remove pin and lift out each lever as it is freed.
7. Remove socket-head setscrew from underdrive shift fork.
8. Move underdrive shift fork and rear output shaft sliding gear forward far enough for gear to clear splines on rear output shaft. Swing fork and gear toward cover opening and lift out gear.
9. Remove rear output shaft bearing retainer and output shaft as an assembly.
10. Remove front output shaft rear cover and shims. Tag shims for reassembly.
11. Remove socket-head setscrew from front wheel drive shift fork.
12. Remove front output shaft bearing retainer with shift bars and gasket.
13. Pull forward on front output shaft as far as possible to permit removal of bearing cup. Remove bearing cone from front output shaft, using suitable puller.
14. Remove front output shaft bearing snap-ring. Using a soft-faced hammer, tap on front end of output shaft and remove it from the rear side of housing. Take out driven gear and sliding gear with shift fork as shaft is withdrawn.
15. Remove shift bars from retainer.

CAUTION

Be sure the poppet balls and springs are secured when withdrawing shift bars. This will prevent possible personal injury.

16. Remove shift bar oil seals.
17. Remove speedometer driven gear.
18. Support inner face of bearing retainer on an arbor press and press output shaft from retainer.
19. Remove oil seal from retainer bore.
20. Remove tapered bearing cone and cup from rear bore of retainer. Remove tapered bearing cup from front bore. Remove O-ring seal.
21. Using a suitable puller, remove bearing cone from output shaft. Remove shims from shaft and tie together before laying aside. Remove speedometer drive gear.
22. Using a puller, remove bearing cone from front output shaft.

Assembly

1. Press bearing cone on rear end of front output shaft.
2. Install speedometer drive gear, shims and bearing cone on output shaft.
3. Position new O-ring seal in bore of rear output shaft bearing retainer. Install tapered bearing cup in front bore of retainer. Install other tapered bearing cup in rear bore of bearing retainer.
4. Place rear output shaft into bearing retainer and support shaft in an arbor press. Position bearing cone over end of shaft and using an adapter slightly larger in diameter than the shaft, press bearing cone on shaft. Locate rear output shaft bearing retainer assembly in a fixed position. Set up a dial indicator and check shaft endplay. Add or remove shims between speedometer drive gear and rear bearing cone to bring endplay within specifications.

It is very important to set end-play correctly, since it controls the seating of the tapered bearings. Incorrect endplay will shorten the lift of bearings.

5. Install new oil seal in rear bore of bearing retainer, using proper adapter.
6. Install speedometer driven gear.

7. Using an adapter of correct size, install shift bar oil seals in front output shaft bearing retainer.

8. Install poppet springs and balls into bearing retainer.

NOTE: Make certain that the heavier loaded spring is installed for the front drive shift bar.

9. Depress poppet balls and insert shift bars into front output shaft bearing retainer.

NOTE: Be sure when installing shift bars that the seal lips are not damaged.

10. Start front output shaft into transfer case from rear. As shaft emerges inside of case, sliding gear with shift fork and front output driven gear can be installed. Hold shaft in position and install bearing cup in rear bore of case. Install front output shaft bearing snap-ring.

11. Support rear end of front output shaft and using an adapter of correct diameter, tap bearing cone onto front end of shaft. With shaft held in position, install bearing cup in front bore of case.

12. Using a new gasket, install front output shaft bearing retainer with shift bars on front of transfer case.

13. Install socket-head setscrew in front wheel drive shaft fork.

14. Install shims and front output shaft rear cover on case. Secure with bolts and torque to specifications. Set up a dial indicator at front end of front output shaft and check end-play. Add or remove shims under rear cover to meet specifications.

NOTE: It is essential to set end-play within specifications, since it controls seating of the tapered bearings. Improper end-play can shorten life of bearings.

15. Install rear output shaft bearing retainer and output shaft as an assembly. Secure with bolts and tighten to specifications.

16. Place rear output shaft sliding gear in underdrive shift fork. Swing fork and gear into case until gear can be positioned on rear output shaft.

17. Install socket-head setscrew in underdrive shift fork.

18. Position shift levers in front output shaft bearing retainer and install shift lever pivot pin. Install pivot pin retaining bolt. Install steady springs on shift levers.

19. Install end yokes on front and rear output shafts and secure with retaining lock nuts.

20. Install spacers and bearings in bore of idler gear. Position idler gear and thrust washers in transfer case. Insert idler shaft into rear of case until slot is flush with case face. Install lock plate and secure with retaining bolt. Tighten to specifications.

21. Install shift bar lock plungers and expansion plugs. Install shift bar poppet spring access hole plugs.

22. Position new gasket on bottom of transfer case and install cover. Secure with bolts and tighten to specifications.

SPECIFICATIONS

END PLAY	
Rear Output Shaft	0.003–0.005 in.
Front Output Shaft	0.000–0.001 in.
BALL POPPET SPRING	
Free Length	
Red	1.028 in.
Yellow	1.078 in
Pressure @ Test Length	
Red @ 59/64 in.	16 lbs.
Yellow @ 49/64 in.	12 lbs.
TORQUE LIMITS (ft. lbs.)	
Rear Output Shaft Bearing Retainer	25–32
Front Output Shaft Rear Bearing Cover	25–32
Front Output Shaft Front Bearing Retainer	25–32
Bottom Cover	10–15
Idler Shaft Lock Bolt	12–17
Companion Flange Nut	225–300

Warner Quadra-Trac®

The Quadra-Trac® transfer case provides full-time, four-wheel drive under all driving conditions. The front and rear driveshafts are driven by a limited slip differential in the transfer case. The limited slip differential is connected to the input shaft by a link-belt type chain. In operation, if the rear axle loses traction, then the engine torque will be transfered through the transfer case differential to the front axle.

The transfer case contains a manually actuated lockout system that locks the front and rear driveshafts together, cancelling the differential action. This feature is used under extreme marginal traction situations.

NOTE: In order to spare the transfer case differential side gears and brake cones from excessive and possibly damaging wear, do not spin the wheels excessively when the vehicle is stuck or bogged down.

An optional gear reduction unit mounted at the rear of the input shaft is available for the Quadra-Trac® unit, making it a two-speed transfer case.

PERFORMANCE CHECKS TRANSFER CASE DIFFERENTIAL TORQUE BIAS CHECK

1. With the lock-out feature *not* engaged and the transmission in Park, raise the vehicle until the front wheels are free of the ground.

2. Disconnect the rear driveshaft from the transfer case.

3. Turn the rear yoke retaining nut with a torque wrench and socket, taking note of how much torque is required to force the cone clutches to slip. They should slip when 110 to 270 ft. lbs. are applied.

Slippage below 10 ft. lbs. indicates replacement of the differential is needed. If no slippage occurs at 270 ft. lbs., improper lubrication is indicated. Drain and refill the transfer case and reduction unit, if so equippped, with the proper lubricant mixture.

DRIVE CHAIN TENSION CHECK

1. Drain the lubricant from the transfer case.

2. Remove the chain inspection plug and insert a steel rule into the hole.

3. A new chain will be 1.575 in. from the outer edge of the plug hole. When the slack in the chain reaches ½–¾ in., the chain should be replaced. No adjustment is possible.

4. Reinstall the drain and chain inspection plugs, and refill the unit with the proper lubricant mixture.

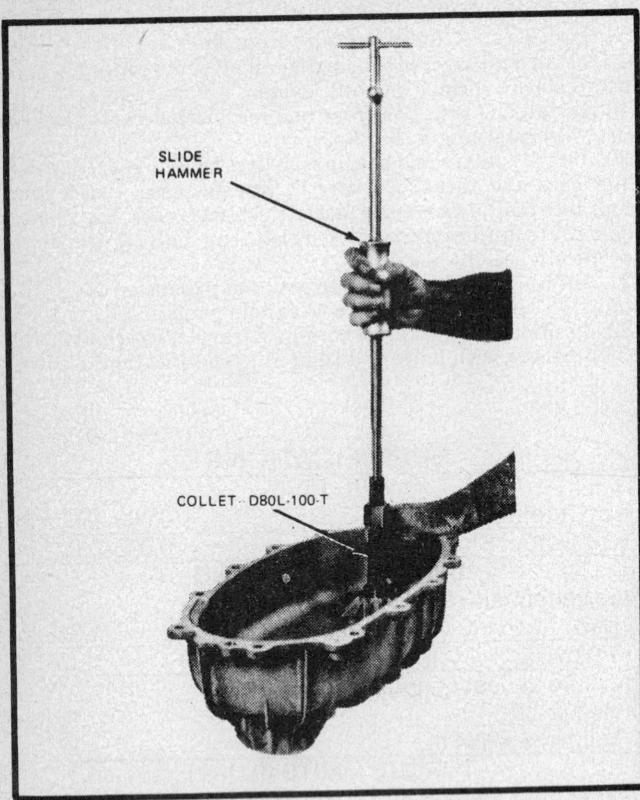

Removing the needle bearing

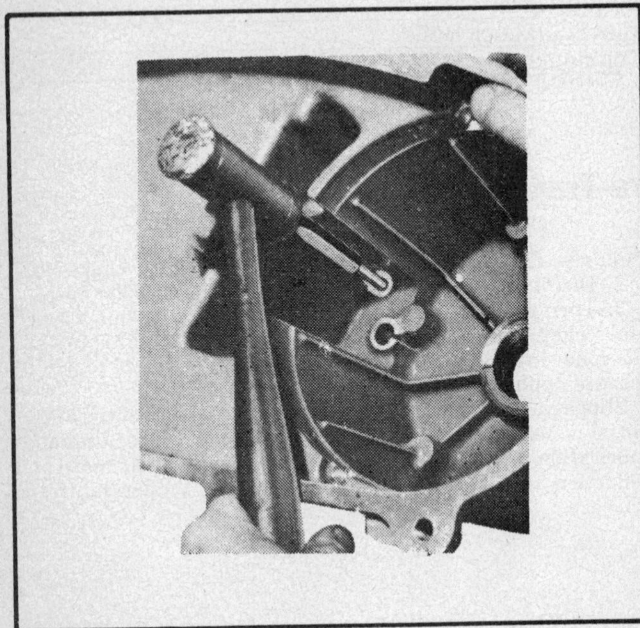

Removing the detent ball

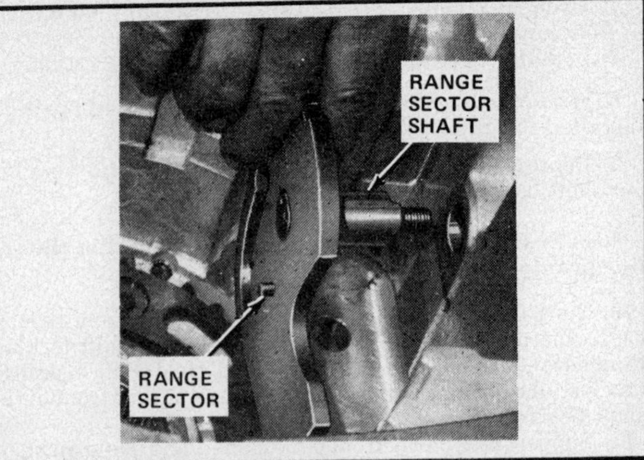

Range sector installation

REAR CASE COVER

Removal

Most Quadra-Trac® components can be serviced without removing the complete unit from the vehicle. To gain access to the rear output shaft, drive sprocket and thrust washer, chain, differential and needle bearing, or the diaphragm control system, just the rear cover has to be removed.

1. Lift and support the vehicle.
2. If the vehicle is equipped with a reduction unit, continue on to the next step for the reduction unit removal procedure. If the vehicle is not equipped with a reduction unit, proceed to Step 7.
3. Loosen all the bolts that attach the reduction unit to the transfer case cover.
4. Move the reduction unit backward just enough to allow the oil to drain from the unit.
5. Loosen the cable retaining bolt at the shift control lever. Loosen the cable clamp bolt and remove the control cable from the clamp bracket and control lever.
6. When the oil has drained, remove the bolts which hold the reduction unit to the transfer case cover. Move the reduction unit rearward to clear the transmission output shaft and pinion cage which is attached to the transfer case drive sprocket. The pinion cage will remain with the transfer case assembly.

NOTE: The pinion cage should not be removed if the transfer case cover assembly is to be removed, but may be removed for inspection or replacement if the transfer case cover assembly is to remain in the vehicle. Removal of the pinion cage involves only removing the snap-ring which holds the cage to the sprocket and sliding the cage backward.

7. Remove the transfer case drain plug and allow the unit to drain.
8. Mark the rear output shaft yoke and universal joint to provide an alignment reference during reassembly. Disconnect the rear drive shaft front universal joint from the transfer case rear yoke.
9. Mark the diaphragm control vacuum hoses for identification during reassembly, then disconnect them. Also remove the lock-up indicator switch wire and the speedometer cable. Remove the indicator switch.
10. Disconnect the parking brake cable guide from the pivot on the right frame side.
11. Remove the bolts which attach the case cover assembly to the case (front housing). Carefully slide the cover assembly backward off the front output shaft and the transmission output shaft.

Disassembly

1. To disassemble the unit, remove the rear output shaft yoke.
2. If the unit is not equipped with a reduction unit, remove the power take-off cover from the rear of the transfer case cov-

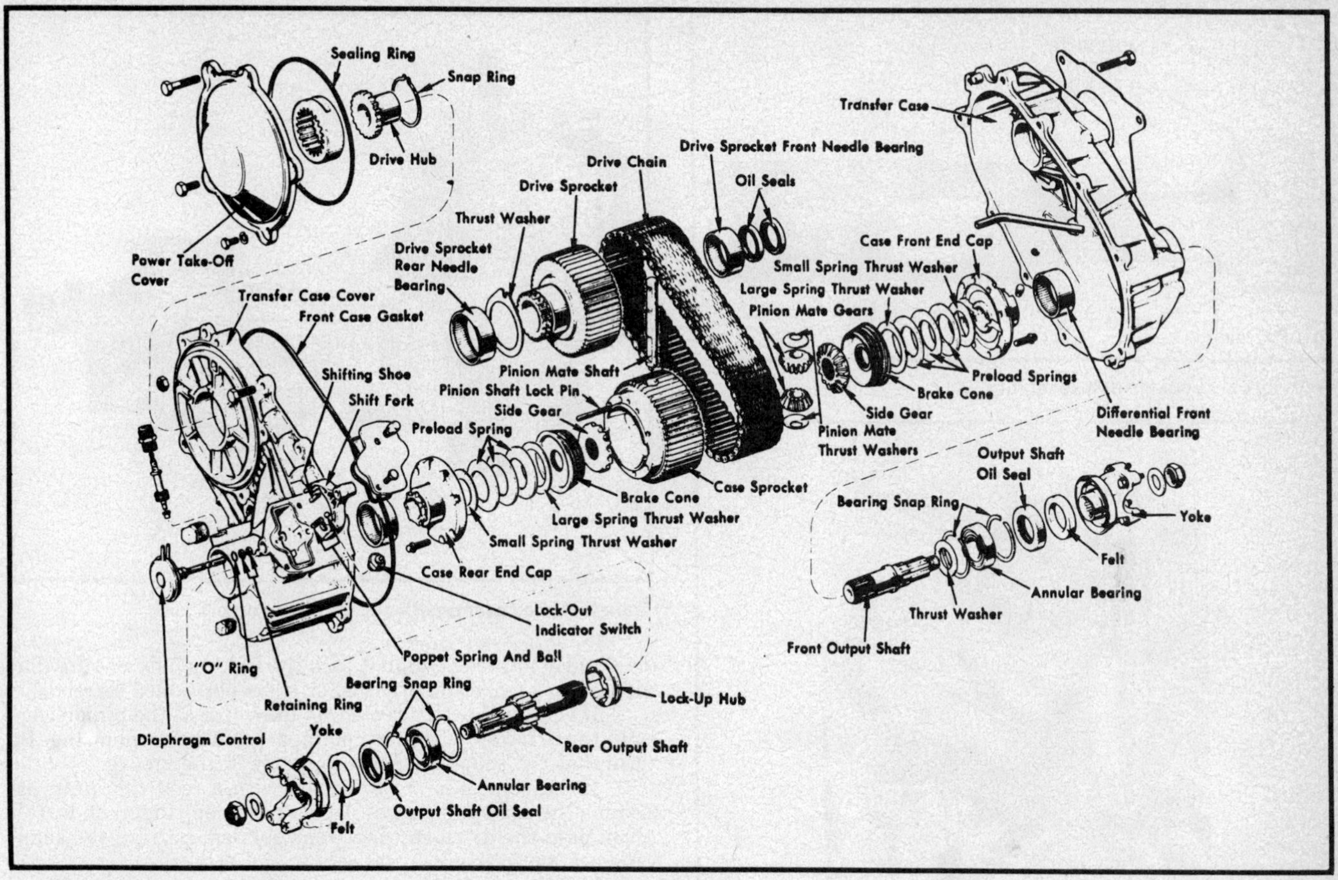

Exploded view of the Warner Quadra-Trac® without the optional reduction unit

er. Remove the sealing ring from the transfer case cover.

3. Using a piece of wood 2 in. × 4 in. and 6 in. long, support the cover and drive sprocket.

4. If not equipped with a reduction unit, remove the drive hub and sleeve from the drive sprocket rear splines by expanding the internal snap-ring. The ring expanding tabs are accessible through a slot in the outside edge of the drive sleeve.

5. If equipped with a reduction unit, remove the pinion cage snap-ring and carrier.

6. Lift the case cover from the drive sprocket and differential. The cover, rear output shaft, bearings and seal, drive sprocket rear needle bearing, and lock-up hub can now be serviced without any further disassembly of other components.

7. Slide the drive sprocket toward the differential unit and remove the chain. The differential unit may now be serviced without any further disassembly of other components.

Assembly

1. Position the drive sprocket on a block of wood 2 in. × 4 in. and 6 in. long.

2. Place the differential assembly about 2 in. from the drive sprocket and with the front end of the differential on the bench.

3. Position the drive chain around the drive sprocket and the differential assembly. Be sure that the chain is properly engaged with the sprocket and differential teeth and that the slack is removed from the chain.

4. Insert the rear output shaft into the differential.

5. Shift the lock-up hub rearward in the case cover. Lubricate the drive sprocket thrust washer and insert it in position on the case cover.

6. Carefully align the case cover and position it onto the drive sprocket and differential. The output shaft may have to

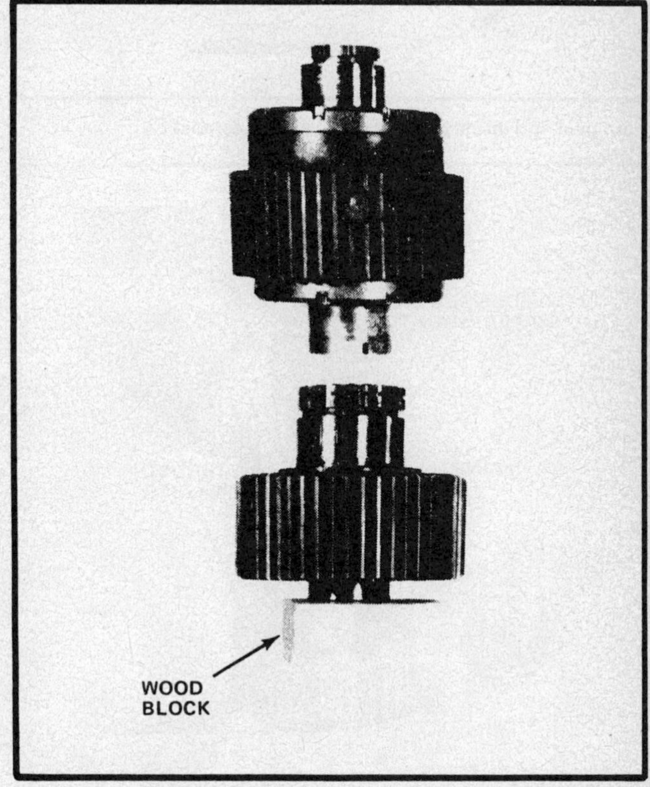

Differential and drive sprocket positioned for chain installation

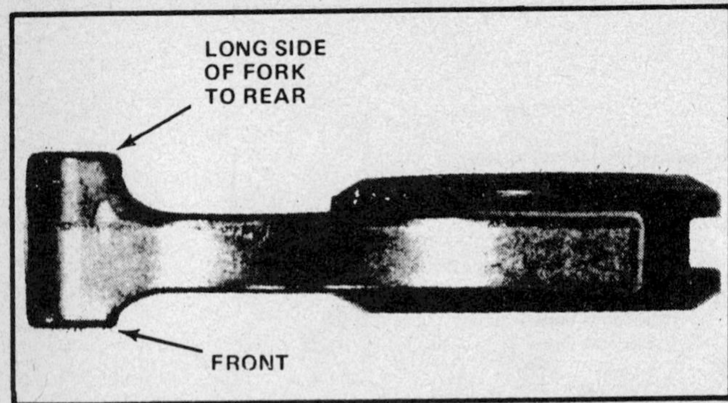

Shift fork and lock-up hub assembly

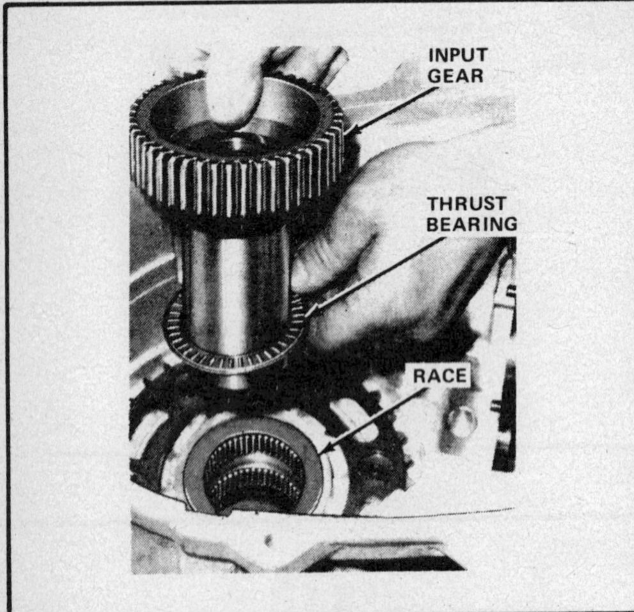

Input gear and thrust bearing removal and installation

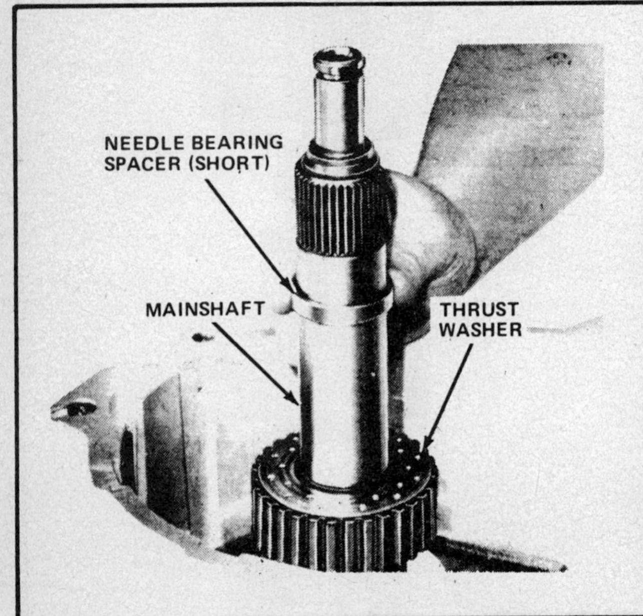

Mainshaft and thrust bearing installation

Transfer case cover positioned for disassembly

be slightly rotated to align it with the lock-up hub. Be sure that the drive sprocket thrust washer stays positioned correctly.

7. If equipped with a reduction unit, install the pinion cage onto the drive sprocket rear splines. Install the snap-ring. Be sure that the snap-ring seats properly in the groove.

8. If the vehicle is not equipped with a reduction unit, assemble the drive hub, drive sleeve, and snap-ring, then install them onto the drive sprocket rear splines. Be sure the snap-ring seats properly.

9. Turn the drive sleeve or pinion cage to make sure the drive sprocket thrust washer did not come out of position. No binding should be present.

10. If not equipped with a reduction unit, install the power take-off sealing ring and cover and tighten the attaching screws.

11. Install the speedometer gear on the rear output shaft.

12. Install the rear output shaft oil seal and the rear yoke and nut. Tighten the nut to specification.

Installation

1. Clean the groove which the front oil seal gasket fits into and install the seal.

2. Install two $^3/_8$ in., 16 × 2 in. long pilot studs into the transfer case front cover housing.

3. Move the cover assembly forward to mesh with the front output shaft and transmission output shaft. It may be necessary to rotate the rear output shaft slightly to allow the two sets of splines to engage.

4. After the cover assembly has been moved forward and is evenly touching the front half of the case, remove the pilot studs and install the rear cover attaching bolts. Tighten the bolts alternately and evenly to specifications.

5. Install the lock out indicator switch and connect the lock out switch wire, diaphragm control vacuum hoses, and the speedometer cable.

6. Install the rear drive shaft.

7. Install the parking brake cable guide to the pivot on the right frame side.

8. Install the reduction unit, if so equipped, as follows:

9. Position the reduction unit to the transfer case and mesh the caged pinions with the sun gear and ring gear, and align the sun gear inner splines with the transmission output shaft splines.

10. Move the reduction unit forward until it touches the sealing ring.

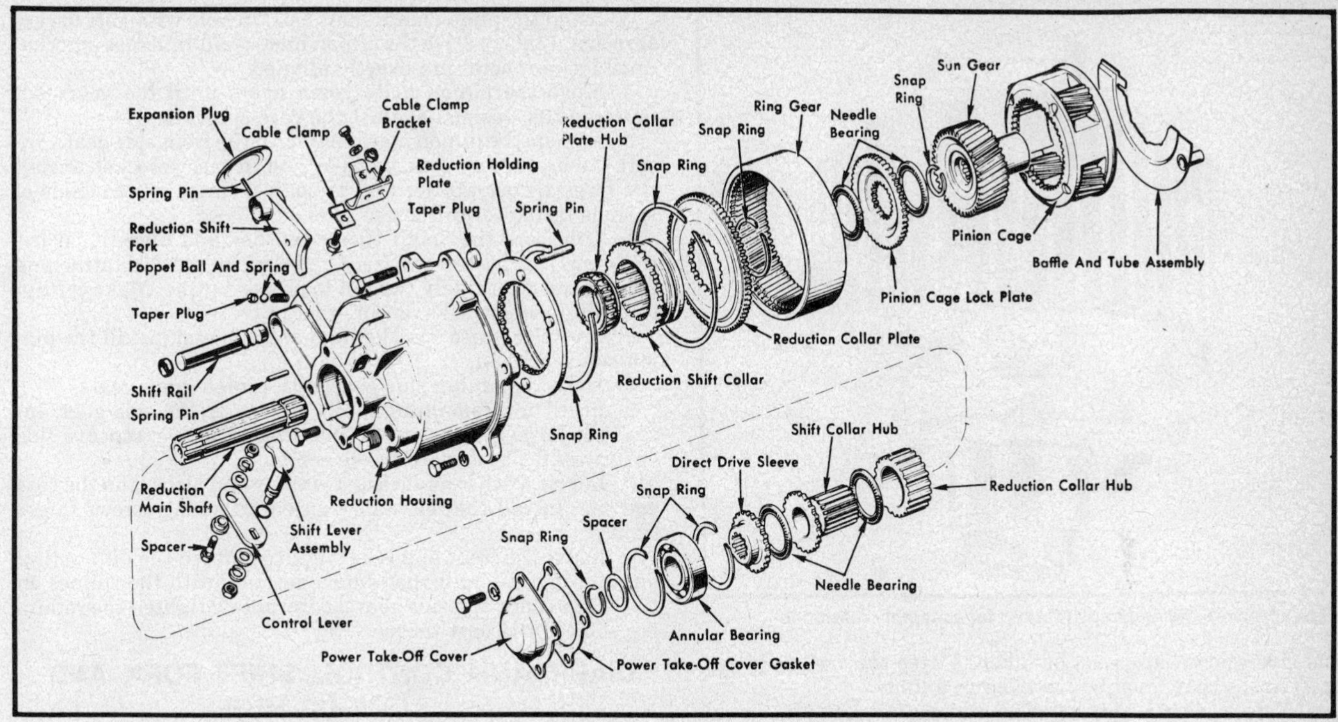

Exploded view of the Warner Quadra-Trac® with the option reduction unit

11. Install the attaching screws loosely, then tighten them alternately to specification.
12. Connect the shift control cable and adjust it by first removing the swivel block from the control lever. Move the control lever to the most forward position. Thread the swivel block in or out on the cable end to obtain the correct length to fit the swivel block in the control lever.
13. Install the proper type and amount of lubricant and lower the vehicle.

NOTE: Use 8 oz. of Jeep Lubricant Concentrate Part No. 8123004 or 5356068 or Lubrizol® 762 (there is no substitute) mixed with SAE 30 non-detergent motor oil. 3.5 pints of the mixture is required to fill the transfer case without a reduction unit, 4.5 pints with a reduction unit.

DIFFERENTIAL ASSEMBLY

Disassembly

1. Mark end caps and case sprocket with paint. Marks must be used to identify front end cap, rear end cap and proper orientation of caps to case sprocket.
2. Remove front end cap. If necessary, tap gently with a soft hammer.
3. Remove thrust washer, preload springs, brake cone and side gears from case sprocket. Care must be taken to keep the various pieces together as they must be installed as a unit.
4. Invert the case sprocket and remove rear cap. If necessary, tap gently with a soft hammer.
5. Remove the thrust washers, preload springs, brake cone

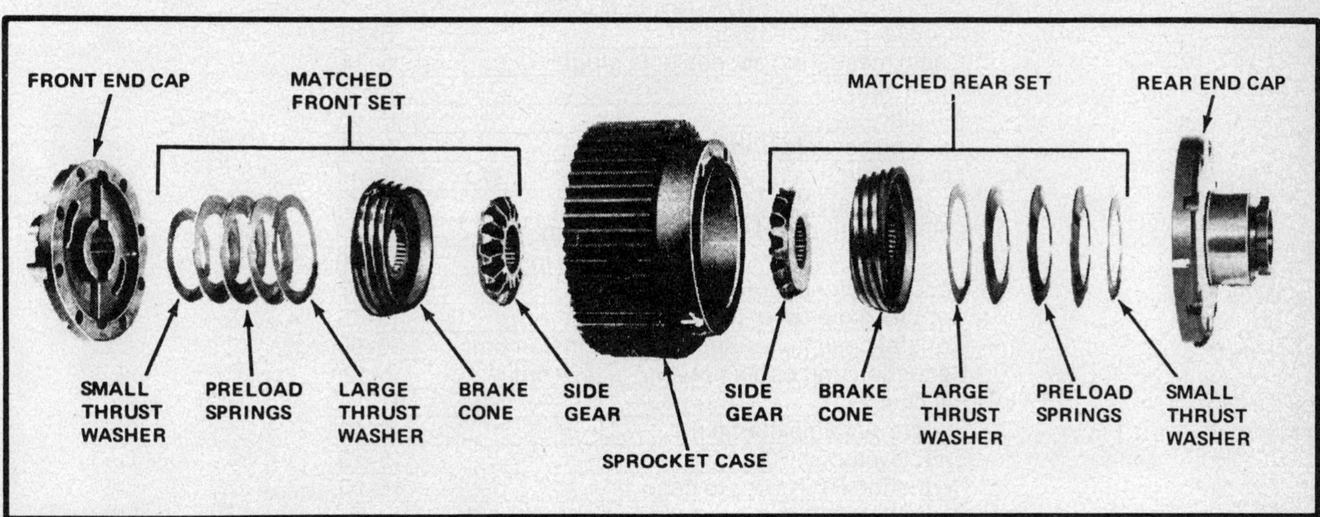

Differential sprocket assembly sequence

Case sprocket and end caps marked for assembly reference

and side gears. Care must be taken to keep the various pieces together as they must be installed as a unit.

6. Raise the case sprocket. The pinion shaft lock pin should fall out. If the pin does not fall, drive the pin out with a ¼ in. pin punch.

7. Drive the pinion mate shaft out of case sprocket, using a brass drift and hammer. Care must be taken to avoid damaging the pinion mate thrust washers.

8. Thoroughly clean and inspect all component parts. Replace any damaged or worn parts with a complete matched set.

Assembly

Prelubricate all bearings and thrust surfaces with Jeep Lubricant Concentrate Part No. 8123004 or 5356068 or Lubrizol® 762 (there is no substitute) prior to installation.

1. Slide the pinion mate shaft in the case sprocket three inches.

2. Install the pinion mate thrust washers and gears on shaft in the proper order.

3. Align the pinion mate shaft lockpin hole with hole in case sprocket. Lightly drive the pinion mate shaft into case sprocket until lockpin holes are exactly aligned.

4. Move the pinion mate gears apart until the gears are pressing the washers against the case sprocket.

5. Engage the pinion mate gear with the front side gears. Insert the brake cone over the gear and in case sprocket. Install the large thrust washer and preload springs, concave side of springs facing toward brake cone.

6. Lubricate the small thrust washer and place it on the front end cap. Install the front end cap, secure with attaching screws and alternately tighten to proper torque. Make certain that alignment marks are in order.

7. Invert the case sprocket and end cap and install the pinion shaft lock pin.

8. Mesh remaining side gear with pinion mate gears.

9. Insert the remaining brake cone over the side gear. Install the large thrust washer and preload spring, concave side of springs facing toward brake cone.

10. Lubricate the small thrust washer and place it on the rear end cap. Install the rear cap, tighten attaching screws finger tight.

11. Insert the front and rear output shafts in the differential and rotate until both shafts have aligned with the splines on the brake cones and side gears. Alternately tighten the retaining screws to proper torque.

DIAPHRAGM CONTROL, SHIFT FORK AND LOCK-UP HUB

Disassembly

1. Remove the vent cover and seal ring.

2. Remove the retaining rings positioning the shift fork on diaphragm. Carefully pry the shift fork forward to gain access to the retaining rings. Remove the spring with a magnet.

3. Caution must be exercised in removal of the diaphragm control rod as it is retained by a spring loaded detent ball. Insert a magnet into the hole to hold the detent ball. Slip the diaphragm control rod out of case. Remove detent ball and spring.

4. Remove shifting fork, plastic shifting shoes and lock-up hub.

Assembly

1. Lubricate the shifting shoes and place them in the shift fork.

SPECIFICATIONS

TORQUE (FT. LBS.)	
Transfer case breather	6–10
Chain measuring access hole plug	6–14
Drain plug	15–25
Fill plug	15–25
Lock-up cover to transfer case	8–10
Lock-out indicator switch	10–15
Output Shaft Nut	90–150
PTO cover to transfer case bolts: 3/8 in.-16	15–25
5/16 in.-18	10–20
Speedometer adapter	20-30
Transfer case cover to transfer case	15–25
Transfer case to transmission extension bolt	30–50
Reduction unit cable housing clamp nut	7–12
Fill plug	15–25
Shift lever cable clamp nut	10–20
Shift lever to shift nut	15–25
Reduction PTO cover to case	15–25
Reduction unit to transfer case bolts: 3/8 in.-16	15–25
5/16 in.-18	8–10

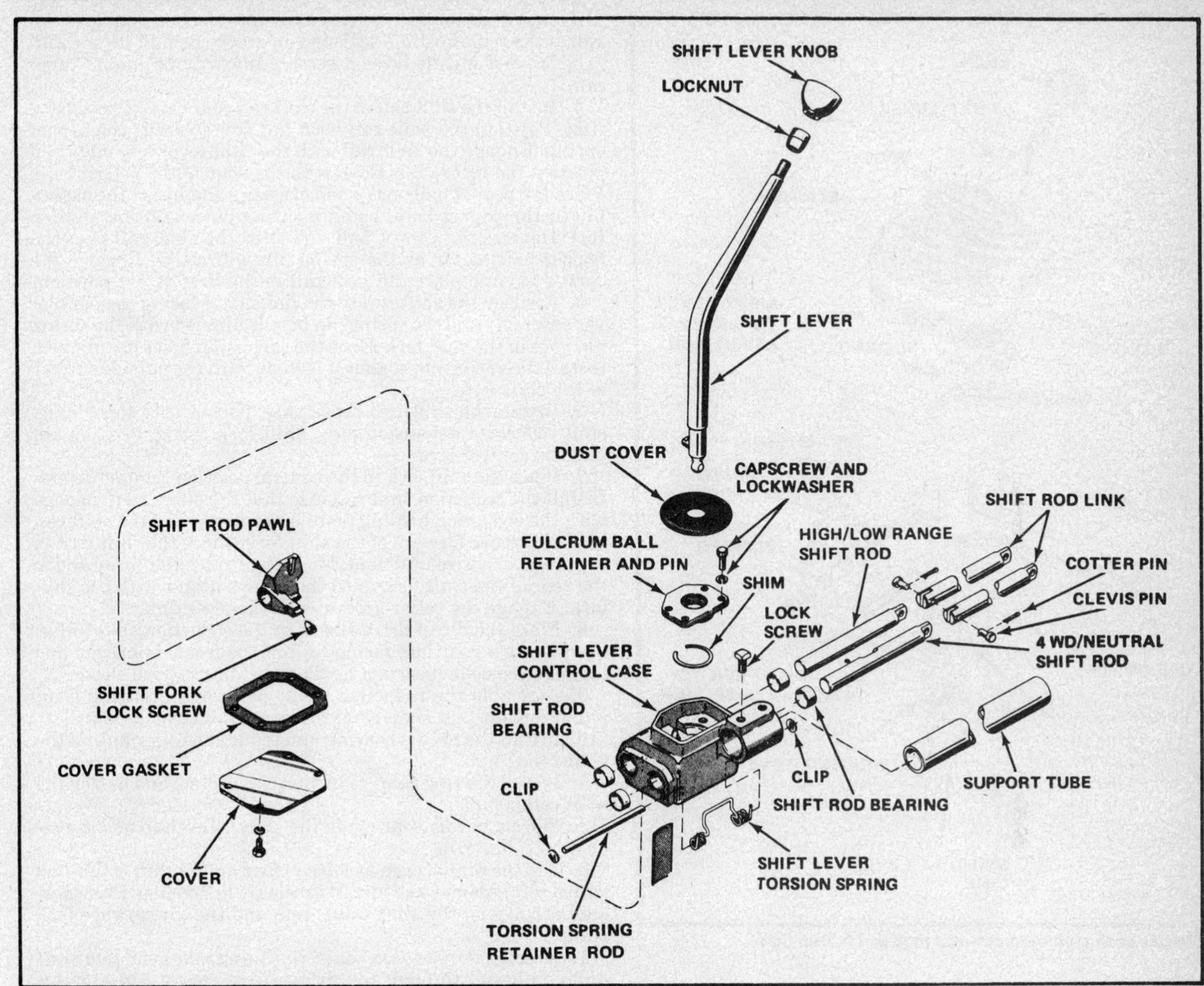

Transfer case shift controls—Cherokee and Wagoneer (© Jeep Corp)

2. Install the shift fork and lock-up hub assembly in the case cover, long end of shift fork first (toward rear). Make certain that the shift fork does not separate from the lock-up hub by reaching through the needle bearings.
3. Insert the diaphragm control rod in the case and shifting fork, stopping before the detent ball hole is reached.
4. Install the detent ball and spring. Depress the detent ball with a ¼ in. pin punch and slide the diaphragm control rod into place.
5. Install the shift fork retaining pin, (clips) and the diaphragm retaining spring, the spring should be below the surface of the bore.
6. Install the vent cover and seal ring.

REDUCTION UNIT

Disassembly

1. Remove PTO cover and gasket.
2. Remove snap-ring from reduction main shaft rear end, slide the reduction main shaft and sun gear assembly forward and out. Remove needle bearings.
3. Remove as an assembly, the ring gear, reduction collar plate, pinion cage lock plate, shift collar hub and reduction collar hub. Using a soft hammer, remove the shift collar hub from the pinion cage lock plate.
4. Remove the pinion cage lock plate, needle bearing, ring gear, reduction collar plate and shift collar hub. Separate the reduction collar hub and needle bearing from shift collar hub.
5. When necessary, separate the reduction collar plate and ring gear by removing retaining snap-ring.
6. Remove needle bearing and direct drive sleeve from the reduction shift collar.
7. Shift the reduction shift collar to the neutral (center) detent with the control lever. Disengage the shift fork. Place the shift in the direct drive detent position (rear), align the collar outer teeth with the inner teeth in the reduction holding plate. Place the fork and collar in the reduction position (front) detent, and remove the reduction shift collar.
8. Remove the annular bearing rear snap-ring and bearing.
9. Remove the shift fork locating spring pin, large expansion plug, shift rail taper plug, and control lever.
10. Drive the spring pin out of the shift fork and rail with a $^3/_{16}$ in. pin punch. Slide the shift rail forward out of the shift fork, and remove the shift fork. Remove the spring shift fork poppet ball. Drive the poppet taper plug into the shift rail bore and remove the plug and spring.
11. Remove the shift lever retaining pin and the shift lever

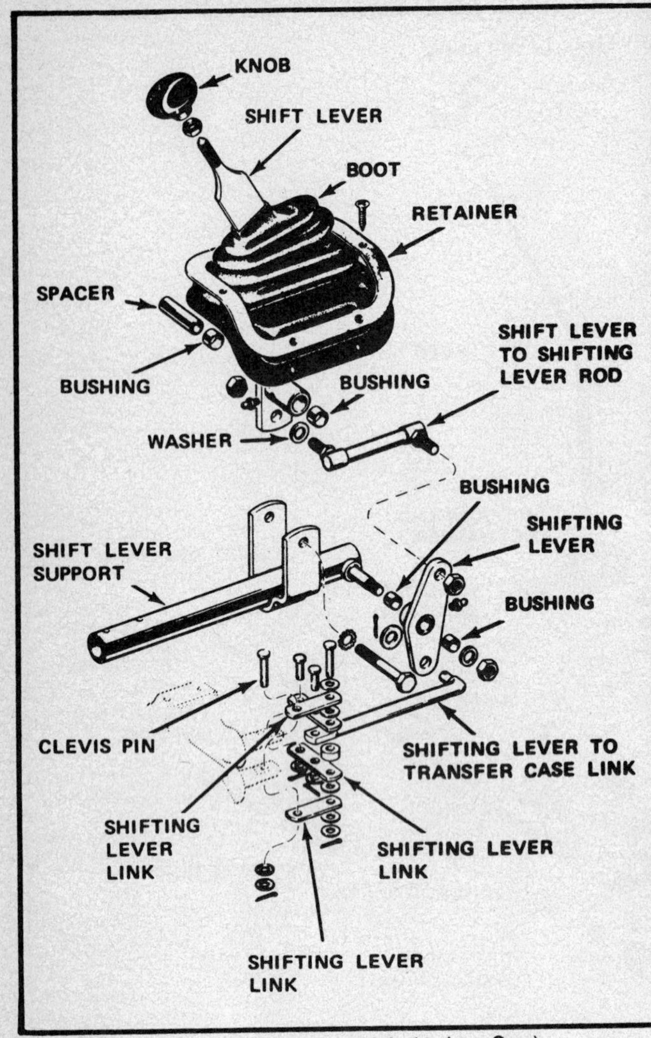

Transfer case shift controls—CJ models (© Jeep Corp)

assembly.

12. Remove the reduction holding plate snap-ring and reduction holding plate.

Assembly

1. Align the shift fork locating spring holes in the reduction holding plate and housing. Install the reduction holding plate. Locating pins should index the plate in the case. Secure the plate with a snap-ring, tabs facing forward.

2. Install the shift lever assembly into the housing, lever towards the rear. Position seal ring on groove in shift lever shaft.

3. Move the shift lever assembly inward and install taper pin.

4. Install the shift rail in the shift rail rear bore, grooved end first. Position the shift rail with flat side towards the poppet spring. Engage the shift rail with the shift lever assembly and position the rail so it is flush with the edge of the poppet bore. Place the poppet ball on the end of spring and insert the assembly in the poppet bore, using a spring pin as an installation tool. Depress the poppet ball and slide the shift rail over the poppet ball as far as the spring pin will allow. Remove the spring pin and place the shift rail in the first detent position.

5. Position the shift rail so the flat side is facing the shift lever assembly and the spring pin bore is aligned with the spring pin bore in the shift fork. Once the spring pin holes are aligned, install the spring pin so that it is flush with the outside surface of the shift fork.

6. Install the shift rail taper plug, poppet bore taper plug, shift rail cover expansion plug, shift fork spring locating pin and the control lever.

7. Place the shift fork in the neutral position (center) detent. Install the reduction shift collar so that the outer teeth engage with the reduction holding plate inner teeth, and the shift collar fork groove forward of the shift fork. Place the shift fork in the direct drive (rear) detent. Move the shift collar away and to the rear of the shift fork until the groove aligns with the shift fork. Engage the collar groove with the shift fork.

8. Place the direct drive sleeve in the reduction shift collar, needle bearing surface facing toward the front. Lubricate and install the needle bearing, against the direct drive sleeve.

9. Assemble the reduction collar plate hub and ring gear. Make certain that snap-rings are seated in their grooves.

10. Install the needle bearing and reduction collar hub on the shift collar hub.

11. Install the ring gear, reduction collar plate and hub on the shift collar hub.

12. Place a needle bearing on the shift collar hub and the reduction collar hub.

13. Tap the pinion cage lock into place on the shift collar hub with a soft hammer and install assembly in housing. Place needle bearings on the shift collar hub and the pinion cage lock plate.

14. Install the reduction main shaft and sun gear into shift collar hub and through the direct drive sleeve and annular bearing. With a brass drift gently tap the assembly as far to the rear as possible. Place the rear spacer on the main shaft and secure with the selective snap-ring which gives the tightest fit, between 0.004–0.009 in. clearance. Snap rings are available in thicknesses ranging from 0.089–0.105 in.

15. Install PTO cover and gasket, tighten attaching bolts to proper torque at the rear of the standard transmission, which provides low and direct gear ranges. It also provides a means of connecting the power to the front axle.

INDEX

DRIVE AXLE SERVICE DIAGNOSIS

Condition	Possible Cause	Correction
Rear Wheel Noise	1. Wheel loose.	1. Tighten loose nuts.
	2. Faulty, brinelled wheel bearing.	2. Faulty or brinelled bearings must be replaced. Check rear axle shaft end play.
	3. Excessive axle shaft end play.	3. Readjust axle shaft end play.
Rear Axle Drive Shaft Noise	1. Misaligned axle housing.	1. Inspect rear axle housing, alignment. Correct as necessary.
	2. Bent or sprung axle shaft.	2. Replace bent or sprung axle shaft.
	3. End play in drive pinion bearings.	3. Refer to Pinion Bearing Pre-load.
	4. Excessive gear lash between ring gear and pinion.	4. Check adjustment of ring gear and pinion. Correct as necessary.
	5. Improper adjustment of drive pinion shaft bearings.	5. Adjust pinion bearings.
	6. Loose drive pinion companion flange nut.	6. Tighten drive pinion flange nut to torque specified.
	7. Improper wheel bearing adjustment.	7. Check axle shaft end play. Readjust as necessary.
	8. Scuffed gear tooth contact surfaces.	8. If necessary, replace scuffed gears.
Rear Axle Drive Shaft Breakage	1. Improperly adjusted wheel bearings.	1. Replace broken shaft and readjust end play.
	2. Misaligned axle housing.	2. Replace broken shaft after correcting rear axle housing alignment.
	3. Vehicle overloaded.	3. Replace broken shaft. Avoid excessive weight on vehicle.
	4. Abnormal clutch operation.	4. Replace broken shaft, after checking for other possible causes. Avoid erratic use of clutch.
	5. Grabbing clutch.	5. Replace broken shaft. Inspect clutch and make necessary repairs or adjustments.
	6. Normal fatigue.	6. Replace broken shaft. Inspect to determine causes or damage.
Differential Case Breakage	1. Improper adjustment of differential bearings.	1. Replace broken case; examine gears and bearings for possible damage. At reassembly, adjust differential bearings.
	2. Excessive ring gear clearance.	2. Replace broken case; examine gears and bearings for possible damage. At reassembly, adjust ring gear and pinion backlash.
	3. Vehicle overloaded.	3. Replace broken case; examine gears and bearings for possible damage. Avoid excessive weight on vehicle.
	4. Erratic clutch operation.	4. Replace broken case. After checking for other possible causes, examine gears and bearings for possible damage. Avoid erratic use of clutch.
Differential Side Gear Broken at Hub	1. Excessive axle housing deflection.	1. Replace damaged gears. Examine other gears and bearings for possible damage. Check rear axle housing alignment.
	2. Misaligned or bent axle shaft.	2. Replace damaged gears. Check axle shafts or alignment. Examine other gears and bearings for possible damage.
	3. Worn thrust washers.	3. Replace damaged gears. Examine other gears and bearings for possible damage. Replace thrust washers that are badly worn.

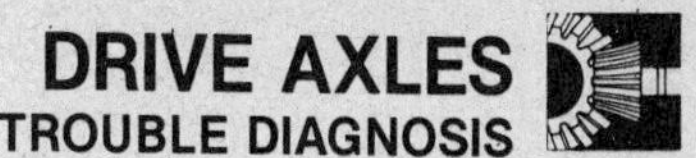

DRIVE AXLE SERVICE DIAGNOSIS

Condition	Possible Cause	Correction
Scoring of Differential Gears	1. Insufficient lubrication.	1. Replace scored gears. Scoring marks on the pressure face of gear teeth or in the bore are caused by instantaneous fusing of the mating surfaces. Scored gears should be replaced. Fill rear axle to required capacity with proper lubricant.
	2. Improper grade of lubricant.	2. Replace scored gears. Inspect all gears and bearings for possible damage. Clean out and refill axle to required capacity with proper lubricant.
	3. Excessive spinning of one wheel.	3. Replace scored gears. Inspect all gears, pinion bores and shaft for scoring, or bearings for possible damage. Service as necessary.
Tooth Breakage (Ring Gear and Pinion)	1. Overloading.	1. Replace gears. Examine other gears and bearings for possible damage. Replace parts as needed. Avoid overloading of vehicle.
	2. Erratic clutch operation.	2. Replace gears, and examine remaining parts for possible damage. Avoid erratic clutch operation.
	3. Ice-spotted pavements.	3. Replace gears. Examine remaining parts for possible damage. Replace parts as required.
	4. Normal fatigue.	4. Replace gears. Examine broken parts to determine cause of normal fatigue.
	5. Improper adjustment.	5. Replace gears. Examine other parts for possible damage. Make sure ring gear and pinion backlash is correct.
Rear Axle Noise	1. Insufficient lubricant.	1. Refill rear axle with correct amount of the proper lubricant. Also check for leaks and correct as necessary.
	2. Improper ring gear and pinion adjustment.	2. Check ring gear and pinion tooth contact.
	3. Unmatched ring gear and pinion.	3. Remove unmatched ring gear and pinion. Replace with a new matched gear and pinion set.
	4. Worn teeth on ring gear or pinion.	4. Check teeth on ring gear and pinion for contact. If necessary, replace with new matched set.
	5. Loose drive pinion bearings.	5. Adjust drive pinion bearings.
	6. Loose differential gear bearings.	6. Adjust differential gear bearings.
	7. Misaligned or sprung ring gear.	7. Check ring gear for runout.
	8. Loose carrier housing bolts.	8. Tighten carrier housing nuts to specifications. Also, check for oil leaks and correct as necessary.
Loss of Lubricant	1. Lubricant level too high.	1. Drain excess lubricant by removing filler plug and allow lubricant to level at lower edge of filler plug hole.
	2. Worn axle shaft oil seals.	2. Replace worn oil seals with new ones. Prepare new seals before replacement.
	3. Cracked rear axle housing.	3. Repair or replace housing as required.
	4. Worn drive pinion oil seal.	4. Replace worn drive pinion oil seal with a new one.
	5. Scored and worn companion flange.	5. Replace worn or scored companion flange and oil seal.

DRIVE AXLE SERVICE DIAGNOSIS

Condition	Possible Cause	Correction
Overheating of Unit	1. Lubricant level too low.	1. Refill rear axle.
	2. Incorrect grade of lubricant.	2. Drain, flush and refill rear axle with correct amount of the proper lubricant.
	3. Bearings adjusted too tightly.	3. Readjust bearings.
	4. Excessive wear in gears.	4. Check gears for excessive wear or scoring. Replace as necessary.
	5. Insufficient ring gear to pinion clearance.	5. Readjust ring gear and pinion backlash and check gears for possible scoring.

DIFFERENTIAL COMPONENT FAILURE DIAGNOSIS

SCORING AND SEIZURE OF SPIDER AND PINION GEARS

The spider arms and pinion gears were badly discolored by heat, caused by the unit operating for a long time after the initial scoring took place. The most probable cause of this type of failure is excessive wheelspin, particularly in off-road or icy road conditions. Other possible causes are inadequate lubrication or overstress. Friction causes the hardened areas to overheat, score, and eventually to seize. The best way to prevent this problem is to avoid wheelspin and overloading under rough terrain or poor traction conditions.

Scoring and seizure of spider and pinion gears

SHOCK FRACTURE

These differential pinion and side gears show a grainy structure which indicates a shock fracture. This type of damage occurs instantaneously. The usual cause is a sudden excessive load, as might be caused by sudden clutch engagement at high engine speed. Another cause is a rapidly spinning wheel suddenly reaching a good traction area. This failure can be prevented by proper clutch operation, and by avoiding wheelspin and overloading under rough terrain or poor traction conditions.

Shock fracture

FATIGUE FRACTURE OF THE DIFFERENTIAL SIDE GEARS

This damage occurs in stages. An initial stress caused a crack, and repeated stresses caused complete failure. Some of the gear teeth were broken off in the later stages. The failures can be seen best at points A and B. All differential gears should be checked when this type of failure is found, very often the other gears will be in the initial stages of failure and must be replaced. This is most often caused by abuse such as sudden clutch engagement or incorrect two-speed axle operation, combined with overloading.

SCORED AND SCUFFED GEAR TEETH

This wear pattern is a result of the gear running without enough lubrication between the tooth surfaces. Either poor quality gear lube or low lubrication level can cause this condition. Excessive torque input to the rear can also cause this wear since it will break down even the best of gear lube. Changing gear lube at regular recommended intervals and keeping excessive torque input to a minimum will usually prevent this problem.

FATIGUE FRACTURED PINION GEAR

This type of fracture develops over a period of time. The fracture works through the gear tooth until the tooth is not strong enough to support the load applied. Failure happens and a section of the tooth breaks away. Continued use of pitted gears is the usual cause of this type of gear failure. As the gear pits, the support area is reduced and must carry the entire load of the gear tooth. As this continues the gear tooth fatigues and the final result is failure of the gear. To prevent this problem the ring and pinion must be replaced if there is any pitting on the gears.

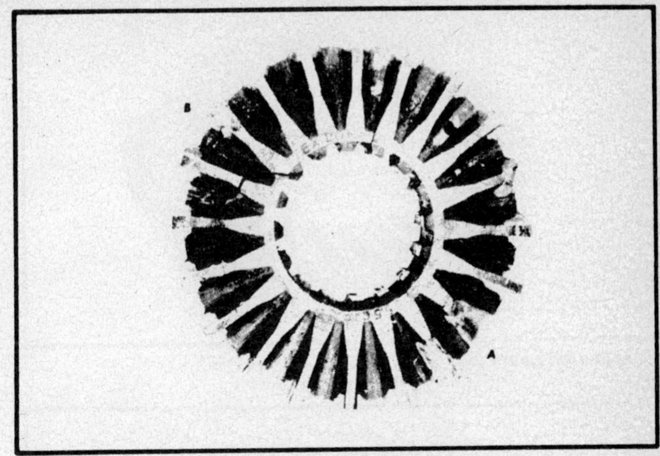

Fatigue fracture of the differential side gears

MISALIGNMENT FATIGUE FRACTURE

This problem comes from misalignment in the axle shaft. This kind of failure can also happen when the axle shaft breaks. If twisted, bent or sprung axle shaft are are not replaced after they are damaged, this kind of failure to the side gears can occur. Bent axle housing can also cause this to happen. In most cases, this type of failure is not instantaneous. It tends to happen over a period of time. The usual cause of this type of failure is abusive operation of the vehicle and severe overloading.

Scored and scuffed gear teeth

OVERHEATED GEAR SET

This problem can be caused by one of three, or any combination of the following circumstances. The causes are low gear lubricant level; improper gear lubricant; or infrequent lubricant change. When one or more of these conditions is present in the rear, it causes the lubricant to break down and allows the gear surface to build up heat because of increased friction. In the failure shown, the gears became so hot the pinion bearing fused to the pinion gear and the pinion gear teeth became distorted. To prevent this problem a good quality gear lubricant must be used in the rear to prevent the breakdown of lubricant under a heavy load.

FRACTURE GEAR TEETH

This problem is caused by improper gear adjustment. The picture on the left shows the result of excessive backlash between the ring and pinion gear. Such backlash allows overloading of the heel section of the gear; gear fracture will follow. The picture on the right shows the result of too little backlash thus allowing the toe section of the gear to overload and become fractured. The best way to eliminate this problem is to correctly adjust the ring and piston gears, when necessary, according to specifications.

Fatigue fractured pinion gear

TWISTED AXLE SHAFT

This problem with the axle comes from abusive and/or extremely severe operation of the vehicle. This is only the first stage of failure where the axle shaft has only twisted, but has not yet started to crack. At this stage the shaft should be replaced. If it is not, the shaft will continue to twist and eventually will break. When this happens it will almost certainly damage other axle parts. To eliminate this problem, the shaft should be replaced if found to be twisted. The driver of the vehicle should be informed to adopt better driving procedures.

Misalignment fatigue fracture

PITTED PINION TEETH

This problem is the result of extremely high pressure on the gear teeth due to severe use. The pitting located at the heel end of the pinion gear teeth happens when overloading of the pinion moves the pinion out of its proper position relative to the ring gear. The result is a concentrated area of contact on the heel part of the gear teeth which will break down the oil film,

Overheated gear set

Fracture gear teeth

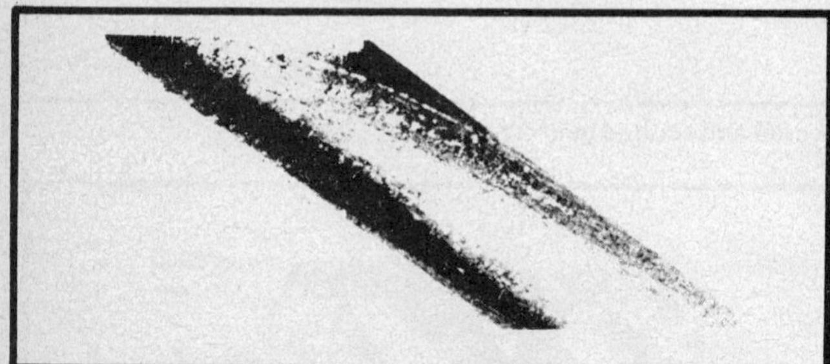

Twisted axle shaft

and thus allow the pinion teeth to pit. Sometimes the ring gear will appear to be undamaged. This is because ring gear damage might not be visible to the naked eye; but the contour of the gear teeth will have changed. The ring and pinion gears must be replaced as a pair, or early failure will occur. The best way to eliminate this problem is to use good quality gear lube. The more severely the vehicle is used the better quality the gear lube should be.

Pitted pinion teeth

Scuffed gear teeth on the coast side only

SCUFFED GEAR TEETH ON THE COAST SIDE ONLY

This wear can be caused by two different things. The first is worn pinion bearing which allows excessive end play in the pinion gear. The result is incorrect contact between the ring and pinion gear teeth on the coast side. This allows excessive pressure to build up on the gear teeth and will break down the oil film, resulting in scoring of the teeth. The second cause is hard, abusive driving in vehicles equipped with a manual transmission. This usually happens when going down a steep grade at high speed and slowing the vehicle by using the clutch to break the speed. The best way to eliminate this problem is to replace the pinion bearing if worn and recommend good driving procedures.

GENERAL AXLE SERVICE

Types of Drive Axles

FULL FLOATING AXLES

Support of the vehicle and the payload weight is by the axle housing. The wheels are driven by splined shafts which "float" within the axle housing.

SEMI–FLOATING AXLE

This axle design provides for the support of the payload and vehicle weight to be carried by the axle shaft through the wheel bearings to the axle housing.

SINGLE REDUCTION AXLE

Final drive ratio is obtained by the use of a single ring gear and pinion set. This type is used for most light and medium duty applications.

DOUBLE REDUCTION AXLE

The final drive ratio is obtained by the use of single ring gear and pinion set in combination with a secondary gear set which is either helical or planetary. This design is used when extreme reduction is necessary and high speeds are not encountered.

2–SPEED AXLES

Final drive ratios are obtained by the use of a single ring gear and pinion set in combination with a secondary gear set, as in the double reduction axles, except the 2-speed axles have the facility to shift from fast ratios to slow ratios. This design is usually found on the medium duty vehicles.

3–SPEED AXLES

Final drive ratios of the 3-speed axles are obtained as follows: 2-speed axles in tandems are operated in either low, intermediate or high range. In low range, the range selector of both axles is shifted to low range. In intermediate range, the range selector of the forward axle is shifted into high and the selector for the rear axle is shifted into low. The power divider unit of the forward axle splits the difference of the ranges and therefore affect the intermediate range. In high range, the range selector for both axles are shifted to high.

LOCK–UP TYPE DIFFERENTIALS

Unlike the standard differential, the locking differential equally divides the torque load between the driving wheels. The vehicle equipped with the locking differential can be operated on any surface (sand, snow, etc.) with a minimum of slippage through one wheel and provides the greatest power to the wheel getting traction. The vehicle with the standard differential provides power to the wheel that's easiest to turn; that is, the one experiencing the poorest traction while the other wheel may be gripping well.

When negotiating a turn, the locking differential allows the outer wheel to turn faster than the inner. When traveling in a straight direction, and the vehicle loses traction over a rough or slippery road, the clutches will lock up and neither wheel will spin. A specified lubricant must be used for locking differentials.

The overhaul procedures are basically the same as for the conventional rear axle assemblies. The noted differences are within the differential carrier case where the lock-up mechanism is located. In some instances where wear is noted within the lock-up mechanism, the lock-up assembly should be replaced as a unit.

AXLE SERVICE AND INSPECTION

Cleaning Bearings

Proper bearing cleaning is important. Bearings should always be cleaned separately from other rear axle parts.

1. Soak all bearings in clean kerosene or diesel fuel oil.

CAUTION

Ordinary gasoline should not be used. Bearings should not be cleaned in hot solution tank.

2. Slush bearings in cleaning solution until all oil lubricant is loosened. Brush bearings with soft bristled brush until ALL dirt has been removed. Remove loose particles of dirt by striking flat against a wood block.
3. Rinse bearings in clean fluid. While holding races to prevent rotation, blow dry with compressed air.

CAUTION

Do not spin bearings while drying.

4. After bearings have been inspected, lubricate thoroughly with regular axle lubricant; then wrap each bearing in clean cloth until ready to use.

Cleaning Parts

Immerse all parts in suitable cleaning fluid and clean thoroughly. Use a stiff bristle brush as required to remove foreign deposits. Clean all lubricant passages or channels in pinion cage, carrier, caps and retainers. Make certain that interior of housing is thoroughly cleaned. Clean vent plugs and breathers.

Small parts such as cap screws, bolts, studs, nuts etc., should be cleaned thoroughly.

Inspection

Magna Flux all steel parts, except ball and roller bearings, to detect presence of wear and cracks.

Checking the drive gear run-out (© General Motors Corp.)

Bearings

Rotate each bearing and check to see if the rollers are worn, chipped, rough or in any other way damaged. Check the cage to see if it is in any way damaged. If either the bearing rollers or the cage are damaged the bearing must be replaced.

Gears

Examine drive gear and drive pinion, differential pinions and differential side gears carefully, for damaged teeth, worn spots in surface hardening, distortion and where drive gear is attached to differential case with rivets, inspect rivets for looseness, replace loose rivets. Check radial clearances between differential side gears and differential case. Check fit of differential pinions on spider.

Differential Case

Inspect case for cracks, distortion or damage, if in good condition, thoroughly clean case and cover; then assemble case with bolts and mount in lathe centers of "V" block stand. If lathe is not available, install differential side bearings and mount case in differential carrier. Install dial indicator and check differential case run out.

Differential case with drive gear installed is checked in the same manner, except that dial indicator reading must be taken at gear instead of at case flange.

Whenever run-out exceeds limits, it may be corrected as later described under "Repair" in this section. However, the support case used in the 2-speed axle cannot be repaired and should be replaced with new case.

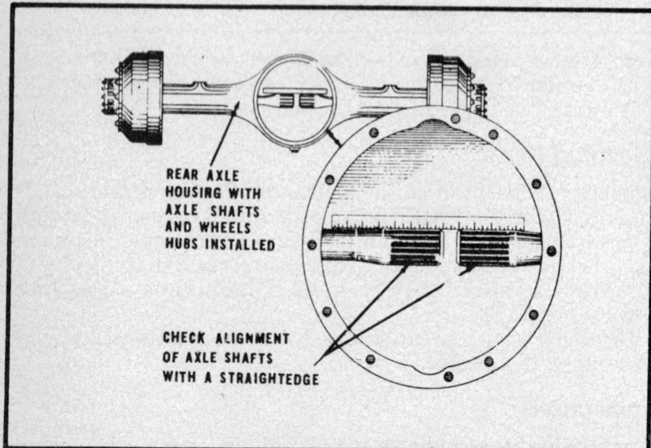

Method of checking the axle housing alignment with full floating axles (© International Harvester Co.)

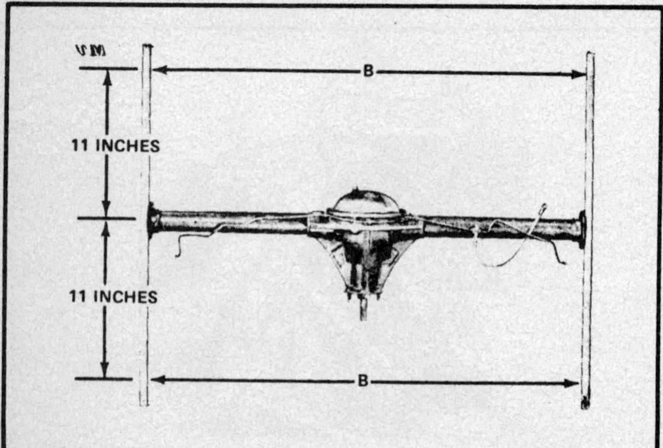

Checking the housing alignment with straight edge bars (© American Motors Corp.)

Axle Shafts

Examine splined end of axle shaft for twisted or cracked splines, twisted shaft, and worn dowel holes in flange. Install new shafts if necessary.

Install axle shaft assembly in lathe centers and check shaft run-out with dial indicator so that indicator shaft end contacts inner surface of flange near outer edge of flange and check flange run-out.

Shims

Carefully inspect shims for uniform thickness. Where various thickness of shims are used in a pack, it is recommended that the thickest shims be used between the thin shims.

Thrust Washers

Replace all thrust washers.

Spider

Carefully inspect spider arms for wear or defects.

Differential Pinion Bushings

Examine bushings (when used) for excessive wear, looseness, or damage. Check fit or gears on spider for excessive clearance.

Axle Housing Sleeves

Sleeves showing damaged threads, wear, or other damage should be replaced if hydraulic press is available, otherwise replace housing.

HOUSING CHECK

Before Removal

A check for bent axle housing can be made with unit in vehicle; however, conventional alignment instruments can be used if available.

1. Raise rear axle with a jack until wheels clear floor. Block up axle under each spring seat.
2. Check wheel bearing adjustment and adjust if necessary, then check wheels for looseness and tighten wheel nuts if necessary.
3. Place a chalk mark on outer side wall of tires at bottom. Measure across tires at chalk marks with a toe-in gauge.
4. Turn wheels half-way around so that chalk marks are positioned at top of wheel. Measure across tires again. If measurement at top is $^1/_3$ in. or more, smaller than measurement at bottom of wheels, axle housing has sagged and is bent. If measurement at top exceeds bottom dimension by $^1/_3$ in. or more, axle housing is bent at ends.
5. Turn chalk marks on both wheels so that marks are level with axle and at rear of vehicle. Take measurement with toe-in gauge at chalk marks; then turn both chalk marks to front and level with axle and take another measurement. If measurement at front exceeds rear dimension by $^1/_3$ in. or more, axle is bent to the rear. If the measurement condition is the reverse, the axle is bent forward.

After Removal

Place two straightedges across the housing flanges and measure the distance between the ends of the straightedges at a point 11 inches from the tube center. Relocate the straightedge 180 degrees and remeasure. If the straightedges are parallel in both measurements within $^3/_{32}$ in., the housing is serviceable.

GENERAL REPAIR

Oil Seal Contact Surfaces

Surface of parts, contacted by oil seals must be free of corrosion, pits and grooves. When abrasive cleaning fails to clean up the seal contact surface and restore smooth finish, a new part must be installed.

OIL SEAL

Removal

Oil seals can be removed with a drift pin. When removing a seal, be careful that it does not become cocked and result in damage to the retainer. Clean surface of retainer carefully, so that seal will seat properly in retainer.

Installation

Coat outer surface of seal retainer with a light coat of sealer, to prevent lubricant leaks. Carefully start seal in retainer. Cutting, scratching, or curling of lip of seal seriously impairs its efficiency and usually results in premature replacement. Lip of seal should be coated with a high temperature grease containing zinc oxide to help prevent scoring and damage to parts during installation.

Seals must always be installed so that seal lip is toward the lubricant.

PINION BEARING ADJUSTMENTS (PRE-LOAD)

Pinion bearing must be adjusted for pre-load before assembly is installed in carrier.

Do not install oil seal until after adjustment is made. Installation of seal would produce false rotating torque.

Cage Type

1. With pinion bearings, and adjusting spacers (or shims) installed in cage, check bearing contact by rotating cage.
2. Using a press, apply pressure (approx. 20,000 lbs.) to outer bearing.
3. Wrap soft wire around cage and pull on horizontal line with spring scale. Rotating (not starting) torque should be within limits recommended by manufacturer.

NOTE: Method of determining inch-pounds torque with scale is to determine radius of cage. Multiply radius in inches by pounds pull required to rotate cage to determine inch-pounds torque. Example: An 8 in. diameter divided by 2 equals 4 in. radius. Multiply 4 in. (radius) by 5 pounds (pull) equals 20 in. pounds torque.

4. If press is not available, check preload torque by installing propeller shaft yoke, washer, and nut and torque to specifications; then check as previously explained. Remove yoke after correct adjustment is obtained.

BEVEL GEAR SHAFT BEARING ADJUSTMENT

Bevel gear shaft bearings must be adjusted for pre-load before pinion and cage assembly and differential assembly are installed in carrier.

1. Wrap several turns of soft wire around gear teeth on cross shaft, then pull on a horizontal line with spring scale. Rotating (not starting) torque should be used.

NOTE: Method of determining inch-pounds torque with scale is to determine radius. Multiply radius in inches by pounds pull required to rotate shaft to determine inch-pounds torque. Example: An 8 in. diameter divided by 2 equals 4 in. radius times 5 pounds (pull) equals 20 inch lbs. torque.

2. Remove or add shims from under cage or cap opposite bevel gear to obtain specified bearing pre-load.

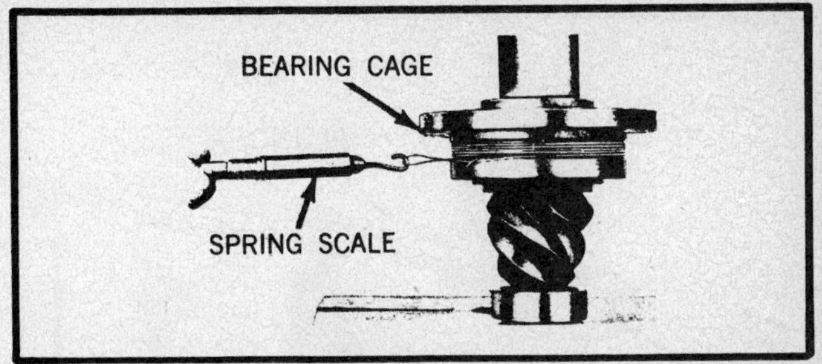

Checking the pinion bearing pre-load (© General Motors Corp.)

Checking the pre-load on bevel gear cross shaft (© General Motors Corp.)

3. When making bevel gear and pinion tooth contact or backlash adjustments it is sometimes necessary to remove or add shims from one side.

NOTE: Always remove or add an equal thickness to the opposite side so to maintain correct pre-load.

GEAR TOOTH CONTACT AND BACKLASH

Pinion Depth Measurement Methods

Methods of adjusting pinions to obtain the proper depths will vary with the axle type and the manufacturers recommendations. Pinion depth settings and gear teeth contact may be determined by the use of pinion setting gauges or by the use of marking dye on the gear teeth.

When using the gauge method, backlash is established after the pinion has been properly set. With the dye method, backlash is obtained first, then the proper pinion tooth contact is established.

The pinion gauge method can be a direct reading micrometer, mounted on or through an arbor bar, set in adapter discs and located in the side carrier bearing cup locations on the differential housing and held in place by the bearing cup caps. The arbor bar coincides and represents the center line of the axle shafts. A reading is taken by the mounted micrometer, from the arbor bar to the head of the pinion to determine the need to add to or remove shims from the shim pack total, to adjust the pinion to the proper nominal assembly dimension or standard pinion depth.

Another method using the arbor bar and discs, is the use of a gauge block with a spring loaded plunger and a thumb screw to lock the plunger upon expansion. A micrometer is used to measure the gauge block after the plunger has been allowed to expand between the arbor bar and the pinion head. As in the mounted micrometer procedure, the shim pack thickness is determined by the reading obtained.

A third method is the use of a gauge block tool, installed in the housing in place of the pinion gear, and a large arbor bar placed in the axle housing differential bearing seats and tightened securely. A measurement is taken between the arbor bar and the pinion tool by either a feeler gauge or the use of individual shims from the shim pack. This measurement represents the shim pack needed for a zero marked pinion.

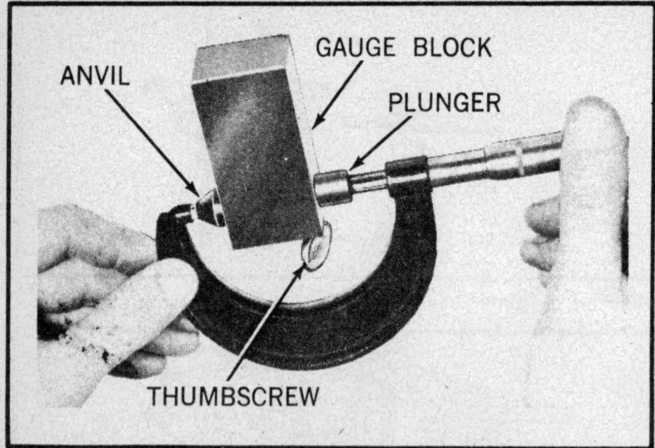

Method of measurement of the gauge block (© Jeep Corp.)

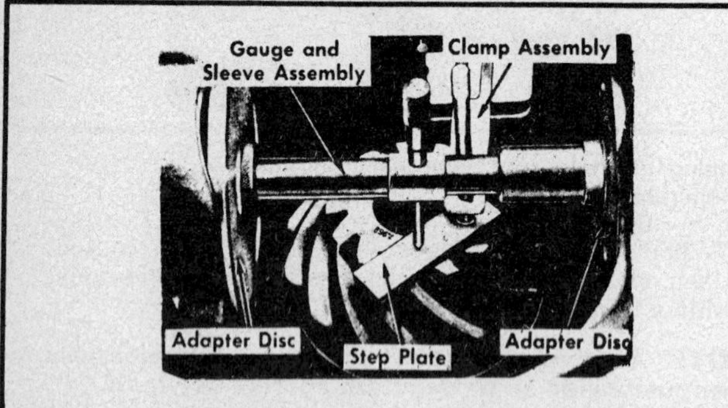

Installment of the pinion gauge—Timken 2-speed (© General Motors Corp.)

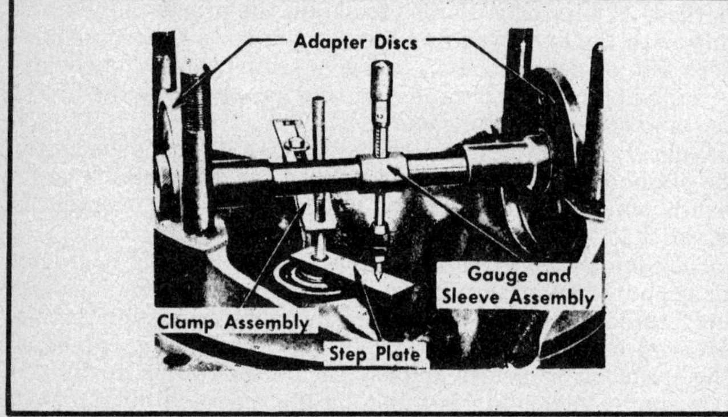

Position of pinion setting gauge (© General Motors Corp.)

Checking the gear backlash-bevel gear (© General Motors Corp.)

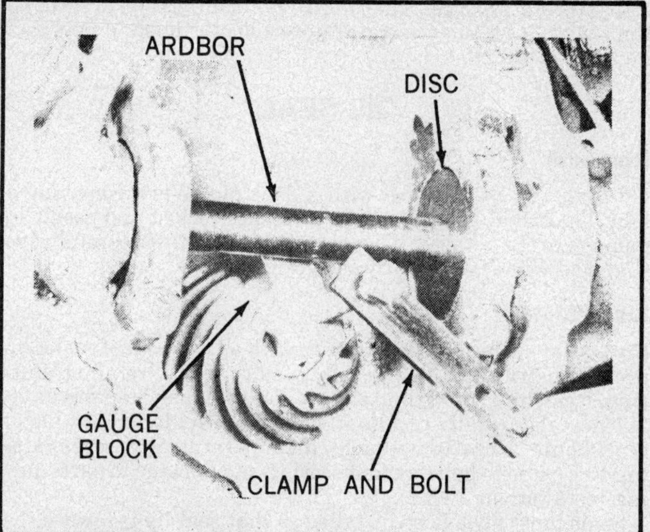

Placement of arbor and gauge block for pinion depth measurement (© Jeep Corp.)

Setting New Pinion (Without Gauge)

Whenever a pinion setting gauge is not available, the approximate thickness of the pinion shim pack at the rear pinion bearing cup, change the sign of the marking (individual variation distance) on the *new* pinion (plus to minus or minus to plus), then add the variation of the old pinion (sign unchanged) which will determine the amount the original shim pack must be changed when installing a new pinion.

On those types of axles where the shims are located between the pinion cage and differential carrier, change the sign of the marking (individual variation distance) on the *old* pinion (plus to minus or minus to plus), then add variation of the new pinion (sign unchanged) which will determine how much the original shim pack must be altered when installing a new pinion.

When the approximate thickness of shim pack has been determined, final check of gear tooth contact must be made using dye method.

Gear Tooth Contact (Dye)

Gear tooth contact cannot be successfully accomplished until pinion and bevel gear bearings are in proper adjustment and gear backlash is within specified limits.

Check for proper tooth contact by painting a few teeth of bevel gear with marking dye. Turn pinion in direction of normal rotation, then check tooth impression on bevel gear.

Gear Backlash

Gears that have been in extended service, form running contacts due to wear of teeth; therefore the original shim pack (between pinion cage and carrier) should be maintained when checking backlash. If backlash exceeds maximum tolerance, reduce backlash only in the amount that will avoid overlap of worn tooth section. Smoothness and roughness can be noted by rotating bevel gear.

If a slight overlap is present at worn tooth section, rotation will be rough.

If new gears are installed, check backlash with dial indicator.

Backlash is increased by moving bevel gear away from pinion, and may be decreased by moving bevel gear toward pinion.

When the drive gear is attached to the differential, backlash is accomplished is differential bearing adjusting rings. It

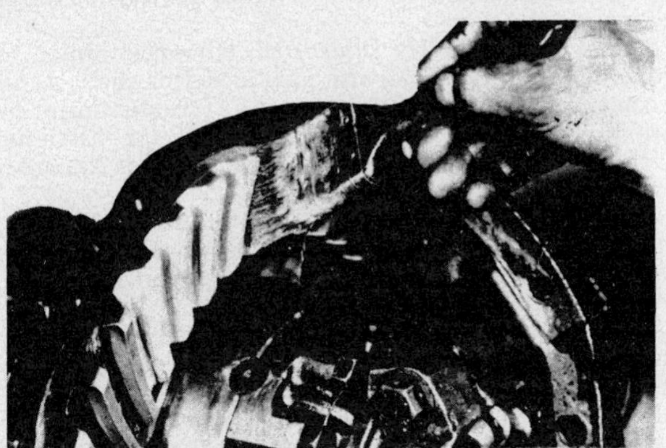

PAINTING GEAR TEETH

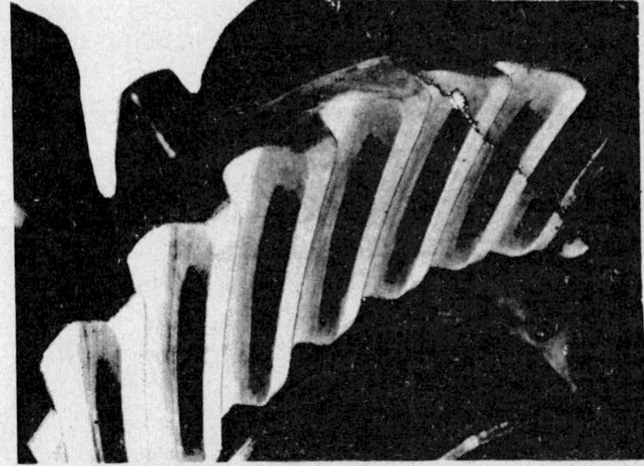

CORRECT TYPE TOOTH CONTACT

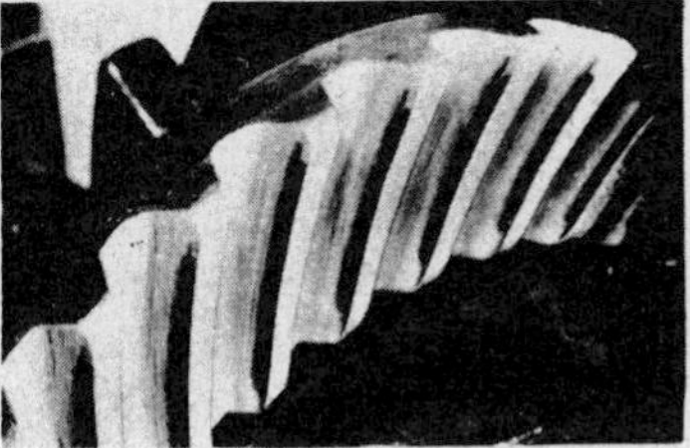

A HIGH NARROW CONTACT is not desirable. If gears are permitted to operate with an adjustment of this kind, noise, galling and rolling over of top edge of teeth will result. To obtain correct contact, move pinion toward bevel gear. This lowers contact area to proper location. This adjustment will decrease the backlash which may be corrected by moving bevel gear away from pinion.

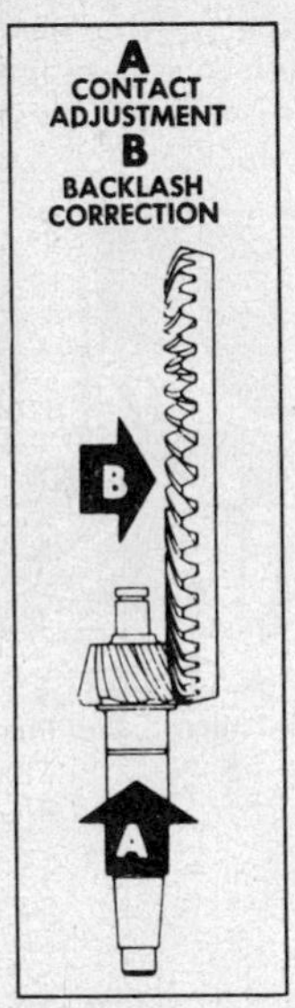

A LOW NARROW CONTACT is not desirable. If gears are permitted to operate with an adjustment of this type, galling, noise and grooving of teeth will result. To obtain correct cc.itact, move pinion away from drive gear. This will raise contact area to proper location. A correct backlash is obtained by moving bevel gear toward pinion.

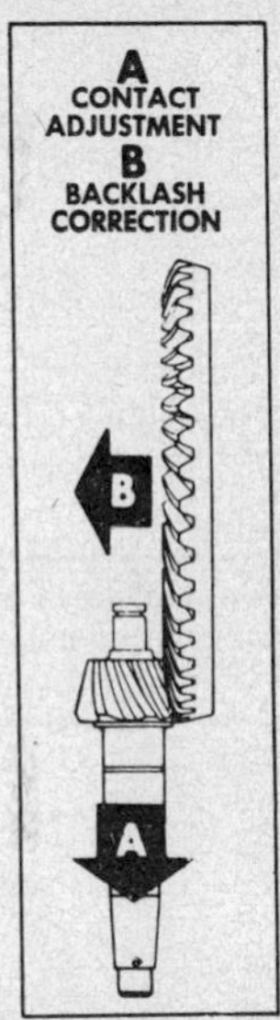

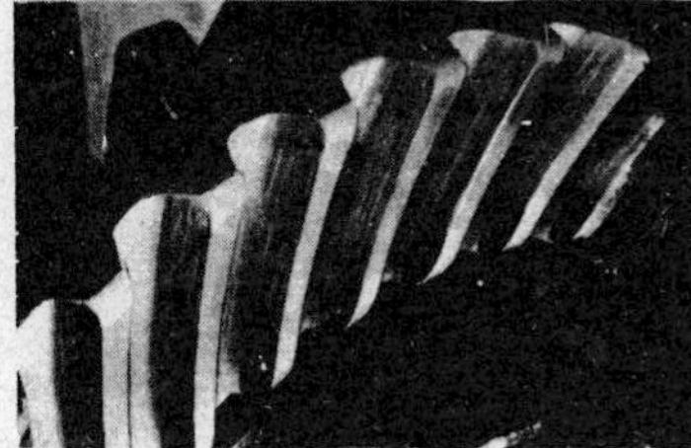

A SHORT TOE CONTACT is not desirable. If gears are permitted to operate with an adjustment of this type, chipping at tooth edges and excessive wear due to small contact area will result. To obtain correct contact, move drive gear from pinion. This will increase the lengthwise contact and move contact toward heel of tooth. Correct backlash is obtained by moving pinion toward bevel gear.

A SHORT HEEL CONTACT is not desirable. If gears are permitted to operate with an adjustment of this type, chipping, excessive wear and noise will result. To obtain correct contact, move drive gear toward pinion to increase lengthwise contact and move contact toward toe. A correct backlash is obtained by moving pinion away from drive gear.

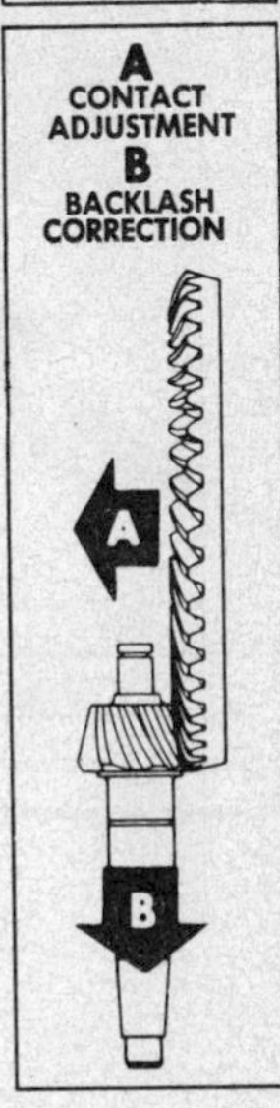

Gear tooth contact chart (© General Motors Corp.)

should be remembered that when one ring is tightened, the opposite ring must be loosened an equal amount to maintain previously established bearing adjustment.

On axles where the bevel gear is supported by cross shaft, backlash is accomplished by adding or removing shims under bearing cages.

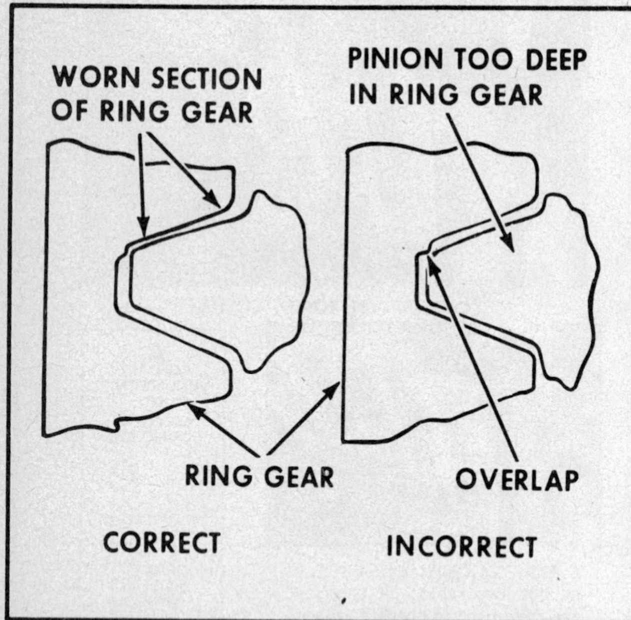

Avoid overlap of worn section of gear teeth during backlash adjustments when using original gears (© International Harvester Co.)

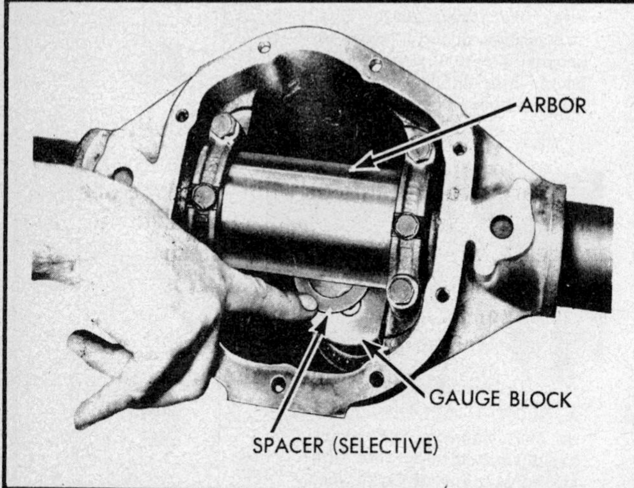

Determining proper shim pack thickness for drive pinion depth of mesh (© Chrysler Corp.)

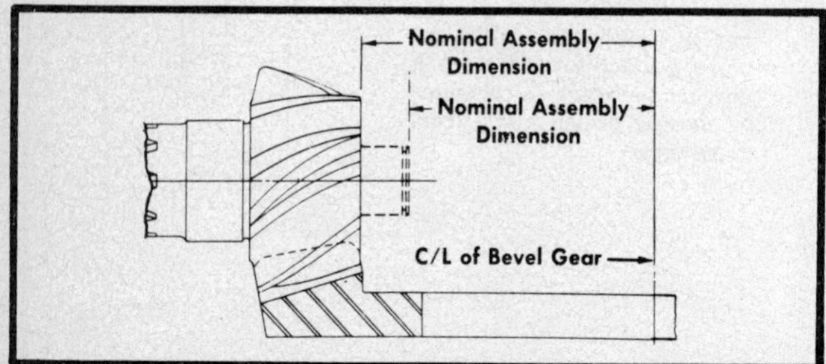

Nominal assembly dimension (© General Motors Corp.)

Terms Used

Certain dimensions must be determined when using the pinion setting gauge:

1. *Nominal Assembly Dimension.* (standard pinion depth) This dimension (varying with axle model) is the distance between the center line of the drive gear (or differential carrier bore) and the end of the drive pinion. This dimension may be marked on the pinion or listed on the Nominal Assembly Dimension and Adapter Disc chart.
2. *Individual Variation Distance,* (pinion depth variance) This dimension is a plus or minus variation of the *Nominal Assembly Dimension* on each individual pinion which may be caused by manufacturing variations.
3. *Corrected Nominal Dimension* (desired pinion depth) This dimension is the *Nominal Assembly Dimension* plus or minus the *Individual Variation Distance.*
4. *Corrected Micrometer Distance is the Corrected Nominal Dimension* less the thickness of the gauge set step plate (0.400") mounted on end of pinion.
5. *Initial Micrometer Reading* is the dimension taken by micrometer to the gauge step plate.
6. *Shim Pack Correction* is determined by the difference between the *Corrected Micrometer Distance* and the *Initial Mi-*

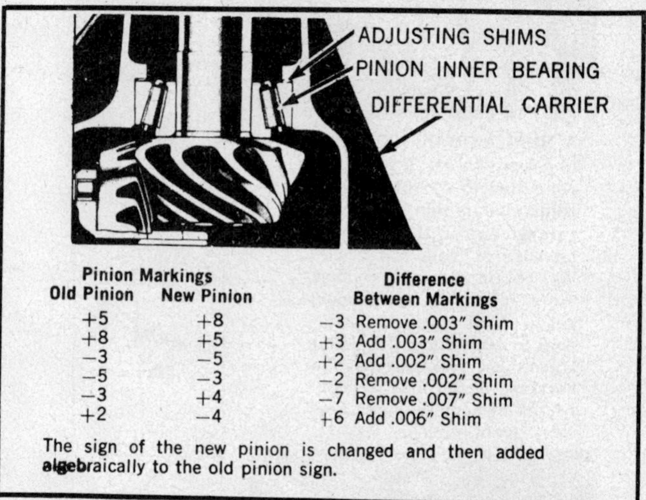

Pinion Markings Old Pinion	New Pinion	Difference Between Markings
+5	+8	−3 Remove .003" Shim
+8	+5	+3 Add .003" Shim
−3	−5	+2 Add .002" Shim
−5	−3	−2 Remove .002" Shim
−3	+4	−7 Remove .007" Shim
+2	−4	+6 Add .006" Shim

The sign of the new pinion is changed and then added algebraically to the old pinion sign.

Determining pinion shim pack thickness, if the shim pack is located at the rear pinion bearing cup (© General Motors Corp.)

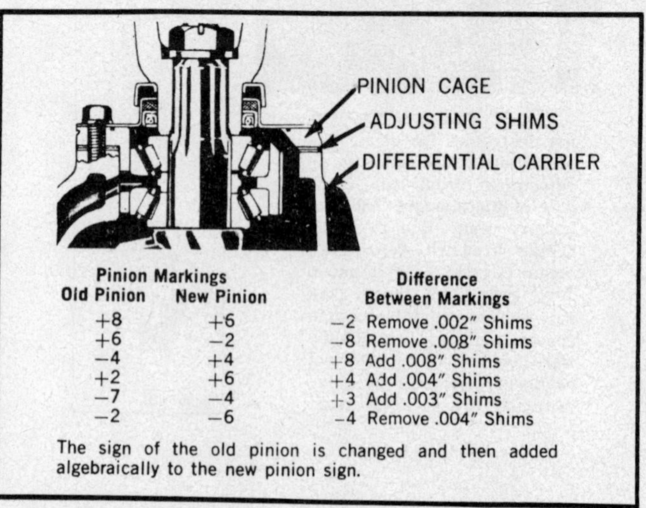

Pinion Markings Old Pinion	New Pinion	Difference Between Markings
+8	+6	−2 Remove .002" Shims
+6	−2	−8 Remove .008" Shims
−4	+4	+8 Add .008" Shims
+2	+6	+4 Add .004" Shims
−7	−4	+3 Add .003" Shims
−2	−6	−4 Remove .004" Shims

The sign of the old pinion is changed and then added algebraically to the new pinion sign.

Determining pinion shim pack thickness, if the shim pack is located between the pinion cage and differential carrier (© General Motors Corp.)

crometer Reading, and represents the amount of shim pack to be added or removed as later explained.

7. *Measured Pinion Depth.* This measurement is the distance between the axle center line and the top of the pinion gear. If a step plate or other type gauge tool is used, this measurement is included in the total.

MARKINGS ON THE PINION AND DRIVE GEARS

Drive gears and pinions are tested at the time of manufacture to detect machining variances and to obtain desirable tooth contact and quietness. When the correct setting is achieved, the gears are considered matched and a set of numbers, along with other identifying marks are etched on the gear set.

A + (plus) or − (minus) sign is used, followed by a digit to represent the factory setting where the tooth contact and quietness were the best. This is called the *Pinion Depth Variance* or *Individual Variation Distance.*

If the pinion is marked +5 for example, this means the distance from the pinion gear rear face to the axle shaft center line is .005 in. more than the standard setting, and if the pinion gear is marked −5, this means that the distance is .005 in. less than the standard setting. To move the pinion to the standard setting, compensating for the variation, shims must be either added to subtracted from the total shim pack, located under the rear pinion bearing cup, between the pinion cage and the dif-

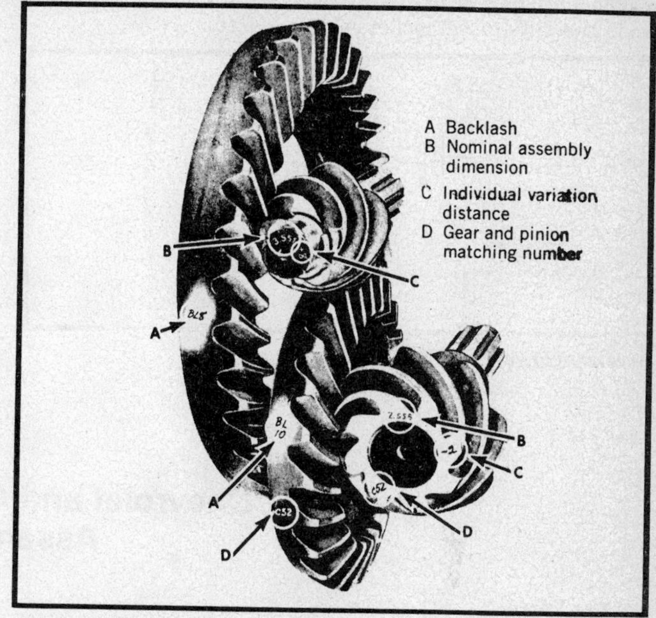

A Backlash
B Nominal assembly dimension
C Individual variation distance
D Gear and pinion matching number
A
B
C
D
Typical pinion and bevel gear markings (© General Motors Corp.)

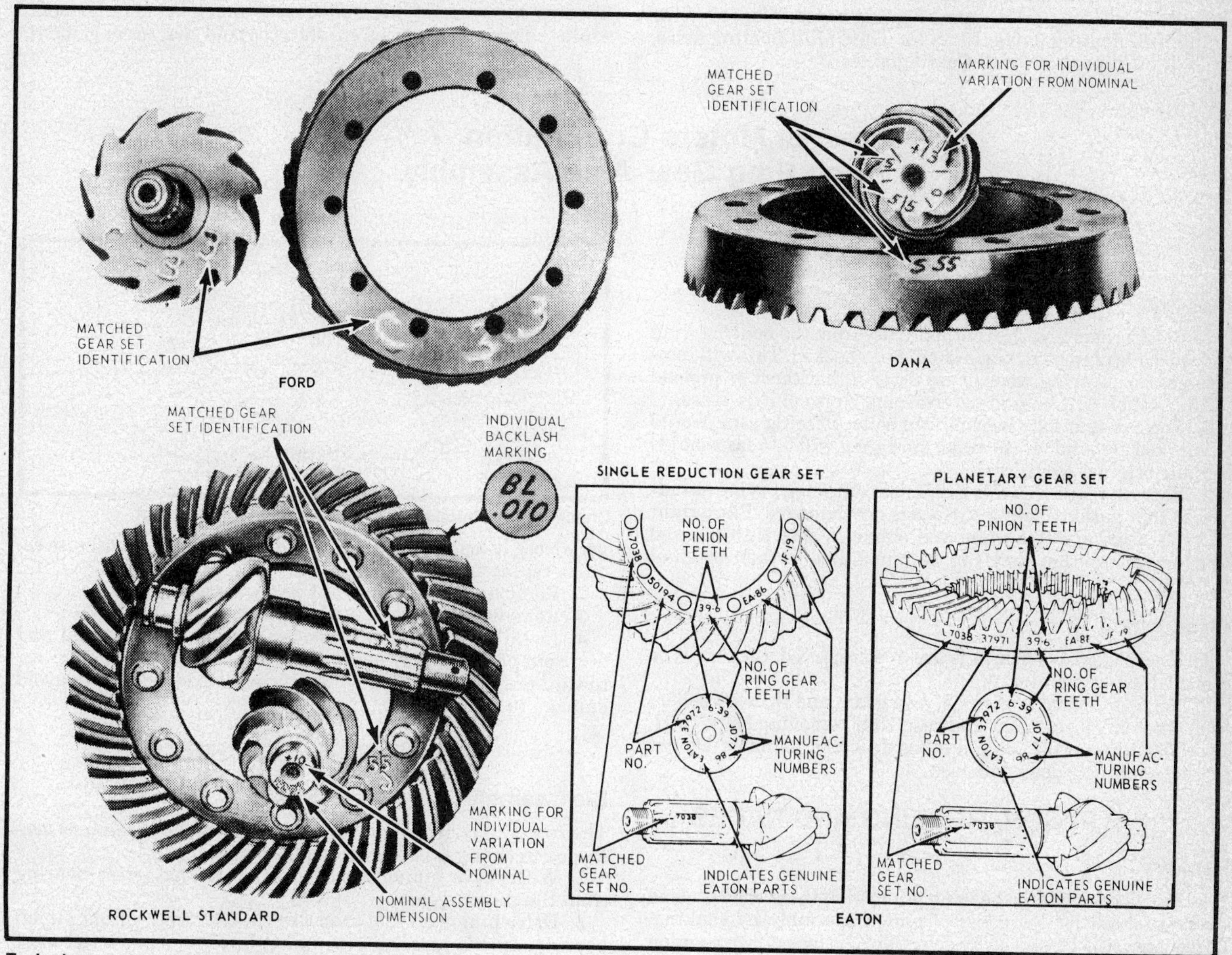

MATCHED GEAR SET IDENTIFICATION
FORD
MATCHED GEAR SET IDENTIFICATION
MARKING FOR INDIVIDUAL VARIATION FROM NOMINAL
DANA
MATCHED GEAR SET IDENTIFICATION
INDIVIDUAL BACKLASH MARKING
BL .010
MARKING FOR INDIVIDUAL VARIATION FROM NOMINAL
NOMINAL ASSEMBLY DIMENSION
ROCKWELL STANDARD
SINGLE REDUCTION GEAR SET
NO. OF PINION TEETH
NO. OF RING GEAR TEETH
PART NO.
MANUFAC-TURING NUMBERS
MATCHED GEAR SET NO.
INDICATES GENUINE EATON PARTS
PLANETARY GEAR SET
NO. OF PINION TEETH
NO. OF RING GEAR TEETH
PART NO.
MANUFAC-TURING NUMBERS
MATCHED GEAR SET NO.
INDICATES GENUINE EATON PARTS
EATON
Typical gear set marking codes (© Ford Motor Co.)

ferential carrier, or under the rear pinion bearing, depending upon the differential model being serviced.

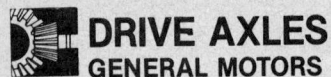

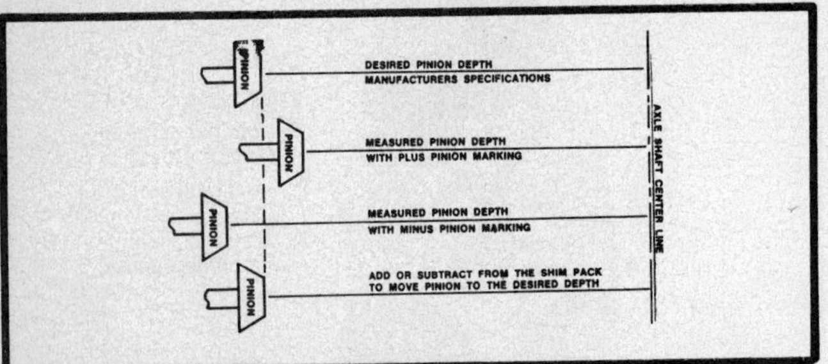

Movement of pinion to obtain desired pinion depth

The procedures to follow in the adjustment of the pinion and drive gears are outlined in the respective differential model disassembly and assembly chapters.

As a rule of thumb on the addition or removal of shims for the pinion depth adjustment, draw a diagram as shown and determine which way the pinion must be moved to obtain the desired pinion depth.

STANDARD TORQUE SPECIFICATIONS AND CAPSCREW MARKINGS

Because of the varied bolt sizes used in the many models of differentials, the torque specifications are not always available to the technician for a specific bolt. By determining the grade of bolt, size, and thread, the proper torque limit can be found in the following chart.

Chevrolet and GMC Rear Axle Assemblies

The single speed rear axles used on the Chevrolet and GMC light and medium trucks are categorized by the ring gear diameter and are identified as follows:
7 $^1/_2$, 8 $^1/_2$, 8 $^7/_8$ in. (GMC) semi-floating axles, 9 $^3/_4$, 10 $^1/_2$ in. (Dana) full floating axles, 10 $^1/_2$ in. (GMC) full floating axles, 12 $^1/_4$ in. (Corporation) full floating axles.

Two speed axles are used by both Chevrolet and GMC trucks that are manufactured by General Motors Corporation or by Eaton Corporation. The Eaton Corporation models can be identified by their use of a spiral bevel pinion gear arrangement, while the remaining axles are of the hypoid gear arrangement.

General Motors Corporation. 7 $^1/_2$ Inch Ring Gear Axle Assembly

REAR AXLE CASE

Removal

1. Before removing the rear axle case from the housing, ring gear to drive pinion backlash should be checked. This will indicate gear or bearing wear or an error in backlash or preload setting which will help in determining cause of axle noise.
2. Remove rear axle bearing cap bolts. Bearing caps should be marked "R" and "L" to make sure they will be reassembled in their original location.
3. Remove rear axle case. Excercise caution in prying on carrier so that gasket sealing surface is not damaged. Place right and left bearing outer races and shims in sets with marked bearing caps so that they can be reinstalled in their original positions.

Disassembly

1. If rear axle side bearings are to be replaced, they must be removed using a puller.
2. Remove rear axle pinions, side gears and thrust washers from case. Mark side gear and case after removing bolts. (L.H. Threads), drive it off using a brass drift and hammer. Do not pry between ring gear and case.

DRIVE PINION, BEARING AND RACES

Removal

1. Check drive pinion bearing pre-load. If there is no preload reading, check for looseness of pinion assembly by shaking. Looseness could be caused by defective bearings or worn pinion flange. If rear axle was operated for an extended period with

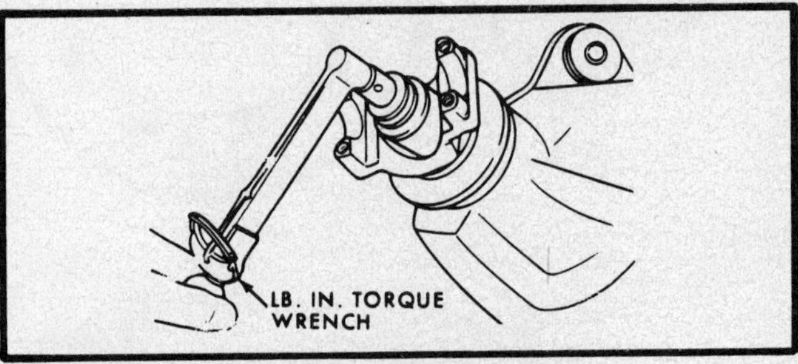

Checking the pinion preload (© General Motors Corp.)

very loose bearings, the ring gear and drive pinion will also require replacement.

2. Remove pinion flange nut and washer.
3. Remove pinion flange.
4. Install drive Pinion Remover J–22536 or its equal and drive out pinion. Apply heavy hand pressure on pinion remover toward rear axle housing to keep front bearing seated to avoid damage to outer race.

BEARING REPLACEMENT

Disassembly

The rear pinion bearing must be removed when it becomes necessary to change the pinion depth adjustment.

1. With drive pinion removed from carrier, press bearing from the pinion gear.
2. Drive pinion oil seal from carrier and remove front pinion bearing. If this bearing is to be replaced, remove outer race from carrier.

STANDARD TORQUE SPECIFICATIONS AND CAPSCREW MARKINGS

Newton-Meter has been designated as the world standard for measuring torque and will gradually replace the foot-pound and kilogram-meter torque measuring standard. Torquing tools are still being manufactured with foot-pounds and kilogram-meter scales, along with the new Newton-Meter standard. To assist the repairman, foot-pounds, kilogram-meter and Newton-Meter are listed in the following charts, and should be followed as applicable.

U.S. BOLTS

SAE Grade Number	1 or 2			5			6 or 7			8		
Capscrew Head Markings Manufacturer's marks may vary. Three-line markings on heads below indicate SAE Grade 5.												
Usage	Used Frequently			Used Frequently			Used at Times			Used at Times		
Quality of Material	Indeterminate			Minimum Commercial			Medium Commercial			Best Commercial		
Capacity Body Size	**Torque**			**Torque**			**Torque**			**Torque**		
(inches)-(thread)	Ft-Lb	kgm	Nm	Ft-Lb	kgm	Nm	Ft-Lb	kgm	Nm	Ft-Lb	kgm	Nm
1/4-20	5	0.6915	6.7791	8	1.1064	10.8465	10	1.3630	13.5582	12	1.6596	16.2698
-28	6	0.8298	8.1349	10	1.3830	13.5582				14	1.9362	18.9815
5/16-18	11	1.5213	14.9140	17	2.3511	23.0489	19	2.6277	25.7605	24	3.3192	32.5396
-24	13	1.7979	17.6256	19	2.6277	25.7605				27	3.7341	36.6071
3/8-16	18	2.4894	24.4047	31	4.2873	42.0304	34	4.7022	46.0978	44	6.0852	59.6560
-24	20	2.7660	27.1164	35	4.8405	47.4536				49	6.7767	66.4351
7/16-14	28	3.8132	37.9629	49	6.7767	66.4351	55	7.6065	74.5700	70	9.6810	94.9073
-20	30	4.1490	40.6745	55	7.6065	74.5700				78	10.7874	105.7538
1/2-13	39	5.3937	52.8769	75	10.3725	101.6863	85	11.7555	115.2445	105	14.5215	142.3609
-20	41	5.6703	55.5885	85	11.7555	115.2445				120	16.5860	162.6960
9/16-12	51	7.0533	69.1467	110	15.2130	149.1380	120	16.5960	162.6960	155	21.4365	210.1490
-18	55	7.6065	74.5700	120	16.5960	162.6960				170	23.5110	230.4860
5/8-11	83	11.4789	112.5329	150	20.7450	203.3700	167	23.0961	226.4186	210	29.0430	284.7180
-18	95	13.1385	128.8027	170	23.5110	230.4860				240	33.1920	325.3920
3/4-10	105	14.5215	142.3609	270	37.3410	366.0660	280	38.7240	379.6240	375	51.8625	508.4250
-16	115	15.9045	155.9170	295	40.7985	399.9610				420	58.0860	568.4360
7/8-9	160	22.1280	216.9280	395	54.6285	535.5410	440	60.8520	596.5520	605	83.6715	820.2590
-14	175	24.2025	237.2650	435	60.1605	589.7730				675	93.3525	915.1650
1-8	236	32.5005	318.6130	590	81.5970	799.9220	660	91.2780	894.8280	910	125.8530	1233.7780
-14	250	34.5750	338.9500	660	91.2780	849.8280				990	136.9170	1342.2420

METRIC BOLTS

Description	Torque ft-lbs. (Nm)			
Thread for general purposes (size x pitch (mm)	**Head Mark 4**		**Head Mark 7**	
6 x 1.0	2.2 to 2.9	(3.0 to 3.9)	3.6 to 5.8	(4.9 to 7.8)
8 x 1.25	5.8 to 8.7	(7.9 to 12)	9.4 to 14	(13 to 19)
10 x 1.25	12 to 17	(16 to 23)	20 to 29	(27 to 39)
12 x 1.25	21 to 32	(29 to 43)	35 to 53	(47 to 72)
14 x 1.5	35 to 52	(48 to 70)	57 to 85	(77 to 110)
16 x 1.5	51 to 77	(67 to 100)	90 to 120	(130 to 160)
18 x 1.5	74 to 110	(100 to 150)	130 to 170	(180 to 230)
20 x 1.5	110 to 140	(150 to 190)	190 to 240	(160 to 320)
22 x 1.5	150 to 190	(200 to 260)	250 to 320	(340 to 430)
24 x 1.5	190 to 240	(260 to 320)	310 to 410	(420 to 550)

CAUTION: Bolts threaded into aluminum require much less torque.

3. If rear pinion bearing is to be replaced, remove outer race from carrier using a punch in slots provided for this purpose.

Cleaning & Inspection

1. Clean all rear axle bearings thoroughly in clean solvent (do not use a brush). Examine bearings visually and by feel. All bearings should feel smooth when oiled and rotated while applying as much hand pressure as possible. Minute scratches and pits that appear on rollers and races at low mileage are due to the initial pre-load, and bearings having these marks should not be rejected.
2. Examine sealing surface of pinion flange for nicks, burrs, or rough tool makrs which would cause damage to the seal and result in an oil leak. Replace if damaged.
3. Examine carrier bore and remove any burrs that might cause leaks around the O.D. of the pinion seal.
4. Examine the ring gear and drive pinion teeth for excessive wear and scoring. If any of these conditions exist, replacement of the gear set will be required.
5. Inspect the pinion gear shaft for unusual wear; also check the pinion and side gears and thrust washers.
6. Check the press fit of the side bearing inner race on the rear axle case hub by prying against the shoulder at the puller recess in the case. Side bearings must be a tight press fit on the hub.
7. Diagnosis of a rear axle failure such as: chipped bearings, loose (lapped-in) bearings, chipped gears, etc., is a warning that some foreign material is present; therefore, the axle housing must be cleaned.

DRIVE PINION

Assembly

1. If a new rear pinion bearing is to be installed, install new outer races.
2. If a new front pinion bearing is to be installed, install new outer race.

SETTING PINION DEPTH

Pinion depth is set with Pinion Setting Gauge J–21777–01. The pinion setting gauge provides in effect, a "Normal" or "zero" pinion as a gauging reference. Instructions are included in gauge set.

1. Make certain all of the gauge parts are clean.
2. Lubricate front and rear pinion bearings liberally with rear axle lubricant.
3. While holding bearings in position, install depth setting gauge assembly.
4. Hold stud stationary with a wrench positioned over the flats on the ends of stud and tighten nut to 2.2 Nm (20 in. lbs.) torque. Rotate gauge plate assembly several complete revolutions to seat the bearings. Then tighten nut until a torque between 1.6 and 2.2 Nm (15 and 25 in. lbs.) is obtained to keep the gauge plate in rotation.
5. Rotate the gauge plate until the gauging areas are parallel with the discs.
6. Make certain rear axle side bearing support bores are clean and free of burrs.
7. Install the correct discs on the gauge shaft.
8. Position the gauge shaft assembly in the carrier so that the dial indicator rod is centered on the gauging area of the gauge block, and the discs seated fully in the side bearing bores. Install side bearing caps and torque bolts to 75 Nm (55 ft. lbs.). Use dial indicator J–8001 or an equivalent indicator reading from 0.0 to 2.5mm (0.00 to 100.0 inch).
9. Set dial indictor at ZERO. Then position on mounting post of the gauge shft with the contact button touching the indicator pad. Push dial indicator downward until the needle rotates approximately $^{3}/_{4}$ turn clockwise. Tighten the dial indicator in this position and recheck.
10. Rotate gauge shaft slowly back and forth until the dial indicator reads the greatest deflection. At the point of greatest deflection, set the dial idicator to ZERO. Repeat rocking action of gauge shaft to verify the ZERO setting.
11. After the ZERO setting is obtained, rotate gauge shaft un-

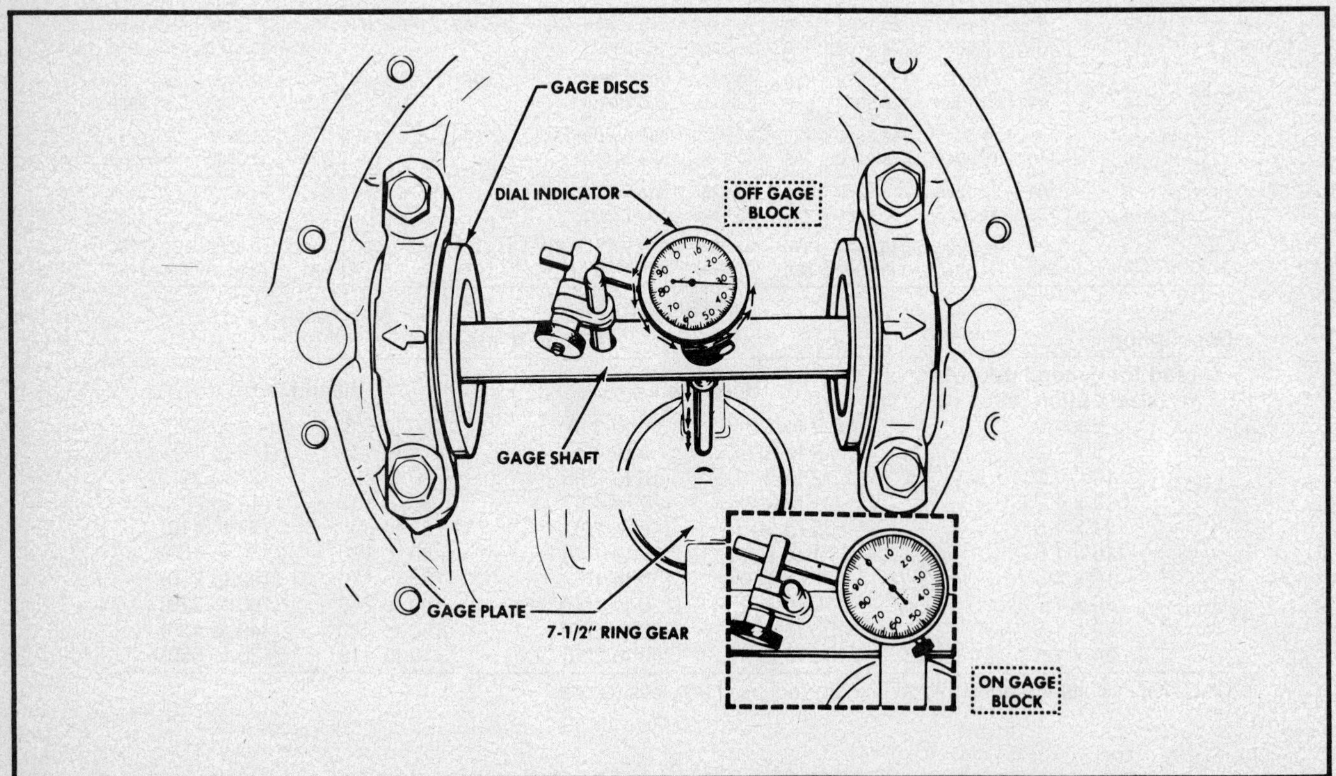

Checking the pinion depth (© General Motors Corp.)

til the dial indicator rod does not touch the gauge block.

12. Record dial reading at pointer position. Example: If pointer moved counterclockwise 1.70mm (0.067 in.) to a dial reading of 0.84mm (0.033 in.) except as follows: Dial indicator reading should be within the range of 0.50–1.27mm (0.020–0.050 in.).

13. Loosen Stud J–21777–43 and remove gauge plate, washer and both bearings from carrier.

14. Position correct shim on drive pinion and install the drive pinion rear bearings.

REAR AXLE CASE

Assembly

Before assembling the rear axle case, lubricate all parts with rear axle lubricant.

1. Place side gear thrust washer over side gear hubs and install side gears in case. If same parts are reused, install in original sides.
2. Position one pinion (without washer) between side gears and rotate gears until pinion is directly opposite from loading opening in case. Place other pinion between side gears so that pinion shaft holes are in line; then rotate gears to make sure holes in pinions will line up with holes in case.
3. If holes line up, rotate pinions back toward loading opening just enough to permit sliding in pinion thrust washers.
4. After making certain that mating surfces of case and ring gear are clean and free of burrs, thread two bolts into opposite sides of ring gear; then install ring gear on case. Install NEW ring gear attaching bolts just snug. NEVER REUSE OLD BOLTS. Torque bolts alternately in progressive stages to 120 Nm (90 ft. lbs.).
5. If case side bearings were removed, re-install bearings.

SIDE BEARING PRE–LOAD ADJUSTMENT

The side bearing pre-load adjustment is to be made before installing the pinion. If the pinion is installed, remove ring gear. Case side bearing pre-load is adjusted by changine the thickness of both the right and left shims by an equal amount. By changing the thickness of both shims equally, the original backlash will be maintained. Production shims are cast iron and vary in thickness from 5.33–6.91mm (0.210–0.272 in.) in increments of 0.05mm (0.002 in.). Standard service spacers are 4.32mm (0.170 in.) thick and steel service shims are available from 1.02–2.08mm (0.040 to 0.082 in.) in increments of 0.05mm (0.002 in.).

Do not attempt to reinstall the production shims as they may break when tapped into place. If service shims were previously installed, they can be reused, but (whether using new or old bearings) adhere to the following procedure in all cases.

1. Before installation of the case assembly, make sure that side bearing surfaces in the carrier are clean and free of burrs. If the same bearings are being reused, they must have the originl outer races in place.
2. Determine the approximate thickness of shims needed by measuring each production shim or each service spacer and shim pack.
3. In addition to the service spacer, a service shim will be needed. To select a starting point in service shim thickness, use the following chart:
4. Place case with bearing outer races in position in carrier. Slip the service spacer between each bearing race and carrier housing with chamfered edge against housing.

Install the left bearing cap loose so that the case may be moved while checking adjustments. Another bearing cap bolt can be added in the lower right bearing cap hole. This will prevent case from dropping while making shim adjustments.

Select one or two shims totaling the amount shown in the right-hand column and position between the right bearing race and the service spacer. Be sure left bearing race and spacer are against left side of housing.

4.32mm (.170") SERVICE SPACER

Total Thickness of Both Prod. Shims Removed	Total Thickness of Service Shims to be Used as a Starting Point
10.57mm .420"	1.52mm .060"
10.92mm .430"	1.78mm .070"
11.18mm .440"	2.03mm .080"
11.43mm .450"	2.29mm .090"
11.68mm .460"	2.54mm .100"
11.94mm .470"	2.79mm .110"
12.19mm .480"	3.05mm .120"
12.45mm .490"	3.30mm .130"
12.70mm .500"	3.56mm .140"
12.95mm .510"	3.81mm .150"
13.21mm .520"	4.06mm .160"
13.46mm .530"	4.32mm .170"
13.97mm .550"	4.83mm .190"

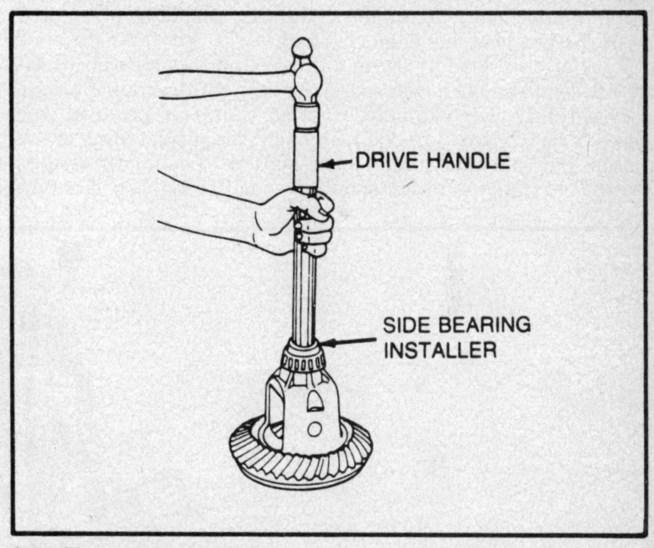

Installing case side bearings (© General Motors Corp.)

5. Insert progressively larger feeler gauge sizes 0.25mm, 0.30mm, 0.36mm, etc. (0.010 in, 0.012 in., 0.014 in., etc.) between the right shim and service spacer until there is noticeable increased drag. Push the feeler gauge downward until the end of the gauge makes contact with the carrier bore so as to obtain a correct reading. The point just before additional drag begins is correct feeler gauge thickness. Rotate case while using feeler gauge to asure an even reading.

The original light drag is caused by weight of the case against the carrier while additional drag is caused by side bearing preload. By starting with a thin feeler gauge; a sense of "feel" is obtained so that the beginning of pre-load can be recognized to obtain Zero clearance. It will be necessary to work case in and out and to the left in order to insert the feeler gauge.

6. Remove left bearing cap and shim from carrier. The total shim pack needed (with no pre-load on side bearings) is the feeler gauge reading found in Step 5 plugs thickness of shims installed in Step 4.
7. Select two shims of approximately equal size whose total thickness is equal to the value obtained in Step 5. These shims will be installed between each side bearing race and service spacer when the case is installed in the carrier. The object of

Step 7 is to obtain the equivalent of a slip fit" of the case in the carrier. For convenience in setting backlash, the "preload will not be added until the final step.

8. If the pinion is in position, install the ring gear, then proceed to REAR AXLE BACKLASH ADJUSTMENT.

DRIVE PINION, BEARING AND RACES

Installtion

1. Install NEW collapsible spacer on pinion and position assembly in carrier. Lubricate pinion bearings with Rear Axle Lubricant before installing pinion.
2. Hold forward on pinion into case assembly.
3. Install front bearing on pinion and drive bering on pinion shaft until sealed in race.
4. Position pinion oil seal in carrier. Install seal.
5. Coat lips of pinion oil seal an seal surface of pinion flange with Lubricant No. 1050169 or equivalent. Install pinion flange on pinionby tapping with a soft hammer until a few pinion threads project through flange.
6. Install pinion washer and nut. Hold pinion flange. While intermittently rotating pinion to seat pinion bearings, tighten pinion flange nut until end play begins to be taken up. When no further end play is detectable and when holder will no longer pivot freely as pinion is rotated, pre-load specifications are being approached. No further tightening should be attempted until the pre-load has been checked.
7. Check pre-load by using an in. pound torque wrench. After pre-load has been checked, final tightening should be done very carefuly. For example, if when checking, pre-load was found to be 0.6 Nm (5 in. lbs.), any additional tightening of the pinion nut can add many additional in. pounds of torque. Therefore, the pinion nut should be further tightened only a little at a time and the pre-load specifications will compress the collapsible spacer too far and require the installation of a new collpsible spacer.

While observing the preceding note, carefully set pre-load at 2.7 to 3.6 Nm (24 to 32 in. lbs.) on new bearings or 1.0 to 1.4 Nm (8 to 12 in. lbs.) on used bearings.

8. Rotate pinion several times to assure that bearings have been seated. Check pre-load again. If pre-load has been reduced by rotating pinion, reset pre-load to specifications.

REAR AXLE BACKLASH ADJUSTMENT

1. Install rear axle case into carrier, using shims as determined by the side bearing pre-load adjustment.
2. Rotate rear axle case several times to seat bearings, then mount dial indicator. Use a small button on the indicator stem so that contct can be made near heel end of tooth. Set dial indicator so that stem is in line as nearly as possible with gear rotation and perpendicular to tooth angle for accurate backlash reading.
3. Check backlash at three or four points around ring gear. Lash must not vary over 0.05mm (0.00 in.) around ring gear. Pinion must be held stationary when checking backlash. If variation is over 0.05mm (0.002 in.) check for burrs, uneven bolting conditions or destorted case flange and make corrections as necessary.
4. Backlash at the point of minimum lash should be between 0.13 and 0.23mm (0.005 and 0.009 in.) for all new gears.
5. If backlash is not within specifications, correct by increasing thickness of one shim and decreasing thickness of other shim the same amount. This will maintain correct rear axle side bearing pre-load. For each 0.03mm (0.001 in.) change in backlash desired, transfer 0.05mm (0.002 in.) in shim thickness. To decrease backlash 0.03mm (0.001 in.), decrease thick-

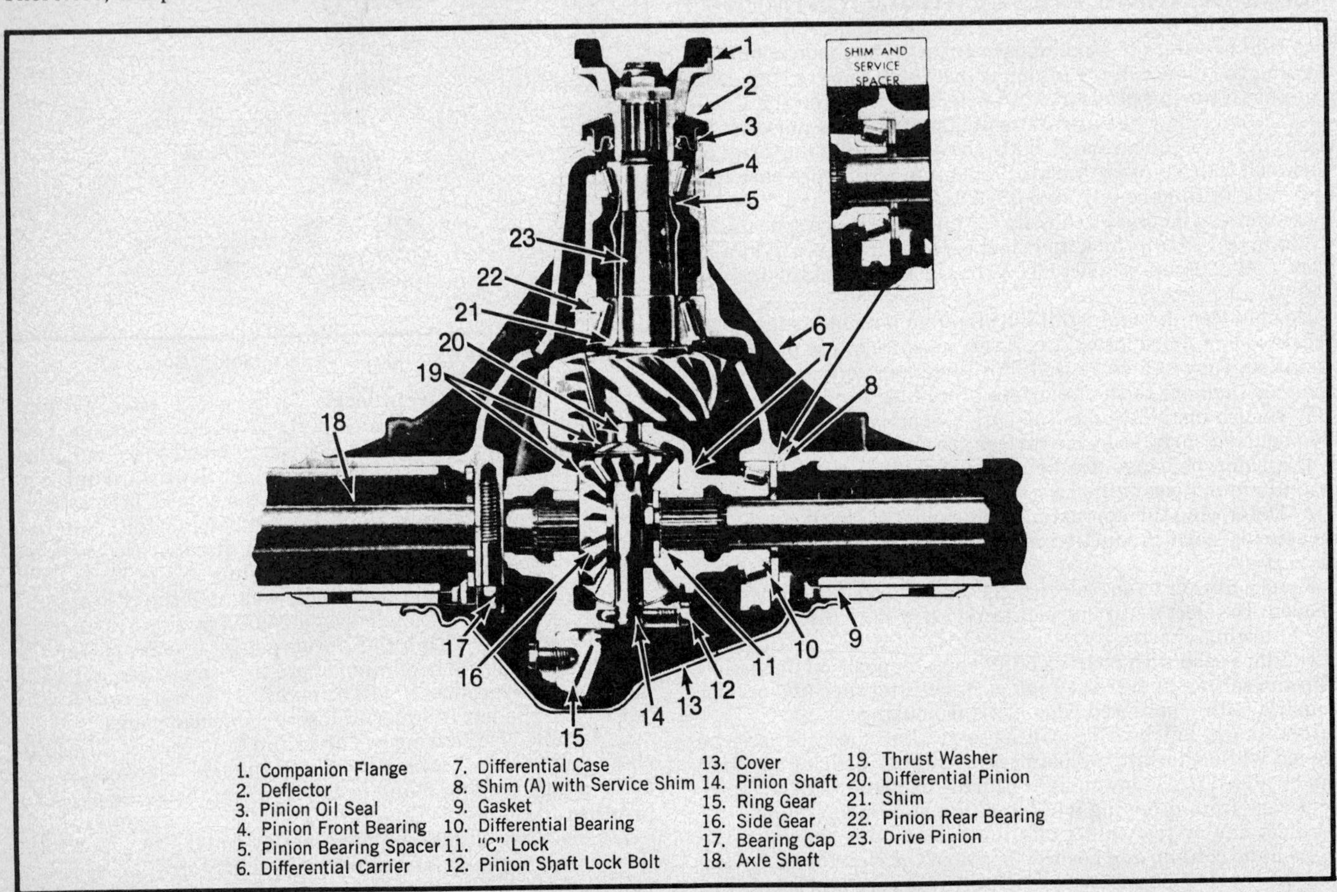

Cross section of the General Motors 8½ and 8⅞ inch rear axle assembly (© General Motors Corp.)

ness of right shim 0.05mm (0.002 in.) and increase thickness of left shim 0.5mm (0.002 in.). To increase backlash 0.05mm (0.002 in.), increase thickness of right shim 0.10mm (0.004 in.) and decrease thickness of left shim 0.10mm (0.004 in.).

6. When backlash is correctly adjusted, remove both bearing caps and both shim packs. Keep packs in their respective position, right or left side.

Select a shim 0.10mm (0.004 in.) thicker than one removed from left side, then insert left side shim pack between the spacer and the left bearing race. Loosely install bearing cap.

7. Select a shim 0.10mm (0.004 in.) thicker than the one removed from right side and insert between the spacer and the right bearing race. It will be necessary to drive the right shim into position.

8. Torque to 75 Nm (55 ft. lbs.).

9. Recheck backlash and correct if necessary.

10. Install axles.

11. Install new cover gasket. Install over and torque cover bolts to 27 Nm (20 ft. lbs.).

12. Fill rear axle to proper level.

General Motors Corporation 8 ½ and 8 ⅞ Inch Ring Gear Axle Assembly

This axle assembly is the semi-floating type with Hypoid type drive pinion and ring gears. The drive pinion gear is supported by two bearings. The differential case contains two pinion gears. The carrier assembly is not removable since it is part of the axle assembly but the design allows for the differential assembly to be serviced while the axle is still in the vehicle. The ring gear is bolted to a one piece differential case that is supported by two preloaded roller bearings.

DIFFERENTIAL CASE

Removal

1. Remove the inspection cover from the axle housing and drain the gear lubricant into a pan.

2. Remove the screw or pin that holds the pinion shaft in place and remove the shaft.

3. Push the axle shaft(s) in a little and remove the "C" locks from the ends of the shafts. Remove the axle shafts from the housing.

4. Before going any further, the backlash should be measured and recorded. This will allow the old gears to be reassembled at the same amount of lash to avoid changing the gear tooth pattern. It also helps to indicate if there is gear or bearing wear, and if there is any error in the original backlash setting.

5. Roll the differential pinions and thrust washers out of the case and also remove the side gears and thrust washers. Make sure to mark the pinions and side gears so they can be reassembled in their original position.

6. Mark the bearing caps and housing and loosen the retaining bolts. Tap the caps lightly to loosen them. When the caps are loose, take the bolts all the way out and then reinstall the bolts just a few turns. This will keep the case from falling out of the housing when it is pried loose.

7. With a pry bar, very carefully pry the case assembly loose. Be careful not to damage the gasket surface on the housing when prying. The case assembly may suddenly come free if the bearings were preloaded, so pry very slowly.

8. When the case assembly is loose, remove the bolts for the bearing caps and remove the caps. Place the caps so they may be reinstalled in the same position. Place any shims that are removed with the cap they were removed from.

DRIVE PINION

Removal

1. With the differential removed, check the pinion preload. Do this by checking the amount of torque needed to turn the pinion gear. For a new bearing, it should be 20–25 in. lbs., and for a used bearing it should be 10–15 in. lbs. If there is no preload reading check the pinion for looseness. If there is any looseness the bearing should be replaced.

2. With a holder assembly installed on the flange, use a socket of the proper size and remove the flange nut and washer.

3. Remove the flange by using a puller assembly and drawing the flange off the pinion splines.

4. Thread the pinion nut a few turns onto the pinion shaft. Using a brass drift and hammer, lightly tap the end of the pinion shaft to remove the pinion from the carrier. Be careful not to allow the pinion to fall out of the carrier after it breaks loose.

5. With the pinion removed from the carrier, discard the old seal pinion nut and collapsible spacer and install new ones when reassembling.

Cleaning & Inspection

1. Clean all parts in solvent and blow dry.

2. Check all of the parts for any signs of wear, chips, cracks or distortion. Replace any parts that are defective.

3. Check the fit of the differential side gears in the case and the fit of the side gear and axle shaft splines.

DIFFERENTIAL BEARING

Replacement

1. With a bearing puller attached to the bearing, pull the bearing from the case.

2. Place the new bearing on the case hub with the thick side of the inner race toward the case. Using a bearing driver, drive the bearing onto the case until it seats against the shoulder on the case.

DRIVE PINION BEARING

Replacement & Adjustment

1. Depending on the bearing that is being replaced, remove the front or rear bearing cup from the carrier assembly.

2. With the pinion gear mounted in a press, press the rear bearing from the pinion shaft. Be sure to record the thickness of the shims that are removed from between the bearing and the gear.

3. Using a bearing driver of the proper size, install a new bearing cup for each one that was removed. Make sure the cups are seated fully against the shoulder in the housing.

4. The pinion depth must now be checked to determine the nominal setting. This allows for machining variations in the housing and enables you to select the proper shim so that the pinion depth can be set for the best bear tooth contact.

5. Clean the housing and carrier assemblies to insure accurate measurement of the pinion depth.

6. Lubricate the front and rear pinion bearings with gear lubricant and install them in their races in the carrier assembly.

7. Using a pinion setting gauge, select the proper clover leaf plate, and install it on the preload stud.

8. Insert the stud through the rear bearing, with the proper size pilot on the stud, and through the front bearing using the proper pilot. Install the hex nut and tighten it until it is just snug.

9. Holding the preload stud with a wrench, tighten the hex nut until 20 in. lbs. of torque are required to rotate the bearings.

10. Install the side bearing discs on the ends of the arbor assembly, using the step of the disc that fits the bore of the carrier.

11. Install the arbor and plunger assembly into the carrier. Make sure the side bearing discs fit properly.

12. Install the bearing caps in the carrier assembly finger tight to make sure the discs do not move.

13. Mount a dial indicator on the mounting post of the arbor. Have the contact button resting on the top surface of the plunger.

14. Preload the dial indicator by turning it one-half revolution and tightening it in this position.

15. Use the button on the gauge plate that corresponds to the ring gear size and turn the plate so the plunger rests on top of it.

16. Rock the plunger rod back and forth across the top of the button until the dial indicator reads the greatest amount of variation. Set the dial indicator to zero at the point of most variation. Repeat the rocking of the plunger several times to check the setting.

17. Turn the plunger until it is removed from the gauging plate button. The dial indicator will now read the pinion shim thickness required to set the nominal pinion depth. Make a note of the reading.

18. Check for the pinion code number on the rear face of the pinion gear being used. This number will indicate the necessary change to the pinion shim thickness. If the pinion is marked with a plus (+) and a number, add that much to the reading you got from the dial indicator. If the pinion has no mark, use the reading from the dial indicator as the correct shim thickness. If the pinion is marked with a minus (−) and a number, subtract that much from the reading on the dial indicator.

19. Remove the depth gauging tools from the carrier assembly and install the proper size shim on the pinion gear.

20. Lubricate the bearing with gear lubricant and using a press, press the bearing into place on the pinion shaft.

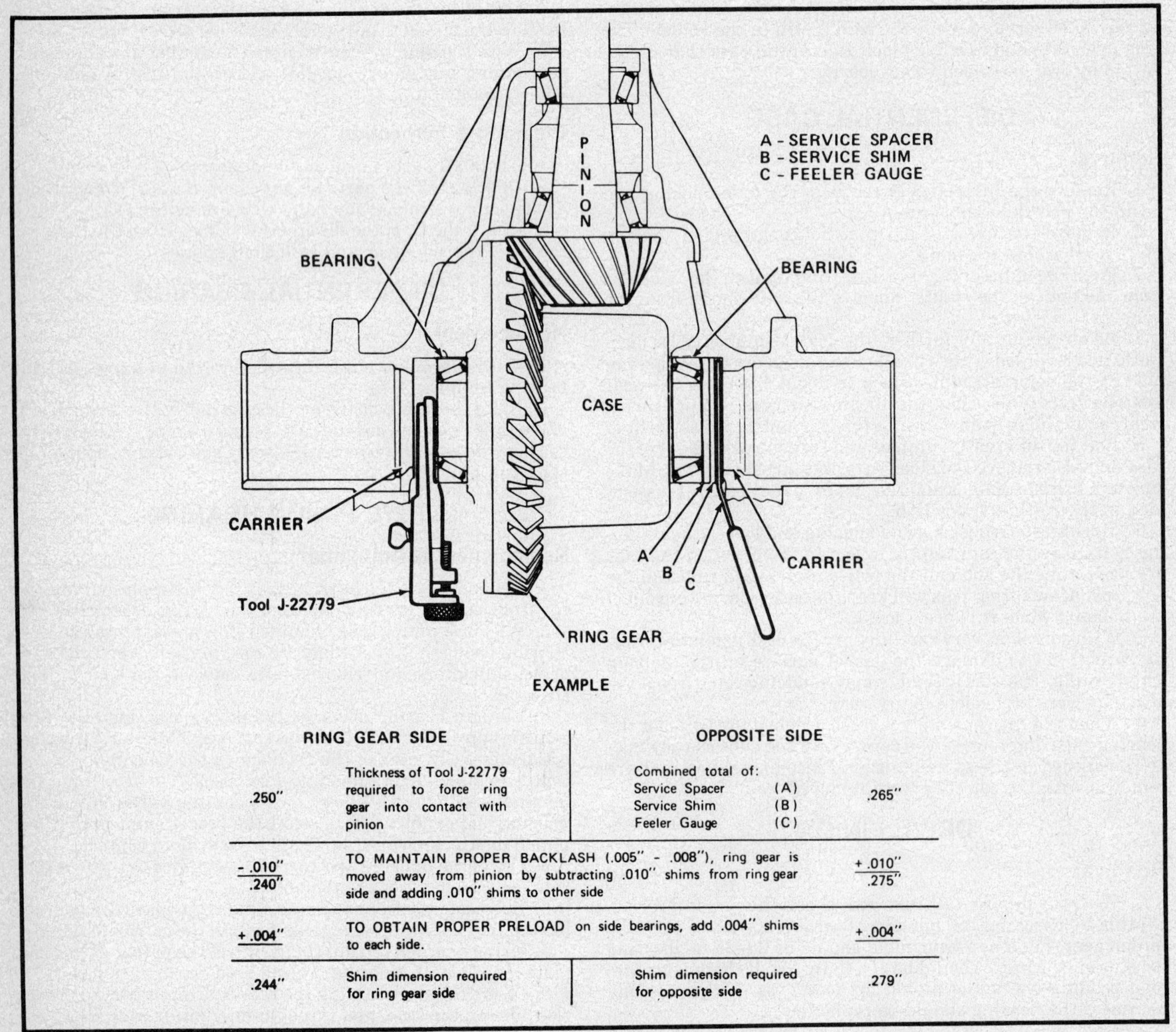

EXAMPLE

RING GEAR SIDE		OPPOSITE SIDE	
.250"	Thickness of Tool J-22779 required to force ring gear into contact with pinion	Combined total of: Service Spacer (A) Service Shim (B) Feeler Gauge (C)	.265"
− .010" / .240"	TO MAINTAIN PROPER BACKLASH (.005" - .008"), ring gear is moved away from pinion by subtracting .010" shims from ring gear side and adding .010" shims to other side		+ .010" / .275"
+ .004"	TO OBTAIN PROPER PRELOAD on side bearings, add .004" shims to each side.		+ .004"
.244"	Shim dimension required for ring gear side	Shim dimension required for opposite side	.279"

Shim pack selection chart (© General Motors Corp.)

PINION GEAR

Installation & Adjustment

1. Lubricate the front bearing with gear lubricant and install it in the front cup.
2. Install the pinion seal in the bore. Using a seal driver and the proper size gauge plate, drive the seal in until the gauge plate is flush with the shoulder of the carrier.
3. Coat the seal lips with gear lubricant and install a new bearing spacer on the pinion gear.
4. Install the pinion gear in the carrier assembly and using a large washer and nut, draw the pinion gear in through the front bearing far enough to get companion flange in place.
5. With the companion flange installed on the pinion shaft, use a holder assembly and tighten the pinion nut until all of the end play is removed from the drive pinion.
6. When there is no more end play the preload should be checked. The preload of the bearing is the amount of torque required to turn the pinion gear. The preload should be 20–25 in. lbs. on new bearings and 10–15 in. lbs. on reused bearings. Tighten the pinion nut until these figures are reached. Do Not over tighten the pinion. This will collapse the spacer too much and make it necessary to replace it.
7. Turn the pinion gear several times to make sure the bearings are seated and recheck the preload.

RING GEAR

Replacement

1. Remove all of the bolts that hold the ring gear to the differential case and with a soft hammer, tap the ring gear off the case.

NOTE: Do not try to pry the ring gear off the case. This will damage the machined surfaces.

2. Clean all dirt from the case assembly and lubricate the case with gear lube. Align the ring gear bolt holes with the holes in the carrier and lightly press the ring gear onto the case assembly. Install all of the bolts and tighten them all evenly, using a criss-cross pattern to avoid cocking the ring gear.
3. When the ring gear is firmly seated against the case, tighten the bolts to 60 ft. lbs.

DIFFERENTIAL CASE ASSEMBLY

Installation & Adjustment

1. Install the thrust washers and side gears into the case assembly. If the original parts are being used, be sure to place them in their original position.
2. Place the pinions in the case so they are 180 degrees apart as they engage the side gears.
3. Turn the pinion gears so the hole in the case lines up with the holes in the gears. When the holes are aligned, install the pinion shaft and lock screw. Do not tighten the lock screw too tightly at this time.
4. Check the bearings, bearing cups, cup seat and carrier caps to make sure they are in good condition.
5. Lubricate the bearings with gear lube. Install the cups on the proper bearings and install the differential assembly in the carrier. Support the carrier assembly to keep it from falling.
6. Install a support strap on the left side bearing and tighten the bearing bolts to an even, snug fit.
7. With the ring gear tight against the pinion gear, insert a gauging tool between the left side bearing cup and the carrier housing.
8. While lightly shaking the tool back and forth, turn the adjusting wheel until a slight drag is felt. Tighten the lock nut.
9. Between the right side bearing and carrier, install a service spacer, 0.170 in. thick, a service shim and a feeler gauge.

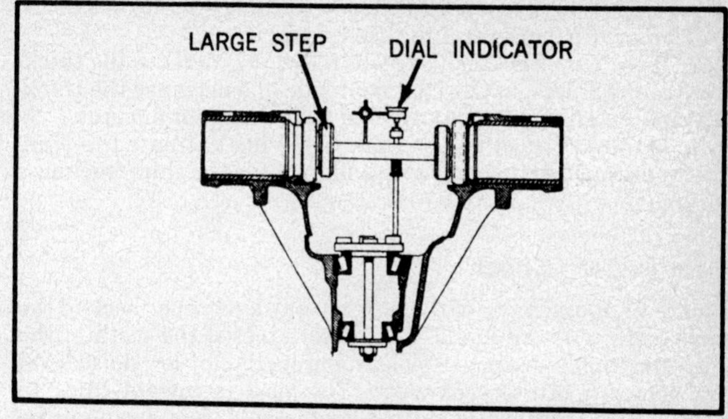

Gauge tools installed in carrier (© General Motors Corp.)

The feeler gauge must be thick enough so a light drag is felt when it is moved between the carrier and the shim.

10. Add the total of the service spacer, service shim and the feeler gauge. Remove the gauging tool from the left side of the carrier and using a micrometer, measure the thickness in at least three places. Average the readings and record the result.
11. Refer to the chart to determine the proper thickness of the shim packs.
12. Install the left side shim first, then install the right side shim between the bearing cup and spacer. Position the shim so the chamfered side is outward or next to the spacer. If there is not enough chamfer around the outside of the shim, file or grind the chamfer a little to allow for easy installation.
13. If there is difficulty in installing the shim, partially remove the case from the carrier and slide both the shim and case back into place.
14. Install the bearing caps and torque them to 60 ft. lbs. Tighten the pinion shaft lock screw.

NOTE: The differential side bearings are now preloaded. If any adjustments are made in later procedures, make sure not to change the preload. Do Not change the total thickness of the shim packs.

15. Mount a dial indicator on the carrier assembly with the indicator button perpendicular to the tooth angle and in line with the gear rotation.
16. Measure the amount of backlash between the ring and pinion gears. The backlash should be between 0.005–0.008 in. Take readings at four different spots on the gear. There should not be variations greater than 0.002 in.
17. If there are variations greater than 0.002 in. between the readings, check the runout between the case and ring gear. The gear runout should not be greater than 0.003 in. If the runout

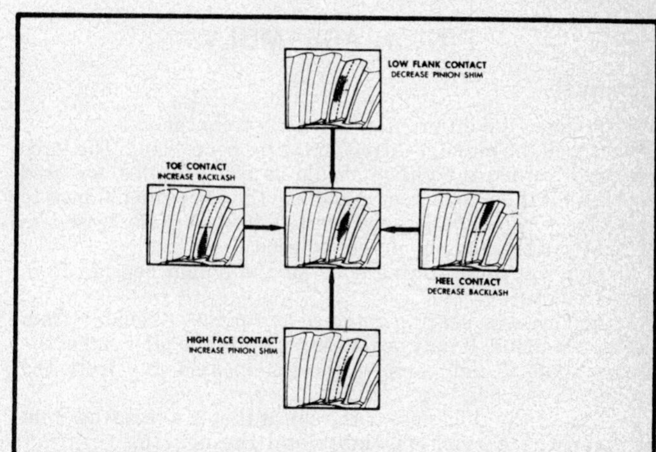

Gear tooth contact check (© General Motors Corp.)

does exceed 0.003 in. check the case and ring gear for the deformation or dirt between the case and gear.

18. If the gear backlash exceeds 0.008 in., increase the thickness of the shims on the ring gear side and decrease the thickness of the shims on the opposite side, an equal amount.

19. If the backlash is less than 0.005 in., decrease the shim thickness on the ring gear side and increase the shim thickness on the opposite side an equal amount.

Gear Pattern Check

Before final assembly of the differential, a pattern check of the gear teeth must be made. This determines if the teeth of the ring and pinion gears are meshing properly, for low noise level and long life of the gear teeth. The most important thing to note is if the pattern is located centrally up and down on the face of the ring gear.

1. Wipe any oil out of the carrier and wipe all dirt and oil from the teeth of the ring gear.
2. Coat the teeth of the ring gear with a gear marking compound.
3. With the bearing caps torqued to 55 ft. lbs., expand the brake shoes until it takes 20–30 ft. lbs. of torque to turn the pinion gear.
4. Turn the companion flange so the ring gear makes one full rotation in one direction, then turn it one full rotation in the opposite direction.
5. Check the pattern on the teeth and refer to the chart for any adjustments necessary.
6. With the gear tooth pattern checked and properly adjusted, install the axle housing cover gasket and cover and tighten securely. Fill the axle with gear lube to the correct level.
7. Road test the vehicle to check for any noise and proper operation of the rear.

General Motors Corporation. 10 1/2 Inch Ring Gear Axle Assembly

This axle is a full floating type that uses special hypoid type drive and pinion gears. The pinion gear is supported by three bearings, two in front of the pinion gear and one behind. The differential assembly has either two or four pinions depending on the application of the axle. This axle assembly must be removed from the vehicle to remove and service the differential.

DIFFERENTIAL

Removal

1. With the axle assembly removed from the vehicle, place the axle assembly in a vise or holding fixture.
2. Remove the bolts that retain the cover assembly and remove the cover, allowing the gear lubricant to drain into a pan.
3. Remove the axle shafts from the axle assembly.

NOTE: Before going any further, check the pinion backlash and record the measurement so that if the same gears are reused they may be installed at the same backlash to avoid changing the gear tooth pattern.

4. From the bearing caps, remove the adjusting nut lock retainers.
5. Mark the bearing caps so they may be reinstalled in the same position and remove the bearing caps.
6. Loosen the side bearing adjusting nut and remove the differential carrier from the axle housing.

PINION ASSEMBLY

Removal

1. Remove the differential assembly from the axle.
2. Check the pinion bearing for the proper preload. The force required to turn the pinion should be 25–35 in. lbs. for used bearings. If there is no reading, shake the companion flange to check for any looseness in the bearing. If there is any looseness present the bearing should be replaced.
3. Remove the retaining bolts for the pinion bearing from the axle housing.
4. Remove the bearing retainer and pinion assembly from the axle housing. It may be necessary to tap the pilot end of the pinion shaft to help remove the pinion assembly from the carrier.
5. Record the thickness of the shims that are removed from between the carrier assembly and the bearing retainer assembly.

DRIVE PINION

Disassembly

1. With the pinion assembly clamped in a vise, install a holder assembly on the flange.
2. Using the proper size socket, remove the pinion nut and washer from the pinion. When reassembling the pinion use a new nut and washer assembly.
3. With the holder assembly still in place, use a puller to remove the flange from the pinion.
4. With the bearing retainer supported in a press, press the pinion out of the retainer assembly. Be careful not to allow the pinion gear to fall onto the floor because this can damage the gear.
5. Separate the pinion flange, oil seal, front bearing and the bearing retainer. If the oil seal needs to be replaced it may have to be driven from the retainer.
6. Using a drift, drive the front and rear bearing cups from the bearing retainer.
7. Support the pinion assembly in a press, with the bearing supported. Press the bearing from the pinion gear.
8. Using a drift, drive the straddle bearing from the carrier assembly.

Cleaning & Inspection

1. Clean off all the parts in solvent and blow dry.
2. Check the pinion gear for signs of wear, chips, cracks or any other imperfections. Check the splines for signs of wear or distortion.
3. Check the bearings for signs of wear or pitting on the rollers and races and check the bearing cage for dents and bends. Check the bearing retainer for any cracks, pits, grooves or corrosion.
4. Check the pinion flange splines for any signs of wear or distortion.
5. Replace parts that show any of the signs mentioned above.

DIFFERENTIAL CASE

Disassembly

1. Scribe a line across the two halves of the differential case so they may be reassembled in the same position, and with the ring gear removed, separate the two halves. To remove the ring gear, remove the ring gear bolts and washers, and using a soft

hammer tap the ring gear from the case.

2. Remove the internal parts from the inside of the case and set them aside in order that they may be reassembled in the same position.

Cleaning & Inspection

1. Check the differential gears, pinions, thrust washers and spider for any signs of unusual wear, chips, cracks or pitting.
2. Check all mating surfaces for signs of wear.
3. Replace parts that show any of the signs mentioned above.

DIFFERENTIAL CASE

Assembly

1. Using a good quality gear lubricant coat all of the parts.
2. Assemble the differential pinions and thrust washers onto the spider and install the assembly into the differential case.
3. Line up the scribe marks on the two halves of the differential case and install the ring gear. Install the ring gear washers and bolts and torque the bolts to approx. 10 ft. lbs.

SIDE BEARING

Replacement

1. Install a bearing puller on the bearing and remove the bearing assembly from the differential case.
2. Check the bearings for any signs of wear on distortion.
3. Install the new bearing by setting it in place on the differential case and, using a bearing driver, drive the bearing onto the case assembly until it seats against the shoulder on the case.

DRIVE PINION

Assembly & Adjustment

1. Coat all of the parts with a good quality gear lubricant.
2. With the pinion gear in a press, press the rear bearings onto the pinion assembly.
3. In the bearing retainer, install the front and rear bearing cups using a driver of the proper size.
4. In the axle housing, install the straddle bearing assembly using the proper size driver.
5. Install the bearing retainer with the bearing cups in place on the pinion gear and install a new collapsible spacer.
6. Press the front bearing onto the pinion gear.
7. Lubricate the oil seal with a good quality high pressure grease and install the seal into the retainer bore. Be sure to press the seal down until it rests against the internal shoulder.

		CODE NUMBER ON ORIGINAL PINION				
		+2	+1	0	-1	-2
CODE NUMBER ON SERVICE PINION	+2	--	ADD .001	ADD .002	ADD .003	ADD .004
	+1	SUBT. .001	–	ADD .001	ADD .002	ADD .003
	0	SUBT. .002	SUBT. .001	–	ADD .001	ADD .002
	-1	SUBT. .003	SUBT. .002	SUBT. .001	–	ADD .001
	-2	SUBT. .004	SUBT. .003	SUBT. .002	SUBT. .001	–

Pinion depth codes and corresponding shim thickness (© General Motors Corp.)

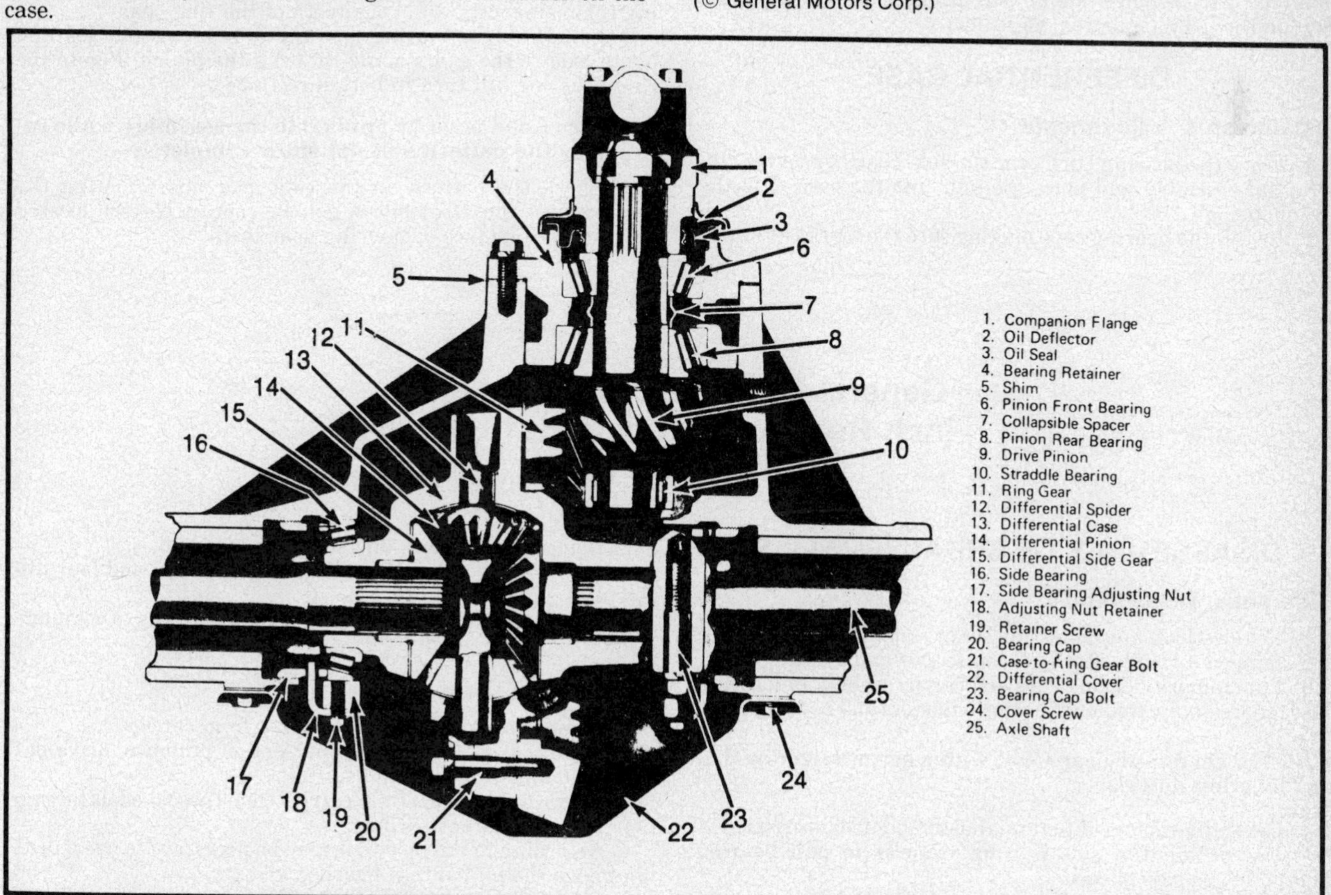

Cross section of General Motors 10½ inch rear assembly (© General Motors Corp.)

8. Install the pinion flange and oil deflector onto the splines of the pinion gear and install a new lock washer and pinion nut.

9. With the pinion flange clamped in a vise and a holder assembly installed on the flange, tighten the nut to obtain the proper preload. Measure the amount of torque required to turn the pinion gear. For a new bearing the torque required is 25–35 in. lbs. and for an old bearing it is 5–15 in. lbs. To preload the bearing, tighten the pinion nut to approx. 350 ft. lbs. and take a reading of the torque required to turn the pinion. Continue tightening the nut until the proper preload is obtained.

CAUTION

Do not tighten the nut too tightly because it will collapse the spacer too much. This will make replacement necessary.

DRIVE PINION ASSEMBLY

Installation

1. If installing a new pinion gear, check the top of the new gear for the depth code number.
2. Compare the new number with the old number on top of the old pinion and check the pinion depth chart for preliminary setting of the pinion depth.
3. Check the thickness of the original shims removed from the pinion and either add or subtract from the shims according to the chart.
4. Place the shim on the carrier assembly and line the holes up with those in the axle housing. Make sure the surfaces are clean of all dirt and grease.
5. Install the retainer and pinion assembly in the housing making sure the holes line up and install the retaining bolts. Torque the bolts to approx. 45 ft. lbs.

DIFFERENTIAL CASE

Installation & Adjustments

1. Place the bearing cups over the side bearings on the differential assembly and place the unit into the carrier in the axle housing.
2. Install the bearing caps making sure the marks are lined up and install the bolts. Tighten the bearing retaining bolts.
3. Loosen the right side nut and tighten the left side nut until the ring gear comes in contact with the pinion gear. Do not force the gears together. This brings the gears to zero lash.
4. Back off the left side adjusting nut about two slots and install the lock fingers into the nut.
5. In this order tighten the right side adjusting nut firmly to force the case assembly into tight contact with the left side adjusting nut and then loosen the right side nut until it is free from the bearing.
6. Again retighten the right side adjusting nut until it comes in contact with the bearing. Tighten the right adjusting nut about two slots if it is an old bearing or three slots if it is a new bearing.
7. Install the lock retainers into the slots and torque the bearing cap bolts to 100 ft. lbs. This procedure now insures that the bearings are preloaded properly. If more adjustments are made, make sure the preload stays the same. To do this, one adjusting nut must be loosened the same amount the other nuts is tightened.
8. Install a dial indicator on the housing and measure the amount of backlash between the ring and pinion gear. The backlash should measure between 0.003 to 0.012 in. with the best figure being between 0.005 to 0.008 in.
9. If the backlash is more than 0.012 in., loosen the right side adjusting nut one slot and tighten the left side one slot. If the backlash is less than 0.003 in., loosen the left side nut one slot and tighten the right side one slot. These adjustments should bring the backlash measurement into an acceptable range.

Pattern Check

1. Clean all the oil off the ring gear and using a gear marking compound, coat all of the teeth of the ring gear.
2. Make sure the bearing caps are torqued to 110 ft. lbs. and apply load to the gears while rotating the pinion. Rotate the ring gear one full turn in both directions.

NOTE: Load must be applied to the assembly while rotating or the pattern will not show completely.

3. Check the pattern on the ring gear and following the chart, adjust the assembly to get the contact pattern located centrally on the face of the ring gear teeth.

General Motors Corporation. 12 1/4 Inch Rear Axle Models H110, H135 H150 and H170

DISASSEMBLY OF SUBASSEMBLIES

Differential Disassembly

1. Remove lock nut, adjusting screw, and thrust block.
2. Remove two adjuster lock cap screws and locks.
3. Punch-mark bearing caps and carrier to help in locating caps for assembly. Remove bearing adjusters and bearing caps.

NOTE: Do not pry caps free with a screwdriver or distort locating dowels.

4. Carefully remove differential assembly from carrier.
5. Use differential side bearing remover to pull bearing cones off each side of case.
6. Make sure that differential case halves are punch-marked so that they can be reassembled in same position.
7. Remove drive gear, and separate case halves.
8. Remove two side gears; differential spider, and four differential pinions.
9. Remove pinion and side gear thrust washers to complete differential disassembly.

Drive Pinion Disassembly

1. Remove seal retainer and gasket from carrier.
2. Use brass drift against inner end of pinion to drive out pinion and bearings assembly.
3. Remove shim pack from carrier from those models having tapered roller outer bearings.
4. According to the model, it may be necessary to use a drift to remove the pinion rear bearing.
5. Clamp yoke in soft-jawed vise. Remove yoke nut and washer and separate drive pinion from yoke.

6. Separate yoke from oil seal retainer.

7. Place retainer in a soft-jawed vise and, using a hammer and chisel, remove oil seal and then the felt oil seal.

8. On models with tapered roller outer bearing, remove bearing cup, outer tapered bearing cone, and bearing spacer from drive pinion.

9. Using bearing remover press plate with press, separate bearing cone (some models) or roller bearing (on all other models) from drive pinion.

10. On models H110 and H135, remove bearing lock ring, and use press plates with arbor press to remove roller bearing from inner end of drive pinion. This completes drive pinion disassembly.

ASSEMBLY OF SUBASSEMBLIES

NOTE: Thoroughly clean and lubricate all components with axle lubricant before reassembling.

Drive Pinion Assembly

1. Clean counterbore of oil seal retainer. Saturate felt seal in oil and install evenly in retainer. Soak oil seal in light engine oil for about one hour before installing. Coat outer surface of seal lightly with sealing compound to prevent oil leaks between seal and retainer.

2. Install oil seal into retainer with lip of seal toward inner side of retainer. Using a seal installer, press oil seal into retainer with face of seal flush with retainer face.

3. Retainer surface must be clean and smooth to prevent oil leaks between retainer and carrier.

4. On models H150 and H170, press bearing into place into carrier bore.

5. On models H110 and H135, press roller bearing into position on drive pinion with chamfered side of inner race facing toward pinion shoulder. Position bearing lock ring to secure bearing on drive pinion.

NOTE: Opposed tapered roller bearing cones, two bearing cups, and spacer used on some models are serviced and replaced as a unit. The spacer is a preselected one to provide proper bearing adjustment.

6. Models with tapered roller bearings:

a. Press inner bearing cone into place with largest side of cone facing pinion gear end.

b. Install original shim pack in carrier. If original ring gear and pinion are reinstalled, use shims that were removed. Shims are available in five thicknesses: 0.012, 0.015, 0.018, 0.021 and 0.024 in. When using new gears, start with one 0.021 in. shim and refer to General Axle Service section for details on checking pinion depth.

c. Insert pinion assembly into carrier (on models H150 and H170), align roller bearing with carrier boss. Install bearing spacer, bearing cup and bearing cone with wide side facing pinion splines.

7. Models with double-row ball bearing: Using a 2 in. pipe or tubing, drive bearing unit into proper seating position.

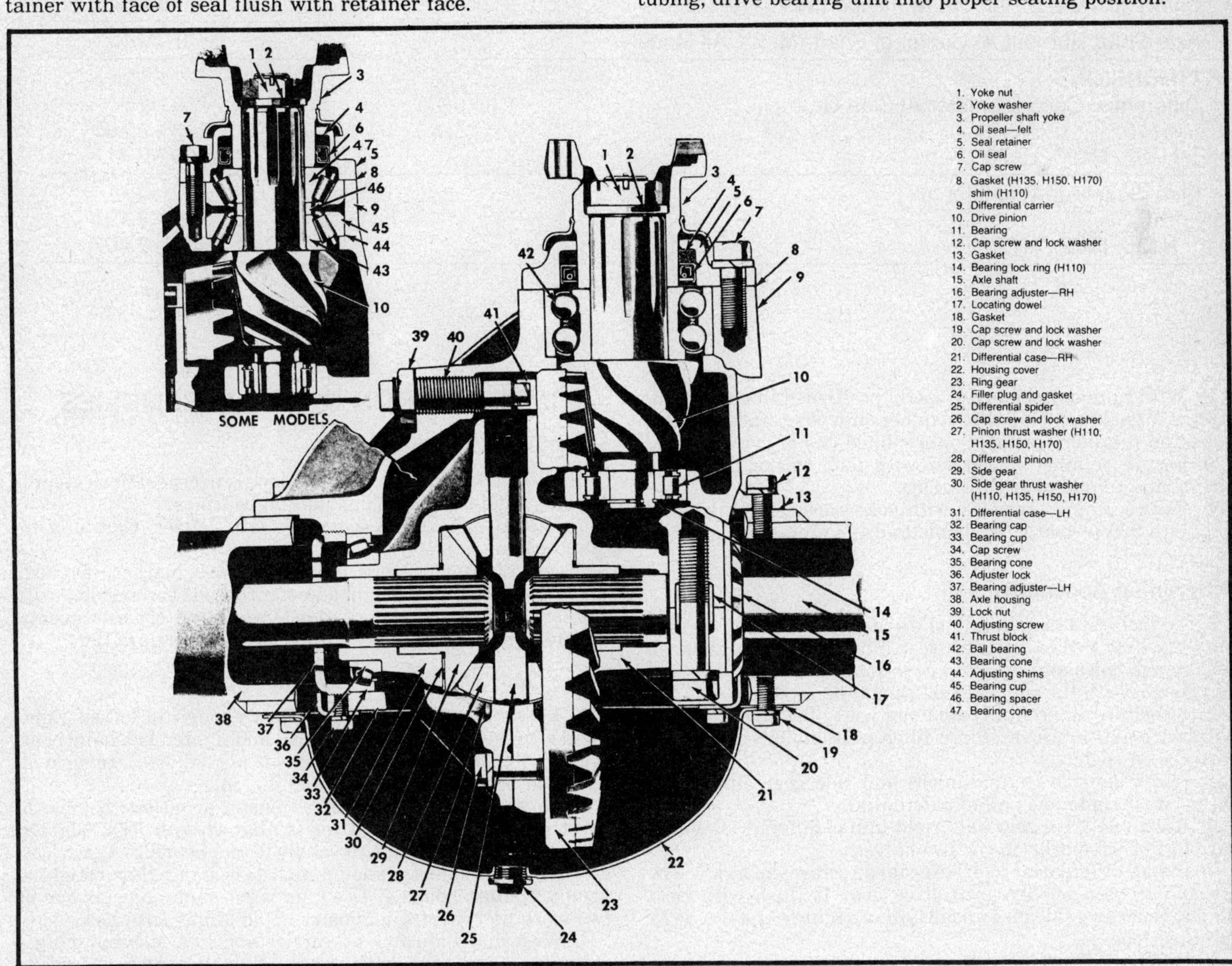

Cross section of the 12¼ inch rear axle assembly (© General Motors Corp.)

12¼ INCH REAR AXLE SPECIFICATIONS Models H110, H135, H150 and H170

TYPE:	Hypoid
ADJUSTMENTS AND CLEARANCES:	
Backlash—Ring Gear To Pinion	0.005″–0.008″
Adjustment Method	See text
Pinion Depth Adjustment:	
Models With Tapered Bearings: Adjustment Method	Shims
Shim Pack Thickness:	
Initial	0.021″
Available	0.012″, 0.015″, 0.018″, 0.021″, 0.024″
Models With Ball Bearings: Adjustment Method	None
Backlash-Side Gear to Pinion Gear	0.007″–0.009″
Thurst Block To Gear Clearance	0.005″–0.007″
TOLERANCES:	
Ring Gear Run-out (Max. when mounted to case)	
H110	0.005″
H135, H150, H170	0.0065″
Differential Case Run-out At Flange (Max.): All Models	0.002″
Axle Shaft Run-out At Center of Shaft (Max.): All Models	0.016″
DIMENSIONS:	
Differential Case Diameter At Side Gear	
H110	2.193″–2.195″
H135, H150, H170	2.409″–2.411″
Side Gear Hub Diameter	
H110	2.189″–2.191″
H135, H150, H170	2.405″–2.407″

8. With pinion assembly properly positioned in carrier, install new gasket. Install seal retainer onto yoke, and assemble yoke and retainer assembly onto splined end of drive pinion.
9. Secure retainer to carrier with lock washers and cap screws and torque to specifications.
10. Secure pinion assembly with yoke washer and nut and torque to 220 ft. lbs. This completes drive pinion assembly.

Differential Assembly

1. To facilitate installation of drive gear, install two guide pins ($^1/_2$ x 20 × 2 in. bolts) in gear. Start guide pins through case flange holes and tap drive gear onto case. If one differential gear is bad, the complete set should be replaced.
2. Lubricate differential case inner walls and all component parts with axle lubricant. Place differential pinions and thrust washers on spider.
3. Assemble side gears, pinions and side gear and pinion thrust washers to left half of differential.
4. Assemble drive gear half (right half of differential, being sure to line up marks on the two halves.
5. Install differential-to-drive gear cap screw and lock washers and tighten evenly until drive gear is flush with case flange. Remove guide pins and install cap screws and torque to specifications.
6. Differential side bearing cones can be installed with special installer tool.

INSTALLATION OF SUBASSEMBLIES

Differential Installation

1. Install bearing cap locating dowels in caps. Lubricate side bearings and place bearing cups on bearings.
2. Install differential assembly into carrier. Carefully install bearing adjusters into carrier.
3. Install bearing caps, aligning punch marks previously made. Be sure that bearing adjuster threads are engaged with carrier and caps. Tighten adjusters alternately and evenly. Tighten bearing cap screws until lock washers are flat.

Drive Gear and Pinion Adjustment

1. Loosen bearing cap screws just enough to loosen right-hand bearing adjuster (pinion side) and tighten left-hand bearing adjuster (opposite pinion side.) Using adjuster, remove all backlash between drive gear and pinion.
2. Back off left-hand bearing adjuster about two notches to point where notch in adjuster is aligned with lock. Tighten right-hand bearing adjuster solidly to seat bearing. Again loosen right-hand adjuster enough to free bearing; then retighten snugly against bearing. Draw up right-hand adjuster one or two more notches until adjuster notch aligns with lock.
3. With dial indicator on carrier adjuster, slowly oscillate drive gear and take backlash reading. Backlash should be 0.005 to 0.008 in.

12¼ INCH REAR AXLE SPECIFICATIONS
Models H110, H135, H150 and H170

TYPE:	Hypoid
Pinion Gear (Inside Diameter)	
H110	0.879″–0.882″
H135, H150, H170	0.9415″–0.9445″
Thrust Washer Thickness: All Models	0.058″–0.062″
Diameter Of Spider Arms	
H110	0.874″–0.875″
H135, H150, H170	0.9365″–0.9375″
Thrust Block Thickness: All Models	0.1845″–0.1885″
Diameter of Axle Shaft Splines	
H110	0.874″–0.875″
H135, H150, H170	0.9365″–0.9375″
TORQUE VALUES:	
Ring Gear Bolts	
H110	118 ft. lbs.
H135, H150, H170	165 ft. lbs.
Differential Bearing Cap Bolts: All Models	205 ft. lbs.
Pinion Yoke Nut: All Models	220 ft. lbs.
Differential Bearing Adjuster Nut Lock Bolt: All Models	15 ft. lbs.
Differential Carrier To Housing Bolts: All Models	83 ft. lbs.
Thrust Block Lock Nut: All Models	128 ft. lbs.
Pinion Bearing Retainer Bolts	
H110	95 ft. lbs.
H135	98 ft. lbs.
H150	93 ft. lbs.
H170	165 ft. lbs.

4. If backlash exceeds 0.008 in., loosen right-hand adjuster one notch; then tighten left-hand adjuster one notch. If less than 0.005 in., loosen left-hand adjuster one notch and tighten right-hand adjuster one notch.
5. After backlash has been adjusted, again tighten bearing cap screws until their respective lock washers flatten out.
6. Check drive gear run-out.
7. Install side bearing adjusting nut lock and secure with cap screws and lock washers.

Checking Pinion Depth (Models with Tapered Roller Bearings Only)

NOTE: Refer to tooth contact chart in the General Axle Service section.

1. Coat drive gear with red lead. Turn pinion shaft several revolutions in both directions while applying considerable drag on drive gear.
2. Pinion depth is determined by shim pack selection. Shim packs are available in thicknesses of: 0.012, 0.015, 0.018, 0.021 and 0.024 in.
3. Changing pinion depth will again require adjusting backlash. After pinion depth and backlash have been adjusted, torque bearing caps to specifications.

Thrust Block Installation

1. Install thrust block and lock nut to adjusting screw. Thread screw and block into carrier until block contacts drive gear. Rotate gear and note change of drag. Adjust these parts until point of greatest drag is reached. Back screw off about a 30 degree turn to provide 0.005 to 0.007 in. clearance between block and gear. Make certain screw does not turn at all when tightening lock nut to 135 ft. lbs. torque.

General Motors Corporation 2–Speed Axle Models T150, T170, and T185

This GMC axle is a 2-speed, planetary type which can be shifted by the driver when desired. Operating the shift control button activates an electric or vacuum shift unit (attached to differential carrier) which, in turn, changes axle speed from low to high or vice-versa.

CAUTION

There is no "Neutral" position. There are just "High" and "Low" ratios. To attempt to coast with axle in a supposedly "Neutral" position could cause serious axle damage.

DIFFERENTIAL CARRIER

Removal

1. Remove all but two cap screws holding carrier to axle housing. Loosen the two remaining cap screws and, with a soft hammer, break carrier loose from housing.

CAUTION

Do not use pin. bar. This might cause damage to carrier or housing.

2. Place a roller jack under carrier, remove the two cap screws and remove carrier and differential assembly from housing.
3. Place carrier and differential assembly in a suitable repair stand.
4. Remove shift unit.

DIFFERENTIAL AND PLANETARY

Removal

1. Remove anchor from end of sun gear.
2. Drive shift lever out of carrier.
3. Remove shift yoke and sleeve assembly. Separate yoke from sleeve.
4. Remove adjusting nut lock.
5. Remove oil trough.
6. Tap bearing caps from carrier.
7. Remove differential and planetary assembly from carrier assembly.

CAUTION

DO NOT drop bearing cones and cups.

DRIVE PINION AND RETAINER

Removal

1. With carrier still in repair stand, use holding bar to hold propeller shaft yoke while removing nut and washer.
2. Using a soft faced hammer or a blunt chisel, work retainer cap and pinion assembly from carrier.
3. Remove pinion adjusting shim pack and record or tag thickness for reassembly information.
4. If necessary, use hammer and drift to remove drive pinion rear bearing from carrier.

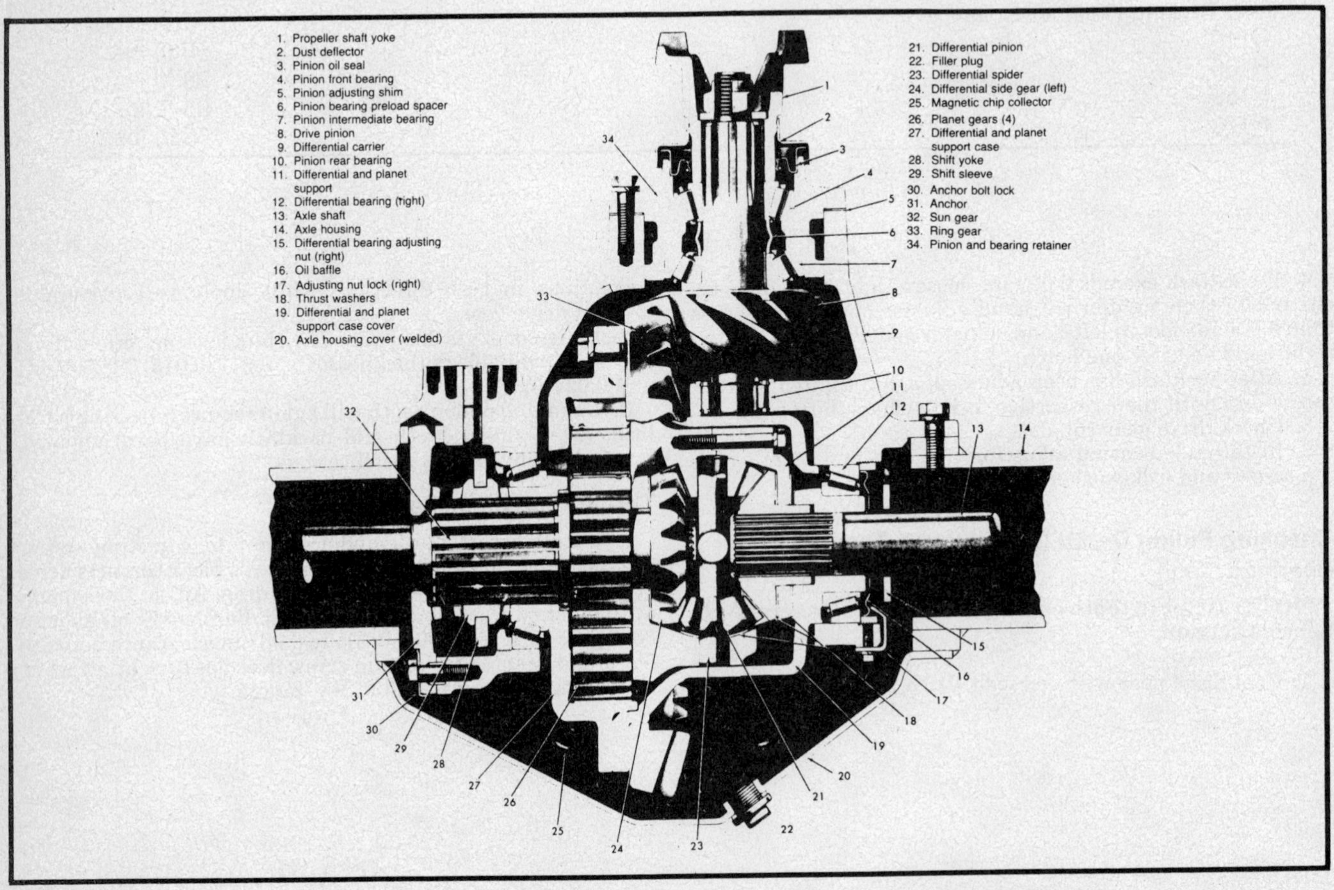

1. Propeller shaft yoke
2. Dust deflector
3. Pinion oil seal
4. Pinion front bearing
5. Pinion adjusting shim
6. Pinion bearing preload spacer
7. Pinion intermediate bearing
8. Drive pinion
9. Differential carrier
10. Pinion rear bearing
11. Differential and planet support
12. Differential bearing (right)
13. Axle shaft
14. Axle housing
15. Differential bearing adjusting nut (right)
16. Oil baffle
17. Adjusting nut lock (right)
18. Thrust washers
19. Differential and planet support case cover
20. Axle housing cover (welded)
21. Differential pinion
22. Filler plug
23. Differential spider
24. Differential side gear (left)
25. Magnetic chip collector
26. Planet gears (4)
27. Differential and planet support case
28. Shift yoke
29. Shift sleeve
30. Anchor bolt lock
31. Anchor
32. Sun gear
33. Ring gear
34. Pinion and bearing retainer

Cross section of a typical General Motors two-speed, single reduction rear axle assembly (© General Motors Corp.)

DRIVE PINION AND RETAINER

Disassembly

1. Carefully pry pinion oil seal from pinion and bearing retainer.
2. Using a press, press downward on end of pinion shaft to separate pinion assembly from retainer. Remove yoke and deflector.
3. Remove pinion front bearing cone from retainer. Pull bearing preload spacer off drive pinion shaft.
4. When necessary, use bearing cup remover to force bearing cups out of retainer cap.
5. Slide pinion bearing remover up over pinion head, and press drive pinion out of intermediate bearing cone.

DIFFERENTIAL AND PLANETARY

Disassembly

1. Punch-mark drive gear, differential support case, and differential cage cover to facilitate proper alignment during reassembly.
2. Remove drive gear and case cover.
3. Tag sun gear and four planetary gears so they may be correctly reassembled. Remove planet gears.
4. Lift differential and planet support assembly away from support case.
5. Punch-mark planet support cover and support and separate.
6. Again mark or tag all pinion and side gears for reassembly to same positions, and remove them along with their respective thrust washers. Slide four pinion gears off differential spider.
7. Remove differential side bearing cups. Insert brass drift through holes in case and cover and drive left and right side bearing cones off hubs.

NOTE: Alternately tap drift from hole on one side to hole on other side to prevent race from binding on hub.

AXLE ASSEMBLY

Before axle is assembled, make sure that all parts have been thoroughly cleaned, especially oil passages. Lightly lubricate all parts while assembling.

When assembling axle unit, it is recommended that new lock washers and gaskets be installed wherever possible. See General Axle Service section for details on cleaning and inspection.

DRIVE PINION AND RETAINER

Assembly

Drive pinion and drive gear must be replaced as a matching set.

1. If it was necessary to remove pinion rear bearing, use a driver handle with bearing installer to bottom bearing into position in carrier.
2. Position pinion intermediate bearing cone and cup in pinion bearing retainer with thicker end of cup facing inward. Use driver handle with bearing cup installer to firmly seat cup in place.
3. Follow step 1 procedure to install pinion front bearing and cup to pinion bearing retainer. Seat cup with handle and cup installer.
4. Use arbor press with a 2 in. inner diameter pipe of suitable length to position pinion intermediate bearing cone with thicker end up against shoulder of drive pinion.
5. Place new pinion bearing spacer on pinion up against bearing cone.
6. Position drive pinion assembly in retainer cap assembly, and install pinion front bearing cone in place. Thicker end of cone should face outward.
7. Again use arbor press with a 2 in. inner diameter pipe of suitable length to press inner race of cone up tightly against spacer.
8. Install pinion oil seal in retainer. See Oil Seal Replacement in the General Axle Service section.

DIFFERENTIAL AND PLANETARY

Assembly

1. Lubricate thrust washers, pinion gears, spider, and side gears. Assemble pinion gears to arms of differential spider and install all above components into planetary support (match up punch-marks made earlier).
2. Align and secure support cover with new lock washers and cap screws. Tighten cap screws to specifications.
3. Install left and right differential bearing cones to support case and support case cover hubs. Use bearing installer for left and right bearings.
4. Install planet gears on journal arms of support. Position sun gear in the planet gears.
5. Align punch-marks and install drive gear to support case cover. Improvised guide pins can be made from drive gear retaining cap screws.
6. Turn differential assembly over so drive gear teeth face downward. Position assembled planet and differential assembly in cover, making sure thrust washer at case bottom is properly positioned.
7. Using lock washers and cap screws, join support case, case cover and drive gear together. Remove guide pins and install rest of lock washers and cap screws. Tighten all cap screws in a cross-wise pattern to specified torque.

DIFFERENTIAL AND PLANETARY

Installation

1. Position left and right side bearing cups over their respective cones. Position differential and planetary assembly into carrier.
2. Install differential adjusting nuts at both sides.
3. Position bearing caps on carrier making certain adjusting nuts properly engage threads in caps. If bearing caps seat flush in place while adjusting nuts turn freely, caps are properly installed. Use soft hammer to seat caps properly. Tap lightly.

CAUTION

Do not force bearing caps on nuts.

4. Tighten cap screws evenly until adjusting nuts turn freely in threads.

DRIVE PINION AND RETAINER

Installation

1. Install original shim pack to carrier, making sure shim holes are aligned with carrier cap screw holes.
2. Properly install pinion and retainer assembly to carrier bore. Make sure pilot end of pinion properly seats in pinion rear bearing.
3. Assemble retainer to carrier with new lock washers and cap screws and torque to specifications.
4. Tap yoke onto pinion shaft splined end, making sure proper spline engagement is made.
5. Install and torque pinion washer and nut to end of drive pinion.
6. Continue tightening nut in small degrees until torque required to rotate drive pinion in carrier is from 25 to 35 inch lbs. (when new pinion bearings are installed). Only 5 to 15 inch lbs. torque is required if same bearings are reinstalled.

DRIVE GEAR AND PINION

Adjustment

1. Loosen right differential adjusting nut. Tighten left adjusting nut. Use differential nut wrench on right side nut and a drift hammer to the left side nut.
2. Tighten left adjusting nut until drive gear contacts pinion and zero lash is obtained; however, do not force gears into contact so as to bind them.
3. Back off left adjusting nut about two notches to a point where nut lock and nut are aligned. Install nut lock and torque to specifications.
4. Tighten right adjusting nut firmly to force the differential and planet assembly into solid contact with left adjusting nut. Loosen right adjusting nut until it no longer contacts its bearing, then retighten until nut contacts bearing. Tighten right adjusting nut from one to two notches more if old bearings are used, and two to three notches if new bearings are used, to a position where nut and nut lock are aligned. Install nut lock and torque to specifications.

NOTE: At this point the differential bearings are properly preloaded. If any additional adjustments are required, make sure that this proper preload remains. If one adjusting nut is loosened, the other nut must be tightened an equal amount to maintain this preload.

5. Mount a dial indicator on the housing and measure the backlash between the drive gear and pinion. Backlash should be from 0.003 to 0.012 in. with 0.005 to 0.008 in. preferred.

NOTE: If backlash is more than 0.012 in., loosen the right adjusting nut one notch and tighten left adjusting nut one notch. If backlash is less than 0.003 in., loosen the left adjusting nut one notch and tighten the right adjusting nut one notch.

Checking Pinion Depth

1. Thoroughly clean drive and pinion gear teeth.
2. Paint drive gear teeth lightly and evenly with a mixture of powdered red lead and oil.
3. Rotate pinion through several revolutions in both directions until a definite contact pattern is developed on drive gear. Apply pressure to drive gear while turning pinion. This will create load on gears to simulate a driving pattern.
4. Examine the pattern on drive gear teeth. If the pinion depth is correct, the tooth pattern will be centered on the pitch line and toward the toe of drive gear.
5. If the pattern is below the pitch line on drive gear teeth, the pinion is too deep and it will be necessary to remove the pinion assembly and increase the shim thickness between the pinion bearing retainer and the carrier.
6. If the pattern is above the pitch line on drive gear teeth, the pinion is too shallow and it will be necessary to remove the pinion assembly and decrease the shim thickness between the pinion bearing retainer and the carrier.
7. Changing the pinion depth will cause some change in backlash. Therefore adjust backlash to maintain correct specifications.
8. Torque bearing cap screws to specifications and recheck drive gear to pinion backlash. Install adjusting nut locks and torque to specifications.
9. Install oil trough to drive gear so that clearance is 0.030–0.090 in. Torque retaining cap screws.

SHIFTER COMPONENTS

Installation

1. Position shift yoke in shift sleeve groove.
2. Slide yoke and sleeve assembly over sun gear. Splines of sleeve and sun gear should properly meash.
3. Install shift lever through carrier housing into yoke mating splines together. Tap end of lever lightly to seat it in yoke.
4. Position the shifter unit and gasket over mounting pad, aligning lever in carrier with shift rod in shift unit.

NOTE: On axles equipped with electrical shift units, shift electrical leads must be connected to shift unit before installing unit to carrier.

5. Install and torque bolts.
6. Install differential assembly into axle housing.

TWO SPEED AXLE SPECIFICATIONS
Models T150, T170 and T185

MAKE	GM Corp.
TYPE	Two-Speed Planetary
ADJUSTMENTS AND CLEARANCES	
Backlash—Ring Gear To Pinion	0.005″–0.008″
Adjustment Method	See text
Backlash—Side Gear To Differential Pinion	0.007″–0.010″
Backlash—Shifter Sleeve	0.004″–0.008″
Backlash—Sun Gear To Planet Gear	0.004″–0.008″
Pinion Depth (Ring Gear-To-Pinion Contact)	See text
Adjustment Method	Shims
Shim Thickness (Starting)	0.021″
Shim Thickness (Available)	0.006″, 0.009″, 0.012″, 0.015″, 0.018″, 0.021″, 0.024″
Pinion Bear Preload (Max., In. Lbs.)	
New Pinion Bearing	30–40 in. lbs.
Old Pinion Bearing	5–15 in. lbs.
Adjustment Method	See text

TWO SPEED AXLE SPECIFICATIONS
Models T150, T170 and T185

MAKE	GM Corp.
TYPE	Two-Speed Planetary
TOLERANCES	
Ring Gear Run-Out (Max. When Mounted To Case)	0.005″
Ring Gear Run-Out (Max. Not Mounted To Case)	0.065″
Differential Case Run-Out (Max.)	0.002″
DIMENSIONS	
Diameter Of Spider Arms	0.9365″–0.9375″
Diameter Of Side Gear Hub	2.405″–2.407″
Diameter (Inside) Of Differential Pinion	0.9415″–0.9445″
Diameter (Inside) Of Planet Gear Bushing	1.3158″–1.3164″
Diameter Of Differential Case Support Arms	1.3122″–1.3132″
Diameter Of Sun Gear, Over Retainer	
Width Of Shifter Yoke	0.395″–0.400″
Width Of Shifter Sleeve At Yoke Groove	0.445″–0.457″
Thrust Washer Thickness (Side Gear, Differential Pinion, Differential Case To Case Cover Thrust Washers)	0.058″–0.062″
FASTENER	
Drive Pinion Yoke Nut	See text①
Planetary Support Case and Cover to Ring Gear	165 ft. lbs.
Differential Bearing-Cap Cap Screws	205 ft. lbs.
Differential Carrier to Housing Cap Screws	150 ft. lbs.
Differential Bearing Lock Cap Screw	10 ft. lbs.
Axle Shaft Cover Cap Screws	19 ft. lbs.
Oil Seal and Pinion Retainer	93 ft. lbs.
Oil Trough to Differential Carrier	10 ft. lbs.
Shift Sleeve Anchor Bolt to Bearing Case	110 ft. lbs.
Differential and Planet Support Case Cover Cap Screws	70 ft. lbs.

① There is no *specific* torque on this nut. The torque applied depends on the force required to rotate the pinion. Refer to Pinion Assembly and Installation.

Dana Corporation

9 $^3/_4$ AND 10 $^1/_2$ Inch RING GEAR AXLE ASSEMBLIES

The Dana Corporation's 9 $^3/_4$ and 10 $^1/_2$ in. ring gear axle assemblies are basically the same, but with certain exceptions. The differential side bearing shims are located between the side bearing cup assembly and the differential case on the 9 $^3/_4$ in. ring gear axle assembly, while on the 10 $^1/_2$ in. ring gear axle assembly, the side bearing shims are located between the side bearing cup and the axle housing. Both axles use inner and outer shims on the pinion gear. The inner shims are used to control the pinion depth in the housing, while the outer shims are used to preload the pinion bearings. The 9$^3/_4$ in. ring gear axle uses a solid differential carrier with a removable side and pinion gear shaft. The 10 $^1/_2$ in. ring gear axle uses a split differential carrier with the side and pinion gears mounted on a cross shaft.

DIFFERENTIAL CASE

Removal

9 $^3/_4$ AND 10 $^1/_2$ INCH RING GEAR ASSEMBLIES

1. The axle assembly can be overhauled either in or out of the vehicle, depending on the repairman's discretion. Either way, the free-floating axles and wheel assemblies must be removed.
2. Drain the lubricant and remove the rear cover and gasket.
3. Matchmark the bearing caps and the housing for reassembly in the same position. Remove the bearing caps and bolts.
4. Using a spreader tool mounted to the carrier housing, spread the housing a maximum of 0.015 in.

CAUTION

Do not exceed this measurement. The housing could be permanently damaged. The use of a dial indicator is recommended to prevent overstretching the housing.

5. Using a pry bar, remove the differential case from the housing. Separate the shims and record the dimensions and location on the 10 $^1/_2$ in. ring gear axle. Remove the spreader tool from the housing.

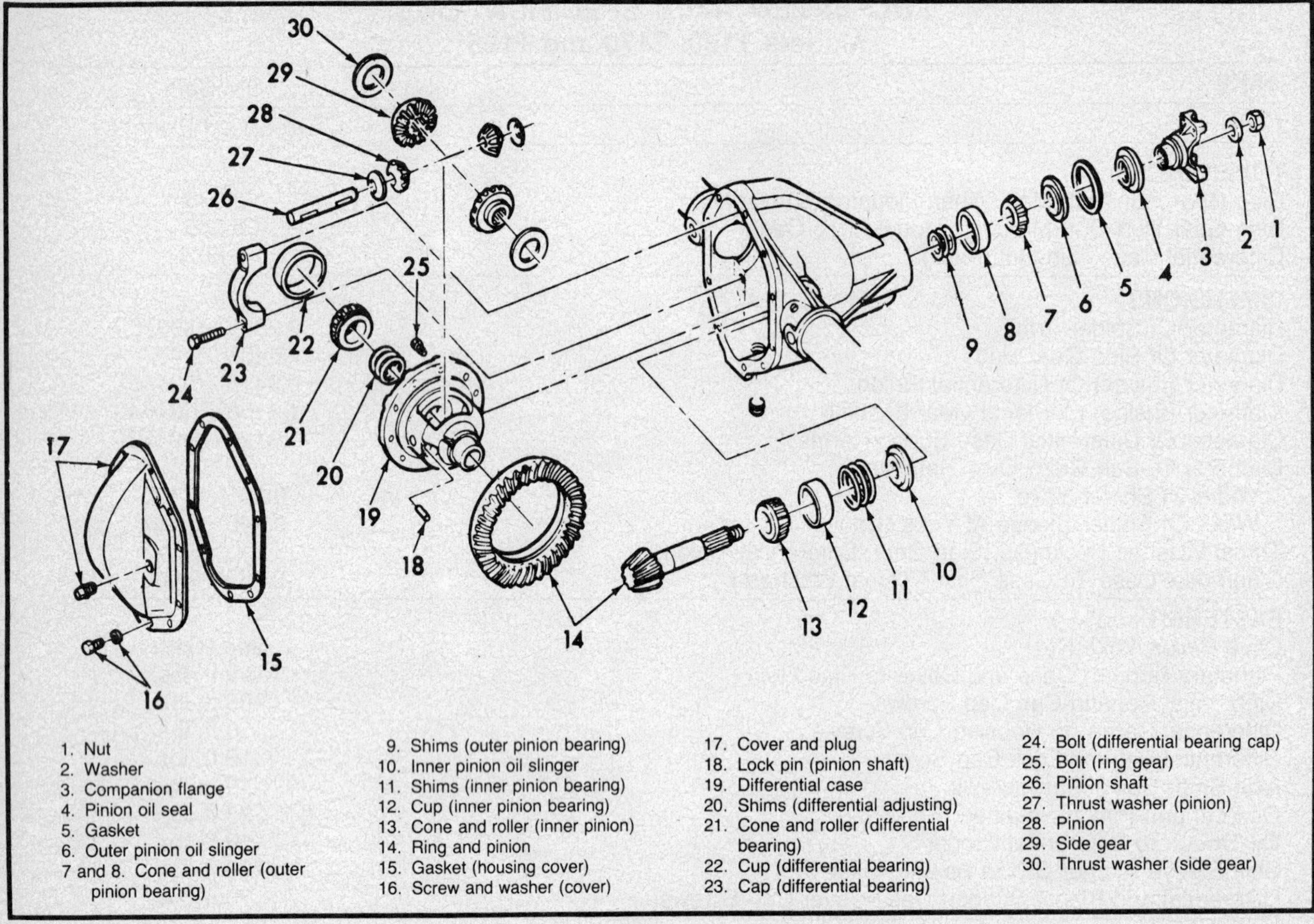

Exploded view of the Dana differential assembly with 9¾ inch ring gear (© General Motors Corp.)

Disassembly

10 ½ in.

1. Remove the differential side bearings from the case, using the necessary puller tools.
2. Remove the ring gear bolts and tap the ring gear from the case with a soft-faced hammer.
3. Scribe the case halves for reassembly and remove the retaining bolts.
4. Tap the top half of the case to separate it from the bottom half. Remove the internal gears, washers and cross.

Inspection

9 ¾ AND 10 ½ INCH

1. Clean the gears, bearings and component parts with solvent and inspect for scoring, chipping or excessive wear.
2. Replace the necessary parts as required.

Assembly

10 ½ INCH

1. Install new thrust washers to the side gears and lubricate the contact surfaces.
2. Assemble the side gears, pinion bears, washers and cross shaft into the flanged half of the case.
3. Install the top half of the case to the bottom half, making sure the scribe marks are lined up.
4. Install the retaining bolts finger tight. Then tighten the bolts alternately to the proper torque specifications.
5. If a new ring gear is to be installed or the old one used, install it to the differential case and align the bolt holes. Tighten the bolts aternately to the proper torque specifications.
6. Install the side carrier bearings by using the proper installation tools.
7. Cover the assembled unit and set aside until ready for the installation into the housing.

Disassembly

9 ¾ INCH

1. Remove the differential side bearing cups and tag to identify the side, if they are to be used again.
2. Remove the differential gear pinion shaft lock pin and remove the shaft. Rotate the side and pinion gears to remove them from the carrier. Remove the thrust bearings.
3. Remove the bearing cones and rollers from the carrier, marking and noting the shim locations.
4. Remove the ring gear retaining bolts and tap the ring gear from the carrier housing.
5. Inspect the components as outlined earlier.

Assembly

9 ¾ INCH

1. Install the differential side gears, the differential pinion gears and new thrust washers into the differential carrier.
2. Align the pinion gear shaft holes and install the pinion shaft into the carrier. Align the lock pin hole in the shaft and

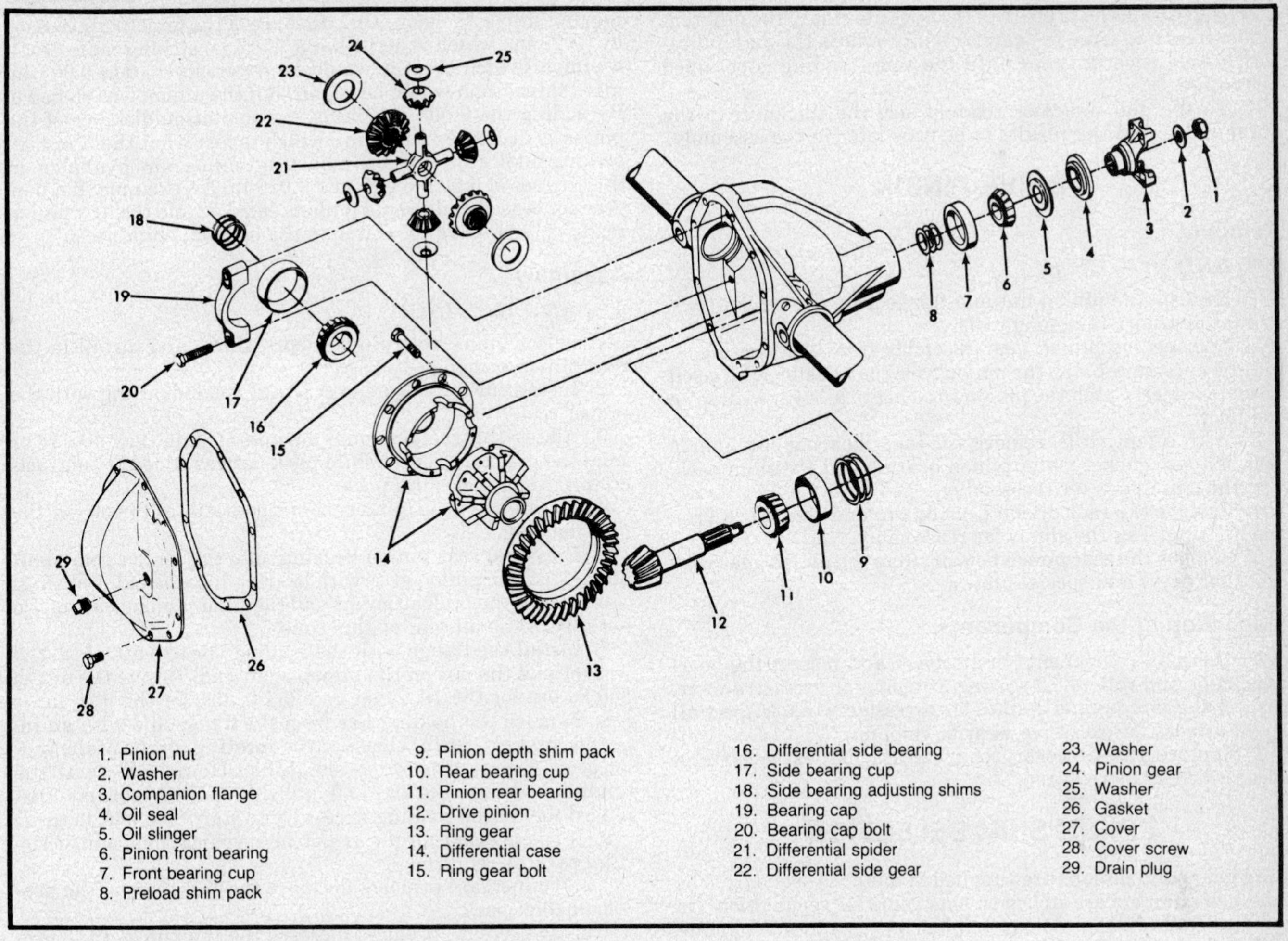

Exploded view of the Dana differential assembly with 10¾ inch ring gear (© General Motors Corp.)

carrier. Install the lock pin and peen the hole to avoid having the pin drop from the carrier.

3. Install the differential case side bearings with the proper installation tools. Do not install the shims at this time.

4. Place the carrier assembly into the axle housing with the bearing cups on the bearing cones. Install the bearing caps in their original position and tighten the bearing cap bolts enough to keep the bearing caps in place.

5. Install a dial indicator on the housing so that the indicator button contacts the carrier flange. Press the differential carrier to prevent side play and center the dial indicator. Rotate the carrier and check the flange for run-out. If the run-out is greater than 0.002 in., the defect is probably due to the bearings or to the carrier and should be corrected.

6. Remove the assembly and install the ring gear. Torque the retaining bolts to specifications and reinstall the assembly into the housing and again install the bearing caps in their original position and tighten the cap bolts enough to keep the bearings caps in place.

7. Again, install the dial indicator and position the indicator button to contact the ring gear back surface. Rotate the assembly and the run-out should be less than 0.002 in. If over 0.002 in., remove the assembly and relocate the ring gear 180 degrees. Reinstall the assembly and recheck. If the run-out remains over the 0.002 in. tolerance, the ring gear is defective. If the measurement is within tolerances, continue on with the assembly.

8. Position two pry bars between the bearing cap and the housing on the side opposite the ring gear. Pull on the pry bars and force the differential carrier as far as possible towards the dial indicator. Rock the assembly to seat the bearings and reset the dial indicator to "O".

9. Reposition the prybars to the opposite side of the carrier and force the carrier assembly as far towards the center of the housing. Read the dial indicator scale. This will be the total amount of shims required for setting the backlash during the reassembly, less the bearing preload. Record the measurement.

10. Remove the differential carrier from the housing and set aside.

SIDE BEARING SHIM SELECTION FOR THE 10 ½ INCH

1. With the pinion gear not in the axle housing, place the bearing cups over the side bearings and install the differential carrier into the axle housing.

2. Place the shim that was originally installed on the ring gear side back into its original position.

3. Install the bearing caps in their proper positions and tighten the bolts enough to keep the bearings in place.

4. Mount a dial indicator on the axle housing with the indicator button contacting the back of the ring gear.

5. Position two prybars between the bearing shim and the housing on the ring gear side of the differential carrier. Force the differential carrier away from the dial indicator and set the indicator to "0".

6. Reposition the prybars to the opposite side of the differential carrier and force the carrier back towards the dial indicator. Repeat several times until the same reading is obtained each time.

7. To the dial indicator reading, add the thickness of the shim and record the results to be used later in the assembly.

DRIVE PINION

Removal

9 3/4 AND 10 1/2 INCH

1. Remove the pinion nut and flange from the pinion gear, using the proper removing tools.
2. Remove the pinion gear assembly from the housing. It may be necessary to tap the pinion from the housing with a soft faced hammer. Catch the pinion so as not to allow it to drop on the floor.
3. With a long drift, remove the inner bearing cup, pinion seal, slinger, gasket, outer pinion bearing and the shim pack. Tag the shim pack for reassembly.
4. Remove the rear pinion bearing cup and shim pack from the housing. Tag the shims for reassembly.
5. Remove the rear pinion bearing from the pinion gear with an arbor press and special plates.

Inspection of the Components

1. Clean all components in a solvent and inspect the bearings, cups and rollers for scoring, chipping or excessive wear. Inspect the flanges and splines for excessive wear. Inspect all gear surfaces for excessive wear or chipping.
2. Replace the necessary bearing assemblies, gears and thrustwashers as required.

PINION SHIM SELECTION

Ring gears and pinions are supplied in matched sets only. The matched numbers are etched on both gears for verification. On the rear face of the pinion, a + (plus) or a – (minus) number will be etched, indicating the best running position for each particular gear set. This dimension is controlled by the shimming behind the inner bearing cup. Whenever baffles or oil slingers are used, they become part of the adjusting shim pack. An example: If a pinion is etched +3, this pinion would require 0.003 in. less shims than a pinion etched 0. This means by removing shims, the mounting distance of the pinion is increased by 0.003 in., which is just what a + (plus) etching indicates. If a pinion is etched -3, it would be necessary to add 0.003 in. more shims than would be required if the pinion was etched 0. By adding the 0.003 in. shims, the mounting distance of the pinion is decreased 0.003 in., which is just what the - (minus) etching indicates. Pinion adjusting shims are available in thicknesses of 0.003, 0.005 and 0.010 in. An example: If a new gear set is used and the old pinion reads +2 and the new pinion reads -2, add 0.004 in. shims to the original shim pack.

Assembly

9 3/4 AND 10 1/2 INCH

1. Select the correct pinion depth shims and install in the rear pinion bearing cup bore.
2. Install the rear bearing cup in the axle housing with the proper tool.
3. Add or subtract an equal amount of shim thickness to or from the preload or outer shim pack, as was added or subtracted from the inner shim pack.
4. Install the front pinion bearing cup into its bore in the axle housing.
5. Press the rear pinion bearing onto the pinion gear shaft and install the pinion gear with bearing into the axle housing.
6. Install the preload shims and the front pinion bearing. Do not install the oil seal at this time.
7. Install the flange with the holding bar tool attached, the washer and the nut on the pinion shaft end. Torque the nut to 250 ft. lbs. for the 10 1/2 in. and 255 ft. lbs. for the 9 3/4 in.
8. Remove the holding bar from the flange and with an in. pound torque wrench, measure the rotating torque of the pinion gear. The rotating torque should be 10 to 20 in. lbs. with the original bearings and 20 to 40 in. lbs. with new bearings. Disregard the torque reading necessary to start the shaft to turn.
9. If the preload torque is not in specifications, adjust the shim pack as required.
   a. To increase preload, decrease the thickness of the preload shim pack.
   b. To decrease preload, increase the thickness of the preload shim pack.
10. When the proper preload is obtained, remove the nut, washer and flange from the pinion shaft.
11. Install a new pinion seal into the housing and reinstall the flange, washer and nut. Using the holder tool, torque the nut to 250 ft. lbs. for the 10 1/2 in. and 255 ft. lbs. for the 9 3/4 in.

Old Pinion Marking	New Pinion Marking								
	- 4	- 3	- 2	- 1	0	+ 1	+ 2	+ 3	+ 4
+ 4	+ 0.008	+ 0.007	+ 0.006	+ 0.005	+ 0.004	+ 0.003	+ 0.002	+ 0.001	0
+ 3	+ 0.007	+ 0.006	+ 0.005	+ 0.004	+ 0.003	+ 0.002	+ 0.001	0	- 0.001
+ 2	+ 0.006	+ 0.005	+ 0.004	+ 0.003	+ 0.002	+ 0.001	0	- 0.001	- 0.002
+ 1	+ 0.005	+ 0.004	+ 0.003	+ 0.002	+ 0.001	0	- 0.001	- 0.002	- 0.003
0	+ 0.004	+ 0.003	+ 0.002	+ 0.001	0	- 0.001	- 0.002	- 0.003	- 0.004
- 1	+ 0.003	+ 0.002	+ 0.001	0	- 0.001	- 0.002	- 0.003	- 0.004	- 0.005
- 2	+ 0.002	+ 0.001	0	- 0.001	- 0.002	- 0.003	- 0.004	- 0.005	- 0.006
- 3	+ 0.001	0	- 0.001	- 0.002	- 0.003	- 0.004	- 0.005	- 0.006	- 0.007
- 4	0	- 0.001	- 0.002	- 0.003	- 0.004	- 0.005	- 0.006	- 0.007	- 0.008

Correction of shims from old pinion to new pinion—Dana 9 3/4 and 10 1/2 inch ring gear (© General Motors Corp.)

Assembly of Differential Carrier Into Axle Housing

9 3/4 INCH

1. As outlined in the Differential Carrier Assembly procedure, the amount of shims required for setting the backlash less bearing preload had been selected and the measurement recorded.
2. With the pinion gear installed and properly set, position the differential carrier assembly into the axle housing and install the bearing caps in their proper positions. Tighten the cap bolts just enough to hold the bearing cups in place.
3. Install a dial indicator on the axle housing with the indicator button contacting the back of the ring gear.
4. Position two prybars between the bearing cup and the axle housing on the ring gear side of the case and pry the ring gear into mesh with the pinion gear teeth, as far as possible. Rock the ring gear to allow the teeth to mesh and the bearings to seat. With the pressure still applied by the prybars, set the dial indicator to "0".
5. Reposition the prybars on the opposite side of ring gear and pry the gear as far as it will go. Take the dial indicator reading. Repeat this procedure until the same reading is obtained each time. This reading represents the necessary amount of shims between the differential carrier and the bearing on the ring gear side.
6. Remove the bearing from the differential carrier on the ring gear side and install the proper amount of shims. Reinstall the bearing.
7. Remove the differential carrier bearing from the opposite side of the ring gear. To determine the amount of shims needed, use the following method.
   a. Subtract the size of the shim pack just installed on the ring gear side of the carrier from the reading obtained and recorded when measurement was taken without the pinion gear in place during the Differential Carrier Assembly procedure. To this figure, add an additional 0.015 in. to compensate for preload and backlash. An example: If the first reading was 0.085 in. and the shims installed on the ring gear side of the carrier were 0.055 in., the correct amount of shims whould be 0.085 − 0.055 + 0.015 = 0.045 in.
8. Install the required shims as determined under step 7 and install the differential side bearing. The installation of the shims should give the proper preload to the bearings and the proper backlash to the ring and pinion gears.

10 1/2 INCH

1. Install the differential carrier, with the side bearings and cups installed, in place in the axle housing.
2. Select the smallest of the original shims as a gauging shim and place it between the bearing cup and the housing on the ring gear side.
3. Install the bearing caps and tighten the bolts enough to hold the cups in place.
4. Mount a dial indicator on the ring gear side of the axle housing and position the indicator button on the rear side of the ring gear.
5. Position two prybars between the bearing cup and the housing on the side opposite the ring gear. With the prybars, force the differential carrier towards the dial indicator and set the indicator dial to "0".
6. Reposition the prybars on the ring gear side of the carrier and force the ring gear into mesh with the pinion gear while observing the dial indicator reading. Repeat this operation until the same reading is obtained each time.
7. Add this indicator reading to the gauging shim thickness to determine the correct shim dimension for installation on the ring gear side of the differential carrier.
8. An example: If the gauging shim was 0.115 in. and the indicator reading was 0.017 in., the correct shim would be 0.115 + 0.017 = 0.172 in.
9. Remove the gauging shim and install the correct shim into position between the bearing cup and the axle housing on the ring gear side of the housing.
10. To determine the correct dimension for the remaining shim, refer to the Side Bearing Shim Selection for the 10 1/2 in. and obtain the recorded shim size. From that figure, subtract the size of the shim installed in step 9 and then add 0.006 in. for the bearing preload and backlash.
11. An example: If the reading of the shim just installed on the ring gear side of the carrier was 0.172 in. and the reading obtained during the checking of clearance without the pinion installed was 0.329, the correct shim dimension would be as follows: 0.329 − 0.172 = 0.157 + 0.006 = 0.163 in.

Installation of Differential Carrier Into Axle Housing

9 3/4 INCH

1. Spread the axle housing with the spreader tool no more than 0.015 in. Install the differential bearing outer cups in their correct locations and install the cups in their respective locations.
2. Install the bolts and tighten finger-tight. Rotate the differential carrier and ring gear and tap with a soft-faced hammer to insure proper seating of the assembly in the axle housing.
3. Remove the spreader tool and torque the cap bolts to specifications.
4. Install a dial indicator and check the ring gear backlash at four equally spaced points of the ring gear circle. The backlash must be within a range of 0.004 to 0.009 in. and must not vary more than 0.002 in. between the points checked.
5. If the backlash is not within specifications, the shim packs must be corrected to bring the backlash within limits.
6. Check the tooth contact pattern and verify.
7. Complete the assembly, fill to proper level with lubricant and operate to verify proper assembly.

10 1/2 INCH

1. Spread the axle housing with a spreader tool, no more than 0.015 in. The carrier assembly is in place in the housing.
2. Assemble the shim, as determined previously, into place between the bearing cup and the housing. Remove the spreader tool.
3. Install the bearing caps in their marked positions and torque the bolts to specifications.
4. Install a dial indicator and check the ring gear backlash at four equally spaced points around the ring gear.
5. The backlash must be within 0.004 to 0.009 in. and must not vary more than 0.002 in. between the positions checked.
6. Whenever the backlash is not within the allowable limits, it must be corrected. Changing of the shim packs is required.
   a. Low backlash is corrected by decreasing the shim on the ring gear side and increasing the opposite side shim an equal amount.
   b. High backlash is corrected by increasing the shim on the ring gear side and decreasing the opposite side shim an equal amount.
7. Check the tooth contact pattern and correct as required.
8. Complete the assembly, fill to the correct level and operate to verify correct repairs.

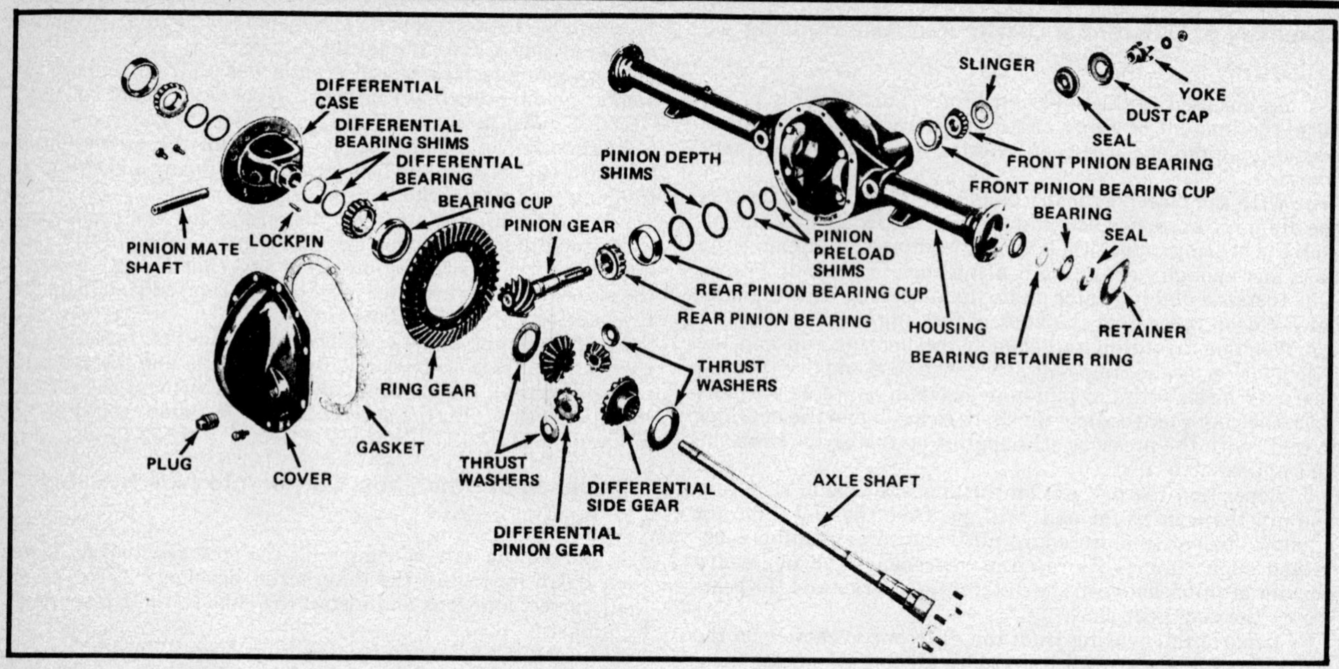

Exploded view of models 30 and 40 rear axles—typical (© Jeep Corp.)

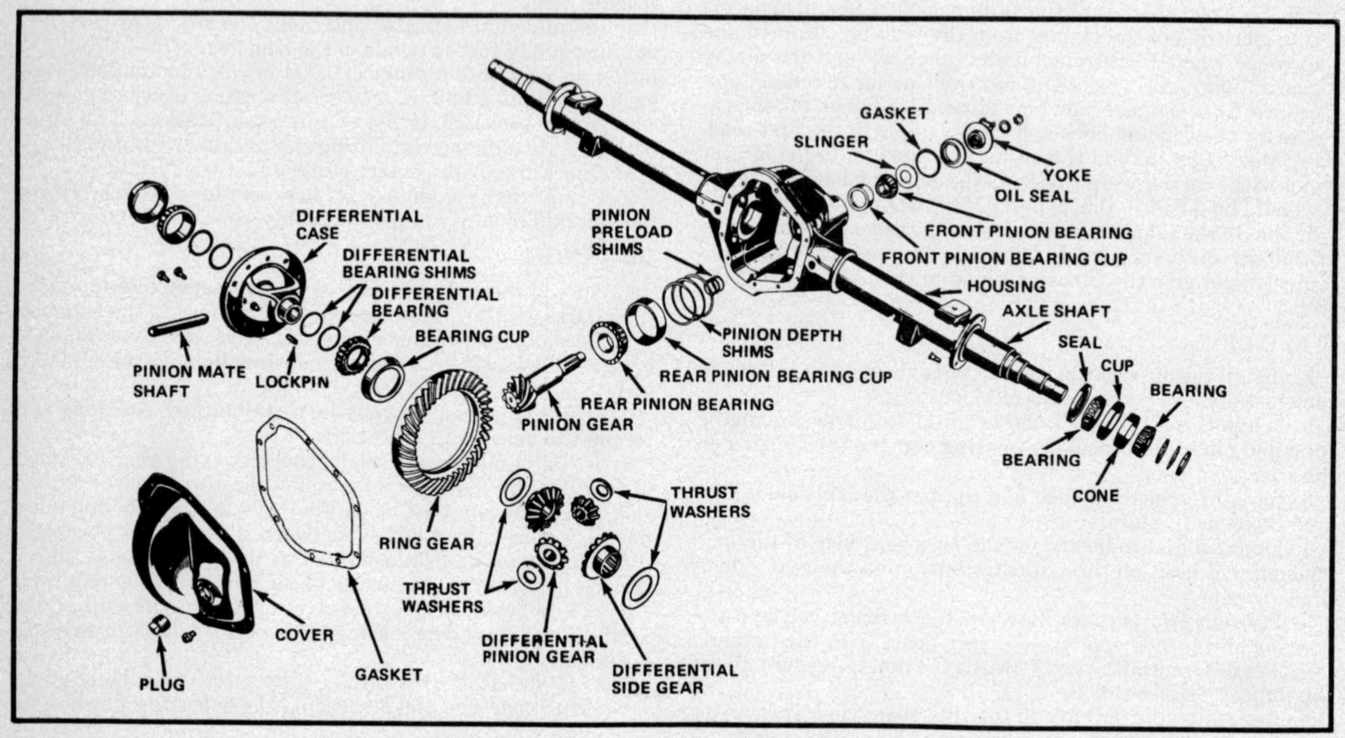

Exploded view of models 60 rear axle—typical (© Jeep Corp.)

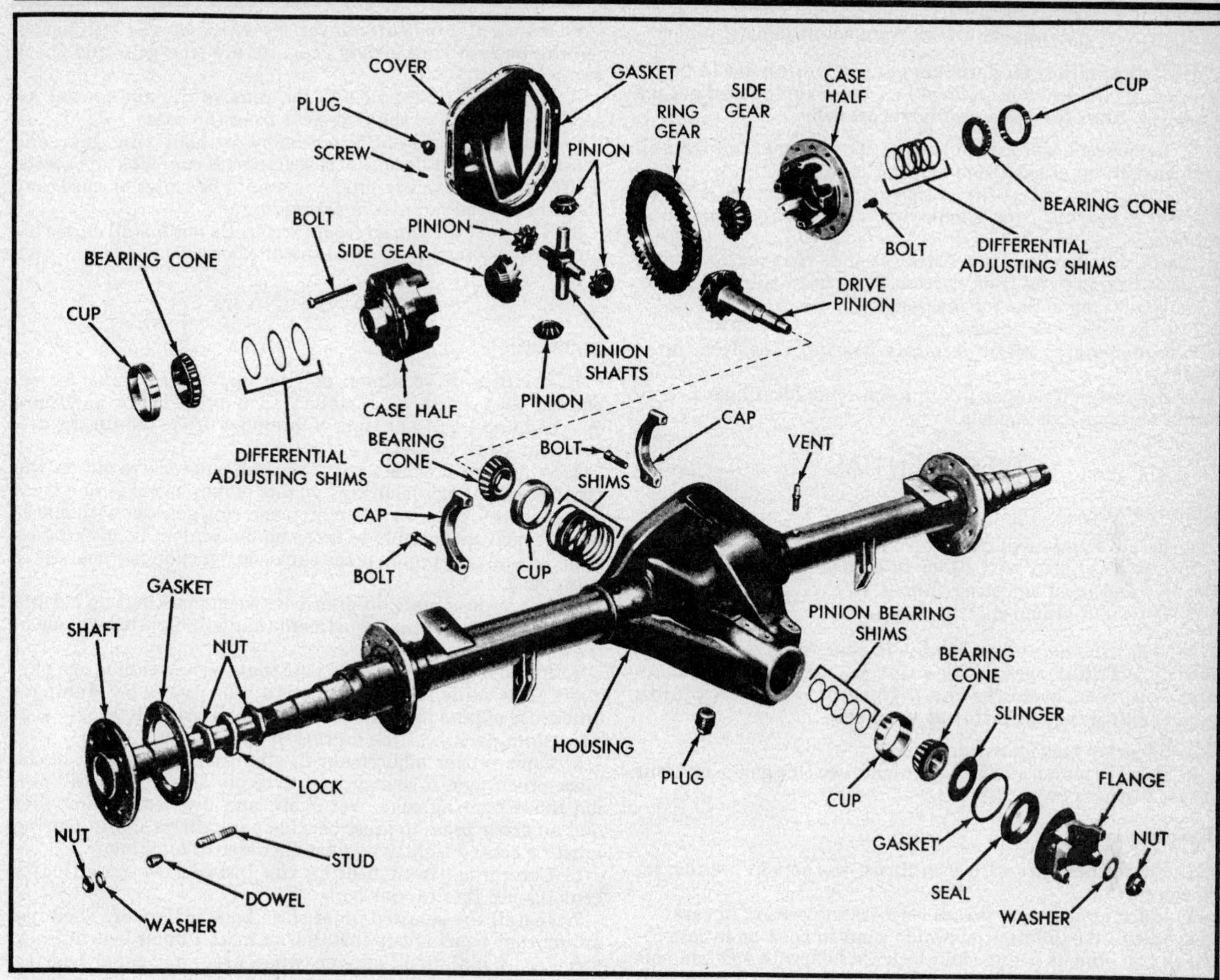

Exploded view of Dana Model 70 rear axle assembly (© Chrysler Corp.)

Dana–Spicer Single Reduction Models 30, 44, 44–1, 60–1–2, 70

DIFFERENTIAL

Removal

1. Drain lubricant.
2. Remove cover and gasket.

NOTE: Attached to a cover bolt is a metal tag which shows the number of teeth on pinion and ring (drive) gear.

3. Remove bearing cap screws. Note the matching marks on cap and carrier and make sure caps are reassembled to correct markings.
4. Using a spreader tool, spread carrier a maximum of 0.020 in. and measure amount of spread with a dial indicator.

CAUTION

Carrier may be permanently damaged if spread more than 0.020 in. Do not attempt differential removal without using a spreader.

5. Carefully lift differential assembly out of carrier.
6. Remove the spreader assembly after removing the differential assembly from the housing.

DRIVE PINION

Disassembly

1. Pull flange (yoke) from shaft splines of drive pinion.
2. Using a press or soft hammer, drive pinion and inner bearing cone assembly out of carrier.

3. Remove and tag shim pack from splined end of pinion.

NOTE: If either ring (drive) gear or pinion are to be replaced, write down markings (+), (-), or (0) located at face end of pinion for reassembly reference.

4. Remove oil seal assembly from carrier bore. This frees oil seal gasket, oil slinger, and bearing cone.
5. If replacement of the pinion tapered bearings is necessary, the bearing cups should be removed from carrier as follows:
   a. Use remover with a driver or slide hammer to remove inner bearing cup from carrier. This frees shim pack. Remove and tag shims for reassembly.
   b. Remove outer bearing cup.
6. Use remover set to separate bearing cone from drive pinion.
7. Separate oil slinger from pinion. This oil slinger is only found on some axle models.

DIFFERENTIAL

Disassembly

1. Remove and label the two bearing cups.
2. Use a suitable type puller to remove the bearing cones. Remove and label adjusting shims.
3. Drive out pinion shaft lock pin.

NOTE: On the Spicer Model 70 rear axle, punch-mark the differential case halves (for reassembly reference) and separate. Remove the differential spider, pinion gears, side gears and thrust washers.

4. Separate ring gear from case.
5. Remove pinion shaft, two pinions, two side gears, and four thrust washers from case.

Assembly

1. Place side gears with new thrust washers in position inside case.
2. Place pinions and thrust washers in position in case.
3. Install the differential pinion shaft in position in case between two pinions. Align shaft lock pin hole with lock pin hole in case and install pinion shaft lock pin. Peen hole to prevent pin from falling out.

NOTE: On the Spicer Model 70 rear axle, install the differential spider along with its pinion gears, side gears and thrust washers into the differential case halves. Bolt the two halves together making sure the punch-marks line up.

4. Place ring (drive) gear in proper position against flange of case and bolt ring gear to case. Alternately tighten these bolts until all bolts are tightened to proper torque.

NOTE: Do not install differential cones or shim packs until pinion depth and bearing preload have been checked out. Differential bearing adjustment is a part of axle assembly procedure.

DIFFERENTIAL BEARING

Adjustment

1. Press fit bearing cones tightly against shoulders on case. Do not install shims at this time.
2. Install bearing cups.
3. Install spreader tool and dial indicator, and spread carrier as described in Differential Removal.
4. Place differential assembly into carrier.
5. Install bearing caps using their respective cap screws. Make sure caps are assembled to their correct markings. Hand tighten bearing cap screws.
6. Install dial indicator at carrier with indicator button contacting back of ring (drive) gear. Rotate ring gear and check run-out.
7. If run-out exceeds 0.002 in., remove the differential assembly and remove the ring gear from the case.
8. Reinstall differential assembly without ring gear and check run-out of differential case flange. If run-out still exceeds 0.002 in., the defect is probably due to bearings or case, and should be corrected before proceeding.
9. Remove differential from carrier. Do not install shims behind the bearings until final installation.

DRIVE PINION

Installation

1. If either drive pinion or ring (drive) gear must be replaced, they must be installed as a set. (These parts are matched and lapped at time of manufacture to obtain the correct gear tooth contact.)
2. Whenever it is necessary to install a new drive pinion, the plus (+) or minus (-) marking on face of rear end of pinion must be considered. Select a new pinion and ring gear set with markings as near as possible to those on old pinion. If marking on both old and new pinion is the same, do not change thickness of shim pack.
3. The approximate difference between markings on old and new drive pinion is the adjustment that will have to be made in the shim packs.
4. In the first listing below note that the new pinion is a plus eight (+8) while the old pinion is a plus five (+5). Making a difference of plus three (+3). This means that the thickness of each shim pack must be decreased by 0.003 in.
5. Once proper adjustment in shim packs has been made, place oil slinger, if so equipped, over pinion shaft. Install pinion inner bearing cone over shaft, and use bearing installer and an arbor press to press bearing onto pinion shaft. Bearing must be seated tightly against shoulder or oil slinger.
6. Use pinion front bearing cup installer to install outer bearing cup into carrier bore.
7. Install the selected inner shim pack in carrier. Then use pinion rear bearing cup installer to install inner bearing cup.
8. Insert pinion, oil slinger (when used) and inner bearing cone assembly into carrier and place the selected shim pack into position on outer end of pinion shaft.
9. Place outer bearing cone over pinion shaft, then use installer to seat bearing tight against shim pack.
10. Install pinion flange (yoke), washer and nut. Hold flange while tightening the nut to proper torque.

Note: Install oil slinger and oil seal only after pinion depth and pinion bearing preload have been checked out.

Checking Pinion Depth Adjustment

1. A pinion depth gauge and correct adapter, which gives a micrometer reading, should be used to determine pinion depth. The actual pinion depth setting can be determined by adding gauge reading to thickness of step plate and comparing result with the nominal dimension of 2.625-in. (models 44/60) or 3.125 in. (model 60), or 3.500 in. (model 70).
2. If the pinion setting is within minus (-) 0.001 in. to plus (+) 0.003 in. of this nominal dimension, the pinion position can be considered satisfactory.
3. If pinion setting exceeds these limits, it must be corrected by adjusting thickness of shim pack behind the pinion inner bearing cup.

Pinion Bearing Preload Adjustment

1. Use a torque wrench to check pinion bearing preload.
2. Rotating torque of pinion should be from 15 to 30 in. lbs.

NOMINAL ASSEMBLY DIMENSION AND ADAPTOR DISC CHART

Axle Model	Nominal Assembly Dimension	Adapter Disc Tool Number
44	2.625″	SE-1065-9-SS
60	3.125″	SE-1065-9-Y
70①	3.500″	SE-1065-9-Y

① Model 70—Use a 0.375 shim under dial pointer

Pinions		Difference Between Markings	Amount To Change Each Shim Pack (in.)
New Pinion	Old Pinion		
+8	+5	+3	Dec. 0.003
+5	+8	−3	Inc. 0.003
−5	−3	−2	Inc. 0.002
−3	−5	+2	Dec. 0.002
+5	−3	+8	Dec. 0.008
−4	+2	−6	Inc. 0.006

Dec. = decrease
Inc. = increase

3. Add or remove shims from pack just behind outer bearing cone to bring preload within these torque limits.

DIFFERENTIAL

Installation

1. Use dial indicator and spreader tool as described in Differential Removal, to spread carrier a maximum of 0.020 in.
2. Install bearing cups and place differential assembly in carrier. Rotate differential and, with a soft hammer, tap ring (drive) gear to assure a proper bearing seating.
3. Reinstall bearing caps in their proper locations as indicated by marks made during the removal procedure. Finger tighten cap screws. Relieve the spreader tool pressure, and tighten cap screws to 70–90 ft. lbs.
4. Move differential assembly tightly against drive pinion.
5. Install dial indicator securely to carrier, then set button at zero and against back of drive gear.
6. Move the differential toward the dial indicator and note the reading. For accuracy, repeat this operation several times.
7. Remove the differential assembly from carrier. Install a shim pack behind differential bearing cone at drive gear side, equal to the dimension indicated by dial indicator.
8. Subtract the indicator reading from the reading previously obtained in paragraph Differential Bearing Adjustment.
9. To the above result should be added 0.015 to 0.020 in. in shims to provide bearing preload.
10. Install the above shim pack behind differential bearing cone at side opposite to drive gear.
11. Spread differential carrier, using spreader tool.
12. Install differential bearing cups then locate differential assembly in carrier.
13. Rotate differential assembly, tapping gear to seat bearings.

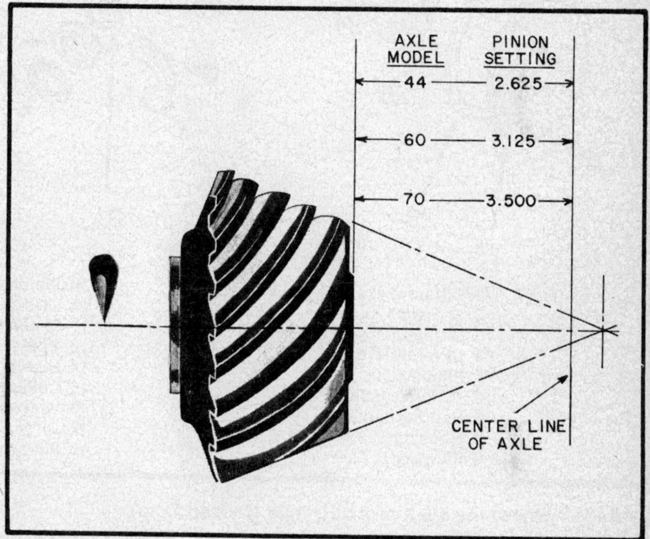

Pinion setting depth measurement (© Chrysler Corp.)

14. Install differential bearing caps in their correct location as indicated by marks made upon disassembly. Finger tighten cap screws.
15. Remove differential carrier spreader tool. Tighten differential bearing cap screws to proper torque.
16. Install dial indicator and check drive gear to drive pinion backlash at four equally spaced points around the drive gear. Backlash must be held to 0.003 to 0.006 in. and must not vary more than 0.002 in. between positions checked.
17. Whenever backlash is not within limits, differential bearing shim pack should be corrected.

AMC/JEEP

All the Jeep, Grand Wagoneer, Comanche and J–10 models are using a Jeep semi-floating type rear axle with flanges axle shafts. Both standard (7 $^{9}/_{16}$ in.) and heavy duty (8 $^{7}/_{8}$ in.) are being used. The J-20 models are using the Dana–Model 60 full-floating rear axle. The standard and heavy duty Jeep rear axle housings are made up of a modular cast iron center section and two steel tubes which are pressed into the center section. The rear drum brake support plates are attached to the mounting flanges at the axle tube outboard ends.

The differential assembly consists of a cast iron case containing two differential side gears, two differential pinion gears and a pinion shaft on which the pinion gears are mounted. The differential side and pinion gears are in constant mesh.

The axle ratio and the ring and pinion gear tooth combinations are stamped on a tag attached to the differential housing cover. On the Jeep rear axles, the axle code letters are stamped on the right side axle housing tube boss.

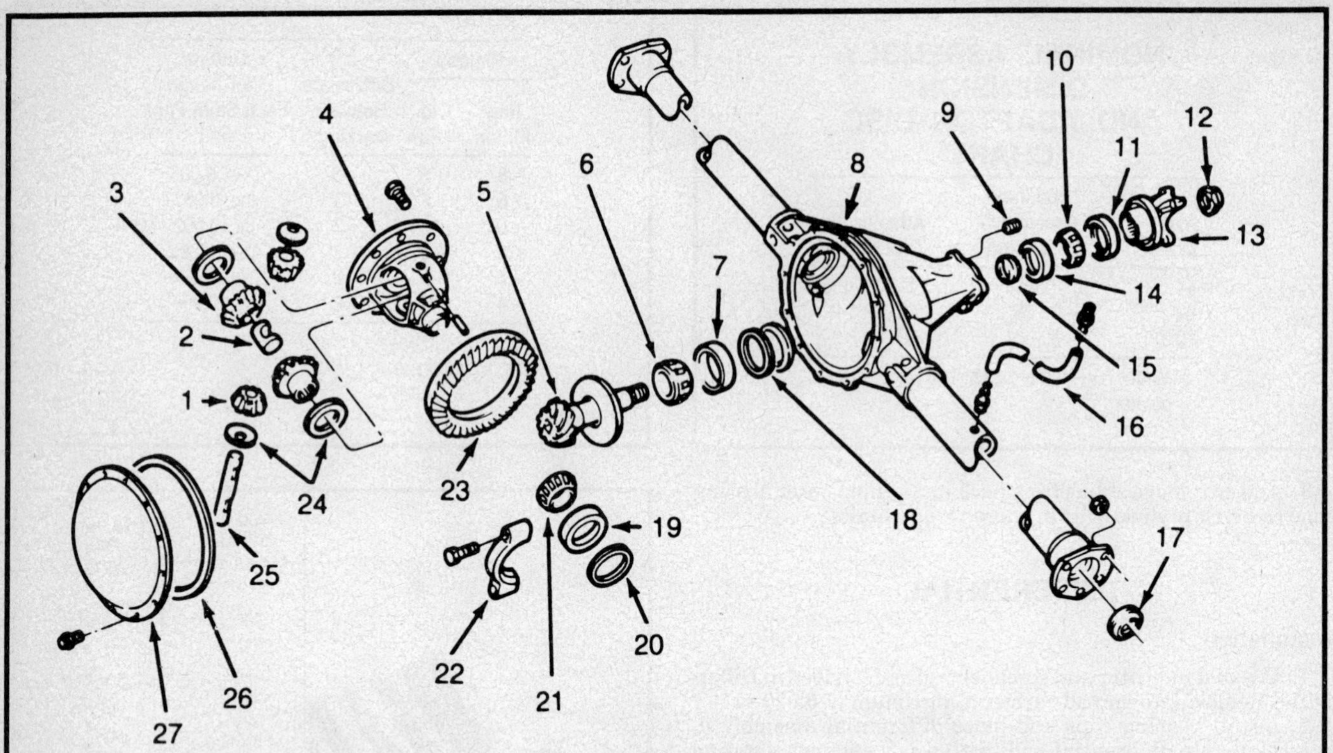

1. Differential pinion gear
2. Thrust block
3. Differential side gear
4. Differential case
5. Pinion gear
6. Pinion rear bearing
7. Bearing cup
8. Housing
9. Fill plug
10. Pinion front bearing
11. Oil seal
12. Pinion nut
13. Yoke
14. Bearing cup
15. Collapsible spacer
16. Vent assembly
17. Oil seal
18. Pinion depth shim
19. Bearing cup
20. Shim
21. Differential bearing
22. Bearing cap
23. Ring gear
24. Thrust washers
25. Pinion mate shaft
26. Gasket
27. Cover

Exploded view of the 8⅞ heavy duty axle (© Jeep Corp)

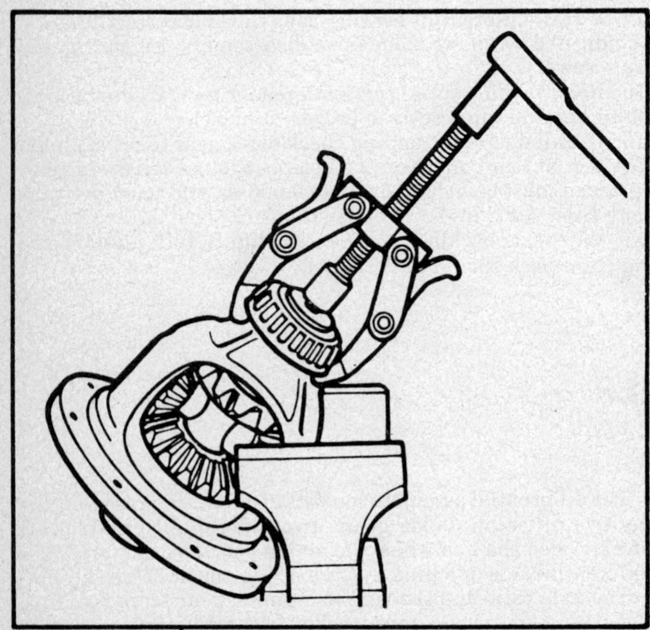

Removing the differential bearing (© Jeep Corp)

NOTE: The Trac–Lok limited slip differentials are available as an option. The Trac–Lok is used only in rear axles and there are two Trac–Lok units used.

7 $^{9}/_{16}$ AND 8 $^{7}/_{8}$ INCH RING GEAR

Removal

NOTE: It is not necessary to remove the rear axle assembly in order to overhaul the differential.

1. Raise and support the vehicle safely. Remove the axle housing cover and drain the lubricant into a suitable drain pan.
2. Remove the wheels, brakedrums, axle shafts and seals. Keep the left and right-side axle parts separated.
3. Mark the bearing caps with a center punch for assembly reference. Loosen the bearing cap bolts until only several threads are engaged, then pull the bearing caps away from the bearings. This will prevent the differential from falling out and sustaining damage when pried from the axle housing.
4. Pry the differential loose in the axle housing. Remove the bearing caps and remove the differential. Tie the differential bearing shims to their respective bearing caps and cups to prevent misplacement.

Differential Disassembly

1. Use Puller J–29721 and adapters or equivalent to remove

the differential bearings. When using this tool, be sure the differential case is secure. When the bearing is removed the differential case can drop if not supported.

2. Remove the ring gear-to-differential case bolts.

NOTE: Do not chisel or wedge the gear from the case.

3. Remove the ring gear from the case. Use a brass drift and hammer to tap the ring gear from the case. Do not nick the ring gear face of the differential case or drop the gear.

4. Remove the pinion mate shaft lockpin using a suitable drift. Remove the pinion mate shaft and remove the thrust block.

5. Rotate the pinion gears on the side gears until the pinion gears are aligned with the case opening. Remove the pinion gears and thrust washers and remove the side gears and thrust washers.

6. Remove the pinion nut using Tool J–8614–01 or equivalent. Remove the axle yoke using Tool J–8614–01, –02, –03 or equivalent.

7. Install the axle housing cover to prevent the pinion gear from falling out when the gear is driven out of the bearings and housing. Loosely attach the cover using two bolts.

8. Remove the pinion seal using tool J–9233 or equivalent. Tap the end of the pinion gear with a soft face mallet to drive the pinion gear out of the front bearing. Remove the front bearing and collapsible spacer. Discard the spacer.

NOTE: The collapsible spacer is used to control pinion bearing preload. Discard this spacer after removal, it is not reusable.

9. Remove the axle housing cover and remove the pinion gear and rear bearing from the housing. Remove the rear bearing cup using Tools J–8092 and J–21786 or equivalent

NOTE: The pinion gear depth adjustment shims are located under the rear bearing cup. Tag these shims for assembly reference.

10. Remove the front bearing cup using Tools J–8092 and J–21787 or equivalent.

NOTE: Keep the bearing cup remover tool seated squarely on the cup to prevent damaging the cup bores during removal.

Differential Axle Housing Alignment

1. Place two straightedges across the tube flanges and measure the distance between the flange ends. If the straightedges are parallel within $^3/_{32}$ in. at a distance of 11 inches from the tube centerline, the axle housing is serviceable.

2. Perform this inspection with the straightedges placed in horizontal and vertical positions.

Pinion Gear Installation and Depth Adjustment

Ring and pinion gear sets are factory tested to detect machining variances. Tests are started at a standard setting which is then varied to obtain the most desirable tooth contact pattern and quiet operation. When this setting is determined, the ring and pinion gear are etched with identifying numbers.
The ring gear receives one number. The pinion gear receives two numbers which are separated by a plus (+) or a minus (-) sign.

The second number on the pinion gear indicates pinion position, in relation to the centerline of the axle shafts, where tooth contact was best and gear operation was most quiet. This number represents pinion depth variance and indicates the amount in thousands of an inch that the gear set varied from the standard setting.

The number on the ring gear and first number on the pinion gear identify the gears as a matched set. Do not attempt to use a ring and pinion set having different numbers. The standard setting for AMC/Jeep axles is 2.547 in. If the pinion is marked

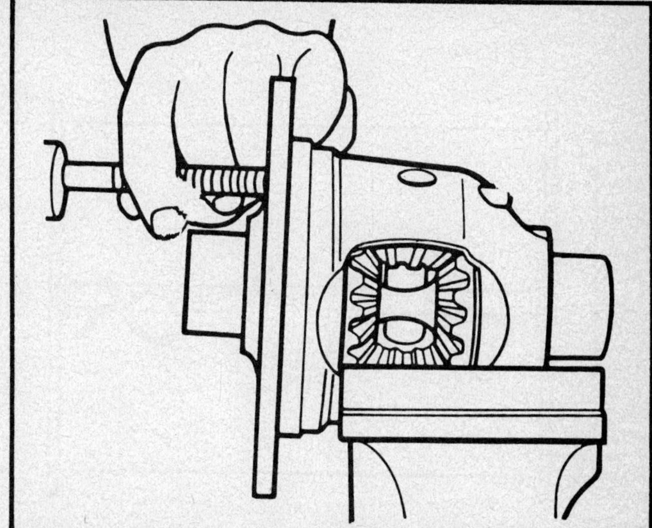

Removing the pinion shaft lock pin (© Jeep Corp)

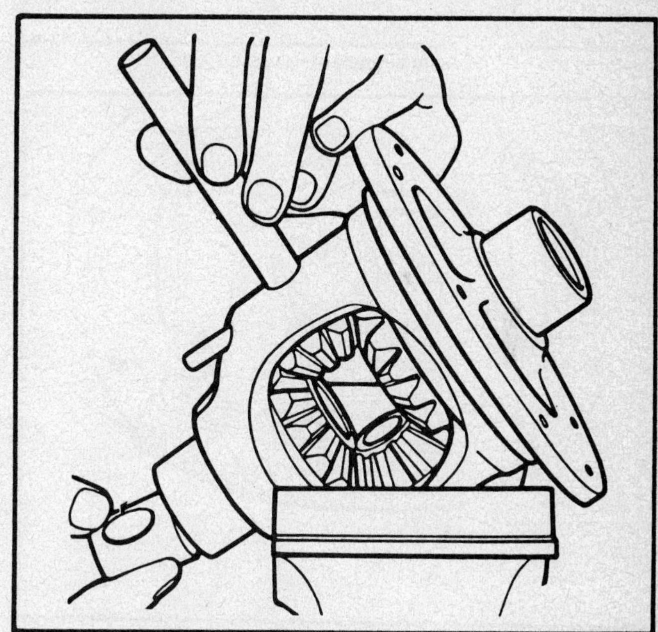

Removing the pinion shaft and thrust block (© Jeep Corp)

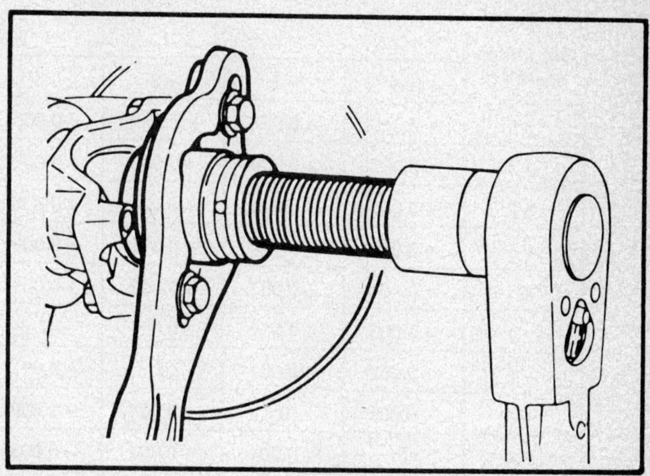

Removing the axle yoke (© Jeep Corp)

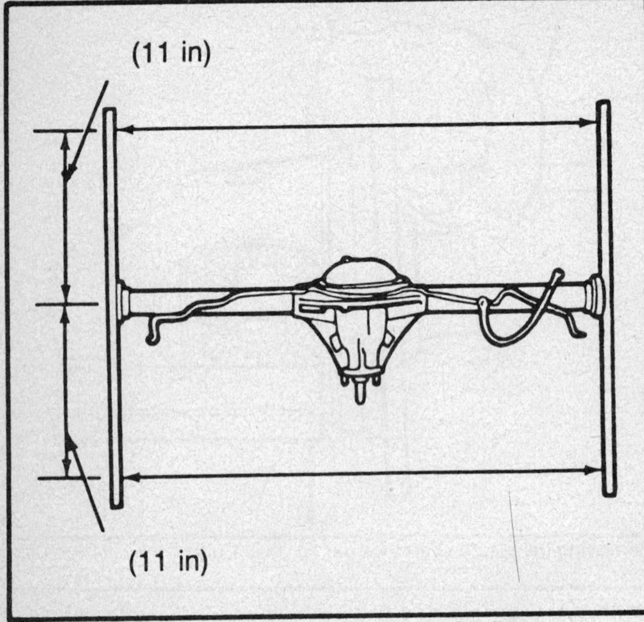

Checking the axle housing alignment (© Jeep Corp)

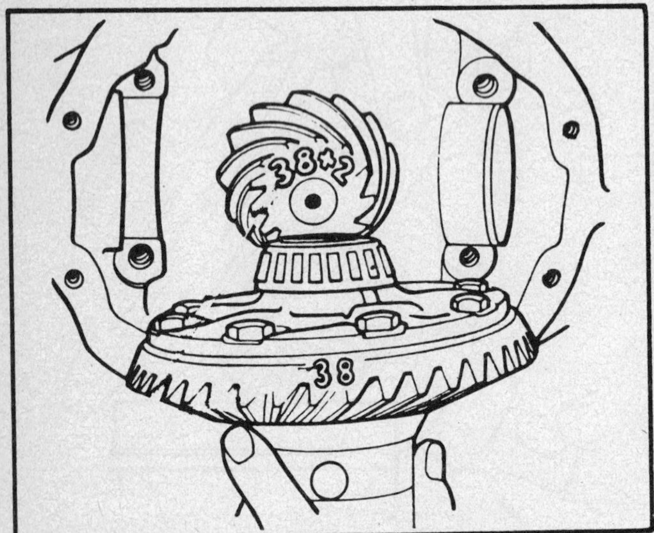

Pinion and ring gear identifying numbers (© Jeep Corp)

+2, the gear set varied from standard by + 0.002 in. and will require 0.002 in. less shims than a gear set marked zero (0).

When a gear set is marked plus (+), the distance from the pinion end face to the axle shaft centerline must be more than the standard setting. If the pinion gear is marked -3, the gear set varied from standard by 0.003 in. more shims than a set marked zero (0). When a set is marked minus (-), the distance from the pinion end face to the axle shaft centerline must be less than the standard setting.

NOTE: On some factory installed gear sets, an additional 0.010 or 0.020 in. may have been machined off the pinion gear bottom face. This does not affect the gear operation but does affect the pinion gear marking and depth measurement.

Pinion gears machined in this fashion have different identifying numbers. For example, if the pinion is marked +23, the number 2 indicates that 0.020 in. was removed from the pinion bottom face and the number 3 indicates that variance from the standard setting is + 0.003 in. If the pinion is marked +16, the number 1 indicates that 0.010 in. was removed from the pinion bottom face and the number 6 indicates that variance from the standard setting is + 0.006 in.

Gear sets with additional amounts machined off the pinion bottom face are factory installed items exclusively. All service replacement gear sets will be machined to standard settings only.

In addition, replacement gear sets marked + or - 0.009 in. or more, or sets with mismatched identifying numbers must be returned to the parts distributor center. Do not attempt to install these gear sets.

The chart provided in this section will help to determine the approximate "starter shim" thickness needed for the initial pinion depth measurement. However, the chart will not provide the exact shim thickness required for final adjustment and must not be used as a substitute for an actual pinion depth measurement. The chart should be used as follows.

1. Measure the thickness of the original pinion depth shim. Note the pinion depth variance numbers marked on the old and new pinion gears.

2. Now use the chart to determine the starter shim thickness. An example of this is as follows:

If the old pinion is marked -3 and the new pinion is marked +2, the chart procedure would be as follows. Go to the old pinion column and locate the -3, then go across the chart until the +2 figure is reached in the new pinion column. The box where the two columns intersect will indicate the amount of starter shim thickness required.

Old Pinion Marking	New Pinion Marking								
	−4	−3	−2	−1	0	+1	+2	+3	+4
+4	+0.008	+0.007	+0.0006	+0.005	+0.004	+0.003	+0.002	+0.001	0
+3	+0.007	+0.006	+0.005	+0.004	+0.003	+0.002	+0.001	0	−0.001
+2	+0.006	+0.005	+0.004	+0.003	+0.002	+0.001	0	−0.001	−0.002
+1	+0.005	+0.004	+0.003	+0.002	+0.001	0	−0.001	−0.002	−0.003
0	+0.004	+0.003	+0.002	+0.001	0	−0.001	−0.002	−0.003	−0.004
−1	+0.003	+0.002	+0.001	0	−0.001	−0.002	−0.003	−0.004	−0.005
−2	+0.002	+0.001	0	−0.001	−0.002	−0.003	−0.004	−0.005	−0.006
−3	+0.001	0	−0.001	−0.002	−0.003	−0.004	−0.005	−0.006	−0.007
−4	0	−0.001	−0.002	−0.003	−0.004	−0.005	−0.006	−0.007	−0.008

Pinion Variance chart for AMC/Jeep 7⁹⁄₁₆ & 8⁷⁄₈ inch ring gear (© Jeep Corp)

Pinion Depth Measurement Adjustment

1. Measure the thickness of the original pinion depth shim. Note the pinion depth variance numbers marked on the old and new pinion gears.

2. Determine the starter shim thickness. With the use of the chart, determine the amount to be added to or subtracted from the original shim thickness for starter shim thickness.

NOTE: The starter shim thickness must not be used as a final shim setting. An actual pinion depth measurement must be performed and the final shim thickness adjusted as necessary.

3. Install the ring bearing on the pinion gear with the large diameter of the bearing cage facing the gear end of the pinion. Press the bearing against the rear face of the gear.

4. Clean the pinion bearing bores in the axle housing thoroughly. This is important in obtaining the correct pinion gear depth adjustment. Install the starter pinion depth shim in the housing rear bearing cup bore. Be sure the shim is centered in the bearing cup bore.

NOTE: If the shim is chamfered, be sure the chamfered side faces the bottom of the bearing cup bore.

5. Install the ring bearing cup using Tools J–8092 and J–8608 or equivalent. Install the front bearing cup using Tools J–8092 and J–8611–01 or equivalent. Install the pinion gear in the rear bearing cup.

6. Install the front bearing, rear universal joint yoke and original pinion nut on the pinion gear. Tighten the pinion nut only enough to remove the bearing end play.

NOTE: Do not install a replacement pinion nut and collapsible spacer at this time as the pinion gear will be removed after depth measurement.

7. Note the pinion depth variance marked on the pinion gear. If the number is preceded by a plus (+) sign, add that amount (in thousandths) to the standard setting for the axle model being overhauled. If the number is preceded by a minus (-) sign, subtract that amount (in thousandths) from the standard setting. The result of this addition or subtraction is the desired pinion depth. Record this figure for future reference.

8. Assemble Arbor tool J–5223–4 and Discs J–5223–23 or equivalent, install the assembled tools in the differential bearing cup bores. Be sure discs are completely seated in bearing cup bores.

9. Install the bearing caps over the discs and install the bearing cap bolts. Tighten the bearing cap bolts securely, but not with the specified torque.

10. Position Gauge Block J–5223–20 or equivalent, on the end face of the pinion gear with the anvil end of the gauge block seated on the gear and the gauge plunger underneath Arbor Tool J–5223–4 or equivalent.

11. Assemble and mount Clamp J–5223–24 and bolt J–5223–29 or equivalent, on the axle housing. Use the axle housing cover bolt to attach the clamp to the housing.

12. Extend the clamp bolt until it presses against the gauge block with enough force to prevent the gauge block from moving. Loosen the gauge block thumbscrew to release the gauge block plunger. When the plunger contacts the arbor tool, tighten the thumbscrew to lock the plunger in position. Do not disturb the plunger position.

13. Remove the clamp and bolt assembly from the axle housing. Remove the gauge block and measure the distance from the end of the anvil to the end of the plunger using a 2–3 in. micrometer. This dimension represents the measured pinion depth. Record this dimension for assembly reference.

14. Remove the bearing caps and remove the arbor tool and discs from the axle housing. Remove the pinion gear, rear bearing cup and pinion depth shim from the axle housing.

15. Measure the thickness or the depth shim. Add this dimension to the measured pinion depth. From this total, subtract the desired pinion depth. The result represents the correct shim thickness required.

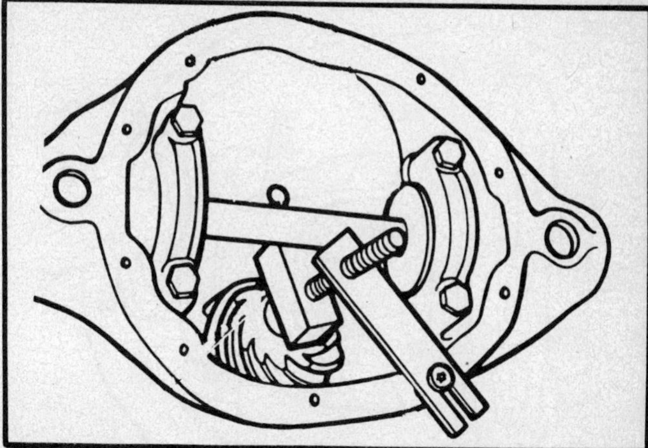

Installing the gauge arbor tool, discs and the gauge block tool (© Jeep Corp)

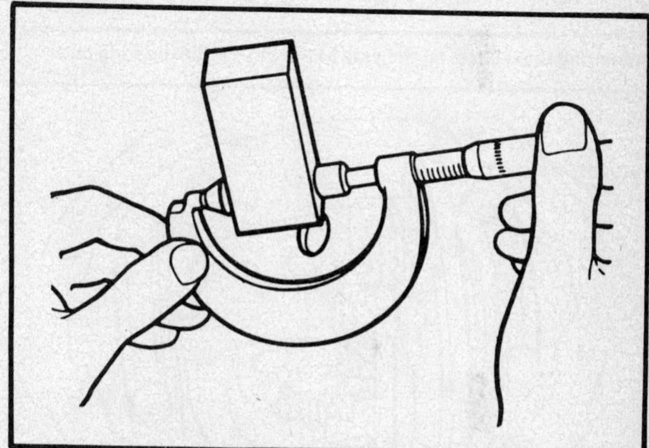

Measuring the anvil with a micrometer (© Jeep Corp)

NOTE: The desired pinion depth is the standard setting plus or minus the pinion depth variance.

Pinion Gear Bearing Preload Adjustment

1. Install the correct thickness pinion depth shim(s) in the axle housing bearing cup bore. Install the rear bearing cup and pinion gear.

NOTE: The collapsible spacer controls the pinion bearing preload. Do not reuse the old spacer. Use a replacement spacer only.

2. Install the replacement collapsible spacer and front bearing on the pinion gear. Install the pinion oil seal using Tool J–22661 or equivalent.

3. Install the pinion yoke and replacement pinion nut. Tighten the pinion nut finger-tight only. Tighten the pinion nut only enough to remove end play and seat the pinion bearings. Use Tool J–22575 or equivalent to tighten the nut and use Tool J–86141–01 or equivalent to hold the yoke while tightening the nut.

4. Rotate the pinion while tightening the nut to seat the bearings evenly. Remove the tools.

NOTE: Do not exceed the specified preload torque and do not loosen the nut to reduce the preload torque if the specified torque is exceeded.

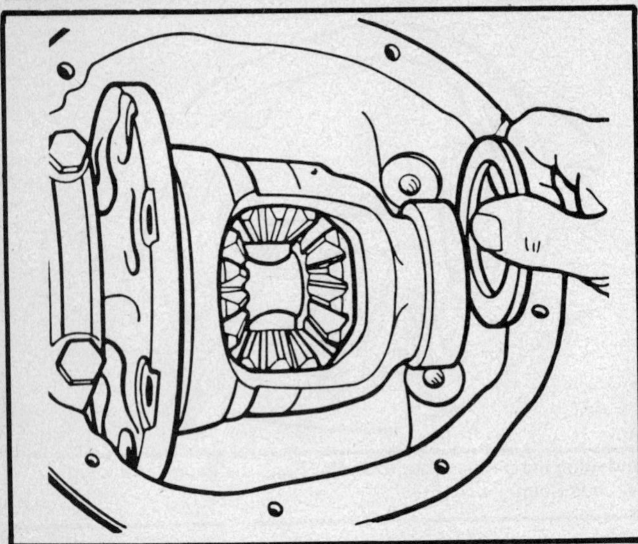

Installing the shim(s) on the side of the differential bearing cup

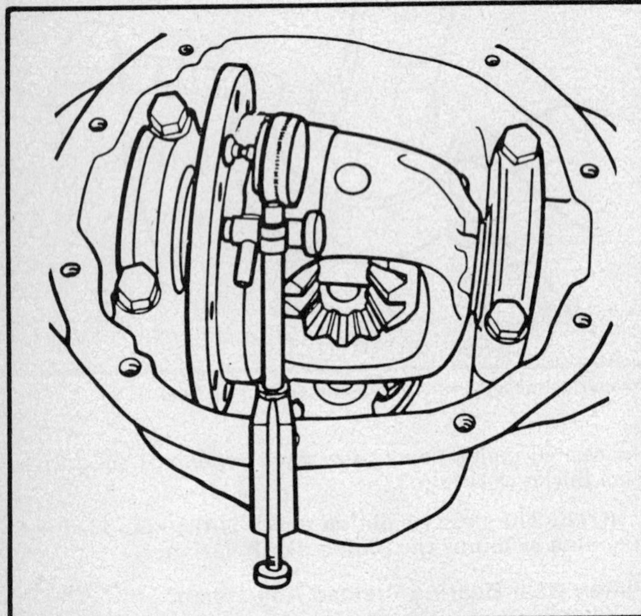

Installation of the dial indicator (© Jeep Corp)

5. Measure the torque required to turn the pinion gear using an inch-pound torque wrench and Tool J–22575 or equivalent. The correct pinion bearing preload torque is 17–25 inch lbs. torque. Continue tightening the pinion nut until the required preload torque is obtained.

6. If the pinion bearing preload torque is exceeded, remove the pinion gear, replace the collapsible spacer and pinion nut and adjust the preload again.

DIFFERENTIAL ASSEMBLY

NOTE: The following items should be done before begining the reassembly of the differential.

Clean each part thoroughly in solvent. Towel dry bearings or allow them to air dry, do not use compressed air to dry bearings as damage might result. Dry all other parts with compressed air or shop towels. If the parts are not to be assembled immediately, cover them to prevent dust or dirt contamination.

Inspect the housing for cracks and sand holes. Replace the housing if it is cracked or porous. Check for burrs and deep

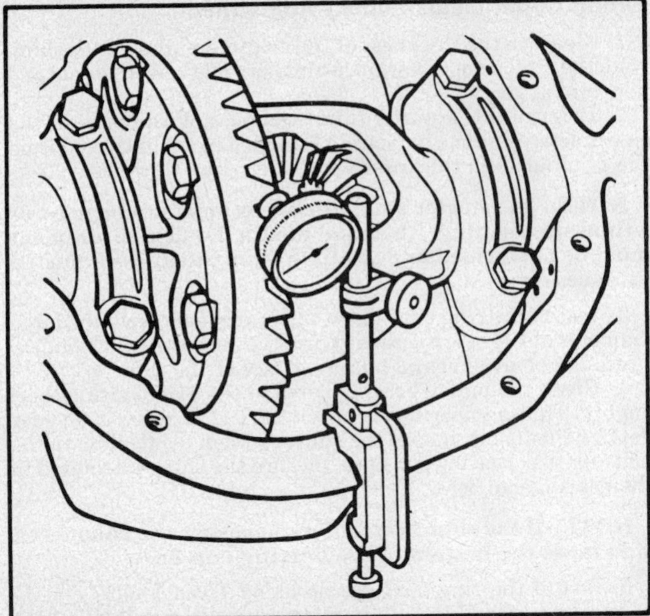

Measuring the ring gear backlash (© Jeep Corp)

scratches or nicks on the gasket and oil seal surfaces. An oil stone or fine tooth file may be used to remove nicks or burrs. The bearing cup bores should be carefully inspected for nicks or burrs that may have been created during bearing cup removal. Inspect and clean the axle tubes. Inspect the vent to be sure that it is not obstructed.

Check housing for bent or loose tubes or other physical damage.

Whenever one rear wheel is stationary and the opposite wheel is spinning, the differential pinion shaft is subject to high torque loads. Inspect the shaft for scoring and wear. The shaft should be a press fit of 0.000–0.010 in. in the case. Replace the shaft if worn or scored.

Inspect the side gears for worn, cracked or chipped teeth. The gears should fit snugly on the axle shaft splines. Also inspect the fit of the gears in the differential case bore. With the gears installed, side clearance must not exceed 0.007 in. Excessive side clearance must be corrected to avoid driveline backlash resulting in a "clunk" noise when the transmission is initially engaged in Drive or Reverse (with automatic transmission).

1. Install the differential bearings on the case using Tools J–21784 and J–8092 or equivalent.

2. Install the thrust washers on the differential side gears and install the gears in the differential case. Install the differential pinion gears in the case. Install the thrust washers behind the pinion gears and align the pinion gear bores.

3. Rotate the differential side and pinion gears until the pinion mate shaft bores in the pinion gears are aligned with the shaft bores in the case.

Install the thrust block in the case. Insert the block through the side gear bore. Align the bore in the block with the pinion mate shaft bores in the pinion gears and case.

4. Install the pinion mate shaft. Align the lockpin bore in the shaft with the bore in the case and install the shaft lockpin.

DIFFERENTIAL BEARING ADJUSTMENT

1. Place the bearing cup over each differential bearing and install the differential case assembly in the axle housing.

2. Install the shim on each side between the bearing cup and the housing. Use 0.080 in. shims as the starting point.

3. Install the bearing caps and tighten the bolts finger-tight. Mount the Dial Indicator J–8001 or equivalent on the housing. Using an appropriate pry tool, pry between the shims and housing. Pry the assembly to one side and zero the indicator,

then pry the assembly to the opposite side and read the indicator.

NOTE: Do not zero or read the indicator while prying.

4. The amount read on the indicator is the shim thickness that should be added to arrive at the zero preload and zero end play. Repeat the procedure to ensure accuracy and adjust if necessary. Shims are available in thicknesses from 0.080 – 0.110 in. in 0.002 in. increments.

5. When sideplay is eliminated, a slight bearing drag will be noticed. Install the bearing caps and tighten the bearing cap bolts with 85 ft. lbs. torque. Attach the dial indicator to the axle housing and check the ring gear mounting face of the differential case for runout. Runout should not exceed 0.002 in.

6. Remove the case from the housing. Retain the shims used to adjust the sideplay.

RING GEAR INSTALLATION

1. Position the ring gear on the differential case. Install the two ring gear bolts in the opposite holes and tighten the bolts to pull the gear into position.

2. Install the remaining ring gear attaching bolts. Tighten the bolts with 105 ft. lbs. torque.

3. Position the shims previously selected to remove the differential bearing sideplay on the bearing cups and install the differential assembly in the axle housing. Install the bearing cap bolts and tighten the bolts with 85 ft. lbs. torque.

4. Attach the dial indicator to the housing. Position the indicator so the indicator stylus contacts the drive side of a ring gear tooth and at a right angle to the tooth. Move the ring gear back and forth and note the movement registered on the dial indicator. The ring gear backlash should be 0.005 – 0.009 in., with 0.008 in. desired.

5. Adjust the backlash as follows: to increase the backlash, install the thinner shim on the ring gear side and the thicker shim on the opposite side. To decrease the backlash, reverse the procedure; however, do not change the total thickness of the shims.

NOTE: The following is an example on how to decrease backlash. The sideplay was removed using 0.090 in. shims on each side totaling 0.180 in. Backlash is checked and found to be 0.011 in. To correct the backlash, add 0.004 in. the the shim on the ring gear side and subtract 0.004 in. from the shim on the opposite side. This will result in 0.094 in. shim on the ring gear side and 0.086 in. shim on the other side. The backlash will be approximately 0.007 – 0.008 in. The total shim thickness remains 0.180 in.

DIFFERENTIAL INSTALLATION AND BEARING PRELOAD ADJUSTMENT

NOTE: The differential bearings must be preloaded to compensate for heat and loads during operation. The differential bearings are preloaded by increasing the shim pack thickness at each side of the differential by 0.004 in. for a total of 0.008 in.

1. Remove the differential assembly from the housing. Be sure to keep the differential bearing shim packs together for the proper assembly. Do not distort the shims in the axle housing bearing bores.

2. Install the differential bearing cups on the differential bearings. The cups should cover the differential bearing rollers completely. Position the differential assembly in the housing so the bearings just start into the housing bearing bores.

Component	Service Set-To Torque	Service Recheck Torque
Wheel Lug Nuts	102 N·m (75 ft-lbs)	81-122 N·m (60-90 ft-lbs)
Brake Support Plate Nuts	43 N·m (32 ft-lbs)	34-54 N·m (25-40 ft-lbs)
U-Joint Strap Bolts	19 N·m (170 in-lbs)	15-23 N·m (140-200 in-lbs)
Differential Bearing Cap Bolts	77 N·m (57 ft-lbs)	70-91 N·m (52-67 ft-lbs)
Ring Gear-to-Case Bolts	70 N·m (52 ft-lbs)	57-88 N·m (42-65 ft-lbs)
Rear Axle Cover Screws	19 N·m (170 in-lbs)	17-21 N·m (150-190 in-lbs)
Rear Axle Filler Plug	34 N·m (25 ft-lbs)	27-41 N·m (20-30 ft-lbs)

7⁹⁄₁₆ inch (standard) ring gear torque specifications (© Jeep Corp)

Component	Service Set-To Torque	Service Recheck Torque
Axle Housing Cover Bolts	19 N·m (14 ft-lbs)	17-21 N·m (12-17 ft-lbs)
Brake Tube-to-Rear Wheel Cylinder	11 N·m (97 in-lbs)	10-12 N·m (90-105 in-lbs)
Differential Bearing Cap Bolts	115 N·m (85 ft-lbs)	102-129 N·m (75-95 ft-lbs)
Ring Gear-to-Case Bolt	142 N·m (105 ft-lbs)	135-149 N·m (95-115 ft-lbs)
Rear Brake Support Plate Bolts	43 N·m (32 ft-lbs)	34-54 N·m (25-40 ft-lbs)
Universal Joint Strap Bolts	19 N·m (170 in-lbs)	16-22 N·m (140-200 in-lbs)

8⁷⁄₈ inch (heavy duty) ring gear torque specifications (© Jeep Corp)

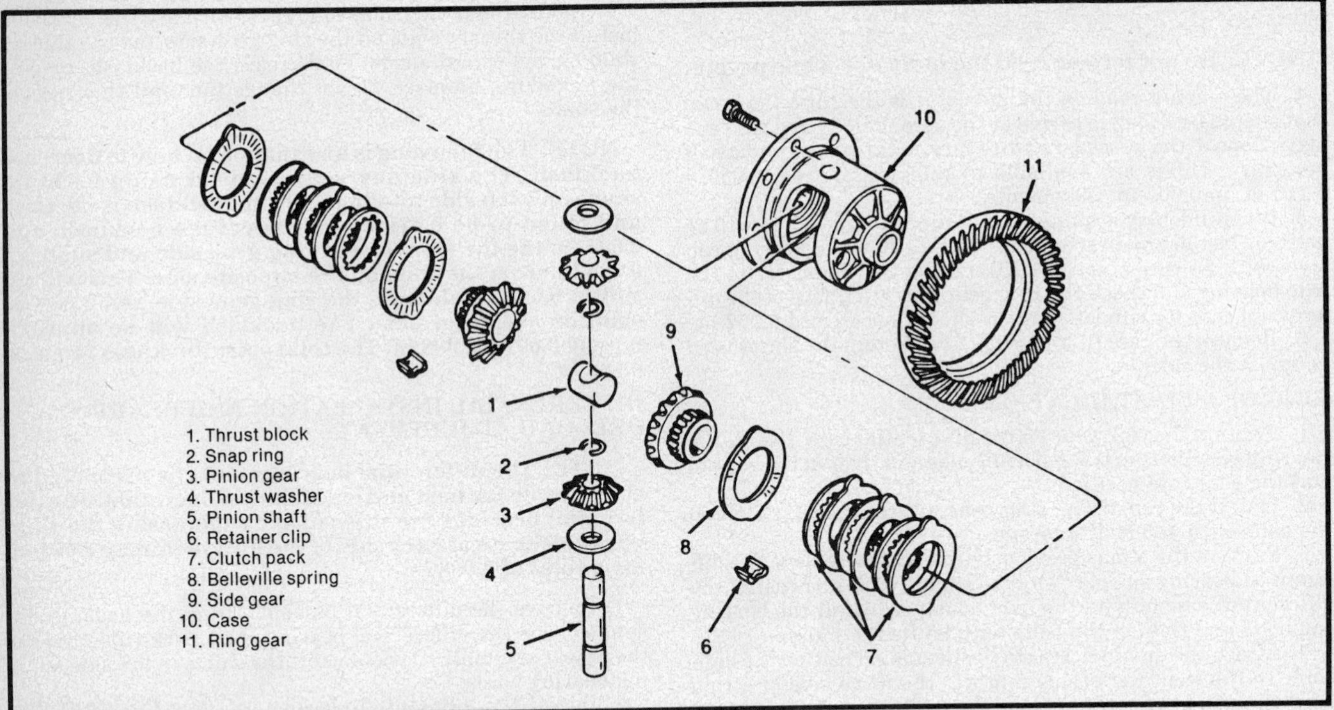

Exploded view of the Trac-Lok differential (© Jeep Corp)

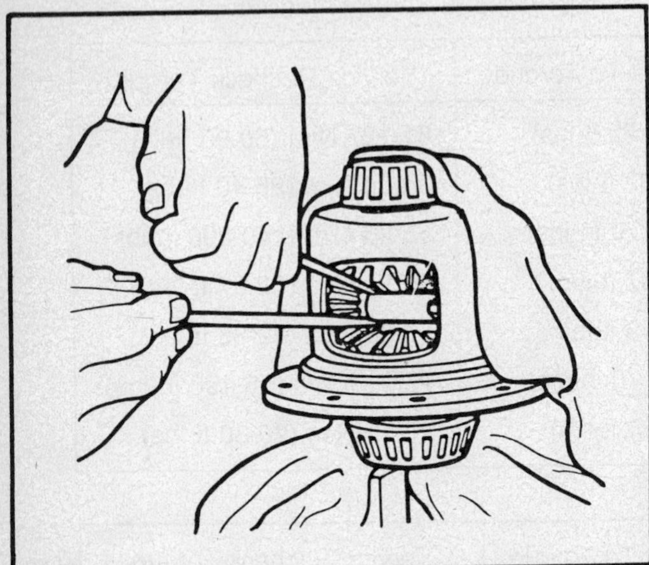

Removing the snap ring from the pinion mate shaft (© Jeep Corp)

NOTE: Slightly tipping the bearing cups will ease starting them into the bores. Also keep the differential assembly square in the housing during installation and push it in as far as possible.

3. Tap the outer edge of the bearing cups until the differential is seated in the housing.
4. Install the differential bearing caps. Position the caps accordingly to the alignment punch marks made at disassembly. Tighten the bearing cap bolts with 85 ft. lbs. torque. Preloading the differential bearings may change the backlash setting. Check and correct the backlash if necessary.
5. Install the propeller shaft, aligning the index marks made at disassembly. Install the axle shafts, bearings, seals and brake support plates. Fill the rear axle with the specified axle lubricant.
6. Check and adjust the axle shaft end play if necessary. Adjust the end play at the left side of the axle shaft only. Install the hubs, drums and wheels.

Lower the vehicle and road test the vehicle to check the rear axle assembly for proper operation.

TRAC–LOK DIFFERENTIAL

Operational Test

If a noisy or rough operation such as a chatter occurs when turning corners, the most probalbe cause of this chatter or noise is incorrect or contaminated lubricant. Before removing the Trac–Lok unit for repair, drain flush and refill the axle with the specified lubricant. A complete lubricant drain and refill with the specified fluid will usually correct the chatter problem. A quick operational test of the Trac–Lok differential can be done easily by performing the following steps.

1. Position one wheel on solid dry pavement and the opposite wheel on ice, mud grease or a similar low traction surface.
2. Gradually increase the engine rpm to obtain the maximum traction prior to a breakaway. The ability to move the vehicle effectively will demonstrate the proper performance.

NOTE: If the test is performed on extremely slick surfaces such as ice or grease coated surfaces, some question may exist as to proper performance. In these extreme cases, a properly performing Trac–Lok will provide greater pulling power by lightly applying the parking brake.

Trac–Lok Differential Dissassembly

1. Remove the differential from the axle housing as previously outlined in this section. Install one axle shaft in the vise with the spline end facing upward and tighten the vise.

2. Do not allow more than 2 $^3/_4$ in. of the shaft to extend above the top of the vise. This prevents the shaft from fully entering the side gear, causing interfernce with the step plate tool used to remove the differential gears.

3. Mount the differential case on the axle shaft with the ring gear bolt heads facing upward. Place some shop towels under the ring gear to protect the gear when it is removed from the case.

4. Remove and discard the ring gear bolts. Remove the ring gear from the case using a rawhide hammer. Remove the differential case from the axle shaft and remove the ring gear and remount the differential case on the axle shaft.

5. Use some suitable tools to disengage the snap rings from the pinion mate shaft. Place a shop towel on the opposite opening of the case to prevent the snap rings from flying out of the case. Remove the pinion mate shaft using a hammer and brass drift.

NOTE: A special gear rotating tool J–23781–3 or equivalent is required to perform the following steps. The tool consists of three parts; the gear rotating tool,forcing screw and step plate.

6. Install step plate tool J–23781–7 or equivalent in the lower differential side gear. Position the pawl end of the gear rotating tool J–23781–7 or equivalent onto the step plate.

7. Insert the forcing screw tool J–8646–2 or equivalent through the top of the case and thread it into the gear rotating tool. Before using the forcing screw tool, apply a small amount of grease to the centering hole in the step plate and oil the threads of the forcing screw.

8. Center the forcing screw in the step plate and tighten the screw to move the differential side gears away from the differential pinion gears. Remove the differential pinion gear thrust washers using a feeler gauge or a shim stock of 0.030 in. thickness. Insert the feeler gauge or shim stock between the washer and the case and withdraw the shim stock with the thrust washer.

9. Tighten the forcing screw until a slight movement of the differential pinion gear is observed. Insert the pawl end of the gear rotating tool between the teeth of one differential side gear.

10. Pull the handle of the tool to rotate the side gears and pinion gears. Remove the pinion gears as they appear in the case opening. It could be necessary to adjust the tension applied on the Belleville springs by the forcing screw before the gears can be rotated in the case.

11. Retain the upper side gear and clutch pack in the case by holding your hand on the bottom of the rotating tool while removing the forcing screw. Remove the rotating tool, upper side gear and clutch pack.

12. Remove the differential case from the axle shaft. Invert the case with the flange or ring gear side up and remove the step plate tool, lower the side gear and clutch pack from the case. Remove the retainer clips from both the clutch packs to allow separation of the plates and discs.

Trac–Lok Differential Assembly

If any one member of either clutch pack shows evidence of excessive wear or scoring, the complete clutch pack must be replaced on both sides.

Clean each part thoroughly in solvent. Towel dry bearings or allow them to air dry, do not use compressed air to dry bearings as damage might result. Dry all other parts with compressed air or shop towels. If the parts are not to be assembled immediately, cover them to prevent dust or dirt contamination.

Inspect the housing for cracks and sand holes. Replace the housing if it is cracked or porous. Check for burrs and deep scratches or nicks on the gasket and oil seal surfaces. An oil stone or fine tooth file may be used to remove nicks or burrs. The bearing cup bores should be carefully inspected for nicks or burrs that may have been created during bearing cup removal.

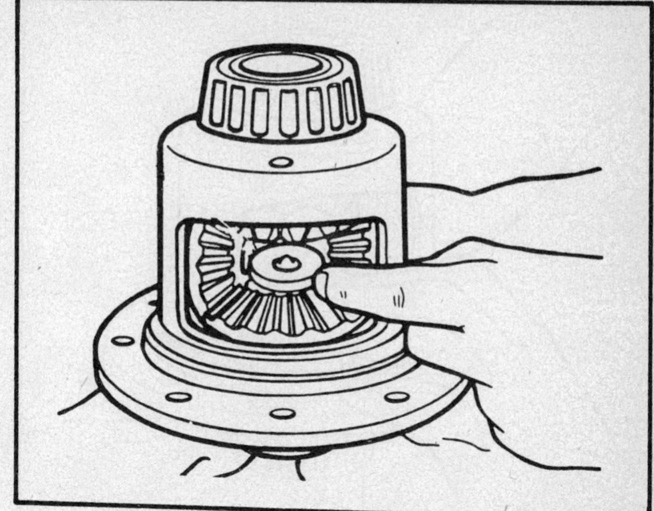

Installing the step plate tool (© Jeep Corp)

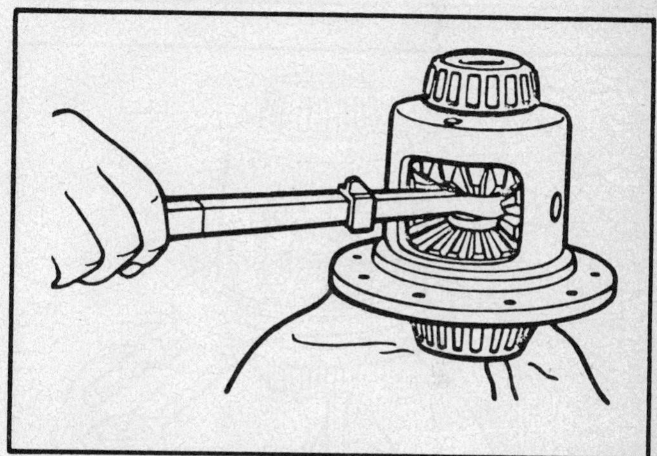

Installing the gear rotating tool (© Jeep Corp)

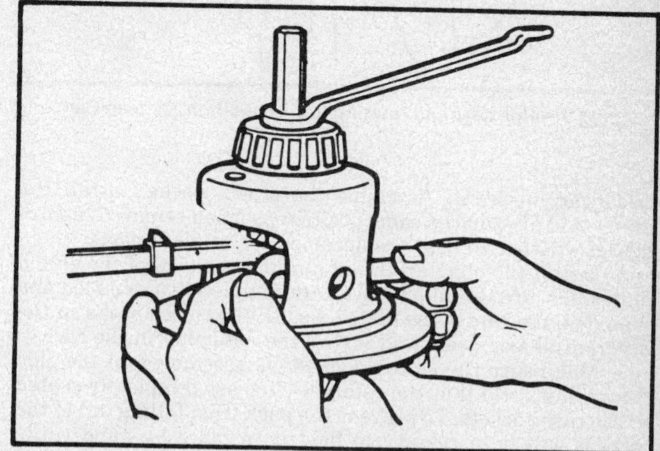

Removing the pinion gear thrust washers (© Jeep Corp)

Inspect and clean the axle tubes. Inspect the vent to be sure that it is not obstructed.

Check housing for bent or loose tubes or other physical damage.

Inspect the side gears for worn, cracked or chipped teeth. The gears should fit snugly on the axle shaft splines. Also inspect the fit of the gears in the differential case bore.

1. Lubricate all the differential components with the speci-

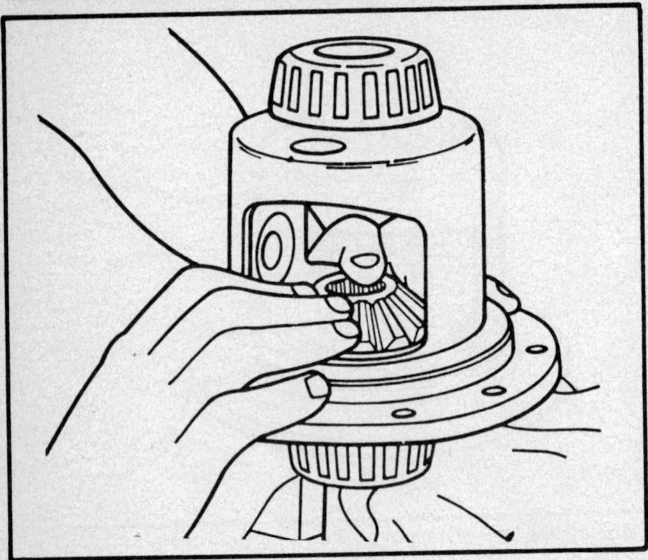

Installing the clutch packs (© Jeep Corp)

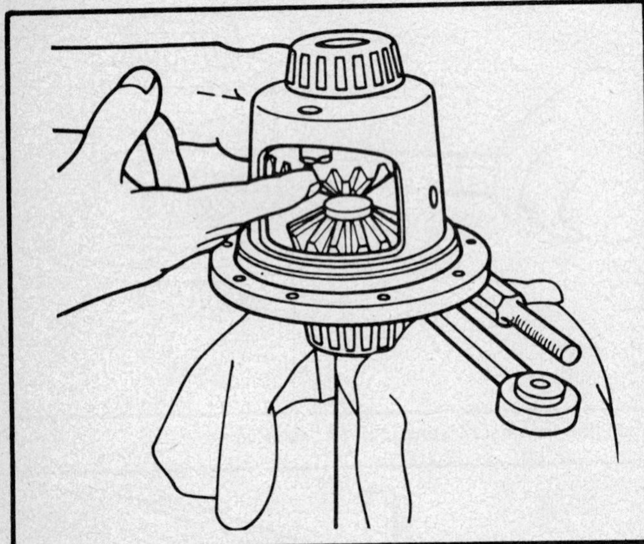

Keeping the side gear and rotating tool in position (© Jeep Corp)

fied gear lubricant. Assemble the clutch packs. Install the plates and discs in the same position as when removed regardless of whether they are replacement or original parts.

2. Install the clutch retainer clips on the ears of the clutch plates. Be sure the clutch packs are completely assembled and seated on the ears of the plates. Install the clutch packs on the differential side gears and install the assembly in the case.

3. Make sure the clutch pack stays assembled on the side gear splines and that the retainer clips are completely seated in the case pockets. To prevent the pack from falling out of the case, it will be necessary to hold it in place by hand while mounting the case on the axle shaft.

NOTE: When installing the differential case on the axle shaft, make sure that the splines of the side gears are aligned with those of the axle shaft. Make sure the clutch pack is still properly assembled in the case after installing the case on the axle shaft.

4. Mount the case assembly on the axle shaft. Install the step plate tool in the side gear and apply a small amount of grease in the centering hole of the step plate.

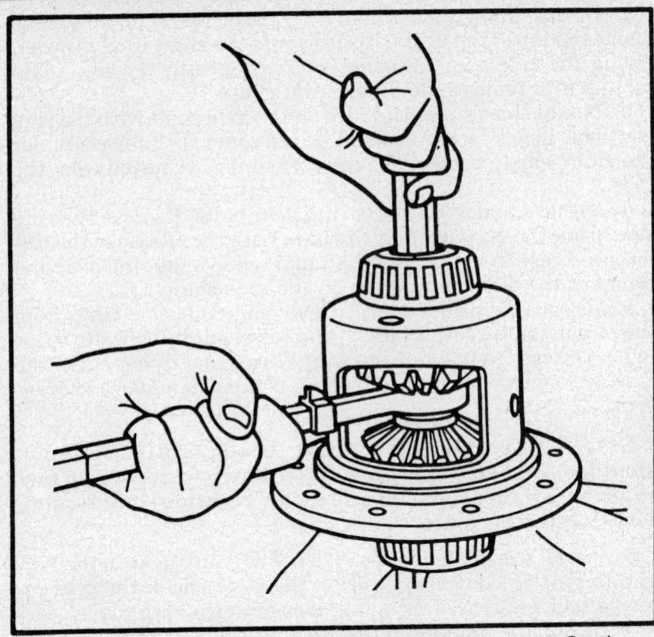

Installing the forcing screw into the rotating tool (© Jeep Corp)

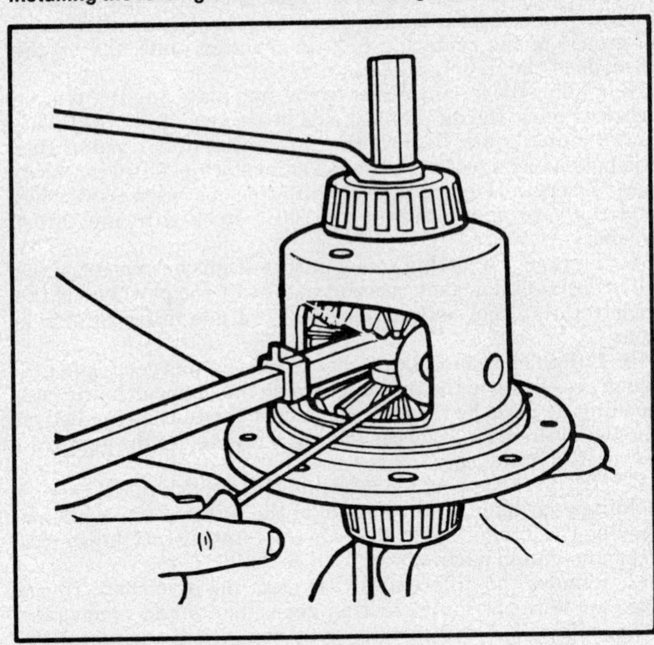

Installing the thrust washers (© Jeep Corp)

5. Install the remaining clutch pack and side gear. Make sure the clutch pack stays assembled on the side gear splines and that the retainer clips are completely seated in the pockets of the case.

6. Position the gear rotating tool in the upper side of the gear. Keep the side gear and rotating tool in position by holding them with your hand. Insert the forcing screw through the top of the case and thread it into the rotating tool.

7. Install both of the differential pinion gears in the case. Be sure the bores of the gears are aligned. Hold the gears in place by hand. Tighten the forcing screw to compress the Belleville springs and provide clearance between the teeth of the pinion gears and the side gears.

8. Position the pinion gears in the case and insert the rotating tool pawl between the side gear teeth. Rotate the side gears by pulling on the tool handle and install the pinion gears.

NOTE: If the side gears will not rotate, the Belleville spring load will have to be adjusted. If adjustment is necessary, loosen or tighten the forcing screw slightly until the gears will rotate.

9. Rotate the side gears, using the rotating tool handle, until the shaft bores in both the pinion gears are aligned with the case bore. Lubricate both sides of the pinion gear thrust washers.

10. Tighten or loosen the forcing screw to permit the thrust washer installation. Install the thrust washers and using a suitable tool, guide
the washers into position. Make sure the shaft bores in the washers and gears are aligned with the case bores.

11. Remove the forcing screw, rotating tool and step plate. Lubricate the pinion mate shaft and seat the shaft in the case. Be sure the snap ring grooves in the shaft are exposed to allow the snap ring installation.

12. Install the pinion mate shaft snap rings, remove the case from the axle shaft and install the ring gear on the case. Be sure to use replacement ring bolts only. Do not reuse the original bolts.

13. Align the ring gear and case bolt holes and install the ring gear bolts finger tight only. Remove the case on the axle shaft and tighten the bolts down evenly to the proper torque specifications.

14. Install the Trac–Lok differential assembly in the axle housing. and follow the procedures previously outline for the other Jeep axles to complete the differential and axle assembly servicing.

Component	Service Set-To Torque	Service Recheck Torque
Wheel Lug Nuts	102 N·m (75 ft-lbs)	81-122 N·m (60-90 ft-lbs)
Brake Support Plate Nuts	43 N·m (32 ft-lbs)	34-54 N·m (25-40 ft-lbs)
U-Joint Strap Bolts	19 N·m (170 in-lbs)	15-23 N·m (140-200 in-lbs)
Differential Bearing Cap Bolts	77 N·m (57 ft-lbs)	64-91 N·m (47-67 ft-lbs)
Ring Gear-to-Case Bolts	70 N·m (52 ft-lbs)	57-88 N·m (42-65 ft-lbs)
Rear Axle Cover Screws	19 N·m (170 in-lbs)	17-21 N·m (150-190 in-lbs)
Rear Axle Filler Plug	34 N·m (25 ft-lbs)	27-41 N·m (20-30 ft-lbs)

7$^{9}/_{16}$ inch (standard) ring gear Trak-Lok differential torque specifications (© Jeep Corp)

Component	Service Set-To Torque	Service Recheck Torque
Axle Housing Cover Bolts	19 N·m (170 in-lbs)	17-21 N·m (150-190 in-lbs)
Brake Tube-to-Rear Wheel Cylinder	11 N·m (97 in-lbs)	10-12 N·m (90-105 in-lbs)
Differential Bearing Cap Bolts	115 N·m (85 ft-lbs)	102-129 N·m (75-95 ft-lbs)
Ring Gear-to-Case Bolt	142 N·m (105 ft-lbs)	135-149 N·m (95-115 ft-lbs)
Rear Brake Support Plate Bolts	43 N·m (32 ft-lbs)	34-54 N·m (25-40 ft-lbs)
Universal Joint Strap Bolts	19 N·m (170 in-lbs)	16-22 N·m (140-200 in-lbs)

8$^{7}/_{8}$ inch (heavy duty) ring gear Trak-Lok differential torque specifications (© Jeep Corp)

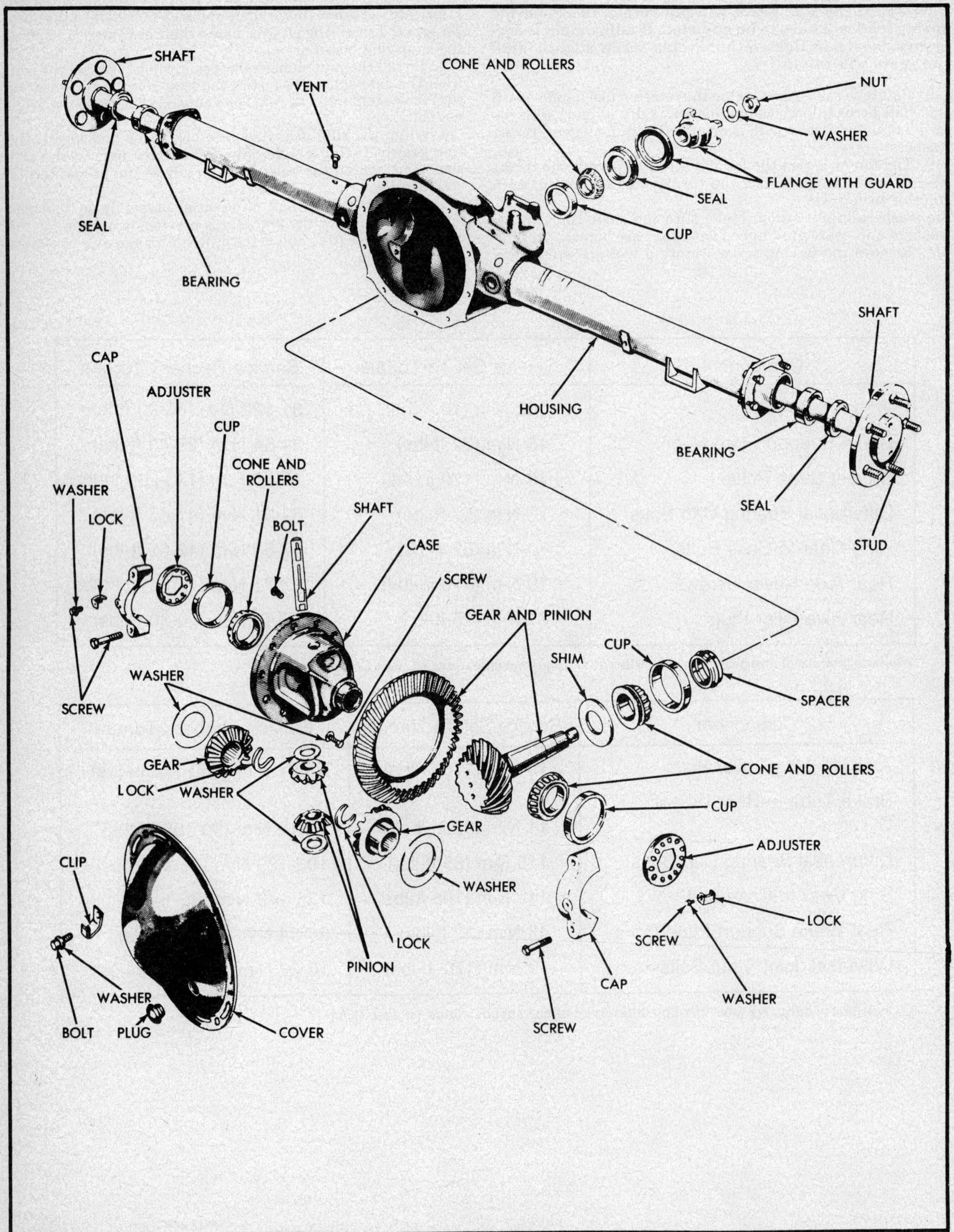

SHAFT
VENT
CONE AND ROLLERS
NUT
WASHER
FLANGE WITH GUARD
SEAL
CUP
SEAL
BEARING
SHAFT
HOUSING
BEARING
SEAL
STUD
CAP
ADJUSTER
CUP
CONE AND ROLLERS
WASHER
LOCK
BOLT
SHAFT
CASE
SCREW
SCREW
GEAR AND PINION
WASHER
CUP
SHIM
SPACER
GEAR
LOCK
WASHER
CONE AND ROLLERS
CUP
GEAR
ADJUSTER
CLIP
WASHER
LOCK
LOCK
SCREW
PINION
WASHER
CAP
BOLT
PLUG
COVER
SCREW

Exploded view of Chrysler Corp. 9¼ inch rear axle assembly (© Chrysler Corp.)

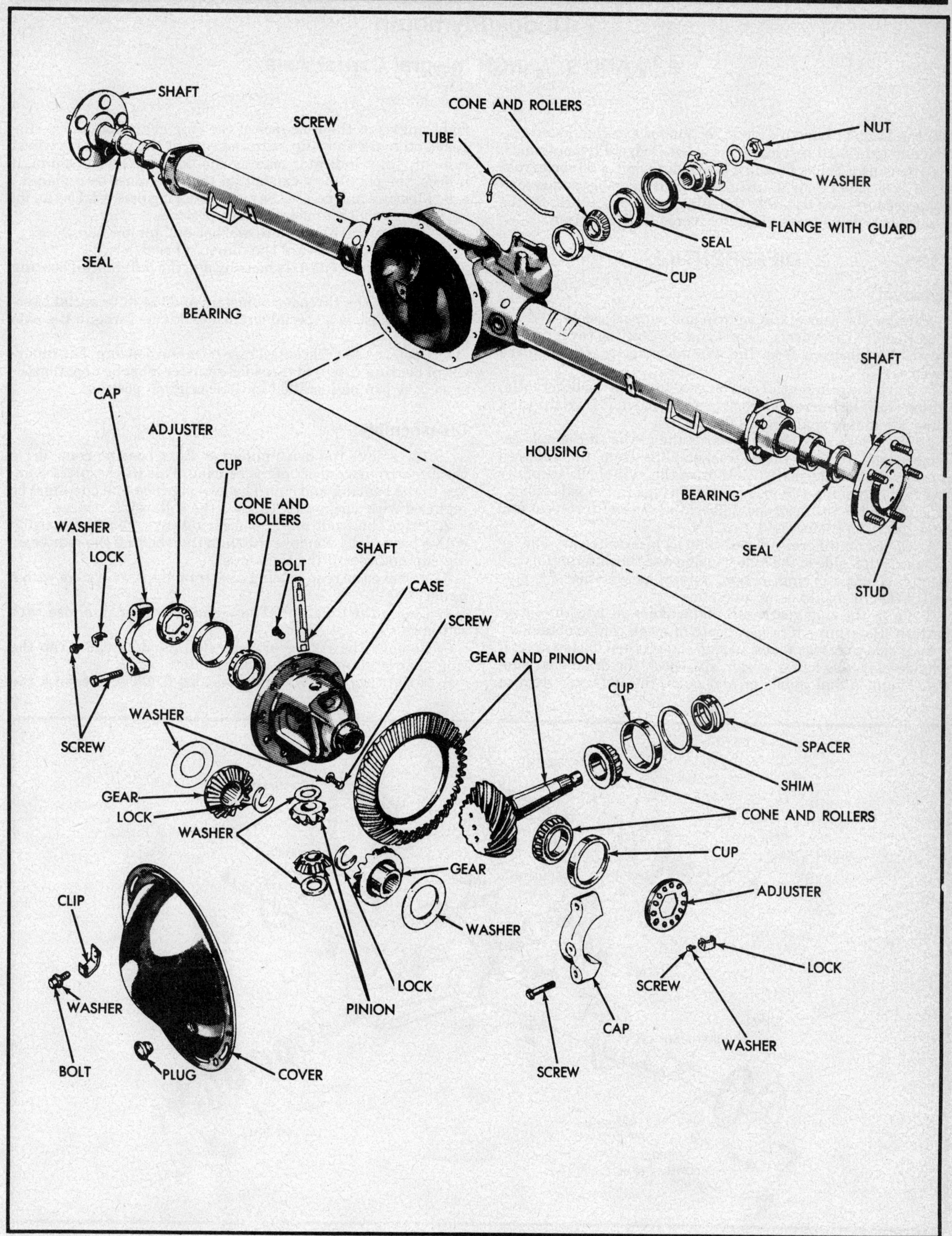

Exploded view of Chrysler Corp. 8⅜ inch rear axle assembly (© Chrysler Corp.)

Dodge/Plymouth

8 3/8 AND 9 1/4 INCH Integral Carrier Axle

See the Dodge/Plymouth truck section for external identification and axle shaft service. Some of the Dodge /Plymouth models are using a Spicer 60 and a heavy duty Spicer 60 series rear drive axle. The removal, installation, disassembly and assembly procedures are basically the same as the procedures for the coventional drive axles already covered in this section.

DIFFERENTIAL

Removal

1. Raise the rear of the vehicle and support safely.
2. Remove the wheels, drums and the housing cover screws. Drain the lubricant from the axle housing by removing the cover.
3. Turn the differential carrier case to make the differential pinion shaft lock screw accessible and remove it from the case. Slide the pinion shaft from the case.
4. Push both axle shafts towards the center of the axle assembly and remove the C-washer clips from the recessed grooves of the axle shafts. Withdraw the axle shafts carefully to avoid damaging the axle shaft bearings in the axle tubes.
5. Clean the inside of the differential case with solvent and blow dry with compressed air.
6. Check for differential side-play by inserting a pry-bar between the left side of the axle housing and the differential case flange. Using a prying motion, determine whether side-play exists. There should be no side-play.
7. Paint the ring gear teeth and make a gear tooth contact pattern. Determine if proper depth of mesh can be obtained.
8. If side-play was found in step six, proceed to step nine. If no side-play was found in step six, check the drive gear run-out. Mount a dial indicator and index the indicator stem at right angles in the rear face of the ring gear. Rotate the ring gear and mark the ring gear and case at the point of greatest run-out. Total indicator reading should not exceed 0.005 in. If it does, the possibility exists that the case must be replaced.
9. Measure and record the pinion bearing preload. Use an in. lb. torque wrench to measure the preload.
10. Remove the pinion nut, washer and pinion flange.
11. Remove and discard the pinion oil seal.
12. Match-mark the axle housing and the differential bearing caps.
13. Remove the threaded adjusters and the differential bearing caps. There is a special wrench to do this through the axle tube.
14. Remove the differential case from the housing. The differential bearing cups and threaded adjuster must be kept together so they can be installed in their original position.

Disassembly

1. To remove the drive pinion or front bearing cone, drive the pinion rearward out of the bearing. This will result in damage to the bearing and cup. The bearing cone and cup must be replaced with new parts. Discard the collapsible spacer.
2. Drive the front and rear bearing cups from the housing with a brass drift. Remove the shim from behind the rear bearing cup and record the thickness.
3. Remove the rear bearing cone from the pinion stem with a puller.
4. Clamp the differential case and ring gear in a vise with soft jaws.
5. Remove the ring gear bolts (left-hand thread). Tap the ring gear loose with a soft-faced mallet.
6. If the ring gear run-out exceeded 0.005 in., recheck the

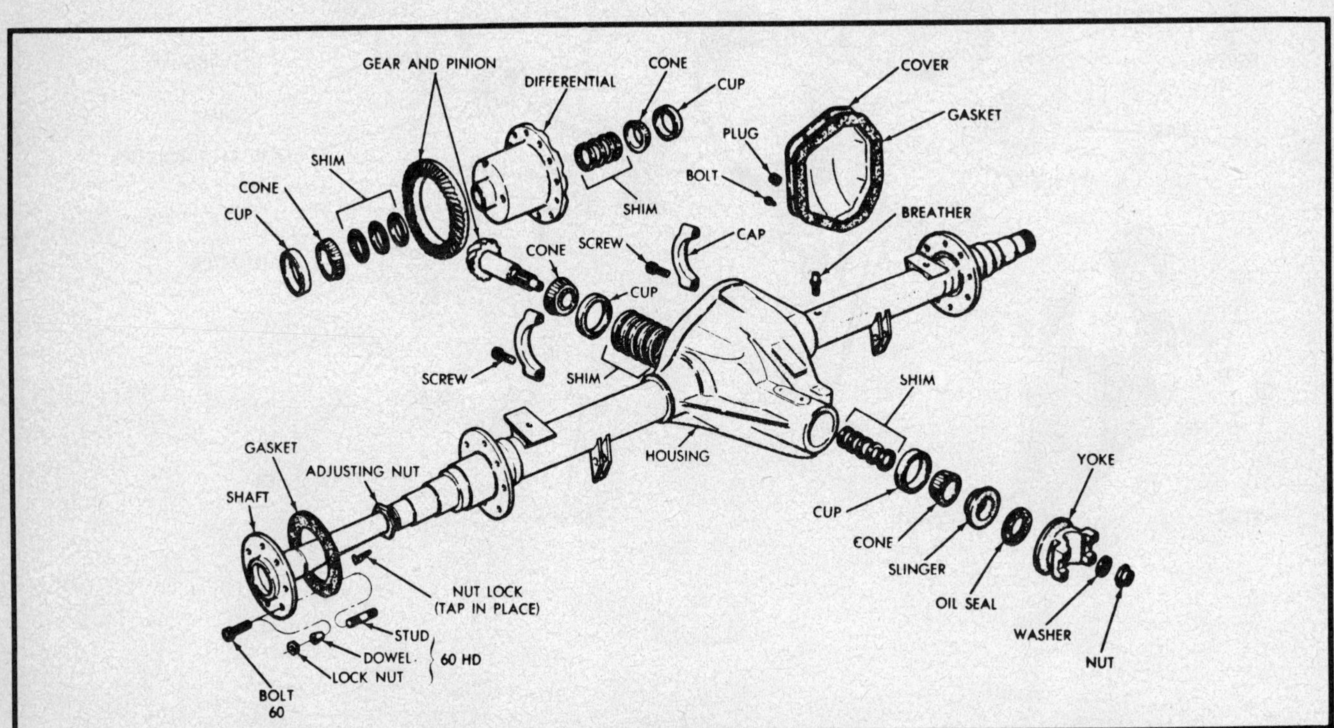

Exploded view of the Spicer 60 and Spicer 60 heavy duty rear axle assembly (© Chrysler Corp.)

case as follows. Install the differential case, cups, caps, and adjusters in the housing. Turn the adjusters to eliminate all sideplay and tighten the differential cap bolts snugly. Measure the run-out at the ring gear flange face. Total indicator reading should not exceed 0.003 in. It is often possible to reduce run-out by removing the ring gear and remounting 180° from its original position. Remove the differential case from the housing.

7. Remove the pinion shaft lock-screw and remove the pinion shaft.

8. Rotate the differential side gears until the differential pinion shafts can be removed through the opening in the case.

9. Remove the differential side gears and thrust washers.

10. Using a puller or a press and press plates, remove the differential side bearings.

Assembly

1. Lubricate all parts, before assembly, with rear axle lubricant.

2. Install the thrust washers on the differential side gears and install the side gears into the case.

3. Place thrust washers on both differential pinions and, working through the opening in the case, mesh the pinion gears with the side gears. The pinions should be exactly 180° apart.

4. Rotate the side gears 90° to align the pinions and thrust washers with the pinion shaft holes.

5. From the pinion shaft lockpin hole side of the case, insert the slotted end of the pinion shaft through the case, conical thrust washer and just through one of the pinion gears.

6. Install a thrust block through the side gear hub, so that the slot is centered between the side gears.

7. Hold all these parts in alignment, and align the lockpin holes in the pinion shaft and case. Install the lockpin from the pinion shaft side of the ring gear flange, temporarily.

8. With a stone, relieve the edge of the chamfer on the inside diameter of the ring gear.

9. Heat the ring gear (fluid bath or heat lamp) to a temperature not exceeding 300°F. Do not heat ring gear with a torch.

10. Align the ring gear with the case. Insert the ring gear screws through the case flange and into the ring gear.

11. Alternately tighten each cap screw to 70 ft. lbs.

12. Position each differential bearing cone on the hub of the differential case (taper away from ring gear) and install the bearing cones. An arbor press may be helpful.

Pinion Depth of Mesh

1. The proper pinion setting (relative to the ring gear) is determined by a shim which has been selected before the pinion is to be installed in the carrier. Pinion bearing shims are available in 0.001 in. increments.

2. The head of the pinion is marked with a "plus" (+) or a "minus" (-) mark that is followed by a number ranging from zero to four. If the old and new pinions have the same marking and the old bearing is being installed, use a shim of the original thickness. If the old pinion is marked zero (0), however, and the new pinion is marked plus two (+2), try a shim that is 0.002 in. thinner. If the new pinion is marked axle housing cup bore and install minus two (-2), try a shim that is 0.002 in. thicker.

3. Position the selected shim in the bore of the rear bearing cup. Install the cup.

NOTE: Special pinion depth measuring tools are available for both the 8 $^3/_8$ and 9 $^3/_8$ in. axles. When using the special tools, follow the manufacturer's recommended procedures. Without the special tools, complete the following procedure and check the pinion depth by examining the pinion to ring gear tooth contact pattern. Correct as required by adding or subtracting shims controlling the pinion depth.

4. Place the rear pinion bearing cone on the pinion stem (small side away from pinion head).

5. Lubricate the front and rear bearing cones and install the rear pinion bearing cone onto the pinion stem with an arbor press.

6. Insert the pinion bearing and collapsible spacer assembly through the carrier and install the front bearing cone. Install the companion flange.

NOTE: During installation of the pinion bearing do not collapse the spacer.

7. Install the drive pinion oil seal into the carrier. Be sure to properly seat the seal.

8. Support the pinion in the carrier.

9. Install the Belleville washer (convex side up) and pinion nut.

10. Hold the companion flange and tighten the pinion nut to remove all end-play, while rotating the pinion to ensure proper bearing seating. Remove the tools and rotate the pinion several revolutions.

11. Torque the pinion nut to 210 ft. lbs. With an in. lbs. torque wrench, measure the pinion bearing preload, which would be 20 to 35 in. lbs. for new bearings or 10 in. lbs. over the original figure if the old pinion bearing is used.

NOTE: The correct preload reading can only be obtained with the carrier nose upright. The final assembly is incorrect if the final pinion nut torque is below 210 ft. lbs. or if the pinion bearing preload is not within specifications. Under no circumstances should the pinion nut be backed off to reduce the pinion bearing preload; if this is done, a new collapsible spacer will have to be installed and the unit adjusted again until proper preload is obtained.

DIFFERENTIAL BEARING PRELOAD AND RING GEAR-TO-PINION BACKLASH

The threaded adjuster uses a hex drive hole, and requires special tool C-4164 to adjust the side bearing preload through the axle tube. An adjuster lock with two pointed teeth which engage in the exposed adjuster thread when the lock is tightened is provided. The shims will range from 0.020–0.038 in. and will be equipped with internal centering tabs. The shims, marked with a number which represents its thickness in thousandths of an in., can be installed with either side against the pinion head.

1. Index the gears so that the same gear teeth are in contact throughout the adjustment.

2. The differential bearing cups will not always move with the adjusters. It is important to seat the bearings by rotating them 5–10 times in each direction, each time the adjusters are moved.

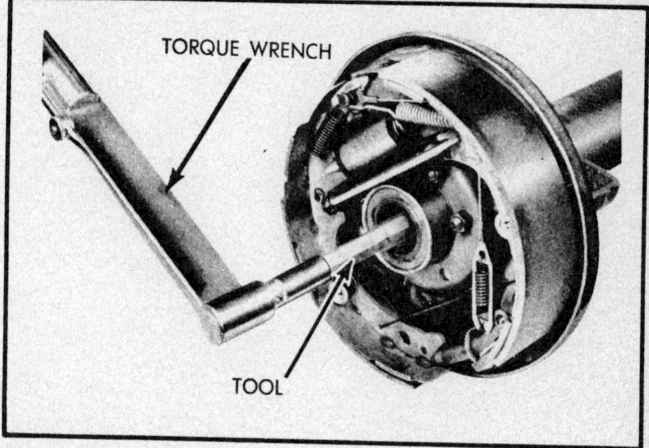

Use of long bar tool with hex end to adjust differential bearing preload and gear backlash (© Chrysler Corp.)

Type	Semi-Floating Hypoid	
Ring Gear Diameter	8.375" (212.7mm)	
Number of Teeth		
Drive Gear	47	45
Pinion	16	14
Ratio to 1	2.94	3.21
Number of Teeth		
Drive Gear	39	39
Pinion	11	10
Ratio to 1	3.55	3.90
PINION BEARINGS		
Type	Taper Roller	
Number Used	Two	
Adjustment	Collapsible Spacer	
Pinion Bearing Preload New Bearings	20-35 in. lbs. (2.25-3.95 N·m)	
Used Rear And New Front	10-25 in. lbs. (1.12-2.82 N·m)	
DIFFERENTIAL	Conventional	
Bearings (Type)	Taper Roller	
Number Used	Two	
Preload Adjustment	Threaded Adjustment	
RING GEAR AND PINION	Hypoid	
Serviced In	Matched Sets	
Pinion Depth Of Mesh Adjustment	Select Shims	
Pinion and Ring Gear Backlash	.005-.008" (.13-.20mm) At Point Of Minimum Backlash	
Runout-Differential Case and Ring Gear Backface	.006" (.15mm) Maximum	
WHEEL BEARINGS		
Type	Straight Roller	
Adjustment	None	
End Play	Built-In	
*Lubrication	Rear Axle Lubricant	
LUBRICATION		
Capacity	4.4 PTS. (3-1/2 Imperial) (2 Liters)	

Type ... Multi-Purpose Lubricant, as defined by MIL-L-2105B (API GL-5) should be used in all rear axle with conventional differentials, such a lubricant is available under Part. No. 4318058 MOPAR Hypoid Gear Lubricant or an equivalent. In Sure-Grip differentials 4 ounces (.1183 liters) of MOPAR Hypoid Gear Oil Additive Friction Modifier, Part No. 4318060 or equivalent must be included with every refill.

8⅜ inch rear axle specifications (© Chrysler Corp.)

TYPE	Semi-Floating Hypoid	
Ring Gear Diameter	9.250" (234.9mm)	
Number of Teeth		
Drive Gear	39	
Pinion	10	
Ratio to 1	3.90	
Number of Teeth		
Drive Gear	45	39
Pinion	14	11
Ratio to 1	3.21	3.55
PINION BEARINGS		
Type	Taper Roller	
Number Used	Two	
Adjustment	Collapsible Spacer	
Pinion Bearing Preload New Bearings	20-35 in. lbs. (2.25-3.95 N·m)	
Used Rear And New Front	10-25 in. lbs. (1.12-2.82 N·m)	
DIFFERENTIAL	Conventional	
Bearings (Type)	Taper Roller	
Number Used	Two	
Preload Adjustment	Threaded Adjustment	
RING GEAR AND PINION	Hypoid	
Serviced In	Matched Sets	
Pinion Depth Of Mesh Adjustment	Selected Shims	
Pinion and Ring Gear Backlash	.005-.008" (.13-.20mm) At Point Of Minimum Backlash	
Runout-Differential Case and Ring Gear Backface	.005" (.127mm) Max.	
WHEEL BEARINGS		
Type	Straight Roller	
Adjustment	None	
End Play	Built-In	
Lubrication	Rear Axle Lubricant	
LUBRICATION		
Capacity	4.5 PTS. (3-3/4 Imperial) (2.1 Liters)	

Type . . . Multi-Purpose Lubricant, as defined by MIL-L-2105B (API GL-5) should be used on all rear axles; such a lubricant is available under Part No. 4318058 MOPAR Hypoid Gear Lubricant or an equivalent. In Sure-Grip Differentials 4 ounces (.1183 liters) of MOPAR Hypoid Gear Oil Additive Friction Modifier, Part No. 4318060 or equivalent must be included with every refill.

9¼ inch rear axle specifications (© Chrysler Corp.)

8-3/8 Inch (212.72mm) Axle	Pounds Foot	N·m
Differential Bearing Cap Bolts	70	95
Ring Gear to Differential Case Bolts (Left Hand Thread)	70	95
Drive Pinion Flange Nut	210 (Min.)	285 (Min.)
Carrier Cover Bolts		
Brake Support Plate Retainer Nuts	30-35	41-47
Propeller Shaft Bolts (Rear)		
Spring Clip (U Bolt) Nuts	45	61

9-1/4 Inch (234.95mm) Axle (HD)	Pounds Foot	N·m
Brake Support Plate Retainer Nuts	75	102
Carrier Cover Bolts		
Differential Bearing Cap Bolts	100	136
Drive Pinion Flange Nut	210 (Min.)	285 (Min.)
Propeller Shaft Bolts (Rear)		
Ring Gear to Differential Case Bolts (Left Hand Thread)	70	95

Spicer 60 and 60HD	Pounds Foot	N·m
Differential Bearing Cap Bolts	70-90	95-122
Differential Case Half Retaining Bolts	35-45	41-47
Ring Gear to Differential Case Bolts (Left Hand Thread)	100-120	136-163
Drive Pinion Flange Nut	250-270	339-366
Carrier Cover Bolts	30-40	41-54
Axle Shaft Retainer Bolts (60), Nuts (60HD)	50-90 (SP60), 55-90 (SP60HD)	68-122 74-122
Propeller Shaft Bolts (Rear)		
Spring Clip (U Bolt) Nuts	125-150-210	169-203-285

Rear axle torque specifications (© Chrysler Corp.)

TYPE	Full-Floating Hypoid	
Ring Gear Diameter	9.750" (247.64mm)	
Number of Teeth		
Drive Gear	46	
Pinion	13	
Ratio to 1	3.54	
Number of Teeth		
Drive Gear	41	41
Pinion	11	10
Ratio to 1	3.73	4.10
PINION BEARINGS		
Type	Taper Roller	
Number Used	2	
Adjustment	Select Shims	
Pinion Bearing Drag Torque (Seal Removed)	10-20 in. lbs. (1.12-2.25 N·m)	
DIFFERENTIAL	Trak-Lok and Standard	
Bearings (Type)	Taper Roller	
Number Used	2	
Preload Adjustment	Select Shims	
RING GEAR AND PINION	Hypoid	
Serviced In	Matched Sets	
Pinion Depth Of Mesh Adjustment	Select Shims	
Pinion and Ring Gear Backlash	.004-.009" (.101-.228mm) at point Of minimum backlash	
Runout-Differential Case and Ring Gear Backface	.006" (.15mm) Maximum	
LUBRICATION		
Capacity	6 Pints (5 Imperial) (2.8 Liters)	
Type	Multi-Purpose Gear Lubricant, as defined by MIL-L-2105B (API GL-5) should be used on all rear axles; such a lubricant is available under Part No. 4318058 MOPAR Hypoid Gear Lubricant or an equivalent. In Trak-Lok Differentials 4 ounces (.1183 liters) of MOPAR Hypoid Gear Oil Additive Friction Modifier, Part No. 4318060 or equivalent must be included with every refill.	

Spicer 60 and 60 heavy duty rear axle specifications (© Chrysler Corp.)

3. With the pinion bearings installed and the preload set, install the differential with adjusters, caps and bearings. Lubricate the bearings and adjuster threads. Check to be sure that there are no crossed threads. Tighten the top cap screws on the right and left to 10 ft. lbs. Tighten the bottom cap screws fingertight until the head is just seated on the bearing cap.
4. Using the tool, check to be sure that the adjuster rotates freely. Turn both adjusters in until bearing play is eliminated with some drive gear backlash (0.010 in.). Seat the bearing rollers.
5. Install and register a dial indicator against the drive side of a gear tooth. Check the backlash at four positions to find the point of minimum backlash. Rotate the gear to the position of least backlash and mark the tooth so that all readings will be taken at the same point.
6. Loosen the right adjuster and turn the right adjuster until the backlash is 0.003–0.004 in. with each adjuster tightened to 10 ft. lbs. Seat the bearings rollers.
7. Tighten the differential bearing cap screws to 100 ft. lbs.
8. Tighten the right adjuster to 70 ft. lbs. and seat the rollers, until the torque remains constant at 70 ft. lbs. Measure the backlash. If the backlash is not 0.006–0.008 in. increase the torque on the right adjusters and seat the rollers until the correct backlash is obtained. Tighten the left adjuster to 70 ft. lbs. and seat the bearings until the torque remains constant.
9. If the assembly is properly done, the initial reading on the left adjuster will be approximately 70 ft. lbs. If it is substantially less, the entire procedure should be repeated.
10. After adjustments are complete, install the adjuster locks. Be sure the teeth are engaged in the adjuster threads. Torque the lockscrews to 90 in. lbs.

Final Assembly

1. Install the axle shafts, C-clips, reinstall the pinion shaft and lock screw and tighten securely.
2. Install the cover on the differential housing, using a new gasket.
3. Refill the rear axle housing with lubricant.

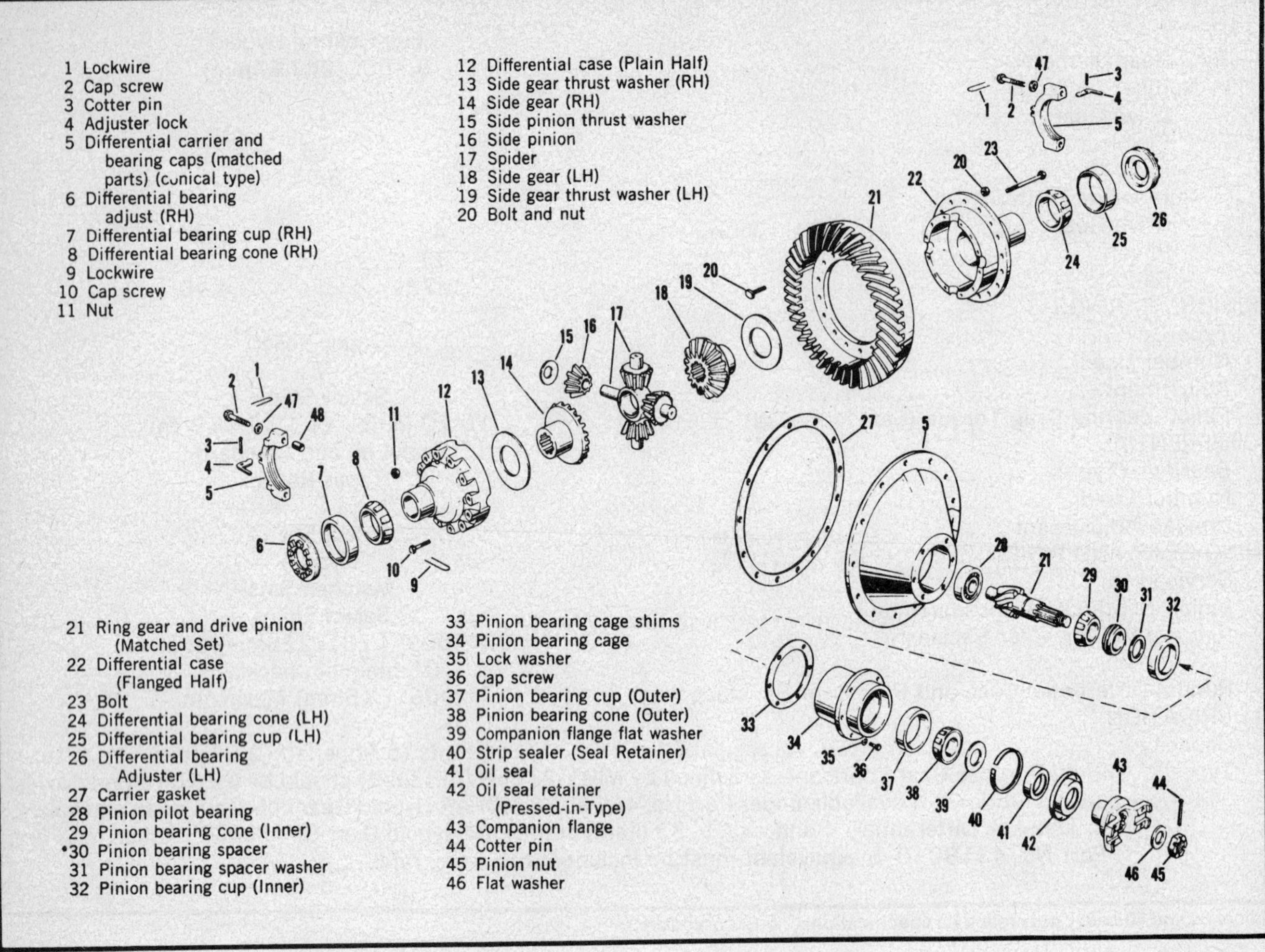

Eaton single-speed, single reduction rear axle (© Eaton Corp.)

Single–Speed, Single Reduction Eaton

MODELS 17120, 18101/18121, 17101/17121

This is a full-floating axle having spiral bevel drive gear and pinion, and using a four-pinion differential assembly. The pinion has three roller bearings—two in front of the pinion teeth and one behind.

Disassembly

1. Remove thrust block screw.
2. Punch mark carrier leg, bearing cap and bearing adjusting nut to aid in reassembly.
3. Remove bearing caps and adjusting nuts.
4. Lift assembly out of carrier housing.
5. Punch mark differential case halves for correct alignment. Separate case halves.
6. Remove pinion shaft pinions, side gears, thrust washers and bearing cones.
7. Separate drive gear from cage.
8. Remove pinion shaft yoke.
9. Using a drift, drive pinion and cage assembly from carrier.

CAUTION

Support bearing cage when driving assembly from carrier.

10. Wire bearing cage shim pack together to facilitate reassembly.
11. Lift bearing cage from pinion and remove cork seal. Remove pinion drive yoke washer and front bearing cone from cage.
12. Remove pinion bearing spacer washer, spacer, inner bearing cone and pilot bearing from pinion shaft.
13. Remove pinion cage bearing cups.
14. Clean all parts thoroughly in a suitable solvent and blow dry with compressed air. The bearings should be immersed in clean solvent and rotated by hand until clean. After cleaning, blow dry with compressed air. Do not spin bearings with air

pressure, as they might score due to absence of any lubrication. Inspect all parts for wear or imperfections. The thrust shoulders must be flat, so that bearing cups will seat properly. Install a new case if cracked or distorted. (For further details, see Cleaning and Inspection in the General Axle Service section).

Assembly

1. Press drive pinion inner bearing cone and rear pilot bearing firmly against pinion shoulder.
2. Stake pilot bearing in at least four places. Install pinion cage bearing cups.
3. Place bearing spacer and washer on pinion shaft. Lubricate bearing cone with SAE 90 oil and position bearing cage on bearing. Lubricate and press outer bearing on pinion shaft. Rotate cage to assure normal bearing contact. If a press is not available, install pinion yoke washer and nut and torque to specifications.
4. While the assembly is in the press under pressure or pinion nut torqued to specifications, check pinion bearing preload. The correct pressures and torques for preload are as follows.
5. Wrap a soft wire around cage and pull on horizontal line with pound scale. Measure diameter of pinion cage. Assuming cage diameter is 6 in., pulling radius would be 3 in.; therefore, 6 pounds pull on scale would equal 18 inch lbs. preload.
6. Use rotating torque, not starting torque. If rotating torque is not within 15 to 35 in. lbs., use thinner spacer to increase pre-load or thicker spacer to decrease pre-load. Torque must be near low limit in. lbs. with original pinion bearings and near high limit when using new bearings.

Staking pinion shaft with bearing ball (© Eaton Corp.)

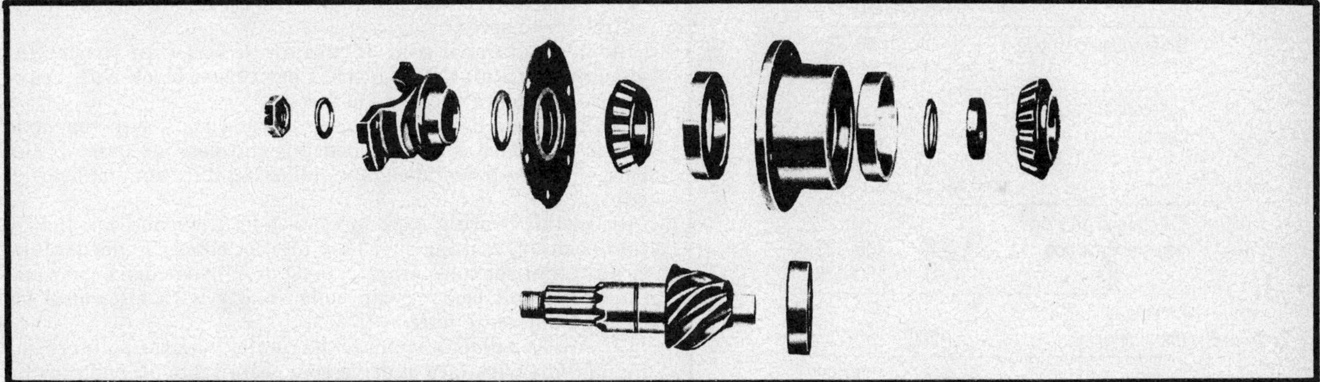

Pinion and cage assembly components (© Eaton Corp.)

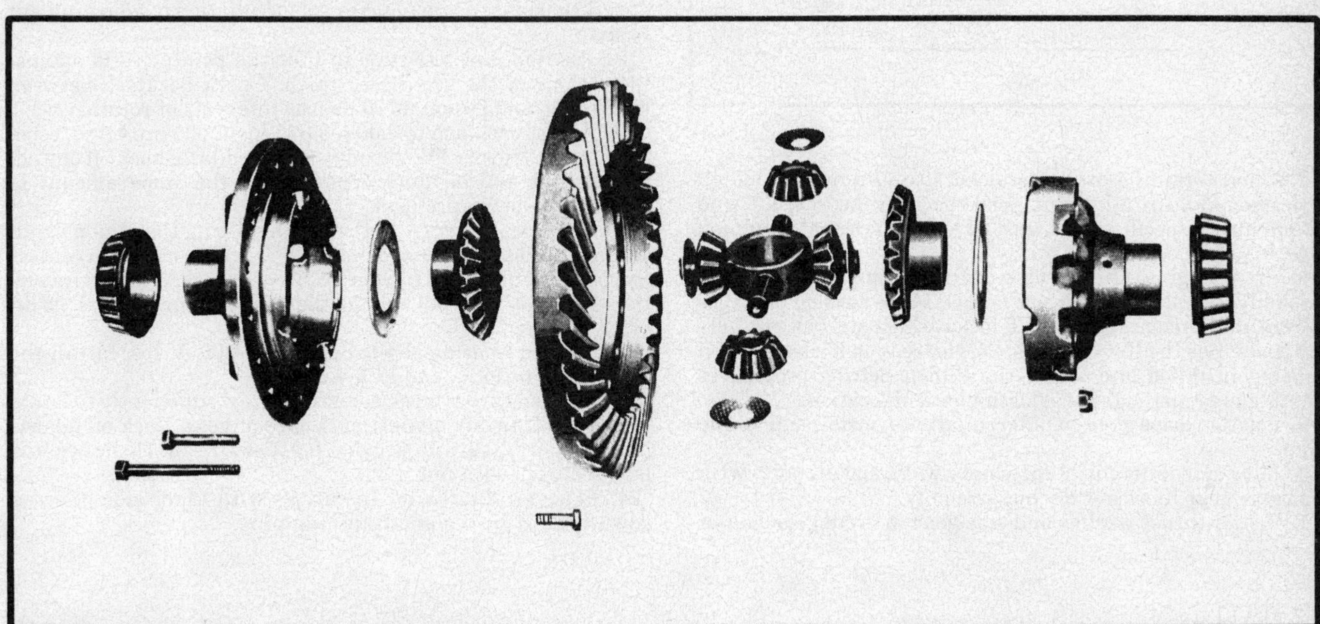

Differential assembly components (© Eaton Corp.)

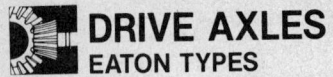

EATON AXLE DRIVE PINION ADJUSTMENT SPECIFICATIONS

		Specifications for Drive Pinion Bearing Preload Adjustment				Drive Pinion Position Adjustment	
	Axle Models	Pinion Bearing Spacer Thickness	Drive Pinion Nut Torque Setting (ft. lbs.)	Arbor Press Preload Pressure Setting (tons)	Spring Scale Reading (lbs.) To obtain 15 to 35 in. lbs. Torque	Pinion Bearing Cage Shim Pack	Depth Gauge Setting
Single Reduction Axles	17101, 17121	0.639	400–600	7–8	6–14	0.030 + 0.125 Spacer	4.2187
	18101, 18121	0.639	400–600	7–8	6–14	0.030 + 0.125 Spacer	4.2187
	19121	0.185	550–850	10–11	5–11	0.024	4.600

TORQUE SPECIFICATIONS

Carrier to housing bolt or stud nut	7/16–14	50–70
	1/2–13	80–100
	5/8–11	150–175
Differential case bolt	7/16–14	50–70
	1/2–13	80–100
Differential bearing cap bolts	5/8–11	150–175
	11/16–11	175–200
	13/16–10	225–250
Differential bearing adjuster lock bolt	9/16–12	100–125
	5/8–11	150–175
Electric shift unit (mounting)	7/16–20	50–70
Pinion cage bolt	9/16–2	100–125
Pinion shaft yoke nut	7/8–16	200–325
	1 1/8–18	325–450
	1 1/4–12	400–600

7. Upon obtaining correct preload, install a new pinion oil seal assembly. Install pinion yoke spacer, yoke and nut, and torque nut to specifications. Install a new cork seal on pinion cage.
8. Place original shim pack on carrier, tap pinion and cage assembly into place with a soft mallet. Make sure oil passages in cage and carrier align. Install lockwashers and bolts at 100–125 ft. lbs. See the General Axle Service section if a new pinion is being installed and follow the Pinion Setting procedures (depth gauge method) for adjusting pinion location.
9. Position drive gear on differential case, install and torque bolts.
10. Lubricate differential case inner walls and all parts with rear axle gear lubricant during assembly.
11. Install thrust washer and side gear in drive gear half of case. Assemble pinions and thrust washers on pinion shaft, and place in case. Place other side and thrust washer on four pinions.
12. Align mating marks and install other case half. Draw case down evenly with four bolts. Check for free rotation of differential gears and correct if necessary. Install remaining bolts at 80–100 ft. lbs. and install lock wire.
13. Press differential bearings squarely and firmly on differential case halves.
14. Thread drive gear thrust block screw in carrier far enough to install thrust block. Coat thrust block with heavy grease and place it on end of screw.
15. Lubricate differential bearings and cups with rear axle lubricant. Place cups over bearing and position assembly in carrier housing. Hand-tighten adjusting nuts against bearing cups.
16. Install bearing caps in correct location and tap lightly into position, making sure they are not cross-threaded. Make certain that some backlash is present between drive gear and pinion. Install bearing cap bolts snugly with allowance for turning adjusting nuts.
17. Attach a dial indicator to the carrier with the pointer resting against back face of drive gear. Eliminate all end play by turning right adjusting nut clockwise.
18. Tighten adjusting nuts, one notch each, to pre-load differential bearings. Align notches for installation of adjusting nut locks.
19. Position dial indicator so that the pointer rests against face of one of the drive gear teeth. Check backlash between drive gear and pinion at 90 degree intervals of rotation.
20. Adjust backlash to 0.008–0.015 in. (0.008 preferred, especially on new gears.) When adjusting backlash, back off one adjusting nut and advance opposite nut the same amount to maintain bearing pre-load.
21. If the depth gauge method for adjusting the pinion depth was not used as mentioned in Step 8, then use the tooth contact method. Then proceed to Step 22. See General Axle Service section. If pinion was adjusted by the depth gauge method, go directly to Step 22.
22. Tighten bearing cap bolts, to 175–200 ft. lbs. Install the adjusting nut locks and lock wires.
23. Tighten thrust block adjusting screw sufficiently to locate thrust block firmly against back face of gear. Back off adjusting screw a 1/4 turn to provide 0.010–0.015 in. clearance and lock securely with nut.
24. Place oil distributor in carrier with taper side of scoop down, install spring and retaining plug.

Eaton Two–Speed and Planetary Double Reduction Axles

The two-speed axle is a full-floating type with bevel drive gear and pinion, and uses a four-pinion differential assembly. The pinion has three roller bearings – two tapered bearings in front of the pinion teeth and one straight roller bearing behind the teeth. An oiling system provides lubrication to the pinion bearings, differential bearings and planetary unit. The planetary double reduction axle combines the ring and pinion and the planetary unit in one axle housing. Procedures for disassembly are the same as the two-speed except the double reduction axle has no shift mechanism and, instead of a sliding clutch gear, it uses a sun gear.

DIFFERENTIAL CARRIER

Disassembly

1. Inspect the carrier before disassembly. (See Cleaning and Inspection paragraph in the General Axle Service section).
2. After removing the oil distributor plug, pull the oil distributor and spring out of the differential carrier.
3. Remove the shift fork shaft plugs, and shaft.
4. Remove the shift fork seal and the shift fork from the housing. Pull the sliding clutch gear out of the differential carrier.
5. Punch the right and left bearing adjusters to aid in relocating the adjustment when reassembling. Remove the differential bearing cap bolts. Back off one bearing adjusting nut to relieve the bearing preload.
6. Remove the right and left bearing caps, bearing adjusters, and locks.
7. Lift the differential and planetary assembly out of the differential side bearing cups.
8. Mark the right and left support cases so that they can be reassembled in the same relative position. Remove the bolts which hold the ring gear to the gear support cases.
9. Clamp the differential assembly (ring gear end up) in a soft-jawed vise.
10. Tap the ring gear with a soft hammer on the gear tooth side until the gear is free of the flange on the right support case.
11. Lift the left support case, thrust washer, oil collector drum, and ring gear from the right support case.
12. Using a soft hammer, remove the high-speed clutch plate from the differential case.
13. Remove the planetary gears and gear pins.
14. Lift the differential assembly and the thrust washer out of the right support case. Mark the two pieces of the differential case for proper assembly.
15. Separate the right and left differential cases. Remove the differential side gears and thrust washers.
16. Remove the differential spider gears, thrust washers, and the differential spider.
17. If the differential support case bearings are to be replaced, they may be removed with a drift. Press on the new bearing so that the ram pressure is against the bearing inner race and not against the roller cage.
18. Hold the pinion shaft flange and remove the pinion shaft nut.
19. Remove the bolts that attach the pinion bearing sleeve to the carrier housing. With a drift, drive the pinion assembly out of the front of the carrier housing.
20. Press the pinion shaft out of the shaft flange and pinion shaft front bearing cone. Remove the bearing preload spacer from the pinion shaft.
21. If the pinion rear bearing cone is to be replaced, remove the pilot bearing, then remove the pinion rear bearing cone with a bearing remover tool.
22. If the pinion bearing cups are to be replaced they may be removed with a small steel bar.

Assembly

1. Press the pilot bearing on the pinion shaft and stake the pinion shaft end at 4 points.
2. Press the pinion rear bearing onto the shaft until seated.
3. To install a new bearing cup, place the pinion bearing retainer sleeve in a press and, using a steel bar, press the cup in the sleeve until it is seated against the recess in the sleeve. Repeat this operation for the other cup.
4. Install the pinion in the bearing retainer sleeve. Place the

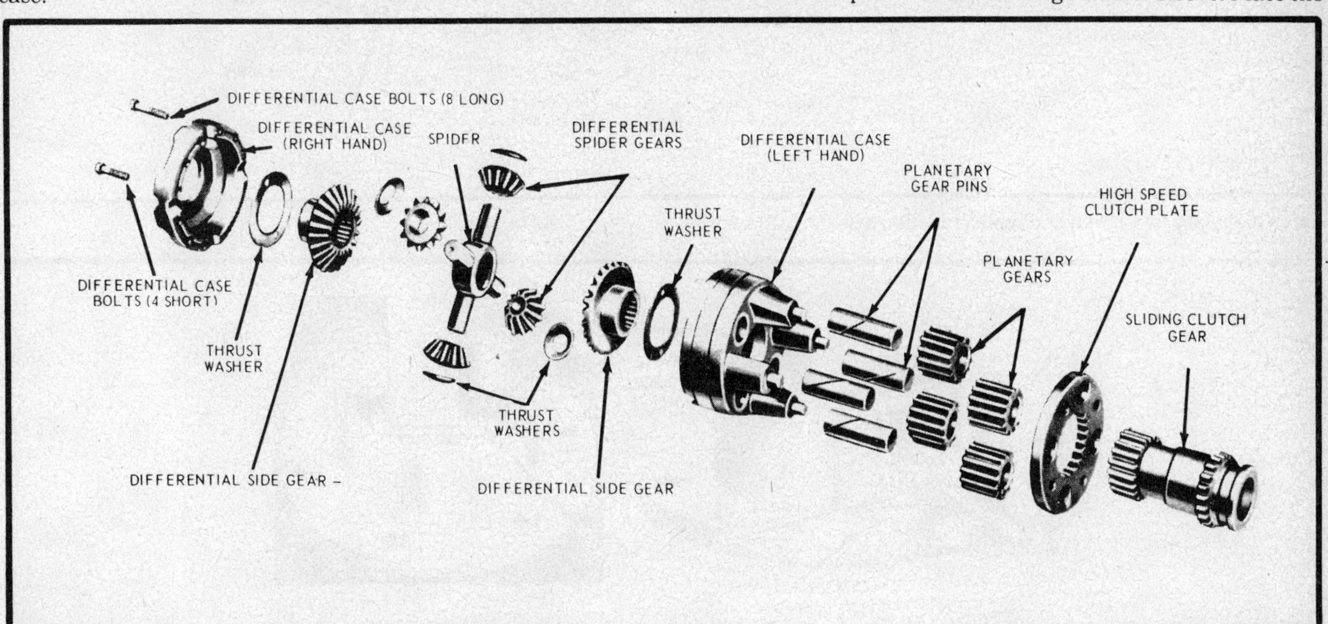

Planetary and differential assembly (© Eaton Corp.)

old spacer on the pinion shaft and install the spacer washer and the pinion front bearing.

5. Check and adjust the pinion bearing preload (see General Axle Service section).

6. Install a new oil seal in the seal retainer or bearing sleeve.

7. Press the universal joint flange on the pinion shaft. Install the flat washer and nut and torque to specifications.

8. If the pinion and ring gear are being replaced, adjust the shim pack between the pinion bearing sleeve and carrier housing as explained in the General Axle Service section.

9. Install a new gasket in the pinion bearing sleeve, if so equipped.

10. Place the shim pack on the bearing sleeve and install the pinion and sleeve assembly in the carrier housing. Install the sleeve to housing bolts and lock washers and torque to specifications.

11. Place the left half of the differential support case in a vise with the planetary side facing downward. Place one of the differential side gear thrust washers in position in the case. Place the differential left-hand side gear (with the short hub) in position in the case.

12. Install the four differential pinions and thrust washers on the differential spider, then place the spider in the differential case. Place the right side gear and thrust washer on the differential pinions.

13. Place the right half of the differential case in position over the differential spider, then install and torque the case bolts.

14. Insert the four planetary gear pins in the holes in the differential case.

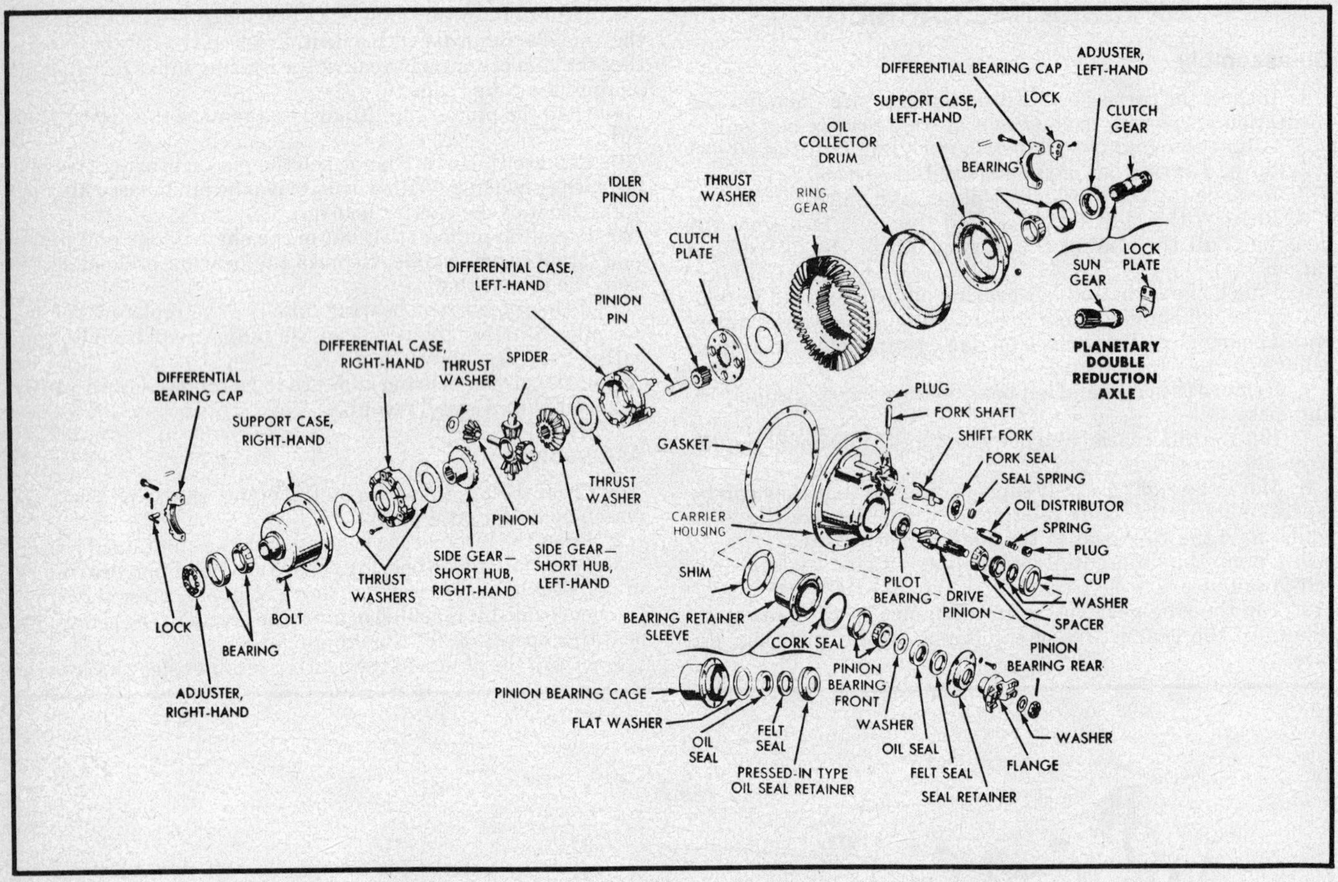

Eaton planetary two-speed or double reduction axle (© Eaton Corp.)

Removal or installation of pinion bearing cup (© Eaton Corp.)

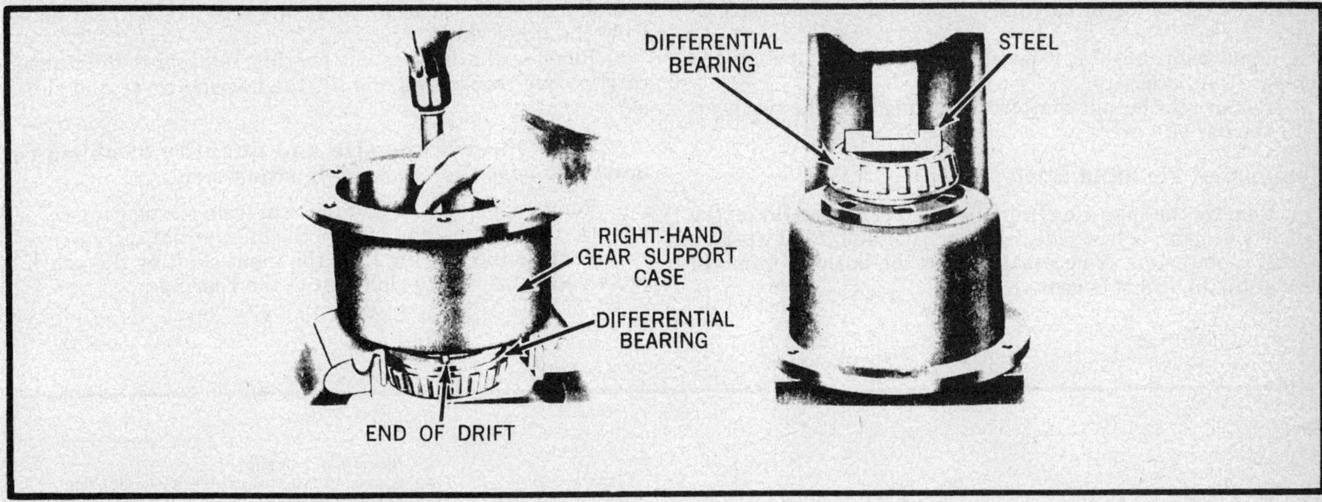

Removing or installing the differential bearing (© Eaton Corp.)

15. Place the four planetary gears on the planetary gear pins. Position the high speed clutch plate on the planetary gear pins with the chamfered teeth facing the planetary gears. Tap the plate in place with a brass hammer.
16. Position the gear support thrust washer in the right gear support case.
17. Place the differential assembly in the gear support case with the planetary end facing upward. Place the ring gear (teeth facing down) over the differential assembly, and engage the planetary gears with the internal teeth on the ring gear.
18. Align the ring gear bolt holes with those in the gear support case. Place the oil collector drum on the ring gear (open side facing gear) with the notches between the bolt holes in the ring gear.
19. Apply oil to each side of the high-speed clutch plate thrust washer and position on the high-speed clutch plate. Place the left gear support case on the ring gear, and line up the bolt holes in the ring gear and both gear support cases.
20. Install the 6 bolts through the gear support cases with the bolt heads against the flange of the right gear support case. Install and torque the nuts and secure with lock wire.
21. Install the differential assembly in the carrier housing and adjust backlash and preload (see General Axle Service section).
22. Check and adjust the gear tooth contact pattern.
23. Install the sliding clutch gear and attach the shift fork to it. Install the shift fork shaft through the hole in the differential carrier and into the shift fork. Install the shift fork shaft plugs. Place the shift fork seal and retainer on the shift fork. Shift the axle into the low range.
24. Place the oil distributor and spring in the carrier. Install the oil distributor plug and gasket.

Eaton Thru–Drive Type Tandem Axles

The Thru-Drive tandem axles are of the single reduction, double reduction, two speed and three speed types.

The three speed axle type is basically a two speed axle unit, electrically controlled by the operator to operate the air or vacuum lock-out mechanism for the power-divider and the speeds are obtained as follows:

1. High Speed: Both axles in high range and in single reduction.
2. Low Speed: Both axles in low range and in double reduction.
3. Intermediate Speed: Forward axle in high range and single reduction and the rear axle in low range and in double reduction, and the inter-axle differential, or power divider, equalizing the differences in RPMs, between the two axles to give a speed midway between the high and low range speeds by the movement of the differential gears in the power divider. A lock-out is used to disengage the power divider and to provide maximum traction and positive drive to both axles during the high and low ranges.

NOTE: This service procedure will cover the forward rear axle of the tandem unit as the rear axle is of the conventional single reduction, two speed or double reduction design and is covered in detail in another chapter.

DIFFERENTIAL CARRIER AND POWER DIVIDER

Disassembly

1. Place the differential carrier and power divider assembly in a repair stand and inspect before disassembly. Refer to the Cleaning and Inspection paragraphs in the General Axle Service section.
2. Remove the carrier cover to differential carrier capscrews and lock washers, and remove the carrier cover assembly.
3. Remove the inner-axle differential off the output shaft side gear.
4. Punch mark the inner-axle differential case before disassembly. Remove the lock nuts and bolts. Separate the cases and remove the thrust washers, side pinions, bushings and spider.

Removal of the Output Shaft

1. Remove the shaft holdout springs and thrust washers if used, and discard. Lift out the output shaft assembly from the carrier assembly by tapping at the companion flange end of the shaft, and remove the bearing cup from the carrier.
2. To disassemble the output shaft, remove the snap-ring

and lift off the side gear assembly. Discard the output shaft O-rings.

3. Remove the bushing from the bore of the output shaft and replace it, if necessary.

4. Remove the output shaft front bearing from the side gear, with the use of a press.

Removal of the Input Shaft

1. Remove the snap-ring from the input shaft and lift off the helical side gear, helical side thrust washer and the D-washer.

2. If replacement is necessary, press the bushing from the bore of the helical side gear.

3. Remove the cotter pin, nut and input companion flange from the input shaft.

4. Remove the input shaft bearing retainer-to-differential carrier cover capscrews and lift the bearing cover and shims off.

NOTE: Observe the size and quantity of shims removed to ease the reassembly adjustment.

5. Remove the oil seal and felt seal from the bearing cover.

6. Drive the input shaft out of the differential carrier cover.

7. Remove the bearing from the input shaft by the use of a press and pressing the shaft out of the bearing.

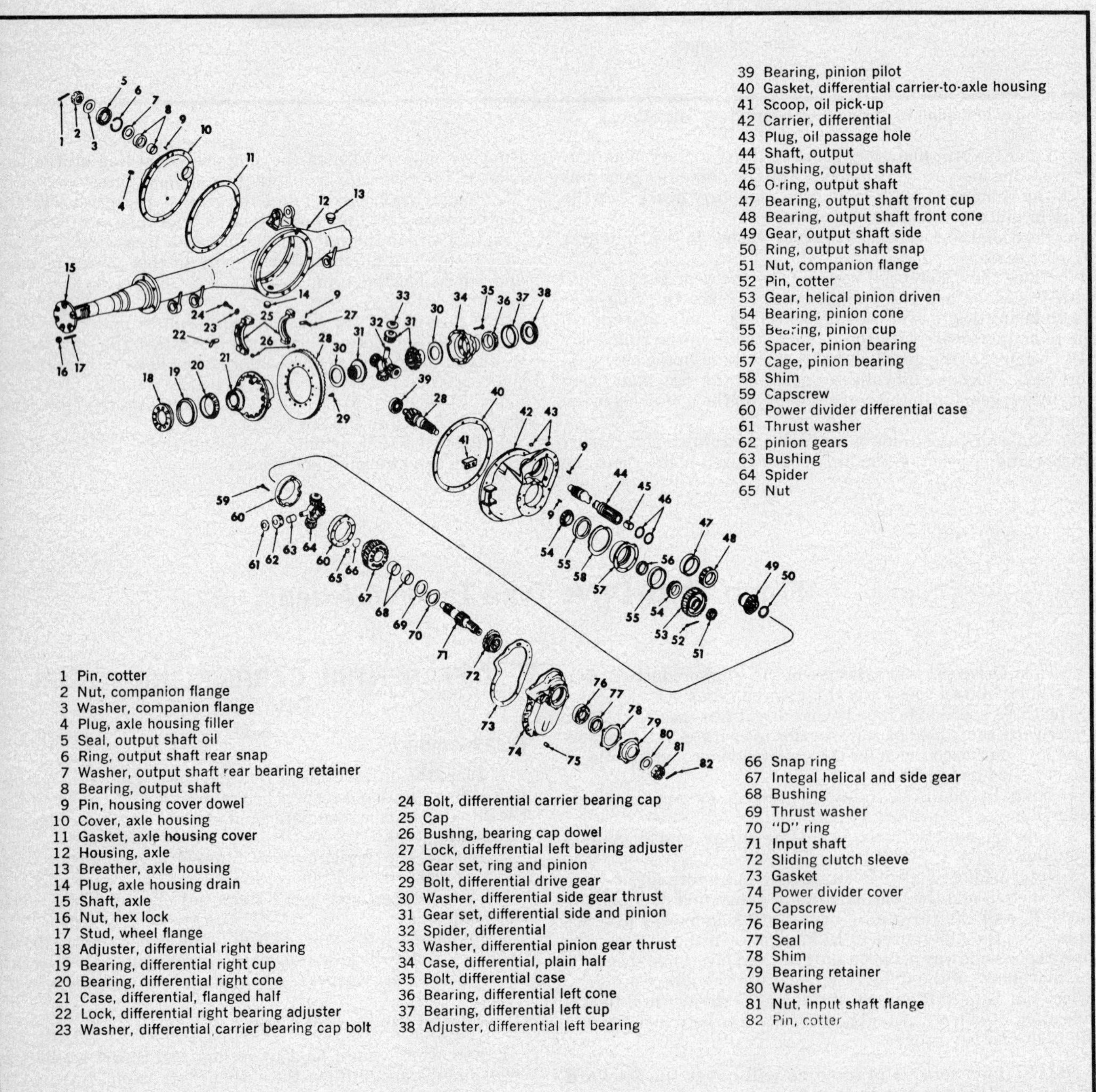

Exploded view of Eaton single reduction forward rear axle—typical (© International Harvester Co.)

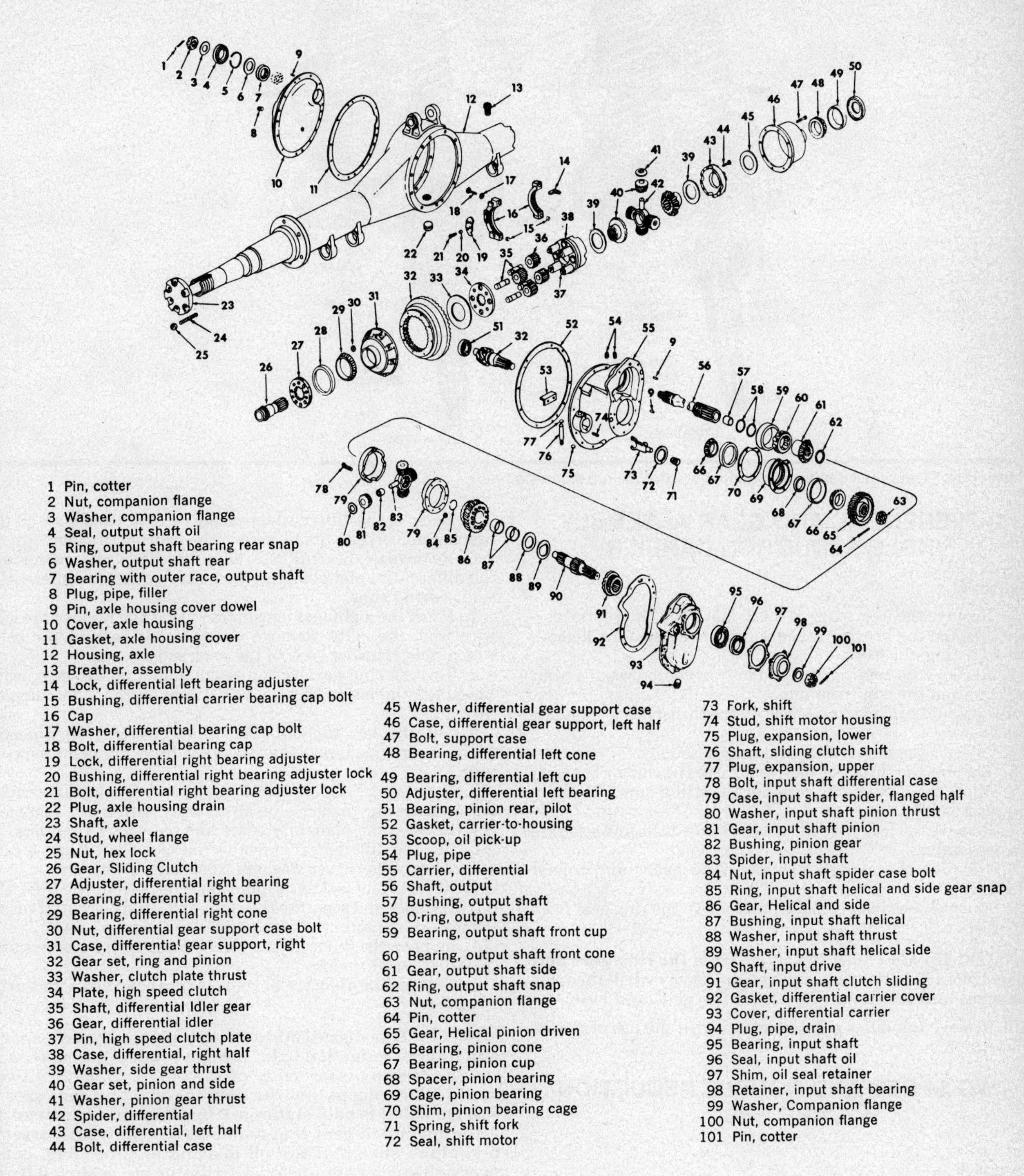
1 Pin, cotter
2 Nut, companion flange
3 Washer, companion flange
4 Seal, output shaft oil
5 Ring, output shaft bearing rear snap
6 Washer, output shaft rear
7 Bearing with outer race, output shaft
8 Plug, pipe, filler
9 Pin, axle housing cover dowel
10 Cover, axle housing
11 Gasket, axle housing cover
12 Housing, axle
13 Breather, assembly
14 Lock, differential left bearing adjuster
15 Bushing, differential carrier bearing cap bolt
16 Cap
17 Washer, differential bearing cap bolt
18 Bolt, differential bearing cap
19 Lock, differential right bearing adjuster
20 Bushing, differential right bearing adjuster lock
21 Bolt, differential right bearing adjuster lock
22 Plug, axle housing drain
23 Shaft, axle
24 Stud, wheel flange
25 Nut, hex lock
26 Gear, Sliding Clutch
27 Adjuster, differential right bearing
28 Bearing, differential right cup
29 Bearing, differential right cone
30 Nut, differential gear support case bolt
31 Case, differential gear support, right
32 Gear set, ring and pinion
33 Washer, clutch plate thrust
34 Plate, high speed clutch
35 Shaft, differential Idler gear
36 Gear, differential idler
37 Pin, high speed clutch plate
38 Case, differential, right half
39 Washer, side gear thrust
40 Gear set, pinion and side
41 Washer, pinion gear thrust
42 Spider, differential
43 Case, differential, left half
44 Bolt, differential case
45 Washer, differential gear support case
46 Case, differential gear support, left half
47 Bolt, support case
48 Bearing, differential left cone
49 Bearing, differential left cup
50 Adjuster, differential left bearing
51 Bearing, pinion rear, pilot
52 Gasket, carrier-to-housing
53 Scoop, oil pick-up
54 Plug, pipe
55 Carrier, differential
56 Shaft, output
57 Bushing, output shaft
58 O-ring, output shaft
59 Bearing, output shaft front cup
60 Bearing, output shaft front cone
61 Gear, output shaft side
62 Ring, output shaft snap
63 Nut, companion flange
64 Pin, cotter
65 Gear, Helical pinion driven
66 Bearing, pinion cone
67 Bearing, pinion cup
68 Spacer, pinion bearing
69 Cage, pinion bearing
70 Shim, pinion bearing cage
71 Spring, shift fork
72 Seal, shift motor
73 Fork, shift
74 Stud, shift motor housing
75 Plug, expansion, lower
76 Shaft, sliding clutch shift
77 Plug, expansion, upper
78 Bolt, input shaft differential case
79 Case, input shaft spider, flanged half
80 Washer, input shaft pinion thrust
81 Gear, input shaft pinion
82 Bushing, pinion gear
83 Spider, input shaft
84 Nut, input shaft spider case bolt
85 Ring, input shaft helical and side gear snap
86 Gear, Helical and side
87 Bushing, input shaft helical
88 Washer, input shaft thrust
89 Washer, input shaft helical side
90 Shaft, input drive
91 Gear, input shaft clutch sliding
92 Gasket, differential carrier cover
93 Cover, differential carrier
94 Plug, pipe, drain
95 Bearing, input shaft
96 Seal, input shaft oil
97 Shim, oil seal retainer
98 Retainer, input shaft bearing
99 Washer, Companion flange
100 Nut, companion flange
101 Pin, cotter

Exploded view of Eaton two and three speed forward rear tandem axle assembly—typical (© International Harvester Co.)

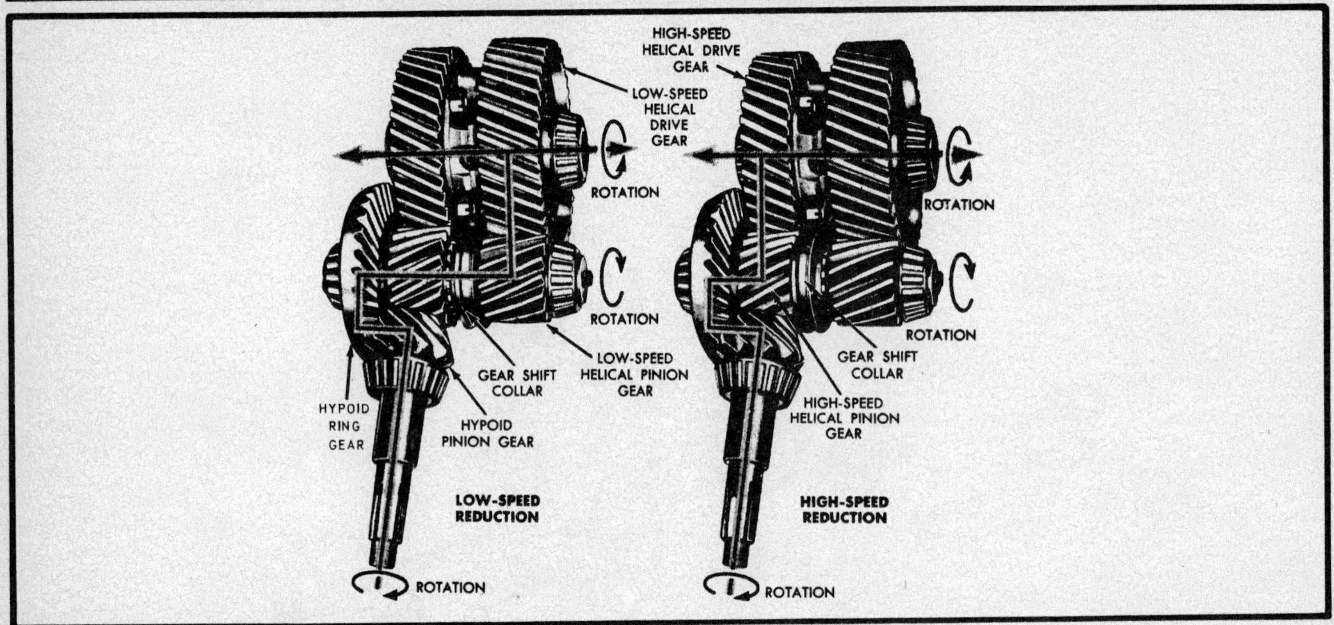

Power flow—two speed double reduction rear axle (© Ford Motor Co.)

DIFFERENTIAL AND GEAR ASSEMBLY SINGLE REDUCTION CARRIER

Removal

1. Remove the lock wires, if used. Mark the differential carrier legs and the bearing caps for proper reassembly. Remove the adjusting nut locks.
2. Remove the bearing cap stud nuts or capscrews, the bearing caps and the adjusting nuts.
3. Loosen the jam nut and back off the thrust block adjusting screw.
4. Lift out the differential and gear assembly.
5. Remove the thrust block from inside the carrier housing.
6. Mark the differential case halves with a punch to aid in the reassembly.
7. Remove the lock wire (if equipped), the bolts and separate the case halves.
8. Remove the spider, pinions, side gears and thrust washers.
9. Remove the rivets or bolts and remove the ring gear from the case.

NOTE: Do not chisel the rivets from the ring gear and case. Damage to the case can result. Always drill through the rivet and press the rivet from the gear and case.

10. Remove the differential bearings with the use of a suitable puller.

TWO SPEED AND DOUBLE REDUCTION CARRIERS

Removal

1. Remove the lock wires. Mark the right and left bearing adjusters to aid in the reassembly. Mark the bearing caps and the differential carrier legs for proper reassembly.
2. Remove the oil distributor plug, if equipped, and pull the oil distributor and spring out of the differential carrier.
3. Remove the shift fork shaft plugs and remove the shaft.
4. Remove the shift fork seal and the shift fork from the housing. Remove the sliding clutch gear from the differential carrier.
5. Remove the differential bearing cap bolts and back off the bearing adjusting nuts to relieve the bearing preload.
6. Remove the bearing caps, adjusters, and locks and remove the differential and planetary assembly out of the differential side bearing cups.
7. Mark the right and left support cases and remove the lock wire from the bolts. Remove the nuts and remove the bolts which hold the ring gear to the gear support case.
8. Tap the ring gear with a soft hammer on the gear tooth side until the gear is free of the flange on the right support case.
9. Lift the left support case, thrust washer, oil collector drum, if equipped, and the ring gear from the right support case.
10. Remove the high-speed clutch plate from the differential case by tapping on each side alternately with a soft hammer.
11. Remove the planetary gears and planetary gear pins.
12. Lift the differential assembly out of the left support case and remove the thrust washers from the support case.
13. Remove the lock wires and capscrews from the differential assembly and separate the right and left differential cases. Remove the differential side gears and thrust washers.
14. Remove the differential spider gears, thrust washers and the differential spider.
15. Remove the differential support case bearings with a drift or puller.

NOTE: The disassembly of the planetary two-speed and double reduction axles used in tandem assemblies is similar to the disassembly of the single planetary two-speed axles except that the double reduction unit uses a sun gear that is held stationary by a lock plate instead of a sliding clutch gear that connects to a shift fork assembly. Make sure that the oil distributor pipe plug, compression spring and the oil distributor are removed from the differential carrier before removing the differential assembly.

DRIVE PINION

Removal

In the single reduction axles, the pinion assembly is removed with the companion flange and pinion end nut in position, but in the tandem assemblies, the pinion end nuts and helical gear

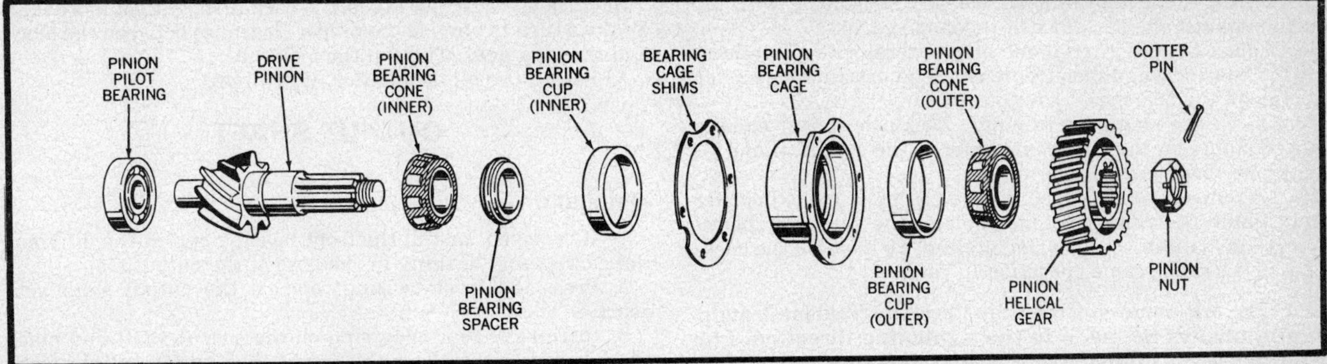

Exploded view of drive pinion—Eaton axle (© International Harvester Co.)

must be removed before the pinion assembly. This is accomplished by first removing the cotter pin and the pinion shaft end nut. With the aid of a puller, remove the helical gear from the pinion shaft. The pinion and pinion cage can then be removed. The bearings can be removed with the aid of a puller or a press.

Inspection

After cleaning and drying the differential parts, examine each part for abnormal wear, cracks, chips, overheating and fractures. Replace the necessary parts needed in the overhaul to return the unit to like-new condition.

DRIVE PINION

Installation

1. Install the necessary bearings and cups on the pinion shaft and the pinion bearing cage.
2. Measure the preload of the pinion bearings by assembling the bearing and pinion shaft without the oil seal in place.
3. Torque the pinion nut to the specified torque and place the universal joint flange in a vise and wrap a strong cord around the pinion bearing retainer.
4. Attach a pound pull scale to the cord and note the pull required to keep the bearing retainer moving.

NOTE: The reading on the pull scale multiplied by one-half the diameter (radius) of the bearing retainer at the point the cord is wrapped (in inches) is the in. lb. torque.

5. The bearing preload is adjusted by the installation of spacers of different lengths.

NOTE: A shorter spacer increases the preload and a longer spacer decreases the preload.

6. If the pinion and ring gear are being replaced, adjust the shim pack accordingly between the pinion bearing sleeve and the carrier housing, as per the shim chart.
7. Install a new gasket in the pinion bearing sleeve, if used.
8. Install the shim pack on the bearing sleeve and install the pinion and sleeve assembly into the carrier housing. Install the bolts and torque to specified tension.

TWO SPEED AND DOUBLE REDUCTION CARRIERS

Installation

1. Place the left half of the differential support case in a vise with the planetary side facing downward.
2. Place one of the side gear thrust washers in position in the case. Position the left hand side gear in the case. (gear with the short hub).
3. Install the four differential pinions and thrust washers on the differential spider and place the spider in the differential case. Install the right side gear and thrust washer on the differential pinions.
4. Place the right half of the differential case over the differential spider and install the case bolts. Tighten to specified torque.
5. Install the four planetary gear pins in the holes in the differential case.
6. Place the four planetary gears on the four planetary gear pins. Position the high speed clutch plate on the planetary gear pins with the chamfered teeth facing the planetary gears. Tap the plate in place with a soft hammer.
7. Place the right gear support case in a vise with the bearing side facing downward. Position the gear support thrust washer in the case.
8. Position the differential assembly in the gear support case with the planetary end facing upward. Place the ring gear over the differential assembly with the teeth facing downward and mesh the planetary gears with the internal teeth on the ring gear.
9. Align the ring gear bolt holes with the holes in the gear support case. Place the oil collector drum on the ring gear with the open side facing the gear, if equipped.
10. Lubricate the high speed clutch plate thrust washer and position it on the high speed clutch plate. Place the left gear support case on the ring gear and align the holes in the ring gear and the gear support cases.
11. Install the bolts through the gear support cases, install the nuts and tighten to specifications.
12. Install the differential into the carrier housing and adjust the backlash and preload by meshing the ring gear with the pinion so that a small amount of backlash exists.
13. Set the differential bearing adjusters in the carrier bearing pocket threads so that they just contact the bearing cups.
14. Position the bearing caps on the carrier and match the marks made upon disassembly. Install the bolts or nuts and tighten to specifications, while moving the adjuster to assure freedom of movement.

NOTE: The bolts or nuts of the bearing caps will have to be loosened to allow the adjusters to move properly upon adjustment of the backlash of the gears.

15. Alternately tighten the bearing adjusters until there is some backlash between the ring gear and pinion, with some preload on the bearings.

NOTE: While the bearings are preloaded, rotate the ring gear several times in each direction to seat the bearing rollers in the cups. This bearing roller seating is most important to assure the bearing rollers of longer life.

16. Loosen the bearing adjusters until they are clear of the bearing cups and then tighten them until they just touch the bearing cups.

17. Install a dial indicator on the carrier housing with the button against the back face of the ring gear.
18. Adjust the differential end play to zero, without preloading the bearings, and then tighten each adjuster nut one notch to preload the bearings.
19. Check the ring gear to pinion backlash at four equally spaced points on the ring gear. Refer to the specifications for the proper back lash clearance.
20. To reduce the back lash, loosen the pinion side adjuster and tighten the ring gear side adjuster the same number of notches to maintain the bearing preload. To increase the backlash, perform the same operation in reverse.

NOTE: When moving the adjusters, the final movement should always be made in the tightening direction. For example, if one adjuster is to be loosened one notch, loosen it two notches, then retighten it one notch. This procedure will assure the adjuster is in contact with the bearing cup and the cup will not shift after being put into service.

21. Adjust the backlash to the best tooth contact pattern within the specification limits.
22. Torque all bolts and nuts to specifications and install the locking wire and secure.
23. Install the sliding clutch gear and position the shift fork on the sliding clutch gear.
24. Install the shift fork shaft through the hole in the differential carrier and into the shift fork. Install the shift fork shaft plugs. Install the shift fork shaft seal and retainer on the shift fork and shift the axle into low range.
25. Install the oil distributor and spring in position in the carrier and install the plug and gasket, if so equipped.

SINGLE REDUCTION CARRIER

Installation

1. Assemble the ring gear to the differential housing and bolt or rivet into place.
2. Install the spider, pinions, side gears and thrust washers into the ring gear half of the case. Align the punch marks and install the other half of the case. Install the bolts and tighten to specifications. Install the lock wires.
3. Install the differential assembly into the carrier and adjust the backlash and bearing preload as outlined in the two speed and double reduction section.
4. Tighten the thrust block screw, if so equipped, until the thrust block touches the ring gear.
5. Back off the screw at least $^1/_{16}$ of a turn, but not more than a $^1/_4$ of a turn to provide the proper clearance between the block and the ring gear. Tighten the lock nut.
6. Install the oil distributor, if equipped.

OUTPUT SHAFT

Installation

1. If removed, install the front bearing cup in the differential carrier and bushing in the bore of the output shaft.
2. Press the front bearing cone on the output shaft side gears.
3. Install the rear snap ring on the output shaft and place the side gear assembly on the output shaft and install the front snap-ring.
4. Install the two O-rings in the grooves of the output shaft.
5. Lubricate the components and install the output shaft assembly in the differential carrier by placing the front bearing cone on the bearing cup in the bore of the carrier.

DIFFERENTIAL CARRIER AND POWER DIVIDER

Installation

1. Lubricate the internal parts of the inter-axle differential and install the bushings, side pinions and thrust washers on the journals of the differential spider.
2. Place the spider assembly into the male differential housing and mate the opposite housing, while aligning the punch marks.
3. Secure the assembly with bolts and nuts and tighten to specifications.
4. Install the inter-axle differential onto the output shaft. Position the differential with the nuts away from the output shaft side gear.

INPUT SHAFT

Installation

1. Press the bearing onto the threaded end of the input shaft.
2. Press the input shaft assembly into the differential carrier cover, and engage the sliding clutch.

NOTE: Assure that the oil drain back holes are properly aligned in the carrier cover, shims and bearing cover.

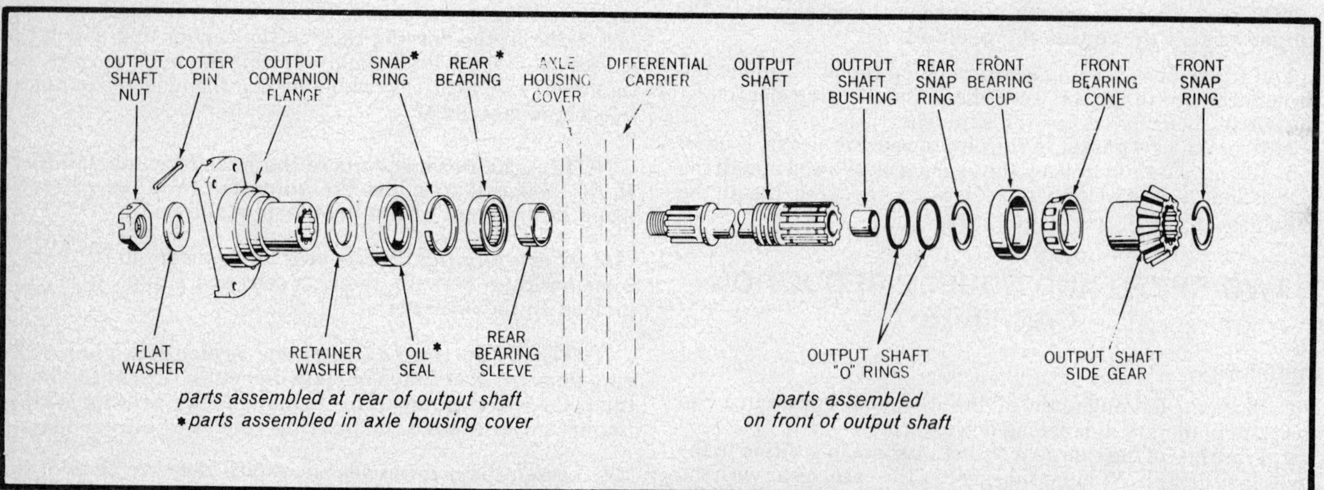

Exploded view of output shaft components—Eaton axles (© International Harvester Co.)

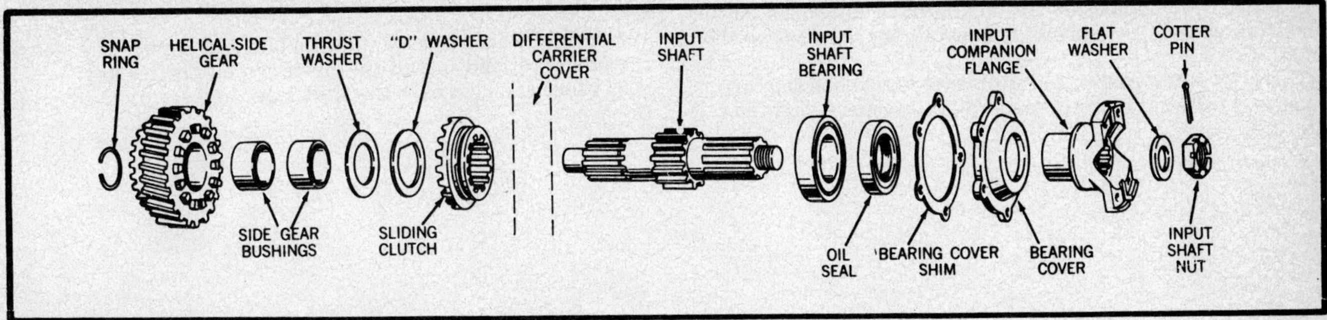

Exploded view of input shaft—Eaton axle (© International Harvester Co.)

3. Install the felt (if used), and oil seal in the input shaft bearing cover.
4. Install the bearing cover and the same amount of shims removed during disassembly. Install the capscrews finger tight.
5. To check bearing adjustment or to determine the thickness of shims required, install the bearing cover on the carrier cover without shims and install and tighten the cap screws finger tight. Using a feeler gauge, measure the clearance between the bearing cover and the carrier cover. This clearance plus 0.001 in. would equal the thickness of the shims required for the correct bearing clearance.
6. Install the companion flange on the input shaft, along with the nut and washer. Tighten the nut to specifications and install the cotter pin.
7. Tighten the bearing cover capscrews to the correct torque.
8. If removed, press the two bushings in the bore of the helical side gear. Place the D-washer, thrust washer and and helical side gear assembly on the input shaft. Install the snap-ring on the input shaft to secure these parts.

DIFFERENTIAL CARRIER COVER

Installation

1. Install a new gasket on the differential carrier and install the cover assembly onto the carrier, aligning the dowel pins with the holes in the cover.

NOTE: Rotate the input shaft slowly to engage the input shaft splines with the splines in the bore of the inter-axle differential spider.

2. Install two cover screws while observing for any binding between the cover and the carrier. If no binding exists, install the remaining cap screws and tighten to specifications.

NOTE: After the assembly, check for the inter-axle differential for operation by rotating the input campanion flange, while holding the output shaft stationary. If the assembly differentiates, the unit is correctly assembled.

AIR OPERATED LOCKOUT

Removal

1. Remove the nuts, washers and cover from the shift cylinder body. Remove the nut and flat washer from the push rod.
2. Remove the cylinder body assembly and compression spring from the carrier cover.

NOTE: Check strainer plate vent screen and felt for a plugged condition. Replace if necessary.

3. Remove the shift fork and push rod assemblies and the input shaft sliding clutch from the carrier cover.

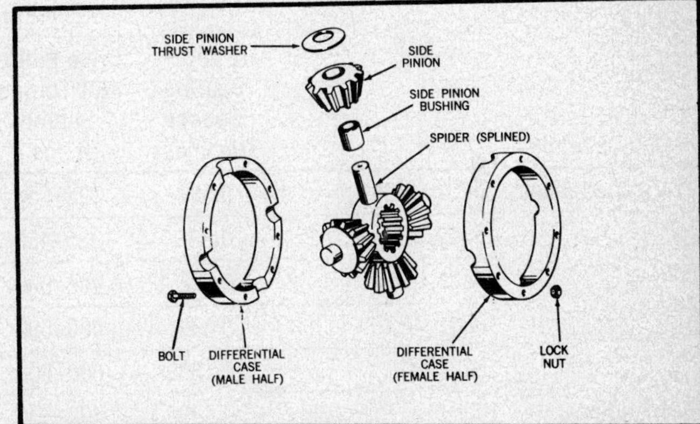

Exploded view of inter-axle differential (© International Harvester Co.)

Installation

1. Install the push rod, seal retainer and felt seal on the carrier cover.
2. Engage the shift fork with the groove in the input shaft sliding clutch and place the assembly into the carrier cover.
3. Install the shift cylinder body, compression spring, and gasket over the push rod and on the carrier cover. Secure the body with capscrews and lockwashers. Tighten to specified torque.
4. Install the felt oilers and gromments on the piston and insert the piston assembly into the body and onto the push rod. Install the flat washer and nut, and tighten to 20 to 26 ft. lbs. torque.
5. Install the gromments on the cylinder body cover and install the cover, lockwashers and nuts.

VACUUM OPERATED LOCKOUT

Removal

1. Remove the boot from the shift lever and remove the clevis pin. Remove the shift lever.
2. Remove the capscrews, lockwashers and shift lever bracket from the carrier cove.
3. Compress the compression spring and remove the pin, retaining washer and spring from the push rod.
4. Remove the shift fork and push rod assembly and input shaft sliding clutch from the carrier cover.

Installation

1. Install the push rod, seal retainer and felt seal on the carrier cover. Engage the lockout shift fork with the groove in the input shaft sliding clutch. Place this assembly into the carrier cover.

2. Place the compression spring and retainer washer on the push rod, depress the spring and install the retainer washer pin.

3. Install a new gasket and shift lever bracket on the carrier cover and install the capscrews and lock washers. Tighten the screws to specifications.

4. Place the shift lever into the bracket, engage the slot in the push rod, and install the clevis pin and cotter key.

5. Place the boot over the shift lever and secure the boot to the bracket.

DRIVE PINION ADJUSTMENT SPECIFICATIONS

Axle Models		Specifications for Drive Pinion Bearing Preload Adjustment: Pinion Bearing Spacer Thickness	Drive Pinion Nut Torque Setting (ft. lbs.)	Arbor Press Preload Pressure Setting (tons)	Spring Scale Reading (lbs.) To obtain 15 to 35 in. lbs. Torque	Drive Pinion Position Adjustment: Pinion Bearing Cage Shim Pack	Depth Gauge Setting
2-speed Axles	13802, 15201	0.530	225–350	4–5	7–16	0.040 + 0.250	3.6244
	16802, 16244, 16221	0.528	325–450	5–6	7–16	0.043	4.125
	17201, 17221	0.638	400–600	7–8	6–14	0.037	4.062
	18201, 18221	0.638	400–600	7–8	6–14	0.037	4.4062
	19221	0.188	600–800	10–11	5–11	0.025	4.7812
Planetary Double Reduction Axles	18301	0.638	400–600	7–8	6–14	0.37	4.4062

TORQUE SPECIFICATIONS

Description		Ft. Lbs.
Differential bearing adjuster lock	Cap screw 9/16-12 (Grade 5)	115–125
	Cap screw 5/8-11 (Grade 5)	160–175
	Cap screw 3/4-10 (Grade 5)	275–300
Differential bearing cap to carrier	Cap screw 5/8-11 (Grade 7)	150–170
	Cap screw 11/16-11 (Grade 7)	210–250
	Cap screw 13/16-10 (Grade 7)	350–425
	Cap screw 7/8-9 (Grade 7)	425–500
Differential carrier to axle housing	Cap screw 7/16-14 (Grade 5)	45–55
	Cap screw 1/2-13 (Grade 5)	75–85
	Cap screw 5/8-11 (Grade 5)	160–175
	Stud nut 1/2-20 (Grade 8)	110–130
	Stud nut 5/8-18 (Grade 8)	220–240
Differential case (axle)	Cap screw 7/16-14 (Grade 7)	55–65
	Cap screw 1/2-13 (Grade 7)	90–105
	Cap screw 9/16-12 (Grade 7)	135–155
Ring gear support case	Bolt/nut 7/16-20 (Grade 7)	60–80
	Bolt/nut 1/2-20 (Grade 7)	90–100
	Bolt/nut 9/16-18 (Grade 7)	130–150
	Bolt/nut 5/8-18 (Grade 7)	190–210
	Locknut 5/8-18	165–190

Description		Ft. Lbs.
Drive pinion	Nut 1-20	225–350
	Nut 1 1/8-18	325–450
	Nut 1 1/4-12	400–600
	Nut 1 1/2-18	500–700
	Nut 1 3/4-12	600–800
Drive pinion bearing cage to carrier	Cap screw 9/16-12 (Grade 5)	115–125
	Cap screw 9/16-12 (Grade 7)	135–155
	Cap screw 5/8-11 (Grade 5)	160–175
	Cap screw 5/8-11 (Grade 7)	170–190
Inspection cover to axle housing	Cap screw 7/16-14 (Grade 3)	35–50
	Cap screw 7/16-14 (Grade 5)	45–55
Shift units to carrier (2-speed)	Stud nut 7/16-20 (Grade 5)	35–45
	Stud nut 1/2-20 (Grade 5)	85–95
Cover plate to carrier (pdr) (At shift unit opening)	Cap screw 7/16-14 (Grade 5)	45–55
	Cap screw 1/2-13 (Grade 5)	75–85
Oil pickup through to carrier	Nylock screw 1/4-20 (Grade 5)	35–50 in.-lbs.

Mack Mid–Liner Rear Axle Disassembly and Assembly

NOTE:Refer to the Mack Mid–Liner section for the removal and installation procedure of the rear axle.

Carrier Disassembly

1. After removing the rear axle, place the rear axle carrier assembly into a suitable support stand.
2. Remove the lubricator tube and match mark the bearing caps for easy assembly reference.
3. Loosen the bearing cap attaching bolts, and loosen (unlock) the adjusting nuts by a $^1/_2$ a turn. Remove the bearing caps and the adjusting nuts.
4. Remove the differential assembly from the carrier case. Remove the bolts from the pinion housing and using a bronze drift or equivalent, drive out the pinion housing. Be sure to remove the pinion depth adjusting shim and set it aside.
5. Clamp the differential gear assembly in a suitable press and remove the assembly ring gear mounting bolts. Using a heavy hammer, remove the ring gear.
6. Remove the bolts assembling the differential case and separate the differential cases. Remove the following components, planet gears, sun gears and friction washers. Drive out the dowel pins.
7. Using a suitable puller, remove the differential carrier bearings.

PINION DISASSEMBLY

1. Now press out the input pinion shaft and be sure to remove the bearing shim. Remove the input shaft seal and pinion front bearing.
2. Press off the rear bearing from the input shaft seal. Remove the snap ring and press off the faucet – type bearing from the end of the input pinion shaft.
3. Remove the bearing cups using a drift and a hammer. Remove the oil deflector and discard it.

PINION ASSEMBLY

NOTE: Clean and check all parts and wash the bearings in clean solvent, allow them to drip dry. Do not apply compressed air to dry bearings and do spin dry the bearings. Be sure lightly grease the bearings before installation.

1. Install bearing races and a new oil deflector. Check them for proper positioning.
2. Press the bearing on the input pinion shaft using driver tool J29476 or equivalent.
3. Oil the rollers of the bearings and install the pinion setting shim. Install the pinion front bearing using driver tool J299476 or equivalent.

NOTE: The following operations are to be performed without installing the oil seal.

4. Install the input flange, washer and nut and torque the pinion flange nut to 531–649 ft. lbs.

SETTING THE PRELOAD ON THE PINION BEARING

NOTE: The preload reading in the Torqometer dial is obtained by smoothly rotating the wrench so as to allow the pointer to stabilize. Do not take into account the high starting torque caused by the inertial load of parts.

1. The new pinion bearing torque should be 1.1–2.1 ft. lbs. and the used pinion bearing torque should be 0.74–0.92 ft. lbs. If the torque is too low, remove and grind the pinion bearing spacer, using a suitable surface grinder.
2. Reassemble as before and carry out a new preload measurement. Repeat these operations until the preload is as close as possible to the maximum value.
3. When a satisfactory preload is obtained, remove the pinion nut, washer and pinion input flange. Install the pinion seal, using pinion seal tool # J29498 or equivalent.
4. Reassemble the input flange , washer and nut . Torque the pinion flange to 531 to 649 ft. lbs. Install the pinion bearing, using driver tool J29477 or equivalent and install the snap ring.

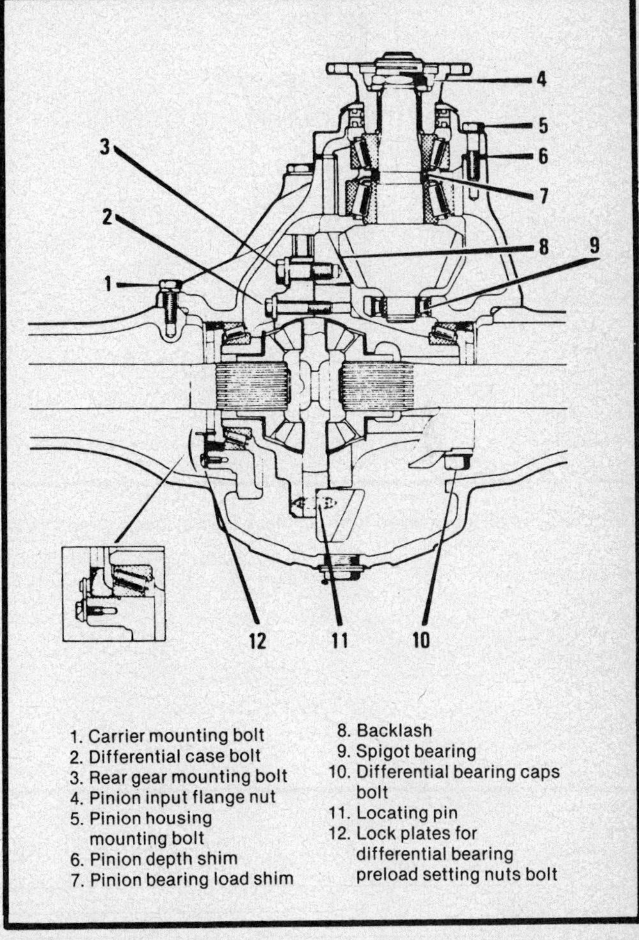

Exploded view of the Mid-Liner carrier assembly (© Mack Trucks, Inc.)

Carrier Assembly

1. Install the differential bearing using driver tool J29478 or equivalent. Install the differential gear inside the differential cases.
2. Install the other half of the differential case by matching the reference marks made during disassembly. Install the bolts and torque them to 80 to 97 ft. lbs.
3. On the differential case, place the ring gear fitted with the two locating pins. Install the O-ring and lubricating plate. Install the ring gear securing bolts and torque them to 221 to 265 ft. lbs. Be sure to use new bolts during reassembly, because the old bolts could snap under the torque.
4. Install the pinion assembly with a shim of 0.16 in. thickness. Carefully position the faucet type bearing in the bore and be sure to observe the oil passage holes.

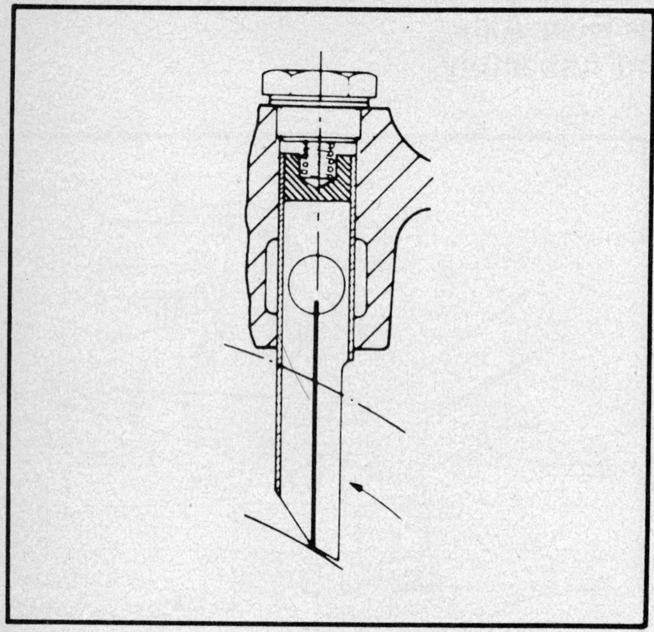

Installing the oil lubrication tube (© Mack Trucks, Inc.)

NOTE: Two shims, sizes 0.157 to 0.142 in. are available for servicing RVI series rear axles.

5. Apply Loctite® 515 sealant or equivalent to both sides of the pinion flange shim. Install the bolts into the pinion assembly and torque them to 66 to 81 ft. lbs.
6. Install the differential carrier and position the bearing caps (be sure to match the reference marks) and adjusting nuts.
7. Establish the backlash adjustment (0.008 to 0.011 in.) by alternately tightening the bearing adjusting nuts with the bearing cap bolts snugly tightened. Check it with a dial indicator for a more accurate reading.
8. Torque the bolts of the bearing caps evenly to 450 to 550 ft. lbs., in increments of a 100 ft. lbs. or less.
9. Mount the torqometer wrench or equivalent to the pinion nut. Apply a preload to the bearing by tightening the adjusting nuts by an equal value, so as to obtain the total preload.

NOTE: To determine the preload, use the charts provided and follow this example: On a vehicle having a carrier ratio of 8 x 41 and a pinion preload set at 13.3 inch lbs., the total preload following the differential gear installation must be within a range of 19.5 to 20.4 inch lbs.

10. After the preload has been completed, install the lubrication tube into its position along with its spring. Torque the lubrication tube to 81 to 96 ft. lbs. Reinstall the carrier assembly into the vehicle, refill axle assembly to the specified amount and road test the vehicle.

TABLE 1 - CARRIER BEARING TOTAL PRELOAD (NEW BEARINGS)

PINION PRELOAD		TOTAL PRELOAD			
		8X41	- CARRIER RATIO		- 9X41
(NM)	(LB. IN.)	(NM)	(LB. IN.)	(NM)	(LB. IN.)
1.5	13.3	2.2 TO 2.3	19.5 TO 20.4	2.2 TO 2.4	19.5 TO 21.3
1.6	14.2	2.3 TO 2.4	20.4 TO 21.3	2.4 TO 2.5	21.3 TO 22.2
1.7	15.1	2.4 TO 2.5	21.3 TO 22.2	2.4 TO 2.6	21.3 TO 23.1
1.8	16.0	2.5 TO 2.6	22.2 TO 23.1	2.6 TO 2.7	23.1 TO 24.0
1.9	16.9	2.6 TO 2.7	23.1 TO 24.0	2.6 TO 2.8	23.1 TO 24.9
2.0	17.8	2.7 TO 2.8	24.0 TO 24.9	2.8 TO 2.9	24.9 TO 25.8
2.1	18.6	2.8 TO 2.9	24.9 TO 25.8	2.8 TO 3.0	24.9 TO 26.6
2.2	19.5	2.9 TO 3.0	25.8 TO 26.6	3.0 TO 3.1	26.6 TO 27.5
2.3	20.4	3.0 TO 3.1	26.6 TO 27.5	3.0 TO 3.2	26.6 TO 28.4
2.4	21.3	3.1 TO 3.2	27.5 TO 28.4	3.2 TO 3.3	28.4 TO 29.3
2.5	22.2	3.2 TO 3.3	28.4 TO 29.3	3.2 TO 3.4	28.4 TO 30.2
2.65	23.5	3.3 TO 3.4	29.3 TO 30.2	3.4 TO 3.5	30.2 TO 31.1

TABLE 2 - CARRIER BEARING TOTAL PRELOAD (NEW BEARINGS)

PINION PRELOAD		TOTAL PRELOAD			
		8X41	- CARRIER RATIO		- 9X41
(NM)	(LB. IN.)	(NM)	(LB. IN.)	(NM)	(LB. IN.)
1.0	8.9	1.3 TO 1.4	11.5 TO 12.4	1.3 TO 1.4	11.5 TO 12.4
1.1	9.8	1.4 TO 1.5	12.4 TO 13.3	1.4 TO 1.5	12.4 TO 13.3
1.25	11.1	1.5 TO 1.6	13.3 TO 14.2	1.6 TO 1.7	14.2 TO 15.1

Pinion bearing preload (determination) chart (© Mack Trucks, Inc.)

Ford Semi–Floating Single Speed Axle, Removable Carrier Type

This is a conventional type axle used on light duty Ford trucks. The axle design uses a removable carrier with the assembly bolted to the axle housing. The axle uses hypoid type gears and has the pinion gear mounted below the center line on the ring gear. The pinion gear is supported by two bearings in front of the gear and one behind. It is important to refer to the tag showing the axle and model number which is secured to the housing to obtain proper replacement parts.

CARRIER ASSEMBLY

Removal

1. With the vehicle raised on a lift, remove the axle shafts from the housing.
2. Remove the drive shaft from the carrier assembly.
3. With a drain pan under the axle, remove the retaining bolts from the carrier and drain the gear lube.
4. Remove the carrier assembly from the axle.

Installation

1. Clean the surfaces of the carrier and the axle housing. Install a new gasket.
2. Position the carrier assembly on the studs in the housing and install the retaining nuts. Torque the nuts to 30–40 ft. lbs.
3. Install the drive shaft and torque the bolts to 13–17 ft. lbs.
4. Install the axles in the housing and secure.
5. Fill the axle housing to the proper level with gear lube and road test for proper operation.

DIFFERENTIAL CASE

Removal & Disassembly

1. Remove the carrier assembly from the axle housing and mount the carrier in a holding fixture.
2. Mark the bearing caps and adjusting nuts so they may be installed in their original positions when assembling.
3. Remove the adjusting nut locks, bearing caps and adjusting nuts.
4. Lift the differential assembly out of the carrier. Using a bearing puller, remove the side bearings from the differential case.
5. Mark the side of the case, the ring gear and the cover so they can be installed in their original positions.
6. Remove the bolts that retain the ring gear to the case and using a soft hammer, tap the ring gear from the case.
7. Using a drift, drive the lock pin from the pinion shaft and separate the halves of the differential case.
8. Drive the pinion shaft out of the case using a brass drift and remove the thrust washers and gears.

DRIVE PINION AND BEARING RETAINER

Removal & Disassembly

1. With a holding fixture installed on the flange, remove the pinion nut and washer. Leave the holding fixture on the flange and using a puller, remove the flange from the pinion shaft.

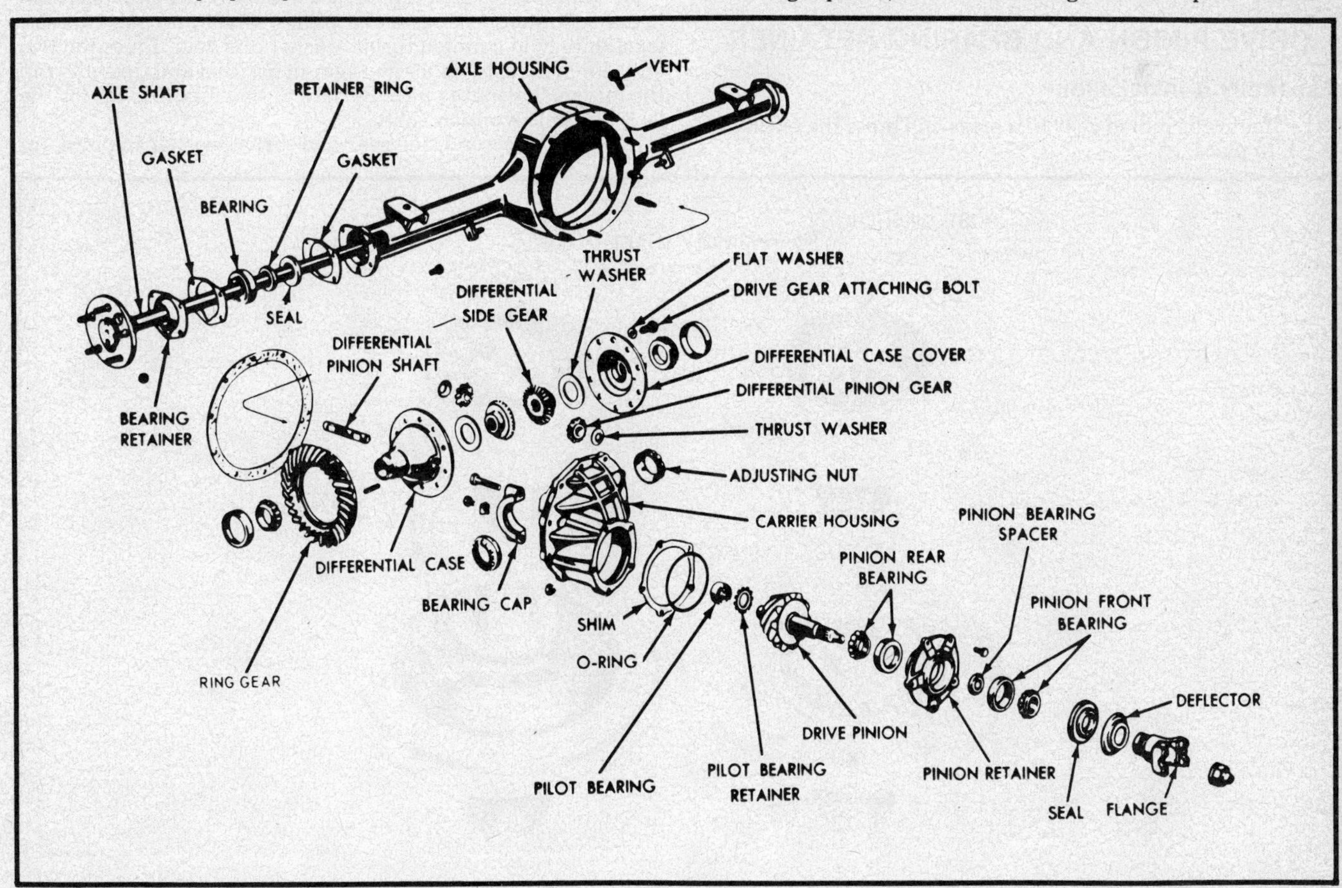

Removable carrier axle—disassembled (© Ford Motor Co.)

2. Using a seal puller, remove the pinion seal from the retainer assembly.

3. Remove the bolts from the retainer assembly and lift the retainer from the carrier. Measure the thickness of the shim that was between the retainer and the carrier assembly. Record the result.

4. Install a piece of hose on the pinion pilot bearing surface in front of the pinion gear. Mount the retainer assembly in a press and press the pinion gear out of the retainer.

5. Mount the pinion shaft in a press and press the rear bearing from the pinion shaft.

PINION BEARING CUP

Replacement

1. With the retainer assembly mounted in a press, using the proper tool, press the front and rear bearing cups from the assembly.

2. Check the inside surfaces of the retainer for any nicks, dirt or distortion.

3. Install the new cups by pressing them into place with the proper tool. When the cups are installed, make sure they are seated in the retainer by trying to fit a 0.0015 in. feeler gauge, between the cup and the bottom of the bore.

PILOT BEARING

Replacement

1. Using a bearing driver, drive the bearing and retainer out of the carrier assembly.

2. Using the same tool, drive the new bearing into place until the driver bottoms against the case.

3. Drive a new retainer into place with the concave side up.

DRIVE PINION AND BEARING RETAINER

Assembly & Installation

1. Mount the pinion gear in a press and press the rear bearing into place.

2. Install the bearing spacer, bearing retainer and front bearing on the pinion shaft and press them into place. Be careful not to crush the bearing spacer.

3. Install a new O-ring in the groove in the retainer assembly. Do not twist the O-ring when fitting it into place.

4. Lubricate both pinion bearings.

5. Check the thickness of the original shim that was recorded earlier. Located on the head of the pinion gear is the shim adjustment number. Compare the number on the old pinion with the one on the new pinion. Refer to the table which indicates the amount of change to the original shim thickness for proper operation.

6. Install the new shim on the housing and install the pinion and retainer assembly, being careful not to damage the O-ring.

7. Install the bearing retainer bolts and torque them to 30–40 ft. lbs.

8. Using a seal driver, install a new pinion seal in the retainer assembly.

9. Position a holding tool on the flange and install the flange on the pinion shaft. With the holding tool still in place, install the washer and nut on the pinion shaft and torque the nut to 175 ft. lbs. Check the pinion bearing preload. The preload should be 8–14 in. lbs. for used bearings and 22–32 in. lbs. for new bearings. *Do not* overtighten the nut. *Do not* back off the nut to obtain the proper preload. If the 175 ft. lbs. initial torque was too much, the collapsible spacer must be replaced. Tighten the pinion only enough to obtain the right preload torque.

DIFFERENTIAL CASE

Assembly & Installation

1. Lubricate all of the differential parts with gear lube before assembling.

2. Install a side gear and thrust washer in the case bore. Using a soft hammer, drive the pinion shaft into the case far enough to hold a pinion thrust washer and gear. Place the second pinion thrust washer and gear in position and carefully tap the pinion shaft into place. Be sure to line up the holes for the lock pin in the pinion shaft.

3. With the second side gear and thrust washer in place, in-

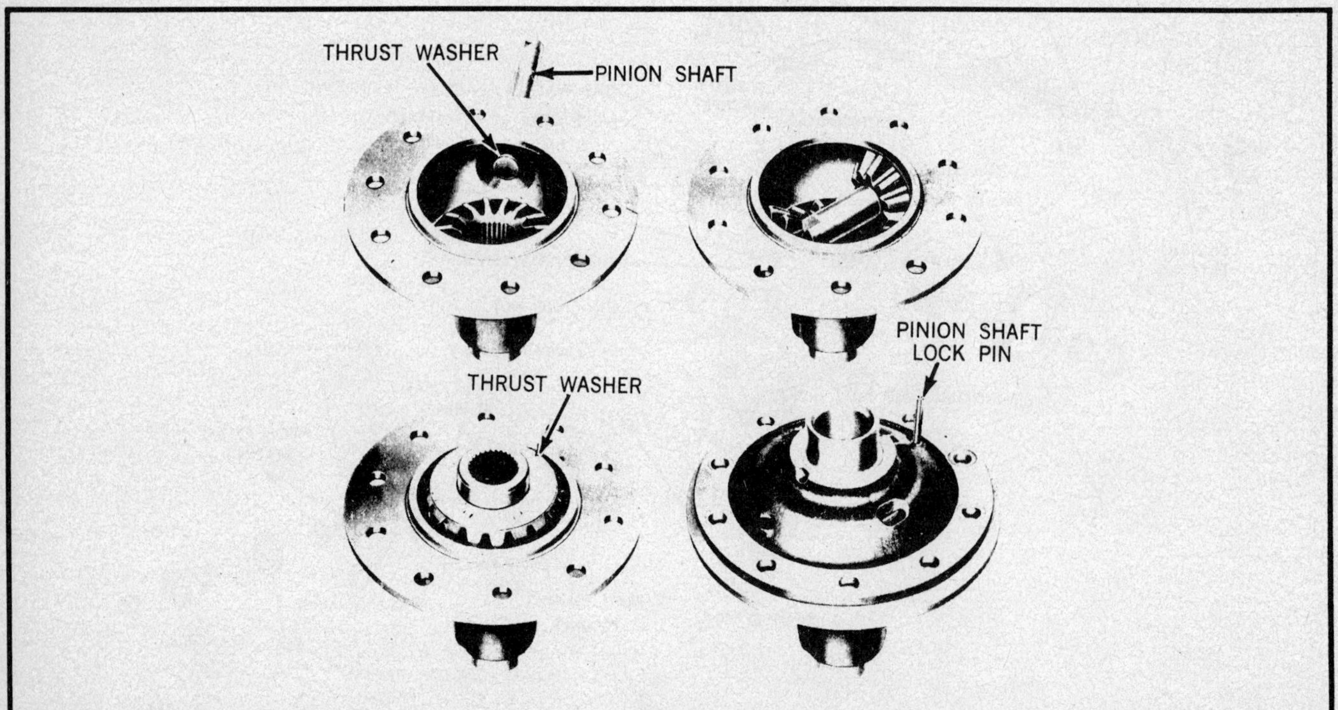

Differential case assembly (© Ford Motor Co.)

stall the cover on the differential case. Drive the pinion lock pin into place. Insert an axle shaft spline into the side gear and check for free rotation of the gears.

4. Install two, two in. long $^7/_{16}$ (N.F.) bolts through the differential case and thread them a little way into the ring gear. These will act as a guide when installing the ring gear on the case. Tap the ring gear into place.

5. Remove the guide pins and install the ring gear bolts. Tighten the bolts evenly to 65–85 ft. lbs.

6. If the differential bearings were removed, install the assembly in a press and press the new bearings into place.

7. Coat the bearing bores in the carrier with gear lube and install the bearing cups on the bearings. Place the differential assembly in the carrier.

8. Slide the differential case in the carrier bore until there is a slight amount of backlash between the gears.

9. Install the adjusting nuts in the carrier so that they just contact the bearing cups. The nuts should be engaged about the same number of threads on each side.

10. Position the bearing caps in the carrier. Be careful to line up the marks. Install the cap bolts and torque them to 70–80 ft. lbs. Make sure the adjusting nuts turn freely as the bolts are being tightened.

11. Adjust the backlash and bearing preload as follows:

a. Loosen the bearing cap bolts then retighten them to 35 ft. lbs.

b. Loosen the adjusting nut on the pinion side so that it is away from the bearing cup. Tighten the nut on the opposite side so that the ring gear is forced into the pinion with no backlash.

c. Recheck the nut on the pinion side to make sure it is still loose. Now tighten this nut until it contacts the bearing cup. After it contacts the cup, turn it two more notches.

d. Rotate the ring gear several times in each direction. This helps to seat the bearings in the cups.

e. Again loosen the nut on the pinion side. If there is any backlash between the gears, tighten the nut on the ring gear side until the backlash is removed.

f. Install a dial indicator on the carrier assembly. Tighten the nut on the pinion side until it just contacts the cup. With the dial indicator set at zero, tighten the pinion side nut until the case is spread 0.008–0.012 in. with new bearings and 0.005–0.008 in. with old bearings. As this preload is applied the ring gear is forced away from the pinion and usually results in the correct backlash.

g. Mount the dial indicator on the ring gear and check the gear for backlash. Make sure the bearing caps are torqued to 75–85 ft. lbs.

h. The backlash should be between 0.008–0.012 in. If the backlash is not correct, loosen one nut and tighten the other an equal amount to move the ring gear in or out to correct the measurement. When making final adjustments, always move the adjusting nuts in a tightening direction. To do this, if a nut had to be loosened one notch, loosen it two notches and tighten it one. This makes certain the nut is in contact with the cup and will not shift when the vehicle is in operation.

i. Coat the ring gear teeth with a marking compound and check the tooth pattern. If the pattern is not correct make the necessary changes to bring it into adjustment.

12. Install the carrier assembly in the vehicle and road test for proper operation.

Ford Bronco II/Ranger 6 $^3/_4$ Inch Ring Gear

Disassembly

1. Raise the vehicle and support it on the underbody, so that the rear axle drops down as far as the springs and shock absorbers permit.

2. Remove the cover from the carrier casting rear face and drain the lubricant. Perform the inspection before disassembly of carrier as directed under the Cleaning and Inspection Section.

3. Remove both rear wheels. Remove the brake drums.

4. Working through the hole provided in the axle shaft flange, remove the nuts that attach the wheel bearing retainers to the axle housing. Pull the axle shafts.

5. Remove the brake backing plate and wire it to the frame rail. Remove both seals with the tool shown.

6. Make scribe marks on the driveshaft end yoke and the axle U-joint flange to ensure proper position of the driveshaft at assembly. Disconnect the driveshaft from the axle U-joint flange. Remove the driveshaft from the transmission extension housing. Install an oil seal replacer tool in the transmission extension housing to prevent transmission leakage.

7. Check and record the ring gear runout and the ring gear backlash.

8. Mark one differential bearing cap and the case to help ensure proper position of the parts during assembly.

9. Loosen the differential bearing cap bolts and bearing caps. Pry the differential case, bearing cups and shims out until they are loose in the bearing caps. Remove the bearing caps and the differential assembly from the carrier.

NOTE: The direction of arrows on bearing caps must be noted. When reassembled, the arrows must be pointing outward.

10. Mark the companion flange in relation to the pinion shaft. Hold the rear axle companion flange with the proper tool and remove the pinion nut. If a new gear set is being installed, the companion flange need not be marked.

11. Remove the companion flange.

12. With a soft-faced hammer, drive the pinion out of the front bearing cone and remove it through the rear of the carrier casting.

13. Remove the pinion seal and front bearing cone from the front of the carrier casting.

DRIVE PINION

Disassembly

1. Remove the drive pinion, front bearing cone, spacer, and seal.

2. Remove the pinion rear bearing cone. Measure the shim found under the bearing cone with a micrometer. Record the thickness of the shim.

NOTE: Before assembling the rear bearing cone to the piston, it will be necessary to adjust Pinion.

DRIVE PINION DEPTH ADJUSTMENT

Individual differences in machining the carrier casting and the gear set and variation in bearing widths require a shim between the pinion rear bearing and pinion head, in order to locate the pinion head, in order to locate the pinion for correct tooth contact with the ring gear. When replacing a ring and pinion gear, the correct shim thickness for the new gear set to

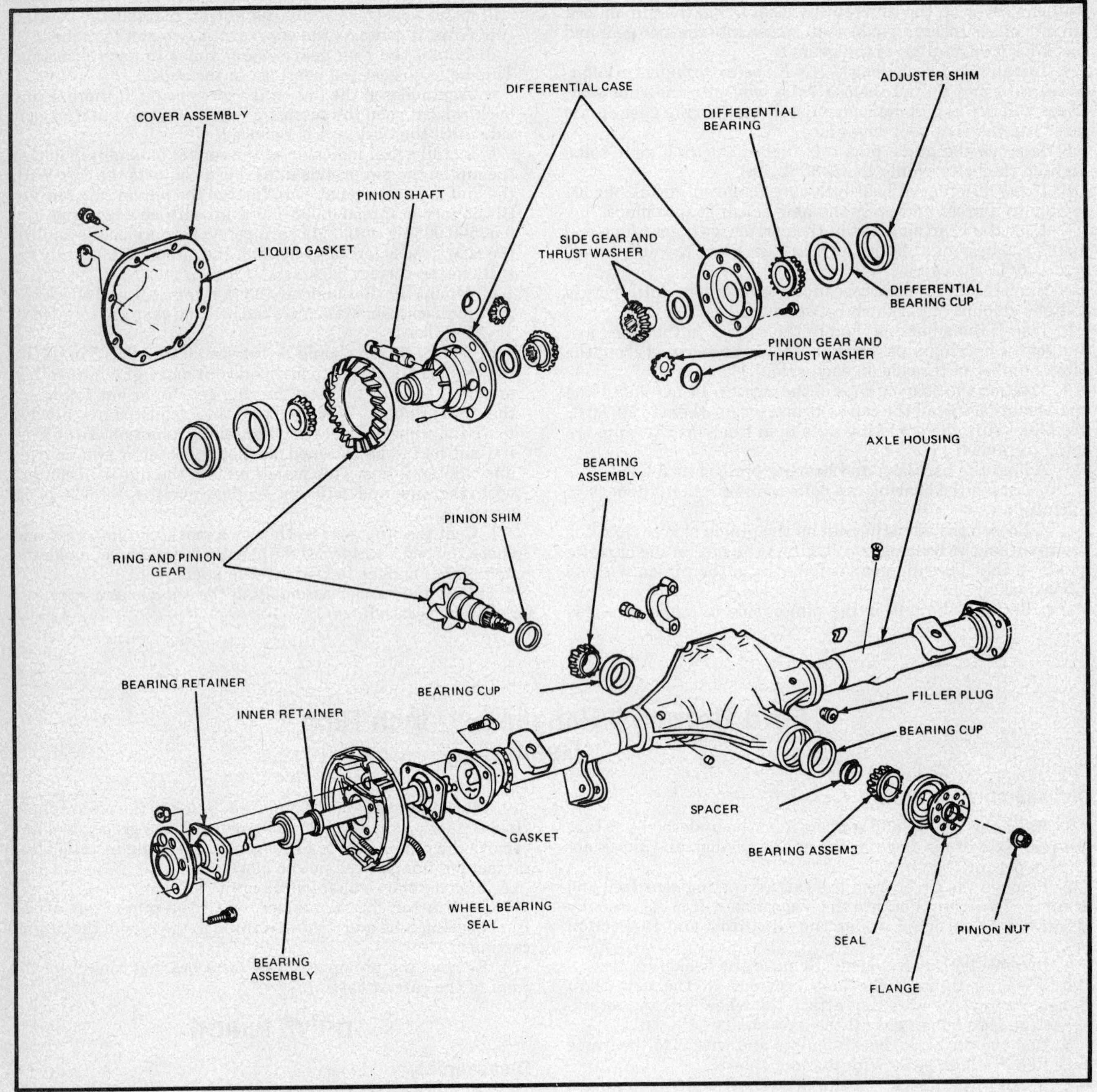

Exploded view 6¾ inch axle assembly (© Ford Motor Co.)

be installed is determined by the following procedure using Tool T79P–4020–A or equivalent.

1. Place the rear pinion bearing (new or used if in good condition) over the aligning disc and insert it into the pinion bearing cup of the carrier. Place the front bearing into the front bearing cup and assemble the tool handle into the screw and tighten to 27 Nm (20 ft. lbs.).

NOTE: The gauge block must be offset to obtain an accurate reading.

2. Center the gauge tube into the differential bearing bore. Install the bearing caps and torque the bolts to specification. (Caps to be installed with the arrows pointing outboard).

3. Make sure that the gauge handle adapter screw, aligning adapter, gauge disc and gauge block assembly are securely mounted between front and rear bearing. Recheck tool handle torque prior to gauging to ensure that bearings are properly seated. This can affect final shim selection when improperly assembled. Clean bearing cups and differential pedestal surfaces thoroughly. Apply only light oil film on bearing assemblies prior to gauging.

4. Gauge block should then be rotated several half turns to ensure rollers are properly seated in bearing cups. Rotational torque on the gauge assembly should be 20 in. lbs. with new bearings. Final position should be approximately 45° across gauge tube to ensure that gauge block is in line with gauge tube high point. This area should be utilized for pinion shim se-

lection. Selection of pinion shim with gauge block not lined up with tube high point will cause improper shim selection and may result in axle noise.

5. Utilize pinion shims as the gauge for shim selection, this will minimize errors in attempting to stack feeler gauge stock together or simple addition errors in calculating correct shim thickness.

NOTE: Shims must be flat. Do not use dirty, bent, nicked or mutilated shims as a gauge.

6. It is important to utilize a light drag on the shim for the correct selection. Do not attempt to force the shim between the gauge block and gauge tube. This will minimize selection of a shim thicker than required, which results in a deep tooth contact in final assembly for integral axles. If the pinion has a plus (+) marking, subtract this amount from the feeler gauge measurement.

7. If the pinion has a minus (-) marking, add this amount to the feeler gauge measurement.

DRIVE PINION REAR BEARING

NOTE: The same rear pinion bearing used in this procedure must be used in final assembly of the axle.

1. Place the selected shim(s) on the pinion shaft and press the pinion bearing until firmly seated on the shaft.

PINION BEARING CUPS

Disassembly and Assembly

Do not remove the pinion bearing cups from the carrier casting unless the cups are to be replaced; drive them out of the carrier casting with a drift. Install the new cups with tool T71P–4616–A or equivalent. Make sure the cups are properly seated in their bores. If a 0.0015 in. feeler gauge can be inserted between a cup and the bottom of its bore at any point around the cup, the cup is not properly seated. Whenever the cups are replaced, the cone and roller assemblies should also be replaced.

DIFFERENTIAL CASE

Disassembly

1. If the differential bearings are to be removed, use tool T77F–4220–B or equivalent. Mark the differential case, cover and ring gear for assembly in the original position.
2. Remove the bolts that attach the ring gear to the differential case and discard them. Press the ring gear from the case or tap it off with a soft-faced hammer.
3. Remove the left side of the differential case.
4. With a drift, drive out the differential pinion shaft lock pin.
5. Drive out the pinion shaft with a brass drift. Remove the gears and thrust washers. Clean and inspect all the parts. Repair or replace all parts as indicated by the inspection.

Assembly

1. Install the differential side gears and thrust washers in their bores.
2. Install the pinion shaft aligning the pinion gears and thrust washers.
3. Install the left case on the right and tap them together.
4. Install the pinion shaft lockpin.
5. Install the differential bearing.

AXLE

Assembly

The drive pinion should be set to the correct depth before final assembly setting is proper. Drive pinion preload requires that a new spacer be used when the pinion is removed. Drive pinion bearing preload is set with the drive pinion assembly installed and the pinion nut tightened to specification. Correct preload is indicted when the rotational torque is 0.9–1.6 Nm (8–14 in. lbs.) with original bearing or 1.8–3.2 Nm (16–29 in. lbs.) for new bearings.

Differential Bearing Preload and Ring Gear Backlash is adjusted with the drive pinion and differential case installed. Adjustment is performed by the installation of shims between the differential bearing cup and axle housing.

DRIVE PINION AND DRIVE PINION BEARING PRELOAD ADJUSTMENT

1. Install the pinion front bearing.
2. Install the pinion seal.
3. Insert the companion flange into the seal and hold it firmly against the pinion front bearing cone. From the rear of the carrier casting, insert the pinion shaft with a new spacer into the flange.
4. Start a new pinion nut. Hold the flange and tighten the pinion shaft nut. As the nut is tightened, the pinion shaft is pulled into the front bearing cone and into the flange.
5. the pinion shaft is pulled into the front bearing cone, pinion shaft end play is reduced. While there is still end play in the pinion shaft, the flange and bearing cone will be felt to bottom on the collapsible spacer.

From this point, a much greater torque must be applied to turn the pinion nut, since the spacer must be collapsed. Very slowly,

BACKLASH CHANGE REQUIRED (INCH)	THICKNESS CHANGE REQUIRED (INCH)	BACKLASH CHANGE REQUIRED (INCH)	THICKNESS CHANGE REQUIRED (INCH)
.001	.002	.009	.012
.002	.002	.010	.014
.003	.004	.011	.014
.004	.006	.012	.016
.005	.006	.013	.018
.006	.008	.014	.018
.007	.010	.015	.020
.008	.010		

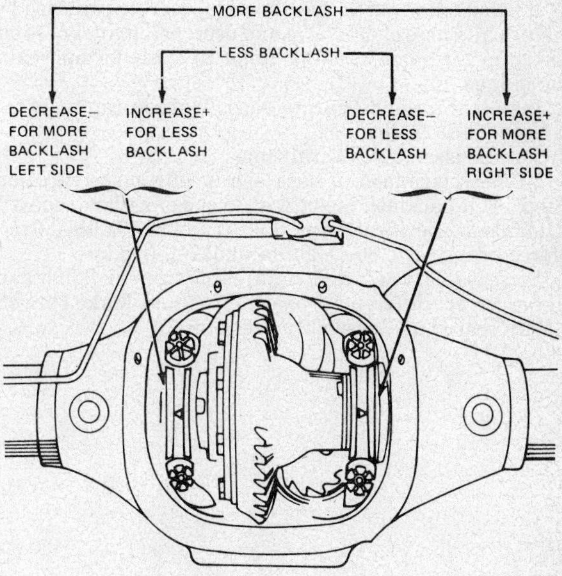

Shim changes for ring gear and pinion backlash (© Ford Motor Co.)

tighten the nut, but check the pinion shaft end play often, to see that the pinion bearing preload does not exceed the limits.

6. If the pinion nut is tightened to the point that the pinion bearing preload exceeds the limits, the pinion shaft must be removed and a new collapsible spacer installed. Do not decrease the preload by loosening the pinion nut. This will remove the compression between the pinion front and rear bearing cones and the collapsible spacer and may permit the front bearing cone to turn on the pinion shaft.

7. As soon as there is a preload on the bearings, turn the pinion shaft in both directions several times to set the bearing rollers.

8. Adjust the bearing preload to specification. Measure the preload with a torque wrench.

DIFFERENTIAL ASSEMBLY

For shim selection after a complete replacement of the rear axle housing, the differential assembly or differential side bearing, use the following instructions. For a ring and pinion replacement only or a backlash adjustment, follow Steps 9 through 13 and Step 15, using the side bearing shims that were originally in the axle.

1. With pinion depth set and pinion installed, place differential case and gear assembly with bearings and cups in carrier.
2. Install a 6.73mm (0.265 in.) shim on left side.
3. Install left bearing cap and tighten bolts finger tight.
4. Install progressively larger shims on the right side until the largest shim selected can be assembled with a slight drag feel.

NOTE: Apply pressure towards left side to ensure bearing cup is seated.

5. Install right side bearing cap and tighten bearing cup bolts to 95–115 Nm (70–85 ft. lbs.).
6. Rotate assembly to ensure free rotation.
7. Check ring gear and pinion backlash. If the backlash is 0.20–0.38mm (0.008–0.015 in.) with 0.30–0.38 (0.012–0.015 in.) preferred, proceed to Step 14. If backlash is not within specifications, go to Step 10, unless zero backlash is measured, then go to Step 8.
8. If a zero backlash condition occurs, add 0.020 in. to the right side and subtract 0.020 in. from the left side to allow backlash indication.
9. Recheck backlash.
10. If backlash is not to specification, correct backlash by increasing thickness of one shim and decreasing thickness on the other shim the same amount. Refer to chart for approximate shim change.
11. Install shim and bearing caps. Tighten cap bolts to 95–110 Nm (70–85 ft. lbs.).
12. Rotate assembly several times.
13. Recheck backlash. If backlash is within specification, go to Step 14. If backlash is not within specification, repeat Step 10. Backlash specification is 0.20–0.38mm (0.008–0.015 in.). Preferred range is 0.30–0.38mm (0.012–0.015 in.).
14. Increase both left and right shim sizes by 0.006 and install for correct differential bearing preload. Make sure shims are fully seated and assembly turns freely.
15. Utilize white marking compound to obtain a tooth mesh contact pattern in your assembly.

NOTE: Reincorporation of pattern inspection is intended to allow technicians the ability to detect gross errors in set up prior to complete reassembly. Pattern contact should be within the primary area of the ring gear tooth surface, avoiding any "narrow" or "hard" contact with outer perimeter of tooth (top to root, toe to heel). Pattern inspection should be on the drive (pull) side. Correct assembly of drive pattern will result in satisfactory coast performance. If gross pattern error is detected, with preferred backlash 0.30–0.38mm (0.012–0.05 in.), recheck pinion shim selection.

16. Install bearing caps and tighten cap bolts to 95–115 Nm (70–85 ft. lbs.).
17. Inspect the machined surfaces of the axle shaft and the axle housing for rough spots, or other irregularities which would affect the sealing action of the oil seal. Check the axle shaft splines for burrs, wear or damage. Carefully remove any burrs or rough spots. Replace worn or damaged parts. Install a new gasket on the housing flange and install the brake backing plate.
18. Carefully slide the axle shaft into the housing so that the rough forging of the shaft will not damage the oil seal. Start the axle splines into the side gar, and push the shaft in until the bearing bottoms in the housing. Install the bearing retainer plate on the mounting bolts t the axle housing, and install the attaching nuts. Tighten the nuts to 27–54 Nm (20–40 ft. lbs.).
19. Remove the oil seal replacer from the transmission extension housing. Align the scribe marks on the flange and driveshaft and connect the driveshaft at the drive pinion flange. Apply Loctite (EOAZ–19554–B) or equivalent to the threads of the attaching bolts and tighten to 95–128 Nm (70–95 ft. lbs.).
20. Install the brake drum and attaching shakeproof retainers. Install the wheel and tire on the brake drum. Install the wheel covers.
21. Clean the gasket mating surface of the rear axle housing and cover. Apply a new continuous bead of silicone rubber sealant (D6AX–19562–B or equivalent) to the carrier casting face.

NOTE: Make sure machined surfaces on both cover and carrier are clean before installing the new silicone sealant. Inside of axle must be covered when cleaning the machined surface to prevent axle contamination.

22. Install cover and tighten cover bolts to 34–47 Nm (25–35 ft. lbs.), except the ratio tag bolt, which is tightened to 20–34 Nm (15–25 ft. lbs.).

NOTE: Cover assembly must be installed within 15 minutes of application of the silicone or new sealant must be applied.

23. Add EOAZ–19580–A (ESP–M2C154–A) lubricant or equivalent through the filler hole until the lubricant level reaches the bottom of the filler hole with the axle in the running position. Install filler plug and tighten to 21–40 Nm (15–30 ft. lbs.).
24. Lower vehicle and road test.

Ford–Bronco II/Ranger

7 1/2 INCH RING GEAR AXLE ASSEMBLY

Disassembly

NOTE: The Aerostar is equipped with a 7 1/2 in. ring gear and the service procedures are the same as outlined below, except for a few minor changes. There are now two new special tools used in the rear axle service procedures. Tool T85L–4067–AH is a driver which is designed to install shims as needed to adjust the ring gear and pinion backlash. The backlash specification is 0.001 to 0.015 in., but 0.012 to 0.015 in. is preferred. Tool T85L–1225–AH is is used to remove the wheel bearing seal from the axle. Both of these tools or their equivalent are needed to complete the rear axle overhaul on the Aerostar. All service operations on the differential case assembly and the drive pinion can be performed with the axle housing installed in the vehicle.

1. Raise the vehicle and place jackstands under the rear frame crossmember. Lower the hoist so that the axle drops down far enough for working ease.
2. Remove the cover from the carrier casting rear face an drain the lubricant. Inspect the case assembly and drive pinion before removal.
3. Remove the rear wheels and brake drums.
4. Remove the axle shafts.
5. Make scribe marks on the driveshaft and yoke and the rear axle companion flange to ensure proper alignment at assembly. Disconnect the driveshaft from the rear axle companion flange. Remove the driveshaft assembly from the vehicle. Insert an oil seal replacement tool in the transmission extension housing to prevent leakage.
6. Check and record the ring gear runout. Check and record the ring gear backlash.
7. Mark on differential bearing cap to help position the caps properly during assembly.
8. Loosen the differential bearing cap bolts and bearing caps.

NOTE: The direction of arrows on bearing caps must be noted. When reassembled, the arrows must be pointing in the same direction as before removal.

9. Pry the differential case, bearing cups and shims out until they are loose in the bearing caps. Remove the bearing caps and remove the differential assembly out of the carrier. On conventional differentials, if the ring is removed, discard the bolts. Install new bolts, coated with Loctite or equivalent. Tighten to 95–115 Nm (70–85 ft. lbs.).

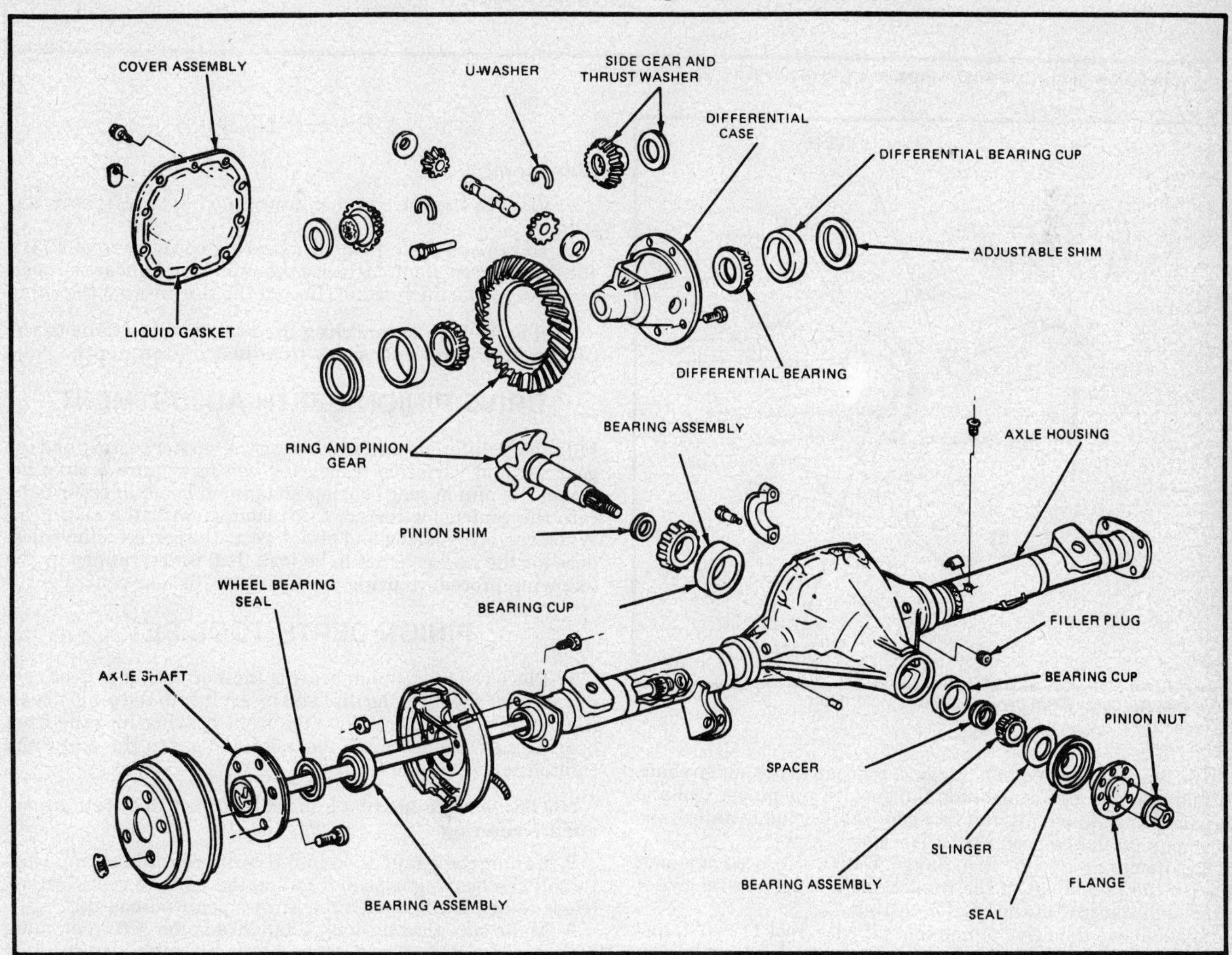

Exploded view 7½ inch axle assembly (© Ford Motor Co.)

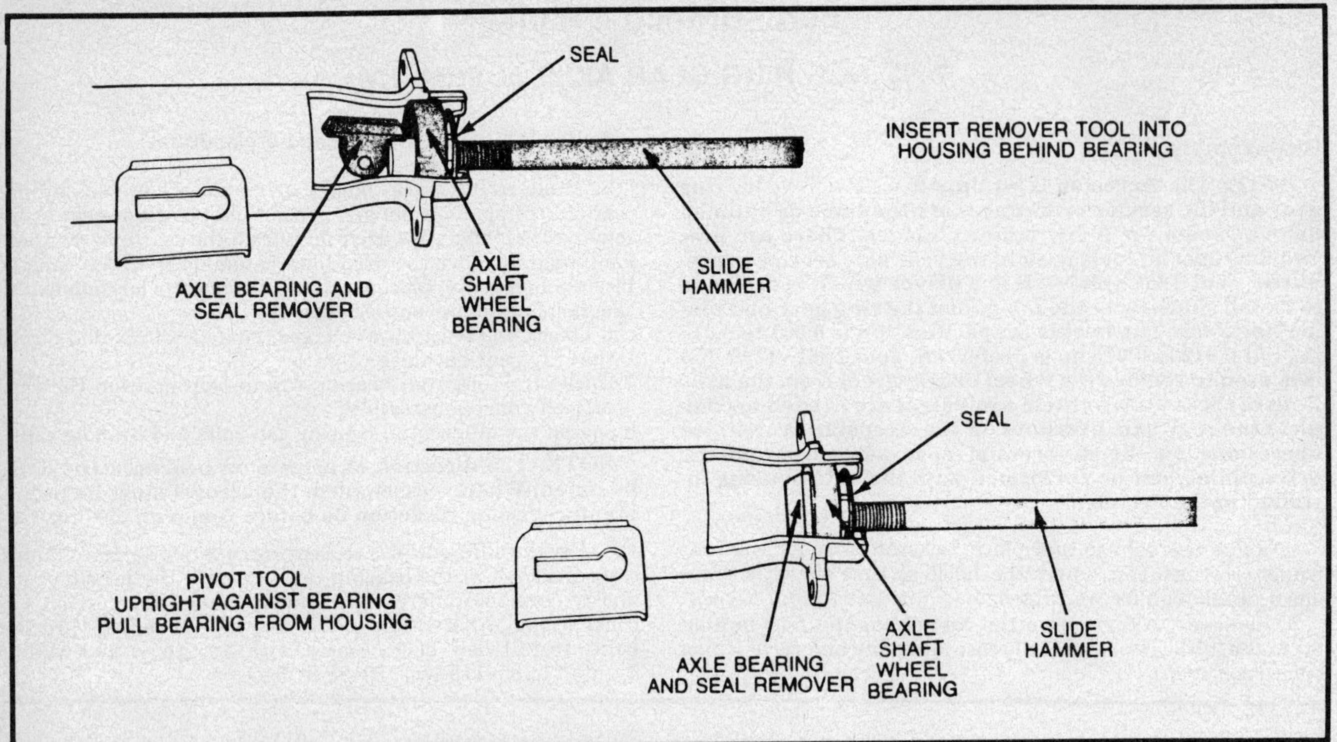

Exploded view of the axle shaft wheel bearing removal (© Ford Motor Co.)

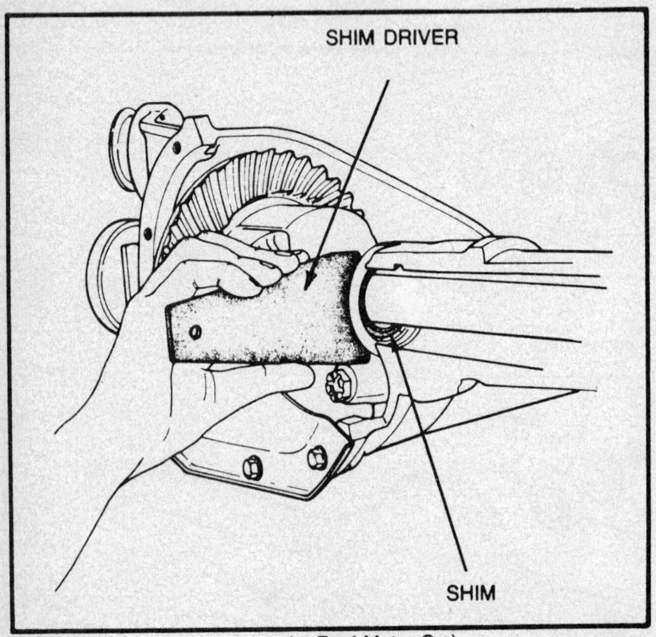

Typical Aerostar shim driver (© Ford Motor Co.)

10. Mark the companion flange in relation to the pinion shaft. Hold the rear axle companion flange with the proper tool and remove the pinion nut. If a new gear set is being installed, the companion flange need not be marked.

11. Remove the companion flange. With a soft-faced hammer, drive the pinion out of the front bearing cone and remove it through the rear of the carrier casting.

12. Remove the drive pinion oil seal with Tool 1125–AC and T50T–100–A or their equivalent. Remove the front pinion bearing cone and roller and slinger from the carrier casting.

DRIVE PINION

Disassembly

1. Remove the drive pinion, front bearing cone, spacer, and seal.

2. To remove the pinion rear bearing cone, use tool T71P–4621–B or equivalent. Measure the shim found under the bearing cone with a micrometer. Record the thickness of the shim.

NOTE: Before assembling the rear bearing cone to the pinion, it will be necessary to adjust pinion depth.

DRIVE PINION DEPTH ADJUSTMENT

Individual differences in machining the carrier casting and the gear set and variation in bearing widths require a shim between the pinion rear bearing and pinion head, in order to locate the pinion for correct tooth contact with the ring gear. When replacing a ring and pinion gear, the correct shim thickness for the new gear set to be installed, is determined by the following procedure using tool T79P–4020–A or equivalent.

PINION DEPTH TOOL SET

1. Place the rear pinion bearing (new or used if in good condition) over the aligning disc and insert it into the pinion bearing cup of the carrier. Place the front bearing into the front bearing cup and assemble the tool handle into the screw and tighten to 27 Nm (20 ft. lbs.).

NOTE: The gauge block must be offset to obtain an accurate reading.

2. Center the gauge tube into the differential bearing bore. Install the bearing caps and torque the bolts to specification. (Caps to be installed with the arrows point outboard.).

3. Make sure that the gauge handle adapter screw, aligning adapter, gauge disc and gauge block assembly are securely mounted between front and rear bearing. Recheck tool handle

torque prior to gauging to ensure that bearings are properly seated. This can affect final shim selection when improperly assembled. Clean bearing cups and differential pedestal surfaces thoroughly. Apply only light oil film on bearing assemblies prior to gauging.

4. Gauge block should then be rotated several half turns to ensure rollers are properly seated in bearing cups. Rotational torque on the gauge assembly should be 20 in. lbs. with new bearings. Final position should be approximately 45° across gauge tube to ensure that gauge block is in line with gauge tube high point. This area should be utilized for pinion shim selection. Selection of pinion shim with gauge block not lined up with tube high point will cause improper shim selection and may result in axle noise.

5. Utilize pinion shims as the gauge for shim selection. This will minimize errors in attempting to stack feeler gauge stock together or simple addition errors in calculating correct shim thickness.

NOTE: Shims must be flat. Do not use dirty, bent, nicked or mutilated shims as a gauge.

6. It is important to utilize a light drag on the shim for the correct selection. Do not attempt to force the shim between the gauge block and gauge tube. This will minimize selection of a shim thicker than required which results in a deep tooth contact in final assembly for integral axles.

7. If the pinion has a plug (+) marking, subtract his amount from the feeler gauge measurement. If the pinion has a minimum (-) marking, add this amount to the feeler gauge measurement.

ASSEMBLY OF DRIVE PINION REAR BEARING CONE

NOTE: The same rear pinion bearing used in this procedure must be used in final assembly of the axle.

1. Place the selected shim(s) on the pinion shaft an depress the pinion bearing until firmly seated on the shaft.

DRIVE PINION BEARING CUPS

Disassembly & Assembly

Do not remove the pinion bearing cups from the carrier casting unless the cups are worn or damaged. If the pinion bearing cups are to be replaced, drive them out of the carrier casting with a drift. Install the new cups. Make sure the cups are properly seated in their bores. If a 0.0015 in. feeler gauge can be inserted between a cup and the bottom of its bore at any point around the cup, the cup is not properly seated. Whenever the cups are replaced, the cone and roller assemblies should also be replaced.

Assembly

The drive pinion must be set to the correct depth before final assembly. Drive pinion preload requires that a new spacer be used when the pinion is removed. Drive pinion bearing preload is set with the drive pinion assembly installed and the pinion nut tightened to specification. Correct preload is indicted when the rotational torque is 0.9–1.6 Nm (8–14 in. lbs.) with the original bearings or 1.8–3.2 Nm (16–29 in. lbs.) for used bearings.

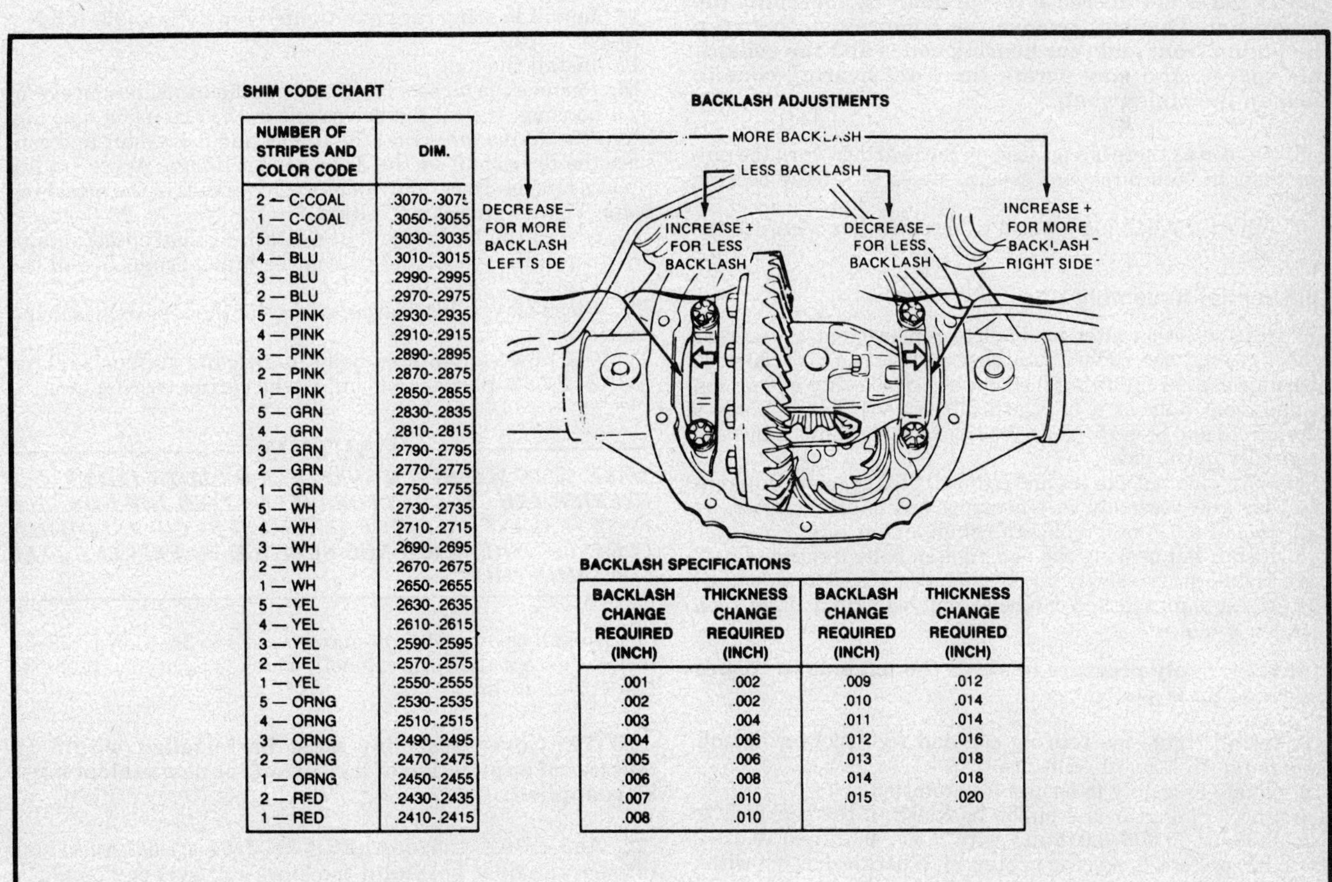

SHIM CODE CHART

NUMBER OF STRIPES AND COLOR CODE	DIM.
2 — C-COAL	.3070-.3075
1 — C-COAL	.3050-.3055
5 — BLU	.3030-.3035
4 — BLU	.3010-.3015
3 — BLU	.2990-.2995
2 — BLU	.2970-.2975
5 — PINK	.2930-.2935
4 — PINK	.2910-.2915
3 — PINK	.2890-.2895
2 — PINK	.2870-.2875
1 — PINK	.2850-.2855
5 — GRN	.2830-.2835
4 — GRN	.2810-.2815
3 — GRN	.2790-.2795
2 — GRN	.2770-.2775
1 — GRN	.2750-.2755
5 — WH	.2730-.2735
4 — WH	.2710-.2715
3 — WH	.2690-.2695
2 — WH	.2670-.2675
1 — WH	.2650-.2655
5 — YEL	.2630-.2635
4 — YEL	.2610-.2615
3 — YEL	.2590-.2595
2 — YEL	.2570-.2575
1 — YEL	.2550-.2555
5 — ORNG	.2530-.2535
4 — ORNG	.2510-.2515
3 — ORNG	.2490-.2495
2 — ORNG	.2470-.2475
1 — ORNG	.2450-.2455
2 — RED	.2430-.2435
1 — RED	.2410-.2415

BACKLASH SPECIFICATIONS

BACKLASH CHANGE REQUIRED (INCH)	THICKNESS CHANGE REQUIRED (INCH)	BACKLASH CHANGE REQUIRED (INCH)	THICKNESS CHANGE REQUIRED (INCH)
.001	.002	.009	.012
.002	.002	.010	.014
.003	.004	.011	.014
.004	.006	.012	.016
.005	.006	.013	.018
.006	.008	.014	.018
.007	.010	.015	.020
.008	.010		

Shim changes for ring gear and pinion backlash (© Ford Motor Co.)

Differential Bearing Preload and Ring Gear Backlash is adjusted with the drive pinion and differential case installed. Adjustment is performed by the installation of shims between the differential bearing cup and axle housing.

DRIVE PINION AND DRIVE PINION BEARING PRELOAD ADJUSTMENT

1. Install the pinion front bearing and slinger.
2. Apply grease, C1AZ–19590–B or equivalent between the lips of the pinion seal and install the pinion seal.
3. Insert the companion flange into the seal and hold it firmly against the pinion front bearing cone. From the rear of the carrier casting, insert the pinion shaft, with a new spacer, into the flange.
4. Start new pinion nut. Hold the flange with special tool T78P–4851–A or equivalent and tighten the pinion nut. As the nut is tightened, the pinion shaft is pulled into the front bearing cone and into the flange.
5. As the pinion shaft is pulled into the front bearing cone, pinion shaft end play is reduced. While there is still end play in the pinion shaft, the flange and bearing cone will be felt to bottom on the collapsible spacer.
6. From this point, a much greater torque must be applied to turn the pinion nut, since the spacer must be collapsed. Very slowly, tighten the nut, but check the pinion shaft end play often to see that the pinion bearing preload does not exceed the limits.
7. If the pinion nut is tightened to the point that pinion bearing preload exceeds the limits, the pinion shaft must be removed and a new collapsible spacer installed.

NOTE: Do not decrease the preload by loosening the pinion nut. This will remove the compression between the pinion front and rear bearing cones and the collapsible spacer, and may permit the front bearing cone to turn on the pinion shaft.

8. As soon as there is a preload on the bearings, turn the pinion shaft in both directions several times to set the bearing rollers.
9. Adjust the bearing preload to specification. Measure the preload.

Differential Assembly

For shim selection after a complete replacement of the rear axle housing, the differential assembly or differential side bearings use the following instructions. For a ring and pinion replacement only or a backlash adjustment, follow Steps 9 through 13 and Step 15, using the side bearing shims that were originally in the axle.

1. With pinion depth set and pinion installed, place differential case gear assembly with bearings and cups in carrier.
2. Install a 6.73mm (0.265 in.) shim on left side.
3. Install left bearing cap and tighten bolts finger tight.
4. Install progressively larger shims on the right side until the largest shim selected can be assembled with a slight drag feel.

NOTE: Apply pressure towards the left side to ensure bearing cup is seated.

5. Install right side bearing cap and tighten bearing cup bolts to 95–15 Nm (70–85 ft. lbs.).
6. Rotate assembly to ensure free rotation.
7. Check ring gear and pinion backlash. If the backlash is 0.20–0.38mm (0.008–0.015 in.) with 0.304–0.381mm (0.012–0.015 in.) preferred, proceed to Step 14. If backlash is not within specifications, go to Step 10, unless zero backlash is measured, then go to Step 8.
8. If a zero backlash conditions occurs, add 0.020 in. to the right side and subtract 0.020 in. from the left side to allow backlash indication.
9. Recheck backlash.
10. If backlash is not to specification, correct backlash by increasing thickness of one shim and decreasing thickness on the other shim the same amount. Refer to chart for approximate shim change.
11. Install shim and bearing caps. Tighten cap bolts to 95–115 Nm (70–85 ft. lbs.).
12. Rotate assembly several times.
13. Recheck backlash. If backlash is within specification, go to Step 14. If backlash is not within specification, repeat Step 10. Backlash specification is 0.20–0.38mm (0.008–0.015 in.). Preferred range is 0.304–0.381mm (0.012–0.015 in.).
14. Increase both left and right shim sizes by 0.006 in. and install for correct differential bearing preload. Make sure shims are fully seated and assembly turns freely.
15. Utilize white marking compound to obtain a tooth mesh contact pattern in your assembly.

NOTE: Reincorporation of pattern inspection is intended to allow technicians the ability to detect gross errors in set up prior to complete reassembly. Pattern contact should be within the primary area of the ring gear tooth surface avoiding any "narrow" or "hard" contact with outer perimeter of tooth (top to root, toe to heel). Pattern inspection should be on the drive (pull) side. Correct assembly of drive pattern will result in satisfactory coast performance. If gross pattern error is detected, the preferred backlash of 0.30–0.38mm (0.012–0.015 in.), recheck pinion shim selection.

16. Install bearing caps and tighten cap bolts to 95–115 Nm (70–85 ft. lbs.).
17. Install the axle shafts.
18. Remove the oil seal replacer from the transmission extension housing. Install the driveshaft in the extension housing. align the scribe marks on the flange and driveshaft and connect the driveshaft at the drive pinion flange. Apply Loctite (EOAZ–19554–B) or equivalent to the threads of the attaching bolts. Tighten attaching bolts to 90–128 Nm (70–95 ft. lbs.).
19. Install the brake drum and attaching shakeproof retainers. Install the wheel and tire on the brake drum. Install the wheel covers.
20. Clean the gasket mating surface of the rear axle housing and cover.

Apply a new continuous bead of silicone rubber sealant (D6AZ–19562–B or equivalent) to the carrier casting face.

CAUTION

MAKE SURE MACHINED SURFACES ON BOTH COVER AND CARRIER ARE CLEAN BEFORE INSTALLING THE NEW SILICONE SEALANT. INSIDE OF AXLE MUST BE COVERED WHEN CLEANING THE MACHINED SURFACE TO PREVENT AXLE CONTAMINATION.

21. Install cover and tighten cover bolts to 34–47 Nm (25–35 ft. lbs.), except the ratio tag bolt, which is tightened to 20–34 Nm (15–25 ft. lbs.).

NOTE: Cover assembly must be installed within 15 minutes of application of the silicone or new sealant must be reapplied.

22. Add EOAZ–19580–A (ESP–MC2154–A) or equivalent through the filler hole until the lubricant level is 9.5mm ($^3/_8$ in.) below the filler hole with the axle in the running position.
23. Lower vehicle and road test.

Ford Bronco, E–150 and F–150

9.0 INCH RING GEAR REAR AXLE

Carrier Removal

1. Raise and support the rear of the vehicle safely, and remove the two rear wheel and tire assemblies.
2. Remove the two brake drums and the axle flange studs. Working through the access hole provided in each axle shaft flange, remove the nuts that secure the rear wheel bearing retainer plate. Pull each axle shaft assembly out of the axle housing, using axle shaft puller adapter tool T66l–4234–A or equivalent. Wire the backing plate to the frame rail . Remove and discard the old gasket if so equipped.
3. Make scribe marks on the drive shaft yoke end and the axle companion flange to insure proper position at assembly. Disconnect the drive shaft at the rear axle U-joint. Hold the cups on the spider with tape. Mark the cups so that they will be in their original position relative to the flange when they are assembled.
4. Remove the drive shaft from the transmission extension housing. Install an oil seal replacer tool or equivalent in the housing to prevent transmission fluid leakage.
5. Clean the area around the carrier with a wire brush and wipe it clean to prevent any dirt from entering the housing. Place a suitable drain pan under the carrier, remove the carrier attaching nuts and washers and drain the axle. Remove the carrier assembly from the axle housing.

Carrier Disassembly

1. Place the carrier assembly into a suitable holding fixture, check and record the ring gear runout and the ring gear backlash.
2. Mark one of the differential bearing cap and the mating bearing support with punch marks to help position the parts during reassembly of the carrier. Remove the adjusting nut locks, bearing caps, (remove the bearing caps with a soft mallet) and adjusting nuts. Lift the differential case assembly out of the carrier.
3. Remove the differential side bearings with special tools T57L–4220–A or T66P–4220–A or their equivalent. Mark the differential case, differential cover and ring gear for assembly in the original position.
4. Separate the differential cover from the differential case. Remove the side gear thrust washer and the side gear. Using a drift, drive out the three diferential pinion shaft lock pins. Drive out the long differential pinion shaft with a brass drift.
5. With a brass drift carefully positioned inside the case, drive out the two short differential pinion shafts. Remove the positioning block, differential pinions and the thrust washers from the differential case.
6. Remove the side gear and side gear thrust washer from the case.
7. Position the carrier assembly in a manner that will permit the removal of the drive pinion shaft nut. Remove the campanion flange from the drive pinion shaft and remove the pinion seal.
8. Remove the pinion and retainer assembly from the carrier housing. If a new pinion bearing and or gear set is installed, a new shim will have to installed. Be very careful not to damage the mounting surfaces of the retainer and the carrier.
9. Place a protective sleeve on the pinion pilot bearing surface. Press the pinion shaft out of the pinion retainer. Press the pinion shaft out of the pinion rear bearing cone, using tool # T71P–4621–B or equivalent.
10. Remove and install a new pinion shaft pilot bearing. Remove the old pinion shaft pilot bearing by pressing it off and install the new one by pressing it on. Install a new pinion shaft pilot bearing retainer, concave side up, on the same press.

NOTE: Do not remove the drive pinion bearing cups from the retainer unless the cups are worn or damaged or if the cone and roller assemblies are damaged.

11. If the cups are worn or damaged, remove them with the use of bearing cup puller T77F–1102–A or T78P–1225–B or equivalent. Install the new bearing cups by pressing them into the retainer with pinion bearing cup replacer T71P–4616–A or eqivalent.
12. After the new cups have been installed, make sure that they are seated in the retainer by trying to insert a 0.0015 in. feeler gauge between the cup and the bottom of the bore. Whenever the cups are replaced, the cone and roller assemblies should also be replaced.

Drive Pinion and Ring Gear Set Assembly

NOTE: When replacing a ring gear and a drive pinion

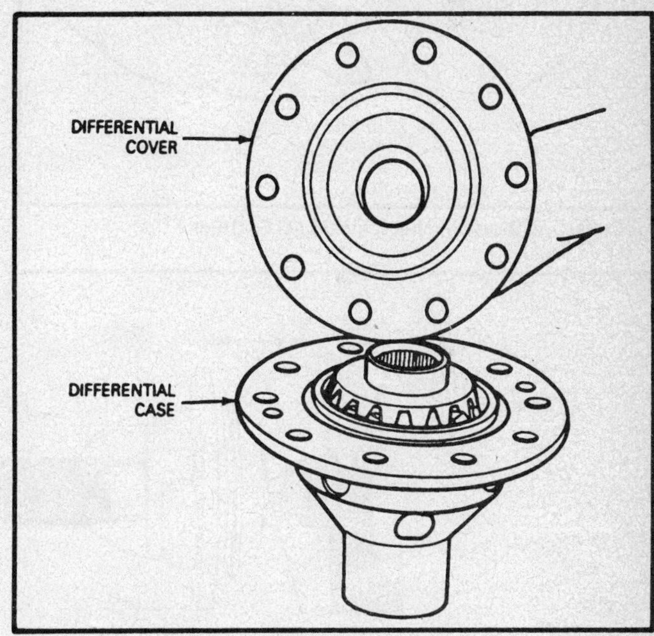

Removing the differential cover (© Ford Motor Co.)

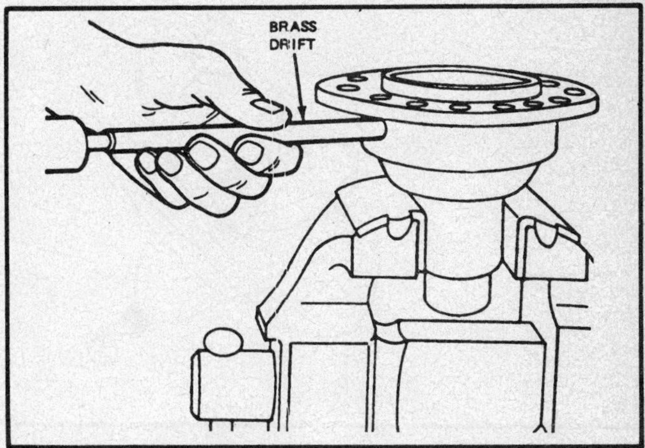

Removing the long differential pinion shaft (© Ford Motor Co.)

or pinion bearings, select the proper pinion shim thickness by using the following procedure and tool T79P–4020–A or equivalent.

1. Select the proper rear pinion bearing aligning adapter and gauge disc to correspond to the axle size (nine in. ring gear). Slide these adapters over the screw or threaded shaft and install the gauge block on the threaded shaft and tighten it securely.

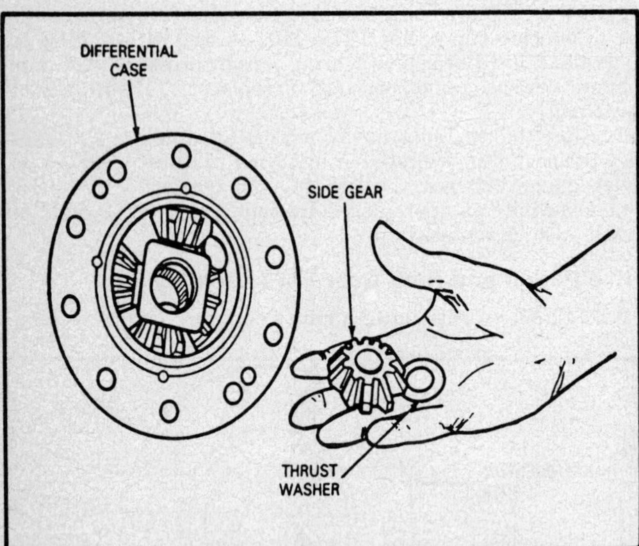

Side gear and thrust washer removal (© Ford Motor Co.)

2. Place this assembly, along with the rear drive pinion bearing, into the pinion bearing retainer assembly. Install the front pinion bearing (new or used, if in good condition) and screw the handle onto the threaded shaft, with the tapered end into the front pinion bearing.

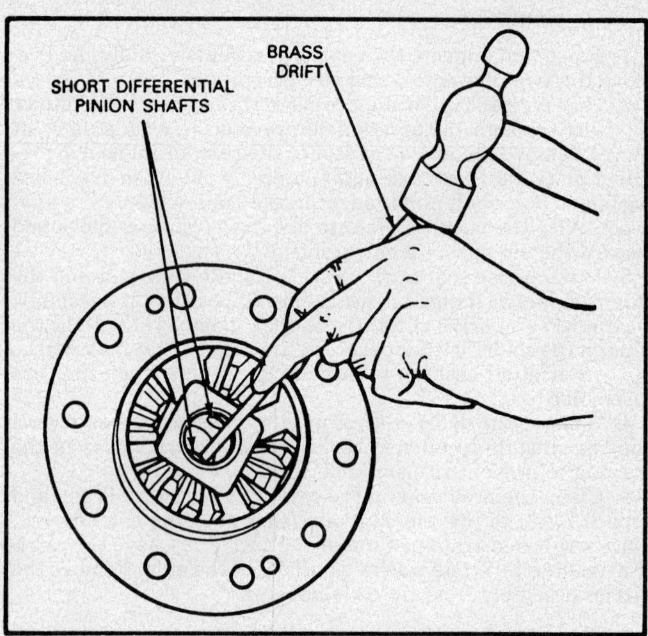

Removing the short differential pinion shaft (© Ford Motor Co.)

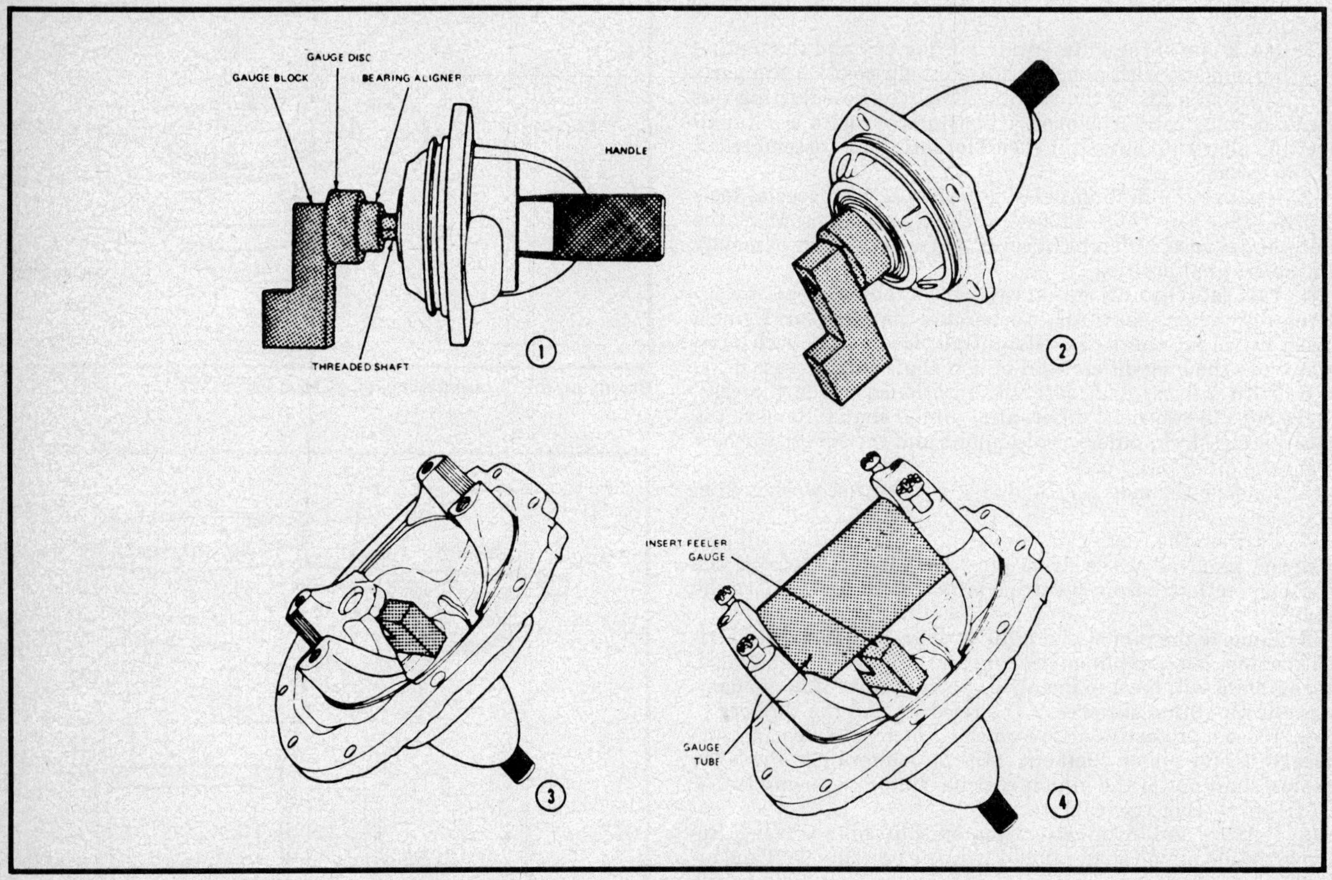

Proper use of the pinion depth gauge tool (© Ford Motor Co.)

3. The flat end of the handle has a $^3/_8$ in. square hole broached in it. This is designed so that an inch pound torque wrench may be used to obtain the proper pinion bearing preload.

4. Install the pinion bearing retainer assembly into the carrier (without a pinion shim) and tighten the attaching bolts to 30 to 45 ft. lbs. Rotate the gauge block so that it rests against the pilot boss.

5. Place the differential gauge tube into the differential bearing bore and tighten the bearing caps to the specified torque. Using a feeler gauge, gauge the space between the differential bearing gauge block and gauge tube. Insert a feeler blade directly along the gauge block top to insure a correct reading. The fit should be a slight drag-type feeling.

6. After a correct feeler gauge is obtained, use the conversion chart provided to find the correct shim thickness needed according to the feeler gauge reading.

7. After determining the correct shim thickness as just outlined in this procedure, assemble the pinion bearing retainer as follows.

NOTE: A new ring gear and drive pinion should always be installed in an axle as a matched set, never separately. Be sure the same matching number appears on the ring gear and on the head of the drive pinion.

8. Install the pinion retainer attaching bolts and torque them to 30 to 45 ft. lbs. . Install the oil slinger, if so equipped.

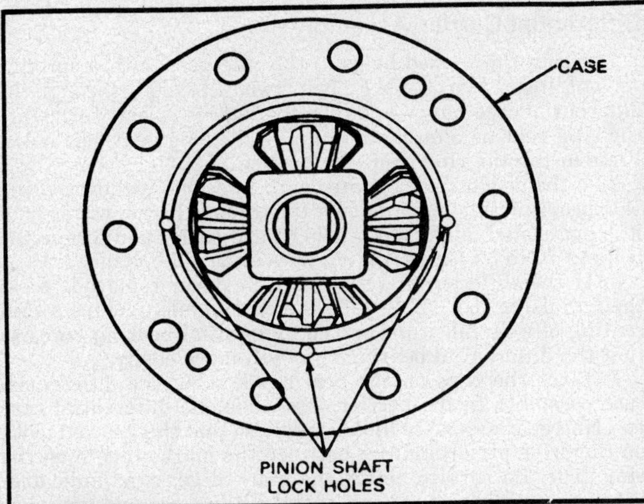

Location of the pinion shaft lock holes

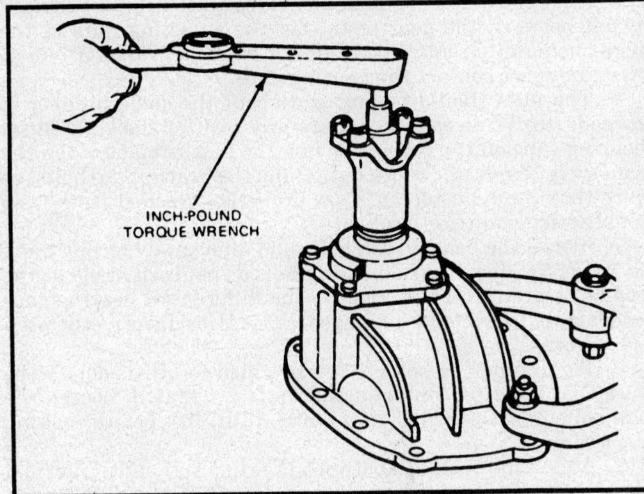

Checking the preload on the pinion bearing (© Ford Motor Co.)

FEELER GAUGE TO SHIM CONVERSION CHART

Feeler Gauge Reading in.	(mm)	Shim Required in.	(mm)
.002	.051	.038	.965
.003	.076	.037	.940
.004	.102	.036	.914
.005	.127	.035	.889
.006	.152	.034	.864
.007	.178	.033	.838
.008	.203	.032	.813
.009	.229	.031	.787
.010	.254	.030	.0762
.011	.279	.029	.737
.012	.305	.028	.711
.013	.330	.027	.686
.014	.356	.026	.660
.015	.381	.025	.635
.016	.406	.024	.610
.017	.432	.023	.584
.018	.457	.022	.559
.019	.483	.021	.533
.020	.508	.020	.508
.021	.533	.019	.483
.022	.559	.018	.451
.023	.584	.017	.432
.024	.610	.016	.406
.025	.635	.015	.381
.026	.660	.014	.356
.027	.686	.013	.330
.028	.711	.012	.305
.029	.737	.011	.279
.030	.762	.010	.254
.031	.787	.009	.229
.032	.813	.008	.208
.033	.838	.007	.178
.034	.864	.006	.152
.035	.889	.005	.127

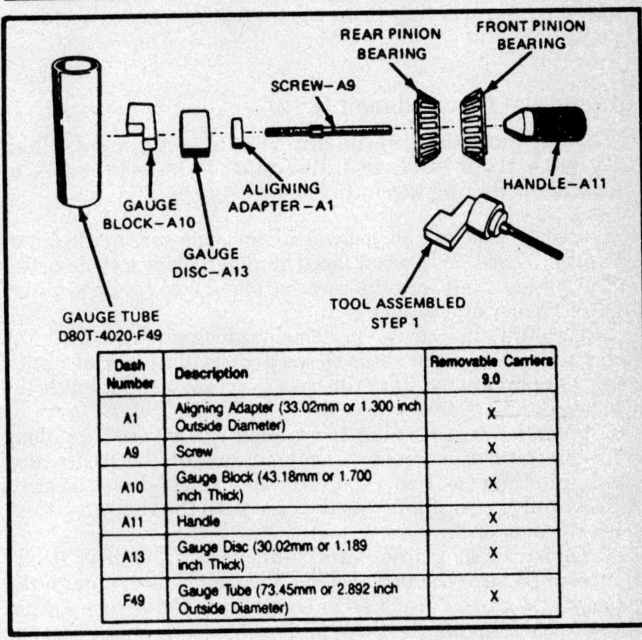

Dash Number	Description	Removable Carriers 9.0
A1	Aligning Adapter (33.02mm or 1.300 inch Outside Diameter)	X
A9	Screw	X
A10	Gauge Block (43.18mm or 1.700 inch Thick)	X
A11	Handle	X
A13	Gauge Disc (30.02mm or 1.189 inch Thick)	X
F49	Gauge Tube (73.45mm or 2.892 inch Outside Diameter)	X

Typical rear axle pinion depth gauge tool (© Ford Motor Co.)

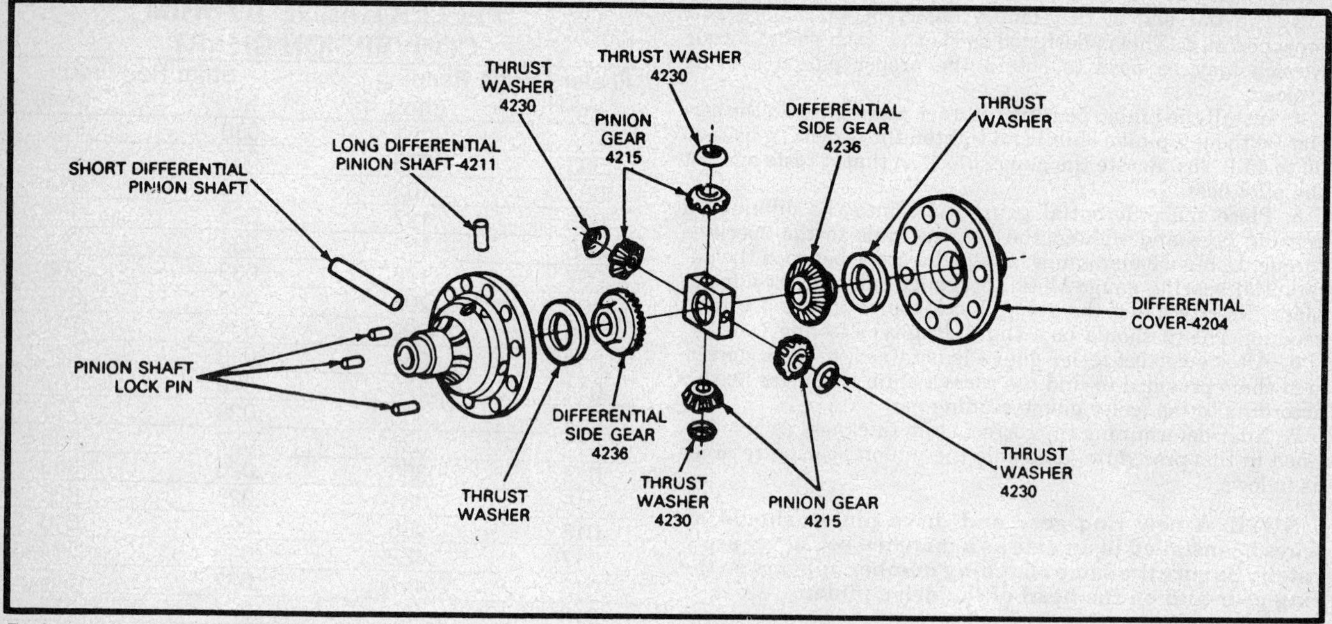

Exploded view of the differential case (© Ford Motor Co.)

9. Install a new pinion oil seal in the bearing retainer,install the companion flange. Start a new pinion nut on the drive pinion shaft and apply a small amount of thread lubricant to the flange side of the nut.

10. Hold the flange with tool T57T–4851–B and tighten the pinion nut. Do not use impact tools. Check the pinion bearing preload, the correct preload will be obtained when the torque required to rotate the pinion in the retainer is as specified in the specifications.

11. If the torque required to rotate the pinion is less than specified, tighten the pinion shaft nut a little at a time until the proper preload is established.

NOTE: Do not over-tighten the pinion nut. If excessive preload is obtained as a result of over tightening, replace the collapsible bearing spacer. Do not back off the pinion shaft nut to establish pinion bearing preload.

Differential Case Assembly

NOTE: Lubricate all the differential components liberally with Hypoid Gear Lubricant, EOAZ–19580–A or equivalent during assembly.

1. Place a side gear thrust washer and side gear in the differential case bore. With a soft faced hammer, drive a short differential pinion shaft into the case far enough to retain a pinion thrust washer and pinion gear.

2. Carefully line up the pinion shaft lock pin holes with the holes provided in the case. Drive a short differential pinion shaft only far enough into the case to retain the pinion thrust washer pinion gear.

3. Install the remaining two pinion thrust washers along with the pinion gears into the case. Install the positioning block into the case. Use a soft face hammer, to drive the short differential pinion shafts into the case until the shafts are flush with the side of the case.

4. Insert the long differential pinion shaft and drive it into the case. Be sure the pinion shaft lock holes line up with the holes in the case. Place a second side gear and thrust washer into position. Install the three pinion shaft lock pins. Press the differential cover on the case.

Differential Carrier Assembly

1. Clean the tapped holes in the ring gear with a suitable solvent. Insert two $^{7}/_{16}$ (N.F.) bolts two inches long through the differential case flange and turn them three or four turns into the ring gear as a quide in aligning the ring gear bolt holes. Press or tap the ring gear into position.

2. If the new bolts are coated with a green or yellow coating of approxitmately $^{1}/_{2}$ in. or over the threaded area, use as is. If it is not coated, apply a suitable thread sealer and torque the bolts to 70 to 85 ft. lbs. Do not re-use the old bolts.

3. If the differential bearings have been removed, press them in using tool T57L–4221–A2 or equivalent. Wipe a thin coating of axle lubricant on the differential bearing bores so that the differential bearing cups will move easily.

4. Place the cups on the bearings and set the differential case assembly in the carrier. Assemble the differential case and ring gear assembly in the carrier so that the marked tooth on the drive pinion indexes between the marked teeth on the ring gear. Be sure to match the marked gears as indicated. When assembled out of time, the result is noise and improper mating.

5. Slide the assembly along the bores until a slight backlash is felt between the gear teeth. Set the adjusting nuts in the bores using differential bearing nut wrench T70P–4067–A so that they just contact the bearing cups.

6. The nuts should be engaged about the same number of threads (turns) on each side. Carefully position the differential bearing caps on the carrier. Match the marks made when the caps were removed. Before tightening the bearing cap bolts, be sure that the adjuster nuts are properly threaded in the cap and carrier and turn freely.

7. Install the bearing cap bolts and alternately torque them to 70 to 85 ft. lbs. If the adjusting nuts do not turn freely as the cap bolts are tightened, remove the differential bearing caps and again inspect for damaged threads or incorrectly positioned caps.

8. Tightening the bolts to the specified torque is done to be sure that the cups and adjusting nuts are seated. Loosen the cap bolts and tighten them to only 25 ft. lbs. before making adjustments.

9. Adjust the backlash between the ring gear and pinion and the differential bearing preload as described in the following section.

Backlash and Differential Bearing Preload Adjustment

1. Remove the adjusting nut locks, loosen the differential bearing cap bolts, then torque the bolts to 15 to 20 ft. lbs. before making adjustments.

2. The left adjusting nut is on the ring gear side of the carrier. The right nut is on the pinion side. Loosen the right nut until it is away from the cup. Tighten the let nut until the ring gear is just forced into the pinion with 0.000 backlash, then rotate the pinion several revolutions to be sure there is no binding. Recheck the right nut at this time to make sure that it is still loose.

3. Install a suitable dial indicator. Tighten the right nut until it first contacts the bearing cups. Set the dial indicator to zero and apply pressure to the bearing by tightening the right nut until the indicator reading shows 0.008 to 0.012 in. case spread.

4. Turn the pinion gear several times in each direction to seat the bearings in the cups and be sure no bind is evident (this step is important). Tighten the bearing cap bolts to 70 to 85 ft. lbs.

5. Measure the backlash on several teeth around the ring gear. If the backlash is out of specification, loosen one adjusting nut and tighten the opposite nut an equal amount, to move the ring gear away from or toward the pinion.

6. Tightening the left nut moves the ring gear into the pinion to decrease the backlash and tightening the right nut moves the ring gear away.

NOTE: When moving the adjusting nuts, the final movement should always be made in a tightening direction. An example of this is, if the left nut had to be loosened one notch, loosen the nut two turns and tighten it one. This insures that the nut is contacting the bearing cup and that the cup can not shift after being put in service. After all such adjustments, check to be sure that the case spread remains as specified for the new or original bearings used.

7. Use a white marking compound to obtain a tooth mesh contact pattern in the assembly. Pattern contact should be within the primary area of the ring gear tooth surface avoiding any narrow or hard contact with the outer perimeter of tooth (top to root, toe to heel).

8. The pattern inspection should be on the drive (pull) side. The correct assembly of the drive pattern will result in a satisfactory coast performance. If gross pattern error is detected with preferred backlash of 0.012 to 0,015 in. recheck the pinion shim selection.

Carrier Installation

NOTE: Any synthetic type wheel bearing seals must not be cleaned, soaked or washed in cleaning solvent. Clean the axle housing and shafts with kerosene and swabs. Do not allow any quantity of solvent to touch the wheel bearings. Clean the mating surfaces of the axle housing and carrier.

1. Position the differential carrier on the studs in the axle housing using a new gasket between the carrier and the housing. Apply a bead of Silicone rubber sealant or equivalent to the gasket. Install the carrier to housing attaching nuts and washers. Torque them to 25 to 40 ft. lbs.

2. Remove the oil seal replacer tool from the transmission extension housing. Position the the drive shaft so that the front U-joint slip yoke splines to the transmission output shaft.

3. Connect the drive shaft to the axle U-joint flange, aligning the scribe marks made on the drive shaft end yoke and the axle U-joint flange during the removal procedure. Install the U-bolts and nuts, tighten the nuts on the U-bolts evenly.

4. Install the two axle shaft assemblies in the axle housing. Be careful not to damage the oil seals. Slowly slide the axle shaft into the housing (Timken bearing axle shafts do not require a gasket). Start the axle splines into the differential side gear and push the shaft until the bearing bottoms in the housing.

5. Install the bearing retainer plates on the attaching bolts on the axle housing flange. Install the nuts on the bolts and alternately torque them to 20 to 40 ft. lbs.

6. Install the two rear brake drums. Install the rear wheel and tire assemblies. If the rear brakes were backed off, readjust them accordingly.

7. Fill the rear axle with 5.5 pints of hypoid gear lubricant EOAZ–19580–A or equivalent. Road test the vehicle and check the rear axle assembly for proper operation.

Identification Tag	Ratio	Ring Gear Dia. (Inches)	Diff. Type	Identification Tag	Ratio	Ring Gear Dia. (Inches)	Diff. Type
320C	3.50:1	9	C4	717P	3.50:1	9	T4
318D	3.50:1	9	C2	705B	3.00:1	9	T4
316D	3.00:1	9	C4	715A	3.50:1	9	T4
319D	3.50:1	9	T2	716P	3.50:1	9	C4
321C	4.11:1	9	T4	714A	3.50:1	9	C4
317D	3.00:1	9	T4	704B	3.00:1	9	C4
Type C4 — Conventional 4-Pinion				Type C2 — Conventional 2-Pinion			
Type T4 — Limited-Slip 4-Pinion							

Rear axle ratios gear and code identifications (© Ford Motor Co.)

Description	mm	Inch	Description	mm	Inch
Backlash Between Ring Gear and Pinion	0.203-0.381	0.008-0.015	Nominal Locating Shim (Continued) Removable Carrier	0.381	0.015
Maximum Backlash Variation Between Teeth	0.102	0.004			
Maximum Runout of Backface of Ring Gear	0.102	0.004	Shims Available (Steps of 0.001) Removable Carrier	0.254-0.736	0.010-0.029
Differential Side Gear Thrust Washer Thickness	0.762-0.812	0.030-0.032	Differential Bearing Preload Used	0.127-0.177	0.005-0.007
Differential Pinion Gear Thrust Washer Thickness	0.762-0.838	0.030-0.033	New	0.203-0.304	0.008-0.012

Rear axle adjustment (© Ford Motor Co.)

Description	ft-lbs	in-lbs	N·m
Pinion Retainer to Carrier Bolts	30-45		41-60
Ring Gear Attaching Bolts	70-85		95-115
Bearing Cap Bolts	70-85		95-115
Carrier to Housing Nuts	25-40		34-54
Adjusting Nut Lock Bolts	12-25		17-33
Axle Shaft Bearing Retainer Nut	20-40		28-54
Pinion Bearing Preload — Original Bearing		8-14	1.0-1.5
Pinion Bearing Preload — New Bearing		16-29	1.8-3.3

Rear axle torque specifications (© Ford Motor Co.)

Rockwell–Standard Single–Speed, Single Reduction

This rear axle is a full floating type with a hypoid drive gear and pinion, and uses a four-pinion differential assembly. The straddle mounted pinion has two tapered roller bearings in front of the pinion teeth and a straight roller bearing behind the pinion teeth. The differential carrier assembly can be removed while the axle remains in the truck.

DIFFERENTIAL CARRIER ASSEMBLY

Removal

1. Remove axle shafts.
2. Drain lubricant. Disconnect propeller shaft at pinion shaft yoke.
3. Remove carrier from axle housing and clean thoroughly.

Disassembly

1. Punch mark carrier leg, bearing cap, and bearing adjusting nut to assist in reassembly.
2. Remove screws, adjusting nut locks, bearing caps and adjusting nuts.
3. Loose lock nut and back off drive gear thrust block adjusting screw.
4. Lift differential out of carrier and remove thrust block from end of adjusting screw inside of carrier.
5. Punch mark differential case halves for correct reassembly alignment and separate case halves.
6. Remove pinion shaft, pinions, side gears, thrust washers and differential bearing cones.
7. To remove drive gear, carefully center punch each rivet to center of rivet head. Use a drill $^{1}/_{22}$ in. smaller than the body of rivet to drill through the rivet head. Press out rivets.
8. Remove pinion shaft nut, washer and yoke. Driving yoke off will cause runout.
9. Remove pinion bearing cover and oil seal assembly and, using puller screws, remove bearing cage. Using a pin. bar to remove cage will damage shims. Driving pinion from inner end with a drift will damage bearing lock ring groove.
10. Wire bearing cage shim pack together to facilitate adjustment when reassembling.
11. Tap pinion shaft out of cage with soft mallet or press shaft from cage. Remove bearing from cage.
12. Remove spacers and inner bearing from shaft.
13. Remove pinion shaft rear pilot bearing lock ring, and then bearing.
14. Remove oil seal assembly from bearing cover.
15. Clean all parts thoroughly in a suitable solvent and blow dry with compressed air. Do not spin bearings with air pressure as they might score due to absence of any lubrication.

Assembly

Inspect all parts for wear or roughness and replace if necessary. (For details, see Cleaning and Inspection in General Axle Service section).

1. Press drive pinion inner bearing cone firmly against pinion shoulder.
2. Press rear pilot bearings firmly against pinion shoulder and install lock ring into pinion shaft groove.
3. Press bearing cups firmly against bearing cage shoulders.
4. Lubricate pinion bearing with SAE 90 oil and insert pinion and bearing assembly into pinion cage.
5. Place original spacers on pinion shaft, and install front bearing and press firmly against spacers. Rotate cage several revolutions to assure normal bearing contact. If a press is not available, install pinion yoke and nut and torque to specifications.
6. While the assembly is in the press under pressure or pinion nut torques to specifications, check pinion bearing preload. The correct pressure and torque for checking pre-load are:
7. Wrap a soft wire around cage and pull on horizontal line with pound scale when determining pinion bearing pre-load, first measure diameter of the pinion cage. Assuming cage diameter is 6 in., the pulling radius would be 3 in.; therefore, 5 pounds pull on the scale would equal 15 inch lbs. pre-load.
8. Use rotating torque, not starting torque. If rotating torque is not within 5 to 15 inch lbs., use thinner spacer to increase pre-load or thicker spacer to decrease pre-load. Torque must be near low limit inch lbs. with original pinion bearings and near high limit when using new bearings. Remove yoke and install new oil seal.
9. Lubricate pinion shaft oil seal and lightly coat outer edge of seal body with non-hardening sealing compound. Press seal against cover shoulder. Install new gasket and bearing cover.
10. Install pinion yoke, washer and nut. Place pinion and cage assembly over carrier studs, hold yoke and tighten nut to specified torque. Install cotter key without backing off nut to align cotter key holes.
11. Place original shim pack on carrier studs with thin shims on both sides to create maximum sealing. Position pinion and cage assembly over studs and tap into position with soft mallet. Install lock washers and nuts. Tighten nuts to specified torque. If a new pinion is being installed, consult the General Axle Service section for correct procedure.
12. Rivet drive gear to differential case using new rivets. Rivets should not be heated, but always upset cold. When correct rivet is used, head being formed will be at least $^{1}/_{8}$ in. larger in diameter than rivet hole and approximately the same height as performed head. Avoid excessive pressure as it might distort

case holes and cause gear eccentricity. Unless shops are equipped to do cold upsetting of rivets properly, replacement bolts should be used.

13. Lubricate differential case inner walls and all component parts with rear axle gear lubricant during assembly.

14. Install thrust washer and side gear in drive gear half of case. Assemble pinions and thrust washers on pinion shaft and position this assembly in the case. Place other side gear and thrust washer in position on the four pinions.

15. Install other case half with mating marks aligned. Draw case down evenly with four bolts. Check for free rotation of differential gears and correct if necessary. Install and torque remaining bolts and then lock wire.

16. Press differential bearings squarely and firmly on differential case halves. Differential bearing cup fit in the pedestal bores should be checked before installing assembly in carrier.

17. Temporarily install bearing cups, threaded adjusting nuts or split ring and bearing caps. Tighten cap bolts to specified torque. Bearing cups must be out of hand push fit in the bores; if not, the bores must be enlarged with a scraper or emery cloth. Use a blued bearing cup as a gauge to check each fit.

18. Lubricate differential bearings and cups with axle lubricant. Place cups over bearings and position assembly in carrier housing. Turn adjusting nuts hand tight against bearing cups.

19. Install bearing caps in correct location as marked, and tap lightly into position. Be sure caps fit over adjusting nuts properly and are not cross-threaded. Some backlash must be present between drive gear and pinion. Install and torque bearing cap bolts.

20. Attach a dial indicator to the carrier with the pointer resting against back face of drive gear. Eliminate all end play by turning right adjusting nut clockwise. Rotate drive gear and check runout. If runout exceeds 0.008 in., remove differential and check the cause.

21. Tighten adjusting nuts, one notch each, to pre-load differential bearings.

Pinion Shaft Thread Size and Number of Threads Per Inch	Required Pressure to Obtain Correct Pre-Load lbs.	Required Torque to Obtain Correct Pre-Load ft. lbs.
1 in. × 20	12,000	300–400
1¼ in. × 18	22,000	700–900
1½ in. × 12	28,000	800–1100
1½ in. × 18	28,000	800–1100
1¾ in. × 12	28,000	800–1100

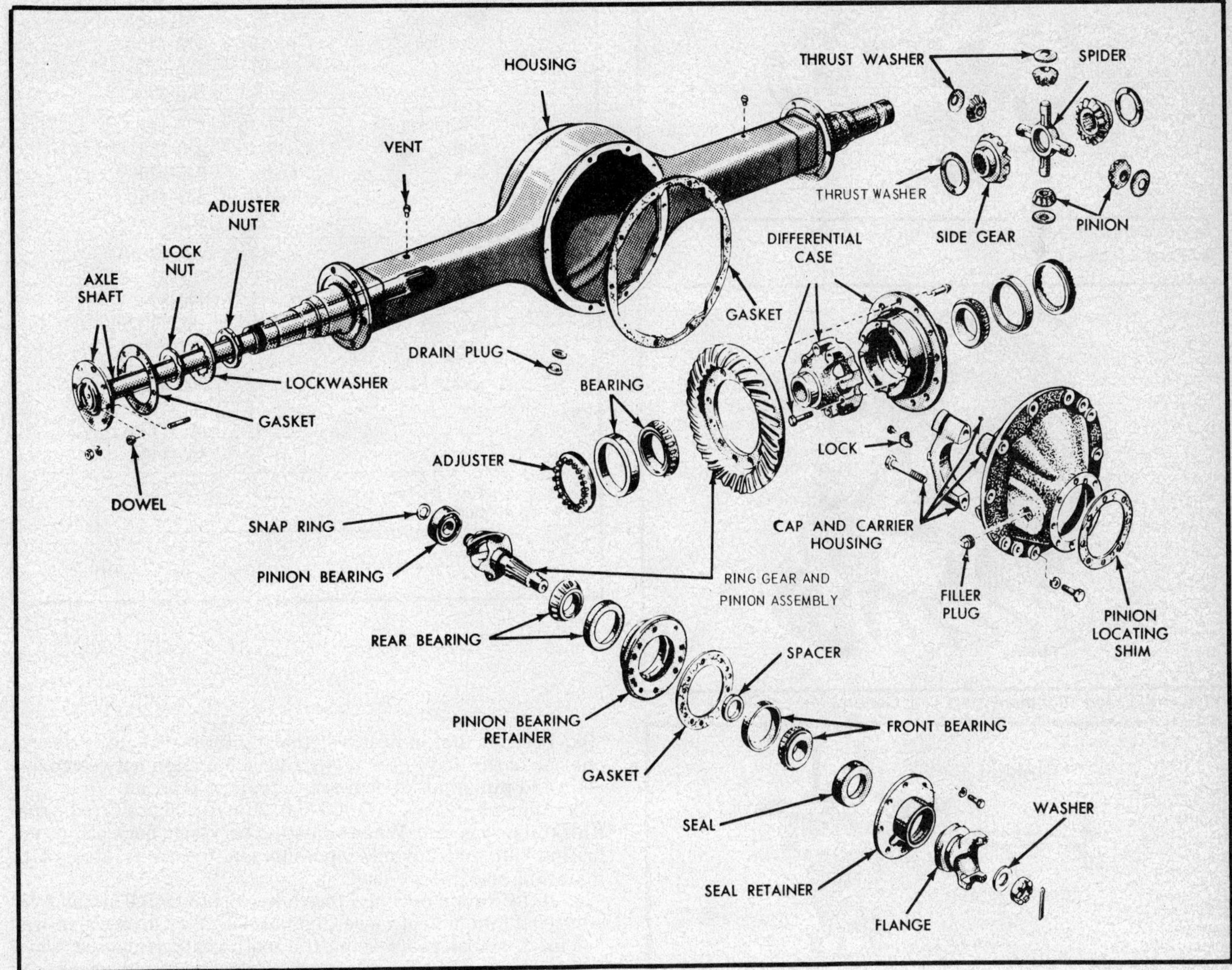

Single-speed, single reduction rear axle (© Ford Motor Co.)

ROCKWELL–STANDARD BEARING PRELOAD

Axle Model	Pinion Shaft Nut–Thread Size and Torque Limits (ft. lbs.)		Press Ram Pressure for Preload Check (Tons)	Pinion and Cross Shaft Bearing Preload (in. lbs.)	Backlash Limits (in.)	Differential Bearing Preload Adjusting Nut Notches Tighten from Zero End Play (each Adjusting Nut)
Single–speed	1–20	300–400	6	5–15	0.005–0.015	1
Single reduction	1¼ × 18	700–900	11	5–15	0.005–0.015	1
	1¼ × 18	800–1100	14	5–15	0.005–0.015	1
	1½ × 12	800–1100	14	5–15	0.005–0.015	1
	1½ × 18	800–1100	14	5–15	0.005–0.015	1

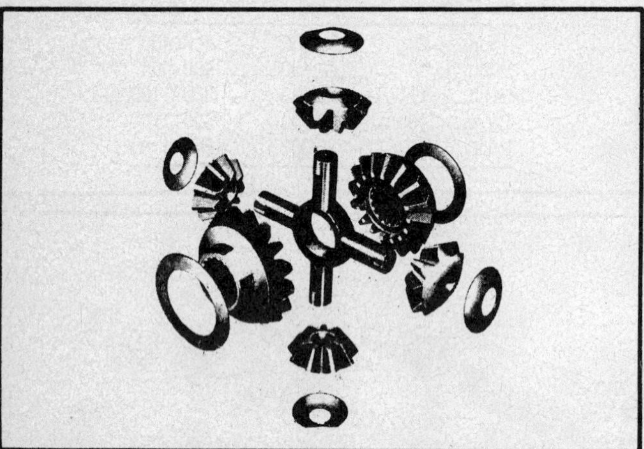
Exploded view of side gear and pinion assembly (© General Motors Corp.)

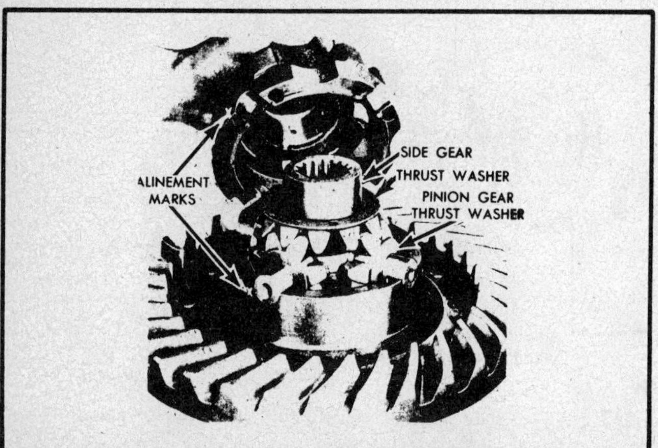

Differential case alignment marks (© General Motors Corp.)

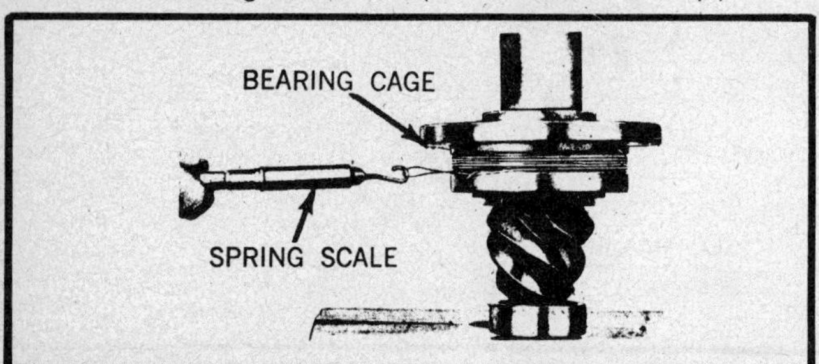

Checking pinion bearing pre-load (© General Motors Corp.)

TORQUE SPECIFICATIONS

Carrier to housing screw or stud nut	½–20	94–102
	⅝–18	186–205
	¾–16	325–360
Differential case bolt	½–20	94–102
	9/16–18	132–145
	⅝–18	186–205
	¾–16	325–360
Differential bearing cap bolt	⅝–11–18	127–140
	¾–10–16	230–250
	⅞–9	345–370
	⅞–14	375–415
	1–12	555–615
Differential bearing adjuster lock bolt	5/16–18	15–17
	½–13	85–91
	9/16–12	120–129
	⅝–11	168–180
Pinion shaft yoke nut	1–20	300–400
	1–¼–18	700–900
	1–½–18	800–1100
	1–½–12	800–1100
	1–¾–12	800–1100
Shaft flange stud	7/16–20	52–58

22. Position dial indicator so the pointer rests against face of one one of the drive gear teeth. Check backlash between drive gear and pinion at 90 degree intervals of rotation.

23. Adjust backlash to 0.006–0.012 in. (0.006 preferred, especially on new gears). When adjusting backlash, back off one adjusting nut and advance opposite nut the same amount to maintain bearing pre-load.

24. If the Pinion Setting Procedures (depth gauge method) for adjusting pinion depth (see General Axle Service section) was not used, adjust gears using the tooth contact method. Then proceed to Step 25. If depth gauge method was used, go directly to Step 25.

25. Torque bearing cap bolts and install and torque adjusting nut locks and cap screws and lock wire.

26. Hold drive gear thrust block on rear face of gear with heavy grease, rotate gear until hole in thrust block aligns with adjusting screw hole in carrier. Install adjusting screw and lock nut, tighten screw enough to locate thrust block firmly against back face of gear. Back off adjusting screw $^1/_4$ turn to create 0.010–0.015 in. clearance and lock securely with nut. Recheck to assure minimum clearance of 0.010 in. during full rotation of drive gear.

Installation

1. Install a new gasket on the axle housing flange. Start carrier into clean housing and hold in place with four equally spaced washers and nuts. Tighten nuts alternately to draw carrier evenly into housing. Install and torque carrier flange lock washers and nuts.
2. Install axle drive shafts and connect universal joint at pinion flange.
3. Fill axle housing to proper level and road test vehicle.

Rockwell–Standard Single–Speed Double Reduction Axles

This axle includes a hypoid helical drive and a two-step gear reduction. The first reduction is through the hypoid pinion and ring gears with the second reduction through the helical gears. The helical pinion gear engages with the helical drive gear. The axle housings are one-piece with full-floating axle shafts.

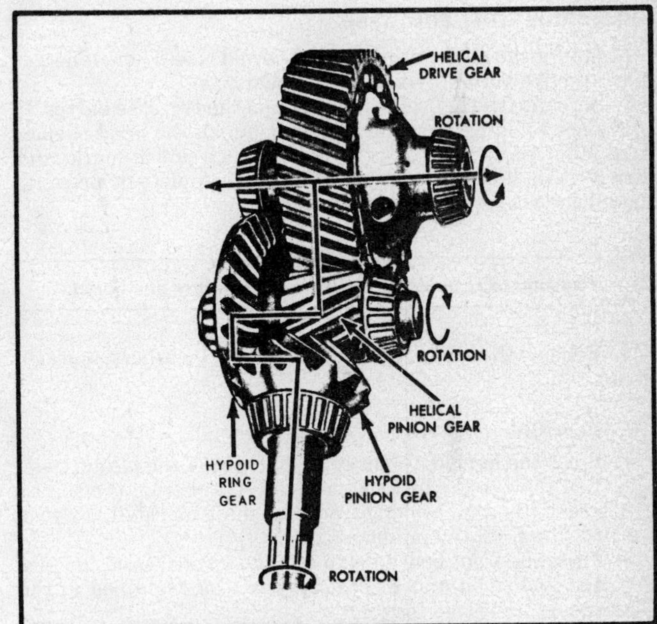

Single-speed double reduction power flow
(© Rockwell International)

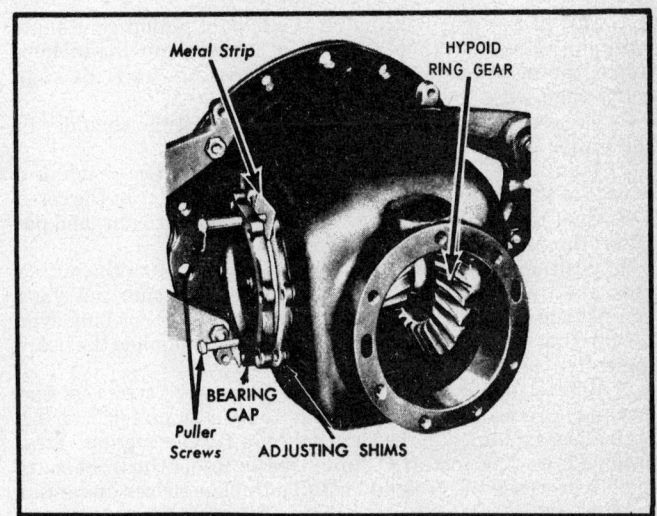

DISASSEMBLY OF REAR AXLE

Differential Carrier

1. Before disassembling, inspect the unit as described in the Cleaning and Inspection paragraph of the General Axle Service section.
2. Punch-mark one differential bearing cap and the corresponding carrier leg. This will be an aid to proper reassembly.
3. Remove the locking wires and bolts from both bearing caps and adjusters and wire together.
5. Lift the differential out of the carrier.
6. Remove the U-joint flange nut and then remove flange with a rawhide mallet. If this is unsuccessful, the flange can be pressed off when the hypoid pinion cage is being disassembled.
7. Using two 3x38x16 puller screws, remove the cage and pinion gear from the carrier.
8. Remove the pinion adjusting shims from the carrier and re-use if the same hypoid gear set is to be used again when the carrier is assembled.
9. Place a wooden block under the helical pinion gear to support the cross shaft. Then remove the bolts from the cross shaft bearing cap mounted on the differential carrier, opposite the hypoid ring gear.
10. Force the bearing cap out of the carrier about $^1/_4$ in. by prying the hypoid ring gear away from the side of the carrier.
11. Place metal strips under both puller screw holes in the bearing cap and, using puller screws, hold them in place against the adjusting shims. do not tighten the screws directly onto the adjusting shims.
12. Tighten the puller screws evenly against the metal strips, and remove the bearing cap and the adjusting shims from the carrier.
13. Carefully remove the hypoid ring gear and cross shaft from the carrier.
14. Replace either cross shaft bearing cup if necessary. Remove the damaged or worn cup from the bearing cap with a suitable puller. To operate the cup in the bearing cap, tap the cap out of the carrier about $^1/_4$ in. with a soft drive and remove from the carrier.

Cross Shaft

1. Remove the locking wire, two screws, and the bearing retaining plate from the hypoid ring gear end of the cross shaft.
2. Press the cross shaft out of the ring gear and the bearing next to the gear. Remove the woodruff key that holds the gear on the shaft.

Removing the cross shaft bearing cap and positioning metal strips (© Rockwell International)

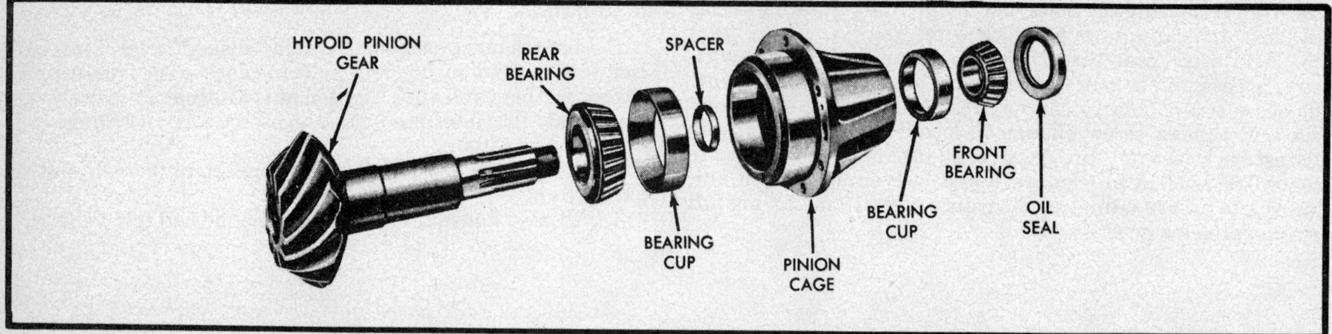

Exploded view of hypoid gear and gage (© Rockwell International)

3. Press the remaining bearing from the cross shaft.

Differential Gear and Case

1. Mount the differential in a soft-jawed vise. Then, if necessary, remove both differential side bearings.

3. Separate the helical drive gear and the two case halves. If rivets are binding these parts, center punch the head of each rivet followed by a $^1/_8$ in. pilot hole at each punch-mark, and then a $^1/_2$ in. hole drilled $^1/_2$ in. deep and complete by pressing out all the rivets with a $^1/_2$ in. punch.

CAUTION

Do not attempt to remove the rivets with a hammer and chisel.

4. Remove the spider, pinion gears, thrust washers, and side gears.

Pinion Cage

1. Press the hypoid pinion gear shaft out of the pinion cage, and then remove the bearing pre-load spacer from the shaft.
2. Press the rear bearing from the shaft and pull the rear bearing cup from the pinion cage.
3. Press the front bearing cup and the oil seal from the pinion cage and clean and inspect all parts as explained in the General Axle Service section

ASSEMBLY OF REAR AXLE

Pinion Cage

1. Install the rear bearing on the hypoid pinion gear shaft against the gear shoulder. Use a 3 in. sleeve about one in. long under the bearing race so that the press ram won't damage roller cage.
2. Press the rear bearing cup firmly against the shoulder in the pinion cage.
3. Install the front bearing cup in the pinion cage making sure that the cup seats firmly against the shoulder in the cage.
4. Coat the pinion rear bearing with axle lubricant, and position the pinion gear in the cage.
5. Position the original bearing preload spacer on the pinion gear shaft and press the pinion front bearing onto the shaft against the spacer. Use a 3 in. sleeve about 5 inches long over the bearing race so that the press ram doesn't damage the bearing roller cage.
6. Rotate the pinion cage several times to be sure that the bearings are properly seated. Then check the pinion bearing preload as explained in the General Axle Service section. If the preload is too low, install a thinner spacer under the front bearing. To decrease the preload, install a thicker spacer under the bearing.
7. When the preload is correct, install the oil seal in the pinion cage.

Differential Gear and Case

1. Check the mating surfaces of the differential case halves and the helical drive gear to be sure they are clean and free of burrs. Then coat all differential parts and the inner walls of the case, with axle lubricant.
2. Install the differential side bearings, making sure they are properly seated. Use a 3 $^1/_4$ in. sleeve about one in. long over the bearing race so that the force of the press ram doesn't damage the bearing roller cage.
3. Position a thrust washer and a side gear in one of the differential case halves. Then place the spider, the pinion gears, and their thrust washers in position. Install the remaining side gear and thrust washer in the case.
4. Position the helical drive gear and install the other case half, aligning the marks on both halves.
5. Install 6 bolts in alternate holes around the case on the side of the gear having the smaller offset. Tighten the bolts and nuts enough to draw the gear and both case halves together. Then check the rotation of the side gears and pinion gears.
6. Install the remaining 6 bolts and nuts, and torque them evenly to specifications and lock wire.

Cross Shaft

1. Place the Woodruff key (tapered end toward pinion gear) in the cross shaft. then press the hypoid ring gear on the shaft, seating it against the shaft shoulder.
2. Carefully press the shaft into the bearing, seating the bearing against the shoulder.
3. Install the remaining bearing on the other end of the shaft. Use a 3 in. sleeve about one in. long over the bearing race so that the press ram won't damage the bearing roller cage.
4. Install the bearing retaining plate and torque and wire the screws.
5. Press the cross shaft bearing cups into the bearing caps. Be sure that the cups are properly seated against the shoulders in the cap bores.

Differential Carrier

1. Coat all parts with axle lubricant before assembly.
2. Position the original shims pack on the right cross shaft bearing cap and install and torque the cap on the differential carrier.
3. Install the cross shaft in the carrier so that the end of the shaft opposite the hypoid ring gear enters the bore at the left baring cap. The right bearing should enter and seat in its bearing cap. Place a wooden block under the helical pinion gear to support the cross shaft.
4. Position the original sham pack on the left cross shaft bearing cap and install and torque the cap on the differential carrier.
5. Rotate the cross shaft to test for normal bearing contact. Then check the cross shaft bearing preload.

NOTE: Do not read the pull required to start the cross

shaft rotating. Read only the steady rotating pull on the scale. To change the scale reading into in. lbs. torque, multiply the scale reading by one-half the diameter of the helical pinion gear at the point where the cord is wound around the gear.

6. If the bearing preload torque is not within 5–15 in. lbs., add shims to decrease the preload, or remove shims to increase the preload.

NOTE: To prevent changing the hypoid ring gear backlash setting, change shims only at the bearing cap opposite the ring gear.

7. Install the pinion cage-filler hole at top. Install and torque the bolts and lock washers. Use the original shim pack between the pinion cage and the differential carrier if the original hypoid gears (ring gear and pinion set) are used. If new hypoid gears are installed, follow the shim selection procedure in the General Axle Service section.
8. Install the U-joint flange, torque the nut and install cotter pin.
9. The backlash can be adjusted by transferring shims from one cross shaft bearing cap to the other. To move the hypoid ring gear away fro the hypoid pinion gear, transfer shims from the right cap to the left cap. To move the ring gear closer to the pinion gear, transfer shims from left to right. For each 0.010 in. movement of the ring gear, the backlash changes about 0.008 in. Adjust backlash to 0.010 in. and check the gear tooth contact pattern. After obtaining a good pattern to 0.020–0.026 in. regardless of the backlash marking on the ring gear.
10. Check the fit of the differential side bearing cups and the bearing adjusters in the bearing caps. The adjusters should thread freely into the caps, and they should move the bearing cups in to the bores with the cap bolts tightened to normal torque.
11. If the cups do not move when the adjusters are hand tightened, remove the caps and clean the bearing surfaces.
12. Position a bearing cup on each differential side bearing. then place the differential on the carrier so that the bearing cups rest in the carrier legs centering the drive gear on the helical pinion gear.
13. Place the bearing adjusters on the threads in the carrier legs, and position the bearing caps on the carrier leg with the matching marks aligned. Check to see that the threads in the caps and legs are matched, if so, install and torque the cap bolts.

Checking the cross shaft bearing pre-load (© Rockwell International)

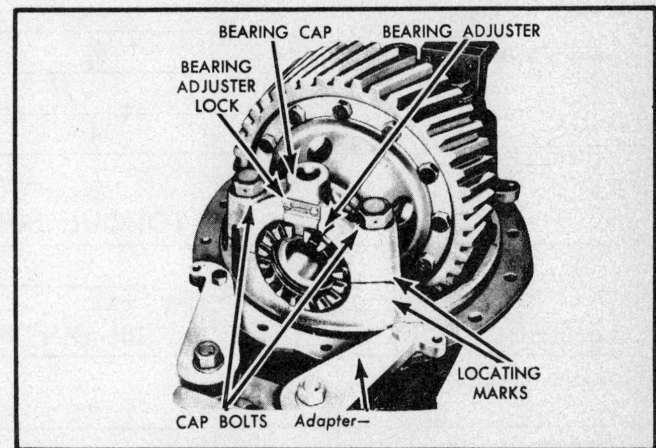

Installation of bearing caps (© Rockwell International)

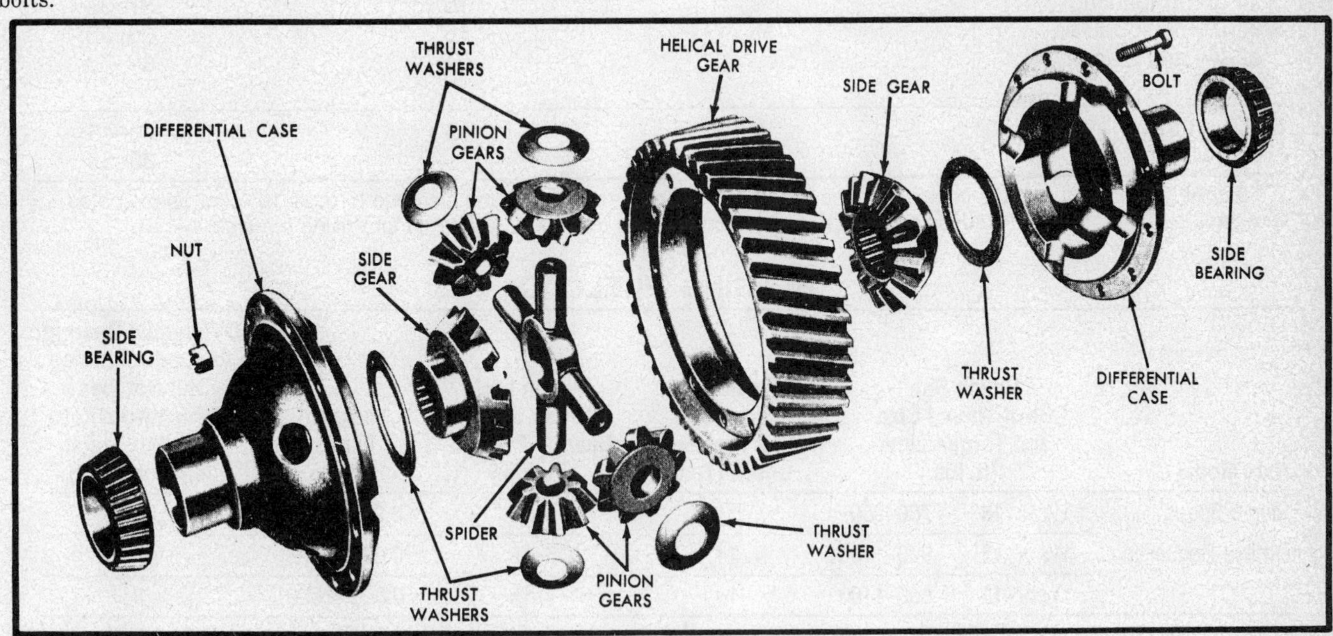

Differential gear and case components (© Rockwell International)

TORQUE SPECIFICATIONS

Location	Cap Screws or Stud Nuts①		
	Diameter	Threads per in.	Torque-Ft. Lb. Min.-Max.
These torques are	3/8	24	38–49
given according	3/8	16	33–43
to diameter and	7/16	14	53–77
threads per inch.	7/16	20	53–67
The torque will	1/2	13	81–104
be the same for	1/2	20	81–104
a specific size	9/16	12	116–149
no matter where	9/16	18	116–149
the bolt or cap	5/8	11	160–205
screw is used	5/8	18	160–205
on the axle	3/4	10	290–370
except for those	3/4	16	290–370
listed below.	7/8	9	470–595
	7/8	14	510–655
	1	14	580–745

TORQUE SPECIFICATIONS

Location	Cap Screws or Stud Nuts①		
	Diameter	Threads per in.	Torque-Ft. Lb. Min.-Max.
Adjusting nut lock	5/16 1/2	18 13	16–20 75–96
Inspection cover	3/8	16	27–35
Shift unit (mounting) Shift unit lock nut, set screw and clamp screw	3/8 3/8 7/16	16 16 14	27–35 30–33 30–33
Shift unit travel limiting screws	1/2 5/8	13 11	40–45 30–33

① Torques given apply to parts coated with machine oil; for dry (as received) parts increase torques 10%; for parts coated with multi-purpose gear oil decrease torques 10%. Nuts on studs to use same torque as for driving the stud.

BEARING PRELOAD

Axle Model	Pinion Shaft Nut-Thread Size and Torque Limits (ft. lbs.)		Press Ram Pressure for Preload Check (Tons)	Pinion and Cross Shaft Bearing Preload (in. lbs.)	Backlash Limits (in.)	Differential Bearing Preload Adjusting Nut Notches Tighten from Zero End Play (each Adjusting Nut)
Single-Speed	1¼ × 18	700–900	11	5–15	0.020–0.026	1
Double Reduction	1½ × 12	800–1100	14	5–15	0.020–0.026	1
	1½ × 18	800–1100	14	5–15	0.020–0.026	1

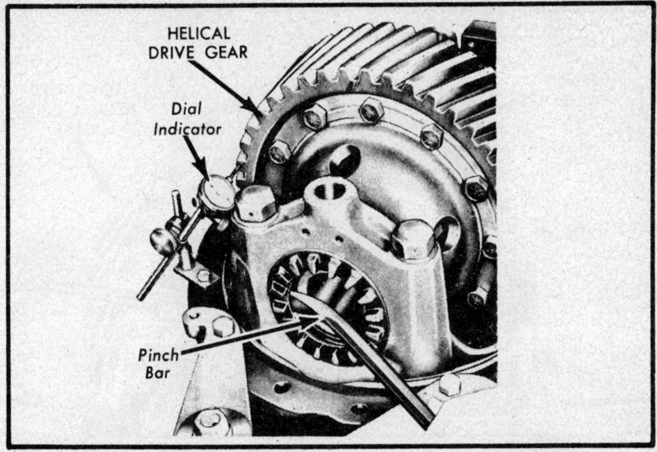

Determining differential end-play (© Rockwell International)

14. Hand tighten the bearing adjusters until they just touch the bearing cups. Then install a dial indicator and check the differential end play using a pin. bar to move the differential away from the indicator. Then tighten the bearing adjuster opposite the dial indicator until there is no side-to-side movement of the differential, and the dial indicator shows no end play.

15. After obtaining the correct end play, adjust the differential bearing preload by tightening the bearing adjusters an additional $^3/_4$–2 $^1/_2$ notches (total for both adjusters).

16. Install the bearing adjuster locks and cap screws.

17. Install locking wires on the lock cap screws and bearing cap bolts.

Rockwell Standard

TWO–SPEED DOUBLE REDUCTION AXLES

This is full floating rear axle having a hypoid drive gear and pinion and using a four-pinion differential assembly. The pinion and cross shaft are each mounted on two tapered roller bearings.

Disassembly

1. Punch-mark one carrier leg and bearing cap for reassembly reference.
2. remove the differential and gear assembly.
3. Punch-mark case halves for correct alignment when assembling.
4. Separate differential case halves. Remove side gears, thrust washers, pinions and pinion shaft.
5. Remove the differential side bearing.
6. Separate gears from case. Center-punch rivets in center of had. Use drill $^1/_{32}$ in. smaller than body of rivet to drill through head, and press out rivets.
7. Remove pinion shaft yoke.
8. Remove pinion bearing cage assembly. If cage is not free, tap loose, or use puller screws in holes provided.
9. Wire bearing cage shim pack together to facilitate adjustment when reassembling.
10. Press pinion shaft out of cage and remove adjusting spacers from shaft. Remove rear bearing from pinion shaft.
11. Press front bearing and pinion shaft oil seal from pinion.
12. Remove two bearing cups from pinion cage.
13. Remove shift fork shaft and shift fork.
14. Tap sleeve from carrier with a soft mallet. Wire shim pack together to facilitate reassembly.
15. Remove screws and force out bearing cage by using a small pin. bar between back of hypoid gear and carrier housing. Wire shim pack together to facilitate reassembly.
16. Remove cross shaft and hypoid gear assembly.
17. Remove cap screws and press cross shaft from bearing and hypoid gear (ring gear). Slide off high speed pinion and remove shaft collar, plungers and springs. Precautions should be taken when removing shift collar as the plungers and spring will fly out. Reinstall shift collar and press shaft through low speed pinion and bearing.
18. Remove cross shaft bearing cups. If cross shaft bearing cover is removed (hypoid gear side), be sure to wire shim pack together.
19. Clean all parts thoroughly in a suitable solvent and blow dry with compressed air. Remove any foreign material from carrier housing. The bearings should be submerged in clean solvent and rotated by hand until clean. After cleaning, blow dry with compressed air.

CAUTION

Do not spin bearings with air pressure, as they might score due to absence of any lubrication. See the General Axle Service section for details on cleaning and inspection.

Assembly

1. Press drive pinion gear rear bearing cone firmly against pinion shoulder.
2. Press pinion cage bearing cups squarely and firmly against cage shoulder.
3. Place bearing spacer on pinion shaft with bevel side toward front bearing. Lubricate bearing cone with axle lubricant and position bearing cage on shaft. Lubricate and press front bearing on pinion shaft. Rotate cage to assure normal bearing contact. If a press is not available, install pinion yoke and nut and torque to specifications.

Differential carrier on a stand (© Rockwell International)

Pinion Shaft Thread Size and Number of Threads Per Inch	Required Pressure to Obtain Correct Pre-Load (lbs.)	Required Torque to Obtain Correct Pre-Load (ft. lbs.)
1 in. × 20	12,000	300–400
1¼ × 18	22,000	700–900
1½ × 12	28,000	800–1100

4. While assembly is in the press under pressure or pinion nut torqued to specifications, check pinion bearing pre-load. The correct pressures and torques for checking pre-load are:

5. Wrap a soft wire around cage and pull on horizontal line with pound scale. When determining pinion bearing pre-load, first measure diameter of pinion cage. Assuming cage diameter is 6 inches, pulling radius would be 3 inches; therefore, 4 pounds pull on scale would equal 12 inch lbs. pre-load.

6. Using rotating torque, not starting torque. If rotating torque is not within 5 to 15 in. lbs., use thinner spacer to increase pre-load or thicker spacer to decrease preload. Torque must be near low limit inch lbs. with original pinion bearings and near high limit when using new bearings.

7. Lubricate a new pinion oil seal and install in pinion cage. Install pinion yoke, washer and nut, tighten to specified torque. Pinion and cage assembly is not installed until after cross shaft and hypoid gear installation. However, if pinion depth gauge tool is being used, install pinion assembly with original shims, then refer to Pinion Setting Procedures in the General Axle Service section. After pinion depth is established, remove pinion and cage assembly.

8. Lubricate inner bearing surfaces on low and high speed pinions with axle lubricant. On some axles (H341, L345), the low speed (small) pinion is located next to the hypoid gear. On the others (Q345, RT340) the high speed (large) pinion is next to the hypoid gear.

9. Position the correct pinion on hypoid gear end of cross shaft, with splined row of teeth toward center of cross shaft. Install key in shaft and start cross shaft into hypoid gear in line with keyway, then press shaft into hypoid gear. Insert feeler gauge between end of helical pinion and thrust surface on cross shaft must be 0.010–0.025 in.

10. Coat the three plungers and springs with axle lubricant, and install in cross shaft. Align the three tapered splines i shift collar with the three plungers, slide collar over plungers with side collar marked LOW SIDE toward low speed (small) pinion.

11. Install remaining pinion on cross shaft with splined row of teeth toward center of shaft. Press cross shaft bearing firmly against cross shaft shoulder. Pinion end play must be 0.010 to 0.026 in.

12. Install bearing retaining washers and torque cap screws to 42–45 ft. lbs. and install lock wire.

13. Press bearing cups firmly against shoulder in the bearing covers.

14. Install cross shaft bearing cover (hypoid gear side) in carrier housing with original shim pack. Torque cap screws.

15. Lubricate bearing cones with axle lubricant, then position cross shaft assembly in bearing cup in carrier. If a front mounted shift unit is used, position shift fork and install shift shaft through its bearings in the carrier and fork. Align hole in fork with detent in shaft. Torque lock screw and install lockwire. Start the other bearing cover and original shim pack in carrier housing (side opposite hypoid gear). Tap cover into position and torque down cap screws. Rotate cross shaft and gear assembly several times to assure normal bearing contact.

16. Lock low speed pinion and cross shaft with shift collar. Wrap a soft wire around the pinion and pull horizontally with a pound scale. To calculate cross shaft bearing preload, first measure diameter of pinion gear. Assuming pinion diameter is 4 in., pulling radius would be 2 in.; therefore, 7 lbs. pull on scale would equal 14 inch lbs. pre-load.

17 Using rotating torque, not starting torque. If rotating torque is not within 5 to 15 inch lbs., use thinner shim under bearing cover (side opposite hypoid gear) to increase pre-load or thicker shim to decrease pre-load.

18. Install drive pinion and cage assembly using correct shim pack if pinion setting gauge was used, or original shim pack if gauge was not used. Install lock washers and torque cap screws.

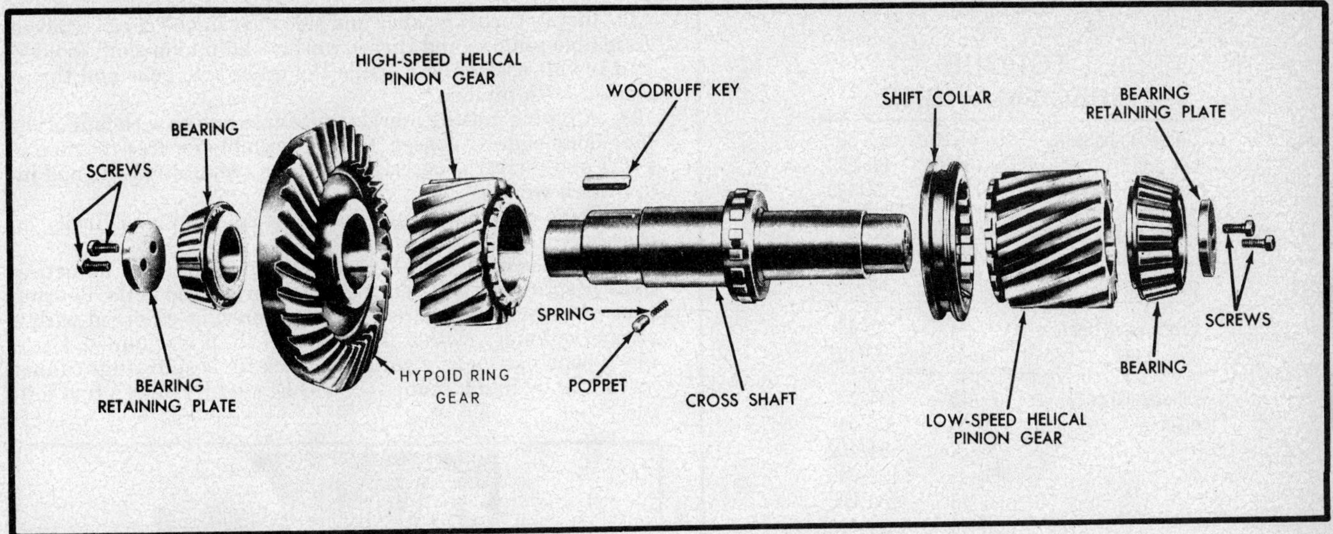

Cross shaft components (© Rockwell International)

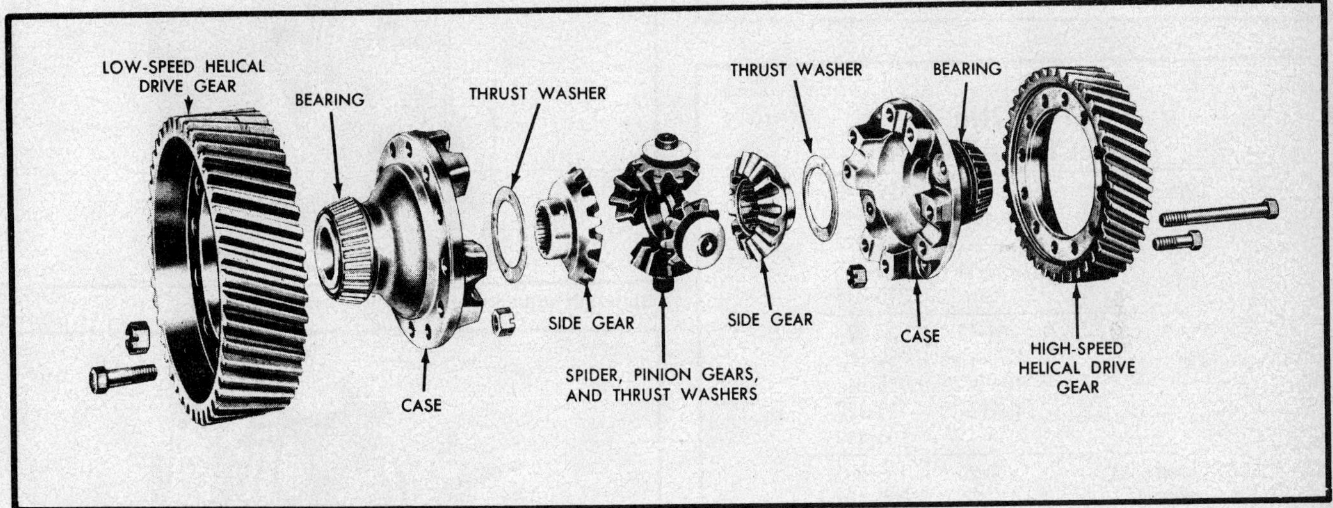

Exploded view of differential gears and case (© Rockwell International)

19. Attach a dial indicator to the carrier with the pointer resting against face of one of the drive gear teeth and adjust backlash temporarily to 0.010 in.

20. To increase backlash, remove sufficient shims from under cross shaft bearing cover (opposite hypoid gear), and insert shims of equal thickness under opposite bearing cover. To decrease backlash, reverse procedure. Following this method cross shaft bearing pre-load will be retained.

21. With backlash temporarily set at 0.010 in., check gear tooth pattern. Refer to "Gear Tooth Contact" in the "General Axle Service" section.

22. After correct tooth contacts have been made, readjust backlash to measure 0.020 to 0.026 in.

23. If axle has a side mounted shift unit, tap shaft unit sleeve into carrier housing with original shim pack. Install lock washers and tighten nuts to 26–29 ft. lbs.

24. If electric shift unit is used, hold shift fork in the collar, lubricate and slide shift shaft through sleeve and into collar. Install and tighten lock screw. Tighten lock nut to 30–35 ft. lbs and install lock wire. Install shift unit.

25. Check clearance of shift fork pads in shift collar. The clearance should be 0.010 minimum on each side of fork in both high and low speed positions. Add or remove shims to achieve correct adjustment.

26. If air shift control is used, hold shift fork in position in the collar, lubricate and slide air shift unit shaft through the sleeve and into the fork. Install lock screw. Tighten lock nut to 30–35 ft. lbs. and install lockwire.

27. On those axles with a front mounted air shift unit, shift both shift unit and shift fork in HI position using no gaskets. Position the shaft unit and bellcrank assembly in slot of shift shaft. Install lock washers and nut and torque to specifications.

28. With collar and fork shifted to engage helical pinion next to hypoid gear, adjust Allen screw and nut in top of carrier to center the fork in the collar within 0.005 in.

29. With collar and fork shifted to engage the helical pinion away from hypoid gear, adjust hex head bolt and lock nut in cross shaft cage to center the fork in the collar within 0.005 in.

NOTE: When checking shift fork clearance, make certain collar is flush with end face of pinion being engaged.

30. Install high and low speed helical gears on their respective differential case halves. If rivets are used, install them cold. Instead of rivets, bolts can be used but must be tightened to specified torque.

31. Lubricate case inner walls and all parts with axle lubricant.

TORQUE SPECIFICATIONS

Carrier to housing bolt or stud nut	7/16–14–20	54–58
	1/2–13–20	85–91
	5/8–11–18	168–180
Cross shaft bearing cage and cover screw	1/2–13–20	85–91
	9/16–12–18	120–129
	5/8–11	168–180
Cross shaft bearing lock screw	7/16–14	42–45
	9/16–12	92–101
Differential case bolts	3/8–16	34–37
	7/16–14	54–58
	1/2–20	94–102
	9/16–18	132–145
	5/8–18	186–205
	3/4–16	325–360

TORQUE SPECIFICATIONS

Differential bearing cap bolt	5/8–11–18	127–140
	3/4–10–16	230–250
	7/8–9–14	345–370
	7/8–14	375–415
	1–14	375–415
Pinion cage bolt	3/8–16	34–37
	7/16–14–20	54–58
	1/2–13–20	85–91
	9/16–12–18	120–129
	5/8–11	168–180
Pinion shaft yoke nut	7/8–20	175–250
	1–20	300–400
	1–1/4–18	700–900
	1–1/2–12–18	800–1100
	1–3/4–12	800–1100

32. Install thrust washer and side gear in one of case halves. Assemble pinions and thrust washers on pinion shaft (spider) and install assembly. Engage the other side gear and thrust washer with pinions.

33. Aligning mating marks, unite case halves with four of the long bolts equally spaced. Check assembly for free rotation of gears and correct if necessary. Torque remaining bolts and install lock wire.

34. Press differential side bearings squarely and firmly on case halves.

35. Temporarily install bearing cups, threaded adjusting nuts or split ring and bearing caps. Torque cap bolts. Bearing cups must be hand pushed into the bores; or enlarged with a scraper or emery cloth until a hand push fit is obtained. Use a blued bearing cup as a gauge to check fit. If split rings cannot be turned by hand, reduce their O.D. slightly with a fine mill file.

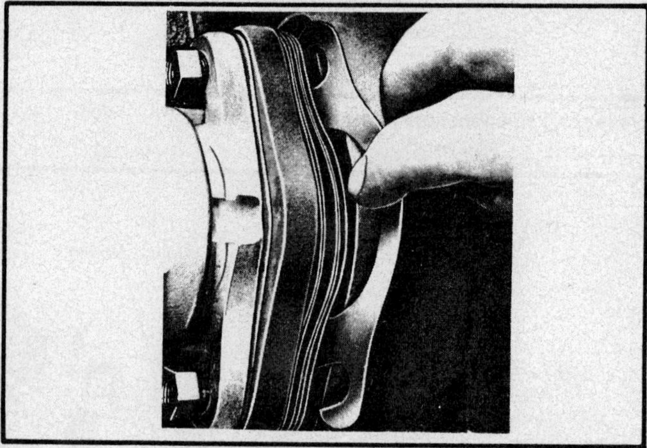

Shift unit adjustment (© Rockwell International)

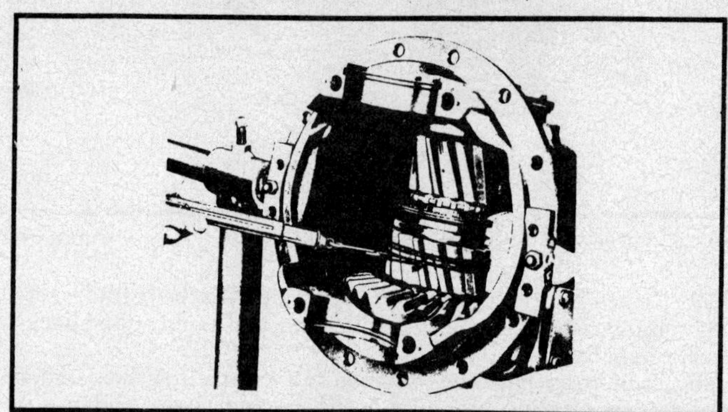

Determining cross shaft preload (© Rockwell International)

BEARING SPECIFICATIONS

Axle Model	Pinion Shaft Nut-Thread Size and Torque Limits (ft. lbs.)		Press Ram Pressure for Preload Check (Tons)	Pinion and Cross Shaft Bearing Preload (in. lbs.)	Backlash Limits (in.)	Differential Bearing Preload Adjusting Nut Notches Tighten from Zero End Play (each Adjusting Nut)
2-Speed	1¾ × 12	800–1100	14	5–15	0.020–0.026	1
Double Reduction	1 × 20	300–400	6	5–15	0.020–0.026	1
	1¼ × 18	700–900	11	5–15	0.020–0.026	1
	1½ × 12	800–1100	14	5–15	0.020–0.026	1

36. Lubricate side bearings with axle lubricant. Place bearing cups in the cones, then position differential assembly between grooves in carrier legs.
37. Insert thin split rings in carrier leg grooves, making certain there is clearance between bearing cup faces and the rings.
38. Attach a dial indicator to the carrier housing with its pointer resting against side surface of one of the drive gears. With a pair of small pin. bars, manipulate assembly back and forth between the split rings and measure the end play.
39. Remove and measure split ring thickness. To the total thickness of the two thin rings, add the end play figure, plus another 0.017 to 0.022 in. to obtain total thickness of two thicker rings required to obtain proper bearing pre-load. For example: If necessary thin rings were 0.290 in. each for a total of 0.580 in., and the end play is 0.005 in., then 0.580 in. plus 0.005 in. equals 0.585 in. Adding an additional 0.020 in. for a total of 0.605 in. thickness for the two split rings would provide 0.020 in. pre-load on the bearings. The 0.605 in. may be divided between the two rings such as 0.300 and 0.305 in.
40. Insert one split ring in carrier leg groove and move differential assembly tightly against ring. Install opposite split ring (with gap upward) by tapping it into the groove with a blunt drift.
41. Tap bearing caps into correct location. Torque cap bolts and install lock wire.

Split ring installation (© Rockwell International)

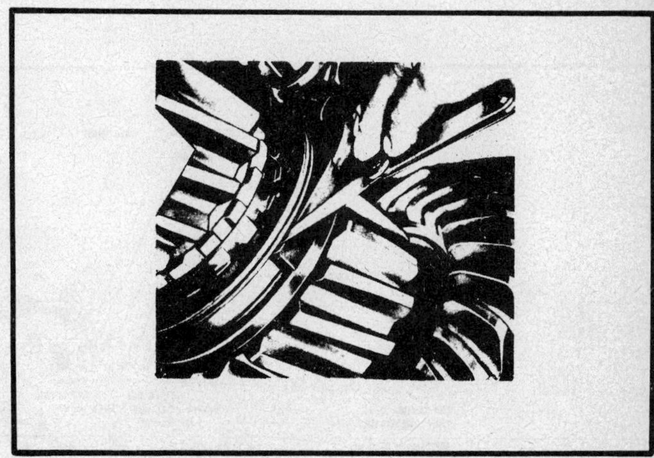

Determining shift fork clearance (© Rockwell International)

Rockwell Standard Tandem Axle

THROUGH–DRIVE TYPE – THREE GEAR TRANSFER TRAIN WITH INTER–AXLE DIFFERENTIAL

NOTE: Before the carrier assembly can be removed from the housing, the through-shaft must be removed from the housing. The removal of the carrier assembly is accomplished in the conventional manner, except for the removal of the through-shaft. The procedure is as follows:

1. Remove the shift shaft housing cap screws and lock washers. Remove the shift shaft housing assembly.
2. Disassemble and remove the shift lever attaching nut, button, lever, cup, and spring. The body fit bolt should not be removed.
3. Remove the through-shaft cage cap screws and lock washers, and remove the through-shaft, cage, and yoke assembly.

NOTE: To free the through-shaft cage from its case bore, it may be necessary to tap the yoke with a soft hammer.

4. Thread the through-shaft assembly from the housing. The sliding clutch must be eased along the shaft at the shift lever opening and when the through-shaft clears the opening, the sliding clutch may be lifted out.
5. Complete the conventional removal of the carrier assembly.

THROUGH–SHAFT ASSEMBLY

Disassembly

1. Remove the through-shaft yoke cotter pin and the nut. Remove the yoke from the shaft.
2. Press the through-shaft from the cage assembly, using a suitable tool against the inner bearing race. Remove the cage snap-ring, if necessary.
3. Tap the radial bearing out of the bore of the cage at the seal end. Discard the seal.

Assembly

1. Install a new bearing into the cage bore and install a new seal.
2. Press the through-shaft into the bearing with the use of suitable tools.
3. Install the yoke, nut, and tighten to specifications, and install the cotter pin.

CARRIER ASSEMBLY

Disassembly

1. Place the carrier assembly into a holding fixture, and remove the adapter case and inter-axle differential assembly by removing the cap screws and separating the assemblies.
2. Remove the inter-axle differential cover cap screws and lift the assembly from the adapter case.
3. Remove the input shaft cotter pin, nut and washer.
4. Press the inter-axle differential assembly from the cover, using suitable press tools.
5. Mark the differential case halves with a punch to assist in the assembly.
6. Remove the lock wire, bolts and separate the case halves and remove the spider, spider pinions, side gears and thrust washers.

NOTE: Do not remove the radial bearing from the case unless replacement is necessary. If the bearing is replaced, install a new oil seal.

7. Remove the lock wire from the bolts in the adapter case assembly and remove the bolts from the bearing cage.
8. Insert two cap screws in the puller holes of the cage and tighten to remove the cage from the adapter case.
9. Lift off the cage and the shim pack. Be sure to keep the shim pack intact for the reassembly.

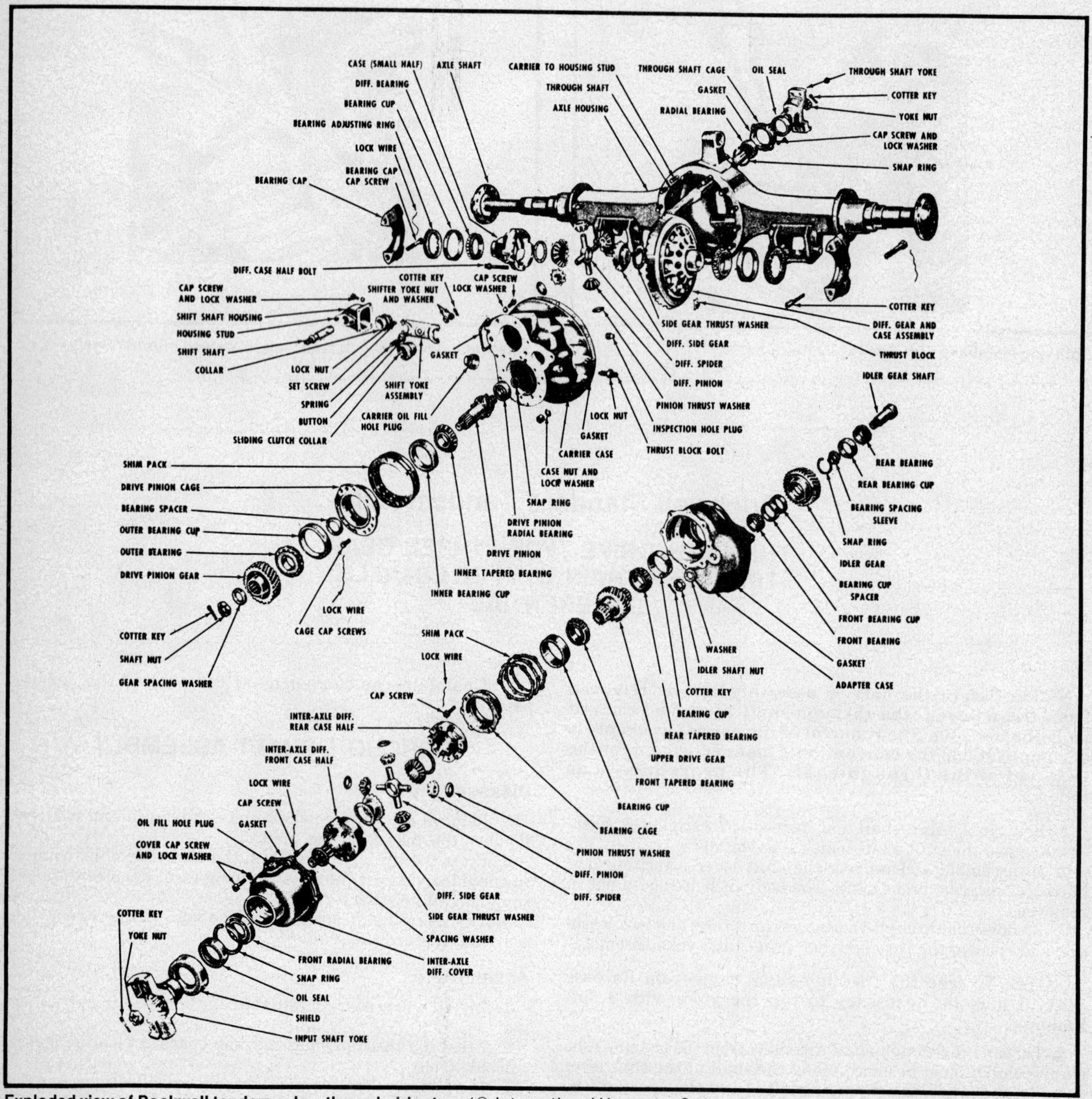

CASE (SMALL HALF)
AXLE SHAFT
CARRIER TO HOUSING STUD
THROUGH SHAFT CAGE
OIL SEAL
THROUGH SHAFT YOKE
DIFF. BEARING
THROUGH SHAFT
GASKET
COTTER KEY
BEARING CUP
AXLE HOUSING
RADIAL BEARING
YOKE NUT
BEARING ADJUSTING RING
CAP SCREW AND LOCK WASHER
LOCK WIRE
SNAP RING
BEARING CAP
BEARING CAP CAP SCREW
DIFF. CASE HALF BOLT
COTTER KEY
CAP SCREW
CAP SCREW AND LOCK WASHER
SHIFTER YOKE NUT AND WASHER
LOCK WASHER
SHIFT SHAFT HOUSING
HOUSING STUD
SHIFT SHAFT
GASKET
COLLAR
LOCK NUT
SET SCREW
SPRING
BUTTON
SLIDING CLUTCH COLLAR
SHIFT YOKE ASSEMBLY
CARRIER OIL FILL HOLE PLUG
COTTER KEY
DIFF. GEAR AND CASE ASSEMBLY
SIDE GEAR THRUST WASHER
DIFF. SIDE GEAR
THRUST BLOCK
DIFF. SPIDER
IDLER GEAR SHAFT
DIFF. PINION
PINION THRUST WASHER
LOCK NUT
INSPECTION HOLE PLUG
GASKET
THRUST BLOCK BOLT
CARRIER CASE
SHIM PACK
REAR BEARING
CASE NUT AND LOCK WASHER
DRIVE PINION CAGE
REAR BEARING CUP
SNAP RING
BEARING SPACER
BEARING SPACING SLEEVE
DRIVE PINION RADIAL BEARING
OUTER BEARING CUP
SNAP RING
OUTER BEARING
DRIVE PINION
IDLER GEAR
DRIVE PINION GEAR
INNER TAPERED BEARING
BEARING CUP SPACER
INNER BEARING CUP
FRONT BEARING CUP
LOCK WIRE
FRONT BEARING
COTTER KEY
CAGE CAP SCREWS
SHIM PACK
WASHER
GASKET
SHAFT NUT
LOCK WIRE
IDLER SHAFT NUT
ADAPTER CASE
GEAR SPACING WASHER
COTTER KEY
CAP SCREW
BEARING CUP
INTER-AXLE DIFF. REAR CASE HALF
REAR TAPERED BEARING
INTER-AXLE DIFF. FRONT CASE HALF
UPPER DRIVE GEAR
LOCK WIRE
FRONT TAPERED BEARING
CAP SCREW
BEARING CUP
OIL FILL HOLE PLUG
GASKET
BEARING CAGE
COVER CAP SCREW AND LOCK WASHER
PINION THRUST WASHER
DIFF. PINION
DIFF. SIDE GEAR
DIFF. SPIDER
COTTER KEY
SIDE GEAR THRUST WASHER
YOKE NUT
SPACING WASHER
FRONT RADIAL BEARING
INTER-AXLE DIFF. COVER
SNAP RING
OIL SEAL
SHIELD
INPUT SHAFT YOKE

Exploded view of Rockwell tandem axle—through-drive type (© International Harvester Co.)

10. From the rear of the adapter case, tap the helical gear assembly with a soft hammer and remove the assembly from the front of the case.
11. If replacement of the bearing cups are necessary, remove them from the cage and adapter case.
12. Remove the tapered bearings from the gear with a suitable puller, if replacement is necessary.
13. Remove the idler gear shaft cotter pin, nut and spacing washer.

NOTE: Flat areas are provided on the idler shaft for holding while removal of the nut is accomplished.

14. Remove the idler shaft, and slide the idler gear from the case.
15. Remove the tapered bearings, cups and spacer or spacers from the idler gear.
16. Loosen the thrust block jam nut and loosen the adjusting screw and back off until the thrust block drops.
17. Check and record the back lash of the ring gear to pinion clearance, unless a new gear set is to be installed.
18. Mark the differential carrier leg and the bearing caps to identify them during the reassembly.
19. Cut the lock wire and remove the adjusting ring nut lock and the bolts from the bearing caps.
20. Remove the bearing caps and the bearing adjusting rings.
21. Lift the differential and gear assembly from the carrier housing.

Removing or installing through-shaft assembly
(© International Harvester Co.)

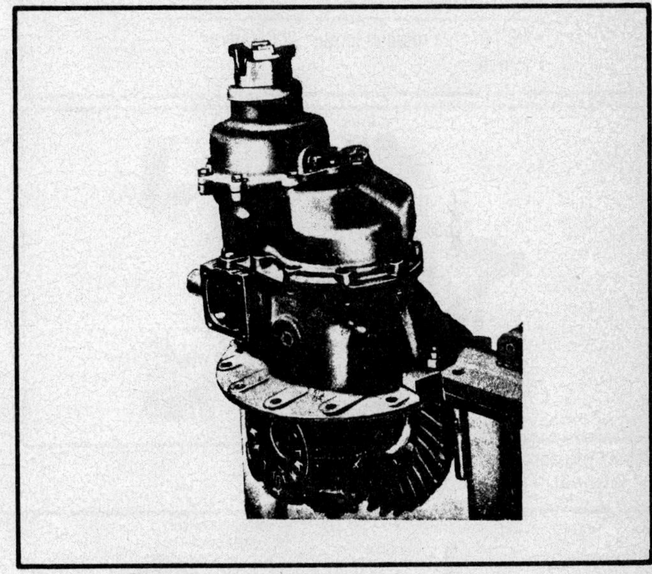

Carrier assembly in holding fixture
(© International Harvester Co.)

DIFFERENTIAL GEAR AND CASE ASSEMBLY

Disassembly

1. Mark the differential case halves for correct alignment during the assembly.
2. Remove the lock wire and cap screws and separate the case halves.
3. Remove the spider, spider pinions, side gears and the thrust washers.
4. If the ring gear is to be replaced, remove the rivets by drilling and press out the rivets.

CAUTION

Never chisel the head of the rivet to remove the ring gear. Damage to the case holes can result.

5. The differential bearings can be removed with the aid of a puller.

Assembly

1. Rivet the ring gear to the case half with new rivets. Tonnage required for squeezing cold rivets is as follows and final pressure should be held for approximately one minute to make sure the rivet has filled the hole.

Diameter of Rivet	Tonnage Required
7/16"	22
1/2"	30
9/16"	36
5/8"	45

NOTE: Differential case bolts are available for service replacement of the rivets to install the ring gear to the case. This eliminates the need for special equipment necessary to correctly cold upset the rivets during the ring gear installation.

2. Lubricate the differential case inner walls and all parts with axle lubricant.
3. Position the thrust washer and side gear in the case half.
4. Place the spider with the pinions and thrust washers in position.
5. Install the second side gear and thrust washer.
6. Align the mating marks on the case halves and assemble the two halves. Install and tighten the cap screws.
7. Install the side differential bearings, if removed, with a suitable sleeve and press.

PINION AND CAGE ASSEMBLY

Disassembly

1. Remove the lock wire and remove the pinion cage cap screws.
2. Remove the pinion cage by tapping the end of the pinion shaft with a soft hammer and brass bar.
3. Remove the pinion cotter pin and nut from the shaft. Remove the gear and spacer.
4. Remove the outer bearing from the cage.
5. Remove the bearing spacer from the pinion shaft.
6. If necessary, remove the pinion inner thrust bearing and remove the radial bearing with a suitable tool.
7. If necessary to replace the pinion bearing cups, remove with a suitable tool.

Assembly

1. Press the rear thrust bearing against the pinion shoulder.

Pinion Shaft Thread Size	Required Not Torque to Obtain Correct Pre-load (ft.lbs.)	Required Pressure to Obtain Correct Pre-load (tons)
1″ × 20	300–400	6
1¼″ × 18	700–900	11
1½″ × 12	800–1100	14
1½″ × 18	800–1100	14
1¾″ × 12	800–1100	14
2″ × 16	800–1100	14

NOTE: Use rotating torque, not starting torque.

Obtaining zero preload differential bearings
(© International Harvester Co.)

2. Press the radial bearing into place on the pinion shaft.
3. Install the radial bearing retaining ring.
4. Install the new cups into the cage using suitable tools. Assure that the cups are firmly against the cage shoulders.
5. Insert the pinion and bearing assembly into the pinion cage and position the spacer over the pinion shaft.
6. Press the forward bearing firmly against the spacer.
7. If a press with a pressure gauge is available, apply pressure to the bearings to check the bearing preload. If a press is not available, torque the pinion nut to specifications and check the preload by wrapping a strong cord or soft wire around the bearing cage and pull on a horizontal line with a pound scale. The preload should be within 5–15 in. lbs. Use a thinner spacer to increase or a thicker spacer to decrease the preload torque.

NOTE: The correct pressures and nut torques for checking the pinion bearing preload are as follows and to find the correct bearing preload, the cage diameter must be measured. An example is as follows: Assuming the pinion cage is 6 in., the radius would be 3 in. With a 5 pound pull, the preload torque would equal 15 inch lbs.

8. Press the drive helical gear against the forward bearing (or spacer where used), and install the washer and pinion shaft nut.
9. Tighten the pinion shaft nut to its proper torque and install the cotter pin.
10. Recheck the pinion bearing preload torque and if not within specifications, repeat the procedure to adjust the bearing preload.
11. If the original gears are to be used, install the original shim pack. If the gears have been replaced, alter the shim pack as follows: Record the variation (etched) and the nominal assembly dimension (stamped) on the head of the new and the old

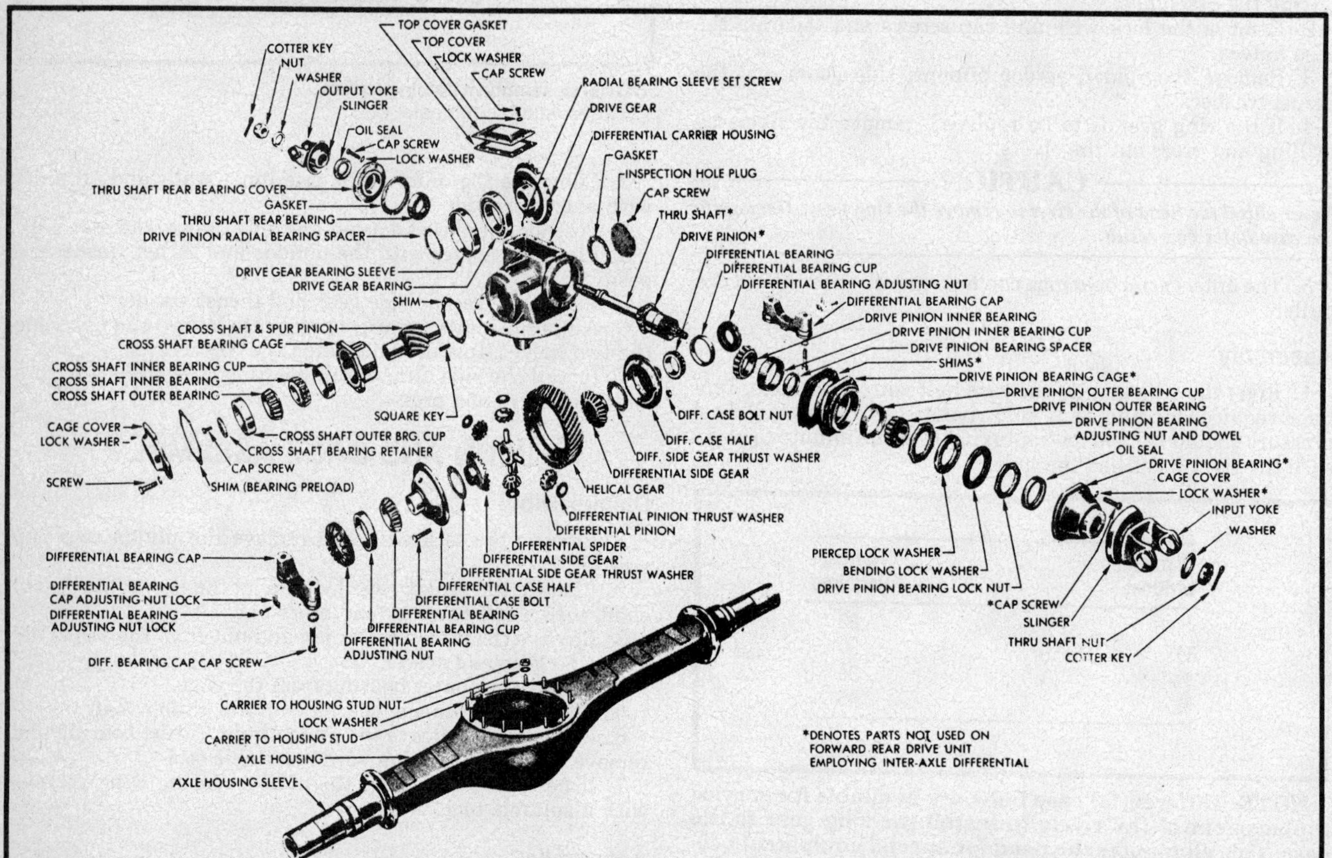

Exploded view of Rockwell SUD, SUDD, STD and STDD series— typical rear axles (© International Harvester Co.)

pinion gear. Increase or reduce the shim pack in regards to the change in the variation from the old to the new pinion. After changing the sign of the old variation, plus to minus or minus to plus, add to the new variation, sign unchanged, and the result will be the shim pack increase or decrease in thousands of an in.

12. Position the pinion and cage assembly in the carrier pinion cage bore and lightly tap into place with a soft hammer.
13. Install the pinion cage screws and torque to specifications. Do not install the lock wire until the final carrier adjustments are made.

CARRIER ASSEMBLY

Assembly

1. Lubricate the differential bearings and cups with axle lubricant.
2. Place the cups over the bearings and position the carrier assembly over the legs of the carrier housing and lower into place.
3. Install the bearing adjusting nuts and turn hand tight against the bearing cups.
4. Install the bearing caps on the carrier legs in relation to the previously made marks.

CAUTION

If the bearing caps do not position properly, the adjusting nuts may be cross-threaded. Remove the bearing caps and reposition the adjusting nuts. Forcing the caps into position may result in irreparable damage to the carrier housing or to the bearing caps.

5. Install the carrier leg cap screw and tighten to specifications.

NOTE: Do not install the adjusting nut locks, cotter keys and lock wire until the final adjustments are made.

6. Install a dial indicator so that the button is mounted on the backface of the gear.
7. Loosen the bearing adjustment nut on the side opposite the ring gear, sufficient to notice end play on the dial indicator.
8. Tighten the same adjusting nut enough to obtain zero end play.
9. Check gear for runout. If the runout exceeds 0.008 in., remove the differential assembly and check for the cause.
10. If the runout is within specifications, tighten the adjusting nuts one notch each from the zero end play, to preload the bearings.
11. If new gears were not used, the established backlash recorded before disassembly should be used. For new gears, the new backlash should be set to 0.010 in. Adjust the backlash by moving the ring gear only. This is done by backing off on one adjusting nut and tightening the opposite adjusting nut the same amount.
12. Check the tooth contact between the ring gear and the pinion as outlined in the beginning of this section.
13. Install the adjuster nut locking cotter pins.
14. Install the lock wire in the appropriate bolts.
15. Install the thrust block in the carrier assembly by firmly tightening the adjusting screw until the thrust block is against the back face of the ring gear.
16. Loosen the adjusting screw a $^1/_4$ turn and lock securely with the lock nut.

ADAPTER CASE

Assembly

1. Install the snap-ring and press the idler gear inner bearing cup squarely against the snap-ring.
2. Install the idler gear cup spacing sleeve against the opposite side of the snap-ring.

Checking ring gear—pinion backlash
(© International Harvester Co.)

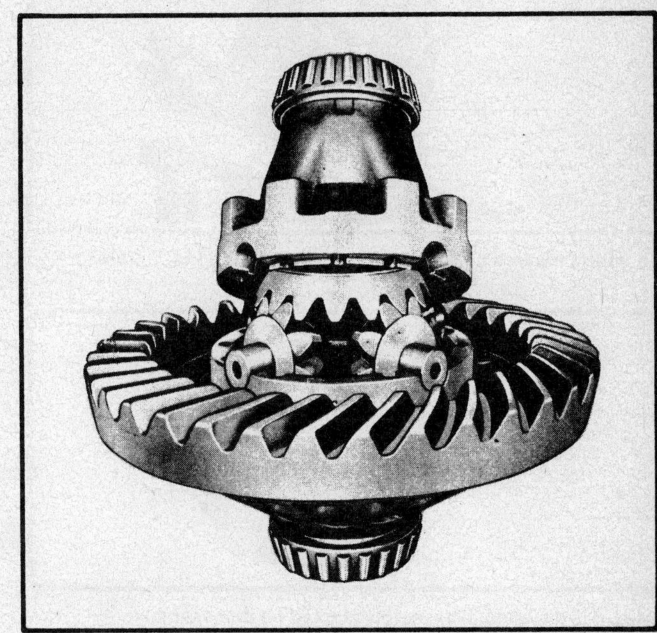

Differential case pinion and side gear assembly
(© International Harvester Co.)

3. Press the idler gear outer bearing cup squarely against the spacing sleeve.
4. Position the idler gear inner and outer bearings into the cups with the spacer or spacers between them.
5. Slide the assembly through the adapter case drive pinion opening and position the assembly so that the bearings are aligned with the adapter case shaft hole.
6. Tap the idler shaft through the idler gear assembly so that the inner bearing is against the idler shaft shoulder.
7. Install the washer and nut and torque to 350–400 ft. lbs.
8. Measure the idler shaft bearing end play by the use of a dial indicator mounted to the adapter case with the stem set against the idler gear face. The correct end play is 0.001–0.005.
9. If the bearing end play does not measure within these limits, use a thinner or thicker spacer or combination of the two spacers as required.

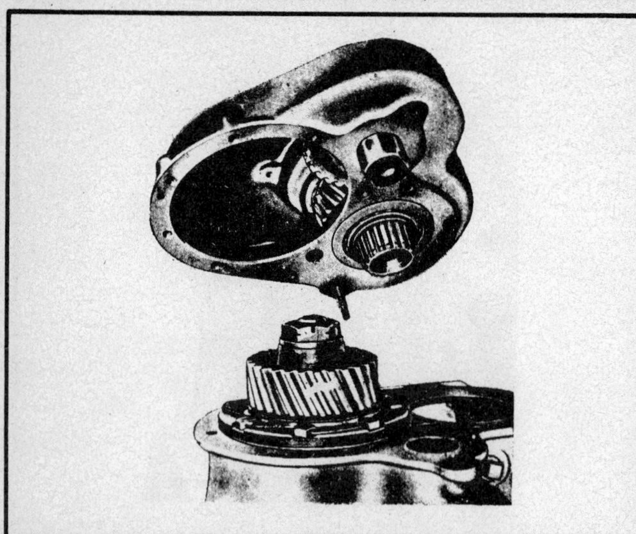

Removing or installing adapter case assembly (© International Harvester Co.)

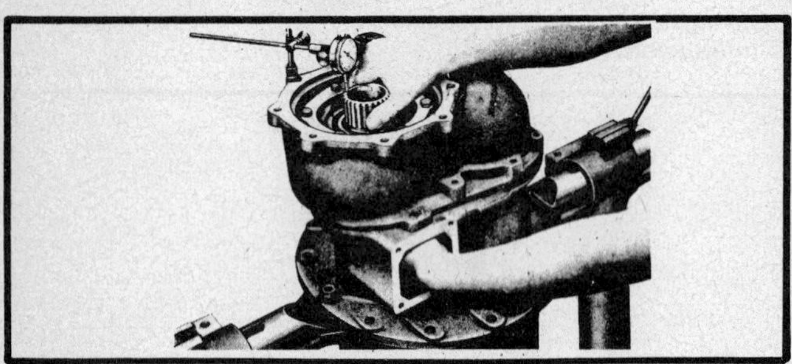

Adjusting tapered bearing end-play (© International Harvester Co.)

Inter-axle differential assembly marked for disassembly (© International Harvester Co.)

Adapter case bearing cage and shim pack (© International Harvester Co.)

10. After the end play has been established, remove the nut and washer and insert the O-ring and reinstall the nut and washer. Torque to 350–400 ft. lbs. and install the cotter pin.

UPPER DRIVE GEAR

Assembly

1. Press the front and rear tapered bearings into the gear.
2. Press the front bearing cup into the bearing cage, if previously removed.
3. Tap the rear bearing into the adapter case and slide the gear assembly into the case.
4. Mount the carrier assembly in the upright position and install the gasket and place the adapter case over the carrier.

NOTE: The idler shaft flat must line up with the corresponding flat in the carrier.

5. Lower the adapter case into position on the carrier and install the lock washers and cap screws. Torque to the proper specifications.
6. Using the original shim pack, install the bearing cage over the upper helical gear with the "TOP" mark up.
7. Install the lock washers and cap screws and tighten to the specified torque.
8. Set a dial indicator button against the end of the gear and check the end play. Adjust the tapered bearing end play to 0.001–0.005 in. by adding or subtracting the shims from the shim pack.
9. Install the lock wire in the respective bolts.

INTER–AXLE DIFFERENTIAL

Assembly

1. Lubricate the differential case walls and all the component parts with lubricant.
2. Position the thrust washer and rear side gear into the case rear half.
3. Place the spider with the pinions and thrust washers in position and install the forward side gear and thrust washer.
4. Align the mating marks and position the forward case half.
5. Install the case cap screws and tighten to the correct torque. Install the lock wire.
6. If the cover assembly was disassembled, install the forward radial bearing and snap-ring.
7. Install the spacer on the input shaft.
8. Position the cover over the input shaft and tap the cover down until the bearing seats against the spacer.
9. Install the gasket and install the cover and differential assembly over the upper drive gear hub. Tap the assembly into position.

NOTE: It will be necessary to line up the splines of the drive gear with those of the side gear.

10. Install the cap screws and lock washers. Tighten to the proper torque.
11. Install the cover oil seal and mount the cover assembly on the adapter case with the gasket in position.
12. Install the cap screws and lock washers and tighten to the specified torque.

CARRIER ASSEMBLY

Installation

1. Using a new gasket, install the carrier assembly onto the housing and secure with the nuts and lock washers. Tighten the nuts evenly to pull the carrier assembly squarely into the housing.

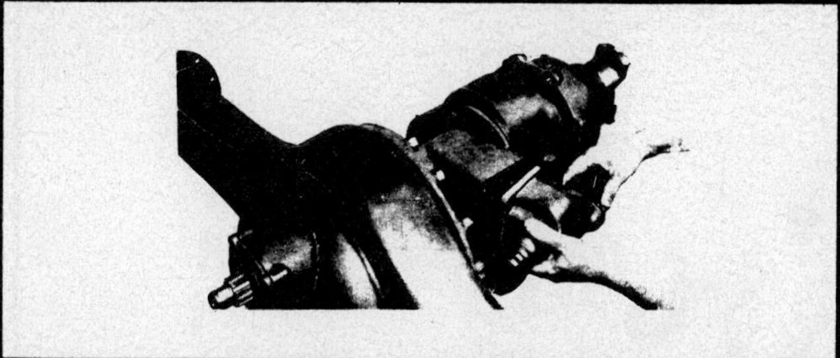

Removing or installing shift shaft housing
(© International Harvester Co.)

2. Install the through-shaft rear radial bearing into the cage and lock in place with the snap ring.
3. Press the cage and bearing assembly on the splined end of the through-shaft with a suitable sleeve.
4. Install the through-shaft cage oil seal.
5. Enter the through-shaft and cage assembly with a new cage gasket into the cage bore in the rear of the axle housing until the forward end of the shaft is even with the shift lever opening.
6. Install the sliding shift collar over the forward end of the shaft through the shift housing opening. Ease the shaft into the forward side gear of the inter-axle differential, while at the same time, passing the shift collar onto the collar splines.
7. Install the through-shaft cage cap screws and lock washers and tighten to the proper torque.
8. Install over the shift lever bolt, the shift lever spring, cup and lever. Locate the lever inner yoke in the collar groove at this time.
9. Install the shift lever button and nut. Tighten the nut securely and install the cotter pin.
10. Positon the shift housing and a new gasket on the carrier assembly.

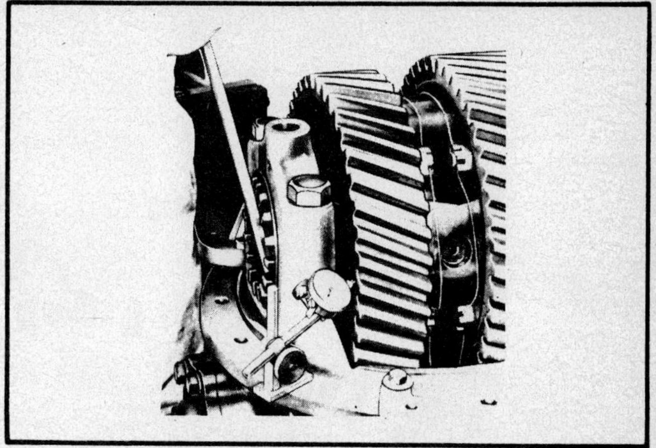

Adjusting differential bearing preload (© Rockwell International)

11. Install the cap screws and lock washers and tighten to the specified torque.
12. Install the through-shaft yoke on the shaft and tighten the nut to the proper torque and install the cotter pin.

SHIFT SHAFT

Adjustment

1. With the shift shaft moved back to its full travel, locking the interaxle differential, turn the adjusting screw in until the end of the screw touches the end of the shift shaft.
2. Move the adjusting screw 1 to 1 $^1/_4$ turn more and lock the adjusting screw with the jam nut. This will allow approximately 0.012 in. clearance between the yoke and the groove of the collar and will thus eliminate yoke or collar wear.

International Harvester Co.

Single Speed, Single Reduction Light and Heavy Duty Rear Axles

The rear axles may vary as to the design and the construction, but the components of the axles perform similarly regardless of the type. The components of the rear axle that the serviceman will be concerned with are the drive gears, the differential assembly and the axle housing. The removal and installation of the carrier assembly is accomplished in the conventional manner, regardless of a single or tandem axle.

CARRIER ASSEMBLY

Disassembly

1. Mount the carrier assembly in a suitable fixture.
2. Remove the cotter pins from the bearing adjuster locks and remove the locks from the bearing caps.
3. Match mark the carrier legs to the bearing caps to identify properly upon reassembly.
4. Remove the ring gear thrust block and adjust screw from the carrier housing.
5. Cut and remove the lock wire. Remove the bearing caps and adjusting nuts.

NOTE: Bearing cap pilot rings may be used on some axle models. Do not lose or damage.

6. Tip the differential assembly away from the pinion and lift the assembly from the housing.

NOTE: Due to the weight of the differential assembly, a lifting device may be may be used to assist in the removal.

DIFFERENTIAL CASE AND GEAR ASSEMBLY

Disassembly

1. Match mark the differential case halves for the proper reassembly.
2. Cut the lock wire and remove the cap screws or stud nuts and separate the case halves.
3. Remove the spider, pinions, side gears and thrust washers from the case halves.
4. Remove the ring gear rivets by center punching each rivet

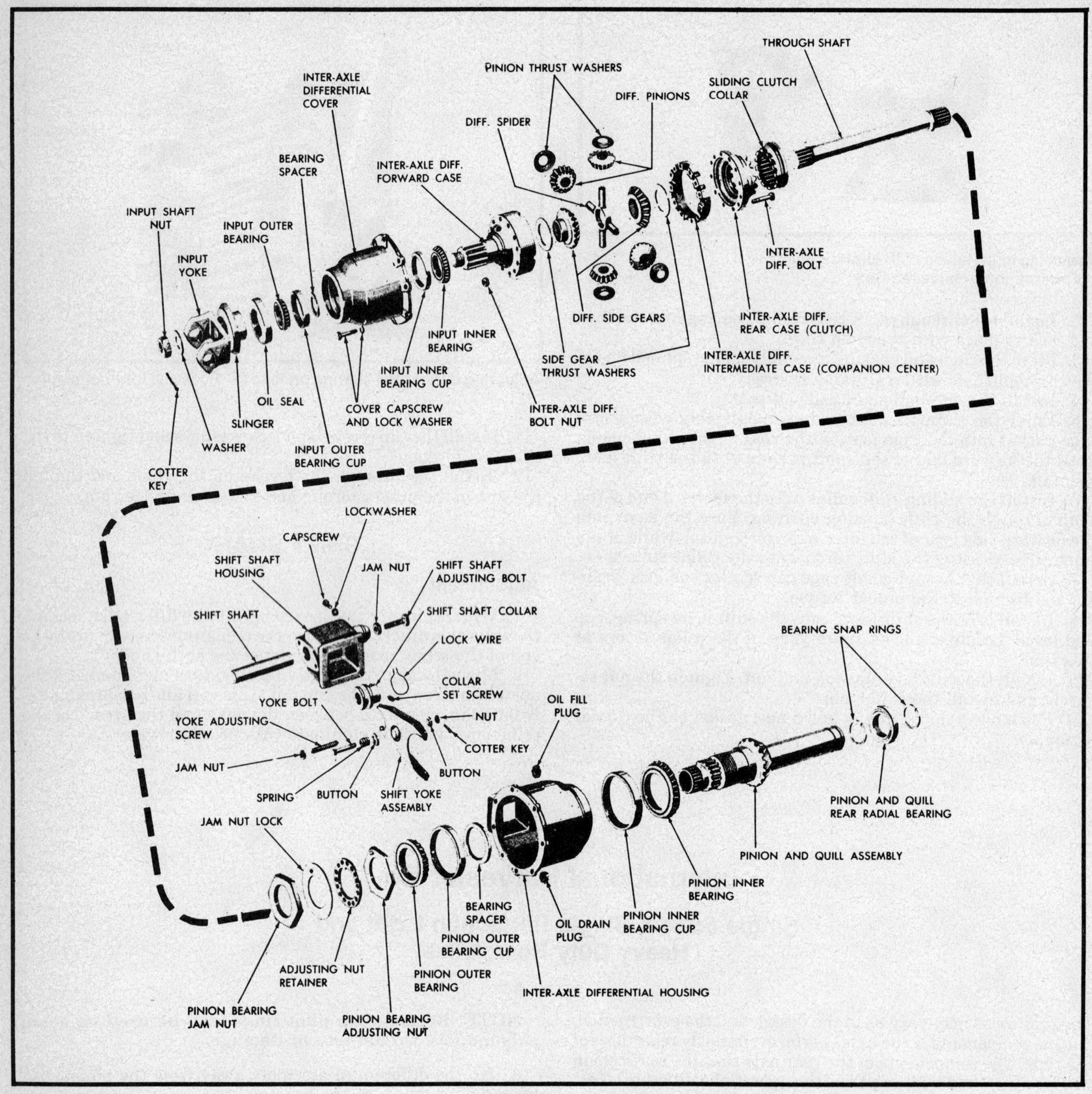

THROUGH SHAFT
PINION THRUST WASHERS
SLIDING CLUTCH COLLAR
INTER-AXLE DIFFERENTIAL COVER
DIFF. PINIONS
DIFF. SPIDER
BEARING SPACER
INTER-AXLE DIFF. FORWARD CASE
INPUT SHAFT NUT
INPUT OUTER BEARING
INPUT YOKE
INTER-AXLE DIFF. BOLT
DIFF. SIDE GEARS
INTER-AXLE DIFF. REAR CASE (CLUTCH)
INPUT INNER BEARING
SIDE GEAR THRUST WASHERS
INTER-AXLE DIFF. INTERMEDIATE CASE (COMPANION CENTER)
INPUT INNER BEARING CUP
OIL SEAL
COVER CAPSCREW AND LOCK WASHER
INTER-AXLE DIFF. BOLT NUT
SLINGER
WASHER
INPUT OUTER BEARING CUP
COTTER KEY
LOCKWASHER
CAPSCREW
SHIFT SHAFT HOUSING
JAM NUT
SHIFT SHAFT ADJUSTING BOLT
SHIFT SHAFT
SHIFT SHAFT COLLAR
BEARING SNAP RINGS
LOCK WIRE
COLLAR SET SCREW
YOKE BOLT
OIL FILL PLUG
NUT
YOKE ADJUSTING SCREW
COTTER KEY
JAM NUT
BUTTON
SPRING
BUTTON
SHIFT YOKE ASSEMBLY
PINION AND QUILL REAR RADIAL BEARING
JAM NUT LOCK
PINION AND QUILL ASSEMBLY
PINION INNER BEARING
BEARING SPACER
PINION INNER BEARING CUP
OIL DRAIN PLUG
PINION OUTER BEARING CUP
ADJUSTING NUT RETAINER
PINION OUTER BEARING
INTER-AXLE DIFFERENTIAL HOUSING
PINION BEARING JAM NUT
PINION BEARING ADJUSTING NUT

Exploded view of single reduction tandem rear axle (© International Harvester Co.)

DRIVE GEAR
RIGHT
DIFFERENTIAL CASE
WRONG

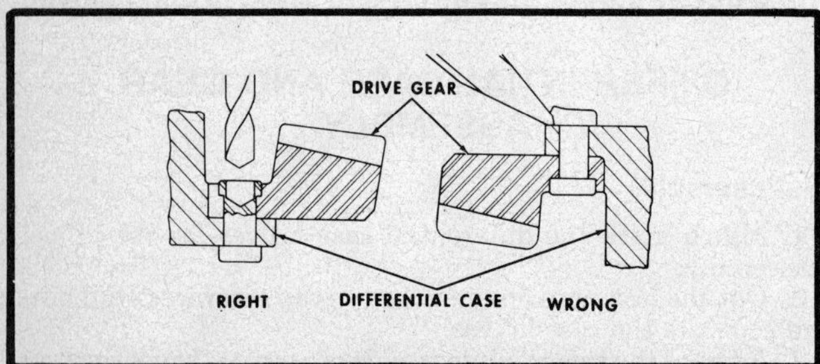

Right and wrong way to remove ring gear rivets (© International Harvester Co.)

head and using a drill, $^1/_{32}$ in. smaller than the rivet body, drill through the rivet head. Use a punch to press out the remaining part of the rivet.

CAUTION

Never use a chisel to cut off the head of the rivets or damage to the differential case can result.

PINION AND CAGE ASSEMBLY

Removal

1. Remove the pinion cage cap screws and remove the pinion cage assembly from the differential carrier.

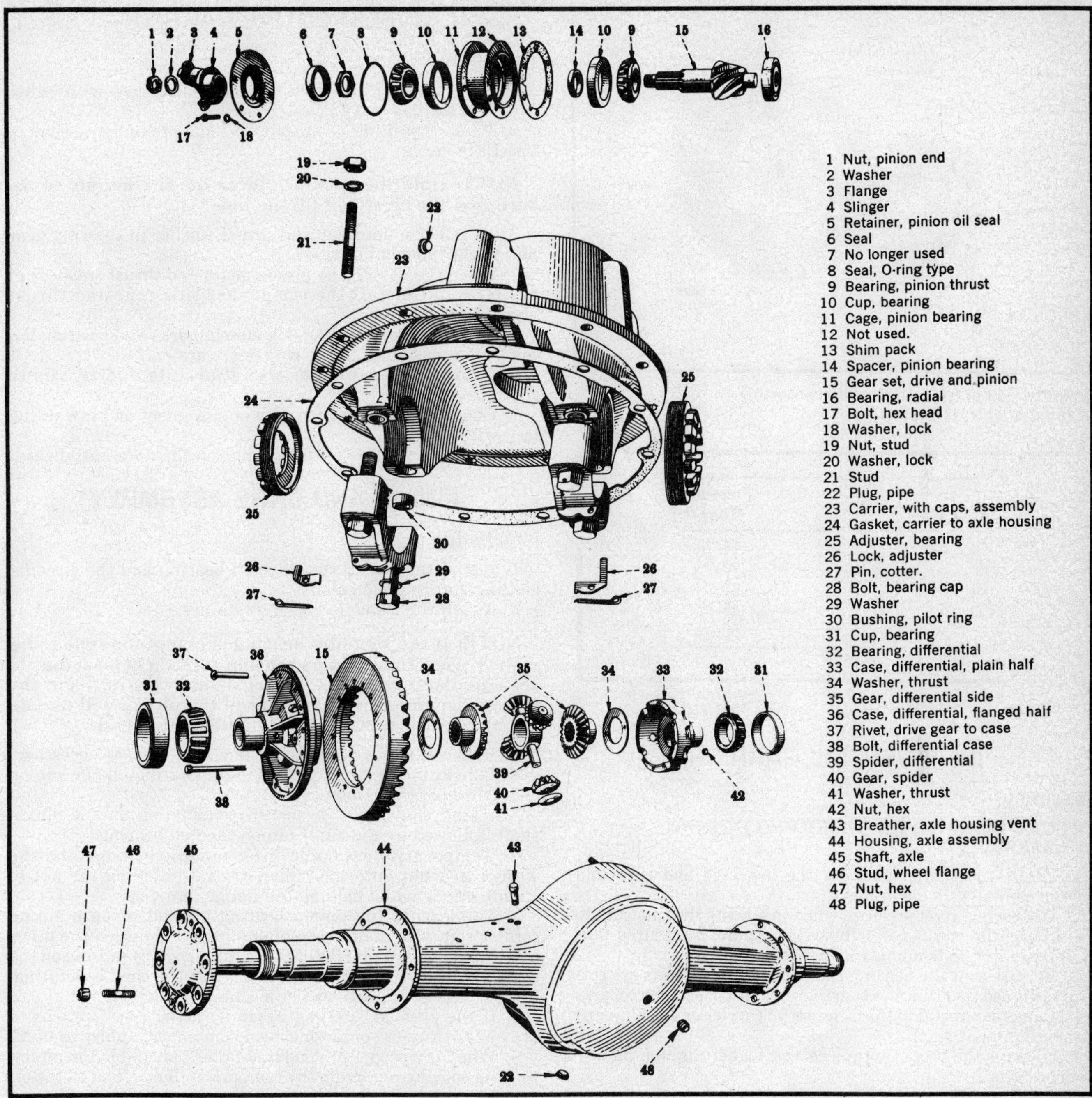

Exploded view of heavy duty single reduction rear axle (© International Harvester Co.)

NOTE: Puller screw holes are provided on some pinion cages, to assist in the removal of the cage from the housing. If not puller screw holes are present, a brass drift can be used on the inner end of the pinion to force the pinion and age assembly from the carrier housing. Do not use a drive on pinion shafts that have the straddle bearing retained by a snap-ring. The snap-ring groove may collapse.

2. Retain the shim pack for use during the reassembly.
3. Remove the companion flange from the pinion shaft, after the removal of the cotter pin and nut.

NOTE: The companion flange may have to be taped off the pinion shaft with a soft hammer.

4. Remove the outer bearing from the cage by holding the cage in a vise and tapping on the pinion shaft end, and forcing the shaft through the cage. Do not allow the component parts to fall.
5. Remove the spacer or spacer combination from the pinion shaft.
6. Remove the rear tapered thrust bearing from the pinion with the aid of a suitable puller.
7. Remove the straddle bearing retainer, if equipped, and remove the bearing with the aid of a suitable puller.

NOTE: The straddle bearing may be retained by staking of the pinion shaft end, by a snap-ring, or by a cap screw and washer.

Exploded view of typical differential assembly
(© International Harvester Co.)

Rivet Size	Pressure Tons
7/16	18–20
1/2	20–25
9/16	36
5/8	45–50
3/4	50

DIFFERENTIAL CARRIER

Assembly

PRECAUTIONS TO BE OBSERVED DURING REASSEMBLY

1. Before assembly, lubricate the bearings and cups and rewrap to maintain cleanliness.
2. Use correct rivet pressure when installing the ring gear to the differential case, or if bolts are available, be assured that the proper torque is applied in tightening.
3. Be sure that the bearing caps and adjusting nuts are correctly aligned and that the bearing cups fit properly. Irreparable damage can result to the differential carrier or bearing caps if the alignment is off.
4. Observe the proper torque settings when tightening any nuts or bolts.

Five Steps in the Reassembly of the Differential Assembly

1. Pinion bearing preload: this is determined by the thickness of the spacer between the two pinion thrust bearings, when tightened in the pinion cage.
2. Establish pinion nominal dimension: Use the manufacturers pinion setting gauge (SE–1065), or use an equivalent tool. Changes to this dimension can be made by adding or removing shims to move the pinion in or out of the carrier housing.
3. Set the ring gear lash: Move the ring gear to or from the pinion by means of the differential bearing adjusters.
4. Preload the differential bearing: This is accomplished by tightening the bearing adjusting nuts after zero end play has been obtained on the bearings.
5. Check the gear tooth contact: Use the paint impression method for this operation.

DIFFERENTIAL CARRIER

Assembly

1. Install the ring gear on the differential case with either the rivet method or by bolts.
2. When installing rivets, observe the pressures needed to upset the rivets.

NOTE: Hold the pressure force for one minute to assure that the rivet will fill the hole.

3. Install the side gear and thrust washer in the ring gear half of the differential case.
4. Place the spider, the pinion gears and thrust washers in position and install the component side gear and thrust washer.
5. Align the previously made match marks and position the component case half to the ring gear case half.
6. Install the cap screws or stud nuts and torque to specifications.
7. Check the gears for freedom of movement and install the lock wire.
8. Install the differential bearings on the differential case.

PINION AND CAGE ASSEMBLY

Installation

1. Install the rear thrust tapered bearing and the straddle bearing on the pinion shaft.
2. Install the straddle bearing retainer.

NOTE: If the straddle bearing is one of the type to be staked, use a blunt pin punch and stake in at least four to six equidistance places, approximately $^1/_8$ in. from the pinion circumference. The size of the pinion will dictate the number of staked points on the pinion end.

3. Renew the bearing cups in the pinion cage, as necessary.
4. Lubricate the bearings and cups and install the pinion shaft through the pinion cage.
5. Install the spacer or spacer combination on the pinion shaft, followed by the outer pinion tapered bearing.
6. Temporarily assemble the companion flange and the washer and nut onto the pinion shaft, tightening the nut to specifications while holding the flange in a vise.
7. To measure the pinion bearing preload, wrap a strong cord or soft wire around the pinion cage and attach the other end to a inch lbs. scale. Rotate the pinion cage by pulling on the spring scale and reading the scale while the cage is rotating. Refer to the specifications list within this chapter.
8. If the preload does not agree with the specifications, a thicker or thinner spacer or spacer combination must be used.
9. When the proper preload is obtained, assemble the pinion bearing cage by removing the companion flange, install the oil seal, cork gasket, reinstall the companion flange, washer and nut. Torque the nut to specifications and install the cotter pin.

PINION NOMINAL DIMENSION

To locate the pinion nominal dimension, refer to the specifications listed within this chapter. Some pinions will have the dimension stamped or etched on the gear end of the shaft. Refer and compare to the specifications. The pinion variation, noted in thousands of an in., will be etched on the gear end of the pinion shaft. This figure will be used in determining the amount of shims needed to locate the pinion gear in the proper relationship to the ring gear centerline.

NOTE: Refer to the beginning of the Rear Axle Drive section for the procedure to follow in the use of the pinion setting gauge tool If the pinion setting gauge tools are not available, the pinion depth will have to be adjusted by as-

Location of pinion setting markings—typical
(© International Harvester Co.)

sembling the carrier assembly, installing the pinion cage assembly and the differential assembly into the carrier housing, and observing the tooth contact pattern on the ring gear. This is a trial and error method and very time consuming.

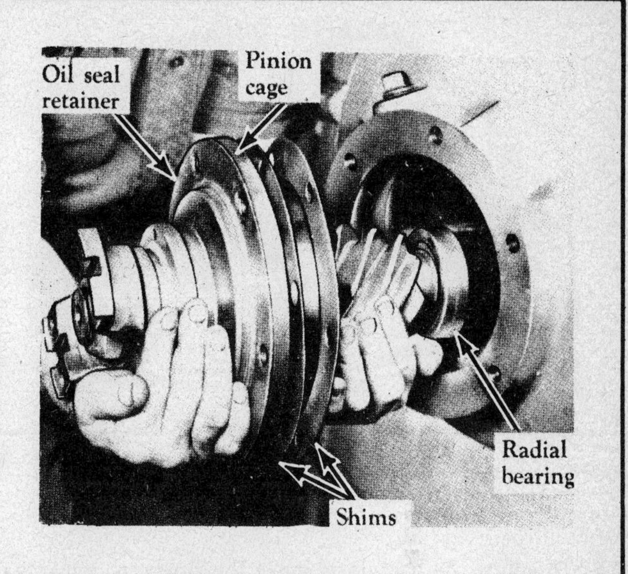

Pinion shaft and cage assembly—typical
(© International Harvester Co.)

DIFFERENTIAL ASSEMBLY

Installation, Preload, Backlash

1. Install the differential assembly with the bearing cups on the differential bearings into the legs of the carrier housing.
2. Install the bearing adjusting nuts and the bearing caps. Install the cap screws or stud nuts and turn the adjusting nuts while tightening the bearing caps to assure freedom of movement of the adjusting nuts.

CAUTION

If the bearing caps are not positioned properly, the adjusting nuts may be crossthreaded, and irreparable damage to the carrier housing or to the bearing cups may result.

3. With the side bearing caps loosened to permit the bearing cup movement, loosen the adjusting nuts only enough to notice end play on a dial indicator, mounted on the carrier assembly with the button contacting the back side of the ring gear.
4. Tighten the adjusting nuts to obtain zero end-play on the indicator.
5. Move the dial indicator to the coast side of the ring gear teeth, and determine the amount of back lash present between the pinion and the ring gear.

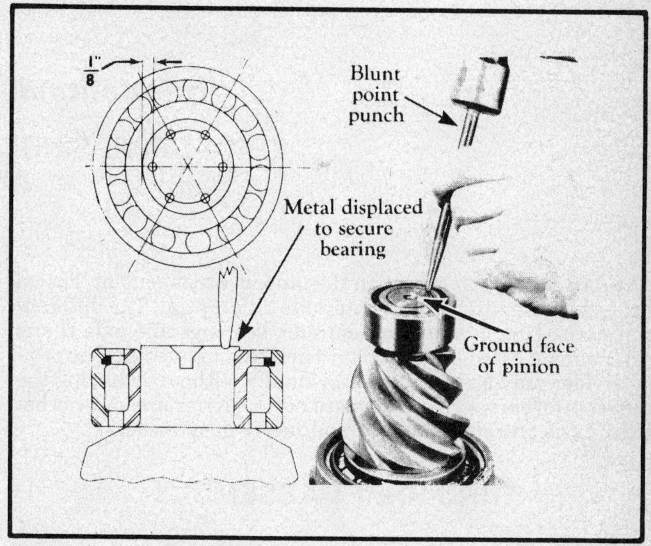

Staking straddle bearing to pinion shaft
(© International Harvester Co.)

SPECIFICATION

Axle Model	Pinion Nominal Dimension (in.)	Differential Bearing Preload (in.)	Pinion Cage Preload (in. lbs.)
RA 9, 18, 23, 28	2.625	0.015	①
RA 16, 17, 83, 84, 53, 54	3.125	0.015	①

① 10–20 in. lbs. for original bearing
20–40 in. lbs. for new bearing

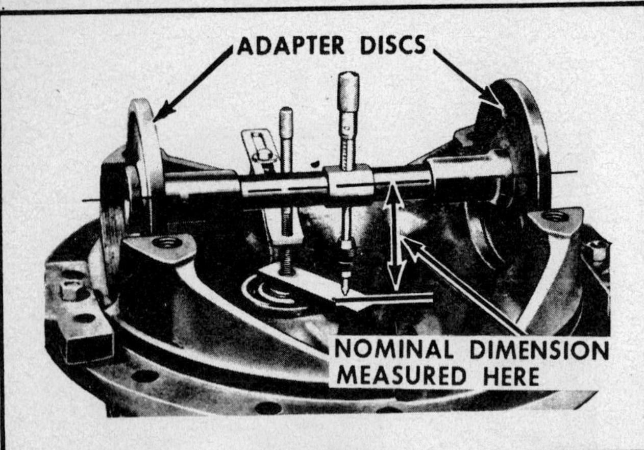

Use of pinion setting gauge—typical
(© International Harvester Co.)

6. To adjust the back lash, move the ring gear towards or away from the pinion by means of the differential bearing adjusting nuts. Move the adjusting nuts the same distance, either in or out to maintain the differential bearing zero-end-play.

7. When the correct backlash clearance is established, tighten each adjusting nut one or two notches (depending upon the axle model), to preload the differential bearings. Tighten the bearing cap screws or stud nuts to the proper torque and recheck the gear backlash. Install the adjusting nut locks and cotter pins.

8. Coat approximately twelve teeth of the ring gear with oiled red lead paint and rotate the pinion in its normal rotation and check the drive side of the ring gear teeth for the tooth contact impression.

NOTE: A sharper tooth contact impression may be obtained by applying a small amount of resistance to the gear with a flat steel bar and using a wrench to turn the pinion.

9. If the area of contact starts near the toe end of the ring gear and extends about $^2/_3$ of the tooth length, the tooth contact is satisfactory.

10. Install the ring gear thrust block, if equipped. Adjust the block firmly against the back face of the ring gear and back off the screw $^1/_4$ turn and lock the jam nut.

11 Install the carrier assembly into the housing, following the reverse procedure of the removal operation.

International Harvester Co.

THRU-DRIVE SINGLE REDUCTION REAR AXLE

The forward rear axle used in the tandem arrangement, has an integral power divider and interaxle differential. The differential parts, ring gear and pinion sets, bearings and axle shafts are common between the forward and rear axle units. The power divider may be removed individually without removing the differential carrier. The overhaul of the carrier assembly is basically the same as the light and heavy duty models.

THRU-SHAFT ASSEMBLY

Removal

1. Disconnect the inter-axle control linkage from the lever at the lock control housing.

NOTE: If equipped with air or vacuum controls, disconnect the air or vacuum lines at the cylinder.

2. Disconnect the drive shaft from the input and thru-shaft flanges.
3. Remove the thru-shaft bearing retainer bolts and loosen the bearing retainer from the housing.
4. Withdraw the bearing cage and the thru-shaft from the axle housing.

POWER DIVIDER ASSEMBLY

Removal

1. Remove the bolts from the inter-axle lock control housing and remove the housing.
2. Remove the inter-axle differential cover bolts and lift the inter-axle assembly from the power divider intermediate case.
3. Remove the intermediate case to differential carrier bolts and lift the intermediate case from the differential carrier.

Disassembly

1. Lift the inter lock clutch ring from the power divider input gear.
2. Remove and disassemble the input gear.

AXLE MODEL RA 341

a. Free the bearing snap-ring and remove by pressing the input shaft to the rear.
b. Remove the input shaft gear and the bearing by pressing forward to free the bearing from the bore.
c. Remove the bearing retainer nut.
d. Pull the bearing from the input gear with a puller tools.

AXLE MODELS RA 351, 355, 386, AND 387

a. Remove the bearing retainer mounting bolts from the rear of the intermediate case and tap the input gear, bearings and retainer assembly out towards the front.
b. Remove the bearing retainer nut and disassemble the retainer and bearing from the input gear.

NOTE: The inner bearing is a press fit and should only be removed if it is to be replaced. Clamp the input gear in a soft jawed vise only, when removing the bearing retainer nut.

3. Loosen and remove the idler shaft end nut while holding the shaft on the flats provided.
4. Support the rear face of the intermediate cover and press the idler shaft from the case.
5. Slide the idler gear and bearings from the cover.
6. Separate the bearings, bearing races, and bearing spacers from the idler gear.

NOTE: Axle models RA 351, 355, 386, and 387 use two bearing spacers.

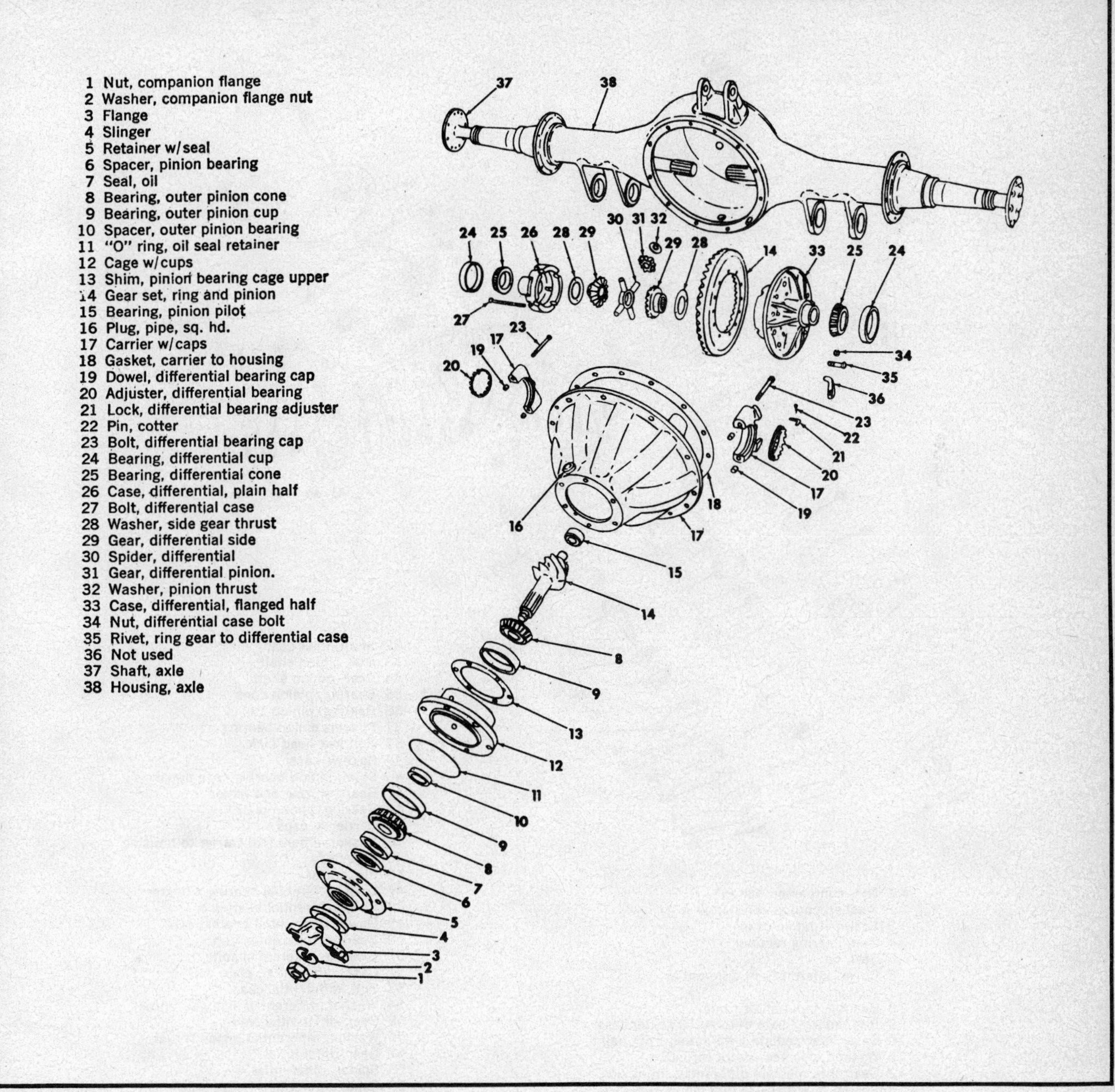

Exploded view of rear axle (© International Harvester Co.)

Assembly

1. Assemble the idler shaft bearings, bearing races and the bearing spacer(s) to the idler gear.

CAUTION

Axle models RA 351,355, 386 and 387, position the bearing spacers correctly to index the oil groove in the rear spacer with the oil passage in the idler shaft.

2. Position the idler shaft in the intermediate case so that the flat on the rear shaft will index with the flats on the differential carrier.
3. Support the front of the intermediate case and press the idler shaft into position.
4. Install the idler shaft end nut and washer and torque to specifications.
5. Using a dial indicator, measure the end play of the idler gear. See specifications for allowable limits.
6. If the end play is not within the allowable limits, increase or decrease the end play by installing a thicker or thinner bearing spacer.
7. Assemble the input gear and install.

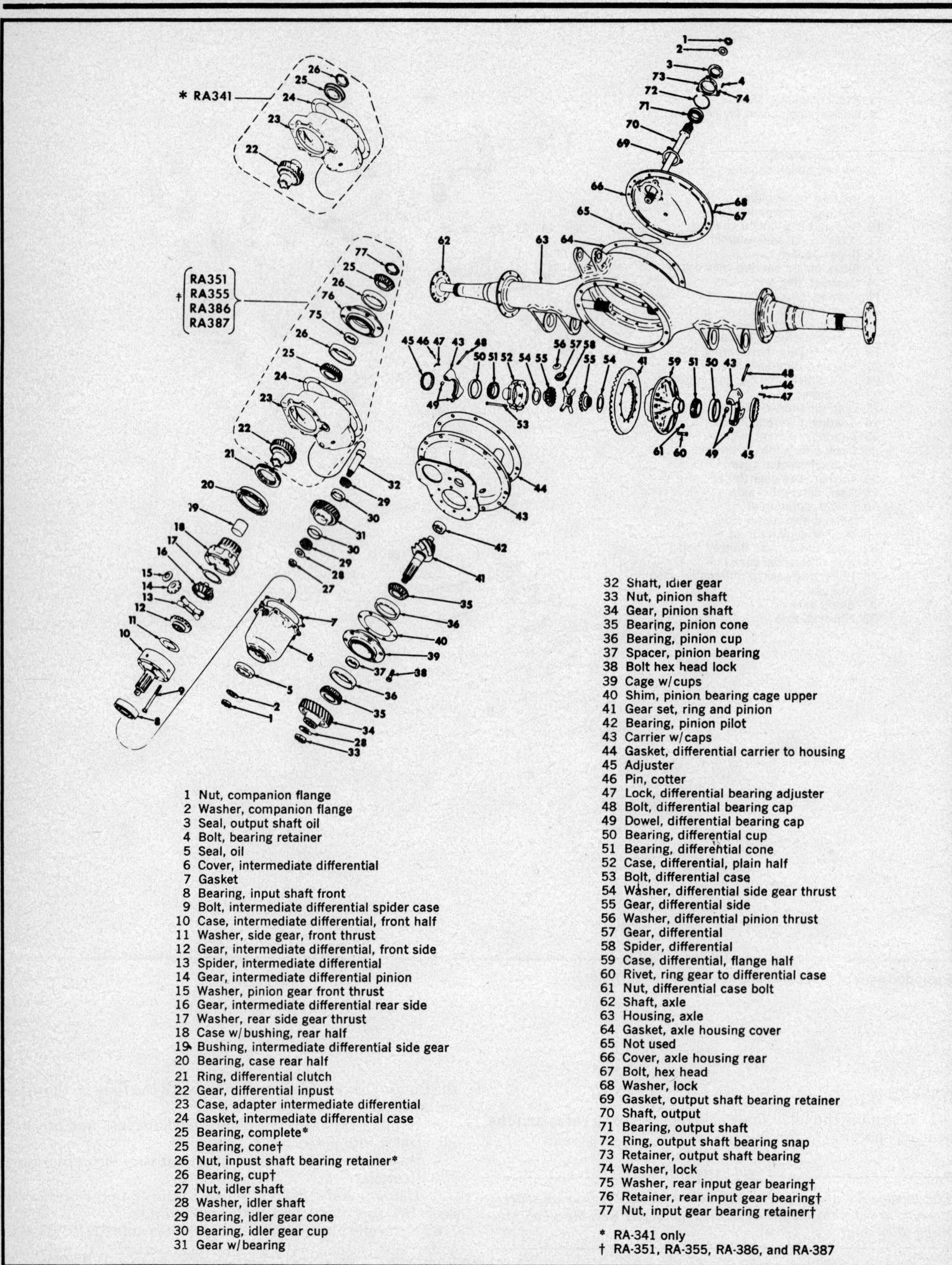

1 Nut, companion flange
2 Washer, companion flange
3 Seal, output shaft oil
4 Bolt, bearing retainer
5 Seal, oil
6 Cover, intermediate differential
7 Gasket
8 Bearing, input shaft front
9 Bolt, intermediate differential spider case
10 Case, intermediate differential, front half
11 Washer, side gear, front thrust
12 Gear, intermediate differential, front side
13 Spider, intermediate differential
14 Gear, intermediate differential pinion
15 Washer, pinion gear front thrust
16 Gear, intermediate differential rear side
17 Washer, rear side gear thrust
18 Case w/bushing, rear half
19 Bushing, intermediate differential side gear
20 Bearing, case rear half
21 Ring, differential clutch
22 Gear, differential inpust
23 Case, adapter intermediate differential
24 Gasket, intermediate differential case
25 Bearing, complete*
25 Bearing, cone†
26 Nut, inpust shaft bearing retainer*
26 Bearing, cup†
27 Nut, idler shaft
28 Washer, idler shaft
29 Bearing, idler gear cone
30 Bearing, idler gear cup
31 Gear w/bearing
32 Shaft, idler gear
33 Nut, pinion shaft
34 Gear, pinion shaft
35 Bearing, pinion cone
36 Bearing, pinion cup
37 Spacer, pinion bearing
38 Bolt hex head lock
39 Cage w/cups
40 Shim, pinion bearing cage upper
41 Gear set, ring and pinion
42 Bearing, pinion pilot
43 Carrier w/caps
44 Gasket, differential carrier to housing
45 Adjuster
46 Pin, cotter
47 Lock, differential bearing adjuster
48 Bolt, differential bearing cap
49 Dowel, differential bearing cap
50 Bearing, differential cup
51 Bearing, differential cone
52 Case, differential, plain half
53 Bolt, differential case
54 Washer, differential side gear thrust
55 Gear, differential side
56 Washer, differential pinion thrust
57 Gear, differential
58 Spider, differential
59 Case, differential, flange half
60 Rivet, ring gear to differential case
61 Nut, differential case bolt
62 Shaft, axle
63 Housing, axle
64 Gasket, axle housing cover
65 Not used
66 Cover, axle housing rear
67 Bolt, hex head
68 Washer, lock
69 Gasket, output shaft bearing retainer
70 Shaft, output
71 Bearing, output shaft
72 Ring, output shaft bearing snap
73 Retainer, output shaft bearing
74 Washer, lock
75 Washer, rear input gear bearing†
76 Retainer, rear input gear bearing†
77 Nut, input gear bearing retainer†

* RA-341 only
† RA-351, RA-355, RA-386, and RA-387

Exploded view of forward tandem axle (© International Harvester Co.)

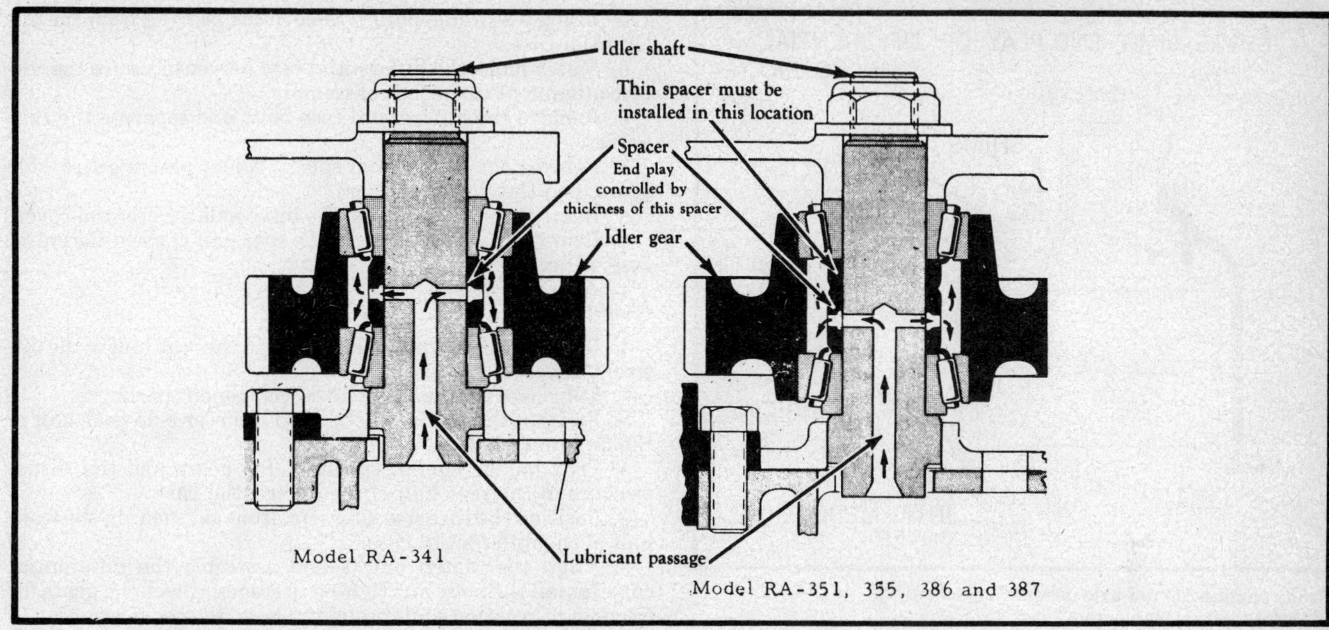

Cross section of idler shaft installation (© International Harvester Co.)

AXLE MODEL RA 341

a. Press the bearing on the input shaft gear.

b. Install the bearing retainer nut, and torque to specifications.

AXLE MODELS RA 351, 355, 386, AND 387

a. Use the original bearing spacer as a trial assembly. Install the bearing and cage on the input shaft and clamp the assembly in a holding fixture.

b. Install the bearing retainer nut and tighten to the specified torque.

c. Measure the input gear bearing end play with a dial indicator. Tolerance should be 0.001–0.003 in.

d. Use bearing spacers as necessary to obtain the correct end play.

e. Stake the retainer nut at the milled slot in the input gear, after the proper end play has been obtained.

f. Install the input gear bearings and cage assembly into the intermediate case and secure with the six hex-headed bolts.

INTER–AXLE DIFFERENTIAL ASSEMBLY

Removal

1. Remove the bolts from the inter-axle lock control housing and remove the housing.
2. Remove the inter-axle differential cover bolts and lift the inter-axle assembly from the power divider intermediate case.

Disassembly

1. Secure the input flange to a holding tool and remove the flange nut.
2. Using a press, force the inter-axle differential assembly from the cover and flange.

CAUTION

Do not allow the differential assembly to fall to the floor

3. Note and retain the shims located between the front bearing and cover.

NOTE: These shims control the end play of the differential assembly in the cover.

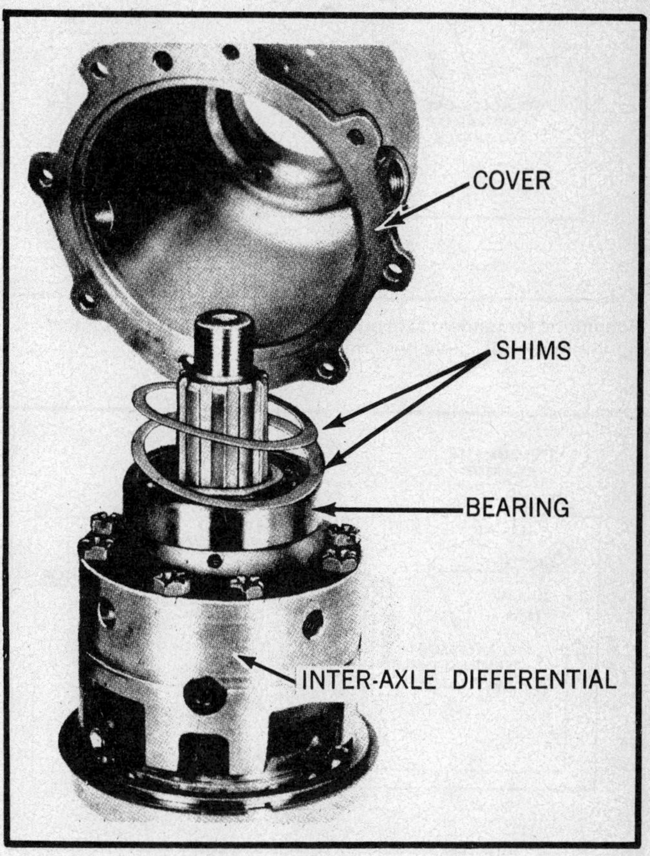

Cover removal—inter-axle differential
(© International Harvester Co.)

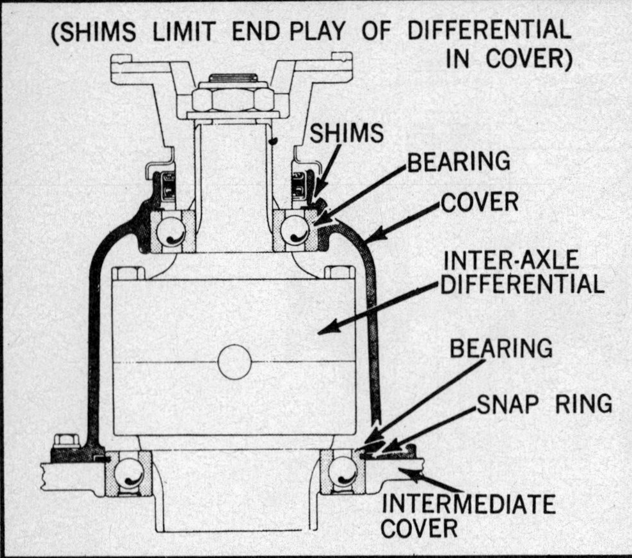

Cross section of inter-axle differential assembly
(© International Harvester Co.)

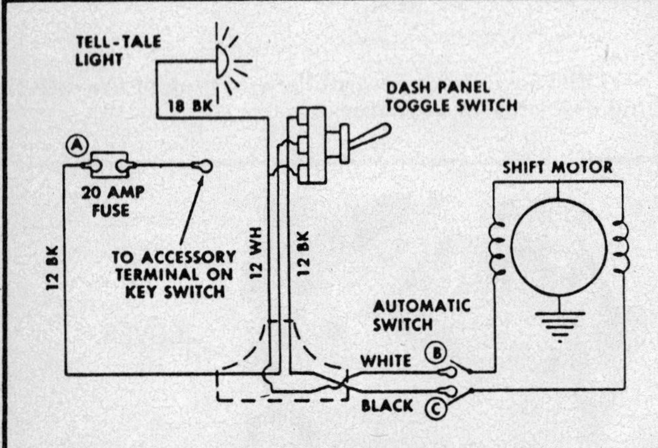

Schematic for tandem axle power divider lock electrical system
(© International Harvester Co.)

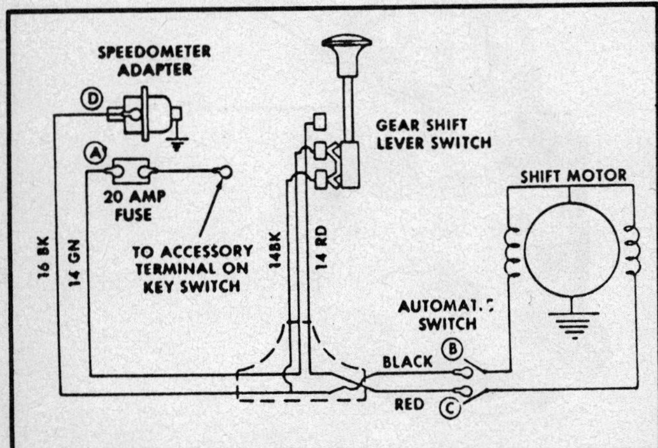

Schematic for two-speed axle shift electrical system
(© International Harvester Co.)

4. Using a suitable puller, remove the bearing from the differential case.
5. Match mark the differential case halves to insure the correct alignment upon the reassembly.
6. Remove the differential case bolts and separate the case halves.
7. Remove the differential spider, spider pinion gears, side gears, and the thrust washers.
8. Remove the oil seal from the inter-axle differential cover.
9. Remove the bushing from the rear half of the differential case, if necessary.

Assembly

1. Install the bushings, if removed, in the rear half of the differential case.
2. Lubricate all the differential component parts.
3. Position the thrust washer and the rear side gear half of the differential case.
4. Position the spider, spider pinion gears and the thrust washers in the rear half of the differential case.
5. Position the thrust washer and front side gear in the front half of the differential case.
6. Align the match marks and assemble the differential case. Install the bolts and tighten in stages. Check the gears for freedom of rotation and torque the bolts to specifications.
7. Press the front and rear bearings into the case.

NOTE: When pressing the front bearing on the case, be certain that the large radius on the inner race of the bearing is next to the case.

THRU–SHAFT ASSEMBLY

Disassembly

1. Remove the end flange nut and washer, and remove the flange from the thru-shaft.
2. Remove the bearing retainer with the seal and snap-ring.
3. Remove the seal and the snap-ring from the bearing retainer.
4. Press the bearing from the shaft.

Assembly

1. Press the bearing onto the shaft.
2. Install a new oil seal into the bearing retainer.
3. Position a new snap-ring into the bearing retainer.
4. Position the bearing retainer assembly onto the shaft.
5. Install the flange, washer and nut. Torque the nut to specifications.

FORWARD AND REAR REAR AXLE CARRIER ASSEMBLIES

Disassembly and Assembly

Because of the similarity of the drive axle assemblies, refer to the light and heavy duty rear axle section for the procedures necessary for the replacement and adjustment of the ring and pinion gears, the overhaul of the differential gear assembly, and the preloading of the pinion and differential bearings. Tolerance and torque specifications will be found in the accompanying charts.

POWER DIVIDER AND INTER–AXLE DIFFERENTIAL ASSEMBLIES

Installation

1. Install a new case gasket on the differential cover.
2. Position the intermediate case assembly on the differen-

tial carrier. Align the flats on the idler shaft to the flats within the carrier.

3. Install the intermediate case bolts and tighten to the specified torque.
4. Position the inter-axle lock clutch ring on the input gear.
5. Place a new gasket in position on the intermediate case.
6. Install the inter-axle differential assembly on the intermediate case, lining up the teeth to mesh properly of the input gear and the gear within the differential case.
7. Install the differential bolts and torque to specifications.
8. Install a new gasket on the lock control housing opening on the intermediate case, and install the lock control housing.
9. Install the lock control housing bolts and torque to specifications.

THRU–SHAFT ASSEMBLY

Installation

1. Place the thru-shaft bearing retainer gasket on the axle housing and insert the thru-shaft into position. Rotate the thru-shaft to mesh the shaft splines with the splines in the inter-axle differential side gears.
2. Install the bearing retainer bolts and tighten to the specified torque.
3. Install the drive shaft to the input and thru-shaft flanges.
4. Connect the inter-axle lock control linkage to the lever at the lock control housing.

NOTE: If equipped with air or vacuum controls, reconnect the air or vacuum lines.

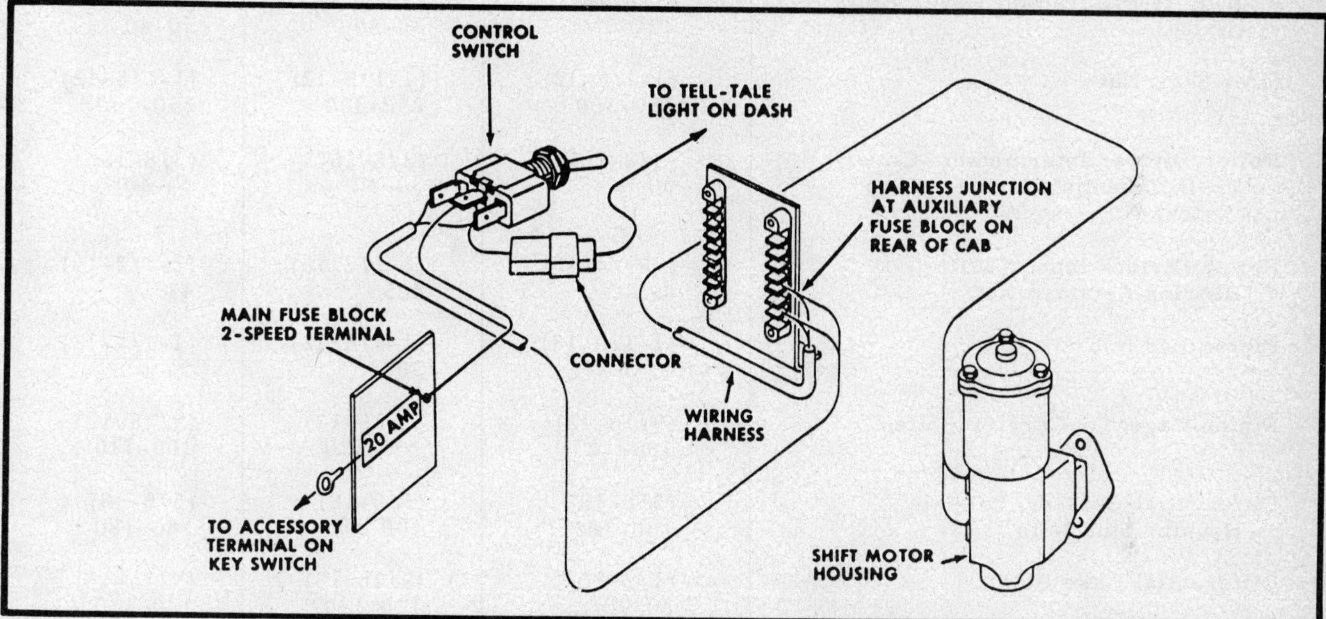

Electric shift system (tandem axle power divider lock type shown) (© International Harvester Co.)

SPECIFICATIONS

Axle Model	Pinion Nominal Dimension (in.)	Differential Bearing Preload	Pinion Cage Preload (in. lbs.)
RA 15, 20	2.9830	One notch each side	5–14
RA 25, 30	3.2530	One notch ech side	6–17
RA 29, 39	3.4725	One notch each side	6–17
RA 42, 44, 47, 48	3.7695	1½ to 3 notches—total both sides	3–8
RA 57, 474	4.2845	1½ to 3 notches—total both sides	3–8
RA 70	①	One notch each side	5–8
RA 71	4.344	One notch each side	5–8
RA 72, 73, 74, 76	4.613	One notch each side	5–8
RA 75, 78	4.600	Two notches from zero end play	
RA 341	3.4725	One notch each side	3–8
RA 351, 355, 472, 386, 387	3.7695	1½ to 3 notch—total	3–8

① Pinion straddle bearing secured with a snap-ring—4.344. Pinion straddle bearing secured with a cap screw—4.596.

TORQUE CHART (Ft. Lbs.)

IH MODEL IH CODE	RA-341 14341	RA-351, 386 14351, 14386	RA-355, 387 14355, 14387
Input Shaft End Nut	(1-1/4-12) 700*	(1-1/4-12) 700*	(1-1/4-12) 700*
Inter-Axle Differential Case Bolts	(1/2-13) 80-100	(1/2-13) 80-100	(1/2-13) 80-100
Inter-Axle Differential Cover Bolts (Nylok)	(3/8-16) 30-40	(3/8-16) 30-40	(3/8-16) 30-40
Idler Shaft Nut	(1-1/8-12) 250-300	(1-1/8-12) 250-300	(1-1/8-12) 250-300
Power Divider Intermediate Cover-To-Differential Carrier Bolts (Nylok)	(3/8-16) 30-40	(3/8-16) 30-40	(3/8-16) 30-40
Power Divider Input Gear Bearing Retainer Nut	(2-1/2-16) 425	(2-1/2-16) 425	(2-1/2-16) 425
Pinion End Nut	(1-1/8-18) 325*	(1-1/4-12) 700*	(1-1/4-12) 700*
Pinion Cage-To-Carrier Bolts	(9/16-12) 100-120	(9/16-12) 100-120	(9/16-12) 100-120
Differential Carrier-To-Axle Housing Stud Nuts	(5/8-18) 160-180	(5/8-18) 160-180	(5/8-18) 160-180
Differential Case Bolts	(1/2-20) 80-90	(9/16-18) 120-130	(9/16-18) 120-130
Differential Bearing Cap-To-Carrier Bolts	(9/16-18) 150-160	(1-14) 400-500	(1-14) 400-500
Axle Flange-To-Wheel Hub Stud Nuts	(5/8-18) 120-140	(5/8-18) 120-140	(3/4-16) 225-250
Inter-Axle Lock Control Housing Bolts (Nylok)	(7/16-14) 30-40	(7/16-14) 30-40	(7/16-14) 30-40
Thru Shaft Rear Bearing Retainer Bolts	(3/8-16) 30-40	(3/8-16) 30-40	(3/8-16) 30-40
Thru Shaft End Nut	(1-1/4-12) 700*	(1-1/4-12) 700*	(1-1/4-12) 700*
Input Gear Bearing Cage Bolts (Nylok)		(3/8-16) 30-40	(3/8-16) 30-40

*Minimum - where cotter pin is used, increase torque as needed to permit installation of cotter pin. Do not back off nut to align cotter pin holes.

Troubleshooting and Diagnosis

OIL LEAK DIAGNOSIS

Diagnosing oil leaks can sometimes be a difficult task if good diagnostic procedures are not followed. Drive train component sealing techniques have changed rapidly in the last few years. The use of anerobic, R.T.V., and other sealers has changed many service procedures in the field. Some things haven't changed, and that is the importance of careful diagnosis and cleanliness of the components during the repairs. This book was developed as an aid to assist you in proper oil leak diagnosis and sealing procedures. The following chapters will provide you with a guide for diagnosing oil leaks in the major components of the vehicle.

HOW TO IDENTIFY LEAKING FLUID

Use the following guide to determine the identity of the leaking fluid

Source	Color* of Fluid
Engine	Amber or Black
Transmission (Auto)	Red
Transaxle (Auto & Man.)	Red
Transmission (A-833)	Red
Transmission (A-435 & 445)	Brown
Rear Axle	Brown
Power Steering	Amber

*Fluids will change color with time and mileage.

OIL LEAK DIAGNOSTIC METHODS

1. VISUAL INSPECTION

- Thoroughly clean suspected leak area. (Use solvent if necessary).
- Blow Dry.
- Start vehicle and operate system* for several minutes or until leak occurs. (Example: If power steering rack is leaking, move rack back and forth several times).

2. LEAK TRACING POWDER

- Thoroughly clean suspected area to be checked, removing all oil and grease.
- Spray leak tracing powder over entire area to be checked.
- Start vehicle and operate system* for several minutes.
- Check for oil leak. Areas where oil is leaking will show up as brown or black spots.
- If leak is not observed, repeat previous two steps.

3. FLUORESCENT DYE OIL ADDITIVE (Do NOT use in power steering systems)

- Add approximately 1 ounce of dye additive to oil. (Some situations will require a second ounce, i.e.: excessively dirty oil, graphite or molybdenum sulfide based oil, or a large capacity crank case).
- Start vehicle and operate suspected system* for several minutes to thoroughly mix and circulate dye into oil. Extremely fine leaks may require a longer time.
- Use "black light" to examine suspected areas for bright yellow glow which will indicate leak path or source.

4. LOW-PRESSURE LEAK TEST

- Attach air hose to: engine-dipstick tube, auto trans.-cooler fitting, manual trans.-vent or fill plug hole, rear axle-vent.
- Regulate air pressure to a maximum of four P.S.I.
- Apply soapy water to suspected area; look for bubbles.
- For non-accessible areas, use a stethoscope with a long probe to listen for escaping air.

5. HIGH-PRESSURE LEAK TEST (ENGINE ONLY)

- Remove oil pressure switch and, with adaptor, attach air hose.
- Regulate air pressure to 80-100 P.S.I.
- Apply soapy water to suspected areas and look for bubbles.
- For non-accessible area, use a stethoscope with a long probe to listen for escaping air.

* NOTE: A road test may be necessary to duplicate conditions that result in oil leaks.

ENGINE OIL LEAKS

TYPICAL HIGH PRESSURE LEAK AREAS

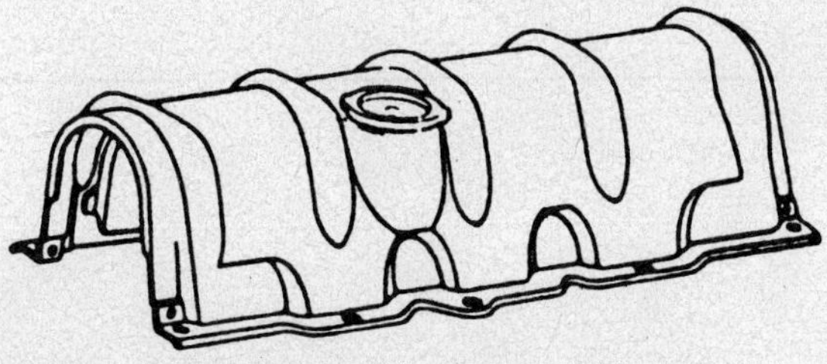

Cylinder Head Cover

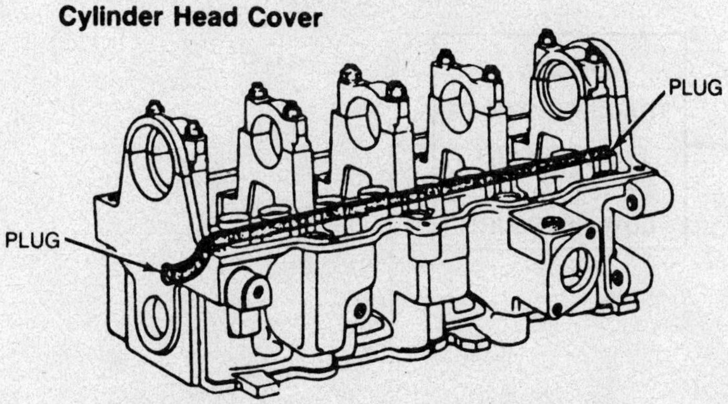

Cylinder Head

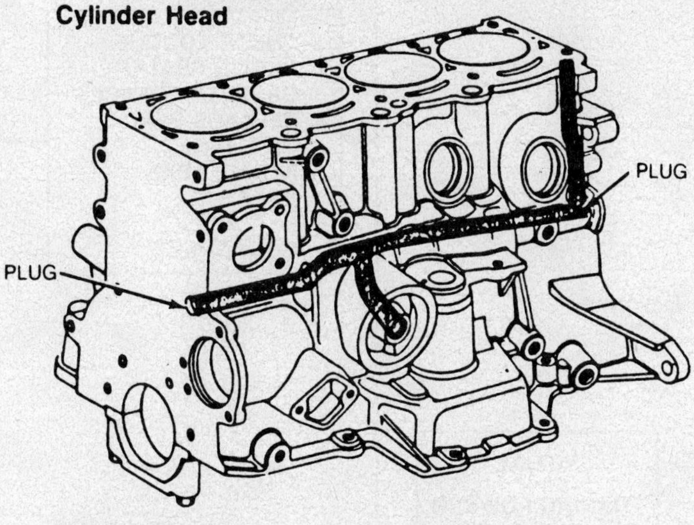

Cylinder Block

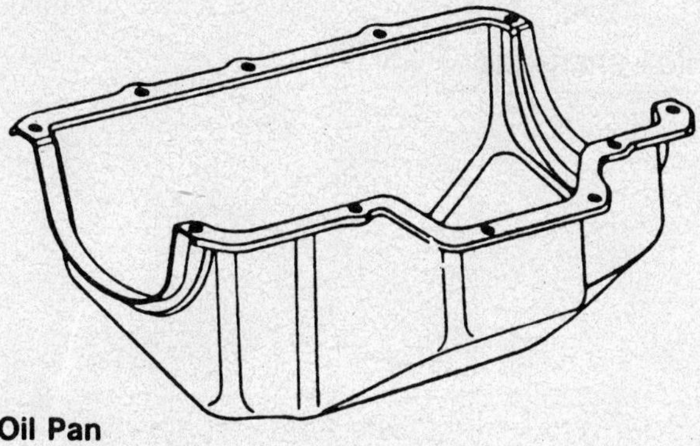

Oil Pan

ENGINE OIL LEAK DIAGNOSIS

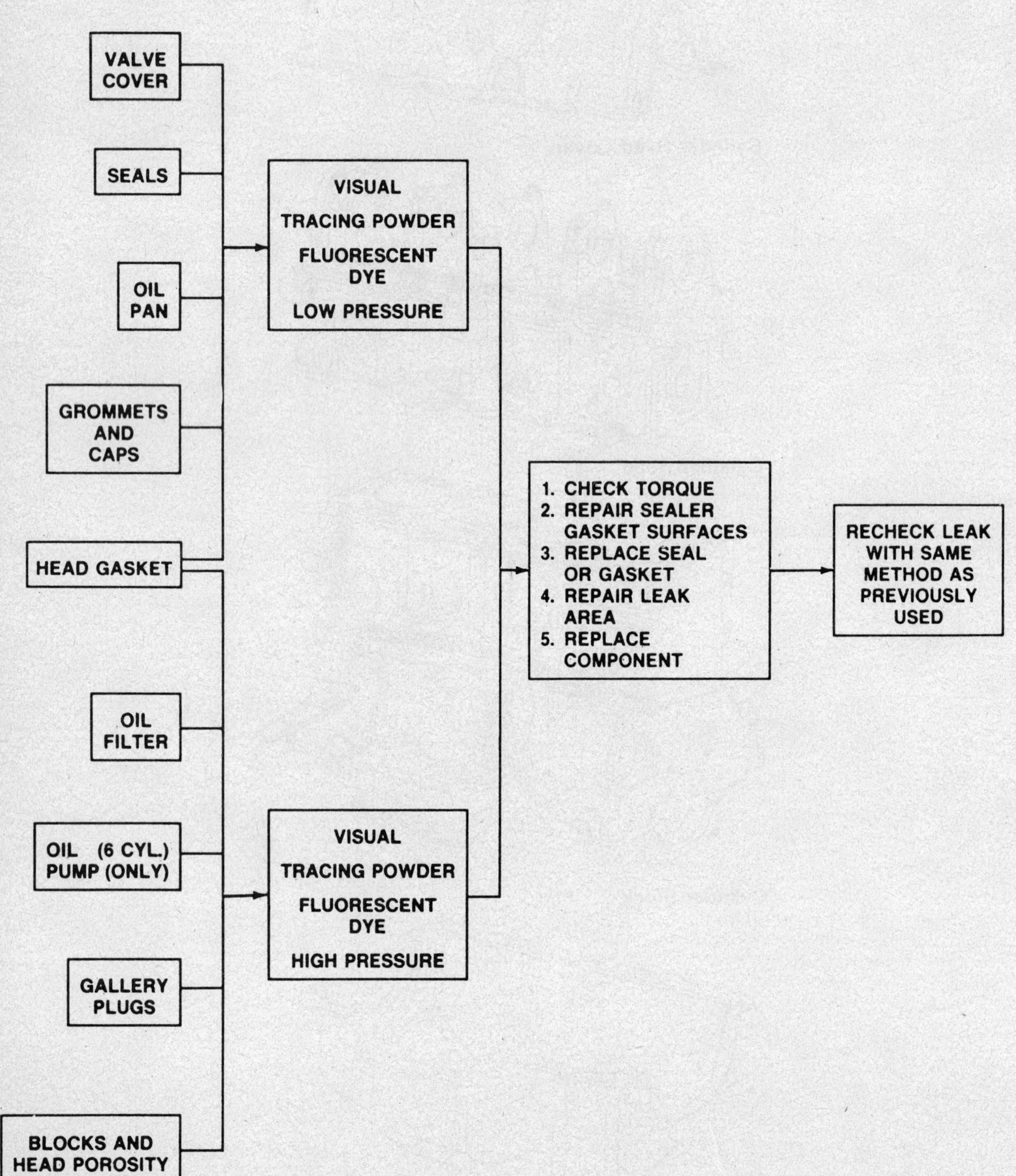
SUSPECTED LEAK SOURCE
DETECTION METHOD
CORRECTIVE ACTION
REPAIR CHECK
VALVE COVER
SEALS
OIL PAN
GROMMETS AND CAPS
HEAD GASKET
OIL FILTER
OIL PUMP (6 CYL.) (ONLY)
GALLERY PLUGS
BLOCKS AND HEAD POROSITY
VISUAL
TRACING POWDER
FLUORESCENT DYE
LOW PRESSURE
VISUAL
TRACING POWDER
FLUORESCENT DYE
HIGH PRESSURE
1. CHECK TORQUE
2. REPAIR SEALER GASKET SURFACES
3. REPLACE SEAL OR GASKET
4. REPAIR LEAK AREA
5. REPLACE COMPONENT
RECHECK LEAK WITH SAME METHOD AS PREVIOUSLY USED

MANUAL TRANSMISSION & TRANSAXLE OIL LEAKS

TYPICAL LEAK AREAS

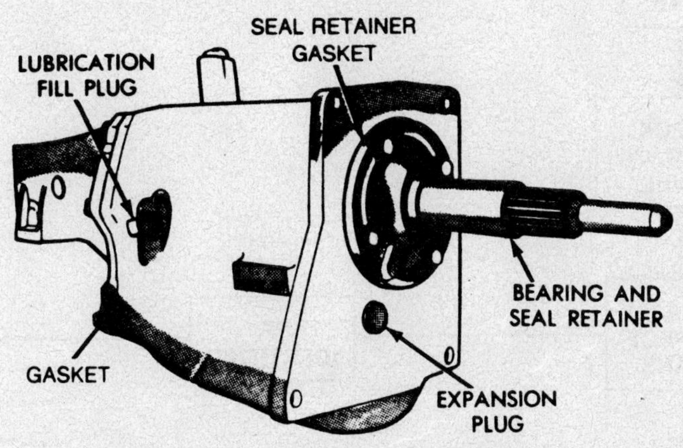

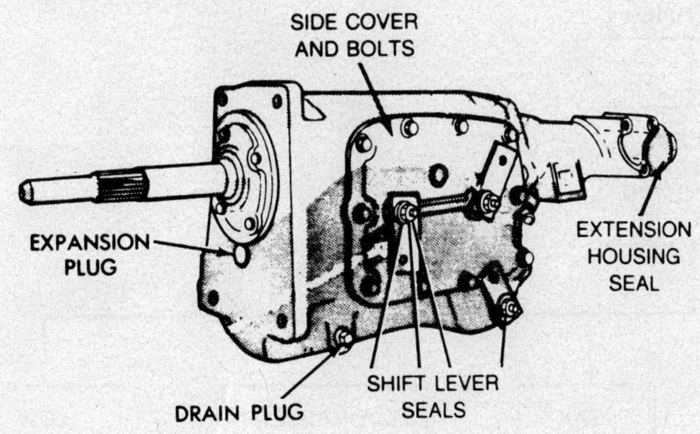

MANUAL TRANSMISSION & TRANSAXLE OIL LEAKS

PRELIMINARY LEAK DIAGNOSIS

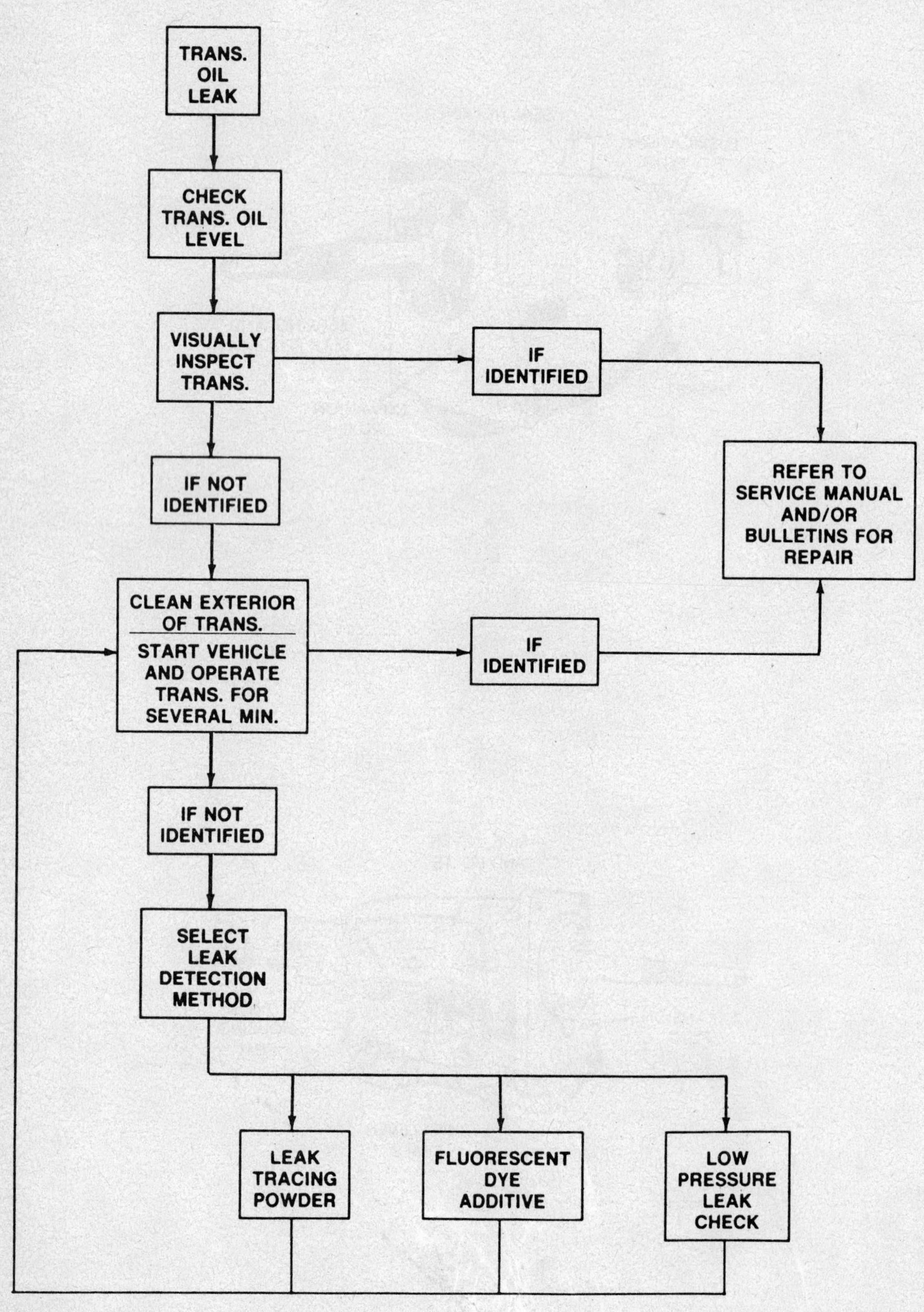

MANUAL TRANSMISSION — LEAK DIAGNOSIS

SUSPECTED LEAK SOURCE	DETECTION METHOD	CORRECTIVE ACTION	REPAIR CHECK
VENT	VISUAL FLUORESCENT DYE TRACING POWDER	CHECK FLUID LEVEL	VERIFY REPAIR OF LEAK WITH SAME METHOD USED FOR DETECTION
BACK-UP LAMP	VISUAL TRACING POWDER FLUORESCENT DYE	CHECK TORQUE HELI-COIL	VERIFY REPAIR OF LEAK WITH SAME METHOD USED FOR DETECTION
SIDE COVER AND BOLTS	VISUAL TRACING POWDER FLUORESCENT DYE	CHECK TORQUE	VERIFY REPAIR OF LEAK WITH SAME METHOD USED FOR DETECTION
SHIFT LEVER SEAL	VISUAL TRACING POWDER LOW PRESSURE FLUORESCENT DYE	REPLACE SEAL	VERIFY REPAIR OF LEAK WITH SAME METHOD USED FOR DETECTION
EXTENSION HOUSING	VISUAL TRACING POWDER FLUORESCENT DYE	CHECK TORQUE RE-SEAL	VERIFY REPAIR OF LEAK WITH SAME METHOD USED FOR DETECTION
EXTENSION HOUSING SEAL	VISUAL TRACING POWDER LOW PRESSURE FLUORESCENT DYE	REPLACE SEAL	VERIFY REPAIR OF LEAK WITH SAME METHOD USED FOR DETECTION
FILL PLUG OR DRAIN PLUG	VISUAL TRACING POWDER FLUORESCENT DYE	CHECK TORQUE HELI-COIL	VERIFY REPAIR OF LEAK WITH SAME METHOD USED FOR DETECTION
CASE POROSITY	VISUAL TRACING POWDER LOW PRESSURE FLUORESCENT DYE	WICK N SEAL	VERIFY REPAIR OF LEAK WITH SAME METHOD USED FOR DETECTION
INPUT SHAFT SEAL AND GASKET	VISUAL TRACING POWDER LOW PRESSURE FLUORESCENT DYE	REPLACE SEAL OR GASKET	VERIFY REPAIR OF LEAK WITH SAME METHOD USED FOR DETECTION

MANUAL TRANSMISSION — TYPICAL LEAK AREAS

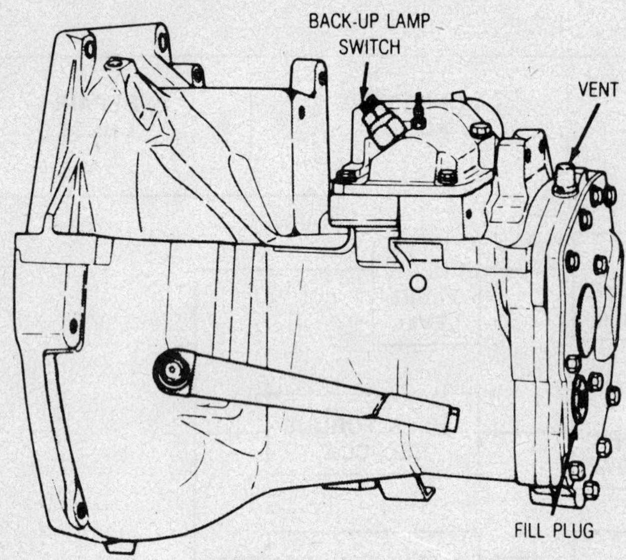

Transaxle—Left Side

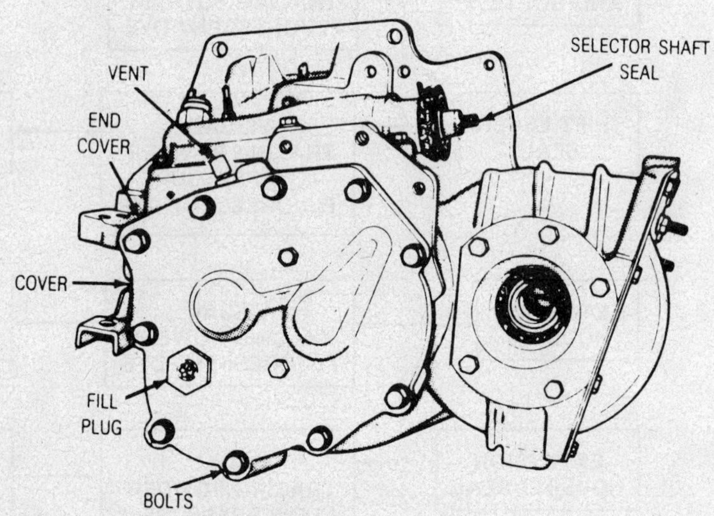

Transaxle—Rear End View

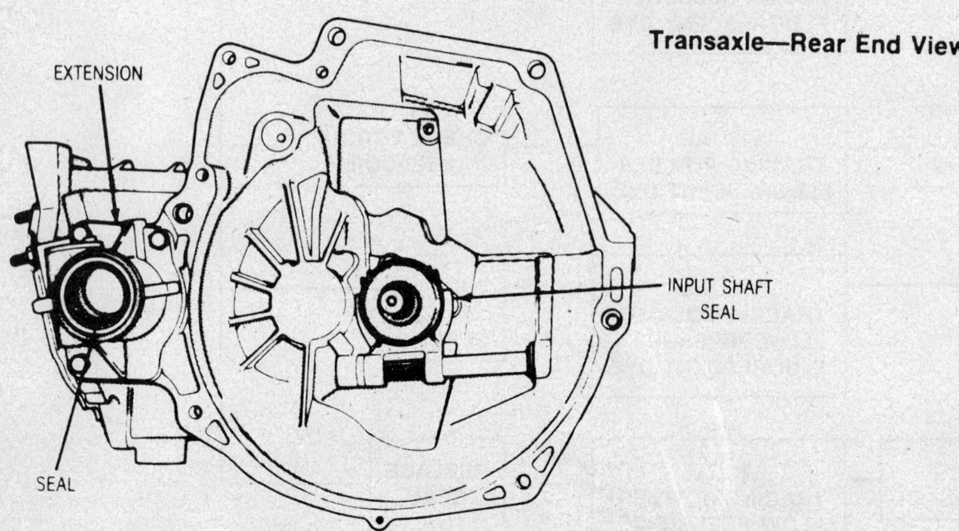

Transaxle—Front End View

MANUAL TRANSAXLE — LEAK DIAGNOSIS

SUSPECTED LEAK SOURCE	DETECTION METHOD	CORRECTIVE ACTION	REPAIR CHECK
VENT	VISUAL FLUORESCENT DYE TRACING POWDER	CHECK FLUID LEVEL	VERIFY REPAIR OF LEAK WITH SAME METHOD USED FOR DETECTION
BACK-UP LAMP	VISUAL TRACING POWDER FLUORESCENT DYE	CHECK TORQUE HELI-COIL	VERIFY REPAIR OF LEAK WITH SAME METHOD USED FOR DETECTION
SHIFT COVER BOLTS	VISUAL TRACING POWDER FLUORESCENT DYE	CHECK TORQUE	VERIFY REPAIR OF LEAK WITH SAME METHOD USED FOR DETECTION
SELECTOR SHAFT SEAL	VISUAL TRACING POWDER LOW PRESSURE FLUORESCENT DYE	REPLACE SEAL	VERIFY REPAIR OF LEAK WITH SAME METHOD USED FOR DETECTION
EXTENSION HOUSING	VISUAL TRACING POWDER FLUORESCENT DYE	CHECK TORQUE RE-SEAL	VERIFY REPAIR OF LEAK WITH SAME METHOD USED FOR DETECTION
DIFF. BRG. RETAINER AND EXTENSION HOUSING SEAL	VISUAL TRACING POWDER LOW PRESSURE FLUORESCENT DYE	REPLACE SEAL	VERIFY REPAIR OF LEAK WITH SAME METHOD USED FOR DETECTION
END & DIFF. COVER	VISUAL TRACING POWDER FLUORESCENT DYE	CHECK TORQUE RE-SEAL	VERIFY REPAIR OF LEAK WITH SAME METHOD USED FOR DETECTION
FILL PLUG	VISUAL TRACING POWDER FLUORESCENT DYE	CHECK TORQUE HELI-COIL	VERIFY REPAIR OF LEAK WITH SAME METHOD USED FOR DETECTION
CASE POROSITY	VISUAL TRACING POWDER LOW PRESSURE FLUORESCENT DYE	WICK N SEAL	VERIFY REPAIR OF LEAK WITH SAME METHOD USED FOR DETECTION
INPUT SHAFT SEAL	VISUAL TRACING POWDER LOW PRESSURE FLUORESCENT DYE	REPLACE SEAL	VERIFY REPAIR OF LEAK WITH SAME METHOD USED FOR DETECTION

AUTOMATIC TRANSMISSION OIL LEAKS

TYPICAL LEAK AREAS

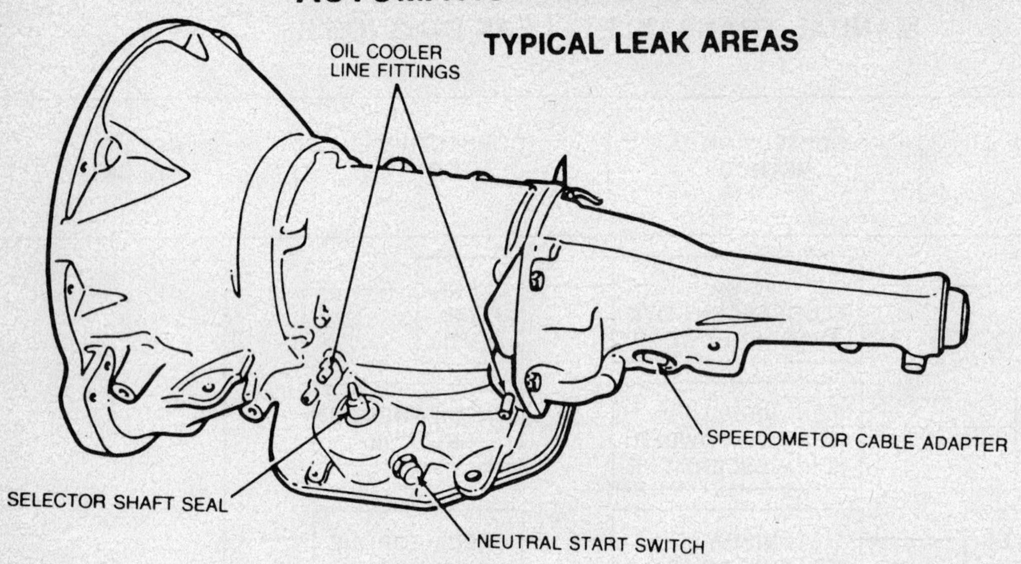

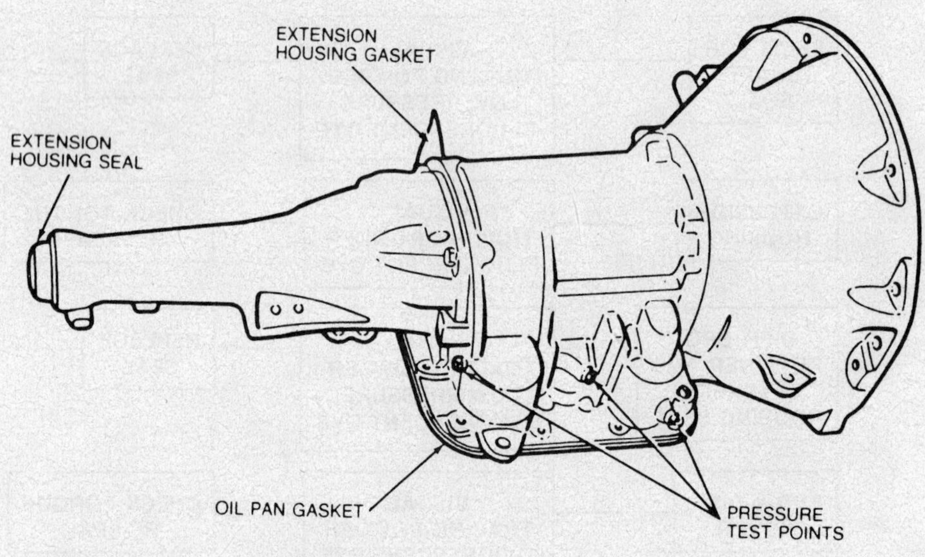

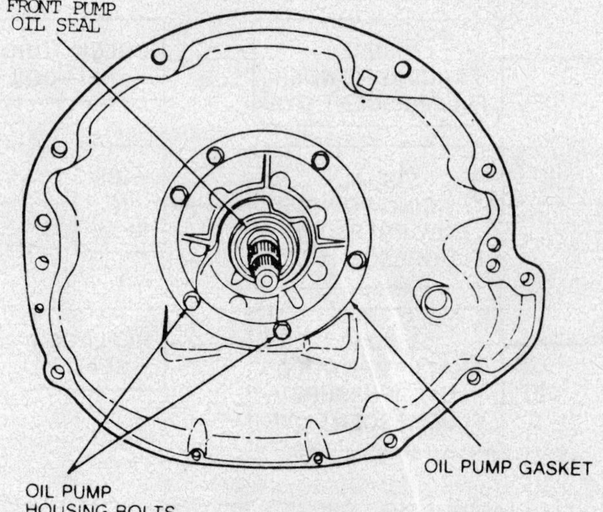

AUTOMATIC TRANSMISSION OIL LEAKS

PRELIMINARY LEAK DIAGNOSIS

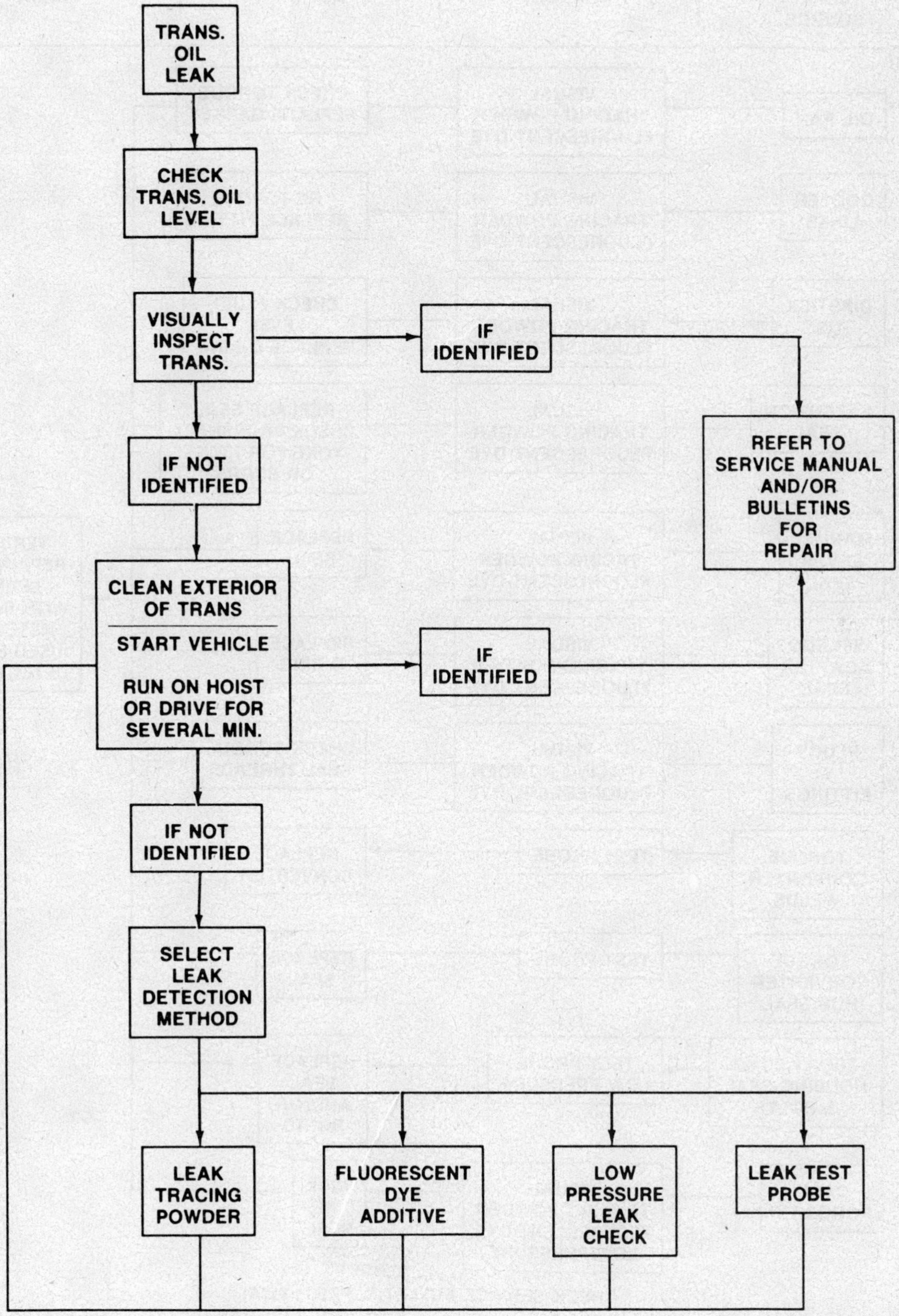

TRANS. OIL LEAK

CHECK TRANS. OIL LEVEL

VISUALLY INSPECT TRANS.

IF IDENTIFIED

IF NOT IDENTIFIED

REFER TO SERVICE MANUAL AND/OR BULLETINS FOR REPAIR

CLEAN EXTERIOR OF TRANS

START VEHICLE

RUN ON HOIST OR DRIVE FOR SEVERAL MIN.

IF IDENTIFIED

IF NOT IDENTIFIED

SELECT LEAK DETECTION METHOD

LEAK TRACING POWDER

FLUORESCENT DYE ADDITIVE

LOW PRESSURE LEAK CHECK

LEAK TEST PROBE

AUTOMATIC TRANSMISSION OIL LEAKS

LEAK DIAGNOSIS

SUSPECTED LEAK SOURCE	DETECTION METHOD	CORRECTIVE ACTION	REPAIR CHECK
OIL PAN	VISUAL TRACING POWDER FLUORESCENT DYE	CHECK TORQUE REPLACE GASKET	VERIFY REPAIR OF LEAK WITH SAME METHOD USED FOR DETECTION
COOLER LINES	VISUAL TRACING POWDER FLUORESCENT DYE	RE-TORQUE REPLACE FITTING	
DIPSTICK TUBE	VISUAL TRACING POWDER FLUORESCENT DYE	CHECK FLUID LEVEL REPLACE O-RING	
EXTENSION SEAL	VISUAL TRACING POWDER FLUORESCENT DYE	REPLACE SEAL CHECK PROPSHAFT YOKE FOR NICKS OR BURRS	
MANUAL LEVER SEAL	VISUAL TACING POWDER FLUORESCENT DYE	REPLACE SEAL	
SPEEDO ADAPTER SEAL	VISUAL TRACING POWDER FLUORESCENT DYE	REPLACE O-RING	
PLUGS & FITTINGS	VISUAL TRACING POWDER FLUORESCENT DYE	CHECK TORQUE SEAL THREADS	
TORQUE CONVERTER WELDS	TEST PROBE	REPLACE CONVERTER	
TORQUE CONVERTER HUB SEAL	TEST PROBE	REPLACE SEAL	
FRONT PUMP HOUSING SEAL & BOLTS	TEST PROBE LOW PRESSURE	REPLACE SEAL AND/OR BOLTS	
CASE POROSITY	VISUAL TRACING POWDER FLOURESCENT DYE LOW PRESSURE	WICK N SEAL	

* CHECK SERVICE BULLETIN #21-11-82(A)

AUTOMATIC TRANSAXLE OIL LEAKS

TYPICAL LEAK AREAS

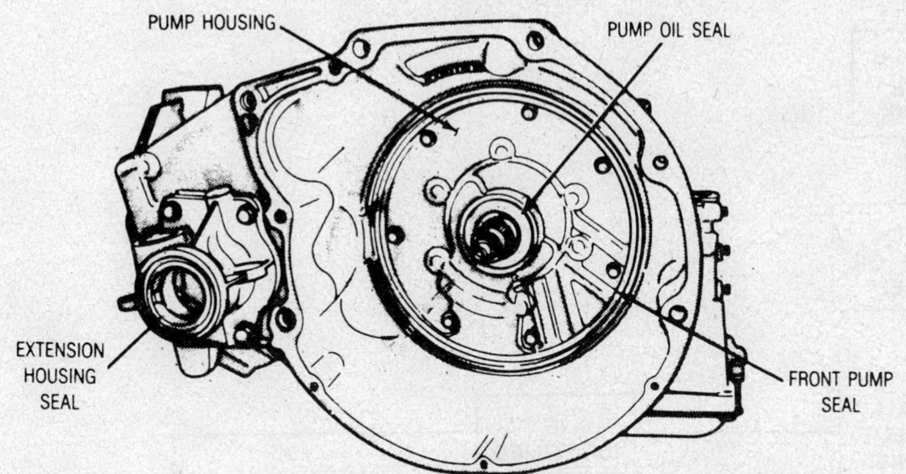

Transaxle—Front End View

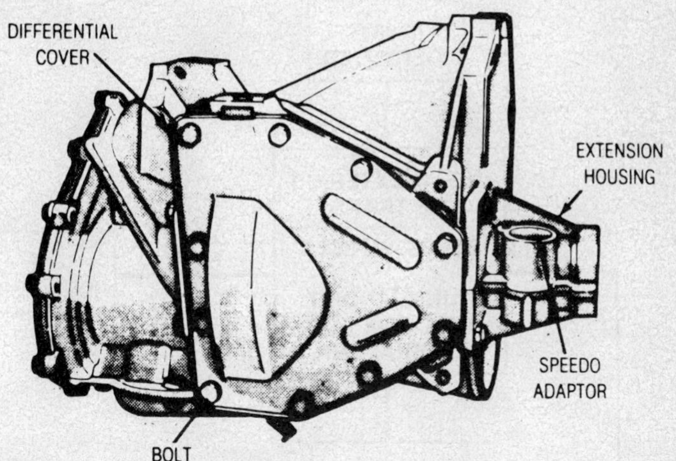

Transaxle—Right Side

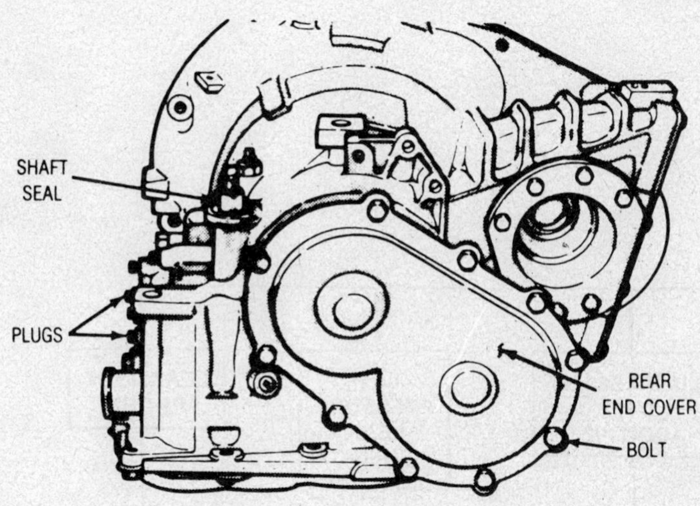

Transaxle—Rear End View

AUTOMATIC TRANSAXLE OIL LEAKS

PRELIMINARY LEAK DIAGNOSIS

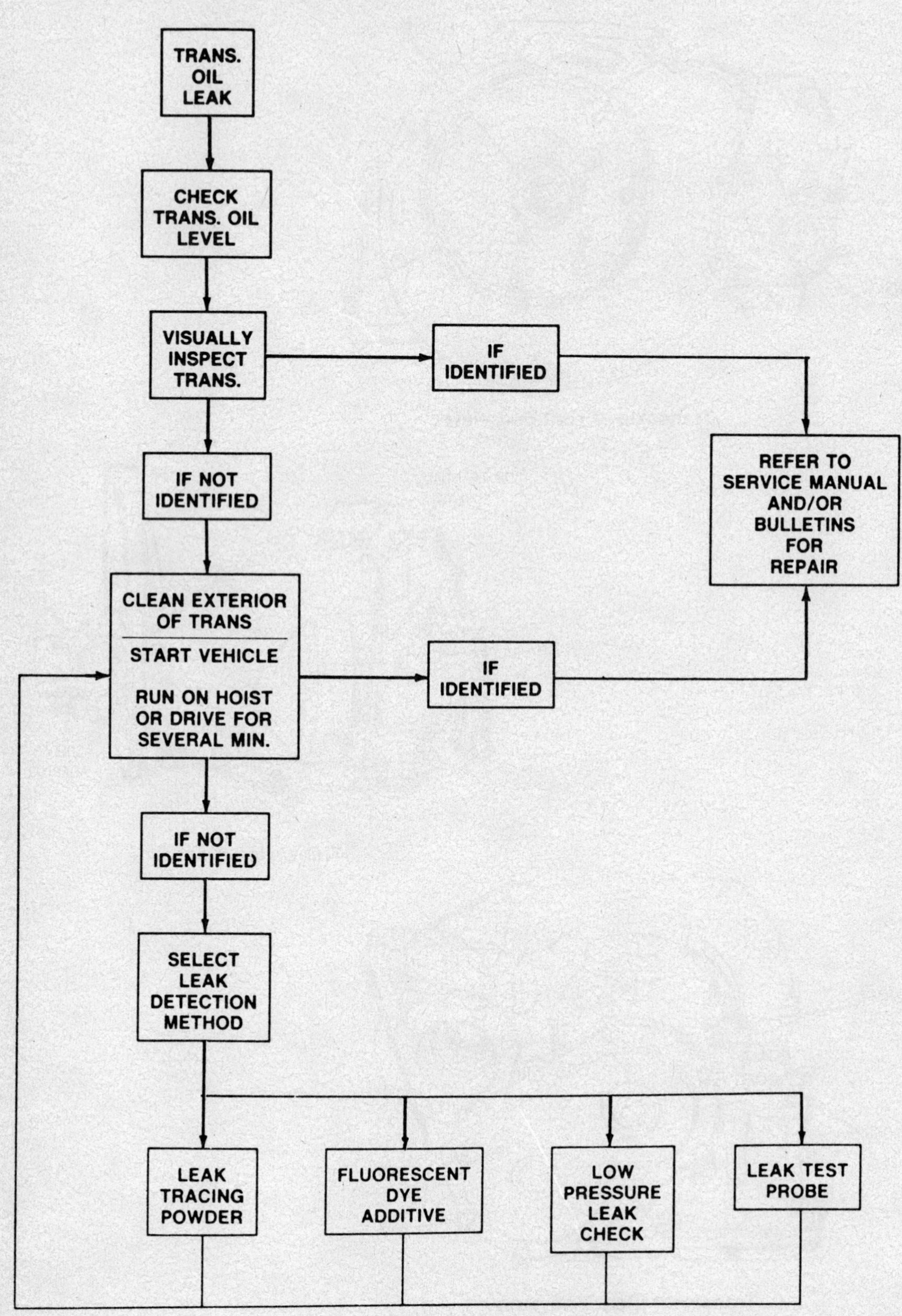

LEAK DIAGNOSIS

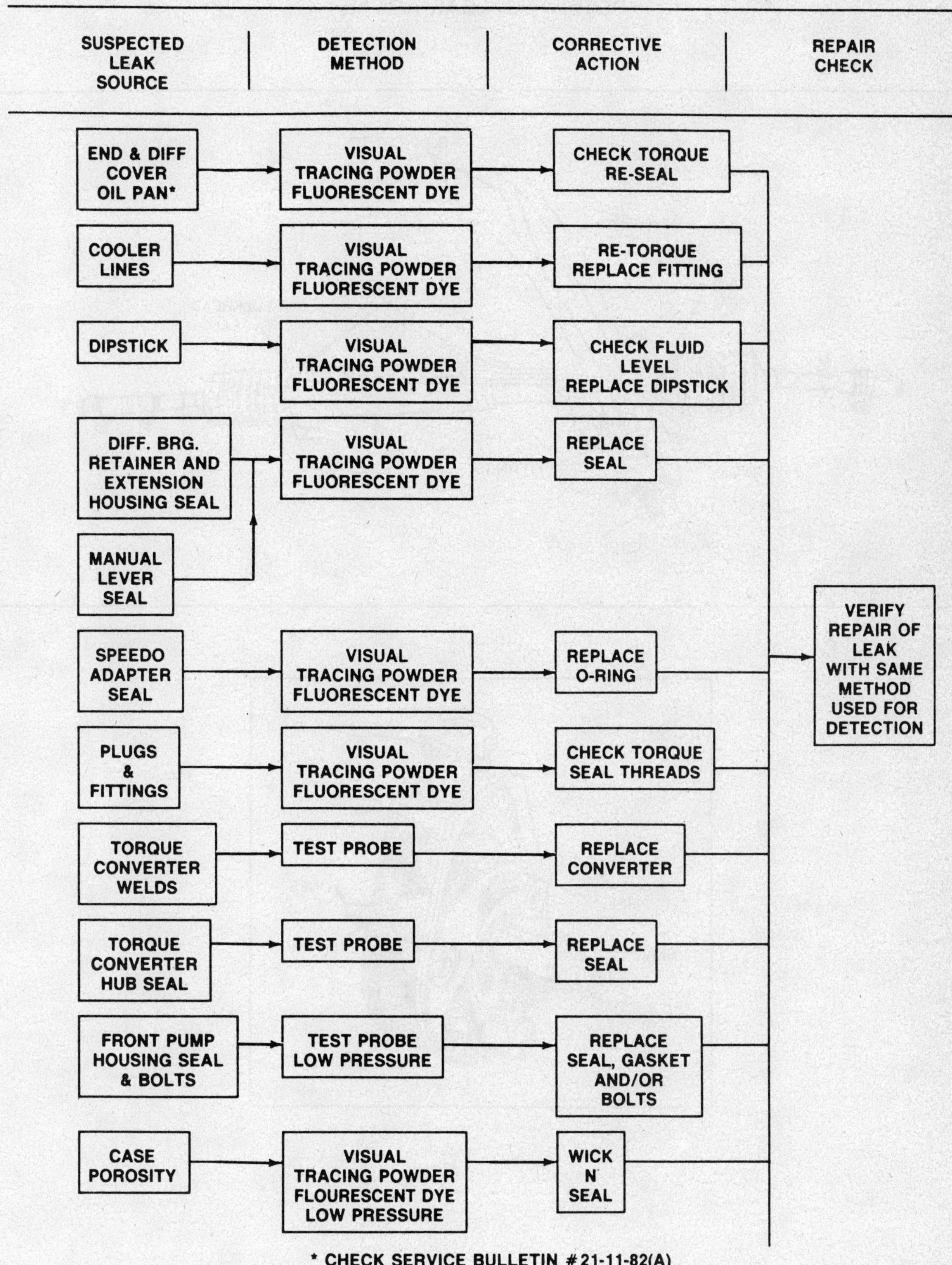
SUSPECTED LEAK SOURCE
DETECTION METHOD
CORRECTIVE ACTION
REPAIR CHECK
END & DIFF COVER OIL PAN*
VISUAL TRACING POWDER FLUORESCENT DYE
CHECK TORQUE RE-SEAL
COOLER LINES
VISUAL TRACING POWDER FLUORESCENT DYE
RE-TORQUE REPLACE FITTING
DIPSTICK
VISUAL TRACING POWDER FLUORESCENT DYE
CHECK FLUID LEVEL REPLACE DIPSTICK
DIFF. BRG. RETAINER AND EXTENSION HOUSING SEAL
MANUAL LEVER SEAL
VISUAL TRACING POWDER FLUORESCENT DYE
REPLACE SEAL
SPEEDO ADAPTER SEAL
VISUAL TRACING POWDER FLUORESCENT DYE
REPLACE O-RING
VERIFY REPAIR OF LEAK WITH SAME METHOD USED FOR DETECTION
PLUGS & FITTINGS
VISUAL TRACING POWDER FLUORESCENT DYE
CHECK TORQUE SEAL THREADS
TORQUE CONVERTER WELDS
TEST PROBE
REPLACE CONVERTER
TORQUE CONVERTER HUB SEAL
TEST PROBE
REPLACE SEAL
FRONT PUMP HOUSING SEAL & BOLTS
TEST PROBE LOW PRESSURE
REPLACE SEAL, GASKET AND/OR BOLTS
CASE POROSITY
VISUAL TRACING POWDER FLOURESCENT DYE LOW PRESSURE
WICK N' SEAL

* CHECK SERVICE BULLETIN #21-11-82(A)

POWER STEERING FLUID LEAK DIAGNOSIS

POTENTIAL LEAK AREAS

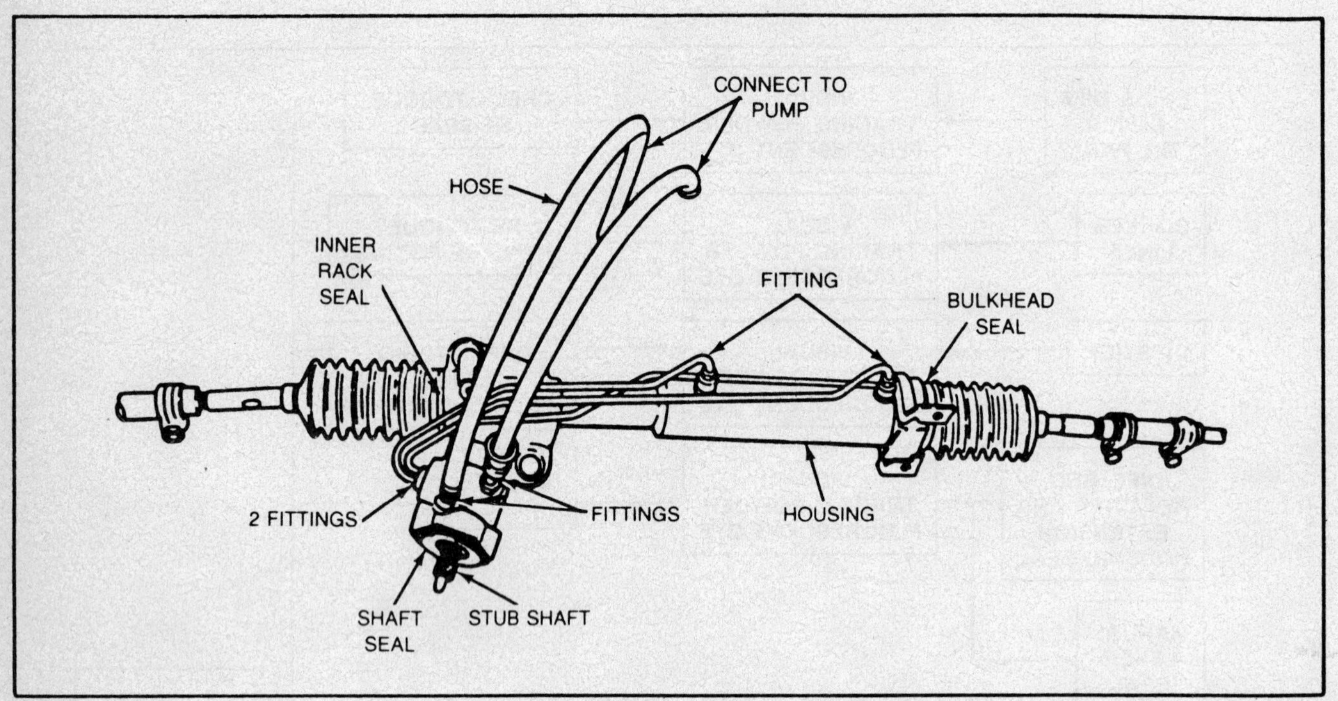

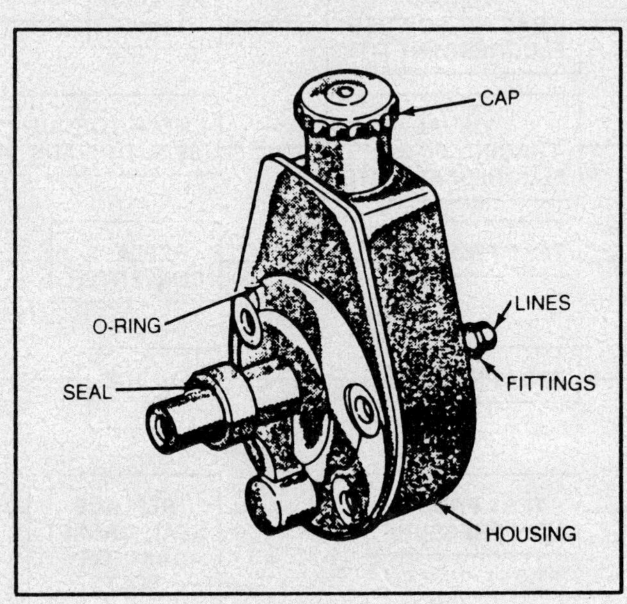

Truck Labor Guide

CONTENTS

This section covers Labor Guide data on standard production line, gasoline and diesel powered vehicles. The time shown does not include interference items unless specified. Where these items cause additional labor, times should be adjusted accordingly.

Chevrolet/GMC Ser 10–30 • 1500 • 3500

GROUP INDEX

ALPHABETICAL INDEX

LABOR 1 TUNE UP 1 LABOR

(Factory Time) Chilton Time

Compression Test

	Chilton Time
Four	
S-series	.6
Astro	.9
Six	.9
V-6	
Vans-Astro	.9
All other models	.7
V-8	1.4
Diesel	1.3

Engine Tune Up, (Electronic Ignition)

Includes: Test battery and clean connections. Tighten manifold and carburetor mounting bolts. Check engine compression, clean and adjust or renew spark plugs. Test resistance of spark plug cables. Inspect distributor cap and rotor. Adjust distributor air gap. Check vacuum advance operation. Reset ignition timing. Adjust idle mixture and idle speed. Service air cleaner. Inspect and adjust drive belts. Inspect choke operation and adjust or free up. Check operation of EGR valve.

	Chilton Time
Four–1982-86	
S-series	1.5
Astro	1.8
Six–1982-86	
Vans	2.5
All other models	2.3
V-6–1982-86	
Vans-Astro	2.3
All other models	2.0
V-8–1982-86	
Vans	3.4
All other models	3.0
w/A.C. add	.5

LABOR 2 IGNITION SYSTEM 2 LABOR

(Factory Time) Chilton Time

GASOLINE ENGINES

Spark Plugs, Clean and Reset or Renew

	Chilton Time
Vans-Astro	
Four (.6)	.8
Six (.4)	*.8
V-6 (.6)	.8
V-8 (.9)	1.3
All Other Models	
Four (.3)	.5
Six (.3)	.6
V-6 (.4)	.6
V-8 (.6)	.9
*w/A.C. add (.5)	.5

Ignition Timing, Reset

	Chilton Time
All models (.3)	.5

Distributor, Renew

Includes: Reset ignition timing.

	Chilton Time
Vans-Astro	
Four (.6)	.9
Six (.3)	*.9
V-6 (.8)	1.1
V-8 (.6)	1.1
All Other Models	
Four	
eng code A (.3)	.5
eng code Y (.6)	.9
eng code E (.6)	.9
Six (.3)	.5
V-6 (.6)	1.0
V-8 (.4)	.6
*w/A.C. add (.5)	.5

Distributor, R&R and Recondition

Includes: Reset ignition timing.

	Chilton Time
Vans-Astro	
Four (.9)	1.5
Six (.5)	*1.4
V-6 (1.1)	1.8
V-8 (.8)	1.6
All Other Models	
Four	
eng code A (.6)	1.0
eng code Y (.9)	1.5
eng code E (.9)	1.5
Six (.8)	1.0
V-6 (.9)	1.5
V-8 (.9)	1.1
*w/A.C. add (.5)	.5

Distributor Points and Condenser, Renew

Includes: Adjust dwell and timing.

	Chilton Time
Vans	
Six (.6)	.8
V-8 (.7)	.9
All Other Models	
Six (.4)	.6
V-8 (.5)	.7

Distributor Cap and/or Rotor, Renew

	Chilton Time
Vans-Astro	
Four (.3)	.5
Six (.3)	*.5
V-6 (.5)	.7
V-8 (.5)	.7
All Other Models	
All engs (.3)	.5
*w/A.C. add (.5)	.5

Ignition Coil, Renew

Includes: Test coil.

	Chilton Time
Four	
eng code Y (2.0)	2.8
eng code E (.6)	.9
eng code A (.3)	.5
Six (.3)	*.5
V-6	
S-series (.7)	1.0
Vans-Astro (.5)	.8
All other models (.4)	.7
V-8 (.5)	.8
*w/A.C. add (.5)	.5

Vacuum Advance Assembly, Renew

Includes: Adjust dwell and timing.

	Chilton Time
Vans	
Six (.3)	*.8
V-6 (.3)	.6
V-8 (.5)	1.0
All Other Models	
Four	
eng code A (.4)	.7
eng code Y (.6)	.9
eng code E (.6)	.9
Six (.3)	.6
V-6 (.6)	.9
V-8 (.4)	.8
*w/A.C. add (.5)	.5

Vacuum Advance Solenoid, Renew

	Chilton Time
All models (.2)	.3

Spark Plug Wires, Renew

	Chilton Time
Vans	
Six (.3)	.7
V-6 (.3)	.6
V-8 (.7)	1.2
All Other Models	
Four	
S-series (.3)	.5
Astro (.5)	.7
Six (.3)	.5
V-6 (.5)	.8
V-8 (.5)	.8
*w/A.C. add (.5)	.5

Ignition Switch, Renew

	Chilton Time
All models (.5)	.9

Ignition Switch Lock Cylinder, Renew

	Chilton Time
All models (.4)	.7
w/Tilt whl add (.1)	.1
Recode cyl add (.3)	.3
Vans, add	.2

ELECTRONIC IGNITION

Distributor Module, Renew

	Chilton Time
Vans	
Six (.3)	*.7
V-6 (.5)	.8
V-8 (.5)	.8
All Other Models	
Four (.3)	.6
Six (.3)	.6
V-6 (.6)	.9
V-8 (.3)	.6
*w/A.C. add (.5)	.5

Distributor Hall Effect Switch, Renew

	Chilton Time
S-series-Astro (.5)	.8

ESC Detonation Sensor, Renew (Knock Sensor)

	Chilton Time
All models (.4)	.6

ESC Module, Renew

	Chilton Time
Vans-Astro (.9)	1.2
All other models (.4)	.4

Distributor Capacitor and/or Module Wiring Harness, Renew

	Chilton Time
Vans	
Six (.4)	*.8
V-6 (.5)	.8
V-8 (.5)	.9
All Other Models	
Four (.4)	.7
Six (.4)	.7
V-6 (.6)	.8

LABOR 2 IGNITION SYSTEM 2 LABOR

(Factory Time)	Chilton Time
V-8 (.5)	.7
•w/A.C. add (.5)	.5
Distributor Pick-Up Coil and/or Pole Piece, Renew	
Includes: R&R distributor and reset ignition timing.	
Vans	
Six (.5)	•1.1
V-6 (.8)	1.3
V-8 (.8)	1.3
All Other Models	
Four	
eng code A (.3)	.6
eng code Y (1.0)	1.5
Six (.5)	.7
V-6	
S-series (.7)	1.1

(Factory Time)	Chilton Time
Astro (.9)	1.3
V-8 (.6)	.8
•w/A.C. add (.5)	.5

DIESEL IGNITION COMPONENTS

(Factory Time)	Chilton Time
Coolant Fast Idle Temperature Switch, Renew	
All models (.3)	.4
Glow Plug Relay, Renew	
Vans (.4)	.6
All other models (.2)	.3
Fast Idle Solenoid, Renew	
Vans (.5)	.7
All other models (.3)	.4

(Factory Time)	Chilton Time
Glow Plugs, Renew	
All models	
Four (.5)	.7
V-8 one	.4
one-each bank	.7
all-both banks	1.3
Glow Plug Module, Renew	
All models (.3)	.5
Glow Plug Control Switch, Renew	
Vans (.5)	.7
All other models (.3)	.4
Fast Idle Relay, Renew	
All models (.3)	.4
Starter Lockout Relay, Renew	
All models (.2)	.3

LABOR 3 FUEL SYSTEM 3 LABOR

GASOLINE ENGINES

(Factory Time)	Chilton Time
Fuel Pump, Test	
Includes: Disconnect line at carburetor, attach pressure gauge.	
All models	.3
Carburetor, Renew	
Includes: Necessary adjustments.	
S-series	
Rochester (.6)	1.0
Isuzu (.8)	1.2
Astro (1.2)	1.7
Vans (.9)	1.4
All other models (.6)	1.0
To perform C.C.C. system test add (.5)	1.0
Carburetor, R&R and Clean or Recondition	
Includes: Necessary adjustments.	
Vans	
1 bbl (2.5)	3.2
2 bbl (2.5)	3.2
4 bbl (2.7)	3.5
All Other Models	
1 bbl (2.3)	3.0
2 bbl (2.3)	3.0
4 bbl (2.5)	3.2
To perform C.C.C. system test add (.5)	1.0
Needle Valve and Seat, Renew	
Includes: R&R carb air horn and floats. Adjust idle speed.	
Vans	
1 bbl (.7)	1.1
2 bbl (.8)	1.2
4 bbl (.9)	1.3
S-series	
Rochester (.9)	1.3
Isuzu (.8)	1.2
All Other Models	
1 bbl (.5)	.9
2 bbl (.7)	1.0
4 bbl (.8)	1.1
To perform C.C.C. system test add (.5)	1.0
Fuel Filter, Renew	
Vans (.4)	.5
All other models (.2)	.3
Anti-Dieseling or Idle Stop Solenoid, Renew	
S-series (.5)	.7
Vans (.4)	.5
All other models (.2)	.3

(Factory Time)	Chilton Time
Automatic Choke Vacuum Diaphragm, Renew (One)	
S-series-Astro	
Rochester (.6)	.8
Isuzu (.9)	1.2
Vans (.6)	.8
All other models (.4)	.6
Carburetor Base Gasket EFE Heater, Renew	
S-series (.6)	1.0
Fuel Pump, Renew	
Four (.6)	•.9
Six (.5)	.7
V-6 (.6)	•.9
V-8 (1.0)	1.4
w/A.I.R. add (.3)	.3
•Astro, add	.4
Fuel Tank, Renew	
Includes: Drain and refill tank.	
Cab Mount	
All models (.5)	1.0
Frame Mount	
side tank-each (1.2)	1.7
Pick-Ups (1.0)	1.8
Vans (.7)	1.2
Suburban & Blazer (.9)	1.4
Jimmy (.9)	1.4
S-series	
rear (1.2)	1.7
left-4X2 (1.0)	1.5
4X4 (1.5)	2.0
Astro (.9)	1.4
w/Fuel tank shield add (.3)	.4
Fuel Gauge (Tank), Renew	
Includes: Drain and refill tank.	
Cab Mounted Tank	
All models (.5)	.9
Frame Mounted Tank	
side tank-each (1.0)	1.5
Pick-Ups (.9)	1.7
Vans (.7)	1.1
Suburban & Blazer (.9)	1.3
Jimmy (.9)	1.3
S-series	
rear (1.3)	1.8
left-4X2 (.9)	1.4
4X4 (1.5)	2.0
Astro (1.0)	1.5
w/Fuel tank shield add (.3)	.4

(Factory Time)	Chilton Time
Fuel Gauge (Dash), Renew	
S-series (.3)	.5
Astro (.9)	1.4
All other models (.5)	.9
Intake Manifold, Renew	
Six	
Vans (1.8)	2.4
All other models (1.2)	1.8
w/P.S. add (.5)	.5
Intake and Exhaust Manifold Gaskets, Renew	
Six	
Vans (1.5)	2.1
All other models (1.4)	2.0
w/P.S. add (.5)	.5
Intake Manifold or Gasket, Renew	
Four	
eng code A (1.7)	2.5
eng code Y (1.9)	2.7
eng code E	
S-series (2.3)	3.2
Astro (2.2)	3.1
w/Cruise control add	.2
Six–All models (1.8)	2.6
V-6	
S-series (3.9)	5.5
Astro (2.6)	3.6
exc Vans (2.0)	2.8
Vans (2.3)	3.2
w/A.C. add (.2)	.2
w/C.C.C. add (.2)	.2
V-8–454 eng	
All models (2.0)	2.7
V-8–All other engs	
exc Vans (2.3)	3.3
Vans (2.4)	3.4
w/A.C. add (.7)	.7
Renew manif add (.3)	.5

FUEL INJECTION

(Factory Time)	Chilton Time
Throttle Body, R&R or Renew	
Astro (.9)	1.3
S-series (.7)	1.1
Renew throttle body kit add (.3)	.3
Renew fuel meter body add (.3)	.3
Throttle Body Fuel Meter Assy., and/or Gasket, Renew	
Astro (.6)	.8
S-series (.4)	.6

LABOR 3 FUEL SYSTEM 3 LABOR

(Factory Time) Chilton Time

Idle Air Control Valve, Renew
Astro (.7) 1.0
S-series (.5) .8

Throttle Body Injector and/or Gasket, Renew
Astro (.9) 1.4
S-series (.7) 1.2

Minimum Idle Speed, Adjust
Astro (.7) 1.0
S-series (.5) .8

Fuel Pressure Regulator and/or Gaskets, Renew
Astro (.9) 1.3
S-series (.7) 1.1

Fuel Pump, Renew (In Tank)
All models (1.3) 1.8

Fuel Pump Relay, Renew
Astro (.7) .9
S-series (.5) .7

DIESEL ENGINE

Air Cleaner, Service
All models (.2) .4

Air Intake Crossover, Renew
All models (.3) .5

Fuel Filter, Renew
All models (.2) .4

Idle Speed, Adjust
All models (.2) .4

Injection Timing, Check and Adjust
All models (.5) .9

Throttle Position Sensor, Renew
All models (.5) .7

Fuel Solenoid, Renew
Vans (2.0) 2.7
All other models (.5) .7

Cold Advance Solenoid, Renew
Vans (2.1) 2.8
All other models (.6) .8

Fuel Injection Head Seal, Renew
Includes: Renew head and drive shaft seals. Renew governor weight retaining ring.
All models
5.7L eng (3.3) 4.7
6.2L eng (4.0) 5.3

Fuel Injection Pump, Renew
Includes: Pressure and electrical tests. Adjust timing.
All models
2.2L eng (1.9) 2.7
5.7L eng (2.6) 3.5
6.2L eng
Vans (3.8) 4.9
All other models (3.3) 4.4

Fuel Return Lines (At Nozzles), Renew
All models-one side (.3) .5
both sides (.4) .7
return hose (.2) .3
w/A.C. add (.2) .2

High Pressure Fuel Lines, Renew
Includes: Flush lines.
Four-one (.4) .7
all (.5) .8
V-8-one (1.2) 1.5
one-each bank (1.4) 1.7
all-both banks (1.5) 2.5

(Factory Time) Chilton Time

Injector Nozzle and/or Seal, Renew
Four
one or all (.6) 1.0
V-8-one (.8) 1.2
one-each bank (1.0) 1.4
all-both banks (1.5) 3.0
w/A.C. add (.2) .2
Clean nozzles add-each .2

Fuel Supply Pump, Renew
All models (.5) .7
w/A.C. add (.2) .2

Fuel Injection Pump Throttle Shaft Seal, Renew
All models
5.7L eng (.9) 1.3
6.2L eng
Vans (2.0) 2.5
All other models (1.7) 2.3

Injection Pump Adapter and/or Seal, Renew
All models
5.7L eng (1.9) 2.4
Locate new timing mark add (.1) .1

Vacuum Pump, Renew
Vans (1.2) 1.6
All other models (.3) .6

Intake Manifold or Gasket, Renew
All models
2.2L eng (.7) 1.2
5.7L eng (2.7) 3.5
6.2L eng (1.4) 2.0
Renew manif add (.2) .5

LABOR 3A EMISSION CONTROLS 3A LABOR

(Factory Time) Chilton Time

GASOLINE ENGINES

Emission Control Check
Includes: Check and adjust engine idle speed, mixture and ignition timing.
All models .6

CRANKCASE EMISSION

Positive Crankcase Ventilation Valve, Renew
All models (.2) .3

Crankcase Vent Filter, Renew
All models (.2) .3

AIR INJECTION REACTOR TYPE

A.I.R. Air Pump Cleaner, Renew
All models (.2) .4

Air Pump, Renew
Four (.4) *.6
Six (.6) .8
V-6 (.4) *.7
V-8 (.8) 1.0
*Astro add .2

Air Pump Relief Valve, Renew
Six (.8) 1.0
V-8 (1.0) 1.2

Diverter or Gulp Valve, Renew
Vans-Astro (.4) .6
All other models (.2) .4

Check Valve, Renew (One)
Vans (.4) .6
All other models (.2) .4
each adtnl .1

Combustion Pipes and/or Extensions, Renew
Vans
Six (.6) .9
V-8-one (.6) .9
both (.8) 1.2
All Other Models
Four (.6) 1.0
Six (.5) .8
V-6-each (.3) .6
V-8-one (.3) .6
both (.5) .9

Vacuum Delay Valve, Renew
All models (.3) .4

Deceleration Valve, Renew
All models (.3) .4

CONTROLLED COMBUSTION TYPE

Air Cleaner Vacuum Motor, Renew
Vans-Astro (.6) .8
All other models (.3) .6

(Factory Time) Chilton Time

Air Cleaner Temperature Sensor, Renew
Vans-Astro (.4) .5
All other models (.3) .4

EGR/EFE Thermal Vacuum Switch, Renew
Vans-Astro (.4) .6
All other models (.3) .5

EVAPORATIVE EMISSION TYPE

Charcoal Canister, Renew
Vans (.7) 1.0
All other models (.2) .4

Canister Purge Thermal Vacuum Switch, Renew
exc Vans (.3) .4
Vans-Astro (.5) .6

TRANSMISSION CONTROLLED SPARK

Transmission Controlled Spark Solenoid, Renew
Vans (.4) .5
All other models (.2) .3

Thermostatic Vacuum Switch or Temperature Switch, Renew
Vans (.5) .6
All other models (.3) .4

LABOR 3A EMISSION CONTROLS 3A LABOR

(Factory Time) Chilton Time

Controlled Spark Relay, Renew (On Firewall)
All models (.2) .3

Thermal Vacuum Switch, Renew
All models (.3) .4

EXHAUST GAS RECIRCULATION SYSTEM

E.G.R. Valve, Renew
Four
eng code A (.8) 1.1
eng code Y (.3) .5
eng code E
Astro (.9) 1.2
S-series (.5) .8
Vans (.5) .8
Diesel
5.7L eng (.6) 1.0
6.2L eng (.2) .4
All other models (.3) .5

E.G.R. Vacuum Delay Valve, Renew
S-series (.2) .3

EARLY FUEL EVAPORATION SYSTEM

E.F.E. Valve, Renew
Six (.3) .6
V-6 & V-8 (.6) 1.0
dual exhaust (.5) .9

E.F.E. Actuator and Rod Assy., Renew
All models (.3) .6

E.F.E. Vacuum Check Valve, Renew
All models (.2) .3

COMPUTER COMMAND CONTROL SYSTEM (C.C.C.)

Computer Command Control System Performance Check
All models (.5) 1.0

Throttle Position Sensor, Adjust
Does not include system performance check.
All models (.4) .9

Manifold Absolute Pressure Sensor, Renew
Does not include system performance check.
S-series (.4) .6
All other models (.5) .7

Engine Speed Sensor, Renew
Does not include system performance check.
Vans (.7) .9
All other models (.5) .7

Calpak, Renew
Does not include system performance check.
All models (.5) .7

Electronic Control Module, Renew
Does not include system performance check.
All models (.5) .6

Mixture Control Solenoid, Renew
Does not include system performance check.
Vans-Astro (1.4) 1.8
All other models-2 bbl (1.1) 1.4
4 bbl (1.2) 1.5

Prom, Renew
Does not include system performance check.
All models (.5) .8

Coolant Temperature Sensor, Renew
Does not include system performance check.
Vans-Astro (.7) .9
All other models (.5) .6

Oxygen Sensor, Renew
Does not include system performance check.
All models (.5) .7

Barometric Sensor, Renew
Does not include system performance check.
All models (.5) .7

Manifold Differential Pressure Sensor, Renew
Does not include system performance check.
All models (.5) .7

Throttle Position Sensor, Renew
Does not include system performance check.
Vans-Astro (1.3) 1.7
All other models-2 bbl (1.1) 1.4
4 bbl (1.2) 1.5

Idle Speed Control Motor, Renew
Does not include system performance check.
All models (.5) .8

Air Control/Air Switching Valve, Renew
Does not include system performance check.
All models (.6) .8

E.G.R. Vacuum Control Solenoid, Renew
Does not include system performance check.
All models (.6) .8

Vehicle Speed Sensor, Renew
Does not include system performance check.
All models (1.0) 1.5

E.G.R. Bleed Control Solenoid, Renew
Does not include system performance check.
Vans-Astro (.5) .7
All other models (.4) .6

EFE/EGR Relay, Renew
Does not include system performance check.
All models (.3) .4

Tachometer Filter, Renew
Does not include system performance check.
All models (.3) .3

COASTING RICHER SYSTEM (C.R.S.)

Engine Speed Sensor, Renew
S-series (.3) .4

Accelerator Switch, Renew
S-series (.3) .4

Clutch Switch, Renew
S-series (.3) .4

Transmission Switch, Renew
S-series (.4) .7

Coasting Valve Solenoid, Renew
S-series (.3) .4

DIESEL ENGINE

Crankcase Depression Regulator Valve, Renew
Vans (.5) .7
All other models (.3) .4

Crankcase Ventilation Filter, Renew
All models (.3) .4

E.G.R. Valve and/or Gasket, Renew
All models
5.7L eng (.6) 1.0
6.2L eng (.2) .4

E.G.R. Control Valve Solenoid, Renew
Vans (.5) .7
All other models (.2) .3

E.P.R. Valve, Renew
Vans (.3) .4
All other models (.6) .8

E.P.R. Control Valve Switch, Renew
All models (.5) .7

E.P.R. Control Valve Solenoid, Renew
Vans (.7) 1.0
All other models (.5) .7

Vacuum Regulator Valve, Renew
Vans (.8) 1.1
All other models (.5) .7

LABOR 4 ALTERNATOR AND REGULATOR 4 LABOR

(Factory Time) Chilton Time

Delcotron Circuits, Test
Includes: Test battery, regulator and Delcotron output.
All models .6

Alternator Drive Belt, Renew
Four
eng code A (.2) .3
w/P.S. add (.2) .2
eng code E (.2) .3
eng code S (.2) .3
w/A.C. add (.1) .1
Six-exc Vans (.2) .3
Vans (.4) .5
w/AIR add (.2) .2
V-6 (.2) .3
w/AIR add (.1) .1
V-8-exc Vans (.2) .3
Vans (.3) .4
w/AIR add (.2) .2
Diesel (.2) .3

Delcotron, Renew
Includes: Transfer fan and pulley.
Four-
eng code A (.6) .8
eng code Y (.3) .5
eng code E (.3) .5
Six-exc Vans (.4) .6
Vans (.5) .7
V-6
Astro (.6) .9
All other models (.4) .6
V8-exc Vans (.6) .8
Vans (.8) 1.0
Diesel-exc Vans (.4) .6
Vans (.7) 1.0
Add circuit test if performed.

Delcotron, R&R and Recondition
Includes: Complete disassembly, replace parts as required, reassemble.
Four-
eng code A (1.5) 2.2
eng code Y (1.3) 2.0
eng code E (1.1) 2.0
Six-exc Vans (1.2) 1.8
Vans (1.3) 1.9

LABOR 4 ALTERNATOR AND REGULATOR 4 LABOR

(Factory Time)	Chilton Time
V-6	
Astro (1.3)	2.2
All other models (1.1)	1.8
V-8-exc Vans (1.2)	2.0
Vans (1.4)	2.2
Diesel-exc Vans (1.3)	2.0
Vans (1.8)	2.7

Add circuit test if performed.

Delcotron Bearings, Renew (Both)

Includes: R&R Delcotron, separate end frames.

(Factory Time)	Chilton Time
Four-	
eng code A (.8)	1.1
eng code Y (.6)	1.0
eng code E (.6)	1.0
Six-exc Vans (.6)	.9
Vans (.7)	1.0
V-6	
Astro (.8)	1.1
All other models (.6)	1.0
V-8-exc Vans (.6)	.9
Vans (.8)	1.1
Diesel-exc Vans (.6)	.9
Vans (1.0)	1.4

Voltage Regulator, Test and Renew

Includes: Disassemble and reassemble Delcotron.

(Factory Time)	Chilton Time
Four-	
eng code A (.7)	1.0
eng code Y (.6)	1.1
eng code E (.6)	1.1
Six-exc Vans (.5)	.8
Vans (.6)	.9
V-6	
Astro (.8)	1.2
All other models (.6)	1.1
V-8-exc Vans (.6)	.9
Vans (.8)	1.1
Diesel-exc Vans (.6)	1.0
Vans (1.0)	1.4

Voltmeter, Renew

(Factory Time)	Chilton Time
S-series (.3)	.6
Astro (.9)	1.4
All other models (.6)	1.0

LABOR 5 STARTING SYSTEM 5 LABOR

Starter Draw Test (On Truck)

(Factory Time)	Chilton Time
All models	.3

Starter, Renew

(Factory Time)	Chilton Time
Four	
eng code A (.6)	1.0
eng code Y (.8)	1.2
eng code E	
4X2 (.7)	1.0
4X4 (1.6)	2.1
Six (.4)	.7
V-6	
4X2 (.6)	1.0
4X4 (1.1)	1.5
V-8 (.6)	.8
Diesel (.8)	1.1

Add draw test if performed.

Starter, R&R and Recondition

Includes: Turn down armature.

(Factory Time)	Chilton Time
Four	
eng code A (1.5)	2.3
eng code Y (2.0)	2.8
eng code E	
4X2 (1.5)	2.3
4X4 (2.4)	3.4
Six (1.2)	2.0
V-6	
4X2 (1.5)	2.3
4X4 (2.0)	2.8
V-8 (1.5)	2.1
Diesel (1.6)	2.2
Renew field coils add (.2)	.5

Add draw test if performed.

Starter Solenoid, Renew

Includes: R&R starter.

(Factory Time)	Chilton Time
Four	
eng code A (.6)	1.0
eng code Y (.9)	1.3
eng code E	
4X2 (.8)	1.1
4X4 (1.6)	2.2
Six (.5)	.8
V-6	
4X2 (.6)	1.0
4X4 (1.1)	1.5
V-8 (.7)	.9
Diesel (.8)	1.0

Starter Drive, Renew

Includes: R&R starter.

(Factory Time)	Chilton Time
Four	
eng code A (.8)	1.2
eng code Y (1.0)	1.4
eng code E	
4X2 (.9)	1.2
4X4 (1.8)	2.4
Six (.7)	1.0
V-6	
4X2 (.8)	1.2
4X4 (1.4)	1.8
V-8 (.8)	1.1
Diesel (1.0)	1.2

Battery Cables, Renew

(Factory Time)	Chilton Time
Positive-exc Vans (.3)	.4
Vans (.4)	.5
Negative (.2)	.3
batt to batt	
Vans (.7)	1.0
All other models (.3)	.4

LABOR 6 BRAKE SYSTEM 6 LABOR

Brakes, Adjust (Minor)

Includes: Adjust brake shoes, fill master cylinder.

(Factory Time)	Chilton Time
two wheels	.4

Bleed Brakes (Four Wheels)

Includes: Fill master cylinder.

(Factory Time)	Chilton Time
All models (.4)	.6

Brake Pedal Free Play, Adjust

(Factory Time)	Chilton Time
All models	.3

Brake Shoes and/or Pads, Renew

Includes: Install new or exchange shoes or pads, adjust service and hand brake. Bleed system.

(Factory Time)	Chilton Time
With Single Rear Wheels	
front-disc (.9)	1.2
rear-drum (1.0)	1.7
All four wheels	2.8
With Dual Rear Wheels	
front-disc (.9)	1.2
rear-drum (2.1)	3.0
All four wheels	4.0
Resurface brake rotor add, each	.9
Resurface brake drum add, each	.5

Brake Drum, Renew (One)

(Factory Time)	Chilton Time
w/Single rear wheels (.3)	.6
w/Dual rear wheels (1.0)	1.4

Free-Up or Renew Brake Self Adjusting Units (One)

(Factory Time)	Chilton Time
w/Single rear wheels (.4)	.7
w/Dual rear wheels (.7)	1.0

Brake Combination Valve and/or Switch, Renew

Includes: Bleed system.

(Factory Time)	Chilton Time
Vans (.8)	1.1
All other models	
w/2 wheel drive (.7)	1.0
w/4 wheel drive (.7)	1.0

BRAKE HYDRAULIC SYSTEM

Wheel Cylinder, Renew

Includes: Bleed system.

(Factory Time)	Chilton Time
With Single Rear Wheels	
one (.8)	1.3
both (1.1)	1.8
With Dual Rear Wheels	
one (1.0)	1.7
both (1.8)	2.6

Wheel Cylinder, R&R and Recondition

Includes: Home cylinder and bleed system.

(Factory Time)	Chilton Time
With Single Rear Wheels	
one (1.0)	1.6
both (1.5)	2.4
With Dual Rear Wheels	
one (1.2)	2.0
both (2.2)	3.2

Brake Hose, Renew

Includes: Bleed system.

(Factory Time)	Chilton Time
All models-front-one (.5)	.8
rear-one (.5)	.8

Master Cylinder, Renew

Includes: Bleed system.

(Factory Time)	Chilton Time
All models (.6)	1.0

Master Cylinder, R&R and Recondition

(Factory Time)	Chilton Time
All models (1.4)	1.8

POWER BRAKES

Power Brake Booster, Renew

(Factory Time)	Chilton Time
S-series (1.2)	1.8
All other models (.6)	1.0

LABOR 6 BRAKE SYSTEM 6 LABOR

(Factory Time) Chilton Time

Power Brake Booster, R&R and Recondition

S-series
single (1.7) 2.5
tandem (1.8) 2.6
All other models (1.3) 1.8

Brake Booster Check Valve, Renew

All models (.3) 3

Hydra-Boost, Renew

Vans (1.2) 1.7
All other models (1.1) 1.6

Hydra-Boost, R&R and Recondition

Vans (1.8) 2.7
All other models (1.5) 2.4

Hydra-Boost Pump, Renew

All models (.7) 1.1
w/A.C. add (.2) 2

Hydra-Boost Pump, R&R and Recondition

All models (1.3) 1.9
w/A.C. add (.2) 2

Hydra-Boost Pump Line, Renew

All models-one (.5) 7

Hydra-Boost Pump Drive Belt, Renew

All models (.2) 3

Accumulator (Hydra-Boost), R&R or Renew

All models (.3) 7

DISC BRAKES

Brake Shoes and/or Pads, Renew

Includes: Install new or exchange shoes or pads, adjust service and hand brake. Bleed system.

With Single Rear Wheels
front-disc (.9) 1.2
rear-drum (1.0) 1.7

COMBINATIONS

Add to Brakes, Renew

See Machine Shop Operations

(Factory Time) Chilton Time

RENEW WHEEL CYLINDER
Each (.3) 4

REBUILD WHEEL CYLINDER
Each (.3) 6

REBUILD CALIPER ASSEMBLY
Each (.5) 6

RENEW BRAKE HOSE
Each 3

RENEW REAR WHEEL GREASE SEALS
Semi-floating axle
one (.2) 3
Full-floating axle
one (.3) 4

RENEW BRAKE DRUM (ONE)
With single rear whls (.4) 5
With dual rear whls (.5) 6

REPACK FRONT WHEEL BEARINGS (BOTH WHEELS)
All models (.6) 6

RENEW DISC BRAKE ROTOR
Each-w/2 whl drive (.3) 5
Each-w/4 whl drive (.6) 8

(Factory Time) Chilton Time

All four wheels 2.8
With Dual Rear Wheels
front-disc (.9) 1.2
rear-drum (2.1) 3.0
All four wheels 4.0
Resurface brake rotor add, each 9
Resurface brake drum add, each 6

(Factory Time) Chilton Time

Disc Brake Pads, Renew

Includes: Install new disc brake pads only.
All models (.9) 1.2

Disc Brake Rotor, Renew

With Two Wheel Drive
All models-one (.7) 1.0
both (1.2) 1.8
With Four Wheel Drive
All models-one (1.0) 1.2
both (1.8) 2.1

Caliper Assembly, Renew

Includes: Bleed system.
All models-one (.7) 1.1
both (1.1) 1.7

Caliper Assembly, R&R and Recondition

Includes: Bleed system.
All models-one (1.2) 1.6
both (2.1) 2.5

PARKING BRAKE

Parking Brake, Adjust

All models (.3) 4

Parking Brake Equalizer, Renew

All models (.3) 6

Parking Brake Control Assembly, Renew

S-series (1.2) 1.7
Vans (.9) 1.5
Astro (1.6) 2.3
All other models (.6) 9
w/Diesel eng add 4

Parking Brake Cables, Renew

Front
All models (.6) 1.0
Intermediate
All models (.3) 5
Rear-one
with single rear whls (.7) 1.0
with dual rear whls (.9) 1.2

LABOR 7 COOLING SYSTEM 7 LABOR

(Factory Time) Chilton Time

Winterize Cooling System

Includes: Run engine to check for leaks, tighten all hose connections. Test radiator and pressure cap, drain radiator and engine block. Add anti-freeze and refill coolant.
All models 8

Thermostat, Renew

All models
Gas engine (.4) 5
Diesel engine (.6) 8
Vans-w/A.C. add (.5) 5

Radiator Assembly, R&R or Renew

Gasoline Engines
All models-w/M.T. (.6) 1.0
w/A.T. (.8) 1.2
Diesel Engines
All models-w/M.T. (.8) 1.2
w/A.T. (1.0) 1.4
w/Eng oil cooler add (.2) 2
w/A.C. add (.3) 3
Renew side tank add
one side (.7) 1.0
both sides (1.1) 1.7

(Factory Time) Chilton Time

ADD THESE OPERATIONS TO RADIATOR R&R

Boil & Repair 1.5
Rod Clean 1.9
Repair Core 1.3
Renew Tank 1.6
Renew Trans. Oil Cooler 1.9
Recore Radiator 1.7

Radiator Hoses, Renew

Vans-Astro
upper (.4) 5
lower (.6) 6
both (.8) 1.0
All other models
upper (.3) 4
lower (.4) 5
both (.5) 7
by-pass (.3) .... *.5
*Vans-Astro add 3

Fan Blade, Renew

exc Vans (.3) 4
Vans (.6) 8

Fan Belt, Renew

All models-one (.2) 3
each adtnl (.2) 3

(Factory Time) Chilton Time

If necessary to R&R fan pulley
add (.2) 3

Water Pump, Renew

Four-
eng code A (.7) 1.3
eng code Y (.9) 1.5
eng code E
S-series (.7) 1.3
Astro (1.1) 1.7
Six (.7) 1.3
V-6
S-series (1.2) 2.0
V-8-exc Vans (.6) 1.5
Vans (.9) 1.7
Diesel
2.2L eng (1.1) 1.9
5.7L eng (1.0) 1.8
6.2L eng
exc Vans (1.6) 2.4
Vans (2.2) 3.0
w/P.S. add (.2) 2
w/A.C. add (.5) 5
w/A.I.R. add (.3) 3

Water Jacket Expansion Plugs, Renew (Engine Block)

All models-each (.3) 7

LABOR 7 COOLING SYSTEM 7 LABOR

(Factory Time)	Chilton Time
Note: If necessary to R&R any component to gain access to plug, add appropriate time.	
Temperature Gauge (Engine Unit), Renew	
All models (.3)	.4
Temperature Gauge (Dash Unit), Renew	
exc Vans (.6)	1.0
Vans (.5)	1.0
S-series (.3)	.6
Astro (.9)	1.4
Heater Hoses, Renew	
Includes: Drain coolant at hose.	
All models-each (.4)	.5
Auxiliary Heater Hoses, Renew (One or All)	
Includes: Drain coolant at hose.	
All models (1.8)	2.4
Hot Water Shut Off Valve, Renew (Auxiliary Heater)	
All models (.7)	1.1
Heater Core, R&R or Renew	
Without Air Conditioning	
exc Vans (.8)	*1.5
Vans-Astro (1.6)	3.0
S-series (.8)	1.5
With Air Conditioning	
exc Vans (1.4)	*2.5
Vans-Astro (2.7)	5.0
S-series (1.5)	3.5
*w/Diesel eng add	1.5
ADD THESE OPERATIONS TO HEATER CORE R&R	
Boil & Repair	1.2
Repair Core	.9
Recore	1.2
Heater Blower Motor, Renew	
Astro (.6)	1.0
All other models (.3)	.5
w/Diesel eng (1.0)	1.5
Heater Blower Motor Switch, Renew	
All models (.4)	.7
Heater Blower Motor Resistor, Renew	
All models (.2)	.4
Heater Control Assembly, Renew	
All models (.5)	.9

LABOR 8 EXHAUST SYSTEM 8 LABOR

(Factory Time)	Chilton Time
Muffler, Renew	
All models-each (.6)	1.0
Tail Pipe, Renew	
All models-each (.5)	.9
Catalytic Converter, Renew	
S-series (.9)	1.3
All other models (.6)	1.0
Catalytic Converter Catalyst, Renew	
All models (.5)	1.0
Front Exhaust Pipe, Renew	
All models	
right side (.7)	.9
left side (.6)	.9
crossover (.5)	1.1
to conv (.6)	.9
Rear Exhaust Pipe, Renew	
All models	
right side (.4)	.9
left side (1.0)	1.3
crossover (.7)	1.3
Intermediate Exhaust Pipe, Renew	
All models (.4)	.7
Resonator and Pipe Assy., Renew	
All models (.4)	.6
E.F.E. Valve (Heat Riser), Renew	
Six (.3)	.6
V-6 & V-8-single exh (.6)	1.0
dual exh (.5)	.9
E.F.E. Actuator and Rod Assy., Renew	
All models (.3)	.6
Exhaust Manifold, Renew	
Four–	
eng codes A-Y (1.0)	1.5
w/A.C. add (.8)	.8
w/P.S. add (.4)	.4
eng code E	
S-series (.7)	1.1
Astro (.9)	1.3
Six–exc Vans (1.1)	1.6
Vans (1.6)	2.1
w/P.S. add (.5)	.5
w/A.I.R. add (.6)	.6
V-6–	
S-series	
right side (.6)	1.0
left side (.9)	1.5
Astro	
right side (1.1)	1.7
left side (.9)	1.5
exc Vans	
right side (1.0)	1.5
left side (.8)	1.2
Vans	
right side (.8)	1.2
left side (1.0)	1.5
w/A.C. add (.3)	.3
w/P.S. add (.3)	.3
w/C.C.C. add (.3)	.3
V-8–454 eng	
right side (1.0)	1.4
left side (.7)	1.1
V-8–All other engs	
exc Vans–right side (1.0)	1.5
left side (.8)	1.2
Vans–right side (1.2)	1.8
left side (1.1)	1.5
w/P.S. add (.2)	.2
w/A.C. add (.7)	.7
w/A.I.R. add (.2)	.2
Diesel	
2.2L eng (.7)	1.2
5.7L eng	
right side (.9)	1.3
left side (.7)	1.1
6.2L eng	
right side (1.1)	1.6
left side (1.3)	1.8
COMBINATIONS	
Muffler, Exhaust and Tail Pipe, Renew	
Four (1.2)	1.7
Six (1.3)	1.9
V-6 (.7)	1.2
V-8-one side (1.1)	1.6

LABOR 9 FRONT SUSPENSION 9 LABOR

(Factory Time)	Chilton Time
Note: On all front suspension operations alignment charges must be added if performed. Time given does not include alignment.	
Check Alignment of Front End	
All models	.5
Note: Deduct if alignment is performed.	
Toe-In, Adjust	
All models (.4)	.6
Align Front End	
Includes: Adjust front wheel bearings.	
S-series	
4X2 (.7)	1.4
4X4 (1.1)	2.0
All other models (1.1)	2.0
Front Wheel Bearings, Clean and Repack	
Two Wheel Drive	
one wheel (.7)	.8
both wheels (1.1)	1.4
Four Wheel Drive	
one wheel (1.2)	1.4
both wheels (2.2)	2.5
Front Wheel Grease Seal, Renew	
Two Wheel Drive	
one wheel (.7)	.7
both wheels (1.1)	1.2
Four Wheel Drive	
one wheel (1.2)	1.3
both wheels (2.2)	2.4
Front Wheel Bearings and Cups, Renew	
Two Wheel Drive	
one wheel (.7)	.9
both wheels (1.1)	1.5
Four Wheel Drive	
one wheel (1.2)	1.5
both wheels (2.2)	2.6
Front Wheel Bearing and Hub Assy., Renew	
S-series-4X4-Astro	
one side (.8)	1.1

(Factory Time) Chilton Time

both sides (1.4) 2.0
Renew inner seal add
one (.4) 4
both (.6) 6

Front Shock Absorber, Renew
S-series 4X4
one (.5) 7
both (.7) 1.1
All other models-one (.3) 5
both (.4) 8

Steering Arm and Knuckle (Integral), Renew
Add alignment charges.
Two Wheel Drive
S-series-one (1.2) 1.6
both (2.2) 3.0
All other models-one (1.0) 1.3
both (1.8) 2.5

Steering Knuckle, Renew
Add alignment charges.
Four Wheel Drive
S-series
one (1.2) 1.6
both (2.2) 3.0
All other models-one (1.6) 1.9
both (3.0) 3.7

Lower Control Arm Assy., Renew
Add alignment charges.
S-series-4X2-one (1.1) 1.6
both (2.1) 3.1
4X4-one (1.5) 2.0
both (2.8) 3.8
All other models-one (.9) 1.3
both (1.7) 2.5

Lower Control Arm Bushings and Shaft, Renew
Add alignment charges.
S-series-4X2-one side (1.2) 1.9
both sides (2.3) 3.5
4X4-one side (1.4) 2.1
both sides (2.5) 4.0
Astro-one side (1.2) 1.9
both sides (2.3) 3.5
All other models-one side (.9) 1.5
both sides (1.7) 2.9

Upper Control Arm Assy., Renew
Add alignment charges.
S-series-4X2-one (.8) 1.3
both (1.2) 2.2
4X4-one (.9) 1.4
both (1.7) 2.7
All other models-one (.6) 1.1
both (1.1) 2.1

Upper Control Arm Bushings and Shaft, Renew
Add alignment charges.
S-series-one side (1.1) 1.7
both sides (2.0) 3.0
Astro-one side (1.0) 1.6
both sides (1.8) 2.8
All other models-one side (.7) 1.4
both sides (1.3) 2.7

Upper Ball Joint, Renew
Add alignment charges.
S-series-4X4
one (.9) 1.3
both (1.6) 2.4
All other models-one (.7) 1.1
both (1.2) 2.1

(Factory Time) Chilton Time

Lower Ball Joint, Renew
Add alignment charges.
S-series-4X4
one (1.1) 1.5
both (2.0) 2.8
All models-one (.7) 1.2
both (1.2) 2.3

Ball Joints or King Pins (Upper and Lower), Renew
Four Wheel Drive
All models-one side (1.8) 2.4
both sides (3.5) 4.7

Front Spring, Renew
Coil
S-series-Astro-one (.8) 1.3
both (1.5) 2.5
All other models-one (.6) 1.2
both (1.0) 2.3
Leaf
All models-one (.7) 1.4
both (1.1) 2.7

Front Spring Shackle or Pin, Renew
All models-one (.4) 7
both (.5) 1.2

Front Spring Eye (Hanger End) Bushings, Renew
All models-one side (.8) 1.5
both sides (1.4) 2.9

Front Stabilizer Shaft, Renew
All models (.5) 9

Front Stabilizer Shaft Bushings, Renew
All models-one (.4) 7
both (.5) 8

FOUR WHEEL DRIVE

K-10-20-30 SERIES

Steering Knuckle Spindle Bearings, Renew
All models-one (1.1) 1.4
both (2.1) 2.7
Renew spindle add,
each (.1) 2
Renew knuckle add,
each (.5) 6

Front Wheel Hub, Renew
All models-one (.6) 9
both (1.1) 1.7

Free Wheeling Hub Control Mechanism, Recondition
All models-one (.3) 5
both (.5) 8
Recond add each (.5) 6

Front Axle Shaft Oil Seals, Renew
All models-one (3.0) 4.0
both (3.1) 4.3

Front Differential Housing Assy., Renew
Includes: R&R drive shaft, transfer all parts as required. Bleed brakes and make all necessary adjustments.
All models (7.4) 10.0

Front Drive Axle Differential Case, R&R or Renew
All models
Corp axle (3.4) 4.2
Dana axle (4.4) 5.4

(Factory Time) Chilton Time

Ring Gear and Pinion Set, Renew
Includes: R&R differential case.
All models
Corp axle (4.3) 5.4
Dana axle (5.5) 6.9

Pinion Bearings, Renew
Includes: R&R differential case.
All models
Corp axle (4.0) 5.5
Dana axle (5.2) 6.6

Differenetial Side Bearings, Renew
Includes: R&R differential case.
All models
Corp axle (3.3) 4.4
Dana axle (4.1) 5.6

Front Axle Housing Cover and/or Gasket, Renew
All models (.4) 7

Pinion Shaft Oil Seal, Renew
All models (.5) 9

Front Drive Shaft, R&R or Renew
All models (.4) 9
w/Transfer case shield add (.1) 1

Front U-Joints, Renew
All models
U-Joint (.6) 1.0
C.V. Joint (1.2) 1.7
w/Transfer case shield add (.1) 1

Front Axle Shaft and/or Universal Joint, Renew (One Side)
Series 10-20 (1.2) 1.7
Series 30 (1.2) 1.7
Renew inner shaft add 4
Renew outer shaft add 4
Renew U-Joint add 4
Renew spindle brg add 1

S-SERIES

Front Torsion Bar, Adjust
S-Series (.3) 5

Front Torsion Bar, Renew
S-Series-one side (.8) 1.2
both sides (1.1) 1.6
w/Skid plate add (.2) 2

Torsion Bar Pivot Arm, Renew
S-Series-one side (.5) 7
both sides (.7) 1.1
w/Skid plate add (.2) 2

Torsion Bar Support Crossmember, Renew
S-Series (1.0) 1.5
w/Skid plate add (.2) 2

Front Differential Vacuum Locking Actuator, Renew
S-series (.3) 5

Front Differential Locking Cable, Renew
S-series (.4) 6
w/Skid plate add (.1) 1

Front Propeller Shaft U-Joints, Renew
S-series
front (.6) 9
rear (1.1) 1.5
both (1.3) 2.0

Front Propeller Shaft Assy., Renew
S-series (.4) 6

LABOR 9 FRONT SUSPENSION 9 LABOR

(Factory Time) — Chilton Time

Output Shaft, Renew
S-Series
right side (1.5) 2.1
left side (1.3) 1.8
both sides (2.7) 3.8
Renew shaft seal add
each (.2) 2

Drive Axle Assy., R&R or Renew
S-Series
one (1.1) 1.5
both (1.9) 2.6
Renew axle shaft, add
each (1.0) 1.0
Renew C/V joint boot, add
each (.2) 2
Renew outer C/V joint, add
each (.3) 3

Renew D.O. joint, add
each (.3) 3
Repack or Recond joints,
add-each (.4) 4

Front Differential Cover or Gasket, Renew
All models (.4) 6

Differential Pinion Shaft Oil Seal and/or Flange, Renew
All models (3.7) 5.2

Differential Output Shaft Tube Assy., R&R or Renew
All models (1.4) 1.9
Renew output shaft seal
add (.1) 1

Renew pilot brg add (.1) 1
Renew shaft assy add (.1) 1
Recond tube assy add (.3) 3

Differential Carrier Assy., Remove & Install
All models (3.1) 4.3
Renew pinion shaft and/or
side pinion gears add (.4) 4
Renew side brgs add (1.0) 1.0
Renew pinion brgs add (1.7) 1.7
Renew ring and pinion
assy, add (1.6) 1.6
Renew case add (1.2) 1.2
Renew carrier add (1.8) 1.8
Renew output shaft brgs add (.9) 9
Renew mount bushs add (.2) 2
Recond complete add (2.2) 3.0
Recond tube add (.3) 3

LABOR 10 STEERING LINKAGE 10 LABOR

(Factory Time) — Chilton Time

Tie Rods or Tie Rod Ends, Renew
Includes: Reset toe-in.
Two Wheel Drive
one (.8) 1.1
both (1.0) 1.6
Four Wheel Drive
one (.7) 9
both (.9) 1.4

Idler Arm, Renew
All models (.7) 1.0
S-series 4X4 add 2

Drag Link, Renew
All models (.4) 9

Intermediate Rod, Renew
Includes: Reset toe-in.
Vans (1.0) 1.4
All other models (.9) 1.3
S-series 4X4 add 2

Pitman, Arm, Renew
All models (.5) 8
S-series 4X4 add 2

Steering Knuckle Arm, Renew
Includes: Reset toe-in.
All models-one (.9) 1.3
both (1.1) 1.7

Steering Damper, Renew
All models (.3) 6
S-series 4X4 add 2

Idler Arm Bracket and Bushing, Renew
All models (.4) 8

LABOR 11 STEERING GEAR 11 LABOR

(Factory Time) — Chilton Time

STANDARD STEERING

Steering Wheel, Renew
All models (.3) 4

Upper Mast Jacket Bearing, Renew
All models-std column (.8) 1.4
tilt column (.9) 1.6
w/Cruise control add (.2) 2

Tilt Column Bearing Housing, Renew
All models (.9) 1.5
w/Cruise control add (.2) 2

Steering Shaft Lower Coupling (Pot Joint), Renew
Includes: R&R intermediate shaft.
S-series (.4) 7
w/P.S. add (.3) 3
All other models (.7) 1.3

Flexible Coupling (Rag Joint), Renew
All models (.6) 1.0

Steering Column Lock Actuator Parts, Renew
All models
std colm (.8) 1.4
tilt colm (.9) 1.6
w/Cruise control add (.2) 2

Steering Gear, Adjust (On Truck)
All models 1.0

Steering Gear, R&R or Renew
All models (.6) 1.0

Steering Gear, R&R and Recondition
Includes: Disassemble, renew necessary parts, reassemble and adjust.
All models (1.5) 2.4

Pitman Shaft Seal, Renew
Does not require gear R&R.
All models (1.1) 1.4

POWER STEERING

Trouble Shoot Power Steering
Includes: Test pump and system pressure. Check pounds pull on steering wheel and check for leaks.
All models 5

Power Steering Belt, Renew
All models (.2) 4

Power Steering Gear, R&R or Renew
S-series (.6) 1.1
All other models (.8) 1.3

Power Steering Gear, R&R and Recondition
S-series (1.6) 2.5
All other models (1.8) 3.0

Valve Body, Recondition
Includes: R&R gear assy.
S-series (.9) 1.4
All other models (1.2) 1.8

Adjuster Plug, Recondition
Includes: R&R gear assy.
S-series (.8) 1.2
All other models (1.0) 1.5

Rack Piston Nut, Recondition
Includes: R&R gear assy.
S-series (1.0) 1.5
All other models (1.2) 1.8

Power Steering Pump, R&R or Renew
All models (.8) 1.2
w/A.C. add (.2) 2
Vans-w/Diesel eng add 2

Power Steering Pump, R&R and Recondition
All models (1.2) 1.8
w/A.C. add (.2) 2
Vans-w/Diesel eng add 2

Power Steering Reservoir and/or 'O' Ring Seal, Renew
All models (1.0) 1.4
w/A.C. add (.2) 2
Vans-w/Diesel eng add 2

Pump Flow Control Valve, Renew
S-series (.3) 7
All other models (.6) 1.0
w/A.C. add (.2) 2

Power Steering Hoses, Renew
All models
pressure (.4) 6
return (.5) 8
w/A.C. add (.2) 2

(Factory Time)	Chilton Time

GASOLINE ENGINES

Compression Test

Four	.6
Six	.9
V-6	.9
V-8	1.4

Cylinder Head Gasket, Renew

Includes: Clean carbon and make all necessary adjustments.

Four	
eng code A (3.4)	4.7
eng code Y (3.7)	5.1
eng code E	
S-series (4.0)	5.6
Astro (4.4)	6.2
w/Cruise control add	.2
w/A.C. add (.8)	.8
w/P.S. add (.4)	.4
Six–exc Vans (3.0)	4.3
Vans (3.9)	5.6
w/P.S. add (.4)	.4
w/A.C. add (.5)	.5
w/A.I.R. add (.6)	.6
w/P.A.I.R. add	.6
V-6–	
S-series-Astro	
one (5.7)	8.1
both (7.6)	10.8
All other models	
one (4.2)	6.0
both (6.5)	9.2
w/A.C. add (.5)	.5
w/P.S. add (.5)	.5
w/C.C.C. add (.3)	.3
V-8–454 eng	
one (4.8)	6.2
both (6.7)	9.1
V-8–all other engs	
exc Vans-one (4.5)	6.2
both (6.4)	8.8
Vans-one (4.8)	6.6
both (7.0)	9.6
w/P.S. add (.2)	.2
w/A.C. add (.7)	.7
w/A.I.R. add (.2)	.2

Cylinder Head, Renew

Includes: Transfer all components, reface valves, clean carbon.

Four	
eng code A (5.7)	7.9
eng code Y (6.2)	8.7
eng code E	
S-series (5.5)	7.7
Astro (5.7)	8.0
w/Cruise control add	.2
w/A.C. add (.8)	.8
w/P.S. add (.4)	.4
Six–exc Vans (5.9)	8.5
Vans (6.0)	8.7
w/P.S. add (.4)	.4
w/A.C. add (.5)	.5
w/A.I.R. add (.6)	.6
w/P.A.I.R. add	.6
V-6–	
S-series-Astro	
one (6.5)	9.2
both (9.0)	12.8
All other models	
one (5.0)	7.1
both (7.6)	10.8
w/A.C. add (.5)	.5
w/P.S. add (.5)	.5
w/C.C.C. add (.3)	.3
V-8–454 eng	
one (5.8)	7.2
both (8.8)	11.2

COMBINATIONS

Add to Valve Job

See Machine Shop Operations

(Factory Time)	Chilton Time

GASOLINE ENGINES

DRAIN, EVACUATE & RECHARGE AIR CONDITIONING SYSTEM	
All models (.7)	1.5
ROCKER ARM STUD, RENEW	
Each (.3)	.3
HYDRAULIC VALVE LIFTERS, DISASSEMBLE AND CLEAN	
Each	.2
DISTRIBUTOR, RECONDITION	
All models (.5)	.9
CARBURETOR, RECONDITION	
1 BBL (1.0)	1.0
2 BBL (1.0)	1.2
4 BBL (.8)	1.5
VALVE GUIDES, REAM OVERSIZE	
Each (.1)	.1

(Factory Time)	Chilton Time
V-8–all other engs	
exc Vans-one (5.4)	7.4
both (8.1)	11.1
Vans-one (5.7)	7.8
both (8.7)	12.0
w/P.S. add (.2)	.2
w/A.C. add (.7)	.7
w/A.I.R. add (.2)	.2

Clean Carbon and Grind Valves

Includes: R&R cylinder heads, grind valves and seats. Minor tune up.

Four	
eng code A (5.2)	7.3
eng code Y (5.3)	7.4
eng code E	
S-series (5.6)	8.0
Astro (6.0)	8.5
w/Cruise control add	.2
w/A.C. add (.8)	.8
w/P.S. add (.4)	.4
Six–exc Vans (5.6)	8.1
Vans (5.7)	8.3
w/P.S. add (.4)	.4
w/A.C. add (.5)	.5
w/A.I.R. add (.6)	.6
w/P.A.I.R. add	.6
V-6–	
S-series-Astro	
one side (7.0)	9.9
both sides (9.4)	13.3
All other models	
one side (5.3)	7.5
both sides (7.8)	11.1
w/A.C. add (.5)	.5
w/P.S. add (.5)	.5
w/C.C.C add (.3)	.3
V-8–454 eng	
one bank (6.1)	7.7
both banks (9.1)	12.2
V-8–all other engs	
exc Vans-one bank (5.8)	8.0
both banks (8.8)	12.1
Vans-one bank (6.1)	8.4
both banks (9.4)	12.9
w/P.S. add (.2)	.2

(Factory Time)	Chilton Time
w/A.C. add (.7)	.7
w/A.I.R. add (.2)	.2

Valves, Adjust

Six (.5)	1.4
V-8 (.8)	1.9
w/A.C. add	.7
w/P.A.I.R. add	.6

Valve Cover Gasket, Renew

Four	
eng code A (.4)	.7
eng code Y (.6)	.9
eng code E	
S-series (.9)	1.3
Astro (1.4)	2.0
Six–exc Vans (.7)	.9
Vans (.8)	1.0
w/A.I.R. add (.3)	.3
w/P.A.I.R. add	.6
V-6–	
S-series-Astro	
one side (.9)	1.3
both sides (1.3)	1.9
exc Vans	
right side (.7)	1.0
left side (.3)	.5
both sides (.9)	1.4
Vans	
right side (.9)	1.3
left side (.5)	.8
both sides (1.1)	1.7
w/A.C. add (.3)	.3
w/C.C.C. add (.3)	.3
V-8–454 eng	
one (.6)	.8
both (1.1)	1.5
V-8–all other engs	
exc Vans-one (.6)	.8
both (1.0)	1.3
Vans-right (.8)	1.3
left (.6)	.8
both (1.2)	1.6
w/A.C. add (.7)	.7
w/A.I.R. add (.2)	.2

Push Rod Side Cover Gasket, Renew

Four	
eng code E	
S-series (1.6)	2.2
Astro (1.8)	2.5
Six–exc Vans	
front (.5)	.7
rear (.3)	.4
both (.7)	1.0
Vans	
front (.6)	.8
rear (.5)	.8
both (.7)	1.2

Valve Push Rods and/or Rocker Arms, Renew

Four	
eng code A-all (.9)	1.2
eng code Y-all (1.0)	1.4
eng code E	
S-series-all (1.4)	2.0
Astro-all (1.9)	2.7
Six–exc Vans	
one or two (.5)	.8
three or more (.7)	1.2
w/A.I.R. add (.3)	.3
w/P.A.I.R. add	.6
Vans	
one or two (.9)	1.2
three or more (1.1)	1.6
V-6–	
S-series-Astro	
one cyl (1.0)	1.5
one cyl-each side (1.8)	2.7

LABOR 12 CYLINDER HEAD & VALVE SYSTEM 12 LABOR

(Factory Time)	Chilton Time
exc Vans	
one cyl-right side (.9)	1.4
one cyl-left side (.5)	1.0
one cyl-both sides (1.2)	1.9
Vans	
one cyl-right side (1.1)	1.7
one cyl-left side (.7)	1.2
one cyl-each side (1.4)	2.2
each adtnl cyl	.1
w/A.C. add (.3)	.3
w/C.C.C. add (.3)	.3
V-8-454 eng	
one cyl (.8)	1.0
one cyl-each bank (1.4)	1.8
all-both banks (1.9)	2.4
V-8-all other engs	
exc Vans	
one cyl (.8)	1.1
one cyl-each bank (1.4)	1.9
all cyls-both banks (1.9)	2.6
Vans	
one cyl (1.0)	1.4
one cyl-each bank (1.5)	2.0
all cyls-both banks (2.1)	2.9
w/A.C. add (.7)	.7
w/A.I.R. add (.2)	.2

Valve Lifters, Renew

Includes: R&R intake manifold on V-6 & V-8 engs. Make all necessary adjustments.

(Factory Time)	Chilton Time
Four	
eng code E	
S-series-all (3.1)	4.3
Astro-all (3.3)	4.6
Six-exc Vans-one (1.0)	1.4
all (1.5)	2.0
Vans-one (1.3)	1.7
all (1.8)	2.3
w/A.I.R. add (.3)	.3
w/P.A.I.R. add	.6
V-6-S-series	
one cyl (4.1)	6.0
one cyl-each side (4.2)	6.2
all cyls-both sides (4.7)	6.9
Astro	
one cyl (3.0)	4.4
one cyl-each side (3.3)	4.8
all cyls-both sides (3.8)	5.5
All other models	
one cyl (2.6)	3.8
one cyl-each side (2.8)	4.1
all cyls-both sides (3.3)	4.8
w/A.C. add (.3)	.3
w/C.C.C. add (.3)	.3
V-8-454 eng	
one (2.5)	3.2
all (3.3)	4.2
V-8-all other engs	
exc Vans-one cyl (2.8)	3.8
all cyls (3.4)	4.6
Vans-one cyl (2.9)	4.0
all cyls (3.5)	4.8
w/A.C. add (.7)	.7
w/A.I.R. add (.2)	.2

Valve Springs or Valve Stem Oil Seals, Renew (Head on Truck)

(Factory Time)	Chilton Time
Four	
eng code A	
one cyl (.8)	1.3
all cyls (1.4)	2.2
eng code Y	
one cyl (1.1)	1.6
all cyls (2.0)	3.0
eng code E	
S-series	
one cyl (1.3)	1.9
all cyls (2.2)	3.1
Astro	
one cyl (1.8)	2.6
all cyls (2.7)	3.8
Six-exc Vans	
one cyl (.7)	1.1
all cyls (1.2)	2.1
Vans	
one cyl (1.1)	1.5
all cyls (1.2)	2.5
w/A.I.R. add (.3)	.3
w/P.A.I.R. add	.6
V-6	
S-series-Astro	
one cyl (1.3)	1.9
one cyl-each side (2.3)	3.4
all cyls-both sides (3.6)	5.3
All other models	
one cyl-right side (1.4)	2.0
one cyl-left side (1.0)	1.5
one cyl-each side (2.0)	2.9
all cyls-both sides (3.2)	4.7
V-8-454 eng	
one cyl (1.1)	1.5
all cyls (3.7)	5.3
V-8-all other engs	
exc Vans	
one cyl (1.1)	1.5
all cyls (3.6)	5.0
Vans	
one cyl (1.4)	1.9
all cyls (4.5)	6.2
w/A.C. add (.7)	.7
w/A.I.R. add (.2)	.2

Valve Rocker Arm Stud, Renew (One)

Includes: Drain and refill cooling system.

(Factory Time)	Chilton Time
Four	
eng code E	
S-series (1.0)	1.5
Astro (1.5)	2.2
Six-exc Vans (.7)	1.0
Vans (1.2)	1.5
w/P.A.I.R. add	.6
V-6	
S-series-Astro (1.3)	1.8
All other models	
right side (1.3)	1.8
left side (.9)	1.4
w/A.C. add (.3)	.3
w/C.C.C. add (.3)	.3
V-8-454 eng (.8)	1.1
V-8-all other engs	
exc Vans (1.1)	1.5
Vans (1.3)	1.8
each adtnl-all engs (.3)	.3
w/A.C. add (.7)	.7
w/A.I.R. add (.2)	.2

DIESEL ENGINE

Compression Test

(Factory Time)	Chilton Time
All models	1.3

Cylinder Head Gasket, Renew

Includes: R&R injector pump and lines. R&R intake manifold and disconnect exhaust manifolds. Clean gasket surfaces, bleed litters and adjust timing. Drain and refill cooling system.

(Factory Time)	Chilton Time
All models-5.7L eng	
right side (5.0)	6.1
left side (4.9)	6.0
both sides (7.2)	9.1
6.2L eng	
one side (5.8)	8.0
both sides (8.1)	11.2
2.2L eng (2.6)	3.8
w/A.C. add (.3)	.3
Vans-w/A.C. add (2.0)	2.0

Cylinder Head, Renew

Includes: R&R injector pump and lines. R&R intake manifold and disconnect exhaust manifolds. Clean gasket surfaces. Transfer parts, reface valves. Bleed lifters and adjust timing. Drain and refill cooling system.

(Factory Time)	Chilton Time
All models-5.7L eng	
right side (5.5)	6.9
left side (5.4)	6.8
both sides (8.1)	10.7
6.2L eng	
one side (6.8)	9.5
both sides (9.6)	13.3
2.2L eng (3.9)	5.7
w/A.C. add (.3)	.3
Vans-w/A.C. add (2.0)	2.0

Clean Carbon and Grind Valves

Includes: R&R injector pump and lines. R&R cylinder heads, clean carbon. Recondition valves and valve seats. Check and adjust valve stem length. Bleed lifters, drain and refill cooling system.

(Factory Time)	Chilton Time
All models-5.7L eng	
right side (5.4)	7.2
left side (5.3)	7.1
both sides (9.1)	12.6
6.2L eng	
one side (7.1)	9.8
both sides (10.4)	14.4
2.2L eng (3.9)	5.7
w/A.C. add (.3)	.3
Vans-w/A.C. add (2.0)	2.0

Rocker Arm Cover or Gasket, Renew

Includes: R&R injector pump and lines.

(Factory Time)	Chilton Time
All models-5.7L eng	
one side (2.0)	2.6
both sides (2.2)	2.9
6.2L eng	
one side (2.6)	3.6
both sides (3.1)	4.3
2.2L eng (.4)	.6
Vans-w/A.C. add (2.0)	2.0

Valve Spring or Valve Stem Oil Seals, Renew (Head on Truck)

Includes: R&R injector pump and lines.

(Factory Time)	Chilton Time
All models-5.7L eng	
one (2.2)	3.1
one-each bank (2.6)	3.7
each adtnl(.3)	.3
6.2L eng	
one cyl (3.0)	4.2
one cyl-each side (3.9)	5.4
each adtnl cyl (.4)	.4
2.2L eng	
one cyl (.8)	1.2
all cyls (1.3)	2.0
Vans-w/A.C. add (2.0)	2.0

Rocker Arm and/or Push Rod, Renew

Includes: R&R injector pump and lines.

(Factory Time)	Chilton Time
All models-5.7L eng	
one cyl (2.1)	3.0
one cyl-each side (2.5)	3.5
each adtnl cyl (.1)	.1
6.2L eng	
one cyl (2.7)	3.7
one cyl-each side (3.3)	4.6
each adtnl cyl (.1)	.1
2.2L eng	
one or all (.7)	1.2
Vans-w/A.C. add (2.0)	2.0

Valve Lifters, Renew

Includes: R&R fuel injection pump and lines.

(Factory Time)	Chilton Time
All models-5.7L eng	
one cyl (3.2)	4.2
one cyl-each side (3.5)	4.5
each adtnl cyl (.1)	.2
6.2L eng-exc Vans	
one cyl (3.4)	4.7
one cyl-each side (4.6)	6.4
each adtnl cyl (.1)	.2
Vans	
one cyl (6.7)	9.3
one cyl-each side (8.8)	12.2
each adtnl cyl (.1)	.1
2.2L eng-all (6.9)	10.0
w/A.C. add (.8)	.8
w/P.S. add (.3)	.3
Vans-w/A.C. add (2.0)	2.0

Valve Clearance, Adjust

(Factory Time)	Chilton Time
All models	
2.2L eng (.6)	1.0

GASOLINE ENGINES

Engine Assembly, R&R

Does not include transfer of any parts or equipment.

(Factory Time)	Chilton Time
Four	5.0
w/A.C. add	.9
w/P.S. add	.4
w/A.T. add	.3
Six–exc Vans	5.1
Vans	7.7
w/P.S. add	.5
w/A.C. add	.5
w/A.I.R. add	.5
w/P.A.I.R. add	.6
V-6	
S-series	
4X2	5.5
4X4	*6.7
*w/M.T. add	2.0
Astro	6.9
exc Vans	4.9
Vans	5.9
w/P.S. add	.3
w/C.C.C. add	.6
w/A.T. add	.4
w/A.C. add	
Vans	1.1
Astro	.9
All other models	.4
V-8–454 eng	6.2
V-8–all other engs	
exc Vans	6.2
Vans	8.6
w/A.C. add	1.5
w/P.S. add	.2
w/A.I.R. add	.4
Vans with Hydra-Boost add	1.1

Engine Assembly, Renew

Includes: R&R engine and transmission assy. Transfer all component parts not supplied with replacement engine. Minor tune up.

(Factory Time)	Chilton Time
Four	
eng code Y	
4X2 (5.4)	8.0
4X4 (8.4)	12.0
w/A.C. add	.4
w/P.S. add	.4
eng code E	
S-series	
4X2 (4.8)	7.0
4X4 (5.6)	8.1
Astro (6.6)	9.6
w/A.C. add	.9
w/P.S. add	.3
w/A.T. add	.3
Six–exc Vans (4.1)	8.2
Vans (5.5)	9.6
w/P.S. add (.4)	.5
w/A.C. add (.5)	.5
w/A.I.R. add (.4)	.5
w/P.A.I.R. add	.6
V-6	
S-series	
4X2 (6.2)	9.0
4X4 (7.1)	*10.2
*w/M.T. add	2.0
Astro (7.2)	10.4
exc Vans (5.8)	8.4
Vans (6.5)	9.4
w/P.S. add (.3)	.3
w/C.C.C. add (.6)	.6
w/A.T. add (.4)	.4
w/A.C. add	
Vans (1.1)	1.1
Astro (.9)	.9
All other models (.4)	.4
V-8–454 eng (6.9)	9.3
V-8–all other engs	
exc Vans (6.0)	8.2
Vans (7.6)	10.5
w/A.C. add (1.3)	1.5
w/P.S. add (.2)	.2
w/A.I.R. add (.4)	.4
Vans with Hydra-Boost add (1.1)	1.1

Cylinder Block, Renew

(w/Internal Parts Less Head(s) and Oil Pan)

Includes: R&R engine and transmission assy. Transfer all components parts not supplied with replacement engine. Clean carbon, grind valves. Minor tune up.

(Factory Time)	Chilton Time
Four	
eng code A	
4X2 (8.0)	12.0
4X4 (8.9)	13.0
eng code Y	
4X2 (9.9)	14.5
4X4 (13.1)	19.0
w/A.C. add (.4)	.4
w/P.S. add (.4)	.4
eng code E	
S-series	
4X2 (9.0)	13.0
4X4 (9.9)	14.4
Astro (10.9)	15.8
w/A.C. add	.9
w/P.S. add	.3
w/A.T. add	.3
Six–exc Vans (9.1)	15.0
Vans (11.4)	17.3
w/P.S. add (.4)	.5
w/A.C. add (.5)	.5
w/A.I.R. add (.4)	.5
w/P.A.I.R. add	.6
V-6	
S-series	
4X2 (11.7)	16.9
4X4 (12.5)	*18.1
*w/M.T. add	2.0
Astro (13.1)	19.0
exc Vans (11.6)	16.8
Vans (12.4)	17.9
w/P.S. add (.3)	.3
w/C.C.C. add (.6)	.6
w/A.T. add (.4)	.4
w/A.C. add	
Vans (1.1)	1.1
Astro (.9)	.9
All other models (.4)	.4
V-8–454 eng (14.9)	20.1
V-8–all other engs	
exc Vans (14.2)	19.5
Vans (14.8)	20.8
w/A.C. add (1.3)	1.5
w/P.S. add (.2)	.2
w/A.I.R. add (.4)	.4
Vans with Hydra-Boost add (1.1)	1.1

Cylinder Block, Renew

(w/Pistons, Rings and Bearings)

Includes: R&R engine and transmission assy. Transfer all component parts not supplied with replacement engine. Clean carbon, grind valves. Minor tune up.

(Factory Time)	Chilton Time
Four	
eng code E	
S-series	
4X2 (11.3)	16.4
4X4 (12.1)	17.5
Astro (13.1)	19.0
w/A.C. add	.9
w/P.S. add	.3
w/A.T. add	.3
Six–exc Vans (12.4)	17.0
Vans (15.0)	19.6
w/P.S. add (.4)	.5
w/A.C. add (.5)	.5
w/A.I.R. add (.4)	.5
w/P.A.I.R. add	.6
V-6	
S-series	
4X2 (14.1)	20.5
4X4 (14.9)	*21.6
*w/M.T. add	2.0
Astro (16.0)	23.2
exc Vans (14.5)	21.0
Vans (15.3)	22.2
w/P.S. add (.3)	.3
w/C.C.C. add (.6)	.6
w/A.T. add (.4)	.4
w/A.C. add	
Vans (1.1)	1.1
Astro (.9)	.9
All other models (.4)	.4
V-8–454 eng (17.7)	23.8
V-8–all other engs	
exc Vans (17.0)	23.4
Vans (17.6)	24.1
w/A.C. add (1.3)	1.5
w/P.S. add (.2)	.2
w/A.I.R. add (.4)	.4
Vans with Hydra-Boost add (1.1)	1.1

Engine Assy., R&R and Recondition

Includes: Rebore block, install new pistons, rings, rod and main bearings. Clean carbon, grind valves. Tune engine.

(Factory Time)	Chilton Time
Four	
eng code A	
4X2 (13.2)	19.7
4X4 (14.1)	21.0
eng code Y	
4X2 (16.0)	23.8
4X4 (18.6)	27.7
w/A.C. add (.4)	.4
w/P.S. add (.4)	.4
eng code E	
S-series	
4X2 (13.5)	19.5
4X4 (14.4)	20.8
Astro (15.4)	22.3
w/A.C. add	.9
w/P.S. add	.3
w/A.T. add	.3
Six–exc Vans (25.0)	32.0
Vans (27.6)	34.6
w/P.S. add (.4)	.5
w/A.C. add (.5)	.5
w/A.I.R. add (.4)	.5
w/P.A.I.R. add	.6
V-6	
S-series	
4X2 (20.7)	28.4
4X4 (22.2)	*29.5
*w/M.T. add	2.0

LABOR 13 ENGINE ASSEMBLY & MOUNTS 13 LABOR

(Factory Time) Chilton Time

Astro (23.4)........ 31.5
exc Vans (20.9)........ 28.8
Vans (21.7)........ 29.2
w/P.S. add (.3)........ .3
w/C.C.C. add (.6)........ .6
w/A.T. add (.4)........ .4
w/A.C. add
Vans (1.1)........ 1.1
Astro (.9)........ .9
All other models (.4)........ .4
V-8-454 eng (32.5)........ 41.9

V-8-all other engs
exc Vans (30.7)........ 43.5
Vans (32.2)........ 45.0
w/A.C. add (1.3)........ 1.5
w/P.S. add (.2)........ .2
w/A.I.R. add (.4)........ .4
Vans with Hydra-Boost add (1.1)........ 1.1

Engine Mounts, Renew

Front

Four-one (.5)........ .7
both (.7)........ 1.0
Six-exc Vans-one (.5)........ 1.1
both (.8)........ 1.4
Vans-one (.7)........ 1.3
both (1.0)........ 1.6
V-6
S-series
one (1.0)........ 1.4
both (1.4)........ 1.9
All other models
one (.8)........ 1.1
both (1.2)........ 1.7

V-8-all engines
one (.8)........ 1.3
both (1.2)........ 1.9

Rear
All models (.4)........ .9

DIESEL ENGINE

Engine Assembly, Remove & Install

Does not include transfer of any parts or equipment.
All models........ 5.0
w/A.C. add........ 1.2
w/A.T. add........ .8

Engine Assembly, Renew (Universal)

Includes: R&R engine assembly. Transfer all component parts not supplied with replacement engine. Make all necessary adjustments.
All models
5.7L eng........ 20.0
6.2L eng........ 22.0
w/A.C. add........ 1.2
w/A.T. add........ .8

Cylinder Block, Renew (Partial)

Includes: Transfer all component parts not supplied with replacement block. Clean carbon, grind valves. Make all necessary adjustments.
All models
2.2L eng (11.1)........ 18.0
5.7L eng........ 21.3
6.2L eng
Vans (17.4)........ 29.5
All other models (15.5)........ 27.6

w/A.C. add........ 1.2
w/A.T. add........ .8

Engine Assembly, R&R and Recondition

Includes: Rebore block, install new pistons, rings, rod and main bearings. Clean carbon, grind valves. Make all necessary adjustments.
All models
2.2L eng........ 27.3
5.7L eng........ 37.2
6.2L eng........ 40.0
w/A.C. add........ 1.2
w/A.T. add........ .8

Engine Assembly, Recondition (In Truck)

Includes: Expand or renew pistons, install new rings, pins, rod and main bearings. Clean carbon, grind valves. Make all necessary adjustments.
All models
2.2L eng........ 20.1
5.7L eng........ 28.5
6.2L eng........ 32.9
w/A.C. add (.3)........ .3

Engine Mounts, Renew

Front
All models-5.7L eng
one (.5)........ .8
both (.6)........ 1.0
6.2L eng
one (.7)........ 1.0
both (1.1)........ 1.5
2.2L eng
one (1.0)........ 1.4
both (1.8)........ 2.6

Rear
All models (.4)........ .6

LABOR 14 PISTONS, RINGS & BEARINGS 14 LABOR

(Factory Time) Chilton Time

GASOLINE ENGINES

Rings, Renew (See Engine Combinations)

Includes: Remove cylinder top ridge, deglaze cylinder walls, replace rod bearings, clean carbon from cylinder heads. Clean piston and ring grooves. Minor tune up.

Four
eng code A
one cyl (5.9)........ 8.5
each adtnl cyl........ .7
4X4 add (.9)........ .9
eng code Y
one cyl (6.9)........ 10.0
each adtnl cyl........ .7
4X4 add (.4)........ .4
w/A.C. add (.4)........ .4
w/P.S. add (.4)........ .4
eng code E
S-series
4X2-one cyl (5.9)........ 8.5
4X4-one cyl (8.5)........ 12.3
Astro-one cyl (6.4)........ 9.3
each adtnl cyl........ .7
w/A.C. add........ .6

Six-exc Vans-one (4.7)........ 6.9
all (6.7)........ 10.3
Vans-one (4.8)........ 7.0
all (6.8)........ 10.4
w/P.S. add (.4)........ .5
w/A.C. add (.5)........ .5
w/A.I.R. add (.6)........ .6
w/P.A.I.R. add........ .6

V-6
S-series-Astro
one cyl (8.4)........ 12.2
one cyl-each side (10.2)........ 14.8
all cyls-both sides (12.1)........ 17.5
All other models
one cyl (6.6)........ 9.5
one cyl-each side (8.8)........ 12.8
all cyls-both sides (10.7)........ 15.5
w/A.C. add (.5)........ .5
w/P.S. add (.5)........ .5
w/C.C.C. add (.3)........ .3
V-8-454 eng-one (6.6)........ 9.1
all (10.9)........ 14.8
V-8-all other engs
exc Vans-one (6.1)........ 8.4
all (10.8)........ 14.9
Vans-one (6.4)........ 8.8
all (11.4)........ 15.7
w/A.C. add (.7)........ .7
w/P.S. add (.2)........ .2
w/A.I.R. add (.2)........ .2

Piston or Connecting Rod, Renew

Includes: Remove cylinder top ridge, deglaze cylinder walls, replace rod bearings, clean carbon from cylinder heads. Minor tune up.

Four
eng code A
one cyl (6.3)........ 9.1
each adtnl cyl........ .7
4X4 add (.9)........ .9
eng code Y
one cyl (7.3)........ 10.5
each adtnl cyl........ .7

4X4 add (.4)........ .4
w/A.C. add (.4)........ .4
w/P.S. add (.4)........ .4
eng code E
S-series
4X2-one cyl (6.6)........ 9.5
4X4-one cyl (9.2)........ 13.3
Astro-one cyl (7.1)........ 10.3
each adtnl cyl........ .7
w/A.C. add........ .6
Six-exc Vans-one (4.7)........ 7.2
all (6.7)........ 11.8
Vans-one (4.8)........ 7.3
all (6.8)........ 11.9
w/P.S. add (.4)........ .5
w/A.C. add (.5)........ .5
w/A.I.R. add (.6)........ .6
w/P.A.I.R. add........ .6
V-6
S-series-Astro
one cyl (8.4)........ 12.5
one cyl-each side (10.2)........ 15.4
all cyls-both sides (12.8)........ 19.3
All other models
one cyl (6.6)........ 9.8
one cyl-each side (8.8)........ 13.4
all cyls-both sides (13.3)........ 17.3
w/A.C. add (.5)........ .5
w/P.S. add (.5)........ .5
w/C.C.C. add (.3)........ .3
V-8-454 eng-one (6.6)........ 9.4
all (10.9)........ 17.2
V-8-all other engs
exc Vans-one (6.1)........ 8.7
all (10.8)........ 17.3

LABOR 14 PISTONS, RINGS & BEARINGS 14 LABOR

(Factory Time)	Chilton Time
Vans-one (6.4)	9.1
all (11.4)	18.1
w/A.C. add (.7)	.7
w/P.S. add (.2)	.2
w/A.I.R. add (.2)	.2

Connecting Rod Bearings, Renew

(Factory Time)	Chilton Time
Four	
eng code A (4.8)	6.7
eng code Y	
4X2 (5.7)	8.0
4X4 (4.7)	6.5
w/A.C. add (.4)	.4
w/P.S. add (.4)	.4
eng code E	
4X2 (2.7)	4.0
4X4 (5.1)	7.4
Six-one (2.0)	2.8
all (3.5)	4.9
w/A.C. add (.7)	.7
V-6	
S-series	
4X2 (6.4)	9.4
4X4 (4.9)	7.3
All other models (3.4)	4.9
w/A.C. add (.2)	.2
w/P.S. add (.2)	.2
w/C.C.C. add (.2)	.2
w/A.T. add (.3)	.3
V-8-454 eng-one (1.8)	2.8
all (3.9)	5.4
V-8-all other engs	
All models-one (1.6)	2.4
all (3.7)	5.2
w/M.T. add (.2)	.2

DIESEL ENGINE

Rings, Renew (See Engine Combinations)

Includes: Remove cylinder to ridge, deglaze cylinder walls. Clean piston and ring grooves. Make all necessary adjustments.

(Factory Time)	Chilton Time
All models	
2.2L eng (10.0)	14.5
w/A.C. add (.8)	.8
w/P.S. add (.3)	.3
5.7L eng (10.6)	14.0
6.2L eng (15.4)	21.5
w/A.C. add (.3)	.3

Piston or Connecting Rod, Renew

Includes: Remove cylinder top ridge, deglaze cylinder walls. Make all necessary adjustments.

(Factory Time)	Chilton Time
All models	
2.2L eng (10.0)	16.3
w/A.C. add (.8)	.8
w/P.S. add (.3)	.3
5.7L eng (10.7)	16.8
6.2L eng (16.5)	23.9
w/A.C. add (.3)	.3

Connecting Rod Bearings, Renew

Includes: Raise engine and clean oil pump screen.

(Factory Time)	Chilton Time
All models	
2.2L eng (7.5)	10.8
w/A.C. add (.8)	.8
w/P.S. add (.3)	.3
5.7L eng (4.0)	5.6
6.2L eng	
Vans (5.6)	7.8
All other models (4.0)	5.8

COMBINATIONS

Add to Engine Work
See Machine Shop Operations

GASOLINE ENGINES

(Factory Time)	Chilton Time
DRAIN, EVACUATE AND RECHARGE AIR CONDITIONING SYSTEM	
All models (.7)	1.5
ROCKER ARM STUD, RENEW	
Each (.3)	.3
HYDRAULIC VALVE LIFTERS, DISASSEMBLE AND CLEAN	
Each	.2
DISTRIBUTOR, RECONDITION	
All models (.5)	.9
CARBURETOR, RECONDITION	
1 BBL (1.0)	1.0
2 BBL (1.0)	1.2
4 BBL (.8)	1.5
VALVE GUIDES, REAM OVERSIZE	
Each (.1)	.1
DEGLAZE CYLINDER WALLS	
Each (.1)	.1
REMOVE CYLINDER TOP RIDGE	
Each (.1)	.1
VALVES, RECONDITION	
Four (1.8)	2.5
Six (2.1)	3.0
V-6 (2.0)	3.0
V-8 (2.7)	3.5
PLASTIGAUGE BEARINGS	
Each (.1)	.1
OIL PUMP, RECONDITION	
All models	.6
w/P.S. add (.2)	.2
w/C.C.C. add (.2)	.2
OIL FILTER, RENEW	
Four (.3)	.4
Six (.2)	.3
V-6 (.3)	.4
V-8 (.3)	.4

LABOR 15 CRANKSHAFT & DAMPER 15 LABOR

GASOLINE ENGINES

Crankshaft and Main Bearings, Renew

Includes: R&R engine, plastigauge bearings.

(Factory Time)	Chilton Time
Four	
eng code A	
4X2 (7.8)	11.3
4X4 (8.9)	12.9
eng code Y	
4X2 (7.8)	11.5
4X4 (10.4)	15.0
w/A.C. add (.4)	.4
w/P.S. add (.4)	.4
eng code E	
S-series	
4X2 (6.4)	9.3
4X4 (7.3)	10.6
Astro (8.3)	12.0
w/A.C. add	.9
w/P.S. add	.3
w/A.T. add	.3
Six-exc Vans (6.5)	8.4
Vans (8.7)	11.8
w/P.S. add (.4)	.5
w/A.C. add (.5)	.5
w/A.I.R. add (.3)	.5
w/P.A.I.R. add	.6
V-6	
S-series	
4X2 (8.5)	12.3
4X4 (9.0)	*13.0
*w/M.T. add	2.0
Astro (10.2)	14.8
exc Vans (9.1)	13.2
Vans (9.7)	14.0
w/P.S. add (.3)	.3
w/C.C.C. add (.6)	.6
w/A.T. add (.4)	.4
w/A.C. add	
Vans (1.1)	1.1
Astro (.9)	.9
All other models (.4)	.4
V-8-454 eng (9.2)	12.4
V-8-all other engs	
exc Vans (8.8)	12.3
Vans (10.3)	14.8
w/A.C. add (1.3)	1.5
w/P.S. add (.2)	.2
w/A.I.R. add (.2)	.2
Vans with Hydra-Boost add (1.1)	1.1

Main Bearings, Renew

Includes: Plastigauge bearings.

(Factory Time)	Chilton Time
Four	
eng code A (5.2)	7.5
eng code Y	
4X2 (5.8)	8.4
4X4 (4.7)	6.8
w/A.C. add (.4)	.4
w/P.S. add (.4)	.4
eng code E	
4X2 (2.9)	4.2
4X4 (5.3)	7.7
Six-exc Vans (3.3)	4.9
Vans (3.5)	5.1
V-6	
S-series	
4X2 (6.1)	9.5
4X4 (4.9)	7.8
All other models (3.1)	4.5
w/A.C. add (.2)	.2
w/P.S. add (.2)	.2
w/C.C.C. add (.2)	.2
w/A.T. add (.3)	.3

LABOR 15 CRANKSHAFT & DAMPER 15 LABOR

(Factory Time)	Chilton Time
V-8–454 eng (3.2)	5.0
V-8–all other engs	
All models (2.9)	4.5
w/M.T. add (.2)	.2

Rear Main Bearing Oil Seal, Renew

(Factory Time)	Chilton Time
Four	
eng code A (4.1)	*6.3
eng code Y	
4X2 (6.7)	*9.7
4X4 (9.2)	*13.3
w/A.C. add (.4)	.4
w/P.S. add (.4)	.4
eng code E	
4X2 (2.4)	3.5
4X4 (3.4)	5.0
w/A.T. add (.3)	.3
w/M.T. add (.4)	.4
Six–exc Vans (1.6)	2.7
Vans (1.8)	2.9
w/A.C. add (.7)	.7
V-6	
S-series	
Full Circle Type	
4X2 (7.3)	10.5
4X4 (7.8)	*11.3
w/A.C. add (.2)	.2
w/P.S. add (.2)	.2
w/C.C.C. add (.6)	.6
*w/M.T. add	2.0
Split Lip Type	
4X2 (3.0)	4.5
4X4 (3.6)	5.5
w/A.T. add (.4)	.4
All other models (2.2)	3.5
V-8–454 eng (2.0)	3.3
V-8–all other engs	
All models (1.6)	3.2
w/M.T. add (.2)	.2

*Includes R&R engine.

Harmonic Balancer (Vibration Damper), Renew

Includes: Renew timing cover oil seal.

(Factory Time)	Chilton Time
Four	
eng code A (.9)	1.5
eng code Y (.7)	1.4
eng code E (.5)	1.1
w/A.C. add (.2)	.2
w/P.S. add (.2)	.2
Six–exc Vans (.8)	1.2
Vans (.9)	1.6
w/P.S. add (.2)	.2
w/A.C. add (.2)	.2
w/A.I.R. add (.2)	.2
V-6	
All models (.8)	1.3
w/A.C. add (.2)	.2
w/P.S. add (.2)	.2
V-8–454 eng (1.2)	1.6
V-8–all other engs	
All models (1.0)	1.5
w/A.C. add (.2)	.2
w/P.S. add (.2)	.2
w/A.I.R. add (.2)	.2

DIESEL ENGINE

Crankshaft and Main Bearings, Renew

Includes: R&R engine, plastigauge bearings.

(Factory Time)	Chilton Time
All models	
2.2L eng (8.9)	13.0
w/A.C. add (.8)	.8
w/P.S. add (.3)	.3
5.7L eng (7.5)	10.9
6.2L eng	
Vans (13.4)	19.5
All other models (8.5)	12.3
w/A.C. add (.3)	.3
w/A.T. add	.8

Main Bearings, Renew

Includes: Plastigauge bearings.

(Factory Time)	Chilton Time
All models	
2.2L eng (7.9)	11.4
w/A.C. add (.8)	.8
w/P.S. add (.3)	.3
5.7L eng (3.5)	5.4
6.2L eng	
Vans (4.9)	7.0
All other models (3.5)	5.0

Main and Rod Bearings, Renew

Includes: Check all bearing clearance.

(Factory Time)	Chilton Time
All models	
2.2L eng (9.1)	12.6
w/A.C. add (.8)	.8
w/P.S. add (.3)	.3
5.7L eng (5.1)	7.8
6.2L eng	
Vans (7.3)	9.4
All other models (5.3)	7.4

Rear Main Bearing Oil Seals, Renew or Repack (Upper and Lower)

Includes: R&R oil pan and rear main bearing cap.

(Factory Time)	Chilton Time
All models	
2.2L eng (1.9)	2.8
5.7L eng (2.8)	4.0
6.2L eng	
Vans (3.7)	5.4
All other models (2.5)	3.6

Harmonic Balancer (Vibration Damper), Renew

(Factory Time)	Chilton Time
All models	
5.7L eng (.9)	1.3
6.2L eng	
Vans (1.2)	1.6
All other models (.8)	1.2
w/A.C. add (.4)	.4

Crankshaft Front Oil Seal, Renew

(Factory Time)	Chilton Time
All models	
5.7L eng (1.0)	1.5
6.2L eng	
Vans (1.2)	1.8
All other models (.8)	1.4
w/A.C. add (.4)	.4

LABOR 16 CAMSHAFT & TIMING GEARS 16 LABOR

GASOLINE ENGINES

Timing Cover Oil Seal, Renew

(Factory Time)	Chilton Time
Four	
eng code A (.9)	1.7
eng code Y (.7)	1.6
eng code E (.5)	1.2
w/A.C. add (.2)	.2
w/P.S. add (.2)	.2
Six–exc Vans (.8)	1.4
Vans (.9)	1.5
w/P.S. add (.2)	.2
w/A.C. add (.2)	.2
w/A.I.R. add (.2)	.2
V-6	
All models (.8)	1.4
w/A.C. add (.2)	.2
w/P.S. add (.2)	.2
V-8–454 eng (1.2)	1.6
V-8–all other engs	
All models (1.0)	1.6
w/A.C. add (.2)	.2
w/P.S. add (.2)	.2
w/A.I.R. add (.2)	.2

Timing Cover Gasket, Renew

Includes: Renew oil seal.

(Factory Time)	Chilton Time
Four	
eng code A (5.6)	8.0
eng code Y (1.7)	2.5
eng code E (1.3)	2.0
w/A.C. add (.4)	.4
w/P.S. add (.4)	.4
Six–all models (1.1)	1.8
w/P.S. add (.2)	.2
w/A.C. add (.2)	.2
w/A.I.R. add (.2)	.2
V-6	
S-series (2.0)	3.0
Astro (1.7)	2.5
exc Vans (1.8)	2.7
Vans (2.1)	3.1
w/A.C. add (.2)	.2
w/P.S. add (.3)	.3
V-8–454 eng (2.2)	2.8
V-8–all other engs	
all models (2.0)	*3.0
w/A.C. add (.5)	.5
w/P.S. add (.2)	.2
w/A.I.R. add (.2)	.2
*Vans w/A.C. add (1.2)	1.2

Timing Chain, Renew

Includes: R&R engine front cover.

(Factory Time)	Chilton Time
Four	
eng code A (5.7)	8.5
eng code Y (2.0)	3.0
w/A.C. add (.4)	.4
w/P.S. add (.4)	.4
V-6	
S-series (2.3)	3.5
Astro (1.8)	3.0
exc Vans (1.9)	3.2
Vans (2.2)	3.6
w/A.C. add (.2)	.2
w/P.S. add (.3)	.3
V-8–454 eng (2.6)	3.3
V-8–all other engs	
all models (2.2)	*3.5
w/A.C. add (.5)	.5
w/P.S. add (.2)	.2
w/A.I.R. add (.2)	.2
*Vans w/A.C. add (1.2)	1.2

Camshaft, Renew

Includes: R&R engine and front cover, where required.

(Factory Time)	Chilton Time
Four	
eng code A (1.0)	1.5

LABOR 16 CAMSHAFT & TIMING GEARS 16 LABOR

(Factory Time) Chilton Time

eng code Y (4.0) 6.0
eng code E
S-series (4.7).... 6.8
Astro (6.0).... 8.7
w/A.C. add 5
w/P.S. add.... .3

Six–exc Vans (3.9).... 6.0
Vans (4.2).... 8.3
w/P.S. add (.4).... .5
w/A.C. add (.5).... .5
w/A.I.R. add (.4).... .5
w/P.A.I.R. add.... .6

V-6
S-series (5.1).... 8.5
Astro (5.7).... 8.8
All other models (6.0).... 9.3
w/C.C.C. add (.3).... .3
w/A.C. add (.3).... .3
w/P.S. add (.3).... .3
V-8–454 eng (6.2).... 9.3
V-8–all other engs
exc Vans (5.8).... 8.0
Vans (6.2).... 9.5
w/A.C. add (1.4).... 1.6
w/P.S. add (.2).... .2
w/A.I.R. add (.4).... .4
Vans with Hydra-Boost add (1.1).... 1.1

Camshaft Timing Gear, Renew
Four
eng code A (.5).... .9
eng code Y (2.0).... 3.0
eng code E
S-series (4.7).... 6.8
Astro (6.0).... 8.7
w/A.C. add.... .5
w/P.S. add.... .3

V-6
S-series (2.3).... 3.5
Astro (1.8).... 3.0
exc Vans (1.9).... 3.2
Vans (2.2).... 3.6
w/A.C. add (.2).... .2
w/P.S. add (.3).... .3

(Factory Time) Chilton Time

DIESEL ENGINE

Timing Cover or Gasket, Renew
Includes: R&R fan blade, crankshaft pulley and balancer. Drain and refill oil and coolant.
All models
2.2L eng (2.5).... 3.6
5.7L eng (2.3).... 3.3
6.2L eng (4.3).... 6.2
w/A.C. add (.4).... .4

Timing Cover Oil Seal, Renew
Includes: R&R fan blade, crankshaft pulley and balancer. Drain and refill oil and coolant.
All models
2.2L eng (1.1).... 2.0
5.7L eng (1.0).... 1.6
6.2L eng
Vans (1.2).... 2.0
All other models (.8).... 1.5
w/A.C. add (.4).... .4

Camshaft Gear and/or Timing Chain, Renew
Includes: R&R fan blades, crankshaft pulley and balancer. Drain and refill oil and coolant.
All models
5.7L eng (3.6).... 4.8
6.2L eng (4.5).... 6.7
w/A.C. add (.4).... .4

Injector Pump Drive Gear, Renew
Includes: R&R timing gear and chain. R&R intake manifold and lifters. Drain and refill oil and coolant, where required.
All models
2.2L eng (.9).... 1.5
5.7L eng (5.2).... 7.2
6.2L eng (4.4).... 6.6
w/A.C. add (.4).... .4

Camshaft, Renew
Includes: R&R radiator, front cover, fuel pump, timing gear and chain. R&R injector pump, intake manifold and lifters. Disconnect exhaust system. Drain and refill oil and coolant. Make all necessary adjustments.
All models
2.2L eng (6.9).... 10.0

(Factory Time) Chilton Time

w/A.C. add (.6).... .6
w/P.S. add (.3).... .3
5.7L eng (6.5).... 10.8
6.2L eng (12.0).... 17.4
w/A.C. add (2.0).... 2.0
w/A.T. add (.3).... .3

Camshaft Bearings, Renew
Includes: R&R radiator, front cover, fuel pump, timing gear and chain. R&R injector pump, intake manifold and lifters. Disconnect exhaust system. Drain and refill oil and coolant. Make all necessary adjustments.
All models
5.7L eng (9.5).... 14.6
w/A.C. add (.2).... .2

Camshaft Rear Bearing Plug, Renew
Note: Use appropriate labor operation for removal of necessary components to gain access to plug.
All models (.3).... .6

Camshaft Timing Gear, Renew
All models
2.2L eng (.9).... 1.6
w/A.C. add (.1).... .1

Crankshaft Timing Gear, Renew
All models
2.2L eng (.9).... 1.6
w/A.C. add (.1).... .1

Camshaft Idler Pulley, Renew
All models
2.2L eng (.4).... .6
w/A.C. add (.1).... .1

Camshaft Drive Belt, Renew
All models
2.2L eng (.8).... 1.5
w/A.C. add (.1).... .1

Camshaft Drive Belt Covers and/or Gaskets, Renew
All models
2.2L eng
upper (.3).... .5
lower or both (.6).... 1.0
w/A.C. add (.1).... .1

LABOR 17 ENGINE OILING SYSTEM 17 LABOR

(Factory Time) Chilton Time

GASOLINE ENGINE

Oil Pan and/or Gasket, Renew
Four
eng code A (3.7).... 5.5
eng code Y
4X2 (4.3).... 6.2
4X4 (3.2).... 4.6
w/A.C. add (.4).... .4
w/P.S. add (.4).... .4
eng code E
4X2 (1.7).... 2.5
4X4 (4.1).... 6.0
Six–exc Vans (1.4).... 2.4
Vans (1.6).... 2.6
w/A.C. add (.7).... .7
V-6
S-series
4X2 (4.9).... 7.3
4X4 (3.4).... 5.1
All other models (1.7).... 2.5
w/A.C. add (.2).... .2

(Factory Time) Chilton Time

w/P.S. add (.2).... .2
w/C.C.C. add (.2).... .2
w/A.T. add (.3).... .3
V-8–454 eng (1.4).... 2.5
V-8–all other engs (1.1).... 2.0
w/M.T. add (.2).... .2

Pressure Test Engine Bearings (Pan Off)
All models.... 1.0

Oil Pump, Renew
Four
eng code A (3.8).... 5.7
eng code Y
4X2 (4.4).... 6.4
4X4 (3.4).... 4.8
w/A.C. add (.4).... .4
w/P.S. add (.4).... .4
eng code E
4X2 (1.9).... 2.7
4X4 (4.2).... 6.2
Six–exc Vans (1.5).... 2.6
Vans (1.8).... 2.8

(Factory Time) Chilton Time

w/A.C. add (.7).... .7
V-6
S-series
4X2 (4.9).... 7.5
4X4 (3.4).... 5.3
All other models (1.8).... 2.7
w/A.C. add (.2).... .2
w/P.S. add (.2).... .2
w/C.C.C. add (.2).... .2
w/A.T. add (.3).... .3
V-8–454 eng (1.5).... 2.7
V-8–all other engs (1.2).... 2.2
w/M.T. add (.2).... .2

Oil Pressure Gauge (Dash), Renew
S-series (.3).... .5
Astro (.9).... 1.4
All other models (.6).... 1.0

Oil Pressure Gauge (Engine Unit), Renew
All models (.2).... .5
w/A.C. add (.2).... .2
w/Cruise control add (.4).... .4

LABOR 17 ENGINE OILING SYSTEM 17 LABOR

(Factory Time) — Chilton Time

Oil Filter By-Pass Valve, Renew

Four-eng code Y (.3)	.4
Six (.2)	.3
V-6 (.3)	.4
V-8 (.3)	.4

Oil Filter Element, Renew

Four (.3)	.4
Six (.2)	.3
V-6 (.3)	.4
V-8 (.3)	.4

DIESEL ENGINE

Oil Pan and/or Gasket, Renew

Includes: Raise engine, R&R and clean oil pump screen.

All models	
2.2L eng (.7)	1.2
5.7L eng (2.1)	3.0
6.2L eng	
Vans (3.2)	4.6
All other models (2.0)	2.9
w/M.T. add (.3)	.3

Pressure Test Engine Bearings (Pan Off)

All models	1.0

Oil Pump, Renew

Includes: Raise engine, R&R and clean oil pump screen.

All models	
2.2L eng (5.9)	8.5
w/A.C. add (.6)	.6
w/P.S. add (.3)	.3
5.7L eng (2.2)	3.2
6.2L eng	
Vans (3.2)	4.8
All other models (2.1)	3.1
w/M.T. add (.3)	.3

Oil Pump, R&R and Recondition

Includes: Raise engine, R&R and clean oil pump screen.

All models	
5.7L eng (2.4)	3.4

Oil Pressure Sending Unit, Renew

All models	
5.7L eng (.3)	.5
6.2L eng (1.4)	1.8

Oil Filter Element, Renew

All models (.3)	.4

Crankcase and/or Gasket, Renew

All models	
2.2L eng (5.8)	8.4
w/A.C. add (.6)	.6
w/P.S. add (.3)	.3

LABOR 18 CLUTCH & FLYWHEEL 18 LABOR

(Factory Time) — Chilton Time

Clutch Pedal Free Play, Adjust

All models (.3)	.4

Bleed Clutch Hydraulic System

All models (.5)	.6

Clutch Master Cylinder, Renew

Includes: Bleed system.

All models (.8)	1.2
Recond cyl add (.4)	.4

Clutch Slave (Actuator) Cylinder, Renew

Includes: Bleed system.

All models (.6)	1.0
Recond cyl add (.4)	.4

Clutch Assembly, Renew

Includes: R&R trans and adjust clutch free play.

3 Speed	
exc Vans	
2 whl drive (2.2)	3.5
4 whl drive (4.0)	5.3
Vans (1.6)	3.0
4 Speed	
exc below	
2 whl drive (3.2)	4.5
4 whl drive (4.7)	6.0
Muncie	
2 whl drive (2.2)	3.0
4 whl drive (3.0)	4.0
S-series	
Isuzu	
Four (2.7)	3.5
V-6 (2.2)	3.0
Warner (2.2)	2.7
Astro (1.9)	2.4
5 Speed	
2 whl drive (2.2)	3.0
4 whl drive (3.5)	4.7
w/Skid plate add (.3)	.3
w/Catalytic converter add (.4)	.4
w/Power take off add (.3)	.3
Renew pilot brg add (.2)	.2

Clutch Release Bearing, Fork and/or Ball Stud, Renew

Includes: R&R trans, and adjust clutch free play.

3 Speed	
exc Vans	
2 whl drive (2.2)	3.3
4 whl drive (4.0)	5.1
Vans (1.6)	2.8
4 Speed	
exc below	
2 whl drive (3.2)	4.3
4 whl drive (4.7)	5.8
Muncie	
2 whl drive (1.7)	2.3
4 whl drive (2.5)	3.4
S-series	
Isuzu	
Four (2.3)	3.1
V-6 (1.9)	2.4
Warner (1.9)	2.4
Astro (1.8)	2.3
5 Speed	
2 whl drive (1.4)	1.9
4 whl drive (2.8)	3.8
w/Skid plate add (.3)	.3
w/Catalytic converter add (.4)	.4
w/Power take off add (.3)	.3

Clutch Cross Shaft Assy., Renew

Includes: Raise vehicle and adjust linkage.

All models (.4)	.9

Flywheel, Renew

Includes: R&R transmission.

3 Speed	
exc Vans	
2 whl drive (2.5)	3.9
4 whl drive (4.3)	5.7
Vans (1.7)	3.4
4 Speed	
exc below	
2 whl drive (3.4)	4.9
4 whl drive (5.0)	6.4
Muncie	
2 whl drive (2.4)	3.2
4 whl drive (3.2)	4.3
S-series	
Isuzu	
Four (2.9)	3.8
V-6 (2.4)	3.3
Warner (2.4)	3.0
Astro (2.1)	2.7
5 Speed	
2 whl drive (2.4)	3.2
4 whl drive (3.7)	4.9
w/Skid plate add (.3)	.3
w/Catalytic converter add (.3)	.4
w/Power take off add (.3)	.3
Renew ring gear add	.5

LABOR 19 STANDARD TRANSMISSION 19 LABOR

(Factory Time) — Chilton Time

Transmission Assy., R&R or Renew

Includes: Raise vehicle and perform necessary adjustments. Transfer all attaching parts.

3 Speed	
exc Vans	
2 whl drive (1.7)	3.2
4 whl drive (3.6)	5.0
Vans (1.4)	2.7
4 Speed	
exc below	
2 whl drive (2.6)	4.2
4 whl drive (4.3)	5.7
New Process (2.3)	3.0
Muncie	
2 whl drive (1.7)	2.3
4 whl drive (2.5)	3.4
S-series	
Isuzu	
Four (2.3)	3.1
V-6 (1.9)	2.6
Warner	
2 whl drive (1.4)	1.9
4 whl drive (2.8)	3.8
Astro	
Muncie (1.4)	1.9

LABOR 19 STANDARD TRANSMISSION 19 LABOR

(Factory Time) — Chilton Time

5 Speed
- 2 whl drive (1.4) 1.9
- 4 whl drive (2.8) 3.8
- w/Skid plate add (.3) 3
- w/Catalytic converter add (.4) 4
- w/Power take off add (.3) 3

Transmission Assy., R&R and Recondition

Includes: Raise vehicle and perform all necessary adjustments.

3 Speed
- exc Vans-w/2 whl drive
  - Muncie (3.0) 4.9
  - Saginaw (3.0) 4.9
  - Tremec (3.8) 5.7
- Vans-w/2 whl drive
  - Muncie (2.7) 4.6
  - Saginaw (2.7) 4.6

4 Speed
- exc below
  - 2 whl drive (5.0) 6.9
  - 4 whl drive (6.7) 8.6
  - New Process (4.2) 5.4
- Muncie
  - 2 whl drive (3.4) 4.7
  - 4 whl drive (5.0) 7.0
- S-series
  - Isuzu
    - Four (3.9) 5.3
    - V-6 (3.5) 4.7
  - Warner
    - 2 whl drive (3.2) 4.5
    - 4 whl drive (4.6) 6.5
- Astro
  - Muncie (3.1) 4.5

5 Speed
- 2 whl drive (3.4) 4.7
- 4 whl drive (4.8) 6.7
- w/Skid plate add (.3) 3
- w/Catalytic converter add (.4) 4
- w/Power take off add (.3) 3

Transmission Shift Cover, Renew or Recondition

Includes: Raise vehicle and adjust linkage.

3 Speed
- exc Vans (.7) 1.3
- Vans (.8) 1.4

4 Speed
- Saginaw (1.9) 2.6
- New Process (.9) 1.4
- Isuzu (.5) 9
- Warner (.8) *1.4
- Muncie
  - 10-30 Series (1.4) 2.0
  - Astro (.6) 8
- *Recond add (.6) 8

5 Speed
- S-series (.8) *1.4
- Astro (1.8) 2.5
- *Recond add (.6) 8

Transmission Rear Oil Seal, Renew

Includes: Raise vehicle, R&R drive shaft.
- All models (.5) 9

Speedometer Driven Gear, Renew
- All models (.3) 6

Speedometer Drive Gear, Renew

4 Speed
- All models (.9) 1.4

5 Speed
- Astro (1.8) 2.5

LABOR 20 TRANSFER CASE 20 LABOR

(Factory Time) — Chilton Time

Transfer Case Assy., R&R or Renew
- Dana (3.1) 4.5
- New Process Model 208 (1.3) 2.0
- New Process Model 207 (1.4) 2.1
- New Process Model 205 (1.4) 2.1
- New Process Model 203 (2.5) 3.8
- w/Power take off add (.3) 3
- w/Skid plate add (.3) 3

Transfer Case Assy., R&R and Recondition
- Dana (5.2) 7.1
- New Process Model 208 (3.5) 5.6
- New Process Model 207 (3.4) 5.5
- New Process Model 205 (3.9) 6.0
- New Process Model 203 (6.8) 8.7
- w/Power take off add (.3) 3
- w/Skid plate add (.3) 3

Transfer Case Oil Seals, Renew

Dana
- front (1.1) 1.7
- rear (.6) 1.0

New Process Model 208
- front (.5) 9
- rear (.3) 6

New Process Model 207
- front (.5) 9
- rear (.4) 7

New Process Model 205
- front (1.1) 1.7
- rear (.6) 1.0

New Process Model 203
- front (.8) 1.4
- rear (.7) 1.3

Transfer Case Power Take Off Cover Gasket, Renew
- All models (.4) 7

Transfer Case Rear Output Shaft Housing Gasket, Renew
- All models-New Process
  - Model 208 (.5) 8
  - Model 207 (.6) 1.0
  - Model 205 (.8) 1.2

Transfer Case Speedometer Drive Gear, Renew
- New Process Model 208 (.5) 7
- New Process Model 207 (.6) 1.0
- New Process Model 205 (.8) 1.1
- New Process Model 203 (.9) 1.2

Rear Output Shaft Housing, Renew
- All models-New Process
  - Model 208 (.5) 9
  - Model 207 (.6) 1.0
  - Model 205 (.8) 1.4

LABOR 21 SHIFT LINKAGE 21 LABOR

(Factory Time) — Chilton Time

STANDARD

Shift Linkage, Adjust
- All models (.3) 4

Gearshift Control Lever, Renew
- All models-column mount (.2) 4
  - floor mount (.3) 6

Transfer Case Gearshift Lever, Renew
- New Process Model 205 (.4) 6
- New Process Model 203 (.3) 5

Transfer Case Shifter Assy., Renew
- New Process Model 203 (1.4) 2.1

Gearshift Control Rods, Renew
- All models-one (.4) 6
  - two (.5) 9

Gear Shift Tube and/or Levers, Renew
- exc Vans (1.7) 2.5
- Vans (1.4) 2.2

AUTOMATIC

Linkage, Adjust

Includes: Adjust neutral safety switch, indicator needle and detent rod, cable or switch.
- All models (.4) 7

Shift Linkage, Adjust (w/Diesel Eng)
- All models
  - Fast idle speed (.2) 3
  - Throttle rod/T.V. cable (.5) 6
  - Trans vacuum valve (.5) 6
  - Complete (.6) 1.0

Note: Does not apply to Vans with THM 400 trans.

Column Shift Selector Lever, Renew
- All models (.2) 3

Shift Control Rods, Renew

Includes: Necessary adjustments.
- All models-one (.3) 5

Cross Shaft Assembly, Renew

Includes: Necessary adjustments.
- All models (.4) 6

Shift Indicator Needle, Renew
- All models (.6) 1.0

(Factory Time) Chilton Time

TURBO HYDRA-MATIC 200C ON TRUCK SERVICES

Drain & Refill Unit
All models........ .9

Oil Pressure Check
All models (.5)........ .7

Check Unit For Oil Leaks
Includes: Clean and dry outside of case and run unit to determine point of leak.
All models........ .9

Neutral Safety Switch, Renew
All models (.3)........ .4

Throttle Valve Control Cable and/or 'O' Ring, Renew
Includes: Adjust cable.
All models (.5)........ .8

Speedometer Driven Gear and/or Seal, Renew
All models (.3)........ .5

Transmission Rear Oil Seal, Renew
Includes: R&R driveshaft.
All models (.4)........ .8

Torque Converter Clutch Switches, Renew
All models
Brake (.2)........ .4
Thermal Vacuum (.3)........ .5
Temp Indicator (.3)........ .5

Governor Assy., R&R or Renew
Includes: Renew governor seal.
All models (1.1)........ 1.7

Governor Assy., R&R and Recondition
Includes: Clean and inspect governor, renew seal and gear.
All models (1.3)........ 2.0

Oil Pan and/or Gasket, Renew
Includes: Clean pan and service screen.
All models (.6)........ .9

Manual Shaft Seal and/or Detent Lever, Renew
Includes: R&R oil pan.
All models (.7)........ 1.1

Valve Body Assembly, Renew
Includes: R&R oil pan and renew filter.
All models (.9)........ 1.5

Valve Body Assy., R&R and Recondition
Includes: R&R oil pan and renew filter. Disassemble, clean, inspect and free all valves. Replace parts as required.
All models (1.6)........ 2.8

Intermediate Servo Assy., R&R or Renew
All models (1.1)........ 1.7
Recond servo add (.2)........ .2

Parking Pawl, Shaft, Rod or Spring, Renew
Includes: R&R oil pan.
All models (1.3)........ 2.0

1-2 Accumulator Piston and/or Spring, R&R or Renew
Includes: R&R oil pan.
All models (.9)........ 1.4
Recond accumulator add (.2)........ .2

SERVICES REQUIRING R&R

Transmission Assembly, R&R or Renew
All models
4X2 (2.6)........ 3.7
4X4 (3.2)........ 4.6

(Factory Time) Chilton Time

Transmission and Converter, R&R and Recondition
Includes: Disassemble transmission completely, including valve body. Clean and inspect all parts. Renew all parts as required. Make all necessary adjustments. Road test.
All models
4X2 (6.2)........ 11.2
4X4 (6.8)........ 11.8

Transmission Assy., R&R and Reseal
Includes: Install all new gaskets and seals.
All models........ 6.5
4X2........ 6.5
4X4........ 7.0

Flywheel (Flexplate), Renew
Includes: R&R transmission.
All models
4X2 (2.8)........ 3.9
4X4 (3.4)........ 4.8

Torque Converter, Renew
Includes: R&R transmission.
All models
4X2 (2.6)........ 3.8
4X4 (3.2)........ 4.7

Front Pump Oil Seal, Renew
Includes: R&R transmission.
All models
4X2 (2.6)........ 3.8
4X4 (3.2)........ 4.7

Front Pump Assy., Renew or Recondition
Includes: R&R transmission.
All models
4X2 (3.0)........ 4.3
4X4 (3.6)........ 5.2
Recond front pump add (.5)........ .8
Renew bushing add (.1)........ .1

Converter Clutch Solenoid Assy., Renew
Includes: R&R transmission, converter and oil pump.
All models
4X2 (2.6)........ 4.0
4X4 (3.2)........ 4.9

Apply and Actuator Valves and/or Bushing, Renew
Includes: R&R transmission, converter and oil pump.
All models
4X2 (2.6)........ 4.0
4X4 (3.2)........ 4.9

Direct, Forward Clutches and Intermediate Band, Renew
Includes: R&R transmission, converter, pump and seal, oil pan, valve body and servo.
All models
4X2 (3.4)........ 4.9
4X4 (4.0)........ 5.8
Recond valve body add (.7)........ 1.0
Recond oil pump add (.5)........ .8
Recond servo add (.2)........ .2
Recond direct clutch add (.3)........ .4
Recond forward clutch add (.4)........ .5
Renew bushings add-each (.1)........ .1

Output Carrier, Sun Gear and Drive Shell, R&R or Renew
Includes: R&R transmission, converter, pump and seal, oil pan, valve body, direct and forward clutches, intermediate band and servo.
All models
4X2 (3.5)........ 5.5
4X4 (4.1)........ 5.9
Recond valve body add (.7)........ 1.0

(Factory Time) Chilton Time

Recond oil pump add (.5)........ .8
Recond servo add (.2)........ .2
Recond direct clutch add (.3)........ .4
Recond forward clutch add (.4)........ .5
Recond sun gear and drum, add (.3)........ .4
Renew output shaft add (.7)........ 1.0
Renew bushings add-each (.1)........ .1

TURBO HYDRA-MATIC '350'

ON TRUCK SERVICE

Drain and Refill Unit
All models (.5)........ .7

Oil Pressure Check
All models (.5)........ .7

Check Unit for Leaks
Includes: Clean and dry outside of case and run unit to determine point of leak.
All models........ .9

Vacuum Modulator, Renew
w/2 whl drive (.3)........ .4
w/4 whl drive (.5)........ .6

Detent Valve Control Cable or Seal, Renew
All models (.5)........ .9

Speedometer Drive Gear, Renew
Includes: R&R extension housing.
w/2 whl drive (.7)........ 1.2
w/4 whl drive (.6)........ 1.1

Speedometer Driven Gear, Renew
All models (.3)........ .5

Governor Assy., R&R or Renew
Includes: R&R cover and gasket.
All models (.3)........ .6

Governor Assy., R&R and Recondition
Includes: R&R cover and gasket.
All models (.6)........ 1.1

Extension Housing Rear Oil Seal, Renew
Includes: R&R drive shaft.
exc Vans (.5)........ .8
Vans (.4)........ .7

Torque Converter Clutch Brake Switch, Renew
All models (.2)........ .4

Torque Converter Clutch Thermal Vacuum Switch, Renew
All models (.3)........ .5

Torque Converter Clutch Vacuum Delay Valve, Renew
All models (.2)........ .3

Engine Low Vacuum Switch, Renew
All models (.2)........ .4

High Vacuum Switch, Renew
All models (.3)........ .5

Oil Pan and/or Gasket, Renew
Includes: Clean oil pan and service screen.
All models (.6)........ 1.0

Parking Pawl, Renew
Includes: R&R oil pan.
All models (1.4)........ 1.9

Intermediate Servo, Renew
Includes: R&R oil pan, valve body and adjust servo.
All models (.9)........ 1.4

(Factory Time) Chilton Time

Governor Pressure Switch and/or Electrical Connector, Renew
Includes: R&R oil pan.
All models (.6)................................ 1.1

Auxiliary Valve Body and/or Apply Valve, Renew
Includes: R&R oil pan.
All models (.8)................................ 1.4
Renew body gskt add (.2)................. .2

Converter Clutch Solenoid, Renew
Includes: R&R oil pan.
All models (.6)................................ 1.1

Intermediate Clutch Accumulator, Renew
All models (.7)................................ 1.2

Valve Body Assy., R&R or Renew
Includes: R&R oil pan and vacuum modulator, clean pan and strainer.
All models (1.0)................................ 1.6

Valve Body, R&R and Recondition
Includes: R&R oil pan and vacuum modulator, clean pan and strainer. Disassemble, clean, inspect, free all valves. Replace parts as required.
All models (1.4)................................ 2.4

SERVICES REQUIRING R&R

Transmission, R&R or Renew
2 whl drive (2.5)........................ 4.6
4 whl drive (4.3)........................ 6.1
w/Skid plate add (.3)........................ .3
Pressure check converter add (.2)..... .2

Transmission and Converter, R&R and Recondition
Includes: Disassemble trans including valve body, clean, inspect and replace parts as required.
2 whl drive (6.5)........................ 11.7
4 whl drive (8.3)........................ 12.3
w/Skid plate add (.3)........................ .3
Pressure check converter add (.2)..... .2

Transmission Assembly, Reseal
Includes: R&R transmission and renew all seals and gaskets.
2 whl drive (3.5)........................ 6.8
4 whl drive (5.3)........................ 8.1
w/Skid plate add (.3)........................ .3

Front Pump Seal, Renew
Includes: R&R transmission.
2 whl drive (2.2)........................ 4.9
4 whl drive (4.0)........................ 6.4
w/Skid plate add (.3)........................ .3

Flywheel (Flexplate), Renew
Includes: R&R transmission.
2 whl drive (2.2)........................ 4.9
4 whl drive (4.0)........................ 6.4
w/Skid plate add (.3)........................ .3

Torque Converter, Renew
Includes: R&R transmission and check end play of converter.
2 whl drive (2.5)........................ 5.2
4 whl drive (4.4)........................ 6.7
w/Skid plate add (.3)........................ .3

Forward, Direct or Intermediate Clutch, R&R or Renew
Includes: R&R transmission, converter and pump seal, intermediate, direct and forward clutches, oil pan, valve body and intermediate servo piston.
2 whl drive (3.4)........................ 5.9
4 whl drive (5.2)........................ 7.4
w/Skid plate add (.3)........................ .3

Forward, Direct or Intermediate Clutch, R&R and Recondition
Includes: R&R transmission, converter and pump seal, intermediate, direct and forward clutches, oil pan, valve body and intermediate servo piston.
2 whl drive (4.3)........................ 7.3
4 whl drive (6.1)........................ 8.8
w/Skid plate add (.3)........................ .3

Front Oil Pump, Renew
Includes: R&R transmission, converter and pump seal.
2 whl drive (2.7)........................ 5.1
4 whl drive (4.5)........................ 6.6
w/Skid plate add (.3)........................ .3

Front Oil Pump, R&R and Recondition
Includes: R&R transmission, converter and pump seal.
2 whl drive (3.2)........................ 5.8
4 whl drive (5.0)........................ 7.3
w/Skid plate add (.3)........................ .3

Low and Reverse Clutch Piston Assembly, R&R or Renew
Includes: R&R trans, converter, pump and seal, intermediate clutch, oil pan, valve body, intermediate servo piston, direct and forward clutches, intermediate band, output carrier, sungear and drive shell, extension housing, speedometer drive gears, governor, output ring gear, low and reverse roller clutch support, reaction carrier and output shell.
2 whl drive (3.9)........................ 6.8
4 whl drive (5.7)........................ 8.1
w/Skid plate add (.3)........................ .3

Low and Reverse Clutch Piston Assembly, R&R and Recondition
Includes: R&R trans, converter, pump and seal, intermediate clutch, oil pan, valve body, intermediate servo piston, direct and forward clutches, intermediate band, output carrier, sungear and drive shell, extension housing, speedometer drive gears, governor, output ring gear, low and reverse roller clutch support, reaction carrier and output shell.
2 whl drive (4.4)........................ 7.6
4 whl drive (6.2)........................ 8.9
w/Skid plate add (.3)........................ .3

Intermediate Band, Renew
Includes: R&R transmission, converter and pump seal, intermediate clutch, oil pan, valve body and intermediate servo piston.
2 whl drive (3.4)........................ 6.1
4 whl drive (5.2)........................ 7.6
w/Skid plate add (.3)........................ .3

TURBO HYDRA-MATIC '400'

ON TRUCK SERVICES

Drain and Refill Unit
All models (.5)................................ .7

Oil Pressure Check
All models (.5)................................ .7

Check Unit for Leaks
Includes: Clean and dry outside of case and run unit to determine point of leak.
All models................................ .9

Vacuum Modulator, Renew
w/2 whl drive (.3)........................ .4
w/4 whl drive (.5)........................ .6

Detent Solenoid, Renew or Adjust
Includes: R&R oil pan.
All models (.6)................................ 1.1

Down Shift Control Switch, Renew
All models (.2)................................ .4

Detent Solenoid Connector, Renew
Includes: R&R oil pan.
All models (.6)................................ 1.1

Speedometer Drive Gear, Renew
Includes: R&R extension housing.
All models (1.0)................................ 1.5

Speedometer Driven Gear, Renew
All models (.3)................................ .5

Governor Assy., R&R or Renew
Includes: R&R cover and gasket.
w/2 whl drive (.3)........................ .6
w/4 whl drive (1.4)........................ 1.9

Governor Assy., R&R and Recondition
Includes: R&R cover and gasket.
w/2 whl drive (.6)........................ 1.1
w/4 whl drive (1.7)........................ 2.4

Extension Housing Rear Oil Seal, Renew
Includes: R&R drive shaft.
All models (.7)................................ 1.0

Oil Pan and/or Gasket, Renew
Includes: Clean oil pan and service screen.
All models (.6)................................ 1.0

Parking Pawl, Renew
Includes: R&R oil pan.
All models (1.0)................................ 1.5

Servos, Renew or Recondition
Includes: R&R oil pan, detent solenoid, servo cover and valve body. Adjust servo.
All models-front (1.3)........................ 1.8
rear (1.5)................................ 2.1

Pressure Regulator Valve, Renew
Includes: R&R oil pan.
All models (.8)................................ 1.4

Valve Body Assy., R&R or Renew
Includes: R&R oil pan and vacuum modulator, clean pan and strainer.
All models (1.1)................................ 1.6

Valve Body, R&R and Recondition
Includes: R&R oil pan and vacuum modulator, clean pan and strainer. Disassemble, clean, inspect, free all valves. Replace parts as required.
All models (1.8)................................ 2.6

SERVICES REQUIRING R&R

Transmission, R&R or Renew
2 whl drive (2.4)........................ 4.7
4 whl drive (4.4)........................ 6.7
w/Skid plate add (.3)........................ .3

Transmission and Converter, R&R and Recondition
Includes: Disassemble trans including valve body, clean, inspect and replace parts as required.
2 whl drive (8.6)........................ 13.7
4 whl drive (10.6)........................ 15.7
w/Skid plate add (.3)........................ .3
Pressure check converter add (.2)..... .2

Transmission Assembly, Reseal
Includes: R&R transmission and renew all seals and gaskets.
2 whl drive (3.6)........................ 6.9

(Factory Time) Chilton Time

4 whl drive (5.6) 8.9
w/Skid plate add (.3) 3

Front Pump Seal, Renew
Includes: R&R transmission.
2 whl drive (2.1) 4.9
4 whl drive (4.1) 6.9
w/Skid plate add (.3) 3

Flywheel (Flexplate), Renew
Includes: R&R transmission.
2 whl drive (2.1) 4.9
4 whl drive (4.1) 6.9
w/Skid plate add (.3) 3

Torque Converter, Renew
Includes: R&R transmission and check end play of converter.
2 whl drive (2.3) 5.3
4 whl drive (4.3) 7.3
w/Skid plate add (.3) 3

Front Oil Pump, Renew
Includes: R&R transmission and converter.
2 whl drive (2.4) 5.5
4 whl drive (4.4) 7.5
w/Skid plate add (.3) 3

Front Oil Pump, R&R and Recondition
Includes: R&R transmission and converter.
2 whl drive (2.9) 6.1
4 whl drive (4.9) 8.1
w/Skid plate add (.3) 3

Forward, Direct or Intermediate Clutch, R&R or Renew
Includes: R&R transmission, converter, oil pan, oil pump and seal.
2 whl drive (2.8) 6.4
4 whl drive (4.8) 8.4
w/Skid plate add (.3) 3

Forward, Direct or Intermediate Clutch, R&R and Recondition
Includes: R&R transmission, converter, oil pan, oil pump and seal, forward clutch, sun gear shaft, front brake band and adjust end play.
2 whl drive (3.4) 7.2
4 whl drive (5.4) 9.2
w/Skid plate add (.3) 3

Center Support and Gear Unit Assy., Renew
Includes: R&R transmission, converter, pump and seal, forward clutch, front brake band, valve body, case extension, speedometer driven gear. Check end play.
2 whl drive (4.0) 8.1
4 whl drive (6.0) 10.1
w/Skid plate add (.3) 3

Center Support and Gear Unit Assy., R&R and Recondition
Includes: R&R transmission, converter, pump and seal, forward clutch, front brake band, valve body, case extension, speedometer driven gear. Check end play.
2 whl drive (4.6) 8.9
4 whl drive (6.6) 10.9
w/Skid plate add (.3) 3

TURBO HYDRA-MATIC 700-R4

ON TRUCK SERVICES

Drain & Refill Unit
All models 9

Oil Pressure Check
All models (.5) 7

(Factory Time) Chilton Time

Check Unit For Oil Leaks
Includes: Clean and dry outside of case and run unit to determine point of leak.
All models 9

Neutral Safety Switch, Renew
All models (.3) 4

Shift Linkage, Adjust
All models (.4) 6

Torque Converter Clutch Switches, Renew
All models
Brake (.2) 4
Thermal Vacuum (.3) 5
Temp Indicator (.3) 5

Detent Valve Control Cable and/or 'O' Ring, Renew
Includes: Adjust cable.
All models (.5) 9

Speedometer Driven Gear and/or Seal, Renew
All models (.3) 5

Extension Housing Rear Oil Seal, Renew
Includes: R&R driveshaft.
All models (.4) 8

Governor Cover and/or Seal, Renew
S-series
4 WD (.6) 8
All other models (.3) 5

Governor Assembly, R&R or Renew
S-series
4 WD (.6) 8
All other models (.4) 7

Governor Assy., R&R and Recondition
S-series
4 WD (.8) 1.2
All other models (.6) 1.0

Oil Pan and/or Gasket, Renew
All models (.6) 9
w/Skid plate add (.3) 3

Governor Pressure Switch, Renew
Includes: R&R oil pan.
All models (.6) 1.1
w/Skid plate add (.3) 3

Converter Clutch Solenoid, Renew
Includes: R&R oil pan.
All models (.6) 1.1
w/Skid plate add (.3) 3

Valve Body Assembly, Renew
Includes: R&R oil pan and renew filter.
All models (.8) 1.5
w/Skid plate add (.3) 3

Valve Body Assy., R&R and Recondition
Includes: R&R oil pan and renew filter. Disassemble, clean, inspect and free all valves. Replace parts as required.
All models (1.7) 2.5
w/Skid plate add (.3) 3

2-4 Servo Assy., R&R or Renew
S-series (1.4) 1.9
All other models (.5) 1.0
w/Skid plate add (.3) 3
Recond servo add (.2) 3

Parking Pawl, Shaft, Rod or Spring, Renew
Includes: R&R oil pan.
All models (.6) 1.1
Renew pawl add (.5) 5
w/Skid plate add (.3) 3

(Factory Time) Chilton Time

1-2 Accumulator Piston and/or Spring, Renew
Includes: R&R oil pan.
All models (.8) 1.5
w/Skid plate add (.3) 3
Recond add (.1) 2

SERVICES REQUIRING R&R

Transmission Assy., R&R or Renew
2 whl drive (2.2) 3.1
4 whl drive (4.0) 4.8
w/Skid plate add (.3) 3

Transmission and Converter, R&R and Recondition
Includes: Disassemble transmission completely, including valve body and overhaul unit. Clean and inspect all parts. Renew all parts as required. Make all necessary adjustments. Road test.
2 whl drive (6.3) 10.1
4 whl drive (7.1) 10.9
w/Skid plate add (.3) 3
Clean and leak check converter add (.2) 4
Check end play add (.2) 3

Transmission Assy., R&R and Reseal
Includes: Install all new gaskets and seals.
2 whl drive 4.7
4 whl drive 5.5
w/Skid plate add 3

Flywheel (Flexplate), Renew
Includes: R&R transmission.
2 whl drive (2.4) 3.3
4 whl drive (4.2) 5.1
w/Skid plate add (.3) 3

Torque Converter, Renew
Includes: R&R transmission.
2 whl drive (2.1) 2.9
4 whl drive (3.9) 4.7
w/Skid plate add (.3) 3

Front Pump Oil Seal, Renew
Includes: R&R transmission.
2 whl drive (2.1) 3.0
4 whl drive (3.9) 4.8
w/Skid plate add (.3) 3

Front Pump Assy., Renew or Recondition
Includes: R&R transmission.
2 whl drive (2.7) 4.0
4 whl drive (4.5) 5.7
w/Skid plate add (.3) 3
Recond front pump add (.5) 6
Renew bushing add (.1) 1

Input Drum, Reverse and Input Clutch, Renew
Includes: R&R transmission.
2 whl drive (3.2) 4.6
4 whl drive (5.0) 6.4
w/Skid plate add (.3) 3
Recond valve body add (.4) 5
Recond front pump add (.5) 6
Renew bushings add-each (.1) 1

Reaction Gear Set, Renew
Includes: R&R transmission.
2 whl drive (3.5) 5.2
4 whl drive (5.3) 7.0
w/Skid plate add (.3) 3
Recond valve body add (.4) 5
Recond front pump add (.5) 6
Renew input clutch drum add (.2) 3
Recond reaction gear set add (.2) 2
Renew bushings add-each (.1) 1

LABOR 23 AUTOMATIC TRANSMISSION 23 LABOR

	(Factory Time)	Chilton Time
Low and Reverse Clutch Piston Assy., Renew		
Includes: R&R transmission.		
2 whl drive	(3.7)	5.7
4 whl drive	(5.5)	7.4
w/Skid plate add	(.3)	.3
Recond valve body add	(.4)	.5
Recond front pump add	(.5)	.6
Recond reverse clutch add	(.4)	.5
Recond input clutch add	(.4)	.5
Renew input clutch drum add	(.2)	.2
Recond reaction gear set add	(.2)	.3
Recond low and reverse clutch add	(.1)	.2
Recond reverse piston add	(.3)	.4
Recond gov or renew gear add	(.2)	.3
Renew gov bushing add	(.4)	.5
Renew bushings add-each	(.1)	.1

LABOR 25 U-JOINTS & DRIVESHAFT 25 LABOR

	(Factory Time)	Chilton Time
Universal Joints, Renew		
All models-one	(.6)	1.0
each adtnl	(.3)	.4
Drive Shaft, R&R or Renew		
One Piece Shaft		
All models	(.3)	.5
Two Piece Shaft		
front shaft	(.4)	.7
rear shaft	(.3)	.5
Center Support Bearing, Renew		
All models	(.5)	1.0

LABOR 26 REAR AXLE 26 LABOR

	(Factory Time)	Chilton Time
Rear Axle, Drain and Refill		
All models		.6
Rear Axle Housing Cover Gasket, Renew		
All models	(.4)	.6
Rear Wheel Hub Assembly, Renew		
All models-one side	(.8)	1.1
both sides	(1.4)	1.8
w/Dual whls add-each side		.1
Rear Wheel Hub Oil Seal, Renew		
All models-one side	(.6)	.9
both sides	(1.0)	1.6
w/Dual whls add-each side		.1
Axle Shaft, Renew		
Semi-Floating Axle		
one	(.6)	.9
both	(.7)	1.2
Full Floating Axle		
one	(.3)	.6
both	(.5)	.8
Axle Shaft Oil Seal, Renew		
Semi-Floating Axle		
one	(.6)	1.1
both	(.8)	1.4
Full Floating Axle		
one	(.7)	1.1
both	(1.2)	1.6
w/Dual whls add, each side	(.1)	.1
Axle Shaft Bearing, Renew		
Semi-Floating Axle		
one	(.7)	1.1
both	(.9)	1.4
Full Floating Axle		
one	(.9)	1.4
both	(1.6)	2.7
w/Dual whls add-each side		.1
Pinion Shaft Oil Seal, Renew		
Includes: Renew pinion flange if necessary.		
All models		
Semi-Floating	(.5)	.8
Full Floating	(.7)	1.1
Differential Case, Renew		
Standard		
Semi-Floating	(2.0)	3.1
Full Floating	(2.2)	3.3
Limited Slip (Semi-Floating)		
Eaton Case	(2.4)	3.5
exc Eaton Case	(2.6)	3.7
Limited Slip (Full Floating)		
Eaton Case	(2.4)	3.5
exc Eaton Case	(2.1)	3.2
Ring and Pinion Gears, Renew		
Semi-Floating Axle	(2.4)	4.1
Full Floating Axle	(2.8)	4.6
Recond diff case add		
std	(.3)	.5
limited slip	(.7)	1.0
Pinion Shaft and/or Side and Pinion Gears, Renew		
Note: Does not require case removal on semi-floating axles.		
Semi-Floating Axle	(1.3)	2.1
Full Floating Axle	(2.0)	3.4
Limited Slip Clutch Plates, Renew		
Semi-Floating Axle		
Eaton Case	(2.4)	3.5
exc Eaton Case	(1.1)	2.0
Full Floating Axle		
Eaton Case	(2.4)	3.5
exc Eaton Case	(2.3)	3.4
Side and Pinion Gear Bearings, Renew		
Semi-Floating Axle	(2.5)	4.1
Full Floating Axle	(3.5)	5.1
Rear Axle Housing, Renew		
Semi-Floating Axle	(4.5)	6.1
Full Floating Axle	(5.1)	6.7
w/Dual whls add	(.2)	.4

LABOR 27 REAR SUSPENSION 27 LABOR

	(Factory Time)	Chilton Time
Rear Spring, Renew		
S-series-one	(.7)	1.1
both	(1.2)	2.0
All other models-one	(.9)	1.3
both	(1.5)	2.1
w/Aux fuel tank add	(.6)	.6
w/Dual whls add-each side		.1
w/Skid plate add	(.3)	.3
Recond add-each side		.5
Rear Spring Shackle, Renew		
exc Vans-one	(.5)	.8
both	(.8)	1.2
Vans-one	(.6)	.9
both	(1.1)	1.7
Rear Spring Eye Bushing, Renew		
Includes: R&R spring.		
All models-one side	(1.0)	1.4
both sides	(1.8)	2.6
w/Dual whls add-each side		.1
w/Skid plate add	(.3)	.3
Rear Shock Absorber, Renew		
All models-one	(.3)	.5
both	(.4)	.8

(Factory Time) Chilton Time

Note: If more than one item requires replacement where evacuation and discharging the system is already included in the operation, deduct 1.0 hour for each additional item to the times listed.

Drain, Evacuate and Recharge System
All models (.7)................................ 1.5

Pressure Test System
All models................................ 1.0

Leak Test
Includes: Check all lines and connections.
All models................................ .6

Refrigerant, Add Partial Charge
All models................................ 1.0

Compressor Belt, Renew
All models (.2)................................ .5
If necessary to R&R fan pulley, add (.3)................................ .3
w/P.S. add (.2)................................ .2
w/AIR add (.2)................................ .2

COMPRESSOR - 6 CYLINDER AXIAL

Compressor Assembly, Renew
Includes: Transfer all necessary attaching parts. Evacuate and charge system.
Six (2.0)................................ 3.1
V-8-exc Vans (1.9)................................ 3.0
Vans (2.3)................................ 3.4

Compressor Assy., R&R and Recondition
Includes: Complete disassembly and overhaul, making all checks and gauging operations. Evacuate and charge system.
Six (3.8)................................ 6.3
V-8-exc Vans (3.8)................................ 6.2
Vans (4.2)................................ 6.8

Compressor Clutch Hub and Drive Plate, Renew
Includes: Check air gap. Does not include R&R compressor.
Six (.8)................................ 1.1
V-8-exc Vans (.5)................................ .8
Vans (.8)................................ 1.1

Compressor Pulley and/or Bearing, Renew
Includes: R&R hub and drive plate.
Six (.9)................................ 1.2
V-8-exc Vans (.6)................................ .9
Vans (.9)................................ 1.2

Compressor Clutch Holding Coil, Renew
Includes: R&R hub and drive plate, pulley and bearing.
Six (1.0)................................ 1.4
V-8-exc Vans (.6)................................ 1.1
Vans (1.0)................................ 1.4

Compressor Shaft Seal Kit, Renew
Includes: R&R clutch hub and drive plate. Evacuate and charge system.
Six (1.7)................................ 2.8
V-8-exc Vans (1.5)................................ 2.6
Vans (1.7)................................ 2.8

Compressor Rear Head, Oil Pump Gears and/or Rear Reed Assembly, Renew
Includes: R&R compressor. R&R rear head and rear reed plate assy. Clean and test parts. Add oil. Evacuate and charge system.
Six (2.0)................................ 3.4
V-8-exc Vans (1.9)................................ 3.3
Vans (2.4)................................ 3.8

Compressor Front Head and/or Front Reed Assembly, Renew
Includes: R&R compressor. R&R rear head and reed plate assy. Disassemble shell to internal mechanism and front head assy. R&R front valve and reed plate and shaft seal assy. Clean and inspect parts. Add oil. Evacuate and charge system.
Six (2.7)................................ 4.5
V-8-exc Vans (2.5)................................ 4.3
Vans (3.1)................................ 4.9

Internal Cylinder and Piston Assy., Renew
Includes: R&R compressor, disassemble, clean and inspect parts. Install new pre-assembled cylinder, pistons and wobble plate unit. Evacuate and charge system.
Six (2.7)................................ 4.3
V-8-exc Vans (2.5)................................ 4.2
Vans (3.1)................................ 4.8

COMPRESSOR - 4 CYLINDER RADIAL

Compressor Assembly, Renew
Includes: Transfer all necessary attaching parts. Evacuate and charge system.
Astro (1.5)................................ 2.5
All other models (1.0)................................ 2.0

Compressor Clutch Hub and Drive Plate, Renew
Includes: Check air gap. Does not include R&R compressor.
All models (.5)................................ .8

Compressor Rotor and/or Bearing, Renew
Astro (1.4)................................ 2.3
All other models (.6)................................ 1.0

Compressor Clutch Coil and/or Pulley Rim, Renew
Astro (1.4)................................ 2.3
All other models (.6)................................ .8

Compressor Shaft Seal Kit, Renew
Includes: R&R clutch hub and drive plate. Evacuate and charge system.
All models (1.3)................................ 2.5

Compressor Front Bearing, Front Head and/or Seal, Renew
Includes: R&R clutch hub and drive plate, rotor, pulley and coil. Evacuate and charge system.
Astro (1.9)................................ 3.0
All other models (1.7)................................ 2.8

Compressor Outer Shell and/or 'O' Rings, Renew
Includes: R&R compressor. R&R clutch hub and drive plate, rotor, pulley and coil. Evacuate and charge system.
Astro (2.1)................................ 3.2
All other models (1.8)................................ 2.9

Compressor Discharge Valve Plate Assy., Renew
Includes: R&R compressor. R&R clutch hub and drive plate, rotor, pulley and coil. Evacuate and charge system.
Astro (2.2)................................ 3.4
All other models (1.8)................................ 2.9
Renew two or more valves add (.1)................................ .2

Compressor Cylinder and Shaft Assy., Renew
Includes: R&R compressor. Transfer clutch hub, drive plate, rotor, pulley, and coil. Inspect front head. Add oil. Evacuate and charge system.
Astro (2.3)................................ 3.5
All other models (1.9)................................ 3.0

COMPRESSOR ASSEMBLY DA-6

Compressor Assembly, Renew
Includes: Transfer parts as required. Evacuate and charge system.
All models (1.1)................................ 2.0

Compressor Clutch Plate and Hub Assy., Renew
Includes: R&R hub and drive plate assy. Check air gap.
Vans-Astro (.4)................................ .7
All other models (.3)................................ .6

Compressor Clutch Coil and/or Pulley Rim, Renew
Includes: R&R hub and drive plate assy.
Vans-Astro (1.0)................................ 1.5
All other models (.8)................................ 1.3

Compressor Rotor and/or Bearing, Renew
Includes: R&R hub and drive plate assy.
Vans-Astro (.9)................................ 1.4
All other models (.7)................................ 1.2

Compressor Shaft Seal Kit, Renew
Includes: Evacuate and charge system.
Vans-Astro (1.2)................................ 2.6
All other models (1.1)................................ 2.5

Compressor Front Head and/or Seal, Renew
Includes: R&R compressor. R&R clutch and pulley assy. R&R shaft seal assy. Clean and inspect parts. Evacuate and charge system.
Vans-Astro (1.6)................................ 3.0
All other models (1.4)................................ 2.8

Compressor Cylinder and Shaft Assy., Renew
Includes: R&R compressor. R&R clutch and pulley assy. R&R shaft seal assy., remove and transfer front head assy. R&R compressor shell and 'O' rings. R&R compressor valve plates. Clean and inspect parts. Evacuate and charge system.
Vans-Astro (2.1)................................ 3.5
All other models (1.9)................................ 3.3

Compressor Relief Valve, Renew
Includes: Evacuate and charge system.
exc Vans (.9)................................ 2.0
Vans-Astro (1.1)................................ 2.3

Condenser, Renew
Includes: Evacuate and charge system.
S-series (1.3)................................ 2.8
exc Vans (1.5)................................ 3.1
Vans-Astro (1.3)................................ 2.8
w/Aux oil cooler add (.3)................................ .3

Evaporator Assembly, Renew
Includes: Evacuate and charge system.
Front Unit
S-series (1.4)................................ 2.8
exc Vans (1.3)................................ 3.2
Vans-Astro (1.5)................................ 3.5
All other models w/Diesel eng (2.9)................................ 4.5
Rear Unit
exc Vans (1.7)................................ 3.6
Vans (2.4)................................ 4.3

Accumulator, Renew
Includes: Evacuate and charge system.
All models (.9)................................ 1.5

Expansion Tube (Orifice), Renew
Includes: Evacuate and charge system.
All models (.7)................................ 1.4

LABOR 28 AIR CONDITIONING 28 LABOR

(Factory Time)	Chilton Time
Pressure Cycling Switch, Renew	
All models (.2)	.3
Receiver - Dehydrator, Renew	
Includes: Evacuate and charge system.	
Vans (1.4)	2.2
Sight Glass and/or 'O' Ring, Renew	
Includes: Evacuate and charge system.	
Vans (.8)	2.0
Expansion Valve, Renew	
Includes: Evacuate and charge system.	
Series 10-20	
rear valve (1.1)	2.2
Vans	
front valve (2.2)	3.3
Vans	
one or both rear valves (2.4)	3.5
Expansion Tube and Screen, Clean and Inspect or Renew	
Includes: Evacuate and charge system.	
All models (.9)	2.0
A.C. Blower Motor, Renew	
Front Unit	
Gas Engine	
S-series (.3)	.5
Astro (.6)	1.0
exc Vans (.2)	.5
Vans (.3)	.6
Diesel Eng	
Vans (.5)	.8
All other models (2.4)	4.0
Rear Unit	
All models (1.1)	1.6
Blower Motor Switch, Renew	
Front unit (.5)	.9
Rear unit (.4)	.8
Temperature Control Assy., Renew	
All models (.5)	.9
Blower Motor Resistor, Renew	
Front unit (.2)	.4
Rear unit (.3)	*.5
*R&R seat add	.2
Blower Motor Relay, Renew	
All models (.3)	.5
Air Conditioning Hoses, Renew	
Includes: Evacuate and charge system.	
Condenser Outlet	
Astro (1.1)	2.2
Comp to Condenser	
exc Vans (1.1)	2.2
Vans (1.3)	2.4
Condenser to Receiver-Dehydrator	
Vans (1.4)	2.5
Receiver-Dehydrator to Exp Valve	
Vans (1.6)	2.7
Condenser to Evaporator	
S-series (.8)	1.7
w/Front A.C. (1.3)	2.4
w/Rear A.C. (1.5)	2.6
Hose, Muffler and Comp Manifold Assy.	
exc Suburban	
w/Rear A.C. (1.3)	2.4
Suburban-w/Rear A.C. (1.0)	2.1
Front to Rear Unit (Under Floor)	
exc Vans-one or both (1.4)	2.6
Vans-one or both (1.5)	2.7
Astro-one or both (1.5)	2.7
Hose and Plate Assy.-Pillar to Overhead	
Series 10-20-Rear Unit (1.3)	2.5
Chevy Van-Rear Unit (1.5)	2.7
Sport Van-Rear Unit (1.7)	2.9
Beauville-Rear Unit (2.9)	4.1

LABOR 30 HEAD AND PARKING LAMPS 30 LABOR

(Factory Time)	Chilton Time
Aim Headlamps	
two	.4
four	.6
Headlamp Sealed Beam Bulb, Renew	
All models-each (.2)	.3
Turn Signal or Parking Lamp Assy., Renew	
All models-each (.2)	.4
Side Marker Lamp Assy., Renew	
All models-each (.2)	.3
Tail and Stop Lamp Assy., Renew	
Includes: Back-up and/or marker lamp assy. on combination units.	
All models-each (.3)	.4
License Lamp Assy., Renew	
All models-each (.2)	.3
Roof Marker Lamp Assy., Renew	
All models-each (.2)	.3
Reflectors, Renew	
All models-each	.2

LABOR 31 WINDSHIELD WIPER & SPEEDOMETER 31 LABOR

(Factory Time)	Chilton Time
Windshield Wiper Motor, Renew	
S-series (.5)	.7
exc Vans (.3)	.6
Vans (1.1)	1.6
w/A.C. add (.1)	.2
Recond motor add (.3)	.5
Wiper Transmission, Renew (One Side)	
All models (.6)	.8
w/A.C. add (.1)	.2
Wiper Switch, Renew	
S-series (1.0)	1.5
Vans	
1982 & later (1.0)	1.5
Delay Wiper Controller Assy., Renew	
All models (.5)	.7
Windshield Washer Pump Assy., Renew	
exc Vans (.2)	.4
Vans	
1982 & later (.2)	.4
w/A.C. add (.1)	.2
Windshield Washer Pump, R&R and Recondition	
exc Vans (.5)	.7
Vans	
1982 & later (.5)	.7
w/A.C. add (.1)	.2
Intermittant Wiper Controller Assy., Renew	
S-series (.3)	.5
All other models (.5)	.8
Pulse Wiper Control Module, Renew	
S-series (.6)	.8
All other models (.3)	.5
Windshield Washer Pump Valve, Renew	
1982-83	
exc Vans (.3)	.4
Vans (1.1)	1.6
1984-86 (.2)	.4
Speedometer Head, R&R or Renew	
S-series (.4)	.8
exc Vans (.6)	1.0
Vans (.5)	.9
Astro (.7)	1.2
Reset odometer add	.2
Speedometer Cable and Casing, Renew	
1982-83	
Without Cruise Control	
upper cable (.4)	.7
lower cable (.3)	.6
one piece (.4)	.8
With Cruise Control	
upper cable (.4)	.6
intermediate cable (.4)	.6
lower cable (.5)	.7
1984-86	
upper cable (.4)	.6
lower cable (.3)	.5
one piece cable	
conv cab (.4)	.6
All other models (.7)	1.1

LABOR 32 LIGHT SWITCHES & WIRING 32 LABOR

	(Factory Time)	Chilton Time
Headlamp Switch, Renew		
S-series	(.6)	.8
exc Vans	(.3)	.4
Vans-Astro	(.5)	.6
w/A.C. add	(.2)	.2
Headlamp Dimmer Switch, Renew		
S-series	(.4)	.6
Vans-Astro	(.5)	.7
All other models	(.3)	.4
Turn Signal and Hazard Warning Switch, Renew		
All models	(.7)	1.1
Back-Up Lamp and Park/Neutral Switch, Renew		
S-series	(.4)	.6
All other models	(.3)	.5
Starter Safety Switch, Renew		
w/A.T.-column mount	(.3)	.5
w/M.T.-clutch mount	(.2)	.4
Back-Up Lamp Switch, Renew		
w/A.T.	(.3)	.5
w/M.T.-floor shift	(.2)	.4
w/M.T.-column shift	(.3)	.5
Stop Light Switch, Renew		
All models	(.2)	.3
Parking Brake Lamp Switch, Renew		
S-series	(.4)	.6
All other models	(.2)	.4
Turn Signal or Hazard Warning Flasher, Renew		
S-series	(.3)	.4
All other models	(.2)	.3
Horn, Renew		
All models	(.2)	.4

LABOR 34 CRUISE CONTROL 34 LABOR

	(Factory Time)	Chilton Time
Regulator Assembly (Transducer), Renew		
Includes: Adjust.		
exc Vans	(.4)	.8
Vans	(.5)	.9
Engagement Switch, Renew		
All models	(.4)	.6
Cruise Control Release Switch, Renew		
All models		
Brake	(.3)	.4
Clutch	(.3)	.4
Cruise Control Servo, Renew		
exc Vans	(.3)	.5
Vans-Astro	(.5)	.7
Renew bracket add	(.1)	.2
Vacuum Hoses, Renew		
exc Vans	(.2)	.3
Vans-Astro	(.4)	.6
Cruise Control Cable or Chain, Renew		
Vans-Astro	(.5)	.7
All other models	(.3)	.5
Power Unit Solenoid, Renew		
All models	(.2)	.3
Cruise Control Vacuum Regulator Valve, Renew		
(w/Diesel eng)		
All models	(.2)	.3
Cruise Control Resume Solenoid, Renew		
All models	(.2)	.3
Cruise Control Module, Renew		
All models	(.3)	.5
Cruise Control Speed Sensor, Renew		
S-series-Vans-Astro	(.6)	.9
All other models	(.7)	1.0
Cruise Control Check Valve, Renew		
All models	(.2)	.4

Chevrolet Trucks Series 40-90

GROUP INDEX

ALPHABETICAL INDEX

LABOR 1 TUNE UP 1 LABOR

(Factory Time) Chilton Time

GASOLINE ENGINES

Compression Test

Six(.6) 9
V-8(.8) 1.1

Engine Tune Up, Minor

Includes: Clean or renew spark plugs. Renew ignition points and condenser, set ignition timing. Adjust carburetor idle speed and mixture. Service air cleaner. Clean or renew fuel filters.

Six(1.3) 1.8
V-8 (2.3) 2.8

Engine Tune Up, Major

Includes: Clean or renew spark plugs. Check compression. Test battery and clean terminals. Renew and adjust distributor points and condenser. Check distributor cap and rotor. Adjust ignition timing and test coil. Tighten manifold bolts, adjust carburetor idle speed and mixture. Inspect and tighten all hose connections. Adjust fan belts. Service air cleaner. Clean or renew fuel filters. Clean or renew PCV valve. Road test.

Six(2.2) 3.0
V-8(3.0) 3.9

DIESEL ENGINES

Compression Test

Detroit Diesel

6-71 (3.0) 3.8
6V-53, 6V-71 (2.9) 3.7
8V-71 (4.1) 5.2
12V-71 (6.0) 7.5

Engine Tune Up, Minor

Includes: Test batteries and clean and tighten terminals. Check and adjust engine idle speed and throttle linkage. Change engine oil. Clean or renew oil, air, fuel and water filters. Tighten radiator hoses and manifold bolts. Check valve lash and adjust tappets. R&R and test injectors. Does not include compression test or injector timing.

Detroit Diesel

6-71 .... 4.4
6V-53, 6V-71 .... 4.5
8V-71 .... 5.0
12V-71 .... 6.0

Engine Tune Up, Major

Includes: Test batteries and clean and tighten terminals. Check and adjust engine idle speed and throttle linkage. Adjust injector timing and injectors. Steam clean engine. Clean or renew air, oil, fuel and water filters. Change engine oil. Check and lubricate shutters. Clean injectors and fuel connections. Inspect for oil, water and fuel leaks. Drain sediment from fuel tanks. Tighten intake manifold, exhaust manifold, turbocharger, blower and engine mounting bolts. Clean fuel pump screen. Adjust crossheads and valves. Check crankshaft end clearance. Adjust fan belts. Tighten and inspect hose connections. Road test.

Does not include compression test.

Detroit Diesel

6-71 .... 10.8
6V-53, 6V-71 .... 11.2
8V-71 .... 12.0
12V-71 .... 13.0

LABOR 2 IGNITION SYSTEM 2 LABOR

(Factory Time) Chilton Time

Spark Plugs, Renew

Six(.3) 6
V-8(.5) 9

Ignition Timing, Reset

All series (.3) 4

Distributor, R&R or Renew

Includes: Reset ignition timing.

Six(.6) 8
V-8–exc below (.6) 1.0
Tilt cab (.8) 1.2

Distributor (Conventional), R&R and Recondition

Includes: Reset ignition timing.

Six(1.0) 1.7
V-8–exc below (1.0) *1.7
Tilt cab (1.3) *1.9
*w/Spinner Type Gov add (1.0) 1.0

Distributor (H.E.I.), R&R and Recondition

Six(1.1) 1.7
V-8–exc below (1.1) 1.7
Tilt cab (1.2) 1.9

Distributor Cap and/or Rotor, Renew

Six(.2) 4
V-8(.4) 5

Distributor Module (H.E.I.), Renew

All series (.5) 6

Ignition Coil, Renew

All series (.5) 6

Vacuum Control Unit, Renew

Includes: Reset ignition timing.

Six(.3) 6
V-8–exc below (.6) 9
Tilt cab (.9) 1.1

Ignition Cables, Renew

Six(.3) 6
V-8(.6) 8

Ignition Switch, Renew

All series (.6) 8

Distributor Points and Condenser, Renew

Includes: Adjust dwell and timing.

Six (.4) 7
V-8 (.5) 8

Distributor Capacitor and/or Module Wiring Harness, Renew

All series (.5) 6

Distributor Pick-Up Coil and/or Pole Piece, Renew

All series (.8) 1.1

LABOR 3 FUEL SYSTEM 3 LABOR

(Factory Time) Chilton Time

GASOLINE ENGINES

Fuel Pump, Test

Includes: Disconnect line at carburetor, attach pressure gauge.

All series 3

Carburetor, Adjust (On Truck)

All series (.3) 4

Carburetor, R&R or Renew

Includes: All necessary adjustments. Service air cleaner.

1 bbl (.5) 7
2 bbl (.6) 8
4 bbl (.8) 1.2

Carburetor, R&R and Recondition

Includes: All necessary adjustments. Service air cleaner.

1 bbl (1.4) 2.1
2 bbl (1.5) 2.1
4 bbl–exc below (1.7) 2.4
Holley (4.3) 5.0

Governor, Renew (Spinner Type)

1 bbl (.7) 1.0
2 bbl (.8) 1.1
4 bbl (.9) 1.2

Governor and Throttle Body, R&R and Recondition (Spinner Type)

Does not include overhaul carburetor.

1 bbl (1.3) 1.9
2 bbl (1.5) 2.1
4 bbl (1.7) 2.3

Electronic Governor, Renew

Does not include R&R carburetor.

4 bbl Holley (.5) 7

Electronic Governor, R&R and Recondition

Does not include R&R carburetor.

4 bbl Holley (.9) 1.3

Solenoid Control Valve, Renew

4 bbl Holley (.2) 3

Electronic Governor Controller, Renew

4 bbl Holley (.2) 3

Fuel Pump, Renew

Pump on engine
exc below (.4) 8
Tilt cab V-8 (.6) *1.1
*w/Air comp add (.2) 2
Pump in tank
All series–each (.6) 1.0

LABOR 3 FUEL SYSTEM 3 LABOR

(Factory Time)	Chilton Time
Fuel Tank, Renew	
Series 40-70	
frame mounted (1.2)	1.6
cab mounted (.9)	1.5
step tank (1.2)	1.6
Tilt cab (.7)	1.2
Series 80-90	
frame mounted (.7)	1.2
cab mounted (1.2)	1.7
step tank (1.2)	1.6
Fuel Gauge (Tank), Renew	
Series 40-70	
frame mounted (.6)	1.0
step tank (.4)	.7
cab mounted (.4)	.7
Tilt cab (.4)	.7
Series 80-90	
frame mounted (.4)	.7
cab mounted (.3)	.7
step tank (.3)	.7
Fuel Gauge (Dash), Renew	
All series–exc below (.4)	.9
Tilt cab (.6)	1.2
Intake Manifold Gaskets, Renew	
Includes: R&R all normal interfering parts.	
Six–conventional (2.0)	3.0
Tilt cab (1.7)	2.2
w/P.S. add (.4)	.4
w/AIR add (.1)	.1
Renew manif add	.5
V-8–307, 350 engs	
conv (2.0)	2.8
V-8–366, 427, 454 engs	
conventional (3.0)	3.8
Tilt cab (3.9)	4.5
w/A.C. add	
307-350 engs w/A.I.R. (.4)	.4
307-350 engs wo/A.I.R. (1.0)	1.0
366-427 engs w/A.C. (1.1)	1.1
w/Air comp add (.6)	.6
Renew manif add (.3)	.5
Intake and Exhaust Manifold Gaskets, Renew	
Six–conv cab (1.6)	2.1
Tilt cab (1.7)	2.2
w/P.S. add (.4)	.4
w/AIR add (.1)	.1
DIESEL ENGINES	
Air Cleaner Assembly, R&R and Clean or Renew	
All series (.5)	.7
Engine Idle Speed, Adjust (Governor)	
Detroit (.9)	1.2
Injection Timing, Adjust	
Isuzu Diesel	
All series (.5)	.9
Deutz Diesel	
All series (.8)	1.2
Detroit Diesel	
conv (1.1)	1.5
Tilt cab (2.0)	2.5
High Pressure Fuel Lines, Renew	
Isuzu Diesel	
one (.3)	.5
each adtnl (.2)	.3
all (.7)	1.2
Injectors, Renew	
Includes: R&R all normal interfering parts. Clean and adjust all parts.	
Isuzu & Deutz Diesel	
one (.5)	.8
each adtnl (.5)	.3
all (1.6)	2.2
Renew nozzles add, each (.2)	.2
Detroit Diesel	
6-71-one (.4)	.7
all (1.8)	2.5
6V-53, 6V-71-one (.4)	.7
all (1.9)	2.5
8V-71-one (.4)	.7
all (2.5)	3.3
12V-71-one (.4)	.7
all (3.6)	4.8
R&R control island add (.8)	.8
Injectors, R&R and Recondition	
Includes: R&R all normal interfering parts. Make all required adjustments and tests.	
Detroit Diesel	
6-71-one (1.2)	1.7
all (6.1)	7.8
6V-53, 6V-71-one (1.2)	1.7
all (6.2)	7.9
8V-71-one (1.2)	1.7
all (8.2)	10.4
12V-71-one (1.2)	1.7
all (11.8)	14.3
R&R control island add (.8)	.8
Fuel Injection Pump, Renew	
Includes: R&R all normal interfering parts. Adjust injection timing and governor.	
Isuzu Diesel	
All series (2.8)	3.9
Deutz Diesel	
All series (2.7)	3.8
Detroit Diesel	
exc below (1.0)	1.4
6V-53, 12V-71 (1.5)	1.6
R&R floor mat add (.4)	.4
Turbocharger Assy., Renew	
Isuzu Diesel	
All series (.6)	1.0
Deutz Diesel	
All series (1.5)	2.2
Blower Assembly, R&R or Renew	
Includes: R&R all interfering parts. Drain and refill radiator. Make all required adjustments.	
Detroit Diesel	
exc below (6.6)	8.5
6-71 (4.5)	5.9
12V-71-one (6.8)	8.9
two (8.3)	10.6
Blower Assembly, R&R and Recondition.	
Includes: R&R all interfering parts. Drain and refill radiator. Clean and inspect all parts, replace as necessary. Sand rotors and housing. Make all required adjustments.	
Detroit Diesel	
exc below (10.1)	13.0
6-71 (8.0)	10.0
12V-71-one (10.3)	13.3
two (15.3)	19.7
Fuel Filter, Renew	
Isuzu Diesel	
All series (.4)	.6
Deutz Diesel	
All series (.4)	.6
Detroit Diesel	
each (.5)	.8
Intake Manifold and/or Gasket, Renew	
Isuzu Diesel (1.1)	1.7
Deutz Diesel (.9)	1.4
Fuel Pump, Renew	
Deutz Diesel	
All series (.5)	.7
Isuzu Diesel	
All series–primary (.5)	.8

LABOR 3A EMISSION CONTROLS 3A LABOR

(Factory Time)	Chilton Time
EMISSION CONTROLS	
Positive Crankcase Ventilation Valve, Renew	
Six & V-8 (.2)	.3
AIR INJECTOR REACTOR TYPE	
Air Pump, R&R	
All series (.4)	.5
Air Pump, Renew	
All series (.6)	.7
Air Pump Relief Valve, Renew	
All series (.5)	.6
Air Check Valve, Renew	
All series-one (.2.)	.3
Reactor Valve, Renew	
All series (.2)	.4
Centrifugal Filter, Renew	
All series (.5)	.6
Diverter Valve, Renew	
All series (.3)	.4
CONTROLLED COMBUSTION TYPE	
Air Cleaner Vacuum Motor, Renew	
All series (.2)	.4
Air Cleaner Temperature Sensor, Renew	
All series (.2)	.3
Charcoal Canister, Renew	
All series (.2)	.4

LABOR 4 ALTERNATOR & REGULATOR 4 LABOR

(Factory Time)	Chilton Time
Alternator Circuits Test	
Includes: Test battery, regulator and alternator output.	
All series	.6
each adtnl battery (.2)	.2
Alternator, R&R or Renew	
Gasoline Engines	
All series (.6)	.8
Diesel Engines	
Isuzu Diesel (.5)	.8
Deutz Diesel (1.0)	1.4
Detroit Diesel	
8.2L	
w/vac brks (.8)	1.1
w/air brks (.6)	.9
Caterpillar Diesel	
3208	
w/vac brks (.7)	1.0
w/air brks (.6)	.9
Alternator, R&R and Recondition	
Gasoline Engines	
All series	
Delco (1.2)	1.7
Leece Neville (1.8)	2.5
Diesel Engines	
Isuzu Diesel (1.4)	2.0
Deutz Diesel (1.2)	1.7
Detroit Diesel	
8.2L	
Delco (1.5)	2.1
Leece Neville (2.1)	2.9
Caterpillar Diesel	
3208	
Delco SI 27 (1.3)	1.8
Delco SI 25 (2.3)	3.2
Delco SI 30 (1.9)	2.7
Leece Neville (1.9)	2.7
Alternator Regulator, Test and Renew	
Gasoline Engines	
Delco (1.0)	1.4
Leece Neville (.3)	.6
Diesel Engines	
Isuzu Diesel (.8)	1.2
Deutz Diesel (.9)	1.3
Detroit Diesel (.4)	.6
Caterpillar Diesel	
3208	
Delco SI 27 (1.1)	1.5
Delco SI 25 (1.2)	1.6
Delco SI 30 (1.0)	1.4
Leece Neville (1.0)	1.4

LABOR 5 STARTING SYSTEM 5 LABOR

(Factory Time)	Chilton Time
Starter Draw Test (On Truck)	
All series (.3)	.3
Starter, R&R or Renew	
GASOLINE ENGINES	
Series 40-70 (.4)	.7
Series 80-90 (.6)	.9
DIESEL ENGINES	
Isuzu Diesel	
All series (.5)	.8
DETROIT DIESEL	
Six (.8)	1.2
Bison-V-6-V-8 (1.6)	2.0
Bruin (1.7)	2.1
8.2L (1.1)	1.6
All others (1.3)	1.7
CUMMINS DIESEL	
All series (1.2)	1.6
CATERPILLAR DIESEL	
Series 40-70 (1.9)	2.6
Series 80-90 (2.9)	3.8
DEUTZ DIESEL	
All series (1.2)	1.7
Starter, R&R and Recondition	
Includes: Recondition armature.	
GASOLINE ENGINES	
Series 40-70 (1.6)	2.5
Series 80-90 (1.8)	2.7
DIESEL ENGINES	
Isuzu Diesel	
All series (3.1)	4.5
DETROIT DIESEL	
Six (2.0)	2.9
Bison-V-6-V-8 (2.8)	3.7
Bruin (2.9)	3.8
8.2L (3.6)	4.8
All others (2.5)	3.4
CUMMINS DIESEL	
All series (2.4)	3.3
CATERPILLAR DIESEL	
All series (4.2)	5.8
DEUTZ DIESEL	
All series (3.4)	4.8
Renew field coils add (.5)	.5
Add draw test if performed.	
Starter Drive, Renew	
Includes: R&R starter.	
GASOLINE ENGINES	
Series 40-70 (.8)	1.2
Series 80-90 (1.0)	1.4
DIESEL ENGINES	
Isuzu Diesel	
All series (.8)	1.2
DETROIT DIESEL	
Six (1.0)	1.5
Bison-V-6-V-8 (1.8)	2.4
Bruin (1.9)	2.5
8.2L (1.5)	2.1
All others (1.5)	2.1
CUMMINS DIESEL	
All series (1.4)	2.0
CATERPILLAR DIESEL	
All series (1.9)	2.5
DEUTZ DIESEL	
All series (1.1)	1.5
Starter Solenoid, Renew	
Includes: R&R starter.	
GASOLINE ENGINES	
Series 40-70 (.5)	1.2
Series 80-90 (.8)	1.4
DIESEL ENGINES	
Isuzu Diesel	
All series (.7)	1.1
DETROIT DIESEL	
Six (1.0)	1.5
Bison-V-6-V-8 (1.8)	2.4
Bruin (1.9)	2.5
8.2L (1.2)	1.8
All others (1.5)	2.1
CUMMINS DIESEL	
All series (1.5)	2.1
CATERPILLAR DIESEL	
All series (2.0)	2.6
DEUTZ DIESEL	
All series (1.1)	1.5
Battery Cables, Renew	
Series 40-70-positive (.3)	.5
negative (.2)	.4
Series 80-90 exc below	
positive (.4)	.5
negative (.3)	.4
Bison-positive (.6)	.8
negative (.5)	.7

LABOR 6 BRAKE SYSTEM 6 LABOR

(Factory Time)	Chilton Time
Brakes Adjust, Minor	
Includes: Adjust brake shoes at all wheels. Fill master cylinder. R&R one front drum.	
Series 40-70	
exc below (.6)	.7
tandem (1.0)	1.0
Series 80-90	
exc below (.9)	.9
tandem (1.2)	1.2
Pressure Bleed Brakes	
All models (.4)	.6
w/Tandem axle add (.3)	.3
w/Booster add (.3)	.3
Brake Drum, Renew (One)	
Includes: R&R wheels and adjust bearings and brake shoes.	
Front	
Series 40-70	
hydraulic (.7)	1.0
front drive axle (2.0)	2.7
air brakes	
cast whl (1.2)	1.6
10 stud disc (1.4)	1.9
8 stud disc whl (1.8)	2.4
Series 80-90	
exc below (1.1)	*1.4
10 stud whls (1.8)	*2.5
*w/Berg air parking brake add (.3)	.3
Rear	
Series 40-70	
10 stud-Corp (.7)	1.0
cast spoke (1.7)	2.2

(Factory Time)	Chilton Time
10 stud-Budd (2.1)	2.8
8 stud disc whl (2.6)	3.5
10 stud flange mount (1.5)	2.0
6 stud-Budd (.8)	1.1
Series 80-90	
6 stud-Budd (.8)	1.1
10 stud-Budd (1.3)	1.7
cast spoke (1.3)	1.7
w/Berg air parking brake add (.3)	.3

Stop Light Switch, Renew

Steel Tilt Cab (1.1)	1.5
Medium Conv. Cab (.4)	.6

Brake Shoes, Renew

Includes: R&R wheel and drum assemblies. Clean and inspect all parts. Install new or exchange shoes, adjust brakes. Road test.

Front (both wheels)	
Series 40-70	
hydraulic	
conv (1.3)	2.0
Tilt cab (Isuzu) (2.9)	3.9
front drive axle (3.2)	4.3
air (1.6)	2.1
Series 80-90 (1.6)	2.1
Rear (both wheels)	
Series 40-70	
single axle	
conv (2.2)	4.0
Tilt cab (Isuzu) (4.4)	5.9
tandem axle (6.4)	7.5
Series 80-90	
single axle (3.2)	4.0
tandem axle (6.4)	7.5
All Wheels	
Series 40-70	
Single axle	
hydraulic	
conv	5.0
Tilt cab (Isuzu)	9.5
front drive axle	7.5
air	6.0
Tandem axle	9.5
Series 80-90	
Single axle	6.0
Tandem axle	9.5
Bleed brakes add	
single axle (.3)	.3
tandem axle (.6)	.6
w/Booster add (.6)	.6
w/Berg parking brake add (.3)	.3

DISC BRAKES

Disc Brake Pads, Renew

Includes: Install new disc brake pads only.

All series	
front (.8)	1.1
rear (1.0)	1.5
all four wheels	2.5
Resurface disc rotor, add-each	.9

Caliper Assembly, Renew

Includes: Renew brake pads if necessary. Bleed brake system.

All series	
front-one (.5)	.8
both (.9)	1.4
rear-one (.8)	1.1
both (1.5)	2.0

Caliper Assy., R&R and Recondition

Includes: Renew brake pads if necessary. Recondition caliper and bleed brake system.

All series	
front-one (1.3)	1.6
both (2.5)	3.0
rear-one (1.6)	1.9
both (3.1)	3.6

COMBINATIONS

Add to Brakes, Renew

RENEW WHEEL CYLINDER

Each	.3

RECONDITION WHEEL CYLINDER

Each	.4

REBUILD CALIPER ASSEMBLY

Each	.8

MASTER CYLINDER, RENEW

All series (.5)	.9

MASTER CYLINDER, RECONDITION

Includes: Hone cylinder.

One side (.8)	1.1
Both sides (1.1)	1.7

FRONT WHEEL BEARINGS, REPACK OR RENEW SEALS

All series	
drum brakes	.7
disc brakes	1.0

RENEW FRONT WHEEL BEARINGS (ONE WHEEL)

All series	
drum brakes	.4
disc brakes	.5

RENEW BRAKE AIR CHAMBER

Each (.3)	.5

RELINE BRAKE SHOES

Front Axle Set (.5)	.6
Rear Axle Set (.5)	.6

RESURFACE BRAKE DRUM

Front-each (.5)	.8
Rear-each (.6)	.9

RENEW REAR WHEEL OIL SEAL

Each (.1)	.1

RENEW INNER REAR WHEEL GREASE SEALS (ONE SIDE)

All series (.8)	1.1

Disc Brake Rotor, Renew

Includes: Clean and repack or renew bearings and seals.

(Factory Time)	Chilton Time
All series	
front-one (1.2)	1.6
both (2.3)	3.1
rear-one (1.6)	2.1
both (3.1)	4.1

BRAKE HYDRAULIC SYSTEM

Wheel Cylinders, Renew

Includes: R&R wheel and drum assembly. Clean and inspect parts. Bleed lines and road test.

Front	
Series 40-70	
Conv	
one (.7)	1.0
both (1.4)	1.9
Tilt cab (Isuzu)	
one (2.1)	2.8
both (4.0)	5.4
Front Drive Axle	
one (1.9)	2.5
both (3.6)	4.8
Series 80-90	
one (1.7)	2.0
both (2.9)	3.5
Rear	
Series 40-70	
Conv	
one (1.5)	2.0
both (2.8)	3.7
Tilt cab (Isuzu)	
one (2.8)	3.7
both (5.1)	6.8
Series 80-90	
one (1.9)	2.2
both-same axle (3.3)	4.2
all	8.0
w/Eaton single spd axle add (.8)	.8
w/Booster add (.3)	.3
w/Two cyl type,	
second cyl add (.2)	.2

Wheel Cylinder, R&R and Recondition

Includes: R&R wheel and drum assembly. Clean and inspect all parts. Hone cylinders. Bleed lines and road test.

(Factory Time)	Chilton Time
Front	
Series 40-70	
Conv	
one (.7)	1.4
both (1.4)	2.7
Tilt cab (Isuzu)	
one (2.1)	3.2
both (4.0)	6.2
Front Drive Axle	
one (1.9)	2.6
both (3.6)	5.0
Series 80-90	
one (1.9)	2.3
both (3.3)	4.1
Rear	
Series 40-70	
Conv	
one (1.5)	2.1
both (2.8)	3.9
Tilt cab (Isuzu)	
one (2.8)	4.1
both (5.1)	7.6
Series 80-90	
exc below-one (2.2)	2.5
both (3.9)	4.8
tandem-one (2.2)	2.5
all	9.2
w/Eaton single spd axle add (.8)	.8
w/Booster add (.3)	.3
w/Two cyl type,	
second cyl add (.2)	.3

Brake Hose, Renew

Includes: Bleed lines.

Series 40-70	
exc below (.5)	7
booster (.6)	.8
tandem (.7)	.9
each adtnl (.3)	.3
Series 80-90	
one (.6)	.8
each adtnl (.3)	.3

(Factory Time) Chilton Time

Master Cylinder, Renew

Includes: Bleed complete system. Adjust pedal free play.

Series 40-70
exc below (.8)........ 1.0
booster (1.1)........ 1.5
tandem (1.3)........ 1.8
Series 80-90
conv-single cyl (.6)........ .9
dual cyl (.9)........ 1.2
Tilt cab (.6)........ .9

Master Cylinder, R&R and Recondition

Includes: Hone cylinder. Adjust pedal free play.

Series 40-70
single cyl (1.0)........ 1.4
dual cyl (1.1)........ 1.6
booster (1.6)........ 2.0
tandem (1.8)........ 2.3
Series 80-90
conv-single cyl (.9)........ 1.3
dual cyl (1.2)........ 1.6
Tilt cab (.9)........ 1.3
Bleed system-add
wo/Booster or Tandem........ .3
w/Booster........ .4
w/Tandem........ .6

POWER BRAKES

Vacuum Power Cylinder, R&R or Renew

Series 40-70 (1.0)........ 1.4

Vacuum Power Cylinder, R&R and Recondition

Series 40-70 (2.1)........ 3.0

Vacuum Power Booster, R&R or Renew

Series 40-70 (.7)........ 1.1

Vacuum Power Booster, R&R and Recondition

Series 40-70 (1.8)........ 2.5

Electro-Hydraulic Pump, Renew

All series (.6)........ .9

Electro-Hydraulic Pump Sensor, Renew

All series (.2)........ .3

Electro-Hydraulic Pump Flow Control Switch, Renew

All series (.3)........ .4

Hydraulic Power Brake Pump (At Engine), R&R or Renew

Includes: Bleed system.

Series 40-70
Gas (.7)........ 1.0
Diesel
Detroit 8.2L
wo/Tilt hood (1.3)........ 2.0
w/Tilt hood (1.1)........ 1.8
Caterpillar (1.0)........ 1.4
w/A.C. add (.2)........ .2

Hydraulic Power Brake Pump, R&R and Recondition

Includes: Bleed system.

Series 40-70
Gas (1.7)........ 2.3
Diesel
Detroit 8.2L
wo/Tilt hood (2.3)........ 3.1
w/Tilt hood (2.1)........ 2.9
Caterpillar (1.8)........ 2.4
w/A.C. add (.2)........ .2

Hydraulic Power Brake Cylinder Assy., R&R or Renew

Includes: Bleed system.

Series 40-70 (.6)........ 1.0

Hydraulic Power Brake Cylinder Assy., R&R and Recondition

Includes: Bleed system.

Series 40-70 (1.1)........ 1.8

AIR BRAKES

Air Compressor Belts, Renew

All series-each (.3)........ .4

Air Pressure Gauge, Renew

All series (.5)........ .7

Brake Application (Treadle) Valve, Renew

Series 40-70
conv cab (1.2)........ 1.9
Tilt cab (Isuzu) (2.0)........ 2.6
Series 80-90
wo/WHEEL LOCK CONTROL
conv cab and steel tilt cabs (.8)........ 1.0
alum tilt cab (1.1)........ 1.5
w/WHEEL LOCK CONTROL
Bison (1.6)........ 2.0
All others (1.2)........ 1.6
w/Berk parking brake add (.3)........ .3

Brake Application (Treadle) Valve, R&R and Recondition

Series 40-70
conv cab (2.0)........ 3.0
Tilt cab (Isuzu) (2.8)........ 3.7
Series 80-90
wo/WHEEL LOCK CONTROL
conv and steel tilt cabs (1.6)........ 2.0
alum tilt cab (1.9)........ 2.5
w/WHEEL LOCK CONTROL
Bison (1.8)........ 2.4
All others (2.0)........ 2.7
w/Berk parking brake add (.3)........ .3

Brake Safety Valve, Renew

All series (.2)........ .3

Brake Quick Release Valve, Renew

All series (.5)........ .8
Recond valve add (.3)........ .5
R&R step tank add (1.1)........ 1.1

Brake Relay Valve, Renew

All series (.6)........ .9
w/Wheel lock control (1.3)........ 1.7
Recond valve add (.4)........ .6

Air Tank, Renew

Series 40-70
Main tank (wet)
conv cab (1.0)........ 1.4
tilt cab (1.3)........ 1.7
front service (.7)........ 1.1
rear service (.8)........ 1.2
dual reservoir (1.4)........ 1.8
Series 80-90
Main tank (1.0)........ 1.4
Front Supply Tank
Bison (1.2)........ 1.6
All others-each (.9)........ 1.3

Air Governor, Renew

All series (.3)........ .6

Air Governor, R&R and Recondition

All series (.7)........ 1.2

Air Chamber, R&R or Renew

Front
All series-one (.4)........ .6
both (.6)........ 1.0

Rear per axle
Series 40-70-one (.6)........ .8
both (1.1)........ 1.5
Series 80-90
exc below-one (.4)........ .6
both (.7)........ 1.0
Stop Master-Fail Safe-one
inner chamber (3.1)........ 4.0
outer chamber (.8)........ 1.0
complete (4.0)........ 5.0
w/Berg brake add (.3)........ .3
Renew slack adjuster add (.2)........ .3
Recondition air chamber add........ .4

Air Strainer, Clean or Renew

All series (.2)........ .3

Air Compressor, R&R or Renew

Series 40-70
water cooled (1.5)........ 2.1
air cooled (1.1)........ 1.7
w/8.2L eng (1.3)........ 1.8
Caterpillar Diesel (1.2)........ 2.0
Isuzu Diesel (4.9)........ 6.6
Series 80-90
GASOLINE ENGINES
air cooler (1.1)........ 1.6
water cooled (1.8)........ 2.5
DIESEL ENGINES
Detroit Diesel
conv cab (2.8)........ 3.4
tilt cab (2.1)........ 2.7
Caterpillar Diesel (1.5)........ 2.0
w/A.I.R. add (.2)........ .2

Air Compressor, R&R and Recondition

Series 40-70
water cooled (5.3)........ 6.4
air cooled (5.0)........ 6.1
w/8.2L eng (4.7)........ 6.4
Caterpillar Diesel (5.0)........ 6.6
Isuzu Diesel (6.5)........ 8.8
Series 80-90
GASOLINE ENGINES
air cooled (5.4)........ 6.5
water cooled (6.1)........ 7.5
DIESEL ENGINES
Detroit Diesel
conv cab (7.1)........ 8.4
tilt cab (6.4)........ 7.7
Caterpillar Diesel (5.0)........ 6.6
w/A.I.R. add (.2)........ .2

Tractor Protection (Breakaway) Valve, Renew

Series 40-70 (.5)........ .8
R&R step tank add (1.1)........ 1.1
Series 80-90 (1.0)........ 1.4
Recond valve add (.4)........ .6

Brake Chamber Diaphragm, Renew (Front or Rear)

All series-each (.4)........ .7

Slack Adjuster, Renew

All Series
Automatic (.5)........ *.8
Manual (.3)........ .6
*Recond adj add, each........ .7

AIR BRAKE ANTI-SKID SYSTEMS

Wheel Speed Sensor Rotor, R&R or Renew (One)

Includes: Test system.

Front (.9)........ 1.2
Rear (1.0)........ 1.3

LABOR 6 BRAKE SYSTEM 6 LABOR

(Factory Time) Chilton Time

Wheel Speed Sensor, R&R or Renew (One)
Includes: Test systems.
Front
AC system (.5) 7
Eaton system (1.4) 1.8
Rear
AC system (.5) 7
Eaton system (1.8) 2.3

Wheel Speed Sensor Bracket, Renew (One)
Includes: Test system.
Front
AC system (1.0) 1.4
Eaton system (.9) 1.3
Rear
AC system (.4) 7
Eaton system (.9) 1.3

Wheel Speed Sensor Cables, R&R or Renew (One)
Includes: Test system.
Front or Rear
AC system (1.1) 1.5
Eaton system (1.3) 1.8

Modulator Assembly, R&R or Renew (One)
Includes: Test system.
Series 40-70
Front axle (1.4) 1.8
Rear axle (1.4) 1.8
Series 80-90
Front axle (1.3) 1.7
Rear axle (1.0) 1.4
Renew solenoid add (.2) 2
Renew control valve add (.2) 2

Computer Assembly, Renew
Includes: Test system, does not include R&R modulator assembly.
All series (.6) 8

Skid Control Warning Light, R&R or Renew
Includes: Test system.
All series (.6) 8

Wiring Harness Adapter, R&R or Renew
Includes: Test system and R&R maintenance recorder.
All series (.4) 6

Warning Unit, R&R or Renew
Includes: Test system.
Eaton (.4) 6

Power Cable, R&R or Renew (One)
Includes: Test system.
Series 40-70
Conventional
Front axle (1.1) 1.6
Rear axle (1.1) 1.6
Tilt cab
Front axle (.7) 9
Rear axle (1.5) 1.9
Series 80-90
Front axle (2.1) 2.6
Rear-single axle (1.1) 1.6
Tandem axle-front (1.1) 1.6
rear (1.8) 2.3

Recorder or Monitor(s), Renew (Each)
Series 40-70 (.4) 8
Series 80-90
Bison (.5) 9
conv cab (.4) 8
tilt cab (.3) 6

PARKING BRAKE

Parking Brake, Adjust
All series (.3) 5

Parking Brake Band or Shoes, Renew
Series 40-70
Internal Drum Type (.6) 1.0
Reline brake shoe add (.4) 6
External Drum or Disc Type
Tru-stop - 2 shoe (.7) 1.2
All others (.5) 9

Parking Brake Lever, Renew
Series 40-70 (.5) 9
Series 80-90 (1.1) 1.5

Parking Brake Drum or Disc, Renew
Series 40-70
Tru-stop - 2 shoe (1.0) 1.4
All others (.6) 1.0
Series 80-90
Band type (1.2) 1.8
Tru-stop - 2 shoe (1.0) 1.4
Bendix (1.1) 1.5

Parking Brake Control Valve, Renew
Series 40-70
conv cab (.3) 6
Series 80-90
wo/WHEEL LOCK CONTROL
All series (.4) 8
w/WHEEL LOCK CONTROL
Bison (.6) 1.0
conv cab (.9) 1.3
alum tilt cab (.4) 8

Rear Parking Brake Cable, Renew (One)
Series 40-70
conv cab (1.1) 1.5
Tilt cab (Isuzu) (.9) 1.3

Berg Parking Brake Chamber, Renew (One)
Series 70-90 (.8) 1.2

LABOR 7 COOLING SYSTEM 7 LABOR

(Factory Time) Chilton Time

Thermostat, Renew
GASOLINE ENGINE
Six–conv (.5) 6
Tilt cab (.6) 9
V-8–conv (.5) 6
Tilt cab (.6) 9
DIESEL ENGINE
Detroit Diesel
conv (.5) 1.0
Tilt cab (.7) 1.2

Radiator, R&R or Renew
GASOLINE ENGINES
Series 40-70
Six (.9) 1.5
V-8
350 eng (.8) 1.4
366, 427 engs (1.3) 2.0
w/Tilt hood (1.4) 2.1
Series 80-90
conv cab (2.4) 3.0
w/A.T. add (.4) 4
w/Oil cooler add (.2) 2
w/Surge tank add (.3) 3
DIESEL ENGINES
Isuzu Diesel
All models (1.8) 3.1
Detroit Diesel
conv cab (2.4) 3.4
Bison (3.7) 4.7
Bruin (2.5) 3.5
Alum tilt cab (2.4) 3.4
Alligator hood (1.7) 3.0
Tilt hood (1.1) 2.0
Cummins Diesel
Bison (3.7) 4.7
All others (2.9) 3.9
Caterpillar Diesel
Series 40-70 (1.7) 3.0
Series 80-90 (2.7) 3.7

Radiator Surge Tank, Renew
Series 40-70 (.6) 1.0
Series 80-90 (1.0) 1.4

Radiator Hose, Renew
GASOLINE ENGINES
All series
upper (.5) 7
lower (.5) 7
by-pass (.4) 6
DIESEL ENGINES
Detroit Diesel
Bison-upper (.5) 7
lower (.9) 1.2
8.2L-upper (.5) 7
lower (.7) 9
All others-upper (.7) 9
lower (.8) 1.0
Cummins Diesel
upper (.3) 4
lower (.9) 1.2
Caterpillar Diesel
upper (.4) 6
lower (.5) 9

Water Pump, Renew
GASOLINE ENGINES
Six–conv (.8) 1.3
Tilt cab (1.2) 1.6
V-8–307, 350 engs
conv (.7) 1.3
Tilt cab (1.0) 1.4
V-8–366, 427 engs
conv (1.3) 1.9
Tilt cab (1.1) 1.5
V-8–454 eng
conv (1.2) 1.6
Tilt cab (2.0) 2.6
DIESEL ENGINES
Isuzu Diesel (1.0) 1.5
Detroit Diesel
exc below (1.5) 2.0
6V-53 (1.0) 1.5
12V-71 (2.5) 3.0
w/A.C. add (.2) 2
w/P.S. add (.2) 2
w/Air inj add (.2) 2
w/Air comp add (.2) 2

Air Cooling Blower Assy., Renew
Deutz Diesel
All series (.6) 1.0

Engine Air Blower Temperature Control Thermostat, Renew
Deutz Diesel
All series (.6) 9

LABOR 7 COOLING SYSTEM 7 LABOR

(Factory Time) — Chilton Time

Fan Blades, Renew

GASOLINE ENGINES

	Chilton Time
Six–conv (.3)	.5
Tilt cab (.4)	.6
V-8–conv (.5)	.6
Tilt cab (1.3)	1.7
DIESEL ENGINES	
Isuzu Diesel (.8)	1.1
Detroit Diesel (1.2)	1.6
Bison (.4)	.6
Cummins Diesel	
Bison (.9)	1.3
All others (.8)	1.2
Caterpillar	
Series 40-70	
3208 (1.0)	1.5
Series 80-90	
All models (1.7)	2.4
w/A.C. add (.2)	.2
w/P.S. add (.2)	.2
w/Air inj add (.2)	.2
w/Air comp add (.2)	.2
w/Fan shroud add (.2)	.2

Drive Belt, Renew

GASOLINE ENGINES

	Chilton Time
Six	
A.C. (.3)	.4
A.I.R. (.3)	.4
Fan (.4)	.5
H/Boost (.4)	.5
P.S. (.2)	.3
V-8	
A.C. (1.1)	1.5
A.I.R. (.2)	.3
Air comp (.3)	.4
Fan (.2)	.3
H/Boost (.2)	.3
P.S. (.2)	.3
DIESEL ENGINES	
Isuzu Diesel	
Fan/Generator (.3)	.5
Detroit Diesel	
one (.3)	.5
Cummins Diesel	
one (.8)	1.1
Caterpillar Diesel	
one or both (.8)	1.1

Temperature Gauge (Dash), Renew

	Chilton Time
conv cab (.4)	.7
Tilt cab (.6)	1.0
Bison (.2)	.4

Temperature Gauge (Engine), Renew

	Chilton Time
Six (.3)	.5
V-8 (.4)	.7
Detroit Diesel (.5)	.8
Cummins Diesel (.3)	.5
Caterpillar Diesel (.5)	.8

Radiator Shutter Assembly, R&R or Renew

	Chilton Time
All series (.8)	1.1

Shutterstat, Renew

	Chilton Time
All series (.4)	.6

Shutter Air Cylinder, Renew

	Chilton Time
All series (.4)	.6

Shutter Air Tank, Renew

	Chilton Time
All series (.3)	.5

Heater Core, R&R or Renew

	Chilton Time
Series 40-70	
Conv.	
wo/A.C. (1.1)	2.0
w/A.C. (1.3)	2.5
Tilt cab (Isuzu)	
wo/A.C. (1.7)	3.0
Series 80-90	
Bison (1.7)	3.0
Alum tilt cab (2.5)	4.5
All others (1.5)	2.8

Heater Blower Motor, Renew

	Chilton Time
Series 40-70	
Conv. (.3)	.6
Tilt cab (Isuzu) (1.3)	2.5
Series 80-90	
Bison (.4)	.8
Alum tilt cab (.6)	1.1
Conv and steel tilt cab (.9)	1.6

Heater Blower Motor Switch, Renew

	Chilton Time
Series 40-70 (.5)	.7
Series 80-90	
Bison (.5)	.9
Alum tilt cab (.4)	.7
All others (.2)	.4

Heater Blower Motor Resistor, Renew

	Chilton Time
Series 40-70 (.4)	.6

Heater Control Assembly, Renew

	Chilton Time
Series 40-70	
Conv. (.6)	.9
Tilt cab (Isuzu) (1.2)	1.8

LABOR 8 EXHAUST SYSTEM 8 LABOR

(Factory Time) — Chilton Time

Muffler, Renew

	Chilton Time
Series 40-70	
Six(.6)	.9
V-8–conv-one (.4)	.6
two (.6)	.9
Tilt cab-one (.5)	.8
two (.7)	1.0
Diesel	
Isuzu (.4)	.6
Detroit	
8.2L (.5)	.8
Series 80	
cab mounted-one (1.0)	1.4
frame mounted-one (1.0)	1.4
Bison-cab mounted (.8)	1.2
muffler w/Tail pipe (.3)	.4

Exhaust Pipe, Renew

	Chilton Time
Series 40-70	
Six(.5)	.8
V-8–conv-one (.8)	1.2
two (1.1)	1.7
Tilt cab-one (.5)	.8
two (.7)	1.1
Crossover (.7)	1.1
Diesel	
SINGLE EXHAUST	
one piece	
Conv. (.3)	.5
Tilt (.7)	1.1
three piece-one section (.4)	.7
each adtnl (.4)	.4
DUAL EXHAUST	
three piece-one section (.6)	1.0
Series 80-90	
one-front (.7)	1.1
rear (.4)	.7
both-front (1.0)	1.5
rear (.6)	1.0
Crossover (1.1)	1.7
Alum Tilt	
one piece-one (1.2)	1.5
both (1.8)	2.4
three piece-one section (1.0)	1.4
each adtnl (.5)	.7
Bison	
one piece (1.3)	1.8
three piece-each section (1.5)	2.0

Exhaust Crossover Pipe, Renew

	Chilton Time
All series (.8)	1.1

Intermediate Exhaust Pipe, Renew

	Chilton Time
All series (.4)	.6

Exhaust Pipe Packing, Renew

	Chilton Time
Six (.5)	.9
V-8–one (.5)	.9
both (.7)	1.6

Tail Pipe, Renew

(Short Pipe)

	Chilton Time
All series-each (.2)	.4

Exhaust Manifold, R&R or Renew

	Chilton Time
GASOLINE ENGINES	
Six (1.9)	2.6
w/P.S. add (.4)	.4
w/AIR add (.1)	.1
V-8	
350 eng-right (.6)	1.0
left (.9)	1.4
366, 427 engs-each (.8)	1.2
w/A.C. add (.3)	.3
w/AIR add (.5)	.5
w/Air comp. add (.6)	.6
DIESEL ENGINES	
Isuzu Diesel (2.7)	3.6
Deutz Diesel (2.7)	3.6
Detroit Diesel	
6-71 (1.8)	2.4
6V-53, 6V-71, 8V-71-one (1.0)	1.5
12V-71-one (1.8)	2.4

LABOR 9 FRONT SUSPENSION 9 LABOR

(Factory Time)	Chilton Time
Note: On all front suspension operations alignment charges must be added if performed. Time given does not include alignment.	
Check Alignment of Front End	
All series (.7)	.9
Note: Deduct if alignment is performed.	
Align Front End	
12,000 lb axle (1.5)	2.3
All other models (1.3)	2.0
Toe-In, Adjust	
All series (.4)	.7
Front Wheel Bearings, Clean and Repack or Renew Seals	
Series 40-70	
Conv cab	
Drum Brakes	
one side (.5)	.8
both sides (.9)	1.5
Disc Brakes	
one side (.9)	1.2
both sides (1.7)	2.3
Tilt Cab	
Drum Brakes	
one side (1.1)	1.4
both sides (2.2)	2.7
Series 80-90	
one side (.8)	1.1
both sides (1.5)	1.8
Front Wheel Bearings and Cups, Renew (One Wheel)	
Series 40-70	
Conv Cab	
drum brakes (.6)	1.0
disc brakes (.8)	1.4
Tilt Cab	
drum brakes (1.1)	1.5
Series 80-90	
inner (.9)	1.0
outer (.9)	1.0
both (1.0)	1.3
Front Axle 'I' Beam, Renew	
Add alignment charges.	
Series 40-70	
4,000-5,000-7,000-7,500 lb axle	
w/Drum brakes (4.7)	6.5
w/Disc brakes (3.7)	5.5
8,100-9,000-10,800	
12,000 lb axle	
conv (5.7)	7.9
Tilt cab (Isuzu) (6.6)	9.2
Series 80-90	
exc below (7.3)	9.5
F0-70 axle (4.9)	6.8
F0-90 axle (6.6)	8.5

(Factory Time)	Chilton Time
Front Shock Absorber, Renew	
All series-one (.3)	.5
both (.5)	.8
Steering Knuckles, Renew	
Add alignment charges.	
Series 40-70	
4,000-5,000-7,000-7,500 lb axle	
one (1.4)	2.6
both (2.6)	4.5
8,100-9,000-10,800	
12,000 lb axle	
Conv-one (2.0)	2.8
both (3.8)	5.3
Tilt cab (Isuzu)	
one (3.0)	4.2
both (5.9)	8.2
Series 80-90	
exc below	
right side (3.0)	3.8
left side (3.3)	4.2
both sides (5.8)	7.0
F0-70 axle	
one side (1.8)	2.6
both sides (3.4)	4.5
F0-90 axle	
one side (2.8)	3.6
both sides (5.1)	6.1
Renew knuckle arm, add	
each	.5
King Pins and Bushings, Renew	
Add alignment charges.	
Series 40-70	
4,000-5,000-7,000-7,500 lb axle	
one side (1.5)	2.9
both sides (2.6)	5.1
8,100-9,000-10,800	
12,000 lb axle	
Conv.	
one side (2.0)	2.9
both sides (3.7)	5.3
Tilt cab (Isuzu)	
one side (2.1)	3.0
both sides (3.7)	5.4
Series 80-90	
exc below	
one side (3.3)	4.2
both sides (5.8)	8.0
F0-70 axle	
one side (1.8)	2.6
both sides (3.4)	4.5
F0-90 axle	
one side (2.8)	3.6
both sides (5.1)	6.1

(Factory Time)	Chilton Time
Front Springs, Renew	
Series 40-70-Conv-one (1.4)	1.8
both (2.7)	3.5
Tilt cab (Isuzu)	
one (2.1)	2.9
both (3.9)	5.4
Series 80-90	
exc below-one (1.4)	2.0
both (2.7)	3.8
Tilt cab-one (1.7)	2.5
both (3.3)	4.5
Front Spring Leaves, Renew	
Series 40-70-Conv-one (1.6)	2.3
both (3.0)	4.5
Tilt cab (Isuzu)	
one (2.3)	3.2
both (4.5)	6.3
Series 80-90	
exc below-one (1.9)	2.5
both (3.7)	4.8
Tilt cab-one (2.1)	3.0
both (4.1)	5.5
Front Spring Center Bolt, Renew	
Series 40-70-Conv-one (1.5)	2.0
both (3.0)	3.9
Tilt cab (Isuzu)	
one (2.1)	3.0
both (3.9)	5.5
Series 80-90-one (1,6)	2.5
both (3.2)	4.9
Front Spring Shackle, Renew	
Series 40-70-one (1.2)	1.6
both (2.0)	3.0
Series 80-90	
exc below-one (.7)	1.0
both (1.3)	1.8
Tilt cab-one (1.2)	1.5
both (2.3)	2.8
Renew bushing add (.5)	.8
Front Hub, Renew (One)	
All series	
five & six stud disc whl (1.2)	1.4
8 stud disc whl (2.1)	2.5
ten stud disc whl (1.5)	1.8
cast spoke whl (1.4)	1.6
Front Spring Shackle and/or Pins, Renew (Shackle End Only)	
Series 40-70	
Conv-one side (1.2)	1.7
Tilt-one side (.5)	.8
Series 80-90	
Bison-one side (1.6)	2.1
Tilt cab-one side (1.2)	1.7
All others-one side (.7)	1.2
Renew spring bushing add-each (.3)	.5

LABOR 10 STEERING LINKAGE 10 LABOR

(Factory Time)	Chilton Time
Tie Rods or Ends, Renew	
Includes: Reset toe-in.	
Series 40-70	
one (.7)	1.0
two (1.0)	1.3
Series 80-90	
each side (.7)	1.2
Steering Knuckle Arm, Renew	
Includes: Reset toe-in.	
Series 40-70	
4-5-7-7,500 lb axle (.9)	1.2
8,100-9,000 lb axle (1.1)	1.4

(Factory Time)	Chilton Time
10,800 lb axle (1.0)	1.5
12,000 lb axle (.9)	1.5
Series 80-90	
exc below	
upper (.3)	.6
lower (.7)	1.0
F0-70 axle-right (.9)	1.4
left (1.0)	1.4
F0-90 axle-right (1.0)	1.4
left (1.1)	1.5
Drag Link, Renew or Recondition	
Series 40-70 (.4)	.7

(Factory Time)	Chilton Time
Series 80-90	
exc below (.5)	.9
Alum Tilt (.8)	1.1
Renew pitman arm add (.2)	.2
Pitman Arm, Renew	
Series 40-70	
conv (.4)	.8
Tilt cab (.6)	1.0
Series 80-90	
conv (.4)	.7
Steel Tilt (.5)	.8
Alum Tilt (1.4)	1.8

LABOR 11 STEERING GEAR 11 LABOR

(Factory Time) Chilton Time

STANDARD STEERING

Steering Gear, Adjust (On Truck)

Includes: Steering gear, drag link tie rods, wheel bearings and toe-in adjustments.

Series 40-60
- Conv (1.0) 1.2
- Tilt cab (Isuzu) (.4) 6

Series 70-90 (1.2) 1.5

Steering Gear, R&R

Series 40-70
- conv (.7) 1.3

Series 80-90
- conv (1.9) 2.8
- Steel Tilt (1.2) 1.8
- Alum Tilt (1.5) 2.0

Steering Gear, R&R and Recondition

Includes: Disassemble, inspect, clean, renew necessary parts, reassemble and adjust.

Series 40-70
- conv (1.6) 2.6

Series 80-90
- conv (3.4) 4.7
- Steel Tilt (2.7) 3.7
- Alum Tilt (3.0) 3.9

Upper Mast Jacket Bearings, Renew

Series 40-70 (.7) 1.0

Series 80-90
- exc below (.7) 1.0
- Alum Tilt (1.9) 2.5

Steering Wheel, Renew

All series (.3) 5

Intermediate Steering and/or Lower Coupling Shaft, Renew

Series 40-70
- conv cab (1.0) 1.4

Series 80-90
- Tilt cab (1.2) 1.6
- Bruin (1.0) 1.4

Pitman Shaft Seal, Renew

Does not include reseting toe-in.

Series 40-70
- semi-integral system (.4) 7
- integral system
  - conv (.5) 1.0
  - Tilt cab (Isuzu) (2.0) 2.8

Series 80-90
- alum tilt (2.4) 3.0
- conv cab (2.2) 2.8

(Factory Time) Chilton Time

POWER STEERING

Trouble Shoot Power Steering

Includes: Check pounds pull on steering wheel, install checking gauges, test pump pressure and check for external leaks.

All models (.7) 7

Power Steering Hoses, Renew

Series 40-70
- pump to gear (.6) 7
- gear to cyl (.5) 6
- cooler hoses-one (.5) 7
  - both (.7) 9

Series 80-90
- Bison-with Detroit Diesel (1.0) 1.4

All others-each (.5) 9

Power Steering Pump Flow Control Valve Assy., Renew

Series 40-70
- wo/Integral system (.5) 7
- w/Integral system (1.1) 1.6

Power Cylinder, Renew

All series
- axle mount (.5) 1.1
- frame mount (.6) 1.2

Power Cylinder, R&R and Recondition

All series
- axle mount (1.0) 1.6
- frame mount (1.1) 1.7

Power Steering Gear, Renew

Series 40-70
- conv cab-
  - wo/Integral system (1.3) 2.0
- conv cab-
  - w/Integral system (2.2) 3.3
- Tilt cab (1.5) 2.2

Series 80-90
- conv cab (2.1) 2.7
- alum tilt (2.3) 3.0

Power Steering Gear, R&R and Recondition

Series 40-70
- conv cab-
  - wo/Integral system (2.9) 4.3
- conv cab-
  - w/Integral system (3.8) 5.7
- Tilt cab (3.2) 4.8

Series 80-90
- conv cab (4.7) 5.8
- alum tilt (4.9) 6.0

(Factory Time) Chilton Time

Power Steering Pump, Renew

Series 40-70

Six (.7) 1.2

V-8
- w/Vacuum brks (.7) 1.2
- w/Air brks (1.8) 2.4

Diesel
- Isuzu (.8) 1.2
- Detroit 8.2L
  - w/Vacuum brks (1.5) 2.0
  - w/Air brks (1.9) 2.7
- Caterpillar
  - 3208 (1.0) 1.5
- Deutz (1.2) 1.7
- Series 80-90
  - Bison-w/Detroit Diesel (5.4) 6.0
- All othérs (.8) 1.2

Power Steering Pump, R&R and Recondition

Series 40-70

Six (1.7) 2.2

V-8
- w/Vacuum brks (1.6) 2.1
- w/Air brks (2.6) 3.5

Diesel
- Isuzu (1.9) 2.5
- Detroit 8.2L
  - w/Vacuum brks (2.3) 3.1
  - w/Air brks (2.7) 3.6
- Caterpillar
  - 3208 (1.8) 2.4
- Deutz (2.2) 2,9
- Series 80-90
  - Bison-w/Detroit Diesel (6.0) 7.3
- All others (1.4) 2.1

Power Steering Reservoir, Renew (Remote)

Includes: Bleed hydraulic system.

All series (.5) 9

Power Steering Oil Cooler, Renew

Series 40-70
- Alligator Hood (.9) 1.4
- Tilt Hood (.5) 8

Series 80-90 (.4) 8

w/A.C. add (.3) 3

Pump Drive Belt, Renew

Series 40-70
- Six (.2) 4
- V-8
  - 350 eng (.2) 4
  - 366, 427 engs (1.0) 1.5
- Cat (.3) 5

LABOR 12 CYLINDER HEAD & VALVE SYSTEM 12 LABOR

(Factory Time) Chilton Time

GASOLINE ENGINES

Cylinder Head Gasket, Renew

Includes: R&R all normal interfering parts. Check cylinder head and block flatness. Adjust carburetor, valves (if adjustable) and ignition timing (when distributor is removed.)

Six–conv (3.9) 5.8
- Tilt cab (5.1) 6.8

w/P.S. add (.4) 4

w/AIR add (.6) 6

V-8–307, 350 engs
- conv
  - one (3.9) 6.3
  - both (5.8) 9.5
- Tilt cab
  - one (5.8) 7.3
  - both (7.7) 9.7

(Factory Time) Chilton Time

V-8–366, 427, 454 engs
- conv
  - one (4.4) 7.0
  - both (7.1) 10.7
- Tilt cab
  - one (6.5) 8.2
  - both (9.1) 11.4

w/A.C. add (1.0) 1.0

w/P.S. add (.5) 5

w/Air inj add (.5) 5

w/Air comp add (.5) 5

Cylinder Head, Renew

Includes: R&R all interfering parts. Check cylinder head flatness. Transfer all necessary components. Clean, reface and lap valves. Check valve spring tension, assembled height and valve head runout. Adjust carburetor, valves and distributor.

(Factory Time) Chilton Time

Six–conv (5.9) 7.8
- Tilt cab (6.0) 7.9

w/P.S. add (.4) 4

w/AIR add (.6) 6

V-8–307, 350 engs
- conv
  - one (4.3) 6.9
  - both (6.6) 10.4
- Tilt cab
  - one (6.8) 8.5
  - both (9.6) 12.2

V-8–366, 427, 454 engs
- conv
  - one (5.7) 8.4
  - both (9.4) 14.6

LABOR 12 CYLINDER HEAD & VALVE SYSTEM 12 LABOR

(Factory Time) Chilton Time

Tilt cab
one (7.6)........ 9.6
w/A.C. add (1.0)........ 1.0
w/P.S. add (.5)........ .5
w/Air inj add (.5)........ .5
w/Air comp add (.5)........ .5

Clean Carbon and Grind Valves

Includes: R&R cylinder head and all interfering parts. Check cylinder head and block flatness. Clean, inspect and recondition or renew all necessary components. Check valve spring tension, assembled height and valve runout. Tune engine.

Six–conv (6.8)........ 8.7
Tilt cab (7.6)........ 9.8
w/P.S. add (.4)........ .4
w/AIR add (.6)........ .6
V-8–307, 350 engs
conv (10.5)........ 14.4
Tilt cab (10.7)........ 14.5
V-8–366, 427, 454 engs
conv (10.8)........ 16.5
Tilt cab (14.2)........ 16.9
w/A.C. add (1.0)........ 1.0
w/P.S. add (.5)........ .5
w/Air inj add (.4)........ .4
w/Air comp add (.5)........ .5

Valve Cover Gasket, Renew

Six–conv (.7)........ 1.0
Tilt cab (.9)........ 1.2
V-8–307, 350 engs
conv-one (.4)........ .6
both (.6)........ .9
Tilt cab-one (.4)........ .6
both (.7)........ .9
V-8–366, 427, 454 engs
one (.5)........ .8
both (.8)........ 1.2

Push Rod Cover Gasket, Renew

Six–front (.5)........ .7
rear (.2)........ .4
both (.6)........ 1.0

Push Rods or Rocker Arms, Renew

Six–conv
one cyl(.7)........ 1.2
all cyls (1.0)........ 1.6
Tilt cab
one or two (1.2)........ 1.6
three or more (1.5)........ 2.0
V-8–conv-one cyl (.5)........ 1.0
one cyl-each side (1.0)........ 1.5
all cyls-both sides (1.5)........ 2.2
Tilt cab
one or two
same bank (.5)........ .7
three or more
same bank (.8)........ 1.0
all-both banks (1.4)........ 1.9
w/A.C. add (1.0)........ 1.0
w/Air comp add (.5)........ .5

Valve Lifters, Renew (All)

Includes: R&R intake manifold and all other interfering parts. Adjust valves, carburetor and ignition timing, where required.

Six–conv (1.3)........ 2.0
Tilt cab (2.2)........ 3.5
w/AIR add (.2)........ .2
V-8–307, 350 engs
conv (2.8)........ 4.0
Tilt cab (4.3)........ 5.5
V-8–366, 427, 454 engs
conv (3.7)........ 5.5
Tilt cab (4.7)........ 6.0
w/A.C. add (1.0)........ 1.0
w/Air inj add (.5)........ .5
w/Air comp add (.5)........ .5

COMBINATIONS

(Factory Time) Chilton Time

Add to Valve Job

VALVE GUIDES, REAM FOR OVERSIZE STEMS
Each (.2)........ .2

ROCKER ARM STUD, RENEW
One (.4)........ .4
Each adtnl (.2)........ .2

DISTRIBUTOR, RECONDITION
All series (.6)........ .9
w/Spinney gov on
V-8 add (.5)........ .5

CARBURETOR, RECONDITION
1 BBL (.7)........ 1.0
2 BBL (1.2)........ 1.4
4 BBL-exc below (1.7)........ 1.9
Holley........ 3.5

(Factory Time) Chilton Time

Valve Springs or Seals, Renew (All)

Includes: R&R valve covers and adjust valves.

Six–conv (2.3)........ 3.2
Tilt cab (2.3)........ 3.2
w/AIR add (.2)........ .2
V-8–307, 350 engs
conv (3.7)........ 5.0
Tilt cab (2.8)........ 4.0
V-8–366, 427, 454 engs (2.8)........ 4.0
w/A.C. add (1.0)........ 1.0
w/Air inj add (.5)........ .5
w/Air comp add (.5)........ .5

DIESEL ENGINES

Cylinder Head Gasket, Renew

Includes: R&R all normal interfering parts. Check cylinder head and block for flatness. Adjust valves and crossheads.

Isuzu Diesel (5.8)........ 8.2
Detroit Diesel
6-71 (8.1)........ 10.2
6V-53, 6V-71-one (6.0)........ 7.5
both (11.5)........ 14.5
8V-71-one (6.2)........ 7.8
both (11.9)........ 15.0
12V-71-one (7.2)........ 9.1
both (13.9)........ 17.5
w/A.C. add (.3)........ .3
w/P.S. add (.2)........ .2

Cylinder Head, Renew

Includes: R&R all normal interfering parts clean carbon from pistons and block. Check cylinder head and block flatness. Transfer all necessary components. Clean, lap and reface valves. Check valve spring tension, assembled height and valve runout. Adjust valves and crossheads.

Isuzu Diesel (10.1)........ 14.3
Deutz Diesel
one cyl (4.6)........ 6.2
all cyls (13.0)........ 17.7
Detroit Diesel
6-71 (17.2)........ 21.5
6V-53, 6V-71-one (10.6)........ 13.3
both (20.7)........ 26.0
8V-71-one (12.0)........ 15.0
both (23.4)........ 29.5

COMBINATIONS

DIESEL ENGINES

Add to Valve Job

ROCKER ARM STUD, RENEW
One (.4)........ .4

ROCKER ARM ASSEMBLY, DISASSEMBLE, CLEAN AND REASSEMBLE
Detroit Diesel
Each cyl (.5)........ .7

VALVE GUIDES, REAM FOR OVERSIZE STEMS
One (.2)........ .2
Each adtnl (.1)........ .1

INJECTOR, RENEW
Each (.2)........ .3

INJECTOR, RECONDITION
Each (.4)........ .5

ADJUST GOVERNOR
All series (.5)........ .6

(Factory Time) Chilton Time

12V-71-one (16.8)........ 21.0
both (30.4)........ 38.0
w/A.C. add (.3)........ .3
w/P.S. add (.2)........ .2
Adjust Governor add (.5)........ .5

Clean Carbon and Grind Valves

Includes: R&R head and all normal interfering parts. Check cylinder head and block flatness, magnaflux head. Clean, inspect and recondition all components as necessary. Pressure test head. Check spring tension, assembled height and valve runout. Adjust valves, crossheads and injectors. Road test.

Isuzu Diesel (7.6)........ 10.8
Deutz Diesel
one cyl (4.4)........ 6.0
all cyls (11.5)........ 15.6
Detroit Diesel
6-71 (19.0)........ 23.8
6V-53, 6V-71 (22.9)........ 28.7
8V-71 (26.0)........ 32.5
12V-71 (33.4)........ 42.0
w/A.C. add (.3)........ .3
w/P.S. add (.2)........ .2

Adjust Valves and Crossheads

Detroit Diesel
6-71 (1.2)........ 1.5
6V-53, 6V-71 (1.6)........ 2.0
8V-71 (1.8)........ 2.5
12V-71 (2.2)........ 2.8

Valve Cover Gasket, Renew

Isuzu Diesel (.7)........ 1.0
Deutz Diesel
one (.2)........ .4
each adtnl (.1)........ .2
Detroit Diesel
each (.4)........ .7

Valve Push Rods, Renew

Isuzu Diesel
one cyl (1.2)........ 1.7
all cyls (1.5)........ 2.1
Deutz Diesel
one cyl (.3)........ .5
all cyls (1.5)........ 2.0

LABOR 12 CYLINDER HEAD & VALVE SYSTEM 12 LABOR

(Factory Time)	Chilton Time
Detroit Diesel	
one cyl (1.2)	1.6
six cyls (5.7)	7.2
eight cyls (6.8)	8.5
twelve cyls (12.0)	15.0

Valve Lifters, Renew (All)

(Factory Time)	Chilton Time
Isuzu Diesel (2.0)	2.9
Deutz Diesel	
one cyl (12.6)	17.0
all cyls (12.8)	17.5
Detroit Diesel	
Six (5.7)	7.3
V-6 (5.7)	7.3
V-8 (6.8)	8.4
V-12 (12.0)	14.8

Valve Springs, Caps or Seals, Renew (All)

(Factory Time)	Chilton Time
Isuzu Diesel	
one cyl (1.4)	2.0
all cyls (2.7)	3.8
Deutz Diesel	
one cyl (.4)	.7
all cyls (2.1)	3.0
Detroit Diesel	
Six (7.3)	9.5
V-6 (7.3)	9.5
V-8 (9.3)	12.0
V-12 (13.3)	17.0

Valve Rocker Arms, Renew

(Factory Time)	Chilton Time
Isuzu Diesel	
one cyl (1.1)	1.6
all cyls (1.6)	2.3
Deutz Diesel	
one cyl (.3)	.5
all cyls (1.4)	1.9

Valve Push Rod Guides, Springs and Seals, Renew

(Factory Time)	Chilton Time
Deutz Diesel	
one cyl (2.5)	3.4
all cyls (6.4)	8.7

LABOR 13 ENGINE ASSEMBLY & MOUNTS 13 LABOR

GASOLINE ENGINES

Engine Assembly, Remove and Reinstall

Includes: R&R all normal interfering parts. Does not include transfer of any components.

(Factory Time)	Chilton Time
Six–conv (5.7)	8.8
Tilt cab (7.4)	9.7
w/P.S. add (.4)	.4
w/AIR add (.6)	.6
V-8–307, 350 engs	
conv (4.4)	6.0
Tilt cab (7.2)	9.3
V-8–366, 427, 454 engs	
366 eng	
conv (5.1)	6.5
Tilt cab (7.7)	10.0
427 eng-conv (8.0)	10.2
Tilt cab (9.3)	12.0
454 eng-conv (8.0)	10.2
Tilt cab (9.3)	12.0
w/A.C. add (1.0)	1.0
w/P.S. add (.5)	.5
w/Air inj add (.4)	.4
w/Air comp add (.9)	.9

Engine Assembly, Renew

Includes: R&R all normal interfering parts. Transfer all necessary components. Tune engine and road test.

(Factory Time)	Chilton Time
Six–conv (7.2)	10.2
Tilt cab (8.2)	10.8
w/P.S. add (.4)	.4
w/AIR add (.6)	.6
V-8–307, 350 engs	
conv (5.9)	8.8
Tilt cab (8.7)	11.5
V-8–366, 427, 454 engs	
366 eng	
conv (8.6)	12.0
Tilt cab (9.4)	12.2
427 eng-conv (9.7)	12.8
Tilt cab (11.0)	14.8
454 eng-conv (8.6)	12.8
Tilt cab (11.0)	14.8
w/A.C. add (1.0)	1.0
w/P.S. add (.5)	.5
w/Air inj add (.4)	.4
w/Air comp add (.9)	.9

Engine Assembly, Renew (Universal)

Includes: R&R engine assy. Transfer all component parts not supplied with replacement engine.

(Factory Time)	Chilton Time
V-8–350 eng	
conv cab (7.6)	11.0
V-8–366, 427 engs	
conv cab (9.8)	14.2
w/A.C. add (1.0)	1.0
w/P.S. add (.5)	.5
w/AIR add (.4)	.4
w/Air comp add (.9)	.9
w/Eng oil cooler add (.4)	.4

Cylinder Assembly (Short Engine), Renew & Grind Valves

Includes: R&R all normal interfering parts. Transfer all necessary parts and equipment. Check valve spring tension, valve seat and head runout, head flatness, stem to guide clearance and assembled height. Tune engine and road test.

(Factory Time)	Chilton Time
Six–conv (12.1)	15.9
Tilt cab (14.6)	18.7
w/P.S. add (.4)	.4
w/AIR add (.6)	.6
V-8–307, 350 engs	
conv (14.7)	18.9
Tilt cab (17.1)	21.9
V-8–366, 427, 454 engs	
366 eng	
conv (16.1)	20.6
Tilt cab (18.7)	23.9
427 eng-conv (19.0)	24.2
Tilt cab (19.3)	24.7
454 eng-conv (19.0)	24.2
Tilt cab (19.3)	24.7
w/A.C. add (1.0)	1.0
w/P.S. add (.5)	.5
w/Air inj add (.4)	.4
w/Air comp add (.9)	.9

Engine Assembly, R&R and Recondition (Complete)

Includes: R&R all normal interfering parts. Disassemble and assemble complete engine. Inspect all components. Rebore block. Install new pistons, rings and pins. Align rods. Plastigauge and install new main and rod bearings. Clean carbon and grind valves, test hydraulic tappets, renew if necessary. Renew all gaskets and seals as necessary. Tune engine and road test.

(Factory Time)	Chilton Time
Six–conv (26.5)	34.4
Tilt cab (28.2)	35.4
w/P.S. add (.4)	.4
w/AIR add (.6)	.6
V-8–307, 350 engs	
conv (31.8)	39.8
Tilt cab (34.6)	43.3
V-8–366, 427, 454 engs	
366 eng	
conv (33.1)	41.5
Tilt cab (35.7)	44.7
427 eng-conv (36.0)	45.0
Tilt cab (37.3)	46.7
454 eng-conv (36.0)	45.0
Tilt cab (37.3)	46.7
w/A.C. add (1.0)	1.0
w/P.S. add (.5)	.5
w/Air inj add (.4)	.4
w/Air comp add (.9)	.9

Engine Mounts, Renew (Both)

(Factory Time)	Chilton Time
Front	
Six(.5)	1.0
V-8–307, 350 eng	
conv (.5)	1.0
Tilt cab (.7)	1.2
V-8–366, 427, 454 engs (.5)	1.0
Rear	
Six (.6)	1.0
V-8–307, 350 eng	
conv (.5)	.8
Tilt cab (.7)	1.1
V-8–366, 427, 454 engs	
All series (.8)	1.3

DIESEL ENGINES

Engine Assembly, Remove and Reinstall

Includes: R&R all normal interfering parts. Does not include transfer of any components.

(Factory Time)	Chilton Time
Detroit Diesel	
6-71-conv (11.6)	14.6
Alum Tilt (11.2)	14.1
6V-53-conv (11.0)	13.8
Steel Tilt (10.0)	12.5
6V-71-Steel Tilt (12.0)	15.1
8V-71-conv (14.1)	17.7
Alum Tilt (13.5)	18.0
12V-71-Alum Tilt (19.0)	23.5
w/A.C. add (1.0)	1.0
w/P.S. add (.8)	.8
w/Pwr take off add (.3)	.3

Engine Assembly, Renew

Includes: R&R all normal interfering parts. Transfer all necessary components. Tune engine and road test.

(Factory Time)	Chilton Time
Deutz Diesel	
All series (7.0)	10.0
Detroit Diesel	
6-71-conv (14.1)	17.7
Alum Tilt (13.7)	17.2
6V-53-conv (13.5)	17.0
Steel Tilt (12.5)	15.7
6V-71-Steel Tilt (14.5)	18.2
8V-71-conv (16.6)	20.9
Alum Tilt (16.0)	20.0
12V-71-Alum Tilt (22.2)	27.8

LABOR 13 ENGINE ASSEMBLY & MOUNTS 13 LABOR

(Factory Time)	Chilton Time
w/A.C. add (1.0)	1.0
w/P.S. add (.8)	.8
w/Pwr take off add (.3)	.3

Cylinder Block, Renew

Includes: R&R all normal interfering parts. Transfer all components without disassembly. Install new main and rod bearings. Renew all necessary seals and gaskets. Adjust timing and clearances. Road test.
Does not include reconditioning of any components.

(Factory Time)	Chilton Time
Isuzu Diesel (27.6)	39.2
w/P.S. add (.4)	.4
Detroit Diesel	
6-71-conv (44.6)	50.2
Alum Tilt (44.4)	50.0
6V-53-conv (43.0)	48.4
Steel Tilt (42.0)	47.3
6V-71-Steel Tilt (48.0)	53.9
8V-71-conv (51.1)	57.4
Alum Tilt (50.5)	56.6
12V-71-Alum Tilt (64.0)	71.5
w/A.C. add (1.0)	1.0
w/P.S. add (.8)	.8
w/Pwr take off add (.3)	.3

Engine Assembly, R&R and Recondition (Complete)

Includes: R&R all normal interfering parts. Complete disassembly and assembly of engine. Pressure test block and head. Plastigauge and renew main, rod and camshaft bearings. Install new pistons, rings, pins and liners. Rebore block. Recondition blower or turbocharger, water and injector pump, oil pump, injectors and governor. Clean carbon and grind valves. Check and set all clearances. Tune engine and road test.

(Factory Time)	Chilton Time
Detroit Diesel	
6-71-conv (72.6)	80.0
Alum Tilt (72.2)	79.6
6V-53-conv (73.0)	80.4
Steel Tilt (72.0)	79.3
6V-71-Steel Tilt (76.0)	83.7
8V-71-conv (84.1)	92.7
Alum Tilt (83.5)	92.0
12V-71-Alum Tilt (93.0)	102.5
w/A.C. add (1.0)	1.0
w/P.S. add (.8)	.8
w/Pwr take off add (.3)	.3

Engine Mounts, Renew

(Factory Time)	Chilton Time
Deutz Diesel	
Front (.5)	.8
Rear-one (.5)	.7
both (.9)	1.3
Detroit Diesel	
Front 6-71 (1.2)	1.6
6V-53 (2.8)	3.5
6V-71 (2.3)	2.9
8V-71 (2.3)	2.9
12V-71 (3.0)	3.8
Rear-right (.4)	.7
left (.7)	1.0

LABOR 14 PISTONS, RINGS & BEARINGS 14 LABOR

GASOLINE ENGINES

Rings, Pins and Main Bearings, Renew and Grind Valves

Includes: R&R all normal interfering parts. Remove cylinder top ridge, hone cylinder walls, clean ring grooves, install new rings. Install new pins and align rods. Plastigauge and install new main and rod bearings. Renew gaskets and seals as necessary. Clean carbon and grind valves. Test valve spring tension, valve seat and head runout, stem to guide clearance, head and block flatness and assembled height. Tune engine and road test.

(Factory Time)	Chilton Time
Six-conv (15.5)	19.7
Tilt cab (16.1)	20.3
w/P.S. add (.4)	.4
w/AIR add (.6)	.6
V-8-307, 350 engs	
conv (19.6)	25.8
Tilt cab (21.2)	27.8
V-8-366, 427, 454 engs	
conv (23.1)	30.9
Tilt cab (23.9)	31.3
w/A.C. add (1.0)	1.0
w/P.S. add (.8)	.8
w/Air inj add (.4)	.4
w/Air comp add (.6)	.6

Rings, Pins, Rod and Main Bearings, Renew

Includes: R&R all normal interfering parts. Remove cylinder top ridge, hone cylinder walls, clean ring grooves, install new rings. Install new pins and align rods. Plastigauge and install new main and rod bearings. Renew gaskets and seals as necessary. Tune engine and road test.

(Factory Time)	Chilton Time
Six-conv (14.0)	17.1
Tilt cab (14.6)	17.7
w/P.S. add (.4)	.4
w/AIR add (.6)	.6
V-8-307, 350 engs	
conv (17.6)	22.1
Tilt cab (19.2)	24.1
V-8-366, 427, 454 engs	
conv (21.1)	27.2
Tilt cab (21.9)	27.6
w/A.C. add (1.0)	1.0
w/P.S. add (.8)	.8
w/Air inj add (.4)	.4
w/Air comp add (.6)	.6

COMBINATIONS

(Factory Time)	Chilton Time
VALVE GUIDES, REAM FOR OVERSIZE STEMS	
Each (.2)	.2
ROCKER ARM STUD, RENEW	
One (.4)	.4
Additional (.2)	.2
DISTRIBUTOR, RECONDITION	
All series (.6)	.9
w/Spinner gov on V-8 add (.5)	.5
CARBURETOR, RECONDITION	
1 BBL (.7)	1.0
2 BBL (1.2)	1.4
4 BBL-exc below (1.7)	1.9
Holley	3.5
REMOVE CYLINDER TOP RIDGE	
Each (.1)	.1
DEGLAZE CYLINDER WALLS	
Six (.7)	.8
V-8 (.9)	1.0
OIL PUMP, RECONDITION	
All series (1.0)	1.2
MAIN BEARINGS, RENEW	
Six (2.0)	2.5
V-8 (1.4)	2.0
PLASTIGAUGE BEARINGS	
Each (.1)	.1

Rings, Pins and Rod Bearings, Renew

Includes: R&R all normal interfering parts. Remove cylinder top ridge, hone cylinder walls, clean ring grooves, install new rings. Install new pins and align rods. Plastigauge and install new rod bearings. Renew gaskets and seals as necessary. Tune engine and road test.

(Factory Time)	Chilton Time
Six-conv (11.2)	13.4
Tilt cab (11.8)	14.0
w/P.S. add (.4)	.4
w/AIR add (.6)	.6
V-8-307, 350 engs	
conv (15.6)	18.9
Tilt cab (17.2)	20.9
V-8-366, 427, 454 engs	
conv (19.1)	24.0
Tilt cab (19.9)	24.4
w/A.C. add (1.0)	1.0
w/P.S. add (.8)	.8
w/Air inj add (.4)	.4
w/Air comp add (.6)	.6

Rings, Renew

Includes: R&R all normal interfering parts. Remove cylinder top ridge, hone cylinder walls, clean ring grooves, install new rings. Renew gaskets and seals as necessary.

(Factory Time)	Chilton Time
Six-conv (7.6)	10.0
Tilt cab (8.4)	10.6
w/P.S. add (.4)	.4
w/AIR add (.6)	.6
V-8-307, 350 engs	
conv (10.8)	14.7
Tilt cab (13.0)	16.7
V-8-366, 427, 454 engs	
conv (14.9)	19.8
Tilt cab (15.7)	20.2
w/A.C. add (1.0)	1.0
w/P.S. add (.8)	.8
w/Air inj add (.4)	.4
w/Air comp add (.6)	.6

Piston, Renew (One)

Includes: R&R all normal interfering parts. Remove cylinder top ridge, hone cylinder walls. Install new piston with rings.

(Factory Time)	Chilton Time
Six-conv (5.6)	7.0
Tilt cab (6.9)	8.9

LABOR 14 PISTONS, RINGS & BEARINGS 14 LABOR

(Factory Time)	Chilton Time
w/P.S. add (.4)	.4
w/AIR add (.6)	.6
V-8–307, 350 engs	
conv (6.2)	8.5
Tilt cab (7.3)	9.0
V-8–366, 427, 454 engs	
conv (7.0)	9.9
Tilt cab (8.8)	11.1
w/A.C. add (1.0)	1.0
w/P.S. add (.8)	.8
w/Air inj add (.4)	.4
w/Air comp add (.6)	.6

Rod Bearings, Renew

Includes: R&R oil pan.

Six–conv (2.4)	4.4
Tilt cab (3.0)	4.8
V-8–307, 350 engs	
conv (2.4)	3.9
Tilt cab (3.3)	4.0
V-8–366, 427, 454 engs	
conv (3.4)	5.2
Tilt cab (3.6)	5.4

DIESEL ENGINES

Rings, Pins, and Main Bearings, Renew and Grind Valves.

Includes: R&R all normal interfering parts. Remove cylinder top ridge, hone cylinder liner walls, clean ring grooves, install new rings. Install new pins and align rods. Plastigauge and install new main and rod bearings. Renew gaskets and seals as necessary. Clean carbon and grind valves. Clean oil pump. Set injection timing and valves and crossheads. Road test.

Does not include renew liners.

Isuzu Diesel (16.0)	23.2
Detroit Diesel	
6-71 (32.7)	39.4
6V-53, 6V-71 (36.3)	43.1
8V-71 (42.0)	48.8
12V-71 (60.1)	69.6
w/A.C. add (1.0)	1.0
w/P.S. add (.2)	.2
w/Pwr take off add (.3)	.3

Rings, Pins, Rod and Main Bearings, Renew

Includes: R&R all normal interfering parts. Remove cylinder top ridge, hone cylinder liner walls, clean ring grooves, install new rings. Install new pins and align rods. Plastigauge and install new main and rod bearings. Renew gaskets and seals as necessary. Clean oil pump. Set injection timing and valves and crossheads. Road test.

Does not include renew liners.

Isuzu Diesel (14.2)	20.5
Detroit Diesel	
6-71 (23.6)	28.4
6V-53, 6V-71 (24.0)	30.1
8V-71 (27.8)	32.8
12V-71 (40.2)	48.6
w/A.C. add (1.0)	1.0
w/P.S. add (.2)	.2

COMBINATIONS

Engine Combinations

(Factory Time)	Chilton Time
ROCKER ARM ASSEMBLY, DISASSEMBLE, CLEAN AND REASSEMBLE	
Detroit Diesel	
Each cyl (.5)	.7
VALVE GUIDES, REAM FOR OVERSIZE STEMS	
One (.2)	.2
each adtnl (.1)	.1
INJECTOR, RENEW	
Each (.2)	.3
INJECTOR, RECONDITION	
Each (.4)	.5
ADJUST GOVERNOR	
All series (.5)	.6
PRESSURE TEST HEAD	
Six (1.5)	1.5
V-6–Each (1.0)	1.0
V-8–Each (1.2)	1.2
MAIN BEARINGS, RENEW	
Isuzu Diesel	
Each (.4)	.5
Deutz Diesel	
Each (.4)	.5
Detroit Diesel	
6-71 (3.7)	4.7
6V-53, 6V-71 (2.2)	2.8
8V-71 (2.7)	3.4
12V-71 (3.6)	4.6
PLASTIGAUGE BEARINGS	
Each (.1)	.1
OIL PUMP, RECONDITION	
Detroit Diesel	
Exc below (.4)	.7
6-71 (1.0)	1.4
12V-71 (2.0)	2.6
Isuzu Diesel (.5)	.6

Rings, Pins and Rod Bearings, Renew

Includes: R&R all normal interfering parts. Remove cylinder top ridge, hone cylinder liner walls, clean ring grooves, install new rings. Install new pins and align rods. Plastigauge and install new rod bearings. Renew gaskets and seals as necessary. Clean oil pump. Set injection timing and valves and crossheads. Road test.

Does not include renew liners.

(Factory Time)	Chilton Time
Isuzu Diesel	
all cyls (11.4)	16.5
Deutz Diesel	
one cyl (5.2)	7.0
all cyls (16.5)	22.5
Detroit Diesel	
6-71 (19.9)	23.9
6V-53, 6V-71 (22.6)	27.6
8V-71 (25.1)	29.3
12V-71 (36.6)	44.1
w/A.C. add (1.0)	1.0
w/P.S. add (.2)	.2

Rings, Renew

Includes: R&R all normal interfering parts. Remove cylinder top ridge, hone cylinder liner walls, clean ring grooves, install new rings. Renew gaskets and seals as necessary. Set injection timing and valves and crossheads. Road test.

Isuzu Diesel	
one cyl (7.6)	11.0
all cyls (9.6)	13.9
Deutz Diesel	
one cyl (4.5)	6.0
all cyls (12.3)	16.7
Detroit Diesel	
6-71 (16.0)	20.0
6V-53, 6V-71 (19.8)	24.8
8V-71 (21.5)	25.7
12V-71 (29.8)	37.3
w/A.C. add (1.0)	1.0
w/P.S. add (.2)	.2

Piston and Liner, Renew (One)

Includes: R&R all normal interfering parts. Hone block bore, check liner height, liner bore and O.D. for proper fit. Install new liner, piston with rings and pin. Renew gaskets and seals as necessary. Set injection timing and valves and crossheads.

Isuzu Diesel	
one cyl (8.1)	11.7
all cyls (10.2)	14.8
Deutz Diesel	
one cyl (4.9)	6.6
all cyls (15.0)	20.5
Detroit Diesel	
6-71 (13.0)	16.7
6V-53, 6V-71 (9.2)	11.7
8V-71 (9.6)	12.3
12V-71 (13.0)	17.0
w/A.C. add (1.0)	1.0
w/P.S. add (.2)	.2
w/Pwr take off add (.3)	.3

Rod Bearings, Renew

Includes: R&R oil pan. Clean oil pump.

Isuzu Diesel	
one (1.6)	2.3
all (2.6)	4.8
Deutz Diesel	
one (1.5)	2.0
all (4.8)	6.5
Detroit Diesel	
6-71 (4.1)	5.4
6V-53, 6V-71 (3.6)	5.0
8V-71 (4.2)	5.5
12V-71 (5.5)	7.2

LABOR 15 CRANKSHAFT & DAMPER 15 LABOR

GASOLINE ENGINES

Crankshaft and Main Bearings, Renew

Includes: R&R all normal interfering parts and engine. Plastigauge and install new bearings. Recondition oil pump.

Six–conv (10.0)	13.0
Tilt cab (10.4)	13.5
w/P.S. add (.4)	.4
w/AIR add (.3)	.3
V-8–307, 350 engs	
conv (8.0)	11.6
Tilt cab (10.1)	14.6
V-8–366, 427, 454 engs	
366 eng	
conv (12.0)	15.0
Tilt cab (13.0)	16.3
427, 454 engs–conv (14.8)	18.5
Tilt cab (16.1)	20.2
w/A.C. add (1.0)	1.0
w/P.S. add (.5)	.5
w/Air inj add (.4)	.4
w/Air comp add (.9)	.9

LABOR 15 CRANKSHAFT & DAMPER 15 LABOR

(Factory Time) Chilton Time

Main and Rod Bearings, Renew

Includes: R&R all normal interfering parts. Plastigauge and install new main and rod bearings. Renew gaskets and seals as necessary. Recondition oil pump.

Six–conv (4.6)	6.4
Tilt cab (4.0)	6.2
V-8–307, 350 engs	
conv (4.6)	6.4
Tilt cab (4.9)	7.6
V-8–366, 427, 454 engs	
conv (5.1)	7.0
Tilt cab (4.8)	7.4

Main Bearings, Renew

Includes: R&R all normal interfering parts. Plastigauge and install new main bearings. Renew gaskets and seals as necessary. Recondition oil pump.

Six–conv (3.6)	4.6
Tilt cab (3.4)	4.4
V-8–307, 350 engs	
conv (3.0)	4.0
Tilt cab (4.1)	5.2
V-8–366, 427, 454 engs	
conv (3.0)	4.6
Tilt cab (4.0)	5.0

Rear Main Bearing Oil Seal, Renew

Includes: R&R all normal interfering parts.

Six–conv (1.2)	2.5
Tilt cab (1.8)	2.7
V-8–conv (1.0)	2.5
Tilt cab (1.6)	2.7

Vibration Damper, Renew

Includes: R&R all normal interfering parts.

Six–conv (1.4)	2.0
Tilt cab (.8)	1.2
w/P.S. add (.2)	.2
V-8–307, 350 engs	
conv (1.6)	2.2
Tilt cab (1.4)	2.0
V-8–366, 427, 454 eng	
conv (2.1)	2.9
Tilt cab (2.6)	3.5
w/A.C. add (.2)	.2
w/P.S. add (.2)	.2
w/Air comp add (.2)	.2

DIESEL ENGINES

Crankshaft and Main Bearings, Renew

Includes: R&R all normal interfering parts and engine. Plastigauge and install new main and rod bearings. Recondition oil pump.

Isuzu Diesel (15.8)	22.9
w/P.S. add (.3)	.3
Deutz Diesel	
All series (15.1)	21.5
Detroit Diesel	
6-71 conv (24.7)	31.7
Alum Tilt (24.3)	31.2
6V-53 conv (20.0)	25.6
Steel Tilt (19.0)	24.2
6V-71 Steel Tilt (21.0)	27.0
8V-71 conv (24.4)	31.4
Alum Tilt (23.8)	30.6
12V-71 Alum Tilt (34.0)	43.5
w/A.C. add (1.0)	1.0
w/P.S. add (.8)	.8
w/Pwr take off add (.3)	.3

Main and Rod Bearings, Renew

Includes: R&R all normal interfering parts. Plastigauge and install new main and rod bearings. Recondition oil pump.

Isuzu Diesel (4.2)	6.4
Deutz Diesel	
All series (5.8)	7.9
Detroit Diesel	
6-71 (7.8)	10.0
6V-53, 6V-71 (7.9)	10.2
8V-71 (8.1)	10.3
12V-71 (11.1)	14.4

Main Bearings, Renew

Includes: R&R all normal interfering parts. Plastigauge and install new main bearings. Recondition oil pump.

Isuzu Diesel (3.2)	4.6
Deutz Diesel	
All series (3.6)	5.0
Detroit Diesel	
6-71 (7.2)	9.2
6V-53, 6-71 (7.3)	9.4
8V-71 (7.2)	9.2
12V-71 (9.9)	12.7

Rear Main Bearing Oil Seal, Renew

Includes: R&R all normal interfering parts.

Isuzu Diesel (2.4)	3.5
Deutz Diesel (2.4)	3.5
Detroit Diesel (5.1)	6.6

Front Main Bearing Oil Seal, Renew

Includes: R&R all normal interfering parts.

Isuzu Diesel (.6)	1.0
w/P.S. add (.3)	.3
Deutz Diesel (1.1)	1.6
Detroit Diesel (6.7)	8.5

Crankshaft Damper, Renew

Isuzu Diesel (.5)	.9
w/P.S. add (.3)	.3
Detroit Diesel (3.4)	4.6
w/P.S. add (.2)	.2

Crankshaft Pulley, Renew

Deutz Diesel (1.1)	1.5

LABOR 16 CAMSHAFT & TIMING GEARS 16 LABOR

(Factory Time) Chilton Time

GASOLINE ENGINES

Timing Cover Oil Seal, Renew

Six–conv (1.5)	2.2
Tilt cab (.8)	1.4
w/P.S. add (.2)	.2
V-8–307, 350 engs	
conv (1.7)	2.4
Tilt cab (1.5)	2.2
w/A.C. add (.2)	.2
w/Air comp add (.2)	.2
V-8–366, 427 engs	
conv (2.3)	3.3
Tilt cab (2.5)	3.5
w/A.C. add (.2)	.2
w/P.S. add (.2)	.2
w/A.I.R. add (.2)	.2
w/Air comp add (.2)	.2

Timing Case Cover or Gasket, Renew

Includes: R&R all normal interfering parts.

Six–conv (2.0)	3.1
Tilt cab (2.1)	2.7
w/P.S. add (.2)	.2
V-8–307, 350 engs (2.2)	3.2
w/A.C. add (.2)	.2
w/P.S. add (.2)	.2
w/Air comp add (.2)	.2
V-8–366, 427, 454 engs	
conv (2.6)	3.5
Tilt cab (3.3)	4.2

Timing Chain or Gears, Renew

Includes: R&R all normal interfering parts.

Six–conv (5.1)	7.8
Tilt cab (6.9)	8.7
w/P.S. add (.2)	.2
V-8–307, 350 engs (2.6)	3.7
w/A.C. add (.2)	.2
w/P.S. add (.2)	.2
w/Air comp add (.2)	.2
V-8–366, 427, 454 engs	
conv (3.0)	4.0
Tilt cab (4.5)	5.7

Camshaft, Renew

Includes: R&R all normal interfering parts. Renew gaskets and seals as necessary. Adjust valves.

Six–conv (5.1)	7.4
Tilt cab (6.6)	7.9
w/P.S. add (.2)	.2
w/AIR add (.5)	.5
V-8–307, 350 engs (5.9)	8.0
Tilt cab (6.3)	8.6
V-8–366, 427, 454 engs	
conv (6.7)	10.5
Tilt cab (7.9)	11.2
w/A.C. add (1.2)	1.2
w/P.S. add (.2)	.2
w/Air comp add (.5)	.5
w/Air inj add (.5)	.5

DIESEL ENGINES

Timing Case Cover or Gasket, Renew

Includes: R&R all normal interfering parts.

Isuzu Diesel	
All series (1.3)	2.0
w/P.S. add (.3)	.3
Deutz Diesel	
All series (3.3)	4.5

Timing Gears, Renew

Includes: R&R all normal interfering parts and all required adjustments.

Detroit Diesel	
6-71 conv (18.6)	*23.3
Alum Tilt (18.2)	*22.8
6V-53 conv (18.0)	*22.5
Steel Tilt (17.0)	*21.3
6V-71 Steel Tilt (19.0)	*23.8
8V-71 conv (21.1)	*26.6
Alum Tilt (20.5)	*25.7
12V-71 Alum Tilt (26.0)	*32.5
*Includes R&R engine	
*w/A.C. add (1.0)	1.0
w/P.S. add (.8)	.8
*w/Pwr take off (.3)	.3

Camshaft, Renew

Includes: R&R all normal interfering parts and all required adjustments.

Isuzu Diesel	
All series (6.6)	9.5
w/P.S. add (.3)	.3

LABOR 16 CAMSHAFT & TIMING GEARS 16 LABOR

(Factory Time)	Chilton Time
Dietz Diesel	
All series (12.5)	*17.0
Detroit Diesel	
6-71 conv (19.6)	*24.6
Alum Tilt (19.2)	*24.1
6V-53 conv-one (20.0)	*25.0
both (24.0)	*30.0
Steel Tilt-one (19.0)	*23.8
both (23.0)	*28.8
6V-71 Steel Tilt-one (22.0)	*27.5
both (27.0)	*33.8
8V-71 conv-one (24.6)	*30.8
both (30.6)	*38.3
Alum Tilt-one (24.0)	*30.0
both (30.0)	*37.5
12V-71 Alum Tilt-one (29.0)	*36.3
both (37.0)	*46.3
*Includes R&R engine	
*w/A.C. add (1.0)	1.0
w/P.S. add (.8)	.8
*w/Pwr take off add (.3)	.3

(Factory Time)	Chilton Time
Camshaft Bearings, Renew (Camshaft Removed)	
Detroit Diesel	
one side (.3)	.6
both sides (.5)	.9

LABOR 17 ENGINE OILING SYSTEM 17 LABOR

GASOLINE ENGINES

(Factory Time)	Chilton Time
Oil Pan or Gasket, Renew	
Six–conv (1.1)	2.0
Tilt cab (1.4)	2.2
V-8–307, 350 engs	
conv (1.0)	1.5
Tilt cab (.9)	1.6
V-8–366, 427, 454 engs	
conv (1.0)	1.6
Tilt cab (1.1)	1.8
Oil Pump, Renew	
Six–conv (1.2)	2.3
Tilt cab (1.6)	2.5
V-8–conv (1.1)	1.7
Tilt cab (1.0)	1.8
Recondition add (.5)	.5
Oil Cooler or Gasket, Renew	
All series (1.0)	1.5
Oil Filter Assembly, Renew	
All series (.3)	.4
Pressure Test Engine Bearings (Pan Removed)	
All series	1.0
Oil Pressure Gauge (Dash), Renew	
conv (.4)	.9
Oil Pressure Gauge (Engine), Renew	
All series (.2)	.4

DIESEL ENGINES

(Factory Time)	Chilton Time
Oil Pan or Gasket, Renew	
Isuzu Diesel	
All series (1.2)	1.7
Deutz Diesel	
All series (1.0)	1.4
Detroit Diesel	
6-71 (1.6)	2.3
6V-53 (1.0)	1.4
6V-71 (1.4)	2.1
8V-71 (1.5)	2.2
12V-71 (2.0)	2.6
Oil Pump, Renew	
Isuzu Diesel	
All series (1.4)	2.0
Deutz Diesel	
All series (3.6)	5.0
Detroit Diesel	
exc below (8.2)	10.4
6-71 (2.3)	3.1
Recondition add	
Detroit Diesel	
exc below (1.0)	1.0
6-71, 12V-71 (2.0)	2.0
Oil Cooler or Gasket, Renew	
Isuzu Diesel	
All series (5.6)	8.1
Deutz Diesel	
All series (1.2)	1.8
Detroit Diesel	
exc below (2.6)	3.7
6-71 (2.2)	3.0
Oil Filter Assembly, Renew	
Isuzu Diesel (.3)	.4
Deutz Diesel (.3)	.4
Detroit Diesel (.5)	.6
Pressure Test Engine Bearings (Pan Removed)	
All series	1.0
Oil Pressure Gauge (Dash), Renew	
conv (.4)	.9
Oil Pressure Gauge (Engine), Renew	
All series (.2)	.4

LABOR 18 CLUTCH & FLYWHEEL 18 LABOR

(Factory Time)	Chilton Time
Clutch Pedal Free Play, Adjust	
All series (.3)	.4
Clutch Control Cable, Renew	
Series 40-70 (.6)	.9
Clutch Master Cylinder, Renew	
Series 40-70 (.5)	.8
Series 80-90	
single (.6)	1.3
dual (.9)	1.7
Clutch Master Cylinder, Recondition	
Series 40-70-one side (.9)	1.2
both sides (1.1)	1.8
Series 80-90	
single (1.3)	1.8
dual-one side (1.7)	2.3
both sides (1.9)	2.7
Clutch Slave Cylinder, Renew	
All series	
conv cab (.6)	1.0
Tilt cab (Isuzu) (.8)	1.2
Clutch Slave Cylinder, Recondition	
All series	
conv cab (1.0)	1.6
Tilt cab (Isuzu) (2.0)	2.7
Bleed Clutch Hydraulic System	
All series (.4)	.6
Clutch Assembly, Renew	
Includes: R&R transmission and all normal interfering parts.	
Series 40-60	
CONVENTIONAL CAB	
SM 465-CH 465	
4 Speed (2.7)	3.7
New Process	
540-542 (2.5)	3.6
7550-7590 (2.0)	3.4
Clark	
280V-282-285 (2.1)	3.0
325-327	
390-397 (3.3)	5.0
450-455-457	
Gas (2.8)	3.9
Diesel (2.6)	3.6
551-557 (2.6)	3.6
Spicer	
5052-5252	
5652-5756 (2.6)	4.0
5552-5852-6052	
Gas (3.6)	5.0
Diesel (3.1)	4.3
Fuller	
10 Speed (3.7)	5.2
13 Speed (5.5)	7.7
TILT CAB	
New Process	
435 (2.1)	3.0
540-542 (3.3)	5.0
Spicer	
5052-5252 (1.9)	3.3
5652-5756 (3.3)	5.0
Clark	
280V-282-285 (3.3)	5.0
TILT CAB (ISUZU)	
5 Speed (2.2)	3.3
SERIES 70-90	
70 SERIES-CONV CAB	
Spicer	
5052-5252	
5652-5752 (3.0)	4.1

LABOR 18 CLUTCH & FLYWHEEL 18 LABOR

	(Factory Time)	Chilton Time
Clark		
385-387		
390V-397V	(3.0)	4.1
Fuller		
10 Speed	(3.7)	5.2
13 Speed	(5.5)	7.7
90 SERIES-CONV CAB		
Spicer		
5-6 Speed	(2.4)	3.7
Fuller		
5 Speed	(5.5)	7.7
10-13 Speed		
w/Single exh	(7.2)	9.8
w/Dual exh	(7.2)	9.8
Spicer		
16 Speed	(5.9)	8.5
ALUM TILT CAB		
Spicer		
5-6 Speed	(5.6)	7.5
Fuller		
10 Speed		
RT910-RT1110		
w/Single or dual exh	(5.1)	7.7
10-13 Speed		
RT9513-RT9513		
RT12513-RT012510		
w/Single or dual exh	(4.1)	6.2
9 Speed	(4.1)	6.2
w/P.T.O. add	(.4)	.4
w/Aux trans add	(.5)	.5
w/Bolted trans crossmember add	(1.0)	1.0
R&R Turbo pipe add		1.0

Clutch Release Bearing, Renew

Includes: R&R transmission and all normal interfering parts.

	(Factory Time)	Chilton Time
SERIES 40-60		
CONVENTIONAL CAB		
SM 465-CH 465		
4 Speed	(2.2)	3.0
New Process		
540-542	(2.5)	3.5
7550-7590	(1.7)	2.6
Clark		
280V-282-285	(1.6)	2.2
325-327		
390-397	(2.8)	3.9
450-455-457		
Gas	(1.9)	2.6
Diesel	(1.4)	1.9
551-557		2.5
Spicer		
5052-5252	(1.9)	2.8
5652-5756	(2.4)	3.2
5552-5852-6052		
Gas	(2.8)	3.9
Diesel	(2.3)	3.2
Fuller		
10 Speed	(3.2)	4.5
13 Speed	(5.0)	7.0
TILT CAB		
New Process		
435	(1.3)	2.2
540-542	(1.9)	2.8
Spicer		
5052-5252	(1.6)	2.5
5652-5756	(1.9)	2.8
Clark		
280V-282-285	(1.9)	2.8
TILT CAB (ISUZU)		
5 Speed	(1.9)	2.8
SERIES 70-90		
70 SERIES-CONV CAB		
Spicer		
5052-5252		
5652-5752	(2.5)	3.3
Clark		
385-387		
390V-397V	(2.5)	3.3
Fuller		
10 Speed	(3.2)	4.5
13 Speed	(5.0)	7.0
90 SERIES-CONV CAB		
Spicer		
5-6 Speed	(2.2)	2.9
Fuller		
5 Speed	(5.0)	6.4
10-13 Speed		
w/Single exh	(5.0)	6.4
w/Dual exh	(6.7)	8.3
Spicer		
16 Speed	(5.4)	7.0
ALUM TILT CAB		
Spicer		
5-6 Speed	(5.1)	6.7
Fuller		
10 Speed		
RT910-RT1110		
w/Single or dual exh	(4.6)	6.2
10-13 Speed		
RT9513-RT09513		
RT012513-RT012510		
w/Single or dual exh	(3.8)	5.4
9 Speed	(3.8)	5.4
w/P.T.O. add	(.4)	.4
w/Aux trans add	(.5)	.5
w/Bolted trans crossmember add	(1.0)	1.0
R&R Turbo pipe add		1.0

Flywheel, Renew

Includes: R&R transmission and all normal interfering parts.

	(Factory Time)	Chilton Time
SERIES 40-60		
CONVENTIONAL CAB		
SM 465-CH 465		
4 Speed	(3.3)	4.4
New Process		
540-542	(2.9)	4.4
7550-7590	(2.7)	4.2
Clark		
280V-282-285	(2.6)	3.6
325-327		
390-397	(3.7)	5.5
450-455-457		
Gas	(3.3)	4.4
Diesel	(3.1)	4.1
551-557	(3.1)	4.1
Spicer		
5052-5252	(2.6)	4.8
5652-5756	(3.1)	5.3
5552-5852-6052		
Gas		
single plate	(4.1)	5.7
double plate	(4.5)	6.3
Diesel		
single plate	(3.6)	5.0
double plate	(4.0)	5.6
Fuller		
10 Speed	(4.2)	5.9
13 Speed	(6.2)	8.7
TILT CAB		
New Process		
435	(2.5)	3.8
540-542	(3.7)	5.8
Spicer		
5052-5252	(3.4)	5.8
5652-5756	(3.7)	6.2
Clark		
280V-282-285	(3.7)	6.2
TILT CAB (ISUZU)		
5 Speed	(2.6)	3.8
SERIES 70-90		
70 SERIES-CONV CAB		
Spicer		
5052-5252		
5652-5752	(3.1)	5.3
Clark		
385-387		
390V-397V	(3.7)	5.5
Fuller		
10 Speed	(4.2)	5.8
13 Speed	(6.2)	8.7
90 SERIES-CONV CAB		
Spicer		
5-6 Speed	(3.1)	4.5
Fuller		
5 Speed	(6.2)	8.5
10-13 Speed		
w/Single exh	(8.0)	10.6
w/Dual exh	(8.0)	10.6
Spicer		
16 Speed	(6.6)	9.3
ALUM TILT CAB		
Spicer		
5-6 Speed	(6.3)	9.0
Fuller		
10 Speed		
RT910-RT1110		
w/Single or dual exh	(5.8)	8.5
10-13 Speed		
RT9513-RT09513		
RT012513-RT012510		
w/Single or dual exh	(4.8)	7.0
9 Speed	(4.8)	7.0
Renew ring gear add	(.4)	.6
w/P.T.O. add	(.4)	.4
w/Aux trans add	(.5)	.5
w/Bolted trans crossmember add	(1.0)	1.0
R&R Turbo pipe add		1.0

LABOR 19 STANDARD TRANSMISSION 19 LABOR

Transmission Assembly, R&R or Renew

Includes: Transfer all necessary parts to new trans as required.

	(Factory Time)	Chilton Time
SERIES 40-60		
4 Speed-SM 465-CH 465		
conv cab	(2.6)	3.6
tilt cab	(1.3)	2.0
5 Speed-Conv cab		
New Process		
540-542	(1.9)	2.6
7550-7590	(1.7)	2.4
Clark		
280V-282-285	(2.4)	3.1
390-397	(3.3)	4.6
450-455-457		
Gas	(1.8)	2.5
Diesel	(1.2)	1.7
551-557	(1.7)	2.4
Spicer		
5052-5252		
5652-5756	(2.3)	3.0

(Factory Time)	Chilton Time
5 Speed-Tilt cab	
Isuzu	
MBG5B-MBG5E (2.1)	3.0
New Process	
540-542 (2.9)	4.0
Clark	
280V-282-285 (1.9)	2.6
Spicer	
5052-5252	
5652-5756 (3.3)	4.6
5552-5852-6052	
Gas (2.6)	3.6
Diesel (2.1)	2.9
Fuller	
10 Speed (3.6)	5.0
13 Speed (4.9)	6.8
SERIES 70-90	
70 SERIES-CONV CAB	
Spicer-5 Speed	
5052-5252	
5652-5752 (3.3)	4.6
Clark-5 Speed	
385-387	
390V-397V (3.3)	4.6
Fuller	
10 Speed (3.6)	5.0
13 Speed (4.9)	6.8
90 SERIES-CONV CAB	
Spicer-5-6 Speed	
6052C-6253A-6852S	
6853C-6852K-SST1062C (2.0)	2.7
Fuller	
5 Speed-T905 (4.9)	6.2
10 Speed	
RT910-RT1110	
w/Single exh (3.2)	4.3
w/Dual exh (6.6)	8.1
13 Speed	
RT9513-RT09513-RT012513	
w/Single exh (4.9)	6.2
w/Dual exh (6.6)	8.1
Spicer	
16 Speed-8716-3B (5.3)	6.8
ALUM TILT CAB	
Spicer-5-6 Speed	
6052C-6852S-6853C	
6852K-SST1062B-1062C	
1262A (5.0)	6.5
Fuller	
9 Speed-RT9509 (3.7)	5.2
RT910-RT1110-RT12510 (4.5)	6.0
13 Speed	
RT-RT09513	
RT-RTO-12513 (3.7)	5.2
w/P.T.O. add (.4)	.4
w/Aux trans add (.5)	.5
w/Bolted trans crossmember	
add (1.0)	1.0
R&R Turbo pipe add	1.0

Transmission Assembly, R&R and Recondition

Includes: Complete disassembly of transmission. Inspect and clean all components. Renew parts, gaskets and seals as necessary. Make all normal adjustments. Road test.

(Factory Time)	Chilton Time
SERIES 40-60	
4 Speed-SM 465-CH 465	
conv cab (5.5)	7.7
tilt cab (3.9)	6.0
5 Speed-Conv cab	
New Process	
540-542 (5.4)	7.5
7550-7590 (4.1)	7.2
Clark	
280V-282-285 (5.6)	8.7
390-397 (6.6)	9.2
450-455-457	
Gas (5.1)	7.1
Diesel (4.5)	6.3
551-557 (6.2)	8.6
Spicer	
5052-5252	
5652-5756 (8.4)	12.4
5 Speed-Tilt cab	
Isuzu	
MBG5B-MBG5E (7.1)	9.9
New Process	
540-542 (5.4)	7.5
Clark	
280V-282-285 (5.1)	8.1
Spicer	
5052-5252	
5652-5756 (5.3)	8.3
5552-5852-6052	
Gas (8.0)	11.2
Diesel (7.5)	10.5
Fuller	
10-13 Speed	
RT610-RT613 (12.0)	15.7
SERIES 70-90	
70 SERIES-CONV CAB	
Spicer-5 Speed	
5052-5252	
5652-5752 (8.4)	12.4
Clark-5 Speed	
385-387	
390V-397V (7.3)	11.7
Fuller-10 Speed	
front case (10.1)	14.1
aux case (5.5)	7.7
complete unit (12.3)	18.0
13 Speed	
front case (13.5)	18.9
inter case (8.5)	11.9
aux case (8.4)	11.8
complete (15.1)	21.0
90 SERIES-CONV CAB	
Spicer 5-6 Speed	
6052C-6253A-6852S	
6853C-6852K-SST1062C (8.4)	12.0
Fuller	
5 Speed-T905 (13.7)	18.6
10 Speed-RT910-RT1110	
w/Single exh	
front unit only (10.0)	14.0
rear unit only (6.7)	9.4
complete unit (13.5)	19.0
w/Dual exh	
front unit only (13.4)	18.3
rear unit only (10.1)	14.1
complete unit (16.9)	22.4

(Factory Time)	Chilton Time
13 Speed-RT9513	
RT09513-RT012513	
w/Single exh	
front unit only (11.7)	15.0
rear unit only (8.4)	11.0
complete unit (15.2)	20.7
w/Dual exh	
front unit only (13.4)	16.7
rear unit only (10.1)	13.0
complete unit (16.9)	22.4
Spicer	
16 Speed-8716-3B (14.3)	23.7
ALUM TILT CAB	
Spicer	
5-6 Speed	
6052C-6852S-6853C	
6852K-SST1062B-1062C	
1262A (11.4)	15.0
Fuller	
9 Speed-RT9509	
front unit only (10.5)	14.0
rear unit only (7.2)	10.0
complete unit (14.0)	20.0
10 Speed-RT910-RT1110	
RT12510	
front unit only (11.3)	14.8
rear unit only (8.0)	10.8
complete unit (14.8)	20.8
13 Speed	
RT-RT09513	
RT-RT012513	
front unit only (10.5)	14.0
rear unit only (7.2)	10.0
complete unit (14.0)	20.0
w/P.T.O. add (.4)	.4
w/Aux trans add (.5)	.5
w/Bolted trans crossmember	
add (1.0)	1.0
R&R Turbo pipe add	1.0

Auxiliary Transmission, R&R

(Factory Time)	Chilton Time
Series 40-70 (1.5)	2.5
w/Hyd. brakes add (.5)	.5
Series 80 (2.8)	3.9
Series 90	
8341 (2.5)	3.6
8345 (2.5)	3.6

Auxiliary Transmission, R&R and Recondition

Includes: Disassembly and assembly. Cleaning and inspection of all parts. Renew or recondition all necessary components. Renew gaskets and seals as required. Road test.

(Factory Time)	Chilton Time
Series 40-70	
Fuller 2A92 (7.2)	9.9
6041 (6.0)	7.7
7041 (6.8)	9.0
w/Hyd. brakes add (.5)	.5
Series 80	
6041 (7.2)	9.3
7041 (6.1)	7.9
Series 90	
8341 (6.8)	8.5
8345 (6.8)	8.5

Auxiliary Transmission Rear Oil Seal, Renew

(Factory Time)	Chilton Time
Fuller 2A92 (.7)	1.1
Spicer 7041 (.6)	1.0
w/Hyd. brakes add (.5)	.5

LABOR 20 TRANSFER CASE 20 LABOR

(Factory Time) Chilton Time

Transfer Case Oil Seals, Renew
All series
front (.8) 1.1
rear (.6) 8

Transfer Case Speedometer Drive Gear, Renew
All series (.9) 1.2

Transfer Case P.T.O. Gasket, Renew
All series (.4) 6

Transfer Case Assembly, Remove & Install
All series (1.7) 2.3
Renew assy add (.9) 1.0

Transfer Case Assy., R&R and Recondition
All series (8.2) 11.0

LABOR 23 AUTOMATIC TRANSMISSION 23 LABOR

(Factory Time) Chilton Time

ALLISON–AT540, 543, 545, MT 640, 643, 650, 653, HT 740-750

ON TRUCK SERVICES

Oil Pressure Test
All series (1.2) 1.6

Check Unit for Oil Leaks
Includes: Clean and dry outside of case, run unit to determine point of leak.
All series 7

Manual or Throttle Lever Oil Seals, Renew
Includes: R&R oil pan and adjustments.
All series (1.4) 1.9

Oil Pan or Gasket, Renew
All series (.7) 1.0

Oil Control Valve Body, R&R and Recondition
AT series (1.9) 2.5
MT 640 (2.2) 2.8
MT 650 (2.4) 3.0
HT series (3.5) 4.2

Clutch Pack Clearance, Check
Includes: R&R oil pan.
All series (1.3) 1.9

Shift Linkage, Adjust
All series (.3) 4

Throttle Linkage, Adjust
All series (.5) 7

Retarder Linkage, Adjust
All series (.3) 4

Retarder Valve Body, Recondition
All series (1.3) 1.6

Vacuum Modulator, Renew
All series (.2) 4

Oil Filter, Renew
AT series (1.3) 1.6
MT series (1.0) 1.3

Neutral Safety Switch, Renew
All series (.3) 5

SERVICES REQUIRING R&R

Transmission Assembly, R&R or Renew
Includes: Drain and refill unit. Adjust linkage and road test.
Series 40-70
AT series–conv (4.3) 5.6
Tilt cab (4.7) 5.9
MT series (4.6) 5.9
Series 80-90
MT series (4.6) 5.8
HT series (7.6) 9.0
w/Pwr take off add (.4) 4

Transmission Assembly, R&R and Recondition
Includes: Drain and refill unit, adjust all linkage. Disassemble and assemble complete transmission, inspect all parts. Clean, renew or recondition components. Renew gaskets and seals as necessary. Road test.
Series 40-70
AT series–conv (14.0) 15.9
Tilt cab (14.4) 16.3
MT 640 (17.2) 20.2
MT 650 (18.0) 21.0
Series 80-90
MT 640 (17.2) 20.2
MT 650 (18.0) 21.0
HT 740 (28.4) 31.2
HT 750 CRD (31.9) 37.0
HT 750 DRD (32.4) 37.5
w/Pwr take off add (.4) 4

Torque Converter, R&R and Recondition
Includes: R&R transmission assembly. Drain and refill unit. Adjust linkage and road test.
Series 40-70
AT 540 conv (5.5) 6.9
Tilt cab (5.9) 7.3
MT series (5.8) 7.3
Series 80-90
MT series (5.4) 6.9
AT series (8.4) 10.6

ALLISON (TURBO HYDRA-MATIC) AT 475

ON TRUCK SERVICES

Drain and Refill Unit
All series (.5) 6

Oil Pressure Check
All series (.5) 8

Check Unit for Oil Leaks
Includes: Clean and dry outside of the case and run unit to determine point of leak.
All series (.7) 7

Vacuum Modulator Assembly, Renew
All series (.3) 5

Oil Pan or Gasket, Renew
All series (.6) 1.0

Oil Control Valve Body, R&R or Renew
All series (.9) 1.3

Oil Control Valve Body, R&R and Recondition
All series (1.6) 2.5

Servos, Renew or Recondition
All series–front (1.2) 1.6
rear (1.4) 1.8

Governor Assembly, R&R or Renew
All series (.3) 5

Governor Assembly, R&R and Recondition
All series (.6) 1.0

Detent Solenoid, Renew and Adjust
All series (.6) 1.0

Kickdown Switch, Renew
All series (.2) 4

Pressure Regulator, Renew
All series (.7) 1.1

Parking Pawl, Renew
All series (.9) 1.3

Manual Shaft, Shaft Seal, Detent Lever and Park Actuator Rod, Renew
All series (.9) 1.3

Case Extension Oil Seal, Renew
All series (.9) 1.3

SERVICES REQUIRING R&R

Note: All the following operations include R&R transmission.

Transmission Assembly, R&R or Renew
All series (3.0) 5.3

Transmission and Converter Assembly, R&R and Recondition
All series (10.0) 15.1

Torque Converter, Renew
All series (3.2) 5.5

Front Oil Pump Oil Seal, Renew
All series (3.0) 5.3

Front Oil Pump, Renew
All series (3.3) 5.8

Front Oil Pump, R&R and Recondition
All series (3.9) 6.5

Bands, Renew
All series (4.5) 7.1

Forward, Direct or Intermediate Clutch, R&R or Renew
All series (3.7) 6.3

Forward, Direct or Intermediate Clutch, R&R and Recondition
All series (4.2) 6.8

Low Sprag Unit, Renew
All series (4.6) 7.2

Intermediate Sprag Unit, Renew
All series (4.0) 6.6

LABOR 25 U-JOINTS & DRIVESHAFT 25 LABOR

(Factory Time) Chilton Time

Drive Shaft, R&R or Renew
All Series-exc. Isuzu
front (.5) 9
rear (.5) 9
intermediate (1.5) 2.0
Tilt cab (Isuzu)
front (1.1) 1.4
rear (.4) 6
intermediate (1.2) 1.6

Universal Joint, Renew or Recondition
Includes: R&R drive shaft.
All Series-exc. Isuzu
front (.9) 1.1
w/Hanger bearing (1.9) 2.3
intermediate
w/Slip joint (.8) 1.2
wo/Slip joint (1.0) 1.4
rear (.9) 1.2
Tilt cab (Isuzu)
front (1.0) 1.4
rear (1.0) 1.4
intermediate (1.1) 1.5

Center Support Bearings, Renew
Series 40-70
conv (1.0) 1.5
Tilt cab (.9) 1.1
Tilt cab (Isuzu) (1.2) 1.5

Hanger Bearing Support Assembly, Recondition
All Series
exc below (1.3) 1.8
band type brake (1.8) 2.3
Bendix brake (2.2) 2.7

LABOR 26 REAR AXLE 26 LABOR

(Factory Time) Chilton Time

FRONT DRIVE AXLE

Front Axle Shaft, Renew
All series-one (.8) 1.1
both (1.5) 2.0

Front Axle Shaft Oil Seal, Renew
All series-one (1.4) 1.8
both (2.7) 3.5

Spindle Pivot Bearing, Renew
All series-one (1.9) 2.5
both (3.5) 4.8

Pinion Shaft Oil Seal, Renew
All series (1.0) 1.4

Front Differential Carrier, R&R or Renew
All series (2.8) 3.7

Front Differential Carrier, R&R and Recondition
All series (4.5) 6.0

REAR DRIVE AXLE

Axle Shaft, Renew (One Axle)
Series 40-70
Corp-one (.3) 6
both (.4) 8
Eaton-one (.4) 7
both (.6) 1.2
flange type-one (.4) 6
both (.7) 1.0
Series 80-90
gear type-one (.3) 6
both (.5) 8
flange type-one (.5) 8
both (.8) 1.2

Rear Wheel Bearing or Oil Seal, Renew
Series 40-70
Corp-one (1.0) 1.3
both (1.9) 2.4
Eaton-one (1.3) 1.7
both (2.4) 3.0
flange type
one side (2.0) 2.5
Series 80-90-one (1.5) 2.0
both (2.8) 3.5

Pinion Shaft Oil Seal, Renew
Series 40-70
RO92 (.6) 1.0
Corp axle (1.0) 1.5
Eaton-single speed (1.1) 1.6
Rockwell-single speed (1.0) 1.5
Eaton-two speed (1.2) 1.7
Tandem (1.3) 1.8
Series 80-90
Single axle (1.0) 1.5
Tandem axle (1.3) 1.8

Tandem Drive Line Alignment, Check
Includes: Road test.
All series 1.4

Tandem Drive Line Alignment, Check and Adjust
Includes: Alignment of engine, transmission drive shafts and both axles. Road test.
All series (1.3) 1.9

Differential Carrier Assembly, R&R or Renew
Series 40-70
SINGLE SPEED
SINGLE AXLE
RO92 (2.4) 3.4
H110-H135-H150
H175 (1.7) 2.4
Spicer
G190S-M220S (2.7) 3.8
Eaton
E17101-E17121-E22121
E23121 (2.7) 3.8
Rockwell
R170 (2.7) 3.8
TWO SPEED
SINGLE AXLE
RO92 (2.3) 3.3
T150-T175 (1.7) 2.4
Spicer
M190T-M220T (2.8) 4.0
Eaton
E17201-E17221-E22221 (2.6) 3.6
E23221 (3.0) 4.2
SINGLE SPEED
FRONT TANDEM
Eaton
DS341 (5.0) 7.1
Rockwell
SL100-SQ100 (3.5) 4.9
TWO SPEED
FRONT TANDEM
Eaton
DT341 (4.4) 6.1
REAR TANDEM-SINGLE SPEED
Eaton
DS341 (2.9) 4.1
Rockwell
SL100-SQ100 (3.5) 4.9
REAR TANDEM-TWO SPEED
Eaton
DT341 (3.9) 5.5
Series 80-90
SINGLE REDUCTION OR FRONT TANDEM
R170-E17121-E18121 (2.5) 3.6
E1910-19121-E23121
E23421-E26421-E26121 (3.0) 4.1
DOUBLE REDUCTION
U200 (3.9) 5.0
44DP-50DP-38DPC (4.8) 5.9
TWO SPEED
T185 (2.7) 3.8
E17221-E18221-E19201
E1922-233221-E26221
DT400-38DTC-44DTC
34DT (3.1) 4.2
TANDEM DUAL DRIVING FRONT UNIT
Single Reduction
Forward Axle With Inter-Axle Diff.
E34DSC-SLHD-SQHD
SSHD-E38DSC-SQHP
E34DSE-E34DS-DS380
44DSC-DS340-SUHD
STHD (4.7) 5.8
SINGLE REDUCTION–PUSHER AXLE
R170 (2.5) 3.6
DOUBLE REDUCTION
SQDD-SRDD-SUDD
Front unit (4.4) 5.5
Rear unit (3.4) 4.5
REAR TANDEM
Single Reduction
R170-E17121-E18121 (2.5) 3.6
E23121-E23421-E26421
E26121 (3.0) 4.1
Double Reduction
44DP-50DP-38DPC (3.6) 4.7
Two Speed-Three Speed
E34D3C-E38D3C
Front unit (3.2) 4.3
Rear unit (2.7) 3.8
E17221-E18221-E23221
E26221-DT400-38DTC
44DTC-34DT (3.1) 4.2
TANDEM DUAL DRIVING REAR UNIT
Single Reduction Forward
Axle With Inter-Axle Diff.
E34DSC-SLHD-SQHD-SSHD
E38DSC-SQHP-E34DSE-E34DS
DS380-44DSC-DS340-SUHD
STHD (2.7) 3.8
R&R fifth wheel add 1.5

LABOR 26 REAR AXLE 26 LABOR

(Factory Time)	Chilton Time
Differential Carrier Assembly, R&R and Recondition	
Includes: Drain and refill unit. R&R all normal interfering parts. Disassemble and assemble complete unit. Inspect, clean, renew or recondition all components. Road test.	
Series 40-70	
SINGLE SPEED	
SINGLE AXLE	
RO92 (7.2)	10.2
H110-H135-H150	
H175 (6.7)	9.5
Spicer	
G190S-M220S (7.3)	10.4
Eaton	
E17101-E17121-E22121	
E23121 (7.3)	10.4
Rockwell	
R170 (8.0)	11.4
TWO SPEED	
SINGLE AXLE	
RO92 (9.7)	13.8
T150-T175 (5.9)	8.4
Spicer	
M190T-M220T (7.9)	11.2
Eaton	
E17201-E17221-E22221 (7.7)	10.9
E23221 (8.1)	11.5
SINGLE SPEED	
FRONT TANDEM	
Eaton	
DS341 (11.6)	16.5
Rockwell	
SL100-SQ100 (8.7)	12.4
TWO SPEED	
FRONT TANDEM	
Eaton	
DT341 (13.0)	18.5
REAR TANDEM-SINGLE SPEED	
Eaton	
DS341 (7.1)	10.0
Rockwell	
SL100-SQ100 (8.4)	11.9
REAR TANDEM-TWO SPEED	
Eaton	
DT341 (9.0)	12.8
Series 80-90	
SINGLE REDUCTION OR FRONT TANDEM	
R170-E17121-E18121 (8.6)	12.6
E1910-19121-E23121	
E23421-E26421-E26121 (10.8)	14.3
DOUBLE REDUCTION	
U200 (11.9)	17.5
44DP-50DP-38DPC (16.3)	21.1
TWO SPEED	
T185 (8.2)	12.3
E17221-E18221-E19201	
E1922-233221-E26221	
DT400-38DTC-44DTC	
34DT (8.2)	14.7
TANDEM DUAL DRIVING FRONT UNIT	
Single Reduction	
Forward Axle With Inter-Axle Diff.	
E34DSC-SLHD-SQHD	
SSHD-E38DSC-SQHP	
E34DSE-E34DS-DS380	
44DSC-DS340-SUHD	
STHD (14.7)	19.5
SINGLE REDUCTION-PUSHER AXLE	
R170 (8.6)	12.6
DOUBLE REDUCTION	
SQDD-SRDD-SUDD	
Front unit (16.3)	22.0
Rear unit (12.7)	18.0
REAR TANDEM	
Single Reduction	
R170-E17121-E18121 (8.6)	12.4
E23121-E23421-E26421	
E26121 (10.8)	14.3
Double Reduction	
44DP-50DP-38DPC (12.7)	16.4
Two Speed-Three Speed	
E34D3C-E38D3C	
Front unit (10.2)	15.0
Rear unit (8.2)	13.3
E17221-E18221-E23221	
E26221-DT400-38DTC	
44DTC-34DT (8.2)	14.7
TANDEM DUAL DRIVING REAR UNIT	
Single Reduction	
Forward Axle With Inter-Axle Diff.	
E34DSC-SLHD-SQHD-SSHD	
E38DSC-SQHP-E34DSC-E34DS	
DS380-44DSC-DS340-SUHD	
STHD (8.8)	14.2
R&R fifth wheel add	1.5
Electric Shift Assembly, Renew	
All series (.4)	.5
Electric Shift Assembly, Recondition	
All series (1.0)	1.2
Axle Shift Control Switch, Renew	
All series (.3)	.4
Axle Shift Motor, Renew	
All series (.6)	1.2
Axle Shift Torsion Spring, Renew	
All series (.4)	.9
Differential Lockout Air Control Valve, Renew	
All series (.6)	1.0
Vacuum Shift Selector Valve Cable, Renew	
All series (.5)	.8
Vacuum Shift Check Valve Assembly, Renew	
All series (.4)	.6
Vacuum or Air Axle Shift Cylinder, Renew	
All series (.3)	.6
Vacuum or Air Axle Shift Cylinder, Recondition	
All series (.8)	1.2
Differential Lockout Chamber, Renew	
Tandem (.3)	.5
Differential Lockout Chamber, Recondition	
Tandem (.8)	1.2

LABOR 27 REAR SUSPENSION 27 LABOR

(Factory Time)	Chilton Time
Rear Spring, Renew	
Series 40-70	
Variable rate-exc Isuzu	
one (1.4)	1.9
both (2.8)	3.9
Hendrickson-one (3.0)	4.0
both (5.7)	7.7
Tilt cab (Isuzu)	
one (1.7)	2.3
both (3.2)	4.4
Series 80-90	
exc below-one (1.7)	2.4
both (3.3)	4.4
Hendrickson-one (3.5)	4.7
both (6.9)	8.9
Page & Page-one (1.6)	2.3
both (3.0)	3.9
w/Radius leaf-one (1.8)	2.5
both (3.5)	4.7
Rear Spring Leaf, Renew	
Series 40-70	
Variable rate-exc Isuzu	
one (1.7)	2.5
both (3.3)	4.6
Hendrickson-one (3.0)	4.6
both (6.3)	8.8
Tilt cab (Isuzu)	
one (1.8)	2.5
both (3.6)	5.0
Series 80-90	
exc below-one (2.3)	2.9
both (4.5)	5.7
Hendrickson-one (4.0)	5.0
both (7.9)	10.0
Page & Page-one (1.6)	2.1
both (3.1)	4.0
w/Radius leaf-one (1.8)	2.3
both (3.5)	4.5
Rear Spring Front Eye Bushings, Renew	
Series 40-70	
Variable rate	
one (.6)	.9
both (1.0)	1.7
Hendrickson-one (1.1)	1.6
both (1.9)	3.0
Series 80-90	
exc below-one (1.9)	2.5
both (3.7)	4.7
Hendrickson-one (3.9)	5.0
both (7.7)	9.7
Page & Page-one (2.0)	2.5
both (4.0)	5.0
w/Radius leaf-one (2.2)	2.8
both (4.3)	5.4
Rear Spring Shackles and/or Pins, Renew	
Tilt cab (Isuzu)	
one side (.6)	.9
both sides (.9)	1.5
Auxiliary Spring, Renew	
Series 40-70	
Variable rate-exc. Isuzu	
one (.7)	1.4
both (1.3)	2.7
Tilt cab (Isuzu)	
one (1.9)	2.6
both (3.6)	5.0
Hendrickson	
one (.6)	1.0
both (1.1)	1.9
Series 80-90	
exc below-one (1.7)	2.2
both (3.3)	4.2
Hendrickson-one (3.5)	4.5
both (6.9)	8.7
Page & Page-one (1.6)	2.1
both (3.0)	4.0
w/Radius leaf-one (1.6)	2.1
both (3.0)	4.0

LABOR 27 REAR SUSPENSION 27 LABOR

	(Factory Time)	Chilton Time
Tandem Suspension Support Beam, R&R		
All series		
one	(4.0)	5.1
both	(8.0)	10.1
Renew add	(2.0)	2.0
Tandem Suspension Torque Arm, Renew		
Series 40-70		
one	(1.1)	1.6
both	(2.3)	3.1
Series 80-90		
exc below		
one	(.5)	.8
both	(.7)	1.0
Tandem-one	(.7)	1.0
both	(1.1)	1.6
Shock Absorbers, Renew		
All series-one	(.3)	.5
both	(.5)	.8

LABOR 28 AIR CONDITIONING 28 LABOR

Note: If more than one item requires replacement where evacuation and discharging the system is already included in the operation, deduct 1.0 hour for each additional item to the times listed.

	(Factory Time)	Chilton Time
Drain, Evacuate and Recharge System		
All Series	(.7)	2.0
Pressure Test System		
All Series		1.2
Refrigerant, Add Partial Charge		
All Series		1.4
Compressor Belt, Renew		
All series	(.2)	.5
Compressor Assembly, Renew		
Includes: Transfer all necessary attaching parts. Evacuate and charge system.		
Series 40-70	(2.0)	3.2
Series 80-90		
Bruin	(2.0)	3.3
All others	(1.2)	2.5
Clutch Hub and Drive Plate, Renew		
Includes: Check air gap.		
Series 40-70	(.6)	1.0
Series 80-90	(.8)	1.3
Compressor Pulley and/or Bearings, Renew		
Includes: R&R clutch hub and drive plate.		
Series 40-70	(.8)	1.2
Series 80-90	(.9)	1.5
Clutch Holding Coil, Renew		
Includes: R&R clutch hub and drive plate.		
Series 40-70	(.9)	1.3
Series 80-90	(1.0)	1.6
Compressor Shaft Seal Kit, Renew		
Includes: R&R clutch hub and drive plate. Evacuate and charge system.		
All series	(2.3)	3.0
Compressor Assy., R&R and Recondition		
Includes: Complete disassembly and overhaul, making all checks and gauging operations. Evacuate and charge system.		
Series 40-70	(2.9)	4.4
Series 80-90		
Bruin	(3.0)	4.5
All others	(2.9)	4.4
Compressor Relief Valve, Renew		
Includes: Evacuate and charge system.		
All series	(.9)	1.6
Condenser Assembly, Renew		
Includes: Evacuate and charge system.		
Series 40-70	(2.5)	3.5
Series 80-90		
conv cab	(1.2)	2.6
alum tilt cab	(1.7)	3.1
Receiver-Dehydrator, Renew		
Includes: Evacuate and charge system.		
Series 40-70	(1.6)	3.0
Series 80-90		
conv cab	(1.0)	2.4
alum tilt cab	(1.1)	2.5
Evaporator Core, Renew		
Includes: Evacuate and charge system.		
Series 40-70	(2.1)	4.0
Series 80-90		
Bison	(2.6)	4.1
Bruin	(3.2)	4.7
All others	(3.4)	4.9
Renew exp valve add	(.1)	.2
Expansion Valve, Renew		
Includes: Evacuate and charge system.		
Series 40-70	(1.3)	2.7
Series 80-90		
conv cab	(1.7)	3.1
alum tilt cab	(1.9)	3.3
Pilot Operated Absolute (P.O.A.) Valve, Renew		
Includes: Evacuate and charge system.		
Series 40-70	(1.3)	2.7
Series 80-90		
conv cab	(1.4)	2.8
alum tilt cab	(1.7)	3.1
Accumulator, Renew		
Includes: Evacuate and charge system.		
All series	(2.0)	2.5
Renew filter dryer add	(.3)	.3
Filter Dryer, Renew		
Includes: Evacuate and charge system.		
All series	(.9)	1.4
Orifice Tube, Renew		
Includes: Evacuate and charge system.		
All series	(1.6)	2.2
Renew filter dryer add	(.3)	.3
Pressure Cycling Switch, Renew		
All series	(.2)	.3
EEVIR Assembly, R&R		
Includes: Evacuate and charge system.		
Bison	(1.5)	2.9
Renew dessicant bag add	(.2)	.3
Renew expansion valve capsule and/or moisture indicator sleeve add	(.3)	.4
Renew POA valve add	(.3)	.4
Renew sight glass add	(.1)	.2
A.C. Blower Motor, Renew		
Series 40-70	(.3)	.6
A.C. Blower Motor Switch, Renew		
Series 40-70	(.5)	.9
Series 80-90	(.4)	.8
A.C. Temperature Control Assy., Renew		
All series	(1.0)	1.4
A.C. Blower Motor Relay, Renew		
All series	(.2)	.4
Air Condition Hoses, Renew		
Includes: Evacuate and charge system.		
All series-one	(1.3)	2.1
each adtnl	(.3)	.5
Renew filter dryer add	(.3)	.3

LABOR 30 HEAD & PARKING LAMPS 30 LABOR

	(Factory Time)	Chilton Time
Aim Headlamps		
two		.4
four		.6
Headlamp Sealed Beam Bulb, Renew		
All series		
single beam unit	(.3)	.4
dual beam unit	(.4)	.5
Directional or Parking Lamp Assy., Renew		
All series		
conv cab	(.2)	.3
tilt cab	(.3)	.4
Directional or Parking Lamp Lens, Renew		
All series	(.2)	.3
Tail or Stop Lamp Lens, Renew		
All series	(.2)	.3
Tail or Stop Lamp Assy., Renew		
All series	(.4)	.5
Reflectors, Renew		
All series-each		.2
License Lamp Assy., Renew		
All series	(.2)	.3
Marker Lamp, Renew		
All series-each	(.4)	.5

LABOR 31 WINDSHIELD WIPER & SPEEDOMETER 31 LABOR

(Factory Time)	Chilton Time
Windshield Wiper Motor, Renew	
Series 40-70	
conv cab (.6)	1.1
Tilt cab (Isuzu) (.9)	1.4
Series 80-90-one side	
Bison (.8)	1.5
conv cab (.5)	.9
tilt cab (.9)	1.4
Recond motor add	.5
Windshield Wiper Switch, Renew	
Series 40-70	
conv cab (.6)	.9
Tilt cab (Isuzu) (.3)	.5
Series 80-90 (.2)	.5
Windshield Washer Pump, Renew	
Series 70-90	
Foot operated (.2)	.5
Windshield Wiper Control Valve, Renew	
Series 70-90	
one side (.5)	.9
Speedometer Head, R&R or Renew	
Series 40-70	
conv cab (.6)	1.1
tilt cab (.5)	1.0
Series 80-90	
Bison (.2)	.4
All others (.4)	.8
Speedometer Cable and Casing, Renew	
Series 40-70	
conv cab (.7)	1.4
tilt cab (.6)	1.2
Series 80-90 (.5)	1.0
Tachometer Cable and Casing, Renew	
Series 40-70 (.6)	1.2
Series 80-90	
Bison (.3)	.7
All others (.2)	.5
Tachometer, R&R or Renew	
Series 40-70	
mechanical (.4)	.8
electric (.6)	1.0
Series 80-90	
Bison (.2)	.4
All others (.4)	.8

LABOR 32 LIGHT SWITCHES & WIRING 32 LABOR

(Factory Time)	Chilton Time
Headlamp Switch, Renew	
Series 40-70 (.3)	.5
Series 80-90	
Bison (.2)	.4
conv cab (.4)	.7
tilt cab (.3)	.6
Headlamp Dimmer Switch, Renew	
All series (.2)	.5
Turn Signal and Hazard Warning Switch, Renew	
Series 40-70	
conv cab (.9)	1.4
tilt cab-direct (.7)	1.1
tilt cab-hazard (.3)	.6
Tilt cab (Isuzu) (.3)	.6
Series 80-90	
Bruin (.4)	.7
All others (.8)	1.2
Turn Signal or Hazard Flasher, Renew	
All series (.2)	.4
Stop Light Switch, Renew	
Series 40-70	
conv cab (.3)	.5
Tilt cab (Isuzu) (1.1)	1.6
Series 80-90	
Bison-w/Alum tilt cab (.6)	1.0
All others (.4)	.7
Starter Safety Switch, Renew	
All series (.3)	.5
Back-Up Lamp Switch, Renew	
All series (.3)	.5
Clearance Light Switch, Renew	
Series 70-90	
Bison (.2)	.4
All others (.3)	.5
Horn, Renew	
Series 40-70	
electric (.4)	.5
air (.2)	.3
Series 80-90	
air or electric (.4)	.6
Horn Relay, Renew	
Series 40-70 (.2)	.3

Vans • Ramcharger • Trailduster • Pick-Ups

GROUP INDEX

ALPHABETICAL INDEX

Dodge/Plymouth Trucks

MODEL IDENTIFICATION CHART

B 100 - DODGE TRADESMAN VAN

B 100 - DODGE SPORTSMAN WAGON

B 200 - DODGE TRADESMAN VAN

B 200 - DODGE SPORTSMAN WAGON

B 300 - DODGE TRADESMAN VAN

B 300 - DODGE SPORTSMAN WAGON

PB 100 - PLYMOUTH VOYAGER WAGON

PB 200 - PLYMOUTH VOYAGER WAGON

PB 300 - PLYMOUTH VOYAGER WAGON

CB 300 - FRONT SECTION - KARY VAN

CB 400 - FRONT SECTION - KARY VAN

AW 100 - RAMCHARGER - 4 WHEEL DRIVE

PW 100 - TRAILDUSTER - 4 WHEEL DRIVE

AD 100 - RAMCHARGER - 2 WHEEL DRIVE

AD 150 - SPORT UTILITY - 2 WHEEL DRIVE

PD 100 - TRAILDUSTER - 2 WHEEL DRIVE

D 100 - DODGE PICK-UP - 2 WHEEL DRIVE

D 150 - DODGE PICK-UP - 2 WHEEL DRIVE

D 200 - DODGE PICK-UP - 2 WHEEL DRIVE

RD 200 - DODGE RAIL-TRACK - 2 WHEEL DRIVE

D 300 - DODGE PICK-UP - 2 WHEEL DRIVE

W 100 - DODGE PICK-UP - 4 WHEEL DRIVE

AW 150 - SPORT UTILITY - 4 WHEEL DRIVE

W 200 - DODGE PICK-UP - 4 WHEEL DRIVE

W 300 - DODGE PICK-UP - 4 WHEEL DRIVE

W 400 - DODGE PICK-UP - 4 WHEEL DRIVE

LABOR 1 TUNE UP 1 LABOR

(Factory Time) Chilton Time

Compression Test

	Chilton Time
Six(.6)	.9
V-8–318-360 engs (.7)	1.0

Engine Tune Up, (Electronic Ignition)

Includes: Test battery and clean connections. Tighten manifold and carburetor mounting bolts. Check engine compression, clean and adjust or renew spark plugs. Test resistance of spark plug wires. Inspect distributor cap and rotor. Adjust distributor air gap. Check vacuum advance operation. Reset ignition timing. Adjust idle mixture and idle speed. Service carburetor air cleaner. Inspect crankcase ventilation system. Inspect and adjust drive belts. Inspect choke operation, adjust or free up as necessary. Check operation of E.G.R. valve.

	Chilton Time
Six	2.8
V-8–318-360 engs	3.2
w/A.C. add	.6

LABOR 2 IGNITION SYSTEM 2 LABOR

(Factory Time) Chilton Time

Spark Plugs, Clean and Reset or Renew

	Chilton Time
Six(.4)	.7
V-8–318-360 eng (.5)	.8

Ignition Timing, Reset

	Chilton Time
B-PB-CB Models (.5)	.7
All other models (.3)	.5

Distributor, Renew

Includes: Adjust ignition timing and renew oil seal if required.

	Chilton Time
Six–B-PB-CB Models (.7)	1.0
All other models (.6)	.9
V-8–318-360 engs	
B-PB-CB Models (.7)	1.0
All other models (.6)	.9

Distributor, R&R and Recondition

Includes: Adjust ignition timing and renew oil seal if required.

	Chilton Time
Six–B-PB-CB Models (1.4)	2.0
All other models (1.3)	1.9
V-8–318-360 engs	
B-PB-CB Models (1.4)	2.0
All other models (1.3)	1.9

Distributor Pick-Up Plate and Coil Assembly, Renew

Includes: R&R distributor, reset ignition timing.

	Chilton Time
Six–B-PB-CB Models (.9)	1.3
All other models (.8)	1.2
V-8–318-360 engs	
B-PB-CB Models (.9)	1.3
All other models (.8)	1.2

Electronic Distributor Reluctor, Renew

Includes: R&R distributor and reset ignition timing.

	Chilton Time
Six–B-PB-CB Models (.8)	1.2
All other models (.7)	1.1
V-8–318-360 engs	
B-PB-CB Models (.8)	1.2
All other models (.7)	1.1

Vacuum Control Unit, Renew

Includes: R&R distributor and reset ignition timing.

	Chilton Time
Six–B-PB-CB Models (.8)	1.2
All other models (.7)	1.1
V-8–318-360 engs	
B-PB-CB Models (.8)	1.2
All other models (.7)	1.1

Distributor Cap, Renew

	Chilton Time
B-PB-CB Models (.4)	.5
All other models (.3)	.4

Electronic Ignition Control Unit, Renew

	Chilton Time
B-PB-CB Models (.3)	.5
All other models (.2)	.4

Spark Control Computer, Renew

	Chilton Time
B-PB-CB models (.7)	1.1
All other models (.6)	1.0

Ignition Cables, Renew

	Chilton Time
Six(.5)	.8
V-8–318-360 engs (.6)	.9

Ignition Coil, Renew

	Chilton Time
B-PB-CB Models (.4)	.6
All other models (.3)	.5

Electronic Ignition Ballast Resistor, Renew

	Chilton Time
B-PB-CB Models (.3)	.5
All other models (.2)	.4

Ignition Switch, Renew

Includes: Renew lock cylinder if required.

	Chilton Time
1982-86	
std colm (.8)	1.2
tilt colm (.4)	.7

LABOR 3 FUEL SYSTEM 3 LABOR

(Factory Time) Chilton Time

Fuel Pump, Test
Includes: Disconnect line at carburetor, attach pressure gauge.
All models.................................... .3

Carburetor, Adjust (On Truck)
All models (.6).............................. .8

Air Cleaner Vacuum Diaphragm, Renew
All models (.5).............................. .8

Air Cleaner Vacuum Sensor, Renew
All models (.5).............................. .8

Coolant Temperature Sensor/Switch, Renew
B-PB-CB models (.7) 1.1
All other models (.6) 1.0

Carburetor, Renew
Includes: All necessary adjustments.
1 bbl (.7).................................... 1.1
2 bbl (.7).................................... 1.1
4 bbl (.8).................................... 1.2

Carburetor, R&R and Clean or Recondition
Includes: All necessary adjustments.
Holly-1 bbl (1.9)........................ 2.5
Carter-2 bbl (2.3)...................... 3.1
Holly-2 bbl (1.9)........................ 2.5
Carter-4 bbl (2.6)...................... 3.5

Fuel Pump, Renew
Six-B-PB-CB Models (.6)................. .9
All other models (.5) 8
V-8-318-360 engs (.5) 8
Add pump test if performed.

Fuel Tank, Renew
Includes: Drain and refill, test and renew tank gauge if necessary.
Main Tank
frame mount (1.0)...................... 1.5
cab mount (.7)............................ 1.2
plastic tank (1.0)........................ 1.5
Auxiliary Tank
cab mount (1.2).......................... 1.7
frame mount (1.0)...................... 1.5
w/Skid plate add (.3)..................... .3

Fuel Gauge (Tank), Renew
Main Tank
frame mount (.7)......................... 1.2
cab mount (.5)............................ .9
plastic tank (1.0)........................ 1.4
Auxiliary Tank
cab mount (.5)............................ .9
frame mount (.6).......................... 1.0
w/Skid plate add (.3)..................... .3

Fuel Gauge (Dash), Renew
1982-86
B-PB-CB Models (.6).................. 1.1
All other models (1.0) 1.5

Intake and Exhaust Manifold Gaskets, Renew
Six
B-PB-CB Models (2.0)................ 3.0
All other models (1.8) 2.8
w/A.C. add (.4) 4
Renew manif add.............................. .5

Intake Manifold Gasket, Renew
V-8
318-360 engs (2.5)...................... 3.5
w/A.C. add (.4) 4
w/Air inj add 6
Renew manif add.............................. .5

LABOR 3A EMISSION CONTROLS 3A LABOR

(Factory Time) Chilton Time

CRANKCASE EMISSION

Positive Crankcase Ventilation Valve, Renew
All models (.2).............................. .3

EVAPORATIVE EMISSION

Vapor Canister, Renew
All models (.3).............................. .5

Vapor Canister Hoses, Renew
All models-one (.2)........................ .3

Vapor Canister Filter, Renew
All models (.2).............................. .3

Vapor Separator, Renew
All models (.9).............................. 1.2

AIR INJECTION SYSTEM

Air Pump, Renew
Six (.9) 1.2
V-8 (.8).. 1.1

Aspirator, Renew
All models (.3).............................. .4

Diverter/Control Valve, Renew
Six (.3) 6
V-8 (.4).. .7

Injection Tube and Check Valve Assy., Renew
Six (.4) 7
V-8 (.5).. .8

Orifice Spark Advance Control Valve, Renew
All models (.2).............................. .4

HEATED AIR SYSTEM

Air Cleaner Vacuum Diaphragm, Renew
1982-86 (.5).................................. .8

Air Cleaner Vacuum Sensor, Renew
1982-86 (.5).................................. .8

EXHAUST GAS RECIRCULATION SYSTEM

E.G.R. Valve, Renew
Six (.4) 6
V-8 (.5).. .7

E.G.R. Coolant Control Valve, Renew
All models (.3).............................. .5

E.G.R. Vacuum Amplifier, Renew
All models (.3).............................. .5

E.G.R. Time Delay Timer, Renew
All models (.2).............................. .4

E.G.R. Time Delay Solenoid, Renew
All models (.2).............................. .4

Change Temperature Switch, Renew
All models (.2).............................. .3

E.F.C. SYSTEM

Oxygen Sensor, Renew
All models (.3).............................. .5

Emission Maintenance Reminder Module, Renew
All models (.2).............................. .4

LABOR 4 ALTERNATOR AND REGULATOR 4 LABOR

(Factory Time) Chilton Time

Alternator Circuits, Test
Includes: Test battery, regulator and alternator output.
All models.................................... .6

Alternator, Renew
Six(.7) 1.2
V-8-318-360 engs
B-PB-CB Models (.9) 1.4
All other models (.7) 1.2
Add circuit test if performed.

Alternator, R&R and Recondition
Six(2.0) 3.1
V-8-318-360 engs
B-PB-CB Models (2.2) 3.3
All other models (2.0) 3.1
Add circuit test if performed.

Alternator Drive End Frame Bearing, Renew
Six(1.0) 1.5
V-8-318-360 engs
B-PB-CB Models (1.2) 1.7
All other models (1.0) 1.5
Renew rear brg add 2

Voltage Regulator, Test and Renew
All models (.2).............................. .6

LABOR 5 STARTING SYSTEM 5 LABOR

(Factory Time) Chilton Time

Starter Draw Test (On Truck)
All models .3

Starter, Renew
Six(.6) 1.0
V-8-318-360 engs (.7) 1.2
Add draw test if performed.

Starter, R&R and Recondition
Six(1.8) 2.7
V-8-318-360 engs (1.9) 2.8
Renew field coils add .5
Add draw test if performed.

Starter Drive, Renew
Includes: R&R starter.
Six(1.1) 1.5
V-8-318-360 engs (1.2) 1.7

Starter Solenoid, Renew
Includes: R&R starter.
Six(1.1) 1.5
V-8-318-360 engs (1.2) 1.7

Starter Relay, Renew
All models (.3) .5

Battery Cables, Renew
All models-positive (.4) .6
ground (.2) .4
starter to relay (.3) .5

LABOR 6 BRAKE SYSTEM 6 LABOR

(Factory Time) Chilton Time

Brakes, Adjust (Minor)
Includes: Adjust brakes, fill master cylinder.
two wheels .5
four wheels .8

Brake Pedal Free Play, Adjust
All models .4

Bleed Brakes (Four Wheels)
Includes: Fill master cylinder.
All models (.4) .6

Brake Drum and Hub Assy., Renew
Includes: Repack and/or renew wheel bearings.
front-one (1.0) 1.6
rear-one (.8) 1.4
w/Dual rear whls add .3

Rear Brake Drum, Renew (One)
All models
semi-floating axle (.3) .6
full floating axle (1.8) 2.3
w/Dual rear whls add (.2) .3

Brake System Indicator Switch, Renew
All models (.3) .5

Brake Shoes and/or Pads, Renew
Includes: Install new or exchange shoes or pads. Service adjusters. Adjust service and hand brake. Bleed system.
front-disc (.6) 1.2
rear-drum
semi-floating axle (.7) 1.4
full floating axle (1.5) 2.5
All four wheels
semi-floating axle 2.5
full floating axle 4.4
Resurface brake rotor add, each 1.0
Resurface brake drum add, each .6

BRAKE HYDRAULIC SYSTEM

Wheel Cylinder, Renew (Standard Brakes)
Includes: Bleed brake system.
front-one (1.4) 1.8
both (2.1) 2.9
rear-one (1.4) 1.8
both (2.1) 2.9
All four wheels 5.0

Wheel Cylinder, R&R and Recondition (Standard Brakes)
Includes: Hone cylinder, bleed brake system.
front-one (1.7) 2.1
both (2.7) 3.3
rear-one (1.7) 2.1
both (2.7) 3.3
All four wheels 6.0

COMBINATIONS

Add to Brakes, Renew
See Machine Shop Operations

(Factory Time) Chilton Time

RENEW WHEEL CYLINDER
Each (.3) .4

REBUILD WHEEL CYLINDER
Each .6

RENEW BRAKE HOSE
Each (.4) .5

REBUILD CALIPER ASSEMBLY
Each (.4) .6

RENEW BRAKE DRUM
Front
Each .3
Rear
Full Floating Axle-each .3
Semi-FLoating Axle-each 1.0

RENEW DISC BRAKE ROTOR
Each (.3) .4

RENEW REAR WHEEL GREASE SEALS OR BEARINGS
Full Floating Axle-each .2
Semi-Floating Axle-each .8

RENEW FRONT WHEEL BEARINGS
(One Wheel) one or both
Drum Brakes .2
Disc Brakes .4

FRONT WHEEL BEARINGS, REPACK OR RENEW SEALS
(Both Wheels)
Drum Brakes .4
Disc Brakes .8

(Factory Time) Chilton Time

Wheel Cylinder, Renew (Disc Brakes)
rear-one (1.1) 1.5
both (2.1) 2.9
w/Dual rear whls add .3

Wheel Cylinder, R&R and Recondition (Disc Brakes)
Includes: Hone cylinder, bleed brake system.
rear-one (1.4) 1.8
both (2.7) 3.5
w/Dual rear whls add .3

Brake Hose, Renew (Flex)
Includes: Bleed brake system.
front-one (.4) .6
rear (.5) .7

Master Cylinder, Renew
Includes: Bleed brake system.
B-PB-CB Models (.8) 1.2
All other models (.5) 1.0

Master Cylinder, R&R and Recondition
Includes: Bleed brake system.
B-PB-CB Models 1.9
All other models 1.7

Brake Line Metering Valve, Renew
Includes: Bleed brake system.
All models (.5) .9

Brake System Combination Valve, Renew
Includes: Bleed brake system.
B-PB-CB models (.9) 1.3
All other models (.8) 1.2

(Factory Time) Chilton Time

POWER BRAKES

Power Brake Unit, Renew
All models
wo/Hydraboost (.5) 1.1
w/Hydraboost (.7) 1.3
w/A.C. add (.1) .3

Power Brake Check Valve, Renew
All models (.2) .4

Power Brake Vacuum Hose, Renew
All models (.3) .4

DISC BRAKES

Brake Shoes and/or Pads, Renew
Includes: Install new or exchange shoes or pads. Service adjusters. Adjust service and hand brake. Bleed system.
front-disc (.6) 1.2
rear-drum
semi-floating axle (.7) 1.4
full floating axle (1.5) 2.5
All four wheels
semi-floating axle 2.5
full floating axle 4.4
Resurface brake rotor add, each 1.0
Resurface brake drum add, each .6

Disc Brake Pads, Renew
Includes: Install new disc brake pads only.
All models (.6) 1.2

LABOR 6 BRAKE SYSTEM 6 LABOR

(Factory Time) Chilton Time

Disc Brake Rotor (w/Hub), Renew (One)
Includes: Repack and/or renew bearings.
2 WD
All models (.8) 1.4
4 WD
44 FBJ front axle (1.1) 2.0
60 F front axle (.9) 1.7

Disc Brake Caliper, Renew (One)
Includes: Bleed front brake lines only.
All models (.5) 1.0

Disc Brake Caliper, R&R and Recondition (One)
Includes: Renew parts as required, bleed front brake lines only.
All models (.8) 1.6

PARKING BRAKE

Parking Brake, Adjust
All models (.3) 5

Parking Brake Lever Assembly, Renew
All models (.6) 9

Parking Brake Cables, Renew
Front
All models (.6) 8
Intermediate
All models (.3) 5
Rear
2 wd-each (.6) 8
4 wd-each (1.0) 1.4
w/Dual rear whls add 3

LABOR 7 COOLING SYSTEM 7 LABOR

(Factory Time) Chilton Time

Winterize Cooling System
Includes: Run engine to check for leaks, tighten all hose connections. Test radiator and pressure cap, drain radiator and engine block. Add anti-freeze and refill coolant.
All models 5

Thermostat, Renew
All models (.5) 8
w/A.C. add (.3) 3

Radiator Assembly, R&R or Renew
B-PB-CB Models (1.0) 1.5
All other models (.7) 1.3
w/A.C. add (.4) 5
w/A.T. add (.1) 2

ADD THESE OPERATIONS TO RADIATOR R&R

Boil & Repair 1.5
Rod Clean 1.9
Repair Core 1.3
Renew Tank 1.6
Renew Trans. Oil Cooler 1.9
Recore Radiator 1.7

Radiator Hoses, Renew
All models-upper (.3) 5
lower (.4) 6
by-pass (.5) 7

Fan Belt, Renew
All models (.3) 5
w/Air inj add (.1) 1

Fluid Fan Drive Unit, Renew
B-PB-CB Models
w/225-318-360 engs (.8) 1.1
All other models
w/225-318-360 engs (.5) 7

Idler Pulley, Renew
All models (.3) 5

Fan Pulley, Renew
B-PB-CB Models
w/225-318-360 engs (.6) 8
All other models
w/225-318-360 engs (.4) 7

Coolant Reserve Tank, Renew
All models (.2) 3

Water Pump, Renew
Six-1982-86
B-PB-CB Models (.9) 1.4
D-AD-PD Models (.7) 1.3
AW-PW-W Models (1.0) 1.6
w/A.C. add (.3) 3
V-8-318-360 engs
B-PB-CB Models
1982-86
wo/A.C. (1.3) 1.8
w/A.C. (1.8) 2.6
w/P.S. add (.2) 2
w/100 Amp alt add (.6) 6
AD-PD-D-W Models
1982-86 (1.1) 1.5
w/A.C. add (.4) 6
w/P.S. add (.2) 2
w/Air inj add (.2) 2

Water Jacket Expansion Plugs, Renew
Engine Block
Six-All models
left side-one (1.9) 2.3
V-8-318-360 engs
All models
front-right or left-one (.6) 1.1
center-right or left-one (.6) 1.1
rear-right side (.5) 1.0
rear-left side (.8) 1.2

Water Jacket Expansion Plugs, Renew
Cylinder Head
V-8-318-360 engs
front-one-all models (.3) 6
Rear-one
B-PB-CB Models (.3) 6
All other models (3.1) 4.2

Temperature Gauge (Engine Unit), Renew
All models (.5) 7

Temperature Gauge (Dash Unit), Renew
B-PB-CB Models
1982-86 (.6) 1.2
All other models
1982-86 (.6) 1.2

Heater Core, R&R or Renew
Without Air Conditioning
Front
B-PB-CB Models
1982-86 (.7) 1.6
All other models
1982-86 (1.3) 2.2
Rear
1982-86-All models (.8) 1.5
With Air Conditioning
Front
B-PB-CB Models
1982-86 (2.7) *5.0
All other models
1982-86 (2.1) *4.0
Rear
1982-86-All models (.6) 1.2
w/Front and rear A.C. add (.3) 5
*Includes Recharge A.C. System.

ADD THESE OPERATIONS TO HEATER CORE R&R

Boil & Repair 1.2
Repair Core 9
Recore 1.2

Heater Water Valve, Renew
All models
w/Heater (.4) 7
w/A.C. (.5) 8

Heater Hoses, Renew
All models-one or both (.4) 6

Heater Blower Motor, Renew
Front
1982-86-All models (.5) 9

Heater Blower Motor Resistor, Renew
All models (.3) 5
Rear
1982-86-All models (.4) 9

Heater Blower Motor Switch, Renew
B-PB-CB Models
1982-86 (.4) 6
All other models
1982-86 (.4) 7

Heater Temperature Control Assembly, Renew
All models (.5) 8

LABOR 8 EXHAUST SYSTEM 8 LABOR

(Factory Time) Chilton Time

Muffler, Renew
All models (.7) 1.1

Tail Pipe, Renew
All models (.4) 7

Exhaust Pipe, Renew
Six(.6) 1.0
V-8-318-360 engs (.8) 1.2

Exhaust Pipe Extension, Renew
All models (.7) 1.1

Exhaust Pipe Flange Gasket, Renew
Six(.2) 5

Catalytic Converter, Renew
All models (.6) 1.1

LABOR 8 EXHAUST SYSTEM 8 LABOR

(Factory Time) Chilton Time

Catalytic Converter Heat Shield, Renew
upper (.4) 9
lower (.2) 4
intermediate (.2) 5

Exhaust Manifold Heat Control Valve, Recondition
Six(2.7) 3.4
w/A.C. add (.3) 3
V-8–318-360 engs (1.2) 1.9

Intake and Exhaust Manifold Gaskets, Renew
Six
B-PB-CB Models (2.0) 3.0
All other models (1.8) 2.8
w/A.C. add (.4) 4
Renew manif add 5

Exhaust Manifold or Gaskets, Renew
Six
B-PB-CB Models
1982-86 (2.1) 2.7
D-AD-PD Models
1982-86 (1.9) 2.5

W-AW-PW Models
1982-86 (1.9) 2.5
V-8–1982-86-318-360 engs
right side (.5) 1.1
left side (.7) 1.3

COMBINATIONS

Muffler, Exhaust and Tail Pipe, Renew
Six 1.6
V-8 .... 1.8

Muffler and Tail Pipe, Renew
All models 1.2

LABOR 9 FRONT SUSPENSION 9 LABOR

(Factory Time) Chilton Time

Note: On all front suspension operations alignment charges must be added if performed. Time given does not include alignment.

Check Alignment of Front End
All models 8
Note: Deduct if alignment is performed.

Toe-In, Adjust
All models 7

Align Front End
Includes: Adjust front wheel bearings.
All models (1.4) 2.0

Wheels, Balance
one 5
each adtnl 3

Front Wheel Bearings, Clean and Repack (Both Wheels)
All models
w/Drum Brakes 1.0
w/Disc Brakes 1.5
w/4 wd 2.0

Front Wheel Bearings and Cups, Renew (One Wheel)
Drum Brakes (.6) 9
Disc Brakes
w/2 wd (.7) 1.1
w/4 wd (1.2) 1.7

Front Wheel Grease Seals, Renew (One Wheel)
All models
w/2 wd (.6) 8
w/4 wd (1.1) 1.5

Front Shock Absorbers, Renew
1982-86-one (.3) 6
both (.5) 9

Steering Knuckle, Renew (One)
w/2 WD
1982-86 (1.1) 1.7
w/4 WD
1982-86
w/44 FBJ Axle (1.5) 2.1
w/60 F Axle (1.2) 1.8

Lower Control Arm, Renew (One)
Add alignment charges.
1982-86 (1.3) 1.9

Lower Ball Joint, Renew (One)
Add alignment charges.
1982-86
w/2 wd (1.4) 2.0
w/4 wd (1.9) 2.7

Lower Control Arm Strut Bushings, Renew (One Side)
Add alignment charges.
1982-86 (.3) 6

Lower Control Arm Bushings, Renew (One Side)
Add alignment charges.
1982-86 (1.5) 2.3

Upper Control Arm, Renew (One)
Includes: Align front end.
1982-86 (1.9) 2.7

Upper Ball Joint, Renew (One)
Add alignment charges.
1982-86
w/2 wd (.9) 1.4
w/44 FBJ Axle (2.0) 3.2
w/60 F Axle (1.8) 3.0

Upper Control Arm Bushings, Renew (One Side)
Includes: Align front end.
1982-86 (1.8) 2.6

Front Sway Bar Bushings, Renew (One or All)
D-AD-PD 150
D-RD 250
D350-450 models (.6) 8
All other models (.4) 6

Front Sway Bar, Renew
All models (.4) 6

Front Spring, Renew (One)
Coil
1982-86 (1.2) 1.7
Leaf
1982-86 (.7) 1.1

Front Spring Shackle, Renew (One)
Includes: Renew bushings.
1982-86 (.8) 1.3

FOUR WHEEL DRIVE

Front Axle Shaft, R&R or Renew (One or Both–One Side)
1982-86
44 FBJ Axle (1.2) 1.8
60 F Axle (1.3) 1.9
Recond U-Joint add-each 2

Front Axle Inner Oil Seals, Renew (Both Sides)
1982-86
44 FBJ Axle (4.1) 6.0
60 F Axle (3.5) 5.0

Front Axle Shaft Spindle, Renew
All models
44 FBJ Axle (.9) 1.3
60F Axle (.8) 1.2

Locking Hub Assy., Renew or Recondition
All models
44 FBJ Axle
Spicer (.5) 9
Auto (.4) 8
60F Axle
Dualmatic (.2) 5

Drive Pinion Oil Seal, Renew
1982-86 (.5) 9

Front Axle Housing Cover and/or Gasket, Renew or Reseal
All models (.4) 8

Front Drive Shaft, Renew (Transfer Case To Front Axle)
1982-86 (.4) 7
w/Skid plate add (.3) 3

Front Drive Shaft Universal Joint, Renew
At Transfer Case
Dana-CV Type (.8) 1.3
Saginaw-CV Type (1.3) 2.0
At Front Axle(.6) 1.0

Front Axle Shaft Outer Oil Seal, Renew
All models-each (.9) 1.2

Front Axle Assy., R&R or Renew
Includes: Renew oil seals, transfer axle shafts and brake assemblies.
All models
44 FBJ Axle (3.8) 5.6
60 F Axle (3.7) 5.5
Renew axle shafts add-each 5

Differential Side Bearings, Renew
Includes: R&R ring and pinion, if necessary. Renew axle inner oil seals and adjust side bearing preload and backlash.
All models
44 FBJ Axle (5.5) 8.1
60 F Axle (4.9) 7.2

LABOR 9 FRONT SUSPENSION 9 LABOR

(Factory Time)	Chilton Time
Differential Case, Renew	
Includes: R&R ring and pinion, if necessary. Renew bearings and gears. Renew pinion seal and axle inner oil seals. Adjust backlash.	
All models	
44 FBJ Axle (5.8)	8.5
60 F Axle (5.4)	7.9
Differential Side Gears, Renew	
Includes: Renew axle inner oil seals if required.	
All models	
44 FBJ Axle (4.5)	6.6
60 F Axle (3.8)	5.5
Ring Gear and Pinion Set, Renew	
Includes: Renew pinion bearing, side bearings and all seals. Make all necessary adjustments.	
All models	
44 FBJ Axle (6.5)	9.6
60 F Axle (5.8)	8.5
Renew diff case add (.3)	.5

LABOR 10 STEERING LINKAGE 10 LABOR

(Factory Time)	Chilton Time
Tie Rods or Tie Rod Ends, Renew	
Includes: Reset toe-in.	
1982-86-each (.7)	1.0
Steering Knuckle Arm, Renew (One)	
w/2 wd	
1982-86 (1.1)	1.5
w/4 wd	
1982-86 (.6)	.9
Center Link, Renew	
B-PB-CB Models	
1982-86 (.6)	.8
All other models	
1982-86 (.4)	.6
Idler Arm, Renew	
1982-86-one (.3)	.5
both (.5)	.7
Pitman Arm, Renew	
B-PB-CB Models	
1982-86 (.4)	.7
All other models	
1982-86 (.5)	.8
Drag Link, Renew	
B-PB-CB models (.3)	.6
All other models (.5)	.8

LABOR 11 STEERING GEAR 11 LABOR

(Factory Time)	Chilton Time
STANDARD STEERING	
Steering Gear, Adjust (On Truck)	
All models (.9)	1.1
Steering Gear Assembly, Renew	
B-PB-CB Models	
1982-86 (1.3)	1.9
D-AD-PD-RD Models	
1982-86 (.6)	1.2
Steering Gear Assy., R&R and Recondition	
Includes: Disassemble, renew necessary parts, reassemble and adjust.	
B-PB-CB Models	
1982-86 (1.9)	2.9
D-AD-PD-RD Models	
1982-86 (1.3)	2.2
Steering Column Mast Jacket, Renew	
Does not include painting.	
B-PB-CB Models	
1982-86	
column shift (1.4)	2.0
floor shift (1.1)	1.6
All other models	
1982-86	
column shift (1.6)	2.4
floor shift (1.1)	1.6
Tilt Column	
All models (2.3)	3.3
Upper Mast Jacket Bearing, Renew	
All models	
w/Std column (.5)	1.0
w/Tilt column (1.1)	1.5
Steering Column Shift Housing, Renew	
All models	
w/Std column (.9)	1.5
w/Tilt column (2.2)	3.3
Steering Gear Cross Shaft Oil Seal, Renew	
All models (.8)	1.4
Steering Wheel, R&R or Renew	
All models (.3)	.5
POWER STEERING	
Trouble Shoot Power Steering	
Includes: Test pump and system pressure. Check pounds pull on steering wheel and check for leaks.	
All models	.5
Power Steering Belt, Renew	
All models (.3)	.5
w/Air inj add (.1)	.1
Power Steering Gear Assy., Renew	
B-PB-CB Models	
1982-86 (1.2)	1.7
All other models	
1982-86 (1.1)	1.6
Power Steering Gear, R&R and Recondition	
B-PB-CB Models	
1982-86 (2.7)	3.9
All other models	
1982-86 (2.2)	3.2
Power Steering Gear Assy., Renew (w/Remanufactured Unit)	
B-PB-CB Models	
1982-86 (1.2)	1.7
Steering Gear Cross Shaft Oil Seals, Renew (Inner and Outer)	
B-PB-CB Models	
1982-86 (.9)	1.6
All other models	
1982-86 (1.2)	1.9
Gear Control Valve Assy., Renew	
B-PB-CB Models	
1982-86 (.5)	.9
All other models	
1982-86 (1.5)	2.2
Pressure Control Valve, Renew	
B-PB-CB Models	
1982-86 (.4)	.8
Power Steering Pump, Test and Renew	
Includes: Transfer or renew pulley.	
B-PB-CB Models	
1982-86 (1.1)	1.5
All other models	
1982-86 (.9)	1.4
Power Steering Pump, R&R and Recondition	
B-PB-CB Models	
1982-86 (1.6)	2.5
All other models	
1982-86 (1.1)	2.3
Pump Flow Control Valve, Test and Clean or Renew	
B-PB-CB models (1.1)	1.6
All other models (.9)	1.3
w/Air inj add (.2)	.2
Power Steering Pump Reservoir and/or Seals, Renew	
B-PB-CB models (.8)	1.1
All other models (.7)	1.0
w/Air inj add (.2)	.2
Pump Drive Shaft Oil Seal, Renew	
All models (.9)	1.3
Power Steering Hoses, Renew	
All models	
pressure-each (.4)	.7
return-each (.3)	.6

LABOR 12 CYLINDER HEAD & VALVE SYSTEM 12 LABOR

(Factory Time) Chilton Time

Compression Test

Six(.6) 9
V-8
318-360 engs (.7) 1.0

Cylinder Head Gasket, Renew

Includes: Clean gasket surfaces, clean carbon, make all necessary adjustments.

Six
B-PB-CB Models
1982-86 (3.6) 5.0
All other models
1982-86 (2.5) 4.0
V-8–318-360 engs
B-PB-CB Models
1982-86-one (3.7) 4.5
both (4.9) 6.6
All other models
1982-86-one (3.1) 4.3
both (4.2) 5.9
w/100 Amp alt add (.6) 6
w/Air inj add (.6) 6
w/A.C. add (.4) 4

Cylinder Head, Renew

Includes: Transfer all parts, reface valves, make all necessary adjustments.

Six
B-PB-CB Models
1982-86 (5.9) 8.2
All other models
1982-86 (5.0) 7.0
V-8–318-360 engs
B-PB-CB Models
1982-86-one (5.0) 6.5
both (7.4) 9.6
All other models
one (4.2) 6.3
both (6.7) 8.9
w/100 Amp alt add (.6) 6
w/Air inj add (.6) 6
w/A.C. add (.4) 4

Clean Carbon and Grind Valves

Includes: R&R cylinder heads, clean gasket surfaces, clean carbon, reface valves and seats. Minor tune up.

Six
B-PB-CB Models
1982-86 (5.4) 7.8
All other models
1982-86 (4.9) 7.8
V-8–318-360 engs
B-PB-CB Models
1982-86 (7.0) 10.6
All other models
1982-86 (6.2) 9.9

COMBINATIONS

Add to Valve Job

See Machine Shop Operations

GASOLINE ENGINES

(Factory Time) Chilton Time

DRAIN, EVACUATE AND RECHARGE AIR CONDITIONING SYSTEM
All Models 1.4

ROCKER ARMS & SHAFT ASSY., DISASSEMBLE AND CLEAN OR RECONDITION
Six (.5) 6
V-8-one side (.5) 6
both sides (.9) 1.1

HYDRAULIC VALVE LIFTERS, DISASSEMBLE AND CLEAN
Each 2

DISTRIBUTOR, RECONDITION
All Models (.7) 1.0

CARBURETOR, RECONDITION
1 BBL (.9) 1.4
2 BBL (1.1) 1.6
4 BBL (1.6) 2.1

VALVE GUIDES, REAM OVERSIZE
Each (.2) 3

VALVES, RECONDITION (ALL)
Cylinder Head Removed
Six (2.2) 3.0
V-8 (2.7) 4.0

(Factory Time) Chilton Time

w/100 Amp alt add (.6) 6
w/Air inj add (.6) 6
w/A.C. add (.4) 4

Valves, Adjust

Six
B-PB-CB Models (.8) 1.2
All other models (.7) 1.1

Valve Cover Gasket, Renew

Six
B-PB-CB Models
1982-86 (.9) 1.2

(Factory Time) Chilton Time

All other models
1982-86 (.8) 1.1
V-8–318-360 engs
B-PB-CB Models
1982-86-one (.5) 8
both (.8) 1.2
All other models
1982-86-one (.5) 8
both (.8) 1.2
w/Air inj add (.2) 2

Valve Push Rod and/or Rocker Arm, Renew

Six
B-PB-CB Models
1982-86-one or all (1.0) 1.7
All other models
1982-86-one or all (.8) 1.5
V-8–318-360 engs
B-PB-CB Models
1982-86-one side (.6) 1.1
both sides (1.0) 2.1
All other models
1982-86-one side (.5) 9
both sides (.9) 1.6
w/Air inj add (.2) 2

Valve Tappets, Renew (SEE NOTE)

Includes: R&R cylinder head on 6 cyl engine, where required.

Six
B-PB-CB Models
1982-86-one (1.6) 2.1
each adtnl (.1) 1
All other models
1982-86-one (1.5) 2.0
each adtnl (.1) 1
V-8–318-360 engs-all models
1982-86-one (1.0) 3.1
one-each bank (1.5) 3.6
all-both banks (2.4) 4.4
w/A.C. add (.2) 2

NOTE: Factory time for V-8 engines is based on using magnetic tool through push rod opening to remove lifters. Chilton experience finds it better and safer to R&R intake manifold, since the lifters have a tendency to stick in the block and sometimes come apart.

Valve Spring and/or Valve Stem Oil Seals, Renew (Head on Truck)

Six–1982-86
All models-one (1.0) 1.4
all (2.6) 3.6
V-8–318-360 engs-all models
1982-86-one (1.1) 1.5
one-each bank (1.7) 2.4
all-both banks (4.4) 5.2

LABOR 13 ENGINE ASSEMBLY & MOUNTS 13 LABOR

(Factory Time) Chilton Time

Engine Assembly, R&R

Does not include transfer of any parts or equipment.

Six
B-PB-CB Models
1982-86-w/M.T. 8.7
w/A.T. 7.8
All other models
1982-86-w/M.T. 7.8
w/A.T. 6.6
V-8–318-360 engs
B-PB-CB Models
1982-86-w/M.T. 9.6
w/A.T. 9.2
All other models
1982-86-w/M.T. 7.7

(Factory Time) Chilton Time

w/A.T. 6.5
w/P.S. add (.2) 2
w/Skid plate add (.3) 3
V-8–w/A.C. add (1.7) .... °1.7
°Includes recharge A.C. system.

(G) Rebuilt Engine Assembly, Renew (w/Cyl. Head(s) and Oil Pan)

Includes: R&R engine assy. Transfer all component parts not supplied with replacement engine.

Six
B-PB-CB models
1982-86-w/M.T. 11.7
w/A.T. 10.8

(Factory Time) Chilton Time

All other models
1982-86-w/M.T. 10.8
w/A.T. 9.6

V-8
318-360 engs
B-PB-CB models
1982-86-w/M.T. 12.6
w/A.T. 12.2
All other models
1982-86-w/M.T. 10.7
w/A.T. 9.5
w/A.C. add 1.0
w/P.S. add 2
w/Air inj add 3
w/Skid plate add 3

LABOR 13 ENGINE ASSEMBLY & MOUNTS 13 LABOR

(Factory Time)	Chilton Time
V-8–w/A.C. add	*1.7

*Includes: Recharge A.C. system.

Short Engine Assy., Renew

(w/All Internal Parts Less Cylinder Head(s) and Oil Pan)

Includes: R&R engine, transfer all component parts not supplied with replacement engine. Clean carbon, grind valves. Tune engine.

(Factory Time)	Chilton Time
Six	
B-PB-CB Models	
1982-86-w/M.T. (13.7)	18.5
w/A.T. (12.8)	17.6
All other models	
1982-86-w/M.T. (11.0)	16.6
w/A.T. (10.1)	15.7
V-8–318-360 engs	
B-PB-CB Models	
1982-86-w/M.T. (15.2)	21.0
w/A.T. (14.3)	20.1
All other models	
1982-86-w/M.T. (13.4)	19.2
w/A.T. (12.5)	18.3
w/P.S. add (.2)	.2
w/Skid plate add (.3)	.3
V-8–w/A.C. add (1.7)	*1.7

*Includes recharge A.C. system.

Cylinder Block, Renew

(w/Pistons and Rings)

Includes: R&R engine, transfer all component parts not supplied with replacement engine, clean carbon, grind valves. Tune engine.

(Factory Time)	Chilton Time
Six	
B-PB-CB Models	
1982-86-w/M.T. (15.5)	22.7
w/A.T. (14.7)	21.8
All other models	
1982-86-w/M.T. (14.6)	21.6
w/A.T. (13.7)	20.7

Engine Assembly, R&R and Recondition

Includes: Rebore block, install new pistons, rings, rod and main bearings. Clean carbon, grind valves. Tune engine.

(Factory Time)	Chilton Time
Six	
B-PB-CB Models	
1982-86-w/M.T. (30.0)	35.2
w/A.T. (29.1)	34.3
All other models	
1982-86-w/M.T. (28.6)	33.0
w/A.T. (27.4)	32.6
V-8–318-360 engs	
B-PB-CB Models	
1982-86-w/M.T. (36.3)	41.5
w/A.T. (35.9)	40.1
All other models	
1982-86-w/M.T. (33.7)	38.9
w/A.T. (32.5)	37.7
w/P.S. add (.2)	.2
w/Skid plate add (.3)	.3
V-8–w/A.C. add (1.7)	*1.7

*Includes recharge A.C. system.

Engine Mounts, Renew

(Factory Time)	Chilton Time
Front	
Six–all models	
1982-86-one (.4)	1.0
V-8–318-360 engs	
B-PB-CB Models	
1982-86-one (.9)	1.2
All other models	
1982-86-one (.4)	.8
Rear	
Six–1982-86 (.5)	1.0
V-8	
B-PB-CB Models	
1982-86 (.6)	1.0
All other models	
1982-86 (1.0)	1.4

LABOR 14 PISTONS, RINGS & BEARINGS 14 LABOR

Rings, Renew (See Engine Combinations)

Includes: R&R pistons, remove cylinder top ridge, hone cylinder walls.

(Factory Time)	Chilton Time
Six	
B-PB-CB Models	
1982-86 (6.8)	9.5
All other models	
1982-86 (7.5)	10.1
V-8–318-360 engs	
B-PB-CB Models	
1982-86 (9.6)	13.4
All other models	
1982-86 (9.7)	13.2
w/100 Amp alt add (.6)	.6
w/Air inj add (.6)	.6
w/A.C. add (.4)	.4

Pistons (w/Pin), Renew

Includes: Remove cylinder top ridge, hone cylinder walls, renew connecting rod bearings if required.

(Factory Time)	Chilton Time
Six	
B-PB-CB Models	
1982-86 (8.5)	11.3
All other models	
1982-86 (8.8)	11.2
V-8–318-360 engs	
B-PB-CB Models	
1982-86 (12.1)	15.8
All other models	
1982-86 (9.4)	12.9
w/100 Amp alt add (.6)	.6
w/Air inj add (.6)	.6
w/A.C. add (.4)	.4

Connecting Rod Bearings, Renew

(Factory Time)	Chilton Time
Six	
B-PB-CB Models	
1982-86-one (1.6)	2.3
all (3.1)	4.5
All other models	
1982-86-one (2.3)	3.3
all (4.1)	5.9
V-8–318-360 engs	
B-PB-CB Models	
1982-86-one (2.5)	3.6
all (4.6)	6.6
All other models	
1982-86-one (1.3)	2.4
all (3.4)	5.1

COMBINATIONS

Add to Engine Work

See Machine Shop Operations

GASOLINE ENGINES

(Factory Time)	Chilton Time
DRAIN, EVACUATE AND RECHARGE AIR CONDITIONING SYSTEM	
All models	1.4
ROCKER ARMS & SHAFT ASSY., DISASSEMBLE AND CLEAN OR RECONDITION	
Six (.5)	.6
V-8-one side (.5)	.6
both sides (.9)	1.1
HYDRAULIC VALVE LIFTERS, DISASSEMBLE AND CLEAN	
Each	.2
DISTRIBUTOR, RECONDITION	
All Models (.7)	1.0
CARBURETOR, RECONDITION	
1 BBL (.9)	1.4
2 BBL (1.1)	1.6
4 BBL (1.6)	2.1
VALVE GUIDES, REAM OVERSIZE	
Each (.2)	.3
VALVE, RECONDITION (ALL)	
Cylinder Head Removed	
Six (2.2)	3.0
V-8 (2.7)	4.0
DEGLAZE CYLINDER WALLS	
Each (.1)	.2
REMOVE CYLINDER TOP RIDGE	
Each (.1)	.1
PLASTIGAUGE BEARINGS	
Each (.1)	.1
OIL PUMP, RECONDITION	
Six (.2)	.4
V-8 (.2)	.4
OIL FILTER ELEMENT, RENEW	
All Models (.2)	.3

LABOR 15 CRANKSHAFT & DAMPER 15 LABOR

(Factory Time)	Chilton Time
Crankshaft and Main Bearings, Renew	
Includes: R&R engine assembly, plastigauge all bearings.	
Six	
B-PB-CB Models	
1982-86-w/M.T. (10.5)	13.6
w/A.T. (9.6)	12.7
All other models	
1982-86-w/M.T. (7.3)	10.4
w/A.T. (6.1)	9.6
V-8–318-360 engs	
B-PB-CB Models	
1982-86-w/M.T. (10.0)	14.7
w/A.T. (9.1)	14.2
All other models	
1982-86-w/M.T. (8.8)	12.2
w/A.T. (7.6)	11.0
w/P.S. add (.2)	.2
w/Skid plate add (.3)	.3
V-8–w/A.C. add (1.7)	°1.7
°Includes recharge A.C. system.	
Main Bearings, Renew	
Includes: Plastigauge bearings.	
Six	
B-PB-CB Models	
1982-86-one (2.7)	3.9
all (4.2)	6.0
All other models	
1982-86-one (1.6)	2.7
all (3.2)	5.2
V-8–318-360 engs	
B-PB-CB Models	
1982-86-one (2.6)	3.7
all (3.2)	4.6
All other models	
1982-86-one (1.8)	3.2
all (3.2)	5.4
Rod and Main Bearings, Renew	
Includes: Plastigauge bearings.	
Six	
B-PB-CB Models	
1982-86 (6.0)	8.7
All other models	
1982-86 (4.2)	6.4
V-8–318-360 engs	
B-PB-CB Models	
1982-86 (5.6)	8.1
All other models	
1982-86 (4.5)	7.2
Rear Main Bearing Oil Seals, Renew (Upper & Lower)	
Six	
B-PB-CB Models	
1982-86 (1.4)	2.0
All other models	
1982-86 (1.6)	2.8
V-8–318-360 engs	
B-PB-CB Models	
1982-86 (1.9)	2.7
All other models	
1982-86 (1.4)	3.1
NOTE: Upper seal removed with special tool. If necessary to R&R crankshaft, use Crankshaft and Main Bearings, Renew.	
Vibration Damper, Renew	
Six	
B-PB-CB Models	
1982-86 (.9)	1.4
D-AD-PD Models	
1982-86 (.8)	1.2
W-AW-PW Models	
1982-86 (.8)	1.4
V-8–318-360 engs	
B-PB-CB Models	
1982-86 (.7)	1.3
All other models	
1982-86 (.4)	.7
w/A.C. add (.4)	.4
Crankshaft Pulley, Renew	
All models	
1982-86 (.5)	.9

LABOR 16 CAMSHAFT & TIMING GEARS 16 LABOR

(Factory Time)	Chilton Time
Timing Chain Case Cover Gasket, Renew	
Six	
All models	
1982-86 (1.4)	2.5
V-8–318-360 engs	
B-PB-CB Models	
1982-86 (2.0)	2.9
All other models	
1982-86 (1.8)	2.6
w/P.S. add (.2)	.2
w/A.C. add (.2)	.2
w/100 Amp alt add (.5)	.5
w/Air inj add (.2)	.2
Timing Chain Case Cover Oil Seal, Renew	
Six	
B-PB-CB Models	
1982-86 (1.1)	1.7
D-AD-PD Models	
1982-86 (.9)	1.2
W-AW-PW Models	
1982-86 (.9)	1.2
V-8–318-360 engs	
All models	
1982-86 (.9)	1.3
w/P.S. add (.2)	.2
w/A.C. add (.4)	.4
Timing Chain or Gear, Renew	
Includes: Renew cover oil seal and crankshaft gear if necessary.	
Six	
1982-86 (2.2)	2.9
V-8–318-360 engs	
B-PB-CB Models	
1982-86 (2.4)	3.5
All other models	
1982-86 (2.3)	3.0
w/P.S. add (.2)	.2
w/A.C. add (.4)	.4
w/100 Amp alt add (.5)	.5
w/Air inj add (.2)	.2
Camshaft, Renew	
Includes: Renew valve tappets and adjust valve clearance when required.	
Six	
B-PB-CB Models	
1982-86 (4.4)	6.4
w/A.C. add (.8)	.8
V-8–318-360 engs	
B-PB-CB Models	
1982-86 (5.3)	7.6
All other models	
1982-86 (4.7)	7.1
w/A.C. add (.8)	.8
w/P.S. add (.2)	.2
w/A.T. add (.3)	.3
w/100 Amp alt add (.5)	.5
w/Air inj add (.8)	.8
Camshaft Bearings, Renew	
(Engine Removed and Disassembled)	
All models (2.0)	2.6

LABOR 17 ENGINE OILING SYSTEM 17 LABOR

(Factory Time)	Chilton Time
Oil Pan or Gasket, Renew	
Six	
B-PB-CB Models	
1982-86 (1.1)	1.7
All other models	
1982-86 (1.4)	2.0
V-8–318-360 engs	
B-PB-CB Models	
1982-86 (1.4)	2.0
All other models	
1982-86 (1.0)	1.6
Oil Pump, Renew	
Six	
B-PB-CB models	
1982-86 (.6)	1.2
All other models	
1982-86 (.9)	1.3
V-8–318-360 engs	
B-PB-CB Models	
1982-86 (1.7)	2.3
All other models	
1982-86 (1.1)	1.8
Oil Pump, R&R and Recondition	
Six	
B-PB-CB Models	
1982-86 (.8)	1.5
All other models	
1982-86 (1.4)	1.8
V-8–318-360 engs	
B-PB-CB Models	
1982-86 (2.1)	2.7
All other models	
1982-86 (1.6)	2.2
Pressure Test Engine Bearings (Pan Off)	
All models	1.2
Oil Pressure Gauge (Dash), Renew	
B-PB-CB Models	
1982-86 (.6)	1.1
All other models	
1982-86 (.6)	1.1
Oil Pressure Gauge (Engine), Renew	
one cyl (2.6)	3.8
All models (.4)	.6
Oil Filter Element, Renew	
All models (.2)	.3

LABOR 18 CLUTCH & FLYWHEEL 18 LABOR

(Factory Time)	Chilton Time
Clutch Pedal Free Play, Adjust	
All models (.3)	.5
Clutch Assembly, Renew	
4 Speed	
w/2 wheel drive (2.9)	4.1
w/4 wheel drive (3.9)	5.1
w/Skid plate add (.3)	.3
w/P.T.O. add (.3)	.5
Clutch Release Bearing, Renew	
4 Speed	
w/2 wheel drive (2.5)	3.9
w/4 wheel drive (3.5)	4.9
w/Skid plate add (.3)	.3
w/P.T.O. add (.3)	.5
Clutch Release Fork, Renew	
4 Speed	
B-PB-CB Models (.3)	.6
D-AD-PD-RD Models (.8)	1.2
W-AW-PW Models (.4)	.7
Clutch Torque Shaft, Renew	
Includes: Renew bearings.	
B-PB-CB Models (.3)	.6
All other models (.6)	.9
Flywheel Assembly, Renew	
4 Speed	
1982-86	
w/Overdrive (2.0)	3.7
w/NP-435-445 and 2/wd (3.2)	4.4
w/NP-435-445 and 4/wd (4.6)	5.8
Renew ring gear add (.6)	.9
w/Skid plate add (.3)	.3

LABOR 19 STANDARD TRANSMISSION 19 LABOR

(Factory Time)	Chilton Time
Transmission Assy., R&R or Renew	
4 Speed	
NP-A833 (2.0)	3.2
NP-435-445	
w/2 wheel drive (2.7)	3.9
w/4 wheel drive (3.7)	4.9
w/Skid plate add (.3)	.3
w/P.T.O. add (.3)	.5
Transmission Assy., R&R and Recondition	
4 Speed	
NP-A833 (4.9)	7.0
NP-435-445	
w/2 wheel drive (5.4)	7.5
w/4 wheel drive (6.4)	8.5
w/Skid plate add (.3)	.3
w/P.T.O. add (.3)	.5
Transmission, Recondition (Off Truck)	
NP-A833 (2.9)	3.9
NP-435-445 (2.7)	3.6
Transmission Front Oil Seal, Renew	
Includes: R&R transmission.	
4 Speed	
NP-A833 (2.5)	3.9
NP-435-445	
w/2 wheel drive (2.8)	4.2
w/4 wheel drive (3.8)	5.2
w/Skid plate add (.3)	.3
w/P.T.O. add (.3)	.5
Extension Housing Oil Seal, Renew	
All models (.5)	.7
Speedometer Drive Pinion, Renew	
All models (.3)	.6

LABOR 20 TRANSFER CASE 20 LABOR

(Factory Time)	Chilton Time
Transfer Case Assy., R&R or Renew	
All models (1.6)	2.5
w/Skid plate add (.3)	.3
Transfer Case Assy., R&R and Recondition	
All models (4.6)	6.7
w/Skid plate add (.3)	.3
Transfer Case Adapter, Renew	
All models (2.7)	3.6
w/Skid plate add (.3)	.3
Transfer Case Adapter Gasket, Renew	
All models (1.8)	2.4
w/Skid plate add (.3)	.3
Transfer Case Shift Lever, Renew	
All models (.4)	.7
Rear Output Shaft Seal, Renew	
All models (1.2)	1.6
Transfer Case Shift Rod, Renew	
All models-one (.3)	.5
both (.4)	.7
Transfer Case Front Yoke, Renew	
All models (.9)	1.2
Front Output Shaft Bearing and/or Gasket, Renew	
All models (1.2)	1.6
w/Skid plate add (.3)	.3
Speedometer Drive Pinion, Renew	
All models (.8)	1.1
Power Take Off Assy., R&R or Renew	
1982-86 (1.4)	2.5
Power Take Off Assy., R&R and Recondition	
1982-86 (3.1)	4.9
Power Take Off Mounting Gasket, Renew	
1982-86 (1.3)	2.4
Power Take Off Cover Gasket, Renew	
1982-86 (.4)	.7
Power Take Off Control Cable, Renew	
1982-86 (.6)	1.0

LABOR 21 SHIFT LINKAGE 21 LABOR

(Factory Time)	Chilton Time
STANDARD	
Shift Linkage, Adjust	
All models (.3)	.5
Gearshift Lever, Renew	
All models	
Overdrive (.2)	.4
NP435-445 (.5)	.7
Gearshift Control Rod and/or Swivels, Renew	
All models-one (.5)	.7
both (.7)	1.0
Gearshift Mechanism, Renew (4 Speed)	
All models-w/Overdrive (.6)	1.1
AUTOMATIC	
Throttle Linkage, Adjust	
All models (.3)	.5
Gearshift Lever, Renew	
All models (.4)	.6
Gearshift Control Rod, Renew	
All models (.4)	.6
Gear Selector Indicator, Renew	
All models	
inst panel mount (.7)	1.0
column mount (.2)	.4
Steering Column Shift Housing, Renew	
1982-86	
w/Std column (.9)	1.5
w/Tilt column (2.2)	3.3

	(Factory Time)	Chilton Time
ON TRUCK SERVICES		
Drain and Refill Unit		
All models		.7
Oil Pressure Test		
Note: Using 3 pressure test points.		
All models		1.5
Check Unit For Oil Leaks		
Includes: Clean and dry outside of case and run unit to determine point of leak.		
All models		1.0
Neutral Safety Switch, Renew		
All models	(.3)	.4
Oil Cooler Lines, Renew		
Includes: Cut and form to size.		
All models-one	(.6)	1.0
Transmission Auxiliary Oil Cooler, Renew		
All models	(.7)	1.2
Throttle Linkage, Adjust		
All models	(.3)	.5
Kickdown Band, Adjust		
All models	(.3)	.5
Throttle Valve Lever Shaft Seal, Renew		
All models	(.3)	.7
Valve Body Manual Lever Shaft Seal, Renew		
All models	(.4)	.8
Extension Housing Oil Seal, Renew		
All models	(.5)	1.1
Extension Housing or Adapter Gasket, Renew		
All models		
w/2 wheel drive	(1.3)	2.0
w/4 wheel drive	(2.7)	3.4
w/Skid plate add	(.3)	.3
Governor Assy., R&R or Recondition		
Includes: R&R extension housing.		
All models		
w/2 wheel drive	(1.6)	2.5
w/4 wheel drive	(3.0)	3.9
w/Skid plate add	(.3)	.3
Parking Lock Sprag, Renew		
Includes: R&R extension housing.		
All models		
w/2 wheel drive	(1.3)	2.2
w/4 wheel drive	(2.7)	3.6
w/Skid plate add	(.3)	.3
Output Shaft Bearing and Oil Seal, Renew		
Includes: R&R extension housing.		
All models		
w/2 wheel drive	(1.4)	2.3
w/4 wheel drive	(2.8)	3.7
w/Skid plate add	(.3)	.3
Oil Pan Gasket, Renew		
All models	(.5)	1.0
Oil Filter, Renew		
All models	(.6)	1.1
Parking Lock Sprag Control Rod, Renew		
Includes: R&R oil pan and remove valve body.		
All models	(.9)	1.9
Accumulator Piston, Renew or Recondition		
Includes: R&R oil pan and adjust band.		
All models	(.6)	1.7
Kickdown Servo, Renew or Recondition		
Includes: R&R oil pan and adjust band.		
All models	(.9)	1.9
Reverse Servo, Renew or Recondition		
Includes: R&R oil pan and adjust band.		
All models	(.8)	1.8
Valve Body Assembly, Renew		
Includes: R&R oil pan and replace filter.		
All models	(.9)	1.7
Valve Body Assy., R&R and Recondition		
Includes: R&R oil pan and replace filter. Disassemble, clean, inspect, free all valves. Replace parts as required.		
All models	(1.7)	2.4
Bands, Adjust		
Includes: R&R oil pan.		
All models		
reverse	(.6)	1.4
SERVICES REQUIRING R&R		
Transmission Assembly, Remove and Reinstall		
B-PB-CB Models		
1982-86	(2.0)	4.7
D-AD-PD-RD Models		
1982-86	(2.3)	5.0
W-AW-PW Models		
1982-86	(4.1)	6.9
Renew trans add	(.4)	.5
Flush converter and lines add	(.5)	.7
w/Skid plate add	(.3)	.3
Transmission Assembly, Renew (w/Remanufactured Unit)		
Includes: Remove and install all necessary interfering parts. Transfer all parts not supplied with replacement unit. Road test.		
B-PB-CB Models		
1982-86	(2.3)	5.2
D-AD-PD-RD Models		
1982-86	(2.6)	5.5
W-AW-PW Models		
1982-86	(4.5)	7.4
Pressure test governor add	(.7)	1.1
w/Skid plate add	(.3)	.3
Transmission Assembly, Reseal		
Includes: R&R trans and renew all seals and gaskets.		
B-PB-CB Models		
1982-86	(4.2)	6.8
D-AD-PD-RD Models		
1982-86	(4.5)	7.1
W-AW-PW Models		
1982-86	(6.3)	8.9
w/Skid plate add	(.3)	.3
Transmission and Converter, R&R and Recondition		
Includes: Disassemble trans including valve body, clean, inspect and replace parts as required.		
B-PB-CB Models		
1982-86	(6.5)	11.8
D-AD-PD-RD Models		
1982-86	(6.8)	12.1
W-AW-PW Models		
1982-86	(8.6)	13.9
w/Skid plate add	(.3)	.3
Flush converter and lines add	(.5)	.7
Torque Converter, Renew		
Includes: R&R transmission.		
B-PB-CB Models		
1982-86	(2.2)	5.1
D-AD-PD-RD Models		
1982-86	(2.5)	5.4
W-AW-PW Models		
1982-86	(4.3)	7.3
w/Skid plate add	(.3)	.3
Kickdown Band, Renew		
Includes: R&R transmission.		
B-PB-CB Models		
1982-86	(2.7)	6.1
D-AD-PD-RD Models		
1982-86	(3.0)	6.4
W-AW-PW Models		
1982-86	(4.8)	8.3
w/Skid plate add	(.3)	.3
Reverse Band, Renew		
Includes: R&R transmission.		
B-PB-CB Models		
1982-86	(3.1)	6.7
D-AD-PD-RD Models		
1982-86	(3.4)	7.0
W-AW-PW Models		
1982-86	(5.2)	8.9
w/Skid plate add	(.3)	.3
Transmission Case, Renew		
Includes: R&R transmission.		
B-PB-CB Models		
1982-86	(3.9)	7.7
D-AD-PD-RD Models		
1982-86	(4.2)	8.0
W-AW-PW Models		
1982-86	(6.0)	9.9
w/Skid plate add	(.3)	.3
Front Pump Assembly, Renew or Recondition		
Includes: R&R trans, replace reaction shaft if necessary.		
B-PB-CB Models		
1982-86	(2.6)	5.9
D-AD-PD-RD Models		
1982-86	(2.9)	6.2
W-AW-PW Models		
1982-86	(4.7)	8.1
w/Skid plate add	(.3)	.3
Front Pump Oil Seal, Renew		
Includes: R&R transmission.		
B-PB-CB Models		
1982-86	(2.2)	5.1
D-AD-PD-RD Models		
1982-86	(2.5)	5.4
W-AW-PW Models		
1982-86	(4.3)	7.3
w/Skid plate add	(.3)	.3

LABOR 25 U-JOINTS & DRIVESHAFT 25 LABOR

(Factory Time) Chilton Time

Drive Shaft, R&R or Renew

All Models
- trans to rear axle (.4) 7
- transfer case bearing to rear axle (.4) 7
- transfer case to front axle (.5) 8
- transfer case to rear axle (.4) 7
- trans to center brg (1.2) 1.7

w/Skid plate add (.3) 3

Universal Joints, Renew or Recondition

Includes: R&R drive shaft.

All Models

Single Piece Shaft

(without center bearing)
- trans to rear axle (.8) 1.3
- at rear axle (.6) 1.1
- transfer case to rear axle (.9) 1.4

(transfer case to front axle)
- Dana CV Type (.8) 1.3
- Saginaw CV Type (1.5) 2.0
- at front axle (.7) 1.3

Two Piece Shaft

(with center bearing)
- any one (.8) 1.3

w/Skid plate add (.3) 3

Drive Shaft Center Bearing, Renew

Includes: Renew insulator if necessary.
- All models (1.0) 1.7

LABOR 26 REAR AXLE 26 LABOR

(Factory Time) Chilton Time

Differential, Drain & Refill
- All models 6

Rear Axle Housing Cover, Renew or Reseal
- All models (.4) 6

Axle Shaft, Renew

Includes: Renew outer oil seal, bearing and gasket on 8 3/8 - 9 1/4 axles.

8 3/8 - 9 1/4 Axles
- 1982-86-one (1.1) 1.5

Spicer 60 - 70 Axle
- 1982-86-one (.5) 1.0

Axle Shaft Bearing, Renew

Includes: Renew oil seal.

8 3/8 - 9 1/4 Axles
- 1982-86-one (1.0) 1.7

Axle Shaft Oil Seal, Renew

8 3/8 - 9 1/4 Axles
- 1982-86-one (.9) 1.6

Pinion Shaft Oil Seal, Renew
- All models (.6) 1.0

Rear Axle Housing, Renew

Includes: Renew pinion oil seal, inner and outer axle shaft or wheel bearing oil seals and gaskets.

8 3/8 - 9 1/4 Axles
- All models (4.2) 6.3

Spicer 60 - 70 Axles
- All models (5.7) 8.5

Differential Carrier Assembly, Renew

Note: Assembly includes axle housing.

8 3/8 - 9 1/4 Axles
- All models (2.0) 3.1

Spicer 60 - 70 Axles
- All models (3.0) 4.6

Differential Side Bearings, Renew

Includes: Renew pinion oil seal and adjust backlash.

8 3/8 - 9 1/4 Axles
- All models (2.4) 3.6

Spicer 60 - 70 Axles
- All models (3.1) 4.6

Renew pinion bearings, add (.9) 1.4

Differential Case, Renew

Includes: Renew ring gear and pinion, bearings and side gears if necessary.

8 3/8 - 9 1/4 Axles

Std & Sure Grip
- All models (3.0) 4.5

Spicer 60 - 70 Axles
- All models (3.6) 5.4

Differential Side Gears, Renew

Includes: Renew axle shaft oil seals.

8 3/8 - 9 1/4 Axles
- All models (1.1) 2.5

Spicer 60 - 70 Axles
- All models (1.4) 3.0

Ring Gear and Pinion Set, Renew

Includes: Renew wheel bearing or inner axle shaft oil seals, pinion oil seal and gaskets.

8 3/8 - 9 1/4 Axles
- All models (3.7) 7.0

Spicer 60 - 70 Axles
- All models (3.7) 7.0

Renew side bearings add (.3) 7

LABOR 27 REAR SUSPENSION 27 LABOR

(Factory Time) Chilton Time

Rear Spring, Renew
- All models–one (.5) 9
- both (1.0) 1.7

w/Aux. rear spring add,
- each (.5) 5

w/Skid plate add (.3) 3

Auxiliary Rear Spring, Renew
- All models–one (.7) 1.5

Rear Spring Shackle, Renew

Includes: Renew bushings.

B-PB-CB Models
- one (.3) 7

All other models
- one (.6) 1.0

w/Skid plate add (.3) 3

Rear Shock Absorbers, Renew
- All models–one (.2) 5
- both (.4) 9

LABOR 28 AIR CONDITIONING 28 LABOR

(Factory Time) Chilton Time

Note: If more than one item requires replacement where evacuation and discharging the system is already included in the operation, deduct 1.0 hour for each additional item to the times listed.

Drain, Evacuate, Leak Test and Charge System
- All models 1.7

Partial Charge

Includes: Leak test.

All models
- w/Front unit (.6) 1.1
- w/Front and rear unit (.9) 1.4

Performance Test
- All models 8

Vacuum Leak Test
- All models 9

ON TRUCK SERVICES

Compressor Belt, Renew
- B-PB-CB Models (.4) 6
- All other models (.3) 5

w/Air inj add (.1) 1

Compressor Clutch Field Coil, Renew

Includes: Renew pulley w/Hub, if necessary.

B-PB-CB Models
- w/C-171 comp (.5) 9

All other models (.5) 9

Compressor Clutch Assembly, Renew

B-PB-CB Models
- w/C-171 comp (.5) 8

All other models (.5) 8

C-171 COMP

Compressor Assembly, Renew

Includes: Transfer parts as required. Pressure test and charge system.

Six
- All models (1.8) 3.2

V-8
- B-PB-CB models (2.1) 3.5

LABOR 28 AIR CONDITIONING 28 LABOR

(Factory Time)	Chilton Time
All other models (1.7)	3.1
w/Rear A.C. add (.3)	.3
Compressor Front Cover and/or Seal, Renew	
Includes: Pressure test and charge system.	
Six	
All models (2.2)	3.5
V-8	
B-PB-CB models (2.5)	3.8
All other models (2.1)	3.4
Compressor Rear Cover and/or Seal, Renew	
Includes: Pressure test and charge system.	
Six	
All models (2.1)	3.4
V-8	
B-PB-CB models (2.4)	3.7
All other models (2.0)	3.3
Compressor Center Seal, Renew	
Includes: Pressure test and charge system.	
Six	
All models (2.3)	3.6
V-8	
B-PB-CB models (2.6)	3.9
All other models (2.2)	3.5
Compressor Shaft Gas Seal, Renew	
Includes: Pressure test and charge system.	
Six	
All models (2.2)	3.5
V-8	
B-PB-CB models (2.5)	3.8
All other models (2.1)	3.4
Expansion Valve, Renew	
Includes: Pressure test and charge system.	
B-PB-CB Models	
front unit (1.1)	2.0
rear unit (1.9)	2.8
All other models (1.0)	1.9
Receiver Drier, Renew	
Includes: Add partial charge, leak test and charge system.	
B-PB-CB Models	
w/Front unit (1.1)	1.9
w/Front and rear unit (1.5)	2.3
All other models (1.1)	1.9
Low Pressure Cut Off Switch, Renew	
Includes: Evacuate and charge system.	
B-PB-CB Models	
w/Front unit (1.0)	1.8
w/Front and rear unit (1.3)	2.1
All other models (1.0)	1.8
Clutch Cycling (Thermostatic Control) Switch, Renew	
All models (.3)	.5
Condenser Assembly, Renew	
Includes: Add partial charge, leak test and charge system.	
B-PB-CB Models	
w/Front unit (1.6)	2.5
w/Front and rear unit (1.9)	3.0
All other models (1.2)	2.2
Evaporator Coil, Renew	
Includes: Add partial charge, leak test and charge system.	
B-PB-CB Models	
Front Unit	
1982-86 (2.9)	5.4
Front Unit-Front and Rear Unit Equipped	
1982-86 (3.2)	6.0
Rear Unit (1.6)	2.8
All other models (2.3)	4.7
Blower Motor, Renew	
B-PB-CB Models	
1982-86	
Front (.9)	1.5
Rear (.4)	.9
All other models	
1982-86 (.4)	.9
Blower Motor Resistor, Renew	
All models (.3)	.4
Blower Motor Switch, Renew	
All models	
Front unit (.5)	.9
Rear unit (.3)	.6
Temperature Control Assembly, Renew	
B-PB-CB Models	
1982-86 (.6)	1.0
All other models	
1982-86 (.5)	.9
A.C. Push Button Vacuum Switch, Renew	
All models (.6)	1.0
Air Conditioning Hoses, Renew	
Includes: Evacuate and charge system.	
SUCTION ASSY	
B-PB Models (1.2)	*2.0
All other models (1.1)	1.9
DISCHARGE ASSY	
All models (1.1)	*1.9
REAR UNIT TUBE ASSY	
B-PB Models (3.7)	5.0
SUCTION HOSE	
Rear unit to rear evap. (1.3)	2.1
DISCHARGE HOSE	
Rear unit to rear evap. (1.3)	2.1
SUCTION HOSE	
Rear unit to front tube (1.3)	2.1
DISCHARGE HOSE	
Rear unit to front tube (1.3)	2.1
*w/Rear A.C. add (.3)	.3

LABOR 30 HEAD AND PARKING LAMPS 30 LABOR

(Factory Time)	Chilton Time
Aim Headlamps	
two	.4
four	.6
Headlamp Sealed Beam Bulb, Renew	
Does not include aim headlamps.	
All models-one (.3)	.3
Parking Lamp or Turn Signal Lamp Lens or Bulb, Renew	
All models-one (.2)	.3
Tail and Stop Lamp Lens or Bulb, Renew	
All models-one (.2)	.3
Reflectors, Renew	
All models-one (.2)	.2

LABOR 31 WINDSHIELD WIPER & SPEEDOMETER 31 LABOR

(Factory Time)	Chilton Time
Windshield Wiper Motor, Renew	
B-PB-CB Models	
1982-86 (.8)	1.2
All other models	
1982-86 (.6)	1.1
Windshield Wiper Pivot, Renew	
All models-one (.5)	.7
Wiper Link, Renew	
All models-one (.5)	.8
Wiper Switch, Renew	
B-PB-CB Models	
1982-86 (.3)	.7
All other models	
1982-86 (.4)	.6
Wiper Delay Control Module, Renew	
All models (.3)	.5
Windshield Washer Pump, Renew	
All models (.3)	.5
Speedometer Head, R&R or Renew	
B-PB-CB Models	
1982-86 (.3)	.6
All other models	
1982-86 (.4)	.7
Reset odometer add	.2
Speedometer Cable and Casing, Renew	
All models-each (.5)	.7

LABOR 32 LIGHT SWITCHES & WIRING 32 LABOR

	(Factory Time)	Chilton Time
Headlamp Switch, Renew		
B-PB-CB Models		
1982-83	(.7)	1.0
1984-86	(.4)	1.0
All other models		
1982-86	(.4)	.7
Headlamp Dimmer Switch, Renew		
All models	(.3)	.5
Back-Up Lamp Switch, Renew		
(w/Manual Trans)		
All models	(.3)	.4
Neutral Safety Switch, Renew		
All models	(.3)	.4
Stop Light Switch, Renew		
All models	(.3)	.4
Turn Signal Switch, Renew		
1982-86		
w/Std column	(.5)	.9
w/Tilt column	(.9)	1.4
Turn Signal or Hazard Warning Flasher, Renew		
All models	(.2)	.3

LABOR 34 CRUISE CONTROL 34 LABOR

	(Factory Time)	Chilton Time
Cruise Control Servo, Renew		
All models	(.4)	.6
Cruise Control Cable, Renew		
All models	(.3)	.5
Cruise Control Vacuum Hoses, Renew		
All models	(.2)	.3
Cruise Control Switch (Turn Signal Lever), Renew		
1982-86		
w/Std column	(.5)	.9
w/Tilt column	(.9)	1.4
Cruise Control Cut-Off Safety Switch, Renew		
All models	(.3)	.4

Dodge Rampage/Plymouth Scamp Front Drive Pick-Ups

GROUP INDEX

ALPHABETICAL INDEX

LABOR — SERVICE BAY OPERATIONS — LABOR

(Factory Time) — Chilton Time

COOLING

Winterize Cooling System

Includes: Run engine to check for leaks, tighten all hose connections. Test radiator and pressure cap, drain radiator and engine block. Add anti-freeze and refill system.

	Chilton Time
All models	.5

Thermostat, Renew

All models (.4)	.6

Radiator Hoses, Renew

All models-upper (.3)	.4
lower (.5)	.6

Drive Belt, Adjust

All models-one	.3
each adtnl	.1

FUEL

Carburetor Air Cleaner, Service

All models (.3)	.3

Carburetor Float Level, Adjust

All models (.7)	1.1

Fuel Filter, Renew

All models	
in line (.2)	.3
in tank (.5)	.8

BRAKES

Brakes, Adjust (Minor)

Includes: Adjust brakes, fill master cylinder.

two wheels	.4

Bleed Brakes (Four Wheels)

Includes: Fill master cylinder.

All models (.4)	.6

Parking Brake, Adjust

All models (.3)	.4

LUBRICATION SERVICE

Lubricate Chassis, Change Oil & Filter

Includes: Inspect and correct all fluid levels.

All models	.6
Install grease fittings add	.1

Lubricate Chassis

Includes: Inspect and correct all fluid levels.

All models	.4
Install grease fittings add	.1

Engine Oil & Filter, Change

Includes: Inspect and correct all fluid levels.

All models	.4

WHEELS

Wheel, Renew

one	.5

Wheel, Balance

one	.3
each adtnl	.2

Wheels, Rotate (All)

All models	.5

ELECTRICAL

Aim Headlamps

All models (.3)	.4

Headlamp Sealed Beam Bulb, Renew

Does not include aim headlamps.

All models-each (.2)	.3

Battery Cables, Renew

All models-ground (.2)	.2
positive (.5)	.6

Headlamp Switch, Renew

All models (.3)	.4

Headlamp Dimmer Switch, Renew (Column Mounted)

All models (.3)	.6

Stop Light Switch, Renew

All models (.3)	.4
w/Cruise control add (.1)	.1

Back-Up Lamp Switch, Renew (w/Manual Trans)

All models (.2)	.4

Neutral Safety Switch, Renew

All models (.3)	.4

Turn Signal Switch, Renew

All models (.5)	1.0

License Lamp Lens, Renew

All models (.2)	.2

Tail Lamp Lens, Renew

All models-one (.2)	.3

Side Marker Lamp Assy., Renew

All models (.2)	.3

License Lamp Assembly, Renew

All models (.2)	.2

Turn Signal or Hazard Warning Flasher, Renew

All models (.2)	.3

Horn Relay, Renew

All models (.2)	.3

Horns, Renew

All models-one (.2)	.4

LABOR — 1 TUNE UP 1 — LABOR

(Factory Time) — Chilton Time

Compression Test

All models	.6

Engine Tune Up, (Electronic Ignition)

Includes: Test battery and clean connections. Tighten manifold and carburetor mounting bolts. Check engine compression, clean and adjust or renew spark plugs. Test resistance of spark plug cables. Inspect distributor cap and rotor. Adjust air gap. Check vacuum advance operation. Reset ignition timing. Adjust idle mixture and idle speed. Service air cleaner. Inspect and adjust drive belts. Inspect choke operation and adjust or free up. Check operation of EGR valve.

All models	1.5

LABOR — 2 IGNITION SYSTEM 2 — LABOR

(Factory Time) — Chilton Time

Spark Plugs, Clean and Reset or Renew

All models (.5)	.6

Ignition Timing, Reset

All models (.3)	.4

Spark Control Computer, Renew

All models (.3)	1.0

Distributor, Renew

Includes: Reset ignition timing.

All models (.4)	.6

Distributor, R&R and Recondition

Includes: Reset ignition timing.

All models (.9)	1.5

Distributor Pick-Up Plate and Coil Assy., Renew

Includes: R&R distributor and reset ignition timing.

All models (.5)	.8

Distributor Pick-Up Plate and Coil Assy., Renew (Hall Effect)

Does not require R&R of distributor.

All models (.3)	.6

Vacuum Advance Unit, Renew

Includes: R&R distributor and reset ignition timing.

All models (.6)	.9

Distributor Cap, Renew

All models (.2)	.4

Ignition Coil, Renew

All models (.2)	.4

Ignition Cables, Renew

All models (.2)	.5

Ignition Switch, Renew

All models (.4)	.8

Ignition Key Buzzer Switch, Renew

All models (.3)	.5

Ignition Key Warning Buzzer, Renew

All models (.2)	.3

Ignition Lock Housing, Renew

Does not include painting.

All models (.9)	1.6

LABOR 3 FUEL SYSTEM 3 LABOR

(Factory Time) Chilton Time

Fuel Pump, Test
Includes: Disconnect line at carburetor, attach pressure gauge.
All models 3

Carburetor Air Cleaner, Service
All models (.3) 3

Heated Air Door Sensor, Renew
All models (.2) 3

Automatic Choke, Renew
All models (.7) 1.0

Choke Vacuum Kick, Adjust
All models (.2) 3

Choke Vacuum Kick Diaphragm, Renew
All models (.2) 4

Accelerator Pump, Renew
All models (.4) 8

Needle Valve and Seat, Renew
Includes: Adjust float level and idle speed and mixture.
All models (.7) 1.1

Carburetor Assembly, Renew
Includes: All necessary adjustments.
All models (.8) 1.2

Carburetor, R&R and Clean or Recondition
Includes: All necessary adjustments.
All models (1.6) 2.4

Fuel Filter, Renew
All models
in line (.2) 3
in tank (.5) 8

Fuel Pump, Renew
All models (.5) 9
Add pump test if performed.

Fuel Tank, Renew
Includes: Drain and refill tank.
All models (.9) 1.5

Fuel Gauge (Dash), Renew
All models (.2) 5

Fuel Gauge (Tank), Renew
All models (.6) 1.0

Intake Manifold, Renew
All models (2.0) 3.7

Intake and Exhaust Manifold Gaskets, Renew
All models (1.9) 3.5

LABOR 3A EMISSION CONTROLS 3A LABOR

(Factory Time) Chilton Time

AIR INJECTION SYSTEM

Air Pump, Renew
All models (.5) 7

Injection Tube and Check Valve Assy., Renew
All models
ex manif mount (.5) 8
to conv
one or both (.4) 6

Air Pump Diverter/Switching Valve, Renew
All models (.4) 7

Aspirator, Renew
All models (.2) 4

Aspirator Tube, Renew
All models (.7) 1.0

Orifice Spark Advance Control Valve, Renew
All models (.3) 5

EVAPORATIVE EMISSION

Vapor Canister, Renew
All models (.4) 6

Vapor Canister Filter, Renew
All models (.2) 3

CRANKCASE EMISSION

Crankcase Vent Valve, Renew
All models (.2) 3

Crankcase Vent Hose, Renew
All models-one (.2) 2

E.G.R. SYSTEM

E.G.R. Valve, Renew
All models (.6) 8

E.G.R. Coolant Valve, Renew (CCEGR)
All models-one (.3) 5

Coolant Controlled Engine Vacuum Switch, Renew (CCEVS)
All models (.3) 5

HEATED INLET AIR SYSTEM

Carburetor Air Cleaner, Service
All models (.3) 3

Heated Air Door Sensor, Renew
All models-one (.2) 3

EFC SYSTEM

Oxygen Sensor, Renew
All models (.2) 4

LABOR 4 ALTERNATOR & REGULATOR 4 LABOR

(Factory Time) Chilton Time

Alternator Circuits, Test
Includes: Test battery, regulator and alternator output.
All models 6

Alternator Assy., Renew
Includes: Transfer pulley if required.
All models (.8) 1.2
w/A.C. add (.5) 5
Add circuit test if performed.

Alternator, R&R and Recondition
Includes: Test and disassemble, renew parts as required.
All models (1.5) 2.1
w/A.C. add (.5) 5

Alternator Front Bearing or Retainer, Renew
Includes: R&R alternator.
All models (.8) 1.3
w/A.C. add (.5) 5

Renew rear brg. add 2

Alternator Regulator, Test and Renew
All models
External type (.2) 6

Alternator Gauge, Renew
All models (.2) 5

Instrument Cluster Voltage Limiter, Renew
All models (.2) 5

LABOR 5 STARTING SYSTEM 5 LABOR

Starter Draw Test (On Truck)
All models 3

Starter Assembly, Renew
Includes: Test starter relay, starter solenoid and amperage draw.
All models (1.0) 1.6

Starter, R&R and Recondition
Includes: Test relay, starter solenoid and amperage draw. Turn down armature.
All models (1.5) 2.5
Renew field coils add (.4) 5

(Factory Time) Chilton Time

Starter Drive, Renew
Includes: R&R starter.
All models (1.6) 2.0

Starter Solenoid, Renew
Includes: R&R starter.
All models (1.1) 1.8

Starter Relay, Renew
All models (.2) 3

Neutral Safety Switch, Renew
All models (.3) 4

Ignition Switch, Renew
All models (.4) 8

Battery Cabies, Renew
All models-ground (.2) 2
positive (.5) 6

LABOR 6 BRAKE SYSTEM 6 LABOR

(Factory Time) Chilton Time

Brake Pedal Free Play, Adjust
All models 3

Brakes, Adjust (Minor)
Includes: Adjust brakes, fill master cylinder.
two wheels 4

Bleed Brakes (Four Wheels)
Includes: Fill master cylinder.
All models (.4) 6

Brake Shoes and/or Pads, Renew
Includes: Install new or exchange shoes or pads, adjust service and hand brake. Bleed system.
All models
Front-disc (.5) 8
Rear-drum (.8) 1.5
All four wheels 2.2
Resurface rotor, add-each 9
Resurface brake drum, add-each 5

Rear Brake Drum, Renew
All models-one (.5) 6

BRAKE HYDRAULIC SYSTEM

Wheel Cylinder, Renew
Includes: Bleed system.
All models-one (.7) 1.1
both (1.3) 2.1

Wheel Cylinder, R&R and Recondition
Includes: Hone cylinder and bleed system.
All models-one 1.2
both 2.3

Brake Hose, Renew (Flex)
Includes: Bleed system.
All models-front-one (.4) 8
rear-one (.4) 8

Master Cylinder, Renew
Includes: Bleed complete system.
All models (.5) 9

Master Cylinder, R&R and Recondition
Includes: Bleed complete system.
All models 1.6

COMBINATIONS
Add to Brakes, Renew

See Machine Shop Operations

(Factory Time) Chilton Time

RENEW WHEEL CYLINDER
Each (.3) 3

REBUILD WHEEL CYLINDER
Each 4

REBUILD CALIPER ASSEMBLY
Each 5

RENEW MASTER CYLINDER
All models (.5) 6

REBUILD MASTER CYLINDER
All models 8

RENEW BRAKE HOSE
Each (.3) 3

RENEW REAR WHEEL GREASE SEALS
One side (.2) 3

RENEW BRAKE DRUM
Each (.3) 3

RENEW DISC BRAKE ROTOR
Each (.2) 2

DISC BRAKE ROTOR STUDS, RENEW
Each 1

(Factory Time) Chilton Time

Master Cylinder Reservoir, Renew
Includes: Bleed complete system.
All models (.6) 1.0

Brake System Combination Valve, Renew
Includes: Bleed complete system.
All models (.7) 1.0

Load Sensing Proportioning Valve, Renew
Includes: Adjust valve and bleed brakes.
All models (.7) 1.1

(Factory Time) Chilton Time

POWER BRAKES

Brake Booster Assembly, Renew
All models (.8) 1.2

Brake Booster Check Valve, Renew
All models (.2) 2

DISC BRAKES

Brake Shoes and/or Pads, Renew
Includes: Install new or exchange shoes or pads, adjust service and hand brake. Bleed system.
All models
Front-disc (.5) 8
Rear-drum (.8) 1.5
All four wheels 2.2
Resurface rotor, add-each 9
Resurface brake drum, add-each 5

Disc Brake Rotor w/Hub, Renew
All models-each (1.0) 1.4

Disc Brake Rotor, Renew
All models (.3) 6

Caliper Assembly, Renew
Includes: Bleed system.
All models-each (.5) 9

Caliper Assembly, R&R and Recondition
Includes: Bleed system.
All models-each (.8) 1.4

PARKING BRAKE

Parking Brake, Adjust
All models (.3) 4

Parking Brake Warning Lamp Switch, Renew
All models (.2) 3

Parking Brake Lever, Renew
All models (.4) 7

Parking Brake Cables, Renew
All models-front (.7) 1.0
rear-each (.4) 6

LABOR 7 COOLING SYSTEM 7 LABOR

(Factory Time) Chilton Time

Winterize Cooling System
Includes: Run engine to check for leaks, tighten all hose connections. Test radiator and pressure cap, drain radiator and engine block. Add anti-freeze and refill system.
All models 5

Thermostat, Renew
All models (.4) 6

Radiator Assembly, R&R or Renew
Includes: Drain and refill coolant.
All models (.5) 9
w/A.T. add (.1) 1

ADD THESE OPERATIONS TO RADIATOR R&R

Boil & Repair 1.5
Rod Clean 1.9
Repair Core 1.3
Renew Tank 1.6
Renew Trans. Oil Cooler 1.9
Recore Radiator 1.7

(Factory Time) Chilton Time

Coolant Reserve Tank, Renew
All models (.5) 7

Radiator Fan Motor, Renew
All models (.4) 5

Radiator Fan Motor Relay, Renew
All models (.2) 3

Radiator Fan Switch, Renew
All models (.3) 6

Radiator Hoses, Renew
All models-upper (.3) 4
lower (.5) 6

Water Pump, Renew
Includes: Drain and refill coolant.
All models (1.1) 1.6
w/A.C. add (.5) 7

Drive Belt, Adjust
All models-one 3
each adtnl 1

(Factory Time) Chilton Time

Drive Belt, Renew
All models
A.C. (.2) 3
Fan & Alter (.3) 4
P/Str (.5) 6

Transaxle Auxiliary Oil Cooler, Renew
All models (.3) 6

Temperature Gauge (Engine Unit), Renew
All models (.3) 4

Heater Hoses, Renew
All models-one (.4) 4
both (.5) 6

Heater Core, R&R or Renew
All models-wo/A.C. (1.0) 1.7
w/A.C. (2.5) *4.2
*Includes recharge A.C. system.

LABOR 7 COOLING SYSTEM 7 LABOR

(Factory Time) Chilton Time

ADD THESE OPERATIONS TO HEATER CORE R&R

Boil & Repair 1.2
Repair Core 9
Recore 1.2

Heater Control Assembly, Renew
All models (.4) 7

Heater Blower Motor, Renew
All models (.4) 6

Heater Blower Motor Resistor, Renew
All models (.2) 3

Heater Blower Motor Switch, Renew
All models (.4) 7

Water Valve, Renew (w/A.C.)
All models (.3) 5

LABOR 8 EXHAUST SYSTEM 8 LABOR

(Factory Time) Chilton Time

Muffler, Renew
All models (.4) 8
Cut exhaust pipe add 2

Catalytic Converter, Renew
All models-one (.7) 9

Exhaust Pipe Extension, Renew
All models (.6) 1.0

Exhaust Pipe, Renew
All models (.7) 1.1
Cut at muffler add 2

Intake and Exhaust Manifold Gaskets, Renew
All models (1.9) 3.5

Exhaust Manifold, Renew
All models (2.7) 3.7

Exhaust Pipe Flange Gasket, Renew
All models (.4) 6

COMBINATIONS

Muffler, Exhaust and Tail Pipe, Renew
All models (1.0) 1.5

LABOR 9 FRONT SUSPENSION 9 LABOR

(Factory Time) Chilton Time

Note: On all front suspension operations alignment charges must be added if performed. Time given does not include alignment.

Wheel, Renew
one (.3) 5

Wheels, Rotate (All)
All models 5

Wheel, Balance
one 3
each adtnl 2

Check Alignment of Front End
All models 5
Note: Deduct if alignment is performed.

Toe-Out, Adjust
All models 6

Align Front End
Includes: Adjust camber, toe-out and center steering wheel.
All models (.8) 1.4

Steering Knuckle, Renew (One)
Add alignment charges.
All models (1.0) 1.6

Front Strut Assembly, R&R or Renew (One)
Add alignment charges.
All models (.8) 1.4

Lower Control Arm, Renew (One)
Add alignment charges.
All models (1.1) 1.6

Lower Ball Joint, Renew (One)
Includes: Reset toe-in.
All models (.8) 1.2

Front Coil Spring or Strut Bearing, Renew (One)
Add alignment charges.
All models (.8) 1.5

Steering Knuckle Bearing, Renew (One) (Wheel Bearing)
All models (1.2) 1.6

Front Sway Bar, Renew
All models (.4) 7

Front Suspension Strut (Dual Path) Mount Assy., Renew
Includes: Renew bearing.
1984-86 (.8) 1.5

K-Frame Assembly, Renew
Add alignment charges.
All models (2.5) 4.0

Drive Shaft Boot, Renew
Includes: Clean and lubricate C/V joint.
All models
one-inner or outer (.7) 1.0
both-one side (1.0) 1.4
Renew shaft seal, add
right side (.1) 1
left side (.3) 3

Drive Shaft C/V Joint, Renew
All models
one-inner or outer (.7) 1.0
both-one side (1.0) 1.4
inter shaft U-joint (.6) 1.0
Renew shaft seal, add
right side (.1) 1
left side (.3) 3

Front Wheel Drive Shaft Assy., Renew
All models
inter spline yoke (.6) 1.0
inter stub shaft (.6) 1.0
all others-each (1.0) 1.4
Renew shaft seal, add
right side (.1) 1
left side (.3) 3

Intermediate Shaft Support Bearing, Renew
All models-each (.6) 1.0

Drive Shaft Oil Seal, Renew
All models
right side (.5) 8
left side (.7) 1.1

LABOR 11 STEERING GEAR 11 LABOR

(Factory Time) Chilton Time

Tie Rod Ends, Renew
Includes: Adjust toe, replace tie rod if necessary.
All models
outer-one (.9) 1.2
Inner and Outer
w/P.S.-one (1.9) 2.5

STANDARD STEERING

Horn Contact, Renew
All models (.2) 3

Steering Wheel, Renew
All models (.2) 3

Steering Column Jacket, Renew
Does not include painting.
All models (1.0) 1.9

Upper Mast Jacket Bearing, Renew
Includes: Replace insulators if necessary.
All models (.8) 1.7

LABOR 11 STEERING GEAR 11 LABOR

(Factory Time) Chilton Time

Steering Column Lower Shaft Bearing, Renew
Includes: Replace support if necessary.
All models (.4)....... .7

Steering Column Shaft, Renew
All models (.8)....... 2.0

Steering Column Flexible Coupling, Renew
All models (.5)....... .9

Steering Gear Assembly, Renew
All models (1.7)....... 3.0

POWER STEERING

Power Steering Pump Pressure Check
All models....... .5

Power Steering Pump Belt, Renew
All models (.5)....... .6
w/A.C. add (.1)....... .1

Power Steering Gear Assembly, Renew
All models (2.3)....... 3.1

Steering Gear Oil Seals, Renew
Includes: R&R gear assy. and reset toe-in.
All models (3.5)....... 5.1

Upper and Lower Valve Pinion Seals, Renew
All models (1.4)....... 2.0
Renew brgs add (.3)....... .5

Power Steering Pump, Renew
Includes: Test pump and transfer pulley.
All models (1.2)....... 1.9

Power Steering Pump, R&R and Recondition
All models (1.5)....... 2.8

Pump Flow Control Valve, Test and Clean or Renew
All models (.6)....... 1.0

Power Steering Reservoir or Seals, Renew
All models (.9)....... 1.4

Pump Drive Shaft Oil Seal, Renew
All models (1.1)....... 1.9

Power Steering Hoses, Renew
All models-each (.4)....... .5

LABOR 12 CYLINDER HEAD & VALVE SYSTEM 12 LABOR

(Factory Time) Chilton Time

Compression Test
All models....... .6

Cylinder Head Gasket, Renew
Includes: Clean carbon.
All models (3.4)....... 4.8
w/A.C. add (.1)....... .1
w/Air inj add (.2)....... .2

Cylinder Head, Renew
Includes: Transfer all necessary parts. Clean carbon. Make all necessary adjustments.
All models (5.3)....... 8.0
w/A.C. add (.1)....... .1
w/Air inj add (.2)....... .2

Clean Carbon and Grind Valves
Includes: R&R cylinder head, adjust valve clearance when required. Minor engine tune up.
All models (4.8)....... 6.8
w/A.C. add (.1)....... .1
w/Air inj add (.2)....... .2

Cylinder Head Cover Gasket, Renew or Reseal
All models (.8)....... 1.1

Valve Rocker Arms or Shaft, Renew
All models (1.2)....... 1.6

Valve Springs and/or Valve Stem Oil Seals, Renew (Head on Car)
All models (1.9)....... 2.9

Valve Tappets, Renew
All models-one (1.0)....... 1.5
all (1.9)....... 2.9

LABOR 13 ENGINE ASSEMBLY & MOUNTS 13 LABOR

(Factory Time) Chilton Time

Engine Assembly, Remove and Install
Includes: R&R engine and transmission as a unit.
Does not include transfer of any parts or equipment.
All models....... 4.5
w/A.C. add (.5)....... .5
w/Air inj add (.3)....... .3

Engine Support, Renew
All models
Engine-right side (.3)....... .5
left side (.3)....... .5
center (.4)....... .6
Trans/Axle
Roll rod (.3)....... .5

Engine Assy., R&R and Recondition
Includes: Rebore block, install new pistons, rings, rod and main bearings. Clean carbon, grind valves, replace valve stem oil seals. Tune engine.
All models (17.8)....... 22.6
w/A.C. add (.5)....... .5
w/Air inj add (.3)....... .3

Short Engine Assembly, Renew
(w/All Internal Parts Less Cyl. Head and Oil Pan)
Includes: R&R engine and transmission as a unit. Transfer all necessary parts not supplied with replacement engine. Clean carbon, grind valves. Minor tune up.
All models (9.1)....... 15.0
w/A.C. add (.5)....... .5
w/Air inj add (.3)....... .3

LABOR 14 PISTONS, RINGS & BEARINGS 14 LABOR

COMBINATIONS

Add to Engine Work

See Machine Shop Operations

DRAIN, EVACUATE & RECHARGE AIR CONDITIONING SYSTEM
All models....... 1.4

DISTRIBUTOR, RECONDITION
All models (.7)....... .7

CARBURETOR, RECONDITION
All models....... 2.0

RECONDITION CYL. HEAD (HEAD REMOVED)
All models (1.4)....... 2.0

CAMSHAFT, RENEW (HEAD DISASSEMBLED)
All models (.1)....... .2

DEGLAZE CYLINDER WALLS
Each (.1)....... .1

REMOVE CYLINDER TOP RIDGE
Each (.1)....... .1

VALVES, RECONDITION (HEAD REMOVED)
All models (1.4)....... 2.0

MAIN BEARINGS, RENEW (PAN REMOVED)
All models (.9)....... 1.4

OIL PUMP, RENEW
All models (.2)....... .3

OIL FILTER ELEMENT, RENEW
All models (.2)....... .3

LABOR 14 PISTONS, RINGS & BEARINGS 14 LABOR

(Factory Time) Chilton Time

Pistons or Connecting Rods, Renew
Includes: Replace rings and connecting rod bearings, deglaze cylinder walls, clean carbon. Minor tune up.
All models
one cyl (4.9) 7.2
all cyls (7.0) 9.3
w/A.C. add (.2) 2
w/Air inj add (.2) 2

Rings, Renew (See Engine Combinations)
Includes: Replace connecting rod bearings, deglaze cylinder walls, clean carbon. Minor tune up.
All models
one cyl (4.6) 6.9
all cyls (5.9) 8.1
w/A.C. add (.2) 2
w/Air inj add (.2) 2

Connecting Rod Bearings, Renew
All models (2.1) 3.0

LABOR 15 CRANKSHAFT & DAMPER 15 LABOR

(Factory Time) Chilton Time

Crankshaft and Main Bearings, Renew
Includes: R&R engine assy.
All models (6.7) 11.2
w/A.C. add (.2) 2
w/P.S. add (.3) 3

Main Bearings, Renew (All)
Includes: R&R engine assy.
All models (7.0) 11.0
w/A.C. add (.2) 2
w/P.S. add (.3) 3

Main and Rod Bearings, Renew (All)
Includes: R&R engine assy.
All models (7.7) 12.0
w/A.C. add (.2) 2
w/P.S. add (.3) 3

Rear Main Bearing Oil Seals, Renew (Complete)
All models (3.5) 5.4
w/Cruise control add (.2) 2

Crankshaft Rear Bearing Oil Seal Retainer, Renew
Includes: Replace oil seal, complete.
All models (4.1) 6.3
w/Cruise control add (.2) 2

Crankshaft Front Oil Seal, Renew
All models (1.3) 2.0
w/A.C. add (.2) 2
w/P.S. add (.2) 2

Crankshaft Pulley, Renew
All models (.5) 8
w/A.C. add (.1) 1
w/P.S. add (.1) 1

LABOR 16 CAMSHAFT & TIMING GEARS 16 LABOR

(Factory Time) Chilton Time

Intermediate Shaft, Renew
All models (1.3) 2.5
w/A.C. add (.2) 2
w/P.S. add (.1) 1

Intermediate Shaft Oil Seal, Renew
All models (1.1) 1.8
w/A.C. add (.2) 2
w/P.S. add (.2) 2

Intermediate Shaft Sprocket, Renew
All models (1.7) 2.7
w/A.C. add (.5) 5
w/P.S. add (.2) 2
w/Air inj add (.2) 2

Camshaft, Renew
All models (1.7) 2.8
Renew valve springs add (1.1) 1.1

Camshaft Sprocket, Renew
Includes: Replace cover oil seal.
All models (1.7) 2.4
w/A.C. add (.5) 5
w/P.S. add (.2) 2
w/Air inj add (.2) 2

Timing Belt, Renew
All models (1.6) 2.3
w/A.C. add (.5) 5
w/P.S. add (.2) 2
w/Air inj add (.1) 1

Timing Belt Cover, Renew
All models-upper (.2) 4
lower (.6) 1.0
w/A.C. add (.2) 2
w/P.S. add (.1) 1

Timing Belt Tensioner, Renew
All models (.9) 1.5
w/A.C. add (.2) 2
w/P.S. add (.2) 2

Camshaft Oil Seal, Renew
All models-front (.7) 1.1
rear (.4) 8

LABOR 17 ENGINE OILING SYSTEM 17 LABOR

(Factory Time) Chilton Time

Oil Pan or Gasket, Renew
All models (1.0) 1.4

Pressure Test Engine Bearings (Pan Off)
All models 1.0

Oil Pump, Renew
All models (1.3) 1.7

Oil Pump, R&R and Recondition
All models (1.7) 2.2

Oil Pressure Gauge (Engine), Renew
All models (.3) 4

Oil Filter Element, Renew
All models (.2) 3

LABOR 18 CLUTCH & FLYWHEEL 18 LABOR

(Factory Time) Chilton Time

Clutch Assembly, Renew
All models (3.3) 4.6
Renew input seal add (.2) 2
w/Cruise control add (.2) 2

Clutch Release Bearing, Renew
All models (3.2) 4.4
w/Cruise control add (.2) 2

Clutch Self Adjusting Mechanism, Renew
All models (.3) 6

Clutch Release Cable, Renew
All models (.3) 5

Flywheel, Renew
All models (3.4) 4.7
w/Cruise control add (.2) 2
Renew ring gear add 5

LABOR 19 STANDARD TRANSMISSION 19 LABOR

	(Factory Time)	Chilton Time
Front Wheel Drive Shaft Assy., Renew		
All models-each	(1.0)	1.5
Renew shaft seal, add		
right side	(.1)	.1
left side	(.3)	.3
Drive Shaft Boot, Renew		
Includes: Clean and lubricate C/V joint.		
All models		
one-inner or outer	(.7)	1.0
both-one side	(1.0)	1.4
Renew shaft seal, add		
right side	(.1)	.1
left side	(.3)	.3
Drive Shaft C/V Joint, Renew		
All models		
one-inner or outer	(.7)	1.0
both-one side	(1.0)	1.4
Renew shaft seal, add		
right side	(.1)	.1
left side	(.3)	.3
Drive Shaft Oil Seal, Renew		
All models-right side	(.5)	.7
left side	(.8)	1.1
Manual Trans/Axle, Remove & Install		
Does not include transfer of any parts or equipment.		
All models	(3.1)	4.3
Manual Trans/Axle Assy., Renew		
Includes: Transfer all necessary parts not supplied with replacement unit.		
All models	(3.5)	4.9
Manual Trans/Axle Assy., R&R and Recondition (Complete)		
All models		
w/A460	(5.6)	8.0
w/A465	(5.9)	8.5

LABOR 21 SHIFT LINKAGE 21 LABOR

	(Factory Time)	Chilton Time
MANUAL		
Gearshift Control Rod and/or Swivel, Renew		
All models	(.3)	.4
Crossover Rod, Renew		
All models	(.3)	.4
Gearshift Lever, Renew		
All models-floor shift	(.4)	.6
Gearshift Mechanism, Renew		
All models	(.6)	.9
w/Console add	(.1)	.1
Gearshift Selector Tube Assy., Renew		
All models	(.4)	.6
Selector Shaft Seal, Renew		
All models	(.8)	1.1
Trans/Axle Selector Shaft, Renew		
All models	(1.3)	1.7
AUTOMATIC		
Throttle Linkage, Adjust		
All models	(.2)	.4
Gearshift Lever, Renew		
All models	(.3)	.5
Gearshift Mechanism, Renew		
Includes: Replace knob and push button if necessary.		
All models	(.5)	.8
Gearshift Control Cable, Renew		
All models	(.7)	1.0
Throttle Lever Control Cable, Renew		
Includes: Adjust cable.		
All models	(.3)	.6

LABOR 23 AUTOMATIC TRANSMISSION 23 LABOR

	(Factory Time)	Chilton Time
ON CAR SERVICES		
Drain & Refill Unit		
All models		.6
Oil Pressure Check		
All models		.8
Check Unit For Oil Leaks		
Includes: Clean and dry outside of case and run unit to determine point of leak.		
All models		.8
Neutral Safety Switch, Renew		
All models	(.3)	.4
Oil Cooler Lines, Renew		
Includes: Cut and form to size.		
All models	(.4)	.6
Throttle Linkage, Adjust		
All models	(.2)	.4
Kickdown Band, Adjust		
All models	(.2)	.4
Throttle Valve Lever Shaft Seal, Renew		
All models	(.5)	.8
Valve Body Manual Lever Shaft Seal, Renew		
All models	(.3)	.6
Differential Gear Cover, Renew		
All models	(.8)	1.2
Drive Shaft Boot, Renew		
Includes: Clean and lubricate C/V joint.		
All models		
one-inner or outer	(.7)	1.0
both-one side	(1.0)	1.4
Renew shaft seal, add		
right side	(.1)	.1
left side	(.3)	.3
Drive Shaft C/V Joint, Renew		
All models		
one-inner or outer	(.7)	1.0
both-one side	(1.0)	1.4
inter shaft U-joint	(.6)	1.0
Renew shaft seal, add		
right side	(.1)	.1
left side	(.3)	.3
Front Wheel Drive Shaft Assy., Renew		
All models		
inter spline yoke	(.6)	1.0
inter stub shaft	(.6)	1.0
all others-each	(1.0)	1.4
Renew shaft seal, add		
right side	(.1)	.1
left side	(.3)	.3
Intermediate Shaft Support Bearing, Renew		
All models-each	(.6)	1.0
Drive Shaft Seal, Renew		
All models-right side	(.5)	.8
left side	(.8)	1.1
Transfer Gear Cover, Renew		
All models	(.5)	.7
Governor Assy., Renew or Recondition		
Includes: R&R oil pan.		
All models	(1.3)	2.4
Governor Support and Parking Gear, Renew		
Includes: R&R oil pan.		
All models	(1.9)	2.9
Oil Pan and/or Gasket, Renew		
All models	(.6)	1.2
Oil Filter, Renew		
Includes: R&R oil pan.		
All models	(.7)	1.4
Parking Lock Sprag, Renew		
Includes: R&R oil pan.		
All models	(1.5)	2.6
Accumulator Piston, Renew or Recondition		
Includes: R&R oil pan.		
All models	(1.1)	2.2
Kickdown Servo, Renew		
Includes: R&R oil pan.		
All models	(1.4)	2.5
Reverse Servo, Renew		
Includes: R&R oil pan.		
All models	(1.2)	2.2
Valve Body, Renew		
Includes: R&R oil pan and renew filter.		
All models	(1.0)	2.1

LABOR 23 AUTOMATIC TRANSMISSION 23 LABOR

(Factory Time) Chilton Time

Valve Body, R&R and Recondition
Includes: R&R oil pan and renew filter.
All models (1.7) 3.2

SERVICES REQUIRING R&R

Trans/Axle Assy., Remove & Install
All models (3.1) 4.5

Trans/Axle Assembly, Reseal
Includes: R&R trans axle and renew all seals and gaskets.
All models (5.0) 7.0

Trans/Axle Assembly, Renew
Includes: Remove and install all necessary interfering parts. Transfer any parts not supplied with replacement unit. Road test.
All models (3.5) 4.9

Trans/Axle Assy., R&R and Recondition
Includes: Disassemble complete, clean, inspect and replace all parts as required.
All models (9.4) 12.7
Flush converter and cooler lines, add (.5) 5

Kickdown Band, Renew
All models (4.0) 6.2

Reverse Band, Renew
All models (4.2) 6.5

Trans/Axle Case, Renew
All models (7.7) 10.0

Front and Rear Clutch Seals, Renew
All models (4.2) 6.5

Torque Converter, Renew
All models (3.3) 5.2

Torque Converter Drive Plate, Renew (With Ring Gear)
All models (3.3) 5.2

Front Oil Pump, Renew
All models (3.7) 6.0

Front Oil Pump Seal, Renew
All models (3.3) 5.2

Reaction Shaft and/or Bushing, Renew
Includes: Renew front pump if necessary.
All models (3.7) 6.0

LABOR 26 REAR AXLE & SUSPENSION 26 LABOR

(Factory Time) Chilton Time

Rear Wheel Bearing, Renew or Repack
Includes: Replace bearing cups and grease seal.
All models-each (.6) 9

Rear Wheel Grease Seal, Renew
All models-each (.4) 7

Rear Spring, Renew
All models-one (.6) 9
both (1.1) 1.7

Rear Shock Absorbers, Renew
All models-one (.3) 4
both (.4) 6

Rear Spring Bushing and/or Shackle, Renew
All models-one (.4) 6

Stub Axle Spindle, Renew
All models-one (.5) 8

Rear Spring Hanger, Renew
All models-one (.7) 1.1

LABOR 28 AIR CONDITIONING 28 LABOR

(Factory Time) Chilton Time

Note: If more than one item requires replacement where evacuation and discharging the system is already included in the operation, deduct 1.0 hour for each additional item to the times listed.

Drain, Evacuate, Leak Test and Charge System
All models 1.4

Partial Charge
Includes: Leak test.
All models (.6) 8

Performance Test
All models 8

Vacuum Leak Test
All models 8

Compressor Drive Belt, Renew
All models (.2) 3

C-171 COMPRESSOR

Compressor Clutch Field Coil, Renew
Includes: Replace pulley w/hub if necessary.
All models (.6) 9

Compressor Clutch Pulley (W/Hub), Renew
All models (.4) 7

Compressor Clutch Assembly, Renew
All models (.6) 9

Compressor Assembly, Renew
Includes: Pressure test and charge system.
All models (1.4) 2.5

Compressor Front Cover or Seal, Renew
Includes: R&R compressor. Pressure test and charge system.
All models (2.1) 3.4

Compressor Rear Cover or Seal, Renew
Includes: R&R compressor. Pressure test and charge system.
All models (2.0) 3.3

Compressor Center Seal, Renew
Includes: R&R compressor. Pressure test and charge system.
All models (2.2) 3.5

Compressor Shaft Gas Seal, Renew
Includes: R&R compressor. Pressure test and charge system.
All models (2.1) 3.4

Expansion Valve, Renew
Includes: Pressure test and charge system.
All models (1.0) 1.7

Receiver Dryer, Renew
Includes: Add partial charge, leak test and charge system.
All models (.9) 1.6

Low Pressure Cut Off Switch, Renew
Includes: Charge system.
All models (.9) 1.4

Clutch Cycling (Thermostatic Control) Switch, Renew
All models (.3) 6

Condenser Assembly, Renew
Includes: Add partial charge, leak test and charge system.
All models (1.5) 2.2

Temperature Control Assembly, Renew
All models (.4) 7

Push Button Vacuum Switch, Renew
All models (.5) 9

Temperature Control Cable, Renew
All models (.6) 9

Vacuum Hose Control Assy., Renew
All models
main assy (2.0) 3.0

Evaporator Coil, Renew
Includes: Add partial charge, leak test and charge system.
All models (2.7) 3.9

Vacuum Actuator, Renew
All models
outside air door (.3) 6
heater/defroster door (.3) 6
A/C mode door (.6) 1.0

Blower Motor, Renew
All models (.6) 9

Blower Motor Resistor, Renew
All models (.3) 4

Blower Motor Switch, Renew
All models (.4) 8

Air Conditioning Hoses, Renew
Includes: Add partial charge, leak test and charge system.
All models-one (1.1) 1.5
each adtnl (.3) 5

LABOR 30 HEAD AND PARKING LAMPS 30 LABOR

(Factory Time) Chilton Time

Aim Headlamps
All models (.3) 4

Headlamp Sealed Beam Bulb, Renew
Does not include aim headlamps.
All models-each (.2) 3

Side Marker Lamp Assy., Renew
All models (.2) 3

License Lamp Assembly, Renew
All models (.2) 2

License Lamp Lens, Renew
All models (.2) 2

Tail Lamp Lens, Renew
All models-one (.2) 3

LABOR 31 WINDSHIELD WIPER & SPEEDOMETER 31 LABOR

(Factory Time) Chilton Time

Windshield Wiper Motor, Renew
All models (.4) 7

Windshield Wiper Switch, Renew
All models (.4) 9

Wiper Pivot, Renew (One)
All models (.3) 5

Wiper Links, Renew
All models (.3) 6

Windshield Washer Pump, Renew
All models (.3) 4

Speedometer Head, R&R or Renew
Does not include reset odometer.
All models (.4) 7

Speedometer Cable and Casing, Renew
All models
speed control to trans (.2) 6
speed control to speedo (.3) 6
trans to speedo (.4) 9

Speedometer Cable (Inner), Renew or Lubricate
All models
speed control to trans (.2) 5
speed control to speedo (.3) 5
trans to speedo (.3) 7

Speedometer Drive Pinion, Renew
Includes: Replace oil seal.
All models (.2) 4

Radio, R&R
All models (.3) 7

LABOR 32 LIGHT SWITCHES & WIRING 32 LABOR

(Factory Time) Chilton Time

Headlamp Switch, Renew
All models (.3) 4

Headlamp Dimmer Switch, Renew (Column Mounted)
All models (.3) 6

Stop Light Switch, Renew
All models (.3) 4
w/Cruise control add (.1) 1

Back-Up Lamp Switch, Renew (w/Manual Trans)
All models (.2) 4

Neutral Safety Switch, Renew
All models (.3) 4

Turn Signal Switch, Renew
All models (.5) 1.0

Turn Signal or Hazard Warning Flasher, Renew
All models (.2) 3

Horn Relay, Renew
All models (.2) 3

Horns, Renew
All models-one (.2) 4

LABOR 34 CRUISE CONTROL 34 LABOR

(Factory Time) Chilton Time

Speed Control Switch (Turn Signal Lever), Renew
All models (.3) 6

Speed Control Servo Assy., Renew
All models (.3) 5

Speed Control Cable, Renew
All models (.4) 7

Speed Control Vacuum Hose, Renew
All models (.2) 3

Cruise Control Clutch Safety Cut-Out Switch, Renew
All models (.3) 4

Ford Trucks—Ser F100—300 Vans • Bronco • Pick-Ups

GROUP INDEX

ALPHABETICAL INDEX

LABOR 1 TUNE UP 1 LABOR

(Factory Time) Chilton Time

Compression Test

	Chilton Time
Four	.5
Six	.6
V-6	.7
V-8	.9

Engine Tune Up, (Electronic Ignition)

Includes: Test battery and clean connections. Tighten manifold and carburetor mounting bolts. Check engine compression, clean and adjust or renew spark plugs. Test resistance of spark plug cables. Inspect distributor cap and rotor. Adjust air gap. Reset ignition timing. Adjust idle mixture and idle speed. Service air cleaner. Inspect and adjust drive belts. Inspect choke operation and adjust or free up. Check operation of EGR valve.

	Chilton Time
Four	1.5
Six	2.1
V-6	2.0
V-8	2.7
w/A.C. add	.6

LABOR 2 IGNITION SYSTEM 2 LABOR

(Factory Time) Chilton Time

Spark Plugs, Clean and Reset or Renew

	Chilton Time
RANGER-BRONCO	
Four (.3)	.4
Six (.4)	.6
V-6 (.6)	.8
V-8 (.6)	.8
AEROSTAR	
Four (.5)	.7
V-6 (1.0)	1.4
ECONOLINE-Six (.5)	.7
V-8 (.6)	.8
F100-350-Six (.4)	.8
V-6 (.4)	.6
V-8 (.6)	.8

Ignition Timing, Reset

	Chilton Time
All models (.3)	.4

Distributor, R&R or Renew

Includes: Reset ignition timing.

	Chilton Time
RANGER (.8)	1.1
AEROSTAR	
Four (.6)	1.0
V-6 (.8)	1.3
BRONCO (.4)	.8
BRONCO II (.8)	1.1
ECONOLINE (.5)	.9
F100-350-Six (.5)	.9
V-6 (.5)	.9
V-8 (.6)	1.0

Distributor, R&R and Recondition

Includes: Reset ignition timing.

	Chilton Time
BRONCO-Six (1.2)	1.7
V-8 (1.5)	2.0
ECONOLINE-Six (1.4)	1.9
V-8 (1.6)	2.1
F100-350-Six (1.2)	1.7
V-6 (1.5)	2.0
V-8 (1.7)	2.2

Distributor Cap and/or Rotor, Renew

	Chilton Time
RANGER (.5)	.6
BRONCO (.3)	.5
ECONOLINE (.4)	.6
F100-350 (.3)	.5
AEROSTAR (.4)	.6

Distributor Points and Condenser, Renew

	Chilton Time
BRONCO (.4)	.7
ECONOLINE (.5)	.8
F100-350-Six (.4)	.7
V-8 (.5)	.8

Distributor Vacuum Control Valve, Renew

	Chilton Time
All models (.3)	.5

Vacuum Control Unit, Renew

Includes: R&R distributor and reset ignition timing.

	Chilton Time
BRONCO (.7)	1.2
ECONOLINE (.8)	1.2
F100-350-Six (.8)	1.2
V-8 (.9)	1.3

Ignition Coil, Renew

Includes: Test.

	Chilton Time
AEROSTAR (.3)	.5
RANGER (.4)	.5
BRONCO I & II (.4)	.5
ECONOLINE (.5)	.6
F100-350 (.4)	.5

Ignition Module Assembly, Renew

	Chilton Time
All models	
Dura-Spark II (.2)	.4
TFI (.5)	.7
Perform system test add (.3)	.3

Distributor Armature, Renew

	Chilton Time
All models (.3)	.6

Distributor Stator, Renew

Includes: R&R armature.

	Chilton Time
All models (.4)	.8

Ignition Cables, Renew

Includes: Test wiring.

	Chilton Time
AEROSTAR	
Four (.5)	.7
V-6 (.7)	1.0
RANGER (.6)	.8
BRONCO (.5)	.7
ECONOLINE (.5)	.8
F100-350 (.4)	.7

Ignition Switch, Renew

	Chilton Time
All models (.3)	.7

LABOR 3 FUEL SYSTEM 3 LABOR

(Factory Time) Chilton Time

GASOLINE ENGINES

Fuel Pump, Test

Includes: Disconnect line at carburetor, attach pressure gauge.

	Chilton Time
All models	
mechanical	.4
electric	.5

Fuel Filter, Renew

	Chilton Time
RANGER-BRONCO (.3)	.4
AEROSTAR	
Four (.7)	.9
V-6 (.3)	.4
ECONOLINE-Six (.4)	.5
V-8 (.3)	.4
F100-350	
Six (.4)	.5
V-8 (.3)	.4

Carburetor, Adjust (On Truck)

	Chilton Time
All models (.3)	.4

Carburetor, R&R or Renew

Includes: Necessary adjustments.

	Chilton Time
RANGER-BRONCO I & II	
Four (.4)	.7
Six (.5)	.9
V-6 (.6)	1.0
V-8 (.6)	1.0
AEROSTAR	
V-6 (.7)	1.1
ECONOLINE-Six (.8)	1.2
V-8 (.5)	.9
F100-350-Six (.5)	.9
V-6 (.5)	.9
V-8 (.8)	1.2

Carburetor, R&R and Clean or Recondition

Includes: Necessary adjustments.

	Chilton Time
RANGER-BRONCO I & II	
Four (1.7)	2.5
Six (1.1)	1.7
V-6 (2.2)	3.0
V-8 (1.6)	2.2
AEROSTAR	
V-6 (2.3)	3.1
ECONOLINE-Six (1.4)	2.0
V-8 (1.5)	2.1
F100-350-Six (1.1)	1.7
V-6 (1.3)	2.2
V-8-2 bbl	
w/Auto choke (1.8)	2.5
w/Manual choke (1.3)	1.9
4 bbl	
Motorcraft (1.8)	2.5
Holly (2.0)	2.7

Fuel Pump, R&R or Renew

	Chilton Time
RANGER-Four (.3)	.5
V-6 (.5)	.8
AEROSTAR	
V-6 (.8)	1.1
BRONCO (.5)	.8
ECONOLINE (.4)	.7
F100-350 (.4)	.7

Add pump test if performed.

LABOR 3 FUEL SYSTEM 3 LABOR

(Factory Time)	Chilton Time
Fuel Tank, Renew	
RANGER	
aft tank (.8)	1.4
mid tank (1.0)	1.8
AEROSTAR (1.1)	1.7
BRONCO (.7)	1.5
BRONCO II (2.1)	3.0
ECONOLINE (.9)	1.5
F100-350	
aft tank (.9)	1.5
mid tank (1.2)	2.0
Auxiliary Fuel Tank, R&R or Renew	
BRONCO (.7)	1.3
ECONOLINE (.9)	1.5
F100-350 (.9)	1.5
Fuel Gauge (Tank), Renew	
RANGER	
aft tank (.7)	1.1
mid tank (.8)	1.2
AEROSTAR (1.0)	1.5
BRONCO	
aft tank (.9)	1.3
mid tank (.7)	1.1
BRONCO II (2.1)	3.0
ECONOLINE	
rear mounted (.3)	.6
side mounted (1.1)	1.9
F100-350	
cab mounted (.3)	.6
rear mounted (1.1)	1.9
side mounted (.5)	.9
Fuel Gauge (Dash), Renew	
RANGER (.6)	1.0
AEROSTAR (.6)	1.0
BRONCO (.6)	1.0
BRONCO II (.6)	1.0
ECONOLINE (.5)	.9
F100-350 (.5)	.9
Intake Manifold or Gaskets, Renew	
RANGER-BRONCO I & II-AEROSTAR	
Four	
2.0 L eng (1.2)	2.0
w/P.S. add (.2)	.2
Six	
1983 & earlier (1.1)	1.6
1984 & later (3.4)	4.7
V-6 (2.8)	3.8
V-8 (1.9)	2.7
ECONOLINE-Six	
1983 & earlier (.9)	1.8
1984 & later (3.4)	4.9
V-8	
302-351 engs (1.6)	2.2
460 eng (2.3)	3.3
F100-350	
Six	
1983 & earlier (1.1)	1.6
1984 & later (3.4)	4.7
V-6 (2.3)	3.3
V-8	
255-302 351W engs (1.5)	2.2
351M-400 engs (1.9)	2.7
460 eng (2.0)	2.5
Renew manif add (.4)	.5

ELECTRONIC FUEL INJECTION (EFI)

(Factory Time)	Chilton Time
Fuel Injector Assy., Renew	
Four–one (.9)	1.3
all (1.0)	1.6
V-8–right side-all (1.4)	1.9
left side-all (.8)	1.1
both sides-all (1.7)	2.3
Air Intake Charge Throttle Body, Renew	
Four–All models (.6)	1.1
Fuel Charging Wiring Assy., Renew	
Four (.3)	.6
V-8 (1.2)	1.7
Fuel Charging Pressure Regulator Assy., Renew	
Four (1.0)	1.5
V-8 (.8)	1.3
Fuel Pump, Renew	
Four	
Ranger (.5)	.8
Aerostar (.6)	.9
w/P.S. add (.2)	.2
V-8 (.5)	.8
Fuel Injection Manifold, Renew	
Four	
Ranger (.8)	1.2
Aerostar (.9)	1.3
V-8–right side (1.3)	1.8
left side (.8)	1.3
both sides (1.7)	2.8
Intake Manifold and/or Gasket, Renew	
Four	
upper (1.1)	1.5
lower (2.2)	3.1
w/P.S. add (.2)	.2
V-8	
upper (1.1)	1.5
lower (3.0)	4.0

DIESEL ENGINE

(Factory Time)	Chilton Time
Glow Plugs, Renew	
Four–one (.2)	.4
all (.3)	.7
V-8–one (.4)	.6
all (.8)	1.2
Glow Plug Module, Renew	
Four (.3)	.4
Glow Plug Relay, Renew	
Econoline (.4)	.6
All other models (.3)	.4
Fuel/Water Separator, Renew	
V-8	
F series (.4)	.6
Econoline (.8)	1.0
Fuel Pump, Renew	
V-8	
All models (.5)	.7
Fuel Filter Element, Renew	
All models	
Four & V-8 (.3)	.4
Intake Manifold and or Gaskets, Renew	
Four	
2.2L eng (1.4)	2.2
2.3L eng (2.4)	3.3
V-8	
F series (2.4)	3.3
Econoline (2.6)	3.6
Renew manif add (.2)	.5
Fuel Injection Pump Nozzles, Renew	
Four–2.3L eng	
one (.8)	1.1
each adtnl (.2)	.2
all (1.2)	1.7
V-8	
one (.3)	.5
each adtnl (.5)	.6
all (1.5)	2.1
Fuel Injection Pump, Renew	
Four	
2.2L eng (1.6)	2.4
2.3L eng (1.4)	1.9
V-8	
F series (2.0)	2.7
Econoline (2.8)	3.8
Injection Pump Drive Gear, Renew	
Four (1.9)	2.9
2.2L eng (1.9)	2.9
2.3L eng (1.4)	2.0
V-8	
F series (1.8)	2.5
Econoline (3.4)	4.7

LABOR 3A EMISSION CONTROLS 3A LABOR

(Factory Time)	Chilton Time
Emission Control Check	
Includes: Check and adjust engine idle speed and mixture, reset ignition timing. Check PCV valve.	
All models (.4)	.6

CRANKCASE EMISSION

(Factory Time)	Chilton Time
Positive Crankcase Ventilation Valve, Clean or Renew	
All models-clean (.4)	.5
renew (.2)	.3

EVAPORATIVE EMISSION TYPE

(Factory Time)	Chilton Time
Canister, Renew	
Bronco (.2)	.4
Econoline (.2)	.4
F100-350 (.4)	.6
Vapor Separator, Renew	
Bronco (.2)	.4
Econoline (.2)	.4
F100-350	
cab mounted (.2)	.4
frame mounted (.3)	.5

CONTROLLED COMBUSTION TYPE

(Factory Time)	Chilton Time
Air Cleaner Motor, Renew	
All models (.2)	.3
Air Cleaner Sensor, Renew	
All models (.2)	.3

(Factory Time) Chilton Time

THERMACTOR TYPE

Thermactor Air Pump, Renew
Four (.3) 5
V-6 (.5) .... *.7
Six (.3) 5
V-8-302-351 W engs (.5) 7
351M, 400 engs (.7) 1.0
460 eng (.4) 7
*Aerostar add 2

Thermactor Drive Belt, Renew
All models (.3) 5

Anti-Backfire Valve, Renew
All models (.3) 4

Relief Valve, Renew
All models (.3) 4

Thermactor Air By-Pass Valve, Renew
All models (.4) 6

TRANSMISSION CONTROLLED SPARK

Controlled Spark Solenoid, Renew
All models (.2) 3

Thermostatic Vacuum Switch, Renew
All models (.2) 3

Temperature Switch, Renew
All models (.3) 5

Spark Relay, Renew
All models (.2) 3

Transmission Controlled Spark Switch, Renew
All models (.3) 5

E.G.R. TYPE

E.G.R. Valve, Renew
Four (.3) .... *.5
Six (.4) 6
V-6 (.3) 5
V-8 (.5) 7
*Aerostar add 2

E.G.R. Switch, Renew
All models (.3) 4

Vacuum Switch, Renew
All models (.3) 4

Air Supply Pump, Renew
All models (.3) 4

Thermostatic Exhaust Control Valve, Renew
Econoline-Six (1.7) 2.4
F100-350-Six (1.5) 2.2

ELECTRONIC EMISSION CONTROL

EEC System, Test
BRONCO (.7) 1.0

EGR Cooler, Renew
Does not include system test.
BRONCO (.6) 1.0

Power Relay, Renew
Does not include system test.
BRONCO (.3) 4

Calibrator Assembly, Renew
Does not include system test.
BRONCO (.2) 4

Processor Assembly, Renew
Does not include system test.
BRONCO (.3) 6

Feedback Carburetor Actuator, Renew
Does not include system test.
BRONCO (.3) 4

Exhaust Gas Oxygen Sensor, Renew
Does not include system test.
BRONCO (.4) 7

Barometric Manifold Absolute Pressure Sensor, Renew
Does not include system test.
BRONCO (.3) 5

Thermactor Air Bypass and Air Diverter Solenoid, Renew
Does not include system test.
BRONCO (.3) 5

MCU SYSTEM

MCU System, Test
All models (.4) 6

Oxygen Sensor, Renew
Does not include system test.
All models (.3) 7

Thermactor Air Valve, Renew
Does not include system test.
All models (.5) 7

Ported Vacuum Switch, Renew
Does not include system test.
All models (.1) 2

Fuel Control Solenoid, Renew
Does not include system test.
All models (.1) 2

E.G.R. Valve, Renew
Does not include system test.
All models (.3) 4

TAB/TAD Solenoid, Renew
Does not include system test.
All models (.1) 2

Canister Purge Solenoid, Renew
Does not include system test.
All models (.1) 2

Vacuum Switch, Renew
Does not include system test.
All models (.3) 4

MCU/ECU Module, Renew
Does not include system test.
All models (.3) 5

Low Temperature Switch, Renew (Electric or Vacuum)
Does not include system test.
All models
2 port (.4) 5
3 port (.3) 4

Feedback Carburetor Actuator, Renew
Does not include system test.
All models (.4) 6

Solenoid, Renew
Does not include system test.
All models-one (.3) 4

Mid Temperature Switch, Renew (Electric or Vacuum)
Does not include system test.
All models (.3) 4

ELECTRONIC ENGINE CONTROL IV

E.E.C. System, Test
All models (.6) 1.0

Throttle Position Sensor, Renew
Does not include system test.
Four
All models (.6) 8
V-6
All models (.3) 5
Six
Econoline (.4) 6
All other models (.2) 4
V-8
Econoline (.4) 6
All other models (.3) 5

Idle Tracking Switch, Renew
Does not include system test.
All models (.2) 4

Air Change Temperature Sensor, Renew
Does not include system test.
All models (.1) 3

Exhaust Gas Oxygen Sensor, Renew
Does not include system test.
Four
All models (.2) 4
V-6
All models (.1) 3
Six
Econoline (.2) 4
All other models (.1) 3
V-8
All models (.2) 5

Knock Sensor, Renew
Does not include system test.
All models (.2) 4

Processor Assembly, Renew
Does not include system test.
All models (.2) 3

Electronic Control Power Relay, Renew
Does not include system test.
Four
All models (.1) 3
V-6
All models (.2) 4
Six & V-8
All models (.1) 3

Choke Cover, Renew
Does not include system test.
V-6
All models (.6) 1.0

E.G.R. Shut-Off Solenoid, Renew
Does not include system test.
Econoline (.2) 3
All other models (.1) 2

Fuel Pump Relay, Renew
Does not include system test.
Four
All models (.1) 2

Fuel Pump Inertia Switch Assy., Renew
Does not include system test.
Four
All models (.1) 2

Throttle Positioner Assembly, Renew
Does not include system test.
All models
Six (.5) 7
V-6 (.4) 6

LABOR 3A EMISSION CONTROLS 3A LABOR

(Factory Time)	Chilton Time
Fuel Injector Assembly, Renew	
Does not include system test.	
Four	
Ranger-one (.7)	.9
all (.8)	1.3
Aerostar-one (1.1)	1.3
all (1.2)	1.7
Knock Sensor, Renew	
Does not include system test.	
All models	
Four (.1)	.3
V-6 (.1)	.3
Air Change Temperature Sensor, Renew	
Does not include system test.	
V-6	
All models (.1)	.3
Canister Purge Valve, Renew	
Does not include system test.	
V-6	
All models (.1)	.2
Six	
Econoline (.2)	.3
All other models (.1)	.2
V-8	
All models (.2)	.3
Engine Coolant Temperature Sensor, Renew	
Does not include system test.	
All models (.2)	.4
Feedback Control Solenoid, Renew	
Does not include system test.	
V-6	
All models (.3)	.4
Six	
Econoline (.4)	.6
All other models (.2)	.3
V-8	
Econoline (.3)	.4
All other models (.5)	.7
Manifold Absolute Pressure Sensor, Renew	
Does not include system test.	
All models (.1)	.3
E.G.R. Valve Position Sensor, Renew	
Does not include system test.	
All models (.2)	.4
Thermactor Air Diverter Valve, Renew	
Does not include system test.	
Econoline (.3)	.5
All other models (.2)	.4
Thick Film Ignition Module, Renew	
Does not include system test.	
Four	
All models (.4)	.6
V-6	
All models (.5)	.7
Six & V-8	
Econoline (.4)	.6
All other models (.3)	.4
Thermactor Air By-Pass Valve, Renew	
Does not include system test.	
All models (.2)	.3
E.G.R. Valve, Renew	
Does not include system test.	
Four	
Ranger (.3)	.4
Aerostar (.5)	.7
V-6	
All models (.2)	.4
V-8	
Econoline (.4)	.6
All other models (.3)	.5
E.G.R. On-Off Solenoid, Renew	
Does not include system test.	
All models (.2)	.3
Throttle Kicker Actuator, Renew	
Does not include system test.	
All models (.3)	.4
Tab/Tad Solenoids, Renew	
Does not include system test.	
All models (.2)	.3
E.G.R. Control Solenoids, Renew	
Does not include system test.	
All models (.2)	.3
Throttle Kicker Solenoid, Renew	
Does not include system test.	
All models (.2)	.3
Profile Ignition Pick-Up Sensor, Renew	
Does not include system test.	
Econoline (.6)	.8
All other models (.5)	.7

LABOR 4 ALTERNATOR AND REGULATOR 4 LABOR

(Factory Time)	Chilton Time
Alternator Circuits, Test	
Includes: Test battery, regulator and alternator output.	
All models (.4)	.6
Alternator, R&R or Renew	
Four (.4)	.7
Six	
Econoline (1.1)	1.5
All other models (.4)	.7
V-6 (.5)	.9
V-8	
Econoline-w/460 eng (1.2)	•1.6
All other models (.5)	.9
•w/Dual Therm. pumps add	.5
Renew brushes add	.3
Renew drive brg add	.3
Renew end brg add	.2
Renew rectifier assy add	.4
Renew stator assy add	.4
Alternator Regulator, Renew	
All models (.3)	.5
Add circuit test if performed.	
Ammeter, Renew	
All models (.5)	.9
Instrument Cluster Voltage Regulator, Renew	
All models (.5)	.7

LABOR 5 STARTING SYSTEM 5 LABOR

(Factory Time)	Chilton Time
Starter Draw Test (On Truck)	
All models (.3)	.3
Starter, R&R or Renew	
Gas Engines	
All models (.4)	.7
Diesel Engines	
Four (.8)	1.1
V-8 (.5)	.8
Renew brushes add	
TK	.5
Motorcraft	.6
Delco	.2
Renew starter drive add	.6
Recond complete add	
TK	1.5
Motorcraft & Delco	1.0
Renew field coils add	.5
Add draw test if performed.	
Starter Solenoid Relay, Renew	
All models (.3)	.5
Battery Cables, Renew	
All models-each (.3)	.4

LABOR 6 BRAKE SYSTEM 6 LABOR

(Factory Time) — Chilton Time

Brake Pedal Free Play, Adjust
- All models (.3) 4

Brakes, Adjust (Minor)

Includes: Adjust brakes, fill master cylinder.
- two wheels 4
- four wheels 7

Bleed Brakes (Four Wheels)

Includes: Fill master cylinder.
- All models (.3) 6

Brake Shoes, Renew

Includes: Install new or exchange shoes, service self adjustors. Adjust service and hand brake. Bleed system.
- BRONCO-front (1.5) 2.0
  - rear (1.3) 1.8
  - All four wheels (2.2) 3.7
- ECONOLINE-F100-350
  - front (1.1) 1.5
  - rear (1.7) 2.2
  - All four wheels (2.3) 3.5
- F100-250 4X4
  - front (1.3) 1.8
  - rear (1.7) 2.2
  - All four wheels (2.5) 3.7
- Resurface brake drum add, each 5

Brake Shoes and/or Pads, Renew

Includes: Install new or exchange brake shoes or pads. Adjust service and hand brake. Bleed system.
- RANGER-AEROSTAR
  - front-disc (.7) 1.1
  - rear-drum (1.1) 1.8
  - All four wheels (1.6) 2.8
- BRONCO-front-disc (.7) 1.1
  - rear-drum ((1.1) 1.8
  - All four wheels (1.6) 2.8
- ECONOLINE 100-150, F100-150
  - front-disc (.7) 1.2
  - rear-drum (1.1) 1.8
  - All four wheels (1.5) 2.9
- F100-250 4X4
  - front-disc (.7) 1.1
  - rear-drum (1.1) 1.8
  - All four wheels (1.5) 2.8
- Resurface brake rotor add, each 9
- Resurface brake drum add, each 5

Front Brake Drum and Hub Assy., Renew
- BRONCO-one (.7) 9
  - both (1.2) 1.6
- ECONOLINE-one (.5) 8
  - both (.7) 1.1
- F100-350-one (.5) 8
  - both (.8) 1.2

Rear Brake Drum, Renew
- All models
- Semi-Floating Axle
  - one (.4) 6
  - both (.6) 9
- Dana Axle (Full Floating)
  - one (.7) 1.1
  - both (1.1) 1.9

Brake Pressure Warning Light Switch, Renew
- All models (.3) 5

BRAKE HYDRAULIC SYSTEM

Wheel Cylinder, Renew

Includes: Bleed system.

Front
- BRONCO-one (1.1) 1.5
  - both (2.1) 2.9
- ECONOLINE, F100-350
  - one (.9) 1.3
  - both (1.7) 2.5

COMBINATIONS

Add to Brakes, Renew

See Machine Shop Operations

(Factory Time) — Chilton Time

RENEW WHEEL CYLINDER
- Each (.3) 4

REBUILD WHEEL CYLINDER
- Each (.3) 6

REBUILD CALIPER ASSEMBLY
- Each (.5) 8

RENEW MASTER CYLINDER
- All models (.4) 7

REBUILD MASTER CYLINDER
- All models 1.3

RENEW BRAKE HOSE
- Each (.3) 3

RENEW REAR WHEEL GREASE SEALS
- One side (.2) 4

FRONT WHEEL BEARINGS, REPACK OR RENEW SEALS (BOTH WHEELS)
- Drum brakes (.3) 6
- Disc brakes (.4) 7
- 4X4 (.6) 8

RENEW BRAKE DRUM
- Each (.2) 3

RENEW DISC BRAKE ROTOR
- Each (.3) 5

(Factory Time) — Chilton Time

- F100-250 4X4
  - one (1.0) 1.4
  - both (1.9) 2.7

Rear
- RANGER-AEROSTAR-one (.8) 1.4
  - both (1.5) 2.6
- BRONCO-one (1.0) 1.5
  - both (1.9) 2.9
- ECONOLINE, F100-350
  - one (1.2) 1.6
  - both (2.3) 3.0
- F100-250 4X4
  - one (1.2) 1.6
  - both (2.3) 3.0

Wheel Cylinder, R&R and Recondition

Includes: Hone cylinder and bleed system.

Front
- BRONCO-one (1.1) 1.8
  - both (2.1) 3.5
- ECONOLINE, F100-350
  - one (.9) 1.6
  - both (1.7) 3.1
- F100-250 4X4
  - one (1.0) 1.7
  - both (1.9) 3.3

Rear
- RANGER-AEROSTAR-one (.8) 1.6
  - both (1.5) 3.0
- BRONCO-one (1.0) 1.8
  - both (1.9) 3.5
- ECONOLINE, F100-350
  - one (1.2) 1.9
  - both (2.3) 3.7
- F100-250 4X4
  - one (1.2) 1.9
  - both (2.3) 3.7

(Factory Time) — Chilton Time

Brake Hose, Renew

Includes: Bleed system.

Front
- RANGER-AEROSTAR-one (.5) 8
  - both (.6) 1.0
- BRONCO, F100-350, F100-250 4X4
  - one (.5) 8
  - both (.6) 1.0
- ECONOLINE 100-350
  - one (.6) 9
  - both (.8) 1.1

Rear
- RANGER-AEROSTAR-one (.5) 8
- BRONCO, F100-250 4X4
  - one (.5) 8
- ECONOLINE 100-350, F100-350
  - one (.6) 9

Master Cylinder, Renew

Includes: Bleed complete system.
- Aerostar (.7) 1.1
- All other models
  - wo/Booster (.6) 1.0
  - w/Booster (.5) 9

Master Cylinder, R&R and Recondition

Includes: Hone cylinder and bleed complete system.
- Aerostar (1.0) 1.6
- All other models
  - wo/Booster (.8) 1.5
  - w/Booster (.7) 1.4

Vacuum Pump, Renew

(w/Diesel Eng)
- ECONOLINE-F-series (.6) 9
- All other models (.4) 6

Brake Differential Valve, R&R or Renew

Includes: Bleed complete system and transfer switch.
- All models (.7) 1.2

POWER BRAKES

Power Brake Booster, R&R or Renew
- AEROSTAR (1.0) 1.5
- BRONCO, F100-250 4X4 (.5) 8
- ECONOLINE (.4) 1.0
- F100-350 (.5) 8
- w/Cruise control add (.2) 2

DISC BRAKES

Brake Shoes and/or Pads, Renew

Includes: Install new or exchange brake shoes or pads. Adjust service and hand brake. Bleed system.
- RANGER
  - front-disc (.7) 1.1
  - rear-drum (1.1) 1.8
  - All four wheels (1.6) 2.8
- BRONCO-front-disc (.7) 1.1
  - rear-drum (1.1) 1.8
  - all four wheels (1.6) 2.8
- ECONOLINE 100-150, F100-150
  - front-disc (.7) 1.2
  - rear-drum (1.1) 1.8
  - all four wheels (1.5) 2.9
- F100-250 4X4
  - front-disc (.7) 1.1
  - rear-drum (1.1) 1.8
  - all four wheels (1.5) 2.8
- Resurface brake rotor add, each 9
- Resurface brake drum add, each 5

LABOR 6 BRAKE SYSTEM 6 LABOR

(Factory Time)	Chilton Time
Disc Brake Rotor, Renew	
Includes: Renew front wheel bearings and grease retainer and repack bearings.	
4X2 models	
one (.6)	.9
both (1.0)	1.6
4X4 models	
one (.7)	1.0
both (1.1)	1.8
w/8 lug whl add	
each side	.1
Caliper Assembly, Renew	
Includes: Bleed complete system.	
All models	
one (.6)	1.0
both (.9)	1.4
w/8 lug whl add	
each side	.1
Caliper Assembly, R&R and Recondition	
Includes: Bleed complete system.	
All models	
Single Piston	
one (.8)	1.5
both (1.2)	2.4
Dual Piston	
one (.9)	1.6
both (1.3)	2.5
w/8 lug whl add	
each side	.1

PARKING BRAKE

(Factory Time)	Chilton Time
Parking Brake, Adjust	
All models (.3)	.5
Parking Brake Control, Renew	
AEROSTAR (.4)	.7
RANGER (.5)	.8
ECONOLINE, F100-350 (.5)	.8
BRONCO, F100-250 4X4 (.6)	.9
BRONCO II (.5)	.8
Parking Brake Cable, Renew	
Front–All models (.6)	1.0
Rear	
Semi-Floating Axle	
one (.5)	.8
both (.8)	1.1
Full Floating Axle	
one (.8)	1.1
both (1.4)	2.0

LABOR 7 COOLING SYSTEM 7 LABOR

(Factory Time)	Chilton Time
Winterize Cooling System	
Includes: Run engine to check for leaks, tighten all hose connections. Test radiator and pressure cap, drain radiator and engine block. Add anti-freeze and refill system.	
All models	.5
Thermostat, Renew	
Gas Engines	
Four (.5)	.6
Six (.4)	.6
V-6 (.7)	.9
V-8 (.6)	.8
Diesel Engines	
Four (.5)	.6
V-8 (1.1)	1.4
Radiator Assembly, R&R or Renew	
Includes: Drain and refill cooling system.	
RANGER-AEROSTAR	
Gas (.6)	1.0
Diesel (.6)	1.0
BRONCO I & II	
Gas (.6)	1.0
ECONOLINE-Six (1.0)	1.5
V-8 (.6)	1.2
Diesel (.9)	1.5
F100-350	
Gas (.6)	1.0
Diesel (1.4)	2.0

ADD THESE OPERATIONS TO RADIATOR R&R

Boil & Repair	1.5
Rod Clean	1.9
Repair Core	1.3
Renew Tank	1.6
Renew Trans. Oil Cooler	1.9
Renew Side Tank	.7
Recore Radiator	1.7
Radiator Hoses, Renew	
RANGER-upper (.3)	.4
lower (.4)	.5
both (.5)	.6
BRONCO, F100-250 4X4	
upper (.5)	.6
lower (.5)	.6
ECONOLINE	
upper (.4)	.5
lower (.6)	.7
F100-350	
upper (.5)	.6
lower (.6)	.7
Water Pump, Renew	
RANGER	
Four (1.2)	1.7
w/A.C. add (.3)	.3
w/P.S. add (.2)	.2
V-6 (1.4)	2.0
w/A.C. add (.4)	.4
Diesel	
2.2L eng (1.1)	1.7
2.3L eng (1.6)	2.3
AEROSTAR	
Four (1.1)	1.7
V-6 (1.3)	2.0
w/A.C. add (.3)	.3
w/P.S. add (.2)	.2
BRONCO-Six (.9)	1.5
V-6 (1.4)	2.0
w/A.C. add (.4)	.4
V-8 (1.1)	1.9
w/A.C. add (.2)	.2
ECONOLINE-Six (1.0)	1.6
V-8 (1.5)	2.1
Diesel (1.4)	2.0
F100-350-Six (1.0)	1.6
V-6 (1.1)	1.7
V-8	
302-351W engs (1.1)	1.7
351M-400 engs (1.3)	2.0
460 eng (1.5)	2.1
Diesel (1.9)	2.7
w/P.S. add	.3
w/A.C. add	.3
Fan Blade, Renew	
V-8-Diesel (.7)	1.0
All other engs	
wo/Viscous drive (.4)	.6
w/Viscous drive (.5)	.7
Drive Belt, Adjust	
All models-one (.3)	.4
each adtnl (.2)	.3
Temperature Gauge (Engine), Renew	
All models (.3)	.5
Temperature Gauge (Dash), Renew	
All models (.6)	1.0
Water Jacket Expansion Plugs, Renew (Side of Block)	
All models-each	.5
Add time to gain accessibility.	
Heater Core, R&R or Renew	
Without Air Conditioning	
AEROSTAR-Main (.6)	1.0
Auxiliary (.8)	1.4
RANGER (.5)	.9
BRONCO (.8)	1.6
BRONCO II (.5)	.9
ECONOLINE-Main (1.1)	1.0
Auxiliary (.8)	1.4
F100-350 (.8)	2.3
WITH AIR CONDITIONING	
1980 & later	
Econoline (1.1)	2.0
All other models (.5)	1.1

ADD THESE OPERATIONS TO HEATER CORE R&R

Boil & Repair	1.2
Repair Core	.9
Recore	1.2
Heater Water Control Valve, Renew	
All models (.3)	.6
Heater Blower Motor, Renew	
AEROSTAR-Main (.5)	.9
Auxiliary (.4)	.7
RANGER (.3)	.7
BRONCO (.3)	.7
ECONOLINE-Main (.3)	.6
Auxiliary (.4)	.7
F100-350	
1980 & later (.3)	.6
Heater Control Assembly, Renew	
All models (.6)	1.1
Heater Blower Motor Switch, Renew	
AEROSTAR	
main (.6)	.9
front (.6)	.9
rear (.4)	.6
RANGER (.5)	.9
BRONCO (.4)	.7

LABOR 7 COOLING SYSTEM 7 LABOR

(Factory Time)	Chilton Time
BRONCO II (.5)	.9
ECONOLINE (.3)	.6
F100-350 (.5)	.9

(Factory Time)	Chilton Time
Heater Blower Motor Resistor, Renew	
RANGER, BRONCO (.3)	.6
ECONOLINE (.3)	.6

(Factory Time)	Chilton Time
F100-350 (.4)	.7
AEROSTAR-Main (.3)	.6
Auxiliary (.5)	.8

LABOR 8 EXHAUST SYSTEM 8 LABOR

(Factory Time)	Chilton Time
Catalytic Converter, Renew	
Four (.6)	.9
Six (.8)	1.2
V-6 (.8)	1.2
V-8 (.9)	1.6
Muffler, Renew	
RANGER-AEROSTAR	
Four (.4)	.7
V-6 (.6)	.9
Diesel (.5)	.8
BRONCO, F100-250 4X4 (.8)	1.4
BRONCO II (.6)	.9
ECONOLINE (.8)	1.4
F100-350	
Std W/B wo/Catalyst (.8)	1.4
w/Catalyst (.8)	1.4
Long W/B (.8)	1.4
V-6 (.7)	1.0
Intermediate Exhaust Pipe, Renew	
RANGER-AEROSTAR	
All models (.7)	1.2
BRONCO, F100-250 4X4	
Six (.5)	1.1
V-8 (.8)	1.4
BRONCO II (.7)	1.0

(Factory Time)	Chilton Time
ECONOLINE-Six (.6)	1.2
V-8 (.9)	1.5
F100-350-Six (.6)	1.2
V-6 (.6)	.9
V-8-351M-400 engs	
Std W/B wo/Catalyst (1.6)	2.3
w/Catalyst (1.9)	2.6
Long W/B (.8)	1.4
460 eng-one (.7)	1.3
both (1.0)	1.9
Diesel (.6)	1.0
Tail Pipe, Renew	
BRONCO (.5)	.7
ECONOLINE (.5)	.7
F100-350 (.4)	.6
Exhaust Manifold, Renew	
Four	
Gas	
2.0L eng (.9)	1.5
2.3L eng (1.4)	2.0
Diesel	
2.2L eng (.9)	1.6
2.3L eng (2.4)	3.4
Six	
1983 & earlier (2.3)	3.0
1984 & later (3.1)	4.4

(Factory Time)	Chilton Time
V-6	
right (1.5)	2.1
left (1.4)	*2.0
both (2.4)	*3.6
V-8	
302-351W engs	
one side (.7)	1.1
both sides (1.1)	1.9
351M-400 engs	
one side (.8)	1.3
both sides (1.2)	2.3
460 eng	
one side (.9)	1.6
both sides (1.3)	2.3
Diesel	
right side (1.7)	2.3
left side (1.6)	2.2
both sides (2.6)	3.8
* w/A.C. add (.3)	.3

COMBINATIONS

Muffler, Exhaust and Tail Pipe, Renew	
RANGER	1.1
BRONCO	1.9
ECONOLINE	1.9
F100-350-one side	1.8
both sides	2.7

LABOR 9 FRONT SUSPENSION 9 LABOR

Note: On all front suspension operations alignment charges must be added if performed. Time given does not include alignment.

(Factory Time)	Chilton Time
Check Alignment of Front End	
All models (.5)	.6
Note: Deduct if alignment is performed.	
Toe-In, Adjust	
All models (.4)	.7
Align Front End	
Includes: Adjust front wheel bearings.	
Aerostar (1.2)	1.5
All other models (1.9)	2.5
Front Wheel Bearings, Clean and Repack (Both Wheels)	
drum brakes	1.0
disc brakes	1.4
4 wheel drive	2.5
Front Wheel Bearings and Cups, Renew (One Wheel)	
Drum Brakes	
Bronco, F100-250 4X4 (.8)	1.1
Econoline, F100-150 (.6)	.9
F250-350 (.7)	1.0
Disc Brakes	
Aerostar (.7)	1.1
Ranger (.8)	1.1
Bronco, F100-250 4X4 (.8)	1.1
Econoline 100-150, F100-150 (.7)	1.0

(Factory Time)	Chilton Time
Econoline 250-350, F250-350 (.8)	1.1
Front Wheel Grease Seal, Renew (One Wheel)	
Drum Brakes	
Bronco (.6)	.8
Econoline (.4)	.6
F100-250 4X4 (.5)	.7
Disc Brakes	
Aerostar (.5)	.8
Ranger (.6)	.8
Bronco, F100-250 4X4 (.6)	.8
Econoline 100-150, F100-150 (.6)	.8
Econoline 250-350, F250-350 (.7)	.9
Front Shock Absorber or Bushings, Renew	
All models-one (.4)	.6
both (.5)	.8
Upper Control Arms, Renew	
Add alignment charges.	
Aerostar-one (1.0)	1.3
both (1.5)	2.0
Upper Control Arm Bushings, Renew	
Add alignment charges.	
Aerostar-one side (1.6)	2.2
both sides (2.5)	3.4
Lower Control Arms, Renew	
Add alignment charges.	
Aerostar-one side (1.5)	2.0
both sides (2.4)	3.2

(Factory Time)	Chilton Time
Front Axle 'I' Beam, Renew	
Includes: R&R wheels and brake backing plates.	
Add alignment charges.	
STAMPED AXLE 4X2	
one side (2.3)	3.1
both sides (3.9)	5.3
FORGED AXLE 4X2	
one side (1.8)	2.4
both sides (2.7)	3.6
Renew ball joints	
add-each (.2)	.3
Renew pivot bushings	
add-each (.2)	.3
Front Spindle Assembly, Renew	
CONTROL ARM AXLE	
one side (1.4)	1.9
both sides (1.9)	2.9
STAMPED AXLE 4X2	
one side (1.6)	2.1
both sides (2.3)	3.1
FORGED AXLE 4X2	
one side (1.4)	1.9
both sides (1.9)	2.5
STAMPED AXLE 4X4	
one side (.6)	.9
both sides (.9)	1.3
FORGED AXLE 4X4	
one side (1.4)	1.9
both sides (1.9)	2.5
Rebush spindle, add each side (.4)	.5

LABOR 9 FRONT SUSPENSION 9 LABOR

(Factory Time)	Chilton Time
Renew needle brgs, add	
each (.1)	.2

Steering Shock Absorber, Renew

(Factory Time)	Chilton Time
BRONCO, F100-250 4X4 (.3)	.6

Track Bar Assembly, Renew

(Factory Time)	Chilton Time
BRONCO, F100-250 4X4 (.6)	1.0

Radius Arm, Renew

(Factory Time)	Chilton Time
All models-one (1.4)	1.9
both (2.1)	2.8

Front Spring, Renew

(Factory Time)	Chilton Time
AEROSTAR	
one (.9)	1.2
both (1.6)	2.1
4X2	
All models	
one (.4)	.7
both (.7)	1.3
4X4	
Ranger-Bronco II	
one (.4)	.7
both (.7)	1.3
F series-Bronco	
one (.7)	1.1
both (1.1)	2.0
Renew tie bolt	
add-each (.5)	.5

Front Stabilizer Bushings, Renew

(Factory Time)	Chilton Time
All models (.5)	.7

Front Stabilizer Bar, Renew

(Factory Time)	Chilton Time
All models (.5)	.7

FRONT WHEEL DRIVE

Front Axle Housing and Differential Assy., R&R (Complete)

Includes: Drain and refill axle, R&R wheels, hubs and axle shafts. Road test.

(Factory Time)	Chilton Time
BRONCO (3.9)	5.4
F100 (3.7)	5.2
F250 (2.8)	4.2

Front Axle Housing, Renew (One Piece Assy)

Includes: R&R housing and differential assy. Transfer all parts. Adjust ring gear and pinion. Does not include disassembly of differential case.

(Factory Time)	Chilton Time
BRONCO (8.0)	9.6
F100 (7.4)	9.0
F250 (7.2)	9.0

Axle Housing Cover or Gasket, Renew

(Factory Time)	Chilton Time
All models (.5)	.7

Front Axle Arm (Beam), Renew (Independent Front Suspension)

(Factory Time)	Chilton Time
w/coil springs	
left side (3.8)	5.1
right side (2.9)	3.9
both sides (5.9)	7.9
w/leaf springs	
left side (3.8)	5.1
right side (3.0)	4.0
both sides (6.1)	8.2
monobeam (4.8)	6.5
Renew ball joints	
add-each (.2)	.3
Renew pivot bushings	
add-each (.2)	.3

Front Axle Shaft, Renew

(Factory Time)	Chilton Time
RANGER-BRONCO II	
right side (1.2)	2.1
left side (.6)	.8
both sides (1.6)	2.5
BRONCO-F150	
one side (.9)	1.4
both sides (1.3)	1.9
F250-350	
one side (.6)	1.1
both sides (1.2)	1.8
O/haul or renew U-Joints,	
add-each (.3)	.3

Front Axle Housing Oil Seals, Renew

(Factory Time)	Chilton Time
RANGER-BRONCO II	
right side (2.1)	2.7
left side (.7)	1.0
both sides (2.1)	2.8
BRONCO-F150	
right side (2.2)	2.8
left side (.8)	1.1
both sides (2.3)	3.0
F250-350	
right side (1.2)	1.5
left side (.6)	1.1
both sides (1.6)	2.2

Front Axle Pinion Oil Seal, Renew

(Factory Time)	Chilton Time
All models (.6)	1.0

Front Axle Pivot Bushings, Renew

(Factory Time)	Chilton Time
All models-one side (.5)	.8
both sides (.7)	1.3

Front Drive Shaft, R&R

(Factory Time)	Chilton Time
All models (.5)	.7
Recond U-Joint, Add	
one (.3)	.4
all (.5)	.6

Differential Carrier, R&R or Reseal

(Factory Time)	Chilton Time
All models	
w/coil springs (2.3)	3.2
w/leaf springs (2.4)	3.3
w/monobeam (3.0)	4.2

Ring Gear Backlash, Adjust

(Factory Time)	Chilton Time
All models	
w/coil springs (3.1)	4.3
w/leaf springs (3.2)	4.4
w/monobeam (3.8)	5.3

Ring Gear and Pinion Set, Renew

(Factory Time)	Chilton Time
All models	
w/coil springs (3.9)	5.4
w/leaf springs (4.0)	5.6
w/monobeam (4.6)	6.4
Renew pinion brgs add (.2)	.4
Recond diff assy add (.2)	.5

Differential Case, Renew

(Factory Time)	Chilton Time
All models	
w/coil springs	
std (3.2)	4.5
locker (3.5)	4.9
w/leaf springs	
std (3.3)	4.6
locker (3.6)	5.0
w/monobeam	
std (3.9)	5.4
locker (4.2)	5.8
Renew diff brgs add (.2)	.4

LABOR 10 STEERING LINKAGE 10 LABOR

Tie Rod Ends, Renew (One Side)

Includes: Reset toe-in.

(Factory Time)	Chilton Time
All models (.8)	1.1

Tie Rod, Renew (One)

Includes: Reset toe-in.

(Factory Time)	Chilton Time
All models (1.2)	1.5

Drag Link, Renew

Does not require toe-in adjustment.

(Factory Time)	Chilton Time
All models (.5)	.9

Pitman Arm, Renew

(Factory Time)	Chilton Time
All models (.4)	.9

Front Spindle Arm, Renew

Includes: R&R wheel hub and brake drum/rotor where required. Reset toe-in.

(Factory Time)	Chilton Time
BRONCO-Part Time Hub	
one (1.0)	1.4
both (1.9)	2.7
Full Time Hub	
one (.9)	1.3
both (1.6)	2.4
ECONOLINE-one (.6)	1.0
both (1.0)	1.8
F100-350-one (1.1)	1.5
both (1.6)	2.2
F100-250 4X4	
Part Time Hub-one (1.0)	1.4
both (1.9)	2.7
Full Time Hub-one (.9)	1.3
both (1.6)	2.4

LABOR 11 STEERING GEAR 11 LABOR

(Factory Time) Chilton Time

STANDARD

Steering Wheel, Renew

All models (.3) 5

Upper Mast Jacket Bearing, Renew

All models
std colm (.5) 9
tilt colm (.6) 1.0

Steering Column Lock Actuator, Renew

All models
std colm (1.0) 1.5
tilt colm (.9) 1.4

Steering Gear, Adjust (On Truck)

Includes: Bearing preload and gear mesh adjustments.
All models (.7) 1.0

Steering Gear, R&R or Renew

All models (.7) 1.2

Steering Gear, R&R and Recondition

Includes: Disassemble, renew necessary parts, reassemble and adjust.
All models (1.4) 2.2

POWER STEERING

Trouble Shoot Power Steering

Includes: Test pump and system pressure. Check pounds pull on steering wheel and check for leaks.
All models (.7) 1.0

Power Steering Belt, Renew

Four
Gas (.3) 5
Diesel (.3) 5
Six (.5) 7
V-6 (.3) 5
V-8
302-351 engs (.4) 6
460 eng (.8) 1.0
Diesel (.4) 6

Power Steering Gear, R&R or Renew

All models (.8) 1.4

Power Steering Gear, R&R and Recondition

Includes: Disassemble, renew necessary parts, reassemble and adjust.
ECONOLINE
Saginaw (2.5) 4.2
XR50 (2.2) 3.9
All other models (2.2) 3.8

Power Steering Cylinder Assembly, R&R or Renew

ECONOLINE (1.6) 2.1
F250 4X4 (.7) 1.1

Power Steering Pump, R&R or Renew

Includes: Transfer pulley where required.
Aerostar-Four (1.1) 1.5
V-6 (1.0) 1.4
All other models
Four
Gas (.7) 1.0
Diesel
2.2L eng (.8) 1.2
2.3L eng (1.2) 1.6
Six (.6) 1.0
V-6 (.8) 1.2
V-8
302-351W engs (.6) 1.0
351M-400 engs (.8) 1.3
460 eng (.5) 1.0
Diesel (1.0) 1.4

Power Steering Pump, R&R and Recondition

Aerostar-Four (1.5) 2.3
V-6 (1.4) 2.2
All other models
Four
Gas (1.1) 1.8
Diesel
2.2L eng (1.2) 2.0
2.3L eng (1.6) 2.4
Six (1.1) 1.8
V-6 (1.3) 2.2
V-8
302-351W engs (1.1) 1.8
351M-400 engs (1.4) 2.0
460 eng (1.0) 1.8
Diesel (1.6) 2.2

Power Steering Pump Shaft Seal, Renew

Includes: R&R pump.
Aerostar-Four (1.2) 1.7
V-6 (1.1) 1.6
All other models
Four
Gas (.7) 1.2
Diesel
2.2L eng (.9) 1.4
2.3L eng (1.3) 1.8
Six (.7) 1.2
V-6 (.9) 1.4
V-8
302-351W engs (.6) 1.2
351M-400 engs (.9) 1.5
460 eng (.6) 1.2
Diesel (1.1) 1.6

Power Steering Control Valve, R&R or Renew

ECONOLINE (2.0) 2.7
F250 4X4 (.9) 1.3

Power Steering Control Valve, R&R and Clean or Recondition

ECONOLINE (2.8) 3.9
F250 4X4 (1.7) 2.4

Power Steering Hoses, Renew

AEROSTAR
pressure (.5) 7
return (.4) 6
BRONCO, F100-250 4X4
pressure (.4) 6
return (.5) 7
ECONOLINE-Six (.7) 1.0
V-8 (.8) 1.1
RANGER, F100-350
pressure (.4) 6
return (.4) 6
cooling (.3) 5
V-8–Diesel
cooling (.5) 7
return (.7) 9
pressure (.6) 8

RACK AND PINION STEERING

Steering Gear, R&R or Renew

All models
manual (.8) 1.3
power (1.0) 1.6
Purge system add (.3) 3

Steering Gear, R&R and Recondition

All models
manual (2.4) 3.8
power (3.0) 4.8
Purge system add (.3) 3

Steering Gear, Adjust (On Truck)

All models (.3) 5

Tie Rod Ball Joint Sockets and Bellows, Renew

All models
manual (1.2) 1.9
power (1.5) 2.4
Purge system add (.3) 3

Input Shaft and Valve Assy., Recondition

All models
manual (1.4) 2.2
power (1.6) 2.5
Purge system add (.3) 3

LABOR 12 CYLINDER HEAD & VALVE SYSTEM 12 LABOR

(Factory Time) Chilton Time

GASOLINE ENGINES

Compression Test

Four 5
Six 6
V-6 7
V-8 9

Cylinder Head Gasket, Renew

Includes: Check cylinder head and block flatness. Clean carbon and make all necessary adjustments.
RANGER-BRONCO I & II
Four
2.0L eng (3.7) 5.2
2.3L eng (4.3) 6.0
w/A.C. add (.3) 3
w/P.S. add (.2) 2
Six (2.1) 3.8
V-6-one (4.3) 6.0
both (5.3) 7.4
V-8-302-351W engs
one (3.0) 4.3
both (4.2) 6.6
351M-400 engs
one (3.3) 4.6
both (4.5) 6.9
AEROSTAR
Four (4.4) 6.1
V-6-one (4.4) 6.1
both (5.4) 7.5
w/A.C. add (.4) 4
w/A.T. add (.1) 1
ECONOLINE-Six (3.4) 5.1
V-8-302-351W engs
one (3.6) 4.8
both (5.4) 7.6
351M-400 engs
one (3.2) 4.4
both (4.4) 5.9
460 eng
one (3.9) 5.0
both (5.7) 7.9

(Factory Time)	Chilton Time
w/P.S. add (.3)	.3
w/A.C. add (.7)	.7
F100-350	
Six (2.8)	3.9
V-6-one (4.7)	6.6
both (6.4)	8.8
V-8-255-302-351W engs	
one (3.0)	4.1
both (4.0)	6.2
351M-400 engs	
one (3.2)	4.3
both (4.4)	6.6
460 eng	
one (4.3)	5.4
both (6.1)	8.3
w/P.S. add (.3)	.3
w/A.C. add (2.0)	2.0

Cylinder Head, Renew

Includes: Transfer all components, clean carbon. Reface valves, check valve spring tension, assembled height and valve head runout.

(Factory Time)	Chilton Time
RANGER-BRONCO I & II	
Four	
2.0L eng (5.8)	8.1
w/A.C. add (.3)	.3
w/P.S. add (.2)	.2
Six (5.0)	6.7
V-6-one (4.5)	6.3
both (5.6)	7.8
V-8-302-351W engs	
one (4.2)	5.8
both (6.7)	9.6
351M-400 engs	
one (4.7)	6.1
both (7.3)	9.8
AEROSTAR	
V-6-one (4.8)	6.7
both (5.9)	8.2
w/A.C. add (.4)	.4
w/A.T. add (.1)	.1
ECONOLINE-Six (6.1)	8.6
V-8-302-351W engs	
one (4.8)	6.3
both (7.9)	10.6
351M-400 engs	
one (4.6)	5.9
both (7.2)	8.9
460 eng	
one (5.3)	7.0
both (8.5)	11.1
w/P.S. add (.3)	.3
w/A.C. add (.7)	.7
F100-350	
Six (5.4)	6.7
V-6-one (5.7)	8.0
both (8.3)	11.5
V-8-255-302-351W engs	
one (4.4)	5.7
both (6.8)	9.4
351M-400 engs	
one (4.6)	5.9
both (7.2)	9.8
460 eng	
one (5.7)	7.0
both (8.9)	11.5
w/P.S. add (.3)	.3
w/A.C. add (2.0)	2.0

Clean Carbon and Grind Valves

Includes: R&R cylinder heads, check valve spring tension, valve seat and head runout, stem to guide clearance and spring assembled height. Minor tune up.

(Factory Time)	Chilton Time
RANGER-BRONCO I & II	
Four	
2.0L eng (6.3)	8.9
w/A.C. add (.3)	.3

COMBINATIONS

Add to Valve Job

(Factory Time)	Chilton Time
DRAIN, EVACUATE & RECHARGE AIR CONDITIONING SYSTEM	
All models (.7)	1.5
ROCKER ARMS OR SHAFT ASSY. DISASSEMBLE AND CLEAN OR RECONDITION	
Six (.6)	1.0
V-8-One side (.5)	.7
Both sides (1.0)	1.3
HYDRAULIC VALVE LIFTERS, DISASSEMBLE AND CLEAN	
Each (.2)	.2
ROCKER ARM STUD, RENEW	
Each (.3)	.3
DISTRIBUTOR, RECONDITION	
All models (.7)	1.0

(Factory Time)	Chilton Time
CARBURETOR, RECONDITION	
1 BBL (.9)	1.2
2 BBL (1.0)	1.3
4 BBL	
Ford (1.0)	1.5
Holly (1.3)	2.0
VALVE GUIDES, REAM OVERSIZE	
Each (.1)	.2
VALVE SEAT INSERT, RENEW	
DIESEL	
V-8-one (.2)	.3
each adtnl (.2)	.2
VALVE GUIDES, RENEW	
DIESEL	
V-8-one (.5)	.6
each adtnl (.5)	.5

(Factory Time)	Chilton Time
w/P.S. add (.2)	.2
Six (4.9)	7.5
V-6	
one side (6.7)	9.4
both sides (8.4)	11.7
V-8-302-351W engs	
one side (4.8)	6.3
both sides (7.8)	10.6
351M-400 engs	
one side (5.1)	6.6
both sides (8.1)	10.9
AEROSTAR	
V-6-one side (6.2)	9.6
both sides (8.5)	11.9
w/A.C. add (.4)	.4
w/A.T. add (.1)	.1
ECONOLINE-Six (6.1)	8.6
V-8-302-351W engs	
one side (5.4)	6.8
both sides (9.0)	11.6
351M-400 engs	
one side (5.0)	6.4
both sides (8.0)	9.9
460 eng (9.3)	11.9
w/P.S. add (.3)	.3
w/A.C. add (.7)	.7
F100-350	
Six (5.5)	8.1
V-6 (9.4)	12.9
V-8-255-302	
351W engs (7.6)	10.2
351M-400 engs (8.0)	10.6
460 eng (9.7)	12.3
w/P.S. add (.3)	.3
w/A.C. add (2.0)	2.0

Rocker Arm Cover or Gasket, Renew

(Factory Time)	Chilton Time
RANGER-BRONCO I & II	
Four	
2.0L eng (.7)	1.0
2.3L eng (1.3)	1.8
Six (.7)	1.0
V-6-one (.8)	1.2
both (1.2)	1.7
V-8-302-351W engs	
one (.4)	.6
both (.6)	1.0
351M-400 engs	
one (.6)	.8
both (.9)	1.3

(Factory Time)	Chilton Time
AEROSTAR	
Four (1.2)	1.7
V-6-right (1.3)	1.8
left (1.5)	2.1
both (2.5)	3.5
ECONOLINE-Six (1.0)	1.3
V-8-302-351W engs	
right (.7)	.9
left (.5)	.7
both (.9)	1.3
351M-400 engs	
one (.6)	.8
both (.8)	1.2
460 eng	
one (.7)	.9
both (1.0)	1.3
F100-350	
Six (.6)	.8
V-6-one (.4)	.6
both (.6)	1.0
V-8-255-302-351W	
351M-400 engs	
one (.4)	.6
both (.6)	1.0
460 eng	
one (.5)	.7
both (.7)	1.1

Rocker Arm Shaft Assy., Recondition

Includes: R&R rocker arm cover.

(Factory Time)	Chilton Time
BRONCO-Six (1.1)	1.6

Valve Push Rod and/or Rocker Arm, Renew

Includes: R&R rocker arm cover.

(Factory Time)	Chilton Time
RANGER-BRONCO I & II	
Four	
2.0L eng	
one (.8)	1.2
all (1.1)	1.7
2.3L eng	
one (1.8)	2.5
all (2.3)	3.2
Six-one (.8)	1.1
all (1.1)	1.5
V-6-one (1.0)	1.4
all-one side (1.2)	1.7
all-both sides (2.1)	2.9
V-8-302-351W engs-one (.5)	.7
all (.9)	1.3
351M-400 engs	
one (.7)	.9
all (1.3)	1.7

LABOR 12 CYLINDER HEAD & VALVE SYSTEM 12 LABOR

(Factory Time)	Chilton Time
AEROSTAR	
Four	
one (1.7)	2.4
all (2.2)	3.1
V-6	
one-right side (1.7)	2.4
one-left side (1.9)	2.7
all-both sides (3.4)	4.8
ECONOLINE-Six-one (1.1)	1.6
all (1.4)	1.9
V-8-302-351W engs	
right side-one (.8)	1.0
left side-one (.6)	.8
all-both sides (1.2)	1.6
351M-400 engs	
one (.7)	.9
all (1.2)	1.6
460 eng	
one (.8)	1.2
all-one side (.9)	1.4
all-both sides (1.4)	2.0
F100-350	
Six-one (.8)	1.1
all (1.1)	1.5
V-8-255-302-351W	
one (.5)	.9
all-one side (.7)	1.2
all-both sides (1.1)	1.9
351M-400 engs	
one (.5)	.9
all-one side (.6)	1.1
all-both sides (1.0)	1.7
460 eng	
one (.6)	1.0
all-one side (.8)	1.3
all-both sides (1.1)	1.9

Valve Tappets, Renew (All)

Includes: R&R intake manifold where required. Adjust carburetor and ignition timing.

RANGER-BRONCO I & II	
Four	
2.0L eng (1.2)	1.7
2.3L eng (1.6)	2.2
Six (1.7)	3.0
V-6 (5.1)	7.1
V-8-302 eng (2.8)	4.5
w/A.C. add (.4)	.4
w/A.T. add (.2)	.2
AEROSTAR	
Four (5.0)	7.0
V-6 (6.1)	8.5
w/A.C. add (.3)	.3
ECONOLINE-Six (2.1)	3.5
V-8-302-351W engs (2.8)	4.0
F100-350	
Six (1.7)	3.2
V-6 (2.6)	4.5
V-8-255-302	
351W engs (2.7)	4.4
460 eng (3.3)	5.0

Valve Tappets, Renew (Without Removing Intake Manifold)

BRONCO-F100-350-V-8	
351M-400 engs	
one (.6)	1.1
one-each side (.9)	1.6
Each adtnl (4) tappets add (.2)	.4

Valve Spring or Valve Stem Oil Seals, Renew (Head on Truck)

Includes: R&R rocker arms or assy. and adjust valves, if adjustable.

RANGER-BRONCO I & II	
Four	
2.0L eng	
one (.9)	1.4
all (1.7)	2.7
2.3L eng	
one (1.5)	2.1
all (3.1)	4.3
Six-one (.9)	1.3
all (2.1)	2.8
V-6-one (1.0)	1.5
each adtnl (.2)	.3
all (3.0)	4.2
V-8-302-351W engs-one (.6)	.9
each adtnl (.1)	.1
all-both sides (2.4)	3.5
AEROSTAR	
Four-one (1.4)	1.9
all (3.0)	4.2
V-6	
right side-one (1.5)	2.1
left side-one (1.7)	2.3
both sides-all (4.3)	6.0
ECONOLINE-Six-one (1.2)	1.6
all (2.4)	3.2
V-8-302-351W engs	
right side-one (.9)	1.2
left side-one(.7)	1.0
all-both sides (2.7)	3.6
351M-400 engs	
one (.8)	1.1
all (2.6)	3.5
460 eng	
one (.9)	1.3
one-each side (1.4)	1.8
all-both sides (2.8)	3.6
F100-350	
Six-one (.7)	1.0
all (2.0)	2.9
V-6-one (.6)	.9
all (2.0)	3.2
V-8-255-302-351W engs	
one (.6)	1.0
one-each side (.9)	1.3
all-both sides (2.2)	2.9
351M-400 engs	
one (.6)	1.0
one-each side (1.1)	1.5
all-both sides (2.6)	3.3
460 eng	
one (.7)	1.1
one-each side (1.1)	1.5
all-both sides (2.8)	3.5

Valve Clearance, Adjust

FOUR	1.8
V-6	2.7

DIESEL ENGINE

Compression Test

FOUR	1.0
V-8	1.8

Cylinder Head Gasket, Renew

Four	
2.2L eng (2.8)	3.9
2.3L eng (6.2)	8.8
V-8	
F series	
right side (6.0)	8.4
left side (5.4)	7.5
both sides (8.5)	12.0
Econoline	
right side (7.3)	10.2
left side (6.3)	8.8
both sides (9.4)	13.1
w/A.C. add (.4)	.4
w/P.S. add (.5)	.5

Cylinder Head, Renew

Includes: Transfer all components. Clean, replace and lap valves. Make all necessary adjustments.

Four	
2.2L eng (4.4)	6.1
2.3L eng (8.0)	11.3
V-8	
F series	
right side (6.2)	9.0
left side (5.6)	8.1
both sides (8.9)	12.9
Econoline	
right side (7.5)	10.8
left side (6.5)	9.4
both sides (9.8)	14.2
w/A.C. add (.4)	.4
w/P.S. add (.5)	.5

Clean Carbon and Grind Valves

Includes: R&R cylinder head. Reface valves and seats. Make all necessary adjustments.

Four	
2.2L eng (5.9)	8.0
2.3L eng (8.7)	12.3
V-8	
F series	
right side (7.9)	11.4
left side (7.3)	10.5
both sides (12.2)	17.6
Econoline	
right side (9.2)	13.3
left side (8.2)	11.8
both sides (13.1)	18.9
w/A.C. add (.4)	.4
w/P.S. add (.5)	.5

Rocker Arm Cover and/or Gasket, Renew

Four	
2.2L eng (.4)	.7
2.3L eng (.5)	.8
V-8	
F series	
right side (.7)	1.0
left side (.6)	.9
both sides (1.0)	1.6
Econoline	
right side (.9)	1.2
left side (.8)	1.1
both sides (1.3)	1.9

Valve Push Rods and/or Rocker Arms, Renew

Four	
2.2L eng-one (.7)	1.2
all (.9)	1.6
2.3L eng-one (.7)	1.0
all (1.2)	1.7
V-8	
F series	
right side (1.0)	1.4
left side (.9)	1.3
both sides (1.5)	2.3
Econoline	
right side (1.2)	1.6
left side (1.1)	1.5
both sides (1.6)	2.6
Note: If necc to tilt eng to renew rods for # 3 & 5 cyls add	2.0

Valve Springs and/or Valve Stem Oil Seals, Renew (Head on Truck)

Four	
2.2L eng-one (.9)	1.6
all (1.4)	2.4
2.3L eng-one (.7)	1.1
all (1.7)	2.4

LABOR 12 CYLINDER HEAD & VALVE SYSTEM 12 LABOR

(Factory Time)	Chilton Time
V-8	
F series	
one cyl (.9)	1.3
one cyl-each side (1.4)	2.2
all cyls-both sides (3.4)	4.9
Econoline	
one cyl (1.1)	1.5
one cyl-each side (1.7)	2.5
all cyls-both sides (3.7)	5.4

Valve Tappets, Renew

(Factory Time)	Chilton Time
Four	
2.2L eng	
all (6.1)	8.8
V-8	
F series	
one cyl (2.9)	4.2
all cyls-one side (3.2)	4.6
all cyls-both sides (4.0)	5.8
Econoline	
one cyl (4.0)	5.8
all cyls-one side (4.3)	6.2
all cyls-both sides (5.0)	7.2
w/A.C. add (.4)	.4
w/P.S. add (.5)	.5

LABOR 13 ENGINE ASSEMBLY & MOUNTS 13 LABOR

GASOLINE ENGINES

Engine Assembly, Remove & Install

Includes: R&R hood and radiator, adjust carburetor and linkage.
Does not include transfer of any parts or equipment.

(Factory Time)	Chilton Time
RANGER-BRONCO I & II	
Four	
2.0L eng	
w/M.T. (3.1)	4.4
w/A.T. (3.4)	4.7
2.3L eng	
w/M.T. (4.5)	6.3
w/A.T. (3.4)	4.7
w/P.S. add (.2)	.2
w/A.C. add (1.0)	1.0
Six (3.3)	4.8
V-6 (5.3)	7.2
V-8-302-351W engs	
w/M.T. (2.9)	4.2
w/A.T. (3.3)	4.8
351M-400 engs	
w/M.T. (2.6)	3.8
w/A.T. (3.3)	4.8
AEROSTAR	
Four (5.8)	8.1
V-6 (6.9)	9.6
w/A.C. add (.9)	.9
ECONOLINE	
Six-w/M.T. (6.3)	8.8
w/A.T. (5.8)	8.1
V-8-302-351W engs (3.9)	5.6
351M-400 engs (5.6)	7.8
460 eng (5.6)	7.1
F100-250-Six	
std trans (2.4)	3.9
auto trans (2.8)	4.3
V-6 (4.4)	6.2
V-8-255-302	
351W engs (2.9)	4.4
351M-400 engs (3.1)	4.6
460 eng (3.9)	5.4
F350	
w/Std trans (2.6)	4.1
351-400 engs	
auto trans (3.1)	4.6
w/P.S. add (.4)	.4
w/A.C. add (.6)	.6

Engine Assembly, Replace With New or Rebuilt Unit (With Cyl. Heads and Oil Pan)

Includes: R&R hood and radiator. R&R engine assembly, transfer all necessary parts, fuel and electrical units. Tune engine. Road test.

(Factory Time)	Chilton Time
BRONCO	
Six (5.0)	7.2
V-8-302-351W engs	
w/M.T. (6.2)	9.7
w/A.T. (6.6)	10.3
ECONOLINE	
Six-w/M.T. (8.0)	11.2
w/A.T. (7.5)	10.7
V-8-302-351W engs (6.2)	9.0
460 eng (8.9)	11.1
F100-250-Six	
std trans (5.1)	7.3
auto trans (5.5)	7.7
V-8-255-302	
351W engs (5.8)	8.0
351M-400 engs (6.0)	8.2
460 eng (7.2)	9.4
F350	
w/Std trans (5.5)	7.7
351-400 engs	
auto trans (6.0)	8.2
w/P.S. add (.4)	.4
w/A.C. add (.6)	.6

Cylinder Assembly, Renew

(w/All Internal Parts Less Head(s) and Oil Pan)

Includes: R&R hood and radiator. R&R engine, transfer all component parts not supplied with replacement engine, clean carbon, grind valves, Minor tune up. Road test.

(Factory Time)	Chilton Time
RANGER-BRONCO I & II	
Four	
2.0L eng	
w/M.T. (9.7)	14.0
w/A.T. (10.0)	14.3
2.3L eng	
w/M.T. (11.4)	16.5
w/A.T. (10.3)	14.9
w/P.S. add (.2)	.2
w/A.C. add (1.0)	1.0
Six (10.7)	15.8
V-6 (13.2)	17.9
V-8-302-351W engs	
w/M.T. (10.8)	15.9
w/A.T. (11.2)	16.5
351M-400 engs	
w/M.T. (10.8)	15.9
w/A.T. (11.5)	16.9
AEROSTAR	
Four (12.7)	18.4
V-6 (14.5)	21.0
w/A.C. add (.9)	.9
ECONOLINE	
Six-w/M.T. (13.7)	20.2
w/A.T. (13.0)	19.5
V-8-302-351W engs (12.6)	18.6
351M-400 engs (14.6)	20.6
460 eng (15.5)	19.4
F100-250-Six	
std trans (14.8)	18.4
auto trans (15.2)	18.8
V-6 (11.3)	16.0
V-8-255-302	
351W engs (11.7)	15.4
351M-400 engs (12.2)	15.9
460 eng (13.8)	17.7
F350	
w/Std trans (12.1)	15.6
351-400 engs	
auto trans (12.2)	15.9
w/P.S. add (.4)	.4
w/A.C. add (.6)	.6

Engine Assembly, R&R and Recondition (Complete)

Includes: R&R hood and radiator. Rebore block, install new pistons, rings, rod and main bearings. Clean carbon, grind valves. Tune engine. Road test.

(Factory Time)	Chilton Time
RANGER-BRONCO I & II	
Four	
2.0L eng	
w/M.T. (16.4)	23.2
w/A.T. (16.7)	23.5
2.3L eng	
w/M.T. (16.9)	23.8
w/A.T. (15.8)	22.2
w/P.S. add (.2)	.2
w/A.C. add (1.0)	1.0
Six (19.1)	27.3
V-6 (19.5)	26.9
V-8-302-351W engs	
w/M.T. (24.5)	31.8
w/A.T. (24.9)	32.2
351M-400 engs	
w/M.T. (24.2)	31.5
w/A.T. (24.9)	32.2
AEROSTAR	
Four (17.1)	24.1
V-6 (20.4)	28.7
w/A.C. add (.9)	.9
ECONOLINE	
Six-w/M.T. (22.1)	29.3
w/A.T. (21.4)	29.6
V-8-302-351W engs (25.5)	31.8
351M-400 engs (27.2)	34.0
460 eng (34.7)	41.4
F100-250-Six	
std trans (23.9)	30.0
auto trans (24.3)	33.4
V-6 (23.8)	32.0
V-8-255-302	
351W engs (29.5)	37.3
351M-400 engs (29.7)	37.5
460 eng (31.2)	39.1
F350	
w/Std trans (29.2)	37.3
351-400 engs	
auto trans (29.7)	37.8
w/P.S. add (.4)	.4
w/A.C. add (.6)	.6

Engine Mounts, Renew

(Factory Time)	Chilton Time
Front	
RANGER-BRONCO-AEROSTAR	
Four	
2.0L eng-one (.4)	.6
both (.5)	.9

LABOR 13 ENGINE ASSEMBLY & MOUNTS 13 LABOR

(Factory Time)	Chilton Time
2.3L eng-one (1.4)	1.9
both (1.5)	2.0
Six-one (.4)	.7
both (.5)	1.1
V-6-right (.7)	1.0
left (.6)	.9
both (.9)	1.4
V-8-302-351W engs	
one (.4)	.6
both (.6)	1.0
351M-400 engs	
right (.7)	.9
left (.5)	.8
both (.8)	1.3
ECONOLINE	
Six-one (.4)	.7
both (.4)	1.0
V-8-302-351-400 engs	
right (.8)	1.1
left (.7)	1.0
both (1.0)	1.5
F100-350	
Six-one (.4)	.7
both (.5)	.9
V-6-right (.7)	1.0
left (.5)	.7
both (.9)	1.4
V-8-255-302-351W engs	
one (.4)	.7
both (.6)	1.0
351M-400 engs-one (.7)	1.2
both (.9)	1.5
460 eng-one (.6)	.8
both (.7)	1.1

Rear

(Factory Time)	Chilton Time
Ranger (.4)	.6
Bronco (.6)	.8
Aerostar (.5)	.7
Econoline (.4)	.7

(Factory Time)	Chilton Time
F100-350	
one (.4)	.7
both (.5)	1.1

DIESEL ENGINE

Engine Assembly, Remove & Install

Includes: R&R hood and radiator. Does not include transfer of any parts or equipment.

(Factory Time)	Chilton Time
Four	
2.2L eng (3.7)	5.1
2.3L eng (4.6)	6.5
w/A.C. add (.4)	.4
w/P.S. add (.5)	.5
V-8	
F series (5.7)	7.9
w/A.T. add (.6)	.6
4X4 add (.2)	.2
Econoline (6.5)	9.1
w/A.C. add	
F series (.3)	.3
Econoline (1.0)	1.0

Cylinder Assembly, Renew (w/All Internal Parts Less Head(s) and Oil Pan)

Includes: R&R hood and radiator. R&R engine, transfer all component parts not supplied with replacement engine. Clean carbon, grind valves. Make all necessary adjustments.

(Factory Time)	Chilton Time
Four	
2.2L eng (12.6)	17.3
2.3L eng (11.6)	16.5
w/A.C. add (.4)	.4
w/P.S. add (.5)	.5
V-8	
F series (14.9)	20.8
w/A.T. add (.6)	.6
4X4 add (.2)	.2
Econoline (15.7)	21.9

(Factory Time)	Chilton Time
w/A.C. add	
F series (.3)	.3
Econoline (1.0)	1.0

Engine Assembly, R&R and Recondition (Complete)

Includes: R&R hood and radiator. Install new cylinder sleeves, pistons, rings, rod and main bearings. Clean carbon, grind valves. Make all necessary adjustments.

(Factory Time)	Chilton Time
Four	
2.2L eng (17.7)	24.7
2.3L eng (16.6)	23.5
w/A.C. add (.4)	.4
w/P.S. add (.5)	.5
V-8	
F series (27.2)	38.0
w/A.T. add (.6)	.6
4X4 add (.2)	.2
Econoline (28.0)	39.2
w/A.C. add	
F series (.3)	.3
Econoline (1.0)	1.0

Engine Mounts, Renew

(Factory Time)	Chilton Time
Front	
Four-one (.6)	.8
both (.9)	1.2
V-8	
F series	
right (1.8)	2.4
left (1.6)	2.1
both (1.9)	2.6
Econoline	
right (1.9)	2.5
left (1.8)	2.3
both (2.1)	2.8
Rear	
Four (.4)	.6
V-8 (.4)	.6

LABOR 14 PISTONS, RINGS & BEARINGS 14 LABOR

GASOLINE ENGINES

Rings, Renew (All)

Includes: Remove cylinder top ridge, deglaze cylinder walls, replace rod bearings, clean carbon. Minor tune up.

(Factory Time)	Chilton Time
RANGER-BRONCO I & II	
Four	
2.0L eng (8.2)	12.8
2.3L eng (7.9)	12.5
w/A.C. & P.S. add (.6)	.6
Six (7.5)	11.1
V-6 (10.9)	15.2
V-8-302-351W engs (10.2)	15.0
351M-400 engs (10.3)	15.1
AEROSTAR	
Four (8.0)	11.9
V-6 (10.8)	15.2
w/A.C. add (.3)	.3
ECONOLINE-Six (8.5)	12.7
V-8-302-351W engs (14.5)	18.0
460 eng (17.3)	20.8
F100-350	
Six (8.5)	11.6
V-6 (10.1)	14.3
V-8-255-302	
351W engs (9.6)	13.1
351M-400 engs (11.1)	14.6
460 eng (13.6)	17.1

COMBINATIONS

Add to Engine Work

(Factory Time)	Chilton Time
DRAIN, EVACUATE & RECHARGE AIR CONDITIONING SYSTEM	
All models (.7)	1.5
ROCKER ARMS OR SHAFT ASSY. DISASSEMBLE AND CLEAN OR RECONDITION	
Six (.6)	1.0
V-8-One side (.5)	.7
Both sides (1.0)	1.3
HYDRAULIC VALVE LIFTERS, DISASSEMBLE AND CLEAN	
Each (.2)	.2
ROCKER ARM STUD, RENEW	
Each (.3)	.3
DISTRIBUTOR, RECONDITION	
All models (.7)	1.0
CARBURETOR, RECONDITION	
1 BBL (.9)	1.2
2 BBL (1.0)	1.3
4 BBL	
Ford (1.0)	1.5
Holly (1.3)	2.0
TIMING CHAIN, RENEW (COVER REMOVED)	
All models (.3)	.5
VALVE GUIDES, REAM OVERSIZE	
Each (.1)	.2
DEGLAZE CYLINDER WALLS	
Each (.1)	.2
REMOVE CYLINDER TOP RIDGE	
Each (.1)	.1
MAIN BEARINGS, RENEW (PAN REMOVED)	
Four (1.9)	2.9
Six (1.6)	2.5
V-6 (1.5)	2.0
V-8 (1.9)	2.9
PLASTIGAUGE BEARINGS	
Each (.1)	.1
OIL PUMP, RECONDITION	
All models (.4)	.6
OIL FILTER ELEMENT, RENEW	
All models (.3)	.4

LABOR 14 PISTONS, RINGS & BEARINGS 14 LABOR

Piston or Connecting Rod, Renew (One)

Includes: Remove cylinder top ridge, deglaze cylinder walls, replace rod bearings, clean carbon. Minor tune up.

(Factory Time)	Chilton Time
RANGER-BRONCO I & II	
Four	
2.0L eng (7.2)	10.0
2.3L eng (7.2)	10.0
w/A.C. & P.S. add (.6)	.6
Six (5.2)	7.6
V-6 (7.8)	10.9
V-8-302-351W engs (5.6)	8.2
351M-400 engs (5.3)	7.8
AEROSTAR	
Four (7.3)	10.0
V-6 (7.9)	10.9
w/A.C. add (.3)	.3
ECONOLINE-Six (5.7)	7.4
V-8-302-351W engs (8.8)	10.7
460 eng (9.8)	11.7
F100-350	
Six (5.7)	7.4
V-6 (6.3)	8.9
V-8-255-302	
351W engs (4.6)	6.8
351M-400 engs (5.8)	7.5
460 eng (7.2)	9.0

Connecting Rod Bearings, Renew

Includes: R&R oil pan, plastigauge and install new bearings. Clean oil pump pick up tube and screen. Renew oil filter.

(Factory Time)	Chilton Time
RANGER-BRONCO	
Four	
2.0L eng	
w/M.T. (3.1)	4.4
w/A.T. (3.5)	4.8
2.3L eng	
w/M.T. (3.9)	5.4
w/A.T. (3.3)	4.6
Six (3.5)	4.8
V-6	
4X2	
w/M.T. (3.3)	4.6
w/A.T. (3.4)	4.8
4X4	
w/M.T. (4.5)	6.3
w/A.T. (4.7)	6.5
V-8-302-351W engs (4.0)	5.7
351M-400 engs (4.2)	5.9
AEROSTAR	
Four (2.6)	3.6
V-6 (3.2)	4.4
ECONOLINE	
Six (3.9)	5.7
V-8-302-351W engs (6.3)	8.0
351M-400 engs (5.1)	6.9
460 eng (4.4)	5.4
F100-350 4X2	
Six (3.5)	4.5
V-6 (3.2)	4.6
V-8-255-302	
351W engs (3.1)	4.1
351M-400 engs	
std trans (3.4)	4.4
auto trans (3.7)	4.7
F100-250 4X4	
351-400 engs (3.6)	4.6
460 eng (4.0)	5.0

DIESEL ENGINE

Rings, Renew (All)

Includes: Remove cylinder top ridge, deglaze cylinder walls, replace rod bearings, clean carbon. Make all necessary adjustments.

(Factory Time)	Chilton Time
Four	
2.2L eng (8.8)	12.3
2.3L eng (8.8)	12.3
V-8	
F series (15.3)	22.1
Econoline (15.8)	22.9
w/A.C. add	
F series (.3)	.3
Econoline (1.0)	1.0

Piston or Connecting Rod, Renew (One)

Includes: Remove cylinder top ridge, deglaze cylinder wall, replace rod bearing, clean carbon. Make all necessary adjustments.

(Factory Time)	Chilton Time
Four	
2.2L eng (7.9)	11.0
2.3L eng (7.7)	11.0
V-8	
F series (11.6)	16.8
Econoline (12.1)	17.5
w/A.C. add	
F series (.3)	.3
Econoline (1.0)	1.0

Connecting Rod Bearings, Renew

(Factory Time)	Chilton Time
Four	
2.2L eng (4.2)	6.0
2.3L eng (3.7)	5.2
V-8	
F series	
4X2 (4.7)	6.8
4X4 (5.2)	7.5
Econoline (5.4)	7.8

LABOR 15 CRANKSHAFT & DAMPER 15 LABOR

GASOLINE ENGINES

Crankshaft and Main Bearings, Renew

Includes: R&R hood and radiator. R&R engine, check all bearing clearances.

(Factory Time)	Chilton Time
RANGER-BRONCO I & II	
Four	
2.0L eng	
w/M.T. (6.9)	9.7
w/A.T. (7.3)	10.3
2.3L eng	
w/M.T. (8.1)	11.4
w/A.T. (7.0)	10.3
w/P.S. add (.2)	.2
w/A.C. add (1.0)	1.0
Six (7.9)	12.0
V-6 (8.9)	12.9
V-8-302-351W engs	
w/M.T. (6.7)	10.2
w/A.T. (6.1)	9.2
351M-400 engs	
w/M.T. (6.8)	10.3
w/A.T. (7.5)	11.3
AEROSTAR	
Four (9.4)	13.6
V-6 (10.5)	15.2
w/A.C. add (.9)	.9
ECONOLINE	
Six-w/M.T. (10.9)	16.5
w/A.T. (10.4)	15.7
V-8-302-351W engs (7.7)	11.6
351M-400 engs (9.8)	14.8
460 eng (10.0)	13.4
F100-250-Six	
std trans (7.0)	10.4
auto trans (7.4)	10.8
V-6 (7.7)	10.8
V-8-255-302	
351W engs (6.8)	11.3
351M-400 engs (7.3)	11.8
460 eng (8.3)	12.8
F350	
w/Std trans (7.0)	11.0
351-400 engs	
auto trans (7.3)	11.8

Main Bearings, Renew

Includes: R&R oil pan, plastigauge and install new main bearings. Recondition oil pump and renew oil filter.

(Factory Time)	Chilton Time
RANGER-BRONCO I & II	
Four	
2.0L eng	
w/M.T. (4.1)	5.9
w/A.T. (4.5)	6.3
2.3L eng	
w/M.T. (4.8)	6.9
w/A.T. (4.2)	6.0
Six (3.7)	5.5
V-6 (7.8)	*11.3
w/A.C. add (.4)	.4
w/A.T. add (.2)	.2
V-8-302-351W engs (4.1)	6.2
351M-400 engs (4.3)	6.4
AEROSTAR	
Four (3.5)	5.0
ECONOLINE	
Six (4.1)	6.4
V-8-302-351W engs (6.4)	8.5
351M-400 engs (5.2)	7.4
460 eng (4.6)	5.8
F100-350 4X2	
Six-std trans (6.6)	*10.0
auto trans (7.0)	*10.4
V-6 (3.3)	4.6
V-8-255-302	
351W engs (3.3)	4.7
351M-400 engs	
std trans (3.6)	5.1
auto trans (4.0)	5.5
F100-250 4X4	
351-400 engs (3.8)	5.3
460 eng (4.2)	5.6

*Includes R&R engine.

Main and Rod Bearings, Renew

Includes: R&R oil pan, plastigauge and install new rod and main bearings. Recondition oil pump and renew oil filter.

(Factory Time)	Chilton Time
RANGER-BRONCO I & II	
Four	
2.0L eng	
w/M.T. (5.0)	7.1
w/A.T. (5.4)	7.5

LABOR 15 CRANKSHAFT & DAMPER 15 LABOR

(Factory Time)	Chilton Time
2.3L eng	
w/M.T. (5.8)	8.1
w/A.T. (5.2)	7.2
Six (5.1)	7.3
V-6 (8.8)	*12.5
w/A.C. add (.4)	.4
w/A.T. add (.2)	.2
V-8-302-351W engs (5.9)	8.6
351M-400 engs (6.1)	8.8
AEROSTAR	
Four (4.5)	6.8
ECONOLINE	
Six (5.5)	8.2
V-8-302-351W engs (8.2)	10.9
351M-400 engs (7.0)	9.8
460 eng (6.3)	7.9
F100-350 4X2	
Six-std trans (8.2)	*11.6
auto trans (8.6)	*12.0
V-6 (4.7)	6.4
V-8-255-302	
351W engs (5.0)	6.8
351M-400 engs	
std trans (5.3)	7.3
auto trans (5.7)	7.7
F100-250 4X4	
351-400 engs (5.5)	7.4
460 eng (5.9)	7.7

*Includes R&R engine.

Rear Main Bearing Oil Seal, Renew (Upper & Lower)

Split Lip Type

Includes: R&R transmission on all 6 cyl models. Includes R&R oil pan on all V-8 models.

(Factory Time)	Chilton Time
RANGER-BRONCO-AEROSTAR	
Four	
2.0L eng	
w/M.T. (3.0)	4.2
w/A.T. (3.4)	4.7
2.3L eng	
4X2-w/M.T. (2.0)	2.8
w/A.T. (3.3)	4.6
4X4-w/M.T. (3.4)	4.7
V-6	
4X2-w/M.T. (3.3)	4.6
w/A.T. (3.6)	5.0
4X4 (4.2)	5.9
Six (4.4)	6.1
V-8-302-351W engs (2.9)	4.3
351M-400 engs (3.1)	4.5
ECONOLINE	
Six-w/M.T. (1.6)	2.2
w/A.T. (2.7)	3.4
V-8-302-351W engs (5.2)	6.6
351M-400 engs (4.0)	5.5
460 eng (3.5)	4.2
F100-250-Six	
3 spd (1.9)	2.5
4 spd (2.4)	3.1
auto trans (2.3)	3.0
V-6 (2.5)	3.5
V-8-255-302	
351W engs (2.2)	2.9
351M-400 engs	
std trans (2.5)	3.2
auto trans (2.8)	3.5
F350	
351-400 engs (2.7)	3.4
460 eng (3.1)	3.8

Crankshaft Front Oil Seal, Renew

Does not require R&R of front cover on V-6 & V-8 engines.

(Factory Time)	Chilton Time
RANGER-BRONCO II-AEROSTAR	
Four-2.0L eng	
Crank (1.7)	2.3
Cam (1.7)	2.3
Aux Shaft (1.8)	2.5
w/A.C. add (.3)	.3
2.3L eng	
Crank (1.6)	2.2
Cam (1.5)	2.1
Aux shaft (1.5)	2.1
All (1.9)	2.7
V-6	
w/M.T. (1.0)	1.6
w/A.T. (1.1)	1.7
BRONCO-F150-350 4X4	
351M-400 engs (.8)	1.3
V-6 (1.0)	1.5
w/A.T. add (.1)	.1

DIESEL ENGINE

Crankshaft and Main Bearings, Renew

Includes: R&R engine assy., check all bearing clearances.

(Factory Time)	Chilton Time
Four	
2.2L eng (7.4)	10.7
2.3L eng (8.0)	11.6
V-8	
F series (11.8)	17.1
w/A.T. add (.6)	.6
4X4 add (.2)	.2
Econoline (12.6)	18.7
w/A.C. add	
F series (.3)	.3
Econoline (1.0)	1.0

Main Bearings, Renew

Includes: Check all bearing clearances.

(Factory Time)	Chilton Time
Four	
2.2L eng (5.0)	7.0
2.3L eng (4.6)	6.6
V-8	
F series	
4X2 (5.4)	7.8
4X4 (5.9)	8.5
Econoline (6.1)	8.8

Main and Rod Bearings, Renew

Includes: Check all bearing clearances.

(Factory Time)	Chilton Time
Four	
2.2L eng (6.0)	8.2
2.3L eng (5.6)	7.8
V-8	
F series	
4X2 (7.5)	10.2
4X4 (8.0)	10.9
Econoline (8.2)	11.2

Crankshaft Front Oil Seal, Renew

(Factory Time)	Chilton Time
Four	
2.2L eng (.9)	1.4
2.3L eng (1.7)	2.5
V-8	
F series (1.7)	2.5
Econoline (1.2)	1.8
w/A.C. add (.4)	.4
w/P.S. add (.5)	.5

Crankshaft Rear Oil Seal, Renew

(Factory Time)	Chilton Time
Four	
2.2L eng (1.9)	2.7
2.3L eng (3.4)	4.7
V-8	
F series	
4X2-w/M.T. (3.3)	4.8
w/A.T. (3.0)	4.3
4X4-w/M.T. (4.3)	6.2
w/A.T. (4.0)	6.0
Econoline (3.1)	4.5

Crankshaft and/or Camshaft Sprockets, Renew

(Factory Time)	Chilton Time
Four	
2.2L eng (1.9)	2.7
2.3L eng (1.1)	1.6
V-8	
F series (4.1)	5.9
Econoline (4.7)	6.8
w/A.C. add (.4)	.4
w/P.S. add (.5)	.5

Vibration Damper or Pulley, Renew

(Factory Time)	Chilton Time
Four	
2.2L eng (.8)	1.2
2.3L eng (.4)	.7
V-8	
F series (1.5)	2.1
Econoline (1.1)	1.5
w/A.C. add (.1)	.1

LABOR 16 CAMSHAFT & TIMING GEARS 16 LABOR

GASOLINE ENGINES

Timing Case Cover, Gasket or Oil Seal, Renew

Includes: R&R radiator. Does not require oil pan removal on 6 cyl (200) or 302 CID engines.

(Factory Time)	Chilton Time
RANGER-BRONCO-AEROSTAR	
Four	
2.0L eng (2.0)	2.9
2.3L eng (1.9)	2.7
w/P.S. add (.2)	.2
w/A.C. add (.3)	.3
Six (2.4)	3.4
V-6 (4.6)	6.4
V-8-302-351W engs (2.0)	2.8
351M-400 engs (3.8)	5.3
ECONOLINE	
Six (3.2)	4.9
V-8-302-351W engs (3.9)	5.5
351M-400 engs (3.9)	5.5
460 eng (3.0)	3.9
F100-350	
Six (2.4)	3.3
V-6 (3.7)	5.2
V-8-255-302	
351W engs (2.0)	2.9
351M-400 engs (3.4)	4.3
460 eng (2.3)	3.4

Timing Belt, Renew

(Factory Time)	Chilton Time
RANGER-AEROSTAR	
Four	
2.0L eng (1.6)	2.5
2.3L eng (1.3)	2.2
w/P.S. add (.2)	.2
w/A.C. add (.3)	.3

Timing Chain or Gears, Renew (SIX)

Includes: R&R timing case cover and radiator, renew gears or chain. Reset ignition timing.

(Factory Time)	Chilton Time
BRONCO-Six (2.7)	3.9
ECONOLINE-Six (3.5)	5.4

LABOR 16 CAMSHAFT & TIMING GEARS 16 LABOR

(Factory Time) Chilton Time

F100-350
Six (2.7) 4.0

CRANKSHAFT GEAR ONLY. FOR CAMSHAFT FIBER GEAR USE CAMSHAFT, RENEW

Timing Chain or Gears, Renew (V-6 & V-8)

Includes: R&R timing case cover and radiator. Renew gears or chain. Reset ignition timing.

RANGER-BRONCO-AEROSTAR
V-6 (4.9) 6.9
V-8
302-351W engs (2.3) 3.3
351M-400 engs (4.1) 5.8
ECONOLINE
V-8
302-351W engs (4.2) 5.8
351M-400 engs (4.2) 5.8
460 eng (3.3) 4.4
F100-350
V-8
255-302-351W engs (2.3) 3.4
351M-400 engs (3.6) 4.8
460 eng (2.7) 3.9

Camshaft or Camshaft Gear, Renew

Includes: R&R radiator, timing case cover. Adjust carburetor and ignition timing. Does not require oil pan removal on 302-360-390 CID engines.

RANGER-BRONCO
Four
2.0L eng (2.2) 3.3
2.3L eng (4.2) 5.9
w/P.S. add (.2) 2
w/A.C. add (.3) 3
Six (5.5) 8.0
V-6 (8.9) 12.5
V-8-302-351W engs (5.0) 7.5
351M-400 engs (5.0) 7.5
AEROSTAR
Four (5.4) 7.5
V-6 (9.6) 13.5
w/A.C. add (.2) 2
w/P.S. add (.2) 2

(Factory Time) Chilton Time

ECONOLINE
Six (6.5) 9.6
V-8-302-351W engs (5.6) 8.3
351M-400 engs (6.7) 9.9
F100-350
Six (5.5) 8.0
V-6 (6.9) 9.8
V-8-255-302
351W engs (5.0) 7.5
351M-400 engs (5.0) 7.5
460 eng (5.6) 8.3

Camshaft Bearings, Renew

Includes: R&R hood, radiator and engine assembly where required. R&R camshaft and renew bearings. Adjust carburetor and ignition timing.

RANGER-BRONCO
Four
2.0L eng (2.7) 4.1
w/P.S. add (.2) 2
w/A.C. add (.3) 3
Six (7.2) 10.8
V-6 (10.5) 14.7
V-8-302-351W engs
w/M.T. (7.7) 11.5
w/A.T. (8.1) 12.1
351M-400 engs
w/M.T. (7.8) 11.6
w/A.T. (8.5) 12.7
AEROSTAR
V-6 (11.9) 17.2
w/A.C. add (.9) 9
ECONOLINE
Six-w/M.T. (10.2) 15.3
w/A.T. (9.7) 14.5
V-8-302-351W engs (8.7) 13.0
351M-400 engs (10.8) 16.2
460 eng (11.4) 15.5
F100-250-Six
std trans (6.2) 7.8
auto trans (6.6) 8.2
V-6 (11.4) 16.0
V-8-255-302
351W engs (7.7) 9.3
351M-400 engs (8.3) 9.9

(Factory Time) Chilton Time

F350
w/Std trans (7.8) 9.4
351-400 engs
auto trans (8.3) 9.9

DIESEL ENGINE

Timing Cover Gasket, Renew

Four
2.2L eng (5.5) 7.9
2.3L eng (2.0) 3.0
V-8
F series (3.9) 5.6
Econoline (4.5) 6.5
w/A.C. add (.4) 4
w/P.S. add (.5) 5

Camshaft, Renew

Four
2.2L eng (6.1) 8.8
2.3L eng (1.5) 2.2
V-8
F series (8.5) 12.3
Econoline (9.5) 13.7
w/A.C. add
F series (.3) 3
Econoline (1.0) 1.0

Camshaft and/or Crankshaft Sprockets, Renew

Four
2.2L eng (1.9) 2.7
2.3L eng (1.1) 1.6
V-8
F series (4.1) 5.9
Econoline (4.7) 6.8
w/A.C. add (.4) 4
w/P.S. add (.5) 5

Camshaft Idler Gear, Renew

Four
2.2L eng (2.0) 2.7
2.3L eng (1.0) 1.5
w/A.C. add (.4) 4
w/P.S. add (.5) 5

Timing Belt, Renew

Four
2.3L eng (1.0) 1.5

LABOR 17 ENGINE OILING SYSTEM 17 LABOR

(Factory Time) Chilton Time

GASOLINE ENGINES

Oil Pan or Gasket, Renew

Includes: Clean oil pick up tube and screen. Renew oil filter.

RANGER-BRONCO
Four
2.0L eng
w/M.T. (2.2) 3.0
w/A.T. (2.6) 3.6
2.3L eng
4X2-w/M.T. (2.9) 4.0
w/A.T. (2.3) 3.2
4X4-w/M.T. (3.4) 4.7
w/A.T. (3.6) 5.0
Six (2.1) 3.0
V-6
4X2
w/M.T. (2.2) 3.0
w/A.T. (2.3) 3.2
4X4
w/M.T. (3.4) 4.8
w/A.T. (3.6) 5.0

(Factory Time) Chilton Time

V-8-302-351W engs (2.2) 3.3
351M-400 engs (2.4) 3.5
AEROSTAR
Four (1.6) 2.2
V-6 (2.2) 3.0
ECONOLINE
Six (2.5) 3.9
V-8-302-351W engs (4.5) 5.6
351M-400 engs (3.3) 4.5
460 eng (2.7) 3.8
F100-350 4X2
Six (1.9) 2.9
V-6 (1.8) 2.5
V-8-255-302
351W engs (1.4) 2.4
351M-400 engs
std trans (1.7) 2.8
auto trans (2.0) 3.1
F100-250 4X4
351-400 engs (1.9) 2.9
460 eng (2.3) 3.4

(Factory Time) Chilton Time

Oil Pump, R&R or Renew

Includes: R&R oil pan, clean oil pump pick up tube and screen. Renew oil filter.

RANGER-BRONCO
Four
2.0L eng
w/M.T. (2.4) 3.2
w/A.T. (2.8) 3.8
2.3L eng
4X2-w/M.T. (3.0) 4.2
w/A.T. (2.4) 3.4
4X4-w/M.T. (3.5) 4.9
w/A.T. (3.7) 5.2
Six (2.2) 3.2
V-6
4X2
w/M.T. (2.3) 3.2
w/A.T. (2.4) 3.4
4X4
w/M.T. (3.5) 5.0
w/A.T. (3.7) 5.2
V-8-302-351W engs (2.3) 3.5
351M-400 engs (2.5) 3.7

LABOR 17 ENGINE OILING SYSTEM 17 LABOR

(Factory Time)	Chilton Time
AEROSTAR	
Four (1.7)	2.4
V-6 (2.3)	3.2
ECONOLINE	
Six (2.6)	4.1
V-8-302-351W engs (4.6)	5.8
351M-400 engs (3.4)	4.7
460 eng (2.7)	4.0
F100-350 4X2	
Six (2.1)	3.1
V-6 (.7)	1.1
V-8-255-302	
351W engs (1.5)	2.6
351M-400 engs	
std trans (1.9)	3.0
auto trans (2.1)	3.3
F100-250 4X4	
351-400 engs (2.0)	3.1
460 eng (2.4)	3.6
Recond pump add (.4)	.5

Pressure Test Engine Bearings (Pan Off)

All models	1.0

Oil Pressure Gauge (Engine), Renew

All models (.3)	.5

Oil Pressure Gauge (Dash), Renew

RANGER (.6)	1.0
BRONCO (.4)	.7
BRONCO II (.6)	1.0
AEROSTAR (.6)	1.0
ECONOLINE (.5)	.8
F100-350 (.5)	1.0

Oil Filter Element, Renew

All models (.3)	.4

DIESEL ENGINE

Oil Pan and/or Gasket, Renew

Four	
2.2L eng (3.2)	4.5
2.3L eng (2.7)	3.7
V-8	
F series	3.6
4X2 (2.6)	3.6
4X4 (3.1)	4.3
Econoline (3.3)	4.7

Pressure Test Engine Bearings (Pan Off)

All models	1.0

Oil Pump, Renew

Four	
2.2L eng (3.4)	4.8
2.3L eng (1.4)	1.9
V-8	
F series	
4X2 (2.8)	3.9
4X4 (3.3)	4.6
Econoline (3.5)	5.0
Recond pump add	.5

Oil Cooler Assembly, Renew

V-8 (1.6)	2.3

Oil Filter Element, Renew

All models (.3)	.4

LABOR 18 CLUTCH & FLYWHEEL 18 LABOR

Clutch Pedal Free Play, Adjust

(Factory Time)	Chilton Time
All models (.3)	.4

Clutch Master Cylinder Control Assy., Renew

RANGER (.6)	1.0

Clutch Assembly, Renew

Includes: R&R trans and transfer case as a unit. Adjust clutch pedal free play.

RANGER	
4 Speed	
4X2	
Four (2.0)	2.8
V-6 (2.5)	3.3
4X4	
Four (2.9)	3.9
V-6 (3.8)	5.2
5 Speed	
4X2	
Four (2.0)	2.8
V-6 (2.7)	3.6
4X4 (3.8)	5.2
AEROSTAR	
Four-TK-5 (2.0)	2.8
V-6-TK-5 (2.3)	3.1
BRONCO	
3 Speed (3.1)	4.1
4 Speed	
Warner T-18 (4.1)	5.4
SROD (3.3)	4.3
New Process 435 (4.2)	5.5
5 Speed	
TK-5 (3.8)	4.9
ECONOLINE	
3 Speed (1.4)	2.7
4 Speed (2.3)	3.5
4 Speed O.D. (1.6)	2.9
4 Speed	
New Process 435 (2.4)	3.6
F100-350 4X2	
3 Speed	
column shift (2.2)	3.3
floor shift (1.5)	2.4
4 Speed	
Overdrive (1.6)	2.5
SROD (1.6)	2.5
TOD (2.2)	3.0
Warner T-18 (2.4)	3.5
Warner T-19 (3.0)	4.0
New Process 435 (2.4)	3.5
F100-350 4X4	
4 Speed	
TOD (3.9)	5.3
Warner T-18 (4.1)	5.4
New Process 435 (4.2)	5.5
SROD (3.3)	4.3
Warner T-19 (3.9)	5.1
w/Skid plate add (.2)	.3
w/Full carpet add (.7)	1.0
w/P.T.O. add (.6)	.8
w/Coupling shaft add (.2)	.3

Clutch Release Bearing, Renew

Includes: R&R trans and transfer case as a unit. Adjust clutch pedal free play.

RANGER	
4 Speed	
4X2	
Four (1.7)	2.5
V-6 (1.7)	3.0
4X4	
Four (3.4)	3.6
V-6 (3.4)	4.9
5 Speed	
4X2	
Four (1.7)	2.5
V-6 (1.7)	3.3
4X4 (3.4)	4.9
AEROSTAR	
Four-TK-5 (2.1)	2.7
V-6-TK-5 (2.1)	3.0
BRONCO	
3 Speed (2.4)	3.4
4 Speed	
Warner T-18 (3.4)	4.7
New Process 435 (3.5)	4.8
SROD (2.6)	3.6
5 Speed	
TK-5 (2.6)	4.8
ECONOLINE	
3 Speed (.8)	2.0
4 Speed (1.7)	2.6
4 Speed O.D. (1.0)	2.0
4 Speed	
New Process 435 (1.7)	2.8
F100-350 4X2	
3 Speed (.8)	1.7
4 Speed	
Overdrive (1.0)	1.8
SROD (.9)	1.8
TOD (1.6)	2.2
Warner T-18 (1.7)	2.8
Warner T-19 (2.2)	3.0
New Process 435 (1.7)	2.8
F100-350 4X4	
4 Speed	
TOD (3.3)	4.5
Warner T-18 (3.4)	4.7
New Process 435 (3.5)	4.8
SROD (2.6)	3.6
Warner T-19 (3.1)	4.5
w/Skid plate add (.2)	.3
w/Full carpet add (.7)	1.0
w/P.T.O. add (.6)	.8
w/Coupling shaft add (.2)	.3

Flywheel, Renew

Includes: R&R trans and transfer case as a unit. R&R clutch and adjust free play.

RANGER	
4 Speed	
4X2	
Four (2.3)	3.1
V-6 (2.8)	3.6
4X4	
Four (3.2)	4.2
V-6 (4.1)	5.5
5 Speed	
4X2	
Four (2.3)	3.1
V-6 (3.0)	3.9
4X4 (4.1)	5.5
AEROSTAR	
Four-TK-5 (1.2)	3.1
V-6-TK-5 (2.8)	3.7
BRONCO	
3 Speed (3.2)	4.4
4 Speed	
Warner T-18 (4.2)	5.7
SROD (3.4)	4.6
New Process 435 (4.4)	5.8
5 Speed	
TK-5 (4.0)	5.2

LABOR 18 CLUTCH & FLYWHEEL 18 LABOR

(Factory Time)	Chilton Time
ECONOLINE	
3 Speed (1.5)	3.0
4 Speed (2.4)	3.8
4 Speed O.D. (1.6)	3.2
4 Speed	
New Process 435 (2.5)	3.9
F100-350 4X2	
3 Speed	
column shift (2.3)	3.6
floor shift (1.7)	3.0
4 Speed	
Overdrive (1.8)	2.8
SROD (1.7)	2.8
TOD (2.4)	3.3
Warner T-18 (2.5)	3.8
Warner T-19 (4.0)	5.4
New Process 435 (2.5)	3.8
F100-350 4X4	
4 Speed	
TOD (4.1)	5.6
Warner T-18 (4.2)	5.7
New Process 435 (4.3)	5.8
SROD (3.4)	4.6
Warner T-19 (4.2)	5.4
w/Skid plate add (.2)	.3
w/Full carpet add (.7)	1.0
Renew ring gear add (.2)	.4
w/P.T.O. add (.6)	.8
w/Coupling shaft add (.2)	.3

LABOR 19 STANDARD TRANSMISSION 19 LABOR

Transmission Assy., Remove and Reinstall

Includes: R&R transmission and transfer case as a unit.

(Factory Time)	Chilton Time
RANGER	
4 Speed	
4X2	
Four (1.7)	2.5
V-6 (2.2)	3.0
4X4	
Four (2.6)	3.6
V-6 (3.5)	4.9
5 Speed	
4X2	
Four (1.7)	2.5
V-6 (2.4)	3.3
4X4 (3.5)	4.9
AEROSTAR	
Four-TK-5 (1.7)	2.5
V-6-TK-5 (2.0)	2.8
BRONCO	
3 Speed (2.4)	3.2
4 Speed	
Warner T-18 (3.4)	4.5
SROD (2.6)	3.4
New Process 435 (3.5)	4.6
5 Speed	
TK-5 (3.5)	4.6
ECONOLINE	
3 speed (.8)	1.8
4 speed (1.7)	2.6
4 speed O.D. (.9)	1.8
4 Speed	
New Process 435 (1.7)	2.6
F100-350 4X2	
3 Speed (.8)	1.5
4 Speed	
Overdrive (.9)	1.6
SROD (.9)	1.6
TOD (1.5)	2.1
Warner T-18 (1.7)	2.6
Warner T-19 (2.2)	3.0
New Process 435 (1.7)	2.6
F100-350 4X4	
4 Speed	
TOD (3.2)	4.4
Warner T-18 (3.4)	4.5
New Process 435 (3.5)	4.6
SROD (2.6)	3.4
Warner T-19 (3.1)	4.3
w/Skid plate add (.2)	.3
w/Full carpet add (.7)	1.0
w/P.T.O. add (.6)	.8
w/Coupling shaft add (.2)	.3

Transmission Assy., R&R and Recondition

Includes: R&R trans and transfer case as a unit. Separate and overhaul transmission only.

(Factory Time)	Chilton Time
RANGER	
4 Speed	
4X2	
Four (3.9)	5.5
V-6 (4.4)	6.1
4X4	
Four (4.8)	6.7
V-6 (5.7)	8.0
5 Speed	
4X2	
Four (3.9)	5.5
V-6 (4.6)	6.4
4X4 (5.7)	8.0
AEROSTAR	
Four-TK-5 (6.0)	8.4
V-6-TK-5 (6.3)	8.8
BRONCO	
3 Speed (4.5)	6.1
4 Speed	
Warner T-18 (5.3)	7.3
SROD (4.4)	6.1
New Process 435 (5.5)	7.6
5 Speed	
TK-5 (7.8)	10.9
ECONOLINE	
3 Speed (2.9)	4.5
4 Speed O.D. (3.6)	5.0
4 Speed	
New Process 435 (3.9)	5.5
F100-350 4X2	
3 Speed (2.9)	4.0
4 Speed	
Overdrive (2.8)	3.9
SROD (2.7)	3.8
TOD (3.3)	4.6
Warner T-18 (3.6)	4.9
New Process 435 (3.7)	5.1
F100-350 4X4	
4 Speed	
TOD (5.0)	7.0
Warner T-18 (5.2)	7.2
New Process 435 (5.5)	7.6
SROD (4.4)	6.1
Warner T-19 (5.0)	7.0
w/Skid plate add (.2)	.3
w/Full carpet add (.7)	1.0
w/P.T.O. add (.6)	.8
w/Coupling shaft add (.2)	.3

Transmission, Recondition (Off Truck)

(Factory Time)	Chilton Time
3 Speed (2.1)	3.2
4 Speed	
TOD (1.8)	2.5
New Process (2.3)	3.4
Warner (1.9)	3.0
Overdrive (2.3)	3.4
SROD (1.9)	3.0
TK (2.2)	3.0
5 Speed	
TK-5 (4.3)	6.0
MMC5 (4.2)	5.9

Extension Housing, Bearing Retainer or Gasket, Renew

Includes: Renew oil seal.

(Factory Time)	Chilton Time
All models 4X2	
3 Speed (1.2)	1.7
4 Speed-O/D (1.3)	1.8
4 Speed-TOD (1.3)	1.8
4 Speed-SROD (1.4)	1.9
4 Speed-TK (1.2)	1.7
4 Speed-Warner T-19 (1.1)	1.7
4 Speed-Warner T-18 (2.4)	3.0
New Process 435 (1.3)	1.8
5 Speed-TK (1.2)	1.7
4X4	
TK (2.2)	2.8
TOD (2.2)	2.8
Warner T-18 (2.4)	3.0
New Process 435 (2.4)	3.0
Warner T-19 (2.0)	2.8
w/Coupling shaft add (.2)	.3

Transmission Rear Oil Seal and/or Bushing, Renew

(Factory Time)	Chilton Time
BRONCO (.7)	1.0
All other models (.5)	.8
w/Coupling shaft add (.2)	.3

LABOR 20 TRANSFER CASE 20 LABOR

(Factory Time) Chilton Time

Transfer Case Assembly, R&R or Renew
All models (1.8).............................. 2.5
Renew assy add.............................. .5
w/P.T.O. add (.6).............................. .8
w/Coupling shaft add (.2).............................. .3

Transfer Case, R&R and Recondition
Includes: R&R trans and/or transfer case. Separate units and overhaul transfer case only.
All models
New Process 203
Full Time (5.0).............................. 8.3
New Process 205
Part Time (4.3).............................. 6.0
New Process 208
Part Time (4.7).............................. 6.4
Borg Warner 1345
Part Time (3.8).............................. 5.3
Borg Warner 1350
Part Time (3.8).............................. 5.3
w/P.T.O. add (.6).............................. .8
w/Coupling shaft add (.2).............................. .3

LABOR 21 SHIFT LINKAGE 21 LABOR

(Factory Time) Chilton Time

STANDARD

Shift Linkage, Adjust
All models (.3).............................. .4

Gear Shift Tube Assy., Renew
(3 SPEED)
Bronco (.5).............................. 1.1
ECONOLINE (.6).............................. 1.1
F100-250 (1.1).............................. 1.7

Gear Shift Rods, Renew
Includes: Adjust shift linkage.
BRONCO (.4).............................. .7
ECONOLINE-3 spd (.5).............................. .7
F100-250-3 spd (.5).............................. .7

Transfer Case Control Lever, Renew
All models (.5).............................. .7

AUTOMATIC

Manual Shift Linkage, Adjust
Includes: Adjust neutral safety switch.
All models
C-4 (.2).............................. .6
C-5 (.4).............................. .6
C-6 (.3).............................. .6
AOD (.3).............................. .6
A4LD (.3).............................. .6

Gear Shift Tube Assembly, Renew
F100-350 (.7).............................. 1.5

Gear Selector Lever, Renew
All models (.3).............................. .5

LABOR 23 AUTOMATIC TRANSMISSION 23 LABOR

(Factory Time) Chilton Time

ON TRUCK SERVICES

Drain and Refill Unit
All models (.7).............................. .7

Oil Pressure Check
All models (.3).............................. .5

Check Unit for Oil Leaks
Includes: Clean and dry outside of case, run unit to determine point of leak.
All models (.7).............................. .9

Neutral Safety Switch, Renew
All models (.3).............................. .4

Vacuum Modulator, Renew
All models (.4).............................. .6

Vacuum Modulator, Adjust
Includes: Pressure check.
All models (.5).............................. .9

Manual and Throttle Linkage, Adjust
Includes: Adjust dashpot, idle speed and accelerate pedal height if adjustable.
All models (.4).............................. .7

Front Servo, Recondition
Includes: Adjust band.
RANGER-AEROSTAR
C-3 (.4).............................. .7
C-5 (.6).............................. 1.1
A4LD (.6).............................. 1.1
BRONCO-C-4 (.7).............................. 1.3
BRONCO II-C-5 (.6).............................. 1.1
ECONOLINE, F100-350
C-4 (.6).............................. 1.1
C-5 (.6).............................. 1.1
C-6 (1.0).............................. 1.9
AOD (1.0).............................. 1.5

Rear Servo, Recondition
RANGER-C-5 (.5).............................. 1.0
BRONCO-C-4 (.7).............................. 1.3
ECONOLINE, F100-350
C-4 (.5).............................. 1.0
AOD (1.0).............................. 1.5

Extension Housing and/or Gasket, Renew
C-3 (.9).............................. 1.5
C-5
4X2 (.9).............................. 1.5
4X4 (1.0).............................. 1.6
C-6
4X2 (1.0).............................. 1.6
4X4 (2.2).............................. 3.0
AOD (1.5).............................. 2.3
A4LD (1.5).............................. 2.3
w/Coupling shaft add (.2).............................. .2

Extension Housing Rear Oil Seal, Renew
All models (.5).............................. .8
w/Coupling shaft add (.2).............................. .2

Front Band, Adjust
Includes: R&R oil pan and renew gasket on MX-FMX.
C-3 (.3).............................. .7
C-4 (.3).............................. .7
C-5 (.3).............................. .7
C-6 (.2).............................. .6
A4LD (.3).............................. .7

Rear Band, Adjust
A4LD (.2).............................. .6
C-4 (.2).............................. .6
C-5 (.2).............................. .6

Front and Rear Bands, Adjust
Includes: R&R oil pan and renew gasket on MX-FMX.
A4LD (.3).............................. .9
C-4 (.3).............................. .9
C-5 (.3).............................. .9

Oil Pan or Gasket, Renew
A4LD (.9).............................. 1.2
C-3 (.7).............................. 1.2
C-5 (.7).............................. 1.2
C-4 & C-6-exc below (.6).............................. 1.1
C-6-w/460 eng (1.2).............................. 1.7
AOD (.7).............................. 1.2

Valve Body Assembly, Renew
Includes: R&R oil pan.
A4LD (1.2).............................. 1.7
C-3 (1.0).............................. 1.5
C-5 (.9).............................. 1.5
C-4 & C-6-exc below (1.1).............................. 1.5
C-6-w/460 eng (1.7).............................. 2.2
AOD (1.3).............................. 1.9

Valve Body Assy., R&R and Recondition
Includes: R&R oil pan and replace filter. Disassemble, clean, inspect, free all valves. Replace parts as required.
A4LD (1.7).............................. 2.5
C-3 (1.5).............................. 2.5
C-4 (1.7).............................. 2.5
C-5 (1.4).............................. 2.5
C-6-exc below (1.6).............................. 2.4
C-6-w/460 eng (2.2).............................. 3.0
AOD (1.7).............................. 3.0

Parking Pawl, Renew
Includes: R&R oil pan or trans assy., as required.
A4LD
4X2 (1.0).............................. 1.6
4X4 (2.4).............................. 3.2
C-3 (1.0).............................. 1.6
C-5
4X2 (3.4).............................. 4.5
4X4 (5.0).............................. 6.7

(Factory Time)	Chilton Time
C-6	
4X2 (3.9)	5.2
4X4 (5.3)	7.1
AOD (1.5)	2.4
w/Coupling shaft add (.2)	.2

Governor and Counterweight Assy., Renew

Includes: Road test.

(Factory Time)	Chilton Time
C-3 (1.0)	1.7
C-5	
4X2 (3.4)	4.7
4X4 (5.0)	7.0
C-6	
4X2 (3.9)	5.3
4X4 (5.3)	7.4
AOD (1.7)	2.6
w/Coupling shaft add (.2)	.2

Governor (Less Counterweight), Renew

Includes: Road test.

(Factory Time)	Chilton Time
C-4 (1.6)	2.4
C-3 (.9)	1.6
C-5	
4X2 (1.3)	1.9
4X4 (2.3)	3.2
C-6	
4X2 (1.2)	1.7
4X4 (2.2)	3.1
AOD (1.6)	2.5
A4LD	
4X2 (1.0)	1.6
4X4 (1.8)	2.6
w/Coupling shaft add (.2)	.2

SERVICES REQUIRING R&R

Transmission Assembly, R&R

Includes: R&R transmission and converter assembly. Drain and refill unit. Adjust linkage.

(Factory Time)	Chilton Time
RANGER-AEROSTAR	
C-3 (2.3)	4.0
C-5	
4X2 (2.3)	4.0
4X4 (3.9)	5.4
A4LD	
4X2 (2.2)	3.1
4X4 (3.9)	5.4
BRONCO (4.9)	6.9
BRONCO II 4X4 (3.9)	5.4
ECONOLINE (2.7)	4.8
F100-350 4X2	
C-4 (2.9)	5.0
C-5 (2.4)	4.2
C-6-exc below (3.4)	5.5
C-6-w/460 eng (4.1)	6.2
AOD (2.9)	4.4
F100-150 4X4 (4.9)	6.9
F250-350 4X4 (4.2)	6.2
w/Skid plate add (.2)	.3
w/P.T.O. add (.6)	.8
w/Coupling shaft add (.2)	.3

Transmission and Converter Assy., R&R and Recondition

Includes: Drain and refill unit. Disassemble trans including valve body, clean, inspect and replace parts as required. Adjust linkage. Road test.

(Factory Time)	Chilton Time
RANGER-AEROSTAR	
C-3 (6.3)	11.5
C-5	
4X2 (6.4)	11.5
4X4 (8.0)	12.4
A4LD	
4X2 (9.1)	12.3
4X4 (10.8)	14.5
BRONCO (9.1)	13.9
BRONCO II 4X4 (8.0)	12.4
ECONOLINE (6.9)	12.0
F100-350 4X2	
C-4 (7.1)	12.3
C-5 (6.5)	11.3
C-6-exc below (7.6)	12.8
C-6-w/460 eng (8.3)	13.2
AOD (7.8)	12.5
F100-150 4X4 (9.1)	13.9
F250-350 4X4 (8.4)	13.4
Clean and check converter add (.5)	.5
Flush oil cooler and lines add (.2)	.2
w/Skid plate add (.2)	.3
w/P.T.O. add (.6)	.8
w/Coupling shaft add (.2)	.3

Transmission Assembly, Renew

Includes: R&R transmission, transfer all necessary parts. Drain and refill unit. Adjust linkage. Road test.

(Factory Time)	Chilton Time
RANGER-AEROSTAR	
C-3 (2.5)	4.5
C-5	
4X2 (2.8)	4.5
4X4 (4.4)	6.0
A4LD	
4X2 (2.7)	3.7
4X4 (4.4)	6.0
BRONCO (5.4)	7.4
BRONCO II 4X4 (4.1)	6.0
ECONOLINE (3.2)	5.3
F100-350 4X2	
C-4 (3.4)	5.5
C-5 (2.9)	5.0
C-6-exc below (3.9)	6.0
C-6-w/460 eng (4.6)	6.7
AOD (3.4)	5.5
F100-150 4X4 (5.4)	7.4
F250-350 4X4 (4.7)	6.7
w/Skid plate add (.2)	.3
w/P.T.O. add (.6)	.8
w/Coupling shaft add (.2)	.3

Transmission Assembly, Reseal

Includes: R&R transmission, drain and refill unit. Renew all seals and gaskets. Adjust linkage. Road test.

(Factory Time)	Chilton Time
RANGER-AEROSTAR	
C-3 (4.1)	6.0
C-5	
4X2 (4.1)	6.0
4X4 (5.7)	7.4
A4LD	
4X2 (4.0)	5.1
4X4 (5.7)	7.4
BRONCO (6.7)	8.2
BRONCO II 4X4	7.4
ECONOLINE (4.5)	6.5
F100-350 4X2	
C-4 (4.7)	6.8
C-5 (4.4)	6.5
C-6-exc below (5.2)	7.3
C-6-w/460 eng (5.9)	8.0
AOD	6.0
F100-150 4X4 (6.7)	8.2
F250-350 4X4 (6.0)	7.7
w/Skid plate add (.2)	.3
w/P.T.O. add (.6)	.8
w/Coupling shaft add (.2)	.3

Torque Converter, Renew

Includes: R&R transmission. Drain and refill unit. Adjust linkage. Road test.

(Factory Time)	Chilton Time
RANGER-AEROSTAR	
C-3 (2.8)	3.7
C-5	
4X2 (2.8)	3.7
4X4 (4.4)	5.9
A4LD	
4X2 (2.7)	3.6
4X4 (4.4)	5.9
BRONCO (5.0)	6.7
BRONCO II 4X4 (4.4)	5.9
ECONOLINE (2.8)	3.7
F100-350 4X2	
C-4 (3.0)	4.0
C-5 (2.9)	3.9
C-6-exc below (3.5)	4.7
C-6-w/460 eng (4.2)	5.6
AOD (3.0)	4.0
F100-150 4X4 (5.0)	6.7
F250-350 4X4 (4.3)	5.8
w/Skid plate add (.2)	.3
w/P.T.O. add (.6)	.8
w/Coupliong shaft add (.2)	.3

Bands, Renew (One or Both)

Includes: R&R transmission. Drain and refill unit. Renew gaskets and seals as necessary. Adjust linkage. Road test.

(Factory Time)	Chilton Time
RANGER	
C-3 (3.8)	5.5
C-5	
4X2 (3.6)	5.3
4X4 (5.2)	8.0
BRONCO	
C-4 (6.2)	8.3
C-6 (6.6)	8.7
BRONCO II 4X4 (5.2)	8.0
ECONOLINE	
C-4 (4.0)	6.5
C-6 (4.4)	6.9
F100-350 4X2	
C-4 (4.2)	6.3
C-5 (3.7)	6.4
C-6-exc below (5.1)	7.3
C-6-w/460 eng (5.8)	8.0
F100-150 4X4 (6.6)	8.7
F250-350 4X4 (5.9)	8.2
w/Skid plate add (.2)	.3
w/P.T.O. add (.6)	.8
w/Coupling shaft add (.2)	3

Front Oil Pump Seal, Renew

Includes: R&R transmission. Drain and refill unit. Adjust linkage. Road test.

(Factory Time)	Chilton Time
RANGER-AEROSTAR	
C-3 (2.4)	4.2
C-5	
4X2 (2.4)	4.2
4X4 (4.0)	6.2
A4LD	
4X2 (2.8)	3.8
4X4 (4.5)	6.1
BRONCO (5.0)	7.1
BRONCO II 4X4 (4.0)	6.2
ECONOLINE (2.8)	4.9
F100-350 4X2	
C-4 (3.0)	5.2
C-5 (2.5)	4.3
C-6-exc below (3.5)	5.7
C-6-w/460 eng (4.2)	6.4
AOD (3.0)	4.6
F100-150 4X4 (5.0)	7.1
F250-350 4X4 (4.3)	6.6
w/Skid plate add (.2)	.3
w/P.T.O. add (.6)	.8
w/Coupling shaft add (.2)	.3

Front Oil Pump, R&R and Recondition

Includes: R&R transmission. Drain and refill unit. Renew gaskets and seals as necessary. Adjust linkage. Road test.

(Factory Time)	Chilton Time
RANGER-AEROSTAR	
C-3 (2.9)	4.0
C-5	
4X2 (2.9)	4.0
4X4 (4.6)	6.4
A4LD	
4X2 (2.8)	3.9
4X4 (4.5)	6.3

LABOR 23 AUTOMATIC TRANSMISSION 23 LABOR

(Factory Time)	Chilton Time
BRONCO	
C-4 (5.6)	7.8
C-6 (6.1)	8.5
BRONCO II 4X4 (4.6)	6.4
ECONOLINE	
C-4 (3.4)	4.7
C-6 (3.9)	5.4
F100-350 4X2	
C-4 (3.6)	5.0
C-5 (3.1)	4.3
C-6-exc below (4.6)	6.4
C-6-w/460 eng (5.3)	7.4
AOD (3.5)	4.9
F100-150 4X4 (6.1)	8.5
F250-350 4X4 (5.4)	7.5
w/Skid plate add (.2)	.3
w/P.T.O. add (.6)	.6
w/Coupling shaft add (.2)	.3

Flywheel and Ring Gear Assy., Renew

Includes: R&R transmission. Drain and refill unit. Adjust linkage. Road test.

(Factory Time)	Chilton Time
RANGER-AEROSTAR	
C-3 (2.6)	4.3
C-5	
4X2 (2.6)	4.3
4X4 (4.2)	6.5
A4LD	
4X2 (2.5)	3.4
4X4 (4.2)	5.7
BRONCO (5.2)	7.4
BRONCO II 4X4 (4.2)	6.5
ECONOLINE (3.0)	5.3
F100-350 4X2	
C-4 (3.2)	5.5
C-5 (2.7)	4.7
C-6-exc below (3.7)	6.0
C-6-w/460 eng (4.4)	6.7
AOD (3.2)	4.8
F100-150 4X4 (5.2)	7.4
F250-350 4X4 (4.5)	6.7
w/Skid plate add (.2)	.3
w/P.T.O. add (.6)	.8
w/Coupling shaft add (.2)	.3

Parking Pawl, Renew

Includes: R&R transmission. Drain and refill unit. Renew gaskets and seals as necessary. Adjust linkage. Road test.

(Factory Time)	Chilton Time
BRONCO	
C-4 (6.3)	8.7
C-6 (6.6)	9.0
ECONOLINE	
C-4 (4.1)	6.3
C-6 (4.4)	6.6
F100-350 4X2	
C-4 (4.3)	6.8
C-5 (3.8)	6.6
C-6-exc below (5.1)	7.3
C-6-w/460 eng (5.8)	8.0
AOD (3.3)	4.9
F100-150 4X4 (6.6)	8.7
F250-350 4X4 (5.9)	8.0
w/Skid plate add (.2)	.3
w/P.T.O. add (.6)	.8
w/Coupling shaft add (.2)	.3

LABOR 25 U-JOINTS & DRIVESHAFT 25 LABOR

Drive Shaft, Renew

(Factory Time)	Chilton Time
RANGER-AEROSTAR (.4)	.6
BRONCO (.4)	.6
ECONOLINE, F100-350	
one piece shaft (.3)	.5
w/Coupling shaft (.6)	.9

Universal Joints, Recondition or Renew

Includes: R&R drive shaft.

(Factory Time)	Chilton Time
Without Coupling Shaft	
front (.8)	1.0
rear (.7)	.9
all (1.1)	1.4
With Coupling Shaft	
front (1.0)	1.4
center (1.0)	1.4
rear (.9)	1.3
all (1.6)	2.0

Drive Shaft Center Support Bearing, Renew

(Factory Time)	Chilton Time
All models (.8)	1.2

LABOR 26 REAR AXLE 26 LABOR

Rear Axle, Drain and Refill

(Factory Time)	Chilton Time
All models (.5)	.6

Axle Housing Cover or Gasket, Renew (Integral Type)

(Factory Time)	Chilton Time
All models (.4)	.6

Axle Shaft, Renew

(Factory Time)	Chilton Time
All models	
Removable Carrier	
one (.5)	.8
both (.8)	1.3
Integral Carrier	
one (.7)	1.0
both (.9)	1.4

Rear Wheel Bearing or Oil Seal, Renew (One Wheel)

(Factory Time)	Chilton Time
All models	
6.75 axle (.6)	.9
7.5 axle (.6)	.9
ball bearing (.6)	.9
roller brg (1.0)	1.3
tapered roller brg (.7)	1.0
full floating axle (.7)	1.0

Rear Axle Shaft Gasket or Outer Oil Seal, Renew

(Factory Time)	Chilton Time
All models	
Semi-Floating Axle	
one side (.5)	.7
both sides (.6)	.9
Full Floating Axle	
one side (.4)	.6
both sides (.6)	.9
Integral Carrier	
one side (.8)	1.1
both sides (1.2)	1.6
Removable Carrier	
one side (.6)	.9
both sides (.9)	1.3

Pinion Shaft Oil Seal, Renew

(Factory Time)	Chilton Time
All models (1.0)	1.2

INTEGRAL CARRIER

Rear Axle Housing, Renew

Includes: Drain and refill axle. R&R wheels, hubs and axle shafts. Renew inner oil seals, remove brake backing plates without disconnecting brake lines. Transfer all parts and adjust ring gear and pinion. Does not include disassembly of differential assembly.

(Factory Time)	Chilton Time
All models	
Ford 7.5 (3.5)	5.0
Dana 60 Semi-Float (6.6)	9.5
Dana 60-61 Full Float (6.9)	10.0
Dana 70 (6.3)	9.1
w/Dual whls add (.3)	.5

Ring Gear and Pinion, Adjust

Includes: Drain and refill axle. Adjust ring and pinion backlash. Road test.

(Factory Time)	Chilton Time
All models	
std axle (1.5)	2.2
limited slip/Trac-Lok (1.8)	2.6

Ring and Pinion Gear, Renew

Includes: Drain and refill axle. Adjust backlash. Road test.

(Factory Time)	Chilton Time
All models	
Ford axle (2.8)	4.0
Dana axle (2.4)	3.5
w/Limited slip add (.1)	.2
Renew pinion brgs and cups add (.6)	.8
Recond diff assy add	
Ford 7.5 (.4)	.6
Dana-std (.5)	.7
Trac-Lok 2 pinion (.6)	.8
Trac-Lok 4 pinion (.7)	1.0

REMOVABLE CARRIER

Differential Carrier, Remove & Install

Includes: Remove or renew axle shafts. Drain and refill axle. Renew oil seal and housing gasket.

(Factory Time)	Chilton Time
All models	
one piece shaft (1.7)	[obscured]
two piece shaft (1.8)	[obscured]
Adjust ring gear add (.2)	[obscured]
Check case run out add (.3)	[obscured]
Renew ring gear & pinion ad[obscured]	
std (1.1)	[obscured]
limited slip/Trac-L[obscured]	
Renew pinion brg cup[obscured]	
Renew case add (1[obscured]	
Renew diff brg ad[obscured]	

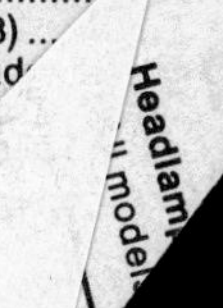

LABOR 27 REAR SUSPENSION 27 LABOR

(Factory Time) Chilton Time

Rear Spring, Renew
4 lug wheel
Aerostar
one (.5) 8
both (.8) 1.4
All other models
one (.9) 1.3
both (1.6) 2.4
5 lug wheel
one (1.0) 1.5
both (1.8) 2.8
8 lug wheel
one (1.1) 1.6
both (1.9) 3.0
Renew spring bushings
add-each (.2) 2

Rear Spring Shackle and/or Bushing, Renew
RANGER-one (1.0) 1.5
both (1.6) 2.6
ALL OTHER MODELS
one (.8) 1.2
both (1.2) 2.1

Rear Shock Absorbers, Renew
All models-one (.3) 6
both (.4) 8

Rear Stabilizer Bar, Renew
All models (.5) 9

Upper Control Arm Bushings, Renew
Aerostar
one side (.7) 1.0
both sides (1.1) 1.7

LABOR 28 AIR CONDITIONING 28 LABOR

(Factory Time) Chilton Time

Note: If more than one item requires replacement where evacuation and discharging the system is already included in the operation, deduct 1.0 hour for each additional item to the times listed.

Drain, Evacuate and Recharge System
Includes: Check for leaks.
All models (.7) 1.5

Pressure Test System
All models 8

Compressor Belt, Renew
Four (.5) 7
All other engs (.3) 6

Compressor Assembly, Renew
Includes: Evacuate and charge system.
Four
Gas
2.0L eng (2.0) 3.0
2.3L eng
Ranger (2.1) 3.1
Aerostar (2.6) 3.7
Diesel
2.3L eng (1.3) 2.3
Six (1.6) 2.4
V-6 (1.5) 2.3
V-8
Gas (1.5) 2.3
Diesel (1.7) 2.5
Recond comp add (.7) 1.0

Compressor Shaft Seal Kit, Renew
Includes: Evacuate and charge system.
Four
Gas
2.0L eng (2.5) 3.5
2.3L eng
Ranger (2.4) 3.4
Aerostar (3.1) 4.2
Diesel (2.2) 3.0
Six (1.9) 2.6
V-6 (2.0) 2.8
V-8
Gas (1.8) 2.5
Diesel (2.1) 2.9

Condenser Assembly, Renew
Includes: Evacuate and charge system.
RANGER (1.0) 2.0
AEROSTAR (1.0) 2.0
BRONCO (1.1) 2.3
BRONCO II (1.0) 2.0
ECONOLINE (1.3) 2.7
F100-350 (1.1) 2.4

Expansion Valve, Renew
Includes: Evacuate and charge system.
All models (1.1) 2.4

Evaporator Core, Renew
Includes: Evacuate and charge system.
RANGER (1.4) 2.7
AEROSTAR (1.5) 2.9
BRONCO (1.9) 3.1
BRONCO II (1.4) 2.7
ECONOLINE (2.4) 3.6
F100-350
1980 & later (1.2) 2.4

Dehydrator Receiver Tank, Renew
Includes: Evacuate and charge system.
BRONCO (1.1) 2.2
ECONOLINE (1.4) 2.5
F100-350 (1.1) 2.2

Accumulator Assembly, Renew
Includes: Evacuate and charge system.
RANGER-BRONCO II (1.0) 1.5
AEROSTAR (1.3) 1.8
BRONCO-F100-350 (.9) 1.5

Orifice Valve, Renew
Includes: Evacuate and charge system.
RANGER-BRONCO II (1.1) 1.7
AEROSTAR
main (1.0) 1.5
auxiliary (1.3) 1.8
BRONCO-F100-350 (.9) 1.4

Blower Motor, Renew
RANGER (.4) 6
AEROSTAR
main (.4) 7
auxiliary (.4) 7
BRONCO
1980 & later (.3) 6
BRONCO II (.4) 6
ECONOLINE (.4) 1.0
F100-350
1980 & later (.3) 6

Blower Motor Switch, Renew
RANGER (.5) 7
AEROSTAR (.6) 9
BRONCO (.5) 7
ECONOLINE (.3) 6
F100-350 (.5) 7

Evaporator Thermostatic Switch, Renew
BRONCO (.6) 1.0
ECONOLINE (.3) 6
F100-350 (.7) 1.2

A/C Clutch Cycling Pressure Switch Assy., Renew
All models (.2) 4

Compressor Service Valve or Gasket, Renew
Includes: Evacuate and charge system.
All models (1.0) 1.9

Air Conditioning Hoses, Renew
Includes: Evacuate and charge system.
All models-one (.8) 1.7
each adtnl (.3) 5

LABOR 30 HEAD AND PARKING LAMPS 30 LABOR

(Factory Time) Chilton Time

…im Headlamps
…two 4
…our 6

…p Sealed Beam Bulb, Renew
…s-each (.2) 3

Parking Lamp Assembly, Renew
RANGER (.2) 3
AEROSTAR (.3) 4
BRONCO-ECONOLINE (.2) 3
F100-350 (.4) 5

Rear Lamp Assembly, Renew
All models (.2) 3

License Lamp Assembly, Renew
All models (.3) 4

Reflector, Renew
All models-each 2

LABOR 31 WINDSHIELD WIPER & SPEEDOMETER 31 LABOR

	(Factory Time)	Chilton Time
Wiper Motor, Renew		
RANGER-BRONCO II	(.4)	.6
AEROSTAR		
front	(.9)	1.4
rear	(.7)	1.1
BRONCO	(.9)	1.4
ECONOLINE	(.9)	*1.4
F100-350	(.9)	1.4
*w/Cruise control add	(.3)	.3
Wiper Switch, Renew		
All models		
front	(.4)	.6
rear	(.2)	.4
Wiper Pivot, Renew		
RANGER-BRONCO II-one	(.4)	.7
both	(.5)	.9
BRONCO-each	(.8)	1.1
AEROSTAR-both	(.4)	.7
ECONOLINE	(.6)	.9
F100-350-each	(.8)	1.1
Washer Pump, Renew		
Aerostar		
front	(.6)	.9
rear	(.3)	.5
All other models-front	(.3)	.4
rear	(.8)	1.1
Windshield Wiper Governor Assy., Renew		
Aerostar	(.5)	.7
All other models	(.4)	.6
Speedometer Head, R&R or Renew		
All models		
Standard	(.6)	1.2
Electronic	(.7)	1.3
Reset odometer add		.2
Speedometer Cable and Casing, Renew		
RANGER-BRONCO II	(.4)	.7
AEROSTAR	(.4)	.7
BRONCO		
one piece	(.5)	.9
upper	(.6)	1.1
lower	(.4)	.7
ECONOLINE		
wo/Sensor	(.4)	.7
w/Sensor-each	(.3)	.5
one piece	(.7)	1.3
upper or lower	(.5)	.9
F100-350	(.5)	.9
Speedometer Cable (Inner), Renew or Lubricate		
RANGER-BRONCO II	(.4)	.7
AEROSTAR	(.4)	.7
BRONCO		
one piece	(.4)	.8
upper	(.6)	1.0
lower	(.4)	.6
ECONOLINE		
one piece	(.6)	1.1
upper	(.6)	1.1
lower	(.4)	.7
F100-350	(.5)	.8

LABOR 32 LIGHT SWITCHES & WIRING 32 LABOR

	(Factory Time)	Chilton Time
Headlamp Switch, Renew		
All models	(.4)	.6
Headlamp Dimmer Switch, Renew		
All models		
floor mount	(.3)	.5
column mount	(.5)	.9
Turn Signal Switch Assy., Renew		
RANGER	(.4)	1.0
AEROSTAR	(.5)	1.0
BRONCO-std whl	(.5)	1.1
tilt whl	(.6)	1.2
BRONCO II-std whl	(.5)	1.1
tilt whl	(.6)	1.2
ECONOLINE-std whl	(.6)	1.2
tilt whl	(.7)	1.3
F100-350-std whl	(.5)	1.1
tilt whl	(.6)	1.2
Turn Signal or Hazard Warning Flasher, Renew		
ECONOLINE	(.4)	.6
All other models	(.3)	.4
Stop Light Switch, Renew		
All models	(.3)	.5
Emergency Flasher Switch Assy., Renew		
BRONCO	(.3)	.6
Parking Brake Indicator Lamp Switch, Renew		
All models	(.3)	.4
Back-Up Lamp Switch, Renew (w/Manual Trans)		
All models	(.3)	.4
Neutral Safety Switch, Renew		
All models	(.3)	.4
Horns, Renew		
All models-each	(.2)	.3
Horn Relay, Renew		
All models	(.3)	.4

LABOR 34 CRUISE CONTROL 34 LABOR

	(Factory Time)	Chilton Time
Cruise Control System Diagnosis		
All models	(.4)	.6
Cruise Control Chain/Cable, Renew		
All models	(.2)	.4
Speed Control Servo Assy., Renew		
All models	(.4)	.6
Road test add	(.3)	.3
Speed Control Relay, Renew		
All models	(.3)	.5
Speed Control Sensor Assy., Renew		
All models	(.3)	.6
Road test add	(.3)	.3
*Econoline		
w/V-8 Diesel add		.3
Speed Control Amplifier Assy., Renew		
All models	(.3)	.6
Road test add	(.3)	.3
Speed Control Actuator Switch Assy., Renew		
All models	(.3)	.6
Road test add	(.3)	.3
Speed Control Metering (Dump) Valve, Renew		
All models	(.2)	.3
Speed Control Clutch Switch, Renew		
All models	(.3)	.4
Road test add	(.3)	.3

Ford Trucks—Series F500-9000

GROUP INDEX

ALPHABETICAL INDEX

LABOR 1 TUNE UP 1 LABOR

(Factory Time) Chilton Time

GASOLINE ENGINE

Compression Test

Six–exc below (.6) 8
N series (.7) 9
V-8–exc below (.9) 1.1
N series (1.1) 1.3

Engine Tune Up, Minor

Includes: Clean or renew spark plugs, renew ignition points and condenser, set ignition timing. Adjust carburetor idle speed and mixture. Service carburetor air cleaner. Clean or renew fuel filter.

Six–F series (1.4) 1.9
N series (1.8) 2.4
C series (1.5) 2.0
L series (1.5) 2.0
V-8–330, 361, 370, 389, 391, 429 engs
F series (1.7) 2.3
N series (1.9) 2.5
C series (1.6) 1.9
L series (1.4) 1.9
V-8–401, 475, 477, 534 engs
F series (1.7) 2.3
N series (1.9) 2.5
C series (1.4) 1.9
L series (1.4) 1.9

Engine Tune Up, Major

Includes: Clean or renew spark plugs. Check compression. Test battery and clean terminals. Renew or adjust distributor points and condenser. Check distributor cap and rotor. Adjust ignition timing and test coil. Free up manifold heat valve. Tighten manifold bolts. Adjust carburetor idle speed and mixture. Inspect and tighten all hose connections. Adjust fan belts. Service air cleaner and fuel filter. Clean or renew PCV valve (if equipped).

Six–F series (2.2) 3.2
N series (2.5) 3.5
C series (2.2) 3.2
L series (2.2) 3.2
V-8–330, 361, 370, 389, 391, 429 engs
F series (2.7) 3.7
N series (2.9) 3.9
C series (2.5) 3.5
L series (2.5) 3.5
V-8–401, 475, 477, 534 engs
F series (2.7) 3.7
N series (2.9) 3.9
C series (2.5) 3.5
L series (2.5) 3.5

DIESEL ENGINES

Compression Test

Includes: R&R injectors and other interfering parts, attach compression gauge and adjust injectors.

Caterpillar
3208
F & LN series (3.3) 4.0
C & L series (3.0) 3.7
3406
All series (2.3) 3.0
Cummins
Six (5.1) 6.1
V-8 (5.6) 7.3
Detroit
6V-71-6V-92 (4.8) 6.0
6-71 (3.8) 4.8
8V-71-8V-92 (5.0) 6.3

Engine Tune Up, Minor

Includes: Test batteries and clean and tighten terminals. Check and adjust engine idle speed and throttle linkage. Change engine oil. Clean or renew oil, air, fuel and water filters. Tighten radiator hoses and manifold bolts. Check valve lash and adjust tappets. R&R and test injectors.
Does not include compression test or injector timing.

Caterpillar
3208
F & LN series (4.5) 5.3
C & L series (4.2) 5.0
3406
All series (3.5) 4.3
Cummins
NH743-855 (3.0) 3.8
NT855 (3.5) 4.5
V-VT555 (3.1) 4.0
V-VT903 (3.5) 4.5
KT(A)1150 (3.5) 4.5
Detroit
6V-53-6V-92 (2.7) 3.5
6-71 (2.2) 3.0
8V-71-8V-92 (3.2) 4.0

Engine Tune Up, Major

Includes: Test batteries and clean and tighten terminals. Check and adjust engine idle speed and throttle linkage. Adjust injector timing and injectors. Steam clean engine. Change engine oil. Clean or renew air, oil, fuel and water filters. Check and lubricate shutters. Clean injectors and fuel connections. Inspect for oil, water and fuel leaks. Drain sediment from fuel tanks. Tighten intake manifold, exhaust manifold, turbocharger and engine mounting bolts. Clean turbocharger impeller and diffuser and fuel pump screen. Adjust crossheads and valves. Check crankshaft and clearance. Adjust and check fan belts. Road test.

Caterpillar
3208
F & LN series (9.4) 11.5
C & L series (9.1) 11.2
3406
All series (8.4) 10.5
Cummins
NH743, 855 (11.2) 14.3
NT855 (12.2) 15.3
V-VT555 (9.8) 12.9
V-VT903 (10.4) 13.5
KT(A)1150 (11.2) 14.3
Detroit
6V-53-6V-92 (9.6) 11.7
6-71 (9.0) 11.1
8V-71-8V-92 (9.8) 11.9

LABOR 2 IGNITION SYSTEM 2 LABOR

(Factory Time) Chilton Time

Spark Plugs, Renew

Six (.5) 7
V-8 (.6) 8

Ignition Timing, Reset

All series (.4) 6

Distributor, R&R or Renew

Includes: Reset ignition timing.

exc below (.6) 8
C & L series (.5) 7

Distributor, R&R and Recondition

Includes: Reset ignition timing.

Six–exc below (1.3) 1.7
C & L series (1.2) 1.6
V-8–exc below (1.7) 2.2
C & L series (1.6) 2.1

Distributor Cap and/or Rotor, Renew

All series (.4) 6

Ignition Coil, Renew

All series (.5) 7

Vacuum Control Unit, Renew

Includes: R&R distributor and reset ignition timing.

exc below (.9) 1.2
C & L series (.8) 1.0

Ignition Module, Renew

All series (.4) 6

Distributor Armature, Renew

All series 7

Ignition Cables, Renew

exc below (.5) 7
401, 475, 477, 534 engs (.6) 8

Ignition Switch, Renew

exc below (.4) 6
F series (.6) 8
CL series (.5) 7

LABOR 3 FUEL SYSTEM 3 LABOR

(Factory Time)	Chilton Time
GASOLINE ENGINES	
Fuel Pump, Test	
Includes: Disconnect line at carburetor, attach pressure gauge.	
All series	.3
Carburetor, Adjust (On Truck)	
All series (.4)	.6
Carburetor, R&R or Renew	
Includes: All necessary adjustments.	
Six–exc below (.7)	.9
C series (.5)	.7
L series (.6)	.8
V-8–330, 361, 389, 391 engs	
All series (.8)	1.0
V-8–370, 429 engs	
All series (.7)	1.1
V-8–401, 475, 477, 534 engs	
All series (.9)	1.2
Carburetor, R&R and Recondition	
Includes: All necessary adjustments.	
Six–exc below (1.3)	1.7
C series (1.1)	1.5
L series (1.2)	1.6
V-8–331, 361, 389, 391 engs	
All series (1.3)	2.0
V-8–370-429 engs	
All series	
2 bbl (1.4)	2.0
4 bbl (1.9)	3.0
V-8–401, 475, 477, 534 engs	
All series (1.4)	3.5
Fuel Pump, Renew	
Pump on engine	
Six–F series (.5)	.7
C & L series (.4)	.6
V-8–330, 361, 389, 391 engs	
All series (.5)	.7
V-8–370, 429 engs	
All series (.6)	.9
Pump in tank	
Drum tank (1.0)	1.4
Frame tank (.5)	.7
Rectangular tank	
w/Batt,s (1.5)	*2.0
All others (1.0)	1.4
*Includes: R&R batteries.	
Fuel Tank, Renew	
Includes: Transfer all necessary parts.	
Rectangular-each (1.3)	1.7
Rectangular-w/Battery each (2.0)	2.7
All other tanks (1.5)	2.0
Fuel Gauge (Tank), Renew	
Rectangular	
w & wo/Step	
Gas (.9)	1.2
Diesel (1.0)	1.3
All other tanks (.4)	.6

(Factory Time)	Chilton Time
Fuel Gauge (Dash), Renew	
F-L-LN series (.6)	.9
C series (.5)	.8
CL series (.4)	.7
w/2 spd shift add (.1)	.1
Intake Manifold Gasket, Renew	
Six (1.1)	1.6
V-8–330, 361, 389, 391 engs	
exc below (2.8)	3.3
L series (3.1)	3.6
V-8–370, 429 engs	
All series (2.5)	3.4
V-8–401, 475, 477, 534 engs	
exc below (2.7)	3.2
C series (2.1)	2.6
L series (2.6)	3.1
LN models (3.3)	3.9
Renew manif add (.4)	.5
DIESEL ENGINES	
Air Cleaner Assembly, R&R and Clean or Renew	
All series (.4)	.6
Engine Idle Speed, Adjust (Governor)	
All series (.9)	1.3
Injectors, Adjust	
Includes: R&R all normal interfering parts.	
exc below (1.5)	2.2
Caterpillar (2.0)	2.6
Cummins	
NT-743, 855 (2.8)	3.7
V-VT 785, V903 (4.4)	5.8
Injectors, Renew	
Includes: R&R all normal interfering parts.	
Caterpillar	
3208	
F & LN series-one (1.7)	2.5
all (2.8)	4.0
C & L series-one (1.0)	2.3
all (2.5)	3.7
3406	
All series-one (1.1)	1.9
all (2.0)	3.2
Cummins	
All engines	
One (2.2)	3.0
Six (4.5)	5.5
Eight (4.8)	6.0
Detroit	
All	
6V-53-6V-92 (3.2)	*4.3
6-71 (2.6)	*3.7
8V-72-8V-92 (3.4)	*4.6
*w/Jacobs brk add each (.1)	.1
Recondition add	
exc below-each (.5)	.5
Cummins-each (.8)	.8
Detroit	
S inj-each (.5)	.5
N inj-each (.8)	.8

(Factory Time)	Chilton Time
Injection Pump, Renew	
Includes: R&R all normal interfering parts.	
Caterpillar	
All series	
3208 (3.3)	4.4
3406 (2.2)	3.3
Cummins	
NT-NH743, 855 (1.7)	2.4
V-VT555, 903 (2.6)	3.5
KT(A)1150 (1.6)	2.3
Detroit	
6-71 (.7)	.9
6V-53, 8V-71 (1.0)	1.9
6V-92, 8V-92 (1.0)	1.3
Injection Pump, R&R and Recondition	
Includes: R&R all normal interfering parts.	
Caterpillar	
All series	
3208 (5.6)	7.0
3406 (6.4)	7.9
Cummins	
All series (3.4)	5.2
Detroit	
6-71 (1.7)	2.2
6V-53, 8V-71 (2.0)	2.5
6V-92, 8V-92 (2.0)	2.5
Turbocharger, Renew	
exc below-one (1.4)	2.1
both (2.1)	2.8
Caterpillar-3406 (1.3)	2.1
Cummins	
NT855 (1.1)	2.6
VT555, 903 (2.3)	3.5
KT(A)1150 (1.4)	2.4
Supercharger, Renew	
Cummins	
NH743, 855 (4.8)	6.2
Shutdown Valve, Renew	
exc below (.5)	.8
Caterpillar (.2)	.3
Cummins (1.0)	1.5
Aneroid Valve, Adjust	
All series (1.1)	1.5
Fuel Filter, Renew	
Cummins (.5)	.7
Caterpillar (.2)	.3
Detroit (.3)	.4
Intake Manifold Gaskets, Renew	
Caterpillar	
All series	
3208 (1.6)	2.2
3406 (1.4)	2.0
Cummins	
NH743, 855 (1.6)	2.3
V-VT785, 903-one (2.3)	3.1
both (2.8)	4.0
V-555-one (1.9)	2.7
both (2.4)	3.6
KT(A)1150 (1.4)	1.9

LABOR 3A EMISSION CONTROLS 3A LABOR

(Factory Time)	Chilton Time
Thermactor Air By-Pass Valve, Renew	
All series (.4)	.6
E.G.R. Vacuum Control Valve, Renew	
All series (.3)	.5

(Factory Time)	Chilton Time
E.G.R. Valve, Renew	
All series (.5)	.7
Thermactor Air Pump, Renew	
All series (.5)	.9
Renew belt add (.2)	.2

LABOR 4 ALTERNATOR & REGULATOR 4 LABOR

(Factory Time)	Chilton Time
Alternator Circuits Test	
Includes: Test battery, regulator and alternator output.	
All models (.6)	.6
Test each adtnl battery add (.2)	.2
Alternator, R&R or Renew	
GAS	
All series	
Motorcraft (.5)	.8
Leece Neville (.6)	.9
Delco (1.2)	1.5
DIESEL	
All series (.6)	1.1
Recondition add	
Ford (.6)	.8
Leece Neville (1.8)	2.0
Delco (1.2)	1.4
Transfer pulley add (.1)	.1
Alternator Regulator, Renew	
exc below (.4)	.7
Delco (1.0)	1.5
Add circuit test if performed.	
Alternator Regulator, Adjust	
Ford (.8)	1.1
Leece Neville (1.0)	1.3
Instrument Cluster Voltage Regulator, Renew	
All series (.6)	.9

LABOR 5 STARTING SYSTEM 5 LABOR

(Factory Time)	Chilton Time
Starter Draw Test (On Truck)	
All models (.3)	3
Starter, R&R or Renew	
MOTORCRAFT	
All series (.4)	.6
PRESTOLITE	
All series (.6)	.8
DELCO	
F series (1.3)	1.7
L-LN series (1.2)	1.6
CL series (1.9)	2.5
CUMMINS	
L-LN series (1.0)	1.3
CL series (2.3)	3.0
CATERPILLAR	
F-C series (1.1)	1.4
L series (1.5)	1.9
LN-CL series (1.8)	2.3
Renew starter drive	
add (.3)	.3
Renew brushes add (.6)	.6
Renew armature add (.3)	.3
Recond complete add (1.5)	2.0
Starter Solenoid Relay, Renew	
GAS ENGINES	
F-L series (.4)	.8
CL series (.5)	.9
Ammeter, Renew	
F series (.6)	.9
C series (.5)	.8
CL series (.4)	.7
L-LN series	
Line Haul (.4)	.7
City Deliv. (.6)	.9
Battery Cables, Renew	
GAS ENGINES	
F series-each (.4)	.5
C series-each (.5)	.7
L series-each (.6)	.8
CL series-each (.4)	.5

LABOR 6 BRAKE SYSTEM 6 LABOR

(Factory Time)	Chilton Time
Brakes, Adjust (Minor)	
Includes: Adjust brake shoes at all wheels. Fill master cylinder. R&R one front drum.	
single axle (.8)	1.0
tandem axle (1.0)	1.2
Bleed Brakes (Four Wheels)	
single axle (.6)	.8
tandem axle (.7)	.9
Brake Pedal Free Play, Adjust	
All models (.3)	.4
Brake Drum or Hub, Renew	
Includes: R&R wheel, renew bearings and adjust brakes.	
FRONT	
F600 4x4	
one (1.1)	1.6
both (1.9)	2.7
500-9000 series	
Disc-6 hole	
one (1.1)	1.6
both (2.0)	2.8
Disc-10 hole	
one (1.7)	2.1
both (3.2)	4.0
Cast wheel	
one (1.3)	1.7
both (2.4)	3.2
REAR	
500-9000	
Disc-6 hole	
one (1.6)	2.2
both (2.9)	3.8
Disc-10 hole	
one (2.2)	2.8
both (4.0)	5.2
Cast wheel	
one (1.7)	2.3
both (2.9)	3.8
Brake Shoes, Renew	
Includes: R&R wheels, hubs and drums. Clean and inspect all parts. Install new or exchange shoes. Adjust brakes and road test.	
F600 4WD-front (2.3)	2.9
rear (3.1)	4.0
all four wheels (5.0)	6.3
500-750 hydraulic	
front (1.8)	2.3
rear	
one axle (3.1)	4.0
both axles (5.7)	7.2
all wheels	
one rear (4.5)	5.7
tandem rear (7.0)	8.8
Air brakes	
front (2.3)	2.9
rear	
one axle (3.1)	4.0
both axles (5.7)	7.2
all wheels	
one rear (4.9)	6.2
tandem rear (7.5)	9.5
800-900 hydraulic	
front (1.9)	2.5
rear	
one axle (3.2)	4.2
both axles (5.9)	7.5
all wheels	
one rear (4.6)	5.9
tandem rear (7.3)	9.2
Air brakes	
front (2.3)	2.9
rear	
one axle (3.1)	4.0
both axles (5.7)	7.2
all wheels	
one rear (4.9)	6.2
tandem rear (7.5)	9.5
Bleed system add	
single axle (.4)	.6
tandem axle (.5)	.7

BRAKE HYDRAULIC SYSTEM

(Factory Time)	Chilton Time
Wheel Cylinder, Renew	
Includes: R&R wheels, hubs and drums. Clean and inspect parts. Bleed lines, adjust brakes and road test.	
F600 4WD	
front-one (1.7)	2.2
both-one wheel (1.9)	2.5
all (3.5)	4.5
rear-one wheel (2.3)	2.9
both wheels (4.2)	5.3
500-750 hydraulic	
front-one wheel (1.7)	2.2
both wheels (2.9)	3.7
rear	
one axle-one wheel (2.3)	2.9
both wheels (4.2)	5.3
both axles (7.6)	9.5
800-900 hydraulic	
front-one wheel (1.8)	2.3
both wheels (3.0)	3.8

(Factory Time)	Chilton Time
rear	
one axle-one wheel (2.4)	3.1
both wheels (4.3)	5.4
both axles (8.0)	10.0
Recondition, each add (.2)	.5

Brake Hose, Renew

Includes: Bleed lines.

Front	
single axle-one (.8)	1.3
both (1.0)	1.5
tandem axle-one (.9)	1.4
both (1.1)	1.7
air hose-one (.3)	.4
both (.4)	.6
Rear	
single axle-one (.9)	1.4
tandem axle-one (1.0)	1.5
two (1.1)	1.7
three (1.3)	2.0
all (1.5)	2.3

Master Cylinder, Renew

Includes: Bleed complete system, adjust pedal free play.

Standard Cylinder	
All series (.8)	1.2
Hydra-Max	
C-series (2.5)	3.5
All other series (1.0)	1.4

Brake Differential Valve, Renew

Includes: Bleed system and transfer switch.

L series (.6)	1.0

BRAKE BOOSTER

Brake Booster Assembly, Renew

Midland diaphragm	
dash mtg (.7)	1.2
frame mtg (.6)	1.1
Bendix	
diaphragm (1.0)	1.5
piston (1.0)	1.5
air hyd (.8)	1.3
Hydra-Max	
F-series (1.8)	2.5
All other series (2.5)	3.5

Brake Booster, R&R and Recondition

Midland diaphragm	
dash mtg (1.2)	2.7
frame mtg (1.1)	2.6
Bendix	
diaphragm (2.1)	3.6
piston (3.1)	4.6
air hyd (2.2)	3.7
Hydra-Max	
F-series (2.9)	4.0

AIR BRAKES

Air Compressor Belts, Renew

All models (.3)	.5

Air Pressure Gauge, Renew

exc below (.8)	1.1
C & L series (.6)	.9
CL series (.4)	.7

Air Brake Pedal Control Valve, Adjust

All series (.5)	.8

Air Brake Pedal Control Valve, Renew

exc below (1.4)	2.0
CL series (.8)	1.2

COMBINATIONS

Add To Brakes, Renew

(Factory Time)	Chilton Time
RENEW WHEEL CYLINDER	
Each (.3)	.4
RECONDITION WHEEL CYLINDERS	
Includes: Hone cylinder.	
Each (.5)	.6
MASTER CYLINDER, RENEW	
All models (.6)	.7
MASTER CYLINDER, RECONDITION	
All models	1.0
REAR WHEEL GREASE SEAL, RENEW	
One side (.3)	.4
FRONT WHEEL BEARINGS, RENEW	
One wheel (.7)	.8
FRONT WHEEL BEARINGS, REPACK	
All models (.6)	.7
RELINE BRAKE SHOES	
Each axle set (.7)	1.0
BRAKE DRUM OR ROTOR, RENEW	
Each (.5)	.6
REBUILD CALIPER ASSEMBLY	
Each (.6)	.6
AIR BRAKE ACTUATOR, RENEW	
Each (.3)	.4
DISC BRAKE ROTOR, MACHINE	
Each (1.0)	1.0

(Factory Time)	Chilton Time

Slack Adjuster, Renew (One Wheel)

All series (.6)	.8

Air Compressor, Renew

Gas	
6.1-7.0L engs	
All series (1.5)	2.2
7.8-8.8L engs	
C-series (2.4)	3.3
L-LN series (1.8)	2.5
Diesel	
Caterpiller	
3208 (1.3)	1.8
3406 (1.2)	1.7
Detroit	
Six-L-series (2.5)	3.5
LN series (3.0)	4.2
6V-8V-92 (3.0)	4.2
8.2L (1.7)	2.4
6V-8V-71 (1.5)	2.2
Cummins (2.5)	3.2
Recondition add (3.8)	5.0

Air Brake Chamber, R&R or Renew

Includes: Adjust slack adjuster.

one-front or rear (.7)	1.0

Air Brake Chamber, R&R and Recondition

Includes: Adjust slack adjuster.

one-front or rear (1.0)	1.5

(Factory Time)	Chilton Time

DISC BRAKES

Disc Brake Rotor, Renew

Includes: Renew or transfer wheel bearings and repack.

All series-one (1.2)	1.7
both (2.3)	3.3

Caliper Assembly, Renew

Includes: Bleed system.

All series-one (1.0)	1.5
both (1.5)	2.5

Caliper Assy., R&R and Recondition

Includes: Bleed system.

All series-one (1.6)	2.1
both (2.7)	3.7

Disc Brake Pads, Renew

Includes: Install new disc brake pads only.

All series (1.2)	1.5

AIR BRAKE ANTI-SKID SYSTEM

Skid Control Monitor Assy., Renew

All series	
Kelsey Hayes (.4)	.7
Eaton (.3)	.6

Skid Control Sensor Ring, R&R or Renew

All series (.9)	1.3

Skid Control Wheel Sensor, R&R or Renew

All series (1.1)	1.7

Skid Control Modulator Valve, R&R or Renew

All series	
Eaton-one (1.1)	1.4
each adtnl (1.0)	1.0
Kelsey-Hayes-one (1.1)	1.4
each adtnl (1.0)	1.0

Skid Control Modulator Controller, Renew

All series	
Kelsey Hayes-one (.5)	.7
each adtnl (.4)	.4
Eaton-one (.7)	1.0
each adtnl (.6)	.6

PARKING BRAKE

Parking Brake, Adjust

All models (.4)	.5

Parking Brake Cable, Renew (To Equalizer)

F-series (.5)	.8
C-series (.8)	1.1
L-LN series (.6)	.9

Parking Brake, Reline

band type (1.1)	1.6
shoe type (1.2)	1.7
w/Coupled shaft, add (.2)	.2

Parking Brake Control, Renew

L series (.4)	.7
C-series	
in cowl (1.4)	1.8
All series-floor lever (.6)	1.0

Parking Brake Drum, Renew

band type (.7)	1.1
shoe type (.7)	1.1
Transmatic (1.8)	2.5
w/Coupled shaft, add (.2)	.2

Thermostat, Renew

(Factory Time)	Chilton Time
GAS	
Six–F series (.4)	.6
C series (.6)	.9
L series (.5)	.8
V-8–330, 361, 389, 391 engs	
All series (.5)	.8
V-8–370, 429 engs	
All series (.5)	.8
V-8–401, 475, 477, 534 engs	
F-series	
Front (.8)	1.1
Rear (.7)	1.0
Both (.9)	1.2
All other series (.6)	.9
DIESEL	
Cummins	
KT1150-NH855 (1.4)	2.0
V-555 (.6)	1.0
VT903-one (1.4)	2.0
both (2.8)	3.8
Detroit	
Six (.8)	1.2
V-8 (.9)	1.3
Caterpillar	
3208 (1.0)	1.4
3406 (.7)	1.1

Radiator Shutter and Cylinder Assembly, Renew

(Factory Time)	Chilton Time
C series (.8)	1.2
F series	
w/Caterpillar V-8 (1.5)	2.2
CL series (.9)	1.3

Shutter Thermostat, Renew

(Factory Time)	Chilton Time
All series (.8)	1.1

Intercooler, Renew

(Factory Time)	Chilton Time
Detroit (1.0)	1.4
Cummins	
F series (3.3)	4.5
C-L series (2.9)	3.8

Radiator, R&R or Renew

(Factory Time)	Chilton Time
GAS	
SIX	
F-C series (1.3)	1.8
L series (.8)	1.2
V-8–330, 361, 389, 391 engs	
F series (1.4)	2.0
C series (1.6)	2.2
L series (1.0)	1.6
V-8–370, 429 engs	
F series (1.0)	1.6
C series (1.6)	2.2
L-LN series (1.4)	2.0
V-8–401, 475, 477, 534 engs	
C series (2.0)	2.8
L series (1.5)	2.3
DIESEL	
F series	
Cat V-8 (1.6)	2.6
C series	
Cat V-8 (1.3)	2.1
L-LN series	
Cat-Six (3.0)	4.3
V-8 (1.0)	1.5
Detroit (1.7)	2.7
Cummins (1.9)	2.9
CL series	
All engs (4.0)	5.5
w/Shutters add (.5)	.5
w/Rad mount A.C. condenser add (1.0)	1.0

Radiator Hose, Renew

(Factory Time)	Chilton Time
GAS	
Six–exc below-upper (.6)	.7
lower (.7)	.9
both (1.0)	1.3
L series-upper (.5)	.7
lower (.5)	.7
both (.6)	.9
V-8–330, 361, 389, 391 engs	
exc below-upper (.6)	.7
lower (.9)	1.1
both (1.1)	1.4
L series-upper (.5)	.7
lower (.6)	.8
both (.7)	1.1
V-8–370, 429 engs	
upper (.5)	.7
lower (.5)	.7
both (.7)	1.0
V-8–401, 475, 477, 534 engs	
exc below-upper (1.0)	1.3
lower (1.0)	1.4
both (1.2)	1.6
L series-upper (.7)	.9
lower (.8)	1.0
both (.9)	1.3
DIESEL	
F series	
exc below-upper (.6)	.8
lower (.7)	.9
both (.9)	1.2
F 8000-upper (.7)	.9
lower (.9)	1.2
both (1.0)	1.4
C series	
exc below-upper (.5)	.7
lower (.6)	.8
both (.8)	1.0
C 8000-upper (.5)	.7
lower (.6)	.8
both (.8)	1.0
L series-upper (.5)	.7
lower (.7)	.8
both (.8)	1.0
CL series	
upper (.7)	.9
lower (.7)	.9
both (.9)	1.3

Fan Blades, Renew

(Factory Time)	Chilton Time
GAS	
Six(.3)	.6
V-8–exc below (.8)	1.2
C series (1.1)	1.5
DIESEL	
F series (.6)	.9
C series	
exc below (.9)	1.3
C 8000 (1.6)	2.1
Caterpillar V-8 (.5)	.8
L series (.4)	.7
CL series (.8)	1.2

Fan Belts, Renew

(Factory Time)	Chilton Time
GAS	
F series-one (.3)	.5
each adtnl (.2)	.3
C series-one (.4)	.6
each adtnl (.2)	.3
L series-one (.3)	.5
each adtnl (.2)	.3
DIESEL	
F series	
exc below-one (.6)	.8
each adtnl (.3)	.5
F 8000-one (1.2)	1.5
each adtnl (.8)	1.0
C series-one (.5)	.7
each adtnl (.3)	.5
L series-one (.4)	.6
each adtnl (.2)	.3
V-8-one (.9)	1.2
each adtnl (.5)	.7
CL series-one (.9)	1.2
each adtnl (.5)	.7

Water Pump, Renew

(Factory Time)	Chilton Time
GAS	
Six(1.0)	1.5
V-8–330, 361, 389, 391 engs	
F series (1.9)	2.5
C series (1.3)	2.0
L series (1.4)	2.0
V-8–370, 429 engs	
F-C series (1.8)	2.5
V-8–401, 475, 477, 534 engs	
F series	
housing & pump (1.6)	2.2
pump only (1.2)	1.7
C series	
housing & pump (1.1)	1.9
pump only (.9)	1.4
L series	
housing & pump (1.7)	2.2
pump only (1.0)	1.7
DIESEL	
Cummins	
KT1150 (2.4)	2.9
V-903 (3.7)	4.7
NH855-V555 (2.5)	3.2
Detroit	
6-71 (1.0)	1.6
All V-8's (1.5)	2.1
Caterpillar	
3208	
F-series (1.9)	2.7
All other series (1.2)	2.0
3406	
All series (3.0)	4.0

Temperature Gauge (Engine), Renew

(Factory Time)	Chilton Time
All series (.4)	.6

Temperature Gauge (Dash), Renew

(Factory Time)	Chilton Time
F series	
exc below (.5)	.8
diesel w/A.C. (.8)	1.0
C series (.6)	1.0
L series	
city delivery (.6)	1.0
line haul (1.0)	1.3
CL series (.4)	.7

Heater Core, R&R or Renew

(Factory Time)	Chilton Time
F series	
wo/A.C. (.9)	1.5
w/A.C. (.6)	1.1
C series (1.0)	1.5
L series (.8)	1.2
CL series (.5)	1.0

Heater Blower Motor, Renew

(Factory Time)	Chilton Time
F-C series (.5)	.7
L series (.6)	.9
CL series (.5)	.9

Heater Switch, Renew

(Factory Time)	Chilton Time
F series (.6)	.9
C series (.3)	.5
L series (.5)	.7
CL series (.6)	.9

Heater Water Valve, Renew

(Factory Time)	Chilton Time
All series-Gas (.6)	.9
Diesel (1.1)	1.5

Blower Motor Resistor, Renew

(Factory Time)	Chilton Time
F-C series (.4)	.6
L series (.3)	.5
CL series (.3)	.5

LABOR 8 EXHAUST SYSTEM 8 LABOR

(Factory Time) Chilton Time

Muffler, Renew

Gas

All series-one (1.0) 1.4
two (1.4) 1.9

Diesel

Six (1.0) 1.4
V-6-V-8
single (1.5) 1.9
dual (1.9) 2.4
Renew inlet pipe add (.3) .3
Renew outlet pipe add (.3) .3

Exhaust Pipe, Renew (Outlet)

Gas

6.1-7.0L engs
right (.8) 1.1
left (.8) 1.1
both (1.3) 1.9
7.8-8.8L engs
single (1.0) 1.4
dual (1.7) 2.2

Diesel

Six
single inlet (1.5) 2.0
connector (.6) .9
extension (.6) .9
dual inlet (1.0) 1.4
V-6-V-8
inlet (.8) 1.1
connector (.8) 1.1
both (1.3) 1.9
dual inlet (1.5) 2.0

Outlet Pipe, Renew

Gas

single (.4) .6
dual (.5) .7

Diesel

single (.4) .6
dual (.6) .8

Exhaust Manifold, R&R or Renew

GAS

Six–L series (1.3) 1.8
F-C series (1.5) 2.0
V-8–330, 361, 389, 391 engs
F series-one (1.3) 1.8
both (2.4) 3.0
C series-one (.9) 1.4
both (1.7) 2.2
L series-right (.8) 1.3
left (.9) 1.4
both (1.5) 2.2
V-8–401, 475, 477, 534 engs
F series-one (1.1) 1.6
both (1.9) 2.4
C series-one (.8) 1.3
both (1.5) 2.0
L series-one (.9) 1.4
both (1.5) 2.0
V-8–370, 429 engs
C-LN series
one (.9) 1.4
both (1.5) 2.0

DIESEL

Caterpillar
F series-one (1.0) 1.6
both (1.6) 2.8
C series-one (.7) 1.3
both (1.2) 2.4
L series-3208-one (.7) 1.3
both (1.2) 2.4
3406 (2.0) 2.9
LN series-one (1.0) 1.6
both (1.6) 2.8
CL series (2.0) 2.9
Cummins
NH743, 855 (1.5) 2.7
NT855 (2.0) 3.2
V555-one (1.6) 2.4
both (2.5) 4.1
V-VT 903-one (2.4) 3.2
both (3.1) 4.7
KT (A) 1150 (1.8) 3.0
Detroit
6V-53-6V-92-each (.6) 1.1
6-71 (1.0) 1.6
8V-71-8V-92-each (.8) 1.3

LABOR 9 FRONT SUSPENSION 9 LABOR

(Factory Time) Chilton Time

Note: On all front suspension operations alignment charges must be added if performed. Time given does not include alignment.

Check Alignment of Front End

All series .8
Note: Deduct if alignment is performed.

Toe-In, Adjust

All series (.4) .7

Front Wheel Grease Seal, Renew

DRUM BRAKES
Disc Wheel
one side (1.0) 1.4
both sides (1.6) 2.2
Cast Spoke Wheel
one side (.9) 1.3
both sides (1.4) 1.9
DISC BRAKES
one side (1.1) 1.5
both sides (2.0) 2.8

Front Wheel Bearings and Cups, Clean and Repack or Renew

DRUM BRAKES
Disc Wheel
one side (1.0) 1.5
both sides (1.8) 2.8
Cast Spoke Wheel
one side (.9) 1.4
both sides (1.5) 2.5
DISC BRAKES
one side (1.3) 1.7
both sides (2.3) 3.1

Front Axle, Renew

Add alignment charges.
5000, 5500 lb axles (4.2) 5.3
6000 lb axle (5.1) 6.5
7000-9000 lb (5.2) 6.6
12000-15000 lb (5.9) *7.5
16000-22000 lb (6.1) 7.7
*w/Linkage type P.S. add (.3) .3

Front Shock Absorbers, Renew

All series-one (.4) .5
both (.6) .8

Steering Knuckle, Renew

Add alignment charges.
F600 4 x 4-one (1.3) 1.7
both (2.0) 2.5
6000 lb axle-right (2.1) 2.8
left (2.2) 2.9
both (3.5) 4.7
7000, 9500 lb axle
right (2.1) 2.9
left (2.4) 3.2
both (3.9) 5.2
12000-15000 lb axle
right (2.6) 3.5
left (2.7) 3.6
both (4.3) 5.8
16000-22000 lb axle
right (2.6) 3.5
left (2.8) 3.7
both (4.6) 6.2

Steering Knuckle, Rebush

Add alignment charges.
6000 lb axle-right (2.5) 3.3
left (2.6) 3.5
both (4.3) 5.8
7000, 9500 lb axle
right (2.6) 3.5
left (2.8) 3.7
both (4.7) 6.3
12000-15000 lb axle
right (3.0) 4.0
left (3.1) 4.1
both (5.1) 6.8
16000-22000 lb axle
right (3.0) 4.0
left (3.2) 4.3
both (5.4) 7.2
F600 4WD-one (1.5) 2.0
both (2.3) 3.1

King Pins and Bushings, Renew (Both Wheels)

5000, 5500 lb axle (4.4) 5.9
7000-15000 lb (5.2) 7.0
16000-22000 lb (5.5) 7.4
F600 4WD (2.5) 3.3

Front Spring, Renew

5000-7000 lb axle-one (1.2) 1.7
both (2.3) 3.2
9000-22000 lb axle
one (1.5) 2.1
both (2.6) 3.9
CL series
one (3.3) 4.6
both (6.5) 9.1
Ream spring bush add,
each .2

Spring Leaf or Tie Bolt, Renew

5000-7000 lb axle-one (1.6) 2.2
both (3.1) 4.3
9000-22000 lb axle
one (1.9) 2.6
both (3.4) 4.7

Spring Shackle and Bushing, Renew

5000-7000 lb axle-one (2.1) 2.9
both (3.9) 5.4
9000-22000 lb axle
one (2.4) 3.3
both (4.2) 5.8

LABOR 9 FRONT SUSPENSION 9 LABOR

FRONT WHEEL DRIVE

Front Axle Shaft or Universal Joint, Renew

(Factory Time)	Chilton Time
F600 4WD-one (1.3)	1.8
both (2.4)	3.0

Differential Carrier Assembly, R&R

Includes: R&R axle shafts, housing gasket. Drain and refill axle.

(Factory Time)	Chilton Time
F600 4WD (3.0)	4.0

Differential Carrier Assembly, R&R and Recondition

Includes: R&R axle shafts, housing gasket. Drain and refill axle. Inspect, clean, renew or recondition all necessary parts.

(Factory Time)	Chilton Time
F600 4WD (6.4)	8.0

Pinion Shaft Oil Seal, Renew

(Factory Time)	Chilton Time
F600 4WD (1.0)	1.5

Front Drive Shaft, Renew

(Factory Time)	Chilton Time
F600 4WD (.6)	1.0

Front Universal Joint, Renew (One)

(Factory Time)	Chilton Time
F600 4WD (1.0)	1.5

LABOR 10 STEERING LINKAGE 10 LABOR

Tie Rod or Tie Rod End, Renew

Includes: Toe-in adjustment.

(Factory Time)	Chilton Time
exc below (1.1)	1.3
F600 4WD (.9)	1.2

Drag Link, Renew

Does not require resetting toe-in.

(Factory Time)	Chilton Time
All series-one (.6)	.9

Drag Link, Adjust

(Factory Time)	Chilton Time
All series (.4)	.5

Pitman Arm, Renew

(Factory Time)	Chilton Time
exc below (.7)	1.0
CL series (.6)	1.0

Spindle Arm, Renew

Includes: Toe-in adjustment.

(Factory Time)	Chilton Time
tapered arm-one (1.3)	1.7
both (1.7)	2.2
bolt on arm-one (1.5)	2.0
both (2.1)	2.7
F600 4WD-one (1.8)	2.3
both (3.1)	4.0

LABOR 11 STEERING GEAR 11 LABOR

STANDARD STEERING

Steering Gear, Adjust (On Truck)

(Factory Time)	Chilton Time
All series (1.1)	1.5

Steering Gear, R&R or Renew

(Factory Time)	Chilton Time
F-C series (1.0)	1.8
L-LN series (.6)	1.4

Steering Gear, R&R and Recondition

Includes: Disassemble, inspect, clean, renew necessary parts, reassemble and adjust.

(Factory Time)	Chilton Time
F-C series (1.9)	3.2
L-LN series (1.5)	2.7

Steering Mast Jacket Bearing, Renew

Includes: R&R steering column.

(Factory Time)	Chilton Time
exc below (.9)	1.2
C series (.7)	.9
CL series (.8)	1.0

Steering Wheel, Renew

(Factory Time)	Chilton Time
All series (.4)	.6

POWER STEERING

Trouble Shoot Power Steering

Includes: Check pounds pull on steering wheel, install checking gauges, test pump pressure and check for external leaks.

(Factory Time)	Chilton Time
exc below (.8)	.8
C-CT series (.7)	.7

Power Steering Hoses, Renew

(Factory Time)	Chilton Time
F500-900	
pressure (.7)	1.0
return (.9)	1.3
F series	
Cat V-8-each (.6)	.9
C series	
Cat V-8-each (.5)	.8
L series-each (.4)	.7
CL series-each (.5)	.8

Power Steering Control Valve Assy., Renew

(Factory Time)	Chilton Time
F500-800 (.6)	1.0
C series (.9)	2.0
L-LN series (.8)	1.8
CL series (1.0)	2.0
Recond add (.8)	.8

Power Steering Cylinder, Renew

(Factory Time)	Chilton Time
All series (.7)	1.5
Recond add (.8)	.8

Power Steering Gear, R&R or Renew

(Factory Time)	Chilton Time
F series	
Gas (1.0)	1.5
Diesel (1.5)	2.0
C series (1.2)	1.7
L-LN series (1.5)	2.0
CL series (1.8)	2.3
Renew sector shaft seals add (.7)	1.0

Power Steering Gear, R&R and Recondition

Includes: Disassemble, inspect, clean, renew necessary parts, reassemble and adjust.

(Factory Time)	Chilton Time
F series	
Gas (2.7)	3.6
Diesel (3.2)	4.4
C series (2.9)	3.9
L-LN series (3.2)	4.4
CL series (3.5)	4.8

Power Steering Pump, R&R or Renew

(Factory Time)	Chilton Time
F series-Gas (.7)	1.1
F series-Detroit (1.3)	1.7
F7000-Cat-V-8 (.9)	1.4
C series-Gas (.7)	1.2
C series-Diesel (.7)	1.2
L series	
Gas (.8)	1.3
Detroit (1.1)	1.6
Caterpillar (.6)	1.1
Cummins (.7)	1.2
CL series	
Detroit (1.0)	1.5
Caterpillar (.7)	1.2
Cummins (2.4)	3.4

Power Steering Pump, R&R and Recondition

(Factory Time)	Chilton Time
F series-Gas (1.3)	1.9
F series-Detroit (1.9)	2.5
F7000-Cat-V-8 (2.4)	3.3
C series-Gas (2.2)	3.1
C series-Diesel (2.2)	3.1
L series	
Gas (2.3)	3.2
Detroit (2.6)	3.5
Caterpillar (2.1)	3.0
Cummins (2.2)	3.1
CL series	
Detroit (1.6)	2.3
Caterpillar (1.3)	2.2
Cummins (3.0)	4.2

Pump Drive Belt, Renew

(Factory Time)	Chilton Time
Gas (.4)	.7
Diesel	
Cummins (.4)	.7
Caterpillar (.5)	.9
Detroit	
CL series (.8)	1.2
All other series (.4)	.7

(Factory Time) Chilton Time

GASOLINE ENGINES

Cylinder Head Gasket, Renew

Includes: R&R all normal interfering parts. Check cylinder head and block flatness. Adjust carburetor, valves (if adjustable) and ignition timing (when distributor is removed).

Six–C series (3.1)	4.2
F series (3.3)	4.5
L series (2.8)	3.8
V-8–330, 361, 389, 391 engs	
F series-one (3.5)	4.8
both (4.4)	6.0
C series-one (3.3)	4.5
both (4.0)	5.5
L series-one (4.5)	6.0
both (5.3)	7.0
V-8–370, 429 engs	
one (3.9)	5.4
both (5.7)	7.8
V-8–401, 475, 477, 534 engs	
F series-one (6.1)	7.5
both (8.4)	10.0
C series-one (5.6)	7.0
both (7.7)	9.5
L series-exc below	
one (6.7)	8.5
both (9.4)	11.5
LN models	
one (8.2)	10.3
both (11.5)	14.5

Cylinder Head, Renew

Includes: R&R all interfering parts. Check cylinder block flatness. Transfer all necessary components. Clean, reface and lap valves. Check valve spring tension, assembled height and valve head runout. Adjust carburetor, valves and distributor.

Six–C series (5.7)	7.2
F series (5.9)	7.5
L series (5.4)	6.8
V-8–330, 361, 389, 391 engs	
F series-one (4.9)	6.3
both (7.2)	9.0
C series-one (4.7)	6.0
both (6.8)	8.5
L series-one (5.9)	7.5
both (8.1)	10.0
V-8–370, 429 engs	
one (5.1)	7.0
both (8.2)	11.3
V-8–401, 475, 477, 534 engs	
F series-one (7.8)	9.3
both (11.2)	13.6
C series-one (7.0)	8.8
both (10.9)	13.1
L series-exc below	
one (8.1)	10.3
both (11.6)	15.1
LN models	
one (9.6)	12.0
both (14.7)	18.5

Clean Carbon and Grind Valves

Includes: R&R cylinder head and all interfering parts. Check cylinder head and block flatness. Clean, inspect and recondition or renew all necessary components. Check valve spring tension, assembled height and valve runout. Tune engine.

Six–C series (6.8)	8.7
F series (7.0)	9.0
L series (6.5)	8.3
V-8–330, 361, 389, 391 engs	
F series (9.0)	11.4
C series (8.6)	10.9
L series (9.9)	12.4
V-8–370, 429 engs (9.4)	12.9

COMBINATIONS

Add to Valve Job

(Factory Time) Chilton Time

VALVE GUIDES, REAM FOR OVERSIZE STEMS	
One (.1)	.2
Twelve (.7)	.9
Sixteen (1.0)	1.2
ROCKER ARMS, RENEW OR DISASSEMBLE AND CLEAN	
Six (.8)	1.0
ROCKER ARM STUD, RENEW	
Each (.3)	.3
DISTRIBUTOR, RECONDITION	
Six (.9)	1.1
V-8 (1.0)	1.2
CARBURETOR, RECONDITION	
Six (.7)	1.2
V-8 (.9)	1.5

(Factory Time) Chilton Time

V-8–401, 475, 477, 534 engs	
F series (13.7)	16.1
C series (13.0)	15.6
L series	
exc below (14.7)	17.6
LN models (16.8)	21.0

Valve Cover Gasket, Renew

Six–F-L series (.8)	1.0
C series (.7)	.9
V-8–330, 361, 389, 391 engs	
F series-one (.5)	.7
both (.7)	.9
C series-one (.4)	.6
both (.6)	.8
L series-one (.6)	.7
both (.9)	1.2
V-8–370, 429 engs	
right (.7)	.9
left (.5)	.7
both (1.0)	1.4
V-8–401, 475, 477, 534 engs	
F series-one (.6)	.8
both (.8)	1.0
C series-one (.4)	.6
both (.6)	.8
L series-exc below	
one (.9)	1.0
both (1.1)	1.5
LN models	
one (1.0)	1.3
both (1.3)	1.7

Push Rod Cover Gasket, Renew

Six(.6)	.9
V-8–401, 475, 477, 534 engs	
F series (2.9)	3.5
C series (2.3)	2.7
L series	
exc below (3.2)	4.0
LN models (3.8)	4.8

Push Rods, Renew

Six–F-L series-one (1.0)	1.3
all (1.3)	1.7
C series-one (.9)	1.2
all (1.2)	1.6
V-8–330, 361, 389, 391 engs	
F series-one (.6)	.8
all (1.0)	1.3

(Factory Time) Chilton Time

C series-one (.5)	.7
all (.9)	1.2
L series-one (.7)	.9
all (1.2)	1.6
V-8–370, 429 engs	
right side-one (.8)	1.1
left side-one (.6)	.8
all-both sides (1.4)	1.9
V-8–401, 475, 477, 534 eng	
F series-one (.9)	1.2
all (1.7)	2.2
C series-one (.7)	.9
all (1.5)	2.0
L series-exc below	
one (1.2)	1.6
all (2.0)	2.5
LN models	
one (1.3)	1.7
all (2.2)	2.8

Rocker Arm Assembly, R&R and Recondition

V-8–330, 361, 389, 391 engs	
F series-one (1.0)	1.5
both (1.7)	2.6
C series-one (.9)	1.4
both (1.6)	2.5
L series-one (1.1)	1.5
both (1.9)	2.6
V-8–401, 475, 477, 534 engs	
F series-one (5.9)	7.4
both (8.0)	9.9
C series-one (5.3)	6.7
both (7.5)	9.2
L series-exc below	
one (6.5)	8.3
both (9.3)	11.5
LN models	
one (8.0)	10.0
both (11.3)	14.2

Valve Lifters, Renew (All)

Includes: R&R intake manifold (V-8) and all interfering parts. Adjust valves, carburetor and ignition timing.

Six–F-L series (1.8)	3.4
C series (1.6)	3.2
V-8–330, 361, 389, 391 engs	
F series (2.8)	3.5
C series (3.2)	4.2
L series (3.2)	4.2
V-8–370, 429 engs (3.6)	5.0
V-8–401, 475, 477, 534 engs	
F series (4.3)	5.8
C series (3.7)	5.2
L series	
exc below (4.6)	6.0
LN models (5.6)	7.0

Valve Springs or Seals, Renew (All)

Includes: R&R valve covers and adjust valves.

Six–F-C series (2.0)	2.5
L series (2.3)	2.9
V-8–330, 361, 389, 391 engs	
F series (2.8)	3.5
C series (2.5)	*3.2
L series (2.7)	3.5
V-8–401, 475, 477, 534 engs	
F series (3.0)	3.8
C series (3.2)	*4.3
L series	
exc below (3.4)	4.5
LN models (3.5)	4.7
*R&R aux water tank add (.5)	.5

LABOR 12 CYLINDER HEAD & VALVE SYSTEM 12 LABOR

(Factory Time) Chilton Time

DIESEL ENGINES

Cylinder Head, R&R or Renew Gasket

Includes: R&R all normal interfering parts. Check cylinder head and block for flatness. Adjust valves and crossheads.

Caterpillar
- F series-one (7.5) 10.8
- both (11.4) 14.4
- C series-one (6.4) 9.6
- both (9.4) 12.8
- L series 3208-one (6.4) 8.9
- both (9.4) 11.6
- 3406 (11.8) 14.8
- LN series-one (7.5) 10.8
- both (11.4) 14.4
- CL series (11.8) 14.8

Cummins
- NH & NT 743-855-one (7.3) 9.3
- all (15.0) 19.2
- V555-one (12.6) 16.1
- all (20.5) 26.0
- V & VT 785, 903
- one (14.1) 16.5
- all (24.4) 30.8
- KT(A)1150-one (6.8) 8.5
- all (14.3) 17.0

Detroit
- 6V-53-one (4.8) 6.4
- both (8.0) 10.2
- 6V-92-one (5.0) 6.6
- both (8.5) 10.7
- 6-71 (8.0) 10.0
- 8V-71-8V-92-one (5.5) 7.0
- both (9.5) 12.0
- w/Jacobs brk add (.5) 5

Clean Carbon and Grind Valves

Includes: R&R head and all normal interfering parts. Check cylinder head and block flatness, magnaflux head. Clean, inspect and recondition all components as necessary. Pressure test head. Check spring tension, assembled height and valve runout. Adjust valves, crossheads and injectors. Road test.

Caterpillar
- F series (15.4) 19.2
- C series (13.4) 17.2
- L series 3208 (13.4) 17.2
- 3406 (16.6) 20.4
- LN series (15.4) 19.2
- CL series (16.6) 20.4

COMBINATIONS

Add to Valve Job

(Factory Time) Chilton Time

INJECTOR SLEEVES, RENEW
- One (.8) 1.0
- Six (2.0) 2.5
- Eight (2.8) 3.5

INJECTOR, RECONDITION
- One (.7) 1.0
- each adtnl (.3) 5

(Factory Time) Chilton Time

Cummins
- NH & NT 743, 855 (23.0) 29.5
- V555 (28.9) 37.0
- V & VT 785, 903 (26.4) 32.9
- KT(A)1150 (17.1) 21.2

Detroit
- 6V-53 (23.0) 29.5
- 6V-92 (25.7) 31.2
- 6-71 (21.0) 25.6
- 8V-71-8V-92 (24.2) 31.0
- w/Jacobs brk add (.5) 5

Adjust Valves and Crossheads

Includes: R&R all normal interfering parts.

Caterpillar
- F & LN series (1.7) 2.1
- C & L series-3208 (1.4) 1.8
- L & CL series-3406 (1.3) 1.7

Cummins
- NH & NT743, 855 (2.8) 3.5
- V & VT785, 903 (4.4) 5.5
- V-555 (3.0) 4.1
- KT(A)1150 (2.3) 3.0

Detroit
- exc below (1.5) 2.0
- 6-71 (1.2) 1.6

Valve Cover Gasket, Renew

Caterpillar
- All series-3208
- one (.3) 5
- both (.6) 9
- 3406 (.9) 1.2

(Factory Time) Chilton Time

CUMMINS
- KT(A)1150-one (.2) 4
- all (1.0) 1.5
- NH & NT743, 855-one (1.1) 1.6
- each adtnl (.9) 1.0
- V & VT 555, 903-one (1.7) 2.2
- each adtnl (1.5) 1.6

Detroit
- each (.3) 5

Valve Push Rods, Renew (All)

Includes: R&R all normal interfering parts. All necessary adjustments.

Caterpillar
- 3208
- F & LN series (2.1) 2.7
- C & L series (1.8) 2.4
- 3406
- All series (2.9) 3.6

CUMMINS
- KT(A)1150 (3.1) 3.8
- NH & NT743, 855 (5.3) 6.0
- V & VT555, 903 (5.7) 6.4

Detroit
- 6V-53-6V-92 (2.9) 3.4
- 6-71 (2.8) 3.3
- 8V-71-8V-92 (3.6) 4.1

Valve Lifters, Renew (All)

Includes: R&R of all normal interfering parts. All necessary adjustments.

Caterpillar
- F series (11.4) 14.5
- C series (9.7) 13.2
- L series-3208 (9.7) 13.2
- 3406 (3.5) 4.7
- LN series (11.4) 14.5
- CL series (3.5) 4.7

Cummins
- NH & NT743, 855 (10.0) 12.5
- V-8 785, V903 (14.6) 18.3
- KT(A)1150 (4.1) 6.4
- V-VT555-903 (16.7) 20.4

Detroit
- 6V-53-6V-92 (4.2) 5.3
- 6-71 (3.8) 4.8
- 8V-71-8V-92 (4.8) 6.0

LABOR 13 ENGINE ASSEMBLY & MOUNTS 13 LABOR

(Factory Time) Chilton Time

GASOLINE ENGINES

Engine Assembly, Remove and Reinstall

Includes: R&R of all normal interfering parts. Does not include transfer of any components.

- **Six**–F-C series (3.0) 4.0
- L series (2.6) 3.7
- **V-8**–330, 361, 389, 391 engs
- F series
- std trans (3.8) 5.0
- auto trans (5.8) 7.5
- C series (3.9) 5.2
- L series
- exc below (3.2) 4.3
- LN models (5.2) 6.8
- **V-8**–370, 429 engs
- F series
- w/M.T. (8.0) 10.4
- w/A.T. (9.8) 12.7

(Factory Time) Chilton Time

- C-L series
- w/M.T. (5.5) 7.1
- w/A.T. (7.0) 9.1
- LN series
- w/M.T. (6.6) 8.5
- w/A.T. (8.5) 11.0
- **V-8**–401, 475, 477, 534 engs
- F series (9.9) 11.8
- C series (7.8) 10.2
- L series
- exc below (7.4) 9.5
- LN models (8.8) 11.2
- w/A.C. add (1.0) 1.0
- w/P.S. add (.4) 4
- w/Air brks add 6

(Factory Time) Chilton Time

Engine Assembly, Renew (Remanufactured Engine)

Includes: R&R engine and all normal interfering parts. Transfer all necessary components. Tune engine and road test.

- **Six**–F-C series (5.7) 7.5
- L series (5.3) 7.0
- **V-8**–330, 361, 389, 391 engs
- F series
- std trans (7.9) 10.0
- auto trans (9.9) 12.0
- C series (8.0) 10.0
- L series
- exc below (7.3) 9.5
- LN models (9.3) 11.5
- **V-8**–370, 429 engs
- F series
- w/M.T. (11.5) 14.9
- w/A.T. (13.3) 17.2

	(Factory Time)	Chilton Time
C-L series		
w/M.T.	(9.0)	11.7
w/A.T.	(10.5)	13.6
LN series		
w/M.T.	(10.8)	13.1
w/A.T.	(12.0)	15.6
V-8–401, 475, 477, 534 engs		
F series	(15.6)	19.0
C series	(13.5)	15.5
L series		
exc below	(13.1)	17.9
LN models	(14.5)	18.7
w/A.C. add	(1.0)	1.0
w/P.S. add	(.4)	.4
w/Air brks add		.6

Cylinder Assembly (Short Engine), Renew & Grind Valves

Includes: R&R engine and all normal interfering parts. Transfer all necessary parts and equipment. Check valve spring tension, valve seat and head runout, head flatness, stem to guide clearance, assembled height. Tune engine and road test.

	(Factory Time)	Chilton Time
Six–F-C series	(11.4)	14.5
L series	(11.0)	14.0
V-8–330, 361, 389, 391 engs		
F series		
std trans	(13.8)	16.0
auto trans	(15.8)	18.0
C series	(13.4)	16.9
L series		
exc below	(13.6)	16.5
LN models	(15.6)	18.5
V-8–370, 429 engs		
F series		
w/M.T.	(13.7)	19.1
w/A.T.	(15.5)	21.7
C-L series		
w/M.T.	(11.2)	15.6
w/A.T.	(12.7)	17.7
LN series		
w/M.T.	(16.0)	22.4
w/A.T.	(17.9)	25.0
V-8–401, 475, 477, 534 engs		
F series	(22.8)	26.0
C series	(20.3)	23.4
L series		
exc below	(19.9)	24.9
LN models	(21.3)	25.7
w/A.C. add	(1.0)	1.0
w/P.S. add	(.4)	.4
w/Air brks add		.6

Engine Assembly, R&R and Recondition (Complete)

Includes: R&R of all normal interfering parts. Disassemble and assemble complete engine. Inspect all components. Rebore block. Install new pistons, rings and pins. Align rods. Plastigauge and install new main, rod and camshaft bearings. Clean carbon and grind valves, test hydraulic tappets, renew if necessary. Renew all gaskets and seals as necessary. Tune engine and road test.

	(Factory Time)	Chilton Time
Six–F-C series	(25.9)	31.0
L series	(24.5)	29.4
V-8–330, 361, 389, 391 engs		
F series		
std trans	(32.8)	38.2
auto trans	(34.8)	40.2
C series	(32.3)	37.7
L series		
exc below	(33.9)	40.5
LN models	(35.9)	42.5
V-8–370, 429 engs		
F series		
w/M.T.	(20.0)	27.0
w/A.T.	(21.8)	29.4
C-L series		
w/M.T.	(17.5)	23.6
w/A.T.	(19.0)	25.6
LN series		
w/M.T.	(18.6)	25.1
w/A.T.	(20.5)	27.6
V-8–401, 475, 477, 534 engs		
F series	(45.6)	51.2
C series	(42.8)	48.2
L series		
exc below	(44.9)	50.3
LN models	(46.3)	53.0
w/A.C. add	(1.0)	1.0
w/P.S. add	(.4)	.4
w/Air brks add		.6

Engine Mounts, Renew

	(Factory Time)	Chilton Time
Front		
Six–one	(.4)	.7
both	(.5)	.9
V-8–exc below–one	(.5)	.8
both	(.8)	1.2
V-8–370, 429 engs	(1.5)	2.2
Rear		
All series	(.5)	.9

DIESEL ENGINES

Engine Assembly, Remove and Reinstall

Includes: R&R of all normal interfering parts. Does not include transfer of any components.

	(Factory Time)	Chilton Time
Caterpillar		
F series	(11.2)	13.4
C series	(8.1)	10.4
L series–3208	(10.2)	12.4
3406	(20.4)	24.6
LN series	(10.8)	13.1
CL series	(12.7)	16.0
Cummins		
NH & NT743, 855	(25.5)	31.6
V555	(24.4)	30.5
V & VT 785, 903	(24.0)	30.0
N927	(19.5)	24.5
Detroit		
6V-53-6V-92	(22.2)	27.8
6-71	(24.6)	30.8
8V-71-8V-92	(23.4)	29.4

Cylinder Block, Renew

Includes: R&R engine and all normal interfering parts. Transfer all components without disassembly. Install new main and rod bearings. Renew all necessary seals and gaskets. Adjust timing and clearances. Road Test.

Does not include reconditioning of any component.

	(Factory Time)	Chilton Time
Caterpillar		
F series	(33.2)	44.5
C series	(31.0)	38.6
L series-3208	(32.2)	40.2
3406	(53.9)	62.8
LN series	(34.4)	43.3
CL series	(46.2)	55.1
Cummins		
NH & NT743, 855	(55.8)	64.3
V555	(55.7)	65.5
V & VT 785, 903	(54.8)	64.5
N927	(49.8)	59.5
Detroit		
6V-53	(54.2)	62.8
6V-92	(56.2)	64.8
6-71	(58.6)	67.8
8V-71-8V-92	(60.4)	69.4

Engine Assembly, R&R and Recondition (Complete)

Includes: R&R of all normal interfering parts. Complete dissassembly and assembly of engine. Pressure test block and head. Plastigauge and renew main, rod and camshaft bearings. Install new pistons, rings, pins and liners. Rebore block. Recondition blower or turbocharger, water and injector pump, oil pump, injectors, governor and other sub-assemblies. Clean carbon and grind valves. Check and set all clearances. Tune engine and road test.

	(Factory Time)	Chilton Time
Caterpillar		
F series	(41.6)	55.9
C series	(38.5)	49.9
L series-3208	(40.6)	53.7
3406	(50.8)	63.9
LN series	(41.2)	54.3
CL series	(43.1)	56.2
Cummins		
NH & NT743, 855	(59.1)	74.1
V555	(62.4)	78.0
V & VT785, 903	(60.5)	75.7
N927	(57.0)	71.3
Detroit		
6V-53	(82.2)	102.8
6V-92	(87.2)	107.8
6-71	(84.6)	105.9
8V-71-8V-92	(93.4)	117.0

Engine Mounts, Renew

	(Factory Time)	Chilton Time
Front		
exc below–one	(.6)	.9
F series–Cat-V-8–one	(.7)	1.0
C series–Cat-V-8	(1.7)	2.4
Rear		
one	(1.0)	1.5
both	(2.0)	2.5

GASOLINE ENGINES

Rings, Pins, Rod and Main Bearings, Renew and Grind Valves

Includes: R&R of all normal interfering parts. Remove cylinder top ridge, hone cylinder walls, clean ring grooves, install new rings. Install new pins and align rods. Plastigauge and install new main and rod bearings. Renew gaskets and seals as necessary. Clean carbon and grind valves. Test valve spring tension, valve seat and head run-out, stem to guide clearance, head and block flatness and assembled height. Tune engine and road test.

(Factory Time)	Chilton Time
Six–F series (17.8)	*22.3
C series (18.1)	*22.7
L series (17.0)	*21.3
V-8–330, 361, 389, 391 engs	
F series (19.2)	24.6
C series (19.6)	23.9
L series (20.4)	25.0
V-8–370, 429 engs	
F-C-L-LN series (18.5)	25.7
V-8–401, 475, 477, 534 engs	
F series (26.6)	32.5
C series (25.2)	31.7
L series	
exc below (27.0)	33.9
LN models (28.9)	36.7
w/A.C. add (1.0)	1.0
w/P.S. add (.4)	.4

*Includes R&R engine.

Rings, Pins, Rod and Main Bearings, Renew

Includes: R&R of all normal interfering parts. Remove cylinder top ridge, hone cylinder walls, clean ring grooves, install new rings. Install new pins and align rods. Plastigauge and install new main and rod bearings. Renew gaskets and seals as necessary. Tune engine and road test.

(Factory Time)	Chilton Time
Six–F series (15.1)	*18.8
C series (15.4)	*19.2
L series (14.3)	*17.8
V-8–330, 361, 389, 391 engs	
F series (16.5)	20.1
C series (15.9)	19.4
L series (16.8)	20.5
V-8–370, 429 engs	
F-C-L-LN series (14.8)	20.4
V-8–401, 475, 477, 534 engs	
F series (22.3)	27.3
C series (21.6)	26.5
L series	
exc below (23.4)	28.7
LN models (25.3)	31.5
w/A.C. add (1.0)	1.0
w/P.S. add (.4)	.4

*Includes R&R engine.

Rings, Pins and Rod Bearings, Renew

Includes: R&R of all normal interfering parts. Remove cylinder top ridge, hone cylinder walls, clean ring grooves, install new rings. Install new pins and align rods. Plastigauge and install new rod bearings. Renew gaskets and seals as necessary. Tune engine and road test.

(Factory Time)	Chilton Time
Six–F series (11.5)	13.6
C series (11.8)	14.0
L series (10.7)	12.6
V-8–330, 361, 389, 391 engs	
F series (14.6)	17.2
C series (14.0)	16.5
L series (14.9)	17.6
V-8–370,429 engs	
F-C-L-LN series (13.9)	19.1

COMBINATIONS

(Factory Time)	Chilton Time
VALVE GUIDES, REAM FOR OVERSIZE STEMS	
One (.1)	.2
Twelve (.7)	.9
Sixteen (1.0)	1.2
ROCKER ARM STUD, RENEW	
Each (.3)	.3
ROCKER ARMS, RENEW OR DISASSEMBLE AND CLEAN	
Six (.8)	1.0
DISTRIBUTOR, RECONDITION	
Six (.9)	1.1
V-8 (1.0)	1.3
CARBURETOR, RECONDITION	
Six (.7)	1.2
V-8 (.9)	1.5
REMOVE CYLINDER TOP RIDGE	
Each (.1)	.1
DEGLAZE CYLINDER WALLS	
Six (1.2)	1.2
V-8 (1.5)	1.5
OIL PUMP, RECONDITION	
All (.4)	.6
MAIN BEARINGS, RENEW (PAN REMOVED)	
V-8 (2.0)	2.9
PLASTIGAUGE BEARINGS	
Each (.1)	.1

(Factory Time)	Chilton Time
V-8–401, 475, 477, 534 engs	
F series (20.3)	24.4
C series (19.6)	23.6
L series	
exc below (21.4)	25.8
LN models (23.3)	28.6
w/A.C. add (1.0)	1.0
w/P.S. add (.4)	.4

Rings, Renew

Includes: R&R all normal interfering parts. Remove cylinder top ridge, hone cylinder walls, clean ring grooves, install new rings. Renew gaskets and seals as necessary.

(Factory Time)	Chilton Time
Six–F series (8.1)	10.2
C series (8.4)	10.6
L series (7.3)	9.2
V-8–330, 361, 389, 391 engs	
F series (10.4)	13.0
C series (9.8)	12.3
L series (10.7)	13.4
V-8–370, 429 engs	
F-C-L-LN series (11.0)	15.6
V-8–401, 475, 477, 534 engs	
F series (16.1)	20.2
C series (15.4)	19.4
L series	
exc below (17.2)	21.6
LN models (19.1)	24.4
w/A.C. add (1.0)	1.0
w/P.S. add (.4)	.4

Piston, Renew (One)

Includes: R&R of all normal interfering parts. Remove cylinder top ridge, hone cylinder walls. Install new piston with rings.

(Factory Time)	Chilton Time
Six–F series (5.0)	6.1
C series (5.2)	6.6
L series (4.2)	5.4
V-8–370, 429 engs	
F-C-L-LN series (6.2)	8.8
V-8–330, 361, 389, 391 engs	
F series (5.3)	6.6
C series (5.1)	6.6
L series (5.6)	6.9
V-8–401, 475, 477, 534 engs	
F series (8.6)	10.6
C series (7.7)	9.1
L series	
exc below (8.9)	11.1
LN models (10.0)	12.4
w/A.C. add (1.0)	1.0
w/P.S. add (.4)	.4

Rod Bearings, Renew

Includes: R&R oil pan, recondition oil pump.

(Factory Time)	Chilton Time
Six–F series (3.4)	4.6
C series (3.7)	4.9
L series (3.1)	4.3
V-8–330, 361, 389, 391 engs	
exc below (3.6)	5.5
C series (3.3)	5.2
L series (3.3)	5.2
V-8–370, 429 engs	
F-LN series (3.2)	4.4
C-L series (2.9)	4.0
V-8–401, 475, 477, 534 engs	
All series (3.9)	5.8

DIESEL ENGINES

Rings, Pins, Rod and Main Bearings, Renew and Grind Valves

Includes: R&R of all normal interfering parts. Hone cylinder liner walls, clean ring grooves, install new rings. Install new pins and align rods. Plastigauge and install new main and rod bearings. Renew gaskets and seals as necessary. Clean carbon and grind valves. Clean oil pump. Set injection timing and valves and crossheads. Road test.

Does not include renew liners.

(Factory Time)	Chilton Time
Caterpillar	
F series (24.7)	31.6
C series (23.3)	30.2
L series-3208 (23.3)	30.2
3406 (26.5)	33.8
LN series (24.7)	31.6
CL series (26.5)	33.8
Cummins	
NH & NT743, 855 (37.8)	47.3
V555 (39.5)	49.0
V & VT785, 903 (38.9)	48.7
N927 (29.2)	36.6
KT(A)1150 (35.1)	44.6
Detroit	
6V-53 (40.4)	50.6
6V-92 (42.7)	52.9
6-71 (37.9)	47.5
8V-71-8V-92 (44.3)	55.4

Rings, Renew

Includes: R&R all normal interfering parts. Hone cylinder liner walls, clean ring grooves, install new rings. Renew gaskets and seals as necessary. Set injection timing and valves and crossheads. Road test.

(Factory Time)	Chilton Time
Caterpillar	
F series (17.1)	21.5
C series (15.7)	20.1
L series-3208 (15.7)	20.1
3406 (20.5)	24.9
LN series (17.1)	21.5
CL series (20.5)	24.9

LABOR 14 PISTONS, RINGS & BEARINGS 14 LABOR

(Factory Time)	Chilton Time
Cummins	
NH & NT743, 855 (21.2)	25.9
V555 (29.6)	34.3
V & VT785, 903 (36.4)	41.1
N927 (18.3)	22.9
Detroit	
6V-53 (18.2)	22.8
6V-92 (19.9)	24.5
6-71 (17.6)	22.1
8V-71-8V-92 (20.8)	26.0

Piston and Liner, Renew (One)

Includes: R&R all normal interfering parts. Hone block bore, check liner height, liner bore and O.D. for proper fit. Install new liner, piston with rings and pin. Renew gaskets and seals as necessary. Set injection timing and valves and crossheads.

(Factory Time)	Chilton Time
Caterpillar	
All series	
3406 (17.7)	22.0
Cummins	
NH & NT743, 855 (16.0)	20.6
V555 (18.6)	23.1
V & VT 785, 903 (21.5)	25.9
N927 (17.9)	22.6
KT(A)1150 (14.1)	18.5
each adtnl	2.0
Detroit	
6V-53 (8.0)	10.2
6V-92 (8.1)	10.4
6-71 (11.8)	15.7
8V-71-8V-92 (9.2)	11.8

COMBINATIONS

(Factory Time)	Chilton Time
INJECTOR SLEEVES, REAM	
One (.8)	1.0
Six (2.0)	2.5
Eight (2.8)	3.5
INJECTORS, RECONDITION	
One (.7)	1.0
each adtnl (.3)	.5
GRIND VALVES, HEAD REMOVED	
Caterpillar 3208-each (2.0)	2.7
3406 (4.8)	5.7
Cummins	
NH & NT-one (2.1)	2.9
all (6.2)	8.0
N927 (5.1)	6.7
V555 (8.2)	10.5
V & VT 785, 903	
One (4.3)	5.8
Both (8.5)	11.1
Detroit	
V-6-each (7.5)	9.9
Six (13.0)	17.0
V-8-each (9.0)	11.5
PRESSURE TEST HEAD	
Six (1.5)	2.0
V-6-each (1.0)	1.5
V-8-each (1.2)	1.8

Rod Bearings, Renew

Includes: R&R all normal interfering parts. Clean oil pump.

(Factory Time)	Chilton Time
Caterpillar	
All series	
3208 (3.7)	4.5
3406 (3.5)	4.3
Cummins	
NH & NT743, 855 (3.1)	4.2
V555 (6.7)	8.8
V & VT 785, 903 (5.7)	7.6
N927 (6.3)	8.3
KT(A)1150 (11.4)	13.8
Detroit	
6V-53 (4.3)	5.8
6V-92 (4.4)	5.9
6-71 (4.9)	6.6
8V-71-8V-92 (5.8)	7.7

LABOR 15 CRANKSHAFT & DAMPER 15 LABOR

GASOLINE ENGINES

Crankshaft and Main Bearings, Renew

Includes: R&R all normal interfering parts and engine. Plastigauge and install new bearings. Recondition oil pump.

(Factory Time)	Chilton Time
Six–F-C series (7.9)	10.4
L series (7.5)	10.3
V-8–330, 361, 389, 391 engs	
F series	
std trans (8.9)	11.6
auto trans (10.9)	14.1
C series (9.0)	11.8
L series	
exc below (8.3)	11.1
LN models (10.3)	13.6
V-8–370, 429 engs	
F series	
w/M.T. (12.7)	17.5
w/A.T. (14.5)	20.0
C-L series	
w/M.T. (10.2)	14.0
w/A.T. (11.7)	16.1
LN series	
w/M.T. (11.3)	15.5
w/A.T. (13.2)	18.2
V-8–401, 475, 477, 534 eng	
F series (15.4)	20.3
C series (13.3)	18.7
L series	
exc below (12.9)	18.0
LN models (14.3)	19.7
w/A.C. add (1.0)	1.0
w/P.S. add (.4)	.4
w/Air brks add	.6

Main and Rod Bearings, Renew

Includes: R&R all normal interfering parts. Plastigauge and install new main and rod bearings. Renew gaskets and seals as necessary. Recondition oil pump.

(Factory Time)	Chilton Time
Six–F-C series (9.2)	*11.8
L series (8.7)	*11.4
V-8–330, 361, 389, 391 engs	
exc below (5.5)	8.2
C series (5.2)	7.9
L series (5.2)	7.9
V-8–370, 429 engs	
F-LN series (5.1)	6.9
C-L series (4.8)	6.5
V-8–401, 475, 477, 534 engs	
All series (5.8)	8.2

*Includes: R&R engine.

Main Bearings, Renew

Includes: R&R all normal interfering parts. Plastigauge and install new main bearings. Renew gaskets and seals as necessary. Recondition oil pump.

(Factory Time)	Chilton Time
Six–F-C series (7.5)	*9.8
L series (7.4)	*9.4
V-8–330, 361, 389, 391 engs	
exc below (3.8)	6.0
C series (3.5)	5.7
V-8–370, 429 engs	
F-LN series (3.4)	4.5
C-L series (3.1)	4.1
V-8–401, 475, 477, 534 engs	
All series (3.8)	6.0

*Includes: R&R engine.

Rear Main Bearing Oil Seal, Renew

Includes: R&R all normal interfering parts.

(Factory Time)	Chilton Time
Six–F-C series	3.8
L series (2.2)	3.1
V-8–330, 361, 389, 391 engs	
exc below (2.3)	3.5
C series (2.0)	3.2
L series (2.0)	3.2
V-8–370, 429 engs	
F-LN series (2.3)	3.5
C-L series (2.0)	3.2
V-8–401, 475, 477, 534 engs	
F series (13.2)	*16.0
C series (10.7)	*13.0
L series	
exc below (10.3)	*12.6
LN models (11.7)	*14.0

*Includes: R&R engine.

Crankshaft Damper or Pulley, Renew

(Factory Time)	Chilton Time
V-8–370, 429 engs (1.9)	2.5

Front Crankshaft Seal, Renew

Does not require R&R of front cover.

(Factory Time)	Chilton Time
V-8–370, 429 engs (2.3)	3.2

DIESEL ENGINES

Crankshaft and Main Bearings, Renew

Includes: R&R all normal interfering parts and engine. Plastigauge and install new main bearings, recondition oil pump.

(Factory Time)	Chilton Time
Caterpillar	
F series (31.7)	40.7
C series (28.6)	36.7
L series-3208 (30.7)	38.1
3406 (47.3)	54.7
LN series (31.3)	40.7
CL series (39.6)	47.0
Cummins	
NH743, 855 (33.6)	42.1
NT855 (34.1)	42.7
V555 (48.0)	60.0

LABOR 15 CRANKSHAFT & DAMPER 15 LABOR

(Factory Time)	Chilton Time
N927 (31.1)	39.0
V & VT785, 903 (45.0)	56.3
KT(A)1150 (25.9)	34.0
Detroit	
6V-53 (29.7)	37.2
6V-92 (26.9)	34.4
6-71 (35.4)	44.4
8V-71-8V-92 (32.7)	40.9

Main and Rod Bearings, Renew

Includes: R&R all normal interfering parts. Plastiguage and install new main and rod bearings. Recondition oil pump.

(Factory Time)	Chilton Time
Caterpillar	
All series	
3208 (4.4)	6.5
3406 (6.8)	8.9
Cummins	
NH & NT743, 855 (8.1)	10.4
V555 (11.4)	15.3
V & VT785, 903 (10.4)	13.8
N927 (10.4)	13.8
KT(A)1150 (12.1)	16.0
Detroit	
6V-53 (6.4)	8.5
6V-92 (6.8)	8.9
6-71 (8.1)	10.4
8V-71-8V-92 (8.5)	11.1

Main Bearings, Renew

Includes: R&R all normal interfering parts. Plastigauge and install new main bearings. Recondition oil pump.

(Factory Time)	Chilton Time
Caterpillar	
All series	
3208 (2.5)	4.6
3406 (4.9)	7.0
Cummins	
NH & NT743, 855 (6.9)	9.1
V555 (9.6)	12.5
V & VT785, 903 (8.6)	11.2
N927 (9.2)	11.8
KT(A)1150 (10.3)	13.0
Detroit	
6V-53 (3.4)	4.8
6V-92 (3.8)	5.2
6-71 (5.1)	6.7
8V-71-8V-92 (4.5)	6.1

Rear Main Bearing Oil Seal, Renew

Includes: R&R all normal interfering parts.

(Factory Time)	Chilton Time
Caterpillar	
3208	
All series (5.3)	7.9
3406	
L series (7.7)	10.0
CL series (5.0)	7.4
Cummins	
NH & NT743, 855 (13.1)	16.9
V555 (10.3)	13.3
V & VT785, 903 (9.3)	11.9
N927 (9.1)	11.6
KT(A)1150 (8.5)	11.0
Detroit	
All series (6.8)	8.7

Crankshaft Damper, Renew

Includes: R&R all normal interfering parts.

(Factory Time)	Chilton Time
Caterpillar	
All series	
3208 (2.8)	3.7
3406 (3.5)	4.6
Cummins	
F series (3.3)	4.4
C, L, W series (.7)	1.0
Detroit	
All series (6.5)	8.4

LABOR 16 CAMSHAFT & TIMING GEARS 16 LABOR

GASOLINE ENGINES

Timing Case Cover, Gasket or Oil Seal, Renew

Includes: R&R all normal interfering parts.

(Factory Time)	Chilton Time
Six–F series (2.6)	3.5
C series (2.4)	3.3
L series (2.0)	2.9
V-8–330, 361, 389, 391 engs	
F series (4.1)	5.0
C series (4.2)	5.0
L series (3.4)	4.5
V-8–370, 429 engs (3.9)	5.4
V-8–401, 475, 477, 534 engs	
F series (5.0)	5.9
C series (3.6)	4.5
L series	
exc below (3.7)	5.0
LN models (4.1)	5.3
w/A.C. add (1.0)	1.0
w/P.S. add (.4)	.4

Timing Chain or Gears, Renew

Includes: R&R all normal interfering parts.

(Factory Time)	Chilton Time
Six–F series (3.1)	4.1
C series (2.9)	3.9
L series (2.5)	3.5
V-8–330, 361, 389, 391 engs	
F series (4.4)	5.6
C series (4.5)	5.6
L series (3.7)	5.1
V-8–370, 429 engs (4.2)	5.7
V-8–401, 475, 477, 534 engs	
F series (5.5)	6.6
C series (4.1)	5.2
L series	
exc below (4.2)	5.7
LN models (4.6)	6.0
w/A.C. add (1.0)	1.0
w/P.S. add (.4)	.4

Camshaft, Renew

Includes: R&R all normal interfering parts. Adjust timing and valves.

(Factory Time)	Chilton Time
Six–F-C series (5.5)	7.2
L series (5.1)	6.8
V-8–330, 361, 389, 391 engs	
F series (6.5)	8.2
C series (6.8)	8.2
L series (7.4)	9.0
V-8–370, 429 engs (7.4)	10.0
V-8–401, 475, 477, 534 engs	
F series (10.4)	12.6
C series (8.8)	10.2
L series	
exc below (9.4)	11.3
LN models (10.5)	12.6
w/A.C. add (1.0)	1.0
w/P.S. add (.4)	.4

Camshaft Bearings, Renew

Includes: R&R engine assembly and other parts for access. Install new camshaft bearings. Adjust valves, carburetor and ignition timing.

(Factory Time)	Chilton Time
Six–F-C series (6.8)	8.4
L series (6.4)	8.0
V-8–330, 361, 389, 391 engs	
F series	
std trans (9.8)	11.5
auto trans (11.8)	13.5
C series (9.9)	11.4
L series	
exc below (9.2)	11.0
LN models (11.2)	13.0
V-8–370, 429 engs	
F-LN series	
w/M.T. (13.9)	18.6
w/A.T. (15.7)	21.1
C-L series	
w/M.T. (11.4)	15.3
w/A.T. (12.9)	17.4
V-8–401, 475, 477, 534 engs	
F series (15.5)	18.5
C series (12.9)	14.8
L series	
exc below (13.0)	16.1
LN models (14.4)	17.8
w/A.C. add (1.0)	1.0
w/P.S. add (.4)	.4

DIESEL ENGINES

Cylinder Front Cover or Gasket, Renew

Includes: R&R all interfering parts.

(Factory Time)	Chilton Time
Caterpillar	
All series-3208 (10.3)	12.6
3406 (9.2)	11.5
Cummins	
NH-NT 743, 855 (8.7)	10.9
V & VT785, 903 (16.5)	19.7
V-555 (16.5)	19.7
KT(A)1150 (9.2)	11.4
Detroit	
exc below (8.7)	10.9
6V-53 (8.1)	10.2

Camshaft, Renew

Includes: R&R engine and all interfering parts. Adjust valves and injection timing.

(Factory Time)	Chilton Time
Caterpillar	
F seriess (19.8)	26.9
C series (18.4)	22.7
L series-3208 (18.4)	22.7
3406 (15.5)	19.8
LN series (19.8)	26.9
CL series (15.5)	19.8
Cummins	
NH & NT743, 855 (23.0)	29.5
V555	38.0
V & VT785, 903 (28.7)	36.7
N927	24.5
KT(A)1150 (19.9)	26.5
Detroit	
6V-53-one (8.5)	10.9
6V-92-one (9.5)	11.9
6-71-one (12.5)	16.2
8V-71-8V-92-one (10.3)	13.3

LABOR 17 ENGINE OILING SYSTEM 17 LABOR

(Factory Time)	Chilton Time
GASOLINE ENGINES	
Oil Pan or Gasket, Renew	
Six–F series (1.4)	2.3
C series (1.7)	2.6
L series (1.1)	2.0
V-8–330, 361, 389, 391 engs	
exc below (1.5)	2.5
C & L series (1.2)	2.2
V-8–370, 429 engs	
F-LN series (1.5)	2.1
C-L series (1.2)	1.8
V-8–401, 475, 477, 534 engs	
All series (1.5)	2.5
Oil Pump, Renew	
Six–F series (1.6)	2.6
C series (1.9)	2.9
L series (1.3)	2.3
V-8–330, 361, 389, 391 engs	
exc below (1.6)	2.7
C & L series (1.3)	2.4
V-8–370, 429 engs	
F-LN series (1.7)	2.3
C-L series (1.4)	2.0
V-8–401, 475, 477, 534 engs	
All series (1.6)	2.7
Oil Pump, R&R and Recondition	
Six–F series (1.8)	3.2
C series (2.1)	3.5
L series (1.5)	2.9
V-8–330, 361, 389, 391 engs	
exc below (1.9)	3.3
C & L series (1.6)	3.0
V-8–370, 429 engs	
F-LN series (2.1)	2.9
C-L series (1.8)	2.6
V-8–401, 475, 477, 534 engs	
All series (1.9)	3.3
Oil Cooler or Gasket, Renew	
V-8–401, 475, 477, 534 engs	
F series (1.5)	2.1
C series (1.2)	1.7
L series (1.1)	1.5
370, 429 engs	
All series (1.0)	1.4

(Factory Time)	Chilton Time
Oil Filter, Renew	
All series (.3)	.4
Pressure Test Engine Bearings (Pan Removed)	
All series	1.0
Oil Pressure Gauge (Dash), Renew	
exc below (.6)	1.0
CL series (.4)	.8
Oil Pressure Sending Unit, Renew	
All series (.3)	.5
DIESEL ENGINES	
Oil Pan or Gasket, Renew	
Caterpillar	
All series	
3208 (1.3)	1.9
3406 (1.7)	2.3
Cummins	
NH & NT743, 855 (3.1)	4.2
V555 (4.6)	6.2
V & VT785, 903 (3.0)	4.0
N927 (4.2)	5.5
KT (A) 1150 (9.6)	12.0
Detroit	
6V-53 (1.0)	1.5
6V-92 (1.4)	2.3
6-71 (1.6)	2.5
8V-71-8V-92 (1.5)	2.4
Oil Pump, Renew	
Caterpillar	
All series	
3208 (10.2)	13.0
3406 (2.3)	3.0
Cummins	
NH & NT743, 855 (1.6)	2.5
V555 (4.5)	6.3
V & VT 785, 903 (3.6)	4.8
N927	5.1
KT(A)1150 (9.7)	12.5
Detroit	
6V-53 (9.0)	11.5
6V-92 (9.6)	12.5
6-71 (5.8)	7.2
8V-71-8V-92 (9.6)	12.5

(Factory Time)	Chilton Time
Oil Pump, R&R and Recondition	
Caterpillar	
All series	
3208 (11.5)	14.5
3406 (3.1)	4.0
Cummins	
NH & NT743, 855 (2.7)	4.0
V555 (5.7)	7.8
V & VT 785, 903 (4.8)	6.3
N927	6.6
KT(A)1150 (11.8)	15.0
Detroit	
6V-53 (10.0)	13.0
6V-92 (10.6)	14.0
6-71 (7.8)	9.7
8V-71-8V-92 (10.6)	14.0
Oil Cooler, Renew	
Caterpillar	
All series	
3208 (1.7)	2.2
3406 (1.6)	2.1
Cummins	
NH & NT743, 855 (2.8)	3.9
V-VT 555, 903 (2.8)	3.9
KT(A)1150 (4.0)	5.4
Detroit	
6V-53 (2.6)	3.7
6V-92 (2.6)	3.7
6-71 (2.2)	3.0
8V-71-8V-92 (5.6)	7.5
Oil Filter, Renew	
Caterpillar	
All series	
3208 (.3)	.6
3406 (.4)	.7
Cummins (.9)	1.2
Detroit (.8)	1.0
Oil Pressure Gauge (Dash), Renew	
exc below (.8)	1.2
C series (.6)	1.0
Oil Pressure Sending Unit, Renew	
exc below (.4)	.6
Cummins (.6)	.8

LABOR 18 CLUTCH & FLYWHEEL 18 LABOR

(Factory Time)	Chilton Time
Clutch Pedal Free Play, Adjust	
All series (.4)	.5
Clutch Master Cylinder, Renew	
All series (.6)	.8
Clutch Master Cylinder, R&R and Recondition	
All series (.8)	1.2
Clutch Slave Cylinder, Renew	
All series (.6)	.9
Clutch Slave Cylinder, R&R and Recondition	
All series (.8)	1.2
Bleed Clutch Hydraulic System	
All series (.4)	.5
Clutch Assembly, Renew	
Includes: R&R transmission.	
4 Speed	
New Process 435 (2.6)	3.4
Borg Warner T-19 (2.7)	3.4

(Factory Time)	Chilton Time
5 Speed	
Clark	
280VO-282V-282VHD 285V-285VHD-390/550 397/557 (2.6)	3.4
Fuller	
T-905A-T-905B (3.5)	4.5
New Process	
542FD-542FL 542FO (3.0)	3.9
Spicer	
5052A-5252A (3.0)	3.9
6052A-6052B-6052C	
C series (3.2)	4.2
L-LN series (4.2)	5.6
6 Speed	
Fuller	
RT-906 (3.7)	4.9
Spicer	
1062	
L-LN series (3.7)	4.9
CL series (5.3)	7.1

(Factory Time)	Chilton Time
9 Speed	
Fuller	
RT-9509A-RT-9509B-RT-12509	
L-LN series (4.2)	5.6
CL series (5.6)	7.5
10 Speed	
Fuller	
RT-610 (4.5)	5.9
RT-910-RTO-910	
RT-1110-RT-12510	
L-LN series (4.2)	5.6
CL series (5.6)	7.5
13 Speed	
Fuller	
RT-613 (4.2)	5.6
RT/RTO-9513-RT-12513	
L-LN series (4.2)	5.6
CL series (5.6)	7.5
16 Speed	
Spicer	
RP8516-3A	
w/Aux (5.4)	7.2
w/P.T.O. add (.6)	.6
w/Coupling shaft add (.2)	.2

LABOR 18 CLUTCH & FLYWHEEL 18 LABOR

(Factory Time) Chilton Time

w/Detroit Diesel add (.5) .5
w/Full carpet add (.7) .7
w/Cat V-8 add 1.0

Clutch Release Bearing, Renew

Includes: R&R transmission assembly.

4 Speed
New Process 435 (1.9) 2.7
Borg Warner T-19 (2.0) 2.7

5 Speed
Clark
280VO-282V-282VHD
285V-285VHD-390/550
397/557 (1.9) 2.7
Fuller
T-905A-T-905B (2.8) 3.8
New Process
542FD-542FL
542FO (2.3) 3.2
Spicer
5052A-5252A (2.3) 3.2
6052A-6052B-6052C
C series (2.5) 3.5
L-LN series (3.5) 4.9

6 Speed
Fuller
RT-906 (3.0) 4.2
Spicer
1062C
L-LN series (3.0) 4.2
CL series (4.6) 6.4

9 Speed
Fuller
RT-9509A-RT-9509B-RT-12509
L-LN series (3.5) 4.9
CL series (4.9) 6.8

10 Speed
Fuller
RT-610 (3.8) 5.2
RT-910-RTO-910
RT-1110-RT-12510
L-LN series (3.5) 4.9
CL series (4.9) 6.8

13 Speed
Fuller
RT-613 (3.5) 4.9
RT/RTO-9513-RT-12513
L-LN series (3.5) 4.9
CL series (4.9) 6.8

16 Speed
Spicer
RP8516-3A
w/Aux (4.7) 6.5
w/P.T.O. add (.6) .6
w/Coupling shaft add (.2) .2
w/Detroit Diesel add (.5) .5
w/Full carpet add (.7) .7

Flywheel, Renew

Includes: R&R transmission.

4 Speed
New Process 435 (3.3) 4.2
Borg Warner T-19 (3.4) 4.2

5 Speed
Clark
280VO-282V-282VHD
285V-285VHD-390/550
397/557 (3.3) 4.2
Fuller
T-905A-T-905B (4.2) 5.3
New Process
542FD-542FL
542FO (3.7) 4.7
Spicer
5052A-5252A (3.7) 4.7
6052A-6052B-6052C
C series (3.9) 5.0
L-LN series (4.9) 6.4

6 Speed
Fuller
RT-906 (4.4) 5.7
Spicer
1062C
L-LN series (4.4) 5.7
CL series (6.0) 7.9

9 Speed
Fuller
RT-9509A-RT-9509B-RT-12509
L-LN series (4.9) 6.4
CL series (6.3) 8.3

10 Speed
Fuller
RT-610 (5.2) 6.6
RT-910-RTO-910
RT-1110-RT-12510
L-LN series (4.9) 6.4
CL series (6.3) 8.3

13 Speed
Fuller
RT-613 (4.9) 6.4
RT/RTO-9513-RT-12513
L-LN series (4.9) 6.4
CL series (6.3) 8.3

16 Speed
Spicer
RP8516-3A
w/Aux (6.1) 7.9
w/P.T.O. add (.6) .6
w/Coupling shaft add (.2) .2
w/Detroit Diesel add (.5) .5
w/Full carpet add (.7) .7
w/Cat V-8 add 1.0

Flywheel Ring Gear, Renew (Flywheel Removed)
All series (.2) .5

LABOR 19 STANDARD TRANSMISSION 19 LABOR

(Factory Time) Chilton Time

Transmission Assembly, R&R

4 Speed
New Process 435 (1.9) 2.7
Borg Warner T-19 (2.0) 2.7

5 Speed
Clark
280VO-282V-282VHD
285V-285VHD-390/550
397/557 (1.9) 2.7
Fuller
T-905A-T-905B (2.8) 3.8
New Process
542FD-542FL
542FO (2.3) 3.2
Spicer
5052A-5252A (2.3) 3.2
6052A-6052B-6052C
C series (2.5) 3.5
L-LN series (3.5) 4.9

6 Speed
Fuller
RT-906 (3.0) 4.2
Spicer
1062C
L-LN series (3.0) 4.2
CL series (4.6) 6.4

9 Speed
Fuller
RT-9509A-RT-9509B-RT-12509
L-LN series (3.5) 4.9
CL series (4.9) 6.8

10 Speed
Fuller
RT-610 (3.8) 5.2
RT-910-RTO-910
RT-1110-RT-12510
L-LN series (3.5) 4.9
CL series (4.9) 6.8

13 Speed
Fuller
RT-613 (3.5) 4.9
RT/RTO-9513-RT-12513
L-LN series (3.5) 4.9
CL series (4.9) 6.8

16 Speed
Spicer
RP8516-3A
w/Aux (4.7) 6.5
w/P.T.O. add (.6) .6
w/Coupling shaft add (.2) .2
w/Detroit Diesel add (.5) .5
w/Full carpet add (.7) .7

Transmission Assembly, R&R and Recondition

Includes: Complete disassembly and assembly of transmission. Inspect and clean all components. Renew parts, gaskets and seals as necessary. Make all normal adjustments. Road test.

4 Speed
New Process 435 (4.2) 5.8
Borg Warner T-19 (4.0) 5.8

5 Speed
Clark
280V-280VO-282VHD
285V (4.3) 5.9
285HD-285VHD (4.6) 6.3
390V/550-397V/557 (4.9) 6.7
Fuller
T-905A-T-905B (9.5) 13.1
New Process
542FD-542FL
542FO (7.1) 9.8
Spicer
5052A-5252A (5.0) 6.9
6052A-6052B-6052C
C series (7.4) 10.3
L-LN series (8.4) 11.6

6 Speed
Fuller
RT-906 (9.7) 14.5
Spicer
1062C
L-LN series (7.9) 11.0
CL series (9.5) 13.3

9 Speed
Fuller
RT-9509A-RT-9509B-RT-12509
L-LN series (11.5) 16.1
CL series (12.9) 18.0

10 Speed
Fuller
RT-610 (15.3) 21.1

LABOR 19 STANDARD TRANSMISSION 19 LABOR

(Factory Time) Chilton Time

RT-910-RTO-910
L-LN series
complete (12.3).................... 16.5
front section (11.1).............. 14.9
rear section (7.1) 9.1
CL series
complete (13.7).................... 19.1
front section (12.5)............... 17.5
rear section (8.5) 11.9
RT-1110-RT-12510 (15.0)........ 20.7

13 Speed
Fuller
RT-613 (12.9) 17.8
RT/RTO-9513-RT-12513
L-LN series
complete (12.9).................... 17.8
front section (10.9).............. 15.0
rear section (6.9) 9.5
CL series
complete (13.8).................... 19.0
front section (11.8).............. 16.2
rear section (7.8) 10.7

16 Speed
Spicer
RP8516-3A
w/Aux (15.3)........................ 23.4
w/P.T.O. add (.6) 6
w/Coupling shaft add (.2) 2
w/Detroit Diesel add (.5).................. .5
w/Full carpet add (.7) 7

Auxiliary Transmission, R&R
All series (1.5)............................ 2.0

Auxiliary Transmission, Renew
Includes: R&R assembly, transfer all necessary components.
All series (3.1)............................ 4.3

Auxiliary Transmission, R&R and Recondition
Includes: Assembly and disassembly. Cleaning and inspection of all parts. Renew or recondition all necessary components. Renew gaskets and seals as required. Road test.
All series
Spicer-7231 (5.1) 7.4
8341 (6.6)............................... 8.8
7041 (6.5)............................... 8.8

LABOR 23 AUTOMATIC TRANSMISSION 23 LABOR

(Factory Time) Chilton Time

ON TRUCK SERVICES

Oil Pressure Test
Allison-MT (1.2).......................... 1.6
Ford-C6 (.9)............................... 1.3

Check Unit for Oil Leaks
Includes: Clean and dry outside of case, run unit to determine point of leak.
All series.................................... .9

Manual and Throttle Linkage, Adjust
Includes: Adjust dashpot, idle speed and accelerator pedal height (if adjustable).
Ford-C6 (.4)................................ .7
Allison (.7).................................. 1.0

Vacuum Modulator, Renew
Ford-C6 (.3)................................ .6
Road test add (.3) 3

Transmission Rear Oil Seal or Bushing, Renew
Ford-C6 (.5)................................ .9

Transmission Oil Filter Element, Renew
Allison-MT (.5) 8
AT (.2) 5

Front Servo, Recondition
Includes: Adjust band.
Ford-C6 (1.0).............................. 1.7

Governor Assembly, Renew (Less Counterweight)
Ford-C6 (1.4).............................. 2.1

Front Band, Adjust
Ford-C6 (.2)................................ .6

Oil Pan or Gasket, Renew
Ford-C6 (.6)................................ 1.0
Allison-MT (1.0).......................... 1.4
Allison-AT (.6)............................. 1.0

Valve Body Assembly, Renew
Includes: R&R oil pan.
Ford-C6 (1.1).............................. 1.7
Allison-MT (1.6).......................... 2.2
Allison-AT (1.6)........................... 2.2

Valve Body Assy., R&R and Recondition
Includes: R&R oil pan and replace filter. Disassemble, clean, inspect, free all valves. Replace parts as required.
Ford-C6 (1.6).............................. 2.6
Allison-MT (3.0).......................... 4.0
Allison-AT (1.9)........................... 2.9

Throttle and Manual Seals and/or Levers, Renew
Includes: R&R oil pan and valve body.
Ford-C6 (.9)................................ 1.3
Allison-MT (1.4).......................... 1.8

SERVICES REQUIRING R&R

Transmission Assembly, R&R
Includes: Drain and refill unit. Adjust linkage and road test.
Ford-C6 (4.1).............................. 5.3
Allison-AT (5.2)........................... 6.4
Allison-MT
C-F series (4.8) 6.0
L series (2.9) 3.7
w/P.T.O. add (.6) 6

Transmission Assembly, R&R and Recondition
Includes: Drain and refill unit, adjust all linkage. Disassemble and assemble complete transmission, inspect all parts. Clean, renew or recondition all components. Renew gaskets and seals as necessary. Road test.
Ford-C6 (8.3).............................. 10.6
Allison-AT (14.9)......................... 19.2
Allison-MT
C-F series (18.2) 24.0
L series (16.3)......................... 22.2
w/P.T.O. add (.6) 6

Torque Converter, R&R and/or Recondition
Includes: R&R transmission assembly. Drain and refill unit. Adjust linkage and road test.
Ford-C6 (4.6).............................. 6.0
Allison-MT
C-F series (6.0) 7.5
L series (4.1)........................... 5.2
w/P.T.O. add (.6) 6

Front Oil Pump, R&R and/or Recondition
Includes: R&R transmission assembly. Drain and refill unit. Adjust linkage and road test.
Ford-C6 (5.3).............................. 6.8
Allison-MT
C-F series (6.8) 8.5
L series (4.9)........................... 6.2
w/P.T.O. add (.6) 6

Rear Oil Pump, R&R and Recondition
Includes: R&R transmission assembly. Drain and refill unit. Adjust linkage and road test.
Allison-MT
C-F series (6.9) 8.7
L series (5.0)........................... 6.4
w/P.T.O. add (.6) 6

Front Pump Oil Seal, Renew
Includes: R&R transmission assembly. Drain and refill unit. Adjust linkage and road test.
Ford-C6 (4.2).............................. 5.5
w/P.T.O. add (.6) 6

LABOR 25 U-JOINTS & DRIVESHAFT 25 LABOR

(Factory Time) Chilton Time

Drive Shaft, R&R or Renew

One piece shaft (.9) 1.1
Splined at coup shaft (.7) 1.0
Yoke at coup shaft (1.2) 1.5
Power divider to
Rearward axle (.6) 1.0

Universal Joint, Recondition or Renew

Does not include R&R drive shaft.
exc below-front (.4) 6
two (.3) 5
three (.3) 5
rear (.3) 5
all (1.1) 1.9
Tandem
500-700-front (.4) 6
two (.3) 5
rear (.3) 5
all (.9) 1.5
750-900-front (.2) 3
rear (.2) 3
all (.4) 6
w/Coupling shaft
front (.2) 3
two (.3) 5
rear (.2) 3
all (.6) 1.0
Inner-trans shaft
front (.6) 8
rear (.4) 6
all (.9) 1.3
Main to aux trans shaft
one (.7) 1.0
both (1.1) 1.5

Center Support Coupling Shaft Bearing, Renew

All series-one (.8) 1.2
each adtnl (.7) 7

Center Support, Renew

All series-one (.8) 1.0
each adtnl (.6) 6

Coupling Shaft, Renew

All series
snap ring type (1.4) 1.8
each adtnl (1.2) 1.2
bolt end type (1.1) 1.5
each adtnl (.9) 9

LABOR 26 REAR AXLE 26 LABOR

(Factory Time) Chilton Time

Rear Axle Housing Cover Gasket, Renew or Reseal

rear tandem (.8) 1.2
forward tandem (1.2) 1.5
Renew output shaft seal
add (.2) 2

Rear Axle Shaft Outer Oil Seal and/or Gasket, Renew

6 hole wheel 8
one (.5) 8
each adtnl (.3) 3
10 hole wheel
one (.6) 9
each adtnl (.5) 5
cast wheel
one (.5) 8
each adtnl (.4) 4

Axle Shaft, Renew

All series-one (.5) 8
two (.8) 1.3

Rear Wheel Bearings, Renew

All series-one axle-one (1.3) 1.9
both (2.2) 3.1
all-both axles (3.9) 5.6

Rear Wheel Bearing Oil Seal, Renew

All series-one axle-one (1.3) 1.8
both (2.2) 3.0
all-both axles (3.9) 5.5

Tandem Drive Line Alignment, Check

Includes: Road test.
All series (1.1) 1.5

Tandem Drive Line Alignment, Check and Adjust

Includes: Alignment of engine, transmission, drive shafts and both axles. Road test.
All series (4.5) 5.5

Pinion Shaft Oil Seal, Renew

All series
Rockwell-front (1.0) 1.5
Rockwell-rear (1.8) 2.7
Eaton-front (1.2) 1.8
Eaton-rear (1.8) 2.7

Differential Carrier Assy., Remove and Install

Includes: Drain and refill axle, renew gasket.
Eaton
single speed (3.3) 4.6
two speed (3.5) 4.9
Dana-Spicer
two speed (3.5) 4.9
Rockwell
single speed (3.0) 4.2
Tandem Eaton
single speed-single reduction
DS341
forward (4.2) 5.9
rearward (3.8) 5.3
DS381-DS460P
forward (5.0) 7.0
rearward (3.8) 5.3
Tandem Eaton
single speed-double reduction
DP381-DP460P
forward (5.0) 7.0
rearward (3.8) 5.3
Tandem Eaton
two speed-single reduction
DT341
forward (4.4) 6.1
rearward (4.0) 5.6
Tandem Rockwell
single speed-single reduction
SL-100
forward (4.2) 5.9
rearward (3.8) 5.3
SQ-100-SSHD-SQHP
forward (5.0) 7.0
rearward (3.8) 5.3

Differential Carrier Assembly, R&R and Recondition

Includes: Drain and refill unit. R&R all normal interfering parts. Disassemble and assemble complete unit. Inspect, clean, renew or recondition all components. Road test.
Eaton
single speed (9.1) 12.8
two speed (9.7) 13.6
Dana-Spicer
two speed (9.7) 13.6
Rockwell
single speed (8.4) 11.8
Tandem Eaton
DS341
forward (11.0) 15.5
rearward (9.6) 13.5
DS381-DS460P
forward (11.8) 16.6
rearward (9.6) 13.5
Tandem Eaton
single speed-double reduction
DP381-DP460P
forward (10.1) 14.2
rearward (8.4) 11.8
Tandem Eaton
two speed-single reduction
DT341
forward (11.6) 16.3
rearward (10.2) 14.3
Tandem Rockwell
single speed-single reduction
SL-100
forward (10.6) 14.9
rearward (8.9) 12.5
SQ-100-SSHD-SQHP
forward (11.4) 16.0
rearward (8.9) 12.5
Renew wheel brgs add
one side (.7) 7
both sides (1.2) 1.2

Electric Shift Assembly, Renew

Eaton-two spd (.4) 6

Electric Shift Assembly, R&R and Recondition

Eaton-two spd (1.1) 1.7

Two Speed Axle Switch, Renew

All series (.4) 6

Two Speed Axle Shift Motor, Renew

All series (.7) 1.0

Power Divider Lockout Cylinder Assembly, Renew

tandem (.6) 9

Power Divider Lockout Cylinder Diaphragm, Renew

tandem (.7) 1.1

LABOR 27 REAR SUSPENSION 27 LABOR

(Factory Time)	Chilton Time
Rear Spring, R&R or Renew	
SINGLE AXLE	
one (1.6)	2.2
both (2.9)	4.0
TANDEM AXLE	
Hendrickson	
one (2.3)	3.2
both (4.2)	5.8
Neway	
one (1.1)	1.5
both (1.9)	2.6
Reyco	
1 axle	
one (1.8)	2.5
both (3.2)	4.4
2 axles	
all (6.1)	8.5
Renew spring bushings add, each (.3)	.3
Renew aux spring leaf add (.6)	.6
Renew aux tie bolt add (.4)	.4
Renew spring leaf or tie bolt add-each side (.7)	7
Rear Spring Shackle and/or Bushings, Renew	
All series	
one-one side (.9)	1.3
one-both sides (1.6)	2.4
Rear Spring Front Shackle Bolt and/or Bushing, Renew	
All series	
one (1.0)	1.5
two (1.7)	2.7
Auxiliary Spring, R&R or Renew	
All series (1.1)	1.5
Auxiliary Spring Leaf, Renew	
All series (1.8)	2.6
Tandem Suspension Support Beam, Renew	
Hendricson	
one (6.5)	8.2
both (10.7)	13.4
Reyco	
one (1.0)	1.4
both (1.7)	2.5
Tandem Suspension Torque Arm Assembly, Renew	
All series-front (1.7)	2.4
rear (1.1)	1.6
both (2.6)	3.5
Center Support Beam Bushings and/or Bar, Renew	
Hendrickson	
tandem axle (3.2)	5.0
Tandem Support Beam Bushings, Renew	
Hendrickson	
tandem axle	
one side (3.5)	5.5
both sides (6.1)	10.0
Tandem Suspension Load Insulators, Renew	
Hendrickson	
one (2.6)	3.8
two (3.9)	5.8
Renew bushings or saddle, add-each (.4)	.5

LABOR 28 AIR CONDITIONING 28 LABOR

(Factory Time)	Chilton Time
Drain, Evacuate and Recharge System	
Includes: Check for leaks.	
All series (.7)	1.5
Note: Models equipped with 2 or more evaporators, require additional time to evacuate and charge the system. Labor charges for operations which require evacuation and recharging the system should be adjusted accordingly.	
Pressure Test System	
All series	.9
Compressor Assembly, Renew	
Includes: Evacuate and charge system.	
F series (1.5)	2.6
L series (1.5)	2.6
CL series (2.2)	3.3
Compressor Shaft Seal Kit, Renew	
Includes: Evacuate and charge system.	
F series (1.2)	2.3
L series (1.4)	2.5
CL series (1.6)	2.7
Compressor Valve Plate Kit, Renew	
Includes: Evacuate and charge system.	
F series (1.5)	2.6
L series (1.6)	2.7
CL series (2.2)	3.3
Compressor Clutch Pulley Bearing, Renew	
CL series (1.0)	1.4
All other series (.6)	1.0
Compressor Clutch Brush Assy., Renew	
L series (.6)	1.0
A.C. Clutch Pressure Switch Assy., Renew	
F series (.2)	.3
Accumulator Assy., Renew	
Includes: Evacuate and charge system.	
F series (1.0)	1.5
Orifice Valve, Renew	
Includes: Evacuate and charge system.	
F series (.9)	1.5
Evaporator Thermostatic Switch, Renew	
All series (.5)	.9
Condenser Assembly, Renew	
Includes: Evacuate and charge system.	
F series (1.4)	2.5
L series (1.3)	2.5
CL series (1.2)	2.3
Expansion Valve, Renew	
Includes: Evacuate and charge system.	
L series (1.4)	2.5
CL series (1.3)	2.4
Evaporator Core, Renew	
Includes: Evacuate and charge system.	
F series (1.4)	2.6
L-LN series (1.4)	2.6
CL series (1.6)	3.0
Dehydrator-Receiver Tank, Renew	
Includes: Evacuate and charge system.	
L series (1.1)	2.1
CL series (.9)	2.0
A.C. Blower Motor, Renew	
F series (.4)	.7
L-LN series (.6)	1.0
CL series (.5)	1.0
A.C. Blower Motor Switch, Renew	
CL series (.6)	1.0
City Deliv (.4)	.7
Line Haul (.5)	.8
Air Conditioning Hoses, Renew	
Includes: Evacuate and charge system.	
All series-one (1.2)	2.3
Fabricate hose add (.2)	.3

LABOR 30 HEAD & PARKING LAMPS 30 LABOR

(Factory Time)	Chilton Time
Aim Headlamps	
All series	.6
Headlamp Sealed Beam Bulb, Renew	
All series-each (.3)	.3
Turn Signal Lamp Assy., Renew	
F series (.3)	.5
C series (.4)	.6
L series (.4)	.6
CL series (.3)	.5
Exterior Bulb, Renew	
All series-each (.3)	4
Reflector, Renew	
All series-each	.2

LABOR 31 WINDSHIELD WIPER & SPEEDOMETER 31 LABOR

(Factory Time)	Chilton Time
Windshield Wiper Motor, Renew	
F series (.9)	1.2
C series-each (.6)	1.1
L series-elec (.6)	1.0
air (.6)	1.1
CL series (.5)	1.0
Windshield Wiper Switch, Renew	
F series (.4)	.7
C series (.4)	.9
L series (.3)	.7
CL series (.7)	1.0
Windshield Washer Pump, Renew	
All series (.3)	.5
Wiper Pivot, Renew	
F series-each (.9)	1.1
C series (.4)	1.0
L series-each (.6)	.9
Speedometer Head, R&R or Renew	
F series (.6)	1.0
C series (.7)	1.4
L-LN series (.6)	1.2
CL series (.4)	.9
Speedometer Cable and Casing, Renew	
F series	
one piece (.6)	1.1
upper (.4)	.7
lower (.4)	.7
C series	
one piece (.8)	1.5
upper (.4)	.7
lower (.3)	.6
mid cable (.3)	.3
L-LN series-upper (.5)	.9
lower (.4)	.7
CL series-upper (.4)	.7
lower (.7)	1.3
Tachometer, Renew	
F series (.6)	1.1
C series (.6)	1.1
L-LN series (.6)	1.1
CL series (.4)	.8
Tachometer Cable and Casing, Renew	
F series (.5)	1.0
C series (.7)	1.4
L-LN series-upper (.3)	.7
lower (.3)	.6
CL series-upper (.4)	.8
lower (.5)	1.0

LABOR 32 LIGHT SWITCHES & WIRING 32 LABOR

(Factory Time)	Chilton Time
Headlamp Switch, Renew	
F series (.4)	.6
C series (.5)	.8
L series (.4)	.6
CL series (.4)	.6
Headlamp Dimmer Switch, Renew	
All series (.3)	.6
Turn Signal Switch Assy., Renew	
F series (.4)	.8
C series (.4)	.8
L-LN series (.6)	1.1
CL series(.4)	.8
Turn Signal or Hazard Flasher, Renew	
All series (.3)	.5
Stop Light Switch, Renew	
F series-wo/Air (.4)	.7
w/Air (.3)	.6
C series-wo/Air (.5)	.7
w/Air (.3)	.6
L series (.3)	.6
CL series (.3)	.6
Back-Up Light Switch, Renew	
All series (.3)	.5
Marker Light or Blinker Emergency Flasher Switch Assy., Renew	
All series (.4)	.6
Horns, Renew	
All series-each (.3)	.5

GMC Trucks—Series 4500-9500

GROUP INDEX

ALPHABETICAL INDEX

LABOR 1 TUNE UP 1 LABOR

(Factory Time) Chilton Time

GASOLINE ENGINES

Compression Test

Six(.6) 9
V-8(.8) 1.1

Engine Tune Up, Minor

Includes: Clean or renew spark plugs. Renew ignition points and condenser, set ignition timing. Adjust carburetor idle speed and mixture. Service air cleaner. Clean or renew fuel filters.

Six(1.3) 1.8
V-8(2.3) 2.8

Engine Tune Up, Major

Includes: Clean or renew spark plugs. Check compression. Test battery and clean terminals. Renew and adjust distributor points and condenser. Check distributor cap and rotor. Adjust ignition timing and test coil. Tighten manifold bolts, adjust carburetor idle speed and mixture. Inspect and tighten all hose connections. Adjust fan belts. Service air cleaner. Clean or renew fuel filters. Clean or renew PCV valve. Road test.

Six(2.2) 3.0
V-8(3.0) 3.9

DIESEL ENGINES

Compression Test

Detroit Diesel

6-71 (3.0) 3.8
6V-53, 6V-71 (2.9) 3.7
8V-71 (4.1) 5.2
12V-71 (6.0) 7.5

(Factory Time) Chilton Time

Engine Tune Up, Minor

Includes: Test batteries and clean and tighten terminals. Check and adjust engine idle speed and throttle linkage. Change engine oil. Clean or renew oil, air, fuel and water filters. Tighten radiator hoses and manifold bolts. Check valve lash and adjust tappets. R&R and test injectors. Does not include compression test or injector timing.

Detroit Diesel

6-71 .... 4.4
6V-53, 6V-71 .... 4.5
8V-71 .... 5.0
12V-71 .... 6.0

Engine Tune Up, Major

Includes: Test batteries and clean and tighten terminals. Check and adjust engine idle speed and throttle linkage. Adjust inject or timing and injectors. Steam clean engine. Clean or renew air, oil, fuel and water filters. Change engine oil. Check and lubricate shutters. Clean injectors and fuel connections. Inspect for oil, water and fuel leaks. Drain sediment from fuel tanks. Tighten intake manifold, exhaust manifold, turbocharger, blower and engine mounting bolts. Clean fuel pump screen. Adjust crossheads and valves. Check crankshaft end clearance. Adjust fan belts. Tighten and inspect hose connections. Road test.

Does not include compression test.

Detroit Diesel

6-71 .... 10.8
6V-53, 6V-71 .... 11.2
8V-71 .... 12.0
12V-71 .... 13.0

LABOR 2 IGNITION SYSTEM 2 LABOR

(Factory Time) Chilton Time

Spark Plugs, Renew

Six(.3) 6
V-8(.5) 9

Ignition Timing, Reset

All series (.3) 4

Distributor, R&R or Renew

Includes: Reset ignition timing.

Six(.6) 8
V-8–exc below (.6) 1.0
Tilt cab (.8) 1.2

Distributor (Conventional), R&R and Recondition

Includes: Reset ignition timing.

Six(1.0) 1.7
V-8–exc below (1.0) *1.7
Tilt cab (1.3) *1.9
*w/Spinner Type Gov add (1.0) 1.0

(Factory Time) Chilton Time

Distributor (H.E.I.), R&R and Recondition

Six(1.1) 1.7
V-8–exc below (1.1) 1.7
Tilt cab (1.2) 1.9

Distributor Cap and/or Rotor, Renew

Six (.2) 4
V-8 (.4) 5

Distributor Module (H.E.I.), Renew

All series (.5) 6

Ignition Coil, Renew

All series (.5) 6

Vacuum Control Unit, Renew

Includes: Reset ignition timing.

Six (.3) 6
V-8–exc below (.6) 9
Tilt cab (.9) 1.1

(Factory Time) Chilton Time

Ignition Cables, Renew

Six(.3) 6
V-8 (.6) 8

Ignition Switch, Renew

All series (.6) 8

Distributor Points and Condenser, Renew

Includes: Adjust dwell and timing.

Six(.4) 7
V-8 (.5) 8

Distributor Capacitor and/or Module Wiring Harness, Renew

All series (.5) 6

Distributor Pick-Up Coil and/or Pole Piece, Renew

All series (.8) 1.1

LABOR 3 FUEL SYSTEM 3 LABOR

(Factory Time) Chilton Time

GASOLINE ENGINES

Fuel Pump, Test

Includes: Disconnect line at carburetor, attach pressure gauge.

All series 3

(Factory Time) Chilton Time

Carburetor, Adjust (On Truck)

All series
Slow & Fast Idle (.3) 4
Idle Mixture (.6) 8

(Factory Time) Chilton Time

Carburetor, R&R or Renew

Includes: All necessary adjustments. Service air cleaner.

1 bbl (.5) 7
2 bbl (.6) 8
4 bbl (.8) 1.2

(Factory Time) Chilton Time

Carburetor, R&R and Recondition

Includes: All necessary adjustments. Service air cleaner.

1 bbl (1.4) 2.1
2 bbl (1.5) 2.1
4 bbl exc below (1.7) 2.4
Holley (4.3) 5.0

Governor, Renew (Spinner Type)

1 bbl (.7) 1.0
2 bbl (.8) 1.1
4 bbl (.9) 1.2

Governor and Throttle Body, R&R and Recondition (Spinner Type)

Does not include overhaul carburetor.

1 bbl (1.3) 1.9
2 bbl (1.5) 2.1
4 bbl (1.7) 2.3

Electronic Governor, Renew

Does not include R&R carburetor.

All series (.5) 7

Electronic Governor, R&R and Recondition

Does not include R&R carburetor.

All series (.9) 1.3

Solenoid Control Valve, Renew

All series (.2) 3

Electronic Governor Controller, Renew

All series (.2) 3

Fuel Pump, Renew

Pump on engine
exc below (.4) 8
Tilt cab V-8 (.6) *1.1
*w/Air comp add (.2) 2
Pump in tank
All series-each (.6) 1.0

Fuel Tank, Renew

Series 4500-7000
frame mounted (1.1) 1.6
cab mounted (.9) 1.5
step tank (1.2) 1.6
Tilt cab (.7) 1.2

Series 8000-9000
frame mounted (1.3) 1.7
cab mounted (1.2) 1.7
step tank (1.2) 1.7

Fuel Gauge (Tank), Renew

Series 4500-7000
frame mounted (.6) 1.0
step tank (.4) 7
cab mounted (.4) 7
Tilt cab (.4) 7

Series 8000-9000
frame mounted (.3) 7
cab mounted (.3) 7
step tank (.7) 1.1

Fuel Gauge (Dash), Renew

All series-exc below (.4) 9
Tilt cab (.6) 1.2
Brigadier (.5) 9
General (.2) 4

(Factory Time) Chilton Time

Intake Manifold Gaskets, Renew

Includes: R&R all interfering parts.

Six–conventional (2.0) 3.0
Tilt cab (1.7) 2.2
w/P.S. add (.4) 4
w/AIR add (.1) 1
Renew manif add 5

V-8–307, 350 engs
conventional (2.0) 2.8
V-8–366, 427, 454 engs
conventional (3.0) 3.8
Tilt cab (3.9) 4.5

w/A.C. add
307-350 engs
w/A.I.R. (.4) 4
307-350 engs
wo/A.I.R. (1.0) 1.0
366-427 engs
w/A.C. (1.1) 1.1
w/Air comp add (.6) 6
Renew manif add (.3) 5

Intake and Exhaust Manifold Gaskets, Renew

Six–conv cab (1.6) 2.1
Tilt cab (1.7) 2.2
w/P.S. add (.4) 4
w/AIR add (.1) 1

DIESEL ENGINES

Air Cleaner Assembly, R&R and Clean or Renew

All series (.5) 7

Engine Idle Speed, Adjust (Governor)

Detroit (.9) 1.2

Injection Timing, Adjust

Isuzu Diesel
All series (.5) 9
Deutz Diesel
All series (.8) 1.2
Detroit Diesel
conv (1.1) 1.5
Tilt cab (2.0) 2.5

High Pressure Fuel Lines, Renew

Isuzu Diesel
one (.3) 5
each adtnl (.2) 3
all (.7) 1.2

Injectors, Renew

Includes: R&R all normal interfering parts. Clean and adjust all parts.

Isuzu & Deutz Diesel
one (.5) 8
each adtnl (.2) 3
all (1.6) 2.2
Renew nozzles add,
each (.2) 2

Detroit Diesel
6-71-one (.4) 7
all (1.8) 2.5
6V-53, 6V-71-one (.4) 7
all (1.9) 1.3
8V-71-one (.4) 7
all (2.5) 3.3
12V-71-one (.4) 7
all (3.6) 4.8
R&R control island add (.8) 8

(Factory Time) Chilton Time

Injectors, R&R and Recondition

Includes: R&R all normal interfering parts. Make all required adjustments and tests.

Detroit Diesel
6-71-one (1.2) 1.7
all (6.1) 7.8
6V-53, 6V-71-one (1.2) 1.7
all (6.2) 7.9
8V-71-one (1.2) 1.7
all (8.2) 10.4
12V-71-one (1.2) 1.7
all (11.8) 14.3
R&R control island add (.8) 8

Fuel Injection Pump, Renew

Includes: R&R all normal interfering parts. Adjust injection timing and governor.

Isuzu Diesel
All series (2.8) 3.9
Deutz Diesel
All series (2.7) 3.8
Detroit Diesel
exc below (1.0) 1.4
6V-53, 12V-71 (1.5) 1.6
R&R floor mat add (.4) 4

Turbocharger Assy., Renew

Isuzu Diesel
All series (.6) 1.0
Deutz Diesel
All series (1.5) 2.2

Blower Assembly, R&R or Renew

Includes: R&R all interfering parts. Drain and refill radiator. Make all required adjustments.

Detroit Diesel
exc below (6.6) 8.5
6-71 (4.5) 5.9
12V-71-one (6.8) 8.9
two (8.3) 10.6

Blower Assembly, R&R and Recondition.

Includes: R&R all interfering parts. Drain and refill radiator. Clean and inspect all parts, replace as necessary. Sand rotors and housing. Make all required adjustments.

Detroit Diesel
exc below (10.1) 13.0
6-71 (8.0) 10.0
12V-71-one (10.3) 13.3
two (15.3) 19.7

Fuel Filter, Renew

Isuzu Diesel
All series (.4) 6
Deutz Diesel
All series (.4) 6
Detroit Diesel
each (.5) 8

Fuel Pump, Renew

Isuzu Diesel
All series-primary (.5) 8
Deutz Diesel
All series (.5) 7

Intake Manifold and/or Gasket, Renew

Isuzu Diesel
All series (1.1) 1.7
Deutz Diesel
All series (.9) 1.4

LABOR 3A EMISSION CONTROLS 3A LABOR

(Factory Time) — Chilton Time

Positive Crankcase Ventilation Valve, Renew
Six & V-8 (.2) 3

AIR INJECTOR REACTOR TYPE

Air Pump, R&R
All series (.4) 5

Air Pump Relief Valve, Renew
All series (.6) 7

Reactor Valve, Renew
All series (.2) 4

Centrifugal Filter, Renew
All series (.5) 6

Diverter Valve, Renew
All series (.3) 4

Air Check Valve, Renew
All series-one (.2) 3

CONTROLLED COMBUSTION TYPE

Air Cleaner Vacuum Motor, Renew
All series (.2) 4

Air Cleaner Temperature Sensor, Renew
All series (.2) 3

Charcoal Canister, Renew
All series (.2) 4

LABOR 4 ALTERNATOR AND REGULATOR 4 LABOR

(Factory Time) — Chilton Time

Alternator Circuits Test
Includes: Test battery, regulator and alternator output.
All series 6
each adtnl battery (.2) 2

Alternator, R&R or Renew
Gasoline Engines
All series (.6) 8
Diesel Engines
Isuzu Diesel (.5) 8
Deutz Diesel (1.0) 1.4
Detroit Diesel
8.2L
w/vac brks (.8) 1.1
w/air brks (.6) 9
6V-53 (.8) 1.2
6-71 (.6) 8
6V-92 (.9) 1.3
8V-71-8V-92 (.9) 1.3
Cummins Diesel
Astro (1.6) 2.0
Brigadier (.9) 1.3
General (.7) 1.0
Caterpillar Diesel
All series (.7) 1.0
Recond alter add
Delco SI 27 (.7) 1.0
Delco SI 25 (1.7) 2.5
Delco SI 30 (1.3) 2.0
Leece Neville (1.3) 2.0

Alternator Regulator, Test and Renew
Gasoline Engines
Delco (1.0) 1.4
Leece Neville (.3) 6
Diesel Engines
Isuzu Diesel (.8) 1.2
Deutz Diesel (.9) 1.3
Detroit Diesel
All series (.4) 6
Cummins Diesel
Astro (2.0) 2.8
Brigadier (1.2) 1.8
General (1.1) 1.6
Caterpillar Diesel
All series (1.1) 1.6

LABOR 5 STARTING SYSTEM 5 LABOR

(Factory Time) — Chilton Time

Starter Draw Test (On Truck)
All series (.3) 3

Starter, R&R or Renew

Gasoline Engines
All series (.4) 6
Renew solenoid add (.2) 3
Renew drive assy add (.4) 5
Recond motor add (1.2) 1.5
Renew field coils add (.3) 5
Recond armature add (.9) 1.0

Diesel Engines
Isuzu Diesel
All series (.5) 8
Deutz Diesel (1.2) 1.7
Detroit Diesel
8.2L (1.1) 1.6
6V-53 (1.1) 1.6
6-71-exc below (1.6) 2.3
Brigadier (2.5) 3.5
8V-71
Astro (1.6) 2.3
Brigadier (2.4) 3.4
General (1.9) 2.7
6V92-exc below (1.9) 2.7
Astro (2.3) 3.3
8V-92
Astro (1.8) 2.5
General (1.3) 1.8
Cummins Diesel
Astro (1.2) 1.7
Brigadier (1.7) 2.4
General (.8) 1.2
Caterpillar Diesel
3208 (2.0) 2.9
3406 (1.1) 1.6
Renew solenoid add (.3) 4
Renew drive assy add (.3) 4
Recond motor add (1.6) 2.5
Recond armature add (1.0) 1.2
Renew field coils add (.4) 5

Battery Cables, Renew
Series 4500-7000 pos (.3) 4
neg (.2) 4
Series 8000-9000-exc below
pos (.4) 5
neg (.3) 4
General-pos (.6) 8
neg (.5) 7

LABOR 6 BRAKE SYSTEM 6 LABOR

(Factory Time) — Chilton Time

Brakes Adjust, Minor
Includes: Adjust brake shoes at all wheels. Fill master cylinder. R&R one front drum.
Series 4500-7000
exc below (.7) 7
tandem (1.0) 1.0
Series 8000-9000
exc below (.9) 9
tandem (1.2) 1.2

Pressure Bleed Brakes
All models (.4) 6
w/Tandem axle add (.3) 3
w/Booster add (.3) 3

Front Brake Drum, Renew (One)
Includes: R&R wheels and adjust bearings and brake shoes.

Front
Series 4500-7000
hydraulic (.7) 1.0
front drive axle (2.0) 2.7
air brakes
cast whl (1.2) 1.6
10 stud disc (1.4) 1.9
8 stud disc whl (1.8) 2.4

(Factory Time)	Chilton Time
Series 8000-9000	
exc below (1.5)	2.0
10 stud whls (1.8)	2.5

Rear Brake Drum, Renew (One)

(Factory Time)	Chilton Time
Series 4500-7000	
10 stud-corp (.7)	1.0
cast spoke (1.7)	2.2
10 stud-Budd (2.1)	2.8
Series 8000-9000	
6 stud-Budd (.8)	1.1
10 stud-Budd (1.3)	1.7
cast spoke (1.6)	2.0
Berg air brake add (.3)	.3
Eaton single spd axle add (.8)	.8

Stop Light Switch, Renew

(Factory Time)	Chilton Time
All series-each-exc. below (.4)	.6
Astro (.9)	1.2
Steel Tilt Cab (1.1)	1.5

Brake Shoes, Renew

Includes: R&R wheel and drum assemblies. Clean and inspect all parts. Install new or exchange shoes, adjust brakes. Road test.

(Factory Time)	Chilton Time
Front (both wheels)	
Series 4500-7000	
hydraulic	
conv (1.3)	2.0
Tilt cab (Isuzu) (2.9)	3.9
front drive axle (3.2)	4.3
air (1.6)	2.1
Series 8000-9000 (2.0)	3.0
Rear (both wheels)	
Series 4500-7000	
single axle	
conv (2.2)	4.0
Tilt cab (Isuzu) (4.4)	5.9
tandem axle (6.4)	7.5
Series 8000-9000	
single axle (3.2)	4.0
tandem axle (6.4)	7.5
All Wheels	
Series 4500-7000	
Single axle	
hydraulic	5.0
conv	5.0
Tilt cab (Isuzu)	9.5
front drive axle	7.5
air	6.0
Tandem axle	9.5
Series 8000-9000	
Single axle	6.0
Tandem axle	9.5
Bleed brakes add	
single axle (.3)	.3
tandem axle (.6)	.6
w/Booster add (.6)	.6
w/Berg parking brake add (.3)	.3

DISC BRAKES

Disc Brake Pads, Renew

Includes: Install new disc brake pads only.

(Factory Time)	Chilton Time
Series 4500-7000	
front (.8)	1.1
rear (1.0)	1.5
all four wheels	2.5
Series 8000-9000	
front (1.6)	2.1
rear (2.3)	3.0
all four wheels	5.0
Resurface disc rotor, add-each	.9

Caliper Assembly, Renew

Includes: Renew brake pads if necessary. Bleed brake system.

(Factory Time)	Chilton Time
Series 4500-7000	
front-one (.5)	.8
both (.9)	1.4
rear-one (.8)	1.1
both (1.5)	2.0
Series 8000-9000	
front-one (1.1)	1.5
both (2.0)	2.8
rear-one (1.6)	2.1
both (3.0)	4.0

Caliper Assy., R&R and Recondition

Includes: Renew brake pads if necessary. Recondition caliper and bleed brake system.

(Factory Time)	Chilton Time
Series 4500-7000	
front-one (1.3)	1.6
both (2.5)	3.0
rear-one (1.6)	1.9
both (3.1)	3.6
Series 8000-9000	
front-one (3.2)	4.2
both (6.2)	8.0
rear-one (3.7)	4.8
both (7.2)	9.0

Disc Brake Rotor, Renew

Includes: Clean and repack or renew bearings and seals.

(Factory Time)	Chilton Time
Series 4500-7000	
front-one (1.2)	1.6
both (2.3)	3.1
rear-one (1.6)	2.1
both (3.1)	4.1
Series 8000-9000	
front-one (1.6)	2.1
both (2.9)	4.0
rear-one (2.9)	3.8
both (5.6)	7.4

COMBINATIONS

Add to Brakes Renew

(Factory Time)	Chilton Time
RENEW WHEEL CYLINDER	
Each	.3
RECONDITION WHEEL CYLINDER	
Each	.4
MASTER CYLINDER, RENEW	
All series (.5)	.9
MASTER CYLINDER, RECONDITION	
Includes: Hone cylinder.	
One side (.8)	1.1
Both sides (1.1)	1.7
FRONT WHEEL BEARINGS, CLEAN AND REPACK	
Drum brakes (.5)	.7
RENEW FRONT WHEEL BEARINGS (ONE WHEEL)	
Drum brakes (.3)	.4
RENEW BRAKE AIR CHAMBER	
Each (.3)	.5
RELINE BRAKE SHOES	
Front axle set (.5)	.6
Rear axle set (.5)	.6
RESURFACE BRAKE DRUM	
Front-each (.5)	.8
Rear-each (.6)	.9
RENEW REAR WHEEL OIL SEAL	
Each (.1)	.1
RENEW INNER REAR WHEEL GREASE SEALS (ONE SIDE)	
All series (.8)	1.1
REBUILD CALIPER ASSEMBLY	
Series 4500-7000-each	.8
Series 8000-9000-each	2.1

BRAKE HYDRAULIC SYSTEM

Wheel Cylinders, Renew

Includes: R&R wheel and drum assembly. Clean and inspect parts. Bleed lines and road test.

(Factory Time)	Chilton Time
Front	
Series 4500-7000	
Conv.	
one (.7)	1.0
both (1.4)	1.9
Tilt cab (Isuzu)	
one (2.1)	2.8
both (4.0)	5.4
front drive axle	
one (1.9)	2.5
both (3.6)	4.8
Series 8000-9000	
one (1.7)	2.0
both (2.9)	3.5
Rear	
Series 4500-7000	
Conv.	
one (1.5)	2.0
both (2.8)	3.7
Tilt cab (Isuzu)	
one (2.8)	3.7
both (5.1)	6.8
Series 8000-9000	
one (1.9)	2.2
both-same axle (3.3)	4.2
all	8.0
w/Eaton single spd axle add (.8)	.8
w/Booster add (.3)	.3
w/Two cyl type, second cyl add (.2)	.2

Wheel Cylinder, R&R and Recondition

Includes: R&R wheel and drum assembly. Clean and inspect all parts. Hone cylinders. Bleed lines and road test.

(Factory Time)	Chilton Time
Front	
Series 4500-7000	
Conv.	
one (.7)	1.4
both (1.4)	2.7
Tilt cab (Isuzu)	
one (2.1)	3.2
both (4.0)	6.2
front drive axle	
one (1.9)	2.6
both (3.6)	5.0
Series 8000-9000	
one (1.9)	2.3
both (3.3)	4.1
Rear	
Series 4500-7000	
Conv.	
one (1.5)	2.4
both (2.8)	4.5
Tilt cab (Isuzu)	
one (2.8)	4.1
both (5.1)	7.6
Series 8000-9000	
exc below-one (2.2)	2.5
both (3.9)	4.8
tandem-one (2.2)	2.5
all	9.2
w/Eaton single spd axle add (.8)	.8
w/Booster add (.3)	.3
w/Two cyl type, second cyl add (.2)	.3

LABOR 6 BRAKE SYSTEM 6 LABOR

(Factory Time)	Chilton Time
Brake Hose, Renew	
Includes: Bleed lines.	
Series 4500-7000	
exc below (.5)	.7
booster (.6)	.8
tandem (.7)	.9
additional (.3)	.3
Series 8000-9000	
one (.6)	.8
each adtnl (.3)	.3
Master Cylinder, Renew	
Includes: Bleed complete system. Adjust pedal free play.	
Series 4500-7000	
exc below (.8)	1.0
booster (1.1)	1.5
tandem (1.3)	1.8
Series 8000-9000	
conv-single cyl (.6)	.9
dual cyl (.9)	1.2
Tilt cab (.6)	.9
Master Cylinder, R&R and Recondition	
Includes: Hone cylinder. Adjust pedal free play.	
Series 4500-7000	
single cyl (.8)	1.3
dual cyl (1.1)	1.6
booster (1.6)	2.0
tandem (1.8)	2.3
Series 8000-9000	
conv single cyl (.9)	1.3
dual cyl (1.2)	1.6
Tilt cab (.9)	1.3
Bleed system-add	
wo/Booster or Tandem	.3
w/Booster	.4
w/Tandem	.6

POWER BRAKES

(Factory Time)	Chilton Time
Vacuum Power Brake Cylinder, R&R or Renew	
Series 4500-7000 (1.0)	1.4
Vacuum Power Brake Cylinder, R&R and Recondition	
Series 4500-7000 (2.1)	3.0
Vacuum Power Brake Booster, R&R or Renew	
Series 4500-7000 (.8)	1.1
Vacuum Power Brake Booster, R&R and Recondition	
Series 4500-7000 (1.8)	2.5
Electro-Hydraulic Pump, Renew	
All series (.6)	.9
Electro-Hydraulic Pump Sensor, Renew	
All series (.2)	.3
Electro-Hydraulic Pump Flow Control Switch, Renew	
All series (.3)	.4
Hydraulic Brake Booster Pump, R&R or Renew	
Includes: Bleed system.	
Series 4500-7000	
Gas Engines	
Six (.7)	1.2
V-8 (.7)	1.2
Diesel Engines	
Detroit 8.2L	
wo/Tilt hood (1.3)	2.0
w/Tilt hood (1.1)	1.8
Caterpillar 3208 (1.0)	1.5
Renew pump seals add (.3)	.4
Recond pump add (1.0)	1.0
Hydraulic Power Brake Cylinder Assy., R&R or Renew	
Includes: Bleed system.	
Series 4500-7000 (.6)	1.0
Hydraulic Power Brake Cylinder Assy., R&R and Recondition	
Includes: Bleed system.	
Series 4500-7000 (1.1)	1.8

AIR BRAKES

(Factory Time)	Chilton Time
Air Compressor Belts, Renew	
All series each (.3)	.4
Air Pressure Gauge, Renew	
All series (.5)	.7
Brake Application (Treadle) Valve, Renew	
Series 4500-7000	
conv cab (1.2)	1.9
Tilt cab (Isuzu) (2.0)	2.6
Series 8000-9000	
wo/WHEEL LOCK CONTROL	
conv cab and steel tilt cabs (.8)	1.0
alum tilt cab (1.1)	1.5
w/WHEEL LOCK CONTROL	
General (1.6)	2.0
All others (1.2)	1.6
w/Berg parking brake add (.3)	.3
Brake Application (Treadle) Valve, R&R and Recondition	
Series 4500-7000	
conv cab (2.0)	3.0
Tilt cab (Isuzu) (2.8)	3.7
Series 8000-9000	
wo/WHEEL LOCK CONTROL	
conv and steel tilt cabs (1.6)	2.0
alum tilt cabs (1.9)	2.5
w/WHEEL LOCK CONTROL	
General (1.8)	2.4
All others (2.0)	2.7
w/Berg parking brake add (.3)	.3
Brake Safety Valve, Renew	
All series (.2)	.3
Brake Quick Release Valve, Renew	
Series 4500-7000 (.5)	.8
Series 8000-9000 (.7)	.9
Recond valve add (.4)	.6
R&R step tank add (1.1)	1.1
Brake Relay Valve, Renew	
Series 4500-7000 (.6)	.9
Series 8000-9000 (.7)	1.0
w/Wheel lock control (1.3)	1.7
Recond valve add (.4)	.6
Air Tank, Renew	
Series 4500-7000	
main tank (wet)	
conv cab (1.0)	1.4
tilt cab (1.3)	1.7
front service (.7)	1.1
rear service (.6)	1.0
dual reservoir (1.4)	1.8
Series 8000-9000	
main tank (1.0)	1.4
front supply tank	
General (1.2)	1.6
All others-each (.9)	1.3
Air Governor, Renew	
All series (.3)	.6
Air Governor, R&R and Recondition	
All series (.7)	1.2
Air Chamber, R&R or Renew	
Front	
All series-one (.4)	.6
both (.6)	1.0
Rear per axle	
Series 4500-7000-one (.6)	.8
both (1.1)	1.5
Series 8000-9000	
exc below-one (.4)	.6
both (.7)	1.0
Stop Master-Fail Safe-one	
inner chamber (3.1)	4.0
outer chamber (.8)	1.0
complete (4.0)	5.0
w/Berg brake add (.3)	.3
Renew slack adjuster add (.2)	.3
Recondition air chamber add	.4
Air Strainer, Clean or Renew	
All series (.2)	.3
Air Compressor, R&R or Renew	
Gasoline Engines	
V-8-350 eng (1.1)	1.5
V-8-366, 427 engs (1.5)	2.0
Diesel Engines	
Isuzu Diesel (4.9)	6.6
Detroit Diesel	
8.2L (1.3)	1.8
6V-53 (1.4)	1.9
6-71-exc below (1.6)	2.1
Brigadier (2.0)	2.7
6V-92	
Astro (1.3)	1.7
Brigadier (2.8)	3.7
General (1.9)	2.5
8V-71-exc below (1.6)	2.1
General (2.1)	2.8
8V-92	
Astro (2.1)	2.8
General (3.7)	4.9
Caterpillar Diesel	
All series (1.2)	2.0
Cummins Diesel	
All series	5.5
Recond comp add	
Isuzu	2.2
All other series (3.8)	5.0
Tractor Protection (Breakaway) Valve, Renew	
Series 4500-7000 (.5)	.8
R&R step tank add (1.1)	1.1
Series 8000-9000	
Astro (2.2)	3.0
Brigadier (.9)	1.4
Recond valve add (.4)	.6
Brake Champer Diaphragm, Renew (Front or Rear)	
All series-each (.4)	.7
w/Parking brake add (.3)	.3
Slack Adjuster, Renew	
Automatic (.5)	*.8
Manual (.3)	.6
*Recond adj add, each	.7

AIR BRAKE ANTI-SKID SYSTEMS

(Factory Time)	Chilton Time
Wheel Speed Sensor Rotor, R&R or Renew (One)	
Includes: Test system.	
Front (.9)	1.2
Rear (1.0)	1.3

LABOR 6 BRAKE SYSTEM 6 LABOR

(Factory Time) Chilton Time

Wheel Speed Sensor, R&R or Renew (One)
Includes: Test system.
Front
AC system (.5) 7
Eaton system (1.4) 1.8
Rear
AC system (.5) 7
Eaton system (1.8) 2.3

Wheel Speed Sensor Bracket, Renew (One)
Includes: Test system.
Front
AC system (1.0) 1.4
Eaton system (.9) 1.3
Rear
AC system (.4) 7
Eaton system (.9) 1.3

Wheel Speed Sensor Cables, R&R or Renew (One)
Includes: Test system.
AC system (1.1) 1.5
Eaton system (1.3) 1.8

Modulator Assembly, R&R or Renew (One)
Includes: Test system.
Series 4500-7000
Front axle (1.4) 1.8
Rear axle (1.4) 1.8
Series 8000-9000
Front axle (1.3) 1.7
Rear axle (1.0) 1.4
Renew solenoid add (.2) 2
Renew control valve add (.2) 2

Computer Assembly, Renew
Includes: Test system. Does not include R&R modulator assembly.
All series (.6) 8

Skid Control Warning Light, R&R or Renew
Includes: Test system.
All series (.6) 8

Wiring Harness Adapter, R&R or Renew
Includes: Test system and R&R the maintenance recorder.
Eaton system (.4) 6

Power Cable, R&R or Renew (One)
Includes: Test system.
Series 4500-7000
Conventional
Front axle (1.1) 1.6
Rear axle (1.1) 1.6
Tilt cab
Front axle (.7) 9
Rear axle (1.5) 1.9
Series 8000-9000
Front axle (2.1) 2.6
Rear-single axle (1.1) 1.6
Tandem axle-front (1.1) 1.6
rear (1.8) 2.3

Recorder or Monitor(s), Renew (Each)
Series 4500-7000 (.4) 8
Series 8000-9000
General (.5) 9
conv cab (.4) 8
Tilt cab (.3) 6

PARKING BRAKE

Parking Brake, Adjust
All series (.3) 5

Parking Brake Lever, Renew
Series 4500-7000 (.5) 9
Series 8000-9000 (1.1) 1.5

Parking Brake Band or Shoes, Renew
Series 4500-7000
Internal drum type (.6) 1.0
Reline brake shoe add (.4) 6
External drum or disc type
Tru-stop-2 shoe (.7) 1.2
All others (.5) 9
Reline brake shoes add (.6) 8
Renew drum or disc add (.5) 5
Series 8000-9000
Band type (.6) 1.1
Tru-stop-2 shoe (.7) 1.2
Bendix (1.6) 2.4
Reline band or shoe add (.4) 6
Renew drum or disc add (.6) 6

Parking Brake Drum or Disc, Renew
Series 4500-7000
Tru-stop-2 shoe (1.0) 1.4
All others (.6) 1.0
Series 8000-9000
Band type (1.2) 1.8
Tru-stop-2 shoe (1.0) 1.4
Bendix (1.1) 1.5

Parking Brake Control Valve, Renew
Series 4500-7000
conv cab (.3) 6
Tilt cab (.4) 8
Series 8000-9000
wo/WHEEL LOCK CONTROL
All series (.4) 8
w/WHEEL LOCK CONTROL
General (.6) 1.0
conv cab (.9) 1.3
alum tilt cab (.4) 8

Rear Parking Brake Cable, Renew (One)
Series 4500-7000
conv cab (1.1) 1.5
Tilt cab (Isuzu) (.9) 1.3

Berg Parking Brake Chamber, Renew (One)
Series 8000-9000 (.8) 1.2

LABOR 7 COOLING SYSTEM 7 LABOR

(Factory Time) Chilton Time

Thermostat, Renew
GASOLINE ENGINE
Six–conv (.5) 6
Tilt cab (.6) 9
V-8–conv (.5) 6
Tilt cab (.6) 9
DIESEL ENGINE
Detroit Diesel
conv (.5) 1.0
Tilt cab (.7) 1.2

Radiator, R&R or Renew
GASOLINE ENGINES
Series 4500-7000
Six (.9) 1.5
V-8
350 eng (.8) 1.4
366, 427 engs (1.3) 2.0
w/Tilt hood (1.4) 2.1
Series 8000-9000
conv cab (2.4) 3.0
w/Oil cooler add (.2) 2
w/Surge tank add (.3) 3
w/A.T. add (.4) 4
DIESEL ENGINES
Isuzu Diesel
All series (1.8) 3.1
Detroit Diesel
conv cab (2.4) 3.4
General (3.7) 4.7
Brigadier (2.5) 3.5
Alum tilt cab (2.4) 3.4
Alligator hood (1.7) 3.0
Tilt hood (1.1) 2.0
All others (3.5) 4.9
Cummins Diesel
Astro (4.2) 5.9
All others (3.7) 5.2
Caterpillar Diesel
Series 4500-7000 (1.7) 2.7
Series 8000-9000 (2.7) 3.7

Radiator Surge Tank, Renew
Series 4500-7000 (.6) 1.0
Series 8000-9000 (1.0) 1.4

Radiator Hose, Renew
GASOLINE ENGINES
All series
upper (.5) 7
lower (.5) 7
by-pass (.4) 6
DIESEL ENGINES
Detroit Diesel
General-upper (.5) 7
lower (.9) 1.2
8.2L-upper (.5) 7
lower (.7) 9
All others-upper (.7) 9
lower (.8) 1.0
Cummins Diesel
upper (.3) 4
lower (.9) 1.2
Caterpillar Diesel
upper (.4) 6
lower (.7) 9

Water Pump, Renew
GASOLINE ENGINES
Six–conv (.8) 1.3
Tilt cab (1.2) 1.6
V-8–307, 350 engs
conventional (.7) 1.3
Tilt cab (1.0) 1.4
V-8–366, 427, 454 engs
conventional (1.3) 1.9
Tilt cab (2.0) 2.6
DIESEL ENGINES
Isuzu Diesel
All series (1.0) 1.5
Detroit Diesel
exc below (1.5) 2.0
6V-53 (1.0) 1.5
12V-71 (2.5) 3.0
w/A.C. add (.2) 2
w/P.S. add (.2) 2
w/Air inj add (.2) 2
w/Air comp add (.2) 2

LABOR 7 COOLING SYSTEM 7 LABOR

(Factory Time)	Chilton Time
Fan Blade, Renew	
GASOLINE ENGINES	
Six–conv (.3)	.5
Tilt cab (.4)	.6
V-8–conv (.5)	.6
Tilt cab (1.3)	1.7
DIESEL ENGINES	
Isuzu Diesel	
All series (.8)	1.1
Detroit Diesel	
Astro (1.2)	1.6
Brigadier (.7)	1.0
General (.4)	.6
Cummins Diesel	
General (.9)	1.3
All others (.8)	1.2
w/A.C. add (.2)	.2
w/P.S. add (.2)	.2
w/Air inj add (.2)	.2
w/Air comp add (.2)	.2
w/Fan shroud add (.2)	.2
Drive Belt, Renew	
Six	
A.C. (.3)	.4
A.I.R. (.3)	.4
Fan (.4)	.5
H/Boost (.4)	.5
P.S. (.2)	.3
V-8	
A.C. (1.1)	1.5
A.I.R. (.2)	.3
Air comp (.3)	.4
Fan (.2)	.3
H/Boost (.2)	.3
P.S. (.2)	.3
DIESEL ENGINES	
Isuzu Diesel	
Fan/Generator (.3)	.5
Detroit Diesel	
one (.3)	.5
Cummins Diesel	
one (.8)	1.1
Caterpillar Diesel	
one or both (.5)	1.1
Temperature Gauge (Dash), Renew	
conventional cab (.4)	.7
Tilt cab (.6)	1.0
General (.2)	.4
Brigadier (.5)	.9
Temperature Gauge (Engine), Renew	
Six (.3)	.5
V-8 (.4)	.7
Detroit Diesel (.5)	.8
Cummins Diesel (.3)	.5
Caterpillar Diesel (.5)	.8
Radiator Shutter Assembly, R&R or Renew	
All series (.8)	1.1
Shutterstat, Renew	
All series (.4)	.6
Shutter Air Cylinder, Renew	
All series (.4)	.6
Shutter Air Tank, Renew	
All series (.3)	.5
Heater Core, R&R or Renew	
Series 4500-7000	
Conv.	
wo/A.C. (1.1)	2.0
w/A.C. (1.3)	2.5
Tilt cab (Isuzu)	
wo/A.C. (1.7)	3.0
Series 8000-9000	
Astro	
Heater (2.5)	4.8
A.C. (2.6)	5.0
Sleeper (2.0)	3.7
Brigadier	
Heater (1.5)	2.9
A.C. (1.8)	3.5
General	
Heater (2.3)	4.7
A.C. (2.5)	4.8
Sleeper (1.8)	3.5
Heater Blower Motor, Renew	
Series 4500-7000	
conv cab (.3)	.6
Tilt cab (Isuzu) (1.3)	2.5
Series 8000-9000	
General (.6)	1.0
Brigadier (.6)	1.0
Astro (.9)	1.6
Heater Blower Motor Switch, Renew	
Series 4500-7000 (.5)	.7
Series 8000-9000	
General (.5)	.9
Astro (.4)	.7
Brigadier (.8)	1.3
Heater Blower Motor Resistor, Renew	
All series (.4)	.6
Heater Control Assembly, Renew	
Series 4500-7000	
conv cab (.6)	.9
Tilt cab (Isuzu) (1.2)	1.8
Series 8000-9000	
Astro (1.3)	1.7
Brigadier (1.2)	1.6
General (.7)	1.0

LABOR 8 EXHAUST SYSTEM 8 LABOR

(Factory Time)	Chilton Time
Muffler, Renew	
Series 4500-7000	
Six(.6)	.9
V-8–conv-one (.4)	.6
two (.6)	.9
Tilt cab-one (.5)	.8
two (.7)	1.0
Diesel	
Isuzu (.4)	.6
Detroit	
8.2L (.5)	.8
Series 8000-9000	
cab mounted-one (1.0)	1.4
frame mounted-one (1.0)	1.4
horizontal-one (1.0)	1.4
vertical-one (.8)	1.2
General-cab mounted (.8)	1.2
muffler w/Tail pipe (.3)	.4
Exhaust Pipe, Renew	
Series 4500-7000	
Six(.5)	.8
V-8–conv-one (.8)	1.2
two (1.1)	1.7
Tilt cab-one (.5)	.8
two (.7)	1.1
Crossover (.7)	1.1
Diesel	
SINGLE EXHAUST	
one piece	
conv (.3)	.5
tilt (.7)	1.1
three piece-one section (.4)	.7
each adtnl (.4)	.4
DUAL EXHAUST	
three piece-one section (.6)	1.0
Series 8000-9000	
one-front (.7)	1.1
rear (.4)	.7
both-front (1.0)	1.5
rear (.6)	1.0
Crossover (1.1)	1.7
Alum Tilt	
one piece-one (1.2)	1.5
both (1.8)	2.4
three piece-one section (1.0)	1.4
each adtnl (.5)	.7
General-one piece (1.3)	1.8
three piece-each section (1.5)	2.0
Exhaust Manifold, R&R or Renew	
GASOLINE ENGINES	
Six(1.9)	2.6
w/P.S. add (.4)	.4
w/AIR add (.1)	.1
V-8	
350 eng-right (.6)	1.0
left (.9)	1.4
366, 427 engs-each (.8)	1.2
w/A.C. add (.3)	.3
w/AIR add (.5)	.5
w/Air comp. add (.6)	.6
DIESEL ENGINES	
Isuzu Diesel (2.7)	3.6
Deutz Diesel (2.7)	3.6
Detroit Diesel	
6-71 (1.8)	2.4
6V-53, 6V-71, 8V-71-one (1.0)	1.5
12V-71-one (1.8)	2.4
Exhaust Pipe Packing, Renew	
Six(.4)	.9
V-8–one (.4)	.9
both (.7)	1.6
Tail Pipe, Renew	
(Short Pipe)	
All series-each (.2)	.4

LABOR 9 FRONT SUSPENSION 9 LABOR

(Factory Time) Chilton Time

Note: On all front suspension operations alignment charges must be added if performed. Time given does not include alignment.

Check Alignment of Front End

All series (.7) 9

Note: Deduct if alignment is performed.

Toe-In, Adjust

All series (.4) 7

Align Front End

12,000 lb axle (1.5) 2.3
All other models (1.3) 2.0

Front Wheel Bearings, Clean and Repack or Renew Seals

Series 4500-7000
Conv cab
Drum Brakes
one side (.5) 8
both sides (.9) 1.5
Disc Brakes
one side (.9) 1.2
both sides (1.7) 2.3
Tilt Cab
Drum Brakes
one side (1.1) 1.4
both sides (2.2) 2.7
Series 8000-9000
one side (.8) 1.1
both sides (1.5) 1.8

Front Wheel Bearings and Cups, Renew (One Wheel)

Series 4500-7000
Conv Cab
drum brakes (.6) 1.0
disc brakes (.8) 1.4
Tilt Cab
drum brakes (1.1) 1.5
Series 8000-9000
inner (.9) 1.0
outer (.9) 1.0
both (1.0) 1.3

Front Shock Absorber, Renew

All series-one (.3) 5
both (.5) 8

Front Axle 'I' Beam, Renew

Add alignment charges.
All series
4,000-5,000
7,000, 7,500 lb axle
w/Drum brakes (4.7) 6.5
w/Disc brakes (3.7) 5.5
8,100-9,000-10,800
12,000-18,000 lb axle
exc Isuzu (5.7) 7.5
Isuzu (6.6) 9.2
Rebush knuckles, add
each (.4) 5

Front Wheel Hub Assy., Renew (One Side)

All series
five & six stud disc (1.2) 1.4
8 stud disc (2.1) 2.5
ten stud disc (1.5) 1.8
cast spoke (1.4) 1.6

Steering Knuckle Assy., Renew

Add alignment charges.
All series
4,000-5,000-7,000-7,500 lb axle
one (1.4) 2.6
both (2.6) 4.5
8,100-9,000-10,800-12,000 lb axle
exc Isuzu
one (2.2) 3.1
both (3.8) 5.3
Isuzu
one (3.0) 4.2
both (5.9) 8.2
16,000-18,000 lb axle
one (2.9) 3.8
both (5.1) 6.6
Renew knuckle arm, add
each 5

King Pins and Thrust Bearings, Renew

Does not include rebush steering knuckles.
All series
4,000-5,000-7,000-7,500 lb axle
one side (1.5) 2.9
both sides (2.6) 5.1
8,100-9,000-10,800-12,000 lb axle
exc Isuzu
one side (2.2) 2.8
both sides (3.7) 5.0
Isuzu
one side (2.1) 3.0
both sides (3.7) 5.4
16,000-18,000 lb axle
one side (2.3) 3.1
both sides (4.2) 5.4
Renew tie rod, add-each 3
Rebush knuckle, add-each 5

Front Leaf Spring Assy., R&R or Renew

All series
conv cab
one (1.4) 1.8
both (2.7) 3.5
Tilt cab-exc Isuzu
one (1.7) 2.1
both (3.3) 4.1
Tilt cab (Isuzu)
one (2.1) 2.9
both (3.9) 5.4
Renew center bolt, add-each 4
Recond spring assy, add-each 6

Front Spring Eye Bushing, Renew

Series 4500-7000
hanger end-each (.6) 9
shackle end-each (1.3) 1.8
Series 8000-9000
hanger end-each (1.0) 1.5
shackle end-each
exc below (1.2) 1.7
General (2.2) 3.0

Front Spring Shackle and/or Pin, Renew (Shackle End Only)

Astro-each (.9) 1.3
Brigadier-each (.7) 1.1
General-each (.6) 1.0
Isuzu-each (.5) 8

LABOR 10 STEERING LINKAGE 10 LABOR

(Factory Time) Chilton Time

Tie Rod End, Renew

Includes: Reset toe-in.
All series
one side (.7) 1.1
both sides (1.0) 1.5

Tie Rod Assembly, Renew

Includes: Reset toe-in.
All series (1.0) 1.4

Pitman Arm, Renew

Series 4500-7000
exc Isuzu (.4) 7
Isuzu (.6) 1.0
Series 8000-9000
Astro (.5) 8
Brigadier (.9) 1.3
General (.4) 7

Drag Link, Renew

All series (.5) 8
Renew pitman arm add 3

Steering Knuckle Arm, Renew

Includes: Reset toe-in. Does not include reset caster or camber.
4,000-5,000-7,000-7,500 lb axle
each (.9) 1.2
8,100-9,000 lb axle
each (1.1) 1.4
10,800 lb axle
each (1.0) 1.5
12,000-16,000-18,000 lb axle
right (.9) 1.2
left (.9) 1.2
left upper (1.5) 2.0

LABOR 11 STEERING GEAR 11 LABOR

STANDARD STEERING

Steering Gear, Adjust (On Truck)

Includes: Steering gear, drag link tie rods, wheel bearings and toe-in adjustments.
Series 4500-7000 (1.0) 1.2
Series 8000-9000 (1.2) 1.5

Steering Gear, R&R

Series 4500-7000
conv (.7) 1.3
Tilt cab (1.0) 1.7
Series 8000-9000
conv (1.9) 2.8
Steel Tilt (1.2) 1.8
Alum Tilt (1.5) 2.0

LABOR 11 STEERING GEAR 11 LABOR

(Factory Time)	Chilton Time
Steering Gear, R&R and Recondition	
Includes: Disassemble, inspect, clean, renew necessary parts, reassemble and adjust.	
Series 4500-7000	
conv (1.6)	2.6
Tilt cab (1.9)	3.0
Series 8000-9000	
conv (3.4)	4.7
Steel Tilt (2.7)	3.7
Alum Tilt (3.0)	3.9
Upper Mast Jacket Bearings, Renew	
Series 4500-7000 (.7)	1.0
Series 8000-9000	
exc below (.5)	.7
Astro (1.5)	2.0
General (1.0)	1.5
Steering Wheel, Renew	
All series (.3)	.5
Intermediate Steering and/or Lower Coupling Shaft, Renew	
Series 4500-7000	
conv cab (1.0)	1.4
tilt cab (.8)	1.2
Series 8000-9000	
Tilt cab (1.2)	1.6
Brigadier (1.0)	1.4
Pitman Shaft Seal, Renew	
Does not include resetting toe-in.	
Series 4500-7000	
semi-integral (.4)	.7
integral system	
exc Isuzu (.5)	1.0
Isuzu (2.0)	2.8
Series 8000-9000	
Astro (.4)	.7
Brigadier (.7)	1.0
General (.3)	.6

POWER STEERING

(Factory Time)	Chilton Time
Trouble Shoot Power Steering	
Includes: Check pounds pull on steering wheel, install checking gauges, test pump pressure and check for external leaks.	
All models (.7)	.7
Power Steering Hoses, Renew	
Series 4500-7000	
pump to gear (.6)	.7
gear to cyl (.5)	.6
cooler hoses-one (.5)	.7
both (.7)	.9
Series 8000-9000	
General-w/Detroit Diesel (1.0)	1.4
All others-each (.5)	.9
Power Steering Pump Flow Control Valve Assy., Renew	
Series 4500-7000	
wo/Integral system (.5)	.7
w/Integral system (1.1)	1.6
Power Cylinder, Renew	
All series	
axle mount (.5)	1.1
frame mount	
exc. below (.6)	1.0
Brigadier (1.0)	1.4
Power Cylinder, R&R and Recondition	
All series	
axle mount (.8)	1.4
frame mount	
exc. below (1.0)	1.5
Brigadier (1.4)	1.9
Power Steering Gear, Renew	
Series 4500-7000	
conv cab-wo/Integral system (1.3)	2.0
conv cab-w/Integral system (2.2)	3.3
tilt cab (1.5)	2.2
Series 8000-9000	
Astro (1.8)	2.6
Brigadier (1.4)	2.2
General (1.6)	2.4
Power Steering Gear, R&R and Recondition	
Series 4500-7000	
conv cab-wo/Integral system (2.9)	4.3
conv cab-w/Integral system (3.8)	5.7
tilt cab (3.2)	4.8
Series 8000-9000	
Astro (3.9)	5.0
Brigadier (3.8)	4.9
General (4.2)	5.4
Power Steering Pump, R&R Renew	
Series 4500-7000	
Six (.7)	1.2
V-8	
w/Vacuum brks (.7)	1.2
w/Air brks (1.8)	2.4
Diesel	
Isuzu (.8)	1.2
Detroit 8.2L	
w/Vacuum brks (1.5)	2.0
w/Air brks (1.9)	2.7
Caterpillar	
3208 (1.0)	1.5
Deutz (1.2)	1.7
Series 8000-9000	
Detroit Diesel	
6V-53 (.9)	1.5
6-71-exc below (.8)	1.4
Brigadier (1.8)	2.4
6V-92-exc below (1.7)	2.3
Brigadier (4.4)	5.5
8V-71 (1.9)	2.5
8V-92 (1.8)	2.4
Cummins Diesel (.7)	1.2
Caterpillar Diesel	
3208 (1.0)	1.5
3406 (.9)	1.5
Deutz Diesel (1.2)	1.7
Recond pump add (1.0)	1.3
Power Steering Reservoir, Renew (Remote)	
Includes: Bleed hydraulic system.	
All series (.6)	.9
Power Steering Oil Cooler, Renew	
Series 4500-7000	
Alligator hood (.9)	1.4
Tilt hood (.5)	.8
Series 8000-9000 (.4)	.8
w/A.C. add (.3)	.3
Pump Drive Belt, Renew	
Series 4500-7000	
Six (.2)	.4
V-8	
350 eng (.2)	.4
366, 427 engs (1.0)	1.5
Cat (.3)	.5

LABOR 12 CYLINDER HEAD & VALVE SYSTEM 12 LABOR

GASOLINE ENGINES

(Factory Time)	Chilton Time
Cylinder Head Gasket, Renew	
Includes: R&R all normal interfering parts. Check cylinder head and block flatness. Adjust carburetor, valves (if adjustable) and ignition timing (when distributor is removed.)	
Six-conv (4.2)	5.8
Tilt cab (5.1)	6.8
w/P.S. add (.4)	.4
w/A.I.R. add (.6)	.6
V-8-307, 350 engs	
conv	
one (3.9)	6.3
both (5.8)	9.5
Tilt cab	
one (5.8)	7.3
both (7.7)	9.7
V-8-366, 427, 454 engs	
conv	
one (4.4)	7.0
both (7.1)	10.7
Tilt cab	
one (6.5)	8.2
both (9.1)	11.4
w/A.C. add (1.0)	1.0
w/P.S. add (.5)	.5
w/Air inj add (.5)	.5
w/Air comp add (.5)	.5
Cylinder Head, Renew	
Includes: R&R all interfering parts. Check cylinder head flatness. Transfer all necessary components. Clean, reface and lap valves. Check valve spring tension, assembled height and valve head runout. Adjust carburetor, valves and distributor.	
Six-conv (5.9)	7.8
Tilt cab (6.0)	7.9
w/P.S. add (.4)	.4
w/A.I.R. add (.6)	.6
V-8-307, 350 engs	
conv	
one (4.3)	6.9
both (6.6)	10.4
Tilt cab	
one (6.8)	8.5
both (9.6)	12.2
V-8-366, 427, 454 engs	
conv	
one (5.7)	8.4
both (9.4)	14.6
Tilt cab	
one (7.6)	9.6
both (12.3)	15.0
w/A.C. add (1.0)	1.0
w/P.S. add (.5)	.5
w/Air inj add (.5)	.5
w/Air comp add (.5)	.5

Clean Carbon and Grind Valves

Includes: R&R cylinder head and all interfering parts. Check cylinder head and block flatness. Clean, inspect and recondition or renew all necessary components. Check valve spring tension, assembled height and valve runout. Tune engine.

(Factory Time)	Chilton Time
Six–conv (6.8)	8.7
Tilt cab (7.6)	9.8
w/P.S. add (.4)	.4
w/A.I.R. add (.6)	.6
V-8–307, 350 engs	
conv (10.5)	14.4
Tilt cab (10.7)	14.5
V-8–366, 427, 454 engs	
conv (10.8)	16.5
Tilt cab (14.2)	16.9
w/A.C. add (1.0)	1.0
w/P.S. add (.5)	.5
w/Air inj add (.5)	.5
w/Air comp add (.5)	.5

Valve Cover Gasket, Renew

(Factory Time)	Chilton Time
Six–conv (.7)	1.0
Tilt cab (.9)	1.2
V-8–307, 350 engs	
conv-one (.4)	.6
both (.6)	.9
Tilt cab-one (.4)	.6
both (.7)	.9
V-8–366, 427, 454 engs	
conv-one (.6)	.8
both (.9)	1.2
Tilt cab-one (.5)	.8
both (.7)	1.1

Push Rod Cover Gasket, Renew

(Factory Time)	Chilton Time
Six–front (.5)	.7
rear (.2)	.4
both (.6)	1.0

Push Rods or Rocker Arms, Renew

(Factory Time)	Chilton Time
Six–conv	
one cyl (.7)	1.2
all cyls (1.0)	1.6
Tilt cab	
one or two (1.2)	1.6
three or more (1.5)	2.0
V-8–conv	
one cyl (.5)	1.0
one cyl-each side (1.0)	1.5
all cyls-both sides (1.5)	2.2
Tilt cab	
one or two same bank (.5)	.7
three or more same bank (.8)	1.0
all-both banks (1.4)	1.9
w/A.C. add (1.0)	1.0
w/Air comp add (.5)	.5

Valve Lifters, Renew (All)

Includes: R&R intake manifold and all other interfering parts. Adjust valves, carburetor and ignition timing, where required.

(Factory Time)	Chilton Time
Six–conv (1.3)	2.0
Tilt cab (2.2)	3.5
w/A.I.R. add (.2)	.2
V-8–307, 350 engs	
conv (2.8)	4.0
Tilt cab (4.3)	5.5
V-8–366, 427, 454 engs	
conv (3.7)	5.5
Tilt cab (4.7)	6.0
w/A.C. add (1.0)	1.0
w/Air inj add (.5)	.5
w/Air comp add (.5)	.5

Valve Springs, or Seals, Renew (All)

Includes: R&R valve covers and adjust valves.

(Factory Time)	Chilton Time
Six–conv (2.3)	3.2
Tilt cab (2.3)	2.9
w/A.I.R. add (.2)	.2
V-8–307, 350 engs	
conv (3.7)	5.0
Tilt cab (2.8)	3.5
V-8–366, 427, 454 engs (2.8)	4.0
w/A.C. add (1.0)	1.0
w/Air inj add (.5)	.5
w/Air comp add (.5)	.5

COMBINATIONS

Add to Valve Job

(Factory Time)	Chilton Time
VALVE GUIDES, REAM FOR OVERSIZE STEMS	
Each (.2)	.2
ROCKER ARM STUD, RENEW	
One (.4)	.4
Each adtnl (.2)	.2
DISTRIBUTOR, RECONDITION	
w/Spinney gov on V-8 add (.5)	.5
CARBURETOR, RECONDITION	
1 BBL (.7)	1.0
2 BBL (1.2)	1.4
4 BBL exc below (1.7)	1.9
Holley (2.0)	3.5

DIESEL ENGINES

COMBINATIONS

Add to Valve Job

(Factory Time)	Chilton Time
ROCKER ARM STUD, RENEW	
One (.4)	.4
ROCKER ARM ASSEMBLY, DISASSEMBLE, CLEAN AND REASEMBLE	
Detroit Diesel	
Each cyl (.5)	.7
VALVE GUIDES, REAM FOR OVERSIZE STEMS	
One (.2)	.2
Each adtnl (.1)	.1
INJECTOR, RENEW	
Each (.2)	.3
INJECTOR, RECONDITION	
Each (.4)	.5
ADJUST GOVERNOR	
All series (.5)	.6

Cylinder Head Gasket, Renew

Includes: R&R all normal interfering parts. Check cylinder head and block for flatness. Adjust valves and crossheads.

(Factory Time)	Chilton Time
Isuzu Diesel (5.8)	8.2
Detroit Diesel	
6-71 (8.1)	10.2
6V-53, 6V-71-one (6.0)	7.5
both (11.5)	14.5
8V-71-one (6.2)	7.8
both (11.9)	15.0
12V-71-one (7.2)	9.1
both (13.9)	17.5
w/A.C. add (.3)	.3
w/P.S. add (.2)	.2

Cylinder Head, Renew

Includes: R&R all normal interfering parts clean carbon from pistons and block. Check cylinder head and block flatness. Transfer all necessary components. Clean, lap and reface valves. Check valve spring tension, assembled height and valve runout. Adjust valves and crossheads.

(Factory Time)	Chilton Time
Isuzu Diesel (10.1)	14.3
Deutz Diesel	
one cyl (4.6)	6.2
all cyls (13.0)	17.7
Detroit Diesel	
6-71 (17.2)	21.5
6V-53, 6V-71-one (10.6)	13.3
both (20.7)	26.0
8V-71-one (12.0)	15.0
both (23.4)	29.5
12V-71-one (16.8)	21.0
both (30.4)	38.0
w/A.C. add (.3)	.3
w/P.S. add (.2)	.2
Adjust Governor add (.5)	.5

Clean Carbon and Grind Valves

Includes: R&R head and all normal interfering parts. Check cylinder head and block flatness, magnaflux head. Clean, inspect and recondition all components, as necessary. Pressure test head. Check spring tension, assembled height and valve runout. Adjust valves, crossheads and injectors. Road test.

(Factory Time)	Chilton Time
Isuzu Diesel (7.6)	10.8
Deutz Diesel	
one cyl (4.4)	6.0
all cyls (11.5)	15.6
Detroit Diesel	
6-71 (19.0)	23.8
6V-53, 6V-71 (22.9)	28.7
8V-71 (26.0)	32.5
12V-71 (33.4)	42.0
w/A.C. add (.3)	.3
w/P.S. add (.2)	.2

Adjust Valves and Crossheads

(Factory Time)	Chilton Time
Detroit Diesel	
6-71 (1.2)	1.5
6V-53, 6V-71 (1.6)	2.0
8V-71 (1.8)	2.5
12V-71 (2.2)	2.8

Valve Cover Gasket, Renew

(Factory Time)	Chilton Time
Isuzu Diesel (.7)	1.0
Deutz Diesel	
one (.2)	.4
each adtnl (.1)	.2
Detroit Diesel	
each (.4)	.7

Valve Push Rods, Renew

(Factory Time)	Chilton Time
Isuzu Diesel	
one cyl (1.2)	1.7
all cyls (1.5)	2.1
Deutz Diesel	
one cyl (.3)	.5
all cyls (1.5)	2.0
Detroit Diesel	
one cyl (1.2)	1.6
six cyls (5.7)	7.2
eight cyls (6.8)	8.5
twelve cyls (12.0)	15.0

LABOR 12 CYLINDER HEAD & VALVE SYSTEM 12 LABOR

(Factory Time) Chilton Time

Valve Lifters, Renew (All)

Isuzu Diesel (2.0) 2.9

Deutz Diesel

one cyl (12.6) 17.0

all cyls (12.8) 17.5

Detroit Diesel

Six (5.7) 7.3

V-6 (5.7) 7.3

V-8 (6.8) 8.4

V-12 (12.0) 14.8

Valve Springs, Caps or Seals Renew (All)

Isuzu Diesel

one cyl (1.4) 2.0

all cyls (2.7) 3.8

Deutz Diesel

one cyl (.4) 7

all cyls (2.1) 3.0

All series (.6) 9

Detroit Diesel

Six (7.3) 9.5

V-6 (7.3) 9.5

V-8 (9.3) 12.0

V-12 (13.3) 17.0

Valve Rocker Arms, Renew

Isuzu Diesel

one cyl (1.1) 1.6

all cyls (1.6) 2.3

Deutz Diesel

one cyl (.3) 5

all cyls (1.4) 1.9

Valve Push Rod Guides, Springs and Seals, Renew

Deutz Diesel

one cyl (2.5) 3.4

all cyls (6.4) 8.7

LABOR 13 ENGINE ASSEMBLY & MOUNTS 13 LABOR

(Factory Time) Chilton Time

GASOLINE ENGINES

Engine Assembly, Remove and Reinstall

Includes: R&R all normal interfering parts. Does not include transfer of any components.

Six–conv (5.7) 8.8

Tilt cab (7.4) 9.7

w/P.S. add (.4) 4

w/A.I.R. add (.6) 6

V-8–307, 350 engs

conv (4.4) 6.0

Tilt cab (7.2) 9.3

V-8–366, 427, 454 engs

366 eng

conv (5.1) 6.5

Tilt cab (7.7) 10.0

427 eng-conv (8.0) 10.2

Tilt cab (9.3) 12.0

454 eng-conv (8.0) 10.2

Tilt cab (9.3) 12.0

w/A.C. add (1.0) 1.0

w/P.S. add (.5) 5

w/Air inj add (.4) 4

w/Air comp add (.9) 9

Engine Assembly, Renew

Includes: R&R all normal interfering parts. Transfer all necessary components. Tune engine and road test.

Six–conv (7.2) 10.2

Tilt cab (8.2) 10.8

w/P.S. add (.4) 4

w/A.I.R. add (.6) 6

V-8–307, 350 engs

conv (6.9) 9.5

Tilt cab (8.7) 11.5

V-8–366, 427, 454 engs

366 eng

conv (8.6) 12.0

Tilt cab (9.4) 12.2

427 eng-conv (8.6) 12.8

Tilt cab (11.0) 14.8

454 eng-conv (9.7) 12.8

Tilt cab (11.0) 14.8

w/A.C. add (1.0) 1.0

w/P.S. add (.5) 5

w/Air inj add (.4) 4

w/Air comp add (.9) 9

Engine Assembly, Renew (Universal)

Includes: R&R engine assy. Transfer all component parts not supplied with replacement engine.

V-8–350 eng

conv cab (7.6) 11.0

V-8–**366, 427 engs**

conv cab (9.8) 14.2

w/A.C. add (1.0) 1.0

w/P.S. add (.5) 5

w/AIR add (.4) 4

w/Air comp add (.9) 9

w/Eng oil cooler add (.4) 4

Cylinder Assembly (Short Engine), Renew & Grind Valves

Includes: R&R all normal interfering parts. Transfer all necessary parts and equipment. Check valve spring tension, valve seat and head runout, head flatness, stem to guide clearance and assembled height. Tune engine and road test.

Six–conv (12.1) 15.9

Tilt cab (14.6) 18.7

w/P.S. add (.4) 4

w/A.I.R. add (.6) 6

V-8–307, 350 engs

conv (14.7) 18.9

Tilt cab (17.1) 21.9

V-8–366, 427, 454 engs

366 eng

conv (16.1) 20.6

Tilt cab (18.7) 23.9

427 eng-conv (19.0) 24.2

Tilt cab (19.3) 24.7

454 eng-conv (19.0) 24.2

Tilt cab (19.3) 24.7

w/A.C. add (1.0) 1.0

w/P.S. add (.5) 5

w/Air inj add (.4) 4

w/Air comp add (.9) 9

Engine Assembly, R&R and Recondition (Complete)

Includes: R&R all normal interfering parts. Disassemble and assemble complete engine. Inspect all components. Rebore block. Install new pistons, rings and pins. Align rods. Plastigauge and install new main and rod bearings. Clean carbon and grind valves, test hydraulic tappets, renew if necessary. Renew all gaskets and seals as necessary. Tune engine and road test.

Six–conv (26.5) 34.4

Tilt cab (28.2) 35.4

w/P.S. add (.4) 4

w/A.I.R. add (.6) 6

V-8–307, 350 engs

conv (31.8) 39.8

Tilt cab (34.6) 43.3

V-8–366, 427, 454 engs

366 eng

conv (33.1) 41.5

Tilt cab (35.7) 44.7

427 eng-conv (36.0) 45.0

Tilt cab (37.3) 46.7

454 eng-conv (36.0) 45.0

Tilt cab (37.3) 46.7

w/A.C. add (1.0) 1.0

w/P.S. add (.5) 5

w/Air inj add (.4) 4

w/Air comp add (.9) 9

Engine Mounts, Renew (Both)

Front

Six (.5) 1.0

V-8–307, 350 engs

conv (.5) 1.0

Tilt cab (.7) 1.2

V-8–366, 427, 454 engs (.5) 1.0

Rear

Six (.6) 1.0

V-8–307, 350 engs

conv (.5) 8

Tilt cab (.7) 1.1

V-8–366, 427, 454 engs

All series (.8) 1.3

DIESEL ENGINES

Engine Assembly, Remove and Reinstall

Includes: R&R all normal interfering parts. Does not include transfer of any component.

Detroit Diesel

6-71-conv (11.6) 14.6

Alum Tilt (11.2) 14.1

6V-53-conv (11.0) 13.8

Steel Tilt (10.0) 12.5

6V-71-Steel Tilt (12.0) 15.1

8V-71-conv (14.1) 17.7

Alum Tilt (13.5) 18.0

12V-71-Alum Tilt (19.0) 23.5

w/A.C. add (1.0) 1.0

w/P.S. add (.8) 8

w/Pwr take off add (.3) 3

Engine Assembly, Renew

Includes: R&R normal interfering parts. Transfer all necessary components. Tune engine and road test.

Deutz Diesel

All series (7.0) 10.0

Detroit Diesel

6-71-conv (14.1) 17.7

Alum Tilt (13.7) 17.2

6V-53-conv (13.5) 17.0

Steel Tilt (12.5) 15.7

6V-71-Steel Tilt (14.5) 18.2

8V-71-conv (16.6) 20.9

Alum Tilt (16.0) 20.0

12V-71-Alum Tilt (22.2) 27.8

LABOR 13 ENGINE ASSEMBLY & MOUNTS 13 LABOR

(Factory Time)	Chilton Time
w/A.C. add (1.0)	1.0
w/P.S. add (.8)	.8
w/Pwr take off add (.3)	.3

Cylinder Block, Renew

Includes: R&R all normal interfering parts. Transfer all components without disassembly. Install new main and rod bearings. Renew all necessary seals and gaskets. Adjust timing and clearances.
Does not include reconditioning of any component.

(Factory Time)	Chilton Time
Isuzu Diesel (27.6)	39.2
w/P.S. add (.4)	.4
Detroit Diesel	
6-71-conv (44.6)	50.2
Alum Tilt (44.4)	50.0
6V-53-conv (43.0)	48.4
Steel Tilt (42.0)	47.3
6V-71-Steel Tilt (48.0)	53.9
8V-71-conv (51.1)	57.4
Alum Tilt (50.5)	56.6
12V-71-Alum Tilt (64.0)	71.5
w/A.C. add (1.0)	1.0
w/P.S. add (.8)	.8
w/Pwr take off add (.3)	.3

Engine Assembly, R&R and Recondition (Complete)

Includes: R&R of all normal interfering parts. Complete disassembly and assembly of engine. Pressure test block and head. Plastigauge and renew main, rod and camshaft bearings. Install new pistons, rings, pins and liners. Rebore block. Recondition blower or turbocharger, water and injector pump, oil pump, injectors and governor. Clean carbon and grind valves. Check and set all clearances. Tune engine and road test.

(Factory Time)	Chilton Time
Detroit Diesel	
6-71-conv (72.6)	80.0
Alum Tilt (72.2)	79.6
6V-53-conv (73.0)	80.4
Steel Tilt (72.0)	79.3
6V-71-Steel Tilt (76.0)	83.7
8V-71-conv (84.1)	92.7
Alum Tilt (83.5)	92.0
12V-71-Alum Tilt (93.0)	102.5
w/A.C. add (1.0)	1.0
w/P.S. add (.8)	.8
w/Pwr take off add (.3)	.3

Engine Mounts, Renew

(Factory Time)	Chilton Time
Deutz Diesel	
Front (.5)	.8
Rear-one (.5)	.7
both (.9)	1.3
Detroit Diesel	
Front 6-71 (1.2)	1.6
6V-53 (2.8)	3.5
6V-71 (2.3)	2.9
8V-71 (2.3)	2.9
12V-71 (3.0)	3.8
Rear-right (.4)	.7
left (.7)	1.0

LABOR 14 PISTONS, RINGS & BEARINGS 14 LABOR

GASOLINE ENGINES

Rings, Pins and Main Bearings, Renew and Grind Valves

Includes: R&R all normal interfering parts. Remove cylinder top ridge, hone cylinder walls, clean ring grooves, install new rings. Install new pins and align rods. Plastigauge and install new main and rod bearings. Renew gaskets and seals as necessary. Clean carbon and grind valves. Test valve spring tension, valve seat and head run-out, stem to guide clearance, and assembled height. Check head and block flatness. Tune engine and road test.

(Factory Time)	Chilton Time
Six-conv (15.5)	19.7
Tilt cab (16.1)	20.3
w/P.S. add (.4)	.4
w/A.I.R. add (.6)	.6
V-8-307, 350 engs	
conv (19.6)	25.8
Tilt cab (21.2)	27.8
V-8-366, 427, 454 engs	
conv (23.1)	30.9
Tilt cab (23.9)	31.3
w/A.C. add (1.0)	1.0
w/P.S. add (.8)	.8
w/Air inj add (.4)	.4
w/Air comp add (.6)	.6

Rings, Pins, Rod and Main Bearings, Renew

Includes: R&R all normal interfering parts. Remove cylinder top ridge, hone cylinder walls, clean ring grooves, install new rings. Install new pins and align rods. Plastigauge and install new main and rod bearings. Renew gaskets and seals as necessary. Tune engine and road test.

(Factory Time)	Chilton Time
Six-conv (14.0)	17.1
Tilt cab (14.6)	17.7
w/P.S. add (.4)	.4
w/A.I.R. add (.6)	.6
V-8-307, 350 engs	
conv (17.6)	22.1
Tilt cab (19.2)	24.1
V-8-366, 427, 454 engs	
conv (21.1)	27.2
Tilt cab (21.9)	27.6
w/A.C. add (1.0)	1.0
w/P.S. add (.8)	.8
w/Air inj add (.4)	.4
w/Air comp add (.6)	.6

COMBINATIONS

(Factory Time)	Chilton Time
VALVE GUIDES, REAM FOR OVERSIZE STEMS	
Each (.2)	.2
ROCKER ARM STUD, RENEW	
One (.4)	.4
Each adtnl (.2)	.2
DISTRIBUTOR, RECONDITION	
All series (.6)	.9
w/Spinner gov on	
V-8 add (.5)	.5
CARBURETOR, RECONDITION	
1 BBL (.7)	1.0
2 BBL (1.2)	1.4
4 BBL-exc below (1.7)	1.9
Holley (2.0)	3.5
REMOVE CYLINDER TOP RIDGE	
Each (.1)	.1
DEGLAZE CYLINDER WALLS	
Six (.7)	.8
V-8 (.9)	1.0
OIL PUMP, RECONDITION	
All series (1.0)	1.2
MAIN BEARINGS, RENEW	
Six (2.0)	2.5
V-8 (1.4)	2.0
PLASTIGAUGE BEARINGS	
Each (.1)	.1

Rings, Pins and Rod Bearings, Renew

Includes: R&R all normal interfering parts. Remove cylinder top ridge, hone cylinder walls, clean ring grooves, install new rings. Install new pins and align rods. Plastigauge and install new main and rod bearings. Renew gaskets and seals as necessary. Tune engine and road test.

(Factory Time)	Chilton Time
Six-conv (11.2)	13.4
Tilt cab (11.8)	14.0
w/P.S. add (.4)	.4
w/A.I.R. add (.6)	.6
V-8-307, 350 engs	
conv (15.6)	18.9
Tilt cab (17.2)	20.9
V-8-366, 427, 454 engs	
conv (19.1)	24.0
Tilt cab (19.9)	24.4
w/A.C. add (1.0)	1.0
w/P.S. add (.8)	.8
w/Air inj add (.4)	.4
w/Air comp add (.6)	.6

Rings, Renew

Includes: R&R all normal interfering parts. Remove cylinder top ridge, hone cylinder walls, clean ring grooves, install new rings. Renew gaskets and seals as necessary.

(Factory Time)	Chilton Time
Six-conv (7.6)	10.0
Tilt cab (8.4)	10.6
w/P.S. add (.4)	.4
w/A.I.R. add (.6)	.6
V-8-307, 350 engs	
conv (10.8)	14.7
Tilt cab (13.0)	16.7
V-8-366, 427, 454 engs	
conv (14.9)	19.8
Tilt cab (15.7)	20.2
w/A.C. add (1.0)	1.0
w/P.S. add (.8)	.8
w/Air inj add (.4)	.4
w/Air comp add (.6)	.6

Piston, Renew (One)

Includes: R&R all normal interfering parts. Remove cylinder top ridge, hone cylinder walls. Install new piston with rings.

(Factory Time)	Chilton Time
Six-conv (5.6)	7.0
Tilt cab (6.9)	8.9
w/P.S. add (.4)	.4
w/A.I.R. add (.6)	.6
V-8-307, 350 engs	
conv (6.2)	8.5
Tilt cab (7.3)	9.0
366, 427, 454 engs	
conv (7.0)	9.9
Tilt cab (8.8)	11.1

LABOR 14 PISTONS, RINGS, PINS & BEARINGS 14 LABOR

(Factory Time)	Chilton Time
w/A.C. add (1.0)	1.0
w/P.S. add (.8)	.8
w/Air inj add (.4)	.4
w/Air comp add (.6)	.6

Rod Bearings, Renew

Includes: R&R oil pan.

(Factory Time)	Chilton Time
Six–conv (2.4)	4.4
Tilt cab (3.0)	4.8
V-8–307, 350 engs	
conv (2.4)	3.0
Tilt cab (3.3)	5.4
V-8–366, 427, 454 engs	
conv (3.4)	5.2
Tilt cab (3.6)	5.4

DIESEL ENGINES

Rings, Pins, and Main Bearings, Renew and Grind Valves

Includes: R&R all normal interfering parts. Remove cylinder top ridge, hone cylinder walls, clean ring grooves, install new rings. Install new pins and align rods. Plastigauge and install new main and rod bearings. Renew gaskets and seals as necessary. Clean carbon and grind valves. Cean oil pump. Set injection timing and valves and crossheads. Road test.
Does not include renew liners.

(Factory Time)	Chilton Time
Isuzu Diesel (16.0)	23.2
Detroit Diesel	
6-71 (32.7)	39.4
6V-53, 6V-71 (36.3)	43.1
8V-71 (42.0)	48.8
12V-71 (60.1)	69.6
w/A.C. add (1.0)	1.0
w/P.S. add (.2)	.2
w/Pwr take off add (.3)	.3

Rings, Pins, Rod and Main Bearings, Renew

Includes: R&R all normal interfering parts. Remove cylinder top ridge, hone cylinder liner walls, clean ring grooves, install new rings. Install new pins and align rods. Plastigauge and install new main and rod bearings. Renew gaskets and seals as necessary. Clean oil pump. Set injection timing and valves and cross heads. Road test.
Does not include renew liners.

(Factory Time)	Chilton Time
Isuzu Diesel (14.2)	20.5
Detroit Diesel	
6-71 (23.6)	28.4
6V-53, 6V-71 (24.0)	30.1
8V-71 (27.8)	32.8
12V-71 (40.2)	48.6
w/A.C. add (1.0)	1.0
w/P.S. add (.2)	.2

Rings, Pins and Rod Bearings, Renew

Includes: R&R all normal interfering parts. Remove cylinder top ridge, hone cylinder liner walls, clean ring grooves, install new rings. Install new pins and align rods. Plastigauge and install new main and rod bearings. Renew gaskets and seals as necessary. Clean oil pump. Set injection timing and valves and crossheads. Road test.
Does not include renew liners.

(Factory Time)	Chilton Time
Isuzu Diesel	
all cyls (11.4)	16.5
Deutz Diesel	
one cyl (5.2)	7.0
all cyls (16.5)	22.5

COMBINATIONS

(Factory Time)	Chilton Time
ROCKER ARM ASSEMBLY, DISASSEMBLE, CLEAN AND REASSEMBLE	
Detroit Diesel	
Each cyl (.5)	.7
VALVE GUIDES, REAM FOR OVERSIZE STEMS	
One (.2)	.2
Each adtnl (.1)	.1
INJECTOR, RENEW	
Each (.2)	.3
INJECTOR, RECONDITION	
Each (.4)	.5
ADJUST GOVERNOR	
All series (.5)	.6
PRESSURE TEST HEAD	
Six (1.5)	1.5
V-6 Each (1.0)	1.0
V-8 Each (1.2)	1.2
MAIN BEARINGS, RENEW	
ISUZU DIESEL	
Each (.4)	.5
Deutz Diesel	
Each (.4)	.5
Detroit Diesel	
6-71 (3.7)	4.7
6V-53, 6V-71 (2.2)	2.8
8V-71 (2.7)	3.4
12V-71 (3.6)	4.6
PLASTIGAUGE BEARINGS	
Each (.1)	.1
OIL PUMP, RECONDITION	
Detroit Diesel	
Exc below (.4)	.7
6-71 (1.0)	1.4
12V-71 (2.0)	2.6
ISUZU DIESEL (.5)	.6

(Factory Time)	Chilton Time
Detroit Diesel	
6-71 (19.9)	23.9
6V-53, 6V-71 (22.6)	27.6
8V-71 (25.1)	29.3
12V-71 (36.6)	44.1
w/A.C. add (1.0)	1.0
w/P.S. add (.2)	.2

Rings, Renew

Includes: R&R all normal interfering parts. Remove cylinder top ridge, hone cylinder liner walls, clean ring grooves, install new rings. Renew gaskets and seals as necessary. Set injection timing and valves and crossheads. Road test.

(Factory Time)	Chilton Time
Isuzu Diesel	
one cyl (7.6)	11.0
all cyls (9.6)	13.9
Deutz Diesel	
one cyl (4.5)	6.0
all cyls (12.3)	16.7
Detroit Diesel	
6-71 (16.0)	20.0
6V-53, 6V-71 (19.8)	24.8
8V-71 (21.5)	25.7
12V-71 (29.8)	37.3
w/A.C. add (1.0)	1.0
w/P.S. add (.2)	.2

Piston and Liner, Renew (One)

Includes: R&R all normal interfering parts. Hone block bore, check liner height, liner bore and O.D. for proper fit. Install new liner, piston with rings and pin. Renew gaskets and seals as necessary. Set injection timing and valves and crossheads.

(Factory Time)	Chilton Time
Isuzu Diesel	
one cyl (8.1)	11.7
all cyls (10.2)	14.8
Deutz Diesel	
one cyl (4.9)	6.6
all cyls (15.0)	20.5
Detroit Diesel	
6-71 (13.0)	16.7
6V-53, 6V-71 (9.2)	11.7
8V-71 (9.6)	12.3
12V-71 (13.0)	17.0
w/A.C. add (1.0)	1.0
w/P.S. add (.2)	.2
w/Pwr take off add (.3)	.3

Rod Bearings, Renew

Includes: R&R oil pan. Clean oil pump.

(Factory Time)	Chilton Time
Isuzu Diesel	
one (1.6)	2.3
all (2.6)	4.8
Deutz Diesel	
one (1.5)	2.0
all (4.8)	6.5
Detroit Diesel	
6-71 (4.1)	5.4
6V-53, 6V-71 (3.6)	5.0
8V-71 (4.2)	5.5
12V-71 (5.5)	7.2

LABOR 15 CRANKSHAFT & DAMPER 15 LABOR

GASOLINE ENGINES

Crankshaft and Main Bearings, Renew

Includes: R&R all normal interfering parts and engine. Plastigauge and install new bearings. Recondition oil pump.

(Factory Time)	Chilton Time
Six–conv (10.0)	13.0
Tilt cab (10.4)	13.5
w/P.S. add (.4)	.4
w/A.I.R. add (.6)	.6
V-8–307, 350 engs	
conv (8.0)	11.6
Tilt cab (10.1)	14.6
V-8–366, 427, 454 engs	
366 eng	
conv (12.0)	15.0
Tilt cab (13.0)	16.3
427, 454 eng conv (14.8)	18.5
Tilt cab (16.1)	20.2
w/A.C. add (1.0)	1.0
w/P.S. add (.5)	.5
w/Air inj add (.4)	.4
w/Air comp add (.9)	.9

LABOR 15 CRANKSHAFT & DAMPER 15 LABOR

Main and Rod Bearings, Renew

Includes: R&R all normal interfering parts. Plastigauge and install new main and rod bearings. Renew gaskets and seals as necessary. Recondition oil pump.

(Factory Time)	Chilton Time
Six–conv (4.6)	6.4
Tilt cab (4.0)	6.2
V-8–307, 350 engs	
conv (4.6)	6.4
Tilt cab (4.9)	7.6
V-8–366, 427, 454 engs	
conv (5.1)	7.0
Tilt cab (4.8)	7.4

Main Bearings, Renew

Includes: R&R all normal interfering parts. Plastigauge and install new main bearings. Renew gaskets and seals as necessary. Recondition oil pump.

(Factory Time)	Chilton Time
Six–conv (3.6)	4.6
Tilt cab (3.4)	4.4
V-8–307, 350 engs	
conv (3.0)	4.0
Tilt cab (4.1)	5.2
V-8–366, 427, 454 engs	
conv (3.0)	4.6
Tilt cab (4.0)	5.0

Rear Main Bearing Oil Seal, Renew

Includes: R&R all normal interfering parts.

(Factory Time)	Chilton Time
Six–conv (1.2)	2.5
Tilt cab (1.8)	2.7
V-8–conv (1.0)	2.5
Tilt cab (1.6)	2.7

Vibration Damper, Renew

Includes: R&R all normal interfering parts.

(Factory Time)	Chilton Time
Six–conv (1.4)	2.0
Tilt cab (.8)	1.2
w/P.S. add (.2)	.2
V-8–307, 350 engs	
conv (1.6)	2.2
Tilt cab (1.4)	2.0
V-8–366, 427, 454 engs	
conv (2.1)	2.9
Tilt cab (2.6)	3.5
R&R each additional drive belt	
add (.2)	.2

DIESEL ENGINES

Crankshaft and Main Bearings, Renew

Includes: R&R all normal interfering parts and engine. Plastigauge and install new main and rod bearings. Recondition oil pump.

(Factory Time)	Chilton Time
Isuzu Diesel (15.8)	22.9
w/P.S. add (.3)	.3
Deutz Diesel	
All series (15.1)	21.5
Detroit Diesel	
6-71 conv (24.7)	31.7
Alum Tilt (24.3)	31.2
6V-53 conv (20.0)	25.6
Steel Tilt (19.0)	24.2
6V-71 Steel Tilt (21.0)	27.0
8V-71 conv (24.4)	31.4
Alum Tilt (23.8)	30.6
12V-71 Alum Tilt (34.0)	43.5
w/A.C. add (1.0)	1.0
w/P.S. add (.8)	.8
w/Pwr take off add (.3)	.3

Main and Rod Bearings, Renew

Includes: R&R all normal interfering parts. Plastigauge and install new main and rod bearings. Recondition oil pump.

(Factory Time)	Chilton Time
Isuzu Diesel (4.2)	6.4
Deutz Diesel	
All series (5.8)	7.9
Detroit Diesel	
6-71 (7.8)	10.0
6V-53, 6V-71 (7.9)	10.2
8V-71 (8.1)	10.3
12V-71 (11.1)	14.4

Main Bearings, Renew

Includes: R&R all normal interfering parts. Plastigauge and install new main bearings. Recondition oil pump.

(Factory Time)	Chilton Time
Isuzu Diesel (3.2)	4.6
Deutz Diesel	
All series (3.6)	5.0
Detroit Diesel	
6-71 (7.2)	9.2
6V-53, 6-71 (7.3)	9.4
8V-71 (7.2)	9.2
12V-71 (9.9)	12.7

Rear Main Bearing Oil Seal, Renew

Includes: R&R all normal interfering parts.

(Factory Time)	Chilton Time
Isuzu Diesel (2.4)	3.5
Deutz Diesel (2.4)	3.5
Detroit Diesel (5.1)	6.6

Front Main Bearing Oil Seal, Renew

Includes: R&R all normal interfering parts.

(Factory Time)	Chilton Time
Isuzu Diesel (.6)	1.0
w/P.S. add (.3)	.3
Deutz Diesel (1.1)	1.6
Detroit Diesel (6.7)	8.5

Crankshaft Damper, Renew

(Factory Time)	Chilton Time
Isuzu Diesel (.5)	.9
w/P.S. add (.3)	.3
Detroit Diesel(3.4)	4.6
w/P.S. add (.2)	.2

Crankshaft Pulley, Renew

(Factory Time)	Chilton Time
Deutz Diesel (1.1)	1.5

LABOR 16 CAMSHAFT & TIMING GEARS 16 LABOR

GASOLINE ENGINES

Timing Cover Oil Seal, Renew

(Factory Time)	Chilton Time
Six–conv (1.5)	2.2
Tilt cab (.8)	1.4
w/P.S. add (.2)	.2
V-8–307, 350 engs	
conv (1.7)	2.4
Tilt cab (1.5)	2.2
w/A.C. add (.2)	.2
w/Air comp add (.2)	.2
V-8–366, 427 engs	
conv (2.3)	3.3
Tilt cab (2.5)	3.5
w/A.C. add (.2)	.2
w/P.S. add (.2)	.2
w/A.I.R. add (.2)	.2
w/Air comp add (.2)	.2

Timing Case Cover or Gasket, Renew

Includes: R&R all normal interfering parts.

(Factory Time)	Chilton Time
Six–conv (2.0)	3.1
Tilt cab (2.1)	2.7
V-8–307, 350 engs (2.2)	3.2
V-8–366, 427, 454 engs	
conv (2.6)	3.5
Tilt cab (3.3)	4.2
R&R each additional drive	
belt add (.2)	.2

Timing Chain or Gears, Renew

Includes: R&R all normal interfering parts.

(Factory Time)	Chilton Time
Six–conv (5.1)	7.8
Tilt cab (6.9)	8.7
V-8–307, 350 engs (2.6)	3.7
V-8–366, 427, 454 engs	
conv (3.0)	4.0
Tilt cab (4.5)	5.7
R&R each additional drive	
belt add (.2)	.2

Camshaft, Renew

Includes: R&R all normal interfering parts. Renew gaskets and seals as necessary. Adjust valves.

(Factory Time)	Chilton Time
Six–conv (5.1)	7.4
Tilt cab (6.6)	7.9
w/P.S. add (.2)	.2
w/A.I.R. add (.5)	.5
V-8–307, 350 engs	
conv (5.9)	8.0
Tilt cab (6.3)	8.6
V-8–366, 427, 454 engs	
conv (6.7)	10.5
Tilt cab (7.9)	11.2
w/A.C. add (1.2)	1.2
w/P.S. add (.2)	.2
w/Air comp add (.5)	.5
w/Air inj add (.5)	.5

DIESEL ENGINES

Timing Case Cover or Gasket, Renew

Includes: R&R all normal interfering parts.

(Factory Time)	Chilton Time
Isuzu Diesel	
All series (1.3)	2.0
w/P.S. add (.3)	.3
Deutz Diesel	
All series (3.3)	4.5

Timing Gears, Renew

Includes: R&R all normal interfering parts and all required adjustments.

(Factory Time)	Chilton Time
Detroit Diesel	
6-71 conv (18.6)	*23.3
Alum Tilt (18.2)	*22.8
6V-53 conv (18.0)	*22.5
Steel Tilt (17.0)	*21.3
6V-71 Steel Tilt (19.0)	*23.8
8V-71 conv (21.1)	*26.6
Alum Tilt (20.5)	*25.7
12V-71 Alum Tilt (26.0)	*32.5
*Includes R&R engine	
*w/A.C. add (1.0)	1.0
w/P.S. add (.8)	.8
*w/Pwr take off (.3)	.3

Camshaft, Renew

Includes: R&R all normal interfering parts and all required adjustments.

(Factory Time)	Chilton Time
Isuzu Diesel	
All series (6.6)	9.5
w/P.S. add (.3)	.3
Deutz Diesel	
All series (12.5)	*17.0
Detroit Diesel	
6-71 conv (19.6)	*24.6
Alum Tilt (19.2)	*24.1
6V-53 conv-one (20.0)	*25.0
both (24.0)	*30.0

LABOR 16 CAMSHAFT & TIMING GEARS 16 LABOR

(Factory Time)	Chilton Time
Steel Tilt-one (19.0)	*23.8
both (23.0)	*28.8
6V-71 Steel Tilt-one (22.0)	*27.5
both (27.0)	*33.8
8V-71 conventional-one (24.6)	*30.8
both (30.6)	*38.3
Alum Tilt-one (24.0)	*30.0
both (30.0)	*37.5
12V-71 Alum Tilt-one (29.0)	*36.3
both (37.0)	*46.3
*Includes R&R engine	
*w/A.C. add (1.0)	1.0
w/P.S. add (.8)	.8
*w/Pwr take off add (.3)	.3

Camshaft Bearings, Renew (Camshaft Removed)

(Factory Time)	Chilton Time
Detroit Diesel	
one side (.3)	.6
both sides (.5)	.9

LABOR 17 ENGINE OILING SYSTEM 17 LABOR

GASOLINE ENGINES

(Factory Time)	Chilton Time
Oil Pan or Gasket, Renew	
Six–conv (1.1)	2.0
Tilt cab (1.4)	2.2
V-8–307, 350 engs	
conv (1.0)	1.5
Tilt cab (.9)	1.6
V-8–366, 427, 454 engs	
conv (.9)	1.6
Tilt cab (1.1)	1.8
Oil Pump, Renew	
Six–conv (1.2)	2.3
Tilt cab (1.6)	2.5
V-8–307, 350 engs	
conv (1.1)	1.6
Tilt cab (1.0)	1.8
V-8–366, 427, 454 engs	
conv (1.0)	1.7
Tilt cab (1.2)	2.0
Recondition add (.5)	.5
Oil Cooler or Gasket, Renew	
All series (1.0)	1.5
Oil Filter Assembly, Renew	
All series (.3)	.4
Pressure Test Engine Bearings (Pan Removed)	
All series	1.0
Oil Pressure Gauge (Dash), Renew	
conv (.4)	.9
Oil Pressure Gauge (Engine), Renew	
All series (.2)	.4

DIESEL ENGINES

(Factory Time)	Chilton Time
Oil Pan or Gasket, Renew	
Isuzu Diesel	
All series (1.2)	1.7
Deutz Diesel	
All series (1.0)	1.4
Detroit Diesel	
6-71 (1.6)	2.3
6V-53 (1.0)	1.4
6V-71 (1.4)	2.1
8V-71 (1.5)	2.2
12V-71 (2.0)	2.6
Oil Pump Renew	
Isuzu Diesel	
All series (1.4)	2.0
Deutz Diesel	
All series (3.6)	5.0
Detroit Diesel	
exc below (8.2)	10.4
6-71 (2.3)	3.1
Recondition add,	
Detroit Diesel	
exc below (1.0)	1.0
6-71, 12V-71 (2.0)	2.0
Oil Cooler or Gasket, Renew	
Isuzu Diesel	
All series (5.6)	8.1
Deutz Diesel	
All series (1.2)	1.8
Detroit Diesel	
exc below (2.6)	3.7
6-71 (2.2)	3.0
Oil Filter Assembly, Renew	
Isuzu Diesel (.3)	.4
Deutz Diesel (.3)	.4
Detroit Diesel (.5)	.6
Pressure Test Engine Bearings (Pan Removed)	
All series	1.0
Oil Pressure Gauge (Dash), Renew	
conv (.4)	.9
Oil Pressure Gauge (Engine), Renew	
All series (.2)	.4

LABOR 18 CLUTCH & FLYWHEEL 18 LABOR

(Factory Time)	Chilton Time
Clutch Pedal Free Play, Adjust	
Astro (.6)	.8
All other models (.3)	.4
Clutch Control Cable, Renew	
Series 4500-7000 (.6)	.9
Clutch Master Cylinder, Renew	
Series 4500-7000 (.5)	.8
Series 8000-9000	
single (.6)	1.3
dual (.9)	1.7
Clutch Master Cylinder, Recondition	
Series 4500-7000-one side (.9)	1.2
both sides (1.1)	1.8
Series 8000-9000	
single (1.3)	1.8
dual-one side (1.7)	2.3
both sides (1.9)	2.7
Clutch Slave Cylinder, Renew	
All series	
conv cab (.6)	1.0
Tilt cab (Isuzu) (.8)	1.2
Clutch Slave Cylinder Recondition	
All series	
conv cab (1.0)	1.6
Tilt cab (Isuzu) (2.0)	2.7
Bleed Clutch Hydraulic System	
All series (.4)	.6

Clutch Assembly, Renew

Includes: R&R transmission and all normal interfering parts.

(Factory Time)	Chilton Time
4 Speed	
SM 465-CH 465 (2.7)	3.7
5 Speed	
Clark	
282-285 (2.1)	3.0
390-397	
Gas (3.3)	5.0
Diesel (2.3)	3.2
450-455-457	
Gas (2.8)	3.9
Diesel (2.6)	3.6
551-557 (2.6)	3.6
NP 542 (3.0)	4.2
Isuzu	
MGB5B-MGB5E (2.3)	3.3
Spicer	
5052-5252-5552	
5852-6052-6253	
Gas (3.6)	5.0
Diesel (3.1)	4.3
Fuller	
T905A-T11605 (4.7)	6.5
6 Speed	
Spicer	
SST1062-SST1362C (2.7)	3.7
Fuller	
T1056-RT-11606	
RT906 (5.7)	8.0
7 Speed	
Spicer	
SS1007-2A-SS1107-2A	
SS1372A	
Astro (4.5)	6.3
Brigadier (6.3)	8.8
Fuller	
TO955ALL-TO955DLL (6.2)	8.7
8 Speed	
Fuller	
RT-9508-RTO-1157DL	
RT-11608-TS-1308 (5.7)	8.0
9 Speed	
Fuller	
RTO-1157DLL-RT-11509	
RTO-11607-RT-RTO-11609A	
RT-RTO-9509 (4.4)	6.1
RT-14609-RT-12509 (7.3)	10.2

	(Factory Time)	Chilton Time
10 Speed		
Fuller		
RTO-1258LL-RT-6610-RTO-958LL		
RT-1110-RTO-11608LL-RTO-14610		
4500-7000 Series	(3.7)	5.2
8000-9000 Series		
General	(6.7)	9.4
All other models	(5.2)	7.3
13 Speed		
Fuller		
RT-6613-RT-RTO-11613		
RT-RTO-9513-RT-RTO-12513		
RT-RTO-14613		
4500-7000 Series	(5.5)	7.7
8000-9000 Series		
Astro	(4.2)	5.9
Brigadier	(6.3)	8.8
General	(7.0)	9.8
14 Speed		
Spicer		
SST1214-3A	(6.3)	8.8
15 Speed		
Fuller		
RT-915-RT-RTO-12515		
RT-11615-RT-RTO-14615		
Brigadier	(6.2)	8.7
General	(7.0)	9.8
w/P.T.O. add		.4
w/Aux trans add		.5
w/Bolted C/member add		1.0
w/Dual exhaust add		1.0
R&R turbo pipe add		1.0
Renew pilot brg add		.2

Clutch Release Bearing, Renew

Includes: R&R transmission and all normal interfering parts.

	(Factory Time)	Chilton Time
4 Speed		
SM 465-CH 465	(2.2)	3.0
5 Speed		
Clark		
282-285	(1.6)	2.2
390-397		
Gas	(2.8)	3.9
Diesel	(1.8)	2.5
450-455-457		
Gas	(1.9)	2.6
Diesel	(1.4)	1.9
551-557	(1.8)	2.5
NP 542	(2.5)	3.5
Isuzu		
MGB5B-MGB5E	(1.9)	2.8
Spicer		
5052-5252-5552		
5852-6052-6253		
Gas	(2.8)	3.9
Diesel	(2.3)	3.2
Fuller		
T905A-T11605	(4.2)	5.8
6 Speed		
Spicer		
SST1062-SST1362C	(2.2)	3.0
Fuller		
T1056-RT-11606		
RT906	(5.2)	7.2
7 Speed		
Spicer		
SS1007-2A-SS1107-2A		
SS1372A		
Astro	(5.2)	7.2
Brigadier	(5.8)	8.1
Fuller		
TO955ALL-TO955DLL	(5.7)	7.9
8 Speed		
Fuller		
RT-9508-RTO-1157DL		
RT-11608-TS-1308	(5.2)	7.2
9 Speed		
Fuller		
RTO-1157DLL-RT-11509		
RTO-11607-RT-RTO-11609A		
RT-RTO-9509	(3.8)	5.3
RT-14609-RT-12509	(6.7)	9.3
10 Speed		
Fuller		
RTO-1258LL-RT-6610-RTO-958LL		
RT-1110-RTO-11608LL-RTO-14610		
4500-7000 Series	(3.2)	4.5
8000-9000 Series		
General	(6.2)	8.6
All other models	(4.7)	6.5
13 Speed		
Fuller		
RT-6613-RT-RTO-11613		
RT-RTO-9513-RT-RTO-12513		
RT-RTO-14613		
4500-7000 Series	(5.0)	7.0
8000-9000 Series		
Astro	(3.7)	5.1
Brigadier	(5.8)	8.1
General	(6.5)	9.0
14 Speed		
Spicer		
SST1214-3A	(5.8)	8.1
15 Speed		
Fuller		
RT-915-RT-RTO-12515		
RT-11615-RT-RTO-14615		
Brigadier	(5.7)	8.0
General	(6.5)	9.0
w/P.T.O. add		.4
w/Aux trans add		.5
w/Bolted C/member add		1.0
w/Dual exhaust add		1.0
R&R turbo pipe add		1.0

Flywheel, Renew

Includes: R&R transmission and all normal interfering parts.

	(Factory Time)	Chilton Time
4 Speed		
SM 465-CH 465	(3.4)	4.4
5 Speed		
Clark		
282-285	(2.8)	4.0
390-397		
Gas	(4.0)	5.6
Diesel	(3.0)	4.2
450-455-457		
Gas	(3.3)	4.4
Diesel	(3.1)	4.1
551-557	(3.1)	4.1
NP 542	(3.7)	5.2
Isuzu		
MGB5B-MGB5E	(2.6)	3.8
Spicer		
5052-5252-5552		
5852-6052-6253		
Gas		
single plate	(4.1)	5.7
double plate	(4.5)	6.3
Diesel		
single plate	(3.6)	5.0
double plate	(4.0)	5.6
Fuller		
T905A-T11605	(5.4)	7.6
6 Speed		
Spicer		
SST1062-SST1362C	(3.4)	4.8
Fuller		
T1056-RT-11606		
RT906	(6.4)	9.0
7 Speed		
Spicer		
SS1007-2A-SS1107-2A		
SS1372A		
Astro	(5.2)	7.3
Brigadier	(7.0)	9.9
Fuller		
TO955ALL-TO955DLL	(6.9)	9.7
8 Speed		
Fuller		
RT-9508-RTO-1157DL		
RT-11608-TS-1308	(6.4)	9.0
9 Speed		
Fuller		
RTO-1157DLL-RT-11509		
RTO-11607-RT-RTO-11609A		
RT-RTO-9509	(5.1)	7.2
RT-14609-RT-12509	(7.3)	10.3
10 Speed		
Fuller		
RTO-1258LL-RT-6610-RTO-958LL		
RT-1110-RTO-11608LL-RTO-14610		
4500-7000 Series	(4.4)	6.2
8000-9000 Series		
General	(7.4)	10.4
All other models	(5.9)	8.3
13 Speed		
Fuller		
RT-6613-RT-RTO-11613		
RT-RTO-9513-RT-RTO-12513		
RT-RTO-14613		
4500-7000 Series	(6.2)	8.7
8000-9000 Series		
Astro	(4.9)	6.9
Brigadier	(7.0)	9.9
General	(7.7)	10.8
14 Speed		
Spicer		
SST-1214-3A	(7.0)	9.9
15 Speed		
Fuller		
RT-915-RT-RTO-12515		
RT-11615-RT-RTO-14615		
Brigadier	(6.9)	9.7
General	(7.7)	10.8
w/P.T.O. add		.4
w/Aux trans add		.5
w/Bolted C/member add		1.0
w/Dual exhaust add		1.0
R&R turbo pipe add		1.0
Renew ring gear add		.6

LABOR 19 STANDARD TRANSMISSION 19 LABOR

(Factory Time)	Chilton Time
Transmission Assembly, R&R	
4 Speed	
SM 465-CH 465 (2.0)	2.8
5 Speed	
Clark	
282-285 (1.4)	1.9
390-397	
w/Gas eng (2.6)	3.6
w/Diesel eng (1.6)	2.2
450-455-457	
Gas (1.8)	2.5
Diesel (1.2)	1.7
551-557 (1.6)	2.4
NP 542 (2.3)	3.2
Isuzu	
MBG5B-MBG5E (2.1)	3.0
Spicer	
5052-5252-5552	
5852-6052-6253	
Gas (2.6)	3.6
Diesel (2.1)	2.9
Fuller	
T905A-T11605 (4.0)	5.6
6 Speed	
Spicer	
SST1062-SST1362C (2.0)	2.8
Fuller	
T1056-RT-11606	
RT-906 (5.0)	7.0
7 Speed	
Spicer	
SS1007-2A-SS1107-2A	
SS1372A	
Astro (3.8)	5.3
Brigadier (5.6)	7.8
Fuller	
TO955ALL-TO955DLL (5.5)	7.7
8 Speed	
Fuller	
RT-9508-RTO-1157DL	
RT-11608-TS-1308 (5.0)	7.0
9 Speed	
Fuller	
RTO-1157DLL-RT-11509	
RTO-11607-RT-RTO-11609A	
RT-RTO-9509 (3.7)	5.1
RT-14609-RT-12509 (6.6)	9.2
10 Speed	
Fuller	
RTO-1258LL-RT-6610-RTO-958LL	
RT-1110-RTO-11608LL-RTO-14610	
4500-7000 Series (3.0)	4.2
8000-9000 Series	
General (6.0)	8.4
All other models (4.5)	6.3
13 Speed	
Fuller	
RT-6613-RT-RTO-11613	
RT-RTO-9513-RT-RTO-12513	
RT-RTO-14613	
4500-7000 Series (4.8)	6.7
8000-9000 Series	
Astro (3.5)	4.9
Brigadier (5.6)	7.8
General (6.3)	8.8
14 Speed	
Spicer	
SST1214-3A (5.6)	7.8
15 Speed	
Fuller	
RT-915-RT-RTO-12515	
RT-11615-RT-RTO-14615	
Brigadier (5.5)	7.7
General (6.3)	8.8
w/P.T.O. add	.4
w/Aux trans add	.5
w/Bolted C/member add	1.0
w/Dual exhaust add	1.0
R&R turbo pipe add	1.0

Transmission Assembly, R&R and Recondition

Includes: Complete disassembly of transmission. Inspect and clean all components. Renew parts, gaskets and seals as necessary. Make all normal adjustments. Road test.

(Factory Time)	Chilton Time
4 Speed	
SM 465-CH 465 (5.5)	7.7
5 Speed	
Clark	
282-285 (4.7)	6.5
390-397	
Gas (6.6)	9.2
Diesel (5.6)	7.8
450-455-457	
Gas (5.1)	7.1
Diesel (4.5)	6.3
551-557 (6.2)	8.6
NP 542 (5.4)	7.5
Isuzu	
MBG5B-MBG5E (7.1)	9.9
Spicer	
5052-5252-5552	
5852-6052-6253	
Gas (8.0)	11.2
Diesel (7.5)	10.5
Fuller	
T905A-T11605 (11.2)	15.6
6 Speed	
Spicer	
SST1062-SST1362C (7.8)	10.9
Fuller	
T1056-RT-11606-RT-906	
front case (11.7)	16.3
aux case (8.9)	12.4
complete (14.2)	19.8
7 Speed	
Spicer	
SS1007-2A	
Astro	
front case (13.0)	18.2
rear case (7.6)	10.6
complete (13.6)	19.0
Brigadier	
front case (14.8)	20.7
rear case (9.4)	13.1
complete (15.4)	21.5
Fuller	
TO955All-TO955DLL	
front case (12.6)	17.6
aux case (8.0)	11.2
complete (14.7)	20.5
8 Speed	
Fuller	
RT-9508-RTO-1157DL	
RT-11608-TS-1308	
front case (12.1)	16.9
aux case (7.5)	10.5
complete (14.2)	19.8
9 Speed	
Fuller	
RTO-1157DLL-RTO-11607	
front case (10.8)	15.1
aux case (6.2)	8.6
complete (12.9)	18.0
RT-RTO-9509	
RT-11509-RT-RTO-11609A	
front case (10.4)	14.5
aux case (7.6)	10.6
complete (12.9)	18.0
RT-14609-RT-12509	
front case (13.3)	18.6
aux case (10.5)	14.7
complete (15.8)	22.1
10 Speed	
RTO-1258LL	
4500-7000 Series	
front case (9.7)	13.5
aux case (6.9)	9.6
complete (12.2)	17.0
8000-9000 Series	
General	
front case (12.7)	17.7
aux case (9.9)	13.8
complete (15.2)	21.2
All other models	
front case (11.2)	15.6
aux case (8.4)	11.7
complete (13.7)	19.1
RT-6610-RTO-958LL	
4500-7000 Series	
front case (10.1)	14.1
aux case (5.5)	7.7
complete (12.2)	17.0
8000-9000 Series	
General	
front case (13.1)	18.3
aux case (8.5)	11.9
complete (15.2)	21.2
All other models	
front case (11.6)	16.2
aux case (7.0)	9.8
complete (13.7)	19.1
13 Speed	
Fuller	
RT-6613	
4500-7000 Series	
front case (13.5)	18.9
int case (8.5)	11.9
aux case (8.4)	11.7
complete (15.1)	21.1
8000-9000 Series	
Astro	
front case (12.2)	17.0
int case (7.2)	10.0
aux case (7.1)	9.9
complete (13.8)	19.3
Brigadier	
front case (14.3)	20.0
int case (9.3)	13.0
aux case (9.2)	12.9
complete (15.9)	22.2
General	
front case (15.0)	21.0
int case (10.0)	14.0
aux case (9.9)	13.9
complete (16.6)	23.2
RT-RTO-9513-RT-RTO-11613	
RT-RTO-12513-RT-RTO-14613	
4500-7000 Series	
front case (11.9)	16.6
aux case (9.3)	13.0
complete (15.9)	22.2
8000-9000 Series	
Astro	
front case (10.6)	14.8
aux case (8.0)	11.2
complete (14.6)	20.4
Brigadier	
front case (12.7)	17.7
aux case (10.1)	14.1
complete (16.7)	23.3
General	
front case (13.4)	18.7
aux case (10.8)	15.1
complete (17.4)	24.3
14 Speed	
Spicer	
SST1214-3A	
front case (14.9)	20.8
rear case (9.4)	13.1
complete (15.4)	21.5
15 Speed	
Fuller	
RT-915-RT-RTO-12515	
RT-11615-RT-RTO-14615	
Brigadier	
front case (12.6)	17.6

LABOR 19 STANDARD TRANSMISSION 19 LABOR

(Factory Time)	Chilton Time
aux case (10.0)	14.0
complete (16.6)	23.2
General	
front case (13.4)	18.7
aux case (10.8)	15.1
complete (17.4)	24.3
w/P.T.O. add	.4
w/Aux trans add	.5
w/Bolted C/member add	1.0
w/Dual exhaust add	1.0
R&R turbo pipe add	1.0

Auxiliary Transmission, R&R

Series 4500-7000 (1.5)	2.5
w/Hyd. brakes add (.5)	.5
Series 7500-8500 (2.8)	3.9
Series 9500	
8341 (2.5)	3.6
8345 (2.5)	3.6

Auxiliary Transmission, R&R and Recondition

Includes: Disassembly and assembly. Cleaning and inspection of all parts. Renew or recondition all necessary components. Renew gaskets and seals as required. Road test.

Series 4500-7000	
6041 (6.0)	7.7
7041 (6.8)	9.0
Fuller 2A92 (7.2)	9.9
w/Hyd. brakes add (.5)	.5
Series 7500-8500	
6041 (7.2)	9.3
7041 (6.1)	7.9
Series 9500	
8341 (6.8)	8.5
8345 (6.8)	8.5

Auxiliary Transmission Rear Oil Seal, Renew

Fuller 2A92 (.7)	1.1
Spicer 7041 (.6)	1.0
w/Hyd. brakes add (.5)	.5

LABOR 20 TRANSFER CASE 20 LABOR

(Factory Time)	Chilton Time

Transfer Case Oil Seals, Renew

All series	
front (.8)	1.1
rear (.6)	.8

Transfer Case Speedometer Drive Gear, Renew

All series (.9)	1.2

Transfer Case P.T.O. Gasket, Renew

All series (.4)	.6

Transfer Case Assembly, Remove & Install

All series (1.7)	2.3
Renew assy add (.9)	1.0

Transfer Case Assy., R&R and Recondition

All series (8.2)	11.0

LABOR 23 AUTOMATIC TRANSMISSION 23 LABOR

(Factory Time)	Chilton Time

Allison–AT540, 543, 545, MT640, 643, 650, 653, 654, HT740-750-754

ON TRUCK SERVICES

Oil Pressure Test

All series (1.2)	1.6

Check Unit for Oil Leaks

Includes: Clean and dry outside of case, run unit to determine point of leak.

All series	.7

Manual or Throttle Lever Oil Seals, Renew

Includes: R&R oil pan and adjustments.

All series (1.4)	1.9

Oil Pan or Gasket, Renew

All series (.7)	1.0

Oil Control Valve Body, R&R and Recondition

AT series (1.9)	2.5
MT 640 (2.2)	2.8
MT 650 (2.4)	3.0
HT series (3.5)	4.2

Clutch Pack Clearance, Check

Includes: R&R oil pan.

All series (1.3)	1.9

Shift Linkage, Adjust

All series (.3)	.4

Throttle Linkage, Adjust

All series (.5)	.7

Retarder Linkage, Adjust

All series (.3)	.4

Retarder Valve Body, Recondition

All series (1.3)	1.6

Vacuum Modulator, Renew

All series (.2)	.4

Oil Filter, Renew

AT series (.9)	1.3
MT series (1.0)	1.3
HT series (1.3)	1.6

Neutral Safety Switch, Renew

All series (.3)	.5

SERVICES REQUIRING R&R

Transmission Assembly, R&R or Renew

Includes: Drain and refill unit. Adjust linkage and road test.

Series 4500-7000	
AT 540-conv (4.3)	5.6
Tilt cab (4.7)	5.9
MT 640-650 (4.6)	5.9
Series 8000-9000	
MT 640-650 (4.6)	5.8
HT 740-750 (7.6)	9.0
w/Pwr take off add (.4)	.4

Transmission Assembly, R&R and Recondition

Includes: Drain and refill unit, adjust all linkage. Disassemble and assemble complete transmission, inspect all parts. Clean, renew or recondition components. Renew gaskets and seals as necessary. Road test.

Series 4500-7000	
AT 540-conv (14.0)	15.9
Tilt cab (14.4)	16.3
MT 640 (17.2)	20.2
MT 650 (18.0)	21.0
Series 8000-9000	
MT 640 (17.2)	20.2
MT 650 (18.0)	21.0
HT 740 (28.4)	31.2
HT 750 CRD (31.9)	37.0
HT 750 DRD (32.4)	37.5
w/Pwr take off add (.4)	.4

Torque Converter, R&R and Recondition

Includes: R&R transmission assembly. Drain and refill unit. Adjust linkage and road test.

Series 4500-7000	
Series 8000-9000	
AT 540 conv (5.5)	6.9
Tilt cab (5.9)	7.3
MT 640-650 (5.8)	7.3
Series 7500-8500	
MT 640-650 (5.4)	6.9
HT 740-750 (8.4)	10.6

ALLISON (TURBO HYDRA-MATIC) AT 475

ON TRUCK SERVICES

Drain and Refill Unit

All series (.5)	.6

Oil Pressure Check

All series (.5)	.8

Check Unit for Oil Leaks

Includes: Clean and dry outside of the case and run unit to determine point of leak.

All series (.7)	.7

Vacuum Modulator Assembly, Renew

All series (.3)	.5

LABOR 23 AUTOMATIC TRANSMISSION 23 LABOR

	(Factory Time)	Chilton Time
Oil Pan or Gasket, Renew		
All series	(.6)	1.0
Oil Control Valve Body, R&R or Renew		
All series	(.9)	1.3
Oil Control Valve Body, R&R and Recondition		
All series	(1.6)	2.5
Servos, Renew or Recondition		
All series-front	(1.2)	1.6
rear	(1.4)	1.8
Governor Assembly, R&R or Renew		
All series	(.3)	.5
Governor Assembly, R&R and Recondition		
All series	(.6)	1.0
Detent Solenoid, Renew and Adjust		
All series	(.6)	1.0
Kickdown Switch, Renew		
All series	(.2)	.4
Pressure Regulator, Renew		
All series	(.7)	1.1
Parking Pawl, Renew		
All series	(.9)	1.3
Manual Shift, Shaft Seal, Detent Lever and Park Actuator Rod, Renew		
All series	(.9)	1.3
Case Extension Oil Seal, Renew		
All series	(.9)	1.3

SERVICES REQUIRING R&R

Note: All the following operations include R&R transmission.

	(Factory Time)	Chilton Time
Transmission Assembly, R&R or Renew		
All series	(3.0)	5.3
Transmission and Converter Assembly, R&R and Recondition		
All series	(10.0)	15.1
Torque Converter, Renew		
All series	(3.2)	5.5
Front Oil Pump Oil Seal, Renew		
All series	(3.0)	5.3
Front Oil Pump, Renew		
All series	(3.3)	5.8
Front Oil Pump, R&R and Recondition		
All series	(3.9)	6.5
Bands, Renew		
All series	(4.5)	7.1
Forward, Direct or Intermediate Clutch, R&R or Renew		
All series	(3.7)	6.3
Forward, Direct or Intermediate Clutch, R&R and Recondition		
All series	(4.2)	6.8
Low Sprag Unit, Renew		
All series	(4.6)	7.2
Intermediate Sprag Unit, Renew		
All series	(4.0)	6.6

LABOR 25 U-JOINTS & DRIVESHAFT 25 LABOR

	(Factory Time)	Chilton Time
Drive Shaft, R&R or Renew		
All series-exc Isuzu		
front	(.5)	.9
rear	(.5)	.9
intermediate	(1.2)	2.0
Tilt cab (Isuzu)		
front	(1.1)	1.4
rear	(.4)	.6
intermediate	(1.2)	1.6

Universal Joint, Renew or Recondition
Includes: R&R drive shaft.

	(Factory Time)	Chilton Time
All series-exc Isuzu		
front	(.8)	1.1
w/Hanger bearing	(1.8)	2.3
intermediate		
w/Slip joint	(.8)	1.2
wo/Slip joint	(1.0)	1.4
rear	(.9)	1.2
Tilt cab (Isuzu)		
front	(1.0)	1.4
rear	(1.0)	1.4
intermediate	(1.1)	1.5
Center Support Bearings, Renew		
Series 4500-7000		
conv	(1.1)	1.5
Tilt cab	(.9)	1.1
Tilt cab (Isuzu)	(1.2)	1.5
Hanger Bearing Support Assembly, Recondition		
All series		
exc below	(1.3)	1.8
band type brake	(1.8)	2.3
Bendix brake	(2.2)	2.7

LABOR 26 REAR AXLE 26 LABOR

FRONT DRIVE AXLE

	(Factory Time)	Chilton Time
Front Axle Shaft, Renew		
All series-one	(.8)	1.1
both	(1.5)	2.0
Front Axle Shaft Oil Seal, Renew		
All series-one	(1.4)	1.8
both	(2.7)	3.5
Spindle Pivot Bearing, Renew		
All series-one	(1.9)	2.5
both	(3.5)	4.8
Pinion Shaft Oil Seal, Renew		
All series	(1.0)	1.4
Front Differential Carrier, R&R or Renew		
All series	(2.8)	3.7
Front Differential Carrier, R&R and Recondition		
All series	(4.5)	6.0

REAR DRIVE AXLE

	(Factory Time)	Chilton Time
Axle Shaft, Renew (One Axle)		
Series 4500-7000		
Corp-one	(.3)	.6
both	(.4)	.8
Eaton-one	(.4)	.7
both	(.6)	1.2
flange type-one	(.4)	.6
both	(.7)	1.0
Series 8000-9000		
gear type-one	(.3)	.6
both	(.5)	.8
flange type-one	(.5)	.8
both	(.8)	1.2
Rear Wheel Bearing or Oil Seal, Renew		
Series 4500-7000		
Corp-one	(1.0)	1.3
both	(1.9)	2.4
Eaton-one	(1.3)	1.7
both	(2.4)	3.0
flange type		
one side	(2.0)	2.5
Series 8000-9000-one	(1.5)	2.0
both	(2.8)	3.5
Pinion Shaft Oil Seal, Renew		
Series 4500-7000		
RO92	(.6)	1.0
Corp axle	(1.0)	1.5
Eaton-single speed	(1.1)	1.6
Rockwell-single speed	(1.0)	1.5
Eaton-two speed	(1.2)	1.7
tandem	(1.3)	1.8
Series 8000-9000		
single axle	(1.0)	1.5
tandem axle	(1.3)	1.8

Tandem Drive Line Alignment, Check
Includes: Road test.

	(Factory Time)	Chilton Time
All series		1.4

Tandem Drive Line Alignment, Check and Adjust
Includes: Alignment of engine, transmission drive shafts and both axles. Road test.

	(Factory Time)	Chilton Time
All series	(1.3)	1.9

Differential Carrier Assembly, R&R or Renew
SERIES 4500-7000
SINGLE SPEED

(Factory Time)	Chilton Time
SINGLE AXLE	
RO92 (2.4)	3.4
H110-H135-H150	
H175 (1.7)	2.4
Spicer	
G190S-M220S (2.7)	3.8
Eaton	
E17101-E17121-E22121	
E23121 (2.7)	3.8
Rockwell	
R170 (2.7)	3.8
TWO SPEED	
SINGLE AXLE	
RO92 (2.3)	3.3
T150-T175 (1.7)	2.4
Spicer	
M190T-M220T (2.8)	4.0
Eaton	
E17201-E17221-E22221 (2.6)	3.6
E23221 (3.0)	4.2
SINGLE SPEED	
FRONT TANDEM	
Eaton	
DS341 (5.0)	7.1
Rockwell	
SL100-SQ100 (3.5)	4.9
TWO SPEED	
FRONT TANDEM	
Eaton	
DT341 (4.4)	6.1
REAR TANDEM-SINGLE SPEED	
Eaton	
DS341 (2.9)	4.1
Rockwell	
SL100-SQ100 (3.5)	4.9
REAR TANDEM-TWO SPEED	
Eaton	
DT341 (3.9)	5.5
SERIES 8000-9000	
SINGLE REDUCTION OR FRONT TANDEM	
R170-E17121-E18121 (2.5)	3.6
E1910-19121-E23121-E23421	
E26421-E26121 (3.0)	4.1
DOUBLE REDUCTION	
U200 (3.9)	5.0
44DP-50DP-38DPC (4.8)	5.9
TWO SPEED	
T185 (2.7)	3.8
E17221-E18221-E1920-199221-	
E23221-E26221-DT400-38DTC-	
44DTC-34DT (3.1)	4.2
TANDEM DUAL DRIVING–FRONT UNIT	
Single Reduction Forward Axle With Inter-Axle Diff	
E34DSC-SLHD-SQHD-SSHD-E38DSC	
SQHP-E34DSE-E34DS-DS380-44DSC-	
DS340-SUHD-STHD (4.7)	5.8
SINGLE REDUCTION–PUSHER AXLE	
R170 (2.5)	3.6
DOUBLE REDUCTION	
SQDD-SRDD-SUDD	
front unit (4.4)	5.5
rear unit (3.4)	4.5
REAR TANDEM	
Single Reduction	
R170-E17121-E18121 (2.5)	3.6
E23121-E23421-E26421	
E26121 (3.0)	4.1
Double Reduction	
44DP-50DP-38DPC (3.6)	4.7
Two Speed-Three Speed	
E34D3C-E38D3C	
front unit (3.2)	4.3
rear unit (2.7)	3.8
E17221-E18221-E23221	
E26221-DT400-38DTC	
44DTC-34DT (3.1)	4.2
TANDEM DUAL DRIVING–REAR UNIT	
Single Reduction Forward Axle With Inter-Axle Diff.	
E34DSC-SLHD-SQHD-SSHD-E38DSC	
SQHP-E34DSE-E34DS-DS380-44DSC	
DS340-SUHD-STHD (2.7)	3.8
R&R fifth wheel add	1.5

Differential Carrier Assembly, R&R and Recondition

Includes: Drain and refill unit. R&R all normal interfering parts. Disassemble and assemble complete unit. Inspect, clean, renew or recondition all components. Road test.

(Factory Time)	Chilton Time
SERIES 4500-7000	
SINGLE SPEED	
SINGLE AXLE	
RO92 (7.2)	10.2
H110-H135-H150	
H175 (6.7)	9.5
Spicer	
G190S-M220S (7.3)	10.4
Eaton	
E17101-E17121-E22121	
E23121 (7.3)	10.4
Rockwell	
R170 (8.0)	11.4
TWO SPEED	
SINGLE AXLE	
RO92 (9.7)	13.8
T150-T175 (5.9)	8.4
Spicer	
M190T-M220T (7.9)	11.2
Eaton	
E17201-E17221-E22221 (7.7)	10.9
E23221 (8.1)	11.5
SINGLE SPEED	
FRONT TANDEM	
Eaton	
DS341 (11.6)	16.5
Rockwell	
SL100-SQ100 (8.7)	12.4
TWO SPEED	
FRONT TANDEM	
Eaton	
DT341 (13.0)	18.5
REAR TANDEM-SINGLE SPEED	
Eaton	
DS341 (7.1)	10.0
Rockwell	
SL100-SQ100 (8.4)	11.9
REAR TANDEM-TWO SPEED	
Eaton	
DT341 (9.0)	12.8
SERIES 8000-9000	
SINGLE REDUCTION OR FRONT TANDEM	
R170-E17121-E18121 (8.6)	12.6
E1910-19121-E23121-E23421-	
E26421-E26121 (10.8)	14.3
DOUBLE REDUCTION	
U200 (11.9)	17.5
44DP-50DP-38DPC (16.3)	21.1
TWO SPEED	
T185 (8.2)	12.3
E17221-E18221-E1920-199221-	
E23221-E26221-DT400-38DTC-	
44DTC-34DT (8.2)	14.7
TANDEM DUAL DRIVING–FRONT UNIT	
Single Reduction Forward Axle With Inter-Axle Diff	
E34DSC-SLHD-SQHD-SSHD-E38DSC	
SQHP-E34DSE-E34DS-DS380-44DSC-	
DS340-SUHD-STHD (14.7)	19.5
SINGLE REDUCTION–PUSHER AXLE	
R170 (8.6)	12.6
DOUBLE REDUCTION	
SQDD-SRDD-SUDD	
front unit (16.3)	22.0
rear unit (12.7)	18.0
REAR TANDEM	
Single Reduction	
R170-E17121-E18121 (8.6)	12.4
E23121-E23421-E26421	
E26121 (10.8)	14.3
Double Reduction	
44DP-50DP-38DPC (12.7)	16.4
Two Speed-Three Speed	
E34D3C-E38D3C	
front unit (10.2)	15.0
rear unit (8.2)	13.3
E17221-E18221-E23221	
E26221-DT400-38DTC	
44DTC-34DT (8.2)	14.7
TANDEM DUAL DRIVING–REAR UNIT	
Single Reduction Forward Axle With Inter-Axle Diff	
E34DSC-SLHD-SQHD-SSHD	
E38DSC-SQHP-E34DSC-E34DS	
DS380-44DSC-DS340-SUHD	
STHD (8.8)	14.2
R&R fifth wheel add	1.5

Electric Shift Assembly, Renew

All series (.4)	.5

Electric Shift Assembly, Recondition

All series (1.0)	1.2

Axle Shift Control Switch, Renew

All series (.3)	.4

Axle Shift Motor, Renew

All series (.9)	1.2

Axle Shift Torsion Spring, Renew

All series (.4)	.9

Differential Lockout Air Control Valve, Renew

All series (.6)	1.0

Vacuum Shift Selector Valve Cable, Renew

All series (.5)	.8

Vacuum Shift Check Valve Assembly, Renew

All series (.4)	.6

Vacuum or Air Axle Shift Cylinder, Renew

All series (.3)	.6

Vacuum or Air Axle Shift Cylinder, Recondition

All series (.8)	1.2

Differential Lockout Chamber, Renew

Tandem (.3)	.5

Differential Lockout Chamber, Recondition

Tandem (.8)	1.2

LABOR 27 REAR SUSPENSION 27 LABOR

(Factory Time)	Chilton Time
Rear Spring, Renew	
Series 4500-7000	
Variable rate-exc Isuzu	
one (1.4)	1.9
both (2.8)	3.9
Isuzu	
one (1.7)	2.3
both (3.2)	4.4
Hendrickson-one (3.0)	4.0
both (5.7)	7.7
Series 8000-9000	
exc below-one (1.9)	2.4
both (3.8)	4.4
Hendrickson-one (2.7)	3.7
both (5.1)	7.1
Page & Page-one (1.6)	2.3
both (3.0)	3.9
w/Radius leaf-one (1.8)	2.5
both (3.5)	4.7
Reyco	
one spring (.9)	1.4
two springs (1.6)	2.5
Rear Spring Leaf, Renew	
Series 4500-7000	
Variable rate-exc Isuzu	
one (1.7)	2.5
both (3.3)	4.6
Isuzu	
one (1.8)	2.5
both (3.6)	5.0
Hendrickson-one (3.0)	4.6
both (6.3)	8.8
Series 8000-9000	
exc below-one (2.3)	2.9
both (4.5)	5.7
Hendrickson-one (3.2)	5.0
both (6.3)	8.8
Page & Page-one (1.6)	2.1
both (3.1)	4.0
w/Radius leaf-one (1.8)	2.3
both (3.5)	4.5
Reyco	
one spring (1.7)	2.4
two springs (3.2)	4.6
Rear Spring Front Eye Bushings, Renew	
Series 4500-7000	
exc below-one (1.1)	1.6
both (1.9)	3.0
Tandem-one (2.8)	3.5
both (5.5)	7.0
Series 8000-9000	
exc below-one (1.9)	2.5
both (3.7)	4.7
Hendrickson-one (1.1)	1.6
both (1.9)	3.0
Page & Page-one (2.0)	2.5
both (4.0)	5.0
w/Radius leaf-one (2.2)	2.8
both (4.3)	5.4
Rear Spring Shackles and/or Pins, Renew	
Tilt cab (Isuzu)	
one side (.6)	.9
both sides (.9)	1.5
Auxiliary Spring, Renew	
Series 4500-7000	
Variable rate-exc Isuzu	
one (.7)	1.4
both (1.3)	2.7
Isuzu	
one (1.9)	2.6
both (3.6)	5.0
Series 8000-9000	
exc below-one (1.5)	2.2
both (3.0)	4.2
Hendrickson-one (3.5)	4.5
both (6.9)	8.7
Page & Page-one (1.6)	2.1
both (3.0)	4.0
w/Radius leaf-one (1.6)	2.1
both (3.0)	4.0
Tandem Suspension Support Beam, R&R	
All series (4.0)	5.1
Tandem Suspension Torque Rod, Renew	
All series	
one (1.1)	1.6
both (2.3)	3.1
Shock Absorbers, Renew	
All series-one (.3)	.5
both (.5)	.8

LABOR 28 AIR CONDITIONING 28 LABOR

Note: If more than one item requires replacement where evacuation and discharging the system is already included in the operation, deduct 1.0 hour for each addditional item to the times listed.

(Factory Time)	Chilton Time
Drain, Evacuate and Recharge System	
All series (.7)	2.0
Pressure Test System	
All series	1.2
Refrigerant, Add Partial Charge	
All series	1.4
Compressor Belt, Renew	
All series (.2)	.5
Compressor Assembly, Renew	
Includes: Transfer all necessary attaching parts. Evacuate and charge system.	
Series 4500-7000 (2.0)	3.2
Series 8000-9000	
Brigadier (2.0)	3.3
All others (1.2)	2.5
Clutch Hub and Drive Plate, Renew	
Includes: Check air gap.	
Series 4500-7000 (.6)	1.0
Series 8000-9000 (.8)	1.3
Compressor Pulley and/or Bearings, Renew	
Includes: R&R clutch hub and drive plate.	
Series 4500-7000 (.8)	1.2
Series 8000-9000 (.9)	1.5
Clutch Holding Coil, Renew	
Includes: R&R clutch hub and drive plate.	
Series 4500-7000 (.9)	1.3
Series 8000-9000 (1.0)	1.6
Compressor Shaft Seal Kit, Renew	
Includes: R&R clutch hub and drive plate. Evacuate and charge system.	
All series (2.3)	3.0
Compressor Assy., R&R and Recondition	
Includes: Complete disassembly and overhaul, making all checks and gauging operations. Evacuate and charge system.	
Series 4500-7000 (2.9)	4.4
Series 8000-9000	
Brigadier (3.0)	4.5
All others (2.9)	4.4
Compressor Relief Valve, Renew	
Includes: Evacuate and charge system.	
All series (.9)	1.6
Condenser Assembly, Renew	
Includes: Evacuate and charge system.	
Series 4500-7000 (1.3)	2.7
Series 8000-9000	
conv cab (1.2)	2.6
alum tilt cab (1.7)	3.1
Receiver-Dehydrator, Renew	
Includes: Evacuate and charge system.	
Series 4500-7000 (1.6)	3.0
Series 8000-9000	
conv cab (1.0)	2.4
alum tilt cab (1.1)	2.5
Evaporator Core, Renew	
Includes: Evacuate and charge system.	
Series 4500-7000 (2.1)	4.0
Series 8000-9000	
General (2.6)	4.1
Brigadier (3.2)	4.7
All others (3.4)	4.9
Renew exp valve add (.1)	.2
Expansion Valve, Renew	
Includes: Evacuate and charge system.	
Series 4500-7000 (1.3)	2.7
Series 8000-9000	
conv cab (1.7)	3.1
alum tilt cab (1.9)	3.3
Pilot Operated Absolute (POA) Valve, Renew	
Includes: Evacuate and charge system.	
Series 4500-7000 (1.3)	2.7
Series 8000-9000	
conv cab (1.4)	2.8
alum tilt cab (1.7)	3.1
Accumulator, Renew	
Includes: Evacuate and charge system.	
All series (2.0)	2.5
Renew filter dryer add (.3)	.3
Filter Dryer, Renew	
Includes: Evacuate and charge system.	
All series (.9)	1.4
Orifice Tube, Renew	
Includes: Evacuate and charge system.	
All series (1.6)	2.2
Renew filter dryer add (.3)	.3

LABOR 28 AIR CONDITIONING 28 LABOR

(Factory Time)	Chilton Time
Pressure Cycling Switch, Renew	
All series (.2)	.3
Receiver Assembly, R&R	
Includes: Evacuate and charge system.	
General (1.5)	2.9
Renew dessicant bag add (.2)	.3
Renew exp valve capsule and/or moisture indicator sleeve add (.3)	.4
Renew POA valve add (.3)	.4
Renew sight glass (.1)	.2
A.C. Blower Motor, Renew	
Series 4500-7000 (.3)	.6
A.C. Blower Motor Switch, Renew	
Series 4500-7000 (.5)	.9
Series 8000-9000 (.4)	.8
A.C. Temperature Control Assy., Renew	
All series (.9)	1.4
A.C. Blower Motor Relay, Renew	
All series (.2)	.4
Air Conditioning Hoses, Renew	
Includes: Evacuate and charge system.	
All series-one (1.3)	2.1
each adtnl (.3)	.5
Renew filter dryer add (.3)	.3

LABOR 30 HEAD AND PARKING LAMPS 30 LABOR

(Factory Time)	Chilton Time
Aim Headlamps	
two	.4
four	.6
Headlamp Sealed Beam Bulb, Renew	
All series	
single beam unit (.3)	.4
dual beam unit (.4)	.5
Directional or Parking Lamp Assy., Renew	
All series	
conv cab (.2)	.3
Tilt cab (.3)	.4
Directional or Parking Lamp Lens, Renew	
All series (.2)	.3
Tail or Stop Lamp Lens, Renew	
All series (.2)	.3
Tail or Stop Lamp Assy., Renew	
All series (.4)	.5
Reflector, Renew	
All series-each	.2
License Lamp Assy., Renew	
All series (.2)	.3
Marker Lamp, Renew	
All series-each (.4)	.5

LABOR 31 WINDSHIELD WIPER & SPEEDOMETER 31 LABOR

(Factory Time)	Chilton Time
Windshield Wiper Motor, Renew	
Series 4500-7000	
conv cab (.6)	1.1
Tilt cab (Isuzu) (.9)	1.4
Series 8000-9000-one side	
General (.6)	1.1
Astro (.6)	1.1
Brigadier (.4)	.7
Recond motor add	.5
Windshield Wiper Switch, Renew	
Series 4500-7000	
conv cab (.6)	.9
Tilt cab (Isuzu) (.3)	.5
Series 8000-9000 (.6)	.9
Windshield Washer Pump, Renew	
Series 8000-9000	
foot operated (.2)	.5
Windshield Wiper Control Valve, Renew	
Series 8000-9000	
one side (.5)	.9
Speedometer Head, R&R or Renew	
Series 4500-7000	
conv cab (.6)	1.1
tilt cab (.5)	1.0
Series 8000-9000	
General (.3)	.6
Astro (.4)	.7
Brigadier (.6)	1.1
Speedometer Cable and Casing, Renew	
Series 4500-7000 (.7)	1.4
Series 8000-9000 (.5)	1.0
Tachometer Cable and Casing, Renew	
Series 4500-7000 (.6)	1.2
Series 8000-9000	
Astro (.6)	1.2
All others (.3)	.5
Tachometer, R&R or Renew	
Series 4500-7000	
mechanical (.4)	.8
electric (.6)	1.0
Series 8000-9000	
General (.2)	.4
All others (.4)	.8

LABOR 32 LIGHT SWITCHES & WIRING 32 LABOR

(Factory Time)	Chilton Time
Headlamp Switch, Renew	
Series 4500-7000 (.3)	.5
Series 8000-9000	
General (.2)	.4
conv cab (.5)	.8
tilt cab (.3)	.6
Headlamp Dimmer Switch, Renew	
All series (.2)	.5
Turn Signal and Hazard Warning Switch, Renew	
Series 4500-7000	
conv cab (.9)	1.4
tilt cab-direct (.7)	1.1
tilt cab-hazard (.3)	.6
Tilt cab (Isuzu) (.3)	.6
Series 8000-9000	
Brigadier (.4)	.7
All others (.8)	1.2
Turn Signal or Hazard Flasher, Renew	
All series (.2)	.4
Stop Light Switch, Renew	
Series 4500-7000	
conv cab (.3)	.5
Tilt cab (Isuzu) (1.1)	1.6
Series 8000-9000	
General-w/Alum tilt cab (.6)	1.0
Astro (.9)	1.3
All others (.4)	.7
Starter Safety Switch, Renew	
All series (.3)	.5
Back-Up Lamp Switch, Renew	
All series (.2)	.5
Clearance Light Switch, Renew	
Series 8000-9000	
General (.2)	.4
All others (.3)	.5
Horn, Renew	
Series 4500-7000	
electric (.4)	.5
air (.2)	.3
Series 8000-9000	
air or electric (.4)	.6
Horn Relay, Renew	
Series 4500-7000 (.2)	.3

GROUP INDEX

ALPHABETICAL INDEX

LABOR 1 TUNE UP 1 LABOR

(Factory Time) Chilton Time

Compression Test

	Chilton Time
Four (.6)	.8
Six (.7)	1.0
V-8 (.9)	1.2

Engine Tune Up, (Minor)

Includes: Clean or renew spark plugs, renew ignition points and condenser, set ignition timing, set carburetor idle speed and mixture. Service carburetor air cleaner. Clean or renew fuel filter.

	Chilton Time
Four	1.8
Six	2.0
V-8	2.3

Engine Tune Up, (Major)

Includes: Check engine compression, clean or renew spark plugs. Test battery, clean terminals. Renew or adjust distributor points and condenser, check distributor cap and rotor. Set ignition timing, test coil, free up manifold heat valve. Tighten manifold bolts. Adjust carburetor idle speed and mixture. Inspect and tighten all hose connections. Adjust fan belt. Service air cleaners (carburetor, vapor canister and air pump). Renew or clean PCV valve.

	Chilton Time
Four	3.0
Six	3.3
V-8	3.8

Engine Tune Up, (Electronic Ignition)

Includes: Test battery and clean connections. Tighten manifold and carburetor mounting bolts. Check engine compression, clean and adjust or renew spark plugs. Test resistance of spark plug cables. Inspect distributor cap and rotor. Adjust air gap. Check vacuum advance operation. Reset ignition timing. Adjust idle mixture and idle speed. Service air cleaner. Inspect crankcase ventilation system. Inspect and adjust drive belts. Inspect choke operation and adjust or free up. Check operation of EGR valve.

	Chilton Time
Four	2.5
Six	2.9
V-8	3.4

LABOR 2 IGNITION SYSTEM 2 LABOR

(Factory Time) Chilton Time

Spark Plugs, Clean and Reset or Renew

	Chilton Time
Four (.4)	.6
Six (.6)	.8
V-8 (.7)	1.0

Ignition Timing, Reset

	Chilton Time
All models (.3)	.4

Distributor, R&R or Renew

Includes: Reset ignition timing.

	Chilton Time
Standard Ignition	
All models (.7)	1.0
Electronic Ignition	
All models (.6)	.9
w/Governor add (.1)	.1

Distributor, R&R and Recondition

Includes: Reset ignition timing.

	Chilton Time
Standard Ignition	
Four (2.0)	2.5
Six (1.7)	2.2
V-8 (2.0)	2.5
Electronic Ignition	
All models (2.1)	2.6
w/Governor add (.4)	.5

Distributor Points and Condenser, Renew

Includes: R&R distributor, reset timing and dwell.

	Chilton Time
All models (1.1)	1.4

Distributor Cap, Renew

	Chilton Time
All models (.2)	.4

Distributor Sensor Assembly, Renew (Electronic Ignition)

Includes: R&R distributor and reset ignition timing.

	Chilton Time
All models (1.3)	1.9

Electronic Ignition Control, Renew

Includes: Test ignition system in chassis.

	Chilton Time
All models (.8)	1.3

Ignition Coil, Renew

Includes: Test coil in chassis, transfer mounting bracket.

	Chilton Time
All models (.6)	.9

Vacuum Control Unit, Renew

Includes: R&R distributor and reset timing and dwell.

	Chilton Time
All models	.9

Spark Plug Cables, Renew

	Chilton Time
Four (.2)	.5
Six (.3)	.7
V-8 (.4)	.8

Ignition Switch, Renew

	Chilton Time
SCOUT II (.9)	1.5
100-200-500 Series (.6)	1.0

LABOR 3 FUEL SYSTEM 3 LABOR

(Factory Time) Chilton Time

GASOLINE ENGINES

Fuel Pump, Test

Includes: Disconnect line at carburetor, attach pressure gauge.

	Chilton Time
All models (.4)	.4

Carburetor, Adjust (On Truck)

	Chilton Time
All models (.2)	.3

Governor R.P.M., Adjust (w/Tachometer)

	Chilton Time
All models (.6)	.8

Carburetor, Renew

Includes: All necessary adjustments.

	Chilton Time
Four (.7)	1.0
Six (.7)	1.0
V-8 (.9)	1.2

Carburetor, R&R and Clean or Recondition

Includes: All necessary adjustments.

	Chilton Time
Four (2.2)	3.2
Six (2.2)	3.2
V-8-2 bbl (2.4)	3.5
4 bbl (2.7)	3.9

Fuel Pump, Renew

	Chilton Time
Four (.4)	.7
Six (.5)	.8
V-8 (.6)	.9

Add pump test if performed.

Fuel Tank, Renew

Includes: Drain and refill tank. Test evaporative loss system.

	Chilton Time
SCOUT II (1.8)	2.6
Under Cab Mount	
100-150-200 Series	
right side-front fill (1.3)	2.0
rear fill (1.1)	1.8
left side-front fill (1.1)	1.8
rear fender mount (1.0)	1.7

Fuel Gauge (Tank Unit), Renew

Includes: Drain and refill tank. R&R tank, test and renew gauge.

	Chilton Time
SCOUT II (1.5)	2.3
Under Cab Mount	
100-150-200 Series	
right side-front fill (1.2)	1.9
rear fill (1.1)	1.8
left side-front fill (1.1)	1.8
rear fender mount (.7)	1.4

Fuel Gauge (Dash Unit), Renew

	Chilton Time
SCOUT II (.4)	.7
100-150-200 Series (.6)	1.0

Intake Manifold or Gaskets, Renew

	Chilton Time
Four (1.6)	2.0
Six (1.4)	1.8
V-8 (2.0)	2.6
Renew manif add (.8)	.8

DIESEL ENGINE

Fuel Injection Lines, R&R or Renew

	Chilton Time
All models-one (.2)	.3
each adtnl (.1)	.2
all (.7)	1.2

Glow Plugs, Renew

	Chilton Time
All models-one (.2)	.3
all (.4)	.7

Fuel Injection Nozzles, Renew

	Chilton Time
All models-one (.5)	.6
each adtnl (.3)	.4
all (1.8)	2.4

LABOR 3 FUEL SYSTEM 3 LABOR

(Factory Time) Chilton Time

Fuel Injection Nozzles, Test
(Nozzles Removed)
All models-one (.4)........................ .6
each adtnl (.2)........................... .3
all (1.4).. 2.0

Fuel Injection Nozzles, Recondition
(Nozzles Removed)
All models-each (.6)........................ .8

Fuel Filter, Renew
All models-primary (.3).................. .4

Fuel Injection Pump, Renew
All models (2.7)................................ 3.8

Fuel Injection Pump, R&R and Recondition
All models (11.3)............................ 15.0

Intake Manifold and/or Gasket, Renew
All models (.7)................................. 1.2

LABOR 3A EMISSION CONTROLS 3A LABOR

(Factory Time) Chilton Time

Emission Control Check
Includes: Check and adjust engine idle speed, mixture and ignition timing. Check PCV valve and air pump filter.
All models.. 1.0

Positive Crankcase Ventilation Valve, Renew or Clean
All models
renew.. .3
clean.. .4

EVAPORATIVE LOSS CONTROL

Canister, Renew
All models.. .5

Canister Filter, Renew
All models.. .3

Liquid Vapor Separator, Renew
SCOUT II.. 1.3

AIR INJECTION SYSTEM

Air Pump, Renew
All models.. .6

Diverter Valve, Renew
All models.. .8

EXHAUST GAS RECIRCULATION SYSTEM

Anti Back-Fire Valve, Renew
All models.. .4

E.G.R. Valve, Renew
All models.. .5

CONTROLLED COMBUSTION TYPE

Air Cleaner Element, Renew
All models.. .2

Air Cleaner Sensor, Renew
All models.. .4

Air Cleaner Vacuum Chamber, Renew
All models.. .5

LABOR 4 ALTERNATOR AND REGULATOR 4 LABOR

(Factory Time) Chilton Time

Alternator Circuits, Test
Includes: Test battery, regulator and alternator output.
All models (.6)................................. .8

Alternator, Renew
Includes: Transfer pulley and fan.
All models (.9)................................. 1.2
w/A.C. add (.2)................................. .2

Alternator, R&R and Recondition
Includes: Disassemble, clean, inspect and test alternator parts. Renew parts as required, reassemble and test.
All models (2.2)................................ 3.0
w/A.C. add (.2)................................. .2

Alternator Drive End Frame Bearing, Renew
Includes: R&R alternator, separate end frames.
All models (1.1)................................ 1.4
w/A.C. add (.2)................................. .2

Voltage Regulator, Renew
All models
w/Integral reg (1.5).................... 1.8
w/External reg (.6)..................... 1.0

LABOR 5 STARTING SYSTEM 5 LABOR

(Factory Time) Chilton Time

Starter Draw Test (On Truck)
All models (.3)................................. .3

Starter, Renew
Six (1.1).. 1.6
Four & V-8 (1.2).............................. 1.7
Diesel (1.0).................................... 1.5
Add draw test if performed.

Starter, R&R and Recondition
Includes: Turn down armature.
Six (2.2).. 2.6
Four & V-8 (2.4).............................. 2.8
Diesel (2.2).................................... 3.0
Renew field coils add (.5)................. .5
Add draw test if performed.

Starter Drive, Renew
Includes: R&R starter.
Six (1.3).. 1.8
Four & V-8 (1.5).............................. 1.9
Diesel (1.3).................................... 1.8

Starter Solenoid, Renew
Includes: R&R starter.
Six (1.1).. 1.7
Four & V-8 (1.3).............................. 1.8
Diesel (1.1).................................... 1.6

Battery Cables, Renew
All models
positive (.4)................................. .6
negative (.3)................................. .4

LABOR 6 BRAKE SYSTEM 6 LABOR

(Factory Time) Chilton Time

Brakes, Adjust (Minor)
Includes: Adjust brakes, fill master cylinder.
All models
2 wheels...................................... .5
4 wheels...................................... .9

Bleed Brakes (Four Wheels)
Includes: Fill master cylinder.
All models (.8)................................. 1.0

Brake Pedal Free Play, Adjust
All models (.3)................................. .4

LABOR 6 BRAKE SYSTEM 6 LABOR

(Factory Time) Chilton Time

Brake Shoes, Renew

Includes: Install new or exchange brake shoes, adjust service and hand brake. Bleed system.

Front–drum (2.0) 2.8
w/Locking hubs add (.3) 4
Rear–drum
semi-floating axle (1.5) 2.4
full floating axle (2.6) 3.4
All Four Wheels
semi-floating axle (3.0) 4.2
full floating axle (4.6) 5.8

Brake Shoes and/or Pads, Renew

Includes: Install new or exchange brake shoes or pads. Adjust service and hand brake. Bleed system.

Front–disc (1.0) 1.4
Rear–drum
semi-floating axle (1.5) 2.4
full floating axle (2.6) 3.4
All Four Wheels
semi-floating axle (2.2) 3.5
full floating axle (3.2) 4.4

Brake Drum, Renew (One)

Includes: Transfer hub to new drum, clean and repack front wheel bearings.

Front–4x2 (1.6) 1.8
4X4 (1.8) 2.0
Rear
Scout II (.5) 7
100-200-500 Series
semi-floating axle (.7) 9
full floating axle (1.7) 2.0

BRAKE HYDRAULIC SYSTEM

Wheel Cylinder, Renew (One)

Includes: Bleed lines.

Front
Scout II 4X2 (1.6) 2.2
4X4 (1.8) 2.4
100-200 Series
4x2 (1.8) 2.4
4X4 (1.9) 2.5
500 Series (2.1) 2.7
Rear
Scout II (1.4) 2.0
Semi-floating axle (1.5) 2.1
Full Floating Axle
100-200 Series (2.0) 2.6
500 Series (2.5) 3.1

Wheel Cylinder, Recondition (One)

Includes: Hone cylinder and bleed lines.

Front
Scout II 4X2 (2.0) 2.6
4X4 (2.2) 2.8
100-200 Series
4x2 (2.2) 2.8
4X4 (2.3) 2.9
500 Series (2.7) 3.3
Rear
Scout II (1.8) 2.4
Semi-floating axle (1.9) 2.5
Full Floating Axle
100-200 Series (2.4) 3.0
500 Series (3.2) 3.8

Master Cylinder, Renew

Includes: Bleed complete system.

All models
wo/Pwr brakes (1.2) 1.6
w/Pwr brakes (1.3) 1.7

COMBINATIONS
Add to Brakes, Renew

(Factory Time) Chilton Time

RENEW WHEEL CYLINDER
Each (.3) 4

REBUILD WHEEL CYLINDER
Each (.4) 6

RENEW BRAKE HOSE
Each (.4) 5

RENEW REAR AXLE GREASE SEALS
Semi-floating
Inner (1.1) 1.4
Outer (.4) 6
Full floating (.2) 4

RENEW FRONT WHEEL BEARINGS (ONE WHEEL)
w/Drum brakes 3
w/Disc brakes 4

FRONT WHEEL BEARING, REPACK OR RENEW SEAL (ONE WHEEL)
w/Drum brakes 2
w/Disc brakes 4

RENEW MASTER CYLINDER
All models (1.0) 1.4

REBUILD MASTER CYLINDER
All models (1.5) 2.0

REBUILD CALIPER ASSEMBLY
Each (.5) 8

RELINE BRAKE SHOES
Each axle set (.4) 6

(Factory Time) Chilton Time

Master Cylinder, R&R and Recondition

Includes: Hone cylinder and bleed system.

All models
wo/Pwr brakes (1.9) 2.4
w/Pwr brakes (2.0) 2.5

Brake Hose, Renew

Includes: Bleed line.

All models–one (.8) 1.1

POWER BRAKES

Power Brake Booster, Renew

Includes: Transfer mounting brackets. Bleed brake system and adjust linkage.

Scout II (1.5) 2.2
100-200 Series (1.6) 2.3
500 Series (1.8) 2.5

Power Brake Booster, R&R and Recondition (Diaphragm Type)

Includes: Bleed brake system and adjust linkage.

100-200 Series (2.0) 2.9
500 Series (2.2) 3.1

DISC BRAKES

Disc Brake Pads, Renew

Includes: Install new disc brake pads only.

All models (1.0) 1.4

Disc Brake Rotor, Renew (One)
two wheel drive (.7) 1.0
four wheel drive (.9) 1.2

Caliper Assembly, Renew (One)

Includes: Bleed lines.

All models (1.1) 1.5

Caliper Assy., R&R and Recondition (One)

Includes: Bleed lines.

All models (1.5) 2.0

PARKING BRAKE

Parking Brake, Adjust
All models (.2) 4

Parking Brake Lever Assy., Renew
Scout II (1.0) 1.4

Drive Line Brake Lining, Renew
open band type (1.0) 1.4
closed band type (1.3) 1.8

LABOR 7 COOLING SYSTEM 7 LABOR

(Factory Time) Chilton Time

Winterize Cooling System

Includes: Run engine to check for leaks, tighten all hose connections. Test radiator and pressure cap, drain radiator and engine block. Add anti-freeze and refill system.

All models 5

Thermostat, Renew
All models (.3) 5

Radiator Assembly, R&R or Renew
All models (.8) 1.2

(Factory Time) Chilton Time

ADD THESE OPERATIONS TO RADIATOR R&R

Boil & Repair 1.5
Rod Clean 1.9
Repair Core 1.3
Renew Tank 1.6
Renew Trans. Oil Cooler 1.9
Recore Radiator 1.7

Radiator Hoses, Renew
All models
upper (.3) 4
lower (.4) 5

(Factory Time) Chilton Time

Fan Belt, Renew
All models–one (.3) 5
each adtnl (.3) 3
w/P.S. add (.2) 2
w/A.C. add (.3) 3

Fan Belt, Adjust
All models (.2) 3

Water Pump, Renew
Four (1.0) 1.6
Six (1.1) 1.7
V-8
304-345-392 engs (1.1) 1.7

LABOR 7 COOLING SYSTEM 7 LABOR

(Factory Time) Chilton Time

400 eng (1.3) 2.0
w/P.S. add (.2) 2
w/A.C. add (.3) 3
w/Modulated fan drive add (.4) 4

Fan Blade or Pulley, Renew
Four (.4) 6
Six (.5) 7
V-8 (.7) 9

Temperature Gauge (Engine Unit), Renew
All models (.3) 5

Temperature Gauge (Dash Unit), Renew
Scout II (.4) 1.0

100-200-500 Series (.6) 1.1

Heater Core, R&R or Renew
Without Air Conditioning
Scout II (.5) 1.2
100-200-500 Series (.8) 1.7
With Air Conditioning
100-200-500 Series (.7) 1.5

ADD THESE OPERATIONS TO HEATER CORE R&R
Boil & Repair 1.2
Repair Core 9

Recore 1.2

Heater Temperature Control Valve, Renew
All models (.3) 6

Heater Blower Motor, Renew
Includes: Transfer blower wheel.
Scout II (.5) 1.0
100-200-500 Series (.6) 1.2

Heater Blower Motor Switch, Renew
Scout II (.4) 7
100-200-500 Series (.7) 1.1

LABOR 8 EXHAUST SYSTEM 8 LABOR

(Factory Time) Chilton Time

Exhaust Pipes, Renew
SCOUT II
Four
front exh pipe (1.0) 1.4
crossover pipe (.9) 1.3
Six(.8) 1.1
V-8
front exh pipe-each (1.0) 1.4
crossover pipe (1.2) 1.7

100-200-500 Series
Six
front pipe (.9) 1.2
intermediate pipe (1.2) 1.7
rear pipe (1.2) 1.7

V-8–Single Exhaust
left pipe (1.2) 1.6
crossover pipe (1.5) 2.1
rear pipe (1.6) 2.2
Dual Exhaust
front pipe (1.0) 1.3
intermediate pipe (1.3) 1.8

Muffler, Renew
All models-each (1.0) 1.4

Catalytic Converter, Renew
All models (.7) 1.4

Tail Pipe, Renew
All models (.8) 1.1

Exhaust Manifold or Gaskets, Renew
Four (.9) 1.4
Six (1.3) 1.8
V-8-one side (1.0) 1.5
both sides (1.7) 2.7

COMBINATIONS

Muffler, Exhaust and Tail Pipes, Renew
Four (1.5) 2.2
Six (1.3) 2.0
V-8-single exh (1.9) 2.6
dual exh-each side (1.2) 1.9
Diesel (.9) 1.4

LABOR 9 FRONT SUSPENSION 9 LABOR

(Factory Time) Chilton Time

Note: On all front suspension operations alignment charges must be added if performed. Time given does not include alignment.

Check Alignment of Front End
All models (.5) 8
Note: Deduct if alignment is performed.

Toe-In, Adjust
SCOUT II (.8) 1.1
100-200-500 Series (.5) 8

Align Front End
Includes: Adjust front wheel bearings.
Coil Spring Suspension
All models (2.3) 3.0

Front Wheel Bearings, Clean and Repack (Both Wheels)
SCOUT II
w/Drum brakes (1.2) 1.6
w/Disc brakes (1.7) 2.1
100-200-500 Series
Drum Brakes
4X2 (1.1) 1.5
4X4 (1.3) 1.7
Disc Brakes
4X2 (1.5) 1.9
4X4 (1.7) 2.1
w/Locking hubs add (.3) 4

Front Wheel Bearings and Cups, Renew (One Wheel)
SCOUT II
w/Drum brakes (.9) 1.2
w/Disc brakes (1.1) 1.4

100-200-500 Series
w/Drum brakes (1.2) 1.5
w/Disc brakes (1.3) 1.6
w/Locking hubs add (.1) 2

Front Wheel Grease Seal, Renew (One Wheel)
SCOUT II
w/Drum brakes (.8) 1.0
w/Disc brakes (1.0) 1.2
100-200-500 Series
w/Drum brakes (.9) 1.1
w/Disc brakes (1.1) 1.3
w/Locking hubs add (.1) 2

Front Shock Absorber, Renew
All models-one (.4) 6
both (.5) 8

Front Axle Assembly, R&R
SCOUT II
w/Drum brakes (2.9) 4.5
w/Disc brakes (2.6) 4.2

Front Axle Tube Assy., Renew
SCOUT II
w/Drum brakes (6.2) 9.1
w/Disc brakes (6.6) 9.5

Spindle Assembly, Renew (One)
SCOUT II
w/Drum brakes (1.3) 2.1
w/Disc brakes (1.5) 2.3
100-200-500 Series
w/Drum brakes (1.4) 2.2
w/Disc brakes (1.7) 2.5
w/Locking hubs add (.2) 2

Ball Sockets, Renew (One Side)
SCOUT II
w/Drum brakes (2.5) 3.9
w/Disc brakes (2.7) 4.1
100-200-500 Series
w/Drum brakes (2.5) 3.9
w/Disc brakes (2.9) 4.3
w/Locking hubs add (.2) 2

Steering Knuckle, Renew (One)
SCOUT II
w/Drum brakes (3.3) 5.1
w/Disc brakes (3.6) 5.4
100-200-500 Series
w/Drum brakes (2.7) 4.5
w/Disc brakes (2.9) 4.7
w/Locking hubs add (.2) 2

Front Spring Assembly, Renew (One)
SCOUT II (.9) 1.5
100-200-500 Series (1.2) 1.7

Front Spring Shackle, Renew (One)
Includes: Renew spring shackle only.
SCOUT II (.4) 8
100-200-500 Series (.7) 1.3

I BEAM SUSPENSION

Axle I Beam, Renew
Add alignment charges.
All models (3.1) 5.5

King Pins and Bushings, Renew (Both Sides)
Add alignment charges.
All models (3.2) 4.7

LABOR 9 FRONT SUSPENSION 9 LABOR

(Factory Time) Chilton Time

Steering Knuckle, Renew (One)
Add alignment charges.
All models (1.5)........ 2.7
Renew bushings add (.7)........ 1.0

Steering Arm, Renew (One)
Add alignment charges.
All models (1.3)........ 1.8

COIL SPRING SUSPENSION

Steering Knuckle, Renew (One)
Add alignment charges.
100-200-500 Series (1.9)........ 2.7

Upper Control Arm, Renew (One)
Add alignment charges.
100-200-500 Series (.9)........ 1.7

Ball Joints, Renew
Add alignment charges.
Series 100-200-500
one upper (1.0)........ 1.8
one lower (2.4)........ 3.2
upper & lower
one side (2.8)........ 3.6

Lower Control Arm, Renew (One)
Add alignment charges.
100-200-500 Series (2.1)........ 2.9

Lower Control Arm Bushings, Renew (One Side)
Add alignment charges.
100-200-500 Series (2.2)........ 3.2

Upper Control Arm Bushings, Renew (One Side)
Add alignment charges.
100-200-500 Series (1.3)........ 2.1

Coil Spring, Renew (One)
Add alignment charges.
100-200-500 Series (2.0)........ 2.9

Lower Control Arm Rod Assy., Renew
100-200-500 Series (.6)........ .9

Sway Bar, Renew
100-200-500 Series (.5)........ 1.0

FOUR WHEEL DRIVE

Front Drive Axle Assy., R&R
SCOUT II
w/Drum brakes (3.5)........ 6.1
w/Disc brakes (3.1)........ 5.7
100-200 Series
w/Drum brakes (3.6)........ 6.2
w/Disc brakes (3.2)........ 5.8
w/Locking hubs add (.3)........ .3

Front Drive Axle Assy., R&R and Recondition
SCOUT II
w/Drum brakes (13.1)........ 16.6
w/Disc brakes (13.5)........ 17.0
100-200 Series
w/Drum brakes (13.6)........ 17.1
w/Disc brakes (13.4)........ 16.9
w/Locking hubs add (.3)........ .3

Front Axle Shaft U-Joint, Renew or Recondition
SCOUT II
w/Drum brakes (1.7)........ 3.0
w/Disc brakes (1.9)........ 3.2
100-200 Series
w/Drum brakes (1.9)........ 3.2
w/Disc brakes (2.1)........ 3.4

Front Axle Drive Shaft, Renew (One) (Inner or Outer)
SCOUT II
w/Drum brakes (1.5)........ 2.6
w/Disc brakes (1.7)........ 2.8
100-200 Series
w/Drum brakes (1.6)........ 2.7
w/Disc brakes (1.9)........ 3.0
w/Locking hubs add (.2)........ .3

Front Differential Assy., R&R and Recondition
Includes: Renew ring gear and pinion.
SCOUT II
w/Drum brakes (9.9)........ 13.4
w/Disc brakes (10.3)........ 13.8
100-200 Series
w/Drum brakes (9.5)........ 13.0
w/Disc brakes (9.3)........ 12.8
w/Locking hubs add (.2)........ .3

Front Drive Axle Housing, Renew
All models
w/Drum brakes (10.0)........ 13.4
w/Disc brakes (10.4)........ 13.7
w/Locking hubs add (.2)........ .3

Front Drive Shaft, R&R or Renew
All models (.8)........ 1.2

Front Universal Joint, Renew or Recondition
Includes: R&R drive shaft.
All models (.8)........ 1.5

LABOR 10 STEERING LINKAGE 10 LABOR

(Factory Time) Chilton Time

Tie Rod, Renew
Includes: Transfer tie rod ends and reset toe-in.
SCOUT II (1.4)........ 2.0
100-200-500 Series (1.0)........ 1.5

Tie Rod Ends, Renew
Includes: Reset toe-in.
SCOUT II-one (1.2)........ 1.7
both (1.4)........ 1.9
100-200-500 Series-one (.8)........ 1.0
both (1.0)........ 1.4

Pitman Arm, Renew
SCOUT II (.5)........ .9
100-200-500 Series (.6)........ 1.0

Idler Arm, Renew
All models (.6)........ .9
Renew bushing add (.1)........ .2

Center Link Assembly, Renew
100-200-500 Series (.9)........ 1.3

Drag Link, Renew
SCOUT II (.4)........ .7
100-200-500 Series (.6)........ 1.0

LABOR 11 STEERING GEAR 11 LABOR

(Factory Time) Chilton Time

STANDARD STEERING

Steering Wheel, Renew
SCOUT II (.4)........ .6
100-200-500 Series
w/Std horn button (.5)........ .7
Custom or Deluxe (.6)........ .8

Energy Absorbing Steering Column, Renew
Includes: Disconnect battery, R&R column, transfer mounting bracket, lock cylinder, ignition switch and steering wheel.
SCOUT II (1.6)........ 2.5

Energy Absorbing Steering Column, Recondition
Includes: Disconnect battery, R&R column, disassemble, clean, inspect and renew parts as required. Reassemble and align steering wheel.
SCOUT II (2.0)........ 3.1

Steering Column Lock Cylinder, Renew
Includes: Disconnect battery. R&R steering wheel and turn signal switch.
SCOUT II (.7)........ 1.3

Steering Gear, Adjust (On Truck)
All models (.4)........ .8

Steering Gear, R&R or Renew
SCOUT II (.9)........ 1.9
100-200-500 Series (1.0)........ 2.0

Steering Gear, R&R and Recondition
Includes: Disassemble, renew necessary parts, reassemble and adjust.
SCOUT II (1.9)........ 2.9
100-200-500 Series (2.3)........ 3.3

POWER STEERING

Trouble Shoot Power Steering
Includes: Check pounds pull on steering wheel, install checking gauge. Test pump pressure and check for external leaks.
All models (.5)........ .8

Power Steering Belt, Renew
All models (.3)........ .5

LABOR 11 STEERING GEAR 11 LABOR

(Factory Time) Chilton Time

Power Steering Hoses, Renew
Includes: Bleed system.
All models - each (.6) .9

Power Steering Gear, R&R or Renew
SCOUT II (1.5) 2.6
100-200-500 Series (1.4) 2.5

Power Steering Gear, R&R and Recondition
Includes: Disassemble, renew necessary parts, reassemble and adjust.
SCOUT II (3.6) 5.0
100-200-500 Series (3.7) 5.1

Power Steering Pump, Renew
Includes: Transfer pulley and bleed system.
SCOUT II (.9) 1.3
100-200-500 Series
Six (1.1) 1.5
V-8-304-345-392 engs (1.0) 1.4
400 eng (1.3) 1.9

Power Steering Pump, R&R and Recondition
Includes: Bleed system.
SCOUT II (1.7) 3.1
100-200-500 Series
V-8-304-345-392 engs (1.8) 3.2
400 eng (2.1) 3.5

LABOR 12 CYLINDER HEAD & VALVE SYSTEM 12 LABOR

(Factory Time) Chilton Time

GASOLINE ENGINES

Compression Test
Four (.6) .8
Six (.7) 1.0
V-8 (.9) 1.2

Cylinder Head Gasket, Renew
Four (3.2) 4.6
Six (3.5) 4.9
V-8-one (3.2) 4.6
both (4.9) 7.7
w/P.S. add (.3) .3
w/A.C. add (.6) .6
w/Pwr brks add (.8) .8

Cylinder Head (With Valves), Renew
Four (4.7) 5.8
Six (4.9) 6.0
V-8-one (5.2) 6.7
both (7.0) 8.4
w/P.S. add (.3) .3
w/A.C. add (.6) .6
w/Pwr brks add (.8) .8

Clean Carbon and Grind Valves
Includes: R&R cylinder head(s), clean gasket surfaces, clean carbon, reface valves and seats. Minor tune up.
Four (8.3) 10.5
Six (9.7) 12.0
V-8 (13.4) 16.3
w/P.S. add (.3) .3
w/A.C. add (.6) .6
w/Pwr brks add (.8) .8

Rocker Arm Cover and/or Gasket, Renew
Four (.3) .5
Six (.7) 1.0
V-8-left (.5) .8
right (.7) 1.0
w/P.S. add (.3) .3
w/A.C. add (.6) .6
w/Pwr brks add (.8) .8

Valve Push Rod or Rocker Arm, Renew (One or All)
Four (.8) 1.1
Six (1.0) 1.3
V-8-left bank (.8) 1.1
right bank (.9) 1.2
both banks (1.3) 1.9

COMBINATIONS
Add To Valve Job
See Machine Shop Operations

(Factory Time) Chilton Time

DRAIN, EVACUATE AND RECHARGE AIR CONDITIONING SYSTEM
All models 1.8

HYDRAULIC VALVE LIFTERS, DISASSEMBLE AND CLEAN
Each (.2) .2

DISTRIBUTOR, RECONDITION
All models (1.5) 1.9

CARBURETOR, RECONDITION
1 BBL (1.3) 1.8
2 BBL (1.6) 2.1
4 BBL (1.9) 2.4

VALVE GUIDES, RENEW
Each (.2) .3

ROCKER ARMS, DISASSEMBLE AND CLEAN OR RENEW
Four (.8) 1.0
Six (.6) .8
V-8 (1.2) 1.4

(Factory Time) Chilton Time

Valve Lifters, Renew (One or All)
Includes: R&R 6 cylinder head.
Four (.9) 1.7
Six (4.9) 6.3
V-8-304-345-392 engs
one cyl (.9) 1.7
one bank (1.3) 2.1
all-both banks (2.1) 3.0
400 eng
one cyl (2.1) 3.0
one bank (2.5) 3.4
all-both banks (3.0) 4.3
w/P.S. add (.3) .3
w/A.C. add (.6) .6
w/Pwr brks add (.8) .8

Valve Spring or Valve Stem Oil Seal, Renew (One) (Head on Truck)
Four (.9) 1.2
Six (1.3) 1.6
V-8-left side (.8) 1.1
right side (.9) 1.2
each adtnl-all engs (.1) .2

(Factory Time) Chilton Time

w/P.S. add (.3) .3
w/A.C. add (.6) .6
w/Pwr brks add (.8) .8

Rocker Arm Assy., R&R and Recondition
Four (1.2) 1.8
Six (1.6) 2.2
V-8-both (2.2) 2.8
w/P.S. add (.3) .3
w/A.C. add (.6) .6
w/Pwr brks add (.8) .8

Valve Push Rod Cover and/or Gasket, Renew
Four (2.8) 3.5
V-8 (2.8) 3.5

DIESEL ENGINE

Compression Test
All models 2.0

Cylinder Head Gasket, Renew
All models (4.4) 6.3

Cylinder Head (With Valves), Renew
Does not include recondition fuel injectors.
All models (6.5) 9.4

Cylinder Head (Less Valves), Renew
Includes: Transfer parts as required. Does not include recondition fuel injectors.
All models (7.9) 11.5

Clean Carbon and Grind Valves
Includes: R&R cylinder head. Check valve guide and stem clearance. Reface valves, stems and seats.
All models (9.9) 14.4

Rocker Arm Assembly, Recondition
Includes: R&R, disassemble, clean. Renew required parts, reassemble.
All models (1.9) 3.0

Valve Push Rods, Renew (One or All)
All models (1.5) 2.1

Valve Tappets, Renew (All)
Includes: Disassemble engine as required.
All models (12.2) 21.0

Rocker Arm Cover and/or Gasket, Renew
All models (.6) 1.0

Valve Clearance, Adjust
All models (1.2) 1.8

LABOR 13 ENGINE ASSEMBLY & MOUNTS 13 LABOR

(Factory Time)	Chilton Time
GASOLINE ENGINES	
Engine Assembly, Remove & Install	
Does not include transfer of any parts or equipment.	
Four–w/M.T. (4.4)	5.8
w/A.T. (5.0)	6.5
Six–w/M.T. (4.9)	6.4
w/A.T. (5.5)	7.2
V-8–w/M.T. (5.0)	6.5
w/A.T. (5.6)	7.3
w/P.S. add (.3)	.3
w/A.C. add (.6)	.6
Engine Assembly, Renew	
Includes: R&R engine assembly, transfer all necessary parts, fuel and electrical units.	
Four–w/M.T. (10.4)	14.0
w/A.T. (10.7)	14.3
Six–w/M.T. (10.6)	14.2
w/A.T. (10.9)	14.5
V-8–w/M.T. (11.9)	15.5
w/A.T. (12.2)	15.8
w/P.S. add (.3)	.3
w/A.C. add (.6)	.6
Cylinder Assembly, Renew (w/All Internal Parts Less Cylinder Heads and Oil Pan)	
Includes: R&R engine assembly, transfer all component parts not supplied with replacement engine, clean carbon, grind valves. Tune engine.	
Four–w/M.T. (16.9)	21.9
w/A.T. (17.2)	22.2
Six–w/M.T. (18.6)	23.6
w/A.T. (18.8)	23.8
V-8–w/M.T. (22.7)	27.7
w/A.T. (23.0)	28.0
w/P.S. add (.3)	.3
w/A.C. add (.6)	.6
Engine Assy., R&R and Recondition	
Includes: Rebore block, install new pistons, rings, pins, rod and main bearings. Clean carbon, grind valves. Tune engine.	
Four–w/M.T. (27.7)	32.5
w/A.T. (27.9)	32.7
Six–w/M.T. (33.1)	39.7
w/A.T. (33.4)	41.0
V-8–w/M.T. (37.8)	47.5
w/A.T. (38.1)	47.8
w/P.S. add (.3)	.3
w/A.C. add (.6)	.6
Engine Mounts, Renew	
Front	
Four (.6)	1.0
Six (.7)	1.1
V-8 (.7)	1.2
Rear	
Four (.6)	1.0
Six (.7)	1.1
V-8 (.5)	.9
DIESEL ENGINE	
Engine Assembly, Remove & Install	
Does not include transfer of any parts or equipment.	
All models–w/M.T. (5.7)	8.5
w/A.T. (6.3)	9.0
Engine Assembly, Renew (w/Complete Engine)	
Includes: R&R engine assembly, transfer all necessary parts, fuel and electrical units.	
All models–w/M.T. (8.6)	12.8
w/A.T. (9.2)	13.3
Engine Assy., R&R and Recondition	
Includes: Install new pistons, rings, pins, rod and main bearings. Clean carbon, grind valves. Recondition rocker arms. Make all necessary adjustments.	
All models–w/M.T. (31.6)	46.7
w/A.T. (31.9)	47.2
Engine Mounts, Renew	
All models–front (.7)	1.1
rear (.6)	1.0

LABOR 14 PISTONS, RINGS & BEARINGS 14 LABOR

(Factory Time)	Chilton Time
GASOLINE ENGINES	
Rings, Renew (See Engine Combinations)	
Includes: Remove cylinder top ridge, deglaze cylinder walls. Minor tune up.	
SCOUT II	
Four (9.5)	12.5
Six (11.7)	15.0
V-8 (14.4)	17.8
100-200-500 Series	
Six–w/M.T. (15.1)	18.9
w/A.T. (15.6)	19.4
V-8–304-345-392 engs (15.8)	19.7
400 eng–w/M.T. (18.2)	21.9
w/A.T. (18.7)	22.4
w/P.S. add (.3)	.3
w/A.C. add (.6)	.6
w/Pwr brks add (.8)	.8
Piston or Connecting Rod, Renew (One)	
Includes: Remove cylinder top ridge, deglaze cylinder walls. Minor tune up.	
SCOUT II	
Four (8.2)	10.3
Six (9.3)	11.8
V-8 (8.6)	11.1
100-200-500 Series	
Six–w/M.T. (12.9)	15.5
w/A.T. (13.4)	16.0
V-8–304-345-392 engs (10.2)	12.8
400 eng–w/M.T. (13.3)	16.0
w/A.T. (13.8)	16.5
w/P.S. add (.3)	.3
w/A.C. add (.6)	.6
w/Pwr brks add (.8)	.8
Connecting Rod Bearings, Renew	
Includes: Check bearing clearances.	
SCOUT II	
Four (2.5)	3.4
Six (3.7)	4.9
V-8 (3.4)	4.6
100-200-500 Series	
Six–w/M.T. (7.8)	10.2
w/A.T. (8.2)	10.8
V-8–304-345-392 engs (5.0)	6.5
400 eng–w/M.T. (8.3)	10.9
w/A.T. (8.7)	11.3
w/P.S. add (.3)	.3
w/A.C. add (.6)	.6
DIESEL ENGINE	
Rings, Renew (See Engine Combinations)	
Includes: Remove cylinder top ridge, deglaze cylinder walls.	
All models (11.9)	17.7
Piston or Connecting Rod, Renew (One)	
Includes: Remove cylinder top ridge, hone cylinder as required. Install new piston rings and pin.	
All models (9.1)	13.5
Connecting Rod Bearings, Renew	
All models (3.4)	5.0

COMBINATIONS
Add to Engine Work

GASOLINE ENGINES

DRAIN, EVACUATE AND RECHARGE AIR CONDITIONING SYSTEM	
All models	1.8
HYDRAULIC VALVE LIFTERS, DISASSEMBLE AND CLEAN	
Each (.2)	.2
DISTRIBUTOR, RECONDITION	
All models (1.5)	1.9
CARBURETOR, RECONDITION	
1 BBL (1.3)	1.8
2 BBL (1.6)	2.1
4 BBL (1.9)	2.4
VALVE GUIDES, RENEW	
Each (.2)	.3
REMOVE CYLINDER TOP RIDGE	
Each (.1)	.1
DEGLAZE CYLINDER WALLS	
Each (.1)	.2
ROCKER ARMS, DISASSEMBLE AND CLEAN OR RENEW	
Four (.8)	1.0
Six (.6)	.8
V-8 (1.2)	1.4
MAIN BEARINGS, RENEW	
Four (1.6)	2.5
Six (1.9)	2.8
V-8 (1.6)	2.5
PLASTIGAUGE BEARINGS	
Each (.1)	.1
OIL PUMP, RECONDITION	
All models (.6)	.9
OIL FILTER ELEMENT, RENEW	
All models (.3)	.4

LABOR 14 PISTONS, RINGS & BEARINGS 14 LABOR

COMBINATIONS

Add To Engine Work

DIESEL ENGINE

(Factory Time) Chilton Time

DRAIN, EVACUATE AND RECHARGE AIR CONDITIONING SYSTEM
All models 1.8

VALVE GUIDES, RENEW
Each (.2) 3

ROCKER ARMS, DISASSEMBLE AND CLEAN OR RENEW
All models (.6) 8

TIMING GEARS, RENEW (COVER REMOVED)
All models (1.1) 1.4

DEGLAZE CYLINDER WALLS
Each (.1) 2

REMOVE CYLINDER TOP RIDGE
Each (.1) 1

ROD BEARINGS, RENEW (PAN REMOVED)
All models (1.9) 2.5

MAIN BEARINGS, RENEW (PAN REMOVED)
All models (2.7) 3.5

PLASTIGAUGE BEARINGS
Each (.1) 1

PISTON SLEEVES, RENEW
One (1.2) 1.5
Each adtnl (.4) 5

OIL PUMP, RECONDITION
All models (.6) 8

LABOR 15 CRANKSHAFT & DAMPER 15 LABOR

(Factory Time) Chilton Time

GASOLINE ENGINES

Crankshaft and Main Bearings, Renew

Includes: R&R engine assembly and plastigauge bearings.

Four–w/M.T. (11.9) 16.0
w/A.T. (12.1) 16.3
Six–w/M.T. (13.0) 17.0
w/A.T. (13.2) 17.5
V-8–w/M.T. (13.9) 18.4
w/A.T. (14.1) 18.9
w/P.S. add (.3) 3
w/A.C. add (.6) 6
w/Pwr brks add (.8) 8

Main Bearings, Renew

Includes: Plastigauge bearings.

SCOUT II
Four (3.1) 4.5
Six (3.4) 4.8
V-8 (3.1) 4.5
100-200-500 Series
Six–w/M.T. (8.4) 10.2
w/A.T. (8.9) 10.8
V-8–304-345-392 engs (4.7) 6.5
400 eng–w/M.T. (7.9) 9.8
w/A.T. (8.4) 10.3

Rear Main Bearing Oil Seal, Renew

Includes: R&R transmission and clutch or converter, except six cylinder.

SCOUT II–Manual trans
Four & V-8
4X2 (4.5) 5.9
4X4 (5.4) 6.8
Six (3.2) 4.3
Auto trans
Four & V-8
4X2 (5.4) 6.8
4X4 (5.9) 7.3
100-200-500 Series–Manual trans
V-8 (5.3) 6.7
Auto trans
V-8 (5.2) 6.6

Crankshaft Pulley, Renew

SCOUT II
All engs (.4) 8
100-200-500 Series
All engs (1.4) 2.0
w/P.S. add (.2) 2

DIESEL ENGINE

Crankshaft and Main Bearings, Renew

Includes: R&R engine assembly and plastigauge bearings.

All models–w/M.T. (14.2) 21.3
w/A.T. (14.4) 21.8

Main Bearings, Renew

Includes: Plastigauge bearings.

All models (4.1) 5.3

Main and Rod Bearings, Renew

Includes: Plastigauge bearings.

All models (6.0) 7.8

Rear Main Bearing Oil Seal, Renew (Lower Half Only)
All models (1.9) 2.8

Crankshaft Pulley, Renew
All models (1.6) 2.2

LABOR 16 CAMSHAFT & TIMING GEARS 16 LABOR

(Factory Time) Chilton Time

GASOLINE ENGINES

Timing Case Cover or Gasket, Renew

SCOUT II
Four (3.3) 4.7
Six (3.7) 4.9
V-8 (3.6) 4.8
100-200-500 Series
Six (5.1) 6.7
V-8 (5.4) 7.0
w/P.S. add (.2) 2

Timing Case Cover Oil Seal, Renew
All engs–exc below (1.4) 1.9
400 eng (5.4) 7.0

Timing Gears and/or Chain, Renew

SCOUT II
Four (3.9) 5.5
Six (4.3) 5.7
V-8 (4.2) 5.6
100-200-500 Series
Six (5.7) 7.5
V-8 (5.9) 7.8
w/P.S. add (.2) 2

Camshaft, Renew

SCOUT II
Four (7.8) 9.7
Six (10.7) 12.6
V-8 (8.8) 10.7
100-200-500 Series
Six (11.0) 13.0
V-8 (10.1) 12.4

Camshaft Bearings, Renew (Engine Removed and Disassembled)
All models (.5) 1.0

DIESEL ENGINE

Timing Case Cover Oil Seal, Renew
All models (1.7) 2.5

Timing Case Cover or Gasket, Renew

Includes: R&R oil pan and renew cover oil seal.

All models (4.0) 5.6

Timing Gears, Renew
All models (4.8) 6.6

Camshaft, Renew

Includes: Disassemble engine as required.

All models (12.0) 17.8

Camshaft Bearings, Renew (Engine Removed and Disassembled)
All models (.5) 1.0

LABOR 17 ENGINE OILING SYSTEM 17 LABOR

(Factory Time) Chilton Time

GASOLINE ENGINES

Oil Pan or Gasket, Renew

SCOUT II

Four (1.4) 2.0
Six (2.4) 3.2
V-8 (1.4) 2.0

100-200-500 Series

Six–w/M.T. (6.2) 8.0
w/A.T. (6.7) 8.5
V-8–304-345-392 engs (3.0) 3.9
400 eng–w/M.T. (6.4) 8.4
w/A.T. (6.9) 8.9

Oil Pump, Renew

Includes: Clean oil pan and pump screen.

SCOUT II

Four (1.7) 2.3
Six (2.5) 3.4
V-8 (1.7) 2.3

100-200-500 Series

Six–w/M.T. (6.5) 8.3
w/A.T. (6.9) 8.8
V-8–304-345-392 engs (3.2) 4.1
400 eng (1.0) 1.6

Pressure Test Engine Bearings (Pan Off)

All models (1.0) 1.2

Oil Pressure Gauge (Dash), Renew

All models (.6) 1.0

Oil Pressure Gauge (Engine), Renew

All models (.2) 5

Oil Filter Element, Renew

All models (.3) 4

DIESEL ENGINE

Oil Pan and/or Gasket, Renew

All models (1.6) 2.3

Pressure Test Engine Bearings (Pan Off)

All models 1.2

Oil Pump, Renew

All models (1.7) 2.7

Oil Pump, R&R and Recondition

All models (2.2) 3.3

Oil Filter Element, Renew

All models (.3) 4

LABOR 18 CLUTCH & FLYWHEEL 18 LABOR

(Factory Time) Chilton Time

Clutch Pedal Free Play, Adjust

All models (.2) 4

Clutch Assembly, Renew

SCOUT II

4X2 (4.0) 5.4
4X4 (5.0) 6.6

100-200-500 Series

304-345-392 engs (4.4) 5.8
258-400 engs (4.7) 6.1
w/258 eng add (.3) 3
Renew pilot brg add (.2) 3

Clutch Release Bearing, Renew

SCOUT II

4X2 (2.9) 4.3
4X4 (3.9) 5.2

100-200-500 Series

floor shift (3.7) 5.0
column shift (3.0) 4.3

Clutch Release Fork, Renew

SCOUT II

4X2 (3.5) 4.9
4X4 (4.5) 5.8

100-200-500 Series

304-345-392 engs (4.3) 5.6
258-400 engs (4.5) 5.8
w/258 eng add (.3) 3

Flywheel, Renew

SCOUT II

4X2 (4.4) 6.0
4X4 (5.3) 7.2

100-200-500 Series

304-345-392 engs (5.2) 6.4
258-400 engs (5.5) 6.7
w/258 eng add (.3) 3
Renew ring gear add (.5) 6

LABOR 19 STANDARD TRANSMISSION 19 LABOR

(Factory Time) Chilton Time

Transmission Assy., Remove & Reinstall

Includes: R&R transmission and transfer case as a unit.

SCOUT II

4X2 (2.6) 4.0
4X4 (3.5) 4.9

100-200-500 Series

3 speed (2.7) 4.1
4 & 5 speed (3.3) 4.7

Transmission Assembly, Renew

Includes: R&R transmission and transfer case as a unit. Transfer drive gear or flange and transfer case where applicable.

SCOUT II

4X2 (3.2) 4.6
4X4 (4.5) 5.9

100-200-500 Series

3 speed (3.2) 4.7
4 & 5 speed (3.9) 5.4

Transmission Assy., R&R and Recondition

Includes: R&R transmission and transfer case as a unit. Separate units and overhaul transmission only.

SCOUT II

3 Speed
4X2 (6.0) 8.1
4X4 (7.3) 9.4
4 Speed
4X2 (7.1) 9.2
4X4 (8.4) 10.5

100-200-500 Series

3 Speed
column shift (7.0) 9.1
floor shift (7.7) 9.8
4 Speed (8.8) 10.5
5 Speed (8.7) 10.5

Transmission, Recondition (Off Truck)

SCOUT II

3 speed (3.2) 4.1
4 speed (4.5) 5.4

100-200-500 Series

3 speed (4.2) 5.1
4 speed (5.3) 6.2
5 speed (5.1) 6.0

Transmission Rear Oil Seal, Renew

All models (1.0) 1.6

LABOR 20 TRANSFER CASE 20 LABOR

Transfer Case Assy., Remove & Reinstall

Includes: R&R transfer case only.

SCOUT II

w/M.T. (2.6) 4.0
w/A.T. (2.9) 4.3

100-200-500 Series

N P Single Lever (2.6) 4.0
Chain Drive (2.1) 3.5
Travelalls add (.2) 2

Transfer Case Assy., Renew

Includes: R&R transfer case from transmission, install a new transfer case.

SCOUT II

w/M.T. (3.0) 4.4
w/A.T. (3.2) 4.7

100-200-500 Series

N P Single Lever (3.9) 5.3
Chain Drive (2.6) 4.0
Travelalls add (.2) 2

Transfer Case, Recondition (Off Truck)

Chain Drive (3.0) 4.0
Spicer No. 20 (3.9) 4.9
N P Single Lever (5.4) 6.4

Transfer Case Assy., R&R and Recondition

SCOUT II

Chain Drive
w/M.T. (5.7) 8.2
w/A.T. (6.0) 8.5
Spicer No. 20
w/M.T. (6.7) 9.2
w/A.T. (6.9) 9.4

100-200-500 Series

N P Single Lever (8.2) 10.7
Chain Drive (5.3) 7.8
Travelalls add (.2) 2

LABOR 23 AUTOMATIC TRANSMISSION 23 LABOR

(Factory Time) Chilton Time

Drain and Refill Unit
All models (.5) .7

Oil Pressure Check
All models (.5) .7

Check Unit For Oil Leaks
Includes: Clean and dry outside of case, run unit to determine point of leak.
All models (.8) 1.0

Adjust Transmission (Complete)
Includes: Drain and refill unit. R&R oil pan, gasket and screen. Adjust front and rear bands and vacuum control solenoid. Clean pan and screen.
All models (1.5) 2.3

Oil Pan and/or Gasket, Renew
All models (.6) 1.1

Transmission Assy., Remove & Reinstall
Includes: R&R transmission and transfer case as a unit.
SCOUT II
13039 - 13049
4X2 (2.6) 4.1
4X4 (3.5) 5.0
13407
4X2 (4.2) 5.7
4X4 (4.8) 6.3
100-200-500 Series
Six (4.3) 5.9
V-8 (4.0) 5.6

Transmission Assy., Renew
Includes: R&R transmission. Drain and refill unit. Transfer flange or drive gear and transfer case where applicable.
SCOUT II
13039-13049
4X2 (4.4) 5.9
4X4 (5.5) 7.0
13407
4X2 (5.1) 6.6
4X4 (6.1) 7.6
100-200-500 Series
Six (5.1) 6.7
V-8 (4.8) 6.4

Transmission Assy., R&R and Recondition
Includes: R&R transmission and transfer case as a unit. Separate units and overhaul transmission only.
SCOUT II
13039-13049
4X2 (12.1) 15.0
4X4 (13.2) 16.1
13407
4X2 (13.6) 16.5
4X4 (14.7) 17.6
100-200-500 Series
Six (13.8) 16.7
V-8 (13.5) 16.4

Converter Assembly, Renew
Includes: R&R transmission and transfer case as a unit. Drain and refill trans.
SCOUT II
13039-13049
4X2 (4.7) 6.2
4X4 (5.4) 6.9
13407
4X2 (4.6) 6.1
4X4 (5.2) 6.7
100-200-500 Series
Six (4.8) 6.4
V-8 (4.5) 6.1

LABOR 25 U-JOINTS & DRIVESHAFT 25 LABOR

(Factory Time) Chilton Time

Drive Shaft, R&R or Renew
All models (.8) 1.1

Universal Joint, Renew (One)
All models (.8) 1.1

Universal Joint, Recondition (One)
All models (1.1) 1.4

Stub Shaft, Renew
All models (1.2) 1.6

Center Bearing, Renew or Recondition
All models (1.0) 1.4

Tighten Drive Shaft Flange (One)
All models (.5) .7

LABOR 26 REAR AXLE 26 LABOR

(Factory Time) Chilton Time

Rear Axle, Drain and Refill
All models (.3) .6

Axle Housing Cover Gasket, Renew
All models (.6) .9

Axle Shaft, Renew
Includes: Renew axle shaft inner and outer seals. Transfer or renew wheel studs and bearing. Adjust axle shaft end play, where applicable.
SCOUT II
right side (1.5) 2.1
left side (1.7) 2.3
100-200-500 Series
Axle Codes
14015-14016-14017
14020-14025-14184
each (.3) .6
Axle Codes
14018-14028-14063
14083-14084
right side (1.5) 2.1
left side (1.7) 2.3

Axle Shaft Bearing and/or Seal, Renew
SCOUT II
right side (1.4) 2.0
left side (1.6) 2.2
100-200-500 Series
right side (1.5) 2.1
left side (1.7) 2.3

Inner and Outer Axle Shaft Oil Seals, Renew
All models
right side (1.4) 2.0
left side (1.6) 2.2

Pinion Shaft Oil Seal, Renew
SCOUT II (.9) 1.3
100-200-500 Series
Axle Codes
14015-14020-14025 (1.1) 1.5
14016-14017-14018
14028-14063-14083
14084 (.9) 1.3
14184 (1.0) 1.4

Rear Axle Assy., Remove & Reinstall
Includes: R&R wheels and brake drums. R&R brake lines at frame. R&R brake cable at backing plate. R&R rear spring pins. Bleed and adjust brakes.
SCOUT II (3.1) 4.6
100-200-500 Series
Axle Codes
14015-14016-14017
14020-14025 (3.7) 5.2
14018-14028-14063
14083-14084 (2.8) 4.3
14184 (4.3) 5.8

Rear Axle Assy., R&R and Recondition
Includes: Recondition differential and pinion assemblies. Renew ring gear and pinion set. Renew bearings and axle shaft oil seals. Make all necessary adjustments. Bleed and adjust brakes.
SCOUT II
Axle Codes
14018 (9.9) 12.0
14028 (10.3) 12.5
100-200-500 Series
Axle Codes
14016 (8.8) 11.0
14017 (9.4) 11.6
14018-14083 (9.2) 11.4
14028-14063, 14084 (10.0) 12.0

Differential Carrier Assy., R&R or Renew
Includes: R&R carrier assy. from axle housing. Drain and refill unit.
100-200-500 Series
Axle Codes
14015-14020-14025 (2.2) 3.0
14184 (3.0) 3.8

Differential Carrier Assy., R&R and Recondition
Includes: R&R carrier from axle housing. Overhaul differential as required, including ring gear and pinion set. Make all necessary adjustments. Drain and refill unit.
100-200-500 Series
Axle Codes
14015-14020 (7.7) 9.3
14025 (7.8) 9.4
14184 (8.3) 10.1

Pinion Shaft Bearings, Renew
Includes: Renew pinion bearings and cups. Make all necessary adjustments. Drain and refill unit.
SCOUT II (7.0) 8.6
100-200-500 Series
Axle Codes
14015-14020-14025 (5.2) 6.8
14016-14017 (6.8) 8.4
14018-14028-14063
14083-14084 (6.6) 8.2
14184 (6.2) 7.8

LABOR 27 REAR SUSPENSION 27 LABOR

(Factory Time) — Chilton Time

Rear Spring, Renew (One)
SCOUT II (.9) ... 1.5
100-200-500 Series (1.3) ... 1.9

Rear Spring, R&R and Recondition (One)
SCOUT II (1.6) ... 2.5
100-200-500 Series (1.8) ... 2.7

Front and Rear Bushings, Renew (Rear Spring)
Includes: R&R spring and shackles. Install new spring and shackle bushings.
SCOUT II-one (1.5) ... 2.0
100-200-500 Series-one (1.7) ... 2.2

Rear Spring Shackle, Renew
Includes: Renew shackle only, one spring.
SCOUT II (.4) 9
100-200-500 Series
rubber mounted (.5) 9
bushing mounted (.8) ... 1.4

Shackle Bushing, Renew (One Spring)
Includes: Renew shackle bushing only.
SCOUT II (.5) ... 1.0
100-200-500 Series
rubber mounted (.6) ... 1.0
bushing mounted (.9) ... 1.5

Rear Shock Absorbers, Renew
All models-one (.4) 5
both (.5) 8

LABOR 28 AIR CONDITIONING 28 LABOR

(Factory Time) — Chilton Time

Drain, Evacuate and Recharge System
All models ... 1.8

Pressure Test System
All models 6

Add Partial Charge to System
All models ... 1.0

Compressor Belt, Renew
SCOUT II
All engs (.6) 8
100-200-500 Series
Six (.5) 7
V-8-304-345-392 engs (.6) 8
400 eng (.3) 5

Compressor Assembly, Renew
Includes: Transfer all necessary attaching parts. Evacuate and charge system.
SCOUT II (2.0) ... 3.1
100-200-500 Series (1.9) ... 3.0

Compressor Magnetic Clutch, Renew
All models (.3) 6

Electric Clutch Brush Assy., Renew
Includes: R&R magnetic clutch.
All models (.4) 7

Dehydrator Filter, Renew
Includes: Evacuate and charge system.
SCOUT II (2.0) ... 2.8
100-200-500 Series (1.5) ... 2.3

Condenser Assembly, Renew
Includes: Evacuate and charge system.
SCOUT II (2.5) ... 3.7
100-200-500 Series (2.2) ... 3.4

Evaporator Core, Renew
Includes: Evacuate and charge system.
SCOUT II (3.0) ... 4.4
100-200-500 Series (2.9) ... 4.3

Expansion Valve Assembly, Renew
Includes: Evacuate and charge system.
SCOUT II (2.6) ... 3.9
100-200-500 Series (3.0) ... 4.4

Evaporator Core Freeze Control Switch, Renew
SCOUT II (1.3) ... 2.1

Evaporator Relay, Renew
100-200-500 Series (.3) 5

Electric Clutch Override Switch, Renew
100-200-500 Series (1.4) ... 2.2

Blower Motor, Renew
SCOUT II (3.0) ... 4.2
100-200-500 Series (2.9) ... 4.1

Blower Motor Switch, Renew
All models (.7) ... 1.0

Air Conditioner Relay Switch, Renew
SCOUT II (.6) 8

Air Conditioning Hoses, Renew
Includes: Evacuate and charge system.
Compressor to Evaporator
All models (2.7) ... 3.5
Compressor to Condenser
All models (2.5) ... 3.5
Hose with Sight Glass, to Evaporator
All models (2.1) ... 3.2
Dehydrator Filter to Sight Glass
All models (1.6) ... 2.7

LABOR 30 HEAD AND PARKING LAMPS 30 LABOR

(Factory Time) — Chilton Time

Aim Headlamps
All models (.3) 4

Headlamp Sealed Beam Bulb, Renew
All models-each (.2) 2

Parking Lamp Assy. or Lens, Renew
All models (.2) 3

Back-Up, Stop, Tail/Turn Signal Lamp or Lens, Renew
All models-each (.2) 3

License Lamp Assy. or Lens, Renew
All models (.2) 2

Reflector, Renew
All models-each 1

LABOR 31 WINDSHIELD WIPER & SPEEDOMETER 31 LABOR

(Factory Time) — Chilton Time

Wiper Motor, Renew
SCOUT II
Early production (.7) ... 1.1
Late Scout II- Terra-Traveler (.5) ... 1.0
100-200-500 Series (.7) ... 1.1

Wiper Switch, Renew
All models 6

Windshield Washer Pump, Renew
All models 4

Speedometer Head, R&R or Renew
All models ... 1.4

Speedometer Cable and Casing, Renew
wo/Cruise Control
All models (1.0) ... 1.6
w/Cruise Control
Trans to Speed Sensor
All models (.6) ... 1.1
Speed Sensor to Speedo
All models (.7) ... 1.3

Speedometer Cable (Inner), Renew or Lubricate
Does not include fabricate core from bulk stock.
wo/Cruise Control
All models (1.1) ... 1.7
w/Cruise Control
Trans to Speed Sensor
All models (.6) ... 1.0
Speed Sensor to Speedo
All models (.7) ... 1.2

LABOR 1 TUNE UP 1 LABOR

(Factory Time) Chilton Time

GASOLINE ENGINES

Compression Test

Six	1.0
V-8	1.2

Engine Tune Up, (Minor)

Includes: Clean or renew spark plugs, renew ignition points and condenser, set ignition timing, set carburetor idle speed and mixture. Service carburetor air cleaner. Clean or renew fuel filter.

Six	2.4
V-8–V engs	2.7
V-8–VS engs	2.9

Engine Tune Up, (Major)

Includes: Check engine compression, clean or renew spark plugs, test battery, clean terminals, renew and adjust distributor points and condenser. Check distributor cap and rotor. Set ignition timing, test coil. Tighten manifold bolts. Adjust idle speed and mixture. Inspect and tighten all hose connections. Adjust fan belts. Service air cleaner.

Six	3.9
V-8–V engs	4.2
V-8–VS engs	4.4
Check fuel pump pressure and vacuum add	.3

Engine Tune Up, (Electronic Ignition)

Includes: Test battery and clean connections. Tighten manifold and carburetor mounting bolts. Check engine compression, clean and adjust or renew spark plugs. Test resistance of spark plug cables. Inspect distributor cap and rotor. Adjust air gap. Check vacuum advance operation. Reset ignition timing. Adjust idle mixture and speed. Service air cleaner. Inspect crankcase ventilation system. Inspect and adjust drive belts. Inspect choke operation and adjust or free up.

V-8	3.2

DIESEL ENGINES

Engine Tune Up, (Minor)

Includes: Test batteries, clean and tighten terminals. Check and adjust engine idle speed and throttle linkage. Change engine oil. Clean or renew oil, air, fuel and water filters. Tighten radiator hoses and manifold bolts. Check valve lash and adjust tappets. R&R and test injectors.
Does not include compression test or injection timing.

IHC Diesel	
Six	4.3
V-8	6.8
Cummins	
Six	4.0
V-8	5.5
Detroit	
6-71	6.0
6V-53, 6V-71	6.2
8V-71	6.5
12V-71	7.7
Caterpillar	
Six	4.3
V-8	5.3

Engine Tune Up, (Major)

Includes: Test batteries, clean and tighten terminals. Check and adjust engine idle speed and throttle linkage. Adjust injector timing and injectors. Steam clean engines. Change engine oil. Clean or renew air, oil, fuel and water filters. Check and lubricate shutters. Clean injectors and fuel connections. Inspect for oil, water, and fuel leaks. Drain sediment from fuel tanks. Tighten intake manifold, exhaust manifold, turbocharger and engine mounting bolts. Clean turbocharger impeller, diffuser and fuel pump screen. Adjust crossheads and valves. Check crankshaft end play. Check and adjust fan belts. Road test.
Does not include compression test.

IHC Diesel	
Six	10.5
V-8	14.8
Cummins Diesel	
Six	10.5
V-8	15.5
Detroit Diesel	
6-71	14.2
6V-53, 6V-71	14.8
8V-71	17.0
12V-71	18.0
Caterpillar	
Six	10.5
V-8	11.5

Compression Test

Includes: R&R injectors and other interfering parts, attach compression gauge and adjust injectors.

IHC Diesel	
Six	5.5
V-8	7.0
Cummins Diesel	
Six	5.0
V-8	8.0
Detroit Diesel	
6-71	4.0
6V-53, 6V-71	3.8
8V-71	6.5
12V-71	7.5
Caterpillar	
Six	3.0
V-8	3.5

LABOR 2 IGNITION SYSTEM 2 LABOR

(Factory Time) Chilton Time

POINT TYPE IGNITION

Spark Plugs, Clean and Reset or Renew

Six(.6)	.8
V-8(.7)	1.0

Ignition Timing, Reset

Six(.3)	.5
V-8(.4)	.6

Distributor, Renew

Includes: Reset ignition timing.

Six(.6)	.8
V-8–V engs (.7)	1.0
V-8–VS engs (.9)	1.2

Distributor, R&R and Recondition

Includes: Reset ignition timing.

Six(1.6)	2.1
V-8–V engs	
wo/Gov and tach (1.9)	2.4
w/Governor (2.2)	2.7
w/Gov and tach (2.4)	2.9
V-8–VS engs	
wo/Gov and tach (2.1)	2.6
w/Governor (2.4)	2.9
w/Gov and tach (2.6)	3.1

Distributor Cap, Renew

Six(.2)	.4
V-8(.3)	.5

Distributor Points and Condenser, Renew

Includes: R&R distributor and reset timing and dwell.

Six(.9)	1.2
V-8–V engs (1.1)	1.4
V-8–VS engs (1.3)	1.6

Ignition Coil, Renew

LOADSTAR-S1600-2100 (.5)	.7
All others (.6)	.8

Vacuum Control Unit, Renew

Includes: R&R distributor and reset timing and dwell.

Six(.8)	1.1
V-8–V engs (.9)	1.3
V-8–VS engs (1.1)	1.5

Ignition Cables, Renew

Six(.4)	.7
V-8–V engs (.5)	.8
V-8–VS engs (.6)	.9

Ignition Switch, Renew

All series (.3)	.6

ELECTRONIC IGNITION

Electronic Ignition Control Module, Renew

Includes: Test system in chassis.

All series (1.2)	1.6

Distributor Sensor Assembly, Renew

Includes: Test system in chassis. R&R distributor and reset ignition timing.

All series (1.5)	2.0

Distributor, R&R and Recondition

Includes: Reset ignition timing.

All series (2.4)	2.9

LABOR 3 FUEL SYSTEM 3 LABOR

(Factory Time) Chilton Time

GASOLINE ENGINES

Fuel Pump, Test

Includes: Disconnect line at carburetor, attach pressure gauge.

All series 3

Carburetor, Adjust (On Truck)

All series 4

Governor R.P.M., Adjust (with Tachometer)

All series (.6) 8

Carburetor Air Cleaner, Service

RD and VS engs (.5) 6
All others (.2) 3

Carburetor, Renew

Includes: All necessary adjustments.

Six(.9) 1.1
V-8-V engs
2210C (1.4) 1.9
2300 (.8) 1.1
2300G-4150G (.9) 1.2
2300 EG-4150 EG (1.6) 2.1
V-8-VS engs
2140G (.9) 1.2
V-8-MV engs
2210G (1.3) 1.6
2300G-4150G (1.4) 1.7

Carburetor, R&R and Clean or Recondition

Includes: All necessary adjustments.

Six
852-885-FFG (2.7) 3.8
2140G (3.1) 4.2
V-8-V engs
2210C (2.8) 4.0
2300 (2.0) 3.1
2300G (2.4) 3.5
2300EG (3.2) 4.4
4150G (2.6) 3.7
4150EG (3.5) 4.8
V-8-VS engs
2140G (3.1) 4.2
852-FFG (2.6) 3.7
V-8-MV engs
2210C (2.8) 3.9
2300G (2.9) 4.0
4150G (3.1) 4.2

Fuel Pump, Renew

Six(.6) 8
V-8-on engine (.5) 8
in tank-step tank (.8) 1.1
All others (.6) 9

Fuel Tank, Renew

under cab mount (.9) 1.7
side mount (1.0) 1.8
step tank (1.1) 1.9
standard mount (1.0) 1.8

Fuel Gauge (Tank), Renew

under cab mount (.5) 8
side mount (.4) 7
step tank (.5) 8
standard mount (.4) 7

Fuel Gauge (Dash), Renew

All series (.5) 8

Intake Manifold Gaskets, Renew

Six(1.4) 2.1
V-8-V engs (2.9) 3.8
V-8-VS engs (1.2) 2.1
V-8-MV engs (2.8) 3.8
V-8-537-605 engs (3.1) 4.0
w/Steel hood add (.4) 4
w/Air brakes add (.5) 5

DIESEL ENGINES

Air Cleaner Assembly, R&R and Clean or Renew

All series 7

Engine Idle Speed, Adjust (Governor)

All series 1.0

Injectors, Renew

Includes: R&R all normal interfering parts, all required cleaning and adjustment.

IHC Diesel
Six-one 8
all 3.4
V-8-one 4
all 2.0
Cummins Diesel
one 1.0
each adtnl 7
Detroit Diesel
one 6
each adtnl 4
Caterpillar
Six-one 1.9
all 3.2
V-8-one 2.5
all 4.0
Recondition add each
IHC Diesel 1.0
Cummins 6

Detroit
S type 7
N type 1.0

Injection Pump, Renew

IHC Diesel
Six 1.2
V-8 .... 2.0
Cummins Diesel
All series 2.2
Detroit Diesel
exc below 1.5
6V-53, 12V-71 .... 2.0
Caterpillar
Six 3.3
V-8 .... 4.4

Blower Assembly, Renew

Cummins Diesel
All series 6.0
Detroit Diesel
exc below 8.0
6-71 .... 5.7
12V-71-one 8.2
two 10.0

Turbocharger, R&R or Renew

IHC DIESEL
DT-466 (1.4) 2.2
Cummins Diesel
All series 3.8
Caterpillar
Six 2.1

Turbocharger, R&R and Recondition

IHC DIESEL
DT-466 (4.3) 6.5

Turbocharger Bearing Housing, Renew

IHC DIESEL
DT-466 (2.0) 3.5

Shutdown Valve, Renew

exc below 8
Cummins Diesel 1.4

Fuel Filter, Renew

All series 7

Intake Manifold Gasket, Renew

IHC Diesel
Six 9
V-8-one 2.0
both 3.2
Cummins Diesel
Six 1.6
Caterpillar
Six 2.0
V-8 .... 2.2

LABOR 4 ALTERNATOR & REGULATOR 4 LABOR

(Factory Time) Chilton Time

Alternator Circuits Test

Includes: Test battery, regulator and alternator output.

All series 8
Test additional battery add 2

Alternator, Renew

All series (1.0) 1.4

Alternator, R&R and Recondition

All series
37, 61 amp (2.3) 2.8
55, 62 amp (2.6) 3.2
65, 85 amp (2.9) 3.8
75 amp (2.5) 3.0
105, 130 amp (2.7) 3.3
145 amp (2.3) 2.8

Alternator Brushes, Renew

All series
37, 61 amp (1.6) 2.1
55, 62 amp (1.9) 2.5
65, 85 amp (2.2) 3.1
75 amp (1.8) 2.3
105, 130 amp (2.0) 2.6
145 amp (1.6) 2.1

Voltage Regulator, Renew

All series
external (.8) 1.1
integral (1.0) 1.5

Voltage Regulator, Test and Adjust

All series-external (.6) 8

LABOR 5 STARTING SYSTEM 5 LABOR

Starter Draw Test (On Truck)

(Factory Time)	Chilton Time
All series	.3

Starter, Renew

(Factory Time)	Chilton Time
LOADSTAR-CARGOSTAR-S1600-2100	
RD-6V53 engs (1.1)	1.5
V engs (1.1)	1.5
VS-D354 engs (1.2)	1.6
DV engs (1.6)	2.1
FLEETSTAR-S2200-2600	
Gasoline engines	
Six (1.2)	1.6
V-8 (1.4)	1.8
Diesel engines	
Six (1.3)	1.8
V-8 (1.5)	2.0
TRANSTAR	
All engs (1.2)	1.7

Starter, R&R and Recondition

Includes: Disassemble, clean, inspect, and test components. Renew parts as necessary and reassemble.

(Factory Time)	Chilton Time
LOADSTAR-CARGOSTAR-S1600-2100	
RD engs (2.6)	3.5
V engs (2.1)	3.0
VS-D354 engs (2.8)	3.7
DV engs (3.7)	4.6
6V53 eng (3.2)	4.1
FLEETSTAR-S2200-2600	
Gasoline Engines	
Six (2.9)	3.8
V-8 (3.1)	4.0
Diesel engines	
Six (3.6)	4.5
V-8 (3.8)	4.7
TRANSTAR	
All engs (3.3)	4.2
Renew field coils add (1.0)	1.0

Starter Drive, Renew

Includes: R&R starter.

(Factory Time)	Chilton Time
LOADSTAR-CARGOSTAR-S1600-2100	
RD engs (1.9)	2.6
V engs (1.4)	2.1
VS-D354 engs (1.9)	2.6
DV engs (2.8)	3.5
6V53 engs (2.3)	3.0
FLEETSTAR-S2200-2600	
Gasoline engines	
Six (2.2)	2.9
V-8 (2.7)	3.4
Diesel engines	
Six (2.4)	3.1
V-8 (3.0)	3.7
TRANSTAR	
All engs (2.3)	3.0

Starter Solenoid or Magnetic Switch, Renew

Includes: R&R starter.

(Factory Time)	Chilton Time
LOADSTAR-CARGOSTAR-S1600-2100	
RD-6V53 engs (1.4)	1.9
V engs (1.2)	1.7
VS-D354 engs (1.6)	2.1
DV engs (1.8)	2.3
FLEETSTAR-S2200-2600	
Gasoline engines	
Six (1.3)	1.8
V-8 (1.5)	2.0
Diesel engines	
Six (1.6)	2.1
V-8 (1.8)	2.3
TRANSTAR	
All engs (1.0)	1.5

Voltmeter or Ammeter, Renew

(Factory Time)	Chilton Time
S1600-2600	
All models (.4)	.6

Battery Cables, Renew

(Factory Time)	Chilton Time
All series-positive	
cowl mount (.4)	.5
frame rail mount (.7)	.9
negative (.3)	.4

LABOR 6 BRAKE SYSTEM 6 LABOR

Brakes, Adjust (Minor)

Includes: Adjust brakes at all wheels, fill master cylinder.

(Factory Time)	Chilton Time
single axle	
hydraulic	1.0
air	.8
tandem axle	
hydraulic	1.2
air	1.0

Bleed Brakes (All Wheels)

Includes: Fill master cylinder.

(Factory Time)	Chilton Time
single axle	.8
tandem axle	1.0

Brake Pedal Free Play, Adjust

(Factory Time)	Chilton Time
All models	.4

Front Brake Shoes, R&R or Renew

Add .6 per axle to reline shoes.

(Factory Time)	Chilton Time
LOADSTAR-S1600-2100	
'I' Beam axle-w/Single rear axle	
hydraulic (2.5)	3.6
air wedge (2.5)	3.6
air cam (2.4)	3.5
'I' Beam axle-w/Tandem rear axle	
hydraulic (2.8)	3.9
air wedge (2.8)	3.9
air cam (2.5)	3.6
w/Front drive axle-02054	
hydraulic (3.3)	4.4
w/Front drive axle-02057-02059	
hydraulic (4.8)	5.9
CARGOSTAR-CO & COF	
hydraulic (2.5)	3.6
air wedge (2.7)	3.8
air cam (2.4)	3.5
FLEETSTAR-S2200-2600	
hydraulic (2.9)	4.0
air wedge (2.9)	4.0
air cam (2.6)	3.7
TRANSTAR	
w/Single rear axle	
air wedge (2.6)	3.7
air cam (2.4)	3.5
w/Tandem rear axle	
air wedge (2.9)	4.0
air cam (2.5)	3.6

Rear Brake Shoes, R&R or Renew

Add .6 per axle to reline shoes.

(Factory Time)	Chilton Time
LOADSTAR-S1600-2100	
w/Single rear axle	
hydraulic (3.1)	4.3
air wedge (3.0)	4.2
air cam (2.8)	4.0
w/Tandem rear axle	
hydraulic (5.6)	7.5
air wedge (5.4)	7.3
air cam (5.2)	7.1
CARGOSTAR	
w/Single rear axle	
hydraulic (3.0)	4.2
air wedge (2.9)	4.1
air cam (2.6)	3.8
w/Tandem rear axle	
hydraulic (5.5)	7.4
air wedge (5.3)	7.2
air cam (4.7)	6.6
FLEETSTAR-S2200-2600	
w/Single rear axle	
hydraulic (3.1)	4.3
air wedge (3.1)	4.3
air cam (2.8)	4.0
w/Tandem rear axle	
hydraulic (5.5)	7.4
air wedge (5.5)	7.4
air cam (5.1)	7.0
TRANSTAR	
w/Single rear axle	
air wedge (3.1)	4.3
air cam (2.9)	4.1
w/Tandem rear axle	
air wedge (5.6)	7.5
air cam (5.3)	7.2

Brake Shoes (All Wheels), R&R or Renew

Add .6 per axle to reline shoes.

(Factory Time)	Chilton Time
LOADSTAR-S1600-2100	
'I' Beam axle-w/Single rear axle	
hydraulic (4.7)	7.3
air wedge (4.7)	7.3
air cam (4.6)	7.2
'I' Beam axle-w/Tandem rear axle	
hydraulic (7.2)	10.0
air wedge (7.0)	9.8
air cam (6.9)	9.7
w/Front drive axle-02054 and single rear axle (5.3)	7.9
w/Front drive axle-02054 and tandem rear axle (7.8)	10.6
w/Front drive axle-02057-02059 and single rear axle (6.8)	9.4
w/Front drive axle-02057-02059 and tandem rear axle (9.3)	12.0
CARGOSTAR	
w/Single rear axle	
hydraulic (4.5)	7.1
air wedge (4.5)	7.1
air cam (4.4)	7.0
w/Tandem rear axle	
hydraulic (6.9)	9.7
air wedge (6.8)	9.6
air cam (6.6)	9.4
FLEETSTAR-S2200-2600	
w/Single rear axle	
hydraulic (4.6)	7.4
air wedge (4.6)	7.4
air cam (4.3)	7.1
w/Tandem rear axle	
hydraulic (7.0)	9.8
air wedge (7.0)	9.8
air cam (6.6)	9.4
TRANSTAR	
w/Single rear axle	
air wedge (4.8)	7.6
air cam (4.6)	7.4
w/Tandem rear axle	
air wedge (7.3)	10.1
air cam (7.0)	9.8

(Factory Time)	Chilton Time

Stop Light Switch, Renew

All series (.3) 5

BRAKE HYRAULIC SYSTEM

Front Wheel Cylinder(s), Renew (One Wheel)

Includes: Bleed lines.

LOADSTAR-S1600-2100
'I' Beam axle
w/Single rear axle (2.4) 3.5
w/Tandem rear axle (2.5) 3.6
w/Front drive axle-02054 and single rear axle (2.7) 3.8
w/Front drive axle-02054 and tandem rear axle (2.8) 3.9
w/Front drive axle-02057-02059 and single rear axle (3.4) 4.5
w/Front drive axle-02057-02059 and tandem rear axle (3.5) 4.6
CARGOSTAR
w/Single rear axle (2.2) 3.3
w/Tandem rear axle (2.4) 3.5
FLEETSTAR-S2200-2600
w/Single rear axle (2.4) 3.5
w/Tandem rear axle (2.5) 3.6

Rear Wheel Cylinder(s), Renew (One Wheel)

Includes: Bleed lines.

All series
w/Single rear axle (2.7) 3.9
w/Tandem rear axle (2.8) 4.0

Recondition Wheel Cylinder(s) (Off Truck)

Includes: Hone cylinder.

All series-each (.1) 4

Master Cylinder, Renew

Includes: Bleed system.

LOADSTAR-S1600-2100
single cyl (1.4) 1.9
dual cyl (1.5) 2.0
CARGOSTAR
CO series (1.1) 1.7
COF series (1.3) 1.9
FLEETSTAR-S2200-2600
single axle (1.2) 1.8
tandem axle (1.4) 2.0

Master Cylinder, R&R and Recondition

Includes: Hone cylinder and bleed lines.

LOADSTAR-S1600-2100
single cyl (1.9) 2.7
dual cyl (2.2) 3.0
CARGOSTAR
single axle (1.5) 2.5
tandem axle (1.6) 2.7
FLEETSTAR-S2200-2600
single axle (1.9) 2.6
tandem axle 2.8

Brake Hose, Renew (One)

Includes: Bleed lines.

LOADSTAR-S1600-2100
single axle (.9) 1.3
tandem axle (1.1) 1.5
CARGOSTAR-FLEETSTAR-S2200-2600
single axle (.9) 1.3
tandem axle (1.0) 1.4

Brake Booster, Renew

Includes: Bleed brake system.

LOADSTAR
cowl mounted (1.6) 2.2
frame mounted (1.8) 2.4
S1600-2100
Hy-Power (1.1) 1.5
Dual Power (.8) 1.1
Dual Vacuum (.9) 1.2

COMBINATIONS

Add to Brakes, Renew

(Factory Time)	Chilton Time

RENEW WHEEL CYLINDER
Each (.1) 3

REBUILD WHEEL CYLINDER
Each (.2) 4

RENEW MASTER CYLINDER
Single cylinder (1.0) 1.4
Dual cylinder (1.1) 1.5

REBUILD MASTER CYLINDER
Single cylinder (.6) 1.0
Dual cylinder (.8) 1.2

RENEW BRAKE HOSE
Hydraulic (.8) 1.0
Air (.3) 5

RELINE BRAKE SHOES
Each axle set 6

RELINE PARKING BRAKE SHOES OR BAND
All series (.3) 5

REPACK FRONT WHEEL BEARINGS (BOTH WHEELS)
All series 6

RENEW FRONT WHEEL BEARINGS AND SEALS
All series-each whl 4

RENEW REAR WHEEL GREASE SEAL
All series-each (.2) 3

RENEW AXLE SHAFT OIL SEAL
All series-inner (1.1) 1.4
Full floating (.2) 4

(Factory Time)	Chilton Time

CARGOSTAR
single axle (1.6) 2.2
tandem axle (1.7) 2.3
FLEETSTAR-S2200-2600
single axle (1.5) 2.1
tandem axle (1.6) 2.2

Brake Vacuum Power Cylinder, Renew

Includes: Bleed brake system.

S1600-2100
single axle (1.5) 2.0
tandem axle (1.6) 2.2

AIR BRAKES

Air Compressor, Renew

LOADSTAR-S1600-2100
gas engs (2.1) 2.8
CARGOSTAR-FLEETSTAR
gas engs (1.6) 2.3
S2200-2600
V-537-3208-DT-466
V-800-3406 engs (2.0) 3.1
6-71N-8V-71-6V-92 engs (2.8) 4.0
NH series engs (3.1) 4.3
TRANSTAR
Belt Driven
All engs (1.6) 2.3
Gear Driven
Cummins
NH engs (2.5) 3.4
V903
conv cab (2.4) 3.3
tilt cab (1.7) 2.4

(Factory Time)	Chilton Time

Detroit
conv cab (2.7) 3.6
tilt cab (2.0) 2.6
Rear eng mount comp add (.7) 1.0

Compressor Belt, Renew

All series (.5) 7
additional belt (.3) 4

Treadle Valve, Renew

conventional (1.2) 1.6
tilt cab (1.8) 2.3
S2200-2600
All models (2.1) 3.0

Relay Valve, Renew

All series (1.2) 1.6

Safety Valve, Renew

All series (.4) 6

Pressure Gauge, Renew

All series (.5) 7

Governor, Renew

All series (.6) 9

Brake Chamber, Renew (One)

All series
single wedge (.8) 1.1
double wedge (1.2) 1.7
air cam (.7) 1.0

Brake Chamber, R&R and Recondition

All series
single wedge (1.1) 1.6
double wedge (1.5) 2.2
air cam (1.0) 1.5

Air Brake Chamber Diaphragm, Renew

All series-each (.3) 7
w/Parking brake chamber add (.2) 3

Brake Wedge Cylinders, Renew (One)

FRONT
All models
single wedge (1.9) 2.7
double wedge (2.4) 3.3
REAR
single axle (2.5) 3.2
tandem axle (2.6) 3.4

Brake Wedge Cylinders, R&R and Recondition (One)

FRONT
All models
single wedge (1.9) 3.2
double wedge (2.4) 3.8
REAR
All series (2.7) 3.8

Slack Adjuster, R&R and Recondition (One)

Includes: All necessary adjustments.

All series (2.1) 2.8

Brake Camshaft, Recondition (Wheels Removed)

FRONT
LOADSTAR-CARGOSTAR
FLEETSTAR-S1600-2600
All models (1.8) 2.5
TRANSTAR
All models (2.0) 2.7
REAR
LOADSTAR-CARGOSTAR-S1600-2100
single axle (2.1) 2.8
tandem axle (4.0) 5.3
FLEETSTAR-S2200-2600
single axle (2.2) 2.9
tandem axle (4.2) 5.5
TRANSTAR
single axle (2.4) 3.1
tandem axle (4.3) 5.6

LABOR 6 BRAKE SYSTEM 6 LABOR

	(Factory Time)	Chilton Time
PARKING BRAKE		
Parking Brake, Adjust		
All series	(.3)	.5
Parking Brake Lever, Renew		
All series	(.9)	1.3
Parking Brake Shoes, Renew		
closed drum type	(1.0)	1.5
open band type	(.7)	1.1
Fleetstar series	(1.3)	2.1
Parking Brake Control Valve, Renew		
All series	(.7)	1.0
AIR BRAKE ANTI-SKID SYSTEM		
Exciter Ring, Renew (One)		
All series-front	(1.5)	2.1
rear	(1.7)	2.4
Wheel Sensor, Renew (One)		
All series-front	(1.2)	1.7
rear	(1.3)	1.9
Computer Module, Renew		
All series-each	(.6)	1.0
Control (Module) Valve, Renew		
All series-each	(.6)	1.0

LABOR 7 COOLING SYSTEM 7 LABOR

	(Factory Time)	Chilton Time
Thermostat, Renew		
LOADSTAR-S1600-2100		
All engs	(.4)	.6
CARGOSTAR		
D354 eng	(.6)	.9
All other engs	(.4)	.6
FLEETSTAR-S2200-2600		
V-537-605 engs	(.5)	.8
All other engs	(.4)	.6
TRANSTAR		
V-800 engs	(1.1)	1.4
VS-DV engs	(.4)	.6
Radiator Assembly, R&R or Renew		
LOADSTAR-S1600-2100		
All engs	(.9)	1.7
CARGOSTAR		
V-engs	(2.8)	3.7
VS-DV-D354 engs	(3.0)	4.2
MV engs	(2.7)	3.7
FLEETSTAR-S2200-2600		
All engs	(4.8)	5.9
TRANSTAR		
conv cab	(5.0)	6.4
tilt cab	(7.1)	8.5
Radiator Hoses, Renew		
LOADSTAR-S1600-2100		
All engs-upper	(.3)	.5
lower	(.4)	.7
CARGOSTAR		
All engs-upper	(.4)	.7
lower	(.5)	.8
FLEETSTAR-S2200-2600		
All engs-upper	(.4)	.7
lower	(.5)	.8
Water Pump, Renew		
LOADSTAR-S1600-2200		
All engs	(1.4)	2.0
CARGOSTAR		
VD-354 engs	(.8)	1.5
VS-DV engs	(1.0)	1.7
MV engs	(1.2)	1.9
FLEETSTAR-S2200-2600		
All engs	(1.4)	2.0
TRANSTAR		
VS engs	(1.4)	2.2
DV engs	(1.5)	2.4
V-800 engs	(1.2)	2.0
Fan Belts, Renew		
All series	(.4)	.6
Temperature Gauge (Dash), Renew		
S1600-2600		
All models	(.4)	.6
TRANSTAR		
conv cab	(.8)	1.4
tilt cab	(1.4)	2.0
All other series	(.5)	1.0
Temperature Gauge (Engine), Renew		
All series	(.4)	.6
Heater Core, R&R or Renew		
LOADSTAR-CARGOSTAR		
All models	(1.8)	2.8
S1600-2600		
All models	(.9)	1.7
FLEESTAR		
All models	(1.0)	1.9
TRANSTAR		
All models	(.8)	1.5
Heater Blower Motor, Renew		
LOADSTAR		
All models	(.3)	.6
S1600-2600		
All models	(.6)	1.0
CARGOSTAR		
All models	(1.6)	2.3
FLEETSTAR		
All models	(.4)	.8
TRANSTAR		
floor mount	(.7)	1.2
side mount	(.4)	.7
Blower Motor Switch, Renew		
All series	(.5)	.7

LABOR 8 EXHAUST SYSTEM 8 LABOR

	(Factory Time)	Chilton Time
Muffler, Renew (Each)		
LOADSTAR		
Six	(1.1)	1.5
V-8 engs	(.7)	1.1
DV-6V53 engs	(.7)	1.1
S1600-2100		
w/single exh	(1.1)	1.5
w/dual exh	(1.4)	1.9
CARGOSTAR		
All engs	(.8)	1.2
FLEETSTAR		
Six	(1.1)	1.5
All other engs	(.8)	1.2
S2200-2600		
Horizontal System		
w/Single pipe	(1.1)	1.5
w/Dual pipes	(1.4)	1.9
Vertical System		
each	(1.0)	1.5
TRANSTAR		
All engs	(.8)	1.2
Silencer muffler	(1.3)	1.9
Tail Pipe, Renew (Each)		
LOADSTAR		
Six	(.8)	1.2
V-8 engs	(.4)	.7
DV engs	(.4)	.7
6V53 eng	(.6)	1.0
S1600-2100		
Horizontal	(.4)	.6
Vertical	(.7)	.9
CARGOSTAR		
short pipe	(.5)	.8
vertical pipe	(.9)	1.2
FLEETSTAR		
short pipe	(.5)	.7
long pipe	(.7)	1.3
vertical pipe	(.7)	1.3
S2200-2600		
All models-each	(.4)	.6
TRANSTAR		
All models	(.4)	.6
Exhaust Pipes, Renew		
LOADSTAR		
Single exhaust		
Six-one	(.7)	1.1
both	(1.3)	2.0
V-8 engs-left	(1.0)	1.4
right	(1.3)	1.7
rear	(.8)	1.2
DV engs-left	(1.1)	1.5
right	(1.4)	1.8
rear	(.8)	1.2
6V53 eng		
left or right	(.6)	1.0
intermediate	(.9)	1.3
rear junction	(1.2)	1.6

LABOR 8 EXHAUST SYSTEM 8 LABOR

(Factory Time)	Chilton Time
Dual exhaust	
V-8 engs-front (.7)	1.1
rear (.8)	1.2
DV engs-front (.7)	1.1
rear (.9)	1.3
6V53 eng	
front (.5)	9
intermediate (.7)	1.1
rear (.8)	1.2
S1600-2100	
V-537-DT-466 engs	
each (.7)	1.1
All other engs	
each (.9)	1.3
CARGOSTAR	
V-8 engs	
left (.6)	1.0
right (.9)	1.3
D354 eng (.9)	1.3
Diesel engs	
left (.7)	1.1
right (1.0)	1.4
FLEETSTAR	
Six-each (.7)	1.1
dual system-each (.7)	1.1
cross over system-each (1.3)	1.7
intermediate (.7)	1.1
flexible (.7)	1.1
rear (.7)	1.1
S2200-2600	
All models-each (.7)	1.1
TRANSTAR	
front-each (1.0)	1.4
crossover (.7)	1.1
intermediate (.8)	1.2
flexible (.8)	1.2
rear (.8)	1.2

Exhaust Manifold Gaskets, Renew

(Factory Time)	Chilton Time
S1600-2600	
V-345 eng	
one (.7)	1.1
both (1.2)	2.0
MV-404-446 engs	
one (.8)	1.2
both (1.5)	2.2
V-537 eng	
left (.9)	1.3
right (1.1)	1.5
both (1.8)	2.7

LABOR 9 FRONT SUSPENSION 9 LABOR

Note: On all front suspension operations alignment charges must be added if performed. Time given does not include alignment.

Check Alignment of Front End

(Factory Time)	Chilton Time
LOADSTAR-CARGOSTAR-S1600-2100	
All models (.7)	.9
FLEETSTAR-TRANSTAR-S2200-2600	
All models (1.0)	1.2

Toe-In, Adjust

(Factory Time)	Chilton Time
LOADSTAR-CARGOSTAR-S1600-2100	
All models (.5)	.6
FLEETSTAR-TRANSTAR-S2200-2600	
All models (.8)	1.0

Front Wheel Bearings, Clean and Repack (Both Wheels)

(Factory Time)	Chilton Time
LOADSTAR-S1600-2100	
'I' beam axle (1.3)	1.7
Dana driving axle (1.8)	2.5
Coleman driving axle (3.3)	4.0
CARGOSTAR	
All models (1.1)	1.5
FLEETSTAR-TRANSTAR-S2200-2600	
All models (1.3)	1.7

Front Wheel Bearings, Renew (One Wheel)

(Factory Time)	Chilton Time
All series	
'I' beam axle (1.0)	1.2
drive axle (1.1)	1.6

Front Wheel Grease Seal, Renew (One Wheel)

(Factory Time)	Chilton Time
All series	
'I' beam axle (.8)	1.0
drive axle (.9)	1.4

Front Shock Absorber or Rubber Bushing, Renew

(Factory Time)	Chilton Time
All series-one (.3)	.5
both (.6)	.9

Axle 'I' Beam, Renew

(Factory Time)	Chilton Time
LOADSTAR	
Axle Codes	
02048-02068-02072	
hydraulic or air (3.4)	4.9
02089-02091-02098	
hydraulic or air (4.2)	5.7
02105-02109-02136-02139	
02208-02215-02218	
hydraulic (4.6)	6.1
air (4.0)	5.5
S1600-2100	
Axle Codes	
02071-02073-02101 (4.9)	6.8
02109-02118-02127	
02139-02309-02329	
02339 (5.2)	7.2
CARGOSTAR	
Axle Codes	
02069	
hydraulic or air (3.3)	4.8
02099	
hydraulic or air (4.2)	5.7
02209-02219	
hydraulic (4.7)	6.2
air (3.9)	5.4
FLEETSTAR	
Axle Codes	
02098-02099	
hydraulic (4.6)	6.1
air wedge (5.0)	6.5
air cam (4.8)	6.3
02109-02112-02136	
02139-02182-02228	
02309-02329-02339	
hydraulic (5.0)	6.5
air wedge (5.3)	6.8
air cam (5.2)	6.7
S2200-2600	
All axle codes (5.3)	7.5
TRANSTAR	
Axle Codes	
02212-02136-02182	
02183-02215-02218 (3.9)	5.4
02139-02228 (4.1)	5.6

King Pins and Bushings, Renew (Both Wheels)

(Factory Time)	Chilton Time
LOADSTAR	
Axle Codes	
02048-02068-02072	
hydraulic or air (3.3)	4.7
02089-02091-02098-bronze bushings	
hydraulic or air (3.9)	5.3
02089-02091-02098-nylon bushings	
hydraulic or air (3.2)	4.6
02105-02109-02136	
02139-02208-02215	
02218-bronze bushings	
hydraulic (4.0)	5.4
air (3.5)	4.9
nylon bushings	
hydraulic (3.5)	4.9
air (3.0)	4.4
S1600-2100	
Axle Codes	
02071-02073-02101	
02109-02118-02127	
02139-02309-02329	
02339	
bronze bushings-hyd brakes (4.5)	6.7
02101-02109-02118	
02127-02139-02309	
02329-02339	
bronze bushings-air cam (4.0)	6.0
CARGOSTAR	
Axle Codes	
02069	
hydraulic or air (3.5)	4.9
02099-bronze bushings	
hydraulic or air (4.1)	5.5
02099-nylon bushings	
hydraulic or air (3.3)	4.7
02209-02219-bronze bushings	
hydraulic (4.3)	5.7
air (3.5)	4.9
02209-02219-nylon bushings	
hydraulic (3.7)	5.1
air (3.0)	4.4
FLEETSTAR	
Axle Codes	
02098-02099	
bronze or nylon bushings	
hydraulic (3.8)	5.2
air wedge (4.2)	5.6
air cam (4.1)	5.5
02109-02139-02228	
02309-02329-02339	
bronze or nylon bushings	
hydraulic (4.1)	5.5
air wedge (4.5)	5.9
air cam (4.3)	5.7
02112-02136-02182	
bronze or nylon bushings	
hydraulic (4.0)	5.4
air wedge (4.3)	5.7
air cam (4.2)	5.6
S2200-2600	
All axle codes (4.4)	6.7
TRANSTAR	
Axle Codes	
02112-02136-02182	
02183-02215-02218	
bronze bushings (3.5)	4.9
nylon bushings (3.0)	4.4
02139-02228	
bronze bushings (3.7)	5.1
nylon bushings (3.1)	4.5

	(Factory Time)	Chilton Time
Steering Knuckle, Renew (One)		
LOADSTAR		
Axle Codes		
02048-02068-02972		
hydraulic or air	(1.5)	2.6
02090-02091-02098		
hydraulic or air	(1.9)	3.0
02105-02109-02136		
02139-02208-02215-02218		
left or right		
hydraulic	(3.6)	4.7
air	(3.1)	4.2
S1600-2100		
All axle codes		
hyd brakes	(3.3)	5.1
air cam	(2.9)	4.5
CARGOSTAR		
Axle Codes		
02069		
hydraulic or air	(1.7)	2.8
02099		
hydraulic or air	(2.0)	3.1
02209-02219		
left or right		
hydraulic	(3.9)	5.0
air	(3.1)	4.2
FLEETSTAR		
Axle Codes		
02098-02099		
hydraulic	(2.3)	3.4
air wedge	(2.5)	3.6
air cam	(2.4)	3.5
02109-02112-02136		
02139-02182-02228		
02309-02329-02339		
left or right		
hydraulic	(3.0)	4.1
air wedge	(3.2)	4.3
air cam	(3.1)	4.2
S2200-2600		
All axle codes		
left side	(3.0)	5.1
right side	(2.7)	4.8
TRANSTAR		
Axle Codes		
02112-02136-02182		
02183-02215-02218		
left or right	(3.1)	4.2
02139-02228		
left or right	(2.9)	4.0

FRONT AXLE IDENTIFICATION CHART

Code No.	New Designation	Old Designation
02048	FA-48	IH 4700#
02054	FA-54	#70 HDF 6000# Driving
02057	FA-57	#9 Coleman 9000# Driving
02059	FA-59	Coleman Driving w/Loc
02064	FA-64	Napco 9000# Driving
02068	FA-68	IH 5000-5500#
02069	FA-69	IH 6000# Wide Tread
02071	FA-71	IH 5000#
02072	FA-72	IH 5500#
02073	FA-73	IH 6000#
02078	FA-78	Napco 9000# Driving
02079	FA-79	Napco 7500# Driving
02089	FA-89	IH 5500#
02098	FA-98	IH 7000-7500#
02099	FA-99	IH 7000# Wide Tread
02101	FA-101	IH 7500#
02105	FA-105	FD-900 RS 9000# Wide Tread
02109	FA-109	IH 9000# Wide Tread
02112	FA-112	FE-970 RS 12000#
02127	FA-127	IH 10,800#
02136	FA-136	FH-901 RS 16000#
02139	FA-139	IH 12000# Wide Tread
02182	FA-182	FL-901 RS 18000#
02183	FA-183	FL-901 RS 20000#
02208	FA-208	FD-208 RS 9000#
02209	FA-209	Timken 9000# Wide Tread
02215	FA-215	FD-215 RS 12000# Wide Tread
02218	FA-218	FD-218 RS 12000#
02219	FA-219	Timken 12000#
02228	FA-228	FF-921 RS 12000# SLD KP
02231	FA-231	RS 16000# FL-931
02232	FA-232	RS 18000# FL-931
02309	FA-309	IH 9000# Wide Track
02329	FA-329	IH 10800# Wide Track
02339	FA-339	IH 12000# Wide Track
02341	FA-341	IH 10800# Wide Track Alum. I Beam

	(Factory Time)	Chilton Time
Steering Knuckle Bushings, Renew (Knuckle Removed)		
All Axle Codes		
bronze bushings	(.7)	1.1
nylon bushings	(.2)	.4
Front Spring, Renew (One)		
LOADSTAR		
All models	(1.2)	1.7
S1600-2100		
w/Draw key	(1.5)	2.0
wo/Draw key	(1.0)	1.5
CARGOSTAR		
All models	(1.0)	1.5
FLEETSTAR		
All models	(1.2)	1.7
S2200-2600		
2200-2500 Models	(1.6)	2.1
2600 Models	(1.4)	2.0
TRANSTAR		
conv cab	(2.2)	2.7
tilt cab	(2.0)	2.5
Front Spring, R&R and Recondition (One)		
LOADSTAR		
All models	(1.9)	2.7
S1600-2100		
w/Draw key	(2.0)	2.5
wo/Draw key	(1.5)	2.0
CARGOSTAR		
All models	(1.7)	2.5
FLEETSTAR		
All models	(2.1)	2.9
S2200-2600		
2200-2500 Models	(2.2)	2.9
2600 Models	(2.0)	2.8
TRANSTAR		
conv cab	(3.0)	3.8
tilt cab	(2.8)	3.6
Front Spring Shackle Bushings, Renew (Spring and Shackle)		
LOADSTAR		
each spring	(1.6)	2.4
S1600-2100		
w/Draw key	(2.0)	2.8
wo/Draw key	(1.5)	2.3
CARGOSTAR		
each spring	(1.4)	2.2
FLEETSTAR		
each spring	(1.6)	2.4
S2200-2600		
2200-2500 Models	(2.1)	2.8
2600 Models	(1.9)	2.7
Front Spring Shackle, Renew		
LOADSTAR		
each	(.7)	1.1
S1600-2100		
w/Draw key	(.7)	1.2
wo/Draw key	(.5)	1.0
CARGOSTAR-FLEETSTAR		
each	(.6)	1.0
S2200-2600		
All models	(.9)	1.4

FRONT WHEEL DRIVE

	(Factory Time)	Chilton Time
Front Drive Axle Assembly, R&R		
LOADSTAR		
Axle Codes		
02054	(3.8)	5.7
02057	(3.1)	5.0
02059	(3.2)	5.1
S1600-2100		
All axle codes	(3.8)	5.9

LABOR 9 FRONT SUSPENSION 9 LABOR

	(Factory Time)	Chilton Time
Front Drive Axle Assy., R&R and Recondition		
LOADSTAR		
Axle Codes		
02054	(13.2)	16.6
02057	(18.4)	25.0
02059	(18.5)	25.2
S1600-2100		
All axle codes	(15.6)	23.6
Front Drive Axle Shaft U-Joint, R&R and Recondition		
LOADSTAR		
Axle Codes		
02054	(1.7)	2.4
S1600-2100		
All axle codes	(2.0)	2.9
Front Drive Axle Shaft Assy., Renew		
LOADSTAR		
Axle Codes		
02054-inner or outer	(1.5)	2.1
02057	(1.0)	1.6
02059	(1.1)	1.7
S1600-2100		
All axle codes	(1.6)	2.2
Front Drive Axle Differential, R&R and Recondition		
LOADSTAR		
Axle Codes		
02054	(9.7)	13.0
02057	(8.5)	11.8
02059	(8.7)	12.0
S1600-2100		
All axle codes	(9.4)	14.3
Front Drive Axle Steering Knuckle Assembly, R&R and Recondition		
LOADSTAR		
Axle Codes		
02054	(2.9)	3.7
02057-02059	(5.3)	6.7
S1600-2100		
All axle codes	(3.6)	5.5

LABOR 10 STEERING LINKAGE 10 LABOR

	(Factory Time)	Chilton Time
Tie Rod, Renew		
FLEETSTAR		
All axle codes	(1.3)	1.7
S1600-2600		
All axle codes	(1.2)	1.5
All other series		
All axle codes	(1.0)	1.4
Tie Rod Ends, Renew		
FLEETSTAR		
All axle codes-one	(1.1)	1.4
both	(1.3)	1.8
S1600-2600		
02591-05327	(.6)	1.0
All axle codes		
one	(1.0)	1.4
both	(1.2)	1.7
All other series		
All axle codes-one	(.8)	1.1
both	(1.0)	1.5
Pitman Arm, Renew		
LOADSTAR		
Steering Code		
05031-05063-05165	(.3)	.6
05219-05243	(.4)	.7
05276-05277-05299		
05301-05302	(.5)	.9
05290	(.6)	1.0
S1600-2600		
All steering codes	(.5)	.9
CARGOSTAR		
All steering codes	(.5)	.9
FLEETSTAR		
Steering Codes		
05031-05044-05320-05321-05322		
05323-05326-05329	(.5)	.9
05236-05267-05268-05270		
05271-05272-05273-05290		
TRANSTAR		
All steering codes	(.6)	1.0
Drag Link, Renew		
LOADSTAR		
socket type ends	(.3)	.6
ball type ends	(.5)	.9
S1600-2600		
All steering codes	(.5)	.9
CARGOSTAR		
All models	(.3)	.6
FLEETSTAR-TRANSTAR		
All models	(.4)	.8
Drag Link End, Renew		
Fleetstar	(.6)	1.1
Drag Link Plugs, Seats and Springs, Renew		
Fleetstar	(.3)	.6
Drag Link, Adjust		
All series	(.2)	.5

LABOR 11 STEERING GEAR 11 LABOR

	(Factory Time)	Chilton Time
Steering Wheel, Renew		
All series	(.5)	.6
Horn Button, Renew		
All series	(.2)	.3
Steering Gear, Adjust		
manual	(.5)	.7
power		
pressure relief screw	(.5)	.8
relief valve plungers	(.4)	.4
Wormshaft Grease Seal, Renew		
Includes: R&R gear assy.		
S1600-2100		
Steering Code		
05057-05058-05165	(1.3)	2.0
Steering Gear, Renew		
LOADSTAR		
Steering Code		
05031-05063-05165	(1.0)	1.9
05219-05243	(1.8)	2.7
05261-05276-05277		
05299-05301-05302	(1.6)	2.5
05290	(2.5)	3.4
S1600-2100		
Steering Code		
05057-05058-05165	(1.1)	1.8
05333-05335-05345	(2.2)	2.9
05332	(2.6)	3.4
CARGOSTAR		
manual	(1.0)	1.9
power		
not integral	(1.5)	2.4
integral	(2.5)	3.4
FLEETSTAR		
Steering Code		
05031-05044	(1.2)	2.1
05236-05267-05268-05270		
05271-05272-05273	(2.9)	3.8
05320-05321-05322		
05323-05326-05329	(2.0)	2.9
05290-05291-05327		
Dual-left	(3.1)	4.0
right	(2.8)	3.7
both	(5.0)	6.7
S2200-2600		
Steering Code		
05057-05058	(1.1)	1.8
05332-05339-05342	(2.4)	3.4
05335-05336	(2.2)	2.9
05337-05338		
dual-left	(2.4)	3.2
right	(2.1)	2.8
both	(3.7)	5.5
05334		
dual-left	(2.8)	3.7
right	(2.5)	3.4
both	(4.5)	6.5
TRANSTAR		
Steering Code		
05044		
CO-4070A	(2.8)	3.7
CO-4070B	(1.7)	2.6
conv cab	(1.7)	2.6
05270-05271-05272		
05273-05283-05284		
05285-05286-05287		
05293	(3.3)	4.2
Steering Gear, R&R and Recondition		
LOADSTAR		
Steering Code		
05031-05063	(3.1)	4.7
05165	(2.2)	3.8
05219-05243	(4.0)	5.6
05261-05276-05277		
05299-05301-05302	(3.8)	5.4
05290	(5.5)	7.1
S1600-2100		
Steering Code		
05057-05058-05165	(2.5)	4.0
05333	(4.1)	5.5

STEERING GEAR

IDENTIFICATION CHART

Code No.	New Designation	Old Designation
05031	S-31	TD-67 Ross, Manual Aluminum Case
05044	S-44	TD-70 Ross, Manual Aluminum Case
05057	S-57	533 Saginaw, Manual
05058	S-58	555 Saginaw, Manual
05063	S-63	TE-70 Manual
05165	S-165	#378 Gemmer, Manual
05219	S-219	HPS 52 Ross, Power Not Integral
05236	S-236	M-39 Sheppard, Power Vickers Pump, Gear Driven
05243	S-243	HPS 70 Ross, Power Not Integral
05261	S-261	HF 64 Ross, Integral Power Gear
05267	S-267	M-39 Sheppard, Power Vickers Pump, Belt Driven
05268	S-268	M-39 Sheppard, Power Eaton Pump, Belt Driven
05270	S-270	M-491 Sheppard, Power Eaton Pump, Belt Driven
05271	S-271	M-59 Sheppard, Power Eaton Pump, Belt Driven
05272	S-272	M-491 Sheppard, Power Vickers Pump, Gear Driven
05273	S-273	M-59 Sheppard, Power Vickers Pump, Gear Driven
05276	S-276	HF 54 Ross, Integral Power Gear
05277	S-277	HF 64 Ross, Integral Power Gear
05283	S-283	M-492 Sheppard, Power Vickers Pump, Belt Driven
05284	S-284	M-492 Sheppard, Power Vickers Pump, Gear Driven
05285	S-285	M-49 Sheppard, Power Vickers Pump, Belt Driven
05286	S-286	M-592 Sheppard, Power Eaton Pump, Belt Driven
05287	S-287	M-592 Sheppard, Power Vickers Pump, Gear Driven
05290	S-290	M-39 Sheppard, Power Dual-Belt Driven Pump
05291	S-291	M-39 Sheppard, Power Dual-Gear Driven Pump
05332	S-332	M-292 Sheppard, Power-Gear Driven Pump
05333	S-333	HFB-52 Ross, Power-Belt Driven Pump
05335	S-335	HFB-64 Ross, Power-Belt Driven Pump
05336	S-336	HFB-64 Ross, Power-Gear Driven Pump
05337	S-337	HFB-64 Ross, Power-Dual Left RCB-52 Right-Belt Driven Pump
05338	S-338	HFB-64 Ross, Power-Dual Left RCB-52 Right-Gear Driven Pump
05339	S-339	M-252 Sheppard, Power-Gear Driven Pump
05342	S-342	M-252 Sheppard, Power, Belt Driven Pump
05344	S-344	M-372 Sheppard, Power-Dual Left
05345	S-345	710 Saginaw, Power-Belt Driven Pump

(Factory Time)	Chilton Time
05335-05345 (4.3)	5.8
05332 (5.6)	7.0
CARGOSTAR	
manual (3.1)	4.7
power	
not integral (3.9)	5.5
integral (5.4)	7.0
FLEETSTAR	
Steering Code	
05031-05044 (3.3)	4.9
05236-05267-05268-05270 05271-05272-05273 (5.9)	7.5
05320-05321-05322 05323-05326-05329 (4.5)	6.1
05290-05291-05327	
Dual-left (6.0)	7.6
right (5.1)	6.7
both (10.3)	13.3
S2200-2600	
Steering Code	
05057-05058 (2.5)	4.0
05332-05339-05342 (5.4)	7.2
05335-05336 (4.4)	5.8
05337-05338	
dual-left (4.6)	6.0
right (3.9)	5.4
both (7.6)	11.0
05334	
dual-left (5.7)	7.0
right (4.8)	6.5
both (9.6)	13.0
TRANSTAR	
Steering Code	
05044	
CO-4070A (4.8)	6.4
CO-4070B (3.8)	5.4
conv cab (3.8)	5.4
05270-05271-05272 05273-05283-05284 05285-05286-05287 05293 (6.2)	7.8

POWER STEERING

Trouble Shoot Power Steering

Includes: Check pounds pull on steering wheel, install checking gauge, test pump pressure and check for leaks.

conv cab	.7
tilt cab	.5

Sector Shaft Seals, Renew (In Chassis)

S1600-2100	
Steering Code	
05335 (.6)	1.1
05345 (.7)	1.2

Power Steering Pump, Renew

LOADSTAR-S1600-2100	
Eaton pump (1.3)	2.0
Saginaw pump (1.2)	1.9
Vickers pump (1.5)	2.2
CARGOSTAR	
with reservoir (1.1)	1.8
without reservoir (1.1)	1.8
FLEETSTAR	
BELT DRIVEN	
Vickers pump (1.3)	2.0
Eaton pump	
with reservoir (1.4)	2.1
without reservoir (1.1)	1.8
GEAR DRIVEN	
All models (1.3)	2.0
S2200-2600	
BELT DRIVEN	
All models (1.3)	2.0
GEAR DRIVEN	
Eaton pump (1.5)	2.2
Vickers pump (1.4)	2.1

LABOR 11 STEERING GEAR 11 LABOR

(Factory Time)	Chilton Time
TRANSTAR	
Eaton pump (1.5)	2.2
BELT DRIVEN	
Vickers pump (1.4)	2.1
Eaton pump	
with reservoir (1.7)	2.4
without reservoir (1.4)	2.1
GEAR DRIVEN	
V-903 eng (1.6)	2.3
V-800 eng (1.7)	2.4
All other engs (1.8)	2.5

Power Steering Pump, R&R and Recondition

(Factory Time)	Chilton Time
LOADSTAR-S1600-2100	
Eaton pump (2.2)	3.3
Saginaw pump (1.9)	3.0
Vickers pump (2.4)	3.5
CARGOSTAR	
with reservoir (2.0)	3.1
without reservoir (1.9)	3.0
FLEETSTAR	
BELT DRIVEN	
Vickers pump (2.1)	3.2
Eaton pump	
with reservoir (2.2)	3.3
without reservoir (1.9)	3.0
GEAR DRIVEN	
All models (2.2)	3.3
S2200-2600	
BELT DRIVEN	
Eaton pump (2.1)	3.2
Saginaw pump (1.9)	3.0
GEAR DRIVEN	
Eaton pump (2.3)	3.4
Vickers pump (2.3)	3.4
TRANSTAR	
BELT DRIVEN	
Vickers pump (2.2)	3.3
Eaton pump	
with reservoir (2.4)	3.5
without reservoir (2.2)	3.3
GEAR DRIVEN	
V-903 eng (2.5)	3.6
V-800 eng (2.7)	3.8
All other engs (2.7)	3.9

Power Steering Control Valve, Renew

(Factory Time)	Chilton Time
All series (1.1)	1.6

Power Steering Control Valve, R&R and Recondition

(Factory Time)	Chilton Time
All series (1.6)	2.3

Power Cylinder, Renew

(Factory Time)	Chilton Time
All series (.8)	1.5

Power Cylinder, R&R and Recondition

(Factory Time)	Chilton Time
All series (1.5)	2.6

Power Steering Hoses, Renew

(Factory Time)	Chilton Time
All series-each (.6)	.9

LABOR 12 CYLINDER HEAD & VALVE SYSTEM 12 LABOR

GASOLINE ENGINES

Cylinder Head Gasket, Renew

Includes: Clean carbon from cylinder heads.

(Factory Time)	Chilton Time
Six (5.6)	7.2
V-8-V engs	
one (4.4)	6.4
both (6.3)	9.1
V-8-VS engs	
left (4.2)	5.8
right (4.3)	5.9
both (6.2)	8.5
V-8-MV engs	
left (3.1)	4.7
right (3.9)	5.5
both (5.6)	7.9
V-8-537, 605 engs	
left (5.2)	6.8
right (5.4)	7.0
both (7.7)	10.0

Cylinder Head Assy., Renew (With Valves)

Includes: Clean carbon from top of pistons. Minor tune up.

(Factory Time)	Chilton Time
Six (8.2)	10.8
V-8-V engs	
one (6.3)	9.1
both (9.2)	13.3
V-8-VS engs	
left (6.8)	8.5
right (6.9)	8.6
both (9.5)	11.8
V-8-MV engs	
left (6.3)	9.0
right (7.1)	9.8
both (9.3)	13.0
V-8-537, 605 engs	
left (8.4)	10.0
right (8.3)	9.9
both (11.2)	15.0

Clean Carbon and Grind Valves

Includes: R&R cylinder heads. Clean carbon, grind valves, reface seats. Tune engine.

(Factory Time)	Chilton Time
Six (12.8)	15.4
V-8-V engs (14.5)	18.6
V-8-VS engs (16.2)	19.0
V-8-MV engs (14.8)	17.5
V-8-537, 605 engs (16.7)	20.5

Valve Cover and/or Gasket, Renew

(Factory Time)	Chilton Time
Six (.4)	.7
V-8-V engs	
one (.7)	1.0
both (.9)	1.5
V-8-VS engs	
one (.6)	.9
both (1.0)	1.5
V-8-MV engs	
one (.5)	.8
both (.9)	1.5
V-8-537, 605 engs	
one (.6)	.9
both (1.0)	1.6

COMBINATIONS

Add to Valve Job

(Factory Time)	Chilton Time
DRAIN, EVACUATE & RECHARGE AIR CONDITIONING SYSTEM	
All series	1.5
DISTRIBUTOR, RECONDITION	
Six (1.2)	1.8
V-8-Standard Ign. (1.9)	2.5
V-8-Electronic Ign. (1.6)	2.2
CARBURETOR, RECONDITION	
All series (2.2)	3.0
RECONDITION CYLINDER HEADS (HEADS REMOVED)	
Six (4.8)	6.3
V-8-each (3.0)	4.5
VALVE GUIDES, RENEW	
Each (.2)	.3
RECONDITION ROCKER ARM ASSY. (REMOVED)	
Each (.6)	1.0
HYDRAULIC VALVE LIFTERS, DISASSEMBLE AND CLEAN	
Each (.2)	.2

Valve Push Rods, Renew (One or All)

(Factory Time)	Chilton Time
Six (1.1)	1.4
V-8-V engs	
one bank (1.0)	1.4
both banks (1.5)	2.1
V-8-VS engs	
one bank (.7)	1.1
both banks (1.2)	1.8
V-8-MV engs	
one bank (1.0)	1.4
both banks (1.6)	2.2
V-8-537, 605 engs	
one bank (1.0)	1.4
both banks (1.6)	2.2

Valve Lifters (Tappets), Renew

(Factory Time)	Chilton Time
V-8-V engs	
one (.9)	1.3
all (2.1)	3.0
V-8-VS engs	
one (.9)	1.3
all (2.1)	3.0
V-8-MV engs	
one (1.7)	2.3
all (3.1)	4.0
V-8-537, 605 engs	
one (1.0)	1.4
all (2.9)	3.8

Valve Spring, Renew (One)

(Factory Time)	Chilton Time
Six (1.0)	1.5
V-8-V engs (1.0)	1.5
V-8-VS engs (1.0)	1.5
V-8-MV engs (.8)	1.3
V-8-537, 605 engs (1.1)	1.6

Rocker Arm Assy., R&R and Recondition

(Factory Time)	Chilton Time
Six (2.9)	4.0
V-8-V engs	
one (1.2)	1.8
both (2.8)	3.5
V-8-VS engs	
one (1.2)	1.8
both (2.3)	3.5
V-8-MV engs	
one (1.1)	1.7
both (2.0)	3.3
V-8-537, 605 engs	
one (1.3)	1.9
both (3.0)	3.7

Valves, Adjust

(Factory Time)	Chilton Time
Six (.8)	1.2

LABOR 12 CYLINDER HEAD & VALVE SYSTEM 12 LABOR

(Factory Time) Chilton Time

DIESEL ENGINES

Cylinder Head, R&R or Renew Gasket

Includes: R&R all normal interfering parts. Check cylinder head and block for flatness. Adjust valves and crossheads.

	Chilton Time
IHC Diesel	
Six	8.3
V-8-exc below-one	7.5
both	13.0
Fleetstar series	
one	7.0
both	12.5
Cummins Diesel	
Six-one	7.9
all	13.3
V-8-one	13.2
all	21.0
Detroit Diesel	
6-71	10.4
6V-53, 6V-71-one	7.7
both	15.5
8V-71-one	8.0
both	15.8
12V-71-one	9.3
both	18.4
Caterpillar Diesel	
Six	14.8
V-8-one	8.9
both	11.6

Clean Carbon and Grind Valves

Includes: R&R all normal interfering parts. R&R head. Check cylinder head and block flatness, magnaflux head. Clean, inspect and recondition all parts as necessary. Pressure test heads. Check spring tension, assembled height and valve runout. Adjust valves, crossheads and injectors. Road test. Does not include renew valve seats.

	Chilton Time
IHC Diesel	
Six	15.9
V-8-exc below	21.5
Fleetstar series	21.8
Cummins Diesel	
Six	22.0
V-8	32.5
Detroit Diesel	
6-71	24.5
6V-53, 6V-71	30.0
8V-71	33.7
12V-71	43.5
Caterpillar Diesel	
Six	20.4
V-8	17.2

Adjust Valves and Crossheads

Includes: R&R all normal interfering parts.

	Chilton Time
IHC Diesel	
Six	1.8
V-8	2.4
Cummins Diesel	
Six	3.7
V-8	6.0
Detroit Diesel	
6-71	1.8
6V-53, 6V-71	2.5
8V-71	2.7
12V-71	3.0
Caterpillar Diesel	
Six	1.7
V-8	2.1

COMBINATIONS

Add to Valve Job

(Factory Time) Chilton Time

	Chilton Time
VALVE GUIDES, REAM FOR OVERSIZE STEMS	
One	.3
each adtnl	.2
INJECTOR, RENEW	
IHC Diesel	
Six	.8
V-8	.5
Cummins Diesel	1.0
Detroit Diesel	.5
Caterpillar Diesel	
Six	1.4
V-8	2.0
INJECTOR, RECONDITION (REMOVED)	
IHC Diesel	1.0
Cummins Diesel	.7
Detroit Diesel	
S type	.8
N type	1.1
Caterpillar Diesel	.8
ADJUST GOVERNOR	
All series	.7
ROCKER ARM STUD, RENEW	
Each	.6
GRIND VALVES (HEADS REMOVED)	
IHC Diesel	
Six	6.5
V-8-each	4.0
Cummins Diesel	
Six-all	8.0
V-8-all	10.5
Detroit Diesel	
6-71	16.0
6V-53, 6V-71	18.0
8V-71	22.5
12V-71	27.0
Caterpillar Diesel	
Six	5.6
V-8-each	2.8
PRESSURE TEST HEAD (ONE)	
Six	2.0
V-6	1.5
V-8	1.8
V-12	2.0

Valve Cover Gasket, Renew

	Chilton Time
IHC Diesel	
Six	.8
V-8-one	.7
both	1.0
Cummins Diesel	
Six	2.0
V-8-one	2.5
both	3.2
Detroit Diesel	
each	.7
Caterpillar Diesel	
Six	1.2
V-8-one	.5
both	.9

Valve Push Rods, Renew

Includes: R&R all normal interfering parts. Perform all required adjustments.

	Chilton Time
IHC Diesel	
Six	2.1
V-8-one side	1.6
both sides	2.8
Cummins Diesel	
Six	3.5
V-8	4.2
Detroit Diesel	
Six & V-6	7.2
V-8	11.7
V-12	15.0
Caterpillar Diesel	
Six	3.6
V-8	2.7

Valve Lifters, Renew

Includes: R&R all normal interfering parts. Perform all required adjustments.

	Chilton Time
IHC Diesel	
Six	3.3
V-8	3.7
Cummins Diesel	
Six	11.9
V-8	17.5
Detroit Diesel	
Six & V-6	9.5
V-8	11.9
V-12	15.9
Caterpillar Diesel	
Six	4.7
V-8	13.2

LABOR 13 ENGINE ASSEMBLY & MOUNTS 13 LABOR

(Factory Time) Chilton Time

GASOLINE ENGINES

Engine Assembly, Remove & Reinstall

Does not include transfer of any parts or equipment.

	Chilton Time
Six–exc Fleetstar (6.8)	10.2
Fleetstar (9.4)	12.8
V-8–V engs (5.9)	9.3
V-8–VS engs	
exc Fleetstar (6.1)	9.5
Fleetstar (9.4)	12.8
V-8–MV engs (6.3)	9.7
V-8–537, 605 engs (8.7)	12.1

Engine Assembly, Renew (Service Engine)

Includes: R&R engine assembly. Transfer all component parts not supplied with replacement engine. Minor tune up.

	Chilton Time
Six–exc Fleetstar (16.2)	21.9
Fleetstar (19.3)	25.0
V-8–V engs (13.7)	19.4
V-8–VS engs	
exc Fleetstar (16.4)	22.1
Fleetstar (20.5)	26.2
V-8–MV engs (15.5)	21.2
V-8–537, 605 engs (20.3)	26.0

Cylinder Assy., (Skeleton Engine), Renew

Includes: R&R engine. Transfer all component parts not supplied with replacement engine. Clean carbon, grind valves. Tune engine.

	Chilton Time
Six–exc Fleetstar (24.4)	30.7

LABOR 13 ENGINE ASSEMBLY & MOUNTS 13 LABOR

(Factory Time)	Chilton Time
Fleetstar (27.6)	33.9
V-8–V engs (24.7)	31.0
V-8–VS engs	
exc Fleetstar (28.8)	35.1
Fleetstar (32.9)	39.2
V-8–MV engs (26.6)	32.9
V-8–537, 605 engs (33.6)	39.9

Engine Assy., R&R and Recondition

Includes: Rebore block, install new pistons, pins, rings, rod and main bearings. Clean carbon, grind values. Tune engine.

(Factory Time)	Chilton Time
Six–exc Fleetstar (36.6)	47.8
Fleetstar (39.9)	51.1
V-8–V engs (39.4)	50.6
V-8–VS engs	
exc Fleetstar (45.3)	56.5
Fleetstar (49.4)	60.6
V-8–MV engs (43.7)	54.9
V-8–537, 605 engs (49.7)	60.9

Engine Mounts, Renew

(Factory Time)	Chilton Time
FRONT	
All series (.7)	.9
REAR	
Six (1.0)	1.4
V-8 (.8)	1.2

DIESEL ENGINES

Engine Assembly, R&R
(Clutch and Transmission Removed)

Includes: R&R all normal interfering parts. Perform all required adjustments. Road test.

(Factory Time)	Chilton Time
IHC Diesel	
Six	6.0
V-8–exc below	6.3
Fleetstar series	*11.8
Cummins Diesel	
Six	10.2
V-8	10.2
Detroit Diesel	
6-71	9.3
6V-53	9.0
6V-71	10.0
8V-71	10.0
12V-71	10.5
Caterpillar Diesel	
Six	24.6
V-8	13.4
*w/Steel hood and fenders add (.6)	.6

Cylinder Block, Renew
(Clutch and Transmission Removed)

Includes: R&R all normal interfering parts. Transfer all components without disassembly. Install new main and rod bearings. Renew gaskets and seals as necessary. Adjust timing and clearances. Road test.
Does not include reconditioning of any components.

(Factory Time)	Chilton Time
IHC Diesel	
Six	23.8
V-8–exc below	32.0
Fleetstar series	*39.0
Cummins Diesel	
Six	48.5
V-8	49.0
Detroit Diesel	
6-71	52.0
6V-53	50.5
6V-71	54.5
8V-71	58.5
12V-71	68.8
Caterpillar Diesel	
Six	62.8
V-8	43.3
*w/Steel hood and fenders add	.6

Engine Assembly, R&R and Recondition
(Complete, Clutch and Transmission Removed)

Includes: R&R all normal interfering parts. Complete disassembly and assembly of engine. Pressure test block and head. Plastigauge and install new main, rod and camshaft bearings. Install new pistons, rings, pins and liners. Rebore block. Recondition governor and other subassemblies. Clean carbon and grind valves. Check and set all clearances. Tune engine and road test.

(Factory Time)	Chilton Time
IHC Diesel	
Six	43.5
V-8–exc below	52.0
Fleetstar series	*59.0
Cummins Diesel	
Six	58.5
V-8	61.0
Detroit Diesel	
6-71	77.0
6V-53	88.0
6V-71	89.0
8V-71	90.5
12V-71	97.5
Caterpillar Diesel	
Six	63.9
V-8	54.3
*w/Steel hood and fenders add	.6

Engine Mounts, Renew

(Factory Time)	Chilton Time
Front	
exc below	.8
Transtar series	1.1
Rear	
exc below	1.0
Transtar series	1.5

LABOR 14 PISTONS, RINGS & BEARINGS 14 LABOR

GASOLINE ENGINES

Piston Rings, Renew

Includes: Remove cylinder top ridge, deglaze cylinder walls. Clean ring grooves. Minor tune up.

(Factory Time)	Chilton Time
Six–exc Fleetstar (14.5)	20.5
Fleetstar (14.9)	20.9
V-8–V engs (16.1)	21.5
V-8–VS engs	
exc Fleetstar (16.7)	22.7
Fleetstar (17.8)	23.8
V-8–MV engs (17.8)	23.8
V-8–537, 605 engs (18.6)	24.6

Piston, Renew (One)

Includes: Remove cylinder top ridge, deglaze cylinder walls. Minor tune up.

(Factory Time)	Chilton Time
Six (12.4)	17.4
V-8–V engs (9.6)	14.6
V-8–VS engs (11.6)	16.6
V-8–MV engs (10.5)	15.5
V-8–537, 605 engs (12.6)	17.6

Connecting Rod Bearings, Renew

Includes: R&R oil pan and check bearing clearances.

(Factory Time)	Chilton Time
Six (3.4)	4.8
V-8–V engs (3.3)	4.7
V-8–VS engs (3.4)	4.8
V-8–MV engs (3.9)	5.3
V-8–537, 605 engs (3.7)	5.0

COMBINATIONS

Engine Combinations

(Factory Time)	Chilton Time
DRAIN, EVACUATE & RECHARGE AIR CONDITIONING SYSTEM	
All series	1.5
DISTRIBUTOR, RECONDITION	
Six (1.2)	1.8
V-8–Standard Ign. (1.9)	2.5
V-8–Electronic Ign. (1.6)	2.2
CARBURETOR, RECONDITION	
All series (2.2)	3.0
VALVE GUIDES, RENEW	
Each (.1)	.3
RECONDITION ROCKER ARM ASSY. (REMOVED)	
Each (.6)	1.0
HYDRAULIC VALVE LIFTERS, DISASSEMBLE AND CLEAN	
Each (.2)	.2
DEGLAZE CYLINDER WALLS	
Six (.6)	1.0
V-8 (.8)	1.2
REMOVE CYLINDER TOP RIDGE	
Each (.1)	.1
MAIN BEARINGS, RENEW	
Six (3.2)	4.2
V-8 (2.0)	3.0
CONNECTING ROD BEARINGS, RENEW	
Six (2.0)	3.0
V-8 (2.5)	3.5
PLASTIGAUGE BEARINGS	
Each (.1)	.1
OIL PUMP, RECONDITION	
All series (.6)	.9
OIL FILTER ELEMENT, RENEW	
All series (.3)	.3

LABOR 14 PISTONS, RINGS & BEARINGS 14 LABOR

DIESEL ENGINES

Rings, Pins, Rod and Main Bearings, Renew and Grind Valves

Includes: R&R all normal interfering parts. Remove cylinder top ridge, hone cylinder liner walls, clean ring grooves, install new rings. Install new pins and align rods. Plastigauge and install new main and rod bearings. Renew gaskets and seals as necessary. Clean carbon and grind valves. Clean oil pump. Set injection timing, valves and crossheads. Road test.

(Factory Time)	Chilton Time
IHC Diesel	
Six	32.5
V-8-exc below	40.4
Fleetstar series	40.0
Cummins Diesel	
Six	38.0
V-8	48.5
Detroit Diesel	
6-71	47.5
6V-53, 6V-71	51.9
8V-71	55.9
12V-71	65.7
Caterpillar Diesel	
Six	33.8
V-8	31.6

Rings, Pins, Rod and Main Bearings, Renew

Includes: R&R all normal interfering parts. Remove cylinder top ridge, hone cylinder liner walls, clean rings grooves, install new rings. Install new pins and align rods. Plastigauge and install new main and rod bearings. Renew gaskets and seals as necessary. Clean oil pump. Set injection timing and valves and crossheads. Road test.

(Factory Time)	Chilton Time
IHC Diesel	
Six	26.0
V-8-exc below	32.4
Fleetstar series	32.0
Cummins Diesel	
Six	30.0
V-8	38.0
Detroit Diesel	
6-71	20.7
6V-53, 6V-71	25.7
8V-71	28.4
12V-71	38.7
Caterpillar Diesel	
Six	28.2
V-8	26.0

Rings, Renew

Includes: R&R all normal interfering parts. Remove cylinder top ridge, hone cylinder liner walls, clean ring grooves, install new rings. Renew gaskets and seals as necessary. Set injection timing, valves and crossheads. Road test.

(Factory Time)	Chilton Time
IHC Diesel	
Six	16.5
V-8-exc below	21.6
Fleetstar series	21.3
Cummins Diesel	
Six	21.0
V-8	26.5
Detroit Diesel	
6-71	20.7
6V-53, 6V-71	25.7
8V-71	28.4
12V-71	38.7
Caterpillar Diesel	
Six	24.9
V-8	21.5

Rod Bearings, Renew

Includes: R&R all normal interfering parts. Clean oil pump.

(Factory Time)	Chilton Time
IHC Diesel	
All series	4.8
Cummins Diesel	
Six	4.2
V-8	7.7
Detroit Diesel	
exc below	6.0
6V-53, 6V-71	6.5
12V-71	7.4
Caterpillar Diesel	
Six	4.3
V-8	4.5

Piston and Liner, Renew (One)

Includes: R&R all normal interfering parts. Hone block bore, check liner height, liner bore and O.D. for proper fit. Install new liner, piston with rings and pin. Renew gaskets and seals as necessary. Set injection timing, valves and crossheads. Road test.

(Factory Time)	Chilton Time
IHC Diesel	
Six	13.8
V-8-exc below	*11.4
Fleetstar series	*11.0
Cummins Diesel	
Six	22.0
V-8	22.8
Detroit Diesel	
6-71	15.7
6V-53, 6V-71	11.8
8V-71	12.5
12V-71	17.0
Caterpillar Diesel	
Six	22.0

*No liner.

COMBINATIONS

Engine Combinations

(Factory Time)	Chilton Time
VALVE GUIDES, REAM FOR OVERSIZE STEMS	
One	.3
each adtnl	.2
INJECTOR, RENEW	
IHC Diesel	
Six	.8
V-8	.5
Cummins Diesel	1.0
Detroit Diesel	.5
Caterpillar Diesel	
Six	1.4
V-8	2.0
INJECTOR, RECONDITION (REMOVED)	
IHC Diesel	1.0
Cummins Diesel	.7
Detroit Diesel	
S type	.8
N type	1.1
Caterpillar Diesel	.8
ADJUST GOVERNOR	
All series	.7
ROCKER ARM STUD, RENEW	
Each	.6
GRIND VALVES (HEADS REMOVED)	
IHC Diesel	
Six	6.5
V-8-each	4.0
Cummins Diesel	
Six-all	8.0
V-8-all	10.5
Detroit Diesel	
6-71	16.0
6V-53, 6V-71	18.0
8V-71	22.5
12V-71	27.0
Caterpillar Diesel	
Six	5.6
V-8-each	2.8
PESSURE TEST HEAD (ONE)	
Six	2.0
V-6	1.5
V-8	1.8
V-12	2.0
PLASTIGAUGE BEARINGS (ONE)	
All series	.1

LABOR 15 CRANKSHAFT & DAMPER 15 LABOR

GASOLINE ENGINES

Crankshaft and Main Bearings, Renew

Includes: R&R engine assy. Check all bearing clearances.

(Factory Time)	Chilton Time
Six–exc Fleetstar (16.8)	21.2
Fleetstar (19.4)	23.8
V-8–V engs (15.4)	20.3
V-8–VS engs	
exc Fleetstar (16.5)	20.5
Fleetstar (20.3)	25.8
V-8–MV engs (16.4)	20.7
V-8–537, 605 engs (21.7)	27.1

Main Bearings, Renew

Includes: R&R oil pan and check bearing clearances.

(Factory Time)	Chilton Time
Six(4.6)	6.4
V-8–V engs (3.1)	4.9
V-8–VS engs (3.2)	5.0
V-8–MV engs (3.0)	4.9
V-8–537, 605 engs (4.4)	6.2

Main and Rod Bearings, Renew

Includes: R&R oil pan and check all bearing clearances.

(Factory Time)	Chilton Time
Six(6.6)	8.9

LABOR 15 CRANKSHAFT & DAMPER 15 LABOR

(Factory Time) Chilton Time

V-8–V engs (5.3) 7.0
V-8–VS engs (5.4) 7.8
V-8–MV engs (5.5) 7.9
V-8–537, 605 engs (6.6) 8.9

Rear Main Bearing Oil Seals, Renew (Engine Removed)

Six(3.5) 4.5
V-8–V engs (1.2) 2.0
V-8–VS engs
exc Fleetstar (6.0) 7.2
Fleetstar (7.1) 8.3
V-8–MV engs (1.4) 2.2
V-8–537, 605 engs (1.5) 2.3

Lower Rear Main Bearing Oil Seal, Renew

Includes: Renew lower seal only.

Six(1.8) 2.8
V-8–VS engs (1.7) 2.7
V-8–537, 605 engs (.9) 1.6

Crankshaft Pulley, Renew

Six–exc Fleetstar (1.6) 2.4
Fleetstar (2.4) 3.6
V-8–V engs (.4) .9
V-8–VS engs
exc Fleetstar (1.7) 2.5
Fleetstar (2.4) 3.6
V-8–MV engs (.4) .9
V-8–537, 605 engs (2.6) 3.8

DIESEL ENGINES

Crankshaft and Main Bearings, Renew (Clutch and Transmission Removed)

Includes: R&R all normal interfering parts and engine. Plastigauge and install new main bearings, recondition oil pump.

IHC Diesel
Six 18.0
V-8–exc below 25.5
Fleetstar series 32.3

Cummins Diesel
Six 26.0
V-8 40.5

Detroit Diesel
6-71 26.5
6V-53 22.0
6V-71 23.0
8V-71 24.3
12V-71 30.0

Caterpillar Diesel
Six 54.7
V-8 40.7

Main Bearings, Renew

Includes: R&R all normal interfering parts. Plastigauge and install new main bearings, recondition oil pump.

IHC Diesel
Six 6.2
V-8 5.4

Cummins Diesel
Six 8.7
V-8 10.0

Detroit Diesel
exc below 9.5
12V-71 13.0

Caterpillar Diesel
Six 7.0
V-8 4.6

Rear Main Bearing Oil Seal, Renew

IHC Diesel
Six *1.8
V-8 *1.2

Cummins Diesel
Six 14.4
V-8 10.0

Detroit Diesel
All series 6.5

Caterpillar Diesel
Six 10.0
V-8 7.9

*Clutch and transmission removed.

Vibration Damper or Pulley, Renew

IHC Diesel
All series 3.8

Cummins Diesel
All series 2.1

Detroit Diesel
All series 4.6

Caterpillar Diesel
Six 4.6
V-8 3.7

LABOR 16 CAMSHAFT & TIMING GEARS 16 LABOR

(Factory Time) Chilton Time

GASOLINE ENGINES

Timing Case Cover or Gasket, Renew

Includes: Renew front seal and R&R oil pan where required.

Six–exc Fleetstar (3.6) 4.9
Fleetstar (4.3) 5.7
V-8–V engs (3.9) 5.2
V-8–VS engs
exc Fleetstar (5.2) 6.6
Fleetstar (7.4) 8.9
V-8–MV engs (2.7) 4.0
V-8–537, 605 engs (7.3) 8.8

Engine Front Cover Oil Seal, Renew

Six–exc Fleetstar (1.6) 2.4
Fleetstar (2.4) 3.6
V-8–V engs (1.6) 2.4
V-8–VS engs
exc Fleetstar (1.7) 2.5
Fleetstar (2.4) 3.6
V-8–MV engs (1.7) 2.5
V-8–537, 605 engs (2.6) 3.8

Timing Gears, Renew

Includes: R&R front cover and oil pan.

Six–exc Fleetstar (4.1) 5.9
Fleetstar (4.9) 6.7
V-8–V engs (4.5) 6.2
V-8–VS engs
exc Fleetstar (5.1) 7.6
Fleetstar (7.3) 9.9
V-8–MV engs (3.2) 5.0
V-8–537, 605 engs (7.0) 9.8

Camshaft, Renew

Includes: R&R radiator and make all necessary adjustments.

Six–exc Fleetstar (8.1) 13.4
Fleetstar (8.9) 14.2
V-8–V engs (8.9) 12.5
V-8–VS engs
exc Fleetstar (8.9) 14.2
Fleetstar (10.9) 16.2
V-8–MV engs (7.6) 12.9
V-8–537, 605 engs (10.1) 15.4

DIESEL ENGINES

Timing Case Cover or Gasket, Renew

Includes: R&R all normal interfering parts.

IHC Diesel
Six 6.8
V-8–exc below 9.3
Fleetstar series 12.5

Cummins Diesel
Six 10.2
V-8 20.0

Caterpillar Diesel
Six 11.5
V-8 12.6

Timing Gears, Renew

Includes: R&R all normal interfering parts. Perform all required adjustments.

IHC Diesel
Six
SM 465 (2.2) 3.0
V-8–exc below 13.0
Fleetstar series 12.7

Cummins Diesel
Six 12.5
V-8 19.8

Detroit Diesel
6-71 *18.5
6V-53 *18.0
6V-71 *18.5
8V-71 *21.8
12V-71 *27.0

*Includes: R&R engine, clutch and transmission removed.

Camshaft, Renew

Includes: R&R all normal interfering parts and engine where necessary. Perform all required adjustments.

IHC Diesel
Six 10.0
V-8–exc below 16.8
Fleetstar series *16.3

Cummins Diesel
Six 29.5
V-8 38.0

Detroit Diesel
6-71 †18.3
6V-53 †25.8
6V-71 †27.1
8V-71 †30.2
12V-71 †32.7

Caterpillar Diesel
Six 19.8
V-8 26.9

*w/Steel hood and fenders add (.6) .6
†Both camshafts.

LABOR 17 ENGINE OILING SYSTEM 17 LABOR

(Factory Time)	Chilton Time
GASOLINE ENGINES	
Oil Pan and/or Gasket, Renew	
Six (1.5)	2.3
V-8–V engs (1.4)	2.2
V-8–VS engs (1.4)	2.2
V-8–MV engs (1.4)	2.2
V-8–537, 605 engs (1.6)	2.4
Oil Pump, Renew	
Six (2.1)	2.7
V-8–V engs (1.6)	2.5
V-8–VS engs (1.6)	2.5
V-8–MV engs (1.6)	2.5
V-8–537, 605 engs (2.2)	2.8
Oil Pump, R&R and Recondition	
Six (2.5)	3.2
V-8–V engs (2.1)	3.3
V-8–VS engs (2.1)	3.3
V-8–MV engs (2.0)	3.3
V-8–537, 605 engs (2.7)	3.8
Oil Pressure Relief Valve Assy., Renew	
V-8–VS engs (.4)	.8
V-8–537, 605 engs (1.8)	2.5
Pressure Test Engine Bearings, (Pan Off)	
All series	1.2
Oil Pressure Gauge (Engine), Renew	
All series (.2)	.4
Oil Pressure Gauge (Dash), Renew	
All series (.5)	1.0
Oil Filter Element, Renew	
All series (.3)	.4
DIESEL ENGINES	
Oil Pan or Gasket, Renew	
IHC Diesel	
All series	2.0
Cummins Diesel	
Six	3.9
V-8	4.2
Detroit Diesel	
exc below	2.2
6V-53	1.5
12V-71	2.7
Caterpillar Diesel	
Six	2.3
V-8	1.9
Oil Pump, Renew	
IHC Diesel	
Six	2.8
V-8	2.3
Cummins Diesel	
Six	2.5
V-8	5.0
Detroit Diesel	
exc below	10.5
6-71	7.5
Caterpillar Diesel	
Six	3.0
V-8	13.0
Recondition add	
IHC Diesel	.8
Cummins Diesel	1.5
Detroit Diesel	
exc below	1.3
6-71, 12V-71	2.5
Caterpillar Diesel	1.0
Oil Filter, Renew	
IHC Diesel	.6
Cummins Diesel	.8
Detroit Diesel	.7
Caterpillar Diesel	.7
Pressure Test Engine Bearings (Pan Off)	
All series	1.2
Oil Cooler, Renew	
IHC Diesel	
All series	3.5
Cummins Diesel	
Six	3.5
V-8	2.3
Detroit Diesel	
exc below	3.5
6-71	3.0

LABOR 18 CLUTCH & FLYWHEEL 18 LABOR

(Factory Time)	Chilton Time
Clutch Pedal Free Play, Adjust	
single plate clutch (.3)	.4
two plate clutch (.6)	.8
Clutch Master Cylinder, Renew	
All series (1.1)	1.5
Clutch Master Cylinder, Recondition	
All series (1.6)	2.0
Clutch Slave Cylinder, Renew	
All series (.9)	1.2
Clutch Slave Cylinder, Recondition	
All series (1.2)	1.6
Clutch Assembly, Renew	
Trans Codes (see chart)	
Loadstar	
13017-13018-13034	
13035-13036-13054	
13057-13401-13402	
13403-13411-13412	
13413-13425 (4.1)	5.5
13068-13088	
13223-13298 (4.9)	6.0
13365-13448 (5.3)	6.5
S1600-2100	
13017-13425-13495	
13496 (3.4)	4.7
13422-13448 (6.0)	7.8
13672-13673-13674 (4.9)	6.1
13690-13691-13696	
13697 (3.8)	5.1
Cargostar	
13017 (3.2)	4.5
13034-13035-13036	
13054-13057	
single plate (4.5)	5.7
13401-13402-13403	
13411-13412-13413	
double plate (4.7)	5.9
13068-13088	
13223-13298	
single plate (5.0)	6.5
double plate (5.3)	6.8
13365-13448	
single plate (5.8)	7.3
double plate (6.0)	7.5
Fleetstar	
13048-13129-13135	
13347-13422-13424	
13448-13459-13463	
13466	
single plate (5.6)	7.1
double plate (5.8)	7.5
13053-13054-13057-13401	
13402-13403-13404-13411	
13412-13413-13414-13415	
13429-13430	
single plate (4.8)	6.0
double plate (5.0)	6.4
13066-13068-13088	
13204-13223-13298	
13320	
single plate (5.1)	7.0
double plate (5.3)	7.4
13110-13111-13112	
13118-13121-13122	
13361-13464-13465	
13488-13489	
single plate (6.6)	8.0
double plate (6.8)	8.4
13351-13352-13353	
13354-13439-13478	
single plate (6.3)	7.6
double plate (6.5)	8.0
13365	
single plate (5.3)	8.0
double plate (5.5)	8.4
S2200-2600	
13128-13129-13196	
13197-13316-13422	
13448-13449-13455	
13456-13459-13462	
13467-13468-13470	
13471-13473-13681	
single plate (5.9)	8.3
double plate (6.0)	8.5
13463-13673-13674	
13683	
single plate (4.6)	6.3
double plate (4.7)	6.5
Transtar	
13128-13129-13345-13349-13368	
13373-13420-13441-13447-13449	
13450-13452-13455-13456-13457	
13459-13460-13462-13463-13466	
13468-13471-13480-13481 (6.0)	9.0
13135-13136-13252	
13320-13356-13371	
13375-13376-13377	
13379-13380 (5.5)	8.0
13130-13388-13389	
13390-13391-13392	
13393-13399-13405 (6.3)	9.5
13334-13347-13348 (5.7)	7.5
13415 (5.3)	7.0
Clutch Release Bearing, Renew (Transmission Removed)	
All series (.3)	.4
Flywheel, Renew (Clutch and Transmission Removed)	
All series (.8)	1.2

Transmission Assembly, R&R or Renew

Trans Code (see chart)

(Factory Time)	Chilton Time
Loadstar	
13017-13018-13425 (3.2)	4.6
13034-13035-13036-13054	
13057-13401-13402-13403	
13411-13412-13413 (3.3)	4.7
13068-13088	
13223-13298 (4.7)	6.1
13365 (5.0)	6.7
13448 (5.6)	7.3
13451-13454 (6.9)	8.6
S1600-2100	
13017-13425-13495	
13496 (2.3)	3.6
13422-13448 (4.7)	6.5
13672-13673-13674 (3.6)	4.8
13690-13691-13696	
13697 (2.5)	3.8
Cargostar	
13017 (2.6)	4.0
13034-13035-13036-13054	
13057-13401-13402-13403	
13411-13412-13413 (2.7)	4.1
13068-13088	
13223-13298 (5.0)	6.7
13365 (4.8)	6.5
13448 (6.2)	7.9
Fleetstar	
13048-13129-13135	
13347-13422-13424	
13448-13459-13463	
13466 (5.8)	7.5
13053-13054-13057-13401	
13402-13403-13404-13411	
13412-13413-13414-13415	
13429-13430 (3.7)	5.1
13066-13068-13088	
13204-13223-13298	
13320 (4.3)	5.7
13351-13352-13353	
13354-13439-13478 (6.4)	8.1
13365 (5.0)	6.7
S2200-2600	
13128-13129-13196	
13197-13316-13422	
13448-13449-13455	
13456-13459-13462	
13467-13468-13470	
13471-13473-13681 (5.2)	7.0
13463-13673-13674	
13683 (3.9)	5.0
Transtar	
13128-13129-13345-13349	
13368-13373-13420-13441	
13447-13449-13450-13452	
13455-13456-13457-13459	
13460-13462-13463-13466	
13468-13471-13480-13481 (6.2)	8.5
13135-13136-13252	
13320-13356-13371	
13375-13376-13377	
13379-13380 (4.9)	6.6
13130-13388-13389	
13390-13391-13392	
13393-13399-13405 (6.5)	8.8
13334-13347-13348 (5.1)	7.3
13415 (4.2)	6.5

Transmission Assy., R&R and Recondition

Includes: Disassemble trans completely, clean, inspect or renew all parts. Install all new gaskets and seals.

Trans Codes (see chart)

(Factory Time)	Chilton Time
Loadstar	
13017-13018 (7.8)	10.4
13034-13035-13036 (8.2)	10.8
13054-13057-13401-13402	
13403-13411-13412-13413 (8.9)	11.5
13068-13088	
13223-13298 (10.2)	13.7
13365	
front section (12.0)	16.0
rear section (9.8)	13.0
complete unit (15.0)	20.0
13425 (7.4)	10.0
13448	
front section (15.8)	20.8
rear section (10.1)	13.4
complete unit (18.8)	25.0
13451-13454 (21.3)	28.4
S1600-2100	
13017 (5.2)	8.0
13442 (16.0)	21.6
13425 (5.9)	9.0
13448 (14.8)	20.0
13495-13496 (5.7)	9.0
13672-13673-13674 (7.7)	11.5
13690-13691 (6.5)	10.0
13696-13697 (6.3)	10.0
Cargostar	
13017 (7.1)	9.4
13034-13035-13036 (7.5)	9.9
13054-13057-13401-13402	
13403-13411-13412-13413 (8.2)	10.9
13068-13088	
13223-13298 (10.4)	13.8
13365	
front section (11.0)	14.5
rear section (8.8)	11.7
complete unit (14.0)	18.7
13348 (18.7)	24.9
Fleetstar	
13048-13129-13448	
13463-13466 (15.9)	21.2
13053-13054-13057-13401	
13402-13403-13404-13411	
13412-113414-13415	
13429-13430 (7.4)	9.9
13066-13068-13088	
13204-13223-13298	
13320 (7.7)	10.2
13135 (8.8)	11.7
13351-13352-13353	
13354-13429-13478	
front section (10.4)	13.9
rear section (10.1)	13.6
complete unit (13.6)	18.0
13347 (10.8)	14.4
13365	
front section (8.4)	11.2
rear section (7.7)	10.3
complete unit (11.1)	14.8
13422-13424 (16.7)	22.3
13459 (16.4)	22.0
13464-13488 (20.1)	26.8
13465-13489 (20.9)	27.6
S2200-2600	
13128 (16.5)	22.1
13129-13196-13471	
13473 (15.6)	21.0
13197-13316 (15.4)	20.9
13422 (16.5)	22.1
13448 (15.3)	20.5
13449-13683 (16.2)	22.0
13455-13456	
front section (12.7)	18.4
rear section (5.8)	7.8
complete unit (15.5)	21.0
13459-13462-13467	
13468-13470 (16.1)	22.0
13463 (13.2)	17.8
13673-13674 (8.4)	12.0
13681 (12.5)	18.2
Transtar	
13128 (19.0)	25.3
13129-13345 (18.1)	24.4
13130	
front section (14.3)	19.1
rear section (10.0)	13.3
complete unit (17.3)	23.0
13135-13136-13252 (10.4)	13.9
13320 (10.1)	13.4
13334-13347-13348 (12.7)	16.9
13349-13368-13373	
13459-13460-13462	
13468 (18.2)	24.2
13356 (10.7)	14.3
13371 (13.5)	18.0
13375-13376-13377	
13379-13380 (14.5)	19.0
13388-13389-13390-13391	
13392-13393-13399-13405	
front section (16.4)	21.8
rear section (12.0)	16.0
complete section (21.4)	28.5
13415 (9.1)	12.1
13420-13463-13466 (17.4)	23.2
13441-13471 (17.7)	23.5
13447-13449	
13450-13452 (14.7)	19.6
13455-13456-13457	
front section (15.5)	20.6
rear section (5.0)	8.0
complete section (18.1)	24.1
13480 (15.2)	20.2
13481	
front section (16.0)	21.3
rear section (5.0)	8.0
complete section (18.6)	24.8

Auxiliary Transmission, R&R

Trans Codes (see chart)

(Factory Time)	Chilton Time
Loadstar	
All codes (2.1)	3.1
S1600-2100	
All codes (2.2)	3.5
Fleetstar-S2200-2600	
All codes (2.2)	3.2
Transtar	
13522-13530-13536	
13540-13546-13551	
13556 (2.2)	3.2
13566-13567 (2.7)	3.7

Auxiliary Transmission, Renew

Trans Codes (see chart)

(Factory Time)	Chilton Time
Loadstar	
All codes (3.1)	4.1
S1600-2100	
All codes (3.1)	4.5
Fleetstar-S2200-2600	
All codes (3.2)	4.2
Transtar	
13522-13530-13536	
13540-13546-13551	
13556 (3.0)	4.0
13566-13567 (3.5)	4.5

Auxiliary Transmission, R&R and Recondition

Trans Codes (see chart)

(Factory Time)	Chilton Time
Loadstar	
13501-13524 (7.1)	10.8
13510 (6.5)	9.6
13522-13523 (6.6)	9.7
13536 (7.0)	10.0
S1600-2100	
13536 (7.4)	10.4
13552-13554 (7.7)	10.7
13601 (6.4)	9.4
Fleetstar-S2200-2600	
13510 (6.6)	9.6
13522-13523 (7.2)	10.2
13530-13536-13556 (7.4)	10.4
13538 (6.7)	9.7
13540 (9.4)	12.4
13546-13551 (10.0)	13.0
13552-13554 (7.7)	10.7
13601 (6.2)	9.2

TRANSMISSION, TRANSFER CASE AND AUXILIARY TRANSMISSION IDENTIFICATION CHART

Code No.	New Designation	Old Designation
13001	T-1	HNS
13002	T-2	HNS w/OD
13004	T-4	IHC 3 spd.
13005	T-5	T87E Remote Control
13007	T-7	T87E Tower Lvr. Control
13008	T-8	IHC 3 spd. w/OD
13010	T-10	T9
13011	T-11	T9 w/Dual PTO
13012	T-12	Austin 4 spd.
13013	T-13	Scout II 4 x 2 WG
13014	T-14	Scout II 4 x 4 WG
13015	T-15	T98A
13016	T-16	T98A w/LH PTO
13017	T-17	NP435 w/RH PTO
13018	T-18	N.P.-435 L.H. PTO
13019	T-19	NP540 Dir. in 5th
13022	T-22	NP540 w/OD
13026	T-26	WGASZ-5G
13027	T-27	WGAS4-7F & ASZ-7F
13028	T-28	WG w/over run clutch
13030	T-30	F51 w/OD
13031	T-31	F51C Dir. in 5th
13034	T-34	OD Syncro
13035	T-35	Dir. in 5th Syncro
13036	T-36	5 spd.—Dir. in 5th Syncro
13039	T-39	WG-11 w/11" Conv.
13040	T-40	4753 w/OD Spicer
13041	T-41	4652 Dir. in 5th Spicer
13044	T-44	WG 4 spd. 1.41 in 3rd
13045	T-45	WG-4 Speed 1.41 in 3rd 4 x 4
13048	T-48	RT-510
13049	T-49	WG 11 w/Oil Cooler
13050	T-50	F-52 w/OD
13051	T-51	F-52C Dir. in 5th
13053	T-53	5W430 AT OD
13054	T-54	5W 43 BT Dir. in 5th
13057	T-57	5W 43 DT Dir. in 5th
13059	T-59	F54 w/OD .88 Ratio
13060	T-60	F54 w/OD .77 Ratio
13061	T-61	F54B Dir. in 5th
13062	T-62	F54C Dir. in 5th 1.38 Ratio
13063	T-63	F54C Dir. in 5th 1.69 Ratio
13064	T-64	F54C Dir. in 5th 6.23 Ratio
13066	T-66	5753 Overdrive
13068	T-68	5652 Dir. in 5th
13070	T-70	F55 w/OD
13071	T-71	F55 B Dir. in 5th
13072	T-72	Dir. in 5th 1.38 Ratio
13073	T-73	F-55B Dir. in 5th 1.69 Ratio
13074	T-74	R 35 Roadranger
13075	T-75	R 45 Roadranger
13076	T-76	Roadranger
13078	T-78	F55C Dir. in 5th
13080	T-80	10CB—650
13081	T-81	10CB—65
13082	T-82	8125 12 spd.
13083	T-83	3152 12 Spicer Sel. w/13" CV
13084	T-84	4652 12 Spicer Sel. w/13" CV
13085	T-85	3556 12 Spicer Sel. w/13" CV
13086	T-86	4756A Spicer Sel. w/13" CV
13088	T-88	5752C Dir. in 5th
13089	T-89	8125U 12 spd.
13093	T-93	3152 Spicer Sel. w/14" CV
13094	T-94	4652 Spicer Sel. w/14" CV
13095	T-95	3556A Spicer Sel. w/14" CV
13096	T-96	4756A Spicer Sel. w/14" CV 5.51 Ratio
13100	T-100	5632 Select O-Matic
13104	T-104	5-H-74 Dir. in 5th
13105	T-105	5-HA-74 Dir. in 5th
13106	T-106	5-H-75 Dir. in 5th
13107	T-107	5-HA-75 Dir. in 5th
13109	T-109	MT30 Allison
13110	T-110	MT40 Allison 3.5
13111	T-111	MT41 Allison 2.5
13112	T-112	MT42 Allison 3.5
13114	T-114	MT30 Allison
13118	T-118	MT41 Allison 3.5
13121	T-121	MT41 Allison 3.0
13122	T-122	MT42 Allison 3.0
13126	T-126	5-H-74 w/OD
13128	T-128	RT510
13129	T-129	RT910
13130	T-130	RT96T
13135	T-135	5H74T
13136	T-136	5H740T
13140	TC-140	NP
13141	TC-141	ND Sgl. Lever
13142	TC-142	N.P. Single Lever
13143	TC-143	Chain Drive
13144	TC-144	Spicer #18
13145	TC-145	Spicer #20
13150	TC-150	T32 Std. Mtg.
13151	TC-151	T32 Fwd. Mtg.
13152	TC-152	T223A6 Std. Mtg.
13153	TC-153	T223 Fwd. Mtg.
13155	TC-155	T223 H Fwd. Mtg.
13163	TC-163	T226L
13164	TC-164	T226K
13165	TC-165	T226E
13188	TC-188	2 Speed
13196	TC-196	RT-1110
13197	TC-197	TO-955DLL
13204	T-204	6352B
13209	T-209	5C-720 w/OD .75 OD Ratio
13210	T-210	5C-720 w/OD .080 OD Ratio
13211	T-211	5C-72 Dir. in 5th 1.69 Ratio
13212	T-212	5C-72 Dir. in 5th 1.38 Ratio
13213	T-213	5C-72 Dir. in 5th 1.27 Ratio
13214	T-214	5W-74 Dir. in 5th
13215	T-215	5CA-720 w/OD .80 OD Ratio
13216	T-216	5CA-72 Dir. in 5th 1.69 Ratio
13219	T-219	5WA-72 Dir. in 5th
13220	T-220	5A-1120

TRANSMISSION, TRANSFER CASE AND AUXILIARY TRANSMISSION IDENTIFICATION CHART

Code No.	New Designation	Old Designation	Code No.	New Designation	Old Designation
13223	T-223	6352 Dir. in 5th	13368	T-368	RTO1213
13224	T-224	6452 Dir. in 5th	13371	T-371	8542A 4 spd.
13225	T-225	6453	13373	T-373	RTOO 913
13226	T-226	6455A	13375	T-375	8552A Dir. in 5th
13227	T-227	R-660	13376	T-376	8554A Dir. in 5th Alum.
13228	T-228	R-63	13377	T-377	8553A 5 spd.
13230	T-230	R-96C	13379	T-379	8553B 5 spd.
13231	T-231	R-960C	13380	T-380	8553B 5 spd. Alum.
13233	T-233	RA-96 Alum. Case & Bell	13388	T-388	8516-4A 16 spd.
13234	T-234	RA-960 Alum. Case & Bell	13389	T-389	85.16-3A 16 spd.
13237	T-237	R-660 Alum. Case & Bell	13390	T-390	8516-5A 16 spd.
13238	T-238	R-63A Alum. Case & Bell	13391	T-391	8516-3B 16 spd.
13239	T-239	10A-1120-.744 Ratio	13392	T-392	8516-3B, 16 spd.
13240	T-240	10B-1120-.636 Ratio	13393	T-393	8716-3B 16 spd.
13245	T-245	8041	13399	T-399	8516-5B 16 spd.
13247	T-247	10A-1120-.636 Ratio	13401	T-401	5CW62 1.16 Ratio
13248	T-248	10B-1120-.744 Ratio	13402	T-402	5CW62 1.37 Ratio
13250	T-250	8041 Alum.	13403	T-403	5CW62 1.57 Ratio
13252	T-252	5H-74T	13404	T-404	5CW620 .86 Ratio
13255	T-255	8241	13405	T-405	8516-3B Air Shift
13259	T-259	8254B Alum. Case	13406	T-406	MT-31 2.8 HD PTO Gear
13260	T-260	8241 Alum.	13407	T-407	3 Speed Fully Automatic
13263	T-263	8051C 5 spd.	13411	T-411	5CW65 1.16 Ratio
13265	T-265	8051/A	13412	T-412	5CW65 1.37 Ratio
13266	T-266	8052 Dir. in 5th	13413	T-413	5CW65 1.57 Ratio
13270	T-270	8055A Alum.	13414	T-414	5CW650 .86 Ratio
13275	T-275	8251	13415	T-415	5CW65 At Dir. in 5th
13276	T-276	8251A	13418	T-418	4 spd. WG T18 RH PTO
13278	T-278	8251F 5 spd.	13419	T-419	4 spd. WG T18 LH PTO
13279	T-279	8252B Dir. in 5th	13420	T-420	RT906 6 spd.
13280	T-280	8255A Alum.	13422	T-422	RT-613
13283	T-283	8555F 5 spd.	13424	T-424	RTO-613
13287	T-287	6852E	13425	T-425	NP-4590 4 Speed 1.66
13294	T-294	6858B	13427	T-427	4 Speed W.G. T-19 L & R PTO
13296	T-296	6854B	13428	T-428	4 Speed W.G. T-19A L & R PTO
13298	T-298	6852G	13429	T-429	MP-7590 Dir. in 5th
13316	T-316	T-955ALL	13430	T-430	MP-7550 Dir. in 5th
13320	T-320	6853C	13439	T-439	8516-3A
13322	T-322	8016-3A 16 spd.	13441	T-441	RT909A 9 spd.
13324	T-324	8016-5B 16 spd.	13445	T-445	4 spd. WG 1.41 in 3rd RH PTO
13331	T-331	3 Speed T-15D W.G. Col. Shift	13447	T-447	SST-6 1263A
13332	T-332	3 Speed T-15D W.G. Floor Shift	13448	T-448	RT610 10 spd.
13334	T-334	T-905J 5 spd.	13449	T-449	SST-6 1062B
13337	T-337	8012-3A 12 spd.	13450	T-450	SST-6 1062A
13338	T-338	8012-5A 12 spd.	13451	T-451	AT-540 Allison 4 Speed
13339	T-339	8016-3D 16 spd.	13452	T-452	SST-6 1262A
13345	T-345	R10-#910	13454	T-454	AT-540 Allison 4 Speed
13347	T-347	T-509-A 5 spd.	13455	T-455	SST-6+1 1007-2A
13348	T-348	T-509-B 5 spd.	13456	T-456	SST-6+1 1007-3A
13349	T-349	RTOF913 13 spd. w/OD	13457	T-457	SST-11 1211A
13351	T-351	7016-3A	13459	T-459	RTO 9513
13352	T-352	7016-3B	13460	T-460	RTOO 9513
13353	T-353	7216-3A	13462	T-462	RT-9513 Dir.
13354	T-354	7216-3B	13463	T-463	T-955
13356	T-356	7452-B 5 spd.	13464	T-464	MT-640 Allison 4 Speed
13361	T-361	MT40 Allison 3.0	13465	T-465	MT-650 Allison 5 Speed
13365	T-365	R463T Roadranger	13466	T-466	TO-955

LABOR 19 STANDARD TRANSMISSION 19 LABOR

TRANSMISSION, TRANSFER CASE AND AUXILIARY TRANSMISSION IDENTIFICATION CHART

Code No.	New Designation	Old Designation	Code No.	New Designation	Old Designation
13467	T-467	RT, RTF-12513	13528	AT-528	3H65 8C-3G65
13468	T-468	RTO 12513	13529	AT-529	3A65-3B65 7C
13470	T-470	RTO-958LL	13530	AT-530	3A65-3B65 8C
13471	T-471	RTF 9509A	13536	AT-536	7041
13473	T-473	RTOF-9509B	13538	AT-538	R-8031R
13474	T-474	HT-740	13539	AT-539	8031-C-F-C7C
13475	T-475	HT-750	13540	AT-540	8031-C-F-C8C
13478	T-478	PR-8516-3A	13546	AT-546	8341A
13480	T-480	SST-10 1010-2A	13551	AT-551	8354A
13481	T-481	SST-20 1020-2A	13552	AT-552	R-8341 CGF
13486	T-486	HT-750	13554	AT-554	R-8341GFL 4 Spd.
13488	T-488	MT-640 Allison 4 Speed	13556	AT-556	4D 4E-75
13489	T-489	MT-650 Allison 5 Speed	13566	AT-566	1314C
13494	T-494	IH 5 Speed Const. Mesh OD	13567	AT-567	1241D
13495	T-495	IH 5 Speed Const. Mesh Dir. in 5th	13601	AT-601	2A-92
13496	T-496	IH 5 Speed Const. Mesh Dir. in 5th	13672	AT-672	CM-5052A
13501	AT-501	5831	13673	AT-673	CM-5052B
13510	AT-510	2A45	13674	AT-674	CM-5252A
13519	AT-519	6231-6231A/B7C	13681	AT-681	RT-1056
13520	AT-520	6231-6231A/B8C	13683	AT-683	SST-6
13522	AT-522	7231-7231A/B7C	13690	AT-690	NP-7591
13523	AT-523	7231-7231A/B8C	13691	AT-691	NP-7551
13524	AT-524	6041-7C	13696	AT-696	Clark 285V
13527	AT-527	3H65 7C-3G65	13697	AT-697	Clark 282V

	(Factory Time)	Chilton Time
Transtar		
13522	(6.6)	**9.6**
13530-13536-13556	(7.3)	**10.3**
13540	(9.2)	**12.2**
13546-13551	(9.4)	**12.4**
13566-13567	(10.2)	**14.0**

	(Factory Time)	Chilton Time
Transfer Case, Renew		
All series	(4.1)	**5.5**
Transfer Case, R&R and Recondition		
All series	(9.8)	**13.5**

LABOR 23 AUTOMATIC TRANSMISSION 23 LABOR

	(Factory Time)	Chilton Time
Transmission Assy., R&R		
Trans Codes (see chart)		
Loadstar-S1600-2100		
13109-13110-13111		
13121-13122-13464		
13465-13488-13489	(4.3)	**5.8**
Cargostar		
13109-13110-13111		
13112-13121-13122		
13406	(5.2)	**6.7**
Fleetstar-S2200-2600		
13110-13111-13112-13118		
13121-13122-13361-13464		
13465-13488-13489	(4.8)	**6.3**
Pressure Check System		
All series	(.8)	**1.3**
Transmission Assy., Renew		
Trans Codes (see chart)		
Loadstar-S1600-2100		
13109-13110-13111		
13121-13122-13464		
13465-13488-13489	(6.6)	**8.0**
Cargostar		
13109-13110-13111		
13112-13121-13122		
13406	(7.6)	**9.7**
Fleetstar-S2200-2600		
13110-13111-13112-13118		
13121-13122-13361-13464		
13465-13488-13489	(7.2)	**9.5**
Transmission Assy., R&R and Recondition		
Includes: Disassemble trans, including valve body, inspect and replace parts as required.		
Trans Codes (see chart)		
Loadstar-S1600-2100		
13109-13110-13111		
13121-13122-13464		
13465-13488-13489	(28.6)	**37.9**
Cargostar		
13109-13110-13111		
13112-13121-13122		
13406	(28.8)	**38.1**
Fleetstar-S2200-2600		
13110-13111-13112		
13118-13121-13122		
13361	(27.6)	**36.9**
13464-13488		
13465-13489	(20.9)	**27.6**
Converter Assembly, Renew		
Includes: R&R transmission.		
Trans Codes (see chart)		

LABOR 23 AUTOMATIC TRANSMISSION 23 LABOR

	(Factory Time)	Chilton Time
Loadstar-S1600-2100		
13109-13110-13111		
13121-13122-13464		
13465-13488-13489	(7.0)	8.5
13451-13454	(5.7)	7.2
Cargostar		
13109-13110-13111		
13112-13121-13122		
13406	(8.4)	9.7
Fleetstar-S2200-2600		
13110-13111-13112		
13118-13121-13122		
13361	(8.0)	9.5
13465-13466		
13488-13489	(6.3)	7.8

Valve Body Assembly, Renew

Includes: R&R and clean oil pan, drain and refill unit.

	(Factory Time)	Chilton Time
Trans Codes (see chart)		
Loadstar-S1600-2100		
13109-13110-13111		
13121-13122-13464		
13465-13488-13489		
13451-13454	(1.8)	2.5
Cargostar		
13109-13110-13111		
13112-13121-13122		
13406	(1.8)	2.5
Fleetstar-S2200-2600		
13110-13111-13112-13118		
13121-13122-13361-13465		
13466-13488-13489	(2.1)	3.0

Valve Body Assy., R&R and Recondition

Includes: Disassemble, clean, inspect and replace parts as required. Drain and refill unit.

	(Factory Time)	Chilton Time
Trans Codes (see chart)		
Loadstar-S1600-2100		
13109-13110-13111		
13121-13122-13464		
13465-13488-13489	(5.3)	7.0
13451-13454	(4.2)	5.9
Cargostar		
13109-13110-13111		
13112-13121-13122		
13406	(5.3)	7.0
Fleetstar-S2200-2600		
13110-13111-13112		
13118-13121-13122		
13361	(5.6)	7.5
13465-13466		
13488-13489	(4.6)	6.3

LABOR 25 U-JOINTS & DRIVESHAFT 25 LABOR

	(Factory Time)	Chilton Time
Universal Joint, Recondition		
Each	(1.0)	1.2
Universal Joint, Recondition (Removed)		
Each	(.5)	.7
Driveshaft, Renew		
All series	(1.0)	1.2
Tighten Drive Shaft Yoke		
All series	(.7)	.9
Stub Shaft, Renew		
Pre Lube center brg	(1.9)	2.7
Ball Bearing	(1.2)	1.6
Single row needle brg	(1.1)	1.5
Silent Spin brg	(1.2)	1.7
w/slip yoke	(.8)	1.2
w/bolted yoke	(1.2)	1.6
Fleetstar series	(1.2)	1.8
Universal Joint, Renew		
All series-each	(.8)	1.1
Center Bearing Assembly, Renew		
All series	(1.3)	1.7
w/slip yoke	(1.0)	1.4
w/bolted yoke	(1.4)	1.7
Center Bearing Assembly, R&R and Recondition		
All series	(1.4)	2.0
w/slip yoke	(1.0)	1.7
w/bolted yoke	(1.4)	2.0
Center Bearing Assy., Recondition (Removed)		
All series	(.4)	.6

LABOR 26 REAR AXLE 26 LABOR

REAR AXLE CODE CHART

Code No.	New Designation	Old Designation
14001	RA-1	Semi-Floating
14002	RA-2	Semi-Floating
14003	RA-3	Semi-Floating w/Power-Lok
14004	RA-4	Dana 2300#
14005	RA-5	R-1060
14006	RA-6	R-1060-w/Power-Lok
14009	RA-9	Spicer #44
14010	RA-10	R-1070
14011	RA-11	R-1070-w/Power-Lok
14012	RA-12	Spicer #27A
14013	RA-13	Spicer #27A w/Power-Lok
14014	RA-14	Dana 2300# w/Power-Lok
14015	RA-15	R-1165
14016	RA-16	Spicer #60
14017	RA-17	Spicer #60 w/Power-Lok
14018	RA-18	Spicer #44
14019	RA-19	Spicer #44 Wide Tred
14020	RA-20	R-1170
14021	RA-21	Spicer #23
14023	RA-23	Spicer #44 w/Power-Lok
14024	RA-24	Spicer #44 w/Power-Lok
14025	RA-25	R-1440
14026	RA-26	R-1440-Induction Hardened
14028	RA-28	Spicer #44 w/Power-Lok
14029	RA-29	IH 15500#
14030	RA-30	R-1470-Cast
14031	RA-31	R-1470-Budd
14032	RA-32	R-1470-Cast Hrd. Hsg.
14033	RA-33	R-1470-Disc Hrd. Hsg.
14035	RA-35	R-1530/31
14039	RA-39	R-1530/31 17000#
14040	RA-40	R-1530/31 Mod. Hsg.
14042	RA-42	IH 17500#
14043	RA-43	Pusher Axle 1HX 190A
14044	RA-44	X-190-18500#
14045	RA-45	R-1572/73-E 1790/91
14046	RA-46	X-190-22000#
14047	RA-47	X-190-23000#
14050	RA-50	R-1632/33-E-1892/93
14051	RA-51	Spicer #30
14053	RA-53	Dana #60 3700#
14054	RA-54	Dana #60 w/Power-Lok
14055	RA-55	E-1911
14056	RA-56	X-200-22000#
14057	RA-57	X-200-22000#
14060	RA-60	R-1547/48-L-101

REAR AXLE CODE CHART

Code No.	New Designation	Old Designation
14063	RA-63	Dana #70 7500# w/Power-Lok
14065	RA-65	Q-101
14067	RA-67	Timkin R-140
14070	RA-70	R-1740/41-R-100
14071	RA-71	R-160
14072	RA-72	Timkin R-170
14073	RA-73	Timkin R-170 Alum. Diff.
14076	RA-76	R-170 Trac. Eq. & Alum. Diff.
14079	RA-79	#44 Eaton w/Drop Box
14083	RA-83	60-2 Dana Unit Bearing
14084	RA-84	60-2 Dana Unit Bearing w/Lok
14120	RA-120	R-2366-E-1350
14125	RA-125	R-2465-E-13600
14126	RA-126	E-13600 13500#
14127	RA-127	
14130	RA-130	R-2466-E-13600-Cast
14131	RA-131	R-2466-E-13600-Budd
14135	RA-135	R-2585/C-E-1600/01
14140	RA-140	H-300-Mod. 190 Hsg.
14143	RA-143	E-16600 170 Air
14145	RA-145	R-2575/76-E-17800#
14146	RA-146	E-17810/11-18500#
14150	RA-150	E-18802/03
14151	RA-151	E-18812/13-22000#
14152	RA-152	E-18812/13-23000#
14154	RA-154	Timkin H 370
14155	RA-155	E-19502/03
14156	RA-156	E-19512/13-22000#
14157	RA-157	E-19512/13-23000#
14158	RA-158	Eaton 198001
14160	RA-160	R-2595/96-LT-301
14161	RA-161	LT-340-Mod. 190 Hsg.
14162	RA-162	L-365 18500#
14165	RA-165	R-2610/11-QT-301
14167	RA-167	QT-365 23000#
14170	RA-170	R-2795/96-R-300
14172	RA-172	RT-365 2300#
14173	RA-173	R-320
14175	RA-175	R-2800/01-U-300
14180	RA-180	E-22501 Alum.
14181	RA-181	E-22501
14184	RA-184	E-15201 13500#
14186	RA-186	18500# Clark Hsg.
14187	RA-187	E-15201 15000#
14189	RA-189	E-16220 w/17000#
14190	RA-190	R-330
14191	RA-191	R-390
14192	RA-192	23000# Timkin Hsg.
14193	RA-193	E-23221 23000#
14197	RA-197	23000# Timkin Hsg.
14199	RA-199	E-16244-17500#
14245	RA-245	R-1540/41-E-2613/14
14246	RA-246	E-7810 18500#
14250	RA-250	R-1640/41-E-2695/96
14252	RA-252	E-8812 23000#
14255	RA-255	R-1640/41-E-2731
14257	RA-257	23000# Timkin Hsg. E 9512
14262	RA-262	w/18000 Clark Hsg. Timkin L
14270	RA-270	R-1760/16-R-200
14272	RA-272	RT-265-23000#
14273	RA-273	R-220
14275	RA-275	R-1819/11-U-200
14276	RA-276	R-1810/11-U-200 Stl. Hsg.
14277	RA-277	U-240 R/Std. 29,000#
14290	RA-290	R-230
14292	RA-292	23000# Timkin Hsg. E-18202 & 22
14298	RA-298	E-35327 35000, 45000#
14301	RA-301	RF-1475-22R
14302	RA-302	Eaton 34DSB
14303	RA-303	Eaton 34DTB
14305	RA-305	RF-1575-28R
14306	RA-306	Eaton 34D3B
14310	RA-310	34R
14312	RA-312	34D (Emeryville Models)
14313	RA-313	34DT
14314	RA-314	34DP
14315	RA-315	SLDD
14316	RA-316	SLDD A-321 36FWC
14317	RA-317	SLD
14318	RA-318	SLHD
14320	RA-320	RF-1685/90-36R
14321	RA-321	36FWC
14323	RA-323	38DS
14324	RA-324	Eaton 38DT
14325	RA-325	38DP
14326	RA-326	42DP
14328	RA-328	SLAD Timkin
14330	RA-330	SQDD
14332	RA-332	SQHD (Emeryville Models)
14333	RA-333	SQHD Timkin
14334	RA-334	SQHD Timkin
14336	RA-336	RA-336 SRDD L/Susp.
14340	RA-340	SQW (Emeryville Models)
14341	RA-341	XF-3014 30000#
14346	RA-346	SQHD Timkin
14348	RA-348	SQHD Timkin
14351	RA-351	XF-351 34000#
14355	RA-355	XF-3816 38000#
14356	RA-356	42-DP
14360	RA-360	Eaton 34D3
14364	RA-364	SUDD Timkin 55000#
14368	RA-368	STDD Timkin 50000#
14371	RA-371	SFDD 4600
14372	RA-372	SFD 4640
14373	RA-373	SFDD Timkin 65000#
14375	RA-375	464
14386	RA-386	IH34000
14387	RA-387	IH38000
14388	RA-388	SLHD Timkin
14390	RA-390	Eaton 38DSC & 38DSE
14391	RA-391	Eaton 38DTC & 38DTE
14392	RA-392	Eaton 38DPC & 38DPE
14393	RA-393	Eaton 38D3C & 38D3E
14399	RA-399	SSHD Timkin 44,000
14418	RA-418	Dead Axle Drop
14423	RA-423	Dead Axle Straight
14446	RA-446	Eaton Sgl. Spd. 44DS
14449	RA-449	Eaton 44DP
14467	RA-467	Eaton E 44 DS 44000# Sqr. Hsg.
14472	RA-472	IH-16 40000#
14474	RA-474	IH-18 46000#

(Factory Time) — Chilton Time

Inspection Cover Gasket, Renew
All series (.5) 7

Axle Shaft, Renew (One)
full floating (.3) 7
semi floating (1.7) 2.5

Axle Shaft Bearing, Renew
semi floating 2.7

Rear Wheel Bearings, Repack
full floating-one whl (1.2) 1.4

Axle Shaft Seal, Renew
semi floating-one side
inner (1.9) 2.3
outer (.9) 1.2

Rear Wheel Bearing, Renew
full floating-one side (1.3) 1.6

Rear Axle Assy., R&R or Renew
Add .8 if necessary to bleed brake system.
Axle Codes (see chart)

Loadstar-Cargostar
14025-14030-14039 (4.6) 7.0
14043-14044-14047 (4.9) 7.3
14057-14126-14127 (5.1) 7.5
14184-14186-14187
14189-14192 (5.2) 7.6
14197 (5.3) 7.7
14302
front (6.6) 9.0
rear (5.7) 8.1
14303-14328
14341-14351
front (6.8) 9.2
rear (5.9) 8.3

S1600-2100
14029-14030-14039
hydraulic (4.5) 7.0
air cam (3.9) 5.8
14042-14044-14047
14187-14199-14192
hydraulic (4.9) 7.3
air cam (4.2) 6.3
14057-14186-14192
14197
hydraulic (5.0) 7.5
air cam (4.5) 6.7
4 Spring Suspension
14341-14351-14355
front (5.6) 8.4
14472-rear (5.2) 7.8
Equalizer Beam Suspension-
Adapter Type
14341-14351-14355
front (6.7) 10.0
14472-rear (6.3) 9.4
Equalizer Beam Suspension-
Tube Type
14341-14351-14355
front (6.1) 9.1
14472-rear (5.6) 8.4

Fleetstar
14044-14047
14272-14292 (4.6) 7.0
14057-14172-14175
14186-14192 (4.8) 7.2
14197 (5.0) 7.4
14302-14303-14306-14328
14341-14351-14355-14386
14387-14388-14399-14446
14333
front (5.6) 8.0
rear (5.1) 7.5
14303-14306
rear (5.2) 7.6

S2200-2600
14044 (4.2) 6.3
14057-14186-14193
14197-14277-14298 (4.5) 6.7
4 Spring Suspension
Front
14351-14355-14399
14446-14467-14472
14474 (5.6) 8.4
Rear
14351-14355-14399
14446-14467-14472
14474 (5.2) 7.8
Equalizer Beam Suspension
Adapter Type-Front
14351-14355-14399
14446-14467-14472
14474 (6.7) 10.0
Adapter Type-Rear
14351-14355-14399
14446-14467-14472
14474 (6.3) 9.4
Equalizer Beam Suspension
Tube Type-Front
14351-14355-14399
14446-14467-14472
14474 (6.1) 9.1
Tube Type-Rear
14351-14355-14399
14446-14467-14472
14474 (5.6) 8.4

Transtar
14047 (3.5) 5.9
14057-14071-14072
14073-14076 (3.6) 6.0
14079 (4.1) 6.5
14192-14197-14273 (3.8)
14302-14390-14446
front (4.5) 6.9
14302-14303-14306-14351
14355-14386-14387-14390
14391-14392-14393-14446
14449
rear (4.0) 6.4
14303-14306-14328-14333
14334-14346-14348-14349
14388-14391-14393
front (4.6) 7.0
14328-14333-143334-14346
14348-14349-14388
rear (3.9) 6.3
14351-14355-14386
14387-14399
front (4.7) 7.1
14364-14386-14373
front (4.9) 7.3
rear (4.4) 6.8
14399-rear (4.1) 6.5
14392-14449-front (4.4) 6.8

Differential Assy., R&R and/or Renéw Gasket
Axle Codes (see chart)

Loadstar-Cargostar
14025-14030-14039 (2.6) 4.0
14043-14044-14057
14126-14127-14187
14189 (2.9) 4.3
14047 (2.7) 4.1
14186-rear (3.1) 4.5
14192-14197-14341
rear (3.1) 4.5
14302
front (3.6) 5.0
rear (3.1) 4.5
14303
front (3.7) 5.1
rear (3.1) 4.5
14328
front (4.2) 5.6
rear (2.9) 4.3
14341-14351
front (4.4) 5.8
rear (3.1) 4.5

S1600-2100
14029-14039 (2.7) 4.0
14030 (2.3) 3.4
14042-14044-14047
14057-14186-14192
14199-14292 (2.8) 4.2
14187 (2.5) 3.7
14197 (3.0) 4.5
14341-14351-14355
front (3.8) 5.7
14472-rear (3.2) 4.8

Fleetstar
14044 (2.7) 4.1
14047 (2.6) 4.0
14057-14192
14272-14292 (2.8) 4.2
14172-14197-14341
14351-14355-14386
14387 (3.0) 4.4
14175 (3.4) 4.8
14186-14446
rear (2.9) 4.3
14302-14328
14333-14388
front (4.2) 5.6
14302-14303-14306
rear (3.1) 4.5
14303-14306
front (4.3) 5.7
14328-14333
14388-14399
rear (3.2) 4.6
14341-14351-14355
14386-14387
front (3.7) 5.1
14399-front (3.9) 5.3
14446-front (4.1) 5.5

S2200-2600
14044-14057 (2.8) 4.2
14186 (2.9) 4.3
14193-14197-14298
14446-14467-rear (3.0) 4.5
14277 (3.1) 4.6
14351-14355-14472
14474-front (3.8) 5.7
14351-14355-14399
14472-14474-rear (3.2) 4.8
14399-front (4.0) 6.0
14446-14467-front (4.2) 6.3

Transtar
14047 (2.4) 3.8
14057 (2.5) 3.9
14071-14072-14073
14076-14192-14197 (2.7) 4.1
14079 (3.3) 4.7
14273 (2.8) 4.2
14302-14390-14392
14446-14449 (3.6) 5.0
14302-14303-14306-14351
14355-14386-14387-14390
14391-14392-14393-14446
14449-rear (2.8) 4.2
14303-14306
14391-14393
front (3.7) 5.1
14328-14333-14334-14346
14348-14349-14388-14399
front (4.2) 5.6
rear (2.9) 4.3
14351-14355
14386-14387
front (3.7) 5.1
14364-14368-14373
front (6.9) 8.3
rear (6.4) 7.8
14399-front (3.9) 5.3

LABOR 26 REAR AXLE 26 LABOR

(Factory Time)	Chilton Time
Differential Assy., R&R and Recondition	
Includes: Disassemble, clean, inspect and replace parts, including ring gear, as necessary. Reassemble, make all necessary adjustments, refill lubricant.	
Axle Codes (see chart)	
Loadstar-Cargostar	
14025-14030-14039 (8.3)	12.2
14043-14044	
14047-14057 (9.2)	13.1
14126-14127-14184	
14187-14189 (8.1)	12.0
14186-14197 (8.4)	12.3
14192 (8.3)	12.2
14303	
front (13.7)	19.6
rear (8.5)	12.4
14302	
front (13.6)	19.5
rear (8.5)	12.4
14328	
front (15.6)	21.5
rear (9.5)	13.4
14341	
front (14.7)	20.6
rear (8.9)	12.8
14351	
front (15.2)	21.1
rear (9.2)	13.1
S1600-2100	
14029-14039 (8.7)	13.0
14030 (8.4)	12.6
14042-14044-14047	
14057-14341-14472	
rear (9.9)	14.8
14186-14199 (9.2)	13.8
14187 (8.5)	12.7
14192 (9.0)	13.5
14197 (9.4)	14.1
14292 (8.8)	13.2
14351-14355	
front (15.6)	23.4
14351-14355	
rear (10.2)	15.3
14341-14472	
front (15.2)	22.8
Fleetstar	
14044 (9.8)	13.7
14047 (9.7)	13.6
14057 (9.9)	13.8
14172 (12.2)	17.1
14175 (12.5)	17.4
14186 (9.2)	13.1
14192 (9.0)	12.9
14197 (9.4)	13.3
14272 (11.1)	15.0
14292 (8.8)	12.7
14302	
front (14.3)	19.2
rear (9.6)	13.5
14303-14306	
front (14.0)	18.9
rear (9.3)	13.2
14328-14333-14388	
front (16.4)	22.3
rear (10.6)	14.5
14341	
front (15.1)	21.0
rear (9.9)	13.8
14351-14355	
14386-14355	
14386-14387	
front (15.6)	21.5
rear (10.0)	13.9
14399	
front (14.8)	20.7
rear (10.5)	14.4
14446	
front (14.8)	20.7
rear (9.5)	13.4
S2200-2600	
14044-14057-14472	
14474-rear (9.9)	14.8
14186-14298 (9.2)	13.8
14193-14197 (9.4)	14.1
14277 (10.8)	16.2
14351-14355-front (15.6)	23.4
14351-14355-rear (10.2)	15.3
14399-front (14.8)	22.2
14399-rear (10.5)	15.7
14446-14467-front (15.0)	22.5
14446-14467-rear (9.7)	14.5
14472-14474-front (15.2)	22.8
Transtar	
14047 (9.0)	12.9
14071 (9.4)	13.3
14079 (11.3)	15.2
14192-14197 (8.5)	15.2
14273 (9.7)	18.5
14302-14390-14446	
front (13.6)	18.5
rear (8.5)	12.4
14303-14306	
14391-14393	
front (13.7)	18.6
rear (8.4)	12.3
14328-14333-14334-14346	
14348-14349-14388	
front (15.6)	21.5
rear (9.5)	13.4
14351-14355	
14386-14387	
front (15.2)	21.1
rear (9.2)	13.1
14364-14368	
front (15.6)	21.5
rear (11.0)	14.9
14373	
front (15.4)	21.3
rear (11.6)	15.5
14392-14449	
front (13.0)	17.9
rear (8.2)	12.1
14399	
front (13.5)	18.4
rear (9.4)	13.3
Pinion, Imput or Output Shaft Oil Seal, Renew	
All series-each (1.1)	1.5
Shift Unit, Renew	
(Electric or Air)	
All series (.5)	.9
Shift Unit, R&R and Recondition	
(Electric or Air)	
All series (1.4)	2.0

LABOR 27 REAR SUSPENSION 27 LABOR

(Factory Time)	Chilton Time
Rear Spring, Renew (One)	
All series	
single axle (1.2)	1.8
tandem axle (2.0)	2.7
IH suspension (1.4)	2.0
Hendrickson suspension (1.9)	2.6
air suspension (.7)	1.1
Reyco suspension (1.5)	2.1
Equalizer Beam Suspension	
w/Cast wheels (2.8)	3.7
w/Budd wheels (3.2)	4.3
4 Spring Suspension	
each (1.1)	1.5
Rear Spring, R&R and Recondition (One)	
All series	
single axle (2.1)	3.0
tandem axle (2.9)	4.0
IH suspension (2.0)	3.0
Hendrickson suspension (2.8)	4.0
Reyco suspension (2.1)	3.0
Equalizer Beam Suspension	
w/Cast wheels (3.1)	4.3
w/Budd wheels (3.5)	4.9
4 Spring Suspension	
each (1.5)	1.9
Rear Spring Center Bolt, Renew (One)	
All series	
single axle (1.4)	2.0
tandem axle (2.1)	2.9
IH suspension (1.5)	2.2
Hendrickson suspension (2.1)	2.8
Reyco suspension (1.6)	2.3
Equalizer Beam Suspension	
w/Cast wheels (2.9)	4.0
w/Budd wheels (3.4)	4.6
4 Spring Suspension	
each (1.3)	1.8
Rear Spring Pin, Renew (One)	
All series	
single axle (.7)	1.1
tandem axle (1.1)	1.5
w/Cast wheels (.7)	1.0
w/Budd wheels (.9)	1.2
Auxiliary Rear Spring, Renew (One)	
All series (.7)	1.2
Rear Shock Absorbers, Renew	
All series-one (.3)	.5
both (.6)	9
Equalizing Beam, Renew (One)	
All series (3.3)	4.0
Adapter Type Hanger	
w/Beam Center Sleeve (6.2)	8.2
wo/Beam Center Sleeve (7.4)	9.8
Tube Type Hanger	
w/Beam Center Sleeve (5.6)	7.5
wo/Beam Center Sleeve (6.7)	8.9
Torque Rod Assembly, Renew (One)	
All series (.5)	.8
Rubber Cushion (Air Suspension), Renew (One)	
All series (2.4)	3.0
Trailing Air (Air Suspension), Renew (One)	
All series (2.1)	2.7
Equalizer Beam Bushings, Renew (One beam-removed)	
All series (1.2)	1.9
Trailing Arm (Air Suspension) Bushings, Renew (One arm-removed)	
All series	
front or rear-each (.7)	1.2

LABOR 28 AIR CONDITIONING 28 LABOR

	(Factory Time)	Chilton Time
Drain, Evacuate & Recharge System		
All series		
full charge	(1.3)	1.5
partial charge	(.6)	.8
Check & Correct Compressor Oil Level		
All series	(.3)	.3
Compressor Assembly, Renew		
All series	(2.3)	3.7
Compressor Drive Clutch, Renew		
All series	(.5)	.6
Dehydrator Filter, Renew		
All series	(1.6)	2.6
Condenser, Renew		
Kysor Kombo	(1.8)	3.4
CO series (blend air)	(2.2)	3.8
Blower Motor, Renew		
side mount	(.4)	.8
floor mounted	(.7)	1.4
Evaporator Core, Renew		
Blend air	(2.5)	4.6
Kysor Kombo	(2.0)	4.1
Expansion Valve, Renew		
Blend Air	(2.5)	4.4
Kysor Kombo	(2.0)	4.1
Thermostatic Control Switch, Renew		
Blend Air	(.3)	.5
Kysor Kombo	(.5)	.7
Refrigerant Low Pressure Switch, Renew		
S1600-2600	(.5)	.8
All other series	(1.7)	2.6
Refrigerant High Pressure Switch, Renew		
All series	(.4)	.6
Refrigerant Hoses, Renew		
evaporator to compressor	(1.8)	3.4
compressor to condenser	(.6)	.8
Add: Charge A/C System.		
full charge	(1.3)	1.5
partial charge	(.6)	.8

LABOR 30 HEAD & PARKING LAMPS 30 LABOR

	(Factory Time)	Chilton Time
Aim Headlamps		
All series	(.3)	.4
Headlamp Sealed Beam Bulb, Renew		
All series	(.3)	.3
Parking (Marker) Lamp Lens, Renew		
All series	(.2)	.3
License Lamp Lens or Assy., Renew		
All series	(.2)	.3
Back-Up Lamp or Lens, Renew		
All series	(.2)	.3
Tail and Stop Lamp Lens, Renew		
All series	(.2)	.3
Reflectors, Renew		
All series-each		.2

LABOR 31 WINDSHIELD WIPER & SPEEDOMETER 31 LABOR

	(Factory Time)	Chilton Time
Windshield Wiper Motor, Renew		
LOADSTAR-S1600-2100		
electric	(.6)	1.0
air	(.7)	1.1
CARGOSTAR		
electric	(1.1)	1.5
air	(1.3)	1.7
FLEETSTAR-S2200-2600		
electric	(.5)	.9
air	(.6)	1.0
TRANSTAR		
All models	(.6)	1.0
Windshield Washer Pump, Renew (w/Reservoir)		
S1600-2600		
All models	(.3)	.4
Speedometer or Tachometer, R&R or Renew		
All series	(.6)	1.1
Speedo or Tach Cable and Casing, Renew		
All series-each	(1.0)	1.6

LABOR 32 LIGHT SWITCHES & WIRING 32 LABOR

	(Factory Time)	Chilton Time
Headlamp Switch, Renew		
All series	(.4)	.5
Headlamp Dimmer Switch, Renew		
All series	(.3)	.6
Ignition Switch, Renew		
All series	(.3)	.6
Stop Light Switch, Renew		
All series	(.3)	.5
Horn, Renew		
All series-each	(.4)	.5
Turn Signal Switch, Renew		
inside column	(.7)	1.2
outside column	(.2)	.6
Turn Signal or Hazard Warning Flasher, Renew		
All series-each	(.2)	.3
Back-Up Lamp Switch, Renew		
All models	(.2)	.4

Jeep Vehicles—CJ Series • Wagoneer • Cherokee • Commanche

GROUP INDEX

ALPHABETICAL INDEX

LABOR — SERVICE BAY OPERATIONS — LABOR

(Factory Time) — Chilton Time

COOLING

(M) Winterize Cooling System

Includes: Run engine to check for leaks, tighten all hose connections. Test radiator and pressure cap, drain radiator and engine block. Add anti-freeze and refill system.

- All models .5

(M) Thermostat, Renew

- All models (.5) .6

(M) Radiator Hoses, Renew

- All models
  - upper (.4) .5
  - lower (.5) .6

FUEL

(M) Carburetor Air Cleaner, Service

- All models .3

(M) Carburetor, Adjust (On Truck)

- All models .4

BRAKES

(G) Brake Pedal Free Play, Adjust

- All models .4

(G) Brakes, Adjust (Minor)

- two wheels .4

(G) Bleed Brakes (Four Wheels)

Includes: Fill master cylinder.

- All models (.4) .5

(M) Parking Brake, Adjust

- All models (.3) .4

LUBRICATION SERVICE

(M) Lubricate Chassis, Change Oil & Filter

Includes: Inspect and correct all fluid levels.

- All models .6
- Install grease fittings add .1

(M) Lubricate Chassis

Includes: Inspect and correct all fluid levels.

- All models .4
- Install grease fittings add .1

(M) Engine Oil & Filter, Change

Includes: Inspect and correct all fluid levels.

- All models .4

WHEELS

(M) Wheel, Renew

- one .5

(G) Wheel, Balance

- one .3
- each adtnl .2

(G) Front Wheel Bearings, Clean and Repack (Both Wheels)

- w/Disc brakes 1.2
- w/4 whl drive 2.3

(M) Front Wheel Bearings, Adjust

- All models .4

ELECTRICAL

(G) Aim Headlamps

- two .4
- four .6

(M) Headlamp Sealed Beam Bulb, Renew

- All models-one .3
  - each adtnl .2

(M) Park and Turn Signal Lamp Lens or Bulb, Renew

- All models-one (.3) .4

(M) Tail Lamp Lens or Bulb, Renew

- All models-one (.3) .4

(M) License Lamp Assembly, Renew

- All models-one (.3) .4

LABOR — 1 TUNE UP 1 — LABOR

(Factory Time) — Chilton Time

(G) Compression Test

- Four (.4) .5
- Six (.4) .6
- V-6 (.6) .7
- V-8 (.7) .9

(G) Engine Tune Up (Electronic Ignition)

Includes: Test battery and clean connections. Tighten manifold and carburetor mounting bolts. Check engine compression, clean and adjust or renew spark plugss. Test resistance of spark plug cables. Inspect distributor cap and rotor. Adjust air gap. Check vacuum advance operation. Reset ignition timing. Adjust idle mixture and idle speed. Service air cleaner. Inspect crankcase ventilation system. Inspect and adjust drive belts. Inspect choke operation and adjust or free up. Check operation of EGR valve.

- **Four**–1982-86 (2.0) 2.8
- **Six**–1982-86 (1.4) 2.0
- **V-6**–1984-86 (2.1) 3.0
- **V-8**–1982-86 (1.9) 2.5
- w/A.C. add .6

LABOR — 2 IGNITION SYSTEM 2 — LABOR

(Factory Time) — Chilton Time

(G) Spark Plugs, Clean & Reset or Renew

- Four (.3) .4
- Six (.3) .5
- V-6 (.5) .6
- V-8 (.6) .8

(G) Ignition Timing, Reset

- CJ/Scrambler
  - Four (.5) .6
  - Six (.2) .3
- All other models (.3) .4

(G) Distributor Assy., R&R or Renew

Includes: Reset ignition timing.

- All models (.5) .7
- Renew driven gear add (1.0) 1.0

(G) Distributor, R&R and Recondition

Includes: Reset ignition timing.

- All models (.9) 1.3

(G) Distributor Sensor, Renew

- All models (.5) .7

(G) Distributor Trigger Wheel, Renew

- All models (.4) .6

(G) Ignition Pick-Up Coil, Renew

- CJ/Scrambler
  - Four (.8) 1.1
  - Six (.3) .5
- Cherokee/Grand Wagoneer/Truck
  - Six (.3) .5
- Che/Wag/Comanche
  - Four (.3) .5
  - V-6 (.8) 1.1

(G) Vacuum Control Unit, Renew

Includes: R&R distributor and reset ignition timing.

- CJ/Scrambler
  - Four (.9) 1.2
  - Six (.4) .6
- Cherokee/Grand Wagoneer/Truck
  - Six (.4) .6
- Che/Wag/Comanche
  - Four (.4) .6
  - V-6 (.9) 1.2

(G) Ignition Cables, Renew

- All models (.4) .7

(G) Ignition Coil, Renew

- All models (.3) .5

(G) Ignition Control Unit, Renew

- All models (.5) .7

(G) Spark Knock Sensor, Renew

- All models (.3) .5

(G) Distributor Cap and/or Rotor, Renew

- All models (.3) .5

(G) Ignition Switch, Renew

- All models (.4) .7

LABOR 3 FUEL SYSTEM 3 LABOR

(Factory Time)	Chilton Time
(G) Fuel Pump, Test	
Includes: Disconnect line at carburetor, attach pressure gauge.	
All models	.3
(G) Carburetor Air Cleaner, Service	
All models	.3
(G) Carburetor, Adjust (On Truck)	
All models	.4
(G) Carburetor Assembly, Renew	
Includes: All necessary adjustments.	
Four	
150 eng (.5)	.8
151 eng (.9)	1.3
Six (.8)	1.2
V-6 (.7)	1.1
V-8 (.9)	1.3
(G) Carburetor, R&R and Clean or Recondition	
Includes: All necessary adjustments.	
Four	
150 eng (1.7)	2.5
151 eng (1.6)	2.4
Six (1.6)	2.4
V-6 (1.5)	2.3
V-8 (1.6)	2.4
(G) Idle Speed Solenoid, Renew	
All models (.4)	.5
(G) Carburetor Float Level, Adjust	
Includes: Renew needle valve and seat if required.	
Four-150 eng (.6)	.8
(G) Choke Vacuum Diaphragm, Renew	
All models (.4)	.6
(G) Vacuum Delay Valve, Renew	
All models (.2)	.3
(G) Electric Choke Relay, Renew	
All models (.3)	.4
(G) Fuel Pump, Renew	
Four (.5)	.7
Six (.5)	.7
V-6 (.5)	.7
V-8 (.7)	.9
(G) Fuel Filter, Renew	
All models (.3)	.4

(Factory Time)	Chilton Time
(G) Fuel Tank, Renew	
CJ/Scrambler (1.0)	1.3
Cherokee/Grand Wagoneer/Truck (1.4)	1.7
Cke/Wag/Comanche (.8)	1.1
(G) Fuel Gauge (Tank Unit), Renew	
CJ/Scrambler (1.3)	1.6
Cherokee/Grand Wagoneer/Truck (1.2)	1.5
Cke/Wag/Comanche (.7)	1.0
(G) Fuel Gauge (Dash Unit), Renew	
CJ/Scrambler (1.3)	1.7
Cherokee/Grand Wagoneer/Truck (.9)	1.2
Cke/Wag/Comanche (.6)	1.0
(G) Intake Manifold and/or Gaskets, Renew	
Four	
150 eng (2.5)	3.6
151 eng (1.4)	2.0
Six (1.4)	2.0
V-6 (3.4)	4.9
V-8 (1.5)	2.2
Renew manif add	.5

THROTTLE BODY INJECTION

(Factory Time)	Chilton Time
(G) Injection System Electrical Test	
All models (.3)	.5
(G) Throttle Plate Assy., Renew	
Includes: System test.	
All models (.7)	1.1
(G) Fuel Injectors, Renew	
Includes: System test.	
All models-one (.7)	1.0
each adtnl	.3
(G) Throttle Body Assy., R&R or Renew	
All models (.4)	1.0
(G) Fuel Meter Assembly, Renew	
All models (.5)	.7
(G) Fuel Pressure Regulator, Renew	
All models (.7)	.9
(G) Fuel Pressure Regulator, Adjust	
All models (.4)	.6

(Factory Time)	Chilton Time
(G) Manifold Pressure Sensor, Renew	
All models (.3)	.4
(G) Wide Open Throttle Switch, Renew	
All models (.4)	.5
(G) Idle Speed Control Motor, Renew	
All models (.4)	.6
(G) Manifold Air Temperature Sensor, Renew	
All models (.3)	.4
(G) Coolant Temperature Sensor, Renew	
All models (.4)	.7
(G) Throttle Position Sensor, Renew	
All models (.5)	.8
(G) Electronic Control Module (ECU), Renew	
All models (.3)	.4
(G) Oxygen Sensor, Renew	
All models (.3)	.5

DIESEL ENGINE

(Factory Time)	Chilton Time
(G) Turbocharger Assy., R&R or Renew	
All models (1.6)	2.5
(G) Intercooler, Renew	
All models (.8)	1.2
(G) Fuel Injector, Renew	
All models-one (.4)	.6
all (1.1)	1.5
(G) Fuel Injection Pump, Renew	
All models (3.7)	5.4
(G) Glow Plug Timer, Renew	
All models (.2)	.4
(G) Glow Plugs, Renew	
All models-one (.4)	.6
all (.7)	1.1
(G) Injection Timing, Adjust	
All models (1.2)	1.5
(G) Intake Manifold and/or Gasket, Renew	
All models (.6)	1.1
Renew manif add (.2)	.5

LABOR 3A EMISSION CONTROLS 3A LABOR

AIR INJECTION SYSTEM

(Factory Time)	Chilton Time
(G) Air Pump, Renew	
CJ/Scrambler	
Four (.9)	1.2
Cke/Wag/Comanche	
V-6 (.5)	.8
All other models	
wo/Serpentine belt (.6)	1.0
w/Serpentine belt (.7)	1.1
(G) Exhaust Check Valve, Renew	
All models (.4)	.5
(G) Air Injection Manifold, Renew	
Four (.5)	.9
Six	
w/V-belt (1.0)	1.6
w/Serpentine belt (1.2)	1.8
V-6-each (.3)	.6
V-8-each (.5)	.9
(G) Diverter Valve, Renew	
Cke/Wag/Comanche	
V-6 (.5)	.7
All other models (.4)	.6
(G) Deceleration Valve, Renew	
Cke/Wag/Comanche	
Four (.4)	.5
All other models (.2)	.3
(G) Air Control Valve, Renew	
All models (.4)	.5

EXHAUST GAS RECIRCULATION

(Factory Time)	Chilton Time
(G) E.G.R. Valve, Renew	
All models (.5)	.6

FUEL VAPOR RECIRCULATION

(Factory Time)	Chilton Time
(M) P.C.V. Valve, Renew	
All models (.3)	.3
(M) Charcoal Canister, Renew	
Cke/Wag/Comanche (.5)	.6
All other models (.3)	.4

ELECTRONIC EMISSION CONTROLS

(Factory Time)	Chilton Time
(G) Microprocessor (MCU), Renew	
All models (.3)	.4
(G) Oxygen Sensor, Renew	
All models (.3)	.5

LABOR 3A EMISSION CONTROLS 3A LABOR

(Factory Time) Chilton Time

(G) Idle Cut-Off Solenoid, Renew

All models (.3)	.4

(G) Electric Choke Relay, Renew

All models (.3)	.4

(G) Enrichment Actuator, Renew

All models	
stepper motor (.4)	.6
duty cycle solenoid (.4)	.6

LABOR 4 ALTERNATOR AND REGULATOR 4 LABOR

(Factory Time) Chilton Time

(G) Alternator Circuits, Test

Includes: Test battery, regulator and alternator output.

All models	.6

(G) Alternator Assy., Renew

Cke/Wag/Comanche	
Four (.4)	.6
V-6 (.3)	.5
Diesel (1.1)	1.6
All other models (.4)	.6

Add circuit test if performed.

(G) Alternator, R&R and Recondition

Cke/Wag/Comanche	
Four (1.0)	1.7
V-6 (.8)	1.5
Diesel (2.0)	3.0
All other models (.9)	1.6

Add circuit test if performed.

(G) Alternator Regulator, Renew

Cke/Wag/Comanche	
Four (.6)	1.0
V-6 (.7)	1.1
Diesel (1.3)	2.0
All other models (.6)	1.0

Add circuit test if performed.

(G) Voltmeter, Renew

CJ/Scrambler (.5)	.9

(G) Ammeter, Renew

Cherokee/Grand Wagoneer/ Truck (.8)	1.3

LABOR 5 STARTING SYSTEM 5 LABOR

(Factory Time) Chilton Time

(G) Starter Draw Test (On Truck)

All models	.3

(G) Starter Assy., Renew

All models	
Gas (.4)	.6
Diesel (2.0)	2.9

Add draw test if performed.

(G) Starter, R&R and Recondition

Includes: Turn down armature.

All models	
Gas (1.0)	2.0
Diesel (2.6)	4.0
Renew field coils add	.5

Add draw test if performed.

(G) Starter Drive, Renew

Includes: R&R starter.

All models	
Gas (.6)	.9
Diesel (2.2)	3.2

(G) Starter Solenoid, Renew

Includes: R&R starter.

All models	
Gas (.9)	1.2
Diesel (2.5)	3.5

(G) Starter Relay, Renew

All models (.3)	.4

(M) Battery Cables, Renew

All models	
positive	.3
negative	.3

(M) Battery Terminals, Clean

All models	.3

LABOR 6 BRAKE SYSTEM 6 LABOR

(Factory Time) Chilton Time

(G) Brake Pedal Free Play, Adjust

All models	.4

(G) Bleed Brakes (Four Wheels)

Includes: Fill master cylinder.

All models (.4)	.5

(G) Brake Shoes and/or Pads, Renew

Includes: Install new or exchange brake shoes or pads. Adjust service and hand brake. Bleed system.

front-disc (.7)	1.1
rear	
semi-float axle (.9)	1.5
full float axle (1.2)	1.9
Resurface disc rotor, add-each	.9
Resurface brake drum, add-each	.5

(G) Rear Brake Drum, Renew

All models-one (.3)	.5

(G) Pressure Limiting Valve, Renew

Includes: Bleed system.

All models (1.0)	1.4

BRAKE HYDRAULIC SYSTEM

(G) Wheel Cylinders, Renew

Includes: Bleed system.

All models-one (.9)	1.3
both (1.5)	2.3

(G) Wheel Cylinders, R&R and Recondition

Includes: Bleed system.

All models-one (.9)	1.6
both (1.5)	2.9

(G) Master Cylinder, Renew

Includes: Bleed system.

CJ/Scrambler (.9)	1.4
All other models (.7)	1.2

(G) Master Cylinder, R&R and Rebuild

Includes: Bleed system.

CJ/Scrambler (1.4)	2.0
All other models (1.2)	1.8

(G) Brake Hose, Renew (Flex)

Includes: Bleed system.

All models-one (.6)	.9

(G) Brake System, Flush and Refill

All models	1.2

DISC BRAKES

(G) Disc Brake Pads, Renew

Includes: Install new disc brake pads only.

All models (.7)	1.1

(G) Disc Brake Rotor, Renew

Cke/Wag/Comanche	
one (.3)	.5
both (.6)	.9
All other models	
one (.6)	1.0
both (1.2)	1.8

(G) Caliper Assembly, Renew

Includes: Bleed system.

All models-one (.6)	1.0
both (1.0)	1.8

LABOR 6 BRAKE SYSTEM 6 LABOR

	(Factory Time)	Chilton Time
(G) Caliper Assy., R&R and Recondition		
Includes: Bleed system.		
All models-one	(.9)	1.5
both	(1.5)	2.8
POWER BRAKES		
(G) Power Brake Booster, Renew		
All models	(.6)	1.0
(G) Vacuum Check Valve, Renew		
All models	(.2)	.3
PARKING BRAKE		
(G) Parking Brake, Adjust		
All models	(.3)	.4
(G) Parking Brake Lever, Renew		
All models	(.5)	.7
(G) Parking Brake Cables, Renew		
All models		
primary	(.7)	1.0
secondary		
semi-float axle	(.7)	1.0
full float axle	(1.2)	1.5

Combinations

ADD TO BRAKES, RENEW

	(Factory Time)	Chilton Time
(G) RENEW WHEEL CYLINDER		
Each		.2
(G) REBUILD WHEEL CYLINDER		
Each		.3
(G) RENEW MASTER CYLINDER		
All models		1.0
(G) REBUILD MASTER CYLINDER		
All models		1.5
(G) RENEW BRAKE HOSE		
Each		.3
(G) RENEW REAR WHEEL GREASE SEALS		
Semi-floating axle		1.4
Full floating axle		.6
(G) REPACK FRONT WHEEL BEARINGS (BOTH WHEELS)		
Drum brake		.6
Disc brake		.8
(G) RENEW BRAKE DRUMS		
Each		.2
(G) RENEW DISC BRAKE ROTOR		
Each		.3
(G) CALIPER ASSEMBLY, RENEW		
Each		.3
(G) CALIPER ASSEMBLY, REBUILD		
Each		.5

LABOR 7 COOLING SYSTEM 7 LABOR

	(Factory Time)	Chilton Time
(M) Winterize Cooling System		
Includes: Run engine to check for leaks, tighten all hose connections. Test radiator and pressure cap, drain radiator and engine block. Add anti-freeze and refill cooling system.		
All models		.5
(M) Thermostat, Renew		
All models	(.5)	.6
(M) Radiator Assy., R&R or Renew		
Includes: Drain and refill cooling system.		
Cke/Wag/Comanche		
wo/A.C.	(.8)	1.2
w/A.C.	(1.5)	2.2
All other models	(.5)	.9
ADD THESE OPERATIONS TO RADIATOR R&R		
(G) Boil & Repair		1.5
(G) Rod Clean		1.9
(G) Repair Core		1.3
(G) Renew Tank		1.6
(G) Renew Trans. Oil Cooler		1.9
(G) Recore Radiator		1.7
(M) Radiator Hoses, Renew		
All models		
upper	(.4)	.5
lower	(.5)	.6
(M) Viscous Fan Assembly, Renew		
All models	(.5)	.7
(G) Water Pump, Renew		
CJ/Scrambler		
Four		
150 eng	(1.1)	1.7
151 eng	(.7)	1.2
Six	(1.0)	1.5
Cherokee/Grand Wagoneer/Truck		
Six	(1.0)	1.5
V-8		
wo/A.C.	(1.3)	2.0
w/A.C.	(1.9)	2.8
Cke/Wag/Comanche		
Four	(1.1)	1.7
V-6	(1.3)	2.0
Diesel	(3.0)	4.5
(G) Temperature Gauge (Dash Unit), Renew		
CJ/Scrambler	(1.3)	1.6
Cke/Wag/Comanche	(.6)	1.0
(G) Temperature Gauge (Engine Unit), Renew		
All models	(.3)	.4
w/Diesel eng add		.1
(G) Water Jacket Expansion Plugs, Renew		
each		.5
Add time to gain accessibility.		
(G) Heater Hoses, Renew		
Includes: Drain and refill cooling system.		
All models		
one or all	(.5)	.7
(G) Heater Core, R&R or Renew		
CJ/Scrambler	(1.2)	2.3
Cherokee/Grand Wagoneer/Truck	(.8)	1.5
Cke/Wag/Comanche		
wo/A.C.	(1.7)	3.3
w/A.C.	(2.0)	3.9
ADD THESE OPERATIONS TO HEATER CORE R&R		
(G) Boil & Repair		1.2
(G) Repair Core		.9
(G) Recore		1.2
(G) Heater Water Control Valve, Renew		
All models	(.4)	.5
(G) Temperature Control Head, Renew		
Cke/Wag/Comanche	(.4)	.7
All other models	(.7)	1.1
(G) Heater Blower Motor, Renew		
CJ/Scrambler	(1.0)	1.6
All other models	(.4)	.7
(G) Blower Motor Switch, Renew		
CJ/Scrambler		
Heater	(.3)	.5
A.C.	(.6)	1.1
Cherokee/Grand Wagoneer/Truck		
Heater	(.7)	1.2
A.C.	(.6)	1.1
Cke/Wag/Comanche	(.4)	.7

LABOR 8 EXHAUST SYSTEM 8 LABOR

	(Factory Time)	Chilton Time
(G) Exhaust Pipe Seal, Renew		
Cke/Wag/Comanche	(.7)	1.2
All other models	(.4)	.7
(G) Front Exhaust Pipe, Renew		
Cke/Wag/Comanche	(.9)	1.3
All other models	(.7)	1.1
(G) Rear Exhaust Pipe, Renew		
All models	(.4)	.5

LABOR 8 EXHAUST SYSTEM 8 LABOR

	(Factory Time)	Chilton Time
(G) Muffler, Renew		
Cke/Wag/Comanche	(.9)	*1.4
All other models	(.6)	.9
*Includes R&R tail pipe and converter.		
(G) Tail Pipe, Renew		
Cke/Wag/Comanche	(.9)	*1.4
All other models	(.6)	.8
*Includes R&R tail pipe and converter.		
(G) Catalytic Converter, Renew		
Cke/Wag/Comanche	(.8)	1.2
CJ/Scrambler	(.8)	1.2
All other models	(.7)	1.1
(G) Manifold Heat Valve (Heat Riser), Renew		
All models		
V-8	(1.0)	1.5
(G) Exhaust Manifold, Renew		
Four		
150 eng	(2.8)	3.9
151 eng	(1.5)	2.1
Six	(1.7)	2.4
V-6-each	(.9)	1.4
V-8-each	(.9)	1.4
Diesel	(2.3)	*3.5
*Includes R&R turbo.		

LABOR 9 FRONT SUSPENSION 9 LABOR

Note: On all front suspension operations alignment charges must be added if performed. Time given does not include alignment.

	(Factory Time)	Chilton Time
(M) Wheel, Renew		
one		.5
(G) Wheel, Balance		
one		.3
each adtnl		.2
(G) Check Alignment of Front End		
All models		.5
Note: Deduct if alignment is performed.		
(G) Toe-In, Adjust		
All models	(.3)	.4
(G) Align Front End		
Includes: Adjust front wheel bearings.		
All models	(.9)	1.4
(G) Lower Control Arm, Renew		
Add alignment charges.		
Cke/Wag/Comanche		
one side	(.4)	.7
(G) Upper and Lower Ball Joints, Renew		
Add alignment charges.		
Cke/Wag/Comanche		
one side	(.8)	1.2
both sides	(1.4)	2.2
(G) Upper Control Arm Bushings, Renew		
Add alignment charges.		
Cke/Wag/Comanche		
in axle housing	(.6)	1.0
(G) Front Spring, Renew		
CJ/Scrambler		
one	(.7)	1.0
both	(.9)	1.5
Cherokee/Grand Wagoneer/Truck		
one	(.9)	1.3
both	(1.2)	1.9
Cke/Wag/Comanche		
one or both	(1.3)	2.0
(G) Front Spring Center Bolt, Renew		
All models-one	(.7)	1.1
(G) Front Spring Shackle Bracket, Renew		
All models-one	(.5)	.8
(G) Front Spring Eye Bushing, Renew		
Includes: Renew shackle and bolt.		
All models-one	(.7)	1.2
(G) Front Spring, R&R and Recondition		
CJ/Scrambler		
one side	(1.8)	2.5
both sides	(3.0)	4.4
All other models		
one side	(1.2)	1.8
both sides	(1.8)	2.9
(G) Front Shock Absorbers, Renew		
Cke/Wag/Comanche		
one	(.2)	.4
both	(.3)	.5
All other models		
one	(.4)	.5
both	(.5)	.7
(G) Front Stabilizer Bar, Renew		
All models	(.5)	.7
(G) Front Stabilizer Bar Bushings, Renew		
Cke/Wag/Comanche	(.4)	.6
All other models	(.7)	1.0

4 WHEEL DRIVE FRONT AXLE

	(Factory Time)	Chilton Time
(G) Front Differential Cover, Renew or Reseal		
All models		.6
(G) Front Axle Shaft, R&R or Renew		
Cke/Wag/Comanche	(.5)	.9
All other models	(.7)	1.2
Renew shaft joint add-		
U-Joint, each	(.3)	.3
C/V Joint, each	(.6)	.6
Renew outer oil seal add,		
each	(.2)	.2
Renew C/V Joint boot add	(.4)	.4
(G) Front Axle Outer Shaft Oil Seals, Renew		
All models		
w/Select-Trac	(1.0)	1.7
Renew outer brg add	(.1)	.1
(G) Front Axle Bearing and Hub Assy., Renew		
Cke/Wag/Comanche		
one side	(.5)	.8
Renew roller brg and/or seal add	(.4)	.4
(G) Pinion Shaft Oil Seal, Renew		
All models	(.9)	1.2
(G) Steering Knuckle, Renew		
All models		
one side	(1.1)	1.7
Renew oil seal add	(.2)	.2
(G) Steering Spindle and/or Bearing, Renew		
All models-one side	(.6)	.9
(G) Front Axle Assy., R&R or Renew		
Cke/Wag/Comanche		
2 WD	(1.7)	2.5
4 WD	(1.9)	2.7
All other models	(2.5)	3.4
(G) Front Axle Assy., R&R and Recondition		
All models	(5.6)	7.8
Renew axle brgs and seals add	(.3)	.5

LABOR 10 STEERING LINKAGE 10 LABOR

	(Factory Time)	Chilton Time
(G) Steering Damper, Renew		
All models	(.3)	.5
(G) Tie Rod Assy., Renew		
Does not include reset toe-in.		
All models-one	(.7)	.9
(G) Pitman Arm, Renew		
Does not include reset toe-in.		
All models	(.5)	.7
(G) Steering Center Link, Renew		
Does not include reset toe-in.		
Cke/Wag/Comanche	(.5)	.8

LABOR 11 STEERING GEAR 11 LABOR

	(Factory Time)	Chilton Time
(G) Steering Wheel, Renew		
All models	(.4)	.5
(G) Horn Contact, Renew		
All models	(.3)	.4
(G) Pitman Shaft Seal, Renew		
All models	(.8)	1.2
(G) Flexible Coupling, Renew		
All models	(.7)	1.0
STANDARD STEERING		
(G) Steering Gear, Adjust (On Truck)		
All models	(.4)	.5
(G) Steering Gear, R&R or Renew		
All models	(.8)	1.2
(G) Steering Gear, R&R and Recondition		
Includes: Remove, disassemble, renew necessary parts, reassemble, reinstall and adjust.		
All models	(1.4)	2.5
POWER STEERING		
(G) Power Steering Oil Pressure Check		
All models		.5
(G) Power Steering Gear, Adjust (On Truck)		
All models	(.4)	.6
(G) Power Steering Gear, R&R or Renew		
All models	(1.0)	1.7
(P) Power Steering Gear, R&R and Recondition		
Includes: Remove, disassemble, renew necessary parts, reassemble, reinstall and adjust.		
All models	(2.2)	3.5
(G) Power Steering Pump, Renew		
Cke/Wag/Comanche		
Four	(1.1)	1.6
V-6	(.6)	1.0
Diesel	(.7)	1.2
All other models	(1.0)	1.5
Recond pump add	(.9)	1.0
(G) Pump Flow Control Valve, Renew		
All models	(.4)	.7
(G) Pump Reservoir, Renew		
All models	(1.3)	1.8
(M) Power Steering Hoses, Renew		
All models-one	(.8)	1.1

LABOR 12 CYLINDER HEAD & VALVE SYSTEM 12 LABOR

	(Factory Time)	Chilton Time
GASOLINE ENGINES		
(G) Compression Test		
Four	(.4)	.5
Six	(.4)	.6
V-6	(.6)	.7
V-8	(.7)	.9
(G) Cylinder Head Gasket, Renew		
Includes: Clean carbon.		
Four		
150 eng	(3.8)	5.5
151 eng	(2.4)	3.3
Six	(3.9)	5.6
V-6-right side	(4.1)	5.8
left side	(3.8)	5.4
both sides	(4.4)	6.3
V-8-right side	(2.8)	4.0
left side	(3.7)	5.3
both sides	(4.4)	6.3
(G) Cylinder Head, Renew		
Includes: Transfer parts as required. Clean carbon.		
Four		
150 eng	(4.2)	6.0
151 eng	(2.8)	4.0
Six	(4.2)	6.0
V-8-one side	(3.7)	5.3
both sides	(5.4)	7.7
(P) Clean Carbon and Grind Valves		
Includes: R&R cylinder head(s). Grind valves and seats. Minor tune up.		
Four		
150 eng	(4.9)	6.8
151 eng	(4.4)	6.4
Six	(5.2)	9.5
V-6	(5.0)	9.0
V-8	(7.1)	10.0
(G) Rocker Arm Cover Gasket, Renew or Reseal		
Four		
150 eng	(1.0)	1.4
151 eng	(.7)	1.0

Combinations

ADD TO VALVE JOB
SEE MACHINE SHOP OPERATIONS

	(Factory Time)	Chilton Time
(G) DRAIN, EVACUATE & RECHARGE AIR CONDITIONING SYSTEM		
All models	(.9)	1.3
(G) ROCKER ARMS, PUSH RODS AND/OR PIVOTS, CLEAN OR RENEW		
Six	(.6)	.8
V-8	(.5)	.8
(G) HYDRAULIC VALVE LIFTERS DISASSEMBLE AND CLEAN		
Each		.2
(G) DISTRIBUTOR, RECONDITION		
All models	(1.0)	1.4
(G) CARBURETOR, RECONDITION		
1 bbl	(1.3)	1.6
2 bbl	(1.5)	2.1
4 bbl	(1.5)	2.1
(P) VALVE GUIDES, REAM OVERSIZE		
Each	(.1)	.2

	(Factory Time)	Chilton Time
Six	(1.5)	1.8
V-6-one side	(1.0)	1.4
both sides	(2.0)	2.8
V-8-one side	(.7)	1.0
both sides	(1.0)	1.4
(G) Valve Tappets (Lifters), Renew (All)		
Four		
150 eng	(1.2)	1.8
151 eng	(2.1)	2.7
Six	(3.6)	5.5
V-6	(4.1)	5.8
V-8	(2.6)	3.7
(G) Valve Clearance, Adjust		
V-6-one side	(1.3)	1.8
both sides	(2.6)	3.6
(G) Valve Springs and/or Valve Stem Oil Seals, Renew (Head on Truck)		
Includes: Renew valve push rods, rocker arms and pivots if required.		
Four		
one or all cyls	(1.7)	2.6
Six		
one cyl	(1.7)	2.2
all cyls	(2.6)	3.7
V-6		
all cyls	(3.2)	4.6
V-8		
one cyl	(.7)	1.2
all cyls	(2.1)	3.7
DIESEL ENGINE		
(G) Compression Test		
All models	(1.3)	1.8
(G) Cylinder Head Gasket, Renew		
Includes: Clean carbon and make all necessary adjustments.		
All models	(7.4)	10.5
(G) Cylinder Head, Renew		
Includes: Transfer parts as required. Make all necessary adjustments.		
All models	(9.2)	13.0
(P) Clean Carbon and Grind Valves		
Includes: R&R cylinder head, grind valves and seats. Make all necessary adjustments.		
All models	(8.8)	12.5
(G) Valve Cover and/or Gasket, Renew		
All models	(.6)	1.0
(G) Valve Clearance, Adjust		
All models	(.8)	1.4

LABOR 13 ENGINE ASSEMBLY & MOUNTS 13 LABOR

(Factory Time) Chilton Time

GASOLINE ENGINES

(G) Engine Assembly, Remove and Install

Does not include transfer of any parts or equipment.

Four
- CJ/Scrambler
  - 150 eng (3.8) 5.4
  - 151 eng (2.6) 3.7
- Cke/Wag/Comanche (5.7) 8.0

Six
- w/M.T. (3.5) 5.0
- w/A.T. (3.9) 5.5

V-6 (5.7) 8.1

V-8
- w/M.T. (3.7) 5.3
- w/A.T. (3.9) 5.5

w/A.C. add (.7) 7

(G) Engine Assembly, Renew (Less Head)

Includes: R&R engine assy. Transfer all component parts not supplied with replacement engine. Minor tune up.

Four
- CJ/Scrambler
  - 150 eng (6.5) 9.2
  - 151 eng (5.3) 7.5
- Cke/Wag/Comanche (8.4) 11.9

Six
- w/M.T. (7.8) 11.1
- w/A.T. (8.2) 11.6

V-6 (9.3) 13.2

V-8
- w/M.T. (8.9) 12.6
- w/A.T. (9.1) 12.9

w/A.C. add (.7) 7

(P) Engine Assembly, R&R and Recondition (Complete)

Includes: Rebore block, remove cylinder top ridge, deglaze cylinder walls, replace pistons, rings, rod and main bearings. Clean carbon, grind valves. Tune engine.

Four
- CJ/Scrambler
  - 150 eng (17.5) 24.8
  - 151 eng (16.3) 23.1
- Cke/Wag/Comanche (19.4) 27.5

Six
- w/M.T. (18.2) 25.8
- w/A.T. (18.6) 26.4

V-6 (19.9) 28.3

V-8
- w/M.T. (20.8) 29.5
- w/A.T. (21.0) 29.8

w/A.C. add (.7) 7

(G) Engine Mounts, Renew

Cke/Wag/Comanche
- right side (.9) 1.2
- left side (.5) 8

All other models
- one side (.5) 8

DIESEL ENGINE

(G) Engine Assembly, Remove & Install

Does not include transfer of any parts or equipment.

All models (6.1) 8.7

w/A.C. add (.7) 7

(P) Cylinder Block, Renew

Includes: R&R engine assy. Transfer all component parts not supplied with replacement engine. Make all necessary adjustments.

All models (19.5) 27.6

Renew cyl head add (1.8) 2.4

w/A.C. add (.7) 7

(P) Engine Assy., R&R and Recondition

Includes: Renew cylinder liners, pistons and rings. Renew main and rod bearings. Clean carbon and grind valves. Make all necessary adjustments.

All models (22.6) 32.0

w/A.C. add (.7) 7

(G) Engine Mounts, Renew

All models
- right side (.9) 1.2
- left side (.5) 8

LABOR 14 PISTONS, RINGS & BEARINGS 14 LABOR

(Factory Time) Chilton Time

GASOLINE ENGINES

(P) Rings, Renew

(See Engine Combinations)

Includes: Remove cylinder top ridge, deglaze cylinder walls, replace rod bearings, clean carbon. Minor tune up.

Four
- CJ/Scrambler
  - 150 eng (7.4) 10.0
  - 151 eng (5.6) 8.1
- Cke/Wag/Comanche (7.8) 11.0

Six (6.4) 9.9

V-6 (8.6) 12.2

V-8 (8.5) 12.0

w/A.C. add (.3) 3

(P) Piston or Connecting Rod, Renew (One)

Includes: Remove cylinder top ridge, deglaze cylinder wall, replace rod bearing, clean carbon. Minor tune up.

Four
- CJ/Scrambler
  - 150 eng (6.7) 9.5
  - 151 eng (4.8) 6.9
- Cke/Wag/Comanche (7.0) 9.9

Six (5.8) 8.2

V-6 (6.6) 9.4

V-8 (6.0) 8.5

(P) Connecting Rod Bearings, Renew

Four
- CJ/Scrambler
  - 150 eng (2.2) 3.2
  - 151 eng (1.8) 2.8
- Cke/Wag/Comanche (3.0) 4.3

Six (2.2) 3.1

V-6 (3.4) 4.8

V-8 (2.5) 3.6

COMBINATIONS

Add to Engine Work

See Machine Shop Operations

(G) DRAIN, EVACUATE & RECHARGE AIR CONDITIONING SYSTEM

All models (.9) 1.3

(G) ROCKER ARMS, PUSH RODS AND/OR PIVOTS, CLEAN OR RENEW

Four (.4) 7

Six (.6) 8

V-8 (.5) 8

(G) HYDRAULIC VALVE LIFTERS, DISASSEMBLE & CLEAN

Each 2

(G) DISTRIBUTOR, RECONDITION

All models (1.0) 1.4

(G) CARBURETOR, RECONDITION

1 bbl (1.3) 1.6

2 bbl (1.5) 2.1

4 bbl (1.5) 2.1

(G) DEGLAZE CYLINDER WALLS

Four (.7) 1.0

Six (.9) 1.3

V-8 (1.2) 1.5

(G) REMOVE CYLINDER TOP RIDGE

Each (.1) 1

(G) TIMING CHAIN, RENEW (COVER REMOVED)

All models (.4) 6

(G) MAIN BEARINGS, RENEW (PAN REMOVED)

Four (.7) 1.2

Six (.9) 1.5

V-8 (.7) 1.2

(G) PLASTIGAUGE BEARINGS

Each (.1) 1

(G) OIL PUMP RECONDITION

Six (.2) 4

(M) OIL FILTER ELEMENT, RENEW

All models (.3) 3

(Factory Time) Chilton Time

DIESEL ENGINE

(P) Pistons and Liners, Renew

Includes: R&R cylinder head and oil pan. Renew pistons, rings and cylinder liners. Make all necessary adjustments.

All models (12.5) 17.7

w/A.C. add (.3) 3

(P) Connecting Rod Bearings, Renew

All models (2.9) 4.1

LABOR 15 CRANKSHAFT & DAMPER 15 LABOR

(Factory Time) Chilton Time

GASOLINE ENGINES

(P) Crankshaft and Main Bearings, Renew

Includes: R&R engine assembly.

Four
CJ/Scrambler
150 eng (5.6) 8.0
151 eng (4.7) 6.7
Cke/Wag/Comanche (7.1) 10.0
Six
w/M.T. (6.0) 8.5
w/A.T. (6.4) 9.0
V-6 (7.2) 10.2
V-8
w/M.T. (6.6) 9.4
w/A.T. (6.8) 9.6
w/A.C. add (.7) 7

(G) Rear Main Bearing Oil Seals, Renew

Four (2.9) 4.1
Six (1.6) 2.5
V-6
split lip (3.0) 4.3
full circle (8.5) *12.0
V-8 (1.6) 2.5
*w/A.C. add (.7) 7

DIESEL ENGINE

(P) Crankshaft and Main Bearings, Renew

Includes: R&R engine assembly.

All models (14.8) 21.0
w/A.C. add (.7) 7

(G) Rear Main Bearing Oil Seal, Renew

All models (2.9) 4.2

(G) Crankshaft Front Oil Seal, Renew

All models (2.0) 2.9

LABOR 16 CAMSHAFT & TIMING GEARS 16 LABOR

(Factory Time) Chilton Time

GASOLINE ENGINES

(G) Timing Cover Oil Seal, Renew

Four
150 eng (.9) 1.5
151 eng (.6) 1.0
Six (.9) 1.5
V-6 (.8) 1.4
V-8 (.9) 1.5
w/A.C. add (.3) 3

(G) Timing Cover and/or Gasket, Renew

Four
150 eng (1.2) 1.7
151 eng (.9) 1.3
Six (1.4) 2.0
V-6 (1.9) 2.7
V-8 (3.2) 4.5
w/A.C. add (.3) 3

(G) Timing Chain, Renew

Four
150 eng (1.5) 2.0
151 eng (1.3) 1.8
Six (1.7) 2.5
V-6 (2.2) 3.2
V-8 (3.5) 5.0
w/A.C. add (.3) 3

(G) Camshaft, Renew

Four (3.4) 4.8
Six (6.0) 8.5
V-6 (5.4) 7.7
V-8 (4.9) 7.1
w/A.C. add (.3) 3

DIESEL ENGINE

(G) Timing Belt Cover, R&R or Renew

All models (1.6) 2.3

(G) Timing Belt, Renew

All models (1.9) 2.7
Renew tensioner add (.1) 1

(G) Camshaft Front Oil Seal, Renew

All models (2.2) 3.1

(G) Camshaft, Renew

All models (2.5) 3.5

LABOR 17 ENGINE OILING SYSTEM 17 LABOR

(Factory Time) Chilton Time

(G) Oil Pan and/or Gasket, Renew

Cke/Wag/Comanche
All engs (2.3) 3.3
All other models
All engs (1.2) 1.7

(P) Pressure Test Engine Bearings (Pan Off)

All models 1.0

(G) Oil Pump, Renew

Cke/Wag/Comanche
All engs (2.4) 3.4
All other models
All engs (1.4) 1.9

(G) Oil Pump, R&R and Recondition

Cke/Wag/Comanche
All engs (2.7) 3.8
All other models
All engs (1.8) 2.6

(G) Oil Pressure Gauge (Dash), Renew

CJ/Scrambler (1.3) 1.7
Cherokee/Grand Wagoneer/
Truck (.8) 1.2
Cke/Wag/Comanche (.6) 1.0

(G) Oil Pressure Gauge (Engine), Renew

All models (.3) 4

(M) Oil Filter Element, Renew

All models (.2) 3

DIESEL ENGINE

(G) Oil Pan and/or Gasket, Renew

All models (2.5) 3.5

(P) Pressure Test Engine Bearings (Pan Off)

All models 1.0

(G) Oil Pump, Renew

All models (2.7) 3.8

(G) Oil Pump, R&R and Recondition

All models (3.2) 4.5

(M) Oil Filter Element, Renew

All models (.2) 3

LABOR 18 CLUTCH & FLYWHEEL 18 LABOR

(Factory Time) Chilton Time

(G) Clutch Pedal Free Play, Adjust

All models (.3) 4

(G) Clutch Master Cylinder, Renew

Includes: Bleed system.

All models (1.0) 1.4

(G) Clutch Slave Cylinder, Renew

Includes: Bleed system.

All models (.7) 1.1

(G) Clutch Reservoir, Renew

All models (.3) 5

(G) Clutch Assembly, Renew

Includes: R&R trans. Renew T.O. brg, clutch plate and disc. Make all necessary adjustments.

CJ/Scrambler (2.7) 3.7
Cherokee/Grand Wagoneer/
Truck (3.4) 4.7
Cke/Wag/Comanche
2 WD (1.9) 2.6
4 WD (2.9) 4.0
Diesel (3.0) 4.2
Renew f/wheel add (.3) 3
Renew ring gear add (.3) 3
Renew pilot bush add (.2) 2

LABOR 19 STANDARD TRANSMISSION 19 LABOR

(Factory Time) Chilton Time

JEEP

(G) Transmission & Transfer Case, Remove & Reinstall (As A Unit)

	Chilton Time
1982-83-3 spd	
exc below (2.3)	3.0
CJ series (1.8)	2.5
4 spd-exc below (1.9)	2.6
CJ series (1.6)	2.3
5 spd (1.3)	2.0
1984-86	
CJ series (2.0)	2.8
Cherokee-Wagoneer (2.7)	3.7
Renew front seal add	.3
Renew assy add	.6
w/Diesel eng add (.2)	.5

(G) Transmission, R&R and Recondition

Includes: Remove trans and transfer case as a unit, separate sections and overhaul transmission only.

	Chilton Time
1982-83-3 spd	
exc below (4.7)	6.5
CJ series (4.2)	6.0
4 spd-exc below (4.9)	6.7
CJ series (4.6)	6.5
5 spd (4.1)	6.0
1984-86	
CJ series	
T-4 (4.8)	6.7
T-5 (4.6)	6.4
Cherokee-Wagoneer	
T-4 (5.0)	7.0
T-5 (5.3)	7.4
AX-4 (4.8)	6.7
AX-5 (4.6)	6.4
w/Diesel eng add (.2)	.5

(G) Transmission, Recondition (Off Truck)

	Chilton Time
T-4 (2.8)	3.9
T-5 (2.6)	3.7
T-18A (2.3)	3.5
T-176 (2.3)	3.5
SR-4 (2.1)	3.5
AX-4 (2.1)	3.5
AX-5 (1.9)	3.0

(G) Speedometer Driven Gear, Renew

	Chilton Time
1982-86 (.3)	.5

TRANSFER CASE

MODEL 300

(G) Rear Bearing Cap and/or Gasket, Renew

	Chilton Time
All models (1.0)	1.2

(G) Transfer Case Bottom Cover and/or Gasket, Renew

	Chilton Time
All models (.8)	1.1

(G) Transfer Case Assy., R&R or Renew

	Chilton Time
All models (1.1)	1.9
Renew case assy. add (.3)	.5

(G) Transfer Case Assy., R&R and Recondition

	Chilton Time
All models (3.7)	4.9

MODEL 208 & 219

(G) Lockout Switch, Renew

	Chilton Time
All models (.4)	.6

(G) Output Shaft Flange, Renew (Front or Rear)

	Chilton Time
All models (.5)	.7
Renew seal add (.3)	.3

(G) Speedometer Driven Gear, Renew

	Chilton Time
All models (.4)	.4

(G) Transfer Case Assy., R&R or Renew

	Chilton Time
All models	
Six (1.3)	2.1
V-8 (.9)	1.7
Renew case assy. add (.3)	.5

(G) Transfer Case Assy., R&R and Recondition

Includes: Disassemble, clean and inspect all parts. Renew all internal component parts as required.

	Chilton Time
All models	
Six (4.3)	6.2
V-8 (3.9)	5.8

MODEL 229

(G) Transfer Case Vacuum Motor, Renew

	Chilton Time
All models (.4)	.6

(G) Vacuum Check Valve, Renew

	Chilton Time
All models (.3)	.4

(G) Transfer Case Assy., R&R or Renew

	Chilton Time
All models (1.4)	2.0
Renew assy. add (.3)	.5

(G) Transfer Case Assy., R&R and Recondition

	Chilton Time
All models (4.2)	5.9

(G) Speedometer Driven Gear, Renew

	Chilton Time
All models (.3)	.5

(G) Output Shaft Flange, R&R or Renew (Front or Rear)

	Chilton Time
All models (.6)	.8
Renew oil seal add (.1)	.2

MODEL 207

(G) Transfer Case Assy., R&R or Renew

	Chilton Time
All models (1.1)	1.5
Renew assy. add (.3)	.5

(G) Transfer Case Assy., R&R and Recondition

	Chilton Time
All models (2.8)	3.9

(G) Speedometer Driven Gear, Renew

	Chilton Time
All models (.3)	.5

(G) Output Shaft Flange, R&R or Renew (Front or Rear)

	Chilton Time
All models (.6)	.8
Renew oil seal add (.1)	.2

LABOR 21 SHIFT LINKAGE 21 LABOR

(G) Gearshift Lever, Renew

	Chilton Time
Cke/Wag/Comanche	
w/M.T. (.6)	.8
w/A.T. (.7)	.9
All other models	
w/M.T. (.6)	.8
w/A.T. (.4)	.6

(G) Transfer Case Shifter Assy., R&R or Renew

	Chilton Time
CJ/Scrambler (1.1)	1.6
All other models	
w/M.T. (1.1)	1.6
w/A.T. (.4)	.8

LABOR 25 U-JOINTS & DRIVESHAFT 25 LABOR

(G) Propeller Shaft, R&R or Renew

	Chilton Time
CJ/Scrambler	
front (.5)	.7
rear (.6)	.8
Cke/Wag/Comanche	
front (.6)	.8
rear (.4)	.6
All other models	
front (.7)	.9
rear (.6)	.8
Recond U-joint add	
single carden (.4)	.5
double joint (1.1)	1.5

JEEP–MODEL 727

ON CAR SERVICES

(G) Drain & Refill Unit
All models 8

(G) Oil Pressure Check
All models 6

(G) Check Unit For Oil Leaks
Includes: Clean and dry outside of case and run unit to determine point of leak.
All models 9

(G) Neutral Safety Switch, Renew
1982-86 (.3) 5

(G) Oil Cooler Lines, Renew
1982-86–one (.4) 6
both (.5) 8

(G) Extension Housing, R&R or Renew
CJ Series
1982-86 (1.1) 1.6
WAG-CKE-TRK
1982-86–Six (1.4) 1.9
V-8 (1.0) 1.5
Renew output shaft brg add (.1) 2

(G) Oil Pan Gasket, Renew
1982-86 (.5) 8

(G) Oil Filter, Renew
1982-86 (.6) 9

(G) Valve Body Assembly, Renew
Includes: R&R oil pan.
1982-86 (.7) 1.2

(P) Valve Body, R&R and Recondition
Includes: R&R oil pan and filter. Disassemble, clean, inspect, free all valves. Replace parts as required.
1982-86 (1.7) 2.8

(G) Low and Reverse Band, Adjust
Includes: R&R oil pan.
1982-86 (.6) 1.0

(G) Throttle Valve Lever Shaft Seal, Renew
Includes: R&R oil pan.
1982-86 (.6) 9

(G) Kickdown Servo, Renew or Recondition
Includes: R&R oil pan.
1982-86 (.9) 1.5

(G) Accumulator Piston, Renew or Recondition
Includes: R&R oil pan.
1982-86 (.6) 1.1

(G) Low and Reverse Servo, Renew or Recondition
Includes: R&R oil pan.
1982-86 (.8) 1.4

(G) Throttle and Regulator Valves, Adjust
Includes: R&R oil pan.
1982-86 (.6) 1.0

(G) Throttle Valve Linkage, Adjust
Includes: R&R oil pan.
1982-86 (.6) 1.0

(G) Kickdown Band, Adjust
Includes: R&R oil pan.
1982-86 (.6) 1.0

SERVICES REQUIRING R&R

(G) Transmission and Transfer Case, R&R or Renew
1982-86–Six (2.4) 3.9
V-8 (2.0) 3.5
Renew trans add (.2) 5

(P) Transmission and Converter, R&R and Recondition
Includes: Disassemble trans completely, including valve body. Clean and inspect all parts. Renew parts as required. Reassemble and test.
1982-86–Six (8.6) 11.9
V-8 (8.2) 11.5
Clean and pressure test converter, add 7

(G) Transmission Assembly, Reseal
Includes: R&R trans and renew all seals and gaskets.
1982-86–Six 5.9
V-8 .... 5.5

(G) Torque Converter, Renew
Includes: R&R trans and transfer case
1982-86–Six (2.6) 4.1
V-8 (2.2) 3.7

(G) Converter Drive Plate, Renew
Includes: R&R trans and transfer case.
1982-86–Six (2.6) 4.2
V-8 (2.2) 3.8

(G) Front Pump Assembly, Renew or Recondition
Includes: R&R trans and transfer case.
1982-86–Six (2.7) 4.5
V-8 (2.3) 4.1

(G) Front Pump Oil Seal, Renew
Includes: R&R trans and transfer case.
1982-86–Six (2.6) 4.2
V-8 (2.2) 3.8

JEEP–MODEL 904 & 999

ON CAR SERVICES

(G) Drain & Refill Unit
All models 8

(G) Oil Pressure Check
All models 6

(G) Check Unit For Oil Leaks
Includes: Clean and dry outside of case and run unit to determine point of leak.
All models 9

(G) Neutral Safety Switch, Renew
1982-86 (.3) 5

(G) Oil Cooler Lines, Renew
1982-86–one (.4) 6
both (.5) 8

(G) Extension Housing, R&R or Renew
CJ Series
1982-86 (1.1) 1.6
WAG-CKE-TRK
1982-86–Six (1.4) 1.9
V-8 (1.0) 1.5
Renew output shaft brg add (.1) 2

(G) Oil Pan Gasket, Renew
1982-86 (.5) 8

(G) Valve Body Assembly, Renew
Includes: R&R oil pan.
1982-86 (.7) 1.2

(P) Valve Body, R&R and Recondition
Includes: R&R oil pan and filter. Disassemble, clean, inspect, free all valves. Replace parts as required.
1982-86 (1.7) 2.8

(G) Low and Reverse Band, Adjust
Includes: R&R oil pan.
1982-86 (.6) 1.0

(G) Throttle Valve Lever Shaft Seal, Renew
Includes: R&R oil pan.
1982-86 (.6) 9

(G) Kickdown Servo, Renew or Recondition
Includes: R&R oil pan.
1982-86 (.9) 1.5

(G) Accumulator Piston, Renew or Recondition
Includes: R&R oil pan.
1982-86 (.6) 1.1

(G) Kickdown Band, Adjust
Includes: R&R oil pan.
1982-86 (.6) 1.0

(G) Low and Reverse Servo, Renew or Recondition
Includes: R&R oil pan.
1982-86 (.8) 1.4

(G) Throttle and Regulator Valves, Adjust
Includes: R&R oil pan.
1982-86 (.6) 1.0

SERVICES REQUIRING R&R

(G) Transmission and Transfer Case, R&R or Renew
Six–1982-86 (2.0) 3.5
V-8–1982-86 (2.4) 3.9
Renew trans add (.2) 5

(P) Transmission and Converter, R&R and Recondition
Includes: Disassemble trans completely, including valve body. Clean and inspect all parts. Renew all parts as required. Reassemble and test.
Six–1982-86 (7.8) 11.0
V-8–1982-86 (8.2) 11.5
Clean and pressure test converter, add 7

(G) Transmission Assembly, Reseal
Includes: R&R trans and renew all seals and gaskets.
Six–1982-86 .... 5.4
V-8–1982-86 .... 5.9

(G) Torque Converter, Renew
Includes: R&R trans and transfer case.
Six–1982-86 (2.2) 3.7
V-8–1982-86 (2.6) 3.9

(G) Converter Drive Plate, Renew
Includes: R&R trans and transfer case.
Six–1982-86 (2.2) 3.8
V-8–1982-86 (2.6) 4.0

(G) Front Pump Assembly, Renew or Recondition
Includes: R&R trans and transfer case.
Six–1982-86 (2.3) 4.1
V-8–1982-86 (2.7) 4.5

(G) Front Pump Oil Seal, Renew
Includes: R&R trans and transfer case.
Six–1982-86 (2.2) 3.8
V-8–1982-86 (2.6) 4.0

LABOR 26 REAR AXLE 26 LABOR

(Factory Time)	Chilton Time
(M) Differential, Drain & Refill	
All models	.6
(G) Inspection Cover Gasket, Renew or Reseal	
All models	.6
(G) Pinion Shaft Oil Seal, Renew	
All models (1.0)	1.2
(G) Axle Shaft Bearings, Renew	
CJ/Scrambler	
right side (1.8)	2.4
left side (1.4)	1.8
both sides (2.0)	2.7
All other models	
semi-float axle	
one side (1.0)	1.3
both sides (1.7)	2.3
full float axle	
each side (.4)	.6
(G) Axle Shaft Oil Seal, Renew (Outer)	
semi-float axle	
one side (.7)	.9
both sides (1.1)	1.5
full float axle	
each side (.4)	.6
(G) Axle Shaft Oil Seal, Renew (Inner & Outer)	
CJ/Scrambler	
right side (1.8)	2.4
left side (1.4)	1.8
both sides (2.0)	2.7
(G) Axle Shaft, Renew	
CJ/Scrambler	
right side (1.6)	2.2
left side (1.2)	1.6
both sides (1.7)	2.3
All other models	
semi-float axle	
one side (.5)	.8
both sides (.8)	1.2
full float axle	
one side (.3)	.5
both sides (.4)	.7
(G) Rear Axle Assy., R&R or Renew	
Cherokee/Grand Wagoneer/Truck (2.3)	3.2
All other models (3.1)	4.3
(P) Rear Axle Assembly, R&R and Recondition (Complete)	
All models (4.0)	5.5
(P) Differential Case, R&R and Recondition	
Includes: Renew side bearings, gears and thrust washers.	
All models (2.8)	3.9
(G) Rear Axle Housing Assy., Renew	
CJ/Scrambler (6.3)	8.7
All other models (5.7)	7.9

LABOR 27 REAR SUSPENSION 27 LABOR

(Factory Time)	Chilton Time
(G) Rear Springs, Renew	
Cke/Wag/Comanche	
one (.9)	1.3
both (1.5)	2.3
All other models	
one (.9)	1.3
both (1.8)	2.6
(G) Rear Spring Shackle, Renew (One)	
Cke/Wag/Comanche (.7)	1.0
(G) Rear Springs, R&R and Recondition	
CJ/Scrambler	
one (1.8)	2.4
both (3.1)	4.2
All other models	
one (1.3)	1.8
both (1.9)	2.6
(G) Rear Spring Center Bolt, Renew	
All models-one (.7)	1.0
(G) Rear Spring Eye Bushing, Renew	
Includes: Renew shackle and pivot bolt.	
All models-one side (.6)	.9
both sides (.7)	1.2
(G) Rear Shock Absorbers, Renew	
Cke/Wag/Comanche	
one (.2)	.4
both (.3)	.5
All other models	
one (.4)	.5
both (.5)	.7
(G) Rear Stabilizer Bar, Renew	
Cke/Wag/Comanche (.5)	.8

LABOR 28 AIR CONDITIONING 28 LABOR

Note: If more than one item requires replacement where evacuation and discharging the system is already included in the operation, deduct 1.0 hour for each additional item to the time listed.

(Factory Time)	Chilton Time
(G) Drain, Evacuate and Recharge System	
All models (.8)	1.3
(G) Refrigerant, Add (Partial Charge)	
All models (.5)	.8
(G) Compressor Drive Belt, Renew	
All models	
V-Belt (.3)	.4
Serpentine (.5)	.6
(G) Compressor Assembly, Renew	
Includes: Transfer parts as required. Evacuate and charge system.	
V-8 engs (2.0)	3.0
All other engs (1.0)	2.0
Recond comp add (1.8)	2.5
(G) Compressor Clutch and/or Pulley, Renew	
Does not include R&R compressor.	
All models (.4)	.6
(G) Condenser Assembly, Renew	
Includes: Evacuate and charge system.	
Cke/Wag/Comanche (1.8)	2.5
All other models (1.4)	2.0
(G) Expansion Valve, Renew	
Includes: Evacuate and charge system.	
All models (1.1)	1.7
(G) Evaporator Core, Renew	
Includes: Evacuate and charge system.	
CJ/Scrambler (1.6)	2.9
Cherokee/Grand Wagoneer/Truck (1.5)	2.7
Cke/Wag/Comanche (2.1)	3.9
(G) A.C. Control Assembly, Renew	
Cke/Wag/Comanche (.4)	.6
(G) Evaporator Fan Motor, Renew	
Does not include evacuate and charge A.C. system.	
CJ/Scrambler (.6)	1.0
All other models (.4)	.6
(G) Receiver Drier Assembly, Renew	
Includes: Evacuate and charge system.	
CJ/Scrambler (1.2)	1.7
Cherokee/Grand Wagoneer/Truck (1.4)	2.0
Cke/Wag/Comanche (1.8)	2.5
(G) A.C. Low Pressure Switch, Renew	
All models (.3)	.5
(G) Air Conditioning Hoses, Renew	
Includes: Evacuate and charge system.	
All models-one	1.7
each adtnl	.3

LABOR 30 HEAD AND PARKING LAMPS 30 LABOR

(Factory Time)	Chilton Time
(G) Aim Headlamps	
two	.4
four	.6
(M) Headlamp Sealed Beam Bulb, Renew	
All models-one	.3
each adtnl	.2
(M) Park and Turn Signal Lamp Lens or Bulb, Renew	
All models-one (.3)	.4
(M) Park and Turn Signal Lamp Assy., Renew	
All models-one (.4)	.5
(M) Tail Lamp Lens or Bulb, Renew	
All models-one (.3)	.4
(M) Tail Lamp Assembly, Renew	
Cherokee/Grand Wagoneer/Truck-one (.5)	.6
All other models-one (.4)	.5
(M) License Lamp Assembly, Renew	
All models-one (.3)	.4
(M) Side Marker Lamp Assembly, Renew	
All models-one (.3)	.4

LABOR 31 WINDSHIELD WIPER & SPEEDOMETER 31 LABOR

(Factory Time)	Chilton Time
(G) Windshield Wiper Motor, Renew	
Cke/Wag/Comanche (.4)	.6
All other models (.6)	.9
(G) Wiper Timer/Governor, Renew	
All models (.3)	.5
(G) Rear Window Wiper Motor, Renew	
Cke/Wag/Comanche (.3)	.5
(G) Wiper Linkage, Renew	
Cherokee/Grand Wagoneer/Truck (1.1)	1.7
CJ/Scrambler (.6)	.9
Cke/Wag/Comanche (.4)	.7
(G) Windshield Washer Pump, Renew	
Cke/Wag/Comanche (.2)	.3
All other models (.4)	.5
(G) Rear Window Washer Pump, Renew	
Cke/Wag/Comanche (.2)	.3
(G) Wiper Switch, Renew (Front or Rear)	
All models (.4)	.7
(G) Speedometer Head, R&R or Renew	
CJ/Scrambler (1.2)	1.8
Cherokee/Grand Wagoneer/Truck (.8)	1.2
Cke/Wag/Comanche (.6)	1.0
Reset odometer add	.2
(G) Speedometer Cable, Renew	
All models	
one or two piece cable and core (.4)	.7
one piece cable and core (.6)	1.0
(G) Radio, R&R	
All models (.7)	1.0
(G) Rear Window Defogger Switch, Renew	
All models (.4)	.6
(G) Liftgate Wiper Switch, Renew	
Cke/Wag/Comanche (.4)	.6

LABOR 32 LIGHT SWITCHES & WIRING 32 LABOR

(Factory Time)	Chilton Time
(G) Turn Signal Switch, Renew	
Cke/Wag/Comanche (.6)	1.0
All other models (.8)	1.1
(M) Turn Signal or Hazard Warning Flasher, Renew	
All models (.2)	.3
(G) Hazard Warning Switch, Renew	
All models (.8)	1.1
(G) Headlamp Dimmer Switch, Renew	
All models (.3)	.4
(G) Headlamp Switch, Renew	
All models (.4)	.6
(G) Stoplight Switch, Renew	
All models (.3)	.4
(G) Back-Up Lamp or Neutral Switch, Renew	
All models	
w/M.T. (.5)	.6
w/A.T. (.4)	.5
(G) Parking Brake Switch, Renew	
All models (.3)	.4
(G) Horn, Renew	
All models-one (.4)	.4
each adtnl	.2
(G) Horn Relay, Renew	
All models (.3)	.4

LABOR 34 CRUISE CONTROL 34 LABOR

(Factory Time)	Chilton Time
(G) Cruise Control Switch, Renew	
Cke/Wag/Comanche (.7)	1.1
All other models (.5)	.9
(G) Cruise Control Speed Sensor, Renew	
All models (.4)	.6
(G) Cruise Control Regulator, Renew	
Cke/Wag/Comanche (.3)	.4
All other models (.5)	.7
(G) Cruise Control Chain/Cable, Renew	
All models (.4)	.5
(G) Cruise Control Vacuum Bleed Switch, Renew	
All models (.3)	.5
(G) Cruise Control Servo, Renew	
All models (.5)	.7
(G) Cruise Control Brake Release Switch, Renew (Vacuum Dump)	
All models (.4)	.6
(G) Cruise Control Wiring Harness, Renew	
All models (.5)	.9

Mack Trucks

GROUP INDEX

ALPHABETICAL INDEX

LABOR 1 TUNE UP 1 LABOR

	(Factory Time)	Chilton Time
DIESEL ENGINE		
Compression Test		
Includes: R&R injectors and interfering parts. Attach compression gauge and test.		
Six		3.8
V-8		5.0
Engine Tune Up, Minor		
Includes: Test batteries and clean and tighten terminals. Check and adjust engine idle speed and throttle linkage. Change engine oil. Clean or renew oil, air, fuel and water filters. Tighten radiator hoses and manifold bolts. Check valve lash and adjust valves. R&R and test injectors. Road test.		
Does not include compression test or injection pump timing.		
Six		7.3
V-8		8.5
Engine Tune Up, Major		
Includes: Test batteries, clean end tighten terminals. Check and adjust engine idle speed and linkage. Adjust injector timing. Steam clean engine. Change engine oil. Clean or renew air, oil, fuel and water filters. Check and lubricate shutters. Clean injectors and fuel connections. Inspect for oil, water and fuel leaks. Drain sediment from fuel tanks. Tighten intake manifold, exhaust manifold, turbocharger and engine mounting bolts. Clean turbo charger impeller and diffuser and fuel pump screen. Adjust valves. Check crankshaft end clearance. Adjust and check fan belts. Road test.		
Does not include compression test.		
Six–exc below		10.7
MB series		11.3
V-8		13.2

LABOR 3 FUEL SYSTEM 3 LABOR

	(Factory Time)	Chilton Time
Injection Pump Timing, Adjust		
Six–exc below		3.0
MB series		3.4
V-8		4.0
Injection Pump, Renew		
Six–exc below		5.4
MB series		6.5
V-8		7.0
Injectors, Renew		
Six–one		.4
all		2.4
V-8–one		.4
all		3.2
Injector, R&R and Recondition		
each		1.3
Turbocharger, Renew		
Includes: Road test.		
Six		2.2
V-8		2.5
Turbocharger, R&R and Recondition		
Includes: Clean, inspect and renew parts as necessary. Road test.		
Six		6.0
V-8		6.5
Fuel Filter, Renew		
each		.4
Intake Manifold Gasket, Renew		
Six–exc below		3.5
MB & F series		2.9
V-8–one		1.9
both		2.5
Fuel Tank, Renew		
DM, U series		2.0
MB & F series		2.4
40 gal tank add		.9
50 gal tank add		1.2
60 gal tank add		1.5
70 gal tank add		1.6
100 gal tank add		2.1
Fuel Gauge (Tank), Renew		
All series		.5
Fuel Gauge (Dash), Renew		
DM, U series		1.5
MB series		1.9
F series		1.0

LABOR 4 ALTERNATOR AND REGULATOR 4 LABOR

	(Factory Time)	Chilton Time
Alternator or Generator Circuits, Test		
Includes: Test battery, regulator and generator or regulator output.		
All series		1.0
Test each adtnl battery add (.2)		.2
Alternator, Renew		
Six–exc below		2.2
END475, ENDT475		2.0
R series		2.0
V-8		1.8
Alternator, R&R and Recondition		
Six–exc below		4.7
END475, ENDT475		4.5
R series		4.5
V-8		4.3
Generator, Renew		
Six		2.3
V-8		2.0
Generator, R&R and Recondition		
Six		4.0
V-8		3.7
Voltage Regulator, Renew		
All series		.9

LABOR 5 STARTING SYSTEM 5 LABOR

	(Factory Time)	Chilton Time
Starter Draw Test (On Truck)		
All series		.5
Starter (Electric), Renew		
Six–exc below		2.6
F & R series		2.3
V-8		1.9
Starter (Electric), R&R and Recondition		
Six–exc below		5.0
F & R series		4.7
V-8		4.3
Starter Solenoid Switch, Renew		
All series		1.0
Air Starter, Renew		
exc below		2.0
F & R series		1.5
Air Starter Control, Renew		
All series		.9
Air Starter Reservoir, Renew		
All series		2.0
Battery Cables, Renew		
exc below		
left side		1.2
right side		.8
both sides		1.5
w/Series parallel switch		4.5
END 673, T673 T675		
left side		.8
right side		.6
both sides		1.0
DM & U series		
left side		2.4
right side		1.7
both sides		3.5

LABOR 6 BRAKE SYSTEM 6 LABOR

(Factory Time) Chilton Time

Brake Pedal Free Play, Adjust

All series	.5
Free up add	.3

Brakes, Adjust (Minor)

Includes: Check air line pressure, adjust brake chamber push rods and slack adjusters.

single axle	2.9
tandem axle	3.6

Brakes, Renew

Includes: R&R wheels and drums. Clean and adjust linkage. Renew oil seals and repack bearings. Adjust brakes and road test.

front-both	
500 series axle	5.3
600 series axle	6.0
rear-per axle	
All series	5.5

Air Compressor, R&R or Renew

Six	4.5
V-8	2.7

Treadle Valve, Renew

F, R, MB series	2.2
DM & U series	2.5

Relay Valve, Renew

All series	.7

Safety Valve, Renew

All series	.4

Quick Release Valve, Renew

Front or Rear	
All series	.7

Air Reservoir, Renew

All series	1.2

Front Wheel Limiting Valve or Switch, Renew

All series	.7

Low Pressure Indicator, Renew

All series	.5

Governor, Renew

All series	.8

Brake Chamber, Renew

All series-one	1.5

Slack Adjuster, R&R and Recondition

Includes: Adjustments.

All series	2.1

Brake Camshaft, Renew

Includes: R&R wheel, drum and shoes. Rebush bracket, adjustments.

All series	
front	2.6
rear	3.3

PARKING BRAKE

Parking Brake, Adjust

All series	1.3

Parking Brake Lever, Renew

All series	1.6

Parking Brake Shoe, Renew

All series	2.1

Parking Brake Drum, Renew

All series	1.6

Parking Brake, R&R and Recondition

Includes: Renew all required parts.

All series	4.7

Parking Brake Lever Pawl Rod and Spring, Renew

All series	1.8

Parking Brake Sector, Renew

All series	1.7

LABOR 7 COOLING SYSTEM 7 LABOR

(Factory Time) Chilton Time

Thermostat, Renew

Six-exc below	1.4
ENDT 675 (ESI)	2.0
V-8-one	1.4
both	2.1

Radiator Assembly, R&R or Renew

Includes: R&R all normal interfering parts.

DM, R & U series	
600 models	
Fiberglass hood	5.0
Sheet metal hood	5.7
700 models	
Fiberglass hood	6.4
Sheet metal hood	7.5
800 models	8.8
MB series	5.0
F & FL series	
Six-exc below	*3.2
CA38, CAS39, CAS40	8.5
V-8	*5.8
*w/A.C. add	.4

Radiator Hoses, Renew

All series-one	1.2
additional	.5

Water Pump, Renew

Six-exc below	1.9
MB & F series	2.3
V-8	2.9

Temperature Gauge (Dash), Renew

exc below	1.5
MB series	1.9
F series	.9

Temperature Gauge (Engine), Renew

All series	.7

Blower Motor Switch, Renew

DM, R, U series	.8
F series	1.5
MB series	1.1

Heater Switch, Renew

DM, U series	.9
F series	1.6
MB series	1.5

Heater Blower Motor, Renew

DM, R, U series	1.1
F series	1.9
MB series	2.0

Heater Core, R&R or Renew

Includes: Drain and refill cooling system.

DM, R, U series	1.8
F series	2.2
MB series	3.5

Heater Control Valve and Cables, Renew

Includes: Drain and refill cooling system.

DM, R, U series	1.5
F series	1.6
MB series	2.5

Shutterstat, Renew

Includes: Drain and refill radiator.

Six	1.8
V-8	.8

LABOR 8 EXHAUST SYSTEM 8 LABOR

(Factory Time) Chilton Time

Muffler, Renew

exc below-each	1.5
MB series-each	1.8

Exhaust Pipe, Renew

Six-exc below	1.4
MB series	1.7
V-8-one	1.5
both	2.5

Exhaust Manifold Gaskets, Renew

Six-exc below	2.7
w/Turbo	3.7
MB series	2.9
w/Turbo	4.2
V-8-one	1.1
both	1.8

LABOR 9 FRONT SUSPENSION 9 LABOR

(Factory Time) Chilton Time

Check and Correct Caster
500 series axle........ 5.5
600 series axle........ 6.5

Check and Correct Toe-In
All series........ 1.5

Front Wheel Bearings, Clean and Repack (Both Wheels)
All series........ 2.8

Front Wheel Bearings and Cups, Renew (One Wheel)
All series........ 2.0

Front Shock Absorber, Renew
one........ .4
both........ .6

Front Axle Assembly, Renew
Includes: R&R all normal interfering parts. Adjust caster, toe-in and wheel bearings. Road test.
500 series axle........ 13.9
600 series axle........ 15.5

Steering Knuckle, Renew
Includes: Adjust toe-in and road test.
500 series axle-left........ 5.3
right........ 4.9
both........ 9.7
600 series axle
left........ 6.4
right........ 6.0
both........ 10.8

King Pins and Bushings, Renew
Includes: Adjust toe-in and road test.
500 series axle........ 8.5
600 series axle........ 9.7

Front Spring, Renew
500 series axle........ 3.8
600 series axle........ 4.4

Front Spring, R&R and Recondition
500 series axle........ 5.0
600 series axle........ 5.6

LABOR 10 STEERING LINKAGE 10 LABOR

(Factory Time) Chilton Time

Tie Rod Ends, Renew
Includes: Toe-in adjustment.
one........ 1.5
two........ 2.1

Drag Link, Renew
Includes: Adjustment and check end play.
All series........ 1.9

Pitman Arm, Renew
Standard steering
exc below........ 1.0
MB series........ 1.8
Power steering
exc below........ 1.6
DM series........ 2.4

Cross Tube, Renew
Includes: Adjust toe-in.
All series........ 2.1

Steering Stops, Renew or Adjust
All series........ .9

LABOR 11 STEERING GEAR 11 LABOR

(Factory Time) Chilton Time

Steering Wheel, Renew
All series........ .9

Steering Gear, Adjust
Includes: Lubricate complete steering mechanism. Adjust worm shaft thrust, lever shaft, drag link and tie rod ends. Tighten steering gear housing to frame and pitman arm to shaft. Adjust front wheel bearings and toe-in.
exc below........ 3.0
DM series........ 4.5

Steering Gear, Renew
DM, U series........ 2.9
F series........ 2.5
MB series........ 5.8

Steering Gear, R&R and Recondition
Includes: Renew all necessary parts.
DM, U series........ 5.6
F series........ 5.2
MB series........ 8.5

Steering Column and Shaft, Renew
DM, U series........ 2.7
F series........ 2.4
MB series........ 3.3

Universal Joint, Renew (Shaft Removed)
All series........ .6

POWER STEERING

Power Steering Control Valve, Renew
All series........ 1.3

Power Steering Pump, Renew
exc below........ 3.5
w/ESI eng........ 2.5
MB series........ 2.1
w/ESI eng........ 2.8
w/END475 eng........ 2.2

Power Steering Gear, Renew
DM, U series........ 4.2
F series........ 3.3

Power Steering Gear, R&R and Recondition
DM, U series........ 7.5
F series........ 6.7

Power Steering Hoses, Renew
exc below........ 2.4
w/ESI eng........ 2.0
MB series........ 2.0
w/ESI eng........ 1.8

LABOR 12 CYLINDER HEAD & VALVE SYSTEM 12 LABOR

(Factory Time) Chilton Time

Cylinder Head Gasket, Renew
Includes: R&R all normal interfering parts. Adjust valves and road test.
Six-R series
one head........ 11.0
two heads........ 13.6
DM & U series
one head........ 12.5
two heads........ 15.3
F & MB series
one head........ 10.1
two heads........ 12.7
V-8-exc below
one head........ 10.4
all heads........ 23.4
F series
one head........ 10.6
all heads........ 24.5

Cylinder Head, Renew
Includes: R&R all normal interfering parts. Transfer all necessary parts. Reface valves and test springs. Adjust clearances. Road test.
Six-R series
one head........ 12.8
two heads........ 16.9
DM & U series
one head........ 14.5
two heads........ 18.6
F & MB series
one head........ 14.5
two heads........ 17.9
V-8-exc below
one head........ 12.3
all heads........ 28.2
F series
one head........ 12.4

LABOR 12 CYLINDER HEAD & VALVE SYSTEM 12 LABOR

(Factory Time) Chilton Time

	Chilton Time
all heads	29.5

Clean Carbon and Grind Valves

Includes: R&R all normal interfering parts. R&R cylinder head. Clean carbon. Resurface valves and reseat head. Clean and inspect lifters. Make all required adjustments and road test.

	Chilton Time
Six–R series	
one head	15.5
two heads	21.5
DM & U series	
one head	16.9
two heads	23.0
F & MB series	
one head	14.7
two heads	19.5
V-8–exc below	
one head	13.1
all heads	33.0
F series	
one head	13.3
all heads	34.5

Valve Cover Gaskets, Renew

	Chilton Time
Six	1.1
V-8	1.8

COMBINATIONS

Add to Valve Job

(Factory Time)	Chilton Time
VALVE GUIDES, RENEW	
Each	.6
VALVE SEAT INSERTS, RENEW	
One	.9
Each adtnl	.4
GRIND VALVES (HEAD REMOVED)	
Six-one head	3.3
Two heads	6.3
V-8-one head	2.0
All heads	7.7
ROCKER ARM ASSEMBLY, DISASSEMBLE, CLEAN AND REASSEMBLE	
Six	5.2
V-8	7.8
INJECTOR, RENEW	
Each	.4
INJECTOR, RECONDITION	
Each	.8
ADJUST GOVERNOR	
All series	1.0

(Factory Time) Chilton Time

Push Rods, Renew

Includes: Adjust valves and road test.

	Chilton Time
Six	3.7
V-8	6.2

Rocker Arm Assembly, R&R and Recondition

Includes: Adjust valves and road test.

	Chilton Time
Six	11.2
V-8	17.5

LABOR 13 ENGINE ASSEMBLY & MOUNTS 13 LABOR

(Factory Time) Chilton Time

Engine Assembly, R&R

Includes: R&R all normal interfering parts. Make all required adjustments and road test. Does not include transfer of any parts or equipment.

	Chilton Time
Six–R series	26.2
DM & U series	31.4
MB series	33.5
F series	
CA47, CAS48	23.4
CA38, CAS39, CAS40	28.3
V-8–exc below	35.9
F series	37.4

Engine Assembly, Recondition (In Chassis)

Includes: R&R all normal interfering parts. Clean carbon and grind valves. Test valve springs, valve guide wear and valve seat run-out. Renew pistons, pins and bushings. Renew cylinder liners. Align rods, plastigauge and install new main and rod bearings. Recondition oil pump. Adjust clearances. Set injection timing. Renew hoses, oil lines, filter elements etc., as necessary. Road test.

Does not include cylinder liner rebore, renew valve seats or guides.

	Chilton Time
Six–R series	40.4
DM & U series	42.7
MB series	38.5
F series	37.6
V-8–exc below	50.7
F series	52.6

Engine Assembly, Recondition (Engine Removed)

Includes: Complete disassembly and assembly of engine. Renew pistons, rings, pins and bushings. Plastigauge and install new main and rod bearings. Renew camshaft bearings. Align rods. Recondition auxiliary drive, turbocharger, water pump and engine oil pump. Renew timing gears as necessary. Renew cylinder liners. Check and adjust clearances and reset injection timing.

Does not include recondition fuel injection pump, injectors, air compressor or renew valve seats.

	Chilton Time
Six	60.0
V-8	75.0

LABOR 14 PISTONS, RINGS & BEARINGS 14 LABOR

COMBINATIONS

(Factory Time)	Chilton Time
VALVE GUIDES, RENEW	
Each	.6
VALVE SEAT INSERTS, RENEW	
One	.9
Additional	.4
GRIND VALVES (HEAD REMOVED)	
Six-one head	3.3
Two heads	6.3
V-8-one head	2.0
All heads	7.7
DEGLAZE CYLINDER WALLS	
Six	1.2
V-8	1.6
REMOVE CYLINDER TOP RIDGE	
Each	.2
ROCKER ARM ASSEMBLY, DISASSEMBLE, CLEAN AND REASSEMBLE	
Six	5.2
V-8	7.8
INJECTOR, RENEW	
Each	.4
INJECTOR, RECONDITION	
Each	.8
ADJUST GOVERNOR	
All series	1.0
MAIN BEARINGS, RENEW	
Six	4.0
V-8	6.0
OIL PUMP, RECONDITION	
All series	1.2

LABOR 14 PISTONS, RINGS, PINS & BEARINGS 14 LABOR

(Factory Time) Chilton Time

Rings, Pins, Rod and Main Bearings, Renew and Grind Valves

Includes: R&R all normal interfering parts. Remove cylinder top ridge and clean ring grooves. Plastigauge and install new main bearings. Fit pins and align rods. Clean carbon and grind valves. Reset injection timing and adjust valves. Road test.

Six–R series	47.5
DM & U series	49.5
MB series	46.5
F series	44.4
V-8–exc below	61.0
F series	58.9

Rings, Pins, Rod and Main Bearings, Renew

Includes: R&R all normal interfering parts. Remove cylinder top ridge and clean ring grooves. Plastigauge and install new main and rod bearings. Fit pins and align rods. Reset injection timing and adjust valves. Road test.

Six–R series	39.6
DM & U series	41.6
MB series	38.6
F series	36.5
V-8–exc below	51.3
F series	49.2

Rings, Renew

Includes: R&R all normal interfering parts. Remove cylinder top ridge and clean ring grooves. Reset injection timing and adjust valves. Road test.

Six–R series	32.2
DM & U series	34.3
MB series	31.8
F series	29.9
V-8–exc below	41.7
F series	39.8

Rod Bearings, Renew

Includes: R&R all normal interfering parts. Plastigauge and install new rod bearings. Road test.

Six–exc below	8.0
MB series	8.9
V-8	12.5

Pistons, Renew

Includes: R&R all normal interfering parts. Remove cylinder top ridge. Road test.

Six–R series	32.6
DM & U series	31.8
MB series	31.8
F series	29.9
V-8–exc below	41.7
F series	39.8

LABOR 15 CRANKSHAFT & DAMPER 15 LABOR

(Factory Time) Chilton Time

Crankshaft and Bearings, Renew

Includes: R&R all normal interfering parts. R&R engine assembly. Transfer all necessary parts and equipment. Plastigauge and install new main and rod bearings. Adjust valves and road test.

Six–R series	36.5
DM & U series	42.0
MB series	44.1
F series	
CA47, CAS48	34.0
CAS38, CAS39, CAS40	38.4
V-8–exc below	50.7
F series	52.6

Main Bearings, Renew

Includes: R&R all normal interfering parts. Plastigauge and install new main bearings. Road test.

Six–exc below	6.2
MB series	6.7
V-8	8.3

Rear Main Bearing Oil Seal, Renew (Transmission Removed)

Includes: R&R all normal interfering parts.

Six–exc below	4.9
MB series	5.2

Front Crankshaft Oil Seal, Renew

Includes: R&R all normal interfering parts.

Six–R, DM & U series	
600	7.7
700	9.9
800	11.4
MB series	9.9
F series	
CAS38, CAS39, CAS40	11.2
CA47, CAS48	6.6
V-8	10.1

Vibration Damper or Pulley, Renew

Includes: R&R all normal interfering parts.

Six–R, DM & U series	
600	6.7
700	7.9
800	10.4
MB series	7.7
F series	
CAS38, CAS39, CAS40	10.4
CA47, CAS48	5.5
V-8	9.0

LABOR 16 CAMSHAFT & TIMING GEARS 16 LABOR

(Factory Time) Chilton Time

Timing Gear Cover Gasket, Renew

Includes: R&R all normal interfering parts.

Six–R, DM & U series	
600	8.3
700	9.6
800	12.1
MB series	9.6
F series	
CAS38, CAS39, CAS40	9.2
CA47, CAS48	7.3
V-8	10.5

Timing Gears, Renew

Includes: R&R all normal interfering parts.

Six–R, DM & U series	
600	9.9
700	11.1
800	13.9
MB series	11.1
F series	
CAS38, CAS39, CAS40	13.6
CA47, CAS48	8.7
V-8	13.3

Camshaft, Renew

Includes: R&R all normal interfering parts. Check injection pump timing, adjust valves and road test.

Six–DM, R, U series	20.3
MB series	24.0
F series	21.6
V-8	30.2

Camshaft Bearings, Renew (Engine Removed and Disassembled)

All series	2.4

LABOR 17 ENGINE OILING SYSTEM 17 LABOR

(Factory Time) Chilton Time

Oil Pan Gasket, Renew

Six–exc below	2.5
MB series	3.5
V-8	2.9

Oil Pump, Renew

Six–exc below	3.3
MB series	4.2
V-8	3.7

Oil Pump, R&R and Recondition

Six–exc below	4.2
MB series	5.4
V-8	4.8

LABOR 17 ENGINE OILING SYSTEM 17 LABOR

(Factory Time)	Chilton Time
Pressure Test Engine Bearings (Pan Removed)	
All series	1.8
Oil Pressure Gauge (Dash), Renew	
exc below	1.7
MB series	2.3
F series	1.0
Oil Pressure Sending Unit, Renew	
All series	1.0
Oil Cooler, Renew	
exc below	2.5
MB series	4.0
F & R series	3.3
Oil Filters, Renew	
All series	1.0

LABOR 18 CLUTCH & FLYWHEEL 18 LABOR

(Factory Time)	Chilton Time
Clutch Pedal Free Play, Adjust	
All series	.9
Clutch Assembly, Renew	
DM, U series	11.4
Maxitorque	11.4
TRQ7220, TRT722/7220	12.2
TRD670, TRD7220	10.3
TRTX670	10.0
MB & F series	
Maxitorque	9.9
TRQ7220, TRT722/7220	10.2
TRD67/670	8.9
Fuller-DM, R, U series	12.4
F & MB series	11.7
Clutch Release Bearing, Renew	
DM, U series	
Maxitorque	10.4
TRQ7220, TRT722/7220	11.2
TRD670, TRD7220	9.3
TRTX670	9.0
MB & F series	
Maxitorque	8.9
TRQ7220, TRT722/7220	9.2
TRD67/670	7.9
Fuller-DM, R, U series	11.4
F & MB series	10.7
Flywheel, Renew (Transmission Removed)	
Six	2.3
V-8	3.7
Clutch Cable, Renew	
DM, U series	2.1
MB series	2.9
F series	1.5
Treadle Valve, Renew	
All series	1.2
Clutch Brake Valve, Renew	
All series	.5
Clutch Release Cylinder, Renew	
All series	.8
Clutch Air Reservoir or Chamber, Renew	
All series	1.2

LABOR 19 STANDARD TRANSMISSION 19 LABOR

(Factory Time)	Chilton Time
Transmission, R&R or Renew	
DM, U series	
Maxitorque	10.3
TRQ7220, TRT722/7220	10.9
TRD670, TRD7220	9.2
TRTX670	10.0
MB & F series	
Maxitorque	8.4
TRQ7220, TRT722/7220	9.0
TRD67/670	7.7
Fuller-DM, R, U series	11.0
MB & F series	10.4

Transmission, R&R and Recondition

Includes: Complete disassembly and assembly of transmission. Inspect and clean all components. Renew parts, gaskets and seals as necessary. Make all required adjustments. Road test.

(Factory Time)	Chilton Time
DM, U series	
TRL-107, TRL-1078	26.7
TRL-1076	26.4
TRDXL-107	30.3
TRDXL-1070, TRDXL-1071	28.9
TRTX670	33.9
TRTD722	26.5
TRD7220	29.2
TRQ7220	38.6
TRT722/7220	34.7
MB & F series	
TRL107, TRL1078	24.9
TRL-1076	24.4
TRDXL-107	28.1
TRDXL-1070, TRDXL-1071	27.0
TRXL-1070, TRXL-1071	29.3
TRD67	30.5
TRQ7220	36.7
TRT722/7220	34.0
Fuller-DM, R, U series	29.3
MB & F series	28.7

LABOR 21 SHIFT LINKAGE 21 LABOR

(Factory Time)	Chilton Time
Shift Lever, Renew (One)	
DM, U series	
MB series	.6
F series	.7
Shift Linkage, Renew	
MB & F series	.6
Shift Universal Joint, Renew (One)	
All series	.6
Shift Tower Bracket, Renew	
MB series	3.0
F series	2.5

LABOR 25 U-JOINTS & DRIVESHAFT 25 LABOR

Universal Joint, Renew (Drive Shaft Removed)	
each	.6
Drive Shaft, R&R or Renew	
single	2.3
front	3.5
rear	2.3
inter-axle	2.3
Stub Shaft, Renew	
each	1.7
Drive Shaft Yoke, Renew	
each	2.6
Center Bearing, Renew	
All series	3.5

LABOR 26 REAR AXLE 26 LABOR

(Factory Time) Chilton Time

Axle Shaft, Renew
one .8

Rear Wheel Bearings, Renew (One Wheel)
All series 2.5

Rear Wheel Oil Seal, Renew (One Wheel)
All series 1.4

Check Tandem Drive Line Alignment
Includes: Road test.
All series 1.6

Tandem Drive Line Alignment, Check and Adjust
Includes: Alignment of engine, transmission, drive shafts and both axles. Road test.
All series 5.7

Differential Carrier Assembly, R&R or Renew
exc below 7.2
CRD92, 95, 112 7.6

Differential Carrier Assembly, R&R and Recondition
Includes: Drain and refill unit. R&R all normal interfering parts. Disassemble and assemble complete unit. Inspect, clean, renew or recondition all components. Road test.
exc below 22.0
CRD92, 95, 112 25.3

Rear Axle Housing, Renew
single axles 16.2
tandem axles
exc below-front 23.6
rear 21.4
both 39.3
56 series
front 21.5
rear 19.4
both 38.9
57 series
front 22.0
rear 20.0
both 40.0
75 series
front 22.4
rear 18.9
both 37.9

Inter-Axle Power Divider, Renew
All series 5.0

Inter-Axle Power Divider Lockout Fork and Clutch, Renew
All series 2.8

Inter-Axle Power Divider Lockout, Renew
All series 6.3

Axle Shift Assembly, Renew
All series .6

Axle Shift Assembly, R&R and Recondition
All series 1.6

Axle Shift Motor, Renew
All series 1.2

LABOR 27 REAR SUSPENSION 27 LABOR

(Factory Time) Chilton Time

Rear Spring, Renew (One)
single axles 3.5
tandem axles
exc below 6.7
56 series 5.5
57 series 6.3
75 series 5.0

Rear Spring Leaf, Renew (One) (Spring Removed)
exc below 2.1
59, 68 series 3.2

Rear Spring Bushing, Renew (One Spring)
exc below 4.2
56 series 3.8
75 series 2.2

Walking Beam, Renew
one 4.0
two 7.5

LABOR 28 AIR CONDITIONING 28 LABOR

(Factory Time) Chilton Time

Compressor Assembly, Renew
Includes: R&R clutch assy., suction and discharge valves.
All models 2.3
Add: Recharge system 1.0

Clutch Assembly Only, Renew
All models 1.5

LABOR 30 HEAD AND PARKING LAMPS 30 LABOR

(Factory Time) Chilton Time

Aim Headlamps
All series .8

Headlamp Sealed Beam Bulb, Renew
MB series 1.0
All other series 1.4

Tail and Stop Lamp Assy., Renew
All series .5

Marker Light Assembly, Renew
All series .7

Back-Up Light Assy., Renew
All series .6

Turn Signal Lamp Assy., Renew
F, MB series .9
DM, U series 1.1

LABOR 31 WINDSHIELD WIPER & SPEEDOMETER 31 LABOR

(Factory Time) Chilton Time

Speedometer Head, R&R or Renew
DM, U series 2.0
F series 2.1
MB series 2.4

Speedometer Cable, Renew
DM, U series 1.9
F series 2.3
MB series 2.2

Speedometer Pencil Gear, Renew
All series .6

Tachometer, R&R or Renew
DM, U series 2.0

LABOR 31 WINDSHIELD WIPER & SPEEDOMETER 31 LABOR

	(Factory Time)	Chilton Time
F series		2.1
MB series		2.4
Tachometer Cable, Renew		
DM, U series		1.2
MB series		2.1
Tachometer Drive, Renew		
All series-Six		.6
Windshield Wiper Motor, Renew		
DM, U series		1.5
F series		
left		1.5
right		1.7
MB series		1.4
Wiper Control Valve, Renew		
F series		2.2
All other series		1.8
Windshield Washer Control, Renew		
All series		.8
Windshield Washer Pump, Renew		
All series		1.0

LABOR 32 LIGHT SWITCHES & WIRING 32 LABOR

	(Factory Time)	Chilton Time
Headlamp Switch, Renew		
DM, U series		.7
F series		.9
MB series		1.1
Headlamp Dimmer Switch, Renew		
All series		.6
Back-Up Light Switch, Renew		
All series		.8
Marker Light Switch, Renew		
All series		.7
Ignition Switch, Renew		
DM, U series		.7
F series		.8
MB series		.9
Horns, Renew		
Electric		.7
Air		1.5
Turn Signal Switch, Renew		
All series		1.0
Turn Signal or Hazard Flasher, Renew		
All series		.4

GENERAL CONVERSION TABLE

Multiply By	To Convert	To	
		Length	—
2.54	Inches	Centimeters	.3937
25.4	Inches	Millimeters	.03937
30.48	Feet	Centimeters	.0328
.304	Feet	Meters	3.28
.914	Yards	Meters	1.094
1.609	Miles	Kilometers	.621
		Volume	
.473	Pints	Liters	2.11
.946	Quarts	Liters	1.06
3.785	Gallons	Liters	.264
.016	Cubic inches	Liters	61.02
16.39	Cubic inches	Cubic cms.	.061
28.3	Cubic feet	Liters	.0353
		Mass (Weight)	
28.35	Ounces	Grams	.035
.4536	Pounds	Kilograms	2.20
		Area	
.645	Square inches	Square cms.	.155
.836	Square yds.	Square meters	1.196
		Force	
4.448	Pounds	Newtons	.225
.138	Ft./lbs.	Kilogram/meters	7.23
1.36	Ft./lbs.	Newton-meters	.737
.112	In./lbs.	Newton-meters	8.844
		Pressure	
.068	Psi	Atmospheres	14.7
6.89	Psi	Kilopascals	.145
		Other	
1.104	Horsepower (DIN)	Horsepower (SAE)	.9861
.746	Horsepower (SAE)	Kilowatts (KW)	1.34
1.60	Mph	Km/h	.625
.425	Mpg	Km/1	2.35
—	**To obtain**	**From**	**Multiply by**

TAP DRILL SIZES

NATIONAL COARSE OR U.S.S.						NATIONAL FINE OR S.A.E.					
Screw & Tap Size	Threads Per Inch	Use Drill Number	Screw & Tap Size	Threads Per Inch	Use Drill Number	Screw & Tap Size	Threads Per Inch	Use Drill Number	Screw & Tap Size	Threads Per Inch	Use Drill Number
No. 5	40	39	1/2	13	27/64	No. 5	44	37	1/2	20	29/64
No. 6	32	36	9/16	12	31/64	No. 6	40	33	9/16	18	33/64
No. 8	32	29	5/8	11	17/32	No. 8	36	29	5/8	18	37/64
No. 10	24	25	3/4	10	21/32	No. 10	32	21	3/4	16	11/16
No. 12	24	17	7/8	9	49/64	No. 12	28	15	7/8	14	13/16
1/4	20	8	1	8	7/8	1/4	28	3	1 1/8	12	1 3/64
5/16	18	F	1 1/8	7	63/64	5/16	24	1	1 1/4	12	1 11/64
3/8	16	5/16	1 1/4	7	1 7/64	3/8	24	Q	1 1/2	12	1 27/64
7/16	14	U	1 1/2	6	1 11/32	7/16	20	W			

BRAKE SYSTEM OPERATIONS

Resurface Disc Brake Rotor .... each .9

Resurface Brake Drums:
- Pass car and Lt. trucks .... each .5
- Heavy Truck up to 16½" dia. .... per in. .2
- Over 16½" dia. .... per in. .3

Remove Hub and Press into New Drum .... each .5

Press in New Hub and True-up Drum .... each .6

Reline Brake Shoes (Riveted):
- Pass cars & Light trucks .... each .1
- Heavy trucks to 3¼" dia. .... each .2
- over 3¼" dia. .... each .3

Cam Grind Brake Shoes .... each .2

Emergency Brake Bands Install:
- Light Trucks .... each .4
- Med. & H.D. Trucks .... each .6

FRONT SUSPENSION OPERATIONS

Fit King Bolts and Install Bushings:
- Up to 1" dia. .... pair .6
- Over 1" to 1⅛" dia. .... pair .8
- Over 1⅛" dia. .... pair 1.0

Fit King Bolts and Install Bushings:
- Volkswagen .... pair 1.3
- Fiat & M.G. (Stepped) .... pair 1.3
- Mercedes Benz .... pair 1.8
- Volvo .... pair 1.8

Tapered Spindles .... pair 2.0

CYLINDER HEAD & VALVE OPERATIONS

Resurface (Grind) Cylinder Head:
- Pass cars & trucks—4 cyl 1.0
- 6 cyl 1.5
- V8—each 1.0
- Diesel Engines .... (Time Quote)
- Grinding over .030 add .... per cyl. .2
- Grinding to Specific Size Request, add .... per cyl. .2

Special Tool Cut Volkswagen Head—Per Cyl 2

Overhaul Cylinder Head:

Includes: Disassemble, clean, reface valves, reseat head, grinding valves to seats, reassemble ready for installation.
- Pass car engines. 4 cyl. 1.6
- 6 cyl 2.3
- V8 .... each 1.6
- F-heads .... each 1.2
- Volkswagen .... each 1.2
- H.D. truck engines, 6 cyl 2.8
- V6 .... each 1.6
- V8 .... each 1.8
- All Diesel engines .... (Time Quote)

NOTE: EXTRA CHARGE TO BE ADDED FOR RESEATING STELLITE VALVE SEATS OR REFACING STELLITE VALVES.

Cylinder Head Clean and Degrease
- Four cyl .... each .4
- Six cyl .... each .5
- V6 .... pair .6
- V8 .... pair .8

Heli Coil, Install .... one 1.0
- Additional .... each .6

VALVE RESEATING

(Includes: Cleaning Valve Ports.)

Grind 1 or 2 Iron or Steel Seats:
- Up to 2 7/16" ID. .... each .4

Grind 3 or More Seats, Add .... each .1

Grind 1 or 2 Iron or Steel Seats:
- Over 2 7/16" ID. .... each .5

Grind 3 or More Seats, Add .... each .2

Grind One Stellite Seat .... each .6

Grind 2 or More Stellite Seats, Add .... each .3

Grind All Import Car Seats .... each .7

Note: Service charge to shop add 7

VALVE GUIDE REAMING

Valve Guides, Ream for Oversize Stems
- Pass cars and Lt. trucks .... One .1
  - Eight .6
  - Twelve .8
  - Sixteen .9
- Med. and H.D. Trucks .... each .2

Valve Guides, Knurl
- Each 3

Valve Guides, Bronze Wall
- Each 6

VALVE SEAT RINGS

Install Steel or Cast Iron Valve Seat Rings
- 1 seat up to 2" ID .... each .8
- Additional seats, add .... each .5
- Complete sets .... each .4
- Seats over 2" ID .... (Special Quote)

NOTE: If Stellite seat rings are installed add charges for grinding.

VALVE ROCKER ARMS AND STUDS

Reface Valve Rocker Arms .... each .1

Remove and Replace One Stud (Drill) 8
- 4 or more studs (drill) addtnl, add .... each .4

Remove and Replace One Stud (Pull) 4
- 4 or more studs (pull) addtnl, add .... each .2

VALVE REFACING

(Includes: Cleaning Valves.)

Reface Valves up to ⅜" stem .... each .1
- Over ⅜" stem .... each .2

Reface Stellite Valves .... each .3

Reface Valves over ½" Stem .... (Special Quote)

Reface Valve Tappets .... each .1

ENGINE BLOCK OPERATIONS

RESURFACE ENGINE BLOCK

- 4 cyl 2.0
- 6 cyl 3.0
- V8-each side 2.0

REBORING CYLINDERS:

Note: Boring blocks to customers specifications, or blocks with hard sleeves, add additional charges:

Passenger Car & Lt. Truck .... one 2.0
- Additional cylinders .... each 1.0

Med. and H.D. Trucks up to 4½" Cyl .... one 2.5
- Additional cylinders .... each 1.5

Over 5" Cylinder .... (Special Quote)

HONING CYLINDERS

Hone or Deglaze Cylinders	per cyl	.2
Remove Cylinder Ridge	per cyl	.2

CYLINDER SLEEVES, INSTALL

(Includes Finishing to any oversize required.)

Pass Cars & Lt. Trucks	one	2.8
2 or 3 sleeves	per cyl	2.5
4 or more sleeves	per cyl	2.1
Angle Block	one	3.8
2 or 3 sleeves	per cyl	3.1
4 or more sleeves	per cyl	2.3
Trucks to 5″ Dia	One	3.2
2 or 3 sleeves	per cyl	3.1
4 or more sleeves	per cyl	2.3
Sleeves over 5″ Dia		(Special Quote)

Note: Engine in chassis and extra charge.

ENGINE BLOCK CLEAN & DEGREASE OR STEAM CLEAN

Small blocks	1.9
Large blocks	2.4

PISTONS, RINGS, PINS & BEARINGS OPERATIONS

Fit Pins

Includes: Disassembly, hone, fitting, assembly and align rod.

	per rod	.3
Align Rods	each	.1
Clean Piston & Install Rings	each	.2
Grind Piston:		
Pass cars & lt. trucks	each	.4
Med. & H.D. trucks	each	.5
Regroove Piston Top Ring Land		
Pass cars & lt. trucks	each	.3
Med. & H.D. trucks	each	.4
Expand or Knurl Pistons	each	.3

CRANKSHAFT OPERATIONS

(Shaft Removed)

Crankshaft Grind (Connecting Rod Throws)

1 con. rod throw		.8
2 con. rod throws	both	1.2
3. con. rod throws	All	1.6
4 con. rod throws	All	1.8
6 con. rod throws	All	2.0
8 con. rod throws	All	2.8

Crankshaft Grind (Main Bearing Throws)

2 main brg. throws	both	1.2
3 main brg. throws	All	1.8
4 main brg. throws	All	2.0
5 main brg. throws	All	2.2
6 main brg. throws	All	2.4
7 main brg. throws	All	2.6

Crankshaft Grind (Connecting Rod & Main Bearing Throws)

4 con. rod and 2 main brg. throws	2.5
4 con. rod and 3 main brg. throws	3.2
4 con. rod and 4 main brg. throws	3.4
4 con. rod and 5 main brg. throws	3.6
6 con. rod and 3 main brg. throws	3.2
6 con. rod and 4 main brg. throws	3.4
6 con. rod and 7 main brg. throws	4.4
8 con. rod and 4 main brg. throws	4.2
8 con. rod and 5 main brg. throws	4.9

(in Chassis)

Rod Journals Grind

Pass car & lt. truck	one	4.0
Additional journals	each	2.0
Med. & H.D. trucks	one	5.0
Additional journals	each	2.5
Throws over 2½″ dia.		(Special Quote)

Crankshaft Micro Finish

Pass car & lt. truck	1.2
Med. & H.D. trucks	2.0

CAMSHAFT AND GEAR OPERATIONS

Camshaft Gear, Press off and Renew	.5
Camshaft Bearings, Renew and Align Bore	
1 or 2 Bearings	2.0
3 Bearings	2.3
4 Bearings	2.7
5 Bearings	3.1
6 Bearings	3.8
7 Bearings	4.6

CLUTCH AND FLYWHEEL OPERATIONS

Adjust Clutch Pressure Plate Levers	(Finger Type)	.6
	(Diaphragm Type)	.7
Clutch Disc Facings, Install		.5
Recondition Clutch Pressure Plate	(Finger Type)	1.2
	(Diaphragm Type)	1.5
Resurface clutch pressure plate, add		.6
Flywheel, Reface (Grind)		
Flat up to 13″		1.2
14″		1.4
15″ to 17″		2.3
Concave-stepped up to 11″		1.4
12″ & 13″		2.0
14″		2.2
15″ to 17″		2.4
Flywheel Ring Gear, Renew		
Shrink		.7
Weld		1.1
Machine		2.0

REAR AXLE OPERATIONS

Rear Axle Bearings, Press off and Renew		
All exec below	each	.4
Chrysler products	each	.5
Pinion Shaft Rear Bearing Press off And Renew	each	.4

MAGNAFLUX OPERATIONS

Cylinder Heads		
Flat head - 4 cyl	each	1.5
6 cyl.	each	1.7
V8	each	1.5
O.H.V. - 4 cyl	each	1.8
6 cyl	each	2.0
V8	each	1.8
Engine Blocks		
4 cyl		2.0
6 cyl		2.5
V8		3.0
Camshaft caps add		1.0
Crankshafts		
4 cyl		1.5
6 cyl		1.7
V8		2.0

Chilton's LABOR CALCULATOR

For dollar rates ending with 50 cents or 1.00 add to the appropriate rate column.

TIME	.50 per hr.	$1.00 per hr.	$10.00 per hr.	$12.00 per hr.	$14.00 per hr.	$16.00 per hr.	$18.00 per hr.	$20.00 per hr.	$22.00 per hr.	$24.00 per hr.	$26.00 per hr.	$28.00 per hr.	$30.00 per hr.	$32.00 per hr.	$34.00 per hr.	$36.00 per hr.	$38.00 per hr.	$40.00 per hr.	$42.00 per hr.	$44.00 per hr.	$46.00 per hr.	$48.00 per hr.	$50.00 per hr.	$55.00 per hr.
.1	.05	.10	$1.00	$1.20	$1.40	$1.60	$1.80	$2.00	$2.20	$2.40	$2.60	$2.80	$3.00	$3.20	$3.40	$3.60	$3.80	$4.00	$4.20	$4.40	$4.60	$4.80	$5.00	$5.50
.2	.10	.20	2.00	2.40	2.80	3.20	3.60	4.00	4.40	4.80	5.20	5.60	6.00	6.40	6.80	7.20	7.60	8.00	8.40	8.80	9.20	9.60	10.00	11.00
.3	.15	.30	3.00	3.60	4.20	4.80	5.40	6.00	6.60	7.20	7.80	8.40	9.00	9.60	10.20	10.80	11.40	12.00	12.60	13.20	13.80	14.40	15.00	16.50
.4	.20	.40	4.00	4.80	5.60	6.40	7.20	8.00	8.80	9.60	10.40	11.20	12.00	12.80	13.60	14.40	15.20	16.00	16.80	17.60	18.40	19.20	20.00	22.00
.5	.25	.50	5.00	6.00	7.00	8.00	9.00	10.00	11.00	12.00	13.00	14.00	15.00	16.00	17.00	18.00	19.00	20.00	21.00	22.00	23.00	24.00	25.00	27.50
.6	.30	.60	6.00	7.20	8.40	9.60	10.80	12.00	13.20	14.40	15.60	16.80	18.00	19.20	20.40	21.60	22.80	24.00	25.20	26.40	27.60	28.80	30.00	33.00
.7	.35	.70	7.00	8.40	9.80	11.20	12.60	14.00	15.40	16.80	18.20	19.60	21.00	22.40	23.80	25.20	26.60	28.00	29.40	30.80	32.20	33.60	35.00	38.50
.8	.40	.80	8.00	9.60	11.20	12.80	14.40	16.00	17.60	19.20	20.80	22.40	24.00	25.60	27.20	28.80	30.40	32.00	33.60	35.20	36.80	38.40	40.00	44.00
.9	.45	.90	9.00	10.80	12.60	14.40	16.20	18.00	19.80	21.60	23.40	25.20	27.00	28.80	30.60	32.40	34.20	36.00	37.80	39.60	41.40	43.20	45.00	49.50
1.0	.50	1.00	10.00	12.00	14.00	16.00	18.00	20.00	22.00	24.00	26.00	28.00	30.00	32.00	34.00	36.00	38.00	40.00	42.00	44.00	46.00	48.00	50.00	55.00
1.1	.55	1.10	11.00	13.20	15.40	17.60	19.80	22.00	24.20	26.40	28.60	30.80	33.00	35.20	37.40	39.60	41.80	44.00	46.20	48.40	50.60	52.80	55.00	60.50
1.2	.60	1.20	12.00	14.40	16.80	19.20	21.60	24.00	26.40	28.80	31.20	33.60	36.00	38.40	40.80	43.20	45.60	48.00	50.40	52.80	55.20	57.60	60.00	66.00
1.3	.65	1.30	13.00	15.60	18.20	20.80	23.40	26.00	28.60	31.20	33.80	36.40	39.00	41.60	44.20	46.80	49.40	52.00	54.60	57.20	59.80	62.40	65.00	71.50
1.4	.70	1.40	14.00	16.80	19.60	22.40	25.20	28.00	30.80	33.60	36.40	39.20	42.00	44.80	47.60	50.40	53.20	56.00	58.80	61.60	64.40	67.20	70.00	77.00
1.5	.75	1.50	15.00	18.00	21.00	24.00	27.00	30.00	33.00	36.00	39.00	42.00	45.00	48.00	51.00	54.00	57.00	60.00	63.00	66.00	69.00	72.00	75.00	82.50
1.6	.80	1.60	16.00	19.20	22.40	25.60	28.80	32.00	35.20	38.40	41.60	44.80	48.00	51.20	54.40	57.60	60.80	64.00	67.20	70.40	73.60	76.80	80.00	88.00
1.7	.85	1.70	17.00	20.40	23.80	27.20	30.60	34.00	37.40	40.80	44.20	47.60	51.00	54.40	57.80	61.20	64.60	68.00	71.40	74.80	78.20	81.60	85.00	93.50
1.8	.90	1.80	18.00	21.60	25.20	28.80	32.40	36.00	39.60	43.20	46.80	50.40	54.00	57.60	61.20	64.80	68.40	72.00	75.60	79.20	82.80	86.40	90.00	99.00
1.9	.95	1.90	19.00	22.80	26.60	30.40	34.20	38.00	41.80	45.60	49.40	53.20	57.00	60.80	64.60	68.40	72.20	76.00	79.80	83.60	87.40	91.20	95.00	104.50
2.0	1.00	2.00	20.00	24.00	28.00	32.00	36.00	40.00	44.00	48.00	52.00	56.00	60.00	64.00	68.00	72.00	76.00	80.00	84.00	88.00	92.00	96.00	100.00	110.00
2.1	1.05	2.10	21.00	25.20	29.40	33.60	37.80	42.00	46.20	50.40	54.60	58.80	63.00	67.20	71.40	75.60	79.80	84.00	88.20	92.40	96.60	100.80	105.00	115.50
2.2	1.10	2.20	22.00	26.40	30.80	35.20	39.60	44.00	48.40	52.80	57.20	61.60	66.00	70.40	74.80	79.20	83.60	88.00	92.40	96.80	101.20	105.60	110.00	121.00
2.3	1.15	2.30	23.00	27.60	32.20	36.80	41.40	46.00	50.60	55.20	59.80	64.40	69.00	73.60	78.20	82.80	87.40	92.00	96.60	101.20	105.80	110.40	115.00	126.50
2.4	1.20	2.40	24.00	28.80	33.60	38.40	43.20	48.00	52.80	57.60	62.40	67.20	72.00	76.80	81.60	86.40	91.20	96.00	100.80	105.60	110.40	115.20	120.00	132.00
2.5	1.25	2.50	25.00	30.00	35.00	40.00	45.00	50.00	55.00	60.00	65.00	70.00	75.00	80.00	85.00	90.00	95.00	100.00	105.00	110.00	115.00	120.00	125.00	137.50
2.6	1.30	2.60	26.00	31.20	36.40	41.60	46.80	52.00	57.20	62.40	67.60	72.80	78.00	83.20	88.40	93.60	98.80	104.00	109.20	114.40	119.60	124.80	130.00	143.00
2.7	1.35	2.70	27.00	32.40	37.80	43.20	48.60	54.00	59.40	64.80	70.20	75.60	81.00	86.40	91.80	97.20	102.60	108.00	113.40	118.80	124.20	129.60	135.00	148.50
2.8	1.40	2.80	28.00	33.60	39.20	44.80	50.40	56.00	61.60	67.20	72.80	78.40	84.00	89.60	95.20	100.80	106.40	112.00	117.60	123.20	128.80	134.40	140.00	154.00
2.9	1.45	2.90	29.00	34.80	40.60	46.40	52.20	58.00	63.80	69.60	75.40	81.20	87.00	92.80	98.60	104.40	110.20	116.00	121.80	127.60	133.40	139.20	145.00	159.50
3.0	1.50	3.00	30.00	36.00	42.00	48.00	54.00	60.00	66.00	72.00	78.00	84.00	90.00	96.00	102.00	108.00	114.00	120.00	126.00	132.00	138.00	144.00	150.00	165.00
3.1	1.55	3.10	31.00	37.20	43.40	49.60	55.80	62.00	68.20	74.40	80.60	86.80	93.00	99.20	105.40	111.60	117.80	124.00	130.20	136.40	142.60	148.80	155.00	170.50
3.2	1.60	3.20	32.00	38.40	44.80	51.20	57.60	64.00	70.40	76.80	83.20	89.60	96.00	102.40	108.80	115.20	121.60	128.00	134.40	140.80	147.20	153.60	160.00	176.00
3.3	1.65	3.30	33.00	39.60	46.20	52.80	59.40	66.00	72.60	79.20	85.80	92.40	99.00	105.60	112.20	118.80	125.40	132.00	138.60	145.20	151.80	158.40	165.00	181.50
3.4	1.70	3.40	34.00	40.80	47.60	54.40	61.20	68.00	74.80	81.60	88.40	95.20	102.00	108.80	115.60	122.40	129.20	136.00	142.80	149.60	156.40	163.20	170.00	187.00
3.5	1.75	3.50	35.00	42.00	49.00	56.00	63.00	70.00	77.00	84.00	91.00	98.00	105.00	112.00	119.00	126.00	133.00	140.00	147.00	154.00	161.00	168.00	175.00	192.50
3.6	1.80	3.60	36.00	43.20	50.40	57.60	64.80	72.00	79.20	86.40	93.60	100.80	108.00	115.20	122.40	129.60	136.80	144.00	151.20	158.40	165.60	172.80	180.00	198.00
3.7	1.85	3.70	37.00	44.40	51.80	59.20	66.60	74.00	81.40	88.80	96.20	103.60	111.00	118.40	125.80	133.20	140.60	148.00	155.40	162.80	170.20	177.60	185.00	203.50
3.8	1.90	3.80	38.00	45.60	53.20	60.80	68.40	76.00	83.60	91.20	98.80	106.40	114.00	121.60	129.20	136.80	144.40	152.00	159.60	167.20	174.80	182.40	190.00	209.00
3.9	1.95	3.90	39.00	46.80	54.60	62.40	70.20	78.00	85.80	93.60	101.40	109.20	117.00	124.80	132.60	140.40	148.20	156.00	163.80	171.60	179.40	187.20	195.00	214.50
4.0	2.00	4.00	40.00	48.00	56.00	64.00	72.00	80.00	88.00	96.00	104.00	112.00	120.00	128.00	136.00	144.00	152.00	160.00	168.00	176.00	184.00	192.00	200.00	220.00
4.1	2.05	4.10	41.00	49.20	57.40	65.60	73.80	82.00	90.20	98.40	106.60	114.80	123.00	131.20	139.40	147.60	155.80	164.00	172.20	180.40	188.60	196.80	205.00	225.50
4.2	2.10	4.20	42.00	50.40	58.80	67.20	75.60	84.00	92.40	100.80	109.20	117.60	126.00	134.40	142.80	151.20	159.60	168.00	176.40	184.80	193.20	201.60	210.00	231.00
4.3	2.15	4.30	43.00	51.60	60.20	68.80	77.40	86.00	94.60	103.20	111.80	120.40	129.00	137.60	146.20	154.80	163.40	172.00	180.60	189.20	197.80	206.40	215.00	236.50
4.4	2.20	4.40	44.00	52.80	61.60	70.40	79.20	88.00	96.80	105.60	114.40	123.20	132.00	140.80	149.60	158.40	167.20	176.00	184.80	193.60	202.40	211.20	220.00	242.00
4.5	2.25	4.50	45.00	54.00	63.00	72.00	81.00	90.00	99.00	108.00	117.00	126.00	135.00	144.00	153.00	162.00	171.00	180.00	189.00	198.00	207.00	216.00	225.00	247.50
4.6	2.30	4.60	46.00	55.20	64.40	73.60	82.80	92.00	101.20	110.40	119.60	128.80	138.00	147.20	156.40	165.60	174.80	184.00	193.20	202.40	211.60	220.80	230.00	253.00
4.7	2.35	4.70	47.00	56.40	65.80	75.20	84.60	94.00	103.40	112.80	122.20	131.60	141.00	150.40	159.80	169.20	178.60	188.00	197.40	206.80	216.20	225.60	235.00	258.50
4.8	2.40	4.80	48.00	57.60	67.20	76.80	86.40	96.00	105.60	115.20	124.80	134.40	144.00	153.60	163.20	172.80	182.40	192.00	201.60	211.20	220.80	230.40	240.00	264.00
4.9	2.45	4.90	49.00	58.80	68.60	78.40	88.20	98.00	107.80	117.60	127.40	137.20	147.00	156.80	166.60	176.40	186.20	196.00	205.80	215.60	225.40	235.20	245.00	269.50
5.0	2.50	5.00	50.00	60.00	70.00	80.00	90.00	100.00	110.00	120.00	130.00	140.00	150.00	160.00	170.00	180.00	190.00	200.00	210.00	220.00	230.00	240.00	250.00	275.00
5.1	2.55	5.10	51.00	61.20	71.40	81.60	91.80	102.00	112.20	122.40	132.60	142.80	153.00	163.20	173.40	183.60	193.80	204.00	214.20	224.40	234.60	244.80	255.00	280.50
5.2	2.60	5.20	52.00	62.40	72.80	83.20	93.60	104.00	114.40	124.80	135.20	145.60	156.00	166.40	176.80	187.20	197.60	208.00	218.40	228.80	239.20	249.60	260.00	286.00
5.3	2.65	5.30	53.00	63.60	74.20	84.80	95.40	106.00	116.60	127.20	137.80	148.40	159.00	169.60	180.20	190.80	201.40	212.00	222.60	233.20	243.80	254.40	265.00	291.50
5.4	2.70	5.40	54.00	64.80	75.60	86.40	97.20	108.00	118.80	129.60	140.40	151.20	162.00	172.80	183.60	194.40	205.20	216.00	226.80	237.60	248.40	259.20	270.00	297.00
5.5	2.75	5.50	55.00	66.00	77.00	88.00	99.00	110.00	121.00	132.00	143.00	154.00	165.00	176.00	187.00	198.00	209.00	220.00	231.00	242.00	253.00	264.00	275.00	302.50

Chilton's LABOR CALCULATOR

For dollar rates ending with 50 cents or 1.00 add to the appropriate rate column.

TIME	.50 per hr.	$1.00 per hr.	$10.00 per hr.	$12.00 per hr.	$14.00 per hr.	$16.00 per hr.	$18.00 per hr.	$20.00 per hr.	$22.00 per hr.	$24.00 per hr.	$26.00 per hr.	$28.00 per hr.	$30.00 per hr.	$32.00 per hr.	$34.00 per hr.	$36.00 per hr.	$38.00 per hr.	$40.00 per hr.	$42.00 per hr.	$44.00 per hr.	$46.00 per hr.	$48.00 per hr.	$50.00 per hr.	$55.00 per hr.
5.6	2.80	5.60	56.00	67.20	78.40	89.60	100.80	112.00	123.20	134.40	145.60	156.80	168.00	179.20	190.40	201.60	212.80	224.00	235.20	246.40	257.60	268.80	280.00	308.00
5.7	2.85	5.70	57.00	68.40	79.80	91.20	102.60	114.00	125.40	136.80	148.20	159.60	171.00	182.40	193.80	205.20	216.60	228.00	239.40	250.80	262.20	273.60	285.00	313.50
5.8	2.90	5.80	58.00	69.60	81.20	92.80	104.40	116.00	127.60	139.20	150.80	162.40	174.00	185.60	197.20	208.80	220.40	232.00	243.60	255.20	266.80	278.40	290.00	319.00
5.9	2.95	5.90	59.00	70.80	82.60	94.40	106.20	118.00	129.80	141.60	153.40	165.20	177.00	188.80	200.60	212.40	244.20	236.00	247.80	259.60	271.40	283.20	295.00	324.50
6.0	3.00	6.00	60.00	72.00	84.00	96.00	108.00	120.00	132.00	144.00	156.00	168.00	180.00	192.00	204.00	216.00	228.00	240.00	252.00	264.00	276.00	288.00	300.00	330.00
6.1	3.05	6.10	61.00	73.20	85.40	97.60	109.80	122.00	134.20	146.40	158.60	170.80	183.00	195.20	207.40	219.60	231.80	244.00	256.20	268.40	280.60	292.80	305.00	335.50
6.2	3.10	6.20	62.00	74.40	86.80	99.20	111.60	124.00	136.40	148.80	161.20	173.60	186.00	198.40	210.80	223.20	235.60	248.00	260.40	272.80	285.20	297.60	310.00	341.00
6.3	3.15	6.30	63.00	75.60	88.20	100.80	113.40	126.00	138.60	151.20	163.80	176.40	189.00	201.60	214.20	226.80	239.40	252.00	264.60	277.20	289.80	302.40	315.00	346.50
6.4	3.20	6.40	64.00	76.80	89.60	102.40	115.20	128.00	140.80	153.60	166.40	179.20	192.00	204.80	217.60	230.40	243.20	256.00	268.80	281.60	294.40	307.20	320.00	352.00
6.5	3.25	6.50	65.00	78.00	91.00	104.00	117.00	130.00	143.00	156.00	169.00	182.00	195.00	208.00	221.00	234.00	247.00	260.00	273.00	286.00	299.00	312.00	325.00	357.50
6.6	3.30	6.60	66.00	79.20	92.40	105.60	118.80	132.00	145.20	158.40	171.60	184.80	198.00	211.20	224.40	237.60	250.80	264.00	277.20	290.40	303.60	316.80	330.00	363.00
6.7	3.35	6.70	67.00	80.40	93.80	107.20	120.60	134.00	147.40	160.80	174.20	187.60	201.00	214.40	227.80	241.20	254.60	268.00	281.40	294.80	308.20	321.60	335.00	368.50
6.8	3.40	6.80	68.00	81.60	95.20	108.80	122.40	136.00	149.60	163.20	176.80	190.40	204.00	217.60	231.20	244.80	258.40	272.00	285.60	299.20	312.80	326.40	340.00	374.00
6.9	3.45	6.90	69.00	82.80	96.60	110.40	124.20	138.00	151.80	165.60	179.40	193.20	207.00	220.80	234.60	248.40	262.20	276.00	289.80	303.60	317.40	331.20	345.00	379.50
7.0	3.50	7.00	70.00	84.00	98.00	112.00	126.00	140.00	154.00	168.00	182.00	196.00	210.00	224.00	238.00	252.00	266.00	280.00	294.00	308.00	322.00	336.00	350.00	385.00
7.1	3.55	7.10	71.00	85.20	99.40	113.60	127.80	142.00	156.20	170.40	184.60	198.80	213.00	227.20	241.40	255.60	269.80	284.00	298.20	312.40	326.60	340.80	355.00	390.50
7.2	3.60	7.20	72.00	86.40	100.80	115.20	129.60	144.00	158.40	172.80	187.20	201.60	216.00	230.40	244.80	259.20	273.60	288.00	302.40	316.80	331.20	345.60	360.00	396.00
7.3	3.65	7.30	73.00	87.60	102.20	116.80	131.40	146.00	160.60	175.20	189.80	204.40	219.00	233.60	248.20	262.80	277.40	292.00	306.60	321.20	335.80	350.40	365.00	401.50
7.4	3.70	7.40	74.00	88.80	103.60	118.40	133.20	148.00	162.80	177.60	192.40	207.20	222.00	236.80	251.60	266.40	281.20	296.00	310.80	325.60	340.40	355.20	370.00	407.00
7.5	3.75	7.50	75.00	90.00	105.00	120.00	135.00	150.00	165.00	180.00	195.00	210.00	225.00	240.00	255.00	270.00	285.00	300.00	315.00	330.00	345.00	360.00	375.00	412.50
7.6	3.80	7.60	76.00	91.20	106.40	121.60	136.80	152.00	167.20	182.40	197.60	212.80	228.00	243.20	258.40	273.60	288.80	304.00	319.20	334.40	349.60	364.80	380.00	418.00
7.7	3.85	7.70	77.00	92.40	107.80	123.20	138.60	154.00	169.40	184.80	200.20	215.60	231.00	246.40	261.80	277.20	292.60	308.00	323.40	338.80	354.20	369.60	385.00	423.50
7.8	3.90	7.80	78.00	93.60	109.20	124.80	140.40	156.00	171.60	187.20	202.80	218.40	234.00	249.60	265.20	280.80	296.40	312.00	327.60	343.20	358.80	374.40	390.00	429.00
7.9	3.95	7.90	79.00	94.80	110.60	126.40	142.20	158.00	173.80	189.60	205.40	221.20	237.00	252.80	268.60	284.40	300.20	316.00	331.80	347.60	363.40	379.20	395.00	434.50
8.0	4.00	8.00	80.00	96.00	112.00	128.00	144.00	160.00	176.00	192.00	208.00	224.00	240.00	256.00	272.00	288.00	304.00	320.00	336.00	352.00	368.00	384.00	400.00	440.00
8.1	4.05	8.10	81.00	97.20	113.40	129.60	145.80	162.00	178.20	194.40	210.60	226.80	243.00	259.20	275.40	291.60	307.80	324.00	340.20	356.40	372.60	388.80	405.00	445.50
8.2	4.10	8.20	82.00	98.40	114.80	131.20	147.60	164.00	180.40	196.80	213.20	229.60	246.00	262.40	278.80	295.20	311.60	328.00	344.40	360.80	377.20	393.60	410.00	451.00
8.3	4.15	8.30	83.00	99.60	116.20	132.80	149.40	166.00	182.60	199.20	215.80	232.40	249.00	265.60	282.20	298.80	315.80	332.00	348.60	365.20	381.80	398.40	415.00	456.50
8.4	4.20	8.40	84.00	100.80	117.60	134.40	151.20	168.00	184.80	201.60	218.40	235.20	252.00	268.80	285.60	302.40	319.20	336.00	352.80	369.60	386.40	403.20	420.00	462.00
8.5	4.25	8.50	85.00	102.00	119.00	136.00	153.00	170.00	187.00	204.00	221.00	238.00	255.00	272.00	289.00	306.00	323.00	340.00	357.00	374.00	391.00	408.00	425.00	467.50
8.6	4.30	8.60	86.00	103.20	120.40	137.60	154.80	172.00	189.20	206.40	223.60	240.80	258.00	275.20	292.40	309.60	326.80	344.00	361.20	378.40	395.60	412.80	430.00	473.00
8.7	4.35	8.70	87.00	104.40	121.80	139.20	156.60	174.00	191.40	208.80	226.20	243.60	261.00	278.40	295.80	313.20	330.60	348.00	365.40	382.80	400.20	417.60	435.00	478.50
8.8	4.40	8.80	88.00	105.60	123.20	140.80	158.40	176.00	193.60	211.20	228.80	246.40	264.00	281.60	299.20	316.80	334.40	352.00	369.60	387.20	404.80	422.40	440.00	484.00
8.9	4.45	8.90	89.00	106.80	124.60	142.40	160.20	178.00	195.80	213.60	231.40	249.20	267.00	284.80	302.60	320.40	338.20	356.00	373.80	391.60	409.40	427.20	445.00	489.50
9.0	4.50	9.00	90.00	108.00	126.00	144.00	162.00	180.00	198.00	216.00	234.00	252.00	270.00	288.00	306.00	324.00	342.00	360.00	378.00	396.00	414.00	432.00	450.00	495.00
9.1	4.55	9.10	91.00	109.20	127.40	145.60	163.80	182.00	200.20	218.40	236.60	254.80	273.00	291.20	309.40	327.60	345.80	364.00	382.20	400.40	418.60	436.80	455.00	500.50
9.2	4.60	9.20	92.00	110.40	128.80	147.20	165.60	184.00	202.40	220.80	239.20	257.60	276.00	294.40	312.80	331.20	349.60	368.00	386.40	404.80	423.20	441.60	460.00	506.00
9.3	4.65	9.30	93.00	111.60	130.20	148.80	167.40	186.00	204.60	223.20	241.80	260.40	279.00	297.60	316.20	334.80	353.40	372.00	390.60	409.20	427.80	446.40	465.00	511.50
9.4	4.70	9.40	94.00	112.80	131.60	150.40	169.20	188.00	206.80	225.60	244.40	263.20	282.00	300.80	319.60	338.40	357.20	376.00	394.80	413.60	432.40	451.20	470.00	517.00
9.5	4.75	9.50	95.00	114.00	133.00	152.00	171.00	190.00	209.00	228.00	247.00	266.00	285.00	304.00	323.00	342.00	361.00	380.00	399.00	418.00	437.00	456.00	475.00	522.50
9.6	4.80	9.60	96.00	115.20	134.40	153.60	172.80	192.00	211.20	230.40	249.60	268.80	288.00	307.20	326.40	345.60	364.80	384.00	403.20	422.40	441.60	460.80	480.00	528.00
9.7	4.85	9.70	97.00	116.40	135.80	155.20	174.60	194.00	213.40	232.80	252.20	271.60	291.00	310.40	329.80	349.20	368.60	388.00	407.40	426.80	446.20	465.60	485.00	533.50
9.8	4.90	9.80	98.00	117.60	137.20	156.80	176.40	196.00	215.60	235.20	254.80	274.40	294.00	313.60	333.20	352.80	372.40	392.00	411.60	431.20	450.80	470.40	490.00	539.00
9.9	4.95	9.90	99.00	118.80	138.60	158.40	178.20	198.00	217.80	237.60	257.40	277.20	297.00	316.80	336.60	356.40	376.20	396.00	415.80	435.60	455.40	475.20	495.00	544.50
10.0	5.00	10.00	100.00	120.00	140.00	160.00	180.00	200.00	220.00	240.00	260.00	280.00	300.00	320.00	340.00	360.00	380.00	400.00	420.00	440.00	460.00	480.00	500.00	550.00
11.0	5.50	11.00	110.00	132.00	154.00	176.00	198.00	220.00	242.00	264.00	286.00	308.00	330.00	352.00	374.00	396.00	418.00	440.00	462.00	484.00	506.00	528.00	550.00	605.00
12.0	6.00	12.00	120.00	144.00	168.00	192.00	216.00	240.00	264.00	288.00	312.00	336.00	360.00	384.00	408.00	432.00	456.00	480.00	504.00	528.00	552.00	576.00	600.00	660.00
13.0	6.50	13.00	130.00	156.00	182.00	208.00	234.00	260.00	286.00	312.00	338.00	364.00	390.00	416.00	442.00	468.00	494.00	520.00	546.00	572.00	598.00	624.00	650.00	715.00
14.0	7.00	14.00	140.00	168.00	196.00	224.00	252.00	280.00	308.00	336.00	364.00	392.00	420.00	448.00	476.00	504.00	532.00	560.00	588.00	616.00	644.00	672.00	700.00	770.00
15.0	7.50	15.00	150.00	180.00	210.00	240.00	270.00	300.00	330.00	360.00	390.00	420.00	450.00	480.00	510.00	540.00	570.00	600.00	630.00	660.00	690.00	720.00	750.00	825.00
16.0	8.00	16.00	160.00	192.00	224.00	256.00	288.00	320.00	352.00	384.00	416.00	448.00	480.00	512.00	544.00	576.00	608.00	640.00	672.00	704.00	736.00	768.00	800.00	880.00
17.0	8.50	17.00	170.00	204.00	238.00	272.00	306.00	340.00	374.00	408.00	442.00	476.00	510.00	544.00	578.00	612.00	646.00	680.00	714.00	748.00	782.00	816.00	850.00	935.00
18.0	9.00	18.00	180.00	216.00	252.00	288.00	324.00	360.00	396.00	432.00	468.00	504.00	540.00	576.00	612.00	648.00	684.00	720.00	756.00	792.00	828.00	864.00	900.00	990.00
19.0	9.50	19.00	190.00	228.00	266.00	304.00	342.00	380.00	418.00	456.00	494.00	532.00	570.00	608.00	646.00	684.00	722.00	760.00	798.00	836.00	874.00	912.00	950.00	1045.00
20.0	10.00	20.00	200.00	240.00	280.00	320.00	360.00	400.00	440.00	480.00	520.00	560.00	600.00	640.00	680.00	720.00	760.00	800.00	840.00	880.00	920.00	960.00	1000.00	1100.00

Mechanic's Data

TAP DRILL SIZES

NATIONAL COARSE OR U.S.S.

Screw & Tap Size	Threads Per Inch	Use Drill Number
No. 5	40	39
No. 6	32	36
No. 8	32	29
No. 10	24	25
No. 12	24	17
1/4	20	8
5/16	18	F
3/8	16	5/16
7/16	14	U
1/2	13	27/64
9/16	12	31/64
5/8	11	17/32
3/4	10	21/32
7/8	9	49/64
1	8	7/8
1 1/8	7	63/64
1 1/4	7	1 7/64
1 1/2	6	1 11/32

NATIONAL FINE OR S.A.E.

Screw & Tap Size	Threads Per Inch	Use Drill Number
No. 5	44	37
No. 6	40	33
No. 8	36	29
No. 10	32	21
No. 12	28	15
1/4	28	3
5/16	24	1
3/8	24	Q
7/16	20	W
1/2	20	29/64
9/16	18	33/64
5/8	18	37/64
3/4	16	11/16
7/8	14	13/16
1 1/8	12	1 3/64
1 1/4	12	1 11/64
1 1/2	12	1 27/64

DECIMAL EQUIVALENT SIZE OF THE NUMBER DRILLS

Drill No.	Decimal Equivalent	Drill No.	Decimal Equivalent	Drill No.	Decimal Equivalent
80	.0135	53	.0595	26	.1470
79	.0145	52	.0635	25	.1495
78	.0160	51	.0670	24	.1520
77	.0180	50	.0700	23	.1540
76	.0200	49	.0730	22	.1570
75	.0210	48	.0760	21	.1590
74	.0225	47	.0785	20	.1610
73	.0240	46	.0810	19	.1660
72	.0250	45	.0820	18	.1695
71	.0260	44	.0860	17	.1730
70	.0280	43	.0890	16	.1770
69	.0292	42	.0935	15	.1800
68	.0310	41	.0960	14	.1820
67	.0320	40	.0980	13	.1850
66	.0330	39	.0995	12	.1890
65	.0350	38	.1015	11	.1910
64	.0360	37	.1040	10	.1935
63	.0370	36	.1065	9	.1960
62	.0380	35	.1100	8	.1990
61	.0390	34	.1110	7	.2010
60	.0400	33	.1130	6	.2040
59	.0410	32	.1160	5	.2055
58	.0420	31	.1200	4	.2090
57	.0430	30	.1285	3	.2130
56	.0465	29	.1360	2	.2210
55	.0520	28	.1405	1	.2280
54	.0550	27	.1440		

DECIMAL EQUIVALENT SIZE OF THE LETTER DRILLS

Letter Drill	Decimal Equivalent	Letter Drill	Decimal Equivalent	Letter Drill	Decimal Equivalent
A	.234	J	.277	S	.348
B	.238	K	.281	T	.358
C	.242	L	.290	U	.368
D	.246	M	.295	V	.377
E	.250	N	.302	W	.386
F	.257	O	.316	X	.397
G	.261	P	.323	Y	.404
H	.266	Q	.332	Z	.413
I	.272	R	.339		

DECIMAL EQUIVALENTS OF THE COMMON FRACTIONS

Fraction	Decimal	Fraction	Decimal	Fraction	Decimal
1/64	.0156	21/64	.3281	43/64	.6719
1/32	.0313	11/32	.3438	11/16	.6875
3/64	.0469	23/64	.3594	45/64	.7031
1/16	.0625	3/8	.3750	23/32	.7188
5/64	.0781	25/64	.3906	47/64	.7344
3/32	.0938	13/32	.4063	3/4	.7500
7/64	.1094	27/64	.4219	49/64	.7656
1/8	.1250	7/16	.4375	25/32	.7813
9/64	.1406	29/64	.4531	51/64	.7969
5/32	.1563	15/32	.4688	13/16	.8125
11/64	.1719	31/64	.4844	53/64	.8281
3/16	.1875	1/2	.5000	27/32	.8438
13/64	.2031	33/64	.5156	55/64	.8594
7/32	.2188	17/32	.5313	7/8	.8750
15/64	.2344	35/64	.5469	57/64	.8906
1/4	.2500	9/16	.5625	29/32	.9063
17/64	.2656	37/64	.5781	59/64	.9219
9/32	.2813	19/32	.5938	15/16	.9375
19/64	.2969	39/64	.6094	61/64	.9531
5/16	.3125	5/8	.6250	31/32	.9688
		41/64	.6406	63/64	.9844
		21/32	.6563		